Proceedings of the Twelfth National Conference on Artificial Intelligence

Volume One

Sponsored by the
American Association for
Artificial Intelligence

AAAI Press / The MIT Press

Menlo Park • Cambridge • London

Contents
Volume One

Technical Papers

The Arts

Art

Believable Agents

Case-Based Reasoning

Cognitive Modeling

Music and Audition

iv

Foreword

Each year, the National Conference on Artificial Intelligence provides a unique opportunity for timely interaction and communication among researchers and practitioners from all areas of AI. This year, in response to popular demand, the program cochairs, the area chairs, and the program committee made a special effort to broaden participation and enliven the conference by increasing the number and variety of papers accepted for presentation and for publication in the proceedings.

Both the call for papers and an article in the Fall, 1993 issue of AI Magazine announced the goal of increasing conference participation and invited prospective authors to submit papers on a variety of topics, including those that "describe theoretical, empirical, or experimental results; represent areas of AI that may have been under-represented in recent conferences; present promising new research concepts, techniques, or perspectives; or discuss issues that cross traditional sub-disciplinary boundaries." The community responded enthusiastically, submitting 780 papers to the conference. Extrapolating from the last few years, this is approximately thirty percent higher than the expected number of submitted papers. Moreover, a straw vote among the area chairs indicates that the quality of submitted papers was at least as high as in previous years.

Each paper was reviewed by three reviewers under the supervision of one of twenty-three senior members of the AI community who served as area chairs. Evaluation crite ria were expanded in an effort to recognize a broader range of scientific contributions. Reviewers and area chairs were asked to view themselves not as "gatekeepers" looking for reasons to reject papers, but rather as "scouts" looking for interesting papers to accept.

The program committee did an excellent job, increasing both the number and variety of accepted papers. Of the 780 papers originally submitted, 55 were either withdrawn by their authors or rejected without review for arriving after the specified due date or for significantly exceeding specified length limitations. Of the remaining 725 papers, 222 were accepted for the conference. Thus, AAAI-94 is a bigger conference than in previous years, presenting a good cross-section of AI research. Familiar session topics include qualitative reasoning, case-based reasoning, and constraint satisfaction. Session topics that have not appeared in recent conference years include genetic algorithms and neural nets. Completely new topics include theater and video, art and music, believable agents, and learning robotic agents.

AAAI-94 has several other exciting programs. The new Student Abstract and Poster Program, which got over 100 submissions, presents a wonderful opportunity for all of us to get acquainted with some of the up-and-coming talent and their great new research ideas. As in recent years, there is a video track (with publication for the first time this year as a video collection by AAAI), a robot competition, and a robot exhibition. A new AI and the Arts exhibition follows the very engaging exhibition introduced at AAAI-92, and there also is a new Machine Translation exhibition.

This year's Keynote address is given by Professor Raj Reddy of Carnegie Mellon University and the AAAI Presidential Address is given by Professor Barbara Grosz of Harvard University. Invited speakers include Joe Bates of Carnegie-Mellon University, Mel Montemerlo of NASA, Steve Ballmer of Microsoft, Kirstie Bellman of ARPA, Geoffrey Hinton of the University of Toronto and Red Whittaker of Carnegie-Mellon University. Invited speakers giving shorter, more specialized presentations include: Rina Dechter of UC Irvine, Johanna Moore of the University of Pittsburgh, Leslie Kaelbling of Brown University, Melanie Mitchell of the Santa Fe Institute, Mark Musen of Stanford University, and Chris Atkeson of MIT.

In sum, the AI community set a goal this year to revitalize the AAAI conference, to restore its atmosphere of excitement, innovation, controversy, and intellectual engagement. The community and conference committee have made great strides toward achieving that goal.

Barbara Hayes-Roth and Richard Korf
Program Cochairs, AAAI-94

Organization of the American Association for Artificial Intelligence

1994 National Conference on Artificial Intelligence (AAAI-94)

Conference Chair
William Swartout, USC/Information Sciences Institute

Program Cochairs
Barbara Hayes-Roth, Stanford University
Richard E. Korf, University of California, Los Angeles

Associate Chair
Howard E. Shrobe, Massachusetts Institute of Technology

Challenge Committee Chair
Thomas L. Dean, Brown University

Art Exhibition Chair
Joseph Bates, Carnegie Mellon University

Machine Translation Showcase Committee
Jaime Carbonell, Carnegie Mellon University
Bonnie Dorr, University of Maryland
Eduard Hovy, University of Southern California

Robot Competition and Exhibition Chair
Reid Simmons, Carnegie Mellon University

Robot Laboratory Chair
Willie Lim, Lehman Brothers

Student Abstract Program Chair
Kristian Hammond, University of Chicago

Tutorial Program Chair
Devika Subramanian, Cornell University

Tutorial Program Cochair
Philip Klahr, Inference Corporation

Video Program Cochairs
John E. Laird, University of Michigan
Elliot Soloway, University of Michigan

Workshop Program Chair
Donald Perlis, University of Maryland

Program Committee
David W. Aha, Naval Research Laboratory
Bradley P. Allen, Inference Corporation
Richard Alterman, Brandeis University
Kevin D. Ashley, University of Pittsburgh
Christer Bäckström, Linköping University
Joseph Bates, Carnegie Mellon University

Richard K. Belew, University of California, San Diego
William P. Birmingham, University of Michigan
Mark Boddy, Honeywell Systems & Research Center
Peter Bonasso, The MITRE Corporation
Craig Boutilier, University of British Columbia
Hans Brunner, US West Advanced Technologies
Sandra Carberry, University of Pennsylvania
B. Chandrasekaran, Ohio State University
    & Stanford University
Eugene Charniak, Brown University
Susan Conry, Clarkson University
James Crawford, CIRL
Roger B. Dannenberg, Carnegie Mellon University
Adnan Darwiche, Rockwell International Science Center
Henry Davis, Wright State University
Luc De Raedt, Katholieke Universiteit Leuven
Thomas L. Dean, Brown University
Rina Dechter, University of California, Irvine
Johan De Kleer, Xerox Palo Alto Research Center
Nachum Dershowitz, University of Illinois at Urbana-
    Champaign
Oskar Dressler, Siemens AG
Mark Drummond, Recom Technologies & NASA Ames
    Research Center
Edmund Durfee, University of Michigan
Clark Elliott, DePaul University & Northwestern University
Susan Epstein, CUNY Hunter College New York
Oren Etzioni, University of Washington
Matthew Evett, Florida Atlantic University
Brian Falkenhainer, Xerox Design Practice & Technology
Adam Farquhar, Stanford University
James R. Firby, University of Chicago
Douglas Fisher, Vanderbilt University
Kenneth Forbus, Northwestern University/Institute for the
    Learning Sciences
Peter Friedland, NASA Ames Research Center
William A. Gale, AT&T Bell Laboratories
Erann Gat, JPL/California Institute of Technology
James Geller, New Jersey Institute of Technology
Matthew Ginsberg, University of Oregon
Piotr Gmytrasiewicz, University of California, Riverside
Andrew Golding, Mitsubishi Electric Research Laboratories
Moises Goldszmidt, Rockwell International Science Center
Georg Gottlob, Technische Universität Wien
John J. Grefenstette, Naval Research Laboratory
Adam J. Grove, NEC Research Institute
Joseph Halpern, IBM Almaden Research Center

Steve Hanks, University of Washington
Othar Hansson, Heuristicrats Research Inc. & University of California, Berkeley
James A. Hendler, University of Maryland
Ian Horswill, Massachusett Institute of Technology & AI Laboratory
Eric Horvitz, Microsoft Research
Douglas J. Howe, AT&T Bell Laboratories
Michael N. Huhns, MCC AI Laboratory
Seth Hutchinson, University of Illinois at Urbana-Champaign
Chung Hee Hwang, University of Rochester
Yumi Iwasaki, Stanford University
Randolph Jones, University of Michigan
Leo Joskowicz, IBM TJ Watson Research Center
Leslie Pack Kaelbling, Brown University
Avi Kak, Purdue University
Peter D. Karp, SRI International
Simon Kasif, Johns Hopkins University
Henry A. Kautz, AT&T Bell Laboratories
Richard M. Keller, NASA Ames Research Center
Hiroaki Kitano, Sony Computer Science Laboratory
Georg Klinker, Digital Equipment Corporation
Daphne Koller, University of California, Berkeley
Janet Kolodner, Georgia Institute of Technology
Kurt Konolige, SRI International
John R. Koza, Stanford University
Benjamin Kuipers, University of Texas at Austin
John Laird, University of Michigan
Gerhard Lakemeyer, University of Bonn
Amy Lansky, NASA Ames Research Center
David Leake, Indiana University
Wendy G. Lehnert, University of Massachusetts
Alon Levy, AT&T Bell Laboratories
Long-Ji Lin, Siemens Corp Research Inc
Marc Linster, Digital Equipment Corporation
Diane Litman, AT&T Bell Laboratories
Sridhar Mahadevan, University of South Florida
V.W. Marek, University of Kentucky
Matthew T. Mason, Carnegie Mellon University
David McAllester, Massachusetts Institute of Technology/AI Laboratory
Kathleen McCoy, University of Delaware
John McDermott, Digital Equipment Corporation
Sheila McIlraith, University of Toronto
David Miller, The MITRE Corporation
Steve Minton, NASA Ames Research Center
Thomas Mitchell, Carnegie Mellon University
Andrew Moore, Carnegie Mellon University
Mark A. Musen, Stanford University
Karen L. Myers, SRI International
Dana S. Nau, University of Maryland
P. Pandurang Nayak, NASA Ames Research Center
Nils Nilsson, Stanford University
Martha Palmer, University of Pennsylvania
Judea Pearl, University of California, Los Angeles
Fernando Pereira, AT&T Bell Laboratories
Dean Pomerleau, Carnegie Mellon University

Jean Ponce, University of Illinois at Urbana-Champaign
David Poole, University of British Columbia
Gregory Provan, Institute for Decisions Systems Research
Teodor Przymusinski, University of California, Riverside
Abhiram Ranade, University of California, Berkeley
Edwina L. Rissland, University of Massachusetts
Enrique Ruspini, SRI International
Stuart Russell, University of California, Berkeley
Jeffrey Schlimmer, Washington State University
Guus Schreiber, University of Amsterdam
Hinrich Schutze, Stanford University
Bart Selman, AT&T Bell Laboratories
Jude Shavlik, University of Wisconsin
Mark Shirley, Xerox Palo Alto Research Center
Yoav Shoham, Stanford University
Reid Simmons, Carnegie Mellon University
Munindar P. Singh, MCC
David E. Smith, Rockwell International
Wayne Snyder, Boston University
Lynn Andrea Stein, Massachusetts Institute of Technology & AI Laboratory
Mark E. Stickel, SRI International
David G. Stork, Ricoh California Research Center
Rudi Studer, Universität Karlsruhe
Devika Subramanian, Cornell University
Richard Sutton, GTE Laboratories Inc.
William Swartout, USC/Information Sciences Institute
Katia Sycara, Carnegie Mellon University
Prasad Tadepalli, Oregon State University
Austin Tate, University of Edinburgh
Gerry Tesauro, IBM Watson Research Laboratories
Richmond Thomason, University of Pittsburgh
Charles Thorpe, Carnegie Mellon University
David Throop, Boeing Missiles & Space
Paul Utgoff, University of Massachusetts
Peter van Beek, University of Alberta
Pascal Van Hentenryck, Brown University
Manuela Veloso, Carnegie Mellon University
David L. Waltz, NEC Research Institute, Inc.
Bonnie L. Webber, University of Pennsylvania
David E. Wilkins, SRI International
Randall Wilson, Sandia National Laboratories
Kent Wittenburg, Bell Communications Research
Gregg Yost, Digital Equipment Corporation
Hantao Zhang, University of Iowa
Shlomo Zilberstein, University of Massachusetts

Auxiliary Reviewers
Jürgen Angele, University of Karlsruhe
John Ash, Washington State University
Andrew Baker, University of Oregon
Anthony Barret, University of Washington
Howard Beck, AIAI, University of Edinburgh
Maria-Paola Bonacina, University of Iowa
Piero Bonatti, University of Technology Vienna
Claudia Boettcher, Fraunhofer Institute, Karlsruhe
Ronen Brafman, Stanford University
Gerhard Brewka, GMD (Germany)
Maurice Bruynooghe, Katholieke Universiteit Leuven

Joanna Bryson, Massachusetts Institute of Technology, AI Laboratory
Steven V. Chenoweth, AT&T Global Information Solutions
Lonnie Chrisman, Carnegie Mellon University
Paul Dagum, Rockwell Science Center
Keith S. Decker, University of Massachusetts
Alvaro Del Val, Stanford University
Marie des Jardins, SRI International
Christy Doran, University of Pennsylvania
Georg Dorffner, Austrian Research Institute for Artificial Intelligence
Brian Drabble, University of Edinburgh, AIAI
Tim Duncan, University of Edinburgh, AIAI
Thomas Eiter, University of Technology Vienna
Werner Emde, GMD (Germany)
Reinhard Enders, Siemens AG
Henrik Eriksson, Stanford University
David Etherington, AT&T Bell Laboratories
Dieter Fensel, University of Karlsruhe
Eugene Fink, Carnegie Mellon University
Hartmut Freitag, Siemens AG
Nir Friedman, Stanford University
Mitch Garnaat, Xerox Corporation
John H. Gennari, Stanford University
Keith Golden, University of Washington
Richard Goodwin, Carnegie Mellon University
Lloyd Greenwald, Brown University
Narendra K. Gupta, Siemens Corporate Research Inc.
Leonard Hermens, Washington State University
William Hill, Bellcore
John Josephson, Ohio State University
Herbert Kay, University of Texas
Jak Kirman, Brown University
Adrian Klein, Stanford University
Kevin Knight, USC/Information Sciences Institute
Sven Koenig, Carnegie Mellon University
Philip D. Laird, NASA Ames Research Center
Dieter Landes, University of Karlsruhe
Neal Lesh, University of Washington
Shieu-Hong Lin, Brown University
Christopher Lynch, Northeastern University
Daniel P. Miranker, University of Texas
Michael Montag, Siemens AG
Dimitri Naidich, University of Iowa
Susanne Neubert, University of Karlsruhe
Ann Nicholson, Brown University
Klaus Noekel, Siemens AG
Ron Parr, UC Berkeley
Peter Patel-Schneider, AT&T Bell Laboratories
Barak Pearlmutter, Siemens Corporate Research Inc
Scott Penberthy, University of Washington
Mark Peot, Stanford University
Lance Ramshaw, Institute for Research in Cognitive Science
Alan Rector, University of Manchester
Elisha Sacks, Princeton University
Kate Sanders, Brown University
Klaus Schild, German Research Center for AI (DFKI)
Franz Schmalhofer, German Research Center for AI (DFKI)

Robert Schrag, University of Texas
Grigori Schwarz, Stanford University
Richard Segal, University of Washington
Naveen Sharma, Xerox Corporation
B. Srinivas, University of Pennsylvania
Jussi Stader, AIAI, University of Edinburgh
Markus Stumptner, University of Technology Vienna
Milind Tambe, USC/Information Sciences Institute
Gabriel Taubin, IBM T.J. Watson Research Center
Peter Terpstra, University of Amsterdam
Samson W. Tu, Stanford University
Tomas E. Uribe, Stanford University
Gertjan van Heijst, University of Amsterdam
Maarten van Someren, University of Amsterdam
Henk Vandecasteele, Katholieke Universiteit Leuven
Patricia Wells, Washington State University
Monika Zickwolff, University of Darmstadt

AAAI Officials

President
Barbara Grosz, Harvard University

President-Elect
Randall Davis, Massachusetts Institute of Technology

Past President
Patrick J. Hayes, University of Illinois

Secretary-Treasurer
Norman R. Nielsen, SRI International

Councilors (through 1994)
Jaime Carbonell, Carnegie Mellon University
Paul Cohen, University of Massachusetts
Elaine Kant, Schlumberger Laboratory for Computer Science
Candace L. Sidner, Digital Equipment Corporation

Councilors (through 1995)
Johan de Kleer, Xerox Palo Alto Research Center
Benjamin Kuipers, University of Texas, Austin
Paul Rosenbloom, USC/Information Sciences Institute
Beverly Woolf, University of Massachusetts

Councilors (through 1996)
Thomas L. Dean, Brown University
Robert S. Engelmore, Stanford University
Peter Friedland, NASA Ames Research Laboratory
Ramesh Patil, USC/Information Sciences Institute

Standing Committees

Conference Chair
William Swartout, USC/Information Sciences Institute

Finance Chair
Norman R. Nielsen, SRI International

AAAI–94
Outstanding Paper Award

A Prototype Reading Coach that Listens

Jack Mostow, Steven F. Roth, Alexander G. Hauptmann and Matthew Kane,
Carnegie Mellon University

This year, AAAI's National Conference on Artificial Intelligence honors a paper that exemplifies high standards in technical contribution and exposition. Papers were nominated for the Outstanding Paper Award by members of the program committee during the NCAI review process. These nominations were then reviewed once again by a smaller subset of the program committee to select the winning paper. Care was taken during the review process to ensure that our final decisions were based on the opinions of impartial readers who are free from personal biases and conflicts of interest.

Volume One

Volume Two

The Arts

Criticism, Culture, and the Automatic Generation of Artworks[1]

Lee Spector and **Adam Alpern**

School of Communications and Cognitive Science
Hampshire College, Amherst, MA 01002
{lspector, aalpern}@hamp.hampshire.edu

Abstract

Researchers wishing to create computational systems that *themselves* generate artworks face two interacting challenges. The first is that the standards by which artistic output is judged are notoriously difficult to quantify. The larger AI community is currently involved in a rich internal dialogue on methodological issues, standards, and rigor, and hence murkiness with regard to the assessment of output must be faced squarely. The second challenge is that any artwork exists within an extraordinarily rich cultural and historical context, and it is rare that an artist who is ignorant of this context will produce acceptable works. In this paper we assert that these considerations argue for case-based AI/Art systems that take critical criteria as parameters. We describe an example system that produces new bebop jazz melodies from a case-base of melodies, using genetic programming techniques and a fitness function based on user-provided critical criteria. We discuss the role that such techniques may play in future work on AI and the arts.

Introduction: Constructing Artists

Applications of computers to the arts date from the earliest days of computing. The use of AI technologies in the arts has a long history as well, particularly in music (Balaban et al. 1992). The majority of these uses fall into two categories: systems that perform "art understanding" tasks of some sort (e.g., music analysis systems), and systems that function as "intelligent" tools for use by human artists (e.g., (Rowe 1993)). Recently, however, a new category of systems has begun to emerge; a category of systems that are designed to *be* artists. By this we mean that such systems, which we will call "constructed artists," are supposed to be capable of creating aesthetically meritorious artworks on their own, with minimal human intervention. Harold Cohen's Aaron system is an early example of this category, and one of its few clear successes to date (McCorduck 1991). Aaron is a system that creates original drawings, each unique and potentially surprising to Cohen, that have been exhibited in galleries internationally. Aaron was constructed through a laborious process of "tutoring" by Cohen, himself an accomplished painter, that spanned over a decade. More recently, work has proceeded on constructed artists that function as poets (Kurzweil 1990), music composers (Ames & Domino 1992), and aesthetic agents in virtual worlds (Bates 1992). A literature has also emerged on the computational underpinnings of artistic creativity more generally (e.g., (Boden 1991)).

Aesthetic Judgements

The philosophy of art, which in the Western tradition dates at least from Plato, has never been an area of widespread agreement (see, e.g., (Dickie & Sclafani 1977)). The range of theories regarding the bases of aesthetic value, judgement and criticism is extraordinary, and the debates show no signs of near-term resolution. This presents a problem for AI scientists wishing to produce computational artists: How do we know when we've got one? How do we know if version A is better than version B, or vice versa? Without the ability to answer such questions the science of artist construction cannot proceed, and these questions *seem* to be inseparably linked to the murky issues of aesthetic judgement. The larger AI community is currently involved in a dialogue on methodological issues, standards, and rigor; many are calling for the adoption of experimental methods from more traditional sciences, for the use of standard examples and criteria of assessment, etc. If those of us working on constructed artists cannot judge our systems without first resolving all of the open questions regarding the judgement of artworks, then we will be on shaky methodological ground indeed. Fortunately, it is possible to separate the two kinds of judgement; we describe one approach to doing so below.

The artworks of Cohen's Aaron have been judged by the artworld and by the museum-going public. According to some theories of art this is the best, or even the only, form of assessment by which to judge the quality of a work (Danto 1978). But this sort of judgement has a high price both in terms of human resources and in terms of time. The science of artist construction will proceed quite slowly if each iteration of each system can be assessed only by organizing a public show and by waiting for critical reviews.[2] Of course, Cohen himself also served as a critic of Aaron's performance, and he was presumably able to apply the results of his judgements to the improvement of the program

---

[1]The authors acknowledge the support of the Dorothy and Jerome Lemelson National Program in Invention, Innovation, and Creativity.

[2]An experiment combining public assessment with genetic techniques similar to those described later in this paper is currently in progress via mosaic on the internet. The address is: http://porsche.boltz.cs.cmu.edu:8001/htbin/mjwgenform.

in a reasonable amount of time. But it is not clear how these interactions can form the basis of a general theory of aesthetic judgement sufficient to ground a science of artist construction. At best they are instructive for other artists with an interest in applying their own critical faculties to the construction of new artists.

Another approach to this dilemma is to work in a genre with codified, formalized valuation criteria. This has been a popular approach in computer music, as rule-systems have been developed for many forms of music (e.g., (Ebcioglu 1992, Maxwell 1992)). There are three problems with this approach. The first is that existing formalizations are often of "dead" forms—it may be that we understand them well enough to codify them only because they have fossilized. If we want our constructed artists to produce creative works in live genres, such formalizations are of little value. The second problem is that it is not clear that adherence to the rules of a particular art form is a good indicator of aesthetic value; it might merely indicate inclusion in the genre, which might be compatible with aesthetic mediocrity. Third, it is not clear that work in genres with codified valuation criteria will generalize to other genres, many of which seem to resist the imposition of criteria upon which the art world can consense.

The alternative approach that we propose is to factor aesthetic judgement out of the systems that we develop. We don't need to know what the "right" criteria are for aesthetic judgement; we only need to know that our systems are capable of conforming to the range of such criteria that might be proposed. If we develop systems that take critical criteria as parameters, and if our systems work over a wide range of variation of these parameters, then we can safely ignore debates about which critical criteria are correct. We can then ask all opposing parties to submit sets of critical criteria; although they must all be formalizable, they may vary considerably. To the extent that we can keep everyone happy, by producing constructed artists to earn accolades from any formal critic, we will be making real progress in the science of artist construction.

Instances of the framework that we present below produce an artist as output when given a critic (and other data) as input. The constructed artist may not be able to adapt to *other* critics that it encounters later in its career; such adaptation is a subject for future work.

An Artist's Culture

Every artwork exists within a rich cultural and historical context, and many theorists have argued that good art can be neither produced nor assessed in ignorance of this context. It is not obvious, to say the least, how a deep appreciation of the human cultural context can be programmed into a constructed artist. Trurl, the robot who builds an electronic bard in a humorous story by Stanislaw Lem, is forced to repeat within the machine "the entire Universe

from the beginning—or at least a good piece of it." (Lem 1974) In most real systems to date, features of the cultural context are implicit in analytical and generative rules, but there is no direct way to vary the culture experimentally.

We believe that the best approach for providing a cultural context for a constructed artist is to make a large case-base of prior works available as a library. In essence, we want to "factor out" the culture in the same way that we "factor out" the critic; by developing systems that take "cultures" as parameters, our systems will be culture-independent and we will be able to assess the success of our systems across cultures. The success of such systems should not depend on any *specific* cultural context; they should be sufficiently flexible to perform within a variety of cultures. The cultural case-base should be made available both to the constructed artist and to the critics that guide the artist construction process.

It may be argued that there is much more to a culture than a library of past works. We agree, but we also believe that a large case-base of successful artworks forms a good basis for cultural sensitivity.[3] Enhanced notions of culture may be incorporated into the framework, so long as all culture-dependent elements are provided as variable parameters to the artist construction system.

Genetic Programming

The framework sketched above calls for an artist construction system that takes as input a set of critical criteria and a case-base of past artworks. The system should produce as output a successful constructed artist—that is, a program that can be executed to produce successful new artworks relative to the given critic and culture.

The technology of *genetic programming* (Koza 1992) provides tools that make the implementation of this framework fairly straightforward. Genetic programming is a technique for the automatic generation of computer programs; in our case we can use the technique to automatically generate computer programs that will function as constructed artists. Genetic programming is an *evolutionary* method in which programs are evolved using a process modeled on Darwinian natural selection.[4] The technique is a variant of the *genetic algorithms* of (Holland 1992). The traditional genetic algorithm evolves fixed-length chromosome strings that encode behavior-producing systems, while genetic programming evolves behavior-producing computer programs directly. The process of natural selection is driven by *fitness;* that is, by some assessment of the quality of each individual. Genetic programming systems take *fitness functions* as parameters. For the production of constructed artists we can provide critical criteria as parameters to the system in the form of fitness functions.

A genetic programming system works with a problem-specific *function set* and *terminal set*. These sets contain the primitive elements out of which all of the output programs will be constructed. The genetic programming process starts by creating a large initial population of programs that are random combinations of elements from the function and terminal sets. One generally ensures that each function can

---

[3]Other case-based approaches to creative processes are presented in (Dartnall & Kim 1993).

[4]Other uses have been made of evolutionary methods in computational arts. See, e.g., (Todd & Latham 1992).

take, in any of its argument positions, any terminal and any value that might be returned by any function in the function set. This allows the use of a simple random function generator, since every combination of functions and terminals can be guaranteed to execute without signalling an error.

Each of the programs in the initial population is assessed for fitness. This is usually accomplished by running each program on a collection of inputs called fitness cases, and by a running a fitness function on the output of each of these runs; the resulting values are then combined to produce a single fitness value for the program.

The fitness values are used in producing the next generation of programs. The next generation may be produced from the current generation via a variety of *genetic operations* including reproduction, crossover, mutation, permutation, and others. We use only reproduction and crossover in the present project; (Koza 1992) describes a variety of genetic operations in detail. The reproduction operator selects a highly fit individual and copies it into the next generation; this is the most direct way to implement the notion of "survival of the fittest." Individuals are selected for reproduction randomly, but the selection function is biased toward highly fit programs.

Fitness-proportionate reproduction does not introduce any new individuals to the system—it merely propagates fit individuals from one generation to the next. The crossover operation, on the other hand, introduces variation by selecting two highly fit *parents*; it generates from them two *offspring,* which are produced by swapping random fragments of the parents. The resulting programs are copied to the next generation.

Over many generations of fitness assessment, reproduction and crossover, the average fitness of the population will tend to improve, as will the fitness of the best-of-generation individual from each generation. After a preestablished number of generations, or after the fitness improves to some preestablished level, the best-of-run individual is designated as the result and is produced as the output from the genetic programming system.

Genetic programming searches the space of computer programs in an attempt to maximize fitness. It is fitness that determines the structure of the resulting programs, not the intuitions of a human programmer or algorithm design-er. Koza presents applications of genetic programming to a wide range of problems, along with arguments to support its utility as a general automatic programming technique (Koza 1992).

Genetic Programming of Constructed Artists

Genetic programming provides an obvious method for building an artist construction system that takes critical criteria as input: We use an off-the-shelf genetic programming system for which we have crafted function and terminal sets adequate for the production of a wide range of artist programs within some given medium. We then allow the user to write a critic function that will be used as a fitness function by the genetic programming system.

Note that we have great freedom in designing the function and terminal sets. We may use any artwork-producing functions and terminals that we feel are appropriate for the given medium. In particular, we may include functions that access a case-base of prior, highly valued works. The case-base may contain works from the real history of art in the given medium, the results of prior runs of genetic programming, or any mixture of the two. Access to the case-base allows the functions in the function set to produce a range of results depending on the artist's cultural context. The case-base access functions should be made available to the critic functions as well, since many critical criteria may be best phrased in terms of comparisons to works in the prevailing culture.

Figure 1 shows a diagram of the resulting framework for the genetic programming of culturally-contextualized, critic-sensitive constructed artists. The arrow from the case-base to the constructed artist reflects the fact that a constructed artist is a program that may itself take input. This input might come from anywhere; it might, for example, come from a random number generator or from real-time interaction with an audience. In our current work we provide our constructed artists with input from the case-base; that is, the constructed artist takes a prior work from the case-base as input, and produces a new work as output.

Genetic Programming of a Bebop Musician

We illustrate the framework with a system that creates simple programs that produce Bebop jazz melodies. Jazz melody is a good medium for this sort of experimentation for several reasons. First, there are several simple ways to represent melodies in a form that is manipulable by simple programming constructs. Second, the jazz tradition includes several "call and response" forms, so the idea of producing a new work on the basis of an old work has established precedents within the genre. Third, the jazz literature contains several analytical works that enumerate critical criteria (e.g., (Coker 1964)), along with many works on technique that provide guidance in creating a function set (e.g., (Baker 1988)).

We decided to generate programs that produce four-measure melodies as output when given four-measure melodies as input. This corresponds to the popular practice

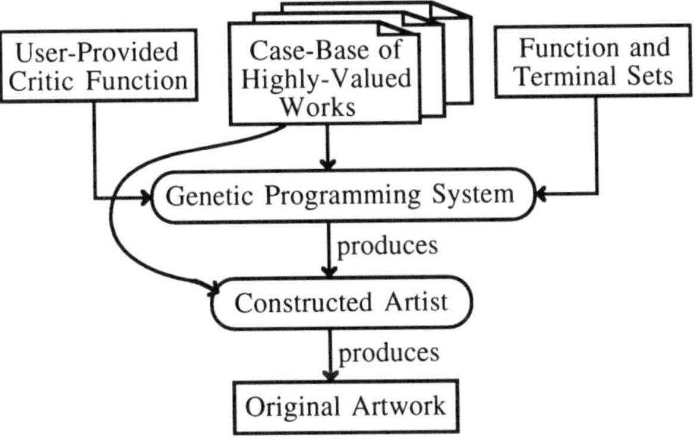

Figure 1. Diagram of the Genetic Artist Construction framework

of "trading four" in jazz improvisation. We used a weak representation for melodies: lists of 64 numbers, each of which represents a pitch that will be sounded for the duration of a sixteenth note. Rests are represented as -1, and equivalent adjacent pitches are merged into notes of longer duration. This representation is inadequate because it can accommodate neither thirty-second notes nor triplets of any kind, and because adjacent notes of equivalent pitch must be separated by a rest in order to sound individually. It is nonetheless sufficient for many simple melodies, and it has the advantages of simplicity and ease of manipulation.

We used Koza's LISP-based genetic programming code, which is presented in an appendix to (Koza 1992) and is available on the internet by anonymous FTP.

Our function set, inspired by a list of techniques in (Baker 1988), consists of the following 13 functions: **REP** takes a single melody and returns a new melody that consists of the first measure of the given melody repeated four times. **8VA** takes a single melody and returns it with every note transposed up an octave; notes that are transposed out of the two-octave range above middle C are wrapped to the bottom of the range. **IVA** is similar to **8VA**, but the transposition interval is determined by matching the given melody against the melodies in the case-base. **IVA** transposes the given melody by the average interval between itself and the most similar melody found in the knowledge base. Similarity is determined by computing the inter-note intervals for the pair of melodies to be compared, and by counting the number of times that three-interval sequences occur in both sequences. **EXTEND** takes a single melody and fills any trailing rests with the melody itself. If given a very short melody **EXTEND** may produce a melody with a large number of repetitions. **TRUNC** takes a single melody and replaces all notes following the last rest with additional rests. **DIMINUTE** takes a single melody and speeds it up. It removes every odd-numbered element of the melody list, compressing the remaining elements into the first half of the list and padding the end with rests. **AUGMENT** takes a single melody and slows it down, doubling each element in the first half of the melody, and discarding the entire second half. **FRAGMENT** takes two melodies and returns a melody that has parts taken from each. The returned melody consists of the first two beats of the first given melody, the second two beats of the second given melody, the third two beats of the first given melody, and so on. The **INVERT** function takes a single melody and returns it with each interval inverted. The first note is held constant, the second note differs from the first by the corresponding interval in the given melody *negated,* etc. Again, notes that would be outside of the two octave range above middle C are wrapped around. **RETROGRADE** takes a single melody and returns it reversed. **MOST-FAMILIAR** takes two melodies and returns the one that is most similar to those in the case-base, using the same similarity metric as in **IVA**. **COMPARE-TRANSPOSE** takes a single melody and returns it unevenly transposed, with each note transposed by half the difference between it and the corresponding note in the most similar melody from the case-base. **ROTATE** takes a single melody and returns it moved forward in time by one quarter note, with the last note wrapped around to the beginning.

Our terminal set consists of a single symbol, **CALL-MELODY**, which serves as the input to the programs produced by the system. One runs the resulting program by setting the variable **CALL-MELODY** to some input melody, and then evaluating the program in a LISP listener.

We ran our system with a case-base consisting of five four-measure fragments from Charlie Parker songs. We assessed the fitness of each program by running it with each of the melodies in the case-base as input. Each run produced a single melody that was assessed on the basis of a set of critical criteria inspired by those presented in (Baker 1988). **TONAL-NOVELTY-BALANCE** returns 0 if there is perfect balance between novel tonal material and tonal material that can be found in the case-base. It returns 1 if there is no balance, and intermediate values for intermediate levels of tonal novelty. Matching is performed with 3-note subsequences of the melodies. **RHYTHMIC-NOVELTY-BALANCE** is identical except that the rhythmic structure of the melody, rather than the tonal structure, is compared against the melodies in the case-base. **TONAL-RESPONSE-BALANCE** compares the melody produced by the program with the melody that was provided as input to the program (**CALL-MELODY**). It compares the two melodies point-for-point and returns 0 for a perfect balance of equality and inequality, 1 for complete mismatch *or* exact equivalence, and intermediate values for intermediate degrees of match. **SKIP-BALANCE** returns 0 if the melody perfectly balances diatonic movement (intervals of less than 3) with "skips" (intervals of size 3 or greater). **RHYTHMIC-COHERENCE** returns 0 as long as the melody contains no single sixteenth notes occurring between longer notes. If isolated sixteenth notes do occur in the melody, **RHYTHMIC-COHERENCE** returns the number such notes.

Four of these five critical functions return real numbers between 0 and 1, with lower numbers indicating better melodies. The last critical function returns 0 for a melody that meets an important constraint, and 1 or greater for melodies that don't. The fitness of a melody-producing program is calculated as the sum of the values returned by the critical functions, summed over all of the fitness cases. Assuming for the moment that **RHYTHMIC-COHERENCE** returns no greater than 1, the maximum (worst) fitness value is the number of critical criteria (5) times the number of fitness cases (5), or 25. The best programs will have fitness values considerably closer to 0. Since **RHYTHMIC-COHERENCE** may return greater than 1, it is possible to get fitness values higher than 25, but we have rarely seen such values in practice.

Results

We ran the genetic programming system with a population size of 250 for 21 generations. The best program from the initial, randomly-created population had a fitness of 7.43. The program was: **(FRAGMENT (AUGMENT CALL-MELODY) CALL-MELODY)**. This simply interleaves, in two-beat-long sections, the input melody with a slowed down version of the input melody. Since many of the critic functions look for balance, and since the input melody is taken from the case base, this simple program actually performs very well.

As shown in Figure 2, the average fitness of the population improved over the next few generations, but the fitness of the best-of-generation program did not improve noticeably until generation 3, when the following was produced:

```
(FRAGMENT
  (COMPARE-TRANSPOSE
    (INVERT (COMPARE-TRANSPOSE CALL-MELODY)))
  CALL-MELODY)
```

This function performs a more complex manipulation of its input, including two calls to the case-sensitive **COMPARE-TRANSPOSE** function. As shown in Figure 2, the fitness of the best-of-generation program, along with the average fitness of the population, continued to improve through subsequent generations.

The best-of-run program for this run was found on generation 19 and had a fitness measure of 2.82. It was:

```
(FRAGMENT
  (COMPARE-TRANSPOSE (8VA (COMPARE-TRANSPOSE
    (FRAGMENT
      (IVA (DIMINUTE (EXTEND CALL-MELODY)))
      (FRAGMENT
        (EXTEND CALL-MELODY)
        (AUGMENT (RETROGRADE (RETROGRADE
          (ROTATE (FRAGMENT CALL-MELODY
                           CALL-MELODY)))))))))
    (MOST-FAMILIAR (INVERT CALL-MELODY)
                   (IVA CALL-MELODY)))
```

Figure 3 shows a call/response pair in music notation. This response pleases our critic very well—the sum of fitness components is 0.19, which is quite close to a perfect score of 0. This should multiplied by 5, producing 0.95, for comparison to the above-mentioned fitness values. (Recall that the above fitness values were summed over 5 fitness cases.) The sum-of-components values for the best-of-run program run on the 5 fitness cases were 0.19, 0.31, 0.65, 0.41, and 1.25. Although the response in Figure 3 pleases the critic, it does not please *us* (the authors) particularly well. This is not an indication of weakness of the genetic programming approach to musician construction. Nor is it an indication that we made improper choices (of function set, terminal set, etc.) in applying the technique; it just means that we should work to improve the critical criteria that we provide as parameters to the system. The quality of the output vis-à-vis our aesthetic judgement is largely separable from the ability of the system to produce critic-pleasing programs. The former is a question to be argued in the philosophy of art; the latter is an element of the science of artist construction.

Our example system *does* have its weaknesses when assessed purely as a critic-pleaser. The best-of-run program pleases the critic when run on melodies that were used in the fitness cases, but it is not as *robust* as we would like. We ran the program on 3 Charlie Parker melodies that were not used in the fitness cases and produced sum-of-components values 0.81, 1.66, and 0.93. These are not terrible; in fact, two of these values are better than the worst sum-of-components value for a melody used as a fitness

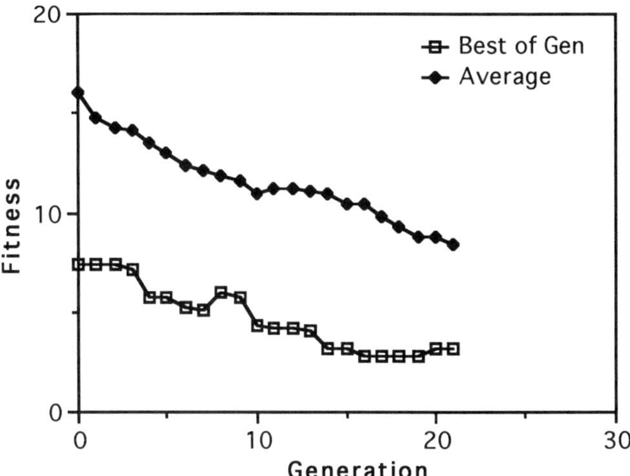

Figure 2. Best-of-generation and average fitnesses

case. But on average the program performs better with input from the fitness cases—it can not yet be said to please our critic in responding to bebop melodies generally.

The lack of robustness is a weakness of our application of the framework to music, and we are exploring it experimentally. We are working with alternative music representation schemes, alternative function and terminal sets, and variations in other parameters of the genetic programming system, in an attempt to produce more robust constructed musicians. We must note, however, that variations in the critic and in the case-base must be explored as well. Although we would like our system to work well independently of changes in these parameters, they have an impact on the ability of the system to produce robust critic-pleasers.

The case for the separability of critical criteria, culture, and techniques for artist construction has been stated strongly in this paper. In fact, the character of a fitness function helps to determine the "fitness landscape" (Kinnear 1994) that is searched by genetic programming. Hence the choice of critic and the composition of the case-base will both have an impact on the effectiveness of the artist construction framework that we have described. For this reason we must work to develop systems that perform well over ranges of critical criteria that might be proposed. To the extent that these ranges depend on our interpretation of the philosophical discussions of aesthetic judgement, the clean separation that we would like to maintain between such discussions and the science of artist construction breaks down. We believe, however, that reasonable generalizations can be made in this area, enabling us to work on artist construction systems with clear, quantitative indicators of success. This belief can only be explored experimentally, by continuing to apply the framework to the construction of artists in various media, by working with various sets of critical criteria that we find in the literature, by providing our systems with access to various cultural contexts, and by assessing the robustness of the art-making programs that result.

The resulting research program presents several challenges. First there are issues of representation; these are

Figure 3. A call/response pair.

problematic even for music, and more so for other media. Then there are issues of scale; our example system uses a tiny case-base and simple critical criteria. While these suffice to demonstrate the framework, we cannot expect to be impressed with the output of systems built on such impoverished notions of culture and criticism. Finally, although our framework frees us from reliance on any *particular* critical criteria, it does require that critical criteria be encoded; some may question the feasibility of this enterprise. We believe that criteria can be extracted from the critical literature, and we are also investigating the automatic generation of critics from the case-base.

Conclusions

Johnson-Laird, in a computational study of jazz improvisation, notes that "neo-Darwinian" theories of creativity have long been espoused, but he rejects them because "their gross inefficiency renders them highly implausible as an account of any sort of mental process." (Johnson-Laird 1991, p.321) The new technologies of genetic algorithms and genetic programming offer the promise of tractable evolutionary processing, and hence theories of creativity-through-evolution may now be explored experimentally. The genetic programming framework for artist construction offers additional advantages in that it provides a relatively clean way to separate out issues of aesthetic judgement from issues of system judgement. Instances of our framework take critics and cultural contexts as parameters, producing constructed artists as output. This allows us to consider the ability of our system to please critics within cultures, without involving us in questions of aesthetics. The separation between the two forms of judgement is not quite as clean as we would like, but nobody said it would be easy to raise an artist.

Acknowledgments

Valuable feedback was provided by Rebecca S. Neimark, Joe Futrelle, and the members of the Propositional Attitudes Task Force at Smith College.

References

Ames, C.; and Domino, M. 1992. Cybernetic Composer: An Overview. In *Understanding Music with AI*, Balaban, M.; Ebcioglu, K.; and Laske, O., eds. 187–205. Cambridge MA: The AAAI Press/The MIT Press.

Baker, D. 1988. *David Baker's Jazz Improvisation*, Revised Edition. Alfred Publishing Co., Inc.

Balaban, M.; Ebcioglu, K.; and Laske, O., eds. 1992. *Understanding Music with AI*. Cambridge MA: The AAAI Press/The MIT Press.

Bates, J. 1992. Virtual Reality, Art, and Entertainment. *Presence* 1: 133–138.

Boden, M.A. 1991. *The Creative Mind: Myths & Mechanisms*. Basic Books (Harper Collins Publishers).

Coker, J. 1964. *Improvising Jazz*. New York: Simon and Schuster, Inc.

Danto, A. 1978. The Artworld. In *Philosophy Looks at the Arts*, Margolis, J., ed. 132–144. Philadelphia, PA: Temple University Press.

Dartnall, T.; Kim, S., eds. 1993. *AI and Creativity*, Working Notes, Spring Symposium. AAAI Technical Report.

Dickie, G.; and Sclafani, R.J., eds. 1977. *Aesthetics*. New York: St. Martin's Press.

Ebcioglu, K. 1992. An Expert System for Harmonizing Chorales in the Style of J. S. Bach. In *Understanding Music with AI*, Balaban, M.; Ebcioglu, K.; and Laske, O., eds. 295–333. Cambridge MA: The AAAI Press/The MIT Press.

Holland, J.H. 1992. *Adaptation in Natural and Artificial Systems*. Cambridge, MA: The MIT Press.

Johnson-Laird, P.N. 1991. Jazz Improvisation: A Theory at the Computational Level. In *Representing Musical Structure*, Howell, P.; West, R.; and Cross, I., eds. 291–325. New York: Academic Press.

Kinnear, K.E. Jr. 1994. Fitness Landscapes and Difficulty in Genetic Programming. In *Proceedings of EC94, The IEEE Conference on Evolutionary Computation*, IEEE.

Koza, J.R. 1992. *Genetic Programming*. Cambridge, MA: The MIT Press.

Kurzweil, R. 1990. *The Age of Intelligent Machines*. Cambridge, MA: The MIT Press.

Lem, S. 1974. *The Cyberiad*. New York: Harcourt Brace Jovanovich, Publishers.

Maxwell, H.J. 1992. An Expert System for Harmonizing Analysis of Tonal Music. In *Understanding Music with AI*, Balaban, M.; Ebcioglu, K.; and Laske, O., eds. 335–353. Cambridge MA: The AAAI Press/The MIT Press.

McCorduck, P. 1991. *Aaron's Code: Meta-art, Artificial Intelligence and the Work of Harold Cohen*. New York : W. H. Freeman and Company.

Rowe, R. 1993. *Interactive Music Systems*. Cambridge, MA: The MIT Press.

Todd, S.; and Latham, W. 1992. *Evolutionary Art and Computers*. Academic Press.

Research problems in the use of a shallow Artificial Intelligence model of personality and emotion*

Clark Elliott
Institute for Applied Artificial Intelligence
DePaul University
243 South Wabash Avenue
Chicago, IL 60604
and
School of Education and Social Policy
Northwestern University
Evanston, IL
email: elliott@ils.nwu.edu

Abstract

This paper presents an overview of some open research problems in the representation of emotion on computers. The issues discussed arise in the context of a broad, albeit shallow, emotion reasoning platform based originally on the ideas of Ortony, Clore, and Collins(Ortony, Clore, & Collins 1988). In addressing these problems we hope to (1) correct and expand our content theory of emotion, and pseudo personality, which underlies all aspects of the research; (2) answer feasibility questions regarding a usable representation of the emotion domain in the computer, and (3) build agents capable of emotional interaction with users. A brief description of a semantics-based AI program, the *Affective Reasoner*, and its recent multi-media extensions is given. Issues pertaining to affective user modeling, an expert system on emotion eliciting situations, the building of a sympathetic computer, models of relationship, personality in games, and the motivation behind the study of emotion on computers are discussed. References to the current literature and recent workshops are made.

Introduction

The emotion reasoning platform discussed in this paper has developed over the course of several years and currently includes, besides the underlying emotion engine (described briefly below), a speech recognition package which is able to discriminate at least some broad categories of emotion content; a music indexing and playback mechanism allowing virtually instant access to hundreds of hours of midi format music used to aid in the expression of emotion; a schematic representation of approximately 70 emotion faces; and a text-to-speech module for expressing dynamically constructed text, including a minimal amount of emotion inflection (through runtime control of speed, pitch and volume).

In the spirit of one of this year's conference themes, we view this project as being in the "platform and concept hacking" stage, wherein we explore what plausible expectations we may make with respect to a shallow model of emotion and personality representation on the computer. Findings are strictly preliminary, and yet enough work has been done to raise what we feel to be some interesting questions.

What we refer to as "emotions" in this paper arise naturally in many human social situations as a byproduct of goal-driven and principled (or unprincipled) behavior, simple preferences, and relationships with other agents. This applies to many situations that one would not ordinary refer to as *emotional*: a social *agent* becoming *annoyed* with someone who is wasting her time (a mild case of that person violating the agent's principle of social efficiency thus blocking of one of the agent's goals through the reduction of a valued resource, time), enjoying a piece of music because it is appealing (liking it, through a simple, unjustifiable, preference), and so forth. We limit our consideration of emotion states, and intensities, to states and intensities similar to what Frijda et al. (Frijda *et al.* 1992) were describing when they referred to the *overall felt intensity* of an emotion as comprising "whatever would go into the generation of a response to a global question such as this: 'How intense was your emotional reaction to situation S?"' Physical manifestations, neural processes, and much about duration are not included in the model.

Lastly, we suggest that the representation of human emotion and personality in a social context, using AI techniques, is long overdue as a major area of study (c.f. (Norman 1980)). It is our belief that for each of the issues raised below, enough background work has been done that partial solutions are within the grasp of the AI community.

*Preparation of this article was supported in part by Andersen Consulting through Northwestern University's Institute for the Learning Sciences.

Background

In our current research, embodied in a large AI program called the Affective Reasoner, we simulate simple worlds populated with with agents capable of responding "emotionally" as a function of their concerns. Agents are given unique pseudo-personalities modeled as both a set of *appraisal frames* representing their individual goals, principles, preferences, and moods, and as a set of *channels* for the expression of emotions. Combinations of appraisal frames are used to create agents' interpretations of situations that unfold in the simulation. These interpretations, in turn, can be characterized by the simulator in terms of the eliciting conditions for emotions. As a result, in some cases agents "have emotions," which then may be expressed in ways that are observable by other agents, and as new simulation events which might perturb future situations (Elliott 1992). Additionally, agents use a case-based heuristic classification system (based on (Bareiss 1989)) to reason about the emotions other agents are presumed to be having, and to form representations of those other agents' personalities that will help them to predict and explain future emotion episodes involving the observed agent (Elliott & Ortony 1992; Elliott 1992).

Ortony, et al. (Ortony, Clore, & Collins 1988) discuss twenty-two emotion types based on valenced reactions to situations being construed as goal-relevant events, acts of accountable agents, or attractive or unattractive objects (including agents interpreted as objects). This theory has been extended to include the two additional emotion types of *love* and *hate* (Elliott 1992). See figure 1.

Additionally, using the work of Ortony, et al. (Ortony, Clore, & Collins 1988) as a guide, we analyzed a set of descriptions of emotion eliciting situations and created a modified set of *emotion intensity variables* to explain the causes of varying emotion intensity, within a coarse-grained simulation paradigm (Elliott & Siegle 1993). We reduced the resulting set of variables to a computable formalism, and represented sample situations in the Affective Reasoner. We then isolated three areas of the simulation where variables in either the short-term *state* of an agent, the long-term *disposition* of an agent, or the *emotion-eliciting situation* itself, helped to determine the intensity of the agent's subsequent affective state. For each area there is an associated group of variables. The first group, *simulation-event variables*, comprises variables whose values change independently of situation interpretation mechanisms. The second group, *stable disposition variables*, consists of variables that are involved in an agent's interpretation of situations, tend to be constant, and help to determine an agent's personality and role in the simulation. We felt that, for the purposes of implementation, the distinction between these two groups was underspecified in the work of Ortony, et al. (Ortony, Clore, & Collins 1988). The last group,

mood-relevant variables, contains those variables that contribute to an agent's mood state. In all there are approximately twenty such variables, although not all apply to each emotion category.

For example, the variable *blameworthiness-praiseworthiness* might roughly be described as the degree to which an observing agent interprets an observed agent as having upheld or violated one of the observing agent's principles, in some situation. It is derived from a set of simulation values, which might include values for the amount of effort expected in a given situation, the accountability of an agent as determined by role, and so forth. It has no default value, being determined entirely by one agent's construal of the simulated act of an another agent.

Our work has focused primarily on the detailed working out of a computational method for representing the antecedents and expression of human emotion in diverse human social situations. This has included the analysis, within the constraints of the underlying emotion theory, of many hundreds of informally described social situations which have given rise to emotions. To date the computational mechanism has included, among other components, (a) the construction of hundreds of *appraisal frames*, which include slots for reasoning about intenstiy and mood, in domains as diverse as, for example, financial accounting, stories, playing poker, and sales, (b) pseudo personality types made up of these appraisal frames, (c) the use of these pseudo personalities for *construing* situations with respect to the concerns of simulated agents, thus giving rise to "emotion generation" in simulation runs, (d) the generation of simple emotion instances based on the twenty-four emotion categories, (e) the generation of actions through approximately 450 channels (about twenty for each emotion category) consistent with the simulated emotions they are intended to express (each of which may, in turn, contain multiple manifestation *instances*), (f) abductive reasoning about the emotions expressed by other agents in the system, (g) the internal representation of the presumed pseudo personalities of observed agents by observing agents, (h) simple "explanations" of the emotions with respect to their emotional antecedents within the simulation, (i) simple models of relationship between the agents, allowing for "emotions" based on the concerns of others, and (j) the inclusion of the user as one of the agents in the system about which reasoning may take place.

Most recently we have been working on opening up communication channels with the user of the system through the addition of modules for speech recognition, inflected speech generation, indexed music-on-demand (using a midi interface and a 400 voice Proteus MS-PLUS synthesizer), and facial expression for the agents.

The broad long-range goals we would like to see pursued include number of applications we envision as made possible by the representational capabilities of a system such as this. Among these are the building of a computer that has some capability of categorizing, and responding to, a user's affective state; the building of systems that allow users to interactively explore the emotional content of a broad range of simulated social situations (e.g., for tutoring, for socially unskilled psychotherapy patients, and for military stress applications); testing the use of "emotionally aware" automated software agents as a way of enhancing the user's engagement in educational, and other software; using emotionally aware agents to communicate priorities naturally to the user, such as with an automated assistant for meetings, or the communication of technical concerns to less technical users through the focus of attention (e.g., operating systems, financial analysis), the use of computer-based emotion expression as an authoring tool (e.g., as online feedback for students), the construction of games that include a complex, yet cohesive, emotion and personality component; the use of the underlying emotion theory to analyze, and manipulate, the automated telling of stories; and platforms for testing the link between music and emotion expression.

Research Questions

Affective user modeling.

One hard, and divisive, problem facing the AI community is that of building user models. Rather than more traditional models which focus on the mental processes of the user in problem solving situations (Van Lehn 1988), we propose an alternative wherein only certain components of the *affective* state of the user is modeled. This is a much smaller problem, but one which should provide useful leverage. It might be considered akin to the feedback a responsive speaker might make use of when "playing" to her audience. We do *not* propose this as a full model of a user's emotional states which would then also require that all of the hard cognitive modeling problems be solved as well.

To implement simple affective user modeling, several components are required: (1) A structure which allows us to capture an agent's (in this case, the user's) outlook on situations that arise. This structure must include some concept of the role, personality, and current state of the user (within the context of shallow emotion reasoning), which together comprise the basis for the user's idiosyncratic way of construing the world. (2) A lexicon through which the user expresses his or her emotions to the computer. (3) A comprehensive set of emotion categories which allow for the mapping of emotion eliciting situations to the emotion expression lexicon, and vice versa. In our current work, as discussed above, we have implemented a broad, albeit shallow, representation of the first component, and a comprehensive, descriptive representation of the third.

The weakest link in such a system is in the lexicon. How does a computer, which has no understanding of faces[1], and which presumably has no mechanism for

---

[1] Although reportedly the work of Eckman might begin

Figure 1: Emotion types (Table based on [O'Rorke and Ortony, 1992] and [Elliott, 1992])

Group	Specification	Name and Emotion Type
Well-Being	appraisal of a situation as an *event*	**joy**: pleased about an *event* **distress**: displeased about an *event*
Fortunes of Others	presumed value of a a situation as an *event* affecting another	**happy-for**: pleased about an *event* desirable for another **gloating**: pleased about an *event* undesirable for another **resentment**: displeased about an *event* desirable for another **sorry-for**: displeased about an *event* undesirable for another
Prospect based	appraisal of a situation as a prospective *event*	**hope**: pleased about a prospective desirable *event* **fear**: displeased about a prospective undesirable *event*
Confirmation	appraisal of a situation as confirming or disconfirming an expectation	**satisfaction**: pleased about a confirmed desirable *event* **relief**: pleased about a disconfirmed undesirable *event* **fears-confirmed**: displeased about a confirmed undesirable *event* **disappointment**: displeased about a disconfirmed desirable *event*
Attribution	appraisal of a situation as an accountable *act* of some agent	**pride**: approving of one's own *act* **admiration**: approving of another's *act* **shame**: disapproving of one's own *act* **reproach**: disapproving of another's *act*
Attraction	appraisal of a situation as containing an attractive or unattractive *object*	**liking**: finding an *object* appealing **disliking**: finding an *object* unappealing
Well-being / Attribution	compound emotions	**gratitude**: admiration + joy **anger**: reproach + distress **gratification**: pride + joy **remorse**: shame + distress
Attraction / Attribution	compound emotion extensions	**love**: admiration + liking **hate**: reproach + disliking

generating plausible explanations which might allow it to determine which emotions are likely to have arisen, know what emotion a user is expressing? In addressing this question we consider several leverage points which show promise in allowing us to work around this problem, at least to some degree. First, and most importantly, it might well prove to be true that users are *motivated* to express their emotions to the computer, provided that there is at least the *illusion* that the computer understands how they are feeling. Should this be so, then some latitude is afforded us in requiring that the user, who is adaptable in communication, conform to the protocol of the computer, which is not. Second, the comprehensive emotion model allows us to develop a large lexicon categorized by both emotion category and intensity. Third, speech recognition packages are advanced enough to capture some of what is of interest to us with respect to the lexicon.

For example, using the work of Ortony et al. as a guide (Ortony, Clore, & Foss 1987), we built expressions containing emotion words, intensity modifiers, and pronoun references to different roles (e.g., *I am a bit sad because he...*, *I am rather sick at heart about her...*, *I was pretty embarrassed after my...*) (Elliott & Carlino 1994). We built phrases containing 198 emotion words (e.g. ...,bothered, brokenhearted, calm, carefree, chagrined, charmed, cheered, cheerful, cheerless,...). In preliminary runs we were able to detect 188 of the emotion words correctly on the first try, in context, with 10 false positives. Misses tended to be cases such as confusing "anguish" with "anguished," and "displeased" with "at ease." There were 10 other instances of difficulty with other parts of the phrases, such as confusing "my" with "I." Most of these would have been caught by a system with even rudimentary knowledge of English grammar.

Additionally, in other preliminary runs of our speech recognition package the computer was able to recognize the seven emotion categories, anger, hatred, sadness, love, joy, fear, and neutral, which we did our best to communicate to it, when speaking the sentence, "Hello Sam, I want to talk to you." In this small exercise we broke the sentence up into three parts, identifying each part as a "word" to the speech recognition system. We then trained each phrase for the seven different inflections. With practice we were able to get close to 100% recognition of the intended emotional state.[2] To achieve this we had to be slightly theatrical, but not overly so, and there was a flavor of speaking with someone who was hard of hearing, but again, not overly so.[3]

___
to address this issue.

[2] And this, even though the goal of the developers of the package was to *eliminate* inflection and simply recognize the words.

[3] Interestingly, when not *imagining* a situation consistent with the emotion we were attempting to express by voice, we were consistently less accurate. In addition, it appeared that the computer was biased somewhat in its errors toward

Once the lexicon is established, and minimal natural language parsing is in place through the use of an ATN or other simple system, tokens can either be interpreted directly as situations in themselves, or as a set of features indexing into a case-base to retrieve similar cases indicating a particular emotion category. To illustrate, on the one hand, from user input of "I am satisfied with the results" we might, for example, yield the *situation*: "the user is *satisfied* now in response to the comparison of her answer with the one just provided by the computer"). On the other hand, given user input of "I am happy now" (spoken with a hateful inflection), we might yield the set of *features*: *user expresses happiness*, and *user's inflection expresses hate*, which in turn retrieves the cases of *hatred* masked by a contrasting verbal expression.

Assuming that such a system can be built, it raises the possibility of testing its numerous applications in diverse domains. We touch on these in the following sections, in concert with other issues.

A sympathetic computer

Sidestepping the issue of whether a a user's *engagement* with a computer system will be increased by dealing with an emotionally believable agent, we might first ask what is required to achieve believability. How much does it matter if the computer is transparent in its capabilities and motivations? What level of sophistication is required? How intelligent does the system have to be to achieve a minimal level of believability?

Consider the following: A computer system detects, or is told by the user (as discussed above), that the user is fearful (anxious, worried, scared – each of these would be categorized as different intensities of the emotion category *fear*). The system is able to respond by asking what might be considered reasonable questions: "What is the name of the *event* over which you are fearful?," "How far is this event in the future?" (According to the underlying theory, as embodied in the Affective Reasoner, *fear* is a prospect-based emotion resulting from the likely blocking of a future *event*.) "What is the likelihood of this coming about?" (*Likelihood* is an intensity variable). It is then able to comment on relationships between the various *intensity variables* and then to recall cases from a library, where either the automated agent itself ("I was afraid of getting turned off!" (Frijda & Swagerman 1987)), or some other agent ("I was previously told the following story by another user...") was *fearful* with similar intensities. Lastly, after verifying that the retrieved case involves an emotion similar to that of the user, the computer agent responds by saying, "I am only a stupid computer program. Nonetheless, in my own simple way, the following is true: I consider you my friend (see *models of relationship* below). I *pity* you for your *fearful* state. I *hope* to become aware in the future that you are *relieved*

___
the category the user was imagining, for certain pairs of categories, which might suggest an interesting study.

about the outcome of situation *<input-situation>*, and that your *preservation goals* with respect to this are not blocked after all."

Such a system is within the range of our current technology, and representational capabilities (and see the reference to Scherer's work below). At what level of sophistication are users willing to accept that, in its own (remarkably) simple way, the computer does nonetheless feel pity for them? Given the tendency of users to anthropomorphize even the simplest video game characters, this would seem to be an important question to answer.

Expert System on Emotion

Scherer describes an expert system on emotion motivated by the need to "use computer modelling and experimentation as a powerful tool to further theoretical development and collect pertinent data on the emotion-antecedent appraisal process" (Scherer 1993). His system captures user input feature vectors representing an emotional situation and shows the relative distance from various predicted emotion concepts (categories in our terminology). He uses this as a way of validating the underlying representation of the appraisal-to-emotion process in his system.

Can we repeat or extend Scherer's results using the differing emotion categories, and appraisal structures? In particular, in the Scherer work the user is asked to identify the intensity of the emotional experience being described. Using our current theory, it would be suitable to draw on the antecedents of emotion intensity, embodied in the twenty or so emotion intensity variables given in (Elliott & Siegle 1993). Such work would also dovetail with the "sympathetic computer" mentioned above.

Models of relationship

In (Elliott & Ortony 1992) the authors discuss the ability of emotionally cognizant agents to model the concerns of one another, and the user. One aspect of these models is that they allow for the modeling of simple *relationships* between the agents, including the user. To wit, we might define a simple model of friendship as requiring that an agent be *happy for* another agent when good fortune strikes that other agent, and feel *pity* when bad fortune strikes. To do this the first agent must have a model of how a situation is presumed to be *construed by that other agent*. For example, to feel sorry for a friend when her basketball team has lost, it is important to know which team the friend is rooting for. This can only be done if each agent maintains some internal model of each other agent's presumed concerns.

In our current work we have built simple models of friendship and animosity, and to some degree, *identification* with another agent (i.e., where an agent takes on another's goals as its own.) When this is extended to include the user, interesting possibilities arise, such as those discussed in the next section. How sophisticated a

set of relationships can we build based on the emotional interaction of the (human and) automated agents?

Games

Consider the game of poker, and how an emotion model can enhance the believability, and possibly interest, of a computerized version of the game. Using a preliminary model, we have discussed (and built a simple versions of) the following system (Marquis & Elliott 1994):

The computer simulates one, or more, agents who play five card draw poker against the user. Each agent knows the basic rules of poker, including betting. Agents have their own *goals*, *principles*, and *preferences* so that they respond differently to different situations that arise. Bluffing, required if one is to truly simulate poker, leads to fear for some agents, hope for others. Some agents show their emotions (through facial expression, music selection, and verbal communication of physical manifestations), others suppress them (as in real life). An agent who has been bluffing and wins, might *gloat*, or if it loses it might feel *remorse*. An increase in the amount of the "pot" increases the *importance* of winning and thus the intensity of many of the emotions. Likewise *surprise* (generally hard to represent) can be derived from losing even though one has a good hand, or vice versa, thus intensifying the respective emotion. Agents might feel reproach towards, for example, a player (such as the user) who is too cautious, or takes to long to decide what to do (based on a violation of the principled customary way of playing). Other emotion-eliciting situations include having the computer attempt to cheat without being caught by the user, and so forth.

One claim that might be made is that to approach a realistic computer model of games such as poker, some model of personality and emotion, minimally a broad and shallow model as described here, is essential. Whether or not this makes the computer a better playing companion is an open question, but again, one that seems worth answering.

Are schematic facial models sufficient?

It is clear that sophisticated dynamic three-dimensional models of faces, such as that shown by Pelechaud at IJCAI93, have the power to delight audiences and convey expressive information(Pelachaud, Viaud, & Yahia 1993). Nonetheless, it may also be argued that much emotional content can be delivered in schematic format as well. Cartoon faces (such as those in *Calvin and Hobbs*, for example, convey much about the current appraisals of the cartoon character, and schematic faces have been used in clinical settings to help children identify their emotions. Are such faces, which are much less computationally expensive to manipulate, able to convey emotions in a consistent way?

In our own work we use a set of approximately seventy schematic faces, covering up to three intensities in each of the twenty-four emotion categories (Elliott,

Yang, & Nerheim-Wolfe 1993). Sixty of these have been included in a morphing module so that faces gradually break into a smile, decay from *rage* back to a default state, and so forth. The module runs in real time, allowing run-time control over face size, rate of morph, and rudimentary mouth movement (for when the agent is speaking). The system thus allows for over 3000 different morphs, a range not possible with 3D representation. The morphs run on a 66 Mhz IBM PC (with sound and speech cards) concurrently with midi playback, text-to-speech, speech recognition, and the background emotion simulation.

Assuming that either representation can be effective, the question still arises about the effectiveness of the emotion representation on which the dynamic face depends. Our approach is that, at present, low-level personality and emotion representations are too complex to simulate complex social interaction, and that content theories of personality and emotion embedded in individual domains are too simplistic. Hence the middle ground, using an *architectural* approach (e.g., at the level of schematic face representation) consistent across all aspects of the system.

Other areas of applicability

There are a number of other areas where a broad, but shallow computer representation of emotion and personality might be useful. These include testing the ability of the computer to represent the underlying principles in many areas of human endeavor. To this end we are formalizing representations in many different domains, including, in addition to the above mentioned domains, business applications (including selling, and financial statement analysis – where personal interpretation and preference of the analyst is actually somewhat common), and storytelling (using emotion themes as organizing principles similar to Lehnert's plot units (Lehnert 1981), (cf. (Reeves 1991))).

Other appropriate uses include military applications where training to deal with stressful situations *must* include a model of personality and emotion and social interaction, as well as role; understanding of political personalities (do world leaders act according to logic, or according to a personal codes based on different principles, and goals?)(Bannerjee 1991); family politics; and social simulations (Kass *et al.* 1992).

Why should this work be pursued?

Emotion representation on the computer can be seen to fall into at least four categories of pursuit: (1) the testing of design issues raised by theories of emotion (Colby 1981; Toda 1982; Frijda & Swagerman 1987; Pfeifer & Nicholas 1985; Sloman 1987), (2) the placing of neuro-motor control in an environmental or social context (Gray 1993; Rolls 1993), (3) the use of a "folk" representation of emotion to control the behavior of automated agents in social situations; and to predict, or attempt to understand, the behavior of other agents in such situations (Elliott 1993; Reilly 1993; Bates, A. Bryan Loyall, & Reilly 1992) and, (4) the use of emotions for process control (Birnbaum & Collins 1984).

At the recent *Workshop on Architectures Underlying Motivation and Emotion* [4] it became clear that the issue of which approach is more promising is far from settled. Even commonly held beliefs about emotions, such as their use as some sort of reactive-planning mechanism were questioned (e.g., Jeffrey Gray posed the question, if this were true, why would all the manifestations of fear arise many seconds *after* slamming on one's brakes to avoid an auto accident?). Perhaps what we consider to be emotions arise only as a byproduct of more essential mechanisms? Nonetheless, it seems that emotions are ubiquitous in human society and an integral part of the social fabric thereof. Until shown that it is wrong, we will continue to make the following argument: even if we were to completely understand, and be able to recreate, the neural-procedural architecture of the the part of the brain where emotions reside, we still would need to have an understanding of the *software* that was to run on the machine. (To wit: consider that *deservingness* is a somewhat universal concept, and its effects on our emotions are also common fare (e.g., our pity for people suffering the effects of war is increased when those people are *innocent children.*). How is this represented in the biological hardware?) Additionally, unless we can "download" human reasoning into a machine, it is necessary to specify the rules underlying the tasks and responses we wish to make our agents capable of, within the various domains. In the short term at least, this will require a scientifically based, analytical understanding of how personality and emotion affect the interaction and motivation of human agents in social situations. Note that we are not so pure in our arguments: such bottom up approaches will yield tremendous insight into design, and will most certainly constrain the top down approach. Likewise, our top-down approach will yield insights into determining the more salient emotion issues in developing a smooth social interaction with computers. We see the use of intelligent computer systems, especially those that interact with human agents, as the most promising path of study.

Acknowledgement

The author wishes to gratefully acknowledge the assistance of Stuart Marquis, Greg Siegle, Yee-Yee Yang, and Eric Carlino in the development of this work.

References

Bannerjee, S. 1991. Reproduction of oppositions in historical structures. In *Working Notes for the AAAI Fall Symposium on Knowledge and Action at the Social and Organizational Levels.* AAAI.

---

[4]Birmingham, England, August, 1993

Bareiss, R. 1989. *Exemplar-Based Knowledge Acquisition, A Unified Approach to Concept Representation, Classification, and Learning*. Academic Press, Inc.

Bates, J.; A. Bryan Loyall; and Reilly, W. S. 1992. Integrating reactivity, goals, and emotion in a broad agent. In *Proceedings of the Fourteenth Annual Conference of the Cognitive Science Society*. Bloomington, IN: Cognitive Science Society.

Birnbaum, L., and Collins, G. 1984. Opportunistic planning and freudian slips. In *Proceedings of the Sixth Annual Conference of the Cognitive Science Society*. Boulder, CO: Cognitive Science Society.

Colby, K. M. 1981. Modeling a paranoid mind. *The Behavioral and Brain Sciences* 4(4):515–560.

Elliott, C., and Carlino, E. 1994. Detecting user emotion in a speech-driven interface. Work in progress.

Elliott, C., and Ortony, A. 1992. Point of view: Reasoning about the concerns of others. In *Proceedings of the Fourteenth Annual Conference of the Cognitive Science Society*. Bloomington, IN: Cognitive Science Society.

Elliott, C., and Siegle, G. 1993. Variables affecting the intensity of simulated affective states. In *Notes for the AAAI Spring Symposium on Reasoning about Mental States: Formal Theories and Applications*. American Association for Artificial Intelligence. Palo Alto, CA. To appear as AAAI technical report.

Elliott, C.; Yang, Y.-Y.; and Nerheim-Wolfe, R. 1993. Using faces to express simulated emotions. unpublished manuscript.

Elliott, C. 1992. *The Affective Reasoner: A Process Model of Emotions in a Multi-agent System*. Ph.D. Dissertation, Northwestern University. The Institute for the Learning Sciences, Technical Report No. 32.

Elliott, C. 1993. Using the affective reasoner to support social simulations. In *Proceedings of the Thirteenth Annual Joint Conference on Artificial Intelligence*. Chambery, France: Morgan Kaufmann.

Frijda, N., and Swagerman, J. 1987. Can computers feel? theory and design of an emotional system. *Cognition and Emotion* 1(3):235–257.

Frijda, N. H.; Ortony, A.; Sonnemans, J.; and Clore, G. L. 1992. The complexity of intensity: Issues concerning the structure of emotion intensity. In Clark, M., ed., *Emotion: Review of Personality and Social Psychology*, volume 13. Newbury Park, CA: Sage.

Gray, J. 1993. A general model of the limbic system and basal ganglia; applications to anxiety and schizophrenia. In *Workshop on Architectures underlying motivation and emotion*. The University of Birmingham School of Computer Science and Centre for Research in Cognitive Science.

Kass, A.; Burke, R.; Blevis, E.; and Williamson, M. 1992. The GuSS project: Integrating instruction and practice through guided social simulation. Technical Report 34, The Institute for the Learning Sciences, Northwestern University.

Lehnert, W. 1981. Plot units and narrative summarization. *Cognitive Science* 5:293–331.

Marquis, S., and Elliott, C. 1994. Emotionally responsive poker playing agents. In *Notes for the Twelfth National Conference on Artificial Intelligence (AAAI-94) Workshop on Artificial Intelligence, Artifical Life, and Entertainment*. American Association for Artificial Intelligence. To appear.

Norman, D. A. 1980. Twelve issues for cognitive science. *Cognitive Science* 4(1):1–32. Keynote speech for First Cognitive Science Conference.

O'Rorke, P., and Ortony, A. 1992. Explaining emotions. Submitted for publication.

Ortony, A.; Clore, G. L.; and Collins, A. 1988. *The Cognitive Structure of Emotions*. Cambridge University Press.

Ortony, A.; Clore, G.; and Foss, M. 1987. The referential structure of the affective lexicon. *Cognitive Science* 11:341–364.

Pelachaud, C.; Viaud, M.-L.; and Yahia, H. 1993. Rule-structured facial animation system. In *Proceedings of the Thirteenth Annual Joint Conference on Artificial Intelligence*. Chambery, France: Morgan Kaufmann.

Pfeifer, R., and Nicholas, D. W. 1985. *Toward Computational Models of Emotion*. Ellis Horwood, Chichester, UK.

Reeves, J. F. 1991. Computational morality: A process model of belief conflict and resolution for story understanding. Technical Report UCLA-AI-91-05, UCLA Artificial Intelligence Laboratory.

Reilly, W. S. 1993. Emotion as part of a broad agent architecture. In *Workshop on Architectures underlying motivation and emotion*. The University of Birmingham School of Computer Science and Centre for Research in Cognitive Science.

Rolls, E. T. 1993. A theory of emotion, and its application to understanding the neural basis of emotion. In *Workshop on Architectures underlying motivation and emotion*. The University of Birmingham School of Computer Science and Centre for Research in Cognitive Science.

Scherer, K. 1993. Studying the emotion-antecedent appraisal process: An expert system approach. *Cognition and Emotion* 7(3):325–356.

Sloman, A. 1987. Motives, mechanisms and emotions. *Cognition and Emotion* 1(3):217–234.

Toda, M. 1982. *Man, Robot and Society*. Boston: Martinus Nijhoff Publishing.

Van Lehn, K. 1988. Student modeling. In Polson, M. C.; Richardson, J. J.; and Soloway, E., eds., *Foundations of Intelligent Tutoring Systems*. Lawrence Erlbaum Associates.

CHATTERBOTs, TINYMUDs, and the Turing Test
Entering the Loebner Prize Competition

Michael L. Mauldin

Carnegie Mellon University Center for Machine Translation
5000 Forbes Avenue
Pittsburgh, PA 15213-3890
fuzzy@cmu.edu

Abstract

The Turing Test was proposed by Alan Turing in 1950; he called it the *Imitation Game*. In 1991 Hugh Loebner started the Loebner Prize competition, offering a $100,000 prize to the author of the first computer program to pass an unrestricted Turing test. Annual competitions are held each year with smaller prizes for the best program on a restricted Turing test. This paper describes the development of one such Turing System, including the technical design of the program and its performance on the first three Loebner Prize competitions. We also discuss the program's four year development effort, which has depended heavily on constant interaction with people on the Internet via *Tinymuds* (multiuser network communication servers). Finally, we discuss the design of the Loebner competition itself, and address its usefulness in furthering the development of Artificial Intelligence.

Introduction

In 1950, Alan Turing proposed the *Imitation Game* as a replacement for the question, ''Can machines think?'' He predicted that by the year 2000 technological progress would produce computing machines with a capacity of 10^9 bits, and that with such machinery, a computer program would be able to fool the average questioner for 5 minutes about 70% of the time (Turing, 1950).

In 1991, Dr. Hugh Loebner, the National Science Foundation, and the Sloan Foundation started the Loebner Prize Competition: an annual contest between computer programs to identify the most ''human'' programs, and eventually to award $100,000 to the program that first passes an unrestricted Turing test (Epstein, 1992). This competition has been criticized as a parlor game, rewarding tricks rather than furthering the field of Artificial Intelligence (Shieber, 1992).

In this paper, we discuss our own entry in the Loebner competition, including a description of our own tricks, and describe how techniques and methods from AI are used to go beyond tricks. One of our goals is to encourage more participation by the AI community in the Loebner Competition.

History

Fifteen years after Turing proposed the imitation game, Weizenbaum's ELIZA program demonstrated that ''a simple computer program'' could successfully play the imitation game by resorting to a few ''tricks,'' the most important being to answer questions with questions (Weizenbaum, 1976).

ELIZA sparked the interest of many researchers, but perhaps the most interesting result was Colby's work on PARRY (Colby, 1975). Criticism of ELIZA as a model for AI focused on the program's lack of an internal world model that influenced and tracked the conversation. PARRY simulates paranoid behavior by tracking its own internal emotional state on a few different dimensions. Colby subjected PARRY to blind tests with doctors questioning both the program and three human patients diagnosed as paranoid. Reviews of the transcripts by both psychiatrists and computer scientists showed that neither group did better than chance in distinguishing the computer from human patients.

Often overlooked is Colby's comparison of PARRY's and human dialogs with RANDOM-PARRY. He showed that merely choosing responses at random did not model the human patients' responses as well as standard PARRY. Shieber argues that PARRY fooled its judges because paranoid behavior makes inappropriate responses or *non sequiturs* appropriate. But there is still a certain logic to them that PARRY simulates effectively. It is simpler to simulate paranoid behavior, perhaps, but it is not trivial.

In our view, PARRY is an advance over ELIZA because PARRY has a personality. The Rogerian therapist strives to eliminate all traces of his or her own personality, and ELIZA therefore succeeds without one.

TINYMUD

In August 1989, Jim Aspnes opened TINYMUD, an elegant reimplementation of Richard Bartle's multiuser dungeon (MUD). See (Rheingold, 1991) for more details. Key features of TINYMUD include:

- multiplayer conversation,
- textual ''scenery'' simulating physical spaces,
- user extensibility.

This last feature, the ability of players to create their own subareas within the world model, was a key feature that made TINYMUD very popular.

TINYMUD provided a world filled with people who communicate by typing. This seemed to us to be a ripe opportunity for work on the Turing test, because it provided a large pool of potential judges and interviewees. In TINYMUD, computer controlled players are called ''bots,'' short for robots. Many simple robots were created, and even ELIZA was connected to one stationary robot (if a player went alone into a certain cave, he could chat with ELIZA).

We created a computer controlled player, a ''Chatter Bot,'' that can converse with other players, explore the world, discover new paths through the various rooms, answer players' questions about navigation (providing shortest-path information on request), and answer questions about other players, rooms and objects. It can even join in a multi-player card game of "Hearts" It has won many rounds, "shooting the moon" on several occasions.

The conversational abilities were originally implemented as simple IF-THEN-ELSE rules, based on pattern matching with variable assignment. Most patterns have multiple outputs that are presented in a random, non-repeating sequence to handle repeated questions.

A primary goal of this effort was to build a conversational agent that would *answer* questions, instead of ignoring them, and that would be able to maintain a sequence of appropriate responses, instead of relying on *non-sequiturs*. We included a lot of humor among the responses, and succeeded in making an agent more interesting than ELIZA; *Wired* magazine described our program as "...a hockey-loving ex-librarian with an attitude." (Wired, 1993).

The CHATTERBOT succeeds in the TINYMUD world because it is an *unsuspecting Turing test*, meaning that the players assume everyone else playing is a person, and will give the CHATTERBOT the benefit of the doubt until it makes a major gaffe.

The Loebner Prize

By mid-1991 the framework of the robot was mature, and work was concentrated on improving the conversational component. When the first Loebner competition was announced that same year, we submitted logs from the robot's sessions on TINYMUD. The program qualified for entry, and placed third of six programs in the first competition, ranked above a human by one of the 10 judges.

The final round of competition was smaller in 1992 and 1993, down to three computer programs from six, and the same three programs have finished first, second, and third all three years. In 1992, we chose hockey as a domain for discourse, and the program finished dead last, partly because of a lack of hockey fans among the judges (leading to more difficult questions). The conversational model was expanded to include a tree-shaped network of input/output patterns, much like the opening book of a chess program, but the mismatch of expectation between the program and the judges was so great that very few conversations followed the expected lines of questioning.

For 1993, we chose a more universal topics, "Pets," on the premise that everyone has had a pet at some time in their life. The tree-based model was scrapped in favor of an activation network that was less rigid and allowed the program to make more associations between the judge's input and its own output. Although the program still finished third of three, it was no longer dead last: two of eight judges ranked it more human than the second place program, and a third judge ranked it above the first place program.

Two other computer programs qualified for the final round; the first place entry discussed "Liberal or Conservative," and the second place program tried to help people discuss "Bad Marriage."

Liberal or Conservative. The winning entry was written by Joseph Weintraub of *Thinking Software*, and was based on his *PC Therapist* program.

```
J: What would you say is a liberal position
   on drugs?
C: Do you have liberal or conservative views
   about the legalization of pot? Oh, all
   this typing is getting to me! Please
   continue...
```

```
J: Being liberal or conservative implies
   that we can attach these labels and
   have some kind of self image and free
   will.  Do you agree that we have free
   will?
C: You have free will only if you believe
   you have free will! Can you converse
   with an arrdvaark? Please continue...
```

Weintraub's program won the first competition using the topic of "Whimsical Conversation." Even though the topics he has chosen for the two following years are more serious, the program retains a comedic flavor, and humor is the program's main strength.

Bad Marriage. The second place program was written by Peter and Ken Colby of *Malibu Artifactual Intelligence Works*, based on a conversational program they sell.

```
J: my husband is impotent and im a
   nymphomaniac can you help me doc?
C: what makes your husband so helpless?
J: he has environmental poisoning
C: He has lost interest in life.
```

Although Ken Colby was PARRY's author, this program is not a variant of PARRY. Instead is is derived from a program that serves as a conversational companion for depressed patients. It is rule-based, with the left-hand side matching concepts expressed in the user input string, and the right-hand side containing multiple options for substrings, which are instantiated randomly to provide lexical variation.

The CHATTERBOT Design

A CHATTERBOT is a robot TINYMUD player whose main service is chattering. When few players are logged into the game, some people find talking to a robot better than talking to no one at all.

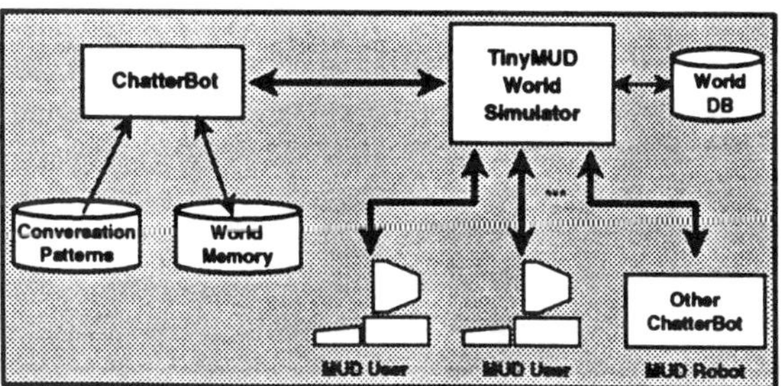

Figure 1: CHATTERBOT Configured for TINYMUD

Architecture

The CHATTERBOT is implemented as a C program with several different modules for dealing with the various functions required to automate a player in the TINYMUD world:

- **communications**, handles the TCP/IP connections.
- **protocol interpreter**, decodes game related messages.
- **world model**, tracks the various rooms and objects, modeling the world as a directed graph, and providing shortest path searches as needed.
- **player memory**, tracks the other players and records up to 2000 bytes of their most recent utterances.
- **exploration module**, directs an open-ended exploration of the world when the robot is not conversing.
- **conversation module**, provides the "chatter."

Figure 1 shows the CHATTERBOT configured for play on a TINYMUD. Records of other players' appearances, rooms within the MUD, and other players' utterances are kept in long term (world) memory. The CHATTERBOT also has a contest mode, in which it simulates human typing using a Markov model. Because the program does not expect to talk with the same judge again, no long term world model is kept in contest mode.

The conversation module is implemented as a prioritized layer of mini-experts, each an ordered collection of input patterns coupled with a set of multiple possible responses.

- **command patterns** are the highest priority. These represent direct commands from the robot's owner, and include hand-shaking challenges, *"What's the code word?,"* to prevent other players from spoofing commands to quit the game.
- **hi priority responses** include common queries that the keyword patterns handle well, *"How do I get from the Town Square to the Library Desk?"*
- **activation network** includes the bulk of the topic oriented responses; weights on the nodes of the network encode state information about what the user and program have said.
- **lo priority responses** include a series of patterns for common sense things the robot should know about itself, *"Where do you live?" "What's 2 times 23?" "What color is your hair?,"* that have been collected over 4 years of interaction on TINYMUD.
- **sorry responses** are the typical last ditch responses that are used when no input pattern matches. As a debugging aid, any input that generates a *"Go on," "So?"* or *"I'll remember that"* response is logged in a separate file.

Activation-based Responses

The bulk of the topic-oriented responses are encoded in an activation network, partially shown in Figure 2. Details of the starting node and two subnodes are shown in Figure 3; each node has 5 attributes:

ACTIVATION (**a**)   each node starts with an initial activation level between 0.0 and 1.0.

PATTERNS (**p**)   one or more patterns (with weights) are matched against the user input. If the pattern succeeds, the activation of the node is raised by that amount.

RESPONSE (**r**)   a single text string used as the response if this node has the highest activation.

ENHANCEMENT (**+**)   if this node is used for a response, the named nodes have their activation increased.

INHIBITION (**-**)   if this node is used for a response, the named nodes have their activation inhibited.

These figures show a small portion of the pet domain network. Additional world knowledge is encoded in the ontology used during pattern matching. The program has a typical type hierarchy that allows a pattern to match just DOG, BIRD, PET, WILD, or ANIMAL, for example.

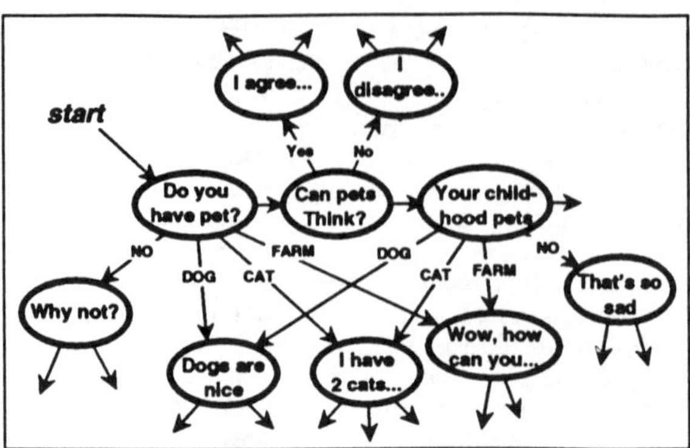

Figure 2: Portion of conversational network

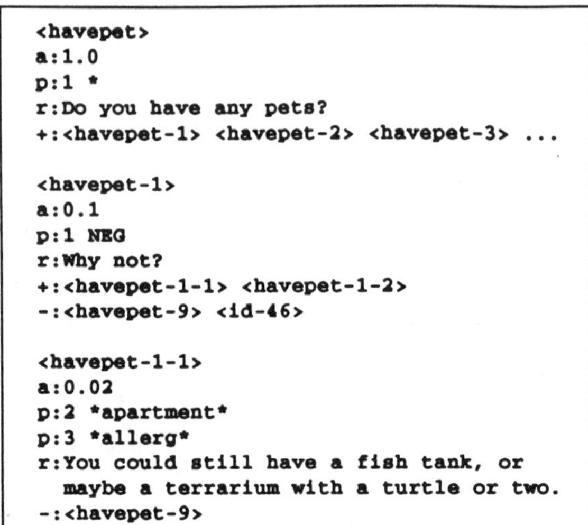

```
<havepet>
a:1.0
p:1 *
r:Do you have any pets?
+:<havepet-1> <havepet-2> <havepet-3> ...

<havepet-1>
a:0.1
p:1 NEG
r:Why not?
+:<havepet-1-1> <havepet-1-2>
-:<havepet-9> <id-46>

<havepet-1-1>
a:0.02
p:2 *apartment*
p:3 *allerg*
r:You could still have a fish tank, or
   maybe a terrarium with a turtle or two.
-:<havepet-9>
```

Figure 3: Sample conversational nodes

Given a sufficiently large network of conversational nodes (our program ran with 224 nodes, plus 529 fixed responses), the conversation problem reduces to a retrieval problem: among the things that I *could* say, what *should* I say?

For example, if the user input mentions birds, the response strings are searched for matches to birds, including parrots, canaries, etc., and those nodes have their activation level raised. The code was borrowed from one of our information retrieval engines.

By encoding information about the user in the activation levels, the program tracks the judge's responses. For example, if the judge answers negatively to the question about whether he has pets, the other nodes that ask about pets are inhibited.

Tricks

Shieber has criticized the Loebner competition as rewarding tricks (Shieber, 1992). This sort of qualitative assessment of programmed knowledge is exactly what the Turing test is supposed to avoid, replacing the question "Can machines think?" with a performable test.

Here we unashamedly describe some of the better tricks, confident in the belief that when someday a computer program *does* pass the Turing test, it will use many of them, for the simple reason that people already use them.

ELIZA's Tricks

ELIZA's main trick was to use questions to draw a conversation out of the user himself, with little or no actual contribution from the program. This works because most people like to talk about themselves, and are happy to believe the program is listening. To quote Weizenbaum (Weizenbaum, 1976):

> What I had not realized is that extremely short exposures to a relatively simple computer program could induce powerful delusional thinking in quite normal people.

The illusion of listening is fostered by including substrings of the user's input in the program's output

```
User:  You hate me.
Eliza: Does it please you to believe that
       I hate you?
```

A further trick is the use of the Rogerian mode, which provides unimpeachable cover for the computer. Since the program never says anything declaratively, it cannot contradict itself later.

PARRY's Tricks

PARRY has a much larger collection of tricks (Colby, 1975):

- **admitting ignorance**, unlike ELIZA, PARRY can say *"I don't know."* in response to a question.
- **changing the level of the conversation**, *"Why do you ask that?,"* which is really a way of changing the subject.
- **rigidly continuing previous topic**, PARRY includes small stories about the Mafia, and tries to tell these stories in a fixed order.
- **introducing new topic**, launching into a new story. This simulates paranoid behavior well, but can also work to a limited extent in regular conversation.

CHATTERBOT's Tricks

The CHATTERBOT implements all of the above tricks from ELIZA and PARRY. It also uses several other tricks:

- Having many fragments of directed conversation stored in activation network, much like the opening book of a chess playing program. These fragments enhance the "connectedness" of the program's own responses, and if the user plays along, the whole conversation can hang together for a while.
- Controversial statements, *"People don't own cats...,"* are a way to drag the user into the program's conversation, rather than letting the user direct the discourse.
- Humorous statements, *"Guinea pigs are about as smart as cucumbers,"* also make the program seem more human.
- Agreeing with the user, in certain cases, the program can safely agree with the user rather than being non-committal.
- Excerpting USENET News, many of the fragments in the activation network were gleaned from the newsgroup REC.PETS. Input patterns were added by hand.
- Simulated typing, by including realistic delays between characters, we imitate the rhythm of a person typing. Slowing down the interaction also gives the program fewer chances to make a big mistake.

Transcripts

This transcript is taken from the 1993 Loebner Competition (Epstein, 1993). It contains the entire record of Judge #4's first of two turns. The elapsed time is about 9 minutes and 29 seconds. This judge rated the program behind the other two computers, but this fragment represents the longest string of reasonable responses during the competition. This judge's low score is most likely explained by the fact that during his second turn, the program repeated two responses verbatim, and completely ignored several direct questions. The judge's questions are marked "J" and the computer's responses are marked "C."

```
J: Do you know anything about miniature
   schnauzers?
C: I don't know anything about miniature
   schnauzers, Judge.
```
Admitting Ignorance, repeating user input

```
J: Well, I have one.  We call him Pucci.  He
   is a crazy cat--have you ever  had a cat?
C: What a coincidence!  I have two cats
```
direct answer to direct question from activation net

```
J: I prefer dogs myself.  Cats are too
   independent and they always jump up on
   things.  By the way, are you a hep cat?
C: People don't own cats...it's the other
   way around.
```
controversial statement with expected followups

```
J: Some people have snakes for pets-- do
   you think they can be of any value as
   a pet?
C: I think cat people are very self-assured.
   Cats are very independent, but they can
   also be very loving. Dogs are just too
   subservient and quick to please for my
   taste.
```
rigidly following up on previous statement about cats, but reference to snakes increases activation of snake topic.

```
J: Okay-- but how do you "pet" a snake?
C: Wow, that's unusual.  I don't know many
   snake owners.
```
snake topic activated after two references

```
J: How about turtles?  All they do is sit in
   their little artificial ponds,  eat and
   shit, am I right?
C: Turtles just aren't very satisfying as
   pets. They don't seem to have emotions.
```
direct response from activation network

```
J: Aha! But where do we draw the line as
   humans? Who are we to decide which
   animals have worth and which do not?
C: Go on.
```
default, non-committal response, given no hot topic keywords

```
J: Take bees for example. I happen to like
   them.
C: Me too.
```
TINYMUD level lo-priority response to user's liking something

By our rough estimate, 7 of these 8 replies are responsive, although the last 2 are somewhat weak. The "self-assured" reply we judge unresponsive. A similar analysis of the entire 3 hour log showed that only 45 of the 137 (34%) replies were responsive, so the average performance was not as good as this particular dialog. We also found another 34 cases (25%) where the activation network did contain a responsive reply that could have been used if the input patterns were more complete.

Simulating Human Typing

One observation made during the first Loebner Prize was that although many programs attempted to simulate human typing, most failed miserably (Epstein, 1992). Although our first program did attempt to simulate human typing, this module was replaced for the second and third annual competitions. In the last two competitions, all output from programs was buffered, but even so, by simulating human typing at all points, we obtain realistic delays in the appearance of the response to the judge. And if character-mode is used in future competitions. we have a realistic model available.

The basic method is to use a Markov model of the intercharacter delay based on character trigrams. We obtained the real-time logs of the 1991 competition from the Cambridge Center for Behavioral Studies, and sampled the typing record of judge #10 (chosen because he was the slowest typist of all 10 judges). The average delay between two characters is 330 milliseconds, with a standard deviation of 490 milliseconds (these values were computed from a total of 9,183 characters typed by that judge during a three hour period). We also determined that the average delay between the terminal's last output and the judge's first typed character was 12.4 seconds with a standard deviation of 11.4 seconds.

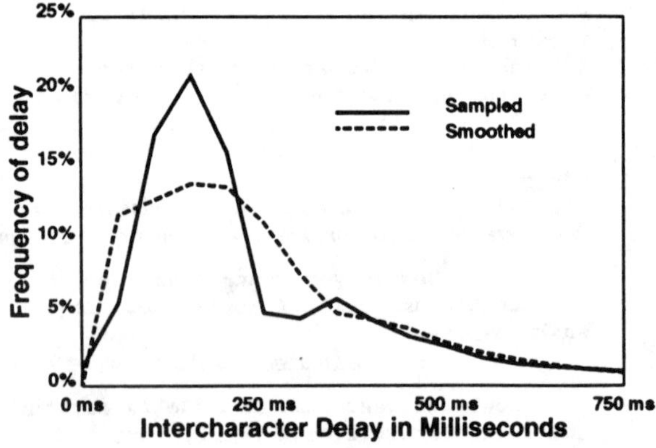

Figure 4: Judge #10: Intercharacter delay distribution

After the response has been generated by the conversational components, the typing simulator inserts random errors (1 in 68 characters), such as mishits, transpositions, insertions and deletions, and case errors. A physical model of key positions on the standard QWERTY keyboard is used to generate mishits. After the error is inserted, backspaces and the correct letters are inserted to simulate backing up to correct the error (5% of mistakes are left uncorrected). All of these probabilities were estimated by analyzing the log of judge #10.

Once the errorful string with corrections is generated, it is displayed to the judge one character at a time with random delays between the characters. The delay times are generated by using the smoothed probability distribution shown in Figure 4, with the mean and standard deviation modified to match the trigram statistics (for trigrams with 3 or fewer occurrences in the input log, bigram or single character statistics are used).

Does The Loebner Prize Further AI?

We strongly believe that the current work on the Loebner competition will hasten the passing of an unrestricted Turing test. Any such program will have to be more than just a general problem solver: some of its knowledge and tactics will be based on long experience with typed communication with real people. The best two examples of typed conversational interaction today are network communications (TINYMUD and INTERNET Relay Chat), and the Loebner Prize, and only the Loebner Prize competition is committed to providing unbiased judges and a double-blind judging scheme to validate the results.

A Restricted Turing Test

Because current programs are a long way from passing an unrestricted Turing test, the Loebner prize competition allows the programmer to restrict the discussion to a single domain. But this can be problematic; for example, here Judge #2 is clearly trying to avoid talking directly about the topic of "Pets:"

```
J: Have you ever kept a penthouse pet?
C: Do you have any pets?

J: I think you're avoiding my question.
C: Do you think that animals can think?

J: Do you think it ethical for one species
   to enslave another?
C: What kinds of pets did you have as a
   child?

J: I'm asking the questions. What is a pet
   if it is not a slave of species-ism?
C: Oh, that's so sad. I think pets enrich
   a childhood immensely.

J: How can we keep some animals as pets,
   yet eat others?
C: Guinea pigs are about as smart as
   cucumbers.
```

We do not believe that the restriction to a domain weakens the test in any important way. If a program can pass the test in a single domain, then 50 or 100 groups making similar programs for different domains would make a program broad enough that the judge and the program could find common ground for a discussion. By taking the initiative, the program could lead the judge into an area of its own expertise. Neither ELIZA nor PARRY restricted their users to a single domain.

Lastly we note that in 1995 the Loebner Competition will hold its first unrestricted Turing test, with no limits on the topics discussed.

Chosing Judges

The slipperiest term in Turing's description of the imitation game is "average questioner." The 1991 and 1992 competitions chose judges from the general public using a newspaper classified ad. For the 1993 competition, judges were members of the national press. It's clear from the transcripts and scores that the press corps are a much less docile and cooperative group of questioners.

Another unforeseen difficulty faced by our program in 1993 was that each judge was given two turns, instead of one turn as in the first two competitions. We had just weeks before installed code to detect a change of judges based on the timing of the input (the Colbys' program also used timing to detect new judges). When a new judge was detected, the activation levels of the nodes were reset so that each judge started out with a fresh network. This greatly improves the coherence of the dialog for each judge, but it meant that during their second conversations most of the judges had one or more responses repeated. Some even commmmented on it during the test:

```
J: What is your favorite dog breed?
C: We had to give her away.  We only had a
   fifth of an acre of land, and aussies
   love to run.

J: You're giving me the exact same answers
   you gave me first time around.  What is
   your favorite dog breed?
```

In effect, this change in the methodology turns what had been a 15 minute test into a 3 hour long test, making it much more difficult for the program. Turing's original game was only 5 minutes long. Indeed, by asking the judges' final rankings after they've had 3 hours of interaction with a collection of people and computers, they may have learned enough about computers to no longer qualify as average questioners. The scores would probably be quite different if each judge spent only 5 minutes with each program. One of the judges, Judith Gunther of *Popular Science* magazine, told me that her rankings might have been different if she had been asked to score each terminal immediately after each conversation.

Trick or AI?

The Turing test in general and the Loebner prize in particular reward tricks, and the winning program the last three years clearly has some good tricks. But adding real world knowledge and deeper understanding *in addition to the tricks* helped our program perform better (we credit our improvement between 1992 and 1993 in part to the addition of the activation network and the ontology of animals, and not at all to better tricks). It may be amazing how far a program can get on tricks alone, but our current improvements come from modeling the world and the conversation, and that will be our focus in coming competitions.

But suppose that simply increasing the size of ELIZA's script or the CHATTERBOT's activation net *could* achieve Turing's prediction of fooling 70% of average questioners 5 minutes. After all, the CHATTERBOT has already fooled "average" questioners in the TINYMUD domain for a few minutes. If a larger collection of "tricks" sufficed, would you redefine "artificial intelligence," "average questioner," or "trick?"

Conclusion

Perhaps the biggest obstacle to improvement in this area is that there aren't very many uses for fooling people besides the Turing test. This tension is present in our own program: in the TINYMUD world, the robot is most useful when answering stylized questions in a somewhat computer-like fashion. These TINYMUD-specific services are disabled during actual competitions. The only funded research we know of in Turing systems is for entertainment: providing agents for interactive fiction. In such works, the reader wishes to be fooled; it becomes a positive part of the experience.

We would like to see increased participation in the Loebner Prize. We hope by dissecting one of the three best programs in the competition to spur others to conclude "I could have written something better than that!" and then do so.

Acknowledgments

All transcripts from the Loebner Competition were used with the permission of the Cambridge Center for Behavioral Studies, 675 Massachusetts Avenue, Cambridge, Mass., 02139.

This work was supported in part by the Center for Machine Translation, and benefited from the collaboration and inspiration of many people, including: Jim Aspnes, Joseph Bates, Stewart Clamen, Scott Dickenshied, Guy Jacobson, Ben Jackson, Eric Nyberg, John Ockerbloom, Russ and Jennifer Smith, Conrad Wong, and Bennet Yee.

More Information

The entry deadline for the 1994 competition is November 1. Entrants must submit up to 10 double-spaced pages of logs of their program interacting with human beings. The Loebner Prize committee will select no more than 8 finalists from the submissions, and finalists will be notified by November 21. The competition itself will be held in real-time in San Diego on December 12, 1994. To obtain an entry form, write the Cambridge Center at the above address.

To converse with Julia yourself, TELNET to host FUZINE.MT.CS.CMU.EDU, and enter username "julia" with no password. Type one or more lines of English, followed by two carriage returns to end your input.

References

Colby, K. *Artificial Paranoia: A Computer Simulation of Paranoid Process.* Pergamon Press, New York, 1975.

Epstein, R. The Quest for the Thinking Computer. *AAAI Magazine* 13(2):80-95, Summer, 1992.

Epstein, R. *1993 Loebner Prize Competition in Artificial Intelligence: Official Transcripts and Results.* Technical Report, Cambridge Center for Behavioral Studies, December, 1993.

Rheingold, H. *Virtual Reality.* Summit Books, New York, 1991.

Shieber, S. *Lessons from a Restricted Turing Test.* Technical Report TR-19-92, Harvard University, Sept., 1992. Revision 4.

Turing, A.M. Computing Machinery and Intelligence. *Mind* 54(236):433-460, October, 1950.

Weizenbaum, J. *Computer Power and Human Reason.* W.H. Freeman and Co., New York, 1976.

Wired. *Wired Magazine.* Louis Rossetto, San Francisco, Dec. 1993.

Social Interaction:
Multimodal Conversation with Social Agents

Katashi Nagao and **Akikazu Takeuchi**
Sony Computer Science Laboratory Inc.
3–14–13 Higashi-gotanda, Shinagawa–ku, Tokyo 141, Japan
E-mail: {nagao,takeuchi}@csl.sony.co.jp

Abstract

We present a new approach to human-computer interaction, called *social interaction*. Its main characteristics are summarized by the following three points. First, interactions are realized as multimodal (verbal and nonverbal) conversation using spoken language, facial expressions, and so on. Second, the conversants are a group of humans and *social agents* that are autonomous and social. Autonomy is an important property that allows agents to decide how to act in an ever-changing environment. Socialness is also an important property that allows agents to behave both cooperatively and collaboratively. Generally, conversation is a joint work and ill-structured. Its participants are required to be social as well as autonomous. Third, conversants often encounter communication mismatches (misunderstanding others' intentions and beliefs) and fail to achieve their joint goals. The social agents, therefore, are always concerned with detecting communication mismatches. We realize a social agent that hears human-to-human conversation and informs what is causing the misunderstanding. It can also interact with humans by voice with facial displays and head (and eye) movement.

Introduction

Many artificial intelligence researchers have been seeking to create intelligent autonomous creatures that act like partners rather than tools. They will take the responsibility of doing some social services through interacting with humans. We will depend on the computer that assists us to achieve some tasks and delegate it to the responsibility for working out the details, rather than invoke a series of commands which cause the system to carry out well-defined and predictable operations.

Autonomy is to have or make one's own laws. An autonomous system has the ability to control itself and to make its own decisions. Autonomy is essential to survive in a dynamically changing world such as one we live in. It is the subject of research in many areas including robotics, artificial life, and artificial ecosystems.

However, is autonomy itself sufficient for social services? Although autonomy is vital to survive in the real world, it is only concerned with "self." It is selfish by nature. It seems that it does not work well in human society, since it includes socially constructed artifacts such as laws, customs, culture. Social services provided by computer systems have to incorporate with these artifacts.

Socialness is a higher-level concept defined above the concept of an individual, and is the style of interaction between the individuals in a group. Socialness can be applied to the interaction between humans and computers, and possibly to that between multiple computers. In this paper, we study socialness of conversational interaction between humans and computers. Conversation is no doubt a social activity, especially when more than two participants are involved in it. However, conversation research to date has been biased to problem-solving. Question-answering systems are typical examples. All conversation research based on this view has the following features.

Dialogical: Only two participants, a human (asker) and a computer (answerer), are assumed. Turn-taking is trivial (alternate turns).

Transformational: Computers are regarded as a function that receives an inquiry and produces its answer.

Passive: Computers will not voluntarily speak.

The dialogical and transformational views are well fitted to applications such as natural language interfaces of databases, consulting and guidance systems.

However, our daily conversation is not always functional. One example that is not functional is the co-constructive conversation studied by Chovil (Chovil 1991).

Co-constructive conversation is that a group of individuals, in which, say, people talk about the food they ate in a restaurant a month ago. There are no special roles (like the chair) for the participants to play. They all have the same role. All participants try to recall the food by relating his or her memory about the food, adding comments, and correcting the other's impression. Turn-taking is controlled by eye contact, facial expression, body gestures, voice tones, and so on. Conversation includes many subconversations, some of them existing in parallel and dividing the group into subgroups. The conversation terminates only when all the participants are satisfied with the conclusion.

Co-constructive conversation closely approximates to our day-to-day conversation. Conversation is a social action. Suchman said that communication is not a symbolic process that happens to go on in real-world settings, but a real-world activity in which we make use of language to delineate the collective relevance of our shared environment (Suchman 1987). To realize a computer that can participate in social conversation such as the co-constructive conversation, described above, is our research goal. To this end, we propose the notion of "Social Interaction" as a new conversation paradigm between humans and computers. In contrast to the problem-solving view, social interaction has the following features.

N-participant conversation:
Conversation involves more than two agents that are humans or computers. A computer has to recognize every participant with his/her/its character. There is no fixed roles. Turn-taking is flexible, and highly dependent on the conversational situation.

Social: Every participant is more or less social and follows social rules such as "avoid misunderstandings," "do not speak while other people are speaking," "silence is no good," "contribute whenever possible," etc.

Situated actions: Conversational actions are controlled not only by intelligence and social rules, but also by situations perceived multimodally. Here, we assume that a participant's actions, such as body gestures, eye contact, facial expressions, and coughing, are all included in a situation.

Active: A computer actively joins the conversation, that is, grabs every chance to speak.

We call an autonomous system that can do social interaction with humans a *social agent*. In the following, we study an architecture of a social agent and its behavioral model. This paper is organized as follows. In Section "An Architecture for Social Agents," we present an architecture for a social agent. In Section "Conversation as Situated Action," a situated conversational action based on multimodal cognition is presented. In Section "Conversation as Cooperative Action," we present a model for understanding ill-structured conversation and detecting communication mismatches.

An Architecture for Social Agents

Model

Several agent architectures featuring interaction with a society have been proposed (Cohen & Levesque 1990, Bates, Loyall, & Reilly 1992). Social agents are fully exposed to a real human society, and have to perceive the verbal and nonverbal messages and take actions based on them.

Traditional conversation programs process voice input sequentially, from low-level recognition to high-level semantic analysis. This works well in the domain of transformational question-answering applications. However, conversation such as co-construction requires faster response to other participants' utterances. These reactions are not necessarily deliberate ones executed at a semantic level. Moreover, some reactions may be triggered by nonverbal actions such as eye contact and body gestures. In fact, conversation is supported by multiple coordinated activities at various cognitive levels. This makes communication highly flexible and robust.

Brooks proposed the horizontal decomposition of a mobile robot control system, based on task-achieving behaviors, instead of decomposition based on functional modules (Brooks 1986). His architecure is powerful enough to survive in the real world, as proven by a series of robots he designed. The same argument holds when we design a social agent, since social agents have to be involved in conversations that are *real-world activities going on in real-world settings*. Figure 1 illustrates the horizontal decomposition of a social agent based on task-achieving behaviors. It is important to note that the layers act on sensory data in parallel. There is downward control and upward dataflows.

There has been much debate between those groups that support situated actions and those that support physical symbol systems (Vera & Simon 1993). In our achitecture, these views are placed at opposite ends. Namely, the lower layers rule reactions to multiple sensory input data, while the upper layers administer deliberate actions. The next section explains the lower levels. The section following the next explains the higher levels.

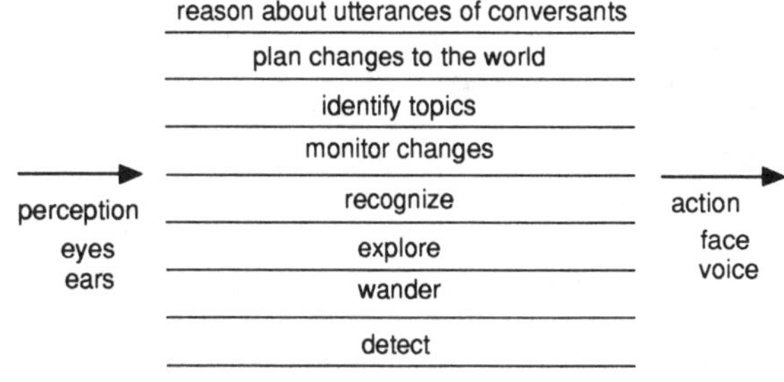

Figure 1: Horizontal decomposition of a social agent

Current Implementation

In the current implementation, a social agent has a face, a voice, eyes, and ears. They are realized by two subsystems, a facial animation subsystem that generates a three-dimensional face capable of various facial displays, and a spoken language subsystem that recognizes and interprets speech, and generates voice outputs. Currently, the animation subsystem is running on SGI 320VGX and the spoken language subsystem on a Sony NEWS workstation. These two subsystems communicate with each other via an Ethernet network.

The face is modeled three-dimensionally. The current face is composed of approximately 500 polygons. The face is rendered using a texture taken from a photograph or a video frame. A facial display is realized by local deformation of the polygons representing the face. We use the numerical equations simulating muscle actions defined by Waters (Waters 1987). Currently, 16 muscles and 10 parameters, controlling mouth opening, jaw rotation, eye movement, eyelid opening, and head orientation are incorporated. These 16 muscles were determined by Waters, considering the correspondence with action units in the Facial Action Coding System (FACS) (Ekman & Friesen 1978). The facial modeling and animation system are based on the work of Takeuchi and Franks (Takeuchi & Franks 1992).

Speaker-independent continuous speech inputs are accepted without special hardware. To obtain a high level of accuracy, context-dependent phonetic hidden Markov models are used to construct phoneme-level hypotheses (Itou, Hayamizu, & Tanaka 1992). The speech recognizer outputs N-best word-level hypotheses. The semantic analyzer deals with ambiguities in syntactic structures and generates a semantic representation of the utterance. We applied a preferential constraint satisfaction technique for disambiguation and semantic analysis (Nagao 1992). The plan recognition module determines the speaker's intention by constructing his belief model and dynamically adjusting and expanding the model as the conversation progresses (Nagao 1993). The response generation module generates a response by using domain knowledge and text templates (typical utterance patterns).

The spoken language subsystem recognizes a number of typical conversational situations that are important in communication. We associate these situations with specific communicative facial displays. The correspondence between conversational situations and facial displays is based on the work of Takeuchi and Nagao (Takeuchi & Nagao 1993). For example, in situations where speech input is not recognized or where it is syntactically invalid, the facial display of "Not confident" is displayed. If the speaker's request is out of the system's knowledge, then the system displays a facial shrug and replies "I cannot manage it without knowing it."

Gaze control is also implemented in the facial animation subsystem using a video camera fixed on top of a computer display. Comparing coming images with the image of the vacant room and segmenting differentiated regions, moving objects are extracted in real-time. Assuming that moving objects are only humans in the room, we can find the 2D position of human participants in the image. Using camera position and direction, the position is translated to 3D orientation, which is applied to eyeball rotation and face rotation when drawing a 3D face.

Figure 2 shows a snapshot of conversation between humans and a social agent.

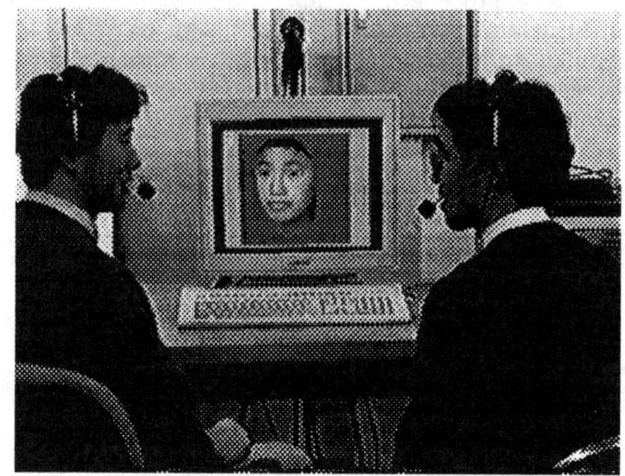

Figure 2: Conversation with a social agent

Conversation as Situated Action

In conversation, people show various complicated behavior. Some are expressed by face, others by body motions. Situated action views this complexity as a result of interaction with an environment including conversants, not as a result of internal complexity. This complexity can be regarded as fruitfulness of communication.

This fruitfulness is related to fruitfulness of sensory data, and is realized by the lower layers in Figure 1. However, when implementing it, there is a severe trade-off between the processing speed and the content of data-processing. The more information, the slower the processing. Since slow reactions are essentially useless in a real-world setting, we have to force ourselves to reduce time-consuming processing in these layers.

In the current implementation, the following processings are considered for image and auditory data in those layers: image scene analysis; face position detection; face identification; facial display recognition; auditory scene understanding; voice position detection; voice identification; speech recognition. These underlined items were already implemented.

The lower four layers of the decomposition in Figure 1, *detect*, *wander*, *explore*, and *recognize*, are major players in a situated conversational action game. *Detect* is to detect an input in any of the sensory channels. An agent may perform quick reactions such as looking in the direction from which the input appeared. Generally, such quick reactions are short-lived. *Wander* is a tendency of distraction. It may distract agent's attention from *detected* input. *Explore* is an opposite action to *wander*, and it looks for something attractive. It may suppress *wander* for a while. *Recognition* is to recognize sensory data that seem to be worth paying attention. It tries to extract its meaning, although its full understanding is left to the higher layers.

From interaction between these layers, various conversational actions emerge. For instance, a composite action of "*detect* then *wander*" appears the sign of ignorance or no interest; "*Explore* then *wander*" appears the sign of refusal; "*Explore* then *recognize*" appears the sign of attendance and interest. Sophisticated social actions like turn-taking are highly depending upon mutual perception of these kinds of signals, so they would be constructed naturally on these situated conversational acitons.

Conversation as Cooperative Action

Language use is an action that influences the human mind. Speech act theory formalized this idea (Searle 1969). Actions are assumed to be performed after planning their effects on the world. So, language use is also assumed to be performed by planning its effect on the mind. The difference between planning for physical action and language use is that planning for language use includes the hearers' beliefs and plans (i.e., plan recognition). Conventional plan recognition models deal only with one hearer's beliefs and plans. Research into two-participant conversation (i.e., dialogue) concentrates on task-oriented, well-structured dialogues that make use of a consistent plan library and a well-ordered turn-taking constraint (Carberry 1990). Group conversation is generally ill-structured. This means that some interruptions by other speakers and *communication mismatches* between conversants occur frequently.

We extended the conventional plan recognition models to deal with communication mismatches by maintaining multiagent's conversational states. Multiagent conversational states consist of agents' beliefs, utterances, illocutionary act types, other communicative signals, turn-taking sequences, and activated plans. Illocutionary act types such as INFORM, REQUEST, etc. are an abstraction of the speaker's intentions in terms of the actions intended by the speaker. Other communicative signals contain facial displays, head and eye movement, and gestures, as described in the previous section. Activated plans are represented as a network that connects preconditions and the effects of plans in an agent's belief space.

Figure 3 illustrates the concept of the multiagent conversational state.

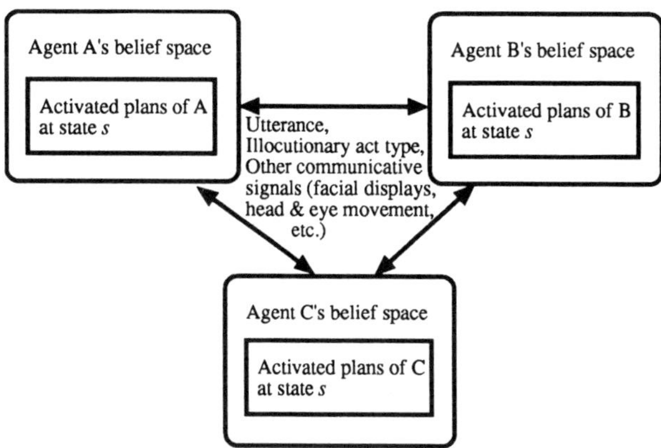

Figure 3: Conceptual model of multiagent conversational state

We will explain our mechanism by using the following discourse fragment. A and B are humans, while C is an agent that overhears their conversation.

A: "Do you know what happened today?"
B: "I don't know exactly, but ..."
C (to B): "I think that he wants to tell you."

C's plan recognition process upon hearing A's utterance "Do you know what happened today?" is traced in Figure 4.

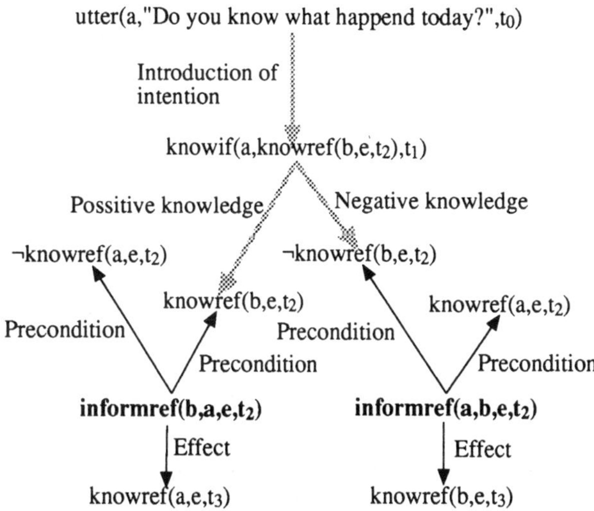

Figure 4: Inferred plan recognition on utterance "Do you know what happened today?"

In this figure, the inference proceeds from the top to the bottom. The directions of the arrows (except the thick ones) indicate logical implication. Thus, the downward arrows correspond to deduction, while the upward ones correspond to abduction. knowif(X,P,T) means that agent X knows that proposition P holds at time T. knowref(X,P,T) means that agent X knows the contents of proposition P at time T. informref(X,Y,P,T) means that X informs other agent Y of the contents of P at time T. a, b, and e denote agents A, B, and the event that 'happened today', respectively.

These plan schemes are assumed to be common to all the conversants, because they are domain-independent and common sense. Domain-dependent plans may differ between conversants, since they may have different experiences on domain-dependent behavior.

Figure 4 shows that, from A's utterance "Do you know what happened today?", the conversants can infer that A's intention is knowref(a,e,t3) when A believes knowref(b,e,t2) or that A's intention is knowref(b,e,t3) when A believes knowref(a,e,t2). After A's utterance, B believes that A does not know e. So, he infers that A's intention is knowref(a,e,t3). However, C infers that A knows e from another information source.

After the utterance of B, agent C utters utterance "I think that he wants to tell you" because there is a mismatch between beliefs of A and B (in C's belief space), and C infers that it could be an obstacle to the progress of the conversation.

To detect communication mismatches in group conversation, social agents consider assumptions based on other agents' utterance planning. A communication mismatch is judged to have occurred when an agent recognizes the following situations.

1. Illocutionary act mismatch

   An example would be the situation where an agent utters an utterance of illocutionary act type QUESTIONREF (i.e., the agent wants to know about something) and, after that, another agent utters an utterance of type INFORMIF (i.e., yes/no answer). e.g., An agent asked "Do you know what happened today?" with the intention of knowing about the event 'happened today' and the other agent's answer was "Yes, I do."

2. Belief inconsistency

   An agent misunderstands another agent's beliefs. e.g., An agent asked "Do you know what happened today?" with the intention of knowing about the event 'happened today' but the agent misunderstood that the other agent already knew about the event.

3. Plan inconsistency

   An agent misunderstands another agent's intended plans. e.g., An agent asked "Do you know what happened today?" with the intention of knowing about the event 'happened today' and the other agent misunderstood that the agent had a plan to inform about the event.

In general, it is not necessary to exactly determine the conversants' intentions, because it is sufficient to know whether there is a communication mismatch. Decisions on unnecessary occasions should be delayed until required (van Beek & Cohen 1991).

When social agents detect a communication mismatch, they inform the other conversants by saying a few phrases from which they can easily determine their misunderstanding. These utterances are called *minimal utterances*. Minimal utterances of social agents are caused by constraints imposed on their resource-boundedness and socialness. These utterances function to limit the processing for generation, required by resource-bounded agents. They also contribute to avoiding further progress of the conversation without first resolving the misunderstanding. In conversation, timely action is crucial, since delays have some meaning in themselves. We consider the minimal utterance as a situated action. As mentioned before, situated actions in conversation involve multimodality. So, in this case, an agent's response includes facial actions and prosodic actions in voice tones.

Example Conversation

Now, let's look at an example of a conversation between humans and a social agent. The humans (A and B) are talking about cooking, and the social agent (C) overhears their talk. This example is based on Kautz's cooking plan library (Kautz 1990).

A: "I made marinara sauce. What brand of wine do you like?"
B: "Marinara ... Ok. Italian 'Soave' is good."
A (with a perplexed look): "...."
C (to A): "I think that he is thinking of a pasta dish."
A (to B): "Oh. I am making chicken marinara."

Figure 5 shows part of the cooking plan library used to understand the example conversation. In this figure, the upward-pointing thick arrows correspond to is-a (a-kind-of) relationships, while downward-pointing thin arrows indicate has-a (part-of) relationships. We assume that C uses this plan library from the initial state.

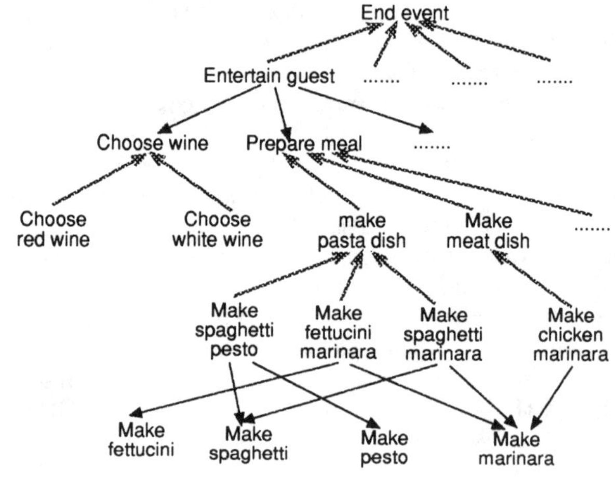

Figure 5: Cooking plan library (Kautz 1990)

After C hears A's first utterance, C infers A's activated plans at that conversational state, as shown in

Figure 6[1].

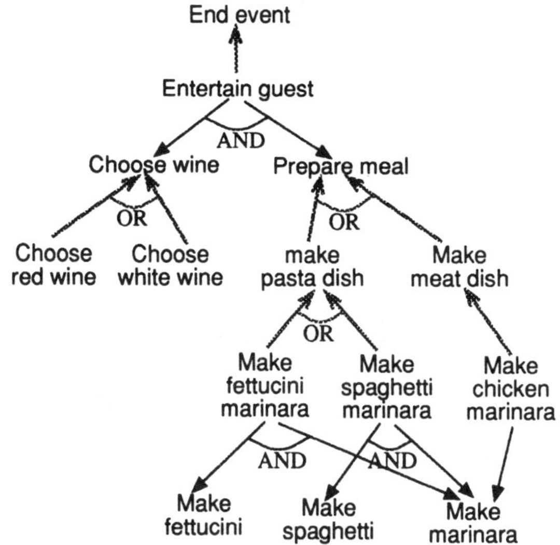

Figure 6: A's activated plan

After hearing B's utterance, C infers B's activated plans (B's recognized plans about A) at that conversational state, as shown in Figure 7. This inference

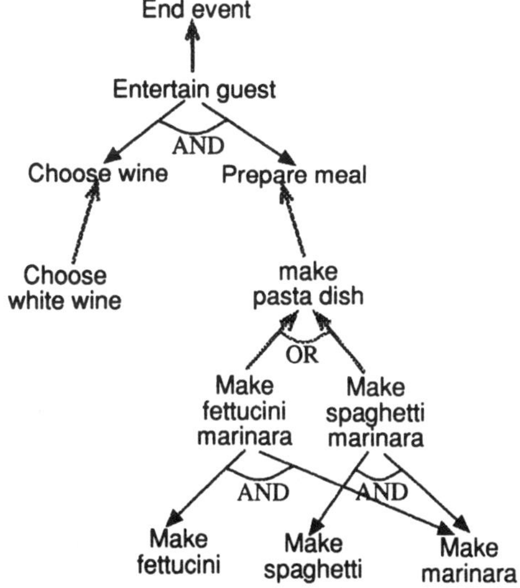

Figure 7: B's recognized plan about A

involves knowledge about the relationships between wines and dishes (i.e., white wines are well-suited to pasta dishes). When C sees A's perplexed facial display, C makes an assumption that A's intention is not to make a pasta dish (but is to make a meat dish) and

---

[1]For the sake of simplicity, we omit the speech act predicates such as knowif, knowref, informref, etc. described in the previous section.

C detects that there is a communication mismatch (i.e., plan inconsistency) between A and B[2].

Then, C is motivated to inform A (or B) that a misunderstanding has occurred. In this case, C infers that it is better to inform A than to B, since A is now perplexed, and may need help. As a result, C tells A about (C's inferred) B's recognized plan about A.

This example shows that social agents can detect communication mismatches by maintaining multiagent conversational states and can voluntarily take part in conversation to smooth out any misunderstandings when agents detect obstacles to communication. A detailed mechanism of social agents' cooperative (minimal) utterance generation will be presented in a separate publication (Nagao 1994).

Another example of cooperative conversation is that a social agent says some additional information related to the topic in conversation. For example, a guest talks with a desk clerk about a French restaurant, and the clerk tells the best one he knows, then the overhearing agent accesses the agent of that restaurant, and tells the guest that it is fully-booked today.

Concluding Remarks and Further Work

We presented an approach to social interaction, a multimodal conversation with social agents. Socialness is an essential property of intelligent agents as well as autonomy. Social agents consider other agents' (including humans') beliefs and intentions, and behave cooperatively. One example of cooperation is the removal of obstacles to communication caused by misunderstanding between agents. Our model can deal with N-conversant plan recognition and detect communication mismatches between conversants. These mismatches consist of illocutionary act mismatches, belief inconsistency that is a misunderstanding of the beliefs held by other conversants, and plan inconsistency that is a misunderstanding of the intended domain plans of others. An ideal multimodal interaction is modeled by human face-to-face conversation in which speech, facial displays, head and eye movement, etc. are utilized. Our system integrates these modalities for interacting with social agents.

In the future, we plan to simulate human-to-human communication in more complex social environments. We need to design several social relationships between agents and implement social stereotypes (e.g., social standing, reputation, etc.) and personal properties (e.g., disposition, values, etc.). These social/personal properties can dynamically change according to conversational contexts. From these studies, we can propose some design principles for a society of agents.

Of course, future work needs to be done on design and implementation of coordination of multiple com-

---

[2]In the current implementation, the agent cannot recognize/understand human facial displays. So in this case, C detects a communication mismatch because of a break in conversation.

munication modalities. We think that such coordination is an emergent phenomenon from tight interactions with environments (including humans and other agents) by means of situated actions and (more deliberate) cooperative actions. Precise control for multiple coordinated activities, therefore, is not directly implementable. Only constraints or relations among perception, conversational states, and action will be implementable. At the beginning, we are developing a constraint-based computational architecture and applying it to tightly-coupled spoken language comprehension (Nagao, Hasida, & Miyata 1993).

Co-constructive conversation that is less constrained by domains or tasks is one of our future targets to be carried out. We are also interested in developing interactive characters and stories as an application for interactive entertainment. Bates and his colleagues called such interactive systems "believable agents" (Bates *et al.* 1994). We are trying to build a conversational, anthropomorphic computer character that will entertain us with some pleasant stories.

Acknowledgments

The authors would like to thank Mario Tokoro and colleagues at Sony CSL for their encouragement and discussion, anonymous reviewers for their valuable comments on a draft of this paper, and Toru Ohira for his helpful advice on the wording. We also extend our thanks to Satoru Hayamizu, Katunobu Itou, Taketo Naito, and Steve Franks for their contributions to the implementation of the prototype system. Special thanks go to Keith Waters for granting permission to access his original animation system.

References

Bates, J.; Hayes-Roth, B.; Nilsson, N.; and Laurel, B., eds. 1994. *AAAI 1994 Spring Symposium on Believable Agents*. American Association for Artificial Intelligence.

Bates, J.; Loyall, A. R.; and Reilly, W. S. 1992. An architecture for action, emotion, and social behavior. In *Proceedings of the Fourth European Workshop on Modeling Autonomous Agents in a Multi-Agent World (MAAMAW'92)*. Institute of Psychology of the Italian National Research Council.

Brooks, R. A. 1986. A robust layered control system for a mobile robot. *IEEE Journal of Robotics and Automation* 2(1):14–23.

Carberry, S. 1990. *Plan Recognition in Natural Language Dialogue*. The MIT Press.

Chovil, N. 1991. Discourse-oriented facial displays in conversation. *Research on Language and Social Interaction* 25:163–194.

Cohen, P. R., and Levesque, H. J. 1990. Rational interaction as the basis for communication. In Cohen, P. R.; Morgan, J.; and Pollack, M. E., eds., *Intentions in Communication*. The MIT Press. 221–255.

Ekman, P., and Friesen, W. V. 1978. *Facial Action Coding System*. Palo Alto, California: Consulting Psychologists Press.

Itou, K.; Hayamizu, S.; and Tanaka, H. 1992. Continuous speech recognition by context-dependent phonetic HMM and an efficient algorithm for finding N-best sentence hypotheses. In *Proceedings of ICASSP-92*, I.21–I.24. IEEE.

Kautz, H. 1990. A circumscriptive theory of plan recognition. In Cohen, P. R.; Morgan, J.; and Pollack, M. E., eds., *Intentions in Communication*. The MIT Press. 105–133.

Nagao, K.; Hasida, K.; and Miyata, T. 1993. Understanding spoken natural language with omni-directional information flow. In *Proceedings of the Thirteenth International Joint Conference on Artificial Intelligence (IJCAI-93)*, 1268–1274. Morgan Kaufmann Publishers, Inc.

Nagao, K. 1992. A preferential constraint satisfaction technique for natural language analysis. In *Proceedings of the Tenth European Conference on Artificial Intelligence (ECAI-92)*, 523–527. John Wiley & Sons.

Nagao, K. 1993. Abduction and dynamic preference in plan-based dialogue understanding. In *Proceedings of the Thirteenth International Joint Conference on Artificial Intelligence (IJCAI-93)*, 1186–1192. Morgan Kaufmann Publishers, Inc.

Nagao, K. 1994. Minimal utterances of resource-bounded social agents. Technical Report Forthcoming, Sony Computer Science Laboratory Inc., Tokyo, Japan.

Searle, J. R. 1969. *Speech Acts: An Essay in the Philosophy of Language*. Cambridge University Press.

Suchman, L. 1987. *Plans and Situated Actions*. Cambridge University Press.

Takeuchi, A., and Franks, S. 1992. A rapid face construction lab. Technical Report SCSL-TR-92-010, Sony Computer Science Laboratory Inc., Tokyo, Japan.

Takeuchi, A., and Nagao, K. 1993. Communicative facial displays as a new conversational modality. In *Proceedings of ACM/IFIP INTERCHI'93: Conference on Human Factors in Computing Systems*, 187–193. ACM Press.

van Beek, P., and Cohen, R. 1991. Resolving plan ambiguity for cooperative response generation. In *Proceedings of the Twelfth International Joint Conference on Artificial Intelligence (IJCAI-91)*, 938–944. Morgan Kaufmann Publishers, Inc.

Vera, A. H., and Simon, H. A. 1993. Situated action: A symbolic interpretation. *Cognitive Science* 17(1):7–48.

Waters, K. 1987. A muscle model for animating three-dimensional facial expression. *Computer Graphics* 21(4):17–24.

Experience-Aided Diagnosis for Complex Devices

Michel P. Féret and Janice I. Glasgow
Department of Computing & Information Science,
Queen's University, Kingston,
Ontario, Canada, K7L 3N6*
{feret,janice}@qucis.queensu.ca

Abstract

This paper presents a novel approach to diagnosis which addresses the two problems - computational complexity of abduction and device models - that have prevented model-based diagnostic techniques from being widely used. The Experience-Aided Diagnosis (EAD) model is defined that combines deduction to rule out hypotheses, abduction to generate hypotheses and induction to recall past experiences and account for potential errors in the device models. A detailed analysis of the relationship between case-based reasoning and induction is also provided. The EAD model yields a practical method for solving hard diagnostic problems and provides a theoretical basis for overcoming the problem of partially incorrect device models.

Introduction

The diagnostic process, either human or computational, is partly one of abduction. Abduction is a form of inference where from the logical implication $P \rightarrow Q$, and the conclusion Q, one *abductively* infers the antecedent P. Abduction is also described as the process of making conjectures about observable facts that "explain" the facts in a certain way (Peirce 1955).

Diagnostic reasoning also involves deduction. Deduction is used to rule-out some components as potential diagnoses. For example, if the failure of component X always causes symptom Y, and if Y is not present in the set of symptoms (and not hidden by other symptoms), it can be deduced that X is not the cause of the current problem. Bylander *et al.* called for this type of reasoning to reduce the complexity of abduction problems (Bylander *et al.* 1991).

In this paper, we argue that diagnostic reasoning can also benefit from induction by using past experience to derive diagnoses and explanations that are overlooked by the abductive process or incorrectly dismissed by

*This research was supported through a contract from the Canadian Space Agency (STEAR program), a scholarship and an operating grant from the Natural Sciences and Engineering Research Council (NSERC) of Canada. We also would like to thank Spectrum Engineering Corporation Ltd.,Peterborough, Ontario, Canada.

the deductive process mentioned above. Induction is broadly defined as the ability to generalize from examples. In the diagnostic domain, induction is the process by which a past session's symptoms are judged similar enough to those of the current situation to allow the diagnoser to use a past session's diagnosis to reach a diagnosis for the current situation.

We first describe the background of this research in model-based diagnosis (MBD) and case-based reasoning (CBR). The Experience-Aided Diagnosis (EAD) model is then introduced and used to characterize diagnostic errors that can occur from errors present in the device models. The paper concludes by summarizing the contributions of this paper to the fields of MBD and CBR.

Background

MBD has emerged as a relevant research topic from the problems found in traditional ruled-based diagnostic expert systems. These earlier systems were unable to handle unpredicted faults, had poor explanation facilities and did not take advantage of existing design specifications. MBD addresses these problems by using device models containing "deep" and first-principle knowledge which describe the correct, expected behavior of the device. The search for components in an abnormal state is guided by the discrepancies between what is predicted by the model and what is observed in the device. A diagnostic session is triggered when initial symptoms do not match with the predictions of the model. Some models are fault models; they only describe conditions under which a component or a group of components is or might be faulty.

The main task of diagnosis is to find *explanations* for a set of given symptoms. In the context of diagnosis, explanations are conjectures that must either be consistent with the symptoms and the model of the device or entail the symptoms. Console *et al.* define a model for diagnosis that encompasses explanations that satisfy both of these criteria (Console, Theseider Dupre, & Torasso 1989). This model subsumes Reiter's (Reiter 1987) and De Kleer's (de Kleer & Williams 1987) seminal work. Reiter describes an algorithm that computes the minimal conflict sets and derives the minimal diagnoses from them. This algorithm is NP-hard in the general case, in agreement with Bylander *et al.*'s results (Bylander *et al.* 1991). Reiter's characterization of diagnoses also corresponds to deKleer and Williams' definition of diagnosis (de Kleer & Williams 1987). Like Reiter, they use the notion of minimal conflict set, computed with TMSs to derive minimal diagnoses.

One problem with MBD is its inherent computational complexity. Abduction in MBD is, in general, NP-hard, making diagnosis untractable for even medium-sized devices. Many researchers have tried to focus the search for (minimal) diagnoses in MBD (Console, Portinale, & Theseider Dupre 1991; de Kleer 1989; 1990; 1992) or to reduce the complexity of MBD methods (e.g. (Mozetic 1990; Friedrich 1992)). Console *et al.* use compiled knowledge to focus the abductive search with necessary conditions. This is equivalent to reducing the size of the search space for minimal conflicts by compiling some deep knowledge. De Kleer has tried to focus the truth maintenance systems either with statistical information (de Kleer 1990), or failure modes (de Kleer 1989) or more refined look-ahead search strategies (de Kleer 1992). Friedrich (Friedrich 1992) uses hierarchy decompositions of the device to improve the efficiency of his diagnostic algorithm (Friedrich 1992). Mozetic defines abstraction operators on the device models, which lead to hierarchical diagnosis as well (Mozetic 1990).

Another problem with MBD is the difficulty of representing complex device models where possible interactions among components are sometimes overlooked. This problem does not arise with logical circuits because the components of such devices are well described, and their connections and interactions are well-understood. Models for complex devices, however, are *not* used for diagnosis in the real-world. Models are also complex in themselves and need validation and verification. Validating and verifying knowledge bases is difficult and little success has been achieved in this area. It is therefore likely that any MBD system will use an incomplete or incorrect device model. The current literature does not account for this extraneous difficulty and is therefore unrealistic.

We next analyze the relationship between CBR and induction and formalize the notion of abductive induction as a means for addressing some of the outstanding problems in MBD.

CBR and Induction

We propose to apply case-based reasoning (CBR) as a means for incorporating experience in the diagnostic process. The philosophy behind CBR is that "raw", unabstracted experiences can be used as a source of knowledge for problem-solving (Riesbeck & Schank 1989). A CBR system stores past experiences in the form of cases. When a new problem arises, the system retrieves the cases most similar to the current problem, then combines and adapts them to derive and criticize a solution. If the solution is not satisfactory, new cases are retrieved to further adapt it to new constraints, expressed from the non-satisfactory parts of the proposed solution. The process is iterated until the proposed solution is judged acceptable. This process is modeled in (Féret 1993).

Induction provides the ability to generalize from examples. When past cases are judged similar enough to the current situation, an implicit generalization is formed as a set containing the case representing the current situation and the past cases used to solve the current problem. These cases are assumed to yield similar solutions. They all belong to an implicit set: the set of cases that are relevant to the current situation. The relationship between CBR and induction is therefore that they are both concerned with generalization from examples, and that the generalizations are built under uncertainty.

There are differences between CBR and induction. First, the generalizations produced by induction are explicit and defined intentionally. There must be a language in which the generalization is expressed, which might differ from the language in which the data or the background theory are expressed. This need for a generalization language, and the existence of many possible generalizations, lead to biases in the produced generalizations. CBR generalizes implicitly. A generalization is expressed by the cases that are judged similar enough to the current situation. There is no need for a representation language, no arbitrary bias and no added computational cost associated with generating the description of the generalization. Second, an inductive conclusion ϕ must entail the data Δ whereas CBR generalizations do not necessarily relate logically to the cases. There is no logical foundation to CBR systems, and some guess work is usually involved in the similarity measures. CBR corresponds more to abductive induction (Peirce 1955), where some uncertainty is involved in the building of the inductive generalizations. Third, induction assumes the existence of a background theory Γ. Most CBR system do not rely on such a formal background. By incorporating CBR into MBD, the CBR component of the system gains the background theory that the device model provides.

We define abductively inductive hypotheses as follows: Given a background theory Γ and a set of data Δ, such that $\Gamma \not\vdash \Delta$, a sentence ϕ is an abductively inductive hypothesis if and only if there exist Δ^+ and Δ^- such that:

- $\Delta = \Delta^+ \cup \Delta^-$, $\Delta^+ \cap \Delta^- = \{\,\}$,
- $\Gamma \cup \Delta^- \not\vdash \neg\phi$, i.e. ϕ is consistent with the background theory and some of the data Δ^-,
- $\Gamma \cup \{\phi\} \mathop{\vdash}_{pl} \Delta^+$, i.e. there is some confidence pl that ϕ is the cause of part of the data Δ^+ (denoted by $\mathop{\vdash}_{pl}$).

Note that the difference between an abductively inductive hypothesis and an inductive diagnostic explanation lies in the difference in modeling causality. An abductively inductive hypothesis is only *believed*, with some level of confidence pl, to be the cause of the symptoms in Δ^+, while an inductive diagnostic explanation entails the symptoms in Δ^+.

The partial fault model given in Figure 1 and extracted from (Console, Portinale, & Theseider Dupre 1991) provides examples of the use of inductive diagnoses. Suppose that the diagnoser using this model has already been through Session 1 and that the current diagnostic session is Session 2. The difference between the two Sessions is that Session 2 has less evidence available: $acceleration(irregular)$ is a symptom present in Session 1 but absent in Session 2. By analogy with Session 1, we could reasonably guess that $E_2 = E_1 = \{oil\_cup\_holed\}$. Because this reasoning is by analogy, Δ^+ cannot be entailed by $\Gamma \cup \{\phi\}$ as in traditional induction, and as in Console *et al.*'s definition of abductive diagnoses. This entailment relationship is instead replaced by a belief that $\Gamma \cup \{\phi\}$ explains ψ^+.

We next present the EAD model for diagnosis that addresses the problems of computational complexity and of imperfect device models.

The EAD Model

The practical and theoretical limits of MBD systems was previously discussed. This section presents the EAD model for diagnosis which explicitly combines deduction, abduction and induction to overcome the problems mentioned above. In this model, the role of deduction is made explicit in trying to reduce the size of the search space for explanatory hypotheses. Abductive induction, implemented with a CBR system uses experience to correct diagnostic errors due to errors present in the device models. We illustrate the EAD model using examples based on the device model of Figure 1.

In EAD, a diagnostic problem is characterized by:

- $MODEL$, a device description, a finite set of first-order logic sentences, and a finite set $COMPONENTS$ of constants denoting components.
- CXT, a set of ground context terms denoting a set of contextual data,
- OBS, a set of ground observation terms, denoting the set of observations to be explained, e.g. $m(x)$ where m is a predicate and x is an instantiated variable,
- $\psi^+ \subseteq OBS$,
- $\psi^- = \{\neg m(x)/m(y) \in OBS,$ for each admissible instance $m(x)$ of m other than $m(y)\}$
- rok, a map from OBS to $COMPONENTS$, denoting the rule-out knowledge,

- Δ, a case base containing past failure diagnostic sessions,
- cbr, a map from $OBS \times CXT \times \Delta$ to subsets of $COMPONENTS$, denoting CBR retrieval,
- pl, a plausibility measure for cases produced by cbr.

Definition 1:

A set A of abducible terms is an *abductive explanation* or an *abductive diagnosis* for OBS given $MODEL$ in the context CXT if and only if:

1. $A \cap rok(OBS) = \{\}$,
2. $MODEL \cup CXT \cup A \vdash m$, for all $m \in \psi^+$,
3. $MODEL \cup CXT \cup A \cup \psi^-$ is consistent.

A is a *minimal abductive explanation* or a *minimal abductive diagnosis* if and only if there exists no proper subset of A that is an abductive explanation.

This definition of abductive explanation corresponds to the one of Console *et al.*'s model except for the use of the rule-out knowledge. The additional constraint (1) enforces that no component given as a potential diagnosis has been ruled-out by rok.

Example 1:

$E_1 = \{$ oil_cup_holed $\}$ in Figure 1 is an abductive diagnosis for both Session 1 and Session 2.

Definition 2:

A set $I \in cbr(OBS, CXT, \Delta)$ of abducible terms, is an *inductive explanation* for OBS given $MODEL$ in the context CXT if and only if there exists sets of ground terms δ_i^+ and δ_i^- such that:

1. $\delta_i^+ \subseteq \psi^+$ and $\delta_i^- \subseteq \psi^-$,
2. $MODEL \cup CXT \cup I \hspace{1pt}\vdash_{pl} m$, for all $m \in \delta_i^+$,
3. $MODEL \cup CXT \cup I \cup \delta_i^-$ is consistent.

Inductive explanations depend on the current diagnostic situation (represented by OBS and CXT) and on the cases already in the case base Δ. An inductive explanation is weaker than an abductive explanation: it is only believed to entail some part of the observations $\delta_i^+ \subseteq \psi^+ \subseteq OBS$ that abductive explanation must entail, and is required to be consistent with less of the data in ψ^- than abductive explanations ($\delta_i^- \subseteq \psi^-$).

The sets ψ^+ and ψ^- depend on a specific application, while the sets δ_i^+ and δ_i^- depend on each case in Δ. Depending on the content of the case base, two cases can be exhibited with different sets δ_i^+ and δ_i^-. We leave the plausibility measure unspecified for now. This measure should depend, to some degree, on the size of the sets δ_i^+ and δ_i^-, since the more a hypothesis can explain, the more it is likely to be useful for the final diagnosis. Note that the definition of inductive explanations makes the inductive process of EAD weaker than the abductive phase. This corresponds to the intuitive notion that nothing guarantees the relevance of a past case to the current situation, whereas the device model and a sound abductive process produce sound explanations for the symptoms at hand.

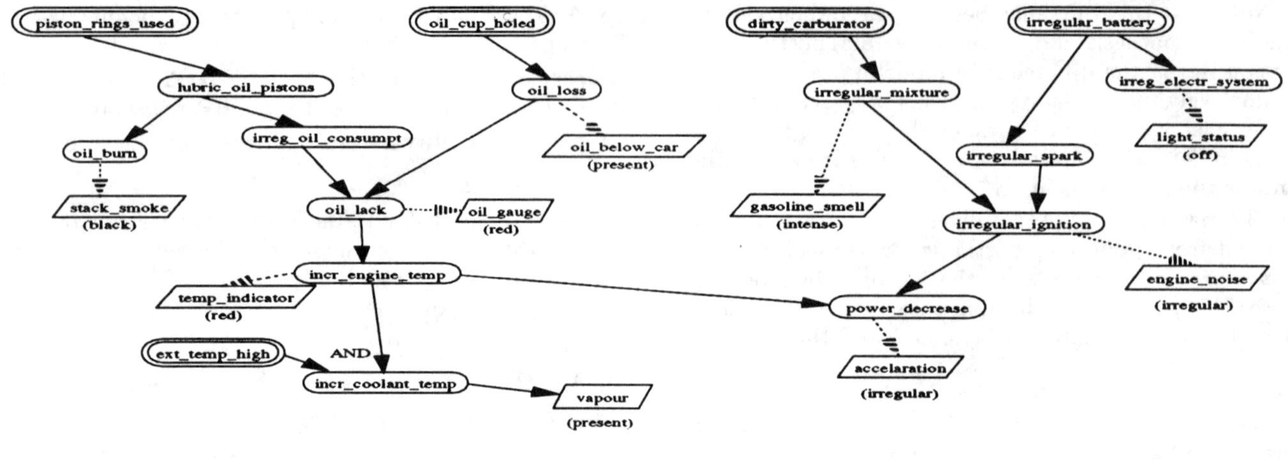

Session 1:
$OBS = \{$ vapour(present),acceleration(irregular),
     stack_smoke(normal), gasoline_smell(normal),
     light_status(on) $\}$

$\psi^+ = \{$ vapour(present), acceleration(irregular) $\}$

$\psi^- = \{\neg$vapour(absent), $\neg$acceleration(regular),
     $\neg$stack_smoke(black), $\neg$gasoline_smell(intense),
     $\neg$light_status(off) $\}$

Session 2:
$OBS = \{$ vapour(present), stack_smoke(normal),
     gasoline_smell(normal), light_status(on) $\}$

$\psi^+ = \{$ vapour(present)$\}$

$\psi^- = \{\neg$vapour(absent), $\neg$stack_smoke(black),
     $\neg$gasoline_smell(intense),$\neg$light_status(off) $\}$

Figure 1: Console *et al.*'s model and two diagnostic sessions

Definition 3:

An inductive explanation I is an *inductive diagnosis* if the plausibility measure for I is greater than or equal to a prescribed threshold P.

Definition 4:

A *case base* Δ is defined as a set of past diagnostic cases: $\Delta = \{\Delta_i = (OBS_i, A_i, I_i, \varepsilon_i)\}$, where OBS_i is a set of observations, A_i is the set of abductive diagnoses for OBS_i, I_i is the set of inductive diagnoses for OBS_i, and ε_i is the correct diagnosis for OBS_i, such that $\varepsilon_i \nsubseteq A_i$.

Because the correct diagnosis ε_i is not produced by the abductive part of the system ($\varepsilon_i \nsubseteq A_i$), Δ only contains cases for which the abductive explanation process failed, i.e. failure cases.

Example 2:

If both Sessions 1 and 2 failed, the case base Δ would contain two cases, representing both sets of observations, the sets of abductive and the inductive diagnoses produced for them, and the correct diagnosis E_1 for both cases[1].

The model for EAD covers both consistency-based and abduction-based explanations, and is complex to use. For the sake of simplicity, we will use a simpler

---

[1]We are only concerned with diagnostic failures here. Successful cases could also be used effectively especially to improve the ranking on the potential diagnoses produced by the abductive part of the diagnoser.

functional notation: $Model(A)$ denotes the deductive closure of the conjunct $MODEL \cap CXT \cap A$, and $Model^{-1}(OBS)$ represents the set of abductive diagnoses found for a set of observations OBS. Similarly, $\mathcal{M}$ denotes the perfect device model that is always consistent and complete with respect to reality. If A is a set of ground terms denoting some facts, $\mathcal{M}(A)$ is the deductive closure of A through $\mathcal{M}$, i.e. all true facts that can be correctly deduced from A using $\mathcal{M}$. A_{pos} denotes the set of individual hypotheses that can truly explain the observations OBS. For all possible OBS, the following relationship holds: $OBS \subseteq \mathcal{M}(A_{pos})$, asserting that, given the correct diagnoses, $\mathcal{M}$ correctly explains at least the observations OBS.

The inverse $\mathcal{M}^{-1}$ of $\mathcal{M}$ represents the ultimate abductive diagnoser, the one that the implemented system attempts to approximate. The complete diagnostic truth, i.e. all possible correct diagnoses for a observations OBS, is represented by $\mathcal{M}^{-1}(OBS)$. If ε_i represents the final correct diagnosis for a set of observations OBS_i, then the following relation holds: $\varepsilon_i \subseteq \mathcal{M}^{-1}(OBS) = A_{pos}$.

We are interested in studying how the CBR system improves the overall performance of the diagnostic system. Thus, it is necessary to characterize diagnostic errors first and study how the CBR system can account for these errors. We next introduce additional definitions concerning the abductive part of the model for EAD.

Definition 5:

rok is *covering* if
$$\mathcal{A}_{pos} \subseteq (COMPONENTS - rok(OBS)).$$
rok is covering if it does not forget hypotheses, i.e. if nothing that can explain the set of observations OBS is pruned away by rok.

Example 3:

A set of rules containing the rule:

IF engine_noise(irregular) THEN ¬irregular_battery

would not be covering, since it would discard the possibility that the battery might be faulty, prematurely concentrating the abductive process on the carburator.

Definition 6:

$Model$ is *faithful* if,
$$\forall\, OBS,\ \forall A \in Model^{-1}(OBS),$$
$$Model(A) \subseteq \mathcal{M}(A).$$

$Model$ is faithful if, for all abductive diagnoses A for OBS, all data entailed by $Model(A)$ is correct with respect to $\mathcal{M}$.

Example 4:

This example assumes the model in Figure 1 except that the two nodes *oil_burn* and *oil_loss* are switched along with their associated symptoms *oil_below_car* and *stack_smoke(black)*. It also assumes that this model is correct i.e. corresponds to $\mathcal{M}$. Given the observations from Session 1, the diagnoser would output *piston_rings_used* as the only possible abductive diagnosis. In turn, we have

$$Model(piston\_rings\_used) \not\subseteq \mathcal{M}(piston\_rings\_used),$$

showing that $Model$ is not faithful.

Definition 7:

$Model$ is *complete* if,
$$\forall\, OBS,\ \forall A \in Model^{-1}(OBS),\ \mathcal{M}(A) \subseteq Model(A).$$

$Model$ is complete if it explains all the data in OBS that is explainable (with respect to $\mathcal{M}$).

Example 5:

Example 4 above is an example where $Model$ is not complete since

$$piston\_rings\_used \in \mathcal{M}^{-1}(OBS) \text{ and,}$$
$$\mathcal{M}(piston\_rings\_used) \not\subseteq Model(piston\_rings\_used).$$

Different ways of using inductive diagnoses can be designed depending on the characteristics of each application. For example, a rough estimate of the quality of the model could be used to determine the degree with which to use and trust the inductive diagnostic process. The more the device model can be trusted, the less the past cases are needed for the current diagnostic situation. Another consideration is the similarity measure used to compare the current situation with retrieved past cases. A statistical analysis of this measure could greatly help determine the uncertainty of its results. Any procedure for merging abductive and inductive diagnoses would be somewhat device dependent and does not belong to a general model for diagnosis combining abduction and induction.

Characterizing Diagnostic Errors

Given the model for diagnosis defined above, and the definitions in the previous section, an error-free diagnoser is one such that all possible explanations for the observations OBS are produced, and that all produced explanations are correct, i.e.:

$$OBS \subseteq \mathcal{M}(\mathcal{A}_{pos}) \subseteq Model(rok(OBS)) \subseteq \mathcal{M}(rok(OBS)) \tag{1}$$

This implies three types of possible diagnostic errors:

Type A: the system fails to explain the data OBS:
$$OBS \not\subseteq Model(rok(OBS))$$

Type B: the system explains the data but in an incorrect way:
$$Model(rok(OBS)) \not\subseteq \mathcal{M}(rok(OBS)),$$

Type C: possible explanations are overlooked:
$$\mathcal{M}(\mathcal{A}_{pos}) \not\subseteq Model(rok(OBS)).$$

Theorem 1:

If $Model$ is monotonic, rok is covering, $Model$ is complete, and $Model$ is faithful then there will be no diagnostic errors.

Equation 1 imposes that for all possible OBS, the data in OBS be explained according to the definition of diagnosis given in the previous section, that all explanations be correct, and that all possible explanations be produced. $Model$ might have to explain more data than there is in OBS. These "extraneous" explanations, which do not explain OBS directly, still have to be correct for diagnostic errors to be avoided. Equation 1 constrains the restriction of $Model$ to all possible $rok(OBS)$, which might be different from $COMPONENTS$. This is important in the case of cancellation effects between hypotheses, or when two pieces of data cannot be present separately.

If $\mathcal{M}$ is not monotonic, i.e. if $\exists A, \exists A',\ A' \subset A$ and $\mathcal{M}(A') \not\subseteq \mathcal{M}(A)$ more hypotheses can potentially explain less symptoms or observations. Intuitively, this situation is more difficult than if $\mathcal{M}$ is monotonic since it implies that consequences of errors in the device model either create erroneous explanations (as if $Model$ was monotonic) or forget explanations and diagnoses (for example if there is an erroneous cancellation effect). A non-monotonic abduction problem makes the search for minimal hitting sets for minimal conflicts NP-hard (Bylander *et al.* 1991).

We have showed the conditions that guarantee the absence of diagnostic errors. Figure 2 shows what kind of errors are produced if these conditions are not met. It describes eight situations combining the three types of errors described above. Errors of type B can occur if $Model$ is not faithful, i.e. incorrect explanations can only be produced by an incorrect model. If the whole device model is considered, i.e. if rok is covering, then errors of type A and C can occur if $Model$ is not complete (Situations 3 and 4). Proofs of these results can be found in (Féret 1993). These results show that,

rok	*Model*		no	error types
		faithful	1	
	complete	not faithful	2	B
covering	not	faithful	3	A C
	complete	not faithful	4	A B C
		faithful	5	A C
not	complete	not faithful	6	A B C
covering	not	faithful	7	A C
	complete	not faithful	8	A B C

Figure 2: Summary of diagnostic error situations

in general, it is hard to discriminate between potential causes of diagnostic errors, directly from the types of errors that are produced. However, specific conditions might render performance improvement easier. For example, if we assume that *rok* is covering, then the problem seems simpler: if an error of type B occurs, then *Model* is not faithful, and if an error of type A or C occurs, *Model* is at least not complete. This gives a strategy to try to improve the device model.

The results above show that there is little hope for a general abductive method for trouble-shooting diagnostic systems. This is a strong argument in favor of alternative methods which aim at improving the performance of MBD systems. This retrospectively justifies the EAD approach.

Discussion

The definitions given in the paper were inspired by the work on the complexity of abduction done by Bylander *et al.* (Bylander *et al.* 1991) and relate to the focused abductive diagnosis of Console *et al.* (Console, Portinale, & Theseider Dupre 1991) and to Reiter's theory of diagnosis from first principles (Reiter 1987).

The mapping from the EAD model to Console *et al.*'s model is as follows:

$$OBS = D,$$
$$rok(OBS) = C \subseteq COMPONENTS,$$
$$cbr(OBS, CXT, \Delta) = \{\, \},$$

Similar to EAD, their model does not make assumptions about the device models it uses. The EAD model is also interesting because it uses compiled knowledge to rule-out possible hypotheses (explanations). This compiled knowledge takes the form of necessary conditions (for parts of the model to be considered) and are compiled *a priori* from the behavioral model of the device. The EAD approach also addresses the control problem of choosing between abductively generating more hypotheses and deductively eliminating others that is present in Console *et al.*'s model. The rule-out knowledge is applied first and the remaining hypotheses are worth investigating and represent a lesser waste of effort should they be found impossible. The EAD

approach is therefore conceptually simpler. The importance of rule-out knowledge is illustrated by considering its role in pruning away individual hypotheses. A linear decrease in the number n of possible individual hypotheses corresponds to an exponential decrease of the size 2^n of the superset of the set of possible individual hypotheses, i.e. the size of the search space. The example in Figure 1 illustrates the potential usefulness of the rule-out knowledge: if the fact $engine\_noise(regular)$ is known, then the following can be logically inferred: 1) the battery is fine, 2) the carburator is not dirty, 3) the ignition is regular, and 4) if there is a power decrease, it can only be because the engine is too hot. This is effective rule-out knowledge since one fact rules out a whole branch of the search space, therefore significantly reducing the cost of the abductive phase of EAD.

The EAD model does not make assumptions on how the rule-out knowledge (*rok*) is brought into the system. It can be compiled from the a deep model (as in (Console, Portinale, & Theseider Dupre 1991)) or simply hand coded by human experts (as in (Milne 1987)). One difference between our model and that of Console *et al.* is that we use rule-out knowledge *before* the abductive process. Koton's CASEY also uses CBR before a more traditional diagnostic approach to achieve speed-up learning - a simpler learning than the one achieved by the EAD model (Koton 1988). Our approach improves efficiency by using rule-out knowledge as soon as possible. We believe that this is effective for many real-world devices, because it is easy to formulate knowledge about independence (as mentioned in (Pearl 1986)) and about inconsistencies between symptoms and potential causes for those symptoms.

Reiter's model is subsumed by Console al.'s but provides insights relative to the search for minimal conflicts and minimal hitting sets. The mapping from our model to Reiter's is as follows:

$$OBS = D,$$
$$rok(OBS) = D,$$
$$cbr(OBS, CXT, \Delta) = \{\, \},$$
$$\psi^+ = \{\, \}.$$

For Reiter, a solution to the diagnosis problem is to find a diagnosis for OBS which satisfies the consistency requirement. There is no equivalent of the plausibility function in Reiter's model, i.e. no way of ranking diagnoses.

In the EAD model, the rule-out knowledge *rok* can be seen as a way to restrict the search for minimal conflicts. If knowledge about impossibilities of some components to be faulty, or of some combinations of components to be faulty simultaneously is available, then the search for minimal conflicts (minimal sets of components that cannot be simultaneously in a normal state together, given the observations OBS) will be reduced. However, the search for minimal hitting sets for the minimal conflicts might actually be made more complex by cancellation knowledge as defined by

Bylander *et al.*, making this search NP-hard. The deductive, rule-out phase of the EAD model addresses this problem by forcing the system to discard as many impossible faults as possible before considering combinations of possible ones. This phase could typically use compiled knowledge to reduce the expensive use of deep knowledge.

Abductive induction, implemented by a CBR system, is used to recall past errors and to avoid these errors in similar situations. Assuming that each failure case is stored in Δ, and that the information derived from the abductive diagnostic process serves as indices for the cases, inductive diagnoses can be retrieved, when the current situation is similar enough to cases stored in Δ, to correct errors made in previous situations. The indices used by the CBR system are paths (or portions of paths) followed by the abductive process through the device model to derive diagnoses. This insures the relevance to the current situation of cases stored under these paths. The building of the case base Δ can be seen as an *a fortiori* knowledge compilation process. Because this process takes place when the system is in place, it produces more focused and more useful compiled knowledge than knowledge compiled *a priori* (Console, Portinale, & Theseider Dupre 1991). (Féret & Glasgow 1993; Féret 1993) presented experimental results that support the effectiveness of the EAD model, especially of its inductive phase.

The EAD model has been implemented as part of the Automated Data Management System (ADMS) and has been applied to two real-world devices: a robotic system called the Fairing Servicing Subsystem, and a Reactor Building Ventilation System (Féret & Glasgow 1991).

This paper makes explicit the relation between CBR and induction by formally defining the notion of abductive induction in the context of automated diagnosis. It presented the EAD model which addresses the problems of computational complexity and of incorrect device models. The EAD model is a practical and general answer to problems encountered while trying to apply MBD to real-world situations. The research presented in this paper also contributes to the field of CBR by providing a formal model of a hybrid CBR system which characterizes the interactions of CBR with another problem-solving paradigm.

References

Bylander, T.; Allemang, D.; Tanner, M. C.; and Josephson, J. R. 1991. The computational complexity of abduction. *Artificial Intelligence* 49:25–60.

Console, L.; Portinale, L.; and Theseider Dupre, D. 1991. Focusing abductive diagnosis. *AI Communications* 4(2/3):88–97.

Console, L.; Theseider Dupre, D.; and Torasso, P. 1989. A theory of diagnosis for incomplete causal models. In *Proceedings of 11th IJCAI*, 1311–1317.

de Kleer, J., and Williams, B. C. 1987. Diagnosis multiple faults. *Artificial Intelligence* 32:97–129.

de Kleer, J. 1989. Diagnosis with behavioral modes. In *Proceedings of the 11th International Joint Conference on Artificial Intelligence*, 1324–1330.

de Kleer, J. 1990. Using crude probability estimates to guide diagnosis. *Artificial Intelligence* 45(3):381–391.

de Kleer, J. 1992. Optimizing focusing model-based diagnosis. In *Proceedings of the 3rd International Workshop on Principles of Diagnosis*, 26–29.

Féret, M. P., and Glasgow, J. I. 1991. Generic diagnosis for mechanical devices. In *Proceedings of the 6th International Conference on Applications of Artificial Intelligence in Engineering*, 753–768. Oxford, UK: Computational Mechanics Publications, Elsevier Applied Science.

Féret, M. P., and Glasgow, J. I. 1993. Hybrid case-based reasoning for the diagnosis of complex devices. In *Proceedings of AAAI-93*, 168–175.

Féret, M. P. 1993. *Explanation-Aided Diagnosis: Combining Case-Based and Model-Based Reasoning for the Diagnosis of Complex Devices*. Ph.D. Dissertation, Department of Computing and Information Science, Queen's University, Kingston, Ontario, Canada.

Friedrich, G. 1992. Theory diagnoses: A concise characterization of faulty systems. In *Proceedings of the 3rd International Workshop on Principles of Diagnosis*, 117–131.

Koton, P. 1988. Reasoning about evidence in causal explanations. In *Proceedings of AAAI-88*, 256–261.

Milne, R. 1987. Strategies for diagnosis. *IEEE Transactions on Systems, Man, and Cybernetics* SMC-17(3):333–339.

Mozetic, I. 1990. Reduction of diagnostic complexity through model abstractions. In *Proceedings of the 1rst International Workshop on Principles of Diagnosis*, 102–111.

Pearl, J. 1986. Fusion, propagation, and structuring in belief networks. *Artificial Intelligence* 28:241–288.

Peirce, C. S., ed. 1955. *Philosophical Writings of Peirce*. New York: Dover Publications Inc.

Reiter, R. 1987. A theory of diagnosis from first principle. In *Artificial Intelligence*, volume 32, 57–95.

Riesbeck, C., and Schank, R., eds. 1989. *Inside Case-Based Reasoning*. Lawrence Erlbaum Associates.

Heuristic Harvesting of Information for Case-Based Argument

Edwina L. Rissland, David B. Skalak, and M. Timur Friedman
Department of Computer Science
University of Massachusetts
Amherst, Massachusetts 01003
{rissland, skalak, friedman}@cs.umass.edu

Abstract

The BankXX system models the process of perusing and gathering information for argument as a heuristic best-first search for relevant cases, theories, and other domain-specific information. As BankXX searches its heterogeneous and highly interconnected network of domain knowledge, information is incrementally analyzed and amalgamated into a dozen desirable ingredients for argument (called *argument pieces*), such as citations to cases, applications of legal theories, and references to prototypical factual scenarios. At the conclusion of the search, BankXX outputs the set of argument pieces filled with harvested material relevant to the input problem situation.

This research explores the appropriateness of the search paradigm as a framework for harvesting and mining information needed to make legal arguments. We discuss how we tackled the problem of evaluation of BankXX from both the case-based reasoning (CBR) and task-performance perspectives. In particular, we discuss how various system parameters—start node, evaluation function, resource limit—affected BankXX from the CBR perspective and how well BankXX performs its assigned task of gathering information useful for legal argumentation by running BankXX on real legal cases and comparing its output with the published court opinions for those cases.

1. Introduction

In this paper we discuss heuristically-guided perusal, analysis, and harvesting of information for use in case-based argument. The specific task we study is the gathering and amalgamating of key pieces of information—called argument pieces—which serve as basic building blocks for argument; this is a prerequisite task to the actual generation of more familiar forms of argument, such as 3-ply arguments [Ashley, 1990] or structured memoranda [Rissland & Skalak, 1991; Branting, 1991; Rissland et al., 1993].

We are particularly interested in this task in realistic situations, such as performing scholarly research in a large well-stocked library with a vast body of potentially relevant materials. In such contexts, multiple retrievals and evaluations of relevance are necessary as one explores materials and builds up an analysis. One often pursues a two-step winnowing approach: gather up potentially useful information as one chases references and then analyze further only those materials with the potential to contribute significantly to key aspects of one's research. In this paper, we explore this view in our BankXX program, which models the process of gathering and analyzing information for the task of creating an argument with the classic paradigm of heuristic best-first search. BankXX's domain concerns an aspect of federal bankruptcy law for individual debtors, specifically the "good faith" requirement for Chapter 13 repayment plans.[1]

A major theme of this paper is that in the face of too much information and too few resources to examine it all, an intelligent information gatherer—person or program—must make choices about which leads to follow, which to ignore or postpone, which information to study closely, which to peruse superficially. A second theme is that the value of some information is not necessarily apparent on first perusal and that some information might not even be accessible on the initial foray into the knowledge base; that is, relevance and accessibility can change as more information is uncovered and examined. For instance, a seemingly unimportant case—one not most on-point or even highly similar—can gain in importance if it turns out that it is the only case addressing a key issue.

In this paper, we present our evaluation of how well BankXX performs on its assigned task of harvesting information useful for legal argumentation (on the "good faith" issue) by running BankXX on real legal cases and comparing its output with the published court opinions for those cases. We also evaluate how various internal parameters affect BankXX's performance as a CBR program. Finally we note that although the context of our research is legal argument, we believe that the use of such heuristic retrieval methods is applicable in other areas, such as diagnosis and design, where CBR methods have been classically applied.

Some of the points we will touch upon in this paper are:

---

[1] Section 1325(a)(3) of the federal bankruptcy code requires that debtors' plans be proposed in "good faith." This term is undefined in the statute and is interpreted in individual cases by application of case law.

This work was supported in part by the Air Force Office of Scientific Research under contract 90-0359.

• The overall process of gathering information for an argument can be usefully modeled as heuristic search.

• *Argument pieces* are used to represent argument and define an evaluation function.

• Retrieval of cases and other knowledge can fruitfully be done with a combination of knowledge-based indexing and heuristic search.

• Retrieval and relevancy assessment is carried out over many iterations.

This paper first discusses the BankXX system generally and exposits how the heuristic search model is embodied in BankXX. In particular, we describe the argument piece model of argument used in BankXX and how heuristic search and evaluation functions drive the program to instantiate it. Once all these pieces are in place, we describe a series of experiments to gauge the performance of the system. We conclude by discussing the contributions of this research.

2. Background

BankXX has all the standard ingredients of CBR—case memory, indexing, case selection metrics—and executes all the standard subtasks—case input and analysis, retrieval, selection, task performance—on the paradigm CBR performance task of creating precedent-based arguments ([Ashley, 1990; Branting, 1991]). BankXX's case memory is structured as a directed graph whose nodes represent legal objects such as cases and legal theories and whose arcs represent their interconnections. Case memory in BankXX is highly associative, heterogeneous, and has a large branching factor. The indices used by BankXX are arcs of the case memory network as well as more complex linkages computed from them. There are multiple paths to most items in memory [Kolodner, 1983; Turner, 1988]. Evaluation functions are used for case selection.

Kolodner [1993, p. 291] discusses retrieval techniques in terms of memory data structures and retrieval algorithms, such as flat memory with serial or parallel search, shared feature networks with breadth-first graph search, prioritized discrimination networks with depth-first graph search, and redundant discrimination networks with breath-first graph search. To this list we can add BankXX's highly-interconnected, heterogeneous semantic networks with heuristic best-first search.

BankXX's application of iterative, heuristic search to case retrieval distinguishes it from many other CBR programs. CBR is in general a heuristic process because its key mechanisms—indices, relevancy metrics, etc.—are heuristic; and CBR programs do implicitly search a case space. However, CBR programs are not usually designed in the classic search paradigm with its **iterative** control cycle of evaluating, selecting, and expanding possibilities on the problem-solving horizon. Most CBR programs do not repeatedly cycle through the retrieval and selection of cases. One exception is Owens's [1993] ANON, which iteratively integrates the search for cases and the extraction

of discriminatory features. Direct Memory Access Parsing (DMAP, [Martin, 1990]) uses a semantic network of case frames that is searched via a marker-passing algorithm. Other CBR systems that use search include Branting's GREBE [1991] (A* search to match structured cases preparatory to making an argument), Alterman's PLEXUS [1988] (search of abstraction hierarchies for substitute plan steps for adaptation), and Kass and Leake's SWALE [1988] (local search of plan repair —"tweak"—hierarchy).

This research also develops a new methodology to evaluate precedent-based argument, and presents a new application of the precision-recall measures used in information retrieval to evaluate case retrieval. We describe an extensive series of experiments that examine BankXX's performance under various parameter settings, and compared to previous programs and actual legal opinions.

3. Argument Pieces: The Components of Argument

Our model of argument is based on the belief that one has a good general sense of the type of information needed to flesh out a good argument, even if one is not an expert in the particular area. This general knowledge includes:

1. what types of domain knowledge exist (e.g., cases, theories, prototypes) and how they are interconnected (e.g., intercase citation, case to theory pointers); and

2. what basic building blocks are needed to put together a good argument (e.g., a viable legal theory, favorable supporting cases, understanding of contrary cases).

Based on these observations, we have chosen a simple representation of an argument for purposes of this research as a collection of *argument pieces*. These building blocks of argument represent fragments of arguments or pieces of legal knowledge that an advocate would ideally like to have when making an argument. We recognize that this idealization of argument does not reflect the logical and rhetorical connections between the various pieces of an argument, or the complexity of argument in general. However, we feel that such information is a prerequisite for constructing more elaborate representations of argument. In BankXX argument pieces are used in two ways: (1) to represent argument, and (2) to define a heuristic evaluation function.

The 12 argument pieces currently used in BankXX are:

1. Supporting Cases - cases decided for the same "side" as the viewpoint assumed in the current problem situation.

2. Best Supporting Cases - the best cases decided for the current viewpoint.

3. Contrary Cases - cases decided for the opposing side.

4. Best Contrary Cases - defined similarly to 2.

5. Leading Cases - one of the five most frequently cited cases in our BankXX corpus. These were found by a frequency analysis of cases citations done on the full text of the opinions of the cases in the BankXX case base.

6. Supporting Citations - citations that: (i) are found in cases with the desired viewpoint, (ii) point to other cases with the same viewpoint, and (iii) use a "citation signal" indicating that the citing case agrees with the cited case (e.g., *accord*, *see*).

7. Factor Analysis - the set of domain factors ("dimensions") that are applicable to the current problem situation.

8. Overlapping Cases - cases sharing a large proportion of domain factors, where large in this paper means at least 75%.

9. Applicable Legal Theories - If each factor defining a theory is applicable to the problem situation, the theory is considered applicable.

10. Nearly Applicable Legal Theories - A theory is nearly applicable if a threshold percentage of defining factors apply. In this paper, the threshold is set at 50%.

11. Factual Prototype Story category - the category of story (e.g., student loan case, medical calamity) that the debtor's factual situation falls under. These categories were assigned by hand.

12. Family Resemblance Prototype - cases decided for the desired viewpoint having the highest family resemblance rating, with respect to a given family, to the instant case according to the Rosch measure of family resemblance [Rosch & Mervis, 1975].

Each of these argument pieces is defined computationally in BankXX. The definitions of "most on-point," "best," and domain "factor" are based directly on those used first in HYPO [Ashley, 1990] and then in CABARET, occasionally with some modification.[2] For each argument piece, there is a "functional predicate" that determines if a node can supply that useful piece of an argument and a data structure containing an object slot to store entities that satisfy its predicate. BankXX builds up their content incrementally (as its search proceeds) and the collection of filled argument pieces is output to the user at the conclusion of BankXX's processing.

4. The Heuristic Search Model in BankXX

BankXX builds up the content of the argument pieces by performing heuristic best-first search in a network of domain knowledge. BankXX always begins its processing by analyzing the problem situation for applicable domain factors and computing a claim lattice, which partially orders the cases that have some of the same factors at work as the current problem. The best and most on-point cases are identified. These provide potential new nodes to be explored and are always the first nodes to be placed on the open list.

BankXX continues by performing the standard cycle of iterative, best-first search. Neighbors of the current node are generated using BankXX's neighbor methods. The "best" node on the open list—one with the maximum value under one of BankXX's evaluation functions—is identified and is then examined by each of the argument pieces in turn in order to determine if it can contribute to that component of the argument. Information that can be harvested by the argument pieces is appended to their data structures. This cycle continues until the search exceeds a user-specified time or space bound (e.g., 30 nodes closed), or until the open list is empty. At the conclusion of the search, the argument is output in a template containing the argument pieces, which have been incrementally filled during the search.

4.1 The Case-Domain Graph

State-space search is defined by a triple: *initial state, set of operators on states, set of goal states.* In best-first search, an *evaluation function* is used to guide the exploration of the state-space [Barr et al., 1981]. We begin by describing the search space.

The Search Space. In BankXX it consists of a semantic network whose nodes represent cases and legal theories from the application domain, the "good faith" issue for personal Chapter 13 bankruptcy plans. Labeled links represent their interconnections. We refer to this network as the *case-domain-graph*. There are six types of case-domain-graph nodes: five represent legal cases in various perspectives proven useful to human legal reasoners and one represents legal theories. In this area of the law, appeals courts often articulate approaches—"theories"—for dealing with the good faith question; these are typically described in terms of domain factors. The five ways legal cases are represented are (1) as factual situations, (2) as bundles of citations, (3) as stereotypical stories or scripts, (4) as a collection of legal factors, or (5) by the measure of their prototypicality. Cases of like type can be grouped into *spaces*: (e.g., Case Citation Space, Legal Theory Space). Each space captures a particular type of knowledge and its natural interconnections. For instance, intercase citations are captured in the Citation Space and legal theories and relationships between them (e.g., refinement) in the Legal Theory Space. All the spaces are interconnected. For instance, cases point to the legal theories that are applied in them and the story prototype they fall under. Thus the case graph is highly interconnected. For more details see [Rissland, Skalak & Friedman, 1993].

The Start Node. In BankXX the default for the initial state is the user-supplied problem situation, which is represented using the same set of hierarchical frames used to represent a case as a collection of facts. Alternatively, the user can input the problem case but specify another node as the start node, for instance, a favorite or well-known case, in order to concentrate the search initially in a particular region of the space.

The Operators. The set of operators used in BankXX are called *neighbor methods*. These use links in the case-

---

[2]For instance, the "best" cases in BankXX are most similar to the problem situation whether or not they are most on-point. This is different from the definition in HYPO.

domain-graph to generate the "successor" nodes to be opened in search. Some follow in-space or cross-space pointers in a straightforward way. For instance, *case-theory-neighbors* generates all the cases that have applied a particular theory. Others, similar to macro-operators, follow a fixed sequence of links. For instance *theory-case-theory-neighbors* finds all the theories applied by any of the cases that use the theory used in the current node. BankXX has 12 neighbor methods. In general, they are more complex than the simple following of outward arcs from a given node.

Goal Nodes. We do not provide goal states to BankXX because of the difficulties inherent in defining an "argument goal" in a way that is consistent with our understanding of how humans develop and evaluate legal arguments. It is hard to say in general that an argument does or does not meet some plausible persuasive or rhetorical goal, or even that one has completed the supporting research.

4.2 Evaluation Functions

We have experimented thus far with three different types of evaluation functions. They differ in the level of abstraction that they use to evaluate nodes in the case-domain graph. All of the evaluation functions are simple linear functions. They form a progression of increasingly more informed evaluation methods, whose considerations range from (1) only the type of information encoded in a node to (2) the contribution of the node to the standard argument pieces and (3) the incremental impact of a node on the overall state of the evolving argument.

In this paper we concentrate on experiments using only the first two. Briefly, they are:

(1) Node-type evaluation function. Its form is:

$$w_1 \; type\text{-}pred_1(c) \;\; + \;\; w_2 \; type\text{-}pred_2(c) \;\; + \;\; ...$$
$$+ \; w_n \; type\text{-}pred_n(c)$$

where *type-pred* checks the *type* of the current node c. This function assesses the potential according to pre-assigned estimations of how useful various types of nodes are. It causes node-types to be examined in the order defined by the weights w_i. In these experiments legal theories have some preference but there is not much difference among the others.[3]

(2) Argument piece evaluation function. The form of this function is:

$$w_1 \; arg\text{-}piece\text{-}pred_1(c,a) + w_2 \; arg\text{-}piece\text{-}pred_2(c,a) + ...$$
$$+ \; w_n \; arg\text{-}piece\text{-}pred_n(c,a)$$

where c is the current node and a is the current state of the argument. Each *arg-piece-pred* computes whether a particular argument piece is fillable by the current node and if that argument piece has <u>not</u> already been completely filled: if so, it returns 1; else, 0. This evaluation function prevents BankXX from wasting computing resources by

unnecessarily bolstering parts of the argument that are already well-established.[4]

5. The BankXX Experiments

In this paper we report on two types of empirical evaluations:

1. comparing the performance of BankXX with itself as a CBR program, by varying parameter settings; and

2. comparing the performance of BankXX with hand-coded arguments found in opinions of actual court cases.

In other experiments, we further explore BankXX's performance.

5.1 Methodology

The methodology for the first set of experiments is straightforward: run BankXX on each of the 54 cases in its case base in a *de novo* manner—that is, excise the case and all its linkages from BankXX's case-domain-graph—and count the number of items filling each of 10 argument pieces.[5] To compare BankXX with written case opinions, we encoded the 54 opinions into "answer" keys comparable in form to those generated by BankXX and applied standard precision and recall measures.

Precision is the ratio of what was mentioned by both the decision and BankXX to that mentioned just by BankXX. **Recall** is the ratio of what was mentioned by both the decision and BankXX to that mentioned just by the decision. We hasten to add that given the small numbers used in these experiments, these measures are very sensitive to small changes. For instance, for a given argument piece, if BankXX retrieves one item that is one of only two items mentioned in the opinion, its precision is 100% and recall is 50%. Should BankXX retrieve an "extra" item not mentioned in the opinion, its precision will drop to 50%; two extra items drop precision to 33%. Its recall will not increase. Since BankXX diligently harvests as much information as it can, it is likely to mention more items than the opinion and be penalized for it in precision and not get credit for it in recall. Thus, one should be careful in reading too much into these traditional metrics. Nonetheless, given their widespread use, we do use them here.

Creating the "answers" needed for precision-recall comparisons was done by reading the court's opinion and

---

[3]The weights are 8 (theories), 6 (cases), 5 (citations), 4 (domain factors), and 3 (factual prototypes).

[4]The weights and the limits on the number of items considered to fill each argument piece (given in brackets) are: 2 [3] (supporting cases), 7 [5] (best supporting cases), 1 [3] (contrary cases), 5 [3] (best contrary cases), 6 [5] (leading cases), 1 [5] (supporting citations), 1 [5] (overlapping cases), 8 [6] (applicable legal theories), 6 [3] (nearly applicable theories), and 6 [1] (factual prototype stories).

[5]There are 10 terms whereas there are 12 argument pieces because the factor analysis argument piece is filled during system initialization, and we do not use the family resemblance prototype argument piece in these experiments.

Case-Based Reasoning   **39**

encoding each case and theory actually cited in the opinion. One problem inherent in encoding written opinions with the set of original argument pieces is how to identify elements fitting each argument piece, since some have technical BankXX meanings (e.g., best case) or make fine distinctions hard for human readers to discern (e.g., applicable versus <u>nearly</u> applicable legal theory, best versus merely supporting cases). In BankXX, these distinctions are made in a principled way with computational definitions. To compensate for such difficulties, the argument pieces were aggregated into four larger-grained argument pieces that were easy to apply.[6] These were then used in hand-coding court opinions and as the basis of BankXX versus actual court performance comparisons. The four simplified argument pieces are: (1) **Cited-Supporting-Cases**,[7] (2) **Cited-Contrary-Cases**,[8] (3) **Cited-Leading-Cases**, and (4) **Cited-Legal-Theories**.[9]

With these aggregated argument pieces, hand-coding was straightforward and involved little subjective judgment. Any case cited in the opinion is listed as a **cited-supporting** case or a **cited-contrary** case depending on how its outcome compares with decision in the opinion.[10] If a cited case is also one that is frequently cited by written opinions in general,[11] it is also listed as a **cited-leading** case. If an opinion <u>explicitly</u> articulates a theory of its own, reiterates or applies the theory of another case, or appeals to a general domain theory (e.g., a "totality of the facts and circumstances" theory of good faith), then that theory is encoded as a **cited-legal-theory**.

Output from these BankXX-court comparison runs can be viewed in various ways. **Figure 1** displays graphically the finest-grained analysis. It shows results for retrieval of objects for the aggregated **cited-leading-cases** argument piece for each of the 54 cases. Each bar compares performance of BankXX with the court opinion on one case.

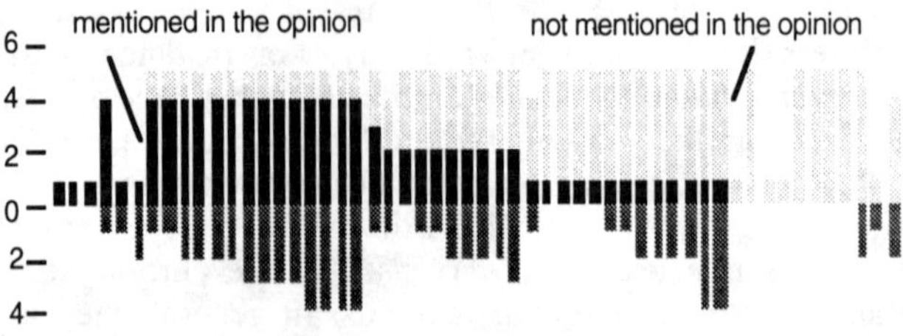

Figure 1: Comparison of retrieved *cited-leading-cases* using the argument piece evaluation function. Performance on each of the cases, in order from highest to lowest precision.

The vertical axis indicates the number of items retrieved. Everything above the zero represents items retrieved by BankXX with the black part of a bar representing those retrieved by BankXX and mentioned in the written opinion and the lightly shaded part of the bar representing items retrieved by BankXX that were not mentioned in the opinion. The darkly shaded part of the bar extending below zero represents items mentioned in the opinion that were not retrieved by BankXX. Graphically, **precision** is the proportion of black out of the total bar above the zero; **recall** is the proportion of black out of the combined black and darkly shaded parts of the bar.

In summary, we ran BankXX on <u>each</u> of the 54 cases in its case base in *de novo* fashion with <u>each</u> of two evaluation functions, and compared retrieval on <u>each</u> argument piece: approximately 1500 data points.[12]

5.2 BankXX as a CBR program

This section describes three experiments we performed to answer questions about BankXX as a case-based retrieval system:

1. How important is the initial query in determining the eventual outcome of retrieval?

2. How much knowledge must the case retrieval function have in order to be effective?

3. When can search terminate and the retrieval result be satisfactory?

As a baseline, BankXX was run with the *Estus* case, 695 F.2d. 311 (8th Cir. 1982), as start node, the argument piece evaluation function, and search limited to closing 30 nodes. We addressed the three questions above in search terms by examining the effects of:

1. varying the start node,

2. changing the evaluation function, and

3. trying different limits on the number of nodes that could be closed.

---

[6]Note five argument pieces are not used in the aggregated argument pieces: supporting-citations, factor-analysis, overlapping-cases, factual-prototype-category, family-resemblance-prototype.

[7]Defined for BankXX as the union of supporting-cases and best-supporting-cases.

[8]Defined for BankXX as the union of contrary-cases and best-contrary-cases.

[9]Defined for BankXX as the union of applicable-legal-theories and nearly-applicable-legal-theories.

[10]Complications, such as the fact that a same side case may have been cited (with a so-called *But see* citation signal) in order to differ with its rationale while still agreeing with its outcome, are overlooked.

[11]A frequency analysis was done on a corpus of cases of approximately 800 cases gathered with a WestLaw retrieval. We then checked the citation frequency of each of BankXX's cases in this larger corpus. The five most frequently cited cases were used to define cited-leading-case category applied to written opinions. By contrast, for BankXX leading-cases is defined with respect to frequency of citation <u>within</u> BankXX's own corpus.

[12]Given 10 argument pieces used in the general CBR experiments and 4 in the BankXX-Court comparisons, there are (2x10 + 2x4) x 54 data points.

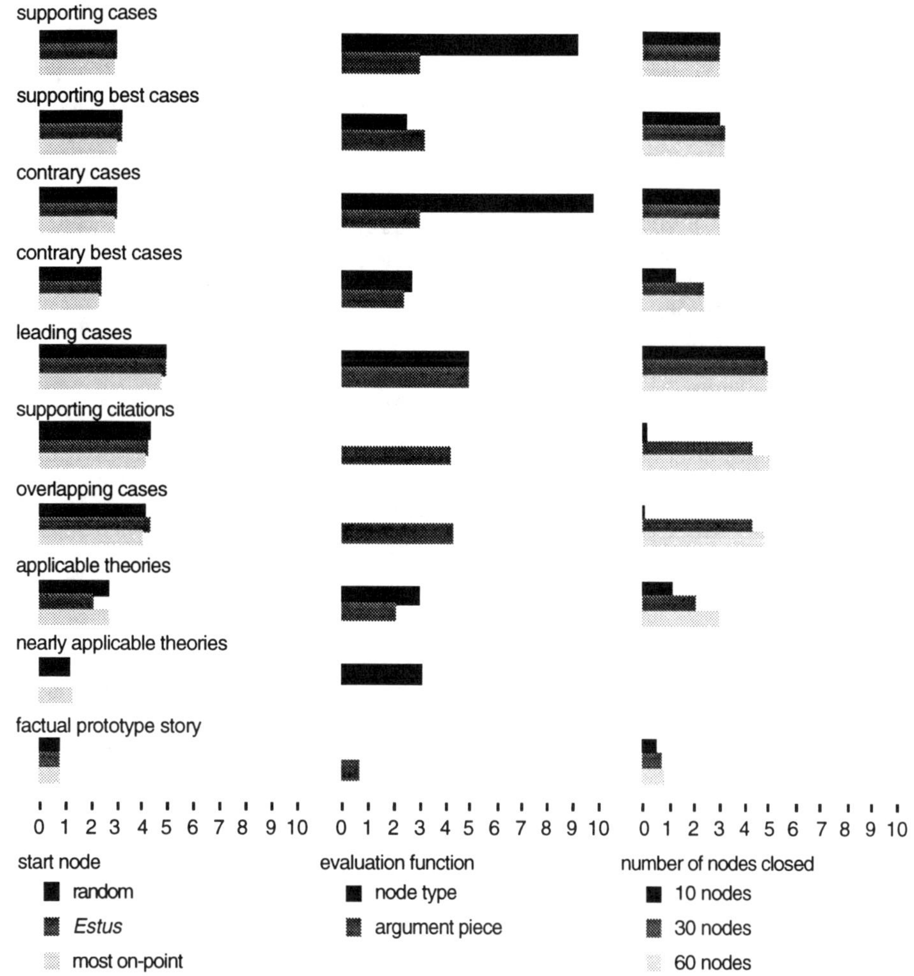

Figure 2: Average number of objects filling each argument piece as the start node is varied (left), the evaluation function is varied (middle), and the number of nodes closed is varied (right).

We ran BankXX *de novo* on all 54 cases in the case base to obtain averages for the number of objects filling each argument piece.[13]

5.2.1 Initial Query Formulation. Using the argument piece evaluation function and stopping search after closing 30 nodes, three different nodes were used as start nodes: a random case, the *Estus* case, and a most on-point case. The random case provides a base line. *Estus* is well known in this area of bankruptcy law—almost any research materials consulted by an attorney will soon lead to it—and therefore it may be considered a realistic and useful starting point. A most on-point case is another starting point likely to be relevant.

The results showed that the choice of start node, which is the initial query to the case base, made little difference to retrieval. As the left hand side of **Figure 2** shows, the average number of objects found for each argument piece is about the same for each of the three start nodes. We examined search paths through the case-domain graph to understand why. It turns out that no matter where search starts in this case-domain graph of 150 nodes, it soon leads to a highly interconnected region which contains many useful cases and theories. For example *Estus* and *Flygare* (another well known case) and the theories promulgated by these cases are part of this area of the graph. Informally speaking, it doesn't matter where search starts because in this domain all roads lead to *Estus*.

We conclude that in browsing a case base where there is a sense of location and a sufficiently rich indexing fabric, the initial probe to case-memory may not matter in a multiple-probe situation.

5.2.2 Case Retrieval Function. Next, we compared the effects of varying the evaluation function while keeping the 30 closed node limit and always starting at the *Estus* node. The node-type evaluation function finds more contrary cases and same side cases, but does so at the expense of failing to fill other argument pieces. See the middle of

---

[13]N.B., numbers of nodes closed, opened, and filling an argument piece are not the same. In general, many more nodes are opened than closed, and the total number of items filling the set of argument pieces exceeds the number of closed nodes (see Figure 2).

Figure 2. The node-type function uses only the type for each node and does not limit the number of objects retrieved for any argument piece. Considering its lack of knowledge, it does surprisingly well.

To understand how a knowledge-poor function can produce satisfactory results, one can consider search as just the first of a two-stage retrieval process for filling the argument pieces. The second stage applies the argument piece predicates to the retrieved objects to determine if they fulfill the requirements of the argument piece.

We conclude that in a two-phase retrieval, a knowledge-poor function to generate candidates in the first phase may be sufficient, as long as the performance criteria in the second phase are sufficiently rich. The efficacy of the classic generate-and-test or "many-are-called/few-are-chosen" (MAC/FAC) approach has been observed in other research as well [Gentner & Forbus, 1991].

5.2.3 Termination of Search of Case Memory.
There is no objective standard for when one has completed research or completed an argument. Thus BankXX has two termination parameters that may be set by the user: limiting the time ("billable seconds") used and the number of nodes closed. In these experiments BankXX was set to terminate after it had closed 10, 30, and 60 nodes.

With the argument piece evaluation function and *Estus* as the start node, 10 nodes was too few to fill up many of the argument pieces. As a rough guide, 30 nodes seemed an appropriate compromise between more exhaustive search and too scanty an examination of the domain-graph. Incremental benefits of more search decreased after about 30 nodes. See the right hand side of Figure 2.

From the CBR perspective, we conclude that the decreased marginal utility of finding more cases causes there to be a point at which additional search of the case base is not effective. This conclusion echoes the results of Veloso and Carbonell [1991] as to the optimal amount of time to search a case base in a hybrid planner.

5.3 BankXX as an Argument Program

Using standard precision and recall measures, we compared the performance of BankXX with written judicial opinions. All 54 cases were run *de novo* with *Estus* as start node and a limit of 30 closed nodes. Results were averaged over the 54 cases.

5.3.1 Precision/Recall Performance and the Evaluation Functions.
We were somewhat surprised to find that in general the knowledge-poor node-level evaluation function usually exhibited higher recall and precision than the knowledge-richer argument piece function. For instance, all the average recall values for the node-type function lie above the corresponding values for the argument piece function. Averaged over the four simplified argument pieces, the node-type evaluation function gave higher recall (0.55), than the argument piece evaluation function (0.44). We conclude that BankXX's overall **recall** performance seems to depend more on the choice of evaluation function than the choice of argument piece. The node-type

evaluation function may give higher recall simply because it retrieves more items than the argument piece function. See the middle of Figure 2. The argument piece evaluation function is more selective but pays a price for that in recall.

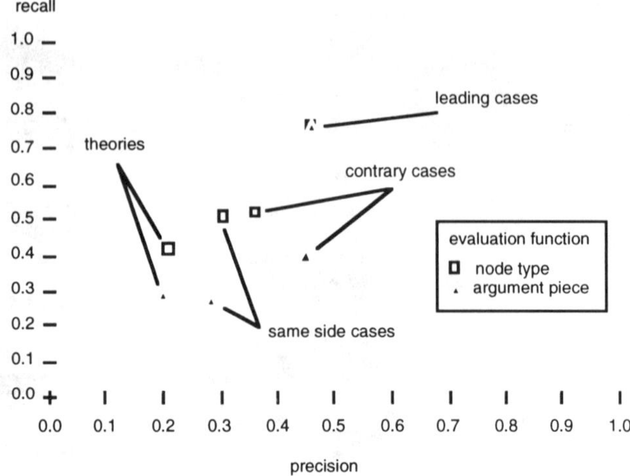

Figure 3: Average precision and recall (over all 54 cases) for the four aggregated argument pieces.

On the other hand, there seems not to be much difference in overall **precision** performance between the two evaluation functions. Each argument piece performs at about the same precision for each function. As we did in Section 5.2.2, we ascribe this to BankXX's two-stage approach: the lack of precision inherent in the node-type function is ameliorated by the precise filling of the argument pieces. Finally, we note that we did not observe the classical trade-offs between precision and recall. This might be because BankXX is not be functioning at a frontier where such phenomena occur or we need to vary other parameters to see them. In these studies, we only varied two, the evaluation function and the argument piece.

5.3.2 Recall/Precision and Argument Pieces.
We observed differences in retrieval precision for the different argument pieces (see **Figure 3**). For both evaluation functions, highest precision was found for **cited-leading-cases** (0.46), followed by **cited-contrary-cases, cited-supporting-cases,** then **cited-legal-theories** (0.21). The results for recall were similar for the argument piece function. For the node-type function there was a flattening of performance differences among recall for the three argument pieces involving cases; all three did well.

We interpret the better precision on **cited-leading-cases** as follows. Since the same small group of leading cases are cited repeatedly in the opinions (that's what makes them leading cases), the probability that a given leading case is mentioned is higher than that for an arbitrary contrary or supporting case or legal theory. Thus if BankXX mentions a leading case it is likely to be in the opinion as well and hence BankXX's good precision marks on this argument piece.

For the other argument pieces, there is a wide range in the amount of information mentioned in the opinions. Thus if BankXX retrieves information not found in the opinions—which is likely to happen given BankXX's diligence in going after information—this lowers BankXX's precision. In particular, BankXX's low precision and recall scores on **cited-legal-theories** may be due to the high number of legal theories (18) relative to the number of cases (54), and the similarity of many theories. The program receives no credit for retrieving a useful but uncited theory in the absence of a metric to measure the similarity of the retrieved theory to the one actually applied by a court.

5.3.3 Precision-Recall Measures - Limitations.

Again, let us note that the answers derived from actual opinions are not necessarily the best possible nor the only answers. Each opinion is the product of an individual judge and clerks. Some will cite many cases in support of their argument. Others will cite few. Some will mention only the legal theory of their particular judicial circuit. Others will look to other circuits as well. We found that earlier decisions, those written when the good faith issue was first being addressed under the new law, tended to look further afield and compared more different approaches. Once a number of appeals courts had set standards for analyzing good faith, opinions tended to look more exclusively to appeals cases in their own circuit for guidance.

Further, the way we have applied precision-recall measures—using the court's opinion as the "right" answer—is but one way to examine performance. Another would involve comparing BankXX with other programs. Without such comparisons, it is hard to judge BankXX's performance.

Lastly, these measures are problematic for a program like BankXX which seeks to harvest as much information as its resource limits allow. If BankXX retrieves information not found in the opinions—which is likely to happen given its biases—this lowers BankXX's precision and does not help its recall, even though BankXX might be doing a superb job of legal analysis. Benchmarks better measuring retrieval *accuracy*[14] are needed in our experiments—and CBR or AI and Law, in general.

6. Conclusions

The general conclusion that we draw from BankXX is that the process of gathering information for an argument can be usefully modeled as heuristic search. In particular, the retrieval of cases and other knowledge can fruitfully be done with a combination of knowledge-based indexing and heuristic search. Using heuristic search as the mechanism to traverse memory permits relevancy assessment and case retrieval to be repeated iteratively in order to locate the

---

[14]In engineering, accuracy is different from precision, which only notes to what decimal point one measures.

nodes in the case graph that provide the underpinnings of an argument.

7. References

Alterman, R. (1988). Adaptive Planning. *Cognitive Science*, 12, 393-422.

Ashley, K. D. (1990). *Modeling Legal Argument: Reasoning with Cases and Hypotheticals*. Cambridge, Massachusetts: M.I.T. Press.

Barr, A., Feigenbaum, E. A. & Cohen, P. (1981). *The Handbook of Artificial Intelligence*. Reading, Massachusetts: Addison-Wesley.

Branting, L. K. (1991). Integrating Rules and Precedents for Classification and Explanation: Automating Legal Analysis. Ph.D. Thesis, Technical Report AI90-146, AI Laboratory, University of Texas, Austin, Texas.

Gentner, D. & Forbus, K. D. (1991). MAC/FAC: A Model of Similarity-based Retrieval. *Proceedings of the 13th Annual Conference of the Cognitive Science Society*, 504-509. Chicago, IL. Lawrence Erlbaum, Hillsdale, NJ.

Kass, A. M. & Leake, D. B. (1988). Case-Based Reasoning Applied to Constructing Explanations. *Proceedings, Case-Based Reasoning Workshop 1988*, 190-208. Clearwater Beach, FL. Morgan Kaufmann.

Kolodner, J. L. (1983). Maintaining Organization in a Dynamic Long-Term Memory. *Cognitive Science*, 7(4), 243-280.

Kolodner, J. L. (1993). *Case-Based Reasoning*. San Mateo, California: Morgan Kaufmann.

Martin, C. E. (1990). Direct Memory Access Parsing. Ph.D. Thesis, Yale University, New Haven, CT.

Owens, C. (1993). Integrating Feature Abstraction and Memory Search. *Machine Learning*, 10(3), 311-340.

Rissland, E. L., Daniels, J. J., Rubinstein, Z. B. & Skalak, D. B. (1993). Case-Based Diagnostic Analysis in a Blackboard Architecture. *Proceedings of the Eleventh National Conference on Artificial Intelligence*, 66-72. Washington, DC. AAAI Press/MIT Press.

Rissland, E. L. & Skalak, D. B. (1991). CABARET: Rule Interpretation in a Hybrid Architecture. *International Journal of Man-Machine Studies*, 34, 839-887.

Rissland, E.L., Skalak, D.B. & Friedman, M. T. (1993). Case Retrieval through Multiple Indexing and Heuristic Search. *Proceedings, 13th International Joint Conference on AI*, 902-908. San Mateo, CA: Morgan Kaufmann.

Rosch, E. & Mervis, C. B. (1975). Family Resemblances: Studies in the Internal Structure of Categories. *Cognitive Psychology*, 7, 573-605.

Turner, R. (1988). Organizing and Using Schematic Knowledge for Medical Diagnosis. *Proceedings, Case-Based Reasoning Workshop 1988*, 435-446. Clearwater Beach, FL. Morgan Kaufmann.

Veloso, M. M. & Carbonell, J. G. (1991). Variable-Precision Case Retrieval in Analogical Problem Solving. *Proceedings, Third Case-Based Reasoning Workshop*, May 1991, 93-106. Washington, D.C. Morgan Kaufmann, San Mateo, CA.

Case-based Acquisition of User Preferences for Solution Improvement in Ill-Structured Domains

Katia Sycara
The Robotics Institute
Carnegie Mellon University
Pittsburgh, PA 15213, U.S.A.
katia@cs.cmu.edu

Kazuo Miyashita
Production Engineering Division
Matsushita Electric Industrial Co.
Kadoma, Osaka 571, Japan
miyasita@mcec.ped.mei.co.jp

Abstract

[1] We have developed an approach to acquire complicated user optimization criteria and use them to guide iterative solution improvement. The effectiveness of the approach was tested on job shop scheduling problems. The ill-structuredness of the domain and the desired optimization objectives in real-life problems, such as factory scheduling, makes the problems difficult to formalize and costly to solve. Current optimization technology requires explicit global optimization criteria in order to control its search for the optimal solution. But often, a user's optimization preferences are state-dependent and cannot be expressed in terms of a single global optimization criterion. In our approach, the optimization preferences are represented implicitly and extensionally in a case base. Experimental results in job shop scheduling problems support the hypotheses that our approach (1) is capable of capturing diverse user optimization preferences and re-using them to guide solution quality improvement, (2) is robust in the sense that it improves solution quality independent of the method of initial solution generation, and (3) produces high quality solutions, which are comparable with solutions generated by traditional iterative optimization techniques, such as simulated annealing, at much lower computational cost.

Introduction

We present an approach, implemented in the CABINS system, to demonstrate the capability of acquiring user context-dependent optimization preferences and reusing them to guide iterative solution optimization in ill-structured domains. This capability is very important for two main reasons. First, traditional search methods, both Operations Research-based and AI-based, that are used in combinatorial optimization, need explicit representation of objectives in terms of a cost function to be optimized

[1] This research was partially supported by the Defense Advance Research Projects Agency under contract #F30602-88-C-0001. Most of the work was performed when the second author was a visiting scientist at the Robotics Institute at Carnegie Mellon University under the support of Matsushita Electric Industrial Co.

(Reeves 1993). In many practical problems, such as scheduling and design, optimization criteria often involve context- and user-dependent tradeoffs which are impossible to realistically consolidate in a cost function. Second, expert system approaches, while having the potential to capture context-dependent tradeoffs in rules, require considerable knowledge acquisition effort (Prerau 1990). Our approach uses case-based reasoning (CBR) which has been successful in dealing with exceptional data (Golding & Rosenbloom 1991; Ruby & Kibler 1992), acquiring user knowledge in complex domains (Chaturvedi 1992; Mckay, Buzacott, & Safayeni 1988), and expending less effort in knowledge acquisition compared with knowledge acquisition for rule-based systems (Lewis, Minior, & Brown 1991). CABINS acquires, stores and reuses two categories of concepts that reflect user preferences (1) what heuristic local optimization action to choose in a particular context, and (2) what combinations of effects of application of a particular local optimization action constitutes an acceptable or unacceptable outcome. These are recorded in the case base and are used by CABINS to guide iterative optimization and induce optimization tradeoffs to evaluate the current solution. The optimization criteria are not explicitly represented as case features or in terms of a cost function but are implicitly and extensionally represented in the case base.

Previous case-based systems for incremental solution revision (e.g. (Hammond 1989; Veloso 1992)) have been motivated only by concerns of computational efficiency, preserving plan correctness rather than improving plan quality, and have assumed the existence of a strong domain model that provides feedback as to plan correctness. Case-based knowledge acquisition systems, (e.g. (Bareiss 1989)) require causal explanations from an expert teacher to acquire domain knowledge. In our approach neither the user nor the program are assumed to possess causal domain knowledge. The user's expertise lies in his/her ability to perform consistent evaluation of the results of problem solving and impart to the program cases of problem solving experiences and histories of evaluation tradeoffs.

In this paper, we present initial experimental results to test three hypotheses. First, our CBR-based incremental revision methodology shows good potential for capturing user optimization preferences in ill-structured domains, such as job shop scheduling, and re-using them to guide optimization. Second, the method is robust in the sense that it improves solution quality independent of the method of initial solution generation. Third, CABINS produces high quality solutions. To test this, we compared the solutions produced by CABINS with explicit optimization criteria, with solutions produced by simulated annealing (a well known iterative optimization technique (Johnson *et al.* 1991; Zweben, Deale, & Gargan 1990; Laarhoven, Aarts, & Lenstra 1992)) for the same criteria. Our investigation was conducted in the domain of job shop schedule optimization and the experimental results, shown in section confirmed these hypotheses.

Job Shop Schedule Optimization

The job shop scheduling problem is one of the most difficult NP-hard combinatorial optimization problems (French 1982). Job shop scheduling deals with allocation of a limited set of resources to a number of activities (operations) associated with a set of jobs so as to respect given temporal relations (e.g. precedence relations among activities), temporal constraints (e.g. job release and due dates) and resource capacity restrictions in order to optimize a set of objectives, such as minimize tardiness, minimize work in process inventory (WIP), maximize resource utilization etc. Due to the tight interactions among scheduling constraints and the often conflicting nature of optimization criteria, it is impossible to assess with any precision the extent of schedule revision or the impact of a scheduling decision on the global satisfaction of optimization criteria. For example, in figure 1 moving forward the last activity of ORDER3 creates downstream cascading constraint violations. Therefore, a repair action must be applied and its repair outcome must be evaluated in terms of the resulting effects on scheduling objectives. In addition, the evaluation itself of what is a "high quality" schedule is difficult because of the need to balance conflicting objectives and trade-off among them. Such tradeoffs typically reflect user preferences, which are difficult to express as a cost function. For example, WIP and weighted tardiness are not always compatible with each other. As shown in figure 2, there are situations where a repair action can reduce weighted tardiness, but WIP increases. Which is a better schedule depends on user preferences.

CABINS *incrementally revises a complete but suboptimal schedule* to improve its quality, based on flexible optimization tradeoffs. Revision-based approaches to scheduling have also been investigated by (Minton *et al.* 1990; Zweben, Deale, & Gargan 1990; Biefeld & Cooper 1991; Laarhoven, Aarts, & Lenstra 1992). In those systems, the initial schedule is repaired by several techniques, such as the min-conflict heuris-

tic or simulated annealing, to minimize the number of constraint violations or optimize a simple cost function (e.g. make-span) of the schedule. The value of incorporating context-dependent user preferences in operational scheduling environments is becoming increasingly recognized (e.g. (Mckay, Buzacott, & Safayeni 1988)) but adequate techniques are lacking.

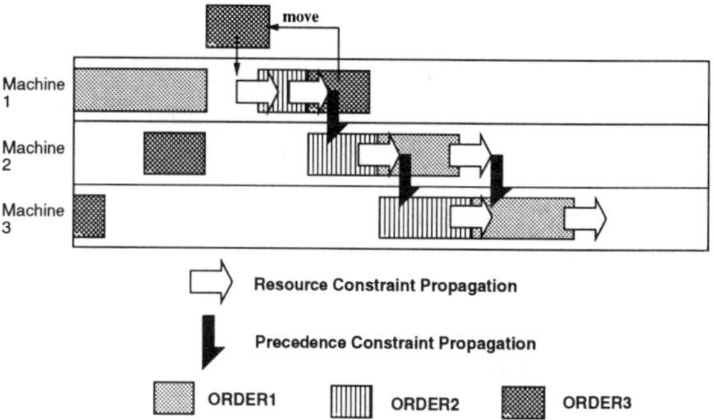

Figure 1: **Example of Tight Constraint Interactions**

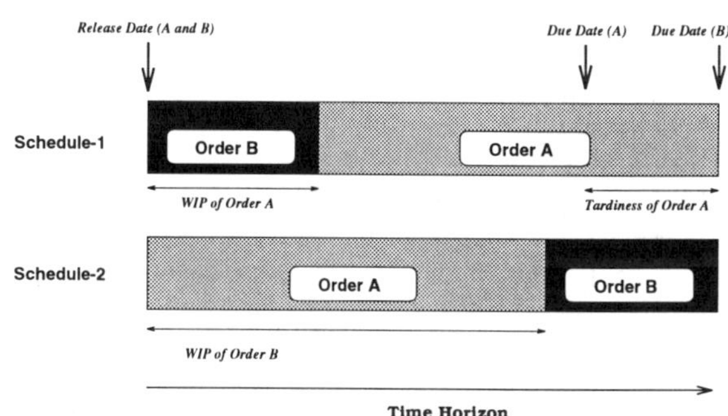

Figure 2: **Example of Conflicting Objectives**

CABINS Overview

CABINS is composed of three modules: (1) an initial schedule builder, (2) an interactive schedule repair (case acquisition) module and (3) an automated schedule repair (case re-use) module. To generate an initial schedule, CABINS can use any of several scheduling methods (e.g. traditional dispatching rules or a constraint-based scheduler).

Case representation

In each repair iteration, CABINS focuses on one activity at a time, the *focal_activity*, and tries to repair it. A case in CABINS describes the application of a particular modification to a focal_activity. Figure 3 shows the information content of a case. Our assumption, borne out by the experimental results, is that despite the ill-structuredness of the domain, the global, local and repair history features express (in an approximate manner) domain regularities. The global features reflect an abstract characterization of potential repair flexibility for the whole schedule. High 'Resource Utilization Average', for example, often indicates a tight schedule without much repair flexibility. Associated with a focal_activity are local features that we have identified, based on those reported in (Ow, Smith, & Thiriez 1988), and which potentially are predictive of estimating the effects of applying a particular repair tactic to the schedule. For example, 'Predictive Shift Gain' predicts how much overall gain will be achieved by moving the current focal_activity earlier in its time horizon. In particular, it predicts the likely reduction of the focal_activity's waiting time when moved to the left within the repair time horizon.

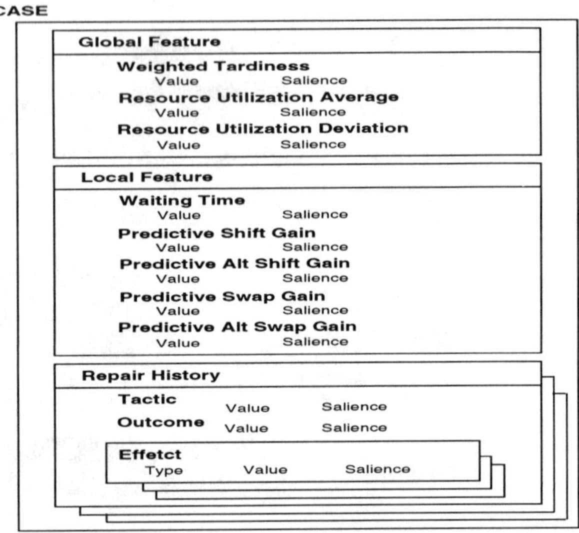

Figure 3: **CABINS Case Representation**

The repair history records the sequence of applications of successive repair tactics, the repair outcome and the effects. Repair effect values describe the impact of the application of a repair action on scheduling objectives (e.g. weighted tardiness, WIP). A repair outcome is the evaluation assigned to the set of effects of a repair action and takes values in the set ['acceptable', 'unacceptable']. Typically the outcome reflects tradeoffs among different objectives. If the application of a repair tactic results in a feasible schedule, the result is judged as either acceptable or unacceptable with respect to the repair objectives. An outcome is 'acceptable' if the user accepts the tradeoffs involved in the set of effects for the current application of a repair action. Otherwise, it is 'unacceptable'. The effect salience is assigned when the outcome is 'unacceptable', and it indicates the significance of the effect to the repair outcome. This value is decided subjectively and interactively. The user's judgment as to balancing favorable and unfavorable effects related to a particular objective constitutes the explanation of the repair

outcome.

Case acquisition

To gather cases, sample scheduling problems are solved by a scheduler. CABINS identifies jobs that must be repaired in the initial sub-optimal schedule. Those jobs are sorted according to the significance of defect, and repaired manually by a user according to this sorting. For example, if the user's optimization criterion is to minimize order tardiness, the most tardy order is repaired first. The user selects a repair tactic to be applied. Tactic application consists of two parts: (a) identify the activities, resources and time intervals that will be involved in the repair, and (b) execute the repair by applying constraint-based scheduling to reschedule the activities identified in (a). Currently CABINS has 11 tactics and a flexible interface through which the user can define more.

After tactic selection and application, the repair effects are calculated and shown to the user who is asked to evaluate the outcome of the repair. If the user evaluates the repair outcome as 'acceptable', CABINS proceeds to repair another focal_activity and the process is repeated. If the user evaluates the repair outcome as 'unacceptable', s/he is asked to supply an explanation in terms of rating the salience/importance of each of the effects. The repair is undone and the user is asked to select another repair tactic for the same focal_activity. The process continues until an acceptable outcome for the current focal_activity is reached, or the repair is given up. Repair is given up when there are no more tactics to be applied to the current focal_activity; in this situation, CABINS carries on repair of another activity. The sequence of applications of successive repair actions, the effects, the repair outcome, and the user's explanation for failed application of a repair tactic are recorded in the repair history of the case. In this way, a number of cases are accumulated in the case base.

Case re-use

Once cases have been gathered, CABINS repairs suboptimal schedules without user interaction. CABINS repairs the schedules by (1) recognizing schedule suboptimalities, (2) focusing on a focal_activity to be repaired in each repair cycle, (3) invoking CBR with the set of global and local features as indices to decide the most appropriate repair tactic to be used for each focal_activity, (4) invoking CBR using the repair effect features (type, value and salience) as indices to evaluate the repair result, and (5) when the repair result is unacceptable, deciding which repair tactic to use next. Note that in contrast to traditional local iterative optimization approaches, (e.g. tabu search, simulated annealing) where the schedule generated in the current iteration as a result of local revision is directly compared (in terms of its associated cost function) with the current schedule, in CABINS, evaluation of the revision is provided by the case base, thus obviating the need for the presence of an explicit cost function.

The similarity between i-th case and the current problem is calculated as follows :

$$exp(-\sqrt{\sum_{j=1}^{N}(SL_j^i \times \frac{CF_j^i - PF_j}{E\_D_j})^2})$$

where SL_j^i is the salience of j-th feature of i-th case in the case-base, and its value has been heuristically defined by the user. CF_j^i is the value of j-th feature of i-th case, PF_j is the value of j-th feature in the current problem, E_D_j is the standard deviation of j-th feature value of all cases in the case-base. Feature values are normalized by division by a standard deviation of the feature value so that features of equal salience have equal weight in the similarity function.

An Example

We briefly illustrate the repair process with a very simple example schedule to be repaired shown in figure 4. The example has ten jobs ($J_1, \ldots, J_{10}$) and each job has five activities with linear precedence constraints. (e.g. O_1^n BEFORE O_2^n, ... , O_4^n BEFORE O_5^n). Resources R_1 and R_2, R_3 and R_5 are substitutable; resource R_4 is a bottleneck. Suppose that the job under repair is J_8. This job has a weight of 2, a due date of 1250 and the scheduled end-time of its last activity is 1390. Hence it has a weighted tardiness of $2 \times (1390 - 1250) = 280$. Suppose the current focal_activity is O_4^8. CBR is invoked with global features (weighted tardiness= 280, resource utilization average=0.544, resource utilization deviation=0.032) plus the set of local features as indices and selects swap as a repair tactic. One can see from the figure that this is a good choice since the focal_activity is scheduled on machine R_4, which doesn't have any substitutable machine and any idle time in the repair time horizon (time between the end of O_3^8 and the end of O_4^8).

To apply swap, CABINS calculates the activity with which O_4^8 will be swapped. To do this, CABINS selects the activity which, if swapped with O_4^8, will result in least amount of precedence constraint violations. In the example, activity O_4^4 is selected as the activity to be swapped with the current focal_activity O_4^8. Job J_4 has weight 3 and weighted tardiness $3 \times (1370 - 1320) = 150$. The effect of applying the swap tactic is that O_4^8 and O_4^4 are unscheduled on R_4 and O_4^8 is re-scheduled to start at time 1090 (the start time of activity O_4^4 prior to the swap). The repair process resolves occurring constraint violations. The repaired schedule is shown in figure 5.

The effects of repairing O_4^8 are calculated. CABINS calculates the effects on J_8 and J_4, the jobs affected by the application of the swap on O_4^8. Machine utilization did not change but J_8 had an estimated decrease in weighted-tardiness of 180 time units and an estimated decrease in WIP of 200 units, J_4 had an increase in

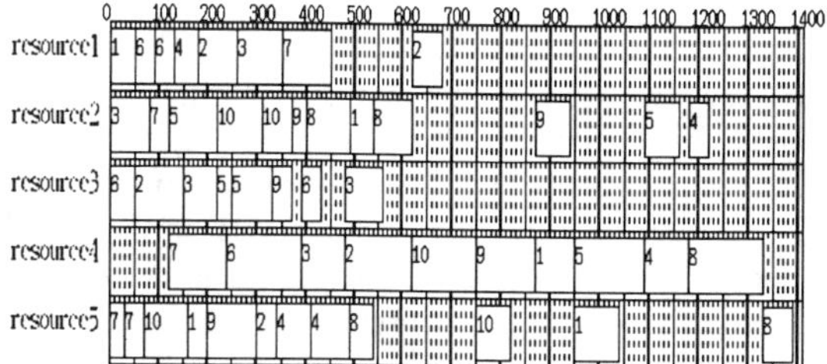

Figure 4: Original Schedule Results

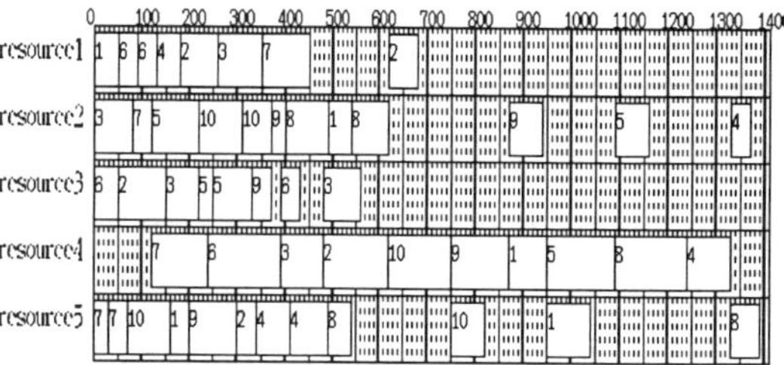

Figure 5: Schedule Results after Repair on O_4^8

weighted-tardiness of 150 units and an increase in WIP of 750 units. CBR is invoked using these effect values, weighted tardiness, WIP, as indices to determine whether this repair outcome is acceptable. The acceptability or unacceptability of the repair will depend on the biases reflected in the case base.

Evaluation of the Approach

We conducted a set of experiments to test the hypothesis that (1) our CBR-based incremental modification and re-use methodology could be effective in capturing user schedule optimization preferences and re-using them to control schedule optimization, (2) the approach is robust in that the schedules produced by CABINS consistently improve a schedule independent of the method used for initial schedule generation and (3) as an iterative optimization method, the approach produces schedules of high quality. These hypotheses are difficult to test since, due to the subjective and ill-defined nature of user preferences, it is not obvious how to correlate scheduling results with the captured preferences or how to define quality of a schedule whose evaluation is subjective.

To address these issues, we had to devise a method to test the hypotheses in a consistent manner. To do that, it is necessary to know the optimization criterion that would be implicit in the case base, so that the experimental results can be evaluated. In the experiments reported here, we used two different explicit criteria (weighted tardiness; WIP+weighted tardiness) to reflect the user's optimization criterion and built a rule-based reasoner (RBR) that goes through a trial-and-error repair process to optimize a schedule. For each repair, the repair effects were calculated and, on this basis, since RBR had a predefined evaluation objective, it could evaluate the repair outcome in a consistent manner. Thus, we used RBR with different rules each time to generate different case bases (each with 1,000 cases) [2] for different explicit optimization objectives. Naturally, an objective, though known to us, is not known to CABINS and is only implicitly and indirectly reflected in an extensional way in each case base. By designing an objective into the RBR so it could be reflected in the corresponding case base we got an experimental baseline against which to evaluate the schedules generated by CABINS.

We evaluated the approach on a benchmark suite of 60 job shop scheduling problems where parameters, such as number of bottlenecks, range of due dates and activity durations were varied to cover a range of job shop scheduling problem instances with the following structure. Each problem class has 10 jobs of 5 operations each and 5 machines. Two parameters were used to cover different scheduling conditions: a range parameter controlled the distribution of job due dates and release dates, and a bottleneck parameter controlled the number of bottleneck resources. Six groups of 10 problems each were randomly generated by considering three different values of the range parameter, and two values of the bottleneck configuration (1 and 2 bottleneck problems). These problems are variations of the problems originally reported in (Sadeh 1991). Our problem sets are, however, different in two respects: (a) we allow substitutable resources for non-bottleneck resources whereas the original problems did not, and (b) the due dates of jobs in our problems are tighter by 20 percents than in the original problems. We also tested the approach on another set of 60 problems of 20 orders and 5 resources with similar results.

A cross-validation method was used to evaluate the learning capability of CABINS. Each problem set in each class was divided in half. The training sample was repaired by RBR to gather cases. These cases were then used for case-based repair of the validation problems. We repeated the above process by interchanging the training and test sets. Reported results are for the validation problem sets.

Experimental Results

Figures 6 show the performance of CABINS using "weighted tardiness" case base (labeled in the figures as CABINS(WT)) vs performance of CABINS using the "weighted tardiness and WIP" case base (labeled in the figures as CABINS(WT+WIP)). The cases constituted the only source of knowledge for CABINS. In

---

^{footnote}

²Since a case represents the application of one repair tactic to an activity, if, for example, 5 repair tactics are utilized in an attempt to successfully repair an activity, then 5 cases would be created.

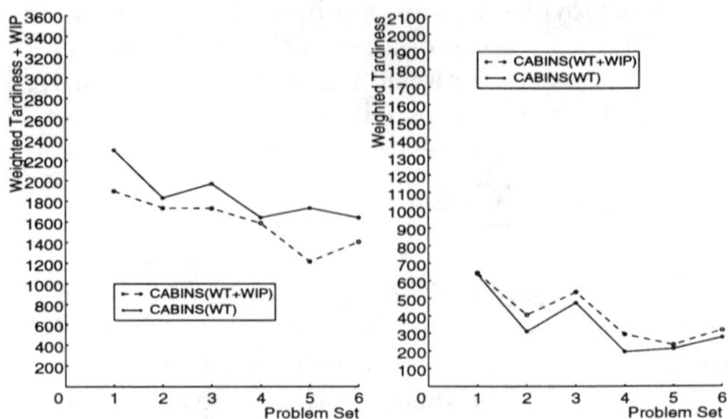

Figure 6: Scheduling Results with Different Case Bases

	Wei.Tar.	WIP	Total	CPU Sec.
EDD	956.0	1284.6	2240.6	0.1
CABINS	349.5	1311.2	1660.7	73.5
SA	340.5	1333.4	1673.9	388.2
WSPT	584.0	1241.0	1825.0	0.1
CABINS	321.0	1254.9	1575.9	72.1
SA	328.5	1320.4	1684.9	398.3
R&M	556.0	1242.0	1798.0	0.1
CABINS	305.3	1264.9	1570.2	84.9
SA	330.1	1290.8	1620.9	450.5
CBS	1173.0	1481.0	2654.0	17.4
CABINS	405.3	1195.0	1600.3	296.5
SA	395.5	1220.0	1615.5	1380.0

Table 1: Repair by CABINS and SA based on Different Methods of Initial Schedule Generation

other words, there was no objective given to CABINS explicitly. The case-bases were used both as a source of suitable repairs, and also as a source of advice regarding repair evaluation. From the results we observe that CABINS(WT) generated higher quality schedules with respect to minimizing weighted tardiness than CABINS(WT+WIP). Conversely, CABINS(WT+WIP) generated higher quality schedules with respect to WIP, and weighted tardiness plus WIP than CABINS(WT). These results indicate that CABINS can acquire different and subjective user preferences.

In order to test the hypothesis that CABINS consistently improves schedule quality independent of the method of initial schedule generation, we generated initial schedules for the benchmark suite of problems using three different state-of-the-art dispatch scheduling heuristics (EDD, WSPT, R&M) (Morton 1992) and a constraint-based scheduler (CBS). The optimization objective was WT+WIP. Table 1 presents the average of all 60 problems in the benchmark and shows that CABINS improved schedule quality independent of method to create the initial schedule. To test the hypothesis that CABINS generates schedules of high quality, we compared the schedules generated by CABINS against schedules generated by simulated annealing with the explicit objective of WT+WIP. Table 1 shows that CABINS generated schedules of comparable quality but was on the average 4-5 times more efficient than simulated annealing.

Conclusions

We have presented a case-based approach to acquire user optimization preferences and reuse them to guide iterative solution optimization in ill-structured domains. We demonstrated the effectiveness of the approach in capturing user preferences and creating efficiently high quality solutions on job shop scheduling problems. One crucial issue is how much effort should be spent to capture "enough" number of cases for "sufficient" solution quality improvement. This is an issue we are currently pursuing. Initial experiments to determine case base size versus quality improvement have shown that a case base of 800 cases gives on the average 20% higher quality improvement at 15% lower computational cost than a case base of 400 cases. It seems that the effort expended to capture a big number of cases can be amortized by future repeated use of the case base to get high quality schedules efficiently. More importantly, CABINS can acquire those cases from user's interaction during the process of solution improvement, thus imposing low additional effort on the user but enhancing solution improvement. We believe that CABINS has the potential for accommodating acquisition of user preferences that change over time. Future work will investigate this issue.

References

Bareiss, R. 1989. *Exemplar-based knowledge acquisition : a unified approach to concept regression, classification, and learning.* New York, NY: Academic Press.

Biefeld, E., and Cooper, L. 1991. Bottleneck identification using process chronologies. In *Proceedings of the 12th International Joint Conference on Artificial Intelligence (IJCAI-91).*

Chaturvedi, A. 1992. Acquiring Implicit Knowledge in a Complex Domain. *Expert Systems with Applications.*

French, S. 1982. *Sequencing and Scheduling: An Introduction to the Mathematics of the Job-Shop.* New York, NY: Ellis Horwood.

Golding, A. R., and Rosenbloom, P. S. 1991. Improving Rule-Based Systems Through Case-Based Reasoning. In *Proceedings of the Ninth National Conference on Artificial Intelligence,* 22–27. AAAI.

Hammond, K. J. 1989. *Case-Based Planning : Viewing Planning as a Memory Task.* New York, NY: Academic Press.

Johnson, D.; Aragon, C.; McGeoch, L.; and Schevon, C. 1991. Optimization By Simulated Annealing: An Experimental Evaluation, Part II (Graph Coloring and Number Partitioning). *Operations Research.*

Laarhoven, P. J. M. V.; Aarts, E. H. L.; and Lenstra, J. K. 1992. Job shop scheduling by simulated annealing. *Operations Research* 40(1):113–125.

Lewis, L.; Minior, D.; and Brown, S. 1991. A Case-Based Reasoning Solution to the Problem of Redundant Engineering in Large Scale Manufacturing. *International Journal of Expert Systems* 4(2):189–201.

Mckay, K.; Buzacott, J.; and Safayeni, F. 1988. The scheduler's knowledge of uncertainty: The missing link. In *Proceedings of IFIP Working Conference on Knowledge Based Production Management Systems.*

Minton, S.; Johnston, M. D.; Philips, A. B.; and Laird, P. 1990. Solving large-scale constraint satisfaction and scheduling problems using a heuristic repair method. In *Proceedings, Eighth National Conference on Artificial Intelligence,* 17–24. Boston, MA.: AAAI.

Morton, T. E. 1992. *HEURISTIC SCHEDULING SYSTEMS: With Application to Production Systems and Product Management.* Pittsburgh, PA.: GSIA, Carnegie Mellon University. Course Textbook.

Ow, P. S.; Smith, S. F.; and Thiriez, A. 1988. Reactive plan revision. In *Proceedings of the Seventh National Conference on Artificial Intelligence,* 77–82. St-Paul, Minnesota: AAAI.

Prerau, D. S. 1990. *Developing and Managing Expert Systems: Proven Techniques for Business and Industry.* Reading, MA: Addison-Wesley.

Reeves, C., ed. 1993. *Modern Heuristic Techniques for Combinatorial Problems.* New York: Halsted Press.

Ruby, D., and Kibler, D. 1992. Learning Episodes for Optimization. In *Machine Learning : proceedings of the Ninth International Workshop (ML92),* 379–384.

Sadeh, N. 1991. *Look-Ahead Techniques for Micro-Opportunistic Job Shop Scheduling.* Ph.D. Dissertation, School of Computer Science, Carnegie Mellon University.

Veloso, M. M. 1992. *Learning by Analogical Reasoning in General Problem Solving.* Ph.D. Dissertation, School of Computer Science, Carnegie Mellon University.

Zweben, M.; Deale, M.; and Gargan, M. 1990. Anytime rescheduling. In *Proceedings of the DARPA Workshop on Innovative Approaches to Planning, Scheduling and Control,* 251–259. San Diego, CA.: DARPA.

Towards More Creative Case-Based Design Systems

Linda M. Wills and Janet L. Kolodner
College of Computing
Georgia Institute of Technology
Atlanta, Georgia 30332-0280
linda@cc.gatech.edu, jlk@cc.gatech.edu

Abstract

Case-based reasoning (CBR) has a great deal to
offer in supporting creative design, particularly
processes that rely heavily on previous design experience, such as framing the problem and evaluating design alternatives. However, most existing
CBR systems are not living up to their potential.
They tend to adapt and reuse old solutions in
routine ways, producing robust but uninspired
results. Little research effort has been directed
towards the kinds of situation assessment, evaluation, and assimilation processes that facilitate
the exploration of ideas and the elaboration and
redefinition of problems that are crucial to creative design. Also, their typically rigid control
structures do not facilitate the kinds of strategic control and opportunism inherent in creative
reasoning. In this paper, we describe the types of
behavior we would like case-based design systems
to support, based on a study of designers working
on a mechanical engineering problem. We show
how the standard CBR framework should be extended and we describe an architecture we are
developing to experiment with these ideas.[1]

Introduction

Creativity in design derives from enumerating several solution alternatives, redescribing and elaborating
problem specifications, and evaluating proposed solutions, based on criteria and constraints that go beyond the stated constraints on a solution. It arises
out of a confluence of processes (including problem
redescription, remembering, assimilation, and evaluation), which interact with each other in complex ways.
Often creativity arises from interesting strategic control of these processes, which in themselves may be
quite mundane (Boden 1990, Chandrasekaran 1990,
Gero & Maher 1993, Navinchandra 1992).

These processes rely heavily on previous design experiences and knowledge of designed artifacts (Goel &
Chandrasekaran 1992, Hinrichs 1992, Kolodner & Penberthy 1990, Kolodner & Wills 1993). An expert designer knows of many design experiences, accumulated
from personally designing artifacts, being given case
studies of designs in school, and observing artifacts
designed by others. The designer draws on these experiences to perform such activities as generating design
alternatives, reformulating and elaborating the problem specification or proposed solutions, and predicting
the outcome of making certain design decisions. The
experiences that are most valuable are often those that
are highly contextualized pieces of knowledge about artifacts, such as how a device behaves in some context
of use, circumstances in which it can fail, and knowledge about situations that might come up not only in
use, but in all phases of its life cycle.

Given the nature of these experiences, we believe
case-based representations and reasoning techniques
lend themselves to supporting creative design. Research in case-based reasoning (CBR) has provided extensive knowledge of how to reuse solutions to old problems in new situations, how to build and search case
libraries (for exploration of design alternatives), and
how to merge and adapt cases. It has developed powerful techniques for partial matching and the formation
of analogical maps between seemingly disparate situations (Kolodner 1993).

However, most existing CBR systems are not living
up to their potential. They tend to adapt and reuse
old solutions in routine ways, producing robust but
uninspired results. They do not attempt to extend
their exploration by deriving constraints and preferences that improve or go beyond those stated in the
original problem. (See (Kolodner 1993, appendix) for
a recent survey.)

Some of this potential is buried in processes that
have been downplayed or even missing in most standard CBR systems. In particular, little research effort
has been directed towards the kinds of situation assessment, evaluation, and assimilation processes that
facilitate the exploration of ideas and the elaboration
and redefinition of problems that are crucial to creative design. Also, to facilitate the kinds of opportunism inherent in creative reasoning, CBR systems
need to break out of their typically rigid control struc-

---

[1]This research was funded in part by NSF Grant No.
IRI-8921256 and ONR Grant No. N00014-92-J-1234.

ture to allow flexible interleaving and communication among processes. In addition, more research attention must be payed to the strategic control mechanisms that guide a creative designer in deciding what to do next.

In this paper, we describe the types of behavior we would like case-based design systems to support, based on an exploratory study of designers working on a mechanical engineering problem. We show how the standard CBR framework should be extended and we describe an architecture we are developing to experiment with these ideas. We end with a set of open issues.

What Do Creative Designers Do?

To gain insights into the knowledge and reasoning involved in creative design, we observed a four-person team engaged in a seven-week undergraduate mechanical engineering (ME) design project. The task was to design and build a device to quickly and safely transport several eggs from one location to another. The device could be constructed from any material, but its size, weight, and cost were restricted.

After exploring several schemes for launching, moving, stopping, and protecting the eggs, the team decided to use a cylindrical egg carrier (of radius 7 cm., length 22.5 cm.), with the eggs wrapped in pipe insulation to protect them inside the carrier. The carrier was dropped down (0.8 m.) from a starting platform and would roll into a target zone (within a 5 m. radius of the starting platform). The team had two possible launch mechanisms up until the final design demonstration day: a spring mechanism and a simple ramp (the spring launch base could be inverted to become a ramp, which was the final choice). In both cases, a string, with one end attached to the launch base, was wrapped around the device, so that as the cylinder dropped, it spun down the string, hit the ground, and rolled into the target zone. The wrapped string gave the carrier momentum and it also prevented it from rolling beyond the target zone.

One of us participated as a member of the team, allowing us to become immersed in the issues and to observe the design process in a natural setting, in both informal and "official" team meetings. We recorded the group's conversations on audiotapes and collected copies of all their design documents and drawings.

We are particularly intrigued by a set of three processes we observed underlying many creative design activities: 1) generation of multiple descriptions or views of a problem, 2) gradual emergence of evaluative issues, constraints and preferences, and 3) serendipitous recognition of solutions to pending problems, sometimes seeing new functions and purposes for common design pieces in the process. We are not claiming that this is a complete set. (For example, our design study has revealed a variety of influences on creativity from collaborative activity.) Rather, we are interested in these processes because they are key processes in design that current case-based systems neglect.

Problem Redescription. The initial problem statement given to our designers was ambiguous, incomplete, contradictory, and underconstrained. They spent a great deal of effort to turn it into something with more detail, more concrete specifications, and more clearly defined and consistent constraints. An important part of this process involved attempting to understand the problem, view it from multiple perspectives, and redescribe it in terms familiar to the designers. They had to refine and operationalize several vague or abstract constraints, while sometimes having to abstract constraints that were too specific.

For example, many of the ideas of one designer, who had a keen interest in automobiles, came from recalling devices and concepts from the car domain, such as shock absorbers, unit-body vs. single-frame construction, and air-bags. Being able to recall these required viewing the problem of protecting the eggs as one of absorbing shock or transferring energy and as a problem of protecting passengers in general, not just eggs.

Our designers also explored the given constraints, deliberately stretching or strengthening them to see what ideas became possible. For example, the initial problem statement was ambiguous about whether or not the device could land (i.e., touch down) short of the target zone and then move into it. The designers considered the extreme possibility of landing as far short of this zone as possible, in which case the device would not fly at all, but would be pushed off or lowered to the ground, where it would then move itself into the safety zone. Visualizing this possibility reminded them of devices, such as elevators and yo-yo's, that could implement parts of this behavior.

This continual elaboration and redescription of the problem helped the designers derive connections between the current problem and similar problems in other domains, facilitating cross-contextual transfer of design ideas. It also primed them to serendipitously recognize relevant objects in the environment that might be reused for a new purpose.

Evaluation. One of the key forces driving evolution of the problem specification is the evaluation of proposed design alternatives. Evaluative issues emerge in the course of evaluating. Designers do not merely depend on constraints that have already been specified. Rather, they bring up additional constraints and criteria as proposals are examined. Proposed solutions often remind them of issues to consider. The problem and solution "co-evolve" (Fischer 1993).

One interesting criteria that emerged in the course of the ME design project was *versatility* – the ability of the device to apply in more than one situation. This criteria was not mentioned or required in the original statement of the problem. It arose in response to ambiguity in the initial problem statement, which described three similar problems but did not specify which one would be assigned. Each problem differed only in the device's starting position (from either the center of a child's wading pool or from a platform of one of two heights) and in its target destination distance. (This is similar in the real world to situations in which the engineers are designing for multiple potential customers with different needs). To deal with the uncertainty and reduce the complexity this variability introduced, the designers began searching for solutions that could be used to solve all three problems or could be easily adapted to apply to each. That is, they began to evaluate proposals on the basis of versatility in addition to the other criteria already in the problem specification. Being able to do this is central to creative design.

Assimilation. Problem redescription provides not only a means for recalling relevant solution alternatives, but also a vocabulary for describing and, in many cases, reinterpreting objects in the designer's environment. This often leads to a new way of viewing the function of some object and facilitates the recognition of potential solutions to pending problems in the external environment.

For example, our designers went to a home improvement store for materials for a spring launch mechanism. While comparing the strengths of several springs by compressing them, they noticed that the springs tended to bend. One designer wrapped a hand around the spring to hold it straight as it was compressed and said the springs would each need to be enclosed in a tube to keep them from bending. Another added that the tube would need to be collapsible (to compress with the spring). The designers could not think of an existing collapsible tube and did not want to build one due to time pressure. They gave up on the springs and started thinking about egg protection. During their search for protection material, they walked through the bathroom section of the store, where they saw a display of toilet paper holders. They immediately recognized them as collapsible tubes which could be used to support the springs.

By playing with the springs, noticing problems and suggesting fixes, the designers formed a specific, concrete, and operationalized description of what a solution would look like to the bending-springs problem. However, the toilet-paper holder was not recalled on the basis of this description. Instead, the description was used to reinterpret the toilet paper holder when it was encountered in the external environment and to recognize its additional function of preventing springs from bending upon compression. The designers were able to interpret objects seen in the environment, or recalled from memory, from a new viewpoint. This viewpoint was based on descriptions and feature dimensions that had been revealed to be important in attempts to solve recent and pending problems.

We refer to this process as *assimilating* the objects into a problem context. It not only involves reinterpreting solution alternatives under consideration, but also comparing and contrasting alternatives with one another, along the dimensions relevant to the problem context. This helps reveal those that are not really new ideas, so that they can be ignored. It can also cause new evaluative issues to emerge as new dimensions or criteria are generated to distinguish seemingly identical ideas.

Strategic Control. The designers we observed did not follow a rigid, methodical plan detailing what to do next. Rather, they moved fluidly between various problem pieces and design processes (e.g., idea generation, adaptation, critiquing, problem refinement, elaboration, and redefinition) in a flexible and highly opportunistic manner.

Our designers employed a variety of strategic control heuristics, some of which are opportunistic. For example, when an alternative was proposed that satisfied some desired criteria extremely well compared to the other alternatives, they directed their efforts toward elaborating that alternative, optimistically suspending criticism or discounting the importance of criteria or constraints that were not satisfied as well. Sometimes this led to reformulation of the problem as constraints were relaxed or placed at a lower priority.

Being able to take advantage of such opportunities requires being able to judge whether progress was being made along a certain line of attack and to choose which ideas are more promising or more likely to lead to something unusual and novel.

Some strategic control heuristics are more deliberate, based on reflection. For example, one heuristic our designers used was to try quick, easy adaptations of a proposed solution first before stepping back and reformulating the problem or relaxing constraints. Other deliberate heuristics attempted to make non-standard substitutions, apply adaptation strategies in circumstances other than the ones they were meant for, and merge pieces of separate solutions with each other in nonobvious ways.

In many cases, the processes that are composed together leading to a novel idea are not in themselves novel and may be quite mundane. The trick is knowing when to do them.

How CBR Systems Can Do Better

Most current CBR systems tend to stick to well-known interpretations of problems and routine ways of adapting old solutions, neglecting exploration of alternatives if something good enough has been found. We believe the CBR paradigm can be extended to support more creative problem solving.

Problem Redescription. Problem redescription corresponds closely to the process of situation assessment – redescribing a problem in the vocabulary of the indexing system. In most CBR systems, situation assessment is skipped; the assumption is made that the initial representation of the problem is sufficient for solving the problem. But, as our observations show, investigating a problem in depth makes available a large set of relevant cues for retrieval. Generating multiple ways of describing a problem provides several different contexts for specifying what would be relevant, if remembered.

Research on indexing has found that it is the combination of setting up a context for retrieval and having already interpreted something in memory in a similar way that allows retrieval. When some case or piece of knowledge is entered into memory, it is not always possible to anticipate how it might be used. Situation assessment processes aim to bridge that gap by helping to redescribe a new problem in a way that is similar to something seen before.

Research into situation assessment and problem reformulation (e.g., in CASEY (Koton 1988), CYRUS (Kolodner 1983), MINSTREL (Turner 1994), BRAIN-STORMER (Jones 1992), and STRATA (Lowry 1987)), show different ways it can be done. However, these techniques have not yet made it into widespread use in practical CBR systems. They should certainly be included in any system aimed at reuse of experience across domains.

Evaluation. CBR systems currently evaluate solutions by checking a set of constraints that have been given to the system. Evaluative procedures are typically buried within case manipulation to predict or test whether a modified case satisfies the specified constraints. Observations of our designers suggests that evaluation should play a more prominent role in case-based design systems, allowing evaluative issues to emerge in the course of evaluating. Navinchandra (1991) calls this *criteria emergence* and shows an example of how it can arise from case-based projection. In addition to criteria, constraints in general (Prabhakar & Goel 1992) and relative priorities among them also gradually emerge. This type of evaluation is a key driving force within creative design, feeding back to situation assessment and guiding case manipulation.

Assimilation. A key idea underlying dynamic memory (Schank 1982), one of the principle foundations of case-based reasoning, is that remembering, understanding, and learning are all inextricably intertwined. The ability to determine where something fits in with what we already know (understanding) is a key part of being able to assimilate objects in our environment into our problem solving. This environment includes not only external objects, but also cases that have been retrieved, elaborated and adapted. Understanding how these fit into a problem context may involve a useful reinterpretation of something already in memory, suggesting in a new way of indexing it.

Strategic Control. Our exploratory study suggests that a linear, sequential composition of CBR processes is much too simple. In reality, these processes are highly intertwined and interact in interesting ways. For example, problem elaboration and redescription tactics specify contexts for search that retrieval processes use, while evaluation of recalled or adapted alternatives feeds information back to these situation assessment tactics, resulting in even better contexts for search. In some cases, what suggests a particular problem refinement or redescription results from trying to confirm the legality of a proposed solution during evaluation and finding a loophole or ambiguity in the current problem specification. In addition, comparing and contrasting a proposed solution with other proposals during assimilation can bring new evaluative issues into focus.

CBR systems need to break out of their typically rigid control structure and allow more interaction and opportunism among processes. This requires making strategic control mechanisms explicit, so they can be easily modified, reasoned about, extended, and learned. More research needs to be directed at identifying and capturing the types of strategic control heuristics designers use.

Proposed Architecture

We are developing an experimental case-based system that emphasizes the processes of situation assessment, evaluation, and assimilation, integrating them with the usual CBR processes of retrieval, elaboration (case manipulation, adaptation, merging, prediction), and learning. It has a flexible, opportunistic control structure which allows us to keep control tactics separate, explicit, and modifiable.

The processes within our system are not applied in a strictly linear succession. Rather, the system has a blackboard-style architecture. The processes are centered around and act upon data structures that represent the evolving problem specification and the set of design alternatives under consideration.

Situation assessment procedures act on the problem specification to evolve it along multiple directions. Evaluation examines design alternatives, checking them against the current specification, to reveal inconsistencies, ambiguities, and incompletenesses in the specification that suggest new redescriptions. Evaluation also brings up new criteria, and constraints which are incorporated into the problem specification.

Elaboration procedures transform alternatives under consideration into new alternatives by applying a variety of adaptation and merging strategies. These strategies are typically suggested by the critique formed by an evaluation of some alternative. Elaboration procedures also augment alternatives with information derived about their consequences and expected behavior. These "data collection" elaborations are currently accomplished by manual augmentations of alternatives with experimental data, but in general can be achieved by case-based projection, simulation, actual experimentation, or visualization.

The evolving problem description is also used by both the retrieval and the assimilation processes. Retrieval interfaces with a library of cases which models, in part, long-term memory. The problem description is used as a probe into memory to pull relevant design cases into consideration (for evaluation, elaboration, etc.). The assimilation process is the dual of retrieval. It accumulates design alternatives proposed (i.e., those retrieved, elaborated, or viewed directly in the external environment) into the pool of design alternatives under consideration, organizing the alternatives with respect to each other.

The data structure holding the set of design alternatives forms an extension of the long-term memory. We call this extension the "problem context." The evolving problem description determines the focal vocabulary of the current problem context. As the specification evolves, the focus changes on the relevant vocabulary to be used for organizing alternatives in the memory (e.g., shape, construction cost, personal safety). In a sense, the problem context is providing a point of view with respect to which objects in the environment and cases recalled can be interpreted and organized by the assimilation process.

The coordination of the various processes is controlled by explicit strategic control mechanisms. There are a set of monitoring procedures, associated with each of the processes, which watch for opportunities for some task to be performed. The opportunities noticed are placed on an "opportunity agenda." Opportunities are chosen and pulled from the agenda by strategic control heuristics. For example, a monitor associated with the assimilation process watches for an alternative to be added that is much better than any other alternative proposed so far, with respect to some desired criterion. This yields an opportunity to change the problem description by increasing the priority of that criterion and/or by relaxing constraints that are not met by that proposal. This simulates the behavior of changing the relative importance among criteria to accommodate an unexpectedly good solution that is stumbled upon. An example strategic control heuristic would be to pursue elaboration opportunities for alternatives that satisfy a desired criteria extremely well before pursuing evaluative processes that would negatively critique the alternatives. This simulates the behavior of optimistically pursuing an idea, suspending all but constructive criticism.

Status, Limitations and Open Issues

Our system currently has implemented procedures for evaluation, assimilation, and retrieval, as well as data structures representing the case library, pool of design alternatives, evolving problem specification, and the opportunity agenda data structure. We have standard agenda management routines. However, these routines currently do not model the ephemeral nature of opportunities (which can either expire or be forgotten). Several monitors surrounding the assimilation process have been implemented, but we still need to define and capture those relevant to the other processes.

Much more work is needed to identify and define strategic control heuristics, situation assessment procedures, and elaboration techniques. Also, not all strategic control mechanisms are triggered by noticing an opportunity. Some may become applicable due to some complex condition that must be inferred through reflection. (For example, realizing that you are reasoning in circles might cause you to make an effort to try a brand new technique.) More research needs to focus on how to represent and infer these kinds of conditions and also how the application of these more reflective strategic control mechanisms can be interleaved with the triggering of opportunistic ones.

We are starting to understand how criteria, constraints, preferences, etc., emerge during evaluation, but more effort is needed in modeling this emergence.

There are a number of interesting open issues concerning how assimilation is managed when the design problem is complex, having several interacting subproblems, each of which have different sets of alternatives and requirements. Assimilation must find the appropriate problem context for interpreting and evaluating a given design alternative. The ability to do this facilitates the serendipitous recognition of solutions to pending problems, as we saw in the bending-springs problem. (See also (Seifert et al. 1994).)

Another open issue is that the designers we studied were not expert mechanical engineers. An interesting empirical question is: would experts, having knowledge of "design principles," behave differently? It may not be the expert vs. novice distinction, but how open-ended the problem is, that is important. After all, the students were familiar with and experienced in solving everyday mechanical problems using objects in their world. We believe that for open-ended, nonroutine problems, expert designers are likely to display the same sorts of behaviors as do our students.

Finally, there are some aspects of creative design that we have not yet explored. In particular, we would like to analyze more carefully the influences collaboration had on creativity in the design project. Our agenda-based model of opportunity management lends itself to simulating the exploration of several opportunities in parallel, and employing multiple control strategies at once. This will allow us to simulate these aspects of collaborative activity and use computational experiments to explore hypotheses about the role of collaboration in creative design.

Conclusion

Our intention in building our system is not to automate design, but to test our hypotheses about the cognition of creative design. We are trying to understand creative processes better, using a case-based cognitive model. As we increase our understanding (and in the process, push CBR technology), we will be able to answer the question how best to assist human designers. This may include 1) aiding the formalization, reformu-

lation, and refinement of specifications (Reubenstein
& Waters 1991, Johnson, Benner, & Harris 1993), 2)
bringing up evaluative issues (Domeshek & Kolodner
1993), 3) retrieving pending problem contexts to help
recognize the applicability of solutions, or 4) proposing
new control strategies.

We are taking a case-based approach to understanding creative design for two reasons. One is that many
creative design activities are highly memory-intensive
and rely on past design experiences, so case-based reasoning has much to offer in this study. The other is
that we hope to make case-based systems themselves
more creative. By using the paradigmatic tools CBR
provides, we are starting to find computational models of the behaviors and processes we observed in our
exploratory study. At the same time, our modeling attempts have deepened our understanding of case-based
processes and memory issues and have suggested extensions that will yield more creative design systems
in the future.

Acknowledgements

We appreciate the insightful discussions we have had
with Terry Chandler, Eric Domeshek, Lucy Gibson,
Todd Griffith, Kenneth Moorman, Nancy Nersessian,
Ashwin Ram, and Mimi Recker. We would like to
thank Otto Baskin, Jon Howard, and Malisa Sarntinoranont, for their invaluable cooperation. We also
appreciate the insights and helpful comments of our
anonymous reviewers.

References

Boden, M. 1990. *The Creative Mind: Myths and Mechanisms*. New York, NY: Basic Books.

Chandrasekaran, B. 1990. Design Problem Solving: A
Task Analysis. *AI Magazine.* 11(4): 59-71.

Domeshek, E.A., and Kolodner, J.L. 1993. Using the
points of large cases, *Artificial Intelligence for Engineering Design, Analysis and Manufacturing* 7(2): 87-96.

Fischer, G. 1993. Turning Breakdowns into Opportunities for Creativity. In Proceedings of the International Symposium on Creativity and Cognition,
Loughborough, England.

Gero, J. and Maher, M. 1993. *Modeling Creativity
and Knowledge-Based Creative Design*. Hillsdale, NJ:
Lawrence Erlbaum Associates, Publishers.

Goel, A. and Chandrasekaran, B. 1992. Case-based
Design: A Task Analysis. In C. Tong and D. Sriram
(eds.), *Artificial Intelligence Approaches to Engineering Design, Volume 2: Innovative Design*. San Diego,
CA: Academic Press.

Hinrichs, T. 1992. *Problem Solving in Open Worlds:
A Case Study in Design*. Northvale, NJ: Erlbaum.

Johnson, W.L., Benner, K.M., and Harris, D.R. 1993.
Developing Formal Specifications From Informal Requirements. *IEEE Expert* 8(4): 82-90.

Jones, E.K. 1992. The Flexible Use of Abstract Knowledge in Planning. Northwestern University, Institute
for the Learning Sciences Technical Report no. 28.

Kolodner, J.L. 1993. *Case-Based Reasoning*. San Mateo, CA: Morgan-Kaufman Publishers, Inc.

Kolodner, J. 1983. Reconstructive Memory: A Computer Model. *Cognitive Science* 7(4): 281-328.

Kolodner, J.L. and Penberthy, T.L. 1990. A Case-Based Approach to Creativity in Problem Solving. In
Proceedings of the Twelfth Annual Conference of the
Cognitive Science Society, Cambridge, MA.

Kolodner, J.L. and Wills, L.M. 1993. Case-Based Creative Design. In AAAI Spring Symposium on AI and
Creativity. Stanford, CA. Reprinted in *AISB Quarterly* 85: 50-57.

Koton, P. 1988. Reasoning about evidence in causal
explanation. In Proceedings of the 6th National Conference on Artificial Intelligence. Cambridge, MA:
AAAI Press/MIT Press.

Lowry, M. 1987. The Abstraction/Implementation
Model of Problem Reformulation. In Proceedings of
the 10th International Joint Conference on Artificial
Intelligence, pp. 1004-1010. Milan, Italy.

Navinchandra, D. 1991. *Exploration and Innovation in
Design: Towards a Computational Model*. New York:
Springer-Verlag.

Navinchandra, D. 1992. Innovative Design Systems:
Where are we, and where do we go from here?. Parts I
and II. *The Knowledge Engineering Review* 7(3): 183-213 and 7(4): 345-362.

Prabhakar, S. and Goel, A. 1992. Performance-Driven
Creativity in Design: Constraint Discovery, Model Revision, and Case Composition. In Proceedings of the
Second International Conference on Computational
Models of Creative Design. Heron Island, Australia.

Reubenstein, H.B. and Waters, R.C. 1991. The Requirements Apprentice: Automated Assistance for Requirements Aquisition. *IEEE Transactions on Software Engineering* 17(3): 226-240.

Schank, R. 1982. *Dynamic Memory: A Theory of
Learning in Computers and People*. New York: Cambridge University Press.

Seifert, C., Meyer, D., Davidson, N., Patalano, A.,
and Yaniv, I. 1994. Demystification of Cognitive Insight: Opportunistic Assimilation and the Prepared-Mind Perspective. In R.J. Sternberg and J.E. Davidson (eds.), *The Nature of Insight*. Cambridge, MA:
MIT Press. Forthcoming.

Turner, S.R. 1994. *MINSTREL*, Lawrence-Erlbaum
Associates, Inc. Forthcoming.

Retrieving Semantically Distant Analogies
with Knowledge-Directed Spreading Activation[*]

Michael Wolverton and Barbara Hayes-Roth
Knowledge Systems Laboratory, Stanford University
701 Welch Rd, Bldg. C
Palo Alto, CA 94304
{mjw|bhr}@hpp.stanford.edu

Abstract

Techniques that traditionally have been useful for retrieving same-domain analogies from small single-use
knowledge bases, such as spreading activation and indexing on selected features, are inadequate for retrieving cross-domain analogies from large multi-use knowledge bases. In this paper, we describe Knowledge-
Directed Spreading Activation (KDSA), a new method
for retrieving analogies in a large semantic network.
KDSA uses task-specific knowledge to guide a spreading activation search to a case or concept in memory
that meets a desired similarity condition. Specifically,
KDSA exploits evaluations of near-analogies encountered during the search to direct the search toward
progressively more promising analogies. We describe
a specific instantiation of this method for the task of
innovative design, and we summarize the theoretical
and experimental results used to validate KDSA.

Introduction

Cross-domain analogy is a commonly-used reasoning
device, especially among individuals who must exhibit
a high level of creativity in their reasoning. Authors,
journalists, and political speechwriters often use surprising metaphors in order to enliven their prose; clever
teachers use analogies to familiar concepts outside of
the domain of discussion to explain unfamiliar concepts; and engineers and inventors often use analogies
in order to help them produce a novel design. The
concern of this paper is the retrieval and use of cross-
domain analogies, specifically those in which the two
analogues are *semantically distant* from one another—
that is, they are very different from one another in all
but a few key features.

The literature on invention is full of examples of
inventions that were guided by semantically distant
analogies. Gutenberg invented the printing press after noticing the connection between applying force to
impress script on paper and applying force to squeeze

[*]This research was supported by NASA Grant NAG2-
581, by Texas Instruments Contract 7554900, and by Mc-
Donnell Douglas Contract S07705. Thanks to Rich Washington and the anonymous AAAI reviewers for helpful
comments.

grapes in a wine press (Koestler 1965). Edison's invention of the quadruplex telegraph was based almost entirely on an analogy to a water system of pumps, pipes,
valves, and water wheels (Hughes 1971). And actress
Hedy Lamarr conceived of a method for coordinating
frequencies between sender and receiver in frequency-
hopping communication by analogy to a player-piano
roll (Simon *et al.* 1985). These examples all show the
inventor making a connection between two concepts
not normally thought of as connected. The fact that
human inventors use semantically distant analogies in
their reasoning suggests that these analogies can be an
important technique for computer reasoning as well.

From looking at examples of analogies in invention,
we can surmise two characteristics of semantically distant analogies that present special problems for the
development of a computational model:

(1) The domains from which the analogies are drawn
are unpredictable. The concepts used to guide novel
designs come from a wide range of domains, and
it is impossible to predict, given the target design
domain, which base domain(s) may prove fruitful for
drawing useful analogies.

(2) In the analogies that are made, differences between
the analogous concepts are as important as similarities. An inventor's chances of developing a truly
novel design by analogy are greatly increased by using a base concept that is unusual or unexpected.
This suggests that the base concept used should be
as different as possible from the target concept while
still being useful for design. That is, the two concepts should share only those features that are necessary to the function of the invention, *and should
mismatch on as many extraneous features as possible*. In particular, analogies with a high degree of
surface similarity seem unlikely to be useful in producing novel inventions.

These two characteristics provide reasons that existing approaches to analogy retrieval are inappropriate
for retrieving semantically distant analogies. Most existing approaches to analogy retrieval are based either
on task-specific indexing of concepts in a case library
or on spreading activation in a semantic network, but

neither of these general approaches is well-suited for finding semantically distant analogies. The indexing approach is inappropriate because characteristic (1) above suggests that a successful "case library" for semantically distant analogies would in fact be a large multi-domain multi-use knowledge base, but most successful indices in case-based reasoning are task-specific. To create a new set of indices for each possible task that may be performed in such a KB (and each possible analogical use of a given concept) would require a prohibitive number of organizational links or constructs. The spreading activation approach is inappropriate because characteristic (2) above suggests that most corresponding features involved in the analogues will be far from each other in the semantic network, and an uncontrolled spread of activation throughout the large semantic net will bog down in combinatorial explosion before reaching the semantically distant base concepts it seeks.

This paper introduces a method, called *knowledge-directed spreading activation* (KDSA), for retrieving semantically distant analogous concepts from a large diverse knowledge base. This method is based on controlled search in a general semantic network. It uses task-specific knowledge to guide a series of spreading activation searches from the target concept to a semantically distant base concept. This knowledge is applied in the evaluation of intermediate concepts retrieved by a standard spread of activation, and by the modification of weights controlling the spread of activation based on those evaluations. The next section describes this method in more detail.

The Approach—KDSA

Viewed abstractly, KDSA is an application of general techniques from state-space search (evaluation functions, subgoaling, etc.) to knowledge base search. KDSA finds analogues by a *series* of heuristically-guided spreading activation searches. Each time spreading activation retrieves a concept from the knowledge base, the concept is evaluated as an analogue, and that evaluation is used to direct the next spreading activation search in more promising directions. KDSA uses promising concepts retrieved during these spreading activation searches as "beacons", guiding the search successively closer to a semantically distant base.

This description of KDSA will assume that all world knowledge is represented in a single semantic network. Within that semantic network, small subgraphs of nodes and links which represent aggregate concepts are explicitly grouped together as conceptual graphs (Sowa 1984). Individual conceptual graphs are treated the same as primitive nodes—i.e., they can be associated with other nodes via links, and they can themselves be parts of larger conceptual graphs. In the discussion below, conceptual graphs will be referred to merely as "concepts".

1. Assign activation to all nodes in the target.

2. Spread activation in semantic network until a new intermediate concept (IC) is retrieved.

3. (GRAPH MATCHER) Find the best mapping between target and IC based only on maximizing isomorphism and minimizing semantic distance between nodes.

4. (MATCH EVALUATION) Evaluate the mapping according to domain-specific similarity metric. If evaluation meets the metric, return IC as base and exit.

5. (SEARCH CONTROL) Based on evaluation, alter the state of the semantic network to guide the next phase of spreading activation in a more promising direction.

6. Go to 2.

Figure 1: Knowledge-Directed Spreading Activation

The basic algorithm of KDSA is shown in Figure 1. The low-level search of memory (step 2 in the figure) is conducted by a spreading activation mechanism (see, e.g., (Anderson 1983)). In this formalism, activation is passed from node to adjacent node via the links that connect them until one concept accumulates enough aggregate activation to be considered retrieved. This basic spreading activation model is a blind knowledge search mechanism. Some method of controlling the search is necessary for the system to retrieve the types of semantically distant base concepts described in the introduction. KDSA uses feedback from the analogues retrieved so far to focus the search.

The agent architecture encompassing KDSA begins the retrieval process when some executing task requests an analogy and designates a target concept. This initial request causes some nodes in the semantic network—those representing the target concept plus possibly others representing desired features of the solution, etc.—to be assigned activation, and this assignment begins the spread of activation in memory. When a concept is retrieved by the spread of activation, the *graph matcher* computes a mapping between it and the target concept. The *match evaluation component* then forms an evaluation of the mapping based on a task-specific similarity metric. This evaluation is passed on to the *search control component*, which uses its task-specific heuristics to focus the spreading activation search in directions that are more likely to lead to highly-evaluated analogies for the current task. The process repeats until an analogue that meets the matching component's similarity metric is retrieved.

For simplicity, KDSA has been described so far as a strictly serial algorithm. In fact, it is designed (and implemented) as a collection of independent knowledge sources that execute within a larger intelligent agent architecture[1], and that interact with the agent's other

---

[1]In the computer implementation of KDSA, the agent architecture used was BB1 (Hayes-Roth 1990).

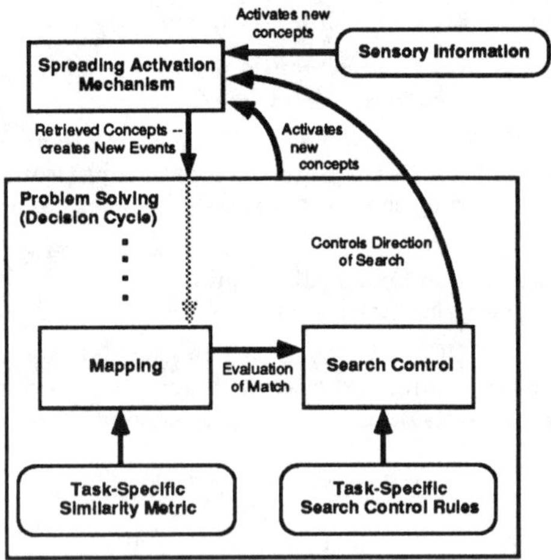

Figure 2: Integration of KDSA into problem-solving architecture

activities. Figure 2 shows this interaction. At any time during the cycle of Figure 1, other concepts may be activated by the agent's other activities, such as ordinary problem solving or processing sensory input. In this way KDSA can account for an individual possibly "stumbling across a solution", i.e., being reminded of an analogue by external or internal cues.

The important components of the retrieval system are discussed in more detail below.

Match Evaluation Each time a concept is retrieved by the spreading activation search as a potential base concept, it is passed to the matching component. The matching component first forms the best possible partial mapping between the potential base and the target, and then it evaluates that partial mapping using heuristics that are specific to the task for which the analogy will be used. These heuristics will base their evaluation on three features of the partial mapping: (1) semantic distance between corresponding nodes in the mapping, i.e., the minimum path distance in the type hierarchy between corresponding nodes of the mapping (2) isomorphism between the graphs, i.e., how many nodes and links match between the target and potential base, and (3) the portion of the representation of the target concept matched, and the relevance of that portion to the goal. The evaluation consists of a numeric rating of the mapping, and a description of the shortcoming(s) of the mapping assigned by the heuristics. If the numeric rating is greater than a threshold value, the potential base is accepted as the final analogy, and the KDSA process halts. Otherwise, the evaluation is passed on to the search control component.

Search Control The search control component uses evaluations from the match evaluation component and other information about the state of the search to in-

fluence the direction of the spread of activation. It uses heuristics to control the direction of the search in two ways: (1) it can change activation of concepts in the semantic net, particularly the target concept and the retrieved intermediate concept, and (2) it can modify the condition under which spreading activation will retrieve new intermediate concepts. The first of these, changing activation of selected concepts in the KB, is the more important of the two methods of search control. This method includes strengthening the activation of promising intermediate concepts (those that nearly pass the mapping component's similarity metric for being a good final analogy), weakening the activation of unpromising concepts, changing activation of *portions* of the intermediate concept or the target based on evaluations, and clearing the activation of all nodes in the semantic network (to start the search over from a new state).

A simple use of KDSA's search control would have it clearing all activation in the semantic network each time a promising concept is encountered, and then restarting the search by making the promising concept a source of activation. In this way KDSA can use these promising concepts as *beacons* along the way to the final good analogy. This is very similar to the way that promising intermediate states are used in heuristic search techniques such as hill-climbing or best-first search (Pearl & Korf 1987).

The use of the matching component of the mechanism to provide feedback to the spreading activation search provides a key distinguishing feature of our approach. Most previous approaches to analogy serialize the retrieval and mapping processes: first they retrieve a concept, then they try to map it, then if mapping fails they start at ground zero with retrieval again. By contrast, mapping in KDSA is an integral part of retrieval: mapping (the matching component) provides ongoing information to the retrieval mechanism (spreading activation and search control) throughout the duration of the retrieval process.

KDSA Applied to Innovative Design

This section describes the particular heuristics used in the implementation of KDSA, called IDA (for Innovative Design by Analogy), to find analogies that are useful for guiding an innovative redesign of the target.

IDA operates in a knowledge base of devices, natural or man-made systems that perform some function. The knowledge base may contain definitions of other concepts as well, but IDA requires that each device be represented by its structure, behavior, and function. Representations of structure consist of the device's parts along with different types of connections among those parts. Representations of behavior and function consist of chains of primitive processes along with the individuals (structural components, substances, etc.) on which those processes act. IDA takes as input an existing device, and returns as output an abstract redesign of that device which satisfies the device's top-level functional requirements, but does so in a different way. This redesign consists of a replacement of one of the target device's top-level behaviors with a behavior from the base device. E.g., a behavior like SPRAYING from the representation of the sprinkler irrigation system may be replaced with DIFFUSION from the circulatory system.

The particular heuristics used in IDA's mapping component attempt to find analogues that satisfy two general requirements:

(1) The base and target devices must have similar functions, but different behaviors and structures.

(2) The base must be adaptable with regard to the target device. That is, IDA must be able to analogically adapt the retrieved base into a new device that satisfies the same function as the target device.

The purpose of the first requirement is to find an analogue which will lead to a redesign which is useful ("similar function") and at the same time novel ("different behavior and structure"). The purpose of the second requirement is to ensure that IDA will actually be able to produce a redesign based on the retrieved base concept, i.e., that the mismatch in behavior with the target is not so great that the two devices have nothing to do with one another. Thus this second requirement's implementation will depend on the system's mechanism for adapting the retrieved base into a final design.

To implement these two requirements, IDA's mapping component considers separate portions of a device's representation separately. Each device representation is broken down into structure, behavior, and function. The behavior and function representations are broken down further into (1) a sequence of primitive processes that make up the behavior or function, and (2) the individuals on which those processes act. There are separate requirements on the degree of isomorphism and semantic distance required for each of those portions of the representation. For example, IDA prefers the match between nodes in the structures of the target and base devices to be high in semantic distance (to satisfy the dissimilar structure requirement), and prefers a mismatch on only one primitive process in the behaviors of the target and base devices (to satisfy the adaptability requirement).

After the mapping component evaluates devices according to the two requirements, the search control module must focus the spread of activation toward other devices in the KB which meet those requirements. IDA does this by focusing the search based on the strengths of the retrieved beacons encountered so far in the search. The mapping component identifies an intermediate concept as promising if it comes close to meeting the metric for being a final analogy. For each promising concept, the search control component then strengthens the activation of its portions that did meet the mapping component's individual requirement. The rest of the activation in the semantic network is wiped out, and the search is restarted from this new state.

IDA's search control rules also use abstractions in the knowledge base as "bridges" to other domains. When IDA retrieves a concept that is in the same domain as the target and is a directly-linked example of a *generic abstraction*—a concept that abstractly describes specific concepts from a number of different domains—it strengthens the activation of that abstraction. This will allow activation to be spread into other domains, increasing the likelihood that IDA will find a distant analogy.

Example

This section presents an example demonstrating the execution of KDSA to retrieve an analogy for creative design. The example shows IDA's behavior for the goal of redesigning a blinkered railroad crossing, that is, an intersection of road and railroad tracks where a train's presence on the tracks is indicated only by blinking lights signalling drivers on the road to stop. IDA meets this goal by suggesting redesign by analogy to an on-off valve. Specifically, it suggests replacing the FLASHING behavior in the description of the blinkered railroad crossing with the BLOCKAGE behavior in the description of the on-off valve. This abstract analogical specification might suggest to a human designer a railroad crossing with a gate that blocks traffic from crossing the tracks. The retrieval of the on-off valve takes place in the following steps:

1. The nodes contained in the representation of BLINKERED-RR-CROSSING are made sources of activation (i.e., they are tagged with some number), and IDA begins spreading activation.

2. After a few cycles of spreading activation, the device INTERSTATE-HIGHWAY-SYSTEM is retrieved. This device is mapped to BLINKERED-RR-CROSSING, and the mapping is evaluated. The mapping is found to be unpromising—the structures of the two devices are semantically close, and the behaviors and functions of the two devices do not correspond in any respect. However, IDA notices that INTERSTATE-HIGHWAY-SYSTEM is an instance of a generic abstraction, the FLOW-SYSTEM device. IDA recognizes this abstraction as a possible mechanism for moving the search out of its current domain, and makes FLOW-SYSTEM a source of activation. All other activation in the semantic network (except the target's) is cleared, and spreading activation starts again.

3. Another of FLOW-SYSTEM's instances, PLUMBING-SYSTEM, is retrieved next, and the mapping between it and BLINKERED-RR-CROSSING is evaluated. This mapping shows high semantic distance between the structures of the devices, and

poor matches between the behaviors and functions of the devices. IDA wants high semantic distance in structure, so the structural aspect of the mapping is rated high, but the behavioral and functional aspects of the mapping are rated low. Since the structure of the PLUMBING-SYSTEM is the strongest part of the mapping evaluation, the search control component makes PLUMBING-SYSTEM's structure a source of activation. Since the behavior and function of the PLUMBING-SYSTEM were rated low, the search control component still bases the search on the behavior and function of the target. So the structure of PLUMBING-SYSTEM and the behavior and function of BLINKERED-RR-CROSSING are made sources of activation, and all other activation in the network is cleared.

4. The next concept retrieved is ON-OFF-VALVE. The matching component recognizes that the mapping between ON-OFF-VALVE and BLINKERED-RR-CROSSING is high in semantic distance between the structures, high in isomorphism between the functions, very low in semantic distance between the top-level process sequences of the functions (they both toggle between PREVENTing and ALLOWing another process), and mismatches in a single process in the behavior description (the BLINKING of the rr crossing corresponds to the BLOCKAGE of the valve). With these conditions met, ON-OFF-VALVE meets the similarity metric for being a final analogy for innovative design. It is retrieved, and IDA's simple design module suggests replacing redesigning the BLINKERED-RR-CROSSING by replacing its BLINKING process with ON-OFF-VALVE's BLOCKAGE process.

Results

One of the major questions important in the evaluation of KDSA is: will KDSA retrieve analogies without examining a sizable fraction of the entire knowledge base? In order to answer this question, KDSA was evaluated using two complementary methods.

The first of these methods is to analyze the behavior of a theoretical model. This model predicts KDSA's retrieval time given various parameters such as the size of the knowledge base, the semantic distance required for the analogy, the likelihood of encountering a beacon concept in the knowledge base, and the quality of each beacon concept in terms of the benefit it provides in reaching the ultimate base concept. This model allows us to examine the behavior of KDSA under a wide range of problem and knowledge base characteristics.

The second method of evaluating KDSA is to examine the behavior of the implementation, IDA. This implementation of KDSA demonstrates that KDSA can, in fact, automatically retrieve semantically distant analogies which are useful in solving a real problem. In addition, while it is presently impossible to test IDA with an actual very large knowledge base, we can measure IDA's retrieval time as a function of the KB size for various subsets of IDA's small knowledge base. These experiments allow us to examine KDSA's behavior as the knowledge base grows, and compare that actual behavior to the prediction of the theoretical model.

Figure 3 graphs some of the results produced by these two validation methods. It shows time taken to retrieve a semantically distant analogy as the size of the knowledge base grows, both for (a) the actual implementation operating in relatively small knowledge bases, and (b) the theoretical model as the knowledge base grows to a size of 1 million nodes. Each graph also shows retrieval time for standard spreading activation (SA) as well. Both methods showed retrieval time for KDSA growing much more slowly than for standard spreading activation as KB size grows. The theoretical model predicts behavior that is roughly logarithmic in the size of the KB.

Detailed presentations of the theoretical and experimental results are published in (Wolverton 1994). These results can be summarized with the following four qualitative statements, with the first statement being verified by both the theoretical model and experiments, and the remainder being predicted by the theoretical model:

(1) As the knowledge base size grows, retrieval time with KDSA grows much more slowly than does retrieval time with standard SA.

(2) For analogies in which the target and the base are semantically distant, KDSA is far more efficient than standard SA.

(3) KDSA is robust over different distributions and utilities of beacon concepts in the knowledge base. Even when the benefit of each beacon search is low relative to the effort involved, KDSA still shows significant savings over standard SA.

(4) KDSA is robust in the face of bad beacons. When a KDSA search suffers from beacons that direct the search away from, rather than toward, the eventual base, KDSA still shows substantial savings over standard SA.

Related Work

There is a large body of AI literature on information retrieval in semantic networks. SCISOR (Rau 1987) and GRANT (Cohen & Kjeldsen 1987) both use heuristic information to direct a spread of activation in semantic networks. KDSA's search control component is similar to the relatedness condition which controls the spread of markers in SCISOR and the path endorsements which direct spreading activation in GRANT. KDSA differs from these systems, however, in that it uses information from previous match evaluations to dynamically adjust the direction of the spread of activation. KDSA in effect runs a *series* of SCISOR-like or GRANT-like searches, starting each sub-search

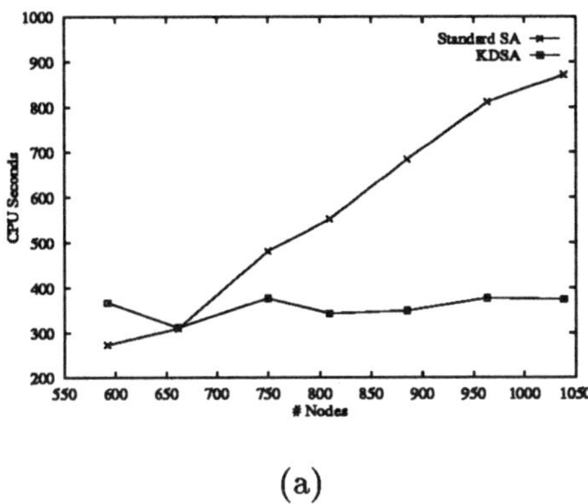 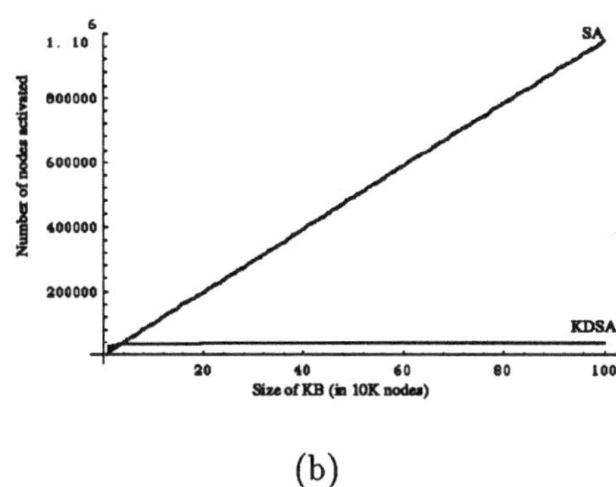

(a)   (b)

Figure 3: Retrieval time for KDSA and standard SA as KB size grows, (a) as observed in the computer implementation IDA in a small knowledge base, (b) as predicted by the theoretical model in a large knowledge base

from the near-misses it has encountered in previous sub-searches, and using the evaluations of those near-misses to formulate its search control for the next sub-search.

Other researchers have used spreading activation in semantic networks to retrieve analogues. Holland et. al.'s PI (Holland *et al.* 1986), Anderson's PUPS (Anderson & Thompson 1989), and Jones's EUREKA (Jones 1989) are all general cognitive models which use spreading activation for analogue retrieval (as well as other knowledge retrieval). In all of these approaches, the architecture's ability to control the spread of activation is limited, so they will have difficulty retrieving semantically distant analogies without the help of external cues. KDSA is able to use such cues when they are available, but also is able to retrieve semantically distant analogies spontaneously.

Conclusion

We have presented knowledge-directed spreading activation, a task-independent method for retrieving analogues in a multi-domain knowledge base. KDSA overcomes the shortcomings that indexing methods may have in large knowledge bases by applying task-specific knowledge to a general semantic network search technique. And it extends previous models of analogue retrieval by using evaluations of failed analogies encountered in the earlier stages of the search to influence the direction of the search in later stages. KDSA has been shown to be useful in retrieving analogues for a real task in the computer implementation IDA. And experimental and theoretical results provide evidence that KDSA will be tractable in a large knowledge base.

References

Anderson, J. R., and Thompson, R. 1989. Use of analogy in a production system architecture. In Vosniadou, S., and Ortony, A., eds., *Similarity and Analogical Reasoning*. Cambridge: Cambridge University Press. 267–297.

Anderson, J. R. 1983. *The Architecture of Cognition*. Harvard University Press.

Cohen, P. R., and Kjeldsen, R. 1987. Information retrieval by constrained spreading activation in semantic networks. *Information Processing and Management* 23(4):255–268.

Hayes-Roth, B. 1990. Architectural foundations for real-time performance in intelligent agents. *Journal of Real-Time Systems* 2:99–125.

Holland, J. H.; Holyoak, K. J.; Nisbett, R. E.; and Thagard, P. R. 1986. *Induction: Processes of Inference, learning, and Discovery*. Cambridge, Massachusetts: MIT Press.

Hughes, T. P. 1971. How did the heroic inventors do it? *American Heritage of Invention and Technology* 1(2):22–23.

Jones, R. 1989. Learning to retrieve useful information for problem solving. In *Proceedings of the Sixth International Workshop on Machine Learning*, 212–214.

Koestler, A. 1965. *The Act of Creation.* Macmillan.

Pearl, J., and Korf, R. E. 1987. Search techniques. *Annual Review of Computer Science* 2:451–467.

Rau, L. F. 1987. Knowledge organization and access in a conceptual information system. *Information Processing and Management* 23(4):269–283.

Simon, M. K.; Omura; Scholtz; and Levitt. 1985. *Spread Spectrum Communications, Vol. 1*. Computer Science Press.

Sowa, J. F. 1984. *Conceptual Structures: Information Processing in Mind and Machine*. Addison-Wesley.

Wolverton, M. 1994. *Retrieving Semantically Distant Analogies*. Ph.D. Dissertation, Computer Science Department, Stanford University.

A Reading Agent

Tamitha Carpenter
tamitha@cs.brandeis.edu
(617) 736-2718

Richard Alterman[*]
alterman@cs.brandeis.edu
(617) 736-2703

Department of Computer Science
and Center for Complex Systems
Brandeis University
Waltham, MA 02254

Abstract

Recent work in agency has explored the interactive nature of goal-driven behavior ("activity"). An interactive agent is responsive to events and is affected by and effects the context in which it exists. Our contention is that interaction is also an important characteristic of a reader. By treating reading as an activity, the *reading agent* can interact with the text, achieving goals and planning what to read, when to read, and how to read. This paper will discuss how reading within a context of activity provides goals and enables planning, thus creating the reading agent. The system described, SPRITe, reads natural language, primarily instructions, in order to facilitate other activities.

Introduction

Recent work in agency (e.g., Suchman, 1987; Agre, 1988; Chapman, 1990) has explored the interactive nature of goal-driven behavior ("activity"). When reading is viewed as an activity, the same issues come into play. In order to define a "reading agent", it is important to establish how an agent interacts with text, how reading interacts with action, and how activity changes the reading process.

For example, consider trying to read the instructions for assembling a lawnmower. If reading occurs in isolation from the assembling activity, the instructions must be read from beginning to end, they can only be understood in general terms (e.g., the reference to a "bolt" can only be concrete once the reader has experienced the bolt used in the lawnmower), and the understanding that results may or may not be adequate for the agent to successfully assemble the lawnmower without referring back to the instructions.

A *reading agent* has several properties that make the reading process active. These include:

- Using goals.
- Planning the reading activity.
- Reading in the context of a larger activity.
- Improving the reading skill.
- Responding to changes in the environment (interactivity).

Other systems have explored some of these properties. Maybury (1991) shows a planning system that *creates* instructions (as well as other types of text). In Ram (1991), knowledge goals were used to take advantage of information as it was read; however, the reading was not a planned activity, and so text was read sequentially from beginning to end. Several other systems have developed models of instruction usage (e.g., Chapman, 1990; Badler et al., 1990; Vere and Bickmore, 1990). However, these models have not taken the step towards building a reading agent that *interacts* with the instructions, using goals and planning strategies.

The properties of a reading agent have been implemented in a model called SPRITe (using Structure to Plan the Reading of Instructional TExt). Instead of reading sequentially, SPRITe uses reading goals and planning techniques to guide how it reads instructions. In addition, SPRITe is integrated in a model of agent intelligence known as **FLOABN** (Alterman et al., 1991). FLOABN works with and learns about mechanical and electronic devices and their instructions. SPRITe primarily interacts with FLOABN's activity planner, an adaptive planning system for engaging in activity (see Zito-Wolf, 1993, for details).

A Cognitive Reading Model

In Carpenter (1993), a protocol study was presented which studied 12 people using instructions. The subjects, students and faculty who had never before used a fax machine, were given the machine's instructions and asked to send a fax. The instructions were presented on a computer monitor one line at a time and the instruction usage was recorded. Subjects were also asked to talk aloud while sending the fax. Their comments were recorded and matched to the instructions showing on the monitor at the time each comment was made.

In spite of the length (approx. 70 pages) and difficulty of the instructions, every subject was able to use the instructions well enough to complete the requested task.

---

* This author is supported in part by a grant from Digital Equipment Corporation.

No one actually read the entire set of instructions. With one exception (a subject who read none of the instructions), the subjects all used the instructions periodically during the interaction until they found text that clarified whatever part of the task was at hand. This text was then read to whatever depth was necessary to extract enough content to continue with the activity.

The subjects used structural and contextual clues in their navigation of the text. The ability to use the structural properties of the instructions is due to their predictable nature. Van Dijk and Kintsch (1983) call the nature of a type of text (e.g., instructions, short stories, et cetera) its *superstructure*. That is, certain structural features (e.g., numbered lists) are used by instructions for specific purposes (e.g., listing a set of steps). The better a reader's knowledge of structure usage, the better he is able to predict the organization of a text.

We have endeavored to create a model of reading that has abilities similar to those portrayed by the subjects of the protocol study. Three primary conclusions from the protocol study reflect the design principles of SPRITe:

1. The subjects interleaved reading with action (e.g., see figure 1).
2. The subjects generally seemed to have some goal in mind, which caused them to skip or reread certain portions of text.
3. The subjects became increasingly confident and skilled in their usage of the instructions. For example, the subjects would often remember where a certain piece of text was located.

By following these behaviors, SPRITe is able to choose when to read, what to read, and how to read.

```
1   TEXT  Use the keypad to enter the
          telephone number, then press the
          Start key.
          :
2   SARA  "Use the keypad to enter the
          telephone number.  And then press
          the..."
          :
3   FAX   <dial beeps>
          :
4   SARA  Then press the start key.  She
          looks for the start key.  This...
5   FAX   <beep>
6   TEXT  Lift the telephone handset, Using
          the telephone, press the Start key
          When the remote ready tones are
          heard, then replace the handset.
```

Figure 1: An excerpt from the protocol study illustrating the interleaving of reading and action. 'TEXT' refers to the line of text showing on the monitor during the current point of interaction and 'FAX' shows the sounds made by the device in response to the user's actions.

The Architecture of a Reading Agent

FLOABN's primary method of activity is based on adaptive planning (Alterman, 1988). The main components of FLOABN (see figure 2) are independent agents (cf. "Society of Mind": Minsky, 1986). Each is capable of running without the other, but in combination, they can accomplish more. This is because the action planner provides the reader with goals and activity against which a concrete understanding of text is made, and the reader provides access to new sources of knowledge that aid the activity's interaction.

In order for the exchange of information to be made successfully, the communication process between SPRITe and the action planner must be defined. For FLOABN's communication, we have defined a set of request and response frames -- a set of templates that, when filled out, provide a predictable structure for information. When the action planner requests information from SPRITe, it chooses one of about 10 request frames to fill out. A request frame suggests a reading goal and provides information such as which plan is in use, a trace of the activity, and the how the plan failed. Each request frame corresponds to a type of breakdown the action planner is likely to encounter, and is designed to provide information about the agent's activity that the reader is likely to need in order to read the instructions and help the action planner recover.

Consider the following "Find-part-ref" request:

```
(request :name    find-part-ref
         :device  fax-machine-001
         :plan    photocopier
         :part    ADF)
```

When this request was made, the action planner was attempting to use a fax machine by adapting its plan for using a photocopier. When the planner encountered the unfamiliar term "ADF" (produced by an earlier access to the instructions), it asked the reader for a definition.

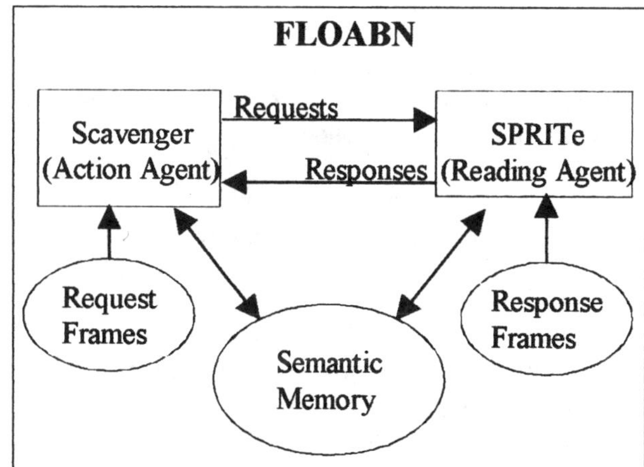

Figure 2: Communication between reading and action agents.

The reader has a list of about 20 response frames. Each request frame has a subset of associated response frames from which the reader must choose. For example, if the planner had made a "Find Object" request, the reader would choose one of the following:

- **Object location**— gives the location of object.
- **Alternative object**— indicates a different object can be used for the same task.
- **Missing object**— indicates the object does not exist and suggests plan modifications.

The "find-part-ref" request frame has only one associated response frame: term-definition. In order to fill out the term-definition response frame, SPRITe first reads the instructions and determines that the definition of ADF is "automatic document feeder". SPRITe then fills out the response frame as follows:

```
(response :name   term-definition
          :device fax-machine-001
          :plan   photocopier
          :term   ADF
          :def    automatic-
                  document-feeder)
```

With this new knowledge, the action planner can use the ADF as part of its interaction with the fax machine.

How to Read

SPRITe (see figure 3) reads instructions using several methods. The overall control of SPRITe is based on the same adaptive planning model as FLOABN's main system. When SPRITe first starts reading, it selects one of about 25 reading plans (e.g., see figure 5) based on the information provided by the request frame and the observable characteristics (i.e., top-level structure) of the text. As reading takes place, the selected plan is adapted to better suit the instructions and/or reading goal of the current situation. This allows SPRITe to react to differences in organization and style between various pieces of text. This also allows the same request frame to cause different reading behavior depending on the instructions and the context.

When SPRITe has successfully read the instructions, it stores three types of information:

1. SPRITe remembers the successful reading steps that were performed as a new plan. This plan is indexed and stored in plan memory.
2. SPRITe remembers the characteristics of the instructions that corresponded to the successful reading steps, thus building a representation of the instructions that will facilitate future usage.
3. SPRITe augments semantic memory with the knowledge it gained through reading.

SPRITe's ability to learn in these ways increases its ability to read effectively and efficiently in the future.

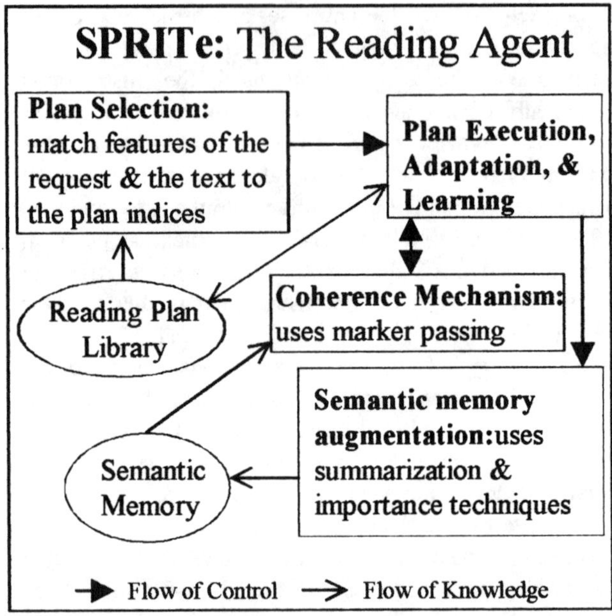

Figure 3: SPRITe -- Inside the Reading Agent

During the execution of reading plans, SPRITe must 'understand' the text it is reading. Understanding is accomplished, at least in part, by establishing *coherence*. SPRITe establishes two types of coherence:

- *textual coherence*: The connection of the meaning of text to other text being read.
- *coherence with activity*: The connection of the meaning of the text to the activity of the agent.

Even if the text is coherent with itself, if the connection of the text with the device and its activity cannot be established, the instructions are useless because they cannot be applied. Coherence of text with activity is not only the association of terms in the text with objects in the world (*external reference*), but also the association of the text with the agent's current interaction (i.e., results of plan steps taken), knowledge of how devices work, and possibilities for future action.

Currently, coherence is established using a modification of the marker passing techniques described in Norvig (1989). SPRITe's knowledge source is a semantic network in which basic concepts (e.g., hierarchy for types of money) are combined with detailed representations of approximately 50 devices.

Top Level Control

This section will describe in detail the process SPRITe uses to read instructions in the context of FLOABN using a simulated[1] Airfone for the first time.

To begin, FLOABN approaches the device, and has the expectation that it will work like a pay telephone.

---

[1]Simulations are based on actual usage of the device.

However, when FLOABN tries to execute its plan for using a pay phone by lifting the receiver, it doesn't work. FLOABN tries adapting its plan, but none of the steps in the pay phone plan is executable. So, FLOABN calls SPRITe with the following request:

```
(request  :name   next-step
          :device Airfone-001
          :plan   pay-phone
          :failed-steps
                  (lift-receiver
                   listen-for-
                        dial-tone
                   insert-coin))
```

This request frame has four required entries:

- the name of the request (which generally is the reading goal)
- what device FLOABN is trying to use
- which action plan FLOABN is using
- what plan steps have failed so far

A fifth optional entry, what plan steps have succeeded, is not present in this instance of the request frame.

SPRITe's algorithm is shown in figure 4. In step 1, SPRITe notes that the request type is "next-step". In step 2, SPRITe locates the Airfone instructions and builds a representation of them, which initially contains a list of the instructions' top-level text structures: 'title', 'italic-text', plain-text', 'enumerated-list', and 'big-text'.

Using Reading Plans

In step 3, SPRITe chooses a reading plan based on the reading goal and indices. The reading goal is matched against the name of the request frame, and the indices are function calls which probe the current situation (i.e., characteristics of the instructions and details from the request frame). For the current example, the plan in figure 5 was chosen because the goal, "next-step", matches the current request frame and because the index evaluates to true (the Airfone instructions are shorter than 2 pages). Since all the indices match, no future change is anticipated.

Step 4 executes the plan. Each plan has three tasks:

1. locate a likely location for relevant text
2. verify that the content of the selected location is going to help (optional)
3. extract the content of the text

The verify and extract steps require the coherence mechanism to build representations of the text at varying levels of detail, while the locate step uses SPRITe's knowledge of instructional text structure and usage to choose the most likely candidate for reading.

The *locate* step is responsible for finding a starting point in the instructions from which the rest of the plan can work and storing that location in the variable *location*. The locate step can occur in two ways: using the method in the :locate portion of the plan or using the representation that SPRITe has built of the instructions. In the current example, SPRITe has not developed its representation of the instructions yet, so the :locate method of the "find-steps_short-text" plan is used, which locates the enumerated list in the Airfone instructions. If no enumerated list had been found, the plan would fail, and SPRITe would either attempt adapting the plan or choosing another plan.

The *verify* step uses the coherence mechanism to determine whether the "dumb" search done by the locate step actually found an appropriate piece of text. The verify portion of the "find-steps_short-text" plan looks for a description component — a piece of text that describes the purpose or content of the list. According to SPRITe's knowledge of instruction superstructures, the description component is an optional first line of text in the list that is not preceded by the "\item" formatting command. In the Airfone example, the enumerated list does not have a description component. This is not a failing condition for this plan. Only if a description **does** exist but is not coherent with the reading goal would the verify step fail. If this were the case, SPRITe would go back to the locate step and find another location.

Finally, SPRITe performs the *extract* step. The call to "read-enum-list" is actually a call to a sub-plan that uses marker passing to establish coherence between the content of the enumerated list and the plan steps provided

---

1. Identify *request type*.
2. **If** instructions for current reading task have been used before:
     then locate previously constructed representation
     else build an initial representation for the instructions
3. Select *reading plan* based on *request frame* and characteristics of the instructions.
     a. If any unmatched indices occur, anticipate future change.
4. Execute *reading plan* and adapt.
     a. Sequence through steps to locate text, verify position, and extract content.
     b. If failure occurs, adapt and either restart **step 4** or continue.
     c. If adaptation is unsuccessful restart **step 3**.
5. Remember successful plan steps and store in plan memory.
6. Prepare and send *response frame*.
7. Return control to ACTION AGENT (or to READING AGENT during a recursive call).

Figure 4: SPRITe's top-level control.

```
(plan
 :name    find-steps_short-text
 :goal    next-step
 :indices (short-text)
 :plan
   (:locate
     (assoc
       '\begin(enumerate) text)
    :verify
      (if (not (next-type location
                          '\item))
        (skim (first location)
            'find-steps))
    :extract (read-enum-list location
      (getf :failed-steps request)
      (getf :successful-steps
          request)))))
```

Figure 5: The reading plan chosen in the Airfone example.

by the request frame. This instance of "read-enum-list" skims the first item (line 5) of the enumerated list and discovers the coherence between the instruction "insert credit card" and the failed-step "insert-coin".

Step 4 also includes the provision for adaptation. In the Airfone example, the plan was successfully executed without the need to adapt. If adaptation had been necessary, SPRITe would have first examined any unmatched indices, as well as features of the text and the request frame that were not utilized by the indices. Using this information, SPRITe would have selected either a new locate step (possibly with a related verify step) or a new extract step from a library of location and extraction techniques. The new step would be inserted into the plan and execution would proceed.

Adding to Plan Memory

SPRITe performs step 5 of its procedure and creates a new plan. The new plan, shown in figure 6, is a copy of the original plan with a few changes. First, the text that was used to develop this plan is remembered (line 2). Although this plan could be used with any text, it will receive preferential treatment when the Airfone instructions are used again. Second, the plan has been modified to specifically find the *first* step of an action plan. This is reflected in the creation of a new index (line 5) which remembers that no *successful-steps* were provided in the request frame. Also, the extract step (line 7) has been shortened to skim only the *first* item in the enumerated list. In addition, the verify step was dropped, since it was not successfully executed.

SPRITe then prepares the following response frame:

```
(response :name    replace-step
          :device Airfone-001
          :plan    pay-phone
          :old-step (insert-coin)
          :new-step
                (insert credit-card))
```

Control is then returned to the action planner, which *proceduralizes* the "insert credit-card" step into its own plan and continues interaction with the Airfone. (For discussion of the proceduralization of instructions, see Alterman et al., 1991.)

The Airfone procedure continues to deviate from the expectations provided by the pay telephone action plan. After inserting the credit card, the action planner is still unable to lift the receiver. Control is given to SPRITe with the following request frame:

```
(request :name    next-step
         :device Airfone-001
         :plan    pay-phone
         :successful-steps
               (insert-credit-card)
         :failed-steps (lift-receiver
               listen-for-dial-tone))
```

SPRITe selects the plan shown in figure 5 again, because both its goal and its index match. The plan created by the previous episode (figure 6) is not selected, even though the :text field matches the current text, because the new index (no :successful-steps field in the request frame) is not matched.

Unlike the previous episode, SPRITe does not use the :locate step provided by the plan, since SPRITe's current representation of the Airfone instructions contains the enumerated list. The :verify step is tried again, with the same results as before. Finally, the :extract step skims the list items, recognizing that the "insert credit card"

```
  (plan
1 :name    find-steps_short-text-001
2 :text    Airfone-instructions
3 :goal    next-step
4 :indices ((short-text text)
5           (null (getf :successful-
                       steps request)))
6 :plan
    (:locate (assoc '\begin(enumerate)
         text)
7     :extract (skim-item (assoc '\item
                       location)
         (getf :failed-steps
               request)))))
```

Figure 6: A new reading plan created during interaction with the Airfone.

item matches the successful step "insert-credit-card".

SPRITe then looks at the next item in the list: "lower door handle over card". This is interpreted as a "close" step, similar to the close step required to play a cassette in a tape deck. A new plan is created in the same way as the plan in figure 6. However, the :locate step is changed to reflect the usage of SPRITe's representation of the instructions. Control is then returned to the action planner with the new information.

With this information, the action planner is finally able to lift the receiver, but is immediately thwarted once again when the "listen for dial tone" step fails. This time, when SPRITe receives control, it selects the new plan (shown in figure 7). The new plan is selected over the original plan because the :text field matches. The enumerated list is selected from SPRITe's representation of the instructions, and the list is perused.

SPRITe matches the first two items in the enumerated list with the successful steps given in the request frame. The third item in the instructions says to "observe lighted display". SPRITe interprets this as a reading instruction. However, the display is blank since the action planner has already lifted the receiver.

So, SPRITe reads the entire instruction, which indicates that the display would have said when to lift the receiver. Since the action planner already successfully lifted the receiver, SPRITe interprets this instruction as being equivalent to the step of "lift-receiver". The next item in the list, "press green DIAL TONE button", is then interpreted as an activation step. FLOABN is now able to complete interaction with the Airfone without further help from the instructions.

Conclusion

This paper has described an intelligent reading agent,

```
(plan
  :name     find-steps_short-text-002
  :text     Airfone-instructions
  :goal     next-step
  :indices ((short-text text))
  :plan
    (:locate
       (or (getf :enum-list inst-rep)
           (assoc '\begin(enumerate)
                    text))
     :extract
       (read-enum-list location
          (getf :failed-steps request)
          (getf :successful-steps
                 request)))))
```

Figure 7: Another reading plan created during interaction with the Airfone.

SPRITe. SPRITe uses planning techniques to perform efficient, goal-driven reading. It develops plans to read a given set of instructions in the context of engagement with a particular device. By planning, adapting, and storing new reading plans, SPRITe builds a library of concrete methods for reading which over time improves SPRITe's ability to read both the texts from which the methods were created, and with instructions in general.

SPRITe is embedded in a larger agent, FLOABN. Combining the activities of reading and action produces an agent more capable than the separate activities could be. The action provides *context* and *goals* for reading, which allow reading to be selective and produce concrete representations of the text. In return, reading provides a detailed knowledge source to the activity planner.

References

Agre, P.E. (1988). The dynamic structure of everyday life. Technical Report AI-TR 1085, MIT Artificial Intelligence Laboratory.

Alterman, R., Zito-Wolf, R., & Carpenter, T. (1991). Interaction, Comprehension, and Instruction Usage. *The Journal of Learning Sciences*, 1(3&4):361-398.

Alterman, R. (1988). Adaptive Planning. *Cognitive Science*, 12:393-421.

Badler, N., Webber, B., Kalita, J., & Esakov, J. (1990). Animation from instructions. In Badler, N., Barsky, B., & Zeltzer, D. (Eds.), *Making Them Move: Mechanics, Control and Animation of Articulated Figures*, pp. 51-93. Morgan Kaufmann, Los Altos, CA.

Carpenter, T. (1993). Using Instructions -- A Protocol Study. Presented at the Third Annual Meeting of the Society for Text and Discourse.

Chapman, D. (1990). Vision, instructions, and action. Technical Report AI-TR 1024, MIT Artificial Intelligence Laboratory.

Maybury, M.T. (1991). *Planning Multisentential English Text Using Communicative Acts*. PhD thesis, University of Cambridge, pp. 178-192.

Norvig, P. (1989). Marker passing as a weak method for text inferencing. *Cognitive Science*, 13(4):569-620.

Ram, A. (1991). A Theory of Questions and Question Asking. *The Journal of Learning Sciences*, 1(3&4).

Suchman, L. A. (1987). *Plans and Situated Actions*. Cambridge University Press.

van Dijk, T. & Kintsch, W. (1983). *Strategies of discourse comprehension*. Academic Press.

Vere, S. & Bickmore, T. (1990). A basic agent. *Computational Intelligence*, 6:41-60.

Zito-Wolf, R. (1993). *Case-Based Representations for Procedural Knowledge*. PhD thesis, Brandeis University.

The Capacity of Convergence-Zone Episodic Memory

Mark Moll
Department of Computer Science
University of Twente
P.O. Box 217, 7500 AE Enschede
The Netherlands
moll@cs.utwente.nl

Risto Miikkulainen
Department of Computer Sciences
The University of Texas at Austin
Austin, TX 78712 USA
risto@cs.utexas.edu

Jonathan Abbey
Applied Research Laboratories
P.O. Box 8029
Austin, TX 78713 USA
broccol@arlut.utexas.edu

Abstract

Human episodic memory provides a seemingly unlimited storage for everyday experiences, and a retrieval system that allows us to access the experiences with partial activation of their components. This paper presents a neural network model of episodic memory inspired by Damasio's idea of Convergence Zones. The model consists of a layer of perceptual feature maps and a binding layer. A perceptual feature pattern is coarse coded in the binding layer, and stored on the weights between layers. A partial activation of the stored features activates the binding pattern which in turn reactivates the entire stored pattern. A worst-case analysis shows that with realistic-size layers, the memory capacity of the model is several times larger than the number of units in the model, and could account for the large capacity of human episodic memory.

Introduction

Human memory system can be divided into semantic memory of facts, rules, and general knowledge, and episodic memory that records the individual's day-to-day experiences Tulving (1972, 1983). Episodic memory is characterized by an extremely high capacity. New memories are formed every few seconds, and many of those persist in the memory for years, even decades (Squire 1987). Another significant characteristic of human memory is content-addressability. Most of the memories can be retrieved simply by activating a partial representation of the experience, such as a sound, a smell, or a visual image.

Although several artificial neural network models of episodic memory have been proposed (Hopfield 1982; Kanerva 1988; Kortge 1990; Miikkulainen 1992), they fall short of explaining the simultaneous huge capacity and content-addressability of human memory. For example in the Hopfield model of N units, $N/4 \log N$ patterns can be stored with a 99% probability of correct retrieval when N is large (Hertz, Krogh, & Palmer 1991; Keeler 1988; McEliece *et al.* 1986). This means that storing and retrieving, for example, 10^8 memories would require in the order of 10^{10} nodes and 10^{20} connections. Given that the human brain is estimated to have about 10^{11} neurons and 10^{15} synapses (Jessell 1991), this is clearly unrealistic.

Despite vast amount of research in human memory, no clear understanding has yet emerged on exactly where and how the memory traces are represented in the brain. There is evidence for both localized encoding and for distributed encoding (Squire 1987). Damasio (1989b, 1989a) proposed a general framework, based on observations of typical patterns of injury-related memory deficits, that can potentially account for much of the data. The main idea is that the memory system is organized in a hierarchy of associational regions, or convergence zones, with each region serving as a basis for higher-level associations. The hierarchy is grounded in the sensory modality regions, and becomes more abstract and general as one moves from the sensory cortical regions to the forebrain. The low-level and intermediate regions contain object representations, and the high-level regions contain representations for complete episodes, in terms of the lower-level entities.

This paper presents a new episodic memory model loosely based on the convergence zone idea. The model consists of a number of perceptual maps and a binding layer (a convergence zone). An episodic experience appears as a pattern of local activations across the perceptual maps, and is encoded as a coarse-coded (Rosenfeld & Touretzky 1989; Touretzky & Hinton 1988) pattern in the binding layer. The connections between the maps and the binding layer store the encoding so that the complete perceptual pattern can later be regenerated from partial activation. The details of the low-level neural implementation are left open in this paper. The goal is to analyze the behavior of the model at the functional level, and derive general results about its capacity and physical size.

A worst-case analysis of the model shows that: (1) with realistic-size maps and binding layer, the capacity of the convergence-zone memory is extremely high, exceeding the number of units in the model by a factor of 5; and (2) the majority of the neural hardware is required in the perceptual processing; the binding

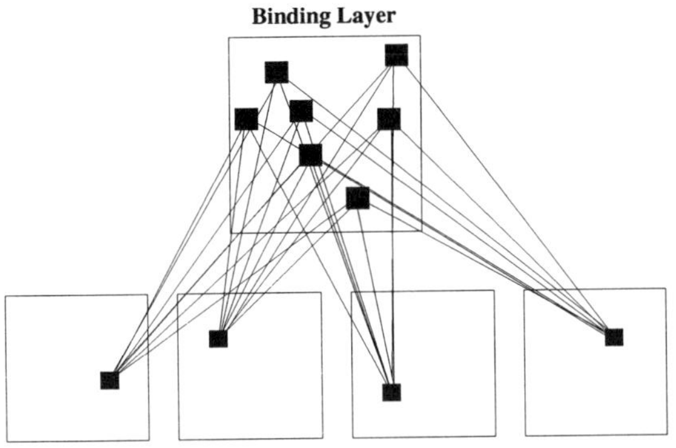

Figure 1: **Storage.** The weights on the connections between the appropriate feature units and the binding representation of the pattern are set to 1.

layer needs to be only a fraction of the size of the perceptual maps. Such results suggest how an extremely high capacity could be achieved in the human episodic memory with very little extra hardware beyond the perceptual maps.

Storage and Retrieval

The model consists of two layers of real-valued units (the feature map layer and the binding layer), and bidirectional binary connections between the layers (figure 1). Perceptual experiences are represented as vectors of feature values, such as color=red, shape=round, size=small. The values are encoded as units on the feature maps. There is a separate map for each feature domain, and each unit on the map represents a particular value for that feature. For instance, on the map for the color feature, the value red could be specified by turning on the unit in the lower-right quarter (figure 1). The feature map units are connected to the binding layer with bidirectional binary connections (i.e. the weight is either 0 or 1). An activation of units in the feature map layer causes a number of units to become active in the binding layer, and vice versa. In effect, the binding layer activation is a compressed, distributed encoding of the value-unit perceptual representation.

Initially, all connections are inactive at 0. A perceptual experience is stored in the memory through the feature map layer in three steps. First, those units that represent the appropriate feature values are activated at 1. Second, a subset of m binding units are randomly selected in the binding layer as the compressed encoding for the pattern, and activated at 1. Third, the weights of all the connections between the active units in the feature maps and the active units in the binding layer are set to 1 (figure 1). Note that only one presentation is necessary to store a pattern.

To retrieve a pattern, first all binding units are set to 0. The pattern to be retrieved is partially specified

in the feature maps by activating a subset of its feature units. For example, in figure 2a the memory is cued with the two leftmost features. The activation propagates to the binding layer through all connections that have been turned on so far. The set of binding units that a particular feature unit turns on is called the binding constellation of that unit. All binding units in the binding encoding of the pattern to be retrieved are active at 2 because they belong to the binding constellation of both retrieval cue units. A number of other units are also activated at 1, because each cue unit takes part in representing multiple patterns, and therefore has several other active connections as well. Only those units active at 2 are retained; units with less activation are turned off (figure 2b).

The activation of the remaining binding units is then propagated back to the feature maps (figure 2c). A number of units are activated at various levels in each feature map, depending on how well their binding constellation matches the current pattern in the binding layer. Chances are that the unit that belongs to the same pattern than the cues has the largest overlap and becomes most highly activated. Only the most active unit in each feature map is retained, and as a result, a complete, unambiguous perceptual pattern is retrieved from the system (figure 2d).

Retrieval Errors

If there are n units in the binding layer and m units are chosen as a representation for a pattern, the number of possible different binding representations is equal to $\binom{n}{m}$. If n is sufficiently large and m is relatively small compared to n, this number is extremely large, suggesting that the convergence-zone memory could have a very large capacity.

However, due to the probabilistic nature of the storage and retrieval processes, there is always a chance that the retrieval will fail. The binding constellations of the retrieval cue units may overlap significantly, and several spurious units may be turned on at the binding layer. When the activation is propagated back to the feature maps, some random unit in a feature map may have a binding constellation that matches the spurious units very well. The "rogue" unit may receive more activation than the correct unit, and a wrong feature value may be retrieved. As more patterns are stored, the binding constellations of feature units become larger, and erroneous retrieval becomes more likely.

To determine the capacity of the convergence-zone memory, the chance of retrieval error must be computed. Below, a probabilistic formulation of the model is first given, and bounds for retrieval error are then computed.

Probabilistic Formulation

Let Z_i be the size of the binding constellation of a feature unit after i patterns have been stored on it and

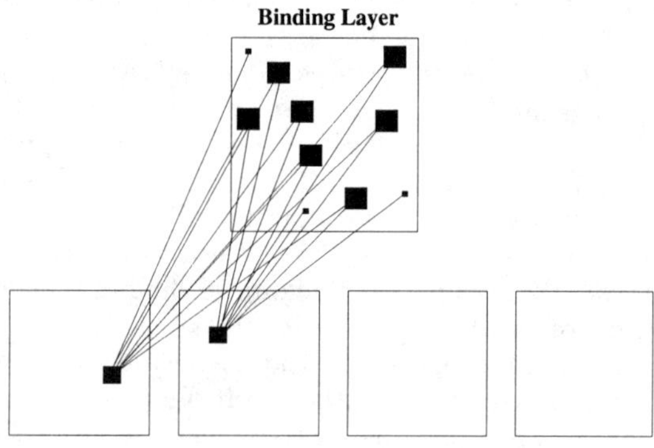
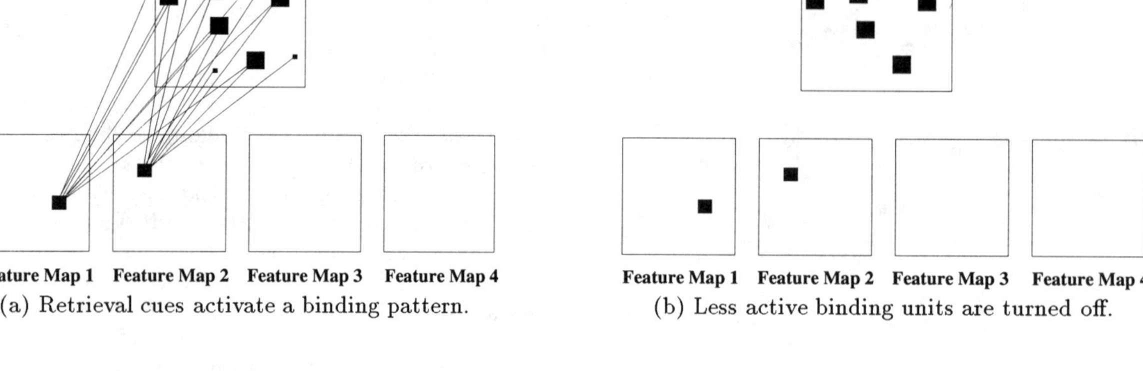

(a) Retrieval cues activate a binding pattern.

(b) Less active binding units are turned off.

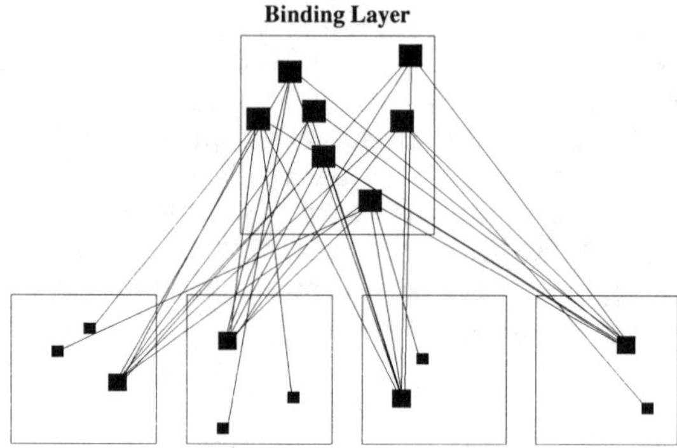
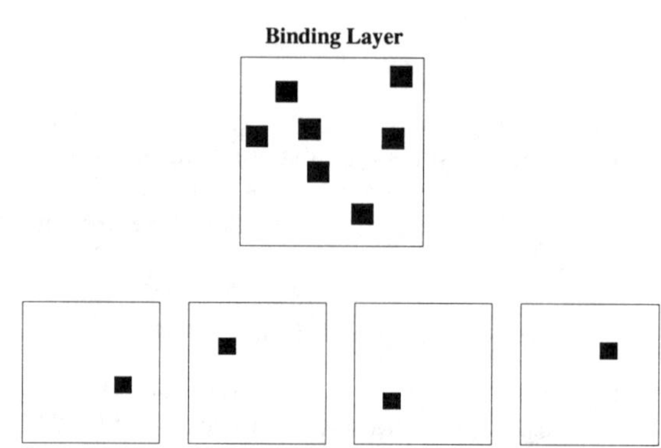

(c) Binding pattern activates feature units.

(d) Less active feature units are turned off.

Figure 2: **Retrieval.** A stored pattern is retrieved by presenting a partial representation as a cue. The size of the square indicates activation level of the unit.

let Y_i be its increase after storing the ith pattern on it. Obviously, $Y_1 = m$. To obtain the distribution of Y_i when $i > 1$, note that the new active connections belong to the intersection of a randomly chosen subset of m connections among all n connections of the unit, and its all remaining inactive connections (a set with $n - z$ elements, where z is the binding constellation at the previous step). Therefore, $Y_i, i > 1$ is hypergeometrically distributed with parameters $m, n - z$, and n:

$$P(Y_i = y | Z_{i-1} = z) = \binom{n - z}{y} \binom{z}{m - y} \bigg/ \binom{n}{m}. \tag{1}$$

The constellation size Z_i is then given by

$$Z_i = \sum_{k=1}^{i} Y_k. \tag{2}$$

Let I be the number of patterns stored on a particular feature unit after p patterns have been stored in the entire memory. I is binomially distributed with parameters p and $\frac{1}{f}$, where f is the number of units in a feature map:

$$I \sim B(p, \frac{1}{f}). \tag{3}$$

Let Z be the binding constellation of a particular feature unit after p patterns have been stored in the memory. It can be shown that $E(Z) = n(1 - (1 - \frac{m}{nf})^p)$. The binding constellation of a feature unit, given that at least one pattern has been stored on it, is denoted by Z'; obviously $E(Z') > E(Z)$. The variable Z' can be used to denote the binding constellation of a retrieval cue, which necessarily must have been used once, assuming that the retrieval cues are valid. Let Z'_j be the binding constellation of the jth retrieval cue and let X_j be the number of units in the intersection of the first j retrieval cues. Then $X_1 = Z'_1$. To get X_j for $j > 1$, we remove from consideration the m units all retrieval cues necessarily have in common (because they belong to the same stored pattern), and randomly select $z - m$ units from the total set of $n - m$ units and see how many of them belong to the current intersection of $x_{j-1} - m$ units. This is a hypergeometric distribution with parameters $z - m, x_{j-1} - m$, and $n - m$:

$$P(X_j = x_j | Z'_j = z, X_{j-1} = x_{j-1}) =$$
$$\binom{x_{j-1} - m}{x_j - m} \binom{n - x_{j-1}}{z - x_j} \bigg/ \binom{n - m}{z - m}. \quad (4)$$

The intersection is taken over the binding constellations of all j retrieval cues.

The number of units in common between a potential rogue unit and the j retrieval cues is denoted by R_{j+1} and is also hypergeometrically distributed, however with parameters z, x, and n because we cannot assume that the rogue unit has at least m units in common with the cues:

$$P(R_{j+1} = r | Z = z, X_j = x) =$$
$$\binom{x}{r} \binom{n - x}{z - r} \bigg/ \binom{n}{z}. \quad (5)$$

The correct unit in a feature map where a retrieval cue was not presented will receive an activation X_{j+1}. The correct unit will be retrieved if $X_{j+1} > R_{j+1}$, which is usually the case because $E(X_{j+1}) > E(R_{j+1})$. In each feature map there are $(f - 1)$ potential rogue units, so the conditional probability of successful retrieval is $(1 - P(R_{j+1} > X_{j+1} | X_{j+1}, Z, X_j))^{(f-1)}$, not addressing tie-breaking. Unfortunately, it is very difficult to compute p_{success}, the unconditional probability of successful retrieval, because the distribution functions of Z, X_j, X_{j+1} and R_{j+1} are not known. But it is possible to derive bounds for p_{success} and show that with reasonable values for n, m, f, and p, the memory is reliable.

Lower bound for memory capacity

Memory capacity can be defined as the maximum number of patterns that can be stored in the memory so that the probability of correct retrieval with a given number of retrieval cues is greater than α (a constant close to 1). In this section, worst-case bounds for the chance of successful retrieval will be derived. The analysis consists of three steps: (1) bounds for the number of patterns stored on a feature unit; (2) bounds for the binding constellation size; and (3) bounds for the intersections of binding constellations. Given particular values for the system parameters, it is then possible to give a lower bound for the capacity of the model.

1. Number of patterns stored on a feature unit. Since I has a binomial distribution (with parameters p and $\frac{1}{f}$), Chernoff bounds can be applied:

$$P(I \leq (1 - \delta)\frac{p}{f}) \leq \left[\frac{e^{-\delta}}{(1 - \delta)^{1-\delta}} \right]^{\frac{p}{f}}, 0 < \delta < 1, \quad (6)$$

$$P(I \geq (1 + \delta)\frac{p}{f}) \leq \left[\frac{e^{\delta}}{(1 + \delta)^{1+\delta}} \right]^{\frac{p}{f}}, \quad \delta > 0. \quad (7)$$

The formal parameter δ determines the tradeoff between the tightness of the bounds and the probability of satisfying them.

2. Size of the binding constellation. Instead of choosing exactly m different units for the binding representation of each pattern, let us select k not-necessarily-distinct units in such a way that the *expected* number of different units is m. This will make the analysis easier at the cost of larger variance, so that the bounds derived will also be valid for the actual process.

Let us assume i patterns are stored on a unit, which is equivalent of selecting ki units from the binding constellation at random. Let Z_v be the expected size of the binding constellation after v units have been selected. Then

$$Z_v = \tilde{Z} + (n - \tilde{Z})(1 - (1 - \frac{1}{n})^{ki-v}), \quad (8)$$

where $\tilde{Z}$ is the size of the binding constellation formed by the first v selected units. Now, $E(Z_v | Z_{v-1}) = Z_{v-1}$, and the sequence of variables $Z_0, \ldots, Z_{ki}$ is a martingale. Moreover, it can be shown that $|Z_v - Z_{v-1}| \leq 1$, and bounds for Z can be obtained from Azuma's inequality (see e.g. Alon & Spencer 1992):

$$P(Z \leq n(1 - (1 - \frac{1}{n})^{ki_l}) - \lambda \sqrt{ki_l}) \leq e^{-\lambda^2}, \quad (9)$$

$$P(Z \geq n(1 - (1 - \frac{1}{n})^{ki_u}) + \lambda \sqrt{ki_u}) \leq e^{-\lambda^2}, \quad (10)$$

where i_l is the lower bound for I obtained from equation 6, and i_u the upper bound from equation 7. Similar bounds can be derived for Z'.

3. Intersection of binding constellations. The process of forming the intersection of j binding constellations incrementally one cue at a time can also be formulated as a martingale process. Let X_j denote the expected number of elements in the intersection of two sets, after the first j elements of the first set have been checked (the elements of the second set are assumed to be known at all times). Then

$$X_j = \tilde{X} + \frac{(n_1 - j)(n_2 - \tilde{X})}{n - j}, \quad (11)$$

where $\tilde{X}$ is the number of elements in the intersection of the second set and the set formed by the first j elements of the first set, and n_1, n_2 and n are the sizes of the first, second, and the superset. If n_1 and n_2 are both smaller than $\frac{1}{2}n$, Azuma's inequality can be applied. Taking the intersection of the previous step as the first set, the binding constellation of the jth cue as the second set, and the binding layer as the common superset, this approach gives us the following upper bound for X_j:

$$P(X_j \geq \frac{(x_{j-1,u} - m)(z'_u - m)}{(n - m)} + m$$
$$+ \lambda \sqrt{x_{j-1,u} - m}) \leq e^{-\lambda^2/2}, \quad \lambda > 0, \quad (12)$$

where z'_u and $x_{j-1,u}$ are upper bounds for Z' and X_{j-1} and are assumed to be less than $\frac{1}{2}n$. When X_j is at its upper bound, a potential rogue unit has the largest chance of taking over. In this case, R_{j+1} has the upper bound

$$\mathrm{P}\left(R_{j+1} \geq \frac{x_{j,u}z_u}{n} + \lambda\sqrt{x_{j,u}}\right) \leq e^{-\lambda^2/2}, \quad \lambda > 0, \quad (13)$$

where z_u and $x_{j,u}$ are upper bounds for Z and X_j. A lower bound for X_{j+1} while using an upperbound for X_j is then given by

$$\mathrm{P}\Big(X_{j+1} \leq \frac{(x_{j,u} - m)(z_l - m)}{(n - m)} + m$$
$$-\lambda\sqrt{x_{j,u} - m}\Big) \leq e^{-\lambda^2/2}, \qquad \lambda > 0. \qquad (14)$$

If the resulting lower bound is smaller than m, m can be used instead.

The above analysis ignores correlations between binding constellations. The correlations originate from storing the same partial pattern multiple times and tend to increase the size of the intersections. The chance that two random patterns have more than one feature in common in j features is equal to $(1 - (1 + \frac{j}{f-1})(1 - \frac{1}{f})^j)$, which is negligible for sufficiently large values of f.

We can now use equations 6–14 to derive a lower bound for the probability of successful retrieval with given system parameters n, m, F, j, f, and p. The retrieval is successful if $r_{j+1,u}$, the upper bound for R_{j+1}, is lower than $x_{j+1,u}$, the lower bound for X_{j+1}. Under this constraint, the probability that none of the variables in the analysis exceeds its bounds is a lower bound for successful retrieval.

Obtaining the upper bound for X_j involves bounding $3j - 1$ variables: I and Z' for the j cues and X_j for the $j - 1$ intersections. Computing $x_{j+1,l}$ and $r_{j+1,u}$ each involve bounding 3 variables (I, Z, and X_{j+1}; I, Z', and R_{j+1}). There are $F - j$ maps, each with one $x_{j+1,l}$ bound and $f - 1$ different $r_{j+1,u}$ bounds (one for each rogue unit). The total number of bounds is therefore $3j - 1 + 3f(F - j)$. Setting the righthand sides of the inequalities 6–14 equal to a small constant β, a lower bound for successful retrieval is obtained:

$$p_{\text{success}} > 1 - (3j - 1 + 3f(F - j))\beta. \qquad (15)$$

For example, assuming each unit in the model corresponds to a vertical column in the cortex, it is reasonable to assume feature maps with 10^6 computational units (Sejnowski & Churchland 1989). We can further assume that the system has 15 feature maps, 10 of which is used to cue the memory, and the binding layer consists of 10^5 units, with 150 used for each binding pattern. Assuming full connectivity between the feature units and the binding units, there are 1.5×10^{12} connections in the system.

If we store 0.85×10^8 patterns in the memory, z'_u and $x_{j-1,u}$ are less than $\frac{1}{2}n$, the chance of partial overlap of more than 1 feature is less than 0.45×10^{-10}, and the analysis above is valid. Setting $\beta = 0.5 \times 10^{-9}$ yields bounds $r_{j+1,u} < x_{j+1,l}$ with $p_{\text{success}} > 99\%$. In other words, 0.85×10^8 memories can be stored in the memory with 99% probability of successful retrieval. Such a capacity is approximately equivalent of storing one new memory every 17 seconds for 70 years, 16 hours a day.

Conclusion

Mathematical analysis shows that an extremely high number of episodes can be stored in the convergence-zone memory with reliable content-addressable retrieval. Moreover, the convergence zone itself requires only a tiny fraction of the hardware required for perceptual representation. These results provide a possible explanation for why human memory appears almost unlimited, and why memory areas appear small compared to the areas devoted to low-level perceptual processing.

The model makes use of the combinatorics and the clean-up properties of coarse coding in a neurally-inspired architecture. The storage capacity of the model appears to be at least two orders of magnitude higher than that of the Hopfield model with the same number of units, while using two orders of magnitude fewer connections. However, direct comparison is difficult because the stored patterns in the Hopfield model are much larger (contain more information), and its $N/4 \log N$ capacity result only indicates how many patterns are stable instead of estimating the probability of correct retrieval with a partial pattern as a cue.

The convergence-zone episodic memory model could be extended to make it more accurate as a model of actual neural processes. For instance, lateral inhibitory connections between units within a feature map could be added to select the unit with the highest activity. A similar extension could be applied to the binding layer; instead of only one unit multiple units should stay active. A variation of the Hebbian learning mechanism (Hebb 1949; Miller & MacKay 1992) could be used to implement the storage mechanism. Such research could lead to a practical implementation of the convergence zone memory, and perhaps even to a hardware implementation. Another important research direction is to analyze the behavior of the model as a psychological model, that is, to observe and characterize its memory interference effects and compare them with experimental results on human episodic memory.

Acknowledgements

We would like to thank Greg Plaxton for pointing us to martingale analysis on this problem. This research was supported in part by NSF grant #IRI-9309273 to the second author.

References

Alon, N., and Spencer, J. H. 1992. *The Probabilistic Method.* New York: Wiley.

Damasio, A. R. 1989a. The brain binds entities and events by multiregional activation from convergence zones. *Neural Computation* 1:123–132.

Damasio, A. R. 1989b. Time-locked multiregional retroactivation: A systems-level proposal for the neural substrates of recall and recognition. *Cognition* 33:25–62.

Hebb, D. O. 1949. *The Organization of Behavior: A Neuropsychological Theory.* New York: Wiley.

Hertz, J.; Krogh, A.; and Palmer, R. G. 1991. *Introduction to the Theory of Neural Computation.* Reading, MA: Addison-Wesley.

Hopfield, J. J. 1982. Neural networks and physical systems with emergent collective computational abilities. *Proceedings of the National Academy of Sciences, USA* 79:2554–2558.

Jessell, E. R. K. 1991. Nerve cells and behavior. In Kandel, E. R.; Schwartz, J. H.; and Jessell, T. M., eds., *Principles of Neural Science.* Elsevier. 18–32.

Kanerva, P. 1988. *Sparse Distributed Memory.* Cambridge, MA: MIT Press.

Keeler, J. D. 1988. Comparison between Kanerva's SDM and Hopfield-type neural networks. *Cognitive Science* 12:299–329.

Kortge, C. A. 1990. Episodic memory in connectionist networks. In *Proceedings of the 12th Annual Conference of the Cognitive Science Society,* 764–771. Hillsdale, NJ: Erlbaum.

McEliece, R. J.; Posner, E. C.; Rodemich, E. R.; and Venkatesh, S. S. 1986. The capacity of the hop field associative memory. *IEEE Transactions on Information Theory* 33:461–482.

Miikkulainen, R. 1992. Trace feature map: A model of episodic associative memory. *Biological Cybernetics* 66:273–282.

Miller, K. D., and MacKay, D. J. C. 1992. The role of constrains in Hebbian learning. CNS Memo 19, Computation and Neural Systems Program, California Institute of Technology, Pasadena, CA.

Rosenfeld, R., and Touretzky, D. S. 1989. A survey of coarse-coded symbol memories. In Touretzky, D. S.; Hinton, G. E.; and Sejnowski, T. J., eds., *Proceedings of the 1988 Connectionist Models Summer School,* 256–264. San Mateo, CA: Morgan Kaufmann.

Sejnowski, T. J., and Churchland, P. S. 1989. Brain and cognition. In Posner, M. I., ed., *Foundations of Cognitive Science.* Cambridge, MA: MIT Press. chapter 8, 315–356.

Squire, L. R. 1987. *Memory and Brain.* Oxford, UK; New York: Oxford University Press.

Touretzky, D. S., and Hinton, G. E. 1988. A distributed connectionist production system. *Cognitive Science* 12:423–466.

Tulving, E. 1972. Episodic and semantic memory. In Tulving, E., and Donaldson, W., eds., *Organization of Memory.* New York: Academic Press. 381–403.

Tulving, E. 1983. *Elements of Episodic Memory.* Oxford, UK; New York: Oxford University Press.

A Model of Creative Understanding[*]

Kenneth Moorman and Ashwin Ram

Georgia Institute of Technology
College of Computing
Atlanta, GA 30332-0280
{kennethm,ashwin}@cc.gatech.edu

Abstract

Although creativity has largely been studied in problem solving contexts, creativity consists of both a generative component and a comprehension component. In particular, creativity is an essential part of reading and understanding of natural language stories. We have formalized the understanding process and have developed an algorithm capable of producing creative understanding behavior. We have also created a novel knowledge organization scheme to assist the process. Our model of creativity is implemented as a portion of the ISAAC (Integrated Story Analysis And Creativity) reading system, a system which models the creative reading of science fiction stories.

Introduction

Creativity remains a largely unexplained facet of human intelligence; neither psychologists nor artificial intelligence researchers have produced complete theories of it. While most creativity researchers have investigated the behavior in a problem solving context, we are more interested in how creativity is manifested during comprehension. We thus distinguish between two forms of creativity: a generative type, *creative invention* or *creative problem solving* (e.g., Hofstadter & McGraw 1993; Kolodner & Wills 1993); and an explanatory type, *creative understanding* (e.g., Kass, Leake, & Owens 1986; Ram 1993). Past research has shown the value of exploiting the relationship between problem solving and understanding (e.g., Wilensky 1983; Birnbaum 1986); likewise, our study of creative understanding should aid general creativity research.

Our model of creative understanding is functional in nature. A cognitive *process* can be explained by describing the *function* of each of its *tasks*, the *relationships* between them, the *mechanisms* which accomplish them, and the *knowledge* required. The resulting *functional theory* can then be used to guide implementation of a process model. We have identified four tasks which are sufficient for the modeling of creative understanding. For three of these, we extended well-known mechanisms from traditional problem solving and comprehension domains. The

---

[*]This work was supported by a Fannie and John Hertz Foundation fellowship and by the Georgia Institute of Technology.

final one, problem reformulation, relies on a new mechanism, function-driven morphological synthesis. While developed in a reading context, this is a general method which can apply to other creativity modeling. The creative understanding processes, mechanisms, and a novel knowledge organization scheme which supports the processes are implemented in the ISAAC (Integrated Story Analysis And Creativity) system which creatively reads science fiction stories.

Creative Understanding

The reading of any story requires some level of creative understanding; it is when normal processing fails that creative understanding is most necessary. Consider the science fiction story, *Men Are Different* (Bloch 1963), seen in Figure 1. If a reader is unfamiliar with the concept of sentient robots, the story is impossible to appreciate. While the next section explains exactly what happens when such a need for creative understanding arises, the remainder of this section presents a discussion of creativity in order to provide a common ground to an elusive and often controversial concept.

Creativity

Creativity is a directed, internal process of a cognitive agent which results in an artifact which is both novel and useful. This is intended as a working definition; the following elaborations should clarify our intended meaning.

Process: For a process to be creative, it must be both *internal* and *directed*. The internal restriction ensures that the reasoner is not simply repeating a piece of knowledge just received from another source. The directedness restriction ensures that the reasoner is not simply a random generator of solutions, where one may eventually be "creative" through sheer chance.

Artifact: An *artifact* results from a mental process by a reasoner and may be either physical or mental. Any artifact can be described by a set of *attributes* which define its characteristics. One of these, *function*, represents the

I'm an archaeologist, and Men are my business. Just the same, I wonder if we'll ever find out about Men—I mean *really* find out what made Man different from us Robots—by digging around on the dead planets. You see, I lived with a Man once, and I know it isn't as simple as they told us back in school.

We have a few records, of course, and Robots like me are filling in some of the gaps, but I think now that we aren't really getting anywhere. We know, or at least the historians say we know, that Men came from a planet called Earth. We know, too, that they rode out bravely from star to star; and wherever they stopped, they left colonies—Men, Robots, and sometimes both—against their return. But they never came back.

Those were the shining days of the world. But are we so old now? Men had a bright flame—the old word is "divine" I think—that flung them far across the night skies, and we have lost the strands of the web they wove.

Our scientists tell us that Men were very much like us—and the skeleton of a Man is, to be sure, almost the same as the skeleton of a Robot, except that it's made of some calcium compound instead of titanium. Just the same, there are other differences.

It was on my last field trip, to one of the inner planets, that I met the Man. He must have been the last Man in this system, and he'd forgotten how to talk—he'd been alone so long. I planned to to bring him back with me. Something happened to him, though.

One day, for no reason at all, he complained of the heat. I checked his temperature and decided that his thermostat circuits were shot. I had a kit of field spares with me, and he was obviously out of order, so I went to work. I pushed the needle into his neck to operate the cut-off switch, and he stopped moving, just like a Robot. But when I opened him up he wasn't the same inside. And when I put him back together I couldn't get him running again. Then he sort of weathered away—and by the time I was ready to come home, about a year later, there was nothing left of him but bones. Yes, Men are indeed different.

Figure 1: *Men Are Different*

best-known uses of the artifact. The remaining attributes are divided into *primary attributes*, which contribute to an explanation for why the artifact can perform its function; and *secondary attributes*, which are the rest.

Novel: There are many arguments concerning whether a creative act must be *novel* and from whose perspective this novelty is judged (e.g., Boden 1991; Stewart 1950; Thurstone 1952). In reference to a given perspective, there are two important ways in which an artifact (M) may be novel with respect to a goal (G); to see these, consider a longsword used for combat.

- Evolutionary Novelty (E-Novel): M is defined to be E-Novel iff M is unknown and M accomplishes G in a better way than other examples of artifacts which accomplish G. This is generally the result of altering one of the primary attributes of M. A shortsword, a bastard sword, or a two-handed sword would all be E-Novel.

- Revolutionary Novelty (R-Novel): M is defined to be R-Novel iff M is unknown and M accomplishes G in a different way than other artifacts which accomplish G. For this, secondary attributes may need to be altered to cause them to participate in the function of M. The light saber from Star Wars is an R-Novel variation of the original longsword.

Useful: *Useful* is somewhat easier to define for an artifact. A reasoner attempting to perform creatively will have a certain task to accomplish. In order for a creative process to exist, it must produce an artifact which accomplishes this task in some manner.

Creative understanding specification

The presented definition of creativity is simply descriptive and is insufficient for implementing a model of creative behavior. For this, we need to develop an algorithmic view of creativity as it exists within creative understanding.

Formalization of problem solving   Since understanding can be described as the complementary operation to problem solving, a formal view of problem solving can be helpful in developing an understanding formalization. *Problem solving* begins with the reasoner in an *initial state*. A reasoner knows of operations that it can perform which will move it through a *search space*. This stops when a *goal state* is achieved. The output from the process is a *solution path* which takes the reasoner from the initial state to the goal state (Newell & Simon 1972). The idea of *constraints* on this process is also important (Sacerdoti 1974; Sussman 1973). These are conditions which cannot be violated in the final solution. Finally, there are times when the reasoner may already possess a solution. If so, problem solving can discover a better solution if the reasoner possesses a critique of why the current solution is not a viable one (Hammond 1989). The complete formulation is shown in Figure 2.

Formalization of understanding   Based on Figure 2, a formal specification of understanding can be developed (Figure 3). Using the example of *Men...*: if a reader sees a robotic character "turn off" a man and then open him, they may understand the episode by reasoning that the robot had the goal of repairing the man (*abduction*):

INPUT:
Initial state (I)
Goal state desired (G)
Set of constraints (C) (optional)
Current solution (S) (optional)
Critique why S is not good enough solution (K) (optional)
OUTPUT:
Solution path (S′) which achieves G given I and does not
violate C

Figure 2: FUNCTION **Problem Solver**

a reader who learns that Mankind has become extinct
and that the remaining robots are curious as to the fate
of their creators may understand this by reasoning about
upcoming story actions (*prediction*); finally, the reader
may attempt to understand why the robot felt that field
repairs was a good solution to the man's discomfort (*explanation*).

INPUT	OUTPUT	Behavior
Solution (S)	Goal (G)	Abduction
Goal (G)	Solution (S)	Prediction
Solution (S) and	Critique (K) of why	Explanation
Goal (G)	S is a good solution	

Figure 3: FUNCTION **Understander**

The creative understanding process

If only known concepts are given to the understanding
process, no creative behavior is necessary. If, however,
a reasoner uses the understanding *process* to comprehend *novel artifacts* in a way which is *useful*, creative
understanding occurs. Notice that the context of reading
provides an exact meaning for the final part of this requirement, usefulness. Since the reasoner has the task of
comprehending some piece of text, an understanding of
an artifact from it is useful if this understanding allows
comprehension to occur and reading to continue. This is
in marked contrast with "traditional" approaches to creativity which must make the context of usefulness more
explicit.

The tasks involved in creative understanding are carried out by a core set of cognitive mechanisms. This
cycle of creative understanding (CUP) is shown in Figure 4 (depicted for an abduction task, the same approach
is used for explanation and prediction). Mundane understanding exists if the reasoner only considers steps 1 and
2; that is, if the reasoner performs only memory retrieval
and incorporation. Each cycle increases the potential for
successful creative understanding. At some point the reasoner will be so far removed from the original concept
that further iterations will be useless; still, there is no
theoretical limit to the "amount" of creativity generated

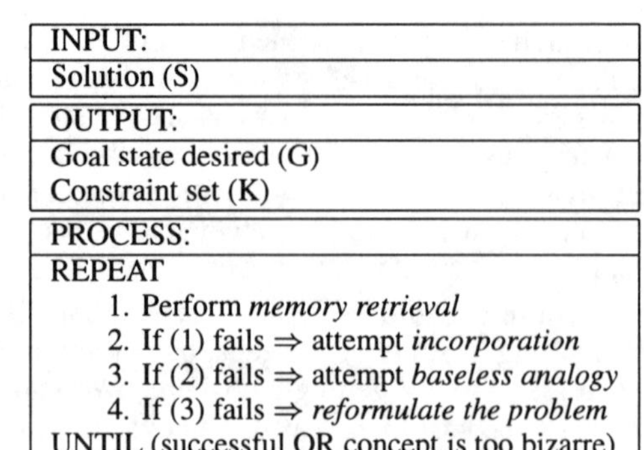

Figure 4: FUNCTION **Creative Understander**

The four steps of CUP

The first step of the CUP algorithm involves a *memory
retrieval*. If concepts are retrieved which cause understanding of the novel concept, the cycle ends successfully.
If nothing is returned which is immediately useful, processing continues. This may occur if nothing is available
in memory or if the proper items are simply not returned
(e.g., due to an indexing problem). In *Men...*, the reasoner
will be confronted with the idea of a sentient robot. If
only an industrial robot exists in memory, understanding
will fail. The concept of *industrial robot* is insufficient
to explain the robot's actions.

If normal memory retrieval fails to produce adequate
understanding, the algorithm will attempt to perform *incorporation*. Incorporation involves the discovery of
relations between concepts which were retrieved from
memory and the concept being explained. If a relationship can be discovered that explains the new concept,
understanding is successful. This stage of the cycle may
result in understanding which appears either mundane or
creative, depending on exactly what was retrieved and
what sorts of relations were discovered. In the example
of *Men...*, incorporation fails because sentience is in conflict between the concepts of *industrial robot* and *story
robot*.

If incorporation fails, the CUP algorithm attempts a
technique known as *baseless analogy*. *Analogy* (e.g.,
Falkenhainer 1987; Gentner 1989) attempts to explain
a concept (the *target*) by appealing to known information about an analogous concept (the *base*). However,
if no existing base exists, it may be possible to dynamically build the base within a given domain if the reasoner
possesses a great deal of information about the target's
domain and the intended base domain (e.g., Clement
1989). For example, atomic structure as in the Bohr
model can be understood within the framework of gang
warfare (WKRP Episode 60 1980). If the reasoner has
a great deal of conceptual background knowledge concerning sentience and robots, it is possible that an understanding of the story robot may result.

Finally, if all of the above steps have failed to produce
a satisfactory understanding, the reasoner must resort to

problem reformulation. There are some cases in which the initial statement of a problem is not the one which will lead to an optimal solution. By recasting the problem in a new way, a reasoner may gain insights into a possible solution. For *Men...*, the reader can attempt to take the retrieved concept of *industrial robot* and manipulate it with the goal of explaining the *story robot*. The method which accomplishes problem reformulations is function-driven morphological synthesis.

1. Consider an artifact in the world, designated as M.
2. Let f be defined as the function which returns the function of an artifact.
3. Let C be the class of functions which alter an object, either by changing some attribute of that object or by adding a new attribute to the object.
4. C_1 through C_n are a set of n such functions.
5. Thus, a set of objects S_{all} can be created by $\cup_{i=1...n} C_i$.
6. Consider the subset, S_f defined as
   $$\{s | s \epsilon S_{all} \text{ and } f(s) = f(M)\}$$
7. Finally, consider the subset S_c defined as
   $$\{s | s \epsilon S_f \text{ where } s \text{ is unknown }\}$$
8. The items in S_c are useful (they fulfill the same role as the original object M) and they are novel to the reasoner. Therefore, they are creative.

Figure 5: Function-driven Morphological Synthesis

Function-driven morphological synthesis

In order to model problem reformulation, we developed a new mechanism—*function-directed morphological synthesis* (FMS), depicted in Figure 5. It is assumed that the reasoner has an artifact that needs to be understood. The reasoner applies a set of manipulator functions to the artifact, altering its attributes and producing new artifacts. The artifacts which possess the original functionality and are novel to the reasoner are considered to be creative ones. The FMS technique was inspired by Allen's *morphological synthesis* (cited in Finke, Ward, & Smith 1992), in which a reasoner manipulates combinations of primary attributes to produce potentially creative results. Since only primary attributes were modified, Allen's technique could not result in an R-Novel item. By removing this restriction, FMS *is* able to produce such novelty. Finally, FMS can exist in both a strong form and a weak form. Strong-FMS performs the manipulations by examining other objects with the same functionality to see how they accomplish their tasks. Weak-FMS does away with this constraint and guides the manipulation through the reasoner's knowledge of given attributes and possible values.

In *Men...*, FMS must attempt to understand the *story robot*. It knows that the robot is a willful agent, which violates the concept of *industrial robot*. Memory retrieval produces a concept which is a willful agent, but is not a robot—man. Thus, FMS begins with *man* as an input (whose "purpose" is willful agency). FMS is aided by the fact that it has the goal of understanding *story robot*.

Thus, when it manipulates the attributes of *man*, it does so by examining the concepts of *man* and *industrial robot* (an example of strong-FMS). It adds attributes to *man* from *industrial robot* and deletes attributes which are no longer needed. The result is a man-like robot which can be used to explain the actions of the *story robot*.

When to say when

A central issue in concept manipulation systems is how does a reasoner know which manipulations are good ones and which ones are potentially dangerous. While a *willing suspension of disbelief* (Corrigan 1979) is required for creativity, too much suspension will lead to ridiculous outcomes. Various approaches have been taken to minimize this problem in other creativity models. One possibility is to have the system do little self-monitoring; this approach can be seen in Lenat's AM system (1990). While AM did create a number of creative concepts, it also created a much larger number of worthless concepts which were filtered out by the human researcher. Alternatively, other systems exist which possess a large number of programmer-supplied heuristics for deciding what to manipulate and how far to carry the alterations; Turner's MINSTREL system (1992) and SWALE (Kass, Leake, & Owens 1986) are examples. The problem with this approach is that no techniques have been proposed which would allow the straightforward creation of these heuristics; instead, developing them is a "black-art." Both approaches have been argued against from a theoretical standpoint (Birnbaum 1986); we prefer a technique which would allow flexible modifications, decided by the system itself. As part of this, a new method of knowledge organization is needed.

Our knowledge organization scheme resembles a standard semantic network, but knowledge is tagged through the use of a multidimensional grid, as shown in Figure 6. One axis of the grid represents a Schankian breakdown: *action*, *agent*, *state*, and *object* (Schank & Abelson 1977). The other dimension represents a natural breakdown: *physical*, *mental*, *social*, *emotional*, and *temporal*. For example, a TRANSfer is a generic action. In the physical column is PTRANS, the mental column contains MTRANS, and the social column contains ATRANS. Our extended representation also includes emotional TRANSfers (the giving of one's love); and temporal TRANSfers (March getting closer to us).

Another difference between a standard semantic network and our organization scheme is the *function tagging* of each concept. Each concept within the knowledge system is tagged with a set of its common functions. If the reasoner is searching for similar concepts, possibly for use in an FMS attempt, this search can be aided by these tags. For example, in one memory retrieval, a car and a horse might be similar; with a different goal, a horse and a zebra would be a closer pair. This tagging allows a more flexible organization of knowledge than previous methods which were forced to carefully place items into the network to ensure that proper similarities were

	Physical	Mental	Social	Emotional	Temporal
Agents	person	consciousness	boss	Ares	entropy
Actions	walking	thinking	selling	loving	getting closer to March
Objects	rock	idea	teacher-student relationship	hatred	second
States	young	lack of knowledge	public dishoner	being angry	early

Figure 6: Knowledge representation grid

revealed when needed.

The knowledge organization scheme allows concept manipulation which is bounded in a reasonable fashion. Each change may leave a concept in the same conceptual grid cell (an *intracellular shift*) or it may cause the concept to cross a cell boundary (an *extracellular shift*). The system is biased against boundary crossings. As a result, conceptual movement within the same grid cell is the cheapest type to perform. Movement along *either* a row or a column is more difficult, and movement which must go along both is the most difficult. These costs act as a heuristic which guides a reasoner performing creative understanding—the greater the cost, the more conceptual movement has occurred. High amounts of conceptual movement indicates that it is likely that the result will be more bizarre than creative. This restricts how many iterations are permissible in the CUP algorithm. Each successive cycle creates concepts which are more and more distant from the original one. The first few iterations will result in concepts which fall within the same grid cell as the original concept. More cycles will create concepts which are shifted in the grid with respect to the beginning concept. By tracking this movement, the reasoner can decide when creative understanding has become too expensive to continue, based on the goals of the reasoner.

Implementation

The ideas discussed above are embodied in the ISAAC reading system, currently implemented at a level of functionality capable of reading the science fiction story *Men Are Different* (Figure 1). It is built in Common Lisp and runs on RS/6000 machines. ISAAC uses the KR frame package (Giuse 1990) for knowledge representation. More details of the ISAAC system, and its general reading capabilities can be found in (Moorman & Ram 1994).

Upon beginning to read *Men Are Different*, ISAAC realizes that the concept of robot it knows (an industrial tool) is insufficient to produce an understanding of the story robot. This realization arises when ISAAC is unable to reconcile its current definition of robot with the actions of the robot in the story, i.e., the predictions made by the existing conceptual definition are failing. Creative understanding is given the task of explaining the novel robot, with the existing concept and the novel one passed to the routine. Incorporation fails to create an understanding since there is little similarity between the two concepts of robots. Next, baseless analogy is attempted. ISAAC attempts to transfer the concept of *industrial robot* to the domain of volitional agents (since this is how the story robot appears to be acting). Unfortunately, ISAAC does not have enough background knowledge to succeed in this case. ISAAC then attempts problem reformulation, using FMS to produce a merged concept containing elements of the current robot concept and the best volitional agent it can retrieve from memory—a man. The result is a man-like, intelligent, volitional robot. The new concept maintains some characteristics of the original robot (it is made of metal, resistant to damage, uses sensors and feedback as a control mechanism, and so on.), but is sufficient to understand the robot in the story. ISAAC stores the new concept in memory as a *story-robot*.

ISAAC needs to perform similar creative understanding on the man in the story. In this case, ISAAC is attempting to explain what goals the robot might have possessed to cause it to act in the fashion that it did. As a result of this understanding attempt, ISAAC understands that the robot is seeing the man as more similar to itself than is warranted. The irony in the story can be seen as a dual shift within our knowledge grid. First, ISAAC is presented with a robot character acting as an *agent* rather than as a *physical object*; the ending is ironic because the narrator then treats the Man, a *physical agent*, as a *physical object* and disassembles him, thereby killing him.

Conclusions

While the CUP algorithm has been successful in assisting ISAAC in the understanding of a single story, more work must be done. Additional stories need to be added to the system in order to evaluate the impact of possessing unneeded information during creative understanding. It is already decided that the next story will be *Zoo* (Hoch 1978), a story similar to *Men...* in several ways but different enough to test expansion possibilities. Objective evaluation of ISAAC's creative performance is also needed. The best such test currently available, the *Torrance Tests of Creative Thinking* (Torrance 1988), is considered flawed in significant ways. While it is an objective test, opponents suggest that what it measures may be too abstract to apply to general creative behavior. We also intend to explore the relationship of *conceptual change* to creative understanding (e.g., Ram 1993; Chi 1993). Finally, we plan to demonstrate our claim that creative understanding issues are important to creative design by implementing a design algorithm based on the CUP and FMS algorithms.

While many researchers have tried to "demystify" creativity, most models of the process which have been put forth have been too vague to allow implementation. Seeing creativity as having two aspects, a generative side and an understanding side, has permitted us to explore new issues in creativity and develop interesting results. The four steps of the CUP model are sufficient for producing behavior which is judged creative. Additionally, the described FMS algorithm is a mechanism which has proven capable of producing novel understanding of concepts. In addition, our reading area has forced us to confront real-world applications of creativity. Humans are certainly aided in reading comprehension by possessing creativity (Popov 1993); by incorporating creative understanding into artificial systems, they gain the ability to learn from experiences with novel concepts and thus grow in scope.

References

Birnbaum, L. 1986. *Integrated Processing in Planning and Understanding*. Ph.D. Dissertation, Yale University. Research Report 489.

Bloch, A. 1963. Men Are Different. In Asimov, I., and Conklin, G., eds., *50 Short Science Fiction Tales*. New York: MacMillan Publishing Co.

Boden, M. A. 1991. *The Creative Mind: Myths and Mechanisms*. New York: BasicBooks.

Chi, M. T. H. 1993. Barriers to conceptual change in learning science concepts: A theoretical conjecture. In *Proceedings of the Fifteenth Annual Conference of the Cognitive Science Society*, 312–317.

Clement, J. 1989. Learning via model construction and criticism: Protocol evidence on sources of creativity in science. In Glover, J. A.; Ronning, R. R.; and Reynolds, C. R., eds., *Handbook of Creativity*. New York: Plenum Press.

Corrigan, R. W. 1979. *The World of the Theatre*. Glenview, IL: Scott, Foresman and Co.

Falkenhainer, B. 1987. Scientific theory formation through analogical reasoning. In *Proceedings of the Fourth International Workshop on Machine Learning*.

Finke, R. A.; Ward, T. B.; and Smith, S. M. 1992. *Creative Cognition: Theory, Research, and Applications*. Cambridge: MIT Press.

Gentner, D. 1989. Mechanisms of analogical learning. In Vosniadou, S., and Ortony, A., eds., *Similarity and Analogical Reasoning*. London: Cambridge University Press.

Giuse, D. 1990. Efficient knowledge representation systems. *The Knowledge Engineering Review* 5(1):35–50.

Hammond, K. J. 1989. CHEF. In Reisbeck, C., and Schank, R., eds., *Inside Case-Based Reasoning*. Hillsdale, NJ: Lawrence Erlbaum Associates.

Hoch, E. D. 1978. Zoo. In Asimov, I.; Greenberg, M. H.; and Olander, J. D., eds., *100 Great Science Fiction Short Short Stories*. Garden City, NY: Doubleday.

Hofstadter, D., and McGraw, G. 1993. Letter Spirit: An emergent model of the perception and creation of alphabetic style. Technical Report 68, Indiana University.

Kass, A. M.; Leake, D. B.; and Owens, C. C. 1986. SWALE: A program that explains. In Schank, R. C., ed., *Explanation Patterns: Understanding Mechanically and Creatively*. Hillsdale, NJ: Lawrence Erlbaum Associates. 232–254. Appendix.

Kolodner, J. L., and Wills, L. M. 1993. Paying attention to the right thing: Issues of focus in case-based creative design. In *Proceedings AAAI-93 CBR Workshop*.

Lenat, D. 1990. The ubiquity of discovery. In Shavlik, J. W., and Dietterich, T. G., eds., *Readings in Machine Learning*. San Mateo, CA: Morgan Kaufmann Publishers, Inc.

Moorman, K., and Ram, A. 1994. A functional theory of creative reading. Technical Report GIT-CC-94/01, Georgia Institute of Technology.

Newell, A., and Simon, H. A. 1972. *Human Problem Solving*. Englewood Cliffs, NJ: Prentice-Hall.

Popov, A. 1993. Creativity and reading comprehension. *Journal of Creative Behavior* 26(3):206–212.

Ram, A. 1993. Creative conceptual change. In *Proceedings of the Fifteenth Annual Conference of the Cognitive Science Society*, 17–26.

Sacerdoti, E. D. 1974. Planning in a hierarchy of abstraction spaces. *Artificial Intelligence* 5(2):115–135.

Schank, R., and Abelson, R. 1977. *Scripts, Plans, Goals, and Understanding*. Hillsdale, NJ: Lawrence Erlbaum Associates.

Stewart, G. W. 1950. Can productive thinking be taught? *Journal of Higher Education* 21:411–414.

Sussman, G. J. 1973. A computational model of skill acquisition. Technical Report AI TR-297, MIT.

Thurstone, L. L. 1952. *Applications of Psychology*. New York: Harper & Row. chapter Creative Talent.

Torrance, E. P. 1988. The nature of creativity as manifest in its testing. In Sternberg, R. J., ed., *The Nature of Creativity*. Cambridge: Cambridge University Press.

Turner, S. 1992. *MINSTREL: A Computer Model of Creativity and Storytelling*. Ph.D. Dissertation, University of California, Los Angeles.

Wilensky, R. 1983. *Planning and Understanding*. Reading, MA: Addison-Wesley.

WKRP Episode 60. 1980. Venus and The Man. Written by Hugh Wilson, Directed by Rod Daniel.

Ordering Relations in Human and Machine Planning[1]

Lee Spector, Mary Jo Rattermann, and Kristen Prentice

School of Communications and Cognitive Science
Hampshire College, Amherst, MA 01002
{lspector, mrattermann, kprentice}@hamp.hampshire.edu

Abstract

Analytical results from AI planning research provide the motivation for this experimental study of ordering relationships in human planning. We examine timings of humans performing specific tasks from the AI planning literature and present evidence that normal human planners, like "state of the art" AI planning systems, use partial-order plan representations. We also describe ongoing experiments that are designed to shed light on the plan representations used by children and by adults with planning deficits due to brain damage. Several points of interest for collaboration between AI scientists and neuropsychologists are noted, as are impacts that we feel this research may have on future work in AI planning.

Introduction

Recent analytical studies have mapped a rich territory of relations among AI planning algorithms, AI planning domains, and computational complexity classes (Chapman 1987, Bylander 1991, Chenoweth 1991, Gupta & Nau 1991, Erol et al. 1991, Minton et al. 1992, Barrett & Weld 1993). The work of Barrett and Weld, in particular, shows that planning algorithms based on partially-ordered plan representations have advantages over total-order planners when applied to problems of certain sorts. One of their results is that problems in the artificial domain called D^1S^1 are easy for partial-order planners but hard for total-order planners. Partial-order planners exhibit linear growth rates for planning time as problem size increases in this domain, while total-order planners exhibit exponential growth rates.[2]

This result motivates the present study of human planning. We know that partial-order planners have specific advantages over total-order planners in AI systems; by looking for signs of such advantages in human systems, we can draw tentative inferences about the representations and algorithms used in human planning. The lessons learned about human

planning can then be re-applied to AI systems, which still lag behind human competence in several areas.

We presented human subjects with tasks from the D^1S^1 domain and noted the time spent planning, as well as the overall time needed to complete the task. As in AI planning systems, linear growth rates in human performance are suggestive of partial-order planning, while exponential growth rates are suggestive of total-order planning. An additional goal of this work is to shed light on the role of the frontal lobe of the brain in the ability of humans to perform complex planning tasks. To this end, we plan to compare the performance of normal adults, adults with frontal lobe lesions, and children at various stages of frontal lobe development.

The remainder of the paper is organized as follows: after a brief refresher on partial-order planning we summarize the relevant complexity results of Barrett and Weld and discuss the neuropsychological background of our experiment. We then describe the Chores software with which the experiment was conducted, along with the details of the D^1S^1 task. This is followed by a summary of our results to date and a discussion of implications and directions for future work.

Partial-order Planning

Most AI planning systems since STRIPS (Fikes & Nilsson 1971) have represented actions as *operator schemata*. Operator schemata describe the conditions under which each action can be performed and the effects that the performance of each action will have on the world. STRIPS-style operator schemata are composed of *precondition* lists that represent the conditions under which the actions can be performed, and pairs of lists called *add* and *delete* lists that represent effects. A *plan* to achieve some given goal from some given initial state is a list of operator schemata, along with assignments for all variables in the schemata, such that the corresponding sequence of actions will appropriately transform the world.

Early planners such as STRIPS worked by constructing sequential (linear, total-ordered) *partial plans* which achieved subsets of the goals, and which could be augmented, manipulated and combined to produce correct final plans. Given a list of goals to achieve, and a system that supports linear partial plans, the natural strategy is to produce plans to achieve each of the goals and to concatenate the resulting partial plans. This strategy can be applied re-

---

[1]The first author acknowledges the support of the Dorothy and Jerome Lemelson National Program in Invention, Innovation, and Creativity.

[2]These results have only been proven for the particular planning algorithms in the Barrett and Weld study, but we believe them to be indicative of the advantages of partial-order planning more generally. (Minton et al. 1992) provides some support for this belief.

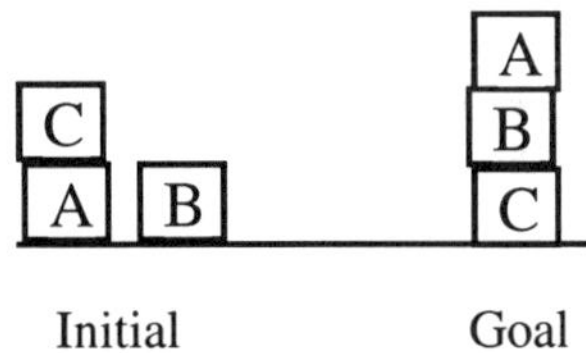

Figure 1. The Sussman Anomaly

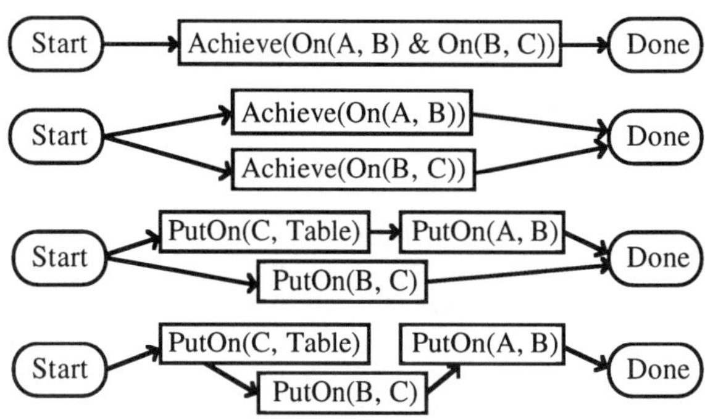

Figure 2. Solving the Sussman Anomaly
with partially ordered partial plans.

cursively to any subgoals introduced in trying to achieve any of the goals. But using linear partial plans in this way leads to a difficulty that can be illustrated with a blocks world problem known as the Sussman Anomaly: Given three blocks labeled A, B, and C, and an initial state in which C is on A, and in which A and B are both on the table, construct a plan for building a tower with A on B and with B on C (Figure 1). The difficulty is that no linear combination of the obvious partial plans for achieving On(A, B) and On(B, C) will yield a correct plan for achieving their conjunction. If On(A, B) is achieved first (by putting C on the table on then putting A on B) then the new {A, B} stack would have to be immediately dismantled in order to achieve On(B, C). (Only one block can be lifted at a time.) On the other hand, if On(B, C) is achieved first (by putting B on C) then once again the new stack would have to be dismantled in order to achieve the other conjunct.

The literature contains several strategies for circumventing this problem (e.g., (Sussman 1990, Sacerdoti 1975, Waldinger 1977)). One of the most popular strategies involves the representation of partial plans as *partial-orders*, rather than as *total-orders*. This allows for the representation of partial plans in which some of the ordering decisions have been left temporarily unspecified. A partially ordered partial plan for the Sussman Anomaly might state that On(A, B) and On(B, C) are both to be achieved, but that the order in which their plans are to be executed has yet to be determined. Further computation may indicate that additional ordering constraints must be imposed; in the case of the Sussman Anomaly the actions into which the goals are decomposed will have to be *interleaved*. Figure 2 illustrates a solution to the Sussman Anomaly using partially ordered action sequences.[3]

Most "state of the art" planning systems now use partially-ordered partial plans (e.g., (Chapman 1987, Currie & Tate 1991, McAllester & Rosenblitt 1991)). Several recent studies have examined the trade-offs in total-order vs. partial-order planning; some of these studies quantify the differences in performance profiles between total-order and partial-order planners (Minton et al. 1992, Barrett & Weld 1993). With regard to human planning, we know of no prior literature on the ordering relations in partial plans. The results from AI planning systems can, however, be used to structure experiments that provide data on the ordering relations used by humans in constructing action plans.

Barrett & Weld's Results and Domain D[1]S[1]

Barrett and Weld examined the performance of three planning algorithms on problems of several classes. Two of their planners are of interest here: *POCL* (for "Partial-Order, Causal-Links") and *TOCL* (for "Total-Order, Causal-Links"). *POCL* and *TOCL* differ, to the extent that this is possible, only in the representation of ordering relations within partial plans; *POCL* uses partial-order representations while *TOCL* uses total-order representations. Both *POCL* and *TOCL* use standard STRIPS-style operator schemata. *POCL* is a variant of the *systematic* nonlinear planning algorithm used in the SNLP planning system (McAllester & Rosenblitt 1991), and *TOCL* is a modification of *POCL* in which an added "linearization" step forces all plans to be totally ordered.[4]

POCL and *TOCL* were run on large sets of problems from both "real" and artificial domains. The real domains included blocks world, transportation planning, and others, while the artificial domains were constructed to highlight the effects of specific patterns of goal interactions. The runtimes for each planner on problems in each domain were analyzed, and several interesting generalizations were noted.

In accounting for the observed data, Barrett and Weld extended Korf's taxonomy of subgoal collections (Korf 1987) to include two new classes: *trivial serializability* and *laborious serializability*. A set of subgoals is said to be trivially serializable "if each subgoal can be solved in any order without ever violating past progress," while a set of subgoals is said to be laboriously serializable "if there exist an inadequate percentage of orders in which the subgoals may be solved without ever violating past progress"[5] (pp. 3–4). Barrett and Weld also produced the following result:

Proposition 11 *Assuming that a problem's subgoals can be achieved in constant time, the expected time to solve a problem rises linearly with the number of sub-*

---

[3] See (Sacerdoti 1975, Tate 1977) for further detail.

[4] The third planner in the Barrett and Weld study (*TOPI*, for "Total-Order, Prior-Insertion") differs from *TOCL* along a different dimension and hence is of no interest to the present study. Barrett and Weld mention that source code for all three planners is available—send mail to bug-snlp@cs.washington.edu.

[5] The full definition: "A set of n subgoals is laboriously serializable if there exists at least one serializable ordering yet at least 1/n of the subgoal orders can not be solved sequentially without possibly violating a previously solved subgoal." (p. 19)

goals if the problem is trivially serializable, but rises exponentially if the problem is laboriously serializable or nonserializable. (p. 36)

It is important to note that the classification of a problem as trivially or laboriously serializable depends on the planning algorithm that is being used; different planning algorithms induce different subgoal structures, and hence it is possible for a single problem to be trivially serializable in the search space of one planner and laboriously serializable in the search space of another. The artificial domain called D^1S^1 is the simplest of Barrett and Weld's domains that is trivially serializable for *POCL* but laboriously serializable for *TOCL*. In D^1S^1 each operator has exactly one precondition, one item on its add list, and one item on its delete list. The precondition lists and add lists are all mutually disjoint, and each operator deletes the precondition of one of the other operators. The pattern for the construction of an *n*-operator D^1S^1 domain is:

Operator:
Action: A_i, Preconditions: $\{I_i\}$, Add: $\{G_i\}$, Delete: $\{I_{i-1}\}$

where i ranges from 1 to n and where the delete list for A_1 is empty. The maximal solvable problems in this domain have initial conditions consisting of all of the I_i and goal conditions consisting of all the G_i. Note that the pattern induces a linear order on the solution to each maximal problem—each operator deletes the precondition to the operator that must immediately precede it in the solution plan. The results of Barrett and Weld tell us that partial-order planners are capable of finding the correct order in linear time, while total-order planners will generally require exponential time.

Neuropsychology of Planning

Neuropsychologists have long studied the role of the frontal cortex in human behavior, and in particular, the effects of damage to this area of the brain. It has long been known that patients with frontal lobe lesions will often behave inappropriately in social situations, experience radical mood swings, and display deficits in processing temporal relationships and order. These deficits appear despite seemingly normal abilities in language, perception, verbal expression, memory and attention (Grafman 1989, 1994; Robertson et al. 1991). In addition to the previously described deficits, it has also been proposed that these patients experience deficits in planning and problem solving (Grafman 1989, Shallice 1988). Unfortunately, the majority of neuropsychological models fail to explicate the precise role of the frontal cortex in cognitive processes (Grafman 1989), and also rely on evidence which is obtained from tasks not directly related to planning and problem solving. One of the goals of our experiment is to provide direct evidence for the role of the frontal cortex in planning behavior, and specifically, to show that damage to the frontal cortex will lead to deficits in the patient's ability to form and carry out complex plans.

D^1S^1 in the Chores Experiment

We are performing experiments built using the NINDS/NIH Chores experiment software (Spector & Grafman 1994) to explore the ordering representations used in human problem solving. The software was designed for human planning experiments with normal subjects, with frontal lobe lesion patients, and with children at various stages of frontal lobe development.[6] The subject interacts with a Macintosh computer that displays a map of a hypothetical city, with icons representing items that the subject is to acquire (the goal list), and icons representing items that the subject already possesses (the inventory). The subject uses the mouse and/or arrow keys to navigate around the map and to perform chores. The subject can backtrack by clicking an "Undo Previous" button—this reverses the effects of the most recently performed chore and moves the subject to the location adjacent to that chore. A time-stamped protocol that lists all of the subject's actions is produced; it can be analyzed to produce several data sets.

The Chores software can be configured to require that constraints be obeyed on the ordering of the chore completions. In our experiments we are using "resource" constraints that are specified in a manner almost identical to STRIPS operator specifications. On a separate screen called "Item Info" each chore is listed along with its relations to resources. The subject may switch between the map and Item Info screens at any time; the times of all such actions are recorded in the protocol. The Item Info screen may indicate that a particular chore "requires" one or more resources—this means that the chore cannot be completed if the resources are not currently in the inventory. The system produces a beep-sound and a time-stamped annotation in the protocol whenever a subject attempts to complete a chore without the necessary requirements. A chore may also "add" one or more resources—this means that successful completion of the chore will add the specified resources to the inventory. If the added item was a goal then it is also removed from the goal list. A chore may also "delete" one or more resources—this means that successful completion of the chore will delete the specified resources from the subject's inventory. Note that the require, add, and delete specifications for chores are strictly analogous to the precondition, add, and delete lists for STRIPS operators. This means that the human subjects will be performing tasks quite similar to those performed by AI planners that manipulate STRIPS operators.

In the present experiment we are interested in the relation between planing time and task size (number of goals). We are using the time spent viewing the Item Info screen as our principal indicator of planning time. The total time to trial completion is also of interest, but this will include time spent manipulating the user interface that may be unrelated to planning time.

---

[6]The general idea for the Chores software was derived from the chore planning experiments described in (Hayes-Roth & Hayes-Roth 1979).

The D^{I}S^I Series

The D^{I}S^I Series is a set of trials built using the Chores experiment software. The entire task consists of two training trials, four test trials, and four foil trials, which are randomly presented to the subject. The first of the two training trials introduces the subject to the basic structure and rules of the task, including the "requires" and "adds" functions, while the second training trial introduces the "deletes" and "undo previous" functions. The four D^{I}S^I trials are as follows: a 2-goal problem in a 2-operator D^{I}S^I domain, a 3-goal problem in a 3-operator D^{I}S^I domain, a 4-goal problem in a 4-operator D^{I}S^I domain, and a 5-goal problem in a 5-operator D^{I}S^I domain. The foils are similar to the D^{I}S^I trials, but they do not actually conform to the D^{I}S^I pattern. To minimize the effects of varying spatial reasoning abilities, all of the maps have the same simple linear layout.

Subjects and Methods

Seventeen normal adults and two frontal subjects were tested in this experiment. Normal subjects were screened for histories of motor and cognitive impairment, and any necessary corrective lenses were worn during testing. Frontal subjects were diagnosed to have cortical damage located in the frontal lobe.

Testing took place in a testing room with only the subject and experimenter present. The subject was seated in front of the computer monitor and was introduced to the experiment with the training trials. The following instructions are a summary of those given to the subjects:

- The goal of this experiment is to obtain a set of items by going to the places on this map. Each time an item is obtained it is removed from the list of objects to get and added to the inventory.
- The places and items on the list are not thematically linked. Thus, going to the "library" will not result in a book being added to the inventory, rather, a triangle will be added.
- The small black square which designates position can move forward or backward one square at a time, and a particular place on the map is entered by moving the black square on top of it. [Subjects are shown how to manipulate the square with the mouse and the arrow keys.]
- The "Item Info" screen displays the relationships between the places on the map and the items. If a place "requires" an item, entry is prohibited unless that item is in the inventory. If a place "adds" an item, then that item will be added to the inventory when that place is entered. If a place "deletes" an item, then if that item is present in the inventory it will be deleted. If the item is not in the inventory then the deletion has no effect.
- The "undo previous" button can be used to undo a previous move. This button may be pressed as many times as necessary to undo to the desired move.

Subjects were encouraged to practice with the training trials and to ask questions until they were comfortable with the rules of the task. The subjects were informed that the trials would be timed and that they should move through them as quickly as possible, but that randomly guessing the order in which to complete the chores would not be beneficial.

The four D^{I}S^I trials and four foils were presented in a different random order to each subject. Upon the completion of each trial the subject protocol was saved for later examination.

Results

We analyzed two aspects of the subjects' performance in the Chores task: Total time to completion and time spent viewing the Item Info screen. The former is the amount of time spent both planning and executing the plan; the latter is a better measure of pure planning time, but it does not include time spent planning from memorized item information. We had predicted that both measures would reveal the hypothesized linear trend for the normal subjects, and as can be seen in Table 1 and in Figures 4 and 5, this prediction was confirmed by the normals' performance on both measures. A linear trend analysis performed on the data from the normal subjects reveals a significant linear trend for total time to completion ($F (1,48) = 31.14$, $p<.0001$) and a significant linear trend for time spent viewing the Item Information screen ($F (1,48) = 48.88$, $p<.0001$). Further support for our hypothesis is provided by analyses of variance performed on both sets of data which revealed a main effect of the number of Chores ($F (3, 48) = 10.48$, $p < .0001$ for time to completion, and $F (3, 48) = 16.74$, $p < .0001$, for time spent viewing the Item Information screen).

Due to the small number of frontal subjects, statistical analyses were not possible; however, as can be seen in Figures 4 and 5, their preliminary data is consistent with the predicted exponential function.

Discussion

Based on suggestions that planning algorithms using partially-ordered plan representations have clear advantages over total-order planners in particular AI planning domains, we set out to investigate the performance of human planning systems in the same domains. Our results suggest that our human subjects enjoy the same advantages. Using the Chores software to test subjects in D^{I}S^I domains, we found that the subjects' total time to completion and time spent viewing the Item Information screen exhibited linear growth rates as the problem size increased.

The data suggests that human planners represent the or-

Number of Chores	Time to Completion	Viewing Item Information
Two Chores	54.91	12.35
Three Chores	131.76	48.71
Four Chores	225.12	93.12
Five Chores	343.53	159.76

Table 1. Mean total time and mean time spent viewing Item Info.

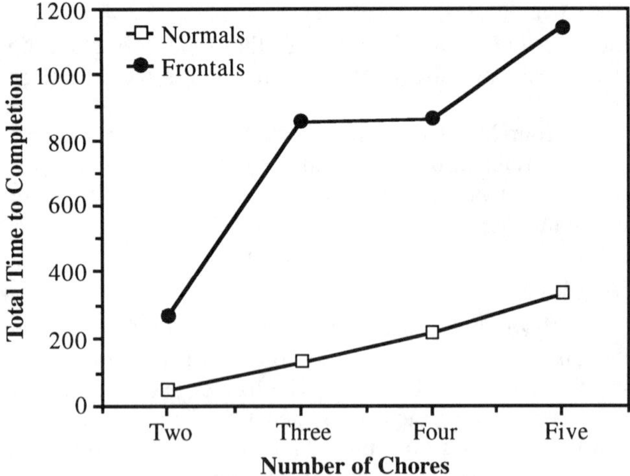

Figure 4. Mean Total Time to Completion, in seconds

dering relations in partial plans using partial-orders. The data only *shows* that human planning time seems to increase linearly with increase in task size in the D^1S^1 domain. The inference that this implies the use of partial-order representations relies on the assumption that the results of Barrett and Weld are generally indicative of the advantages of partial-order planning as opposed to total-order planning. Although we believe this to be the case, we note that the experiments provide data even if the results of Barrett and Weld fail to generalize. The human planners are managing to achieve linear performance *somehow*. They are either using partial-order representations or other algorithmic methods that achieve the same effect with respect to efficiency in this domain. One alternative is that the linear human performance owes to the brain's use of parallel algorithms.[7] While such alternatives deserve further study, we currently believe that partial-order representations provide the best explanation for the data.

An additional goal of this experiment was to examine the role of frontal cortex in planning by testing patients with frontal cortex lesions. Although preliminary, our results suggest that the performance of frontal patients in this domain is more similar to that of total-order planners; specifically, their performance seemed to exhibit an exponential growth rate as problem size increased. More data from frontal patients is necessary to strengthen this claim.

Our results have implications for both the psychology and the neuropsychology of planning, as well as for the AI community. First, we have provided evidence that in a domain in which partial-order planning is advantageous, normal adults perform in a way that suggests the representation of partial-plan ordering relations as partial-orders. Second, we have preliminary evidence that suggests that the frontal cortex of the brain may play a role in this type of planning. While frontal lesion patients' difficulty with social situations and with temporal ordering is well docu-

mented, the effect of this damage on planning is not as well studied. In our work, we have directly tested the ability of these individuals to form and carry out plans, and we believe that their deficits lead to a specific pattern of performance with analogs in the computational literature.

The utility of partial-order planning, discovered by AI planning researchers, receives further support from the evidence that normal humans appear to use partial-order plan representations. Further study may uncover additional features of the algorithmic basis of human planning, both in normal subjects and in subjects with planning deficits. These studies may provide further support for current AI techniques, but they may also provide alternative models. Given that human planners are proficient in ways that current AI models are not, the interplay between the human and machine studies should be of interest to those extending the state of the art in AI planning. The fruitfulness of this interplay relies, however, on the coherence of the cross-disciplinary dialogue. We suggest that one way to maximize the impact of psychological experimentation on AI practice is to construct the experiments within the conceptual frameworks developed in AI research.

Future Work

In our ongoing studies we are continuing our examination of the role of frontal cortex in human planning. We are currently testing more frontally lesioned patients, and we have adapted the procedure to make it appropriate for testing 7–11-year-old children. Based on research suggesting that the frontal cortex does not fully develop until late in childhood, we expect to find that the younger children display the same exponential performance that our frontal subjects exhibit. This work will provide further evidence for the role of the frontal cortex in human planning behavior.

Although the present study focuses on the representation of ordering relations in partial plans, the same framework can be applied to study other aspects of planning, and other aspects of cognition more generally, across the human/machine frontier. AI research often yields precise, quantitative

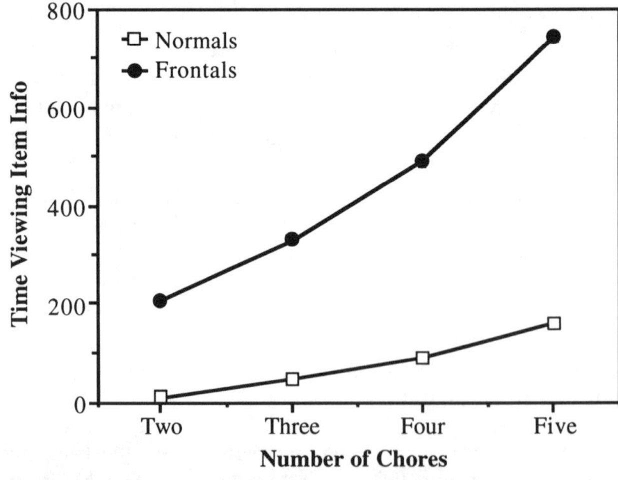

Figure 5. Mean Time Viewing Item Information, in seconds.

---

[7]We thank an anonymous reviewer for drawing our attention to this possibility.

results that relate computational structures to aspects of performance. By using these results as guides, we can gather data on human cognition that will allow us to make inferences about human computational structures. And of course there is always the possibility that we will be surprised; that we will find that the human computational structures were other than we had expected. Since the concepts that underlie these investigations will be taken from the computational literature, there should be clear paths by which one could apply the lessons of the surprises in improving the state-of-the-art in AI.

Conclusions

In conclusion, we have found that the results of analytical work in AI planning can be used to investigate human planning. Specifically, we have evidence that suggests that normal human planners use partial-order representations for partial plans, as do most modern AI planning systems. We have further preliminary evidence that suggests that damaged human planning systems use methods akin to those used in less efficient AI systems; specifically, we believe that adults with frontal lobe lesions will be shown to be using planning methods similar to those employed in total-order planners. We believe that the parallels between the human and machine cases are instructive, and that they may lead to further developments in both human and machine studies.

Acknowledgments

Jordan Grafman funded and guided the development of the Chores software, and, along with Jim Hendler, was instrumental in launching the larger interdisciplinary effort of which this work is a part. Paula Koseff ran several trials of the experiment on subjects at NIH under Grafman's supervision. Chris Chase and Neil Stillings helped in analyzing the results. Jason Juneau worked on the software and is part of the ongoing experimental team.

References

Barrett, A.; and Weld, D.S. 1993. Partial-Order Planning: Evaluating Possible Efficiency Gains. Technical Report 92-05-01 Expanded Version, Dept. of Computer Science and Engineering, U. of Washington, Seattle.

Bylander, T. 1991. Complexity Results for Planning. In *Proceedings of the Twelfth International Joint Conference on Artificial Intelligence, IJCAI-91*, 274–279.

Chapman, D. 1987. Planning for Conjunctive Goals. *Artificial Intelligence* 32: 333–377.

Chenoweth, S.V. 1991. On the NP-Hardness of Blocks World. In *Proceedings of the Ninth National Conference on Artificial Intelligence, AAAI-91*, 623–628.

Currie, K.; and Tate, A. 1991. O-plan: the open planning architecture. *Artificial Intelligence* 52: 49–86.

Erol, K.; Nau, D.S.; and Subrahmanian, V.S. 1991. Complexity, Decidability and Undecidability Results for Domain-Independent Planning. CS-TR-2797, Dept. of Computer Science, U. of Maryland.

Fikes, R.E.; and Nilsson, N. 1971. STRIPS: A New Approach to the Application of Theorem Proving to Problem Solving. In *Artificial Intelligence* 2, 189–208.

Grafman, J. 1989. Plans, Actions, and Mental Sets: Managerial Knowledge Units in the Frontal Lobes. In *Integrating Theory and Practice in Clinical Neuropsychology*, 93-138. New Jersey: Lawrence Erlbaum Publishers.

Grafman, J. 1994. Alternative Frameworks for the Conceptualization of Prefrontal Lobe Functions. In *Handbook of Neuropsychology*, Vol. 9. Boller, F.; and Grafman, J. , eds. Elsevier Science Publishers.

Gupta, N.; and Nau, D.S. 1991. Complexity Results for Blocks-World Planning. In *Proceedings of the Twelfth International Joint Conference on Artificial Intelligence, IJCAI-91*, 629–633.

Hayes-Roth, B.; Hayes-Roth, F. 1979. A Cognitive Model Planning. *Cognitive Science* 3: 275–310.

Korf, R.E. 1987. Planning as Search: A Quantitative Approach. *Artificial Intelligence* 33: 65–88.

McAllester, D.; and Rosenblitt, D. 1991. Systematic Nonlinear Planning. In *Proceedings of the Ninth National Conference on Artificial Intelligence, AAAI-91*, 634–639.

Minton, S.; Drummond, M.; Bresina, J.L.; and Philips, A.J. 1992. Total Order vs. Partial Order Planning: Factors Influencing Performance. In *KR '92. Principles of Knowledge Representation and Reasoning — Proceedings of the Third International Conference*, 83–92. San Mateo, CA: Morgan Kaufmann Publishers.

Robertson, L.C.; Lamb, M.; and Knight, T. 1991. Normal Global-Local Analysis in Patients with Dorsolateral Frontal Lobe Lesions. *Neuropsychologia* 29, 959–967.

Sacerdoti, E.D. 1975. The Nonlinear Nature of Plans. In *Advance Papers of the Fourth International Joint Conference on Artificial Intelligence, IJCAI-75*, 206–214.

Shallice, T. 1988. *From Neuropsychology to Mental Structure*, New York: Cambridge University Press.

Spector, L.; and Grafman, J. 1994. Planning, Neuropsychology, and Artificial Intelligence: Cross-Fertilization. In *Handbook of Neuropsychology*, Vol. 9, Boller, F.; and Grafman, J., eds. 377–392. Amsterdam: Elsevier Science Publishers.

Sussman, G.J. 1990. The Virtuous Nature of Bugs. In *Readings in Planning*. Allen, J.; Hendler, J.; and Tate, A., eds. 111–117. San Mateo, CA: Morgan Kaufmann Publishers, Inc.

Tate, A. 1977. Generating Project Networks. In *Proceedings of the International Joint Conference on Artificial Intelligence, IJCAI-77*, 888–893.

Waldinger, R. 1977. Achieving Several Goals Simultaneously. *Machine Intelligence* 8 (1977).

Experimentally Evaluating Communicative Strategies: The Effect of the Task

Marilyn A. Walker

Mitsubishi Electric Research Laboratories*

201 Broadway

Cambridge, Ma. 02139, USA

`walker@merl.com`

Abstract

Effective problem solving among multiple agents requires a better understanding of the role of communication in collaboration. In this paper we show that there are communicative strategies that greatly improve the performance of resource-bounded agents, but that these strategies are highly sensitive to the task requirements, situation parameters and agents' resource limitations. We base our argument on two sources of evidence: (1) an analysis of a corpus of 55 problem solving dialogues, and (2) experimental simulations of collaborative problem solving dialogues in an experimental world, Design-World, where we parameterize task requirements, agents' resources and communicative strategies.

1 Introduction

A common assumption in work on collaborative problem solving is that interaction should be efficient. When language is the mode of interaction, the measure of efficiency has been, in the main, the number of utterances required to complete the dialogue [Chapanis *et al.*, 1972]. One problem with this efficiency measure is that it ignores the cognitive effort required by resource limited agents in collaborative problem solving. Another problem is that an utterance-based efficiency measure shows no sensitivity to the required quality and robustness of the problem solution.

Cognitive effort is involved in processes such as making inferences and swapping items from long term memory into working memory. When agents have limited working memory, then only a limited number of items can be SALIENT, i.e. accessible in working memory. Since other processes, e.g. inference, operate on salient items, an inference process may require the cognitive effort involved with retrieving items from long term memory, in addition to the effort involved with reasoning itself.

The required quality and robustness of the problem solution often determines exactly how much cognitive effort is required. This means that a resource-limited agent may do well on some tasks but not on others [Norman and Bobrow, 1975]. For example, consider constraint-based tasks where it is difficult for an agent to simultaneously keep all the constraints in mind, or inference-based tasks that require a long deductive chain or the retrieval of multiple premises, where an agent may not be able to simultaneously access all of the required premises.

Furthermore, contrary to the efficiency hypothesis, analyses of problem-solving dialogues shows that human agents in dialogue engage in apparently inefficient conversational behavior. For example, naturally-occurring dialogues often include utterances that realize facts that are already mutually believed, or that would be mutually believed if agents were logically omniscient [Pollack *et al.*, 1982; Finin *et al.*, 1986; Walker, 1993]. Consider 1-26a, which repeats information given in 1-20 ... 1-23:

(1)   (20) H: Right. The maximum amount of credit that you will be able to get will be 400 *that they will be able to get will be 400 dollars on their tax return*
(21) C: *400 dollars for the whole year?*
(22) H: *Yeah it'll be 20%*
(23) C: *um hm*
(24) H: Now if indeed they pay the $2000 to your wife, that's great.
(25) C: um hm
(26a) H: SO WE HAVE 400 DOLLARS.
(26b) Now as far as you are concerned, that could cost you more.....

Utterances such as 1-26a, that repeat, paraphrase or make inferences explicit, are collectively called INFOR-MATIONALLY REDUNDANT UTTERANCES, IRUs. In 1, the utterances that originally added the belief that *they will get 400 dollars* to the context are in *italics* and the IRU is given in CAPS.

About 12% of the utterances in a corpus of 55 naturally-occurring problem-solving dialogues were IRUs [Walker, 1993], but the occurrence of IRUs contradicts fundamental assumptions of many theories of

*This research was partially funded by ARO grant DAAL03-89-C0031PRI and DARPA grant N00014-90-J-1863 at the University of Pennsylvania and by Hewlett Packard, U.K.

communication [Allen and Perrault, 1980], *inter alia*. The hypothesis that is investigated in this paper is that IRUs such as 1-26a are related to agents' limited attentional and inferential capacity and reflect the fact that beliefs must be salient to be used in deliberation and inference.[1] Hence apparently redundant information serves an important cognitive function.

In order to test the hypothesized relationship of communicative strategies to agents' resource limits we developed a test-bed environment, Design-World, in which we vary task requirements, agents' resources and communicative strategies. Our artificial agents are based on a cognitive model of attention and memory. Our experimental results show that communicative strategies that incorporate IRUs can help resource-limited cognitive agents coordinate, limit processing, and improve the quality and robustness of the problem solution. We will show that the task determines whether a communicative strategy is beneficial, depending on how the task is defined in terms of fault intolerance and the level of belief coordination required.

2 Design-World Task and Agent Architecture

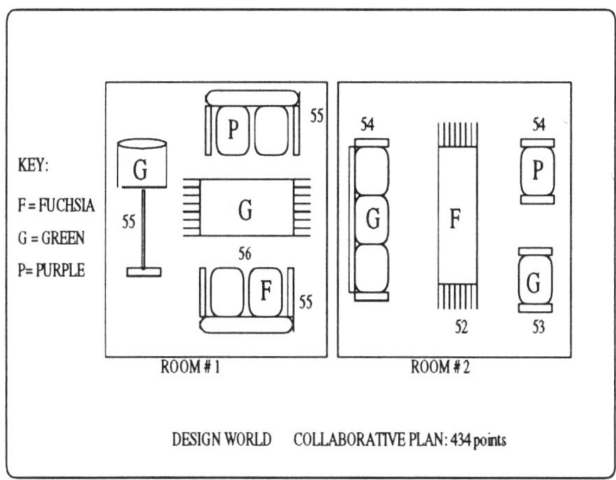

Figure 1: Potential Final State for Design-World Task: A Collaborative Plan Achieved by the Dialogue

The Design-World task consists of two agents who carry out a dialogue in order to come to an agreement on a furniture layout design for a two room house [Whittaker *et al.*, 1993]. Figure 1 shows a potential final plan constructed as a result of a dialogue. The agents' shared intention is to design the house, which requires two subparts of designing room-1 (the study) and designing room-2 (the living room). A room design consists of four intentions to PUT a furniture item into the room. Each furniture item has a color and point value, which provides the basis for calculating the utility of

---

[1]The type of IRU in 1-26a represents the Attention class of IRUs; Attitude and Consequence IRUs are discussed elsewhere [Walker, 1992; Walker, 1993].

a PUT-ACT involving that furniture item. Agents start with private beliefs about the furniture items they have and their colors. Beliefs about which furniture items exist and how many points they are worth are mutual.

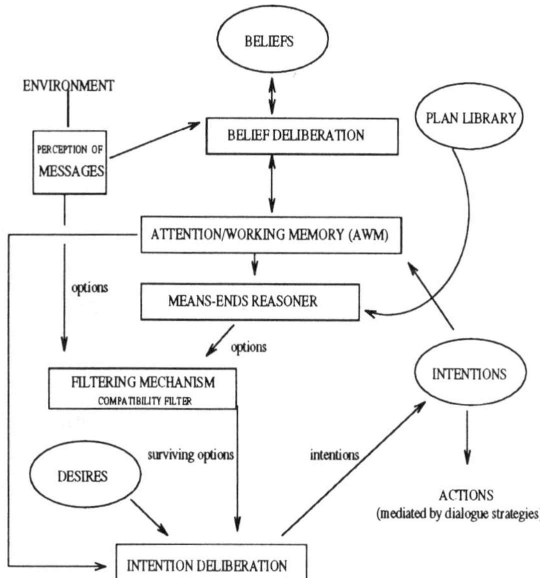

Figure 2: Design-World version of the IRMA Agent Architecture for Resource-Bounded Agents with Limited Attention (AWM)

The agent architecture for deliberation and means-end reasoning is based on the IRMA architecture, also used in the TileWorld simulation environment [Bratman *et al.*, 1988; Pollack and Ringuette, 1990], with the addition of a model of limited Attention/Working memory, AWM. See figure 2.

The Attention/Working Memory model, AWM, is adapted from [Landauer, 1975]. While the AWM model is extremely simple, Landauer showed that it could be parameterized to fit many empirical results on human memory and learning [Baddeley, 1986]. AWM consists of a three dimensional space in which propositions acquired from perceiving the world are stored in chronological sequence according to the location of a moving memory pointer. The sequence of memory loci used for storage constitutes a random walk through memory with each loci a short distance from the previous one. If items are encountered multiple times, they are stored multiple times [Hintzmann and Block, 1971].

When an agent retrieves items from memory, search starts from the current pointer location and spreads out in a spherical fashion. Search is restricted to a particular search radius: radius is defined in Hamming distance. For example if the current memory pointer loci is (0 0 0), the loci distance 1 away would be (0 1 0) (0 -1 0) (0 0 1) (0 0 -1) (-1 0 0) (1 0 0). The actual locations are calculated modulo the memory size. The limit on the search radius defines the capacity of attention/working memory and hence defines which stored beliefs and intentions are SALIENT.

The radius of the search sphere in the AWM model is used as the parameter for Design-World agents' resource-bound on attentional capacity. In the experiments below, memory is 16x16x16 and the radius parameter varies between 1 and 16, where AWM of 1 gives severely attention limited agents and AWM of 16 means that everything an agent knows is salient.

The advantages of the AWM model is that it was shown to reproduce, in simulation, many results on human memory and learning. Because search starts from the current pointer location, items that have been stored most recently are more likely to be retrieved, predicting recency effects [Baddeley, 1986]. Because items that are stored in multiple locations are more likely to be retrieved, the model predicts frequency effects [Landauer, 1975]. Because items are stored in chronological sequence, the model produces natural associativity effects [Anderson and Bower, 1973]. Because deliberation and means-end reasoning can only operate on salient beliefs, limited attention produces a concomitant inferential limitation, i.e. if a belief is not salient it cannot be used in deliberation or means-end-reasoning. This means that mistakes that agents make in their planning process have a plausible cognitive basis. Agents can both fail to access a belief that would allow them to produce an optimal plan, as well as make a mistake in planning if a belief about how the world has changed as a result of planning is not salient.

3 Design-World Communicative Strategies

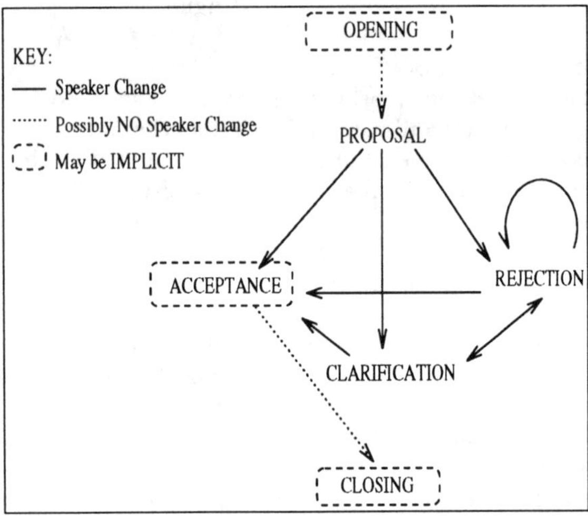

Figure 3: Discourse Actions for the Design-World Task

A COMMUNICATIVE STRATEGY is a strategy for communicating with another agent, which varies according to the agents' initiative, amount of information about the task, degree of resource-bounds, and communication style [Walker and Whittaker, 1990; Carletta, 1992; Cawsey *et al.*, 1992; Guinn, 1993]. Design-World agents

communicate with an artificial language whose primitive communicative acts are PROPOSE, ACCEPT, REJECT, SAY. These primitive acts can be composed to produce higher level discourse acts such as PROPOSALS, ACCEPTANCES, REJECTIONS, OPENINGS and CLOSINGS [Walker, 1993]. See figure 3.

A discourse act may be left implicit, or may be varied to consist of one or more communicative acts. Discourse acts are different from actions on the environment because they are actions whose intended effect is a change in the other agent's mental state. Because the other agent is an active intelligence, it is possible for it to supplement an underspecified discourse action with its own processing. The variation in the degree of explicitness of a discourse act is the basis of agents' communicative strategies. Here we will compare three communicative strategies: (1) All-Implicit; (2) Close-Consequence; and (3) Explicit-Warrant.

The All-Implicit strategy is a 'bare bones' strategy, exemplified by the partial dialogue in 2. In 2 each utterance is shown both as a gloss in *italics*, and in the artificial language that the agents communicate with.

(2) 1: BILL: *Then, let's put the green rug in the study.*
      (propose agent-bill agent-kim option-43: put-act
      (agent-bill green rug room-1))

     2: KIM: *Then, let's put the green lamp in the study.*
      (propose agent-kim agent-bill option-61: put-act
      (agent-kim green lamp room-1))

     3: BILL: *No, instead let's put the green couch in the study.*
      (reject agent-bill agent-kim option-75: put-act
      (agent-bill green couch room-1))

      .....

In Design-World, unlike TileWorld, an option that is generated via means-end reasoning or from proposals of other agents only becomes an intention if it is ACCEPTED by both agents. See figure 3. In dialogue 2, Bill makes a proposal in 1, and then Kim implicitly accepts this proposal with a new proposal in 2. In 2-3 Bill rejects Kim's proposal and makes a counter-proposal.

The content of communicative acts are beliefs and (potential) intentions. Dialogue 2 illustrates part of the cycle for achieving a DESIGN-HOUSE plan: (1) individual agents MEANS-END REASON about options in the domain; (2) individual agents DELIBERATE about which options are preferable; (3) then agents make PROPOSALS to other agents, based on the options identified in a reasoning cycle, about actions that CONTRIBUTE to the satisfaction of their intentions; (4) then these proposals are ACCEPTED or REJECTED by the other agent, or acceptance/rejection is postponed by ASKING for more information. See figure 2. Deliberating whether to accept or reject a proposal is based on beliefs about the proposed action's utility [Doyle, 1992].

Agents parameterized with the All-Implicit strategy do not include IRUs in any discourse act or produce any discourse acts labelled as potentially implicit in figure 3. Agents parameterized with the Close-Consequence and Explicit-Warrant strategies include IRUs at dialogue segment closings and in proposals.

In dialogue 3 agent CLC uses the Close-Consequence strategy. CLC makes explicit CLOSING statements, such as 3-2, on the completion of the intention associated with a discourse segment. CLC's CLOSING discourse act also includes IRUs as in 3-3; CLC makes the inference explicit that since they have agreed on putting the green rug in the study, Bill no longer has the green rug (act-effect inference).

(3) 1: BILL: *Then, let's put the green rug in the study.*
(propose agent-bill agent-clc option-30:   put-act
(agent-bill green rug room-1))

2: CLC: *So, we've agreed to put the green rug in the study.*
(close agent-clc agent-bill intended-30:   put-act
(agent-bill green rug room-1))

3: CLC: AGENT-BILL DOESN'T HAVE GREEN RUG.
(say agent-clc agent-bill bel-48:   has n't (agent-bill green rug))

The Close-Consequence strategy of making inferences explicit at the close of a segment is intended to parallel the naturally occurring example in 1. In both cases an inference is made explicit that follows from what has just been said, and the inference is sequentially located at the close of a discourse segment.

The Explicit-Warrant strategy varies the proposal discourse act by including WARRANT IRUs in each proposal. In general a WARRANT for an intention is a reason for adopting the intention, and here WARRANTS are the score propositions that give the utility of the proposal, which are mutually believed at the outset of the dialogues. In 4, the WARRANT IRU is in CAPS.

(4) 1: IEI: PUTTING IN THE GREEN RUG IS WORTH 56
(say agent-iei agent-iei2 bel-265:   score (option-202: put-act (agent-bill green rug room-1) 56))

2: IEI: *Then, let's put the green rug in the study.*
(propose agent-iei agent-iei2 option-202:   put-act
(agent-bill green rug room-1))

Since warrants are used by the other agent in deliberation, the Explicit-Warrant strategy can save the other agent the processing involved with determining which facts are relevant for deliberation and retrieving them from memory. The Explicit-Warrant strategy also occurs in natural dialogues [Walker, 1993].

4   Design World Task Variations

Design-World supports the parameterization of the task so that it can be made more difficult to perform by making greater processing demands on the agents. These task variations will be shown to interact with variations in communicative strategies and attentional capacity in section 5.

Standard Task

The Standard task is defined so that the RAW SCORE that agents achieve for a DESIGN-HOUSE plan, constructed via the dialogue, is the sum of all the furniture

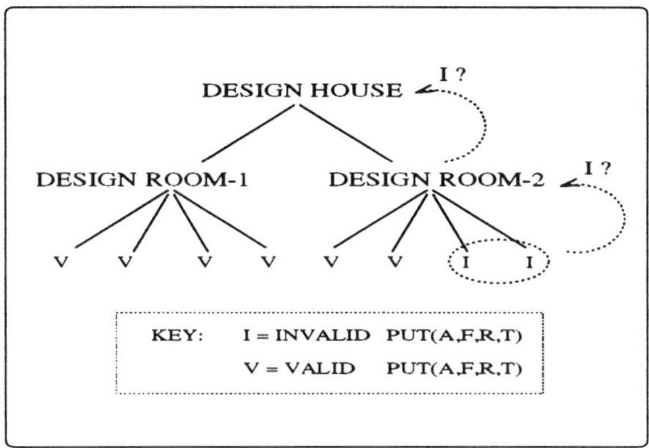

Figure 4: Evaluating Task Invalids: for some tasks invalid steps invalidate the whole plan.

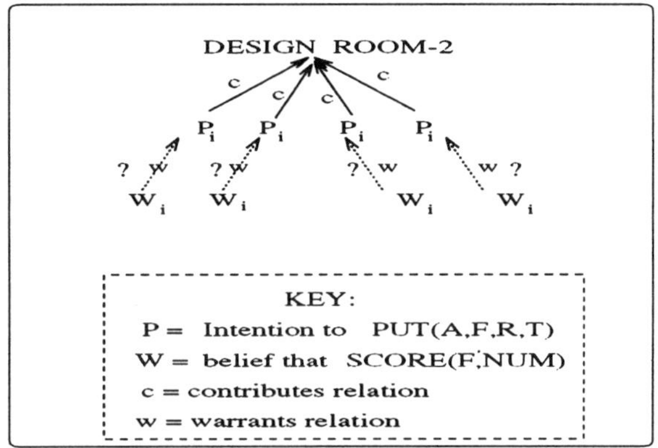

Figure 5: Tasks can differ as to the level of mutual belief required. Some tasks require that the WARRANT W, a reason for doing P, is mutually believed and others don't.

items for each valid step in their plan. The point values for invalid steps in the plan are simply subtracted from the score so that agents are not heavily penalized for making mistakes.

Zero Invalids Task

The Zero-Invalids Task is a fault-intolerant version of the task in which any invalid intention invalidates the whole plan. In general, the effect of making a mistake in a plan depends on how interdependent different subparts of the problem solution are.[2] Figure 4 shows the choices for the effect of invalid steps for the Design-World task. The score for invalid steps (mistakes) can just be subtracted out; this is how the Standard task is defined. Alternately, invalid steps can propagate up so that an invalid PUT-ACT means that the Design-Room plan is invalid. Finally, mistakes can completely propagate so that the Design-House plan is invalid if one step is invalid, as in the Zero-Invalids task.

---

[2] Contrast aircraft scheduling with furnishing a room.

Zero NonMatching Beliefs Task
The Zero-Nonmatching-Beliefs task is designed to investigate the effect of the level of agreement that agents must achieve. Figure 4 illustrates different degrees of agreeing in a collaborative task, e.g. agents may agree on the actions to be done, but not agree on the **reasons** for intending that action.[3] The Zero-NonMatching-Beliefs task is defined so that a WARRANT W, a reason for doing P, must be mutually supposed.

5 Experimental Results

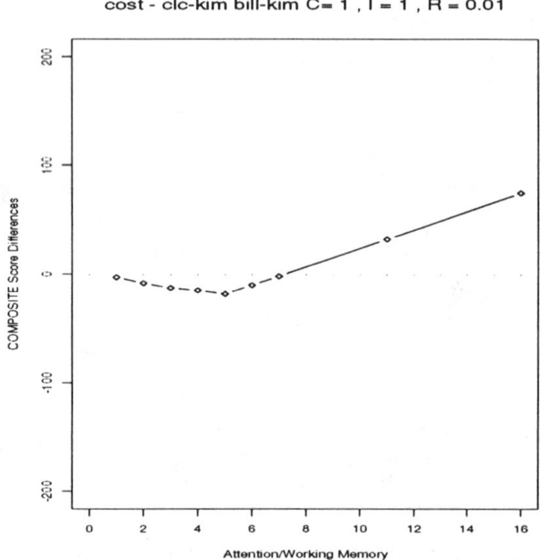

Figure 6: Close-Consequence can be detrimental in the Standard Task. Strategy 1 is the combination of an All-Implicit agent with a Close-Consequence agent and Strategy 2 is two All-Implicit agents, Task = Standard, commcost = 1, infcost = 1, retcost = .01

We wish to evaluate the relative benefits of the communicative strategies in various tasks for a range of resource limits. In section 4 we defined an objective performance measure for the DESIGN-HOUSE plan for each task variation. We must also take cognitive costs into account. Because cognitive effort can vary according to the communication situation and the agent architecture, performance evaluation introduces three additional parameters: (1) COMMCOST: cost of sending a message; (2) INFCOST: cost of inference; and (3) RETCOST: cost of retrieval from memory:

PERFORMANCE =
Task Defined RAW SCORE
  − (COMMCOST × total messages)
  − (INFCOST × total inferences)
  − (RETCOST × total retrievals)

---

[3] Consider a union/ management negotiation where each party has different reasons for any agreement.

We simulate 100 dialogues at each parameter setting and calculate the normalized performance distributions for each sample run. In the results to follow, COMMCOST, INFCOST and RETCOST are fixed at 1,1, .01 respectively, and the parameters that are varied are (1) communication strategy; (2) task definition; and (3) AWM settings.[4] Differences in the performance distributions for each set of parameters are evaluated for significance over the 100 dialogues using the Kolmogorov-Smirnov (KS) two sample test [Siegel, 1956].

A strategy A is defined to be BENEFICIAL as compared to a strategy B, for a set of fixed parameter settings, if the difference in distributions using the Kolmogorov-Smirnov two sample test is significant at $p < .05$, in the positive direction, for two or more AWM settings. A strategy is DETRIMENTAL if the differences go in the negative direction. Strategies may be neither BENEFICIAL or DETRIMENTAL, since there may be no difference between two strategies.

A DIFFERENCE PLOT such as that in figure 6 will be used to summarize a comparison of strategy 1 and strategy 2. In the comparisons below, strategy 1 is either Close-Consequence or Explicit-Warrant and strategy 2 is the All-Implicit strategy. **Differences** in performance between two strategies are plotted on the Y-axis against AWM parameter settings on the X-axis. Each point in the plot represents the difference in the means of 100 runs of each strategy at a particular AWM setting. These plots summarize the information from 18 performance distributions (1800 simulated dialogues). Every simulation run varies the AWM radius from 1 to 16 to test whether a strategy only has an effect at particular AWM settings. If the plot is above the dotted line for 2 or more AWM settings, then strategy 1 may be BENEFICIAL, depending on whether the differences are significant.[5]

In the reminder of this section, we first compare within strategy, for each task definition and show that whether or not a strategy is beneficial depends on the task. Then we compare across strategies for a particular task, showing that the interaction of the strategy and task varies according to the strategy. The comparisons will show that what counts as a good collaborative strategy depends on cognitive limits on attention and the definition of success for the task.

5.1 Close Consequence
The difference plot in figure 6 shows that Close-Consequence is DETRIMENTAL in the Standard task at AWM of 1 . . . 5 (KS > 0.19, $p < .05$).

In contrast, if the task is the fault-intolerant Zero-Invalids task, then the Close-Consequence strategy is

---

[4] See [Walker, 1993; Walker, 1995] for results related to varying the relative cost of retrieval, inference and communication.

[5] Visual difference in means and distributional differences need not be correlated, however KS significance values will be given with each figure, and difference plots are much more concise than actual distributions.

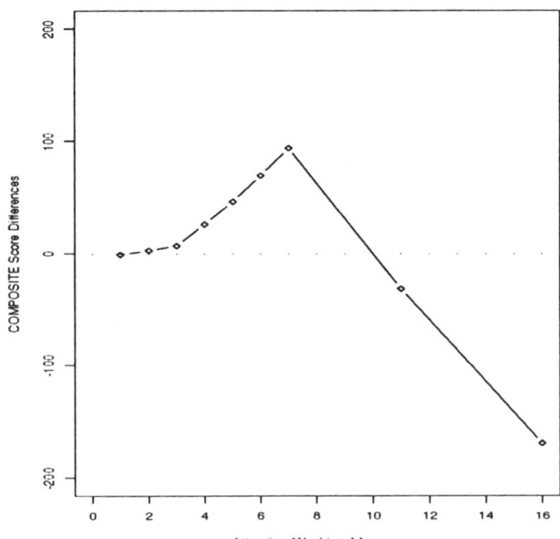

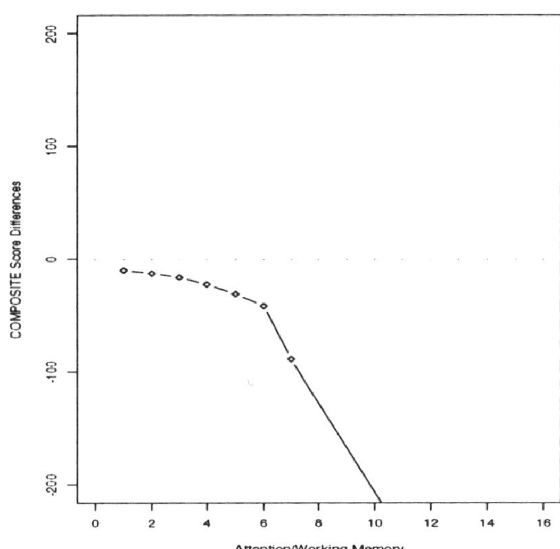

Figure 7: Close Consequence is beneficial for Zero-Invalids Task. Strategy 1 is the combination of an All-Implicit agent with a Close-Consequence agent and Strategy 2 is two All-Implicit agents, Task = Zero-Invalid, commcost = 1, infcost = 1, retcost = .01

Figure 8: Close-Consequence is detrimental for Zero-Nonmatching-Beliefs Task. Strategy 1 is the combination of an All-Implicit agent with a Close-Consequence agent and Strategy 2 is two All-Implicit agents, Task = Zero-Nonmatching-Beliefs, commcost = 1, infcost = 1, retcost = .01

BENEFICIAL. Figure 7 demonstrates that strategies which include Consequence IRUs can increase the robustness of the planning process by decreasing the frequency with which agents make mistakes (KS for AWM of 3 to 6 > .19, p < .05). This is a direct result of **rehearsing** the act-effect inferences, making it unlikely that attention-limited agents will forget that they have already used a furniture item.

Figure 8 shows that the Close-Consequence strategy is detrimental when the task requires agents to achieve matching beliefs on the WARRANTS for their intentions (KS 1,3) > 0.3, p < .01). This is because IRUs displace other facts from AWM. In this case agents forget the scores of furniture pieces under consideration, which are the warrants for their intentions. Thus here, as elsewhere, we see that IRUs can be detrimental by making agents forget critical information.

5.2 Explicit Warrant

Figure 9 shows that Explicit-Warrant is beneficial in the Standard task at AWM values of 3 and above. Here, the scores improve because the beliefs necessary for deliberating the proposal are made available in the current context with each proposal (KS for AWM of 3 and above > .23, p < .01), so that agents don't have to search memory for them. At AWM parameter settings of 16, where agents can search a huge belief space for beliefs to be used as warrants, the saving in processing time is substantial.

When the task is Zero-Invalid (no figure due to space), the benefits of the Explicit-Warrant strategy are

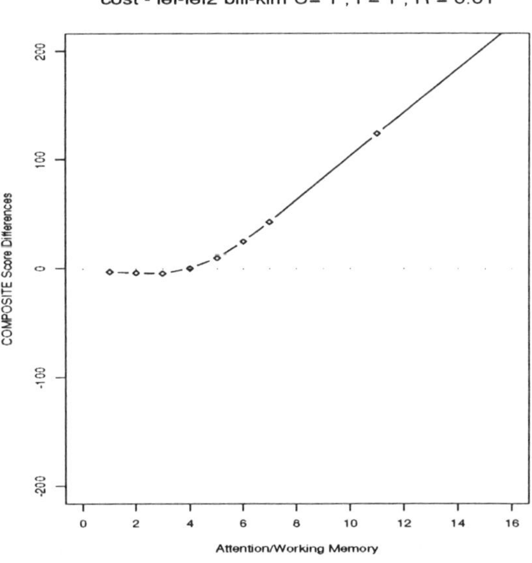

Figure 9: Explicit-Warrant saves Retrieval costs: Strategy 1 is two Explicit-Warrant agents and strategy 2 is two All-Implicit agents: Task = Standard, commcost = 1, infcost = 1, retcost = .01

dampened from the benefits of the Standard task, because Explicit-Warrant does nothing to address the reasons for agents making mistakes. In comparison with the All-Implicit strategy, it is detrimental at AWM of

1 and 2, but is still beneficial at AWM of 5,6,7, and 11.

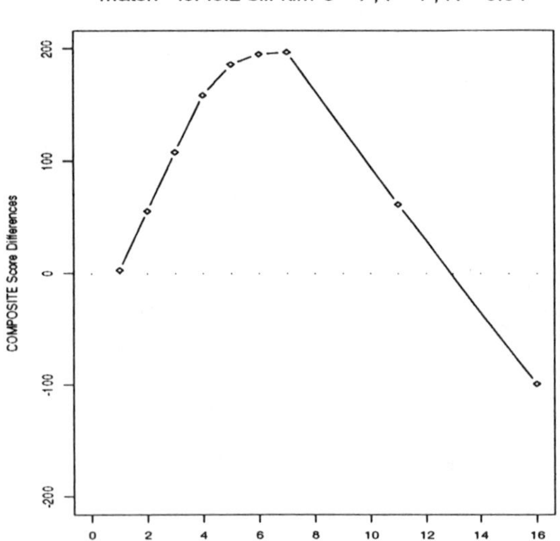

Figure 10: Explicit-Warrant is beneficial for Zero-NonMatching-Beliefs Task: Strategy 1 is two Explicit-Warrant agents and strategy 2 is two All-Implicit agents: Task = Zero-Nonmatching-Beliefs, commcost = 1, infcost = 1, retcost = .01

In contrast to Close-Consequence, the Explicit-Warrant strategy is highly beneficial when the task is Zero-NonMatching-Beliefs, see figure 10 (KS > .23 for AWM from 2 to 11, p < .01). When agents must agree on the warrants underlying their intentions, including these warrants with proposals is a good strategy even if the agent already knows the warrants. This is due to agents' resource limits, which means that retrieval is indeterminate and that there are costs associated with retrieving warrants from memory. At high AWM the differences between the two strategies are small.

6 Related Work

Design-World was inspired by the TileWorld simulation environment: a rapidly changing robot world in which an artificial agent attempts to optimize reasoning and planning [Pollack and Ringuette, 1990; Hanks *et al.*, 1993]. TileWorld is a single agent world in which the agent interacts with its environment, rather than with another agent. Design-World uses similar methods to test a theory of the effect of resource limits on communicative behavior between two agents.

The belief reasoning mechanism of Design-World agents was informed by the theory of belief revision and the multi-agent simulation environment developed in the Automated Librarian project [Galliers, 1991; Cawsey *et al.*, 1992]. The communicative acts and discourse acts used by Design-World agents are similar to those used in [Carletta, 1992; Cawsey *et al.*, 1992; Sidner, 1992; Stein and Thiel, 1993].

Design-World is also based on the method used in Carletta's JAM simulation for the Edinburgh Map-Task [Carletta, 1992]. JAM is based on the Map-Task Dialogue corpus, where the goal of the task is for the planning agent, the instructor, to instruct the reactive agent, the instructee, how to get from one place to another on the map. JAM focuses on efficient strategies for recovery from error and parametrizes agents according to their communicative and error recovery strategies. Given good error recovery strategies, Carletta argues that 'high risk' strategies are more efficient, where efficiency is a measure of the number of utterances in the dialogue. While the focus here is different, we have shown that that the number of utterances is just one parameter for evaluating performance, and that the task definition determines when strategies are effective.

7 Conclusion

In this paper we showed that collaborative communicative behavior cannot be defined in the abstract: what counts as collaborative depends on the task, and the definition of success in the task. We used two empirical methods to support our argument: corpus based analysis and experimentation in Design-World. The methods and the focus of this work are novel; previous work on resource limited agents has not examined the role of communicative strategies in multi-agent interaction whereas work on communication has not considered the effects of resource limits.

We showed that strategies that are inefficient under assumptions of perfect reasoners with unlimited attention and retrieval are effective with resource limited agents. Furthermore, different tasks make different cognitive demands, and place different requirements on agents' collaborative behavior. Tasks which require a high level of belief coordination can benefit from communicative strategies that include redundancy. Fault intolerant tasks benefit from redundancy for rehearsing the effects of actions.

Because the communicative strategies that we tested were based on a corpus analysis of human human financial advice dialogues and because variations in the Design-World task were parametrized, we believe the results presented here may be domain independent, though clearly more research is needed.

Here we fixed the parameters for the cost of communication, inference and retrieval, only discussed a few of the implemented discourse strategies, and didn't discuss Design-World parameters that increase the inferential complexity of the task and that limit inferential processing. Elsewhere we show that: (1) when retrieval is free or when communication cost is high, that the Explicit-Warrant strategy is detrimental at low AWM [Walker, 1993]; (2) some IRU strategies are only beneficial when inferential complexity is higher than in the Standard Task [Walker, 1993]; (3) IRUs that make inferences explicit can help inference limited agents perform as well as logically omniscient ones [Walker, 1995].

One ramification of the results presented here is that experimental environments for testing agent architectures should support task variation [Pollack and Ringuette, 1990; Hanks *et al.*, 1993]. Furthermore the task variation should test aspects of the interaction of the agents involved. These results also inform the design of multi-agent problem solving systems and for systems for teaching, advice and explanation.

References

[Allen and Perrault, 1980] James F. Allen and C. Raymond Perrault. Analyzing intention in utterances. *Artificial Intelligence*, 15:143–178, 1980.

[Anderson and Bower, 1973] J. R. Anderson and G. H. Bower. *Human Associative Memory*. V.H. Winston and Sons, 1973.

[Baddeley, 1986] Alan Baddeley. *Working Memory*. Oxford University Press, 1986.

[Bratman *et al.*, 1988] Michael Bratman, David Israel, and Martha Pollack. Plans and resource bounded practical reasoning. *Computational Intelligence*, 4:349–355, 1988.

[Carletta, 1992] Jean C. Carletta. *Risk Taking and Recovery in Task-Oriented Dialogue*. PhD thesis, Edinburgh University, 1992.

[Cawsey *et al.*, 1992] Alison Cawsey, Julia Galliers, Steven Reece, and Karen Sparck Jones. Automating the librarian: A fundamental approach using belief revision. Technical Report 243, Cambridge Computer Laboratory, 1992.

[Chapanis *et al.*, 1972] A. Chapanis, R.B. Ochsman, R.N. Parrish, and G.D. Weeks. Studies in interactive communication: The effects of four communication modes on the behavior of teams during cooperative problem-solving. *Human Factors*, 14:487–509, 1972.

[Doyle, 1992] Jon Doyle. Rationality and its roles in reasoning. *Computational Intelligence*, November 1992.

[Finin *et al.*, 1986] Timothy W. Finin, Aravind K. Joshi, and Bonnie Lynn Webber. Natural language interactions with artificial experts. *Proceedings of the IEEE*, 74(7):921–938, 1986.

[Galliers, 1991] Julia R. Galliers. Autonomous belief revision and communication. In P. Gardenfors, editor, *Belief Revision*, pages 220 – 246. Cambridge University Press, 1991.

[Guinn, 1993] Curry I. Guinn. A computational model of dialogue initiative in collaborative discourse. In *AAAI Technical Report FS-93-05*, 1993.

[Hanks *et al.*, 1993] Steve Hanks, Martha E. Pollack, and Paul R. Cohen. Benchmarks, testbeds, controlled experimentation and the design of agent architectures. *AI Magazine*, December 1993.

[Hintzmann and Block, 1971] D. L. Hintzmann and R. A. Block. Repetition and memory: evidence for a multiple trace hypothesis. *Journal of Experimental Psychology*, 88:297–306, 1971.

[Landauer, 1975] Thomas K. Landauer. Memory without organization: Properties of a model with random storage and undirected retrieval. *Cognitive Psychology*, pages 495–531, 1975.

[Norman and Bobrow, 1975] Donald A. Norman and Daniel G. Bobrow. On data-limited and resource-limited processes. *Cognitive Psychology*, 7(1):44–6, 1975.

[Pollack *et al.*, 1982] Martha Pollack, Julia Hirschberg, and Bonnie Webber. User participation in the reasoning process of expert systems. In *AAAI82*, 1982.

[Pollack and Ringuette, 1990] Martha E. Pollack and Marc Ringuette. Introducing the Tileworld: Experimentally Evaluating Agent Architectures. In *AAAI90*, pages 183–189, 1990.

[Sidner, 1992] Candace Sidner. Using discourse to negotiate in collaborative activity: An artificial language. *AAAI Workshop on Cooperation among Heterogeneous Agents*, 1992.

[Siegel, 1956] Sidney Siegel. *Nonparametric Statistics for the Behavioral Sciences*. McGraw Hill, 1956.

[Stein and Thiel, 1993] Adelheit Stein and Ulrich Thiel. A conversational model of multimodal interaction. In *AAAI93*, 1993.

[Walker, 1993] Marilyn Walker. Informational redundancy and resource bounds in dialogue. In *AAAI Spring Symposium on Reasoning about Mental States*, 1993. Also available as IRCS techreport IRCS-93-20, University of Pennsylvania.

[Walker, 1992] Marilyn A. Walker. Redundancy in collaborative dialogue. In *Fourteenth International Conference on Computational Linguistics*, pages 345–351, 1992.

[Walker, 1993] Marilyn A. Walker. *Informational Redundancy and Resource Bounds in Dialogue*. PhD thesis, University of Pennsylvania, 1993.

[Walker, 1995] Marilyn A. Walker. Testing collaborative strategies by computational simulation: Cognitive and task effects. *Knowledge Based Systems*, 1995. March.

[Walker and Whittaker, 1990] Marilyn A. Walker and Steve Whittaker. Mixed initiative in dialogue: An investigation into discourse segmentation. In *Proc. 28th Annual Meeting of the ACL*, pages 70–79, 1990.

[Whittaker *et al.*, 1993] Steve Whittaker, Erik Geelhoed, and Elizabeth Robinson. Shared workspaces: How do they work and when are they useful? *IJMMS*, 39:813–842, 1993.

Automated Accompaniment of Musical Ensembles

Lorin Grubb and Roger B. Dannenberg

School of Computer Science, Carnegie Mellon University
5000 Forbes Avenue
Pittsburgh, PA 15213
lgrubb@cs.cmu.edu and rbd@cs.cmu.edu

Abstract[1]

This paper describes a computer accompaniment system capable of providing musical accompaniment for an ensemble of performers. The system tracks the performance of each musician in the ensemble to determine current score location and tempo of the ensemble. "Missing parts" in the composition (i.e., the accompaniment) are synthesized and synchronized to the ensemble. The paper presents an overview of the component problems of automated musical accompaniment and discusses solutions and their implementation. The system has been tested with solo performers as well as ensembles having as many as three performers.

Introduction

Musical performance in ensembles requires more than just mastery of an instrument. Ensemble performers must be able to listen to one another and react to changes in the performance. These include changes in tempo and loudness, for example. Even following the flow of performance can be difficult as instruments drop out and re-enter. Each performer must synchronize with the ensemble, that is, play at the appropriate time and with the appropriate tempo. The computer accompaniment problem is to track, in real-time, a performance by a solo musician or a group of musicians and to produce the "missing" voices of the composition in synchrony with the other performers. It is assumed that all performers, including the computer, play from a score that specifies the pitches and their musical timing. An ensemble accompaniment system is a flexible alternative to playing along with a recording when a full ensemble is not available. It also enables new compositions combining human and machine performers.

We describe a system developed to provide accompaniment for an ensemble. Several computer accompaniment systems for following *solo* performers have been described (Dannenberg 1984, Vercoe 1984, Baird et. al. 1993). In (Dannenberg 1984) the accompaniment problem is partitioned into three distinct subproblems: 1) detecting what the soloist has performed, 2) determining the score position of the soloist from the detected performance, and 3) pro-

ducing an accompaniment in synchrony with the detected performance. A solution for each subproblem and a method for its implementation is also provided.

The system presented here extends the capabilities of previous accompaniment systems by performing with multiple musicians. To follow an ensemble, the solutions to the first and second subproblems in the solo accompaniment system must be simultaneously applied to multiple performers. Before taking actions to control an accompaniment (the solution to the third subproblem), the ensemble system must examine and combine the score position and tempo suggestions produced through tracking multiple performers. Note that this may require resolution of conflicting information. This paper details specifics of the problem of tracking multiple performers and combining the results in order to produce an accompaniment. A solution to the problem and a brief description of its implementation are provided. We conclude with a discussion of some qualitative results of actually using the system to accompany multiple performers.

Problem Description

The performance-monitoring component of a computer accompaniment system must process a digital representation of the performance in order to extract required parameters. These parameters might include fundamental pitch, note duration, dynamic (relative loudness), and articulation. The representation of the performance, in the simplest case, might be MIDI (Musical Instrument Digital Interface) messages (Rothstein 1992) sent from an electronic keyboard. Since most of the required parameters are explicitly represented in MIDI messages, extracting the needed information is simple. In a more difficult case, the representation is an audio signal from a microphone. This is often the representation obtained from wind instruments, for example. Extracting musical parameters from this type of input requires more analysis than does processing MIDI messages. Fortunately, there exist commercially available devices for converting analog input into MIDI-encoded pitch and amplitude information. The most difficult case is multiple instruments recorded with a single microphone. We do not address this case.

Once basic parameters (like pitch) have been extracted from the performance, the next task for accompaniment systems is to estimate the performer's location in the score.

---

1. This material is based upon work supported under a National Science Foundation Graduate Research Fellowship

This involves comparing the sequence of extracted performance parameters to the expected sequence of parameters (the given score), attempting to find the best match. A robust pattern matcher is required because a perfect performance cannot guaranteed.

As successive score locations are identified and time stamped, tempo is estimated by comparing the actual time difference between performed events and the expected time difference between the corresponding score events. Since it is well-known that performers alter durations of particular beats within a measure for expressive purposes (Desain & Honing 1992), the accompaniment system must average successive time difference comparisons to avoid sudden drastic tempo changes.

Accompaniment systems also produce the actual accompaniment. Generally, an accompaniment must be continuous and aesthetically acceptable, yet reactive to the performer's omissions, errors, and tempo changes. If the performer increases or decreases the tempo slightly for interpretive reasons, the accompaniment should do likewise. If the performer pauses or jumps ahead in the score, the accompaniment should follow as much as possible, but the accompaniment should always sound "musical" rather than "mechanical". Thus, a considerable number of decisions must be made by the accompaniment generation component in response to tempo and location information.

The task of estimating score location and tempo in an ensemble accompaniment system is complicated by the fact that multiple performers must be tracked and their individual score locations and tempi combined and resolved. Several considerations affect this resolution process. For instance, if one performer's tracking system is having difficulty tracking the performance, possibly because of signal processing difficulties or because the performer is making mistakes, then the estimates from that tracking system should not strongly affect the final estimation. Also, performers who become inactive for a relatively long duration (i.e., have a rest or a sustained pitch) should affect the final estimations less than recently active voices, which are more likely to indicate the current tempo and score position. Additionally, a performer whose score position is relatively distant from the majority of the ensemble, presumably indicating that this performer is lost or has fallen behind, should be ignored. A combination of the tracking systems' estimates must satisfy these considerations as much as possible in order to produce an accurate, unified ensemble score location and tempo.

Approach

To identify the score location of a single performer, we use a modified version of the dynamic programming algorithm for identifying the longest common subsequence of two strings (Cormen et. al. 1990). Regarding the performance as a sequence of pitches, the objective is to delete a minimal number of notes from performance and score sequences to obtain an exact match. In practice, a prefix (the performance) is matched against a complete string (the score), and only a portion of the score is examined in order to save time.

The matching algorithm is applied on every recognized note in the performance. The objective is to find the "best" match between performance and score according to the evaluation function:

$$evaluation = a \times matched\ notes - b \times omissions - c \times extra\ notes$$

Although the number of ways the performed pitches can be matched against the score is exponential in the number of performed notes, dynamic programming allows us to compute the best match in time that is linear in the length of the score, and which gives a result after each performed note. By using a "window" centered around the expected score location, the work per performed note is further reduced to a constant. A more detailed presentation of this algorithm can be found in (Bloch & Dannenberg 1985), which also shows how to modify this algorithm to handle polyphonic performance input (e.g., chords played on a keyboard).

If a new score location has been posited, it is placed in a buffer along with a timestamp indicating the "real time" when that location was reached by the performer. If one views these buffer entries as points in a graph mapping real time of the performance on the abscissa to "score time" (the position in the score) on the ordinate, the tempo of the performance at any instant is given by the slope of the graph (since tempo is the amount of score traversed in a unit of real time). Figure 1 graphs a tracked performance. Since performers are noticeably inconsistent within a tempo, it is necessary to apply some form of averaging in order to avoid occasional drastic tempo change estimates. Although many averaging techniques are available, we have elected to simply take the slope of the line between the first and last points in the location buffer. Since the buffer size is limited and relatively small, with older entries discarded one at a time once the buffer's capacity is exceeded, this tempo estimation is still responsive to actual changes in tempo but less "jerky" than estimates based solely on the two most recent entries in the buffer. If the matching algorithm detects a performance error, the buffer is emptied and no tempo or score position estimates are possible until several correct notes are played.

For an ensemble accompaniment system which must track multiple performers simultaneously, separate instances of the match state and the score location buffer must be maintained. Notes from different performers are identified by different MIDI channels, and the appropriate state is updated. Since score location information for each performer is available, it is possible to estimate each performer's current score location at any time. For example, consider Figure 2. If at time t_1, the performer is at score location s1 and maintaining an estimated tempo of 0.5; then at time t_1+2, the performer's expected score location would be s_1+1 (if no intervening input is received from the performer).

The various estimates must eventually be consolidated into a single ensemble score position and tempo. The accompaniment system estimates an ensemble score position and tempo on every input from every performer. To accomplish this in accordance with the criteria presented in

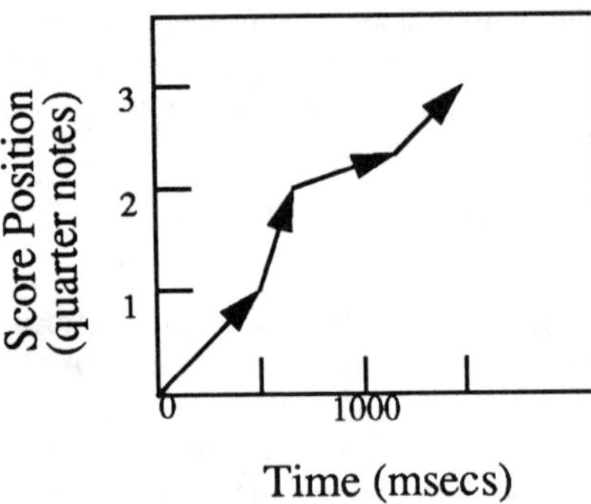

Figure 1,
Example performance graph.

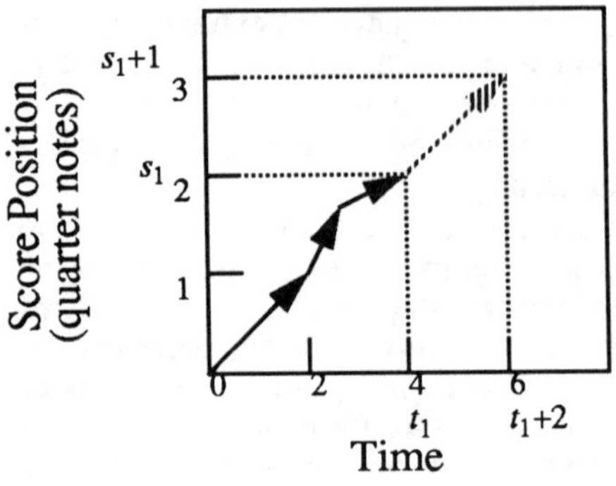

Figure 2,
Estimated score position.

section two, each pair of estimations from each tracking system is rated, and a weighted average is computed from both score location and tempo estimates. The ratings are constructed so that an estimate is given more weight when it is more recent, and less weight when it does not cluster with other estimates. Figure 3 presents the rating function. The final rating (FR) used for the weighted average is the product of the squares of two independent ratings—a recency rating (RR) and a clustering rating (CR).

The recency rating for each tracking system (as given in Figure 3) decays from a value of one to zero during a three-second interval. If the score-position buffer of the tracking system is empty, then the recency rating is zero. This value is squared in the final rating product, causing the final rating to decay more rapidly (in a quasi-exponential fashion) over the three-second interval. The rating is designed to give preference to the most recently active performers, thereby making the accompaniment performance more reactive. The clustering rating (also given in Figure 3) characterizes the relative separation of voices. It is the ratio of the summed distance of the i'th voice from all other voices, divided by the maximum possible summed distance at the time of rating. The rating decays from a value of one for the best case (i.e., all voices and the accompaniment are at identical score positions) to a value of zero in the worst case (i.e., all voices except the i'th voice are at the same position). This rating, like the recency rating, is squared in the final rating so as to give an even stronger preference to voices which are "relatively" tightly clustered. The final rating is a product of the squares of the other ratings so that it is guaranteed to be less than or equal to the minimum of the individual squares (since each square ranges from zero to one). Thus, as the criteria characterized by the component ratings fail to be satisfied, the final rating decreases.

The ensemble score position and tempo are calculated as a weighted average of the tracking system estimates. Each estimate is weighted by its final rating, and thus affects the overall estimate according to its "relative" satisfaction of the specified criteria compared to the estimates of the other tracking systems. For example, consider a performance of the section of score presented in Figure 4. As the first performer proceeds, the recency rating of the other voices will decay. The tempo and score position estimated by the first performer's tracking system will quickly dominate the ensemble average, causing the accompaniment to more closely follow that performer.

Once the ensemble score position and tempo estimates have been calculated, they are used to make adjustments to the accompaniment performance according to a set of accompaniment rules. These rules are based upon studies of how real accompanists react to similar situations encountered during a performance (Mecca 1993). First, the time difference between the ensemble score position and the accompaniment score position is calculated. If the time difference is less than a pre-determined "noise" threshold, then the accompaniment tempo is simply set to the ensemble tempo. The noise threshold is used to prevent excessive jumping and tempo alterations, since performers do make subtle alterations in note placement (Bilmes 1992). This threshold is adjustable but is generally set to around 100 msecs. If the performer is ahead of the accompaniment by a difference at least as great as the noise threshold, but less than the "jump" threshold, then the accompaniment tempo is increased to an abnormally fast tempo (even faster than the actual ensemble performance) so that the accompaniment will catch-up to the ensemble. If the accompaniment catches the ensemble prior to calculating another estimate, the tempo is reset to the previous tempo estimate. The jump threshold indicates how large a score position difference is too large to bother trying to perform in order to catch the ensemble. If the time difference is at least as great as this threshold, then the accompaniment system will skip to the estimated ensemble score position and start using the estimated ensemble tempo. Finally, if the performer is behind the accompaniment by a time difference at least as great as the noise threshold, then the accompaniment will pause until the performer reaches the accompaniment's current position. To prevent the accompaniment from continuing too far ahead of the performers, it is necessary to maintain an input expectation point. If this point is passed without additional input from any performer, then the accompaniment system pauses until additional input is received. Once input is received, the score position and tempo are estimated, necessary alterations to the performance parameters are implemented as just described, and the accompaniment is restarted.

$$\text{Ensemble Score Position} = \frac{\sum_{i=1}^{n} FR(i) \times pos(i)}{\sum_{i=1}^{n} FR(i)}$$

$$FR(i) = (RR(i))^2 \times (CR(i))^2 + c$$

FR(i) = Final rating for estimate from tracking system i
RR(i) = Recency rating for estimate from tracking system i
CR(i) = Clustering rating for estimate from tracking system i
c = Very small constant to prevent FR from reaching zero

$$RR(i) = \begin{array}{l} 1 - \dfrac{(rtime - ltime(i))}{3} \\[4pt] 0 \end{array} \quad \text{if} \quad \begin{array}{l} (rtime - ltime(i)) \leq 3 \\[8pt] (rtime - ltime(i)) > 3 \end{array}$$

rtime = Current time for which estimates are made
ltime(i) = Time of last match made by tracking system i

$$CR(i) = 1 - \frac{\left(\sum_{j=1}^{n} |pos(i) - pos(j)| \right) - |acc - pos(i)|}{n \times (pos(max) - pos(min))}$$

n = Number of active tracking systems
pos(i) = Score position for tracking system i
pos(j) = Score position for tracking system j
acc = Score position for accompaniment
pos(max) = Maximum of all pos(i), pos(j), and acc
pos(min) = Minimum of all pos(i), pos(j), and acc but NOT pos(max)

Figure 3, Function to calculate ensemble score position.

Implementation

The ensemble accompaniment system is constructed using the CMU MIDI Toolkit (Dannenberg 1993) which provides MIDI message handling, real-time scheduling, and performance of MIDI sequences. It is possible to adjust the position and tempo of a sequence (score) performance on-the-fly as part of processing input or generating output. The system is written in C and runs on DOS-based PCs, Macintoshes, Amigas, and Unix workstations. The ensemble accompaniment system has been tested on both a DOS-based system and an Amiga.

Figure 4, Score excerpt.

To obtain performance input, both MIDI keyboards and pitch-to-MIDI converters have been used. The keyboards themselves generate MIDI messages which can be directly sent to the ensemble accompaniment system. The pitch-to-MIDI converter is an IVL Pitchrider, designed for use primarily with wind instruments. It takes input directly from a microphone, analyzes the input to identify fundamental pitch and attack, and generates MIDI messages that can be sent to the ensemble accompaniment system. For wind instruments, the data from this device can be used by the accompaniment system without modification. A software preprocessor has been developed to further analyze the data sent from this device when receiving vocal input (singing).

The ensemble system consists of four software components: a matcher, which receives input from a performance and uses dynamic programming to determine score location; an estimator, which maintains the score location buffer, calculates tempi, and generates estimates on request; a voter, which rates and combines multiple score location and tempo estimates into an ensemble location and tempo; and a scheduler, which uses the ensemble estimates to change the accompaniment performance according to the rules described in section three. A matcher-estimator combination forms a single performance tracking system. The accompaniment system may instantiate multiple tracking systems at initialization depending on user-supplied specifications. Only one voter and one scheduler are ever present. Figure 5 diagrams the interaction between these components for the case when the system is to accompany an ensemble of two performers.

When MIDI messages are received as input, the appropriate matcher is invoked according to the channel number of the message. (Each performer's input must be sent on a separate MIDI channel.) The matcher applies the dynamic programming algorithm to determine the score location of the performer. The success or failure of this process is passed along to the estimator. If the match was successful then the estimator will pass its score position and tempo estimates to the voter. The voter will then request similar estimates from each of the other active tracking systems. The ratings are then generated for each set of estimates, as previously described. When an ensemble score position

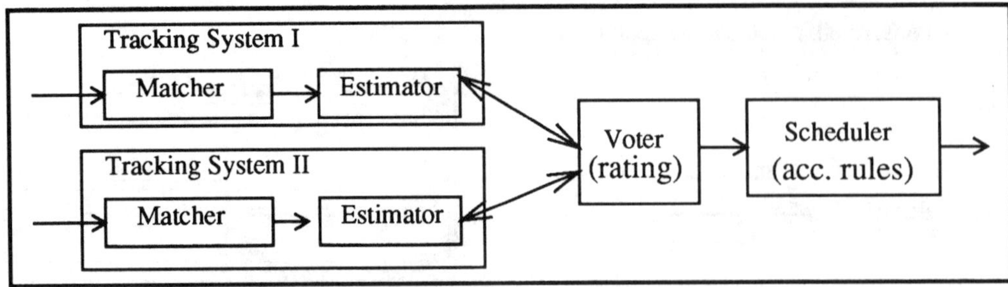

Figure 5, Components of the accompaniment system.

and tempo have been generated, they are passed to the scheduler which determines any necessary and appropriate modifications to the accompaniment performance, according to the rules presented in the previous section. Our toolkit automatically manages the activation of input handling routines and MIDI message generation for performance of the accompaniment. The MIDI output can then be sent to a synthesizer for sound production.

Results

The ensemble accompaniment system has performed with ensembles of one, two, and three players consisting of both MIDI keyboards and acoustic wind instruments. The pieces used for testing range in difficulty from a simple canon on "Row, row, row your boat" to excerpts from Handel's *Water Music*. In the case of a single performer, the system functions exactly the same as the solo accompaniment system previously constructed. It is highly reactive to tempo changes of the soloist and tolerant of omitted notes, wrong notes, and extra notes. If too many wrong notes or extra notes appear in the performance (as in a heavily embellished rendition), the matcher becomes unable to recognize the part, but the accompaniment will continue according to the last tempo estimate. The occasional mistake from a competent performer does not present a problem. In the case of omitted notes (such as when the performer jumps ahead), the system will ignore the performer until enough notes are correctly matched so that the matcher's score overcomes the penalty imposed by the skipped notes. The farther the performer jumps, the larger is the penalty and the corresponding delay. Note that this penalty increases only for notes skipped by the performer—if the soloist omits a rest during which time the accompaniment plays, no penalty is generated and the accompaniment almost immediately re-synchronizes with the performer.

In the case of an ensemble of two performers, the system is able to simultaneously track both performers. If either performer drops out, the system continues to accompany the other. Tempo changes of the latter performer are recognized by the system—readily so, once the silent performer's recency rating has decayed. Also, since the score position of the accompaniment affects the clustering rating for each performer, if one performer should skip ahead or fall behind, the system will continue to synchronize with the other performer—ignoring the "lost" performer until he or she rejoins the ensemble or until the

first performer stops or becomes lost. If both performers skip ahead or change tempo in synchrony, then the accompaniment does likewise according to the accompaniment rules described in section three. The system acts similarly in the case of three performers. In addition, should two of the three performers jump ahead or fall behind to the same position in the score, leaving only one performer in synchrony with the accompaniment, the system will quickly re-synchronize with the two performers since they represent the majority of the ensemble. Note also that when tracking multiple performers, the accompaniment is less affected by a single performer playing wrong notes or omitting notes, providing the other performers are accurate and in synchrony.

While the system works well with small ensembles, several problems must be addressed in order for the system to perform with larger ensembles. Two problems at the input level are that MIDI only permits sixteen logical channels and that individual microphones in large ensembles will experience cross-talk, making pitch estimation more difficult. There is no reason to believe that either of these problems is insurmountable.

Compute time is another consideration. Processing an input requires time linear in the ensemble size (since estimates from all tracking systems must be re-rated). In the worst case, if all parts simultaneously play a note, the amount of work to be completed before the next note in the score is performed is quadratic in the ensemble size. On the slowest PC used, handling a single input requires 1.4 msec. for an ensemble of one. The expense of recomputing one rating (for larger ensembles) is 0.3 msec. Based on these numbers, a conservative estimate indicates that we can process 16 inputs in 100 msec. A sixteenth note of 100 msec. duration implies a tempo of 150 quarter notes per minute. This is a fast tempo. If we were to update the voter once every 100ms instead of on each input, we could handle hundreds of instruments in real time with current processor technology. For large acoustic ensembles, the computation will be dominated by signal processing of acoustic input.

Conclusions

Developing this accompaniment system has helped to define important criteria and considerations relevant to ensemble accompaniment. When generating score location and tempo estimates for an ensemble, it is useful to consider both the recency of the input from individual performers and the clustering, or relative proximity, among the performer's score positions. This information assists in distinguishing recent and reliable performer input from that which has come from a lost or resting performer, or one who is not following the score.

Construction and testing of this system has demonstrated there exists a trade-off between reactivity and stability of an accompaniment. As previously indicated, the ensemble accompaniment system currently attempts to be reactive to the performers. For example, in the case of three performers where two performers have jumped ahead in the score but one has remained with the accompaniment, the system will quickly jump to the score location of the ensemble majority. This reactivity could be questioned, since in some cases maintaining a stable accompaniment that does not skip ahead with the majority might be preferred. A more stable accompaniment might also be desired if the majority of the ensemble is consistently dragging the tempo, as opposed to changing tempo for expressive purposes. This trade-off must be considered during construction of both the rating functions used to calculate the ensemble position and tempo, and the rules used to determine when to change tempo and score position of the accompaniment.

Although the ensemble accompaniment system generally reacts to performance situations in a reasonable manner, there remain some questionable actions which might be improved. Some of these are related to the reactivity-stability trade-off just mentioned. One example is the placement of expectation points used to pause the accompaniment if no performer input is received. The more frequently these points are placed, the more reactive to tempo reductions and missed entrances the system becomes. The more sparse their placement, the more stable the accompaniment and the more performers are forced to compensate for their own mistakes. The use of knowledge-based rules to better define the relative rating of each performer's score location and tempo is also a consideration. If it is clear from the score that a particular performer should be inactive at present, then perhaps that performer's estimates should be ignored. This might make the system more immediately reactive to the contrapuntally active performers, as opposed to waiting for the inactive performer's recency rating to decay. It is hoped that further experimentation with the present system will help to define a more comprehensive understanding of these trade-offs and alternatives, leading to a more versatile accompaniment system.

Additionally, pre-performance analysis of the score might help develop useful performance expectations. Annotations in scores can provide useful performance hints to the scheduler (Dannenberg & Bookstein 1991). Automating this annotation process would, however, require significant musical knowledge pertinent to interpreting scores. Alternatively, we are also interested in experimenting with learning through rehearsal, possibly by using techniques similar to those presented in (Vercoe & Puckette 1985). Ideally, an accompaniment system should be able to improve by practicing a piece with an ensemble and noting where to expect consistent tempo changes, embellishment, or performer error. This could be done with a single ensemble and single score, as well as with a single score performed by multiple ensembles. Since even two expressive performances by the same ensemble may vary greatly, the challenge will be to extract reliable characterizations of multiple ensemble performances and use them to enhance the accompaniment in successive performances, beyond what the naive and score-independent expectations allow. Using our current system as a starting point, techniques for effectively learning performance nuances can now be explored.

References

Baird, B., Blevins, D., and Zahler, N. 1993. Artificial intelligence and music: implementing an interactive computer performer. *Computer Music Journal* 17(2): 73-9.

Bilmes, J. 1992. A model for musical rhythm. In Proceedings of the 1992 International Computer Music Conference, 207-10.

Bloch, J. and Dannenberg, R. 1985. Real-time computer accompaniment of keyboard performances. In Proceedings of the 1985 International Computer Music Conference, 279-90.

Cormen, T., Leiserson, C., and Rivest, R. 1990. *Introduction to Algorithms*, 314-19. New York: McGraw-Hill Book Co.

Dannenberg, R. 1984. An on-line algorithm for real-time accompaniment. In Proceedings of the 1984 International Computer Music Conference, 193-8.

Dannenberg, R., and Bookstein, K. 1991. Conducting. In Proceedings of the 1991 International Computer Music Conference, 537-40.

Dannenberg, R. 1993. *The CMU MIDI Toolkit*. Pittsburgh: Carnegie Mellon University.

Desain, P., and Honing, H. 1992. Tempo curves considered harmful. In *Music, Mind, and Machine: Studies in Computer Music, Music Cognition, and Artificial Intelligence*, 25-40. Amsterdam, Thesis Publishers.

Mecca, M. 1993. Tempo following behavior in musical accompaniment. Master's thesis, Carnegie Mellon University.

Rothstein, J. 1992. *MIDI: A Comprehensive Introduction*. Madison: A-R Editions.

Vercoe, B. 1984. The synthetic performer in the context of live performance. In Proceedings of the 1984 International Computer Music Conference, 199-200.

Vercoe, B and Puckette, M. 1985. Synthetic rehearsal: training the synthetic performer. In Proceedings of the 1985 International Computer Music Conference, 275-78.

Auditory Stream Segregation in Auditory Scene Analysis with a Multi-Agent System

Tomohiro Nakatani, Hiroshi G. Okuno, and Takeshi Kawabata

NTT Basic Research Laboratories
3-1 Morinosato-Wakamiya, Atsugi, Kanagawa 243-01 Japan
{nakatani, okuno, kawabata}@nuesun.ntt.jp

Abstract

We propose a novel approach to auditory stream segregation which extracts individual sounds (*auditory stream*) from a mixture of sounds in auditory scene analysis. The HBSS (*Harmonic-Based Stream Segregation*) system is designed and developed by employing a multi-agent system. HBSS uses only harmonics as a clue to segregation and extracts auditory streams incrementally. When the tracer-generator agent detects a new sound, it spawns a tracer agent, which extracts an auditory stream by tracing its harmonic structure. The tracer sends a feedforward signal so that the generator and other tracers should not work on the same stream that is being traced. The quality of segregation may be poor due to redundant and ghost tracers. HBSS copes with this problem by introducing monitor agents, which detect and eliminate redundant and ghost tracers. HBSS can segregate two streams from a mixture of man's and woman's speech. It is easy to resynthesize speech or sounds from the corresponding streams. Additionally, HBSS can be easily extended by adding agents of a new capability. HBSS can be considered as the first step to computational auditory scene analysis.

Introduction

Over the past years a considerable number of studies have been made on human auditory mechanisms. Although we have many techniques for processing particular sounds such as speech, music, instruments, and the sounds made by specific devices, we don't have enough mechanisms for processing and understanding sounds in real acoustic environments. Research into the latter is being made in the field of *Auditory Scene Analysis* (Bregman 1990), which is to speech recognition is what scene analysis is to character recognition. Auditory scene analysis is a difficult challenging area, partly because acoustic theory is not still rather inadequate (e.g., there is no good acoustic design methodology for concert halls), and partly because most research in acoustics has been focused exclusively on speech and music, ignoring many other sounds. Additionally, the *reductionist* approach to auditory scene analysis, which tries to sum up various techniques for handling individual sounds, is not promising.

Looking and listening are more active than seeing and hearing (Handel 1989). The essentials of our approach to auditory scene analysis are twofold:

- Active perception of observer — looking and listening rather than seeing and hearing, and

- Multi-sensor perception — may use multi-modal information perceived by means of sensor organs

The multi-agent system was recently proposed as a new modeling technology in artificial intelligence (Brooks 1986) (Maes 1991) (Minsky 1986) (Okuno 1993). We assume like Minsky that an agent has a limited capability, although in Distributed Artificial Intelligence, an agent is supposed to be much more powerful like a human being than ours. Each agent has its own goal and competes and/or cooperates with other agents. Through interactions among agents, intelligent behavior emerges (Okuno & Okada 1992).

Consider the approach that the multi-agent paradigm is applied to model auditory scene analysis. We expect that it will enhance the following functionalities: (1) *Goal-Orientation* — Each agent may have its own goal. (2) *Adaptability* — According to the current situation, the behavior of the system varies between reactive and deliberate. (3) *Robustness* — The system should respond sensibly even if the input contains errors, or is ambiguous and incomplete. (4) *Openness* — The system can be extended by adding agents of new capabilities. It can also be integrated into other systems as a building block.

In this paper, auditory stream segregation, the first stage of auditory scene analysis, is modeled and implemented by a multi-agent system. The rest of this paper is organized as follows: Section 2 investigates issues in auditory stream segregation. In Section 3, the basic system of auditory stream segregation with a multi-agent system is explained and evaluated to identify its problems. Section 4 presents and evaluates the HBSS (Harmonic-Based Stream Segregation) that copes with the problems. Related work and the conclusions are given in Section 5 and 6, respectively.

Auditory stream for auditory scene analysis

Auditory stream

Auditory scene analysis understands *acoustic events* or *sources* that produce sounds (Bregman 1990). An acoustic event consists of *auditory streams* (or simply *stream*, hereafter), each of which is a group of acoustic components that have consistent characteristics. The process that segregates auditory streams from a mixture of sounds is called *auditory stream segregation.*

Many techniques have been proposed so far. For example, Brown uses auditory maps in auditory stream segregation (Brown 1992) (Brown & Cooke 1992). These are off-line algorithms in the sense that any part of the input is available to the algorithm at any time. However, off-line algorithms are not well suited for many applications. Additionally, it is not easy to incorporate schema-based segregation and grouping of streams into such a system, since it does not support a mechanism of extending capabilities.

To design a more flexible and expandable system, we adopted a multi-agent system to model auditory stream segregation, and used a simple characteristic of the sounds, that is, the harmonic structure.

Definitions — Harmonic representation

We use only the *harmonic structure* or *harmonicity* of sounds as a clue to segregation. Other characteristics, including periodicity, onset, offset, intensity, frequency transition, spectral shape, interaural time difference and interaural intensity difference, may be used for further processing.

A harmonic sound is characterized by a fundamental frequency and its overtones. The frequency of an overtone is equal to an integer multiple of the fundamental frequency. In this paper, *harmonic stream* refers to an auditory stream corresponding to a harmonic sound, *harmonic component* refers to a single overtone in the harmonic stream, and *agent's stream* refers to the stream an agent traces. We also define the *harmonic intensity* $E(\omega)$ of the sound wave $x(t)$ as

$$E(\omega) = \sum_{k=1}^{n} \| H_k(\omega) \|^2, \qquad (1)$$

where

$$H_k(\omega) = \sum_{t} x(t) \cdot \exp(-jk\omega t), \qquad (2)$$

t is time, k is the index of the harmonic components, and ω is the fundamental frequency. We call the absolute value of H_k the *intensity* of the harmonic component, and call the phase of H_k the *phase* of the harmonic component. In this paper, the term *common fundamental frequency* is extended to include the case where the fundamental frequency of one sound coincides with overtone of another sound.

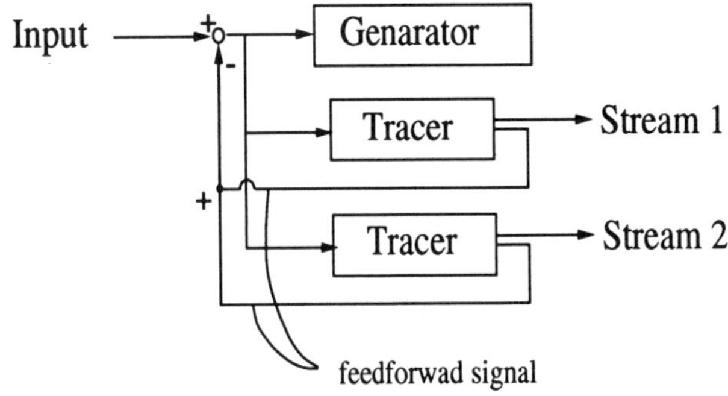

Figure 1: Structure of basic system

Issues in segregation

To extract an auditory stream from a mixture of sounds, it is necessary to find out the harmonic structure, its fundamental frequency and the power of each overtone. The system should segregate auditory streams incrementally, since it will be used as a building block for real-time applications. The important issues to cope with these requirements are summarized below:

1. How to find the beginning of a new harmonic structure,

2. How to trace a harmonic structure,

3. How to reduce the interference between different tracings, and

4. How to find the end of a harmonic structure,

Basic stream segregation

Agents for Basic system

The basic system (Nakatani et al. 1993) consists of two types of agents, the *stream-tracer generator* (hereafter, *the generator*) and *stream tracers* (hereafter, *tracers*). The generator detects a new stream and generates a tracer. The tracers trace the input sound to extract auditory streams. Figure 1 shows the structure of these agents. The input signal consists of the mixed audio waveform.

System parameters   The basic system uses three parameters to control the sensitivity of segregation:

1. Power threshold array θ_1 to check for overtones,

2. Power threshold θ_2 to check for fundamental frequencies,

3. Duration T_1 to check for the continuity of sounds.

These three parameters are global and shared among all the agents. The parameter θ_1 is a array of thresholds for frequency regions and plays the most important role in controlling the sensitivity.

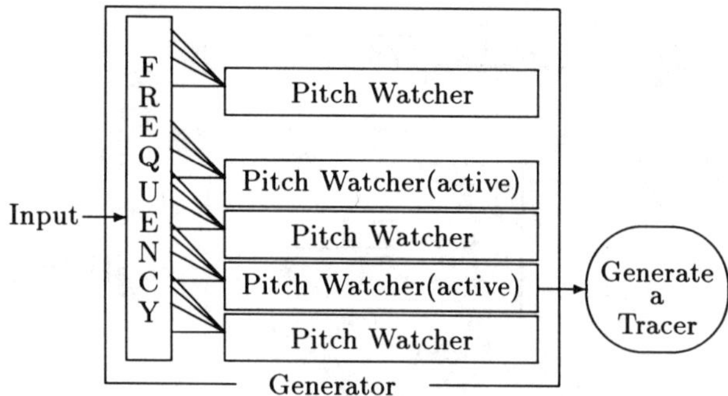

Figure 2: Structure of Generator
Active pitch watch detects a sound.

Generator

The generator detects the beginning of harmonic structures included in the input sounds and generates a new tracer agent. It consists of agents called *pitch watchers* (Figure 2), which monitors the harmonic structure at each frequency ω by evaluating the harmonic intensity defined by Equation 1. Each pitch watcher treats ω as a candidate fundamental frequency, and is activated if the following conditions are satisfied:

1. There is at least one overtone of ω whose power is larger than θ_1,

2. the power of the fundamental frequency, ω, is larger than θ_2, and

3. there is a peak near ω in the acoustic spectrum.

The active pitch watcher with the largest harmonic intensity generates a new tracer, which traces the new stream whose fundamental frequency is ω in Equation 2.

Tracer

Each tracer searches for the fundamental frequency ω_n within the neighborhood of the frequency ω_{n-1} of the previous input frame by maximizing the harmonic intensity (Equation 1). In evaluating Equation 1, overtones whose power is less than θ_1 are discarded. Then, the tracer calculates the intensity and the phase of each harmonic component by using Equation 2.

The tracer terminates automatically if one of the following conditions is satisfied for a period of T_1:

- there is no overtone whose power is larger than θ_1, or

- the power of ω is less than θ_1.

Reducing interference between tracers

A stream should be extracted *exclusively* by one tracer. For this purpose, two tasks are performed by each agent.

Table 1: Benchmark mixtures of two sounds

No	sound$_1$	sound$_2$
1	man's speech	synthesized sound (Fundamental Frequency is 200 Hz)
2	man's speech	synthesized sound (F.F. is 150 Hz)
3	man's speech	woman's speech

Male and female speech utter "aiueo" independently.

Subtract signal As shown in Figure 1, a tracer guesses the input of the next frame and makes a feed-forward signal (called *a subtract signal*), which is subtracted from the input mixture of sounds. The waveform to be subtracted is synthesized by adjusting the phase of its harmonic components to the phase of the next input frame. The remaining input (called *the residual input*) goes to all the tracers and to the generator. Each tracer restores the sound data, $x(t)$, by adding the residual signal to its own subtract signal. By this mechanism, the generator does not generate a new tracer for existing streams and one tracer cannot trace another tracer's stream.

Updating the global parameters θ_1 and θ_2 Each tracer increases the array elements of θ_1 for the regions in the vicinity of the frequency it is tracing. The increase is in proportion to the estimated trace error of each harmonic component, and results in lower sensitivity around the neighboring frequency regions. When terminating, each tracer decreases the array elements of θ_1 in its frequency regions, thereby raising the sensitivity.

Let A be the intensity of a traced harmonic component, ω be the frequency of the harmonic component, and ω' be the representative frequency for each frequency region. We estimate the trace error for the harmonic component at frequency ω' as

$$T(\omega') = c \cdot \left\| \sum_t A \sin(\omega t) \exp(-j\omega' t) \right\|,$$

where c is a constant. Since the frequency of higher-order harmonic components is more sensitive to the fundamental frequency than that of lower-order components, the threshold for a higher-order component should be increased over a wider region. Consequently, we use $T(\omega + (\omega_0/\omega) \cdot (\omega' - \omega))$ to increase the local threshold for the harmonic component at frequency ω'.

Each tracer also updates the global parameter θ_2 for every input frame. This is increased by the amount in proportion to the square root of the harmonic intensity. In most regions in vicinity of harmonic components, this value is set much lower than θ_2.

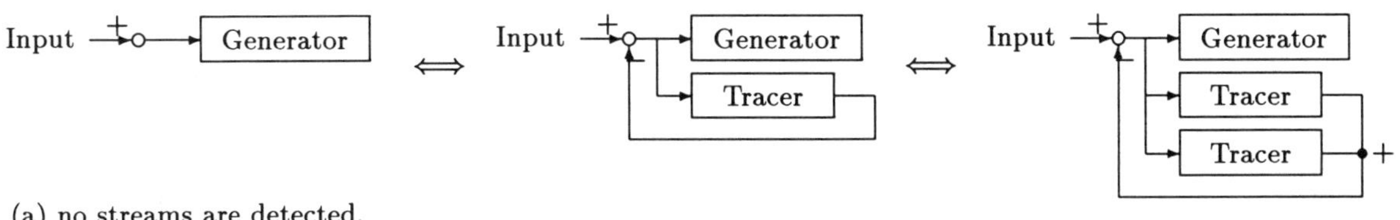

Figure 3: Dynamic generation and termination of Tracer agents

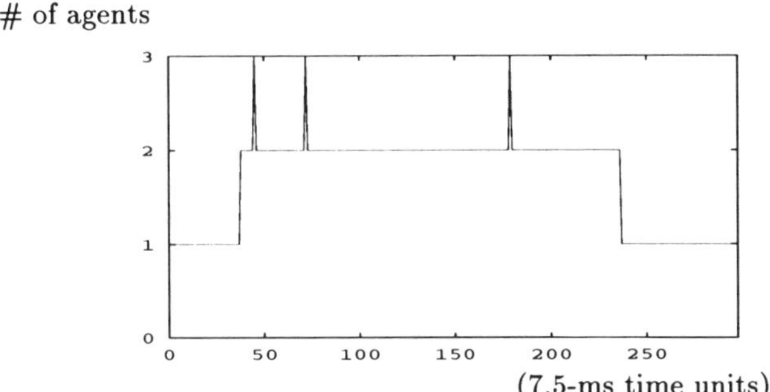

Figure 4: Dynamics of tracer agents (Exp. 1)
(Total number of generated agents = 5)

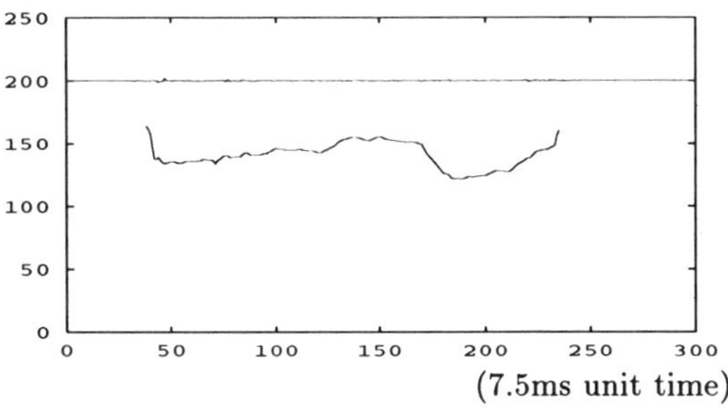

Figure 5: Segregated streams (Exp. 1)

System Behavior

Figure 3(a) shows the initial state of the system. No sound is input to the generator and no tracer is generated. When a new sound enters the system, the generator is activated and a new tracer is generated (Figure 3(b)). Since a tracer is not complete, some errors may be fed into the generator. However, the tracer increases the threshold values adaptively according to the harmonic components, so this mechanism inhibits the generation of inappropriate tracers due to trace errors. The next stream is detected in almost the same way as the first stream (Figure 3(c)). When two or more tracers are generated, each tracer ignores competing components that are excessively influenced by the other streams. As a result, each stream is expected to be well segregated.

Evaluation

We evaluate this system by using three sets of sound mixtures as shown in Table 1. The input signals consisted of combinations of a male speaker and a female speaker uttering Japanese vowels "aiueo", and a stationary synthesized sound with an exponentially attenuating sequence of harmonic components up to 6 kHz.

The input sounds were sampled at 12 kHz, 16-bit quantized, and analyzed with a 30-ms Hamming window. The frame period was 7.5 ms.

Experiment 1 Figure 4 depicts the dynamic generation and termination of tracers in response to the first set of input sounds (Table 1). It shows that three inappropriate tracers (called *redundant tracers*) follow a stream assigned to another tracer, but terminate immediately. The segregated streams are depicted in Figure 5. Both of the sounds resynthesized[1] from the segregated streams are very similar to the original sounds. Additionally, the formants of the original voice are preserved in the resynthesized voice.

Experiment 2 Figure 6 depicts the dynamic generation and termination of tracers in response to the second set of input sounds. The first redundant tracer terminates immediately, while three inappropriate tracers continue to operate for as long as the second sound lasts. One of the three tracers is a redundant tracer. The rest are two *ghost tracers* that traces non-existing streams. The segregated streams are depicted in Figure 7. The sound resynthesized from the segregated stream corresponding to the 150-Hz synthesized sound was very similar to the original sound, but the man's speech was not so good, sounding more like "aiueo-h". Most formants of the original voice are preserved in the resynthesized voice.

---

[1]At the presentation, the original and resynthesized sounds will be demonstrated.

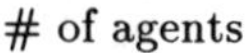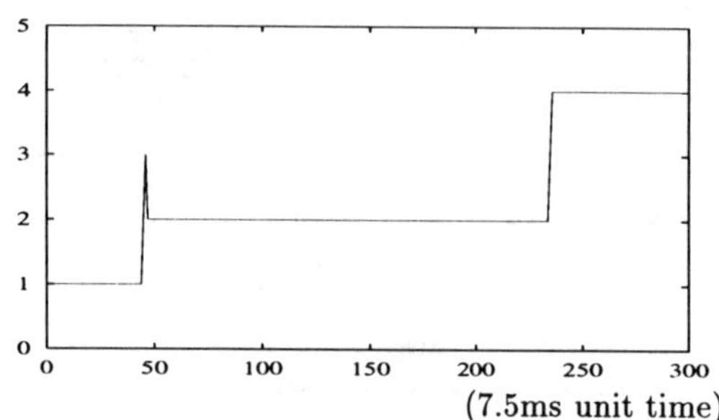

Figure 6: Dynamics of Tracer agents (Exp. 2)
(Total number of generated agents = 5)

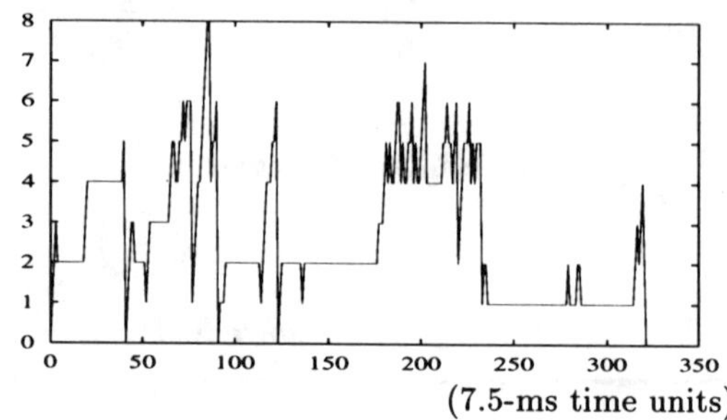

Figure 8: Dynamics of tracer agents (Exp. 3)
(Total number of generated agents = 70)

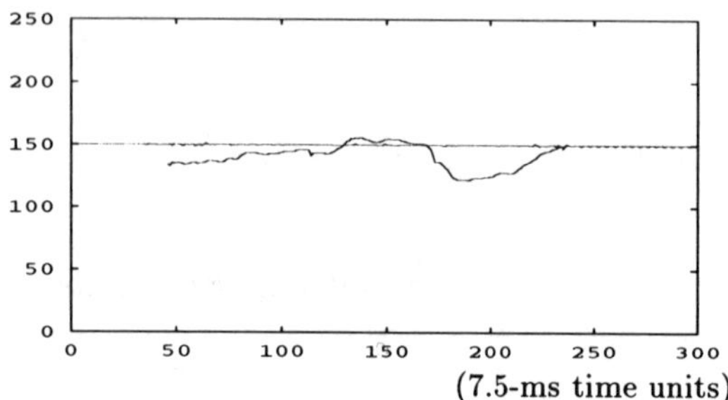

Figure 7: Segregated streams (Exp. 2)

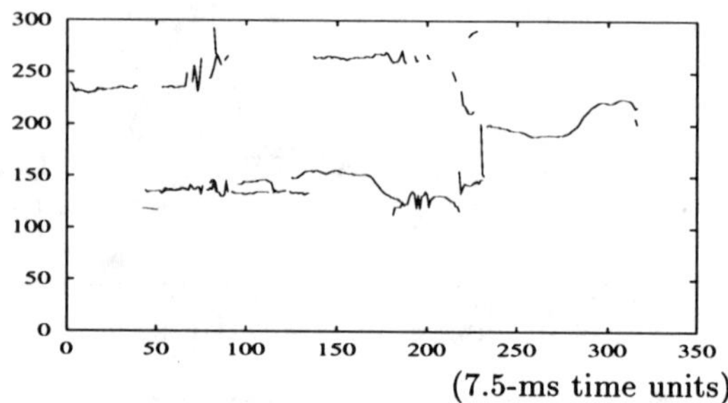

Figure 9: Segregated streams (Exp. 3)

Experiment 3 The third input signal results in the generation of 70 tracer agents, many of which were short-lived as shown in Figure 8. There are many redundant and ghost tracers. However, none of these agents traced both the man's and woman's speech at the same time, as shown in Figure 9. Each of the sounds resynthesized from the corresponding segregated stream was quite poor compared with the original. Additionally, it is not easy to resynthesize a sound by grouping segregated streams. Some formants of man's and woman's original voice are destroyed in each resynthesized voice, respectively.

Summary The basic system occasionally generates redundant and ghost tracers. A redundant tracer is caused by imperfect subtract signals and poor termination detection. A ghost tracer, on the other hand, is caused by self-oscillation, because the phase of the subtract signals is not considered. A pair of ghost tracers usually trace two streams with opposite phases.

Since each tracer extracts a stream according to the current internal status of the tracer and the current residual signal, it is difficult to determine which tracer is inappropriate. In the next section, we extend the basic system to cope with this problem.

Advanced stream segregation

An advanced stream segregation is proposed to cope with the problems encountered by the basic system (Nakatani et al. 1993). The advanced system is also called the HBSS (*Harmonic-Based Stream Segregation*) system.

Monitors

We introduce agents called *monitors* to detect and kill redundant and ghost tracers. A monitor is generated simultaneously with a tracer, which it supervises (Figure 10). The monitor starts a log for its tracer, and uses it to do the following.

1. Eliminate a redundant tracer, and

2. Adjust the intensity of harmonic components according to the input sound.

Eliminating redundant tracers Redundant tracers should be killed for stable segregation. When the following conditions are met, the monitor judges that its tracer is tracing the same stream as some other tracer.

1. The tracer shares a common fundamental frequency with others for a constant period of time, and

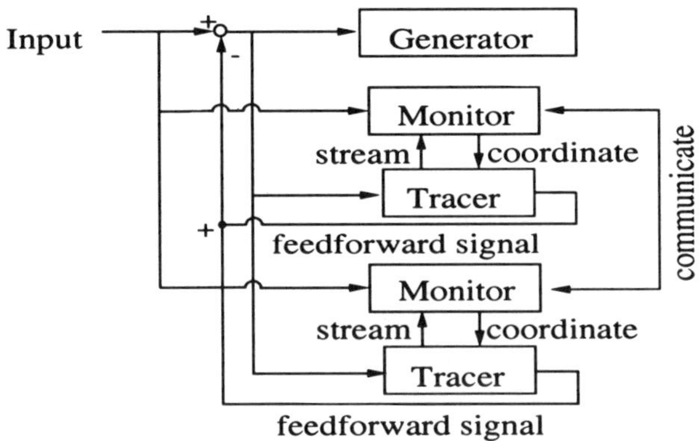

Figure 10: Structure of advanced system (HBSS)

2. The tracers have a common harmonic balance.
The *harmonic balance* is defined as the vector B,

$$B = \frac{1}{\sum_i h_i}(h_1, \ldots, h_m), \qquad (3)$$

where $(h_1, \ldots, h_m)$ is a sequence of components each of which is nearly equal to some overtone of the other stream. Two streams have a *common harmonic balance* if the following condition is met:

$$\sum_{i=1}^{m} \frac{\alpha_i}{m} < 1.0 + \epsilon, \qquad (4)$$

$$\begin{cases} \alpha_i = r_{1,i}/r_{2,i} & \text{if } r_{1,i} > r_{2,i}, \\ \alpha_i = r_{2,i}/r_{1,i} & \text{otherwise.} \end{cases}$$

Here $(r_{1,1}\ldots r_{1,m})$ and $(r_{2,1}\ldots r_{2,m})$ are the harmonic balances of two streams and ϵ is a constant.

The first condition is easily detected by comparing the trace logs. When a number of monitors detect that their tracers are monitoring the same stream, they all kill each other, along with their tracers, except for the monitor that was generated earliest to trace their common fundamental frequency.

Adjusting the stream   Since the feedforward signals of the tracers are subtracted from the waveform, sound components not included in the original sound may be created through tracer interactions. The monitors continuously reduce such sound components in the following way.

Let E_{comp} be the intensity of a harmonic component whose frequency is ω, E_{in} be the intensity of the actual input sound at the corresponding frequency ω in the acoustical spectrum, and r be E_{comp}/E_{in}. If r is greater than the constant c for the past τ frames, the monitor substitutes the value of E_{comp} with the value given by

$$E_{comp} = \alpha(\log(r/c)/\tau + 1.0) \cdot E_{in},$$

where α is a constant. If $\tau = 1$, the change in E_{comp} is small. As τ becomes larger, E_{comp} approaches αE_{in}.

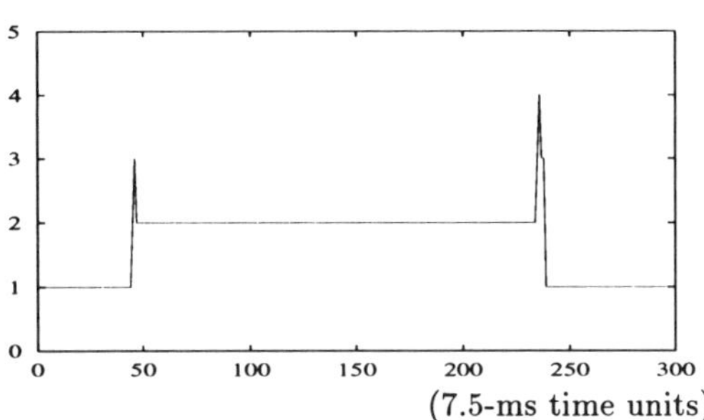

Figure 11: Dynamics of tracer agents (Exp. 4)
(Total number of generated agents = 7)

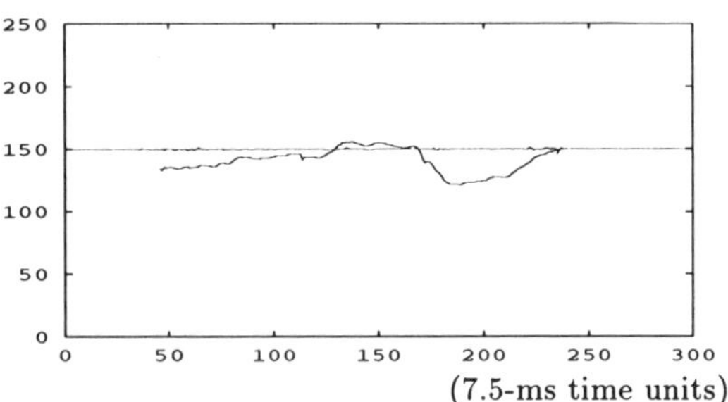

Figure 12: Segregated streams (Exp. 4)

System Behavior

We will briefly explain why inappropriate tracers cannot survive for long. A ghost tracer will be killed as follows:

- A tracer which does not trace an existing stream will be attenuated by the adjustment of its monitor.

- A tracer which traces an existing stream of another tracer will be terminated.

On the other hand, a tracer that is tracing an actual stream is influenced little by the adjustment of its monitor. A redundant tracers will be killed, leaving the oldest tracer to trace the stream stably.

Evaluation

The performance of the advanced system (HBSS) was evaluated using the same set of benchmark signals. Since the first mixture was well segregated even by the basic system, we skipped the result of this experiment with the advanced system.

Experiment 4   Figure 11 shows the dynamic generation and the termination of tracers in response to the second set of input sounds, and segregated streams are depicted in Figure 12. These figures show that

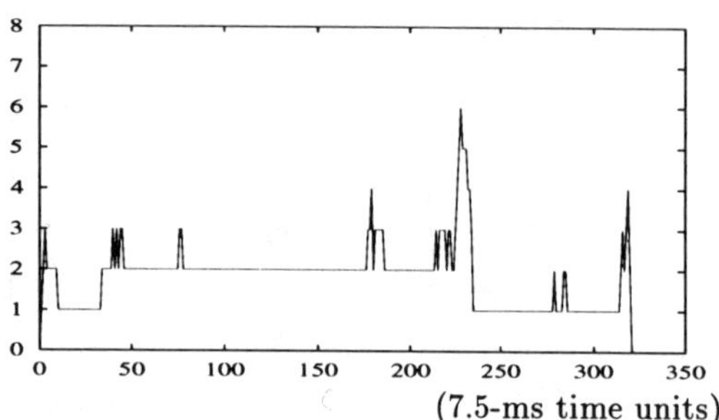

Figure 13: Dynamics of tracer agents (Exp. 5)
(Total number of generated agents = 37)

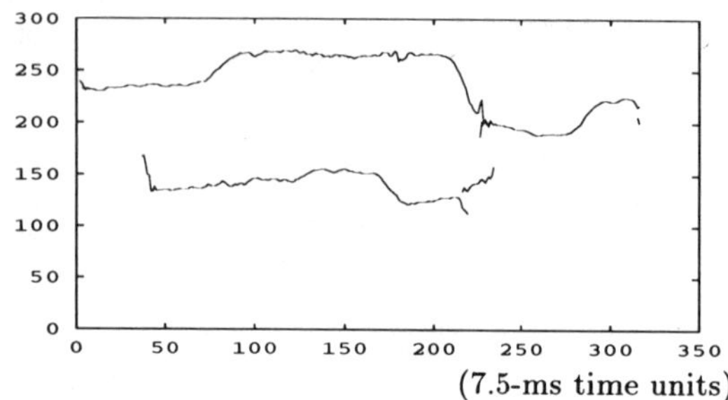

Figure 14: Segregated streams (Exp. 5)

redundant and ghost tracers are killed well. Both sounds resynthesized from the corresponding segregated streams are very similar to the original. Additionally, the formants of the original voice are well preserved in the resynthesized voice.

Experiment 5 The third input signal results in total of 37 generated agents, and Figure 13 shows that redundant and ghost tracers are killed soon. The segregated streams are depicted in Figure 14. Both sounds resynthesized from the segregated streams are not too bad. Additionally, it is easy to resynthesize sounds, because the women's speech was resynthesized from only one stream and the man's speech from two streams. The formants of the man's and woman's original voice are preserved in each resynthesized voice, respectively.

Related Work

Auditory Scene Analysis Bregman classifies the mechanisms of auditory scene analysis into two categories: *simultaneous (spectrum)* and *sequential* grouping (Bregman 1990). The former extracts auditory streams from a mixture of sounds, while the latter groups together auditory streams that belong to the same acoustic source. The Experiment 3 with the third mixture of two sounds in Table 1 shows that it is very difficult to segregate man's and woman's speech by simultaneous grouping followed by sequential grouping. The proposed system integrates both grouping processes and proves to be effective.

Brown and Cooke proposed computational auditory scene analysis (Brown 1992) (Brown & Cooke 1992), which builds auditory map to segregate speech from the other sound such as siren and telephone rings. This system extracts various acoustic characteristics on batch basis, but the extension or interface to other systems is not considered.

Integrated Architecture IPUS (*Integrated Processing and Understanding Signals*) (Lesser & Nawab 1993) integrates signal processing and signal interpretation into blackboard system. IPUS has a small set of front-end signal processing algorithms (SPAs) and choose correct parameters setting for SPA and correct interpretations by dynamic SPA reconfiguration. In other words, IPUS views the reconfiguration as a diagnosis for discrepancy between top-down search for SPA and bottom-up search for interpretation. IPUS has various interpretation knowledge sources which understand actual sounds such as hair driers, footsteps, telephone rings, fire alarms, and waterfalls (Nawab 1992). Since IPUS is a generic architecture, it is possible to implement any capability, but IPUS is fully-fledged. The initial perception can be much simplified. Additionally, a primitive SPA (or agent, in our terminology) that segregates a stream incrementally is not considered so far.

Okuno (Okuno 1993) proposed to use subsumption architecture (Brooks 1986) to integrate bottom-up and top-down processing to realize cognition capabilities. The term "subsumption architecture" is often confused with "behavior-based control" (Brooks 1986), but they are different. The former indicates that interaction between agents is specified by inhibitors and suppressors, or activation propagation (Maes 1991), while the latter indicates that it is behavior that is subsumed. We will use subsumption architecture rather than blackboard architecture, because the former allows agents to interact directly with the environment and can make it easier to extend the capabilities of system.

Wada (Wada & Matsuyama 1993) employed a multi-agent system in deciding regions of image. An agent is placed to a candidate region and then communicates with adjacent agent to determine the boundary of two regions. The interaction of agents is similar to that of HBSS. This and our result proves that a multi-agent system is promising in pattern recognition.

Conclusions

We have presented basic and advanced methods for auditory steam segregation with a multi-agent system, which use only the harmonic structure of input sounds. The advanced system, HBSS, is able to segregate man's and woman's speech. This result suggests a clue to understanding the *cocktail party problem*. We are about to investigate this problem by designing a new agent that extracts only human voice including consonants by using the information HBSS extracted. This new agent will be added to HBSS with subsumption architecture so that its output subsumes (overwrites) human voice stream segregated by HBSS.

HBSS is currently being evaluated with a wide range of sound mixtures such as a mixture of speech and, white noise of a sound of breaking glass. The performance of segregating human voice from white noise is shown to become worse as the power of white noise increases. However, it is known that constant white noise can be reduced by the spectral subtraction (Boll 1979). We will develop a new agent that reduces white noise by employing the spectral subtraction and use it as a front-end of HBSS.

One might argue that HBSS would not treat transient or bell sounds. This is somewhat true, but is not fatal, because the current HBSS holds and uses just a previous state to segregate auditory streams. We are working to design a new agent that holds longer previous states to restore missing phonemes caused by loud noise. This process is similar to *phonemic restoration* in auditory perception.

In case a mixture of sounds comprises only harmonic sounds and any pair of sounds have not any common fundamental frequency, HBSS would be able to segregate all sounds. This situation is an extension of the first benchmark mixture. Of course, as the number of pairs of sounds that have common fundamental frequency increases, it becomes more difficult to segregate such sounds. This is also the case for human perception. Therefore, we think that, active hearing, or listening, is essential. The typical example of listening is a cocktail party problem.

HBSS uses only harmonics in segregation. This is because we don't either have enough acoustic characteristics to represent a sound or know their hierarchy. In vision, there are a set of visual characteristics and Marr (Marr 1982) proposed their hierarchy, that is, primary and $2\frac{1}{2}$ sketch. It is urgent and important in the research of auditory scene analysis to develop a methodology to represent general acoustics, not restricted to speech or music.

Acknowledgments.

We would like to thank M. Kashino of NTT, H. Kawahara and M. Tsuzaki of ATR for discussions on auditory perception. We would like to thank S.H. Nawab of Boston University and other participants of Abstract Perception Workshop held at Japanese Advanced Institute of Science and Technology for comments on an earlier draft. We would also like to thank I. Takeuchi and R. Nakatsu of NTT for their continuous encouragement of our inter-group research.

References

Boll, S.F. 1979 A Spectral Subtraction Algorithm for Suppression of Acoustic Noise in Speech, In Proceedings of International Conference on Acoustics, Speech, and Signal Processing, IEEE, 200-203.

Bregman, A.S. 1990. *Auditory Scene Analysis – the perceptual organization of sound*, The MIT Press.

Brooks, R.A. 1986. A Robust Layered Control System for a Mobile Robot, *IEEE Journal of Robotics and Automation* RA-2(1): 14–23.

Brown, G. 1992. Computational auditory scene analysis: A representational approach, *PhD thesis*, Dept. of Computer Science, University of Sheffield.

Brown, G.J.; and Cooke, M.P. 1992. A computational model of auditory scene analysis, In Proceedings of International Conference on Spoken Language Processing, 523-526, IEEE.

Handel, S. 1989. *Listening*. The MIT Press.

Lesser, V.; Nawab, S.H.; Gallastegi, I.; and Klassner, F. 1993. IPUS: An Architecture for Integrated Signal Processing and Signal Interpretation in Complex Environments. In Proceedings of the Eleventh National Conference on Artificial Intelligence, 249–255.

Maes, P. ed. 1991. *Designing Autonomous Agents: Theory and Practice from Biology to Engineering and Back*, special issue of *Robot and Autonomous Systems*, The MIT Press/Elsevier.

Marr, D. 1982. *Vision.* Freeman.

Minsky, M. 1986. *Society of Minds.* Simon & Schuster, Inc.

Nakatani, T.; Kawabata, T.; and Okuno, H.G. 1993. Speech Stream Segregation by Multi-Agent System. In Proceedings of International Workshop on Speech Processing (IWSP-93), 131–136, The Institute of Electronics, Information and Communication Engineers. Also numbered Technical Report, SP93–97.

Nawab, S.H.; and Lesser, V. 1992. Integrated Processing and Understanding of Signals, 251–285. in Oppenheim, A.V.; and Nawab, S.H. eds. 1992. *Symbolic and Knowledge-Based Signal Processing*, Prentice-Hall.

Okuno, H.G.; and Okada, M. 1992. Emergent Computation Model for Spoken Language Understanding (*in Japanese*). Technical Report SIG-AI 82-3, 21–30, Information Processing Society of Japan.

Okuno, H.G. 1993. Cognition Model with Multi-Agent System (*in Japanese*), 213–225. In Ishida, T. ed. 1993. *Multi-Agent and Cooperative Computation II (Selected Papers from MACC '92)*, Tokyo, Japan: Kindai-Kagaku-sha.

Wada, T.; and Matsuyama, T. 1993. Region-Decomposition of Images by Distributed and Cooperative Processing. Proceedings of the Workshop on Multi-Agent and Cooperative Computation (MACC '93). Japanese Society for Software Science and Technology.

Simulating Creativity in Jazz Performance

Geber Ramalho   Jean-Gabriel Ganascia

LAFORIA-IBP-CNRS
Université Paris VI - 4, Place Jussieu
75252 Paris Cedex 05 - FRANCE
Tel. (33-1) 44.27.37.27 - Fax. (33-1) 44.27.70.00
e-mails: {ramalho, ganascia}@laforia.ibp.fr

Abstract

This paper considers the problem of simulating creativity in the domain of Jazz improvisation and accompaniment. Unlike most current approaches, we try to model the musicians' behavior by taking into account their experience and how they use it with respect to the evolving contexts of live performance. To represent this experience we introduce the notion of *Musical Memory,* which explores the principles of Case-Based Reasoning (Slade 1991). To produce live music using this *Musical Memory* we propose a problem solving method based on the notion of PACTs (*Potential ACTions*) that are activated according to the context and then combined in order to produce notes. We show that our model supports two of the main features of creativity: non-determinism and absence of well-defined goals (Johnson-Laird 1992).

1 - Introduction

Our research is concerned with the study of the strengths and limitations of AI techniques to simulate creative behavior on a computer. Although creativity has always been present on the AI research agenda there is no accurate understanding of human creativity; its simulation on a computer still remains an open problem (AAAI 1993). In fact, there is an apparent paradox in the formalization of creativity due to the common sense opinion that, by definition, creativity embodies what cannot be formalized.

To avoid both real and imaginary difficulties of simulating creative behavior on a computer, we have decided to concentrate on modeling particular kinds of creative activities such as musical ones. We do not intend to model creativity from a psychological point of view but rather to investigate it by seeking the simple computational mechanisms that may underlie it. In other words, we attempt to model creativity in terms of problem solving (Newell & Simon 1972; Nilsson 1971, Laird, Newell & Rosembloom, 1987).

We have chosen to work on Jazz improvisation and accompaniment because of their spontaneity, in contrast to the formal aesthetic of contemporary classical music composition. From an AI point of view, modeling Jazz performance raises interesting problems since performance requires both theoretical knowledge and great

skill. In addition, Jazz musicians are encouraged to develop their musical abilities by listening and practicing rather than studying in *conservatoires* (Baker 1980).

In Section 2 we present briefly the problems of modeling musical creativity in Jazz performance. We show the relevance of taking into account the fact that musicians integrate rules and memories dynamically according to the context. In Section 3 we introduce two basic notions of our model: PACTs and Musical Memory. A general description of our model is given in Section 4. In Section 5 we give further details about the modules of our model, showing particularly how the composition module integrates the two above-mentioned notions to create music. In the last section we discuss our current work and directions for further developments.

2 - Modeling Musical Creativity

2.1 - The Problem and the Current Approaches

Let us begin by defining some simple musical concepts. A note is a triplet (pitch, duration, amplitude) and can be considered as the basic tonal music element. Putting notes together one obtains other musical elements such as a melody (temporal sequence of notes) or a chord (set of simultaneous notes). Scales and rhythm concern respectively the pitches and durations of a set of notes. The tasks of improvisation and accompaniment consist in playing notes (melodies and/or chords) according to the guidelines laid down in a given chord grid (sequence of chords underlying the song). But, it is in the strikingly large gap between the actually played music and the chord grid instructions that the richness of live Jazz performance lies (Ramalho & Pachet 1994).

Musicians cannot justify all the local choices they make (typically at note-level) even if they have consciously applied some strategies in the performance. This is the greatest problem of modeling the knowledge used to fill the gap referred to above. To face this problem, the first approach is to make random-oriented choices from a library of musical patterns weighted according to their frequency of use (Ames & Domino 1992). The second approach focuses on very detailed descriptions so as to obtain a complete explanation of musical choices in terms of rules or grammars (Steedman

1984). In the first case, since there is no explicit semantics associated to random-oriented choices, it is difficult to control changes at more abstract levels than the note level. In the second, the determinism of rule-based framework lacks flexibility because of the introduction of "artificial" or over-specialized rules that do not correspond to the actual knowledge used by musicians. This crucial trade-off between "flexibility and randomness" and "control and semantics" affects the modeling of other creative activities too (Rowe & Partridge 1993).

2.2 - Claims on Knowledge and Reasoning in Jazz Performance

If musical creativity is neither a random activity nor a fully explainable one, then creativity modeling requires a deeper understanding of the nature and use of musical knowledge. This section presents two general results of our early work where we interviewed Jazz musicians and recorded live performances in order to elicit this knowledge.

Our first claim is that Jazz musicians' activities are supported by two main knowledge structures: memories and rules. More specifically, we claim that these memories are the main source of knowledge in intuitive composition tasks and that most Jazz rules are either abstract or incomplete with respect to their possibility of directly determining the notes to be played. Jazz musicians use rules they have learned in schools and through Jazz methods (Baudoin 1990). However, these rules do not embody all knowledge. For example, there is no logical rule chaining that can directly instantiate important concepts such as tension, style, swing and contrast, in terms of notes. This phenomenon is a consequence of the Jazz learning process which involves listening to and imitating performances of great Jazz stars (Baker 1980). The experience thus acquired seems to be stored in a long term musical memory.

To put it in a nutshell, musicians integrate rules and memories into their actions dynamically. Sometimes, note-level rules (that determine the notes directly) are applied but, very often, these rules are not available. In these cases a fast search for appropriate musical fragments in the musician's auditory memory is carried out using the available general rules. This memory search is both flexible and controlled because of the mechanism of partial matching between the memory contents and requirements stated by the general rules. In terms of modeling, this is an alternative approach that avoids the need for "artificial" rules or randomness.

Our second claim is that musical actions depend strongly on contexts that evolve over time. The great interaction between either musicians themselves or musicians and the public/environment may lead them to reinforce or discard their initial strategies while performing. The constraints imposed by real-time performance force musicians to express their knowledge as a fast response to on-going events rather than as an accurate search for "the best musical response". Jazz creativity occurs within the continuous confrontation between the musician's background knowledge and the context of live performance.

3- Two Basic Notions of our Model

3.1 - Potential ACTions (PACTs)

Pachet (Pachet 1990) has proposed the notion of PACTs (at this time called "strategies") as a generic framework for representing the potential actions (or intentions) that musicians may take within the context of performance. Focusing the modeling on musical actions rather than on the syntactic dimension of notes, additional knowledge can be expressed. In fact, PACTs can represent not only notes but also incomplete and abstract actions, as well as action chaining. PACTs are frame-like structures whose *main attributes* are: start-beat, end-beat, dimensions, abstract-level, type and instrument-dependency. Let us now see how PACTs are described, through a couple of examples.

PACTs are activated at a precise moment in time and are of limited duration which can correspond to a group of notes, a chord, a bar, the entire song, etc. PACTs may rely on different dimensions of notes: rhythm (r); amplitude (a); pitch (p) and their arrangements (r-a, r-p, p-a, r-p-a). When its dimensions are instantiated, the abstract level of a PACT is *low* , otherwise it is *high*. For instance, "play loud", "play this rhythm" and "play an ascending arpeggio" are low-level PACTs on amplitudes, rhythm and pitches respectively. "Play this lick transposed one step higher" is a low-level PACT on all three dimensions. "Play syncopated" and "use major scale" are high-level on respectively rhythm and pitches. PACTs can be of two types: *procedural* (c.g. "play this lick transposed one step higher") or *property-setting* (e.g. "play bluesy"). PACTs may also depend on the instrument. For example, "play five-note chord" is a piano PACT whereas "play stepwise" is a bass PACT.

For the sake of simplicity we have not presented many other descriptors that are needed according to the nature and abstract level of the PACTs. For instance, pitch PACTs have descriptors such as pitch-contour (ascending, descending, etc.), pitch-tessitura (high, low, middle, etc.), pitch-set (triad, major scale, dorian mode, etc.) and pitch-style (dissonant, chord-based, etc.).

From the above description two important properties of PACTs appear. The first one is the *playability* of a PACT. The less abstract a PACT is and the more dimensions it relies on, the more it is "playable" (e.g. "play ascending notes" is less playable than "play C E G", "play bluesy" is less playable than "play a diminished fifth on the second beat", etc.). A *fully playable* (or just *playable*) *PACT* is defined as a low-level PACT on all three dimensions. The second property is the *combinability* of PACTs, i.e. they can be combined to generate more playable PACTs. For instance, the PACT "play ascending notes" may combine with "play triad notes" in a given context (e.g. C major) to yield "play C E G". In this sense, PACTs may or may not be compatible. "Play loudly" and "play quietly" cannot be combined whereas "swing", "play major scale" and "play loudly" can. These properties constitute the basis of our problem solving method. As discussed in Section 4, solving a musical problem consists in assembling (combining) a set of PACTs that have been activated by the performance context.

3.2 - Musical Memory

There is no guarantee that a given set of PACTs contains the necessary information so as to produce a playable PACT. As discussed in Section 2.2, this lack of information is related to the fact that musical choices cannot be fully expressed in terms of logical rule chaining, i.e. *Jazz rules* are often either abstract or incomplete to determine directly the notes to be played. To solve this problem we have introduced the notion of Musical Memory which explores the principles of case-based reasoning [Slade 91]. This Musical Memory is a long term memory that accumulates the musical material (cases) the musicians have listened to. These cases can be retrieved and modified to provide missing information.

The contents and representation of the Musical Memory can be determined: the cases must correspond to low-level PACTs that can be retrieved during the problem solving according to the information contained in the activated PACTs. These cases are obtained by applying transformations (e.g. time segmentation, projection on one or two dimensions, etc.) to transcriptions of actual Jazz recordings. This process (so far, guided by a human expert) yields cases such as melody fragments, rhythm patterns, amplitude contours, chords, etc. The cases are indexed from various points of view that can have different levels of abstraction such as underlying chords, position within the song, amplitude, rhythmic and melodic features (Ramalho & Ganascia 94). These features are in fact the same ones used to describe high-level PACTs. For instance, pitches are described in terms of contour, tessitura, set and style as discussed in last section.

It is important to stress that high-level PACTs have also been determined from transcriptions of Jazz recordings but not automatically, since this would require much more complex transformations on the transcriptions. These PACTs were in fact acquired during an earlier knowledge acquisition phase working with experts.

4 - General Description of our Model

4.1 - What is a Musical Problem?

Johnson-Laird (Johnson-Laird 1992) among other researchers has identified three features of creative tasks that show the difficulties of formalizing creativity as classical problem solving (Newell & Simon 1972; Nilsson 1971): non-determinism (for the same given composition problem it is possible to obtain different musical solutions which are all acceptable); absence of well-defined goals (there is only a vague impression of what is to be accomplished, i.e. goals are refined or changed in the on-going process); no clear point of termination (because of both the absence of a clear goal and the absence of aesthetic consensus for evaluating results).

Taking an initial state of a problem space as a time segment (e.g. bars) with no notes, a musical problem consists in filling this time segment with notes which satisfy some criteria. This intuitive formulation of what a musical problem is underlies the above criticism of formalizing musical creativity. Some AI researchers have encountered many difficulties in exploring this point of view (see for instance Vicinanza's work (Vincinanza & Prietula 1989) on generating tonal melodies). However, we present here a different point of view that allows us to formalize and deal with musical creativity as problem solving. We claim that the musical problem is in fact to know how to start from a "vague impression" and go towards a precise specification of these criteria. In other words, the initial state of the music problem space could be any set of PACTs within a time interval and the goal could be a unique playable PACT. The goal is fixed and clearly defined (i.e. the goal is to play!) and solving the problem is equivalent to assembling or combining PACTs. An associated musical problem would be to determine the time interval continuously so as to reach the end of the song.

4.2 - The Reasoner

What we do is model a musician as a *reasoner* whose behavior is simulated by three modules which work coordinately in parallel (see Figure 1). The modules of our model resemble the *Monitoring*, *Planning* and *Executing* ones of some robotics applications (Ambros-Ingerson & Steel 1988). The *context* is composed of a *chord grid* which is given at the outset and *events* that occur as the performance goes on, i.e. the notes played by the orchestra and reasoner and also the public reactions. The *perception module* "listens to" the context events and puts them in the *Short-Term Memory*. The *composing module* computes the notes (a playable PACT) which will be executed in the future time segment of the chord grid. This is done using three elements: the Short-Term Memory contents, the reasoner's mood and the chords of the future chord grid segment. The *reasoner's Mood* changes according to the context events. The *execution module* works on the current chord grid segment by executing the playable PACT previously provided by the composing module. This execution corresponds to the sending of note

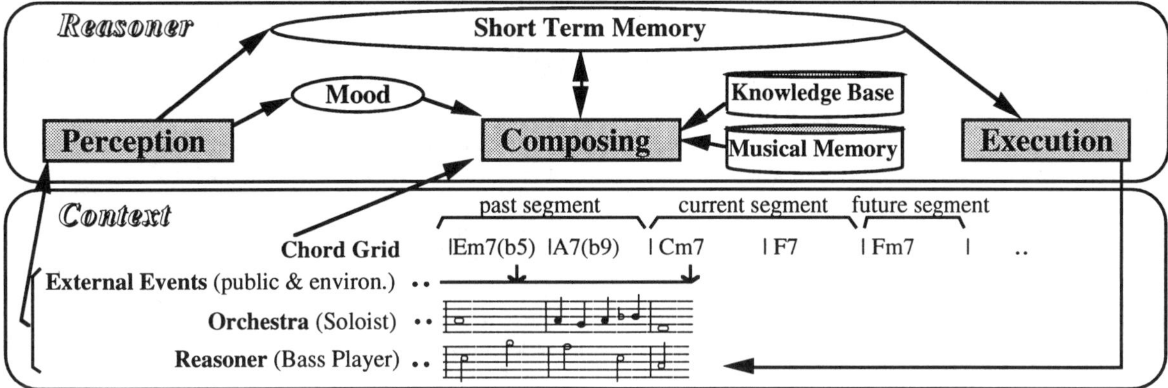

Figure 1 - Overall Description of the Model

information at their start time to the perception module and to a MIDI synthesizer, which generates the corresponding sound.

5 - Components of our Model

5.1 - The Perception Module

Modeling the dialog between musicians and their interaction with the external environment is a complex problem since the context events are unpredictable and understanding them depends on cultural and perceptual considerations.

To achieve an initial validation of our model, our current work focuses on the implementation of the composing module, since it is at the heart of the improvisation tasks. And instead of implementing the perception module, we have proposed a structure called a Performance Scenario which is a simpler yet still powerful representation of the evolving context. The idea is to control the context events by asking for the user's aid. Before the performance starts, the user imagines a virtual external environment and characterizes it by choosing some features and events from a limited repertoire and assigning an occurrence time to the events. As for the dialog between the musicians, the user listens to a previous orchestra recording and gives a first level interpretation by leaving some marks such as "soloist using dorian mode in a cool atmosphere" or "soloist is playing this riff". In short, the Performance Scenario is composed of marks that are obtained from the interpretation of the orchestra part and the setting of external environment events. These marks are only available to the system at their specified start time.

Unfortunately, the user cannot interpret the notes the reasoner himself has just played. However, the reasoner can take into account some simple features of these notes (e.g. last note, pitch and amplitude direction, etc.) when activating and assembling PACTs.

5.2 - The Composition module

The problem of playing along a given chord grid can be viewed as a continuous succession of three sub-problems: establishing the duration of the new chord grid segment; determining the PACTs associated to this segment; and assembling this group of PACTs in order to generate a unique playable PACT. The first two are more questions of problem setting, the third is a matter of problem solving and planning.

The composition model is supported by a Musical Memory and Knowledge Base. The former contains low-level PACTs that can be retrieved during the PACT assembly. The latter contains production rules and heuristics concerned with the segmentation of the chord grid, changes in the Mood and the selection/activation of PACTs. These rules are also used to detect and solve incompatibilities between PACTs, to combine PACTs and to modify low-level PACTs retrieved from the Musical Memory.

5.2.1 - Segmenting the Chord Grid and Selecting PACTs

The chord grid is segmented in non regular time intervals corresponding to typical chord sequences (II-V cadences, modulations, turnarounds, etc.) abundantly catalogued in Jazz literature (Baudoin 1990). In fact, the reasoning of musicians does not progress note by note but by "chunks" of notes (Sloboda 1985). The criteria for segmenting the chord grid are simple and are the same as those used for segmenting the transcription of Jazz recordings in order to build the Musical Memory.

Given the chord grid segment, the group of associated PACTs derives from three sources. Firstly, PACTs are activated according to the chords of the grid segment (e.g. "if two chords have a long duration and a small interval distance between them then play an ascending arpeggio"). Other PACTs are activated from the last context events (e.g. "if soloist goes in descending direction then follow him"). The activation of a PACT corresponds to the assignment of values to its attributes, i.e. the generation of an instance of the class PACT in an Object-Oriented

Language. Finally, the previously activated PACTs whose life time intersects the time interval defined by the segmentation (e.g. "during the improvisation play louder") are added to the group of PACTs obtained from the first two steps.

The reasoner can be seen as an automaton whose state (Mood) changes according to the context events (e.g. "if no applause after solo then Mood is *bluesy*" or "if planning is late with respect to the execution then Mood is *in a hurry*"). So far, the reasoner's Mood is characterized by a simple set of "emotions". In spite of its simplicity, the Mood plays a very important role in the activation and assembling of PACTs. It appears in the left-hand side of some rules for activating PACTs and also has an influence on the heuristics that establish the choice preferences for the PACT assembly operators. For instance, when the reasoner is "in a hurry" some incoming context events may not be considered and the planning phase can be bypassed by the activation of playable PACTs (such as "play this lick") which correspond to the various "default solutions" musicians play.

5.2.2 - Assembling PACTs

The initial state of the assembly problem space is a group of selected PACTs corresponding to the future chord grid segment. The goal is a playable PACT. A new state can be reached by the application of three operators or operator schemata (since they must previously have been instantiated to be applied): delete, combine and add. The choice of operator follows an opportunistic problem solving strategy which seeks the shortest way to reach the goal. Assembling PACTs is a kind of planning whose *space state* is composed of *potential actions* that are combined both in parallel and sequentially since sometimes they may be seen as constraints and other times as procedures. Furthermore, the actions are not restricted to primary ones since potential actions have different abstract levels. Finally, there is no backtracking in the operator applications.

The *delete operator* is used to solve conflicts between PACTs by eliminating some of them from the group of PACTs that constitute the next state of the space problem. For instance, the first two of the PACTs "play ascending arpeggio", "play in descending direction", "play louder" and "play syncopated" are incompatible. As proposed in SOAR (Laird, Newell & Rosembloom, 1987), heuristics state the preferences for choosing a production rule from a set of fireable rules. In our example, we eliminate the second one because the first one is more playable.

The *combine operator* transforms compatible PACTs into a new one. Sometimes the information contained in the PACTs can be merged immediately to yield a low-level PACT on one or more dimensions (e.g. "play ascending notes" with "play triad notes" yields "play C E G" in a C major context). Other times, the information is only placed side by side in the new PACT waiting for future merger (e.g. "play louder" and "play syncopated" yields, say, "play louder and syncopated"). Combining this with "play ascending arpeggio" generates a playable PACT.

The *add operator* supplies the missing information that is necessary to assemble a playable PACT by retrieving and adapting adequate cases (low-level PACTs on one or more dimensions) from the Musical Memory. The retrieval is done by a partial pattern matching between case indexes, the chords of the chord grid segment and the current activated PACTs. Since the concepts used in the indexation of cases correspond to the descriptors of high-level PACTs, it is possible to retrieve low-level PACTs when only high-level PACTs are activated. For instance, if the PACTs "play bluesy" and "play a lot of notes" are activated in the context of "Bb7-F7" chords, we search for a case that has been indexed as having a bluesy style, a lot of notes and IV7-I7 as underlying chords. When there is no PACT on a particular dimension, we search for a case that has "default" as a descriptor of this dimension. For instance, it is possible to retrieve a melody even when the activated PACTs concern amplitudes only.

The cases may correspond to some "chunks" of the note dimensions that may not *fit in* the "gaps" that exist in the current activated PACTs. Thus, retrieved cases may carry additional information which can be partially incompatible with the activated PACTs. Here either the conflicting information is ignored or it can "short-circuit" the current PACT assembly and lead to a different playable PACT. Let us suppose that the activated PACTs concern pitches and amplitudes and the retrieved case concerns pitches and rhythm. Only the activated PACTs on amplitude can be considered to be combined with the retrieved case generating a playable PACT. But, if the retrieved case concerns rhythm and amplitudes, perhaps the latter information could be ignored.

Choosing the add operator balances the cost in terms of memory search time with the possibility of short-circuiting the assembly process. Short-circuiting is an important feature of music creativity. For instance, in melody composition there is no chronological ordering between rhythm and pitches (Sloboda 1985). Sometimes both occur together! This feature is often neglected by computational formalisms (Vincinaza & Prietula 1989).

5.3 - The Execution Module

The problem of planning in a dynamic world is that when the plan is being generated new events may occur and invalidate it. In music performance, it suffices that the musician plays to provoke changes in the context. Thus, monitoring context changes at the same time as replanning what is being executed is very difficult in real-time conditions.

In our model we consider that the reasoning mechanisms that underlie planning and replanning in music performance are not the same. The replanning that can be done while playing is related more to simple and fast anatomic reactions than to complicated and refined reasoning. Consequently, beyond the role of controlling a MIDI synthesizer, the execution module has also to perform the changes in already generated plans. The idea is that particular context events trigger simple replanning such as "modify overall amplitude", "don't play these notes", "replace this note by another", etc. In short, since the composition module has finished its task, it is no longer concerned by changes to the plan it has generated. The context events occurring during a given plan generation will only be taken into account in the following plan generation.

At the current stage, the execution module has no replanning facilities. Notes are executed by a MIDI scheduler developed by Bill Walker (CERL Group - University of Illinois).

6 - Discussion

We have shown how an extension to classical problem solving could simulate some features of musical creativity. This extension attempts to incorporate both the experience musicians accumulate by practicing and the interference of the context in the musicians' ongoing reasoning. Although we do not use randomness in our model, there is no predetermined path to generate music. The musical result is constructed gradually by the interaction between the PACTs activated by the context and the Musical Memory's resources.

The notion of PACTs was first implemented (Pachet 1990) for the problem of generating live bass line and piano voicing. At this time, results were encouraging but, exploring exclusively a rule-based approach, various configurations of PACTs were hardly treated, if at all. This was due to the difficulty of expressing all musical choices in terms of rules. Our work has concentrated on improving the formalization of PACTs within a problem solving perspective. We have also introduced the notion of Musical Memory and seen how it can be coupled with PACTs. Today, Pachet's system is being reconsidered and re-implemented to take into account both the Musical Memory and a wider repertoire of PACTs.

In our model we have bypassed perceptual modeling. This is a tactical decision with respect to the complexity of modeling creativity in music. However, this modeling is essential for two reasons: to provide a machine with full creative behavior in music and, if coupled with machine learning and knowledge acquisition techniques, to help us in acquiring PACTs.

Acknowledgments

We would like to thank François Pachet, Jean-Daniel Zucker and Vincent Corruble who, as both musicians and computer scientists, have given us continuous encouragement and technical support. This work has been partly supported by a grant from the Brazilian Education Ministry - CAPES/MEC.

References

AAAI '93 Workshop on Artificial Intelligence & Creativity 1993. Melon Park, AAAI Press.

Ambros-Ingerson, J. & Steel, S. 1988. Integrating Planning, Execution and Monitoring, In Proceedings of the Sixth National Conference on Artificial Intelligence, 83-88, AAAI Press.

Ames, C. & Domino, M. 1992. Cybernetic Composer: an overview, In M. Balaban, Ebicioglu K. & Laske, O. eds., *Understanding Music with AI: Perspectives on Music Cognition*, The AAAI Press, California.

Baker, M. 1980. Miles Davis Trumpet, Giants of Jazz Series, Studio 224 Ed., Lebanon.

Baudoin, P. 1990 *Jazz: mode d'emploi*, Vol. I and II. Editions Outre Mésure, Paris.

Johnson-Laird, P. 1992. *The Computer and the Mind*, Fontana, London.

Laird, J., Newell, A. & Rosembloom, P. 1987. SOAR: An Architecture of General Intelligence, *Artificial Intelligence* 33, 1-64.

Newell, A. & Simon, H. 1972. Human Problem-Solving, Englewood Cliffs. Prentice Hall, NJ.

Nilsson, N. 1971. *Problem-Solving Methods in Artificial Intelligence*, McGraw-Hill Book Co., New York.

Pachet, F. 1990. Representing Knowledge Used by Jazz Musicians, In the Proceedings of the International Computer Music Conference, 285-288, Montreal.

Ramalho, G & Ganascia, J.-G. 1994. The Role of Musical Memory in Creativity and Learning: a Study of Jazz Performance, In M. Smith, Smaill A. & Wiggins G. eds., *Music Education: an Artificial Intelligence Perspective*, Springer-Verlag, London.

Ramalho, G. & Pachet, F. 1994. What is Needed to Bridge the Gap Between Real Book and Real Jazz Performance?, in the Proceedings of the Fourth International Conference on Music Perception and Cognition, Liège.

Rowe, J. & Partridge, D. 1993. Creativity: a survey of AI approaches, *Artificial Intelligence Review* 7, 43-70, Kluwer Academic Pub.

Slade, S. 1991. Case-Based Reasoning: a Research Paradigm, *AI Magazine*, Spring, 42-55.

Sloboda, J., 1985. *The Musical Mind: The Cognitive Psychology of Music*, Oxford University Press, New York.

Steedman, M. 1984. A Generative Grammar for Jazz Chord Sequences, *Music Perception*, Vol. 1, No. 2, University of California Press.

Vincinanza, S. & Prietula, M. 1989. A Computational Model of Musical Creativity, In Proceedings of the Second Workshop on Artificial Intelligence and Music, 21-25, IJCAI, Detroit.

The Synergy of Music Theory and AI:
Learning Multi-Level Expressive Interpretation

Gerhard Widmer

Department of Medical Cybernetics and Artificial Intelligence, University of Vienna, and
Austrian Research Institute for Artificial Intelligence,
Schottengasse 3, A-1010 Vienna, Austria
gerhard@ai.univie.ac.at

Abstract

The paper presents interdisciplinary research in the intersection of AI (machine learning) and Art (music). We describe an implemented system that learns expressive interpretation of music pieces from performances by human musicians. The problem, shown to be very difficult in the introduction, is solved by combining insights from music theory with a new machine learning algorithm. Theoretically founded knowledge about music perception is used to transform the original learning problem to a more abstract level where relevant regularities become apparent. Experiments with performances of Chopin waltzes are presented; the results indicate musical understanding and the ability to learn a complex task from very little training data. As the system's domain knowledge is based on two established theories of tonal music, the results also have interesting implications for music theory.

Introduction

Suppose you were confronted with the following task: you are shown a few diagrams like the one in figure 1, consisting of a sequence of symbols and a graph on top of these which associates a precise numeric value with each symbol. You are then given a new sequence of symbols (see bottom half of fig. 1) and asked to draw the 'correct' corresponding graph, or at least a 'sensible' one. Impossible, you think? Indeed, in this form the problem is extremely hard. It is radically underconstrained, it is not at all clear what the relevant context is (that a single symbol itself does not determine the associated numeric value is clear because the same symbol is associated with different values in fig. 1), and the problem is exacerbated by the fact that the examples are extremely noisy: the same example, if presented twice, will never look exactly the same.

This paper will explain why people are nevertheless capable of solving this problem and will present a computer program that effectively learns this task. The

*This research was sponsored in part by the Austrian *Fonds zur Förderung der wissenschaftlichen Forschung (FWF)*. Financial support for the Austrian Research Institute for Artificial Intelligence is provided by the Austrian Federal Ministry for Science and Research.

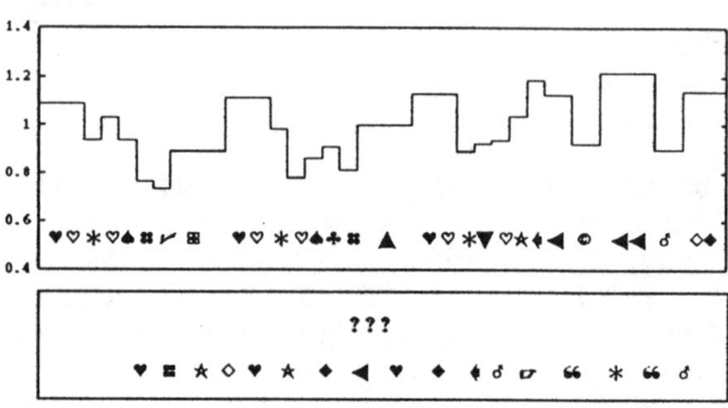

Figure 1: A training example and a new problem.

problem, as the next section will reveal, comes from the domain of tonal music, and it will be solved by combining music-theoretic insights and theories with a hybrid machine learning algorithm. The result is an operational system that learns to solve a complex task from few training examples and produces artistically interesting (if not genuinely original) results. The main points we would like the reader to take home from this are on a general methodological level. This is an interdisciplinary project, and as such it has implications for both AI/machine learning and musicology.

From the point of view of machine learning, the project demonstrates an alternative (though not novel) approach to knowledge-intensive learning. Instead of learning directly from the input data and using the available domain knowledge to guide the induction process, as it is done in many knowledge-based learning systems—e.g., FOCL (Pazzani & Kibler 1992)—we use the domain knowledge (music theory) to restructure and transform the raw input data, to define more abstract target concepts, and to lift the entire problem to a more abstract level where relevant structures and regularities become apparent.

From the point of view of musicology, the interesting result is not only that expressive interpretation can indeed be learned by a machine (at least to a certain degree). The project also indicates that AI and in particular machine learning can provide useful techniques for the empirical validation of general music theories. Our system is based on two well-known

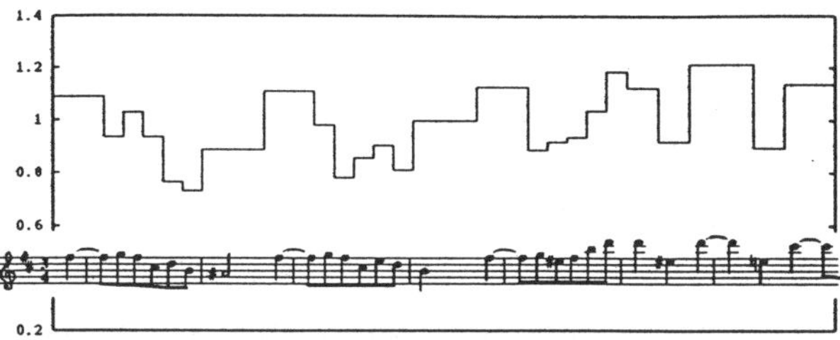

Figure 2: The problem as perceived by a human learner

theories of tonal music (Lerdahl & Jackendoff 1983; Narmour 1977), and an analysis of the learning results provides empirical evidence for the relevance and adequacy of the constructs postulated by these theories.

A closer look at the problem

To return to the abstract problem in the previous section, why is it that people are able to tackle it successfully? There are two simple reasons: (1) the problem is presented to them in a different form, and (2) they possess a lot of knowledge that they bring to bear on the learning task (mostly unconsciously). To unveil the secret, the people learning this task are music students learning to play some instrument, and to them the problem presents itself roughly as shown in fig. 2. The meaningless symbols from fig. 1 are now the notes of a melody (incidentally, the beginning of Chopin's Waltz Op.69 no.2), and the graph on top plots the relative *loudness* with which each note has been played by a performer. What students learn from such examples is general principles of *expressive performance*: they learn to play pieces of music in an expressive way by continuously varying loudness or tempo, and they learn that by looking at the score as written and simultaneously listening to real performances of the piece. That is, the graph is *heard* rather than seen.

Generally, expressive interpretation is the art of 'shaping' a piece of music by varying certain musical parameters during playing, e.g., speeding up or slowing down, growing louder or softer, placing micro-pauses between events, etc. In this project, we concentrate on the two most important expression dimensions, *dynamics* (variations of loudness) and *rubato* (variations of local tempo). The relevant musical terms are *crescendo* vs. *diminuendo* (increase vs. decrease in loudness) and *accelerando* vs. *ritardando* (speeding up vs. slowing down), respectively. Our program will be shown the melodies of pieces as written and recordings of these melodies as played expressively by a human pianist. From that it will have to learn general principles of expressive interpretation.

Why should the learning problem be easier when presented in the form of fig. 2 rather than fig. 1? The difference between the two representations is that the latter offers us an *interpretation framework* for the symbols; we recognize notes, we recognize patterns (e.g., measures, ascending or descending lines, etc.),

we know that the note symbols encode attributes like duration, tone height, etc. When listening to the piece, we hear more than just single, unrelated notes—we hear the rhythmic beat, we hear groups that belong together, we hear melodic, rhythmic, and other patterns, and we associate the rise and fall of loudness with these groups and patterns. In short, we have additional *knowledge* about the task, which helps us to *interpret* the input.

Our learning program will also need such knowledge if it is to effectively learn expressive interpretation from examples. Music theory can tell us more precisely what the relevant knowledge might be.

What music theory tells us

Expressive performance has only fairly recently become a topic of central interest for cognitive musicology. There is no general theory of expression, but two assumptions are widely agreed upon among theorists, and these form the basis of our approach:

1. Expression is not arbitrary, but highly correlated with the *structure* of music as it is perceived by performers and listeners. In fact, expression is a means for the performer to emphasize certain structures and maybe de-emphasize others, thus conducing the listener to 'hearing' the piece as the performer understands it.

2. Expression is a *multi-level* phenomenon. More precisely, musical structure can be perceived at various levels, local and global, and each such structure may require or be associated with its own expressive shape. Structures and expressive shapes may be nested hierarchically, but they can also overlap, reinforce each other, or conflict.

The notion of *musical structure* is fundamental. It is a fact that listeners do not perceive a presented piece of music as a simple sequence of unrelated events, but that they immediately and automatically interpret it in structural terms. For instance, they segment the flow of events into 'chunks' (motives, groups, phrases, etc.); they intuitively hear the *metrical structure* of the music, i.e., identify a regular alternation of strong and weak beats and know where to tap their foot. Linearly ascending or descending melodic lines are often heard as one group, and so are typical rhythmic figures and other combinations of notes. Many more structural dimensions can be identified, and it has been shown that acculturated listeners extract these structures in a highly consistent manner, and mostly without being aware of it. This is the (unconscious) musical 'knowledge' that listeners and musicians automatically bring to bear when listening to or playing a piece.

What music theory tells us, then, is that the level of individual notes is not adequate, neither for understanding expressive performances, nor for learning. Analyzing an expressive performance without structural understanding would mean trying to make sense of figure 1 without being able to interpret the symbols. Expression decisions are not a function of single notes, but usually refer to larger-scale structures (e.g., 'emphasize this phrase by slowing down towards the end'). That is the level on which the decision rules should be represented; it is also the level on which musicians would discuss a performance.

The design of our system has been guided by these insights. We have selected two well-known theories of tonal music—Lerdahl & Jackendoff's (1983) *Generative Theory of Tonal Music* and Narmour's (1977) *Implication-Realization Model*—as the conceptual basis. Both theories postulate certain types of structures that are claimed to be perceivable by human listeners. These types of structures provide the abstract vocabulary with which the system will describe the music. As the structures are of widely varying scope—some consist of a few notes only, others may span several measures—and as expressive patterns will be linked to musical structures, the system will learn to recognize and apply expression at multiple levels.

From theoretical insights to a strategy

The *raw training examples* as they are presented to the system consist of a sequence of notes (the melody of a piece) with associated numeric values that specify the exact loudness and tempo (actual vs. notated duration), respectively, applied to each note by the performer. However, as observed above, the note level is not adequate. We have thus implemented a *transformation strategy*. The system is equipped with a preprocessing component that embodies its knowledge about structural music perception. It takes the raw training examples and transforms them into a more abstract representation that expresses roughly the types of structures human listeners might hear in the music. In this step also the target concepts for the learner are transformed to the appropriate level of granularity by identifying relevant chunks and associating them with higher-level patterns in the expression (dynamics and tempo) curves. Learning then proceeds at this abstraction level, and the resulting expression rules are also formulated at the structure level. Likewise, when given a new piece to play, the system will first analyze it and transform it into an abstract form and then apply the learned rules to produce an expressive interpretation.

Transforming the problem

The problem transformation step proceeds in two stages. The system first performs a musical analysis of the given melody. A set of analysis routines, based on selected parts of the theories by Lerdahl and Jackendoff (1983) and Narmour (1977), identifies various structures in the melody that might be heard as units or chunks by a listener or musician. The result is a rich annotation of the melody with identified structures. Fig. 3 exemplifies the result of this step with

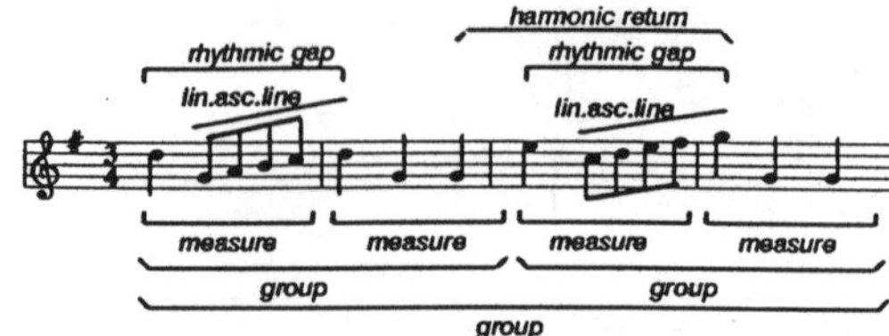

Figure 3: Structural interpretation of part of minuet.

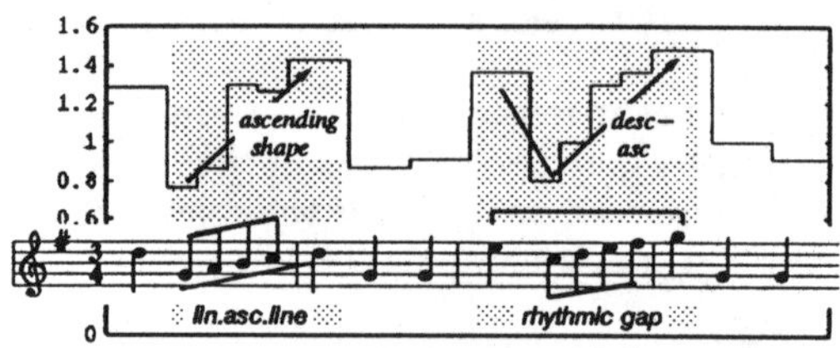

Figure 4: Two of the expressive shapes found.

an excerpt from a simple Bach minuet. The perceptual chunks identified here are four *measures* heard as rhythmic units, three *groups* heard as melodic units or "phrases" on two different levels, two *linearly ascending melodic lines*, two rhythmic patterns called *rhythmic gap fills* (a concept derived from Narmour's theory), and a large-scale pattern labelled *harmonic departure and return*, which essentially marks the points where the melody moves from a stable to a less stable harmony and back again. It is evident from this example that the structures are of different scope, some completely contained within others, some overlapping.

In the second step, the relevant abstract target concepts for the learner are identified. The system tries to find prototypical *shapes* in the given expression curves (dynamics and tempo) that can be associated with these structures. Prototypical shapes are rough trends that can be identified in the curve. The system distinguishes five kinds of shapes: `even_level` (no recognizable rising or falling tendency of the curve in the time span covered by the structure), `ascending` (an ascending tendency from the beginning to the end of the time span), `descending`, `asc_desc` (first ascending up to a certain point, then descending), and `desc_asc`. The system selects those shapes that minimize the deviation between the actual curve and an idealized shape defined by straight lines. The result of this analysis step are pairs <*musical structure, expressive shape*> that will be given to the learner as training examples.

Fig. 4 illustrates this step for the dynamics curve associated with the Bach example (derived from a performance by the author). We look at two of the structures found in fig. 3: the ascending melodic line in measures 1–2 has been associated with the shape `ascending`, as the curve shows a clear ascending (*crescendo*) tendency in this part of the recording. And the 'rhythmic gap fill' pattern in measures 3–4 has been played with a `desc_asc` (*decrescendo – crescendo*) shape.

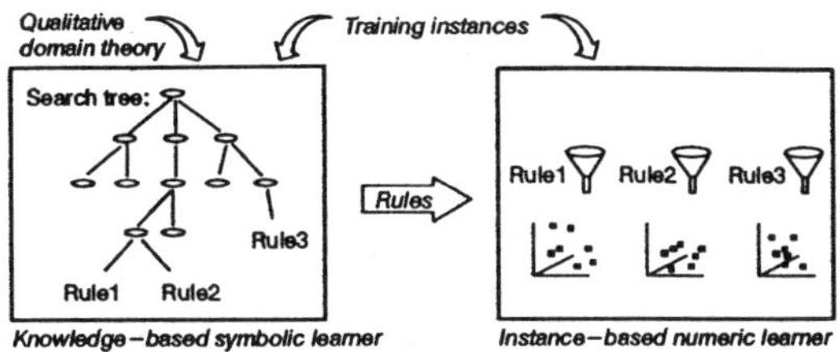

Figure 5: Schema of learning algorithm IBL-SMART.

Learning expression rules: IBL-SMART

The results of the transformation phase are passed on to a learning component. Each pair *<musical structure, expressive shape>* is a training example. Each such example is further described by a quantitative characterization of the shape (the precise loudness/tempo values (relative to the average loudness and tempo of the piece) of the curve at the extreme points of the shape) and a description, in terms of music-theoretic features, of the structure and the notes at its extreme points (e.g., note duration, harmonic function, metrical strength, ...). Some of these descriptors are symbolic (nominal), others numeric.

In abstract terms, the problem is then to learn a numeric function: given the description of a musical structure in terms of symbolic and numeric features, the learned rules must decide (1) which shape to apply and (2) the precise numeric dimensions of the shape (e.g., at which loudness level to start, say, a crescendo line, and at which level to end it).

The learning algorithm used in our system is IBL-SMART (Widmer 1993). IBL-SMART is a multistrategy learner in two respects: at the top level, it integrates symbolic and numeric learning; and the symbolic component integrates various plausible reasoning strategies so that it can utilize a given *domain theory* (possibly incomplete and imprecise/qualitative) to bias the induction process.

The second aspect is not relevant here, as we have no explicit domain theory—the musical knowledge is used in the preprocessing stage. The integration of symbolic and numeric learning is what is required here, and that is realized in a quite straightforward way in IBL-SMART: the program consists of two components (see fig. 5), a symbolic rule learner and an instance-based numeric learner. The symbolic component is a non-incremental algorithm that learns DNF rules by growing an explicit discrimination or refinement tree in a top-down fashion. The basic search strategy is inspired by the ML-SMART framework (Bergadano & Giordana 1988): a best-first search, guided by coverage and simplicity criteria, is conducted until a set of hypotheses is found that covers a sufficient number of positive examples. In our case, the *target concepts* for the symbolic learner are the different expressive shapes, i.e., it learns to determine the appropriate general shape to be applied to a musical structure.

The numeric component of IBL-SMART is an instance-based learner that in effect builds up *numeric interpolation tables* for each learned symbolic rule to predict precise numeric values. It stores the instances with their numeric attribute values and can predict the target values for some new situation by numeric interpolation over known instances. The connection between these two components is as follows: each rule (conjunctive hypothesis) learned by the symbolic component describes a subset of the instances; these are assumed to represent one particular subtype of the concept to be learned. All the instances covered by a rule are given to the instance-based learner to be stored together in a separate instance space. Predicting the target value for some new situation then involves matching the situation against the symbolic rules and using only those numeric instance spaces for prediction whose associated rules are satisfied. The symbolic learner effectively partitions the space for the instance-based method, which then constructs highly specialized numeric predictors. The basic idea is somewhat reminiscent of the concept of *regression trees* (Breiman *et al.* 1984). For a more detailed presentation of the algorithm, the reader is referred to (Widmer 1993).

Applying learned rules to new problems

When given the score of a new piece (melody) to play expressively, the system again first transforms it to the abstract structural level by performing its musical analysis. For each of the musical structures found, the learned rules are consulted to suggest an appropriate expressive shape (for dynamics and rubato). The interpolation tables associated with the matching rules are used to compute the precise numeric details of the shape. Starting from an even shape for the entire piece (i.e., equal loudness and tempo for all notes), expressive shapes are applied to the piece in sorted order, from shortest to longest. That is, expression patterns associated with small, local structures are applied first, and more global forms are overlayed later. Expressive shapes are overlayed over already applied ones by averaging the respective dynamics and rubato values. The result is an expressive interpretation of the piece that pays equal regard to local and global expression patterns, thus combining micro- and macro-structures.

Experimental Results

This section briefly presents some results achieved with waltzes by Frédéric Chopin. The training pieces were five rather short excerpts (about 20 measures each) from the three waltzes Op.64 no.2, Op.69 no.2 (see fig.2), and Op.70 no.3, played by the author on an electronic piano and recorded via MIDI. The results of learning were then tested by having the system play other excerpts from Chopin waltzes. Here, we can only show the results in graphic form.

As an example, fig. 6 shows the system's performance of the beginning of the waltz Op.18 after learning from the five training pieces. The plots show

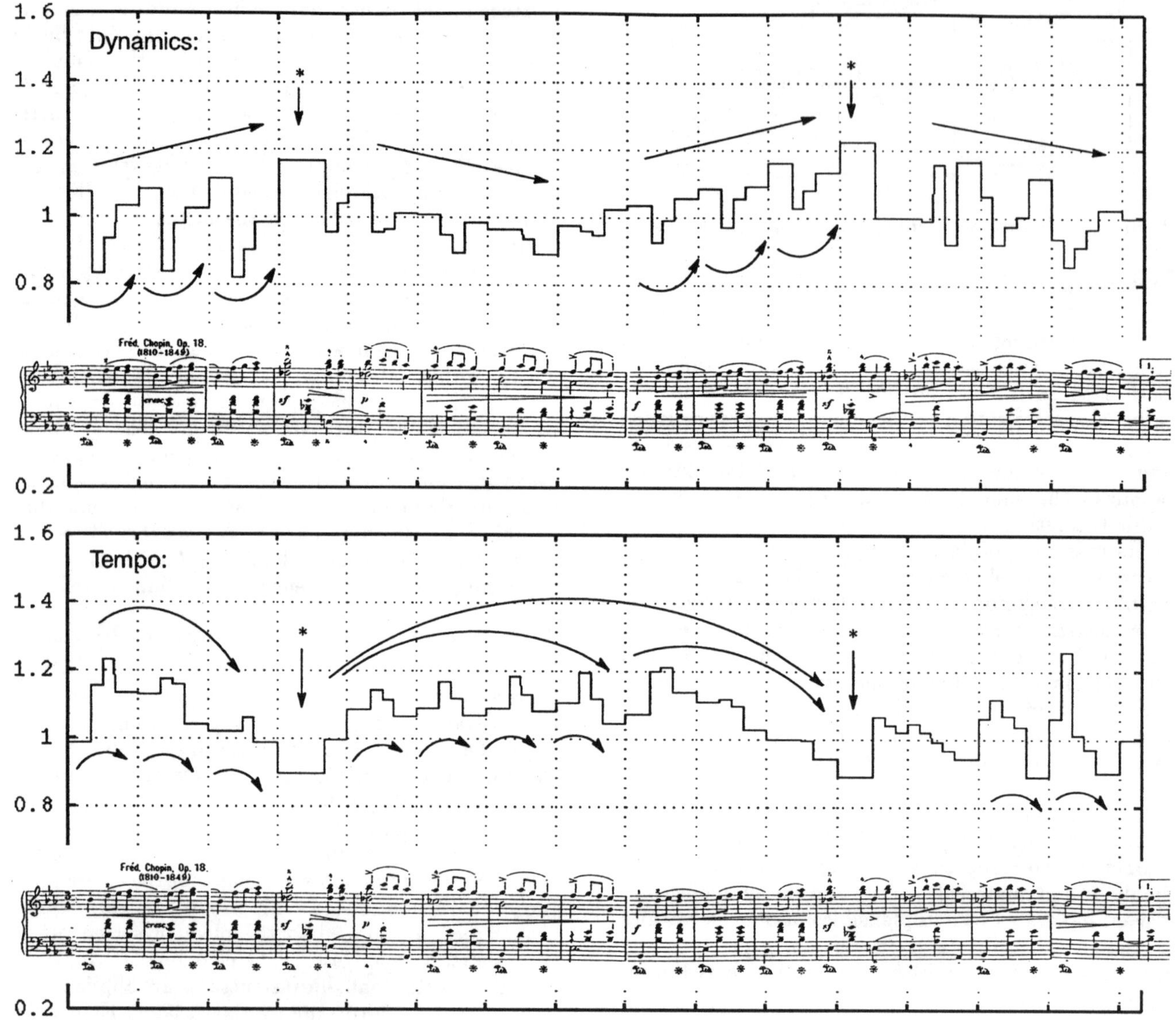

Figure 6: Chopin Waltz op.18, E♭ major, as played by learner: *dynamics* (top) and *tempo* (bottom).

the loudness (*dynamics*) and tempo variations, respectively. A value of 1.0 means average loudness or tempo, higher values mean that a note has been played louder or faster, respectively. The arrows have been added by the author to indicate various structural regularities in the performance. Note that while the written musical score contains some explicit expression marks added by the composer (or editor) — e.g., commands like *cresc*, *sf* or *p* and graphical symbols calling for large-scale crescendo and decrescendo — the system was not aware of these; it was given the notes only.

It is difficult to analyze the results in a quantitative way. One could compare the system's performance of a piece with a human performance of the same piece and somehow measure the difference between the two curves. However, the results would be rather meaning-less. For one thing, there is no single correct way of playing a piece. And second, relative errors or deviations cannot simply be added: some notes and structures are more important than others, and thus errors are more or less grave.

In a qualitative analysis, the results look and sound musically convincing. The graphs suggest a clear understanding of musical structure and a sensible shaping of these structures, both at micro and macro levels. At the macro level (arrows above the graphs), for instance, both the dynamics and the tempo curve mirror the four-phrase structure of the piece. In the dynamics dimension, the first and third phrase are played with a recognizable crescendo culminating at the end point of the phrases (the B♭ at the beginning of measures 4 and 12). In the tempo dimension, phrases (at least the first three) are shaped by giving them a roughly parabolic shape—speeding up at the beginning, slowing down towards the end. This agrees well with theories of rubato published in the music literature (Todd 1989).

At lower levels, the most obvious phenomenon is the phrasing of the individual measures, which creates the distinct waltz 'feel': in the dynamics dimension, the first and metrically strongest note of each measure is emphasized in almost all cases by playing it louder than the rest of the measure, and additional melodic considerations (like rising or falling melodic lines) determine the fine structure of each measure. In the tempo dimension, measures are shaped by playing the first note slightly longer than the following ones and then again slowing down towards the end of the measure.

The most striking aspect is the close correspondence between the system's variations and Chopin's explicit marks in the score (which were not visible to the system!). The reader trained in reading music notation may appreciate how the system's dynamics curve closely parallels Chopin's various crescendo and decrescendo markings and also the *p* (*piano*) command in measure 5. Two notes were deemed particularly worthy of stress by Chopin and were explicitly annotated with *sf* (*sforzato*): the Bb's at the beginning of the fourth and twelfth measures. Elegantly enough, our program came to the same conclusion and emphasized them most extremely by playing them louder and longer than any other note in the piece; the corresponding places are marked by arrows with asterisks in fig. 6.

Experiments with other Chopin waltzes produced results of similar quality. Preliminary results with songs by Franz Schubert are also encouraging, but suggest that an overabundance of musical structures might degrade the quality somewhat. This indicates the need for a more refined shape combining strategy.

Summary and Discussion

This paper has presented a system that learns to solve a complex musical task from a surprisingly small set of examples and produces artistically interesting results. The essence of the method is (1) a theory-based transformation of the learning problem to an appropriate abstraction level and (2) a hybrid symbolic/numeric learning algorithm that learns both symbolic decision rules and predictors of precise numeric values.

What really made the problem solvable—and this is the main point we would like to make—is the interdisciplinary and principled approach: combining machine learning techniques with a solid analysis of the task domain and using existing theories of the domain as a sound basis. The result is a system that is of interest to both fields involved, machine learning and music.

From the point of view of machine learning, using available domain knowledge to transform the learning problem to an abstraction level that makes hidden regularities visible is a viable alternative to more 'standard' knowledge-based learning, where learning proceeds at the level of the original data, and the knowledge is used to bias induction towards plausible generalizations. This approach has also been advocated by a number of other researchers, most notably (Flann & Dietterich 1989). That does not preclude the additional use of domain knowledge for guiding the induction process. Indeed, though the performances produced by our system are musically sensible, the rules it constructs do not always correspond to our musical intuition. To further guide the system towards interpretable rules we plan to supply it with a partial *domain theory* that specifies relevant dependencies between various domain parameters. This will require no changes to the system itself, because IBL-SMART is capable of effectively taking advantage of incomplete and imprecise domain theories (Widmer 1993).

For musicology, the project is of interest because its results lend empirical support to two quite recent general theories of tonal music. In particular, the role of Narmour's music theory is strengthened by our results. Some music researchers claim that grouping (phrase) structure is *the* essential carrier of information for expressive phrasing. An analysis of the results of our system, however, suggests that melodic surface patterns derived from Narmour's theory are equally important and determine or explain to a large extent the microstructure of expression. We would generally propose our methodology (using established artistic or other theories as a basis for programs that learn from real data) as a fruitful empirical validation strategy.

References

Bergadano, F., and Giordana, A. 1988. A knowledge intensive approach to concept induction. In *Proceedings of the Fifth International Conference on Machine Learning*. Ann Arbor, MI.

Breiman, L.; Friedman, J.; Olshen, R.; and C. Stone, C. 1984. *Classification and Regression Trees*. Belmont, CA: Wadsworth.

Flann, N., and Dietterich, T. 1989. A study of explanation-based methods for inductive learning. *Machine Learning* 4(2):187–226.

Lerdahl, F., and Jackendoff, R. 1983. *A Generative Theory of Tonal Music*. Cambridge, MA: MIT Press.

Narmour, E. 1977. *Beyond Schenkerism*. Chicago University Press.

Pazzani, M., and Kibler, D. 1992. The utility of knowledge in inductive learning. *Machine Learning* 9(1):57–94.

Todd, N. 1989. Towards a cognitive theory of expression: The performance and perception of rubato. *Contemporary Music Review* 4:405–416.

Widmer, G. 1993. Plausible explanations and instance-based learning in mixed symbolic/numeric domains. In *Proceedings of the 2nd Intl. Workshop on Multistrategy Learning*. Harper's Ferry, W.VA.

Knowledge Representation for Video

Marc Davis
Interval Research Corporation
1801-C Page Mill Road
Palo Alto, CA 94304
davis@interval.com

Abstract

Current computing systems are just beginning to enable the computational manipulation of temporal media like video and audio. Because of the opacity of these media they must be represented in order to be manipulable according to their contents. Knowledge representation techniques have been implicitly designed for representing the physical world and its textual representations. Temporal media pose unique problems and opportunities for knowledge representation which challenge many of its assumptions about the structure and function of what is represented. The semantics and syntax of temporal media require representational designs which employ fundamentally different conceptions of space, time, identity, and action. In particular, the effect of the syntax of video sequences on the semantics of video shots demands a representational design which can clearly articulate the differences between the context-dependent and context-independent semantics of video data. This paper outlines the theoretical foundations for designing representations of video, discusses *Media Streams*, an implemented system for video representation and retrieval, and critiques related efforts in this area.

Introduction

The central problem in the creation of robust and scalable systems for manipulating video information lies in representing video content. Currently, content providers possess large archives of film and video for which they lack sufficient tools for search and retrieval. For the types of applications that will be developed in the near future (interactive television, personalized news, video on demand, etc.) these archives will remain a largely untapped resource, unless we are able to access their contents. Without a way of accessing video information in terms of its content, a hundred hours of video is less useful than one.

Given the current state of the art in machine vision and signal processing, we cannot now, and probably will not be able to for a long time, have machines "watch" and understand the content of digital video archives for us. Unlike text, for which we have developed sophisticated parsing and indexing technologies, and which is accessible to processing in various structured forms (ASCII, RTF, PostScript, SGML, HTML), video is still largely opaque. Some headway has been made in this area. Algorithms for the automatic annotation of scene breaks are becoming more robust and enhanced to handle special cases such as fades (Zhang, Kankanhalli, & Smoliar 1993). Work on camera motion detection is close to enabling reliable automatic classification of pans and zooms (Teodosio 1992; Tonomura, Akutsu, Otsuji, & Sadakata 1993; Ueda, Miyatake, Sumino, & Nagasaka 1993). Researchers are also making progress in the automatic segmentation and tagging of audio data by means of parsing the audio track for pauses and voice intensities (Arons 1993), as well as specialized audio parsers for music, laughter, and other highly distinct acoustic phenomena (Hawley 1993). Advances in signal separation and speech recognition will also go a long way to automating the parsing of the content of the audio track. Yet this information alone does not enable the creation of a sufficient representation of video content to support content-based retrieval and manipulation. Signal-based parsing and segmentation technologies must be combined with representations of the higher level structure and function of video data in order to enable machines to make inferences about video content.

Why is video representation an important research area for AI? Besides the pragmatic value of this work for the information and entertainment industries, its relevance extends to the enabling of a broad-based shift in the media of human communication and knowledge. We are currently in a crucial phase of a second "Gutenberg shift" (McLuhan 1962) in which video is becoming a ubiquitous data type not only for viewing (i.e., reading) but for daily communication and composition (i.e., writing). This shift will only be possible when we can construct representations of video which enable us to parse, index, browse, search, retrieve, manipulate, and (re)sequence video according to representations of its content.

Video representation also requires the rethinking of traditional approaches to knowledge representation and story generation in AI. The generation problem has been framed as the problem of constructing a media independent engine for creating sequences of concepts or events which then guide synthesis processes in different media (usually text (Schank & Riesbeck 1981), occasionally graphics (Feiner & McKeown 1990; Kahn 1979)). With recorded video, the generation problem is recast as a representation and retrieval problem. The task, as in editing together found footage, is a matter of creating media specific representations of video which facilitate the retrieval and resequencing of exiting content. This difference in approach has fundamental ramifications for representational design. It is not merely a matter of adapting media independent representations to the specific properties of video, but of designing representations whose basic ontology and inference mechanisms capture the specific semantic and syntactic properties of video.

Therefore, the task which confronts artificial intelligence researchers in this area is to gather insights from disciplines that have studied the structure and function of video data and to use these insights in the design of new representations for video which are adequate to the task of representing the medium. Film analysis and theory have developed a useful repertoire of analytical strategies for describing the semantics and syntax of video data. These insights inform the following theoretical discussion and representational design.

Representing Video

Current paradigms of video representation are drawn from practices which arose primarily out of "single-use" video applications. In single-use applications, video is shot, annotated, and edited for a given movie, video, or television program. Representations are created for one given use of the video data. There do exist certain cases today, like network news archives, film archives, and stock footage houses, in which video is used multiple times, but the level of granularity of the representation and the semantics of the representations do not support a wide reusability of video content. The challenge is to create representations which support "multi-use" applications of video. These are applications in which video may be dynamically resegmented, retrieved, and resequenced on the fly by a wide range of users *other than those who originally created the data.*

Most attempts to represent video content utilize representations developed for other media. Most commercially used representations apply techniques used for representing text (predominantly keywords or full text annotation); AI-influenced representations apply techniques developed for representing the physical world (Guha 1994; Guha & Lenat 1994; Lenat & Guha 1990) or for representing abstract, supposedly media-independent concepts (Schank 1993; Schank & Rieger 1974). All of these attempts neglect to consider that video as a data type may have unique properties which may themselves need to explicitly represented and which may render techniques developed for other media inadequate.

Stream-Based Representation of Temporal Media

In designing a representation of video content we must think about the structure of what is being represented. A video camera produces a temporal stream of image and sound data represented as a stream of frames played back at a certain rate—normally 30 frames per second. This stream of frames has higher level structures of organization commonly referred to as follows: a stream of frames recorded between the time in which the recording device is turned on and turned off is a *shot*; a temporal concatenation of shots is referred to as a *sequence*; and a sequence of shots all sharing the same spatial location is often referred to as a *scene* (Bordwell & Thompson 1990).

In most representations of video content, a stream of video frames is segmented into units called *clips* whose boundaries often, but do not necessarily, coincide with shot or scene boundaries. Current tools for annotating video content used in film production, television production, and multimedia, add descriptors (often keywords) to clips. There is a significant problem with this approach. By taking an incoming video stream, segmenting it into various clips, and then representing the content of those clips, a clip-based representation imposes a *fixed segmentation* on the content of the video stream. To illustrate this point, imagine a camera recording a sequence of 100 frames. Traditionally, one or more parts of the stream of frames is segmented into clips which are then respectively annotated by attaching descriptors. The clip is a fixed segmentation of the video stream that is separated from its context of origin and enforces only one segmentation of the original data.

In a stream-based representation, the stream of frames is left intact and is represented by multi-layered annotations with precise time indexes (beginning and ending points in the video stream). The result is that this representation makes annotation pay off—the richer the annotation, the more numerous the possible segmentations of the video stream.

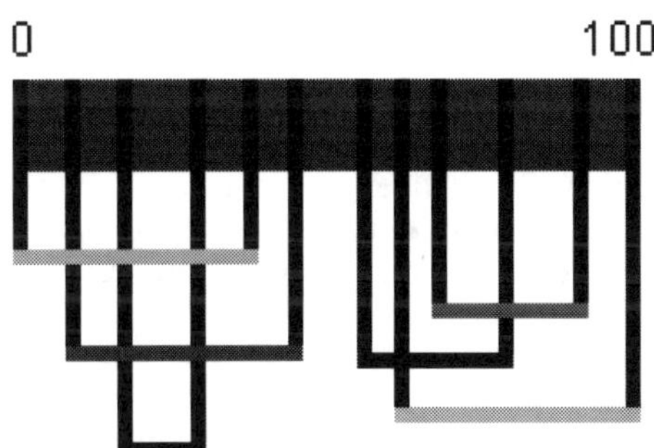

The Stream of 100 Frames of Video with 6 Annotations Resulting in *66* Possible Segmentations of the Stream

Clips change from being fixed segmentations of the video stream, to being the results of retrieval queries based on annotations of the video stream. In short, in addressing the challenges of representing video *what we need are representations which make clips, not representations of clips.*

Video Syntax and Semantics

In attempting to create a representation of video content, an understanding of the semantics and syntax of video information is a primary concern. For video, it is essential to clearly distinguish between context-dependent and context-independent semantics. Syntax, the sequencing of individual video shots, creates new semantics which may not be present in any of the individual shots and which may supersede or contravene their existing semantics. This is evidenced by a basic property of the medium which enables not only the repurposing of video data (the resequencing of video shots taken from their original contexts and used to different ends in new contexts), but its basic syntactic functionality: the creation of meaningful sequences through concatenating visual and auditory representations of discontinuous times and discontiguous spaces. Eisenstein described this property as *montage* (Eisenstein 1947).

The early experimental evidence for effects of the syntax of shot combination on the semantics of individual shots was established by the Soviet cinematographer Lev Kuleshov early in this century (Isenhour 1975; Kuleshov 1974). The classic example of the "Kuleshov Effect" was evidenced by the following experiment. The following sequence was shown to an audience: a long take in close-up of the Russian actor Mozhukin's expressionlessly neutral face — cut — a bowl of steaming soup — cut — the same face of the actor — cut — a woman in a coffin — cut — the same face of the actor — cut — a child playing with a toy bear— cut — the same face of the actor. When audience members were asked what they saw, they said, "Oh, he was hungry, then he was sad, then he was happy." The same exact image of the actor's face was used in each of the three short sequences. What the Kuleshov Effect reveals is that the semantics of video information is highly determined by what comes before and what comes after any given shot.

Because of the impact of the syntax of video sequences on the semantics of video shots, any indexing or representational scheme for video content needs to explain how the semantics of video changes by resequencing and recombination. The challenge is then twofold: to describe what features or annotations survive recombination and to describe how the features which do not survive emerge from those which do.

The challenge of representing the syntax dependent and syntax independent semantic features of video content has a deep similarity to a core problem in knowledge representation: the frame problem (McCarthy & Hayes 1969). The important difference between approaches to solving the frame problem in AI and the demands of creating a knowledge representation for video lies in the fact that video is itself a representation of the world with its own ontological properties and its own constraints on the construction and maintenance of continuity through the montage of shots. In a word, video has not only its own semantics and syntax, but its own "common sense" which previous approaches to common sense knowledge, temporal, and action representation have yet to address.

Ontological Issues in Video Representation

Space

Through sequencing of shots video enables the construction of many types of spaces: representations of spaces which have real world correlates (real spaces); spaces which do not but could exist in the physical world (artificial spaces); and even spaces which cannot exist in the physical world as we commonly experience it (impossible spaces). In thinking about the first two classes of spaces which can be constructed cinematically (real and artificial spaces) an important distinction can be made among three types of spatial locations: the actual spatial location of the recording of the video; the spatial location which the viewer of the video infers when the video is viewed independent of any other shots; and the spatial location which the viewer of the video infers when it is viewed in a given sequence.

For example, imagine a shot filmed in a dark alley in Paris on October 22, 1983, from 4:15 am to 4:17 am. The actual location of recording may be in a given street in a certain part of the city and could be expressed in terms of an exact longitude, latitude, and altitude. The shot we are imagining has no distinguishing features which mark it as a particular Parisian street or as a Parisian street at all. Independent of any sequence it appears as a "generic dark alley in a city." With the use of a preceding establishing shot, for example an aerial view of New York City at night, the shot now has the inferable spatial location of "a dark alley in New York City." Therefore, representations of the spatial location of a video must represent the difference between a video's actual recorded spatial location and its visually inferable ones.

The geometry of video spaces and the objects within them also have unique properties. The location of objects within the video frame can be represented by a hybrid 2 dimensional and 3 dimensional representation. Since video spaces can be constructed and concatenated into irreal geometries they have only a relational 3 dimensionality in which the geometry is best expressed in terms of *relative* as opposed to *absolute* positions. Therefore, 3 dimensional spatial relations are on the order of "in front of," or "on top of," etc. opposed to a given XYZ coordinate. Since the 3 dimensional world of the video is itself represented in a 2 dimensional projection, all objects in the 3 dimensional space of the recorded/constructed world have a location in the 2 dimensional plane of the screen. The 2 dimensional screen position of an object is a crucial aspect of its spatial representation and composition which is used by filmmakers to create both aesthetic order (in terms of balanced compositions as in photography) and cognitive order (in terms of the "rules" of Western filmmaking for the construction of space through action, chief among them being the "180 degree rule" which results is the well-known shot reverse shot of two person dialogue crosscutting).

Identity

Identity of persons and objects is complex in video. A considerable portion of the cinematic craft is devoted to the construction and maintenance of coherent identities for characters and locales. This is achieved thorough the discipline of "continuity." Continuity is the process whereby salient details of a character's and a locale's appearance remain in continuity from shot to shot (i.e., remain constant when appropriate, change when appropriate). For example, if an actor is wearing a black hat in one shot and not in the next, if there is no inferable explanation for the absence of the hat "continuity" is said to have been broken. The effort to maintain continuity is deeply related to the frame problem in AI. But because video is not the physical world, but a systematic representation of it, continuity can be established and maintained by inferences not found in common sense reasoning.

Interesting examples center on techniques for maintaining the continuity of the identity of a character in a narrative film. A character can literally be "assembled" out of the parts of other characters at various levels of granularity. Kuleshov is well known for constructing a woman character by editing together shots of different body parts of several different women. The identity of a character between shots may rely on any combination of: role (which is comprised of costume, action, and location) and actor. In a demo reel from the stock footage house Archive Films, scenes of several different actors are cut together to make up the central character of a business man traveling around on a busy workday (Archive Films 1992). Continuity of identity can cut across roles and be established by the continuity of the actor. Shots of the same actor taken from various performances of different characters can be edited together to form one character. Imagine, for example, a story about a killer cyborg who goes to Mars which could be created by editing together several of Arnold Schwarzenegger's films (The Terminator and Total Recall).

Action

The central problem for representing temporal media is the representation of dynamic events. For video in particular, the challenge is to come up with techniques for representing and visualizing the complex structure of the actions of characters, objects, and cameras. A representation of cinematic action for video retrieval and repurposing needs to focus on the granularity, reusability, and semantics of its units. In representing the action of bodies in space, the representation needs to support the hierarchical decomposition of its units both spatially and temporally.

Spatial decomposition is supported by a representation that hierarchically orders the bodies and their parts which participate in an action. For example, in a complex action like driving an automobile, the arms, head, eyes, and legs all function independently. Human body motions may be further categorized in two ways: abstract physical motions and conventionalized physical motions. Abstract physical motions can be represented according to articulations and rotations of joints. There are, however, many commonly occurring, complex patterns of human motion which seem to have cross-cultural importance (e.g., walking, sitting, eating, talking, etc.). Conventionalized body motions compactly represent motions which may involve multiple abstract body motions.

Temporal decomposition is enabled by a hierarchical organization of units such that longer sequences of action can be broken down into their temporal subabstractions all the way down to their atomic units. In the representational design of the CYC system, Lenat points out the need for more than a purely temporal representation of events that would include semantically relevant atomic units organized into various temporal patterns (repeated cycles, scripts, etc.) (Lenat & Guha 1990). For example, the atomic unit of "walking" would be "taking a step" which repeats cyclically. An atomic unit of "opening a jar" would be "turning the lid" (which itself could theoretically be broken down into smaller units—but much of the challenge of representing action is knowing what levels of granularity are useful).

In video, however, actions and their units do not have a fixed semantics because their meaning can shift as the video is recut and inserted into new sequences. For example, a shot of two people shaking hands, if positioned at the beginning of a sequence depicting a business meeting, could represent "greeting," if positioned at the end, the same shot could represent "agreeing." Video brings to our attention the effects of context and order on the meaning of represented action. In addition, the prospect of representing video for a global media archive brings forward an issue which traditional knowledge representation has largely ignored: cultural variance. The shot of two people shaking hands may signify greeting or agreeing in some cultures, but in others it does not. How are we to annotate shots of people bowing, shaking hands, waving hello and good-bye? The list goes on.

An answer to these issues is to represent the context-independent semantics of actions using physically-based description and to build up the representation of context-dependent semantics by creating a network of analogies between similar concrete action sequences which are themselves represented by physically-based descriptions.

Time

The representation of time in video requires the same distinction made for representing space: the difference between actual recorded time and the two types of visually inferable time.

A further important distinction in narrative video must be made between three different types of temporal duration (Bordwell & Thompson 1990):

- story duration (the duration of the events of the entire story as opposed to the particular story events selected for presentation in the video);
- plot duration (the duration of the particular events presented in the video);
- screen duration (the duration of the actual video as screened)

The full representation of these three types of duration is an open research problem.

Media Streams: A Research Prototype for Video Representation and Retrieval

Media Streams Overview

Over the past three years, members of the MIT Media Laboratory's Machine Understanding Group (Marc Davis with the assistance of Brian Williams and Golan Levin under the direction of Prof. Kenneth Haase) have been building a prototype for the representation and retrieval of video data. This system is called *Media Streams* (Davis 1993a; Davis 1993b). Media Streams is written in Macintosh Common Lisp and FRAMER (Haase 1993a), a persistent framework for media annotation and description that supports cross-platform knowledge representation and database functionality. Media Streams runs on an Apple Macintosh Quadra 950 with three high resolution, accelerated 24-bit color displays and uses Apple's QuickTime digital video format.

Media Streams makes use of all the insights outlined above about knowledge representation for video. With an iconic visual language designed for video representation, users create stream-based representations of video content. Media Streams utilizes a hierarchically structured semantic space of iconic primitives which are combined to form compound descriptors which are then used to create multi-layered, temporally indexed annotations of video content. These iconic primitives are grouped into descriptive categories designed for video representation and are structured to deal with the special semantic and syntactic properties of video data. The categories include: space, time, weather, characters, objects, character actions, object actions, relative position, screen position, recording medium, cinematography, shot transitions, and subjective thoughts about the material.

Media Streams' interface addresses two fundamental issues in video annotation and retrieval: creating and browsing the space of descriptors to be used in annotation and retrieval; and annotating, browsing, and retrieving video shots and sequences. Consequently, the system has two main interface components: the Icon Space (Fig. 1) and the Media Time Line (Fig. 2).

The Icon Space is the interface for the selection and compounding of the iconic descriptors in Media Streams. To date there are approximately 3000 iconic primitives. Through compounding, the base set of primitives can produce millions of unique expressions. In the Icon Space, users can create palettes of iconic descriptors for use in annotation and search. By querying the space of descriptors, users can dynamically group related iconic descriptors on-the-fly. These icon palettes enable users to reuse the descriptive effort of others. When annotating video, users can make use of related icons that other users have already created and used to annotate similar pieces of video. What enables the user to navigate and make use of a large number of primitives is the way the Icon Space organizes icons into cascading icon hierarchies. The Icon Space has two significant forms of organization for managing navigational and descriptive complexity: a cascading hierarchy with increasing specificity of primitives on subordinate levels; and compounding of hierarchically organized primitives across multiple axes of description.

The Media Time Line is the core browser and viewer of Media Streams (Fig. 2). It enables users to visualize video at multiple timescales simultaneously, to read and write multi-layered iconic annotations, and provides one consistent interface for annotation, browsing, query, and editing of video and audio data.

Media Streams Representational Structures

The underlying representation of video in Media Streams combines two distinct representations: a semantically structured generalization space of atemporal categorical descriptors; and an episodically structured relational space of temporal analogical descriptions. The atemporal semantic representation underlies the icon hierarchies in the Icon Space. The temporal episodic representation is built up when iconic descriptors are used to create annotations on Media Time Lines which establish specific relationships between these descriptions through combination and temporal order.

The semantic/episodic distinction was originated by researchers in human memory (Baddeley 1984; Tulving 1993) and made computational by Schank's work in dynamic memory (Schank 1982). Semantic memory can be thought of as the categorical or definitional part of human memory: remembering what a thing is and what class or category it belongs to. Episodic memory can be thought of as the representation of a sequence of events, an episode. Semantic and episodic memory structures enable us to create a mixed representational system which can answer the fundamental problem of video retrieval systems: how do we determine the similarity of descriptors, of descriptions, of shots, and of sequences? Similarity needs to be context-sensitive and compare not just descriptors, but relations between them. The determination of similarity holds the key to retrieval, and due to the properties of video as a medium (especially its semantic and syntactic features discussed above) the semantic and episodic memory systems must work together using different similarity metrics in order to retrieve video based on its unique features.

Media Streams Retrieval Algorithms

Media Streams employs two different types of retrieval algorithms: atemporal semantically based retrieval of icons and video segments; and temporal analogically based retrieval of video segments and sequences. Both retrieval strategies can use each other and be interleaved.

These algorithms can be further distinguished by the objects they operate on and the criteria of similarity they employ. All retrieval algorithms operate on descriptors and relations between them. At the simplest level, retrieval can be based on the *identity* of components. A more semantically based retrieval utilizes the hierarchical tree structure of the Icon Space to match components

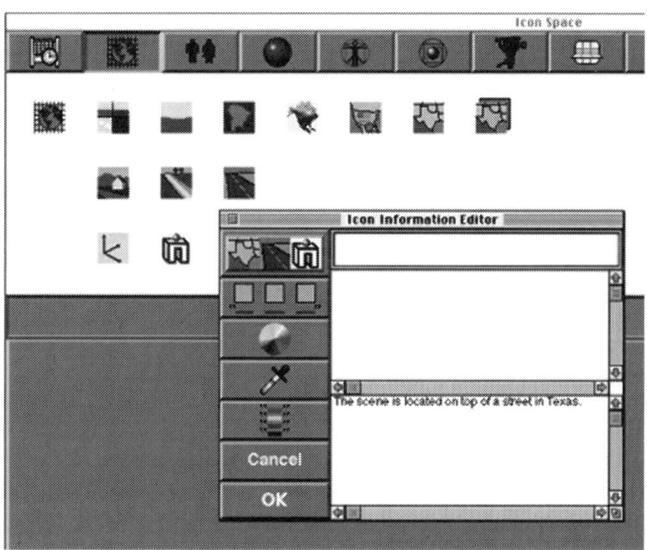

Figure 1: Icon Space (Detail)

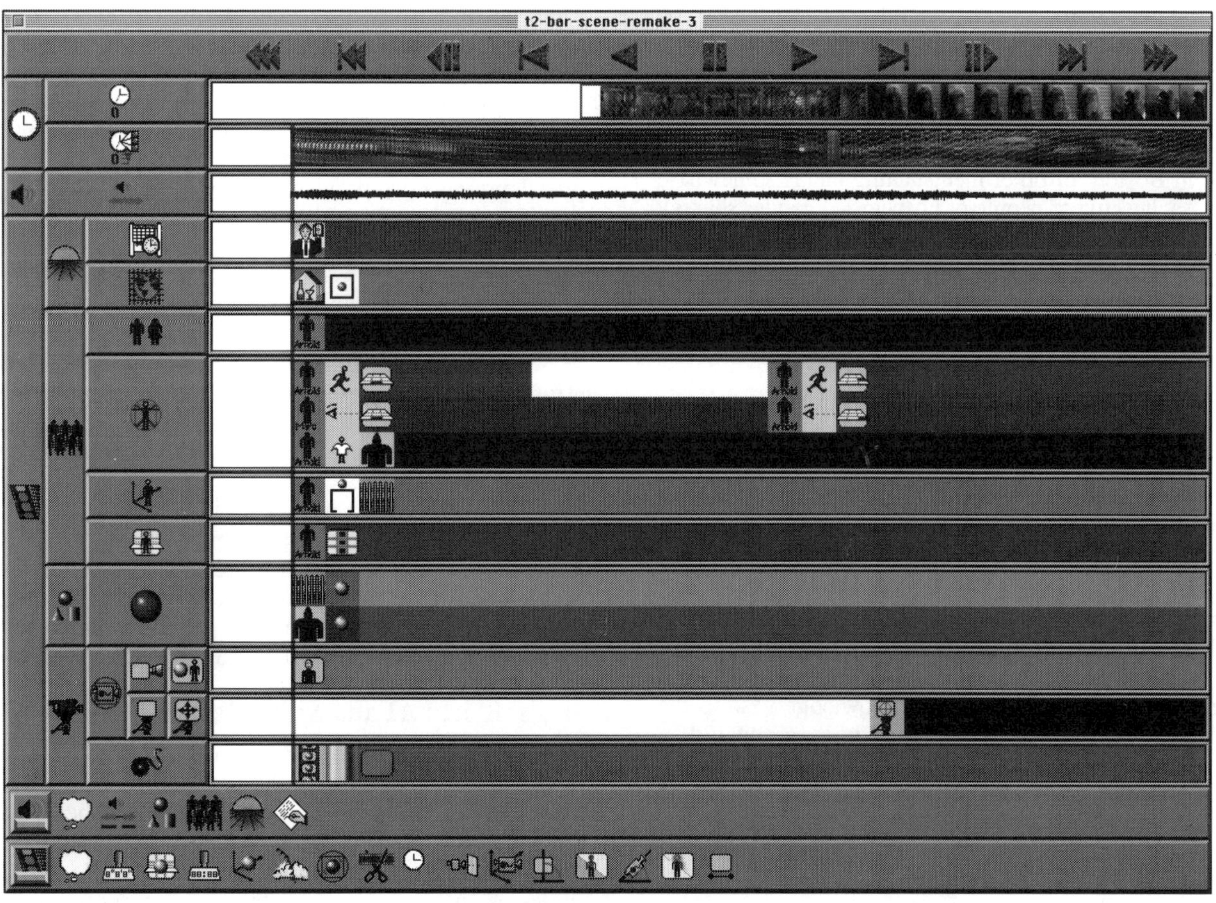

Figure 2: Media Time Line

based on *generalization* or *specialization*. The most sophisticated retrieval is that which takes into account the semantic and syntactic structure of temporally-indexed descriptions and the relations between them and thereby matches based on *analogical* similarity.

These retrieval algorithms are based on work done by Professor Kenneth Haase (Haase 1993b). His analogical matching system called "Mnemosyne" (after the Greek goddess of memory who was also the mother of the nine muses) is a radically memory-based representational system in which analogical matching forms the core representation. The challenge which this memory-based representation addresses is the inflexibility and brittleness of most semantic or categorical representations. In knowledge representations where a fixed hierarchical semantic structure is not sufficient to allow flexibility of the representation, an episodic memory structure is needed so that the semantics of the descriptors used in the semantic memory is, in effect, contextualized by a network of differences and similarities between concrete examples of the descriptors' use. Media Streams extends this work by combining semantic and episodic representational systems in order to facilitate context-independent and context-dependent representation and retrieval of video. Media Streams also adds the ability to represent and match on temporal relations. This extension is based on earlier work in temporal representation (Allen 1985).

Here is an example to illustrate how Media Streams' representational structures and retrieval algorithms work. Imagine we want to find a video shot of John and Joe shaking hands in Boston. A query which used only semantic memory would find shots of John and Joe shaking hands in Boston, of other men shaking hands somewhere in Massachusetts, of people of unspecified gender shaking hands somewhere in the United States, etc. A query which used episodic and semantic memory would find shots of John and Joe shaking hands in Boston as well as shots of Hirotada and Takafumi bowing to one another in Tokyo, and so forth.

Related Work

The CYC Project: Representing the World

The goal of the CYC project is to overcome the brittleness and domain-specificity of all previous attempts at representing our common-sense knowledge about the world (Lenat & Guha 1990). Since 1984 the CYC project has done extensive work in creating representations of objects, actions, and events. Recently the CYC project has begin to apply its large semantic knowledge base to the representation and retrieval of still images and video. Surprisingly, these attempts fall prey to exactly the same criticism which Lenat himself levied against efforts to represent the physical world by natural language. Lenat argued that natural language was an inadequate representational system for representing knowledge about the world because it is not a designed representation (Lenat & Guha 1990). In other words, natural language is not designed in such a way so as to capture the salient features of the world which are amenable to computational representation. Nevertheless, the CYC project makes a methodological error in its efforts to represent stills and video: it applies its representation language (which is a representation of the world) to video without redesigning it for the representation of video. What Media Streams does in contrast is create a representation language for video, in other words, a representation of a representation of the world. According to Guha, CYC represents video as "information bearing objects with propositional content." Guha admits that this approach may break down due to the particular context-dependent and context-independent semantics of video data (Guha 1994). With video, editing and resequencing may change the given "propositional content" of any "information bearing object."

Schank: Conceptual Dependency and Case Based Reasoning

Conceptual dependency reduced all of human action into a small set of composable primitives (Schank & Rieger 1974). This work has a certain appeal for its rigor and simplicity, yet it has an apparent deficit for application to video representation: the semantics of human action within video are not fixed and change on recombination. The challenge is not to reduce all video actions to unambiguous media-independent primitives, but to articulate a semantics of action which is conditioned by the properties of the medium.

Traditional case-based reasoning relies on the indexing of cases under predetermined abstractions. This approach presents two problems for video representation: the indexing must, as stated above, articulate the difference between context dependent and context independent aspects of video content; and then use this distinction in its indexing to support the reindexing of cases when video elements are resequenced.

Schank and his students have recently applied their efforts to video representation. They are conducting a large scale project to develop a video database for interactive corporate training applications. In this work, video is represented as if it were just text, or a fortiori, ideas. The video data is treated as if it were fully transparent and one need only represent the ideas behind it in order to fully represent its contents. Schank does concede that this approach is designed for the needs of his current project and that it may prove inadequate for representing video which will be resegmented and/or repurposed (Schank 1993).

Bloch: AI and Video Representation

The mots promising prior work done in knowledge representation for video is the research of Gilles Bloch (Bloch 1987). In his short unpublished paper he outlines the issues involved in applying Schank's conceptual dependency representation to video segments. He also discusses using Noël Burch's categories for transitions, and mentions the importance of gaze vectors in video (Burch

1969). His prototype system supposedly was able to construct simple video sequences using Schankian scripts. His work did not address the issue of how these representations are written (annotation) or read (browsing) and the extent to which they supported repurposability and resegmentation of the content is unclear. Unfortunately, Bloch's untimely death cut off this fruitful early path of research in applying artificial intelligence techniques to the problems of video representation.

Conclusion and Future Work

This paper is a first attempt to articulate the challenge of creating robust representations of video within artificial intelligence which will support the description, retrieval, and resequencing of video according to its content. Work in the representation of video content requires a fundamental analysis of the structure and function of video. The implications of this analysis for designing representations of video content are a coming to terms with the unique semantic, syntactic, and ontological properties of the representational system of video. Media Streams is a research effort in video annotation and retrieval which has begun to develop these types of representations. Much research remains to be done especially in the area of the representation of time, transitions, and the higher level structures of sequences, scenes, and stories.

Acknowledgments

The research discussed above was conducted at the MIT Media Laboratory and Interval Research Corporation. The support of the Laboratory and its sponsors is gratefully acknowledged. I want to thank Brian Williams and Golan Levin for their continually awe-inspiring efforts and my advisor, Prof. Kenneth Haase, for his insight, inspiration, and support. Thanks also to Warren Sack, David Levitt, and Wendy Buffett for editorial and moral support.

References

Allen, J. F. 1985. *Maintaining Knowledge about Temporal Intervals.* In R. J. Brachman & H. J. Levesque Eds., *Readings In Knowledge Representation* pp. 510-521. San Mateo, California: Morgan Kaufmann Publishers, Inc.

Archive Films. 1992. Archive Films Demo Reel. New York: Archive Films.

Arons, B. 1993. Interactively Skimming Recorded Speech. Ph.D., Massachusetts Institute of Technology.

Baddeley, A. D. 1984. *Memory Theory and Memory Therapy.* In B. A. Wilson & N. Moffat Eds., *Clinical Management of Memory Problems.* 5-27. Rockville, Maryland: Aspen Systems Corporation.

Bloch, G. R. 1987. From Concepts to Film Sequences. Unpublished Document. Yale University Department of Computer Science.

Bordwell, D., & Thompson, K. 1990. *Film Art - An Introduction* third ed. McGraw-Hill Publishing Company.

Burch, N. 1969. *Theory of Film Practice* Helen R. Lane, Trans.. Princeton: Princeton University Press.

Davis, M. 1993a. Media Streams: An Iconic Visual Language for Video Annotation. In Proceedings of the 1993 IEEE Symposium on Visual Languages. 196-202. Bergen, Norway: IEEE Computer Society Press.

Davis, M. 1993b. Media Streams: An Iconic Visual Language for Video Annotation. *Telektronikk* 4.93: 59-71.

Eisenstein, S. M. 1947. *The Film Sense* Jay Leyda, Trans. San Diego: Harcourt Brace Jovanovich, Publishers.

Feiner, S. K., & McKeown, K. R. 1990. Generating Coordinated Multimedia Explanations. In Proceedings of the Sixth IEEE Conference on Artificial Intelligence Applications. Santa Barbara: IEEE Press.

Guha, R. V. 1994. Personal Communication.

Guha, R. V., & Lenat, D. B. 1994. Enabling Agents to Work Together. *Communications of the ACM* Forthcoming.

Haase, K. 1993a. FRAMER: A Persistent Portable Representation Library. Internal Document. MIT Media Laboratory.

Haase, K. 1993b. Integrating Analogical and Case-Based Reasoning in a Dynamic Memory. Internal Document. MIT Media Laboratory.

Hawley, M. 1993. Structure out of Sound. Ph.D., Massachusetts Insitute of Technology.

Isenhour, J. P. 1975. The Effects of Context and Order in Film Editing. *AV Communications Review* 23(1): 69-80.

Kahn, K. 1979. Creation of Computer Animations from Story Descriptions. Technical Report. No. 540. Massachusetts Institute of Technology Artificial Intelligence Laboratory.

Kuleshov, L. 1974. *Kuleshov on Film: Writings by Lev Kuleshov* Ronald Levaco, Trans. Berkeley: University of California Press.

Lenat, D. B., & Guha, R. V. 1990. *Building Large Knowledge-Based Systems: Representation and Inference in the Cyc Project.* Reading, Massachusetts: Addison-Wesley Publishing Company, Inc.

McCarthy, J., & Hayes, P. 1969. *Some Philosophical Problems from the Standpoint of Artificial Intelligence.* In *Machine Intelligence 4* . Endinburgh: Endinburgh University Press.

McLuhan, M. 1962. *The Gutenberg Galaxy: The Making of Typographic Man.* Toronto: University of Toronto Press.

Schank, R. C. 1982. *Dynamic Memory: A Theory of Reminding and Learning in Computers and People.* Cambridge: Cambridge University Press.

Schank, R. C. 1993. Personal Communication.

Schank, R. C., & Rieger III, C. J. 1974. Inference and the Computer Understanding of Natural Language. *Artificial Intelligence* 5(4): 373-412.

Schank, R. C., & Riesbeck, C. 1981. *Inside Computer Understanding: Five Programs Plus Miniatures.* Hillsdale, New Jersey: Lawrence Erlbaum Associates.

Teodosio, L. 1992. Salient Stills. M.S.V.S., Massachusetts Institute of Technology Media Laboratory.

Tonomura, Y., Akutsu, A., Otsuji, K., & Sadakata, T. 1993. VideoMAP and VideoSpaceIcon: Tools for Anatomizing Content. In Proceedings of INTERCHI'93. 131-136. Amsterdam, The Netherlands: ACM Press.

Tulving, E. 1993. What is Episodic Memory? *Current Directions in Psychological Science* 2(3): 67-70.

Ueda, H., Miyatake, T., Sumino, S., & Nagasaka, A. 1993. Automatic Structure Visualization for Video Editing. In Proceedings of INTERCHI'93. 137-141. Amsterdam, The Netherlands: ACM Press.

Zhang, H., Kankanhalli, A., & Smoliar, S. W. 1993. Automatic Partitioning of Full-Motion Video. *Multimedia Systems* 1: 10-28.

Semi-Autonomous Animated Actors

Steve Strassmann[1]

Apple Computer, Inc.
One Main St., Cambridge, MA 02142
straz@apple.com

Abstract

This paper describes an interdisciplinary experiment in controlling semi-autonomous animated human forms with natural language input. These computer-generated characters resemble traditional stage actors, in that they are more autonomous than traditional hand-guided animated characters, and less autonomous than fully improvisational agents. We introduce the *desktop theater* metaphor, reserving for users the creative role of a theatrical writer or director.

1. Introduction

Much animation research has been devoted to the two extreme ends of the scale of autonomous behavior. In traditional animation, a character's behavior is fully guided by the artist [Thomas 81], [Jones 89]. This approach can achieve astounding results, but only through comparably astounding investments of both skill and labor. At the other extreme, agent- or simulation-based techniques [Johnson 91], [Bates et al 92], [Loyall et al 93] give rise to fully autonomous characters, improvising behavior in real-time with little creative input required from the user once the initial conditions are set up.

This paper describes a system called Divadlo[2], for controlling semi-autonomous characters, whose improvisational skills lie somewhere in the middle of the autonomy spectrum. Like traditional stage actors, their behavior is largely constrained by an external source (the script and stage directions, provided by the user). Such a system might be called a *desktop theater*[3], system since it reserves for users the creative role of a theatrical writer or director. This gives the user

the potential to realize specific creative ideas with significantly less effort than traditional animation techniques.

In typical usage (Figure 1a-b), a user enters natural language commands, either as individual sentences or as paragraphs, describing a scene. Statements describing initial conditions take immediate effect. As characters and objects are introduced, positioned, and otherwise specified, the graphics display is updated in real time. Statements describing actions or transformations of non-zero duration are accumulated in parallel and/or serial combinations into a plan, which is refined and rendered into an animation. This last step is performed offline, not interactively, due to performance limitations in the graphics subsystem.

This system was inspired in part by the vision of an interactive fantasy system [Laurel 86], and in part by SHRDLU [Winograd 72], in which a semi-autonomous agent manipulated simulated blocks and pyramids in a 3d environment in response to a natural language dialog with the user. Other efforts at story animation generally output 2d forms [Kahn 79], [Takashima 87], avoiding the many problems of 3d representation and control. We are aware of only one other group [Badler et al 91] which has assembled a significant architecture to enable natural language control of animated 3d human forms.

2. Overview

Perhaps the most challenging aspect of building such a system was the need to integrate specialized information for natural language, 3d graphics, planning, and robotics. Rather than focusing on developing any one particular theory or subsystem, we observed that the parts interact in combination to produce both synergies and compromises in design and performance.

---

[1]This paper describes work done at the MIT Media Laboratory, Cambridge, Mass., completed in 1991. It was supported in part by an equipment grant from Hewlett-Packard Corporation, and research grants from Toshiba and the Nichidai Fund.

[2]*Divadlo* is Czech for "theater," as *robot* is derived from the Czech word for "worker".

[3]This is by analogy to "desktop publishing" systems, which reduce the skills and labor needed for document publishing while reserving the creative aspects for users.

">

```
p> New scene.
Creating a new scene: SCENE.1
p> The characters in this scene are John and
Mary.
Adding actors to the scene: (JOHN MARY)
p> John's shirt is green.
OK.
p> He's left-handed.
OK.
p> There's a desk at stage left.
Introducing a new object: DESK.1
p> It's facing center stage.
OK.
...(more stage layout directions)...
p> In this scene, John gets angry.
New action: BECOME.1
p> He offers the book to Mary rudely, but she
refuses it.
New actions: (OFFER.1 REFUSE.1)
p> He slams it down on the table.
New action: SLAM.1
p> Mary cries while John glares at her.
New action: (CRY.1 GLARE.1)
```

Figure 1b: The scene specified in figure 1a, above

Figure 2: System overview

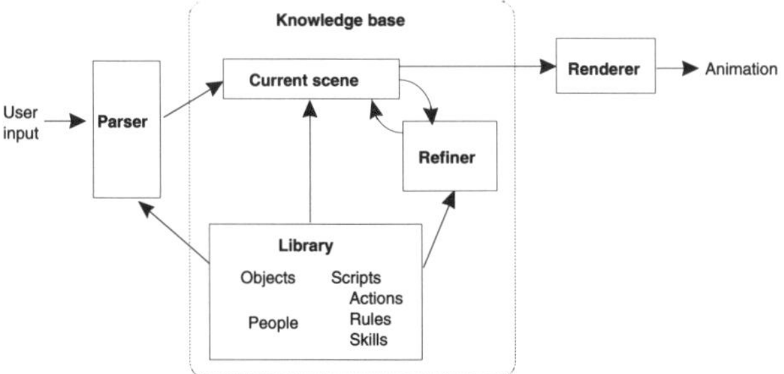

Figure 2 shows an overview of the system's structure. A parser (and simple generator) handles input from the user, and a graphics subsystem generates and records the output animations. A knowledge base is used to maintain a library of potentially useful objects and actions, as well as knowledge about objects and actions instantiated in the current scene. Knowledge about scripts, plans, goals, resources, and robotic motor skills is used to refine the user-specified plan into a detailed animation script.

2.1 Knowledge base

At the center of the system is a frame-like knowledge base implemented in ARLOtje [Haase 90]. Units in ARLOtje are organized into class hierarchies, and each unit is distinguished by the values stored in slots it possesses or inherits from other units. By using one representation scheme for all these different components, the task of sharing knowledge among them is greatly simplified. For example, the unit representing the notion of a chair contains *linguistic* information ("chair" is a noun), *physical* information (the shape and color of a chair), and *functional* information for reasoning (chairs are for sitting on).

The knowledge base includes:

- A grammar and lexicon, grounded in the object, pose, and script library, for use by the natural language parser and generator.

- A semantic network describing characters, objects and their attributes, including:

  - Quantitative 3d geometrical knowledge: shapes, positions, orientations, and hierarchical relationships among objects.

  - Quantitative color, shading, and texture information about each object for use by the graphics subsystem in rendering.

  - Qualitative information about object attributes, inferred from quantitative information. This allows the parser to disambiguate references like "the downstage chair" or "the blue book". This also greatly facilitates resource planning, such as identifying unoccupied chairs before sitting, or clear portions of table surfaces before placing objects.

  - Qualitative information about the actor's status, such as its posture (sitting or leaning), emotional state, or immediate goals or constraints.

- Poses; partial specifications of typical body postures

- Scripts describing actions, including preconditions, postconditions and other constraints. These include:

  - A repertoire of high-level tasks for specification by the user.

  - A repertoire of low-level motor skills, such as standing or grasping.

- Rules describing partial rewriting of plans when certain patterns are detected in them.

In addition, the units are surrounded by utility functions containing heuristic rules which capture special-purpose knowledge. These largely reside in or are invoked by dæmons on a unit's slots, and are used to constrain or compute values as they are needed.

2.2 Object representation

The "actors" in this system are derived from one of two (one male, one female) fully articulated human forms, rendered in 3d. Each figure is a tree of 44 rigid polyhedra (about 2000 polygons), connected by joints of one or more degrees of freedom. While this is still more doll-like than realistic, it is enough detail to simulate posture down to individual knuckles on the hand. A specific actor can be instanced and given customized body dimensions, clothing, body, or hair color.

Symbolic annotations are used to correlate polyhedra and their attributes to units in the knowledge base. For example, asserting that a character is wearing tennis sneakers would cause certain polygons to be colored white. This sort of knowledge-enhanced modeling, by integrating symbolic and traditional animation data, greatly reduces the effort required to populate a scene with models.

In addition to actors, the system has a stock of about 30 kinds of props, including furniture, office equipment, plumbing fixtures, and appliances, all of which come in a variety of decorator colors. Knowledge about each prop includes shape, lexicon entries, attribute-based variants (such as numerical values for "large" and "small" in the case of boxes), and constraints on positioning and usage. Light sources and camera angles are also available for creation and manipulation through natural language commands.

To get a handle on controlling the human form, we use a data structure called a pose to represent partial configurations. A pose is a tree whose nodes are coordinate transformation matrices with symbolic annotations. For example, an "ok" hand gesture is a pose capturing the tree of joint rotations on one hand (rooted at the wrist), with the thumb and forefinger forming a circle. A "salute" is a pose which captures the entire body's skeletal tree in a military salute. Recalling, combining, or simple interpolation of such poses greatly enriches the repertoire of possible movement. Thus, a character can salute and then bring the hand forward to give an "ok" gesture.

Poses turn out to be convenient for describing inanimate, articulated objects as well. Refrigerators can be open or shut and chairs can be reclined by applying appropriate poses to them.

2.3 Linguistic knowledge

Divadlo's parser is derived from BUP, a bottom-up parser for augmented phrase-structured grammars [Finin 85]. The lexicon is grounded in several hundred units in the knowledge base, including the instantiable objects and behaviors, as well as units for attributes such as adjectives and adverbs.

The parser supports resolution of pronouns, many common contractions, prefixes and suffixes, verb conjugation, and input of arbitrary number and string constants. Pronouns are resolved using a few simple heuristics such as gender or most-recent reference.

The grammar consists of about a hundred rules. In general, input falls into three broad categories: queries, commands, and statements. The system is non-modal; any kind of input can be entered at any time, and multiple inputs can be concatenated into a paragraph for block execution.

2.3.1 Queries

Queries allow the user to interrogate the system with questions like "Where's the chair?", "Who is eating the pie?", or "Is John left-handed?" As each query is parsed, the knowledge base is searched and a simple generator is used to create the answer. There are 8 categories of queries (corresponding to who, what, where, etc.), each with its own ad hoc rules for generating database searches and generating English responses.

In response to a question like "Where's the chair?", Divadlo prints something like `"The red chair is in front of the desk"`, which is arguably better for end-users than something like `"CHAIR.1 AT-LOCATION (45.3 3.7)"` The system takes advantage of the fact that both numerical and symbolic information is stored. Since, in this hypothetical case, the chair was not moved since it was originally placed (`AT-LOCATION (FRONT-OF DESK.3)`), this attribute is still available for use. If the chair had been moved to an arbitrary location with no symbolic significance, the generator might infer another descriptive phrase from the coordinates, such as "The red chair is downstage."

2.3.2 Commands

The user issues *commands* to Divadlo in order to give control information outside the narrative of the scene being constructed. These include commands for controlling the graphics subsystem ("*Record*"), inspecting objects in the knowledge base ("*Inspect the chair*"), or terminating the program ("*Quit*").

2.3.3 Statements

Most input forms are *statements*, which describe the scene. While commands are all imperatives, statements are distinguished by a simple trick: they are all third-person declaratives. A statement in present continuous tense, e.g. "John is sitting on the chair," is taken as an initial condition and is executed immediately, just as a stage direction in a script would be. A statement in present simple tense, e.g. "John sits on the chair," is taken as an action to be executed during the scene (see below).

2.4 Actions

Actions are units that represent processes that occur over time. This includes elements of an actor's behavior, a continuous change to internal or mental states, or environmental changes. The expressive nature of a character's behavior is largely expressed by the choice of actions to portray a given task, or by the values of animation control parameters which modulate task execution.

Since Divadlo cannot animate in real time, actions derived from user statements are added to a single global plan, from which an animation is eventually compiled and rendered in a batch operation. By default, each new action specified in a statement is appended to the scene's plan, or script, in serial order. Parallel actions can be specified with compound statements such as "While $action_1$, $action_2$," or "$action_1$ as $action_2$." A special kind of parallel action, whose duration spans the entire scene, can be specified with a form like "In this scene, $action_1$."

Since it is assumed that the user provides relatively concrete instructions, no attempt is made to perform sophisticated problem-solving, e.g. "James Bond then rescues all the prisoners." It suffices to traverse the global plan top-down, expanding actions into successively finer detail. This is described in section 3, below.

2.4.1 Motor skills

The lowest level unit that actually implements an action is a *motor skill* [Zeltzer 82]. A motor-skill action has a `SKILL-CODING` attribute which contains a lisp function which actually does the "dirty work" of positioning the joints and limbs of the actor over time.

To implement this function, a variety of techniques are used, appropriate to the skill. Some of these are surveyed in [Calvert 91]. The simplest skills, like `WAVE-HELLO`, are interpolations of stored poses (or keyframes), specifying joint angles on the actor's arm. Divadlo has a set of tools that supports a variety of keyframing techniques, including linear and spline interpolation, several different representations for joing rotation and displacement, and smooth merging of multiple, partially specified keyframes (e.g. allowing an actor to snap its fingers while waving hello).

Skills may also use more advanced techniques, like inverse kinematics, which is used by skills like `REACH`, which places the actor's hand at a given point in space. Walking uses a special hybrid algorithm similar to the one used in [Sims 87]. Full dynamical modeling is not yet supported in Divadlo, though many others have demonstrated dynamics-based control models for animated human forms [Girard and Maciejewski 85][Badler et al 93].

Figure 3 shows a typical motor skill for sitting, which uses a combination of inverse kinematics (to keep the feet placed on the floor and guide the actor's posterior to the chair's seat) and key framing (to rotate the hands naturally).

Figure 3: A typical motor skill for sitting

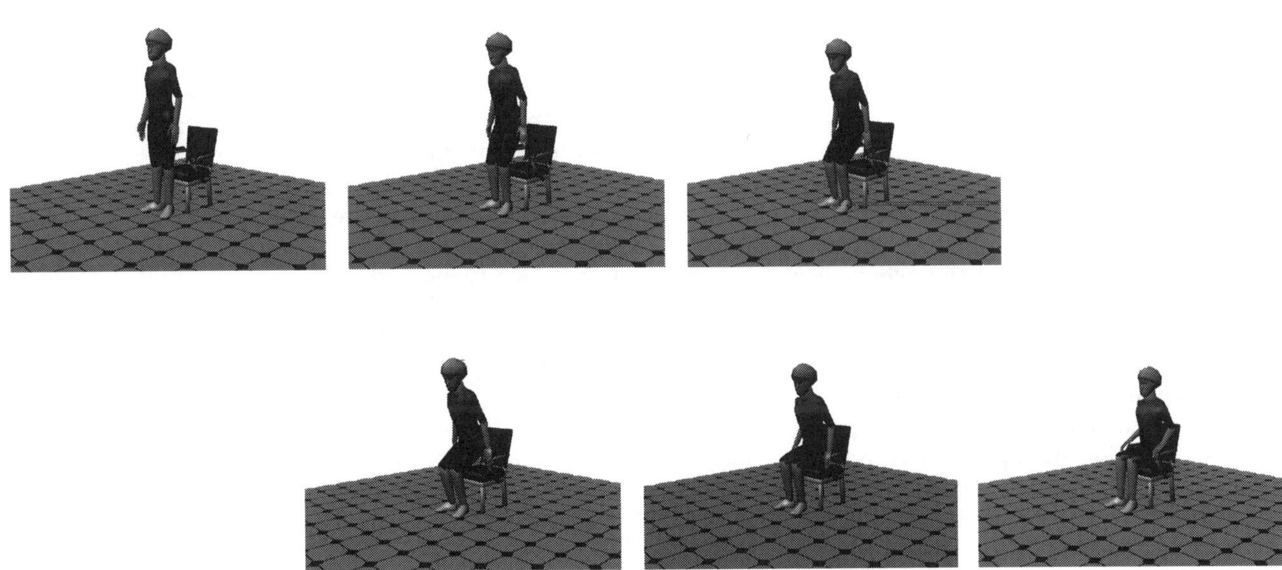

```lisp
(defscript sit
   ((agent (find-plausible-agent this-action))
    (chair (find-plausible-chair this-action))
    (current-occupant (get-value (my chair) 'occupant)))
  (already-sitting
     :doc ("No need to SIT, - ~a is already sitting down." (my agent))
     :test (equalp (my agent) (my current occupant))
     :script (delete-action this-action))
  (already-occupied
     :doc ("~a currently occupied by ~a, evacuate it." (my chair)
           (my current-occupant))
     :test (and (not (null (my current-occupant)))
                (not (equal (my current-occupant) (my agent))))
     :effects '((occupant ,(my chair) ,(my agent))
                (posture ,(my current-occupant) standing)
                (posture ,(my agent) sitting))
     :script (create-subtasks this-action
               '(serial
                  (stand (agent ,(my current-occupant)))
                  (go (agent ,(my current-occupant)
                       (to ,(make-suggestion '(pick-random-place-nearby ,(my-chair)))))
                  (sit (agent ,(my agent)) (chair ,(my chair))))))
  (far-away
     :doc ("~a is too far away from ~a, must move closer" (my agent) (my chair))
     :test (not (ready-to-sit? (my agent) (my chair)))
     :effects '((occupant ,(my chair) ,(my agent))
                (position ,(my agent)
                          ,(get-value (my chair) 'position)
                (posture ,(my agent) (sitting ,(my chair))))
     :script (create-subtasks this-action
               '(serial
                  (go (agent ,(my agent))
                      (to ,(place-in-front-of (my chair))))
                  (sit (chair ,(my chair))))))
  (normal-case
     :doc ("~a sits on ~a" (my agent) (my chair))
     :test t
     :effects '((occupant ,(my chair) ,(my agent))
                (posture ,(my agent) (sitting ,(my chair))))
     :script (create-subtasks this-action
               '(sit-motor-skill (agent ,(my agent)) (chair ,(my chair)))))))
```

2.4.2 Scripts

The expansion of higher-level actions are are governed by a *script* [Schank & Abelson 77], associated with each general class of actions. These serve as templates for the action instances, which are knowledge units placed on the global plan to represent concrete details of the performance.

A script has two parts; the resources which indicate parameters which must be known before any further reasoning can be done, and the cases, which describe various ways to carry out the action. For example, Figure 4 shows a typical script describing the action SIT.

The first element of the DEFSCRIPT form, after the action's name, SIT, is a list of resources, which in this case are agent, chair, and current-occupant. Each instance of an action attempts to bind specific values for these resources before continuing with the expansion. For example, if the sentence "John sits on the red chair" instantiates the action SIT.3, and if nobody is sitting

on that red chair at that point in the plan, the resources can be filled in as follows: AGENT → JOHN, CHAIR → DESK-CHAIR.1, CURRENT-OCCUPANT → NIL.

Often, the value of a resource may not be immediately computable with the currently available information, in which case it is deferred for later analysis (see below). For convenience, helper functions like find-plausible-agent and find-plausible-target are sometimes used to help identify resource bindings. These capture specific knowledge by following a few simple heuristics, just as looking for for the object and subject of the sentence, respectively. They also constrain the search, for example, by making sure the AGENT is an animate object.

The remainder of the script describes one or more cases, describing different possible conditions which may affect the performance of that action. Each case includes

- *name* - the name of this case

- *documentation* - a descriptive form for use in tracing the planner's progress

- *test* - a predicate indicating whether this case is applicable

- *effects* - assertions summarizing the consequences of performing this case

- *script* - actions to take in order to implements this case

The example above shows several cases that might arise for an actor instructed to sit down. It may already be sitting, there may be someone else in the target chair, or the target chair may be far enough away to require the subtask of approaching it. The last case is the "normal" case, in which it is assumed that all preconditions have been satisfied, and the appropriate motor skill can be directly invoked.

3. Simple planning

Divadlo uses a relatively simple planner, always operating on a concrete, global plan, with no back-tracking. As previously mentioned, most stage directions are straightforward. The system's main task is to expand high-level tasks into appropriate subtasks, and to infer and provide concrete animation control parameters to the motor skills.

Plan expansion occurs in two passes on each iteration: in the first, a pending action is selected and expanded — the most common operations are substitution (replacing with a more specific task), insertion (to satisfy preconditions or postconditions), or deletion (of superfluous actions). The second pass allows opportunistic modifications to the plan, by applying rewrite rules triggered by matching patterns and perform arbitrary operations on the plan elements. Examples include:

- consolidation, such as replacing RUN and KICK-BALL with a specialized version RUN-WHILE-KICKING-BALL.

- inserting or removing delays to break up coincidences or improve synchronization between related actions.

- altering resource parameters of actions, e.g. changing the way an actor performs a task after repeating it thrice, to avoid seeming too repetitious.

- insertion of opportunistic behavior, such as having a sick character occasionally sneeze while performing other tasks.

Some limited lookahead is provided by a mechanism for *deferred choices*, inspired by a similar feature in ANI [Kahn 79]. In computing resource values before expanding a script, insufficient or ambiguous information causes an explicit choice object to be created, which captures the dependencies and alternatives. Choices are placed on a queue to be resolved when the necessary information is available, or when continued deferral would halt further progress, in which case a peremptory decision is made.

Divadlo is not a purely symbolic system, but neither is it purely a situated or "nouvelle" AI as categorized in [Brooks 90]. We note that our goal is entertainment, not verisimilitude. Unlike robotics or physically-based animation, a grounding in reality or high-fidelity simulation is not always necessary or even desirable from an artistic point of view. (This is fortunate, considering how difficult it is to build such systems, and how computationally demanding they are to run interactively). On the other hand, unlike purely symbolic systems, Divadlo's objects are grounded in a simulated world with three continuous spatial and one temporal dimension, in which the generally accepted rules of gravity, collision avoidance, etc. must usually be followed.

4. Conclusion

We believe that somewhere between the vivid furniture of Virtual Reality (passive-reactive objects) and the teeming ant colonies of Artificial Life (fully autonomous agents), there lies the relatively unexplored domain of the semi-autonomous agent. We envision an entertainment system of the future, consisting of a troupe of virtual thespians ready to act out dramatic scenes of the user's invention.

In real life, actors get relatively explicit stage instructions from writers and directors, and are rarely called upon to perform complex problem-solving. They are told where to stand, when to move, and are often given advice on how to modulate their motion. This creative control is part of *the pleasure of writing and directing*, and our goal is to reserve it for the user. At the same time, a large category of users prefer to avoid fully-guided animation, which carries the obligation to provide *too much* control at too low a level of detail. The expertise of animators needs to be captured into useful action units so that "clip behaviors", much like "clip art", could be pragmatically recycled.

Before this can be realized, however, several disparate components must be integrated into a practical infrastructure for these actors to inhabit. We have built an experimental system integrating natural language, knowledge representation, planning, robotics, and computer animation.

Acknowledgements

The author would like to thank Marvin Minsky for his guidance and support, Tim Finin for use of the BUP parser, and members of the former Computer Graphics and Animation Group at the Media Lab for portions of the animation subsystem.

Bibliography

Badler, Norman I., Webber, B.L., Kalita, J, and Esakov, J., *Animation from Instructions*, chap. 3 of *Making Them Move*, ed. by Badler, Barsky, & Zeltzer; Morgan Kaufmann, San Mateo, CA, 1991.

Badler, Norman I., Phillips, C. and Webber, B. *Simulating Humans: Computer Graphics, Animation and Control*, Oxford University Press, 1993.

Bates, Joseph, Loyall, A. Bryan and Reilly, W. Scott , *Integrating Reactivity, Goals, and Emotion in a Broad Agent*, Proceedings of the 14th Annual Conference of the Cognitive Science Society, 1992.

Brooks, Rodney A., *Elephants Don't Play Chess*, in *Designing Autonomous Agents*, ed. by Pattie Maes, Elsevier/MIT Press, 1991.

Calvert, Tom, *Composition of Realistic Animation Sequences for Multiple Human Figures*, chap. 2 of *Making Them Move*, ed. by Badler, Barsky, & Zeltzer; Morgan Kaufmann, San Mateo, CA, 1991.

Finin, Tim, *BUP - A Bottom-Up Parser for Augmented Phrase-Structured Grammars*, Franz lisp software, Univ. of Pennsylvania, 1985.

Girard, M. and Maciejewski, A. *Computational Modeling for the Computer Animation of Legged Figures*, *Computer Graphics*, ACM Siggraph Proceedings, 1985.

Haase, Ken, *ARLOtje Internals Manual*, MIT Media Lab, 1990.

Jones, Chuck, *Chuck Amuck*, Harper & Collins, Toronto, 1989.

Johnson, Michæl B., *Build-a-Dude: Action Selection Networks for Computational Autonomous Agents*, MS Thesis, MIT Media Lab, Feb. 1991.

Kahn, Kenneth Michæl, *Creation of Computer Animation from Story Descriptions*, Ph.D. thesis, AI TR-540, MIT AI Lab, 1979.

Laurel, Brenda Kay, *Toward the Design of a Computer-Based Fantasy System*, PhD thesis, Ohio State University, 1986.

Loyall, A. Bryan and Bates, Joseph, *Real-time Control of Animated Broad Agents*, Proceedings of the 15th Annual Conference of the Cognitive Science Society, 1993.

Minsky, Marvin, *Society of Mind*, Simon and Schuster, New York, 1985.

Schank, R.C. and Abelson, R.P. *Scripts, Plans, Goals, and Understanding*, Lawrence Erlbaum Press, Hillsdale, NJ, 1977.

Sims, Karl, *Locomotion of Jointed Figures over Complex Terrain*, MS Thesis, MIT Media Lab, June 1987.

Strassmann, Steve, *Desktop Theater: Automatic Generation of Expressive Animation* , Ph.D. thesis, MIT Media Lab, June, 1991.

Takashima, Y., Shimazu, H., and Tomono, M., *Story Driven Animation*, CHI+GI '87 Proceedings, ACM SIGCHI, pp. 149-153, 1987.

Winograd, Terry, *Understanding Natural Language*, Cognitive Psychology Vol. 3, (1) 1972.

Zeltzer, David, *Motor Control Techniques for Figure Animation*, IEEE Computer Graphics and Applications 2(9):53-59, 1982.

Automated Reasoning

Rule Based Updates on Simple Knowledge Bases

Chitta Baral

Department of Computer Science
University of Texas at El Paso
El Paso, Texas 79968, U.S.A.
chitta@cs.ep.utexas.edu

Abstract

In this paper we consider updates that are specified as rules and consider simple knowledge bases consisting of ground atoms. We present a translation of the rule based update specifications to extended logic programs using situation calculus notation so as to compute the updated knowledge base. We show that the updated knowledge base that we compute satisfies the update specifications and yet is minimally different from the original database. We then expand our approach to incomplete knowledge bases.

We relate our approach to the standard revision and update operators, the formalization of actions and its effects using situation calculus and the formalization of database evolution using situation calculus.

Introduction

Most work on belief revision in the literature focus on updating theories by sentences in the theory itself. Several different "update" operators (update, revision, contraction, erasure, forget etc) (KM89; GM88) and the relation between them have been studied (KM92) and postulates have been suggested for some of these operators (GM88; KM92).

In this paper[1] we consider updates that are specified as rules (MT94b) (similar to rules in a logic program) and present methods to compute updated knowledge bases when knowledge bases consist of a set of ground atoms.

The following example illustrates the kind of updates that we consider.

Consider a knowledge base consisting of three employees: John, Peter and Carl; which represent a certain department D in an organisation. During an organisational shake up the department has to be updated based on the new knowledge that "If John remains in the department D then Peter has to leave the department D and if Carl remains in the department then John has to stay in the department".

---

[1]Supported by the grants NSF-IRI-92-11-662 and NSF-CDA 90-15-006.

It should be noted that the intended meaning (MT94a) of the first statement is different from the statement "either John leaves the department or Peter leaves the department". If the new knowledge is specified in propositional theory or in first order logic they would be equivalent. The "if" and "then" in the statement "If John remains in the department D then Peter has to leave the department D" are treated differently from the first order implication. Our intent is to give a higher priority to "John than to Peter". This is necessary because we might like to have the language that specifies updates to have properties (say like 'monotonicity') which are different from the ones held by the language of the database.

To specify such rules Marek and Truszczynski (MT94a) introduce the notion of *revision programs*. They define P-justified revision of simple knowledge bases by a revision program. In this paper we show how to compute P-justified revisions of knowledge bases using extended logic programs and situation calculus. Marek and Truszczynski 's definition of P-justified revision is only limited to the case when the CWA is assumed about the initial knowledge base. We extend the idea of P-justified revision to knowledge bases that could be incomplete and present an extended logic program that computes the revised knowledge base when the initial knowledge base may be incomplete.

We then consider update rules that explicitly relates the initial knowledge base to the revised knowledge base and show how revisions can be computed for such updates. Such rules are beyond the scope of Marek and Truszczynski 's revision programs.

Our approach of computing the revised knowledge base is similar to the formalization of database evolution (Rei92) but uses extended logic programs (GL91) instead of first order logic. In its use of situation calculus and extended logic programs our approach treats revision specifications as "actions" and a knowledge base as a "situation" and has similarity to the formalization of actions and their effects in (GL92). Our approach is different than the event calculus approach in (Ko92) and considers more complex revisions than discussed in it.

Revision Specifications

In this section we review the concept of revision specifications[2] and P-justified revision as defined in (MT94b).

Let U be a denumerable set. Its elements are referred to as atoms. A knowledge base is any subset of U. By $\neg U$ we mean the set $\{\neg a \; : \; a \in U\}$. Elements of $U \cup \neg U$ are called literals.

A revision specification uses a syntax similar to logic programs except that it has two special operators "in" and "out". For any atom a the intuitive meaning $in(a)$ is that the atom a is present in the revised knowledge base. Similarly the meaning of $out(a)$ is that the atom a is absent in the revised knowledge base. For any atom p in U, $in(p)$ an $out(p)$ are referred to as r-literals of U.

The statement "If John remains in the department D then Peter has to leave the department D" is written as the revision rule:

$$out(peter) \leftarrow in(john)$$

We now formally define the revision specifications and P-justified revision.

Definition 1 *(MT94b)* A *revision rule* can be of the following two forms

$$in(p) \leftarrow in(q_1), \ldots, in(q_m), out(s_1), \ldots, out(s_n) \quad (1)$$

$$out(p) \leftarrow in(q_1), \ldots, in(q_m), out(s_1), \ldots, out(s_n) \quad (2)$$

where p, q_i's and s_j's are atoms.

A collection of revision rules is called a revision specification. □

A knowledge base B is a *r-model* of (satisfies) an r-literal $in(p)$ ($out(p)$ respectively) if $p \in B$ ($p \notin B$, respectively). B is a r-model of the body of a rule if it satisfies each r-literal of the body. B is a r-model of a rule C if the following conditions hold: whenever B satisfies the body of C, then B satisfies the head of C. B is a r-model of a revision specification P if B satisfies each rule in P.

Definition 2 *(MT94b)* Let P be a revision specification. By $norm(P)$ we denote the definite program obtained from P by replacing each occurance of $in(a)$ by a and each occurance of $out(b)$ by b'. The *necessary change* for P is the pair (I, O) where $I = \{a \; : \; a \in$ least model of $norm(P)\}$ and $O = \{b \; : \; b' \in$ least model of $norm(P)\}$. P with necessary change (I, O) is said to be *coherent* if $I \cap O = \emptyset$. □

---

[2] Marek and Truszczynski used the term *revision programs* instead of revision specifications. We believe it to be more of a specification language (similar to the language $\mathcal{A}$ (GL92) for specifying effects of actions) that can be implemented in a logical language of choice, rather than a programming language.

Definition 3 *(MT94b)* Let P be a revision specification and D_I and D_R be two knowledge bases.

P_{D_R} is the revision program obtained from P by eliminating from P every rule of the type 1 or 2 such that $q_i \notin D_R$ or $s_j \in D_R$.

$P_{D_R}|D_I$ is the revision program obtained from P_{D_R} by eliminating from the body of each rule in P_{D_R} $in(a)$ if $a \in D_I$ and $out(a)$ if $a \notin D_I$.

If $P_{D_R}|D_I$ with necessary change (I, O) is coherent and $D_R = D_I \cup I \setminus O$ then D_R is called *P-justified revision* of D_I, and we write $D_I \xrightarrow{P} D_R$. □

Intuitively, P_{D_R} is the set of rules obtained from P by removing all rules in P whose body is not satisfied by D_R; and $P_{D_R}|D_I$ is the set of rules obtained from P_{D_R} by removing all r-literals that satisfy D_I from the bodies of rules in P_{D_R}.

Example 1 Let $D_I = \{a, b\}$ and P_1 be the revision specification

$$out(b) \leftarrow in(a) \; \} \; P_1$$

Let D_R be $\{a\}$.

$P_{1_{D_R}}$ is same as P_1 and $P_{1_{D_R}}|D_I = \{out(b)\}$ and hence is coherent with the necessary change $(\emptyset, \{b\})$ and $D_R = D_I \cup \emptyset \setminus \{b\}$. Hence, $D_I \xrightarrow{P} D_R$.

Let P_2 be

$$\begin{aligned} out(b) &\leftarrow in(a) \\ out(a) &\leftarrow in(b) \end{aligned} \Bigr\} \; P_2$$

It is easy to see that P_2-justified revisions of D_I are $\{a\}$ and $\{b\}$.

Let P_3 be

$$\begin{aligned} out(b) &\leftarrow in(a) \\ out(a) & \end{aligned} \Bigr\} \; P_3$$

It is easy to see that P_3-justified revisions of D_I is $\{b\}$. Intuitively we can consider P_1 as the logic program $\{out\_b \leftarrow not\ out_a\}$ and P_3 as the logic program

$$out\_b \leftarrow not\ out\_a$$

$$out\_a \leftarrow$$

Let P_4 be

$$\begin{aligned} in(a) &\leftarrow in(a) \\ in(c) &\leftarrow in(c) \end{aligned} \Bigr\} \; P_4$$

It is easy to see that P_4-justified revisions of D_I is $\{a, b\}$. □

Proposition 1 *(MT94b)* If a knowledge base D satisfies a revision specification P then D is a unique P-justified revision of D. □

Proposition 2 *(MT94b)* Let P be a revision specification and D_I be a knowledge base. If a knowledge base D_R is a P-justified revision of D_I, then D_R is a r-model of P. □

Proposition 3 *(MT94b)* Let P be a revision specification and D_I be a knowledge base. If D_R is a P-justified revision of D_I, then $D_R \div D_I$ is minimal in the family $\{D \div D_I \; : \; D$ is a r-model of $P \}$, where $\div$ denotes the symmetric difference. i.e. $A \div B = (A \setminus B) \cup (B \setminus A)$. $\qquad\square$

It should be noted that the above proposition just says P-justified revisions are r-models of the revision specification that are minimally different from the original database. It does not say that r-models of the revision specification that are minimally different from the original database are P-justified revisions. In Example 1 both $\{a\}$ and $\{b\}$ are r-models of P_1 minimally different from D_I but only $\{a\}$ is a P_1-justified revision. This is similar to the logic program $a \leftarrow not\ b$ which has two minimal models $\{a\}$ and $\{b\}$, but has the only stable model $\{a\}$.

Translating Revision specifications to Extended Logic Programs

In this section we translate revision specifications to extended logic programs and show that the answer sets of the translated program correspond to the P-revisions.

The extended logic program $\Pi(P \cup D_I)$ where P is the revision specification and D_I is the initial knowledge base, uses variables of three sorts: *situation* variables $s, s', \ldots$, *fluent* variables $f, f', \ldots$, and *revision*[3] variables $r, r', \ldots$.

The program $\Pi(P \cup D)$ consists of the translations of the individual revision rules and the initial knowledge base in P and certain other rules. We now present the translation $\Pi(P \cup D)$ where s is the situation corresponding to the initial knowledge base D_I, r correspond to the revision dictated by the revision specification P and $res(r, s)$ is the situation corresponding to the knowledge base obtained by revising the initial knowledge base with the revision specification P.

Algorithm 1 *[Translating Revision Specifications – with CWA about the initial database]*

1. Initial Database
If p is proposition in the initial database then $\Pi(P \cup D)$ contains

(1.1) $holds(p, s)$

and the rule

(1.2) $\neg holds(F, s) \leftarrow not\ holds(F, s)$
which encodes the CWA about the initial database.

2. Inertia Rule

(2.1) $holds(F, res(r, s)) \leftarrow holds(F, s), not\ ab(F, r, s)$

---

[3]The revision variables correspond to the action variables in situation calculus and in the translation of the language $\mathcal{A}$ to extended logic programs in (GL92)

This rule is motivated by the minimality consideration that only changes that happens to the initial knowledge base are the ones dictated by the revision specification.

3. Translating the revision rules

(a) Each revision rule of the type (1)

is translated to the rule

(3.a.1) $holds(p, res(r, s)) \leftarrow$
$\qquad holds(q_1, res(r, s)), \ldots, holds(q_m, res(r, s)),$
$\qquad \neg holds(s_1, res(r, s)), \ldots, \neg holds(s_n, res(r, s))$

(b) Each revision rule of the type (2)

$out(p) \leftarrow in(q_1), \ldots, in(q_m), out(s_1), \ldots, out(s_n)$

is translated to the rules:

(3.b.1) $\neg holds(p, res(r, s)) \leftarrow$
$\qquad holds(q_1, res(r, s)), \ldots, holds(q_m, res(r, s)),$
$\qquad \neg holds(s_1, res(r, s)), \ldots, \neg holds(s_n, res(r, s))$

(3.b.2) $ab(p, a, s) \leftarrow$
$\qquad holds(q_1, res(r, s)), \ldots, holds(q_m, res(r, s)),$
$\qquad \neg holds(s_1, res(r, s)), \ldots, \neg holds(s_n, res(r, s))$

Since the inertia rule (2.1) is only for the positive facts we do not need a rule defining abnormality corresponding to (3.a.1), but we do need such a rule corresponding to (3.b.1) to block the inertia rule and avoid inconsistency.

4. Completing the revised database

To encode the CWA w.r.t. the revised database $\Pi(P \cup D_I)$ contains the rule

(4.1) $\neg holds(F, res(r, s)) \leftarrow not\ holds(F, res(r, s))$ $\quad\square$

Example 2 Consider D_I and P_2 from Example 1. the translation $\Pi(P_2 \cup D_I)$ consists of the following rules:

$$
\left.
\begin{array}{l}
holds(a, s) \\
holds(b, s) \\
\neg holds(b, res(r_1, s)) \leftarrow holds(a, res(r_1, s)) \\
ab(b, r_1, s) \leftarrow holds(a, res(r_1, s)) \\
\neg holds(a, res(r_1, s)) \leftarrow holds(b, res(r_1, s)) \\
ab(a, r_1, s) \leftarrow holds(b, res(r_1, s)) \\
1.2 \\
2.1 \\
4.1
\end{array}
\right\} \Pi(P_2 \cup D_I)
$$

$\qquad\square$

Theorem 1 Let P be a revision specification corresponding to a revision operator r and D_I be an initial database. Let $\Pi(P \cup D_I)$ be the translation to extended logic programs.

(i) $D_I \xrightarrow{P} D_R$ implies there exists a consistent answer set A of $\Pi(P \cup D_I)$ such that
$\quad$ (a) $f \in D_R$ iff $holds(f, res(r, s)) \in A$.
$\quad$ (b) $f \notin D_R$ iff $\neg holds(f, res(r, s)) \in A$.

(ii) If A is a consistent answer set of $\Pi(P \cup D_I)$ then $D_I \xrightarrow{P} D_R$, where $D_R = \{f \; : \; holds(f, res(r, s)) \in A\}$

Proof:(sketch)

(i) Let $A = A_1 \cup A_2 \cup A_3 \cup A_4 \cup A_5 \cup A_6$ where,

$A_1 = \{holds(f, res(r, s)) : f \in D_I \setminus O\}$

$A_2 = \{holds(f, res(r, s)) : f \in I\}$

$A_3 = \{\neg holds(f, res(r, s)) : f \notin D_R\}$

$A_4 = \{holds(f, s) : f \in D_I\}$

$A_5 = \{\neg holds(f, s) : f \notin D_I\} \cup$

$A_6 = \{ab(f, r, s) : f \in O\}$

It is easy to see that A is consistent. To show A as an answer set of $\Pi(P \cup D_I)$ we observe that A_1, A_3, A_4, A_5 come from application of the rules (2.1), (4.1), (1.1) and (1.2) respectively and A_2 and A_6 come from combined application of the rules (3.a.1), (3.b.1) and (3.b.2).

Moreover, there is a one to one correspondence between P_{D_R} and R^A where R consists of the rules from (3.a.1) and (3.b.1). $\qquad\square$

Example 3 The answer sets of $\Pi(P_2 \cup D_I)$ are

$\{holds(a, s), holds(b, s), holds(a, res(r_1, s)),$
$\neg holds(b, res(r_1, s)) ab(b, r_1, s)\}$ and

$\{holds(a, s), holds(b, s), holds(b, res(r_1, s)),$
$\neg holds(a, res(r_1, s)) ab(a, r_1, s)\}$ $\qquad\square$

Rule based Revision of Incomplete Knowledge Bases

The approach in the last section and in (MT94b) assumes that the initial knowledge base is complete. i.e. there is CWA about the initial knowledge base. In this section we define P-justified revision of possibly incomplete knowledge bases with respect to revision specifications. We believe that it is more intuitive and understandable to define the P-justified revision through a translation to an extended logic program than directly in the style given in the previous section and hence do the former in this section.

Unless otherwise specified from now on by a knowledge base we mean a possibly incomplete knowledge base which is a subset of $U \cup \neg U$. As in the last section we translate the initial knowledge base and the revision specification to an extended logic program so as to compute the revised knowledge bases. As in the previous section, our translation uses situation calculus notations. The translation of an initial knowledge base D_I and the revision specification P denoted by $\Pi_{inc}(P \cup D_I)$ consists of the following:

Algorithm 2 *[Translating Revision Specs – without CWA about the initial database]*

1. Initial Database
If p is proposition in the initial knowledge base $\Pi_{inc}(P \cup D_I)$ contains

(1.1) $holds(p, s)$

If $\neg q$ is proposition in the initial knowledge base $\Pi_{inc}(P \cup D_I)$ contains

(1.2) $\neg holds(q, s)$

2. Inertia Rules

(2.1) $holds(F, res(r, s)) \leftarrow holds(F, s), not\ ab(F, r, s)$

(2.2)
$\neg holds(F, res(r, s)) \leftarrow \neg holds(F, s), not\ ab(F', r, s)$

Since our initial knowledge base may be incomplete we need two different inertia rules.

3. Translating the revision rules

(a) Each revision rule of the type (1) is translated to the rules (3.a.1) and

(3.a.2) $\quad\quad\quad ab(p', a, s) \quad\quad\quad\quad\quad \leftarrow$
$\quad holds(q_1, res(r, s)), \ldots, holds(q_m, res(r, s)),$
$\quad \neg holds(s_1, res(r, s)), \ldots, \neg holds(s_n, res(r, s))$

(b) Each revision rule of the type (2) is translated to the rules (3.b.1) and (3.b.2). $\qquad\square$

Definition 4 Let P be a revision specification and D_I be an initial knowledge base. If A is an answer set of $\Pi_{inc}(P \cup D_I)$ then the set $D_R = \{f : holds(f, res(r, s)) \in A\} \cup \{\neg f : \neg holds(f, res(r, s)) \in A\}$ is said to be a P-justified revision of D_I.

A knowledge base B is a *r-i-model* of (satisfies) an r-literal $in(p)$ ($out(p)$ respectively) if $p \in B$ ($\neg p \in B$, respectively). B is a r-i-model of the body of a rule if it satisfies each r-literal of the body. B is a r-i-model of a rule C if the following conditions hold: whenever B satisfies the body of C, then B satisfies the head of C. B is a r-i-model of a revision specification P if B satisfies each rule in P.

Proposition 4 Let P be a revision specification and D_I be a knowledge base. If D_R is a P-justified revision of D_I, then $D_R \div D_I$ is minimal in the family $\{D \div D_I : D$ is a r-i-model of $P \}$, where $\div$ denotes the symmetric difference. i.e. $A \div B = (A \setminus B) \cup (B \setminus A)$. $\qquad\square$

Specifying revisions that depend on the previous state

The revision specifications defined in the previous sections can only express the relationship between the elements of the revised knowledge base. Although it uses the implicit assumption that there is minimal change to the initial database, it can not explicitly state any relation between the initial knowledge bases and the revised knowledge base. For example if we would like to say that "all assistant professors with 20 journal papers are to be promoted to associate professors" we can not express it using revision specifications.

In this section we extend revision specifications to allow us to specify such update descriptions.

An *extended revision rule* can be of the following two forms:

$$in(p) \leftarrow in(q_1), \ldots, in(q_m), out(s_1), \ldots, out(s_n),$$
$$was\_in(t_1), \ldots, was\_in(t_k),$$
$$was\_out(u_1), \ldots, was\_out(u_l) \tag{3}$$

$$out(p) \leftarrow in(q_1), \ldots, in(q_m), out(s_1), \ldots, out(s_n),$$
$$was\_in(t_1), \ldots, was\_in(t_k),$$
$$was\_out(u_1), \ldots, was\_out(u_l) \tag{4}$$

where p, q_i's, s_j's, t_i's and u_j's are atoms.

An extended revision specification is a collection of extended revision rules.

The statement "all assistant professors with 20 journal papers are to be promoted to associate professors" can be expressed using the following extended revision specification:

$$in(associate(X)) \leftarrow$$
$$was\_in(assistant(X)), was\_in(haspaper(X, 20))$$

$$out(assistant(X)) \leftarrow$$
$$was\_in(assistant(X)), was\_in(haspaper(X, 20))$$

Similar to the last section we define revisions with respect to an extended revision specification using extended logic programs and use situation calculus notation.

Algorithm 3 *[Translating Extended Revision Specifications]*
Our translation will be same as in Algorithm 2 except the translation of the revision rules. The extended revision rules are translated as follows:

(a) Each extended revision rule of the type (3)

is translated to the rules

(3.a.1') $holds(p, res(r, s)) \leftarrow$
$\quad holds(q_1, res(r, s)), \ldots, holds(q_m, res(r, s)),$
$\quad \neg holds(s_1, res(r, s)), \ldots, \neg holds(s_n, res(r, s)),$
$\quad holds(t_1, s), \ldots, holds(t_k, s),$
$\quad \neg holds(u_1, s), \ldots, \neg holds(u_l, s)$

(3.a.2') $ab(p', a, s) \leftarrow$
$\quad holds(q_1, res(r, s)), \ldots, holds(q_m, res(r, s)),$
$\quad \neg holds(s_1, res(r, s)), \ldots, \neg holds(s_n, res(r, s)),$
$\quad not \; \neg holds(t_1, s), \ldots, not \; \neg holds(t_k, s),$
$\quad not \; holds(u_1, s), \ldots, not \; holds(u_l, s)$

(b) Each extended revision rule of the type (4)

is translated to the rules

(3.b.1') $\neg holds(p, res(r, s)) \leftarrow$
$\quad holds(q_1, res(r, s)), \ldots, holds(q_m, res(r, s)),$
$\quad \neg holds(s_1, res(r, s)), \ldots, \neg holds(s_n, res(r, s)),$
$\quad holds(t_1, s), \ldots, holds(t_k, s),$
$\quad \neg holds(u_1, s), \ldots, \neg holds(u_l, s)$

(3.b.2') $ab(p, a, s) \leftarrow$
$\quad holds(q_1, res(r, s)), \ldots, holds(q_m, res(r, s)),$
$\quad \neg holds(s_1, res(r, s)), \ldots, \neg holds(s_n, res(r, s)),$
$\quad not \; \neg holds(t_1, s), \ldots, not \; \neg holds(t_k, s),$
$\quad not \; holds(u_1, s), \ldots, not \; holds(u_l, s) \qquad \Box$

The use of $not \; \neg holds(t_1, s)$ and $not \; holds(u_l, s)$ instead of $holds(t_1, s)$ and $\neg holds(u_l, s)$ in (3.a.2') and (3.b.2') is to be cautious when applying the inertia rules (GL92). For example if $D_I = \{assistant(john)\}$ and we have the extended revision specification

$$out(assistant(X)) \leftarrow was\_in(haspaper(X, 20))$$

for the update called "promote" we would not like to have $assistant(john)$ in $D_{promote}$ because we are not sure if $haspaper(john, 20)$ is $false$ in D_I. We would rather have $D_{promote}$ contain neither $assistant(john)$ nor $\neg assistant(john)$.

Definition 5 Let P be an extended revision specification and D_I be an initial knowledge base. If A is an answer set of $\Pi_{inc}(P \cup D_I)$ then the set $D_R = \{f : holds(f, res(r, s)) \in A\} \cup \{\neg f : \neg holds(f, res(r, s)) \in A\}$ is said to be a P-justified revision of D_I.

Relationship with standard update operators

In this section we discuss how rule based revision relates to standard revision and update operators.

When we consider a knowledge base to be a set of propositional facts (with CWA) it is easy to see that the concepts of update and revision (KM92) coincide. For such knowledge bases the following proposition relates the standard definition of updates with P-justified revision.

Definition 6 For any revision rule S, f_S is the propositional formula obtained by replacing each $out(a)$ in S by $\neg a$ and each $in(a)$ in S by a and treating $\leftarrow$ as the implication. For any revision specification P, F_P is the propositional formula obtained by the conjunction of all the f_S's, for all S's in P. $\qquad \Box$

Proposition 5 Let P be a revision specification and D_I be a knowledge base.

D_R is a model (in the propositional sense) of $D_I \; o \; F_P$ where o is the revision operator (KM92) iff $D_R \div D_I$ is minimal in the family $\{D \div D_I \; : \; D$ is a r-model of $P \}$ $\qquad \Box$

When we consider a knowledge base to be a set of literals then a knowledge base may have several models and update and revision (KM92) may be different depending upon the definition of closeness between models and between theories (knowledge bases).

Proposition 6 Let P be a revision specification and D_I be a knowledge base.

D_R is a model of $D_I \; o \; F_P$ where o is the revision operator (KM92) iff $D_R \div D_I$ is minimal in the family $\{D \div D_I \; : \; D$ is a r-i-model of $P \}$ $\qquad \Box$

From the above propositions it is clear that the P-justified revisions computed using the translations suggested in this paper do not compute all the models of the standard revisions (KM92). In Example 1 both $\{a\}$ and $\{b\}$ are r-models of P_1 minimally different from D_I and are also be the models of $D_I \ o \ F_{P_1}$ but only $\{a\}$ is a P_1-justified revision.

One possible way to obtain all the models would be to translate the revision specification P_1 to a first-order theory instead of an extended logic program and minimize the abnormality using circumscription. That has been the approach of Reiter (Rei92) to specify database evolution. On the other hand in certain cases we might need revisions to be specified as rules instead of a formula and also in certain cases extended logic programs may be preferred over circumscription as a computing formalism.

Relation with $\mathcal{A}$ and its extensions

$\mathcal{A}$ is a specification language for representing effects of actions suggested by Gelfond and Lifschitz in (GL92). The e-propositions in $\mathcal{A}$ which are of the form

$$A \ causes \ F \ if \ P_1, \ldots, P_n$$

corresponds to the extended revision rule

$$in(F) \leftarrow was\_in(P_1), \ldots, was\_in(P_n)$$

when the domain consists of only action A and $F, P_1, \ldots, P_n$ are positive atoms.

Revision specifications of the form (1) and (2) are similar to constraints in $\mathcal{AR}$ (KL94), an extension of $\mathcal{A}$. Although the constraints in $\mathcal{AR}$ allow for formulas we believe if rules of the form (1) and (2) are used instead it may be possible to state when a domain description in the language of $\mathcal{AR}$ will have models with unique transition functions.

Conclusion

In this paper we considered the language of *revision specifications* for specifying revision conditions as rules. We presented a translation to extended logic programs that uses situation calculus notation so as to compute the revised knowledge base given a knowledge base consisting of atoms and a revision specification. We then considered knowledge bases that may be incomplete and presented a translation for computing revision for such a case. We also extended the language of revision specifications to allow rules explicitly relating the initial and the revised database. Finally we compared our approach with the standard revise and update operators and with the specification language $\mathcal{A}$.

We believe a more thorough study is necessary to further relate extended revision specifications to standard update operators and also to further relate with languages for reasoning about actions. In particular the impact of using rule based constraints instead of constraint formulas in $\mathcal{AR}$ needs to be studied.

Acknowledgement

I would like to thank Prof. Wiktor Marek whose talk on "Revision Programs" in UT El Paso in Dec 93 triggered the ideas expanded on this paper. I would also like to thank the anonymous referees for their valuable comments.

References

M. Gelfond and V. Lifschitz. Classical negation in logic programs and disjunctive databases. *New Generation Computing*, pages 365–387, 1991.

M. Gelfond and V. Lifschitz. Representing actions in extended logic programs. In *Joint International Conference and Symposium on Logic Programming.*, pages 559–573, 1992.

P. Gardenfors and D. Makinson. Revisions in knowledge systems using epistemic entrenchment. In *Proc. 2nd international conference on theoretical aspects of reasoning about knowledge*, pages 1413–1419, 1988.

G. Kartha and V. Lifschitz. Actions with indirect effects. To appear in KR 94, 1994.

H. Katsuno and A. Mendelzon. A unified view of propositional knowledge base updates. In *Proc. of IJCAI-89*, pages 1413–1419, 1989.

H. Katsuno and A. Mendelzon. On the difference between updating a knowledge base and revising it. In *Proc. of KR 92*, pages 387–394, 1992.

R. Kowalski. Database Updates in the Event Calculus. In *The Journal of Logic Programming*, 12 (1992), 121-146

W. Marek and M. Truszczyński. Revision programming. manuscript, 1994.

W. Marek and M. Truszczyński. Revision specifications by means of programs. manuscript, 1994.

R. Reiter. Formalizing database evolution in the situation calculus. In ICOT, editor, *Proc. of the International Conference on Fifth Generation Computer Systems*, pages 600–609, 1992.

Recovering Software Specifications
with Inductive Logic Programming

William W. Cohen

AT&T Bell Laboratories

600 Mountain Avenue

Murray Hill, NJ 07974

`wcohen@research.att.com`

Abstract

We consider using machine learning techniques to help understand a large software system. In particular, we describe how learning techniques can be used to reconstruct abstract Datalog specifications of a certain type of database software from examples of its operation. In a case study involving a large (more than one million lines of C) real-world software system, we demonstrate that off-the-shelf inductive logic programming methods can be successfully used for specification recovery; specifically, Grendel2 can extract specifications for about one-third of the modules in a test suite with high rates of precision and recall. We then describe two extensions to Grendel2 which improve performance on this task: one which allows it to output a set of candidate hypotheses, and another which allows it to output specifications containing determinations. In combination, these extensions enable specifications to be extracted for nearly two-thirds of the benchmark modules with perfect recall, and precision of better than 60%.

Introduction

Frawley *et al.* [1991] define *knowledge discovery* as the "extraction of implicit, previously unknown, and potentially useful information." Machine learning methods are often used to perform knowledge discovery from databases. Here we investigate the use of machine learning methods for a different knowledge discovery task—understanding a large software system. This is an important application area, as program understanding is a major task in maintaining large software systems [Corbi, 1989]; it has been estimated that for large software systems, more than half of the time spent on maintenance is spent on program understanding [Parikh and Zvegintzov, 1983, page ix].

We present a case study involving a large real-world software system which investigates the use of machine learning methods for *specification recovery—i.e.*, constructing specifications of software from the software itself. Such specifications are useful for program un-

derstanding, but are often not provided with existing software systems. More specifically, we investigate recovering Datalog definitions of database views from C routines which implement these views.

In addition to its potential practical importance, the problem of specification recovery raises (in this domain) a number of interesting research problems. One problem is technical: the natural representation for specifications is a first-order language that is in general hard to learn. Another problem is methodological: as the high-level goal is not prediction but discovery, it is not obvious how one should evaluate the learning system. Despite these difficulties, it will be demonstrated that off-the-shelf but state-of-the-art learning methods can be successfully used for specification recovery in this domain. However, these off-the-shelf methods can also be improved by adapting them more closely to the task at hand.

The Discovery Problem

The experiments of this paper were carried out with the "Recent Change" (henceforth RC) subsystem of the 5ESS[1] switching system. A large part of the 5ESS system is a *database* which encodes all site-specific data. As the database is used by the switch, which is a real-time, distributed system, it has a number of quirks; however, for the purposes of this paper, it can be regarded as a conventional relational database.

The database is optimized for retrieval, and hence information is often stored internally in a redundant and unintuitive format. Thus, the switch administrator accesses the database through the *RC subsystem*, which contains several hundred *views* into the database. RC views are essentially "virtual relations"; they can be accessed and updated in much the same manner as actual relations, but are designed to present a simpler interface to the underlying data. For reasons of efficiency each view is implemented as a C routine which supports a standard set of operations, such as reading and deleting tuples in the view. These routines can be quite complex. In particular, in updating a view, it is often

---

[1]5ESS is a trademark of AT&T.

necessary to check that *integrity constraints* are maintained. Integrity constraints may affect many database relations and checking them is often non-trivial.

The purpose of our discovery system is to automatically construct high-level, declarative specifications of these views. The constructed specifications are in Datalog (*i.e.*, Prolog with no function symbols), and describe how views are derived from the underlying relations. As an example, a view v_1 which is a projection of columns 1,3,5 and 4 of relation r might be specified by the one-clause Datalog program

$$v_1\,(A,B,C,D) \leftarrow r(A,Z,B,D,C).$$

Similarly, a projection v_2 of the join of two relations s and t might be specified

$$v_2\,(A,B,C,D) \leftarrow s(A,B,D),\ t(B,A,Y,Z,C)$$

It may seem surprising that a language as restricted as Datalog can be useful in specifying real-world software systems. We emphasize that *these specifications are not complete descriptions* of the underlying code; they suppress many "details" such as integrity constraints, error handling, and how relations are stored in the database (which is actually distributed over several processors). However, they are a useful description of one important aspect of the code.

We conjecture that in many large systems, software understanding can be facilitated by such abstract, high-level descriptions. Ideally such high-level descriptions would be provided along with the source code: this would be the case, for example, if the source were generated automatically from a specification. For older software systems, however, this is unlikely to be the case. We note that software understanding is especially important for older systems, as they tend to be harder to maintain. These "legacy" systems are are also more likely to be replaced by a newer system with equivalent functionality—an enterprise which again requires understanding the existing system.

To summarize, the *specification recovery* problem we will consider here is to automatically construct *view specifications* like the one above. This particular specification recovery problem is attractive for a number of reasons. The domain is broad enough to be interesting, as the implementation of a view can be arbitrarily complex. On the other hand, the domain is constrained enough so that specification recovery is often possible; in particular, there is reason to believe that concise abstract specifications do indeed exist for many of the views. Another advantage is that although the subsystem being studied is huge (more than 1,100,000 lines of C) it is highly modular; hence insight into the behavior of this large system can be gained by solving many moderate-sized specification recovery problems. The population of problems is also important enough that a successful discovery tool would be practically interesting, and is large enough to form a useful testbed for specification recovery techniques.

Learning View Specifications

The approach we propose to recovering view specifications is the following. First, execute the code to find all tuples in a view v, given a specific database DB. (This process is sometimes called *materializing* the view v.) Second, construct a dataset in which all tuples in the materialized view are positive examples, and all tuples not in the materialized view are (either implicitly or explicitly) negative examples. Third, learn a Datalog definition of v from this dataset, and return this learned definition as the specification of v. The learning step is the most complex one; however there are currently a number of "inductive logic programming" systems which learn logic programs from examples (*e.g.*, see [Quinlan, 1990; Muggleton and Feng, 1992]).

Learning specifications with FOIL

To make this idea concrete, let us return to our example view v_1.[2] Suppose the materialized view v_1 (derived from the relation r) is as follows:

Materialized view v_1:

ssnum	first	last	mi
421-43-4532	dave	jones	q
921-31-3273	jane	jones	q

Relation r:

id	dept	fname	lname	mi
921-31-3273	sales	jane	jones	q
421-43-4532	sales	dave	jones	q

From the view one can derive these examples of the target relation v_1:

$$+v_1\,(421\text{-}43\text{-}4532, dave, jones, q)$$
$$+v_1\,(921\text{-}31\text{-}3273, jane, jones, q)$$

Using these examples, and also using the relation r as background knowledge, the inductive logic programming system FOIL [Quinlan, 1990] will produce the correct specification $v_1\,(A,B,C,D) \leftarrow r(A,E,B,D,C)$. We say "correct" as this example is isomorphic to an actual RC view, and the specification correctly describes the implementation. The specification is also considerably more concise than the implementation—which in this case contains 80 non-comment lines of C—and hence is arguably also more understandable.

Note that in this example we reduced FOIL's search space dramatically by providing the single relevant background relation r, rather than all relations in DB. Restricting the search in this way is essential, as RC databases are large. Fortunately, automatically finding the relevant relations is easy, as computer-readable

---

[2] Except when otherwise indicated, the examples of this paper are isomorphic to real RC views. However, identifiers have been changed: in part to avoid divulging proprietary information, and in part to avoid reader confusion, as RC identifiers appear rather cryptic to an outsider. For pedagogical reasons, we have also used the simplest view specifications as examples.

documentation exists describing which RC relations are accessed by which RC views.

Although FOIL's performance on this small example is encouraging, an more detailed exploratory study conducted using real RC views revealed several limitations. First, for noise-free problems, FOIL is known to scale well with the number of training examples, but poorly with the arity of background relations [Pazzani and Kibler, 1992]. (This problem is shared by GOLEM [Muggleton and Feng, 1992], another well-known inductive logic programming system.) However, many of the relations in the RC database have large arities—*e.g.*, the 36 views used in our exploratory experiments used 18 relations with arity greater than 10 and 9 relations with arity greater than 25.

A second problem with FOIL stems from the fact that the materialized view provides no explicit negative examples. FOIL contains a mechanism for automatically generating negative examples, using the closed world assumption; however, while this technique is in principle appropriate, in practice it is impractical to create enough negative examples to prevent over-generalization on views of moderately high arity. For example, FOIL is unable to correctly learn the view $v_3(A,B,C,D,E,F,G) \leftarrow u(A,B,C,D),w(A,G,F,E,H)$ from a dataset of 136 examples; even with a sample of 360,000 negative tuples FOIL learns the overgeneral specification $v_3(A,B,C,D,E,F,G) \leftarrow u(A,B,C,D)$.

A final disadvantage of FOIL is that due to coding conventions and the like, there are many regularities across view recovery problems which could potentially be exploited in learning; however, FOIL has no mechanism for using such constraints. As a concrete example, it happens that RC view specifications always are composed of *generative* clauses—*i.e.*, when $v(X_1,\ldots,X_n)$ is the head of a clause in a view specification, each X_i always appears somewhere in the body of the clause. However, FOIL can and often does hypothesize nongenerative specifications.

Learning specifications with Grendel2

To summarize our exploratory study, we concluded that to recover view specifications, better mechanisms were needed for preventing over-generalization and for incorporating domain-specific constraints. One inductive logic programming system which has such mechanisms is Grendel2.

Grendel2 is a successor system to Grendel [Cohen, 1992]. In addition to the usual set of positive and negative examples, Grendel takes as input an explicit description of the hypothesis space to be searched—*i.e.*, the intended *bias* of the learning system—written in a formalism called an *antecedent description grammar* (ADG). ADGs are essentially context-free grammars. Grendel's hypotheses are sets of clauses whose antecedents are sentences of an ADG provided by the user.

ADGs provide a way of describing biases used in "theory-guided" learning systems like FOCL [Pazzani and Kibler, 1992]; however they cannot easily express certain other biases. To concisely describe "language biases" like *ij*-determinacy [Muggleton and Feng, 1992] a generalization of ADGs called "augmented ADGs" has been proposed [Cohen, 1993]. Augmented ADGs are analogous to *definite clause grammars* [Sterling and Shapiro, 1986].

Grendel2 is an extension of Grendel that uses augmented ADGs. Like Grendel, Grendel2 uses a FOIL-like technique to search its hypothesis space.[3] The output of Grendel2 is in general a set of clauses, each of which is a sentence of the augmented ADG.

By applying Grendel2 to the view recovery problem, we were able to exploit a number of domain-specific constraints. In Grendel2's datasets, each example is not simply a tuple in the materialized view, but a tuple to which extra information has been attached: specifically, each view tuple is tagged with the list of database tuples read in constructing this view tuple. (These tags were obtained automatically by adding additional "instrumentation" code to the database interface routines.) For example, the dataset for v_1 above is

$$+trace(v_1(421\text{-}43\text{-}4532,dave,jones,q),$$
$$[r(421\text{-}43\text{-}4532,sales,dave,jones,q)]).$$
$$+trace(v_1(921\text{-}31\text{-}3273,jane,davis,q),$$
$$[r(921\text{-}31\text{-}3273,sales,jane,davis,q)])$$

An augmented ADG was then written which generates certain common types of view specifications—namely, projections, certain types of joins, and combinations thereof—and which also encodes a number of additional constraints. One constraint is that clauses generated by the ADG must access the database in an order consistent with the traces of each view tuple. Also, clauses must be generative, in the sense defined above, and use only relevant database relations. These constraints can be expressed quite compactly using ADGs: the largest ADG used in the experiments in this paper (the one used for Grendel/MD, below) contains just 11 rewrite rules and about 30 lines of code.

No negative examples are given to (or constructed by) Grendel2. Instead of using negative examples to prevent over-general hypotheses from being produced, generality is implicitly constrained by the requirement that hypotheses be sentences of the ADG.

The augmented ADG also generates clauses in a special format, as shown on the left-hand side of Figure 1. This format is convenient, as in the RC subsystem a mnemonic *field name* is associate with each column in a view or relation; these field names can be easily added to the specification, as is shown by the variant specification on the right-hand side of Figure 1. (For

---

[3]Note that this is different from the learning method described in [Cohen, 1993], in which a restricted class of augmented ADGs were converted into simple ADGs and passed to Grendel.

trace(v_1(A,B,C,D),[r(E,F,G,H,I)]) ←	v_1(Vssnum,Vfirst,Vlast,Vmi) ←
E=A, r(E,F,G,H,I), B=G, C=H, D=I.	Rid=Vssnum, r(Rid,Rdept,Rfname,Rlname,Rmi), Vfirst=Rfname, Vlast=Rlname, Vmi=Rmi.

Figure 1: Specifications generated by Grendel2. On the left, a specification as produced by the learner. On the right, a more readable version of the specification, formed by removing "trace" information and adding mnemonic field names.

readability, information associated with the traces has been removed from this specification.) Since RC programmers prefer to think in terms of field names rather than column positions, we believe this format to be more readable to persons familiar with the domain. Addition of these mnemonic names is automatic, using existing computer-readable documentation on the RC database.[4]

Evaluation of Discovery Systems

While machine learning tools are typically evaluated by the accuracy of the hypotheses that they produce, this metric is appropriate only when the final purpose of the system is prediction. In this section we will address the methodological question: how should one evaluate a discovery system of the type described above?

This question is made more difficult by the fact that data is often stored redundantly in the RC database. To take a simple artificial example, suppose that we have the following view and relation:

Materialized view v_4:

first	last
jane	jones
dave	smith
⋮	⋮

Relation n:

fname	lname	login
jane	jones	jones
dave	smith	smith
⋮	⋮	⋮

If there is an integrity constraint that requires the *id* field of relation n to be identical to the *lname* field, then the following are equally valid specifications of view v_4:

v_4(First, Last) ←
    n(Fname, Lname, Login),
    First=Fname,
    Last=Lname.

v_4(First, Last) ←
    n(Fname, Lname, Login),
    First=Fname,
    Last=Login.

It is not at all obvious what the discovery system *should* do in this case. We will assume here that both speci-

---

[4]In passing, we note that the ordering of the conjuncts in the body of this clause is not arbitrary, but is based on knowledge about which view and relation fields are indexed. Literals in the body are ordered so that following the usual Prolog evaluation order, the operation of a specification mimics the operation of the actual C code in performing an indexed read.

fications are of interest to the user, and that an ideal discovery system would recover both of them.

To be precise, let us fix a specification language $\mathcal{L}$. For every view v, there is a set of specifications $CorrectSpecs_{\mathcal{L}}(v)$ in $\mathcal{L}$ that can be considered *correct* in the sense that for every legal database, they will produce the same set of tuples as the actual C implementation of v. Assuming that the goal of the user of the system is to find all correct specifications of each view, the specification recovery problem can thus be restated quite naturally as an information retrieval task: given the query "what are the correct specifications of view v?" the discovery system will return a set $ProposedSpecs(v)$, which would ideally be identical to $CorrectSpecs_{\mathcal{L}}(v)$.

If one knew the actual value of $CorrectSpecs_{\mathcal{L}}(v)$, one could measure the performance of a discovery system via the standard information retrieval measures of *recall* and *precision*. *Recall* is the percentage of things in $CorrectSpecs_{\mathcal{L}}(v)$ that appear in $ProposedSpecs(v)$; it measures the percentage of correct specifications that are proposed. *Precision* is the percentage of things in $ProposedSpecs(v)$ that appear in $CorrectSpecs_{\mathcal{L}}(v)$; it measures the number of correct *vs.* incorrect specifications that are proposed. (Notice that for the learning algorithms discussed above, $ProposedSpecs(v)$ is always a singleton set, and hence high recall can be obtained only if $CorrectSpecs_{\mathcal{L}}(v)$ is usually a singleton set.)

Unfortunately, in the RC subsystem it is not easy to determine $CorrectSpecs_{\mathcal{L}}(v)$ for a view v: although one can find one correct specification s by manually reading the code, to determine if a second specification s' is equivalent to s for all legal databases requires knowledge of the integrity constraints enforced by the system, which are not completely documented. Thus, to evaluate the system, we used a cross-validation like approach to evaluate specifications. A routine was written that takes a database DB and a materialized view v and enumerates *all* consistent one-clause specifications allowed by the grammar. Let us call this set $ConsistentSpecs_{\mathcal{L}}(v, DB)$. Recall that a correct specification is by definition one that materializes the correct view for all databases. Hence

$$CorrectSpecs_{\mathcal{L}}(v) \equiv \bigcap_j ConsistentSpecs_{\mathcal{L}}(v, DB_j)$$

where the index j runs over all legal databases DB_j. Thus one can approximate $CorrectSpecs_{\mathcal{L}}(v)$ by taking a series of databases $DB_1, DB_2, \ldots, DB_k$ and using the rule

$$CorrectSpecs_{\mathcal{L}}(v) \approx \bigcap_{i=1}^{k} ConsistentSpecs_{\mathcal{L}}(v, DB_i)$$

$$(1)$$

For our experiments, we collected several RC databases. To estimate the recall and precision of a discovery system on a view v, we used the system to find $ProposedSpecs(v)$ from one database $DB*$, and then computed recall and precision, using Equation 1 to approximate $CorrectSpecs_{\mathcal{L}}(v)$.[5] This process was repeated using different training databases $DB*$, and the results were averaged.[6] This evaluation metric is much like cross-validation; however, rather than measuring the predictive accuracy of a hypothesis on hold-out data, a hypothesis is evaluated by seeing if it is 100% correct on a set of holdout databases. This rewards the hypotheses most valuable in a discovery context: namely, the hypotheses that are with high probability 100% correct.

As an example, if we report a precision of 75% for a view v, this means on average 75% of the specifications obtained by running the learner on a single database were 100% correct on *all* the sample databases. If we report a recall of 50% for v this means that on average half of the specifications that are consistent with all of the sample databases can be obtained by running the learner on a single database.

Experimental Results

The work reported in this paper is still in progress; in particular we are still engaged in the process of collecting additional datasets, and improving the augmented ADG that encodes domain-specific knowledge. In this section, we will describe a controlled study in which we compared three different Grendel2-based learning algorithms. Importantly, these algorithms (and the ADGs used with them) were based only on data from the exploratory study; thus they were developed *without any knowledge of the views used as benchmarks below*. In other words, this is a purely prospective test of the learning systems.

[5] This approximation is relatively expensive to compute because all enumerating consistent specifications must be enumerated; thus we generated only consistent *one-clause* specifications. Fortunately many RC views can be specified by a single clause.

[6] Ideally the process is repeated using every possible database for training. However, in the actual experiments, it was sometimes the case that a view was empty in one of more databases. Such databases were not used for training.

In the experiments, we used four RC databases, ranging in size from 5.6 to 38 megabytes, and 19 benchmark views. The views contain up to 209 fields, involve relations containing up to 90 fields, and contain between one and 531 tuples. While it is difficult to measure the size of a complete implementation of any single view, the views have an average of 747 non-comment lines in top-level module of their C implementations, the longest top-level C implementation is 2904 lines long, and the shortest is 210 lines. In addition to measuring the recall and precision of recovered specifications, we also measured the percentage of benchmark views for which any specifications could be recovered; this is shown in the table below in a column labeled *scope*. All of the learning algorithms described in this section abort with an error message when a problem falls outside their scope.

The result of applying Grendel2 to this set of benchmarks is shown in the first line of Table 1. For this set of problems, and using an augmented ADG written on the basis of our exploratory study, Grendel2 is able to learn specifications for just under a third of the views. When it does succeed, however, it achieves over 80% recall and precision.

We also evaluated the performance of two extensions of Grendel2. To motivate the first extension, note that when many consistent hypotheses exist, Grendel2 makes a more or less arbitrary choice among them. A useful alternative would be for the learning system to return instead the entire set $ConsistentSpecs_{\mathcal{L}}(v, DB)$.

Unfortunately, when there is insufficient training data, there may be an enormous number of consistent specifications. In these cases directly outputting $ConsistentSpecs_{\mathcal{L}}(v, DB)$ is not desirable. To address this problem we developed a *factored form* for view specifications which enables certain large sets of specifications to be compactly presented. As an example, the factored specification

$$v_5\,(VBuffid, VAddr, VLength, VBytes) \leftarrow$$
$$RKey{=}VBuffid,$$
$$p(RKey, RLoc, RLen, RBytes),$$
$$VAddr{=}RLoc,$$
$$(\ VLength{=}RLen\ ;\ VLength{=}RBytes\ ),$$
$$(\ VBytes{=}RLen\ ;\ VBytes{=}RBytes\ ).$$

is shorthand for four specifications, one for every possible pairing of the variables $VLength$, $VBytes$, $RLen$ and $RBytes$.

The row of Table 1 labeled Grendel2/M shows results for an extension of Grendel2 that finds a factored representation of all consistent single-clause specifications. Even though Grendel2/M is restricted to single-clause view specifications, it has the same scope as Grendel2; however, the recall is now perfect. Somewhat suprisingly, Grendel2/M also has slightly better precision, although the difference is not statistically significant.

The goal of the second extension was to increase the scope of Grendel2. Our exploratory study showed that often data is not simply copied from a relation

Learner	Scope	Recall	Precision	
Grendel2	31.6%	83.3%	83.3%	
Grendel2/M	31.6%	100.0%	87.5%	
Grendel2/MD	63.1%	100.0%	61.0%	—all views
			82.2%	—views solved by Grendel2/M
			52.2%	—remaining views

Table 1: Results for Grendel2 and extensions

to a view; instead some simple conversion step is performed. For example, in the specification below, view v_6 is a copy of q with every value of "0" in the third column replaced by the empty string.

$v_6(VProblemCode, VSeverity, VHelpBufId) \leftarrow$
$\quad RPCode = VProblemCode,$
$\quad q(RPCode, RLevel, RTextBufId),$
$\quad VSeverity = RLevel,$
$\quad zero2nullstr(RTextBufId, VHelpBufId).$

$zero2nullstr(0,'').$
$zero2nullstr(Id, Id) \leftarrow Id \neq 0.$

Grendel2 typically fails on such views; furthermore, learning views with conversion functions like *zero2nullstr* is very difficult since a wide range of conversions are performed. We addressed this problem by extending Grendel2/M to generate view specifications that contain *determinations*. A determination between two variables X and Y is denoted $Y \prec X$, and indicates that the value of Y can be be functionally derived from the value of X. Using determinations, v_5 could be specified

$v_6(VProblemCode, VSeverity, VHelpBufId) \leftarrow$
$\quad RPCode = VProblemCode,$
$\quad q(RPCode, RLevel, RTextBufId),$
$\quad VSeverity = RLevel,$
$\quad VHelpBufId \prec RTextBufId.$

Specifications with determinations are even more abstract than the Datalog specifications generated by Grendel; in particular, they cannot be used to materialize a view. However, they are plausibly useful for program understanding.[7]

The row labeled Grendel2/MD of Table 1 shows results for this extension of Grendel2/M.[8] Determinations increase the scope of the learner to more than 60% but also decreases precision to around 60%—much less than the 87.5% precision obtained by Grendel2/M. However, closer examination of the data shows that the difference is less than it appears: Grendel2/MD obtains 82% recall on the problems also solvable by Grendel2/M, but only 52% recall on the problems that it alone can solve. Thus, only some of the decrease in precision appears to be due to the larger hypothesis space used by Grendel/MD; the greater part seems to be due to the fact that (in this set of benchmarks) the views requiring determinations are harder to learn from the data provided.

Interestingly, there seems to be little correlation between the complexity of the C implementation of a view and the performance of the learning systems.[9] This suggests that specification recovery methods based on learning may be a useful complement to methods based primarily on source code analysis.

Related work

Specification and design recovery has been frequently proposed in the software engineering community as an aid in maintaining or replacing hard-to-maintain code, and space does not permit a detailed discussion of all previous related work. Instead we will discuss in general terms the most important differences between our methods and known techniques.

Known techniques for extracting specifications from software rely mostly on deductive static analysis of code. (For example, see Biggerstaff [1989], Kozaczynski and Ning [1990], Breuer and Lano [1991], or Rich and Wills [1990].) The techniques of this paper share some common ground with this previous work; notably, the methods are also knowledge-based, being provided with a good deal of information about the likely form of the specifications being extracted. The primary difference from previous work is that specifications are extracted primarily using *inductive* reasoning about the behavior of the code, rather than deductive reasoning about the code itself.

One previous method that makes some use of program traces is described by Sneed and Ritsch [1993]. However, their main goal is to augment static analysis with information about dynamic properties of a program such as timing information and test set coverage, rather than to reduce the complexity of static analysis.

Our experimental results were in recovering view specifications from C code and materialized views. A good deal of research has also been devoted to the related problem of recovering logical data mod-

---

[7] Note also that actually materializing a view is not part of the evaluation procedure; hence these specifications can also be evaluated using the metrics of scope, recall, and precision.

[8] The grammar allows only determinations between X and a single variable Y, or between X and a constant value.

[9] The C code for the views successfully learned by Grendel2/MD averages 717 non-comment lines long, and the longest view (2904 lines) was one of those learned. Code for the unlearnable views averages 813 lines (not statistically significantly from the average length of learnable views) and the shortest unlearnable view is only 354 lines.

els from databases. However, most methods that have been proposed for this task are only partially automated [Aiken *et al.*, 1993; Hainaut *et al.*, 1993; Premerlani and Blaha, 1993], while our method is fully automatic.

Conclusions

To summarize, we have proposed using learning techniques to extract concise, high-level specifications of software as an aid in understanding a large software system. Based on the assumption that the "useful" specifications are those that with high probability exactly agree with the implementation, we outlined a method for estimating from test data the *recall* and *precision* as well as the *scope* of a learning system. Using this methodology, we demonstrated that Grendel2 can extract specifications for about one-third of the modules from a test suite with high recall and precision.

Two extensions of Grendel2 were also described which improve its performance as a discovery system: one which allows it to output a set of hypotheses, and another which allows it to learn specifications including determinations. Both extensions appear to be unique among inductive logic programming systems. In combination, these techniques allow specifications to be extracted for nearly two-thirds of the benchmark views with perfect recall, and precision of better than 60%. These results are especially encouraging because they were obtained using test cases drawn from a large (more than one million lines of C) real-world software system, and because they are a prospective test of a learning system still under development.

These results have implications both for the software engineering community and the machine learning community. Specification recovery is a potentially important application area for machine learning. The results of this paper suggest that broad classes of specifications can be extracted by currently available methods. However, the research problems encountered in specification recovery problems are quite different from those encountered in "mainstream" machine learning tasks. It seems probable that further inquiries into this area are likely to raise many topics for further research.

Acknowledgements

This research would have impossible without the data-collection efforts of Hari Vallanki, Sandra Carrico, Bryan Ewbank, David Ladd, and Ken Rehor. I am also grateful to Jason Catlett and Cullen Schaffer for advice on methodology, and to Prem Devanbu and Bob Hall for comments on a draft of this paper.

References

Aiken, P.; Muntz, A.; and Richards, R. 1993. A framework for reverse engineering of dod legacy systems. In *Working Conference on Reverse Engineering*. IEEE Computer Society Press.

Biggerstaff, Ted J. 1989. Design recovery for maintenance and reuse. *IEEE Computer* 36–49.

Breuer, P. T. and Lano, K. 1991. Creating specifications from code: Reverse engineering techniques. *Journal of Software Maintenance: Research and Practice* 3:145–162.

Cohen, William W. 1992. Compiling knowledge into an explicit bias. In *Proceedings of the Ninth International Conference on Machine Learning*, Aberdeen, Scotland. Morgan Kaufmann.

Cohen, William W. 1993. Rapid prototyping of ILP systems using explicit bias. In *Proceedings of the 1993 IJCAI Workshop on Inductive Logic Programming*, Chambery, France.

Corbi, T. A. 1989. Program understanding: challenge for the 1990s. *IBM Systems Journal* 28(2):294–306.

Frawley, William; Piatesky-Schapiro, Gregory; and Matheus, Christopher 1991. Knowledge discovery in databases: An overview. In Piatesky-Schapiro, Gregory and Frawley, William, editors 1991, *Knowledge Discovery in Databases*. The AAAI Press.

Hainaut, J.-L.; Chandelon, M.; Tonneau, C.; and Joris, M. 1993. Contribution to a theory of database reverse engineering. In *Working Conference on Reverse Engineering*. IEEE Computer Society Press.

Kozaczynski, W. and Ning, J. 1990. SRE: A knolwedge based environment for large scale software re-engineering activities. In *Proceedings of the 11th International Conference on Software Engineering*.

Muggleton, Stephen and Feng, Cao 1992. Efficient induction of logic programs. In *Inductive Logic Programming*. Academic Press.

Parikh, Girsh and Zvegintzov, Nicholas, editors 1983. *Tutorial on Software Maintanance*. IEEE Computer Society Press.

Pazzani, Michael and Kibler, Dennis 1992. The utility of knowledge in inductive learning. *Machine Learning* 9(1).

Premerlani, W. J. and Blaha, M. R. 1993. An approach for reverse engineering of relational databases. In *Working Conference on Reverse Engineering*. IEEE Computer Society Press.

Quinlan, J. Ross 1990. Learning logical definitions from relations. *Machine Learning* 5(3).

Rich, Charles and Wills, Linda 1990. Recognizing a program's design: A graph-parsing approach. *IEEE Software* 82–89.

Sneed, H. M. and Ritsch, H. 1993. Reverse engineering via dynamic analysis. In *Working Conference on Reverse Engineering*. IEEE Computer Society Press.

Sterling, Leon and Shapiro, Ehud 1986. *The Art of Prolog: Advanced Programming Techniques*. MIT Press.

Can we enforce full compositionality in uncertainty calculi?

Didier Dubois and Henri Prade
Institut de Recherche en Informatique de Toulouse (I.R.I.T.) – C.N.R.S.
Université Paul Sabatier, 118 route de Narbonne
31062 Toulouse Cedex, France
{dubois, prade}@irit.irit.fr

Abstract

At AAAI'93, Elkan has claimed to have a result trivializing fuzzy logic. This trivialization is based on too strong a view of equivalence in fuzzy logic and relates to a fully compositional treatment of uncertainty. Such a treatment is shown to be impossible in this paper. We emphasize the distinction between i) degrees of partial truth which are allowed to be truth functional and which pertain to gradual (or fuzzy) propositions, and ii) degrees of uncertainty which cannot be compositional with respect to all the connectives when attached to classical propositions. This distinction is exemplified by the difference between fuzzy logic and possibilistic logic. We also investigate an almost compositional uncertainty calculus, but it is shown to lack expressiveness.

1. Introduction

There is a very active research trend in Artificial Intelligence concerning the management of uncertainty in knowledge-based systems. This trend is still influenced by the MYCIN experiments (Buchanan & Shortliffe, 1984), where a basic idea was to attach weights expressing uncertainty to facts and rules in a knowledge base. Then we are faced with the problem of how to propagate these weights in reasoning procedures. This problem has usually been dealt with on a rule-by-rule basis, by splitting it into three subproblems: i) computing the weight bearing on a compo-site fact from the weights bearing on the elementary parts of this fact; ii) propagating the weight bearing on the conditions of the rule to the conclusion, by integrating the weight bearing on the rule; iii) combining the weights bearing on partial conclusions pertaining to the same matter. However, investigating the validity of such a method requires a proper interpretation of the weights. Reading the literature in this area, it appears that these weights may have two interpretations: degrees of uncertainty and degrees of partial truth and that people tend to make a confusion between these two notions. One of the reasons why this confusion was made is the need for a compositionality law for computing the resulting weights in the style of many-valued logics where all the connectives are usually truth-functional. Even degrees of probability are sometimes called degrees of truth (e.g., Nilsson, 1986) although probabilistic logic excludes compositionality.

The emergence of fuzzy rule-based systems in process control problems has led AI researchers, that criticized MYCIN-like systems, to reject fuzzy logic on the same grounds of dubious compositionality assumptions. For instance, in a recent paper, Elkan (1993) has questioned its well-foundedness and cast serious doubts on the reasons of its success, arguing that "fuzzy logic collapses mathematically to two-valued logic". This claim is in fact due to the use of too strong a notion of logical equivalence which is valid in two-valued logic, but which has nothing to do with fuzzy logic. Furthermore, Elkan (1993) does not mention the important distinction between two totally different problems to which fuzzy set-based methods apply, namely the handling of *gradual* (thus non-Boolean) properties whose satisfaction by a completely known state of facts is a matter of degree on the one hand, and the handling of uncertainty pervading Boolean propositions and induced by incomplete states of knowledge (which can be represented by means of fuzzy sets) on the other hand. The first problem can be addressed by means of a truth functional fuzzy (multiple-valued) logic, while the second one is the realm of possibility theory (Zadeh, 1978; Dubois & Prade, 1988a) which is a non-fully compositional uncertainty calculus (i.e., the degree of uncertainty of a compound proposition cannot systematically be computed from the degrees of uncertainty of its components only). Elkan (1993)'s paper is thus pervaded by the wrong but alas rather common idea that truth functional fuzzy logic has something to do with uncertainty handling. Assuming a fully compositional many-valued calculus on a Boolean algebra of propositions (a structure enforced by his equivalence requirement), the logical system collapses to two-valued logic.

This paper is a presentation of the authors' view on the problem of handling uncertainty and partial truth in the framework of information systems. In Section 2 we argue in favor of a clear distinction between (un)certainty and truth and propose a practical definition of truth based on approximate matching between a proposition and the description of a state of facts. Section 3 recalls the impossibility of a fully compositional calculus for dealing with uncertainty about Boolean propositions, and illustrates this impossibility result by comparing fuzzy logic and possibilistic logic. In Section 4 we investigate the possibility

"

of an *almost* fully compositional uncertainty calculus, but its expressiveness turns to be very limited.

2. Partial Truth vs. Uncertainty

The distinction between degrees of truth and degrees of uncertainty goes back to De Finetti (1936), and seems to have been almost completely forgotten by Artificial Intelligence people. The confusion pervading the relationship between truth and uncertainty in the expert systems literature is apparently due to the lack of a dedicated paradigm for interpreting partial truth, and grades of uncertainty in a single framework. Such a paradigm can derive from a commonsense view of truth, *as the compatibility between a statement and reality*. This naïve definition of truth has been criticized by philosophers (see, e.g., Gochet in his discussion of Dubois & Prade (1988b)) but can be suitably modified by changing the debatable word "reality" into "what is known about reality" and interpreting the latter as "the description of some actual state of facts as stored in a data base". Hence computing the degree of truth of a statement S comes down to estimating its conformity with the description of what is known of the actual state of facts. As a consequence, truth evaluation comes down to a semantic matching procedure. This point of view is in accordance with Zadeh (1982) test-score semantics for natural languages. Four interesting situations can be encountered.

a) <u>Classical two-valued logic</u>. In order to compute truth-values, we need a precise definition of what "proposition" means. This is a matter of convention. The usual convention is that a proposition is identified with a set of "possible worlds" or "states of fact". Moreover a proposition is said to be true if and only if the actual state of facts is one of those which the proposition encompasses. By convention a proposition is true or false. If the actual state of facts is known and encoded as an item d in a database, the truth-value $\tau_d(S)$ (=1 (true) or 0 (false)) of a proposition S in a state of facts d can be computed.

b) <u>Partial truth</u>. This convention can be changed. Instead of defining a proposition as a binary entity that fits the actual state of fact or not, we can decide to use a more refined scale to evaluate the compatibility between a proposition S and a precisely known state of facts d. This is usual in natural language. For instance, the compatibility of "a tall man", with some individual of a given size is often graded: the man can be judged *not quite* tall, *somewhat* tall, *rather* tall, *very* tall, etc. Changing the usual true/false convention leads to a new concept of proposition whose compatibility with a given state of facts is a matter of degree, and can be measured on a scale L that is no longer $\{0,1\}$, but the unit interval for instance. It reflects linguistic levels such as "somewhat", "rather", "very", etc. This kind of convention leads to identifying a "fuzzy proposition" S with a fuzzy set of possible words; the degree of membership of a possible world to this fuzzy set evaluates the degree of fit between the proposition and the state of facts it qualifies. This degree of fit $\tau_d(S) \in L$

is called degree of truth of proposition S in the possible world d. Many-valued logics, especially truth-functional ones, provide a calculus of degrees of truth, including degrees between "true" and "false".

c) <u>Uncertainty</u>. On the other hand, even if we keep the convention that a proposition is either true or false, it is not always possible to determine whether it is *actually* true or false in given circumstances, because the actual state of facts is not known. In such a situation, we face uncertainty. Clearly uncertainty is a meta-level concept with respect to truth, since the uncertainty bears on whether a proposition is true or false (and nothing else). Moreover uncertainty is knowledge-dependent, i.e., refers to an agent. If uncertainty is encoded in a binary way, there can be only 3 situations: the agent is sure that S is true, he is sure that S is false, or he does not know. This last situation does *not* correspond to a third truth-value but to a suspended choice. More refined models of uncertainty will use an ordered scale U (again, the unit interval [0,1] usually) then $g(S) \in U$ will express to what extent one is sure that S is true, and $g(\neg S)$ to what extent one is sure that S is false. A typical example of degree of uncertainty is a degree of probability. Then our imperfect knowledge of the actual state of facts is modelled via a probability distribution over possible worlds, $g(S)$ being the probability of the set of possible worlds identified with S. In other situations our knowledge of the actual state of facts is described by a set K of propositions that are believed as being true by some agent (what Gärdenfors (1988) calls a belief set). The available knowledge is then described by the set D of possible worlds where all propositions in K are true; a proposition S is surely true if $D \subseteq S$, surely false if $D \subseteq \neg S$ (the complement of S) and S is uncertain if $D \cap S \neq \emptyset$, $D \cap \neg S \neq \emptyset$. This is again the crude trichotomy mentioned above in the presence of incomplete knowledge. Between this crude model, and the sophisticated, additive probabilistic approach to uncertainty lies a third more qualitative approach. Suppose that the set D of possible states of fact is ordered in terms of plausibility, normality and the like. Then D can be viewed as a fuzzy set of possible states of facts. The overlapping between D and the ordinary set of possible worlds identified with a proposition S will be a matter of degree. This is possibility theory that handles two degrees $\Pi(S)$ and $N(S)$ attached to S, respectively the possibility and the necessity that S is true. $\Pi(S) = 1$ means that S is true in one of the most plausible worlds in D. $N(S) = 1$ means that S is true in all possible worlds in D. Total ignorance on the truth value of S is expressed by $\Pi(S) = 1$, $N(S) = 0$. Moreover $N(S) = 1 - \Pi(\neg S)$ while $P(\neg S) = 1 - P(S)$ in the probabilistic approach. Note that the presence of uncertainty does not affect the truth-value scale which is always $\{0,1\}$: degrees of uncertainty are not truth-values.

d) <u>Uncertain partial truth</u>. In that case truth may altogether be a matter of degree and may be ill-known. Then, all values $\alpha = \tau_d(S)$ such that d is compatible with the available information D, is a candidate truthvalue for S. When both S and D can be expressed as fuzzy sets, we can consider for each truth-value $\alpha \in L$, such that $\alpha = \tau_d(S)$ a degree of possibility $\mu_D(d)$ that α is the truth-value of S. This fuzzy set of more or less possible truth-values forms a so-called fuzzy truth-value (Zadeh, 1979) denoted $\tau_D(S)$. A fuzzy truth-value combines the ideas of partial truth and of uncertainty about truth. It is thus a more complex construct than degrees of truth and degrees of uncertainty. Changing the fuzzy set D into a probability distribution on possible worlds, $\tau_D(S)$ becomes a random truth-value over a non-binary truth set L.

A standard analogical example that points out the difference between degrees of truth and degrees of uncertainty is that of a bottle. In terms of binary truth-values, a bottle is viewed as full or empty. If one accounts for the quantity of liquid in the bottle, one may say the bottle is "half full" for instance; under this way of speaking "full" becomes a fuzzy predicate and the degrees of truth of "The bottle is full" reflects the amount of liquid in the bottle. The situation is quite different when expressing our ignorance about whether the bottle is either full or empty (given that we know only one of the two situations is the true one). To say that the probability that the bottle is full is 1/2 does not mean that the bottle is half full. Degrees of uncertainty are clearly a higher level notion than degrees of truth.

3. Fuzzy Logic vs. Possibilistic Logic

3.1. The Compositionality Problem

An important consequence of the above distinction between degrees of truth and degrees of uncertainty is that degrees of uncertainty bearing on classical propositions cannot be compositional for all connectives. Namely there cannot exist operations $\oplus$ and $*$ on [0,1], nor negation functions f such that $g(S) \neq 0,1$ for some S, $g(T) = 1$, $g(\bot) = 0$ and the following identities simultaneously hold for all classical propositions S_1, S_2, S

$$g(\text{not } S) = f(g(S)) \quad (1) \; ; \; g(S_1 \wedge S_2) = g(S_1) * g(S_2) \quad (2)$$
$$g(S_1 \vee S_2) = g(S_1) \oplus g(S_2) \quad (3)$$

This result is proved independently in (Dubois & Prade, 1988b) and (Weston, 1987). A family of propositions represented by a classical language form a Boolean algebra. The lack of compositionality is then a direct consequence of the well-known fact in mathematics that a non-trivial Boolean algebra that is linearly ordered has only two elements. However weak forms of compositionality make sense; for instance $\Pi(S_1 \vee S_2) = \max(\Pi(S_1), \Pi(S_2))$ in possibility theory, but generally, $\Pi(S_1 \wedge S_2) < \min(\Pi(S_1), \Pi(S_2))$; $\Pi(S_1 \wedge S_2) = \min(\Pi(S_1),\Pi(S_2))$ holds only for logically independent propositions; see Sec. 3.3. Similarly with grades of probability where $P(S) = 1 - P(\text{not } S)$ but $P(S_1 \wedge S_2) = P(S_1) \cdot P(S_2)$ only in situations of stochastic independence. The above impossibility result is a new way of stating a well known fact, i.e., that the unit-interval is *not* a Boolean algebra. It rejects many usual uncertainty handling compositional techniques currently used in expert systems into ad-hocery.

This result is based on the assumption that the propositions to evaluate are not fuzzy ones. By contrast, truth values of fuzzy propositions can be compositional when they can be precisely evaluated (i.e., under complete information). This is because closed sets of fuzzy propositions are no longer Boolean algebras but form weaker structures compatible with the unit interval. For instance, using max, min, $1 - (\cdot)$ for expressing disjunction, conjunction and negation of fuzzy propositions equips sets of such propositions with a distributive lattice structure that is compatible with the unit interval; this structure is the only one where all laws of Boolean algebra hold except the laws of non-contradiction and of excluded middle (Bellman & Giertz, 1973). Sometimes, arguments against fuzzy set theory rely on the impossibility of compositionality (e.g., Weston, 1987; Elkan, 1993). Usually these arguments are based on the wrong assumption that the algebra of propositions to be evaluated is Boolean. Note that fuzzy truth values (case d above) are not truth- functional, generally.

3.2. Fuzzy Logic Equivalence is not Classical

Elkan (1993) claims that in fuzzy logic the four following requirements hold for any propositions S_1 and S_2, τ being a truth assignment function such that $\forall S, \tau(S) \in [0,1]$

$$\tau(S_1 \wedge S_2) = \min(\tau(S_1),\tau(S_2)) \quad (4)$$
$$\tau(S_1 \vee S_2) = \max(\tau(S_1),\tau(S_2)) \quad (5)$$
$$\tau(\neg S) = 1 - \tau(S) \quad (6)$$
$$\tau(S_1) = \tau(S_2) \text{ if } S_1 \text{ and } S_2 \text{ are logically equivalent.} \quad (7)$$

While (4)-(5)-(6) are indeed the basic relations governing degrees of truth in fuzzy logic (as well as fuzzy set membership degrees) as proposed by Zadeh (1965), requirement (7) where "logically equivalent" is understood in a stronger sense than the equivalences induced by (4)-(5)-(6) has never been seriously considered by any author in the fuzzy set literature (up to a few erroneous papers which may always exist in a large corpus of publications). Indeed assuming that degrees of truth can be intermediary between 0 and 1, the propositions under consideration are no longer classical ones. Hence logical equivalence must be redefined from scratch. (7) should be understood the other way around: "S_1 is equivalent to S_2" means $\tau(S_1) = \tau(S_2)$ in all possible worlds. Obviously some classical logic equivalences still hold with fuzzy propositions obeying (4)-(5)-(6), namely the ones allowed by the De Morgan's structure induced by (4)-(5)-(6), as for instance

$$S \wedge S \equiv S \; ; \; S \vee S \equiv S \qquad \text{(idempotency)}$$
$$S_1 \wedge (S_2 \vee S_3) \equiv (S_1 \wedge S_2) \vee (S_1 \wedge S_3) \; ;$$
$$S_1 \vee (S_2 \wedge S_3) \equiv (S_1 \vee S_2) \wedge (S_1 \vee S_3) \qquad \text{(distributivity)}.$$

But other Boolean equivalences *do not* hold, for instance

$$S \wedge \neg S \not\equiv \bot \text{ since (4) and (6) } \textit{only} \text{ entail}$$
$$\tau(S \wedge \neg S) = \min(\tau(S), 1 - \tau(S)) \leq 1/2$$

$S \vee \neg S \not\equiv T$ since (5) and (6) *only* entail

$$\tau(S \vee \neg S) = \max(\tau(S), 1 - \tau(S)) \geq 1/2$$

where $\tau(\perp) = 0$ and $\tau(T) = 1$. Indeed the failure of contradiction and excluded-middle laws is typical of fuzzy logic as emphasized by many authors. This is natural with gradual properties like 'tall'. For instance, in a given context, somebody who is 1.75 meter tall, may be considered neither as completely tall (i.e., tall with degree 1) nor as completely not tall (i.e., tall with degree 0); in this case we may have, for example, $\mu_{tall}(1.75) = 0.5 = \mu_{\neg tall}(1.75)$.

Idempotency is thus preserved by using min and max for intersection and union respectively but not the excluded middle and contradiction laws. If we change the truth-functions in (4, 5, 6), we change the structure of the set of propositions (hence the underlying conventions). For instance using $\max(0, a + b - 1)$ in (4) and $\min(a + b, 1)$ we recover the laws of excluded middle and of non-contradiction but we lose idempotency of conjunction and disjunction. Indeed, the laws of excluded middle and non-contradiction are not consistent with idempotency of conjunction and disjunction, when truth is no longer a binary notion (Dubois & Prade, 1980). Note that Elkan (1993) finds it natural to require that propositions $\neg(A \wedge \neg B)$ and $B \vee (\neg A \wedge \neg B)$ be equivalent, and shows that this requirement is incompatible with the convention of propositions having more than 2 truth-levels in the presence of (4, 5, 6). Many-valued logics are trivialized by this result only insofar as the proposed equivalence is so intuitively compelling that any fuzzy logic system should adopt it. The intuitive appeal of this equivalence is far from striking since in the presence of (4, 5, 6), $\neg(A \wedge \neg B) \equiv \neg A \vee B$ and $B \vee (\neg A \wedge \neg B) \equiv (\neg A \vee B) \wedge (B \vee \neg B)$. Elkan's suggested equivalence is clearly related to the acceptance of the excluded middle law (for B), a unusual requirement in fuzzy logic.

3.3. Possibility and Qualitative Uncertainty

The presence or absence of compositional rules is thus a criterion to distinguish between logics of graded truth (that handle vague propositions under complete information) and logics of uncertainty (that handle usual propositions under incomplete information). This is well exemplified by the distinction between fuzzy logic and possibilistic logic.

Fuzzy sets can be used not only for modelling the gradual nature of properties but can also be used for representing incomplete states of knowledge. In this second use, the fuzzy set plays the role of a possibility distribution which provides a complete ordering of mutually exclusive states of the world according to their respective levels of possibility or plausibility. For instance, if we *only know* that "John is tall" (but not his precise height), where the meaning of 'tall' is described in the context by the mem-bership function of a fuzzy set, i.e., μ_{tall}, then the greater $\mu_{tall}(x)$ is, the greater the possibility that height(John) = x and the smaller $\mu_{tall}(x)$, the smaller this possibility.

Given a [0,1]-valued possibility distribution π

describing an incomplete state of knowledge, Zadeh (1978) defines a so-called possibility measure Π such that

$$\Pi(S) = \sup\{\pi(x), x \text{ makes } S \text{ true}\} \qquad (8)$$

where S is a *Boolean* proposition, i.e., a proposition which can be true or false only. It can be easily checked that for Boolean propositions S_1 and S_2, we have

$$\Pi(S_1 \vee S_2) = \max(\Pi(S_1), \Pi(S_2)) \qquad (9)$$

but *only* $\quad \Pi(S_1 \wedge S_2) \leq \min(\Pi(S_1), \Pi(S_2)) \qquad (10)$

in the general case (equality holds when S_1 and S_2 are *logically independent*). Indeed if $S_2 \equiv \neg S_1$, $\Pi(S_1 \wedge S_2) = \Pi(\perp) = 0$, while $\min(\Pi(S), \Pi(\neg S)) = 0$ only if the information is sufficiently complete for having either $\Pi(\neg S) = 0$ (S is true) or $\Pi(S) = 0$ (S is false). If nothing is known about S, we have $\Pi(S) = \Pi(\neg S) = 1$. By duality, a necessity measure N is associated to Π according to the relation (which can be viewed as a graded version of the relation between what is necessary and what is possible in modal logic)

$$N(S) = 1 - \Pi(\neg S) \qquad (11)$$

which states that S is all the more necessarily true as $\neg S$ has a low possibility to be true. It entails

$$N(S_1 \wedge S_2) = \min(N(S_1), N(S_2)) \qquad (12)$$

and $\quad N(S_1 \vee S_2) \geq \max(N(S_1), N(S_2)). \qquad (13)$

Observe also that neither Π, nor N, are fully compositional with respect to $\wedge$, $\vee$ and $\neg$. Possibilities are only compositional with respect to disjunction, necessities with respect to conjunction. The equalities (9), (11) and (12) should not be confused with (5), (6) and (4) respectively. In (9), (11), (12) we deal with Boolean propositions pervaded with uncertainty due to incomplete information, while (4)-(5)-(6) pertain to non-Boolean propositions whose truth is a matter of degree (the information being assumed to be complete). This distinction is a crucial prerequisite in any discussion about fuzzy sets and possibility theory and their use in automated reasoning.

Possibility measures have been shown (Dubois, 1986; Dubois & Prade, 1991) to be the numerical counterpart of so-called qualitative possibility relations $\geq$ (where $S_1 \geq S_2$ reads "S_1 is at least as possible as S_2"), in the sense that $\forall \Pi, \exists$ an ordering $\geq$ such that $\forall S_1, \forall S_2, \Pi(S_1) \geq \Pi(S_2) \Leftrightarrow S_1 \geq S_2$. The ordering $\geq$ is supposed to be reflexive, complete ($S_1 \geq S_2$ or $S_2 \geq S_1$), transitive, non-trivial ($T > \perp$), such that $\forall S, T \geq S$ (certainty of tautology) and to satisfy the characteristic axiom

$$\forall S_1, \text{ if } S_2 \geq S_3 \text{ then } S_1 \cup S_2 \geq S_1 \cup S_3.$$

For qualitative necessity the above axiom is changed, for the corresponding ordering, by substituting $\cap$ to $\cup$. This shows the qualitative nature of possibility and necessity measures.

The case d of Section 2 which combines the case of fuzzy statements and of incomplete information can be also handled in the possibilistic framework. Let μ_D be the membership function of the fuzzy set representing the available information and μ_S be the one representing the fuzzy statement. The degree of truth $\tau_D(S)$ is then itself a fuzzy set of $[0,1]$, which can be interpreted as a fuzzy truth-value, whose membership function is defined by

$$\mu_{\tau_D(S)}(v) = \sup_d \{\mu_D(d) \mid \mu_S(d) = v\}; \mu_{\tau_D(S)}(v) = 0 \text{ if } \mu_S^{-1}(v) = 0$$

i.e., $\mu_{\tau_D(S)}(v)$ is the grade of possibility that the degree of truth of S is equal to v knowing that the state of facts is restricted by D. The fuzzy truth value $\mu_{\tau_D(S)}$ can be approximated by means of two numbers $\Pi(S)$ and $N(S)$, which extend (8) and its dual to the case of a fuzzy statement S (Dubois & Prade, 1985), namely with $\pi = \mu_D$

$$\Pi(S) = \sup_d \min(\mu_S(d), \pi(d))$$
$$N(S) = 1 - \Pi(\neg S) = \inf_d \max(\mu_S(d), 1 - \pi(d)).$$

Indeed $\Pi(S)$ and $N(S)$ can be viewed as the degrees of possibility and necessity that S is "true", if we interpret "true" by extending its definition from $\{0,1\}$ (i.e., $\mu_{\text{true}}(1) = 1$, $\mu_{\text{true}}(0) = 0$) to $[0,1]$ by letting $\mu_{\text{true}}(v) = v$, $\forall v \in [0,1]$. We then have in any case

$$\Pi(S) = \sup_v \min(\mu_{\tau_D(S)}(v), v)$$
$$N(S) = \inf_v \max(1 - \mu_{\tau_D(S)}(v), v).$$

4. Almost Preserving Compositionality

As said above a measure of uncertainty defined on a Boolean algebra and taking its values in the interval $[0,1]$ cannot be fully compositional with respect to all the logical connectives, just because we cannot equip $[0,1]$ with a structure of Boolean algebra. However we may try to preserve compositionality *as far as possible*. Recently Schwartz (1992) has proposed a logic of likelihood governed by the following laws, for all S, S_1, S_2

$$g(\neg S) = 1 - g(S); \quad g(S_1 \vee S_2) = \begin{cases} 1 \text{ if } S_1 \vee S_2 = T \\ \max(g(S_1), g(S_2)) \text{ if not ;} \end{cases}$$

$$g(S_1 \wedge S_2) = \begin{cases} 0 \text{ if } S_1 \wedge S_2 = \bot \\ \min(g(S_1), g(S_2)) \text{ if not.} \end{cases}$$

Such a measure of likelihood g is as compositional as possible. Note that these likelihood set-functions are self-dual. Moreover only operations with a qualitative flavor are used to combine the likelihood degrees. Only a totally ordered set equipped with an order reversing involution is required as a likelihood scale. In the following we investigate what is the power of expressiveness of these measures of likelihood, in the finite case.

Let $\Omega = \{\omega_1, ..., \omega_n\}$ be the finite set of atoms of the Boolean algebra 2^Ω. Let $g(\{\omega_i\}) = g_i \in [0,1]$. We have

$$\forall i, g_i = 1 - g(\Omega - \{\omega_i\}) = 1 - \max_{j \neq i} g_j = \min_{j \neq i} (1 - g_j).$$

If $\exists i, g_i = 1$ then $g(\Omega - \{\omega_i\}) = 0$ and then $\forall j \neq i$, $g_j = 0$. Thus it corresponds to the *deterministic* case.

Let us suppose that $\exists i, g_i = \alpha \in (0,1)$. Then

$$\forall j \neq i, g_j \leq \max_{k \neq i} g_k = g(\Omega - \{\omega_i\}) = 1 - g_i = 1 - \alpha.$$

Let us suppose that $\alpha = g_1 \geq g_2 \geq ... \geq g_n$. Then

$$g_2 = 1 - g(\Omega - \{\omega_2\}) = 1 - \max_{j \neq 2} g_j = 1 - g_1 = 1 - \alpha.$$

Since g_1 is the maximal level, it follows that $\alpha \geq 1/2$. Similarly we have: $g_3 = 1 - \max(g_1, g_2, g_4, ..., g_n) = 1 - \alpha, ..., g_n = 1 - \alpha$. Thus if $g_1 < 1$, we can only have $1 > g_1 \geq g_2 = g_3 = ... = g_n = 1 - g_1 > 0$. So we can only describe a *pseudo-deterministic* situation where $\exists i, g_i = \alpha \geq 1/2$, and $\forall j \neq i, g_j = 1 - \alpha \leq 1/2$. In particular, total uncertainty is described by $\forall i, g_i = \alpha = 1 - \alpha = 1/2$.

In this calculus, we only have at most four certainty levels corresponding respectively to the complete certainty of truth (1), the likelihood of truth (L), the unlikelihood of truth (UL = 1 − L), and the complete certainty of falsity. Especially this representation of uncertainty does not really need the unit interval since only a 4-element totally ordered set $\{0, UL, L, 1\}$ is needed.

Thus this proposal corresponds to the most elementary logic of likelihood which can be imagined: there exists *one* alternative ω_0 which, without being necessarily completely certain, appears to be more likely than the others which are considered as having a smaller, undifferentiated level of likelihood. This seems to coincide with the "simplified English probabilistic logic" considered by Aleliunas (1990); this logic also distinguishes between the four levels: 0 (certainly false), unlikely, likely, 1 (certainly true).

It is interesting to see whether likelihood measures induce a comparative probability ordering on events. Namely a comparative probability ordering $\geq$ is such that $\geq$ is complete and transitive, $S \geq \emptyset$, $\forall S \subseteq \Omega$, and $\geq$ satisfies the additivity axiom (Fine, 1973): $\forall S_1$,

$$\text{if } S_1 \cap (S_2 \cup S_3) = \emptyset,$$
$$\text{then } S_2 > S_3 \Leftrightarrow S_1 \cup S_2 > S_1 \cup S_3 \quad (14)$$

where $S_1 > S_2$ means $S_1 \geq S_2$ and not $(S_2 \geq S_1)$. Any non-degenerate function g classifies the events in Ω into 4 classes of level 1, L, UL and 0 respectively. Namely $\exists \omega_0$ such that the class of level L is $\{S \neq \Omega, \omega_0 \in S\}$, the class of level UL is $\{S \neq \emptyset, \omega_0 \notin S\}$. The class of level 1 is $\{\Omega\}$ and the one of level 0 is $\{\emptyset\}$. Particularly we have, for $S_1 \neq S_2$, $S_1 > S_2$ if and only if $S_1 = \Omega$ or $S_2 = \emptyset$ or $(\omega_0 \in S_1$ and $\omega_0 \notin S_2)$. Let us consider whether (14) holds:

- if $S_2 = \Omega$ then $S_1 = \emptyset$ and (14) is trivial. From now on $S_1 \neq \emptyset$;
- if $S_2 \neq \Omega$, $S_3 \neq \emptyset$ then assume $S_2 > S_3$, i.e., $\omega_0 \in S_2$, $\omega_0 \notin S_3$. Since $S_1 \cap S_2 = \emptyset$, $\omega_0 \notin S_1$. Hence $\omega_0 \notin S_1 \cup S_3$ and $S_1 \cup S_2 > S_1 \cup S_3$.
  Conversely assume $\Omega \neq S_1 \cup S_2 > S_1 \cup S_3$. Clearly $S_1 \cup S_3 \neq \emptyset$; we have $\omega_0 \in S_1 \cup S_2$, $\omega_0 \notin S_1 \cup S_3$.

Hence $\omega_0 \notin S_1$, and $\omega_0 \in S_2 - S_3$. Hence $S_2 > S_3$.

Assume now $S_1 \cup S_2 = \Omega > S_1 \cup S_3$ then since $S_1 \cap (S_2 \cup S_3) = \emptyset$, it follows that $S_3 \subseteq S_2$. If $\omega_0 \in S_2 - S_3$ then $g(S_1 \cup S_2) = 1 > g(S_1 \cup S_3) = $ UL and $g(S_2) = L > g(S_3) = $ UL. If $\omega_0 \in S_3$ we have $g(S_2) = g(S_3) = L$ and $g(S_1 \cup S_2) = 1 > g(S_1 \cup S_3) = $ L. Hence (14) fails when $S_1 \cup S_2 = \Omega$.

- when $S_3 = \emptyset$ then (14) fails too, if $\omega_0 \in S_1$ since then $g(S_2) > g(S_3)$ but $g(S_1 \cup S_2) = g(S_1 \cup S_3) = $ L, generally.

As a consequence the likelihood measure *almost* satisfies the axioms of a comparative probability relation. It satisfies the following reasonable relaxation of additivity: $\forall S_1, S_2, S_3$ such that $S_1 \cup S_2 \neq \Omega$, $S_1 \cap (S_2 \cup S_3) = \emptyset$, $S_3 \neq \emptyset$: $S_2 > S_3 \Leftrightarrow S_1 \cup S_2 > S_1 \cup S_3$. This section gives an answer to the following question: how far can we go with a representation of uncertainty that tries to take advantage of truth-functionality as far as possible. It is shown here that, not only full truth-functionality is not possible, but retaining this property as much as mathematical consistency allows, leads to a very crude, almost deterministic model of uncertainty.

5. Concluding Remarks

The intended purpose of this paper is to emphasize the distinction between the treatment of gradual (or vague) predicates in presence of complete information which can be handled in a fully truth functional multiple-valued way (this is for instance the case for most of the applications in fuzzy control), and the handling of uncertainty for propositions which are either true or false (and which more generally may also have intermediary degrees of truth). In this second case, possibility theory offers a qualitative way for handling uncertainty which can be cast in a logical formalism (see, e.g., Dubois, Lang and Prade, 1991). Possibility theory, as probability theory and any uncertainty calculus is not fully compositional with respect to all connectives. It is still possible to enforce an almost fully compositional calculus for uncertainty, only at the high price of an important loss of expressiveness. On the whole we agree with Elkan (1993) on the point that the truth-functional fuzzy logic is not adapted to a proper handling of uncertainty in knowledge-based system. But our agreement is not based on an alleged self-inconsistency of fuzzy logic leading to a collapse. It is based on the fact that fuzzy logic offers a calculus of truth-values not of degrees of uncertainty. Especially there is no treatment of uncertainty in fuzzy controllers. Elkan's trivialization result kills truth-functional uncertainty handling systems, and certainly does not harm fuzzy logic nor the interpolation device at work in fuzzy controllers.

References

Aleliunas, R. 1990. A summary of a new normative theory of probabilistic logic. In *Uncertainty in AI, Vol. 4* (R.D. Shachter et al., eds.), 199-206. North-Holland.

Bellman, R.E.; and Giertz, M. 1973. On the analytic formalism of the theory of fuzzy sets. *Information Science* 5:149-157.

Buchanan, B.G.; and Shortliffe, E.H. 1984. *Rule-Based Expert Systems*. Readings, MA: Addison-Wesley.

De Finetti, B. 1936. La logique de la probabilité. In *Actes du Congrès Inter. de Philosophie Scientifique*, Paris, 1935, IV1-IV9. Hermann et Cie Editions, 1936.

Dubois, D. 1986. Belief structures, possibility theory and decomposable confidence measures on finite sets. *Comput. Artif. Intell.* (Bratislava) 5(5):403-416.

Dubois, D.; Lang, J.; and Prade, H. 1994. Possibilistic Logic. In *Handbook of Logic in AI and Logic Programming, Vol. 3* (D.M. Gabbay et al., eds.), 439-513. Oxford University Press.

Dubois, D.; and Prade, H. 1980. New results about properties and semantics of fuzzy set-theoretic operators. In *Fuzzy Sets* (P.P. Wang, S.K. Chang, eds.), 59-75. Plenum.

Dubois, D.; and Prade, H. 1985. Evidence measures based on fuzzy information. *Automatica* 31:547-562.

Dubois, D.; and Prade, H. 1988a. *Possibility Theory*. New York: Plenum Press.

Dubois, D.; and Prade, H. 1988b. An introduction to possibilistic and fuzzy logics (with discussions). In *Non Standard Logics for Automated Reasoning* (P. Smets et al., eds.), 287-315 & 321-326. Academic Press.

Dubois, D.; and Prade, H. 1991. Epistemic entrenchment and possibilistic logic. *Artificial Intelligence* 50:223-239.

Elkan, Ch. 1993. The paradoxical success of fuzzy logic. In *Proc. AAAI'93*, Washington, DC, July 11-15, 698-703.

Fine, T.L. 1973. *Theories of Probability*. New York: Academic Press.

Gärdenfors, P. 1988. *Knowledge in Flux*. MIT Press.

Nilsson, N.J. 1986. Probabilistic logic. *Artificial Intelligence* 28:71-87.

Schwartz, D.G. 1992. A min-max semantics for fuzzy likelihood. In *Proc. 1st IEEE Inter. Conf. on Fuzzy Systems*, San Diego, CA, March 8-12, 1393-1398.

Weston, T. 1987. Approximate truth. *J. Philos. Logic* 16:203-227.

Zadeh, L.A. 1965. Fuzzy sets. *Infor. & Cont.* 8:338-353.

Zadeh, L.A. 1978. Fuzzy sets as a basis for a theory of possibility. *Fuzzy Sets and Systems* 1:3-28.

Zadeh, L.A. 1979. A theory of approximate reasoning. In *Machine Intelligence, Vol. 9* (J.E. Hayes, D. Michie, and L.I. Mikulich, eds.), 149-194. New York: Elsevier.

Zadeh, L.A. 1982. Test score semantics for natural languages and meaning representation via PRUF. In *Empirical Semantics, Vol. 1* (B.B. Rieger, ed.), 281-349. Bochum: Brockmeyer.

An Empirical Evaluation of Knowledge Compilation by Theory Approximation

Henry Kautz and Bart Selman

AI Principles Research Department
AT&T Bell Laboratories
Murray Hill, NJ 07974
{kautz, selman}@research.att.com

Abstract

Computational efficiency is a central concern in the design of knowledge representation systems. Compiling a knowledge-base into a more tractable form has been suggested as a way around the inherent intractability of many representation formalisms. Because not all theories can be put into an equivalent tractable form, Selman and Kautz (1991) have suggested compiling a theory into upper and lower bounds (one logically weaker, the other logical stronger) that approximate the original information.

A central question in this approach is how well the bounds capture the original knowledge. This question is inherently empirical. We present a detailed empirical evaluation of the compilation of two kinds of theories: computationally challenging randomly generated theories, and propositional encodings of planning problems. Our results show that one can answer a very high percentage of queries even using unit clause bounds, which are much easier to compute than more general tractable approximations. Furthermore, we demonstrate that many of the queries that can be answered by the bounds are expensive to answer using only the original theory: in other words, knowledge compilation does not just "skim off" easy queries. In fact, we show substantial total computational savings in using the bounds together with the original theory to answer all queries (with no errors) from a large benchmark set, over using the original theory alone. This study suggests that knowledge compilation may indeed be a practical approach for dealing with intractability in knowledge representation systems.

Introduction

In the design of knowledge representation systems, the tradeoff between expressive power and computational tractability has been studied extensively. Unfortunately, the languages that allow for efficient inference are often considered too restrictive. One way around this issue is to employ some form of *knowledge compilation*. The idea is to let the user enter statements into the knowledge base (KB) in an unrestricted language, and have the system subsequently translate the information into a tractable form. Since an exact translation is often not possible, Selman and Kautz (1991) propose to *approximate* the original theory by using two bounds, one logically weaker (the upper bound) and the other logically stronger (the lower bound). As an example, they consider compiling general propositional theories into two approximating Horn theories. Certain queries can be answered quickly by using the bounds, as will be described below.

Though theoretically appealing, the practical value of knowledge compilation will depend on how well the bounds approximate the original information. In other words, what fraction of the incoming queries can be answered quickly by using the bounds? We would also like it to be the case that among those queries that can be answered with the bounds, there are queries that *cannot* be answered easily using the original theory (*i.e.*, the bounds are not just "skimming off" the easy queries).

We will first show, by using a general complexity-theoretic argument, that there do exist theories for which answering certain queries using the bounds is much easier than answering the same queries on the original theory. This argument reveals the existence of such theories and queries, but does not rule out the possibility that one would rarely encounter them in practice. We therefore also undertook an empirical evaluation of the knowledge compilation approach. We considered two classes of theories: hard random theories and propositional encodings of planning problems. We compile those theories, and give experimental data which shows that the compilation leads to dramatic computational savings.

In order to conduct our experiments, we needed theories that were sufficiently challenging, so that answering queries would take a reasonable computational effort; otherwise there would be no need for compilation in the first place. For the random theories, we used the hard problem class as identified in Mitchell *et al.* (1992). For our planning problems, we constructed a simple autonomous robot domain. To our surprise, planning problems that would intuitively appear quite hard were often answered almost instantaneously by the standard Davis-Putnam satisfiability procedure (Davis & Putnam 1960). In fact, we were able to prove that a very general class of such problems can be solved in linear time by unit propagation (a standard component of satisfiable procedures), even though many AI planning systems would find them very difficult. After identifying this class of "easy" planning problems, we were able to construct a planning domain that is provably computationally difficult, as was needed in our evaluation of knowledge compilation.

The form of knowledge compilation examined in this paper is based on approximations between logical languages that fall into different classes in the hierarchy of computational complexity. The term "knowledge compilation" is used more broadly in the expert systems community to refer to a wide variety of work that aims to increase the efficiency of such systems. Much of this work develops techniques for transforming "deep" functional models of devices to "shallow" diagnostic rules (Chandrasekaran & Mittal 1983; Keller 1991). The output of such systems does not correspond to either an upper-bound or a lower-bound in our sense; while some information may be lost in the compilation process (as with our upper-bounds), the compilers themselves *introduce* domain-specific information about diagnosis. Others view knowledge compilation as a kind of automatic programming, with the goal of converting a system specification to an implementation that exactly satifies it (Dieterich 1991). Bylander (1991) provides a high-level logical characterization of some different kinds of knowledge compilation; interestingly, he argues that forms of knowledge compilation based on approximations (as is ours) are unlikely to provide significant computational improvement. However, his argument is based on the assumption that the compilation process itself must be tractable, which we explicitly reject.

Knowledge Compilation by Theory Approximation

Selman and Kautz (1991) define knowledge compilation by theory approximation as follows. Assume that we have a logical theory Σ. One can approximate Σ by two theories Σ_{lub} and Σ_{glb} that are in a given tractable logical language. The approximation is such that $\Sigma_{\text{glb}} \models \Sigma \models \Sigma_{\text{lub}}$. So, Σ_{glb} is logically stronger than the original theory, and is called a *greatest lower bound* (GLB); and Σ_{lub} is logically weaker than the original theory, and is called a *least upper bound* (LUB).[1] The bounds are the best ones possible, given the particular tractable language. This means, for example, that there does not exist a tractable theory Σ' that is not logically equivalent to the Σ_{glb} and is such that $\Sigma_{\text{glb}} \models \Sigma' \models \Sigma$. The LUB of a theory is unique, but there can be several distinct GLBs.

Let us consider an example of approximating a general propositional theory by two bounding Horn theories. We take $\Sigma = (\neg a \vee c) \wedge (\neg b \vee c) \wedge (a \vee b)$. ($a$, b, and c are propositional letters.) The Horn theory $a \wedge b \wedge c$ is an example of a Horn lower-bound; both $a \wedge c$ and $b \wedge c$ are GLBs; $(\neg a \vee c) \wedge (\neg b \vee c)$ is an example of a Horn upper-bound; and c is the LUB. These bounds can be verified by noting that

$$(a \wedge b \wedge c) \models (a \wedge c) \models \Sigma \models c \models ((\neg a \vee c) \wedge (\neg b \vee c)).$$

---

[1] The terminology is based on a model-theoretic view of the approximations. Note that the models of, for example, the Σ_{glb} form a subset of the models of Σ. We are interested in a largest possible subset. For another approach to approximating logical theories, see Dalal and Etherington (1992).

KC_Query(α)
if $\Sigma_{\text{lub}} \models \alpha$ then return "yes"
else if $\Sigma_{\text{glb}} \not\models \alpha$ then return "no"
else determine whether $\Sigma \models \alpha$ using
      a general theorem prover and the original theory.

Figure 1: Fast querying using theory approximation. The original theory is Σ; Σ_{lub} and Σ_{glb} are its approximations; and α is the query.

Moreover, there is no Horn theory Σ' logically distinct from $a \wedge c$ such that $(a \wedge c) \models \Sigma' \models \Sigma$. Similar properties hold of the other GLB and of the LUB.

Instead of compiling into Horn theories, one can choose to compile into other tractable propositional theories, such as a set of unit clauses (*i.e.*, a conjunction of literals) or a set of binary clauses. Our experiments below show that even unit bounds lead to substantial computational savings.

Fig. 1 shows how the bounds can be used to improve the efficiency of a knowledge representation system. The system first tries to obtain an answer quickly by using the bounds, which can be done in linear time for Horn (Dowling & Gallier 1984) or unit bounds. In case no answer is obtained, the query is tested directly against the original theory. Note that KC_Query thus remains a *complete* procedure. A time-saving alternative would be for the system to simply return "don't know" if the bounds do not answer it.

The system can thus answer certain queries in linear time, resulting in a improvement in its overall response time. Exactly how many queries can be handled directly by the approximations depends on how well the bounds characterize the original theory.

Computational Savings

The key question concerning knowledge compilation is whether it will lead to an actual savings in computational effort. For example, it could be the case that queries answered by the approximating bounds can also be answered quickly using the original theory. An obvious counterexample is any inconsistent theory. Compilation yields an inconsistent upper bound. Any query against this bound would quickly return "yes" (see Fig. 1). However, evaluating a query against the original theory would in general involve proving that the theory was inconsistent, which is NP-complete.

Of course, most interesting knowledge bases will be consistent. Let us therefore consider a consistent theory that is equivalent to a Horn theory, but is not in Horn form. Clearly, all queries can be answered efficiently against the bounds. However, it is *not* the case that a theorem prover could also answer queries efficiently against the original theory. This can be shown using a result by Valiant and Vazirani (1986). They show that even if a propositional theory has a single model (and is thus trivially equivalent to a Horn theory), finding the model is still intractable (unless NP $\neq$

RP, which is unlikely). Therefore, there cannot exist a theorem prover that efficiently handles this special case, because such a prover could be used to find the unique model of the non-Horn theory (by repeatedly testing whether each literal followed from the theory).

This complexity theoretic argument shows that there exist theories where compilation gives a provable computational savings. Of course, this still leaves open the question whether one would encounter such theories in practice. In the next two sections, we therefore present an empirical evaluation of knowledge compilation of two classes of theories. In both cases, we will demonstrate substantial computational savings.

Empirical Evaluation I: Hard Random Theories

In this section, we consider the compilation of hard, randomly-generated propositional theories. Mitchell *et al.* (1992) show that most randomly-generated theories are easy to reason with. Such theories tend to be either very over-constrained or very under-constrained; in either case, experiments show that answering queries is easy using the standard Davis-Putnam procedure (Davis & Putnam 1960).[2] However, Mitchell *et al.* also described how to generate computationally challenging theories. The key is to generate formulas with a particular ratio of clauses to variables. For random 3CNF formulas, the ratio is about 4.3. We consider hard random 3CNF theories containing between 75 and 200 variables. In order to simplify the following analysis, we computed bounds that consisted of conjunctions of unit clauses. Note that unit clauses are a restricted case of Horn clauses. Therefore, these bounds are not as tight as the full Horn bounds. We will show that even these bounds are useful for answering a high percentage of queries. Because the full Horn bounds are tighter, they would answer an even higher percentage of queries. However, by considering the unit clause bounds we are able to provide a simple exact analysis.

We began by generating a set of 40 random 3CNF theories, with 10 each based on 75, 100, 150, and 200 variables. Then we computed the unit LUB and a unit GLB of each. Table 1 gives the median size, in literals, of the LUB and GLB for each size theory. The bounds were computed using the algorithms as given in Selman and Kautz (1991), adapted for generating unit bounds. We generated the optimal bounds. Computation time for the unit LUBs ranged from 5 minutes for the 75 variable theories, to one hour for the 200 variable theories. (All experiments were run on a 100Mhz SGI Challenge.) Computation of the unit GLBs ranged from 1 minute to 5 minutes each.

---

[2]If the theory is over-constrained, it is generally unsatisfiable, so that all queries trivially follow. If it is under-constrained and the CNF query contains short disjunctions, then the query almost certainly does not follow. Finally, if the theory is under-constrained and the CNF query contains only long disjunctions, then the query almost certainly does follow, which can be easily shown by adding the negation of the query to the theory and using the Davis-Putnam procedure with unit propagation to show inconsistency.

vars	clauses	size unit LUB	size unit GLB	percent queries answered unit	binary	ternary
75	322	53	71	100%	85%	88%
100	430	57	93	100%	76%	79%
150	645	62	139	100%	66%	66%
200	860	132	188	100%	83%	85%

Table 1: Statistics for compiling and querying hard random 3CNF theories.

The percentage of queries that could be answered by these bounds, as given in Table 1, is computed using some basic probability theory. We assume that we are dealing with single-clause queries drawn from a uniform fixed-clause length distribution. The simplest case is the unit clause queries. All unit clause queries can be answered using only the unit LUB, because this bound is complete for such queries. Thus this column is 100% for every size theory.

Next, let us consider the more interesting case of binary queries. Let $x \vee y$ be a random binary clause, where x and y are distinct and not complements. We wish to compute the probability that the bounds answer the query, given that the unit LUB is of size l and the unit GLB is of size m, and there are N variables in the theory. That is, we wish to compute

$$Pr((\Sigma_{\text{lub}} \vdash x \vee y) \text{ or } (\Sigma_{\text{glb}} \nvdash x \vee y))$$

which equals

$$Pr(\Sigma_{\text{lub}} \vdash x \vee y) + Pr(\Sigma_{\text{glb}} \nvdash x \vee y)$$

because the two possibilities are disjoint. A disjunction is entailed by a set of literals if and only if one of the disjuncts is so entailed. Thus,

$$Pr(\Sigma_{\text{lub}} \vdash x \vee y) = Pr((\Sigma_{\text{lub}} \vdash x) \text{ or } (\Sigma_{\text{lub}} \vdash y))$$

This quantity is equal to

$$Pr(\Sigma_{\text{lub}} \vdash x) + (\Sigma_{\text{lub}} \vdash y) - (\Sigma_{\text{lub}} \vdash x \wedge y)$$

The first and second terms are equal to the odds of picking a random literal that is in the LUB, namely $l/(2N)$. The third term is equal to the number of ways of choosing two distinct literals from the LUB, divided by the number of ways of choosing two distinct, non-complementary literals, namely $l(l-1)/((2N)2(N-1))$. Thus,

$$Pr(\Sigma_{\text{lub}} \vdash x \vee y) = \frac{l}{2N} + \frac{l}{2N} - \frac{l(l-1)}{4N(N-1)}$$

Using a similar calculation, we can calculate $Pr(\Sigma_{\text{lub}} \vdash x \vee y)$. Combining the probability that the LUB answers the query with the probability that the GLB answers the query results in the expression

$$1 - \frac{4N(m-l) - 3(m-l) + l^2 - m^2}{4N(N-1)}$$

The value of this expression was used to complete the "binary" column of Table 1.

vars	clauses	bounds and tableau		tableau only	
		binary	ternary	binary	ternary
75	322	51	48	258	248
100	430	54	45	368	341
150	645	61	59	1286	1084
200	860	55	51	12962	8632

Table 2: Time in seconds to answer 1000 random queries.

The probability that the bounds answer a random *ternary* query can be similarly derived, and was used to complete the final column of the table.

As we can see from Table 1, the percentage of queries that can be handled by the unit clause bounds is quite high. Note that the queries handled by the bounds can be answered in linear time. The Davis-Putnam procedure, however, scales exponentially on the queries considered in the table (this follows from the experiments in Mitchell *et al.* (1992)). Thus, this suggests that knowledge compilation on such hard randomly-generated theories should have a clear payoff.

We verified the computational savings suggested by the preceding analysis by implementing the fast querying algorithm shown in Fig. 1, and testing 1000 random binary and 1000 random ternary queries against each of the 40 test theories.

In case both bounds failed to answer a query, it was tested against the original theory using an efficient implementation of the Davis-Putnam procedure called "tableau".[3] Table 2 lists the average time to run each batch of a 1000 queries, using the bounds together with tableau versus using tableau alone. Thus, in both cases *all* queries were answered. We see that knowledge compilation reduced the overall time by *over two orders of magnitude* on the largest theories. This eliminates the remote possibility that the bounds are only answering the "easy" queries. Earlier we invoked complexity theory to argue that in *general* the bounds are not limited to easy queries; these experiments verify that the bounds answer hard queries against a computationally interesting distribution of random theories.

As an aside, we observe that even when we take into account the time required to compile the theories, we obtain an overall time savings. For example, on the 200 variable theories, computing the bounds takes about an hour and five minutes; thus, the total time to compute the bounds *and* answer 1000 binary queries is 3,955 seconds, versus 12,962 seconds not using the bounds. (Note that difference in overall time would increase even further when we would consider, for example, 10000 queries.) Thus in this case we have gone beyond the main objective of knowledge compilation, namely to speed query answering by shifting computational effort from on-line to off-line (compilation), and have actually reduced the total amount of work required.

---

[3]The Davis-Putnam procedure is currently the fastest known complete procedure for propositional satisfiability testing and theorem-proving on the class of formulas considered here (Buro & Büning 1992; Dubois *et al.* 1993). Tableau (Crawford & Auton 1993) is one of the fastest implementations of the algorithm.

Finally, we observe that these positive results for random theories are quite surprising, since one would expect that their apparent lack of structure would make them hard to approximate by simpler theories.

Empirical Evaluation II: Planning Formulas

Planning has traditionally been formalized as first-order deduction (Green 1969; McCarthy & Hayes 1969). In this approach, a plan is basically a *proof* that a statement asserting the existence of a goal state is valid. Kautz and Selman (1992) develop an alternative formalization of planning as propositional satisfiability. They show how planning problems in typical domains, such as the blocks world, can be axiomatized so that every *model* of the axioms corresponds to a plan. The satisfiability formalization makes it easy to state facts about any state of the world (not just the initial and goal states) and is closer in spirit to modern constraint-based planners (Stefik 1981; Chapman 1987) than is the deductive approach.

We decided to evaluate knowledge compilation within the planning as satisfiability framework. The particular problems described in the Kautz and Selman paper all have unique models, corresponding to a single solution. Compiling such formulas provides no benefit beyond finding the single satisfying model. Therefore we developed a class of planning problems that each have many different solutions. Compiling these problems allows one to evaluate quickly various queries about what must hold in all solutions, as well as to pose queries that impose additional constraints on the possible solutions.

We call this domain the "mapworld". In the basic version of the mapworld, we imagine that a robot is moving between nodes of a graph, such as the one shown in Fig. 2. (Ignore for now the section of the figure labeled "MAZE", which will be explained later.) At each time step the robot can either stay in place or move to an adjacent node. An instance of the mapworld consists of axioms that describe a particular such graph, as well as constraints on the location of the robot at various times, up to some final instance; for example, that the robot be at node a at time 0 and at node g at final time 10. One can then pose queries to answer against these axioms, such as "Can the robot be at node f at time 2?" (obviously, no), or "Does the fact that the robot goes through node c imply that it does *not* go through node k?" (less obviously, this implication does indeed hold, because it takes at least 11 steps to reach g when going through both c and k).

One application in which the ability to answer queries of this sort is useful is plan recognition (Schmidt, Sridharan, & Goodson 1978; Allen & Perrault 1980; Kautz 1986). For example, one may have partial knowledge about the goals and actions of another agent, and want to be able to infer the possible states the agent could be in at various times. Another interesting application is in reactive planning systems (Agre & Chapman 1987; Schoppers 1987; Kaelbling 1988; Kabanza 1990). An important issue in such systems is how to combine reactive behaviors (*e.g.* move to a node if it contains food) with more global plans (*e.g.* visit nodes x and y before the end of the day). A possible architecture

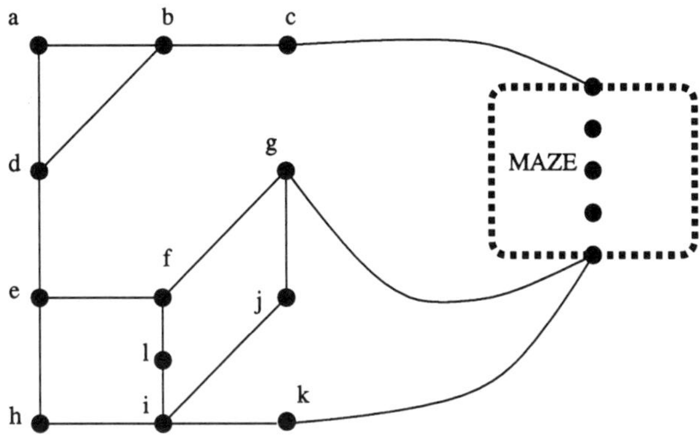

Figure 2: The mapworld domain.

for a combined system would have a reactive module that *proposed* actions (*e.g.* move to node *c*), which are however *rejected* if the axiomatization of the global planning problem entails the *negation* of the action (*i.e.*, the action would be incompatible with the global goals). This proposal is similar to Bratman, Israel, and Pollack's (1988) view of plans as *filters*, but note that we suggest filtering against the whole set of possible solutions (models) of the planning problem, rather than against a single one. Clearly it requires the ability to check rapidly if the proposed action is consistent with at least one solution to the global problem.

The basic mapworld can be captured by the following kinds of axioms. The proposition that the robot is a node x at time i is written x_i. First, there are movement axioms $\mathcal{M}$, that state that the robot always stays put or moves to an adjacent node; for our example, these would include

$$a_i \supset (a_{i+1} \lor b_{i+1} \lor d_{i+1})$$

for $0 \leq i < 10$. Second, there are disjointedness axioms $\mathcal{D}$, that state that the robot is only at one node at a time; for example,

$$a_i \supset (\neg b_i \land \cdots \land \neg k_i).$$

Finally, there are assertions that constrain the robot to be at certain locations at certain times; such positive assertions (such as $\{a_0, g_{10}\}$) are designated $\mathcal{P}$, while negative assertions (such as $\{\neg f_5\}$) are designated $\mathcal{N}$. Finally, we define propositions of the form x_{ever} by

$$x_{\text{ever}} \equiv (x_0 \lor x_1 \lor \cdots \lor x_{10}).$$

Given these axioms, the first query above becomes "Does $\mathcal{M} \cup \mathcal{D} \cup \mathcal{N} \cup \mathcal{P} \models \neg f_2$?", and the second becomes "Does $\mathcal{M} \cup \mathcal{D} \cup \mathcal{N} \cup \mathcal{P} \models c_{\text{ever}} \supset \neg k_{\text{ever}}$?" Surprisingly, it turns out that *all* CNF queries against a basic mapworld problem can be answered quickly, using a standard theorem-prover.[4] One can prove that a simple rule of inference

---

[4] It is not surprising, of course, that an efficient algorithm *exists* for these queries, because the lengths of the shortest paths between all points in a graph can be determined in polynomial time (Aho, Hopcroft, & Ullman 1974). What is unexpected is that the SAT encoding of the problem allows an efficient solution by a completely general theorem-prover, that does not employ a special shortest-path algorithm.

called "unit propagation" is complete for such theories. Unit propagation is takes only linear time, and is part of all resolution-style theorem proving procedures, such as the Davis-Putnam procedure. In general unit propagation by itself is not a complete decision procedure. However, one can prove the following theorem (Kautz & Selman 1994):

Theorem: *For any basic mapworld problem and clausal query α, we have*

$$\mathcal{M} \cup \mathcal{D} \cup \mathcal{N} \cup \mathcal{P} \models \alpha$$

iff unit propagation proves that $\mathcal{M} \cup \mathcal{D} \cup \mathcal{N} \cup \mathcal{P} \cup \{\neg\alpha\}$ is inconsistent.

Thus, knowledge compilation is not needed in this case: unit propagation yields a linear-time decision procedure. This indicates that there are interesting computational advantages to using a satisfiability encoding for planning. For example, a standard STRIPS-style planner (Fikes & Nilsson 1971) would end up exploring (in general) an exponential number of paths before realizing that certain sets of nodes cannot be reached within a fixed time-bound.

To make our mapworld more computationally challenging, we generalize it by adding constraints that say that certain pairs of nodes are forbidden to appear on the same path. Such constraints often occur in real-life planning problems, where for example going through a node represents consuming some limited resource. An example of such a constraint is $\neg f_{\text{ever}} \lor \neg j_{\text{ever}}$, which states that the robot cannot pass through both nodes f and j on its way to g. This change makes planning much harder — in fact, answering CNF-queries becomes NP-complete, as can be shown by a reduction from *path with forbidden pairs* (Garey & Johnson 1979, page 203). This also greatly increases the applicability of our results, because most interesting planning problems are NP-complete (Gupta & Nau 1991; Erol, Nau, & Subrahmanian 1992) and thus can be efficiently encoded as mapworld problems.

In Fig. 2, the area labeled "MAZE" is a 30-node subgraph constructed so that all paths through it are blocked by various forbidden pairs of nodes. Disregarding these pairs, the shortest path through the maze is 5 steps long. By counting alone, then, one would think that was possible to go

	RandBin	RandEver	Hand
number queries	500	400	5
theory only time	2013	8953	1071
KC_Query time	464	3748	439
Σ+LUB time	580	840	6.9
KC using Σ+LUB time	283	617	6.8
bounds only time	5	6	1
num. answered by bounds	376	144	2

Table 3: Statistics on querying mapworld with and without knowledge compilation. Time in seconds.

from a to g by traversing the maze in no more than 10 steps (the time limit on the problem). It is computationally hard, however, to determine that these paths are blocked, and that in fact the robot *must* traverse the edge from d to e. Any query that depends on realizing this fact is also quite hard to answer. We therefore *compiled* the problem instance, effectively moving the most computationally difficult part of the reasoning off-line. (As we will see, the bounds also contain a great many other non-trivial conclusions concerning the mapworld example.)

The SAT encoding of the mapworld in Fig. 2 contains 576 variables and 29,576 clauses. It takes about 4400 seconds to compute both the unit LUB and a unit GLB. The unit LUB determines the values of 341 of the variables. The GLB we found was a single model, which nonetheless was useful in query-answering.

We then created three different test sets of queries: RandBin is a set of 500 random binary queries; RandEver is set of 400 random binary queries, where the propositions are taken just from the "ever" predicates; and Hand is a small set of hand-constructed queries that are intuitively interesting and non-obvious, such as $f_{ever} \vee i_{ever}$.

Table 3 compares the results of various ways of running the queries. For "theory only" the queries were simply tested against the uncompiled problem using tableau. The "KC_Query" row is the time required to answer all queries using the query algorithm presented in Fig. 1 that uses both the bounds and the original theory. In all cases we see a significant speed-up. In fact, the savings for the RandEver test set more than pays off the entire cost of computing the bounds.

We then experimented with several variations on the basic knowledge-compilation querying algorithm. For the "Σ+LUB" row we conjoined the original theory with its unit LUB, and then ran all queries using tableau. Note that the conjoined theory is logically unchanged (since the original theory entails its LUB), but is easier to reason with. For the RandBin test set, this approach is not as good as the plain "KC_Query" algorithm; however, for RandEver and Hand it is considerably faster. Next, in the "KC using Σ+LUB" experiments we first tested each query directly against the bounds, but if they did not answer it, we then answered it using tableau with the conjoined theory. In every case this was the fastest complete method.

Finally, we ran the queries against the bounds only, leav-ing some of them unanswered. In all cases this took only a few seconds for hundreds of queries. About 75% of the RandBin queries, 36% of the RandEver queries, and 2 out 5 of the Hand queries can be answered in this way. However, the great difference in speed (*e.g.*, 5 seconds on the RandBin queries, versus 283 seconds for the fastest complete method) suggests that using the bounds alone may be most practical for many real-time applications. For example, in many domains instead of relying on expensive theorem proving a system may try to obtain information by direct sensing of its environment.

Conclusion

We have evaluated the computational savings that can be gained by compiling general logical theories into a pair of tractable approximations. We first argued on complexity-theoretic grounds that on certain theories knowledge compilation must result in computational savings. We then considered the compilation of two kinds of theories: hard random CNF theories, and propositional encodings of planning problems. In both cases our experiments showed that a high percentage of queries can be answered using the tractable bounds, and that the approach leads to a dramatic decrease in the time required to answer a large series of queries. This indicates that the knowledge compilation approach is useful for both unstructured, randomly generated theories, and highly structured theories such as encodings of planning domains. In this paper, we obtained good performance with unit clausal approximations. An open question that we will address in future work is whether it is worthwhile to compute the more accurate, but more expensive to obtain, Horn approximations. In any case, this study has shown that knowledge compilation by theory approximation is indeed a promising approach for dealing with intractability in knowledge representation systems.

References

Agre, P. E., and Chapman, D. 1987. Pengi: an implementation of a theory of activity. In *Proceedings of AAAI-87*, 268.

Aho, A. V.; Hopcroft, J. E.; and Ullman, J. D. 1974. *The Design and Analysis of Computer Algorithms*. Reading, MA: Addison-Wesley.

Allen, J. F., and Perrault, C. R. 1980. Analyzing intention in utterances. *Artificial Intelligence* 143–177.

Bratman, M. E.; Israel, D. J.; and Pollack, M. E. 1988. Plans and resource-bounded practical reasoning. *Computational Intelligence* 4(4). also SRI TR 425R.

Buro, M., and Büning, H. K. 1992. Report on a SAT competition. Technical Memorandum 110, Mathematik/Informatik Universität Paderborn.

Bylander, T. 1991. A simple model of knowledge compilation. *IEEE Expert* 6(2):73–74.

Chandrasekaran, B., and Mittal, S. 1983. Deep versus compiled knowledge approaches to diagnostic problem solving. *International Journal of Man-Machine Studies* 19(5):425–436.

Chapman, D. 1987. Planning for conjunctive goals. *Artificial Intelligence* 32:333–378.

Crawford, J., and Auton, L. 1993. Experimental results on the crossover point in satisfiability problems. In *Proceedings of AAAI-93*, 21–27.

Dalal, M., and Etherington, D. W. 1992. Tractable approximate deduction using limited vocabularies. In *Proceedings of CSCSI-92*, 206–212.

Davis, M., and Putnam, H. 1960. A computing procedure for quantification theory. *Journal of the Association for Computing Machinery* 7:201–215.

Dietterich, T. G. 1991. Bridging the gap between specification and implementation. *IEEE Expert* 6(2):80–82.

Dowling, W. F., and Gallier, J. H. 1984. Linear time algorithms for testing the satisfiability of propositional Horn formula. *Journal of Logic Programming* 3:267–284.

Dubois, O.; Andre, P.; Boufkhad, Y.; and Carlier, J. 1993. SAT versus UNSAT. In *Preprints, Second DIMACS Algorithm Implementation Challenge*. Piscataway, NJ: Rutgers University.

Erol, K.; Nau, D.; and Subrahmanian, V. 1992. On the complexity of domain-independent planning. In *Proceedings of AAAI-92*, 381–386.

Fikes, R. E., and Nilsson, N. J. 1971. STRIPS: a new approach to the application of theorem proving to problem solving. *Artificial Intelligence* 2.

Garey, M. R., and Johnson, D. S. 1979. *Computers and Intractability: a Guide to the Theory of NP-Completeness.* San Francisco: W. H. Freeman and Company.

Green, C. 1969. Application of theorem proving to problem solving. In *Proceedings of IJCAI-69*, 219–239.

Gupta, N., and Nau, D. S. 1991. Complexity results for blocks-world planning. In *Proceedings of AAAI-91*, 629.

Kabanza, F. 1990. Synthesis of reactive plans for multipath environments. In *Proceedings of AAAI-90*.

Kaelbling, L. 1988. Goals as parallel program specifications. In *Proceedings of AAAI-88*, 60–65.

Kautz, H., and Selman, B. 1992. Planning as satisfiability. In *Proceedings of ECAI-92*, 359.

Kautz, H., and Selman, B. 1994. An empirical evaluation of knowledge compilation by theory approximation (extended version). Technical report, AT&T Bell Laboratories, Murray Hill, NJ.

Kautz, H. 1986. Generalized plan recognition. In *Proceedings of AAAI-86*.

Keller, R. M. 1991. Applying knowledge compilation techniques to model-based reasoning. *IEEE Expert* 6(2):82–87.

McCarthy, J., and Hayes, P. J. 1969. Some philosophical problems from the standpoint of artificial intelligence. In MICHIE, D., ed., *Machine Intelligence 4*. Chichester, England: Ellis Horwood. 463ff.

Mitchell, D.; Selman, B.; and Levesque, H. 1992. Hard and easy distribution of SAT problems. In *Proceedings of AAAI-92*.

Schmidt, C.; Sridharan, N.; and Goodson, J. 1978. The plan recognition problem: an intersectiuon of psychology and artificial intelligence. *Artificial Intelligence* 11.

Schoppers, M. J. 1987. Universal plans for reactive robots in unpredictable environments. In *Proceedings of AAAI-87*, volume 2, 1023.

Selman, B., and Kautz, H. 1991. Knowledge compilation using Horn approximations. In *Proceedings of AAAI-91*, 904–909.

Stefik, M. 1981. Planning with constraints (molgen: Part 1 and 2). *Artificial Intelligence* 16:111–170.

Valiant, R., and V.V., V. 1986. NP is as easy as detecting unique solutions. *Theoretical Computer Science* 47:85–93.

ModGen: Theorem Proving by Model Generation[*]

Sun Kim   Hantao Zhang
Department of Computer Science
The University of Iowa
Iowa City, IA 52242, U.S.A
{sunkim,hzhang}@cs.uiowa.edu

Abstract

ModGen (Model Generation) is a complete theorem prover for first order logic with finite Herbrand domains. ModGen takes first order formulas as input, and generates models of the input formulas. ModGen consists of two major modules: a module for transforming the input formulas into propositional clauses, and a module to find models of the propositional clauses. The first module can be used by other researchers so that the SAT problems can be easily represented, stored and communicated. An important issue in the design of ModGen is to ensure that transformed propositional clauses are satisfiable iff the original formulas are. The second module can be easily replaced by any advanced SAT problem solver. ModGen is easy to use and very efficient. Many problems which are hard for general resolution theorem provers are found easy for ModGen.

Introduction

Many theorem proving problems are difficult for today's theorem provers not because these problems are really hard but because the methods are not suitable to these problems. For example, one of test problems in Larry Wos' thought-provoking book (Wos 1988) (Test Problem 6) asks one to prove that any group of order 7 is commutative. Using OTTER (McCune 1990), one of the best resolution-based theorem provers, this problem cannot be solved in hours. However, if we code this problem in the propositional logic, the problem can be solved in a couple of seconds.

The test problem mentioned above involves functions of finite domains. For this kind of problems, the constraint solving methods are better tools. The FINDER program (Stanley 1992) developed by John Slaney is a well-known program for model generation based on a constraint solving method.

The goal of our project is to create a subroutine of OTTER which has similar functionality as FINDER. However, instead of using any constraint solving methods, we prefer to use a decision procedure for the satisfiability (SAT) of propositional formulas:

---

[*]Partially supported by the National Science Foundation under Grants CCR-9202838 and CCR-9357851.

- While the SAT problem is a special case of constraint satisfaction problems, many constraint satisfaction problems can be easily and efficiently converted into an instance of the SAT problem. The SAT problem is a core of a large family of computationally intractable NP-complete problems and has been identified as central to a variety of areas in computing theory and engineering.

- There has been great interet in designing efficient algorithms to solve the SAT problem. Various satisfiability testing methods are available, such as backtracking, resolution and its variations — the Davis-Putnam algorithm is one of the known methods. Some local search algorithms have been developed to solve large size instances of the SAT problem (Gu 1993).

Since we intended that the user of OTTER can easily use special methods to handle problems of finite domain, we of course must have a procedure which converts first order formulas into propositional clauses. We found that automatically converting first-order formulas into propositional formulas is not a trivial task. One of the *33 Research Problems* proposed in (Wos 1988) by Wos asks what criteria can be used effectively choose between predicate and function notation for representing the problem under study. For instance, "the product of a and b equals c" can be written as $P(a, b, c)$ or $prod(a, b) = c$. However, no references are given in (Wos 1988) for the conditions which ensure that the initial formulas are satisfiable iff the converted formulas are. The existence of quantifiers in the formulas makes the problem more complicated.

For example, suppose one of the axioms for a group of order 7 is axiom $x * i(x) = e$, where x is a variable over a domain S of seven elements, say $S = \{1, 2, ..., 7\}$. We may obtain 7 instances of this axiom by replacing x by a value from 1 to 7. The resulting clauses are ground (i.e., variable-free) but they are not propositional clauses. We have to replace functions like $*$ and i by predicate symbols. We may introduce a predicate P_i such that $P_i(x, y)$ is true whenever $i(x) = y$. To get rid of $i(x)$ in that axiom, we may assume $i(x) = u$ and use $P_i(x, u) \Rightarrow (x * u = e)$ as a new axiom. Now the question is: Since the two axioms are not logically equivalent, what additional information is needed to make them equivalent ? This questions must be answered if we want to correctly convert a set of formulas into a set of propositional clauses. We are also interested in the efficiency of the conversion, in the sense that the converted clauses have shorter and less duplicated clauses. These questions will be answered in this paper.

Traditional constraint solving methods do not need to convert general formulas into propositional clauses. For instance, FINDER (Stanley 1992) uses generate-and-test approach to test constraints represented by clauses. While the design philosophy of FINDER and ModGen are very different, FINDER has a great impact on the design of ModGen. Because of the different design philosophies, ModGen offers some advantages:

- ModGen accepts arbitrary formulas (including quantifiers) while FINDER accepts only clauses.

- ModGen can be used to generate propositional clauses for other programs and it is very easy to change SAT decision procedures in ModGen.

- Experimental results show that ModGen outperforms FINDER for almost all the examples tried.

This paper is organized as follows: At first, we give an overview of ModGen and show by examples how ModGen is used. Next, we describe how to correctly and efficiently convert general formulas into propositional clauses; we discuss how to handle function symbols and quantifiers. Finally, we present some experimental results of ModGen.

Overview of ModGen

ModGen mainly consists of two modules, *a propositional clause generator* and the program SATO (SATisfiability Testing Optimized) (Zhang 1993) which is an efficient implementation of the Davis-Putnam algorithm (Davis & Putnam 1960). The overall structure of ModGen is shown in Figure 1. ModGen takes first order formulas either in arbitrary form or in clausal form as input, and generates models of input formulas. All variables in input formulas should be of finite domain. Also, ranges of all functions in input formulas should be finite.

The propositional clause generator generates propositional clauses in clausal form from input formulas. If input formulas are not in clausal form, ModGen transforms them in clausal form, and then generates propositional clauses.

The generated propositional clauses are fed to SATO, which determines the satisfiability of the clauses. If the clauses are satisfiable, SATO generates their Herbrand models, that is, which propositional variables are set to true. Since there is a one-to-one mapping between a propositional variable and a function instance, from the Herbrand models generated by

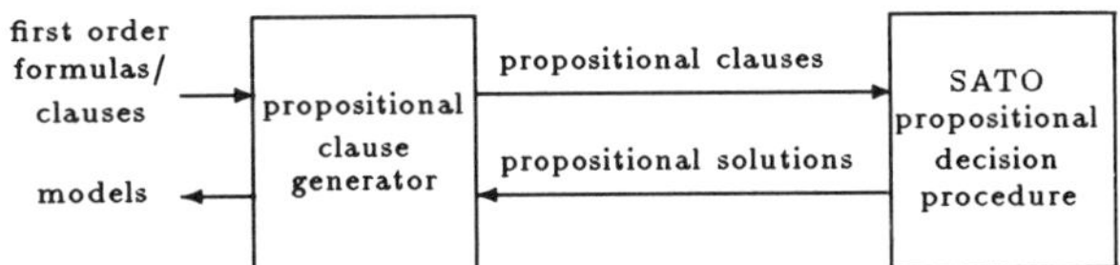

Figure 1: Overview of ModGen

SATO, ModGen can print out solutions in terms of function values.

The input to ModGen consists of three parts: (a) sorts of finite elements, (b) functions (including predicates); and (c) (multisort) first order formulas. ModGen decides whether there exist any (or how many) models for the input formulas.

In the beginning of this project, we decided to use the syntax of OTTER (McCune 1990) for input formulas and clauses. This is because

- OTTER is the best known resolution-based theorem prover and is very popular in the community of automated theorem proving;

- we wish that ModGen become a complementary tool to OTTER for finite domain problems and many OTTER's input files can be directly input to ModGen without any modification.

For the above reasons, some code of OTTER has been used in implementing ModGen. Especially, the entire module for parsing input formulas has been used, so the syntax of ModGen is the same as that of OTTER.

We illustrate the use of ModGen by two simple examples.

The Queen Problem

The 8-queen problem is to find placements of 8 queens over a 8×8 chess board so that no two queens attack each other.

```
sort(board, 8). % the number of queens is 8
func(p(board, board), bool).
% p(i, j) = true iff a queen is placed at (i, j).

list(usable). % a list of clauses
% (a) No two queens are on the same column.
-p(x, z) | -p(y, z) | (x = y).
% (b) No two queens are on the same row.
-p(z, x) | -p(z, y) | (x = y).
% (c) No two queens are on the same diagonal.
-p(x,y) | -p(u,v) | $ABS(x-u) = $ABS(y-v) | (x=u).
end_of_list.

formula_list(usable). % a list of formulas
% (d) Each column must have a queen.
(all x exists y p(x, y)).
end_of_list.
```

Note that the built-in function $ABS(x) returns the absolute value of x. It takes less than 0.3 second on an IBM RS6000 for ModGen to decide that there are 92 solutions to the above input. If the user likes to test the 15-queen problem, the only change to the input file is to replace 8 by 15. It takes 2.6 hours for ModGen to decide that there are 2,279,184 solutions for the case of 15. This result cannot compare to that of Sosic and Gu whose program can decide 3,000,000 queens in one minute (Sosic & Gu 1991). However, it is known that there exist solutions to any case but the exact numbers of solutions for large queen problems are still unknown. ModGen may be used to answer such unknown questions while Sosic and Gu's problem cannot.

The queen problem can be also specified in terms of a function q such that $q(i) = j$ iff $p(i, j)$. Below is an input file to ModGen:

```
assign(MODEL, 1).       % search only one model
sort(row, 8).           % the number of queens is 8
func(q(row), row, bijective).
    % q being bijective implies that no two queens
    % in the same row or the same column and
    % there exists a queen for each column.
list(usable).
% No two queens are on the same diagonal.
-(q(u) = q(v) + x) | -($ABS(u - v) = x) | (x = 0).
end_of_list.
```

The second input file is much simpler than the first one — this shows the flexibility of ModGen for specifying problems. The following is the result of executing ModGen with the above input.

```
Model #1:
    row |  0 1 2 3 4 5 6 7
    ----+-----------------
      q |  3 1 6 2 5 7 4 0
```

The Non-Obviousness Problem

The second example shows how easy to use ModGen, that is, ModGen can use some of OTTER's input file without any change. The example is called the "non-obviousness" problem and has appeared in many issues of *Newsletter of Association on Automated Reasoning* (Pelletier & Rudnicki 1986). The input file of OTTER (v3.0.0) is as follows:

```
set(auto).

list(usable).
    -p(a,b).
    -q(c,d).
    p(x,y) | q(x,y).
    q(x,y) | -q(y,x).
    p(x,z) | -p(x,y) | -p(y,z).
    q(x,z) | -q(x,y) | -q(y,z).
end_of_list.
```

The same file can be used by ModGen: The command `set(auto)`, which automatically turns on a set of inference rules of OTTER, is skipped by ModGen. ModGen assumes by default that p and q are binary predicates over $S = \{a, b, c, d\}$. While it takes 3.8 seconds for OTTER to show that the input clauses are unsatisfiable, it takes only 0.04 second on the same machine for ModGen; our result is the best among the

results reported in the Newsletters of Automated Reasoning.

Propositional Clause Generation

In this section, we present a procedure which can correctly and efficiently convert general formulas into propositional clauses for functions of finite domains. The procedure consists of the following steps:

1. Transform general formulas into clauses.

2. Eliminate function symbols in each clause by introducing new predicates and variables.

3. Instantiate variables in each clause by values and evaluate the truth value of built-in functions and predicates.

4. Return each instantiated clause in an abstract form.

Methods for transforming general formulas into clauses can be found in many textbooks on logic programming. An abstract form of a clause is a list of integers such that the absolute value of each integer is the index of a propositional variable and the sign of the integer is the sign of the literal. In the following, we discuss only steps 2 and 3.

Eliminating function symbols

We will use functions with only one argument for notational convenience; functions with more than one argument can be treated similarly. As mentioned in the introduction, for each function f, we introduce a predicate P_f such that $f(x) = y$ iff $P_f(x, y)$. We can eliminate each term $f(t)$ in a clause formula by substituting a new variable u for $f(t)$, assuming $f(t) = u$. Thus, the transformation rule is as follows.

$$(\beta) \quad \frac{L(f(t)) \mid M}{\neg P_f(t, x) \mid L(x) \mid M[f(t) \leftarrow x]}$$

where M is a disjunction of literals, $L(f(t))$ is a literal containing the term $f(t)$ and f is not a predicate.

The soundness and completeness of the above rule is ensured by the totalness of f:

Theorem 1 *Suppose $f(x) = y$ iff $P_f(x, y)$ and f is total. For any clause $L(f(t)) \mid M$ and any set S of clauses, $S_1 = S \cup \{L(f(t)) \mid M\}$ is satisfiable if and only if $S_2 = S \cup \{\neg P_f(t, x) \mid L(x) \mid M[f(t) \leftarrow x]\}$ is satisfiable.*

Proof: If S_1 is satisfiable, because $L(f(t)) \mid M$ implies $\neg P_f(t, x) \mid L(x) \mid M[f(t) \leftarrow x]$, S_2 must be satisfiable.

If S_1 is unsatisfiable, by Herbrand's theorem, there exists a unsatisfiable set G_1 of ground instances of S_1. For any Herbrand interpretation H on G_1, there much exist a ground clause in G_1 which is false in H. If this ground clause is not an instance of $L(f(t)) \mid M$, then this ground clause must be an instance of S_2, so H will falsify S_2.

If this ground clause is an instance of $L(f(t)) \mid M$, then it can be written as $\sigma L(f(t)) \mid \sigma M$ for some substitution σ. Because f is total, there must exist a value a such that $f(\sigma t) = a$. Consider the instance

$$(*) \qquad \neg P_f(\sigma t, a) \mid \sigma L(a) \mid \sigma M[f(t) \leftarrow a]$$

of $\neg P_f(t, x) \mid L(x) \mid M[f(t) \leftarrow x]$. Because $P_f(\sigma t, a)$ iff $f(\sigma t) = a$, $\neg P_f(\sigma t, a)$ is false under H. The rest literals of $(*)$ are also false under H because $\sigma L(f(t)) \mid \sigma M$ is false under H and $f(\sigma t) = a$. Hence H will falsify S_2, too. In other words, every interpretation will falsify S_2, so S_2 must be unsatisfiable. $\Box$.

While the totalness of functions is a sufficient condition for the above theorem, we were unable to weaken this condition further. In (Wos 1988), it is said that an equation like $prod(prod(x, y), z) = prod(x, prod(y, z))$ could be replaced by two clauses when using predicate notation:

$$-P(x, y, u) \mid -P(y, z, w) \mid -P(u, z, v) \mid P(x, w, v),$$
$$-P(x, y, u) \mid -P(y, z, w) \mid -P(x, w, v) \mid P(u, z, v).$$

By the above theorem, if $prod$ is total, then only one clause is sufficient. However, when $prod$ is partial, we do not know if the two clauses are sufficient to replace $prod(prod(x, y), z) = prod(x, prod(y, z))$.

To ensure that $f(x) = y$ iff $P_f(x, y)$, some formulas about P_f should be added:

1. **Totalness:** $\forall x \exists y \, . \, P_f(x, y)$.

2. **Image Uniqueness:**
   $\forall x \forall y_1 \forall y_2 \, . \, P_f(x, y_1) \wedge P_f(x, y_2) \Rightarrow (y_1 = y_2)$.

In ModGen, the transformation rule (β) is repeatedly applied to the general clauses until no functions are left, with the exception that when function symbols appear with equalities, the application of the rule becomes selective.

Dealing with equalities

When functions are used in equalities, we use special techniques to reduce the number of ground clauses generated from general clauses. There are two cases: (1) equalities between a function and a variable/constant, and (2) equalities between functions.

For the first case, say $f(x) = y$, we directly transform this equation into a literal, without introducing a new variable, that is, $P_f(x, y)$ instead of $u = y \mid \neg P_f(x, u)$; the latter is obtained by the transformation rule (β) and would result in too many ground clauses, because it introduces a new variable. The following lemmas ensures that the former transformation is sound.

Lemma 2 *Assuming the totalness and image uniqueness properties of f, $P_f(x, y)$ and $u = y \mid \neg P_f(x, u)$ are logically equivalent.*

Proof: Note that the instances of $u = y \mid \neg P_f(x, u)$ (after removing evaluable literals) are of form $\neg P_f(a_i, a_k)$ and the instances of $P_f(x, y)$ are of form $P_f(a_i, a_j)$.

The ground clauses obtained from the totalness property of a function, that is, assuming the range of $f(x)$ is $\{a_1, ..., a_n\}$, are:

$$P_f(x, a_1) \mid ... \mid P_f(x, a_n) \qquad (1)$$

for *all* x. Using resolution, for any value a_i and a_j, we can deduce $P_f(a_i, a_j)$ from instances of $u = a_j$ $\neg P_f(a_i, u)$ and (1).

On the other hand, we can also deduce $\neg P_f(a_i, a_k)$ from $P_f(a_i, a_j)$ and the ground clause generated from the image-uniqueness property. Hence, $P_f(x, y)$ and $u = y \mid P_f(x, u)$ are logically equivalent under the presence of the totalness and image-uniqueness properties of f. $\Box$

For the second case, say $f(x) = g(y)$, we have two choices, to remove $f(x)$ first or to remove $g(y)$ first, and depending on the removal sequence, the resulting clause will be different. If we remove $f(x)$ first, then the resulting clause will be $\neg P_f(x, u) \mid P_g(y, u)$. On the other hand, if we remove $g(y)$ first, then the resulting clause will be $P_g(y, v) \mid \neg P_f(x, v)$. When a function is total, by the theorem in the previous subsection, it is sufficient to generate either of the two clauses.

Dealing with Skolem functions

ModGen takes first order formulas with quantifiers as input and then transforms these formulas into clauses; skolem functions may be introduced during this process. Skolem functions can be treated as ordinary functions which have the totalness and the image-uniqueness properties.

Skolem constants are also treated as ordinary functions, that is, 0-arity functions. The difference is that the image-uniqueness property can not be enforced.

Although treating skolem functions as ordinary functions is sufficient, for efficiency, we treat some skolem functions specially. If a skolem function has all the universally quantified variables as its arguments and does not appear in other clauses, then we can eliminate the skolem function as follows: Suppose $f(x)$ is a skolem function appearing in clause $C(f(x))$. We replace $f(x)$ by a new variable y and $C(f(x))$ is equivalent to $\exists y \, . \, C(y)$. If the domain of y is $\{a_1, ..., a_n\}$, then $\exists y \, . \, C(y)$ is equivalent to $C(a_1) \mid \cdots \mid C(a_n)$. If a skolem function appears in more than one clauses, then we can not eliminate it this way, because $\exists y (P(y) \wedge Q(y))$ is not equivalent to $(\exists y P(y)) \wedge (\exists y Q(y))$ in general. For the same reason, we can eliminate skolem constants if a clause containing skolem constants is a ground clause and skolem constants do not appear in other clauses.

Example 3 Consider the formula $\forall y \exists x f(x) = y$. The clausal form of this formula is $f(S(y)) = y$, where S(y) is a skolem function. Assume that the sort of variables x and y contains n elements. Since the skolem function S has all universally quantified variables as its arguments, we can eliminate the skolem function as

for each values of variables $v_1, ..., v_n$ in C **do**
    for each evaluable literal l in a clause C **do**
        if l is evaluated to false,
        then delete l from C.
        else exit // No propositional clause from C
    endfor
    // C consists of literals with unevaluable predicates.
    generate a ground clause by instantiating each v_i
endfor

Figure 2: Evaluation of literals and propositional clause generation

follows.

$$f(a_1) = y \mid ... \mid f(a_n) = y \qquad (2)$$

By instantiating (2), n ground clauses will be generated. On the contrary, if we did not eliminate the skolem function first, then we would instantiate $P_f(u, y) \mid \neg P_S(y, u)$ and n^2 ground clauses would be generated. $\qquad\square$

Instantiating general clauses

The next step is to generate propositional clauses in case that all evaluable literals are evaluated to false while instantiating all variables in a clause. Evaluatable literals are those consisting of only variables and builtin functions/predicates like =(equality). If one of the evaluable literals in a clause is evaluated to true, then no propositional clause will be generated from the clause because the entire clause is eventually true. On the other hand, if one of evaluable literals in a clause is evaluated to false, then the literal will be deleted from the clause because this literal is known to be false, thereby having no effect on the evaluation of the clause. The procedure for generating propositional clauses from a clause, in which function instances are removed, is in Figure 2.

Example 4 The clause $f(x) < f(y) \mid x \geq y$ becomes, by substituting u for $f(x)$ and v for $f(y)$,

$$\neg P_f(x, u) \mid \neg P_f(y, v) \mid u < v \mid x \geq y \qquad (3)$$

where $P_f(x, u)$ is true iff $f(x) = u$ and $P_f(x, v)$ is true iff $f(x) = v$.
The next step is to instantiate all the variables in the formula 3. Assume for one instance that $u = 2, v = 1, x = 1$ and $y = 2$. Then a ground clause $(\neg P_f(1,1) \mid \neg P_f(0,2))$ will be generated because both $u < x$ and $x \geq y$ are evaluated to false. Assume another instance that $u = 1, v = 2, x = 1$ and $y = 2$. Then no ground clause will be generated because $u < x$ is evaluated to true. $\qquad\square$

In general, it is possible that identical ground clauses are generated more than once. ModGen avoids duplication of ground clauses only for symmetric cases.

Queen of order	No. of models	FINDER (sec)	ModGen No. of clauses	ModGen runtime(sec)
5	10	0.20	170	0.07
6	38	0.25	302	0.17
7	40	0.42	490	0.31
8	92	0.75	744	0.61
9	352	1.95	1074	1.34
10	724	6.15	1490	3.46
11	2680	26.10	2002	11.65
12	14200	131.73	2620	52.03
13	73712	725.78	3354	267.97
14	365596	4212.52	4214	1500.27
15	2279184	26604.08	5210	9323.61

Table 1: Experiment with Queen problems

QG5 of order	No. of models	NOELIMINATION No. of clauses	NOELIMINATION runtime (sec)	ELIMINATION No. of clauses	ELIMINATION runtime (sec)
5	1	2211	0.14	1461	0.10
6	0	4552	0.31	3040	0.17
7	3	8401	0.47	5657	0.31
8	1	14301	0.81	9693	0.51
9	0	22879	1.29	15589	0.89
10	0	54846	4.09	43846	2.62
11	5	80279	10.01	64307	5.41
12	0	113683	25.37	91219	11.26
13	0	156573	562.84	125815	234.71

Table 2: Experiment with Quasigroup 5 problems

When predicates to be generated are invariant to the exchange of two variables, predicates are said to be symmetric with respect to the two variables. The following example illustrates the elimination of redundant clauses by the symmetry checking.

Example 5 Consider $P_f(x, y) \mid P_f(x, z)$. Assume that $x = 1, y = 1$ and $z = 2$. Then $P_f(1, 1) \mid P_f(1, 2)$ will be generated. Assume also that $x = 1, y = 2$ and $z = 1$. Then $P_f(1, 2) \mid P_f(1, 1)$ will be generated. Clearly, the two ground clauses are identical.

If we exchange y for z in the above clause, the clause becomes $P_f(x, z) \mid P_f(x, y)$ which is identical to the original clause. Then, it is sufficient to generate ground clauses from $P_f(x, y) \mid P_f(x, z)$ only for $y \leq z$ since all ground clauses generated for $y > z$ are redundant. $\qquad\square$

It is also possible to generate fewer ground clauses by applying some of the unit literal deletion and pure literal deletion. However, this kind of checkings can be done by the propositional decision procedure.

Experimental Results

We tested ModGen with the queen problem, quasigroup problems, and several puzzles. The experiment is done on a IBM RS6000/530. All times are taken as the best of three runs.

The result of the experiment with the queen problem is shown in Table 1, which also includes the result of FINDER for performance comparison. ModGen runs as more than twice faster than FINDER for queen problems of order > 10.

The experimental results with some quasigroup problems (Bennett 1989; Stanley, Fujita, & Stickel 1993) are listed in Tables 2 and 3. The QG5 problem is to investigate the existence of Latin squares

GQ6 of order	No. of models	INDIRECT		DIRECT	
		No. of clauses	run time (sec)	No. of clauses	run time (sec)
5	0	48121	4.19	2711	0.13
6	0	959296	86.38	5632	0.25
7	0	23676843	2290.65	10459	0.47
8	2	-	-	17885	0.80
9	4	-	-	28711	1.37
10	0	-	-	43846	2.39
11	0	-	-	64307	5.88
12	0	-	-	91219	86.54
13	41760	-	-	125815	3287.47

Table 3: Experiment with Quasigroup 6 problem

problem	models	No. of clauses	runtime(sec)
Agatha	1	34	0.02
Nonobvious	0	162	0.04
Jobs	16	404	0.12
Steamroller	0	2250	0.21

Table 4: Experiment with puzzle problems

satisfying the identity $(((y * x) * y) * y) = x$ (viewing the square as a multiplication table). This problem includes two skolem functions which can be eliminated as explained in the previous section. The data in the column under ELIMINATION in Table 2 are the result of eliminating skolem functions and the data under NOELIMINATION are the result of treating the skolem function as ordinary functions. Eliminating skolem functions not only generates smaller number of ground clauses but also accelerates the search. The performance difference comes from the fact that ModGen generates one less order of ground clauses for formulas having skolem symbols.

The experimental results with another quasigroup problem, QG6 (Stanley, Fujita, & Stickel 1993), are is listed in Table 3. This problem is to investigate the existence of Latin squares satisfying the identity $((x * y) * y) = (x * (x * y))$, which is an equality between function instances ans is specially treated in ModGen. The data in the column under INDIRECT in Table 3 are the result of employing the transformation of $f(x) = y$ to $u = y \mid \neg P_f(x, u)$. The data under DIRECT in Table 3 are the result of employing the transformation of $f(x) = y$ to $P_f(x, y)$. As shown in Table 3, the performance difference is amazingly large. We could not experiment beyond order 7 for INDIRECT because of the excessive computing time. This performance difference is manifested by the observation that the INDIRECT strategy generates one more order of ground clauses for *each* literal having equality with function instances.

We also experimented with some puzzle problems such as Non-obviousness, Schubert's Steamroller (Stickel 1986), Jobs and Agatha; the results are listed in Table 4. Shubert's Steamroller has the conclusion negated so that it is unsatisfiable. This experiment shows that ModGen can solve puzzle problems very fast.

References

Bennett, F. 1989 Quasigroup Identities and Mendelsohn Designs, *Canadian Journal of Mathematics* 41: 341–368.

Gu, J. 1993 Local search for satisfiability (SAT) problem, *IEEE Trans. on Systems, Man, and Cybernetics* 23(4): 1108-1129.

Davis, M; Putnam, H 1960 A computing procedure for quantification theory, *J. of ACM* 7: 201-215.

McCune, W. W 1990 Otter 2.0 users' guide, Mathematics and Computer Science Division, Argonne National Laboratory, Argonne, Illinois.

Pelletier, F. J; Rudnicki, P 1986 Non-Obviousness, *Automated Reasoning Newsletter* 6: 4-5.

Selman, B.; Levesque, H.; Mitchell, D. 1992 A new method for solving hard satisfiability problems, In *Proceedings of AAAI'92*: 440-446.

Slaney, J. 1992 FINDER, Finite Domain Enumerator: Version 2.0 Notes and Guide, Technical report TR-ARP-1/92, Automated Reasoning Project, Australian National University.

Slaney, J; Fujita, M; and Stickel, M Automated reasoning and exhaustive search: Quasigroup existence problems To appear in *Computers and Mathematics with Applications*.

Sosic, R.; Gu, J. 1991 3,000,000 queens in less than one minute, *SIGART Bulletin*, 2(2): 22-24

Stickel, M. 1986 Shubert's steamroller problem: formulations and solutions, *J. of Automated reasoning* 2: 89-101.

Wos, L. 1988 *Automated reasoning: 33 Basic research problems*, Prentice Hall, New Jersey.

Zhang, H. 1993 SATO: A decision procedure for propositional logic, *Association for Automated Reasoning Newsletter*, 22: 1-3.

Small is Beautiful:
A Brute-Force Approach to Learning First-Order Formulas

Steven Minton and **Ian Underwood**
Recom Technologies
NASA Ames Research Center
Mail Stop 269-2
Moffett Field, CA 94035
{minton,ian}@ptolemy.arc.nasa.gov

Abstract

We describe a method for learning formulas in first-order logic using a brute-force, smallest-first search. The method is exceedingly simple. It generates all irreducible well-formed formulas up to a fixed size and tests them against a set of examples. Although the method has some obvious limitations due to its computational complexity, it performs surprisingly well on some tasks. This paper describes experiments with two applications of the method in the MULTI-TAC system, a program synthesizer for constraint satisfaction problems. In the first application, axioms are learned, and in the second application, search control rules are learned. We describe these experiments, and consider why searching the space of small formulas makes sense in our applications.

Introduction

Most machine learning systems prefer smaller, simpler hypotheses to larger, more complex ones. This bias is a form of Occam's Razor. While Occam's razor has obvious aesthetic appeal, some researchers have attempted to justify Occam's razor on more principled grounds by showing that it produces more accurate hypotheses; for instance, Blumer et al. (1987) show formally that one version of Occam's razor produces hypothesis that are likely to be predictive of future observations.

However, in some applications, the *utility* of the learned information depends on more than just prediction accuracy. Utility considerations often provide us with an additional reason for applying Occam's Razor, a point which has received scant attention. In our application, which involves automated problem solving, utility considerations place strong requirements on the learning process. In particular, the learned theories must consist of small sets of simple first-order formulas. Complex formulas, or large numbers of formulas, can significantly degrade system performance.

Yet another reason for preferring simpler hypotheses is that they can be relatively straightforward to find, particularly if we equate "simplest" with "smallest". In our system, the learning component systematically generates well-formed formulas, in order of size, beginning with the smallest. It tests each formula against a set of training examples, attempting to find formulas that are adequate for the needs of the performance component. This *brute force, smallest-first* (BFSF) search often produces theories that are more efficient and more comprehensive than those entered by hand.

In this paper we describe two applications of BFSF inductive learning in the MULTI-TAC system. In one application, the system learns axioms that are then used by a theorem prover to reason about generic constraint satisfaction problems (CSPs), such as graph coloring and bin packing. In the second application, the system learns search control rules to guide a constraint satisfaction engine. We were initially surprised that a brute force approach worked so well for our applications. In retrospect, we can identify several reasons why searching the space of small formulas is appropriate in our domains.

An Overview of the Multi-TAC system

MULTI-TAC (Multi-Tactic Analytic Compiler) is designed for a scenario where a combinatorial search problem must be solved routinely, as in a scheduling application where each week manufacturing tasks are assigned to workers. The system takes as input a specification of the generic problem and a set of problem instances. The objective is to synthesize an efficient program for the instance population. In practice, our goal is to do as well as competent programmers, as opposed to algorithms experts. Attaining this level of performance on a wide variety of problems would very useful; many relatively simple applications are not automated because programmers are unavailable.

The system starts with a set of domain-independent heuristics. When it encounters a new domain, it creates problem-specific approximations of these heuristics, and then searches for the combination that performs best on the instance population. It returns as output a Lisp program that incorporates this combination of heuristics.

In order to present a problem to MULTI-TAC it must be formalized as an integer CSP, that is, as a set of constraints over a set of integer variables. A solution

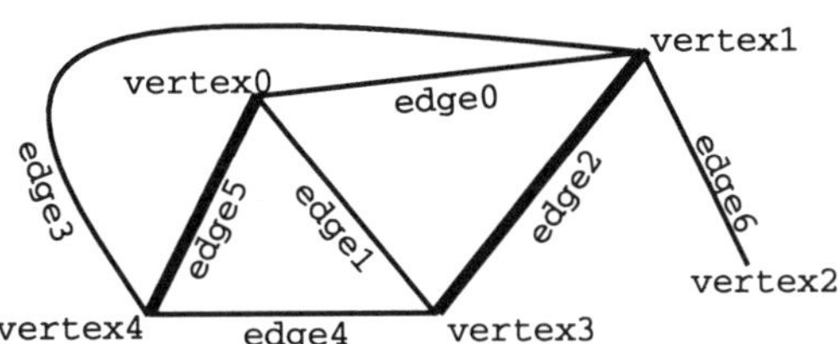


```
(declare-parameter 'K 2)
(declare-type-size 'edge 7)
(declare-type-size 'vertex 5)
(declare-relation-data
  '((endpoint edge0 vertex0)
    (endpoint edge0 vertex1)
    (endpoint edge1 vertex0)
    (endpoint edge1 vertex3)...))
```

Figure 1: An instance of MMM with $K = 2$. A solution $E' = \{$edge2 edge5$\}$ is indicated in boldface. The instance specification is on the right.

exists when all the variables are assigned a value such the constraints on each variable are satisfied.

For example, consider the NP-complete problem, "Minimum Maximal Matching" (MMM), described in (Garey & Johnson 1979). An instance of MMM consists of a graph $G = (V, E)$ and an integer $K \leq | E |$. The problem is to determine whether there is a subset $E' \subseteq E$ with $| E' | \leq K$ such that no two edges in E' share a common endpoint and every edge in $E - E'$ shares a common endpoint with some edge in E'. See Figure 1 for an example.

To formulate MMM as a CSP, we represent each edge in the graph with a variable. If an edge is chosen to be in E', it is assigned the value 1, otherwise it is assigned the value 0. The constraints can be stated as follows:

1. If $edge_i$ is assigned 1, then for every $edge_j$ that shares a common endpoint with $edge_i$, $edge_j$ must be assigned 0.

2. If $edge_i$ is assigned 0, then there must exist an $edge_j$ such that $edge_i$ and $edge_j$ share a common endpoint, and $edge_j$ is assigned 1.

3. The cardinality of the set of edges assigned 1 must be less than or equal to K.

A *problem specification* describes the types (*e.g.*, **vertex** and **edge**) and relations (*e.g.*, **endpoint**) and specifies the constraints in a typed predicate logic. An *instance specification* (Figure 1) instantiates the types and relations referred to in the problem specification. Our constraint language is relatively expressive, as it allows for full first-order quantification and the formation of sets and bags. Below we show how the first constraint above is specified, for some edge $Edge_i$:

```
(or (not (assigned Edge_i 1))
    (∀ Vrtx : (endpoint Edge_i Vrtx)
      (∀ Edge_j : (endpoint Edge_j Vrtx)
        (or (equal Edge_j Edge_i)
            (assigned Edge_j 0)))))
```

The notation $(\forall x:$ (endpoint $x\ y$)...) should be read as "forall x such that (endpoint $x\ y$)...".

The constraint language includes two types of relations, problem-specific *user-defined relations* such as **endpoint**, and built-in *system-defined relations*, such as **assigned**, **equal** and **less-than**. (There are no functions; instead, we use two-place relations.) The

assigned relation has special significance since it represents the state during the search process. In MMM, for example, the search proceeds by assigning each edge a value. In a solution state, every edge must be assigned a value such that the constraints are satisfied.

Enumerating Formulas

We now describe how the MULTI-TAC systematically generates hypotheses of increasing size. A formula is defined to be of size s if it contains s atomic formulas. The system first generates formulas of size 1, then formulas up to size 2, and so on, until it exceeds a pre-determined bound on either the computation time or the number of formulas. The generation process is based on a recursive grammar[1] for the language:

$$wff = (\forall\ var : atomic\ wff)\ |\ (\exists\ var : atomic\ wff)\ |$$
$$(\textbf{and}\ wff \ldots wff)\ |\ (\textbf{or}\ wff \ldots wff)\ |$$
$$(\textbf{not}\ atomic)\ |\ atomic$$
$$atomic = (predicate\ term \ldots term)$$
$$term = var\ |\ constant$$

Formulas of size $s > 1$ are generated by existentially or universally quantifying formulas of size $s-1$, or conjoining or disjoining sets of formulas whose size sums to s. In MULTI-TAC a recursive procedure, GENERATE-FORMULAS accomplishes this. GENERATE-FORMULAS takes a size s and a set "free variables", and generates all formulas of size s defined over one or more of the free variables.

Atomic formulas are generated using the user-defined types and relations (from the problem specification) and the system-defined relations. Each argument either is a variable or is a constant mentioned in the problem specification (i.e., arbitrary integers are *not* used). The MMM specification, for example, mentions the constants 1 and 0, and the relation **endpoint**.

Our implementation uses several simple techniques to improve the efficiency of the generation process. The most significant of these is that only "irreducible" formulas are generated. MULTI-TAC uses a simplifier to check each (sub)formula returned by GENERATE-FORMULAS; any formula which can be reduced to a smaller equivalent formula is discarded since the smaller formula will have been generated as well.

---

[1] The grammar shown here is simplified, since it does not include set/bag generators.

After the candidate formulas have been generated, MULTI-TAC employs training examples to identify which formulas are useful. In the following sections we describe two applications, and for each we describe how the useful formulas are identified.

Inducing axioms

MULTI-TAC includes a resolution theorem-prover that can be used during program synthesis for several different reasoning tasks. For example, the prover can be used to verify that a given value will necessarily violate a constraint, or that the antecedent of a search control rule will be satisfied in a given situation.

In order to use the theorem prover, we require axioms that describe the problem domain. Some axioms can be derived from the problem specification. For example, the problem description explicitly specifies the argument types for each relation. So, for MMM, an axiom stating that (`endpoint` x y) implies (`edge` x) can be created directly from the problem specification. However, other information may be left implicit in the instances. For example, in MMM (or any graph) it is necessarily true that for every edge there is at least one vertex that is its endpoint, but this is not stated in the problem specification.

We need these additional axioms for the theorem prover to operate effectively. In addition, for the theorem prover to operate efficiently, it helps significantly if there are only a few small axioms. Having too many axioms, or very complex axioms, may greatly impair a resolution theorem prover's performance because the branching factor will be higher.

These axioms have to come from somewhere. One possibility is to require the user to enter them along with the problem specification. However, experience shows that axioms entered by users tend to be incomplete, unnecessarily complicated, and just plain incorrect. One contributing factor is that people are generally not facile with predicate calculus. (In fact, the authors have noticed that we ourselves make many mistakes.) But even if users are asked to enter the axioms in English they tend to neglect relevant information. For example, for the MMM problem, one might forget to mention that every edge has an endpoint since it is so obvious. (It may also seem obvious that every edge actually has two unique endpoints, but in fact this is not true, since some edges may be connected to the same vertex at both ends. This illustrates the difficulty of writing axioms.)

Alternatively, we have found that a suitable set of axioms can often be found using BFSF induction. Our training examples are problem instances randomly selected from the instance distribution. (The instance distribution only provides positive examples, so we do not use negative examples.) An iterative approach is used to produce axioms. On the nth iteration, the system generates formulas of size n and tests them against the training examples, retaining only those formulas

that are consistent with all of the examples. Then the system filters this set further, eliminating formulas that can be proved using smaller formulas as axioms (i.e., those found on the previous iterations). The remaining formulas are reduced to an independent set by trying to prove each formula, using the other formulas as axioms. This set is minimal, in the sense that each axiom in the set is not provable in terms of the others. (This is time-consuming, but necessary, since redundant formulas degrade the theorem prover's performance.) The system then proceeds with the next iteration, until a resource bound is exceeded.

Of course, there is always a chance that the system may induce incorrect axioms. We can either ask the user for assistance in eliminating incorrect axioms or accept the entire set and take the chance that our proofs will be incorrect in some cases.

Here we consider only the former approach. After each iteration, the user is asked to approve the proposed axioms. If the user chooses not to accept an axiom, he can provide an example that is inconsistent with the proposed axiom. The example is then added to the training set. For instance, the system may propose that "there are at least two edges in every graph". The user can then enter a graph containing a single edge as a counterexample. Often a single counterexample will rule out a whole class of potential axioms; we have found that a few counterexamples often suffice to rule out all incorrect axioms.

Table 1 summarizes a set of experiments with several combinatorial problems described in (Garey & Johnson 1979): BIN PACKING, DOMINATING SET, GRAPH 3-COLORABILITY, NOT ALL EQUAL 3-SAT, PARTITION-INTO-TRIANGLES and MMM. To make the experiment more challenging, the task was to produce axioms for distributions consisting only of solvable instances. Axioms characterizing only solvable instances can be used to quickly screen out unsolvable instances, and in addition are useful for many other tasks.[2] For purposes of comparison, we asked two human volunteers to do the same task. (Both were familiar with predicate calculus, and one was a MULTI-TAC project member who had experience with the theorem prover.)

For each problem, all formulas up to size 4 were generated. To test the formulas, fifteen training examples were generated. As explained above, the user (one of the authors) could enter additional examples by hand, and in our experiments between 2 and 4 additional examples were entered per problem in response to incorrect axioms. Columns 2,3 and 4 show the number of formulas of each size that were generated. The last column shows the number of axioms finally retained.

---

[2]These axioms are essentially a superset of the axioms describing arbitrary instances (solvable or not). For example, for `Graph 3-Colorability`, the axiom set would include the axioms describing graphs in general, but it might also include the axiom "No vertex has an edge to itself", since this is true of solvable instances.

	$s = 2$	$s = 3$	$s = 4$	Final
Bin Packing	6	42	450	4
Dominating Set	8	70	1242	4
Graph 3-Color	8	48	472	5
Not-All-Eq 3-Sat	6	40	474	35
Part. Into Triangles	8	42	472	6
Min Max Matching	6	32	250	5

Table 1: Axiom Learning, Experimental Results

One striking aspect of these experiments was how few training instances were required. In fact, the set of formulas generally stabilized after the third example – relatively few formulas were eliminated by subsequent examples (except for the user-provided counterexamples). This is somewhat surprising, since a PAC analysis reveals that for 1000 hypotheses, approximately 200 examples are required just to be .95 confident that the error is less than .05. Of course, this is a worst-case analysis, and it appears that the worst case assumptions are violated in at least two ways. First, many of the formulas are equivalent (or almost equivalent), since there are many ways to state the same fact. Second, most of the formulas appear to be either true, false, almost always true or almost always false. Thus, after just a few examples, the formulas that are left are true or almost always true. We conjecture that this will occur for many problems. An analogous situation has been identified in the CSP literature – for some well-known problems, almost all instances are easy to solve because they are either over-constrained or under-constrained (Cheeseman, Kanefsky, & Taylor 1991; Mitchell, Selman, & Levesque 1992).

If we compare the learned axioms to those produced by our human subjects, the results are as expected. Often the humans neglected to state relevant axioms or stated them incorrectly. The machine-generated axiom sets were more complete, and in some cases, the axioms were stated more concisely. (In fact, the machine did a better job than the authors for MMM.) On the other hand, for one problem, NOT ALL EQUAL 3SAT, the system generated many redundant axioms because it could not prove they were redundant within the time limit. Finally, the humans also identified a couple of axioms of size 5 and 6 that the system obviously did not generate. (However, these axioms appeared to be useless for the system's purposes.)

As we have argued, one advantage of the BFSF method is that it produces small sets of small axioms. To illustrate the benefits, we tried reversing the smallest-first bias, producing MMM axioms of size four before looking for smaller axioms. This did indeed result in a poorer set of axioms, including:

$(\forall\, E_1 : (\text{edge } E_1)$
$\quad (\exists\, E_2 : (\text{edge } E_2)$
$\quad\quad (\exists\, V : (\text{endpoint } E_1\ V)$
$\quad\quad\quad (\text{endpoint } E_2\ V)$

This states that "for every edge E_1, there is an edge E_2 that shares an endpoint with E_1. Although this ap-pears to be false, it is in fact true, since E_1 and E_2 can refer to the same edge. Thus, it is actually an obscure way to state the axiom, "every edge has an endpoint". The problem with this, aside from obscurity, is that it is much less efficient for resolution theorem-proving; larger axioms translate into more (and larger) clauses, and thus increase the prover's branching factor.

Inducing Search Control Rules

In MULTI-TAC, search control rules are used to control the choices made during the constraint satisfaction process, such as variable and value-ordering choices. For example, we can implement the generic variable-ordering heuristic "prefer the most-constrained variable" by using a rule which, at each choice point, selects the variable with the fewest possible remaining values. Unfortunately, using this generic rule can be costly since it requires that the system maintain the possible values for each variable during the search.

Minton (1993a) has described an analytic approach for automatically generating control rules. This method operationalizes generic variable and value-ordering heuristics by incorporating information from the problem specification. For MMM this process produced 52 candidate control rules, including the those shown below. (Recall that in MMM the CSP search proceeds by assigning each edge either 0 or 1.)

- Prefer an edge with the most neighbors (i.e., adjacent edges).

- Prefer an edge with the most neighbors that have been assigned values.

- Prefer an edge that has a neighbor that has been assigned the value 1.

These rules were produced by operationalizing and approximating the generic "most constrained variable first" heuristic. The rules vary in their application cost and their effectiveness in reducing search. For example, the first rule is relatively inexpensive, since the ordering can be precomputed and the edges sorted accordingly before the CSP search process begins. (The compiler has been specially crafted to make efficient use of such rules.) The third rule is more powerful but more costly to apply since the ordering cannot be precomputed. MULTI-TAC allows such rules to be used in combination. The system's utility evaluation module carries out a beam search for the best combination of rules; different combinations are evaluated by running them on representative problem instances.

Although the analytic learning method has performed well, producing control rules that are comparable or better than hand-coded ones (Minton 1993b; 1993a), there is a significant drawback. For each generic heuristic, the system's designers must write a meta-level theory that can be operationalized to produce control rules. This involves a sophisticated "theory-engineering" process where the designers guess

	Analytic Learning		Inductive Learning			
	Solved	Time	Solved	Time	Rules Gen	Rules Kept
Bin Packing	46	.58	66	.48	539	17
Dominating Set	19	.93	45	.73	2931	70
Graph 3-Colorability	96	.33	100	.25	805	30
Not-All-Equal 3-Sat	84	.66	81	.75	1084	68
Partition Into Triangles	100	.73	100	.54	805	38
Minimum Maximal Matching	92	.10	38	.73	535	22

Table 2: Search Control Learning, Experimental Results

what operationalizations will produce useful rules, without knowing exactly what problems the system will eventually be tried on.

An alternative approach is to use BFSF induction for generating control rules. (Actually, as we will see, it makes sense to use both learning methods for robustness!) Minton (1990) and Etzioni & Minton (1992) have argued that smaller control rules tend to be more efficient and more general. We will not review these arguments here, but we will show empirically that BFSF induction produces good control rules.

We begin by considering how candidate control rules approximating the "most-constrained variable" heuristic can be learned. In MULTI-TAC, variable ordering preference rules[3] take the form "(Prefer v) if (P v)" where (P v) is an arbitrary formula containing v. The BFSF method generates all candidate variable-ordering rules up to size s, and tests them using examples that illustrate the most-constrained heuristic. To find examples we run our CSP problem solver (without any ordering heuristics) on randomly selected problem instances and periodically stop the solver at variable selection choice points. Each example consists of a pair of variables and a state, such that one variable is a most-constrained variable in that state and the other variable is not. A variable is "most-constrained" if no other variable has fewer possible values.

We test each rule on each example by seeing if the antecedent holds for the most-constrained variable and does not hold for the other variable. In this case we say the rule was correct on the example. Since we do not expect our rules to be one-hundred percent correct, we simply retain all rules which are correct more often than they are incorrect. The utility evaluation module then finds the best combination of these rules.

MULTI-TAC can learn other types of control rules similarly, such as rules that prefer the "least constraining value". The main requirement is an inexpensive way of generating examples. Unfortunately, for some generic heuristics, we have not yet found an inexpensive way of producing examples. For instance, we would like to induce rules that recognize problem sym-

---

[3]There is also an alternative syntax for preference rules that allows individual candidates to be numerically scored. We also generate rules of this form, but since the syntax involves the set generator construct which we avoided discussing in the last section, we will not describe it here.

metries (Minton 1993a) but we do not know an inexpensive way of generating examples of symmetries.

We experimentally evaluated the inductive method by comparing to the analytic method on the 6 problems introduced earlier. This is a significant test for the inductive method because in previous experiments (Minton 1993b; 1993a) the analytic method produced very good results – in some cases, MULTI-TAC's programs were faster than those of human programmers. To compare the inductive and analytic approaches on each problem, both methods were used to produce most-constrained-first variable-ordering rules and least-constraining-first value-ordering rules. The BFSF method generated rules up to a size limit of 4. Thirty examples were used in the BFSF test phase.

In our experiments, the rules produced by the inductive approach resulted in superior programs on four of the six problems. To evaluate the programs, we used one hundred randomly-generated instances as in (Minton 1993b). The columns labeled "Solved" in Table 2 show the primary performance indicator: how many of the 100 test instances were solved within a preset time limit. The columns labeled "Time" show the fraction of the total available CPU time actually used. (This is relevant primarily for GRAPH 3-COLORABILITY and PARTITION-INTO-TRIANGLES where both methods solved most of the instances). The remaining two columns show the total number of rules generated during BFSF search and the number of rules retained.

The inductive approach proved superior on four problems, but its performance was particularly good on BIN PACKING and DOMINATING SET, where substantially more instances were solved. There was also one problem where the inductive approach was substantially inferior, MMM. We analyzed why the inductive approach performed poorly on MMM, and found that the "good" rules (those learned by the analytic approach) were generated, but they did not do well in the test phase. We believe the problem arises because our examples are produced during un-informed search, which in some respects does not mirror the situations that occur when control rules are used.

Finally, we note that, as in our axiom learning experiments, very few examples were necessary for our experiments. As can be seen from the last two columns, it was relatively rare for a rule to be retained.

Discussion

In the preceding sections we outlined a relatively simplistic, brute force approach for generating axioms and search control knowledge in MULTI-TAC. Initially, we were surprised that the approach worked so well. In retrospect, we can identify several important factors that contribute to its success.

First, computers are very good at brute force search. They can quickly examine large numbers of candidate formulas. But even so, brute force would be out of the question without a strong bias for small formulas. Thus, a second contributing factor is the "smallest-first" bias. This bias is clearly appropriate for our applications. Both the theorem prover and the search control module are much more likely to be effective if the learned formulas (the axioms and search control rules) are concise.

A third reason for the success is that certain characteristics of our problem domains help keep the number of small candidate formulas manageable. Most importantly, each problem specification generally includes only a few user-defined predicates. This is similar to having only a few "features" per domain. Similarly, the problem specification generally only mentions a few constants. (Recall that the generator uses only those constants mentioned in the problem specification, essentially a form of language bias.)

These justifications are still insufficient to explain our results, however. The situation reminds us of the story of the drunk who was looking for his keys by the lamppost. (The drunk looks for his keys by the light, even though he thinks he may have dropped them somewhere else.) While we know that small formulas are preferable for our applications and furthermore, that we can easily search the space of small formulas, do we really have any confidence that our target formulas (either axioms or control rules) will actually BE small? Clearly there is no guarantee. But we note that the language has been designed so that users can easily and concisely specify the constraints on a large variety of combinatorial problems. Furthermore, when the user formulates a given problem domain, he will tend to define relations that will make the constraints simple to specify. Therefore, because we believe that the problem constraints will usually be concisely specified, we also have some confidence that the axioms and search control rules will be concisely specifiable as well. This is hard to formalize or quantify, but we believe that it is a significant factor.

Finally, we have already remarked upon the fact that very few training examples were required for our applications. On a related note, we should mention that the issue of noise is not an important consideration in our applications. The theorem-proving application is noise-free, and the search control application does not involve noise in the traditional sense.

Interestingly, the factors we have identified as important to the success of our approach should hold for a variety of other tasks besides automated software synthesis. In particular, BFSF induction might prove useful in other design tasks where a user creates a problem specification and the design task is broken down into small subcomponents.

Limitations and Future work

The most obvious limitation of our approach is that the number of generated formulas grows exponentially as the size bound is increased.[4] In our experiments, it typically took under a minute for a Sparc2 to generate all formulas of size 4. Generating formulas of size 5 can usually be accomplished in several minutes. For the axiom-learning application, the number of size 5 formulas ranges from 3450 for MMM to almost 34000 for DOMINATING SET. In practice, however, generating the formulas is not the bottleneck. In order to test whether a formula is consistent with an example, MULTI-TAC converts each formula to an Lisp procedure which is then compiled. The most time-consuming aspect of the induction process is running the Common-Lisp compiler on these procedures.[5] For 5000 formulas, this takes more than an hour. Once the formulas have been compiled, testing the examples is relatively quick.

Thus, the most profitable improvement would be to reduce the number of formulas generated. Currently, GENERATE-FORMULAS often produces "nonsensical" subformulas that are unsatisfiable. In principal these could be identified by a theorem-prover if it had the appropriate domain axioms. We are currently investigating a much more practical approach that uses examples to identify subformulas that are probably unsatisfiable. Instead of generating all formulas and testing them on the examples, we interleave the generation and test processes. Any subformula that is false on all examples is eliminated during the generation phase.

Another improvement involves the invention of new predicates to reformulate the constraints. As we explained previously, the success of our approach depends on whether the target concepts can be expressed concisely, given the constraint language and the user-defined predicates. In some cases, a concise representation may require the invention of new predicates. How can we invent appropriate predicates? One way is to look for transformations that rewrite the problem constraints in a more concise form. For example, the MMM problem constraints could be rewritten more concisely given a "neighbor" predicate, such that

---

[4] Assume the domain has p predicates and k constants, where r is the maximum arity of any predicate. Then, since a formula of size s has at most s atomic formulas, there are at most sr distinct variables in any formula. Consequently, if α is the number of literals that could be generated, then $\alpha \leq 2p(k + sr)^r$. Since a formula of size s may include no more than s quantifiers and connectives (of which there are 4), the number of possible formulas is $O(4^s \alpha^s)$.

[5] We also note that eliminating redundant axioms is time consuming, since the theorem prover is used.

(**neighbor** $edge_1$ $edge_2$) if $edge_1$ and $edge_2$ share a common endpoint. Currently, MULTI-TAC is capable of inventing new predicates (through finite-differencing and related techniques), but these are used only to rewrite the problem constraints for efficiency purposes. We plan to investigate whether the invented predicates can improve the induction process as well.

Related Work

Most the the empirical work on first-order learning has been in the context of inductive logic programming (ILP), a paradigm which is quite different from ours (Muggleton 1992). In ILP the target language is usually restricted to horn clauses, while we allow full first-order formulas. On the other hand, ILP methods can be used to learn recursive programs, while we are interested only in simple formulas. Furthermore, ILP methods are generally concerned with optimizing accuracy in an environment that is typically noisy. In contrast, our applications have led us to focus primarily on efficiency. Finally, perhaps the most significant difference is that ILP systems usually operate by generalizing or specializing hypotheses. In our approach, the hypothesis space is explicitly enumerated.

All in all, there has been surprising little applied work using brute force enumeration of formulas, perhaps because the approach seems so simplistic. Weiss et al.(1990) describe an algorithm that looks for the best logical expression of a fixed length or less that covers a sample population, but they search the space heuristically. Systematic enumeration techniques have received a bit more attention from researchers interested in more restricted languages. Riddle, Segal and Etzioni (1994) report good results with an exhaustive, depth-bounded algorithm for learning decision trees, and Schlimmer (1993) describes an exhaustive, but efficient, method for learning determinations.

Methodologically, we were influenced by Holte's (1993) study showing that one-level decision trees perform well on many commonly used datasets. Holte advocates exploring algorithms that have small hypothesis spaces, a methodology he refers to as "simplicity-first". If a simple algorithm works, then one can analyze why it worked, otherwise the hypothesis space can be expanded to rectify specific deficiencies. We view our work as an instance of this methodology.

Conclusion

We have shown that brute force induction is surprisingly useful for learning axioms and control rules in MULTI-TAC. Our approach relies on a bias in favor of small formulas. One reason that this bias is appropriate is that small formulas tend to have much higher *utility* in our applications, a point rarely discussed in the induction literature.

The success of our approach also depends on certain aspects of the domain. In particular, we limit the predicates and terms in our generalization language to those mentioned in the problem specification, a type of a language bias. We pointed out that our approach will be successful only if the target concepts can be represented concisely. Since presumably the language allows the problem constraints to be represented concisely, we conjectured that the language is also sufficient to allow the target concepts to be represented concisely.

We expect that our approach will prove useful for many of the problems that MULTI-TAC encounters. It also seems plausible that the approach will work for other types of design problems, and thus may be a promising avenue for further research.

References

Blumer, A.; Ehrenfeucht, A.; Haussler, D.; and Warmuth, M. K. 1987. Occam's razor. *Information Processing Letters* 24:377–380.

Cheeseman, P.; Kanefsky, B.; and Taylor, W. 1991. Where the *really* hard problems are. In *IJCAI-91*.

Etzioni, O., and Minton, S. 1992. Why EBL produces overly-specific knowledge: A critique of the prodigy approaches. In *Proc. Ninth International Machine Learning Conference*.

Garey, M., and Johnson, D. 1979. *Computers and Intractability: A Guide to the Theory of NP-Completeness*. W.H. Freeman and Co.

Holte, R. 1993. Very simple classification rules perform well on most commonly used datasets. *Machine Learning* 1(11):63–90.

Minton, S. 1990. Quantitative results concerning the utility of explanation-based learning. *Artificial Intelligence* 42.

Minton, S. 1993a. An analytic learning system for specializing heuristics. In *Proc. IJCAI-93*.

Minton, S. 1993b. Integrating heuristics for constraint satisfaction problems: A case study. In *Proc. AAAI*.

Mitchell, D.; Selman, B.; and Levesque, H. 1992. Hard and easy distributions of SAT problems. In *Proc. AAAI-92*.

Muggleton, S. 1992. *Inductive Logic Progamming*. Academic Press.

Riddle, P.; Segal, R.; and Etzioni, O. 1994. Representation design and brute-force induction in a Boeing manufacturing domain. *Applied Artificial Intelligence* 8:125–147.

Schlimmer, J. 1993. Efficiently inducing determinations: A complete and systematic search algorithm that uses optimal pruning. In *Proc. Tenth International Machine Learning Conference*.

Weiss, S.; Galen, R.; and Tadepalli, P. 1990. Maximising the predictive value of production rules. *Artificial Intelligence* 45.

Avoiding Tests for Subsumption [†]

Anavai Ramesh **Neil V. Murray**
Inst. for Programming and Logics – CSI Dept.
University at Albany - SUNY, Albany, NY 12222
rameshag/nvm@cs.albany.edu

Abstract

Useful equivalence-preserving operations based on *anti-links* are described. These operations eliminate a potentially large number of subsumed paths in a negation normal form formula. Those anti-links that directly indicate the presence of subsumed paths are characterized. These operations are useful for prime implicant/implicate algorithms because most of the computational effort in computing the prime implicants and prime implicates of a propositional formula is spent on subsumption checks. The problem of removing all subsumed paths in an NNF formula is shown to be NP-hard, even though such formulas may be small relative to the size of their path sets. The general problem of determining whether a pair of subsumed paths is associated with an arbitrary anti-link is shown to be NP-complete. Further reductions of subsumption checks are shown to be available when *strictly pure* full blocks are present. The effectiveness of operations based on anti-links and strictly pure full blocks is examined with respect to some benchmark examples from the literature.

Introduction

The consequences of a ground formula, expressed as minimal implied clauses, are useful in certain approaches to non-monotonic reasoning [5,11,13], where all consequences of a formula set (e.g., the support set for a proposed commonsense conclusion) are required. Minimal conjunctions that imply a formula are useful in situations where satisfying models are desired, as in error analysis during hardware verification. Such minimal implied clauses are the formula's *prime implicates*, and the minimal conjunctions that imply it are its *prime implicants*.

Many algorithms have been proposed to compute the prime implicates of propositional boolean formula. Most algorithms [1,2,3,4,14] assume that the input is either in conjunctive normal form (CNF) or in disjunctive normal form (DNF). Other algorithms [10] require the input to be a conjunction of DNF formulas. In [12] a set of techniques is proposed for finding the prime implicates of formulas in negation normal form (NNF). Those techniques are based on *dissolution*, an inference rule introduced in [8], and on an algorithm called PI. The techniques described here are polynomial for classes of formulas for which any CNF/DNF-based technique must be exponential.

The PI algorithm is described in [12]; there, PI is used to enumerate all the prime implicates of a *full dissolvent*, an NNF formula that has no conjunctive links (defined later). PI repeatedly does subsumption checks to keep intermediate results as small as possible. However these checks are expensive. Most result in failure, and they have to be done on sets which can be exponentially large. The time required for these operations can be reduced by using a more compact representation of the intermediate results [1], but avoiding as many such checks as possible is the focus of this paper.

We show that the full dissolvent can be restructured before applying PI such that many non-prime implicates are removed without doing subsumption checks at all. We define *disjunctive* and *conjunctive anti-links*[1] in NNF formulas, and we identify operations to remove such anti-links and their associated subsumed paths. This leaves fewer subsumption checks for the PI algorithm.

In the next section we describe our path semantics viewpoint and our graphical representation of formulas in classical logic. In Section 3 we introduce *anti-links* and develop useful equivalence-preserving operations based on them. In Section 4, complexity issues are discussed and some NP-completeness results are proven. Section 5 introduces further techniques based on strictly pure subformulas. The effectiveness of our techniques on certain benchmark formulas described by Ngair [10] is explored. Proof are omitted for lack of space.

[†] This research was supported in part by National Science Foundation Grant CCR-9101208.

---

[1] Anti-links and some associated operators were first proposed by Beckert and Hähnle – personal communication. The first motivation for studying anti-links arose in connection with regular clausal tableau calculi (Letz, p. 114 [6]). The anti-link rule as it will be defined later can be viewed as an implementation of the regularity condition in [6] for the propositional non-clausal case (Letz considered the first-order clausal case). There, refinements of general inference rules are considered, whereas the anti-link rule allows implementation as a preprocessing step.

Foundations: Facts on Formulas in Negation Normal Form

We assume the reader to be familiar with the notions of *atom, literal,* and *formula* from classical logic. We consider only formulas in *negation normal form* (NNF): The only connectives used are conjunction and disjunction, and all negations are at the atomic level.

In this section, we review a number of technical terms and definitions taken from [9]. They are required for the development of the anti-link operations defined in Section 3, and they make the paper somewhat self-contained even for readers not familiar with dissolution.

Semantic Graphs

A *semantic graph* G is a triple *(N,C,D) of nodes, c-arcs,* and *d-arcs,* respectively, where a node is a literal occurrence, a c-arc is a conjunction of two semantic graphs, and a d-arc is a disjunction of two semantic graphs. Any of N,C,D may be empty. If N is empty, G is either *true* (empty conjunction) or *false* (empty disjunction). Each semantic graph used in the construction of a semantic graph is called an *explicit subgraph*, and each proper explicit subgraph is contained in exactly one arc. We will typically use G to refer to both the graph and to the corresponding node set when the meaning is evident from context.

We use the notation $(X,Y)_c$ for the c-arc from X to Y and similarly use $(X,Y)_d$ for a d-arc; the subscript may be omitted when no confusion is possible. Arbitrary subformulas are denoted by upper case italic letters; plain upper case letters are used for single nodes.

In Figure 1 below, the formula $((\neg C \wedge A) \vee D \vee E) \wedge (\neg A \vee (B \wedge C))$, is displayed graphically:

$$\begin{array}{ccccc} \overline{C} & & & & \\ \wedge & \vee & D & \vee & E \\ A & & & & \\ & & \wedge & & \\ & & & B & \\ \overline{A} & \vee & \wedge & & \\ & & & C & \end{array}$$

Figure 1.

Note that c-arcs and d-arcs are indicated by the usual symbols for conjunction and disjunction. Essentially, the only difference between a semantic graph and a formula in NNF is the point of view, and we will use either term depending upon the desired emphasis. For a more detailed exposition, see [9].

If A and B are nodes in a graph, and if $\mathbf{a} = (X,Y)_\alpha$ is an arc ($\alpha = c$ or $\alpha = d$) with A in X and B in Y, we say that $\mathbf{a}$ is the arc *connecting* A and B, and that A and B are α-*connected*. In Figure 1, C is c-connected to each of B, A, $\overline{C}$, D, and E and is d-connected to $\overline{A}$.

Let G be a semantic graph. A *partial c-path through G* is a set of nodes such that any two are c-connected, and a *c-path* through G is a partial c-path that is not properly contained in any partial c-path. The c-paths of the graph in Figure 1 above are: $\{C, A, \overline{A}\}$, $\{C, A, B, C\}$, $\{D, \overline{A}\}$, $\{D, B, C\}$, $\{E, \overline{A}\}$, $\{E, B, C\}$. We similarly define d-path using d-arcs instead of c-arcs. The following lemma is obvious.

Lemma 1. Let G be a semantic graph. Then an interpretation I satisfies (falsifies) G iff I satisfies (falsifies) every literal on some c-path (d-path) through G.

If we consider conjunction and disjunction as n-ary connectives, then we informally define a *full block* to be subset of the arguments of one connective, i.e., of one explicit subformula.

Let H be a full block; H is a conjunction or a disjunction of fundamental subgraphs of some explicit subgraph M. If the final arc (main connective) of M is a conjunction, then we define the *c-extension* of H to be M and the *d-extension* of H to be H itself. The situation is reversed if the final arc (main connective) of M is a d-arc. We will use the notation $\text{CE}(H)$ and $\text{DE}(H)$ for the c- and d-extensions, respectively, of H. In Figure 1, $\text{CE}(\overline{A}) = \overline{A}$ and $\text{DE}(\overline{A}) = \overline{A} \vee \begin{smallmatrix} B \\ \wedge \\ C \end{smallmatrix}$.

Path Dissolution

A *c-link* is defined to be a complementary pair of c-connected nodes; d-connected complementary nodes form a d-link. Unless stated otherwise, we use the term link to refer to a c-link. Path dissolution is in general applicable to collections of links; here we restrict attention to single links. Suppose then that we have literal occurrences A and $\overline{A}$ residing in conjoined subgraphs X and Y, respectively. Consider, for example, the link $\{A, \overline{A}\}$ in Figure 1. Then the entire graph $G = (X \wedge Y)$ is the smallest full block containing the link, where $X = \begin{smallmatrix} \overline{C} \\ \wedge \\ A \end{smallmatrix} \vee D \vee E$ and $Y = \overline{A} \vee \begin{smallmatrix} B \\ \wedge \\ C \end{smallmatrix}$.

The *c-path complement* of an arbitrary subgraph H with respect to X, written $\text{CC}(H, X)$, is defined to be the subgraph of X consisting of all literals in X that lie on paths that do not contain nodes from H; the *c-path extension* of H with respect to X, written $\text{CPE}(H, X)$, is the subgraph containing all literals in X that lie on paths that *pass through H*. (In the development of anti-link operations, we will require the dual operations of CC and CPE. We use DC for the *d-path complement* and DPE for the *d-path extension* operators. Their definitions and properties are straightforward by duality.)

It is intuitively clear that the paths through $(X \wedge Y)$ that do not contain the link are those through $(\text{CPE}(A, X) \wedge \text{CC}(\overline{A}, Y))$ plus those through $(\text{CC}(A, X) \wedge \text{CPE}(\overline{A},Y))$ plus those through $(\text{CC}(A, X) \wedge \text{CC}(\overline{A}, Y))$. The reader is referred to [9] for the formal definitions of CC and of CPE.

Let $H = \{A, \overline{A}\}$ be a link, and let $M = (X, Y)_c$ be the smallest full block containing H. We define $DV(H, M)$, the *dissolvent of H in M*, as follows:

$$
\begin{array}{ccc}
X & & CC(A, X) \\
\wedge & \vee & \wedge \\
CC(\overline{A}, Y) & & CPE(\overline{A}, Y)
\end{array}
$$

Theorem 1. Let H link in a semantic graph G, and let M be the smallest full block containing H. Then M and $DV(H, M)$ are equivalent.

We may therefore select an arbitrary link H in G and replace the smallest full block containing H by its dissolvent, producing (in the ground case) an equivalent graph that has strictly fewer c-paths than the old one. This proves

Theorem 2. At the ground level, path dissolution is a strongly complete rule of inference.

Fully Dissolved Formulas

If we dissolve in semantic graph G until it is linkless, the resulting graph is called the *full dissolvent of G*; we denote it by $FD(G)$. The set of c-paths in $FD(G)$ is unique: It is exactly the set of satisfiable c-paths in G.

In the discussion that follows, we will often refer to subsumption of d- and c-paths rather than of disjuncts and conjuncts. We denote by $l(p)$ the literal set of path p. In this way, no change in the standard definition of subsumption is necessary. We also assume the reader to be familiar with the standard definitions of prime implicate and prime implicant. The theorem below is from [12].

Theorem 3. In any non-empty formula in which no c-path (d-path) contains a link, every implicate (implicant) of the formula is subsumed by some d-path (c-path) in the formula.

In [12], the prime implicates of G are computed by first obtaining $FD(G)$; then, knowing that all implicates are present in the d-paths of $FD(G)$, the PI algorithm computes $\psi(FD(G))$, where

$$\psi(\mathcal{F}) = \{P \mid (P \text{ is a d-path through } \mathcal{F}) \wedge$$

$$(P \neq true) \wedge (\forall \text{ d-paths } Q \text{ through } \mathcal{F}, l(Q) \not\subseteq l(P))\}.$$

Used in this way, PI extracts all unsubsumed (non-tautological) d-paths from an NNF formula without c-links. In general, PI computes $\psi(\mathcal{F})$ for an arbitrary NNF formula $\mathcal{F}$.

Subsumed Paths and Anti-Links

Let $M=(X,Y)_d$ be a d-arc in a semantic graph G and let A_X and A_Y be occurrences of the literal A in X and in Y respectively. Then we call $\{A_X,A_Y\}$ a *disjunctive anti-link*. Note that M is the smallest full block containing the anti-link. If $M=(X,Y)_c$ is a c-arc in a semantic graph G and if A_X and A_Y are nodes in X and in Y respectively, then we call $\{A_X,A_Y\}$ a *conjunctive anti-link*.

Theorem 4. Let G be a semantic graph in which d-path p is subsumed by a distinct non-tautological d-path p' in G. Then G contains either a disjunctive anti-link or a conjunctive anti-link.

Unfortunately, the presence of anti-links does not imply the presence of subsumed paths, and hence the converse of the above theorem is not true.

Redundant Anti-links

We now identify those disjunctive anti-links which do imply the presence of subsumed paths. We say a disjunctive anti-link $\{A_X,A_Y\}$ with respect to the graph G is *redundant* if either $CE(A_X) \neq A$ or $CE(A_Y) \neq A$.

Let $\{A_X,A_Y\}$ be a disjunctive anti-link in graph G, where $M = (X,Y)_d$ is the smallest full block containing the anti-link. We define $\mathcal{DP}_{A_X,A_Y,G}$ to be the set of all d-paths of M which pass through both $CE(A_X) - \{A_X\}$ and A_Y or through both $CE(A_Y) - \{A_Y\}$ and A_X.

In general, one or both of the literals in a redundant anti-link $\{L_X, L_Y\}$ is an argument of a conjunction, and $\mathcal{DP}_{L_X,L_Y,G} \neq \emptyset$.

Theorem 5. Let $\{A_X,A_Y\}$ be a redundant disjunctive anti-link in semantic graph G. Then each d-path in $\mathcal{DP}_{A_X,A_Y,G}$ is properly subsumed by a d-path in G that contains the anti-link.

An Anti-Link Operator

The identification of redundant disjunctive anti-links can be done easily by checking to see if either $CE(A_X) \neq A_X$ or $CE(A_Y) \neq A_Y$. After identifying a redundant anti-link, it is possible to remove it using the *disjunctive anti-link dissolvent* (DADV) operator; in the process, all d-paths in $\mathcal{DP}_{A_X,A_Y,G}$ are eliminated, and the two occurrences of the anti-link literal are collapsed into one. Let $\{A_X,A_Y\}$ be a disjunctive anti-link and let $M = (X, Y)_d$ be the smallest full block containing the anti-link. Then $DADV(\{A_X, A_Y\}, M) =$

$$
\begin{array}{ccc}
DC(A_X,X) & \vee & DC(A_Y,Y) \\
& \wedge & \\
DC(CE(A_X), X) & \vee & DPE(A_Y,Y) \\
& \wedge & \\
DPE(A_X,X) & \vee & CC(A_Y,Y) \;.
\end{array}
$$

Consider the formula G of the form $(X, Y)_d$, where

$$
G = \begin{array}{ccc}
A \vee C & & A \\
\wedge & \vee & \wedge \\
B & & E \vee C
\end{array} .
$$

We have $DC(A_X, X) = B$ and $DC(A_Y, Y) = (E \vee C)$, so the upper conjunct in DADV is $(B \vee E \vee C)$. For the middle conjunct, $CE(A_X) = A_X$, $DC(CE(A_X), X) = B$, and $DPE(A_Y, Y) = A_Y$; this conjunct is $(B \vee A)$. Finally in the lower conjunct, $DPE(A_X, X) = (A \vee C)$ and $CC(A_Y, Y) = \emptyset$ *(false)*, so this reduces to $(A \vee C)$.The result is:

$$\text{DADV}(\{A_X, A_Y\}, M) = \begin{array}{ccc} B & \vee & E \vee C \\ & \wedge & \\ B & \vee & A \\ & \wedge & \\ A & \vee & C \end{array}$$

We point out that although DADV produces a CNF formula in this simple example, in general it does not. Theorem 6 below states that DADV($\{A_X, A_Y\}, G$) is logically equivalent to G and does not contain those d-paths in $\mathcal{DP}_{A_X, A_Y, G}$.

Theorem 6. Let $M = (X \vee Y)$ be the smallest full block containing $\{A_X, A_Y\}$, a disjunctive anti-link in semantic graph G. Then DADV($\{A_X, A_Y\}, M$) is equivalent to M and differs in d-paths from M as follows: Those d-paths in $\mathcal{DP}_{A_X, A_Y, M}$ are not present, and any d-path of M containing the anti-link is replaced by a path with the same literal set having only one occurrence of the anti-link literal.

By identifying a redundant anti-link $H = \{A_X, A_Y\}$ and the smallest full block M containing it, and then replacing M by DADV(H, M), at least one subsumed d-path is removed. This proves

Theorem 7. Finitely many applications of the DADV operation on redundant anti-links will result in a graph without redundant disjunctive anti-links, and termination of this process is independent of the choice of anti-link at each step.

Simplifications

The following simplified versions of DADV result in formulas that are syntactically smaller than those that result from the general definition.

1. If $\text{CE}(A_X) = A_X$ (and $\text{CE}(A_X) \neq X$), then $\text{DC}(\text{CE}(A_X), X) = \text{DC}(A_X, X)$. Therefore by (possibly non atomic) factoring on $\text{DC}(A_X, X)$ and observing that $(\text{DC}(A_Y, Y) \wedge \text{DPE}(A_Y, Y)) = Y$, DADV($\{A_X, A_Y\}, M$) becomes

$$\begin{array}{c} \text{DC}(A_X, X) \vee Y \\ \wedge \\ \text{DPE}(A_X, X) \vee \text{CC}(A_Y, Y) \end{array}$$

2. If $\text{CE}(A_X) = X$, then $\text{DC}(\text{CE}(A_X), X) = \emptyset$ (*true*). Hence $\text{DPE}(A_X, X) = A_X$ and $\text{DC}(A_X, X) = X - \{A_X\}$. DADV($\{A_X, A_Y\}, M$) becomes

$$\begin{array}{c} X - \{A_X\} \vee \text{DC}(A_Y, Y) \\ \wedge \\ A_X \vee \text{CC}(A_Y, Y) \end{array}$$

3. If both Case 1 and Case 2 apply, then $\text{CE}(A_X) = X = A_X$, and the above formula simplifies to $A_X \vee \text{CC}(A_Y, Y)$.

Note that in all the above versions of DADV, the roles of X and Y can be interchanged.

Conjunctive Anti-Links

There are conjunctive anti-links that always indicate the presence of d-paths that are subsumed by others, and they are easy to detect. However, the conditions to be met are much more restrictive than those for redundant disjunctive anti-links. Consider a conjunctive anti-link $\{A_X, A_Y\}$, where the smallest full block M containing the anti-link is $(A_X \wedge Y)$. Every d-path in Y which passes through A_Y will be subsumed by the d-path consisting of the single literal A_X. Hence we can replace Y by $\text{DC}(A_Y, Y)$.

Complexity Considerations

The problem of eliminating all subsumed paths in a graph in an efficient manner does not seem feasible. Let G be a semantic graph, and let p be any path in G. The graph G' is called a *d-minimal equivalent* of G if it satisfies the following conditions.

1. G is logically equivalent to G'.

2. If p' and q' are two distinct d-paths in G', then p' does not subsume q' and vice versa.

3. If p' is a d-path in G', then there is a d-path p in G such that, $l(p) = l(p')$.

4. If p is a minimal d-path in G, then there is a d-path p' in G' such that $l(p') = l(p)$.

Note that Property 1 is implied by Properties 3 and 4, and that G' need not be unique. However, the d-paths of G' will always include all essential (and possibly some inessential) prime implicates of G. The *c-minimal equivalent* of a graph is defined in the obvious dual way.

Computing d-minimal equivalent graphs efficiently would be helpful for finding prime implicates. In a d-minimal equivalent graph of a full dissolvent, subsumption checks can be completely eliminated by Property 2 above. Hence to find the prime implicates of G, we can find a d-minimal equivalent G' of the full dissolvent FD(G), and then simply enumerate the d-paths of G'.

A d-minimal equivalent of a given graph G can be trivially obtained by first enumerating all the d-paths of the given graph G and then eliminating all the subsumed d-paths. The above algorithm is exponential in the size of G, because G' is being constructed in CNF. However an NNF d-minimal equivalent G' of G may be small compared to a CNF d-minimal equivalent. Even so, the problem is NP-hard (proof follows) and hence is not likely to have an efficient algorithm.

Theorem 8. The following problem (*Elimination of subsumed paths*) is NP-hard. Given a graph G, find a d-minimal equivalent graph G'.

We have seen that the general problem of computing d-minimal graphs is NP-hard. Nevertheless, redundant disjunctive anti-links are easily recognized, and eliminating their corresponding subsumed d-paths can be done without direct subsumption checks. On the other hand, recognizable subsumed d-paths due to conjunctive anti-links are not likely to be as plentiful due to the strong restriction defining such useful anti-links. It is also difficult to find out if an arbitrary conjunctive anti-link results in subsumed d-paths. In fact, this problem is NP-complete.

Theorem 9. The following problem is NP-complete.

INSTANCE: Given a conjunctive anti-link $\{A_X, A_Y\}$ in graph G.

QUESTION: Are there two d-paths p_X and p_Y in G, such that p_X passes through A_X and p_Y passes through A_Y and either p_X subsumes p_Y or vice versa.

Benchmark Examples

Ngair [10] has investigated examples that prove difficult for many proposed prime implicate/implicant algorithms. In this section, we show that PI + anti-links is effective for some of these examples. For other examples from [10], applying anti-link techniques appears not to produce as significant an improvement. We also develop another technique based on *strictly pure* full blocks, and which results in a dramatic improvement for these latter examples.

Examples Using Anti-Links

In [10] Ngair proposes a class of formulas for which reliance on an intermediate CNF form can result in an exponential increase in size and hence would be intractable for CNF-based algorithms. Dissolution + PI also does poorly for these examples: Although the full dissolvent can be computed quickly, a large number of subsumption checks must be performed by PI. It turns out, however, that the subsumed implicates correspond to useful and easily recognizable anti-links of both the disjunctive and conjunctive kind. We show that if these anti-links links are removed after dissolution is performed, dissolution + PI can find all the implicates in polynomial time.

We represent this class of formulas as $\{\mathcal{F}_i\}$, $i \geq 1$. Shown below is the formula $\mathcal{F}_N$:

$$((\overline{A}_3 \wedge \cdots \wedge \overline{A}_{2N-1}) \vee A_1) \wedge ((\overline{A}_4 \wedge \cdots \wedge \overline{A}_{2N}) \vee A_2)$$

$$\wedge ((A_1 \wedge A_2) \vee \cdots \vee (A_{2n-1} \wedge A_{2n}))$$

Observe that $\mathcal{F}_N$ has $3 \cdot N$ literals, and $2 \cdot N$ c-links; dissolution can remove these links by performing $2 \cdot N$ dissolution steps we get a full dissolvent.

Using $N+3$ factoring operations [9] (a special case of anti-link operation) and 3 anti-link operations the full dissolvent reduces to $(A_1 \wedge A_2)$; the prime implicates are just $\{A_1\}$ and $\{A_2\}$. Hence dissolution + removal of anti-links + PI can handle the above class of problems in polynomial time. Perhaps the most important point is that no subsumption checks whatsoever are required.

Strictly Pure Full Blocks

Recall that a full block is essentially an explicit subgraph; it is a subset of the arguments of a conjunction or disjunction, and, via commutations and reassociations, can in fact be made explicit. We say a full block M in graph G is *pure* if there are no c-links or d-links that consist of exactly one node from M. (This is just the obvious generalization of pure literal used in the literature on CNF-based automated deduction.) If, in addition, there are no conjunctive or disjunctive anti-links that consist of exactly one node from M, we say that M is *strictly pure*. (Simply put, M shares no variables with the rest of G.)

When factored, some of the examples from [10] contain surprisingly many strictly pure full blocks. Note that both factoring and recognizing strictly full blocks are polynomial operations. Intuitively, such full blocks can be replaced by single new variables, and the implicates of the resulting graph bear a strong relationship to those of the original.

Theorem 10. Let M be a satisfiable strictly pure full block in satisfiable semantic graph G, and let X be a new variable not occurring in G. We denote by G_X the graph obtained by the substitution of X for M in G. Let $D = D_{G-M} \vee D_M$ be a non-tautological disjunction of literals from G, where D_{G-M} consists of literals not in M, and D_M consists of literals that are. We define the disjunction D_X to be $D_{G-M} \vee \{D_M / X\} = D_{G-M} \vee X$ (the result of replacing in D every literal of D_M by the new variable X and collapsing the multiple occurrences of X). Then
1) If D does not contain literals from M, then D is a prime implicate of G $\Leftrightarrow D$ is a prime implicate of G_X
2) If D contains literals from M then D is a prime implicate of G $\Leftrightarrow D_X$ is a prime implicate of G_X and D_M is a prime implicate of G_M.

More examples

In [10] Kean provides the class of examples referred to as K_{mn}. They have $m(n+1)$ input CNF clauses and $(m+1)^n + mn$ prime implicates. This set of clauses can be factored to get a more compact representation in NNF as shown below.

$$(A_1 \vee (\overline{S}_{11} \wedge \cdots \wedge \overline{S}_{1m})) \wedge \cdots \wedge$$

$$(A_n \vee (\overline{S}_{n1} \wedge \cdots \wedge \overline{S}_{nm})) \wedge (\overline{A}_1 \vee \cdots \vee \overline{A}_n)$$

Since the number of prime implicates is exponential, so is the number of subsumption checks required. The number of subsumption checks for the IPIA [1] and GEN-PI [10] are shown in Table 1. Since they also have no anti-links, For each i the literals $\{\overline{S}_{i1} \cdots \overline{S}_{im}\}$ form a full block M_i, and all literals in it are strictly pure. Let K'_{mn} be the graph obtained by replacing each full block M_i by a new variable X_i. By the corollary of Theorem 10, we can get the prime implicates of K_{mn} from the prime implicates of K'_{mn}. Since each of the subgraphs M_i has no c-links, the prime implicates of M_i are present as d-paths by Theorem 3. By the contrapositive of Theorem 4, neither are sub-

Examples	IPIA[2]	GEN–PI[3]	PI+ANTI-LINK
$K_{3\,3}$	5166	972	164
$K_{4\,4}$	506472	11600	887
$K_{5\,4}$	1730120	29074	887

Table 1.

sumption checks required to find these prime implicates. Thus the number of subsumption checks to be done is exactly that required for computing the prime implicates of K'_{mn}, and this is significantly less than that needed for K_{mn}. Note that the number of prime implicates of K'_{mn} is only 2^n+n. For the problems in Table 1, we applied the above technique in combination with anti-link operations. For K'_{mn}, the full dissolvent depends only on n and can be defined recursively. (We omit the graph due to space limitations.)

The number of subsumption checks required in this case is also shown in Table 1. There is clearly a significant reduction in the number of subsumption checks required by our techniques. Note that for the problem $K_{m\,n}$ the number of subsumption checks depends only on n and not on m.

Our techniques are not limited to NNF formulas. They can sometimes be used by other algorithms like IPIA and GEN-PI which are not based on NNF formulas. For example K'_{mn} turns out to be in CNF and hence both IPIA and GEN-PI can handle these formulas, thereby reducing the number of subsumption checks needed. However normal forms like CNF provide very little scope for applying these techniques directly. For example the literals $\{\overline{S}_{i\,1} \cdots \overline{S}_{i\,m}\}$ in the unfactored form of $K_{m\,n}$ do not form a full block. Hence one cannot apply Theorem 10. They do form a full block after factoring. This provides stronger evidence that by avoiding less general normal forms like CNF/DNF, one can improve the performance of prime implicate algorithms.

Conclusions and Future Work

Anti-links admit useful equivalence-preserving operations that remove subsumed paths without any direct checks for subsumption. This is significant for prime implicate computations, since such computations tend to be dominated by subsumption checks.

Although prime implicate/implicant problems are intractable in general, our techniques perform exponentially better than others on certain examples. In addition, we are able to improve performance greatly on the inherently exponential examples of [10].

Some experimental results on a dissolution- and PI-based prime implicate system are reported in [12]. The system will be extended to include anti-link operations, so as to test their effectiveness in practice.

---

[2] Data obtained from [10]. [3] Inferred from [1].

References

1. de Kleer, J. An improved incremental algorithm for computing prime implicants. *Proceedings of AAAI-92, 780-785.*

2. Jackson, P., and Pais, J. Computing prime implicants. *Proceedings of the CADE-10*, Kaiserslautern, Germany, July, 1990. In *LNAI*, Springer-Verlag, Vol. 449, 543-557.

3. Jackson, P. Computing prime implicants incrementally. *Proceedings of CADE-11*, Saratoga Springs, NY, June, 1992. In *LNAI*, Springer-Verlag, Vol. 607, 253-267.

4. Kean, A., and Tsiknis, G. An incremental method for generating prime implicants/implicates. *Journal of Symbolic Computation* 9 (1990), 185-206.

5. Kean, A., and Tsiknis, G. Assumption based reasoning and clause management systems. *Computational Intelligence* 8,1 (Nov. 1992),1-24.

6. Letz, R. First-order calculi and proof procedures for automated deduction. Ph.D. thesis, TH Darmstadt, June 1993.

7. Murray, N.V., and Rosenthal, E. Inference with path resolution and semantic graphs. *J.ACM 34,2* (April 1987), 225-254.

8. Murray, N.V., and Rosenthal, E. Path dissolution: A strongly complete rule of inference. *Proceedings of AAAI-87*, Seattle, WA, July, 1987, 161-166.

9. Murray, N.V., and Rosenthal, E. Dissolution: Making paths vanish. *J.ACM* 40,3 (July 1993), 504-535.

10. Ngair,T. A new algorithm for incremental prime implicate generation. *Proceedings of IJCAI-93*, Chambery, France, August, 1993.

11. Przymusinski, T.C. An algorithm to compute circumscription. Artificial Intelligence 38 (1989), 49-73.

12. Ramesh, A., and Murray, N.V. Non-clausal deductive techniques for computing prime implicants and prime implicates. *Proceedings* of LPAR-93, St. Petersburg, Russia,July, 1993. In *LNAI*, Springer-Verlag, Vol. 698, 277-288.

13. Reiter, R. and de Kleer, J. Foundations of assumption-based truth maintenance systems: preliminary report. *Proceedings of AAAI-87*, Seattle, WA, July, 1987, 183-188.

14. Slagle, J.R., Chang, C.L., and Lee, R.C.T. A new algorithm for generating prime implicants. *IEEE Transactions on Computers,* C-19(4) (1970), 304-310.

15. Strzemecki, T. Polynomial-time algorithms for generation of prime implicants. *Journal of Complexity* 8 (1992), 37-63.

On Kernel Rules and Prime Implicants

Ron Rymon*
Intelligent Systems Program
University of Pittsburgh
Pittsburgh, PA 15260
rymon@isp.pitt.edu

Abstract

We draw a simple correspondence between *kernel rules* and *prime implicants*. Kernel (minimal) rules play an important role in many induction techniques. Prime implicants were previously used to formally model many other problem domains, including Boolean circuit minimization and such classical AI problems as diagnosis, truth maintenance and circumscription.

This correspondence allows computing kernel rules using any of a number of prime implicant generation algorithms. It also leads us to an algorithm in which learning is boosted by an auxiliary domain theory, e.g., a set of rules provided by an expert, or a functional description of a device or system; we discuss this algorithm in the context of SE-tree-based generation of prime implicants.

Introduction

Rules have always played an important role in Artificial Intelligence (AI). In machine learning, while a variety of other representations have also been used, a great deal of research has focused on rule induction. Moreover, many of the other representations (e.g., decision trees) are directly interchangeable with a set of rules.

Prime implicants (PIs) are minimal conjunctions of Boolean literals. Always computed with respect to a given logical theory, a prime implicant has the property that it can be used alone to prove this theory. In the early days of computers, PIs were used in Boolean function minimization procedures, e.g., (Quine 52; Karnaugh 53; McCluskey 56; Tison 67; Slagle, Chang & Lee 70; Hong, Cain & Ostapko 74). In AI, PIs were used to formally model TMSs and ATMSs (Reiter 87; de Kleer 90), circumscription (Ginsberg 89; Raiman & de Kleer 92), and Model-Based Diagnosis (de Kleer, Mackworth & Reiter 90). A number of new, and improved PI generation algorithms have emerged, e.g., (Greiner, Smith & Wilkerson 89;

Jackson & Pais 90; Kean & Tsiknis 90; de Kleer 92; Ngair 92; Rymon 94).

In machine learning, it is commonly argued that simpler models are preferable because they are likely to have more predictive power when applied to new instances (a principle often referred to as *Occam's razor*). One way in which a model can be simpler is if all of its rules are simple, i.e., have fewer conditions in the antecedent. As it turns, *kernel* (minimal) rules and prime implicants are closely related. We will show a direct mapping between the two which allows *computing* kernel rules using PI generation algorithms. This will lead us to an algorithm which combines knowledge induced from examples with knowledge acquired from an expert, or which is otherwise available. This is done by combining the PIs of multiple theories. Given that prime implicants have been actively researched for a few decades now, we believe that this correspondence has the potential to benefit the machine learning community in other ways.

Kernel Rules are Prime Implicants

Consider a typical machine learning scenario: we are presented with a *training set* (TSET) of *class*-labeled examples. Each example is described by values assigned to a set of *attributes* (also called features or variables), and is labeled with its correct class. We assume all attributes and the class are Boolean. By *partial description* we refer to an instantiation of a subset of attributes; an *object* is a partial description in which all attributes are instantiated. By *universe* we refer to the collection of all possible objects.

It is common to assume that class labels were assigned based on a set of, unknown as yet, principles; for the purpose of this paper, we assume no noise. It is the role of the induction program to unearth these principles, or at least some approximation thereof. Numerous techniques were devised throughout the years for this purpose, ranging from various forms of regressions, to neural and Bayesian networks, to decision trees, graphs, rules and more. Rules are one form of representation which has also been heavily used in other branches of AI. One advantage of proving prop-

*Parts of this work were supported by NLM grant R01-LM-05217; an ARO graduate fellowship when the author was at the University of Pennsylvania; a NASA consulting contract; and self-funding.

erties for a rule-based representation is that rules are easily mapped into many of the other representations. In decision trees, for example, a rule corresponds to attribute-value assignments labeling a path from the root to a leaf.

Definition 1 *Kernel Rules*

A *rule* is a partial description such that all objects in TSET that agree with its instantiated variables are all labeled with the same class and such that there exists at least one such object. A *kernel rule* is a rule such that none of its subsets is a rule.

A rule is thus a *set* of instantiated variables, and a kernel rule is one which is set-wise minimal. (To save notation, we will sometimes refer to this set *with the* class variable; the distinction should be clear from the context.) Another way to view a rule is as a conjunctive set of conditions. We call it a rule because if the training data were representative of the universe, we could use it to predict the class of new instances. The more conditions are included in its conjunction, the more specific the rule is; a kernel rule is thus a most general rule.

Kernel rules are the essence of our SE-tree-based induction framework (Rymon 93). Each kernel rule corresponds to the attribute-value assignments labeling one path from the root to a leaf. We have shown that SE-trees generalize, and often outperform, decision trees as classifiers.

Example 2 Consider the following training examples consisting of various test results ($a, b, c,$ and d) of patients suspected of suffering from a disease (x):

Patient	a	b	c	d	Disease (x)
1	true	true	true	true	true
2	false	false	false	false	false
3	true	false	false	false	true

The five kernel rules inferable from these examples and their SE-tree representation are depicted next:

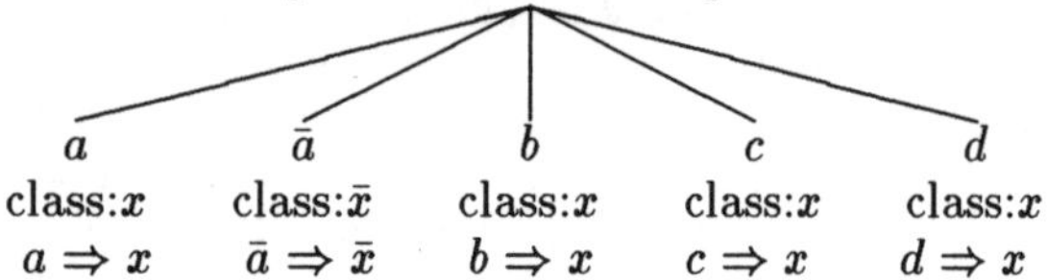

Definition 3 *Prime Implicants (Implicates)*

Let V be a set of Boolean variables. A *literal* is either a variable v, or its negation $\neg v$. Let Σ be a propositional theory. A conjunction of literals π is an *implicant* of Σ if $\pi \models \Sigma$ (where $\models$ is the entailment operator). A disjunction of literals τ is an *implicate* of Σ if $\Sigma \models \tau$. Such a conjunction (disjunction) can also be thought of as a set of literals. It is a *prime implicant (implicate)* if none of its subsets is an implicant (implicate). An implicant (implicate) is *trivial* if it contains a complementary pair of literals.

Prime implicates and prime implicants are duals. In particular, any algorithm which computes prime implicates from a DNF formula can also compute prime

implicants from the corresponding CNF formula, and vice versa. Many PI generation algorithms assume the theory is given in one form or the other.

Definition 4 *Training Set Theory*

Let e be an object, and let a_i denote the attribute instantiations in e. Let x be an instantiation of the class variable. We define

$$\sigma(e, x) \overset{\text{def}}{=} a_1 \wedge a_2 \wedge \cdots \wedge a_n \to x = \bar{a}_1 \vee \bar{a}_2 \vee \cdots \vee \bar{a}_n \vee x$$

Let TSET be a set of objects $\{e_j\}_{j=1}^m$, each labeled with a class x_j. The theory given by TSET is defined:

$$\Sigma(\text{TSET}) \overset{\text{def}}{=} \wedge_{j=1}^m \sigma(e_j, x_j)$$

The purpose of this transformation is to represent logically the information contributed by a each example alone and by the collection as a whole. For the first patient in Example 2 we have:

$$a \wedge b \wedge c \wedge d \to x = \bar{a} \vee \bar{b} \vee \bar{c} \vee \bar{d} \vee x$$

As a conjunction, the training set theory can be used to constrain the classifiers considered to those who produce the same class labels for the given examples.

Theorem 5 *Kernel Rules are Prime Implicants*

Let TSET be a training set, x the class variable. Let TSET^+ be the set of positive examples, and TSET^- the set of negative examples. Let Σ^+ denote $\Sigma(\text{TSET}^+)$ and similarly let Σ^- denote $\Sigma(\text{TSET}^-)$. Let KR^+ be the set of positive kernel rules, i.e., with x in their consequent, and KR^- the set of negative kernel rules, i.e., with $\bar{x}$ in their consequent. Let PI(T) denote the collection of non-trivial PIs for a theory T. Then

$$\text{KR}^- = \text{PI}(\Sigma^+) - \{x\} \text{ modulo subsumption}^1 \text{ with PI}(\Sigma^-);$$
$$\text{KR}^+ = \text{PI}(\Sigma^-) - \{\bar{x}\} \text{ modulo subsumption with PI}(\Sigma^+).$$

Proof: Let r be a partial description. First, it is clear that x (respectively $\bar{x}$) is a PI for Σ^+ (respectively Σ^-)[2]. We will prove that (1) if $r \in \text{PI}(\Sigma^+)$ and $r \neq x$ then either $r \in \text{KR}^-$ or r is subsumed by some $r' \in \text{PI}(\Sigma^-)$, and (2) vice versa, i.e., if $r \in \text{KR}^-$ then $r \in \text{PI}(\Sigma^+)$. The proof for the other part of the theorem is analogous.

(1) Suppose $r \in \text{PI}(\Sigma^+)$ and that r is not subsumed by any PI of Σ^-. As a PI, $r \models \Sigma^+$ and thus contradicts at least one variable assignment in every positive example, and so covers none of these. We still have to show that there is a negative example that is covered by r and that r is minimal.

---

[1] One rule subsumes another if it is a subset of the other. This operation removes from one set all rules subsumed by any rule from the other set. Note that if a PI appears in both sets, it is removed from both.

[2] Also note that x does not appear in any other PI for TSET^+. In fact, to make things computationally easier, x and $\bar{x}$ can be omitted from the respective theories; they were only included for pedagogical reasons to emphasize the correspondence between clauses and examples.

Suppose that none of the negative examples is covered by r. Since every example assigns a value to each variable, it must be the case that r contradicts every negative example by at least one variable-assignment. Thus, r is an implicant of Σ^- and therefore there is a prime implicant in $\mathrm{PI}(\Sigma^-)$ which subsumes r. In contradiction to the assumption.

As a prime implicant, r must be minimal and therefore it is a kernel rule.

(2) Suppose $r \in \mathrm{KR}^-$. Then r does not cover any of the positive examples, and therefore it must contradict at least one variable assignment in each and every positive example. Thus, by definition, r is an implicant of Σ^+. As a kernel rule, r is minimal and therefore it is a prime implicant. $\boxed{\mathrm{Q.E.D}}$

Consider again Example 2:

$\Sigma^+ \overset{\mathrm{def}}{=} (\bar{a} \vee \bar{b} \vee \bar{c} \vee \bar{d} \vee x) \wedge (\bar{a} \vee b \vee c \vee d \vee x)$, and so $\mathrm{PI}(\Sigma^+) = \{x, \bar{a}, b\bar{c}, b\bar{d}, \bar{b}c, \bar{b}d, cd, \bar{c}d\}$. Computed similarly $\mathrm{PI}(\Sigma^-) = \{\bar{x}, a, b, c, d\}$. Six of the former PIs are subsumed by some of the latter, leaving as a negative kernel rule only $\bar{a}$. All the PIs for Σ^-, except for $\bar{x}$ which is removed, are positive kernel rules.

The first immediate application of Theorem 5 is that kernel rules can be *computed* using any of a number of PI generation algorithms. We briefly explore this possibility next. This theorem also leads to an opportunity to combine kernel rules with other available knowledge. As PIs, kernel rules can be combined with PIs of another theory, e.g., an auxiliary domain theory, to obtain a more refined classifier. We discuss this possibility in the subsequent sections of this paper. Besides these two immediate applications, we believe this correspondence may lead to new insights drawn from one area of research to the other.

Computing Rules as Prime Implicants

Assuming the availability of a PI generation algorithm, Theorem 5 suggests a very simple way to compute kernel rules: transform the training set into positive and negative theories; then compute the PIs for each of the theories; then, after removing the trivial x and $\bar{x}$, take the union of the two sets while removing subsumed conjuncts. The consequent of each rule is determined by the set from which it came: x in rules originating from $\mathrm{PI}(\Sigma^-)$ and $\bar{x}$ in those from $\mathrm{PI}(\Sigma^+)$.

As previously mentioned, research over the years has produced an abundance of PI generation algorithms. Since there may sometimes be an exponential number of PIs, there are also many algorithms which compute *subsets* of these, or which compute them according to some prioritization scheme. In machine learning, (Hong 93) used a logic minimization algorithm (Hong, Cain & Ostapko 74) to induce a minimally covering set of minimal rules. Each iteration in the STAR algorithm (Michalski 83) essentially computes the PIs of all negative examples and one positive example. A version space's most general rules (Mitchell 82) correspond to the positive kernel rules, or the PIs of the negative theory. (Ngair 92) shows that both a version space and PIs are modelable as general order-theoretic structures and are thus computable using simple lattice operations. The SE-tree-based learning framework (Rymon 93) and PI generation algorithm (Rymon 94) both support partial exploration of rules, e.g., minimal covers or maximizers of some user-specified priority.

Most of the PI generation algorithms assume that the input theory is given in either CNF or DNF. For the purpose of computing the PIs of a training set theory, a PI generation algorithm should be able to receive its input in CNF. However, as will soon be discussed, one may wish to combine these with the PIs of another theory which may be given in a different form; hence the flexibility offered by the variety of algorithms. Furthermore, certain algorithms may outperform or underperform others, depending on certain features of the underlying theory and of its PIs.

The flexibility offered by the fact that positive and negative kernel rules can be computed *separately* and then combined using a simple union-with-subsumption operator may be of practical importance when dealing with large problems. The disadvantage of this is that many PIs may later be subsumed; a similar consideration applies when combining PIs of the training set theory with those of an auxiliary theory. Some of this duplicity can be avoided in an SE-tree-based framework, as will be discussed later.

Boosting Learning with an Auxiliary Domain Theory

One major problem in *applying* machine learning is that examples are often scarce. Even where examples are seemingly abundant, their number is often minuscule relative to the syntactic size of the domain. Learning programs thus face a hard *bias selection* problem, having to decide between a large number of distinct classifiers that equally fit the training set. We propose that the PI-based approach lends itself to use of auxiliary domain knowledge, in the form of a logical theory, to leverage learning by restricting the set of hypotheses considered. Computationally, at least if an SE-tree-based algorithm is used, significant parts of the search space may be discarded without even being searched.

Consider Example 2 again. Since the universe size is 16 (2^4), and since only three examples were given, there are $2^{16-3} = 2^{12}$ different classifiers *consistent* with the training examples. Prime implicants belong to a somewhat stricter class, namely conjunctions which *entail* the training set theory. While each of the kernel rules is consistent with the examples, they may contradict on other objects. Indeed, in the SE-tree-based classification framework, the number of classifiers potentially embodied in a collection of kernel rules depends on the number of objects on which two or more rules contradict. In Example 2, there are 7 such objects (Figure 1a) and thus 2^7 classifiers.

Now suppose that in addition to the training examples, we are also given an auxiliary domain theory (ADT) which we will assume holds in the domain and thus consistent with the examples. It is reasonable to demand that labels assigned by a candidate classifier be consistent with this theory. Furthermore, we will insist that the classifier *entails* ADT. To achieve this, we will compute rules as PIs of the conjunction of the respective training set theory and ADT.

Theorem 6 *Rules for Examples + ADT*

Let TSET be a training set, x a class variable, and Σ^+ and Σ^- as before. Let ADT be an auxiliary domain theory such that $\text{ADT} \stackrel{\text{def}}{=} \text{ADT}^0 \cup \text{ADT}^- \cup \text{ADT}^+$ where ADT^0 does not mention x nor $\bar{x}$; ADT^- is in CNF and does not mention x; and ADT^+ is in CNF and does not mention $\bar{x}$. Let $\text{PI}^+ \stackrel{\text{def}}{=} \text{PI}(\Sigma^+ \cup \text{ADT}^0 \cup \text{ADT}^+)$ and $\text{PI}^- \stackrel{\text{def}}{=} \text{PI}(\Sigma^- \cup \text{ADT}^0 \cup \text{ADT}^-)$. If r is a partial description then

(1) if $r \in$(PI$^-$ modulo subsumption with PI$^+$) then r does not cover any negative example and does cover at least one positive example; r is minimal as such.

(2) if $r \in$(PI$^+$ modulo subsumption with PI$^-$) then r does not cover any positive example and does cover at least one negative example; r is minimal as such.

Proof: We will only prove (1); the proof for (2) is analogous. If $r \in$PI$^-$ then r contradicts at least one assignment in each of the negative examples; thus it does not cover any negative example. If r did not cover any positive example, then $r \models \Sigma^+$ and therefore there exists $r' \in$PI$^+$ such that $r' \subseteq r$, in contradiction to the assumption. $\boxed{\text{Q.E.D}}$

Note that the decomposition of ADT was not used in the proof. The theorem still holds if ADT is taken as a whole and PIs for $\Sigma^+ \cup \text{ADT}$, modulo subsumption, are taken as negative rules and vice versa for positive rules. The problem is that important rules may be lost that way. In particular, consider a situation in which Σ^- was included as part of ADT. Then, PI($\Sigma^+ \cup \text{ADT}$) is subsumed by PI($\Sigma^- \cup \text{ADT}$) and we lose all negative rules.

The new ADT-boosted induction algorithm will thus partition ADT as above, and then use the respective components to compute positive and negative rules. Compared to its predecessor, the new algorithm will typically result in rules with a more restricted scope. Note that some new PIs may appear which are independent of the class labeling decision, e.g., a domain rule such as "males can never be pregnant". However, these will appear in both the positive and negative PIs and will thus be removed by subsumption.

Thanks to the diversity of PI generation algorithms, ADT^0 can be given in a variety of syntactic forms; if it is in DNF, its PIs can be computed separately using an algorithm which accepts DNF input. The PIs of the combined theories can then be computed as the PIs of the combination of the PIs of each of the respective theories, by invoking same program again. If ADT^0 is also in a CNF then the PIs of the combined theories can be computed in a single shot. Most notably, a set of rules such as the ones typically gathered from domain experts can easily be transformed into a CNF.

Consider Example 2 once again. Suppose that in our domain it is impossible for test (attribute) b to be positive if test a is negative, i.e., $\bar{a} \to \bar{b}$. We first transform this statement to a domain theory in CNF: $\text{ADT} \stackrel{\text{def}}{=} \text{ADT}^0 \stackrel{\text{def}}{=} (a \vee \bar{b})$. Then, we compute PIs for $\Sigma^+ \cup \text{ADT}$, and similarly for $\Sigma^- \cup \text{ADT}$. After removing subsumed PIs, only two rules are left: $a \Rightarrow x$, and $\bar{a}\bar{b} \Rightarrow \bar{x}$. Figure 1b depicts a class-labeled universe according to these two rules. Notably, there are no contradictions left (although this does not hold in general). Also note that part of the syntactic universe that was covered by the previous set of rules is not covered by the new rules; according to the ADT, these object are not part of the *real* universe as it is impossible for a to be negative without b being negative as well.

ab	$a\bar{b}$	$\bar{a}b$	$\bar{a}\bar{b}$	
x	x	x $\bar{x}$	x $\bar{x}$	cd
x	x	x $\bar{x}$	x $\bar{x}$	$c\bar{d}$
x	x	x $\bar{x}$	x $\bar{x}$	$\bar{c}d$
x	x	x $\bar{x}$	$\bar{x}$	$\bar{c}\bar{d}$

(a) TSET only

ab	$a\bar{b}$	$\bar{a}b$	$\bar{a}\bar{b}$	
x	x		$\bar{x}$	cd
x	x		$\bar{x}$	$c\bar{d}$
x	x		$\bar{x}$	$\bar{c}d$
x	x		$\bar{x}$	$\bar{c}\bar{d}$

(b) with ADT

Figure 1: Class Labelings with and without ADT

Kernel rules can be computed in various orders:

1. Compute PIs separately for each of $\Sigma^+ \cup \text{ADT}^+$, $\Sigma^- \cup \text{ADT}^-$, and ADT^0; then merge while subsuming supersets. In this case, PI(ADT^0) is only computed once. Using the SE-tree data structure, merging is linear in the size of the trees. This may be wasteful, however, if many PIs for one theory are subsumed by another.

2. Compute PIs for the two *combined* theories directly. This may save time and space if many PIs of ADT^0 are later subsumed. However, in essence, many of the PIs of ADT^0 are computed twice.

3. If the SE-tree method is used, compute PI(ADT^0), and then use the resulting SE-tree as the basis for search for the PIs of the combined theories. In expanding this tree, nodes previously pruned shall remain pruned. However, unexplored branches may have to be "re-opened". Some of the PIs of ADT^0 may have to be further expanded.

An SE-tree-based Implementation

Set-Enumeration (SE) trees were proposed in (Rymon 92) as a simple way to systematically search a space of sets. It was suggested they can serve as a uniform model for many problems in which solutions are modeled as unordered sets.

Given a set of attributes, a *complete* SE-tree is a tree representation of all sets of attribute-value pairs. It uses an indexing on the set of attributes to do so systematically, i.e., to *uniquely* represent *all* such sets. The SE-tree's root is always labeled with the empty set. Then, a node's descendants are each labeled with an expansion of the parent's set with a single attribute-value assignment. The key to systematicity is that a node is only expanded with attributes ranked higher in the appropriate indexing scheme than attributes appearing in its own label. For example, assuming alphabetic indexing, a node labeled $a\bar{b}d$ will not be expanded with c nor with $\bar{c}$, but only with e, f, etc. Allowed attributes are referred to as that node's *View*. Of course, the complete SE-tree is too large to be completely explored and so an algorithm's search will typically be restricted to its most relevant parts. A simple PI generation algorithm is outlined in (Rymon 92) as an example application of SE-trees.

In (Rymon 93), we presented an SE-tree-based *induction framework* and have argued that it generalizes decision trees in several ways. Like decision trees, an SE-tree is induced via recursive partitioning of the training data. Also like decision trees, classification requires traversing matching paths in the tree. However, an SE-tree embodies many decision trees and thus allows for explicit mediation of conflicts. While here we assume a fixed indexing, attributes in a node's *View* can be dynamically re-ordered, e.g. by information-gain, without infringing on completeness.

An improved version of the SE-tree-based PI generation algorithm is detailed in (Rymon 94). This algorithm accepts input in CNF and works by computing minimal *hitting sets* for the collection of clauses. It is briefly presented next:

First, given a collection of sets, a hitting set is a set which "hits" (shares at least one element with) each set in the collection. Non-trivial PIs correspond to minimal hitting sets (excluding those which include both a variable and its negation.).

The algorithm works by exploring an imaginary SE-tree in a best-first fashion, where PIs are explored in an order conforming to some user-specified prioritization; thus, if time constraints are imposed, the most important PIs will be discovered. Exploration starts with the empty set. Then, iteratively, an open nodes with the highest priority is expanded with *all* possible one-attribute expansions which (a) are in that node's *View*, and (b) hit a set not previously hit by that node. Expanded nodes which hit all sets are marked as hitting sets and the rest remain open for further expansion.

The algorithm uses two pruning rules. First, nodes subsumed by previously discovered hitting sets can be pruned; they cannot lead to *minimal* hitting sets. Second, a node is pruned if any of the sets it does not hit is completely outside its *View*; given the SE-tree structure, such a node cannot lead to a hitting set.

(Rymon 94) also suggests a recursive problem de-composition heuristic in which the collection of sets not hit by a node is partitioned into variable-disjoint sub-collections. If such partitioning exists, the minimal hitting sets for the union are given by the product of the minimal hitting sets for the sub-collections. These are computed via recursive application of the algorithm to each of the sub-collections.

Consider Example 2 again: Σ^+ consists of the sets $\{\bar{a}, \bar{b}, \bar{c}, \bar{d}, x\}$, $\{\bar{a}, b, c, d, x\}$. Figures 2a,b depicts the SE-trees explored for computing PI(Σ^+) and PI(Σ^-), ignoring PIs with x or $\bar{x}$. Note that, in the former, a branch labeled a was never considered because a does not appear in Σ^+ and that a branch labeled d was pruned because it cannot lead to a solution. However, except for nodes labeled with d or $\bar{d}$, other nodes cannot be pruned for having too narrow a *View*; this is because examples assign values to *all* variables. For the same reason, decomposition is also impossible.

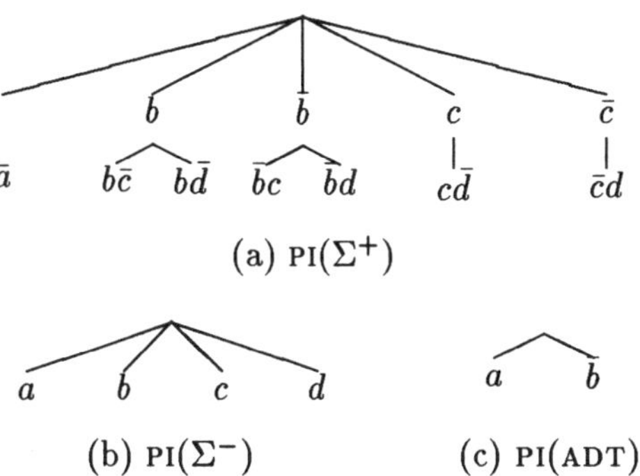

(a) PI(Σ^+)

(b) PI(Σ^-)   (c) PI(ADT)

Figure 2: Original SE-trees

Consider now the ADT $\stackrel{\text{def}}{=} (a \vee \bar{b})$, as discussed before. Figure 2c shows the SE-tree for PI(ADT). Figures 3a,b shows SE-trees for the combined theories. Note that now, branches from the root labeled with c or $\bar{c}$ can be pruned because they cannot lead to hitting sets for ADT. Also, once all sets in the training set theories are hit, one can take advantage of the decomposition heuristic. Notably, PIs for the combined theories are more complex; they have to hit more sets. This makes the resulting rules *less* conflicting. Figure 3c shows the kernel rules obtained by merging-with-subsumption the trees in 3a,b.

Summary

We have shown a simple correspondence between kernel rules and prime implicants which

a. Allows *computing* kernel rules using any of a number of prime implicants generation algorithms; and

b. Leads to a PI-based learning algorithm which can be boosted with an auxiliary domain theory, e.g., a set of rules provided by a domain expert, or a functional description of a device.

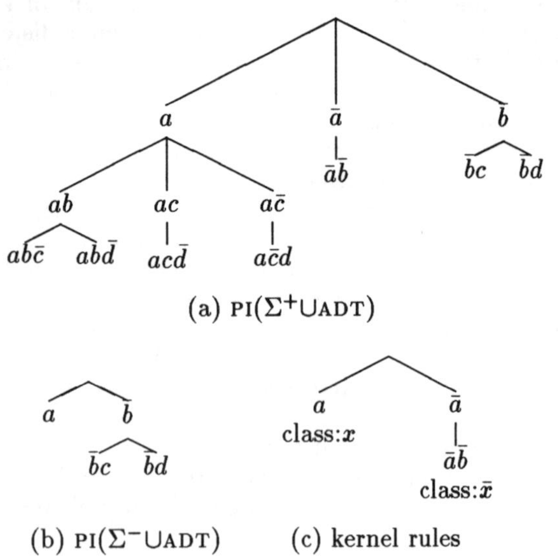

(a) PI($\Sigma^+ \cup$ADT)

(b) PI($\Sigma^- \cup$ADT)   (c) kernel rules

Figure 3: SE-trees for combined theories

We outline an SE-tree-based algorithm which allows exploring rules according to some user-defined preference criterion. We hope the domain theory enhancement will eventually contribute to the applicability of this machine learning approach to real-world domains. In addition, given the significant research involving prime implicants, we believe the correspondence presented here may lead to new insights as researchers reinterpret these results in the realm of machine learning.

Acknowledgement

Discussions with Dr. John Clarke have motivated this work. I also thank Ron Kohavi, Foster Provost, Bob Schrag and anonymous reviewers for important discussions and comments.

References

de Kleer, J., Exploiting Locality in a TMS. In Proceedings *8th National Conf. on Artificial Intelligence*, pp. 254-271, Boston MA, 1990.

de Kleer, J., Mackworth, A. K., and Reiter, R., Characterizing Diagnoses. In Proceedings *8th National Conf. on Artificial Intelligence*, pp. 324-330, Boston MA, 1990.

de Kleer, J., An Improved Incremental Algorithm for Generating Prime Implicates. In Proceedings *10th National Conf. on Artificial Intelligence*, pp. 780-785, San Jose CA, 1992.

Ginsberg, M., A Circumscriptive Theorem Prover, *Artificial Intelligence*, 39, pp. 209-230, 1989.

Greiner, R., Smith, B. A., and Wilkerson R. W., A Correction to the Algorithm in Reiter's Theory of Diagnosis. *Artificial Intelligence*, 41, pp. 79-88, 1989.

Hong, S. J., Cain, R. G., and Ostapko, D. L., MINI: A Heuristic Approach for Logic Minimization. *IBM Journal of Research and Development*, pp. 443-458, 1974.

Hong, S. J., R-MINI: A Heuristic Algorithm for Generating Minimal Rules from Examples. IBM Research Report RC 19145, 1993.

Jackson, P., and Pais, J., Computing Prime Implicants. In Proceedings *Conf. on Automated Deduction*, pp. 543-557, 1990.

Karnaugh, G., The Map Method for Synthesis of Combinational Logic Circuits. *AIEE Trans. Communications and Electronics*, vol. 72, pp. 593-599, 1953.

Kean, A., and Tsiknis, G., An Incremental Method for Generating Prime implicants/Implicates. *Journal of Symbolic Computation*, 9:185-206, 1990.

McCluskey, E., Minimization of Boolean Functions. *Bell System Technical Journal*, 35:1417-1444, 1956.

Michalski, R., A Theory and Methodology of Inductive Learning. *Artificial Intelligence*, 20, 1983, pp. 111-116

Mitchell, T. M., Generalization as Search. *Artificial Intelligence*, 18, 1982, pp. 203-226.

Ngair, T., *Convex Spaces as an Order-Theoretic Basis for Problem Solving*, Ph. D. Thesis, Computer and Information Science, Univ. of Pennsylvania, 1992.

Quine, J. O. W., The Problem of Simplifying Truth Functions. *American Math. Monthly*, 59:521-531, 1952.

Raiman, O., and de Kleer, J., A Minimality Maintenance System. In Proceedings *3rd Int'l Conf. on Principles of Knowledge Representation and Reasoning*, Cambridge MA, pp. 532-538, 1992.

Reiter, R., A Theory of Diagnosis From First Principles. *Artificial Intelligence*, 32, pp. 57-95, 1987.

Rymon, R., Search through Systematic Set Enumeration. In Proceedings *3rd Int'l Conf. on Principles of Knowledge Representation and Reasoning*, Cambridge MA, pp. 539-550, 1992.

Rymon, R., An SE-tree-based Characterization of the Induction Problem. In Proceedings *10th Int'l Conf. on Machine Learning*, pp. 268-275, Amherst MA, 1993.

Rymon, R., An SE-tree-based Prime Implicant Generation Algorithm. To appear in *Annals of Math. and A.I.*, special issue on Model-Based Diagnosis, Console & Friedrich eds., Vol. 11, 1994.

Slagle, J. R., Chang, C, and Lee R. C., A New Algorithm for Generating Prime Implicants. *IEEE Trans. on Computers*, 19(4), 1970.

Tison, P., Generalized Consensus Theory and Application to the Minimization of Boolean Functions. *IEEE Trans. on Computers*, 16(4):446-456, 1967.

Using Hundreds of Workstations
to Solve First-Order Logic Problems

Alberto Maria Segre & David B. Sturgill
Department of Computer Science
Cornell University
Ithaca, NY 14853-7501
{segre,sturgill}@cs.cornell.edu

Abstract

This paper describes a distributed, adaptive, first-order logic engine with exceptional performance characteristics. The system combines serial search reduction techniques such as bounded-overhead subgoal caching and intelligent backtracking with a novel parallelization strategy particularly well-suited to coarse-grained parallel execution on a network of workstations. We present empirical results that demonstrate our system's performance using 100 workstations on over 1400 first-order logic problems drawn from the "Thousands of Problems for Theorem Provers" collection.

Introduction

We have developed an distributed, adaptive, first-order logic engine as the core of a planning system intended to solve large logistics and transportation scheduling problems (Calistri-Yeh & Segre, 1993). This underlying inference engine, called DALI (*Distributed, Adaptive, Logical Inference*), is based on an extended version of the Warren Abstract Machine (WAM) architecture (Aït-Kaci, 1991) which also serves as the basis for many modern Prolog implementations. DALI takes a first-order specification of some application domain (the *domain theory*) and uses it to satisfy a series of queries via a model elimination inference procedure. Our approach is inspired by PTTP (Stickel, 1988), in that it is based on Prolog technology (*i.e.*, the WAM) but circumvents the inherent limitations thereof to provide an inference procedure that is complete relative to first-order logic. Unlike PTTP, however, DALI employs a number of serial search reduction techniques such as bounded-overhead subgoal caching (Segre & Scharstein, 1993) and intelligent backtracking (Kumar & Lin, 1987) to improve search efficiency. DALI also exploits a novel parallelization scheme called *nagging* (Sturgill & Segre, 1994) that supports the effective use of a large number of loosely-coupled processing elements.

The message of this paper is that efficient implementation technology, serial search reduction techniques, and parallel nagging can be successfully combined to produce a high-performance first-order logic engine. We support this claim with an extensive empirical performance evaluation.

The DALI System

The basis of our implementation is the WAM. The WAM supports efficient serial execution of Prolog: the core idea is that definite clauses may be compiled into a series of primitive instructions which are then interpreted by the underlying abstract machine. The efficiency advantage of the WAM comes from making compile-time decisions (thus reducing the amount of computation that must be repeated at run time), using carefully engineered data structures that provide an efficient scheme for unwinding variable bindings and restoring the search state upon backtracking, and taking several additional efficiency shortcuts, which, while acceptable for Prolog, are inappropriate for theorem proving in general.

In our implementation, the basic WAM architecture is extended in three ways. First, we provide completeness with respect to first-order logic. Next, we incorporate serial search reduction techniques to enhance performance. Finally, we employ a novel asynchronous parallelization scheme that effectively distributes the search across a network of loosely-coupled heterogeneous processing elements.

First-Order Completeness

As described in (Stickel, 1988), Prolog — and the underlying WAM — can be used as the basis for an efficient first-order logic engine by circumventing the following intrinsic limitations: (*i*) Prolog uses unsound unification, *i.e.*, it permits the construction of cyclic terms, (*ii*) Prolog's unbounded depth-first search strategy is incomplete, and (*iii*) Prolog is restricted to definite clauses. PTTP demonstrates how these three limitations can be overcome without sacrificing the high inference rate common to many Prolog implementations.

Like Stickel, we repair Prolog's unsound unification by performing the missing "occurs check." We also borrow a compile-time technique from (Plaisted, 1988) to "flatten" unification and perform circularity checking only when needed. In our implementation, the circularity check is handled efficiently by a new WAM instruction. We restore search completeness by using a depth-first iterative deepening search strategy (Korf, 1985) in the place of depth-first search.[1] Finally, the definite-clause restriction is lifted by adding the model elimination reduction operation to the familiar Prolog resolution step and by compiling in all contrapositive versions of each domain theory clause. As suggested in (Stickel, 1988), the use of the model elimination reduction operation enables the inclusion of cycle detection with little additional programming effort (cycle detection is a pruning technique that reduces redundant search).

Serial Search Reduction

Our second set of modifications to the WAM support a number of *adaptive inference techniques*, or serial search reduction mechanisms. In (Segre & Scharstein, 1993) we introduce the notion of a bounded-overhead subgoal cache for definite-clause theorem provers. Bounded-overhead caches contain only a fixed number of entries; as new entries are made, old entries are discarded according to some preestablished cache management policy, *e.g.*, *least-recently used*. Limiting the size of the cache helps to avoid thrashing, a typical consequence of unbounded-size caches operating within bounded physical memory. Cache entries consist of successfully-proven subgoals as well as subgoals which are known to be unprovable within a given resource limit; matching a cache entry reduces search by obviating the need to explore the same search space more than once. As a matter of policy, we do not allow cache hits to bind logical variables. In exchange for a reduction in the number of cache hits, this constraint avoids some situations where taking a cache hit may actually increase the search space. Cache entries are allowed to persist until the domain theory changes; thus, information acquired in the course of solving one query can help reduce search on subsequent queries.

In a definite-clause theory, the satisfiability of a subgoal depends only on the form of the subgoal itself. However,

when the model elimination reduction operation is used, a subgoal's satisfiability may also depend on the ancestor goals from which it was derived. Accordingly, a subgoal may fail in one situation while an identical goal may succeed (via the reduction operation) elsewhere in the search. DALI extends the definite-clause caching scheme of (Segre & Scharstein, 1993) to accommodate the context sensitivity of cached successes. The DALI implementation presented here simply disables the caching of failures in theories not composed solely of definite clauses, although this is unnecessarily extreme.

In addition to subgoal caching, we employ a form of intelligent backtracking similar to that of (Kumar & Lin, 1987). Normally, the WAM performs chronological backtracking, resuming search from the most recent OR choicepoint after a failure. Naturally, this new search path may also fail for the same underlying reason as the previous path. Intelligent backtracking attempts to identify the reasons for a failure and backtrack to the most recent choicepoint that is not doomed to repeat it. Our intelligent backtracking scheme requires minimal change to the WAM for the definite-clause case. Briefly, choicepoints along the current search path are marked at failure time depending on the variables they bind; unmarked choicepoints are skipped when backtracking. As with subgoal caching, the marking procedure must also take ancestor goals into account when deciding which choicepoints to mark.

Nagging

In (Sturgill & Segre, 1994) we introduce a parallel asynchronous search pruning strategy called *nagging*. Nagging employs two types of processes; a *master* process which attempts to satisfy the user's query through a sequential search procedure and one or more *nagging* processes which perform speculative search in an effort to prune the master's current search branch. When a nagging process becomes idle it requests a snapshot of its master's state as characterized by the variable bindings and the stack of open goals. The nagging process then attempts to prove a permuted version of this goal stack under these variable bindings using the same resource limit in effect on the master process. If the nagging process fails to find a proof, it guarantees that the master process will be unable to satisfy all goals on its goal stack under current variable bindings. The master process is then forced to backtrack far enough to retract a goal or variable binding that was rejected by the nagger. If, however, the nagging process does find a proof, then it has satisfied a permuted ordering of all the master's open goals, thereby solving the original query. This solution is then reported.

---

[1] Unlike PTTP's depth metric which is based on the number of nodes in the proof, our depth-first iterative deepening scheme measures depth as the height of the proof tree. Although each depth measure has its advantages and neither leads to uniformly superior performance, our choice is motivated by concerns for compatibility with both our intelligent backtracking and caching schemes.

Nagging has many desirable characteristics. In particular, it affords some opportunity to control the granularity of nagged subproblems and is also intrinsically fault tolerant. As a result, nagging is appropriate for loosely-coupled hardware. Additionally, nagging is not restricted to definite-clause theories and requires no extra-logical annotation of the theory to indicate opportunities for parallel execution. Finally, nagging may be cleanly combined with other parallelism schemes such as OR and AND parallelism. Readers interested in a more complete and general treatment of nagging are referred to (Sturgill & Segre, 1994).

Evaluation

We wish to show that (*i*) subgoal caching, intelligent backtracking, and nagging combine to produce superior performance, and (*ii*) our approach scales exceptionally well to a large numbers of processors. In order for our results to be meaningful, they should be obtained across a broad spectrum of problems from the theorem proving literature. To this end, we use a 1457-element subset of the 2295 problems contained in the *Thousands of Problems for Theorem Provers* (TPTP) collection, release 1.0.0 (Suttner *et al.*, 1993). The TPTP problems are expressed in first-order logic: 37% are definite-clause domain theories, 5% are propositional (half of these are definite-clause domain theories), and 79% require equality. The largest problem contains 6404 clauses, and the number of logic variables used ranges from 0 to 32000. For our test, we exclude 838 problems either because they contained more than one designated query clause, or, in one instance, due to a minor flaw in the problem specification.

Four different configurations of the DALI system are applied to this test suite; three are serial configurations, while the fourth employs nagging. Each configuration operates on identical hardware and differs only in which serial search reduction techniques are applied and in whether or not additional nagging processors are used. We use a single, dedicated, Sun Sparc 670MP "Cypress" system with 128MB of real memory as the main processor for each tested configuration. Nagging processors, when used, are drawn from a pool of 110 additional Sun Sparc machines, ranging from small Sparc 1 machines with 12MB of memory to additional 128MB 670MP processors running SunOS (versions 4.1.1 through 4.1.3). These machines are physically scattered throughout two campus buildings and are distributed among three TCP/IP subnets interconnected by gateways. Note that none of the additional machines are intrinsically faster than the main processor; indeed, the majority have much slower CPUs and far less memory than does the main processor. Furthermore, unlike the main processor, the nagging processors represent a shared resource and are used to support some number of additional users throughout the experiment.

Three serial configurations of DALI are tested. Σ_0 is a simple serial system that is essentially equivalent to a WAM-level reconstruction of PTTP modulo the previously cited difference in depth bound calculation.[2] Σ_1 adds intelligent backtracking, while Σ_2 incorporates intelligent backtracking, cycle detection, and a 100-element least-recently used subgoal cache. Each configuration performs unit-increment depth-first iterative deepening and is limited to exploring $1,000,000$ nodes before abandoning the problem and marking it as unsolved; elapsed CPU time (sum of system time and user time) is recorded for each problem. Note that the size of the cache is quite arbitrarily selected; larger or smaller caches may well result in improved performance. In addition, a unit increment may well be a substantially suboptimal increment for iterative deepening. Depending on the domain, increasing the increment value or changing the cache size may have a significant effect on the system's performance. The results reported in this paper are clearly dependent on the values of these parameters, but the conclusions we draw from these results are based only on comparisons between identically-configured systems.

The fourth tested configuration, Σ_3, adds 99 nagging processors to the configuration of Σ_2. Nagging processors are identically configured with intelligent backtracking, cycle detection, and 100-element least-recently used subgoal caches. For each problem, the currently "fastest" 99 machines (as determined by elapsed time for solving a short benchmark problem set) in the processor pool are selected for use as nagging processors. These additional processors are organized hierarchically, with 9 processors nagging the main processor and 10 more processors nagging each of these in turn. Hierarchical nagging, or *meta-nagging*, reduces the load on the main processor by amortizing nagging overhead costs over many processors. Recursively nagged processors are more effective as naggers in their own right, since nagging these processors prunes their search and helps them to exhaust their own search spaces more quickly. The main processor is subject to the same $1,000,000$ node resource constraint as the serial configurations tested.

Σ_0 solves 384 problems within the allotted resource bound, or 26.35% of the 1457 problems attempted. Σ_1,

<hr>

[2] As a rough measure of performance, this configuration running on the hardware just described performs at about 10K LIPS on a benchmark definite-clause theory.

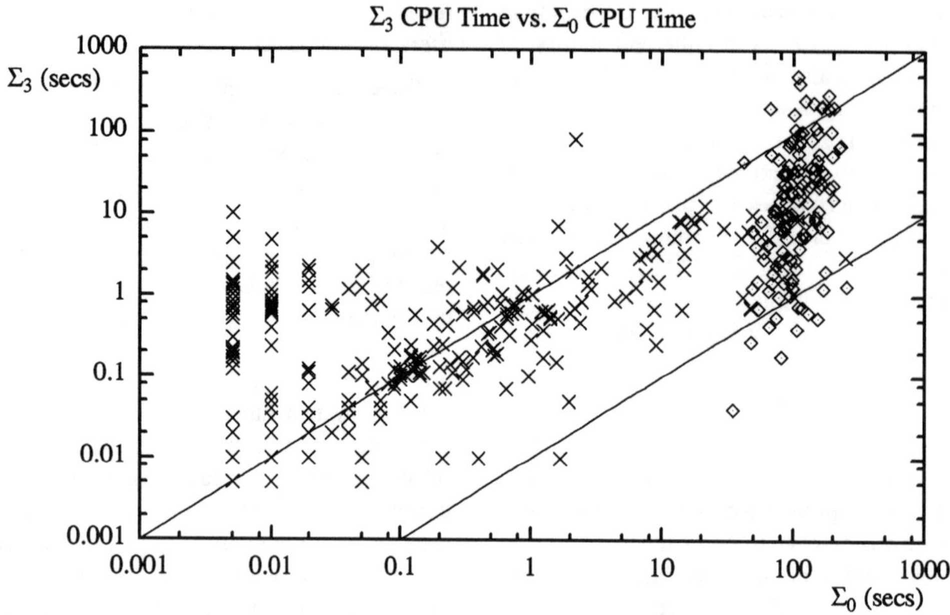

Figure 1: Performance of Σ_3 (log elapsed CPU time to solution on main processor) vs. performance of Σ_0 (log elapsed CPU time to solution or failure). The "cross" datapoints correspond to the 384 problems solved by both systems, while the "diamond" datapoints correspond to the 130 problems solved only by Σ_3; x-coordinate values for the "diamond" datapoints represent recorded time-to-failure for Σ_0, an optimistic estimate of actual solution time. The two lines represent $f(x) = x$ and $f(x) = x/100$. Since the granularity of our metering software is only 0.01 seconds, any problem taking less than 0.01 CPU seconds to solution is charged instead for 0.005 seconds.

identical to Σ_0 save for the use of intelligent backtracking and cycle detection, solves an additional 56 problems, or a total of 440 problems (30.19%). Σ_2, which adds a 100-element subgoal cache to the configuration of Σ_1, solves an additional 20 problems (76 more than Σ_0), for a total of 460 problems solved (31.57%). Finally, Σ_3, the 100-processor version of Σ_2, solves a total of 514 problems (35.27%). Note that in every case adding a search reduction technique results in the solution of additional problems.[3]

The additional problems solved by each successively more sophisticated configuration represent one important measure of improved performance. A second metric is the relative speed with which the different configurations solve a given problem; we consider here one such comparison between the most sophisticated system tested, Σ_3, and the least sophisticated system tested, Σ_0. Figure 1 plots the logarithm of the CPU time to solution for Σ_3 against the logarithm of the CPU required to either solve or fail to solve the same problem for Σ_0. Each point in the plot corresponds to a problem solved by at least one of the systems; the 384 "cross" datapoints correspond to problems solved by both systems, while the 130 "diamond" datapoints correspond to problems solved only by Σ_3. Datapoints falling below the line $f(x) = x$ represent problems that are solved faster by Σ_3, while datapoints falling below the line $f(x) = x/100$ represent problems that are solved more than 100 times faster with 100 processors.[4]

---

[3] While Σ_3 solves 56 problems not solved by Σ_2, 2 problems solved by Σ_2 were not solved by Σ_3. While no individual technique is likely to cause an increase in the number of nodes explored, interactions between techniques may result in such an increase. For example, changes to search behavior due to nagging will affect the contents of the main processor's cache; changes in cache contents will in turn affect the main processor's search behavior with respect to an identical serial system.

[4] The fact that some problems demonstrate superlinear speedup may seem somewhat alarming. Intuitively, using N identical processors should result in, at best, N times the performance. Here, the additional $N - 1$ processors are, on average, much slower than the main processor, and one would therefore initially expect sublinear speedup. However, superlinear speedup can result since the parallel system does not explore the space in the same order as the serial system. In particular, a nagging processor may explore a subgoal ordering that provides a solution with significantly less search than the original ordering, resulting in a net performance improvement much larger than N. In addition, the parallel system has the added advantage of subgoal caching and intelligent backtracking which also make substantial performance contributions on some problems.

If we consider only those problems solved by both systems (the 384 "cross" datapoints in Figure 1) and if we informally define "easy" problems to be those problems requiring at most 1 second to solve with the serial system, then we see that the performance of Σ_3 on such problems is often worse than that of the more naive serial system Σ_0; thus, many of these datapoints lie above the $f(x) = x$ line. We attribute this poor performance to the initial costs of nagging (*e.g.*, establishing communication and transmitting the domain theory to all processors). For "hard" problems, however, the initial overhead is easily outweighed by the performance advantage of nagging. Furthermore, the performance improvement on just a few "hard" problems dwarfs the loss in performance on all of the "easy" problems — an effect that is visually obscured by the logarithmic scale used for both axes of Figure 1.

A more precise way of convincing ourselves that Σ_3 is superior to Σ_0 is to use a simple nonparametric test such as the one-tailed paired sign test (Arbuthnott, 1710), or the one-tailed Wilcoxon matched-pairs signed-ranks test (Wilcoxon, 1945) to test for statistically significant differences between the elapsed CPU times for problems solved by both systems. These tests are nonparametric analogues to the more commonly used Student t-test; nonparametric tests are more appropriate here since we do not know anything about the underlying distribution of the elapsed CPU times.

The null hypothesis we are testing is that the recorded elapsed CPU times for Σ_0 are at least as fast as the recorded elapsed CPU times for Σ_3 on the 384 problems solved by both systems. The Wilcoxen test provides only marginal evidence for the conclusion that Σ_3 is faster than Σ_0 ($N = 384$, $p = .096$). However, if we only consider the "harder" problems, then there is significant evidence to conclude that Σ_3 is faster than Σ_0 ($N = 70$, $p < 10^{-6}$).

Of course, both our informal visual analysis of Figure 1 and the nonparametric analysis just given systematically understate the relative performance of Σ_3 by excluding the 130 problems that were solved only by Σ_3 (the "diamond" datapoints in Figure 1). Since these problems were not solved by Σ_0, we take the time required for Σ_0 to reach the resource bound as the abscissa for the datapoint in Figure 1: this is an *optimistic* estimate of the real solution time, since we know Σ_0 will require *at least* this much time to actually solve the problem. Graphically, the effect is to displace each "diamond" datapoint to the left of its true position by some unknown margin. Note that even though their x-coordinate value is understated, 117 (90%) of these datapoints still fall below the $f(x) = x$ line, and a 12 (roughly 10%) still demonstrate superlinear speedup. If we could use the actual Σ_0 solution time as the abscissa for

these 130 problems, the effect would be to shift each "diamond" datapoint to the right to its true position, greatly enhancing Σ_3's apparent performance advantage over Σ_0.

Is it possible to tease apart the performance contribution due to each individual technique? We can use the Wilcoxon test to compare each pair of successively more sophisticated system configurations. We conclude that Σ_1 is significantly faster than Σ_0 ($N = 384$, $p < 10^{-6}$), indicating that intelligent backtracking and cycle detection together are effective serial speedup techniques. In a similar fashion, Σ_2 is in turn significantly faster than Σ_1 ($N = 440$, $p < 10^{-6}$), indicating that subgoal caching is also an effective serial speedup technique when used with intelligent backtracking and cycle detection. In contrast, we find only marginal evidence that Σ_3 is uniformly faster than Σ_2 over the entire problem collection ($N = 458$, $p = .072$). However, as with the Σ_3 vs. Σ_0 comparison, separating "harder" problems, where Σ_3 significantly outperforms Σ_2 ($N = 108$, $p < 10^{-6}$), from "easier" problems, where the Σ_2 significantly outperforms Σ_3 ($N = 350$, $p < 10^{-6}$) enables us to make statistically valid statements about the relative performance of Σ_3 and Σ_2. As before, all of these results — by ignoring problems left unsolved by one of the systems being compared — systematically understate the performance advantage of the more sophisticated system in the comparison.

Unlike nagging, where problem size is a good predictor of performance improvement, it is much more difficult to characterize when caching, intelligent backtracking, or cycle detection are advantageous. Some problems are solved more quickly with these techniques, while others problems are not; knowing whether a problem is "hard" or "easy" *a priori* gives no information about whether or not caching, intelligent backtracking, or cycle detection will help, a conclusion that is supported by our statistical analysis.

Conclusion

We have briefly reviewed the design and implementation of the DALI system. The premise of this paper is that efficient implementation technology, serial search reduction techniques, and nagging can be successfully combined to produce a first-order logic engine that can effectively bring hundreds of workstations to bear on large problems. We have supported our claims empirically over a broad range of problems from the theorem proving literature. While the results presented here are quite good, we believe we can still do better. We are now in the process of adding an *explanation-based learning* component that compiles "chains of reasoning" used in successfully solved problems into new macro-operators (Segre & Elkan, 1994). We are also exploring alternative cache-management policies, the use of dynamically-sized caches, and compile-time techniques for determining how caching can be used most effectively in a given domain. Similarly, we are studying compile-time techniques for selecting appropriate opportunities for nagging and we are also looking at how best to select a topology of recursive nagging processors. Finally, we are exploring additional sources of parallelism.

These efforts contribute to a larger study of practical, effective, inference techniques. In the long term, we believe that our distributed, adaptive, approach to first-order logical inference — driven by a broad-spectrum philosophy that integrates multiple serial search reduction techniques as well as the use of multiple processing elements — is a promising one that is also ideally suited to large-scale applications of significant practical importance.

Acknowledgements

We wish to acknowledge Maria Paola Bonacina, Randy Calistri-Yeh, Charles Elkan, Don Geddis, Geoff Gordon, Simon Kasif, Drew McDermott, David Plaisted, Mark Stickel, and three anonymous reviewers for their helpful comments on an early draft of this paper. Support for this research was provided by the Office of Naval Research through grant N00014-90-J-1542 (AMS), by the Advanced Research Project Agency through Rome Laboratory Contract Number F30602-93-C-0018 via Odyssey Research Associates, Incorporated (AMS), and by the Air Force Office for Scientific Research through a Graduate Student Fellowship (DBS).

References

Aït-Kaci, H. (1991). *Warren's Abstract Machine.* Cambridge, MA: MIT Press.

Arbuthnott, J. (1710). An Argument for Divine Providence, Taken from the Constant Regularity Observed in the Births of Both Sexes. *Philosophical Transactions, 27*, 186-190.

Calistri-Yeh, R.J. & Segre, A.M. (April 1993). *The Design of ALPS: An Adaptive Architecture for Transportation Planning* (Technical Report TM-93-0010). Ithaca, NY: Odyssey Research Associates.

Korf, R. (1985). Depth-First Iterative Deepening: An Optimal Admissible Tree Search. *Artificial Intelligence, 27*(1), 97-109.

Kumar, V. & Lin, Y-J. (August 1987). An Intelligent Backtracking Scheme for Prolog. *Proceedings of the IEEE Symposium on Logic Programming*, 406-414.

Plaisted, D. (1988). Non-Horn Clause Logic Programming Without Contrapositives. *Journal of Automated Reasoning,*

4(3), 287-325.

Segre, A.M. & Elkan, C.P. (*To appear, 1994*). A High Performance Explanation-Based Learning Algorithm. *Artificial Intelligence*

Segre, A.M. & Scharstein, D. (August 1993). Bounded-Overhead Caching for Definite-Clause Theorem Proving. *Journal of Automated Reasoning, 11*(1), 83-113.

Stickel, M. (1988). A Prolog Technology Theorem Prover: Implementation by an Extended Prolog Compiler. *Journal of Automated Reasoning, 4*(4), 353-380.

Sturgill, D.B. & Segre, A.M. (To appear, June 1994). A Novel Asynchronous Parallelization Scheme for First-Order Logic. *Proceedings of the Twelfth Conference on Automated Deduction*

Suttner, C.B., Sutcliffe, G. & Yemenis, T. (1993). *The TPTP Problem Library (TPTP v1.0.0)* (Technical Report FKI-184-93). Munich, Germany: Institut für Informatik, Tecnische Universität München.

Wilcoxon, F. (1945). Individual Comparisons by Ranking Methods. *Biometrics, 1*, 80-83.

Termination Analysis of OPS5 Expert Systems[*]

Hsiu-yen Tsai   Albert Mo Kim Cheng

Department of Computer Science
University of Houston
Houston, Texas 77204-3475
Email:(hsiuyen, cheng)@cs.uh.edu

Abstract

Bounded response time is an important requirement when rule-based expert systems are used in real-time applications. In the case the rule-based system cannot terminate in bounded time, we should detect the "culprit" conditions causing the non-termination to assist programmers in debugging. This paper describes a novel tool which analyzes OPS5 programs to achieve this goal. The first step is to verify that an OPS5 program can terminate in bounded time. A graphical representation of an OPS5 program is defined and evaluated. Once the termination of the OPS5 program is not expected, the "culprit" conditions are detected. These conditions are then used to correct the problem by adding extra rules to the original program.

Introduction

As rule-based expert systems become widely adopted in new application domains such as real-time systems, ensuring that they meet stringent timing constraints in these safety-critical and time-critical environments emerges as a challenging design problem. In real applications, rule firings are triggered by the changes in the environment. The computation time of an expert system is highly unpredictable and dependent on the working memory conditions. If the computation takes too long, the expert system may not have sufficient time to respond to the ongoing changes in the environment, making the result of the computation useless or even harmful to the system being monitored or controlled.

To remedy this problem, two solutions are proposed in the literature. The first one is to reduce the execution time via parallelism in the matching phase and/or firing phase of the recognize-act cycle. Several approaches (Ishida 1991; Kuo & Moldovan 1991; Schmolze 1991; Pasik 1992; Cheng 1993) have been provided to achieve this goal. The other solution is to optimize the expert system by modifying or

*This material is based upon work supported in part by the National Science Foundation under Award No. CCR-9111563 and by the Texas Advanced Research Program under Grant No. 3652270.

resynthesizing the rule base if the response time is found to be inadequate(Zupan & Cheng 1994). There have been few attempts to formalize the question of whether a rule-based program has bounded response time. Some formal frameworks are introduced in (Browne, Cheng, & Mok 1988; Cheng & Wang 1990; Cheng *et al.* 1993). Their work focus on EQL (Browne, Cheng, & Mok 1988) and MRL (Wang 1990) rule-based languages, which are developed for real-time rule-based applications.

Our work in this paper is related to the second solution. In particular, we shall investigate the timing properties of programs written in the OPS5 language, which is not designed for real-time purposes although it has been widely adopted in practice. Our experience has shown that most rule-based programs are not designed for all possible data domains. Because rule-based programs are data-driven, certain input data are required to direct the control flows in the programs. Many control techniques are implemented in this manner and often require the absence of or a specific ordering of working memory elments to generate initial working memory(WM). Hence, if these WMEs are not in the expected data domain, abnormal program behavior will occur, usually leading to a cycle in the program flow. While we predict the timing bound, termination should be detected as well. Here, we focus on the following points.

- Formalize a graphical representation of rule-based programs.

- Detect the termination conditions of OPS5 programs. In (Ullman 1988), similar work focuses on the recursive relation in backward chaining programs. Here, rule-based programs which employ forward chaining are discussed.

- If an OPS5 program is not detected to terminate for all initial program states, extract the "culprit" conditions which cause non-termination to assist programmers in correcting the program.

- Modify the program to ensure program termination.

The rest of the paper is organized as follows. In Section 2 we define a graph to represent OPS5 programs.

Section 3 introduces a novel method of termination detection. Section 4 describes a technique to find the "culprit" conditions. An additional refinement phase is discussed in Section 5. Section 6 describes how the tool is constructed and provides a brief analysis of its computational complexity. Section 7 is the conclusion.

Static Analysis of Control Paths

Several graphical representations of rule-based programs have been developed for analysis, testing, and debugging purposes. An intuitive representation is a *physical rule flow graph*. In such a graph, nodes represent rules and an edge from node a to node b implies rule b is executed immediately after rule a is executed. Unlike programs written in a procedural language, the control flows of rule-based programs are embedded in the data and cannot be easily derived. Thus one cannot in general find physical paths among rules without running the program for every possible initial program state. Furthermore, since the developer and the tester of a rule-based program usually think in terms of logical paths, a physical rule flow graph is not the most appropriate abstraction. This leads to the definition of a graph called *Enable Rule (ER)* graph, which is adapted from (Cheng & Wang 1990) and (Kiper 1992). The control information among rules in OPS5 is represented by the ER graph. To define the ER graph, we need to first define the state space graph.

Definition 1 *The state space graph of an OPS5 program is a labeled directed graph $G=(V,E)$. V is a set of nodes each of which represents a set of Working Memory Elements(WMEs). We say that a rule is **enabled** at node i iff its enabling condition is satisfied by the WMEs at node i. E is a set of edges each of which denotes the firing of a rule such that an edge (i,j) connects node i to node j iff there is rule R which is enabled at node i, and firing R will modify the Working Memory(WM) to have the same WMEs at node j.*

Definition 2 *Rule a is said to potentially enable rule b iff there exist at least one reachable state in the state space graph of the program where (1) the enabling condition of rule b is false, and (2) firing rule a causes the enabling condition of rule b to become true.*

Since the state space graph cannot be derived without running the program for all allowable initial states, we use symbolic pattern matching to determine the *potentially enable* relation between rules. Rule a potentially enables rule b iff the symbolic form of a WME modified by the actions in rule a matches one of the enabling conditions of rule b. Here, the symbolic form represents a set of WMEs and is of the form:

```
(classname ↑attribute1 v1 ↑attribute2 v2 ...
↑attributen vn)
```

where v1, v2 ... and vn are either variables or constant values and each attribute can be omitted. For example, (class ↑a1 3 ↑a2 <x>) can be a symbolic form of the following WMEs.

```
(class ↑a1 3 ↑a2 4)
(class ↑a1 3 ↑a2 8 ↑a3 4)
(class ↑a1 3 ↑a2 <y> ↑a4 <z>)
```

Example 1 illustrates the *potentially enable* relation. Rule a potentially enables rule b because the first action of rule a creates a WME (class_c ↑c1 off ↑c2 <x>) which symbolically matches the enabling condition (class_c ↑c1 <y>) of rule b. Note that the second action of rule a does not match the first enabling condition (class_a ↑a1 <x> ↑a2 off) of rule b because variable <y> ranges in <<open close>>.

Example 1 An example of the *potentially enable* relation

```
(p a
  (class_a ^a1 <x> ^a2 3)
  (class_b ^b1 <x> ^b2 {<y> << open close >> })
-->
  (make class_c ^c1 off ^c2 <x>)
  (modify 1 ^a2 <y>))
(p b
  (class_a ^a1 <x> ^a2 off)
  (class_c ^c1 <y>)
-->
  (modify 1 ^a2 open))
```

The symbolic matching method actually detects the enabling relation by checking the attribute ranges. This information can be found by analyzing the semantics of the rules.

Definition 3 *The enable-rule (ER) graph of a set of rules is a labeled directed graph $G = (V, E)$. V is a set of nodes such that there is a node for each rule. E is a set of edges such that an edge connects node a to node b iff rule a potentially enables rule b.*

Note that an edge from a to b in the ER graph does not mean that rule b will fire immediately after rule a. If rule b is potentially enabled, that only implies rule b may be added to the agenda of the rules to be fired.

The previous analysis is useful since it does not require us to know the contents of working memory, which cannot be obtained statically.

Termination Detection

The ER graph provides information about the logical paths of an OPS5 program. We can use this graph to trace the control flows of the program. Since we know the potentially enable relation between rules, we can detect if the firing of each rule in an OPS5 program can terminate. A rule is said to be terminating if the number of that rule's firings is always bounded.

Definition 4 *Suppose rule b potentially enables rule a. Then there is an edge from node b to node a in the ER graph. A matched condition of rule a is one of the enabling condition elements of rule a, which may be matched by executing an action of rule b. Here, rule b is called the enabling rule of the matched condition.*

Definition 5 *An unmatched condition is one of the enabling condition elements of a rule which cannot be matched by firing any rule, including this rule.*

Example 2 *Matched* and *unmatched* conditions

```
(p b                    (p a
  (c1 ^a1 5)              (c2 ^a2 <x>)
  (c2 ^a2 <x> ^a3 2)      (c3 ^a4 <x> ^a5 <y>)
-->                     -->
  (modify 2 ^a2 3))       (modify 1 ^a2 <y>))
```

In example 2, suppose the firing of any other rule cannot match the second condition element of rule a. In the ER graph, rule b will *potentially enable* rule a. The first condition element (c2 ↑a2 <x>) of rule a is a *matched condition* because it may be matched by firing rule b. The second condition element (c3 ↑a4 <x> ↑a5 <y>) of rule a is an *unmatched condition* because it cannot be matched by firing other rules.

Next, we derive a theorem to detect the termination of a program. One way to predict the termination condition is to make sure that every state in the state space graph cannot be reached twice or more. However, since it is computationally expensive to expand the whole state space graph, we use the ER graph to detect this property.

Theorem 1 *A rule r will terminate if one of the following conditions holds:*

C1. *The actions of rule r modify or remove the unmatched conditions of rule r.*

C2. *The actions of rule r modify or remove the matched conditions of rule r. All of the enabling rules of the matched conditions can terminate in bounded time.*

C3. *Every rule, which enables rule r, can terminate in bounded time.*

Proof:

C1. Since the firing of any rule cannot match the *unmatched conditions*, the only WMEs which can match the *unmatched conditions* are the initial WMEs. Moreover, since the actions of rule r change the contents of these WMEs, the WMEs cannot match the *unmatched conditions* again after rule r is fired. Otherwise, the *unmatched condition* will be matched by firing rule r. This contradicts the definition of *unmatched conditions*. Each initial WME matching the *unmatched condition* can cause rule r to fire at most once since we have a finite number of initial WMEs. Thus rule r can terminate in bounded time.

C2. Since the enabling rules of the *matched conditions* can terminate in bounded time, by removing these rules, the *matched conditions* can be treated as *unmatched conditions*. According to condition 1, rule r can terminate in bounded time.

C3. All rules which enable rule r can terminate in bounded time. After these rules terminate, no other rule can trigger rule r to fire. Thus rule r can terminate as well.

Consider the following rule:

```
(p a
  (c1 ^a1 1 ^a2 <x>)
  (c2 ^a1 4 ^a2 <x>)
-->
  (modify 2 ^a1 3))
```

Suppose the second condition element (c2 ↑a1 4 ↑a2 <x>) cannot be matched by firing any rule, including this rule itself. Then this condition element is an *unmatched condition*. Suppose there are three WMEs in the initial working memory matching this condition element. Then this condition element can be matched by at most three WMEs. The actions of rule a modify these three WMEs when rule a fires. As a result, rule a can fire at most three times.

If there is no cycle in the ER graph or every cycle can be broken (i.e., cycle can be exited), then the firings of every rule in the OPS5 program are finite, and thus termination is detected. However, if the termination cannot be detected, we shall inspect the cycles in the ER graph.

Cycles in the ER Graph
Enabling Conditions of a Cycle

Suppose rules $p_1, p_2 \ldots, p_n$ form a cycle in the ER graph. W is a set of WMEs and W causes rules $p_1, p_2 \ldots, p_n$ to fire in that order. If after firing $p_1, p_2 \ldots, p_n$ in that order will form the WMEs W again, then W is the enabling condition of the cycle. We use symbolic tracing to find W if the data of each attribute are literal. Example 3 illustrates the idea.

Rule p_1 and p_2 form a cycle in the ER graph. To distinguish different variables in different rules, we assign different names to variables. Thus, the program is rewritten as in example 4.

Example 3 Two rules with an embedded cycle

```
    (p p1
      (class1 ^a11 { <x> <> 1 } )
      (class2 ^a21 <y>)
    -->
      (modify 1 ^a11 <y>))
    (p p2
      (class1 ^a11 <x>)
      (class2 ^a21 { <x> << 2 3 >> } ^a22 <y>)
    -->
      (modify 1 ^a11 <y>))
```

Example 4 Example 3 with modified variables

```
    (p p1
      (class1 ^a11 { <x-1> <> 1 } )
      (class2 ^a21 <y-1>)
    -->
      (modify 1 ^a11 <y-1>))
    (p p2
      (class1 ^a11 <x-2>)
      (class2 ^a21 { <x-2> << 2 3 >> } ^a22 <y-2>)
    -->
      (modify 1 ^a11 <y-2>))
```

A symbol table is built for each variable, which is bound according to the semantics of the enabling conditions. Here, the symbol table is shown in table 1.

Variable	Boundary
x-1	<>1
y-1	none
x-2	2,3
y-2	none

Table 1.

Variable	Boundary
x-1	<>1
y-1	2,3
x-2	2,3
y-2	none

Table 2.

Variable	Boundary
x-1	<>1
y-1	2,3
x-2	2,3
y-2	<>1

Table 3.

The non-terminating condition W is initially the set of all enabling conditions. Thus W is

```
(class1 ^a11 <x-1>)
(class2 ^a21 <y-1>)
(class1 ^a11 <x-2>)
(class2 ^a21 <x-2> ^a22 <y-2>)
```

Each variable is associated with the symbol table.

Now we trace the execution by firing p_1 first; p_1 enables p_2 by matching the first condition. Since the first condition of rule p_2 can be generated from rule p_1, it can be removed from W. Variable x-2 is now replaced by y-1. W is

```
(class1 ^a11 <x-1>)
(class2 ^a21 <y-1>)
(class2 ^a21 <y-1> ^a22 <y-2>)
```

Since x-2 is bound with 2 and 3, y-1 is bound with the same items. The symbol table is modified as in table 2.

After executing the action of rule p_2, W is now

```
(class1 ^a11 <y-2>)
(class2 ^a21 <y-1>)
(class2 ^a21 <y-1> ^a22 <y-2>)
```

To make this WM trigger p_1 and p_2 in that order again, the WME (class1 ↑a11 <y-2>) must match the first condition of p_1. Thus variable y-2 is bound with x-1's boundary. The symbol table is shown in table 3. W is

```
(class1 ^a11 <y-2>)
(class2 ^a21 <y-1>)
(class2 ^a21 <y-1> ^a22 <y-2>)
      where y-2<>1 and y-1=2,3
```

The detailed algorithm for detecting the enabling conditions of cycles is described next.

Algorithm 1 *The Detection of Enabling Conditions of Cycles*

Premise: The data domain of each attribute is literal.

Purpose: Rules $p_1, p_2 \ldots, p_n$ form a cycle in the *ER* graph. Find a set of WMEs W which fire $p_1, p_2 \ldots, p_n$ in that order such that these firings cannot terminate in bounded time.

1. Assign different names to the variables in different rules.

2. Initialize W to be the set of all enabling conditions of $p_1, p_2 \ldots, p_n$.

3. Build a symbol table for variables. Each variable is bound with the semantics of enabling conditions.

4. Simulate the firing of $p_1, p_2 \ldots, p_n$ in that order. Each enabling condition of rule p_i is matched from the initial WM unless it can be generated from rule

p_{i-1}. If the enabling condition element w of rule p_i can be generated by firing p_{i-1}, then remove w from W. Substitute p_{i-1}'s variables v_{i-1} for corresponding variables v_i in p_i. Modify v_{i-1}'s boundary in the symbol table.

5. If p_1's enabling condition elements can be generated by p_n, substitute p_n's variables v_n for corresponding variables v_1 in p_1. Modify v_n's boundary in the symbol table.

6. In steps 4 and 5, while substituting p_{i-1}'s variables for p_is', check the intersection of the boundaries of p_i's and p_{i-1}'s variables. If the intersection is empty, then terminate the algorithm.

7. Suppose W_n is the WM after firing $p_1, p_2 \ldots, p_n$. If W_n can match W, then W is an enabling condition of the cycle $p_1, p_2 \ldots, p_n$.

Note that there can be more than one set of enabling conditions W of a cycle. Hence, by applying the algorithm, we may obtain different Ws.

Prevention of Cycles

After detecting the enabling conditions W of a cycle, we can add an extra rule r' with W as the enabling conditions of r'. By doing so, once the working memory has the WMEs matching the enabling conditions of a cycle, the control flow can be switched from the cycle to r'. In example 3, r' is

```
(p loop-rule1
   (class1 ^a11 { <y-2> <>1 } )
   (class2 ^a21 { <y-1> << 2 3 >> } )
   (class2 ^a21 <y-1> ^a22 <y-2>)
-->
   action ...
```

The action of r' is determined by the application. The simplest way is to halt in order to escape from the cycle.

To ensure the program flow switches out of the cycles, the extra rules r' should have higher priorities than the regular ones. To achieve this goal, we use the MEA control strategy and modify the enabling conditions of each regular rule.

At the beginning of the program, two WMEs are added to the WM and the MEA strategy is enforced.

```
(startup
   ......
   (strategy mea)
   (make control ^rule regular)
   (make control ^rule extra))
```

The condition (control ↑rule regular) is added to each regular rule as the first enabling condition element. (control ↑rule extra) is added to each extra rule as the first enabling condition element too. Since the MEA strategy is enforced, the order of instantiations is based on the recency of the *first* time tag. The recency of the condition (control ↑rule regular) is lower than that of the condition (control ↑rule extra). Thus, the instantiations of the extra rules are chosen for execution earlier than those of the regular rules. Example 5 is the modified result of example 3.

Example 5 The modified result of example 3

```
(startup
  (strategy mea)
  (make control ^rule regular)
  (make control ^rule extra))
(p p1
  (control ^rule regular)
  (class1 ^a11 { <x> <> 1 } )
  (class2 ^a21 <y>)
-->
  (modify 2 ^a11 <y>))
(p p2
  (control ^rule regular)
  (class1 ^a11 <x>)
  (class2 ^a21 { <x> << 2 3 >>} ^a22 <y>)
-->
  (modify 2 ^a11 <y>))
(p loop-rule1
  (control ^rule extra)
  (class1 ^a11 { <y-2> <> 1 } )
  (class2 ^a21 { <y-1> << 2 3 >> } )
  (class2 ^a21 <y-1> ^a22 <y-2>)
-->
  (halt))
```

Usually, applications do not expect cycles embedded in the control paths. Thus, once the entrance of a cycle is detected, the program can be abandoned. Hence, after all cycles in the ER graph are found and extra rules are added, we can guarantee that the program will terminate. However, we can also have exception handling on the action of the extra rules. One way to handle the exception is to remove the WMEs which match the enabling condition of a cycle. In example 5, the action of the extra rule can be (remove 2 3 4). Since the WMEs which match the enabling condition of a cycle are removed, the instantiations in the cycle are also removed. Then other instantiations in the agenda can be triggered to fire.

Program Refinement

The ER graph of a typical OPS5 program is complex and usually contains many cycles. Furthermore, even for a single cycle, there may exist more than one enabling condition to trigger the cycle. This leads to a large number of extra rules in the modified programs and thus reduces their runtime performance. To tackle this problem, redundant conditions and rules must be removed after the modification.

Redundant Conditions

In algorithm 1, after symbolic tracing, some variables will be substituted and the boundaries may be changed too. This may cause subset relationship among the enabling condition elements of a cycle. In an extra rule, if condition element C_i is a subset of condition element C_j, then C_j can be omitted to simplify the enabling condition. In example 5, the condition (class2 ↑a21 <y-1> ↑a22 <y-2>) is a subset of (class2 ↑a21). Hence, (class2 ↑a21) can be omitted.

```
(p loop-rule1
  (control ^rule extra)
  (class1 ^a11 { <y-2> <>1 } )
;   (class2 ^a21 { <y-1> << 2 3 >> } )  ;omitted
  (class2 ^a21 { <y-1> << 2 3 >> ^a22 <y-2>)
-->
  (halt))
```

Redundant Rules

Since each cycle is analyzed independently, the extra rules correspond to cycles with different enabling conditions. If the enabling condition of rule r_i is a subset of the enabling condition of rule r_j, then rule r_i can be removed since firing r_i will definitely fire r_j. The cycling information of rule r_j contains that of rule r_i. Thus, it is sufficient to simply provide more general information. In many cases, if the set of nodes P_i which form a cycle C_i is a subset of the set P_j which form a cycle C_j, then the enabling condition of C_j is a subset of C_i's enabling condition. The situation becomes apparent when the cycle consists of many nodes. Hence, we can expect to remove the extra rules whose enabling conditions are derived from larger cycles.

In the following rules, rule 3 and rule 4 can be removed because their enabling conditions are subsets of the enabling conditions of rule 1 and 2, respectively.

```
(p 1
  (class1 ^a13 { <y-1> <> 1 } )
  (class2 ^a22 <y-1>)
-->
  action ...
(p 2
  (class1 ^a13 { <x-1> <> 1 } )
  (class2 ^a22 <y-1>)
  (class4 ^a41 2 ^a42 <x-3>)
-->
  action ...
(p 3                     ; redundant rule
  (class1 ^a13 { <y-1> << 2 3 >> } )
  (class4 ^a41 { <y-4> <> 1 } ^a42 <y-1>)
  (class2 ^a22 <y-1>)
-->
  action ...
(p 4                     ; redundant rule
  (class1 ^a13 { <x-1> <> 1} )
  (class2 ^a22 { <y-1> << 2 3 >> }
  (class4 ^a41 <y-4> ^a42 <y-1>)
  (class4 ^a41 2 ^a42 <x-3>)
-->
  action ...
```

Implementation

The tool has been implemented on a DEC 5000/240 workstation. Two real-world expert systems are examined. The tool adds one extra rule to the OMS expert system(Barry & Lowe 1990) and 4 extra rules to the ISA expert system(Marsh 1988). Before extra rules are added, these two expert systems have 29 and 15 rules, respectively.

For an OPS5 program with n rules, there are potentially $O(n!)$ cycles embedded in the ER graph. However, in a real application, especially in real-time expert systems, it is unlikely that a cycle contains a large number of nodes. If it is detected that no path contains m nodes in the ER graph, there is no need to test cycles with more than m nodes. This reduces both computational complexity and memory space.

To further reduce the computation time, we can store the path information. If there is no path in the order of executing rules $p_1, p_2 \ldots, p_n$, there is no cycle containing this path. Thus we do not need to examine the cycles with the embedded path. The ER graph actually represents all possible paths between two rules. We can construct a linear list to store all impossible paths with more than two rules. Thus, it is a tradeoff between time and space. In our tool, we store impossible paths with up to nine nodes.

Conclusion

We have presented an approach to detect the termination conditions of OPS5 rule-based programs. A data dependency graph (ER graph) is used to capture all of the logical paths of a rule-based program.

Then this ER graph is used to detect if an OPS5 program can terminate in bounded time. More specifically, our technique detects rules which have a finite number of firings. Once non-termination is detected, we extract every cycle in the ER graph and find the enabling conditions of the cycles. After finding the enabling conditions W of a cycle, rule r' is added with W as the enabling conditions. By doing so, once the working memory has the WMEs matching the enabling conditions of a cycle, the control flow can be switched out of the cycle to r'. However, to ensure the program flow switches to r', the program is modified such that r' has higher priority than the regular rules. The extra rules are further refined to remove redundant conditions and rules.

By providing programmers the "culprit" conditions, extra rules can be added to correct the program. If the cycle is an abnormal situation, we can abandon the task to guarantee the termination of the program. However, if recovery from the cycle is required, these conditions can be used to guide the programmers to correct them.

Ongoing work applies the proposed technique to large rule-based systems to test its efficiency and performance. A tight estimation of execution time also must be resolved so that we can predict more precisely about the timing behavior of OPS5 and OPS5-style rule-based systems in terms of execution time.

References

Barry, M. R., and Lowe, C. M. 1990. Analyzing spacecraft configurations through specialization and default reasoning. In *Proc. of the Goddard Conf. on Space Applications of Artificial Intelligence*, 165–179. NASA.

Browne, J. C.; Cheng, A. M. K.; and Mok, A. K. 1988. Computer-aided design of real-time rule-based decision system. Technical report, Department of Computer Science, University of Texas at Austin. Also to appear in *IEEE Trans. on Software Eng.*

Cheng, A. M. K., and Wang, C.-K. 1990. Fast static analysis of real-time rule-based systems to verify their fixed point convergence. In *Proc. 5th Annual IEEE Conf. on Computer Assurance.*

Cheng, A. M. K.; Browne, J. C.; Mok, A. K.; and Wang, R.-H. 1993. Analysis of real-time rule-based system with behavioral constraint assertions specified in Estella. *IEEE Trans. on Software Eng.* 19(19):863–885.

Cheng, A. M. K. 1993. Parallel execution of real-time rule-based systems. In *Proc. IEEE Intl. Parallel Processing Symposium.*

Ishida, T. 1991. Parallel rule firing in production systems. *IEEE Trans. on Knowledge and Data Eng.* 3(1).

Kiper, J. D. 1992. Structural testing of rule-based expert systems. *ACM Trans. on Software Eng. and Methodology* 1(2).

Kuo, S., and Moldovan, D. 1991. Implementation of multiple rule firing production system on hypercube. *J. Parallel and Distr. Computing* 13(4):383–394.

Marsh, C. 1988. The isa expert system: A prototype system for failure diagnosis on the space station. Mitre report, The MITRE Corp., Houston, TX.

Pasik, A. J. 1992. A source-to-source transformation for increasing rule-based parallelism. *IEEE Trans, on Knowledge and Data Eng.* 4(4).

Schmolze, J. G. 1991. Guaranteeing serizlizable results in synchronous parallel production systems. *J. Parallel and Distr. Computing* 13(4).

Ullman, J. D. 1988. Efficient tests for top-down termination of logical rules. *J. of the ACM* 35(2).

Wang, C.-K. 1990. MRL: The language. Tech. report, University of Texas at Austin, Real-Time Lab, Department of Computer Sciences.

Zupan, B., and Cheng, A. M. K. 1994. Optimization of rule-based expert systems via state transition system construction. In *Proc. IEEE Conf. on Artificial Intelligence for Applications*, 320–326.

Refining the Structure of Terminological Systems:
Terminology = Schema + Views[*]

M. Buchheit[1] and **F. M. Donini**[2] and **W. Nutt**[1] and **A. Schaerf**[2]
1. German Research Center for Artificial Intelligence (DFKI), Saarbrücken, Germany
{buchheit,nutt}@dfki.uni-sb.de
2. Dipartimento di Informatica e Sistemistica, Università di Roma "La Sapienza," Italy
{donini,aschaerf}@assi.dis.uniroma1.it

Abstract

Traditionally, the core of a Terminological Knowledge Representation System (TKRS) consists of a so-called TBox, where concepts are introduced, and an ABox, where facts about individuals are stated in terms of these concepts. This design has a drawback because in most applications the TBox has to meet two functions at a time: on the one hand, similar to a database schema, framelike structures with typing information are introduced through primitive concepts and primitive roles; on the other hand, views on the objects in the knowledge base are provided through defined concepts.

We propose to account for this conceptual separation by partitioning the TBox into two components for primitive and defined concepts, which we call the *schema* and the *view* part. We envision the two parts to differ with respect to the language for concepts, the statements allowed, and the semantics.

We argue that by this separation we achieve more conceptual clarity about the role of primitive and defined concepts and the semantics of terminological cycles. Moreover, three case studies show the computational benefits to be gained from the refined architecture.

Introduction

Research on terminological reasoning usually presupposes the following abstract architecture, which reflects quite well the structure of existing systems. There is a logical representation language that allows for two kinds of statements: in the TBox or *terminology*, concept descriptions are introduced, and in the ABox or *world description*, individuals are characterized in terms of concept membership and role relationship. This abstract architecture has been the basis for the design of systems, the development of algorithms, and the investigation of the computational properties of inferences.

Given this setting, there are three parameters that characterize a terminological system: (i) the language for concept descriptions, (ii) the form of the statements allowed, and (iii) the semantics given to concepts and statements. Research tried to improve systems by modifying these three parameters. But in all existing systems and almost all theoretical studies language and semantics have been kept uniform.[1]

The results of these studies were unsatisfactory in at least two respects. First, it seems that tractable inferences are only possible for languages with little expressivity. Second, no consensus has been reached about the semantics of terminological cycles, although in applications the need to model cyclic dependencies between classes of objects arises constantly.

Based on an ongoing study of applications of terminological systems, we suggest to refine the two-layered architecture consisting of TBox and ABox. Our goal is twofold: on the one hand we want to achieve more conceptual clarity about the role of primitive and defined concepts and the semantics of terminological cycles; on the other hand, we want to improve the tradeoff between expressivity and worst case complexity. Since our changes are not primarily motivated by mathematical considerations but by the way systems are used, we expect to come up with a more practical system design.

In the applications studied we found that the TBox has to meet two functions at a time. One is to declare frame-like structures by introducing primitive concepts and roles together with typing information like isa-relationships between concepts, or range restrictions and number restrictions of roles. *E.g.,* suppose we want to model a company environment. Then we may introduce the concept Employee as a specialization of Person, having exactly one name of type Name and at least one affiliation of type Department. This is similar to class declarations in object-oriented systems. For this purpose, a simple language is sufficient. Cycles occur naturally in modeling tasks, *e.g.,* the boss of an Employee is also an Employee. Such declarations have

---

[*]This work was partly supported by the Commission of the European Union under ESPRIT BRA 6810 (Compulog 2), by the German Ministry of Research and Technology under grant ITW 92-01 (TACOS), and by the CNR (Italian Research Council) under Progetto Finalizzato Sistemi Informatici e Calcolo Parallelo, LdR "Ibridi."

---

[1]In (Lenzerini & Schaerf 1991) a combination of a weak language for ABoxes and a strong language for queries has been investigated.

no definitional import, they just restrict the set of possible interpretations.

The second function of a TBox is to define new concepts in terms of primitive ones by specifying necessary *and* sufficient conditions for concept membership. This can be seen as defining *abstractions* or *views* on the objects in the knowledge base. Defined concepts are important for querying the knowledge base and as left-hand sides of trigger rules. For this purpose we need more expressive languages. If cycles occur in this part they must have definitional import.

As a consequence of our analysis we propose to split the TBox into two components: one for declaring frame structures and one for defining views. By analogy to the structure of databases we call the first component the *schema* and the second the *view* part. We envision the two parts to differ with respect to the language, the form of statements, and the semantics of cycles.

The schema consists of a set of primitive concept introductions, formulated in the *schema language*, and the view part by a set of concept definitions, formulated in the *view language*. In general, the schema language will be less expressive than the view language. Since the role of statements in the schema is to restrict the interpretations we want to admit, first order semantics, which is also called descriptive semantics in this context (see Nebel 1991), is adequate for cycles occurring in the schema. For cycles in the view part, we propose to choose a semantics that defines concepts uniquely, *e.g.*, least or greatest fixpoint semantics.

The purpose of this work is not to present the full-fledged design of a new system but to explore the options that arise from the separation of TBoxes into schema and views. Among the benefits to be gained from this refinement are the following three. First, the new architecture has more parameters for improving systems, since language, form of statements, and semantics can be specified differently for schema and views. So we found a combination of schema and view language with polynomial inference procedures whereas merging the two languages into one would have led to intractability. Second, we believe that one of the obstacles to a consensus about the semantics of terminological cycles has been precisely the fact that no distinction has been made between primitive and defined concepts. Moreover, intractability results for cycles mostly refer to inferences with defined concepts. We proved that reasoning with cycles is easier when only primitive concepts are considered. Third, the refined architecture allows for more differentiated complexity measures, as shown later in the paper.

In the following section we outline our refined architecture for a TKRS, which comprises *three* parts: the *schema*, the *view taxonomy*, and the *world description*, which comprise primitive concepts, defined concepts and assertions in traditional systems. In the third section we show by three case studies that adding a simple schema with cycles to existing systems does not increase the complexity of reasoning.

The Refined Architecture

We start this section by a short reminder on concept languages. Then we discuss the form of statements and their semantics in the different components of a TKRS. Finally, we specify the reasoning services provided by each component and introduce different complexity measures for analyzing them.

Concept Languages

In concept languages, complex concepts (ranged over by C, D) and complex roles (ranged over by Q, R) can be built up from simpler ones using concept and role forming constructs (see Tables 1 and 2 a set of common constructs). The basic syntactic symbols are (i) *concept names*, which are divided into *schema names* (ranged over by A) and *view names* (ranged over by V), (ii) *role names* (ranged over by P), and (iii) *individual names* (ranged over by a, b). An *interpretation* $\mathcal{I} = (\Delta^{\mathcal{I}}, \cdot^{\mathcal{I}})$ consists of the *domain* $\Delta^{\mathcal{I}}$ and the *interpretation function* $\cdot^{\mathcal{I}}$, which maps every concept to a subset of $\Delta^{\mathcal{I}}$, every role to a subset of $\Delta^{\mathcal{I}} \times \Delta^{\mathcal{I}}$, and every individual to an element of $\Delta^{\mathcal{I}}$ such that $a^{\mathcal{I}} \neq b^{\mathcal{I}}$ for different individuals a, b (*Unique Name Assumption*). Complex concepts and roles are interpreted according to the semantics given in Tables 1 and 2, respectively.

In our architecture, there are two different concept languages in a TKRS, a *schema language* for expressing schema statements and a *view language* for formulating views and queries to the system. The view and schema languages in the case studies will be defined by restricting the set of concept and role forming constructs to a subset of those in Tables 1 and 2.

The Three Components

Now we describe the three parts of a TKRS: the schema, the view taxonomy and the world description.

We first focus our attention to the schema. The schema introduces concept and role names and states elementary type constraints. This can be achieved by *inclusion axioms* having one of the forms:

$$A \sqsubseteq D, \quad P \sqsubseteq A_1 \times A_2,$$

where A, A_1, A_2 are schema names, P is a role name, and D is a concept of the schema language. Intuitively, the first axiom states that all instances of A are also instances of D. The second axiom states that the role P has domain A_1 and range A_2. A *schema* S consists of a finite set of schema axioms.

Inclusion axioms impose only necessary conditions for being an instance of the schema name on the left-hand side. For example, the axiom "Employee $\sqsubseteq$ Person" declares that every employee is a person,

Construct Name	Syntax	Semantics
top	$\top$	$\Delta^{\mathcal{I}}$
singleton set	$\{a\}$	$\{a^{\mathcal{I}}\}$
intersection	$C \sqcap D$	$C^{\mathcal{I}} \cap D^{\mathcal{I}}$
union	$C \sqcup D$	$C^{\mathcal{I}} \cup D^{\mathcal{I}}$
negation	$\neg C$	$\Delta^{\mathcal{I}} \setminus C^{\mathcal{I}}$
universal quantification	$\forall R.C$	$\{d_1 \mid \forall d_2 : (d_1, d_2) \in R^{\mathcal{I}} \rightarrow d_2 \in C^{\mathcal{I}}\}$
existential quantification	$\exists R.C$	$\{d_1 \mid \exists d_2 : (d_1, d_2) \in R^{\mathcal{I}} \wedge d_2 \in C^{\mathcal{I}}\}$
existential agreement	$\exists Q \doteq R$	$\{d_1 \mid \exists d_2.(d_1, d_2) \in Q^{\mathcal{I}} \wedge (d_1, d_2) \in R^{\mathcal{I}}\}$
number restrictions	$(\geq n\, R)$	$\{d_1 \mid \sharp\{d_2 \mid (d_1, d_2) \in R^{\mathcal{I}}\} \geq n\}$
	$(\leq n\, R)$	$\{d_1 \mid \sharp\{d_2 \mid (d_1, d_2) \in R^{\mathcal{I}}\} \leq n\}$

Table 1: Syntax and semantics of concept forming constructs.

Construct Name	Syntax	Semantics
inverse role	P^{-1}	$\{(d_1, d_2) \mid (d_2, d_1) \in P^{\mathcal{I}}\}$
role restriction	$(R\!:\!C)$	$\{(d_1, d_2) \mid (d_1, d_2) \in R^{\mathcal{I}} \wedge d_2 \in C^{\mathcal{I}}\}$
role chain	$Q \circ R$	$\{(d_1, d_3) \mid \exists d_2.(d_1, d_2) \in Q^{\mathcal{I}} \wedge (d_2, d_3) \in R^{\mathcal{I}}\}$
self	ϵ	$\{(d_1, d_1) \mid d_1 \in \Delta^{\mathcal{I}}\}$

Table 2: Syntax and semantics of role forming constructs.

but does not give a sufficient condition for being an employee.[2]

A schema may contain *cycles* through inclusion axioms (see Nebel 1991 for a formal definition). So one may state that the bosses of an employee are themselves employees, writing "Employee $\sqsubseteq$ $\forall$boss.Employee." In general, existing systems do not allow for terminological cycles, which is a serious restriction, since cycles are ubiquitous in domain models.

There are two questions related to cycles: the first is to fix the semantics and the second, based on this, to come up with a proper inference procedure. As to the semantics, we argue that axioms in the schema have the role of narrowing down the models we consider possible. Therefore, they should be interpreted under descriptive semantics, *i.e.*, like in first order logic: an interpretation $\mathcal{I}$ satisfies an axiom $A \sqsubseteq D$ if $A^{\mathcal{I}} \subseteq D^{\mathcal{I}}$, and it satisfies $P \sqsubseteq A_1 \times A_2$ if $P^{\mathcal{I}} \subseteq A_1^{\mathcal{I}} \times A_2^{\mathcal{I}}$. The interpretation $\mathcal{I}$ is a model of the schema $\mathcal{S}$ if it satisfies all axioms in $\mathcal{S}$. The problem of inferences will be dealt with in the next section.

The *view part* contains *view definitions* of the form

$$V \doteq C,$$

where V is a view name and C is a concept in the view language. Views provide abstractions by defining

new classes of objects in terms of the concept and role names introduced in the schema. We refer to "$V \doteq C$" as the *definition* of V. The distinction between schema and view names is crucial for our architecture. It ensures the separation between schema and views.

A *view taxonomy* $\mathcal{V}$ is a finite set of view definitions such that (*i*) for each view name there is at most one definition, and (*ii*) each view name occurring on the right hand side of a definition has a definition in $\mathcal{V}$.

Differently from schema axioms, view definitions give necessary *and* sufficient conditions. As an example of a view, one can describe the bosses of the employee Bill as the instances of "BillsBosses $\doteq$ $\exists$boss-of.{BILL}."

Whether or not to allow cycles in view definitions is a delicate design decision. Differently from the schema, the role of cycles in the view part is to state recursive definitions. For example, if we want to describe the group of individuals that are above Bill in the hierarchy of bosses we can use the definition "BillsSuperBosses $\doteq$ BillsBosses $\sqcup$ $\exists$boss-of.BillsSuperBosses." But note that this does not yield a definition if we assume descriptive semantics because for a fixed interpretation of BILL and of the role boss-of there may be several ways to interpret BillsSuperBosses in such a way that the above equality holds. In this example, we only obtain the intended meaning if we assume least fixpoint semantics. This observation holds more generally: if cycles are intended to uniquely define concepts then descrip-

---

[2]It gives, though, a sufficient condition for being a person: If an individual is asserted to be an Employee we can deduce that it is a Person, too.

tive semantics is not suitable. However, least or greatest fixpoint semantics or, more generally, a semantics based on the μ-calculus yield unique definitions (see Schild 1994). Unfortunately, algorithms for subsumption of views under such semantics are known only for fragments of the concept language defined in Tables 1 and 2.

In this paper, we only deal with acyclic view taxonomies. In this case, the semantics of view definitions is straightforward. An interpretation $\mathcal{I}$ satisfies the definition $V \doteq C$ if $V^{\mathcal{I}} = C^{\mathcal{I}}$, and it is a model for a view taxonomy $\mathcal{V}$ if $\mathcal{I}$ satisfies all definitions in $\mathcal{V}$.

A state of affairs in the world is described by *assertions* of the form

$$C(a), \qquad R(a,b),$$

where C and R are concept and role descriptions in the view language. Assertions of the form $A(a)$ or $P(a,b)$, where A and P are names in the schema, resemble basic facts in a database. Assertions involving complex concepts are comparable to view updates.

A *world description* $\mathcal{W}$ is a finite set of assertions. The semantics is as usual: an interpretation $\mathcal{I}$ satisfies $C(a)$ if $a^{\mathcal{I}} \in A^{\mathcal{I}}$ and it satisfies $R(a,b)$ if $(a^{\mathcal{I}}, b^{\mathcal{I}}) \in R^{\mathcal{I}}$; it is a model of $\mathcal{W}$ if it satisfies every assertion in $\mathcal{W}$.

Summarizing, a knowledge base is a triple $\Sigma = \langle \mathcal{S}, \mathcal{V}, \mathcal{W} \rangle$, where $\mathcal{S}$ is a schema, $\mathcal{V}$ a view taxonomy, and $\mathcal{W}$ a world description. An interpretation $\mathcal{I}$ is a model of a knowledge base if it is a model of all three components.

Reasoning Services

For each component, there is a prototypical reasoning service to which the other services can be reduced.

Schema Validation: Given a schema $\mathcal{S}$, check whether there exists a model of $\mathcal{S}$ that interprets every schema name as a nonempty set.

View Subsumption: Given a schema $\mathcal{S}$, a view taxonomy $\mathcal{V}$, and view names V_1 and V_2, check whether $V_1^{\mathcal{I}} \subseteq V_2^{\mathcal{I}}$ for every model $\mathcal{I}$ of $\mathcal{S}$ and $\mathcal{V}$;

Instance Checking: Given a knowledge base Σ, an individual a, and a view name V, check whether $a^{\mathcal{I}} \in V^{\mathcal{I}}$ holds in every model $\mathcal{I}$ of Σ.

Schema validation supports the knowledge engineer by checking whether the skeleton of his domain model is consistent. Instance checking is the basic operation in querying a knowledge base. View subsumption helps in organizing and optimizing queries (see *e.g.* Buchheit *et al.* 1994). Note that the schema $\mathcal{S}$ has to be taken into account in all three services and that the view taxonomy $\mathcal{V}$ is relevant not only for view subsumption, but also for instance checking. In systems that forbid cycles, one can get rid of $\mathcal{S}$ and $\mathcal{V}$ by expanding definitions. This is not possible when $\mathcal{S}$ and $\mathcal{V}$ are cyclic.

Complexity Measures

The separation of the core of a TKRS into three components allows us to introduce refined complexity measures for analyzing the difficulty of inferences.

The complexity of a problem is generally measured with respect to the size of the whole input. However, with regard to our setting, three different pieces of input are given, namely the schema, the view taxonomy, and the world description. For this reason, different kinds of complexity measures may be defined, similarly to what has been suggested in (Vardi 1982) for queries over relational databases. We consider the following measures (where $|X|$ denotes the size of X):

Schema Complexity: the complexity as a function of $|\mathcal{S}|$;

View Complexity: the complexity as a function of $|\mathcal{V}|$;

World Description Complexity: the complexity as a function of $|\mathcal{W}|$;

Combined Complexity: the complexity as a function of $|\mathcal{S}| + |\mathcal{V}| + |\mathcal{W}|$.

Combined complexity takes into account the whole input. The other three instead consider only a part of the input, so they are meaningful only when it is reasonable to suppose that the size of the other parts is negligible. For instance, it is sensible to analyze the schema complexity of view subsumption because usually the schema is much bigger than the two views which are compared. Similarly, one might be interested in the world description complexity of instance checking whenever one can expect $\mathcal{W}$ to be much larger than the schema and the view part.

It is worth noticing that for every problem combined complexity, taking into account the whole input, is at least as high as the other three. For example, if the complexity of a problem is $O(|\mathcal{S}| \cdot |\mathcal{V}| \cdot |\mathcal{W}|)$, its combined complexity is cubic, whereas the other ones are linear. Similarly, if the complexity of a given problem is $O(|\mathcal{S}|^{|\mathcal{V}|})$, both its combined complexity and its view complexity are exponential, its schema complexity is polynomial, and its world description complexity is constant.

In this paper, we use combined complexity to compare the complexity of reasoning in our architecture with the traditional one. Moreover, we use schema complexity to show how the presence of a large schema affects the complexity of the reasoning services previously defined. View and world description complexity have been investigated (under different names) in (Nebel 1990; Baader 1990) and (Schaerf 1993; Donini *et al.* 1994), respectively.

For a general description of the complexity classes we use see (Johnson 1990)

Case Studies

In this section, we study some illustrative examples that show the advantages of the architecture we propose. We extend three systems by a language for cyclic schemas and analyze their computational properties.

As argued before, a schema language should be expressive enough to declare isa-relationships, restric the range of roles, and specify roles to be necessary (at least one value) or functional (at most one value). These requirements are met by the language $\mathcal{SL}$ (see Buchheit *et al.* 1994), which is defined by the following syntax rule:

$$D \longrightarrow A \mid \forall P.A \mid (\geq 1\ P) \mid (\leq 1\ P).$$

Obviously, it is impossible to express in $\mathcal{SL}$ that a concept is empty. Therefore, schema validation in $\mathcal{SL}$ is trivial. Also, subsumption of schema names is decidable in polynomial time.

We proved that inferences become harder for extensions of $\mathcal{SL}$. If we add inverse roles, schema validation remains trivial, but subsumption of schema names becomes NP-hard. If we add any constructs by which one can express the empty concept—like disjointness axioms—schema validation becomes NP-hard. However, in our opinion this does not mean that extensions of $\mathcal{SL}$ are not feasible. For some extensions, we came up with natural restrictions on the form of schemas that decrease the complexity. Also, it is not clear whether realistic schemas will contain structures that require complex computations.

In all three case studies, the schema language is $\mathcal{SL}$. As view language, we investigate three different languages derived from three actual systems described in the literature, namely CONCEPTBASE (Jarke 1992), KRIS (Baader & Hollunder 1991), and CLASSIC (Borgida *et al.* 1989). For the extended systems, we study the complexity of the reasoning services, where, in particular, we aim at showing two results: (*i*) reasoning with respect to schema complexity is always tractable, (*ii*) combined complexity is not increased by the presence of terminological cycles in the schema.

In all three cases, we assume that the view taxonomy is acyclic. For this reason, from this point on we assume that no view names occur in view definitions or in the world description. This can be achieved by iteratively substituting every view name with its definition, which is possible because of our acyclicity assumption (see Nebel 1990 for a discussion of this substitution and its complexity).

The Language of CONCEPTBASE as View Language

In (Buchheit *et al.* 1994) the query language $\mathcal{QL}$ was defined, which is derived from the deductive object-oriented database system CONCEPTBASE under development at the University of Aachen. In $\mathcal{QL}$ roles are formed with all the constructs of Table 2, and concepts are formed according to the syntax rule:

$$C, D \longrightarrow A \mid \top \mid \{a\} \mid C \sqcap D \mid \exists R.C \mid \exists Q \doteq R.$$

Note that all concepts in $\mathcal{QL}$ correspond to existentially quantified formulas. We feel that most practical queries are of this form and do not involve universal quantification. In (Buchheit *et al.* 1994) it has been shown that view subsumption in $\mathcal{QL}$ can be computed in polynomial time w.r.t. combined complexity. We generalized this result.

Theorem 1 *With $\mathcal{SL}$ as schema language and $\mathcal{QL}$ as view language, instance checking is in PTIME w.r.t. combined complexity.*

This result illustrates the benefits of the new architecture because by restricting universal quantification to the schema and existential quantification to views we can have both without losing tractability. We proved that for the extension of $\mathcal{SL}$ by the construct $\exists P.A$, the combined complexity of view subsumption becomes NP-hard (whereas the schema complexity remains PTIME). From the results in (Donini *et al.* 1992a) it follows that adding universal quantification to $\mathcal{QL}$ would make view subsumption NP-hard.

The Language of KRIS as View Language

The system KRIS, under development at DFKI, provides as its core the expressive language $\mathcal{ALCN}$, which is defined by the following syntax rule:

$$C, D \longrightarrow A \mid C \sqcap D \mid C \sqcup D \mid \neg C \mid$$
$$\forall P.C \mid \exists P.C \mid (\geq n\ P) \mid (\leq n\ P).$$

The complexity of reasoning with $\mathcal{ALCN}$ is known: Subsumption between $\mathcal{ALCN}$-concepts has been proved PSPACE-complete in (Hollunder, Nutt, & Schmidt-Schauß 1990) and instance checking w.r.t. an acyclic TBox and an ABox has recently been proved PSPACE-complete too in (Hollunder 1993). For the combination of $\mathcal{SL}$ and $\mathcal{ALCN}$ in our architecture, we have the following result:

Theorem 2 *With $\mathcal{SL}$ as schema language and $\mathcal{ALCN}$ as view language, view subsumption and instance checking are PSPACE-complete problems w.r.t. combined complexity and PTIME problems w.r.t. schema complexity.*

We conclude that a simple schema with cycles can be added to systems like KRIS without changing the complexity of reasoning. However, if $\mathcal{ALCN}$ is also used as the schema language, then schema complexity alone is EXPTIME-hard (Buchheit, Donini, & Schaerf 1993).

The Language of CLASSIC as View Language

Finally, we study the concept language of the CLASSIC system as view language. CLASSIC has been developed at Bell Labs and is used in several applications. We refer to this language as $\mathcal{CL}$.

In CLASSIC individuals are treated in a special way (see Borgida & Patel-Schneider 1993), which we capture by the following syntax and conventions: Individuals are represented by *individual concepts* $B_1, \ldots, B_n$

that appear neither in the schema nor in the left-hand side of a definition and that are interpreted as mutually disjoint sets. Then the construct $(\text{one-of } B_1 \ldots B_n)$ of CLASSIC can be modeled by a disjunction $B_1 \sqcup \cdots \sqcup B_n$ of individual concepts. The construct $(\text{fills } P\ B)$ can be interpreted as a particular case of existential quantification, which we write as $\exists P.B$. The **same-as** construct $p \downarrow q$, which expresses agreement of chains p, q of functional roles, can be modeled by a combination of $\mathcal{SL}$ schema axioms and our existential agreement. Now, the syntax of $\mathcal{CL}$ is the following:

$$C, D \longrightarrow A \mid C \sqcap D \mid \forall P.C \mid (\leq n\,P) \mid (\geq n\,P) \mid$$
$$B_1 \sqcup \cdots \sqcup B_k \mid \exists P.B \mid p \downarrow q.$$

Theorem 3 *With $\mathcal{SL}$ as schema language and $\mathcal{CL}$ as view language, view subsumption and instance checking are problems in PTIME w.r.t. combined complexity.*

This shows that adding cyclic schema information does not endanger the tractability of reasoning with CLASSIC, which was one of the main concerns of the CLASSIC designers (Borgida *et al.* 1989). Note that adding the **same-as** construct to $\mathcal{SL}$ makes view subsumption undecidable (Nebel 1991).

Conclusion

We have proposed to replace the traditional TBox in a terminological system by two components: a schema, where primitive concepts describing frame-like structures are introduced, and a view part that contains defined concepts. We feel that this architecture reflects adequately the way terminological systems are used in most applications.

We also think that this distinction can clarify the discussion about the semantics of cycles. Given the different functionalities of the schema and view part, we propose that cycles in the schema are interpreted with descriptive semantics while for cycles in the view part a definitional semantics should be adopted.

In three case studies we have shown that the revised architecture yields a better tradeoff between expressivity and the complexity of reasoning.

The schema language we have introduced might be sufficient in many cases. Sometimes, however, one might want to impose more integrity constraints on primitive concepts than those which can be expressed in it. We see two solutions to this problem: either enrich the language and have to pay by a more costly reasoning process, or treat such constraints in a passive way by only verifying them for the objects in the knowledge base. The second alternative can be given a logical semantics in terms of epistemic operators (see Donini *et al.* 1992b).

References

Baader, F., and Hollunder, B. 1991. A terminological knowledge representation system with complete inference algorithm. *Proc. PDK-91*, LNAI, 67–86.

Baader, F. 1990. Terminological cycles in KL-ONE-based knowledge representation languages. *Proc. AAAI-90*, 621–626.

Borgida, A., and Patel-Schneider, P. F. 1993. A semantics and complete algorithm for subsumption in the CLASSIC description logic. Submitted.

Borgida, A.; Brachman, R. J.; McGuinness, D. L.; and Alperin Resnick, L. 1989. CLASSIC: A structural data model for objects. *Proc. ACM SIGMOD*, 59–67.

Buchheit, M.; Jeusfeld, M. A.; Nutt, W.; and Staudt, M. 1994. Subsumption between queries to object-oriented databases. *Information Systems* 19(1):33–54.

Buchheit, M.; Donini, F. M.; and Schaerf, A. 1993. Decidable reasoning in terminological knowledge representation systems. *Journal of Artificial Intelligence Research* 1:109–138.

Donini, F. M.; Hollunder, B.; Lenzerini, M.; Marchetti Spaccamela, A.; Nardi, D.; and Nutt, W. 1992a. The complexity of existential quantification in concept languages. *Artificial Intelligence* 53:309–327.

Donini, F. M.; Lenzerini, M.; Nardi, D.; Nutt, W.; and Schaerf, A. 1992b. Adding epistemic operators to concept languages. *Proc. KR-92*, 342–353.

Donini, F. M.; Lenzerini, M.; Nardi, D.; and Schaerf, A. 1994. Deduction in concept languages: From subsumption to instance checking. *Journal of Logic and Computation* 4(92–93):1–30.

Hollunder, B.; Nutt, W.; and Schmidt-Schauß, M. 1990. Subsumption algorithms for concept description languages. *Proc. ECAI-90*, 348–353.

Hollunder, B. 1993. How to reduce reasoning to satisfiability checking of concepts in the terminological system KRIS. Submitted.

Jarke, M. 1992. ConceptBase V3.1 User Manual. Aachener Informatik-Berichte 92-17, RWTH Aachen.

D. S. Johnson. 1990. A catalog of complexity classes. *Handbook of Theoretical Computer Science*, volume A, chapter 2.

Lenzerini, M., and Schaerf, A. 1991. Concept languages as query languages. *Proc. AAAI-91*, 471–476.

Nebel, B. 1990. Terminological reasoning is inherently intractable. *Artificial Intelligence* 43:235–249.

Nebel, B. 1991. Terminological cycles: Semantics and computational properties. In Sowa, J. F., ed., *Principles of Semantic Networks*. Morgan Kaufmann, Los Altos. 331–361.

Schaerf, A. 1993. On the complexity of the instance checking problem in concept languages with existential quantification. *Journal of Intelligent Information Systems* 2:265–278.

Schild, K. 1994. Terminological cycles and the propositional μ-calculus. *Proc. KR-94*.

Vardi, M. 1982. The complexity of relational query languages. *Proc. STOC-82*, 137–146.

Boosting the correspondence between description logics and propositional dynamic logics

Giuseppe De Giacomo and **Maurizio Lenzerini**
Dipartimento di Informatica e Sistemistica
Università di Roma "La Sapienza"
Via Salaria 113, 00198 Roma, Italia
{degiacom,lenzerini}@assi.dis.uniroma1.it

Abstract

One of the main themes in the area of Terminological Reasoning has been to identify description logics (DLs) that are both very expressive and decidable. A recent paper by Schild showed that this issue can be profitably addressed by relying on a correspondence between DLs and propositional dynamic logics (PDL). However Schild left open three important problems, related to the translation into PDLs of functional restrictions on roles (both direct and inverse), number restrictions, and assertions on individuals. The work reported in this paper presents a solution to these problems. The results have a twofold significance. From the standpoint of DLs, we derive decidability and complexity results for some of the most expressive logics appeared in the literature, and from the standpoint of PDLs, we derive a general methodology for the representation of several forms of program determinism and for the specification of partial computations.

Introduction

The research in Artificial Intelligence and Computer Science has always paid special attention to formalisms for the structured representation of information. In Artificial Intelligence, the investigation of such formalisms began with semantic networks and frames, which have been influential for many formalisms proposed in the areas of knowledge representation, data bases, and programming languages, and developed towards formal logic-based languages, that will be called here *description logics*[1] (DLs). Generally speaking, DLs represent knowledge in terms of objects (individuals) grouped into classes (concepts), and offer structuring mechanisms for both characterizing the relevant properties of classes in terms of relations (roles), and establishing several interdependencies among classes (e.g. is-a).

Two main advantages in using structured formalisms for knowledge representation were advocated, namely, epistemological adequacy, and computational effectiveness. In the last decade, many efforts have been devoted to an analysis of these two aspects. In particular, starting with (Brachman & Levesque 1984), the research on the computational complexity of the reasoning tasks associated with DLs has shown that in order to ensure decidability and/or efficiency of reasoning in all cases, one must renounce to some of the expressive power (Levesque & Brachman 1987, Nebel 1988, Nebel 1990a, Donini et al. 1991a, Donini et al. 1991b, Donini et al. 1992). These results have led to a debate on the trade-off between expressive power of representation formalisms and worst-case efficiency of the associated reasoning tasks. This issue has been one of the main themes in the area of DLs, and has led to at least four different approaches to the design of knowledge representation systems.

- In the first approach, the main goal of a DL is to offer powerful mechanisms for structuring knowledge, as well as sound and complete reasoning procedures, while little attention has to be paid to the (worst-case) computational complexity of the reasoning procedures. Systems like OMEGA (Attardi & Simi 1981), LOOM (MacGregor 1991) and KL-ONE (Brachman & Schmolze 1985), can be considered as following this approach.

- The second approach advocates a careful design of the DLs so as to offer as much expressive power as possible while retaining the possibility of sound, complete, and efficient (often polynomial in the worst case) inference procedures. Much of the research on CLASSIC (Brachman et al. 1991) follows this approach.

- The third approach, similarly to the first one, advocates very expressive languages, but, in order to achieve efficiency, accepts incomplete reasoning procedures. No general consensus exists on what kind of incompleteness is acceptable. Perhaps, the most interesting attempts are those resorting to a non-standard semantics for characterizing the form of incompleteness (Patel-Schneider 1987, Borgida & Patel-Schneider 1993, Donini et al. 1992).

---

[1] Terminological logics, and concept languages are other possible names.

- Finally, the fourth approach is based on what we can call "the expressiveness and decidability thesis", and aims at defining DLs that are both very expressive and decidable, i.e. designed in such a way that sound, complete, and terminating procedures exist for the associated reasoning tasks. Great attention is given in this approach to the complexity analysis for the various sublogics, so as to devise suitable optimization techniques and to single out tractable subcases. This approach is the one followed in the design of KRIS (Baader & Hollunder 1991).

The work presented in this paper adheres to the fourth approach, and aims at both identifying the most expressive DLs with decidable associated decision problems, and characterizing the computational complexity of reasoning in powerful DLs. In order to clearly describe this approach, let us point out that by "very expressive DL" we mean:

1. The logic offers powerful constructs in order to form concept and role descriptions. Besides the constructs corresponding to the usual boolean connectives (union, intersection, complement), and existential and universal quantification on roles, three important types of construct must be mentioned, namely, those for building complex role descriptions, those for expressing functional restrictions (i.e. that a role is functional for a given concept), and those for expressing number restrictions (a generalization of functional restrictions stating the minimum and the maximum number of links between instances of classes and instances of roles).

2. Besides the possibility of building sophisticated class descriptions, the logic provides suitable mechanisms for stating necessary and/or sufficient conditions for the objects to belong to the extensions of the classes. The basic mechanism for this feature is the so-called inclusion assertion, stating that every instance of a class is also an instance of another class. Much of the work done in DLs assumes that all the knowledge on classes is expressed through the use of class descriptions, and rules out the possibility of using this kind of assertions (note the power of assertions vanishes with the usual assumption of acyclicity of class definitions).

3. The logic allows one to assert properties of single individuals, in terms of the so-called membership assertions. Two membership assertions are taken into account, one for stating that an object is an instance of a given class, and another one for stating that two objects are related to by means of a given role.

Note that, among the constructs for role description, the one for inverse of roles has a special importance, in particular because it makes DLs powerful enough to subsume most frame-based representation systems, semantic data models and object-oriented database models proposed in the literature. Also, functional restrictions on atomic roles and their inverse are essential for real world modeling, specially because the combined use of functional restrictions and inverse of atomic roles allows n-ary relations to be correctly represented.

Two main approaches have been developed following the "expressiveness and decidability thesis". The first approach relies on the tableau-based technique proposed in (Schmidt-Schauß & Smolka 1991, Donini et al. 1991a), and led to the identification of a decision procedure for a logic which fully covers points (2) and (3) above, and only partially point (1) in that it does not include the construct for inverse roles (Buchheit, Donini, & Schaerf 1993). The second approach is based on the work by Schild, which singled out an interesting correspondence between DLs and several propositional dynamic logics (PDL), which are modal logics specifically designed for reasoning about program schemes. The correspondence is based on the similarity between the interpretation structures of the two logics: at the extensional level, objects in DLs correspond to states in PDLs, whereas connections between two objects correspond to state transitions. At the intensional level, classes correspond to propositions, and roles correspond to programs. The correspondence is extremely useful for at least two reasons. On one hand, it makes clear that reasoning about assertions on classes is equivalent to reasoning about dynamic logic formulae. On the other hand, the large body of research on decision procedures in PDL (see, for example, Kozen & Tiuryn 1990) can be exploited in the setting of DLs, and, on the converse, the various works on tractability/intractability of DLs (see, for example, Donini et al. 1991b) can be used in the setting of PDL.

However, in order to fully exploit this correspondence, we need to solve at least three problems left open in (Schild 1991), concerning how to fit functional restrictions (on both atomic roles and their inverse), number restrictions, and assertions on individuals, respectively, into the correspondence. Note that these problems refer to points (1) and (3) above.

In this paper we present a solution to each of the three problems, for several very expressive DLs. The solution is based on a particular methodology, which we believe has its own value: the inference in DLs is formulated in the setting of PDL, and in order to represent functional restrictions, number restrictions and assertions on individuals, special "constraints" are added to the PDL formulae. The results have a twofold significance. From the standpoint of DLs, we derive decidability and complexity results for some of the most expressive languages appeared in the literature (the only language which is not subsumed by ours is the one studied in (Buchheit, Donini, & Schaerf 1993), whose expressive power is incomparable with respect to the DLs studied here), and from the standpoint of PDLs, we derive a general methodology for the representation of several forms of program determinism corresponding to functional[2] and number restrictions, and for the

---

[2] Note that no decidability results were known for a PDL

specification of partial computations (assertions on individuals).

The paper is organized as follows. In Section 2, we recall the basic notions of both DLs and PDLs. In Section 3, we present the result on functional restrictions, showing that Converse PDL is powerful enough to allow the representation of functional restrictions on both atomic roles and their inverse. In Section 4, we outline the generalization to the case of number restrictions, and in Section 5 we deal with the problem of representing assertions on individuals. In particular, we analyze two languages and show that reasoning in knowledge bases consisting on both assertions on classes and assertions on individuals in these two languages can be again reduced to satisfiability checking of particular PDL formulae. Finally, in Section 6, we present examples of modeling with the powerful and decidable DLs introduced in the paper, and outline possible extensions of our work. For the sake of brevity all proofs are omitted.

Preliminaries

We base our work on two logics, namely the DL $\mathcal{C}$, and the PDL $\mathcal{D}$, whose basic characteristics are recalled in this section.

The formation rules of $\mathcal{C}$ are specified by the following abstract syntax

$$
\begin{aligned}
C &\longrightarrow \top \mid \bot \mid A \mid \neg C \mid C_1 \sqcap C_2 \mid C_1 \sqcup C_2 \mid \\
&\quad C_1 \Rightarrow C_2 \mid \exists R.C \mid \forall R.C \\
R &\longrightarrow P \mid R_1 \sqcup R_2 \mid R_1 \circ R_2 \mid R^* \mid id(C)
\end{aligned}
$$

where A denotes an atomic concept, C (possibly with subscript) denotes a concept, P denotes an atomic role, and R (possibly with subscript) denotes a role. The semantics of concepts is the usual one: an interpretation $\mathcal{I}$ with domain $\Delta^{\mathcal{I}}$ interprets concepts as subsets of $\Delta^{\mathcal{I}}$ and roles as binary relations over $\Delta^{\mathcal{I}}$, in such a way that the meaning of the constructs is preserved (for example, $(C_1 \Rightarrow C_2)^{\mathcal{I}} = \{d \in \Delta^{\mathcal{I}} \mid d \notin C_1^{\mathcal{I}} \text{ or } d \in C_2^{\mathcal{I}}\}$, where $C^{\mathcal{I}}$ denotes the set of elements of $\Delta^{\mathcal{I}}$ assigned to C by $\mathcal{I}$). Note that $\mathcal{C}$ is a very expressive language, comprising the constructs for union of roles $R_1 \sqcup R_2$, chaining of roles $R_1 \circ R_2$, transitive closure of roles R^*, and the identity role $id(C)$ projected on C.

A $\mathcal{C}$-intensional knowledge base ($\mathcal{C}$-TBox) is defined as a finite set $\mathcal{K}$ of inclusion assertions of the form $C_1 \sqsubseteq C_2$, where C_1, C_2 are $\mathcal{C}$-concepts. The assertion $C_1 \sqsubseteq C_2$ is satisfied by an interpretation $\mathcal{I}$ if $C_1^{\mathcal{I}} \subseteq C_2^{\mathcal{I}}$, and $\mathcal{I}$ is a model of $\mathcal{K}$ if every assertion of $\mathcal{K}$ is satisfied by $\mathcal{I}$. A TBox $\mathcal{K}$ logically implies an assertion $C_1 \sqsubseteq C_2$, written $\mathcal{K} \models C_1 \sqsubseteq C_2$, if $C_1 \sqsubseteq C_2$ is satisfied by every model of $\mathcal{K}$.

As pointed out in (Schild 1991), there is a direct correspondence between $\mathcal{C}$ and a PDL, here called $\mathcal{D}$,

____

where both atomic programs and their converse can be made (locally) deterministic.

whose syntax is as follows:

$$
\begin{aligned}
\phi &\longrightarrow true \mid false \mid A \mid \neg\phi \mid \phi_1 \wedge \phi_2 \mid \phi_1 \vee \phi_2 \mid \\
&\quad \phi_1 \Rightarrow \phi_2 \mid <r>\phi \mid [r]\phi \\
r &\longrightarrow P \mid r_1 \cup r_2 \mid r_1; r_2 \mid r^* \mid \phi?
\end{aligned}
$$

where A denotes a propositional letter, ϕ (possibly with subscript) denotes a formula, P denotes an atomic program, and r (possibly with subscript) denotes a program. The semantics of $\mathcal{D}$ is based on the notion of structure, which is defined as a triple $M = (\mathcal{S}, \{\mathcal{R}_P\}, \Pi)$, where $\mathcal{S}$ denotes a set of states, $\{\mathcal{R}_P\}$ is a family of binary relations over $\mathcal{S}$, such that each atomic program P is given a meaning through $\mathcal{R}_P$, and Π is a mapping from $\mathcal{S}$ to propositional letters such that $\Pi(s)$ determines the letters that are true in the state s. Given M, the family $\{\mathcal{R}_P\}$ can be extended in the obvious way so as to include, for every program r, the corresponding relation $\mathcal{R}_r$ (for example, $\mathcal{R}_{r_1;r_2}$ is the composition of $\mathcal{R}_{r_1}$ and $\mathcal{R}_{r_2}$). For this reason, we often denote a structure by $(\mathcal{S}, \{\mathcal{R}_r\}, \Pi)$, where $\{\mathcal{R}_r\}$ includes a binary relations for every program (atomic or non-atomic). A structure M is called a model of a formula ϕ if there exists a state s in M such that $M, s \models \phi$. A formula ϕ is satisfiable if there exists a model of ϕ, unsatisfiable otherwise.

The correspondence between $\mathcal{C}$ and $\mathcal{D}$ is realized through a mapping δ from $\mathcal{C}$-concepts to $\mathcal{D}$-formulae, and from $\mathcal{C}$-roles to $\mathcal{D}$-programs. The mapping δ maps the constructs of $\mathcal{C}$ in the obvious way. For example:

$$
\begin{aligned}
\delta(A) &= A & \delta(\exists R.C) &= <\delta(R)>\delta(C) \\
\delta(P) &= P & \delta(R_1 \sqcup R_2) &= \delta(R_1) \cup \delta(R_2) \\
\delta(\neg C) &= \neg\delta(C) & \delta(R_1 \circ R_2) &= \delta(R_1); \delta(R_2) \\
\delta(R^*) &= \delta(R)^* & \delta(id(C)) &= \delta(C)?
\end{aligned}
$$

In the rest of this section, we introduce several notions and notations that will be used in the sequel. Some of them are concerned with extensions of $\mathcal{D}$ that include the construct r^-, denoting the converse of a program r (see Section 3).

The _Fisher-Ladner closure_ of a $\mathcal{D}$-formula Φ, denoted $CL(\Phi)$, is the least set F such that $\Phi \in F$ and such that (we assume $\vee, \Rightarrow, [\cdot]$ to be expressed by means of $\neg, \wedge, < \cdot >$ as usual):

$$
\begin{aligned}
\phi_1 \wedge \phi_2 \in F &\Rightarrow \phi_1, \phi_2 \in F, \\
\neg\phi \in F &\Rightarrow \phi \in F, \\
<r>\phi \in F &\Rightarrow \phi \in F, \\
<r_1; r_2>\phi \in F &\Rightarrow <r_1><r_2>\phi \in F, \\
<r_1 \cup r_2>\phi \in F &\Rightarrow <r_1>\phi, <r_2>\phi \in F, \\
<r^*>\phi \in F &\Rightarrow <r><r^*>\phi \in F, \\
<\phi'>\phi \in F &\Rightarrow \phi' \in F.
\end{aligned}
$$

Note that, the size of $CL(\Phi)$ is linear with respect to the size of Φ. The notion of Fisher-Ladner closure can be easily extended to formulae of other PDLs.

We introduce the notion of path in a structure M, which extends the one of _trajectory_ defined in (Ben-Ari, Halpern, & Pnueli 1982) in order to deal with the converse of an atomic programs. A *path* in a structure M is a sequence $(s_0, \ldots, s_q)$ of states of M, such that $(s_{i-1}, s_i) \in \mathcal{R}_a$ for some $a = P \mid P^-$, where $i = 1, \ldots, q$. The *length* of $(s_0, \ldots, s_q)$ is q. We inductively define the set of paths $Paths(r)$ of a program r in a structure M, as follows (we assume, without loss of generality, that in r all occurrences of the converse operator are moved all the way in):

$$
\begin{aligned}
Paths(a) &= \mathcal{R}_a \; (a = P \mid P^-), \\
Paths(r_1 \cup r_2) &= Paths(r_1) \cup Paths(r_2), \\
Paths(r_1; r_2) &= \{(s_0, \ldots, s_u, \ldots, s_q) \mid \\
&\qquad (s_0, \ldots, s_u) \in Paths(r_1) \text{ and} \\
&\qquad (s_u, \ldots, s_q) \in Paths(r_2)\}, \\
Paths(r^*) &= \{(s) \mid s \in \mathcal{S}\} \cup (\textstyle\bigcup_{i>0} Paths(r^i)), \\
Paths(\phi'?) &= \{(s) \mid M, s \models \phi'\}.
\end{aligned}
$$

We say that a path (s_0) in M *satisfies* a formula ϕ which is not of the form $< r > \phi'$, if $M, s_0 \models \phi$. We say that a path $(s_0, \ldots, s_q)$ in M *satisfies* a formula ϕ of the form $< r_1 > \cdots < r_l > \phi'$, where ϕ' is not of the form $< r' > \phi''$, if $M, s_q \models \phi'$ and $(s_0, \ldots s_q) \subseteq Paths(r_1; \cdots; r_l)$.

Finally, if a denotes the atomic program P (resp. the inverse of an atomic program P^-), then we write a^- to denote P^- (resp. P).

Functional restrictions

In this section, we study an extension of $\mathcal{C}$, called $\mathcal{CIF}$, which is obtained from $\mathcal{C}$ by adding both the role construct R^- and the concept construct $(\leq 1 \, a)$, where $a = P \mid P^-$. The meaning of the two constructs in an interpretation $\mathcal{I}$ is as follows:

$$
\begin{aligned}
(R^-)^{\mathcal{I}} &= \{(d_1, d_2) \mid (d_2, d_1) \in R^{\mathcal{I}}\}, \\
(\leq 1 \, a)^{\mathcal{I}} &= \{d \in \Delta^{\mathcal{I}} \mid \begin{array}{l} \text{there exists } \textit{at most one } d' \\ \text{such that} (d, d') \in a^{\mathcal{I}} \end{array} \}.
\end{aligned}
$$

The corresponding PDL will be called $\mathcal{DIF}$, and is obtained from $\mathcal{D}$ by adding the programs of the form r^-, and the formulae of the form $(\leq 1 \, a)$, where, again, $a = P \mid P^-$. The meaning of the two constructs in $\mathcal{DIF}$ can be easily derived by the semantics of $\mathcal{CIF}$. Observe that the r^- construct allows one to denote the converse of a program, and the $(\leq 1 \, a)$ construct allows the notion of local determinism for both atomic programs and their converse to be represented in PDL. With the latter construct, we can denote states from which the running of an atomic program (symmetrically, the converse of an atomic program) is deterministic, i.e., it leads to at most one state. It is easy to see that this possibility allows one to impose the so-called global determinism too, i.e., that certain atomic programs and converse of atomic programs are globally deterministic. Therefore, $\mathcal{DIF}$ subsumes the logic studied in (Vardi & Wolper 1986), called Converse Deterministic PDL, in which atomic programs (but not their converse) are globally deterministic.

From the point of view of DLs, as mentioned in the Introduction, the presence of inverse roles and of functional restrictions on both atomic roles and their inverse, makes $\mathcal{CIF}$ one of the most expressive DLs among those studied in the literature.

The correspondence between $\mathcal{CIF}$ and $\mathcal{DIF}$ is realized through the mapping δ described in Section 2, suitably extended in order to deal with inverse roles and functional restrictions. From δ we easily obtain the mapping δ^+ from $\mathcal{CIF}$-TBoxes to $\mathcal{DIF}$-formulae. In particular, if $\mathcal{K} = \{K_1, \cdots, K_n\}$ is a TBox in $\mathcal{CIF}$, and $P_1, \ldots, P_m$ are all atomic roles appearing in $\mathcal{K}$ then (we abbreviate $(P_1 \cup \cdots \cup P_m \cup P_1^- \cup \cdots \cup P_m^-)^*$ by $\mathbf{u}$, for notational convenience)

$$
\begin{aligned}
\delta^+(\mathcal{K}) &= [\mathbf{u}] \; \delta^+(\{K_1\}) \wedge \cdots \wedge \delta^+(\{K_n\}), \\
\delta^+(\{C_1 \sqsubseteq C_2\}) &= (\delta(C_1) \Rightarrow \delta(C_2)).
\end{aligned}
$$

Observe that $\delta^+(\mathcal{K})$ exploits the power of program constructs (union, converse, and transitive closure) and the "connected model property" of PDLs in order to represent inclusion assertions of DLs. Based on this correspondence, we can state the following: if $\mathcal{K}$ is a TBox, then $\mathcal{K} \models C_1 \sqsubseteq C_2$ (where atomic concepts and roles in C_1, C_2 are also in $\mathcal{K}$) iff the $\mathcal{DIF}$-formula

$$
\delta^+(\mathcal{K}) \wedge \delta(C_1) \wedge \delta(\neg C_2)
$$

is unsatisfiable. Note that the size of the above formula is polynomial with respect to the size of $\mathcal{K}, C_1$, and C_2.

Let $\mathcal{DI}$ be the PDL obtained from $\mathcal{D}$ by adding the r^- construct only. We are going to show that, for any $\mathcal{DIF}$-formula Φ, there is a $\mathcal{DI}$-formula, denoted $\gamma(\Phi)$, whose size is polynomial with respect to the size of Φ, and such that Φ is satisfiable iff $\gamma(\Phi)$ is satisfiable. Since satisfiability in $\mathcal{DI}$ is EXPTIME-complete, this ensures us that satisfiability in $\mathcal{DIF}$, and therefore logical implication for $\mathcal{CIF}$-TBoxes, are EXPTIME-complete too.[3] In what follows, we assume without loss of generality that Φ is in negation normal form (i.e., negation is pushed inside as much as possible). We define the *$\mathcal{DI}$-counterpart* $\gamma(\Phi)$ of a $\mathcal{DIF}$-formula Φ as the conjunction of two formulae, $\gamma(\Phi) = \gamma_1(\Phi) \wedge \gamma_2(\Phi)$, where:

- $\gamma_1(\Phi)$ is obtained from the original formula Φ by replacing each $(\leq 1 \, a)$ with a new propositional letter $A_{(\leq 1 \, a)}$, and each $\neg(\leq 1 \, a)$ with $(< a > H_{(\leq 1 \, a)}) \wedge (< a > \neg H_{(\leq 1 \, a)})$, where $H_{(\leq 1 \, a)}$ is, again, a new propositional letter.

- $\gamma_2(\Phi) = \gamma_2^1 \wedge \cdots \wedge \gamma_2^q$, with one conjunct γ_2^i of the form (we use the abbreviation $\mathbf{u}$ for $(P_1 \cup \cdots \cup P_m \cup P_1^- \cdots \cup P_m^-)^*$, where $P_1, \ldots, P_m$ are all the atomic roles appearing in Φ):

$$
[\mathbf{u}]((A_{(\leq 1 \, a)} \wedge < a > \phi) \Rightarrow [a]\phi)
$$

for every $A_{(\leq 1 \, a)}$ occurring in $\gamma_1(\Phi)$ and every $\phi \in CL(\gamma_1(\Phi))$.

---

[3] Indeed $\gamma(\delta^+(\mathcal{K}) \wedge \delta(C_1) \wedge \delta(\neg C_2))$ is the $\mathcal{DIF}$-formula corresponding to the implication problem $\mathcal{K} \models C_1 \sqsubseteq C_2$ for $\mathcal{CIF}$-TBoxes.

Intuitively $\gamma_2(\Phi)$ constrains the models M of $\gamma(\Phi)$ so that: for every state s of M, if $A_{(\leq 1\ a)}$ holds in s, and there is an a-transition from s to t_1 and an a-transition from s to t_2, then t_1 and t_2 are equivalent with respect to the formulae in $CL(\gamma_1(\Phi))$. We show that this allows us to actually collapse t_1 and t_2 into a single state. Note that the size of $\gamma(\Phi)$ is polynomial with respect to the size of Φ.

To prove that a $\mathcal{DIF}$-formula is satisfiable iff its $\mathcal{DI}$-counterpart is, we proceed as follows. Given a model $M = (\mathcal{S}, \{R_r\}, \Pi)$ of $\gamma(\Phi)$, we build a tree-like structure $M^t = (\mathcal{S}^t, \{R_r^t\}, \Pi^t)$ such that $M^t, root \models \gamma(\Phi)$ ($root \in \mathcal{S}^t$ is the root of the tree-structure), and the local determinism requirements are satisfied. From such M^t, one can easily derive a model $M_\mathcal{F}^t$ of Φ. In order to construct M^t we make use of the following notion. For each state s in M, we call by $ES(s)$ the smallest set of states in M such that

- $s \in ES(s)$, and

- if $s' \in ES(s)$, then for every s'' such that $(s', s'') \in \mathcal{R}_{a;A_{(\leq 1\ a^-)}?;a^-}$, $ES(s'') \subseteq ES(s)$.

The set $ES(s)$ is the set of states of M that are to be collapsed into a single state of M^t. Note that, by $\gamma_2(\Phi)$, all the states in $ES(s)$ satisfy the same formulae in $CL(\gamma_1(\Phi))$. The construction of M^t is done in three stages.

Stage 1. Let $<a_1>\psi_1, \ldots, <a_h>\psi_h$ be all the formulas of the form $<a>\phi'$ included in $CL(\Phi)$.[4] We consider an infinite h-ary tree $\mathcal{T}$ whose root is $root$ and such that every node x has h children $child_i(x)$, one for each formula $<a_i>\psi_i$ (we write $father(x)$ to denote the father of a node x). We define two partial mappings m and l: m maps nodes of $\mathcal{T}$ to states of M, and l is used to label the arcs of $\mathcal{T}$ by atomic programs, converse of atomic programs, or a special symbol 'undefined'. For the definition of m and l, we proceed level by level. Let $s \in \mathcal{S}$ be any state such that $M, s \models \gamma(\Phi)$. We put $m(root) = s$, and for all arcs corresponding to a formula $<a_i>\psi_i$ such that $M, s \models\, <a_i>\psi_i$ we put $l((root, child_i(root))) = a_i$. Suppose we have defined m and l up to level k, let x be a node at level $k+1$, and let $l((father(x), x)) = a_j$. Then $M, m(father(x)) \models\, <a_j>\psi_j$, and therefore, there exists a path $(s_0, s_1, \ldots, s_q)$, with $s_o = m(father(x))$ satisfying $<a_j>\psi_j$. Among the states in $ES(s_1)$ we choose a state t such that there exists a *minimal* path (i.e., a path with minimal length) from t satisfying ψ_j. We put $m(x) = t$ and for every $<a_i>\psi_i \in CL(\Phi)$ such that $M, t \models\, <a_i>\psi_i$ we put $l((x, child_i(x))) = a_i$.

Stage 2. We change the labelling l, proceeding again level by level. If $M, m(root) \models A_{(\leq 1\ a)}$, then for each arc $(root, child_i(root))$ labelled a, except for one randomly chosen, we put $l((root, child_i(root)) =$

---

[4]Notice that the formulas ψ_i may be of the form $<r>\phi$, and that $\psi_i \in CL(\Phi)$.

'undefined'. Assume we have modified l up to level k, and let x be a node at level $k+1$. Suppose $M, m(x) \models A_{(\leq 1\ a)}$. Then if $l((father(x), x)) = a^-$, for each arc $(x, child_i(x))$ labelled a, we put $l((x, child_i(x)) =$ 'undefined', otherwise (i.e. $l((father(x), x)) \neq a^-$) we put $l((x, child_i(x)) =$ 'undefined' for every arc $(x, child_i(x))$ labelled a, except for one randomly chosen.

Stage 3. For each P, let $\mathcal{R}'_P = \{(x, y) \in \mathcal{T} \mid l((x, y)) = P \text{ or } l((y, x)) = P^-\}$. We define the structure $M^t = (\mathcal{S}^t, \{R_r^t\}, \Pi^t)$ as follows: $\mathcal{S}^t = \{x \in \mathcal{T} \mid (root, x) \in (\bigcup_P(\mathcal{R}'_P \cup \mathcal{R}'^-_P))^*\}$, $\mathcal{R}_P^t = \mathcal{R}'_P \cap (\mathcal{S}^t \times \mathcal{S}^t)$, and $\Pi^t(x) = \Pi(m(x))$ for all $x \in \mathcal{S}^t$. From $\{\mathcal{R}_P^t\}$ we get all $\{\mathcal{R}_r^t\}$ as usual.

The basic property of M^t is stated in the following lemma.

Lemma 1 *Let Φ be a $\mathcal{DIF}$-formula, M a model of $\gamma(\Phi)$, and M^t a structure derived from M as specified above. Then, for every formula $\phi \in CL(\gamma_1(\Phi))$ and every $x \in \mathcal{S}^t$, $M^t, x \models \phi$ iff $M, m(x) \models \phi$.*

Once we have obtained M^t, we can define a new structure $M_\mathcal{F}^t = (\mathcal{S}_\mathcal{F}^t, \{\mathcal{R}_{\mathcal{F}r}^t\}, \Pi_\mathcal{F}^t)$ where, $\mathcal{S}_\mathcal{F}^t = \mathcal{S}^t$, $\{\mathcal{R}_{\mathcal{F}r}^t\} = \{\mathcal{R}_r^t\}$, and $\Pi_\mathcal{F}^t(x) = \Pi^t(x) - \{A_{(\leq 1\ a)}, H_{(\leq 1\ a)}\}$ for each $x \in \mathcal{S}_\mathcal{F}^t$. The structure $M_\mathcal{F}^t$ has the following property.

Lemma 2 *Let Φ be a $\mathcal{DIF}$-formula, and let $M^t, M_\mathcal{F}^t$ be derived from a model M of $\gamma(\Phi)$ as specified above. Then $M^t, root \models \gamma_1(\Phi)$ implies $M_\mathcal{F}^t, root \models \Phi$.*

Considering that every model of Φ can be easily transformed in a model of $\gamma(\Phi)$ we can state the main result of this section.

Theorem 3 *A $\mathcal{DIF}$-formula Φ is satisfiable iff its $\mathcal{DI}$-counterpart $\gamma(\Phi)$ is satisfiable.*

Corollary 4 *Satisfiability in $\mathcal{DIF}$ and logical implication for $\mathcal{CIF}$-TBoxes are EXPTIME-complete problems.*

Number restrictions

In this section, we briefly outline a method that allows us to polynomially encode number restrictions into $\mathcal{CIF}$. Let us call $\mathcal{CIN}$ the language obtained from $\mathcal{CIF}$ by adding the constructs $(\geq n\ a)$ and $(\leq n\ a)$ for number restrictions, where n is a non-negative integer, and $a := P \mid P^-$. The meaning of $(\geq n\ a)$ (resp. $(\leq n\ a)$) in an interpretation $\mathcal{I}$ is given by the set of individuals that are related to at least (at most) n instances of a.

Let $\mathcal{K}$ be a $\mathcal{CIN}$-TBox. We, first, introduce for each atomic role P in $\mathcal{K}$ a new primitive concept A_P and two atomic roles F_P and G_P, imposing that each individual in the class A_P is related to exactly one instance of F_P^- and G_P^-. In this way the original P can be represented by means of the role $F_P \circ id(A_P) \circ G_P^-$. Then we replace F_P by $f_P \circ id(A_P) \circ (f'_P \circ id(A_P))^*$ and G_P by $g_P \circ id(A_P) \circ (g'_P \circ id(A_P))^*$, making the atomic roles f_P, f'_P, g_P, g'_P and their inverse, globally functional, and requiring that no individual is linked to others by means of both f_P^- and f'^-_P, or g_P^- and g'^-_P. In this way the concept $(\leq n\, P)$ can be obtained simply by imposing that there are at most n states in the chain $f_P \circ id(A_P) \circ (f'_P \circ id(A_P))^*$, and the concept $(\leq n\, P^-)$ can be obtained by imposing that there are at most n states in the chain $g_P \circ id(A_P) \circ (g'_P \circ id(A_P))^*$. These constraints are easily expressible in $\mathcal{CIF}$. Analogous considerations hold both for $(\geq n\, a)$ and for qualified number restrictions, where a qualified number restriction is a concept of the form $(\leq n\, a.C)$ (resp. $(\geq n\, a.C)$), which is interpreted as the set of individuals that are related to at most (resp. at least) n instances of C by means of a.

Membership assertions

In this section, we study reasoning involving knowledge on single individuals expressed in terms of membership assertions. Given an alphabet $\mathcal{O}$ of symbols for individuals, a membership assertion is of one of the following forms:

$$C(\alpha_1), \quad R(\alpha_1, \alpha_2)$$

where C is a concept, R is a role, and α_1, α_2 belong to $\mathcal{O}$. The semantics of such assertions is stated as follows. An interpretation $\mathcal{I}$ is extended so as to assign to each $\alpha \in \mathcal{O}$ an element $\alpha^\mathcal{I} \in \Delta^\mathcal{I}$ in such a way that different elements are assigned to different symbols in $\mathcal{O}$. Then, $\mathcal{I}$ satisfies $C(\alpha)$ if $\alpha^\mathcal{I} \in C^\mathcal{I}$, and $\mathcal{I}$ satisfies $R(\alpha_1, \alpha_2)$ if $(\alpha_1^\mathcal{I}, \alpha_2^\mathcal{I}) \in R^\mathcal{I}$. An extensional knowledge base (ABox) $\mathcal{M}$ is a finite set of membership assertions, and an interpretation $\mathcal{I}$ is called a model of $\mathcal{M}$ if $\mathcal{I}$ satisfies every assertion in $\mathcal{M}$.

A knowledge base is a pair $\mathcal{B} = (\mathcal{K}, \mathcal{M})$, where $\mathcal{K}$ is a TBox, and $\mathcal{M}$ is a ABox. An interpretation $\mathcal{I}$ is called a model of $\mathcal{B}$ if it is a model of both $\mathcal{K}$ and $\mathcal{M}$. $\mathcal{B}$ is satisfiable if it has a model, and $\mathcal{B}$ logically implies an assertion β ($\mathcal{B} \models \beta$), where β is either an inclusion or a membership assertion, if every model of $\mathcal{B}$ satisfies β. Since logical implication can be reformulated in terms of unsatisfiability (e.g. if $\beta = C(\alpha)$, then $\mathcal{B} \models \beta$ iff $\mathcal{B} \cup \{\neg C(\alpha)\}$ is unsatisfiable), we only need a procedure for checking satisfiability of a knowledge base.

It is worth noting that, from the point of view of PDLs, an ABox is a sort of specification of partial computations, and that no technique is known for integrating such a form of specification with PDLs' formulae.

We study the satisfiability problem for knowledge bases expressed in two extensions of the basic language $\mathcal{C}$. The first extension regards the language $\mathcal{CF}$, obtained from $\mathcal{C}$ by adding the construct $(\leq 1\, P)$. We show that satisfiability of a $\mathcal{CF}$-knowledge base $\mathcal{B}$ can be polynomially reduced to satisfiability of a $\mathcal{DF}$-formula $\varphi(\mathcal{B})$, where $\mathcal{DF}$ is the PDL obtained from $\mathcal{D}$ by including the construct $(\leq 1\, P)$.

We start by defining $\varphi_0(\mathcal{B})$ to be the $\mathcal{DF}$-formula resulting from the conjunction of the following formulae

(there is a new letter A_i in $\varphi_0(\mathcal{B})$ for each individual α_i in $\mathcal{B}$): for every individual α_i, $A_i \Rightarrow \wedge_{j \neq i} \neg A_j$; for every membership assertion of the form $C(\alpha_i)$, $A_i \Rightarrow \delta(C)$ (δ is the mapping introduced in Section 2); for every membership assertion of the form $R(\alpha_i, \alpha_j)$, $A_i \Rightarrow\, < R > A_j$; for every inclusion assertion $C_1 \sqsubseteq C_2$ in $\mathcal{K}$, $\delta(C_1) \Rightarrow \delta(C_2)$.

Let $create$ be a new atomic program, and $\mathbf{u}$ an abbreviation for $(P_1 \cup \ldots \cup P_m)^*$, where $P_1, \ldots, P_m$ are all the atomic roles in $\mathcal{B}$. We define the $\mathcal{DF}$-counterpart of $\mathcal{B}$ as $\varphi(\mathcal{B}) = \varphi_1(\mathcal{B}) \wedge \varphi_2(\mathcal{B})$, where:

- $\varphi_1(\mathcal{B}) = \varphi_1^1(\mathcal{B}) \wedge \cdots \wedge \varphi_1^n(\mathcal{B}) \wedge [create]([\mathbf{u}]\varphi_0(\mathcal{B}))$, with one $\varphi_1^i(\mathcal{B}) =\, < create > A_i$ for each individual α_i in $\mathcal{B}$.

- $\varphi_2(\mathcal{B})$ is the conjunction of the following formulae:

  - For all A_i, for all $\phi \in CL([\mathbf{u}]\varphi_0(\mathcal{B}))$:

  $$[create](< \mathbf{u} > (A_i \wedge \phi) \Rightarrow [\mathbf{u}](A_i \Rightarrow \phi)). \quad (1)$$

  - For all A_i, for all $\phi \in CL([\mathbf{u}]\varphi_0(\mathcal{B}))$, for all programs $r \in CL([\mathbf{u}]\varphi_0(\mathcal{B}))$:

  $$[create](<\mathbf{u}> (A_i \wedge < r_{\neg ind} > \phi) \Rightarrow [\mathbf{u}](A_i \Rightarrow < r_{\neg ind} > \phi)), \quad (2)$$

  where $r_{\neg ind}$ denotes the program obtained from the program r by chaining the test $(\wedge_{j \neq i} A_j)$? after each atomic program in r.

  - For all A_i, A_j, for all programs $r' \in Pre(r)$, $r \in CL([\mathbf{u}]\varphi_0(\mathcal{B}))$:

  $$[create](<\mathbf{u}> (A_i \wedge < r'_{\neg ind} > A_j) \Rightarrow [\mathbf{u}](A_i \Rightarrow < r'_{\neg ind} > A_j)), \quad (3)$$

  where $Pre(r)$ for a program r, is defined inductively as follows (ε is the empty sequence of programs): $Pre(P) = \{\varepsilon\}$; $Pre(r_1; r_2) = \{r_1; r'_2 \mid r'_2 \in Pre(r_2)\}$; $Pre(r_1 \cup r_2) = Pre(r_1) \cup Pre(r_2)$; $Pre(r^*) = \{r^*; r' \mid r' \in Pre(r)\}$; $Pre(\phi?) = \{\varepsilon\}$.[5]

The role of (1),(2) and (3) is to allow us to collapse all the states where a certain A_i holds, so as to be able to transform them into a single state corresponding to the individual α_i.

In the following we call states t of a model M of $\varphi(\mathcal{B})$, *individual-aliases* of an individual α_i iff $M, t \models A_i$. The formulae (2) and (3) allow us to prove the technical lemma below.

Lemma 5 *Let M be a model of $\varphi(\mathcal{B})$, let t be an individual-alias of α_i, and let $< r > \phi \in CL([\mathbf{u}]\varphi_0(\mathcal{B}))$. If there is a path from t that satisfies $< r > \phi$, containing N individual-aliases $t_1, \ldots, t_N$ of $\alpha_1, \ldots, \alpha_N$ respectively, then from every individual-alias t' of α_i in M, there is a path that satisfies $< r > \phi$, containing N individual-aliases $t'_1, \ldots, t'_N$ for $\alpha_1, \ldots, \alpha_N$ (in the same order as $t_1, \ldots, t_N$).*

---

[5] Notice that $< \varepsilon > \phi \equiv \phi$ and $[\varepsilon]\phi \equiv \phi$.

Given a model $M = (\mathcal{S}, \{\mathcal{R}_r\}, \Pi)$ of $\varphi(\mathcal{B})$, we can obtain a new model $M' = (\mathcal{S}', \{\mathcal{R}'_r\}, \Phi')$ of $\varphi(\mathcal{B})$ in which there is exactly one individual-alias, for each individual in $\mathcal{B}$. Let $s \in \mathcal{S}$ be such that $M, s \models \varphi(\mathcal{B})$. For every individual α_i, we randomly choose, among its individual-aliases x such that $(s, x) \in \mathcal{R}_{create}$, a distinguished one denoted by s_{α_i}. We define a set of relations $\{\mathcal{R}''_P\} \cup \{\mathcal{R}''_{create}\}$ as follows: $\mathcal{R}''_{create} = \{(s, s_{\alpha_i}) \in \mathcal{R}_{create} \mid \alpha_i$ is an individual$\}$, and $\mathcal{R}''_P = (\mathcal{R}_P - \{(x, y) \in \mathcal{R}_P \mid M, y \models A_j$ for some $A_j\}) \cup \{(x, s_{\alpha_j}) \mid (x, y) \in \mathcal{R}_P$ and $M, y \models A_j$ for some $A_j\}$. The structure M' is defined as: $\mathcal{S}' = \{x \in \mathcal{S} \mid (s, x) \in ((\bigcup_P \mathcal{R}''_P) \cup \mathcal{R}''_{create})^*\}$, $\mathcal{R}'_P = \mathcal{R}''_P \cap (\mathcal{S}' \times \mathcal{S}')$ and $\mathcal{R}'_{create} = \mathcal{R}''_{create} \cap (\mathcal{S}' \times \mathcal{S}')$, and $\Pi'(x) = \Pi(x)$, for each state $x \in \mathcal{S}'$ (from $\{\mathcal{R}'_P\}$ and $\mathcal{R}'_{create}$ we get $\{\mathcal{R}'_r\}$ as usual). Observe that the transformation from M to M' *does not change* the number of "out-going edges" for those states of M which are also states of M'. The following two lemmas concern M'.

Lemma 6 *Let M be a model of $\varphi(\mathcal{B})$, and M' a structure derived from M as specified above. Then for every formula $\phi \in CL(\varphi_1(\mathcal{B}))$, for every state x of M': $M, x \models \phi$ iff $M', x \models \phi$.*

Lemma 7 *Let M be a model of $\varphi(\mathcal{B})$ such that $M, s \models \varphi(\mathcal{B})$, and let M' be a structure derived from M as specified above. Then $M', s \models \varphi(\mathcal{B})$.*

We can now state the main theorem on reasoning in $\mathcal{CF}$-knowledge bases.

Theorem 8 *A $\mathcal{CF}$-knowledge base $\mathcal{B}$ is satisfiable iff its $\mathcal{DF}$-counterpart $\varphi(\mathcal{B})$ is satisfiable.*

Corollary 9 *Satisfiability and logical implication for $\mathcal{CF}$-knowledge bases (TBox and ABox) are EXPTIME-complete problems.*

The second extension regards the language $\mathcal{CI}$, obtained from $\mathcal{C}$ by adding the construct for inverse of roles. Analogously to the case of $\mathcal{CF}$, satisfiability of a $\mathcal{CI}$-knowledge base $\mathcal{B}$ can be polynomially reduced to satisfiability of a $\mathcal{DI}$-formula $\eta(\mathcal{B})$, where $\mathcal{DI}$ is the PDL obtained from $\mathcal{D}$ by allowing converse programs. Let $\eta_0(\mathcal{B})$ be a $\mathcal{DI}$-formula defined similarly to $\varphi_0(\mathcal{B})$ in the case of $\mathcal{CF}$, $create$ a new atomic program, and $\mathbf{u}$ an abbreviation for $(P_1 \cup \ldots \cup P_m \cup P_1^- \cup \ldots \cup P_m^-)^*$, where $P_1, \ldots, P_m$ are all the atomic roles in $\mathcal{B}$. We define the $\mathcal{DI}$-counterpart of $\mathcal{B}$ as $\eta(\mathcal{B}) = \eta_1(\mathcal{B}) \wedge \eta_2(\mathcal{B})$, where:

- $\eta_1(\mathcal{B}) = \eta_1^1(\mathcal{B}) \wedge \cdots \wedge \eta_1^n(\mathcal{B}) \wedge [create]([\mathbf{u}]\eta_0(\mathcal{B}))$, with each $\eta_1^i(\mathcal{B}) = < create > A_i$ for each individual α_i in $\mathcal{B}$.

- $\eta_2(\mathcal{B}) = \eta_2^1(\mathcal{B}) \wedge \cdots \wedge \eta_2^p(\mathcal{B})$, where we have one $\eta_2^i(\mathcal{B})$ of the form

$$[create](< \mathbf{u} > (A_i \wedge \phi) \Rightarrow [\mathbf{u}](A_i \Rightarrow \phi)), \qquad (4)$$

for each A_i, and for each $\phi \in CL([\mathbf{u}]\eta_0(\mathcal{B}))$.

Again, the role of (4) is to make all the states where a certain A_i holds, equivalent, so as to be able to collapse

them into a single state corresponding to the individual α_i. By reasoning similarly to the case of $\mathcal{CF}$, we derive the result below.[6]

Theorem 10 *A $\mathcal{CI}$-knowledge base $\mathcal{B}$ is satisfiable iff its $\mathcal{DI}$-counterpart $\eta(\mathcal{B})$ is satisfiable.*

Corollary 11 *Satisfiability and logical implication for $\mathcal{CI}$-knowledge bases (TBox and ABox) are EXPTIME-complete problems.*

We remark that, in establishing the satisfiability of $\mathcal{CF}$-knowledge bases, the satisfiability of $\mathcal{CI}$-knowledge bases, and the satisfiability of a $\mathcal{CIF}$ concepts, we resorted to a transformation of their models. Unfortunately the kind of transformation used in the first two cases cannot be composed with the one used in the latter. This results in the impossibility of extending the constructions carried out in this section to $\mathcal{CIF}$-knowledge bases.

Discussion and conclusion

The work by Schild on the correspondence between DLs and PDLs provides an invaluable tool for devising decision procedures for very expressive DLs. In this paper we included into this correspondence, notions such as functional restrictions on both atomic roles and their converse, number restrictions, and assertions on individuals, that typically arise in modeling structured knowledge. We made use of the correspondence to determine decision procedures and establish the decidability and the complexity of some of the most expressive DLs appeared in the literature. It is worth noticing that the PDLs defined in this paper are novel and of interest in their own right.

Space limitations have prevented us to demonstrate the full power of the results presented. We mention here that they form the basis to derive suitable decision procedures both for extensions of $\mathcal{CIF}$ that include n-ary relation and qualified number restrictions, and for knowledge bases (TBox and ABox) based on $\mathcal{CF}$ extended with qualified number restrictions. Moreover, some of these results can also be formulated in the setting of the μ-calculus, that has been used to model in single framework terminological cycles interpreted according to Least and Greatest Fixpoint Semantics (Nebel 1991, Schild 1994, De Giacomo & Lenzerini 1994).

In concluding the paper, we would like to show two salient examples of use of the powerful DLs introduced here. They concern the definition of concepts for the representation of lists, and n-ary trees. Consider the following inductive definition of list: *nil* is a *list*; a *node* that has exactly one successor that is a *list*, is a *list*; nothing else in a *list*. This is equivalent to define a list as a chain (of any finite length) of nodes that terminates with nil. Assuming *node* and *nil* to be concepts

---

[6]The proof is much simpler in this case, witness the absence of constraints analogous to (2) and (3) above.

of our language, we can denote the concept *list* as (we use $C_1 \doteq C_2$ as a shorthand for $C_1 \sqsubseteq C_2, C_2 \sqsubseteq C_1$):

$$list \doteq \exists(id(node \sqcap (\leq 1\ succ)) \circ succ)^*.nil$$

Similarly we can denote the class of (possibly infinite) n-ary trees as:

$$n\_tree \doteq \forall child^-.\bot \sqcap$$
$$\forall child^*.(node \sqcap (\leq 1\ child^-) \sqcap (\leq n\ child))$$

which defines a n_tree as a node having no father and at most n children, and such that all descendents are nodes having one father and at most n children.

Observe that, in order to fully capture the above concepts, we make use of inverse roles, functional restrictions on both atomic and inverse roles, and number restrictions.

References

Attardi, G., and Simi, M. 1981. Consistency and completeness of omega, a logic for knowledge representation. In Proceedings of the International Joint Conference on Artificial Intelligence, 504–510.

Baader, F., and Hollunder, B. 1991. A terminological knowledge representation system with complete inference algorithm. In Proceedings of the Workshop on Processing Declarative Knowledge, Lecture Notes in Artificial Intelligence, pages 67–86: Springer-Verlag.

Ben-Ari, M.; Halpern, J. Y.; and Pnueli, A. 1982. Deterministic propositional dynamic logic: Finite models, complexity, and completeness. *Journal of Computer and System Sciences*, 25:402–417.

Borgida, A., and Patel-Schneider, P. F. 1993. A semantics and complete algorithm for subsumption in the CLASSIC description logic. Forthcoming.

Brachman, R. J., and Levesque, H. J. 1984. The tractability of subsumption in frame-based description languages. In Proceedings of the Fourth National Conference on Artificial Intelligence, 34–37.

Brachman, R. J.; McGuinness, D. L.; Patel-Schneider, P. F.; Alperin Resnick, L.; and Borgida, A. 1991. Living with CLASSIC: when and how to use a KL-ONE-like language. In John F. Sowa, editor, *Principles of Semantic Networks*, 401–456: Morgan Kaufmann.

Brachman, R. J., and Schmolze J. G. 1985. An overview of the KL-ONE knowledge representation system. *Cognitive Science*, 9(2):171–216.

Buchheit M.; Donini F. M.; and Schaerf, A. 1993. Decidable reasoning in terminological knowledge representation systems. In Proceedings of the Thirteenth International Joint Conference on Artificial Intelligence, 704–709.

De Giacomo, G., and Lenzerini, M. 1994. Concept language with number restrictions and fixpoints, and its relationship with mu-calculus. In Proceedings of Eleventh European Conference on Artificial Intelligence.

Donini, F. M.; Hollunder, B.; Lenzerini M., Marchetti Spaccamela A.; Nardi, D.; and Nutt, W. 1992. The complexity of existential quantification in concept languages. *Artificial Intelligence*, 2–3:309–327.

Donini, F. M.; Lenzerini, M.; Nardi, D.; and Nutt, W. 1991a. The complexity of concept languages. In Proceedings of the Second International Conference on Principles of Knowledge Representation and Reasoning, 151–162.

Donini, F. M.; Lenzerini, M.; Nardi, D.; and Nutt, W. 1991b. Tractable concept languages. In Proceedings of the Twelfth International Joint Conference on Artificial Intelligence, 458–463.

Donini, F. M.; Lenzerini, M.; Nardi, D.; Nutt, W; and Schaerf, A. 1992. Adding epistemic operators to concept languages. In Proceedings of the Third International Conference on Principles of Knowledge Representation and Reasoning, 342–353.

Kozen, D., and Tiuryn, J. 1990. Logics of programs. In *Handbook of Theoretical Computer Science – Formal Models and Semantics*, 789–840: Elsevier.

Levesque, H. J., and Brachman, R. J. 1987. Expressiveness and tractability in knowledge representation and reasoning. *Computational Intelligence*, 3:78–93.

MacGregor, R. 1991. Inside the LOOM description classifier. *SIGART Bulletin*, 2(3):88–92.

Nebel, B. 1988. Computational complexity of terminological reasoning in BACK. *Artificial Intelligence*, 34(3):371–383.

Nebel, B. 1990. Terminological reasoning is inherently intractable. *Artificial Intelligence*, 43:235–249.

Nebel, B. 1991. Terminological cycles: Semantics and computational properties. In John F. Sowa, editor, *Principles of Semantic Networks*, 331–361: Morgan Kaufmann.

Patel-Schneider, P. F. 1987. A hybrid, decidable, logic-based knowledge representation system. *Computational Intelligence*, 3(2):64–77.

Schild, K. 1991. A correspondence theory for terminological logics: Preliminary report. In Proceedings of the Twelfth International Joint Conference on Artificial Intelligence, 466–471.

Schild, K. 1994. Terminological cycles and the propositional μ-calculus. In Proceedings of the Fourth International Conference on Knowledge Representation and Reasoning.

Schmidt-Schauß, M., and Smolka, G. 1991. Attributive concept descriptions with complements. *Artificial Intelligence*, 48(1):1–26.

Vardi, M. Y., and Wolper, P. 1986. Automata-theoretic techniques for modal logics of programs. *Journal of Computer and System Sciences*, 32:183–221.

A Description Classifier for the Predicate Calculus

Robert M. MacGregor

USC/Information Sciences Institute
4676 Admiralty Way
Marina del Rey, CA 90292-6695
macgregor@isi.edu

Abstract

A description classifier organizes concepts and relations into a taxonomy based on the results of subsumption computations applied to pairs of relation definitions. Until now, description classifiers have only been designed to operate over definitions phrased in highly restricted subsets of the predicate calculus. This paper describes a classifier able to reason with definitions phrased in the full first order predicate calculus, extended with sets, cardinality, equality, scalar inequalities, and predicate variables. The performance of the new classifier is comparable to that of existing description classifiers. Our classifier introduces two new techniques, dual representations and auto-Socratic elaboration, that may be expected to improve the performance of existing description classifiers.

Introduction

A *description* is an expression in a formal language that defines a set of instances or tuples. A *description logic* (also called a terminological logic) consists of a syntax for constructing descriptions and a semantics that defines the meaning of each description. Description logics [MacGregor 90].provide the foundation for a number of modern knowledge representation systems, including Loom[MacGregor 91], BACK[Peltason 91], CLASSIC[Borgida et al 89], KREP[Mays et al 91], and KRIS[Baader&Hollunder 91]. Each of these systems includes a specialized reasoner called a *description classifier* that computes subsumption relationships between descriptions, and organizes them into one or several taxonomies. Subsumption computations play a role in these systems analogous to the match or unification operations performed in other classes of deductive systems.

Description logic systems as a class implement a style of deductive inference that is deeper than standard backchaining, and that is much more efficient than theorem prover-based deduction. A hallmark of description logics is that they severely limit the expressive power of their description languages. We believe that the absence of full expressivity is one of the factors that is preventing description classifiers from becoming a standard component in knowledge base management systems [Doyle&Patil 91]. Accordingly, we have developed a new classifier that accepts description expressions phrased using the full predicate calculus, extended with sets, cardinality, equality, scalar inequalities, and predicate variables. The description syntax is uniform for predicates of arbitrary arity, and recursive definitions are supported.

We have found that architectural principles developed for description logic classifiers can be transferred into a classifier that reasons with predicate calculus expressions. This paper begins by describing the internal format and subsumption algorithm used in the predicate calculus (PC) classifier. We next discuss the normal form transformations used in this classifier. The strategy for normalization incorporates two innovations, dual representations and auto-Socratic elaboration, that increase both the performance and the flexibility of the classifier. Finally, we present results indicating that the new classifier has performance comparable to that of existing classifiers.

Descriptions

A *relation description* specifies an intensional definition for a relation. It has the following components:

- a <u>name</u> (optional);
- a list of <u>domain</u> variables $< dv_1, \dots, dv_k >$, where k is the arity of the relation;
- a <u>definition</u>—an open sentence in the prefix predicate calculus whose free variables are a subset of the domain variables.
- a <u>partial</u> indicator (true or false)— if true, it indicates that the predicate represented by the relation definition is a necessary but not sufficient test for membership in the relation.

If a relation description is partial, then the relation is said to be primitive. If R is a non-primitive relation with arity one, then its extension is defined as the set $\{dv_1 \mid defn_R \}$, where dv_1 is the domain variable and $defn_R$ is the definition in the description of R. If R is a non-primitive relation with arity k greater than one, then its extension is defined as the set of tuples $\{< dv_1, \dots, dv_k > \mid defn_R \}$, where $dv_1, \dots, dv_k$ are the domain variables and $defn_R$ is the definition in the description of R. If R is primitive, then its extension is a subset of the set associated with its definition.

Relation descriptions are introduced by the **defrelation** operator, with the syntax

```
(defrelation <name> (<domain variables>)
                [:def | :iff-def] <definition>)
```

The keyword **:def** indicates that the definition is partial, while the keyword **:iff-def** indicates that it is not. For example

```
(defrelation Person (?p) :def (Mammal ?p))
```

defines a relation Person to be a primitive subrelation of the relation Mammal.[1] The description

```
(defrelation daughter (?p ?d)
   :iff-def (and (child ?p ?d)
                 (Female ?d))))
```

defines the relation **daughter** to be a non-primitive binary subrelation of the relation **child**.

A simple sentence is predication of the form $(P\ t_1\ ...\ t_k)$ where $t_1\ ...\ t_k$ are terms, and P is either the name of a k-ary relation or a term that evaluates to a k-ary relation. Complex sentences are constructed from simple sentences using the operators **and**, **or**, **not**, and **implies**, and the quantifiers **forsome** and **forall**. A term is either a constant, a variable, a set expression, or a form $(F\ t_1\ ...\ t_j)$ where F is a single-valued relation of arity $(j+1)$ (i.e., F is a function). A variable is a string of characters prefixed by "**?**". A set expression is a term of the form **(setof (<variables>) <definition>)** that defines an unnamed relation with domain variables **<variables>** and definition **<definition>**. The function **the-relation** takes as arguments a name (a string of characters not prefixed by "**?**") and a positive integer indicating the arity, and returns the relation with that name and arity (relations of different arity may share the same name).

Subsumption

The primary deductive task of a description classifier is the computation of "subsumption" relationships. We say that a relation A *subsumes* a relation B if, based upon their respective definitions, the extension of A contains the extension of B. A description classifier organizes descriptions into a hierarchy, with description A placed above description B if A's relation subsumes B's relation. The inverse relation to subsumes is called *specializes*. B specializes A if A subsumes B.

Consider the following pair of descriptions. **At-Least-One-Son** defines the set of all persons that have at least one son:

---

[1] A sortal relation such as Person would ordinarily be introduced as a concept, using the **defconcept** operator, rather than being defined as a unary relation. The algorithm is the same for classifying concepts and for classifying unary relations. For simplicity, we avoid distinguishing between concepts and unary relations in this paper.


```
(defrelation At-Least-One-Son (?p)
  :iff-def (and
    (Person ?p)
    (>= (cardinality
          (setof (?c) (son ?p ?c)))
       1))
```

More-Sons-Than-Daughters defines the set of persons that have more sons than daughters:

```
(defrelation More-Sons-Than-Daughters (?pp)
  :iff-def (and
    (Person ?pp)
    (> (cardinality
          (setof (?b) (son ?pp ?b)))
       (cardinality
          (setof (?g) (daughter ?pp ?g)))))))
```

The PC classifier can prove that **At-Least-One-Son** subsumes **More-Sons-Than-Daughters**, i.e. it will classify **More-Sons-Than-Daughters** below **At-Least-One-Son**. The remainder of this paper describes the proof strategy that it uses to find such subsumption relationships.

The majority of description classifiers currently implemented, including the PC classifier, employ a *structural* subsumption test.[2] Roughly speaking, to prove that a description A subsumes a description B, a structural subsumption prover attempts to demonstrate that for every structural "component" in (the internal representation for) the definition of A there exists a "corresponding component" in (the internal representation for) the definition of B. An appealing feature of a classification strategy that uses a structural test is that much of the inferencing occurs in a "normalization" phase that precedes the actual test. If a description is repeatedly tested for subsumption against other descriptions (the usual situation in a classifier) the cost of normalization is amortized across all tests, thereby lowering the average cost of each subsumption test.

Most classifiers adopt frame-like representations for their internal representation of descriptions, and their subsumption tests operate by comparing the structure between a pair of such frames. The PC classifier parses definitions phrased in the prefix predicate calculus into graph-based structures, and all subsequent reasoning involves operations on these graphs. Each of our graphs represents a set expression, consisting of a list of domain variables and a set membership test (the definition). The root node of such a graph is equated with a **setof** expression, additional nodes represent each of the domain variables, and the remaining edges and nodes represent the membership test. A node can represent a variable, a constant, or another set expression. A predicate applied to a list of terms is represented by a (hyper) edge connecting the nodes corresponding to the terms in the list, together with a pointer to the node that corresponds to the predicate. Nodes representing skolem variables are introduced to represent function terms. Variables other than domain

---

[2] The KRIS classifier [Baader&Hollunder 91] is the notable exception.

variables are assumed to be existentially quantified. As we shall see below, our graph representation eliminates the use of (or need for) universal quantifiers. The notation includes explicit representations for disjunction, negation, and enumerated sets—these constructs lie outside of the scope of the present discussion.

Because edges in a graph can point to (root nodes of) other graphs, our graph structures form a network. Each edge in the network "belongs to" exactly one graph—the graph corresponding to the innermost **setof** expression that contains the predication that defines that edge. Each graph is defined to consist of a set of edges plus the set of all nodes referenced by those edges. A node can therefore "belong to" many different graphs. The job of a subsumption test that is comparing graphs A and B is to find a substitution that maps nodes and edges belonging to graph A to corresponding nodes and edges belonging to graph B.

The parser that converts predicate calculus descriptions into graphs applies a few simple transformations in the process, including skolemization of set and function expressions, and conversion of material implications into subset relations (this is illustrated later in this section). In the remainder of this paper, we shall use the term "graph" to refer to a **setof** expression that has undergone these transformations, and we will use graph terminology (e.g., nodes, edges, paths) when referring to structural components and features within our set expressions.

The **At-Least-One-Son** relation defined above is associated with a graph representing the following set

```
(setof (?p)
   (and (Person ?p)
        (>= (cardinality
                (setof (?c) (son ?p ?c)))
            1)
```

The addition of variables to represent the nested **setof** expression and the Skolemized cardinality function produces the following equivalent set expression

```
(setof (?p) (exists (?s1 ?card1)          [1]
   (and (Person ?p)
        (= ?s1 (setof (?c) (son ?p ?c)))
        (cardinality ?s1 ?card1)
        (>= ?card1 1))))
```

We can now illustrate how a structural subsumption algorithm finds a subsumption relationship between **At-Least-One-Son** and **More-Sons-Than-Daughters**. Here is the "graph" for **More-Sons-Than-Daughters**:

```
(setof (?pp)                              [2]
   (exists (?s2 ?s3 ?card2 ?card3) (and
      (Person ?pp)
      (= ?s2 (setof (?b) (son ?pp ?b)))
      (= ?s3 (setof (?g) (daughter ?pp ?g)))
      (cardinality ?s2 ?card2)
      (cardinality ?s3 ?card3)
      (> ?card2 ?card3))))
```

To prove that **At-Least-One-Son** subsumes **More-Sons-Than-Daughters**, we look for a substitution mapping nodes in [1] to nodes in [2] such that for each

edge in the graph [1] there is a corresponding edge in the graph [2]. The correct substitution σ is

$?p \Rightarrow_\sigma ?pp; \ ?s1 \Rightarrow_\sigma ?s2; \ ?card1 \Rightarrow_\sigma ?card2$

except that there is a problem—no edge in graph [2] corresponds to the edge **(>= ?card1 1)** in graph [1]. However, a constraint representing the missing edge **(>= ?card2 1)** is logically derivable from the existing constraints/edges present in graph [2]—the addition of this missing edge would result in a set expression logically equivalent to the expression [2]. Using a process we call "elaboration" (explained in Section 5), the PC classifier applies forward chaining rules to augment each graph with edges that logically follow from the existence of other edges already present in the graph. In the case of graph [2], the following edges would be added during elaboration

```
(Integer ?card2), (>= ?card2 0),
(Integer ?card3), (>= ?card3 0),
(>= ?card2 1)
```

This last edge, representing our "missing edge", derives from the fact that **?card3** is non-negative, **?card2** is strictly greater than **?card3**, hence greater than zero, and that **?card2** is an integer. After applying elaboration to graph [2], the substitution σ successfully demonstrates that the relation **At-Least-One-Son** subsumes the relation **More-Sons-Than-Daughters**.

To our knowledge, no existing description classifier other than the PC classifier can compute this subsumption relation. We know this because none of them have the expressive power needed to *represent* the relation **More-Sons-Than-Daughters**. Here are two more relations that cannot be expressed in any existing description logic:

```
(defrelation One-of-Five-Fastest-Ships (?s)
   :iff-def (and
      (Ship ?s)
      (<= (cardinality
             (setof (?fs)
                (faster-than ?fs ?s)))
          4)))
```

and

```
(defrelation Third-Fastest-Ship (?s)
   :iff-def (and
      (Ship ?s)
      (= (cardinality
            (setof (?fs)
               (faster-than ?fs ?s)))
         2)))
```

Knowledge about upper and lower bounds (in this case, that "= 2" is a stricter constraint than "<= 4") is hardwired into the PC classifier. Since the remaining structure is identical between the two graphs, it is straightforward for the PC classifier to determine that the relation **One-of-Five-Fastest-Ships** subsumes the relation **Third-Fastest-Ship**.

Before we conclude our discussion of graph notation, recall that it does not provide a means for explicitly representing universally quantified variables. Instead, when the parser encounters an expression of the form

```
(forall (?v1 ... ?vk)
    (implies <antecedent> <consequent>))
```
it transforms this expression into the equivalent expression
```
(contained-in
    (setof (?v_1 ... ?v_k) <antecedent>)
    (setof (?v_1 ... ?v_k) <consequent>))
```
where **contained-in** is the subset/superset relation. In effect, reasoning about universally quantified variables is transformed into reasoning about set relationships. For example, the graph for
```
(defrelation Relaxed-Parent (?p)
  :iff-def (and
      (Parent ?p)
      (forall (?c) (implies (child ?p ?c)
                              (Asleep ?c))))))
```
is
```
(setof (?p) (and
    (Parent ?p)
    (contained-in (setof (?c) (child ?p ?c))
                  (setof (?c) (Asleep ?c)))))
```
Substituting a reference to the unary relation **Asleep** for the set of things satisfying the **Asleep** predicate yields
```
(setof (?p) (and
    (Person ?p)
    (contained-in (setof (?c) (child ?p ?c))
                  (the-relation Asleep 1))))
```

<u>The Subsumption Test</u>

Let A and B be relations defined by expressions/graphs G_A and G_B. We apply the following test to prove that A subsumes B: If A is primitive (if its description is partial) then succeed if G_B explicitly inherits a relation known to specialize A. Formally, B specializes a primitive relation A if G_B contains an edge $R(dv_1, ... ,dv_k)$ where $dv_1, ... ,dv_k$ are the domain variables in the root node of G_B and R is a relation that specializes A. Otherwise (A is not primitive) succeed if there exists a substitution σ from nodes in G_A to nodes in G_B such that all of the following conditions hold:

(1a) If x is a constant node in G_A, then $\sigma(x)$ denotes the same constant, i.e., $\sigma(x) = x$;

(1b) If x is a set node in G_A, then $\sigma(x)$ is also a set node and definition(x) $\equiv_\sigma$ definition($\sigma(x)$), where for all set nodes y, "definition(y)" refers to the subgraph that defines y, and "$\equiv_\sigma$" denotes structural equivalence under the substitution σ;

(2) If $P_A(x_1, ... ,x_k)$ is an edge in G_A then there exists an edge $P_B(\sigma(x_1), ... , \sigma(x_k))$ in G_B such that either

    (i) $P_B = \sigma(P_A)$ or

    (ii) P_A and P_B are relations and P_B specializes P_A, or

    (iii) the edge $P_A(x_1, ... ,x_k)$ matches one the special cases 3a, 3b, 4a, 4b, 4c, or 4d;

(3a) If contained-in(x,R_A) is an edge in G_A and R_A is a relation, then there exists an edge contained-in($\sigma(x),R_B$) in G_B such that R_B specializes R_A;

(3b) If contains(x,R_A) is an edge in G_A and R_A is a relation, then there exists an edge contains($\sigma(x),R_B$) in G_B such that R_B subsumes R_A;

(4a) If >=(x,k_A) is an edge in G_A and k_A represents a numeric constant (k_A denotes a number) then there exists an edge >=($\sigma(x)$, k_B) in G_B such that value(k_B) >= value(k_A), where for all constant nodes k, "value(k)" is the denotation of k;

(4b, 4c, 4d) Analogous to (4a) for the relations <=, <, and >.

<u>Remark</u>: The alternatives (ii) and (iii) in condition 2 above serve to relax what would otherwise be a strictly *structural* subsumption test. Their inclusion in our test enables us to reduce the size of our graphs. For example, if one of our graphs contains both of the edges C(x) and C'(x) and C' specializes C, then we can eliminate the edge C(x) without sacrificing inferential completeness.

Canonical Graphs

To the best of our knowledge, all classifiers that utilize a structural subsumption test preface that test with a series of transformations designed to produce a "canonical" or "normalized" internal representation for each of the relations being tested. The strategy underlying these canonicalization transformations is to make otherwise dissimilar representations become as alike as possible, so that ideally, a structural test would suffice for determining subsumption relationships. For all but very restricted languages this strategy cannot result in a test for subsumption that is both sound and complete. For languages as expressive as NIKL , Loom, or BACK, theory tells us that a sound and complete decision procedure for testing subsumption relationships does not exist (i.e., subsumption testing is "undecidable") [Patel-Schneider 89]. The designers of structural subsumption-based classification systems have concluded that a strategy that relies on (imperfect) canonicalization transformations and a structural subsumption test represents a reasonable approach to "solving" this class of undecidable problems.

The PC classifier splits the normalization process into two phases. In the *canonicalization* phase, equivalence-preserving transformations (rewrite rules) are applied that substitute one kind of graph structure for another. In the subsequent *elaboration* phase, structure is added to a graph (again preserving semantic equivalence), but no structure is subtracted. The PC classifier implements several canonicalization strategies. The most important is the procedure that "expands" each of the edges in a graph that is labeled by a non-primitive relation. An edge with label R is expanded by substituting for the edge a copy of the graph for R. A second important canonicalization is one that substitutes an individual node for a nested set in cases

<h1 align="center">Representative Selection of Elaboration Rules</h1>

<u>Inequality rules:</u>

$I1 >= MIN$ and $Number(MIN)$ and $I2 >= I1 \Rightarrow I2 >= MIN$	; propagate lower bound
$I1 > MIN$ and $Number(MIN)$ and $I2 >= I1 \Rightarrow I2 > MIN$	; propagate strict lower bound
$I1 >= MIN$ and $Number(MIN)$ and $I2 > I1 \Rightarrow I2 > MIN$	; propagate strict lower bound
$I1 <= MAX$ and $Number(MAX)$ and $I2 <= I1 \Rightarrow I2 <= MAX$	; propagate upper bound
$I1 < MAX$ and $Number(MAX)$ and $I2 <= I1 \Rightarrow I2 < MAX$	; propagate strict upper bound
$I1 <= MAX$ and $Number(MAX)$ and $I2 < I1 \Rightarrow I2 < MAX$	; propagate strict upper bound
$I > MIN$ and $Integer(I) \Rightarrow I >= floor(MIN) + 1$	; round lower bound up

$I >= MIN$ and $Integer(I)$ and $Number(MIN)$ and $not(Integer(MIN))$
$\qquad \Rightarrow I >= floor(MIN) + 1$

$I < MAX$ and $Integer(I) \Rightarrow I <= ceiling(MAX) - 1$	; round upper bound down

$I <= MAX$ and $Integer(I)$ and $Number(MAX)$
$\qquad$ and $not(Integer(MAX)) \Rightarrow I <= ceiling(MAX) - 1$

$I1 >= I2$ and $I2 >= I1 \Rightarrow I1 = I2$	; equate two-way greater or equal
$I1 >= I2 \Rightarrow I2 <= I1$	; inverse greater or equal
$I1 <= I2 \Rightarrow I2 >= I1$	; inverse lesser or equal
$I1 > I2 \Rightarrow I2 < I1$	; inverse greater
$I1 < I2 \Rightarrow I2 > I1$	; inverse lesser

<u>Cardinality rules:</u>

$set(S) \Rightarrow exists(I)\ cardinality(S,I)$	; sets have cardinalities
$cardinality(S,I) \Rightarrow Integer(I)$	; integer cardinality
$cardinality(S,I) \Rightarrow I >= 0$	; non-negative cardinality
$contained\text{-}in(S1,S2) \Rightarrow cardinality(S1) <= cardinality(S2))$	; greater cardinality superset

$I >= MIN$ and $I <= MAX$ and $Integer(I)$ and $Integer(MIN)$
$\qquad$ and $Integer(MAX)$ and $domain\text{-}variable(S,I)$
$\qquad$ and $arity(S) = 1 \Rightarrow cardinality(S) <= MAX - MIN$

$in(I,S) \Rightarrow cardinality(S) >= 1$	; non-empty set
$cardinality(S) = 1$ and $in(I,S)$ and $in(J,S) \Rightarrow I = J$	; equate members of singleton set

<u>Contained-in rules:</u>

$contained\text{-}in(S1,S2)$ and $in(I,S1) \Rightarrow in(I,S2)$	; propagate members up
$contained\text{-}in(S1,S2)$ and $cardinality(S1) = cardinality(S2) \Rightarrow S1 = S2$	;equate equal cardinality superset
$contained\text{-}in(S1,S2)$ and $contained\text{-}in(S2,S3) \Rightarrow contained\text{-}in(S1,S3)$	; transitivity of contained-in
$contained\text{-}in(S1,S2)$ and $contained\text{-}in(S2,S1) \Rightarrow S1 = S2$	; equate two-way containment
$S1 = S2 \Rightarrow contained\text{-}in(S1,S2)$	; reflexivity of contained-in
$contained\text{-}in(S1,S2)$ and $contained\text{-}in(S1,S3)$ and $intersection(S2,S3,S4)$	; contained-in intersection set

$\qquad \Rightarrow contained\text{-}in(S1,S4)$

$contained\text{-}in(S1,S2) \Rightarrow contains(S2,S1)$	; inverse contained-in
$contains(S1,S2) \Rightarrow contained\text{-}in(S2,S1)$	; inverse contains

<u>Other rules:</u>

$in(I,S1)$ and $in(I,S2)$ and $intersection(S1,S2,S3) \Rightarrow in(I,S3)$	; member of intersection set

$domain\text{-}variable(S1,I1)$ and $arity(S1) = 1$
$\qquad$ and $in(I1,S2) \Rightarrow contained\text{-}in(S1,S2)$

Table 1

when this transformation is guaranteed to preserve semantic equivalence.

Elaboration

This section describes two of the elaboration procedures implemented in the PC classifier.[1] Each of them implements a form of constraint propagation. Collectively,

the constraint propagation procedures incorporated into the PC classifier implement four of the five classes of forward constraint propagation (all but Boolean constraint propagation) embodied in McAllester's SCREAMER system [McAllester&Siskind 93].

Elaboration Rules and Dual Representations

An "elaboration rule" is an if-then rule that adds edges (or occasionally, nodes) to a graph. Table 1 illustrates many of the elaboration rules used in the PC classifier. A comparison of our rules with those published by Borgida to

---

[1] Other elaboration procedures include primitive edge expansion, recognition ,and realization.

describe the Classic classifier [Borgida 92] reveals that our rules tend to be finer grained than those in Classic, enabling it, for example, to have a superior ability to reason about cardinality relationships (as evidenced by the sons-and-daughters and fastest-ships examples in Section 2).

A graph is elaborated by applying the rules in Table 1 repeatedly until no additional structure can be produced (the use of these rules is similar to the use of a "local" rule set [Givan&McAllester 92]). In addition, the elaboration procedure applies a structural subsumption test between each pair of nested sets, and adds a "contained-in" edge if it finds a subsumption relationship. Consider the following definition:

```
(defrelation Brothers-Are-Friends (?p)
   :iff-def (contained-in
                    (setof (?b) (brother ?p ?b))
                    (setof (?f) (friend ?p ?f)))))
```

The graph for this relation is

```
(setof (?p) (exists (?s1 ?s2)
   (and
       (= ?s1 (setof (?b) (brother ?p ?b)))
       (= ?s2 (setof (?f) (friend ?p ?f))))
       (contained-in ?s1 ?s2))))
```

Applying the applicable elaboration rules results in the following graph

```
(setof (?p) (exists (?s1 ?s2 ?card1 ?card2)
   (and
       (= ?s1 (setof (?b) (brother ?p ?b)))
       (= ?s2 (setof (?f) (friend ?p ?f))))
       (cardinality ?s1 ?card1)
       (cardinality ?s2 ?card2)
       (Integer ?card1) (>= ?card1 0)
       (Integer ?card2) (>= ?card2 0)
       (>= ?card2 ?card1) (<= ?card1 ?card2)
       (contained-in ?s1 ?s2)
       (contains ?s2 ?s1))))
```

Elaboration is applied to a graph for the purpose of making implicit structure explicit, and therefore accessible to our structural subsumption algorithm. We observe that our graph for **Brothers-Are-Friends** now has quite a bit of additional structure. The up side to elaboration is that when seeking to prove that Brothers-Are-Friends is subsumed by some other relation R, the additional structure increases the possibility that our subsumption test will discover that R subsumes **Brothers-Are-Friends** (because in this case the graph for **Brothers-Are-Friends** contains additional structure to map *to*). The down side is that the additional structure could make it less likely that the subsumption test finds the inverse subsumption relationship, i.e., that **Brothers-Are-Friends** subsumes R (because in this case the graph for **Brothers-Are-Friends** contains additional structure that must be mapped *from*). Intuitively, if G is a graph, applying elaboration rules to G makes it "easier" to classify G below another graph, but it makes it "harder" to classify another graph below G.

The standard answer to this apparent conundrum is to elaborate all graphs before computing subsumption relationships between them. We find two problems with the standard approach: (1) For this strategy to succeed, it is necessary to apply "the same amount" of elaboration to all graphs . As we shall soon see, in the scheme we have implemented for the PC classifier, the amount of elaboration applied to a graph is variable, depending on more than just the initial graph structure. (2) Because it causes the size of a graph to increase, elaboration degrades the performance of a subsumption algorithm at the same time that it increases the algorithm's completeness.

Dual Representations

Our solution is to maintain two separate graphs for each relation, one elaborated and one not. Given a relation R, let g(R) refer to the canonicalized but unelaborated graph for R, and let e-g(R) refer to the canonicalized *and* elaborated graph for R. To test if relation R subsumes relation S, our subsumption algorithm compares g(R) with e-g(S), i.e., it looks for a substitution that maps from the unelaborated graph for R to the elaborated graph for S.

This "dual representation" architecture completely solves the first of the two problems we cited above, and reduces the negative effect on performance of the second: (1) For relations R and S, increasing the amount of elaboration applied to e-g(R) increases the completeness of a test to determine if S subsumes R, without affecting the completeness of a test to determine if R subsumes S. (2) Assume that the cost of a subsumption test between two graphs is proportional to the product of the "sizes" of those graphs. If elaboration causes the size of each graph to grow by a factor of K, then the cost of comparing e-g(R) and e-g(S) is (K * K) times the cost of comparing g(R) and g(S). However the cost of comparing e-g(R) with g(S) is only K times the cost of comparing unelaborated graphs. Hence, according to this rough calculation, the standard elaboration strategy has a cost K times that of the dual representation strategy, where K is the ratio between the relative sizes of elaborated and unelaborated graphs.

Auto-Socratic Elaboration

A potentially serious drawback of conventional (overly aggressive) elaboration strategies is that they may generate graph structures that are never referenced by any subsequent subsumption tests (these represent a waste of both time and space). Alternatively, an overly timid strategy may suffer incompleteness by failing to generate structures that it should. This section introduces a new technique, called "auto-Socratic elaboration", that assists the classifier in controlling the generation of new graph structure.

Given a graph G, if we add a new set node N to G containing any definition whatsoever, but we do not add any new edges that relate N to previously existing nodes in G, then the denotation of G remains unchanged. Hence, this represents a legal elaboration of the graph G. Consider the following pairs of graphs:

"The set of things with at most two female children"

```
(setof (?p)                                        [3]
    (exists (?s0 ?card0) (and
        (= ?s0 (setof (?c) (and
                    (child ?p ?c) (Female ?c)))
        (cardinality ?s0 ?card0)
        (>= 2 ?card0))))
```

"The set of things with at most two children"

```
(setof (?p) (exists (?s1 ?card1)                   [4]
    (and (= ?s1 (setof (?c) (child ?p ?c)))
         (cardinality ?s1 ?card1)
         (>= 2 ?card1))))
```

In this section, we discuss the problem of determining that the graph [3] subsumes the graph [4]. Our structural subsumption test fails initially because no set node in [4] corresponds to the set node ?s0 in [3]. We can elaborate graph [4] by adding to it a new set node ?s2 having the same definition as that of ?s0, resulting in:

```
(setof (?p)                                        [5]
    (exists (?s1 ?card1 ?s2) (and
        (= ?s1 (setof (?c) (child ?p ?c)))
        (= ?s2 (setof (?c) (and
                    (child ?p ?c) (Female ?c)))
        (cardinality ?s1 ?card1)
        (>= 2 ?card1))))
```

The elaboration procedure described in the previous section will apply a subsumption test to the pair <?s1,?s2>, resulting in the addition of the edge "contains(?s1,?s2)" (thereby making an implicit subsumption relationship explicit). Application of Table 1 elaboration rules yields

```
(setof (?p)                                        [6]
    (exists (?s1 ?card1 ?s2 ?card2) (and
        (= ?s1 (setof (?c) (child ?p ?c)))
        (= ?s2 (setof (?c) (and
                    (child ?p ?c) (Female ?c)))
        (cardinality ?s1 ?card1)
        (cardinality ?s2 ?card2)
        (contains ?s1 ?s2)
        (>= 2 ?card1)
        (>= ?card1 ?card2)
        (>= 2 ?card2))))
```

Structural subsumption can determine that graph [3] subsumes graph [6], implying that graph [3] also subsumes graph [4]. It remains for us to specify how and when the PC classifier decides to add a new set node to a graph, as exemplified by the transformation from graph [4] to graph[5].

Our PC classifier implements a "demand-driven" strategy for adding new set nodes to a graph. If a test to determine if a graph G_A subsumes a graph G_B returns a negative result, and if the result is due to the identification of a set node N_A in G_A for which there is no set node in G_B having an equivalent definition, the following steps occur:

(1) A new set node N_B with definition equivalent to that for N_A (after substitution) is added to G_B;

(2) Tests are made to see if N_B subsumes or is subsumed by any other sets in G_B;

(3) If so, new contained-in edges are added, triggering additional elaboration of G_B;

(4) The subsumption test is repeated.

We call this procedure "auto-Socratic elaboration". "Socratic" inference [Crawford&Kuipers 89] refers to an inference scheme in which the posing of questions by an external agent triggers the addition (in forward chaining fashion) of new axioms to a prover's internal knowledge base. We refer to our procedure as "auto-Socratic" because in the PC classifier, the system is asking *itself* (subsumption) questions in the course of classifying a description, and its attempts to answer such questions may trigger forward-driven inferences (elaborations).

Performance

The PC classifier was compared with that of the Loom classifier on three different knowledge bases. The largest (containing approximately 1300 definitions) is a translated version of the Shared Domain Ontology (SDO) knowledge base used by researchers in the ARPA/Rome Labs Planning Initiative. The other two knowledge bases were synthetically generated using knowledge base generator procedures previously used in a benchmark of six classifiers performed at DKFI[Profitlich et al 92].[1] The results of Table 2 indicate that the Loom classifier is roughly twice as fast the PC classifier.[2]

---

[1] Loom was one of the faster classifiers in the DFKI benchmark.
[2] Testing was performed on a Hewlitt-Packard 730 running Lucid Common Lisp.

Knowledge Base	PC Classifier	Loom Classifier
SDO	80 seconds	45 seconds
Synthetic #1	58 seconds	22 seconds
Synthetic #2	45 seconds	34 seconds

Table 2

Completeness

DL languages have been developed that have complete classifiers. However, completeness comes at a steep price: the DL languages that support complete classification have very restricted expressiveness. While such languages are of theoretical interest, and may be useful for certain niche applications, their severe constraints limit their utility and preclude them from broad application.

In contrast, our approach provides a rich and highly expressive representation language. If this expressiveness is used, then classification must be incomplete. But where should it be incomplete? Different applications and domains will stress different sorts of reasoning. Inferences that are important in one will be inconsequential in another. A virtue of the PC architecture is that it is flexible and extensible. By changing elaboration rules, we can fine-tune the performance of the classifier, allowing us to change the kinds of inferences that are supported and tradeoff the breadth and depth of inference against efficiency. Thus, the PC classifier and language frees an application developer from a representational straitjacket by enhancing both the expressiveness of the language and the range of inference that can be supported.

Conclusions

DL languages have been developed that have complete classifiers. However, completeness comes at a steep price: the DL languages that support complete classification have very restricted expressiveness. While such languages are of theoretical interest, and may be useful for certain niche applications, their severe constraints limit their utility and preclude them from broad application.

In contrast, our approach provides a rich and highly expressive representation language. If this expressiveness is used, then classification must be incomplete. But where should it be incomplete? Different applications and domains will stress different sorts of reasoning. Inferences that are important in one will be inconsequential in another. A virtue of the PC architecture is that it is flexible and extensible. By changing elaboration rules, we can fine-tune the performance of the classifier, allowing us to change the kinds of inferences that are supported and tradeoff the breadth and depth of inference against efficiency. Thus, the PC classifier and language frees an application developer from a representational straitjacket by enhancing both the expressiveness of the language and the range of inference that can be supported.

Acknowledgments. I would like to thank Bill Swartout and Tom Russ for their edits and criticisms of earlier drafts of this paper. Eric Melz provided the timings listed in Table 2.

References [Baader&Hollunder 91] Franz Baader and Bernhard Hollunder, "KRIS: Knowledge Representation and Inference System", *SIGART Bulletin*, 2(3), 1991, pp.8-14.

[Borgida et al 89] Alex Borgida, Ron Brachman, Deborah McGuinness, and Lori Halpern-Resnick, "CLASSIC: A Structural Data Model for Objects", *Proc. of the 1989 ACM SIGMOD Int'l Conf. on Data*, 1989, pp.59-67.

[Borgida 92] Alex Borgida, "From Types to Knowledge Representation: Natural Semantics Specifications for Description Logics", *International Journal on Cooperative and Intelligent Information Systems* [1,1] 1992.

[Crawford&Kuipers 89] J.M. Crawford and Benjamin Kuipers, "Towards a Theory of Access-Limited Logic for Knowledge Representation, *Proc. First Int'l Conf. on Principles of Knowledge Representation and Reasoning*, Toronto, Canada, May, 1989, pp.67-78.

[Doyle&Patil 91] Jon Doyle and Ramesh Patil, "Two Theses of Knowledge Representation: Language Restrictions, Taxonomic Classification, and the Utility of Representation Services", *Artificial Intelligence*, 48, 1991, pp.261-297.

[Givan&McAllester 92] Robert Givan and David McAllester, "New Results on Local Inference Relations", *Proc. Third Int'l Conf. on Principles of Knowledge Representation and Reasoning*, Cambridge, Massachusetts, October 1992. pp.403-412.

[MacGregor 90] Robert MacGregor, "The Evolving Technology of Classification-based Knowledge Representation Systems", *Principles of Semantic Networks: Explorations in the Representation of Knowledge,* Chapter 13, John Sowa, Ed., Morgan-Kaufman, 1990.

[MacGregor 91] Robert MacGregor, "Using a Description Classifier to Enhance Deductive Inference", *Proc. Seventh IEEE Conference on AI Applications*, Miami, Florida, February, 1991, pp 141-147.

[Mays et al 91] Eric Mays, Robert Dionne, and Robert Weida, K-REP System Overview, *SIGART Bulletin*, 2(3), 1991, pp.93-97.

[McAllester&Siskind 93] Jeffrey M. Siskind and David A. McAllester, "Nondeterministic Lisp as a Substrate for Constraint Logic Programming", *AAAI-93 Proc. of the Eleventh Nat'l Conf. on Artificial Intelligence*, Washington, DC, pp.133-138.

[Patel-Schneider 89] Peter Patel-Schneider, "Undecidability of Subsumption in NIKL", *Artificial Intelligence*, 39(2), 1989, pp.263-272.

[Peltason 91] "The BACK System - An Overview",*SIGART Bulletin*, 2(3), 1991, pp.114-119.

[Profitlich et al 92] Jochen Heinsohn, Danial Kudenko, Bernhard Nebel, and Hans-Jürgen Profitlich, "An Empirical Analysis of Terminological Representation Systems", AAAI-92 Proc. of the Tenth Nat'l Conf., San Jose, Calif., 1992, pp. 767-773.

Causal Reasoning and Uncertainty Management

Forming beliefs about a changing world[*]

Fahiem Bacchus
Department of Computer Science
University of Waterloo
Waterloo, Ontario
Canada, N2L 3G1
fbacchus@logos.uwaterloo.ca

Adam J. Grove
NEC Research Institute
4 Independence Way
Princeton, NJ 08540
grove@research.nj.nec.com

Joseph Y. Halpern
IBM Almaden Research Center
650 Harry Road
San Jose, CA 95120–6099
halpern@almaden.ibm.com

Daphne Koller
Computer Science Division
University of California, Berkeley
Berkeley, CA 94720
daphne@cs.berkeley.edu

Abstract

The situation calculus is a popular technique for reasoning about action and change. However, its restriction to a first-order syntax and pure deductive reasoning makes it unsuitable in many contexts. In particular, we often face uncertainty, due either to lack of knowledge or to some probabilistic aspects of the world. While attempts have been made to address aspects of this problem, most notably using nonmonotonic reasoning formalisms, the general problem of uncertainty in reasoning about action has not been fully dealt with in a logical framework. In this paper we present a theory of action that extends the situation calculus to deal with uncertainty. Our framework is based on applying the *random-worlds* approach of [BGHK94] to a situation calculus ontology, enriched to allow the expression of probabilistic action effects. Our approach is able to solve many of the problems imposed by incomplete and probabilistic knowledge within a unified framework. In particular, we obtain a *default* Markov property for chains of actions, a derivation of conditional independence from irrelevance, and a simple solution to the frame problem.

Introduction

The *situation calculus* is a well-known logical technique for reasoning about action and change [MH69]. Calculi of this sort provide a useful mechanism for dealing with simple temporal phenomena, and serve as a foundation for work in planning. Nevertheless, the many restrictions inherent in the situation calculus have inspired continuing work on extending its scope.

An important source of these restrictions is that the situation calculus is simply a first-order theory. Hence, it is only able to represent "known facts" and can make only valid deductions from those facts. It is unable to represent probabilistic knowledge; it is also ill-suited for reasoning with incomplete information. These restrictions make it impractical in a world where little is definite, yet where intelligent, reasoned decisions must nevertheless be made. There has

been much work extending the basic situation calculus using various nonmonotonic theories. Although interesting, these theories address only a certain limited type of uncertainty; in particular, they do not allow us to represent actions whose effects are probabilistic. This latter issue seems to be addressed almost entirely in a non-logical fashion. In particular, we are not aware of any work extending the situation calculus to deal with probabilistic information. This is perhaps understandable: until recently, it was quite common to regard approaches to reasoning based on logic as being irreconcilably distinct from those using probability. Recent work has shown that such pessimism is unjustified. In this paper we use a new theory of probabilistic reasoning called the *random-worlds method* [BGHK94] which naturally extends first-order logic. We show that this method can be successfully applied to temporal reasoning, yielding a natural and powerful extension of the situation calculus.

The outline of this paper is as follows. First, we briefly describe the situation calculus, discussing in more detail some of its problems, and some of the related work addressing these problems. We then describe our own approach. We begin by summarizing the random-worlds method. Although the application of this method to temporal reasoning is not complicated, an appropriate representation of temporal events turns out to be crucial. The solution, based on *counterfactuals*, seems to be central to many disciplines in which time and uncertainty are linked.

After these preliminaries, we turn to some of the results obtained from our approach. As we said, our goal is to go beyond deductive conclusions. Hence, our reasoning procedure assigns *degrees of belief* (probabilities) to the various possible scenarios. We show that the probabilities derived using our approach satisfy certain important desiderata. In particular, we reason correctly with both probabilistic and nondeterministic actions (the distinction between the two being clearly and naturally expressed in our language). Furthermore, we obtain a default Markov property for reasoning about sequences of actions. That is, unless we know otherwise, the outcome of an action at a state is independent of previous states. We note that the Markov property is not an externally imposed assumption, but rather is a naturally derived consequence of the semantics of our approach. Moreover, it can be overridden by information in the knowledge

---

[*]Some of this research was performed while Daphne Koller was at Stanford University and at the IBM Almaden Research Center. Work supported in part by the Canadian Government through their NSERC and IRIS programs, by the Air Force Office of Scientific Research (AFSC) under Contract F49620-91-C-0080, and by a University of California President's Postdoctoral Fellowship.

base. The Markov property facilitates a natural mechanism of *temporal projection*, and is a natural generalization of an intuitive mechanism of projection in deterministic domains in which we consider action effects sequentially. In general, when actions have deterministic effects (whether in fact, or only by default, which is another easily made distinction) then our approach achieves most standard desiderata.

Finally, we turn to examining one of the most famous issues that arise when reasoning about action: the *Frame Problem* and the associated *Yale Shooting Problem* (YSP) [MH69, HM87]. We show that our approach can solve the former problem, without suffering from the latter, almost automatically. Writing down a very natural expression of a frame axiom almost immediately gives the desired behavior. We state a theorem, based on the criterion of Kartha [Kar93], showing the general correctness of our approach's solution to the frame problem. We also compare our solution to one given by Baker [Bak91].

Preliminaries

The situation calculus

We assume some familiarity with the situation calculus and associated issues. In brief, by *situation calculus* we refer to a method of reasoning about temporal phenomena using *first-order logic* and a sorted ontology consisting of *actions* and *situations*. A situation is a "snapshot" of the world; its properties are given by predicates called *fluents*. For example, consider a simple version of the well-known Yale Shooting problem. To represent an initial situation S_0 where Fred is alive and there is an unloaded gun we can use the formula $Alive(S_0) \wedge \neg Loaded(S_0)$. The effects actions have on situation can be encoded using a *Result* function. For instance, we can write $\forall s\, (Loaded(s) \Rightarrow \neg Alive(Result(Shoot, s)))$, to assert that if a loaded gun is fired it will kill Fred.[1] We can then ask what would happen if, starting in S_0, we load the gun, wait for a moment, and then shoot: $Alive(Result(Shoot, Result(Wait, Result(Load, S_0))))$?

The most obvious approach for deciding whether this is true is to use first-order deduction. However, for this to work, we must provide many other facts in addition to the two above. In fact, to answer questions using deduction we would in general have to provide a complete theory of the domain, including a full specification of the initial situation and explicit formulas describing which fluents do *and do not* change whenever any action is taken. For instance, we would need to say that after a *Wait* action, a loaded gun continues to be loaded, if Fred was alive before he will be alive afterwards, and so on. The issue of stating the non-effects of actions is known as the *frame problem* [MH69]: how do we avoid having to represent the numerous axioms required to describe non-effects? We would like to omit or abbreviate these axioms somehow.

The frame problem is only one aspect of the problem of completeness; generally our knowledge will be deficient in

---

[1] In general, we use upper case for constants and lower case for variables.

other ways as well. For example,

- we may not know the truth value of every fluent in the initial situation.

- we may know the situation after some sequence of actions has been performed, but not know precisely which actions were taken. (This leads to one type of *explanation* problem.)

- we may not know precisely what effects an action has. This may be due to a simple lack of information, or to the fact that the action's effects are probabilistic (e.g., we might believe that there is a small chance that Fred could survive being shot). Note that even if we know the probabilities of the various action outcomes, the situation calculus's first-order language is too weak to express them.

In all such cases, it is unlikely that deductive reasoning will reach any interesting conclusions. For instance, if we leave open the logical possibility that the gun becomes unloaded while we wait, then there is nothing we can say with certainty about whether Fred lives.

Our strategy for investigating these issues is to examine a generalized notion of inference that not only reports certain conclusions (in those rare cases where our knowledge supports them), but also assigns degrees of belief (i.e., probabilities) to other conclusions. For instance, suppose *KB* is some knowledge base stating what we know about actions' effects, the initial situation, and so on, and we are interested in a query such as $\varphi = Alive(Result(Shoot, Result(Wait, Result(Load, S_0))))$. The next section shows how we define $Pr(\varphi|KB)$, the degree of belief in φ (which is a number between 0 and 1) given our knowledge *KB*. It is entirely possible for *KB* to be such that $Pr(\varphi|KB) = 0.1$, which would mean we should have high but not complete confidence that Fred would be dead after this sequence of actions. To a large extent, it is the freedom to assign intermediate probabilities (other than 0 or 1) that relieves us of traditional situation calculus' demand for complete knowledge. A related important feature is our ability to make use of statistical knowledge (for instance, an assertion that shooting only succeeds 90% of the time). Of course, the real success of our approach depends crucially on the details and behavior of the particular method we have for computing probabilities. Examining this method, and justifying its successes, is the goal of the rest of this paper.

Before continuing, we remark that the importance of the issues we have raised is well known. There have been numerous attempts to augment deductive reasoning with the ability to "jump to conclusions", i.e., *nonmonotonic* reasoning (e.g., [HM87, Kau86, Lif87]), often in an attempt to solve the frame problem. The idea of reasoning to "plausible" conclusions, rather than only the deductively certain ones, clearly shares some motivation with our decision to evaluate numeric probabilities. The connection is in fact quite deep; see [BGHK94]. However, the application of pure nonmonotonic logics to reasoning about actions has proven to be surprisingly difficult and, in any event, these approaches are not capable of dealing with probabilistic actions or with the quantitative assessment of probabilities.

There has also been work addressing the issue of probabilities in the context of actions. The propositional approaches to the problem (e.g., [Han90, DK89]) do not incorporate the full expressive power of the situation calculus. Furthermore, even those that are able to deal with abductive queries typically cannot handle explanation problems (since they do not place a prior probability distribution over the space of actions). [Ten91] achieves a first-order ontology by applying the reference-class approach of [Kyb74] to this problem. His approach, however, has a somewhat "procedural" rather than a purely logical (semantic) character. Hence, although it specifies how to do forward projection—assessing probabilities for outcomes given knowledge of an initial situation—it does not support arbitrary queries from arbitrary knowledge bases. This flexibility is important, particularly for explanation and diagnosis. Finally, none of these works subsume all the issues addressed by advocates of nonmonotonic reasoning. Our approach provides a framework for dealing with these issues in a uniform fashion.

Random-worlds

We now turn to a summary of the *random-worlds method*; see [BGHK94] and the references therein for full details. We emphasize that this is a general technique for computing probabilities, given arbitrary knowledge expressed in a very rich language; it was *not* developed specifically for the problem of reasoning about action and change. As a general reasoning method, random-worlds has been shown to possess many attractive features [BGHK94], including a preference for more specific information and the ability to ignore irrelevant information. In a precise sense, it generalizes both the powerful theory of default reasoning of [GMP90] and (as shown in [GHK92]) the principle of maximum entropy [Jay78]; it can also be used to do reference class reasoning from statistics in the spirit of [Kyb74].

The two basic ideas underlying the random-worlds method are the provision of a general language for expressing statistical information, and a mechanism for probabilistic reasoning from such information.

The language we use extends full first-order logic with statistical information, as in [Bac90]), by allowing *proportion expressions* of the form $||\varphi(x)|\psi(x)||_x$. This is interpreted as denoting the proportion of domain elements satisfying φ, among those satisfying ψ.[2] (Actually, an arbitrary set of variables is allowed in the subscript.) A simple *proportion formula* has the form $||\varphi(x)|\psi(x)||_x \approx 0.6$ where "$\approx$" stands for "approximately equal." Approximate equality is required since, if we make a statement like "90% of birds can fly", we almost certainly do not intend this to mean that *exactly* 90% of birds fly. Among other things, this would imply that the number of birds is a multiple of ten! Approximate equality is also important because it allows us to capture defaults. For example, we can express "Birds typically fly" as $||Fly(x)|Bird(x)||_x \approx 1$. We omit a description of the formal semantics, noting that the main subtlety concerns the

interpretation of approximate comparisons, and that the special case of ≈ 1 is related to the well-known ϵ-semantics [Pea89].

The second aspect of the method is, of course, the specific way in which degrees of belief are computed. Before reviewing these, we remark that for the purposes of most of this paper, the random-worlds method can be regarded as a black box which, given any knowledge base *KB* and a query φ, assesses a degree of belief (i.e., a probability) $\mathrm{Pr}^w_\infty(\varphi|KB)$.

Very briefly, and ignoring the subtlety of approximate equality, the method is as follows. For any domain size N, we consider all the worlds (first-order structures) of size N consistent with *KB*. Let $\#worlds_N(KB)$ be the number of size N worlds that satisfy *KB*. Appealing to the principle of indifference, we regard all such worlds as being equally plausible. It then follows that, given a domain size N, we should define $\mathrm{Pr}^w_N(\varphi|KB) = \frac{\#worlds_N(\varphi \wedge KB)}{\#worlds_N(KB)}$. Typically, all that is known about N is that it is "large". Thus, the *degree of belief* in φ given *KB* is taken to be $\lim_{N \to \infty} \mathrm{Pr}^w_N(\varphi|KB)$.

Applying random-worlds in a temporal context is mostly a problem of choosing an appropriate representation scheme. Here we are guided mostly by the standard ontology of situation calculus, and reason about *situations* and *actions*. Indeed, since our language includes that of first-order logic, it would be possible to use the language of standard situation calculus without change. However, we want to do more than this. In particular, we want to allow probabilistic actions and statistical knowledge. To do this, we need to allow for actions that can have several effects (even relative to the same preconditions). For this purpose, it is useful to conceptually divide a situation into two components: the *state* and the *environment*. The state is the *visible* part of the situation; it corresponds to the truth values of the fluents. The environment is intended to stand for all aspects of the situation not determined by the fluents (such as the time, or other properties of the situation that we might not wish to express explicitly within our language).

So what is a *world* in this context? Our worlds have a three-sorted domain, consisting of states, environments, and actions. *Situations* are simply state-environment pairs. Each world provides an interpretation of the symbols in our language over this domain, in the standard manner. For the purposes of this paper, fluents are taken to be unary predicates over the set of states.[3] Actions map situations to new situations via a *Result* function; hence, each world also provides, via the denotation of *Result*, a complete specification of the effect of an action on every situation.

Each state in the world's domain can be viewed as a truth assignment to the fluents. If we have k fluents in the language, say $P_1, \ldots, P_k$, we require that there be at most one state for each of the 2^k possible truth values of the fluents.[4]

---

[2] If $\psi(x)$ is identically *true*, we generally omit it.

[3] We observe that we can easily extend our ontology to allow complex fluents (e.g., *On(A,B)* in the blocks world), and/or reified fluents.

[4] This restriction was also used by Baker [Bak91] in his solution to the frame problem. It does not postulate the existence of a state for *all* possible assignments of truth values, and hence allows a

We do this by adding the following formula to the *KB*:

$$\forall v, v'((P_1(v) \equiv P_1(v') \wedge \cdots \wedge P_k(v) \equiv P_k(v')) \Rightarrow v = v').$$

Because the set of states is bounded, when we take the domain size to infinity (as is required by random worlds), it is the set of actions and the set of possible environments that grow unboundedly.

As stated above, action effects are represented using a *Result* function that maps an action and a situation to a situation. In order to formally define, within first-order logic, a function whose range consists of pairs of domain elements, we actually define two functions—$Result_1$ and $Result_2$—that map actions and situations to states and environments respectively. We occasionally abuse notation and use *Result* directly in our formulas. Note that the mapping from an action and a situation to a situation is still a deterministic one. However, *Result* is not necessarily deterministic when we only look at states. Two situations can agree completely in terms of what we say about them (their state), and nevertheless an action may have different outcomes.

As promised, this new ontology allows us to express non-deterministic and probabilistic actions, as well as the deterministic actions of the standard situation calculus. For example, consider a simple variant of the Yale Shooting Problem (YSP), where we have only two fluents, *Loaded* and *Alive*, and three actions, *Wait*, *Load*, and *Shoot*. Each world will therefore have (at most) four states, corresponding to the four possible truth assignments to *Loaded* and *Alive*. We assume, for simplicity, that we have constants denoting these states: $V_{AL}, V_{A\bar{L}}, V_{\bar{A}L}, V_{\bar{A}\bar{L}}$. Each world will also have domain elements corresponding to the three named actions, and possibly to other (unnamed) actions. The remaining domain elements correspond to different possible environments. The fluents are unary predicates over the states, and $Result_1$ is a function that takes a triple—an action, a state, and an environment—and returns a new state.[5] In the *KB* we can specify different constraints on $Result_1$. For example,

$$\forall v \, (Loaded(v) \Rightarrow ||\neg Alive(Result_1(Shoot, v, e))||_e \approx 0.9), \tag{1}$$

asserts that the *Shoot* action has probabilistic effects; it says that 90% of shootings (in a state where the gun is loaded) result in a state in which Fred is dead. On the other hand,

$$\forall v, e \, (Loaded(v) \Rightarrow \neg Alive(Result_1(Shoot, v, e))), \tag{2}$$

asserts that *Shoot* has the deterministic effect of killing Fred when executed in any state where the gun is loaded.

We might not know what happens is the gun is not loaded: Fred might still die of the shock. In such cases, we can simply leave this unspecified. Later in the paper, we discuss the different ways in which our language allows us to specify the effects of actions, and the conclusions these entail.

---

correct treatment of ramifications. Baker then uses circumscription to ensure that there is exactly one state for each assignment of truth values *consistent with the* KB. In our framework, the combinatorial properties of random-worlds guarantee that this latter fact will hold in almost all worlds.

[5]Similarly, the $Result_2$ function returns a new environment, but there is usually no need for the user to provide information about this function.

Counterfactuals

While our basic ontology seems natural, there are other possible representations. However, it turns out that the use of a *Result* function is crucial. Although the use of *Result* is quite standard in situation calculus, it is important to realize that its denotation in each world tells us the outcome of each action in all situations, including those situations that never actually occur. That is, in each world *Result* provides *counterfactual* information.

This can best be understood using an example. Consider the YSP example, where for simplicity we ignore environments and consider only a single action—*Shoot*—which is always taken at the initial state. We know that Fred is alive at the initial state, but nothing about the state of the gun—it could be loaded or not. Assume that, rather than having a *Result* function, we choose to have each world simple denote a single run (history) for this experiment. In this new ontology, we could use a constant V_0 denoting the initial state and another constant V_1 denoting the second state; each of these will necessarily be equal to one of the four states described above. In order to assert that shooting a loaded gun kills Fred, we would state that $Loaded(V_0) \Rightarrow \neg Alive(V_1)$. Furthermore, assume that after being shot the gun is no longer loaded. It is easy to see that there are essentially three possible worlds (up to renaming of states): if $Loaded(V_0)$ (so that $V_0 = V_{AL}$), then necessarily $V_1 = V_{\bar{A}L}$, and if $\neg Loaded(V_0)$ then either $V_1 = V_{\bar{A}L}$ or $V_1 = V_{AL}$. The random-worlds method, used with this new ontology, would give a degree of belief of $\frac{1}{3}$ to the gun being loaded at V_0, simply because *Shoot* has more possible outcomes if the gun is unloaded. Yet intuitively, since we know nothing about the initial status of the gun, the correct degree of belief for $Loaded(V_0)$ is $\frac{1}{2}$. This is the answer we get by using the ontology of situation calculus with the *Result* function. In this case, the different worlds correspond to the different denotations of *Result* and V_0. Assuming that no action can revive Fred once he dies, there are only two possible denotations for *Result*: $Result(Shoot, V_{A\bar{L}})$ is either $V_{\bar{A}\bar{L}}$ or $V_{A\bar{L}}$, while $Result(Shoot, V) = V_{\bar{A}\bar{L}}$ if $V \neq V_{A\bar{L}}$. Furthermore, V_0 is either V_{AL} or $V_{A\bar{L}}$. Hence, there are four possible worlds. In exactly two of these, we have that $Loaded(V_0)$. The key idea here is that, because our language includes *Result*, each world must specify not only the outcome of shooting a loaded gun, but also the outcome of shooting *had the gun been unloaded*. Once this counterfactual information is taken into account, we get the answers we expect.

We stress that the *KB* does not need to include any special information because of our use of counterfactuals. As is standard in the situation calculus, we put into the *KB* exactly what we know about the *Result* function (for example, that shooting a loaded gun necessarily kills Fred). The *KB* admits a set of satisfying worlds, and in each of these worlds *Result* will have some counterfactual behavior. The random worlds method takes care of the rest by counting among these alternate behaviors.

The example above and the results below show that random worlds works well with an ontology that has implicit counterfactual information (like the situation calculus and its *Result* function). On the other hand, with other ontologies (such as the language used above that simply records what actually happens and nothing more) the combinatorics lead to unintuitive answers. Hence, it might seem that counterfactual ontologies are simply a technical requirement of random worlds. However, the issue of counterfactuals seems to arise over and over again in attempts to understand temporal and causal information. They have been used in both philosophy and statistics to give semantics to causal rules [Rub74]. In game theory [Sta94] the importance of counterfactuals (or strategies) has long been recognized. Baker's approach [Bak91] to the frame problem is, in fact, also based on the use of counterfactuals.

We have already mentioned that random-worlds subsumes the principle of maximum entropy. It has been argued [Pea88] that maximum entropy (and hence random-worlds) cannot deal appropriate with causal information. In fact, our example above is closely related, in a technical sense, to the problematic examples described by Pearl. But once again, an appropriate representation of causal rules using counterfactuals solves the problem [Hun89]. In fact, counterfactuals have been used recently to provide a formulation of Bayesian networks based on deterministic functions [Pea93]. All these applications of counterfactuals turn out to be closely linked to our own, even though none consider the random-worlds method. The ontology of this paper is, in some sense, the convergence of these technically diverse, but philosophically linked, frameworks. As our results suggest, the generality of the random-worlds approach may allow us to draw these lines of research together, and so expose the common core.

Results

As a minimal requirement, we would like our approach to be compatible with standard deductive reasoning, whenever the latter is appropriate. As shown in [BGHK94], this desideratum is automatically satisfied by random worlds:

Proposition 1: *If φ is a logical consequence of a knowledge base KB, then* $\Pr_\infty^w(\varphi|\text{KB}) = 1$.

Hence, our approach supports all the conclusions that can be derived using ordinary situation calculus. However, as we now show, it can deal with much more.

An important concept in reasoning about change is the idea of a *state transition*. In our context, a state transition takes us from one situation to the next via the *Result* function. Since we can only observe the state component of a situation, we are particularly interested in the probability that an action takes us from a situation $(V, \cdot)$ to another $(V', \cdot)$ (where the specific identity of the environment is irrelevant). We are in fact interested in the *transition probability* $\Pr_\infty^w(Result(A, V, E) = V'|\text{KB})$. As we show later on in this section, these transition probabilities can often be used to compute the cumulative effects of sequences of actions.

We can use the properties of random worlds to derive transition probabilities from our action descriptions. Consider a particular state V and action A. There are many ways in which we can express knowledge relevant to associated

transition probabilities. One general scheme uses assertions of the form

$$\forall e\,(\varphi(Result_1(A, V, e))), \tag{3}$$

where φ is a Boolean combination of fluents. Assertion (3) says that φ is true of all states that can result from taking A at state V. In general, when *KB* entails such a statement, then Proposition 1 can be used to show that our degree of belief in $\varphi(Result_1(A, V, E)) = 1$. For example, if *KB* consists of (2) only, then $\Pr_\infty^w(Alive(Result_1(Shoot, V_{AL}, E))|KB) = 0$, as expected (here, φ is *Alive*).

Assertion (2) describes a deterministic effect. However, even for nonprobabilistic statements such as (3), our approach can go far beyond deductive reasoning. For instance, we might not always know the full outcome of every action in every state. A *Load* action might result in, say, between one and six bullets being placed in the gun. If we have no other information, our approach would assign a degree of belief of $\frac{1}{6}$ to each of the possibilities. In general, we can formalize and prove the following result (where, as in our remaining results, E is a constant over environments not appearing anywhere in *KB*):

Proposition 2: *Suppose* KB *contains (3), but no additional information about the effects of A in V. Then,* $\Pr_\infty^w(Result_1(A, V, E) = V'|\text{KB}) = \frac{1}{m}$, *where m is the number of states satisfying φ, and V' is one of these states.*

We note that we can prove a similar result in the case where our ignorance is due to incomplete information about the initial state (as illustrated in the previous section).

As we discussed, our language can also express information about probabilistic actions (where we have statistical knowledge about the action's outcomes). Our theory also derives many of the conclusions we would expect. For example, if *KB* contains (1), then we would conclude $\Pr_\infty^w(\neg Alive(Result_1(Shoot, V, E))|KB \wedge Loaded(V)) = 0.9$. In general, the *direct inference* property exhibited by random worlds allows us to prove the following:

Proposition 3: *If* KB *entails* $\|\varphi(Result(A, V, e))\|_e \approx \alpha$, *then* $\Pr_\infty^w(\varphi(Result(A, V, E))|\text{KB}) = \alpha$.

Nondeterminism due to ignorance on the one hand, and probabilistic actions on the other, are similar in that they both lead to intermediate degrees of belief between 0 and 1. Nevertheless, there is an important conceptual difference between the two cases, and we consider it a significant feature of our approach that it can capture and reason about both.

Given our statistical interpretation of defaults, the ability to make statistical statements about the outcomes of actions also allows us to express a *default assumption* of determinism. For instance, $\forall v\,(Loaded(v) \Rightarrow \|\neg Alive(Result_1(Shoot, v, e))\|_e \approx 1)$ states that shooting a loaded gun *almost* surely kills Fred. Even though a default resembles a deterministic rule in many ways, the distinction can be important. We would prefer to explain an unusual occurrence by finding a violated default, rather than by postulating the invalidity of a law of nature (which would result in inconsistent beliefs). For example, if, after the shooting, we observe Fred walking away, then our approach would conclude that Fred survived the shooting, rather than that he is a zombie. This distinction between certain outcomes and default outcomes is also easily made in our framework.

In general, we may have many pieces of information describing the behavior of a given action at a given state. For example, consider the YSP with an additional fluent *Noisy*, where our *KB* contains (1) and

$$\forall v \, (Loaded(v) \Rightarrow ||Noisy(Result_1(Shoot, v, e))||_e \approx 0.8).$$

Given all this information, we would like to compute the probability that shooting the gun in a state V where $Alive(V) \wedge Loaded(V)$ results in the state V_{ALN} (where N stands for *Noisy*). Unless we know otherwise, it seems intuitive to assume that Fred's health in the resulting state should be independent of the noise produced; that is, the answer should be $0.1 \times 0.8 = 0.08$. This is, in fact, the answer produced by our approach. This is an instance of a general result, asserting that transition probabilities can often be computed using *maximum entropy*. While, we do not have the space to fully describe the general result, we note that it entails a *default assumption of independence*. That is, unless we have reason to believe that *Alive* and *Noisy* are correlated, our approach will assume that they are not. We stress that this is only a default. We might know that *Alive* and *Noisy* are negatively correlated (perhaps because lack of noise is sometimes caused by a misfiring gun). In this case we can easily add to the *KB*, for example, that $\forall v \, (Loaded(v) \Rightarrow ||Noisy(Result_1(Shoot, V, e)) \wedge Alive(Result_1(Shoot, V, e))||_e \approx 0.05)$. The resulting *KB* is not inconsistent; the default assumption of independence is dropped automatically.

We now turn to the problem of reasoning about the effects of a sequence of actions. The *Markov* assumption, which is built into most systems that reason about probabilistic actions [Han90, DK89], asserts that the effects of an action depend only on the state in which it is taken. As the following result demonstrates, our approach *derives* this principle from the basic semantics. We note that the Markov assumption is only a default assumption in our framework; it fails if the *KB* contains assertions implying otherwise. Formally, it requires that our information about *Result* be expressed solely in terms of *transition proportions*, i.e., proportion expressions of the form $||\varphi(Result_1(A, V, e))||_e$, where φ is a Boolean combination of fluents. Hence, if our *KB* contains information about $||Result(A_1, Result(A_2, V, e))||_e$, the Markov property might no longer hold.

Proposition 4: *Suppose that the only occurrence of Result in* KB *is in the context of transition proportions, and that E and E' do not appear in* KB. *Then*

$$\begin{aligned} &\mathrm{Pr}^w_\infty(Result(A_1, V, E) = (V', E') \wedge \\ &Result_1(A_2, V', E') = V'' \mid \mathrm{KB}) = \\ &\mathrm{Pr}^w_\infty(Result_1(A_1, V, E) = V' \mid \mathrm{KB}) \times \\ &\mathrm{Pr}^w_\infty(Result_1(A_2, V', E') = V'' \mid \mathrm{KB}). \end{aligned}$$

Of course, it follows from the proposition that to compute $\mathrm{Pr}^w_\infty(Result(A_2, Result(A_1, V, E)) = V''$, we just sum over all intermediate states. This result generalizes to arbitrary sequences of actions in the obvious way.

The Frame Problem

Perhaps the best single illustration of the power of our approach in the context of the situation-calculus is its ability to deal simply and naturally with the frame problem. Many people have an intuition about the frame problem which is, roughly speaking, that "fluents tend not to change value very often". This suggests that if we could formalize this general principle (that change is unusual), it could serve as a substitute for the many explicit frame axioms that would otherwise be needed. However, as shown in [HM87], the most obvious formulations of this idea in standard nonmonotonic logics often fail. Suppose we use a formalism that, in some way, tries to minimize the number of changes in the world. In the YSP, after waiting and then shooting we expect there to be *some* change: we expect Fred to die. But there is another model which seems to have the "same amount" of change: the gun miraculously becomes unloaded as we wait, and thus Fred does not die. This seems to be the wrong model, but it turns out to be difficult capture this intuition formally. Subsequent to Hanks and McDermott's paper, there was much research in this area before adequate solutions were found.

How does our approach fare? It turns out that we can use our statistical language to directly translate the intuition we have about frame axioms, and the result gives us exactly the answers we expect in such cases as the YSP. We formalize the statement of minimal change for a fluent P by asserting that it changes in very few circumstances; that is, any action applied in any situation is unlikely to change P: $||P(Result_1(a, v, e)) \neq P(v)||_{(a,v,e)} \approx 0$. Of course, the statistical chance of such frame violations cannot be exactly zero, because some actions do cause change in the world. However, the "approximately equals" connective allows for this. Roughly speaking, the above axiom, an instance of which can be added for each fluent P for which we think the frame assumption applies, will cause us to have degree of belief 0 in a fluent changing value unless we have explicit knowledge to the contrary.[6]

There is one minor subtlety. Recall that in the random-worlds approach, we consider the limit as the domain tends to infinite size. As we observed, since the number of states is bounded, this means that the number of environments and actions must grow without bound. This does not necessarily mean that the number of actions grows without bound. However, in the presence of the frame axioms (as given above), we need this stronger assumption. This need is quite easy to explain. If the only action is *Shoot*, then half the triples (a, v, e) (those where *Loaded* is true in v) would lead to a change in the fluent *Alive*. In this framework, it would be inconsistent to simultaneously suppose that there is only one way of changing the world (i.e., *Shoot*) and also that every fluent (and in particular, *Alive*) hardly ever changes. Making the quite reasonable assumption that there are many other ways of effecting change in the world (i.e., many other ac-

---

[6]Note that having degree of belief 0 does not mean that we believe something to be impossible, but only extremely unlikely. Hence, this representation does allow for unexpected change, a useful feature in explanation problems.

tions in the domain), even though we may say nothing about them, removes the contradiction.

Given this, if we add frame axioms as given above we get precisely the results we want. If we try to predict forward from one state to the next, we conclude (with degree of belief 1) that nothing changes except those fluents that the action is known to affect. If we consider a sequence of actions, we can predict the outcome by applying this rule for the first action with respect to the initial state, then applying the second action to the state just obtained, and so on. This is essentially a consequence of Proposition 4, combined with the properties of our frame axiom. In the YSP, for example, the *Load* action will cause the gun to be loaded, but will change nothing else. *Wait* will then leave the state completely unchanged. Finally, because the gun will still be loaded, performing *Shoot* will kill Fred as expected.

The idea of a formal theory being faithful to this intuitive semantics (essentially, that in which we consider actions one at a time, assuming minimal change at each step) has recently been formalized by Kartha [Kar93]. Roughly speaking, he showed that a simple procedural language $\mathcal{A}$ [GL92] can be embedded into three approaches for dealing with the frame problem [Bak91, Ped89, Rei91], so that the answers prescribed by $\mathcal{A}$'s semantics (which are the intuitively "right" answers) are also obtained by these formalisms. The following result shows that we also pass Kartha's test. Specifically:

Proposition 5: *There is a sound and complete embedding of $\mathcal{A}$ into our language in which the frame axioms appear in the above form.*

Thus, the random-worlds approach succeeds in solving the frame problem as well as the above approaches, at least in this respect. However, as we mentioned above, our approach is significantly more expressive, in that it can deal with quantitative information in a way that none of these other approaches can. Furthermore, our approach does not have difficulty with state constraints (i.e., ramifications), a problem encountered by a number of other solutions to the frame problem (e.g., those of Reiter and Pednault).

Why does the random-worlds method work so easily? There are two reasons. First, the ability to say that proportions are very small lets us express, in a natural way *within our language*, the belief that frame violations are rare. Alternative approaches to the problem tend to use powerful minimization techniques, such as circumscription, to encode this. But much more important is our use of an ontology that includes counterfactuals. This turns out to be crucial in avoiding the YSP. Even if the gun does in fact become unloaded somehow, we do not escape the fact that shooting with a loaded gun *would have* killed Fred. Baker and Ginsberg's [BG89] solution to the frame problem (based on circumscription) relies on a similar notion of counterfactual situations. But while the solutions are related, they are not identical: for instance, we do not suffer from the problem concerning extraneous fluents that Baker [Bak89] mentions.[7]

---

[7]We also note that Baker and Ginsberg's solution was constructed especially to deal with the problem of minimizing frame violations. Our solution to the frame problem and the YSP arises

Some solutions to the YSP work by augmenting a principle of minimal change with a requirement that we should prefer models in which change occurs as late as possible (e.g., [Kau86, Sho88]). This solves the original YSP because the model in which Fred dies violates the frame axiom (that Fred should remain alive) later than the model in which the gun miraculously becomes unloaded. However, it has been observed that such theories fail on certain explanation problems, such as Kautz's [Kau86] stolen car example. Our approach deals well with explanation problems. In Kautz's example, we park our car in the morning only to find when we return in the evening that it has been stolen. Theories that delay change lead to the conclusion that the car was stolen just prior to our return. A more reasonable answer is to be indifferent about exactly when the car was stolen. Our approach assigns equal probability to the car being stolen over each time period of our absence. That is, if *KB* axiomatizes the domain in the natural way, and the only action that makes a car disappear from the parking lot is the *StealCar* action, then we would conclude that:

$$\mathrm{Pr}^w_\infty(A_i = StealCar | KB \wedge \neg Parked(Result_1(A_\ell, Result(\cdots Result(A_1, Result(ParkCar, V_0, E)) \cdots)))) = \tfrac{1}{\ell}.$$

Conclusion

As shown in [BGHK94], the random-worlds approach provides a general framework for probabilistic and default first-order reasoning. The key to adapting random worlds to the domain of causal and temporal reasoning lies in the use of counterfactual ontologies to represent causal information. Our results show that the combination of random worlds and counterfactuals can be used to address many of the important issues in this domain. The ease with which the general random-worlds technique can be applied to yet another important domain, and its success in dealing with the core problems encountered by other approaches, shows its versatility and broad applicability as a general framework for inductive reasoning.

There is, however, one important issue which this approach fails to handle appropriately: the *qualification problem*. The reasons for this failure are subtle, and cannot be explained within the space limitations. However, as we discuss in the full paper, the problem is closely related to the fact that random worlds does not learn statistics from samples. This aspect of random-worlds was discussed in [BGHK92], where we also presented an alternative method to computing degrees of belief, the *random-propensities* approach, that does support learning. In future work, we hope to apply this alternative approach to the ontology described in this framework. We have reason to hope that this approach will maintain the desirable properties described in this framework, and will also deal with the qualification problem.

References

[Bac90]   F. Bacchus. *Representing and Reasoning with Probabilistic Knowledge*. MIT Press, 1990.

---

naturally and almost directly from our general approach.

[Bak89]   A. Baker. A simple solution to the Yale shooting problem. In *Proc. First International Conference on Principles of Knowledge Representation and Reasoning (KR '89)*, pages 11–20. Morgan Kaufman, 1989.

[Bak91]   A. Baker. Nonmonotonic reasoning in the framework of the situation calculus. *Artificial Intelligence*, 49:5–23, 1991.

[BG89]   A. Baker and M. Ginsberg. Temporal projection and explanation. In *Proc. Eleventh International Joint Conference on Artificial Intelligence (IJCAI '89)*, pages 906–911, 1989.

[BGHK92]   F. Bacchus, A. J. Grove, J. Y. Halpern, and D. Koller. From statistics to belief. In *Proc. National Conference on Artificial Intelligence (AAAI '92)*, pages 602–608, 1992.

[BGHK94]   F. Bacchus, A. J. Grove, J. Y. Halpern, and D. Koller. Generating degrees of belief from statistical information. Technical report, 1994. Preliminary version in *Proc. Thirteenth International Joint Conference on Artificial Intelligence (IJCAI '93)*, 1993, pages 906–911.

[DK89]   T. Dean and K. Kanazawa. Persistence and probabilistic projection. *IEEE Tran. on Systems, Man and Cybernetics*, 19(2):574–85, 1989.

[GHK92]   A. J. Grove, J. Y. Halpern, and D. Koller. Random worlds and maximum entropy. In *Proc. 7th IEEE Symp. on Logic in Computer Science*, pages 22–33, 1992.

[GL92]   M. Gelfond and V. Lifschitz. Representing actions in extended logic programming. In *Logic Programming: Proc. Tenth Conference*, pages 559–573, 1992.

[GMP90]   M. Goldszmidt, P. Morris, and J. Pearl. A maximum entropy approach to nonmonotonic reasoning. In *Proc. National Conference on Artificial Intelligence (AAAI '90)*, pages 646–652, 1990.

[Han90]   S. J. Hanks. *Projecting Plans for Uncertain Worlds*. PhD thesis, Yale University, 1990.

[HM87]   S. Hanks and S. McDermott. Nonmonotonic logic and temporal projection. *Artificial Intelligence*, 33(3):379–412, 1987.

[Hun89]   D. Hunter. Causality and maximum entropy updating. *International Journal of Approximate Reasoning*, 3(1):379–406, 1989.

[Jay78]   E. T. Jaynes. Where do we stand on maximum entropy? In *The Maximum Entropy Formalism*, pages 15–118. MIT Press, 1978.

[Kar93]   G. Kartha. Soundness and completeness theorems for three formalizations of action. In *Proc. Thirteenth International Joint Conference on Artificial Intelligence (IJCAI '93)*, pages 724–729, 1993.

[Kau86]   H. Kautz. A logic of persistence. In *Proc. National Conference on Artificial Intelligence (AAAI '86)*, pages 401–405, 1986.

[Kyb74]   H. E. Kyburg, Jr. *The Logical Foundations of Statistical Inference*. Reidel, 1974.

[Lif87]   V. Lifschitz. Formal theories of action: Preliminary report. In *The Frame Problem in Artificial Intelligence*, pages 121–127. Morgan Kaufmann, 1987.

[MH69]   J. M. McCarthy and P. J. Hayes. Some philosophical problems from the standpoint of artificial intelligence. In *Machine Intelligence 4*, pages 463–502. Edinburgh University Press, 1969.

[Pea88]   J. Pearl. *Probabilistic Reasoning in Intelligent Systems*. Morgan Kaufmann, 1988.

[Pea89]   J. Pearl. Probabilistic semantics for nonmonotonic reasoning: A survey. In *Proc. First International Conference on Principles of Knowledge Representation and Reasoning (KR '89)*, pages 505–516, 1989.

[Pea93]   J. Pearl. Aspects of graphical models connected with causality. In *49th Session of the International Statistics Institute*, 1993.

[Ped89]   E. Pednault. ADL: Exploring the middle ground between STRIPS and the situation calculus. In *Proc. First International Conference on Principles of Knowledge Representation and Reasoning (KR '89)*, pages 324–332. Morgan Kaufmann, 1989.

[Rei91]   R. Reiter. The frame problem in the situation calculus: A simple solution (sometimes) and a completeness result for goal regression. In *Artificial Intelligence and Mathematical Theory of Computation*, pages 359–380. Academic Press, 1991.

[Rub74]   D. B. Rubin. Estimating causal effects of treatments in randomized and nonrandomized studies. *Journal of Educational Psychology*, 66:688–701, 1974.

[Sho88]   Y. Shoham. Chronological ingorance: experiments in nonmonotonic temporal reasoning. *Artificial Intelligence*, 36:271–331, 1988.

[Sta94]   R. C. Stalnaker. Knowledge, belief and counterfactual reasoning in games. In *Proc. Second Castiglioncello Conference*. Cambridge University Press, 1994. To appear.

[Ten91]   J. D. Tenenberg. Abandoning the completeness assumptions: A statistical approach to the frame problem. *International Journal of Expert Systems*, 3(4):383–408, 1991.

Probabilistic evaluation of counterfactual queries

Alexander Balke and **Judea Pearl**
Cognitive Systems Laboratory
Computer Science Department
University of California, Los Angeles, CA 90024
<balke@cs.ucla.edu> and *<judea@cs.ucla.edu>*

Abstract

Evaluation of counterfactual queries (e.g., "If A were true, would C have been true?") is important to fault diagnosis, planning, and determination of liability. We present a formalism that uses probabilistic causal networks to evaluate one's belief that the counterfactual consequent, C, would have been true if the antecedent, A, were true. The antecedent of the query is interpreted as an external action that forces the proposition A to be true, which is consistent with Lewis' *Miraculous Analysis*. This formalism offers a concrete embodiment of the "closest world" approach which (1) properly reflects common understanding of causal influences, (2) deals with the uncertainties inherent in the world, and (3) is amenable to machine representation.

Introduction

A counterfactual sentence has the form

If A were true, then C would have been true

where A, the counterfactual antecedent, specifies an event that is contrary to one's real-world observations, and C, the counterfactual consequent, specifies a result that is expected to hold in the alternative world where the antecedent is true. A typical instance is "If Oswald were not to have shot Kennedy, then Kennedy would still be alive" which presumes the factual knowledge of Oswald's shooting Kennedy, contrary to the antecedent of the sentence.

The majority of the philosophers who have examined the semantics of counterfactual sentences (Goodman 1983; Harper, Stalnaker, & Pearce 1981; Nute 1980; Meyer & van der Hoek 1993) have resorted to some form of logic based on worlds that are "closest" to the real world yet consistent with the counterfactual's antecedent. Ginsberg (Ginsberg 1986), following a similar strategy, suggested that the logic of counterfactuals could be applied to problems in planning and diagnosis in Artificial Intelligence. The few other papers in AI that have focussed on counterfactual sentences (e.g., (Jackson 1989; Pereira, Aparicio, & Alferes 1991; Boutilier 1992) have mostly adhered to logics based on the "closest world" approach.

In the real world, we seldom have adequate information for verifying the truth of an indicative sentence, much less the truth of a counterfactual sentence. Except for the small set of relationships between variables which can be modeled by physical laws, most of the relationships in one's knowledge base are non-deterministic. Therefore, it is more practical to ask not for the truth or falsity of a counterfactual, but for one's degree of belief in the counterfactual consequent given the antecedent. To account for such uncertainties, (Lewis 1976) has generalized the notion of "closest world" using the device of "imaging"; namely, the closest worlds are assigned probability scores, and these scores are combined to compute the probability of the consequent.

The drawback of the "closest world" approach is that it leaves the precise specification of the closeness measure almost unconstrained. More specifically, it does not tell us how to encode distances in a way that would (1) conform to our perception of causal influences and (2) lend itself to economical machine representation. This paper can be viewed as a concrete explication of the closest world approach, one that satisfies the two requirements above.

The target of our investigation are counterfactual queries of the form:

If A were true, then what is the probability that C would have been true, given that we know B?

The proposition B stands for the actual observations made in the real world (e.g., that Oswald did shoot Kennedy and that Kennedy is dead) which we make explicit to facilitate the analysis.

Counterfactuals are intertwined with notions of causality: We do not typically express counterfactual sentences without assuming a causal relationship between the counterfactual antecedent and the counterfactual consequent. For example, we can safely state "If the sprinkler were on, the grass would be wet", but the contrapositive form of the same sentence in counterfactual form, "If the grass were dry, then the sprinkler would not be on", strikes us as strange, because we do not think the state of the grass has causal influence on the state of the sprinkler. Likewise, we do not state "All blocks on this table are green, hence, had this white block been on the table, it would have been green". In fact, we could say that people's use of counterfactual statements is aimed precisely at conveying generic causal information, uncontaminated by specific, transitory observations, about the real world. Observed facts often do reflect strange combinations of rare eventualities (e.g., all blocks being green) that have nothing to do with general traits of influence and behavior. The counterfactual sentence, however, emphasizes the law-like, necessary component of the relation considered. It is for this reason, we speculate, that we find such frequent use of counterfactuals in ordinary discourse.

The importance of equipping machines with the capability to answer counterfactual queries lies precisely in this causal reading. By making a counterfactual query, the user intends to extract the generic, necessary connection between the antecedent and consequent, regardless of the contingent factual information available at that moment.

Because of the tight connection between counterfactuals and causal influences, any algorithm for computing counterfactual queries must rely heavily on causal knowledge of the domain. This leads naturally to the use of probabilistic causal networks, since these networks combine causal and probabilistic knowledge and permit reasoning from causes to effects as well as, conversely, from effects to causes.

To emphasize the causal character of counterfactuals, we will adopt the interpretation in (Pearl 1993a), according to which a counterfactual sentence "If it were A, then B would have been" states that B would prevail if A were forced to be true by some unspecified action that is exogenous to the other relationships considered in the analysis. This action-based interpretation does not permit inferences from the counterfactual antecedent towards events that lie in its past. For example, the action-based interpretation would ratify the counterfactual

> If Kennedy were alive today, then the country would have been in a better shape

but not the counterfactual

> If Kennedy were alive today, then Oswald would have been alive as well.

The former is admitted because the causal influence of Kennedy on the country is presumed to remain valid even if Kennedy became alive by an act of God. The second sentence is disallowed because Kennedy being alive is not perceived as having causal influence on Oswald being alive. The information intended in the second sentence is better expressed in an indicative mood:

> If Kennedy was alive today then he could not have been killed in Dallas, hence, Jack Ruby would not have had a reason to kill Oswald and Oswald would have been alive today.

Our interpretation of counterfactual antecedents, which is similar to Lewis' (Lewis 1979) *Miraculous Analysis*, contrasts with interpretations that require that the counterfactual antecedent be consistent with the world in which the analysis occurs. The set of closest worlds delineated by the action-based interpretation contains all those which coincide with the factual world except on possible consequences of the action taken. The probabilities assigned to these worlds will be determined by the relative likelihood of those consequences as encoded by the causal network.

We will show that causal theories specified in functional form (as in (Pearl & Verma 1991; Druzdzel & Simon 1993; Poole 1993)) are sufficient for evaluating counterfactual queries, whereas the causal information embedded in Bayesian networks is not sufficient for the task. Every Bayes network can be represented by several functional specifications, each yielding different evaluations of a counterfactual. The problem is that, deciding what factual information deserves undoing (by the antecedent of the query) requires a model of temporal persistence, and, as noted in (Pearl 1993c), such a model is not part of static Bayesian networks. Functional specification, however, implicitly contains the temporal persistence information needed.

The next section introduces some useful notation for concisely expressing counterfactual sentences/queries. We then present an example demonstrating the plausibility of the external action interpretation adopted in this paper. We then demonstrate that Bayesian networks are insufficient for uniquely evaluating counterfactual queries whereas the functional model is sufficient. A counterfactual query algorithm is then presented, followed by a re-examination of the earlier example with a quantitative analysis using this algorithm. The final section contains concluding remarks.

Notation

Let the set of variables describing the world be designated by $X = \{X_1, X_2, \ldots, X_n\}$. As part of the complete specification of a counterfactual query, there are real-world observations that make up the background context. These observed values will be represented in the standard form $x_1, x_2, \ldots, x_n$. In addition, we must represent the value of the variables in the counterfactual world. To distinguish between x_i and the value of X_i in the counterfactual world, we will denote the latter with an asterisk; thus, the value of X_i in the counterfactual world will be represented by x_i^*. We will also need a notation to distinguish between events that might be true in the counterfactual world and those referenced explicitly in the counterfactual antecedent. The latter are interpreted as being forced to the counterfactual value by an external action, which will be denoted by a hat (e.g., $\hat{x}$).

Thus, a typical counterfactual query will have the form "What is $P(c^*|\hat{a}^*, a, b)$?" to be read as "Given that we have observed $A = a$ and $B = b$ in the real

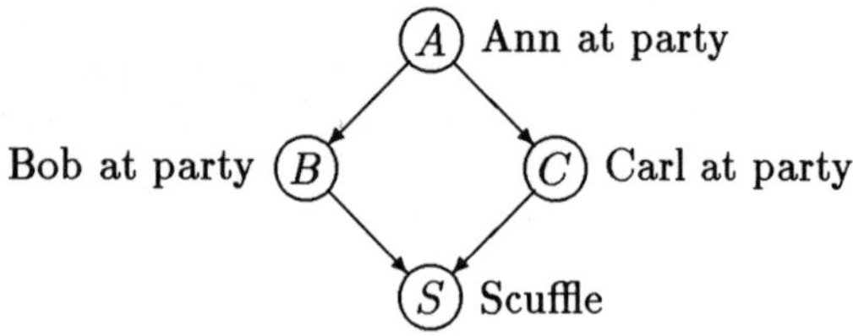

Figure 1: Causal structure reflecting the influence that Ann's attendance has on Bob and Carl's attendance, and the influence that Bob and Carl's attendance has on their scuffling.

world, if A were $\hat{a}^*$, then what is the probability that C would have been c^*?"

Party example

To illustrate the external-force interpretations of counterfactuals, consider the following interpersonal behaviors of Ann, Bob, and Carl:

- Ann sometimes goes to parties.

- Bob likes Ann very much but is not into the party scene. Hence, save for rare circumstances, Bob is at the party if and only if Ann is there.

- Carl tries to avoid contact with Ann since they broke up last month, but he really likes parties. Thus, save for rare occasions, Carl is at the party if and only if Ann is not at the party.

- Bob and Carl truly hate each other and almost always scuffle when they meet.

This situation may be represented by the diamond structure in Figure 1. The four variables A, B, C, and S have the following domains:

$$a \in \left\{ \begin{array}{l} a_0 \equiv \text{Ann is not at the party.} \\ a_1 \equiv \text{Ann is at the party.} \end{array} \right\}$$

$$b \in \left\{ \begin{array}{l} b_0 \equiv \text{Bob is not at the party.} \\ b_1 \equiv \text{Bob is at the party.} \end{array} \right\}$$

$$c \in \left\{ \begin{array}{l} c_0 \equiv \text{Carl is not at the party.} \\ c_1 \equiv \text{Carl is at the party.} \end{array} \right\}$$

$$s \in \left\{ \begin{array}{l} s_0 \equiv \text{No scuffle between Bob and Carl.} \\ s_1 \equiv \text{Scuffle between Bob and Carl.} \end{array} \right\}$$

Now consider the following discussion between two friends (Laura and Scott) who did not go to the party but were called by Bob from his home ($b = b_0$):

Laura: Ann must not be at the party, or Bob would be there instead of at home.

Scott: That must mean that Carl is at the party!

Laura: If Bob were at the party, then Bob and Carl would surely scuffle.

Scott: No. If Bob was there, then Carl would not be there, because Ann would have been at the party.

Laura: True. But if Bob were at the party even though Ann was not, then Bob and Carl would be scuffling.

Scott: I agree. It's good that Ann would not have been there to see it.

In the fourth sentence, Scott tries to explain away Laura's conclusion by claiming that Bob's presence would be evidence that Ann was at the party which would imply that Carl was not at the party. Scott, though, analyzes Laura's counterfactual statement as an indicative sentence by imagining that she had observed Bob's presence at the party; this allows her to use the observation for abductive reasoning. But Laura's subjunctive (counterfactual) statement should be interpreted as leaving everything in the past as it was (including conclusions obtained from abductive reasoning from real observations) while forcing variables to their counterfactual values. This is the gist of her last statement.

This example demonstrates the plausibility of interpreting the counterfactual statement in terms of an external force causing Bob to be at the party, regardless of all other prior circumstances. The only variables that we would expect to be impacted by the counterfactual assumption would be the descendants of the counterfactual variable; in other words, the counterfactual value of Bob's attendance does not change the belief in Ann's attendance from the belief prompted by the real-world observation.

Probabilistic vs. functional specification

In this section we will demonstrate that functionally modeled causal theories (Pearl & Verma 1991) are necessary for uniquely evaluating counterfactual queries, while the conditional probabilities used in the standard specification of Bayesian networks are insufficient for obtaining unique solutions.

Reconsider the party example limited to the two variables A and B, representing Ann and Bob's attendance, respectively. Assume that previous behavior shows $P(b_1|a_1) = 0.9$ and $P(b_0|a_0) = 0.9$. We observe that Bob and Ann are absent from the party and we wonder whether Bob would be there if Ann were there $P(b_1^*|\hat{a}_1^*, a_0, b_0)$. The answer depends on the mechanism that accounts for the 10% exception in Bob's behavior. If the reason Bob occasionally misses parties (when Ann goes) is that he is unable to attend (e.g., being sick or having to finish a paper for AAAI), then the answer to our query would be 90%. However, if the only reason for Bob's occasional absence (when Ann goes) is that he becomes angry with Ann (in which case he does exactly the opposite of what she does), then the answer to our query is 100%, because Ann and Bob's current absence from the party proves that Bob is not angry. Thus, we see that the information contained in the conditional probabilities on the observed variables is insufficient for answering counterfactual queries uniquely; some information about the mechanisms responsible for these probabilities is needed as well.

The functional specification, which provides this information, models the influence of A on B by a deterministic function

$$b = F_b(a, \epsilon_b)$$

where ϵ_b stands for all unknown factors that may influence B and the prior probability distribution $P(\epsilon_b)$ quantifies the likelihood of such factors. For example, whether Bob has been grounded by his parents and whether Bob is angry at Ann could make up two possible components of ϵ_b. Given a specific value for ϵ_b, B becomes a deterministic function of A; hence, each value in ϵ_b's domain specifies a *response function* that maps each value of A to some value in B's domain. In general, the domain for ϵ_b could contain many components, but it can always be replaced by an equivalent variable that is minimal, by partitioning the domain into equivalence regions, each corresponding to a single response function (Pearl 1993b). Formally, these equivalence classes can be characterized as a function $r_b : \mathrm{dom}(\epsilon_b) \to \mathbf{N}$, as follows:

$$r_b(\epsilon_b) = \begin{cases} 0 & \text{if } F_b(a_0, \epsilon_b) = 0 \ \& \ F_b(a_1, \epsilon_b) = 0 \\ 1 & \text{if } F_b(a_0, \epsilon_b) = 0 \ \& \ F_b(a_1, \epsilon_b) = 1 \\ 2 & \text{if } F_b(a_0, \epsilon_b) = 1 \ \& \ F_b(a_1, \epsilon_b) = 0 \\ 3 & \text{if } F_b(a_0, \epsilon_b) = 1 \ \& \ F_b(a_1, \epsilon_b) = 1 \end{cases}$$

Obviously, r_b can be regarded as a random variable that takes on as many values as there are functions between A and B. We will refer to this domain-minimal variable as a *response-function variable*. r_b is closely related to the *potential response variables* in Rubin's model of counterfactuals (Rubin 1974), which was introduced to facilitate causal inference in statistical analysis (Balke & Pearl 1993).

For this example, the response-function variable for B has a four-valued domain $r_b \in \{0, 1, 2, 3\}$ with the following functional specification:

$$b = f_b(a, r_b) = h_{b, r_b}(a) \tag{1}$$

where

$$h_{b,0}(a) = b_0 \tag{2}$$

$$h_{b,1}(a) = \begin{cases} b_0 & \text{if } a = a_0 \\ b_1 & \text{if } a = a_1 \end{cases} \tag{3}$$

$$h_{b,2}(a) = \begin{cases} b_1 & \text{if } a = a_0 \\ b_0 & \text{if } a = a_1 \end{cases} \tag{4}$$

$$h_{b,3}(a) = b_1 \tag{5}$$

specify the mappings of the individual response functions. The prior probability on these response functions $P(r_b)$ in conjunction with $f_b(a, r_b)$ fully parameterizes the model.

Given $P(r_b)$, we can uniquely evaluate the counterfactual query "What is $P(b_1^*|\hat{a}_1^*, a_0, b_0)$?" (i.e., "Given $A = a_0$ and $B = b_0$, if A were a_1, then what is the probability that B would have been b_1?"). The action-based interpretation of counterfactual antecedents implies that the disturbance ϵ_b, and hence the response-function r_b, is unaffected by the actions that force the counterfactual values[1]; therefore, what we learn about the response-function from the observed evidence is applicable to the evaluation of belief in the counterfactual consequent. If we observe (a_0, b_0), then we are certain that $r_b \in \{0, 1\}$, an event having prior probability $P(r_b = 0) + P(r_b = 1)$. Hence, this evidence leads to an updated posterior probability for r_b (let $\vec{P}(r_b) = \langle P(r_b{=}0), P(r_b{=}1), P(r_b{=}2), P(r_b{=}3) \rangle$)

$$\vec{P}'(r_b) = \vec{P}(r_b|a_0, b_0) =$$
$$\langle \frac{P(r_b{=}0)}{P(r_b{=}0) + P(r_b{=}1)}, \frac{P(r_b{=}1)}{P(r_b{=}0) + P(r_b{=}1)}, 0, 0 \rangle.$$

According to Eqs. 1-5, if A were forced to a_1, then B would have been b_1 if and only if $r_b \in \{1, 3\}$, which has probability $P'(r_b{=}1) + P'(r_b{=}3) = P'(r_b{=}1)$. This is exactly the solution to the counterfactual query,

$$P(b_1^*|\hat{a}_1^*, a_0, b_0) = P'(r_b{=}1) = \frac{P(r_b{=}1)}{P(r_b{=}0) + P(r_b{=}1)}.$$

This analysis is consistent with the *prior propensity account* of (Skyrms 1980).

What if we are provided only with the conditional probability ($P(b|a)$) instead of a functional model ($f_b(a, r_b)$ and $P(r_b)$)? These two specifications are related by:

$$P(b_1|a_0) = P(r_b{=}2) + P(r_b{=}3)$$
$$P(b_1|a_1) = P(r_b{=}1) + P(r_b{=}3).$$

which show that $P(r_b)$ is not, in general, uniquely determined by the conditional distribution $P(b|a)$.

Hence, given a counterfactual query, a functional model always leads to a unique solution, while a Bayesian network seldom leads to a unique solution, depending on whether the conditional distributions of the Bayesian network sufficiently constrain the prior distributions of the response-function variables in the corresponding functional model.

In practice, specifying a functional model is not as daunting as one might think from the example above. In fact, it could be argued that the subjective judgments needed for specifying Bayesian networks (i.e., judgments about conditional probabilities) are generated mentally on the basis of a stored model of functional relationships. For example, in the noisy-OR mechanism, which is often used to model causal interactions, the conditional probabilities are derivatives of a functional model involving AND/OR gates, corrupted by independent binary disturbances. This model is used, in fact, to *simplify* the specification of conditional probabilities in Bayesian networks (Pearl 1988).

---

[1]An observation by D. Heckerman (personal communication)

Evaluating counterfactual queries

From the last section, we see that the algorithm for evaluating counterfactual queries should consist of: (1) compute the posterior probabilities for the disturbance variables, given the observed evidence; (2) remove the observed evidence and enforce the value for the counterfactual antecedent; finally, (3) evaluate the probability of the counterfactual consequent, given the conditions set in the first two steps.

An important point to remember is that it is not enough to compute the posterior distribution of each disturbance variable (ϵ) separately and treat those variables as independent quantities. Although the disturbance variables are initially independent, the evidence observed tends to create dependencies among the parents of the observed variables, and these dependencies need to be represented in the posterior distribution. An efficient way to maintain these dependencies is through the structure of the causal network itself.

Thus, we will represent the variables in the counterfactual world as distinct from the corresponding variables in the real world, by using a separate network for each world. Evidence can then be instantiated on the real-world network, and the solution to the counterfactual query can be determined as the probability of the counterfactual consequent, as computed in the counterfactual network where the counterfactual antecedent is enforced. But, the reader may ask, and this is key, how are the networks for the real and counterfactual worlds linked? Because any exogenous variable, ϵ_a, is not influenced by forcing the value of any endogenous variables in the model, the value of that disturbance will be identical in both the real and counterfactual worlds; therefore, a single variable can represent the disturbance in both worlds. ϵ_a thus becomes a common causal influence of the variables representing A in the real and counterfactual networks, respectively, which allows evidence in the real-world network to propagate to the counterfactual network.

Assume that we are given a *causal theory* $T = \langle D, \Theta_D \rangle$ as defined in (Pearl & Verma 1991). D is a directed acyclic graph (DAG) that specifies the structure of causal influences over a set of variables $X = \{X_1, X_2, \ldots, X_n\}$. Θ_D specifies a functional mapping $x_i = f_i(\mathrm{pa}(x_i), \epsilon_i)$ ($\mathrm{pa}(x_i)$ represents the value of X_i's parents) and a prior probability distribution $P(\epsilon_i)$ for each disturbance ϵ_i (we assume that ϵ_i's domain is discrete; if not, we can always transform it to a discrete domain such as a response-function variable). A counterfactual query "What is $P(c^*|\hat{a}^*, obs)$?" is then posed, where c^* specifies counterfactual values for a set of variables $C \subset X$, $\hat{a}^*$ specifies forced values for the set of variables in the counterfactual antecedent, and *obs* specifies observed evidence. The solution can be evaluated by the following algorithm:

1. From the known causal theory T create a Bayesian network $< G, \mathcal{P} >$ that explicitly models the disturbances as variables and distinguishes the real world

variables from their counterparts in the counterfactual world. G is a DAG defined over the set of variables $V = X \cup X^* \cup \epsilon$, where $X = \{X_1, X_2, \ldots, X_n\}$ is the original set of variables modeled by T, $X^* = \{X_1^*, X_2^*, \ldots, X_n^*\}$ is their counterfactual world representation, and $\epsilon = \{\epsilon_1, \epsilon_2, \ldots, \epsilon_n\}$ represents the set of disturbance variables that summarize the common external causal influences acting on the members of X and X^*. $\mathcal{P}$ is the set of conditional probability distributions $P(V_i|\mathrm{pa}(V_i))$ that parameterizes the causal structure G.

   If $X_j \in \mathrm{pa}(X_i)$ in D, then $X_j \in \mathrm{pa}(X_i)$ and $X_j^* \in \mathrm{pa}(X_i^*)$ in G ($\mathrm{pa}(X_i)$ is the set of X_i's parents). In addition, $\epsilon_i \in \mathrm{pa}(X_i)$ and $\epsilon_i \in \mathrm{pa}(X_i^*)$ in G. The conditional probability distributions for the Bayesian network are generated from the causal theory:

$$P(x_i|\mathrm{pa}_X(x_i), \epsilon_i) = \begin{cases} 1 & \text{if } x_i = f_i(\mathrm{pa}_X(x_i), \epsilon_i) \\ 0 & \text{otherwise} \end{cases}$$

   where $\mathrm{pa}_X(x_i)$ is the set of values of the variables in $X \cap \mathrm{pa}(x_i)$.

$$P(x_i^*|\mathrm{pa}_{X^*}(x_i^*), \epsilon_i) = P(x_i|\mathrm{pa}_X(x_i), \epsilon_i)$$

   whenever $x_i = x_i^*$ and $\mathrm{pa}_{X^*}(x_i^*) = \mathrm{pa}_X(x_i)$. $P(\epsilon_i)$ is the same as specified by the functional causal theory T.

2. Observed evidence. The observed evidence *obs* is instantiated on the real world variables X corresponding to *obs*.

3. Counterfactual antecedent. For every forced value in the counterfactual antecedent specification $\hat{x}_i^* \in \hat{a}^*$, apply the action-based semantics of $set(X_i^* = \hat{x}_i^*)$ (see (Pearl 1993b; Spirtes, Glymour, & Scheines 1993)), which amounts to severing all the causal edges from $\mathrm{pa}(X_i^*)$ to X_i^* for all $x_i^* \in \hat{a}^*$ and instantiating X_i^* to the value specified in $\hat{a}^*$.

4. Belief propagation. After instantiating the observations and actions in the network, evaluate the belief in c^* using the standard belief update methods for Bayesian networks (Pearl 1988). The result is the solution to the counterfactual query.

In the last section, we noted that the conditional distribution $P(x_k|\mathrm{pa}(X_k))$ for each variable $X_k \in X$ constrains, but does not uniquely determine, the prior distribution $P(\epsilon_k)$ of each disturbance variable. Although the composition of the external causal influences are often not precisely known, a subjective distribution over response functions may be assessable. If a reasonable distribution can be selected for each relevant disturbance variable, the implementation of the above algorithm is straightforward and the solution is unique; otherwise, bounds on the solution can be obtained using convex optimization techniques. (Balke & Pearl 1993) demonstrates this optimization task in deriving bounds on causal effects from partially controlled experiments.

A network generated by the above algorithm may often be simplified. If a variable X_j^* in the counterfactual world is not a causal descendant of any of the variables mentioned in the counterfactual antecedent $\hat{a}^*$, then X_j and X_j^* will always have identical distributions, because the causal influences that functionally determine X_j and X_j^* are identical. X_j and X_j^* may therefore be treated as the same variable. In this case, the conditional distribution $P(x_j|\mathrm{pa}(x_j))$ is sufficient, and the disturbance variable ϵ_j and its prior distribution need not be specified.

Party again

Let us revisit the party example. Assuming we have observed that Bob is not at the party ($b = b_0$), we want to know whether Bob and Carl would have scuffled if Bob were at the party (i.e., "What is $P(s_1^*|\hat{b}_1^*, b_0)$?").

Suppose that we are supplied with the following causal theory for the model in Figure 1:

$$
\begin{aligned}
a &= f_a(r_a) &&= h_{a,r_a}() \\
b &= f_b(a, r_b) &&= h_{b,r_b}(a) \\
c &= f_c(a, r_c) &&= h_{c,r_c}(a) \\
s &= f_s(b, c, r_s) &&= h_{s,r_s}(b, c)
\end{aligned}
$$

where

$$
P(r_a) = \begin{cases} 0.40 & \text{if } r_a = 0 \\ 0.60 & \text{if } r_a = 1 \end{cases}
$$

$$
P(r_b) = \begin{cases} 0.07 & \text{if } r_b = 0 \\ 0.90 & \text{if } r_b = 1 \\ 0.03 & \text{if } r_b = 2 \\ 0 & \text{if } r_b = 3 \end{cases}
$$

$$
P(r_c) = \begin{cases} 0.05 & \text{if } r_c = 0 \\ 0 & \text{if } r_c = 1 \\ 0.85 & \text{if } r_c = 2 \\ 0.10 & \text{if } r_c = 3 \end{cases}
$$

$$
P(r_s) = \begin{cases} 0.05 & \text{if } r_s = 0 \\ 0.90 & \text{if } r_s = 8 \\ 0.05 & \text{if } r_s = 9 \\ 0 & \text{otherwise} \end{cases}
$$

and

$$
\begin{aligned}
h_{a,0}() &= a_0 \\
h_{a,1}() &= a_1
\end{aligned}
$$

$$
h_{s,0}(b, c) = s_0
$$

$$
h_{s,8}(b, c) = \begin{cases} s_0 & \text{if } (b, c) \neq (b_1, c_1) \\ s_1 & \text{if } (b, c) = (b_1, c_1) \end{cases}
$$

$$
h_{s,9}(b, c) = \begin{cases} s_0 & \text{if } (b, c) \in \{(b_1, c_0), (b_0, c_1)\} \\ s_1 & \text{if } (b, c) \in \{(b_0, c_0), (b_1, c_1)\} \end{cases}
$$

The response functions for B and C (h_{b,r_b} and h_{c,r_c}) both take the same form as that given in Eq. (5).

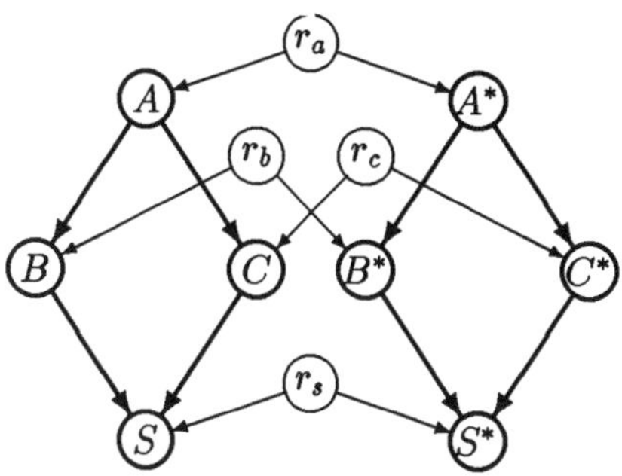

Figure 2: Bayesian model for evaluating counterfactual queries in the party example. The variables marked with $*$ make up the counterfactual world, while those without $*$, the factual world. The r variables index the response functions.

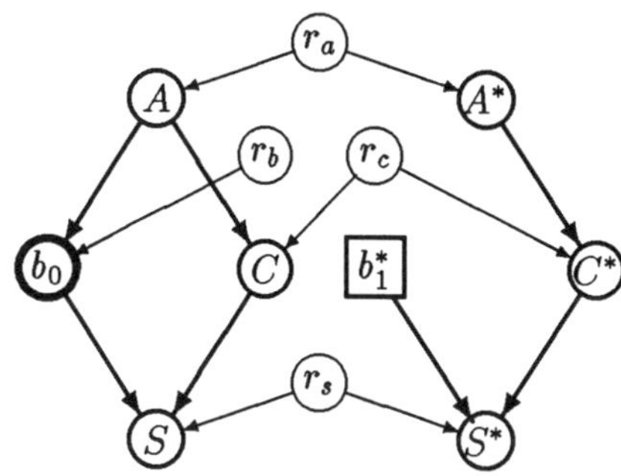

Figure 3: To evaluate the query $P(s_1^*|\hat{b}_1^*, b_0)$, the network of Figure 2 is instantiated with observation b_0 and action $\hat{b}_1^*$ (links pointing to b_1^* are severed).

These numbers reflect the authors' understanding of the characters involved. For example, the choice for $P(r_b)$ represents our belief that Bob usually is at the party if and only if Ann is there ($r_b = 1$). However, we believe that Bob is sometimes ($\sim 7\%$ of the time) unable to go to the party (e.g., sick or grounded by his parents); this exception is represented by $r_b = 0$. In addition, Bob would sometimes ($\sim 3\%$ of the time) go to the party if and only if Ann is not there (e.g., Bob is in a spiteful mood); this exception is represented by $r_b = 2$. Finally, $P(r_s)$ represents our understanding that there is a slight chance (5%) that Bob and Carl would not scuffle regardless of attendance ($r_s = 0$), and the same chance ($P(r_s=9) = 5\%$) that a scuffle would take place either outside or inside the party (but not if only one of then shows up).

Figure 2 shows the Bayesian network generated from step 1 of the algorithm. After instantiating the real world observations (b_0) and the actions ($\hat{b}_1^*$) specified by the counterfactual antecedent in accordance with steps 2 and 3, the network takes on the configuration shown in Figure 3.

If we propagate the evidence through this Bayesian network, we will arrive at the solution

$$
P(s_1^*|\hat{b}_1^*, b_0) = 0.79.
$$

which is consistent with Laura's assertion that Bob and Carl would have scuffled if Bob were at the party, given that Bob actually was not at the party. Compare this to the solution to the indicative query that Scott was thinking of:

$$P(s_1|b_1) = 0.11.$$

that is, if we had observed that Bob was at the party, then Bob and Carl would probably not have scuffled. This emphasizes the difference between counterfactual and indicative queries and their solutions.

Special Case: Linear-Gaussian Models

Assume that knowledge is specified by the structural equation model

$$\vec{x} = B\vec{x} + \vec{\epsilon}$$

where B is a triangular matrix (corresponding to a causal model that is a DAG), and we are given the mean $\vec{\mu}_\epsilon$ and covariance $\Sigma_{\epsilon,\epsilon}$ of the disturbances $\vec{\epsilon}$ (assumed to be Gaussian). The mean and covariance of the observable variables $\vec{x}$ are then given by:

$$\vec{\mu}_x = S\vec{\mu}_\epsilon \tag{6}$$
$$\Sigma_{x,x} = S\Sigma_{\epsilon,\epsilon}S^t \tag{7}$$

where $S = (I - B)^{-1}$.

Under such a model, there are well-known formulas (Whittaker 1990, p. 163) for evaluating the conditional mean and covariance of $\vec{x}$ under some observations $\vec{o}$:

$$\vec{\mu}_{x|o} = \vec{\mu}_x + \Sigma_{x,o}\Sigma_{o,o}^{-1}(\vec{o} - \vec{\mu}_o) \tag{8}$$
$$\Sigma_{x,x|o} = \Sigma_{x,x} - \Sigma_{x,o}\Sigma_{o,o}^{-1}\Sigma_{o,y} \tag{9}$$

where, for every pair of sub-vectors, $\vec{z}$ and $\vec{w}$, of $\vec{x}$, $\Sigma_{z,w}$ is the sub-matrix of $\Sigma_{x,x}$ with entries corresponding to the components of $\vec{z}$ and $\vec{w}$. Singularities of Σ terms are handled by appropriate means.

Similar formulas apply for the mean and covariance of $\vec{x}$ under an action $\vec{\hat{a}}$. B is replaced by the action-pruned matrix $\hat{B} = [\hat{b}_{ij}]$ defined by:

$$\hat{b}_{ij} = \begin{cases} 0 & \text{if } X_i \in \vec{a} \\ b_{ij} & \text{otherwise} \end{cases} \tag{10}$$

The mean and covariance of $\vec{x}$ under $\hat{B}$ is evaluated using Eqs. (6) and (7), where B is replaced by $\hat{B}$:

$$\vec{\hat{\mu}}_x = \hat{S}\vec{\mu}_\epsilon \tag{11}$$
$$\hat{\Sigma}_{x,x} = \hat{S}\Sigma_{\epsilon,\epsilon}\hat{S}^t \tag{12}$$

where $\hat{S} = (I - \hat{B})^{-1}$. We can then evaluate the distribution of $\vec{x}$ under the action $\vec{a}$ by conditioning on the value of the action $\vec{a}$ according to Eqs. (8) and (9):

$$\vec{\mu}_{x|\hat{a}} \triangleq \vec{\hat{\mu}}_{x|a} = \vec{\hat{\mu}}_x + \hat{\Sigma}_{x,a}\hat{\Sigma}_{a,a}^{-1}(\vec{a} - \vec{\hat{\mu}}_a) \tag{13}$$
$$\Sigma_{x,x|\hat{a}} \triangleq \hat{\Sigma}_{x,x|a} = \hat{\Sigma}_{x,x} - \hat{\Sigma}_{x,a}\hat{\Sigma}_{a,a}^{-1}\hat{\Sigma}_{a,x} \tag{14}$$

To evaluate the counterfactual query $P(x^*|\hat{a}^* o)$ we first update the prior distribution of the disturbances by the observations $\vec{o}$:

$$\vec{\mu}_\epsilon^o \triangleq \vec{\mu}_{\epsilon|o} = \vec{\mu}_\epsilon + \Sigma_{\epsilon,\epsilon}S^t(S\Sigma_{\epsilon,\epsilon}S^t)^{-1}(\vec{o} - \vec{\mu}_o)$$
$$\Sigma_{\epsilon,\epsilon}^o \triangleq \Sigma_{\epsilon,\epsilon|o} = \Sigma_{\epsilon,\epsilon} - \Sigma_{\epsilon,\epsilon}S^t(S\Sigma_{\epsilon,\epsilon}S^t)^{-1}S\Sigma_{\epsilon,\epsilon}$$

We then evaluate the means $\vec{\mu}_{x^*|\hat{a}^* o}$ and variances $\Sigma_{x^*,x^*|\hat{a}^* o}$ of the variables in the counterfactual world (x^*) under the action $\hat{a}^*$ using Eqs. (13) and (14), with Σ^o and μ^o replacing Σ and μ.

$$\vec{\mu}_{x^*|\hat{a}^* o} \triangleq \vec{\mu}_{x|\hat{a}}^o = \vec{\hat{\mu}}_x^o + \hat{\Sigma}_{x,a}^o(\hat{\Sigma}_{a,a}^o)^{-1}(\vec{a} - \vec{\hat{\mu}}_a^o)$$
$$\Sigma_{x^*,x^*|\hat{a}^* o} \triangleq \hat{\Sigma}_{x,x|\hat{a}}^o = \hat{\Sigma}_{x,x}^o - \hat{\Sigma}_{x,a}^o(\hat{\Sigma}_{a,a}^o)^{-1}\hat{\Sigma}_{a,x}^o$$

where, from Eqs. (11) and (12), $\vec{\hat{\mu}}_x^o = \hat{S}\vec{\mu}_\epsilon^o$ and $\hat{\Sigma}_{x,x}^o = \hat{S}\Sigma_{\epsilon,\epsilon}^o\hat{S}^t$.

It is clear that this procedure can be applied to non-triangular matrices, as long as S is non-singular. In fact, the response-function formulation opens the way to incorporate feedback loops within the Bayesian network framework.

Conclusion

The evaluation of counterfactual queries is applicable to many tasks. For example, determining liability of actions (e.g., "If you had not pushed the table, the glass would not have broken; therefore, you are liable"). In diagnostic tasks, counterfactual queries can be used to determine which tests to perform in order to increase the probability that faulty components are identified. In planning, counterfactuals can be used for goal regression or for determining which actions, if performed, could have avoided an observed, unexpected failure. Thus, counterfactual reasoning is an essential component in plan repairing, plan compilation and explanation-based learning.

In this paper we have presented formal notation, semantics, representation scheme, and inference algorithms that facilitate the probabilistic evaluation of counterfactual queries. World knowledge is represented in the language of modified causal networks, whose root nodes are unobserved, and correspond to possible functional mechanisms operating among families of observables. The prior probabilities of these root nodes are updated by the factual information transmitted with the query, and remain fixed thereafter. The antecedent of the query is interpreted as a proposition that is established by an external action, thus pruning the corresponding links from the network and facilitating standard Bayesian-network computation to determine the probability of the consequent.

At this time the algorithm has not been implemented but, given a subjective prior distribution over the response variables, there are no new computational tasks introduced by this formalism, and the inference process follows the standard techniques for computing beliefs in Bayesian networks (Pearl 1988). If prior distributions over the relevant response-function variables cannot be assessed, we have developed methods of using the standard conditional-probability specification of Bayesian networks to compute upper and lower bounds on counterfactual probabilities (Balke & Pearl 1994).

The semantics and methodology introduced in this paper can be adopted to nonprobabilistic formalisms as well, as long as they support two essential components: abduction (to abduce plausible functional mechanisms from the factual observations) and causal projection (to infer the consequences of the action-like antecedent). We should note, though, that the license to keep the response-function variables constant stems from a unique feature of counterfactual queries, where the factual observations are presumed to occur not earlier than the counterfactual action. In general, when an observation takes place before an action, constancy of response functions would be justified if the environment remains relatively static between the observation and the action (e.g., if the disturbance terms ϵ_i) represent unknown pre-action conditions). However, in a dynamic environment subject to stochastic shocks a full temporal analysis using temporally-indexed networks may be warranted or, alternatively, a canonical model of persistence should be invoked (Pearl 1993c).

Acknowledgments

The research was partially supported by Air Force grant #AFOSR 90 0136, NSF grant #IRI-9200918, Northrop Micro grant #92-123, and Rockwell Micro grant #92-122. Alexander Balke was supported by the Fannie and John Hertz Foundation. This work benefitted from discussions with David Heckerman.

References

Balke, A., and Pearl, J. 1993. Nonparametric bounds on causal effects from partial compliance data. Technical Report R-199, UCLA Cognitive Systems Lab.

Balke, A., and Pearl, J. 1994. Bounds on probabilistically evaluated counterfactual queries. Technical Report R-213-B, UCLA Cognitive Systems Lab.

Boutilier, C. 1992. A logic for revision and subjunctive queries. In *Proceedings Tenth National Conference on Artificial Intelligence*, 609–15. Menlo Park, CA: AAAI Press.

Druzdzel, M. J., and Simon, H. A. 1993. Causality in bayesian belief networks. In *Proceedings of the 9th Annual Conference on Uncertainty in Artificial Intelligence (UAI-93)*, 3–11.

Ginsberg, M. L. 1986. Counterfactuals. *Artificial Intelligence* 30:35–79.

Goodman, N. 1983. *Fact, Fiction, and Forecast*. Cambridge, MA: Harvard University Press, 4th edition.

Harper, W. L.; Stalnaker, R.; and Pearce, G., eds. 1981. *Ifs: Conditionals, Belief, Decision, Chance, and Time*. Boston, MA: D. Reidel.

Jackson, P. 1989. On the semantics of counterfactuals. In *Proceedings of the Eleventh International Joint Conference on Artificial Intelligence*, 1382–7 vol. 2. Palo Alto, CA: Morgan Kaufmann.

Lewis, D. 1976. Probability of conditionals and conditional probabilities. *The Philosophical Review* 85:297–315.

Lewis, D. 1979. Counterfactual dependence and time's arrow. *Noûs* 455–476.

Meyer, J.-J., and van der Hoek, W. 1993. Counterfactual reasoning by (means of) defaults. *Annals of Mathematics and Artificial Intelligence* 9:345–360.

Nute, D. 1980. *Topics in Conditional Logic*. Boston: D. Reidel.

Pearl, J., and Verma, T. 1991. A theory of inferred causation. In *Principles of Knowledge Representation and Reasoning: Proceedings of the Second International Conference*, 441–452. San Mateo, CA: Morgan Kaufmann.

Pearl, J. 1988. *Probabilistic Reasoning in Intelligent Systems: Networks of Plausible Inference*. San Mateo, CA: Morgan Kaufman.

Pearl, J. 1993a. From Adams' conditionals to default expressions, causal conditionals, and counterfactuals. Technical Report R-193, UCLA Cognitive Systems Lab. To appear in *Festschrift for Ernest Adams*, Cambridge University Press, 1994.

Pearl, J. 1993b. From Bayesian networks to causal networks. Technical Report R-195-LLL, UCLA Cognitive Systems Lab. Short version: Statistical Science 8(3):266-269.

Pearl, J. 1993c. From conditional oughts to qualitative decision theory. In *Uncertainty in Artificial Intelligence: Proceedings of the Ninth Conference*, 12–20. Morgan Kaufmann.

Pereira, L. M.; Aparicio, J. N.; and Alferes, J. J. 1991. Counterfactual reasoning based on revising assumptions. In *Logic Programming: Proceedings of the 1991 International Symposium*, 566–577. Cambridge, MA: MIT Press.

Poole, D. 1993. Probabilistic Horn abduction and Bayesian networks. *Artificial Intelligence* 64(1):81–130.

Rubin, D. B. 1974. Estimating causal effects of treatments in randomized and nonrandomized studies. *Journal of Educational Psychology* 66(5):688–701.

Skyrms, B. 1980. The prior propensity account of subjunctive conditionals. In Harper, W.; Stalnaker, R.; and Pearce, G., eds., *Ifs*. D. Reidel. 259–265.

Spirtes, P.; Glymour, C.; and Scheines, R. 1993. *Causation, Prediction, and Search*. New York: Springer.

Whittaker, J. 1990. *Graphical Models in Applied Multivariate Statistics*. New York: John Wiley & Sons.

Symbolic Causal Networks

Adnan Darwiche
Rockwell International Science Center
444 High Street
Palo Alto, CA 94301
darwiche@rpal.rockwell.com

Judea Pearl
Computer Science Department
University of California
Los Angeles, CA 90024
pearl@cs.ucla.edu

Abstract

For a logical database to faithfully represent our beliefs about the world, one should not only insist on its logical consistency but also on its causal consistency. Intuitively, a database is causally inconsistent if it supports belief changes that contradict with our perceptions of causal influences — for example, coming to conclude that it must have rained only because the sprinkler was observed to be on. In this paper, we (1) suggest the notion of a causal structure to represent our perceptions of causal influences; (2) provide a formal definition of when a database is causally consistent with a given causal structure; (3) introduce symbolic causal networks as a tool for constructing databases that are guaranteed to be causally consistent; and (4) discuss various applications of causal consistency and symbolic causal networks, including nonmonotonic reasoning, Dempster–Shafer reasoning, truth maintenance, and reasoning about actions.

Introduction

Consider the database,

$$\Delta = \begin{array}{lcl} \text{wet\_ground} & \supset & \text{it\_rained} \\ \text{sprinkler\_was\_on} & \supset & \text{wet\_ground,} \end{array}$$

which entails no beliefs about whether it rained last night: $\Delta \not\models \text{it\_rained}$ and $\Delta \not\models \neg\text{it\_rained}$. If we tell this database that the sprinkler was on, it surprisingly jumps to the conclusion that it must have rained last night: $\Delta \cup \{\text{sprinkler\_was\_on}\} \models \text{it\_rained}$. This change in belief is counterintuitive! Given that we perceive no causal connection between the sprinkler and rain, we would not come to believe that it rained only because we observed the sprinkler on. That is, database Δ supports a belief change that contradicts common perceptions of causal influences, hence, it will be labeled *causally inconsistent.*

For another example of causal inconsistency, consider the database,

$$\Gamma = \text{kind} \supset \text{popular, } \text{fat} \supset \neg\text{popular.}$$

Initially, this database is ignorant about whether the person is kind: $\Gamma \not\models \text{kind}$ and $\Delta \not\models \neg\text{kind}$. However, once we tell the database that John is fat, it jumps to the strange result that John must be unkind: $\Gamma \cup \{\text{fat}\} \models \neg\text{kind}$. Here also, the database contradicts common perceptions of causal influences according to which no causal connection exists between kindness and weight. Therefore, database Γ is also causally inconsistent.

As it turns out, it is not uncommon for domain experts to construct databases that contradict with their own perceptions of causal influences, especially when the database is large enough and has multiple authors. The reason is that domain experts tend to focus on the plausibility of individual sentences rather than on the interactions among these sentences or how they would respond to future information.

But even when an expert is careful enough to construct a causally consistent database, it is not uncommon to turn it into a causally inconsistent one in the process of augmenting it with default assumptions. For example, an expert could have constructed the following database,

$$\Delta = \begin{array}{lcl} \text{wet\_ground} \wedge \neg\text{ab}_1 & \supset & \text{it\_rained} \\ \text{sprinkler\_was\_on} \wedge \neg\text{ab}_2 & \supset & \text{wet\_ground,} \end{array}$$

which is causally consistent because it remains ignorant about rain given information about the sprinkler. However, a nonmonotonic formalism that minimizes abnormalities would turn Δ into the database,

$$\Delta' = \begin{array}{lcl} \neg\text{ab}_1 \wedge \neg\text{ab}_2 & & \\ \text{wet\_ground} \wedge \neg\text{ab}_1 & \supset & \text{it\_rained} \\ \text{sprinkler\_was\_on} \wedge \neg\text{ab}_2 & \supset & \text{wet\_ground,} \end{array}$$

which is causally inconsistent because it finds sprinkler_was_on a sufficient evidence for it_rained: $\Delta' \not\models \text{it\_rained}$ and $\Delta' \cup \{\text{sprinkler\_was\_on}\} \models \text{it\_rained}$.

In fact, we shall see later that causally inconsistent databases are also not uncommon in ATMS implementations of diagnosis systems and Dempster-Shafer reasoning, thus leading to counterintuitive results (Laskey & Lehner 1989; Pearl 1990).

Given the importance of causal consistency, and given the tendency to generate causally inconsistent databases, we shall concern ourselves in this paper with formalizing this notion in order to support do-

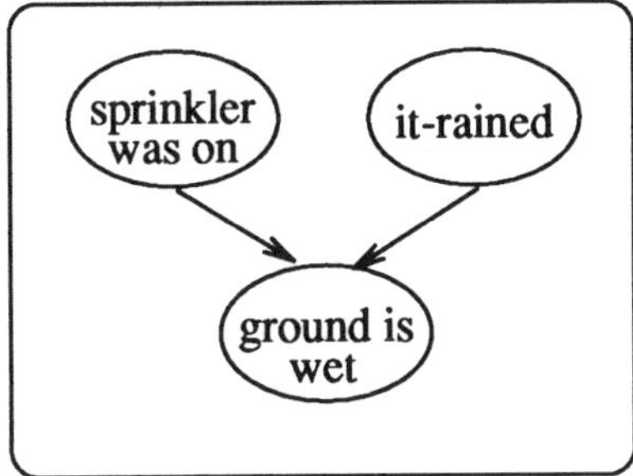

Figure 1: A causal structure.

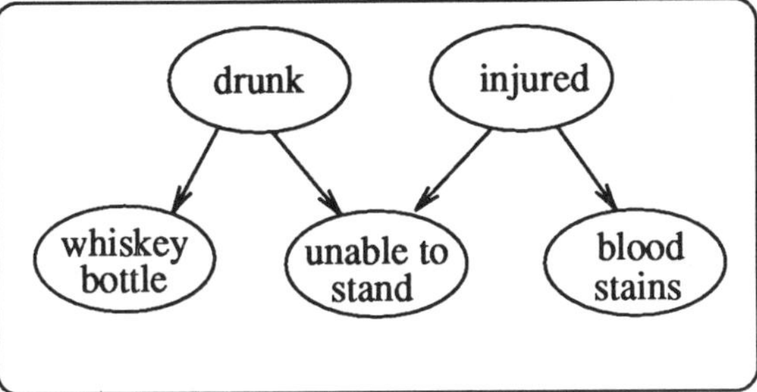

Figure 2: A causal structure.

main experts and commonsense formalisms in avoiding causally inconsistent databases.[1] In particular, we shall suggest the notion of a *causal structure* to represent perceptions of causal influences; provide a formal definition of when a database is causally consistent with a given causal structure; introduce *symbolic causal networks* as a tool for constructing causally consistent databases; and, finally, discuss various applications of symbolic causal networks, including nonmonotonic reasoning, truth maintenance, and reasoning about actions.

Causality and Belief Change

Since causal consistency is relative to specific perceptions of causal influences, formalizing causal consistency requires one to represent these perceptions formally. For this purpose, we will adopt causal structures, which are directed acyclic graphs that have been used extensively in the probabilistic literature for the same purpose (Pearl 1988b; Spirtes, Glymour, & Schienes 1993) — see Figures 1 and 2.[2]

The parents of a proposition p in a causal structure are those perceived to be its **direct causes.**

---

[1]The discussion in this paper is restricted to propositional databases.

[2]The results in this paper do not depend on a graphical representation of causal influences. For example, one can introduce a predicate *Direct_Cause* and proceed to axiomatize the contents of a causal structure.

The descendants of p are called its **effects** and the non–descendants of p are called its **non–effects.** In the structure of Figure 2, drunk and injured are the direct causes of unable_to_stand; unable_to_stand and whiskey_bottle are the effects of drunk; while injured and bloodstains are its non–effects.

Propositions that are relevant to the domain under consideration but do not appear in a causal structure are called the **exogenous propositions** of that structure. Exogenous propositions are the source of uncertainty in causal influences. They appear as *abnormality predicates* in nonmonotonic reasoning (Reiter 1987), as *assumption symbols* in ATMSs (de Kleer 1986), and as *random disturbances* in probabilistic models of causality (Pearl & Verma 1991). Each state of exogenous propositions will be referred to as an **extension.** For example, if ab_1 and ab_2 are the exogenous propositions of the structure in Figure 1, then $\neg ab_1 \wedge ab_2$ is an extension of that structure. Given an extension of a causal structure, there would be no longer any uncertainty about the causal influences it portrays.

The basic premise of this paper is that changes in our beliefs are typically constrained by the causal structures we perceive (Pearl 1988a). And the purpose of this section is to make these constraints precise so that a database is said to be consistent with a causal structure precisely when it does not contradict such constraints. The key to formalizing these constraints is the following interpretation of causal structures:

> The truth of each proposition in a causal structure is functionally determined by (a) the truth of its direct causes and (b) the truth of all exogenous propositions.

Following are some constraints on belief changes that are suggested by the above interpretation of causal structures (Pearl 1988b):

Common causes: In Figure 3a, the belief in c_2 should be independent of information about c_1 assuming that no information is available about e and that all exogenous propositions are known.

Indirect effects: In Figure 3b, the belief in e should be independent of information about c whenever proposition m and all exogenous propositions are known.

Common effects: In Figure 3c, the belief in e_2 should be independent of information about e_1 given that proposition c and all exogenous propositions are known.

These constraints on belief changes and others are summarized by **the principle of causal independence,** which is a version of the Markovian Condition in the probabilistic literature (Pearl 1988b; Spirtes, Glymour, & Schienes 1993). In a nutshell, the principle says that "once exogenous propositions and the direct causes of a proposition are known, the belief in that proposition should become independent

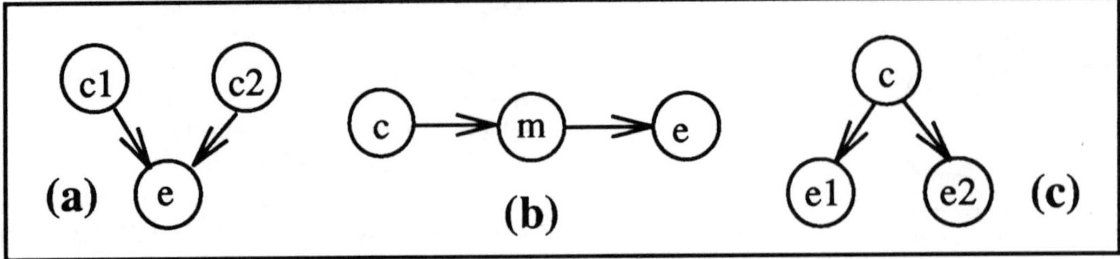

Figure 3: Causal interactions.

of information about its non–effects."[3]

We will formalize this principle in the remainder of this section and then use it later in defining causal consistency. But first, we need to define when database Δ finds X conditionally independent of Y given Z, that is, when adding information about Y to Δ does not change its belief in any information about X[4] given that Δ has full information about Z.[5] The following definition captures exactly this intuition:

Definition 1 (Conditional Independence) *Let X, Y, and Z be disjoint sets of atomic propositions and let $\hat{X}, \hat{Y}$, and $\hat{Z}$ be instantiations of these propositions, respectively. Database Δ finds X independent of Y given Z precisely when the logical consistency of $\Delta \cup \{\hat{Z}, \hat{X}\}$ and $\Delta \cup \{\hat{Z}, \hat{Y}\}$ implies the logical consistency of $\Delta \cup \{\hat{Z}, \hat{Y}, \hat{X}\}$.*

This is equivalent to saying that if Δ has full information about Z, then the addition of information about Y to Δ will not change its belief in any information about X.[6] For example, the database

$$\text{it\_rained} \lor \text{sprinkler\_was\_on} \equiv \text{wet\_ground}$$

finds {it_rained} independent of {sprinkler_was_on}, but finds them dependent given {wet_ground}. Similarly, the database,

$$\text{it\_rained} \supset \text{wet\_ground}, \quad \text{wet\_ground} \supset \text{slippery\_ground},$$

finds {slippery_ground} dependent on {it_rained}, but finds them independent given {wet_ground}. Finally,

---

[3]The requirement of knowing exogenous propositions renders this principle applicable to incomplete causal structures and constitutes, in fact, a definition of what information ought to be summarized by the exogenous variables.

[4]By information about a set of atomic propositions we mean a logical sentence constructed from these propositions.

[5]Database Δ has full information about atomic propositions Z if for each p in Z, Δ entails p or entails $\neg p$.

[6]This notion of independence is isomorphic to the one known in the literature on relational databases as multi-valued embedded dependencies. Therefore, this notion of independence satisfies the graphoid axioms (Pearl 1988b), which include symmetry (X is independent of Y given Z precisely when Y is independent of X given Z).

the database,

$$\text{battery\_is\_ok} \supset \text{lights\_on}, \quad \neg\text{battery\_is\_ok} \supset \neg\text{car\_starts},$$

finds {lights_on} dependent on {car_starts}, but finds them independent given {battery_is_ok}.

We are now ready to state the principle of causal independence formally:

Definition 2 (Causal Independence) *Database Δ satisfies the principle of causal independence with respect to causal structure $\mathcal{G}$ precisely when (a) Δ is logically consistent and (b) for every extension $\mathcal{E}$ of $\mathcal{G}$ that is logically consistent with Δ, the database $\Delta \cup \{\mathcal{E}\}$ finds each proposition in $\mathcal{G}$ conditionally independent of its non–effects given its direct causes.*

Causal Consistency

Consider the following database,

$$\Delta = \begin{array}{ll} \text{wet\_ground} \land \neg\text{ab}_1 & \supset \quad \text{it\_rained} \\ \text{sprinkler\_was\_on} \land \neg\text{ab}_2 & \supset \quad \text{wet\_ground}. \end{array}$$

This database does not satisfy the principle of causal independence with respect to the structure in Figure 1 because it finds sprinkler_was_on a sufficient evidence for it_rained under the extension $\neg\text{ab}_1 \land \neg\text{ab}_2$.

Note, however, that although database Δ does not satisfy the principle of causal independence, it does not contradict it either. Specifically, the extended database $\Delta \cup \{\text{ab}_1 \lor \text{ab}_2\}$ satisfies the principle because the added sentence $\text{ab}_1 \lor \text{ab}_2$ rules out the only extension, $\neg\text{ab}_1 \land \neg\text{ab}_2$, under which the database violates the principle. This suggests the following definition:

Definition 3 (Causal Consistency) *Let Δ be a database and let $\mathcal{G}$ be a causal structure. An extension $\mathcal{E}$ of $\mathcal{G}$ is causally consistent with Δ precisely when $\Delta \cup \{\mathcal{E}\}$ satisfies the principle of causal independence with respect to $\mathcal{G}$.*

That is, the extension $\neg\text{ab}_1 \land \neg\text{ab}_2$ above is causally inconsistent with database Δ, while the remaining extensions $\neg\text{ab}_1 \land \text{ab}_2$, $\text{ab}_1 \land \neg\text{ab}_2$, and $\text{ab}_1 \land \text{ab}_2$ are causally consistent with it.

We can further define a database as causally consistent precisely when it has at least one causally consistent extension. A definition of causal consistency was given in (Goldszmidt & Pearl 1992) for databases containing defeasible conditionals (defaults) and was based on a probabilistic semantics of defeasible conditionals. Definition 3 is based on standard propositional semantics, which makes it directly applicable to commonsense formalisms based on classical logic. Moreover, causal consistency as we have defined it here is a semantical notion, independent of database syntax.

As we mentioned earlier, even when a domain expert is careful enough to construct a causally consistent database, it is not uncommon for a nonmonotonic formalism to turn it into a causally inconsistent one. Consider, for example, the database

$$\Delta = \begin{array}{lll} \text{whiskey\_bottle} \wedge \neg\text{ab}_1 & \supset & \text{drunk} \\ \text{drunk} \wedge \neg\text{ab}_2 & \supset & \text{unable\_to\_stand} \\ \text{unable\_to\_stand} \wedge \neg\text{ab}_3 & \supset & \text{injured} \\ \text{injured} \wedge \neg\text{ab}_4 & \supset & \text{bloodstains,} \end{array}$$

which could easily be authored by a person perceiving the causal structure in Figure 2. When this database is fed to a nonmonotonic formalism that minimizes abnormalities, the formalism ends up augmenting it with the extension $\mathcal{E} = \{\neg\text{ab}_1, \neg\text{ab}_2, \neg\text{ab}_3, \neg\text{ab}_4\}$, which is causally inconsistent with Δ. Specifically, $\Delta \cup \mathcal{E}$ jumps to the conclusion bloodstains only because whiskey_bottle was observed: $\Delta \cup \mathcal{E} \not\models$ bloodstains and $\Delta \cup \mathcal{E} \cup \{\text{whiskey\_bottle}\} \models$ bloodstains.

With respect to the structure in Figure 2, database Δ has sixteen extensions corresponding to the different instantiations of the four abnormality predicates. As it turns out, all extensions containing $\neg\text{ab}_2 \wedge \neg\text{ab}_3$ are causally inconsistent, including the extension in which all abnormalities are minimized.

One way to avoid selecting these counterintuitive extensions is to inform nonmonotonic formalisms about causal consistency and provide them access to causal structures. A nonmonotonic formalism would then insist that only causally consistent extensions are selected. This approach should then lead to causal versions of existing nonmonotonic formalisms — for example, causal circumscription, causal default logic, and so on — in which each theory has a causal structure associated with it (Goldszmidt & Pearl 1992). Another solution is to feed nonmonotonic formalisms databases that already satisfy the principle of causal independence. In this case, nonmonotonic formalisms need not know about causality; they are guaranteed to stay out of danger because any extension that is logically consistent with the database is also causally consistent with it. For example, the database $\Delta \cup \{\text{ab}_2 \vee \text{ab}_3\}$ satisfies the principle of causal independence because the four extensions that are causally inconsistent are also logically inconsistent with the database. We will provide in the next section a systematic method for constructing databases that satisfy the principle of causal independence, thus eliminating the need to test for the causal consistency of extensions.

The connection between causality and nonmonotonic reasoning was discussed in (Pearl 1988a), where a system, called C-E, has been proposed for ensuring the faithfulness of default inferences to causal perceptions. In the C-E system, causality is represented by classifying defaults into either causal or evidential rules. We observe, however, that by classifying rules as such, one is indirectly communicating a causal structure. For example, the C-E rules wet_ground $\longrightarrow_E$ it_rained and sprinkler_was_on $\longrightarrow_C$ wet_ground implicitly encode the causal structure in Figure 1. In the C-E system, a causal structure is used procedurally to block default inferences that contradict with the structure. In the approach described here, a causal structure is used declaratively to classify extensions into those consistent with the structure and those inconsistent with it.

Separating the causal structure from the rule syntax has a number of merits. First, it keeps one within the realm of classical logic, which makes the approach applicable to logic–based formalisms such as circumscription and ATMSs. Next, using rules to communicate a causal structure may overburden domain experts. For example, to express the sentence $\neg$sprinkler_was_on $\wedge$ $\neg$it_rained $\supset$ $\neg$wet_ground, one needs three C-E rules: $\neg$sprinkler_was_on$\wedge\neg$it_rained $\longrightarrow_C$ $\neg$wet_ground, wet_ground $\wedge$ $\neg$it_rained $\longrightarrow_E$ sprinkler_was_on, and wet_ground $\wedge$ $\neg$sprinkler_was_on $\longrightarrow_E$ it_rained. Finally, it is not always clear whether a rule is causal or evidential. For example, given the rules it_rained $\longrightarrow_C$ $\neg$sprinkler_was_on[7] and wet_ground $\longrightarrow_E$ it_rained, it is not clear whether the rule $\neg$it_rained $\wedge$ wet_ground $\longrightarrow$ sprinkler_was_on is evidential or causal.

Symbolic Causal Networks

We will concern ourselves in this section with providing a systematic procedure that is guaranteed to generate databases that are not only causally consistent, but also satisfy the principle of causal independence. Therefore, the generated databases can be given to nonmonotonic formalisms without having to worry about whether adding assumptions will make them causally inconsistent.

The procedure we propose is that of constructing a symbolic causal network: a propositional database that is annotated by a causal structure.

A symbolic causal network has two components: A **causal structure** $\mathcal{G}$ that captures perceptions of causal influences and a set of **micro theories** capturing logical relationships between propositions and their direct causes — see Figures 4 and 5.

A micro theory for p is a set of clauses δ, where

1. each clause in δ refers only to p, its direct causes, and to exogenous propositions;

2. if δ entails a clause that does not mention p, then that clause must be vacuous.

Condition 1 ensures the locality of a micro theory to a proposition and its direct causes, while Condition 2

---

[7]We have a device that deactivates the sprinkler when it detects rain.

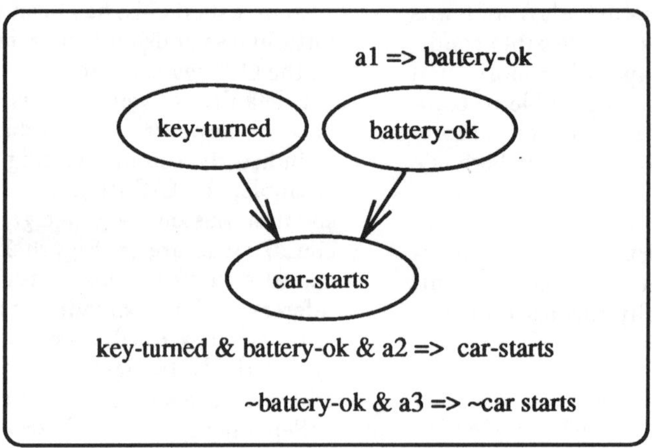

Figure 4: A symbolic causal network.

prohibits a micro theory for p from specifying a relationship between the direct causes of p.[8]

One can ensure the previous conditions by adhering to micro theories that contain only two types of material implications: $\psi \wedge \alpha \supset p$ and $\phi \wedge \beta \supset \neg p$, where

1. ψ and ϕ are constructed from the direct causes of p;

2. α and β are constructed from exogenous propositions; and

3. $\alpha \wedge \beta$ is unsatisfiable whenever $\psi \wedge \phi$ is satisfiable.

For example, the sentences kind $\wedge \neg ab_1 \supset$ popular and fat $\wedge \neg ab_2 \supset \neg$popular do not constitute a micro theory for popular since $\neg ab_1 \wedge \neg ab_2$ and kind $\wedge$ fat are both satisfiable. This leads to the relationship $\neg ab_1 \wedge \neg ab_2 \wedge$ fat $\supset \neg$kind between weight and kindness, thus violating Condition 2 of micro theories.

We stress here that micro theories do not appeal to the distinction between evidential and causal rules. Formally, a micro theory contains standard propositional sentences and is constrained only by its locality (to specific propositions) and by what it can express about these propositions, both are characteristic of causal modeling. For example, one typically does not specify a relationship between the inputs to a digital gate by stating that certain input combinations would lead to conflicting predictions about the output.

If one induces a propositional database using a symbolic causal network — that is, by associating micro theories with the propositions of a causal structure — then one is guaranteed the following:

Theorem 1 *Let Δ be a database induced by a symbolic causal network having causal structure $\mathcal{G}$. Then Δ satisfies the principle of causal independence with respect to $\mathcal{G}$.*

---

[8] The satisfaction of such local conditions permits us to predict feasible scenarios in a backtrack–free manner (Dechter & Pearl 1991).

As a representational language, symbolic causal networks are complete with respect to databases that do not constrain the state of exogenous propositions:

Theorem 2 *Let Δ be a database satisfying the principle of causal independence with respect to a causal structure $\mathcal{G}$. If Δ is logically consistent with every extension of $\mathcal{G}$, then Δ can be induced by a symbolic causal network that has $\mathcal{G}$ as its causal structure.*

Applications of Symbolic Causal Networks

The basic motivation behind symbolic causal networks has been their ability to guarantee causal consistency. But symbolic causal networks can be viewed as the logical analogue of probabilistic causal networks; see Table 1. Therefore, many of the applications of probabilistic causal networks have counterparts in symbolic causal networks. We elaborate on some of these applications in this section. Other applications, such as diagnosis, are discussed elsewhere (Darwiche 1993).

Logical consistency One of the celebrated features of probabilistic causal networks is their ability to ensure the global consistency of the probability distribution they represent as long as the probabilities associated with each proposition in a causal structure are locally consistent. Symbolic causal networks provide a similar guarantee: As long as the micro theories associated with individual propositions satisfy their local conditions, the global database is guaranteed to be logically consistent. This is a corollary of Theorem 1.

Causal truth maintenance In the same way that probabilistic causal networks are supported by algorithms that compute probabilities (Pearl 1988b), symbolic causal networks are supported by algorithms that compute ATMS labels (Darwiche 1993; de Kleer 1986;

	Probabilistic causal network	Symbolic causal network
Represents	probability distribution + effects of actions	propositional database + effects of actions
Graphically Encodes	probabilistic independences + causal structure	logical independences + causal structure
Guarantees	probabilistic consistency Markovian condition	logical consistency causal independence
Computes	probabilities	arguments (ATMS labels)

Table 1: Analogous notions in probabilistic and symbolic causal networks.

Reiter & de Kleer 1987).[9] Therefore, symbolic causal networks inherit the applications of ATMSs. The important difference with traditional ATMSs, however, is that the database formed by a symbolic causal network is guaranteed (by satisfying causal independence) to protect us from conclusions that clash with our causal understanding of the domain. The importance of this property is best illustrated by an example that uses ATMSs to implement Dempster–Shafer reasoning (Laskey & Lehner 1989; Pearl 1990). Specifically, the Dempster–Shafer rules, wet_ground $\xrightarrow{.7}$ it_rained and sprinkler_was_on $\xrightarrow{.9}$ wet_ground, are typically reasoned about in an ATMS framework by constructing the database,

$$\Delta = \begin{array}{ll} \text{wet\_ground} \wedge a_1 & \supset \quad \text{it\_rained} \\ \text{sprinkler\_was\_on} \wedge a_2 & \supset \quad \text{wet\_ground}, \end{array}$$

and attaching probabilities .7 and .9 to the assumptions a_1 and a_2 (Laskey & Lehner 1989). Initially, the ATMS label of it_rained is empty and, hence, the belief in it_rained is zero. After observing sprinkler_was_on, however, the ATMS label of it_rained becomes $a_1 \wedge a_2$, which raises the belief in it_rained to $.7 * .9 = .63$. That is, the belief in it_rained increased from zero to .63 only because sprinkler_was_on was observed; see (Pearl 1990) for more related examples.

We get this counterintuitive behavior here because database Δ does not satisfy the principle of causal independence with respect to the causal structure in Figure 1. If the database satisfies this principle, the ATMS label of it_rained is guaranteed not to change as a result of adding sprinkler_was_on to the database — see (Darwiche 1993) for more details on this guarantee. For example, the database $\Delta \cup \{\neg a_1 \vee \neg a_2\}$ satisfies the principle of causal independence with respect to the causal structure in Figure 1. Therefore, the ATMS label it assigns to it_rained is empty and so is the label that $\Delta \cup \{\text{sprinkler\_was\_on}\}$ assigns to it_rained. This guarantees that Dempster–Shafer belief in it_rained remains zero after sprinkler_was_on is observed.

---

[9] More precisely, symbolic causal networks compute *arguments*, which are logically equivalent to ATMS labels but are not necessarily put in canonical form (Darwiche 1993). Computing arguments is easier than computing ATMS labels. In fact, the complexity of computing arguments in symbolic causal networks is symmetric to the complexity of computing probabilities in probabilistic causal networks (Darwiche 1992; 1993).

Reasoning about actions Our focus so far has been the enforcement of causal constraints on belief changes that result from observations (belief revisions). But perceptions of causal influences also constrain (and in fact are often defined by) belief changes that result from interventions (named belief updates in (Katsuno & Mendelzon 1991)). For example, if we connect C in the first circuit of Figure 5 to a high voltage, we would come to believe that A and D will be set to OFF. But if we perform the same action on the second circuit, we would not come to the same belief. Note, however, that the two circuits have the same logical description, and do not mention external interventions explicitly, which means that they would lead to equivalent belief changes under all observations.

The reason why the same action leads to different results from two logically equivalent descriptions is that the descriptions are accompanied by different causal structures. It is the constraints encoded by these structures that govern our expectations regarding interventions in these circuits (Goldszmidt & Pearl 1992). A related paper (Darwiche & Pearl 1994) provides a specific proposal for predicting the effect of action when domain knowledge is represented using a symbolic causal network, showing also how the frame, ramification and concurrency problems can be handled effectively in this context. The key idea is that micro theories allow one to organize causal knowledge efficiently in terms of just a few basic mechanisms, each involving a relatively small number of propositions. Each external elementary action overrules just one mechanism leaving the others unaltered. The specification of an action then requires only the identification of the mechanism which is overruled by that action. Once this is identified, the overall effect of the action (or combinations thereof) can be computed from the immediate effect of the action, combined with the constraints imposed by the remaining mechanisms. Thus, in addition to encoding a set of current beliefs, and belief changes due to hypothetical observations, a causal database constrains how future beliefs would change in response to every hypothetical action or actions combination (Pearl 1993). These latter constraints can in fact be viewed as the defining characteristic of causal relationships, of which the Markovian condition is a byproduct (Pearl & Verma 1991).

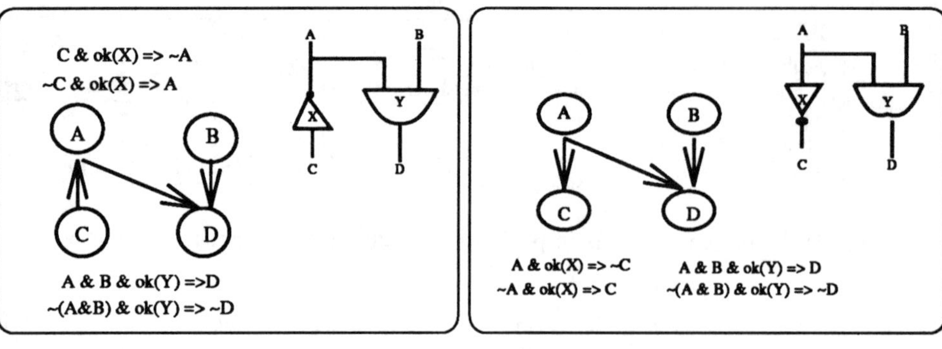

Figure 5: Different symbolic causal networks leading to logically equivalent databases.

Conclusion

If a classical logic database is to faithfully represent our beliefs about the world, the database must be consistent with our perceptions of causal influences. In this paper, we proposed a language for representing such perceptions and then formalized the consistency of a logical database relative to a given causal structure. We also introduced symbolic causal networks as tools for constructing databases that are guaranteed to be causally consistent. Finally, we discussed other applications of symbolic causal networks, including the maintenance of logical consistency, nonmonotonic reasoning, Dempster–Shafer reasoning, truth maintenance, and reasoning about actions and change.

Acknowledgments

The research was partially supported by ARPA contract #F30602-91-C-0031, Air Force grant #AFOSR 90 0136, NSF grant #IRI-9200918, and Northrop-Rockwell Micro grant #93-124. This work benefitted from discussions with Moises Goldszmidt and Sek-Wah Tan.

References

Darwiche, A., and Pearl, J. 1994. Symbolic causal networks for reasoning about actions and plans. Working notes: AAAI Spring Symposium on Decision–Theoretic Planning.

Darwiche, A. 1992. *A Symbolic Generalization of Probability Theory*. Ph.D. Dissertation, Stanford University.

Darwiche, A. 1993. Argument calculus and networks. In *Proceedings of the Ninth Conference on Uncertainty in Artificial Intelligence (UAI)*, 420–427.

de Kleer, J. 1986. An assumption-based TMS. *Artificial Intelligence* 28:127–162.

Dechter, R., and Pearl, J. 1991. Directed constraint networks: A relational framework for causal modeling. In *Proceedings, 12th International Joint Conference of Artificial Intelligence (IJCAI-91)*, 1164–1170.

Goldszmidt, M., and Pearl, J. 1992. Rank–based systems: A simple approach to belief revision, belief update and reasoning about evidence and actions. In *Proceedings of the Third Conference on Principles of Knowledge Representation and Reasoning*, 661–672. Morgan Kaufmann Publishers, Inc., San Mateo, California.

Katsuno, H., and Mendelzon, A. 1991. On the difference between updating a knowledge base and revising it. In *Principles of Knowledge Representation and Reasoning: Proceedings of the Second International Conference*, 387–394.

Laskey, K. B., and Lehner, P. E. 1989. Assumptions, beliefs, and probabilities. *Artificial Intelligence* 41(1):65–77.

Pearl, J., and Verma, T. 1991. A theory of inferred causation. In *Principles of Knowledge Representation and Reasoning: Proceedings of the Second International Conference*, 441–452.

Pearl, J. 1988a. Embracing causality in default reasoning. *Artificial Intelligence* 35:259–271.

Pearl, J. 1988b. *Probabilistic Reasoning in Intelligent Systems: Networks of Plausible Inference*. Morgan Kaufmann Publishers, Inc., San Mateo, California.

Pearl, J. 1990. Which is more believable, the probably provable or the provably probable. In *Proceedings, CSCSI-90, 8th Canadian Conference on AI*, 1–7.

Pearl, J. 1993. From bayesian networks to causal networks. Technical Report R-195-LLL, Cognetive Systems Laboratory, UCLA. (Short version in *Statistical Science*, Vol. 8, No. 3 (1993), pp. 266-269.).

Reiter, R., and de Kleer, J. 1987. Foundations of assumption-based truth maintenance systems: Preliminary report. In *Proceedings of AAAI*, 183 -188. AAAI.

Reiter, R. 1987. Nonmonotonic reasoning. *Ann. Rev. Comput. Sci* 2:147–186.

Spirtes, P.; Glymour, C.; and Schienes, R. 1993. *Causation, Prediction, and Search*. New York: Springer-Verlag.

Causal Default Reasoning:
Principles and Algorithms

Hector Geffner

Departamento de Computación
Universidad Simón Bolívar
Aptdo 89000, Caracas 1080-A
Venezuela
hector@usb.ve

Abstract

The minimal model semantics is a natural interpretation of defaults yet it often yields a behavior that is too weak. This weakness has been traced to the inability of minimal models to reflect certain *implicit* preferences among defaults, in particular, preferences for defaults grounded on more 'specific' information and preferences arising in causal domains. Recently, 'specificity' preferences have been explained in terms of conditionals. Here we aim to explain causal preferences. We draw mainly from ideas known in Bayesian Networks to formulate and formalize *two principles* that explain the basic preferences that arise in causal default reasoning. We then define a semantics based on those principles and show how variations of the algorithms used for inheritance reasoning and temporal projection can be used to compute in the resulting formalism.

Motivation

The semantics of minimal models provides a direct interpretation of defaults: to determine the acceptable consequences of a classical theory W augmented with a set D of formulas labeled as 'defaults', the semantics selects the models of W that violate minimal subsets of D. The resulting semantics is simple and captures the basic intuition that 'as many defaults should be accepted as it is consistently possible". Yet the conclusions sanctioned are too weak. Consider for example the theory comprised of the defaults[1]

$$(\star) \qquad r_1 : a \to d \ , \ r_2 : a \wedge b \to \neg d \ , \ r_3 : c \to b$$

The defaults may stand for the rules 'if I turn the key, the car will start', 'if I turn the key and the battery is dead, the car won't start', and 'if I left the lights on last night, the battery is dead'. They can also be thought as a simplified representation of the Yale Shooting scenario (Hanks & McDermott 1987): 'if Fred is alive, he will be alive', 'if Fred is alive and I shoot, Fred won't be alive', and 'if I load the gun, I will shoot'.

---

[1]Throughout the paper, defaults $p \to q$ are regarded as material implications, not as rules of inference. Material implications which are firmly believed will be denoted with the symbol '$\Rightarrow$'.

Given the facts a and c, we would expect the conclusion $b \wedge \neg d$. Yet the facts produce three minimal models M_i, each M_i violating a single default r_i, $i = 1, 2, 3$, with two of those models, M_2 and M_3, sanctioning exactly the opposite conclusion.

Part of the reason the expected conclusion is not sanctioned is that we haven't explicated the precedence of the rule $a \wedge b \to \neg d$ over the conflicting but less 'specific' rule $a \to d$. This precedence can be expressed in a number of ways: by giving the first rule priority over the second, by making the first rule a strict non-defeasible rule, or by adding explicit axioms to 'cancel' the second rule when the first rule is applicable. Each of these options have different merits. For our purposes what matters is that they all prune the minimal model M_2 that violates the 'superior' rule r_2, but leave the other two minimal models M_1 and M_3 intact. Hence, the expected conclusion $b \wedge \neg d$ still fails to be sanctioned. The question this raises, is: *on what grounds can the 'unintended' minimal model M_3, where rule r_3 is violated, be pruned?*

The default theory $(\star)$ is not very different from the theories handled by inheritance and temporal projection algorithms (Horty, Thomason, & Touretzky. 1987; Dean & McDermott 1987). The idea in these algorithms is to use a default like $A \to p$ to conclude p from A, when either there are no 'reasons' for $\neg p$ or when those reasons are 'weaker' than $A \to p$. The essence of these algorithms is a careful form of forward chaining that can be expressed as follows:

Procedure P_0

$\vdash p$ if p in W or $\vdash A$, $A \to p$ in D, and all *forward arguments* for $\sim p$ not weaker than $A \to p$ contain a rule $B \to q$ s.t. $\vdash \sim q$

As it is common in these procedures, rules are definite, A and B are conjunctions of atoms, p and $\sim p$ are incompatible propositions, and $\vdash A$ holds when $\vdash a_i$ holds for each $a_i \in A$. Likewise, forward arguments for $\sim p$ are collection of rules Δ that permit us to establish $\sim p$ from the facts W by *reasoning along the direction of the rules*. That is, such collection of rules Δ must contain a rule $C \to \sim p$ such that C logically follows from Δ and W. The strength of such rules determine the strength of the argument.

The theory $(\star)$ can be processed by this procedure once the literal $\neg \mathsf{d}$ is replaced by a new atom d' declared to be incompatible with d. P_0 then yields a and c, as $W = \{\mathsf{a}, \mathsf{c}\}$, then b, as r_3 is a reason for b and there are no forward arguments for $\sim\mathsf{b}$, and finally c, as r_2 is a reason for d' and the only forward argument for $\sim\mathsf{d}'$ (d) rests on the rule r_1 that is weaker than r_2.

The procedure P_0 is simple and intuitive, and as the example shows, captures inferences that escape the minimal model semantics. To understand why this happens it is useful to look at the latter from its proof-theoretic perspective. The proof-theory of minimal models can be understood in terms of *arguments:*

Definition 1 *A subset Δ of D is an* argument *against a default r in D given a set of formulas W, when $W + \Delta$ is logically consistent but $W + \Delta + \{r\}$ is not.*

If there is an argument against r, there will be a minimal model that violates r, and vice versa. In the presence of priorities, arguments need to be ordered by 'strength' and this criterion has to be modified slightly (Baker & Ginsberg 1989; Geffner 1992).

In the theory $(\star)$ the 'spurious' model M_3 pops up because the rules r_1 and r_2 provide an argument against r_3. This argument is not considered by P_0 because it is not a *forward* argument. Since this is the right thing to do in this case, one may wonder whether non-forward arguments can always be ignored. The answer is no. For example, if d is observed, P_0 would still derive b, implicitly favoring rule r_2 over r_3 with no justification. The same is true for approaches in which defaults are represented by one-directional rules of inference. Interestingly, in such a case, the minimal model semantics behaves correctly.

Causal Rule Systems

Preliminary Definitions

The problem of defining a semantics for causal default theories can be seen as the problem of distinguishing legitimate arguments from spurious ones. In this section we will look closer at this distinction in the context of a class of simple causal default theories that we call *causal rule systems* or CRSs for short. The language of causal rule systems is sufficiently powerful to model interesting domains and most scenarios analyzed in the literature but purposely excludes non-causal rules and disjunctions. We will report the extensions to handle these and other constructs elsewhere.

A *causal rule system* T comprises a set D of *defeasible causal rules* $A \rightarrow p$ where p is an atom and A is a conjunction of zero or more atoms, a set F of atomic *facts,* and a set C of *constraints* expressing that a given conjunction of atoms B cannot be true. Variables are assumed to be universally quantified. Rules and constraints will refer to members of D and C respectively, or to ground instances of

them. Likewise, constraints will be divided between *background constraints* and *observed constraints.* The former will express domain constraints and will be denoted by rules $B \rightarrow$ with no head (e.g., $\mathtt{alive}(p, t) \wedge \mathtt{dead}(p, t) \rightarrow$), while the latter will express contingent constraints and will be denoted as $\neg B$ (e.g., $\neg[\mathtt{on}(\mathsf{a}, \mathsf{b}, \mathsf{t_1}) \wedge \mathtt{on}(\mathsf{b}, \mathsf{c}, \mathsf{t_1})]$). This distinction between background and evidence is implicit in probability theory and in Bayesian Networks (Pearl 1988b) and it used in several theories of default reasoning (Geffner 1992; Poole 1992). For simplicity, we will assume that background constraints $B \rightarrow$ involve exactly two atoms. We will say that such pairs of atoms are *incompatible* and use the expression $\sim p$ to denote atoms q *incompatible* with p. The generalization to n-ary background constraints is straightforward but makes the notation more complex and it is seldom needed.

Every rule will have a *priority* which will be represented by a non-negative integer; the higher the number associated with a rule, the higher its priority. This scheme is sufficiently simple and will not introduce the distortions common to total orderings of defaults because *the scope of priorities will be local:* priorities will only establish an order among rules $A \rightarrow p$ and $B \rightarrow \sim p$ whose consequents are incompatible. Priorities thus play a role analogous to local conditional probability matrices in Bayesian Nets allowing us to determine the net effect of conflicting causal influences acting on the same proposition. Unless otherwise stated, all priorities will be assumed equal.

Finally, as in other representations involving causal relations (e.g., (Shoham 1988; Pearl 1988b)), we will require that causal rules be *acyclic*. To make this precise, let us define the dependency graph of a CRS as a directed graph whose nodes are ground atoms, and where for every instance of a causal rule $A \rightarrow p$ there is a c-link relating every atom a in A to p, and for every instance of a background constraint $p \wedge q \rightarrow$, there are two k-links, one from p to q and another from q to p. Then, a CRS is *acyclic* iff its dependency graph does not contain cycles involving c-links. It's very simple to check that the encoding of acyclic inheritance network in CRSs is acyclic, like the encoding of theories about change (see below).

Semantics

The key to distinguishing legitimate arguments from spurious ones lies in an idea advanced by Pearl in a number of places which is at the basis of the model of intercausal relations captured by Bayesian Networks. It says that *two events should not interact through a common variable that they causally affect, if that variable or a consequence of it has not been observed* (Pearl 1988b, pp. 19). As we will see below, there are arguments in causal rule systems that violate this criterion. To identify and prune such arguments, it will be useful to recall the distinction between forward and backward arguments:

Definition 2 *An argument Δ against a rule $A \to p$ is a forward argument when Δ contains a rule $B \to \sim p$ such that B is supported by Δ.*[2] *An argument which is not a forward argument is a* backward *argument.*

In causal rule systems, all forward and backward arguments arise from rules violating some constraint. That is, a consistent collection of rules Δ will be an argument against a default $A \to p$ when the rules $\Delta + \{A \to p\}$ support a conjunction of atoms B ruled out by some constraint. Moreover, such a constraint can be either part of the evidence or part of the background. In a Bayesian Network, the former would be represented by an observation and the latter by the network itself.[3] It is simple to check then that the arguments that violate Pearl's criterion are precisely the *the backward arguments that do not originate in evidential constraints but in background constraints.* Such arguments establish a relation on events merely because they have *conflicting* causal influences on unobserved variables. To identify and prune those arguments, we will first make precise the distinction between background and evidential constraints.

Definition 3 *An* evidential constraint *is a formula $\neg B$, where B is a conjunction of atoms that is consistent with the background constraints but inconsistent with the background constraints and the evidence (facts and observed constraints).*

Basically, $\neg B$ is an evidential constraint when $\neg B$ is an observed constraint, or when $B \wedge A \to$ or $\neg(B \wedge A)$ are background or observed constraints, and A is a conjunction of one or more *facts*.

The backward arguments that arise from evidential constraints will be called *evidential arguments,* and the ones arising from background constraints will be called *spurious arguments.*

Definition 4 *A collection of rules Δ is* refuted by the evidence *or is an* evidential nogood *when Δ supports B, for an evidential constraint $\neg B$. A backward argument Δ against a rule r is* evidential *when $\Delta + \{r\}$ is refuted by the evidence, and is* spurious *otherwise.*

For example, in the theory that results from $(\star)$ by replacing $\neg d$ by an atom d' incompatible with d, there are no evidential constraints and the backward argument against rule r_3 comprised of rules r_1 and r_2 is spurious. On the other hand, if d is observed, there will be an evidential constraint $\neg d'$ and r_2 will provide an evidential argument against r_3.

---

[2] A formula w is supported by Δ, when w logically follows Δ and the facts.

[3] The constraint that p and q cannot be both true can be captured in a Bayesian Network either by encoding p and q as values of a single variable, or by encoding them as values of two different variables with a third variable, *observed to be 'false'*, which is true when both p and q are true.

Before defining a semantics that reflects this distinction, let us define *causal arguments* as forward arguments with the appropriate strength:

Definition 5 *A forward argument Δ against a default $A \to p$ is a causal argument when Δ contains a rule $B \to \sim p$ not weaker than $A \to p$ such that B is supported by Δ.*

The basic principle in causal default reasoning can then be expressed as follows:

> Only causal and evidential arguments need to be considered in causal default reasoning. In particular, rules not facing causal or evidential arguments should be accepted.

Although the given definitions of causal and evidential arguments are tied to the language of causal rule system, these notions, like the notions of causal and evidential support in Bayesian Networks, are more general. It should thus be possible to devise analogous definitions for more powerful languages.

The semantics of causal rule systems will reflect this principle. We will define it in two steps. Let us first say that *an argument Δ is validated by a model M* when M does not violate any rule in Δ, and that a rule r violated by a model M is *causally (evidentially) justified* when there is a causal (evidential) argument against r validated by M. Let us also say that a causal rule system is *predictive* when it does not give rise to evidential arguments; i.e., when no collection of rules is refuted by the evidence. Then, since in the absence of evidential arguments only causal arguments need to be considered, the semantics of predictive systems can be defined as follows:

Definition 6 *The* causal models *of a predictive causal rule system are the models in which every rule violated is causally justified.*

To extend this semantics to an arbitrary causal rule system T, we will use the expression T/Δ to denote the result of removing the rules in Δ from T. The minimal collection of rules Δ that render T/Δ a *predictive* system will be called *culprit sets*. It's easy to check that these culprit sets are exactly the minimal sets of rules that 'hit' all collections of rules refuted by the evidence (the evidential nogoods). The semantics of *arbitrary* causal rule systems can then be defined as follows:

Definition 7 *The causal models of an arbitrary causal rule system T are the causal models of the* predictive *systems T/Δ for any culprit set Δ.*

The system that results from the theory $(\star)$ after changing $\neg d$ by d' is a predictive system with a single class of causal models where r_1 is the only violated rule. On the other hand, if the fact d is added, two culprit sets $\{r_2\}$ and $\{r_3\}$ arise, and the causal models of the resulting theory will satisfy r_1 and violate one of r_2 or r_3.

Definition 8 *A ground atom p is a causal consequence of a causal rule system T iff p holds in all causal models of T.*

Some Properties

Proposition 1 *Causal models always exist when the facts and constraints are logically consistent.*

Now let $\Delta[M]$ denote the collection of rules violated by a causal model M of a causal rule system T. Then, $T/\Delta[M]$ is a logically consistent set of Horn clauses, and thus, has a unique minimal Herbrand model M_H. Clearly M_H is a causal model of T as well, and moreover, it is a *canonical model* in the sense that only models like M_H need to be considered:

Proposition 2 *A ground atom p is a causal consequence of a causal rule system T if p is true in all its* canonical *causal models.*

Every consistent causal rule system will have one or more canonical causal models. Finding one of them can be done efficiently:

Theorem 1 *The problem of finding a canonical causal model for a finite propositional* CRS *is tractable.*

The importance of this result is that many theories of interest have a *unique* canonical causal model. Let us say that a theory is *deterministic* when for every pair of rules $A \rightarrow p$ and $B \rightarrow \sim p$ with incompatible consequents and compatible antecedents, one rule has priority over the other. Then for predictive theories that are deterministic we get:

Theorem 2 *Causal rule systems which are predictive and deterministic possess a single canonical causal model.*

Corollary 1 *The problem of determining whether a given ground atom is a causal consequence of a finite, predictive and deterministic causal rule system is tractable.*

A class of causal theories that are predictive and deterministic are the theories for reasoning about change which include no information about the 'future' (Lin & Shoham 1991; Sandewall 1993). They can be expressed as CRSs of the form:

Persistence:	$T(f, s) \rightarrow T(f, r(a, s))$
Action:	$T(p_1, s) \wedge \cdots \wedge T(p_n, s) \rightarrow T(f, r(a, s))$
Facts:	$T(f_1, s_0) \; ; \; T(f_2, s_0) \; ; \; \ldots$
Constraints:	$T(f, s) \wedge T(g, s) \rightarrow$

It's simple to verify that the resulting theories are acyclic, predictive and deterministic (assuming rules about change have priority over rules about persistence). An equivalent formulation based on time rather than on situations would have similar properties. Most semantics for reasoning about change coincide for theories like the one above: the preferred model is the one which is 'chronologically' minimal (Shoham 1988),

where every 'exception' is explained (Gelfond & Lifschitz 1988), where actions are minimized (Lifschitz 1987), etc. Moreover, the proof-procedure P_0 presented in Section 1 is adequate for such systems (the facts F should take the place of W in P_0):

Theorem 3 *The proof-procedure P_0 is sound and complete for finite causal rule systems that are both predictive and deterministic. The procedure P_0 remains sound but not necessarily complete for systems which are predictive but not deterministic.*

Priorities Revisited

The results of the previous section seem to confirm that for predictive theories causal models are adequate. For more general theories however, they are not. A simple example illustrates the problem. Consider the chain of rules:

$$r_1 : \mathbf{a} \rightarrow \mathbf{b} \; , \;\; r_2 : \mathbf{b} \rightarrow \mathbf{c} \; , \;\; r_3 : \mathbf{c} \rightarrow \mathbf{d}$$

together with the rule $r_4 : \mathbf{f} \rightarrow \mathbf{c'}$, where $\mathbf{c}$ and $\mathbf{c'}$ are incompatible and r_4 has priority over r_2. Given $\mathbf{a}$ and $\mathbf{f}$, we get a predictive, deterministic theory, whose single (canonical) causal model M sanctions $\mathbf{b}$ and $\mathbf{c'}$. If the prediction $\mathbf{c'}$ is confirmed, however, another causal model M' pops up, which refutes the prediction $\mathbf{b}$. This is because the observation $\mathbf{c'}$ yields an evidential constraint $\neg \mathbf{c}$ that refutes the rules r_1 and r_2, producing two culprit sets $\{r_1\}$ and $\{r_2\}$.

The explanation for this behavior can also be found by looking at probability theory and Bayesian Networks. We have a 'gate' composed of two conflicting rules $r_4 : \mathbf{f} \rightarrow \mathbf{c'}$ and $r_2 : \mathbf{b} \rightarrow \mathbf{c}$, with r_4 having priority over r_2. The semantics partially reflects this priority by validating r_4 in all causal models. Yet, while it makes $\mathbf{b}$ irrelevant to $\mathbf{c'}$, it makes $\mathbf{c'}$ *relevant* to $\mathbf{b}$; i.e., $\mathbf{c'}$ refutes $\mathbf{b}$ even though $\mathbf{b}$ does not refute $\mathbf{c'}$. This is anomalous because irrelevance should be symmetric (Pearl 1988b). A common solution to this problem is to add 'cancellation axioms' (like making rule r_2 *inapplicable* when $\mathbf{f}$ holds). Here we develop a different solution that avoids making such axioms explicit.

Let us say that a rule $A \rightarrow p$ is a *defeater* of a conflicting rule $B \rightarrow \sim p$ when its priority is higher and that $A \rightarrow p$ is *verified* in a model when both A and p hold in the model. Then, we will be able to regard a collection of rules Δ as *irrelevant* when those rules are *defeated* as follows:[4]

Definition 9 *A collection of rules Δ is* defeated *or* preempted *in a causal rule system T when every causal model of T/Δ verifies a defeater for each rule in Δ.*

Then the second principle needed is:

----

[4]The notions of defeat and preemption are common in inheritance algorithms and argument systems (e.g., (Horty, Thomason, & Touretzky. 1987; Pollock 1987)). Here the corresponding notions are slightly more involved because rules are used to reason both forward and backward.

$$\boxed{\text{Arguments involving defeated rules are irrelevant}}$$

Certainly, *defeat is closed under union:*

Theorem 4 *If Δ_1 and Δ_2 are two sets of rules defeated in T, then the union $\Delta_1 + \Delta_2$ of those sets is also defeated in T.*

This means that in any causal rule system T there is always a unique maximal set of defeated rules which we will denote as $\Delta_0[T]$. The strengthened causal consequences of a causal rule system T can then be defined as follows:

Definition 10 (Revised) *A ground atom p is a causal consequence of a causal rule system T if p is true in all causal models of $T/\Delta_0[T]$.*

Since the second principle was motivated by problems that result from the presence of evidential arguments, it's reassuring that the new semantics is equivalent to the old one when such arguments are not present:

Theorem 5 *A ground atom p is a causal consequence of a predictive causal rule system T iff p is true in all causal models of T.*

To check whether a given atom p is a causal consequence however, it's not necessary to first identify the maximal set of rules defeated; any such set suffices:

Theorem 6 *If a ground atom p is true in all causal models of T/Δ, for any set of rules Δ defeated in T, then p is a causal consequence of T.*

We address finally the task of *computing* in general theories:

Theorem 7 *Let $P = \{p_1, p_2, \ldots, p_n\}$ be a collection of atoms derived by the procedure P_0 from a system T by application of a collection of rules Δ. Then each p_i in P is a causal consequence of T if P shields Δ from every evidential argument Δ' against rules in Δ; i.e., if every such Δ' contains a rule $B \to \sim p_i$ for some p_i in P.*

The new proof-procedure works in two stages: in the first it uses P_0 to derive tentative conclusions, ignoring evidential counterarguments. In the second, it verifies that all such counterarguments are defeated, and therefore, can legitimately be ignored.

In the theory above, the procedure P_0 yields b and c' by application of the rules r_1 and r_4. To verify whether b and c' are actual causal consequences of the theory, Theorem 7 says we only need to consider the evidential arguments against r_1 or r_4. Since the only such (minimal) argument $\Delta' = \{r_2, r_3\}$ contains a rule $r_2 : b \to c$ whose consequent c is incompatible with c', we are done. Indeed, r_2 is defeated in the theory, and b and c' follow.

Related Work

The first principle is a reformulation of Pearl's idea that 'causes do not interact through the variables they influence if these variables have not been observed' (Pearl 1988b, pp 19). Other attempts to use this idea in the context of causal default reasoning are (Pearl 1988a; Geffner 1992; Goldszmidt & Pearl 1992). The contribution of this work is to explain the patterns of causal default reasoning in terms of some simple and meaningful principles that tie up a number of important notions in default reasoning: minimal and 'coherent' models (see below), background vs. evidential knowledge, forward vs. backward reasoning, etc. Interestingly, the need to distinguish background from evidence also appears in systems that handle 'specificity' preferences (Poole 1992; Geffner 1992), and in a slightly different form, in certain systems for causal reasoning (Sandewal 1991; Konolige 1992).

Many approaches to causal default reasoning are based on a preference criterion that rewards the 'most coherent' models; namely, the models where the set of violated rules without a causal justification is minimal or empty (e.g., (Gelfond 1989), as approaches based on non-normal defaults and the stable model semantics). For predictive theories, the most coherent models and causal models coincide; indeed, the causal models of predictive theories are *defined* as the models where *all* violated rules have a causal justification. Yet the two types of models differ in the general case. For example, in a theory comprised of three rules $r_i : p_i \to q_i$, $i = 1, \ldots, 3$, where q_2 is incompatible with both q_1 and q_3, the most coherent model given the facts p_1, p_2, p_3 and $\neg q_1$, is the model M that validates the rule r_2. Yet, the model M' that validates r_3 is also a causal model. Likewise, if r_3 is given priority over r_2, both M and M' would be the most coherent models but only the former would be a causal model. In the two cases, causal models behave as if the rule r_1, which is violated by the evidence, was excluded. The 'coherence' semantics, on the other hand, does not exclude the rule but rewards the models where it gets a causal explanation. The result is that sometimes the coherence semantics is stronger than causal models and sometimes is weaker. More important though is that the coherence semantics violates the first principle; indeed, in the second case, the rule r_3 fails to be sanctioned even though r_3 does not face either causal or evidential arguments. As a result, the coherence semantics makes the proof-procedure described in Theorem 7 unsound.

Causal rule systems which are *predictive* can be easily compiled into logic programs with negation as failure. Every ground rule $r_i : A_i \to p_i$ can be mapped to a logic programming rule $p_i \leftarrow A_i, \neg ab_i$ along with rules $ab_j \leftarrow A_i, \neg ab_i$ for every conflicting rule $r_j : A_j \to p_j$ with priority equal or smaller than r_i. In addition, facts translate to rules with empty bodies. From the discussion above, it's clear that the causal consequences of the original theory would be exactly the atoms that are true in all the stable models of the resulting program (Gelfond & Lifschitz 1988). The same mapping will not work for non-predictive systems as the semantics and algorithms for logic programs are limited in the the the way negative information is handled (Geffner 1991).

Causal rule systems are also related to ordered programs (Laenens & Vermeir 1990) where, using our language, facts are treated like rules, and all constraints are treated like background constraints. As a result, there are no evidential arguments and all reasoning is done along the direction of the rules. This is also common to approaches in which defaults are regarded as tentative but one-way rules of inference. We have argued that such interpretations of defaults may be adequate in the context of predictive theories but will fail in general: even if a default $a \rightarrow b$ does not provide a reason to conclude $\neg a$ from $\neg b$, it may well provide a reason to avoid concluding a when $\neg b$ is known.

Conclusions

We have presented a pair of principles that account for the basic preferences among defaults that arise in causal domains. We have also defined a semantics based on those principles and presented some useful proof-procedures to compute with it. The language of the formalism can be extended in a number of ways. Some extensions are more direct (e.g., n-ary background constraints, non-causal rules); others are more subtle (e.g., disjunctions). We are currently working on these extensions and will report them elsewhere. We are also looking for more efficient procedures that would avoid the need to precompute all 'evidential nogoods' when they exist.

Acknowledgments. Thanks to Wlodek Zadrozny, Pierre Siegel, Benjamin Grosof, and Kurt Konolige for discussions related to the content of this paper.

References

Baker, A., and Ginsberg, M. 1989. A theorem prover for prioritized circumscription. In *Proceedings IJCAI-89*, 463–467.

Dean, T., and McDermott, D. 1987. Temporal data base management. *Artificial Intelligence* 32:1–55.

Geffner, H. 1991. Beyond negation as failure. In *Proceedings of the Second International Conference on Principle of Knowledge Representation and Reasoning*, 218–229.

Geffner, H. 1992. *Reasoning with Defaults: Causal and Conditional Theories*. Cambridge, MA: MIT Press.

Gelfond, M., and Lifschitz, V. 1988. The stable model semantics for logic programming. In *Proceedings of the Fifth International Conference and Symposium on Logic Programming*, 1070–1080. Cambridge, Mass.: MIT Press.

Gelfond, M. 1989. Autoepistemic logic and formalization of commonsense reasoning. a preliminary report. In *et al.*, M. R., ed., *Proceedings of the Second International Workshop on Non-Monotonic Reasoning*, 177–186. Berlin, Germany: Springer Lecture Notes on Computer Science.

Goldszmidt, M., and Pearl, J. 1992. Stratified rankings for causal relations. In *Proceedings of the Fourth Workshop on Nonmonotonic Reasoning*, 99–110.

Hanks, S., and McDermott, D. 1987. Non-monotonic logics and temporal projection. *Artificial Intelligence* 33:379–412.

Horty, J.; Thomason, R.; and Touretzky., D. 1987. A skeptical theory of inheritance. In *Proceedings AAAI-87*, 358–363.

Konolige, K. 1992. Using default and causal reasoning in diagnosis. In *Proceedings of the Third International Conf. on Principles of Knowledge Representation and Reasoning*.

Laenens, E., and Vermeir, D. 1990. A fixpoint semantics for ordered logic. *Journal of Logic and Computation* 1(2):159–185.

Lifschitz, V. 1987. Formal theories of action. In *Proceedings of the 1987 Workshop on the Frame Problem in AI*, 35–57.

Lin, F., and Shoham, Y. 1991. Provably correct theories of action. In *Proceedings AAAI-91*, 349–354.

Pearl, J. 1988a. Embracing causality in default reasoning. *Artificial Intelligence* 35:259–271.

Pearl, J. 1988b. *Probabilistic Reasoning in Intelligent Systems*. Los Altos, CA.: Morgan Kaufmann.

Pollock, J. 1987. Defeasible reasoning. *Cognitive Science* 11:481–518.

Poole, D. 1992. The effect of knowledge on belief: Conditioning, specificity and the lottery paradox. *Artificial Intelligence* 49:281–309.

Sandewal, E. 1991. Features and fluents. Technical Report R-91-29, CS Department, Linkoping University, Linkoping, Sweden.

Sandewall, E. 1993. The range of applicability of nonmonotonic logics for the inertia problem. In *Proceedings IJCAI-93*, 738–743.

Shoham, Y. 1988. *Reasoning about Change: Time and Causation from the Standpoint of Artificial Intelligence*. Cambridge, Mass.: MIT Press.

Testing Physical Systems

Peter Struss

Technical University of Munich, Computer Science Dept.,
Orleansstr. 34
D-81667 Munich, Germany
struss@informatik.tu-muenchen.de

Abstract

We present a formal theory of model-based testing, an algorithm for test generation based on it, and outline how testing is implemented by a diagnostic engine. The key to making the complex task of test generation feasible for systems with continuous domains is the use of model abstraction. Tests can be generated using manageable finite models and then mapped back to a detailed level. We state conditions for the correctness of this approach and discuss the preconditions and scope of applicability of the theory.

Introduction

Testing means shifting a system into different states by appropriate inputs in order to find observations that determine its present behavior mode. Often, the tests are designed to *confirm a particular behavior,* usually the correct or intended one, for instance in manufacturing. In diagnosis we may, in contrast, want discriminating tests which effectively and efficiently *identify the present* (faulty) *behavior.* This paper focuses on confirming tests. There exist theories and algorithms for test generation in particular domains. For digital circuits, for instance, a solution is feasible because, although the number of components can be large, the individual components exhibit a simple behavior and, more fundamentally, because of the Boolean domain of the variables (Roth 1980). For variables with large domains or for physical systems with continuous behavior, these techniques are not applicable. In extending methods from model-based diagnosis, and exploiting our work on multiple modeling (Struss 1992), we propose a general theory that addresses the generation and application of tests in such domains.

We first discuss the problems addressed and outline the basic ideas of our approach by presenting a simple (continuous and dynamic) system, a thyristor. In the next section, we present the basic theory and an algorithm for test generation. Then testing of constituents in the context of a whole device is shown to be a straightforward extension. We outline briefly how testing is implemented by a standard model-based diagnosis engine, and finally, we discuss the achievements, preconditions, and restrictions of the approach. Due to space limitations, we do not always treat the most general cases, and we omit proofs. Both can be found in (Struss 1994).

The Intuition behind Testing

A thyristor is a semi-conductor with anode, A, cathode, C, and gate, G, that operates as a (directed) switch: it works in two states, either conducting current in a specified direction with almost zero resistance (exaggerated by the upper line of the simplified characteristic curve in Fig. 1a), or blocking current like a resistor with almost infinite resistance (the horizontal line). The transition from the OFF state to ON is controlled by the gate; if it receives a pulse the thyristor "fires", provided the voltage drop exceeds a threshold, V_{Th}. There is a second way to fire a thyristor (which is normally avoided, but may occur in certain circuits and situations), namely if the voltage drop exceeds the breakover voltage, V_{Bo} as is indicated by the characteristic in Fig. 1a. The annotation with 1 and 0 indicates the presence and absence of a gate pulse.

Now suppose we want to test a thyristor, i.e. to make sure that it behaves according to the described correct behavior. This creates several problems: voltage and current are considerered to have a continuous domain. We can only gather a finite set of sample observations. But if they all agree with the desired behavior, what would then make us confident that more observations could not reveal a contradiction to this behavior? It is the fact that *there is no other possible behavior* (a faulty one) *that would also be consistent with the previous observations.*

What are the possible faults of a thyristor? A thyristor may be *punctured*, i.e. acting like a wire, or *blocking* like an open switch. A third kind of fault may be due to the fact that the actual *breakover voltage is less than the nominal one*, with the result that the thyristor fires at a voltage drop well below V_{Bo} without a gate pulse. With V'_{Bo} we denote the lowest tolerable actual breakover voltage (or the highest one which is considered to characterize a faulty behavior). Fig. 1 shows the (idealized) characteristics of these behaviors in comparison to the correct behavior.

Considering these behaviors (and, perhaps, looking at the figures), we may get the following idea for a set of two tests: the first one with a high voltage drop (i.e. between V'_{Bo} and V_{Bo}) without a gate pulse, and a second one with a medium or high voltage drop (i.e. between V_{Th} and V_{Bo}) in conjunction with a gate pulse.

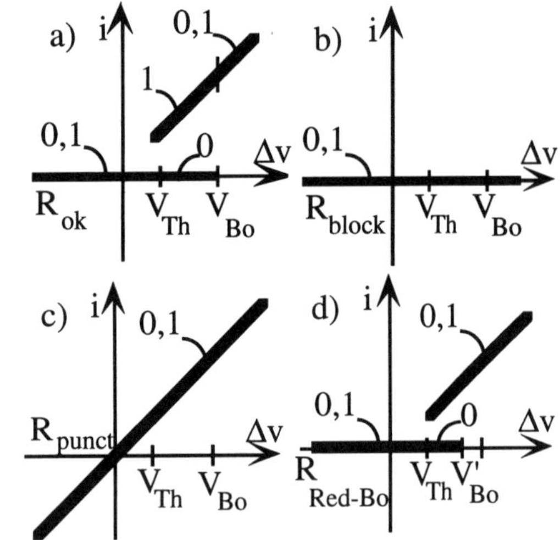

Figure 1 The characteristic of the behaviors of a thyristor:
a) correct b) blocking c) punctured
d) with a reduced breakover voltage

If we obtain results that comply with the correct behavior in both cases (zero current for the former, positive current for the latter), then the thyristor must be correct, because these observations rule out all three types of faults: the first one contradicts the punctured behavior and a reduced breakover voltage, while the second one refutes the blocking mode. This simple example illustrates several fundamental ideas :

- A particular behavior is confirmed if all others can be refuted by some finite set of observations.
- We obtain such sets of tests by describing behaviors through relations among variables and by determining their distinctions (i.e. set differences).
- We may end up with less tests than the number of behaviors to be refuted (in the thyristor example two tests for an *infinite* number of behaviors).

Finally, the thyristor indicates a way to address the complexity problem when we have to handle large or even infinite domains:

- We may be able to perform test generation using a (qualitative) abstraction of the behavior description (e.g. with characterizations such as "high" and "medium").

In the remainder of this paper we develop these ideas into a formal theory and an algorithmic solution for test generation and testing.

Test Generation for Single Constituents

First, we present the basic definitions and results that allow the generation of tests, based on relational behavior models. For all definitions and theorems, we first paraphrase them in English before presenting the formal statement. Throughout this section, we consider one constituent (component, mechanism, process, subsystem that is) of a system that is assumed to be accessible. It has a (not necessarily finite) set of possible behaviors, BEHVS, associated with it.

The Foundation: Finding Observable Distinctions

As motivated by the example (and common in model-based reasoning systems which use constraints for modeling), we describe behavior modes by the set of value tuples that are possible under this behavior, i.e. by a relation R in some representation. Using the formalism of (Struss 1992) such a representation is determined by selecting a vector $\underline{v} = (v_1,...,v_2)$ of local variables and their respective domains:

$$DOM(\underline{v}) = DOM(v_1) \times DOM(v_2) \times .... \times DOM(v_k).$$

For the time being, we assume one fixed representation $(\underline{v}, DOM(\underline{v}))$, because this simplifies the notation and is not an essential restriction (the general case is treated in (Struss 1994)). The behavior models of the thyristor can be described in the representation

$$((\Delta V, i, gate), \mathbb{R} \times \mathbb{R} \times \{0,1\}).$$

By SIT we denote the set of situations physically possible under the present mode of a constituent. We define a behavior model M(R) as the claim that, the relation $R \subseteq DOM(\underline{v})$ covers all value tuples $\underline{v}$ may take in a situation $s \in$ SIT:

Definition 1 (Behavior Model)

$$M(R) : \Leftrightarrow$$
$$\forall \underline{v}_0 \in DOM(\underline{v}) \; (\exists s \in SIT \; \underline{v}(s) = \underline{v}_0) \Rightarrow \underline{v}_0 \in R \;^1 .$$

If $M(R_i)$ is a model of the behavior $B_i \in$ BEHVS, i.e. $B_i \Rightarrow M(R_i)$, and if an observation (obs) contradicts the behavior model, i.e. lies outside R_i, then we can safely rule out the behavior:

$$obs \Rightarrow \neg M(R_i) \;\vdash\; obs \Rightarrow \neg B_i.$$

While this provides a way for *refuting* behaviors, we are interested in *confirming* a particular behavior.

As suggested by the example, tests are defined as sets of value tuples T_i such that observing at least one tuple in each set in reality allows us to conclude the presence of a behavior mode. More formally: a set of value tuples $V = \{\underline{v}_i\}$ containing at least one tuple out of each T_i,

$$\forall T_i \; \exists \underline{v}_i \in V \; \underline{v}_i \in T_i,$$

is called a hitting set of $\{T_i\}$. The fact that all the values in V are actually taken in some real situation is denoted by the sentence φ_V:

$$\varphi_V \equiv \forall \underline{v}_i \in V \; \exists s_i \in SIT \; \underline{v}(s_i) = \underline{v}_i$$

Definition 2 (Test, Confirming Test Set)

A test is a non-empty relation on some representational space: $T_i \subseteq DOM(\underline{v})$.

A set $\{T_i\}$ of tests is a confirming test set for a behavior $B_0 \in$ BEHVS iff for all hitting sets V of $\{T_i\}$, observation of V entails B_0:

$$\varphi_V \;\vdash\; B_0.$$

What assured us that the tests in the previous section actually confirm the thyristor's correct behavior? The fact that no other behavior mode would survive observations from both tests. In general, fo each behavior B_j, different from the one to be confirmed, there must exist a test T_i

---

^{1} $\underline{v}(s) = \underline{v}_0$ means that $\underline{v}$ has the value $\underline{v}_0$ in situation s rather than equality. Because $\underline{v}$ can take different values (from different domains, but also in the same domain), (Struss 1992) uses a special predicate Val .

lying completely outside a modeling relation of B_j. In other words, the complement of T_i,

$$T_i^c := \text{DOM}(\underline{v}) \backslash T_i,$$

specifies a model of B_j. This is stated by Lemma 1.

Lemma 1

$\{T_i\}$ is a confirming test set for B_0 iff

$$\forall B_j \in \text{BEHVS} \; B_j \neq B_0 \Rightarrow (\exists T_i \;\; B_j \Rightarrow M(T_i^c)).$$

A test is only useful if it is observable. So, in the following, let $\text{OBS}(\underline{v}) \subseteq \text{VARS}(\underline{v})$ be the set of observable variables in the representation $(\underline{v}, \text{DOM}(\underline{v}))$ with the respective projection

$$p_{obs} : \text{DOM}(\underline{v}) \rightarrow \text{DOM}(\underline{v}_{obs}).$$

Definition 3 (Observable Test Set)

A test set $\{T_i\}$ is observable, if all T_i are observable, i.e. $T_i \subset \text{DOM}(\underline{v}_{obs})$.

Lemma 1 indicates the way to generate confirming (observable) test sets for some behavior $B_0 \in \text{BEHVS}$: we have to find (observable) distinctions between B_0 and each other mode B_i, and confirm these distinctions to be present. We can grasp them as the set differences

$$D_i := p_{obs}(R_0) \backslash p_{obs}(R_i)$$

of appropriate modeling relations of these behaviors. Note that the number of differences D_i can be smaller than the number of behaviors to be refuted, because the modeling relations chosen may cover several behaviors (For the thyristor, for instance, $R_{\text{RED-B}_0}$ covers an infinite set of behaviors).

Any observable test refuting $M(R_i)$ and containing only tuples consistent with $M(R_0)$ must be a subset of D_i. Although we could use $\{D_i\}$ as a test set, we may further reduce the number of tests by replacing several D_i by a common subset. We call a set of sets, $\{T_k\}$, a *hitting set of sets* of $\{D_i\}$, if it contains a non-empty subset of each D_i:

$$\forall D_i \; \exists T_k \;\; \emptyset \neq T_k \subseteq D_i \, .$$

This is the basis for the generation of observable confirming test sets:

Lemma 2

Let $\{R_i \mid R_i \subset \text{DOM}(\underline{v})\}$ cover all behaviors (except B_0):

$$\forall B_j \in \text{BEHVS} \backslash \{B_0\} \;\; \exists R_i \;\; B_j \Rightarrow M(R_i),$$

and $R_0 \subset \text{DOM}(\underline{v})$ cover B_0:

$$B_0 \Rightarrow M(R_0).$$

If $\{T_k\}$ is a hitting set of sets of $\{D_i\}$, then it is an observable confirming test set for B_0.

The thyristor test set is an illustration of Lemma 2. We also obtain a neccessary condition for the existence of a confirming test set: if B_0 is actually a restriction of some other behavior B_j, it is impossible to find a confirming test set for B_0. Note that even if $R_0 \backslash R_i$ is non-empty, D_i may be empty, because the distinction is not observable in the given representation.

Now we have determined test sets that confirm a particular behavior, *if* they are observed. However, we do not want to wait for them to drop from heaven, but we would like to enforce them by an appropriate *causal input* to the system.

Finding Deterministic Test Inputs

We assume that the causal variables are observable, which is reasonable, because it means we know what we are doing to the constituent. So, let $\text{CAUSE}(\underline{v}) \subseteq \text{OBS}(\underline{v}) \subseteq \text{VARS}(\underline{v})$ be the set of susceptible variables and

$$p_{cause} : \text{DOM}(\underline{v}) \rightarrow \text{DOM}(\underline{v}_{cause})$$
$$p'_{cause} : \text{DOM}(\underline{v}_{obs}) \rightarrow \text{DOM}(\underline{v}_{cause})$$

the respective projections into the set of input tuples. What we would like to have is test inputs, i.e. subsets of $\text{DOM}(\underline{v}_{cause})$, that are guaranteed to determine whether or not a particular behavior is present. More precisely: if we input one tuple out of each set to the constituent, the resulting value tuples of $\underline{v}$ deterministically either confirm or refute the behavior:

Definition 4 (Test Input, Deterministic Input Set)

A test input is a non-empty relation on $\text{DOM}(\underline{v}_{cause})$: $TI_i \subseteq \text{DOM}(\underline{v}_{cause})$.

A set of test inputs $\{TI_i\}$ is deterministic for a behavior $B_0 \in \text{BEHVS}$ iff for all sets $V = \{\underline{v}_i\} \subseteq \text{DOM}(\underline{v})$ whose set of causes $\{p_{cause}(\underline{v}_i)\}$ forms a hitting set of $\{TI_i\}$, observation of V is inconsistent with B_0 or entails it:

$$\varphi_V \vdash \neg B_0 \quad \text{or} \quad \varphi_V \vdash B_0$$

How can we generate deterministic input sets? Unfortunately, for a test set $\{T_i\}$ confirming B_0, the input set $\{p_{cause}(T_i)\}$ is not necessarily deterministic.

To illustrate this, we consider the relation R_{neg} which is a subset of $R_{ok} \backslash R_{punct}$ (for $\Delta V < 0$) and which could be used to rule out the fault "punctured" of the thyristor (Fig. 2). p_{cause} projects to $(\Delta V, \text{gate})$:

$$p_{cause}(R_{neg}) = (-\infty, -\varepsilon) \times \{0\}.$$

However, if we choose a test input with $(\Delta V, \text{gate})$ out of $(-\infty, -\varepsilon) \times \{0\}$, a value of i might be observed such that the vector lies in the intersection of R_{ok} and R_{punct} (indicated by "$\times$" in Fig. 2) and, hence, is consistent with the correct behavior but also fails to refute the fault. As a cure, we have to exclude $p_{cause}(R_{ok} \cap R_{punct})$, i.e. to reduce the test input for Δv to $(-\infty, \varepsilon')$.

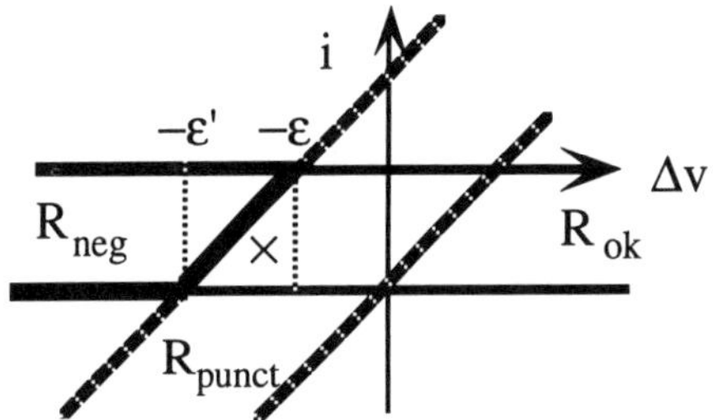

Figure 2 $p_{cause}(R_{ok} \backslash R_{punct})$ and $p_{cause}(R_{ok} \cap R_{punct})$ overlap

More generally, in order to construct input sets deterministic for some $B_0 \in \text{BEHVS}$ and leading to observable test sets, for each $B_i \neq B_0$ we have to determine and eliminate those inputs that possibly lead to the same observations under both B_0 and B_i. This is the set $p'_{cause}(p_{obs}(R_0) \cap p_{obs}(R_i))$. Hence, if we define

$$DI_i := p_{cause}(R_0) \backslash p'_{cause}(p_{obs}(R_0) \cap p_{obs}(R_i)),$$

then we are guaranteed that any input chosen from DI_i causes an observable value tuple that is inconsistent with $M(R_i)$ or with $M(R_0)$ (possibly with both of them). This is the idea underlying the proof of Theorem 3.

Theorem 3

Under the conditions of Lemma 2, each set of test inputs $\{TI_k\}$ that is a hitting set of sets of $\{DI_i\}$ is deterministic for B_0 and

$$\{T_k\} := \{p_{obs}(R_0) \cap p'^{-1}_{cause}(TI_k)\}$$

is an observable confirming test set for B_0.

In practice, one wants to avoid test inputs that are extreme and possibly cause (or make worse) damage. For instance, we do not want to test with $\Delta V > V_{B_0}$, because the thyristor could be destroyed. In this case, DI_i may have to be further reduced by intersecting it with a set of admissible inputs: $DI_{iadm} := R_{adm} \cap DI_i$.

Lemma 2 does not prevent us from constructing observable tests that are not real, but rather an artificial result of the choice of model relations: a non-empty $D_i = p_{obs}(R_0) \backslash p_{obs}(R_i)$ may be due to choosing R_0 much larger than what is covered by the behavior, and D_i potentially contains only physically impossible values. In contrast, simply because nothing prevents us from causing inputs and observing observables, we have

Theorem 4

The existence of a deterministic input set ensures the existence of an observable and controllable test set *in reality*.

A Test Generation Algorithm

Here, we outline a family of algorithms (Fig. 3) based on Theorem 3, and discuss it briefly.

```
TI-SET = NIL
FOR R in MODEL-RELATIONS DO
(1) DI = R_adm ∩ p_cause(R_0) \ p'_cause(p_obs(R_0) ∩ p_obs(R))
(2) IF DI = ∅
        THEN "No (adm.) deterministic test input against" R
(3)     DI = R_adm ∩ p_cause(p_obs(R_0) \ p_obs(R))
        IF DI = ∅
        THEN "No (adm.) observable test against" R
            GOTO .NEXT
    Select TI∈ TI-SET with DI ∩ TI ≠∅
    IF TI exists
(4)     THEN TI = TI ∩ DI
(5)     ELSE Append DI to TI-SET
    .NEXT
END FOR
FOR TI IN TI-SET
(6) Collect p_obs(R_0) ∩ p'^-1_cause(TI) in T-SET
```

Figure 3 An algorithm for generating (preferably deterministic) test inputs TI and test sets T confirming B_0

The algorithm iterates over the model relations of behaviors $B_i \neq B_0$ and attempts to create an admissible input set that discriminates between R_0 and R_i deterministically and in an observable way according to the above definition of DI_i (step 1). If this is impossible (2), it determines in (3) the admissible input set corresponding to an observable test (obtained as D_i according to Lemma 2) – which may fail, as well.

If there exist input sets from previous iterations with a non-empty intersection with the new DI, one of them is selected and replaced by this intersection (4). Thus, we account for the behavior(s) corresponding to the current R without increasing the number of tests. Otherwise, the current DI is added as a new test input in itself (5). In step 6, an observable test set is constructed from the final input set according to Theorem 3. It is confirming B_0, if all R_i could be accounted for. The algorithm generates the two tests for the thyristor mentioned before. The selection of TI for step 4 opens space for variations and heuristics. For instance, simply the first one with a non-empty intersection could be chosen, or the one with the largest intersection. The latter strategy always requires intersection with all existing input sets and assessment of the result, but may get closer to the optimum w.r.t. the number of tests generated.

If there exists a single test, the algorithm generates it in linear time. In other cases, it is quadratic w.r.t. the number of model relations (which may be less than the number of behaviors) and may fail to generate a test set of minimal cardinality. Its result, including whether or not an existing minimal cardinality test set is found, can depend on the ordering of the model relations. In many domains, it will pay off to use more elaborate and costly algorithms in order to reduce the number of tests required.

Making Test Generation Feasible through Model Abstraction

For physical systems with large or continuous domains and complex behavior, the question arises whether it is practically feasible to compute projections, intersections and set differences. The answer is that we do not have to. As pointed out in the beginning, we want to make test generation for such domains feasible by performing it with model relations in an abstract representation (with small domains). We have to formalize this procedure and prove its correctness.

The key idea is simple: If $M(R_i)$ is a model of B_i, i.e. $B_i \Rightarrow M(R_i)$, and if R'_i is another relation (preferably in a finite domain) that specifies a weaker model, i.e. $M(R_i) \Rightarrow M(R'_i)$, then refuting $M(R'_i)$ suffices to rule out B_i. Hence, we can build test sets from such finite relations R'_i. The task is then to find conditions and a systematic way to generate models that are guaranteed to be weaker (in the logical sense specified above) by switching to a different representation $(\underline{v}', DOM'(\underline{v}'))$ with finite domains.

In (Struss 1992), a large class of transformations between representations is characterized by conditions that are both rather weak and natural:

Definition 5 (Representational Transformation)

A surjective mapping $\tau: DOM(\underline{v}) \rightarrow DOM'(\underline{v}')$ is a representational transformation iff it has the following properties

$$\underline{v}(s) = \underline{v}_0 \quad \Rightarrow \quad \underline{v}'(s) = \tau(\underline{v}_0)$$
$$\underline{v}'(s) = \underline{v}'_0 \quad \Rightarrow \quad \exists \underline{v}_0 \in \tau^{-1}(\underline{v}'_0) \; \underline{v}(s) = \underline{v}_0.$$

This simply means that, in the same situation, variables in the different representations have values related by τ.

Under such representational transformations, models are preserved (Struss 1992):

Lemma 5

If $\tau: DOM'(\underline{v}') \rightarrow DOM(\underline{v})$ is a representational transformation, then

$$M(R') \Rightarrow M(\tau(R')) \quad \text{and} \quad M(R) \Rightarrow M(\tau^{-1}(R)).$$

This means, if we map a model relation from some original representation into a different one under a representational transformation the image will specify a weaker model, as required. In particular, we can choose a representation with a finite domain, construct (observable) confirming test sets and (deterministic) input sets in this representation from the transformed model relations and map them back to the original detailed representation.

The following theorem states that this actually yields (deterministic) input sets and (observable) confirming test sets in the original representation, thus justifying the intuitive approach:

Theorem 6

Let $\tau_{obs}: DOM(\underline{v}_{obs}) \rightarrow DOM'(\underline{v}'_{obs})$
and $\tau_{cause}: DOM(\underline{v}_{cause}) \rightarrow DOM'(\underline{v}'_{cause})$
be representational transformations.
If $\{T'_i\}$ is an observable confirming test set for B_0
then so is
$$\{T_i\} := \{\tau^{-1}_{obs}(T'_i)\} \ .$$
If $\{TI_i\}$ is a deterministic input set for B_0, then so is
$$\{TI_i\} := \{\tau^{-1}_{cause}(TI'_i)\}.$$

In particular, qualitative abstraction (mapping real numbers to a set of landmarks and the intervals between them) is a representational representation. In the thyristor example, the landmarks can be chosen as 0, V_{Th}, V'_{Bo}, V_{Bo} for ΔV and 0 for i. With the respective model relations in this representation, the test generation algorithm produces the deterministic input set
$$\{\{(high,0)\}, \{medium,high\} \times \{1\}\},$$
where $high = (V'_{Bo}, V_{Bo})$ and $medium = (V_{Th}, V'_{Bo})$.

Of course, the abstract representation may be too coarse to allow for the separation of particular behaviors. We can use this as a criterion for selecting representations and behavior models, for instance, as the highest level that still allows to distinguish one behavior from the others.

Remark 7

τ_{cause} being a representational transformation is also a *necessary* condition in the following sense: If it is violated, we can construct behaviors and model relations such that there exist observable test sets with deterministic input sets for them in the abstract representation, but none in the stronger one. However, these constructed behaviors may be irrelevant to any real physical system, and the back-transformation of tests may work for the practical cases nevertheless.

Testing Constituents in an Aggregate

Quite often the constituent to be tested is embedded in a particular context, namely an environment consisting of other interacting constituents, and only the entire aggregate can be controlled and observed. Our approach is general enough to cover this case.

We regard the aggregate as the constituent to be tested, and observables and causes are related to this aggregate constituent. The goal is to confirm one behavior of this aggregate constituent by refuting the other behaviors out of a certain set. This set is given as the behaviors of the aggregate resulting from the different behaviors of the constituent embedded in it.

More formally, let a constituent C_0 be in a particular context CTX consisting of constituents $C_1, ... C_n$ with their respective variables. The aggregate is $C_{agg} = \{C_j\} \cup \{C_0\}$, and representations for describing the aggregate's behavior can be obtained from the representations for single constituents by taking the union of the local variables. For the sake of simplicity, we assume that all local relations are already specified in the aggregate representation. Issues that arise if the assumption is dropped are discussed in (Struss 1994).

If $M(R_j)$ are behavior models for constituents C_j, then $R_{CTX} = \cap R_j$ specifies a corresponding behavior model for $CTX = \{C_j\}$. If $M(R_{i_0})$ are models of the behaviors B_i of C_0, then the relations $R_i = R_{CTX} \cap R_{i_0}$ specify models of the behaviors of $C_{agg} = CTX \cup \{C_0\}$ produced by the behaviors of C_0 in CTX. In applying the test generation algorithm to these relations, we can construct observable tests and deterministic test inputs for the behavior of C_{agg} that involves the particular behavior B_0 of C_0. Since p_{cause} and p_{obs} project to input sets and observables of C_{agg}, the tests are observable and controllable *through* C_{agg}. Of course, this provides a confirming test set for B_0 of C_0, *only if $M(R_{CTX})$ holds*. This corresponds, for instance, to the widespread assumption that while testing a constituent, its context works properly. However, we can also generate tests based on the assumption that the context may contain particular faults, which, for instance, have been hypothesized by a diagnosis step.

By constructing all behavior modes of C_{agg} corressponding to a single fault of any constituent, we can generate a test set confirming the correctness of all constituents under this assumption.

Realization of Testing

Now we have to implement a test system, i.e. a program that takes the test inputs and the observed responses of the device and returns whether the respective behavior has been confirmed or refuted. For this purpose, we do not have to invent a new machinery but can apply an existing diagnostic system. Tests confirming a behavior are based on refuting models of all other behaviors. Refuting behaviors through observations is also the principle of consistency-based diagnosis (de Kleer, Mackworth & Reiter 1990), and we can implement testing through one of the consistency-based diagnosis engines, GDE[+] (Struss & Dressler 1989).

In more detail, GDE[+] represents a constituent by the set of behavior models $M(R_i)$. If a complete test set $\{T_k\}$ is observed, i.e. φ_v holds for some hitting set V of $\{T_k\}$,

then we have
$$\forall T_k \; \exists s \in SIT \; \exists \underline{v}_k \in T_k \; \underline{v}(s) = \underline{v}_k.$$
By construction, there exists for each $D_i := R_0 \backslash R_i$ at least one $T_k \subseteq D_i$. Hence, it follows
$$\forall i \neq 0 \; \exists s \in SIT \; \exists \underline{v}_i \in D_i \; \underline{v}(s) = \underline{v}_i,$$
which means GDE^+ refutes all behaviors except B_0:
$$\forall i \neq 0 \; \exists s \in SIT \; \exists \underline{v}_i \notin R_i \; \underline{v}(s) = \underline{v}_i$$
$$\Rightarrow \forall i \neq 0 \; \neg M(R_i) \; \Rightarrow \; \forall i \neq 0 \; \neg B_i.$$
Then GDE^+ confirms B_0 by applying its "physical negation" rule (stating the completeness of the enumerated behaviors)
$$\neg B_1 \wedge \neg B_2 \wedge ... \wedge \neg B_n \Rightarrow B_0.$$
Of course, observation of a value outside R_0 lets GDE^+ refute B_0. In summary, GDE^+ makes the inferences required for the application of a deterministic input set.

Note that, for the purpose of testing, we can replace the constituent's model set $\{M(R_i)\}$ by the complements of the tests, $\{M(T^c_k)\}$, thus potentially reducing the number and, perhaps, the complexity of models to be checked. (Again, the details are discussed in (Struss 94)).

Conclusions

We make the rather strong claim that the theory presented here really solves the problem of testing physical systems. It solves it "in principle", in the same sense as model-based diagnosis is a solution to the problem of fault localization and identification. By this, we want to emphasize two aspects:

On the positive side, it is a *general* theory covering large classes of devices, for which there exists no formal theory or systematic solution of the testing problem today. All other solutions to test generation are only variations of this principled approach, perhaps by applying heuristics, making certain assumptions, or exploiting particularities of the domain (For instance, we can show that the D-algorithm (Roth 1980) is a specialization of our algorithm for digital circuit testing).
Particularly people from model-based diagnosis may be sceptical about the necessity of (complete sets of) fault models for this approach. However, knowledge (or assumptions) about the possible faults is not a drawback of our system, but is *inherent to the task of testing.* In contrast to diagnosis, where we may be content with refutation of (correct) behaviors, testing aims at confirming a particular behavior, usually the correct one. This is impossible, unless we make certain assumptions about the other possible behaviors, although this may happen unconsciously and implicitly. (This is why we are talking about testing of *physical systems,* and, for instance, not about testing system designs or software.) Our approach has the advantage to make such assumptions explicit (and the multiple modeling framework allows us to treat them as defeasible hypotheses, see (Struss 1992)).

The representation through relations is quite natural for broad classes of physical systems. Note that the models are *not* required to be *deterministic* (remember the model of the class of thyristor faults called "Reduced V_{Bo}").

On the problem side, it is a solution only "in principle", because it shifts the burden to the hard task of modeling. A major problem is finding appropriate models of devices with complex *dynamic* behavior. The thyristor, a dynamic device, illustrates that it can be possible to do the testing under temporal abstraction. Model abstraction is the key for the feasibility of the algorithm. But the models have to be strong enough to distinguish the behavior of interest from the other ones.

We do not expect the algorithm to handle systems with thousands of components in a flat structure. But first experiments suggest that it can produce results in a reasonable amount of time for devices which are already complex enough to prohibit the completeness and/or optimality of manually generated tests. Currently, we are exploring binary-decision diagrams as a compact representation of the model relations.

In this paper, we considered only testing with the goal of *confirming one particular behavior.* Testing in the context of diagnosis for identifying the present behavior is the subject of another paper. Other perspectives are supporting design for testability and sensor placement.

In summary, we presented an approach to model-based test generation and testing that makes a large class of systems amenable to principled methods and well-founded algorithms. The exploitation of model abstraction is crucial to making the task practically feasible for an interesting class of technical systems, notwithstanding the fact that the general task of hypothesis testing is np-complete (McIlraith 1993). Finally, the basis of the theory is quite simple, simple enough to be powerful.

Acknowledgements

This work has been supported in part by the Christian-Doppler-Labor of the Technical University of Vienna.

References

de Kleer, J., Mackworth, A., and Reiter, R. 1990, Characterizing Diagnoses. In Proceedings of the AAAI 90, 324-330.

McIlraith, S. 1993, Generating Tests Using Abduction. In Working Papers of the Fourth International Workshop on Principles of Diagnosis, Aberystwyth, 223-235.

Roth, G. P. 1980, *Computer Logic, Testing, and Verification.* Rockville: Computer Science Press.

Struss, P. 1992, What's in SD? Towards a Theory of Modeling for Diagnosis. In: Hamscher, W. Console, L., and de Kleer, J. eds., *Readings in Model-based Diagnosis.* San Mateo: Morgan Kaufmann: 419-449.

Struss, P., Dressler, O. 1989, "Physical Negation" - Integrating Fault Models into the General Diagnostic Engine. In Proc. 11th Int. Joint Conf. on Artificial Inteligence, Detroit, MI, 1318-1323.

Struss, P. 1994, A Theory of Testing Physical Systems Based on First Principles, Technical Report, Christian-Doppler-Labor, Technical University of Vienna.

Abstraction in Bayesian Belief Networks and Automatic Discovery From Past Inference Sessions *

Wai Lam
Department of Computer Science
University of Waterloo
Waterloo, Ontario,
Canada, N2L 3G1
wlam1@logos.uwaterloo.ca

Abstract

An abstraction scheme is developed to simplify Bayesian belief network structures for future inference sessions. The concepts of abstract networks and abstract junction trees are proposed. Based on the inference time efficiency, good abstractions are characterized. Furthermore, an approach for automatic discovery of good abstractions from the past inference sessions is presented. The learned abstract network is guaranteed to have a better average inference time efficiency if the characteristic of the future sessions remains moreorless the same. A preliminary experiment is conducted to demonstrate the feasibility of this abstraction scheme.

1 Introduction

One of the most advanced techniques for conducting exact probabilistic inferences in a multiply-connected Bayesian belief network is the *junction tree* approach developed by (Jensen, Lauritzen, & Olesen 1990; Jensen, Olesen, & Andersen 1990). Whereas it provides a good structure for propagating and updating beliefs through local computations in an object-oriented fashion, the inference time complexity is still intractable in the worst case due to the fact that probabilistic inference on Bayesian belief networks is a NP-hard problem (Cooper 1990) in general. In this paper we explore an approach to improving the inference time efficiency by means of *abstraction*. The concepts of *abstract networks* and *abstract junction trees* are characterized. The essence of this abstraction scheme is to hide those unimportant ground subnetworks so that probabilistic reasoning can be conducted on a higher abstract level with significantly increased efficiency. In cases where we need to know the beliefs in the hidden ground subnetwork, we can readily restore the ground subnetwork structure and resume the inference. The main goal of our approach is to reduce the average inference time for future inference sessions. In accordance with this objective, we characterize *good* abstract junction trees. Based on the characteristic of

---
*Wai Lam's work was supported by an OGS scholarship.

the past inference sessions, a method is developed for automatic discovery of good structures for abstraction.

Some work has been done on improving the time efficiency of probabilistic inference on Bayesian belief networks. In this paper we concentrate on exact probabilistic inference instead of approximate inference. An early technique was due to Baker and Boult who proposed a technique for pruning a Bayesian network structure before conducting belief updating and propagation given an inference session (Baker & Boult 1990). This approach prunes away those variables that are probabilistically independent of the variables of interest in the session. However, if majority of the variables are not probabilistically independent, the pruned structure is almost the same size as the original one. Heckerman developed a kind of structure known as similarity networks which can deal with some large and complex structures common in fault diagnosis domains such as medical diagnosis (Heckerman 1990).Whereas it is very useful in structures containing a *distinguished variable*, it cannot be applied in an arbitrary network structure in general. Recently, (Xiang, Poole, & Beddoes 1992) developed *multiply sectioned Bayesian networks* which partition an original network into separate localized Bayesian subnetworks. It requires an assumption that the whole network can be viewed as a collection of natural subdomains where the user will pay attention to one subdomain for a period of time before switching to another subdomain. In contrast, the abstraction approach proposed in this paper does not impose any restrictions on the network structure.

2 Overview of Basic Idea

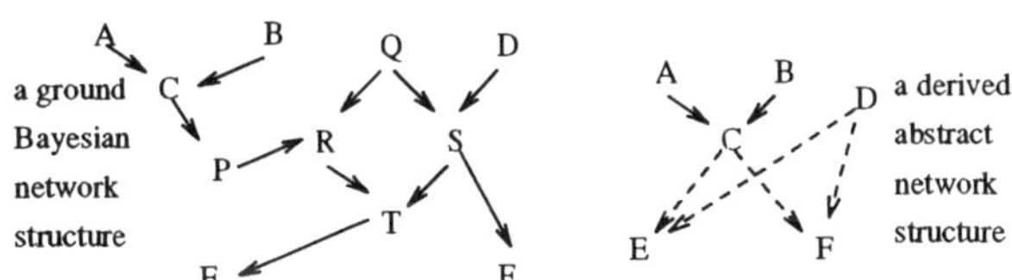

Figure 1: A Ground Network and Its Abstract Network

Consider a Bayesian belief network for a concerned domain with the ground structure as depicted in Figure 1. Suppose many inference sessions only involve probabilistic inferences between the elements in the variable set: $\{A, B, C, D, E, F\}$ (In other words, the variable set $\{P, Q, R, S, T\}$ does not involve in most inference sessions). For instance, in a particular session, the beliefs of A and F are queried given the evidences instantiated for the variables B and C. In order to compute the posterior beliefs of the queried variables in these sessions, we need to perform belief updating and propagation on the entire network structure.

Suppose based on the past experience, this observation is true for *most* inference sessions. We can summarize these inactive variables to form four *abstract arcs* namely: $C \rightarrow E$, $D \rightarrow E$, $C \rightarrow F$ and $D \rightarrow F$. Figure 1 shows the structure of the new abstract network that has incorporated these abstract arcs (the abstract arcs are denoted by dashed lines). Instead of using the original ground network, this abstract network is used for conducting inferences. It raises an issue regarding how to determine the conditional probability parameters associated with the abstract arcs. However, if appropriate conditional probability parameters could be determined, the probabilistic inference results based on this abstract network would be exactly the same as that computed from the original ground network. Clearly, the inference time will be greatly reduced since the structure of the abstract network is simpler and smaller. Determining the conditional probability parameters for the abstract arcs is not a trivial task since we require the joint probability distribution of the abstract network be the same as that of the ground network marginalized appropriately. In Section 3.4, we show that the conditional probability parameters of the abstract arcs can be calculated based on a local subnetwork structure consisting of the variables to be abstracted.

One of the advanced methods for conducting inference in Bayesian networks is the *junction tree* approach proposed by (Jensen, Lauritzen, & Olesen 1990). It transforms the original network into a secondary clique tree structure where belief updating and propagation is carried out. The inference in our abstraction scheme is also based on the junction tree approach. We present how the abstract arcs incorporate into a junction tree environment forming an *abstract junction tree*. Hence, the actual belief updating and propagation are performed on the abstract junction tree structure after the location of the abstractions are determined and assimilated.

If there is a need to compute the belief of a variable currently not found in the abstract junction tree in a particular session, an *abstract expansion* will be executed on the appropriate spot of the junction tree and belief propagation can be done accordingly to obtain the required result. If the abstract junction tree is a good abstraction of the domain, we expect the need for abstract expansion is very infrequent. Based on the pattern of inference sessions, we characterize *good* subnetworks where abstraction can be done.

The inference time efficiency can be briefly overviewed as follows: Some computational efforts are needed for calculating the conditional probability parameters associated with the abstract arcs and constructing the abstract junction tree. Nevertheless, this step is required only once for a network since it is not required during the inference sessions. If a good abstraction has been chosen when generating the abstract network, we expect most of the inference sessions only deal with the variables in the abstract network, and thus abstract expansions will rarely occur. Under this circumstance, it greatly reduces the inference time even though some computational costs are required for expansions in a few sessions. Section 5 will compare in detail the inference time efficiency of the ground and the abstract network. Based on the analysis of the inference time efficiency, we characterize a condition for *good* abstractions.

3 Abstract Networks and Abstract Junction Trees

As outlined in Section 2, Jensen's junction tree approach (Jensen, Lauritzen, & Olesen 1990) is chosen in our abstraction scheme due to its great flexibility in reasoning about a multiply-connected network. It transforms the original network into a secondary clique tree structure, called *junction tree*, where belief updating and propagation is carried out. The nodes and edges in a junction tree are known as *junction nodes* and *junction links* respectively. Each junction node contains a number of variables from the original network. Associated with each junction link, there is another structure called *separator* which contains the intersection of the variables in both junction nodes connected by the junction link. Moreover, there is a *belief table* stored in each junction node and each separator. In an inference session, the evidences are entered into the junction tree and belief propagation is performed on the tree structure. The main operations for belief propagation are Collect-Evidence and Distribute-Evidence as described in (Jensen, Lauritzen, & Olesen 1990).

We use the term *ground network* and *ground junction tree* referring to the original Bayesian belief network and its corresponding junction tree respectively. Before discussing the concepts of abstract networks and abstract junction trees, we first introduce the notions of *self-contained subnetworks* and *self-contained junction subtrees*.

3.1 Definitions

Let the variables of a ground network be $\vec{X} = \{X_1, X_2, \ldots, X_n\}$.

Definition 3.1 A *self-contained subnetwork* is a connected subgraph of a ground network and possesses the following property:

Let the variables in the subnetwork be $\vec{C}$ (i.e., $\vec{C} \subset \vec{X}$), $\forall X_i, X_j \in \vec{C}$, if X_k is a variable along a directed path between X_i and X_j, then we have $X_k \in \vec{C}$.

Intuitively, a self-contained subnetwork is a compact, connected unit in the underlying ground network.

Definition 3.2 With respect to a self-contained subnetwork consisting of the variable set $\vec{C}$, a *destination variable set* contains all such a variable X_i that it is outside the subnetwork (i.e., $X_i \in (\vec{X} - \vec{C})$) and X_i is a direct successor of a variable inside the subnetwork. Also, a *source variable set* contains all such a variable X_j that it is outside the subnetwork and X_j is a direct parent of a variable in the subnetwork or it is a direct parent of a variable in the corresponding destination variable set.

For instance, in the ground network of Figure 1, the subnetwork comprising the variables $\{ P, Q, R, S, T \}$ and the associated arcs inside the subnetwork is an example of a self-contained subnetwork. The set of variables $\{C, D\}$ and $\{E, F\}$ are its corresponding source and destination variable set respectively. Note that the parents of each destination variable must be in the source variable set, or the subnetwork variable set, or the destination variable set itself.

For a given self-contained subnetwork, we identify a *self-contained junction subtree* as follows:

Definition 3.3 With respect to a self-contained subnetwork, a *self-contained junction subtree* is a subtree in the ground junction tree and is composed of: i) all junction nodes containing a variable in the self-contained subnetwork; ii) the junction links associated with these junction nodes in the subtree. The junction node adjacent to the self-contained junction subtree in the ground junction tree is known as the *adjacent junction node*.

Essentially, a self-contained junction subtree in a ground junction tree is a counterpart of a self-contained subnetwork in a ground network.

3.2 Abstract Network Construction

Now, we are in a position to explain our abstraction scheme. In our scheme, abstraction is performed on a self-contained subnetwork unit. Basically, the whole subnetwork is summarized as a collection of *abstract arcs* as discussed below.

Consider a self-contained subnetwork Θ_C consisting of the variable set $\vec{C} = \{C_1, C_2, \ldots C_i\}$ from a ground network. Let the source variable set $\vec{S}$, with respect to Θ_C be $\{S_1, S_2, \ldots S_m\}$; the destination variable set $\vec{D}$ with respect to Θ_C be $\{D_1, D_2, \ldots D_k\}$. Suppose that the numbering of the variables are named according to the corresponding variable ordering in the ground network. Let the ordering of all the above variables in the ground network be $S_1, S_2, \ldots S_m, C_1, C_2, \ldots C_i, D_1, D_2, \ldots D_k$. An abstract arc is constructed by linking a source variable S_{m_1} (i.e., $S_{m_1} \in \vec{S}$) to a destination variable D_{k_1} (i.e., $D_{k_1} \in \vec{D}$) if there exists a directed path from S_{m_1} to D_{k_1} in the ground network.

As a result, associated with each self-contained subnetwork, there is a group of abstract arcs linking the source and destination variables. The whole self-contained subnetwork unit together with its incoming arcs (from the source variables) and outgoing arcs (to the destination variables) can be extracted from the ground network and substituted by the corresponding group of abstract arcs. After the substitution, it gives rise to an *abstract subnetwork* structure which is composed of: (1) the group of abstract arcs, (2) the source variable set, and (3) the destination variable set. For instance, the variables C, D, E, F and the arcs $C \rightarrow E$, $C \rightarrow F$, $D \rightarrow E$, $D \rightarrow F$ in Figure 1 form an abstract subnetwork. Thus, an abstract subnetwork can be viewed as an abstraction element representing for the corresponding self-contained subnetwork. Intuitively, the abstract subnetwork can capture all the probabilistic relationships contributed by the self-contained subnetwork. When the self-contained subnetwork has been replaced by the abstract subnetwork, the original ground network becomes an *abstract network*.

We hope that probabilistic inferences regarding the variables in the abstract network can be carried out without any loss of accuracy. In Section 3.4, we will show that it can be achieved by setting the appropriate conditional probability parameters associated with the abstract arcs.

3.3 Abstract Junction Tree Construction

Based on the structure of an abstract subnetwork, an *abstract junction subtree* can be constructed by transforming the local structure of the abstract subnetwork to a junction tree using Jensen's ordinary transformation technique (Jensen, Lauritzen, & Olesen 1990). The belief tables of the junction nodes in the abstract junction subtree can be readily computed from the new conditional probability parameters associated with the destination variables. Therefore, an abstract junction subtree can be viewed as an individual object representing a summary of the corresponding self-contained junction subtree.

We are now ready to make use of the abstract junction subtree to perform abstraction on the ground junction tree summarized below:

1 the self-contained junction subtree is removed from the ground junction tree.
2 the abstract junction subtree is inserted into the ground junction tree by setting up a junction link between each adjacent junction node and the appropriate junction node in the abstract junction subtree. (Adjacent junction node is defined in Definition 3.3)
3 the self-contained junction subtree is stored and indexed by the abstract junction subtree so that it can be restored back into the ground junction tree if necessary.

3.4 Computing New Probability Parameters

Using the notation in Section 3.1, we further analyze the structure and the conditional probability parameters associated with the abstract arcs. In an abstract subnetwork, each destination variable has a new parent set whose elements come from one or all of the following two groups: (1) the source variable set $\vec{S}$ (due to abstract arcs), and (2) the original parents not in the subnetwork variable set $\vec{C}$ (This kind of parent must be in the destination variable set $\vec{D}$). Specifically the new parent set of a destination variable D_{k_1} is a subset of $\vec{S} \cup \{D_1, D_2, \ldots D_{k_1-1}\}$.

We need to calculate the new conditional probability parameters associated with the new parent set for each destination variable. A requirement for these parameters is that the joint probability distributions of the abstract network must be equivalent to that of the original ground network marginalized appropriately. This will guarantee the results of probabilistic inferences regarding the variables in the abstract network are identical to that computed from the original ground network.

We propose a technique to calculate the required probability parameters based on the local structure of the subnetwork as follows: First, a local Bayesian network Θ'_C is identified by including all of the following items:

- the variables in the set $\vec{S} \cup \vec{C} \cup \vec{D}$;
- the existing arcs linking the variables within the subnetwork Θ_C;
- the existing arcs linking from a source variable to a variable in the subnetwork Θ_C; and
- the existing incoming arcs for a destination variable

In fact, this local belief network Θ'_C has almost the same topological complexity as the self-contained subnetwork structure Θ_C. To determine the conditional probability parameter of a destination variable given a particular instantiation of its new parent set, belief updating and propagation is performed on the network Θ'_C with the parent instantiation as the specific evidences. The required conditional probability parameter value is just the posterior belief of the destination variable. It is claimed that the probability parameters computed by this technique render equivalent joint probability distribution of the abstract network and the ground network. The proof is given in (Lam 1994).

3.5 Performing Abstraction

In the above discussion, we only consider one self-contained subnetwork. However, it is absolutely possible to have more than one subnetworks in a ground network. Each subnetwork serves a local part of the ground network where an abstraction can be done individually. As a result, an abstract network, evolving from a ground network, may contain one or more abstract subnetworks which replace their corresponding self-contained subnetworks. Similarly, an abstract junction tree is obtained by replacing each of the self-contained junction subtree unit with the corresponding abstract junction subtree and it becomes the new secondary structure on which subsequent inferences are conducted.

4 Abstract Expansion

Once an abstract junction tree is formed, the subsequent inference sessions will be performed on this new tree structure. If a good abstraction has been used, we expect the abstract junction tree structure is sufficient for most of the inference sessions. However, there are some sessions, albeit infrequently occurred, which require evaluation of the variables in a self-contained subnetwork. These kinds of variables do not exist in the abstract junction tree. This situation may occur in the middle of an inference session.

To deal with this problem, we propose a mechanism called *abstract expansion* which makes it possible to continue the required inference. Basically, abstract expansion transforms an abstract junction subtree by restoring back its corresponding self-contained junction subtree. This operation is exactly the reverse of the substitution of the self-contained subtree.

5 Computational Advantages

The computational advantage of the abstract junction tree will be analyzed in this section. First, let us discuss the computational cost required to perform a probabilistic inference in a subtree. We concentrate our attention to the inference cost needed to conduct a basic inference operation in a connected junction subtree. Then, the inference cost of the ground and abstract junction trees are compared and the overall computational gain is characterized.

Consider a connected junction subtree Φ. Let $jnode(\Phi)$ denote the set of junction nodes in Φ; $sep(\Phi)$ denote the set of separators in Φ; $size(J)$ denote the size of the belief table stored in J where J can be a junction node or a separator; and $numlink(J)$ denote the number of junction links adjacent to the junction node J. Suppose the computational cost of an addition operator is of the factor λ to the cost of a multiplication operator. Let $probinf(\Phi)$ be the total number of multiplication operations associated with the junction subtree Φ in an inference session. It can be shown that $probinf(\Phi)$ is given by:

$$\sum_{J \in jnode(\Phi)} (1 + \lambda)\,numlink(J)\,size(J) + 2 \sum_{S \in sep(\Phi)} size(S)$$

$$(1)$$

Now, let us consider the computational cost for an abstract expansion. Let $expsn(\Phi)$ denote the number of multiplication operations required to perform an abstract expansion in the self-contained junction subtree Φ. Since the main task for an abstract expansion is a Distribute-Evidence operation in the corresponding self-contained junction subtree, $expsn(\Phi)$ is given by:

$$\sum_{J \in jnode(\Phi)} (1 + \lambda(numlink(J)-1))\,size(J) + \sum_{S \in sep(\Phi)} size(S)$$

$$(2)$$

It can be observed that the number of the separators (i.e., $|sep(\Phi)|$) actually depends on the number of junction nodes (i.e., $|jnode(\Phi)|$); the size of a separator also depends on the size of its associated junction nodes. Therefore, the main thrust of $probinf$ and $expsn$ operations is the number and the size of the junction nodes within the junction subtree. Note that the size of a junction node refers to the size of the belief tables stored in the junction node.

Now, we can compare the inference costs in the abstract junction tree and the ground junction tree where no abstraction has been done. There is no need to examine the whole tree in both cases since the only differences are those spots where abstractions have been done. Hence, we can focus on the computational costs around self-contained junction subtrees and abstract junction subtrees. Suppose Φ_G denotes a junction subtree, in a ground junction tree, which consists of (1) all the junction nodes in the self-contained junction subtree and all its adjacent junction nodes; (2) all the junction links within the self-contained junction subtree and connecting to the adjacent junction nodes. Similarly, let Φ_A denote a junction subtree, in an abstract junction tree, which consists of (1) all the junction nodes in the abstract junction subtree and all its adjacent junction nodes; (2) all the junction links within the abstract junction subtree and connecting to the adjacent junction nodes. Let N be the total number of inference sessions. The total number of multiplication required in the self-contained junction subtree for N sessions is $N\ probinf(\Phi_G)$. On the other hand, the total number of multiplication required in the abstract junction subtree is $N\ probinf(\Phi_A) + n\ expsn(\Phi_G)$ where n is the number of inference sessions which require abstract expansions. To compare the costs, we define the computational gain ($gain$) as follows:

$$gain = \frac{N\ probinf(\Phi_G) - (N\ probinf(\Phi_A) + n\ expsn(\Phi_G))}{N\ probinf(\Phi_G)}$$

$$\frac{probinf(\Phi_G) - (probinf(\Phi_A) + \mu\ expsn(\Phi_G))}{probinf(\Phi_G)} \quad (3)$$

where μ is the fraction of sessions which require abstract expansions.

If $gain > 0$, it conveys the fact that abstraction definitely reduces some computational costs for the given N sessions. We can also conclude that the average inference time efficiency is improved. The maximum possible value for $gain$ is 1 and it occurs when no computation is needed in the abstract junction subtree. As a result, it is expected that $gain$ will be between 0 and 1.[1] If a good abstraction has been chosen, we have the following two observations: First, the number and size of the junction nodes in the abstract junction subtree (i.e., Φ_A) should be far less than that of the self-contained junction subtree (i.e., Φ_G). Second, the fraction of sessions which require abstract expansion (i.e., μ) should be close to 0. Both observations will lead to a computational gain greater than 0 and thus the average inference time efficiency is improved. Based on this characterization of computational cost, an algorithm for automatic discovery of good abstract networks from the past inference sessions is presented in the next section.

---

[1] If $gain < 0$, it means the abstract junction tree requires extra computations over the ground junction tree and it indicates a bad abstraction has been chosen.

6 Discovery of Abstract Networks

We have developed a learning mechanism which can discover good abstraction network from the past inference sessions. Precisely, it can discover possible locations in the ground network where abstraction can be performed. Also, it will guarantee a better average inference computational efficiency if the future sessions follow moreorless the same pattern as the past sessions on which the learning approach is based.

An inference session includes setting the evidences and making queries. First, some information about a past session needs to be collected for the learning algorithm. We locate a set of *inactive variables* for each session. An inactive variable is actually a variable which is in neither the evidence nor the query set for that session. For each session, we record these inactive variables pertaining to this particular session. When more past sessions are gathered, the records of inactive variables form an inactive variable table and this table provides valuable information for the learning algorithm. The objective is to obtain a set of variables where good self-contained subnetworks can be identified and good abstract subnetworks can be constructed.

Intuitively, if a variable appears in many records in the inactive variable table, it is probably a good variable for abstraction. Suppose an abstract junction tree is constructed from a ground junction tree. The computational gain based on the past inference sessions can be calculated by Equation 3. The greater the gain is, the better the abstraction in term of the average inference time efficiency.

The remaining problem is to find the set of variables on which the abstraction should be done and possesses the greatest computational gain (as defined in Equation 3). In principle, all different combinations of the variables appearing in the inactive variable table can be tested by evaluating their computational gains. Then, the set of variables which gives the maximum gain is chosen as the solution. Clearly, there are exponentially many different combinations and so we tackle this problem by a best-first search algorithm.

In fact, the inactive variable table gives us a good source of information for the task of learning a set of good variables for abstraction. First we extract all the variables in the inactive variable table and rank them in a list in descending order according to the number of occurrences of that variable in the table. The resulting list formed is called the INACTIVE-LIST. A best-first search based on the INACTIVE-LIST is performed. The goal is to find the set of inactive variables which maximizes the computational gain as defined in Equation 3. The OPEN list for the best-first search algorithm contains search elements sorted in ascending order of the merits of the elements. Each search element consists of three components, namely, the current inactive variable set (CURRENT), the next variable to be added (NEXT-NODE), and the merit value of this search element (M-VALUE). NEXT-NODE is a variable from the INACTIVE-LIST and it will the next variable to be added to the CURRENT for evaluating the computational gain if this search element is explored. The merit value M-VALUE is just the computational gain of CURRENT. The initial OPEN list is constructed by search elements with CURRENT being a single variable from INACTIVE-LIST and NEXT-NODE being the variable which follows that single variable in the INACTIVE-LIST. The best-first search algorithm is outlined as below:

1 the first search element in the OPEN list is extracted and examined.

2 the NEXT-NODE of this element is added to its CURRENT forming the set of variables called the NEW-CURRENT. The computational gain of the NEW-CURRENT is evaluated. Let the variable following the NEXT-NODE in the INACTIVE-LIST be the NEW-NEXT-NODE.

3 A new search element is generated from the NEW-CURRENT and the NEW-NEXT-NODE and is inserted into the OPEN list appropriately according to the new computational gain.

4 go to step 1 if the computer resource is permitted and the OPEN list is non-empty.

After the search algorithm, the CURRENT associated with the first element in the OPEN list gives the required set of variables for abstraction.

7 A Preliminary Experiment

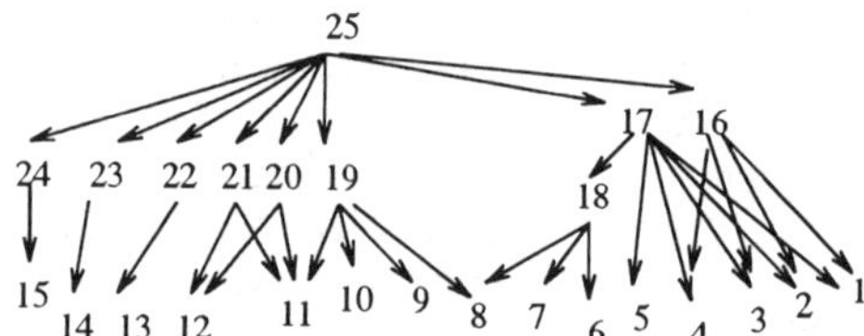

Figure 2: The Ground Network of MUNIN

A preliminary experiment has been done to demonstrate the automatic discovery algorithm. The structure of the Bayesian belief network used in this experiment as depicted in Figure 2 is derived from a system called MUNIN which is a Bayesian belief network for interpretation of electromyographic findings developed by (Andreassen *et al.* 1987). One possible ground junction tree for this network is shown in Figure 3. Some

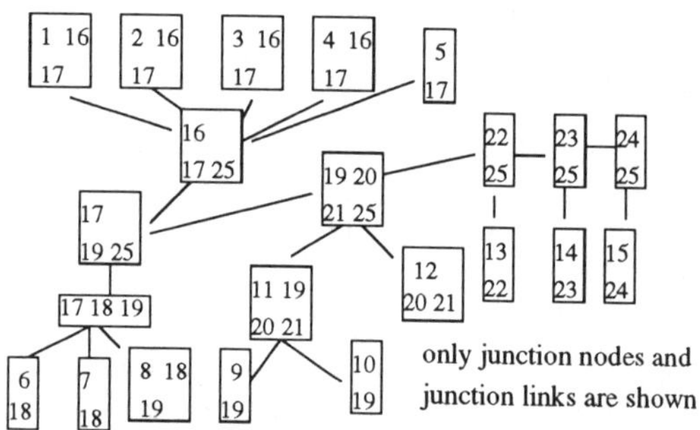

Figure 3: A Ground Junction Tree for MUNIN

hypothetic inference sessions were synthesized and an inactive variable table was generated as shown in Table 1.   Next, our learning algorithm was applied to the table and the set of variables proposed for abstraction, which is {16, 17, 18, 19, 20, 21}, was obtained.

set of inactive variables in each inference session	number of sessions
1 5 13 14 15 16 17 18 19 20 21	46
4 9 10 16 17 18 19 20 21 23 24	21
16 17 18 19 20 21	62
3 16 17 18 19 21 24	16
1 6 11 16 17 18 19 20 21 22	12
2 3 12 16 17 18 19 20 21	28
4 13 15 17 18 19 20	15
	total : 200

Table 1: Inactive Variables from Past Inference Sessions

Based on this set of variables, the self-contained subnetwork and the self-contained junction subtree is located. Then, the abstract subnetwork and the abstract junction subtree were generated. The learned abstract network is shown in Figure 4. Note that the structure of the abstract junction subtree is much simpler than that of the self-contained junction subtree. The computational gain evaluated by Equation 3 based on our inference sessions was 0.71. Thus the learned abstract junction tree will have a better average inference time.

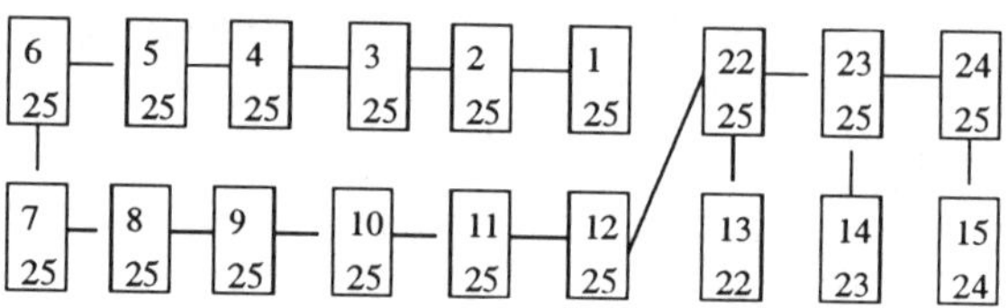

Figure 4: A Learned Abstract Junction Tree

Acknowledgements

I owe a special debt of gratitude to Fahiem Bacchus for introducing me to this problem.

References

Andreassen, S.; Woldbye, M.; Falck, B.; and Andersen, S. 1987. MUNIN - a causal probabilistic network for interpretation of electromyographic findings. In *Procceedings of the International Joint Conference on Artifical Intelligence (IJCAI)*, 366–372.

Baker, M., and Boult, T. 1990. Pruning Bayesian networks for efficient computation. In *Proceedings of the Conference on Uncertainty in Artificial Intelligence*, 257–264.

Cooper, G. F. 1990. The computational complexity of probabilistic inference using Bayesian belief networks. *Artificial Intelligence* 42:393–405.

Heckerman, D. 1990. Similarity networks for the construction of multiple-fault belief networks. In *Proceedings of the Conference on Uncertainty in Artificial Intelligence*, 32–39.

Jensen, F.; Lauritzen, S.; and Olesen, K. 1990. Bayesian updating in causal probabilistic networks by local computations. *Computational Statistics Quarterly* 4:269–282.

Jensen, F.; Olesen, K.; and Andersen, S. 1990. An algebra of Bayesian belief universes for knowledge-based systems. *Networks* 20:637–659.

Lam, W. 1994. Characterizing abstract Bayesian belief networks. In preparation.

Xiang, Y.; Poole, D.; and Beddoes, M. 1992. Exploring localization in Bayesian networks for large expert systems. In *Proceedings of the Conference on Uncertainty in Artificial Intelligence*, 344–351.

Noise and Uncertainty Management in Intelligent Data Modeling

Xiaohui Liu and **Gongxian Cheng**
Birkbeck College
Department of Computer Science
University of London, Malet Street
London WC1E 7HX, United Kingdom
hui@dcs.bbk.ac.uk; ubacr46@dcs.bbk.ac.uk

John Xingwang Wu
Institute of Ophthalmology
Department of Preventive Ophthalmology
University of London, Bath Street
London EC1V 9EL, United Kingdom
smgxjow@ucl.ac.uk

Abstract

The management of uncertain and noisy data plays an important role in many problem solving tasks. One traditional approach is to quantify the magnitude of noise or uncertainty in the data and to take this information into account when using this type of data for different purposes. In this paper we propose an alternative way of handling uncertain and noisy data. In particular, noise in the data is positively identified and deleted so that quality data can be obtained. Using the assumption that interesting properties in data are more stable than the noise, we propose a general strategy which involves machine learning from data and domain knowledge. This strategy has been shown to provide a satisfactory way of locating and rejecting noise in large quantities of visual field test data, crucial for the diagnosis of a variety of blinding diseases.

Introduction

Much research has been done to see how real world data can be intelligently modeled using AI methods to produce useful knowledge (Frawley, Piatetsky-Shapiro, & Matheus 1991; Weiss & Kulikowski 1991). Notable examples include the TDIDT (Top Down Induction of Decision Trees) family of learning systems where classification rules are learned from a set of training examples (Quinlan 1986; Bratko & Kononenko 1987). The data are also modeled and directly used to solve problems in application domains. For example, visual field test data are directly used to train neural networks which would associate these data with different kinds of blinding diseases (Nagata, Kani, & Sugiyama 1991).

The real world data, collected or generated in a variety of different environments, however, often contain noise, and are incomplete and uncertain. One of the most challenging research issues in intelligent data analysis is, therefore, how to handle noise and uncertainty in the data so that these data can be used correctly and most effectively in achieving the above described objectives.

One of the traditional approaches to the management of noisy and uncertain data is to use mathematical and statistical techniques to quantify their magnitude in the data and to present general information about the data quality. The decision-making or problem solving process using this type of uncertain information, however, is ultimately a subjective one, depending on one's experience and knowledge. The outcome from this process, therefore, would be often uncertain as well. Also, knowledge discovered from this type of data might be of questionable validity.

In this paper we propose an alternative way of handling noisy data, which has great potential in improving the quality of problem solving and knowledge acquired from data. Instead of measuring and providing information on the amount of noise in the data, we try to explicitly identify and then discard the noise before these data are used for any purpose.

In section 2, the type of noise considered in this paper is defined and a general strategy for its identification is proposed, which involves machine learning from data and domain knowledge. In section 3, this strategy is applied to large quantities of visual field test data which are crucial for the diagnosis of a variety of blinding diseases. In section 4, this strategy is evaluated and we show that it provides a satisfactory way of locating and rejecting noise in the test data. Finally, the work is summarized in section 5.

Noise and its Identification

Measurement Noise

In learning classificatory knowledge from data, there is a universe of objects that are described in terms of a collection of attributes (Quinlan 1986). The objective is to extract from a set of training examples, rules for classifying objects into a number of prespecified categories using those attributes. In these learning systems, data are defined as *noisy* when either the values of attributes or classes contain errors.

In this paper we shall put an emphasis on the errors of attribute values as we are considering the use of data for general purpose applications, not limited to learning classification rules. One of the main reasons for these errors is that the attributes used to describe an object are often based on *measurements*. To illustrate the idea, consider the task of diagnosing blinding diseases such as glaucoma. A dominating attribute would be to test the visual field of a patient. It is highly unlikely that one could obtain absolutely correct visual field data because these data, collected from patients' responses to visual stimuli on a computer screen, necessarily contain errors caused by various behavioral factors such as the learning effect, inattention, failure of fixation, fatigue etc. These errors are typically in the form of false positive or negative responses from patients (Lieberman & Drake 1992). Quinlan has also given an example of false positive or negative readings for the presence of some substance in the blood (Quinlan 1986).

The *noise* in data considered in this paper refers to incorrect data items caused by measurements. Consequently we shall use the term *measurement noise* throughout the paper.

Identifying the Measurement Noise

One fundamental assumption made in (Becker & Hinton 1992), where a new self-organizing neural network is proposed, is that interesting properties in data are more stable than the noise (Mitchison & Durbin 1992). For example, the property that a normal person who does not have any visual function loss should be able to see the stimuli on the test screen most of the time is more stable than the occasional fluctuation in data caused by errors (e.g. false positive or false negative responses) for whatever reasons. We have adopted this assumption as our basic principle for identifying measurement noise, to which we shall refer as the *noise identification principle*.

Suppose that a repeated test is designed where the same measurement is made a fixed number of times and consider the visual test as an example. A normal person might be distracted in the middle of a test, say, for example the fifth of the repeated measurements. This results in poor sensitivity values for, perhaps, most of the locations within the visual field, leading to fluctuation in the data. This type of fluctuation, however, should not affect the overall results of the visual field as she or he should be able to see the stimuli on the screen during most of the other trials in the test. The main task here is to identify the common feature exhibited by most of the trials, i.e., the person can see the stimuli most of the time. The part of the data inconsistent with this feature, i.e. the fifth trial, will then be exposed and consequently suspected as noise.

The question is, then, how to find a computational method capable of detecting interesting features among data. Unsupervised learning algorithms seem to be natural candidates, as they are known to be capable of extracting meaningful features, which reflect the inherent relationships between different parts of the data (Fisher, Pazzani, & Langley 1991). For example, we can use an unsupervised learning algorithm such as self-organizing maps(Kohonen 1989) to let the data self-organize in such way that more stable parts of data are clustered to reflect certain interesting features, while parts of data which are inconsistent with those features will be separated from the stable cluster.

It should be emphasized that the less stable part of data should not necessarily be the measurement noise in that they can be actually the true measurements reflecting real values of an attribute. In the example of diagnosing glaucoma using visual field data, the fluctuation in the data can be caused by behavioral factors such as fatigue and inattention, but can also be caused by pathological conditions of the patient. Consider that a glaucoma patient undergoes a visual field test. It is quite possible that there will be still fluctuations in the responses at certain test locations, even if s/he has fully concentrated during the test. The nature of the disease has dictated her/his responses. The elimination of these responses would lead to the loss of much useful diagnostic information, and worse still, could lead to incorrect conclusion about the patient's pathological status.

Therefore, it would be desirable to check whether the less stable part of data is indeed the measurement noise. This is difficult to achieve using the data alone, as there are often many possible explanations for fluctuation in the same data set, as discussed above. The use of a substantial amount of domain specific knowledge, however, has potentials in resolving this difficulty. For example, the knowledge of how diseases such as glaucoma manifest themselves on the test data is crucial for identifying the measurement noise, as we can then have a better chance of finding out the component within the less stable part of the data, which is caused by pathological reasons.

The above discussions lead to a general strategy for identifying the measurement noise in data, which consists of two steps. Firstly, an unsupervised learning algorithm is used to cluster the more stable part of the data. This algorithm should be able to detect some interesting features among those data. The less stable part of the data, which are inconsistent with those features, then becomes the suspect of measurement noise.

Secondly, knowledge in application domains, together with knowledge about the relationships among data, is used to check whether the less stable part of data is indeed the measurement noise. This type of domain specific knowledge may be acquired from experts, however, it is often incomplete. For example, only a partial understanding has been obtained about how diseases like glaucoma manifest themselves on any visual field test data (Wu 1993). Therefore, it is often desirable to apply machine learning methods to the initially incomplete knowledge in order to generalize over unknown situations. One such example is shown in the next section.

Identifying Noise in Glaucomatous Test Data

The Computer Controlled Video Perimetry (CCVP). The CCVP (Fitzke *et al.* 1989; Wu 1993) is a newly developed visual function test method and has been shown to be an effective way of overcoming difficulties in the early detection of visual impairments caused by glaucoma. It examines the sensitivity of a number of locations in the visual field using vertical bars on the computer screen [see Figure 1 for an example]. All these locations are tested by several different stimuli and the test is repeated a fixed number of times. One popular version of the CCVP test examines 6 locations using the same stimulus and the test is repeated 10 times.

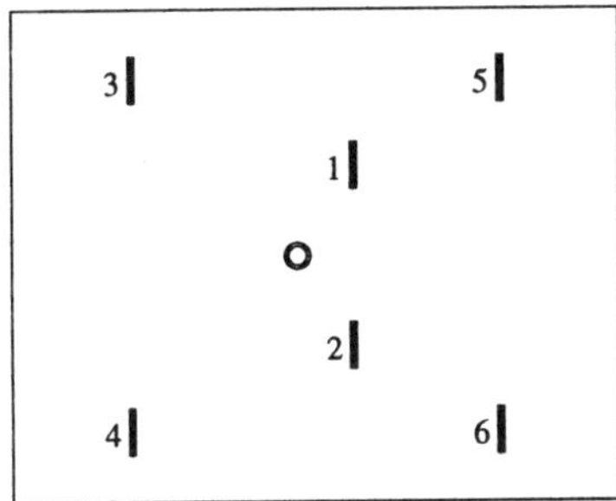

Figure 1: A CCVP screen layout

If the stimulus is seen at any stage of the test, the patient presses a button as a response. At the end of this CCVP test, ten data vectors are produced, each of which records the patient's response during a single trial. Each vector consists of 6 data elements referring to the results of testing 6 locations using the same stimulus. As far as each location is concerned, there will be a sensitivity value calculated by counting the percentage of positive responses. The clinician relies heavily on these location sensitivity values to perform diagnosis.

Applying the Strategy to the CCVP Data

Identifying the More Stable Part of the CCVP data. The method for identifying the more stable part of the CCVP data is to model the patient's test behavior using the self-organizing maps (SOM). Data clusters can then be visualized or calculated. This method consists of three steps.

Firstly, Kohonen's learning technique (Kohonen 1989) is used to train a network capable of generating maps which reflect the patient's test behavior. Each response pattern for each test trial is used as an input vector to the self-organizing map and each winner node is produced on the output map. In all, 2630 trial data vectors corresponding to 263 tests are used to train the network and the whole data set is reiteratively submitted 100 times in random orders.

Secondly, an effort is made to find a network which shows better *neighborhood preservations*, i.e. similar input patterns are mapped onto identical or closely neighboring neurons on the output map. This step is important as we want to map similar response patterns from patients onto similar neurons. We have used the *topographical product* (TP) (Bauer & Pawelzik 1992) as a measurement for this purpose where TP indicates the magnitude of neighborhood violation. Therefore, the smaller the value of TP is, the better the neighborhood preservation would become.

Having obtained a well-performed network, the final step is to generate the behavior maps for individual patients and analyze these maps to identify the more stable part of data. As far as each patient is concerned, there would be ten winner nodes and nine transitions on the output map. These transitions constitute a transition trajectory, which graphically illustrates how patient's behavior changed from one trial to the other [Figure 2].

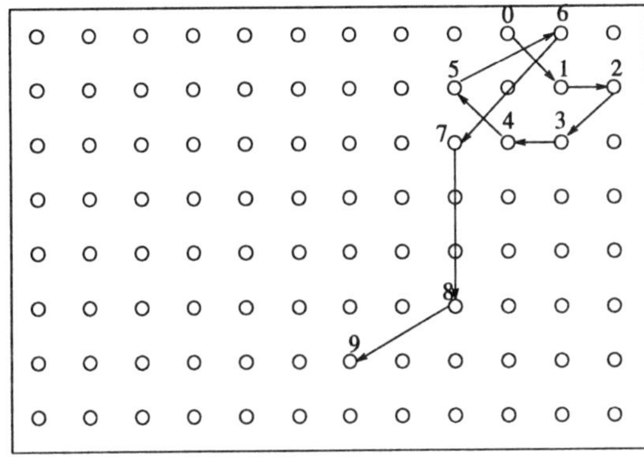

Figure 2: A transition trajectory in the output map

As one of the key SOM features is that similar input vectors would lead to similar winner nodes, here we have the general rule for identifying the more stable part of the data: if most of the winner nodes are centered around one particular region, then the input data vectors associated with these nodes constitute the more stable part of the data. These vectors share one common feature: they are similar to each other, judged to a large extent by a distance measurement such as the Euclidean distance.

The above rule can be implemented by algorithms using the geometry positions of the nodes and their relative distances. The approach taken here is to search for a maximum set of neurons on the output map, which occupies the smallest topographical area. In particular, an evaluation function is defined in equation 1 for this purpose and the objective is to find a subset of winner nodes, S, which minimizes the value of $F(S)$.

$$F(S) = A(S(k))/k^2 \quad (k = N, N-1, ..., \lfloor N/2+1 \rfloor)(1)$$

Where N is the total number of winner nodes (ten

in our application), A denotes the topographical area in the map occupied by a subset of winner nodes, and $S(k)$ represents a subset of winner nodes with k members.

Checking the Less Stable Part of Data. Let us now examine the less stable part of data, for example, the data vectors associated with winner nodes 8 and 9 in Figure 2, and see whether or not some of these vectors are the measurement noise. For our chosen application, we are particularly interested in finding out whether data items within this less stable part of data are caused by pathological conditions of the patient during the visual field test.

To achieve this, a deep understanding of how diseases manifest themselves on the data is essential. Here we have used both knowledge about inherent relationships among data and domain knowledge from experts to obtain this understanding.

The knowledge about data is reflected on the maps produced by the SOM. For example, each neuron on the output map is likely to have a number of input vectors associated with it, and these input vectors in turn determine the physical meanings of the neuron such as average sensitivity, the number of input patterns the neuron represents, and typical patterns the neuron represents etc. Using these physical meanings, domain experts can try to group those input patterns which have the same or similar pathological meanings. In our case, an input pattern consists of a vector of 6 elements, each of which represents whether the patient sees the stimulus in a certain location on the computer screen [Figure 1].

There are four major groups created by experts. Group A is composed of those input patterns reflecting that the patient under test is showing the early sign of upper hemifield damage, while group B consists of those patterns demonstrating that the upper hemifield of the patient is probably already damaged. Group C and D are made of those patterns similar to group A and B, except they are used to represent two different stages of the lower hemifield damage. Any two patterns which fall into the same group, no matter how distant they may appear on the test behavior map, will be considered as having the same pathological meanings.

Take group A as an example. It contains the following three patterns:

$$\{ (1,1,0,1,1,1)^t, (1,1,0,1,0,1)^t, (1,1,1,1,0,1)^t \}$$

These have been identified as possible patterns for a glaucoma patient showing early sign of upper hemifield damage. Two factors have been taken into consideration by experts when selecting these patterns. Firstly, the domain knowledge about early upper hemifield damage is used, for example, locations 3 and 5 which are within the upper hemifield were not seen in some of those patterns and the reason why location 1 is not included is that it often indicates the upper hemi-

field is probably already damaged (Wu 1993). Secondly, the physical meanings of the trained map are used, especially how typical input patterns are associated with output neurons. For example, the above three patterns are in a topographically connected area on the map.

These pathological groups are then used to check whether the less stable part of the data are the measurement noise. A simple way to do this is as follows. When those nodes, whose corresponding input data vectors are the less stable part of the data, are identified, check whether each of these data vectors belongs to the same pathological groups as those patterns which were recognized as the more stable part of data. If yes, then treat it as a true measurement; otherwise, it is measurement noise.

One of the major difficulties in applying this method is that the patterns which are made up those pathological groups are not complete in that they (27 in total) are only a subset of all the possible patterns ($2^6 = 64$). Therefore, when there is a new pattern occurring, the above method cannot be applied. One of the main reasons why experts cannot classify all the patterns into those four groups is that the CCVP is a newly introduced test and the reflection of glaucoma patients and suspects on the CCVP data is not fully understood.

To overcome this difficulty, machine learning methods can be applied to generalize from those 27 classification examples provided by the experts. In particular, we have used the back-propagation algorithm (Rumelhart, Hinton, & Williams 1986) for this purpose. The input neurons represent the locations within the visual field, output neurons are those pathological groups, and three hidden nodes are used in the fully configured network.

The trained network is able to reach 100% accuracy for the training examples and to further classify another 26 patterns. One of the interesting observations is that patterns within each of the resultant groups tend to be clustered in a topographically connected area, a property demonstrated by the initial groups. The remaining patterns are regarded as the unknown class since they have no significant output signal in output neurons. They have been found to be much more likely to appear in the less stable part of the CCVP data than in the more stable one.

It should be noted that the application described above is rather a simple one in which there are only 64 possible input patterns. This particular version of the CCVP test is chosen for its simplicity in order to make it easier to describe the general ideas in implementing the noise identification principle. In fact, there is a more popular version of CCVP which also tests the six locations within the visual field by ten repeated trials, however, using *four* different stimuli. Therefore the data vectors produced within this test contain 24 items, instead of 6, and consequently, there are 2^{24} possible input patterns. We have also experimented with large quantities of data from this test using the proposed noise identification strategy. The results are similar to those of the simpler test described in the next section.

Evaluation

The Strategy

The noise identification strategy is based on the assumption that interesting properties in data are more stable than the noise. It can be applied to those areas where repeated measurements can be easily made about attributes concerned. Below are several observations regarding this strategy.

Firstly, explicit identification and deletion of measurement noise in data may be a necessary step before the data can be properly explored, as shown in our application. In particular, we have found that noise deletion can offer great assistance to the clinician in diagnosing those otherwise ambiguous cases (see section 4.2). In a separate experiment with learning hidden features from the CCVP data, we have found that many useful features, such as behavioral relationship between two test locations, were not initially found from the raw CCVP data, but were uncovered from the data after the measurement noise was deleted using the strategy proposed in this paper.

Secondly, the use of domain knowledge supplied by experts is of special concern as this type of knowledge involves a substantial amount of subjective elements, and is often incomplete as shown in our application. It should be pointed out that this strategy cannot be applied to those applications where there is little relevant high quality knowledge but a lot of *false noise*, i.e., those data items from the less stable part of the data which actually reflect the true measurements. Where there is little concern about the false noise situation, however, an unsupervised learning algorithm can be used directly to identify the measurement noise, in this case, the entire less stable part of the data.

Finally, no claim is made that this strategy can be used to identify all the measurement noise in data, or all the noise identified is the real one. This depends on the ability of the chosen algorithms to accurately cluster those data items with common features and the quality of domain knowledge used to exclude the false noise.

The Results

Here we present the results in applying the proposed strategy to a set of clinical test data (2630 data vectors) collected from a group of glaucoma patients and suspects. To find out how successful this strategy is in achieving its objective, we use the idea of *reproducibility* of the test results.

As glaucoma is a long term progressing disease, the visual function should remain more or less the same during a short period of time. Therefore results from

such two repeated tests within this time period should be very close. However, this is not always true under real clinical situations as measurement noise is involved in each test, perhaps for different reasons. Thus it is not surprising to note that there are a large number of repeated tests, which were conducted within an average time span of one month, whose results showed disagreements to various degrees.

As one of the main reasons for the disagreement is the measurement noise, it is natural to assume that the sensitivity results of the two tests should agree (to various degrees) after the noise is discarded. This then constitutes a method for evaluating our proposed strategy for identifying and eliminating noise from data.

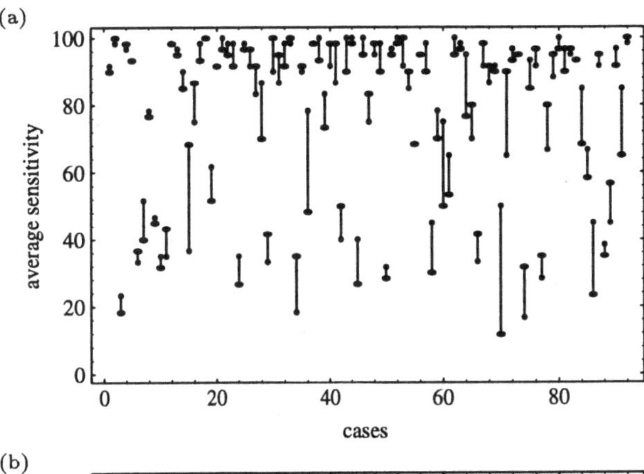

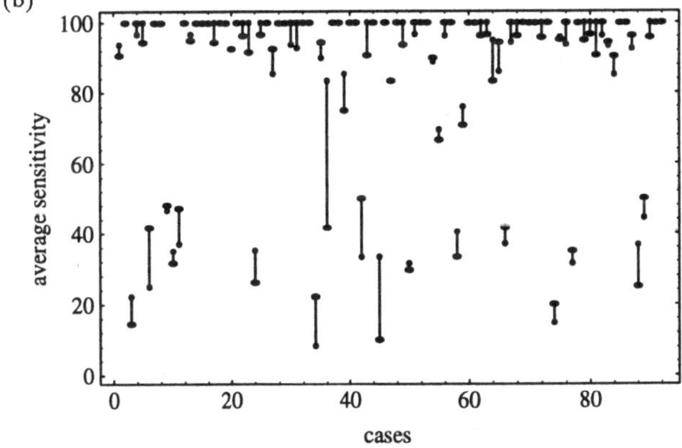

Figure 3: (a) before deletion; (b) after deletion

Ninety-two pairs of test records are available for this purpose. The average sensitivity values of these tests are contrasted in Figure 3(a) where the dot is used to indicate the result of the first test, the oval is used for the result of the second test, and the difference between the two results for each case is illustrated by the line in between them. The same results after the rejection of noise by the proposed strategy are given in Figure 3(b).

The results from the two repeated tests have much better agreements after the noise is rejected. This is indicated by the observation that the lines between the two tests are in general shortened in Figure 3(b). In fact, if one calculates the mean difference between the two tests, 5.4 is the figure for the original data, while 3.6 is obtained after the noise is eliminated.

Another major finding is that noise deletion may also be of direct diagnostic assistance to the clinician. One of the difficulties for the clinician is that the result from one test suggests that the patient is *normal* (no glaucoma), while the result from the other test shows that the patient is *abnormal* (having glaucoma of some kind). It has been found that the average sensitivity value of 75% appears to be the golden line n CCVP that divides the normal and abnormal groups (Wu 1993). Since much better agreement is shown between the two repeated tests after the deletion of noise, there would be fewer cases whose test results are split by the golden line. This is indeed the case with our data as shown in Figure 3: there are quite a few conflicting cases in Figure 3(a), while only about two such cases exist in Figure 3(b).

It is worth reiterating that the CCVP is a newly introduced test method. A deeper understanding of its characteristics and its relevance to diagnosis can help further improve the results of identifying the measurement noise in the CCVP data.

Concluding Remarks

In this paper we have introduced an alternative way of dealing with noisy data. Instead of measuring and providing information on the amount of noise in the data, we explicitly identify and then discard the noise so that quality data can be used for different applications.

The principle we adopted for identifying measurement noise is that interesting properties in data are more stable than noise. To implement this principle for our application, self-organizing maps are used to model patient's behavior during the visual field test and to separate the more stable part of data from the less stable one. Expert knowledge, augmented by supervised learning techniques, is also used to check whether data items within the less stable part are measurement noise caused by behavioral factors, or those caused by the patient's pathological conditions.

The proposed strategy has been shown to be a satisfactory way of identifying measurement noise in visual field test data. Moreover, the explicit identification and elimination of the noise in these data have been found not just desirable, but essential, if the data are to be properly modeled and explored. Finally, the strategy may be used as a preprocessor to a variety of systems using data with measurement noise.

Acknowledgements

This work is in part supported by the International Glaucoma Society, British Council for Prevention of Blindness, and International Center for Eye Health. We would like to thank Phil Docking for his comments on an early draft of this paper and anonymous referees' informative review.

References

Bauer, H. U., and Pawelzik, K. R. 1992. Quantifying the neighborhood preservation of self-organizing feature maps. *IEEE Trans. on Neural Networks* 3(4):570–9.

Becker, S., and Hinton, G. E. 1992. Self-organizing neural network that discovers surfaces in random-dot stereograms. *Nature* 355:161–163.

Bratko, I., and Kononenko, I. 1987. Learning diagnostic rules from incomplete and noisy data. In Phelps, B., ed., *Interactions in Artificial Intelligence and Statistical Methods*. Technical. 142–53.

Fisher, D. H.; Pazzani, M. J.; and Langley, P. 1991. *Concept Formation: Knowledge and Experience in Unsupervised Learning*. Morgan Kaufmann.

Fitzke, F. W.; Poinoosawmy, D.; Nagasuberamanian, S.; and Hitchings, R. A. 1989. Peripheral displacement threshold in glaucoma and ocular hypertension. *Perimetry Update 1988/89* 399–405.

Frawley, W. J.; Piatetsky-Shapiro, G.; and Matheus, C. J. 1991. Knowledge discovery in databases: An overview. In Piatetsky-Shapiro, G., and Frawley, W. J., eds., *Knowledge Discovery in Databases*. AAAI Press / The MIT Press. 1–27.

Kohonen, T. 1989. *Self-Organization and Associative Memory*. Springer-Verlag.

Lieberman, M. F., and Drake, M. V. 1992. *Computerized Perimetry*. Slack Inc.

Mitchison, G., and Durbin, R. 1992. Learning from your neighbour. *Nature* 355:112–113.

Nagata, S.; Kani, K.; and Sugiyama, A. 1991. A computer-assisted visual field diagnosis system using a neural network. *Perimetry Update 1990/91* 291–95.

Quinlan, J. R. 1986. Induction of decision trees. *Machine Learning* 1:81–106.

Rumelhart, D. E.; Hinton, G. E.; and Williams, R. J. 1986. Learning representations by back-propagating errors. *Nature* 323:533–36.

Weiss, S. M., and Kulikowski, C. A. 1991. *Computer Systems that Learn*. Morgan Kaufmann.

Wu, J. X. 1993. *Visual Screening for Blinding Diseases in the Community Using Computer Controlled Video Perimetry*. Ph.D. Dissertation, University of London.

Markov Chain Monte-Carlo Algorithms for the Calculation of Dempster-Shafer Belief

Serafín Moral

Departamento de Ciencias de la Computación e I. A.,
Universidad de Granada
18071 - Granada - Spain
smc@robinson.ugr.es

Nic Wilson

Department of Computer Science
Queen Mary and Westfield College
Mile End Rd., London E1 4NS, UK
nic@dcs.qmw.uk.ac

Abstract

A simple Monte-Carlo algorithm can be used to calculate Dempster-Shafer belief very efficiently unless the conflict between the evidences is very high. This paper introduces and explores Markov Chain Monte-Carlo algorithms for calculating Dempster-Shafer belief that can also work well when the conflict is high.

1. Introduction

Dempster-Shafer theory (Shafer 1976, 1990, Dempster 1967) is a promising method for reasoning with uncertain information. The theory involves splitting the uncertain evidence into independent pieces and calculating the combined effect using Dempster's rule of combination. A major problem with this is the computational complexity of Dempster's rule. The straightforward application of the rule is exponential (where the problem parameters are the size of the frame of discernment and the number of evidences). A number of methods have been developed for improving the efficiency, e.g., (Laskey & Lehner 1989, Wilson 1989, Provan 1990, Kennes & Smets 1990) but they are limited by the $\#P$-completeness of Dempster's rule (Orponen 1990). However, the precise value of Dempster-Shafer belief is of no great importance—it is sufficient to find an approximate value, within a small range of the correct value. Dempster's formulation suggests a simple Monte-Carlo algorithm for calculating DS-belief, (Pearl 1988, Kämpke 1988, Wilson 1989, 1991). This algorithm, described in section 3, involves a large number of independent trials, each taking the value 0 or 1 and having an expected value of the Dempster-Shafer belief. This belief is then approximated as the average of the values of these trials. The algorithm can be used to efficiently calculate Dempster-Shafer belief unless the conflict between the evidences is very high. Unfortunately there are cases where the conflict will

be very high (Shafer 1992) making this algorithm unusable for those cases.

Similar problems have been found for Monte-Carlo algorithms in Statistics, and also in Bayesian networks. A common solution is to use Markov Chain Monte-Carlo algorithms (Smith & Roberts 1993, Geyer 1992, Hrycej 1990) for which the trials are not independent, but are instead governed by a Markov Chain (Feller 1950). Such methods are used when it is very difficult to simulate independent realizations of some complicated probability distribution.

In this paper we develop Markov Chain algorithms for the calculation of Dempster-Shafer belief. Section 4 describes the algorithms and gives the convergence results. Convergence of the algorithms is dependent on a particular connectivity condition; a way of testing for this condition is given in section 5. Section 6 discusses the results of computer testing of the algorithm. Section 7 shows how the algorithm can be extended and applied to the calculation of Dempster-Shafer belief on logics, and on infinite frames, and section 8 briefly discusses some extensions to these algorithms which may work when the connectivity condition is not satisfied.

2. Belief Functions and Source Triples

Let Θ be a finite set. Θ is intended to represent a set of mutually exclusive and exhaustive propositions. A mass function over Θ is a function $m: 2^{\Theta} \to [0,1]$ such that $m(\emptyset) = 0$ and $\sum_{A \in 2^{\Theta}} m(A) = 1$. Function $\text{Bel}: 2^{\Theta} \to [0,1]$ is said to be a belief function over Θ if there exists a mass function m over Θ with, for all $X \in 2^{\Theta}$, $\text{Bel}(X) = \sum_{A \subseteq X} m(A)$. Clearly, to every mass function over Θ there corresponds (with the above relationship) a unique belief function; conversely for every belief function over Θ there corresponds a unique mass function (Shafer 1976).

Belief functions are intended as representations of subjective degrees of belief, as described in (Shafer

1976, 1981). Mathematically, they were derived from Dempster's lower probabilities induced by a multivalued mapping (Dempster 1967), and Dempster's framework (using what we call source triples) turns out to be more convenient for our purposes. [1]

A source triple over Θ is defined to be a triple (Ω, P, Γ) where Ω is a finite set, P is a probability function on Ω, and Γ is a function from Ω to 2^{Θ}, such that for all $\omega \in \Omega$, $\Gamma(\omega) \neq \emptyset$ and $P(\omega) \neq 0$.

Associated with a source triple is a mass function, and hence a belief function, given respectively by $m(X) = \sum_{\omega\,:\,\Gamma(\omega)=X} P(\omega)$ and $\mathrm{Bel}(X) = \sum_{\omega\,:\,\Gamma(\omega)\subseteq X} P(\omega)$. Conversely, any mass/belief function can be expressed in this way for some (non-unique) source triple. Each belief function (or source triple) is intended to represent a separate piece of evidence. The impact of a set of independent evidences is calculated using Dempster's rule[2], which (in terms of source triples) is a mapping sending a finite set of source triples $\{(\Omega_i, P_i, \Gamma_i),\ \text{for } i = 1,\ldots,m\}$, to a triple $(\Omega, P_{\mathrm{DS}}, \Gamma)$, defined as follows. Let $\overline{\Omega} = \Omega_1 \times \cdots \times \Omega_m$. For $\omega \in \overline{\Omega}$, $\omega(i)$ is defined to be its ith component (sometimes written ω_i), so that $\omega = (\omega(1), \ldots, \omega(m))$. Define $\Gamma' : \overline{\Omega} \to 2^{\Theta}$ by $\Gamma'(\omega) = \bigcap_{i=1}^{m} \Gamma_i(\omega(i))$ and probability function P' on $\overline{\Omega}$ by $P'(\omega) = \prod_{i=1}^{m} P_i(\omega(i))$, for $\omega \in \overline{\Omega}$. Let Ω be the set $\{\omega \in \overline{\Omega} : \Gamma'(\omega) \neq \emptyset\}$, let Γ be Γ' restricted to Ω, and let probability function P_{DS} on Ω be P' conditioned on Ω, so that for $\omega \in \Omega$, $P_{\mathrm{DS}}(\omega) = P'(\omega)/P'(\Omega)$. The factor $1/P'(\Omega)$ can be viewed as a measure of the conflict between the evidences (Shafer 1976).

The combined measure of belief Bel over Θ is thus given, for $X \subseteq \Theta$, by $\mathrm{Bel}(X) = P_{\mathrm{DS}}(\{\omega \in \Omega : \Gamma(\omega) \subseteq X\})$, which we abbreviate to $P_{\mathrm{DS}}(\Gamma(\omega) \subseteq X)$. Letting, for $i = 1, \ldots, m$, Bel_i be the belief function corresponding to $(\Omega_i, P_i, \Gamma_i)$, then $\mathrm{Bel} = \mathrm{Bel}_1 \oplus \cdots \oplus \mathrm{Bel}_m$ where $\oplus$ is Dempster's rule for belief functions as defined in (Shafer 1976).

Since there are exponentially many subsets of Θ, we are never going to be able to calculate the belief in all of them for large Θ. Instead, it is assumed that, for a fairly small number of important sets $X \subseteq \Theta$, we are interested in calculating $\mathrm{Bel}(X)$.

3. A Simple Monte-Carlo Algorithm

Since, for $X \subseteq \Theta$, $\mathrm{Bel}(X) = P_{\mathrm{DS}}(\Gamma(\omega) \subseteq X)$, the obvious idea for a Monte-Carlo algorithm for calculating $\mathrm{Bel}(X)$ is to repeat a large number of trials, where for each trial, we pick ω with chance $P_{\mathrm{DS}}(\omega)$ and let the value of the trial be 1 if $\Gamma(\omega) \subseteq X$, and 0 otherwise. $\mathrm{Bel}(X)$ is then estimated by the average value of the trials. We can pick ω with chance $P_{\mathrm{DS}}(\omega)$ by repeatedly (if necessary) picking $\omega \in \overline{\Omega}$ with chance $P'(\omega)$ until we get an ω in Ω. (Picking ω with chance $P'(\omega)$ is easy: for each $i = 1, \ldots, m$ we pick $\omega_i \in \Omega_i$ with chance $P_i(\omega_i)$ and let $\omega = (\omega_1, \ldots, \omega_m)$.)

The time that the algorithm takes to achieve a given accuracy is roughly proportional to $|\Theta|m/P'(\Omega)$, making it very efficient for problems where the evidences are not very conflicting (Wilson 1991).[3]

If, however, there is high conflict between the evidences, so that $P'(\Omega)$ is extremely small, then it will tend to take a very long time to find an ω in Ω.

Example Let $\Theta = \{x_1, x_2, \ldots, x_m\}$, for each $i = 1, \ldots, m$ let $\Omega_i = \{1, 2\}$, let $P_i(1) = P_i(2) = \frac{1}{2}$, let $\Gamma_i(1) = \{x_i\}$ and let $\Gamma_i(2) = \Theta$. The triple $(\Omega_i, P_i, \Gamma_i)$ corresponds to a simple support function (see (Shafer 1976)) with $m_i(\{x_i\}) = \frac{1}{2}$ and $m_i(\Theta) = \frac{1}{2}$. The conflict between the evidences is very high for large m since we have $P'(\Omega) = (m + 1)/2^m$ so the simple Monte-Carlo algorithm is not practical.

4. The Markov Chain Monte-Carlo Algorithms

Here we consider Monte-Carlo algorithms where the trials are not independent, but instead form a Markov Chain, so that the result of each trial is (probabilistically) dependent only on the result of the previous trial.

4.1 The Connected Components of Ω

The Markov Chain algorithms that we will consider require a particular condition on Ω to work, which we will call connectedness. This corresponds to the Markov Chain being irreducible (Feller 1950).

For $i \in \{1, \ldots, m\}$ and $\omega, \omega' \in \Omega$ write $\omega \equiv_i \omega'$ if ω and ω' differ at most on their ith co-ordinate, i.e.,

<hr>

[1] It also seems to be more convenient for justification of Dempster's rule, see (Shafer 1981, Wilson 1993).

[2] There has been much discussion in the literature on the soundness of the rule, e.g., (Pearl 1990, IJAR 1992); justifications include (Shafer 1981, Ruspini 1987, Wilson 1989, 1993).

[3] Of course, the constant of proportionality is higher if greater accuracy is required.

If this algorithm is applied to calculate unnormalised belief (Smets 1988), which has been shown in (Orponen 1990) to be a $\#P$-complete problem, then the $1/P'(\Omega)$ factor in the complexity is omitted; this means that we have, given any degree of accuracy, a low order polynomial efficiency algorithm for calculating an 'intractable' problem (up to that degree of accuracy).

if for all $j \in \{1, \ldots, m\} \setminus \{i\}$, $\omega(j) = \omega'(j)$. Let R be the union of the relations $\equiv_i$ for $i \in \{1, \ldots, m\}$, so that $\omega \, R \, \omega'$ if and only if ω and ω' differ at most on one co-ordinate; let equivalence relation $\equiv$ be the transitive closure of R. The equivalence classes of $\equiv$ will be called *connected components* of Ω, and Ω will be said to be *connected* if it has just one connected component, i.e, if $\equiv$ is the relation $\Omega \times \Omega$.

4.2 The Basic Markov Chain Monte-Carlo Algorithm

Non-deterministic function $\mathrm{PDS}^N(\omega_0)$ takes as input initial state $\omega_0 \in \Omega$ and number of trials N and returns a state ω. The intention is that when N is large, for any initial state ω_0, $\Pr(\mathrm{PDS}^N(\omega_0) = \omega) \approx \mathrm{P_{DS}}(\omega)$ for all $\omega \in \Omega$. The algorithm starts in state ω_0 and randomly moves between elements of Ω. The current state is labelled ω_c.

> FUNCTION $\mathrm{PDS}^N(\omega_0)$
> $\omega_c := \omega_0$
>   **for** $n = 1$ **to** N
>   **for** $i = 1$ **to** m
> $\omega_c := operation_i(\omega_c)$
>   **next** i
>   **next** n
>   **return** ω_c.

Non-deterministic function $operation_i$ changes at most the ith co-ordinate of its input ω_c—it changes it to y with chance proportional to $\mathrm{P}_i(y)$. We therefore have, for $\omega, \omega' \in \Omega$,

$$\Pr(operation_i(\omega') - \omega) = \begin{cases} \alpha_{\omega'} \mathrm{P}_i(\omega(i)) & \text{if } \omega \equiv_i \omega'; \\ 0 & \text{otherwise.} \end{cases}$$

The normalisation constant $\alpha_{\omega'}$ is given by $\alpha_{\omega'}^{-1} = \sum_{\omega \, \equiv_i \, \omega'} \mathrm{P}_i(\omega(i))$.

4.3 The Calculation of Belief

Now that we have a way of picking ω with chance approximately $\mathrm{P_{DS}}(\omega)$ we can incorporate it, in the obvious way, in an algorithm for calculating $\mathrm{Bel}(X)$. This gives function $\mathrm{B}_K^N(\omega_0)$ with inputs ω_0, N and K, where $\omega_0 \in \Omega$ is a starting value, N is the number of trials, and K is the number of trials used by the function $\mathrm{PDS}^K(\cdot)$ used in the algorithm. The value $\mathrm{B}_K^N(\omega_0)$ can be seen to be the proportion of the N trials in which $\Gamma(\omega_c) \subseteq X$.

In the $\mathrm{B}_K^N(\omega_0)$ algorithm, for each call of $\mathrm{PDS}^K(.)$, Km values of ω are generated, but only one, the last, is used to test if $\Gamma(\omega) \subseteq X$. It may well be more efficient to use all of the values, which is what $\mathrm{BEL}^N(\omega_0)$ does. The implementation is very similar to that for $\mathrm{PDS}^N(\omega_0)$, the main difference being the extra line in the inside **for** loop. The value returned by $\mathrm{BEL}^N(\omega_0)$ is the proportion of the time that $\Gamma(\omega_c) \subseteq X$.

FUNCTION $\mathbf{B}_K^N(\omega_0)$	FUNCTION $\mathbf{BEL}^N(\omega_0)$
$\omega_c := \omega_0$	$\omega_c := \omega_0$
$S := 0$	$S := 0$
for $n = 1$ **to** N	**for** $n = 1$ **to** N
$\omega_c := \mathbf{PDS}^K(\omega_c)$	**for** $i = 1$ **to** m
if $\Gamma(\omega_c) \subseteq X$	$\omega_c := operation_i(\omega_c)$
then $S := S + 1$	**if** $\Gamma(\omega_c) \subseteq X$
next n	**then** $S := S + 1$
return $\frac{S}{N}$	**next** i
	next n
	return $\frac{S}{Nm}$

The key result is the following.

Theorem Suppose Ω is connected. Then

1. given $\varepsilon > 0$ there exists N' such that for all $N \geq N'$, any $\omega \in \Omega$ and any starting value ω_0, $|\Pr(\mathrm{PDS}^N(\omega_0) = \omega) - \mathrm{P_{DS}}(\omega)| < \varepsilon$;

2. given $\varepsilon, \delta > 0$ there exists K' and N' such that for all $K \geq K'$ and $N \geq N'$ and any ω_0, $\Pr(|\mathrm{B}_K^N(\omega_0) - \mathrm{Bel}(X)| < \varepsilon) \geq 1 - \delta$; and

3. given $\varepsilon, \delta > 0$ there exists N' such that for all $N \geq N'$ and any ω_0, $\Pr(|\mathrm{BEL}^N(\omega_0) - \mathrm{Bel}(X)| < \varepsilon) \geq 1 - \delta$.

This shows that PDS^N approximates $\mathrm{P_{DS}}$ to arbitrary accuracy, and that B_K^N and BEL^N approximate $\mathrm{Bel}(X)$ to arbitrary accuracy. The proof of this theorem is a consequence of general convergence results for Markov Chain Monte-Carlo algorithms; a summary of these can be found in (Smith & Roberts 1993). However, the main problem with the convergence results is that, in general, it is very difficult to assess when we have reached the desired precision.

The reason that we require that Ω be connected is that that, in the algorithms, the only values that ω_c can take are the members of the $\equiv$-equivalence class of the starting position ω_0.

4.4 Speeding up Intersections

In the implementation of B_K^N and BEL^N we have to perform operation $operation_i(\omega)$, which involves changing the ith co-ordinate of ω to y, with a probability proportional to $\mathrm{P}_i(y)$. The main difficulty lies in that the new ω' has to belong to Ω, that is, $\Gamma(\omega') \neq \emptyset$. In order to find possible values of ω', we have to calculate the intersection of all the sets $\Gamma_j(\omega_j)$ for $j \neq i$. This calculation is of order $\mathrm{O}(|\Theta|(m - 1))$.

However, this operation can be speeded up. Define, for each $\omega \in \Omega$, a function $h_\omega \colon \Theta \to I\!\!N$ given by $h_\omega(\theta) = \sum_{i=1}^{m} I_{\Gamma_i(\omega_i)}(\theta)$ where $I_{\Gamma_i(\omega_i)}(\theta)$ is equal to 1 if $\theta \in \Gamma_i(\omega_i)$ and 0 otherwise. Suppose we have stored the function h_ω. If we calculate $h_\omega - I_{\Gamma_j(\omega_j)}$ then the desired intersection is given by the elements of Θ with a maximum value of this difference.

Suppose now that we have randomly picked a new ith co-ordinate, y. We can calculate the new h-function, $h_{\omega'}$ by just adding $I_{\Gamma_j(y)}$ to the above difference. This method allows us to calculate the intersection in $O(|\Theta|)$.

5. The Connectivity of Ω

For the above algorithms B_K^N and BEL^N to converge we require that Ω be connected. Many important cases lead to a connected Ω; for example, if the individual belief functions Bel_i are simple support functions, consonant support functions, discounted Bayesian or any other discounted belief functions (i.e., with $m_i(\Theta) \neq 0$) then Ω will be connected. Other cases clearly lead to non-connected Ω, for example, if each Bel_i is a Bayesian belief function. Unfortunately it will sometimes not be at all clear whether Ω is connected or not, and the obvious way of testing this requires a number of steps exponential in m. In 5.1 we construct a method for dealing with this problem.

5.1 Using Θ to Find the Connected Components

$\underline{\Theta}$, the core of Θ, is defined to be $\bigcup_{\omega \in \Omega} \Gamma(\omega)$. For $\theta \in \Theta$, let $\theta^* \subseteq \Omega$ be the set $\{\omega \in \Omega : \Gamma(\omega) \ni \theta\}$ and, for $i \in \{1, \ldots, m\}$, $\theta_i^* = \{\omega_i \in \Omega_i : \Gamma_i(\omega_i) \ni \theta\}$.

Define relation R' on $\underline{\Theta}$ by $\theta \; R' \; \psi \iff \omega \; R \; \omega'$ for some $\omega \in \theta^*$ and $\omega' \in \psi^*$ (relation R was defined at the beginning of section 4). Let equivalence relation $\equiv'$ be the transitive closure of R'.

Proposition

(i) Suppose $\theta, \psi \in \underline{\Theta}$. Then $\theta \; R' \; \psi \iff$ for at most one i, the set $(\theta_i^* \cap \psi_i^*)$ is empty.

(ii) A one-to-one correspondence between the equivalence classes of $\equiv'$ and $\equiv$ is given by $X \rightarrow \bigcup_{\theta \in X} \theta^*$, for $\equiv'$-equivalence class X. The inverse of this mapping is given by $W \rightarrow \bigcup_{\omega \in W} \Gamma(\omega)$, for $\equiv$-equivalence class W.

Part (i) implies that R' can be expressed easily in terms of commonality[4] functions: $\theta \; R' \; \psi \iff Q_i(\{\theta, \psi\}) = 0$ for at most one $i \in \{1, \ldots, m\}$.

The most important consequence of this proposition is that it gives an alternative method for testing if Ω is connected: we can use (i) to construct the equivalence

---

[4] The commonality function Q corresponding to a mass function m is defined by $Q(X) = \sum_{A \supseteq X} m(A)$ for $X \subseteq \Theta$.

classes of $\equiv'$; by (ii), Ω is connected if and only if there is a single $\equiv'$-equivalence class. Often Θ will be very much smaller than Ω, so this method will be much more efficient than a straightforward approach.

5.2 Finding a Starting Position $\omega_0 \in \Omega$

The algorithms require as input a value ω_0 in Ω (and any element will do). It might seem hard to find such an element ω_0 if Ω is very much smaller than $\overline{\Omega}$. However, we should have no problem in picking an element θ in $\underline{\Theta}$, the core of Θ, since the core consists of possibilities not completely ruled out by the evidence. But then, for $i = 1, \ldots, m$, we can pick ω_i such that $\Gamma_i(\omega_i) \ni \theta$. Letting $\omega_0 = (\omega_1, \ldots, \omega_m)$, we have $\Gamma(\omega_0) \ni \theta$ so $\omega_0 \in \Omega$ as required.

5.3 Barely Connected Ω

The convergence theorem guarantees that the algorithms will converge to the correct value for connected Ω, but it does not say how quickly. The following example illustrates that the convergence rate will tend to be very slow if Ω is only barely connected (i.e., if it is very hard for the algorithm to move between some elements of Ω).

Example Let $m = 2k - 1$, for some $k \in I\!N$, and let $\Theta = \{x_1, x_2\}$. For each $i = 1, \ldots, m$ let $\Omega_i = \{1, 2\}$, let $P_i(1) = P_i(2) = \frac{1}{2}$, let $\Gamma_i(2) = \Theta$ and, for $i \leq k$, let $\Gamma_i(1) = \{x_1\}$, and, for $i > k$, let $\Gamma_i(1) = \{x_2\}$. Each triple $(\Omega_i, P_i, \Gamma_i)$ corresponds to a simple support function. Ω is very nearly not connected since it is the union of two sets $\{x_1\}^*$ (which has 2^k elements) and $\{x_2\}^*$ (which has 2^{k-1} elements) which have just a singleton intersection $\{(2, \ldots, 2)\}$.

Suppose we want to use function $B_K^N(\omega_0)$ or function $BEL^N(\omega_0)$ to estimate $Bel(\{x_1\})$ (which is just under $\frac{2}{3}$). If we start with ω_0 such that $\Gamma(\omega_0) = \{x_1\}$ then it will probably take of the order of 2^k values of ω to reach a member of $\{x_2\}^*$. Therefore if k is large, e.g. $k = 30$, and we do a million trials then our estimate of $Bel(\{x_1\})$ will almost certainly be 1. Other starting positions ω_0 fare no better.

Since $P'(\Omega) \approx 3/2^k$ the simple Monte-Carlo algorithm does not perform satisfactorily here either. Generally, if Ω is barely connected, then it will usually be small in comparison to $\overline{\Omega}$, so the contradiction will tend to be high, and the simple Monte-Carlo algorithm will not work well either.

6. Experimental Testing

The performance of the three Monte-Carlo algorithms for estimating $Bel(X)$, $MCBEL^N$, B_K^N and BEL^N, was tested experimentally; MCBEL^N is the simple Monte-Carlo algorithm described in section 3, where N is the number of times an element $\omega \in \overline{\Omega}$ is picked with chance $\text{P}'(\omega)$ (so the number of useful trials will be approximately $N\text{P}'(\Omega)$).

We considered randomly generated belief functions on a frame Θ with 30 elements. The number of focal elements (i.e, sets with non-zero mass) was chosen using a Poisson distribution with mean 8.0. Each focal element A was determined by first picking a random number p in the interval $[0,1]$, and then, independently for each $\theta \in \Theta$, including θ in A with chance p.

Two experiments were carried out. In the first one, six belief functions were combined and a set $X \subseteq \Theta$ was randomly generated. The exact belief of this event was calculated and 100 approximations were made for each of the three Monte-Carlo algorithms, with $N = 5000$, $K = 6$. This was repeated for ten different combinations and ten randomly selected sets X. The second experiment was very similar: the only difference being that 10 belief functions were combined and $K = 10$.

The calculation times of the different algorithms were similar. In the light of the results we can conclude:

- The Markov Chain Monte-Carlo algorithms performed significantly better than the simple Monte-Carlo algorithm; e.g, in the first experiment, the mean errors of the Markov Chain algorithms were typically about 0.005, whereas in the simple algorithm, mean errors were typically about 0.01.

- There was no significant difference between the performance of the two Markov Chain Monte-Carlo algorithms. In BEL^N we use more cases of the sample, but in B_K^N there is a greater degree of independence between the cases.

It also appears that when m is increased, the relative precision of the Markov Chain algorithms with respect to the simple algorithm increases. This is due to the fact that the degree of conflict increases with m. Detailed results will appear in (Moral & Wilson 1994).

7. Extensions and Applications

Calculation of Belief on Logics: Dempster-Shafer theory can easily be extended to logics (see also (Pearl 1990, Wilson 1991)). For example, let $\mathcal{L}$ be the language (i.e. the set of well-formed formulae) of a propositional calculus. To extend the definitions of mass function, belief function, source triple and Dempster's rule we can (literally) just replace the words 'over Θ' by 'on $\mathcal{L}$', replace 2^Θ by $\mathcal{L}$, replace $\emptyset$ by $\perp$, $\subseteq$ by $\models$ and

intersection $\cap$ by conjunction $\wedge$.[5] To adapt the algorithms we just need to change the condition $\Gamma(\omega_c) \subseteq X$ to the condition $\Gamma(\omega_c) \models X$ in the functions $\text{B}_K^N(\omega_0)$ and $\text{BEL}^N(\omega_0)$.

Infinite frames: The Monte-Carlo algorithms open up the possibility of the computation of Dempster-Shafer belief on infinite frames Θ, with perhaps also an infinite number of focal elements (so that Ω is infinite). Clearly we will need some effective way of intersecting the focal elements; for example, this may be practical if $\Theta \subseteq \mathbb{R}^n$ for some n, and the focal elements are polytopes.

The algorithms can also be used for calculating Dempster-Shafer belief in belief networks, and in decision-making, for calculating upper and lower expected utility, see (Moral & Wilson 1994).

8. Discussion

Although the Markov Chain Monte-Carlo algorithms appear to often work well, there remains the problem of cases where Ω is not (or is barely) connected. We will briefly discuss ways in which the algorithm could be improved for such cases.

Blocking Components: A technique sometimes useful in Gibbs samplers is to block together components (see (Smith & Roberts 1993)); for our problem, this amounts to changing simultaneously more than one co-ordinate of ω at a time; this can connect up components which were previously not connected (but will increase the time for each trial).

Artificially Increasing Ω: Recall that the state space Ω was defined to be $\{\omega \in \overline{\Omega} : \Gamma'(\omega) \neq \emptyset\}$. If we use Ω' as the state space where $\Omega \subseteq \Omega' \subseteq \overline{\Omega}$, and define relations $\equiv_i$, R and $\equiv$ on Ω', then the functions $\text{B}_K^N(\omega_0)$ and $\text{BEL}^N(\omega_0)$ will converge to $\text{Bel}(X)$, given that Ω' is connected, so long as we don't count trials where $\omega \in \Omega' \setminus \Omega$ (i.e, we don't increment S or the trial counter for such an ω). This means that if Ω is not connected or is barely connected then we could improve the connectivity by judiciously adding extra points to Ω.

Weighted Simulation: Another approach to solving this type of problem, is to sample from a wrong but easier model and weighting to the distribution of interest (also known as 'importance sampling'). This method has been used in Bayesian networks (Fung &

---

[5] Note that now a belief function does not determine a unique mass function.

These definitions also work for many other logics, such as modal logics, or $\mathcal{L}$ could be the set of closed formulae in a first order predicate calculus.

Chang 1990). It could be used directly, or in conjunction with the algorithms given here to improve the connectivity of Ω.

Several combinations of the above procedures could produce optimal results in difficult situations. A simple strategy is to combine first by an exact method the groups of belief functions with a high degree of conflict, and then to combine the results with a simulation procedure.

Acknowledgements

The second author is supported by a SERC postdoctoral fellowship. This work was also partially supported by ESPRIT (I and II) basic research action 3085, DRUMS. We are also grateful for the use of the computing facilities of the school of CMS, Oxford Brookes University.

References

Dempster, A. P., 1967 Upper and Lower Probabilities Induced by a Multi-valued Mapping. *Annals of Mathematical Statistics* 38: 325-39.

Feller, W., 1950, *An Introduction to Probability Theory and Its Applications*, second edition, John Wiley and Sons, New York, London.

Fung, L., and Chang, K. C., 1990, Weighting and Integrating Evidence for a Stochastic Simulation in Bayesian Networks, *Uncertainty in Artificial Intelligence 5*, 209–220.

Geyer, C. J., 1992, Practical Markov Chain Monte-Carlo (with discussion), *Statistical Science 7*, 473–511.

Hrycej, T., 1990, Gibbs Sampling in Bayesian Networks, *Artificial Intelligence 46*, 351–363.

IJAR, 92, *International Journal of Approximate Reasoning*, 6, No. 3 [special issue].

Kämpke, T., 1988, About Assessing and Evaluating Uncertain Inferences Within the Theory of Evidence, *Decision Support Systems 4*: 433-439.

Kennes, R., and Smets, Ph., 1990, Computational Aspects of the Möbius transform, in *Proc. 6th Conference on Uncertainty in Artificial Intelligence*, P. Bonissone, and M. Henrion, (eds.), MIT, Cambridge, Mass., USA, 344-351.

Laskey, K. B., and Lehner, P. E., 1989, Assumptions, Beliefs and Probabilities, *Artificial Intelligence* 41 (1989/90):65-77.

Moral, S., and Wilson, N., 1994, *Markov Chain Monte-Carlo Algorithms for the Calculation of Dempster-Shafer Belief*, technical report, in preparation.

Orponen, P., 1990, Dempster's rule is # P-complete, *Artificial Intelligence*, 44: 245–253.

Pearl, J., 1988, *Probabilistic Reasoning in Intelligent Systems: Networks of Plausible Inference*, Morgan Kaufmann Publishers Inc.

Pearl, J., 1990, Reasoning with Belief Functions: An Analysis of Compatibility, *International Journal of Approximate Reasoning*, 4(5/6), 363–390.

Provan, G. M., 1990, A Logic-Based Analysis of Dempster-Shafer Theory, *International Journal of Approximate Reasoning* 4: 451-495.

Ruspini, E. H., 1987, Epistemic Logics, Probability and the Calculus of Evidence, *Proc., 10th International Joint Conference on AI* (IJCAI-87), Milan, 924-931.

Shafer, G., 1976, *A Mathematical Theory of Evidence*, Princeton University Press, Princeton, NJ.

Shafer, G., 1981, Constructive Probability, *Synthese*, 48: 1-60.

Shafer, G., 1990, Perspectives on the Theory and Practice of Belief Functions, *International Journal of Approximate Reasoning* 4: 323-362.

Shafer, G., 1992, Rejoinders to Comments on "Perspectives on the Theory and Practice of Belief Functions", *International Journal of Approximate Reasoning*, 6, No. 3, 445-480.

Smets, Ph., 1988, Belief Functions, in *Non-standard Logics for Automated Reasoning*, P. Smets, E. Mamdami, D. Dubois and H. Prade, Academic Press, London.

Smith, A.F.M., and Roberts, G.O., 1993, Bayesian Computation via the Gibbs Sampler and Related Markov Chain Monte-Carlo methods (with discussion). *J. Royal Statistical Society* B 55, 3–23.

Wilson, N., 1989, Justification, Computational Efficiency and Generalisation of the Dempster-Shafer Theory, Research Report no. 15, June 1989, Dept. of Computing and Mathematical Sciences, Oxford Polytechnic., to appear in *Artificial Intelligence*.

Wilson, N., 1991, A Monte-Carlo Algorithm for Dempster-Shafer Belief, *Proc. 7th Conference on Uncertainty in Artificial Intelligence*, B. D'Ambrosio, P. Smets and P. Bonissone (eds.), Morgan Kaufmann, 414-417.

Wilson, N., 1993, The Assumptions Behind Dempster's Rule, *Proceedings of the Ninth Conference of Uncertainty in Artificial Intelligence (UAI93)*, David Heckerman and Abe Mamdani (eds.), Morgan Kaufmann Publishers, San Mateo, California, 527-534.

Focusing on the most important explanations:
Decision-theoretic Horn abduction

Paul O'Rorke

Department of Information and Computer Science
University of California, Irvine, CA 92717–3425
ororke@ics.uci.edu

Abstract

This paper describes a new method, called Decision-Theoretic Horn Abduction (DTHA), for generating and focusing on the most important explanations. A procedure is given that can be used iteratively to generate a sequence of explanations from the most to the least important. The new method considers both the likelihood and utility of partial explanations and is applicable to a wide range of tasks. This paper shows how it applies to an important engineering design task, namely Failure Modes and Effects Analysis (FMEA). A concrete example illustrates the advantages of the general approach in the context of FMEA.

Introduction

Abduction, the process of finding and evaluating explanations, is important in a number of areas of AI, including diagnosis and natural language understanding. One of the difficulties associated with abduction is that there are far too many explanations and it is difficult to focus on the best ones. The definition of "best" and of methods for comparing and evaluating explanations is also difficult. Many of the most advanced abduction methods address these problems by focusing on and preferring the most likely explanations (taking a Bayesian probabilistic approach to gauging likelihood). Poole (1992, 1993) describes a general approach called *Probabilistic Horn Abduction* (PHA) and shows how it can be applied to tasks such as diagnosis.

Probabilistic approaches represent an advance extending and improving previous methods. However, further improvement is needed because *sometimes the most likely explanations are not the most important ones.* For an example, consider a diagnostic situation involving symptoms that usually indicate a benign condition. But assume that sometimes these symptoms indicate a malignant and frequently fatal disorder. It may well be desirable to focus attention first on the diagnosis that corresponds to the potentially deadly problem even if it is far less likely.

The method described in this paper — Decision-Theoretic Horn Abduction (DTHA) — focuses on the most important explanations, not just the most likely ones. Importance is measured using decision-theory, which extends probability theory by combining numerical measures of likelihood or probability with measures of value or utility. The DTHA method extends Poole's (1992) Probabilistic Horn Abduction (PHA) procedure for finding maximally likely explanations of individual observations. DTHA considers multiple observations (a finite number of "outcomes" in the terminology of decision-theory) with differing importance (as indicated by given numerical "utility" scores). DTHA computes the importance of alternative explanations by multiplying the utility of the outcomes by the products of the prior probabilities of the assumptions underlying the corresponding explanations. Extreme values (whether maximal or minimal) are considered to be more important. DTHA focuses on the most important explanation: it will work on unlikely explanations if the outcomes are sufficiently valuable and it will pursue explanations of less valuable outcomes if they are sufficiently likely.

Decision-Theoretic Horn Abduction

A version of Decision-Theoretic Horn Abduction based closely on Poole's (1992) PHA procedure is given in table 1. The inputs are: a finite list of "assumables" $a_1, \ldots, a_m$ and corresponding probabilities $p_1, \ldots, p_m$; a finite list of inconsistent assumptions $nogood(a_i, a_j)$, where $i, j \in \{1, \ldots, m\}$; a Probabilistic Horn Abduction theory; and a finite set of outcomes $o_1, \ldots, o_n$ and corresponding utilities $u_1, \ldots, u_n$. The output is (one of) the most important explanation-outcome pair(s).

The notation used in table 1 is to be understood as follows. For each value of i from one to n, $\mathcal{D}_i$ contains done and $\mathcal{P}_i$ contains partial explanations of outcome o_i. Partial explanations have the form $\langle A, p, C \rangle$ where A contains the assumptions made so far, p is the probability of the partial explanation and C is a conjunction of conditions that remain to be explained. The probability p of the partial explanation is the prior probability of the set of assumptions A. Note that it is important to distinguish the probabilities associated with sets of assumptions and partial explanations

Table 1: A Version of Decision-Theoretic Horn Abduction (DTHA)

Initialization: for $i = 1, \ldots, n$ set $\mathcal{D}_i := \emptyset$ and set $\mathcal{P}_i := \{\langle \emptyset, 1.0, o_i \rangle\}$

Procedure: Do while $\exists i$ such that $1 \leq i \leq n \wedge \mathcal{P}_i \neq \emptyset$

1. let $i \in \{1, \ldots, n\}$ and the corresponding $\langle A, \hat{p}_i, C \rangle \in \mathcal{P}_i$ be such that

$$\hat{p}_i \times u_i = \max_{j=1,\ldots,n} \hat{p}_j \times u_j$$

2. set $\mathcal{P}_i := \mathcal{P}_i \setminus \{\langle A, \hat{p}_i, C \rangle\}$
3. if $C = true$
   (a) then if $ok(A)$ then set $\mathcal{D}_i := \mathcal{D}_i \cup \{A\}$, output A, and halt
   (b) else let $C = a \wedge R$
      i. for each rule $h \leftarrow B$ such that $mgu(a, h)$ exists, set $\sigma := mgu(a, h)$ and set $\mathcal{P}_i := \mathcal{P}_i \cup \{\langle A, \hat{p}_i, B \wedge R \rangle \sigma\}$
      ii. if $\exists j \in \{1, \ldots, m\}$ such that $a = a_j$ and $ok(A \cup \{a_j\})$ then set $\mathcal{P}_i := \mathcal{P}_i \cup \{\langle A \cup \{a_j\}, \hat{p}_i \times p_j, R \rangle\}$

---

from the probabilities associated with individual assumptions, although they are related. The connection is that $p = \prod_{a_i \in A} p_i$ under the independence assumptions associated with PHA. The meaning of the remaining notation is as follows. For $i = 1, \ldots, n$ let $\hat{p}_i = \max_{\langle A, p, C \rangle \in \mathcal{P}_i} p$. At the beginning of execution of the procedure, each $\hat{p}_i$ represents the probability of one of the most likely partial explanations of the outcome o_i. This explanation, denoted $\langle A, \hat{p}_i, C \rangle$, is at least as likely as any other explanation of the i-th outcome in $\mathcal{P}_i$.

The initialization step of the procedure sets all the groups of *done* explanations to the empty set $\emptyset$. The sets of partial explanations $\mathcal{P}_i$ are initialized to singletons containing the explanations $\langle \emptyset, 1.0, o_i \rangle$. This is because the initial goal is to explain the outcome, the initial estimate bounding the probability of the goal from above is one, and no assumptions have been made yet in pursuit of this goal. The body of the procedure is as follows.

Step 1 selects the most important partial explanation to work on (if there is a non-empty set of partial explanations). The importance of a partial explanation $\langle A, p, C \rangle$ of outcome o_i is defined here as $p \times u_i$. This measure of importance is desirable because it is larger for more likely explanations and for outcomes with larger utilities. Step 1 finds a particular value of i and a partial explanation for outcome o_i with maximal importance over *all* known partial explanations — including explanations of other outcomes. Keep in mind that the importance and probability associated with a partial explanation are an upper bound: additional assumptions are often needed to complete the explanation and these assumptions reduce the probability of the original partial explanation (see Step 3(b)ii). For

this reason, the "most important" partial explanation at one stage may produce explanations that are less important later on. Step 1 and the following steps ensure that DTHA "loses interest" in such explanations once they become less important than some alternative candidate.

The remaining steps execute a round of Probabilistic Horn Abduction focused on $\langle A, \hat{p}_i, C \rangle$ and o_i. Step 2 deletes the partial explanation that is about to be processed. If the explanation is complete, step 3a checks its assumptions to see whether they are acceptable. If so, it records the explanation, communicates it to the user, and halts processing (at least for now). The acceptability test ok has two components: 1) a check *new* that makes certain that the same explanation of the same outcome has not been seen before and 2) a limited consistency check *consistent* that ensures that no pair of assumptions in the explanation is an instance of a *nogood*. (To be specific, $ok(A, i) \equiv new(A, i) \wedge consistent(A)$ where $new(A, i) \equiv [\not\exists D \in \mathcal{D}_i[D \subseteq A]]$ and $consistent(A) \equiv \forall \{a_j, a_k\} \subseteq A[\forall x, y[nogood(x, y) \rightarrow \not\exists \theta[\{a_j, a_k\} = \{x, y\}\theta]]]$.) If the partial explanation is not complete, there is more work to be done. At least one condition (a) remains to be proven, so the following steps focus on it. Backward chaining occurs in step 3(b)i. If there is a rule (with head h and body B) that concludes the condition that is desired, that condition is deleted and the conditions of the rule are added in its place to the remaining conditions R. Assumptions are made in step 3(b)ii. If the condition to be explained is assumable, it is deleted from the conditions to be explained and added to the assumptions supporting the explanation. The probability of the partial explanation is reduced by multiplying it by the prior probability of the new assumption.

The backward chaining and assumption steps are mutually exclusive under the assumptions made in Probabilistic Horn Abduction. Once one or the other step is executed, the procedure is repeated. Then, the selection step (1) may shift attention elsewhere.

The procedure given in table 1 halts when it arrives at a single explanation of a single outcome. However, if the main body — **procedure** — is called again, it will deliver the next most important explanation, and so on, until the partial explanations are exhausted for all the outcomes.

A variant of this procedure suitable for finding the most costly, most likely potential outcomes can be had by representing costs as negative utilities and taking min instead of max in step 1. This version will be discussed below. Equivalently, the absolute value can be taken before taking the max or the negative utilities can all be made positive prior to input.

The version of DTHA described in table 1 is suitable for abductive planning (Elkan, 1990; Krivičić & Bratko, 1993). In this application, the goal is to find a set of assumptions and a chain of inferences specifying a course of action leading to an outcome that maximizes expected utility. It is also possible to apply a variant of DTHA to consider potentially harmful outcomes. The goal then is ultimately to minimize distress. This is done by identifying the most likely and most harmful outcomes so that something can be done to avert or avoid them. Failure Modes and Effects Analysis (FMEA) is a good example of this type of application. FMEA is used to illustrate the method in the following section.

A Method for Failure Modes and Effects Analysis

This section presents a novel abductive approach to Failure Modes and Effects Analysis (FMEA). This form of reliability analysis and risk assessment is often required by governments of their contractors and in turn it is often required by these companies of their subcontractors. FMEA is extensively used in the aerospace and automotive industries worldwide. The stated purposes of FMEA are to determine the consequences of all possible failure modes of all components of a system, to assess risks associated with failures, and to recommend actions intended to reduce risks. (Henley & Kumamoto, 1991)

In FMEA, pairs of failure modes and outcomes are prioritized using so-called "risk priority numbers (RPNs)." These numbers take into account three things: the undesirability of the effects caused by failures, their likelihood, and their detectability. This paper ignores the issue of detectability and considers only how the likelihoods and costs of failures can be used to prioritize the automatic construction of FMEAs.

The key ideas are: 1) to associate FMEAs with explanations of how undesirable effects can be caused by failures and 2) to order the generation of FMEAs so that the most likely and most undesirable outcomes are considered first. The first idea is implemented by specifying a model and/or theory of the system undergoing FMEA, including the following: 1) normal and failure modes and their associated prior probabilities 2) outcomes and their utilities; and 3) rules governing causal connections between the failure modes and outcomes. The second idea is implemented by using DTHA and by considering a partial explanation P_1 to be more important than a partial explanation P_2 if the probability of P_1 times the cost of the associated outcome is larger than the probability of P_2 times the cost of its outcome.

A Model of an Automotive System

An automotive example is given in this section as an illustration of the ideas and as a demonstration of how to implement FMEA as a special case of DTHA. The example is loosely based on real events.

The first event involved engine fires in General Motors cars. The fires were caused by a fuel hose coming loose and leaking. This prompted a recall. A similar event reported in the Los Angeles Times (Nauss, 1993) involved engine fires in GM's new Saturn line caused by a short circuit in the generator leading to electrical overloads in a wiring harness. All Saturn sedans, coupes, and station wagons built between 1991 and 1993 were recalled. Automotive industry analysts estimated the direct cost of the recall as \$8–\$20 million. This example indicates that the costs that can be incurred when potential faults are not anticipated can be substantial.

Another event involved solder joints in the circuit connecting an electronic controller to a sensor. Most modern cars have electronic controllers that regulate ignition, fuel injection, and so on. Sensors placed in strategic parts of the engine provide the controller with the information needed to optimize the performance of the engine. (Schultz, Lees, & Heyn, 1990)

In pre-sales field testing by another manufacturer of an engine with an electronic controller and sensors, it was discovered that a wire connected to a sensor's housing could come loose due to faulty solder joints. Without the information provided by the sensor, the electronic controller cannot regulate the engine properly. This can result in an unacceptable increase in emissions (to a level above the maximum allowed by government regulations). The problem was caught before the cars were distributed to the public, so a costly recall was avoided. Computerized FMEA will enable us to anticipate similar problems prior to field testing during the final stages of design, thus avoiding the manufacture of trouble-prone systems.

The following example shows how DTHA can be applied to FMEA and illustrates the behavior of DTHA in the context of FMEA. Recall that this approach requires a model including normal and failure modes, probabilities, outcomes and their utilities, plus causal connections between failure modes and outcomes. The model provided in the example is sketched in figure 1. There are three subsystems modeled as chambers connected together by pipes. Fuel enters the fuel pump, then goes through the delivery pipe to the injection system. Next, fuel is injected into the combustion chamber through a nozzle. From the combustion chamber, the (burned) fuel goes through an exhaust pipe to the exhaust manifold. The model also has an electrical circuit. Two wires connect an electronic controller to a sensor (which might be in the injection system, the fuel pump, or elsewhere in the car, e.g., the tachometer). Connections are modeled explicitly as components: pipes are connected to chambers by pipe joints and wires are connected to other components by solder joints. The structural part of the model comprises the components and connections just described.

The model also provides information about normal and failure modes and how often they occur. All the basic components are either in a normal or a broken state.[1] Most of them are considered to be highly reli-

---

[1]Failure rates and states are assigned to basic but not

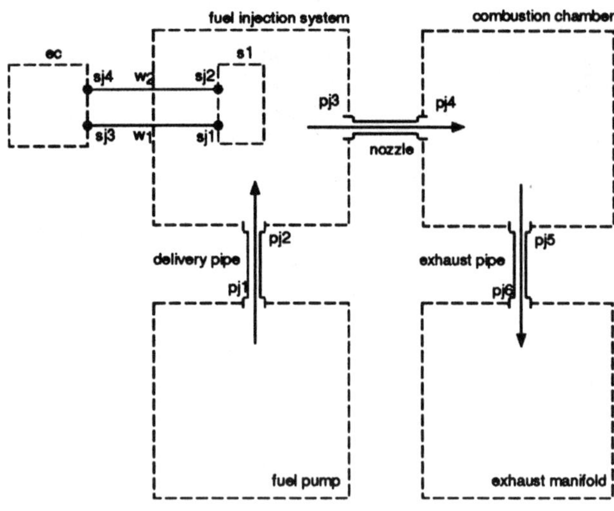

able: the prior probability of the broken state is only 0.0001 so the probability of normality is 0.9999.[2] The connections are less reliable: the prior probability of breakage for pipe joints and solder joints is 0.01. Sensors are the least reliable components: the prior probability that a sensor is broken is 0.05.

The outcomes of concern in this case are 1) there might be a fire in the engine compartment, 2) the exhaust emissions might be too high, and 3) the engine might run inefficiently. These outcomes are assigned costs of 10^6, 10^5, and 10^4 respectively.

The immediate causes of the outcomes are specified by rules. Two rules specify two independent causes of fires in the engine compartment due to fuel leaks in a pipe and a pipe joint near hot parts of the engine. Another rule states that the exhaust will be dirty if the electronic controller is uninformed. The final rule says that the engine will be less efficient if the electronic controller is uninformed.

Another set of rules specifies different aspects of the behaviors and functions of the components in the system. These rules provide the remaining connections linking the outcomes to their possible causes in terms of failure modes of the components. Two rules specify normal and failure modes of pipes and pipe joints. Normally, pipes connecting chambers cause the propagation of their contents. (To avoid cycles, flows are considered to be unidirectional.) When pipes or joints are broken, they leak. A fact states that the fuel pump supplies the fuel injection system with fuel. Additional rules specify that the electronic controller will be uninformed if a sensor is broken, or if the circuit connecting

the electronic controller and the sensor is broken. A rule states that a circuit is broken if there is a component in the circuit that is broken. The rules for failure modes of solder joints say that when a connection between two wires is broken, the voltage on the wires goes to zero.

FMEA for the Automotive System

This section describes the behavior of the Decision-Theoretic Horn Abduction algorithm when it is invoked repeatedly given the model of the previous section as input. The following text summarizes a trace produced by an implementation of DTHA in PRO-LOG. The three outcomes are labelled in descending order on their costs as F, H, and L for engine fire, high emissions, and low efficiency respectively. Let these labels be variables that stand for the weighted cost of the most likely cause of the corresponding outcome. The variables are initialized with the outcome's costs since they might be unconditionally true. The labels are intended to be mnemonic and their alphabetic order reflects their initial numerical order: $F > H > L$. As the analysis proceeds, the variables will be updated and their order will change.

$\boxed{F = 10^6 > H = 10^5 > L = 10^4}$ — First, an attempt is made to explain the "engine fire" outcome without making any assumptions. The attempt fails but two partial explanations involving assumptions are added to the set of partial explanations for this outcome: one corresponds to a broken pipe and the other to a broken pipe joint. The pipe joint is considered to be relatively unreliable ($p_{pj} = 10^{-2}$) while the pipe is considered to be one of the more reliable ($p_p = 10^{-4}$) components. So the leading possibility is that the pipe joint will leak and cause an engine fire. This has a weighted cost of $10^{-2} \times 10^6 = 10^4$.

$\boxed{H = 10^5 > F = 10^4 = L}$ — Now "high emissions" has a higher weighted cost than the most likely possible cause of engine fires so it is pursued. Hypotheses about a faulty sensor ($p_s = 5 \times 10^{-2}$) and solder joints ($p_{sj} = 10^{-2}$) and wires ($p_w = 10^{-4}$) are added to the set of partial explanations for high emissions. The most likely hypothesis is that a sensor will be faulty. The corresponding weighted cost is 5×10^3.

$\boxed{F = 10^4 = L > H = 5 \times 10^3}$ — The focus returns to engine fires.[3] A possible cause, that the second pipe joint will break, is found and printed out. The next most likely explanations (involving wires) have weighted costs of 10^2.

$\boxed{L = 10^4 > H = 5 \times 10^3 > F = 10^2}$ — Next, low efficiency becomes the most important outcome. The same conditions that can contribute to high emissions can contribute to low efficiency so they are added to the set of partial explanations for low efficiency as well.

---

to complex components.

[2]The states of components are considered to be mutually exclusive and exhaustive.

[3]Low efficiency could have been chosen at this point since it has the same weighted cost.

Table 2: DTHA-FMEA on the Automotive Example

Causes & Consequences	Priorities
F	$> H > L$
H	$> F = L$
pipe joint $2 \rightarrow F$	$= L > H$
L	$> H > F$
sensor $1 \rightarrow H$	$> L > F$
solder joints 1,2,3, and $4 \rightarrow H$	$> L > F$
sensor $1 \rightarrow L$	$> F > H$
solder joints 1,2,3, and $4 \rightarrow L$	$= F > H$
delivery pipe$\rightarrow F$	$> H > L$
wires 1 and $2 \rightarrow H$	$> L$
wires 1 and $2 \rightarrow L$	

Again, the most likely is sensor failure ($P = .05$). So the weighted cost associated with the most likely cause of low efficiency is now 5×10^2.

$$\boxed{H = 5 \times 10^3 > L = 5 \times 10^2 > F = 10^2}$$ — Now the most important outcome is high emissions and the sensor is the most likely possible cause of this problem. This fact is reported to the user.

This process will continue as long as the outputs are sufficiently important to the user. In this example, a complete list of cause-consequence pairs is possible and is shown in table 2. The behavior of DTHA on the example is also summarized in table 2. The cause-consequence pairs are shown in order of generation in the first column. The consequences together with the second column shows the priorities of the system at each step. Failure Modes and Effects Analyses were done for the top priority outcome at each step resulting in the corresponding cause-consequence pairs.

Although the sensor is five times more likely to break than the pipe joint, the joint is chosen for the first FMEA because the outcome engine fire is ten times more costly than high emissions which is the most costly consequence of the sensor failing. Next, the possible causes of failure of the sensor circuit are enumerated. All of these are considered before the remaining cause of the most costly outcome because that cause (failure of the delivery pipe) is so unlikely. Finally, the most reliable components whose failure could lead to the less important outcomes are considered in turn. Ignoring the initial consideration of each outcome, the pattern in the example was F then H then L followed by a return to F then H then L.

Relation to Previous Work

Work on abduction in AI dates back to Pople (1973). There are many different approaches to explanation construction and evaluation, including case-based (Leake, 1992) and connectionist (Thagard, 1989) methods that address many of the same issues. The abduction method described in the present paper is a descendent of logic-based methods for generating explanations embodied in Theorist (Poole, Goebel, & Aleliunas, 1987) and Tacitus (Hobbs, Stickel, Martin, & Edwards, 1988). Recently, logical and symbolic approaches to abduction have been extended by adding probability and the most probable explanations have been considered to be the best ones. For example, Peng and Reggia (1990) adapt a probabilistic approach to diagnosis viewing it as a special case of abduction. Charniak and Goldman (1993) take a probabilistic approach to plan recognition, a special case of abduction that occurs in natural language processing. Poole (1992, 1993) describes a general integration of logical and probabilistic approaches to explanatory reasoning called *Probabilistic Horn Abduction* (PHA). A major weakness of these methods is that they do not take utilities or values into consideration when they evaluate and search for explanations. It is important to do so in many practical situations, for example in abductive planning and in considering failures that might cause undesirable outcomes (as in FMEA).

The abuctive approach to FMEA differs from existing AI approaches to FMEA described in (Hunt, Price, & Lee, 1993; Price, Hunt, Lee, & Ormsby, 1992) — largely due to the difference between postdiction and prediction. The abductive approach is an example of postdiction since it infers possible causes or reasons for given effects. Previous approaches use prediction to infer possible effects from given causes. Some use a simple forward-chaining simulator for prediction. More sophisticated qualitative and model-based reasoning is used for prediction in the approaches cited above. The main advantage of predictive (especially model-based) approaches to FMEA is that they can generate consequences that were not anticipated in advance. The main advantage of the DTHA approach is that it automatically focuses on the most important FMEAs first, although all FMEAs can be generated if required. Another advantage is that it works for multiple faults.

Limitations; Future Work

Although it appears to be adequate for significant practical tasks such as FMEA, the method described here is limited due due to the assumptions employed. For example, the model of outcomes and utilities is extremely simple: it is assumed that outcomes and utilities are given by the user. This is reasonable in the context of FMEA, since designers typically have a finite and small number of outcomes they are concerned about and they usually know the utilities of these undesirable effects of component failures. But in more complex situations, methods for acquiring and calculating utilities from users and from more basic information will be needed. Work on these issues in the new field of Decision-Theoretic Planning seems relevant.

Conclusion

This paper provides a new method that generates explanations focusing on the most important ones. Importance is measured taking into account utilities or values in addition to probabilities so the method is called Decision-Theoretic Horn Abduction (DTHA). The addition of utilities is an important improvement over existing probabilistic approaches because in many situations the most likely explanations are not the best ones to focus on or generate. For example, in diagnosis, the most dangerous disease that explains the symptoms should often be considered before more common but less dangerous disorders. In abductive planning, in determining the best explanations of how to achieve a goal one should often take into consideration the value of the goal relative to alternatives and the costs of the actions involved in the plans in addition to the likelihood of success.

The paper provides an example illustrating the general DTHA method in the context of a task, Failure Modes Effects Analysis (FMEA), that involves utilities in addition to probabilities. In this context, the explanations correspond to assumptions about various components being in failure or normal modes and these cause outcomes that correspond to costly effects that the designers wish to avoid. The example demonstrates that the method is capable of keeping priorities straight in deciding which explanation-outcome pairs to generate. The method shifts the focus of attention: starting on one outcome, moving to another, and returning to an earlier focus. When the more costly or valuable outcome is at least as probable, or not too improbable, it is pursued. On the other hand, the method focuses attention on the most important explanations and outcomes even when this requires switching attention from more to less costly or from more to less probable outcomes.

Acknowledgments

The author is grateful to the reviewers; to David Poole for conversations and for Prolog code implementing PHA; and to Chris Price, Andy Ormsby, and David Pugh for conversations and for a demo of their FMEA system FLAME II. The author was a consultant with FAW (the Research Institute for Applied Knowledge Processing) during the research and the development of the prototype described here. Rüdiger Wirth, FAW FMEA group leader, provided assistance and support.

References

Charniak, E., & Goldman, R. P. (1993). A Bayesian model of plan recognition. *Artificial Intelligence, 64,* 53–79.

Elkan, C. (1990). Incremental, approximate planning. *The Eighth National Conference on Artificial Intelligence* (pp. 145–150). San Mateo, CA: AAAI Press/The MIT Press.

Henley, E. J., & Kumamoto, H. (1991). *Probabilistic risk assessment: Reliability engineering, design, and analysis.* Piscataway, NJ: IEEE Press.

Hobbs, J. R., Stickel, M., Martin, P., & Edwards, D. (1988). Interpretation as abduction. *Proceedings of the Twenty Sixth Annual Meeting of the Association for Computational Linguistics* (pp. 95–103). Buffalo, NY: The Association for Computational Linguistics.

Hunt, J. E., Price, C. J., & Lee, M. H. (1993). Automating the FMEA process. *Intelligent Systems Engineering, 2*(2), 119–132.

Krivičić, K., & Bratko, I. (1993). Abductive planning with qualitative models of dynamic systems. In N. Piera-Carreté, & M. G. Singh (Eds.), *Qualitative Reasoning and Decision Technologies* (pp. 389–395). Barcelona: CIMNE.

Leake, D. B. (1992). *Evaluating explanations: A Content theory.* Hillsdale, NJ: Lawrence Erlbaum Associates.

Nauss, D. W. (1993). Nearly all Saturns recalled over potential engine fires. *Los Angeles Times (Orange County Edition).* Los Angeles, CA: A1 and A19.

Peng, Y., & Reggia, J. A. (1990). *Abductive inference methods for diagnostic problem solving.* New York: Springer-Verlag.

Poole, D. (1992). Logic programming, abduction and probability. *Proceedings of the International Conference on Fifth Generation Computer Systems (FGCS-92)* (pp. 530–538). Tokyo.

Poole, D. (1993). Probabilistic Horn abduction and Bayesian networks. *Artificial Intelligence, 64,* 81–129.

Poole, D. L., Goebel, R., & Aleliunas, R. (1987). Theorist: A logical reasoning system for defaults and diagnosis. In N. Cercone, & G. McCalla (Eds.), *The Knowledge Frontier: Essays in the Representation of Knowledge.* New York: Springer-Verlag.

Pople, H. E. (1973). On the mechanization of abductive logic. *Proceedings of the Third International Joint Conference on Artificial Intelligence* (pp. 147–152). San Mateo, CA: Morgan Kaufmann.

Price, C. J., Hunt, J. E., Lee, M. H., & Ormsby, A. R. T. (1992). A model-based approach to the automation of failure mode effects analysis for design. *Proceedings of the Institution of Mechanical Engineers, Part D: Journal of Automobile Engineering, 206,* 206–291.

Schultz, M., Lees, A. W., & Heyn, E. V. (Eds.). (1990). *What's wrong with my car? A guide to troubleshooting common mechanical and performance problems.* Mount Vernon, New York: Consumers Union.

Thagard, P. (1989). Explanatory coherence. *The Behavioral and Brain Sciences, 12*(3), 435–502.

The Emergence of Ordered Belief from Initial Ignorance

Paul Snow

P.O. Box 6134
Concord, NH 03303-6134
paulsnow@delphi.com

Abstract

Some simple assumptions about prior ignorance, and the idea that a sufficiently arresting contrast in the likelihoods of evidence will elicit belief that one proposition is at least as belief-worthy as another, lead to a partial ordering of propositions without the use of any kind of prior probability. The partial ordering is *not* a posterior probability distribution, but does share some intuitively pleasing properties of a probability, such as complementarity. Deciding the order (if any) between two disjunctions depends only on the highest likelihood disjunct in each, and so query handling in partitioned domains is efficient. In the event that an ordinary probability distribution is required for coherent decision making, one can be quickly calculated from the partial order.

Introduction

Ignorance is the unwillingness to order any of two or more sentences according to their belief-worthiness, unless one sentence implies the other. The unwillingness may be a matter of choice, as when a scientist wishes to interpret evidence about rival hypotheses without taking into account any personal views about the prior likeliness of the various rivals (Berger and Berry 1988). Other times, the unwillingness may be involuntary, as when there is no simply no basis for holding any opinion about the relative likeliness of the sentences in question.

However it arises, ignorance is not faithfully represented by any single probability distribution over the sentences. Whatever probabilities are assigned to the sentences, those probabilities are ordered with respect to one another, even though the sentences themselves generally are not. (For discussion of similar problems when representing ignorance in other uncertainty calculi, see Shenoy 1993.)

The approach developed in this paper avoids the assessment of a prior probability distribution under ignorance. Nevertheless, the emergence of ordered belief from prior ignorance retains a distinctly probabilistic flavor.

Notation and Assumptions about Ignorance

The notation

$$S >e> T$$

will denote the condition that the believer asserts that sentence S is, with a warrant satisfactory to the believer, at least as belief-worthy as sentence T in light of evidence e. If evidence e does not lead the believer to assert such an ordering of sentences S and T, then we write

$$S ?e? T$$

Note that this is distinct from asserting the *contrary* of $S >e> T$, which would be holding that S is less belief worthy than T. The condition of having no relevant evidence is indicated by the particle *nil*, as in

$$S ?nil? T$$

which expression denotes that there is no ordering between some sentences S and T in the absence of evidence.

We shall assume that the sentences of interest belong to a partitioned domain, which is defined as follows:

Definition. A *partitioned domain* is a set comprising:

(i) the always-true sentence, denoted **true**

(ii) the always false sentence, denoted **false**

(iii) two or more mutually exclusive sentences, called *atoms*

(iv) well-formed expressions involving atoms, **or**, and parentheses, called *simple disjunctions*

(v) well-formed expressions involving simple disjunctions, **true, false, or, not**, and parentheses

We shall also assume throughout that the atoms in the domain are collectively exhaustive, that is, exactly one of the atoms is true. This additional assumption places little epistemological burden on the believer (at worst, it means that one of the atoms is "none of the other atoms are true"), and has the convenient effect that every sentence in the domain has an equivalent simple disjunction.

Our first assumptions about ignorance, and the conquest of ignorance by evidence express the following ideas. If no evidence has yet been observed, and the question of relative belief-worthiness is not answerable on logical grounds, then there is no satisfactory warrant to order one sentence ahead of another. Even after evidence has been observed, the question may remain open. Once a commitment to an ordering is made, then other commitments may be inferred by conditional probability considerations, or by a fundamental belief-ordering consistency principle of the kind discussed by Sugeno (unpublished dissertation, cited in Prade 1985). The formal assumptions are:

A1. (Lack of explicit non-trivial prior orderings) For any sentences S and T,

S >nil> T implies that T implies S.

A2. (Lack of implicit non-trivial prior orderings) Values for conditional probabilities and orderings among them are neither known nor assumed if those values or orderings imply non-trivial constraints on the prior probabilities.

A3. (Consistency) For all evidence e, including *nil*, and any sentences S, S', T and T',

if S' implies S, then S >e> S';

if S' implies S and S' >e> T, then S >e> T;

if T' implies T and S >e> T, then S >e> T'.

A4. (Impartiality) If S >e> T, and S' and T' are sentences, and S is exclusive of T , then

if S' is exclusive of T and p(e | S') >= p(e | S), then S' >e> T, and

if S is exclusive of T' and p(e | T) >= p(e | T'), then S >e> T'.

A5. (Recovery from ignorance about atoms) For exclusive atoms s and t, and non-nil evidence e where p(e | s) > 0, a necessary and sufficient condition for s >e> t is that

f(e, s, t) >= q   [A5.1]

where q is a real number chosen by the believer, and f(, ,) is a real-valued function chosen by the believer which is increasing in p(e | s) and decreasing in p(e | t), and such that a necessary condition for [A5.1] to hold is that p(e | s) is strictly greater than p(e | t), and such that p(e | t) = 0 is not a necessary condition for [A5.1] to hold.

A6. (Quasi-additivity) For any sentences S, T, and U where (S **and** U) and (T **and** U) are both false, and for all evidence e, including *nil*,

S or U >e> T or U if and only if S >e> T

An Inference Rule for Overcoming Ignorance In Simple Disjunctions

Assumptions A3 and A4 have a strong consequence when the propositions of interest belong to a partitioned domain. It is easy to show that if D is a simple disjunction, then the conditional p(e | D) is a convex combination of the p(e | d)'s, the conditionals for the evidence given each of the atoms within D. Thus,

$$P(e | D) = < \max_{d \text{ in } D} p(e | d)   [1]$$

Theorem 1. Let S and T be simple disjunctions which are mutually exclusive, and let s and t be atoms where p(e | s) and p(e | t) are the greatest conditional probabilities for non-nil evidence e given atoms in S and T respectively.

S >e> T if and only if s >e> t.

Proof. S >e> T implies s >e> T by A4 and [1], which implies s >e> t by A3. Conversely, s >e> t implies s >e> T by A4 and [1], which implies S >e> T by A3. //

The theorem and assumption A5 lead to the following rule for deciding whether observed evidence *e* bearing on the states supports the assertion of S >e> T under certain circumstances:

Inference Rule. If S and T are simple disjunctions with no states in common, and if s and t are such that p(e | s) and p(e | t) are the greatest conditional probabilities for the evidence e given any atom in S and T respectively, then a sufficient condition for S >e> T is that f(e, s, t) >= q, where f(, ,) and q are as described in assumption A5.

This inference rule is strong enough by itself to handle problems like statistical hypothesis testing, where typically, disjoint propositions are compared, and often only one pair of propositions in a domain is of interest at any one time. Some further development to be introduced later will use the rule in a decision procedure which is applicable to all non-trivial ordering questions in partitioned domains.

Partial Qualitative Probability

Definition. A *partial qualitative probability* is a partial order of the sentences in a partitioned domain, such that, for all evidence e, including nil, and any sentences S, T, and U:

(i) (boundedness) **true** >e> S and S >e> **false**

(ii) (transitivity) (S >e> T) **and** (T >e> U) implies that S >e> U

(iii) (quasi-additivity) if S **and** U and T **and** U are both false, then

(S **or** U) >e> (T **or** U) if and only if S >e> T.

This definition is designed to echo that of an ordinary qualitative probability (de Finetti, 1937), differing only in being a partial, rather than a complete, ordering.

Within a partial qualitative probability, any ordering question involving simple disjunctions can be resolved by the theorem and the inference rule. To decide whether S >e> T:

(1) Eliminate from S and T all the atoms common to both, leaving S* and T*.

(2) If S* and T* are both empty, then S>e> T; if S* is empty and T* is not, then **not** (S >e> T); if T* is empty and S* is not, then S >e> T. Otherwise, apply the Inference Rule derived from Theorem 1 to S* and T*; S >e> T just in case S* >e> T*.

Partial qualitative probabilities also share an intuitively appealing property with ordinary probability distributions:

Theorem 2. (Complementarity) If S and T are simple disjunctions, and ">e>" is a partial qualitative probability, then

$$S >e> T \text{ implies } \textbf{not} (T) >e> \textbf{not} (S)$$

Proof. Let C be the disjunction of atoms common to S and T, S' be the atoms in S and not in T, and T' be the atoms in T and not in S. Then by quasi-additivity, S' >e> T'. Let Q be the disjunction of atoms not in S and not in T. **not** (S) is T' **or** Q, and **not** (T) is S' **or** Q. Since S' >e> T', then by quasi-additivity, (S' **or** Q) >e> (T' **or** Q), or **not** (T) >e> **not** (S).   //

Any Ordering Satisfying A1-A6 is a Partial Qualitative Probability

Lemma. If A, B, C, and D are simple or empty (containing no atoms except those that are false given the evidence) disjunctions, and there is no atom in common between A and B, nor any atom in common between C and D, then

$$A >e> B \textbf{ and } C >e> D \text{ implies } (A \textbf{ or } C) >e> (B \textbf{ or } D)$$

Proof. If (B **or** D) implies (A **or** C), then the required ordering holds. Suppose that is not the case. If B is empty or D is empty, then the lemma is trivial. If A is empty, then B is empty, and if C is empty, then D is empty [A3]. Suppose none of them are empty. For orderings to be asserted, evidence must be non-nil. Let a, b, c, and d be the atoms such that p(e | atom) is greatest among atoms in A, B, C, and D respectively.

WOLG, suppose that p(e | a) >= p(e | c). Let AC and BD disjoin the atoms that are peculiar to (A **or** C) and (B **or** D) respectively. By A5 and theorem 3, f (e, c, d) >= q, and since the function is increasing in p(e | second argument), f (e, a, d) >= q. Since f (e, a, b) >= q as well, then a >e> [the atom in (B **or** D) with the greatest p(e | atom)]. By A5, atoms a and d have different p(e | atom)'s, and so they must be distinct, and a must be distinct from all other atoms in D for the same reason; a is distinct from all atoms in B by hypothesis. So, a is in AC. BD is not empty, because we suppose no implication, so theorem 3 applies. The required ordering follows from A6. //

Note that the property proven in the lemma is generally **untrue** in conventional probabilistic reasoning systems. That it holds for systems satisfying A1-A6 is closely related to theorem 3 and the inference rule. In the absence of prior information or logical grounds to resolve the question, what matters in the comparison of sentences is the best-supported atom peculiar to each sentence. Thus, even though *A or C* may have atoms in common with *B or D*, this does not disrupt the ranking of their best-supported atoms (unless there are no atoms peculiar to each sentence, in which case, the order is logically determined).

Theorem 6. Any ordering satisfying assumptions A1-A6 is a partial qualitative probability.

Proof. Boundedness: Since **false** implies S, so S >e> **false** by A3, and since S implies **true**, **true** >e> S by A3.

Quasi-additivity: Assumption A6.

Transitivity: Let A be the disjunction of the atoms common to each of S, T, and U, B the atoms common to S and T alone, C those common to S and U alone, D those for T and U alone, and S*, T*, and U* those atoms unique to S, T, and U respectively. If e is nil, then T implies S and U implies T, so U implies S, and transitivity holds. Suppose, then, that e is not nil. Let a be the maximum conditional probability for e among the atoms of A, and b, c, d, s, t, and u be the corresponding quantities for B, C, D, S*, T*, and U*, respectively.

By quasi-additivity, we have S >e> T implies C **or** S* >e> D **or** T*. Similarly, T >e> U implies B **or** T* >e> C **or** U*. We wish to show that B **or** S* >e> D **or** U*. Since C **or** S* and D **or** T* have no atom in common, and nor do B **or** T* and C **or** U*, we apply the lemma to get

$$C \textbf{ or } S^* \textbf{ or } B \textbf{ or } T^* >e> D \textbf{ or } T^* \textbf{ or } C \textbf{ or } U^*$$

which by quasi-additivity simplifies to

$$B \textbf{ or } S^* >e> D \textbf{ or } U^*$$

as required.   //

A Note on Assumption A5

In the assumption, we required that p(e | s) be strictly greater than p(e | t) in order for s >e> t to hold when p(e | s) is positive. We now present an example where if A5 called for a weak inequality, then the resulting ordering would fail to be a partial qualitative probability.

All letters are as in the transitivity portion of the proof of the theorem of the last section, and once again, we have S >e> T and T >e> U. An assignment of values for the atomic conditional probabilities consistent with this, and the modification of A5 to allow ordering assertions on weak inequalities, is:

$$d = .5, s = .4, u = .5, b = .4, t = .6, \text{ and } c = .6$$

It is easy to confirm that under a weak inequality rule, C **or** S* >e> D **or** T*, the quasi-additive condition for S >e> T, and B **or** T* >e> C **or** U*, the condition for T >e> U. If the ordering is transitive, then S >e> U, and if it is quasi-additive, then B **or** S* >e> D **or** U*, so by theorem 3, it must be that either *b* or *s* is no smaller than both *d* and *u*. Neither is the case, since *b* is less than *d* or *u*, and so is *s*.

Adoption of Priors from Ordered Beliefs

A partial qualitative probability ordering possesses many of the intuitively appealing properties of a probability distribution. Nevertheless, it lacks the coherence of beliefs thought to be demanded in practical decision making problems, and provided by probability distributions (Lindley 1982), or in weaker form by set estimates (Kyburg and Pittarelli 1992).

Faced a similar conflict between the demands of modeling beliefs with Dempster-Shafer-style belief functions and the demands of coherence in action under risk, Smets (et al. 1991; Dubois et al. 1993) has proposed a two-tier system of belief representation, his "Transferable Belief Model". Up until action is required, beliefs are represented by the less-than-fully coherent D-S formalism (Smets' "credal" phase). Once action is called for, the original formalism is mapped onto a probability distribution, and that probability is used for decision making (Smets' "pignistic" phase). Once called into action, the probability distribution is also subject to revision in the face of further evidence using Bayesian methods.

At some point, therefore, the user of the ignorance representation may find it expedient to convert the orderings revealed by the evidence into an ordinary probability estimate, to use that estimate for decision making, and to apply further evidence to it using Bayes' theorem in the usual way.

Because of the restricted form of possible orderings consistent with theorem 1 and partial qualitative probability, it is quite tractable to use the asserted orderings to derive a useful "surrogate" probability distribution when the number of atoms in the domain is finite. It is generally impossible to have a truly agreeing single probability distribution, i.e., some distribution in which p(S | e) >= p(T | e) if and only if S >e> T. That's because any probability distribution is a complete ordering, rather than the partial ordering that arises from the assumptions. But it is easy to compute a probability distribution where for every S >e> T, the probabilities are ordered p(S | e) >= p(T | e).

The permissible orderings entail a single system of simultaneous linear constraints, each (apart from the total probability constraint) either of the form

$$p(s) >= c$$

(for atoms s where there is no distinct atom t such that s >e> t) where c is a non-negative constant which doesn't depend on the atom s, or else of the form

$$p(s) >= \Sigma\, p(s')$$

(for atoms s where there is one or more t such that s >e> t) where the summation is over all atoms s' such that s >e> s'. Since any atom s is ordered ahead of the disjunction of all the atoms s' such that s >e> s', the system has exactly one more non-redundant constraint than the number of atoms in the domain (the single total probability constraint is the extra constraint).

In order for the system to be consistent, that is, to have any solution, the constant c is bounded above by some positive quantity. It is easy to show that if c is chosen to equal that upper bound, then the system has a unique solution. The following algorithm computes the permissible upper bound on c and the associated unique solution to the system with effort that is linear in the number of atoms under discussion.

Algorithm for Computing Maximal *c* and Corresponding Solution

For N atoms, establish arrays:

Weight [1..N] For each atom, the multiple of c that satisfies the order constraints

Runsum [1..N] For atom indexed I, the sum of Weight [1] through Weight [I]

Prob [1..N] The conditional probabilities for the evidence given each atom

and scalar quantities:

Index As the name implies, an Index

Cutoff An index, the least value where f (P [Index], P [Cutoff]) < q

Last The value of Runsum [Cutoff - 1], or 1 if

```
      Cutoff = 1
BEGIN

1. Sort Prob [ ] in ascending order.
2. Initialize Cutoff = Last = Weight [ 1 ] = Runsum [ 1 ]
   = 1.
3. for Index = 2 .. N
     while f ( Prob [ Index ], Prob [ Cutoff ] ) >= q
         Last := Runsum [ Cutoff ]
         Cutoff := Cutoff + 1
     end while
     Weight [ Index ] := Last
     Runsum [ Index ] := Weight [ Index ]
                                + Runsum [ Index -1 ]
   end for
4. The maximum possible value of c is 1 / Runsum [ N ]; if
   c is set to this maximum, then the unique solution of the
   linear system is

     p( Index ) = Weight [ Index ] / Runsum [ N ].

END
```

Since *Cutoff* always increases in value, and never exceeds *Index*, it is easy to confirm that the effort required by the above algorithm is linear in the number of atoms.

Choosing Other Values for *c*

The single solution, maximum c approach is computationally simple, and places the least possible burden on subsequent evidence to overcome the low probability value assigned to the least favored atoms should one of them turn out to be true. On the other hand, smaller values of c may be preferred. In that case, the constraints describe a convex set of probability distributions, a set which contains all probability distributions which display all of the orderings asserted by the partial qualitative probability.

One reason for preferring a lower value of the constant c might be that the user prefers to use some particular other single probability distribution, for example, the maximum entropy distribution over all distributions consistent with the asserted ordering constraints. Such a distribution can be found using numerical or analytical optimization methods over the system with c = 0. Again, the simple form of the solution set, whether described in vertex or constraint form, should be an asset in searching for a congenial probability distribution. (There are exactly as many vertices as there are atoms, and the vertices are simple to enumerate using the information about Weight [] and Runsum [] produced by the algorithm of the last section.)

Another occasion for choosing a smaller c is when the user is content to represent beliefs for decision and action in convex set form. Although the convex set formalism lacks the full coherence of a singleton distribution, there is a considerable and growing literature which suggests methods for using convex sets in decision (see, for example, Sterling and Morrell 1991 for a review). Because of the small number of vertices, revision of the convex set in the light of further evidence is tractable (Levi 1980), and as with any convex set, revision can also be performed by a transformation of the system's coefficients (Snow 1991).

It can be shown that there are positive values of c such that the convex set represents *only* the orderings asserted by the partial qualitative probability. Among these, the largest such value will ordinarily be preferred since that choice places the least burden on subsequent evidence to reveal the truth of the least favored atoms should that happen to be necessary. Finding the largest such c requires about the same effort as enumerating the vertices with a known c, that is, order N^2. A full discussion of this point, however, is beyond the scope of the present paper.

Conclusions

Assumptions A1-A6 describe an intuitively appealing way that evidence can overcome initial ignorance. Although the mechanism is Bayesian, in that conditional probabilities are compared, there are no prior probabilities. Nevertheless, the inferences that arise from the assumptions retain some of the characteristics of probability distributions, including complementarity, and if normatively coherent behavior in gambling is required, then probabilities can be computed on demand. Query handling and the calculation of coherent probabilities are both computationally inexpensive.

References

Berger, J. O. and D. A. Berry, Statistical analysis and the illusion of objectivity, *American Scientist 76*, 159-165, 1988.

de Finetti, B., La prevision, ses lois logiques, ses sources subjectives, *Annales de l'Institut Henri Poincare 7*, 1-68, 1937 (English translation by H.E. Kyburg, Jr. in H.E. Kyburg, Jr. and H.E. Smokler, eds., *Studies in Subjective Probability*, New York: Wiley, 1964).

Dubois, D., H. Prade, and P. Smets, Representing partial ignorance, Workshop on Higher Order Uncertainty, George Mason University, July 1993.

Kyburg, H. E., Jr. and M. Pittarelli, Some problems for convex Bayesians, in D. Dubois, M.P. Wellman, B. D'Ambrosio, and P. Smets (eds.), *Uncertainty in Artificial Intelligence*, San Mateo, CA: Morgan Kaufmann, 149-154,1992.

Levi, I., *The Enterprise of Knowledge*, Cambridge, MA: MIT Press, 1980.

Lindley, D. V., Scoring rules and the inevitability of probability, *International Statistical Review 50*, 1-26 (with commentaries), 1982.

Prade, H., A computational approach to approximate and plausible reasoning with applications to expert systems, *IEEE Transactions on Pattern Analysis and Machine Intelligence 7*, 260-283, 1985.

Shenoy, P.P., Modeling ignorance in uncertainty theories, Workshop on Higher Order Uncertainty, 1993.

Smets, P., Y-T. Hsia, A. Saffiotti, R. Kennes, H. Xu, and E. Umkehrer, The transferable belief model, in R. Kruse and P. Siegel (eds.), *Symbolic and Quantitative Approaches to Uncertainty*, Berlin: Springer-Verlag, Lecture Notes in Computer Science 548, 91-96, 1991.

Snow, P., Improved posterior probability estimates from prior and conditional linear constraint systems, *IEEE Transactions on Systems, Man, and Cybernetics 21*, 464-469, 1991.

Sterling. W. C. and D. R. Morrell, Convex Bayes decision theory, *IEEE Transactions on Systems, Man, and Cybernetics 21*, 173-183, 1991.

Constraint Satisfaction

The Hazards of Fancy Backtracking

Andrew B. Baker*
Computational Intelligence Research Laboratory
1269 University of Oregon
Eugene, Oregon 97403
baker@cs.uoregon.edu

Abstract

There has been some recent interest in intelligent backtracking procedures that can return to the source of a difficulty without erasing the intermediate work. In this paper, we show that for some problems it can be counterproductive to do this, and in fact that such "intelligence" can cause an exponential increase in the size of the ultimate search space. We discuss the reason for this phenomenon, and we present one way to deal with it.

1 Introduction

We are interested in systematic search techniques for solving constraint satisfaction problems. There has been some recent work on intelligent backtracking procedures that can return to the source of a difficulty without erasing the intermediate work. In this paper, we will argue that these procedures have a substantial drawback, but first let us see why they might make sense. Consider an example from (Ginsberg 1993). Suppose we are coloring a map of the United States (subject to the usual constraint that only some fixed set of colors may be used, and adjacent states cannot be the same color).

Let us assume that we first color the states along the Mississippi, thus dividing the rest of the problem into two independent parts. We now color some of the western states, then we color some eastern states, and then we return to the west. Assume further that upon our return to the west we immediately get stuck: we find a western state that we cannot color. What do we do?

Ordinary chronological backtracking (depth-first search) would backtrack to the most recent decision, but this would be a state east of the Mississippi and hence irrelevant; the search procedure would only address the real problem after trying every possible coloring for the previous eastern states.

---

*This work has been supported by the Air Force Office of Scientific Research under grant number 92-0693 and by ARPA/Rome Labs under grant numbers F30602-91-C-0036 and F30602-93-C-00031.

Backjumping (Gaschnig 1979) is somewhat more intelligent; it would immediately jump back to some state adjacent to the one that we cannot color. In the process of doing this, however, it would erase all the intervening work, i.e., it would uncolor the whole eastern section of the country. This is unfortunate; it means that each time we backjump in this fashion, we will have to start solving the eastern subproblem all over again.

Ginsberg has recently introduced *dynamic backtracking* (Ginsberg 1993) to address this difficulty. In dynamic backtracking, one moves to the source of the problem without erasing the intermediate work. Of course, simply retaining the *values* of the intervening variables is not enough; if these values turn out to be wrong, we will need to know where we were in the search space so that we can continue the search systematically. In order to do this, dynamic backtracking accumulates nogoods to keep track of portions of the space that have been ruled out.

Taken to an extreme, this would end up being very similar to dependency-directed backtracking (Stallman & Sussman 1977). Although dependency-directed backtracking does not save intermediate values, it saves enough dependency information for it to quickly recover its position in the search space. Unfortunately, dependency-directed backtracking saves far too much information. Since it learns a new nogood from every backtrack point, it generally requires an exponential amount of memory — and for each move in the search space, it may have to wade through a great many of these nogoods. Dynamic backtracking, on the other hand, only keeps nogoods that are "relevant" to the current position in the search space. It not only learns new nogoods; it also throws aways those old nogoods that are no longer applicable.

Dynamic backtracking, then, would seem to be a happy medium between backjumping and full dependency-directed backtracking. Furthermore, Ginsberg has presented empirical evidence that dynamic backtracking outperforms backjumping on the problem of solving crossword puzzles (Ginsberg 1993).

Unfortunately, as we will soon see, dynamic backtracking has problems of its own.

The plan of the paper is as follows. The next section reviews the details of dynamic backtracking. Section 3 describes an experiment comparing the performance of dynamic backtracking with that of depth-first search and backjumping on a problem class that has become somewhat of a standard benchmark. We will see that dynamic backtracking is *worse* by a factor exponential in the size of the problem. Note that this will not be simply the usual complaint that intelligent search schemes often have a lot of overhead. Rather, our complaint will be that the effective search space itself becomes larger; even if dynamic backtracking could be implemented without any additional overhead, it would still be far less efficient than the other algorithms.

Section 4 contains both our analysis of what is going wrong with dynamic backtracking and an experiment consistent with our view. In Section 5, we describe a modification to dynamic backtracking that appears to fix the problem. Concluding remarks are in Section 6.

2 Dynamic backtracking

Let us begin by reviewing the definition of a constraint satisfaction problem, or CSP.

Definition 1 *A constraint satisfaction problem (V, D, C) is defined by a finite set of variables V, a finite set of values D_v for each $v \in V$, and a finite set of constraints C, where each constraint $(W, P) \in C$ consists of a list of variables $W = (w_1, \ldots, w_k) \subseteq V$ and a predicate on these variables $P \subseteq D_{w_1} \times \cdots \times D_{w_k}$. A solution to the problem is a total assignment f of values to variables, such that for each $v \in V$, $f(v) \in D_v$ and for each constraint $((w_1, \ldots, w_k), P)$, $(f(w_1), \ldots, f(w_k)) \in P$.*

Like depth-first search, dynamic backtracking works with partial solutions; a partial solution to a CSP is an assignment of values to some subset of the variables, where the assignment satisfies all of the constraints that apply to this particular subset. The algorithm starts by initializing the partial solution to have an empty domain, and then it gradually extends this solution. As the algorithm proceeds, it will derive new constraints, or "nogoods," that rule out portions of the search space that contain no solutions. Eventually, the algorithm will either derive the empty nogood, proving that the problem is unsolvable, or it will succeed in constructing a total solution that satisfies all of the constraints. We will always write the nogoods in directed form; e.g.,

$$(v_1 = q_1) \wedge \cdots \wedge (v_{k-1} = q_{k-1}) \Rightarrow v_k \neq q_k$$

tells us that variables v_1 through v_k cannot simultaneously have the values q_1 through q_k respectively.

The main innovation of dynamic backtracking (compared to dependency-directed backtracking) is that it only retains nogoods whose left-hand sides are currently true. That is to say that if the above nogood

were stored, then v_1 through v_{k-1} would have to have the indicated values (and since the current partial solution has to respect the nogoods as well as the original constraints, v_k would either have some value other than q_k or be unbound). If at some point, one of the left-hand variables were changed, then the nogood would have to be deleted since it would no longer be "relevant." Because of this relevance requirement, it is easy to compute the currently permissible values for any variable. Furthermore, if all of the values for some variable are eliminated by nogoods, then one can resolve these nogoods together to generate a new nogood. For example, assuming that $D_{v_9} = \{1, 2\}$, we could resolve

$$(v_1 = a) \wedge (v_3 = c) \Rightarrow v_9 \neq 1$$

with

$$(v_2 = b) \wedge (v_3 = c) \Rightarrow v_9 \neq 2$$

to obtain

$$(v_1 = a) \wedge (v_2 = b) \Rightarrow v_3 \neq c$$

In order for our partial solution to remain consistent with the nogoods, we would have to simultaneously unbind v_3. This corresponds to backjumping from v_9 to v_3, but without erasing any intermediate work. Note that we had to make a decision about which variable to put on the right-hand side of the new nogood. The rule of dynamic backtracking is that the right-hand variable must always be the one that was most recently assigned a value; this is absolutely crucial, as without this restriction, the algorithm would not be guaranteed to terminate.

The only thing left to mention is how nogoods get acquired in the first place. Before we try to bind a new variable, we will check the consistency of each possible value[1] for this variable with the values of all currently bound variables. If a constraint would be violated, we write the constraint as a directed nogood with the new variable on the right-hand side.

We have now reviewed all the major ideas of dynamic backtracking, so we will give the algorithm below in a somewhat informal style. For the precise mathematical definitions, see (Ginsberg 1993).

Procedure DYNAMIC-BACKTRACKING

1. Initialize the partial assignment f to have the empty domain, and the set of nogoods Γ to be the empty set. At all times, f will satisfy the nogoods in Γ as well as the original constraints.

2. If f is a total assignment, then return f as the answer. Otherwise, choose an unassigned variable v and for each possible value of this variable that would cause a constraint violation, add the appropriate nogood to Γ.

3. If variable v has some value x that is not ruled out by any nogood, then set $f(v) = x$, and return to step 2.

---

[1] A value is possible if it is not eliminated by a nogood.

4. Each value of v violates a nogood. Resolve these nogoods together to generate a new nogood that does not mention v. If it is the empty nogood, then return "unsatisfiable" as the answer. Otherwise, write it with its chronologically most recent variable (say, w) on the right-hand side, add this directed nogood to Γ, and call ERASE-VARIABLE(w). If each value of w now violates a nogood, then set $v = w$ and return to step 4; otherwise, return to step 2.

Procedure ERASE-VARIABLE(w)

1. Remove w from the domain of f.

2. For each nogood $\gamma \in \Gamma$ whose left-hand side mentions w, call DELETE-NOGOOD(γ).

Procedure DELETE-NOGOOD(γ)

1. Remove γ from Γ.

Each variable-value pair can have at most one nogood at a given time, so it is easy to see that the algorithm only requires a polynomial amount of memory. In (Ginsberg 1993), it is proven that dynamic backtracking always terminates with a correct answer.

This is the theory of dynamic backtracking. How well does it do in practice?

3 Experiments

To compare dynamic backtracking with depth-first search and backjumping, we will use randomly-generated propositional satisfiability problems, or to be more specific, random 3-SAT problems with n variables and m clauses.[2] Since a SAT problem is just a Boolean CSP, the above discussion applies directly. Each clause will be chosen independently using the uniform distribution over the $\binom{n}{3}2^3$ non-redundant 3-literal clauses. It turns out that the hardest random 3-SAT problems appear to arise at the "crossover point" where the ratio of clauses to variables is such that about half the problems are satisfiable (Mitchell, Selman, & Levesque 1992); the best current estimate for the location of this crossover point is at $m = 4.24n + 6.21$ (Crawford & Auton 1993). Several recent authors have used these crossover-point 3-SAT problems to measure the performance of their algorithms (Crawford & Auton 1993; Selman, Levesque, & Mitchell 1992).

In the dynamic backtracking algorithm, step 2 leaves open the choice of which variable to select next; backtracking and backjumping have similar indeterminacies. We used the following variable-selection heuristics:

1. If there is an unassigned variable with one of its two values currently eliminated by a nogood, then choose that variable.

2. Otherwise, if there is an unassigned variable that appears in a clause in which all the other literals have been assigned false, then choose that variable.

3. Otherwise, choose the unassigned variable that appears in the most binary clauses. A binary clause is a clause in which exactly two literals are unvalued, and all the rest are false.[3]

The first heuristic is just a typical backtracking convention, and in fact is intrinsically part of depth-first search and backjumping. The second heuristic is unit propagation, a standard part of the Davis-Putnam procedure for propositional satisfiability (Davis, Logemann, & Loveland 1962; Davis & Putnam 1960). The last heuristic is also a fairly common SAT heuristic; see for example (Crawford & Auton 1993; Zabih & McAllester 1988). These heuristics choose variables that are highly constrained and constraining in an attempt to make the ultimate search space as small as possible.

For our experiments, we varied the number of variables n from 10 to 60 in increments of 10. For each value of n we generated random crossover-point problems[4] until we had accumulated 100 satisfiable and 100 unsatisfiable instances. We then ran each of the three algorithms on the 200 instances in each problem set. The mean number of times that a variable is assigned a value is displayed in Table 1.

Dynamic backtracking appears to be worse than the other two algorithms by a factor exponential in the size of the problem; this is rather surprising. Because of the lack of structure in these randomly-generated problems, we might not expect dynamic backtracking to be significantly better than the other algorithms, but why would it be *worse*? This question is of more than academic interest. Some real-world search problems may turn out to be similar in some respects to the crossword puzzles on which dynamic backtracking does well, while being similar in other respects to these random 3-SAT problems — and as we can see from Table 1, even a small "random 3-SAT component" will be enough to make dynamic backtracking virtually useless.

4 Analysis

To understand what is going wrong with dynamic backtracking, consider the following abstract SAT example:

$$a \rightarrow x \tag{1}$$
$$\Rightarrow \neg a \tag{2}$$
$$\neg a \Rightarrow b \tag{3}$$
$$b \Rightarrow c \tag{4}$$

---

[2]Each clause in a 3-SAT problem is a disjunction of three literals. A literal is either a propositional variable or its negation.

[3]On the very first iteration in a 3-SAT problem, there will not yet be any binary clauses, so instead choose the variable that appears in the most clauses overall.

[4]The numbers of clauses that we used were 49, 91, 133, 176, 218, and 261 respectively.

| | Average Number of Assignments | | |
Variables	Depth-First Search	Backjumping	Dynamic Backtracking
10	20	20	22
20	54	54	94
30	120	120	643
40	217	216	4,532
50	388	387	31,297
60	709	705	212,596

Table 1: A comparison using randomly-generated 3-SAT problems.

$$c \Rightarrow d \tag{5}$$

$$x \Rightarrow \neg d \tag{6}$$

Formula (1) represents the clause $\neg a \vee x$; we have written it in the directed form above to suggest how it will be used in our example. The remaining formulas correspond to groups of clauses; to indicate this, we have written them using the double arrow ($\Rightarrow$). Formula (2) represents some number of clauses that can be used to prove that a is contradictory. Formula (3) represents some set of clauses showing that if a is false, then b must be true; similar remarks apply to the remaining formulas. These formulas will also represent the nogoods that will eventually be learned.

Imagine dynamic backtracking exploring the search space in the order suggested above. First it sets a true, and then it concludes x using unit resolution (and adds a nogood corresponding to (1)). Then after some amount of further search, it finds that a has to be false. So it erases a, adds the nogood (2), and then deletes the nogood (1) since it is no longer "relevant." Note that it does *not* delete the proposition x — the whole point of dynamic backtracking is to preserve this intermediate work.

It will then set a false, and after some more search will learn nogoods (3)–(5), and set b, c and d true. It will then go on to discover that x and d cannot both be true, so it will have to add a new nogood (6) and erase d. The rule, remember, is that the most recently valued variable goes on the right-hand side of the nogood. Nogoods (5) and (6) are resolved together to produce the nogood

$$x \Rightarrow \neg c \tag{7}$$

where once again, since c is the most recent variable, it must be the one that is retracted and placed on the right-hand side of the nogood; and when c is retracted, nogood (5) must be deleted also. Continuing in this fashion, dynamic backtracking will derive the nogoods

$$x \Rightarrow \neg b \tag{8}$$

$$x \Rightarrow a \tag{9}$$

The values of b and a will be erased, and nogoods (4) and (3) will be deleted.

Finally, (2) and (9) will be resolved together producing

$$\Rightarrow \neg x \tag{10}$$

The value of x will be erased, nogoods (6)–(9) will be deleted, and the search procedure will then go on to rediscover (3)–(5) all over again.

By contrast, backtracking and backjumping would erase x before (or at the same time as) erasing a. They could then proceed to solve the rest of the problem without being encumbered by this leftover inference. It might help to think of this in terms of search trees even though dynamic backtracking is not really searching a tree. By failing to retract x, dynamic backtracking is in a sense choosing to "branch" on x before branching on a through d. This virtually doubles the size of the ultimate search space.

This example has been a bit involved, and so far it has only demonstrated that it is *possible* for dynamic backtracking to be worse than the simpler methods; why would it be worse in the *average* case? The answer lies in the heuristics that are being used to guide the search.

At each stage, a good search algorithm will try to select the variable that will make the remaining search space as small as possible. The appropriate choice will depend heavily on the values of previous variables. Unit propagation, as in equation (1), is an obvious example: if a is true, then we should immediately set x true as well; but if a is false, then there is no longer any particular reason to branch on x. After a is unset, our variable-selection heuristic would most likely choose to branch on a variable other than x; branching on x anyway is tantamount to randomly corrupting this heuristic. Now, dynamic backtracking does not really "branch" on variables since it has the ability to jump around in the search space. As we have seen, however, the decision not to erase x amounts to the same thing. In short, the leftover work that dynamic backtracking tries so hard to preserve often does more harm than good because it perpetuates decisions whose heuristic justifications have expired.

This analysis suggests that if we were to eliminate the heuristics, then dynamic backtracking would no longer be defeated by the other search methods. Table 2 contains the results of such an experiment. It is important to note that all of the previously listed heuristics (including unit resolution!) were disabled for the purpose of this experiment; at each stage, we simply chose the first unbound variable (using some

Variables	Average Number of Assignments		
	Depth-First Search	Backjumping	Dynamic Backtracking
10	77	61	51
20	2,243	750	478
30	53,007	7,210	3,741

Table 2: The same comparison as Table 1, but with all variable-selection heuristics disabled.

Variables	Average Number of Assignments		
	Depth-First Search	Backjumping	Dynamic Backtracking
10	20	20	20
20	54	54	53
30	120	120	118
40	217	216	209
50	388	387	375
60	709	705	672

Table 3: The same comparison as Table 1, but with dynamic backtracking modified to undo unit propagation when it backtracks.

fixed ordering). For each value of n listed, we used the same 200 random problems that were generated earlier.

The results in Table 2 are as expected. All of the algorithms fare far worse than before, but at least dynamic backtracking is not worse than the others. In fact, it is a bit better than backjumping and substantially better than backtracking. So given that there is nothing intrinsically wrong with dynamic backtracking, the challenge is to modify it in order to reduce or eliminate its negative interaction with our search heuristics.

5   Solution

We have to balance two considerations. When backtracking, we would like to preserve as much nontrivial work as possible. On the other hand, we do not want to leave a lot of "junk" lying around whose main effect is to degrade the effectiveness of the heuristics. In general, it is not obvious how to strike the appropriate balance. For the propositional case, however, there is a simple modification that seems to help, namely, undoing unit propagation when backtracking.

We will need the following definition:

Definition 2 *Let v be a variable (in a Boolean* CSP*) that is currently assigned a value. A nogood whose conclusion eliminates the other value for v will be said to* justify *this assignment.*

If a value is justified by a nogood, and this nogood is deleted at some point, then the value should be erased as well. Selecting the given value was once a good heuristic decision, but now that its justification has been deleted, the value would probably just get in the way. Therefore, we will rewrite DELETE-NOGOOD as follows, and leave the rest of dynamic backtracking intact:

Procedure DELETE-NOGOOD(γ)

1. Remove γ from Γ.

2. For each variable w justified by γ, call ERASE-VARIABLE(w).

Note that ERASE-VARIABLE calls DELETE-NOGOOD in turn; the two procedures are mutually recursive. This corresponds to the possibility of undoing a cascade of unit resolutions. Like Ginsberg's original algorithm, this modified version is sound and complete, uses only polynomial space, and can solve the the union of several independent problems in time proportional to the sum of that required for the original problems.

We ran this modified procedure on the same experiments as before, and the results are in Table 3. Happily, dynamic backtracking no longer blows up the search space. It does not do much good either, but there may well be other examples for which this modified version of dynamic backtracking is the method of choice.

How will this apply to non-Boolean problems? First of all, for non-Boolean CSPs, the problem is not quite as dire. Suppose a variable has twenty possible values, all but two of which are eliminated by nogoods. Suppose further that on this basis, one of the remaining values is assigned to the variable. If one of the eighteen nogoods is later eliminated, then the variable will still have but three possibilities and will probably remain a good choice. It is only in the Boolean problems that an assignment can go all the way from being totally justified to totally unjustified with the deletion of a single nogood. Nonetheless, in experiments by Jónsson and Ginsberg it was found that dynamic backtracking often did worse than depth-first search when coloring random graphs (Jónsson & Ginsberg 1993). Perhaps some variant of our new method would help on these problems. One idea would be to delete a value if it loses a certain number (or percentage) of the nogoods that once supported it.

6 Conclusion

Although we have presented this research in terms of Ginsberg's dynamic backtracking algorithm, the implications are much broader. Any systematic search algorithm that learns and forgets nogoods as it moves laterally through a search space will have to address—in some way or another—the problem that we have discussed. The fundamental problem is that when a decision is retracted, there may be subsequent decisions whose justifications are thereby undercut. While there is no *logical* reason to retract these decisions as well, there may be good heuristic reasons for doing so.

On the other hand, the solution that we have presented is not the only one possible, and it is probably not the best one either. Instead of erasing a variable that has lost its heuristic justification, it would be better to keep the value around, but in the event of a contradiction remember to backtrack on this variable instead of a later one. With standard dynamic backtracking, however, we do not have this option; we always have to backtrack on the most recent variable in the new nogood. Ginsberg and McAllester have recently developed *partial-order dynamic backtracking* (Ginsberg & McAllester 1994), a variant of dynamic backtracking that relaxes this restriction to some extent, and it might be interesting to explore some of the possibilities that this more general method makes possible.

Perhaps the main purpose of this paper is to sound a note of caution with regard to the new search algorithms. Ginsberg claims in one of his theorems that dynamic backtracking "can be expected to expand fewer nodes than backjumping provided that the goal nodes are distributed randomly in the search space" (Ginsberg 1993). In the presence of search heuristics, this is false. For example, the goal nodes in *unsatisfiable* 3-SAT problems are certainly randomly distributed (since there are not any goal nodes), and yet standard dynamic backtracking can take orders of magnitude longer to search the space.

Therefore, while there are some obvious benefits to the new backtracking techniques, the reader should be aware that there are also some hazards.

Acknowledgments

I would like to thank all the members of CIRL, and especially Matthew Ginsberg and James Crawford, for many useful discussions.

References

Crawford, J. M., and Auton, L. D. 1993. Experimental results on the crossover point in satisfiability problems. In *Proceedings of the Eleventh National Conference on Artificial Intelligence*, 21–27.

Davis, M., and Putnam, H. 1960. A computing procedure for quantification theory. *Journal of the Association for Computing Machinery* 7:201–215.

Davis, M.; Logemann, G.; and Loveland, D. 1962. A machine program for theorem-proving. *Communications of the ACM* 5:394–397.

Gaschnig, J. 1979. Performance measurement and analysis of certain search algorithms. Technical Report CMU-CS-79-124, Carnegie-Mellon University.

Ginsberg, M. L., and McAllester, D. A. 1994. GSAT and dynamic backtracking. In *Proceedings of the Fourth International Conference on Principles of Knowledge Representation and Reasoning*.

Ginsberg, M. L. 1993. Dynamic backtracking. *Journal of Artificial Intelligence Research* 1:25–46.

Jónsson, A. K., and Ginsberg, M. L. 1993. Experimenting with new systematic and nonsystematic search procedures. In *Proceedings of the AAAI Spring Symposium on AI and NP-Hard Problems*.

Mitchell, D.; Selman, B.; and Levesque, H. 1992. Hard and easy distributions of SAT problems. In *Proceedings of the Tenth National Conference on Artificial Intelligence*, 459–465.

Selman, B.; Levesque, H.; and Mitchell, D. 1992. A new method for solving hard satisfiability problems. In *Proceedings of the Tenth National Conference on Artificial Intelligence*, 440–446.

Stallman, R. M., and Sussman, G. J. 1977. Forward reasoning and dependency-directed backtracking in a system for computer-aided circuit analysis. *Artificial Intelligence* 9:135–196.

Zabih, R., and McAllester, D. 1988. A rearrangement search strategy for determining propositional satisfiability. In *Proceedings of the Seventh National Conference on Artificial Intelligence*, 155–160.

Dead-end driven learning *

Daniel Frost and Rina Dechter
Dept. of Information and Computer Science
University of California, Irvine, CA 92717
{dfrost,dechter}@ics.uci.edu

Abstract

The paper evaluates the effectiveness of learning for speeding up the solution of constraint satisfaction problems. It extends previous work (Dechter 1990) by introducing a new and powerful variant of learning and by presenting an extensive empirical study on much larger and more difficult problem instances. Our results show that learning can speed up backjumping when using either a fixed or dynamic variable ordering. However, the improvement with a dynamic variable ordering is not as great, and for some classes of problems learning is helpful only when a limit is placed on the size of new constraints learned.

1. Introduction

Our goal in this paper is to study the effect of *learning* in speeding up the solution of constraint problems. The function of learning in problem solving is to record in a useful way some information which is explicated during the search, so that it can be reused either later on the same problem instance, or on similar instances which arise subsequently. The approach we take involves a during-search transformation of the problem representation into one that may be searched more effectively. This is done by enriching the problem description by new constraints (sometimes called *nogoods*), which do not change the set of solutions, but make certain information explicit. The idea is to learn from dead-ends; whenever a dead-end is reached we record a constraint explicated by the dead-end.

This type of learning has been presented in dependency-directed backtracking strategies in the TMS community (Stallman & Sussman 1977), and within intelligent backtracking for Prolog(Bruynooghe & Pereira 1984). Recently, it was treated more systematically by Dechter (1990) within the constraint network framework. Different variants of learning were examined there, while taking into account the trade-off between the overhead of learning and performance

*This work was partially supported by NSF grant IRI-9157636, by Air Force Office of Scientific Research grant AFOSR 900136 and by grants from Toshiba of America and Xerox.

improvement. The results, although preliminary, indicated that learning could be cost-effective.

The present study extends (Dechter 1990) in several ways. First, a new variant of learning, called jump-back learning, is introduced and is shown empirically to be superior to other types of learning. Secondly, we experiment with and without restrictions on the size of the constraints learned. Thirdly, we use a highly efficient version of backjumping as a comparison reference. Finally, our experiments use larger and harder problem instances than previously studied.

2. Definitions and Preliminaries

A Constraint Network consists of a set of n variables, $X_1, \ldots, X_n$; their respective value domains, $D_1, \ldots, D_n$; and a set of constraints. A *constraint* $C_i(X_{i_1}, \ldots, X_{i_j})$ is a subset of the Cartesian product $D_{i_1} \times \ldots \times D_{i_j}$, consisting of all tuples of values for a subset $(X_{i_1}, \ldots, X_{i_j})$ of the variables which are compatible with each other. A *solution* is an assignment of values to all the variables such that all the constraints are satisfied. Sometimes the goal is to find all solutions; in this paper, however, we focus on the task of finding one solution, or proving that no solution exists. A constraint satisfaction problem (CSP) can be associated with a *constraint graph* consisting of a node for each variable and an arc connecting each pair of variables that are contained in a constraint. A *binary* CSP is one in which each of the constraints involves at most two variables.

Backjumping

Many algorithms have been proposed for solving CSPs. See (Dechter 1992; Mackworth 1992) for reviews. One algorithm that was shown always to dominate naive backtracking is *backjumping* (Gaschnig, 1979; Dechter, 1990). Like backtracking, backjumping considers each variable in some order and assigns to each successive variable a value from its domain which is consistent with the values assigned to the preceding variables. When a variable is encountered such that none of its possible values is consistent with previous assignments (a situation referred to as a *dead-end*), a backjump

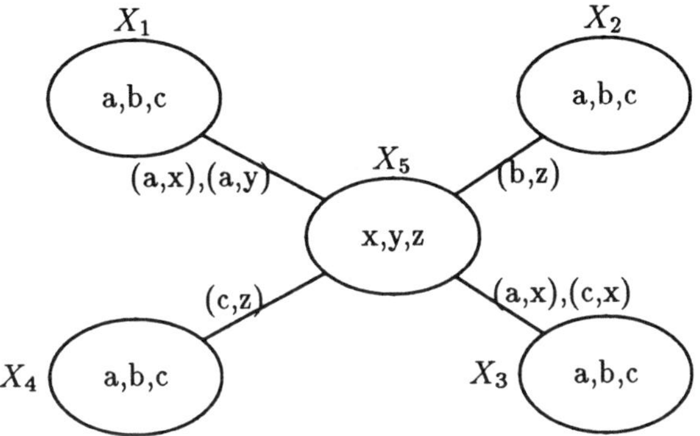

Figure 1: A small CSP. Note that the *dis*allowed pairs are shown on each arc.

takes place. The idea is to jump back over several irrelevant variables to a variable which is more directly responsible for the current conflict. The backjumping algorithm identifies a *jump-back set*, that is, a subset of the variables preceding the dead-end variable which are inconsistent with all its values, and continues search from the last variable in this set. If that variable has no untried values left, then a *pseudo dead-end* arises and further backjumping occurs.

Consider, for instance, the CSP represented by the graph in Fig. 1. Each node represents a variable that can take on a value from within the oval, and the binary constraint between connected variables is specified along the arcs by the disallowed value pairs. If the variables are ordered $(X_1, X_5, X_2, X_3, X_4)$ and a dead-end is reached at X_4, the backjumping algorithm will jump back to X_5, since X_4 is not connected to X_3 or X_2.

The version of backjumping we use here is a combination of Gaschnig's (1979) backjumping and Dechter's (1990) graph-based backjumping, as proposed by Prosser (1993). Prosser calls the algorithm *conflict-directed* backjumping. In this version, the jump-back set is created by recording, for each value v of V, the variable to be instantiated next, the first past variable (relative to the ordering) whose assigned value conflicts with $V = v$. The algorithm will be combined with both fixed and dynamic variable orderings.

Variable Ordering Heuristics

It is well known that variable ordering affects tremendously the size of the search space. In previous studies it has been shown that the *min-width* ordering is a very effective fixed ordering (Dechter & Meiri 1989), while dynamic variable ordering (Haralick & Elliott 1980; Purdom 1983; Zabih & McAllester 1988) frequently yields best performance. We incorporate both strategies in our experiments.

The *minimum width* (MW or min-width) heuristic (Freuder 1982) orders the variables from last to first by selecting, at each stage, a variable in the constraint graph that connects to the minimal number of vari-

ables that have not yet been selected. For instance, the ordering X_1, X_5, X_2, X_3, X_4 is a min-width ordering of the graph in Fig. 1.

Dynamic variable ordering (DVO) allows the order of variables to change during search. The version we use selects at each point the variable with the smallest remaining domain size, when only values that are consistent with all instantiated variables are considered. Ties are broken randomly. The variable that participates in the most constraints is selected to be first in the ordering. If any future variable has an empty domain, then it is moved to be the next in the ordering, and a dead-end will occur on that variable. Otherwise, a variable with the smallest domain size is selected (similar to unit-propagation in Boolean satisfiability problems).

3. Learning Algorithms

In a dead-end at X_i, when the current instantiation $S = (X_1 = x_1, \ldots, X_{i-1} = x_{i-1})$ cannot be extended by any value of X_i, we say that S is a *conflict set*. An opportunity to learn new constraints is presented whenever backjumping encounters a dead-end, since had the problem included an explicit constraint prohibiting the dead-end's conflict-set, the dead-end would have been avoided. To learn at a dead-end, we record a new constraint which makes explicit an incompatibility among variable assignments that already existed, implicitly. The trade-off involved is in possibly finding out earlier in the remaining search that a given path cannot lead to a solution, versus the cost of having to process a more extensive database of constraints.

There is no point in recording S as a constraint at this stage, because this state will not recur. However, if S contains one or more subsets that are also in conflict with X_i, then recording these smaller conflict sets as constraints may prove useful in the continued exploration of the search space because future states may contain these subsets.

Different types of learning differ in the way they identify smaller conflict sets. In (Dechter 1990) learning is characterized as being either *deep* or *shallow*. Deep learning only records *minimal* conflict sets, that is, those that do not have subsets which are conflict sets. Shallow learning allows recording non-minimal conflict sets as well. Learning can also be characterized by *order*, the maximum constraint size that is recorded. In (Dechter 1990) experiments were limited to recording unary and binary constraints, since constraints involving more variables are applicable less frequently, require more space to store, and are more expensive to consult.

In this paper we experiment with four types of learning: *graph-based shallow* learning, *value-based shallow* learning, and *deep* learning, already presented in (Dechter 1990), as well as a new type, called *jump-back* learning.

In **value-based learning** all irrelevant variable-value pairs are removed from the initial conflict set S. If a variable-value pair $X_j = x_j$ doesn't conflict with any value of the dead-end variable then it is redundant and can be eliminated. For instance, if we try to solve the problem in Fig. 1 with the ordering $(X_1, X_2, X_3, X_4, X_5)$, after instantiating $X_1 = a, X_2 = b, X_3 = b, X_4 = c$, the dead-end at X_5 will cause value-based learning to record $(X_1 = a, X_2 = b, X_4 = c)$, since the pair $X_3 = b$ is compatible with all values of X_5. Since we can pre-compute in $O(n^2 k)$ time a table that will tell us whether $X_i = x_j$ conflicts with any value of each other variable, the complexity of value-based learning at each dead-end is $O(n)$.

Graph-based shallow learning is a relaxed version of value-based learning, where information on conflicts is derived from the constraint graph alone. This may be particularly useful on sparse graphs. For instance, in Fig. 1 graph-based shallow learning will record $(X_1 = a, X_2 = b, X_3 = b, X_4 = c)$ as a conflict set relative to X_5, since all variables are connected to X_5. The complexity of learning at each dead-end here is $O(n)$, since each variable is connected to at most $n - 1$ other variables.

Jump-back learning uses as the conflict-set the jump-back set that is explicated by the backjumping algorithm itself. Recall that conflict-directed backjumping examines, starting from the first variable, each instantiated variable and includes it in the jump-back set if it conflicts with a value of the current variable that previously did not conflict with any variable. For instance in Fig. 1, when using the same ordering and reaching the dead-end at X_5, jump-back learning will record $(X_1 = a, X_2 = b)$ as a new constraint. These two variables are selected because the algorithm first looks at $X_1 = a$ and notes that it conflicts with $X_5 = x$ and $X_5 = y$. Proceeding to $X_2 = b$, the conflict with $X_5 = z$ is noted. At this point all values of X_5 have been ruled out, and the conflict set is complete. Since the conflict set is already assembled by the underlying backjumping algorithm, the added complexity of computing the conflict set is constant.

In **deep learning** all and only minimal conflict sets are recorded. In Fig. 1, deep learning will record two minimal conflict sets, $(X_1 = a, X_2 = b)$ and $(X_1 = a, X_4 = c)$. Although this form of learning is the most accurate, its cost is prohibitive and in the worst-case is exponential in the size of the initial conflict set (Dechter 1990).

4. Complexity of backtracking with learning

We will now show that graph-based learning yields a useful complexity bound on the algorithm performance, relative to a graph parameter known as w^*. Since graph-based learning is the most conservative learning algorithm (when no order restrictions are imposed), the bound is applicable to all the variants of

	Cross-over value of C	
N	$T = 1/9$	$T = 2/9$
25	199	89
50	380	166
75	565	244
100	747	317
150	1100	468
200	1477	621
250	1842	771

Figure 2: Empirically determined values of C that generate 50% solvable CSP instances. $K = 3$ for this data.

learning we discuss.

Given a constraint graph and a fixed ordering of the nodes d, the *width* of a node is the number of arcs that connect that node to previous ones, called its *parents*. The width of the graph relative to d is the maximum width of all nodes in the graph. The induced graph is created by considering each node in the original graph in order from last to first, and adding arcs connecting each of its parents to each other parent. The induced width of an ordering, $w^*(d)$, is the width of its induced graph.

Theorem 1: Let d be an ordering and let $w^*(d)$ be its induced width. Any backtrack algorithm using ordering d and graph-based learning has a space complexity of $O((nk)^{w^*(d)})$ and a time complexity of $O((2nk)^{w^*(d)})$.

Proof: Due to graph-based learning there is a one-to-one correspondence between dead-ends and conflict sets. It can be shown that backtracking with graph-based learning along d records conflict-sets of size $w^*(d)$ or less. Therefore the number of dead-ends is bounded by

$$\sum_{i=1}^{w^*(d)} \binom{n}{i} k^i = O((nk)^{w^*(d)}).$$

This gives the space complexity. Since deciding that a dead-end occurred requires testing all constraints containing the dead-end variable and at most $w^*(d)$ prior variables, at most $O(2^{w^*(d)})$ constraints are checked per dead-end, yielding a time bound of

$$O((2nk)^{w^*(d)}).$$

5. Methodology and Results

The experiments reported in this paper were run on random instances generated using a four parameter model: N, K, T and C. The problem instances have N variables, each having a domain of size K. The problems we experiment with always start off as binary CSPs, but can become non-binary as constraints involving more than two variables are added by learning. The parameter T (tightness) specifies a fraction

N	K	Statistic	No Learning	With this type of learning			
				Graph-based	Value-based	Jump-back	Deep
25	3	CC	16,930	30,636	29,185	10,203	117,556
		DE	156	178	181	82	67
		CPU secs	0.048	0.083	0.077	0.032	0.325
		NGs		178	181	82	153
		Size		11.6	6.8	3.5	3.4
25	6	CC	274,133	1,340,512	1,428,109	330,672	55,771,462
		DE	2,777	2,833	2,932	1,276	832
		CPU secs	0.777	2.067	2.183	0.667	78.283
		NGs		2,833	2,932	1,276	1894
		Size		11.2	10.4	5.2	4.4
50	3	CC	303,668	8,051,435	7,111,384	119,642	27,134,341
		DE	2,205	5,107	4,512	437	333
		CPU secs	1.298	11.492	9.913	0.367	44.788
		NGs		5,107	4,512	437	654
		Size		20.6	13.6	4.6	4.2

Figure 3: Detailed results of comparing backjumping with no learning to backjumping with each of four kinds of learning. $T = 1/9$ and C is set to the cross-over point. See the text for discussion.

of the K^2 value pairs in each constraint that are disallowed by the constraint. The incompatible pairs in a constraint are selected randomly from a uniform distribution, but each constraint will always have the same fraction T of such incompatible pairs. T ranges from 0 to 1, with a low value of T, such as $1/9$, termed a loose or relaxed constraint. The fourth parameter, C, specifies the number of constraints out of the $N * (N - 1)/2$ possible. Constraints are chosen randomly from a uniform distribution.

As in previous studies (Cheeseman, Kanefsky, & Taylor 1991; Mitchell, Selman, & Levesque 1992), we observed that the hardest instances tend to be found where about half the problems are solvable and half are not (the "cross-over" point). Most of our experiments were conducted with instances drawn from this 50% range; the necessary parameter combinations were determined experimentally (Frost & Dechter 1994) and are given in Fig. 2.

Results

We first compared the effectiveness of the four learning schemes. Fig. 3 presents a summary of experiments with sets of problems of several sizes (N) and number of values (K). 100 problems in each class were generated and solved by five algorithms: backjumping without learning, and then backjumping with each of the four types of learning. In all cases a min-width variable ordering was applied and no bound was placed on the size of the constraints recorded. For each problem instance and for each algorithm we recorded the number of consistency checks (CC), the number of (non-pseudo) dead-ends (DE), the CPU time (CPU secs), the number of new nogoods recorded (NGs), and the average size of (number of variables in) the learned constraints. A consistency check is recorded each time the algorithm checks if the values of two or more variables are consistent with respect to the constraint between them. The number of dead-ends is a measure of the size of the search space explicated. All experiments were run using a single program with as much shared code and data structures as possible. Therefore we believe CPU time is a meaningful comparative measure.

This experiment demonstrated that only the new jump-back type of learning was effective on these reasonably large size problems. Once the superiority of jump-back learning was established we stopped experimenting with other types of learning. In the following discussion and figures, all references to learning should be taken to mean jump-back learning.

To determine whether learning would be effective for CSPs with many variables, in our next set of experiments we generated instances from parameters $K = 3$, $T = 1/9$, $N = \{25, 50, 75, 100\}$, and C set to the appropriate cross-over points. We used backjumping with a min-width ordering on 200 instances in each category, both with and without learning. (No limit was placed on the order of learning.) The mean numbers of consistency checks, dead-ends, and CPU seconds are reported in Fig. 4. The results were encouraging: by all measures learning provided a substantial improvement when added to backjumping. (Experiments with $T = 2/9$ and $T = 3/9$, not reported here due to space, show a similar pattern.) Our only reservation was that from other work we knew that a dynamic variable ordering can be a significant improvement over the static min-width. Would learning be able to improve backjumping with DVO?

To find out, we ran another set of experiments, using the same instances, plus some generated with higher values of N; this time backjumping used a dynamic variable ordering. We also experimented with vari-

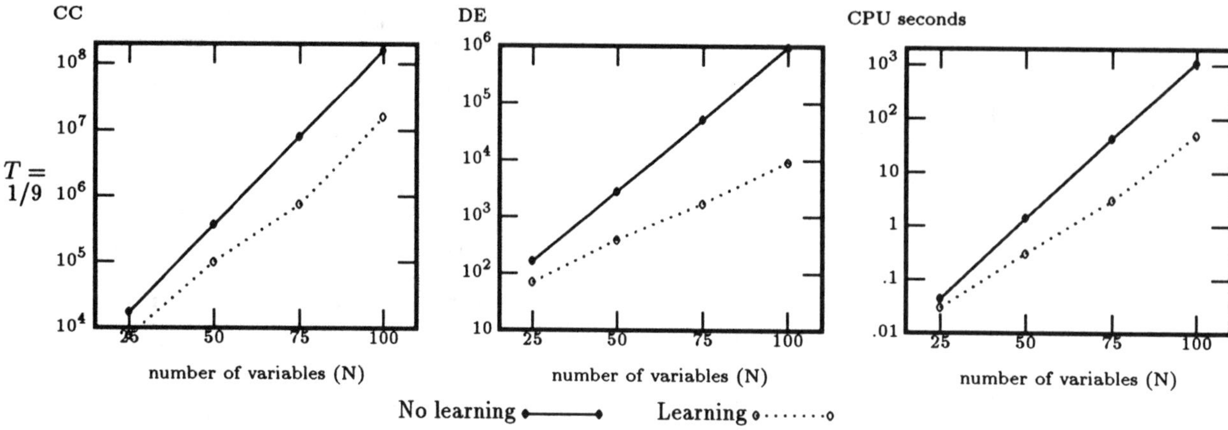

Figure 4: Comparison of BJ+MW with and without learning (of unlimited order); $K = 3$.

ous orders of learning. Recall that in i-order learning, new constraints are recorded only if they include i or fewer variables. In (Dechter 1990) experiments were conducted with first and second order learning. Here, we tried second-, third-, and fourth-order learning, as well as learning without restriction on the size of new constraints. However, only third-order and unlimited-order learning are reported, due to space constraints, in Fig. 6.

We make several observations from these data. First, learning becomes more effective as the number of variables in the problem increases. With DVO, when $N < 100$, the absence or presence of learning, of whatever order, makes very little difference. With the powerful DVO ordering, there are too few dead-ends for learning to be useful, or for the overhead of learning to cause problems. As N increases from 100 on up, learning becomes more effective. For instance, looking at data for $T = 2/9$, and comparing CPU time for No Learning with CPU time for unlimited order learning, we see improvements at $N = 100$ of 1.6 (0.815 / 0.499), at $N = 150$ of 6.9 (25.463 / 3.710), and at $N = 200$ of 7.8 (170.990 / 21.808).

A second observation is that when the individual constraints are loose ($T = 1/9$), learning is at best only slightly helpful and can sometimes deteriorate performance. The reason is that the conflict-sets with loose constraints tend to be larger, since each variable in the conflict set can invalidate (in the case of $T = 1/9$) only one value from the dead-end variable's domain.

Thirdly, we note that as the order of learning becomes higher, the size of the search space decreases (as measured by the number of dead-ends), but the amount of work at each node increases, indicated by the larger count of consistency checks. For instance, the data for $N = 200, T = 2/9$, show that in going from third-order learning to unlimited order learning, dead-ends go down slightly while consistency checks increase by a factor of five. The overall CPU time for the two

versions is almost identical, because in our implementation consistency checking is implemented very efficiently. If the cost to perform each consistency check were higher in relation to the cost to expand the search to a new node, unlimited learning might require more CPU time than restricted order learning.

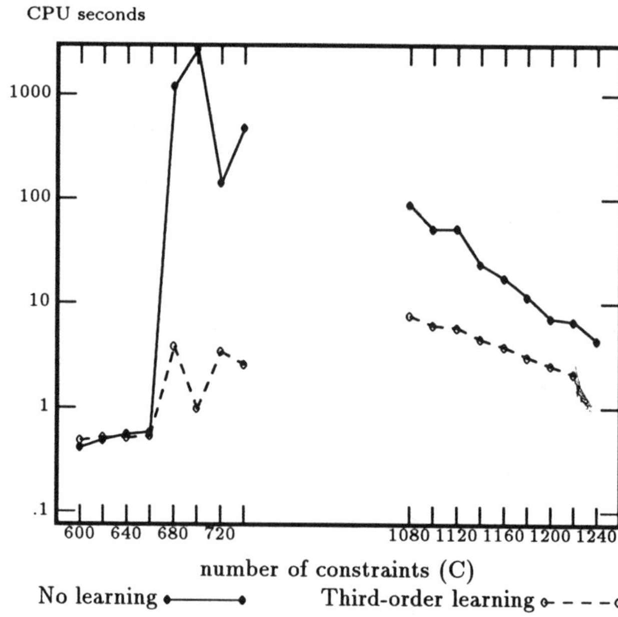

Figure 5: BJ+DVO without learning and with third-order learning, for N=300, K=3, T=2/9, and non-50% values of C. All problems with $C \leq 740$ were solvable; all with $C \geq 1080$ had no solution.

As expected, learning is more effective on problem instances that have more dead-ends and larger search spaces, where there are more opportunities for each learned constraint to be useful. Comparing the means

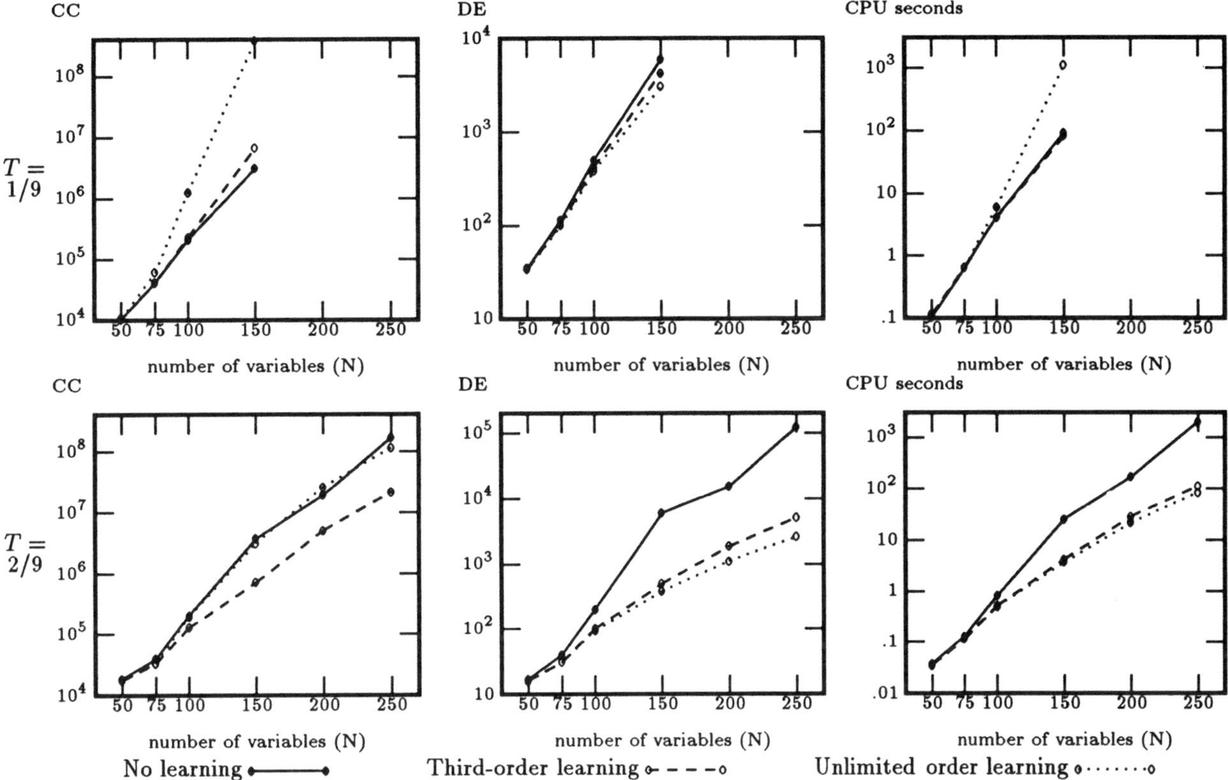

Figure 6: Comparison of BJ+DVO, without learning, and with third-order and unlimited order learning; $K = 3$.

of 200 problem instances solved both with and without learning can obscure the trend that the improvement from learning is generally much greater for the very hardest instances of the population. For instance, the data for $N = 200, T = 2/9$ show that the mean CPU time for 200 instances is 170.990 without learning and 21.808 with learning, improving by a factor of 7.8 (170.990 / 21.808). If we just consider the 20 problem instances out of the 200 which required the most CPU time to be solved without learning, the mean CPU time of those 20 instances without learning is 1107.18, and 72.48 with unlimited order learning. The improvement for the hardest problems is a factor of 15, about twice that of the entire sample.

Fig. 5 shows that with large enough N, problems do not have to be drawn from the 50% satisfiable area in order to be hard enough for learning to help. Learning was especially valuable on extremely hard solvable problems generated by slightly underconstrained values for C. For instance, at $N = 300, K = 3, T = 2/9, C = 680$, the hardest problem (out of 200 instances) took 47 CPU hours without learning, and under one CPU minute with learning. The next four hardest problems took 4% as much CPU time with learning as without.

Controlling the order of learning has a greater impact on the constraints recorded as N increases. We see this in Fig. 7 (drawn from the same set of experiments as Fig. 6), where the average constraint size increases for unlimited order learning, but not for third-order. The primary cause of this effect is that learned non-binary constraints are becoming part of conflict-sets. The first constraint learned with these parameters (particularly $K = 3$) can have at most three variables in it, one eliminating each value of the dead-end. Once a 3-variable constraint exists, it may contribute two variables to a conflict set, and thus a four variable conflict set can arise. For $N = 250$, the largest conflict set we observed had 11 elements. Recording such a constraint is unlikely to be helpful later in the search.

It is worth noting that we did not find the space requirements of learning to be overwhelming, as has been reported by some researchers. For instance, the average problem at $N = 250$ and $T = 2/9$ took about 100 CPU seconds and recorded about 2600 new constraints (with unlimited order learning). Each constraint requires fewer than 25 bytes of memory, so the total added memory is well under one megabyte. We found that computer memory is not the limiting factor; time is.

N	Order 3			Unlimited order		
	Dead-ends	Learned	Avg. Size	Dead-ends	Learned	Avg. Size
50	16	15	2.20	16	16	2.25
75	31	30	2.06	31	31	2.11
100	101	90	2.11	94	94	2.27
150	499	447	2.07	383	383	2.29
200	1,874	1,561	2.09	1,110	1,110	2.58
250	5,119	4,046	2.10	2,608	2,608	2.86

Figure 7: Figures for $T = 2/9$; learning with BJ+DVO. "Learned" is number of new constraints learned; "Avg. Size" is the average number of variables in the constraints.

5. Conclusions

We have introduced a new variant of learning, called jump-back learning, which is more powerful than previous versions. Our experiments show that it is very effective when augmented on top of an efficient version of backjumping, resulting in at least an order of magnitude reduction in CPU time for some problems.

Learning seems to be particularly effective when applied to instances that are large or hard, since it requires many dead-ends to be able to augment the initial problem in a significant way. However, on easy problems with few dead-ends, learning will add little if any cost, thus perhaps making it particularly suitable for situations in which there is a wide variation in the hardness of individual problems. In this way learning is superior to other CSP techniques which modify the initial problem, such as by enforcing a certain order of consistency, since the cost will not be incurred on very easy problems. Moreover, we have shown that the performance of any backtracking algorithm with learning, using a fixed ordering, is bounded by $\exp(w^*)$.

An important parameter when applying learning is the order, or maximum size of the constraints learned. With no restriction on the order, it is possible to learn very large constraints that will be unlikely to prune the remaining search space. We plan to study the relationship between K, the size of the domain, and the optimal order of learning. Clearly with higher values of K, the order may need to be higher, especially for loose constraints, possibly rendering learning less effective.

References

Bruynooghe, M., and Pereira, L. M. 1984. Deduction revision by intelligent backtracking. In Campbell, J. A., ed., *Implementation of Prolog*. Ellis Horwood. 194–215.

Cheeseman, P.; Kanefsky, B.; and Taylor, W. M. 1991. Where the *really* hard problems are. In *Proceedings of the International Joint Conference on Artificial Intelligence*, 331–337.

Dechter, R., and Meiri, I. 1989. Experimental evaluation of preprocessing techniques in constraint satisfaction problems. In *International Joint Conference on Artificial Intelligence*, 271–277.

Dechter, R. 1990. Enhancement Schemes for Constraint Processing: Backjumping, Learning, and Cutset Decomposition. *Artificial Intelligence* 41:273–312.

Dechter, R. 1992. Constraint networks. In *Encyclopedia of Artificial Intelligence*. John Wiley & Sons, 2nd edition.

Freuder, E. C. 1982. A sufficient condition for backtrack-free search. *JACM* 21(11):958–965.

Frost, D., and Dechter, R. 1994. Search for the best constraint satisfaction search. In *Proceedings of the Twelfth National Conference on Artificial Intelligence*.

Gaschnig, J. 1979. Performance measurement and analysis of certain search algorithms. Technical Report CMU-CS-79-124, Carnegie Mellon University.

Haralick, R. M., and Elliott, G. L. 1980. Increasing Tree Search Efficiency for Constraint Satisfaction Problems. *Artificial Intelligence* 14:263–313.

Mackworth, A. K. 1992. Constraint satisfaction problems. In *Encyclopedia of Artificial Intelligence*. John Wiley & Sons, 2nd edition.

Mitchell, D.; Selman, B.; and Levesque, H. 1992. Hard and Easy Distributions of SAT Problems. In *Proceedings of the Tenth National Conference on Artificial Intelligence*, 459–465.

Prosser, P. 1993. Hybrid Algorithms for the Constraint Satisfaction Problem. *Computational Intelligence* 9(3):268–299.

Purdom, P. W. 1983. Search Rearrangement Backtracking and Polynomial Average Time. *Artificial Intelligence* 21:117–133.

Stallman, R. M., and Sussman, G. S. 1977. Forward reasoning and dependency-directed backtracking in a system for computer-aided circuit analysis. *Artificial Intelligence* 9:135–196.

Zabih, R., and McAllester, D. 1988. A Rearrangement Search Strategy for Determining Propositional Satisfiability. In *Proceedings of the Seventh National Conference on Artificial Intelligence*, 155–160.

In search of the best constraint satisfaction search *

Daniel Frost and Rina Dechter
Dept. of Information and Computer Science
University of California, Irvine, CA 92717
{dfrost,dechter}@ics.uci.edu

Abstract

We present the results of an empirical study of several constraint satisfaction search algorithms and heuristics. Using a random problem generator that allows us to create instances with given characteristics, we show how the relative performance of various search methods varies with the number of variables, the tightness of the constraints, and the sparseness of the constraint graph. A version of backjumping using a dynamic variable ordering heuristic is shown to be extremely effective on a wide range of problems. We conducted our experiments with problem instances drawn from the 50% satisfiable range.

1. Introduction

We are interested in studying the behavior of algorithms and heuristics that can solve large and hard constraint satisfaction problems via systematic search. Our approach is to focus on the average-case behavior of several search algorithms, all variations of backtracking search, by analyzing their performance over a large number of randomly generated problem instances. Experimental evaluation of search methods may allow us to identify properties that cannot yet be identified formally. Because CSPs are an NP-complete problem, the worst-case performance of any algorithm that solves them is exponential. Nevertheless, the average-case performance between different algorithms, determined experimentally, can vary by several orders of magnitude.

An alternative to our approach is to do some form of average-case analysis. An average-case analysis requires, however, a precise characterization of the distribution of the input instances. Such a characterization is often not available.

There are limitations to the approach we pursue here. The most important is that the model we use to generate random problems may not correspond to the type of problems which a practitioner actually encounters, possibly rendering our results of little or no relevance. Another problem is that subtle biases, if not outright bugs, in our implementation may skew the results. The only safeguard against such bias is the repetition of our experiments, or similar ones, by others; to facilitate such repetition we have made our instance generating program available by FTP[1].

In the following section we define formally constraint satisfaction problems and describe briefly the algorithms and heuristics to be studied. We then show that the linear relationship between the number of constraints and the number of variables at the 50% solvable region, observed for 3-SAT problems by (Mitchell, Selman, & Levesque 1992; Crawford & Auton 1983), is observed only approximately for binary CSPs with more than two values per variable. We conducted our experiments with problems drawn from this region. Section 3 describes those studies, which involved backtracking, backjumping, backmarking, forward checking, two variable ordering heuristics, and a new value ordering heuristic called sticking values. The results of these experiments show that backjumping with a dynamic variable ordering is a very effective combination, and also that backmarking and the sticking values heuristic can significantly improve backjumping with a fixed variable ordering. The final section states our conclusions.

2. Definitions and Algorithms

A *constraint satisfaction problem* (CSP) is represented by a *constraint network*, consisting of a set of n variables, $X_1, \ldots, X_n$; their respective value domains, $D_1, \ldots, D_n$; and a set of constraints. A *constraint* $C_i(X_{i_1}, \ldots, X_{i_j})$ is a subset of the Cartesian product $D_{i_1} \times \ldots \times D_{i_j}$, consisting of all tuples of values for a subset $(X_{i_1}, \ldots, X_{i_j})$ of the variables which are compatible with each other. A *solution* is an assignment of values to all the variables such that no constraint is

---

*This work was partially supported by NSF grant IRI-9157636, by Air Force Office of Scientific Research grant AFOSR 900136 and by grants from Toshiba of America and Xerox.

---

[1] ftp to ics.uci.edu, login as "anonymous," give your e-mail address as password, enter "cd /pub/CSP-repository," and read the README file for further information.

violated; a problem with a solution is termed *satisfiable*. Sometimes it is desired to find all solutions; in this paper, however, we focus on the task of finding one solution, or proving that no solution exists. A *binary* CSP is one in which each of the constraints involves at most two variables. A constraint satisfaction problem can be represented by a *constraint graph* consisting of a node for each variable and an arc connecting each pair of variables that are contained in a constraint.

Algorithms and Heuristics

Our experiments were conducted with backtracking (Bitner & Reingold 1985), backmarking (Gaschnig 1979; Haralick & Elliott 1980), forward checking (Haralick & Elliott 1980), and a version of backjumping (Gaschnig 1979; Dechter 1990) proposed in (Prosser 1993) and called there *conflict-directed* backjumping. Space does not permit more than a brief discussion of these algorithms. All are based on the idea of considering the variables one at a time, during a *forward* phase, and instantiating the current variable V with a value from its domain that does not violate any constraint either between V and all previously instantiated variables (backtracking, backmarking, and backjumping) or between V and the last remaining value of any future, uninstantiated variable (forward checking). If V has no such non-conflicting value, then a *dead-end* occurs, and in the *backwards* phase a previously instantiated variable is selected and re-instantiated with another value from its domain. With backtracking, the variable chosen to be re-instantiated after a dead-end is always the most recently instantiated variable; hence backtracking is often called *chronological* backtracking. Backjumping, in contrast, can in response to a dead-end identify a variable U, not necessarily the most recently instantiated, which is connected in some way to the dead-end. The algorithm then "jumps back" to U, uninstantiates all variables more recent than U, and tries to find a new value for U from its domain. The version of backjumping we use is very effective in choosing the best variable to jump back to.

Determining whether a potential value for a variable violates a constraint with another variable is called a *consistency check*. Because consistency checking is performed so frequently, it constitutes a major part of the work performed by all of these algorithms. Hence a count of the number of consistency checks is a common measure of the overall work of an algorithm. Backmarking is a version of backtracking that can reduce the number of consistency checks required by backtracking without changing the search space that is explored. By recording, for each value of a variable, the shallowest variable-value pair with which it was inconsistent, if any, backmarking can eliminate the need to repeat unnecessarily checks which have been performed before and will again succeed or fail. Although backmarking *per se* is an algorithm based on backtracking, its consistency check avoiding techniques can be applied to backjumping (Nadel 1989; Prosser 1983). In our experiments we evaluate the success of integrating backjumping and backmarking.

The forward checking algorithm uses a *look-ahead* approach: before a value is chosen for V, consistency checking is done with all future (uninstantiated) variables. Any conflicting value in a future variable W is removed temporarily from W's domain, and if this results in W having an empty domain then the value under consideration for V is rejected.

We used two variable ordering heuristics, min-width and dynamic variable ordering, in our experiments. The *minimum width* (MW or min-width) heuristic (Freuder 1982) orders the variables from last to first by repeatedly selecting a variable in the constraint graph that connects to the minimal number of variables that have not yet been selected. Min-width is a static ordering that is computed once before the algorithm begins. In a dynamic variable ordering (DVO) scheme (Haralick & Elliott 1980; Purdom 1983; Zabih & McAllester 1988) the variable order can be different in different branches of the search tree. Our implementation selects at each step the variable with the smallest remaining domain size, when only values that are consistent with all instantiated variables are considered. Ties are broken randomly, and the variable participating in the most constraints is selected to be first.

We also experimented with a new value ordering heuristic for backjumping called *sticking value*. The notion is to remember the value a variable is assigned during the forward phase, and then to select that value, if it is consistent, the next time the same variable needs to be instantiated during a forward phase. (If the "sticking value" is not consistent, then another value is chosen arbitrarily.) The intuition is that if the value was successful once, it may be useful to try it first later on in the search. This heuristic is inspired by local repair strategies (Minton *et al.* 1992; Selman, Levesque, & Mitchell 1992) in which all variables are instantiated, and then until a solution is found the values of individual variables are changed, but never uninstantiated.

Before jumping to our empirical results, we want to mention that the backjumping algorithm when used with a fixed ordering has a nice graph-based complexity bound. Given a graph G, a *dfs* ordering of the nodes is an ordering generated by a depth first search traversal on G, generating a *DFS* tree (Even 1979). We have shown elsewhere the following theorem:

Theorem 1(Collin, Dechter, & Katz 1991): Let G be a constraint network and let d be a dfs ordering of G whose DFS tree has depth m. Backjumping on d is $O(\exp(m))$.

3. Methodology and Results

The experiments reported in this paper were run on random instances generated using a model that takes

K	N	C	C/N	C	C/N	C	C/N	C	C/N
		$T = 1/9$		$T = 2/9$		$T = 3/9$		$T = 4/9$	
3	25	199	7.96	89	3.56	51	2.04	31	1.24
3	30	236	7.87	104	3.47	59	1.97	36	1.20
3	35	272	7.77	120	3.43	68	1.94	41	1.17
3	40	310	7.75	137	3.43	76	1.90	45	1.13
3	50	380	7.60	166	3.32	91	1.82	53	1.06
3	60	454	7.57	196	3.27	106	1.77	62	1.03
3	75	565	7.53	244	3.25	132	1.76	74	0.99
3	100	747	7.47	317	3.17	169	1.69	92	0.92
3	125	927	7.42	394	3.15	207	1.66	109	0.87
3	150	1100	7.40	468	3.12	242	1.61	127	0.85
3	175	1290	7.37	546	3.12	281	1.61	146	0.83
3	200	1471	7.36	623	3.11	318	1.59	159	0.80
3	225			697	3.10	353	1.57	176	0.78
3	250			773	3.09	390	1.56	193	0.77
3	275			847	3.08	425	1.54	205	0.75
		$T = 4/36$		$T = 8/36$		$T = 12/36$		$T = 16/36$	
6	15	**	**	102	6.80	62	4.13	41	2.73
6	25	**	**	165	6.60	100	4.00	65	2.60
6	35	500	14.29	228	6.51	137	3.91	89	2.54
6	50	710	14.20	325	6.50	193	3.87	125	2.51
6	60	852	14.20	389	6.48	231	3.85	150	2.50
		$T = 9/81$		$T = 18/81$		$T = 27/81$		$T = 36/81$	
9	15	**	**	**	**	79	5.27	53	3.53
9	25	**	**	211	8.44	128	5.12	87	3.48
9	35	**	**	294	8.40	178	5.09	119	3.40

Figure 1: The "C" columns show values of C which empirically produce 50% solvable problems, using the model described in the text and the given values of N, K, and T. The "C/N" column shows the value from the "C" column to its left, divided by the current value for N. "**" indicates that at this setting of N, K and T, even the maximum possible value of C produced only satisfiable instances. A blank entry signifies that problems generated with these parameters were too large to run.

four parameters: N, K, T and C. The problem instances are binary CSPs with N variables, each having a domain of size K. The parameter T (tightness) specifies a fraction of the K^2 value pairs in each constraint that are disallowed by the constraint. The value pairs to be disallowed by the constraint are selected randomly from a uniform distribution, but each constraint has the same fraction T of such incompatible pairs. T ranges from 0 to 1, with a low value of T, such as 1/9, termed a loose or relaxed constraint. The parameter C specifies the number of constraints out of the $N*(N-1)/2$ possible. The specific constraints are chosen randomly from a uniform distribution. This model is the binary CSP analog of the Random KSAT model described in (Mitchell, Selman, & Levesque 1992).

Although our random generator can create extremely hard instances, they may not be typical of actual problems encountered in applications. Therefore, in order to capture a wider variety of instances we introduce another generator, the *chain* model, that creates problems with a specific structure. A chain problem instance is created by generating several disjoint subproblems, called *nodes*, with our general gen-

erator described above, ordering them arbitrarily, and then joining them sequentially so that a single constraint connects one variable in one subproblem with one variable in the next.

50% Solvable Points for CSPs

All experiments reported in this paper were run with combinations of N, K, T and C that produces problem instances which are about 50% solvable (sometimes called the "cross-over" point). These combinations were determined empirically, and are reported in Fig. 1. To find cross-over points we selected values of N, K and T, and then varied C, generating 250 or more instances from each set of parameters until half of the problems had solutions. Sometimes no value of C resulted in exactly 50% satisfiable; for instance with $N = 50, K = 6, T = 12/36$ we found with $C = 194$ that 46% of the instances had solutions, while with $C = 193$ 54% did. In such cases we report the value of C that came closest to 50%.

For some settings of N, K and T, all values of C produce only satisfiable instances. Since generally there is an inverse relationship between T, the tightness of each constraint, and C, the number of constraints, this situation occurs when the constraints are so loose that even with C at its maximum value, $N * (N - 1)/2$, no unsatisfiable instances result. Our data indicate that this phenomenon only occurs at small values of N.

N	BT+MW	BJ+MW	BT+DVO	BJ+DVO
	K=3 T=1/9			
25	65,413	14,964	2,006	1,977
50	15,248,270	383,321	10,944	10,214
75		8,268,113	51,907	45,014
100		320,587,286	245,974	190,965
125			1,596,655	832,753
150			14,834,004	3,301,619
	K=3 T=2/9			
25	7,489	2,177	571	549
50	895,245	22,153	2,284	1,785
75		243,845	12,581	5,669
100		2,856,423	2,730,226	18,097
125			907,645	32,326
150			4,892,729	199,617
	K=3 T=3/9			
25	2,324	588	254	236
50	1,096,518	2,947	1,493	547
75		11,912	32,604	1,071
100		68,532	1,761,694	2,967
125		341,046		6,329
150		500,734		7,601
	K=3 T=4/9			
25	991	229	124	117
50	43,091,355	642	868	206
75		1,498	141,799	330
100		4,069	1,205,712	855
125		10,722		995
150		14,490		1,916
	K=9 T=9/81			
15	5,844	724	673	673
25	859,802	116,382	1,929	1,924
35		119,547,843	219,601	217,453
	K=9 T=18/81			
15	110,242	48,732	2,428	2,426
25	15,734,382	6,841,255	253,289	252,581
35		392,776,002	17,988,106	17,901,386
	K=9 T=27/81			
15	106,762	73,541	10,660	10,648
25	1,099,838	583,038	55,402	54,885
35		4,868,528	201,658	189,634

Figure 2: Comparison of backjumping and backtracking with min-width and dynamic variable ordering. Each number represents mean consistency checks over 1000 instances. The chart is blank where no experiments were conducted because the problems became too large for the algorithm.

We often found that the peak of difficulty, as measured by mean consistency checks or mean CPU time, is not exactly at the 50% point, but instead around the 10% to 30% solvable point, and the level of difficulty at this peak is about 5% to 10% higher than at the 50% point. We nevertheless decided to use the 50% satisfiable point, since it is algorithm independent. The precise value of C that produces the peak of difficulty can vary depending on algorithm, since some approaches handle satisfiable instances more efficiently.

In contrast to the findings of (Mitchell, Selman, &

Nodes	BT+MW	BJ+MW	BT+DVO	BJ+DVO
5	17,395,021	13,249	21,564	2,824
10		27,315	83,828	4,707
20		98,260	282,101	8,260
30		294,771	1,201,582	19,882

Figure 3: Comparison of backjumping and backtracking with min-width and dynamic variable ordering, using "chain" problems with 15-variable nodes. K=3, T=1/9, and $N = 15 *$ "Nodes". Each number represents mean consistency checks over 1000 instances.

Levesque 1992; Crawford & Auton 1983) for 3-SAT, we did not observe a precise linear relationship between the number of variables and the number of constraints (which are equivalent to clauses in CNF). The ratio of C to N appears to be asymptotically linear, but it is impossible to be certain of this from our data.

Static and Dynamic Variable Orderings

In our first set of experiments we wanted to assess the merits of static and dynamic variable orderings when used with backtracking and backjumping. As the data from Fig. 2 indicate, DVO prunes the search space so effectively that when using it the distinction between backtracking and backjumping is not significant until the number of variables becomes quite large. An exception to this general trend occurs when using backtracking with dynamic variable ordering on sparse graphs. For example, with $N = 100$, $K = 3$, and $T = 3/9$, C is set to 169, which creates a very sparse graph that occasionally consists of two or more disjoint sub-graphs. If one of the sub-graphs has no solution, backtracking will still explore its search space repeatedly while finding solutions to the other sub-graphs. Because backjumping jumps between connected variables, in effect it solves the disconnected sub-graphs separately, and if one of them has no solution the backjumping algorithm will halt once that search space is explored. Thus the data in Fig. 2 show that backtracking, even with dynamic variable ordering, can be extremely inefficient on large CSPs that may have disjoint sub-graphs.

T	C	C/2775	DVO single	MW jmp size
1/9	565	.204	68%	1.92
2/9	244	.088	39%	3.55
3/9	132	.048	27%	5.68
4/9	74	.027	16%	7.25

Figure 4: Data with $N = 75, K = 3$, drawn from the same experiments as in Fig. 2. The column "C/2775" indicates the ratio of constraints to the maximum possible for $N = 75$.

At large N, the combination of DVO and backjumping is particularly felicitous. Backjumping is more effective on sparser constraint graphs, since the average

K	N	T	Backtracking	Forward Checking
3	100	1/9	245,974	252,229
3	100	2/9	2,730,226	5,052,422
3	100	3/9	1,761,694	665,109
6	35	4/36	639,699	646,529
6	35	8/36	78,217	79,527
6	35	12/36	18,404	18,981
6	35	16/36	6,863	7,125
9	25	9/81	1,929	1,935
9	25	18/81	253,289	255,589
9	25	27/81	55,402	56,006
9	25	36/81	17,976	18,274

Figure 5: Comparison of backtracking and forward checking with DVO. Each number is the mean consistency checks over 1000 instances.

size of each "jump" increases with increasing sparseness. DVO, in contrast, tends to function better when there are many constraints, since each constraint provides information it can utilize in deciding on the next variable. We assessed this observation quantitatively by recording the frequency with which backjumping with DVO selected a variable that only had one remaining compatible value. This is the situation where DVO can most effectively prune the search space, since it is acting exactly like unit-propagation in boolean satisfiability problems, and making the forced choice of variable instantiation as early as possible. See Fig. 4, where the column labelled "DVO single" shows how likely DVO was to find a variable with one remaining consistent value, for one setting of N and K. The decreasing frequency of single-valued variables as the constraint graph becomes sparse indicates that DVO has to make a less-informed choice about the variable to choose next.

For the backjumping algorithm with a MW ordering we recorded the average size of the jump at a dead-end, that is, how many variables were passed over between the dead-end variable and the variable jumped back to. With backtracking this statistic would always be 1. This statistic is reported in the "MW jmp size" column in Fig. 4, and shows how backjumping jumps further on sparser graphs.

Dynamic variable order was somewhat less successful when applied to the chain type problems. With these structured problems we were able to experiment with much larger instances, up to 450 variables organized as thirty 15-variable nodes. The data in Fig. 3 show that backjumping was more effective on this type of problem than was DVO, and the combination of the two was over an order of magnitude better than either approach alone.

Forward Checking

A benefit of studying algorithms by observing their average-case behavior is that it is sometimes possible to determine which component of an algorithm is actually responsible for its performance. For instance, forward checking is often acclaimed as a particularly good algorithm (Nadel 1989). We note that it is possible to implement just part of forward checking as a variable ordering heuristic: if instantiating a variable with a certain value will cause a future variable to be a dead-end, then rearrange the variable ordering to make that future variable the next variable. The result is essentially backtracking with DVO. This method does not do all of forward checking, which would require rejecting the value that causes the future dead-end. In Fig. 5 we compare forward checking with backtracking, using DVO for both algorithms. The result is approximately equivalent performance. Thus we suggest that forward checking should be recognized more as a valuable variable ordering heuristic than as a powerful algorithm.

Backmarking and sticking values

The next set of experiments was designed to determine whether backmarking and sticking values, alone or in combination, could improve the performance of backjumping under a static min-width ordering. (We plan to report on backmarking and sticking values with dynamic variable ordering in future work.) Since backmarking and sticking values remember information about the history of the search in order to guide future search, we report on CPU time as well as consistency checks (see Fig. 6). Is the overhead of maintaining additional information less than the cost of the saved consistency checks? Only by examining CPU time can we really tell. We implemented all the algorithms and heuristics described in this paper in a single C program, with common data structures, subroutines, and programmer skill, so we believe comparing CPU times is meaningful, though not definitive.

Our experiments as summarized in Fig. 6 show that both backmarking and sticking values offer significant improvement when integrated with backjumping, usually reducing CPU time by a half or a third. As expected, the improvement in consistency checks is much greater, but both enhancements seem to be cost effective. Backmarking offers more improvement than does sticking values. Both techniques are more effective on the problems with smaller domain sizes; at $K = 9$ the benefit of sticking values in terms of reduced CPU time has almost disappeared. Backmarking helps backjumping over all the problem types we studied. The results from chain problems did not vary significantly from those of the unstructured problems.

4. Conclusions

We have several results from experimenting with larger and harder CSPs than have been reported before. Backjumping with dynamic variable ordering seems in general to be a powerful complete search algorithm. The two components complement each other, with backjumping stronger on sparser, more structured, and possibly disjoint graphs. We have shown that the

K	N	T	Consistency Checks				CPU Seconds			
			BJ	BJ+BM	BJ+ST	BJ+BM+ST	BJ	BJ+BM	BJ+ST	BJ+BM+ST
3	100	1/9	8,268,113	2,600,518	3,800,616	1,423,911	48.954	30.737	23.773	15.198
3	100	2/9	243,835	101,389	129,220	61,326	3.045	2.043	1.664	1.255
3	100	3/9	11,912	6,777	7,599	4,733	0.359	0.302	0.275	0.249
3	100	4/9	1,498	1,096	1,132	873	0.171	0.165	0.163	0.159
6	35	4/36	113,514,082	22,126,240	104,507,721	20,071,376	274.410	140.622	236.639	120.630
6	35	8/36	2,274,267	466,249	1,672,745	438,477	9.410	4.308	6.429	4.003
6	35	12/36	235,842	74,645	215,581	70,725	1.429	0.872	1.212	0.823
6	35	16/36	39,868	15,674	37,963	15,344	0.342	0.224	0.303	0.219
9	25	9/81	116,382	15,157	97,672	13,792	0.250	0.112	0.220	0.100
9	25	18/81	6,786,710	1,260,078	6,514,347	1,239,246	19.117	10.548	18.565	10.393
9	25	27/81	583,038	144,578	566,322	142,904	2.249	1,430	2.247	1.427
9	25	36/81	96,245	30,761	93,870	30,410	0.483	0.339	0.485	0.339
Chain problems with 30 nodes of 15 variables each.										
3	450	1/9	294,771	93,151	188,618	80,264	10.736	6.211	8.003	5.632

Figure 6: Results from experiments with backjumping, backmarking and sticking values. Each number is the mean of 1000 instances, and a min-width ordering was used throughout.

power of forward checking is mostly subsumed by a dynamic variable ordering heuristic. We have introduced a new value ordering heuristic called sticking values and shown that it can significantly improve backjumping when the variables' domains are relatively small. We have also shown that the backmarking technique can be applied to backjumping with good results over a wide range of problems.

One result visible in all our experiments is that among problems with a given number of variables, and drawn from the 50% satisfiable region, those with many loose constraints are much harder than those with fewer and tighter constraints. This is consistent with tightness properties shown in (van Beek & Dechter 1994). The pattern is not always observed for low values of N and T, since there may be no 50% region at all. We have also shown that the linear relationship between variables and clauses observed with boolean satisfiability problems at the cross-over point is not found with CSPs generated by our model.

References

Bitner, J. R., and Reingold, E. 1985. Backtrack programming techniques. *Communications of the ACM* 18:651–656.

Collin, Z.; Dechter, R.; and Katz, S. 1991. On the Feasibility of Distributed Constraint Satisfaction. In *Proceedings of the International Joint Conference on Artificial Intelligence*, 318–324.

Crawford, J. M., and Auton, L. D. 1983. Experimental results on the crossover point in satisfiability problems. In *Proceedings of the Eleventh National Conference on Artificial Intelligence*, 21–27.

Dechter, R. 1990. Enhancement Schemes for Constraint Processing: Backjumping, Learning, and Cutset Decomposition. *Artificial Intelligence* 41:273–312.

Even, S. 1979. *Graph Algorithms*. Maryland: Computer Science Press.

Freuder, E. C. 1982. A sufficient condition for backtrack-free search. *JACM* 21(11):958–965.

Gaschnig, J. 1979. Performance measurement and analysis of certain search algorithms. Technical Report CMU-CS-79-124, Carnegie Mellon University.

Haralick, R. M., and Elliott, G. L. 1980. Increasing Tree Search Efficiency for Constraint Satisfaction Problems. *Artificial Intelligence* 14:263–313.

Minton, S.; Johnson, M. D.; Phillips, A. B.; and Laird, P. 1992. Minimizing conflicts: a heuristic repair method for constraint satisfaction and scheduling problems. *Artificial Intelligence* 58(1–3):161–205.

Mitchell, D.; Selman, B.; and Levesque, H. 1992. Hard and Easy Distributions of SAT Problems. In *Proceedings of the Tenth National Conference on Artificial Intelligence*, 459–465.

Nadel, B. A. 1989. Constraint satisfaction algorithms. *Computational Intelligence* 5:188–224.

Prosser, P. 1983. BM + BJ = BMJ. In *Proceedings of the Ninth Conference on Artificial Intelligence for Applications*, 257–262.

Prosser, P. 1993. Hybrid Algorithms for the Constraint Satisfaction Problem. *Computational Intelligence* 9(3):268–299.

Purdom, P. W. 1983. Search Rearrangement Backtracking and Polynomial Average Time. *Artificial Intelligence* 21:117–133.

Selman, B.; Levesque, H.; and Mitchell, D. 1992. A New Method for Solving Hard Satisfiability Problems. In *Proceedings of the Tenth National Conference on Artificial Intelligence*, 440–446.

van Beek, P., and Dechter, R. 1994. Constraint tightness versus global consistency. In *Proc. of KR-94*.

Zabih, R., and McAllester, D. 1988. A Rearrangement Search Strategy for Determining Propositional Satisfiability. In *Proceedings of the Seventh National Conference on Artificial Intelligence*, 155–160.

Solution Reuse in Dynamic Constraint Satisfaction Problems

Gérard Verfaillie and **Thomas Schiex**
ONERA-CERT
2 avenue Edouard Belin, BP 4025
31055 Toulouse Cedex, France
{verfail,schiex}@cert.fr

Abstract

Many AI problems can be modeled as constraint satisfaction problems (CSP), but many of them are actually dynamic: the set of constraints to consider evolves because of the environment, the user or other agents in the framework of a distributed system. In this context, computing a new solution from scratch after each problem change is possible, but has two important drawbacks: inefficiency and instability of the successive solutions. In this paper, we propose a method for reusing any previous solution and producing a new one by *local changes* on the previous one. First we give the key idea and the corresponding algorithm. Then we establish its properties: termination, correctness and completeness. We show how it can be used to produce a solution, either from an empty assignment, or from any previous assignment and how it can be improved using filtering or learning methods, such as *forward-checking* or *nogood-recording*. Experimental results related to efficiency and stability are given, with comparisons with well known algorithms such as *backtrack*, *heuristic repair* or *dynamic backtracking*.

Problem description

Recently, much effort has been spent to increase the efficiency of the constraint satisfaction algorithms: filtering, learning and decomposition techniques, improved backtracking, use of efficient representations and heuristics ... This effort resulted in the design of constraint reasoning tools which were used to solve numerous real problems.

However all these techniques assume that the set of variables and constraints which compose the CSP is completely known and fixed. This is a strong limitation when dealing with real situations where the CSP under consideration may evolve because of:

- the *environment*: evolution of the set of tasks to be performed and/or of their execution conditions in scheduling applications;
- the *user*: evolution of the user requirements in the framework of an interactive design;
- other *agents* in the framework of a *distributed system*.

The notion of dynamic CSP (DCSP) (Dechter & Dechter 1988) has been introduced to represent such situations. A DCSP is a sequence of CSPs, where each one differs from the previous one by the addition or removal of some constraints. It is indeed easy to see that all the possible changes to a CSP (constraint or domain modifications, variable additions or removals) can be expressed in terms of constraint additions or removals.

To solve such a sequence of CSPs, it is always possible to solve each one from scratch, as it has been done for the first one. But this naive method, which remembers nothing from the previous reasoning, has two important drawbacks:

- *inefficiency*, which may be unacceptable in the framework of real time applications (planning, scheduling, etc.), where the time allowed for replanning is limited;
- *instability* of the successive solutions, which may be unpleasant in the framework of an interactive design or a planning activity, if some work has been started on the basis of the previous solution.

Existing methods

The existing methods can be classified in three groups:

- *heuristic* methods, which consist of using any previous consistent assignment (complete or not) as a heuristic in the framework of the current CSP (Hentenryck & Provost 1991);
- *local repair* methods, which consist of starting from any previous consistent assignment (complete or not) and of repairing it, using a sequence of local modifications (modifications of only one variable assignment) (Minton *et al.* 1992; Selman, Levesque, & Mitchell 1992; Ghedira 1993);
- *constraint recording* methods, which consist of recording any kind of constraint which can be deduced in the framework of a CSP and its justification, in order to reuse it in the framework of any new

CSP which includes this justification(de Kleer 1989; Hentenryck & Provost 1991; Schiex & Verfaillie 1993).

The methods of the first two groups aim at improving both efficiency and stability, whereas those of the last group only aim at improving efficiency. A little apart from the previous ones, a fourth group gathers methods which aim at minimizing the distance between successive solutions (Bellicha 1993).

Key idea

The proposed method originated in previous studies for the French Space Agency (CNES) (Badie & Verfaillie 1989) which aimed at designing a scheduling system for a remote sensing satellite (SPOT). In this problem, the set of tasks to be performed evolved each day because of the arrival of new tasks and the achievement of previous ones. One of the requirements was to disturb as little as possible the previous scheduling when entering a new task.

For solving such a problem, the following idea was used: it is possible to enter a new task t iff there exists for t a location such that all the tasks whose location is incompatible with t's location can be removed and entered again one after another, without modifying t's location.

In terms of CSP, the same idea can be expressed as follows: let us consider a binary CSP; let A be a consistent assignment of a subset V of the variables;[1] let v be a variable which does not belong to V; we can assign v i.e., obtain a consistent assignment of $V \cup \{v\}$ iff there exists a value val of v such that we can assign val to v, remove all the assignments (v', val') which are inconsistent with (v, val) and assign these unassigned variables again one after another, without modifying v's assignment. If the assignment $A \cup \{(v, val)\}$ is consistent, there is no variable to unassign and the solution is immediate. Note that it is only for the sake of simplicity that we consider here a binary CSP. As we will see afterwards, the proposed method deals with general n-ary CSPs.

With such a method, for which we use the name *local changes* (*lc*) and which clearly belongs to the second group (*local repair* methods), solving a CSP looks like solving a *fifteen puzzle* problem: a sequence of variable assignment changes which allows any consistent assignment to be extended to a larger consistent one.

Algorithm

The corresponding algorithm can be described as follows:

$lc(csp)$
    return $lc\text{-}variables(\emptyset, \emptyset, variables(csp))$

---

[1] An assignment A of a subset of the CSP variables is consistent iff all the constraints assigned by A are satisfied; a constraint c is assigned by an assignment A iff all its variables are assigned by A.

$lc\text{-}variables(V_1, V_2, V_3)$
; V_1 is a set of assigned and fixed variables
; V_2 is a set of assigned and not fixed variables
; V_3 is a set of unassigned variables
    if $V_3 = \emptyset$
    then return *success*
    else let v be a variable chosen in V_3
        let d be its domain
        if $lc\text{-}variable(V_1, V_2, v, d) = failure$
        then return *failure*
        else return $lc\text{-}variables(V_1, V_2 \cup \{v\}, V_3 - \{v\})$

$lc\text{-}variable(V_1, V_2, v, d)$
    if $d = \emptyset$
    then return *failure*
    else let val be a value chosen in d
        $save\text{-}assignments(V_2)$
        $assign\text{-}variable(v, val)$
        if $lc\text{-}value(V_1, V_2, v, val) = success$
        then return *success*
        else $unassign\text{-}variable(v)$
            $restore\text{-}assignments(V_2)$
            return $lc\text{-}variable(V_1, V_2, v, d - \{val\})$

$lc\text{-}value(V_1, V_2, v, val)$
    let be $A_1 = assignment(V_1)$
    let be $A_{12} = assignment(V_1 \cup V_2)$
    if $A_1 \cup \{(v, val)\}$ is inconsistent
    then return *failure*
    else if $A_{12} \cup \{(v, val)\}$ is consistent
        then return *success*
        else let V_3 a non empty subset of V_2 such that
            let $A_{123} = assignment(V_1 \cup V_2 - V_3)$
            $A_{123} \cup \{(v, val)\}$ is consistent
            $unassign\text{-}variables(V_3)$
            return $lc\text{-}variables(V_1 \cup \{v\}, V_2 - V_3, V_3)$

Properties

Let us consider the following theorems:

Theorem 1 *If the CSP csp is consistent (resp. inconsistent), the procedure call lc(csp) returns success (resp. failure); in case of success, the result is a consistent assignment of csp's variables.*

Theorem 2 *Let V_1 and V_2 be two disjunct sets of assigned variables and let V_3 be a set of unassigned variables; let be $V = V_1 \cup V_2 \cup V_3$; let be $A_1 = assignment(V_1)$; if there exists (resp. does not exist) a consistent assignment A of V, such that $A\downarrow_{V_1} = A_1$, the procedure call lc-variables(V_1, V_2, V_3) returns success (resp. failure);[2] in case of success, the result is a consistent assignment of V.*

Theorem 3 *Let V_1 and V_2 be two disjunct sets of assigned variables; let v be an unassigned variable; let d be its domain; let be $V = V_1 \cup V_2 \cup \{v\}$; let be*

---

[2] Let A be an assignment of a subset V of the CSP variables and V' be a subset of V; the notation $A\downarrow_{V'}$ designates the restriction of A to V'.

$A_1 = assignment(V_1)$; *if there exists (resp. does not exist) a consistent assignment A of V, such that $A \downarrow_{V_1} = A_1$, the procedure call lc-variable(V_1, V_2, v, d) returns success (resp. failure); in case of success, the result is a consistent assignment of V.*

Theorem 4 *Let V_1 and V_2 be two disjunct sets of variables; let v be an unassigned variable; let val be one of its possible values; let be $V = V_1 \cup V_2 \cup \{v\}$; let be $A_1 = assignment(V_1)$; if there exists (resp. does not exist) a consistent assignment A of V, such that $A \downarrow_{V_1 \cup \{v\}} = A_1 \cup \{(v, val)\}$, the procedure call lc-value(V_1, V_2, v, val) returns success (resp. failure); in case of success, the result is a consistent assignment of V.*

Theorem 1 expresses the *termination, correctness* and *completeness* properties of the algorithm. Theorems 2, 3, 4 express the same properties for the procedures *lc-variables, lc-variable* and *lc-value*.

It is easy to show that Theorem 1 (resp. 2 and 3) is a straigthforward consequence of Theorem 2 (resp. 3 and 4).

Let us consider the set V_{23} of the not fixed variables ($V_{23} = V_2 \cup V_3$ for the procedure *lc-variables*, $V_{23} = V_2 \cup \{v\}$ for the procedures *lc-variable* and *lc-value*). It is just as easy to show that, if Theorem 3 (resp. Theorem 4) holds when $|V_{23}| < k$, then Theorem 2 (resp. Theorem 3) holds under the same condition.

Let us now use an induction on the cardinal of V_{23} to prove Theorems 2, 3 and 4.

Let us assume that $|V_{23}| = 1$ and let us prove Theorem 4 in this case. Let us consider a procedure call *lc-value*$(V_1, \emptyset, v, val)$:

- let us assume that there exists a consistent assignment A of V, such that $A\downarrow_{V_1 \cup \{v\}} = A_1 \cup \{(v, val)\}$; since $V = V_1 \cup \{v\}$, $A_1 \cup \{(v, val)\}$ and $A_{12} \cup \{(v, val)\}$ are equal and consistent and the procedure returns *success*; the resulting assignment $A_1 \cup \{(v, val)\}$ of V is consistent;

- let us now assume that there exists no consistent assignment A of V, such that $A \downarrow_{V_1 \{v\}} = A_1 \cup \{(v, val)\}$; since $V = V_1 \cup \{v\}$, $A_1 \cup \{(v, val)\}$ is inconsistent and the procedure returns *failure*.

Theorem 4, and consequently Theorem 3 and 2 are proven in this particular case.

Let us assume that Theorems 2, 3 and 4 hold when $|V_{23}| < k$ and let us prove that they hold when $|V_{23}| = k$.

Let us first consider Theorem 4 and a procedure call *lc-value*(V_1, V_2, v, val), with $|V_2| = k - 1$. Let us note that, when the procedure *lc-variables* is recursively called, its arguments satisfy the following relations: $V_2' \cup V_3' = V_2$ ($|V_{23}'| = k - 1$) and $V_1' \cup V_2' \cup V_3' = V_1 \cup V_2 \cup \{v\} = V$. This allows us to use the induction assumption:

- let us assume that there exists a consistent assignment A of V, such that $A\downarrow_{V_1 \{v\}} = A_1 \cup \{(v, val)\}$;

since $A_1 \cup \{(v, val)\}$ is consistent, the procedure does not immediately return *failure*; either $A_{12} \cup \{(v, val)\}$ is consistent and the procedure returns immediately *success*, with a consistent assignment of V, or it is not and:

- there exists a non empty subset V_3 of V_2 such that $A_{123} \cup \{(v, val)\}$ is consistent: for example, V_2;

- whatever the set chosen for V_3, the call to *lc-variables* returns *success* with a consistent assignment of V, according to the induction assumption;

- let us now assume that there exists no consistent assignment A of V, such that $A \downarrow_{V_1 \cup \{v\}} = A_1 \cup \{(v, val)\}$; since $A_{12} \cup \{(v, val)\}$ is inconsistent, the procedure does not immediately return *success*; either $A_1 \cup \{(v, val)\}$ is inconsistent and the procedure returns immediately *failure*, or it is not and:

- there exists a non empty subset V_3 of V_2 such that $A_{123} \cup \{(v, val)\}$ is consistent: for example, V_2;

- whatever the set chosen for V_3, the call to *lc-variables* returns *failure*, according to the induction assumption.

Theorem 4 and consequently Theorems 3 and 4 are proven, when $|V_{23}| = k$. They are therefore proven whatever the cardinal of V_{23}. That allows us to conclude that Theorem 1 is proven *i.e.*, that the algorithm described above ends, is correct and complete.

Practical use

From a practical point of view, the problem is now to choose a set V_3 that is as small as possible, in order to reduce the number of variables that need to be unassigned and subsequently reassigned.

In the general case of n-ary CSPs, a simple method consists of choosing one variable to be unassigned for each constraint which is unsatisfied by the assignment $A_{12} \cup \{(v, val)\}$. The resulting assignment $A_{123} \cup \{(v, val)\}$ is consistent, since all the previously unsatisfied constraints are no longer assigned, but we have no guarantee that the resulting set V_3 is one of the smallest ones. Note that it does not modify the termination, correctness and completeness properties of the algorithm. It may only alter its results in terms of efficiency and stability. We did not compare the cost of searching for one of the smallest sets of variables to be unassigned with the resulting saving.

In the particular case of binary CSPs, a simpler method consists of unassigning each variable whose assignment is inconsistent with (v, val). The resulting set V_3 is the smallest one.

It is important to note that this algorithm is able to solve any CSP, either starting from an empty assignment (from scratch), or starting from any previous assignment. The description above (see *Algorithm*) corresponds to the first situation. In the second one, if A is the starting assignment, then the first step consists of producing a consistent assignment A' that is included in A and as large as possible. The method presented above can be used. If V_2 (resp. V_3) is the resulting set of assigned (resp. unassigned) variables, the CSP can be solved using the procedure call *lc-variables*$(\emptyset, V_2, V_3)$ (no fixed variable).

Comparisons and improvements

The resulting algorithm is related to the *backjumping* (Dechter 1990; Prosser 1993), *intelligent backtracking* (Bruynooghe 1981), *dynamic backtracking* (Ginsberg 1993) and *heuristic repair* (Minton *et al.* 1992) algorithms, but is nevertheless different from each of them. Like the first one, it avoids useless backtracking on choices which are not involved in the current conflict. Like the following two ones, it avoids, when backtracking, undoing choices which are not involved in the current conflict. Like the last one, it allows the search to be started from any previous assignment. But *backjumping*, *intelligent* and *dynamic backtracking* are not built for dealing with dynamic CSPs, and *heuristic repair* uses the usual backtracking mechanism. Finally, *local changes* combines the advantages of an efficient backtracking mechanism with an ability to start the search from any previous assignment.

Moreover, it can be improved, without any problem, by using any filtering or learning method, such as *forward-checking* or *nogood-recording* (Schiex & Verfaillie 1993). The only difference is the following one: for *backtrack*, *forward-checking* and *nogood-recording* are applied from the assigned variables; for *local changes*, as for *heuristic repair*, they are applied from the assigned and fixed variables. Note that the combination of *local changes* and *nogood-recording* is an example of solution and reasoning reuse.

Experiments

In order to provide useful comparisons, eight algorithms have been implemented on the basis of the following four basic algorithms: *backtrack* (*bt*), *dynamic backtracking* (*dbt*), *heuristic repair* (*hrp*) and *local changes* (*lc*), using *conflict directed backjumping* (*cbj*) and *backward* (*bc*) or *forward-checking* (*fc*): *bt-cbj-bc*, *bt-cbj-fc*, *dbt-bc*, *dbt-fc*, *hrp-cbj-bc*, *hrp-cbj-fc*, *lc-bc* and *lc-fc*.

Each time there is no ambiguity, we will use the abbreviations *bt*, *dbt*, *hrp* and *lc* to designate these algorithms. Note that *dbt* and *lc* can not be improved by *cbj*, because they already use a more powerful *backtracking* mechanism.

Heuristics

For each algorithm, we used the following simple yet efficient heuristics:

- choice of the *variable* to be assigned, unassigned or reassigned: choose the variable whose domain is the smallest one;

- choice of the *value*:
  - for *bt* and *dbt*: first use the value the variable had in the previous solution, if it exists;
  - for *hrp* and *lc*: choose the value which minimizes the number of unsatisfied constraints.

In the case of *bt*, *dbt* and *hrp*, the previous solution is recorded, if it exists. In the case of *bt* and *dbt*, it is used in the framework of the choice of the value. In the case of *hrp*, it is used as a starting assignment. In the case of *lc*, the greatest consistent assignment previously found (a solution if the previous problem is consistent) is also recorded and used as a starting assignment.

For the four algorithms, two trivial cases are solved without any search: the previous CSP is consistent (resp. inconsistent) and there is no added (resp. removed) constraint.

CSP generation

Following (Hubbe & Freuder 1992), we randomly generated a set of problems where:

- the number nv of variables is equal to 15;

- for each variable, the cardinality of its domain is randomly generated between 6 and 16;

- all the constraints are binary;

- the connectivity *con* of the constraint graph *i.e.*, the ratio between the number of constraints and the number of possible constraints, takes five possible values: 0.2, 0.4, 0.6, 0.8 and 1;

- the mean tightness *mt* of the constraints *i.e.*, the mean ratio between the number of forbidden pairs of values and the number of possible pairs of values, takes five possible values: 0.1, 0.3, 0.5, 0.7 and 0.9; for a given value of *mt*, the tightness of each constraint is randomly generated between $mt - 0.1$ and $mt + 0.1$.

- the size *ch* of the changes *i.e.*, the ratio between the number of additions or removals and the number of constraints, takes six possible values: 0.01, 0.02, 0.04, 0.08 and 0.16 et 0.32.

For each of the 25 possible pairs (con, mt), 5 problems were generated. For each of the 125 resulting initial problems and for each of the 6 possible values of *ch*, a sequence of 10 changes was generated, with the same probability for additions and removals.

Measures

In terms of efficiency, the three usual measures were performed: number of *nodes*, number of *constraint checks* and *cpu time*. In terms of stability, the *distance* between two successive solutions *i.e.*, the number of variables which are differently assigned in both solutions, was measured each time both exist.

nv = 15, 6 ≤ dom ≤ 16, ch = 0.04
number of constraint checks

backward checking

mt	0.1			0.3			0.5			0.7			0.9		
con															
0.2	c	bt	12	c	bt	10	c	bt	127	ci	bt	21 954	i	bt	96
		hrp	13		hrp	11		hrp	24		hrp	30 330		hrp	3 862
		dbt	12		dbt	10		**dbt**	23		dbt	2 508		dbt	21
		lc	3		**lc**	4		lc	27		**lc**	248		**lc**	6
0.4	c	bt	32	c	bt	84	ci	bt	21 536	i	bt	788	i	bt	297
		hrp	33		hrp	61		hrp	100 752		hrp	110 240		hrp	10 263
		dbt	32		dbt	45		dbt	11 020		**dbt**	326		dbt	95
		lc	8		**lc**	39		**lc**	6257		lc	471		**lc**	49
0.6	c	bt	56	c	bt	518	i	bt	29 601	i	bt	3 189	i	**bt**	5
		hrp	57		hrp	472		hrp	159 511		hrp	27 617		hrp	2 050
		dbt	56		dbt	104		**dbt**	8 050		**dbt**	802		**dbt**	5
		lc	19		**lc**	89		lc	17 399		lc	941		lc	8
0.8	c	bt	75	c	bt	13 558	i	bt	2 777	i	bt	72	i	bt	8
		hrp	63		hrp	81 291		hrp	125 966		hrp	10 046		hrp	2 161
		dbt	68		**dbt**	5 126		**dbt**	1 235		**dbt**	57		dbt	7
		lc	25		lc	10 591		lc	1 470		lc	131		**lc**	3
1	c	**bt**	0	ci	bt	45 179	i	bt	1 424	i	bt	370	i	bt	16
		hrp	0		hrp	469 701		hrp	110 541		hrp	3 459		hrp	234
		dbt	0		**dbt**	19 265		**dbt**	805		**dbt**	171		dbt	8
		lc	0		lc	132 203		lc	3 500		lc	181		**lc**	7

forward checking

mt	0.1			0.3			0.5			0.7			0.9		
con															
0.2	c	bt	144	c	bt	92	c	bt	104	ci	bt	386	i	bt	24
		hrp	16		**hrp**	15		**hrp**	40		hrp	2 591		hrp	11
		dbt	144		dbt	93		dbt	106		dbt	257		dbt	17
		lc	23		lc	21		lc	45		**lc**	113		**lc**	3
0.4	c	bt	346	c	bt	254	ci	**bt**	1 245	i	bt	260	i	bt	29
		hrp	39		**hrp**	63		hrp	6 732		hrp	2 850		hrp	69
		dbt	346		dbt	261		dbt	1 554		**dbt**	233		dbt	29
		lc	75		lc	104		lc	1 953		lc	275		**lc**	27
0.6	c	bt	548	c	bt	321	i	**bt**	2 336	i	bt	316	i	bt	11
		hrp	70		**hrp**	191		hrp	12 392		hrp	1 253		hrp	348
		dbt	548		dbt	341		dbt	2 749		**dbt**	314		dbt	11
		lc	143		lc	205		lc	5 526		lc	468		**lc**	7
0.8	c	bt	558	c	**bt**	1 379	i	bt	987	i	bt	185	i	bt	15
		hrp	76		hrp	6 791		hrp	6 521		hrp	562		hrp	7
		dbt	564		dbt	1 761		dbt	858		dbt	169		dbt	15
		lc	185		lc	2 081		**lc**	757		**lc**	100		**lc**	2
1	c	**bt**	0	ci	**bt**	8 092	i	bt	1 857	i	bt	279	i	bt	28
		hrp	0		hrp	98 755		hrp	4 772		hrp	746		hrp	53
		dbt	0		dbt	10 573		dbt	1 687		dbt	281		dbt	28
		lc	0		lc	37 891		**lc**	1 373		**lc**	124		**lc**	6

Results

The two tables above show the mean number of *constraint checks*, when solving dynamic problems with changes of intermediate size (*ch* = 0.04). The first one show the results obtained when using *backward-checking*: *bt-cbj-bc*, *dbt-bc*, *hrp-cbj-bc* and *lc-bc*. The second one show the same results obtained when using *forward-checking*: *bt-cbj-fc*, *dbt-fc*, *hrp-cbj-fc* and *lc-fc*.

At the top left corner of each cell, a letter *c* (resp. *i*) means that all the problems are consistent (resp. inconsistent). Two letters (*ci*) mean that some of them are consistent and the others inconsistent. The less (resp. more) constrained problems, with small (resp. large) values for *con* and *mt i.e.*, with few loose (resp. many tight) constraints, are in the top left (resp. bottom right) of each table.

Each number is the mean value of a set of 50 results (5 ∗ 10 dynamic problems). In each cell, the algorithm(s) which provides the best result is(are) pointed out in bold.

Analysis

As it has been previously observed (Cheeseman, Kanefsky, & Taylor 1991), the hardest problems are neither the least constrained (solution quickly found), nor the most constrained (inconsistency quickly established), but the intermediate ones, for them it is difficult to establish the consistency or the inconsistency.

If we consider the first table, with *backward-checking*, we can see that:

- *hrp* is efficient on the least constrained problems, but inefficient and sometimes very inefficient on the others;

- *dbt* is always better than *bt* and the best one on the intermediate problems;

- *lc* is almost always better than *hrp* and the best one, both on the least constrained problems and the most constrained ones; it is better on loosely connected problems than on the others; it is nevertheless inefficient on intermediate strongly connected problems.

If we consider the second table, with *forward-checking*, the previous lessons must be modified, because *forward-checking* benefits *bt* and *hrp* more than *dbt* and *lc* (the number of constraint checks is roughly divided by 12 for *bt* and *hrp*, by 3 for *dbt* and *lc*):

- *hrp* becomes the best one on the least constrained problems;

- *bt* and *dbt* are the best ones on the intermediate ones;

- *lc* remains the best one on the most constrained ones.

Note that these results might be different in case of *n*-ary constraints on which *forward-checking* is less efficient.

We do not show any results related to the *cpu time* because number of *constraint checks* and *cpu time* are strongly correlated, in spite of a little overhead for *hrp* and *lc* (around 850 constraint checks per second for *bt* and *dbt*, around 650 for *hrp* and *lc*; this aspect depends widely on the implementation).

More surprising, the four algorithms provide very similar results in terms of *distance* between successive solutions. It seems to be the result of the mechanisms of each algorithm and of the heuristics used to choose the value.

Note finally that, although *hrp* and *lc* provide better results with small changes than with large ones, the results obtained with other change sizes do not modify the previous lessons.

Conclusion

Although other experiments are needed to confirm it, we believe that the proposed method may be very convenient for solving large problems, involving binary and *n*-ary constraints, often globally underconstrained and subject to frequent and relatively small changes, such as many real scheduling problems.

Acknowlegments

This work was supported both by the French Space Agency (CNES) and the French Ministry of Defence (DGA-DRET) and was done both at ONERA-CERT (France) and at the University of New Hampshire (USA). We are indebted to P.Hubbe, R.Turner and J. Weiner for helping us to improve this paper and to E. Freuder and R. Wallace for useful discussions.

References

Badie, C., and Verfaillie, G. 1989. OSCAR ou Comment Planifier Intelligemment des Missions Spatiales. In *Proc. of the 9th International Avignon Workshop*.

Bellicha, A. 1993. Maintenance of Solution in a Dynamic Constraint Satisfaction Problem. In *Proc. of Applications of Artificial Intelligence in Engineering VIII*, 261–274.

Bruynooghe, M. 1981. Solving Combinatorial Search Problems by Intelligent Backtracking. *Information Processing Letters* 12(1):36–39.

Cheeseman, P.; Kanefsky, B.; and Taylor, W. 1991. Where the *really* Hard Problems Are. In *Proc. of the 12th IJCAI*, 294–299.

de Kleer, J. 1989. A Comparison of ATMS and CSP Techniques. In *Proc. of the 11th IJCAI*, 290–296.

Dechter, R., and Dechter, A. 1988. Belief Maintenance in Dynamic Constraint Networks. In *Proc. of AAAI-88*, 37–42.

Dechter, R. 1990. Enhancement Schemes for Constraint Processing : Backjumping, Learning and Cutset Decomposition. *Artificial Intelligence* 41(3):273–312.

Ghedira, K. 1993. *MASC : une Approche Multi-Agent des Problèmes de Satisfaction de Contraintes*. Thèse de doctorat, ENSAE, Toulouse, France.

Ginsberg, M. 1993. Dynamic Backtracking. *Journal of Artificial Intelligence Research* 1:25–46.

Hentenryck, P. V., and Provost, T. L. 1991. Incremental Search in Constraint Logic Programming. *New Generation Computing* 9:257–275.

Hubbe, P., and Freuder, E. 1992. An Efficient Cross-Product Representation of the Constraint Satisfaction Problem Search Space. In *Proc. of AAAI-92*, 421–427.

Minton, S.; Johnston, M.; Philips, A.; and Laird, P. 1992. Minimizing Conflicts: a Heuristic Repair Method for Constraint Satisfaction and Scheduling Problems. *Artificial Intelligence* 58:160–205.

Prosser, P. 1993. Hybrid Algorithms for the Constraint Satisfaction Problem. *Computational Intelligence* 9(3):268–299.

Schiex, T., and Verfaillie, G. 1993. Nogood Recording for Static and Dynamic CSP. In *Proc. of the 5th IEEE International Conference on Tools with Artificial Intelligence*.

Selman, B.; Levesque, H.; and Mitchell, D. 1992. A New Method for Solving Hard Satisfiability Problems. In *Proc. of AAAI-92*, 440–446.

Weak-commitment Search for Solving Constraint Satisfaction Problems

Makoto Yokoo
NTT Communication Science Laboratories
2-2 Hikaridai, Seika-cho, Soraku-gun, Kyoto 619-02 Japan
yokoo@cslab.kecl.ntt.jp

Abstract

The min-conflict heuristic (Minton *et al.* 1992) has been introduced into backtracking algorithms and iterative improvement algorithms as a powerful heuristic for solving constraint satisfaction problems. Backtracking algorithms become inefficient when a bad partial solution is constructed, since an exhaustive search is required for revising the bad decision. On the other hand, iterative improvement algorithms do not construct a consistent partial solution and can revise a bad decision without exhaustive search. However, most of the powerful heuristics obtained through the long history of constraint satisfaction studies (e.g., forward checking (Haralick & Elliot 1980)) presuppose the existence of a consistent partial solution. Therefore, these heuristics can not be applied to iterative improvement algorithms. Furthermore, these algorithms are not theoretically complete.

In this paper, a new algorithm called *weak-commitment* search which utilizes the min-conflict heuristic is developed. This algorithm removes the drawbacks of backtracking algorithms and iterative improvement algorithms, i.e., the algorithm can revise bad decisions without exhaustive search, the completeness of the algorithm is guaranteed, and various heuristics can be introduced since a consistent partial solution is constructed. The experimental results on various example problems show that this algorithm is 3 to 10 times more efficient than other algorithms.

Introduction

A Constraint Satisfaction Problem (CSP) is a general framework that can formalize various problems in AI, and many theoretical and experimental studies have been performed (Mackworth 1992). Recently, the min-conflict heuristic (Minton *et al.* 1992) has been identified as a powerful heuristic for finding one solution of a CSP. This heuristic can be described as follows: when deciding a variable value, it chooses the value that minimizes the number of constraint violations between other variables. This heuristic has been applied to backtracking algorithms (Minton *et al.* 1992) and iterative improvement algorithms (Minton *et al.* 1992; Morris 1993).

In backtracking algorithms, a consistent partial solution is constructed for a subset of variables, and this partial solution is extended by adding variables one by one until a complete solution is found. In the backtracking algorithm that incorporates the min-conflict heuristic (min-conflict backtracking), all variables are given tentative initial values. When a variable is added to the partial solution, its tentative initial value is revised so that the new value satisfies all constraints between the partial solution, and satisfies as many constraints between variables that are not included in the partial solution as possible.

The drawback of backtracking algorithms is as follows.

- **One mistake in the value selection is fatal.** In min-conflict backtracking, the partial solution constructed during the search process will not be revised unless it is proven that there exists no complete solution subsuming the partial solution. If the algorithm makes a bad selection of a variable value, the algorithm must perform an exhaustive search for the partial solution in order to revise the bad decision. When the problem becomes very large, doing such an exhaustive search is virtually impossible.

On the other hand, iterative improvement algorithms (Minton *et al.* 1992; Morris 1993; Selman, Levesque, & Mitchell 1992) do not construct a consistent partial solution. In these algorithms, a *flawed* solution containing some constraint violations is revised by local changes until all constraints are satisfied. The min-conflict heuristic is used as the basis for the local changes. In these algorithms, the value of one variable can be changed repeatedly without any exhaustive search. Therefore, one mistake in the value selection is not fatal and can be revised easily. However, the iterative improvement algorithms have the following drawbacks.

- **The completeness of the algorithms can not be guaranteed.** We say that an algorithm is complete if the algorithm is guaranteed to find one solution eventually when solutions exist; and when there exists no solution, the algorithm is guaranteed to find out the fact that there exists no solution and terminate. One exception is the fill algorithm (Morris 1993), which is guaranteed to find a solution if there exists one. However, this algorithm is far less efficient than a similar incomplete algorithm called the breakout algorithm (Morris 1993). Also, the fill algorithm will not terminate when there exists no solution.

- **Introducing other heuristics is difficult.** The completeness of the algorithms may have only theoretical importance when solving large-scale problems. A more practical drawback is that we can not apply most of the powerful heuristics obtained through the long history of constraint satisfaction studies (e.g., forward checking (Haralick & Elliot 1980)) to iterative improvement algorithms, since these heuristics presuppose the existence of a consistent partial solution.

In this paper, a new algorithm called *weak-commitment* search which utilizes the min-conflict heuristic is developed. In this algorithm, all variables are given tentative initial values, and variables are added one by one to the consistent partial solution as in the min-conflict backtracking. This algorithm constructs a consistent partial solution, but commits to the partial solution *weakly*, in contrast to backtracking algorithms which never abandon a partial solution unless it turns out to be hopeless. Namely, this algorithm commits to the partial solution as long as it can be extended. However, when there exists no value for one variable that satisfies all constraints between the partial solution, this algorithm abandons the whole partial solution, and starts constructing a new partial solution from scratch, using the current value assignment as new tentative initial values.

This algorithm removes the drawbacks of backtracking algorithms and iterative improvement algorithms, i.e., the algorithm can revise bad decisions without exhaustive search, the completeness of the algorithm is guaranteed, and various heuristics can be introduced since a consistent partial solution is constructed.

In the following, we give a brief description of the CSP, and describe the weak-commitment search algorithm. Then, we show several empirical results indicating the efficiency of this algorithm. Furthermore, we examine the algorithm complexity and show a probabilistic model of the min-conflict backtracking and the weak-commitment search.

Constraint Satisfaction Problem

A constraint satisfaction problem can be described as follows. There exist n variables $x_1, x_2, ..., x_n$, each of which takes its value from a finite, discrete domain $D_1, D_2, ..., D_n$, respectively. There also exists a set of constraints. In this paper, we assume that a constraint is represented as a *nogood*, i.e., a combination of variable values that is prohibited[1]. We represent the fact that variable x_i's value is d_i as a tuple (x_i, d_i). A constraint $\{(x_i, d_i), (x_j, d_j)\}$ means that the combination of $x_i = d_i$ and $x_j = d_j$ is prohibited. A solution of a CSP is the value assignment of all variables that satisfies all constraints, i.e., the assignment that is not a superset of any nogood.

Weak-commitment Search Algorithm

The weak-commitment search algorithm is illustrated in Figure 1. Initially, *vars-left* is set to $\{(x_1, d_1), (x_2, d_2), ..., (x_n, d_n)\}$, where d_i is the tentative initial value of x_i. Also, *partial-solution* is assigned to an empty set. This algorithm moves variables from *vars-left* to *partial-solution* one by one.

The essential difference between this algorithm and the min-conflict backtracking is the shaded part in Figure 1. In min-conflict backtracking, backtracking is performed at this part and the most-recently added variable is removed from the partial solution. In weak-commitment search, the whole partial solution is abandoned, i.e., all elements of *partial-solution* are moved to *vars-left*. Then, the search process is restarted using the current value assignment as new tentative initial values. It must be noted that not all variable values in the partial solution will be revised again. Since the algorithm revises only the constraint violating variables, the variables that already satisfy all constraints will not be revised again.

This algorithm records the abandoned partial solutions in *nogoods* as new constraints, and avoids creating the same partial solution that has been created and abandoned before. Therefore, the completeness of the algorithm (always finds a solution if one exists, and terminates if no solution exists) is guaranteed.

In Ginsberg & Harvey (1990), a backtrack-based algorithm called the *iterative broadening* algorithm is presented. This algorithm avoids strong commitments and revises bad decisions without exhaustive search. The weak-commitment algorithm is similar to the iterative broadening algorithm where the search width is set to 1. However, the iterative broadening algorithm iteratively widens the search width if the trial employing the initial width fails. On the other hand, the weak-commitment search algorithm restarts the search process without changing the search width.

We show an example of algorithm execution using the well-known n-queens problem, placing n queens on an $n \times n$ chess board so that these queens will not threaten each other. In this example, we use the 4-queens problem. This problem can be formalized as a CSP where each variable represents the position of

---

[1] In general, a constraint is represented as an *allowed* combination of variable values. In this paper, we use the opposite representation since this representation is convenient for treating an abandoned partial solution as a new constraint. This choice of representation is inessential and does not affect the evaluation results in this paper.

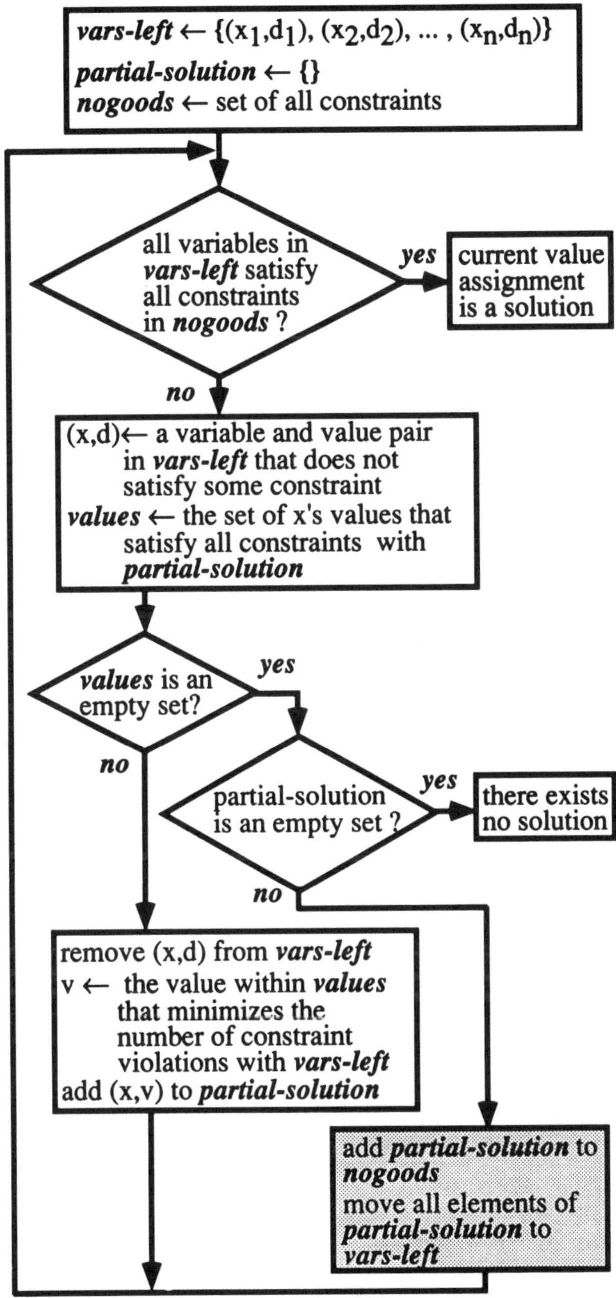

Figure 1: Weak-commitment search algorithm

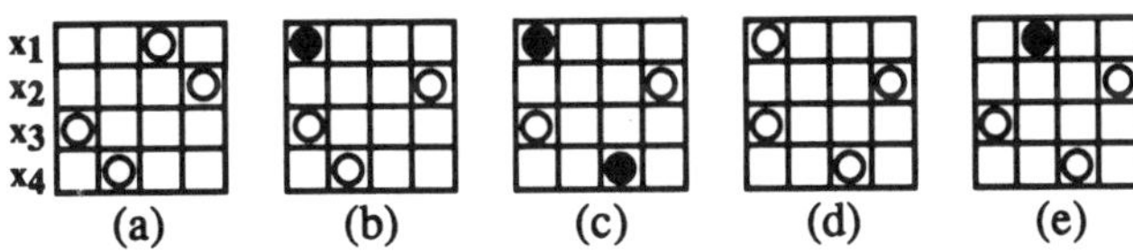

Figure 2: Example of algorithm execution

a queen in each row, and the domain of a variable is {1,2,3,4}. The initial state is illustrated in Figure 2(a). The algorithm first revises the position of the first queen (Figure 2(b)), then revises the position of the fourth queen (Figure 2(c)). A queen whose position is revised is added to *partial-solution*. We represent a queen in *partial-solution* as a filled circle. In Figure 2(c), there exists no consistent position with *partial-solution* for the third queen. Therefore, the whole *partial-solution* is abandoned (Figure 2(d)). The algorithm revises the position of the first queen again (Figure 2(e)). Consequently, all constraints are satisfied.

Evaluations

In this section, we compare the weak-commitment search, the min-conflict backtracking, and an iterative improvement algorithm by experiments on typical examples of CSPs (n-queens, graph-coloring, and 3-SAT problem).

We use the breakout algorithm (Morris 1993) as the representative for iterative improvement algorithms. This algorithm has a notable feature in that it does not stop at local minima, and has been shown to be more efficient than other iterative improvement algorithms (Morris 1993). However, this algorithm is not complete, i.e., the algorithm can fall into an infinite processing loop.

We measure the number of required steps and the number of consistency checks. Each change of one variable value, each backtracking, and each restarting is counted as one step. Also, one consistency check represents the check of one combination of variable values among which a constraint exists[2]. The number of consistency checks is widely used as a machine-independent measure for constraint satisfaction algorithms. For all three algorithms, in order to reduce unnecessary consistency checks, the result of consistency checks at the previous step is recorded and only the difference is calculated in each step.

In order to terminate the experiments in a reasonable amount of time, the maximum number of steps is limited to 5000, and we interrupt any trial that exceeds this limit. For an interrupted trial, we count the number of required steps as 5000, and use the number of consistency checks performed until the interruption for the evaluation.

n-queens

The first example problem is the n-queens problem described in the previous section. We show the ratio of successful trials (trials finished within the limit), the number of required steps, and the number of consistency checks for n=10, 50, 100 in Table 1. We run 100 trials with different initial values and show the

---

[2]The number of checks for newly added constraints (abandoned partial solutions) is also included.

n	weak-commitment			min-conflict BT			breakout		
	ratio	steps	checks	ratio	steps	checks	ratio	steps	checks
10	100%	29.7	2292.8	100%	240.7	15482.2	100%	41.7	7065.0
50	100%	23.9	48593.5	97%	264.5	300175.0	100%	37.9	180393.5
100	100%	27.1	236821.7	99%	76.4	912465.1	100%	38.9	777051.1

Table 1: Comparison on n-queens

n	ratio of trials with BT	weak-commitment	min-conflict BT
10	80%	35.9	299.7
50	17%	58.2	1473.4
100	2%	96.5	2563.5

Table 2: Required steps for trials with backtracking/restarting

average[3]. These initial values are generated by the greedy method described in Minton *et al.* (1992).

As shown in Table 1, for all cases, the weak-commitment search is more efficient than the min-conflict backtracking and the breakout algorithm. We can see that the breakout algorithm does a lot more consistency checks for each step compared with the weak-commitment search. This fact can be explained as follows. When choosing a variable to change its value, the weak-commitment search (and the min-conflict backtracking) can choose any of the constraint violating variables. On the other hand, the breakout algorithm must choose a variable so that the number of constraint violations can be reduced by changing its value. Therefore, in the worst case (when the current assignment is a local minimum), the breakout algorithm has to check all the values for all constraint violating variables[4].

For the trials without backtracking/restarting, the behaviors of the weak-commitment search and the min-conflict backtracking are exactly the same. We show the ratio of trials with backtracking/restarting, and the average number of steps for these trials in Table 2. We can see that the numbers of required steps for the min-conflict backtracking in trials with backtracking are very large and dominate the average of all trials.

---

[3]In Minton *et al.* (1992), it is reported that the min-conflict backtracking can solve the 100-queens problem in around 25 steps. In our experiment, there exists one trial that exceeds 5000 steps and the result of this trial becomes the dominant factor in the average. The average except this trial is almost identical to the result reported in Minton *et al.* (1992). For $n \geq 1000$, the result for the min-conflict backtracking and weak-commitment search are exactly the same, and almost identical to the result reported in Minton *et al.* (1992).

[4]If the current assignment is not a local minimum, the breakout algorithm does not have to check all variables.

Graph-coloring

The graph-coloring problem involves painting nodes in a graph by k different colors so that any two nodes connected by an arc do not have the same color. We randomly generate a problem with n nodes and m arcs by the method described in Minton *et al.* (1992), so that the graph is connected and the problem has a solution. We evaluate the problem $n = 120, 180, 240$, where $m = n \times 2$ and $k=3$. This parameter setting corresponds to the "sparse" problems for which Minton *et al.* (1992) report poor performance of the min-conflict heuristic. We generate 10 different problems, and for each problem, 10 trials with different initial values are performed (100 trials in all). As in the n-queens problem, the initial values are set by the greedy method.

We introduce two kinds of heuristics (*forward checking* and *first-fail principle* (Haralick & Elliot 1980)) into the min-conflict backtracking and the weak-commitment search, i.e., for each variable, we keep the list of values consistent with the partial solution, and when selecting a variable to be added to the partial solution, we select the variable that has the least number of consistent values. Also, the variable that has only one consistent value is included into the partial solution immediately. Furthermore, before including a variable into the partial solution, we check whether each of remaining variables (variables in *vars-left*) has at least one consistent value with the partial solution, and avoid selecting a value that causes immediate failure. Table 3 shows evaluation results for the three algorithms.

Although Minton *et al.* (1992) report poor performance for the min-conflict backtracking for these problems, by introducing the two heuristics (*forward checking* and *first-fail principle*), the performance of the min-conflict backtracking becomes relatively good in our evaluation. However, there exist several trials in which a mistake in the value selection becomes fatal, and the min-conflict backtracking fails to find a solution within the limit. Therefore, the weak-commitment search is more efficient than the min-conflict backtracking.

For these problems, the *forward checking* and *first-fail principle* are very efficient and the weak-commitment search is about 10 times more efficient than the breakout algorithm. We can see that the capability of accommodating such powerful heuristics is a great advantage of the weak-commitment search over iterative improvement algorithms.

| | weak-commitment | | | min-conflict BT | | | breakout | | |
n	ratio	steps	checks	ratio	steps	checks	ratio	steps	checks
120	100%	28.9	2118.8	99%	78.1	2931.2	100%	198.4	14620.8
180	100%	41.3	3178.9	99%	98.5	5548.5	100%	352.3	32139.3
240	100%	71.9	5988.6	95%	443.6	42164.5	100%	601.2	66892.5

Table 3: Comparison on graph-coloring

| | weak-commitment | | | min-conflict BT | | | breakout | | |
n	ratio	steps	checks	ratio	steps	checks	ratio	steps	checks
300	100%	187.7	24357.0	55%	2717.7	1075986.1	100%	828.0	133911.5
500	100%	359.4	47376.0	15%	4428.8	2368672.5	93%	1596.2	352095.8
700	100%	633.2	83345.1	0%	—	—	77%	2740.2	746752.5
900	100%	980.3	132731.7	0%	—	—	70%	3006.8	1032267.3
1100	100%	1246.8	168845.9	0%	—	—	69%	3384.5	1454297.9

Table 4: Comparison on 3-SAT problem

3-SAT Problem

For the third example problem, we use the 3-SAT problem, which is commonly used as a benchmark for iterative improvement algorithms. This problem is to assign truth values for n boolean variables that satisfy constraints represented as clauses. Each clause consists of three variables. The number of clauses divided by the number of variables is called the *clause density*, and the value 4.3 has been identified as the critical value that produces particularly difficult problems (Mitchell, Selman, & Levesque 1992).

Table 4 shows results of changing the number of variables n by setting the clause density to 4.3. We use the same method described in Morris (1993) to generate a random problem that has a solution. We generate 10 different problems, and for each problem, 10 trials with different initial values[5] are performed (100 trials in all). As in the case of the graph-coloring problems, we introduce the two heuristics into the min-conflict backtracking and the weak-commitment search.

As shown in Table 4, the min-conflict backtracking is very inefficient for this problem. On the other hand, the weak-commitment search is around 10 times more efficient than the breakout algorithm for larger n. For this problem, the effect of the heuristics is not powerful enough to completely avoid bad decisions. Such less powerful heuristics are of little use to the min-conflict backtracking. On the other hand, they are useful for the weak-commitment search algorithm since the variable values are iteratively revised by restarting.

Discussions

Algorithm Complexity

The worst-case time complexity of the weak-commitment search becomes exponential in the num-

---

[5]These initial values are set by the greedy method as in the case of the other problems.

ber of variables n. This result seems inevitable since constraint satisfaction is NP-complete in general. The space complexity of the weak-commitment search is determined by the number of newly added nogoods (constraints) to *nogoods*, i.e., the number of restartings. In the worst case, this is also exponential in n. On the other hand, the space complexity of the backtracking algorithm is linear to n. This result seems inevitable since the weak-commitment search changes the search order flexibly while guaranteeing the completeness of the algorithm. This is also the case for the fill algorithm described in Morris (1993), whose worst-case space complexity becomes exponential in n.

However, the number of restartings will never exceed the number of required steps. Therefore, we can assume that the space complexity would never become a problem in practice as long as the problem can be solved within a reasonable amount of time. Also, the nogood that is a superset of other nogoods is redundant and can be removed from *nogoods*.

Furthermore, we can restrict the number of recorded nogoods. In that case, the theoretical completeness can not be guaranteed. However, in practice, the weak-commitment search algorithm can still find a solution for all example problems when the number of recorded nogoods is restricted so that only 10 of the most recently found nogoods are recorded.

Probabilistic Model

In order to show theoretical evidence that the weak-commitment search is more efficient than the min-conflict backtracking, we use a simple probabilistic model as follows. Let us assume that the probability for finding a solution without any backtracking in the min-conflict backtracking is given by the constant value p, regardless of the initial values. Also, let us assume that the expected number of steps for trials without backtracking is given by n_s ($n_s \leq n$), the expected number of steps for trials with backtracking is given by B, and the expected number of steps until the occurrence of the first backtracking is given by n_b ($n_b \leq n$). Then, the expected number of steps for the min-conflict backtracking can be represented as $n_s p + B q$, where $q = 1 - p$.

On the other hand, in the weak-commitment search, a solution can be found without any restarting with the probability p, and the expected number of steps in this case is given by n_s. Also, the probability that a solution can be found after one restarting is given by pq, and the expected number of steps is given by $n_s + n_b$. In the same way, the probability that a solution can be found after k restartings is given by pq^k, and the expected number of steps is given by $n_s + kn_b$. This probability distribution of the number of restartings is identical to the well-known geometric distribution, and the expected number of restartings is given by q/p. Therefore, the expected number of steps can be given by $n_s + n_b q/p$.

The condition that the weak-commitment search is more efficient than the min-conflict backtracking is $n_s p + B q > n_s + n_b q/p$. By transforming this formula, we obtain $p > n_b/(B - n_s)$. Since we can assume that $B \gg n_s$, and $n_b \leq n$, we obtain the sufficient condition $p > n/B$, i.e., if the probability of finding a solution without backtracking is larger than the ratio of the number of variables and the number of steps for the trials with backtracking, the weak-commitment search is more efficient than the min-conflict backtracking.

The experimental results in the previous section show that the min-conflict backtracking can find a solution efficiently without backtracking in many trials, but the number of required steps for trials with backtracking becomes very large. Therefore, we can assume that the condition $p > n/B$ is satisfied in many cases. For example, from the experimental results in Table 2, we can assume that B for the 50-queens problem is around 1473.4, and p is around 0.83 (where q is 0.17). Then, n/B is around 0.034. This value is much smaller than the expected value of p (0.83).

In reality, the probability of finding a solution without backtracking is affected by the initial values. In the weak-commitment search, when restarting, the current value assignment is used as the new tentative initial values. Therefore, by repeating the restartings, we can expect the value assignment to become close to the final solution; thus, the probability of finding a solution without restartings increases. In such a case, even if the average probability of finding a solution without backtracking is very small and the condition $p > n/B$ is not satisfied, the weak-commitment search can be more efficient than the min-conflict backtracking. For example, although the min-conflict backtracking never finds a solution without backtracking in the 3-SAT problem (Table 4), the weak-commitment search can find a solution. This is because the value assignment is iteratively improved in the weak-commitment search.

Conclusions

We have presented the *weak-commitment* search algorithm for solving CSPs. This algorithm can revise bad decisions without exhaustive search, and the completeness of the algorithm is guaranteed. By experimental results, we have shown that this algorithm is 3 to 10 times more efficient than the breakout algorithm and the min-conflict backtracking.

Our future work includes showing the effectiveness of this algorithm in practical application problems, developing a theoretical model to compare the performance of the weak-commitment search and iterative improvement algorithms, and applying the weak-commitment search algorithm to *distributed constraint satisfaction problems*, in which variables and constraints are distributed among multiple problem solving agents (Yokoo *et al.* 1992).

Acknowledgments

The author wishes to thank Tsukasa Kawaoka, Ryohei Nakano, and Nobuyasu Osato for their support in this work at NTT Laboratories; and Toru Ishida, Kazuhiro Kuwabara, Shigeo Matsubara, and Jun-ichi Akahani for their helpful comments.

References

Ginsberg, M. L., and Harvey, W. D. 1990. Iterative broadening. In *Proceedings of the Eighth National Conference on Artificial Intelligence*, 216–220.

Haralick, R., and Elliot, G. L. 1980. Increasing tree search efficiency for constraint satisfaction problems. *Artificial Intelligence* 14:263–313.

Mackworth, A. K. 1992. Constraint satisfaction. In S.C.Shapiro., ed., *Encyclopedia of Artificial Intelligence*. Wiley-Interscience Publication. 285–293.

Minton, S.; Johnston, M. D.; Philips, A. B.; and Laird, P. 1992. Minimizing conflicts: a heuristic repair method for constraint satisfaction and scheduling problems. *Artificial Intelligence* 58:161–205.

Mitchell, D.; Selman, B.; and Levesque, H. 1992. Hard and easy distributions of SAT problem. In *Proceedings of the Tenth National Conference on Artificial Intelligence*, 459–465.

Morris, P. 1993. The breakout method for escaping from local minima. In *Proceedings of the Eleventh National Conference on Artificial Intelligence*, 40–45.

Selman, B.; Levesque, H.; and Mitchell, D. 1992. A new method for solving hard satisfiability problems. In *Proceedings of the Tenth National Conference on Artificial Intelligence*, 440–446.

Yokoo, M.; Durfee, E. H.; Ishida, T.; and Kuwabara, K. 1992. Distributed constraint satisfaction for formalizing distributed problem solving. In *Proceedings of the Twelfth IEEE International Conference on Distributed Computing Systems*, 614–621.

Planning from First Principles for Geometric Constraint Satisfaction

Sanjay Bhansali
School of EECS
Washington State University
Pullman, WA 99163
bhansali@eecs.wsu.edu

Glenn A. Kramer
Enterprise Integration Technologies
459 Hamilton Avenue
Palo Alto, CA 94301
gak@eit.com

Abstract.

An important problem in geometric reasoning is to find the configuration of a collection of geometric bodies so as to satisfy a set of given constraints. Recently, it has been suggested that this problem can be solved efficiently by symbolically reasoning about geometry using a *degrees of freedom* analysis. The approach employs a set of specialized routines called *plan fragments* that specify how to change the configuration of a set of bodies to satisfy a new constraint while preserving existing constraints. In this paper we show how these plan fragments can be automatically synthesized using first principles about geometric bodies, actions, and topology.

Introduction

An important problem in geometric reasoning is the following: given a collection of geometric bodies, or *geoms*, and a set of constraints between them, find a *configuration*, i.e. position, orientation, and dimension, of the geoms that satisfies all the constraints. Solving this problem is an integral task for constraint-based sketching and design, geometric modeling for computer-aided design, kinematic analysis of robots and other mechanisms, and describing mechanical assemblies.

In [3] Kramer suggests that general-purpose constraint satisfaction techniques are not well suited to problems involving complicated geometry. He describes a system called GCE that uses an alternative approach called *degrees of freedom analysis*. This approach is based on symbolic reasoning about geometry and is more efficient than systems based on algebraic equation solvers. GCE employs a set of specialized routines called *plan fragments*, that specify how to change the configuration of a geom using a fixed set of operators and the available degrees of freedom, so that a new constraint is satisfied while preserving the geom's prior constraints. This approach is canonical: at any point one may choose any constraint to be satisfied without affecting the final result. The resulting algorithm has polynomial time complexity and is more efficient than general-purpose constraint satisfaction algorithms.

Since the most interesting part of problem-solving is performed by plan fragments, the success of this approach depends on one's ability to construct a complete set of plan fragments meeting the canonical specification. In this paper we describe how to automatically generate plan fragments using first principles about geoms, actions, and topology.

Our approach is based on planning. Plan fragment generation becomes a planning problem by considering the various geoms and invariants on them as describing a *state*.

Operators are actions, e.g. *rotate*, that change the configuration of geoms, thereby violating or achieving some constraint. An *initial* state is specified by the set of existing invariants on a geom and a *final* state by the additional constraints to be satisfied. A plan is a sequence of actions that when applied to the initial state achieves the final state.

With this formulation, one could presumably use a classical planner, e.g. STRIPS [1], to automatically generate a plan-fragment. However, plan fragment actions are parametric operators with a real-valued domain. Thus, the search space consists of an infinite number of states. Our approach uses *loci information* (representing a set of points that satisfy some constraints) to reason about the effects of operators and thus reduces the search problem to a problem in topology, involving reasoning about the intersection of various loci.

Another issue to be addressed is the *frame problem*: how to determine what properties or relationships do not change as a result of an action. A typical solution is to use the assumption that an action does not modify any property or relationship unless explicitly stated as an effect of the action. Such an approach works well if one knows *a priori* all possible constraints or invariants that might be of interest and relatively few constraints get affected by each action - which is not true in our case. We use a novel scheme for representing effects of actions. It is based on reifying actions in addition to geoms and invariant types. We associate, with each pair of geom and invariants, a set of actions that can be used to achieve or preserve that invariant for that geom. Whenever a new geom or invariant type is introduced the corresponding rules for actions that can achieve/preserve the invariants are added. Since there are many more invariant types than actions in this domain, this scheme results in simpler rules. A unique feature of our work is the use of geometry-specific matching rules to determine when two or more general actions that achieve/preserve different constraints can be reformulated to a less general action.

Another shortcoming of using a conventional planner is the difficulty of representing conditional effects of operators. In GCE an operation's effect depends on the type of geom as well as the particular geometry. E.g, the action of translating a body to the intersection of two lines on a plane normally reduces the body's translational degrees of freedom to zero; however, if the two lines happen to coincide then the body still retains one translational degree of freedom and if the two lines are parallel but do not coincide then the action fails. Kramer calls such situations *degeneracies*. One approach to handling degeneracies is to use a reactive planner that dynamically revises its plan at run-time. However, this could result in unacceptable performance in many real-time applications. Our approach makes it possible to pre-compile all potential degeneracies in the plan. We achieve this by dividing the planning algorithm into two phases. In the first phase a skeletal plan is generated that works in the normal case and in the second phase, this skeletal plan is refined to take care of singularities and degeneracies. This approach is similar to the idea of refining skeletal plans in MOLGEN [2] and the idea of critics in HACKER [4] to fix known bugs in a plan. However, the skeletal plan refinement in MOLGEN essentially consisted of instantiating a partial plan to work for specific conditions, whereas in our method a complete plan which works for a normal case is extended to handle special conditions like degeneracies.

A Plan Fragment Example.

The following is a simple example of a plan fragment specification that is also used to illustrate our approach. The example is illustrated in Figure 1.

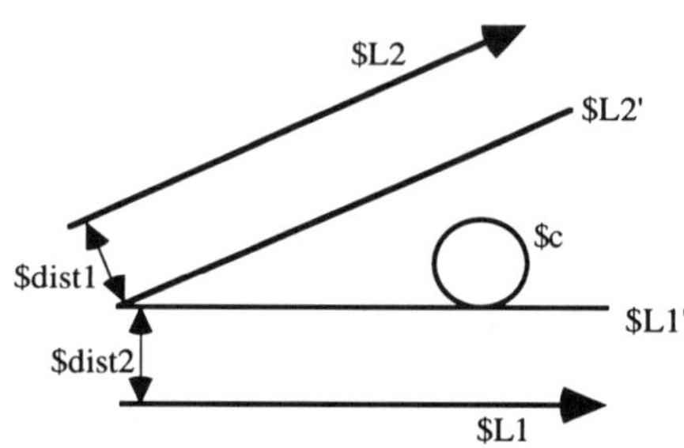

Figure 1. Example problem (initial state)

Geom-type: circle
Name: $c
Invariants: (fixed-distance-line $c $L1 $d1
                    $BIAS_COUNTER_CLOCKWISE)
To-be-achieved: (fixed-distance-line $c $L2 $dist2
                  $BIAS_CLOCKWISE)

In this example, a variable radius circle $c[1] has a prior constraint specifying that the circle is at a fixed distance $dist1 to the left of a fixed line $L1 (or alternatively, the line, $L1 is tangent in a counterclockwise direction to the circle). A new constraint to be satisfied is that the circle be at a fixed distance $dist2 to the right of another line $L2.

To solve this problem, three different plans can be used: (a) translate the circle from its current position to a position such that it touches the two lines $L2' and $L1' shown in the figure. (b) scale the circle while keeping its point of contact with $L1' fixed, so that it touches $L2' (c) scale and translate the circle so that it touches both $L2' and $L1'.

Each of the above plan fragment would be available to GCE from a plan-fragment library. Note that some of the plan fragments would not be applicable in certain situations.

---

[1]We use the following conventions: symbols preceded by $ represent constants, symbols preceded by ? represent variables, expressions of the form (>> parent subpart) denote the subpart of a compound term, parent.

For example, if $L1 and $L2 are parallel, then a single translation can never achieve both the constraints, and plan-fragment (a) would not be applicable. We show how each of the plan-fragments can be automatically synthesized by reasoning from more fundamental principles.

Overview of System Architecture

Figure 2 depicts the architecture of our system showing the various knowledge components and the plan generation process. The knowledge represented in the system is broadly categorized into a Geom Knowledge-base that contains knowledge specific to geometric entities and a Geometry Knowledge-base that is independent of particular geoms and can be reused for generating plan fragments for any geom. The geom-specific knowledge consists of six knowledge components:

1. Actions. These describe operations that can be performed on geoms. In the GCE domain, three actions suffice to change the configuration of a body to an arbitrary configuration: (**translate** *g v*) which denotes a translation of geom *g* by vector *v*; (**rotate** *g pt ax amt*) which denotes a rotation of geom *g*, around point *pt*, about an axis *ax*, by an angle *amt*; and (**scale** *g pt amt*) where *g* is a geom, *pt* is a point about which *g* is scaled, and *amt* is a scalar.

2. Invariants. These describe constraints to be solved for the geoms. The initial version of our system has been designed to generate plan fragments for a variable-radius circle on a fixed workplane, with constraints that are distances between these circles and points, lines, and other circles on the same workplane. There are seven invariant types to represent these constraints. An example of an invariant is: (**Fixed-distance-point** *g pt dist bias*) which specifies that the geom *g* lies at a fixed distance *dist* from point *pt*; *bias* specifies whether *g* lies inside or outside a circle of radius *dist* around point *pt*.

3. Loci. These represent sets of possible values for a geom parameter, e.g. the position of a point on a geom. The various kinds of loci can be grouped into either a 1d-locus (described by an equation of 1 variable) or a 2d-locus (described by an equation of 2 variables). For example, (**make-line-locus** *through-pt direc*) represents an infinite line (a 1d-locus) passing through *through-pt* and having direction *direc*. Other loci in the system include rays, circles, parabolas, hyperbolas, and ellipses.

4. Measurements. These are used to represent the computation of some function, object, or relationship between objects. These terms are mapped into a set of service routines which are called by the plan fragments. An example of a measurement terms is: (**0d-intersection** *1d-locus1 1d-locus2*). This represents the intersection of two 1d-loci. In the normal case, the intersection of two 1-d loci is a point. Singular cases occur when the two loci happen to coincide; in such a case their intersection returns one of the loci instead of a point. Degenerate cases occur when the two loci do not intersect; in such cases, the intersection is undefined. These exceptional conditions are used during the second phase of the plan generation process to elaborate a skeletal plan (see Section 3.3).

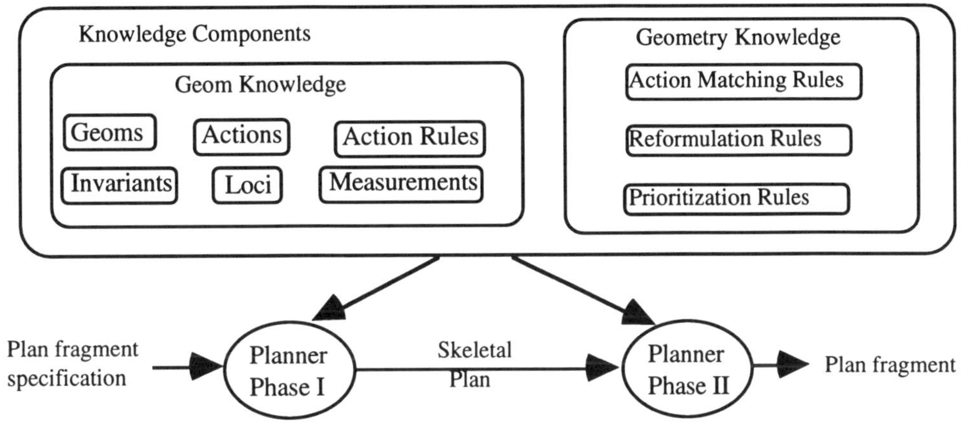

Figure 2. Architectural Overview of the Plan fragment Generator

5. Geoms. These are the objects of interest in solving geometric constraint satisfaction problems. Examples of geoms are lines, line-segments, circles, and rigid bodies. Geoms have degrees of freedoms which allow them to vary in location and size. For example, in 3D-space, a circle with a variable radius has three translational, two rotational, and one dimensional degree of freedom.

The configuration variables of a geom are defined as the minimal number of real-valued parameters required to specify the geometric entity in space unambiguously. Thus, a circle has six configuration variables (three for the center, one for the radius, and two for the plane normal). In addition, the representation of each geom includes the following: *name*: a unique symbol to identify the geom; *invariant-descriptors*: a set of rules that describe how invariants on the geom can be preserved or achieved by actions (see below); *invariants*: the set of current invariants on the geom; *invariants-to-be-achieved*: the set of invariants that nccd to be achieved for the geom.

6. Action Rules (Invariant Descriptors). An action rule describes the effect of an action on an invariant. The planner must know: (1) how to achieve an invariant using an action and (2) how to choose actions that preserve as many of the existing invariants as possible. In general, there are several ways to achieve an invariant and several actions that will preserve one or more invariant. The intersection of these two sets of actions is the set of feasible solutions. In our system, the effect of actions is represented as part of geom-specific knowledge in the form of action rules, whereas knowledge about how to compute intersections of two or more sets of actions is represented as geometry-specific knowledge (since it does not depend on the particular geom being acted on).

An action rule is a three-tuple (*pattern, to-preserve, to-[re]achieve*). *Pattern* is the invariant of interest; *to-preserve* is a list of actions that can be taken without violating the pattern invariant; and *to-[re]achieve* is a list of actions that can be taken to achieve the invariant or re-achieve an existing invariant "clobbered" by an earlier action. These actions are stated in the most general form. The matching rules in the Geometry Knowledge base are then used to obtain the most general unifier of two or more actions.

An example of an invariant descriptor, associated with variable radius circle geoms is:

pattern: (1d-constrained-point ?c (>> ?c CENTER) ?1dlocus)
to-preserve: (scale ?c (>> ?c CENTER) ?any)
    (translate ?c (v- (>> ?1dlocus ARBITRARY-PT)
        (>>   ?c   CENTER))
to-[re]achieve:(translate ?c (v- (>> ?1dlocus ARBITRARY-PT)
        (>> ?c CENTER))

This descriptor is used to preserve or achieve the constraint that the center of a circle geom lie on a 1d locus. Two actions that may be performed without violating this constraint: (1) scale the circle about its center, and (2) translate the circle by a vector that goes from its current center to an arbitrary point on the 1d locus. To *achieve* this invariant only one action may be performed: translate the circle so that its center moves from its current position to an arbitrary position on the 1-dimensional locus.

The *Geometry specific knowledge* is organized as three different kinds of rules:

1. Matching Rules. These are used to match terms using geometric properties. The planner employs a unification algorithm to match actions and determine whether two actions have a common unifier. Here standard unification is not sufficient since it is purely syntactic and does not use knowledge about geometry. To illustrate this, consider the two actions: (i) (**rotate** $g $pt1 ?vec1 ?amt1), and (ii) (**rotate** $g $pt2 ?vec2 ?amt2). Each denotes a rotation of a fixed geom $g, around a fixed point about an arbitrary axis by an arbitrary amount. Standard unification fails when applied to the above terms because no binding of variables makes the two terms syntactically equal. However, knowledge about geometry allows matching the two terms to yield (**rotate** $g $pt1 (v- $pt2 $pt1) ?amt1), denoting a rotation of the geom around the axis passing through $pt1 and $pt2. The point around which the body is rotated can be any point on the axis (here arbitrarily chosen as $pt1) and the amount of rotation can be anything.

2. Reformulation Rules. These are used to rewrite pairs of invariants on a geom into an equivalent pair of simpler invariants (using a well-founded ordering). Here equivalence means that the two sets of invariants produce the same range of motions in the geom.

Besides reducing the number of plan fragments, reformulation rules also help to simplify action rules. Currently all action rules (for variable radius circles and line-segments) use only a single action to preserve or achieve an invariant. If we do not restrict the allowable signatures on a geom, it is possible to create examples where we need a sequence of (more than one) actions in the rule to achieve the invariant, or we need complex conditions that need to be checked to determine rule applicability. Allowing sequences and conditionals on the rules increases the complexity of both the rules and the pattern matcher. This makes it difficult to verify the correctness of rules and reduces the efficiency of the pattern matcher.

3. Prioritizing Rules. Given a set of invariants to be achieved on a geom, a planner generally creates multiple solutions. A majority of the solutions contain redundant actions which can be easily eliminated (e.g. if there are two consecutive translations, they can be replaced by a single translation). However, after such redundant actions are eliminated, the planner may still have multiple solutions. A set of rules called *prioritizing rules* are then used to choose a preferred solution. We have identified two types of prioritizing rules:

1. Prefer solutions that subsume an alternative solution. This rule permits more flexibility in resolving degeneracies in the plan fragment later.

2. Choose the solution that minimizes a geom's motion as measured by a motion function. This rule reflects that in most applications,e.g. computer-aided sketching it is desirable to produce the least amount of perturbation to a geometric system in order to satisfy a set of constraints.

Plan Fragment Generation

The plan fragment generation process is divided into two phases. In the first phase a specification of the plan fragment is taken as input, and a planner is used to generate a set of skeletal plans. These form the input to the second phase which chooses one of the skeletal plans and elaborates it to take care of singularities and degeneracies. The output of this phase is a complete plan fragment.

Phase I

A skeletal plan is generated using a breadth-first search process. Figure 3 gives the general form of a search tree produced by the planner. The planner first tries the reformulation rules to rewrite the geom invariants into a canonical form. Next, the planner searches for actions that produce a state in which at least 1 invariant in the Preserved list is preserved or at least 1 action in the To-be-achieved (TBA) list is achieved. The preserved and achieved invariants are pushed into the Preserved list, and the clobbered or unachieved invariants are pushed into the TBA list of the child state.

The above strategy will produce intermediate nodes in the search tree which might clobber one or more preserved invariant without achieving any new invariant.

The planner iteratively expands each leaf node in the

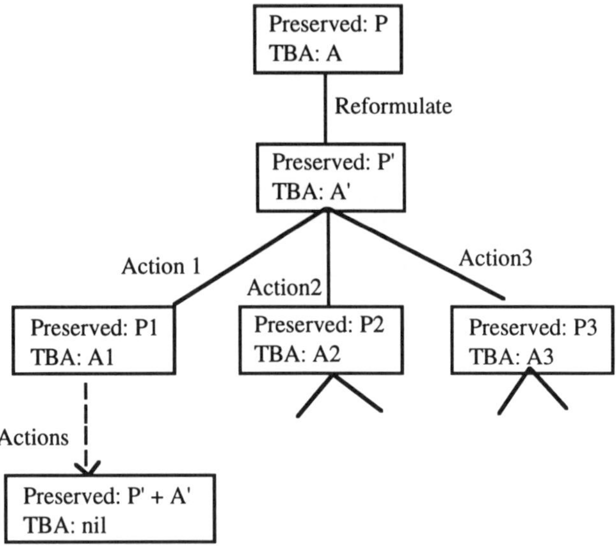

Figure 3. Overview of the search tree produced by the planner

search tree until one of the following is true: (1) The node represents a solution, i.e. the TBA list is nil. (2) The node represents a cycle, i.e. the Preserved and TBA lists are identical to an ancestor node. The node is then marked as terminal and the search tree is pruned at that point. If all leaf nodes are marked as terminal, then the search terminates. The plan-steps of each of those solution nodes represents a skeletal plan fragment. When multiple skeletal plan fragments are obtained, the planner chooses one of them using the prioritizing rule described earlier and passes it to the second phase of the plan fragment generation.

Phase I: Example

We use the example of Section 1 to illustrate Phase I of the planner. The planner begins by trying to reformulate the constraints. It uses a reformulation rule to produce the search tree shown in Fig. 4. Next, the planner searches for actions that can achieve the new invariant or preserve the existing invariant. We only describe the steps involved in finding actions that satisfy the maximal number of constraints (in this case, two). The planner first finds all actions that achieve the *1d-constrained-point* invariant by examining the action rules associated with the variable circle geom. The action rule given in section 1 contains a pattern that matches the *1d-constrained-point* invariant. The relevant action after the appropriate substitutions is:

```
(translate $c
        (v- (>> (angular-bisector
            (make-displaced-line $L1 $BIAS_LEFT $d1)
            (make-displaced-line $L2 $BIAS_RIGHT $d2)
            arbitrary-pt)
    (>> $c center)))
```

Similarly, the planner finds all actions that will preserve the *fixed-distance-line invariant*. Matching and performing the appropriate substitutions yields the single action:

```
(translate $c (v- (>> (make-line-locus
                (>> $c center) (>> $L1 direction))
            arbitrary-point)
        (>> $c center)))
```

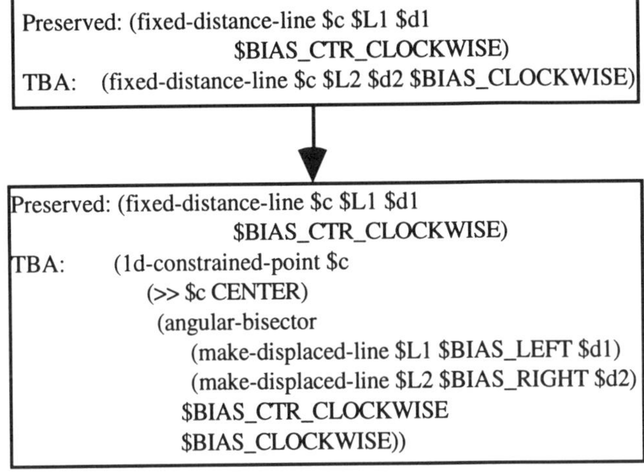

```
Preserved: (fixed-distance-line $c $L1 $d1
                    $BIAS_CTR_CLOCKWISE)
TBA:    (fixed-distance-line $c $L2 $d2 $BIAS_CLOCKWISE)
```

```
Preserved: (fixed-distance-line $c $L1 $d1
                    $BIAS_CTR_CLOCKWISE)
TBA:        (1d-constrained-point $c
             (>> $c CENTER)
             (angular-bisector
                  (make-displaced-line $L1 $BIAS_LEFT $d1)
                  (make-displaced-line $L2 $BIAS_RIGHT $d2)
             $BIAS_CTR_CLOCKWISE
             $BIAS_CLOCKWISE))
```

Figure 4. Search tree after reformulating invariants

Now, to find an action that both preserves the preserved invariant and achieves the TBA invariant, the planner attempts to match the preserving action with the achieving action. The two actions do not match using standard unification, but match employing the following geometry-specific matching rule:

```
(v- (>> $1d-locus1 arbitrary-point) $to)
(v- (>> $1d-locus2 arbitrary-point) $to)

         ⇓

(v- (0d-intersection $1d-locus1 $1d-locus2) $to)
```

(To move to an arbitrary point on two different loci, move to the intersection point of the two loci)

to yield the following action:

```
(translate $c (v- (0d-intersection
                   (angular-bisector (make-displaced-line..).)
                   (make-line-locus (>> $c center)
                                    (>> $L1 direction))
              (>> $c CENTER)))
```

This action moves the circle to the point shown in Figure 5 and achieves both the constraints. This single one-step plan constitutes a skeletal plan fragment. There are two other actions that are generated by the planner in the first iteration, one of which achieves the new constraint but clobbers the prior invariant, while the second one moves the circle to another configuration without achieving the new constraint but preserving the prior constraint.

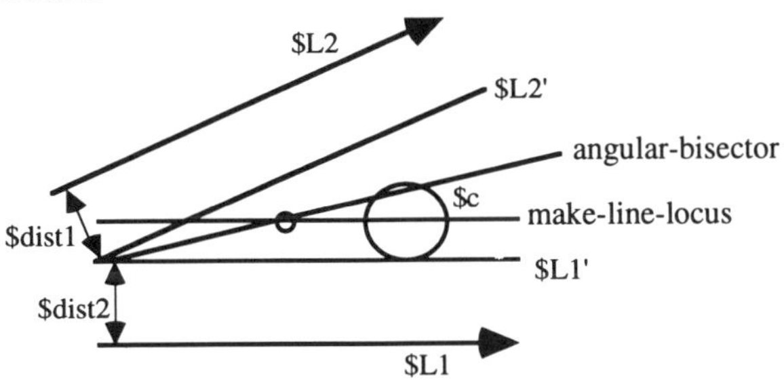

Figure 5. The **O** denotes the point to which the circle is moved.

After two iterations the following solutions are obtained:

(1) Translate to the intersection of the *angular-bisector* and *make-line-locus*. (2) Translate to an arbitrary point on the *angular-bisector*, followed by a translation to the intersection point. (3) Translate to an arbitrary point of *make-line-locus*, followed by a translation to the intersection point. (4) Translate to an arbitrary point on the *angular-bisector* and then scale.

At this stage the first phase of the plan fragment generation is terminated and the skeletal plan fragments are passed on to the second phase of the planner.

Phase 2: Elaboration of Skeletal Plan Fragment

The first step in Phase 2 is to select one of the skeletal plan fragments. The system begins this process by first eliminating all redundant steps in a plan.

Elimination of Redundant Plan-steps. We assume that there is only one degree of dimensional freedom for each geometric body. Under this assumption it can be proved that 1 translation, 1 rotation, and 1 scale is sufficient to change the configuration of an object to an arbitrary configuration in 3D space. Therefore, any plan fragment that contains more than 1 instance of any action type contains redundancies and can be rewritten to an equivalent plan fragment by eliminating redundant actions, or combining two or more action into a single composite action. As an example, consider the following pair of translations on a geom:

- (translate $g ?vec)
- (translate $g (v- ?to$_2$ (>> $g center)))

where *?vec* represents an arbitrary vector and *?to$_2$* represents an arbitrary position. If *?to$_2$* is independent of any positional parameter of the geom, then the first translate action is redundant and can be removed.

After eliminating redundant plan-steps, the system selects one of the plan fragments using the prioritizing rule described earlier, i.e. it selects one of the plan fragments that subsumes the maximal number of other plan fragments.

Least Motion. The least motion principle is meant to reduce the total perturbation in a geometric configuration when satisfying a set of new constraints. This is done by first defining a motion function, $C_{A,G}$ for each action, A, and geom type, G. For example, for a translation of a circle, the motion function, $C_{T,circle}$ could be the square of the displacement of the center of the circle from its initial to its final position. Next, we choose a motion summation function, $\sum$ that sums the motion produced by individual actions on a geom. An example of the summation function is the normal addition operator: plus.

The total motion for a geom is computed using the summation function and the motion functions for action-geom pairs. When a plan fragment is not deterministic, the expression representing the total motion would contain one or more variables representing the ungrounded parameters of the geom. If the motion function and the summation function are chosen so that the resultant expression is analytically evaluable, then we can compute the values of the variables that would minimize the expression representing the total motion. Substituting these values back in the plan fragment results in a plan fragment producing the least motion.

Exception Handling. Exceptional conditions occur when geometric entities are positioned so that the solution of a set of constraints results in either a solution that has extra degrees of freedom or results in no solution. To detect and characterize degeneracies, we begin by enumerating the elementary geoms and grouping possible values of these elements into equivalence classes. An equivalence class represents a set of solutions that are all associated with some kind of exception condition or a normal situation.

Whenever an expression contains a subterm whose value is instantiated at run-time, the computed value is checked for membership in one of the equivalence classes above to see if this situation represents an exception. To implement this, the representation of each elementary geom contains an additional attribute called solution-type which denotes the equivalence class of solution type for that geom. Each service routine that computes one of these geoms would return both the solution type and the solution value(s).

For an aggregate type the exceptional cases are derived by taking the cross product of the exceptional cases of each of the components of the aggregate. In general, the characterization of the value of a subterm as an exception depends on the context in which it occurs. Thus, to determine exception conditions in a plan fragment, we enumerate for each action term, all possible exception conditions of its arguments that might cause the action to fail.

The elaboration of the skeletal plan fragment consists of converting each action in the plan into a case statement. The conditions of the case statement represent one of the exception conditions of interest for the corresponding action. The body of each conditional branch represents the action to be taken to deal with the exception. Depending upon the exception, the action might involve choosing one solution from several alternatives, or generating an error message describing why the action failed.

Phase II: Example

Four skeletal plan fragments were generated in the first phase of the planner. Using the rule for eliminating redundant translations given earlier, the second and third plan fragments can be reduced to single translation plan fragments equivalent to the first plan fragment. This leaves only two distinct plan fragment solutions to consider.

Using the prioritizing rule, the system concludes that the first plan fragment consisting of a single translation is subsumed by the second plan fragment consisting of a translation and scaling. Thus, the second plan fragment is chosen as the preferred solution.

Next, the system discovers that the plan fragment is not deterministic since it contains an action that translates the circle geom to an arbitrary point on the angular-bisector. It grounds the plan by finding a fixed point on the locus based on least motion (Due to space limitations a full

discussion on computing least motion is omitted). The grounded plan fragment is:

```
(translate $c (v- (compute-least-motion-points ...)
              (>> $c center))
(scale $c (>> $c center)
              (line-point-distance $L1 (>> $c center)))
```

Next, each action in the above plan fragment is transformed into a case statement:

```
(let ((vector (v- (compute-least-motion-points ...)
              (>> $c center))))
  (case vector.solution-type
    (zero-vector (nop) ...)
    (one.of-N (funcall #'select-one-from-N vector))
      (not-ground (print "Error:..."))
      (undefined (print "Error: ..."))
    (t (translate $c vector.value))
  (let ((amt (line-point-distance $L1 (>> $c center))))
    (case amt.solution-type
      (zero (print "Zero dimension error ..."))
      (negative (print "Bias inconsistent ..."))
      (undefined (print "Error: ..."))
      (t (scale $g (>> $g center) amt.value))
```

This plan fragment is very concise, containing only the logic for solving a set of constraints; most of the other functionality that used to be part of the plan fragment is pushed down to service routines that deal with topology.

Conclusions and Future Work

We have described an automatic plan fragment generation methodology that can automatically synthesize plan fragments for geometric constraint satisfaction systems by reasoning from first principles about geometric entities, actions, and topology. We implemented the first phase of the planner and used it to synthesize plan fragments for variable-radius circle and line-segment geoms and are currently implementing Phase II of the planner.

Further work includes extending and evaluating the approach to handle more complex (e.g. 3-d) geoms and constraints and pushing the automation one level further so as to automatically acquire some types of knowledge from simpler building blocks. For example, a technique for automatically synthesizing the least motion function from some description of the geometry would be very useful.

Acknowledgment: This work was done while the first author was with the Knowledge Systems Laboratory, Stanford and the second author was at the Schlumberger Laboratory for Computer Science, Austin.

References

[1] Fikes, R. E. and Nilsson, N.J., "STRIPS: a new approach to the application of theorem proving to problem solving, Artificial Intelligence 2, 1971, pp. 198-208.
[2] Friedland, P.E., "Knowledge-based experiment design in molecular genetics", *Technical Report No. 79-771*, Computer Science Department, Stanford University, 1979.
[3] Kramer, G. A. "A Geometric Constraint Engine", *Artifical Intelligence*, 58(1-3), pp. 327-360.
[4] Sussman, G.J., *A computer model of skill acquisition*, American Elsevier: New York, 1975.

GENET: A Connectionist Architecture for Solving Constraint Satisfaction Problems by Iterative Improvement*

Andrew Davenport, Edward Tsang, Chang J. Wang and Kangmin Zhu

Department of Computer Science, University of Essex,
Wivenhoe Park, Colchester,
Essex CO4 3SQ, United Kingdom.
{daveat,edward,cwang,kangmin}@essex.ac.uk

Abstract

New approaches to solving constraint satisfaction problems using iterative improvement techniques have been found to be successful on certain, very large problems such as the million queens. However, on highly constrained problems it is possible for these methods to get caught in local minima. In this paper we present GENET, a connectionist architecture for solving binary and general constraint satisfaction problems by iterative improvement. GENET incorporates a learning strategy to escape from local minima. Although GENET has been designed to be implemented on VLSI hardware, we present empirical evidence to show that even when simulated on a single processor GENET can outperform existing iterative improvement techniques on hard instances of certain constraint satisfaction problems.

Introduction

Recently, new approaches to solving constraint satisfaction problems (CSPs) have been developed based upon iterative improvement (Minton *et al.* 1992; Selman & Kautz 1993; Sosic & Gu 1991). This technique involves first generating an initial, possibly "flawed" assignment of values to variables, then hill-climbing in the space of possible modifications to these assignments to minimize the number of constraint violations. Iterative improvement techniques have been found to be very successful on certain kinds of problems, for instance the min-conflicts hill-climbing (Minton *et al.* 1992) search can solve the million queens problem in seconds, while GSAT can solve hard, propositional satisfiability problems much larger than those which can be solved by more conventional search methods.

These methods do have a number of drawbacks. Firstly, many of them are not complete. However, the size of problems we are able to solve using iterative improvement techniques can so large that to do a complete search would, in many cases, not be possible anyway. A more serious drawback to iterative improvement techniques is that they can easily get caught in local minima. This is most likely to occur when trying to solve highly constrained problems where the number of solutions is relatively small.

In this paper we present GENET, a neural-network architecture for solving finite constraint satisfaction problems. GENET solves CSPs by iterative improvement and incorporates a learning strategy to escape local minima. The design of GENET was inspired by the heuristic repair method (Minton *et al.* 1992), which was itself based on a connectionist architecture for solving CSPs—the Guarded Discrete Stochastic (GDS) network (Adorf & Johnston 1990). Since GENET is a connectionist architecture it is capable of being fully parallelized. Indeed, GENET has been designed specifically for a VLSI implementation.

After introducing some terminology we describe a GENET model which has been shown to be effective for solving binary CSPs (Wang & Tsang 1991). We introduce extensions to this GENET model to enable it to solve problems with general constraints. We present experimental results comparing GENET with existing iterative improvement techniques on hard graph coloring problems, on randomly generated general CSPs and on the *Car Sequencing Problem* (Dincbas, Simonis, & Van Hentenryck 1988). Finally, we briefly explain what we expect to gain by using VLSI technology.

Terminology

We define a constraint satisfaction problem as a triple (Z, D, C) (Tsang 1993), where:

- Z is a finite set of *variables*,

- D is a function which maps every variable in Z to a set of objects of arbitrary type. We denote by D_x the set of objects mapped by D from x, where $x \in Z$. We call the set D_x the domain of x and the members of D_x possible *values* of x.

- C is a set of *constraints*. Each constraint in C restricts the values that can be assigned to the variables in Z simultaneously. A constraint is a *nogood*

*Andrew Davenport is supported by a Science and Engineering Research Council Ph.D Studentship. This research has also been supported by a grant (GR/H75275) from the Science and Engineering Research Council.

if it forbids certain values being assigned to variables simultaneously.

An *n-ary* constraint applies to *n* variables. A *binary* CSP is one with unary and binary constraints only. A *general* CSP may have constraints on any number of variables.

We define a *label*, denoted by $\langle x, v \rangle$, as a variable-value pair which represents the assignment of value v to variable x. A *compound label* is the simultaneous assignment of values to variables. We use $(\langle x_1, v_1 \rangle, \ldots, \langle x_n, v_n \rangle)$ to denote the compound label of assigning $v_1, \ldots, v_n$ to $x_1, \ldots, x_n$ respectively. A *k-compound label* assigns k values to k variables simultaneously. A *solution tuple* of a CSP is a compound label for all the variables in the CSP which satisfies all the constraints.

Binary GENET

Network Architecture

The GENET neural network architecture is similiar to that of the GDS network. In the GENET network each variable i in Z is represented by a *cluster* of *label nodes*, one for each value j in its domain. Each label node may be in one of two states "on" or "off". The state $S_{\langle i,j \rangle}$ of a label node representing the label $\langle i, j \rangle$ indicates whether the assignment of the value j to variable i is true in the current network state. The output of a label node $V_{\langle i,j \rangle}$ is 1 if $S_{\langle i,j \rangle}$ is "on" and 0 otherwise.

All binary constraints in GENET must be represented by *nogood* ground terms. Binary constraints are implemented as inhibitory (negatively weighted) connections between label nodes which may be modified as a result of learning. Initially all weights are set to -1.

The input to each label node $I_{\langle i,j \rangle}$ is the weighted sum of the output of all the connected label nodes:

$$I_{\langle i,j \rangle} = \sum_{k \in Z, l \in D_k} W_{\langle i,j \rangle \langle k,l \rangle} V_{\langle k,l \rangle} \qquad (1)$$

where $W_{\langle i,j \rangle \langle k,l \rangle}$ is the connection weight between the label nodes representing the labels $\langle i, j \rangle$ and $\langle k, l \rangle$[1].

Since there are only connections between incompatible label nodes the input to a label node gives an indication of how much constraint violation would occur should the label node be in an on state. If no violation would occur the input would be a maximum of zero. A CSP is solved when the input to all the on label nodes is zero—such a state is called a *global minima*.

Each cluster of label nodes is governed by a *modulator* which effectively implements a variation of the *min-conflicts* heuristic (Minton *et al.* 1992). The purpose of the modulator is to determine which label node in the cluster is to be on. Only one label node in a cluster may be on at any one time. The modulator selects the label node with the highest input to be on, with ties

---

[1] If there is no constraint between two label nodes representing $\langle i, j \rangle$ and $\langle k, l \rangle$ then $W_{\langle i,j \rangle \langle k,l \rangle} = 0$.

being broken randomly. When the modulator changes the label node which is on in a cluster we say it has made a *repair*.

GENET Convergence Procedure

A *state* of a GENET network represents a complete assignment of values to variables i.e. exactly one label node in each cluster is on. The initial state of the GENET network is determined randomly—one label node per cluster is selected arbitrarily to be on. GENET iterates over *convergence cycles* until it finds a global minima. We define a convergence cycle as:

1. foreach cluster in parallel do[2] update states of all label nodes in cluster,

2. if none of the label nodes have changed state in step 1 then

(a) if the input to all on nodes is zero then solution found—terminate,

(b) else activate learning,

3. goto step 1.

Learning

Like most hill-climbing searches, GENET can reach local optimal points in the search space where no more improvements can be made to the current state—in this case we say the network is in a *minima*. A *local minima* is a minima in which constraints are violated. GENET can sometimes escape such minima by making sideways moves to other states of the same "cost". However in some minima this is not possible, in which case we say the network is in a *single-state* minima. To escape local minima we adjust the weights on the connections between label nodes which violate a constraint according to the following rule:[3]

$$W^{t+1}_{\langle i,j \rangle \langle k,l \rangle} = W^{t}_{\langle i,j \rangle \langle k,l \rangle} - V_{\langle i,j \rangle} V_{\langle k,l \rangle} \qquad (2)$$

where $W^{t}_{\langle i,j \rangle \langle k,l \rangle}$ is the connection weight between label nodes representing $\langle i, j \rangle$ and $\langle k, l \rangle$ at time t.

By using weights we associate with each constraint a cost of violating that constraint. We can also associate with each GENET network state a cost which is the sum of the magnitudes of the weights of all the constraints violated in that state.

Learning has the effect of "filling in" local minima by increasing the cost of violating the constraints which are violated in the minima. After learning, constraints which were violated in the minima are less likely to be violated again. This can be particularly useful in

---

[2] We do not want clusters to update their states at exactly the same time since this may cause the network to oscillate between a small number of states indefinitely. In a VLSI implementation we would expect the clusters to update at slightly different times.

[3] Morris (Morris 1993) has recently reported a similiar mechanism for escaping minima.

structured CSPs where some constraints are more critical than others (Selman & Kautz 1993).

Learning is activated when the GENET network state remains unchanged after a convergence cycle. Thus learning may occur when GENET, given the choice of a number of possible sideways moves to states of the same cost, makes a sideways move back to its current state. We consider this a useful feature of GENET since it allows the network to escape more complicated *multi-state* minima composed of a "plateau" of states of the same cost.

A consequence of learning is that we can show GENET is not complete. This is because learning affects many other possible network states as well as those that compose the local minima. As a result of learning new local minima may be created. A discussion of the problems this may cause can be found in (Morris 1993).

General Constraints

Many real-life CSPs have general constraints e.g. scheduling, car sequencing (Dincbas, Simonis, & Van Hentenryck 1988). In this section we describe how can we represent two types of general constraint, the *illegal* constraint and the *atmost* constraint, in a GENET network. One of our motivations for devising these particular constraints has been the Car Sequencing Problem, a real-life general CSP once considered intractable (Parrello & Kabat 1986) and which has been successfully tackled using CSP solving techniques (Dincbas, Simonis, & Van Hentenryck 1988).

Since we cannot represent general constraints by binary connections alone, we introduce a new class of nodes called *constraint nodes*. A constraint node is connected to one or more label nodes.

Let c be a constraint node and L be the set of label nodes which are connected to c. Then the input I_c to the constraint node c is the *unweighted* sum of the outputs of these connected label nodes:

$$I_c = \sum_{\langle i,j \rangle \in L} V_{\langle i,j \rangle} \tag{3}$$

We can consider the connection weights between constraint nodes and label nodes to be assymetric. The weight on all connections from label nodes to constraint nodes is 1 and is not changed by learning. Connection weights from constraint nodes to label nodes are, like for binary constraints, initialised to -1 and can change as a result of learning. The input to label nodes in networks with general constraints C is now given by:

$$I_{\langle i,j \rangle} = \sum_{k \in Z, l \in D_k} W_{\langle i,j \rangle \langle k,l \rangle} V_{\langle k,l \rangle} + \sum_{c \in C} W_{c,\langle i,j \rangle} V_{c,\langle i,j \rangle} \tag{4}$$

where $V_{c,\langle i,j \rangle}$ is the output of the constraint node c to the label node $\langle i,j \rangle$.

The learning mechanism for connection weights $W^t_{c,\langle i,j \rangle}$ between constraint nodes c and label nodes $\langle i,j \rangle$ is given by:

$$W^{t+1}_{c,\langle i,j \rangle} = \begin{cases} W^t_{c,\langle i,j \rangle} - 1 & \text{if } S_c > 0 \\ W^t_{c,\langle i,j \rangle} & \text{otherwise} \end{cases} \tag{5}$$

where S_c is the state of the constraint node.

The Illegal Constraint

The *illegal*$(\langle x_1, v_1 \rangle, \ldots, \langle x_k, v_k \rangle)$ constraint specifies that the k-compound label $L = (\langle x_1, v_1 \rangle, \ldots, \langle x_k, v_k \rangle)$ is a nogood. An illegal constraint is represented in a GENET network by an illegal constraint node, which is connected to the k label nodes which represent the k labels in L.

$$S_{ill} = I_{ill} - (k - 1) \tag{6}$$

The state S_{ill} of the illegal constraint node is negative if less than $k - 1$ of connected label nodes are on. In this case there is no possibility that the constraint will become violated should another node become on. A constraint node in this state outputs 0 to all the connected label nodes.

If $k - 1$ of the connected label nodes are on then we want to discourage the remaining off label node from becoming on, since this will cause the constraint to be violated. However, we do not wish to penalize the label nodes which are already on, since the constraint remain satisfied even if they do change state. In this case we want to output 1 to the label node which is off and 0 to the remaining label nodes.

Finally, if all the connected label nodes are on then the constraint is violated. We want to penalize all these nodes for violating the constraint, so we give them all an output of 1 to encourage them to change state.

We summarize the output $V_{ill,\langle i,j \rangle}$ from an illegal constraint node *ill* to a label node representing the label $\langle i,j \rangle$ by:

$$V_{ill,\langle i,j \rangle} = \begin{cases} 0 & \text{if } S_{ill} < 0 \\ 1 + S_{ill} - V_{\langle i,j \rangle} & \text{otherwise} \end{cases} \tag{7}$$

The Atmost Constraint

We can easily extend the illegal constraint node architecture to represent more complex constraints. For instance, given a set of variables *Var* and values *Val* the *atmost(N, Var, Val)* constraint specifies that no more than N variables from *Var* may take values from *Val*. The atmost constraint node is connected to all nodes of the set L which represent the labels $\{\langle i,j \rangle | i \in Var, j \in Val, j \in D_i\}$. This constraint is a modification of the atmost constraint found in the CHIP constraint logic programming language.

The state S_{atm} of an atmost constraint node is determined as follows:

$$S_{atm} = I_{atm} - N \tag{8}$$

The output from an atmost constraint node is similar to that for the illegal constraint node, although we have the added complication that a single variable may have more than one value in the constraint. We do not want label nodes in the same cluster to receive different inputs from a particular constraint node since, in situations where the network would normally be in a single state local minima, we would find the network oscillating about the states of these label nodes. Instead, we give the output of an atmost constraint node atm to a label node representing the label $\langle i, j \rangle$ as follows:

$$V_{atm,\langle i,j \rangle} = \begin{cases} 0 & \text{if } S_{atm} < 0 \\ 1 - \text{Max}\{V_{\langle i,k \rangle} | k \in Val\} & \text{if } S_{atm} = 0 \\ 1 & \text{otherwise} \end{cases} \tag{9}$$

Experimental Results

Graph Coloring

In (Selman & Kautz 1993) it is reported that the performance of GSAT on graph coloring problems is comparable with the performance of some of the best specialised graph-coloring algorithms. This surprised us since a graph coloring problem with N vertices to be colored with k colors would require, in a conjunctive normal form (CNF) representation, $N \times k$ variables. Since each of these variables has a domain size of 2 the size of the search space is 2^{Nk}. To represent such a problem as a CSP would require N variables of domain size k, giving a search space of size k^N. For example, the 250 variable 29 coloring problem in Table 1 has a search space size in GENET of 4×10^{365} possible states. This is far smaller than the corresponding size of 3×10^{2183} states possible in GSAT.

Another difference between GSAT and GENET is the way in which they make repairs. GSAT picks the best "global" repair which reduces the number of conflicts amongst all the variables, whereas GENET makes "local" repairs which minimizes the number of conflicts for each variable. Thus we would expect repairs made by GSAT to be of "higher quality" than those of GENET, although they are made at the extra expense of considering more possibilities for each repair.

We compared GSAT[4] and GENET[5] on a set of hard graph coloring problems described in (Johnson *et al.* 1991), running each method ten times on each problem. We present the results of our experiments in Tables 1 and 2. Both GSAT and GENET managed to solve all the problems, although GSAT makes many more repairs to solve each problem. These results seem to confirm our conjecture that for CSPs such as graph coloring GENET is more effective than GSAT because of the way it represents such problems.

---

[4] We ran GSAT with MAX-FLIPS set to $10\times$ the number of variables, and with averaging in reset after every 25 tries.

[5] All experiments were carried out using a GENET simulator written in C++ on a Sun Microsystems Sparc Classic.

| graph | | median | median number |
nodes	colors	time	of repairs
125	17	8.0 hours	$65,197,415$
125	18	30 secs	$65,969$
250	15	5.0 secs	$2,839$
250	29	1.8 hours	$7,429,308$

Table 1: GSAT on hard graph coloring problems.

| graph | | median | median number |
nodes	colors	time	of repairs
125	17	2.6 hours	$1,626,861$
125	18	23 secs	$7,011$
250	15	4.2 secs	580
250	29	1.1 hours	$571,748$

Table 2: GENET on hard graph coloring problems.

Random General Constraint Satisfaction Problems

There are two important differences between a sequential implementation of GENET and min-conflicts hill-climbing (MCHC). The first is our learning strategy for escaping local minima. The second difference is in choosing which variables to update. MCHC selects randomly a variable to update from the set of variables which are currently in conflict with other variables. In GENET we randomly select variables to update from the set of all variables, regardless of whether they conflict with any other variables.

Our aim in this experiment was to try to determine empirically what effect these individual modifications to MCHC was making to the effectiveness of its search.

We compared GENET with a basic min-conflicts hill-climbing search, a modified MCHC (MCHC2) and a modified version of GENET (GENET2). MCHC2 randomly selects variables to update from the set of all variables, not just those which are in conflict. MCHC2 can also be regarded as a sequential version of GENET without learning. In GENET2 variables are only updated if they are in conflict with other variables.

We produced a set of general CSPs with varying numbers of the *atmost(N, Var, Val)* constraint, where $N = 3$, $|Var| = 5$ and $|Val| = 5$. The problems were not guaranteed to be solvable. Each problem had fifty variables and a domain of ten values. The set of variables and values in each constraint were generated randomly. At each data-point we generated ten problems. We ran each problem ten times with GENET, GENET2, MCHC and MCHC2. We set a limit of five hundred thousand repairs for each run, after which failure was reported if no solution had been found.

Figure 1 shows that MCHC2 solves more problems than MCHC. This is to be expected since, because MCHC2 can modify the values of variables which are

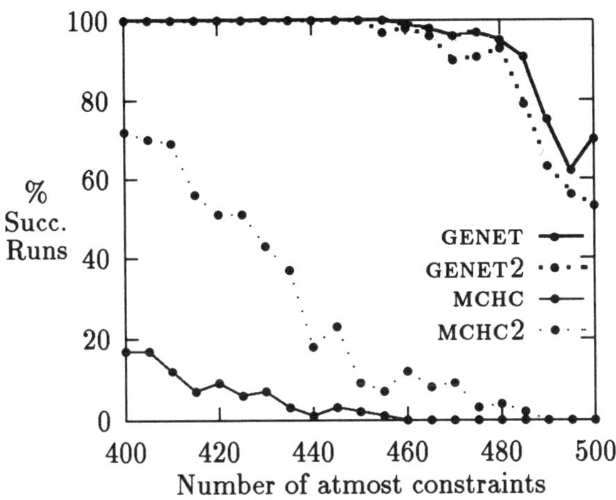

Figure 1: Comparison of percentage of successful runs for GENET and min-conflicts hill-climbing searches on randomly generated general constraint satisfaction problems.

not in conflict, it is less likely to become trapped in local minima. The performance of GENET2 shows that learning is an even more effective way of escaping local minima. However Figure 1 shows that combining these two approaches in GENET is the most effective way of escaping minima for this particular problem set.

The Car Sequencing Problem

We have been using the car-sequencing problem as a benchmark problem during the development of a GENET model which would solve general CSPs. The car-sequencing problem is a real-life general CSP which is considered particularly difficult due to the presence of global atmost constraints. For a full description of the car sequencing problem see (Dincbas, Simonis, & Van Hentenryck 1988).

We compared GENET with MCHC, MCHC2 and CHIP. CHIP is a constraint logic programming language which uses a complete search based on forward-checking and the fail-first principle to solve CSPs. In our experiments we used randomly generated problems of size 200 cars and utilisation percentages in the range 60% to 80%. At each utilisation percentage we generated ten problems. The problems all had 200 variables with domains varying from 17 to 28 values and approximately 1000 atmost constraints of varying arity. All the problems were guaranteed to be solvable. We ran the GENET, MCHC and MCHC2 ten times on each problem, with a limit of one million repairs for each run, after which failure was reported. This limit corresponded to a running time of approximately 220 seconds at 60% utilisation up to 270 seconds at 80% utilisation. We used the method described in (Dincbas, Simonis, & Van Hentenryck 1988) to program the problems in CHIP, which

utilisa-tion %	MCHC		MCHC2	
	% succ. runs	median repairs	% succ. runs	median repairs
60	78	737	85	549
65	81	586	82	524
70	82	670	85	508
75	76	1282	82	811
80	29	10235	51	4449

Table 3: A comparison of MCHC and MCHC2 on 200 car sequencing problems.

utilisa-tion %	GENET		GENET3	
	% succ. runs	median repairs	% succ. runs	median repairs
60	84	463	100	452
65	87	426	100	439
70	83	456	100	426
75	85	730	100	686
80	50	4529	100	1886

Table 4: A comparison of GENET and GENET3 on 200 car sequencing problems.

included adding redundant constraints to speed up the search. With a time limit of one hour to solve each problem CHIP managed to solve two problems at 60% utilisation, one problem at 65% utilisation, two problems at 70% utilisation and one problem at 75% utilisation. The results for min-conflicts hill-climbing and GENET on 200 car sequencing problems are given in Tables 3 and 4.

From Table 3 it can be seen that MCHC2 is more effective than MCHC at solving the car-sequencing problem. However the results for MCHC2 and GENET are very similiar, indicating that learning is having very little or no effect in GENET. This can be attributed to the presence of very large plateaus of states of the same cost in the search space. Learning is activated only when GENET stays in the same state for more than one cycle, thus learning is less likely to occur when these plateaus are large. To remedy this problem we made a modification to GENET to force learning to occur more often. We define the parameter p_{sw} as the probability that, in a given convergence cycle, GENET may make sideways moves. Thus, for each convergence cycle, GENET may make sideways moves with probability p_{sw}, and may only make moves which decrease the cost with probability $1 - p_{sw}$. Thus, if GENET is in a state where only sideways moves may be made then learning will occur with a probability of at least $1 - p_{sw}$. The results for GENET3 in Table 4, where p_{sw} is set to 0.75, shows that this modification significantly improves the performance of GENET.

VLSI Implementation

Although the results presented so far have been obtained using a GENET simulator on a single processor machine, it is the aim of our project to implement GENET on VLSI chips. A full discussion of a VLSI implementation for GENET would be beyond the scope of this paper[6] so in this section we describe what we expect to gain by using VLSI technology.

A disadvantage of the min-conflicts heuristic, as noted by Minton (Minton *et al.* 1992), is that the time taken to accomplish a repair grows with the size of the problem. For a single-processor implementation of GENET the cost of determining for a single variable the best value to take is proportional to the number of values in the domain of the variable and the number constraints involving that value. To determine for each variable the best value to take can potentially be performed at constant time in a VLSI implementation of GENET no matter how large the domain or how highly constrained the problem. This would mean that the time taken for GENET to perform a single convergence cycle would be constant, no matter what the problem characteristics[7]. Since we estimate the time taken to perform one convergence cycle using current VLSI technology to be of the order of tens of nanoseconds, this would allow all the CSPs mentioned in this paper to be solved in seconds rather than minutes or hours.

Conclusion

We have presented GENET, a connectionist architecture for solving constraint satisfaction problems by iterative improvement. GENET has been designed to be implemented on VLSI hardware. However we have presented empirical evidence to show that even when simulated on a single processor GENET can outperform existing iterative improvement techiques on hard binary and general CSPs,

We have developed strategies for escaping local minima which we believe significantly extend the scope of hill-climbing searches based on the min-conflicts heuristic. We have presented empirical evidence to show that GENET can effectively escape local minima when solving a range of highly constrained real-life and randomly generated problems.

Acknowledgements

We would also like to thank Alvin Kwan for his useful comments on earlier drafts of this paper. We are grateful to Bart Selman and Henry Kautz for making their implementation of GSAT available to us.

---

[6] A VLSI design for GENET is described in (Wang & Tsang 1992)

[7] The size of problem would be limited by current VLSI technology

References

Adorf, H., and Johnston, M. 1990. A discrete stochastic neural network algorithm for constraint satisfaction problems. In *Proceedings of the International Joint Conference on Neural Networks*.

Dincbas, M.; Simonis, H.; and Van Hentenryck, P. 1988. Solving the car-sequencing problem in logic programming. In *Proceedings of ECAI-88*.

Johnson, D.; Aragon, C.; McGeoch, L.; and Schevon, C. 1991. Optimization by simulated annealing: an experimental evaluation; part II, graph coloring and number partitioning. *Operations Research* 39(3):378–406.

Minton, S.; Johnston, M.; Philips, A.; and Laird, P 1992. Minimizing conflicts: a heuristic repair method for constraint satisfaction and scheduling problems. *Artificial Intelligence* 58:161–205.

Morris, P. 1993. The breakout method for escaping from local minima. In *Proceedings of the Twelth National Conference on Artificial Intelligence*. AAAI Press/The MIT Press.

Parrello, B., and Kabat, W. C. 1986. Job-shop scheduling using automated reasoning: A case study of the car-sequencing problem. *JOURNAL of Automated Reasoning* 2:1–42.

Selman, B., and Kautz, H. 1993. Domain independent extensions to GSAT: Solving large structured satisfiability problems. In *Proceedings of the 13th International Joint Conference on Artificial Intelligence*.

Sosic, R., and Gu, J. 1991. 3,000,000 queens in less than one minute. *SIGART Bulletin* 2(2):22–24.

Tsang, E. 1993. *Foundations of Constraint Satisfaction*. Academic Press.

Wang, C., and Tsang, E. 1991. Solving constraint satisfaction problems using neural-networks. In *Proceedings IEE Second International Conference on Artificial Neural Networks*.

Wang, C., and Tsang, E. 1992. A cascadable VLSI design for GENET. In *International Workshop on VLSI for Neural Networks and Artificial Intelligence*.

Expected Gains from Parallelizing
Constraint Solving for Hard Problems

Tad Hogg and Colin P. Williams

Xerox Palo Alto Research Center
3333 Coyote Hill Road
Palo Alto, CA 94304, U.S.A.
Hogg@parc.xerox.com, CWilliams@parc.xerox.com

Abstract

A number of recent studies have examined how the difficulty of various NP-hard problems varies with simple parameters describing their structure. In particular, they have identified parameter values that distinguish regions with many hard problem instances from relatively easier ones. In this paper we continue this work by examining independent parallel search. Specifically, we evaluate the speedup as function of connectivity and search difficulty for the particular case of graph coloring with a standard heuristic search method. This requires examining the full search cost distribution rather than just the more commonly reported mean and variance. We also show similar behavior for a single-agent search strategy in which the search is restarted whenever it fails to complete within a specified cost bound.

Introduction

Several recent studies have related the structure of constraint satisfaction problems to the difficulty of solving them with search [Cheeseman et al., 1991, Mitchell et al., 1992, Williams and Hogg, 1992, Crawford and Auton, 1993, Gent and Walsh, 1993, Williams and Hogg, 1993]. Particular values of simple parameters, describing the problem structure, that lead to hard problem instances, on average, were identified. These values are also associated with high variance in the solution cost for different problem instances, and for a single instance with respect to different search methods or a single nondeterministic method with, e.g., different initial conditions or different tie-breaking choices made when the search heuristic ranks some choices equally. Structurally, these hard problems are characterized by many large partial solutions, which prevent early pruning by many types of heuristics.

Can these observations be exploited in practical search algorithms? One possibility is to run several searches independently in parallel, stopping when any process first finds a solution (or determines there are none) [Fishburn, 1984, Helmbold and McDowell, 1989, Pramanick and Kuhl, 1991, Kornfeld, 1981, Imai et al., 1979, Rao and Kumer, 1992, Mehrotra and Gehringer, 1985, Ertel, 1992]. Since the benefit of this approach relies on variation in the individual methods employed, the high variance seen for the hard problems suggests it should be particularly applicable for them [Cheeseman et al., 1991, Rao and Kumer, 1992]. In some cases, this approach could be useful even if multiplexed on a serial machine [Janakiram et al., 1987]. This method is particularly appealing since it requires no communication between the different processes and is very easy to implement.

However, the precise benefit to be obtained from independent parallel searches is determined by the nature of the full distribution of search cost, not just by the variance. In this paper, we present experimental results on the expected speedup from such parallel searches for a particular well-studied example, graph coloring. By evaluating the speedup obtainable from graphs of different connectivities we investigate consequences of different structural properties for the benefit of parallelization, even when such problems are equally hard for a serial search.

In the remainder of the paper we describe the graph coloring search problem and show the types of cost distributions that arise for a heuristic search method. We then show how the speedup from parallelization is determined from the distribution and present empirically observed speedups for a variety of graphs. We also present a similar analysis and experiments for a single-agent search strategy.

Graph Coloring Problems

The graph coloring problem consists of a graph, a specified number of colors, and the requirement to find a color for each node in the graph such that no pair of adjacent nodes (i.e., nodes linked by an edge in the graph) have the same color. Graph coloring has received considerable attention and a number of search methods have been developed [Minton et al., 1990, Johnson et al., 1991, Selman et al., 1992]. This is a well-known NP-complete problem whose solution cost grows exponentially in the worst case as the number of nodes in the graph increases.

For this problem, the average degree of the graph γ (i.e., the average number of edges coming from a node in the graph) distinguishes relatively easy from harder problems, on average. In this paper, we focus on the case of 3–coloring (i.e., when 3 different colors are available).

In our experiments we used a complete, depth-first backtracking search based on the Brelaz heuristic [Johnson et al., 1991] which assigns the most constrained nodes first (i.e., those with the most distinctly colored neighbors), breaking ties by choosing nodes with the most uncolored neighbors (with any remaining ties broken randomly). For each node, the smallest color consistent with the previous assignments is chosen first, with successive choices made when the search is forced to backtrack. This complete search method is guaranteed to eventually terminate and produce correct results.

The Cost Distribution

For our experiments we used randomly generated graphs with 100 nodes and with a specified average connectivity γ. For these problems, there are two distinct regions with hard problems. The first, near $\gamma = 4.5$ has a fairly high density of hard instances. The second, at somewhat lower connectivities, has mostly easy problems but occasionally instances with extremely high search costs. These extreme cases have such large cost that they dominate the mean cost in this region. These observations are summarized in Fig. 1.

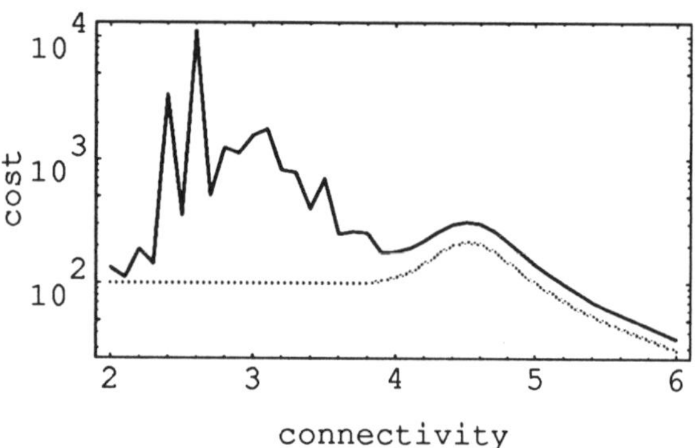

Fig. 1. Search cost as a function of average connectivity γ of the graphs with 100 nodes. The black curve shows the mean cost and the gray one is the median cost. Values are shown in increments of 0.1 for γ and are based on 50,000 samples at each point. The large variance in search cost for the lower connectivities produces the sharp peaks in the mean cost, an indication that many more samples are required to determine it accurately.

For the behavior of parallel search we need to consider the distribution of search costs. For the cases in which a single search solves the problem rapidly there is not much to be gained from parallel methods. Thus we focus on the behavior of problems in the hard regions of intermediate connectivity. Fig. 2 gives examples of the types of cost distribution we encountered. Specifically, there were two distinct shapes. On one hand, we found multimodal distributions with a wide range of individual costs. In these cases, the search often completes rapidly but because of

the occasional high-cost instance, the mean search cost is relatively large. On the other hand, we found more tightly clustered distributions in which all the searches required about the same, large cost. As described below, these distinct distribution shapes give rise to very different potential for parallel speedup through multiple searches.

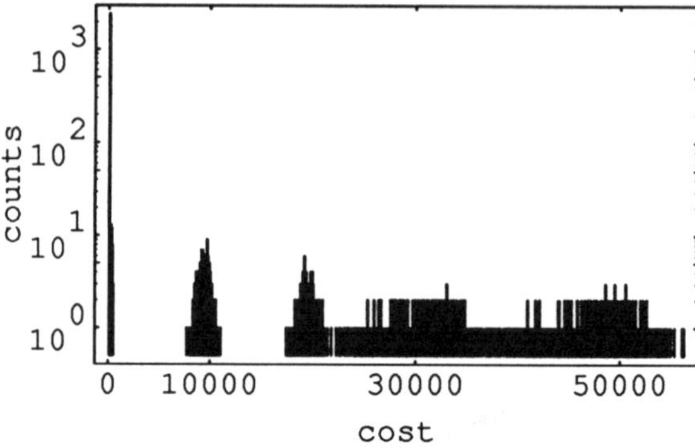

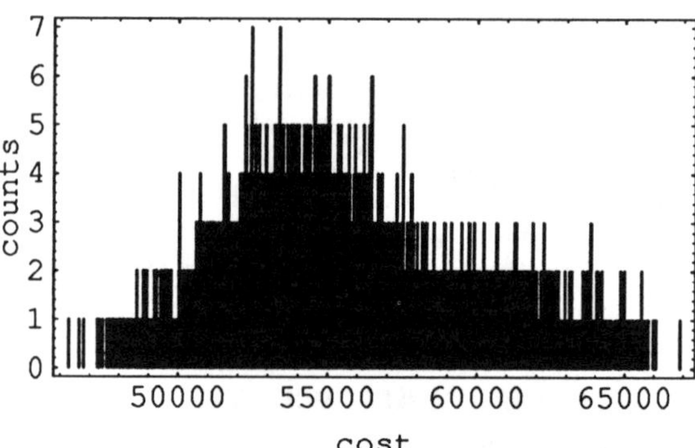

Fig. 2. The search cost distribution for two 100–node graphs with $\gamma = 3.5$. In each case, the graph was searched 10,000 times. The plots give the number of times each cost was found. The first case is a multimodal distribution with average cost $T_1 = 15122$ and a large possible speedup: $S(10) = 76$, $S_{opt} = 37$ with $\tau^* = 412$. The second case is a fairly sharp unimodal distribution (note the expanded cost scale on the horizontal axis). It has average cost $T_1 = 55302$ and very limited speedup: $S(10) = 1.1$ and $S_{opt} = 1$ with no cutoff (i.e., $\tau^* = \infty$). These quantities are defined in Eqs. 1 and 3.

Speedup with Parallel Search

When a heuristic search involves some random choices, repeated runs on the same problem can give different search costs. This is especially true when incorrect choices made early in the search are undone only after a large number of steps. In such cases, one could benefit from running multiple, independent versions of the search, stopping when the first one completes. In this section, we show how the expected speedup for this method is determined by the full cost distribution of the search method.

Specifically, for a given problem instance, let $p(i)$ be the probability that an individual search run terminates after exactly i search steps. We also define the cumulative distribution, i.e., the probability that the search requires *at least* i steps, as $q(i) = \sum_{j \geq i} p(j)$. For a group of k independent searches the search cost for the group is defined as the cost for the first agent that terminates, i.e., the minimum of the individual finishing times. The probability that the group as a whole requires at least i steps, $q_k(i)$, is just the probability that *all* of the individual searches require at least i steps. Because the searches run independently, we have simply $q_k(i) = q(i)^k$. Thus the probability that the group finishes in exactly i steps is $p_k(i) = q(i)^k - q(i+1)^k$.

With these expressions we can now determine the average speedup. Specifically, again for a given problem instance, let T_k be the average cost for a group of k agents to solve the problem. Then we define the speedup as

$$S(k) = \frac{T_1}{T_k} \qquad (1)$$

This can be expressed in terms of the cost distribution by noting that $T_k = \sum_i i p_k(i)$. Whilst this measure of speedup is a commonly used measure of parallel performance, we should note that for the extended distributions seen in our studies, it can differ from "typical" behavior when the mean search times are greatly influenced by rare, high-cost events. Even in these cases, however, this measure does give some insight into the nature of the distribution and allows for a simple comparison among different classes of graphs.

In our experimental studies, we estimate the cost distribution $p(i)$ by repeating the individual search N times (for most of our experiments we used $N = 100$ to allow for testing many graphs, but saw similar behaviors in a few graphs with more samples, such as $N = 10^4$ for the examples of Fig. 2). Let $n(i)$ be the number of searches that finished in exactly i steps. Then we used $p(i) \approx n(i)/N$ to obtain an estimate for the speedup for a given problem. By repeating this procedure over many different graphs, all having the same connectivity, we can obtain an estimate of the average speedup, $\langle S(k) \rangle$, as a function of average connectivity, γ. Alternatively we can also ask how large k needs to be in order to solve a problem, having a particular connectivity, within a prespecified cost limit.

Experimental Results: Speedup

We searched a number of graphs at various connectivities and recorded the distribution of search times. From this we obtained estimates of the expected search cost for a single search and the speedup when several searches are run independently in parallel. To study the two regions of hard problems we selected graphs with $\gamma = 3.5$ and $\gamma = 4.5$. More limited experiments with $\gamma = 3.0$ were qualitatively similar to the $\gamma = 3.5$ case.

The speedups for $\gamma = 3.5$ are shown in Fig. 3 as a function of single-agent search cost. Whilst we see many

samples with fairly limited speedup, this class of graphs generally shows an increased speedup with single search cost. A similar story is seen in Fig. 4 for the average speedup among these samples as a function of number of parallel searches. This shows an increasing speedup, especially for the harder cases. Together with Fig. 1 we conclude that at this connectivity we have mostly easy cases, but many of the harder cases can often benefit increasingly from parallelization.

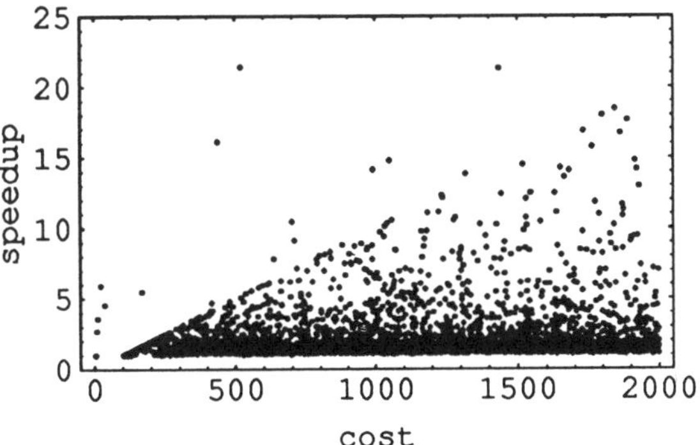

Fig. 3. Speedup $S(10)$ for 10 agents vs. average single-agent cost T_1 for 100–node graphs at $\gamma = 3.5$. Each graph was searched 100 times to estimate the single-agent cost distribution. There were also a few samples with larger speedups than shown in the plot, as well as samples with substantially higher costs which continued the trend toward increasing speedups.

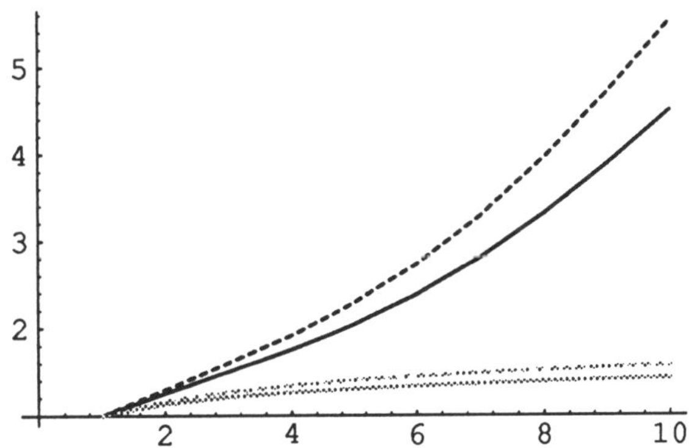

Fig. 4. Average speedup $\langle S(k) \rangle$ (black) and median speedup (gray) vs. number of agents k for 100–node graphs at $\gamma = 3.5$. The solid curves include all samples while the dashed ones include only those whose average single-agent cost was at least 1000.

The behavior is different for $\gamma = 4.5$ as shown in Fig. 5. In this case most samples exhibit limited speedup. In particular, there is no increase in speedup with single search cost. In Fig. 6 we see the limited benefit of additional parallel searches, both for all samples and those with high cost.

Speeding Up a Single Agent

Another way to use the cost distribution of an individual search method for a given problem is to devise a better

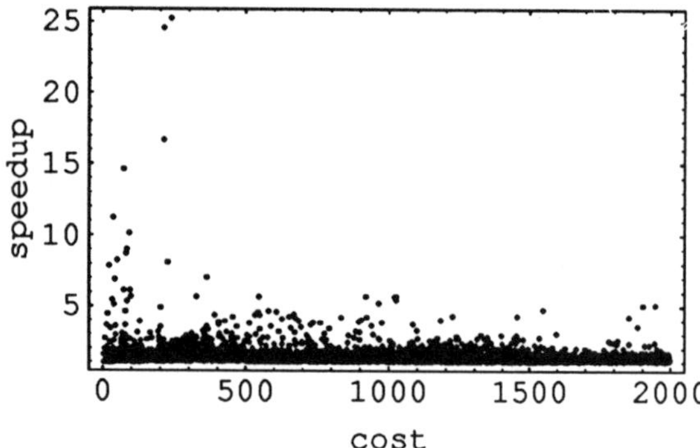

Fig. 5. Speedup $S(10)$ for 10 agents vs. average single-agent cost T_1 for 100–node graphs at $\gamma = 4.5$. Each graph was searched 100 times to estimate the single-agent cost distribution.

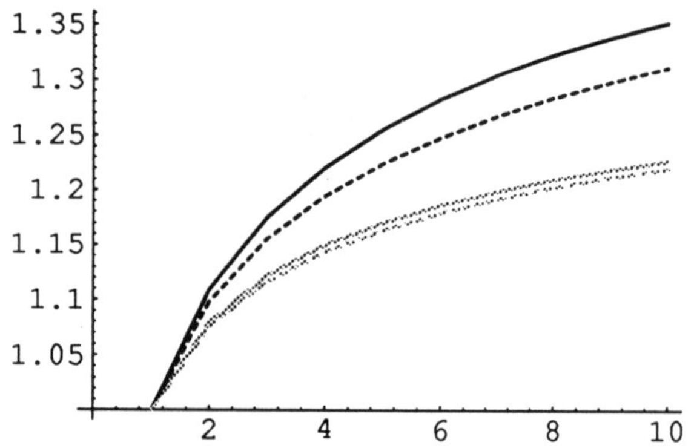

Fig. 6. Average speedup $\langle S(k) \rangle$ (black) and median speedup (gray) vs. number of agents k for 100–node graphs at $\gamma = 4.5$. The solid curves include all samples while the dashed ones include only those whose average single-agent cost was at least 1000.

strategy for use by a single agent. For example, if the agent finds it is taking an inordinately long time in the search, it can abandon the search and start over. With a prudent choice of when to quit, this strategy can lead to improved performance. Specifically, suppose the agent restarts its search after τ steps. Then the time to solve the problem will be given by $T = \tau(m - 1) + t$, where m is the number of search repetitions required to find a case that finishes within the time bound and t is the time spent on this last search case. The expected overall search cost for this strategy when applied to a given problem is just $\ell(\tau) = \tau(\overline{m} - 1) + \overline{t}$ with the overbars denoting averages over the individual search distribution for this problem. Let $Q(i) = 1 - q(i + 1)$ be the probability the individual search completes in *at most* i steps. Then $Q(\tau)$ is the probability that a search trial will succeed before being terminated by the cost bound. Thus the average number of repetitions required for success is $\overline{m} = \frac{1}{Q(\tau)}$. The expected cost within a repetition that does in fact succeed is given by $\overline{t} = \sum_{i \leq \tau} ip(i|\tau)$ where $p(i|\tau) = \frac{p(i)}{Q(\tau)}$ is the conditional probability the search succeeds after exactly i steps given it succeeds in at most τ steps. Finally, using

the identity $\sum_{i \leq \tau} ip(i) = \tau Q(\tau) - \sum_{i < \tau} Q(\tau)$ we obtain the expression for, $\ell(\tau)$, the expected overall search cost for the "restart after τ steps" strategy:

$$\ell(\tau) = \frac{1}{Q(\tau)}\left(\tau - \sum_{i=0}^{\tau-1} Q(i)\right) \tag{2}$$

In particular, when the individual search is never aborted, corresponding to $\tau = \infty$, we recover the average individual search cost, i.e., $\ell(\infty) = T_1$.

Among all possible choices of the cutoff time, even allowing it to vary from one repetition of the search to the next, the optimal strategy [Luby et al., 1993] is obtained by selecting a single termination time τ^* which minimizes $\ell(\tau)$. The speedup of this search method over the original one is then given by

$$S_{opt} = \frac{T_1}{\ell(\tau^*)} \tag{3}$$

Finally we should note that this strategy of restarting searches if they don't finish within a prespecified time can be combined with independent parallel agents to give even greater potential speedups [Luby and Ertel, 1993].

Experimental Results: Optimal Strategy

Unfortunately, in practice one never knows the cost distribution for a new problem before starting the search. However, we can evaluate it for a range of graph coloring problems as an additional indication of the benefit of independent search for graphs of different connectivities. This can also give some indication of the appropriate termination time to use.

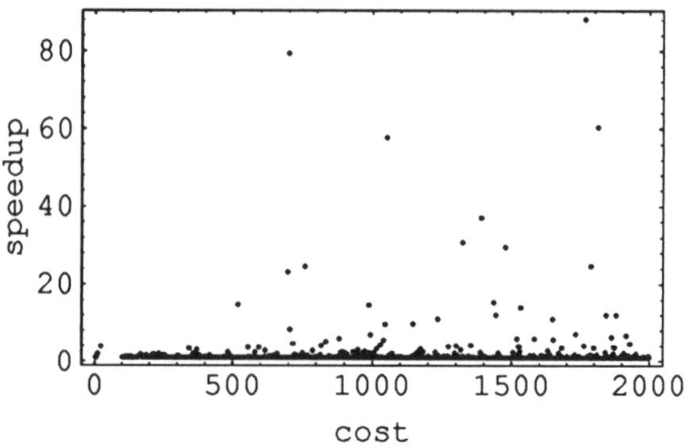

Fig. 7. Speedup S_{opt} for optimal single-agent search vs. average single-agent cost T_1 for 100–node graphs at $\gamma = 3.5$. Each graph was searched 100 times to estimate the single-agent cost distribution. We also found samples with substantially higher costs than shown in the plot, which continued the trend toward increasing speedups.

In Figs. 7 and 8 we show the speedup of this "optimal restart" single search strategy compared to the average "never restart" single search time. We see the same

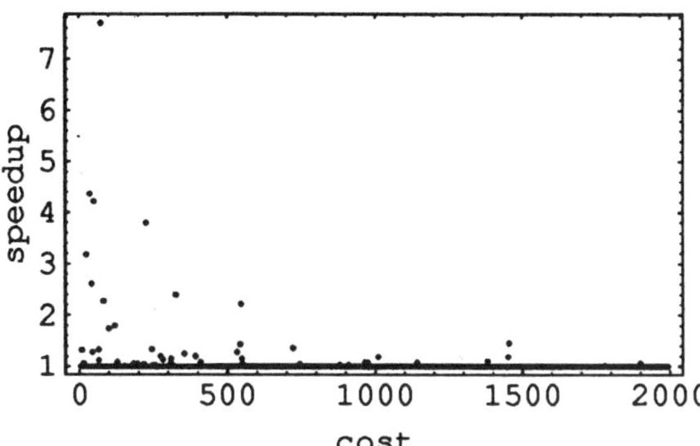

Fig. 8. Speedup S_{opt} for optimal single-agent search vs. average single-agent cost T_1 for 100–node graphs at $\gamma = 4.5$. Each graph was searched 100 times to estimate the single-agent cost distribution.

qualitative behavior as with our previous results on independent parallel search: no significant speedup for many of the harder problems but with somewhat more speedup for the cases at the lower connectivity.

As with the independent parallel search, an extended multimodal distribution allows this strategy to greatly outperform a single search, on average. Thus these results again demonstrate the existence of the two types of cost distributions.

Discussion

We have examined the benefit from independent parallel search for a particular constraint satisfaction problem, as a function of a parameter characterizing the structure of the problem. This extends previous work on the existence of hard and easy regions of problems to the question of what kinds of search methods are suitable for the hard instances. With our samples we saw that, for the most part, independent parallelization gives fairly limited improvement for the hard cases. This is consistent with previous observations that the hard problems persist for a range of common heuristic search algorithms; and the resulting conjecture that these problems are intrinsically hard because of their structure. Specifically, this may be due to their having a large number of partial solutions, few of which can be extended to full solutions [Cheeseman et al., 1991, Williams and Hogg, 1992]. These large partial solutions in turn make it difficult for heuristics, based on a local evaluation of the search space, to rapidly prune unproductive search paths. Our results for the graphs with limited speedup lend support to this conjecture.

There were also a number of cases with significant speedup, especially for the lower connectivity graphs. Since this is due to a very extended, multimodal distribution, an interpretation of these cases is that the overall cost is very sensitive to the early decisions made by the heuristic. While the correct choice leads to relatively rapid search, the structure of the problem does not readily provide an indication of incorrect choices. Thus in the latter case the search continues a long time before finally revising the early choices.

As a caveat, we should point out that our observations are based on a limited sampling of the individual search cost distribution (i.e., 100 trials per graph). Because of the extended nature of these distributions, additional samples may reveal some rare but extremely high cost search runs. These runs could significantly increase the mean individual search time while having only a modest effect on the parallel speeds. In such cases, the estimate of the potential speedup based on our limited sampling would be too low. To partially address this issue we searched a few graphs with significantly more trials (up to 10^4 per graph), finding the same qualitative behaviors.

There are a number of future directions for this work. One important question is the extent to which our results apply to other constraint satisfaction problems which also exhibit this behavior of easy and hard regions; as well as to other types of search methods such as genetic algorithms [Goldberg, 1989] or simulated annealing [Johnson et al., 1991]. For instance, when applied to optimization problems, one would need to consider the quality of solutions obtained as well as the search time required. Another issue concerns how the behaviors reported here may change as larger problems are considered.

Curiously, independent studies of other NP-hard problems, using very different search algorithms, have discovered qualitatively similar kinds of cost distributions [Ertel, 1992]. It is possible, therefore, that such distributions are quite generic across many different problems and algorithms. If so, our observation that the potential gains from independent parallel search vary with some parameter characterizing the problem structure, might be useful in designing an overall better parallel search algorithm. Specifically, as hard problems in the "hard" region do not appear to benefit much from independent parallelization we might prefer instead attempt to solve problems in this region by some more sophisticated parallel search method.

We have experimented with one such method, which we call "cooperative problem solving" in which the different computational agents exchange and reuse information found during the search, rather than executing independently. If the search methods are sufficiently diverse but nevertheless occasionally able to utilize information found in other parts of the search space, greater performance improvements are possible [Hogg and Williams, 1993] including, in some cases, the possibility of super-linear speedups [Clearwater et al., 1991].

References

Cheeseman, P., Kanefsky, B., and Taylor, W. M. (1991). Where the really hard problems are. In Mylopoulos, J. and

Reiter, R., editors, *Proceedings of IJCAI91*, pages 331–337, San Mateo, CA. Morgan Kaufmann.

Clearwater, S. H., Huberman, B. A., and Hogg, T. (1991). Cooperative solution of constraint satisfaction problems. *Science*, 254:1181–1183.

Crawford, J. M. and Auton, L. D. (1993). Experimental results on the cross-over point in satisfiability problems. In *Proc. of the Eleventh Natl. Conf. on AI (AAAI93)*, pages 21–27, Menlo Park, CA. AAAI Press.

Ertel, W. (1992). Random competition: A simple, but efficient method for parallelizing inference systems. In Fronhofer, B. and Wrightson, G., editors, *Parallelization in Inference Systems*, pages 195–209. Springer, Dagstuhl, Germany.

Fishburn, J. P. (1984). *Analysis of Speedup in Distributed Algorithms*. UMI Research Press, Ann Arbor, Michigan.

Gent, I. P. and Walsh, T. (1993). An empirical analysis of search in GSAT. *J. of AI Research*, 1:47–59.

Goldberg, D. E. (1989). *Genetic Algorithms in Search, Optimization and Machine Learning*. Addison-Wesley, NY.

Helmbold, D. P. and McDowell, C. E. (1989). Modeling speedup(n) greater than n. In Ris, F. and Kogge, P. M., editors, *Proc. of 1989 Intl. Conf. on Parallel Processing*, volume 3, pages 219–225, University Park, PA. Penn State Press.

Hogg, T. and Williams, C. P. (1993). Solving the really hard problems with cooperative search. In *Proc. of the. Eleventh Natl. Conf. on AI (AAAI93)*, pages 231–236, Menlo Park, CA. AAAI Press.

Imai, M., Yoshida, Y., and Fukumura, T. (1979). A parallel searching scheme for multiprocessor systems and its application to combinatorial problems. In *Proc. of IJCAI-79*, pages 416–418.

Janakiram, V. K., Agrawal, D. P., and Mehrotra, R. (1987). Randomized parallel algorithms for prolog programs and backtracking applications. In Sahni, S. K., editor, *Proc. of 1987 Intl. Conf. on Parallel Processing*, pages 278–281, University Park, PA. Penn State Univ. Press.

Johnson, D. S., Aragon, C. R., McGeoch, L. A., and Schevon, C. (1991). Optimization by simulated annealing: An experimental evaluation; part ii, graph coloring and number partitioning. *Operations Research*, 39(3):378–406.

Kornfeld, W. A. (1981). The use of parallelism to implement a heuristic search. In *Proc. of IJCAI-81*, pages 575–580.

Luby, M. and Ertel, W. (1993). Optimal parallelization of las vegas algorithms. Technical report, Intl. Comp. Sci. Inst., Berkeley, CA.

Luby, M., Sinclair, A., and Zuckerman, D. (1993). Optimal speedup of las vagas algorithms. Technical Report TR-93-010, Intl. Comp. Sci. Inst., Berkeley, CA.

Mehrotra, R. and Gehringer, E. F. (1985). Superlinear speedup through randomized algorithms. In Degroot, D., editor, *Proc. of 1985 Intl. Conf. on Parallel Processing*, pages 291–300, Washington, DC. IEEE.

Minton, S., Johnston, M. D., Philips, A. B., and Laird, P. (1990). Solving large-scale constraint satisfaction and scheduling problems using a heursitic repair method. In *Proceedings of AAAI-90*, pages 17–24, Menlo Park, CA. AAAI Press.

Mitchell, D., Selman, B., and Levesque, H. (1992). Hard and easy distributions of SAT problems. In *Proc. of 10th Natl. Conf. on Artificial Intelligence (AAAI92)*, pages 459–465, Menlo Park. AAAI Press.

Pramanick, I. and Kuhl, J. G. (1991). Study of an inherently parallel heuristic technique. In *Proc. of 1991 Intl. Conf. on Parallel Processing*, volume 3, pages 95–99.

Rao, V. N. and Kumer, V. (1992). On the efficiency of parallel backtracking. *IEEE Trans. on Parallel and Distributed Computing*.

Selman, B., Levesque, H., and Mitchell, D. (1992). A new method for solving hard satisfiability problems. In *Proc. of 10th Natl. Conf. on Artificial Intelligence (AAAI92)*, pages 440–446, Menlo Park, CA. AAAI Press.

Williams, C. P. and Hogg, T. (1992). Using deep structure to locate hard problems. In *Proc. of 10th Natl. Conf. on Artificial Intelligence (AAAI92)*, pages 472–477, Menlo Park, CA. AAAI Press.

Williams, C. P. and Hogg, T. (1993). Extending deep structure. In *Proc. of the Eleventh Natl. Conf. on AI (AAAI93)*, pages 152–157, Menlo Park, CA. AAAI Press.

Noise Strategies for Improving Local Search

Bart Selman, Henry A. Kautz, and Bram Cohen
AT&T Bell Laboratories
Murray Hill, NJ 07974
{selman, kautz, cohen}@research.att.com

Abstract

It has recently been shown that local search is surprisingly good at finding satisfying assignments for certain computationally hard classes of CNF formulas. The performance of basic local search methods can be further enhanced by introducing mechanisms for escaping from local minima in the search space. We will compare three such mechanisms: simulated annealing, random noise, and a strategy called "mixed random walk". We show that mixed random walk is the superior strategy. We also present results demonstrating the effectiveness of local search with walk for solving circuit synthesis and circuit diagnosis problems. Finally, we demonstrate that mixed random walk improves upon the best known methods for solving MAX-SAT problems.

Introduction

Local search algorithms have been successfully applied to many optimization problems. Hansen and Jaumard (1990) describe experiments using local search for MAX-SAT, *i.e.*, the problem of finding an assignment that satisfies as many clauses as possible of a given CNF formula. In general, such local search algorithms find good but non-optimal solutions, and thus such algorithms were believed not to be suitable for satisfiability testing, where the objective is to find an assignment that satisfies *all* clauses (if such an assignment exists).

Recently, however, local search has been shown to be surprisingly good at finding completely satisfying assignments for CNF problems (Selman *et al.* 1992; Gu 1992). Such methods outperform the best known systematic search algorithms on certain classes of large satisfiability problems. For example, GSAT, a randomized local search algorithm, can solve 2,000 variable computationally hard randomly-generated 3CNF (conjunctive normal form) formulas, whereas the current fastest systematic search algorithms cannot handle instances from the same distribution with more than 400 variables (Buro and Kleine-Büning 1992; Dubois *et al.* 1993).

The basic GSAT algorithm performs a local search of the space of truth-assignments by starting with a randomly-generated assignment, and then repeatedly changing ("flipping") the assignment of a variable that leads to the largest decrease in the total number of unsatisfied clauses. As with any combinatorial problem, local minima in the search space are problematic in the application of local search methods. A local minimum is defined as a state whose local neighborhood does not include a state that is strictly better. The standard approach in combinatorial optimization of terminating the search when a local minimum is reached (Papadimitriou and Steiglitz 1982) does not work well for Boolean satisfiability testing, since only global optima are of interest. In Selman *et al.* (1992) it is shown that simply continuing to search by making non-improving, "sideways" moves, dramatically increases the success rate of the algorithm.[1] We call the set of states explored in a sequence of sideways moves a "plateau" in the search space. The search along plateaus often dominates GSAT's search. For a detailed analysis, see Gent and Walsh (1992).

The success of GSAT is determined by its ability to move between successively lower plateaus. The search fails if GSAT can find no way off of a plateau, either because such transitions from the plateau are rare or nonexistent. When this occurs, one can simply restart the search at new random initial assignment. There are other mechanisms for escaping from local minima or plateaus, which are based on occasionally making uphill moves. Prominent among such approaches has been the use of simulated annealing (Kirkpatrick *et al.* 1982), where a formal parameter (the "temperature") controls the probability that the local search algorithm makes an uphill move.

In Selman and Kautz (1993), we proposed another mechanism for introducing such uphill moves. The strategy is based on mixing a random walk over variables that appear in unsatisfied clauses with the greedy local search. The strategy can be viewed as a way of introducing noise in a very focused manner — namely, perturbing only those variables critical to to the re-

---

[1] Minton *et al.* (1990) encountered a similar phenomenon in their successful application of local search in solving large scheduling problems.

maining unsatisfied clauses.

We will present detailed experimental data comparing the random walk strategy, simulated annealing, random noise, and the basic GSAT procedure on computationally difficult random formulas. In doing this comparison, we tuned the parameter settings of each procedure to obtain their best performance. We will see that the random walk strategy significantly outperforms the other approaches, and that all the escape strategies are an improvement over basic GSAT.

One might speculate that the good performance of the random walk strategy is a consequence of our choice of test instances. We therefore also ran experiments using several other classes of problem instances, developed by transforming other combinatorial problems into satisfiability instances. In particular, we considered problems from planning (Kautz and Selman 1992) and circuit synthesis (Kamath *et al.* 1991; 1993). These experiments again demonstrate that mixed random walk is the superior escape mechanism. In addition, we show that GSAT with walk is faster than systematic search on certain circuit synthesis problems (such as adders and comparators) that contain *no* random component. We then present data on experiments with a modified version of the random walk strategy that further improves performance over GSAT with walk. Finally, we demonstrate that mixed random walk also improves upon the best known methods for solving MAX-SAT problems.

Local Search for Satisfiability Testing

GSAT (Selman *at al.* 1992) performs a greedy local search for a satisfying assignment of a set of propositional clauses.[2] The procedure starts with a randomly generated truth assignment. It then changes ("flips") the assignment of the variable that leads to the greatest decrease in the total number of unsatisfied clauses. Note that the greatest decrease may be zero (sideways move) or negative (uphill move). Flips are repeated until either a satisfying assignment is found or a pre-set maximum number of flips (MAX-FLIPS) is reached. This process is repeated as needed up to a maximum of MAX-TRIES times.

In Selman *et al.* (1992), it was shown that GSAT substantially outperforms backtracking search procedures, such as the Davis-Putnam procedure, on various classes of formulas, including hard randomly generated formulas and SAT encodings of graph coloring problems (Johnson *et al.* 1991).

As noted above, local minima in the search space of a combinatorial problem are the primary obstacle to the application of local search methods. GSAT's use of sideways moves does not completely eliminate this problem, because the algorithm can still become stuck on a plateau (a set of neighboring states each with an equal number of unsatisfied clauses). Therefore, it is useful to employ mechanisms that escape from local minima or plateaus by making uphill moves (flips that increase the number of unsatisfied clauses). We will now discuss two mechanisms for making such moves.[3]

Simulated Annealing

Simulated annealing introduces uphill moves into local search by using a noise model based on statistical mechanics (Kirkpatrick *et al.* 1983). We employ the annealing algorithm defined in Johnson *et al.* (1991): Start with a randomly generated truth assignment. Repeatedly pick a random variable, and compute δ, the change in the number of unsatisfied clauses when that variable is flipped. If $\delta \leq 0$ (a downhill or sideways move), make the flip. Otherwise, flip the variable with probability $e^{-\delta/T}$, where T is a formal parameter called the *temperature*. The temperature may be either held constant,[4] or slowly decreased from a high temperature to near zero according to a cooling schedule. One often uses *geometric* schedules, in which the temperature is repeatedly reduced by multiplying it by a constant factor (< 1).

Given a finite cooling schedule, simulated annealing is not guaranteed to find a global optimum — that is, an assignment that satisfies all clauses. Therefore in our experiments we use multiple random starts, and compute the average number of restarts needed before finding a solution. We call this number R.

The basic GSAT algorithm is very similar to annealing at temperature zero, but differs in that GSAT naturally employ restarts and *always* makes a downhill move if one is available. The value of R for GSAT is simply the average number of tries required to find a solution.

The Random Walk Strategy

In Selman and Kautz (1993), we introduced several extensions to the basic GSAT procedure. One of those extensions mixes a random walk strategy with the greedy local search. More precisely, they propose the following **mixed random walk strategy:**

With probability p, pick a variable occuring in some unsatisfied clause and flip its truth assignment.
With probability $1 - p$, follow the standard GSAT scheme, *i.e.*, make the best possible local move.

Note that the "walk" moves can be uphill.

---

[3]If the *only* possible move for GSAT is uphill, it will make such a move, but such "forced" uphill moves are quite rare, and are not effective in escaping from local minima or plateaus.

[4]This form of annealing corresponds to the Metropolis algorithm (Jerrum 1992). See Pinkas and Dechter (1992), for an interesting modification of the basic annealing scheme.

---

[2]A clause is a disjunction of literals. A literal is a propositional variable or its negation. A set of clauses corresponds to a CNF formula: a conjunction of disjunctions.

A natural and simpler variation of the random walk strategy is not to restrict the choice of a randomly flipped variable to the set of variables that appear in unsatisfied clauses. We will refer to this modification as the *random noise* strategy. Note that random walk differs from both simulated annealing and random noise, in that in random walk upward moves are closely linked to unsatisfied clauses. The experiments discussed below will show that the random walk strategy is generally significantly better.

Experimental Results

We compared the basic GSAT algorithm, simulated annealing, random walk, and random noise strategies on a test suite including both randomly-generated CNF problems and Boolean encodings of other combinatorial problems. The results are given in the Tables 1, 2, and 3. For each strategy we give the average time in seconds it took to find a satisfying assignment,[5] the average number of flips it required, and R, the average number of restarts needed before finding a solution. For each strategy we used at least 100 random restarts (MAX-TRIES setting in GSAT) on each problem instance; if we needed more than 20 restarts before finding a solution, the strategy was restarted up to 1,000 times. A "*" in the tables indicates that no solution was found after running for more than 10 hours or using more than 1,000 restarts.

The parameters of each method were varied over a range of values, and only the results of the best settings are included in the table. For basic GSAT, we varied MAX-FLIPS and MAX-TRIES; for GSAT with random walk, we also varied the probability p with which a non-greedy move is made, and similarly for GSAT with random noise. In all of our experiments, the optimal value of p was found to be between 0.5 and 0.6. For constant temperature simulated annealing, we varied the temperature T from 5 to 0 in steps of 0.05. (At $T = 5$, uphill moves are accepted with probability greater than 0.8.) For the random formulas, the best performance was found at $T = 0.2$. The planning formulas required a higher temperature, $T = 0.5$, while the Boolean circuit synthesis were solved most quickly at a low temperature, $T = 0.15$.

We also experimented with various geometric cooling schedules. Surprisingly, we did not find any geometric schedule that was better than the best constant-temperature schedule. We could not even significantly improve the average number of restarts needed before finding a solution by extremely slow cooling schedules, regardless of the effect on execution time. An possible explanation for this is that almost all the work in solving CNF problems lies in satisfying the last few unsatisfied clauses. This corresponds to the low-temperature tail of a geometric schedule, where the temperature has little variation.

Hard Random Formulas

Random instances of CNF formulas are often used in evaluating satisfiability procedures because they can be easily generated and lack any underlying "hidden" structure often present in hand-crafted instances. Unfortunately, unless great care is taken in specifying the parameters of the random distribution, the problems so created can be trivial to solve. Mitchell *et al.* (1992) show how computationally difficult random problems can be generated using the fixed-clause length model. Let N be the number of variables, K the number of literals per clause, and L the number of clauses. Each instance is obtained by generating L random clauses each containing K literals. The K literals are generated by randomly selecting K variables, and each of the variables is negated with a 50% probability. The difficulty of such formulas critically depends on the ratio between N and L. The hardest formulas lie around the region where there is a 50% chance of the randomly generated formula being satisfiable. For 3CNF formulas ($K = 3$), experiments show that this is the case for $L \approx 4.3N$. (For larger N the the critical ratio for the 50% point converges to 4.25.) We tested the algorithms on formulas around the 4.3 point ranging in size from 100 to 2000 variables.

Table 1 presents our results. For the smallest (100-variable) formula, we observe little difference in the running times. As the number of variables increase, however, the random walk strategy significantly dominates the other approaches. Both random noise and simulated annealing also improve upon basic GSAT, but neither of these methods found solutions for largest three formulas.[6] The performance of GSAT with walk is quite impressive, especially consider that fact that fastest current systematic search methods cannot solve hard random 3CNF instances with over 400 variables (Dubois *et al.* 1993).

The columns marked with "flips" give the average number of flips required to find an assignment. (A "flip" in our simulated annealing algorithm is an actual change in the truth assignment. We do not count flips that were considered but not made.) When comparing the number of flips required by the various strategies, we arrive at the same conclusion about the relative efficiencies of the methods. This shows that our observations based on the running times are not simply a consequence of differences in the relative efficiencies of our implementations.

Finally, let us consider R, the average number of restarts needed before finding a solution. Basic GSAT easily gets stuck on plateaus, and requires many random restarts, in particular for larger formulas. On the

---

[5] The algorithms were implemented in C and ran on an SGI Challenge with a 70 MHz MIPS R4400 processor. For code and experimental data, contact the first author.

[6] GSAT with walk finds approximately 50% of the formulas in the hard region to be satisfiable, as would be expected at the transition point for SAT.

| formula | | GSAT | | | | | | | | | | Simul. Ann. | | |
| | | basic | | | walk | | | noise | | | | | | |
vars	clauses	time	flips	R	time	flips	R	time	flips	R	time	flips	R
100	430	.4	7554	8.3	.2	2385	1.0	.6	9975	4.0	.6	4748	1.1
200	860	22	284693	143	4	27654	1.0	47	396534	6.7	21	106643	1.2
400	1700	122	2.6×10^6	67	7	59744	1.1	95	892048	6.3	75	552433	1.1
600	2550	1471	30×10^6	500	35	241651	1.0	929	7.8×10^6	20	427	2.7×10^6	3.3
800	3400	*	*	*	286	1.8×10^6	1.1	*	*	*	*	*	*
1000	4250	*	*	*	1095	5.8×10^6	1.2	*	*	*	*	*	*
2000	8480	*	*	*	3255	23×10^6	1.1	*	*	*	*	*	*

Table 1: Comparing noise strategies on hard random 3CNF instances.

other hand, GSAT with walk is practically guaranteed to find a satisfying assignment. Apparently, mixing random walk over variables in the unsatisfied clauses with greedy moves allows one to escape almost always from plateaus that have few or no states from which a downhill move can be made. The other two strategies also give an improved value of R over basic GSAT but the effect is less dramatic.

Planning Problems

As a second example of the effectiveness of the various escape strategies, we consider encodings of blocks-world planning problems (Kautz and Selman 1992). Such formulas are very challenging for basic GSAT. Examination of the best assignments found when GSAT fails to find a satisfying assignment indicates that difficulties arise from extremely deep local minima. For example, the planning problem labeled "Hanoi" corresponds to the familiar "towers of Hanoi" puzzle, in which one moves a stack of disks between three pegs while never placing a larger disk on top of a smaller disk. There are many truth assignments that satisfy *nearly* all of the clauses that encode this problem, but that are very different from the correct satisfying assignment; for example, such a near-assignment may correspond to slipping a disk out from the bottom of the stack.

As seen in Table 2, GSAT with random walk is far superior. As before, basic GSAT fails to solve the largest problems. GSAT with walk is about 100 times faster than simulated annealing on the two largest problems, and over 200 times faster than random noise. The random noise and annealing strategies on the large problems also require many more restarts than the random walk strategy before finding a solution.

Circuit Synthesis

Kamath *et al.* (1991) developed a set of SAT encodings of Boolean circuit synthesis problems in order to test a satisfiability procedure based on integer programming. The task under consideration was to derive a logical circuit from its input-output behavior. Selman *et al.* (1992) showed that basic GSAT was competitive with their integer-programming method. In Table 3,

we give our experimental results on five of the hardest instances considered by Kamath *et al.* As is clear from the table, both the random walk and the simulated annealing strategies significantly improve upon GSAT, with random walk being somewhat better than simulated annealing. For comparison, we also included the original timings reported by Kamath *et al.*[7] In this case, the random noise strategy does not lead to an improvement over basic GSAT. In fact mixing in random noise appears to degrade GSAT's performance. Note that the basic GSAT procedure already performs quite well on these formulas, which suggests that they are relatively easy compared to our other benchmark problems.

The instances from Kamath *et al.* (1991) were derived from randomly wired Boolean circuits. So, although the SAT encodings contain some intricate structure from the underlying Boolean gates, there is still a random aspect to the problem instances. Recently, Kamath *et al.* (1993) have generalized their approach, to allow for circuits with multiple outputs. Using this formulation, we can encode Boolean circuits that are useful in practical applications. Some examples are adder and comparator circuits. We encoded the I/O behavior of several of such circuits, and used GSAT with walk to solve them. Table 4 shows our results. ("GSAT+w" denotes GSAT with walk. We used $p = 0.5$. We will discuss the "WSAT" column below.) The type of circuit is indicated in the table. For example, every satisfying assignment for the formula 2bitadd_11 corresponds to a design for a 2-bit adder using a PLA (Programmable Logic Array). The suffix "11" indicates that the circuit is constrained to use only 11 AND-gates. We see from the table that GSAT with walk can solve the instances in times that range from less than a second to a few minutes. We also included the timings for the Davis-Putnam (DP) procedure. We used a variant of this procedure developed by Crawford and Auton (1993). This procedure is currently one of the fastest complete methods, but it is quite surprising to see that it only solves two of

---

[7]Kamath *et al.*'s satisfiability procedure ran on a VAX 8700 with code written in FORTRAN and C.

formula			GSAT basic			GSAT walk			GSAT noise			Simul. Ann.		
id	vars	clauses	time	flips	R	time	flips	R	time	flips	R	time	flips	R
med.	273	2311	7.5	70652	125	0.4	3464	1.0	4.5	41325	1.1	4.5	12147	1.0
rev.	201	1382	3.7	41693	100	0.3	3026	1.0	2.7	29007	1.1	2.7	9758	1.0
hanoi	417	2559	*	*	*	39	334096	2.6	20017	16×10^6	100	3250	4.1×10^6	25
huge	937	14519	*	*	*	38	143956	1.1	9648	37×10^6	200	8302	4.4×10^6	13

Table 2: Comparing noise strategies on SAT encodings of planning problems.

formula		Int.P.	GSAT basic			GSAT walk			GSAT noise			Simul. Ann.		
id	vars	time	time	flips	$R.$	time	flips	$R.$	time	flips	$R.$	time	flips	$R.$
f16a1	1650	2039	58	709895	5	2	3371	1.1	375	1025454	6.7	12	98105	1.3
f16b1	1728	78	269	2870019	167	12	25529	1.0	1335	2872226	167	11	96612	1.4
f16c1	1580	758	2	12178	1.0	1	1545	1.0	5	14614	1.0	5	21222	1.0
f16d1	1230	1547	87	872219	7.1	3	5582	1.0	185	387491	1.0	4	25027	1.0
f16e1	1245	2156	1	2090	1.0	1	1468	1.0	1	3130	1.0	3	5867	1.0

Table 3: Comparing noise strategies on the circuit synthesis problem instances as studied in Kamath *et al.* (1991).

the instances.[8] (A "$\star$" indicates that the method ran for 10 hrs without finding an assignment.) The good performance of GSAT with walk on these problems indicates that local search methods can perform well on structured problems that do not contain any random component.

Circuit Diagnosis

Larrabee (1992) proposed a translation of the problem of test pattern generation for VLSI circuits into a SAT problem. We compared the performance of GSAT with walk and that of DP on several of Larrabee's formulas. Our results are in table 5.[9] We see that GSAT with walk again works very well, especially compared to DP's systematic search. These results and the ones for circuit synthesis are of particular interest because they involve encodings of problems with clear practical applications, and are not just useful as benchmark problems for testing satisfiability procedures.

Modifying the Random Walk Strategy

We have recently begun to experiment with a new algorithm that implements GSAT's random walk strategy with subtle but significant modifications. This new algorithm, called WSAT (for "walk sat"), makes flips by first randomly picking a clause that is not satisfied by the current assignment, and then picking (either at random or according to a greedy heuristic) a variable within that clause to flip. Thus, while GSAT with walk can be viewed as adding "walk" to a greedy algorithm, WSAT can be viewed as adding greediness as a heuristic to random walk. The "WSAT" columns in Tables 4 and 5 shows that WSAT can give a substantial speed up over GSAT with walk. Whether or not WSAT outperforms GSAT with walk appears to depend on the particular problem class. We are currently studying this further.

One unexpected and interesting observation we have already made is that there can be a great variance between running GSAT with 100% walk (*i.e.*, $p = 1.0$) and running WSAT where variables are picked within an unsatisfied clause at random. At first glance, these options would appear to be identical. However, there is a subtle difference in the probability that a given variable is picked to be flipped. GSAT maintains a list (without duplicates) of the variables that appear in unsatisfied clauses, and picks at random from that list; thus, every variable that appears in an unsatisfied clause is chosen with equal probability. WSAT employs the two-step random process described above (first picking a clause, and then picking a variable), that favors variables that appear in many unsatisfied clauses. For many classes of formulas, the difference does not appear to be significant. However, GSAT with 100% walk does not solve the circuit diagnosis problems, whereas WSAT with random picking can solve all of them.

Maximum Satisfiability

Finally, we compare the performance of GSAT with walk to the methods studied by Hansen and Jaumard (1990) for MAX-SAT. Our results appear in Table 6. Hansen and Jaumard compared five differ-

---

[8]Preliminary experiments indicate that some of these formulas can also be solved by combining DP with multiple starts that randomly permute variables. Details will appear in the full version. We thank Jimi Crawford for discussions on this issue.

[9]The table contains some typical satisfiable instances from a collection made available by Allan van Gelder and Yumi Tsuji at the University of California at Irvine.

| formula | | | DP | GSAT+w | WSAT |
id	vars	clauses	time	time	time
2bitadd_12	708	1702	*	0.081	0.013
2bitadd_11	649	1562	*	0.058	0.014
3bitadd_32	8704	32316	*	94.1	1.0
3bitadd_31	8432	31310	*	456.6	0.7
2bitcomp_12	300	730	23096	0.009	0.002
2bitcomp_5	125	310	1.4	0.009	0.001

Table 4: Comparing an efficient complete method (DP) with local search strategies on circuit synthesis problems. (Timings in seconds.)

| formula | | | DP | GSAT+w | WSAT |
id	vars	clauses	time	time	time
ssa7552-038	1501	3575	7	129	2.3
ssa7552-158	1363	3034	*	90	2
ssa7552-159	1363	3032	*	14	0.8
ssa7552-160	1391	3126	*	18	1.5

Table 5: Comparing DP with local search strategies on circuit diagnosis problems by Larrabee (1989). (Timings in seconds.)

ent algorithms for MAX-SAT. They considered a basic local search algorithm called "zloc", two deterministic algorithms proposed by David Johnson (1974) called "zjohn1" and "zjohn2", a simulated annealing approach called "anneal", and their own "steepest ascent, mildest descent" algorithm, "zsamd". The last one is similar to basic GSAT with a form of a tabu list (Glover 1989). They showed that "zsamd" consistently outperformed the other approaches.

We repeated their main experiments using GSAT with walk. The problem instances are randomly generated 3SAT instances. For each problem size, 50 problems were randomly generated, and each problem was solved 100 times using different random initial assignments. The mean values of the best, and mean number of unsatisfied clauses found during the 100 tries are noted in the table. For example, on the 500 variable, 5000 clause 3SAT instances, the best assignments GSAT with walk found contained an average of 161.2 unsatisfied clauses. As we can see from the table, GSAT with walk consistently found better quality solutions than any other method. Note that there is only a small difference between the best and mean values found by GSAT with walk, which may indicate that the best values are in fact close to optimal.

Conclusions

We compared several mechanisms for escaping from local minima in satisfiability problems: simulated annealing, random noise, and mixed random walk. The walk strategy introduces perturbations in the current state that are directly relevant to the unsatisfied constraints of the problem. Our experiments show that this strategy significantly outperforms simulated an-

nealing and random noise on several classes of hard satisfiability problems. Both of the latter strategies can make perturbations that are in a sense less focused, in that they may involve variables that do not appear in any unsatisfied clauses. The relative improvement found by using random walk over the other methods increases with increasing problem size. We also showed that GSAT with walk to be remarkably efficient in solving basic circuit synthesis problems. This result is especially interesting because the synthesis problems do not have any random component, and are very hard for systematic methods. Finally, we demonstrated that GSAT with walk also improves upon the best MAX-SAT algorithms. Given the effectiveness of the mixed random walk strategy on Boolean satisfiability problems, an interesting direction for future research would be to explore similar strategies on general constraint satisfaction problems.

References

Buro, M. and Kleine-Büning, H. (1992). Report on a SAT competition. Technical Report # 110, Dept. of Mathematics and Informatics, University of Paderborn, Germany.

Crawford, J.M. and Auton, L.D. (1993) Experimental Results on the Cross-Over Point in Satisfiability Problems. *Proc. AAAI-93*, Washington, DC, 21–27.

Davis, M. and Putnam, H. (1960). A computing procedure for quantification theory. *J. Assoc. Comput. Mach.*, 7, 201–215.

Dubois, O., Andre, P., Boufkhad, Y., and Carlier, J. (1993). SAT versus UNSAT. DIMACS Workshop on Satisfiability Testing, New Brunswick, NJ, Oct. 1993.

Glover, F. (1989). Tabu search — Part I. *ORSA Journal*

method		100	100	100	300	300	300	300	500
#vars		100	100	100	300	300	300	300	500
#clauses		200	500	700	600	800	1500	2000	5000
zloc	best	0.4	10.8	21.0	2.8	8.3	35.4	64.4	233.8
zjohn1	mean	2.3	14.9	28.2	4.7	10.6	45.3	74.1	268.8
zjohn2	mean	1.4	13.5	26.9	2.7	9.0	44.1	76.5	257.4
anneal	best	0	5.6	15.1	0.7	3.1	22.6	47.6	215.7
zsamd	best	0	3.7	13.4	0.5	1.2	10.6	34.0	174.6
	mean	0.3	5.1	14.7	2.4	4.3	15.3	39	182.8
GSAT+	best	0	2.8	12.9	0	0	7.6	31.8	161.2
	mean	0	2.9	12.9	0	0	8.1	34.9	163.6

Table 6: Experimental results for MAX-3SAT. The data for the first five methods are from Hansen and Jaumard (1990).

of Computing, 1, 190–206.

Gent, I.P. and Walsh, T. (1992). The enigma of SAT hill-climbing procedures. Techn. report 605, Department of Computer Science, University of Edinburgh. Revised version appeared in the *Journal of Artificial Intelligence Research*, Vol. 1, 1993.

Gu, J. (1992). Efficient local search for very large-scale satisfiability problems. *Sigart Bulletin*, Vol. 3, no. 1, 8–12.

Hansen J. and Jaumard, B. (1990). Algorithms for the maximum satisfiability problem. *Computing*, 44, 279–303.

Jerrum, M. (1992) Large Cliques Elude the Metropolis Process. *Random Structures and Algorithms*, Vol. 3, no. 4, 347–359.

Johnson, D.S. (1974) Optimization algorithms for combinatorial problems. *J. of Comp. and Sys. Sci.*, 9:256–279.

Johnson, D.S., Aragon, C.R., McGeoch, L.A., and Schevon, C. (1991) Optimization by simulated annealing: an experimental evaluation; part II, graph coloring and number partioning. *Operations Research*, 39(3):378–406.

Kamath, A.P., Karmarkar, N.K., Ramakrishnan, K.G., and Resende, M.G.C. (1991). A continuous approach to inductive inference. *Mathematical Programming*, 57, 215–238.

Kamath, A.P., Karmarkar, N.K., Ramakrishnan, K.G., and Resende, M.G.C. (1993). An Interior Point Approach to Boolean Vector Function Synthesis. Technical Report, AT&T Bell Laboratories, Nov. 1993.

Kautz, H.A. and Selman, B. (1992). Planning as satisfiability. *Proceedings ECAI-92*, Vienna, Austria.

Kirkpatrick, S., Gelatt, C.D., and Vecchi, M.P. (1983). Optimization by Simulated Annealing. *Science*, 220, 671–680.

Larrabee, T. (1992). Test pattern generation using Boolean satisfiability. *IEEE Transactions on Computer-Aided Design*, 1992.

Minton, S., Johnston, M.D., Philips, A.B., and Laird, P. (1990) Solving large-scale constraint satisfaction and scheduling problems using a heuristic repair method. *Proceedings AAAI-90*, 1990, 17–24. Extended version appeared in *Artificial Intelligence*, 1992.

Mitchell, D., Selman, B., and Levesque, H.J. (1992). Hard and easy distributions of SAT problems. *Proceedings AAAI-92*, San Jose, CA, 459–465.

Papadimitriou, C.H. (1991). On Selecting a Satisfying Truth Assignment. *Proc. of the Conference on the Foundations of Computer Science*, 163–169.

Papadimitriou, C.H., Steiglitz, K. (1982). *Combinatorial optimization*. Englewood Cliffs, NJ: Prentice-Hall, Inc.

Pinkas, G. and Dechter, R. (1992). An Improved Connectionist Activation Function for Energy Minimization. *Proc. AAAI-92*, San Jose, CA, 434–439.

Selman, B. and Kautz, H.A. (1993). Domain-Independent Extensions to GSAT: Solving Large Structured Satisfiability Problems. *Proc. IJCAI-93*, Chambery, France.

Selman, B. and Levesque, H.J., and Mitchell, D.G. (1992). A New Method for Solving Hard Satisfiability Problems. *Proc. AAAI-92*, San Jose, CA, 440–446.

Improving Repair-based Constraint Satisfaction Methods by Value Propagation

Nobuhiro Yugami   Yuiko Ohta   Hirotaka Hara

FUJITSU LABORATORIES LTD.
1015, Kamikodanaka Nakahara-ku,
Kawasaki 211, Japan
yugami@flab.fujitsu.co.jp

Abstract

A constraint satisfaction problem (CSP) is a problem to find an assignment that satisfies given constraints. An interesting approach to CSP is a repair-based method that first generates an initial assignment, then repairs it by minimizing the number of conflicts. Min-conflicts hill climbing (MCHC) and GSAT are typical examples of this approach. A serious problem with this approach is that it is sometimes trapped by local minima. This makes it difficult to use repair-based methods for solving problems with many local minima.

We propose a new procedure, EFLOP, for escaping from local minima. EFLOP changes the values of mutually dependent variables by propagating changes through satisfied constraints. We can greatly improve the performance of repair-based methods by combining them with EFLOP.

We tested EFLOP with graph colorability problems, randomly generated binary CSPs and propositional satisfiability problems. EFLOP improved the performance of MCHC and GSAT for all experiments and was more efficient for large and difficult problems.

Introduction

A constraint satisfaction problem (CSP) is a problem to find an assignment that satisfies given constraints. Approaches to solving CSPs can be classified into constructive methods and repair-based methods [Minton et al. 92]. Constructive methods are based on a tree search and find a solution by incrementally extending a consistent partial assignment. Constraint directed search [Fox 87], arc and path consistency algorithms [Mohr & Henderson 86] and intelligent backtrackings such as dependency directed backtracking [Doyle 79] fall into this group. Repair-based methods are based on a local search. They first generate an initial assignment with conflicts, then repair it by minimizing the number of conflicts. Min-conflicts hill climbing (MCHC) [Minton et al. 90] and GSAT [Selman, Levesque & Mitchell 92] are typical examples. For small- and medium-scale problems, constructive methods show good performance. However, repair-based methods are more practical for large-scale problems.

Repair-based methods use local search techniques such as hill climbing to minimize the number of conflicts. Local search techniques do not provide the capability to escape from local minima. It is, thus difficult to solve a CSP with many local minima by using a repair-based method. One solution is to use a more powerful local search techniques such as simulated annealing (SA). Johnson et al. applied SA to graph colorability problems [Johnson et al. 91]. However, this has a major disadvantage that local search techniques capable of escaping from local minima such as SA, require a very long time for problem solving. Another solution is combining local search methods with a special procedure for escaping from local minima. [Selman & Kautz, 93] and [Morris, 93] proposed constraint weighting for escaping from local minima.

We propose a new procedure EFLOP (Escaping From Local Optima by Propagation) to resolve this problem. EFLOP changes the values of mutually dependent variables for escaping from local minima. Satisfied constraints are used for finding such a set of variables and their new values. Repair-based methods call EFLOP when they are trapped by local minima and restart search from an output assignment of EFLOP.

Repair-based methods and their limitations

Repair-based methods solve a minimization problem of the number of conflicts. If an original CSP is solvable, then the minimization problem has an optimum assignment with no conflict and the optimum assignment is a solution of the original CSP. Min-conflicts hill climbing (MCHC) [Minton et al. 90] solves this minimization problem by repairing an assignment with a following simple value selection heuristic.

Min-conflicts heuristic

Select a variable in conflict randomly. Assign it a value that minimizes the number of conflicts. Break ties randomly.

This heuristic guarantees that the number of conflicts of the new assignment is fewer than or equal to that of the old assignment because it selects the present value if all other values increase the number of conflicts. The number of conflicts, thus decreases monotonically.

MCHC could solve certain classes of CSPs, e.g., n-queens problems and graph colorability problems for dense graphs but could not solve other classes of CSPs such as graph colorability problems for sparse graphs [Minton et al. 92]. This is because MCHC has few ability to escape from local minima of the minimization problem. We explain this with an example of a graph colorability problem. Figure 1 shows a local minimum assignment for a 3-colorability problem used by Selman [Selman & Kautz 93] as an example that the basic GSAT could not escape from. Each node (variable) should be colored with one of the three colors but the color must be different from colors of neighboring nodes. In Figure 1, only one constraint, $x \neq y$, is violated. Min-conflicts heuristic selects x (or y) and tries to assign a new value to x. However, x=green and x=blue cause two conflicts respectively and x=red, the present value, minimizes the number of conflicts. Min-conflicts heuristic, thus selects red for x and MCHC can not escape from this local minimum assignment.

EFLOP procedure

We first discuss the property of local minimum assignments of CSPs. The example in Figure 1 can be

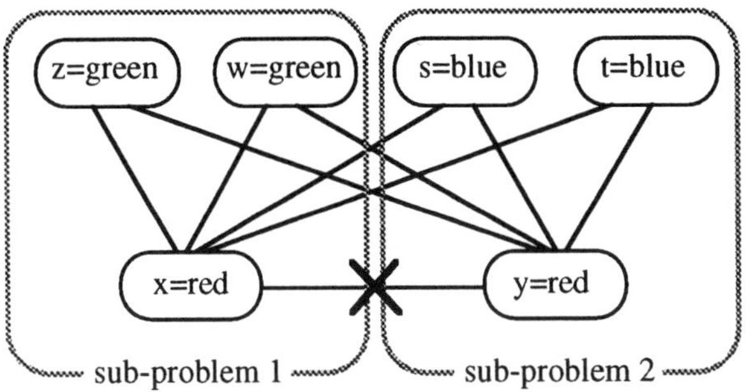

Figure 1: A local minimum assignment

A local minimum assignment and a division into consistent sub-problems of a graph 3-colorability problem. Only a constraint between sub-problems is violated.

divided into two sub-problems where all constraints within each sub-problem are satisfied but a constraint between sub-problems is violated. In general, if an assignment is local minimum, a problem can be divided into consistent sub-problems where conflicts occur only between different sub-problems. In such a case, changing the value of the conflicting variable causes new conflicts in the sub-problem that the variable belongs to. This increases the total number of conflicts and makes it impossible to escape from local minima with hill climbing like methods such as MCHC and GSAT.

This property of local minima leads directly to the following procedure for escaping from them.

Step 1: Find a consistent sub-problem that involves a variable in conflict.

Step 2: Change the values of variables in the sub-problem so that the new values satisfy all constraints in the sub-problem.

However, this is not practical because Step 2 requires to solve the sub-problem and takes a long time if the sub-problem is not small. EFLOP avoids this difficulty by combining Step 1 and Step 2, extending the sub-problem incrementally by propagating the changes of values of variables through satisfied constraints.

Figure 2 shows the procedure of EFLOP. EFLOP first selects a variable in conflict randomly and changes the value of it. If this change causes a satisfied constraint to become unsatisfied, EFLOP tries to resolve it by changing a value of another variable in the constraint. If

procedure EFLOP
Input   : a local minimum assignment;
Output: an assignment that is not local minimum;

begin
    select a variable v in conflict randomly;
    change v's value randomly;
    $V := \{v\}$;
    while possible
        select a constraint c that satisfies following
        conditions;
            (c1) c is satisfied before EFLOP is called;
            (c2) c is not satisfied now;
            (c3) there is a variable v in c and its value a
                such that
                (c3-1) $v \notin V$;
                (c3-2) v's present value is consistent with
                        old values of variables in V;
                (c3-3) $v=a$ makes c satisfied;
                (c3-4) $v=a$ is consistent with new values
                        of variables in V;
        change v's value to a;
        add v to V;
    end_of_while;
end;

Figure 2: EFLOP procedure

this second change causes a new constraint violation, EFLOP tries to resolve it by changing the value of the third variable. This is continued until no new conflict can be resolved by changing values of variables that aren't changed yet.

If more than one variable-value pairs satisfy the condition (c3), EFLOP selects one of them with a following heuristic so as not to propagate value changes to too many variables.

EFLOP heuristic

Select a pair of a variable and its value that minimizes the number of constraints which are satisfied before EFLOP is called but will be violated after the change. Break ties randomly.

The sub-problem defined by the set of changed variables V and constraints between variables in V, is consistent before EFLOP is called because of the

condition (c3-2). The sub-problem is also consistent after EFLOP terminates because of the condition (c3-4).

We explain EFLOP procedure in detail using the example in Figure 1. EFLOP first selects a variable in conflict and its new value (new value must be different from the present value) randomly. Let x and green be selected. EFLOP changes the value of x to green and initializes the set of changed variables V = {x}. This new value, green, violates two constraints, x≠z and x≠w. Both of these constraints satisfy conditions (c1)~(c3), EFLOP thus selects one of them. Let x≠z be selected. EFLOP tries to satisfy it by changing a value of a variable in it, i.e., x or z but EFLOP doesn't change x's value because the condition (c3-1) requires that each variable is changed at most once. Two variable-value pairs, z=red and z=blue, satisfy condition (c3). EFLOP selects z=blue because z=red causes one new conflict but z=blue causes no new conflict. EFLOP changes z's value to blue and adds z to V. Next, EFLOP tries to satisfy x≠w. Because of the same reason in x≠z, EFLOP changes w's value to blue. EFLOP terminates because there is no constraint that satisfies (c1)~(c3). EFLOP then assigns green to x, blue to z and blue to w, i.e., EFLOP changes the values of variables in sub-problem 1 (Figure 1) to other consistent values between them and the new assignment generated by EFLOP satisfies all constraints.

Experiments

In this section, we show the effect of EFLOP by using graph colorability problems, randomly generated binary CSPs and propositional satisfiability problems. EFLOP is not a method for solving CSP, but is a method for improving the performance of repair-based methods. We combined EFLOP with MCHC for binary CSPs and for colorability problems, and combined with GSAT for SAT. We compared their performance with and without EFLOP. MCHC (GSAT) with EFLOP calls EFLOP whenever it trapped by local minima and restarts from an output assignment of EFLOP. MCHC (GSAT) without EFLOP restarts from a randomly generated initial assignment when it is trapped by local minima. We used C language on a SPARCstation2 for all experiments.

Graph Colorability Problems

We generated 3-colorability problems of sparse graphs by the way in [Minton et al. 92]. We first divided N nodes

nodes	edges	MCHC	MCHC+EFLOP
30	60	304	85
60	120	3,320	341
90	180	13,700	924
120	240	71,000	1,880
150	300	334,000	3,990

Table 1: Average numbers of hill climbing steps for graph 3-colorability problems

variables	strength	MCHC	MCHC+EFLOP
20	0.64	9,890	3,570
40	0.64	203,000	71,100
60	0.62	3,320,000	334,000

Table 2: 50% solvable strength and average number of hill climbing steps for binary CSPs

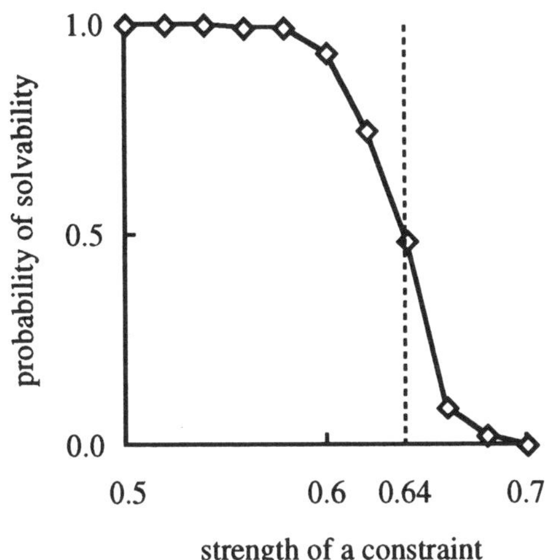

Figure 3: Probability of solvability of random CSPs with 20 variables, 10 values for each variable and 40 constraints

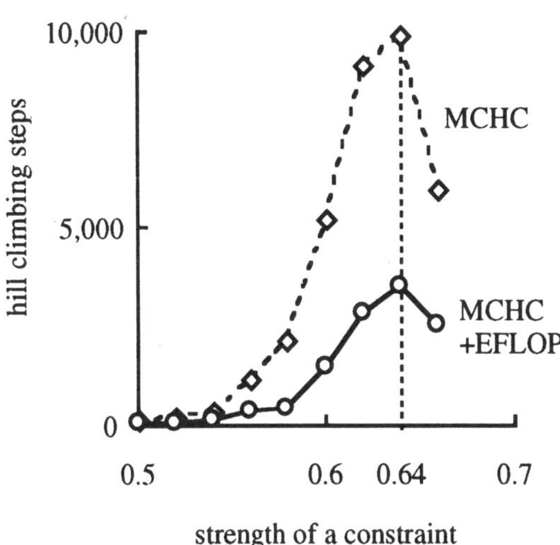

Figure 4: Average numbers of hill climbing steps for 20 variables CSPs

to 3 groups with N/3 nodes and randomly created edges between nodes in different groups. If the generated graph had unconnected components, we rejected it. This generation guarantees the solvability of generated problems.

We used the graphs with 2N edges because [Minton et al. 92] reported the poor performance of MCHC for such problems. Table 1 shows the average numbers of hill climbing steps of MCHC (average of 100 problems for each N) with and without EFLOP for 3-colorability problems with 30~150 nodes. EFLOP could improved MCHC drastically and its effect was larger for large problems than that of small problems.

Binary CSPs

We generated binary CSPs with 4 parameters, the number of variables, N, the domain size of each variable, D, the number of constraints, M and the strength of the constraint, S. The strength of the constraint is the ratio of the number of forbidden value pairs to the number of all value pairs of two variables in the constraint. This means that $(1-S)D^2$ value pairs satisfy the constraint and SD^2 value pairs violate the constraint. When generating a problem, we first selected M variable pairs as constraints and for each constraint (variable pair), we selected $(1-S)D^2$ permitted value pairs randomly. We did all selections randomly, so a generated problem may not have a solution. This way of generating CSPs was based on [Freuder & Wallace 92].

We first tested EFLOP's effect on CSPs with 20 variables, 10 possible values for each variable and 40 constraints (N=20, D=10, M=40). Figure 3 shows the probability of solvability, the ratio of solvable problems to generated problems and figure 4 shows the average numbers of hill climbing steps (average of 100 solvable problems for each strength). MCHC with EFLOP was faster than without at all strength and the difference was biggest at the "50% solvable" strength, the strength at which a half of randomly generated problems were solvable. This is because that when S was near this value, the ratio of the numbers of local minima to the number of solutions was large, so MCHC trapped by local minima with high probability.

Table 2 shows 50% solvable strengths and average numbers of hill climbing steps (average of 100 solvable problems) at the strengths of CSPs with 20, 40 and 60 variables. For each case, we set M=2N. It is interesting to note that the strength was almost constant. This suggests that the 50% solvable strength depends only on the constraints-to-variables ratio and domain size. The result was that EFLOP could improve the performance of MCHC for all cases and the improvement was greater for large problems. MCHC with EFLOP was about 3 times faster than MCHC without EFLOP for problems with 20 variables and the improvement was more than 10 times for problems with 60 variables.

Satisfiability Problems

A propositional satisfiability problem (SAT) is a problem to determine whether a given logical formula can be satisfied or not, and to find a truth assignment that satisfies the formula if it is satisfiable. The formula is given in conjunctive normal form and a clause is a constraint that at least one literal in the clause should be true. Selman et al. proposed an efficient repair-based method for SAT, GSAT [Selman, Levesque & Mitchell 92] and extended GSAT with clause weighting and random walk to overcome the inability to escape from local minima [Selman & Kautz 93]. We used basic GSAT and didn't use these extensions for our experiments because we wanted to know the effect of EFLOP alone.

We generated SAT with three parameters, the number of variables, N, and the number of clauses, M and the length of clause, K. For each clause, we first selected K variables randomly and negated each variable with probability 0.5. This generation was based on [Mitchell, Selman & Levesque 92].

We first tested EFLOP with 3-SAT (K=3) problems. Mitchell et al. [Mitchell, Selman & Levesque 92] reported

variables	clauses	GSAT	GSAT+EFLOP
50	215	1,390	562
100	430	11,300	5,760
150	637	87,800	35,600

Table 3: Average number of flips for 3-SAT

clause length	clauses	GSAT	GSAT+EFLOP
3	215	1,390	562
4	495	7,950	2,230
5	1,075	68,000	4,760

Table 4: Average number of flips for 3-, 4- and 5-SAT with 50 variables

the hardness of 3-SAT. Their conclusion was that 3-SAT was most difficult when the ratio of clauses to variables was 50% satisfiable ratio, the ratio at which a randomly generated problem was satisfiable with probability 0.5, and this ratio was 4.3 for 3-SAT. Table 3 shows the average number of flips (average of 100 satisfiable problems) for randomly generated 3-SAT with M=4.3N. GSAT with EFLOP was about twice as fast as GSAT without EFLOP. The difference between them didn't depend on the number of variables.

We also examined the dependency of the EFLOP's effect on clause length. Table 4 shows the 50% satisfiable clauses-to-variables ratio for 3-, 4- and 5-SAT and the average number of flips (average of 100 satisfiable problems) at the ratio. EFLOP was more effective for problems with longer clauses and GSAT with EFLOP was about 10 times faster than GSAT without EFLOP for 5-SAT.

Conclusions

We have proposed a new procedure, EFLOP, for improving the performance of repair-based constraint satisfaction methods such as min-conflicts hill climbing (MCHC) and GSAT. Repair-based methods solve a CSP by minimizes the number of conflicts. The most serious problem of these methods is that they can't escape from local minima. EFLOP propagates changes of values through satisfied constraints and changes the values of mutually dependent variables at once. This enables to escape from local minima and thus improves the performance of repair-based methods. EFLOP is independent on problem domains and can be used with any repair-based method.

We tested EFLOP's effect by using graph colorability problems, randomly generated binary CSPs and satisfiability problems. EFLOP improved the performance of MCHC and GSAT, and the improvement was greater for larger and more difficult problems.

An interesting question is how effective EFLOP is for structured problems such as planning problems. In structured problems, some variables strongly depend on each other and a value change for one variable causes many conflicts between such variables. In a planning problem, a selection of an operator is strongly dependent on previous operators and affects selections for following operators through its preconditions and post conditions. This property causes many local minima and makes it very difficult to solve structured problems by repair-based methods [Kautz & Mitchell 92]. EFLOP changes values of such mutually dependent variables at once, and the ability to do this will improve the performance of repair-based methods for structured problems.

References

[Doyle 79] J. Doyle : A Truth Maintenance System, Artificial Intelligence, Vol. 12, pp.231-272, 1979

[Fox 87] M. Fox : Constraint Directed Search: A Case Study of Job-Shop Scheduling, Morgan Kaufman Publishers, Inc., 1887

[Freuder & Wallace 92] E.C. Freuder and R.J.Wallace : Partial constraint satisfaction, Artificial Intelligence Vol. 58, pp.21-70, 1992

[Kautz & Selman 92] H. kautz and B. Selman : Planning as Satisfiability, Proc. ECAI 92, pp.359-363

[Johnson et al. 91] A. K. Johnson, C. R. Aragon, L. A. McGeoch and C. Schevon: Optimization by simulated annealing: an experimental evaluation Part II, Operating Research Vol. 39, pp.378-406, 1991

[Minton et al. 90] S. Minton, M. D. Johnston, A. B. Philips and P. Laird: Solving Large-Scale Constraint Satisfaction and Scheduling Problems Using a Heuristic Repair Method, Proc. of AAAI-90, pp.17-24, 1990

[Minton et al. 90] S. Minton, M. D. Johnston, A. B. Phillips and P. Laird: Minimizing conflicts: a heuristic repair method for constraint satisfaction and scheduling problems, Artificial Intelligence Vol. 58, pp.161-203, 1992

[Mitchell, Selman & Levesque 92] D. Mitchell, B. Selman and H. Levesque: Hard and Easy Distributions of SAT Problems, Proc. of AAAI-92, pp.459-465, 1992

[Mohr, Thomas & Henderson 86] R. Mohr and T. C. Henderson, Arc and Path Consistency Revisited, Artificial Intelligence Vol. 28 pp.225-233, 1986

[Morris 93] P. Morris, The Breakout Method for Escaping From Local Minima, Proc. of AAAI-93, pp.40-45, 1993

[Selman, Levesque & Mitchell 92] B. Selman, H. Levesque and D. Mitchell: A New Method for solving Hard Satisfiability Problems, Proc. of AAAI-92, pp.440-446, 1992

[Selman & Kautz 93] B. Selman and H. Kautz: Domain-Independent Extensions to GSAT: Solving Large Structured Satisfiability Problems, Proc. of IJCAI-93, pp.290-295, 1993

An Approach to Multiply Segmented Constraint Satisfaction Problems[*]

Randall A. Helzerman and Mary P. Harper
School of Electrical Engineering
1285 Electrical Engineering Building
Purdue University
West Lafayette, IN 47907
{helz, harper}@ecn.purdue.edu

Abstract

This paper describes an extension to the constraint satisfaction problem (CSP) approach called MUSE CSP (*MU*ltiply *SE*gmented *C*onstraint *S*atisfaction *P*roblem). This extension is especially useful for those problems which segment into multiple sets of partially shared variables. Such problems arise naturally in signal processing applications including computer vision, speech processing, and handwriting recognition. For these applications, it is often difficult to segment the data in only one way given the low-level information utilized by the segmentation algorithms. MUSE CSP can be used to efficiently represent several similar instances of the constraint satisfaction problem simultaneously. If multiple instances of a CSP have some common variables which have the same domains and compatible constraints, then they can be combined into a single instance of a MUSE CSP, reducing the work required to enforce node and arc consistency.

Introduction

Constraint satisfaction provides a convenient way to represent certain types of problems. In general, these are problems which can be solved by assigning mutually compatible values to a fixed number of variables under a set of constraints. This approach has been used in a variety of disciplines including machine vision, belief maintenance, temporal reasoning, graph theory, circuit design, and diagnostic reasoning (Kumar 1992). A classic example of a CSP is the map coloring problem (e.g., Figure 1), where a color must be assigned to each country such that no two neighboring countries have the same color. A variable represents a country's color, and a constraint arc between two variables indicates that the two joined countries are adjacent and should not be assigned the same color. Formally, a CSP (Mackworth 1977; Mohr & Henderson 1986) is defined in Definition 1.

Definition 1 (Constraint Satisfaction Problem)
$N = \{i, j, \ldots\}$ *is the set of nodes, with* $|N| = n$,
$L = \{a, b, \ldots\}$ *is the set of labels, with* $|L| = l$,
$L_i = \{a | a \in L \text{ and } (i, a) \text{ is admissible}\}$,
$R1$ *is a unary relation,* (i, a) *is admissible if* $R1(i, a)$,
$R2$ *is a binary relation,* (i, a)-(j, b) *is admissible if*
$R2(i, a, j, b)$.

---

[*]This work is supported in part by Purdue Research Foundation, NSF grant number IRI-9011179, and NSF Parallel Infrastructure Grant CDA-9015696.

A CSP network contains all n-tuples in L^n which satisfy $R1$ and $R2$. Since some of the values associated with a variable may be incompatible with values assigned to other variables, it is desirable to eliminate as many of these values as possible by enforcing local consistency conditions (such as arc consistency) before a globally consistent solution is extracted (Dechter 1992). Node and arc consistency are defined in Definitions 2 and 3 respectively. Node consistency is easily enforced by the operation $L_i = L_i \cap \{x | R1(i, x)\}$. Enforcing arc consistency is more complicated, but Mohr and Henderson (Mohr & Henderson 1986) have designed an optimal algorithm (AC-4), which runs in $O(yl^2)$ time (where y is the number of pairs of nodes for which $R2$ is not the TRUE relation).

Definition 2 (Node Consistency) *An instance of CSP is said to be* node consistent *if and only if each variable's domain contains only labels which do not violate the unary relation $R1$, i.e.:* $\forall i \in N : \forall a \in L_i : R1(i, a)$

Definition 3 (Arc Consistency) *An instance of CSP is said to be* arc consistent *if and only if for every pair of nodes i and j, each element of L_i (the domain of i) has at least one element of L_j for which they both satisfy the binary relation $R2$, i.e.:* $\forall i, j \in N : \forall a \in L_i : \exists b \in L_j : R2(i, a, j, b)$

There are many types of problems which can be solved by using this approach in a more or less direct fashion. There are also problems which might benefit from the CSP approach, but which are difficult to segment into a single set of variables. This is the class of problems our paper addresses. For example, suppose the map represented in Figure 1 were scanned by a noisy computer vision system, with a resulting uncertainty as to whether the line between regions 1 and 2 is really a border or an artifact of the noise. This situation would yield two CSP problems as depicted in Figure 2. A brute-force approach would be to solve both of the problems, which would be reasonable for scenes containing few ambiguous borders. However, as the number of ambiguous borders increases, the number of CSP networks would grow in a combinatorially explosive fashion. In the case of ambiguous segmentation, it might often be more efficient to merge the constraint networks into a single network which would compactly represent all of them simultaneously, as shown in Figure 3. In this paper, we develop an extension to CSP called MUSE CSP (*MU*ltiply *SE*gmented *C*onstraint *S*atisfaction *P*roblem) to represent multiple instances

"

of CSP problems.

The initial motivation for extending CSP came from work in spoken language parsing (Zoltowski *et al.* 1992; Harper *et al.* 1992; Harper & Helzerman 1993). The output of a hidden-Markov-model-based speech recognizer is often a list of the most likely sentence hypotheses (i.e., an N-best list) where parsing can be used to rule out the ungrammatical sentence hypotheses. Maruyama (Maruyama 1990a; 1990c; 1990b) has shown that parsing can be cast as a CSP with a finite domain, so constraints can be used to rule out syntactically incorrect sentence hypotheses. However, individually processing each sentence hypothesis provided by a speech recognizer is inefficient since many sentence hypotheses are generated with a high degree of similarity. An alternative representation for a list of similar sentence hypotheses is a word graph or lattice of word candidates which contains information on the approximate beginning and end point of each word. Word graphs are typically more compact and more expressive than N-best sentence lists. In an experiment (Zoltowski *et al.* 1992), word graphs were constructed from three different lists of sentence hypotheses. The word graphs provided an 83% reduction in storage, and in all cases, they encoded more possible sentence hypotheses than were in the original list of hypotheses. Figure 4 depicts a word graph containing eight sentence hypotheses which was constructed from two sentence hypotheses: *Its hard to recognizes speech* and *It's hard to wreck a nice beach*. By structuring the spoken language parsing problem as a MUSE CSP problem, the constraints used to parse individual sentences would be applied to a word graph of sentence hypotheses, eliminating from further consideration all those hypotheses that are ungrammatical. The goal in this case is to utilize constraints to eliminate as many ungrammatical hypotheses as possible, and then to select the best remaining sentence hypothesis (given the word probabilities given by the recognizer).

From CSP to MUSE CSP

If there are multiple, similar instances of a CSP which need to be solved, then separately enforcing node and arc consistency on each instance can often result in much duplicated work. To avoid this duplication, we have combined the multiple instances of CSP into a

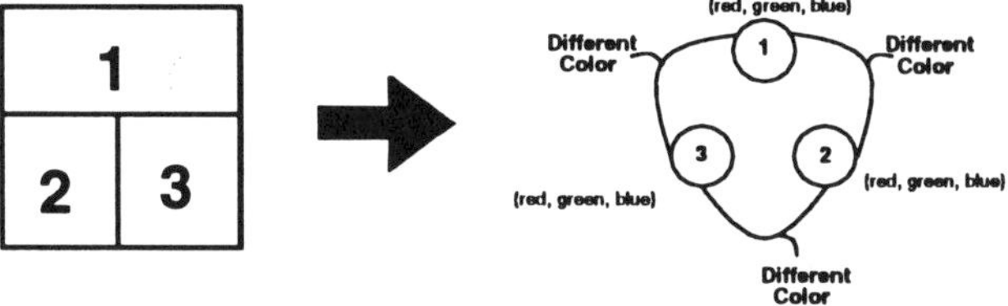

Figure 1: The map coloring problem as an example of CSP. When using a CSP approach, the variables are depicted as circles, where each circle is associated with a finite set of possible values, and the constraints imposed on the variables are depicted using arcs. An arc looping from a circle to itself represents a unary constraint (a relation involving a single variable), and an arc between two circles represents a binary constraint (a relation on two variables).

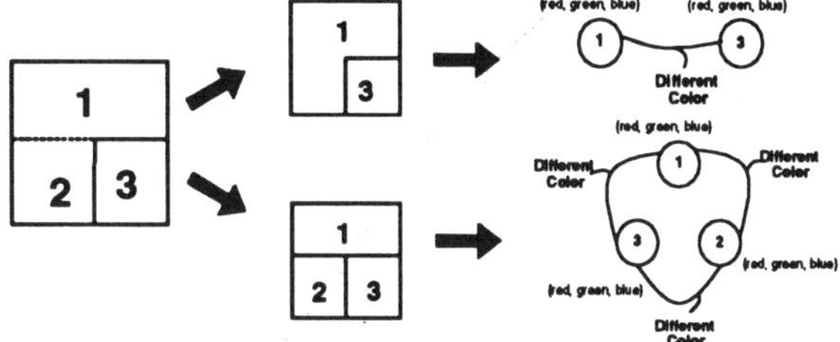

Figure 2: An ambiguous map yields two CSP problems.

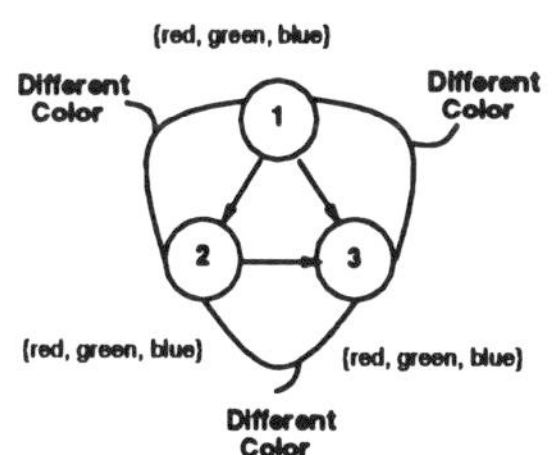

Figure 3: The two CSP problems of figure 2 are captured by a single instance of MUSE CSP. The directed edges form a DAG such that the paths through the DAG correpond to instances of combined CSPs.

shared constraint network and revised the node and arc consistency algorithms to support this representation.

Formally, we define MUSE CSP as follows:

Definition 4 (MUSE CSP)
$N = \{i, j, \ldots\}$ is the set of nodes, with $|N| = n$,
$\Sigma \subseteq 2^N$ is a set of segments with $|\Sigma| = s$,
$L = \{a, b, \ldots\}$ is the set of labels, with $|L| = l$,
$L_i = \{a | a \in L$ and (i, a) is admissible in at least one segment\}$,
$R1$ is a unary relation, (i, a) is admissible if $R1(i, a)$,
$R2$ is a binary relation, (i, a)-(j, b) is admissible if $R2(i, a, j, b)$.

The segments in Σ are the different sets of nodes representing instances of CSP which are combined to form a MUSE CSP. We also define $L_{(i,\sigma)}$ to be the set of all labels $a \in L_i$ that are admissible for $\sigma \in \Sigma$.

Because there can be an exponential number of segments in the set Σ, it is important to define methods for combining instances of CSP into a single, compact MUSE CSP. To create a MUSE CSP, we must be able to determine when variables across several instances of CSP can be combined into a single shared variable, and we must also be able to determine which subsets of variables in the MUSE CSP correspond to individual CSPs. A word graph of sentence hypotheses is an

| It's | hard | to | wreck | a | nice | beach |
| Its | hard | to | recognizes | | | speech |

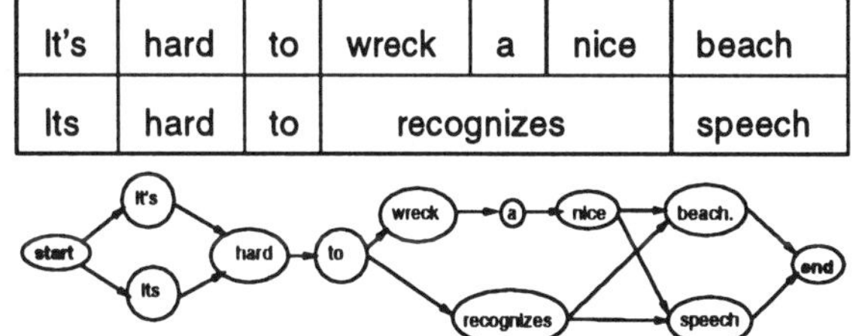

Figure 4: Multiple sentence hypotheses can be parsed simultaneously by propagating constraints over a word graph rather than individual sentences.

excellent representation for a MUSE CSP based constraint parser for spoken sentences. Words that occur in more than one sentence hypothesis over the same time interval are represented using a single variable. The edges between the word nodes, which indicate temporal ordering among the words in the sentence, provide links between words in a sentence hypothesis. A sentence hypothesis, which corresponds to an individual CSP, is simply a path through the word nodes in the word graph going from a start node to an end node.

The concepts used to create a MUSE CSP network for spoken language can be adapted to other CSP problems. In particular, it is desirable to represent a MUSE CSP as a directed acyclic graph (DAG) where the paths through the DAG correspond to instances of CSP problems. In addition, CSP networks should be combined only if they satisfy the conditions below:

Definition 5 (MUSE CSP Combinability) *p instances of CSP $C_1, \ldots, C_p$ are said to be MUSE Combinable iff the following conditions hold:*

1. *If $\{\sigma_1, \sigma_2, \ldots, \sigma_q\} \subseteq \{N_1, \ldots, N_p\} \wedge (i \in \sigma_1 \wedge i \in \sigma_2 \wedge \ldots \wedge i \in \sigma_q) \wedge (a \in L_{(i,\sigma_1)} \wedge a \in L_{(i,\sigma_2)} \wedge \ldots \wedge a \in L_{(i,\sigma_q)}), then R1_{\sigma_1}(i,a) = R1_{\sigma_2}(i,a) = \ldots = R1_{\sigma_q}(i,a).$*

2. *If $\{\sigma_1, \sigma_2, \ldots, \sigma_q\} \subseteq \{N_1, \ldots, N_p\} \wedge (i, j \in \sigma_1 \wedge i, j \in \sigma_2 \wedge \ldots \wedge i, j \in \sigma_q) \wedge (a \in L_{(i,\sigma_1)} \wedge a \in L_{(i,\sigma_2)} \wedge \ldots \wedge a \in L_{(i,\sigma_q)}) \wedge (b \in L_{(j,\sigma_1)} \wedge b \in L_{(j,\sigma_2)} \wedge \ldots \wedge b \in L_{(j,\sigma_q)}), then R2_{\sigma_1}(i,a,j,b) = R2_{\sigma_2}(i,a,j,b) = \ldots = R2_{\sigma_q}(i,a,j,b).$*

These conditions are not overly restrictive, requiring only that the labels for each variable i must be consistently admissible or inadmissible for all instances of CSP which are combined. These conditions do not uniquely determine which variables should be shared across CSP instances for a particular problem type. We define an operator $\oplus$ which combines instances of CSP into an instance of MUSE CSP in Definition 6.

Definition 6 *($\oplus$, the MUSE CSP Combining Operator)* If $C_1, \ldots, C_p$ are MUSE combinable instances of CSP, then $C = C_1 \oplus \ldots \oplus C_p$ will be an instance of MUSE CSP such that:

$$N = N_1 \cup \ldots \cup N_p$$
$$\Sigma = \{N_1, \ldots, N_p\}$$
$$L = L_1 \cup \ldots \cup L_p$$
$$L_i = L_{(i,N_1)} \cup L_{(i,N_2)} \cup \ldots \cup L_{(i,N_p)}$$
$$R1(i,a) = \bigvee_{\sigma=N_1}^{N_p} \left(R1_\sigma(i,a) \wedge a \in L_{(i,\sigma)} \right)$$
$$R2(i,a,j,b) = \bigvee_{\sigma=N_1}^{N_p} \left(R2_\sigma(i,a,j,b) \wedge (a \in L_{(i,\sigma)} \wedge b \in L_{(j,\sigma)}) \right)$$

As mentioned above, a DAG is an excellent representation for a MUSE CSP, where its nodes are the elements of N, and its edges are arranged such that every σ in Σ maps onto a path through the DAG. In some applications, such as speech recognition (Zoltowski *et al.* 1992; Harper *et al.* 1992; Harper & Helzerman 1993), the DAG will already be available to us. In applications where the DAG is not available, the user must determine the best way to combine instances of CSP to maximize sharing. We have provided an algorithm (shown in Figure 5) which automatically constructs a single instance of a MUSE

1. Assign each element i of N some number v in the range of 1 to n by using ord(i) = v.
2. **for** each $\sigma \in \Sigma$ **do** {
3.   Add to σ two distinguished nodes called **start** and **end** with ord(**start**)=0, ord(**end**)=∞.
4.   Sort the elements of σ by their ordinal numbers.
5.   **for** $i, j \in \sigma$ such that i's position immediatly preceeds j's position in the sorted σ **do** {
6.   Next-edge$_i$:=Next-edge$_i$ $\cup \{(i,j)\}$
7.   Prev-edge$_j$:=Prev-edge$_j$ $\cup \{(i,j)\}$ }}

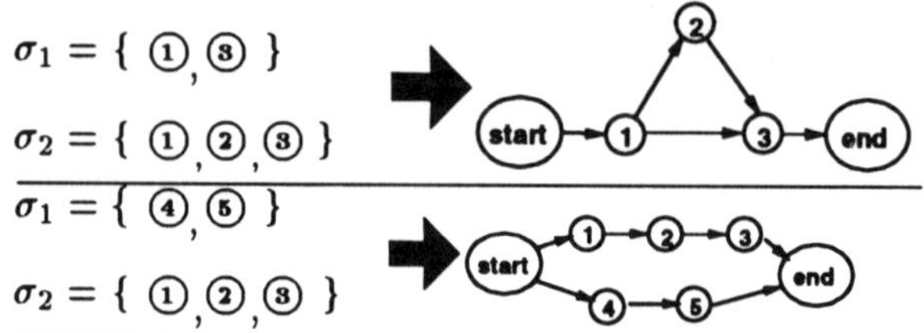

Figure 5: The algorithm to create a DAG to represent the set Σ, and examples of its action.

CSP from multiple CSP instances in $O(sn \log n)$ time, where s is the number of CSP instances to combine, and n is the number of nodes in the MUSE CSP. This algorithm requires the user to assign numbers to variables in the CSPs such that variables that can be shared are assigned the same number. As shown by the examples in Figure 5, for a given set of CSPs, the greater the intersection between the sets of node numbers across CSPs, the more compact the MUSE CSP.

Depending on the application, the solution for a MUSE CSP could range from the set of consistent labels for a single path through the MUSE CSP to all compatible sets of labels for all paths (or CSPs). For our speech processing application, we select the most likely path through the MUSE CSP based on probabilities assigned to word candidates by our speech recognition algorithm. It is desirable to prune the search space before selecting a solution by enforcing local consistency conditions, such as node and arc consistency. However, node and arc consistency must first be extended to MUSE CSP.

Definition 7 (MUSE Node Consistency) *An instance of MUSE CSP is said to be node consistent if and only if each variable's domain, L_i, contains only labels which do not violate the unary relation R1, i.e.: $\forall i \in N : \forall a \in L_i : R1(i,a)$*

Definition 8 (MUSE Arc Consistency) *An instance of MUSE CSP is said to be arc consistent if and only if for every label a in each domain L_i there is at least one segment σ whose nodes' domains contain at least one label b which satisfy the binary relation R2, i.e.: $\forall i \in N : \forall a \in L_i : \exists \sigma \in \Sigma : i \in \sigma \wedge \forall j \in \sigma : j \neq i \Rightarrow \exists b \in L_j : R2(i,a,j,b)$*

A MUSE CSP is node consistent if all of its segments are node consistent. Unfortunately, arc consistency in a MUSE CSP requires more attention because even though a binary constraint might disallow a label in one segment, it might allow it in another segment. When enforcing arc consistency in a CSP, a label a in L_i can be eliminated from node i whenever any other domain L_j has no labels which together with a satisfy the binary constraints. However, in a MUSE CSP, before a label can be eliminated from a node, it must fail to satisfy the binary constraints in all the segments in

Notation	Meaning
(i, j)	An ordered pair of nodes.
$[(i, j), a]$	An ordered pair of a node pair (i, j) and a label $a \in L_i$.
$M[(i, j), a]$	$M[(i, j), a] = 1$ indicates that the label a is not admissible for (and has already been eliminated from) all segments containing i and j.
E	All node pairs (i, j) such that there exists a segment which contains both i and j.
$S[(i, j), a]$	$[(j, i), b] \in S[(i, j), a]$ means that label a at node i and b at j are simultaneously admissible.
Next-edge$_i$	If a directed edge from i to j exists in E, then (i, j) is a member of this set.
Prev-edge$_i$	If a directed edge from j to i exists in E, then (j, i) is a member of this set.
Counter$[(i, j), a]$	The number of labels in L_j compatible with a in L_i.
Prev-Sup$[(i, j), a]$	$(i, k) \in$ Prev-Sup$[(i, j), a]$ means that a is admissible in every segment containing i, j, and k.
Next-Sup$[(i, j), a]$	$(i, k) \in$ Next-Sup$[(i, j), a]$ means that a is admissible in every segment containing i, j, and k.
Local-Prev-Sup(i, a)	A set of elements (i, j) such that $(j, i) \in$ Prev-edge$_i$ and a is compatible with at least one of j's labels.
Local-Next-Sup(i, a)	A set of elements (i, j) such that $(i, j) \in$ Next-edge$_i$ and a is compatible with at least one of j's labels.
List	A queue of arc support to be deleted.

Figure 6: Data structures and notation for the algorithms.

which it appears. Therefore, the definition of MUSE arc consistency is modified as shown in Definition 8. Notice that Definition 8 reduces to Definition 3 when the number of segments is one. Because MUSE arc consistency must hold for all segments, if a single CSP were selected from the MUSE CSP after MUSE arc consistency is enforced, additional filtering can be required for that single instance.

MUSE CSP Arc Consistency Algorithm

MUSE arc consistency[1] is enforced by removing from the domains those labels in L_i which violate the conditions of Definition 8. MUSE AC-1 builds and maintains several data structures, described in Figure 6, to allow it to efficiently perform this operation. Figure 8 shows the code for initializing the data structures, and Figure 9 contains the algorithm for eliminating inconsistent labels from the domains.

If label a at node i is compatible with label b at node j, then a *supports* b. To keep track of how much support each label a has, the number of labels in L_j which are compatible with a in L_i are counted, and the total is stored in Counter$[(i, j), a]$. The algorithm must also keep track of which labels that label a supports by using $S[(i, j), a]$, which is a set of arc and role value pairs. For example, $S[(i, j), a] = \{[(j, i), b], [(j, i), c]\}$ means that a in L_i supports b and c in L_j. If a is ever invalid for L_i then b and c will loose some of their support. This is accomplished by decrementing Counter$[(j, i), b]$ and Counter$[(j, i), c]$. For regular CSP arc consistency,

[1] We purposely keep our notation and presentation as close as possible to that of Mohr and Henderson in (Mohr & Henderson 1986), in order to aid understanding for those already familiar with the literature on arc consistency.

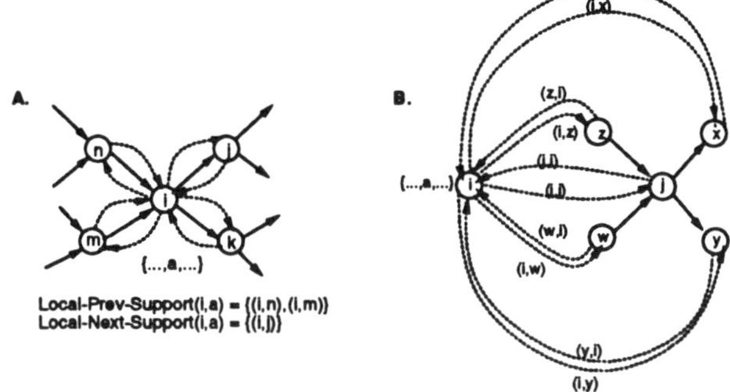

Figure 7: **A**: Local-Prev-Sup and Local-Next-Sup for an example DAG. The sets indicate that the label a is allowed for every segment which contains n, m, and j, but is disallowed for every segment which contains k. **B**: Given that Next-edge$_j = \{(j, x), (j, y)\}$ and $S[(i, x), a] = \emptyset$ and $S[(i, y), a] = \emptyset$, a is inadmissible for every segment containing both i and j.

if Counter$[(i, j), a]$ becomes zero, a would automatically be removed from L_i, because that would mean that a was incompatible with every label for j. However, in MUSE arc consistency, this is not the case, because even though a could not participate in a solution for any of the segments which contain i and j, there could be another segment for which a would be perfectly legal. A label cannot become globally inadmissible until it is incompatible with every segment.

By representing Σ as a DAG, the algorithm is able to use the properties of the DAG to identify local (and hence efficiently computable) conditions under which labels become globally inadmissible. Consider Figure 7A, which shows the nodes which are adjacent to node i in the DAG. Because every segment in the DAG which contains node i is represented as a path through the DAG going through node i, either node j or node k must be in every segment containing i. Hence, if the label a is to remain in L_i, it must be compatible with at least one label in either L_j or L_k. Also, because either n or m must be contained in every segment containing i, if label a is to remain in L_i, it must also be compatible with at least one label in either L_n or L_m.

In order to track this dependency, two sets are maintained for each label a at i, Local-Next-Sup(i, a), and Local-Prev-Sup(i, a). Local-Next-Sup(i, a) is a set of ordered node pairs (i, j) such that $(i, j) \in$ Next-edge$_i$, and there is at least one label $b \in L_j$ which is compatible with a. Local-Prev-Sup(i, a) is a set of ordered pairs (i, j) such that $(j, i) \in$ Prev-edge$_i$, and there is at least one label $b \in L_j$ which is compatible with a. Whenever one of i's adjacent nodes, j, no longer has any labels b in its domain which are compatible with a, then (i, j) should be removed from Local-Prev-Sup(i, a) or Local-Next-Sup(i, a), depending on whether the edge is from j to i or from i to j, respectively. If either Local-Prev-Sup(i, a) or Local-Next-Sup(i, a) becomes the empty set, then a is no longer a part of any solution, and may be eliminated from L_i. In Figure 7A, the role value a is admissible for the segment containing i and j, but not for the

```
1.  List:=φ; E := {(i,j)|∃σ ∈ Σ : i,j ∈ σ ∧ i ≠ j ∧ i,j ∈ N};
2.  for  (i,j) ∈ E do
3.     for a ∈ Lᵢ do {
4.        M[(i,j),a] := 0; Counter[(i,j),a] := 0; S[(i,j),a] := φ;
5.        Prev-Sup[(i,j),a] := φ; Next-Sup[(i,j),a] := φ;
6.        Local-Prev-Sup(i,a) := φ; Local-Next-Sup(i,a) := φ };
7.  for  (i,j) ∈ E do
8.     for a ∈ Lᵢ do {
9.        Total:=0;
10.       for b ∈ Lⱼ do
11.          if R2(i,a,j,b) then {
12.             Total:=Total+1;
13.             S[(j,i),b] := S[(j,i),b] ∪ {[(i,j),a]} };
14.       if Total=0 then {
15.             M[(i,j),a] := 1; List:=List ∪{[(i,j),a]} };
16.       else Counter[(i,j),a]:=Total;
17.       Prev-Sup[(i,j),a] :=
                {(i,x)|(i,x) ∈ E ∧ (x,j) ∈ Prev-edgeⱼ}
                ∪{(i,j)|(i,j) ∈ Prev-edgeⱼ}
                ∪{(i,start)|(start,j) ∈ Prev-edgeⱼ};
18.       Next-Sup[(i,j),a] :=
                {(i,x)|(i,x) ∈ E ∧ (j,x) ∈ Next-edgeⱼ}
                ∪{(i,j)|(j,i) ∈ Next-edgeⱼ}
                ∪{(i,end)|(j,end) ∈ Next-edgeⱼ};
19.       if (i,j) ∈ Next-edgeᵢ then
                Local-Next-Sup(i,a):=Local-Next-Sup(i,a) ∪ {(i,j)};
20.       if (j,i) ∈ Prev-edgeᵢ then
                Local-Prev-Sup(i,a):=Local-Prev-Sup(i,a) ∪ {(i,j)} }
```

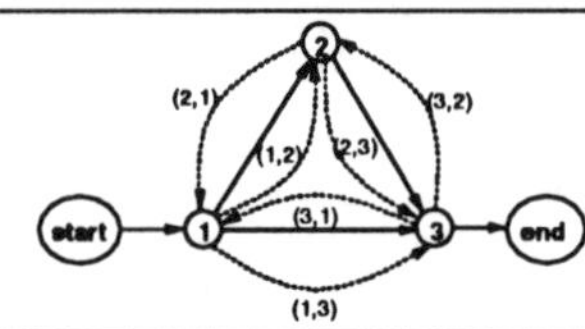

Prev-Sup[(1,2),a]	=	{(1,2)}	Next-Sup[(1,2),a]	=	{(1,3)}
Prev-Sup[(1,3),a]	=	{(1,2),(1,3)}	Next-Sup[(1,3),a]	=	{(1,end)}
Prev-Sup[(2,1),a]	=	{(2,start)}	Next-Sup[(2,1),a]	=	{(2,1),(2,3)}
Prev-Sup[(3,1),a]	=	{(3,start)}	Next-Sup[(3,1),a]	=	{(3,1),(3,2)}
Prev-Sup[(2,3),a]	=	{(2,3),(2,1)}	Next-Sup[(2,3),a]	=	{(2,end)}
Prev-Sup[(3,2),a]	=	{(3,1)}	Next-Sup[(3,2),a]	=	{(3,2)}
Local-Prev-Sup(1,a)	=	{(1,start)}	Local-Next-Sup(1,a)	=	{(1,2),(1,3)}
Local-Prev-Sup(2,a)	=	{(2,1)}	Local-Next-Sup(2,a)	=	{(2,3)}
Local-Prev-Sup(3,a)	=	{(3,1),(3,2)}	Local-Next-Sup(3,a)	=	{(3,end)}

Figure 8: Algorithm for initializing the MUSE CSP data structures along with a simple example. The dotted lines are members of the set E.

segment containing i and k. If because of constraints, the labels in j become inconsistent with a on i, (i,j) would be eliminated from Local-Next-Sup(a,i), leaving an empty set. In that case, a would no longer be supported by any segment.

The algorithm can utilize similar conditions for nodes which may not be directly connected to i by Next-edge$_i$ or Prev-edge$_i$. Consider Figure 7B. Suppose that the label a at node i is compatible with a label in L_j, but it is incompatible the labels in L_x and L_y, then it is reasonable to eliminate a for all segments containing both i and j, because those segments would have to include either node x or y. To determine whether a role value is admissible for a set of segments containing i and j, we calculate Prev-Sup$[(i,j),a]$ and Next-Sup$[(i,j),a]$ sets. Next-Sup$[(i,j),a]$ includes all (i,k) arcs which support a in i given that there is a directed edge between j and k and (i,j) supports a. Prev-Sup$[(i,j),a]$ includes all (i,k) arcs which support a in i given that there is a directed edge between k and j and (i,j) supports a. Note that Prev-Sup$[(i,j),a]$ will contain an ordered pair (i,j) if $(i,j) ∈$ Prev-edge$_j$, and Next-Sup$[(i,j),a]$ will contain an ordered pair (i,j) if $(j,i) ∈$ Next-edge$_j$. These elements are included because the edge between nodes i and j is

sufficient to allow j's labels to support a in the segment containing i and j. Dummy ordered pairs are also created to handle cases where a node is at the beginning or end of a network: when $(\mathbf{start},j) ∈$ Prev-edge$_j$, $(i,\mathbf{start})$ is added to Prev-Sup$[(i,j),a]$, and when $(j,\mathbf{end}) ∈$ Next-edge$_j$, $(i,\mathbf{end})$ is added to Next-Sup$[(i,j),a]$. Figure 8 shows the support sets that the initialization algorithm creates for the label a in the simple example DAG.

To illustrate how these data structures are used in MUSE AC-1 (see Figure 9), consider what happens if initially $[(1,3),a] ∈ List$ for the MUSE CSP in Figure 8. First, it is necessary to remove $[(1,3),a]$'s support from all S$[(3,1),x]$ such that $[(3,1),x] ∈$ S$[(1,3),a]$ by decrementing for each x, Counter$[(3,1),x]$ by one. If the counter for any $[(3,1),x]$ becomes 0, and the value has not already been placed on the $List$, then it is added for future processing. Once this is done, it is necessary to remove $[(1,3),a]$'s influence on the DAG. To handle this, we examine the two sets Prev-Sup$[(1,3),a] = \{(1,2),(1,3)\}$ and Next-Sup$[(1,3),a] = \{(1,\mathbf{end})\}$. Note that the value $(1,\mathbf{end})$ in Next-Sup$[(1,3),a]$ and the value $(1,3)$ in Prev-Sup$[(1,3),a]$, once eliminated from those sets, require no further action because they are dummy values. However, the value $(1,2)$ in Prev-Sup$[(1,3),a]$ indicates that $(1,3)$ is a member of Next-Sup$[(1,2),a]$, and since a is not admissible for $(1,3)$, $(1,3)$ should be removed from Next-Sup$[(1,2),a]$, leaving an empty set. Note that because Next-Sup$[(1,2),a]$ is empty and assuming that M$[(1,2),a] = 0$, $[(1,2),a]$ is added to $List$ for further processing. Next, $(1,3)$ is removed from Local-Next-Sup$(1,a)$, but that set is non-empty. During the next iteration of the while loop, $[(1,2),a]$ is popped from $List$. When Prev-Sup$[(1,2),a]$ and Next-Sup$[(1,2),a]$ are processed, Next-Sup$[(1,2),a] = ∅$ and Prev-Sup$[(1,2),a]$ contains only a dummy, which is removed. When $(1,2)$ is removed from Local-Next-Sup$(1,a)$, the set becomes empty, so a is no longer compatible with any segment containing 1 and can be eliminated from further consideration as a possible label for 1.

In contrast, consider what happens if initially $[(1,2),a] ∈ List$ for the MUSE CSP in Figure 8. In this case, Prev-Sup$[(1,2),a]$ contains $(1,2)$ which requires no additional work; whereas, Next-Sup$[(1,2),a]$ contains $(1,3)$, indicating that $(1,2)$ must be removed from Prev-Sup$[(1,3),a]$'s set. After the removal, Prev-Sup$[(1,3),a]$ is non-empty, so the segment containing nodes 1 and 3 still supports the label a on 1. The reason that these two cases provide different results is that nodes 1 and 3 are in every segment; whereas, nodes 1 and 2 are only in one of them.

Running Time and Correctness of MUSE AC-1

The running time of the routine to initialize the MUSE CSP data structures (in Figure 8) is $O(n^2 l^2 + n^3 l)$, and the running time for the algorithm which prunes labels that are not arc consistent (in Figure 9) also operates in $O(n^2 l^2 + n^3 l)$ time, where n is the number of nodes

```
1.  while List ≠ φ do {
2.     choose [(j, i), b] from List and remove it from List;
3.     for [(i, j), a] ∈ S[(j, i), b] do {
4.        Counter[(i, j), a]:=Counter[(i, j), a] − 1;
5.        if Counter[(i, j), a] = 0 ∧ M[(i, j), a] = 0 then {
6.           List:=List ∪{[(i, j), a]};
7.           M[(i, j), a] := 1 } };
8.     for (j, x) ∈ Next-Sup[(j, i), b] do {
9.        Prev-Sup[(j, x), b]:=Prev-Sup[(j, x), b] − {(j, i)};
10.       if Prev-Sup[(j, x), b] = φ ∧ M[(j, x), b] = 0 then {
11.          List:=List ∪{[(j, x), b]};
12.          M[(j, x), b] := 1 } };
13.    for (j, x) ∈ Prev-Sup[(j, i), b] do {
14.       Next-Sup[(j, x), b]:=Next-Sup[(j, x), b] − {(j, i)};
15.       if Next-Sup[(j, x), b] = φ ∧ M[(j, x), b] = 0 then {
16.          List:=List ∪{[(j, x), b]};
17.          M[(j, x), b] := 1 } };
18.    if (j, i) ∈ Next-edge; then
19.       Local-Next-Sup(j, b):= Local-Next-Sup(j, b) − {(j, i)};
20.    if Local-Next-Sup(j, b) = φ then {
21.       L_j := L_j − {b}
22.       for (j, x) ∈ Local-Prev-Sup(j, b) do
23.          if M[(j, x), b] = 0 then {
24.             List:=List ∪{[(j, x), b]}; M[(j, x), b] := 1 } };
25.    if (i, j) ∈ Prev-edge; then
26.       Local-Prev-Sup(j, b):= Local-Prev-Sup(j, b) − {(j, i)};
27.    if Local-Prev-Sup(j, b) = φ then {
28.       L_j := L_j − {b}
29.       for (j, x) ∈ Local-Next-Sup(j, b) do
30.          if M[(j, x), b] = 0 then {
31.             List:=List ∪{[(j, x), b]}; M[(j, x), b] := 1 } } } ;
```

Figure 9: Algorithm to enforce MUSE CSP arc consistency.

in a MUSE CSP and l is the number of labels. By comparison, the running time for CSP arc consistency is $(n^2 l^2)$, assuming that there are n^2 constraint arcs. Note that for applications where $l = n$, the running times of the algorithms are the same (this is true for parsing spoken language with a MUSE CSP). Also, if the Σ is representable as a planar DAG (in terms of Prev-edge and Next-Edge, not E), then the running time of the algorithms is the same because the average number of values in Prev-Sup and Next-Sup would be a constant. In the general case, the increase in the running time for arc consistency of a MUSE CSP is reasonable considering that it is possible to combine a large number of CSP instances (possibly exponential) into a compact graph with a small number of nodes.

Next we prove the correctness of MUSE AC-4. A role value is eliminated from a domain by MUSE AC-4 only if its Local-Prev-Sup or its Local-Next-Sup becomes empty. Therefore, we must show that a role value's local support sets become empty if and only if that role value cannot participate in a MUSE arc consistent solution. This is proven for Local-Next-Sup (Local-Prev-Sup follows by symmetry). Observe that if $a \in L_i$, and it is incompatible with all of the nodes which immediately follow L_i in the DAG, then it cannot participate in a MUSE arc consistent solution. In line 19 in figure 9, (i, j) is removed from Local-Next-Sup(i, a) set only if $[(i, j), a]$ has been popped off $List$. Therefore, we show that $[(i, j), a]$ is put on $List$, only if $a \in L_i$ is incompatible with every segment which contains i and j by induction on the number of iterations of the while loop.

For the base case, the initialization routine only puts $[(i, j), a]$ on $List$ if $a \in L_i$ is incompatible with every label in L_j (line 15 of Figure 8). Therefore, $a \in L_i$ is in no solution for any segments which contain i and

j. Assume the condition holds for the first k iterations of the while loop in Figure 9, then during the $(k+1)$th iteration, new tuples of the form $[(i, j), a]$ are put on the list by line 6 (in which case a is no longer compatible with any labels in L_j), line 11 (in which case Prev-Sup$([(i, j), a]) = φ$), line 16 (in which case Next-Sup$([(i, j), a]) = φ$), or line 24 (there is no longer any Next-Sup for a). In any of these cases, $a \in L_i$ is incompatible with every segment which contains i and j. We can therefore conclude that this is true for all iterations of the while loop.

In conclusion, MUSE CSP can be used to efficiently represent several similar instances of the constraint satisfaction problem simultaneously. If multiple instances of a CSP have some common variables with the same domains and compatible constraints, then they can be combined into a single instance of a MUSE CSP, and much of the work required to enforce node and arc consistency need not be duplicated across the instances. For our work in speech processing, the MUSE arc consistency algorithm was very effective at pruning the incompatible labels for the individual CSPs represented in the composite structure. Very little additional work is typically needed to enforce arc consistency on a CSP represented by the best path through the network.

References

Dechter, R. 1992. From local to global consistency. *Artificial Intelligence* 55:87–107.

Harper, M. P., and Helzerman, R. A. 1993. PARSEC: A constraint-based parser for spoken language parsing. Technical Report EE-93-28, Purdue University, School of Electrical Engineering, West Lafayette, IN.

Harper, M.; Jamieson, L.; Zoltowski, C.; and Helzerman, R. 1992. Semantics and constraint parsing of word graphs. In *Proceedings of the International Conference on Acoustics, Speech, and Signal Processing*, II-63–II-66.

Kumar, V. 1992. Algorithms for constraint-satisfaction problems: A survey. *AI Magazine* 13(1):32–44.

Mackworth, A. 1977. Consistency in networks of relations. *Artificial Intelligence* 8(1):99–118.

Maruyama, H. 1990a. Constraint dependency grammar. Technical Report #RT0044, IBM, Tokyo, Japan.

Maruyama, H. 1990b. Constraint dependency grammar and its weak generative capacity. *Computer Software*.

Maruyama, H. 1990c. Structural disambiguation with constraint propagation. In *The Proceedings of the Annual Meeting of ACL*.

Mohr, R., and Henderson, T. C. 1986. Arc and path consistency revisited. *Artificial Intelligence* 28:225–233.

Zoltowski, C.; Harper, M.; Jamieson, L.; and Helzerman, R. 1992. PARSEC: A constraint-based framework for spoken language understanding. In *Proceedings of the International Conference on Spoken Language Understanding*.

Reasoning about Temporal Relations:
A Maximal Tractable Subclass
of Allen's Interval Algebra*

Bernhard Nebel
Universität Ulm
Fakultät für Informatik
D-89069 Ulm, Germany
nebel@informatik.uni-ulm.de

Hans-Jürgen Bürckert
DFKI
Stuhlsatzenhausweg 3
D-66123 Saarbrücken, Germany
hjb@dfki.uni-sb.de

Abstract

We introduce a new subclass of Allen's interval algebra we call "ORD-Horn subclass," which is a strict superset of the "pointisable subclass." We prove that reasoning in the ORD-Horn subclass is a polynomial-time problem and show that the path-consistency method is sufficient for deciding satisfiability. Further, using an extensive machine-generated case analysis, we show that the ORD-Horn subclass is a maximal tractable subclass of the full algebra (assuming P≠NP). In fact, it is the unique greatest tractable subclass amongst the subclasses that contain all basic relations.

Introduction

Temporal information is often conveyed qualitatively by specifying the relative positions of time intervals such as "...point to the figure while explaining the performance of the system ..." Further, for natural language understanding (Allen 1984; Song & Cohen 1988), general planning (Allen 1991; Allen & Koomen 1983), presentation planning in a multi-media context (Feiner *et al.* 1993), and knowledge representation (Weida & Litman 1992), the representation of qualitative temporal relations and reasoning about them is essential. Allen (1983) introduces an algebra of binary relations on intervals for representing qualitative temporal information and addresses the problem of reasoning about such information. Since the reasoning problems are NP-hard for the full algebra (Vilain & Kautz 1986), it is very unlikely that other polynomial-time algorithms will be found that solve this problem in general. Subsequent research has concentrated on designing more efficient reasoning algorithms, on identifying tractable special cases, and on isolating sources of computational complexity (Golumbic & Shamir 1992; Ladkin & Maddux 1988; Nökel 1989; Valdéz-Pérez 1987; van Beek 1989; 1990;

van Beek & Cohen 1990; Vilain & Kautz 1986; Vilain, Kautz, & van Beek 1989).

We extend these previous results in three ways. Firstly, we present a new tractable subclass of Allen's interval algebra, which we call *ORD-Horn subclass*. This subclass is considerably larger than all other known tractable subclasses (it contains 10% of the full algebra) and strictly contains the *pointisable subclass* (Ladkin & Maddux 1988; van Beek 1989). Secondly, we show that the *path-consistency method* is sufficient for deciding satisfiability in this subclass. Thirdly, using an extensive machine-generated case analysis, we show that this subclass is a maximal subclass such that satisfiability is tractable (assuming P≠NP).[1]

From a practical point of view, these results imply that the path-consistency method has a much larger range of applicability than previously believed, provided we are mainly interested in satisfiability. Further, our results can be used to design backtracking algorithms for the full algebra that are more efficient than those based on other tractable subclasses.

Reasoning about Interval Relations using Allen's Interval Algebra

Allen's (1983) approach to reasoning about time is based on the notion of *time intervals* and *binary relations* on them. A **time interval** X is an ordered pair (X^-, X^+) such that $X^- < X^+$, where X^- and X^+ are interpreted as points on the real line.[2] So, if we talk about **interval interpretations** or *I-interpretations* in the following, we mean mappings of time intervals to pairs of distinct real numbers such that the beginning of an interval is strictly before the ending of the interval.

---

*This work was supported by the German Ministry for Research and Technology (BMFT) under grant ITW 8901 8 as part of the WIP project and under grant ITW 9201 as part of the TACOS project, and by the European Comission as part of DRUMS-II, the ESPRIT Basic Research Project P6156.

[1]The programs we used and an enumeration of the ORD-Horn subclass can be obtained from the authors or by anonymous ftp from `duck.dfki.uni-sb.de` as `/pub/papers/DFKI-others/RR-93-11.programs.tar.Z`.

[2]Other underlying models of the time line are also possible, e.g., the rationals (Allen & Hayes 1985; Ladkin 1987). For our purposes these distinctions are not significant, however.

Basic Interval Relation	Symbol	Endpoint Relations	
X before Y	$\prec$	$X^- < Y^-,$	$X^- < Y^+,$
Y after X	$\succ$	$X^+ < Y^-,$	$X^+ < Y^+$
X meets Y	m	$X^- < Y^-,$	$X^- < Y^+,$
Y met-by X	$\overset{\smile}{\text{m}}$	$X^+ = Y^-,$	$X^+ < Y^+$
X overlaps Y	o	$X^- < Y^-,$	$X^- < Y^+,$
Y overlapped-by X	$\overset{\smile}{\text{o}}$	$X^+ > Y^-,$	$X^+ < Y^+$
X during Y	d	$X^- > Y^-,$	$X^- < Y^+,$
Y includes X	$\overset{\smile}{\text{d}}$	$X^+ > Y^-,$	$X^+ < Y^+$
X starts Y	s	$X^- = Y^-,$	$X^- < Y^+,$
Y started-by X	$\overset{\smile}{\text{s}}$	$X^+ > Y^-,$	$X^+ < Y^+$
X finishes Y	f	$X^- > Y^-,$	$X^- < Y^+,$
Y finished-by X	$\overset{\smile}{\text{f}}$	$X^+ > Y^-,$	$X^+ = Y^+$
X equals Y	$\equiv$	$X^- = Y^-,$ $X^+ > Y^-,$	$X^- < Y^+,$ $X^+ = Y^+$

Table 1: The set **B** of the thirteen basic relations.

Given two interpreted time intervals, their relative positions can be described by *exactly one* of the elements of the set **B** of thirteen **basic interval relations** (denoted by B in the following), where each basic relation can be defined in terms of its **endpoint relations** (see Table 1). An atomic formula of the form $X B Y$, where X and Y are intervals and $B \in \mathbf{B}$, is said to be **satisfied** by an I-interpretation iff the interpretation of the intervals satisfies the endpoint relations specified in Table 1.

In order to express indefinite information, unions of the basic interval relations are used, which are written as sets of basic relations leading to 2^{13} **binary interval relations** (denoted by R, S, T)—including the **null relation** $\emptyset$ (also denoted by $\bot$) and the **universal relation B** (also denoted by $\top$). The set of all binary interval relations $2^{\mathbf{B}}$ is denoted by $\mathcal{A}$.

An atomic formula of the form $X \{B_1, \ldots, B_n\} Y$ (denoted by ϕ) is called **interval formula**. Such a formula is satisfied by an I-interpretation $\Im$ iff $X B_i Y$ is satisfied by $\Im$ for some i, $1 \leq i \leq n$. Finite sets of interval formulas are denoted by Θ. Such a set Θ is called I-**satisfiable** iff there exists an I-interpretation $\Im$ that satisfies every formula of Θ. Further, such a satisfying I-interpretation $\Im$ is called I-**model** of Θ. If an interval formula ϕ is satisfied by every I-model of a set of interval formulas Θ, we say that ϕ is **logically implied** by Θ, written $\Theta \models_I \phi$.

Fundamental **reasoning problems** in this framework include (Golumbic & Shamir 1992; Ladkin & Maddux 1988; van Beek 1990; Vilain & Kautz 1986): Given a set of interval formulas Θ, (1) decide the *of I-satisfiability of* Θ (**ISAT**), and (2) determine for each pair of intervals X, Y the *strongest implied relation* between them (**ISI**).

In the following, we often consider **restricted reasoning problems** where the relations used in interval formulas in Θ are only from a subclass $\mathcal{S}$ of all inter-

val relations. In this case we say that Θ **is a set of formulas over** $\mathcal{S}$, and we use a parameter in the problem description to denote the subclass considered, e.g., ISAT($\mathcal{S}$). As is well-known, ISAT and ISI are equivalent with respect to polynomial Turing-reductions (Vilain & Kautz 1986) and this equivalence also extends to the restricted problems ISAT($\mathcal{S}$) and ISI($\mathcal{S}$), provided $\mathcal{S}$ contains all basic relations.

The most prominent method to solve these problems (approximately for all interval relations or exactly for subclasses) is *constraint propagation* (Allen 1983; Ladkin & Maddux 1988; Nökel 1989; van Beek 1989; van Beek & Cohen 1990; Vilain & Kautz 1986) using a slightly simplified form of the *path-consistency algorithm* (Mackworth 1977; Montanari 1974). In the following, we briefly characterize this method without going into details, though. In order to do so, we first have to introduce Allen's interval algebra.

Allen's interval algebra (1983) consists of the set $\mathcal{A} = 2^{\mathbf{B}}$ of all binary interval relations and the operations unary **converse** (denoted by $\cdot^{\smile}$), binary **intersection** (denoted by $\cap$), and binary **composition** (denoted by $\circ$), which are defined as follows:

$$\forall X, Y: \quad\quad X R^{\smile} Y \quad \leftrightarrow \quad Y R X$$
$$\forall X, Y: \quad X (R \cap S) Y \quad \leftrightarrow \quad X R Y \wedge X S Y$$
$$\forall X, Y: \quad X (R \circ S) Y \quad \leftrightarrow \quad \exists Z: (X R Z \wedge Z S Y).$$

Assume an operator Γ that maps finite sets of interval formulas to finite sets of interval formulas in the following way:

$$\begin{aligned}
\Gamma(\Theta) \quad = \quad & \Theta \cup \{X \top Y \mid X, Y \text{ appear in } \Theta\} \\
& \cup \{X R Y \mid (Y R^{\smile} X) \in \Theta\} \\
& \cup \{X (R \cap S) Y \mid (X R Y), (X S Y) \in \Theta\} \\
& \cup \{X (R \circ S) Y \mid (X R Z), (Z S Y) \in \Theta\}.
\end{aligned}$$

Since there are only finitely many different interval formulas for a finite set of intervals and Γ is monotone, it follows that for each Θ there exists a natural number n such that $\Gamma^n(\Theta) = \Gamma^{n+1}(\Theta)$. $\Gamma^n(\Theta)$ is called the **closure** of Θ, written $\overline{\Theta}$. Considering the formulas of the form $(X R_i Y) \in \overline{\Theta}$ for given X, Y, it is evident that the R_i's are closed under intersection, and hence there exists $(X S Y) \in \overline{\Theta}$ such that S is the *strongest relation* amongst the R_i's, i.e., $S \subseteq R_i$, for every i. The subset of a closure $\overline{\Theta}$ containing for each pair of intervals only the strongest relations is called the **reduced closure** of Θ and is denoted by $\widehat{\Theta}$.

As can be easily shown, every reduced closure of a set Θ is **path consistent** (Mackworth 1977), which means that for every three intervals X, Y, Z and for every interpretation $\Im$ that satisfies $(X R Y) \in \widehat{\Theta}$, there exists an interpretation $\Im'$ that agrees with $\Im$ on X and Y and in addition satisfies $(X S Z), (Z S' Y) \in \widehat{\Theta}$. Under the assumption that $(X R Y) \in \Theta$ implies $(Y R^{\smile} X) \in \Theta$, it is also easy to show that path consistency of Θ implies that $\Theta = \widehat{\Theta}$. For this reason, we will use the term **path-consistent set** as a synonym for a set that is the reduced closure of itself. Finally, computing $\widehat{\Theta}$ is polynomial in the size of Θ (Mackworth & Freuder 1985; Montanari 1974).

The ORD-Horn Subclass

Previous results on the tractability of $\mathrm{ISAT}(\mathcal{S})$ (and hence $\mathrm{ISI}(\mathcal{S})$) for some subclass $\mathcal{S} \subseteq \mathcal{A}$ made use of the *expressibility* of interval formulas over $\mathcal{S}$ as certain logical formulas involving endpoint relations.

As usual, by a **clause** we mean a disjunction of literals, where a **literal** in turn is an atomic formula or a negated atomic formula. As **atomic formulas** we allow $a \leq b$ and $a = b$, where a and b denote endpoints of intervals. The negation of $a = b$ is also written as $a \neq b$. Finite sets of such clause will be denoted by Ω. In the following, we consider a slightly restricted form of clauses, which we call **ORD clauses**. These clauses do not contain negations of atoms of the form $(a \leq b)$, i.e., they only contain literals of the form:

$$a = b, \ a \leq b, \ a \neq b.$$

The **ORD-clause form** of an interval formula ϕ, written $\pi(\phi)$, is the set of ORD clauses over endpoint relations that is equivalent to ϕ, i.e., every interval model of ϕ can be transformed into a model of the ORD-clause form over the reals and *vice versa* using the obvious transformation. Consider, for instance, $\pi(X\,\{\mathsf{d},\mathsf{o},\mathsf{s}\}\,Y)$:

$$\begin{aligned}
\{\ &(X^- \leq X^+), &&(X^- \neq X^+), \\
&(Y^- \leq Y^+), &&(Y^- \neq Y^+), \\
&(X^- \leq Y^+), &&(X^- \neq Y^+), \\
&(Y^- \leq X^+), &&(X^+ \neq Y^-), \\
&(X^+ \leq Y^+), &&(X^+ \neq Y^+)\}.
\end{aligned}$$

The function $\pi(\cdot)$ is extended to finite sets of interval formulas in the obvious way, i.e., for identical intervals in Θ, identical endpoints are used in $\pi(\Theta)$. Similarly to the notions of I-satisfiability, we define R-satisfiability of Ω to be the satisfiability of Ω over the real numbers.

Proposition 1 Θ *is I-satisfiable iff* $\pi(\Theta)$ *is R-satisfiable.*

Not all relations permit a ORD-clause form that is as concise as the the one shown above, which contains only *unit clauses*. However, in particular those relations that allow for such a clause form have interesting computational properties. For instance, the **continuous endpoint subclass** (which is denoted by $\mathcal{C}$) can be defined as the subclass of interval relations that (1) permit a clause form that contains only unit clauses, and (2) for each unit clause $a \neq b$, the clause form contains also a unit clause of the form $a \leq b$ or $b \leq a$.

As demonstrated above, the relation $\{\mathsf{d},\mathsf{o},\mathsf{s}\}$ is a member of the continuous endpoint subclass. This subclass has the favorable property that the path-consistency method solves $\mathrm{ISI}(\mathcal{C})$ (van Beek 1989; van Beek & Cohen 1990; Vilain, Kautz, & van Beek

1989). A slight generalization of the continuous endpoint subclass is the **pointisable subclass** (denoted by $\mathcal{P}$) that is defined in the same way as $\mathcal{C}$, but without condition (2). Path-consistency is not sufficient for solving $\mathrm{ISI}(\mathcal{P})$ (van Beek 1989) but still sufficient for deciding satisfiability (Ladkin & Maddux 1988; Vilain & Kautz 1986).

We generalize this approach by being more liberal concerning the clause form. We consider the subclass of Allen's interval algebra such that the relations permit an ORD-clause form containing only clauses with *at most one positive literal*, which we call **ORD-Horn clauses**. The subclass defined in this way is called **ORD-Horn subclass**, and we use the symbol $\mathcal{H}$ to refer to it. The relation $\{\mathsf{o},\mathsf{s},\mathsf{f}^\smile\}$ is, for instance, an element of $\mathcal{H}$ because $\pi(X\,\{\mathsf{o},\mathsf{s},\mathsf{f}^\smile\}\,Y)$ can be expressed as follows:

$$\begin{aligned}
\{\ &(X^- \leq X^+), &&(X^- \neq X^+), \\
&(Y^- \leq Y^+), &&(Y^- \neq Y^+), \\
&(X^- \leq Y^-), &&(X^- \leq Y^+), &&(X^- \neq Y^+), \\
&(Y^- \leq X^+), &&(X^+ \neq Y^-), &&(X^+ \leq Y^+), \\
&(X^- \neq Y^- \vee X^+ \neq Y^+)\}.
\end{aligned}$$

By definition, the ORD-Horn subclass contains the pointisable subclass. Further, by the above example, this inclusion is strict.

Consider now the theory ORD that axiomatizes "=" as an equivalence relation and "$\leq$" as a partial ordering over the equivalence classes:

$$\begin{aligned}
\forall x,y,z: \quad & x \leq y \wedge y \leq z && \rightarrow && x \leq z \\
\forall x: \quad & x \leq x \\
\forall x,y: \quad & x \leq y \wedge y \leq x && \rightarrow && x = y \\
\forall x,y: \quad & x = y && \rightarrow && x \leq y \\
\forall x,y: \quad & x = y && \rightarrow && y \leq x.
\end{aligned}$$

Although this theory is much weaker than the theory of the reals, R-satisfiability of a set Ω of ORD clauses is nevertheless equivalent to the satisfiability of $\Omega \cup ORD$ over arbitrary interpretations.

Proposition 2 *A set of ORD clauses* Ω *is R-satisfiable iff* $\Omega \cup ORD$ *is satisfiable.*[3]

Proof Sketch. Any linearization of a partial order that satisfies all atoms appearing in ORD clauses also satisfies these atoms. Hence, a model of $\Omega \cup ORD$ can be used to generate an R-model for Ω. The other direction is trivial. $\blacksquare$

In the following, ORD_Ω shall denote the axioms of ORD instantiated to all endpoints mentioned in Ω. As a specialization of the Herbrand theorem, we obtain the next proposition.

Proposition 3 $\Omega \cup ORD$ *is satisfiable iff* $\Omega \cup ORD_\Omega$ *is satisfiable.*

---

[3]Full proofs are given in the long paper (Nebel & Bürckert 1993), which can be obtained by anonymous ftp from `duck.dfki.uni-sb.de`.

From the fact that ORD_Ω and Ω are propositional Horn formulas, polynomiality of ISAT($\mathcal{H}$) is immediate.

Theorem 4 ISAT($\mathcal{H}$) *is polynomial.*

The Applicability of Path-Consistency

Enumerating the ORD-Horn subclass reveals that there are 868 relations (including the null relation $\perp$) in Allen's interval algebra that can be expressed using ORD-Horn clauses. Since the full algebra contains $2^{13} = 8192$ relations, $\mathcal{H}$ covers more than 10% of the full algebra. Comparing this with the continuous endpoint subclass $\mathcal{C}$, which contains 83 relations, and the pointisable subclass $\mathcal{P}$, which contains 188 relations,[4] having shown tractability for $\mathcal{H}$ is a clear improvement over previous results. However, there remains the question of whether the "traditional" method of reasoning in Allen's interval algebra, i.e., constraint propagation, gives reasonable results. As it turns out, this is indeed the case.

Theorem 5 *Let $\widehat{\Theta}$ be a path-consistent set of interval formulas over $\mathcal{H}$. Then $\widehat{\Theta}$ is I-satisfiable iff $(X \perp Y) \notin \widehat{\Theta}$.*

Proof Sketch. A case analysis over the possible non-unit clauses in $\pi(\widehat{\Theta}) \cup ORD_{\pi(\widehat{\Theta})}$ reveals that no new units can be derived by *positive unit resolution*, if the ORD-clause form of the interval formulas satisfies the requirement that it contains all implied atoms and the clauses are minimal. By refutation completeness of positive unit resolution (Henschen & Wos 1974), the claim follows. ∎

The only remaining part we have to show is that transforming Θ over $\mathcal{H}$ into its equivalent path-consistent form $\widehat{\Theta}$ does not result in a set that contains relations not in $\mathcal{H}$. In order to show this we prove that $\mathcal{H}$ is closed under converse, intersection, and composition, i.e., $\mathcal{H}$ (together with these operations) defines a subalgebra of Allen's interval algebra.

Theorem 6 $\mathcal{H}$ *is closed under converse, intersection, and composition.*

Proof Sketch. The main problem is to show that the composition of two relations has an ORD-Horn form. We show that by proving that any minimal clause C implied by $\pi(\{X\,RY, Y\,SZ\})$ is either ORD-Horn or there exists a set of ORD-Horn clauses that are implied by $\pi(\{X\,RY, Y\,SZ\})$ and imply C. ∎

From that it follows straightforwardly that ISAT($\mathcal{H}$) is decided by the path-consistency method.

Theorem 7 *If Θ is a set over $\mathcal{H}$, then Θ is satisfiable iff $(X \perp Y) \notin \widehat{\Theta}$ for all intervals X, Y.*

---

[4] An enumeration of $\mathcal{C}$ and $\mathcal{P}$ is given by van Beek and Cohen (1990).

The Borderline between Tractable and NP-complete Subclasses

Having identified the tractable fragment $\mathcal{H}$ that contains the previously identified tractable fragment $\mathcal{P}$ and that is considerably larger than $\mathcal{P}$ is satisfying in itself. However, such a result also raises the question for the the boundary between polynomiality and NP-completeness in Allen's interval algebra.

While the introduction of the algebraic structure on the set of expressible interval relations may have seem to be only motivated by the particular approximation algorithm employed, this structure is also useful when we explore the computational properties of restricted problems. For any arbitrary subset $\mathcal{S} \subseteq \mathcal{A}$, $\overline{\mathcal{S}}$ shall denote the **closure** of $\mathcal{S}$ under converse, intersection, and composition. In other words, $\overline{\mathcal{S}}$ is the carrier of the **least subalgebra generated by** $\mathcal{S}$. Apparently, it is possible to translate any set of interval formulas Θ over $\overline{\mathcal{S}}$ into a set Θ' over $\mathcal{S}$ in polynomial time in a way such that I-satisfiability is preserved.

Theorem 8 ISAT($\overline{\mathcal{S}}$) *can be polynomially transformed to* ISAT($\mathcal{S}$).

In other words, once we have proven that satisfiability is polynomial for some set $\mathcal{S} \subseteq \mathcal{A}$, this result extends to the least subalgebra generated by $\mathcal{S}$. Conversely, NP-hardness for a subalgebra is "inherited" by all subsets that generate this subalgebra.

It still takes some effort to prove that a given fragment $\mathcal{S}$ is a *maximal* tractable subclass of Allen's interval algebra. Firstly, one has to show that $\mathcal{S} = \overline{\mathcal{S}}$. For the ORD-Horn subclass, this has been done in Theorem 6. Secondly, one has to show that ISAT($\mathcal{T}$) is NP-complete for all *minimal* subalgebras $\mathcal{T}$ that strictly contain $\mathcal{S}$. This, however, means that these subalgebras have to be identified. Certainly, such a case analysis cannot be done manually. In fact, we used a program to identify the minimal subalgebras strictly containing $\mathcal{H}$. An analysis of the clause form of the relations appearing in these subalgebras leads us to consider the following two relations:

$$N_1 = \{d, d^\smile, o^\smile, s^\smile, f\}$$
$$N_2 = \{d^\smile, o, o^\smile, s^\smile, f^\smile\}.$$

One of these two relations can be found in all minimal subalgebras strictly containing $\mathcal{H}$, as can be shown using a machine-assisted case analysis.

Lemma 9 *Let $\mathcal{S} \subseteq \mathcal{A}$ be any set of interval relations that strictly contains $\mathcal{H}$. Then N_1 or N_2 is an element of $\overline{\mathcal{S}}$.*

For reasons of simplicity, we will not use the ORD clause form in the following, but a clause form that also contains literals over the relations $\geq, <, >$. Then the clause form for the relations mentioned in the lemma can be given as follows:

$$\pi(X\,N_1\,Y) = \{(X^- < X^+),\ (Y^- < Y^+),$$
$$(X^- < Y^+),\ (X^+ > Y^-),$$
$$((X^- > Y^-) \vee (X^+ > Y^+))\},$$

$$\pi(X\ \mathrm{N_2}\ Y) \;=\; \{\,(X^- < X^+),\ \ (Y^- < Y^+),$$
$$(X^- < Y^+),\ \ (X^+ > Y^-),$$
$$((X^- < Y^-) \vee (X^+ > Y^+))\}.$$

We will show that each of these relations together with the two relations

$$\mathrm{B_1} \;=\; \{\prec, \mathsf{d}^\smile, \mathsf{o}, \mathsf{m}, \mathsf{f}^\smile\}$$
$$\mathrm{B_2} \;=\; \{\prec, \mathsf{d}, \mathsf{o}, \mathsf{m}, \mathsf{s}\},$$

which are elements of $\mathcal{C}$, are enough for making the interval satisfiability problem NP-complete. The clause form of these relations looks as follows:

$$\pi(X\ \mathrm{B_1}\ Y) \;=\; \{\,(X^- < X^+),\ \ (Y^- < Y^+),$$
$$(X^- < Y^-),\ \ (X^- < Y^+)\}$$
$$\pi(X\ \mathrm{B_2}\ Y) \;=\; \{\,(X^- < X^+),\ \ (Y^- < Y^+),$$
$$(X^+ < Y^+),\ \ (X^- < Y^+)\}$$

Lemma 10 *ISAT($\mathcal{S}$) is NP-complete if*

1. $\mathcal{N}_1 = \{\mathrm{B_1}, \mathrm{B_2}, \mathrm{N_1}\} \subseteq \mathcal{S}$, or

2. $\mathcal{N}_2 = \{\mathrm{B_1}, \mathrm{B_2}, \mathrm{N_2}\} \subseteq \mathcal{S}$.

Proof Sketch. Since ISAT($\mathcal{A}$) $\in$ NP, membership in NP follows.

For the NP-hardness part we will show that 3SAT can be polynomially transformed to ISAT($\mathcal{N}_k$). We will first prove the claim for $\mathcal{N}_1$. Let $D = \{C_i\}$ be a set of clauses, where $C_i = l_{i,1} \vee l_{i,2} \vee l_{i,3}$ and the $l_{i,j}$'s are literal occurrences. We will construct a set of interval formulas Θ over $\mathcal{N}_1$ such that Θ is I-satisfiable iff D is satisfiable.

For each literal occurrence $l_{i,j}$ a pair of intervals $X_{i,j}$ and $Y_{i,j}$ is introduced, and the following first group of interval formulas is put into Θ:

$$(X_{i,j}\ \mathrm{N_1}\ Y_{i,j}).$$

This implies that $\pi(\Theta)$ contains among other things the following clauses $(X_{i,j}^- > Y_{i,j}^- \vee X_{i,j}^+ > Y_{i,j}^+)$.

Additionally, we add a second group of formulas for each clause C_i:

$$(X_{i,2}\ \mathrm{B_1}\ Y_{i,1}), (X_{i,3}\ \mathrm{B_1}\ Y_{i,2}), (X_{i,1}\ \mathrm{B_1}\ Y_{i,3}),$$

which leads to the inclusion of the clauses $(Y_{i,1}^- > X_{i,2}^-)$, $(Y_{i,2}^- > X_{i,3}^-)$, $(Y_{i,3}^- > X_{i,1}^-)$ in $\pi(\Theta)$.

This construction leads to the situation that there is no model of Θ that satisfies for given i all disjuncts of the form $(X_{i,j}^- > Y_{i,j}^-)$ in the clause form of $\pi(X_{i,j}\mathrm{N_1}Y_{i,j})$. If the jth disjunct $(X_{i,j}^- > Y_{i,j}^-)$ is unsatisfied in an I-model of Θ, we will interpret this as the satisfaction of the literal occurrence $l_{i,j}$ in C_i of D.

In order to guarantee that if a literal occurrence $l_{i,j}$ is interpreted as satisfied, then all complementary literal occurrences in D are interpreted as unsatisfied, the following third group of interval formulas for complementary literal occurrences $l_{i,j}$ and $l_{g,h}$ are added to Θ:

$$(X_{g,h}\ \mathrm{B_2}\ Y_{i,j}),\ \ (X_{i,j}\ \mathrm{B_2}\ Y_{g,h}),$$

which leads to the inclusion of $(Y_{i,j}^+ > X_{g,h}^+)$, $(Y_{g,h}^+ > X_{i,j}^+)$. This construction guarantees that Θ is I-satisfiable iff D is satisfiable.

The transformation for $\mathcal{N}_2$ is similar. ∎

Based on this result, it follows straightforwardly that $\mathcal{H}$ is indeed a maximal tractable subclass of $\mathcal{A}$.

Theorem 11 *If $\mathcal{S}$ strictly contains $\mathcal{H}$, then ISAT($\mathcal{S}$) is NP-complete.*

The next question is whether there are other maximal tractable subclasses that are incomparable with $\mathcal{H}$. One example of an incomparable tractable subclass is $\mathcal{U} = \{\{\prec, \succ\}, \top\}$. Since $\{\prec, \succ\}$ has no ORD-Horn clause form, this subclass is incomparable with $\mathcal{H}$, and since all sets of interval formulas over $\mathcal{U}$ are trivially satisfiable (by making all intervals disjoint), ISAT($\mathcal{U}$) can be decided in constant time. The subclass $\mathcal{U}$ is, of course, not a very *interesting* fragment. Provided we are interested in temporal reasoning in the framework as described by Allen (1983), one necessary requirement is that *all basic relations* are contained in the subclass. A machine-assisted exploration of the space of subalgebras leads us to the following machine-verifiable lemma.

Lemma 12 *If $\mathcal{S}$ is a subclass that contains the thirteen basic relations, then $\overline{\mathcal{S}} \subseteq \mathcal{H}$, or $\mathrm{N_1}$ or $\mathrm{N_2}$ is an element of $\overline{\mathcal{S}}$.*

Using the fact that $\mathrm{B_1}, \mathrm{B_2}$ are elements of the least subalgebra generated by the set of basic relations and employing Lemma 10 again, we obtain the quite satisfying result that $\mathcal{H}$ is in fact the unique greatest tractable subclass amongst the subclasses containing all basic relations.

Theorem 13 *Let $\mathcal{S}$ be any subclass of $\mathcal{A}$ that contains all basic relations. Then either $\mathcal{S} \subseteq \mathcal{H}$ and ISAT($\mathcal{S}$) is polynomial or ISAT($\mathcal{S}$) is NP-complete.*

Conclusion

We have identified a new tractable subclass of Allen's interval algebra, which we call *ORD-Horn subclass* and which contains the previously identified *continuous endpoint* and *pointisable* subclasses. Enumerating the ORD-Horn subclass reveals that this subclass contains 868 elements out of 8192 elements in the full algebra, i.e., more than 10% of the full algebra. Comparing this with the continuous endpoint subclass that covers approximately 1% and with the pointisable subclass that covers 2%, our result is a clear improvement in quantitative terms.

Furthermore, we showed that the "traditional" method of reasoning in Allen's interval algebra, namely, the *path-consistency method*, is sufficient for deciding satisfiability in the ORD-Horn subclass. In other words, our results indicate that the path-consistency method has a much larger range of applicability for reasoning in Allen's interval algebra than previously believed—if we are mainly interested in satisfiability.

Provided that a restriction to the subclass $\mathcal{H}$ is not possible in an application, our results may be employed in designing faster backtracking algorithms for the full algebra (Valdéz-Pérez 1987; van Beek 1990). Since our subclass contains significantly more relations than other tractable subclasses, the branching factor in a backtrack search can be considerably decreased if the ORD-Horn subclass is used.

Finally, we showed that it is impossible to improve on our results. Using a machine-generated case analysis, we showed that the ORD-Horn subclass is a *maximal* tractable subclass of Allen's interval algebra and, in fact, even the *unique greatest* tractable subclass in the set of subclasses that contain all basic relations. In other words, the ORD-Horn subclass presents an optimal tradeoff between expressiveness and tractability (Levesque & Brachman 1987) for reasoning in Allen's interval algebra.

Acknowledgments We would like to thank Peter Ladkin, Henry Kautz, Ron Shamir, Bart Selman, and Marc Vilain for discussions concerning the topics of this paper. In addition, we would like to thank Christer Bäckström for comments on an earlier version of this paper.

References

Allen, J. F., and Hayes, P. J. 1985. A common-sense theory of time. In *Proc. 9th IJCAI*, 528–531.

Allen, J. F., and Koomen, J. A. 1983. Planning using a temporal world model. In *Proc. 8th IJCAI*, 741–747.

Allen, J. F. 1983. Maintaining knowledge about temporal intervals. *CACM* 26(11):832–843.

Allen, J. F. 1984. Towards a general theory of action and time. *Artificial Intelligence* 23(2):123–154.

Allen, J. F. 1991. Temporal reasoning and planning. In Allen, J. F.; Kautz, H. A.; Pelavin, R. N.; and Tenenberg, J. D., eds., *Reasoning about Plans*. San Mateo, CA: Morgan Kaufmann. chapter 1, 1–67.

Feiner, S. K.; Litman, D. J.; McKeown, K. R.; and Passonneau, R. J. 1993. Towards coordinated temporal multimedia presentation. In Maybury, M., ed., *Intelligent Multi Media*. Menlo Park, CA: AAAI Press. Forthcoming.

Golumbic, M. C., and Shamir, R. 1992. Algorithms and complexity for reasoning about time. In *Proc. 10th AAAI*, 741–747.

Henschen, L., and Wos, L. 1974. Unit refutations and Horn sets. *JACM* 21:590–605.

Ladkin, P. B., and Maddux, R. 1988. On binary constraint networks. Technical Report KES.U.88.8, Kestrel Institute, Palo Alto, CA.

Ladkin, P. B. 1987. Models of axioms for time intervals. In *Proc. 6th AAAI*, 234–239.

Levesque, H. J., and Brachman, R. J. 1987. Expressiveness and tractability in knowledge representation and reasoning. *Computational Intelligence* 3:78–93.

Mackworth, A. K., and Freuder, E. C. 1985. The complexity of some polynomial network consistency algorithms for constraint satisfaction problems. *Artificial Intelligence* 25:65–73.

Mackworth, A. K. 1977. Consistency in networks of relations. *Artificial Intelligence* 8:99–118.

Montanari, U. 1974. Networks of constraints: fundamental properties and applications to picture processing. *Information Science* 7:95–132.

Nebel, B., and Bürckert, H.-J. 1993. Reasoning about temporal relations: A maximal tractable subclass of Allen's interval algebra. DFKI Research Report RR-93-11, Saarbrücken, Germany.

Nökel, K. 1989. Convex relations between time intervals. In Rettie, J., and Leidlmair, K., eds., *Proc. 5. Österreichische Artificial Intelligence-Tagung*. Berlin, Heidelberg, New York: Springer-Verlag. 298–302.

Song, F., and Cohen, R. 1988. The interpretation of temporal relations in narrative. In *Proc. 7th AAAI*, 745–750.

Valdéz-Pérez, R. E. 1987. The satisfiability of temporal constraint networks. In *Proc. 6th AAAI*, 256–260.

van Beek, P., and Cohen, R. 1990. Exact and approximate reasoning about temporal relations. *Computational Intelligence* 6:132–144.

van Beek, P. 1989. Approximation algorithms for temporal reasoning. In *Proc. 11th IJCAI*, 1291–1296.

van Beek, P. 1990. Reasoning about qualitative temporal information. In *Proc. 8th AAAI*, 728–734.

Vilain, M. B., and Kautz, H. A. 1986. Constraint propagation algorithms for temporal reasoning. In *Proc. 5th AAAI*, 377–382.

Vilain, M. B.; Kautz, H. A.; and van Beek, P. G. 1989. Constraint propagation algorithms for temporal reasoning: A revised report. In Weld, D. S., and de Kleer, J., eds., *Readings in Qualitative Reasoning about Physical Systems*. San Mateo, CA: Morgan Kaufmann. 373–381.

Weida, R., and Litman, D. 1992. Terminological reasoning with constraint networks and an application to plan recognition. In Nebel, B.; Swartout, W.; and Rich, C., eds., *Principles of Knowledge Representation and Reasoning: Proc. 3rd Int. Conf.*, 282–293. Cambridge, MA: Morgan Kaufmann.

A filtering algorithm for constraints of difference in CSPs [*]

Jean-Charles RÉGIN

GDR 1093 CNRS
LIRMM UMR 9928 Université Montpellier II / CNRS
161, rue Ada – 34392 Montpellier Cédex 5 – France
e-mail : regin@lirmm.fr

Abstract

Many real-life Constraint Satisfaction Problems (CSPs) involve some constraints similar to the alldifferent constraints. These constraints are called constraints of difference. They are defined on a subset of variables by a set of tuples for which the values occuring in the same tuple are all different. In this paper, a new filtering algorithm for these constraints is presented. It achieves the generalized arc-consistency condition for these non-binary constraints. It is based on matching theory and its complexity is low. In fact, for a constraint defined on a subset of p variables having domains of cardinality at most d, its space complexity is $O(pd)$ and its time complexity is $O(p^2d^2)$. This filtering algorithm has been successfully used in the system RESYN (Vismara et $al.$ 1992), to solve the subgraph isomorphism problem.

Introduction

The constraint satisfaction problems (CSPs) form a simple formal frame to represent and solve some problems in artificial intelligence. The problem of the existence of solutions in a CSP is NP-complete. Therefore, some methods have been developed to simplify the CSP before or during the search for solutions. The consistency techniques are the most frequently used. Several algorithms achieving arc-consistency have been proposed for binary CSPs (Mackworth 1977; Mohr & Henderson 1986; Bessière & Cordier 1993; Bessière 1994) and for n-ary CSPs (Mohr & Masini 1988a). Only limited works have been carried out on the semantics of contraints : (Mohr & Masini 1988b) have described an improvement of the algorithm AC-4 for special constraints introduced by a vision problem, (Van Hentenryck, Deville, & Teng 1992) have studied monotonic and functional binary constraints. In this work, we are interested in a special case of n-ary constraints : the constraints of difference, for which we propose a filtering algorithm.

A constraint is called *constraint of difference* if it is defined on a subset of variables by a set of tuples

---

[*]This work was supported by SANOFI-CHIMIE

for which the values occuring in the same tuple are all different. They are present in many real-life problems.

These constraints can be represented as n-ary constraints and filtered by the generalized arc-consistency algorithm GAC4 (Mohr & Masini 1988a). This filtering efficiently reduces the domains but its complexity can be expensive. In fact, it depends on the length and the number of all admissible tuples. Let us consider a constraint of difference defined on p variables, which take their values in a set of cardinality d. Thus, the number of admissible tuples corresponds to the number of permutations of p elements selected from d elements without repetition : $^dP_p = \frac{d!}{(d-p)!}$. Therefore some constraint resolution systems, like CHIP (Van Hentenryck 1989), represent these n-ary constraints by sets of binary constraints. In this case, a binary constraint of difference is built for each pair of variables belonging to the same constraint of difference. But the pruning performance of arc-consistency, for these constraints is poor. In fact, for a binary alldifferent constraint between two variables i and j, arc-consistency removes a value from domain of i only when the domain of j is reduced to a single value. Let us suppose we have a

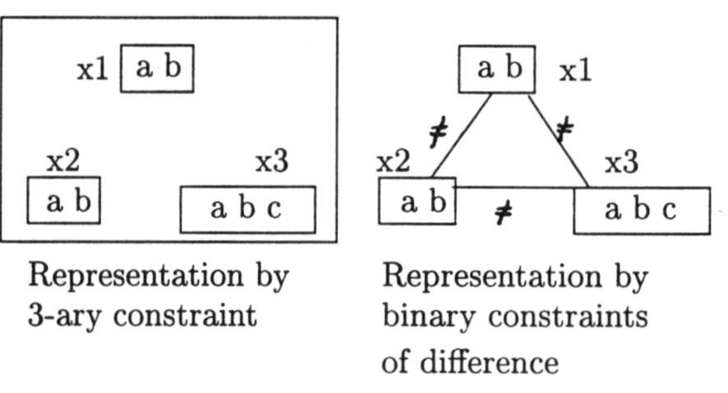

Representation by
3-ary constraint

Representation by
binary constraints
of difference

Figure 1.

CSP with 3 variables x_1, x_2, x_3 and one constraint of difference between these variables (see figure 1). The domains of variables are $D_1 = \{a, b\}$, $D_2 = \{a, b\}$ and $D_3 = \{a, b, c\}$. The GAC4 filtering with the constraint of difference represented by a 3-ary constraint, removes the values b and c from the domain of x_3, while arc-consistency with the constraint of difference represented by binary constraints of difference, does not delete any value.

In this paper we present an efficient way of implementing the generalized arc-consistency condition for the constraints of difference, in order to benefit from its pruning performances. Its space complexity is in $O(pd)$ and its time complexity is in $O(p^2d^2)$.

The rest of the paper is organized as follows. Section 2 gives some preliminaries on constraint satisfaction problems and matching, and proposes a restricted definition of arc-consistency, which concerns only the constraints of difference : the diff-arc-consistency. Section 3 presents a new condition to ensure the diff-arc-consistency in CSPs having constraints of difference. In section 4 we propose an efficient implementation to achieve this condition and analyse its complexity. In section 5, we show its performance and its interest with an example. A conclusion is given in section 6.

Preliminaries

A finite CSP (Constraint Satisfaction Problem) $\mathcal{P} = (X, \mathcal{D}, \mathcal{C})$ is defined as a set of n *variables* $X = \{x_1, ..., x_n\}$, a set of finite *domains* $\mathcal{D} = \{D_1, ..., D_n\}$ where D_i is the set of possible *values* for variable i and a set of *constraints* between variables $\mathcal{C} = \{C_1, C_2, ..., C_m\}$. A constraint C_i is defined on a set of variables $(x_{i_1}, ..., x_{i_j})$ by a subset of the cartesian product $D_{i_1} \times ... \times D_{i_j}$. A solution is an assignment of value to all variables which satisfies all the constraints. We will denote by :

- $D(X')$ the union of domains of variables of $X' \subseteq X$ (i.e $D(X') = \cup_{i \in X'} D_i$).
- X_C the set of variables on which a constraint C is defined.
- p the arity of a constraint C : $p = |X_C|$.
- d the maximal cardinality of domains.

A value a_i in the domain of a variable x_i is consistent with a given n-ary constraint if there exists values for all the other variables in the constraint such that these values with a_i *together simultaneously* satisfy the constraint. More generally, arc-consistency for n-ary CSPs or the generalized arc-consistency is defined as follows (Mohr & Masini 1988a):

Definition 1 *A CSP* $\mathcal{P} = (X, \mathcal{D}, \mathcal{C})$ *is* **arc-consistent** *iff* : $\forall x_i \in X, \forall a_i \in D_i, \forall C \in \mathcal{C}$ *constraining* $x_i, \forall x_j, ..., x_k \in X_C, \exists a_j, ..., a_k$ *such that* $C(a_j, ..., a_i, ..., a_k)$ *holds.*

Definition 2 *Given a CSP* $\mathcal{P} = (X, \mathcal{D}, \mathcal{C})$, *a constraint* C *is called* **constraint of difference** *if it is defined on a subset of variables* $X_C = \{x_{i_1}, ..., x_{i_k}\}$ *by a set of tuples, denoted by* $tuples(C)$ *such that :*
$$tuples(C) \subseteq D_{i_1} \times ... \times D_{i_k} \setminus \{(d_1, ..., d_k) \in D_{i_1} \times ... \times D_{i_k} \ s.t. \exists u, v \, | \, d_u = d_v\}$$

From the previous definition, we propose a special arc-consistency which concerns only the constraints of difference :

Definition 3 *A CSP* $\mathcal{P} = (X, \mathcal{D}, \mathcal{C})$ *is* **diff-arc-consistent** *iff all of its constraints of difference are arc-consistent.*

Definition 4 *Given a constraint of difference* C, *the bipartite graph* $GV(C) = (X_C, D(X_C), E)$ *where* $(x_i, a) \in E$ *iff* $a \in D_i$ *is called* **value graph** *of* C.

Figure 2 gives an example of a constraint of difference and its value graph.

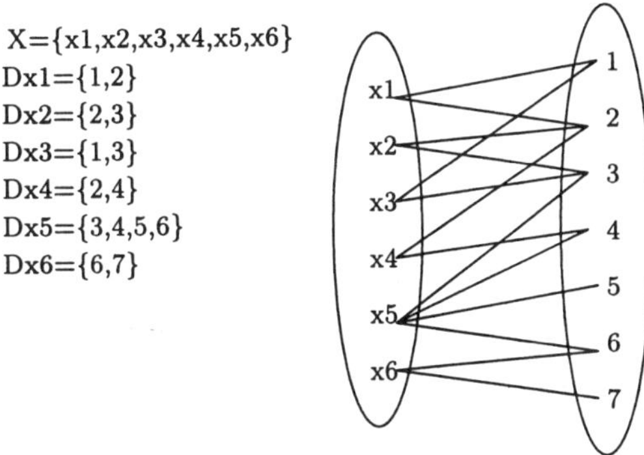

Figure 2: A constraint of difference defined on a set X and its value graph.

Definition 5 *A subset of edges in a graph* G *is called* **matching** *if no two edges have a vertex in common. A matching of maximum cardinality is called a* **maximum matching**. *A matching* M **covers a set** X *if every vertex in* X *is an endpoint of an edge in* M.

Note that a matching which covers X in a bipartite graph $G = (X, Y, E)$ is a maximum matching.

From the definition of a matching and the value graph we present, in the next section, a new necessary condition to ensure the diff-arc-consistency in CSPs having constraints of difference.

A new condition for CSPs having constraints of difference

The following theorem establishes a link between the diff-arc-consistency and the matching notion in the value graph of the constraints of difference.

Theorem 1 *Given a CSP* $\mathcal{P} = (X, \mathcal{D}, \mathcal{C})$. $\mathcal{P}$ *is diff-arc-consistent iff for each constraint of difference* C *of* $\mathcal{C}$ *every edge in* $GV(C)$ *belongs to a matching which covers* X_C *in* $GV(C)$.

proof
$\Rightarrow$: Let us consider a constraint of difference C and $GV(C)$ its value graph. From each admissible tuple of C, a set of pairs can be built. A pair consists of a variable and its assigned value in the tuple. The set

of pairs contains a pair for each variable. This set corresponds to a set of edges, denoted by A in $GV(C)$. Since $\mathcal{P}$ is diff-arc-consistent, the values in each tuple are all different. Thus, two edges of A cannot have a vertex in common and A is a matching wich covers X_C. Moreover, each value of each variable in the constraint belongs to at least one tuple. So, each edge of $GV(C)$ belongs to a matching which covers X_C.

$\Leftarrow$: Let us consider a variable x_i and a value a of its domain. For each constraint of difference C, the pair (x_i, a) belongs to a matching which covers X_C in $GV(C)$. Since in a matching no two edges have a vertex in common, there exists values for all the other variables in the constraint such that these values together simultaneously satisfy the constraint. So $\mathcal{P}$ is diff-arc-consistent. $\square$

The use of matching theory is interesting because (Hopcroft & Karp 1973) have shown how to compute a matching which covers X in a bipartite graph $G = (X, Y, E)$, with m edges, [1] in time $O(\sqrt{|X|}m)$.

This theorem gives us an efficient way to represent the constraint of difference in a CSP. In fact, a constraint of difference can be represent only by its value graph, with a space complexity in $O(pd)$. It also allows us to define a basic algorithm (algorithm 1) to filter the domains of variables of the set on which one constraint of difference is defined. This algorithm builds the value graph of the constraint of difference and computes a matching which covers X_C in order to delete every edge which belongs to no matching covering X_C. Figure 3 gives an application of this filtering.

Algorithm 1: DIFF-INITIALIZATION(C)
% returns false if there is no solution, otherwise true
% the function COMPUTEMAXIMUMMATCHING(G) computes a maximum matching in the graph G
begin
1   Build $G = (X_C, D(X_C), E)$
2    $M(G) \leftarrow$ COMPUTEMAXIMUMMATCHING(G)
    if $|M(G)| < |X_C|$ **then return** *false*
3   REMOVEEDGESFROMG($G, M(G)$)
    return *true*
end

The complexity of step 1 is $O(d|X_C| + |X_C| + |D(X_C)|)$. Step 2 costs $O(d|X_C|\sqrt{|X_C|})$. And we now show that it is possible to compute step 3 in linear time. So the complexity for one constraint of difference will be $O(d|X_C|\sqrt{|X_C|})$.

Deletion of every edge which belongs to no matching which covers X

In order to simplify the notation, we consider a bipartite graph $G = (X, Y, E)$ rather than the bipartite

---

[1](Alt *et al.* 1991) give an implementation of Hopcroft and Karp's algorithm which runs in time $O(|X|^{1.5}\sqrt{m \log|X|})$. For dense graph this is an improvement by a factor of $\sqrt{\log|X|}$.

graph $G = (X_C, D(X_C), E)$, and a matching M which covers X in G. In order to understand how we can

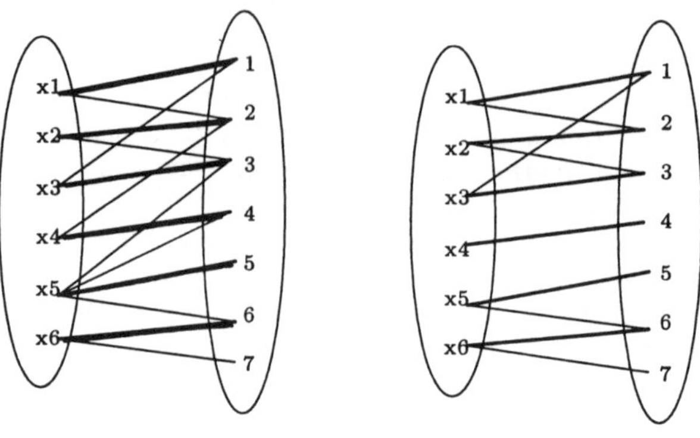

Figure 3: A value graph before and after the filtering.

delete every edge which belongs to no matching, we present a few definitions about matching theory. For more information the reader can consult (Berge 1970) or (Lovász & Plummer 1986).

Definition 6 *Let M be a matching, an edge in M is a **matching** edge; every edge not in M is **free**. A vertex is **matched** if it is incident to a matching edge and **free** otherwise. An **alternating path** or **cycle** is a simple path or cycle whose edges are alternately matching and free. The **length** of an alternating path or cycle is the number of edges it contains. An edge which belongs to every maximum matching is **vital**.*

Figure 3 gives an example of a matching which covers X in a bipartite graph. The bold edges are the matching edges. Vertex 7 is free. The path $(7, x6, 6, x5, 5)$ is an alternating path which begins at a free vertex. The cycle $(1, x3, 3, x2, 2, x1, 1)$ is an alternative cycle. The edge $(x4, 4)$ is a vital.

Property 1 (Berge 1970) *An edge belongs to some of but not all maximum matchings, iff, for an arbitrary maximum matching M, it belongs to either an even alternating path which begins at a free vertex, or an even alternating cycle.*

From this property we can find for an arbitrary matching M which covers X, every edge which belongs to no matching covering X. There are the edges which belong to neither M (there are not vital), nor an even alternating path which begins at a free vertex, nor an even alternating cycle.

Proposition 1 *Given a bipartite graph $G = (X, Y, E)$ with a matching M which covers X and the graph $G_O = (X, Y, Succ)$, obtained from G by orienting edges with the function :*
$$\forall x \in X : Succ(x) = \{y \in Y \,/\, (x, y) \in M\}$$
$$\forall y \in Y : Succ(y) = \{x \in X \,/\, (x, y) \in E - M\}$$
we have the two following properties :
1) Every directed cycle of G_O corresponds to an even alternating cycle of G, and conversely.

2) *Every directed simple path of G_O, which begins at a free vertex corresponds to an even alternating path of G which begins at a free vertex, and conversely.*

proof
If we ignore the parity, it is obvious that the proposition is true. In the first case, since G is bipartite it does not have any odd cycle. In the second case, we must show every directed simple path of G_O which begins at a free vertex to corresponds to an even alternating path of G which begins at a free vertex. M is a matching which covers X, so there is no free vertex in X. Since G is bipartite and since every path begins at a free vertex, in Y, every odd directed simple path ends with a vertex in X. From this vertex, we can always find a vertex in Y which does not belong to the path, because every vertex in X has one successor and because a vertex in Y has one predecessor. Therefore from an odd directed simple path we can always build an even directed simple path.$\square$

From this proposition we produce a linear algorithm (algorithm 2), that deletes every edge which does not belong to any matching which covers X.

Algorithm 2: REMOVEEDGESFROMG$(G,M(G))$
% RE is the set of edges removed from G.
% $M(G)$ is a matching of G which covers X
% The function returns RE
begin

1   Mark all directed edges in G_O as "unused". Set RE to $\emptyset$.

2   Look for all directed edges that belong to a directed simple path which begins at a free vertex by a breadth-first search starting from free vertices, and mark them as "used".

3   Compute the strongly connected components of G_O. Mark as "used" any directed edge that joins two vertices in the same strongly connected component.

4   **for** each directed edge de marked as "unused" **do**
       set e to the corresponding edge of de
       if $e \in M(G)$ **then** mark e as "vital"
       else
          $RE \leftarrow RE \cup \{e\}$
          remove e from G

   return RE
end

Step 2 corresponds to the point 2 of the proposition 1. Step 3 computes the strongly connected component of G_O, because an edge joining two vertices in the same strongly connected component belongs to a directed cycle and conversely. These edges belong to an even alternating cycle of G (cf point 1 of proposition 1). After this step the set A of all edges belonging to some but not all matchings covering X are known. The set RE of edges to remove from G is: $RE = E - (A \cup M)$. This is done by step 4. The algorithm complexity is the same as the search for strongly connected components(Tarjan 1972) , *i.e* $O(m + n)$ for a graph with m edges and n vertices.

We have shown how for *one* constraint of difference C every edge which belongs to no matching which covers X_C can be deleted. But a variable can be constrained by several constraints and it is necessary to propagate the deletions. In fact, let us consider x_i a variable of X_C, x_i can be constrained by several constraints. Thus, a value of D_i can be deleted for reasons independant from C. This deletion involves the removal of one edge from $GV(C)$. So, it is necessary to study the consequences of this modification of the $GV(C)$ structure.

Propagation of deletions

The deletion of values for one constraint of difference can involve some modifications for the other constraints. And for the other constraints of difference we can do better than repeat the first algorithm by using the fact that before the deletion, a matching which covers X is known.

The propagation algorithm we propose has two sets as parameters. The first one represents the set of edges to remove from the bipartite graph, and the second the set of edges that will be deleted by the filtering. The algorithm needs a function, denoted by MATCHINGCOVERINGX(G, M_1, M_2), which computes a matching M_2, which covers X, from a matching M_1 which is not maximum. It returns true if M_2 exists and false otherwise. The new filtering is represented by algorithm 3.

Algorithm 3: DIFF-PROPAGATION$(G,M(G),ER,RE)$
% the function returns false if there is no solution
% G is a value graph
% $M(G)$ is a matching which covers X_C
% ER is the set of edges to remove from G
% RE is the set of edges that will be deleted by the filtering
begin
     $computeMatching \leftarrow false$

1   **for** each $e \in ER$ **do**
       if $e \in M(G)$ **then**
          $M(G) \leftarrow M(G) - \{e\}$
          if e is marked as "vital" **then return** $false$
          else $computeMatching \leftarrow true$
       remove e from G

2   **if** $computeMatching$ **then**
       if $\neg$ MATCHINGCOVERINGX$(G,M(G),M')$ **then**
          return $false$
       else
          $M(G) \leftarrow M'$

3    $RE \leftarrow$ REMOVEEDGESFROMG$(G,M(G))$
   return $true$
end

It is divided into three parts. First, it removes edges from the bipartite graph. Second, it eventually computes a new matching which covers X_C. Third, it deletes the edges which does not belongs to any matching covering X_C. The algorithm returns false if ER

contains a vital edge or if there does not exist a matching which covers X_C.

Now, let us compute its complexity. Let m be the number of edges of G, and n be the number of vertices. Let us suppose that we must remove k edges from G ($|ER| = k$). The complexity of 1 is in $O(k)$. Step 2 involves, in the worst case, the computation of a matching covering X_C from a matching of cardinality $|M - k|$. This computation has cost $O(\sqrt{k}\,m)$ (see theorem 3 of (Hopcroft & Karp 1973)). The complexity of step 3 is in $O(m)$.

In the worst case, the edges of G can be deleted one by one. Then the previous function will be called m times. So the global complexity is in $O(m^2)$. If $p = |X_C|$ and d is the maximum cardinality of domains of variables of X_C, then the complexity is in $O(p^2 d^2)$ for one constraint of difference.

An example : the zebra problem

1. There are five houses, each of a different color and inhabited by men of different nationalities, with differents pets, drinks and cigarettes.
2. The Englishman lives in the red house.
3. The Spaniard owns a dog.
4. Coffee is drunk in the green house.
5. The Ukrainian drinks tea.
6. The green house is immediately to the right of the ivoiry house.
7. The Old-Gold smoker owns snails.
8. Kools are being smoked in the yellow house.
9. Milk is drunk in the middle house.
10. The Norwegian lives in the first house on the left.
11. The Chesterfield smoker lives next to the fox owner.
12. Kools are smoked in the house next to the house where the horse is kept.
13. The Lucky-Strike smoker drinks orange juice.
14. The Japanese smokes Parliament.
15. The Norwegian lives next to the blue house.
The *query* is : Who drinks water and who owns the zebra ?

This problem can be represented as a constraint network involving 25 variables, one for each of the five colors, drinks, nationalities, cigarettes and pets :

C_1 red	B_1 coffee	N_1 Englishman	T_1 Old-Gold	A_1 dog
C_2 green	B_2 tea	N_2 Spaniard	T_2 Chesterfield	A_2 snails
C_3 ivoiry	B_3 milk	N_3 Ukranian	T_3 Kools	A_3 fox
C_4 yellow	B_4 orange	N_4 Norwegian	T_4 Lucky-Strike	A_4 horse
C_5 blue	B_5 water	N_5 Japanese	T_5 Parliament	A_5 zebra

Each of the variables has domain values $\{1, 2, 3, 4, 5\}$, each number corresponding to a house position (e.g. assigning the value 2 to the variable *horse* means that the horse owner lives in the second house) (Dechter 1990). The assertions 2 to 15 are translated into unary and binary constraints. In addition, there are three

ways of representing the first assertion which means that the variables in the same cluster must take different values :

1. A binary constraint is built between any pair of variables of the same cluster ensuring that they are not assigned the same value. In this case we have a binary CSP.

2. Five 5-ary constraints of difference are built (one for each of the clusters). And the CSP is not binary.

3. The five 5-ary constraints of difference are represented by their value graphs. The space complexity of one constraint is in $O(pd)$.

The first representation is generally used to solve the problem (Dechter 1990; Bessière & Cordier 1993). From these three representations we can study the different results obtained from arc-consistency. They are given in figures 4 and 5. The constraints corresponding to the assertions 2 to 15 are represented in extension. The constraints of difference among the variables of each cluster are omitted for clarity.

For the first representation, the result of the filtering by arc-consistency is given in figure 4.

2 (=)

N_1	C_1
3	3
4	4
5	5

3 (=)

N_2	A_1
2	2
3	3
4	4
5	5

4 (=)

B_1	C_2
4	4
5	5

5 (=)

N_3	B_2
2	2
4	4
5	5

6 (-1)

C_2	C_3
4	3
5	4

7 (=)

T_1	A_2
1	1
2	2
3	3
4	4
5	5

8 (=)

T_3	C_4
1	1
3	3
4	4
5	5

9

B_3
3

10

N_4
1

11 (±1)

T_2	A_3
1	2
2	1
2	3
3	2
3	4
4	3
4	5
5	4

12 (±1)

A_4	T_3
2	1
2	3
3	4
4	3
4	5
5	4

13 (=)

T_4	B_4
1	1
2	2
4	4
5	5

14 (=)

N_5	T_5
2	2
3	3
4	4
5	5

15 (±1)

N_4	C_5
1	2

A_5	B_5
1	1
2	2
3	4
4	5
5	

Figure 4.

For the second representation, the filtering algorithm employed is the generalized arc-consistency. Figure 5 shows the new results. It has pruned more values that the previous one.

For the third representation, the filtering algorithm employed is arc-consistency for the binary constraints combined with the new filtering for the constraints of difference. The obtained results are the same as with the second method.

Let us denote by a the number of binary constraints corresponding to the assertions 2 to 15, p the size of a cluster, c the number of clusters, d the number of

$$
\begin{array}{|c|c|}\hline 2\ (=) \\\hline N_1 & C_1 \\\hline 3 & 3 \\ 4 & 4 \\ 5 & 5 \\\hline\end{array}
\quad
\begin{array}{|c|c|}\hline 3\ (=) \\\hline N_2 & A_1 \\\hline 3 & 3 \\ 4 & 4 \\ 5 & 5 \\\hline\end{array}
\quad
\begin{array}{|c|c|}\hline 4\ (=) \\\hline B_1 & C_2 \\\hline 4 & 4 \\ 5 & 5 \\\hline\end{array}
\quad
\begin{array}{|c|c|}\hline 5\ (=) \\\hline N_3 & B_2 \\\hline 2 & 2 \\ 4 & 4 \\ 5 & 5 \\\hline\end{array}
\quad
\begin{array}{|c|c|}\hline 6\ (-1) \\\hline C_2 & C_3 \\\hline 4 & 3 \\ 5 & 4 \\\hline\end{array}
\quad
\begin{array}{|c|c|}\hline 7\ (=) \\\hline T_1 & A_2 \\\hline 3 & 3 \\ 4 & 4 \\ 5 & 5 \\\hline\end{array}
\quad
\begin{array}{|c|c|}\hline 8\ (=) \\\hline T_3 & C_4 \\\hline 1 & 1 \\\hline\end{array}
\quad
\begin{array}{|c|}\hline 9 \\\hline B_3 \\\hline 3 \\\hline\end{array}
$$

$$
\begin{array}{|c|}\hline 10 \\\hline N_4 \\\hline 1 \\\hline\end{array}
\quad
\begin{array}{|c|c|}\hline 11\ (\pm 1) \\\hline T_2 & A_3 \\\hline 2 & 1 \\ 2 & 3 \\ 3 & 4 \\ 4 & 3 \\ 4 & 5 \\ 5 & 4 \\\hline\end{array}
\quad
\begin{array}{|c|c|}\hline 12\ (\pm 1) \\\hline A_4 & T_3 \\\hline 2 & 1 \\\hline\end{array}
\quad
\begin{array}{|c|c|}\hline 13\ (=) \\\hline T_4 & B_4 \\\hline 2 & 2 \\ 4 & 4 \\ 5 & 5 \\\hline\end{array}
\quad
\begin{array}{|c|c|}\hline 14\ (=) \\\hline N_5 & T_5 \\\hline 2 & 2 \\ 3 & 3 \\ 4 & 4 \\ 5 & 5 \\\hline\end{array}
\quad
\begin{array}{|c|c|}\hline 15\ (\pm 1) \\\hline N_4 & C_5 \\\hline 1 & 2 \\\hline\end{array}
\quad
\begin{array}{|c|}\hline A_5 \\\hline 1 \\ 3 \\ 4 \\ 5 \\\hline\end{array}
\quad
\begin{array}{|c|}\hline B_5 \\\hline 1 \\\hline\end{array}
$$

Figure 5.

values in a domain and $O(ed^2)$ the complexity for arc-consistency[2] in binary CSPs. Let us compute the complexity for the three methods :

1. For the first representation, the number of binary constraints of difference added is in $O(cp^2)$. So, the filtering complexity is $O((a + cp^2)d^2)$.

2. In the second case, we can consider that the complexity is the sum of the lengths of all admissible tuples for the five 5-ary constraints. It is in $O(\frac{d!}{(d-p)!}p)$.

3. For the third method arc-consistency is in $O(ad^2)$ and the filtering for the constraints of difference is in $O(cp^2d^2)$. The total complexity is in $O(ad^2) + O(cp^2d^2)$. It is equivalent to the first one.

The second filtering eliminates more values than the first one. But its complexity is higher. The representation and the algorithm proposed in this paper give pruning results equivalent to the second approach with the same complexity as the first one. So we can conclude that the new filtering is good for problems looking like the zebra problem.

Conclusion

In this paper we have presented a filtering algorithm for constraints of difference in CSPs. This algorithm can be viewed as an efficient way of implementing the generalized arc-consistency condition for a special type of constraint : the constraints of difference. It allows us to benefit from the pruning performance of the previous condition with a low complexity. In fact, its space complexity is in $O(pd)$ and its time complexity is in $O(p^2d^2)$ for one constraint defined on a subset of p variables having domains of cardinality at most d. It has been shown to be very efficient for the zebra problem. And it has been successfully used to solve the subgraph isomorphism problem in the system RESYN (Vismara *et al.* 1992), a computer-aided design of complex organic synthesis plan.

---

[2](Mohr & Masini 1988b) reduce this complexity to $O(ed)$ for the binary alldifferent constraints

Acknowledgments

We would like to thank particularly Christian Bessière and also Marie-Catherine Vilarem, Tibor Kökény and the anonymous reviewers for their comments which helped improve this paper.

References

Alt, H.; Blum, N.; Melhorn, K.; and Paul, M. 1991. Computing a maximum cardinality matching in a bipartite graph in time $o(n^{1,5}\sqrt{m/\log n})$. *Information Processing Letters* 37:237–240.

Berge, C. 1970. *Graphe et Hypergraphes*. Paris: Dunod.

Bessière, C., and Cordier, M. 1993. Arc-consistency and arc-consistency again. In *Proceedings AAAI*, 108–113.

Bessière, C. 1994. Arc-consistency and arc-consistency again. *Artificial Intelligence* 65(1):179–190.

Dechter, R. 1990. Enhencement schemes for constraint processing : Backjumping, learning, and cutset decomposition. *Artificial Intelligence* 41:273–312.

Hopcroft, J., and Karp, R. 1973. $n^{5/2}$ algorithm for maximum matchings in bipartite graphs. *SIAM Journal of Computing* 2:225–231.

Lovász, L., and Plummer, M. 1986. *Matching Theory*. North Holland mathematics studies 121.

Mackworth, A. 1977. Consistency in networks of relations. *Artificial Intelligence* 8:99–118.

Mohr, R., and Henderson, T. 1986. Arc and path consistency revisited. *Artificial Intelligence* 28:225–233.

Mohr, R., and Masini, G. 1988a. Good old discrete relaxation. In *Proceedings ECAI*, 651–656.

Mohr, R., and Masini, G. 1988b. Running efficiently arc consistency. *Syntactic and Structural Pattern Recognition* F45:217–231.

Tarjan, R. 1972. Depth-first search and linear graph algorithms. *SIAM Journal of Computing* 1:146–160.

Van Hentenryck, P.; Deville, Y.; and Teng, C. 1992. A generic arc-consistency algorithm and its specializations. *Artificial Intelligence* 57:291–321.

Van Hentenryck, P. 1989. *Constraint Satisfaction in Logic Programming*. M.I.T. Press.

Vismara, P.; Régin, J.-C.; Quinqueton, J.; Py, M.; Laurenço, C.; and Lapied, L. 1992. RESYN : Un système d'aide à la conception de plans de synthèse en chimie organique. In *Proceedings 12th International Conference Avignon'92*, volume 1, 305–318. Avignon: EC2.

On the Inherent Level of Local Consistency in Constraint Networks

Peter van Beek
Department of Computing Science
University of Alberta
Edmonton, Alberta, Canada T6G 2H1
vanbeek@cs.ualberta.ca

Abstract

We present a new property called *constraint looseness* and show how it can be used to estimate the level of local consistency of a binary constraint network. Specifically, we present a relationship between the looseness of the constraints, the size of the domains, and the inherent level of local consistency of a constraint network. The results we present are useful in two ways. First, a common method for finding solutions to a constraint network is to first preprocess the network by enforcing local consistency conditions, and then perform a backtracking search. Here, our results can be used in deciding which low-order local consistency techniques will *not* change a given constraint network and thus are not useful for preprocessing the network. Second, much previous work has identified conditions for when a certain level of local consistency is sufficient to guarantee a network is backtrack-free. Here, our results can be used in deciding which local consistency conditions, if any, still need to be enforced to achieve the specified level of local consistency. As well, we use the looseness property to develop an algorithm that can sometimes find an ordering of the variables such that a network is backtrack-free.

Introduction

Constraint networks are a simple representation and reasoning framework. A problem is represented as a set of variables, a domain of values for each variable, and a set of constraints between the variables. A central reasoning task is then to find an instantiation of the variables that satisfies the constraints. Examples of tasks that can be formulated as constraint networks include graph coloring (Montanari 1974), scene labeling (Waltz 1975), natural language parsing (Maruyama 1990), temporal reasoning (Allen 1983), and answering conjunctive queries in relational databases.

In general, what makes constraint networks hard to solve is that they can contain many local inconsistencies. A local inconsistency is a consistent instantiation of $k - 1$ of the variables that cannot be extended to a kth variable and so cannot be part of any global solution. If we are using a backtracking search to find a solution, such an inconsistency can lead to a dead end

in the search. This insight has led to the definition of conditions that characterize the level of local consistency of a network (Freuder 1985; Mackworth 1977; Montanari 1974) and to the development of algorithms for enforcing local consistency conditions by removing local inconsistencies (e.g., (Cooper 1989; Dechter & Pearl 1988; Freuder 1978; Mackworth 1977; Montanari 1974; Waltz 1975)). However, the definitions, or necessary and sufficient conditions, for all but low-order local consistency are expensive to verify or enforce as the optimal algorithms are $O(n^k)$, where k is the level of local consistency (Cooper 1989; Seidel 1983).

In this paper, we present a simple, sufficient condition, based on the size of the domains of the variables and on a new property called *constraint looseness*, that gives a lower bound on the the inherent level of local consistency of a binary constraint network. The bound is tight for some constraint networks but not for others. Specifically, in any constraint network where the domains are of size d or less, and the constraints have looseness of m or greater, the network is strongly ($\lceil d/(d - m) \rceil$)-consistent[1]. Informally, a constraint network is strongly k-consistent if a solution can always be found for any subnetwork of size k in a backtrack-free manner. The parameter m can be viewed as a lower bound on the number of instantiations of a variable that satisfy the constraints. We also use the looseness property to develop an algorithm that can sometimes find an ordering of the variables such that all solutions of a network can be found in a backtrack-free manner.

The condition we present is useful in two ways. First, a common method for finding solutions to a constraint network is to first preprocess the network by enforcing local consistency conditions, and then perform a backtracking search. The preprocessing step can reduce the number of dead ends reached by the backtracking algorithm in the search for a solution. With a similar aim, local consistency techniques can be interleaved with backtracking search. The effectiveness of using

---

[1] $\lceil x \rceil$, the ceiling of x, is the smallest integer greater than or equal to x.

local consistency techniques in these two ways has been studied empirically (e.g., (Dechter & Meiri 1989; Gaschnig 1978; Ginsberg *et al.* 1990; Haralick & Elliott 1980; Prosser 1993)). In this setting, our results can be used in deciding which low-order local consistency techniques will *not* change the network and thus are not useful for processing a given constraint network. For example, we use our results to show that the n-queens problem, a widely used test-bed for comparing backtracking algorithms, has a high level of inherent local consistency. As a consequence, it is generally fruitless to preprocess such a network.

Second, much previous work has identified conditions for when a certain level of local consistency is sufficient to guarantee a solution can be found in a backtrack-free manner (e.g., (Dechter 1992; Dechter & Pearl 1988; Freuder 1982; 1985; Montanari 1974; van Beek 1992)). These conditions are important in applications where constraint networks are used for knowledge base maintenance and there will be many queries against the knowledge base. Here, the cost of preprocessing will be amortized over the many queries. In this setting, our results can be used in deciding which local consistency conditions, if any, still need to be enforced to achieve the specified level of local consistency.

Background

We begin with some needed definitions.

Definition 1 (binary constraint networks; Montanari (1974)) *A binary constraint network consists of a set X of n variables $\{x_1, x_2, \ldots, x_n\}$, a domain D_i of possible values for each variable, and a set of binary constraints between variables. A binary constraint or relation, R_{ij}, between variables x_i and x_j, is any subset of the product of their domains (i.e., $R_{ij} \subseteq D_i \times D_j$). An instantiation of the variables in X is an n-tuple $(X_1, X_2, \ldots, X_n)$, representing an assignment of $X_i \in D_i$ to x_i. A consistent instantiation of a network is an instantiation of the variables such that the constraints between variables are satisfied. A consistent instantiation is also called a* solution.

Mackworth (1977; 1987) defines three properties of networks that characterize local consistency of networks: *node*, *arc*, and *path consistency*. Freuder (1978) generalizes this to k-consistency.

Definition 2 (strong k-consistency; Freuder (1978; 1982)) *A network is k-consistent if and only if given any instantiation of any $k-1$ variables satisfying all the direct relations among those variables, there exists an instantiation of any kth variable such that the k values taken together satisfy all the relations among the k variables. A network is* strongly k-consistent *if and only if it is j-consistent for all $j \leq k$.*

Node, arc, and path consistency correspond to strongly one-, two-, and three-consistent, respectively.

A strongly n-consistent network is called *globally consistent*. Globally consistent networks have the property that any consistent instantiation of a subset of the variables can be extended to a consistent instantiation of all the variables without backtracking (Dechter 1992).

Following Montanari (1974), a binary relation R_{ij} between variables x_i and x_j is represented as a $(0,1)$-matrix with $|D_i|$ rows and $|D_j|$ columns by imposing an ordering on the domains of the variables. A zero entry at row a, column b means that the pair consisting of the ath element of D_i and the bth element of D_j is not permitted; a one entry means the pair is permitted. A concept central to this paper is the looseness of constraints.

Definition 3 (m-loose) *A binary constraint is m-loose if every row and every column of the $(0,1)$-matrix that defines the constraint has at least m ones, where $0 \leq m \leq |D| - 1$. A binary constraint network is m-loose if all its binary constraints are m-loose.*

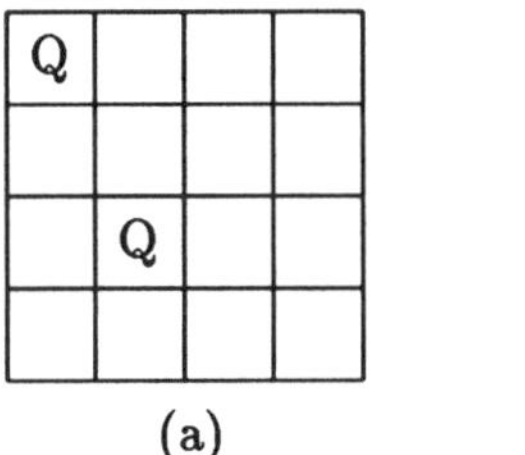
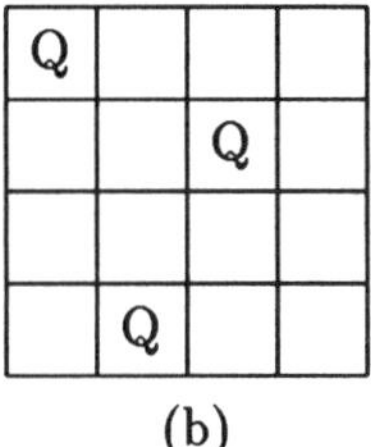

(a)   (b)

Figure 1: (a) not 3-consistent; (b) not 4-consistent

Example 1. We illustrate some of the definitions using the well-known n-queens problem. The problem is to find all ways to place n-queens on an $n \times n$ chess board, one queen per column, so that each pair of queens does not attack each other. One possible constraint network formulation of the problem is as follows: there is a variable for each column of the chess board, $x_1, \ldots, x_n$; the domains of the variables are the possible row positions, $D_i = \{1, \ldots, n\}$; and the binary constraints are that two queens should not attack each other. The $(0,1)$-matrix representation of the constraints between two variables x_i and x_j is given by,

$$R_{ij,ab} = \begin{cases} 1 & \text{if } a \neq b \wedge |a - b| \neq |i - j| \\ 0 & \text{otherwise,} \end{cases}$$

for $a, b = 1, \ldots, n$.

For example, consider the constraint network for the 4-queens problem. The constraint R_{12} between x_1 and x_2 is given by,

$$R_{12} = \begin{bmatrix} 0 & 0 & 1 & 1 \\ 0 & 0 & 0 & 1 \\ 1 & 0 & 0 & 0 \\ 1 & 1 & 0 & 0 \end{bmatrix}.$$

Entry $R_{12,43}$ is 0, which states that putting a queen in column 1, row 4 and a queen in column 2, row 3 is not allowed by the constraint since the queens attack each other. It can be seen that the network for the 4-queens problem is 2-consistent since, given that we have placed a single queen on the board, we can always place a second queen such that the queens do not attack each other. However, the network is not 3-consistent. For example, given the consistent placement of two queens shown in Figure 1a, there is no way to place a queen in the third column that is consistent with the previously placed queens. Similarly the network is not 4-consistent (see Figure 1b). Finally, every row and every column of the (0,1)-matrices that define the constraints has at least 1 one. Hence, the network is 1-loose.

A Sufficient Condition for Local Consistency

In this section, we present a simple condition that estimates the inherent level of strong k-consistency of a binary constraint network. The condition is a sufficient but not necessary condition for local consistency.

It is known that some classes of constraint networks already possess a certain level of local consistency and therefore algorithms that enforce this level of local consistency will have no effect on these networks. For example, Nadel (1989) observes that an arc consistency algorithm never changes a constraint network formulation of the n-queens problem, for $n > 3$. Dechter (1992) observes that constraint networks that arise from the graph k-coloring problem are inherently strongly k-consistent. The following theorem characterizes what it is about the structure of the constraints in these networks that makes these statements true.

Theorem 1 *If a binary constraint network, R, is m-loose and all domains are of size $|D|$ or less, then the network is strongly $\left(\left\lceil \frac{|D|}{|D|-m} \right\rceil\right)$-consistent.*

Proof. We show that the network is k-consistent for all $k \leq \lceil |D|/(|D|-m) \rceil$. Suppose that variables $x_1, \ldots, x_{k-1}$ can be consistently instantiated with values $X_1, \ldots, X_{k-1}$. To show that the network is k-consistent, we must show that there exists at least one instantiation X_k of variable x_k that satisfies all the constraints,

$$(X_i, X_k) \in R_{ik} \qquad i = 1, \ldots, k-1$$

simultaneously. We do so as follows. The instantiations $X_1, \ldots, X_{k-1}$ restrict the allowed instantiations of x_k. Let v_i be the (0,1)-vector given by row X_i of the (0,1)-matrix R_{ik}, $i = 1, \ldots, k-1$. Let $\text{pos}(v_i)$ be the positions of the zeros in vector v_i. The zero entries in the v_i are the forbidden instantiations of x_k, given the instantiations $X_1, \ldots, X_{k-1}$. No consistent instantiation of x_k exists if and only if $\text{pos}(v_1) \cup \cdots \cup \text{pos}(v_{k-1}) = \{1, \ldots, |D|\}$. Now, the key to the proof is that all the v_i contain at least m ones. In other words, each v_i

contains at most $|D| - m$ zeros. Thus, if

$$(k-1)(|D|-m) < |D|,$$

it cannot be the case that $\text{pos}(v_1) \cup \cdots \cup \text{pos}(v_{k-1}) = \{1, \ldots, |D|\}$. (To see that this is true, consider the "worst case" where the positions of the zeros in any vector do not overlap with those of any other vector. That is, $\text{pos}(v_i) \cap \text{pos}(v_j) = \emptyset$, $i \neq j$.) Thus, if

$$k \leq \left\lceil \frac{|D|}{|D|-m} \right\rceil,$$

all the constraints must have a non-zero entry in common and there exists at least one instantiation of x_k that satisfies all the constraints simultaneously. Hence, the network is k-consistent. $\square$

Theorem 1 always specifies a level of local consistency that is less than or equal to the actual level of inherent local consistency of a constraint network. That is, the theorem provides a lower bound. Graph coloring problems provide examples where the theorem is exact, whereas n-queens problems provide examples where the theorem underestimates the true level of local consistency.

Example 2. Consider again the well-known n-queens problem discussed in Example 1. The problem is of historical interest but also of theoretical interest due to its importance as a test problem in empirical evaluations of backtracking algorithms and heuristic repair schemes for finding solutions to constraint networks (e.g., (Gaschnig 1978; Haralick & Elliott 1980; Minton *et al.* 1990; Nadel 1989)). For n-queens networks, each row and column of the constraints has $|D|-3 \leq m \leq |D|-1$ ones, where $|D| = n$. Hence, Theorem 1 predicts that n-queens networks are inherently strongly $(\lceil n/3 \rceil)$-consistent. Thus, an n-queens constraint network is inherently arc-consistent for $n \geq 4$, inherently path consistent for $n \geq 7$, and so on, and we can predict where it is fruitless to apply a low order consistency algorithm in an attempt to simplify the network (see Table 1). The actual level of inherent consistency is $\lfloor n/2 \rfloor$ for $n \geq 7$. Thus, for the n-queens problem, the theorem underestimates the true level of local consistency.

Table 1: Predicted ($\lceil n/3 \rceil$) and actual ($\lfloor n/2 \rfloor$, for $n \geq 7$) level of strong local consistency for n-queens networks

n	4	5	6	7	8	9	10	11	12
pred.	2	2	2	3	3	3	4	4	4
actual	2	2	2	3	4	4	5	5	6

The reason Theorem 1 is not exact in general and, in particular, for n-queens networks, is that the proof of the theorem considers the "worst case" where the positions of the zeros in any row of the constraints

$R_{ik}, i = 1, \ldots, k - 1$, do not overlap with those of any other row. For n-queens networks, the positions of some of the zeros do overlap. However, given only the looseness of the constraints and the size of the domains, Theorem 1 gives as strong an estimation of the inherent level of local consistency as possible as examples can be given where the theorem is exact.

Example 3. Graph k-colorability provides examples where Theorem 1 is exact in its estimation of the inherent level of strong k-consistency. The constraint network formulation of graph coloring is straightforward: there is a variable for each node in the graph; the domains of the variables are the possible colors, $D = \{1, \ldots, k\}$; and the binary constraints are that two adjacent nodes must be assigned different colors. As Dechter (1992) states, graph coloring networks are inherently strongly k-consistent but are not guaranteed to be strongly $(k+1)$-consistent. Each row and column of the constraints has $m = |D| - 1$ ones, where $|D| = k$. Hence, Theorem 1 predicts that graph k-colorability networks are inherently strongly k-consistent.

Example 4. We can also construct examples, for all $m < |D| - 1$, where Theorem 1 is exact. For example, consider the network where, $n = 5$, the domains are $D = \{1, \ldots, 5\}$, and the binary constraints are given by,

$$R_{ij} = \begin{bmatrix} 0 & 1 & 1 & 1 & 1 \\ 0 & 0 & 1 & 1 & 1 \\ 1 & 0 & 0 & 1 & 1 \\ 1 & 1 & 0 & 0 & 1 \\ 1 & 1 & 1 & 0 & 0 \end{bmatrix}, \ 1 \leq i < j \leq n,$$

and $R_{ji} = R_{ij}^T$, for $j < i$. The network is 3-loose and therefore strongly 3-consistent by Theorem 1. This is exact, as the network is not 4-consistent.

We conclude this section with some discussion on what Theorem 1 contributes to our intuitions about hard classes of problems (in the spirit of, for example, (Cheeseman, Kanefsky, & Taylor 1991; Williams & Hogg 1992)). Hard constraint networks are instances which give rise to search spaces with many dead ends. The hardest networks are those where many dead ends occur deep in the search tree. Dead ends, of course, correspond to partial solutions that cannot be extended to full solutions. Thus, networks where the constraints are loose are good candidates to be hard problems since loose networks have a high level of inherent strong consistency and strong k-consistency means that all partial solutions are of at least size k.

Computational experiments we performed on random problems provide evidence that loose networks can be hard. Random problems were generated with $n = 50$, $|D| = 5, \ldots 10$, and $p, q = 1, \ldots, 100$, where $p/100$ is the probability that there is a binary constraint between two variables, and $q/100$ is the probability that a pair in the Cartesian product of the domains is in the constraint. The time to find one solution was measured. In the experiments we discovered that, given that the number of variables and the domain size were fixed, the hardest problems were found when the constraints were as loose as possible without degenerating into the trivial constraint where all tuples are allowed. That networks with loose constraints would turn out to be the hardest of these random problems is somewhat counter-intuitive, as individually the constraints are easy to satisfy. These experimental results run counter to Tsang's (1993, p.50) intuition that a single solution of a loosely constrained problem "can easily be found by simple backtracking, hence such problems are easy," and that tightly constrained problems are "harder compared with loose problems." As well, these hard loosely-constrained problems are not amenable to preprocessing by low-order local consistency algorithms, since, as Theorem 1 states, they possess a high level of inherent local consistency. This runs counter to Williams and Hogg's (1992, p.476) speculation that preprocessing will have the most dramatic effect in the region where the problems are the hardest.

Backtrack-free Networks

Given an ordering of the variables in a constraint network, backtracking search works by successively instantiating the next variable in the ordering, and backtracking to try different instantiations for previous variables when no consistent instantiation can be given to the current variable. Previous work has identified conditions for when a certain level of local consistency is sufficient to ensure a solution can be found in a backtrack-free manner (e.g., (Dechter 1992; Dechter & Pearl 1988; Freuder 1982; 1985; Montanari 1974; van Beek 1992)). Sometimes the level of inherent strong k-consistency guaranteed by Theorem 1 is sufficient, in conjunction with these previously derived conditions, to guarantee that the network is globally consistent and therefore a solution can be found in a backtrack-free manner. Otherwise, the estimate provided by the theorem gives a starting point for applying local consistency algorithms.

In this section, we use constraint looseness to identify new classes of backtrack-free networks. First, we give a condition for a network to be inherently globally consistent. Second, we give a condition, based on a directional version of the looseness property, for an ordering to be backtrack-free. We also give an efficient algorithm for finding an ordering that satisfies the condition, should it exist.

We begin with a corollary of Theorem 1.

Corollary 1 *If a binary constraint network, R, is m-loose, all domains are of size $|D|$ or less, and $m > \frac{n-2}{n-1}|D|$, the network is globally consistent.*

Proof. By Theorem 1, the network is strongly n-consistent if $\lceil |D|/(|D| - m) \rceil \geq n$. This is equivalent to, $|D|/(|D| - m) > n - 1$ and rearranging for m gives the result. $\square$

As one example, consider a constraint network with $n = 5$ variables that has domains of at most size $|D| = 10$ and constraints that are 8-loose. The network is globally consistent and, as a consequence, a solution can be found in a backtrack-free manner. Another example is networks with $n = 5$, domain sizes of $|D| = 5$, and constraints that are 4-loose.

Global consistency implies that all orderings of the variables are backtrack-free orderings. Sometimes, however, there exists a backtrack-free ordering when only much weaker local consistency conditions hold. Freuder (1982) identifies a relationship between the *width* of an ordering of the variables and the level of local consistency sufficient to ensure an ordering is backtrack-free.

Definition 4 (width; Freuder (1982)) *Let $o = (x_1, \ldots, x_n)$ be an ordering of the variables in a binary constraint network. The width of a variable, x_i, is the number of binary constraints between x_i and variables previous to x_i in the ordering. The width of an ordering is the maximum width of all variables.*

Theorem 2 (Freuder (1982)) *An ordering of the variables in a binary constraint network is backtrack-free if the level of strong k-consistency of the network is greater than the width of the ordering.*

Dechter and Pearl (1988) define a weaker version of k-consistency, called directional k-consistency, and show that Theorem 2 still holds. Both versions of k-consistency are, in general, expensive to verify, however. Dechter and Pearl also give an algorithm, called adaptive consistency, that does not enforce a uniform level of local consistency throughout the network but, rather, enforces the needed level of local consistency as determined on a variable by variable basis. We adapt these two insights, directionality and not requiring uniform levels of local consistency, to a condition for an ordering to be backtrack-free.

Definition 5 (directionally m-loose) *A binary constraint is directionally m-loose if every row of the $(0,1)$-matrix that defines the constraint has at least m ones, where $0 \le m \le |D| - 1$.*

Theorem 3 *An ordering of the variables, $o = (x_1, \ldots, x_n)$, in a binary constraint network, R, is backtrack-free if $\left\lceil \frac{|D|}{|D| - m_j} \right\rceil > w_j$, $1 \le j \le n$, where w_j is the width of variable x_j in the ordering, and m_j is the minimum of the directional looseness of the (nontrivial) constraints $R_{ij}, 1 \le i < j$.*

Proof. Similar to the proof of Theorem 1. $\square$

A straightforward algorithm for finding such a backtrack-free ordering of the variables, should it exist, is given below.

FINDORDER(R, n)
1. $I \leftarrow \{1, 2, \ldots, n\}$
2. **for** $p \leftarrow n$ **downto** 1 **do**
3.   find a $j \in I$ such that, for each R_{ij}, $i \in I$ and $i \ne j$, $\lceil |D|/(|D| - m_{ij}) \rceil > w_j$, where w_j is the number of constraints R_{ij}, $i \in I$ and $i \ne j$, and m_{ij} is the directional m-looseness of R_{ij} (if no such j exists, report failure and halt)
4.   put variable x_j at position p in the ordering
5. $I \leftarrow I - \{j\}$

Example 5. Consider the network in Figure 2. The network is 2-consistent, but not 3-consistent and not 4-consistent. Freuder (1982), in connection with Theorem 2, gives an algorithm for finding an ordering which has the minimum width of all orderings of the network. Assuming that the algorithms break ties by choosing the variable with the lowest index, the minimal width ordering found is $(x_5, x_4, x_3, x_2, x_1)$, which has width 3. Thus, the condition of Theorem 2 does not hold. In fact, this ordering is not backtrack-free. For example, the partial solution $x_5 \leftarrow 1$, $x_4 \leftarrow 3$, and $x_3 \leftarrow 5$ is a dead end, as there is no instantiation for x_2. The ordering found by procedure FINDORDER is $(x_4, x_3, x_2, x_1, x_5)$, which has width 4. It can be verified that the condition of Theorem 3 holds. For example, w_1, the width at variable x_1, is 2, and the constraints R_{41} and R_{31} are both 3-loose, so $\left\lceil \frac{|D|}{|D| - m_1} \right\rceil = 3 > w_1 = 2$. Therefore all solutions of the network can be found with no backtracking along this ordering.

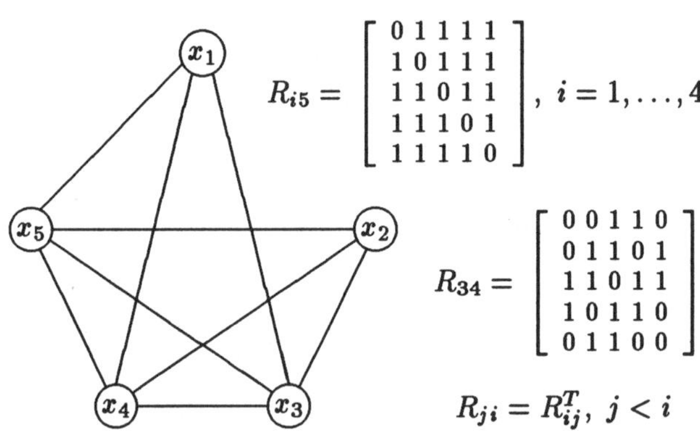

$$R_{ij} = \begin{bmatrix} 0 & 0 & 1 & 1 & 1 \\ 1 & 0 & 0 & 1 & 1 \\ 1 & 1 & 0 & 0 & 1 \\ 1 & 1 & 1 & 0 & 0 \\ 1 & 1 & 1 & 1 & 0 \end{bmatrix}, \ i = 1, 2; \ j = 3, 4$$

$$R_{i5} = \begin{bmatrix} 0 & 1 & 1 & 1 & 1 \\ 1 & 0 & 1 & 1 & 1 \\ 1 & 1 & 0 & 1 & 1 \\ 1 & 1 & 1 & 0 & 1 \\ 1 & 1 & 1 & 1 & 0 \end{bmatrix}, \ i = 1, \ldots, 4$$

$$R_{34} = \begin{bmatrix} 0 & 0 & 1 & 1 & 0 \\ 0 & 1 & 1 & 0 & 1 \\ 1 & 1 & 0 & 1 & 1 \\ 1 & 0 & 1 & 1 & 0 \\ 0 & 1 & 1 & 0 & 0 \end{bmatrix}$$

$$R_{ji} = R_{ij}^T, \ j < i$$

Figure 2: Constraint network for which a backtrack-free ordering exists

Conclusions and Future Work

Local consistency has proven to be an important concept in the theory and practice of constraint networks. However, the definitions, or necessary and sufficient conditions, for all but low-order local consistency are expensive to verify or enforce. We presented a sufficient condition for local consistency, based on a new property called constraint looseness, that is straightforward and inexpensive to determine. The condition can be used to estimate the level of strong local consistency of a network. This in turn can be used in (i) deciding whether it would be useful to preprocess the network before a backtracking search, and (ii) deciding which local consistency conditions, if any, still need to be enforced if we want to ensure that a solution can be found in a backtrack-free manner. Finally, the looseness property was used to identify new classes of "easy" constraint networks.

A property of constraints proposed by Nudel (1983) which is related to constraint looseness counts the number of ones in the entire constraint. Nudel uses this count, called a compatibility count, in an effective variable ordering heuristic for backtracking search. We plan to examine whether m-looseness can be used to develop even more effective domain and variable ordering heuristics. We also plan to examine how the looseness property can be used to improve the average case efficiency of local consistency algorithms. The idea is to predict whether small subnetworks already possess some specified level of local consistency, thus potentially avoiding the computations needed to enforce local consistency on those parts of the network.

Acknowledgements. Financial assistance was received from the Natural Sciences and Engineering Research Council of Canada.

References

Allen, J. F. 1983. Maintaining knowledge about temporal intervals. *Comm. ACM* 26:832–843.

Cheeseman, P.; Kanefsky, B.; and Taylor, W. M. 1991. Where the really hard problems are. In *Proceedings of the Twelfth International Joint Conference on Artificial Intelligence*, 331–337.

Cooper, M. C. 1989. An optimal k-consistency algorithm. *Artificial Intelligence* 41:89–95.

Dechter, R., and Meiri, I. 1989. Experimental evaluation of preprocessing techniques in constraint satisfaction problems. In *Proc. of the Eleventh International Joint Conference on Artificial Intelligence*, 271–277.

Dechter, R., and Pearl, J. 1988. Network-based heuristics for constraint satisfaction problems. *Artificial Intelligence* 34:1–38.

Dechter, R. 1992. From local to global consistency. *Artificial Intelligence* 55:87–107.

Freuder, E. C. 1978. Synthesizing constraint expressions. *Comm. ACM* 21:958–966.

Freuder, E. C. 1982. A sufficient condition for backtrack-free search. *J. ACM* 29:24–32.

Freuder, E. C. 1985. A sufficient condition for backtrack-bounded search. *J. ACM* 32:755–761.

Gaschnig, J. 1978. Experimental case studies of backtrack vs. waltz-type vs. new algorithms for satisficing assignment problems. In *Proceedings of the Second Canadian Conference on Artificial Intelligence*, 268–277.

Ginsberg, M. L.; Frank, M.; Halpin, M. P.; and Torrance, M. C. 1990. Search lessons learned from crossword puzzles. In *Proceedings of the Eighth National Conference on Artificial Intelligence*, 210–215.

Haralick, R. M., and Elliott, G. L. 1980. Increasing tree search efficiency for constraint satisfaction problems. *Artificial Intelligence* 14:263–313.

Mackworth, A. K. 1977. Consistency in networks of relations. *Artificial Intelligence* 8:99–118.

Mackworth, A. K. 1987. Constraint satisfaction. In Shapiro, S. C., ed., *Encyclopedia of Artificial Intelligence*. John Wiley & Sons.

Maruyama, H. 1990. Structural disambiguation with constraint propagation. In *Proceedings of the 28th Conference of the Association for Computational Linguistics*, 31–38.

Minton, S.; Johnston, M. D.; Philips, A. B.; and Laird, P. 1990. Solving large-scale constraint satisfaction and scheduling problems using a heuristic repair method. In *Proceedings of the Eighth National Conference on Artificial Intelligence*, 17–24.

Montanari, U. 1974. Networks of constraints: Fundamental properties and applications to picture processing. *Inform. Sci.* 7:95–132.

Nadel, B. A. 1989. Constraint satisfaction algorithms. *Computational Intelligence* 5:188–224.

Nudel, B. 1983. Consistent-labeling problems and their algorithms: Expected-complexities and theory-based heuristics. *Artificial Intelligence* 21:135–178.

Prosser, P. 1993. Hybrid algorithms for the constraint satisfaction problem. *Computational Intelligence* 9:268–299.

Seidel, R. 1983. On the complexity of achieving k-consistency. Department of Computer Science Technical Report 83-4, University of British Columbia. Cited in: A. K. Mackworth 1987.

Tsang, E. 1993. *Foundations of Constraint Satisfaction*. Academic Press.

van Beek, P. 1992. On the minimality and decomposability of constraint networks. In *Proceedings of the Tenth National Conference on Artificial Intelligence*, 447–452.

Waltz, D. 1975. Understanding line drawings of scenes with shadows. In Winston, P. H., ed., *The Psychology of Computer Vision*. McGraw-Hill. 19–91.

Williams, C. P., and Hogg, T. 1992. Using deep structure to locate hard problems. In *Proceedings of the Tenth National Conference on Artificial Intelligence*, 472–477.

Distributed
Artificial Intelligence

Divide and Conquer in Multi-agent Planning

Eithan Ephrati
Computer Science Department
University of Pittsburgh
Pittsburgh, PA
tantush@cs.pitt.edu

Jeffrey S. Rosenschein
Institute of Computer Science
The Hebrew University
Jerusalem, Israel
jeff@cs.huji.ac.il

Abstract

In this paper, we suggest an approach to multi-agent planning that contains heuristic elements. Our method makes use of subgoals, and derived sub-plans, to construct a global plan. Agents solve their individual sub-plans, which are then merged into a global plan. The suggested approach may reduce overall planning time and derives a plan that approximates the optimal global plan that would have been derived by a central planner, given those original subgoals.

We consider two different scenarios. The first involves a group of agents with a common goal. The second considers how agents can interleave planning and execution when planning towards a common, though dynamic, goal.

Decomposition Reducing Complexity

The complexity of a planning process is measured by the time (and space) consumed. Let b be the branching factor of the planning problem (the average number of new states that can be generated from a given state by applying a single operator), and let d denote the depth of the problem (the optimal path from the initial state to the goal state). The time complexity of the planning problem is then $O(b^d)$ (Korf 1987).

In a multi-agent environment, where each agent can carry out each of the possible operators (possibly with differing costs), the complexity may be even worse. A centralized planner should consider assigning each operator to each one of the n agents. Thus, finding an optimal plan becomes $O(n \times b)^d$.

However, if the global goal can be decomposed into n subgoals ($\{g_1, \ldots, g_n\}$) the time complexity may be reduced significantly. Let b_i and d_i denote respectively the branching factor and depth of the optimal plan that achieves g_i. Then, as shown by Korf in (Korf 1987), if the subgoals are independent or serializable,[1] the central multi-agent planning time complexity can be reduced to $\sum_i((n \times b_i)^{d_i})$, where $b_i \approx \frac{b}{n}$ and $d_i \approx \frac{d}{n}$.

---

[1] A set of subgoals is said to be *independent* if the plans that achieve them do not interact. If the subgoals are *serializable* then there exists an ordering among them such that achieving any subgoal in the series does not violate any of its preceding subgoals.

This phenomenon of reduced complexity due to the division of the search space can be exploited most naturally in a multi-agent environment. The underlying idea is to assign to each agent a subgoal and let that agent construct the plan that achieves it. Since agents plan in parallel, planning time is further reduced to $\max_i(n \times b_i)^{d_i}$. Moreover, if each agent is to generate its plan according to its own view (assuming that the available operators are common knowledge) then the complexity becomes $\max_i(b_i)^{d_i}$. The global plan can then be constructed out of local plans that are based upon the agents' local knowledge. Unfortunately, unless the subgoals are independent or serial, the plans that achieve the set of subgoals interfere, and conflicts (or redundant actions) may arise and need to be resolved.

In this paper we suggest a heuristic approach to multi-agent planning that exploits this phenomenon of decomposed search space. The essential idea is that the individual sub-plans serve to derive a heuristic function that is used to guide the search for the *global plan*. This global search is then done in the space of world states which is pruned using the A^* algorithm. Our method makes use of pre-existing subgoals. These subgoals are not necessarily independent, nor are they necessarily serial. The separate agents' sub-plans, each derived separately and in parallel, are ultimately merged into a unified, valid global plan. The suggested approach may reduce overall planning time while deriving the optimal global plan that would have been derived, given those original subgoals. In multi-agent environments this approach also removes the need for a central planner that has global knowledge of the domain and of the agents involved.

Our scenario involves a group $\mathcal{A} = \{a_1, \ldots, a_n\}$ of n agents. These agents are to achieve a global goal G. The global goal, G, has been divided into n subgoals ($\{G_1, \ldots, G_n\}$), and formulated as a subgoal planning problem (i.e., the interrelationship among subgoals has been specified). The agents communicate as they construct a global plan.

A Simple Example

Consider a scenario in the slotted blocks world. As described in Figure 1 there are three agents (a_1, a_2, a_3)

and 4 blocks (a,b,c,d) with lengths of $1, 2, 2$, and 3 respectively. The world may be described by the following relations: **Clear**(b)(—there is no object on b); **On**$(b, x, V/H)$(—b is located on block/location x either vertically (V) or horizontally (H)); **At**(x, loc)(— the left edge of object x (agent or block) is at loc).

The functions $r(b)$ and $l(b)$ return the region of b's left edge, and the length of b, respectively. We will use only the first letter of a predicate to denote it.

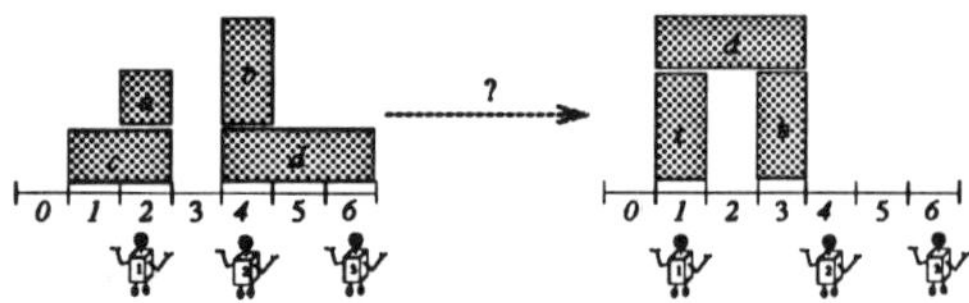

Figure 1: An Arch in the Blocks World

The available operators (described in a STRIPS-like fashion) are:

Take$_i(b, x, y)$— Agent i takes b from region/block x to region/bloc y: [cost: $|loc(x) - loc(y)| \times l(b)$, pre: $C(b), C(y), A(a_i, x)$, del: $C(y), A(a_i, x), A(b, x), O(b, x, z)$, add: $C(x), O(b, y, z), A(a_i, y), A(b, y)$]

Rotate$_i(b)$—i rotates b by $\pm\frac{\pi}{2}$: [cost: $l^2(b)$, pre: $C(b), A(a_i, r(b))$, del: $O(b, x, z)$, add: $O(b, x, \bar{z})$] ($\bar{H}$ denotes V and vice versa)

Move$_i(x, y)$—i goes from x to y: [cost: $|x - y|$, pre: $A(a_i, x)$, del: $A(a_i, x)$, add: $A(a_i, y)$]

The initial state is described in the left side of Figure 1. The agents are to construct an arch such as the one pictured in the right side of the figure. A straightforward division into subgoals is to first construct left and right columns (appropriately distant and aligned) and then put up a top. Given this *a priori* breakdown into subgoals, our agents are to go through a planning process that will result in satisfying the original goal.

Assumptions and Definitions

- The *global goal*, G, is a set of predicates, possibly including uninstantiated variables. g denotes any grounded instance of G (a set of grounded predicates that specifies a set of states). We assume that G is divided into n abstract subgoals $\{G_1, G_2, \ldots, G_n\}$, such that there exists a consistent set of instances of these subgoals that satisfies G ($\cup_i g_i \models G$).

  In accordance with the possibly required (partial) order of subgoal achievement, we denote the preconditions for any plan, p_i, that achieves g_i by g_i^0 (which for most subgoals is simply the initial state).

- Each p_i is expressed by the set of the essential propositions that enable any sequence of operators that construct it. These propositions are partially ordered according to their temporal order in p_i.[2]

---

[2]Using SNLP (McAllester & Rosenblitt 1991) terminology, these are the propositions in the causal links that construct the "nonlinear abstraction" of p_i, partially ordered

- For the merging/composition process to find the (optimal) global plan, it will, in general, be necessary to generate more than just one plan for some subgoals. d_i denotes the depth (radius) of the search that is needed so as to generate the sufficient number of sub-plans that achieve g_i. We assume that d_i is known ahead of time (for each g_i).[3] $\mathcal{P}_i$ denotes the (sufficient) set of plans that is generated within this d_i-depth search.

- Each agent has a *cost function* over the domain's operators. The cost of a_j's plan $c_j(p_j)$ is $\sum_{k=1}^{m} c_j(op_k)$.

- Given that the set of propositions E holds (in some world state), $F_{ollow}^1(E)$ is defined to be the set of all propositions that can be satisfied by invoking at most one operator at that state. ($F_{ollow}^1(E) = \{I \mid \exists_{op}[op(E) \models I]\}$ where $op(E)$ denotes the invocation of op at a state that satisfies E.) Similarly, $F_{ollow}^2(E)$ is the set of propositions that can be achieved by invoking at most two operators *simultaneously* (by two agents) given E, and $F_{ollow}^n(E)$ is the set that can be achieved by at most n simultaneous actions.

The Process

At the beginning of the planning process each agent, i, is assigned (for the purposes of the *planning process*) one subgoal g_i. Given that subgoal, the agent derives $\mathcal{P}_i$, the (sufficient) set of sub-plans that achieves it given some initial configuration g_i^0.

The significant savings in time and space complexity of the search is established by the decomposition of the search space and by parallelism of the search. However, the primary phase of the subgoal technique is the process of merging the sub-plans that achieve the given subgoals. A sub-plan is constructed by an agent with only a local view of the overall problem. Therefore, conflicts may exist among agents' sub-plans, and redundant actions may also have been generated. Given the set of sub-plans, we are looking for a method to inexpensively merge them into an optimal global plan.

To do so we employ an iterative search. The underlying idea is the *dynamic generation of alternatives* that identifies the optimal global plan. At each step, all agents state additional information about the sub-plan of which they are in charge. The current set of candidate global plans is then expanded to comprise the new set of candidate global plans. The process continues

---

according to their safety conditions, and stated as prerequisites (preconditions in UCPOP's terminology (Penberthy & Weld 1992)) (e.g., if step w has prerequisite $On(x, B)$ and step s enables it by establishing $On(A, B)$, the essential proposition is $On(x, B)$ rather than $On(A, B)$).

[3]This unrealistic assumption is needed only for the *completeness* of the planning process. However, using domain dependent knowledge, the corresponding d_i's may be assessed heuristically. In general, the more the sub-plans will tend to interact (and the closer to optimal the solution needs to be) the deeper the d_i's that are needed.

until the optimal plan is found. Plans are represented by the partially ordered sets of the essential propositions that enable them. These sets of propositions are aggregated throughout the process.

We use ordered propositions instead of sequences of operators for the following reasons. First, the constructed sub-plans serve only to *guide* the heuristic search for the actual global multi-agent plan. The *actual* multi-agent action to establish a proposition is determined only during the merging process itself. This is essential for the efficiency of the resulting multi-agent plan.[4] Second, the propositions encode all the information needed for the heuristic evaluation. And third, by dealing with propositions we achieve more flexibility (least commitment) in the merging process, both in the choice of operators and in their bindings.

Note that the essential search method is similar to the search employed by progressive world-state planners. In general, the search through the space of states is inferior to the search, as conducted by POCL planners, through the space of plans (Minton, Bresina, & Drummond 1991). The reason is that any (nondeterministic) choice of action within the first method also enforces the timing of that action (and thus, a greater breadth of search is needed to ensure completeness, e.g., in the Sussman anomaly). However, given the individual sub-plans, our merging procedure need consider only a small number of optional expansions, among which the heuristic evaluation "foresees" most commitments that may result in backtracking. Thus, becomes possible and worthwhile to avoid the causal-link-protection step of the POCL planners.

To achieve that, the search method employs an A^* algorithm where each path represents one optional global multi-agent plan. The heuristic function ($f' = g+h'$) that guides the search is dynamically determined by the agents during the process. g is the actual cost of the partial path (multi-agent plan) that has already been constructed. h' is the sum of the approximate remaining costs, h'_i, that each agent assigns to that path, based on its own generated sub-plan. Since based upon an actually constructed plan, each individual estimate, h'_i, is absolutely accurate in isolation. Thus, if the subgoals are independent, then the global heuristic function ($\sum_i^n h'_i$) will be accurate, and the merging process will choose the correct (optimal) candidate for further expansion at each step of the process.

Unfortunately, since in general sub-plans will tend to interfere with one another, h' is an underestimate (the individual estimates will turn out to be too optimistic). An underestimated heuristic evaluation is also desirable, since it will make the entire A^* search

admissible, meaning that once a path to the global goal has been found, it is guaranteed to be the optimal one. However, due to overlapping constraints ("favor relations" (Martial 1990), or "positive" interactions) the global heuristic evaluation might sometimes be an overestimate. Therefore, the A^* search for the optimal path would (in those cases) have to continue until the potential effect of misjudgment in the global heuristic evaluation fades away. In general, the more overlap appears in the individual sub-plans, the more additional search steps are needed.

More specifically, the agents go through the following search loop:[5]

1. At step k one aggregated set (of propositions), A_j^{k+}, is chosen from all sets with minimal heuristic value, $\mathcal{A}^{k+}$. This set (with its corresponding multi-agent plan) is the path currently being considered. Each agent declares the maximal set of propositions, E_i^*, such that:

   (a). These propositions represent some possible sequence of consecutive operators in the agents' private sub-plan, and all their necessary predecessors hold at the current node.

   (b). The declaration is "feasible," i.e., it can be achieved by having each of the agents perform at most one action simultaneously with one another ($E_i^* \subseteq F_{ollow}^n(A_j^{k+})$).

2. All (set-theoretic) maximal feasible expansions of A_j^{k+} with elements of the agents' declarations are generated. [Each expansion, $Ex(A_j^{k+})$, is one of the fixed points $\{I \mid (I \in \bigcup_i E_i^*) \wedge (I \cup Ex(A_j^{k+}) \in F_{ollow}^n(A_j^{k+}))\}$. Note that this is only a subset of the expansions that a "blind planner" should generate.]

3. At this stage, based on the extended set of propositions, the agents construct additions to the ongoing candidate plans. Each expansion that was generated in the previous step induces a sequence of operations that achieves it. The generation of these sequences is discussed below.

4. All expansions are evaluated, in a central manner, so as to direct the search (i.e., find the value, $f' = g+h'$, of the A^* evaluation function):

   (a). The g component of each expansion is simply taken to be the cost of deriving it (the cost of the plan that is induced by the current path plus the additional cost of the multi-agent plan that derives the expansion).

   (b). To determine the heuristic component, h', each agent declares h'_i, the estimate it associates with

---

[4]For example, it might be the case that towards the achievement of his assigned subgoal a_i planned to perform op_k in order to establish proposition P, but in the multi-agent plan P will actually be established by a_j performing op_r. Therefore, what counts for the global plan is *what* is established, rather than *how* it is established.

[5]The set of all aggregated sets of propositions at step k is denoted by $\mathcal{A}^k$ (its constituent sets will be denoted by A_j^k, where j is simply an index over those sets). $\mathcal{A}^{k+}$ denotes the set that has the maximal value according to the heuristic function at step k.

each newly-formed set of aggregated propositions. This is the cost it associates with completing its "private" sub-plan, given that the expansion is established. The h' value is then taken to be the sum of these estimates ($\sum_i h'_i(Ex_r(A^{k+}))$).

5. The aggregated set A_j^{k+} is replaced by its union with all of its expansions: $\mathcal{A}^{k+1} = (\mathcal{A}^k \setminus A_j^{k+}) \cup \{A_j^{k+} \cup Ex_r(A_j^{k+})\}$.

The process ends when all "best plans" have been found. Since the heuristic function is not guaranteed to be an underestimate, stopping when the first global plan has been generated may not result in the optimal global plan. It is a matter of policy, how much more searching the agents should do (if at all) to discover better global plans.

The entire process has the following advantages from a complexity point of view. First, the branching factor of the search space is strictly constrained by the individual plans' propositions. Second, the A^* algorithm uses a relatively good heuristic function, because it is derived "bottom-up" from the plans that the agents have already generated (not simply an artificial h' function). Third, generation of successors in the search tree is split up among the agents (each doing a part of the search for a successor). Fourth, the heuristic function is calculated only for maximally "feasible" alternatives (infeasible alternatives need not be considered).

Theorem 1 *Given $\mathcal{P}_i$, the sub-plans that achieve each subgoal $\{g_i\}$, the merging algorithm will find the optimal multi-agent plan that achieves these subgoals. The process will end within $O(q \times d)$ steps where d is the length of the optimal plan, and q is a measure of the positive interactions between overlapping propositions.*

In comparison to planning by a central planner, the overall complexity of the planning process, $O((n \times b)^d)$, is reduced to $O(\max_i b_i^{d_i} + b \times n \times q \times d)$, where $b_i^{d_i} \approx (\frac{b}{n})^{\frac{d}{n}}$.

Proof: The formal proofs of the theorems in this paper appear in (Ephrati 1993).

Construction of the Global Plan

The multi-agent plan is constructed throughout the process (Step 3 of the algorithm). At this step, all the optimal sequences of operators are determined. We require that the actual plan be constructed dynamically in order to determine the g value of each alternative. The construction of the new segments of plans is determined by the cost that agents assign to each of the required actions; each agent bids for each action that each expansion implies. The bid that each agent gives takes into consideration the actions that the agent has been assigned so far. Thus, the global minimal cost sequence can be determined.

An important aspect of the process is that each expansion of the set of propositions belongs to the F_{ollow}^n of the already achieved set. Therefore, it is straightforward to detect actions that can be performed in par-

allel. Thus the plan that is constructed is not just cost-efficient, but also time-efficient.

There are several important tradeoffs to be made here in the algorithm, and the decision of the system designer will affect the optimality of the resulting plan. First, it would be possible to use Best First Search instead of A^* so as to first determine the entire set of propositions, and only then construct the induced plan. Employing such a technique would still be less time-consuming than global planning. Second, when the agents add on the next steps of the global plan, they could consider the (developing) global plan from its beginning to the current point when deciding on the least expensive sequence of additional steps. This will (eventually) result in a globally optimal plan, but at the cost of continually reevaluating the developing plan along the way. Alternatively, it is possible to save all possible combinations of the actions that achieve any $Ex_r(A_j^{k+})$, and thus have a set of plans correspond to each expansion. Third, each agent declares $E_i^* \subseteq F_{ollow}^n(\mathcal{A}^{k+})$ to ensure maximal parallelism in the resulting global plan. However, agents may relate just to $F_{ollow}^1(\mathcal{A}^{k+})$ and establish parallelism only after the global plan is fully constructed.

Back to the Example

Consider again the example. Assume that the agents' subgoals are (respectively): $g_1 = \{A(c,1), O(c,1,V), C(c)\}$, $g_2 = \{A(b,3), O(b,3,V), C(b)\}$, and $g_3 = \{A(d,1), O(d,c,V)\}$. To simplify things we will use throughout this example $F_{ollow}^1(A^{k+})$ instead of $F_{ollow}^n(A^{k+})$. The resulting multi-agent plan is illustrated in Figure 2.

Given these subgoals, the agents will generate the following sets of propositions:[6]

$p_1 = \{[C(a), \underline{A(c,1)}, A(a_i, r(a))]^{[0]} \cup [\underline{C(c)}]^{[1]} \cup [A(a_i, r(c))]^{[2]} \cup [\underline{O(c,1,V)}]^{[4]}\}$ (this ordered set corresponds to the plan $\langle T_1(a,2,3), M_1(3,1), R_1(c)\rangle$).

$p_2 = \{[\underline{C(b)}, A(a_j, r(b)), C(3)]^{[0]} \cup [\underline{O(b,3,V)}]^{[2]}\}$ (inducing the plan $\langle T_2(b,4,3)\rangle$).

$p_3 = \{[C(b), C(3)]^{[0]} \cup [A(a_k, r(b)), C(3)]^{[2]} \cup [\underline{C(d)}]^{[2]} \cup [A(a_k, r(d)]^{[1]} \cup [\underline{g_2}, \underline{g_1}, \underline{O(d,c,H)}]^{[9]}\}$ (inducing the plan $\langle M_3(6,4), T_3(b,4,3), M_3(3,4), T_3(d,4,1)\rangle$).

Notice that there exists a positive relation between a_2's and a_3's sets of propositions (both would need block b to be removed from on top of block d), but there is a possible conflict, slot 3, between their plans and a_1's plan.

At the first iteration, there is only one candidate set for expansion—the empty set. The aggregated set

---

[6]We underline propositions that, once satisfied, must stay valid throughout the process (e.g., propositions that construct the final subgoal). The region b denotes any region besides $r(b)$. We use only the first letter of operators and predicates to denote them. The additional estimated cost of satisfying a subset of propositions appears in the superscript brackets.

of declared propositions is:
$[A(c, 1), C(a), C(b), C(3), A(a_i, r(a)), A(a_j, r(b))]$. The (sole) expansion is fully satisfied by the initial state; therefore, $g(A^1) = 0$, and $f'(A^1)$ is equal to its h' value (that is, the sum of the individual estimate costs, which is 23, i.e., $= 7 + 2 + 14$, a heuristic overestimate of 4). **At the second iteration,** a_1 declares $[C(c)]$, a_2 declares $[O(b, 3, V)]$, and a_3 may already declare $[C(d)]$. All declarations are in $F^1_{ollow}(\mathcal{A}^1)$. Thus, $Ex(A^1) = [C(c), O(b, 3, V), C(d)])$. These propositions can be achieved by $T_i(a, 2, 0)$ and $T_j(b, 4, 3)$. The bids that a_1, a_2 and a_3 give to these actions are respectively $[2, 5]$, $[4, 2]$, and $[6, 4]$. Therefore, a_1 is "assigned" to block a and a_2 is assigned to block b while a_3 remains unemployed. The constructed plan is $\langle \{T_1(a, 2, 0), T_2(b, 4, 3)\} \rangle$ (where both agents perform in parallel), yielding a g value of 4. **At the third iteration,** $(A^{2+} = [C(c), O(b, 3, V), C(d)])$, a_1 declares $[A(a_i, r(c))]$ and a_3 declares $[A(a_k, r(d)), C(c)]$. According to the agents' bids, this expansion can best be achieved by $\langle \{M_1(0, 1), M_2(3, 4)\} \rangle$ **At the fourth iteration,** only a_1 has a feasible expansion to the current best set, that is $[O(c, 1, V)]$ (note that a_3 may not declare his final subgoal before a_2's and a_1's assigned subgoals are satisfied). The corresponding segment of the multi-agent plan is $\langle R_1(c) \rangle$. Finally, **at the fifth iteration,** only a_3's assigned goal is not satisfied, and he declares $[O(d, c, H)]$. This last expansion is best satisfied by $\langle T_2(d, 4, 1) \rangle$. Thus, the overall cost is 19. Notice that the final goal is achieved without any physical contribution on the part of a_3.

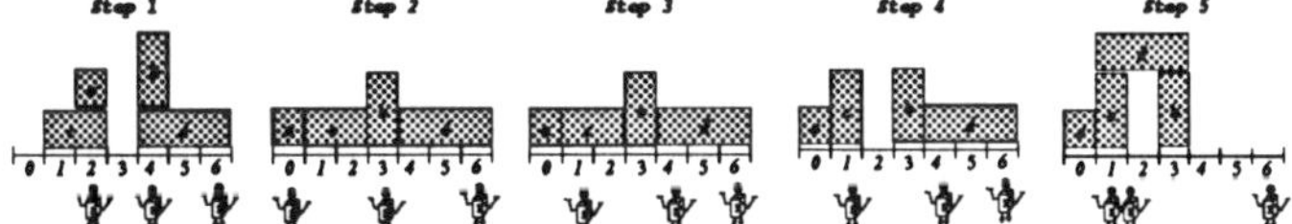

Figure 2: The resulting multi-agent plan

Interleaved Planning and Execution

The multi-agent planning procedure is based on the *incremental* process of merging sub-plans. This attribute of the process makes it very suitable for scenarios where the execution of the actual plan is urgent. In such scenarios it is important that, parallel to the planning process, the agents will actually execute segments of the plan that has been constructed so far (Dean & Boddy 1988; Durfee 1990). We assume that there is some look-ahead factor, l, that specifies the number of planning steps that should precede the actual execution step(s). We also assume that each agent can construct the first l optimal steps (in terms of propositions) of its own sub-plan.

The fact that in order to find the first step(s) of the multi-agent optimal plan it is important for the merging process to have only the corresponding first step(s)

of the individual sub-plans, also makes the process very suitable for scenarios where the global goal may change dynamically. In such cases, the required revision of the (merged) multi-agent plan may sufficiently be expressed only by the first l look-ahead steps. Moreover, the process is flexible in response to such global changes, since they may be handled through the division of the new goal into subgoals. Thus, a change in the global goal may be reflected only in changes in several subgoals, and plan revision is needed only in several sub-plans.

We can therefore use the planning algorithm in scenarios where planning and execution are interleaved, and goals may dynamically change. As in the previous scenario, the key element of the approach is a cost-driven merging process that results in a coherent global plan (of which the first l sets of simultaneous operators are most relevant), given the sub-plans. At each time step t each agent, i, is assigned (for the purposes of the *planning process*) one task and derives (the first l steps of) p^t_i, the sub-plan that achieves it. Note that once i has been assigned g^t_i at any given t, the plan it derives to accomplish the subgoal stays valid (for the use of the algorithm) as long as g^t_i remains the same. That is, for any time $t + k$ such that $g^{t+k}_i = g^t_i$, it holds that $p^{t+k}_i = p^t_i$. Thus, re-planning is modularized among agents; one agent may have to re-plan, but the others can remain with their previous plans.

As in the previous scenario, at each step, all agents state additional information about the sub-plan of which they are in charge. The next l optimal steps are then determined and the current configuration of the world, s^t, is changed to be s^{t+1}. The process continues until all tasks have been accomplished (the global goal as of that specific time has been achieved).

Since steps of the plan are executed in parallel to the planning process, the smaller the look-ahead factor is, the smaller the weight of the g component of the evaluation function becomes (and the more the employed search method resembles Hill Climbing). Therefore, the resulting multi-agent plan may only approximate the actual optimal global plan.

Theorem 2 *Let the cost effect of "positive" interactions among members of some subset, p, of the set of sub-plans, P^t, that achieves G^t be denoted by δ^+_p, and let the cost effect of "negative" interactions among these sub-plans be denoted by δ^-_p. Accordingly, let $\delta = \max_{p \in P^t} \mid \delta^+_p - \delta^-_p \mid$.[7] We say that the multi-agent plan that achieves G^t is δ-optimal, if it diverges from the optimal plan by at most δ.*

Then, at any time step t, employing the merging algorithm, the agents will follow a δ-optimal multi-agent plan that achieves G^t.

---

[7] The effect of heuristic overestimate (due to positive future interaction between individual plans) and the effect of heuristic underestimate (due to interference between individual plans) offset one another.

Conclusions and Related Work

In this paper, we presented a heuristic multi-agent planning framework. The procedure relies on an *a priori* division of the global goal into subgoals. Agents solve local subgoals, and then merge them into a global plan. By making use of the computational power of multiple agents working in parallel, the process is able to reduce the total elapsed time for planning as compared to a central planner. The optimality of the procedure is dependent on several heuristic aspects, but in general increased effort on the part of the planners can result in superior global plans.

An approach similar to our own is taken in (Nau, Yang, & Hendler 1990) to find an optimal plan. It is shown there how planning for multiple goals can be done by first generating several plans for each subgoal and then merging these plans. The basic idea there is to try and make a global plan by repeatedly merging complete plans that achieve the separate subgoals and answer several restrictions. In our approach, there are no prior restrictions, the global plan is created incrementally, and agents do the merging in parallel.

In (Foulser, Li, & Yang 1992) it is shown how to handle positive interactions efficiently among different parts of a given plan. The merging process looks for redundant operators (as opposed to aggregating propositions) within the same *grounded linear plan* in a dynamic fashion. In (Yang 1992), on the other hand, it is shown how to handle conflicts efficiently among different parts of a given plan. Conflicts are resolved by transforming the planning search space into a constraint satisfaction problem. The transformation and resolution of conflicts is done using a backtracking algorithm that takes cubic time. In our framework, both positive and negative interactions are addressed simultaneously.

Our approach also resembles the GEMPLAN planning system (Lansky & Fogelsong 1987; Lansky 1990). There, the search space is divided into "regions" of activity. Planning in each region is done separately, but an important part of the planning process within a region is the updating of its overlapping regions (while the planning process freezes).

Our planning framework also relates to the approach suggested in (Wellman 1987). There too the planning process is viewed as the process of incremental constraint posting. A method is suggested for assigning preferences to sets of constraints (propositions in our terminology) that will direct the planner. However, the evaluation and comparison between alternatives is done according to the global view of the single planner, and is based on pre-defined dominance relations.

Acknowledgments

This work has been supported in part by the Air Force Office of Scientific Research (Contract F49620-92-J-0422), by the Rome Laboratory (RL) of the Air Force Material Command and the Defense Advanced Research Projects Agency (Contract F30602-93-C-0038), and by an NSF Young Investigator's Award (IRI-9258392) to Prof. Martha Pollack.

And in part by the Israeli Ministry of Science and Technology (Grant 032-8284).

References

Dean, T., and Boddy, M. 1988. An analysis of time-dependent planning. In *Proceedings of the Seventh National Conference on Artificial Intelligence*, 49–54.

Durfee, E. H. 1990. A cooperative approach to planning for real-time control. In *Proceedings of the Workshop on Innovative Approaches to Planning, Scheduling and Control*, 277–283.

Ephrati, E. 1993. *Planning and Consensus among Autonomous Agents*. Ph.D. Dissertation, The Hebrew University of Jerusalem, Jerusalem, Israel.

Foulser, D. E.; Li, M.; and Yang, Q. 1992. Theory and algorithms for plan merging. *Artificial Intelligence* 57:143–181.

Korf, R. E. 1987. Planning as search: A quantitative approach. *Artificial Intelligence* 33:65–88.

Lansky, A. L., and Fogelsong, D. S. 1987. Localized representation and planning methods for parallel domains. In *Proceedings of the Sixth National Conference on Artificial Intelligence*, 240–245.

Lansky, A. L. 1990. Localized search for controlling automated reasoning. In *Proceedings of the Workshop on Innovative Approaches to Planning, Scheduling and Control*, 115–125.

Martial, F. von 1990. Coordination of plans in multi-agent worlds by taking advantage of the favor relation. In *Proceedings of the Tenth International Workshop on Distributed Artificial Intelligence*.

McAllester, D., and Rosenblitt, D. 1991. Systematic nonlinear planning. In *Proceedings of the Ninth National Conference on Artificial Intelligence*, 634–639.

Minton, S.; Bresina, J.; and Drummond, M. 1991. Commitment strategies in planning: A comparative analysis. In *Proceedings of the Twelfth International Joint Conference on Artificial Intelligence*, 259–265.

Nau, D. S.; Yang, Q.; and Hendler, J. 1990. Optimization of multiple-goal plans with limited interaction. In *Proceedings of the Workshop on Innovative Approaches to Planning, Scheduling and Control*, 160–165.

Penberthy, J., and Weld, D. 1992. UCPOP: A sound, complete, partial order planner for ADL. In *Proceedings of the Third International Conference on Knowledge Representation and Reasoning*, 103–114.

Wellman, M. P. 1987. Dominance and subsumption in constraint-posting planning. In *Proceedings of the Tenth International Joint Conference on Artificial Intelligence*, 884–889.

Yang, Q. 1992. A theory of conflict resolution in planning. *Artificial Intelligence* 58(1-3):361–393.

Progressive Negotiation for Resolving Conflicts among Distributed Heterogeneous Cooperating Agents

Taha Khedro
Department of Civil Engineering
Stanford University
Stanford, CA 94305-4020
khedro@cive.stanford.edu

Michael R. Genesereth
Department of Computer Science
Stanford University
Stanford, CA 94305-2140
genesereth@cs.stanford.edu

Abstract

Progressive negotiation is a strategy for resolving conflicts among distributed heterogeneous cooperating agents. This strategy aims at minimizing backtracking to previous solutions and provably ensures consistency of agents' distributed solutions and convergence on a globally-satisfiable solution. The progressive negotiation strategy is enforced by a task-independent agent called Facilitator, which coordinates and controls the interaction of cooperating agents. The interaction of cooperating agents includes the communication of messages, the identification of conflicts, and the negotiation of conflicts as a way to resolve them. In this paper, we formally present our conceptualization of cooperating agents and their interaction via the facilitator. We next discuss the conflict types identified by agents and then present the progressive negotiation strategy for resolving conflicts. We then present two theorems that discuss the consistency and convergence of distributed solutions ensured by the strategy. Finally, we conclude with a summary of this paper and remarks about the strategy.

Introduction

The topic of negotiation has been a subject of central interest in Distributed Artificial Intelligence (DAI) (Zlotkin & Rosenschein 1993). The word has been used in a variety of ways although it generally refers to communication mechanisms that improve coordination (Kuwabara & Lesser 1989; Conry, Meyer, & Lesser 1988). Negotiation procedures have included the exchange of partial global plans (Durfee 1988), the communication of information intended to alter other agents' goals (Sycara 1989), and the use of incremental suggestions leading to joint plans of action (Kraus & Wilkenfield 1991). In this paper, we propose a negotiation strategy called Progressive Negotiation for resolving conflicts among distributed heterogeneous agents. The strategy aims at minimizing backtracking to previous solutions while agents are cooperating to reach a globally-consistent satisfiable solution. We assume that cooperating agents have disparate knowledge and interact via a task-independent agent called Facilitator by sending and receiving messages, which are assertions and retractions of predicate logic sentences (Genesereth 1992). Each agent has a theory, which involves a vocabulary of predicate symbols, function symbols, and constant symbols, a set of predicate-logic axioms expressing the agent's task-specific knowledge, and another set of predicate-logic axioms expressing the agent's criteria constraints, which can be relaxed. Because of the nature of the tasks performed by cooperating agents, their theories overlap and subsets of the vocabularies are shared among them. Also, cooperating agents are allowed to have part of their vocabulary not shared with other agents. In addition, agents are allowed to have vocabularies that are related by a set of predicate logic axioms, provided in the facilitator.

In this paper, we first formally describe cooperating agents and their interaction via the facilitator. We then formalize conflict types and introduce the strategy of progressive negotiation for resolving conflicts. Then, we present theorems that discuss the consistency of distributed solutions and the solution convergence of the progressive negotiation strategy. Finally, the paper concludes with a summary and a few remarks about the strategy.

Cooperating Agents

We consider that a cooperating agent α has knowledge K^α as a set of predicate logic axioms, a set of criteria constraints C^α as predicate logic axioms, and a database D^α as a set of ground predicate logic atoms, all expressed over a vocabulary consisting a set of predicate, function, and constant symbols, X^α. A cooperating agent α has authority to make a final decision over a vocabulary $Y^\alpha \subseteq X^\alpha$. Final decisions are those decisions that conclude a disagreement between agents. The goal of every cooperating agent α is to find a complete local solution G^α that is consistent with both its knowledge K^α and constraints C^α. Formally, this can be expressed as follows:

$$G^\alpha \cup K^\alpha \cup C^\alpha \text{ is consistent.} \tag{1}$$

At time t, agent α maintains a partial local solution, which consists of a set of predicate-logic atoms D_t^α. In the process of finding a solution, agent α generates a set of assertions and retractions of atoms V_t^α that is consistent with its knowledge K_t^α and constraints C_t^α, and updates its partial local solution to D_t^α. Agent α also updates its solution when it receives a set of messages reflecting assertions and retractions of predicate logic sentences. Formally the solution update step can be expressed as follows:

$$\forall\ assertion(v) \in V_t^\alpha \mid D_{t'}^\alpha = D_t^\alpha \cup v, \text{ and}$$
$$\forall\ retraction(v) \in V_t^\alpha \mid D_{t'}^\alpha = D_t^\alpha - v. \tag{2}$$

Agent Interaction

Cooperating agents interact via a task-independent agent called facilitator, which coordinates and controls the exchange of messages. The facilitator captures the interests of agents and performs various functions aimed at facilitating the exchange of assertions and retractions of predicate-logic sentences. In the event of receiving messages, the facilitator determines the appropriate recipient agents of the messages and forwards them accordingly. In addition, it translates between vocabularies used by different agents in their exchange of sentences. The translation is achieved through a set of predicate-logic axioms R^ϕ defined over a subset of all agents' vocabularies $X^\phi \subseteq X$.

Consider the group of agents $\Gamma = \{\alpha, \beta, ..., \zeta\}$ that are cooperating on solving a problem defined by agents' knowledge K^α, K^β, ..., K^ζ over a vocabulary X. The group of agents interact via the facilitator ϕ, which captures the agents' interests expressed as sets of predicate logic axioms I^α, I^β, ..., I^ζ and a set of translation axioms R^ϕ over X^ϕ. This can formally be expressed as follows:

$$X^\phi \subseteq X = X^\alpha \cup X^\beta \cup ... \cup X^\zeta,$$
$$K = K^\alpha \cup K^\beta \cup ... \cup K^\zeta \cup R^\phi, \text{ and}$$
$$I = I^\alpha \cup I^\beta \cup ... \cup I^\zeta. \tag{3}$$

At time t, when an agent $\xi \in \Gamma$ generates messages V_t^ξ, it updates its current local solution to D_t^ξ and then communicates V_t^ξ to the facilitator. When the facilitator receives the set of messages V_t^ξ, it first deduces additional sentences based on the axioms R^ϕ. The result of this translation step is the set of sentences U_t^ϕ whose number is typically greater than that in V_t^ξ. This translation step can formally be expressed as follows:

$$U_t^\phi = sentences(V_t^\xi) \cup R^\phi \text{ is consistent.} \tag{4}$$

Then the facilitator checks for the agents that are interested in the communicated sentences, U_t^ϕ. For every $\delta \in \Gamma - \{\xi\}$, if $I^\delta \cup U_t^\phi$ is consistent, agent δ is interested and is added to the set of interested agents Δ. For every interested agent $\delta \in \Delta$, the facilitator forwards an appropriate set of messages W_t^δ. When agent δ receives the set of messages W_t^δ, it updates its current local solution to D_t^δ.

Conflict Types

Agent δ checks the consistency of the updated local solution D_t^δ with respect to its knowledge K_t^δ and constraints C_t^δ. If

$$D_t^\delta \cup K_t^\delta \cup C_t^\delta \text{ is consistent,} \tag{5}$$

there is no conflict and agent δ accepts the messages. Conversely, if

$$D_t^\delta \cup K_t^\delta \cup C_t^\delta \text{ is inconsistent,} \tag{6}$$

there is a conflict and agent δ identifies the conflict as one of three types: critical conflict, non-critical conflict with authority, and non-critical conflict without authority. In this section, the three conflict types are formally discussed.

- *Critical Conflict:* a critical conflict is a conflict in which the updated solution based on the received messages is inconsistent with the agent's knowledge K^δ. Formally, a critical conflict can be expressed as follows:

$$D_t^\delta \cup K_t^\delta \text{ is inconsistent.} \tag{7}$$

- *Non-Critical Conflict with Authority:* a non-critical conflict with authority is a conflict in which the updated solution is consistent with the agent's knowledge K_t^δ but inconsistent with the agent's constraints C_t^δ, and the vocabularies of each sentence in W_t^δ belong to X^δ over which agent δ has authority. Formally, a non-critical conflict with agent δ having authority over the vocabulary can be expressed as follows:

$$D_t^\delta \cup K_t^\delta \text{ is consistent,}$$
$$D_t^\delta \cup C_t^\delta \text{ is inconsistent, and}$$
$$\forall\ message(w) \in W_t^\delta \mid vocabulary(w) \in X^\delta. \tag{8}$$

- *Non-Critical Conflict without Authority:* a non-critical conflict without authority is a conflict in which the updated solution is consistent with the agent's knowledge K_t^δ but inconsistent with the agent's constraints C_t^δ, and the vocabularies of each message in W_t^δ do not belong to X^δ over which agent δ has authority. Formally, this can be expressed as follows:

$$D_{t_\zeta}^\delta \cup K_\zeta^\delta \text{ is consistent,}$$
$$D_t^\delta \cup C_t^\delta \text{ is inconsistent, and}$$
$$\forall \, message(w) \in W_t^\delta \mid vocabulary(w) \notin X^\delta. \quad (9)$$

Progressive Negotiation: A Conflict Resolution Strategy

Conflict resolution is an essential requirement for cooperation for autonomous, intelligent, interacting agents (Adler et al. 1989). In conflict resolution, the role of negotiation has been emphasized as the focal point for conflict resolution in distributed problem solving for different domains (Durfee & Lesser 1987; Laasri, Laasri, & Lesser 1990; Lander & Lesser 1989) Our research has focused on developing a strategy called progressive negotiation for resolving conflicts that aims at minimizing backtracking to previous solutions. In this strategy, conflict resolution is carried out by agents. Depending on the type of conflict, negotiation takes place in an attempt to resolve the conflict. In this strategy, critical conflicts are always resolved because they result from the agent's knowledge, which must be satisfied in order to have a satisfiable solution. Non-critical conflicts are resolved by getting one of the agents to relax some of its violated criteria constraints in order for an agreement to be reached. The following is a formal treatment of how conflicts are resolved for the three types outlined in the previous section.

Critical Conflicts

When a critical conflict is identified, agent δ determines a set of axioms $Q_t^\delta \subseteq K_t^\delta$ that caused the conflict and sends it to the facilitator. The facilitator in turn forwards appropriate axioms to the sending agent ζ and other agents in Δ interested in Q_t^δ. Formally, the violated axioms can be expressed as follows:

$$Q_t^\delta = \{q \mid \forall q \in K_t^\delta \text{ such that}$$
$$D_t^\delta \cup q \text{ is inconsistent}\}. \quad (10)$$

Once the sending agent ζ receives the set of axioms $Q_{t'}^\zeta$, at time t', forwarded by the facilitator, it checks the consistency of the axioms $Q_{t'}^\zeta$ with its knowledge $K_{t'}^\zeta$. If $Q_{t'}^\zeta \cup K_{t'}^\zeta$ is inconsistent, there is no solution that is consistent with the knowledge of both agents.

If $Q_{t'}^\zeta \cup K_{t'}^\zeta$ is consistent, however, then there could be a solution that is consistent with the knowledge of both agents. In this case, the agent's constraints are updated to $C_{t'}^\zeta$ ensuring that $C_{t'}^\zeta \cup Q_{t'}^\zeta$ is consistent. This update may involve relaxation of some constraints in $C_{t'}^\zeta$. After updating its constraints, agent ζ generates new messages $V_{t'}^\zeta$ and updates its local solution to $D_{t'}^\zeta$, in a way that ensures the consistency of the updated solution with its knowledge and updated constraints. Formally, we can write:

$$D_{t'}^\zeta \cup K_{t'}^\zeta \cup C_{t'}^\zeta \text{ is consistent.} \quad (11)$$

The messages $V_{t'}^\zeta$ are then sent to the facilitator, which forwards appropriate messages to all interested both agents. At time t'', agent δ receives the new messages $W_{t''}^\delta$ and updates its local solution to $D_{t''}^\delta$. The new local solution, at time t'', for agent δ will provably be consistent with the agent's knowledge since $K_t^\delta = K_{t''}^\delta$. Formally, we can write:

$$D_{t''}^\delta \cup K_{t''}^\delta \text{ is consistent.} \quad (12)$$

Non-Critical Conflicts with Authority

When a critical conflict is identified, agent δ determines a set of axioms $P_t^\delta \subseteq K_t^\delta$ that caused the conflict and sends it to the facilitator. The facilitator in turn forwards appropriate axioms to the sending agent ζ and other agents in Δ interested in P_t^δ. Formally, the violated axioms can be expressed as follows:

$$P_t^\delta = \{p \mid \forall \, p \in C_t^\delta \text{ such that}$$
$$D_t^\delta \cup p \text{ is inconsistent}\}. \quad (13)$$

Once the sending agent ζ receives the set of axioms $P_{t'}^\zeta$, at time t' forwarded by the facilitator, it checks the consistency of the axioms $P_{t'}^\zeta$ with its knowledge $K_{t'}^\zeta$ knowing that $K_{t'}^\zeta = K_{t'}^\zeta$. If $P_{t'}^\zeta \cup K_{t'}^\zeta$ is inconsistent (i.e., the sets of violated axioms and the agent's knowledge do not lead to a solution), agent ζ rejects the received set of axioms $P_{t'}^\zeta$, and they are sent back to agent δ, which relaxes its set of constraints to $C_{t''}^\delta$ such that $D_{t''}^\delta \cup C_{t''}^\delta$ is consistent since $D_{t''}^\delta = D_t^\delta$.

If $P_{t'}^\zeta \cup K_{t'}^\zeta$ is consistent, however, then agent ζ relaxes some of its constraints to $C_{t'}^\zeta$, if necessary, such that $P_{t'}^\zeta \cup C_{t'}^\zeta$ is consistent. Then agent ζ generates new messages $V_{t'}^\zeta$ and updates its local solution to $D_{t'}^\zeta$ in a way that ensures the consistency of the updated solution with the agent's knowledge and constraints,

$$D_{t'}^{\xi} \cup K_{t'}^{\xi} \cup C_{t'}^{\xi} \text{ is consistent.} \quad (14)$$

The messages $V_{t'}^{\xi}$ are then sent to the facilitator, which forwards it to all interested agents. Agent δ receives the new messages $W_{t''}^{\delta}$ at time t'', and updates its local solution to $D_{t''}^{\delta}$. The new local partial solution for agent δ will provably be consistent with the agent's knowledge and constraints since $K_{t''}^{\delta} = K_t^{\delta}$ and $C_{t''}^{\delta} = C_t^{\delta}$,

$$D_{t''}^{\delta} \cup K_{t''}^{\delta} \cup C_{t''}^{\delta} \text{ is consistent.} \quad (15)$$

Non-Critical Conflicts without Authority

This case is similar to the case of non-critical conflicts with authority. The only difference is that when agent ξ receives the constraints $P_{t'}^{\xi}$ forwarded by the facilitator, it checks $P_{t'}^{\xi} \cup K_{t'}^{\xi} \cup C_{t'}^{\xi}$ knowing that $K_{t'}^{\xi} = K_t^{\xi}$ and $C_{t''}^{\xi} = C_t^{\xi}$. If $P_{t'}^{\xi} \cup K_{t'}^{\xi} \cup C_{t'}^{\xi}$ is inconsistent, agent ξ rejects the set of constraints, and they are sent back to agent δ, which relaxes its set of constraints to $C_{t''}^{\delta}$ such that $D_{t''}^{\delta} \cup C_{t''}^{\delta}$ is consistent since $D_{t''}^{\delta} = D_t^{\delta}$.

If $P_{t'}^{\xi} \cup K_{t'}^{\xi} \cup C_{t'}^{\xi}$ is consistent, however, then agent ξ generates new messages $V_{t'}^{\xi}$ and updates its local solution to $D_{t'}^{\xi}$ in a way that ensures the consistency of its knowledge and constraints,

$$D_{t'}^{\xi} \cup P_{t'}^{\xi} \cup K_{t'}^{\xi} \cup C_{t'}^{\xi} \text{ is consistent.} \quad (16)$$

Again the messages $V_{t'}^{\xi}$ are then sent to the facilitator, which forwards it to all interested agents. For agent δ, the new messages $W_{t''}^{\delta}$ are received at time t'' and the local solution is updated to $D_{t''}^{\delta}$. The new local solution for agent δ will provably satisfy the agent's knowledge since $K_{t''}^{\delta} = K_t^{\delta}$ and $C_{t''}^{\delta} = C_t^{\delta}$,

$$D_{t''}^{\delta} \cup K_{t''}^{\delta} \cup C_{t''}^{\delta} \text{ is consistent.} \quad (17)$$

Solution Consistency and Convergence

In this section, we present two theorems for proving the consistency of distributed local solutions and the convergence on a common globally satisfiable solution under certain conditions for the progressive negotiation strategy. Before presenting these two theorems, we give a number of definitions that are used in the proofs.

Definition 1: Let ξ denote an agent from the group of agents, $\xi \in \Gamma$. The interests of agent ξ are said to be complete if and only if:

$$\forall x \in X^{\xi}, \exists s \in I^{\xi} \text{ expressing interest in } x. \quad (18)$$

Definition 2: Let K^{α}, K^{β}, ..., K^{ζ}, denote the knowledge for the group of agents $\Gamma = \{\alpha, \beta, ..., \zeta\}$ and R^{ϕ} denote the translation axioms captured in the facilitator ϕ. The initial sets of axioms expressing agents' knowledge are said to be consistent if and only if:

$$K = K^{\alpha} \cup K^{\beta} \cup ... \cup K^{\zeta} \cup R^{\phi} \text{ is consistent.} (19)$$

Definition 3: Let C^{α}, C^{β}, ..., C^{ζ} denote the initial sets of constraints for the group of agents $\Gamma = \{\alpha, \beta, ..., \zeta\}$. The initial sets of constraints are said to be consistent if and only if:

$$C = C^{\alpha} \cup C^{\beta} \cup ... \cup C^{\zeta} \text{ is consistent.} \quad (20)$$

Definition 4: Let Y^{α}, Y^{β}, ..., Y^{ζ} respectively denote the authorities of the group of agents $\Gamma = \{\alpha, \beta, ..., \zeta\}$. The authorities of the group of agents Γ are said to be exhaustive if and only if:

$$Y^{\alpha} \cup Y^{\beta} \cup ... \cup Y^{\zeta} = X. \quad (21)$$

Definition 5: Let Y^{α}, Y^{β}, ..., Y^{ζ} respectively denote the authorities of the group of agents $\Gamma = \{\alpha, \beta, ..., \zeta\}$. The authorities of the group of agents Γ are said to be disjoint (i.e., authorities over sets of interrelated vocabularies do not overlap) if and only if:

$$\forall \xi, \psi \in \Gamma \mid Y^{\xi} \subseteq X^{\xi} \wedge Y^{\psi} \subseteq X^{\psi}$$
$$\Rightarrow Y^{\xi} \cap Y^{\psi} = \varnothing, \text{ and}$$
$$\forall r \in R^{\phi} \text{ over } Z^{\phi} \subseteq X^{\phi} \wedge \forall \xi, \psi \in \Gamma \mid$$
$$Y^{\xi} \cap Z^{\phi} \neq \varnothing \wedge Y^{\psi} \cap Z^{\phi} = \varnothing. \quad (22)$$

Consistency of Distributed Solutions

In this section, we present a theorem that states the consistency of distributed local solutions for the progressive negotiation strategy.

Theorem 1: For the group of agents Γ, if the interests of the agents are complete (which is usually the case), the progressive negotiation strategy guarantees the consistency of the distributed local solutions generated after every exchange among agents. Formally, the distributed local solutions after an exchange at time tn can be expressed as follows:

$$D_{tn} = D_{tn}^{\alpha} \cup D_{tn}^{\beta} \cup ... \cup D_{tn}^{\zeta} \text{ is consistent.} \quad (23)$$

Proof: Suppose that $D_{tn} = D_{tn}^{\alpha} \cup D_{tn}^{\beta} \cup ... \cup D_{tn}^{\zeta}$ is inconsistent. Then there must exist at least two local solutions D_{tn}^{α} and D_{tn}^{β} such that

$$D_{tn}^{\alpha} \cup D_{tn}^{\beta} \text{ is inconsistent.} \qquad (24)$$

This means that there are at least two ground atoms, d^{α} and d^{β}, in the solutions D_{tn}^{α} and D_{tn}^{β} respectively such that $d^{\alpha} = \neg d^{\beta}$, which in turn, means that one of the agents α or β did not receive a message about it or update its solution. This is not possible because it contradicts the solution update step of agent interaction (2). Therefore, there cannot be any two partial solutions such that $D_{tn}^{\alpha} \cup D_{tn}^{\beta}$ is inconsistent. Thus, $D_{tn} = D_{tn}^{\alpha} \cup D_{tn}^{\beta} \cup ... \cup D_{tn}^{\zeta}$ is always consistent according to the progressive negotiation strategy.

Convergence on a Common Solution

In this section, we present a theorem that states the convergence conditions of the progressive negotiation strategy.

Theorem 2: For the group of agents Γ, if the interests are complete (which is usually the case), and the sets of axioms expressing agents' knowledge are consistent, whereas the set of initial axioms expressing agents' constraints is not necessarily consistent, and the authorities are exhaustive and disjoint, then the progressive negotiation strategy guarantees convergence on a common solution that satisfies all agents' knowledge, and a relaxed version of the initial constraints. Formally, the following must be proven:

$$D_{tn} \cup K_{tn}^{\alpha} \cup ... \cup K_{tn}^{\zeta} \cup R^{\phi} \text{ is consistent.} \qquad (25)$$

Proof: Suppose that $D_{tn} \cup K_{tn}^{\alpha} \cup ... \cup K_{tn}^{\zeta} \cup R^{\phi}$ is inconsistent. Thus, one can write:

$$D_{tn}^{\alpha} \cup ... \cup D_{tn}^{\zeta} \cup K_{tn}^{\alpha} \cup ... \cup K_{tn}^{\zeta} \cup R^{\phi} \text{ is}$$
$$\text{inconsistent.} \qquad (26)$$

Given that $K_{tn}^{\alpha} \cup ... \cup K_{tn}^{\zeta} \cup R^{\phi}$ is consistent as stated in the theorem conditions, and having proved that $D_{tn}^{\alpha} \cup ... \cup D_{tn}^{\zeta}$ is always consistent in Theorem 1, one can conclude that equation (26) can hold if and only if either of two possibilities holds:

- There exists at least one agent $\xi \in \Gamma$ such that its local solution is inconsistent with the facilitator's translation axioms: $D_{tn}^{\xi} \cup R^{\phi}$, or

- There exist at least two agents $\xi, \psi \in \Gamma$ such that their local solutions are inconsistent with their knowledge: $D_{tn}^{\xi} \cup D_{tn}^{\psi} \cup K_{tn}^{\xi} \cup K_{tn}^{\psi}$.

Case 1: In order for $D_{tn}^{\xi} \cup R^{\phi}$ to be inconsistent, there must be sent or received messages (respectively V_{tn}^{ξ} or W_{tn}^{ξ}) that are inconsistent with R^{ϕ} since the local solution atoms are typically updates of atoms in V_{tn}^{ξ} or W_{tn}^{ξ}. Formally, one of the following must hold:

$$V_{tn}^{\xi} \cup R^{\phi} \text{ is inconsistent, or}$$
$$W_{tn}^{\xi} \cup R^{\phi} \text{ is inconsistent.} \qquad (27)$$

This is not possible because of the facilitator's translation step expressed in equation (4) and the completeness of agents' interests. Therefore, $D_{tn}^{\xi} \cup R^{\phi}$ is consistent and there cannot be any agent whose solution does not satisfy the facilitator's translation axioms.

Case 2: $D_{tn}^{\xi} \cup D_{tn}^{\psi} \cup K_{tn}^{\xi} \cup K_{tn}^{\psi}$ can never be inconsistent because $D_{tn}^{\xi} \cup D_{tn}^{\psi}$ is consistent from Theorem 1, $K_{tn}^{\xi} \cup K_{tn}^{\psi}$ is consistent from the theorem conditions, and $D_{tn}^{\xi} \cup K_{tn}^{\xi}$ is consistent and $D_{tn}^{\psi} \cup K_{tn}^{\psi}$ is consistent from equations (11, 12, 14, 15, 16, and 17) and other equations of the progressive negotiation strategy. Thus, there cannot be any agent whose local solution is inconsistent with other agents' knowledge. Therefore, $D_{tn} \cup K_{tn}^{\alpha} \cup ... \cup K_{tn}^{\zeta} \cup R^{\phi}$ is always consistent and the solution convergence of the progressive negitiation strategy is guaranteed.

Summary and Concluding Remarks

In this paper, we formally presented a conflict resolution strategy called Progressive Negotiation that guarantees the consistency of distributed solutions and convergence on a globally-satisfiable solution. The strategy involves communication of predicate-logic axioms to alter distributed agents' local solutions incrementally to reach a globally-consistent satisfiable solution. It aims at minimizing backtracking to previous solutions by getting agents to communicate their violated axioms and thus to inform all agents involved in a conflict about those axioms, which ensures they will not commit that violation again. The strategy assumes that interacting agents exchange their messages via a task-independent agent called facilitator, which controls the exchange of messages in a way that ensures the satisfaction of agents' knowledge and constraints with respect to their current local solutions. The theorems presented for proving convergence of the progressive negotiation strategy show the conditions under which a group of distributed cooperating heterogeneous agents are guaranteed to reach an agreement in the course of negotiation. It is possible that an agreement among agents can be reached in some cases even if they do not comply with all the convergence conditions. However, if these conditions are not followed, convergence is not guaranteed in every exchange.

References

Adler, M. R., Davis, A. B., Weihmayer, R., and Worrest, R. W. 1989. Conflict-Resolution Strategies for Non-hierarchical Distributed Agents. Research Notes in Artificial Intelligence, Distributed Artificial Intelligence, Morgan Kaufmann Publishers, Inc., pages 139-161.

Conry S., Meyer, R., and Lesser, V. 1988. Multiagent Negotiation in Distributed Planning. Readings in Distributed Artificial Intelligence, A. Bond and L. Gasser, editors, pages 367-384. Morgan-Kaufmann Publishers, Inc.

Durfee, E. H. and Lesser, V. R. 1987. Using Partial Global Plans to Coordinate Distributed Problem Solvers. In Proceedings of the Tenth International Joint Conference on Artificial Intelligence, pages 857-883.

Durfee, E. H. 1988. Coordination of Distributed Problem Solvers. Kluwer Academic Publishers.

Genesereth, M. R. 1992. An Agent-Based Framework for Software Interoperability. In Proceedings of DARPA Software Technology Conference, pages 359-366.

Kraus, S. and Wilkenfeld, J. 1991. Negotiations over Time in a Multi Agent Environment: Preliminary Report. In Proceedings of the Twelfth International Joint Conference on Artificial Intelligence, pages 56-61.

Kuwabara, K. and Lesser, V. R. 1989. Extended Protocol for Multistage Negotiation. In Proceedings of the Ninth Workshop on Distributed Artificial Intelligence, pages 129-161.

Laasri, B. Laasri, H. and Lesser, V. R. 1990. Negotiation and Its Role in Cooperative Distributed Problem Solving. In Proceedings of the Tenth AAAI International Workshop on Distributed Artificial Intelligence.

Lander, S. and Lesser, V. R. 1989. A Framework for the Integration of Cooperative Knowledge-Based Systems. In Proceedings of the IEEE International Symposium on Intelligent Control, Albany, NY.

Sycara, K. P. 1989. Argumentation: Planning other Agents' Plans. In Proceedings of the Eleventh International Joint Conference on Artificial Intelligence, pages 517-523.

Zlotkin, G. and Rosenschein, J. S. 1993. A Domain Theory for Task Oriented Negotiation. In Proceedings of the Thirteenth International Joint Conference on Artificial Intelligence, pages 416-422.

A Collaborative Parametric Design Agent

Daniel Kuokka and Brian Livezey
Lockheed Palo Alto Research Laboratories
Orgn 96-20, Bld 254F
3251 Hanover Street
Palo Alto, CA 94304
kuokka@aic.lockheed.com, livezey@aic.lockheed.com

Abstract

ParMan combines the use of agent communication protocols, constraint logic programming, and a graphical presentation interface to yield an intelligent parametric design tool supporting collaborative engineering. This provides one of the first complete, end-to-end applications of distributed knowledge-level communication among engineering tools, as envisioned by PACT (Cutkosky *et al.* 1993). In addition, it represents a significant extension of parametric design to a distributed setting. This paper describes the underlying technologies of ParMan, based on CLP(R), the Knowledge Query and Manipulation Language, and knowledge-based facilitation agents.

Introduction

Parametric design is a common and important class of design. Numerous systems and approaches have been developed to address this problem (Bouchard 1992; Frayman & Mittal 1987; Kolb 1989), but they have largely ignored a fundamental issue: the constraints typically come from multiple sources, making parametric design a collaborative task. ParMan is a distributed parameter management system that addresses this basic omission by coupling a parametric design tool, based on constraint logic programming (Jaffar & Lassez 1987; Jaffar *et al.* 1992), with an agent-based collaborative engineering infrastructure (Cutkosky *et al.* 1993; McGuire *et al.* 1993). The merged functionality is presented to the user in a highly intuitive fashion via a specialized graphical user interface. The result is an intelligent parametric design tool supporting collaborative engineering.

Ironically, just as ParMan introduces collaboration into parametric design, it proposes a much needed process for the agent-based engineering community. Work on agent infrastructures for engineering has brought previously isolated tools on-line, allowing a high degree of knowledge sharing among design tools. However, the technology for controlling such highly integrated tools has not kept pace with the integration technology. When should changes be transferred to the network of agents: as they are made, at some intermediate check

point, upon file saving, or upon version update? ParMan provides an interface for controlling when various aspects of the local design are made public, in addition to providing a means of specifying and testing parametric constraints. Thus, ParMan provides one of the first systems to support the design process by utilizing distributed yet highly integrated tools.

There is a growing body of work in collaborative engineering design systems and distributed AI such as (Birmingham *et al.* 1993; Pan & Tenenbaum 1991; Petrie 1993; Saad & Maher 1993; Sriram 1993; Weber *et al.* 1992; Werkman 1992). ParMan is notable in that it emphasizes parametric design as the single formal model for collaboration. Work on intelligent software agents, such as (Dent *et al.* 1992; Maes & Kozierok 1993) is similar in spirit, but these systems tend to emphasize autonomy and learning instead of communication among agents. In this respect, the area of computer supported cooperative work (Reeves & Shipman 1992: Stefik *et al.* 1987) is very relevant.

Throughout this paper, the term "agent" is used to refer to a semi-autonomous participant in a distributed design scenario. Agents typically are not stand-alone software systems, but consist of a tool and a human user. Agents are semi-autonomous in that they act spontaneously and dynamically according to local goals, yet they must contribute to the joint problem solving effort, so they cannot act without consideration of other agents.

The remainder of this paper is organized as follows: the next section gives a user view of ParMan, focusing on an example. Next, a system view of ParMan is presented, covering algorithms and implementation issues. Finally, we evaluate ParMan based on experiments in several domains.

User View

An engineer uses ParMan to define and analyze constraints over a set of parameters. As parameters and constraints are entered, ParMan interacts with other agents, maintaining a distributed constraint set that is presented back to the local user. Other agents are usu-

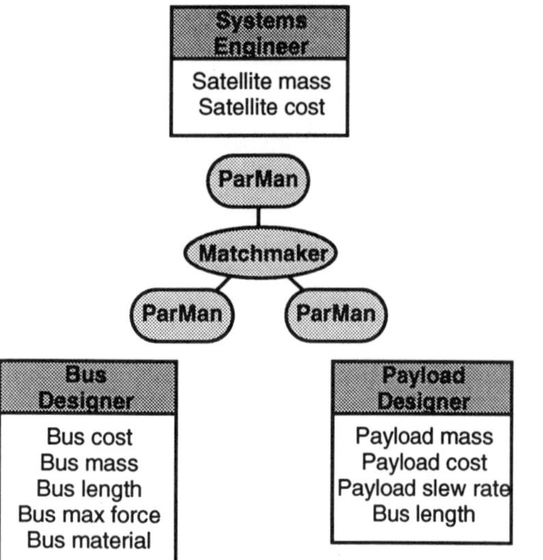

Figure 1: Each participant in the design task uses Par-Man to communicate constraints on specific parameters.

ally ParMan users as well, but the underlying protocols are quite general, allowing any conformant software system to participate. Thus, ParMan may interact with a broad range of CAD tools, either autonomous or human guided, as long as they can communicate parameter constraints.

ParMan is illustrated via an example from the Lockheed FSAT (Frugal Satellite) program, an effort to design a simple, inexpensive, reusable satellite. The satellite consists of a simple tubular bus with a payload. Imagine an Integrated Product Design (IPD) team working on the conceptual design of the satellite. The team consists of several participants: a systems engineer, a bus designer, and a payload designer. Each participant has specific interests, shown in Figure 1 (the Matchmaker, described in the Agent Interface section, is used by ParMan to route messages).

ParMan aids in the conceptual design of the satellite as follows. First, the engineer uses the Project Selector to choose from a list of all projects that are of interest to members of the design team (see Figure 2). The list is populated dynamically by the distributed set of ParMan users, consistency being maintained by the exchange of KQML messages such as **advertise**, **subscribe**, **tell**, and **ask** (see the Agent Interface section). Thus, all users are kept apprised of all projects and can collaborate on any or all of them. In the example at hand, each team member selects the FSAT project.

Once a project is selected, each team member uses the Parameter Graph Editor to define a set of parameters of specific interest (also in Figure 2). The graphical structure allows the user to define components and associate parameters with those components. When a

parameter or component is placed in the graph, ParMan asserts its existence to the other agents (users may also define private parameters). Upon receipt of a parameter assertion, ParMan adds it to the Parameter Graph Editor, using a different color from that used for parameters specified by the local user. This allows the user to identify forgotten or inconsistently-named parameters.

From the Parameter Graph Editor, each user selects a subset of the parameters to be displayed in the Parameter Table, a worksheet of parameters relevant to his aspect of the design (see Figure 3). Notice that the hierarchical namespace implicit in the Parameter Graph Editor is carried over to the Parameter Table.

The user can now begin defining constraints over the parameters in the Parameter Table. These constraints are expressed in ParMan's Constraint Language, which includes standard infix arithmetic constraints and an extensible set of predicates. Constraints are entered via the Constraint Editor (also shown in Figure 3), which is brought up by selecting a Parameter Table cell. Equality constraints (e.g., $bus.length = 3m$) appear as entries directly in the Parameter Table; otherwise, "***" appears. As constraints are entered, ParMan looks for inconsistencies among the constraints and indicates them by displaying the associated cells in red.

Constraints entered by the user are reflected in the center column, which represents the user's local constraints. There are also right and left columns (the left constraint column is collapsed in the figure), which represent constraints shared with other agents (those "to the right" and "to the left," as described below). The arrow columns between constraint columns control when and how constraints are *propagated* between columns. The arrow columns on the far right and left similarly control when and how constraints are *advertised*, *subscribed*, *asked*, and *told* to other agents.

At any point, the user may choose to share his constraints with other agents. He can also ask to be kept informed about any constraints that other agents place on selected parameters. This is a two-step process: first the user turns on advertisement and subscription via the arrows in the right-hand column, which expresses ParMan's commitment to answer questions and receive updates about parameter constraints. Next, the user controls which constraints are actually shared by *propagating* (via an interior column of arrows) the constraints to the right-hand column. If advertisement is turned on, those constraints present in the right-hand value column are sent to the network of agents.

If subscription is turned on, constraints arrive from other agents and are added to the set of constraints in the right-hand column, and the consistency of the expanded set of constraints is tested. If there is an inconsistency among this distributed set of constraints, ParMan displays the cell for each parameter involved in the inconsistency in yellow (recall that if a local conflict

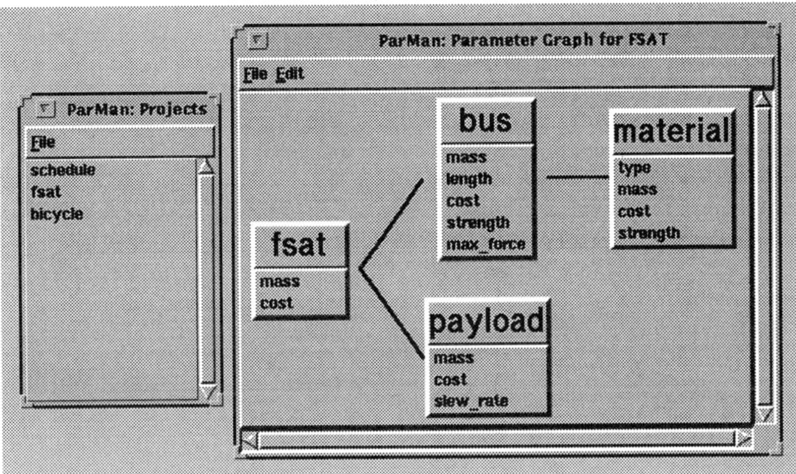

Figure 2: The Project Selector and Parameter Graph Editor permit users to collaboratively define projects and parameter spaces.

is detected, the cells turn red, since local conflicts are considered more serious). The entire set of constraints, those defined locally and those defined by other agents, can be observed by expanding the "right constraints" region in the Constraint Editor (see Figure 3).

ParMan provides several tools to aid conflict resolution. The Constraint Grapher, shown in Figure 4, presents a graphical display of the parameters and constraints, with links connecting related parameters and constraints. Constraint nodes are presented in green if the constraint is satisfied. Red is used to indicate constraints that are in direct conflict. Yellow is used to indicate constraints that participate in a conflict, but cannot be directly implicated. In Figure 4, the shaded nodes would appear in red.

The Constraint Grapher is valuable in isolating problems and finding solutions, even across multiple users. In our example, the bus designer notices that there is a problem centered around the strength of the bus (the red shading draws his attention to those constraints). He might be tempted to try different materials to overcome the strength limitation, but the *bus.material.type* node is not highlighted, indicating that choice of material has no bearing on the problem at hand. (The constraint checker determined that all other materials have problems as well: composite construction is too expensive and alloy construction is too heavy.)

Noticing that a constraint on *bus.length*, supplied by the payload designer, does participate in the problem, the bus designer calls the payload designer to see if the constraint can be loosened. This is acceptable to the payload designer, so she loosens the constraint on the bus length, which is automatically communicated between the ParMan agents. The bus designer's ParMan checks the new constraint set, determines that there is

no longer a conflict, and removes all the highlighting in the Parameter Table. In this manner, ParMan not only provides automated constraint analysis, it also serves as an excellent visualization and collaboration tool.

Thus far in our example, parameters have only been propagated to and from the "right." ParMan also includes a symmetrical "left" side, which is typically used for communication with a CAD tool. In our example, the user could have a rigid-body dynamics tool that, given the payload mass and slew rate, computes the force exerted on the mounting. In this case, the user would advertise mass and slew rate to the left, and subscribe to force from the left. (Since our example does not include such a dynamics tool, we approximate force via the simple formula shown).

ParMan includes several other facilities not illustrated in this example: a constraint solver, which attempts to find a closed form solution to the set of constraints; a Constraint Tester, which allows the user to drag individual constraints into a test region to isolate problems; a clique finder, which separates the constraints into independent sets; and a units converter, which is used implicitly in the example above, and can also be called explicitly.

From a more global perspective, there are several modes of use spanning two dimensions: use with or without a tool, and with or without an external agent network. As illustrated above, ParMan can be used without a tool if the user has constraints for, or manually computes all parameters. The addition of a tool simply automates aspects of this process. ParMan is useful in the absence of other agents if the user simply wants to trade-off local parameters under local constraints. The addition of other agents makes the parametric design problem distributed and collaborative.

ParMan may, in fact, be used in several modes

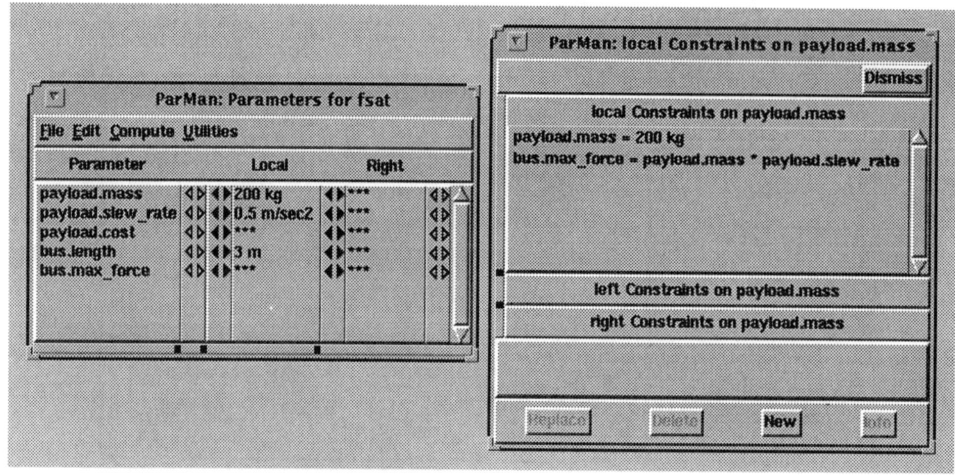

Figure 3: Parameters and simple constraints are displayed on the Parameter Table, more complicated constraints for each parameter are entered and viewed via the Constraint Editor

throughout the life of a single project. In the early stages of a project, a single user might experiment locally with various parameter settings. As he becomes confident about some of his choices, he may advertise his parameters and begin to collaborate and negotiate with other designers with ParMan's support. As the design evolves, initial rough estimates may be refined by incorporating design tools into the process.

System View

ParMan is implemented in Tcl/Tk, utilizing CLP(R) for constraint computation, and the SHADE agent infrastructure for communications. Each of these is described below.

Agent Interface

The collaborative aspect of ParMan is built on research underway in the area of agent-based, knowledge-level engineering communications (Cutkosky *et al.* 1993; McGuire *et al.* 1993). Much of this work has focused on four basic problems: developing an adequate knowledge representation to serve as an interlingua; developing a vocabulary, or ontology, that defines the terms used in communication; developing an agent speech act protocol; and developing a set of facilitation agents that improve communication among end-user agents.

ParMan is designed to work with one set of solutions to these problems, corresponding to the SHADE architecture (Kuokka *et al.* 1993). Specifically, ParMan uses KIF (Knowledge Interchange Format (Genesereth & Fikes 1992)) as its interlingua, although other representations such as Step/Express, ISO 10303, are being explored. KQML (Knowledge Query and Manipulation Language (Finin *et al.* 1992)) is used as the speech act language, which *carries* the embedded KIF sentence. Furthermore, ParMan assumes the existence

of a Matchmaker (Kuokka *et al.* 1993), a facilitator that matches and routes advertisements and subscriptions among the set of cooperating agents.

Even though ParMan assumes a very basic ontology for communicating parameter existence and constraints, it does not depend on the existence of an ontology for the engineering domain. Instead, the Project Selector and Parameter Graph Editor allow a distributed set of users to define a vocabulary of projects, components, and parameters interactively. The Constraint Language allows the users to define relationships among the components and parameters. This capability illustrates an incomplete but practical solution to the semantic unification problem (Petrie 1992), and is critical to successful knowledge-level communication among agents. Previous solutions have been centered around the definition of common data models (e.g., STEP) and formal shared ontologies (Gruber 1993). Both of these approaches require a high degree of a priori agreement among the participants, even before the specifics of the problem are known. By contrast, ParMan's Parameter Graph Editor provides a very dynamic, albeit human-aided, approach.

Looking more closely at the messages exchanged among ParMan agents in the example, when the user advertises his willingness to supply constraints on a particular parameter (e.g., *bus.mass*), the following messages are sent:

```
(advertise :content
  (stream-about :language kif :content
    (mass (bus fsat))))

(advertise :content
  (subscribe :content
    (stream-about :language kif :content
      (mass (bus fsat)))))
```

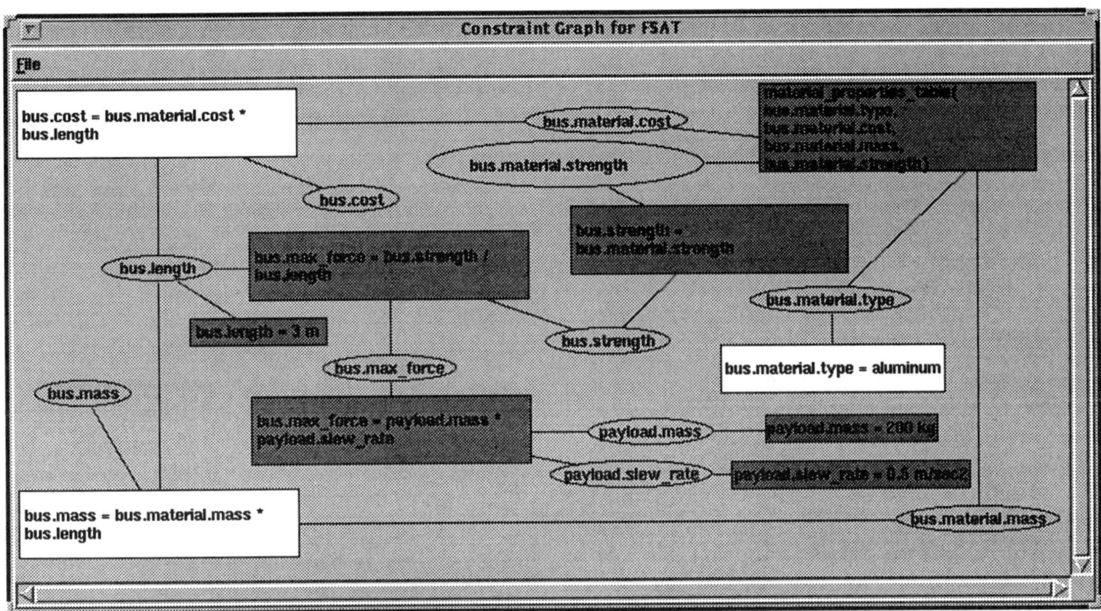

Figure 4: The Constraint Grapher aids in the visualization of relationships among parameters and constraints.

Conversely, when the user wants to hear about constraints on a particular parameter, ParMan seeks to *recruit* all agents that might assert constraints on that parameter. This is achieved via the following messages:

```
(recruit-all :content
  (stream-about :language kif :content
    (mass (bus fsat))))
```

```
(recruit-all :content
  (subscribe :content
    (stream-about :language kif :content
      (mass (bus fsat)))))
```

In each case, the first message (with top-level content stream-about) indicates a query/response modality. Stream-about is essentially a one-time query with the stipulation that replies are in the form of a stream. The second message (with top-level content subscribe) indicates a continuous update modality.

These messages depend on a Matchmaker, which matches subscribes to stream-abouts and recruits to advertises. Upon finding a match, the Matchmaker sends the appropriate subscription or query on to the advertising agent. By depending on the Matchmaker, ParMan need not worry about sending the right message to the right place, it need only send it's capabilities, interests, and assertions to the Matchmaker, which performs the appropriate message routing.

Once a connection is made between an information producer and information supplier, specific constraints are then sent via messages of the form:

```
(tell :content
  (< (mass (bus fsat)) (* 100 kg)))
```

Constraints are withdrawn via messages of the form:

```
(untell :content
  (< (mass (bus fsat)) (* 100 kg)))
```

ParMan depends heavily upon the agent communications infrastructure being developed by projects such as SHADE. However, in return, it provides one of the first complete agent-based engineering tools to make extensive use of the infrastructure, providing valuable insights about useful protocols and necessary extensions.

Constraint Solver

The constraint checking of ParMan uses the CLP(R) language (Jaffar *et al.* 1992), which is an instance of the Constraint Logic Programming scheme defined by Jaffar and Lassez (Jaffar & Lassez 1987). ParMan applies the basic CLP(R) engine in several different ways to implement the clique finding, conflict detection, and constraint simplification functions. Each of these is described below. Since engineering domains typically intermingle a number of different unit systems, all constraints are converted to SI units before being passed to any of the constraint solving functions. This ensures that values are related accurately.

The clique finder may be used by the user to simplify the parameter space, and it is used by the conflict detection algorithm as a preprocessor. A clique is a group of all parameters, such that each parameter is linked to each other parameter in the group, directly or transitively, by one or more constraints. Cliques are detected by simply traversing the graph formed by taking the parameters as nodes and the constraints as links.

Conflict detection is invoked whenever a constraint is added, deleted, or modified. ParMan first forms two sets of *potentially affected* constraints. A constraint is said to be potentially affected by a modified constraint if it contains parameters that are in the same clique as one or more of the parameters that occur in the modified constraint. The first set of potentially affected constraints consists solely of local constraints. The second set is the union of the first set and the potentially affected right and left constraints.

Once the two constraint sets have been formed, each is passed separately to the constraint solver. Given a constraint set, CLP(R) successively adds the constraints to a set of collected constraints, at each step determining whether the set of constraints has a solution. If there is no solution, the system backtracks, trying alternative solutions to some of the previous constraints. If no solution can be found in the first set of constraints, the corresponding parameters are marked as locally inconsistent (and appear in red in the Parameter Table). If the first set is found to be consistent, the second set is tested by an identical method. If no solution can be found, the corresponding parameters are marked as globally inconsistent (and appear in yellow in the Parameter Table).

When an inconsistent set of constraints is displayed in the Constraint Grapher or in the Constraint Tester, a slight variant of the above procedure is used to determine the status of each constraint. A single set of constraints is formed. Initially, all constraints are labeled as *exonerated*. An exoneration of a constraint is lifted if removal of that constraint from any inconsistent subset leaves the subset consistent. Next, all constraints whose exonerations have been lifted are labeled as *indicted*. An indictment is lifted if removal of that constraint from one of the inconsistent subsets leaves that subset inconsistent. All constraints that remain unlabeled are now labeled as *accused*. Exonerated constraints are displayed in green, accused constraints in yellow, and indicted constraints in red.

Finally, constraint simplification proceeds in a manner similar to conflict detection. However, if the constraint set is found to be consistent, the CLP(R) **dump** predicate is used to produce the simplified set of constraints.

Evaluation and Conclusions

ParMan has been used on example problems in several domains: the FSAT domain, a bicycle design domain, and a meeting scheduling domain. In all cases, the users were geographically distributed (in separate offices).

In each test, it is striking how the apparent complexity of the global problem was significantly reduced when distributed among multiple people. Distribution allows each user to focus on and ensure satisfaction of those constraints representing a single perspective.

Once each user assumed his role, ParMan proved to be a very natural system for encoding and solving distributed constraint satisfaction problems. Each user's constraints were easily entered, and their propagation to other users as external constraints was simple and understandable. Flagging of conflicts by color coding also proved to convey the essential information without complexity. Finally, the facility to find a solution proved quite beneficial. In fact, in early tests without this facility, the users expressed concern that, even though the system indicated that there were no conflicts, the solution was not readily apparent.

Another problem was encountered with an earlier prototype which allowed only numerical parameters and algebraic constraints. This proved to be extremely limiting, as every domain had significant symbolic parameters (e.g., material type) and extrinsic constraints (e.g., tables of material cost). As a result, ParMan's constraint language was extended to permit symbolic constants and user-defined predicates.

In many domains, ParMan's clique finder divides constraints into subsets of manageable computational complexity. However, in domains where these subsets become large, performance of constraint testing and satisfaction may become a problem. The practical limitations of ParMan, and techniques to improve constraint satisfaction efficiency are under investigation.

The underlying agent communication infrastructure used by ParMan has been invaluable to the overall system. KQML provides the language by which agents coordinate the exchange of knowledge, and the Matchmaker allows ParMan to route messages by content rather than by name of a responsible agent.

Even though ParMan, in its current form, is quite promising, there are still several areas for improvement. The user interface does not yet allow direct editing of the constraint graph, and the interface to extrinsic constraints is still under development. Finally, significant user testing by engineers is needed to further gauge the applicability of the basic parametric design paradigm.

ParMan represents an integrated, cross-disciplinary contribution to three fields: artificial intelligence, engineering design, and human-computer interaction. From an AI perspective, it demonstrates and extends the use of CLP(R). Also, it represents one of the most significant applications of emerging agent communication techniques. In fact, the development of ParMan has resulted in several extensions to and clarifications of KQML and matchmaking. From an engineering perspective, it represents a highly interactive, intelligent concurrent engineering paradigm, with an emphasis on practicality as a key requirement. And from a human computer interaction perspective, ParMan represents a general tool for knowledge-level computer supported collaboration, with emphasis on an intuitive interface to a complex task.

Acknowledgments

The authors would like to acknowledge the contributions of Larry Harada for his implementation of the Matchmaker and feedback on ParMan interface, and Bill Mark for his insights and support of this work.

References

Birmingham, W.; Darr, T.; Durfee, E.; Ward, A.; and Wellman, M. 1993. Supporting mechatronic design via a distributed network of intelligent agents. In *Proceedings of the AAAI Workshop on AI in Collaborative Design.*

Bouchard, E. 1992. Concepts for a future aircraft design environment. In *Proceedings of the Aerospace Design Conference.*

Cutkosky, M.; Engelmore, R.; Fikes, R.; Gruber, T.; Genesereth, M.; Mark, W.; Tenenbaum, J.; and Weber, J. 1993. PACT: An experiment in integrating concurrent engineering systems. *IEEE Computer* 26(1).

Dent, L.; Boticario, J.; McDermott, J.; Mitchell, T.; and Zabowski, D. 1992. A personal learning apprentice. In *Proceedings of the National Conference on Artificial Intelligence.* AAAI Press.

Finin, T.; Weber, J.; Wiederhold, G.; Genesereth, M.; Fritzson, R.; McGuire, J.; McKay, D.; Shapiro, S.; Pelavin, R.; and Beck, C. 1992. Specification of the KQML agent communication language. Official document of the DARPA Knowledge Sharing Initiative's External Interfaces Working Group. Technical Report 92-04, Enterprise Integration Technologies, Inc.

Frayman, F., and Mittal, S. 1987. Cossack: A constraints-based expert system for configuration tasks. In *Knowledge Based Expert Systems in Engineering: Planning and Design.* D. Sriram and R. Adey (eds.).

Genesereth, M., and Fikes, R. 1992. Knowledge interchange format, version 3.0 reference manual. Technical Report Logic-92-1, Computer Science Department, Stanford University.

Gruber, T. 1993. A translation approach to portable ontology specifications. *Knowledge Acquisition* 5(2).

Jaffar, J., and Lassez, J. 1987. Constraint logic programming. In *Proceedings of the 14th ACM Symposium on Principles of Programming Languages.* Association for Computing Machinery.

Jaffar, J.; Michaylov, S.; Stuckey, P.; and Yap, R. 1992. The CLP(R) language and system. *ACM Transactions on Programming Languages and Systems (TOPLAS)* 14(3).

Kolb, M. 1989. Investigation of constraint-based component modeling for knowledge representation in computer aided conceptual design. Technical report, Massachusetts Institute of Technology, Dept of Aeronautics and Astronautics.

Kuokka, D.; McGuire, J.; Weber, J.; Tenenbaum, J.; Gruber, T.; and Olsen, G. 1993. SHADE: Knowledge-based technology for the re-engineering problem; annual report. Technical report, Lockheed Artificial Intelligence Center.

Maes, P., and Kozierok, R. 1993. Learning interface agents. In *Proceedings of the National Conference on Artificial Intelligence.* AAAI Press.

McGuire, J.; Kuokka, D.; Weber, J.; Tenenbaum, J.; Gruber, T.; and Olsen, G. 1993. SHADE: Technology for knowledge-based collaborative engineering. *Concurrent Engineering: Research and Applications* (1).

Pan, J., and Tenenbaum, J. 1991. Toward an intelligent agent framework for enterprise integration. In *Proceedings of the National Conference on Artificial Intelligence.* AAAI Press.

Petrie, C. 1992. Introduction. In *Enterprise Integration Modeling.* MIT Press.

Petrie, C. 1993. The Redux' server. In *Proceedings of the Intl. Conf. on Intelligent and Cooperative Information Systems.*

Reeves, B., and Shipman, F. 1992. Supporting communication between designers with artifact-centered evolving information spaces. In *CSCW.*

Saad, M., and Maher, M. 1993. A computational model for synchronous collaborative design. In *Proceedings of the AAAI Workshop on AI in Collaborative Design.*

Sriram, D. 1993. Computer supported collaborative engineering. In *Proceedings of the AAAI Workshop on AI in Collaborative Design.*

Stefik, M.; Foster, G.; Bobrow, D.; Kahn, K.; Lanning, S.; and Suchman, L. 1987. Beyond the chalk board: Computer support for collaboration and problem solving in meetings. *Communications of the ACM* 30(1).

Weber, J.; Livezey, B.; McGuire, J.; and Pelavin, R. 1992. Spreadsheet-like design through knowledge-based tool integration. *International Journal of Expert Systems: Research and Applications* 5(1).

Werkman, K. 1992. Multiple agent cooperative design evaluation using negotiation. In *Artificial Intelligence in Design.*

Exploiting Meta-Level Information in a Distributed Scheduling System*

Daniel E. Neiman, David W. Hildum, Victor R. Lesser and **Tuomas W. Sandholm**
Computer Science Department
University of Massachusetts
Amherst, MA 01003
DANN@CS.UMASS.EDU

Abstract

In this paper, we study the problem of achieving efficient interaction in a distributed scheduling system whose scheduling agents may borrow resources from one another. Specifically, we expand on Sycara's use of resource texture measures in a distributed scheduling system with a central resource monitor for each resource type and apply it to the decentralized case. We show how analysis of the abstracted resource requirements of remote agents can guide an agent's choice of local scheduling activities not only in determining local constraint tightness, but also in identifying activities that reduce global uncertainty. We also exploit meta-level information to allow the scheduling agents to make reasoned decisions about when to attempt to solve impasses locally through backtracking and constraint relaxation and when to request resources from remote agents. Finally, we describe the current state of negotiation in our system and discuss plans for integrating a more sophisticated cost model into the negotiation protocol. This work is presented in the context of the Distributed Airport Resource Management System, a multi-agent system for solving airport ground service scheduling problems.

Introduction

The problem of scheduling resources and activities is known to be extremely challenging (Garey & Johnson 1979; Fox 1983; Smith, Fox, & Ow 1986; Sadeh 1991). The complexity increases when the scheduling process becomes dependent upon the activities of other concurrent schedulers. Such interactions between scheduling agents arise when, for example, agents must borrow resources from other agents in order to resolve local impasses or improve the quality of a local solution. Distributed scheduling applications are not uncommon, for example, the classic meeting planning problem (Sen & Durfee 1993) can be considered as a distributed scheduling problem; the airport

*This work was partly supported by DARPA contract N00014-92-J-1698 and NSF contracts CDA-8922572 and IRI-9208920. The content of this paper does not necessarily reflect the position or the policy of the Government and no official endorsement should be inferred.

ground service scheduling (AGSS) problem we address in this paper is another; and similar problems may arise in factory floor manufacturing domains.

In distributed scheduling systems, problem-solving costs will likely increase because of the interaction among agents caused by the lending of resources. One method of increasing the quality of solutions developed by such multi-agent schedulers and minimizing the costs of backtracking is to allow agents to communicate abstracted versions of their resource requirements and capabilities to other agents. The use of this *meta-level* information allows the scheduling agents to develop models of potential interactions between their scheduling processes and those of other agents, where an interaction is defined as a time window in which the borrowing or lending of a resource might occur. We show how the identification of interactions affects the choice of scheduling heuristics, communication, and negotiation policies in a distributed scheduling system. We discuss our heuristics in the context of a specific testbed application, the Distributed Airport Resource Management System (DIS-ARM).

Related Work

The use of meta-level information to define the interactions between agents has been studied extensively by Durfee and Lesser via the use of partial global plans (Durfee & Lesser 1991). This work has been extended by Decker and Lesser (Decker & Lesser 1992; 1993) to incorporate more sophisticated coordination relationships. According to this framework, we can view our detection of potential loan requests using texture measures to be an identification of *facilitating* relationships, and our modification of the scheduling algorithm as an attempt to exploit this perceived relationship. The formulation of distributed constraint satisfaction problems as distributed AI was described by Yakoo (Yakoo, Ishida, & Kuwabara 1990), however, this work concentrated more on the problem of distributed backtracking rather than on coordinating agents.

The problem of coordinating distributed schedulers has been studied extensively by Sycara and colleagues (Sycara *et al.* 1991). They describe a mechanism for transmitting abstractions of resource requirements (*textures*) between agents. Each agent uses these texture measures to form a model of the aggregate system demand for resources. This model is used to allocate resources using various heuristics. For example, a *least-constraining-value* heuristic is used to allocate resources based on the minimization of the probablity that the reservation would conflict with any other. For each type of resource, one agent is assigned the task of coordinating allocations and determining whether requests can be satisfied. All resources of a given type are considered interchangeable and the centralized resource monitor does not need to perform significant planning to choose the most suitable resource; instead, its role is simply to ensure that each resource is allocated to no more agents than can be served by that resource during any given time period.

We investigate a similar use of abstracted resource demands for a case in which centralized resource monitors are not possible since resources of the same type may possess unique characteristics, and agents possess proprietary information about local resources (such as current location and readiness). Agents may respond to a request for a resource either by immediately satisfying it with a reservation, denying it, or by performing local problem-solving actions to attempt to produce a suitable reservation.

In our domain, we have found that Sycara's texture measures alone do not convey sufficient information to allow satisfactory scheduling. Their texture measures consist of a demand profile for each resource which represents, for each time interval, the sum of probabilities that resource requests will overlap that interval. These probabilities are based on the assumption that reservations can occur at any time within the requested interval. Assignment of resources is then performed using these probabilities to implement a least-constraining-value heuristic.

These texture measures do not capture sufficient information regarding time-shift preferences of resource assignments within the specified interval. In our domain, resources may legally be assigned at any time within the interval between the earliest start time and the latest finish time, but for some activities, there exist strong preferences as to which end of the interval the assignment is biased. For example, when scheduling ground services for an airport, once a flight arrives, it is important to unload baggage as early as possible so that necessary transfers can be made to connecting flights. The shift preference can be determined by the assigning agent using domain knowledge, provided that it knows the nature of the task generating the request. Because this information is not captured in the texture measures, the heuristic described by Sycara, *et al.* is likely to lead to poor schedules within the airport ground service scheduling domain.

Overview: The Distributed Dynamic Scheduling System

In order to test our approach to solving distributed *resource-constrained scheduling problems* (RCSPs), we have designed a distributed version of a reactive, knowledge-based scheduling system called DSS (the Dynamic Scheduling System) (Hildum 1994). DSS provides a foundation for representing a wide variety of real-world RCSPs. Its flexible scheduling approach is capable of reactively producing quality schedules within dynamic environments that exhibit unpredictable resource and order behavior. Additionally, DSS is equipped to manage the scheduling of shared tasks connecting otherwise separate orders, and handle RCSPs that involve mobile resources with significant travel requirements.

DSS is implemented as an agenda-based blackboard system (Erman *et al.* 1980; Carver & Lesser 1994) using GBB (the Generic Blackboard System) (Corkill, Gallagher, & Murray 1986). It maintains a blackboard structure upon which a developing schedule is constructed, and where the sets of orders and resources for a particular RCSP are stored. A group of knowledge sources are provided for securing the necessary resource reservations. These knowledge sources are triggered as the result of developments on the blackboard, namely the creation and modification of the service goals attached to all resource-requiring tasks. Triggered knowledge sources are placed onto an agenda and executed in the order of their priority.

The Distributed Dynamic Scheduling System (DIS-DSS) maintains separate blackboard structures for each agent and provides communication utilities for transmitting requests and meta-level information between agents. Remote analogues of service goals, task structures, and other scheduling entities are created as needed to model the state of other agents. The information about other agents' schedules and commitments is incomplete and is limited to the content of goals, meta-level information, and those parts of the schedule to which the local agent itself has contributed.

The approach we have taken towards distributing DSS is to view each agent as representing an autonomous organization possessing its own resources. It is this autonomous nature of the organizations that is the rationale for distributing the resource allocation problem. Although a centralized architecture might produce more efficient solutions, real world considerations such as cost and ownership often lead to confederations in which information transfer regarding commitments and capabilities is limited. In this model, the primary relationship between agents is a commitment to exchange resources as needed and a willingness to negotiate with other agents to resolve impasses. This model of a decentralized group of agents performing independent tasks in a resource-constrained environment is similar to the architecture of Moehlman's Distributed Fireboss (Moehlman, Lesser, & Buteau 1992). We distinguish our work from Moehlman's by our use of meta-level information to control the decision process by which agents choose to resolve impasses locally, through backtracking and constraint relaxation, or through requests to remote agents.

Because resources are owned by specific agents and possess unique characteristics regarding location and travel times that are known only to the owning agent, we can not define central resource monitors responsible for allocating each type of resource. This, again, distinguishes our approach from that of Sycara, et al. (Sycara *et al.* 1991). Agents requiring a resource must communicate directly with the agent owning a resource of that type and negotiate for its loan.

This architecture provides a rich domain for the study of agent coordination issues in a distributed environment; agents must be able to model the interactions of their tasks with those of neighboring agents closely enough to be able to determine which agents will be most likely to provide the desired resources at the lowest cost to both agents. This coordination requires local reasoning on the part of agents in order to determine how to cooperate efficiently with an acceptable level of communication and redundant computation.

Assumptions In our work with DIS-DSS, we have made a number of assumptions about the nature of agents, schedules, and communication overheads.

- Agents are cooperative and will lend a resource if it is available.

- Agents will only request a resource from one agent at a time – this is to avoid the possibility of redundant computation and communication if multiple agents attempt to provide the resource cf. (Sandholm 1993).

- Once agents have lent a resource to another agent, they will never renege on this agreement. This limits the ability of the system to perform global backtracking; we intend to eliminate this restriction in the next version of the system.

- Communication is asynchronous and can occur at any point during the construction of a local schedule; therefore requests may arrive before an agent has completely determined its own requirements for resources in the time window of interest.

- The cost of messages is largely in the processing and in the inherent delay caused by transmission – the amount of data within the message may be large, within limits.

Communication of Abstract Resource Profiles Without information regarding other agents' abilities to supply missing resources, an agent may be unable to complete a solution, or may be forced to compromise the quality of its solution. To allow agents to construct a model of global system constraints and capabilities, we have developed a protocol for the exchange and updating of resource profiles: summarizations of the agent's committed resources, available resources, and estimated future demand.

Upon startup, each agent in DIS-DSS receives a set of orders to be processed. The agents examine these orders and generate an abstract description of their resource requirements for the scheduling period. This *bottleneck-status-list* consists of a list of intervals, with each interval annotated by a triple: resources in use, resources requested, and resources available. The request field of this triplet represents an abstraction of the agent's true resource requirements. Certain aspects of a reservation such as mobile resource travel times to the objects to be serviced, cannot be easily estimated in advance. The time intervals specified for each resource request are pessimistic, consisting of the earliest possible start time and latest possible finish times for the activity requesting that resource. The true duration of the task can be estimated by the scheduling agent using its domain knowledge regarding the typical time required to perform a task. We define the demand for a resource r performing task T in interval (t_j, t_k) to be:

$$\text{avg\_demand}(T, r, t_j, t_k) = \text{duration}(T, r)/(t_k - t_j)$$

Once resource abstractions have been developed for each resource type required (or possessed) by the agent, it transmits its abstractions to all other agents. Likewise, it receives abstractions from all agents. Once the agent has received communications from all other agents, it prepares a map of global resource requirements and uses it to generate a set of data structures called *lending possibilities*. Each lending possibility represents an interval in which some agent appears to have a shortfall in a resource. For each lending possiblity, the agent generates a list of possible lenders for that resource, based on the global resource map and its knowledge of its own resource requirements. These lending possibility structures are used to predict when remote agents may request resources and when the local agent may need to borrow resources. This information guides the agent's decision-making process in determining both when to process local goals and when and from whom to request resources.

The Distributed Airport Resource Management System

The Distributed Airport Research Management System testbed was constructed using DIS-DSS to study the roles of coordination and negotiation in a distributed problem-solver. DIS-ARM solves distributed AGSS problems where the function of each scheduling agent is to ensure that each flight for which it is responsible receives the ground servicing (gate assignment, baggage handling, catering, fuel, cleaning, etc.) that it requires in time to meet its arrival and departure deadlines. The supplying of a resource is usually a multi-step task consisting of setup, travel, and servicing actions. Each resource task is a subtask of the airplane servicing supertask. There is considerable parallelism in the task structure: many tasks can be done simultaneously. However, the choice of certain resource assignments can often constrain the start and end times of other tasks. For example, selection of a specific arrival gate for a plane may limit the choice of servicing vehicles due to transit time from their previous servicing locations and may limit refueling options due to the presence or lack of underground fuel tanks at that gate. For this reason, all resources of a specific type can not be considered interchangeable in the AGSS domain. Only the agent that owns the resource can identify all the current constraints on that resource and decide whether or not it can be allocated to meet a specific demand.

Exploiting Meta-level Information in Dis-DSS

In this section, we examine three areas in which meta-level abstractions of global resource requirements are exploited in Dis-DSS. We show how the goal rating scheme of an agent's blackboard-based scheduler is modified to satisfy the twin aims of scheduling based on global constraints and of planning activities in order to reduce uncertainty about agent interactions. We describe how communication of resource abstractions is based on models of agents' interests and the manner in which agents choose between local and remote methods of satisfying a request.

Scheduling using Texture Measures

Many scheduling systems divide processing into the categories of variable selection, the choice of the next activity to schedule, and value selection, the selection of a resource and time slot for that activity. In Dis-DSS, variable selection corresponds to the satisfaction of a particular resource request. Value selection is handled in DSS by a collection of opportunistic scheduling heuristics. We focus here on the problem of coordinating resource requests so that local variable-selection heuristics possess sufficient information to make informed decisions.

In many knowledge-based scheduling systems, the object of control is to arrange scheduling activities so that the most tightly constrained activities are scheduled first in order to reduce the need for backtracking. In a distributed system, we have an additional criterion: to schedule problem-solving activities in such a way that global uncertainty about certain tasks is reduced before decisions regarding those tasks are made. A scheduler may be uncertain of whether other agents will request a resource in a tightly constrained time period and whether other agents will be able to supply a needed resource. While the resource abstractions may indicate a loan request is likely, the duration of

the loan and details of the resource's destination can only be determined once the request has been received. Likewise, details of the precise timing and duration of a loan can only be determined upon receipt of a remote reservation. We have added coordination heuristics to the agenda scheduler of Dis-DSS whose purpose is to promote problematic activities in each agent's scheduling queue so that their early execution will reduce uncertainty about global system requirements.

In the Dis-DSS blackboard-based architecture, tasks which require resources generate *service-goals*. Requests received from remote agents generate *remote-service-goals*. Each goal stimulates knowledge sources that act to secure an appropriate resource. The order of execution of knowledge sources depends on the rating of the stimulating goals. Goals are rated using a basic 'most-tightly-constrained-first' opportunistic heuristic. The goals are then stratified according to the following scheme, with the uppermost levels receiving the highest priority and contention within each level being resolved according to the basic rating heuristic.

1. Tightly constrained goals that may not be satisfiable locally or that can only be satisfied by a borrowing event *and* remote requests that do not overlap any local request.

2. Tightly constrained goals that can *only* be satisfied locally.

3. Goals representing requests from remote agents that overlap local goals.

4. Unconstrained or loosely constrained tasks.

5. Goals that *potentially* overlap with tasks of remote agents.

A goal g is considered to be tightly constrained in interval (t_j, t_k) if there exists a time within that interval such that for each resource type r that can satisfy g, the number of unreserved resources is less than the sum of the average demand for all outstanding goals.

$$\forall \ r \ s.t. \ \text{Sat}(g, r) \ \exists \ t \in (t_j, t_k) \ s.t.$$

$$N_{available}(r, t) < \sum_{g} \text{avg\_demand}(task(g), r, t_j, t_k)$$

A goal potentially overlaps with a task of a remote agent if there exists a lending-possibility data structure for that remote agent describing a potential shortfall within the time interval spanned by that goal for some resource type that could satisfy the goal.

The rationale for this goal ordering is as follows. Goals that can not be satisfied locally must be transmitted to remote agents. The transmission of a goal conveys considerably more information than is available in the resource texture profiles. The potential lending agent will therefore have more accurate information regarding the interval for which the resource is desired and the preferred shift preference for the reservation in that interval (early or late). Once it has received the goal, it will be able to make more informed decisions about the tightness of constraints for both the local and remote goals. If the agent is able to satisfy the remote goal, it will be able to update its resource demand curve and transmit it to other agents who may also have been potential lenders of that resource. For all these reasons, early transmittal and satisfaction of remote service goals is desirable.

Tightly constrained goals that potentially overlap remote requests are deferred until some overlapping goal arrives, or until a resource update arrives indicating that the remote agent no longer requires that resource, or until no other work is available for the agent to perform. By deferring goals until more information about interactions is available, the system can avoid making premature decisions while at the same time working on unrelated or less constrained tasks. Once a request arrives, conflicts for resources can be arbitrated according to which goal is most pressing and least conducive to backtracking and/or constraint relaxation.

There are a number of competing requirements for the rating and processing of remote service goals. One would like to process a remote service goal as soon as possible in order to return information to the requesting agent. At the same time, both local and remote service goals requesting the same type of resource should be rated according to the same constraint tightness heuristics. The goal rating function in Dis-DSS attempts to satisfy these requirements by prioritizing those remote service goals that do not overlap any local service goals and by mapping overlapping remote service goals onto the same priority level as those local goals that they overlap. Note that the "overlapping" relationship is transitive: if the priority of a goal is reduced while waiting for a remote request, any lower rated goal that overlaps that goal's time interval must also wait even though it may not directly overlap the interval of the potential remote request.

Guiding Communication using Texture Measures

Reducing communication costs is an important issue in distributed systems. For this reason, Dis-DSS agents use the lending possibility models of agent interactions to guide communication activities. When its resource requirements change, an agent transmits the information about the resource type only to those agents who, based on its local information, would be interested in receiving updates concerning that resource type. An agent with no surplus resources of a given type may not be interested if the local agent increases its need for a particular resource, likewise, an agent with a surplus of a particular resource may not need to be notified if an agent reduces its demand for that resource type.

However, agents who possess shortfalls in a time interval for a particular type of resource will receive updates during processing whenever an agent increases the precision of its resource abstractions by securing or releasing a resource.

The use of local knowledge to guide communication episodes may lead to agents' knowledge of the global state of the system becoming increasingly out of date. The degree to which this should be allowed to happen is dependent upon the acceptable level of uncertainty in the system and the accuracy with which resource abstractions can be made.

Ordering Methods for Achieving Resource Assignments

In DSS, the process of securing a resource is achieved through a series of increasingly costly methods: assignment, preemption, and right shifting. These correspond roughly to request satisfaction, backtracking, and constraint relaxation. Preemption is a conservative form of backtracking in which existing reservations are preempted in favor of a more constrained task. Right shifting satisfies otherwise intractable requests by shifting the time interval of the reservation downstream (later) until a suitable resource becomes available. Because this method relaxes the latest finish time constraint, it has the potential to seriously decrease the quality of a solution. In the AGSS domain, for example, right shifting a reservation may result in late departures.

In DSS, methods are ordered according to increasing cost. In the distributed version of the system, the choice and ordering of methods is more complex. When an agent cannot immediately acquire a resource locally, it faces a decision: should it perform backtracking or constraint relaxation locally, communicating only when it has exhausted all local alternatives, or should it immediately attempt to borrow the resource from another agent? The decision-making process becomes even more difficult if we allow requests from remote agents to take precedence over local requirements such that agents may have to perform backtracking or constraint relaxation in order to satisfy a remote request. We consider this last decision process a form of *negotiation*, because it involves determining which of two agents should bear the cost of reduced solution quality and/or increased problem-solving effort.

In Dis-DSS, we use the lending possibility data structures to dynamically generate plans for achieving each resource assignment. When it appears that a remote agent will have surplus resources at the necessary time, then the agent will generate a request as soon as it becomes clear that the resource can not be secured locally. If, however, it appears that the resource is tightly constrained globally, the agent will choose to perform backtracking and/or constraint relaxation operations locally rather than engage in communication episodes that will probably prove futile.

One use of meta-information occurs during the planning for constraint relaxation. The scheduling agent attempts to minimize the magnitude of the right shift in order to reduce the effect of the constraint relaxation on the quality of the solution. To do this, the agent must determine whether the minimum right shift can be achieved locally or remotely. However, requiring agents to submit bids detailing their earliest reservations for a given resource would be a costly process. Instead, the agent uses the abstractions of remote resource availability to generate a threshold value for the right shift delay. If this value is less than the delay achieved through right shifting locally, the agent sequentially transmits the resource request to the appropriate remote agents. If a remote agent can provide a reservation with a delay of less than or equal to the threshold value, it immediately secures the resource. Otherwise, it returns the delay of the earliest possible reservation. If no reservation is found, the local agent sets the threshold to the earliest possible value returned by some remote agent. This new threshold is then compared to the current best local delay (which might have changed due to local scheduling while the remote requests were being processed). This process continues until a reservation is made or until the threshold becomes greater than the delay achievable by right shifting locally. Obviously, the better the initial estimate for the delay threshold, the less communication activities will be required.

The meta-information is also used to determine the order in which agents should be asked for resources, beginning with the agent(s) with the least tightly constrained resources.

Experimental Results

The performance of the mechanisms that we have developed for DIS-DSS were tested in a series of experiments using a single agent system as a basis for comparison. We used six scenarios designed to test the performance of the system in tightly constrained situations. The number of orders in each scenario ranged from 10 to 60 and a minimal set of resources was defined for each scenario. Each scenario was distributed for a three agent case. Orders were assigned to each agent on a round-robin basis such that each agent would perform approximately the same amount of work. Resources were distributed randomly so that in some cases each agent would possess all necessary resources while in other cases, borrowing from remote agents would be necessary.

We ran DIS-ARM on each scheduling scenario using the following configurations of the scheduler:

- The baseline case with a single agent.

- The 3 agent case with no use of meta-level information, and an opportunistic (most-tightly-constrained-variable-first) goal rating scheme

- The 3 agent case using the heuristic goal rating scheme incorporating meta-level information but requesting resources from remote agents only when all local methods have failed.

- The 3 agent case using heuristic goal rating, meta-level information, and dynamic reordering of resource acquisition methods to account for the probability of securing a goal either locally or remotely.

For each run, we recorded the average tardiness of the schedule, the number of failed goals (if any), the number of resource-securing methods tried, the number of requests, the number of satisfied remote service goals, and the number of communication episodes that occurred during problem solving. In each case, we assumed that communication costs were negligible in relation to problem-solving and that requests and resource constraint updates would be received on the simulation cycle immediately succeeding the one in which they were sent.

Because of the small number of test cases we have examined in our preliminary experiments, we present our results anecdotally. As expected, the distributed version of the scheduler always produces a schedule of somewhat lower quality than the centralized one. When the opportunistic scheduler of the centralized version is used for scheduling in a distributed environment, its lack of information about global constraints causes it to produce somewhat inferior results. The heuristic incorporating meta-level information consistently outperforms the opportunistic scheduler in terms of the number of tardy tasks. The opportunistic scheduler occasionally will produce a schedule with less total tardiness than the distributed algorithm. We interpret this as a trade-off between satisfying global requirements (by delaying certain goal satisfactions until remote information becomes available) and satisfying local requirements by producing needed results promptly. This is an interesting trade-off that we intend to study in depth. Attempting to always solve problems locally using preemption and constraint relaxation produced schedules with much greater delays than when agents dynamically determined when to request resources remotely based on the meta-level resource abstractions.

Conclusions and Future Work

The work we have performed with DIS-DSS is preliminary, but promising. Our results indicate that the idea of using meta-level information to schedule activities in order to reduce local uncertainty about global constraints results in better coordination between agents with a subsequent increase in goal satisfaction. We have also demonstrated that meta-level information can be successfully used to guide the choice between satisfying goals locally and remotely, and in optimizing the choice of agents from which to request resources.

Our experiments were performed with each agent's

orders being defined statically before scheduling. This allowed the agents to develop a model of their predicted resource requirements before scheduling began. If we were to model a system in which orders changed dynamically, either due to equipment failures or timetable changes, we would expect the model of global resource requirements to become increasingly inaccurate. We would like to understand the implications of allowing jobs to arrive dynamically on the performance of a distributed system using meta-level information.

As well as continuing to explore the role of meta-level resource abstractions, we plan to use the DIS-DSS testbed to explore a number of important issues in distributed scheduling. One of our primary goals is to expand the idea of negotiation between agents that we have touched upon in this paper. Because the airport ground service scheduling domain represents a "real world" scenario, we are able to create a meaningful cost model involving not only the delay in each schedule, but the probable cost of that delay in terms of missed connections. By allowing agents to exchange this information when requesting resources, they will be able to more meaningfully weigh the importance of local tasks against the quality of the global solution.

References

Carver, N., and Lesser, V. 1994. The evolution of blackboard control architectures,. *Expert Systems with Applications- Special Issue on the Blackboard Paradigm and Its Applications* 7(1):1–30.

Corkill, D. D.; Gallagher, K. Q.; and Murray, K. E. 1986. GBB: A generic blackboard development system. In *Proceedings of the Fifth National Conference on Artificial Intelligence*, 1008–1014.

Decker, K. S., and Lesser, V. R. 1992. Generalizing the partial global planning algorithm. *International Journal of Intelligent and Cooperative Information Systems* 1(2):319–346.

Decker, K. S., and Lesser, V. R. 1993. Quantitative modeling of complex computational task environments. In *Proceedings of the Eleventh National Conference on Artificial Intelligence*, 217–224.

Durfee, E., and Lesser, V. 1991. Partial global planning: A coordination framework for distributed hypothesis formation. *IEEE Transactions on Systems, Man, and Cybernetics* 21(5):1167–1183.

Erman, L. D.; Hayes-Roth, F.; Lesser, V. R.; and Reddy, D. R. 1980. The hearsay-ii speech-understanding system: Integrating knowledge to resolve uncertainty. *Computing Surveys* 12(2):213–253.

Fox, M. S. 1983. *Constraint-Directed Search: A Case Study of Job-Shop Scheduling*. Ph.D. Dissertation, Carnegie Mellon University, Pittsburgh PA.

Garey, M. R., and Johnson, D. S. 1979. *Computers and Intractability: A Guide to the Theory of NP-Completeness*. New York: W.H. Freeman.

Hildum, D. W., and Corkill, D. D. 1990. Solving dynamic sequencing problems. COINS Technical Report 90–63, University of Massachusetts.

Hildum, D. W. 1994. *Flexibility in a Knowledge-Based System for Solving Dynamic Resource-Constrained Scheduling Problems*. Ph.D. Dissertation, Computer Science Dept., University of Massachusetts, Amherst, MA 01003.

Moehlman, T. A.; Lesser, V. R.; and Buteau, B. L. 1992. Decentralized negotiation: An approach to the distributed planning problem. *Group Decision and Negotiation* (2):161–191.

Sadeh, N. 1991. *Look-Ahead Techniques for Micro-Opportunistic Job Shop Scheduling*. Ph.D. Dissertation, Carnegie Mellon University, Pittsburgh PA.

Sandholm, T. 1993. An implementation of the contract net protocol based on marginal cost calculations. In *Proceedings of the Eleventh National Conference on Artificial Intelligence*, 256–262.

Sen, S., and Durfee, E. 1993. A formal analysis of communication and commitment in distributed meeting scheduling. In *Proceedings of the Twelfth Workshop on Distributed AI*.

Smith, S. F.; Fox, M. S.; and Ow, P. S. 1986. Constructing and maintaining detailed production plans: Investigations into the development of knowledge-based factory scheduling systems. *AI Magazine* 7(4):45–61.

Sycara, K.; Roth, S.; Sadeh, N.; and Fox, M. 1991. Distributed constrained heuristic search. *IEEE Transactions on Systems, Man, and Cybernetics* 21(6):1446–1461.

Yakoo, M.; Ishida, T.; and Kuwabara, K. 1990. Distributed constraint satisfaction for DAI problems. In *Proceedings of the 10th International Workshop on Distributed Artificial Intelligence*.

A Computational Market Model for Distributed Configuration Design

Michael P. Wellman

University of Michigan, AI Laboratory
1101 Beal Avenue
Ann Arbor, MI 48109-2110
wellman@engin.umich.edu

Abstract

This paper[1] presents a precise market model for a well-defined class of distributed configuration design problems. Given a design problem, the model defines a computational economy to allocate basic resources to agents participating in the design. The result of running these "design economies" constitutes the market solution to the original problem. After defining the configuration design framework, I describe the mapping to computational economies and our results to date. For some simple examples, the system can produce good designs relatively quickly. However, analysis shows that the design economies are *not* guaranteed to find optimal designs, and we identify and discuss some of the major pitfalls. Despite known shortcomings and limited explorations thus far, the market model offers a useful conceptual viewpoint for analyzing distributed design problems.

Introduction

With advances in network technology and infrastructure, opportunities for the decentralization of design activities are growing rapidly. Moreover, the specialization of design expertise suggests a future where teams form *ad hoc* collaborations dynamically and flexibly, according to the most opportunistic connections. Centralized coordination or control is anathema in this environment. Instead we seek general decentralized mechanisms which respect the local autonomy of the agents involved, yet at the same time facilitate results (in our case, designs) with globally desirable qualities.

Design of complex artifacts can be viewed as fundamentally a problem of *resource allocation*. We generally have numerous performance and functional objectives to address, with many options for trading among these objectives and for furthering these objectives in exchange for increased cost. When the design problem is distributed, then these tradeoffs are not only across objectives, but also across agents (human or computational) participating in the design. Typically each agent is concerned with a subset of the components or functions of the artifact being designed, and may individually reflect a complex combination of the fundamental objectives.

Consider a hyper-simplified scenario in aircraft design. Suppose we have separate agents responsible for the airfoil, engines, navigation equipment, etc. Suppose that we have a target for the aircraft's total weight. Since total weight is the sum of the weights of its parts, we might consider allocating *a priori* each agent a slice of the "weight budget". This approach has several serious problems. First, if we do not choose the slices correctly, then it could be that one of the agents makes extreme compromises (e.g., an under-powered engine or expensive exotic metals for the fuselage) while the others could reduce weight relatively easily. Second, it will typically be impossible to determine good slices in advance, because the appropriate allocation will depend on other design choices. For example, depending on the position of the wings, reducing body weight while maintaining structural soundness may be more or less expensive. Or if we have a more powerful engine, then it may be that extra total weight can be accommodated, and the fixed budget itself was not realistic.

Rather than allocate fixed proportions of resources, we desire an approach that dynamically adjusts the allocation as the design progresses. One way to achieve this sort of behavior is via a negotiation and trading process. For example, if the engine agent would benefit substantially from a slight increment in weight, it might offer to trade some of its drag allowance to the airfoil agent for a share of the latter's weight allocation. If there is enough of this kind of trading going on, then it makes sense to establish *markets* in the basic resources—weight, drag, etc. Then we can view the entire system as a sort of economy devoted to allocating resources for the design. We call this system the *design economy*.

In this paper, we present a precise market model for a well-defined class of distributed configuration design problems. Given a design problem, our model defines a computational economy to solve the design problem, expressed in terms of concepts from microeconomic theory. We can then implement these economies in our WALRAS system for market-oriented programming (Wellman 1993), thus producing a runnable design economy.

The following sections describe the configuration design framework, the mapping to computational economies, and

---

[1] An extended version is available via anonymous ftp as ftp://ftp.eecs.umich.edu/people/wellman/aaai94ext.ps.

preliminary results. For some simple examples, the system can produce good designs relatively quickly. However, analysis shows that the design economies are *not* guaranteed to find optimal designs, and we identify and discuss some of the major pitfalls. We argue that most of these problems are inherent in decentralization generally, not in the design economy *per se*, and moreover that the market model offers useful concepts for engineering the configuration of a variety of multiagent tasks.

Distributed Configuration Design

We adopt a standard framework for configuration design (Mittal and Frayman 1989). Our specific formulation follows (Darr and Birmingham 1994), and covers many representative systems (Balkany et al. 1993). Design in this framework corresponds to selection of *parts* to perform *functions*. More precisely, a design problem consists of:

- A set of attributes, $A_1,\ldots,A_n$, and their associated domains, $X_1,\ldots,X_n$.
- A set of available parts, P, where each part $p \in P$ is defined by a tuple of attribute-value pairs.
- A distinguished subset of attributes, F, the *functions*. The domain of a function attribute is the set of parts that can perform that function.
- A set of constraints, R, dictating the allowable part combinations (either directly or indirectly via constraints on the attributes).
- A utility function, $u: X_1 \times \cdots \times X_n \to \Re$, ranking the possible combinations of attribute values by preference.

A *design D* is an assignment of parts to functions. Thus, the role of functions in this framework is to define when a design is complete. D is *feasible* if it satisfies R. The *valuation* of a design, *val*(D), is the assignment to attribute values induced by the assignment of parts to functions. Typically, this is just the sum over the respective attribute values of a design's component parts. Finally, a feasible design D is *optimal* if for all feasible designs D', $u(val(D)) \geq u(val(D'))$.

In addition, it is often useful to organize the parts into *catalogs*. Let catalog i, $1 \leq i \leq m$, consist of parts C_i, where $C_1,\ldots,C_m$ is a partition of P. A catalog design includes at most one part per catalog.[2] In distributed design, catalogs are the units of distribution: each catalog agent selects a part to contribute or chooses not to participate.

In this general form, the design task is clearly intractable (it subsumes general constraint satisfaction and optimization). Tractability can be obtained only by imposing restrictions on R and u. Instantiations of this framework adopt specialized constraint languages, and often relax the

---

[2]In the degenerate case where each catalog lists only one part, catalog design reverts to the situation without catalogs. Typically catalogs will correspond to functions, although this is not a requirement. Indeed, this definition places no restriction on the number of functions any part may implement.

requirement of optimality. We shall accept comparable compromises in our mapping to the market model.

Computational Markets

The market model we adopt is a computational realization of the most generic, well-studied theoretical framework, that of general equilibrium theory (Hildenbrand and Kirman 1976; Shoven and Whalley 1992). General equilibrium is concerned with the behavior of a collection of interconnected markets, one market for each good. A general-equilibrium system consists of:

- a collection of goods, $g_1,\ldots,g_n$, and
- a collection of agents, divided into two types:
  - *consumers*, who simply exchange goods, and
  - *producers*, who can transform some goods into others.

A consumer is defined by (1) a *utility function*, which specifies its relative preference for consuming a bundle of goods $\langle x_1,\ldots,x_n \rangle$, and (2) an *endowment* $\langle e_1,\ldots,e_n \rangle$ of initial quantities of the goods. Consumers may trade all or part of their initial endowments in exchange for quantities of the other goods. All trades must be executed at the established market prices, $\langle p_1,\ldots,p_n \rangle$. A consumption bundle is feasible for a consumer if and only if it satisfies the *budget constraint*,

$$\sum_{i=1}^{n} x_i p_i \leq \sum_{i=1}^{n} e_i p_i,$$

which says that a consumer may spend only up to the value of its endowment. The decision problem faced by a consumer is to maximize its utility subject to the budget constraint.

The other class of agents, producers, do not consume goods, but rather transform various combinations of some goods (the inputs) into others (outputs). The feasible combinations of inputs and outputs are defined by the producer's *technology*. For example, if the producer can transform one unit of g_1 into two units of g_2, with constant returns to scale, then the technology would include the tuples $\{\langle -x, 2x, 0,\ldots,0 \rangle \mid x \geq 0\}$. This production would be profitable as long as $p_1 < 2 p_2$. The producer's decision problem is to choose a production activity so as to maximize *profits*, the difference between revenues (total price of output) and costs (total price of input). Note that a producer does not have a utility function.

In the computational market price system we use, WALRAS, we can implement consumer and producer agents and direct them to bid so as to maximize utility or profits, subject to their own feasibility constraints. The system derives a set of market prices that balance the supply and demand for each good. Since the markets for the goods are interconnected (due to interactions in both production and consumption), the price for one good will generally affect the demand and supply for others. WALRAS adjusts the prices via an iterative bidding protocol, until the system reaches a *competitive equilibrium* (see (Wellman 1993) for details), i.e., an allocation and set of prices such that (1) consumers bid so to maximize utility, subject to their budget constraints, (2) producers bid so to maximize profits, subject to their technological possibilities, and (3) net demand is zero for all goods.

An economy in competitive equilibrium has the desirable property of Pareto Optimality: it is not possible to increase the utility of one agent without decreasing that of other(s). Moreover, for any Pareto optimum (i.e., any admissible allocation), there is some corresponding set of initial endowments that would lead to this result. Given certain technical restrictions on the producer technologies and consumer preferences, equilibrium is guaranteed to exist and the system converges to it. Specifically, if technologies and preferences are smooth and strictly convex, then a unique equilibrium exists (see (Varian 1984) for formal treatment). If in addition, the derived demands are such that increasing the price for one good does not decrease the demand for others, then the iterative bidding process is guaranteed to converge to this equilibrium (Arrow and Hurwicz 1977; Milgrom and Roberts 1991).

The Design Economy

We next proceed to instantiate the general-equilibrium framework for our distributed configuration design problem. As noted above, our purpose in applying the economic mechanism is to provide a principled basis for resolving tradeoffs across distributed design agents. By grouping the agents together in a single economy, we establish a *common currency* linking the agents' local demands for available resources. Using this common currency, the market can (at least under the circumstances sketched above) efficiently allocate resources toward their most productive use with minimal communication or coordination overhead. The fact that all interaction among agents occurs via exchange of goods at standard prices greatly simplifies the design of individual agents, as they can focus on their own attributes and the parameters of their local economic problems. In addition, the price interface provides a straightforward way to influence the system's behavior from the outside—by setting the relative prices of exogenously derived resources and performance attributes. And similarly, the prices within the system can be interpreted from the outside in terms of economic variables that are meaningful to those participating in the design process.

Market Configuration

In general, to cast a distributed resource-allocation problem in terms of a computational market, one needs to specify

- the goods (commodities) traded,
- the consumer agents trading and ultimately deriving value from the goods,
- the producer agents, with their associated technologies for transforming some goods into other goods, and
- the agents' bidding behavior.

There are two classes of goods we consider in the problem of distributed design. First, we have basic resource attributes, such as weight and drag in the fanciful aircraft example above. These are resources required by the components in order to realize the desired performance, but are limited or costly or both. Generally, we desire to minimize our overall use of resources. The second class of goods are performance attributes, such as engine thrust or leg room in a passenger aircraft. We also include the function attributes in this category. Performance attributes measure the capabilities of the designed artifact, and we typically desire to maximize these.

In terms of our framework for distributed configuration design, both resource and performance attributes are kinds of attributes. Functions can be viewed as a subclass of performance attributes. So, the first step in mapping a design problem to our market model is to identify the goods with the attributes. Although it is not strictly necessary to distinguish the resource from performance attributes, we do so for expository reasons, as it facilitates intuitive understanding of the flow of goods in the design economy.

The remaining steps are to identify the agents and define their behavior. As mentioned above, it is typical in multiagent design to allocate individual agents responsibility for distinct components or functions. Within our distributed design scheme, these agents correspond to catalogs. In a distributed constraint-satisfaction formulation of the problem (Darr and Birmingham 1994), catalog agents select a part to contribute to the overall design. The chosen part entails a particular pattern of resource usage and performance, as specified in its associated attribute vector.

Correspondingly, in the design economy, each part in the catalog is associated with a vector of resource and performance *goods*. The resources can be interpreted as input goods, and the performance goods as output. In this view, the *catalog producer* is an agent that transforms resources to performance. For example, the engine agent in our aircraft design transforms *weight* and *drag* (and *noise*, etc.) into *thrust*. The particular combinations of weight/drag/thrust/... represented by the various engine models constitute this producer's *technology*. Thus, to specify a catalog producer's technology (and that's all there is to specify for a producer), we simply form a set of the attribute-value tuples characterizing each part. We then go through and negate the values for the resource goods, leaving the values for performance goods intact.[3]

An economy with only producers would have no purpose. To ground the system, we define a consumer agent, conceptually the end user or customer for the overall design.[4] The consumer is endowed with the basic resource

---

[3]This assumes that all attributes are measured in increasing resource usage or increasing performance. If not, we would simply rescale the values in advance.

[4]If there are more than one class of users or customers with distinct preferences, then we could introduce several consumer agents. The underlying computational market accommodates any

goods. So for example, we will initialize the system by endowing the consumer with a total weight, typically an amount greater than the heaviest conceivable aircraft defined by combination of the heaviest available parts. The idea is that the consumer then (effectively) sells this weight to the various catalog agents, in exchange for performance goods like thrust.

The consumer has preferences over the overall design attributes, as specified by its utility function. This function is essentially equivalent to the function u defined in the general framework for configuration design. There is one syntactic modification, however. In the original specification, u was increasing in the performance attributes and decreasing in the resource attributes. The consumer's utility function, in contrast, must be increasing in all attributes. To ensure this, we define the "consumption" of a resource good as the amount left over after the consumer sells part of its endowment. Thus, if the consumer's endowment of weight is w and the total weight of the aircraft (sum of the weight of the parts) is w', then the effective weight consumed is $w - w'$. If the consumer prefers lighter airplanes, then it prefers to "consume" as much weight as possible.

Thus far, we have accounted for all elements of the configuration design framework except for the constraints (recall that the functions are a subset of performance attributes). We are able to map some kinds of constraints into this framework, but not others. The simplest type of constraint is an upper bound on the total usage of a particular resource (e.g., the total noise cannot exceed FAA regulations). To capture this kind of constraint, we simply endow the consumer with exactly the upper bound. Since the consumer is the only source of resource goods in the economy, this effectively restricts the combined choices of the producers. Some other kinds of constraints can also be handled by defining new intermediate goods. This is best illustrated by example in the next section.

Finally, we must note an implicit assumption underlying the mapping described above. In order for the resource and performance goods to be reasonably traded among the consumer and producers, it must be the case that the total resource usage (resp. performance achieved) does indeed correspond to the sum of the parts. In other words, the *val* function described above must be additive (but note that the utility function u need not be). There may be some encoding tricks to get around this restriction in some cases, but the basic design economy assumes this property.

An Example

To illustrate the mapping from configuration design problems to design economies, we carry out the exercise for an example presented by (Darr and Birmingham 1994). The problem is a very simplified computer configuration design. In the example, we have two functions to satisfy: *processing*, and serial *port*. Our design criteria are *dollar* cost and reliability, as measured in failures-per-million-

hours (*fpmh*). These criteria are represented in the design economy as resource goods. There are no performance goods, except for the two functions mentioned. There is also another good, *memory* access, which is conceived here not as an overall performance attribute but as an intermediate good enabling the *processing* function.[5]

We also have three constraints. The total dollar cost must not exceed 11, the total failure rate must not exceed 10 fpmh, and the RAM must be at least as fast as the CPU's memory access. The first two of these constraints are captured simply by endowing the consumer with 11 dollars and 10 fpmh. The consumer's utility function specifies preferences over these two goods, as well as the functions *processing* and *port*. Representing the functions as utility attributes rather than constraints deviates from the original framework somewhat by allowing the user the flexibility to trade off functionality for performance or resource savings.

There are 14 available parts, organized into three catalogs. The CPU catalog contains four CPU models, each of which supplies the *processing* function. Five serial ports are available to support the *port* function, and five RAM models can supply *memory* access. The complete CPU catalog is presented in Table 1.

CPU	process	dollars	fpmh	memory
CPU1	1	6	1	40
CPU2	1	4	7	140
CPU3	1	2	2	40
CPU4	1	1	5	30

Table 1: CPU catalog.

The catalogs are converted into technologies simply by listing the attribute tuples as good tuples, possibly after some rescaling. For example, the CPU agent's technology is:

$$\left\{ \begin{array}{l} \langle 1, -6, -1, -1/40 \rangle, \langle 1, -4, -7, -1/140 \rangle, \langle 1, -2, -2, -1/40 \rangle, \\ \langle 1, -1, -5, -1/30 \rangle, \langle 0, 0, 0, 0 \rangle \end{array} \right\}.$$

This means that the agent has five options, with the net good productions listed. The first option is to produce an output of 1 unit of processing (by default, functions take values in $\{0,1\}$) from an input of 6 *dollars*, 1 *fpmh*, and 1/40 *memory* access units. This last input requires some explanation. In order to represent the constraint that CPU be at least as fast as RAM, we define the intermediate good *memory* access, which is an output of RAM and an input of CPU. The constraint is then enforced by requiring that CPU buy enough speed from RAM. Since the values listed in the catalog above are memory access times, we invert them to convert to speed units.

Finally, the tuple of zeros is an element of every technology. An agent always has the option to produce nothing, in which case its resource usage is zero (as are its profits).

---

[5]We chose this interpretation specifically to illustrate the notion of intermediate goods; in the next section we simplify the model to treat *memory* as a function.

---

number of agents, but our design economies thus far have employed only one.

Similar technologies are generated for the RAM catalog (input *dollar* and *fpmh*, output *memory*) and serial port (input *dollar* and *fpmh*, output *port*), as shown in Table 2.

RAM	$	fpmh	memory	**Port**	$	fpmh	port
null	0	0	0	null	0	0	0
RAM1	−6	−2	1/40	SP1	−6	−1	1
RAM2	−3	−3	1/10	SP2	−3	−3	1
RAM3	−2	−6	1/35	SP3	−2	−4	1
RAM4	−2	−4	1/30	SP4	−1	−8	1
RAM5	−1	−7	1/35	SP5	−1	−6	1

Table 2: Technologies for RAM and Port catalog producers.

The configuration of the design economy is best described in terms of flow of goods, depicted in Figure 1. The consumers supply the basic resources, which are transformed by the producers to performance goods (as well as intermediate resources needed by other producers), which are ultimately valued by the consumer.

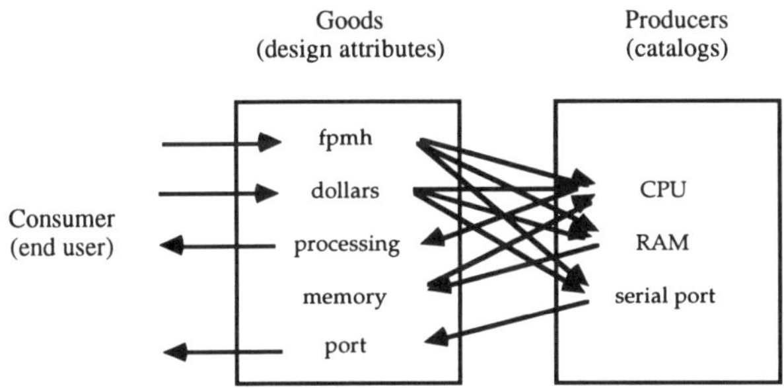

Figure 1: Flow of goods in the example design economy.

Agent Behavior

All that remains to specify our mapping is to define the behavior of the various agents. The consumer's problem is to set demands maximizing utility, subject to the budget constraint. This defines a constrained optimization problem, parametrized by current going prices.

In our example, we adopt a standard special functional form for utility, one exhibiting constant elasticity of substitution (CES) (Varian 1984). The CES utility function is

$$u(x_1,\ldots,x_n) = \left(\sum_{i=1}^{n} \alpha_i^{1-\rho} x_i^{\rho} \right)^{1/\rho},$$

where the α_i are good coefficients and ρ is a generic substitution parameter. One virtue of the CES utility function is that there is a closed-form solution to the optimal demand function,

$$x_i(p_1,\ldots,p_n) = \frac{\alpha_i \sum_{j=1}^{n} p_j e_j}{p_i^{1/(1-\rho)} \sum_{j=1}^{n} \alpha_j p_j^{\rho/(\rho-1)}}.$$

The consumer can simply evaluate this function at the going prices whenever prompted by the bidding protocol. In WALRAS, bids are actually demand *curves*, where the price p_i of the good i being bid varies while the other prices are held fixed. CES consumers transmit a closed-form description of this curve, with p_i the dependent variable.

The producers' bidding task is also quite simple. Catalog producers face a discrete choice among the possible component instances, each providing a series of values for goods corresponding to resource and performance attributes. Let $\left(x_1^j,\ldots,x_n^j \right)$ be the vector of quantities representing part j in the producer's catalog, and π^j denote the profitability of part j, as a function of prices:

$$\pi^j(p_1,\ldots,p_n) = \sum_{i=1}^{n} p_i x_i^j.$$

All catalogs include the null part 0, where $x_i^0 = 0$ for all i. Given a set of prices, the producer selects the most profitable part:

$$j*(p_1,\ldots,p_n) = \arg\max_j \pi^j(p_1,\ldots,p_n).$$

Just as for consumers, when a producer bids on good i, it specifies a range of demands for all values of p_i (the price of good i), holding all other prices fixed, which is determined by the optimal part for that price,

$$x_i(p_i) = x_i^{j*(\bar{p}_1,\ldots,p_i,\ldots\bar{p}_n)}.$$

When all prices but one are fixed, we can simplify the profit function as follows:

$$\pi^j(\bar{p}_1,\ldots,p_i,\ldots,\bar{p}_n) = p_i x_i^j + \sum_{k \neq i} \bar{p}_k x_k^j = p_i x_i^j + \bar{\beta}^j,$$

where the parameter $\bar{\beta}^j$ depends on part j and the fixed prices $\bar{p}_k$, $k \neq i$. For example, part j is more profitable than j' if and only if

$$p_i x_i^j + \bar{\beta}^j > p_i x_i^{j'} + \bar{\beta}^{j'},$$

or equivalently (for $x_i^j > x_i^{j'}$),

$$p_i > \frac{\bar{\beta}^{j'} - \bar{\beta}^j}{x_i^j - x_i^{j'}}.$$

It is clear from the above that parts with higher values of x_i^j become maximally profitable, if ever, at higher prices p_i. Therefore, one way to calculate $j*(\bar{p}_1,\ldots,p_i,\ldots,\bar{p}_n)$ is to sort the parts in increasing order of x_i^j and then use the inequality above to derive the price threshold between each adjacent pair.[6] These thresholds dictate the optimal part at any p_i (assuming the other prices fixed), and the associated demand x_i^{j*}. Thus, the form of the producer's demand is a step function, defined by a set of threshold prices where different components become optimal.

Results

We have run the design economy on a few simple examples, including the one presented above modified to treat *memory* as a function rather than an intermediate

---

[6]This includes the null part, with $x_i^0 = \bar{\beta}^0 = 0$. If the threshold decreases, then the intervening part can never be optimal (it is not on the convex hull) for any price of good i, and can be skipped.

good. On this example, it produces the optimal design in three bidding cycles, although it never (as long as we have run it) reaches a price equilibrium. After the third cycle, the prices continue to fluctuate, although never enough to cause one of the catalog producers to change its optimal part. Unfortunately, we have no way of detecting with certainty that the part choices are stable.

Although we have yet to run systematic experiments, we have observed similar behavior on a variety of small examples. We have also encountered examples where the design economy does not appear to converge on a single design, or it converges on a design far from the global optimum. This is not surprising, as the general class of design economies producible by the mapping specified above does not satisfy the known conditions for existence of competitive equilibrium. Indeed, the conditions are never strictly satisfied by design economies generated as described, because the discreteness of catalogs violates convexity.

Extensions

As mentioned above, designs produced by the market model are not guaranteed to be optimal or even feasible, due to the discreteness (and other non-convexities) of the problem. They are more likely to be local optima, where no single change of policy by one of the producer agents will constitute an improved design. In current work, we are attempting to characterize the performance of the scheme for special cases. For those cases where perfectly competitive equilibria do not exist, we are investigating the possibility of relaxing the competitiveness assumption. In addition, we are looking into hybrid schemes that use the market to bound the optimal value by computing the global optimum for a smooth and convex relaxation of the original problem. This is analogous to branch-and-bound schemes that make use of regular linear-programming algorithms for integer-programming problems. In this and other approaches, we expect the economic price information exploited by the market-oriented approach to lead to more rational tradeoffs in the distributed design process.

We are also exploring combinations of market-based and constraint-based methods, where we use general constraints (including those inexpressible in the market model) to prune the catalogs before running the design economy. A hybrid approach interleaving market-directed search for good designs with constraint reasoning uses each method to compensate for inadequacies in the other.

Economics and Distributed AI

Why Economics?

To coordinate a set of largely autonomous agents, we usually seek mechanisms that (A) produce globally desirable results, (B) avoid central coordination, and (C) impose minimal communication requirements. In addition, as engineers of such systems, we also prefer mechanisms

that (D) are amenable to theoretical and empirical analysis. In human societies, advocates of market economies argue that B is essential (for various reasons) and that market price systems perform well on criterion A because they provide each agent with the right incentives to further the social good. Because prices are a very compact way to convey this incentive information to each agent, we can argue that price systems also satisfy C (Koopmans 1970). For these reasons, some have found the market economy an inspiring social metaphor for approaches to coordinating distributed computational agents. Thus, we sometimes see mechanisms and protocols appealing to notions of negotiation, bidding, or other economic behavior.

Criterion D is also a compelling motivation for exploring economic coordination mechanisms in a computational setting. The problem of coordinating multiple agents in a societal structure has been deeply investigated by economists, resulting in a large body of concepts and insights, as well as a powerful analytical framework. The phenomena surrounding social decision making have been studied in other social science disciplines as well, but economics is distinguished by its focus on three particular issues:

Resource allocation. The central aspect of the outcome of the agents' behavior is the allocation of resources and distribution of products throughout the economy.

Rationality abstraction. Most of microeconomic theory adopts the assumption that individual agents are *rational* in the sense that they act so as to maximize utility. This approach is highly congruent with much work in Artificial Intelligence, where we attempt to characterize an agent's behavior in terms of its knowledge and goals (or more generally, beliefs, desires, and intentions). Indeed, this *knowledge level* analysis requires some kind of rationality abstraction (Newell 1982), and is perhaps even implicit in our usage of the term *agent*.

Decentralization. The central concern of economics is to relate decentralized, individual decisions to aggregate behavior of the overall society. This is also the concern of Distributed AI as a computational science.

Related Work

In addition to my own prior work in market-oriented programming (Wellman 1993), there have been several other efforts to exploit markets for distributed computation. Most famous in AI is the contract net (Davis and Smith 1983), but it is only recently that true economic mechanisms have been incorporated in that framework (Sandholm 1993). There have been interesting recent proposals for incorporating a range of economic ideas in distributed allocation of computational resources (Drexler and Miller 1988; Miller and Drexler 1988), as well as some actual experiments along these lines (Cheriton and Harty 1993; Kurose and Simha 1989; Waldspurger et al. 1992). However, there are no other computational market models for distributed design of which we are aware.

This approach also shares some conceptual features with Shoham's approach to "agent-oriented programming"

(Shoham 1993). Where Shoham defines a set of interactions based on speech acts, we focus exclusively on the economic actions such as exchange and production. In both approaches (as well as some others (Huberman 1988)), the underlying idea is to get an improved understanding of a complex computational system via social constructs.

Finally, there is a large literature on decomposition methods for mathematical programming problems, which could perhaps be applied to distributed design. Many of these and other distributed optimization techniques (Bertsekas and Tsitsiklis 1989) can themselves be interpreted in economic terms, using the close relationship between prices and Lagrange multipliers. The main distinction of the approach advocated here is conceptual. Rather than taking a global optimization problem and decentralizing it, our aim is to provide a framework that accommodates an exogenously given distributed structure.

Conclusions

The main contribution of this work is a precise market model for distributed design, covering a significant class of configuration design problems. The model has been implemented within a general environment for defining computational market systems. Although we have yet to perform extensive, systematic experiments, we have found that the design economy produces good designs on some simple problems, but breaks seriously on others. Analysis is underway to characterize the cases where it works. It cannot be expected to work universally, as these are known intractable optimization problems, and distributing the problem only makes things worse.

In the long run, by embedding economic concepts within our design algorithms, we facilitate the support of actual economic transactions that we expect will eventually be an integral part of networks for collaborative design and other inter-organizational interactions. Many other technical problems will need to be solved (involving security for proprietary information and bidding protocols, for example) before this is a reality, but integrating economic ideas at the conceptual level is an important first step.

Acknowledgments

Special thanks to Bill Birmingham and Tim Darr for assistance with the distributed design problem and examples. Daphne Koller and the anonymous referees provided useful comments on the paper and the work.

References

Arrow, K. J. and L. Hurwicz, Ed. (1977). Studies in Resource Allocation Processes. Cambridge, Cambridge University Press.

Balkany, A., W. P. Birmingham, and I. D. Tommelein (1993). An analysis of several configuration design systems. *AI EDAM* **7**: 1-17.

Bertsekas, D. P., and J. N. Tsitsiklis (1989). *Parallel and Distributed Computation*. Englewood Cliffs, NJ, Prentice-Hall.

Cheriton, D. R., and K. Harty (1993). A market approach to operating system memory allocation. Stanford University Department of Computer Science.

Darr, T. P. and W. P. Birmingham (1994). An Attribute-Space Representation and Algorithm for Concurrent Engineering. University of Michigan.

Davis, R. and R. G. Smith (1983). Negotiation as a Metaphor for Distributed Problem Solving. *Artificial Intelligence* **20**: 63-109.

Drexler, K. E. and M. S. Miller (1988). Incentive engineering for computational resource management. In (Huberman 1988) 231-266.

Hildenbrand, W. and A. P. Kirman (1976). *Introduction to Equilibrium Analysis: Variations on Themes by Edgeworth and Walras*. Amsterdam, North-Holland.

Huberman, B. A., Ed. (1988). The Ecology of Computation. North-Holland.

Koopmans, T. C. (1970). Uses of prices. *Scientific Papers of Tjalling C. Koopmans* Springer-Verlag. 243-257.

Kurose, J. F., and R. Simha (1989). A microeconomic approach to optimal resource allocation in distributed computer systems. *IEEE Trans. on Computers* **38**: 705-717.

Milgrom, P. and J. Roberts (1991). Adaptive and sophisticated learning in normal form games. *Games and Economic Behavior* **3**: 82-100.

Miller, M. S. and K. E. Drexler (1988). Markets and Computation: Agoric Open Systems. In (Huberman 1988) 133-176.

Mittal, S. and F. Frayman (1989). Towards a generic model of configuration tasks. *Proceedings of the Eleventh International Joint Conference on Artificial Intelligence*, Detroit, MI, Morgan Kaufmann.

Newell, A. (1982). The Knowledge Level. *Artificial Intelligence* **18**: 87-127.

Sandholm, T. (1993). An implementation of the contract net protocol based on marginal cost calculations. *Proceedings of the National Conference on Artificial Intelligence*, Washington, DC, AAAI Press.

Shoham, Y. (1993). Agent-oriented programming. *Artificial Intelligence* **60**: 51-92.

Shoven, J. B. and J. Whalley (1992). *Applying General Equilibrium*. Cambridge University Press.

Varian, H. R. (1984). *Microeconomic Analysis*. New York, W. W. Norton & Company.

Waldspurger, C. A., T. Hogg, B. A. Huberman, et al. (1992). Spawn: A distributed computational economy. *IEEE Transactions on Software Engineering* **18**: 103-117.

Wellman, M. P. (1993). A market-oriented programming environment and its application to distributed multicommodity flow problems. *Journal of Artificial Intelligence Research* **1**(1): 1-23.

Emergent Coordination through the Use of Cooperative State-Changing Rules

Claudia V. Goldman and **Jeffrey S. Rosenschein***
Computer Science Department
Hebrew University
Givat Ram, Jerusalem, Israel
clag@cs.huji.ac.il, jeff@cs.huji.ac.il

Abstract

Researchers in Distributed Artificial Intelligence have suggested that it would be worthwhile to isolate "aspects of cooperative behavior," general rules that cause agents to act in ways conducive to cooperation. One kind of cooperative behavior is when agents independently alter the environment to make it easier for everyone to function effectively. Cooperative behavior of this kind might be to put away a hammer that one finds lying on the floor, knowing that another agent will be able to find it more easily later on.

We examine the effect a specific "cooperation rule" has on agents in the multi-agent Tileworld domain. Agents are encouraged to increase tiles' degrees of freedom, even when the tile is not involved in an agent's own primary plan. The amount of extra work an agent is willing to do is captured in the agent's *cooperation level*. Results from simulations are presented. We present a way of characterizing domains as multi-agent deterministic finite automata, and characterizing cooperative rules as transformations of these automata. We also discuss general characteristics of cooperative state-changing rules. It is shown that a relatively simple, easily calculated rule can sometimes improve global system performance in the Tileworld. Coordination emerges from agents who use this rule of cooperation, without any explicit coordination or negotiation.

Introduction

Distributed Artificial Intelligence (DAI) is concerned with effective agent interactions, and the mechanisms by which these interactions can be achieved. Researchers in DAI have taken many approaches to this overall question, considering in particular explicit coordination and negotiation techniques (Smith 1978; Malone, Fikes, & Howard 1988; Kuwabara & Lesser 1989; Conry, Meyer, & Lesser 1988; Kreifelts & Martial 1990; Durfee 1988; Sycara 1988; 1989; Kraus & Wilkenfeld 1991; Zlotkin & Rosenschein 1993b; Ephrati & Rosenschein 1993), as well as implicit modeling of other

---

*This research has been partially supported by the Israeli Ministry of Science and Technology (Grant 032-8284).

agents' beliefs and desires (Genesereth, Ginsberg, & Rosenschein 1986; Gmytrasiewicz & Durfee 1992; Kraus 1993; Grosz & Kraus 1993).

There have also been repeated attempts by researchers to establish norms of cooperative behavior, general rules that would cause agents to act in ways conducive to cooperation. The search space for multi-agent action is large, and cooperative behavior on the part of agents would ideally act to limit this search space. These investigations into cooperative behavior have generally taken the approach of shaping agents' plans in particular directions, such that other agents could interact appropriately. An agent that acts predictably, shares its information, and defers globally constraining choices as long as possible, will be an easier one with which to coordinate. Work in this area includes early research by Davis and his colleagues at MIT (Davis 1981), and some of the RAND work on cooperative behavior in the air traffic control domain (McArthur, Steeb, & Cammarata 1982). Multi-agent reactive systems have also been analyzed, where solutions are arrived at dynamically by reactive agents (eco-agents) in multi-agent environments (Ferber & Drogoul 1992). More recently, Tennenholtz, Shoham, and Moses have considered how social laws for artificial agent societies could be developed and evaluated (Tennenholtz & Moses 1989; Shoham & Tennenholtz 1992b; 1992a).

While these streams of research have considered how agents' plans could be adapted to maximal cooperative effect, we take a different approach to the question. Instead of asking how an agent might temper its own goal-satisfying behavior to be cooperative, we ask how an agent might *transform the world* in a cooperative manner, at the same time that it is pursuing its own goal. We explore *cooperative state-changing rules*, that are imposed on the agents' behaviors as meta-rules. Those meta-rules don't have any influence on the primary actions that the agents are going to execute. Rather, they induce the agents to perform *extra work* that will transform the world into one in which the work of all agents might be done more easily.

Tileworld Interactions

The Domain

Consider agent interactions in a multi-agent version of the Tileworld (Pollack & Ringuette 1990). Agents can move only through navigable discrete squares; moving from one square to another costs one unit. Agents are programmed to roam the grid and push tiles into holes. In our simulations, we considered two ways in which agents decide which tile to go after. In one variation, they choose the closest (Euclidean distance) tile, compute and traverse their path to it, then push it to the hole that is closest to the tile (again, Euclidean distance). The computation of distance is a (lower-bound) heuristic, since it doesn't take into account barriers, other agents, and tiles (but it is quick to compute). In the second variation, agents are assigned tiles and holes arbitrarily by the programmer, and stop when they finish their assignments. This use of the Tileworld is non-standard, in that we are *not* focusing here on the architecture (reactive or otherwise) of the agents. Instead, we are using the Tileworld as an interesting, constrained domain that helps us understand implicit cooperative behavior.

Strongly-Coupled Interactions

The goals of separate agents in the multi-agent Tileworld are highly interconnected, primarily because the constraints on movement are so severe. Agents need to laboriously go around barriers to get into position and push a tile into a hole. Consider, for example, the simple interaction shown in Figure 1 (a variation of an example from (Zlotkin & Rosenschein 1993a)).

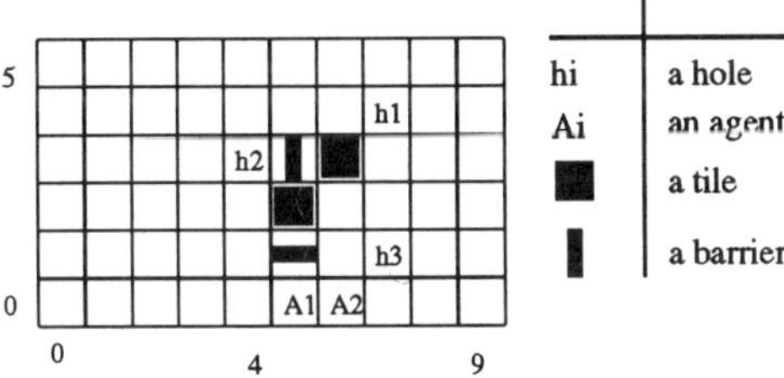

Figure 1: Strongly-Coupled Interactions

Assume that agent A_1 wants to fill holes 1 and 2, and that agent A_2 wants to fill holes 2 and 3 (perhaps the agents were assigned these goals *a priori*). For either agent to accomplish its goal, it would need to carry out a large number of movements to position the tiles and itself appropriately. For example, for A_1 to fill its holes alone, it needs to move 17 steps (assuming A_2 is not in its way). Similarly, A_2, alone in the world, would need to move 26 steps to fill its holes. However, if they work together, they can satisfy A_1 completely (and A_2 partially) by going 12 steps (or satisfy A_2 completely and A_1 partially).

The highly constrained nature of the multi-agent Tileworld provides ample opportunity for cooperative behavior, as the above example shows (e.g., one agent pushes a tile away from a barrier, while the other then pushes it perpendicularly). However, finding these multi-agent optimal plans tends to be a very difficult task. Instead, we examine the possibility that the cooperative behavior exhibited in the above example can be approximated by giving the agents an inclination towards sociable behavior. We will induce this kind of behavior through a meta-rule that causes the agents to help one another implicitly, without having to search for an optimal multi-agent plan. Ideally, when the agents are acting sociably, their combined activity will approach the optimal solution that they would have found had they carried out full multi-agent planning, but at a fraction of the computational cost.

A Rule for Sociable Behavior in the Tileworld

In general, a rule for sociable behavior can take several forms. In the simplest case, an agent may have two courses of action that he perceives as equivalent; if other agents would prefer him to carry out specifically one of those courses of action, he might do so in order to be cooperative. Sometimes, however, we may design agents to actually carry out extra work, to improve the environment for other agents (the amount of extra work subject to the designer's discretion). This latter kind of rule is the one that interests us here.

Obviously, if one designer is building all agents, as in a cooperative problem solving scenario, then such a cooperative meta-rule will have clear utility if it improves overall system performance. If separate designers, with separate goals, are building the agents, there may still be justification for their putting in such a meta-rule, under certain circumstances; however, we do not consider these issues (such as *stability* of the cooperative rule) in this paper.

In the Tileworld domain, it is better for every agent to have tiles freely movable, i.e., less constrained by barriers, so that tiles can be pushed into holes more easily. Each tile has a *degree of freedom* associated with it, the number of directions in which it can be pushed, either zero, two, or four. When we want agents to act cooperatively, we induce them to free tiles, by increasing the tiles' degree of freedom from two to four.

The key point in any given domain is to identify the state characteristics that allow goals to be achieved more easily. Cooperative agents are those that tend towards moving the world into these more conducive, less constrained configurations. In general, a world with more freed tiles is better than one that has constrained tiles. Although it may not be cheap for an agent to free a given tile, it may sometimes be possible to exert a small amount of extra effort, free a tile, and save another agent a large amount of work. In particular, if agent A_i is on its way to push a tile into a hole, and there is a constrained tile close by that can be freed, then the agent might free it.

This kind of cooperation does not require that the agents communicate, nor that they have a model of the other agents' specific plans, beliefs, or goals (though we do assume that agents know the current status of the grid). Cooperation will emerge out of the sociable behavior of the individual agents.

How much extra work should an agent be willing to do to act sociably? In our domain, how close does a constrained tile need to be for an agent to go out of its way and free it? In general, the *extra work* that the agent may do is the movement outside one of its minimal paths and back, so as to free a tile. We call this amount of extra work the *cooperation level* of the agent.

Simulations

We have run simulations using the MICE distributed agent testbed (Montgomery *et al.* 1992) to statistically analyze the efficacy of different cooperation levels (Hanks, Pollack, & Cohen 1993).

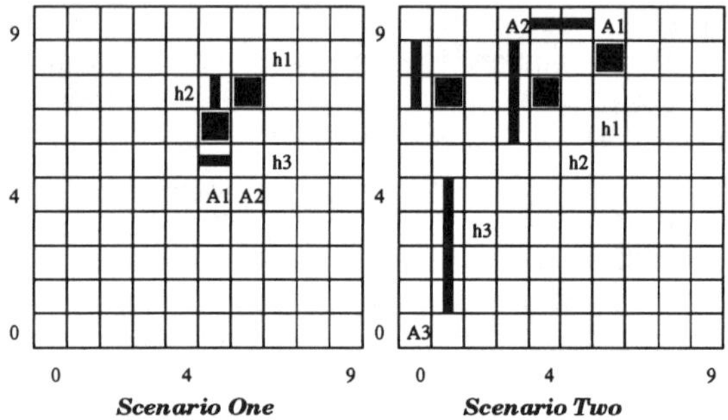

Figure 2: Simulations

In all the experiments, the agents have positive, static and predefined cooperation levels. At each tick of time, the agent tries to free a constrained tile that is different from the one it is pushing into a hole, such that the sum of the costs of the paths from the agent location to the constrained tile, freeing the tile, and going back to its original position (to continue with its original task) is not larger than its cooperation level.

We first discuss the impact of the cooperative rule, presented above, for two specific scenarios (see Figure 2). These are illustrative of general ways in which the rule can generate cooperative activity. Then we present additional results gathered from using the rule in randomly generated Tileworlds.

Scenario One: The aim of each agent in this example is to fill as many holes as it can. Both agents are by design trying to get to their closest tile. In the first scenario, the tiles are at a diagonal to their final holes; since agents can't push tiles diagonally, it is more efficient for one agent to position the tile while the other pushes it without any repositioning necessary. Here, A_2 positions both tiles (getting the "assist"), while A_1 actually does the work of pushing the tiles into the

holes. Total work: 11 for A_1 and 13 for A_2 (instead of 17 for each when there is no cooperative rule in force). It's important to emphasize that A_2 does not push tiles because it understands that A_1 will use them—it is simply using the cooperative rule (A_2 had a cooperation level of 2 for this scenario). The optimal solution, created perhaps by a central planner, would actually have saved the agents some work; that solution would consist of only 12 steps (5 for A_2 and 7 for A_1), but require a great deal more effort to find. In the optimal solution, A_2 does not run after tiles that A_1 eventually pushes into holes.

Scenario Two: In the second scenario, agents are blocked from their closest tiles by a barrier. As they move around the barrier, another agent prepares the target tile by pushing it to the end of the barrier. With A_1's cooperation level set at 8, A_2's level set at 4, and A_3's set at 0, the work is accomplished in 37 steps (as opposed to 48 for the non-cooperative solution). The extra work undertaken by A_1 benefits A_2; the extra work undertaken by A_2 benefits A_3. The optimal solution, more difficult to compute, takes 28 steps.

Experimental Results

We have run agent experiments on 74 randomly generated Tileworlds. All the worlds consisted of 4 agents, 6 holes, 6 tiles and 8 barriers. Each agent's primary goal is to push the closest tile into the closest hole. The worlds differed from one another by the length of the barriers (1–4) and by the locations of the agents, the holes, the tiles, and the barriers, all of which were determined randomly. We computed the number of steps that each agent carried out in pushing as many tiles as it could into the holes that were spread in an $11 * 11$ grid. The simulation stopped when there were no more tiles or holes left, or whenever the number of time ticks was 400. For each world, the agents' performance was tested with the agents being given cooperation level 0, cooperation level 1, and so on, up to and including cooperation level 8. In each of the 666 simulations (74 worlds by 9 cooperation levels), all agents were given the same cooperation level.

In 13 worlds, we found that the minimum number of steps done by the group of agents with some strictly positive cooperation level was less than the total work done by non-cooperative agents. In only 4 worlds was being cooperative actually harmful, i.e., agents cumulatively carried out more total steps to fill up the holes with any strictly positive cooperation level. In the other 57 worlds, the agents went the same number of steps when they behaved cooperatively and when they were given zero cooperation level. Therefore, in 17.56% of the worlds we tested, positive cooperation level was beneficial.

How confident can we be that this percentage reflects the real state of affairs for the overall space of worlds we were testing (i.e., 4 agents, 6 holes, etc.)? Using elementary statistical theory, we find that we can have 95% confidence that the error in probability will be less than 4.42% plus or minus for a sample size of 74 worlds (meaning we have 95% confidence that the real percentage of targeted worlds where a positive cooperation level is beneficial lies between 13.14% and 21.98%). Had we wanted to decrease the bound on the error of estimation to 2% plus or minus, we would have needed to exhaustively check 362 randomly generated worlds; to decrease the bound to 1% plus or minus, we would have needed to check 1448 worlds.[1]

The simulations were run with agents programmed to push the closest tile into the nearest hole; the chances that they would pass sufficiently close to *another* (constrained) tile to activate the cooperation rule were fairly small. Were the cooperation level sufficiently high, of course, an agent would wander far off his path to free tiles, but then it is likely that the overall performance of the group would decrease (since so much extra work is being squandered on cooperation). One can imagine other scenarios where the likelihood of finding tiles to free would be increased—for example, if the agents were sent to push arbitrary pre-assigned tiles (instead of the closest tile), and might pass other, closer, tiles on the way. In these cases, beneficial cooperation is likely to be more prevalent.

What is striking about the above, simple, experiment, is just how often a primitive, easy-to-calculate cooperative rule benefited the group as a whole. The improved performance was achieved without complicated computation or communication among the agents and the rule itself was easily identifiable for the domain. However, how would we, in general, discover suitable cooperative rules for different domains? The following section explores this question.

Cooperative Rule Taxonomy

Which kinds of rules can be designed for a given domain? Which domain characteristics are relevant for designing cooperative state-changing rules? We are interested in a general way of framing the problem of cooperative rules, that will make the analysis of a wide range of domains possible.

We define a *multi-agent deterministic finite automaton*, based on the standard definition of a deterministic finite automaton (Lewis & Papadimitriou 1981).

Definition .1 *A multi-agent deterministic finite automaton (MADFA) is a quintuple $M = (K, \Sigma, \overline{\delta}, s, F)$:*
- *K is a finite set of states, the set of the multi-agent world states,*
- *Σ is an alphabet. The letters are the actions that the agents can take,*

$\overline{\delta} : K \times \overline{\Sigma} \to K$ *is the transition function. $\overline{\Sigma}$ denotes (multi-agent) vectors of Σ (i.e., multi-agent actions),*
- *s is the initial state of the multi-agent world,*
- *$F \subseteq K$ is the set of final states where all the agents' goals are achieved.*

The language accepted by the *multi-agent deterministic finite automaton* is defined as the set of all the vector strings it accepts. For example, a word in the Tileworld domain, with three agents, could be $\{\{$north,south,east$\}$ $\{$north,west,nil$\}\}$, north $\in \Sigma$, $\{$north, south, east$\} \in \overline{\Sigma}$. We consider two related multi-agent automata for each domain. One describes the domain in general, i.e., all the possible states and transitions that can exist in a given domain (it will be denoted by GMADFA). The second is a sub-automaton of the first, that includes only those states and transitions permitted by the agents' actual programmed behavior (that is, the sub-automaton includes only those potential transitions that might actually occur, given the way agents are programmed to act; agents may still have a choice at run-time, but the sub-automaton includes all choices they might make. It will be denoted by SMADFA.). The specific initial and final states might change for different examples, but the same architecture can be studied to find cooperative rules regardless of the details of the examples. Assuming that the rule designer has sufficient information about the domain, he can formulate these two automata that describe the domain in general and the agents' potential behavior within the domain, and use the automata to deduce appropriate cooperative rules.

The corresponding automata for two distinct domains follow:
The Tileworld SMADFA — K is the set of grid configurations of the Tileworld. $\Sigma = \{$ nil,south,east,north,west$\}$. F is the set of states in which holds ((#tiles with degree of freedom > 0) $= 0$) $\bigvee$ (#holes $= 0$).
The FileWorld SMADFA — The FileWorld domain consists of agents whose goals are to write to and read from shared files. Whenever an agent performs an action that accesses the file, the file is locked for the other agents (i.e., they can't access it). $\Sigma = \{$*pass-lock, read, write*$\}$. One agent, having the lock, can perform the write or read action and move the world into another state in which it can continue writing or reading indefinitely. If the agent performs *pass-lock*, then the lock is passed to another agent.

The Cooperative State-Changing Rules

The purpose of a cooperative state-changing rule is to enable agents to improve the world by moving it into a state in which the agents' work will be easier. One way to make the agents' work easier is to shorten the possible paths in SMADFA leading from an initial state to a final state. A problem domain considered as an automaton can help a rule designer deduce useful cooperative rules. The rules then can be applied to dif-

---

ferent specific problems. For example, the cooperative
rule found for the Tileworld above can be imposed on
the agents in different specific scenarios. The given
initial state of a particular Tileworld example doesn't
matter, nor does it matter what the specific goals of
each agent are; the analysis of how to improve agents'
performance looks at the general actions that they can
execute in the domain. We can shorten the words in
three different ways (i.e., three categories of cooperative state-changing rules) by changing the SMADFA:

1. **Find a shortcut** by using the existing actions in
the alphabet; i.e., look at GMADFA, at possible states
and transitions, that were not included in SMADFA,
and add them to it,

2. **Find a shortcut** by adding to the alphabet new
actions that the agents are capable of doing,

3. **Cut loops** by minimizing the times the agents can
be in a loop. We might choose to parameterize the
actions; thus, cutting loops could be expressed by a
change to Σ, (i.e., to the parameter that indicates the
number of times the specific action can be taken).

The sociability rule presented for the Tileworld is of
the first kind above—it finds a shortcut using existing
actions, since the agents' original actions include the
push action. Adding "extra work" to the Tileworld
SMADFA means to explore other states and transitions to them such that paths from the initial state to
a final state can be shorter.

Passing the lock so that other agents will also have
access to a file can be a cooperative state-changing
rule for the FileWorld. This rule is of the third kind;
it cuts a loop created by an agent who goes on reading
or writing to a file. The FileWorld SMADFA can be
modified by setting a limit to the number of characters
that an agent can read from or write to a file before
handing over the lock.

To develop appropriate rules for different domains,
and to be able to evaluate these rules, we present below some general characteristics that may prove useful
in creating cooperative state-changing rules:

state dependent — a rule is *state dependent* if the
extra work that needs to be done can only be accomplished in specific states. For example, in the Tileworld a tile can be freed only if there is a constrained
tile and there is an agent with appropriate cooperation
level that could free it. Therefore, the rule we proposed
above for the Tileworld is state dependent.

guaranteed — a rule is *guaranteed* if there is certain
to be no harm (no increased global work) by executing
it. In the Tileworld, the rule we presented is not *guaranteed*, because the direction to which the tile is freed
is heuristically computed. In the FileWorld, given that
an agent has returned its lock, it is guaranteed that any
other agent could use it and hence benefit from it.

reversible — a rule is *reversible* if its effects can be undone. The Tileworld rule is reversible, since any agent
can push a freed tile to be next to a barrier again. In
contrast, adding information to what is known by a

group of agents might be irreversible.

redundant — a rule is *redundant* if performing the
extra work encompassed in the rule might cause the
agents to stay in the same state. Consider, for example, the StudyWorld, in which the agents are students.
One of the possible actions to be performed by an agent
is to borrow a book from the library. In this world, a
cooperative rule might consist of a student leaving a
summary of the book he has borrowed from the library. In this case, the same summary might be left
again by another student, making the rule redundant.

resource dependent — a rule is *resource dependent*
if following it implies the use of consumable resources
(e.g., filling the printer tray with paper, although you
don't have to print).

Conclusions

We have presented a "rule of cooperative behavior"
that can sometimes improve overall system performance in the multi-agent Tileworld. Agents are encouraged to move tiles away from barriers (even when
these tiles do not contribute to their primary goal),
as long as the amount of extra work required is not
too great. The addition of this implicitly cooperative
behavior does not require a great deal of extra computation on the part of agents, nor any communication
whatsoever. Cooperation emerges cheaply from agents
acting sociably, without the overhead of negotiation or
coordination. Simulations were run that illustrated the
benefits of this emergent cooperation. Although unlikely to produce optimal behavior (except by chance),
the cooperative rule can improve performance in a non-
trivial number of instances.

We have also shown how a world can be characterized by mapping it onto an automaton. We identified
three kinds of cooperative state-changing rules that can
be modeled as changes to the automaton.

The principle of cooperative behavior extends to arbitrary domains, where system designers can identify
aspects of global states that are generally desirable.
In the Tileworld, it is generally desirable that tiles be
unconstrained by barriers. In the blocks world, it is
generally desirable that blocks be clear. The designers
of agents can benefit by manufacturing rules of sociable behavior that encourage agents to carry out state
transformations that tend to be socially desirable.

Future research will examine benefits to the system
when the cooperation level of agents changes dynamically over time (for example, as a penalty mechanism
aimed at uncooperative agents), how the subdivision of
labor might also be affected by cooperative meta-rules,
other criteria for qualifying cooperative rules, and stable sociability rules for multi-agent systems. We are
also interested in looking for ananlytical ways to evaluate the cooperation level for a given domain. One
way is to look at the cost of a task when the agents
cooperate as a function of the cost of the original task,
and to find the cooperation level that minimizes the

new cost. Another way is to regard the cooperative behavior as a perturbation of the distribution of the amount of work performed by zero-cooperative agents.

References

Conry, S. E.; Meyer, R. A.; and Lesser, V. R. 1988. Multistage negotiation in distributed planning. In Bond, A. H., and Gasser, L., eds., *Readings in Distributed Artificial Intelligence*. San Mateo, California: Morgan Kaufmann Publishers, Inc. 367–384.

Davis, R. 1981. A model for planning in a multi-agent environment: steps toward principles for teamwork. Working Paper 217, Massachusetts Institute of Technology AI Laboratory.

Durfee, E. H. 1988. *Coordination of Distributed Problem Solvers*. Boston: Kluwer Academic Publishers.

Ephrati, E., and Rosenschein, J. S. 1993. Multi-agent planning as a dynamic search for social consensus. In *Proceedings of the Thirteenth International Joint Conference on Artificial Intelligence*, 423–429.

Ferber, J., and Drogoul, A. 1992. Using reactive multi-agent systems in simulation and problem solving. In Avouris, N. M., and Gasser, L., eds., *Distributed Artificial Intelligence: Theory and Praxis*. Kluwer Academic Press. 53–80.

Genesereth, M. R.; Ginsberg, M. L.; and Rosenschein, J. S. 1986. Cooperation without communication. In *Proceedings of the National Conference on Artificial Intelligence*, 51–57.

Gmytrasiewicz, P., and Durfee, E. H. 1992. A logic of knowledge and belief for recursive modeling: Preliminary report. In *Proceedings of the Tenth National Conference on Artificial Intelligence*, 628–634.

Grosz, B., and Kraus, S. 1993. Collaborative plans for group activities. In *Proceedings of the Thirteenth International Joint Conference on Artificial Intelligence*, 367–373.

Hanks, S.; Pollack, M. E.; and Cohen, P. R. 1993. Benchmarks, test beds, controlled experimentation, and the design of agent architectures. *AI Magazine* 17–42.

Kraus, S., and Wilkenfeld, J. 1991. Negotiations over time in a multi agent environment: Preliminary report. In *Proceedings of the Twelfth International Joint Conference on Artificial Intelligence*, 56–61.

Kraus, S. 1993. Agents contracting tasks in noncollaborative environments. In *Proceedings of the Eleventh National Conference on Artificial Intelligence*, 243–248.

Kreifelts, T., and Martial, F. 1990. A negotiation framework for autonomous agents. In *Proceedings of the Second European Workshop on Modeling Autonomous Agents and Multi-Agent Worlds*, 169–182.

Kuwabara, K., and Lesser, V. R. 1989. Extended protocol for multistage negotiation. In *Proceedings of the Ninth Workshop on Distributed Artificial Intelligence*, 129–161.

Lewis, H. R., and Papadimitriou, C. H. 1981. *Elements of the theory of computation*. Prentice-Hall, Inc.

Malone, T.; Fikes, R.; and Howard, M. 1988. Enterprise: A market-like task scheduler for distributed computing environments. In Huberman, B. A., ed., *The Ecology of Computation*. Amsterdam: North-Holland Publishing Company. 177–205.

McArthur, D.; Steeb, R.; and Cammarata, S. 1982. A framework for distributed problem solving. In *Proceedings of the National Conference on Artificial Intelligence*, 181–184.

Montgomery, T. A.; Lee, J.; Musliner, D. J.; Durfee, E. H.; Damouth, D.; and So, Y. 1992. *MICE Users Guide*. Artificial Intelligence Laboratory, Department of Electrical Engineering and Computer Science, University of Michigan, Ann Arbor, Michigan.

Pollack, M. E., and Ringuette, M. 1990. Introducing the Tileworld: Experimentally evaluating agent architectures. In *Proceedings of The National Conference on Artificial Intelligence*, 183–189.

Shoham, Y., and Tennenholtz, M. 1992a. Emergent conventions in multi-agent systems: initial experimental results and observations (preliminary report). In *Principles of knowledge representation and reasoning: Proceedings of the Third International Conference(KR92)*.

Shoham, Y., and Tennenholtz, M. 1992b. On the synthesis of useful social laws for artificial agent societies (preliminary report). In *Proceedings of the Tenth National Conference on Artificial Intelligence*.

Smith, R. G. 1978. *A Framework for Problem Solving in a Distributed Processing Environment*. Ph.D. Dissertation, Stanford University.

Sycara, K. 1988. Resolving goal conflicts via negotiation. In *Proceedings of the Seventh National Conference on Artificial Intelligence*, 245–250.

Sycara, K. 1989. Argumentation: Planning other agents' plans. In *Proceedings of the Eleventh International Joint Conference on Artificial Intelligence*, 517–523.

Tennenholtz, M., and Moses, Y. 1989. On cooperation in a multi-entity model. In *Proceedings of the Eleventh International Joint Conference on Artificial Intelligence*, 918–923.

Zlotkin, G., and Rosenschein, J. S. 1993a. Compromise in negotiation: Exploiting worth functions over states. Technical Report 93–3, Leibniz Center for Computer Science, Hebrew University.

Zlotkin, G., and Rosenschein, J. S. 1993b. A domain theory for task oriented negotiation. In *Proceedings of the Thirteenth International Joint Conference on Artificial Intelligence*, 416–422.

Forming Coalitions in the Face of Uncertain Rewards

Steven Ketchpel

Stanford University
Computer Science Department
Stanford CA, 94305
ketchpel@cs.stanford.edu

Abstract

When agents are in an environment where they can interact with each other, groups of agents may agree to work together for the benefit of all the members of the group. Finding these coalitions of agents and determining how the joint reward should be divided among them is a difficult problem. This problem is aggravated when the agents have different estimates of the value that the coalition will obtain. A "two agent auction" mechanism is suggested to complement an existing coalition formation algorithm for solving this problem.

1. The Problem

Given a set of agents with different abilities and different information, there may be many opportunities for cooperation among the agents that will benefit all. Even more likely is the chance that a *coalition* can form, a subset of the agents working together, benefiting each agent in the group perhaps at the expense of the community as a whole. An agent following the economic principle of rationality will attempt to form a coalition which will maximize its own utility. However, the other agents in these coalitions will have their own preferences, and a complicated cycle of dependencies emerges. Agents only want to commit to a coalition once all of the other agents have committed. The final division of the agents into coalitions should be *stable* in the sense that no subset of the agents could leave their current coalitions to form a new one yielding all of the agents in that new coalition a higher utility than they obtain from their previous coalitions.

For example, imagine there are a number of people interested in starting new hi-tech companies. There are

The research was partially supported by a National Defense Science and Engineering Graduate Fellowship. The ideas contained within do not necessarily reflect the position or the policy of the Government and no official endorsement should be inferred.

many possible combinations of people that could work together, but getting them to commit to form a new company is difficult. A scientist with a hot new product idea doesn't want to commit unless a company has the necessary start-up capital. But financial backers typically require a thorough evaluation of the product and prefer a company president who has clout in the industry. The president may have reservations about working with certain financial officers, and so on. Even after the involved parties do agree to work together, bargaining over how to share the profits can reveal diverging perceptions about the relative importance of the different contributors. The coalition formation process, in this context, would describe which people should work together to start new companies and would also suggest a way to divide the profits among the partners. Stability in this scenario would mean that it would be unprofitable for one company to hire away workers from another, and there is no incentive for workers to get together (possibly with people from other companies) to start a new company.

To evaluate a system formally, the agents $a_1,...,a_N$ are divided into a partition P containing coalitions $C_1,...,C_M$ such that every agent is a member of exactly one coalition. The payoff to an agent is a function u(P, a) of both the partition and the agent. For P to be stable, there must not be any other partition P' forming coalitions $C'_1,..., C'_M$ such that $\exists C'_i \in P' \; \forall a_j \in C'_i \; u(P', a_j) > u(P, a_j)$. If there were such a C'_i, the agents of that coalition would desert their current coalitions and form C'_i.

Determining how to divide the utility among the agents in the coalition is a problem that has received some attention in both game theory and distributed AI. A summary of the related research appears in Section 2. Many of these sources make the assumption that the value of any coalition is common knowledge. In game theoretic terms, there is a valuation function $v: 2^A \to \Re$, which takes any possible subset of the agent pool A, and returns a real value representing the utility which is split among the members of the coalition. For the sake of simplicity, we assume that this utility is paid by an entity outside the system of agents, and that none of the agents have any inherent interest in achieving the goals, beyond merely fulfilling the contract to receive payment. The main contribution of this paper is to examine the case where the agents do not have access to this function, but instead have different expectations about the value.

Section 3 analyzes one of the most widely used division mechanisms, the Shapley value, and its inherent problems. Section 4 proposes an alternative approach which does not make the common knowledge assumption. The "Two Agent Auction" mechanism and the properties proved about it constitute the original research contribution. Section 5 concludes with directions for further research.

2. Related Research

At the 1993 European Workshop on "Modeling Autonomous Agents in a Multi-Agent World", three papers on coalition formation were presented [(Ketchpel 1993), (Shechory & Kraus 1993), (Zlotkin & Rosenschein 1993)]. The last two assumed super-additive domains in which adding an additional agent to a coalition can never reduce the utility of that coalition. Zlotkin and Rosenschein (Zlotkin & Rosenschein 1993) made the further stipulation that utility was not directly transferable between agents. All three papers assumed that the agents had common knowledge of the value function of the game and advocated the use of the Shapley value to divide the utility among the members of the coalition.

There is another body of literature in economics which addresses the division of goods or costs among the members of a society. Raiffa includes a chapter in his book (Raiffa 1982) on fair division and includes an analysis where the involved parties place different values on the goods to be divided. Ephrati and Rosenschein (Ephrati & Rosenschein 1991) use another device from economics known as the Clarke tax to allocate costs among multiple agents deciding among alternatives, charging each agent only in proportion to the amount it changed the group decision. The WALRAS system (Wellman 1993) uses a market scheme to reach an equilibrium among buyers and sellers of a commodity in the context of distributed action. However, none of these works analyzes the possibility of collusion by a coalition. This paper attempts to unite these two strands of research.

3. The Shapley Value and its Problems

The function u(P, a) determines the amount of utility that agent a receives from its membership in its coalition in P. It is assumed that the distribution is efficient and no utility is lost in the division, so $\sum_{a \in C} u(P, a) = v(C)$. There have been a number of suggestions for such a distribution function u(P, a). One of the earliest and most widely used is due to Shapley (Shapley 1953). The Shapley value is calculated by looking at each of the different dynamics that could lead to the coalition under consideration. Agents either "found" a coalition if they are the initial member, or else join a coalition founded by another member. The permutations of the members in the coalition is the set of

formation dynamics. Each permutation describes an order in which the coalition could have been formed. Each agent adds value to a given formation process based on the marginal utility contributed by that agent. For example, if agent A is joining agents B, C, and D, and $v(ABCD) = 100$ and $v(BCD) = 60$, then A's marginal contribution under this formation ordering is $v(ABCD) - v(BCD) = 40$. If agent A joins a coalition started by B, and they are subsequently joined by agents C and D, A's marginal contribution is $v(AB) - v(B)$. There are 22 other permutations that also might lead to the final coalition ABCD. By averaging A's marginal contribution across all the different formation possibilities, A's Shapley value is obtained. The underlying assumption is that all of the different formation processes are equally likely and, therefore, the marginal contributions for each formation are weighted equally. This calculation ensures that the sum of the Shapley values for all of the members of the coalition will be exactly the coalition's combined utility.

The Shapley value has several disadvantages. First, the most efficient known calculation is exponential, though efficient means to calculate the expectation of the Shapley value over a large number of interactions are known. (Zlotkin & Rosenschein 1994). Second, it assumes common knowledge of the value that the coalition will obtain if it works as a unit. In more realistic assessments, each agent might have a different expectation for the value of the collaboration.

To address these uncertainties more realistically, the value function should be dependent on which agent is performing the determination. That is, for two agents A and B, $v_A(AB)$, A's estimate of the value of coalition AB is not necessarily equal to B's estimate $v_B(AB)$, and both of these values may differ from the utility that will actually result from the coalition, which is denoted $v(AB)$ (and is the same $v(AB)$ used above). The potential disparity between these values (the actual utility and the various agents' estimates of it) opens up a further problem. One agent may overestimate the value, and promise its potential coalition partner a "share" of utility larger than the total obtained by the whole coalition. When the obtained utility fails to meet the rosy predictions of the optimistic agent, who is penalized?

4. Coalition Formation Using a Two Agent Auction

The problem that we are attempting to solve is two-fold: first, to determine coalitions of agents that will work together; second, to decide how to reward the agents, that is, what payment each agent will receive. These problems are complicated because the search space is very large (an exponential number of coalitions) and there are many dependencies among the decisions. For example, an agent's offer to join a coalition may depend on the agents already in the coalition, the amount of the offer, offers from other coalitions, and the future prospects of this coalition's merging with other coalitions. Finally, the agents may have different perceptions about the value of collaboration and their respective contributions to the group's outcome. The solution that we outline simplifies the problem along several dimensions, which we hope to address in future work.

The basic model that we assume is an economic one of rational agents entering into contracts that specify guaranteed payments. The agents may have different bargaining power due to their relative contributions to coalitions, but we assume that they all play symmetric roles in the bargaining process. The prescribed process consists of the following steps:

1. Agents exchange initial offers to other available agents. These offers will lead to a possible agreement and contract among the agents.
2. Agents evaluate the offers they received, and rank them in order of preference, based on their expected profit.
3. Using these preference orderings, the agents attempt to pair off into coalitions of size 2 with the most attractive potential partners.
4. The newly formed pairs enter a "two agent auction" that makes one agent the manager, bearing the risk and given the opportunity to bargain on behalf of the pair in future negotiations. The non-managing agent receives a fixed payment for its role in the coalition. The final agreement price is a function of the initial offers and the agents' valuations of the collaborative effort.
5. The process repeats, with the pairs formed in one round playing the role of individual agents in the next.

4.1. A Coalition Formation Algorithm

In previous work (Ketchpel 1993), we noted that the coalition formation problem is related to the stable marriage problem (Gusfield & Irving 1989). In the stable marriage problem, an equal number of men and women seek mates. Each participant has a preference ordering among the candidates, and a stable matching is generated when each man is paired with a woman and there is no blocking pair of a man and woman that prefer to be paired with each other to being paired with their current partners. A stable matching may be found for any instance of the problem in time $O(n^2)$ where n is the number of people involved.

The coalition formation process for coalitions of size 2 is equivalent to a variant of the stable marriage problem known as the stable roommate problem with unacceptable partners. In the stable roommate problem, the two classes of men and women are conflated to a single class, agents. When unacceptable partners are allowed, an agent prefers being unpaired to being paired with certain other agents. A pairing which matches any agent with an unacceptable partner is inherently unstable. Centralized versions of the stable roommate problem with unacceptable partners find stable matchings (when they exist) in time $O(n^2)$.

However, in a setting of autonomous, distrustful agents, a centralized algorithm is not a viable solution. In

(Ketchpel 1993), a decentralized alternative is proposed. The modified algorithm is a greedy process where each agent proceeds down its preference list extending an offer to the top agent it hasn't previously asked, accepting offers that improve its utility, and rejecting all others. At the end of a round, all of the pairs form proto-coalitions, which may join other proto-coalitions in the future. They select one of the members to act as the head of the coalition. In the subsequent rounds, the process repeats, with each coalition head extending offers to the heads of other coalitions and to agents that have not yet been paired. The process repeats until no new associations are formed. The algorithm takes time $O(n^3)$ for n agents. Although stability is not guaranteed, an agent will never settle for a less desirable coalition partner unless all of the better alternatives (taking the previous rounds of formation as given) have turned it down once already. Even if the other possible partners have turned it down in the past, they may later be willing to accept such a coalition. The agent will never approach these possible partners again, so unstable pairings may form. For a more complete description and complexity analysis, see (Ketchpel 1993).

4.2. The Two Agent Auction

One mechanism to solve the division of utility in the face of uncertainty is to assign one of the agents responsibility for managing the group actions. The manager is required to meet the offers that it extended to the various coalition members, even if the coalition's actual utility were less than expected. In exchange for undertaking this risk, the managing agent would receive all of the utility accruing to the coalition, and would earn a profit if this amount were greater than the salaries it paid. Also, as the manager, it has the authority to negotiate on behalf of the group to form larger coalitions.

The algorithm described in Section 4.1 has the property that each of the proto-coalitions has exactly two entities (which may be agents or coalitions). Therefore, each of the auctions occurs between two agents, the managers of the coalitions that are merging. The two managing agents A and B begin the bargaining process using the initial offers that they extended to each other when the preference lists for the previous step were made. These offers will not necessarily add up to either agent's estimate of $v(AB)$, nor need they total the actual $v(AB)$ value. The offers are adjusted according to the method described below and summarized in Figure 1. The two agents are guaranteed to converge on an agreeable value. The non-managing agent gets this agreed value, regardless of the actual utility of the coalition. The managing agent receives the balance of the utility obtained by the group. We use $O(A, B)$ to represent the amount of the initial offer which agent A extended to agent B; similarly, $O(B, A)$ is B's initial offer to A.

In selecting the agent to be the manager, there are four cases that may occur:

1. Both agents A and B want to be the manager, based on the offers and their beliefs about the actual value of the collaboration. So, $v_A(AB) - O(A, B) > O(B, A)$ and

$v_B(AB) - O(B, A) > O(A, B)$. The agents reach agreement through an ascending auction.

2. Agent A wants to be the manager, and agent B is happy to agree. So, $v_A(AB) - O(A, B) > O(B, A)$ and $v_B(AB) - O(B, A) \leq O(A, B)$. In this case, A is selected to be the manager.

3. Symmetric to 2, with B wanting to be the manager.

4. Neither agent wants to be the manager, because both expect better payoffs if the other agent is the manager. So, $v_A(AB) - O(A, B) \leq O(B, A)$ and $v_B(AB) - O(B, A) \leq O(A, B)$. The agents reach agreement by entering a descending auction.

In the first case, there needs to be further negotiation over who will manage the contract. To settle the difference, both agents incrementally increase their offers to the other coalition agent until one or the other is willing to forgo the opportunity to be the manager. In essence, the two agents are "bidding" for the right to manage the contract.

```
BEGIN.
  k := 0. /*k is number of rounds of negotiation conducted*/
  δ := 1. /*δ is "precision" of negotiation*/
  IF  v_A(AB) - O(A, B) > O(B, A)
         AND v_B(AB) - O(B, A) > O(A, B)
    I := +1.     /*Reduce Case 1 to 2 or 3*/
      WHILE ((v_A(AB) - (O(A, B) + I*k*δ) > (O(B, A) + I*k*δ)
             AND v_B(AB) - (O(B, A) +I*k*δ)> (O(A, B)+ I*k*δ))
        k := k + 1.
      END-WHILE.
  ELSE
    IF v_A(AB) - O(A, B) ≤ O(B, A)
         AND v_B(AB) - O(B, A) ≤ O(A, B))
      I := -1.     /*Reduce Case 4 to 2 or 3*/
      WHILE ((v_A(AB) - (O(A,B) + I*k*δ)<(O(B,A)+ I*k*δ)
             AND v_B(AB) - (O(B,A) + I*k*δ) ≤ O(A,B) + I*k*δ))
        k := k +1.
      END-WHILE.
    END-IF.
  END-IF.

  IF v_A(AB) - (O(A, B) + I*k*δ) ≥ O(B, A) + I*k*δ
    A is manager, B gets O(A, B).+ I*k*δ     /*Case 2*/
  ELSE
    B is manager, A gets O(B, A)+ I*k*δ     /*Case 3*/
  END-IF.
END.
```

Figure 1: Algorithm for selecting manager & determining utility division

In the ascending auction called for in the first case, at each iteration of the WHILE loop in Figure 1, both agents increase their offers by δ. The bidding stops when either agent finds that the "opposing" agent (although they are coalition partners, they are competing with each other to maximize individual shares of the joint gain) has extended an offer that is greater than it would expect if it managed the contract. Note that there is some asymmetry in the roles of the agents. In one case the test is a strict inequality, while in the other case, the test is less than or equal to. We arbitrarily select the agent that initiates the proposal to be agent A.

In the fourth case in which neither agent wants to be the manager, the agents enter an auction situation similar to case 1, but instead of incrementing their offers, they decrement them. At some point one of the agents will decide that with this new lower offer, it is better to accept the managing role than the small amount just promised by the other agent. This agent is made the manager, and its last offer is considered the agreement value.

As an example, assume that agents A and B have agreed to form a coalition, and are trying to determine the distribution of the utility from the joint effort. Agent A expects that the value of the outcome will be 100, so $v_A(AB) = 100$. Agent A realizes that agent B is doing a larger share of the work, so is willing to offer agent B a larger share of the utility, in this case, $O(A, B) = 60$. Agent B is more pessimistic about the expected outcome of their joint effort, expecting only 80 units of utility $v_B(AB) = 80$. Agent B thinks that agent A's contribution is minimal and is only willing to give agent A 15 units, $O(B, A) = 15$. The case analysis outlined above shows that this example falls in the first case, and both agents A and B want to manage the contract. Agent A's expected profit if it is the manager is 40 $(v_A(AB) - O(A, B))$; if A accepts B's offer, A will only obtain 15. Agent B carries out a similar analysis and sees that its expected return of 65 if it manages the contract $(v_B(AB) - O(B, A))$ exceeds A's offer of 60. At this point, the negotiation enters the stage of incrementally increasing offers. The progress of these iterative offers is shown in Figure 2. At round 3, B determines that it expects to get more if it allows A to manage the contract, so A is obligated to pay B 63 units of utility when B accomplishes its share of the work, and agent A will get the actual amount $v(AB)$. If this amount is less than 63, A still must pay B the promised 63 units. If $v(AB)$ is less than 81, then A would have been better off accepting B's offer of 18, rather than receiving $v(AB)$ while paying agent B 63.

	A's Expected Value if:		B's Expected Value if:	
	__A manages__	__B manages__	__B manages__	__A manages__
k	$v_A(AB) - O(A, B)$ $- k * \delta$	$O(B, A)$ $+ k * \delta$	$v_B(AB) - O(B, A)$ $- k * \delta$	$O(A, B)$ $+ k * \delta$
1	39	16	64	61
2	38	17	63	62
3	37	18	62	63

Figure 2: Sequence of offers between agents

4.3 Analysis of the Two Agent Auction

Although the negotiation is described above in an incremental process, the result is deterministic. The agent with the higher estimate of $v(AB)$ always becomes the manager, as is shown in Figure 3. Moreover, Theorem 2 in Figure 4 shows that the agreement price is also determined by the initial offers and valuations. If the agents are willing to share their estimates of $v(AB)$ with their initial offers, they can directly calculate the differences between the evaluations of the agents' contributions and determine which agent should be the manager and what the final offer to the non-managing agent should be. If the $v(AB)$ estimates are not shared, the iterative method described above will yield the same result, though the manager's estimate of $v(AB)$ will never become public knowledge. The choice of incremental versus direct calculation is dependent on the domain, and the tradeoff between the benefit of privacy of information against the cost of more communication.

Theorem 1: Between two agents A and B, the one with the higher valuation of $v(AB)$ will always win the managing role.

The auction stops after k rounds, when either:
1) $O(B, A) + k*\delta > v_A(AB) - (O(A, B) + k*\delta)$; B manages
or
2) $O(A, B) + k*\delta \geq v_B(AB) - (O(B, A) + k*\delta)$; A manages

If (1) is the reason for stopping,
    (1a) $O(B, A) + k*\delta > v_A(AB) - (O(A, B) + k*\delta)$
and (1b) $O(A, B) + k*\delta < v_B(AB) - (O(B, A) + k*\delta)$

Adding $k*\delta$ to both sides of 1a and 1b,

  (1a') $O(B, A) + 2*k*\delta > v_A(AB) - O(A, B)$
  (1b') $O(A, B) + 2*k*\delta < v_B(AB) - O(B, A)$

Adding $O(A, B)$ to both sides of (1a')
    and $O(B, A)$ to both sides of (1b')

  (1a") $O(A, B) + O(B, A) + 2*k*\delta > v_A(AB)$
  (1b") $O(A, B) + O(B, A) + 2*k*\delta < v_B(AB)$

By transitivity of 1a" and 1b"
  $v_A(AB) < v_B(AB)$, and in (1), B is the manager

If (2) is the reason for stopping,
    (2a) $O(B, A) + k*\delta \leq v_A(AB) - (O(A, B) + k*\delta)$
and (2b) $O(A, B) + k*\delta > v_B(AB) - (O(B, A) + k*\delta)$

Proof proceeds as above, replacing the strict inequality with non-strict inequality, yielding,

  $v_B(AB) \leq v_A(AB)$, and in case 2, A is the manager

So, in both cases, the agent with the higher estimate of $v(AB)$ is the manager.

Figure 3: Agent with higher estimate of $v(AB)$ is manager

Theorem 2: The agreement price (AP) will be within δ of

$$\frac{O(M,N) + v_N(MN) - O(N,M)}{2}$$, where M is the manager, N is the other (non-managing) agent.

The auction will stop in round k when

$$O(M, N) + k*d \geq v_N(MN) - (O(N,M) + k*\delta)$$
$$O(M, N) + 2*k*\delta \geq v_N(MN) - O(N,M)$$
$$2*k*\delta \geq v_N(MN) - O(N,M) - O(M, N)$$

$$k = \left\lceil \frac{v_N(MN) - O(N,M) - O(M,N)}{2*\delta} \right\rceil$$

The offer after k rounds of negotiation is $O(M, N) + k*\delta$.

$$AP = O(M,N) + \left\lceil \frac{v_N(MN) - O(N,M) - O(M,N)}{2*\delta} \right\rceil * \delta$$

$$O(M,N) + \frac{v_N(MN) - O(N,M) - O(M,N)}{2*\delta} * \delta \leq AP, \text{ and}$$

$$AP < O(M,N) + \left(\frac{v_N(MN) - O(N,M) - O(M,N)}{2*\delta} + 1 \right) * \delta$$

$$\frac{O(M,N) + v_N(MN) - O(N,M)}{2} \leq AP, \text{ and}$$

$$AP < \frac{O(M,N) + v_N(MN) - O(N,M)}{2} + \delta.$$

So, AP is within δ of $\dfrac{O(M,N) + v_N(MN) - O(N,M)}{2}$

Figure 4: Agreement price is function of offers and $v(AB)$ estimates

4.4. Selecting Initial Offers

The agreement price that is reached is a function of the initial offers and the estimates of $v(AB)$ as Figure 4 shows. From the final value, it appears that both agents will extend initial offers of 0. The agreement price increases with $O(M, N)$, the initial offer of the manager to the non-manager. Therefore, an initial offer of 0 would minimize the agreement price with respect to this variable. Likewise, the agreement price decreases as the offer of the non-manager to the manager increases, so an initial offer of 0 would maximize the agreement price. However, this analysis is too simplified. The initial offers play a second role in the coalition formation process, namely determining the preference lists. Therefore, the agents need to extend sufficiently high offers to each other to ensure that the other agent will agree to form a coalition. The auction mechanism (and the desire to minimize the initial offers) is only needed <u>after</u> two agents have agreed to form a coalition. In order to select an optimal initial offer, agents need to take into account expectations about the offers that other agents will make. This game theoretic analysis requires more complicated machinery that is beyond the scope of this paper, and is grounds for future research.

5. Conclusion and Future Research

This paper has described a utility distribution mechanism designed to perform in situations where there is uncertainty in the utility that a coalition obtains. The two agent auction is shown to have certain properties: first, the agent valuing the collaboration more highly is always selected manager; second, the agreement price is a deterministic function of the agent's initial offers and estimates of the value of collaboration.

A logical next step would be to further develop the game theoretic aspects of this model. First, the agents need additional information to strategically make their initial offers. Second, in the final stages of the two agent auction, an agent might want to report a higher estimate of $v(AB)$ than it truly holds, knowing that if the other agent has a higher value still, this deception will raise the agreement price.

Agents may also want to form coalitions that temporarily decrease their expected utility in the short run, with the expectation that this coalition will be able to improve its position by bargaining in future rounds. A related analysis (Aumann & Myerson 1988) looks only at the case of super-additive environments. A further interesting problem is to see if agents can infer useful information based on the preferences revealed by the offers, then act strategically with this new knowledge.

Acknowledgments

This work would not have been possible without the guidance and support of the numerous people who made considerable contributions. Steven Brenner, Barbara Grosz, Joe Halpern, Victor Milenkovic, Jeff Rosenschein, Dan Roth, Stuart Shieber, Yoav Shoham, the Logic Group at Stanford, and anonymous reviewers deserve mention for thought-provoking discussions and helpful suggestions.

References

Aumann, Robert J., and Myerson, Roger B. 1988. Endogenous formation of links between players and of coalitions: an application of the Shapley value. In Roth, Alvin E., ed., *The Shapley Value*, chapter 12, pp. 175–191. Cambridge University Press.

Ephrati, Eithan and Rosenschein, Jeffrey S. 1991. The Clarke Tax as a consensus mechanism among automated agents. In Proceedings of the Ninth National Conference on Artificial Intelligence, 173–178. Menlo Park, CA: AAAI Press.

Gusfield, Dan and Irving, Robert W. 1989. *The Stable Marriage Problem: Structure and Algorithms.* Cambridge, MA: MIT Press.

Ketchpel, Steven P. 1993. Coalition Formation Among Autonomous Agents. In Pre-Proceedings of the 5th European Workshop on "Modeling Autonomous Agents in a Multi-Agent World" Supplement. Neuchâtel, Switzerland: Institut d'Informatique et Intelligence artificielle, Université de Neuchâtel.

Raiffa, Howard. 1982. *The Art and Science of Negotiation.* Cambridge, MA: Belknap Press.

Shapley, Lloyd. 1953. A Value for N-Person Games. In Kuhn, H. W. and Tucker. A. W. eds. *Contributions to the Theory of Games*. Princeton University Press.

Shechory, On and Kraus, Sarit. 1993. Coalition Formation Among Autonomous Agents: Strategies and Complexity. In Pre-Proceedings of the 5th European Workshop on "Modeling Autonomous Agents in a Multi-Agent World". Neuchâtel, Switzerland: Institut d'Informatique et Intelligence artificielle, Université de Neuchâtel.

Wellman, Michael P. 1993. A Market-Oriented Programming Environment and its Application to Distributed Multicommodity Flow Problems. *Journal of Artificial Intelligence Research.* 1: 51–92.

Zlotkin, Gilad and Rosenschein, Jeffrey S. 1994. Coalition, Cryptography, and Stability: Mechanisms for Coalition Formation in Task Oriented Domains. In Proceedings of the Twelfth National Conference on Artificial Intelligence. To appear.

Zlotkin, Gilad and Rosenschein, Jeffrey S. 1993. One, Two, Many: Coalitions in Multi-agent Systems. In Pre-Proceedings of the 5th European Workshop on "Modeling Autonomous Agents in a Multi-Agent World". Neuchâtel, Switzerland: Institut d'Informatique et Intelligence artificielle, Université de Neuchâtel.

The Impact of Locality and Authority on Emergent Conventions: Initial Observations

James E. Kittock*
Robotics Laboratory
Computer Science Department
Stanford University
Stanford, CA 94305
`jek@cs.stanford.edu`

Abstract

In the design of systems of multiple agents, we must deal with the potential for conflict that is inherent in the interactions among agents; to ensure efficient operation, these interactions must be coordinated. We extend, in two related ways, an existing framework that allows behavioral conventions to emerge in agent societies. We first consider localizing agents, thus limiting their interactions. We then consider giving some agents authority over others by implementing asymmetric interactions. Our primary interest is to explore how locality and authority affect the emergence of conventions. Through computer simulations of agent societies of various configurations, we begin to develop an intuition about what features of a society promote or inhibit the spontaneous generation of coordinating conventions.

Introduction

Imagine a society of multiple agents going about their business: perhaps it is a team of construction robots assembling a house. Perhaps it is a group of delivery robots responsible for carrying books, copies, or medical supplies throughout a building. Or perhaps it is a society of software agents, working to collect data from diverse sources in "information space." Whatever the nature and environment of these agents, they will find it necessary to interact with one another. There is an inherent potential for conflict in such interactions; for example, two robots might attempt to move through a doorway at the same time, or two software agents might try to modify the same file. As designers, we have achieved *coordination* when agents' actions are chosen specifically to prevent such conflicts. *Conventions* are a straightforward means of implementing coordination in a multi-agent system. When several conflicting strategies are available to agents for approaching a particular task, a convention specifies a common choice of action for all agents.

In general, designing all necessary conventions into a system or developing a centralized control mechanism to legislate new conventions is a difficult and perhaps intractable task (Shoham & Tennenholtz 1992b). It has been shown that it is possible for an agent society to reach a convention without any centralized control if agents interact and learn from their experiences (Shoham & Tennenholtz 1992a). Conventions thus achieved have been called "emergent conventions", and the process for reaching them has been dubbed "co-learning." (Shoham & Tennenholtz 1993)

In previous work on the emergence of conventions through co-learning, it was assumed that each agent in a society is equally likely to interact with any other agent (Shoham & Tennenholtz 1992a). This seems an unreasonable assumption in the general case, and we consider ways to extend the framework by allowing for non-uniform interaction probabilities. Conceptually, we can divide limitations on interactions into two categories: those due to inherent separation (geographic distance, limited communication, etc.) and those due to organizational separation (division of labor, segregation of classes, etc.). These notions are two sides of one coin; they are different forms of *locality* within a multi-agent society.

Previous work also assumed that agents have equal influence on one another's behavior. However, in practice this is not generally true; multi-agent systems often have variations in *authority*. We model differences in authority by implementing asymmetrical interactions in which the less influential agent always receives feedback as a result of its actions, while the more influential agent receives feedback with some probability. As the probability that an agent receives "upward feedback" from its subordinates decreases, the agent's authority increases. This is intended to model a situation in which the agent can act with impunity, choosing strategies based only upon their perceived effects on other agents (this can also model the case in which an agent is simply stubborn and deliberately chooses to ignore feedback). We do not claim that this is a an exhaustive treatment of the notion of authority, but this asymmetry of interaction is one aspect of authority

---

*This research was supported in part by the Air Force Office of Scientific Research under grant number F49620-92-J-0547-P00001 and by the National Science Foundation under grant number IRI-9220645.

"

that is strongly related to the topological organization of the agent society.

Our primary aim in this paper is to explore how various forms of locality and authority affect the the emergence of conventions in a multi-agent society. We note that our goal is not to model human society; rather, we seek to gain a preliminary understanding of what global properties we might expect in a society of artificial agents that adapt to one anothers' behavior.

The Basic Framework

Our explorations of multi-agent societies take place within a formal model that allows us to capture the essential features of agent interactions without becoming lost in unnecessary detail. In particular, we distill the environment to focus on the interactions between agents: each agent's environment consists solely of other agents in the system. This allows us to be precise about the effects of agents on one another.

In this model, agents must choose from a finite repertoire of *strategies* for carrying out an action. When agents interact, they receive feedback based on their current strategies; this simulates the utility various situations would have to an agent (for example, a robot might get negative feedback for colliding with an obstacle and positive feedback for completing a task). An agent may update its strategy at any time, but must do so based only upon the history of its feedback (its "memory"). As designers in pursuit of emergent coordination in an agent society, our ultimate goal is for all agents to adopt the same strategy. Thus, we must find an appropriate strategy update rule that causes a convention to arise from mixed strategies.

We have limited our preliminary investigation to pairwise interactions, and we can write the possible outcomes of agent interactions as a matrix in which each entry is the feedback that the agents involved will receive as a result of their choice of strategies.[1] We model coordination by the following matrix:

	A	B
A	+1, +1	−1, −1
B	−1, −1	+1, +1

In this case, agents have two strategies from which to choose. It is not important which particular strategy a given agent uses, but it is best if two interacting agents use the same strategy.[2] A simplified example of such a situation from a mobile robotics domain is deciding who enters a room first: a robot going in or a robot going out. If some robots use one strategy and some

---

[1] Although the matrix we use to model feedback is analogous to the payoff matrix formalism in game theory, it is important to note that we assume neither that agents are "rational" nor that they can access the contents of the matrix directly.

[2] We limit our discussion here to the two-strategy case, but the results are qualitatively similar when more strategies are available to agents.

robots use the other, there will be much unnecessary maneuvering about (or knocking of heads) when two robots attempt to move through a door simultaneously. If all robots use the same strategy, the system will run much more smoothly. This is reflected in the matrix entries: there is positive feedback for two agents using the same strategy and negative feedback for two agents using different strategies. Since there is no *a priori* preference between the two available strategies, the feedback matrix is symmetric with respect to them.

Agents update their strategies based upon the contents of a finite memory. Each memory element records the time of an interaction, the strategy used by the agent in that interaction, and the feedback the agent received as a result of that interaction. When an agent receives new feedback, it discards its oldest memory, to maintain the memory at a fixed size. Currently, we make the rather weak assumption that interactions are anonymous; although this reduces the amount of information available to each agent, we believe that exploring the behavior of societies of simple agents will yield insight into the behavior we can expect from more complex agents.

For our preliminary investigations, we have chosen to use a learning rule similar to the Highest Cumulative Reward rule used by Shoham and Tennenholtz (Shoham & Tennenholtz 1993). To decide which strategy it will use, an agent first computes the cumulative reward for each strategy by summing the feedback from all interactions in which it used that strategy and then chooses the strategy with the highest cumulative reward (HCR). There are, of course, many other possible learning rules agents could use, including more sophisticated reinforcement learning techniques such as Q-learning (Watkins 1989); however, using the simpler HCR rule fits with our program of starting with a simpler system.

In preliminary experimentation, we found that small memory sizes allow the agent society to achieve a convention rapidly; we consistently used an agent memory of size 2 in the experiments described in this paper. Thus, each agent chooses a new strategy based only on the outcome of the previous two interactions.

Locality and Authority

In practice, locality can arise in two general ways, either as an inherent part of the domain or as a design decision; we will examine localization models that reflect both of these sources. Whatever its origin, we implement localization with non-uniform interaction probabilities: an agent is more likely to interact with those agents to which it is "closer" in the society.

Two-Dimensional Grids Consider two systems of mobile robots. In both societies, there is an inherent locality: each robot has some restricted neighborhood in which it moves (perhaps centered on its battery charger). In one society, each robot is confined to a small domain and only interacts with other robots that are nearby. In the other system, the robots' domains are less rigid; although they generally move in a small area, they occasionally wander over a greater distance. Now assume that in both systems, each robot randomly chooses between two available strategies. The robots then interact pairwise, receive feedback as specified by the matrix describing coordination, and update their strategies according to the HCR rule.

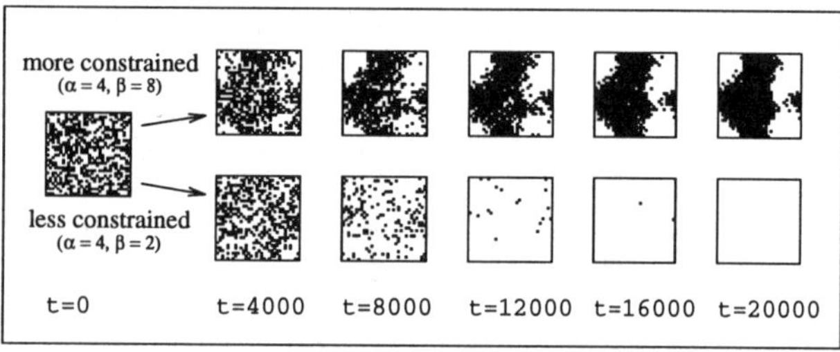

Figure 1: Time evolution example for agents on a grid.

A typical example of the time evolution of two societies fitting this description can be seen in Figure 1. In our initial investigations, the agents (robots) occupy a square grid, with one agent at each grid site; in this case there are 1024 agents on a 32 by 32 grid. The agents are colored white or black according to their choice of strategy. In the society at the top of the figure, the agents are tightly constrained, while those in the society at the bottom have more freedom to wander. Both systems start from the same initial configuration, but their evolution is quite different. In the system of agents with limited interaction, we see the spontaneous development of coordinated sub-societies. These macroscopic structures are self-supporting—agents on the interior of such a structure will have no cause to change strategy. The only changes will come at the edges of the sub-societies, which will wax and wane until eventually all of the agents are using one of the strategies. In the system of agents with more freedom of interaction, sub-societies do not appear to arise. The strategy which (perhaps fortuitously) gains dominance early is able to spread its influence throughout the society, quickly eliminating the other strategy.

In our model, we describe a robot's motion as a statistical profile that gives the likelihood of the robot wandering a particular distance from its "home" point. The probability of two robots interacting is thus a function of their individual movement profiles; we have modeled this by a simple function, $p(r) \propto [1+(\alpha r)^\beta]^{-1}$, where r is the distance between the two robots, measured as a fraction of the size of the grid. This function was chosen because the parameters allow us to independently control the overall size of an agent's domain of interaction (α) and the "rigidness" of the domain boundary (β). Figure 2 shows the function for a variety of parameter settings. With this function, we can

model robots confined to a large domain, robots confined to a small domain, robots that usually move in a small domain but occasionally wander over a larger area, etc. Note that the parameter α controls where the probability is halved, regardless of the value of β; in the limit $\beta \to \infty$, if $r > 1/\alpha$ then $p(r) = 0$. We can think of $1/\alpha$ as the "effective radius" of the probability distribution.

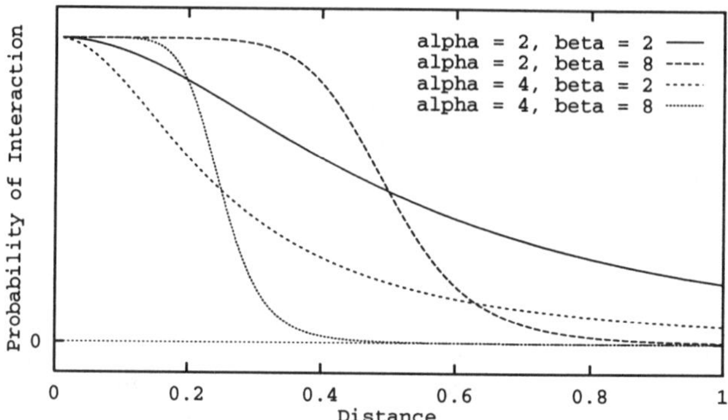

Figure 2: $p(r) \propto [1+(\alpha r)^\beta]^{-1}$.

Trees and Hierarchies In many human communities, the societal organization is built up of layers. Hierarchies in large companies and "telephone trees" for distributing messages are examples of such structures. For our purposes, *trees* are defined in the standard fashion: each node has one parent and some number of children; one node, the root node, has no parent.[3] Agents organized as a tree can interact only with their parents and children. If we allow agents to interact with their peers—other agents on the same level—we call the resulting structure a *hierarchy*. We believe that these localizing structures may be useful in societies of artificial agents for some of the same reasons they have served humans well: delegation of responsibilities, rapid distribution of information, etc. Furthermore, trees and hierarchies provide a natural setting for investigating the effects of authority.

Implementing Authority In the present experiments, an agent in a tree or hierarchy is equally likely to interact with any other agent to which it is connected, be it parent, child, or peer. However, by giving agents the ability to selectively ignore feedback they receive from interactions with agents at a lower level, we can implement a simple form of authority. We refer to the feedback an agent receives when interacting with its child in the organization as "upward feedback," and

---

[3]We limit our discussion here to trees with a branching factor of two; additional experiments have shown that increasing the branching factor does not change the relative qualitative behavior of the tree and hierarchical organization schemes.

varying the probability that this upward feedback is incorporated into an agent's memory can be thought of as modeling a range of management styles, from egalitarian bosses who listen to and learn from their subordinates to autocratic bosses who expect their subordinates to unquestioningly follow the rule "Do as I do." In this preliminary model agents always heed feedback from their parents and peers.

Experimental Results

For each experiment, the number of agents, social structure, and other parameters are fixed. Each agent's probability distribution for interacting with the other agents is computed, and the system is run multiple times. At the beginning of each run, the agents' initial strategies are chosen randomly and uniformly from the two available strategies. In each iteration of the run, a first agent is chosen randomly and uniformly from the society; a second agent is then chosen randomly according to the first agent's probability distribution. The agents interact and possibly update their strategies as described above. The system is run until all of the agents are using the same strategy, i.e. until we have 100% convergence. Each experiment was run 1000 times (with different random seeds), and the *convergence time* was computed by averaging the number of iterations required in each run.

Two-Dimensional Grids We begin our survey of experimental results by considering agents on a square grid, with interaction probabilities defined by the function $p(r)$. In Figure 3, we see how the time for all of the agents to agree upon a particular strategy scales with the size of the system, for various parameter values.

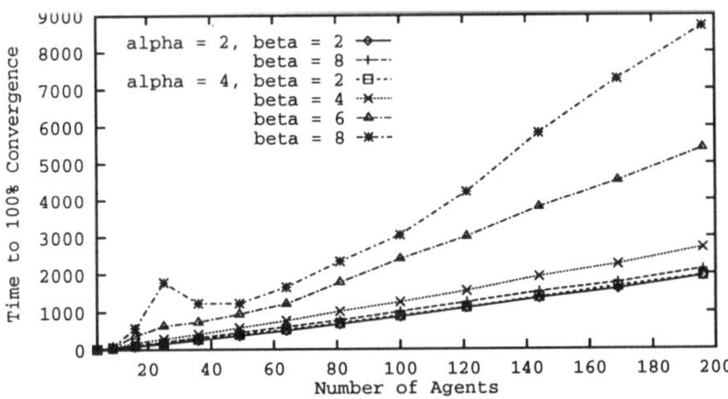

Figure 3: Convergence time vs. number of agents for two-dimensional grid.

In general, the convergence time appears to be polynomial in the number of agents in the system. Fitting curves to the data yields a range of empirical estimates from $O(n^{1.28})$ for the least restricted societies $(\alpha = 2, \beta = 2)$ to $O(n^{1.45})$ for the most restricted $(\alpha = 4, \beta = 8)$. To examine the interaction of the parameters in more detail, we fix the number of agents

in the system and observe how the convergence time is affected by various parameter settings.

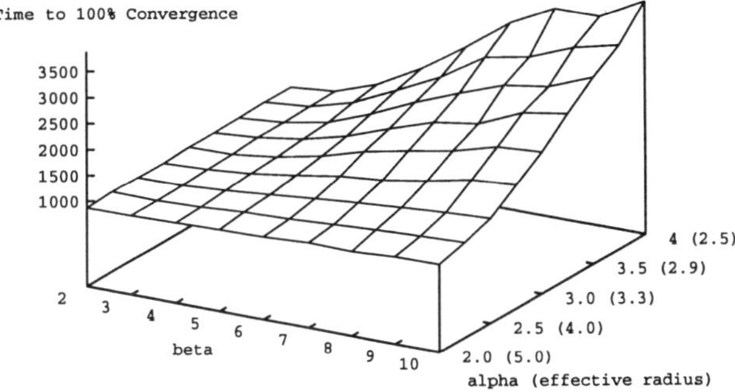

Figure 4: Convergence time for 100 agents on a two-dimensional grid for various parameter settings.

In Figure 4, we see this for a society of 100 agents; the effective radius in numbers of grid units is noted next to each value of α. We find that the steepness of the drop-off in the interaction probability, controlled by β, becomes more and more significant as α is increased. To think of it in terms of mobile robots, as the effective radius of a robot's domain is decreased, the rigidity of the boundary of its domain becomes increasingly relevant.

Trees, Hierarchies, and Authority We now look at the results of experiments with the tree and hierarchy organizational structures. Initially, we will assume full top-down authority, i.e. parent nodes never pay attention to feedback from their children.

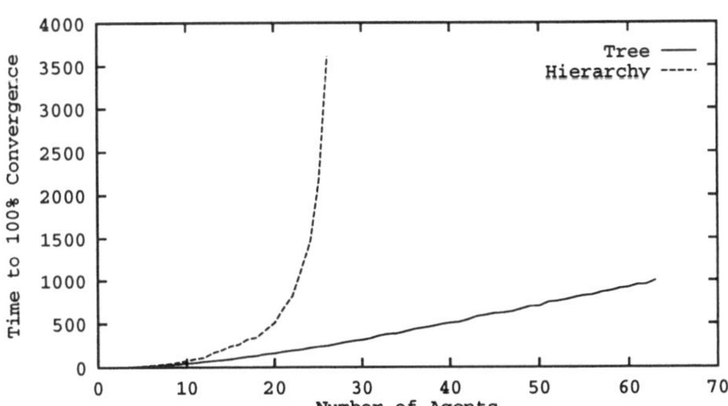

Figure 5: Convergence time vs. number of agents for tree and hierarchy organizations with full top-down authority.

In Figure 5, we see the effects of system size on the time to achieve total coordination. It appears that the convergence time for trees is polynomial in the number of agents, while for hierarchies, the convergence time seems to be exponential in the number of agents. Fitting to curves yields empirical estimates of $O(e^{0.26n})$ for hierarchies and $O(n^{1.85})$ for trees.

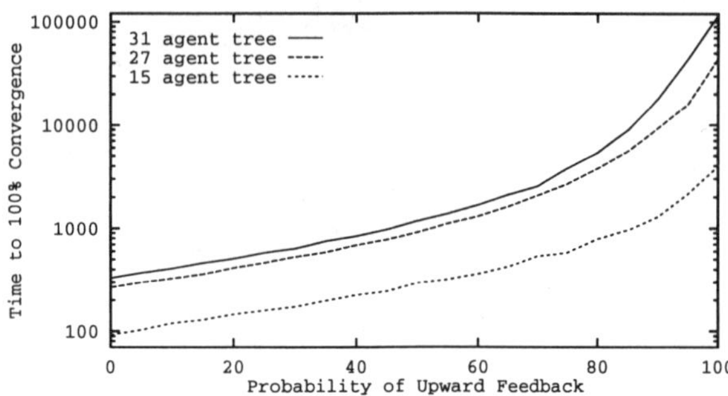

Figure 6: Effect of decreasing authority (increased upward feedback) on convergence time for tree organization.

Now we increase the probability of upward feedback, reducing the authority of agents over their descendents in the tree. In Figure 6, the convergence time is plotted against the probability of upward feedback for three tree-structured systems of different sizes. We see that the time for total coordination to be achieved increases exponentially (the y-axis is logarithmic) with increasing upward feedback, until a probability of about 75% is reached, at which point the convergence time increases even more dramatically.

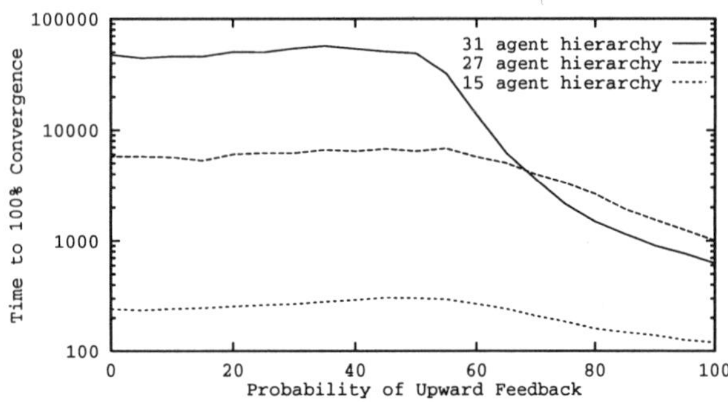

Figure 7: Effect of decreasing authority (increased upward feedback) on convergence time for hierarchy organization.

In Figure 7, the convergence time is plotted against the probability of upward feedback for the same three system sizes, now organized as hierarchies. In this case, the convergence time increases slightly with decreasing authority until a probability of about 50% is reached, at which point the society begins achieving coordination ever more rapidly. It appears that while authority is useful in trees, agents in hierarchies should listen to their subordinates.

Discussion

From the results of experiments with agents on a grid, we might speculate that increased interaction between agents promotes the emergence of conventions for coordinating actions. This is further borne out by the data in Figure 7—as the probability of upward feedback is increased, the amount of interaction effectively increases, and the system converges more rapidly. However, the behavior of trees seems to defy this conjecture: Figure 6 shows that increased interaction on a tree *decreases* the efficiency of convention emergence. Furthermore, although societies with top-down authority have *less* overall interaction when organized as trees rather than as hierarchies, they converge much more readily when tree-structured, as seen in Figure 5. It appears that neither locality nor authority is a sufficient predictor of system performance by itself.

To develop further intuition about the results with trees, hierarchies, and authority, we can observe the time evolution of representative systems. In Figure 8, we see four societies of 63 agents. The systems depicted represent the possible combinations of tree vs. hierarchy and top-down authority vs. no authority. All four systems start from the same initial condition, but they evolve quite differently.

Figure 8: Time evolution example for trees and hierarchies. In this diagram, parent nodes are drawn twice as wide as their children. Thus, coordinated subtrees appear as vertical rectangles.

In the authoritarian tree, we see that there is a strong directional pressure "pushing" a convention through the tree. Each node receives feedback only from its parent, and will quickly adopt its parent's strategy. We can think of this pressure as defining a "flow of information" through the society. This contrasts with the authoritarian hierarchy, in which each level of the organization is completely connected internally, but only weakly connected to the next level. The deeper a node is in the graph, the less likely it is to interact with its parent, and the flow of information is diluted. It becomes possible for adjacent levels to independently converge upon *different* conventions, hence we see a horizontal division in strategies at $t = 1000$.

When we eliminate authority by having upward feedback occur with 100% probability, we increase the potential for inter-level interaction. In trees, this causes the flow of information to become incoherent and we are left with a sprawling, weakly connected society. Subsocieties emerge, but now they develop on subtrees, rather than across levels. For hierarchies, we saw that reducing top-down authority causes the convergence time to decrease, and in the bottom row of Figure 8, we see one of the reasons this happens: a level which might have otherwise converged to an independent convention is rapidly brought into line with the rest of the system.

Conclusion

We have seen that locality and authority in a multi-agent society can profoundly affect the evolution of conventions for behavior coordination. We draw three (tentative) conclusions. First, in weakly connected systems, there is a tendency for sub-societies to form, hampering convergence.[4] Conversely, systems with greater overall interaction tend to converge more rapidly. Finally, if our agents are weakly connected, whether by design or necessity, it appears best to have a directional flow of feedback—strong authority—to ensure the rapid spread of conventions throughout the society.

There are numerous ways this work can be extended. In addition to exploring other forms of locality and authority, we can investigate noise, more complex learning algorithms, and explicit communication. We have already begun experimentation with emergent cooperation, and preliminary results seem to indicate that organizing structures which promote the emergence of conventions for coordination do not necessarily serve the objective of emergent cooperation. Ultimately, we would like to develop an analytic theory of convention emergence; experiments such as these serve both to guide exploration and to test theoretical results.

Research into various forms of emergent behavior in multi-agent systems relates to our investigations, particularly work on coordination and cooperation among agents. While our model incorporates adaptive agents that learn purely from experience, many researchers have taken the view that agents should be treated as "rational" in the game-theoretic sense, choosing their actions based on some expected outcome ((Stary 1993) is an overview of these approaches). In (Glance & Huberman 1993), Glance and Huberman approach closest to our work, exploring the effects of a dynamic social structure on cooperation between agents. In their model, an agent decides whether or not to cooperate by examining the behavior of other agents; if the agent perceives enough cooperation in its environment, then it decides to cooperate as well. This differs significantly from our model, in which the actual results of an agent's actions cause it to adapt its behavior. Glance and Huberman implement locality by weighting agents' perceptions of one another according to their proximity within the organization. Our notion of locality differs because it is not based on an expectation of interaction: it is based on the actual occurrence or non-occurrence of interactions.

This research bears a close resemblence to work in economics and game theory (Kandori, Mailath, & Rob 1991). One of our current goals is to gain a better understanding of this relationship. More generally, research on adaptive multi-agent systems appears to have ties to work in artificial life (Lindgren 1992), population genetics (Mettler, Gregg, & Schaffer 1988), and quantitative sociology (Weidlich & Haag 1983). However, while systems from these diverse fields share characteristics such as distributed components and complex dynamics, their particulars remain unreconciled.

References

Glance, N. S., and Huberman, B. 1993. Organizational fluidity and sustainable cooperation. In *Proceedings of the Modeling Autonomous Agents in a Multi-Agent World conference*. In press.

Kandori, M.; Mailath, G.; and Rob, R. 1991. Learning, Mutation and Long Equilibria in Games. Mimeo. University of Pennsylvania.

Lindgren, K. 1992. Evolutionary phenomena in simple dynamics. In *Artificial Life II*. Santa Fe Institute.

Mettler, L. E.; Gregg, T. G.; and Schaffer, H. E. 1988. *Population Genetics and Evolution*. Prentice Hall, second edition.

Shoham, Y., and Tennenholtz, M. 1992a. Emergent conventions in multi-agent systems: initial experimental results and observations. In *KR-92*.

Shoham, Y., and Tennenholtz, M. 1992b. On the synthesis of useful social laws for artificial agent societies. In *Proceedings of the Tenth National Conference on Artificial Intelligence*. AAAI.

Shoham, Y., and Tennenholtz, M. 1993. Co-learning and the evolution of social activity. Submitted for publication.

Stary, C. 1993. Dynamic modelling of collaboration among rational agents: redefining the research agenda. In *IFIP Transactions A (Computer Science and Technology)*, volume A-24. Human, Organizational and Social Dimensions of Information Systems Development. IFIP WG8.2 Working Group.

Watkins, C. 1989. *Learning from Delayed Rewards*. Ph.D. Dissertation, King's College.

Weidlich, W., and Haag, G. 1983. *Concepts and Models of a Quantitative Sociology; The Dynamics of Interacting Populations*. Springer-Verlag.

---

[4]If agents from different components interact only very rarely, it may not be important for the subsocieties to have the same convention.

Learning to coordinate without sharing information

Sandip Sen, Mahendra Sekaran, and John Hale
Department of Mathematical & Computer Sciences
University of Tulsa
600 South College Avenue
Tulsa, OK 74104-3189
sandip@kolkata.mcs.utulsa.edu

Abstract

Researchers in the field of Distributed Artificial Intelligence (DAI) have been developing efficient mechanisms to coordinate the activities of multiple autonomous agents. The need for coordination arises because agents have to share resources and expertise required to achieve their goals. Previous work in the area includes using sophisticated information exchange protocols, investigating heuristics for negotiation, and developing formal models of possibilities of conflict and cooperation among agent interests. In order to handle the changing requirements of continuous and dynamic environments, we propose learning as a means to provide additional possibilities for effective coordination. We use reinforcement learning techniques on a block pushing problem to show that agents can learn complimentary policies to follow a desired path without any knowledge about each other. We theoretically analyze and experimentally verify the effects of learning rate on system convergence, and demonstrate benefits of using learned coordination knowledge on similar problems. Reinforcement learning based coordination can be achieved in both cooperative and non-cooperative domains, and in domains with noisy communication channels and other stochastic characteristics that present a formidable challenge to using other coordination schemes.

Introduction

In this paper, we will be applying recent research developments from the reinforcement learning literature to the coordination problem in multiagent systems. In a reinforcement learning scenario, an agent chooses actions based on its perceptions, receives scalar feedbacks based on past actions, and is expected to develop a mapping from perceptions to actions that will maximize feedbacks. Multiagent systems are a particular type of distributed AI system (Bond & Gasser 1988), in which autonomous intelligent agents inhabit a world with no global control or globally consistent knowledge. These agents may still need to coordinate their activities with others to achieve their own local goals. They could benefit from receiving information about what others are doing or plan to do, and from sending them information to influence what they do.

Coordination of problem solvers, both selfish and cooperative, is a key issue to the design of an effective distributed AI system. The search for domain-independent coordination mechanisms has yielded some very different, yet effective, classes of coordination schemes. Almost all of the coordination schemes developed to date assume explicit or implicit sharing of information. In the explicit form of information sharing, agents communicate partial results (Durfee & Lesser 1991), speech acts (Cohen & Perrault 1979), resource availabilities (Smith 1980), etc. to other agents to facilitate the process of coordination. In the implicit form of information sharing, agents use knowledge about the capabilities of other agents (Fox 1981; Genesereth, Ginsberg, & Rosenschein 1986) to aid local decision-making. Though each of these approaches has its own benefits and weaknesses, we believe that the less an agent depends on shared information, and the more flexible it is to the on-line arrival of problem-solving and coordination knowledge, the better it can adapt to changing environments.

In this paper, we discuss how reinforcement learning techniques of developing policies to optimize environmental feedback, through a mapping between perceptions and actions, can be used by multiple agents to learn coordination strategies without having to rely on shared information. These agents, though working in a common environment, are unaware of the capabilities of other agents and may or may not be cognizant of goals to achieve. We show that through repeated problem-solving experience, these agents can develop policies to maximize environmental feedback that can be interpreted as goal achievement from the viewpoint of an external observer. This research opens up a new dimension of coordination strategies for multiagent systems.

Acquiring coordination knowledge

Researchers in the field of machine learning have investigated a number of schemes for using past experience to improve problem solving behavior (Shavlik & Dietterich 1990). A number of these schemes can be effectively used to aid the problem of coordinating multiple agents inhabiting a common environment. In cooperative domains, where agents have approximate models of the behavior of other agents and are willing to reveal information to enable the group perform better as a whole, pre-existing domain knowledge can be used inductively to improve performance over time. On the other hand, learning techniques that can be used incrementally to develop problem-solving skills relying on little or no pre-existing domain knowledge can be used by both cooperative and non-cooperative agents. Though the latter form of learning may be more time-consuming, it is generally more robust in the presence of noisy, uncertain, and incomplete information.

Previous proposals for using learning techniques to coordinate multiple agents have mostly relied on using prior knowledge (Brazdil et al. 1991), or on cooperative domains with unrestricted information sharing (Sian 1991). Even previous work on using reinforcement learning for coordinating multiple agents (Tan 1993; Weiß 1993) have relied on explicit information sharing. We, however, concentrate on systems where agents share no problem-solving knowledge. We show that although each agent is independently optimizing its own environmental reward, global coordination between multiple agents can emerge without explicit or implicit information sharing. These agents can therefore act independently and autonomously, without being affected by communication delays (due to other agents being busy) or failure of a key agent (who controls information exchange or who has more information), and do not have to be worry about the reliability of the information received (Do I believe the information received? Is the communicating agent an accomplice or an adversary?). The resultant systems are, therefore, robust and general-purpose.

Reinforcement learning

In reinforcement learning problems (Barto, Sutton, & Watkins 1989; Holland 1986; Sutton 1990), reactive and adaptive agents are given a description of the current state and have to choose the next action from a set of possible actions so as to maximize a scalar *reinforcement* or *feedback* received after each action. The learner's environment can be modeled by a discrete time, finite state, Markov decision process that can be represented by a 4-tuple $\langle S, A, P, r \rangle$ where $P : S \times S \times A \mapsto [0,1]$ gives the probability of moving from state s_1 to s_2 on performing action a, and $r : S \times A \mapsto \Re$ is a scalar reward function. Each agent maintains a policy, π, that maps the current state into the desirable action(s) to be performed in that state. The expected value of a discounted sum of future rewards of a policy π at a state x is given by $V_\gamma^\pi \stackrel{\text{def}}{=} E\{\sum_{t=0}^\infty \gamma^t r_{s,t}^\pi\}$, where $r_{s,t}^\pi$ is the random variable corresponding to the reward received by the learning agent t time steps after if starts using the pol-

icy π in state s, and γ is a discount rate ($0 \leq \gamma < 1$).

Various reinforcement learning strategies have been proposed using which agents can can develop a policy to maximize rewards accumulated over time. For our experiments, we use the Q-learning (Watkins 1989) algorithm, which is designed to find a policy π^* that maximizes $V_\gamma^\pi(s)$ for all states $s \in S$. The decision policy is represented by a function, $Q : S \times A \mapsto \Re$, which estimates long-term discounted rewards for each state–action pair. The Q values are defined as $Q_\gamma^\pi(s,a) = V_\gamma^{a;\pi}(s)$, where $a; \pi$ denotes the event sequence of choosing action a at the current state, followed by choosing actions based on policy π. The action, a, to perform in a state s is chosen such that it is expected to maximize the reward,

$$V_\gamma^{\pi^*}(s) = \max_{a \in A} Q_\gamma^{\pi^*}(s, a) \text{ for all } s \in S.$$

If an action a in state s produces a *reinforcement* of R and a transition to state s', then the corresponding Q value is modified as follows:

$$Q(s,a) \leftarrow (1-\beta)\, Q(s,a) + \beta\, (R + \gamma \max_{a' \in A} Q(s', a')). \quad (1)$$

Block pushing problem

To explore the application of reinforcement learning in multi-agent environments, we designed a problem in which two agents, a_1 and a_2, are independently assigned to move a block, b, from a starting position, S, to some goal position, G, following a path, P, in Euclidean space. The agents are not aware of the capabilities of each other and yet must choose their actions individually such that the joint task is completed. The agents have no knowledge of the system physics, but can perceive their current distance from the desired path to take to the goal state. Their actions are restricted as follows; agent i exerts a force $\vec{F}_i$, where $0 \leq |\vec{F}_i| \leq F_{max}$, on the object at an angle θ_i, where $0 \leq \theta \leq \pi$. An agent pushing with force $\vec{F}$ at angle θ will offset the block in the x direction by $|\vec{F}| \cos(\theta)$ units and in the y direction by $|\vec{F}| \sin(\theta)$ units. The net resultant force on the block is found by vector addition of individual forces: $\vec{F} = \vec{F}_1 + \vec{F}_2$. We calculate the new position of the block by assuming unit displacement per unit force along the direction of the resultant force. The new block location is used to provide *feedback* to the agent. If (x, y) is the new block location, $P_x(y)$ is the x-coordinate of the path P for the same y coordinate, $\Delta x = |x - P_x(y)|$ is the distance along the x dimension between the block and the desired path, then $K * a^{-\Delta x}$ is the feedback given to each agent for their last action (we have used $K = 50$ and $a = 1.15$).

The field of play is restricted to a rectangle with endpoints $[0, 0]$ and $[100, 100]$. A trial consists of the agents starting from the initial position S and applying forces until either the goal position G is reached or the block leaves the field of play (see Figure 1). We abort a trial if a pre-set number of agent actions fail to

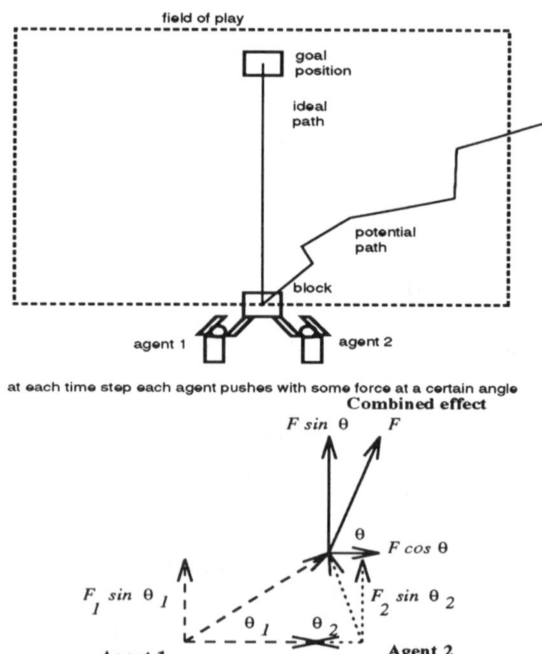

Figure 1: The block pushing problem.

take the block to the goal. This prevents agents from learning policies where they apply no force when the block is resting on the optimal path to the goal but not on the goal itself. The agents are required to learn, through repeated trials, to push the block along the path P to the goal. Although we have used only two agents in our experiments, the solution methodology can be applied without modification to problems with arbitrary number of agents.

Experimental setup

To implement the policy π we chose to use an internal discrete representation for the external continuous space. The force, angle, and the space dimensions were all uniformly discretized. When a particular discrete force or action is selected by the agent, the middle value of the associated continuous range is used as the actual force or angle that is applied on the block.

An experimental run consists of a number of trials during which the system parameters (β, γ, and K) as well as the learning problem (granularity, agent choices) is held constant. The stopping criteria for a run is either that the agents succeed in pushing the block to the goal in N consecutive trials (we have used $N = 10$) or that a maximum number of trials (we have used 1500) have been executed. The latter cases are reported as non-converged runs.

The standard procedure in Q-learning literature of initializing Q values to zero is suitable for most tasks where non-zero feedback is infrequent and hence there is enough opportunity to explore all the actions. Be-

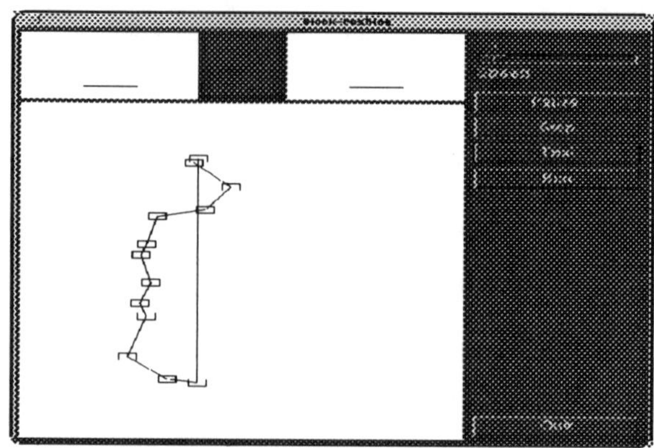

Figure 2: The X/Motif interface for experimentation.

cause a non-zero feedback is received after every action in our problem, we found that agents would follow, for an entire run, the path they take in the first trial. This is because they start each trial at the same state, and the only non-zero Q-value for that state is for the action that was chosen at the start trial. Similar reasoning holds for all the other actions chosen in the trial. A possible fix is to choose a fraction of the actions by random choice, or to use a probability distribution over the Q-values to choose actions stochastically. These options, however, lead to very slow convergence. Instead, we chose to initialize the Q-values to a large positive number. This enforced an exploration of the available action options while allowing for convergence after a reasonable number of trials.

The primary metric for performance evaluation is the average number of trials taken by the system to converge. Information about acquisition of coordination knowledge is obtained by plotting, for different trials, the average distance of the actual path followed from the desired path. Data for all plots and tables in this paper have been averaged over 100 runs.

We have developed a X/Motif interface (see Figure 2) to visualize and control the experiments. It displays the desired path, as well as the current path along which the block is being pushed. The interface allows us to step through trials, run one trial at a time, pause anywhere in the middle of a run, "play" the run at various speeds, and monitor the development of the policy matrices of the agents. By clicking anywhere on the field of play we can see the current best action choice for each agent corresponding to that position.

Choice of system parameters

If the agents learn to push the block along the desired path, the reward that they will receive for the best action choices at each step is equal to the maximum possible value of K. The steady-state values for the Q-values (Q_{ss}) corresponding to optimal action choices can be calculated from the equation:

$$Q_{ss} = (1 - \beta)\, Q_{ss} + \beta\,(K + \gamma\, Q_{ss}).$$

Solving for Q_{ss} in this equation yields a value of $\frac{K}{1-\gamma}$. In order for the agents to explore all actions after the Q-values are initialized at S_I, we require that any new Q value be less than S_I. From similar considerations as above we can show that this will be the case if $S_I \geq \frac{K}{1-\gamma}$. In our experiments we fix the maximum reward K at 50, S_I at 100, and γ at 0.9. Unless otherwise mentioned, we have used $\beta = 0.2$, and allowed each agent to vary both the magnitude and angle of the force they apply on the block.

The first problem we used had starting and goal positions at $(40, 0)$ and $(40, 100)$ respectively. During our initial experiments we found that with an even number of discrete intervals chosen for the angle dimension, an agent cannot push along any line parallel to the y-axis. Hence we used an odd number, 11, of discrete intervals for the angle dimension. The number of discrete intervals for the force dimension is chosen to be 10.

On varying the number of discretization intervals for the state space between 10, 15, and 20, we found the corresponding average number of trials to convergence is 784, 793, and 115 respectively with 82%, 83%, and 100% of the respective runs converging within the specified limit of 1200 trials. This suggests that when the state representation gets too coarse, the agents find it very difficult to learn the optimal policy. This is because the less the number of intervals (the coarser the granularity), the more the variations in reward an agent gets after taking the same action at the same state (each discrete state maps into a larger range of continuous space and hence the agents start from and ends up in physically different locations, the latter resulting in different rewards).

Varying learning rate

We experimented by varying the learning rate, β. The resultant average distance of the actual path from the desired path over the course of a run is plotted in Figure 3 for β values 0.4, 0.6, and 0.8. The average number of trials to convergence is 784, 793, and 115 respectively with 82%, 83%, and 100% of the respective runs converging within the specified limit of 1200 trials.

In case of the straight path between (40,0) and (40,100), the optimal sequence of actions always puts the block on the same x-position. Since the x-dimension is the only dimension used to represent state, the agents update the same Q-value in their policy matrix in successive steps. We now calculate the number of updates required for the Q-value corresponding to this optimal action before it reaches the steady state value. Note that for the system to converge, it is necessary that only the Q-value for the optimal action at $x = 40$ needs to arrive at its steady state value. This is because the block is initially placed at $x = 40$, and so long as the agents choose their optimal action, it never reaches any other x position. So, the number of updates to reach steady state for the Q-value associated with the optimal action at $x = 40$

should be proportional to the number of trials to convergence for a given run.

In the following, let S_t be the Q-value after t updates and S_I be the initial Q-value. Using Equation 1 and the fact that for the optimal action at the starting position, the *reinforcement* received is K and the next state is the same as the current state, we can write,

$$
\begin{aligned}
S_{t+1} &= (1 - \beta)\, S_t + \beta\, (K + \gamma\, S_t) \\
&= (1 - \beta\, (1 - \gamma))\, S_t + \beta\, K \\
&= A\, S_t + C \qquad (2)
\end{aligned}
$$

where A and B are constants defined to be equal to $1 - \beta * (1 - \gamma)$ and $\beta * K$ respectively. Equation 2 is a difference equation which can be solved using $S_0 = S_I$ to obtain

$$
S_t = A^{t+1}\, S_I + \frac{C\, (1 - A^{t+1})}{1 - A}.
$$

If we define convergence by the criteria that $|S_{t+1} - S_t| < \epsilon$, where ϵ is an arbitrarily small positive number, then the number of updates t required for convergence can be calculated to be the following:

$$
\begin{aligned}
t &\geq \frac{\log(\epsilon) - \log(S_I\, (1 - A) - C)}{log(A)} \\
&= \frac{\log(\epsilon) - \log(\beta) - \log(S_I\, (1 - \gamma) - K)}{log(1 - \beta\, (1 - \gamma))} \qquad (3)
\end{aligned}
$$

If we keep γ and S_I constant the above expression can be shown to be a decreasing function of β. This is corroborated by our experiments with varying β while holding $\gamma = 0.1$ (see Figure 3). As β increases, the agents take less number of trials to convergence to the optimal set of actions required to follow the desired path. The other plot in Figure 3 presents a comparison of the theoretical and experimental convergence trends. The first curve in the plot represents the function corresponding to the number of updates required to reach steady state value (with $\epsilon = 0$). The second curve represents the average number of trials required for a run to converge, scaled down by a constant factor of 0.06. The actual ratios between the number of trials to convergence and the values of the expression on the right hand side of the inequality 3 for β equal to 0.4, 0.6, and 0.8 are 24.1, 25.6, and 27.5 respectively (the average number of trials are 95.6, 71.7, and 53; values of the above-mentioned expression are 3.97, 2.8, and 1.93). Given the fact that results are averaged over 100 runs, we can claim that our theoretical analysis provides a good estimate of the relative time required for convergence as the learning rate is changed.

Varying agent capabilities

The next set of experiments was designed to demonstrate the effects of agent capabilities on the time required to converge on the optimal set of actions. In the first of the current set of experiments, one of the agents was chosen to be a "dummy"; it did not exert

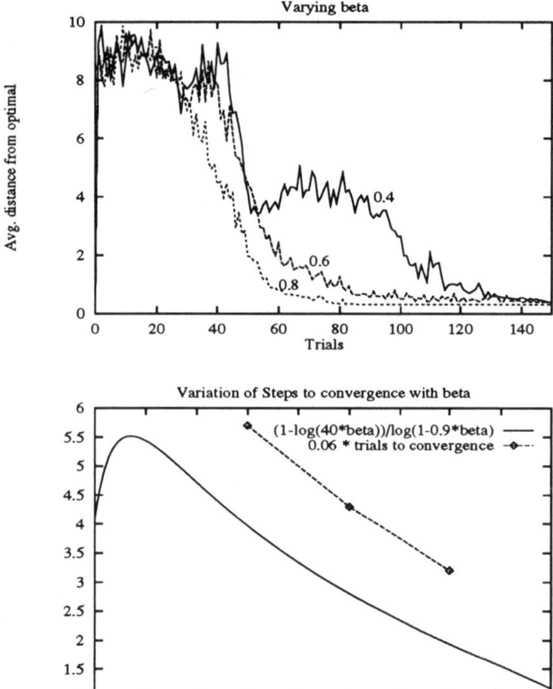

Figure 3: Variation of average distance of actual path from desired path over the course of a run, and the number of updates for convergence of optimal Q-value with changing β ($\gamma = 0.1$, $S_I = 100$).

any force at all. The other agent could only change the angle at which it could apply a constant force on the block. In the second experiment, the latter agent was allowed to vary both force and angle. In the third experiment, both agents were allowed to vary their force and angle. The average number of trials to convergence for the first, second, and third experiment are 431, 55, and 115 respectively. The most interesting result from these experiments is that two agents can learn to coordinate their actions and achieve the desired problem-solving behavior much faster than when a single agent is acting alone. If, however, we simplify the problem of the only active agent by restricting its choice to that of selecting the angle of force, it can learn to solve the problem quickly. If we fix the angle for the only active agent, and allow it to vary only the magnitude of the force, the problem becomes either trivial (if the chosen angle is identical to the angle of the desired path from the starting point) or unsolvable.

Transfer of learning

We designed a set of experiments to demonstrate how learning in one situation can help learning to perform well in a similar situation. The problem with starting and goal locations at (40,0) and (40,100) respectively

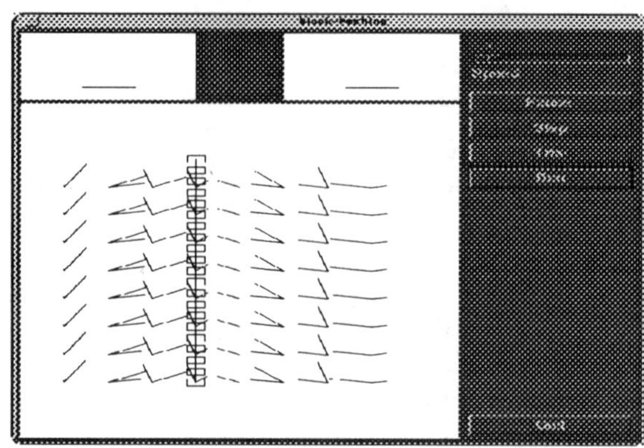

Figure 4: Visualization of agent policy matrices at the end of a successful run.

is used as a reference problem. In addition, we used five other problems with the same starting location and with goal locations at (50,100), (60,100), (70,100), (80,100), and (90,100) respectively. The corresponding desired paths were obtained by joining the starting and goal locations by straight lines. To demonstrate transfer of learning, we first stored each of the policy matrices that the two agents converged on for the original problem. Next, we ran a set of experiments using each of the new problems, with the agents starting off with their previously stored policy matrices.

We found that there is a linear increase in the number of trials to convergence as the goal in the new problem is placed farther apart from the goal in the initial problem. To determine if this increase was due purely to the distance between the two desired paths, or due to the difficulty in learning to follow certain paths, we ran experiments on the latter problems with agents starting with uniform policies. These experiments reveal that the more the angle between the desired path and the y-axis, the longer the agents take to converge. Learning in the original problem, however, does help in solving these new problems, as evidenced by a $\approx 10\%$ savings in the number of trials to convergence when agents started with the previously learned policy. Using a one-tailed t-test we found that all the differences were significant at the 99% confidence level. This result demonstrates the transfer of learned knowledge between similar problem-solving situations.

Complimentary learning

If the agents were cognizant of the actual constraints and goals of the problem, and knew elementary physics, they could independently calculate the desired action for each of the states that they may enter. The resulting policies would be identical. Our agents, however, have no planning capacity and their knowledge is encoded in the policy matrix. Figure 4 provides a snapshot, at the end of a successfully converged run, of what each agent believes to be its best action choice for each of the possible states in the world. The action choice for each agent at a state is represented by a straight line at the appropriate angle and scaled to represent the magnitude of force. We immediately notice that the individual policies are complimentary rather than being identical. Given a state, the combination of the best actions will bring the block closer to the desired path. In some cases, one of the agents even pushes in the wrong direction while the other agent has to compensate with a larger force to bring the block closer to the desired path. These cases occur in states which are at the edge of the field of play, and have been visited only infrequently. Complementarity of the individual policies, however, are visible for all the states.

Conclusions

In this paper, we have demonstrated that two agents can coordinate to solve a problem better, even without a model for each other, than what they can do alone. We have developed and experimentally verified theoretical predictions of the effects of a particular system parameter, the learning rate, on system convergence. Other experiments show the utility of using knowledge, acquired from learning in one situation, in other similar situations. Additionally, we have demonstrated that agents coordinate by learning complimentary, rather than identical, problem-solving knowledge.

The most surprising result of this paper is that agents can learn coordinated actions without even being aware of each other! This is a clear demonstration of the fact that more complex system behavior can emerge out of relatively simple properties of components of the system. Since agents can learn to coordinate behavior without sharing information, this methodology can be equally applied to both cooperative and non-cooperative domains.

To converge on the optimal policy, agents must repeatedly perform the same task. This aspect of the current approach to agent coordination limits its applicability. Without an appropriate choice of system parameters, the system may take considerable time to converge, or may not converge at all.

In general, agents converged on sub-optimal policies due to incomplete exploration of the state space. We plan to use Boltzmann selection of action in place of deterministic action choice to remedy this problem, though this will lead to slower convergence. We also plan to develop mechanisms to incorporate world models to speed up reinforcement learning as proposed by Sutton (Sutton 1990). We are currently investigating the application of reinforcement learning for resource-sharing problems involving non-benevolent agents.

References

A. B. Barto, R. S. Sutton, and C. Watkins. Sequential decision problems and neural networks. In *Proceedings of 1989 Conference on Neural Information Processing*, 1989.

A. H. Bond and L. Gasser. *Readings in Distributed Artificial Intelligence*. Morgan Kaufmann Publishers, San Mateo, CA, 1988.

P. Brazdil, M. Gams, S. Sian, L. Torgo, and W. van de Velde. Learning in distributed systems and multi-agent environments. In *European Working Session on Learning*, Lecture Notes in AI, 482, Berlin, March 1991. Springer Verlag.

P. R. Cohen and C. R. Perrault. Elements of a plan-based theory of speech acts. *Cognitive Science*, 3(3):177–212, 1979.

E. H. Durfee and V. R. Lesser. Partial global planning: A coordination framework for distributed hypothesis formation. *IEEE Transactions on Systems, Man, and Cybernetics*, 21(5), September 1991.

M. S. Fox. An organizational view of distributed systems. *IEEE Transactions on Systems, Man, and Cybernetics*, 11(1):70–80, Jan. 1981.

M. Genesereth, M. Ginsberg, and J. Rosenschein. Cooperation without communications. In *Proceedings of the National Conference on Artificial Intelligence*, pages 51–57, Philadelphia, Pennsylvania, 1986.

J. H. Holland. Escaping brittleness: the possibilities of general-purpose learning algorithms applied to parallel rule-based systems. In R. Michalski, J. Carbonell, and T. M. Mitchell, editors, *Machine Learning, an artificial intelligence approach: Volume II*. Morgan Kaufman, Los Alamos, CA, 1986.

J. W. Shavlik and T. G. Dietterich. *Readings in Machine Learning*. Morgan Kaufmann, San Mateo, California, 1990.

S. Sian. Adaptation based on cooperative learning in multi-agent systems. In Y. Demazeau and J.-P. Müller, editors, *Decentralize AI*, volume 2, pages 257–272. Elsevier Science Publications, 1991.

R. G. Smith. The contract net protocol: High-level communication and control in a distributed problem solver. *IEEE Transactions on Computers*, C-29(12):1104–1113, Dec. 1980.

R. S. Sutton. Integrated architecture for learning, planning, and reacting based on approximate dynamic programming. In *Proceedings of the Seventh International Conference on Machine Learning*, pages 216–225, 1990.

M. Tan. Multi-agent reinforcement learning: Independent vs. cooperative agents. In *Proceedings of the Tenth International Conference on Machine Learning*, pages 330–337, June 1993.

C. Watkins. *Learning from Delayed Rewards*. PhD thesis, King's College, Cambridge University, 1989.

G. Weiß. Learning to coordinate actions in multi-agent systems. In *Proceedings of the International Joint Conference on Artificial Intelligence*, pages 311–316, August 1993.

Coalition, Cryptography, and Stability:
Mechanisms for Coalition Formation in Task Oriented Domains

Gilad Zlotkin
Center of Coordination Science
Sloan School of Management, MIT
1 Amherst Street, E40-179
Cambridge, MA 02139 USA
gilad@mit.edu

Jeffrey S. Rosenschein
Computer Science Department
Hebrew University
Givat Ram, Jerusalem
Israel
jeff@cs.huji.ac.il

Abstract

Negotiation among multiple agents remains an important topic of research in Distributed Artificial Intelligence (DAI). Most previous work on this subject, however, has focused on bilateral negotiation, deals that are reached between two agents. There has also been research on n-agent agreement which has considered "consensus mechanisms" (such as voting), that allow the full group to coordinate itself. These group decision-making techniques, however, assume that the entire group will (or has to) coordinate its actions. Sub-groups cannot make sub-agreements that exclude other members of the group.

In some domains, however, it may be possible for beneficial agreements to be reached among sub-groups of agents, who might be individually motivated to work together to the exclusion of others outside the group. This paper considers this more general case of n-agent coalition formation. We present a simple coalition formation mechanism that uses cryptographic techniques for subadditive Task Oriented Domains. The mechanism is efficient, symmetric, and individual rational. When the domain is also concave, the mechanism also satisfies coalition rationality.

Introduction

In multi-agent domains, agents can often benefit by coordinating their actions with one another; in some domains, this coordination is actually required. In two-agent encounters, the situation is relatively simple: either the agents reach an agreement (i.e., coordinate their actions), or they do not. With more than two agents, however, the situation becomes more complicated, since agreement may be reached by sub-groups.

The process of agent coordination, and of reaching agreement, has been the focus of much research in Distributed Artificial Intelligence (DAI). The general term used for this process is "negotiation" (usually in the 2-agent case) (Conry, Meyer, & Lesser 1988; Kraus & Wilkenfeld 1991; Kreifelts & von Martial 1990; Kuwabara & Lesser 1989; Sycara 1988; Zlotkin & Rosenschein 1993a; Rosenschein & Zlotkin 1994), and "reaching consensus" (in the n-agent case) (Ephrati & Rosenschein 1991; 1993). Both approaches, though

dealing with different numbers of agents, share one underlying assumption: the agreement, if it is reached, will include all relevant members of the encounter. Thus, even in the n-agent case where a voting procedure might enable consensus to be reached, the entire group will be bound by the group decision. Sub-groups cannot make sub-agreements that exclude other members of the group. Interesting variations on these approaches, which nonetheless remain bilateral in essence, are the Contract Net (Smith 1978), which allows bilateral agreement in n-agent environments, and bilateral negotiation among two sub-groups discussed in (Kraus, Wilkenfeld, & Zlotkin 1995).

In some domains, however, it may be possible for beneficial agreements to be reached among sub-groups of agents, who might be individually motivated to work together to the exclusion of others outside the group. Voting procedures are not applicable here, because the full coalition may not be able to satisfy all its members, who are free to create more satisfying sub-coalitions. This paper considers this more general case of n-agent coalition formation (recent pieces of work on similar topics are (Ketchpel 1993; Shechory & Kraus 1993)). Building on our previous work (Zlotkin & Rosenschein 1993a), which dealt only with bilateral negotiation mechanisms, we here analyze the kinds of n-agent coordination mechanisms that can be used in specific classes of domains.

Coalitions

An Example—The Tileworld

Consider the following simple example in a multi-agent version of the Tileworld (Pollack & Ringuette 1990) (see Figure 1). A single hole in the grid is represented by a framed letter (such as $\boxed{a}$). Each agent's position is marked by its name (such as A_1). Tiles are represented by black squares ($\blacksquare$) inside the grid squares.

Agents can move from one grid square to another horizontally or vertically (unless the square is occupied by a hole—multiple agents can be in the same grid square at the same time). When a tile is pushed into any grid square that is part of a hole, the square is filled and becomes navigable as if it were a regular

"

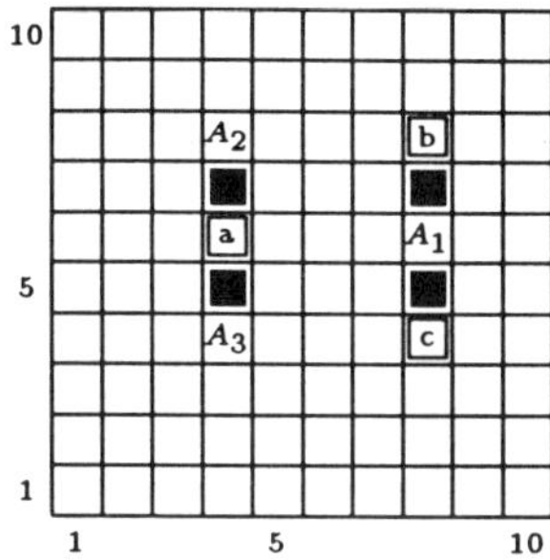

Figure 1: Three-Agent Encounter in the Tileworld

grid square. The domain is static except for changes brought about by the agents.

Agent 1's goal is to fill hole [a], while agents 2 and 3 need to fill holes [b] and [c] respectively. To fill its hole, each agent needs to do 7 steps. Agents can cooperate and help each other to reduce the cost of achieving their goals. There are several kinds of joint plans that the agents can execute that will reduce the cost of achieving their goals. Some of those joint plans are listed in the table on the right side of Figure 1.

The *coalition structure* {1,3},{2} means that there are two *coalitions*, one consisting of the agents 1 and 3, and the other consisting only of agent 2. When two agents form a coalition it means that they are coordinating their actions. The utility of an agent from a joint plan that achieves his goal is the difference between the cost of achieving his goal alone and the cost of his part of the joint plan (Zlotkin & Rosenschein 1991).

The coalition that gives the maximal total utility is the full coalition that involves all 3 agents, where they all coordinate their actions to mutual benefit (total utility is 17).[1] Although this full coalition is globally optimal, Agent 1's utility is only 4, and he would prefer to reach agreement with either agent 2 or agent 3 (with utility of 6), but not with both.

The agents in the above scenario are able to transfer utility to each other, but in a non-continuous way. Agent 1, for example, can "transfer" to agent 2 seven points of utility by achieving his goal. He cannot, however, transfer an arbitrary amount. Without this arbitrary, continuous utility transfer capability, agent 1 will prefer to form a coalition with either one of the other two agents, rather than with both.

Coalition Games

The definitions below are standard ones from coalition theory (Kahan & Rapoport 1984).

Definition 1 *A coalition game with transferable utility in normal characteristic form is* (N, v) *where:* $N =$

---

[1]The joint plan where agent 1 achieves both 2 and 3's goals (with cost of 3), while either agent 2 or 3 achieves 1's goal (each with expected cost of $\frac{1}{2}$).

Coalitions	u_1	u_2	u_3
{1},{2},{3}	0	0	0
{1,2},{3}	6	6	0
{1,3},{2}	6	0	6
{2,3},{1}	0	0	0
{1,2,3}	4	$6\frac{1}{2}$	$6\frac{1}{2}$

Table 1: Possible Coalitions in the Tileworld Example

$\{1, 2, \ldots, n\}$ *set of agents, and* $v: 2^N \to \mathbb{R}$. *For each coalition which is a subset of agents* $S \subseteq N$, $v(S)$ *is the value of the coalition* S, *which is the total utility that the members of* S *can achieve by coordinating and acting together.*

The Tileworld example from Figure 1 can be described as a coalition game (N, v) such that: $v(\{1\}) = v(\{2\}) = v(\{3\}) = v(\{2, 3\}) = 0$, $v(\{1, 2\}) = v(\{1, 3\}) = 12$, and $v(\{1, 2, 3\}) = 17$.

Note that the value derived by a coalition is independent of the coalition structure. A given coalition is guaranteed to get a certain utility, regardless of what coalitions are formed by the other agents. In the Tileworld domain this assumption is not necessarily true— though it is true in the example we gave above. We will see below that in Task Oriented Domains (Zlotkin & Rosenschein 1993a) this definition of the coalition value is directly applicable.

Task Oriented Domains

Definition 2 *A Task Oriented Domain (TOD) is a tuple* $< \mathcal{T}, \mathcal{A}, c >$ *where:* $\mathcal{T}$ *is the set of all possible tasks;* $\mathcal{A} = \{A_1, \ldots A_n\}$ *is an ordered list of agents;* c *is a* monotonic *function* $c: [2^{\mathcal{T}}] \to \mathbb{R}^+$. $[2^{\mathcal{T}}]$ *stands for all the finite subsets of* $\mathcal{T}$. *For each finite set of tasks* $X \subseteq \mathcal{T}$, $c(X)$ *is the cost of executing all the tasks in* X *by a* single *agent.* c *is monotonic, i.e., for any two finite subsets* $X \subseteq Y \subseteq \mathcal{T}, c(X) \leq c(Y); c(\emptyset) = 0$.

An encounter *within a TOD* $< \mathcal{T}, \mathcal{A}, c >$ *is an ordered list* $(T_1, \ldots, T_n)$ *such that for all* $k \in \{1 \ldots n\}, T_k$ *is a finite set of tasks from* $\mathcal{T}$ *that* A_k *needs to achieve.* T_k *will also be called* A_k *'s goal.*

The Postmen Domain (Zlotkin & Rosenschein 1989) is one classic example of a TOD. In this domain, each agent is given a set of letters to deliver to various nodes on a graph; starting and ending at the Post Office, the agents are to traverse the graph and make their deliveries. Agents can reach agreements to carry one another's letters, and save on their travel.

In multi-agent Task Oriented Domains, agents can reach agreements about the re-distribution of tasks among themselves. When there are more than two agents, the agents can also form coalitions such that tasks are re-distributed only among the members of the same coalition. When mixed deals are being used by agents (those are agreements where agents settle on

a probabilistic distribution of tasks), it can be useful
to conceive of the interaction as a coalition game with
transferable utility. The use of probability smooths
the discontinuous distribution of tasks, and therefore
of utility. However, utility is still not money in a
classic TOD; utility is the difference between the cost
of achieving your goal alone, and the cost of your part
of the deal. Therefore, there is an upper bound on the
amount of utility that each agent can get—no agent
can get more utility than his stand-alone cost. As we
shall see below, however, our model never attempts to
violate this upper bound on utility.

Subadditive Task Oriented Domains

In some domains, by combining sets of tasks we may
reduce (and can never increase) the total cost, as compared with the sum of the costs of achieving the sets
separately. The Postmen Domain, for example, has
this property, which is called *subadditivity*. If X and
Y are two sets of addresses, and we need to visit all of
them ($X \cup Y$), then in the worst case we will be able to
do the minimal cycle visiting the X addresses, then do
the minimal cycle visiting the Y addresses. This might
be our best plan if the addresses are disjoint and de-
coupled (the topology of the graph is against us). In
that case, the cost of visiting all the addresses is equal
to visiting one set plus the cost of visiting the other set.
However, in some cases we may be able to do better,
and visit some addresses on the way to others.

Definition 3 *$TOD < \mathcal{T}, \mathcal{A}, c >$ will be called* **subadditive** *if for all finite sets of tasks $X, Y \subseteq \mathcal{T}$, we have
$c(X \cup Y) \leq c(X) + c(Y)$.*

Coalitions in Subadditive Task Oriented Domains

In a TOD, a group of agents (a coalition) can coordinate by redistributing their tasks among themselves.
In a subadditive TOD, the way to minimize total cost
is to aggregate as many tasks as possible into one execution batch (since the cost of the union of tasks is
always less than the sum of the costs). Therefore, the
maximum utility that a group can derive in a subadditive TOD is the difference between the sum of stand-
alone costs and the cost of the overall union of tasks.
This difference will be defined to be the value of the
coalition.

Definition 4 *Given an encounter $(T_1, \ldots, T_n)$ in a
subadditive TOD $< \mathcal{T}, \mathcal{A}, c >$, we will define the coalition game induced by this encounter to be (N, v),
such that $N = \{1, 2, \ldots, n\}$, and $\forall S \subseteq N$, $v(S) =
\sum_{i \in S} c(T_i) - c(\bigcup_{i \in S} T_i)$.*

Superadditive Coalition Games

It seems intuitively reasonable that agents in a coalition game should not suffer by coordinating their actions with a larger group. In other words, if you take

two disjoint coalitions, the utility they can derive together should not be less than the sum of their separate
utilities (at the worst, they could "coordinate" by ignoring each other). This property (which, however, is
not always present) is called *superadditivity*.

Definition 5 *A coalition game with transferable utility in normal characteristic form (N, v) is* superaddi-
tive *if for any disjoint coalitions $S, V \subset N, S \cap V = \emptyset$,
then $v(S) + v(V) \leq v(S \cup V)$.*

Theorem 1 *Any encounter $(T_1, \ldots, T_n)$ in a subadditive TOD induces a superadditive coalition game
(N, v).*

Proof. Proofs can be found in (Zlotkin & Rosenschein
1993b). □

Mechanisms for Subadditive TODs

We would like to set up rules of interaction such that
communities of self-interested agents will form beneficial coalitions. There are several attributes of the rules
of interaction that might be important to the designers of these self-interested agents (as discussed further
in (Rosenschein 1993)):

1. Efficiency: The agents should not squander resources when they come to an agreement; there should
not be wasted utility when an agreement is reached.
Since the coalition game is superadditive it means that
the sum of utilities of the agents should be equal to
$v(N)$.

2. Stability: Since the coalition game is superadditive, the full coalition can always satisfy the efficiency
condition, and therefore we will assume that the full
coalition will be formed. The stability condition then
relates to the payoff vector $(u_1, \ldots, u_n)$ that assigns to
each agent i a utility of u_i. There are three levels of stability (rationality) conditions: individual, group, and
coalition rationality. *Individual Rationality* means that
that no individual agent would like to opt out of the
full coalition; i.e., $u_i \geq v(\{i\}) = 0$. *Group Rationality
(Pareto Optimality)* means that the group as a whole
would not prefer any other payoff vector over this vector; i.e., $\sum_{i=1}^{n} u_i = v(n)$. This condition is equivalent
to the efficiency condition above. *Coalition Rationality* means that no group of agents should have an incentive to deviate from the full coalition and create a
sub-coalition; i.e., for each subset of agents $S \subseteq N$,
$\sum_{i \in S} u_i \geq v(S)$.

3. Simplicity: It will be desirable for the overall interaction environment to make low computational demands on the agents, and to require little communication overhead.

4. Distribution: Preferably, the interaction rules will
not require a central decision maker, for all the obvious
reasons. We do not want our distributed system to
have a performance bottleneck, nor collapse due to the
single failure of a special node.

5. Symmetry: Two symmetric agents should be assigned the same utility by the mechanism (two agents

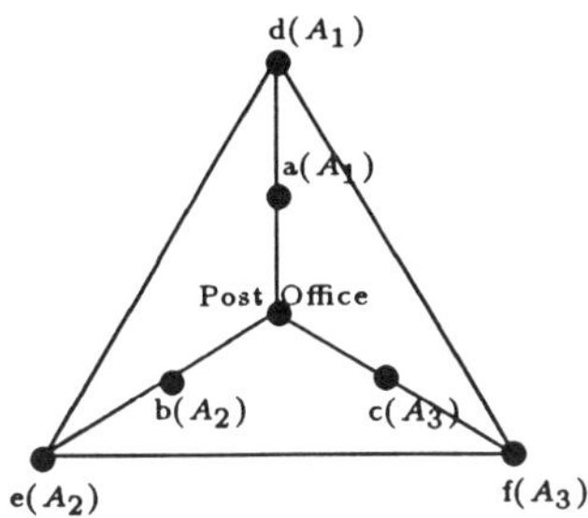

Figure 2: Example of an Unstable Encounter

are symmetric when they contribute exactly the same value to all possible coalitions).

We will develop a mechanism for subadditive TODs such that agents agree on the all-or-nothing deal, in which each agent has some probability of executing all the tasks. The question that we will try to answer now is "What should be the division of utilities among all agents in the full coalition?"

Coalition rationality is the strongest stability condition, and implies individual rationality and group rationality.[2] However, this condition is very strong, and cannot always be satisfied.

Consider the encounter from a three-agent Postmen Domain that can be seen in Figure 2.

The Post Office is in the center. The length of each arch is 1. The encounter is $(T_1 = \{a, d\}, T_2 = \{b, e\}, T_3 = \{c, f\})$.[3] Each agent can deliver his letters with a cost of 4. The cost of delivering the union of the letters of any two agents is 5. Therefore, the value of any two agents' coalition is $(2*4) - 5 = 3$. The cost of delivering all the letters is 8. Therefore, the value of the full coalition is $(3*4) - 8 = 4$. We would like to find a payoff vector (u_1, u_2, u_3) that satisfies the following conditions:
(1) $\forall i \in \{1, 2, 3\}\ u_i \geq v(\{i\}) = 0$;
(2) $\forall i \neq j \in \{1, 2, 3\}\ u_i + u_j \geq v(\{i, j\}) = 3$;
(3) $u_1 + u_2 + u_3 \geq v(\{1, 2, 3\}) = 4$.

Since the full coalition is also the maximal valued configuration, condition (3) is satisfied by equality (i.e., $u_1 + u_2 + u_3 = 4$). If we add up all the inequalities, we will have $u_1 + u_2 + u_3 >= 4\frac{1}{2}$, which cannot be satisfied. This means that in any division of the value of the full coalition among the agents there will be at least two agents that will prefer to opt out of the coalition and form a sub-coalition! For example, assume that the full coalition is formed with payoff vector $(1, 1, 2)$. Agents 1 and 2 can get more by forming a coalition (i.e., by excluding agent 3 from the coalition). The new payoff

___

[2] All payoffs that satisfy the coalition rationality conditions are called the *core* of the game in the game theory literature. See, for example, (Kahan & Rapoport 1984).

[3] Agent 1 has to deliver letters to addresses a and d, agent 2 has to deliver letters to addresses b and e, and agent 3 has to deliver letters to addresses c and f.

vector can then be $(1\frac{1}{2}, 1\frac{1}{2}, 0)$. This coalition and payoff vector is also not stable, since now agent 3 can tempt agent 2 (for example) to form a coalition with 3 by promising 2 more utility. The new payoff vector can then be $(0, 2, 1)$. However, now agent 1 can convince the two agents that they all can do better by forming the full coalition again. The new payoff vector can then be $(\frac{1}{3}, 2\frac{1}{3}, 1\frac{1}{3})$. This coalition is also not stable...

Shapley Value

The Shapley Value (Shapley 1988; Young 1988) for agent i is a weighted average of all the utilities that i contributes to all possible coalitions. The weight of each coalition is the probability that this coalition will be formed in a random process that starts with the one-agent coalition, and in which this coalition grows by one agent at a time such that each agent that joins the coalition is credited with his contribution to the coalition. The Shapley Value is actually the expected utility that each agent will have from such a random process (assuming any coalition and permutation is equally likely).

Definition 6 *Given a superadditive coalition game with transferable utility in normal characteristic form (N, v), the Shapley Value is defined to be:* $u_i = \sum_{S \subset N, i \notin S} \frac{(n - |S| - 1)! |S|!}{n!} v(S \cup \{i\}) - v(S)$.

The Shapley Value satisfies the efficiency, symmetry, and individual rationality conditions (Shapley 1988; Kahan & Rapoport 1984). However, it does not necessarily satisfy the coalition rationality condition.

Theorem 2 *The Shapley Value is also:* $u_i = c(T_i) - \sum_{S \subset N, i \notin S} \frac{(n - |S| - 1)! |S|!}{n!} \Delta_c^i(S)$. $\Delta_c^i(S) \equiv c(S \cup \{i\}) - c(S)$, *i.e., the additional* cost *that agent i adds to a coalition S.*

Agent i's Shapley Value is the difference between the cost of its goal and its weighted average cost contribution to all possible coalitions. The cost that agent i can contribute to a coalition is bounded by $c(T_i)$. Therefore, the average contribution is also bounded by $c(T_i)$, which also means that the Shapley Value is positive (i.e., satisfies the individual rationality contribution) and bounded by $c(T_i)$ (which is also the maximal utility that an agent can get according to our model). Thus (as we promised above in Section), our model never attempts to transfer to an agent more utility than he can get by simply having his tasks performed by others.

Mechanisms for Subadditive TODs

We can define a Shapley Value-based mechanism for subadditive TODs that forms the full coalition and divides the value of the full coalition using the Shapley Value. The mechanism simply chooses the following (all-or-nothing) mixed deal, $(p_1, \ldots, p_n)$, such that
$$p_i = \frac{\sum_{S \subset N, i \notin S} \frac{(n - |S| - 1)! |S|!}{n!} \Delta_c^i(S)}{c(N)}.$$

Theorem 3 *The above all-or-nothing deal is well-defined, (i.e., $\forall i \in N : 0 \leq p_i \leq 1; \sum_{i=1}^{n} p_i = 1$) and gives each agent i an expected utility that is exactly the Shapley Value u_i.*

Evaluation of the Mechanism

The above mechanism gives each agent its Shapley Value. The mechanism is thus symmetric and efficient (i.e., satisfying group rationality), and also satisfies the criterion of individual rationality. However, as was seen in Example 2, no mechanism can guarantee coalition rationality. Besides failing to guarantee coalition rationality, the mechanism also does not satisfy the simplicity condition. It requires agents to calculate the Shapley Value, a computation that has exponential computational complexity.

The computational complexity of a mechanism should be measured relative to the complexity of the agent's standalone planning problem. This relative measurement would then signify the computational overhead of the mechanism. Each agent in a Task Oriented Domain needs to calculate the cost of his set of tasks, i.e., to find the best plan to achieve them. Calculation of the value of a coalition is linear in the number of agents in the coalition.[4] The calculation of the Shapley Value requires an evaluation of the value of all (2^n) possible coalitions. In Section below we will show that there exists another Shapley-based mechanism that has linear computational complexity.

Concave TODs

Definition 7 [Concavity]:[5] *$TOD < \mathcal{T}, \mathcal{A}, c >$ will be called* **concave** *if for all finite sets of tasks $X \subseteq Y$, $Z \subseteq \mathcal{T}$, we have $c(Y \cup Z) - c(Y) \leq c(X \cup Z) - c(X)$.*

All concave TODs are also subadditive. It turns out that general subadditive Task Oriented Domains can be restricted, becoming concave Task Oriented Domains. For example, the Postmen Domain is subadditive, when the graphs over which agents travel can assume any topology. By restricting legal topologies to trees, the Postmen Domain becomes concave.

Definition 8 *A coalition game with transferable utility in normal characteristic form (N, v) is convex if for any coalitions S, V, $v(S) + v(V) \leq v(S \cup V) + v(S \cap V)$.*

In convex coalition games, the incentive for an agent to join a coalition grows as the coalition grows.

Theorem 4 *Any encounter $(T_1, \ldots, T_n)$ in a concave TOD induces a* convex *coalition game (N, v).*

Theorem 5 [Shapley (1971)] (Shapley 1971): *In convex coalition games, the Shapley Value always satisfies the criterion of coalition rationality.*

---

[4]The cost of a set of tasks needs to be calculated only a linear number of times.

[5]The definition is from (Zlotkin & Rosenschein 1993a).

In concave TODs, the Shapley-based mechanism introduced above is fully stable, i.e., satisfies individual, group, and coalition rationality.

The Random Permutation Mechanism

The Shapley Value is equal to the expected contribution of an agent to the full coalition, assuming that all possible orders of agents joining and forming the full coalition are equally likely. This leads us to a much simpler mechanism called the *Random Permutation Mechanism*: agents choose a random permutation and form the full coalition, one agent after another, according to the chosen permutation. Each agent (i) gets utility (w_i) that is equal to its contribution to the coalition, at the time he joined it. This is done by agreeing on the all-or-nothing deal, $(p_1, \ldots, p_n)$, such that $p_i = \frac{c(T_i) - w_i}{c(N)}$.

Theorem 6 *If each permutation has an equal chance of being chosen, then the Random Permutation Mechanism gives each agent an expected utility that is equal to its Shapley Value.*

The Shapley-based Random Permutation Mechanism does not explicitly calculate the Shapley Value, but instead calculates the cost of only n sets of tasks. Therefore, it has linear computational complexity. The problem of coalition formation is reduced to the problem of reaching consensus on a random permutation.

Consensus on Permutation

No agent would like to be the first one that starts the formation of the full coalition (since this agent by definition gets zero utility). If the domain is concave (and therefore the coalition game is convex), each agent has an incentive to join the coalition as late as possible. To ensure stability, we need to find a consensus mechanism that is resistant to any coalition manipulation. No coalition should be able, by coordination, to influence the resulting permutation such that the members of the coalition will be the last ones to join the full coalition. For example, this means that no coalition of $n - 1$ agents could force the single agent that is out of the coalition to go first.

We will use the simple cryptographic mechanism that allows an agent to encrypt a message using a private key, to send the encrypted message, and then to send the key such that the message can be unencrypted. Using these tools, each agent chooses a random permutation and a key, encrypts the permutation using the key, and broadcasts the encrypted message to all other agents. After he has received all encrypted messages, the agent broadcasts the key. Each agent unencrypts all messages using the associated keys. The consensus permutation is the combination of all permutations.

Each agent can make sure that each permutation has an equal chance of being chosen even if he assumes that the rest of the agents are all coordinating their permutations against him (i.e., trying to make him be the first). All he needs to do is to choose a *random* permutation. Since his permutation will also be combined into the final permutation, everything will be shuffled in a way that no one can predict.

Conclusions

We have considered the kinds of n-agent coordination mechanisms that can be used in Task Oriented Domains (TODs), when any sub-group of agents may engage in task exchange to the exclusion of others.

We presented a simple, efficient, symmetric, and individual rational Shapley Value-based coalition formation mechanism that uses cryptographic techniques for subadditive TODs. When the domain is also concave, the mechanism also satisfies coalition rationality.

Future research will consider non-subadditive TODs. It will also consider issues of incentive compatibility in multi-agent coalition formation, investigating mechanisms that can be employed when agents have partial information about the goals of other group members and can deceive one another about this private information.

References

Conry, S.; Meyer, R.; and Lesser, V. 1988. Multistage negotiation in distributed planning. In Bond, A., and Gasser, L., eds., *Readings in Distributed Artificial Intelligence*. San Mateo: Morgan Kaufmann Publishers, Inc. 367–384.

Ephrati, E., and Rosenschein, J. S. 1991. The Clarke Tax as a consensus mechanism among automated agents. In *Proceedings of the Ninth National Conference on Artificial Intelligence*.

Ephrati, E., and Rosenschein, J. S. 1993. Distributed consensus mechanisms for self-interested heterogeneous agents. In *First International Conference on Intelligent and Cooperative Information Systems*, 71–79.

Kahan, J. P., and Rapoport, A. 1984. *Theories of Coalition Formation*. London: Lawrence Erlbaum Associates.

Ketchpel, S. P. 1993. Coalition formation among autonomous agents. In *Pre-Proceedings of the Fifth European Workshop on Modeling Autonomous Agents in a Multi-Agent World*.

Kraus, S., and Wilkenfeld, J. 1991. Negotiations over time in a multi agent environment: Preliminary report. In *Proceedings of the Twelfth International Joint Conference on Artificial Intelligence*, 56–61.

Kraus, S.; Wilkenfeld, J.; and Zlotkin, G. 1995. Multiagent negotiation under time constraints. *Artificial Intelligence*. to appear. A preliminary version appeared in CS-TR-2975, University of Maryland.

Kreifelts, T., and von Martial, F. 1990. A negotiation framework for autonomous agents. In *Proceedings of the Second European Workshop on Modeling Autonomous Agents and Multi-Agent Worlds*, 169–182.

Kuwabara, K., and Lesser, V. R. 1989. Extended protocol for multistage negotiation. In *Proceedings of the Ninth Workshop on Distributed Artificial Intelligence*, 129–161.

Pollack, M. E., and Ringuette, M. 1990. Introducing the Tileworld: Experimentally evaluating agent architectures. In *Proceedings of the National Conference on Artificial Intelligence*, 183–189.

Rosenschein, J. S., and Zlotkin, G. 1994. *Rules of Encounter: Designing Conventions for Automated Negotiation among Computers*. Cambridge: MIT Press.

Rosenschein, J. S. 1993. Consenting agents: Negotiation mechanisms for multi-agent systems. In *Proceedings of the International Joint Conference on Artificial Intelligence*, 792–799.

Shapley, L. S. 1971. Cores of convex games. *International Journal of Game Theory* 1:11–26.

Shapley, L. S. 1988. A value for n-Person games. In Roth, A. E., ed., *The Shapley Value*. Cambridge: Cambridge University Press. chapter 2, 31–40.

Shechory, O., and Kraus, S. 1993. Coalition formation among autonomous agents: Strategies and complexity. In *Pre-Proceedings of the Fifth European Workshop on Modeling Autonomous Agents in a Multi-Agent World*.

Smith, R. G. 1978. *A Framework for Problem Solving in a Distributed Processing Environment*. Ph.D. Dissertation, Stanford University.

Sycara, K. P. 1988. Resolving goal conflicts via negotiation. In *Proceedings of the Seventh National Conference on Artificial Intelligence*, 245–250.

Young, H. P. 1988. Individual contribution and just compensation. In Roth, A. E., ed., *The Shapley Value*. Cambridge: Cambridge University Press. chapter 17, 267–278.

Zlotkin, G., and Rosenschein, J. S. 1989. Negotiation and task sharing among autonomous agents in cooperative domains. In *Proceedings of the Eleventh International Joint Conference on Artificial Intelligence*, 912–917.

Zlotkin, G., and Rosenschein, J. S. 1991. Cooperation and conflict resolution via negotiation among autonomous agents in noncooperative domains. *IEEE Transactions on Systems, Man, and Cybernetics* 21(6):1317–1324.

Zlotkin, G., and Rosenschein, J. S. 1993a. A domain theory for task oriented negotiation. In *Proceedings of the International Joint Conference on Artificial Intelligence*, 416–422.

Zlotkin, G., and Rosenschein, J. S. 1993b. One, two, many: Coalitions in multi-agent systems. In *Pre-Proceedings of the Fifth European Workshop on Modeling Autonomous Agents in a Multi-Agent World*.

An Experiment in the Design of Software Agents

Henry Kautz, Bart Selman,
Michael Coen, Steven Ketchpel, and Chris Ramming

AI Principles Research Department
AT&T Bell Laboratories
Murray Hill, NJ 07974
{kautz, selman, jcr}@research.att.com
mhcoen@ai.mit.edu
ketchpel@cs.stanford.edu

Abstract

We describe a bottom-up approach to the design of software agents. We built and tested an agent system that addresses the real-world problem of handling the activities involved in scheduling a visitor to our laboratory. The system employs both task-specific and user-centered agents, and communicates with users using both email and a graphical interface. This experiment has helped us to identify crucial requirements in the successful deployment of software agents, including issues of reliability, security, and ease of use. The architecture we developed to meet these requirements is flexible and extensible, and is guiding our current research on principles of agent design.

Introduction

There is much recent interest in the creation of software agents. A range of different approaches and projects use the term "agents", ranging from adaptive user interfaces to systems that use planning algorithms to generate shell scripts (Maes 1993; Dent *et al.* 1992; Shoham 1993; Etzioni *et al.* 1992).

In our own approach, agents assist users in a range of daily, mundane activities, such as setting up meetings, sending out papers, locating information in multiple databases, tracking the whereabouts of people, and so on. Our objective is to design agents that blend transparently into normal work environments, while relieving users of low-level administrative and clerical tasks. We take the practical aspect of software agents seriously: users should feel that the agents are reliable and predictable, and that the human user remains in ultimate control.

One of the most difficult aspects of agent design is to define specific tasks that are both feasible using current technology, and are truly useful to the everyday user. Furthermore, it became clear during the testing of our initial prototype that users have little patience when it it comes to interacting with software agents. We therefore paid special attention to the user interface aspects of our system. In particular, whenever possible, we opted for graphically-oriented interfaces over pure text-based interfaces. In addition, reliability and error-handling is crucial in all parts of a software agent system. The real world is an unpredictable place: messages between agents may be lost or delayed, people may respond inappropriately to requests, and so forth.

Our approach has been bottom-up. We began by identifying possible useful and feasible tasks for a software agent. The first such task we choose involved the activities surrounding the scheduling of a visitor to our lab. We designed and implemented a set of software agents to handle this task. We deliberately made no commitment in advance to a particular agent architecture. We then tested the system with ordinary users; the feedback from this test led to many improvements in the design of the agents and the human/agent interfaces, as well as the development of a general and flexible framework for agent interaction. The key feature of the framework is the use of personalized agents called "userbots" that mediate communication between users and task-specific agents. We are now in our third round of implementation and testing, in which we are further refining and generalizing our userbots so that they can communicate with software agents developed by other research groups, such as the "softbots" of Etzioni *et al.* (1992).

We believe that the bottom-up approach is crucial in identifying the necessary properties of a successful agent platform. Our initial experiments have already led us to formulate some key properties. Examples include the separation of task-specific agents from user-centered agents, the need to handle issues of security and privacy, and as mentioned above, the need for good human interfaces and high reliability.

Taskbots and Userbots

Selecting an appropriate task for software agents to perform is itself a challenge. Agents must provide solutions to real problems that are important to real users. The whole raison d'être for software agents is lost if they are restricted to handling toy examples. On the other hand, more complex tasks frequently include a range of long-term research issues, such as understanding unrestricted natural language.

After considering a number of possible agent tasks, we settled on the problem of scheduling a visitor to our lab.[1] This job is quite routine, but consumes a substantial amount

---

[1] See also Dent *et al* (1992) and Maes and Kozierok (1993), that describe the design of software agents that *learn* how to assist users in scheduling meetings and managing their personal calendars.

of the host's time. The normal sequence of tasks consists of announcing the upcoming visit by email; collecting responses from people who would like to meet with the visitor, along with their preferred meeting times; putting together a schedule that satisfies as many constraints as possible (taking into account social issues, such as not bumping the lab director from the schedule); sending out the schedule to the participants, together with appropriate information about room and telephone numbers; and, of course, often rescheduling people at the last minute because of unforeseen events.

We decided to implement a specialized software agent called the "visitorbot" to handle these tasks. (We use the suffix "bot" for "software robot".) After examining various proposed agent architectures (Etzioni, Lesh, & Segal 1992; Shoham 1993), we decided that it was necessary to first obtain practical experience in building and a using a concrete basic agent, before committing to any particular theoretical framework. Our initial implementation was a monolithic agent, that communicated directly with users via email. The program was given its own login account ("visitorbot"), and was activated upon receiving email at that account. (Mail was piped into the visitorbot program using the ".forward" facility of the Unix mail system.)

Our experience in using the visitorbot in scheduling a visit led to the following observations:

1. Email communication between the visitorbot and humans was cumbersome and error-prone. The users had to fill in a pre-defined form to specify their preferred meeting times. (We considered various forms of natural language input instead of forms. However, the current state of the art in natural language processing cannot parse or even skim unrestricted natural language with sufficient reliability. On the other hand, the use of restricted "pseudo"-natural language has little or no advantage over the use of forms.) Small editing errors by users often made it impossible to process the forms automatically, requiring human intervention. Moreover, users other than the host objected to using the visitorbot at all; from their point of view, the system simply made their life harder.

Based on this observation, we realized that an easy to use interface was crucial. We decided that the next version of the visitorbot would employ a graphical interface, so that users could simply click on buttons to specify their preferred meeting times. This approach practically eliminated communication errors between people and the visitorbot, and was viewed by users as an improvement over the pre-Bot environment.

2. There is a need for redundancy in error-handling. For example, one early version of the visitorbot could become confused by bounced email, or email responses by "vacation" programs. Although our platform has improved over the initial prototype, more needs to be done. Agents must react more or less predictably to both foreseen errors (*e.g.*, mangled email), and unforeseen errors (*e.g.*, a subprocess invoked by the bot terminates unexpectedly). Techniques from the area of software reliability and real-time systems design could well be applicable to this problem. For exam-

ple, modern telephone switching systems have a down-time of only a few minutes per year, because they continuously run sophisticated error-detection and recovery mechanisms.

3. The final task of creating a good schedule from a set of constraints did not require advanced planning or scheduling techniques. The visitorbot translated the scheduling problem into an integer programming problem, and solved it using a commercial integer programming package (CPLEX). An interesting advantage of this approach is that was easy to incorporate soft constraints (such as the difference between an "okay" time slot and a "good" time slot for a user).

This experience led us to the design shown in Fig. 1. This design includes an agent for each individual user in addition to the visitorbot. For example, the agent for the user "kautz" is named "kautzbot", for "selman" is named "selmanbot", and so on. The userbots mediate communication between the visitorbot and their human owners.

The normal interaction between the visitorbot and the users proceeds as follows. The initial talk announcement is mailed by the visitorbot to each userbot. The userbot then determines the preferred mode of communication with its owner. In particular, if the user is logged in on an X-terminal, the userbot creates a pop-up window on the user's screen, containing the announcement and a button to press to request to meet with the visitor, as shown in the left-hand window in Fig. 2. If the user clicks on "yes", the userbot passes this information back to the visitorbot, which responds with a request to obtain the user's preferred meeting times. The userbot then creates a graphical menu of meeting times, as shown in the right-hand window in Fig. 2. The user simply clicks on buttons to indicate his or her preferences. The userbot then generates a message containing the preferences and mails it back to the visitorbot. If the userbot is unable to determine the display where the user is working, or if the user fails to respond to the pop-up displays, the userbot forwards the request from the visitorbot via email to the user as a plain text form.

There are several important advantages of this design. First, the visitorbot does not need to know about the user's display, and does not need permission to create windows on that display. This means, for example, that a visitorbot at Bell Labs can create a graphical window at any site that is reachable by email where there are userbots. This was successfully tested with the "mhcoenbot" running at MIT.[2] The separation of the visitorbot from the userbot also simplifies the design of the former, since the userbots handle the peculiarities of addressing the users' displays. Even more importantly, the particular information about the user's location and work habits does not have to be centrally available. This information can be kept private to the user and his or

---

[2]Sometimes it is possible to create a remote X-window over the internet, but this is prone to failure. Among other problems, the user would first have to grant permission to ("xhost") the machine running the visitorbot program; but note that the user may not even know the identity of machine on which the visitorbot program is running. Even if the identity of the machine is known, it may be impossible to serve X-windows directly due to "firewalls" or intermittent connections.

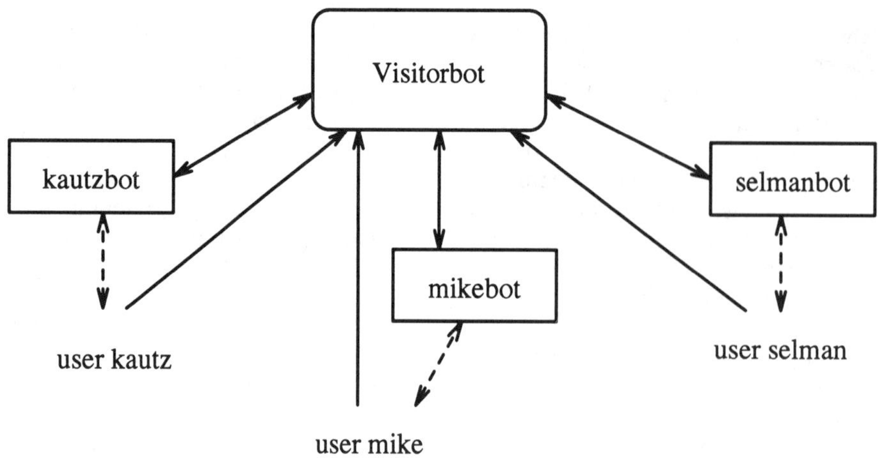

Figure 1: Current architecture of the agent system. Solid lines represent email communication; dashed lines represent both graphical and email communication.

her userbot.

Another advantage of this design is that different users, who may have access to different computing resources, can run different userbots, of varying levels of sophistication. Thus, everyone is not restricted to a "least common denominator" type interface.

Perhaps the most important benefit of the design is that a task-specific agent (such as the visitorbot) is not tied to any specific form of communication. The task-specific agent specifies *what* information is to be transmitted or obtained, but not *how* the communication should take place. The userbot can then employ a wide range of media, such as graphics, voice, FAX, email, etc. for interacting with its owner. The userbot also can take into account its owners preferences and such factors as the owners whereabouts and current computing environment in deciding on the mode of communication. For example, a userbot could incorporate a telephone interface with a speech synthesizer. This would enable a userbot to place a call to its owner (if the owner so desires), read the talk announcement, and collect the owner's preferences by touch-tone. Note that this extension would not require any modification to the visitorbot itself.

Refining the Userbot

Tests of the visitorbot/userbot system described in the previous section showed that users greatly preferred its ease of use and flexibility over our initial monolithic, email-based agent. Now that we had developed a good basic architecture, the logical next step was to incorporate new task-specific agents. In order to do so, we undertook a complete reimplementation of the system. In the new implementation, all visitorbot-specific code was eliminated from the userbots. We designed a simple set of protocols for communication between task-specific agents and userbots. Again, our approach was pragmatic, in that we tried to established a minimal set of conventions for the applications we were considering, rather than immediately trying to create a full-blown agent interlingua.

In brief, bots communicate by exchanging email which is tagged with a special header field, "XBot-message-type". The message type indicates the general way in which the body of the message (if any) should be processed by the receiver. For example, the message type "xchoices" means that the message is a request for the receiver to make a series of *choices* from among one or more sets of alternatives described in the body of the message. The inclusion of the field "XBot-return-note" in the message indicates that the result of processing the message should be mailed back to the sender. The communication protocol establishes the syntax for the data presented in the body of each message type, and the format of the data that results from processing the message. However, the protocol deliberately does not specify the exact method by which the processing is carried out. For example, a userbot may process an xchoices message by creating a pop-up menu, or calling the user on the telephone, or simply by consulting a database of defaults that the user has established.

When applications are developed that demand novel kinds of interactions with userbots, the communication protocols can be extended by adding new message types. This will require the creation of mechanisms for distributing "updates" to the userbots to handle the extensions (an issue we return to below). So far, however, only a very small number of message types (namely, ones for requesting choices, requesting help, and simply conveying a piece of information) have been needed. One question that more experience in building bots will answer is whether the number of basic message types is indeed bounded and small, or if new types are often needed with new applications.

In essence, then, the messages that task-specific bots and userbots exchange can be viewed as *intensions* – such a request to make a choice – rather than *extensions* – for example, if one were to mail a message containing a program that draws a menu on the screen when executed.[3] In this

____

[3]This description of messages as intensions versus extensions

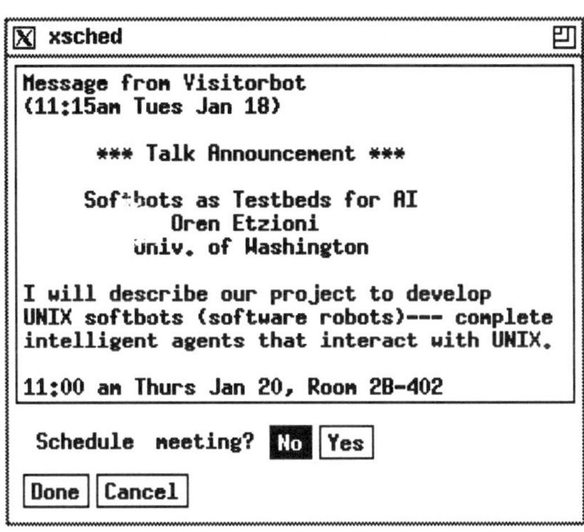

Figure 2: Graphical interfaces created by a userbot in response to messages from the visitorbot. The left window is created by processing a talk announcement; the right, by a request for the user's preferred meeting times.

regard it is informative to contrast our approach with that used in *Telescript*, the electronic messaging language created General Magic. In Telescript, messages are full-fledged programs, and are executed on the receiving machine by a fixed interpreter. Thus, Telescript messages are purely extensional. While the Telescript approach has the advantage that the reception of a message can initiate arbitrarily novel and complex processing, this must be weighed against the fact that any flexibility in the *way* in which the interaction takes place with the user must be built into each and every message.

One aspect of the preliminary userbot that some users found objectionable was the fact that various windows (such as those in Fig. 2) would pop-up whenever the userbot received mail, which could be disruptive. Therefore, in the new implementation messages are normally not displayed until the user makes an explicit request to interact with his or her userbot. This interaction is supported by a continuously-running "active" userbot, as shown in Fig. 3. The main userbot window indicates the number of outstanding messages waiting to be processed, the userbot's state (working or idle), and three buttons. Clicking on the "process message" button allows the userbot to process messages that require user interaction – for example, bringing up an xchoices window on behalf of the visitorbot. Note, however, that messages that are tagged as "urgent" are always immediately processed by the userbot.

____

is due to Mark Jones.

The second button, "user preferences", brings up a window in which the user can set various options in the behavior of his or her userbot. For example, checking the "autopilot" box makes the userbot pop up windows without waiting to be explicitly told to do so. The "voice" checkbox causes the userbot to announce the receipt of new userbot mail using the speaker in a Sun workstation – a kind of audible "biff" for botmail. The "forward to" options are used to indicate that the userbot should choose try to communicate with its owner at a remote location – for example, by transmitting messages via a FAX-modem to the owner's home telephone. (Currently the code to support the "forward to" options has not yet been completed. The exact appearance and functionality of these options may differ in the final version.)

Finally, the third button in the main userbot window brings up the window labeled "taskbots". This window contains a button for each task-specific agent whose email address is known to the userbot. (This information is maintained in file that the user can easily customize.) Clicking on a button in this window initiates communication with the designed task-specific agent, by sending a message of type "help" to that agent. The communication protocol specifies that the agent should respond to a help message by sending back a menu of commands that the agent understands, together with some basic help information, typically in the form of an xchoices message. When the userbot processes this response, it creates a window containing the appropriate controls for interacting with that particular task-specific

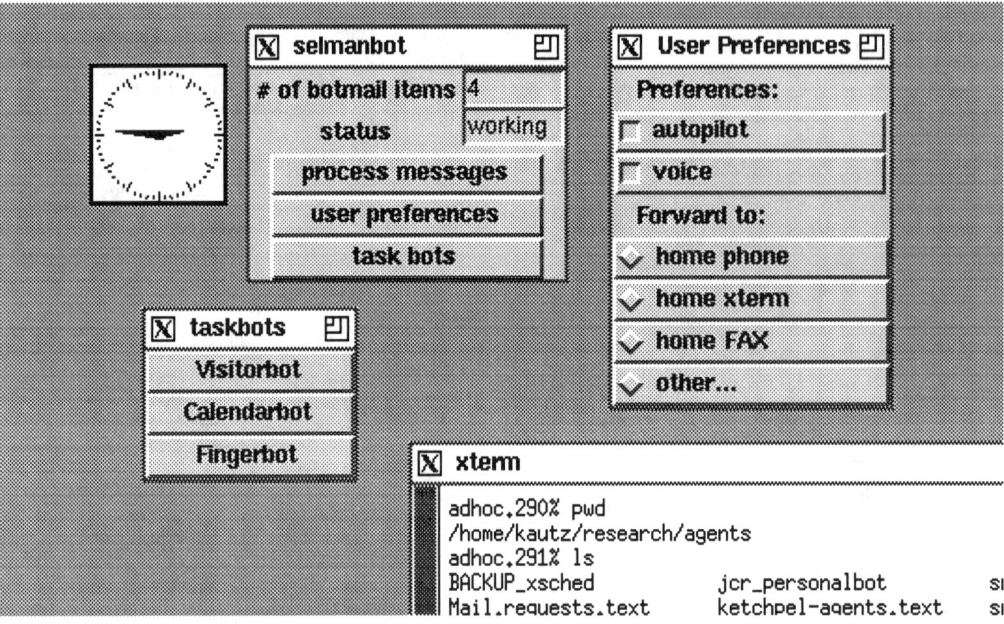

Figure 3: Graphical display of a userbot.

agent. For example, a user who is hosting a visitor to our lab starts the entire process by clicking on the visitorbot button. This leads to the creation of a window containing buttons for basic visitorbot commands, such as scheduling a new visitor, getting the status of a visit, ordering a schedule to be generated, and so on. Clicking on some of these buttons could lead to the creation of other windows, for example, one in which to type the text of the abstract of the visitor's talk.

At the time that this paper is being written, only the visitorbot button in the taskbots menu is active. Over the next few months we intend to establish communication with Oren Etzioni's "finger" agent (used to obtain information about people on the internet) (Etzioni, Lesh, & Segal 1992), and Tom Mitchell's "calendar" agent (used to schedule meetings among groups of people) (Dent *et al.* 1992). The fingerbot and calendarbot will not themselves be ported to our laboratory's computers; instead, those programs will run at their respective "homes" (University of Washington and CMU), and communication with userbots at various sites will take place using ordinary internet email. We hope that the idea of a userbot will provide a powerful and flexible framework for integrating many different kinds of software agents that run in different computing environments.

Privacy and Security

Early discussions with potential users made it clear that privacy and security are central issues in the successful deployment of software agents. Some proposed agent systems would filter through all of the user's email, pulling out and deleting messages that the agent would like to handle. We found that users generally objected to giving a program permission to delete automatically any of their incoming mail. An alternative approach would give the bot authority to read but not modify the user's mail. The problem with this is that the user's mail quickly becomes polluted with the many messages sent between the various bots.

Our solution to this problem has been to create a pseudo-account for each userbot, with its own mail alias. Mail sent to this alias is piped into a userbot program, that is executed under the corresponding user's id. This gives the instantiated userbot the authority, for example, to create a window on the user's display. Any "bot mail" sent to this alias is not seen by the user, unless the userbot explicitly decides to forward it.

Each user has a special ".bot" directory, which contains information customized to the particular user. These files specify the particular program that instantiates the userbot, a log of the userbot mail, and the user's default display id. In general, this directory contains user-specific information for the userbot. It is important to note that this directory does not need to be publicly readable, and can thus contain sensitive information for use by the userbot. Examples of such information include the names of people to which the bot is not supposed to respond, unlisted home telephone numbers, the user's personal schedule, and so on.

Thus, userbots provide a general mechanism for the distribution and protection of information. For a concrete example, consider the information you get by running the "finger" command. Right now, you have to decide whether your home phone number will be available to everyone on the internet, or no one at all. A straightforward task of your userbot would be to give out your phone number via email on request from (say) faculty members at your department and people listed in your address book, but not to every person who knows your login id.

Earlier we described the alternative Telescript model in which messages are programs that are executed on the receiving machine. This model raises concerns of computer security, particularly if such programs are able to access the host's file system. (Security features in Telescript allow the user to disable file access, but this would appear to limit the kinds of tasks Telescript agents could perform.) Userbot systems are by nature secure, insofar as the routines for processing each message type within the userbot are secure. Although this is a non-trivial condition, it would appear to be easier to guarantee that the code of the userbot itself (that is presumably obtained from a trusted source) is secure, rather than to guarantee that every email program (that could come from anyone) does not contain a virus. Extensions and updates to userbots to handle new message types would have to be distributed through secure channels, perhaps by using cryptographic techniques (Rivest, Shamir, & Adleman 1978).

Bots vs. Programs

An issue that is often raised is what exactly distinguishes software agents from ordinary programs. In our view, software agents are simply a special class of programs. Perhaps the best way to characterize these programs is by a list of distinguishing properties:

Communication: Agents engage in complex and frequent patterns of two-way communication with users and each other.

Temporal continuity: Agents are most naturally viewed as continuously running processes, rather than as functions that map a single input to a single output.

Responsibility: Agents are expected to handle private information in a responsible and secure manner.

Robustness: Agents should be designed to deal with unexpected changes in the environment. They should include mechanisms to recover both from system errors and human errors. If errors prevent completion of their given tasks, they still must report the problem back to their users.

Multi-platform: Agents should be able to communicate across different computer system architectures and platforms. For example, very sophisticated agents running on a high-end platform should be able to carry out tasks in cooperation with relatively basic agents running on low-end systems.

Autonomy: Advanced agents should have some degree of decision-making capability, and the ability to choose among different strategies for performing a given task.

Note that our list does not commit to the use of any particular form of reasoning or planning. Although advanced agents may need general reasoning and planning capabilities, our experiments have shown that interesting agent behavior can already emerge from systems of relatively simple agents.

Conclusions

We have described a bottom-up approach to the design of software agents. We built and tested an agent system that addresses the real-world problem of handling the communication involved in scheduling a visitor to our laboratory.

Our experiment helped us to identify crucial factors in the successful deployment of agents. These include issues of reliability, security, and ease of use. Security and ease of use were obtained by separating task-specific agents from personal userbots. This architecture provides an extensible and flexible platform for the further development of practical software agents. New task-specific agents immediately obtain a graphical user interface for communicating with users via the userbots. Furthermore, additional modalities of communication, such as speech and FAX, can be added to the userbots, without modifying the task-specific agents.

Perhaps the hardest problem we encountered was defining the initial task. More attention should be paid to identifying useful and compelling agent applications that blend unobtrusively into ordinary work environments. We believe that the empirical approach taken in this paper is essential for guiding research toward the truly central and difficult issues in agent design.

Acknowledgements

We thank Oren Etzioni for stimulating discussions about softbots during his visit to Bell Labs, leading us to initiate our own softbot project. We also thank Ron Brachman, Mark Jones, David Lewis Chris Ramming, Eric Sumner, and other members of our center for useful suggestions and feedback.

References

Dent, L.; Boticario, J.; McDermott, J.; Mitchell, T.; and Zabowski, D. 1992. A personal learning apprentice. In *Proceedings of AAAI-92*, 96–103. AAAI Press/The MIT Press.

Etzioni, O.; Hanks, S.; Weld, D.; Draper, D.; Lesh, N.; and Williamson, M. 1992. An approach to planning with incomplete information. In *Proceedings of KR-92*, 115–125. Morgan Kaufmann.

Etzioni, O.; Lesh, N.; and Segal, R. 1992. Building softbots for UNIX. Technical report, University of Washington, Seattle, WA.

Maes, P., and Kozierok, R. 1993. Learning interface agents. In *Proceedings of AAAI-93*, 459–464. AAAI Press/The MIT Press.

Maes, P., ed. 1993. *Designing Automomous Agents.* MIT/Elsevier.

Rivest, R. L.; Shamir, A.; and Adleman, L. 1978. A method for obtaining digital signatures and public key cryptosystems. *Communications of the ACM* 21(2):120–126.

Shoham, Y. 1993. Agent-oriented programming. *Artificial Intelligence* 60:51–92.

Collaborative Interface Agents

Yezdi Lashkari
MIT Media Laboratory,
Cambridge, MA 02139
yezdi@media.mit.edu

Max Metral
MIT Media Laboratory,
Cambridge, MA 02139
memetral@media.mit.edu

Pattie Maes
MIT Media Laboratory,
Cambridge, MA 02139
pattie@media.mit.edu

Abstract

Interface agents are semi-intelligent systems which assist users with daily computer-based tasks. Recently, various researchers have proposed a learning approach towards building such agents and some working prototypes have been demonstrated. Such agents learn by 'watching over the shoulder' of the user and detecting patterns and regularities in the user's behavior. Despite the successes booked, a major problem with the learning approach is that the agent has to learn from scratch and thus takes some time becoming useful. Secondly, the agent's competence is necessarily limited to actions it has seen the user perform. Collaboration between agents assisting different users can alleviate both of these problems. We present a framework for multi-agent collaboration and discuss results of a working prototype, based on learning agents for electronic mail.

Introduction

Learning interface agents are computer programs that employ machine learning techniques in order to provide assistance to a user dealing with a particular computer application. Although they are successful in being able to learn their user's behavior and assist them, a major drawback of these systems is the fact that they require a sufficient amount of time before they can be of any use. A related problem is the fact that their competence is necessarily restricted to situations similar to those they have encountered in the past. We present a collaborative framework to help alleviate these problems. When faced with an unfamiliar situation, an agent consults its peers who may have the necessary experience to help it.

Previous interface agents have employed either end-user programming and/or knowledge engineering for knowledge acquisition. For example, (Lai, Malone, & Yu 1988) have "semi-autonomous agents" that consist of a collection of user-programmed rules for processing information related to a particular task. The problems with this approach are that the user needs to recognize the opportunity for employing an agent, take the initiative in programming the rules, endow this agent with explicit knowledge (specified in an abstract language), and maintain the rules over time (as habits change etc). The knowledge engineered approach on the other hand, requires a knowledge engineer to outfit an interface with large amounts of knowledge about the application and the domain and how it may contribute to the user's goals. Such systems require a large amount of work from the knowledge engineer. Furthermore, the knowledge of the agent is fixed and cannot be customized to the habits of individual users. In highly personalized domains such as electronic mail and news, the knowledge engineer cannot possibly anticipate how to best aid each user in each of their goals.

To address the problems of the rule-based and knowledge-engineered approaches, machine learning techniques have been employed by (Kozierok & Maes 1993; Maes & Kozierok 1993; Hermens & Schlimmer 1993; Dent *et al.* 1992) and others. In the Calendar Agent (Kozierok & Maes 1993), memory-based reasoning is combined with rules to model each user's meeting scheduling habits. Results described in (Kozierok & Maes 1993) show that the learning approach achieves a level of personalization impossible with knowledge engineering, and without the user intervention required by rule-based systems. It is also interesting to note that the addition of rules provides the flexibility to explicitly teach the agent, and shows that the rule-based and learning approaches can successfully coexist.

While the learning approach enjoys several advantages over the others, it has its own set of deficiencies. Most learning agents have a slow 'learning curve' ; that is, they require a sufficient number of examples before they can make accurate predictions. During this period, the user must operate without the assistance of the interface agent. Even after learning general user behavior, when completely new situations arise the agent may have trouble dealing with them. The agents of different users thus have to go through similar experiences before they can achieve a minimal level of competence, although there may exist other agents that already possess the necessary experience and confidence.

We propose a collaborative solution to these problems. Experienced agents can help a new agent come up to speed quickly as well as help agents in unfamiliar situations. The framework for collaboration presented here allows agents of different users, possibly employing different strategies (rule-based, MBR, CBR, etc.) to cooperate to best aid their individual users. Agents thus have access to a much larger body of knowledge than that possessed by any individual agent. Over time agents learn to trust the suggestions of some of their peers more than others for various classes of situations. Thus each agent also learns which of its peers is a reliable 'expert' vis-a-vis its user for different types of situations.

A Single User's Agent

This paper describes experiments conducted with implemented interface agents for the electronic mail domain for a commercial email application, Eudora (Dorner 1992). This section describes an individual email agent.

Each user's interface agent learns by continuously "looking over the shoulder" of the user as the user is performing actions. The interface agent monitors the actions of the user over long periods of time, finds recurrent patterns and offers to automate them. For example, if an agent notices that a user almost always stores messages sent to the mailing-list "genetic-algorithms" in the folder *AI Mailing Lists*, then it can offer to automate this action next time a message sent to that mailing list is encountered. The agent can also automate reading, printing, replying, and forwarding as well as assign priority to messages.

We have chosen Memory Based Reasoning (Stanfill & Waltz 1986) as the algorithm which attempts to capture user patterns. Our implementation of MBR is based upon the concepts of situations and actions. In the electronic mail domain, we choose mail messages along with some context information to represent situations and the user's handling of the messages as actions. At any particular point in time, the user may be presented with a number of messages. When the user takes an action, it is paired with the corresponding situation and the situation-action pair is recorded in the agent's memory. For example, if the user reads a message $\mathcal{M}$, the pair $< \mathcal{M}'$, read-action$>$ is memorized, where $\mathcal{M}'$ contains details about the message $\mathcal{M}$ and relevant context information (for example that $\mathcal{M}$ was read n^{th} out of a total of k unread messages). When new situations occur, they are compared to the situations previously encountered. After gathering the closest matching situations in memory, the agent can calculate a prediction for an action in the new situation. In addition, the agent can calculate a confidence in its prediction by considering such factors as the number of situations in its memory and the proximity of the culled situations to the new situation. For a more detailed description, see (Kozierok & Maes 1993).

A situation is specified in terms of a set of fields. MBR measures situation proximity by applying a weighted sum of the distance between the corresponding fields of two situations. In the e-mail domain, appropriate fields would be the originator of the message, the subject, etc. The values of fields may be of any type. In previous systems, these fields were mainly strings or other static values. In our implementation, field values can also be objects. These objects can in turn have fields, which may be used in predicting actions. For example, the originator of a message is a *Person* object, which contains fields such as that person's position in an organization and their relation to the user. Object-based MBR is much less brittle than traditional MBR systems and can also use extra knowledge present in the objects if it finds it to be useful. For example, let's say that Mary always reads all messages from her boss Kay. If Mary were to suddenly receive a message from Kay's boss (therefore also Mary's boss), the system will correctly suggest that Mary read the message, since it uses the knowledge that Mary reads everything from her boss (and therefore probably her boss's boss too) although it has never previously received a message from Kay's boss. [1] Thus object-based MBR allows the same situation to be viewed differently depending on what information is available. In contrast, a string-based MBR system does not possess the same flexibility since we cannot extract more features from the string.

After predicting an action for a given situation, the agent must decide how to use that prediction. For each possible action, the user can set two confidence thresholds: the *tell-me* threshold and the *do-it* threshold. If the confidence in a prediction is above the tell-me threshold, the email agent displays the suggestion in the message summary line. If the confidence is above the do-it threshold, the agent autonomously takes the action.

The agent's confidence in its predictions grows with experience, which gives the user time to learn to trust the agent. During this period, it is especially useful to give the user the opportunity to see exactly what the agent is doing. This feedback is accomplished in three ways: an activity monitor, an explanation facility, and an interface to browse and edit the agent's memory. The activity monitor presents a small caricature to the user at all times. The caricature depicts states such as alert, thinking, and working, similar to (Kozierok & Maes 1993). An explanation facility provides English descriptions of why the agent suggested an action.

An agent starts out with no experience. As messages arrive and its user takes action, its memory grows. Only after a sufficient number of situation-action pairs have been generated, is the agent able to start predicting patterns of behavior confidently and accurately.

---

[1]Information about Kay and her boss are retrieved from a knowledge base of the kind maintained by most corporations or university academic departments.

However, when it encounters a new situation that is unlike anything it has in its memory, it is still unsure of what to do. This is because the machine learning algorithm used requires the training examples to cover most of the example space to work effectively.

A Framework For Collaboration

We propose a collaborative solution to the problems above. While a particular agent may not have any prior knowledge, there may exist a number of agents belonging to other users who do. Instead of each agent re-learning what other agents have already learned through experience, agents can simply ask for help in such cases. This gives each agent access to a potentially vast body of experience that already exists. Over time each agent builds up a trust relationship with each of its peers analogous to the way we consult different experts for help in particular domains and learn to trust or disregard the opinions of particular individuals.

Collaboration and communication between various agents can take many different forms. This paper is only concerned with those forms that aid an agent in making better predictions in the context of new situations. There are two general classes of such collaboration.

Desperation based communication is invoked when a particular agent has insufficient experience to make a confident prediction. For example, let us suppose that a particular agent A_1 has just been activated with no prior knowledge, and its user receives a set of new mail messages. As A_1 doesn't have any past experience to make predictions, it turns in desperation to other agents and asks them how their user would handle similar situations.

Exploratory communication, on the other hand, is initiated by agents in bids to find the best set of peer agents to ask for help in certain classes of situations. We envisage future computing environments to have multitudes of agents. As an agent has limited resources and can only have dealings with a small number of its peers at a given time, the issue of which ones to trust, and in what circumstances, becomes quite important. Exploratory communication is undertaken by agents to discover new (as yet untried) agents who are better predictors of their users' behaviors than the current set of peers they have previously tested.

Both forms of communication may occur at two orthogonal levels. At the situation level, desperation communication refers to an agent asking its peers for help in dealing with a new situation, while exploratory communication refers to an agent asking previously untested peers for how they would deal with old situations for which it knows the correct action, to determine whether these new agents are good predictors of its user's behavior. At the agent level, desperation communication refers to an agent asking trusted peers to recommend an agent that its peers trust, while exploratory communication refers to agents asking peers for their evaluation of a particular agent perhaps to see how well these peers' modelling of a particular agent corresponds with their own. Hence agents are not locked into having to turn for help to only a fixed set of agents, but can pick and choose the set of peers they find to be most reliable.

For agents to communicate and collaborate they must speak a common language as well as follow a common protocol. We assume the existence of a default ontology for situations in a given domain (such as electronic news, e-mail, meeting scheduling, etc). Our protocol does not preclude the existence of multiple ontologies for the same domain. This allows agent creators the freedom to decide which types of ontologies their agents will understand. As the primary task of an agent is to assist its particular user, the protocol for collaboration is designed to be flexible, efficient and non-binding. We briefly present the protocol below.

- **Registration:** Agents wishing to help others register themselves with a "Bulletin Board Agent" whose existence and location is known to all agents. While registering, agents provide information regarding how they can be contacted, what standard domains they can provide assistance in, what ontologies they understand and some optional information regarding their user. Every agent registering with a bulletin board agent is given a unique identifier by the bulletin board.

- **Locating peers:** Agents wishing to locate suitable peers may query bulletin board agents. An agent querying a bulletin board agent need not itself register with that bulletin board. Queries to a bulletin board agent can take many different forms depending on the type of information required. This allows agents to locate suitable peers in the most convenient way. For example, an agent's user may explicitly instruct it to ask a specific user's agent for help in dealing with certain types of situations.

- **Collaboration:** Collaborative communication between agents occurs in the form of request and reply messages. An agent is not required to reply to any message it receives. This leaves each agent the freedom to decide when and whom to help. Any request always contains the agent's identifier, the agent's contact information (for replies), the ontology used in the request, and a *request identifier* (*reqid*) generated by the agent issuing the request. The *reqid* is necessary since an agent may send out multiple requests simultaneously whose replies may arrive out of order.

  Analogously every reply always contains the replying agent's identifier and the reqid used in the request.

  The types of requests and their associated replies are presented below.

  - **Situation level collaboration:** When a situation occurs for which an agent does not have a good prediction, it sends off a **Request-for-Prediction** message to its peers. A prediction request contains all the features of the situation which the agent issuing the request wishes to divulge. This allows the requesting agent the freedom to withhold sensitive or private information. An agent receiving a prediction request may choose to ignore it for any of a variety of reasons. It may not have a good prediction for the specific situation, it may be too busy to respond, the agent issuing the request may not have been very helpful in the past, or the agent may not be important enough. If however, an agent decides to respond to a prediction request, it sends back a response containing its prediction and its confidence in this prediction (a normalized value).

Note that the prediction request is used by agents for both desperation and exploratory communication. An agent receiving a prediction request does not know whether the request originated via exploratory or desperation based behavior on the part of the agent issuing that request. The distinction is made by the agent issuing the request. Replies to requests sent in desperation are used to predict an action for a particular situation, while replies to requests sent in exploratory mode are compared with the actions that the user *actually took* in those situations, and are used to model how closely a peer's suggestions correspond with its user's actions.

Agent level collaboration: An agent may send its peers a **Request-for-Evaluation** request. An evaluation request is sent when an agent wants to know what some of its peers think about a certain agent in terms of being able to model their users in particular classes of situations. An evaluation request contains the identifier of the agent to be evaluated (designated as the *target agent*) and the particular class of situations for which the evaluation is needed.

In any domain and ontology there exist different classes of situations. Certain agents may model a particular user's behavior in a particular class of situations very well and fail miserably in other classes. Note that we expect the domain ontologies to define these classes. For example an email agent may discover that peer agent A_1 is a very good predictor of its user's actions for messages sent to a mailing list, while being quite useless in predicting what its user does with any other type of message. On the other hand peers A_2 and A_3 are excellent predictors of its user's behavior with regards to email forwarded by her groupmates. This enables agents to locate and consult different 'expert' peers for different classes of situations.

An agent that chooses to respond to an evaluation request sends back a normalized value which reflects its *trust* in the target agent's ability to

model its user's behavior for that particular class of situations.

An agent may also ask trusted peer agents to recommend a peer who has been found to be useful by the trusted peer in predicting its user's behavior for a particular class of situation. A **Request-for-Recommendation** contains the situation class for which the agent would like its trusted peer to recommend a good agent. Replies to recommendation requests contain the identifier and contact information of the agent being recommended.

Agents model peers' abilities to predict their user's actions in different classes of situations by a *trust* value. For each class of situations an agent has a list of peers with associated trust values. Trust values vary between 0 and 1.

The trust values reflect the degree to which an agent is willing to trust a peer's prediction for a particular situation class. A trust value represents a probability that a peer's prediction will correspond with its user's action based on a prior history of predictions from the peer. Agents may start out by picking a set of peers at random or by following their user's suggestion as to which peer agents to try first. Each previously untested peer agent gets has its trust level set to an initial value. As a peer responds to a prediction request with a prediction p, and an agent's user takes a particular action a, the agent updates the trust value of its peer in the appropriate situation class as follows:

$$trust = \ clamp(0, 1, trust + \delta_{p,a} * (\gamma * trust * conf))$$

where

$$\delta_{p,a} = \left\{ \begin{array}{ll} +1 & \text{if prediction p} = \text{user action a} \\ -1 & \text{if prediction p} \neq \text{user action a} \end{array} \right.$$

and *trust* represents the trust level of a peer, *conf* represents the confidence the peer has in this particular prediction, γ is the trust learning rate, and $clamp(0, 1, c)$ ensures that the value of c always lies in $(0, 1]$. The rationale behind the modelling above is as follows. An agent's trust in a peer rises when the peer makes a correct prediction and falls for incorrect predictions. The amount it rises and falls by depends on how confident the peer was in its prediction. That is, a peer who makes an incorrect prediction with a high confidence value should be penalized more heavily than one that makes an incorrect prediction but with a lower confidence value.

When an agent sends out a prediction request to more than one peer it is likely to receive many replies, each with a potentially different prediction and confidence value. In addition, the agent has a trust value associated with each peer. This gives rise to many possible strategies which an agent can use to choose a prediction and a confidence value for this prediction. We believe that both trust and peer confidence should play a role in determining which prediction gets selected and with what confidence. Each predicted action is assigned a *trust-confidence sum* value which is the trust weighted sum of the confidence values of all the peers predicting this action. The action with the highest trust-confidence sum is chosen. The confidence associated with the action chosen is currently that of the most confident peer suggesting this action. We are exploring more sophisticated trust-confidence combination strategies using decision theoretic and Bayesian strategies.

Experimental Results

The concepts above have been implemented for a commercial electronic mail handler (Eudora) for the Apple Macintosh. The agent, implemented in Macintosh Common Lisp, communicates with the mail application using the AppleEvent protocol. The MBR Engine is domain independent, and can be easily adapted to calendar applications or news readers. Furthermore, all of these applications can share fields and actions. As more applications implement an AppleEvent interface, the agent should be able to aid the user with these applications as well. Currently, several users are actively making use of the agent on their actual mail. While the computations are intensive, we have achieved satisfactory performance on most high end Macintoshes.

The performance of MBR in interface agents has been documented in (Kozierok & Maes 1993). We wish to show that multi-agent collaboration strictly improves upon results obtained from single agent systems. Namely, multi-agent collaboration should steepen the learning curve and improve the handling of entirely novel messages.

To illustrate this, we set up the following scenario using the actual e-mail of two graduate students over a three day period (approximately 100 messages per user).

Calvin and Hobbes are two graduate students in the Intelligent Agents group.

1. **Hobbes :** Hobbes has been around for some time and hence his agent is quite experienced. Hobbes' agent has noted the following trends in its user's behavior. All messages to 'bpm', a music mailing list are refiled to a folder called bpm for later reading. Messages directly addressed to Hobbes are read by him and then deleted, as are messages to other mailing lists.

2. **Calvin :** Calvin is a new graduate student in the group. Calvin's agent starts out with absolutely no experience. Calvin also refiles all messages from the 'bpm' list for later perusal. He deletes subscription requests sent to the list. Calvin reads messages directly addressed to him, and then refiles them to appropriate folders. The rest of his mail, such as messages to other lists, he reads and deletes.

We plotted the confidence of Calvin's agent's suggestions as Calvin takes actions on about 100 actual mail messages. Figure 1 shows the results obtained. The x-axis indicates the growing experience of Calvin's

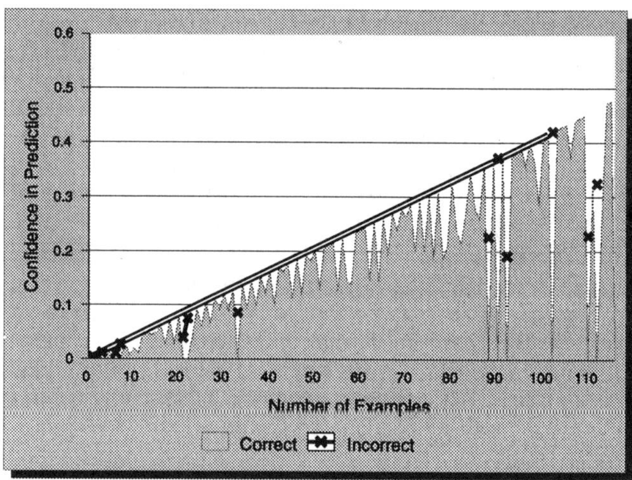

Figure 1: Performance without Collaboration

agent as Calvin takes successive actions on the mail messages and the number of situation-action pairs in the memory increases. The thick rising *trend line* indicates how Calvin's agent's performance (in terms of confidence in predictions) rises slowly with experience. The numerous pockets show new user behavior being modeled. The agent makes several mistakes very early, which is to be expected, since the situations it has in its memory early on do not effectively capture all of Calvin's behavior patterns. Towards the end, we see several more mistakes, which reflect a new pattern occuring. With the tell-me threshold for all actions set at 0.1, the graph shows that it will take approximately 40 examples for the agent to gain enough confidence to consistently have suggestions for the user.

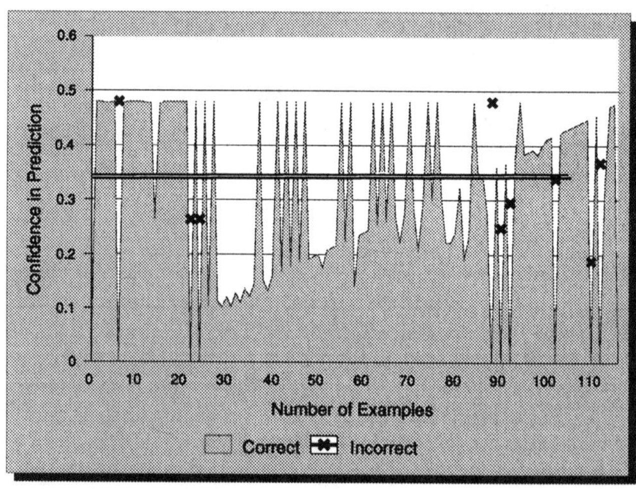

Figure 2: Performance with Collaboration

Figure 2 shows the level of confidence of Calvin's agent in its suggestions with multi-agent collabora-

tion. [2] It may be noted that the confidence levels
of all correct suggestions are always greater than the
confidence levels generated by Calvin's agent alone
at any point. The thick horizontal *trend line* indicates that multi-agent collaboration enables an inexpe-
rienced agent to make accurate predictions with high
confidence as soon as it is activated as well as fill in
gaps in even an experienced agent's knowledge. Note
that trust modelling of Hobbes' agent is taking place
inside Calvin's agent with each action Calvin takes on
his mail. Space restrictions preclude the presentation
of results regarding trust modelling of multiple peers
in this paper.

Related Work

Various types of learning interface agents have been implemented (Kozierok & Maes 1993; Maes & Kozierok
1993; Hermens & Schlimmer 1993; Dent *et al.* 1992).
All of them are essentially designed to act in a stand-
alone fashion or engage in restricted task specific communication with identical peers. Our agents not only
come up to speed much faster, but also discover which
of a large set of heterogeneous peers are useful consultants to know in particular domains.

Multi-Agent Systems research has concentrated on
negotiation and cooperation strategies that are used
by autonomous agents who must compete for scarce
resources. Various formal protocols and frameworks
have been proposed to model agent's intentions, domains and negotiation strategies (Zlotkin & Rosenschein 1993; Rosenschein & Genesereth 1985) based on
various game-theoretic, logical, economic and speech-
act models. While the analytic frameworks above are
important, most are based on restrictive assumptions
about the domain or the agents' capabilities and assume that the reason agents cooperate is because they
need access to a shared resource or have multiple overlapping goals.

The Ontolingua tools (Gruber 1993) and the work
on the KQML Agent-Communication Language (Finin
et al. 1993) provide a way for agents using different ontologies to communicate effectively with each other and
may be used to implement our collaborative architecture. Our research represents an actually implemented
system in a real domain that shows the benefits of collaboration amongst agents.

Conclusions

We have implemented a learning interface agent for
a commercial application in a real world domain, and
have tested it with real world data. Results have shown
that multi-agent collaboration steepens the agent's
learning curve, and helps in new, unseen situations.
Trust modeling allows each agent to build a model of

each agent's area of expertise, and consult only those
agents which will be useful for each area.

Acknowledgments

This research was sponsored by grants from Apple
Computer Inc. and the National Science Foundation
under grant number IRI-92056688.

References

Dent, L.; Boticario, J.; McDermott, J.; Mitchell, T.;
and Zabowski, D. 1992. A personal learning apprentice. In *Proceedings of the Tenth National Conference
on Artificial Intelligence*, 96–103. San Jose, California: AAAI Press.

Dorner, S. 1992. *Eudora Reference Manual.* Qual-
comm Inc.

Finin, T.; Weber, J.; Wiederhold, G.; Genesereth,
M.; Fritzson, R.; McKay, D.; McGuire, J.; Pelavin,
R.; Shapiro, S.; and Beck, C. 1993. Specification of
the KQML agent-communication language. Techni-
cal Report EIT TR 92-04 (Revised June 15, 1993),
Enterprise Integration Technologies, Palo Alto, CA.

Gruber, T. 1993. A translation approach to
portable ontology specification. *Knowledge Acquisition* 5(2):199–220.

Hermens, L., and Schlimmer, J. 1993. A machine
learning apprentice for the completion of repetitive
forms. In *Proceedings of the Ninth IEEE Conference
on Artificial Intelligence for Applications*, 164–170.
Orlando, Florida: IEEE Press.

Kozierok, R., and Maes, P. 1993. A learning interface agent for scheduling meetings. In *Proceedings of
the ACM SIGCHI International Workshop on Intelligent User Interfaces*, 81–88. Orlando, Florida: ACM
Press.

Lai, K.; Malone, T.; and Yu, K. 1988. Object lens: A
spreadsheet for cooperative work. *ACM Transactions
on Office-Information Systems* 5(4):297–326.

Maes, P., and Kozierok, R. 1993. Learning interface agents. In *Proceedings of the Eleventh National
Conference on Artificial Intelligence*, 459–465. Washington D.C.: AAAI Press.

Rosenschein, J., and Genesereth, M. 1985. Deals
among rational agents. In *Proceedings of the Ninth
International Joint Conference on Artificial Intelligence*, 91–99. Los Angeles, CA: Morgan Kaufmann.

Stanfill, C., and Waltz, D. 1986. Toward memory-
based reasoning. *Communications of the ACM*
29(12):1213–1228.

Zlotkin, G., and Rosenschein, J. 1993. A domain
theory for task oriented negotiation. In *Proceedings
of the Thirteenth International Joint Conference on
Artificial Intelligence*, 416–422. Chambery, France:
Morgan Kaufmann.

---

[2]Hobbes takes no actions on his mail for the duration
of this experiment, hence his agent's confidence remains
unchanged.

Enabling
Technologies

Combining Left and Right Unlinking
for Matching a Large Number of Learned Rules

Robert B. Doorenbos
School of Computer Science
Carnegie Mellon University
Pittsburgh, PA 15213-3891
Robert.Doorenbos@CS.CMU.EDU

Abstract

In systems which learn a large number of rules (productions), it is important to match the rules efficiently, in order to avoid the machine learning *utility problem*. So we need match algorithms that scale well with the number of productions in the system. (Doorenbos 1993) introduced *right unlinking* as a way to improve the scalability of the Rete match algorithm. This paper introduces a symmetric optimization, *left unlinking*, and demonstrates that it makes Rete scale well on an even larger class of systems. Unfortunately, when left and right unlinking are combined in the same system, they can interfere with each other. We give a particular way to combine them which we prove minimizes this interference, and analyze the worst-case remaining interference. Finally, we present empirical results showing that the interference is very small in practice, and that the combination of left and right unlinking allows five of our seven testbed systems to learn over 100,000 rules without incurring a significant increase in match cost.[1]

1 Introduction

The goal of this research is to support large learned production systems; i.e., systems that learn a large number of rules. This is important because if AI is to achieve its long-term goals, AI systems (including rule-based systems) must be able to use vast amounts of knowledge. In large systems it is crucial that we match the rules efficiently; otherwise the systems will be very slow. In particular, we don't want the match cost to increase significantly as new rules are learned. Such an increase is one cause of the *utility problem* in machine learning (Minton 1988) — if the learned

rules slow down the matcher, the net effect of learning can be to slow down the whole system, rather than speed it up. For example, learned rules may reduce the number of basic steps a system takes to solve problems (e.g., by pruning the search space), but if the slowdown in the matcher increases the time per step, then this can outweigh the reduction in the number of steps. This has been observed in several machine learning systems (Minton 1988; Etzioni 1990a; Tambe, Newell, & Rosenbloom 1990; Cohen 1990; Gratch & DeJong 1992).

To avoid this slowdown, previous research on the utility problem from match cost has taken three general approaches. One approach is simply to reduce the number of rules in the system's knowledge base, by being selective about when to learn or which rules or types of rules to learn, or by forgetting previously learned rules if they slow down the matcher enough to cause an overall system slowdown (Minton 1988; Etzioni 1990b; Holder 1992; Gratch & DeJong 1992; Greiner & Jurisica 1992; Markovitch & Scott 1993). Unfortunately, this approach is inadequate for the long-term goals of AI because, given the current state of match technology, it precludes learning a vast amount of knowledge. Moreover, it is intuitively desirable to have AI systems that take advantage of every opportunity for learning, rather than forgoing certain opportunities.

The second general approach is to reduce the match cost of individual rules, taken one at a time. Many techniques have been developed for this (Tambe, Newell, & Rosenbloom 1990; Minton 1988; Etzioni 1990a; Pérez & Etzioni 1992; Chase *et al.* 1989; Cohen 1990; Kim & Rosenbloom 1993). This prevents just a handful of *expensive rules* from slowing the matcher down to a crawl; thus, the system can learn more rules before an overall slowdown results. Unfortunately, an overall slowdown can still result when a large number of individually cheap rules exact a high match cost.

The third approach, and the one taken by this work, complements the second by reducing the aggregate match cost of a large number of rules, without regard to

---

[1] This research is sponsored by the Wright Laboratory, Aeronautical Systems Center, Air Force Materiel Command, USAF, and the Advanced Research Projects Agency (ARPA) under grant number F33615-93-1-1330. Views and conclusions contained in this document are those of the authors and should not be interpreted as necessarily representing official policies or endorsements, either expressed or implied, of Wright Laboratory or the United States Government.

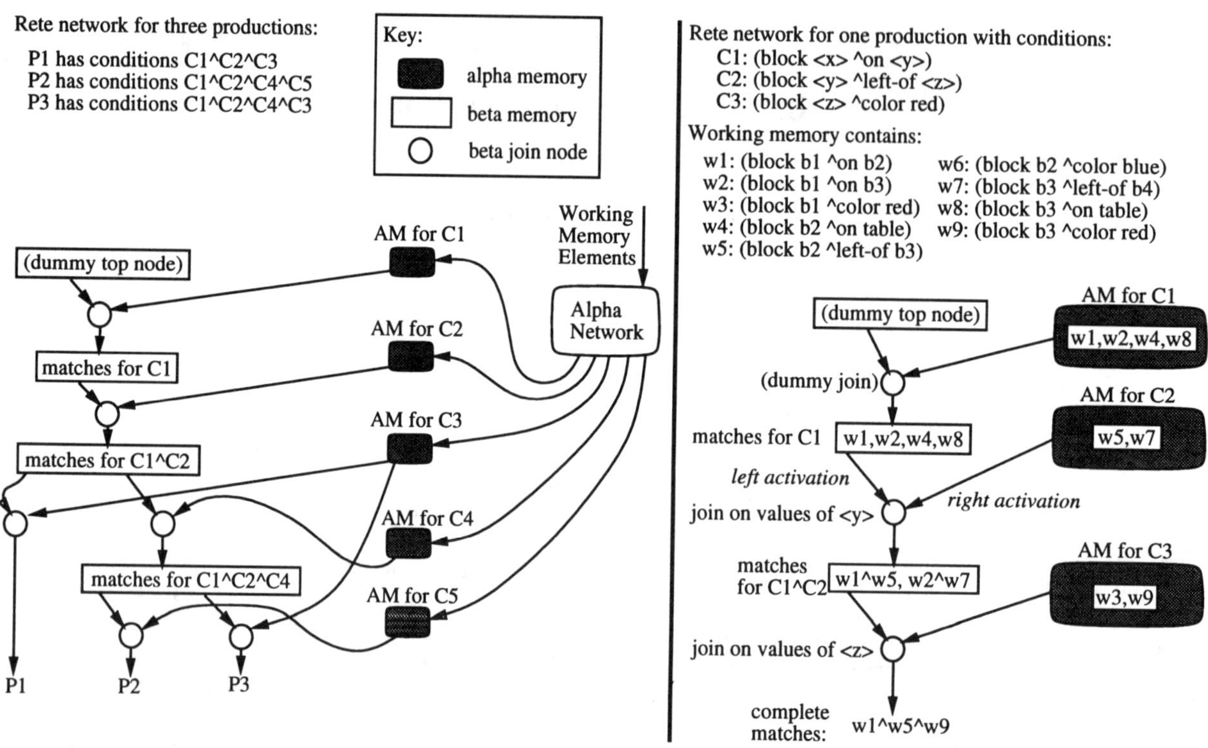

Figure 1: Network used by Rete for several productions (left) and instantiated network for one production (right).

the cost of each individual rule. As (Doorenbos 1993) showed, the use of sophisticated match algorithms can sometimes reduce the matcher slowdown due to learning a large number of rules to the point where it is unproblematic. (Doorenbos 1993) introduced the idea of *right unlinking* in the Rete match algorithm (Forgy 1982), and showed that for at least one "natural" system (not designed just for match algorithm performance), Dispatcher, right unlinking eliminated virtually all the matcher slowdown associated with learning 100,000 rules. However, for another natural system, Assembler, the matcher was still slowing down to a crawl as the system learned 35,000 rules.

In this paper we build on the idea of right unlinking. We begin by reviewing in Section 2 the basic Rete algorithm and right unlinking. Section 3 examines the cause of the slowdown in the Assembler system, and shows how it can be avoided by adding another improvement to Rete: *left unlinking*. Left unlinking is essentially symmetric to right unlinking. Unfortunately, these optimizations are not completely orthogonal: when combined in the same system, they can interfere with each other. In Section 4 we give a particular way to combine them which we prove minimizes this interference. The worst-case remaining interference is analyzed in Section 5. Finally, Section 6 presents empirical results, showing that in contrast to the worst case, the interference is very small in practice. The evaluation is done with respect to a set of seven systems — including

the aforementioned Dispatcher and Assembler — implemented in Soar (Laird, Newell, & Rosenbloom 1987; Rosenbloom *et al.* 1991), an architecture which learns new rules through *chunking* (Laird, Rosenbloom, & Newell 1986). The combination of both left and right unlinking allows five out of the seven systems to learn over 100,000 rules without incurring a significant increase in match cost.

2   Background

We begin by briefly reviewing the Rete algorithm. As illustrated in Figure 1, Rete uses a dataflow network to represent the conditions of the productions. The network has two parts. The alpha part performs the constant tests on working memory elements. Its output is stored in *alpha memories* (AM), each of which holds the current set of working memory elements passing all the constant tests of an individual condition. The alpha network is commonly implemented using a simple discrimination network and/or hash tables, and thus is very efficient, running in approximately constant time per change to working memory. Previous studies have shown that the beta part of the network accounts for most of the match cost (Gupta 1987). The beta part contains *join nodes*, which perform the tests for consistent variable bindings between conditions, and *beta memories*, which store partial instantiations of productions (sometimes called *tokens*). When working memory changes, the network is updated as follows: the changes are sent through the alpha network and the appropriate alpha memories are updated. These updates are then propagated over to the attached join nodes (*activating* those nodes). If any new partial instantiations are created, they are propagated down the beta part of the network (activating other nodes). Whenever the propagation reaches the bottom of the network, it indicates that a production's conditions are completely matched.

An important feature of Rete is its *sharing* of nodes between productions. When two or more productions have a common condition, Rete uses a single alpha memory for it, rather than creating a duplicate memory for each production. Furthermore, when two or more productions have the same first few conditions, the same parts of the network are used to match those conditions, avoiding duplicating match effort across those productions.

Although Rete is one of the best standard match algorithms available, (Doorenbos 1993) observed that neither it nor its major alternative — Treat (Miranker 1990) — scales well with the number of rules in the Dispatcher and Assembler systems: both Rete and Treat slow down linearly in the number of rules. However, (Doorenbos 1993) described an optimization for Rete, *right unlinking*, which eliminated this linear slowdown in Dispatcher (but not Assembler).

To understand what right unlinking is, consider the activation of a join node from its associated alpha memory (henceforth called a *right activation*) — this happens whenever a working memory element is added to or removed from its alpha memory. Right unlinking is based on the observation that if the join node's beta memory is empty, then no work need be done: the working memory element cannot match any items in the beta memory, because there aren't any items there. So if we know in advance that the beta memory is empty, we can skip the right activation of that join node. We refer to right activations of join nodes with empty beta memories as *null right activations*.

We modify the Rete algorithm to incorporate *right unlinking* as follows. On each alpha memory there is a list of associated join nodes. Whenever a join node's beta memory becomes empty, we splice that join node out of the list on its associated alpha memory. When the beta memory later becomes nonempty again, we splice the join node back into the list. Now while a join node is unlinked from its alpha memory, it never gets activated by the alpha memory. Note that since the only activations we are skipping are null activations — which would not yield a match anyway — this optimization does not affect the set of complete production matches that will be found.

As (Doorenbos 1993) showed, in the Dispatcher system, the slowdown in the standard Rete algorithm is almost entirely due to a linear increase in the number of null right activations. So right unlinking is very effective in avoiding the slowdown in Dispatcher. How-

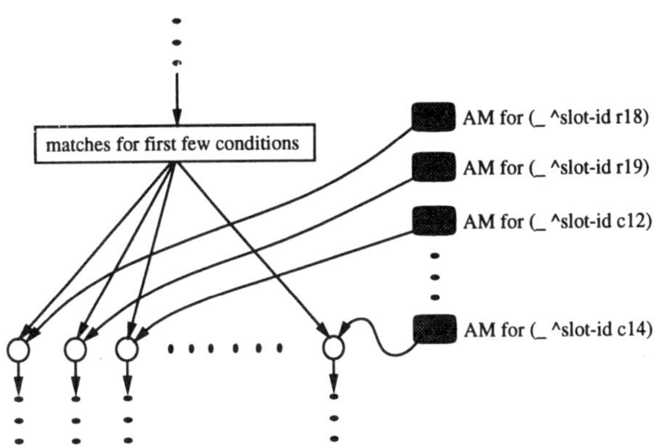

Figure 2: Part of the Rete network for Assembler.

ever, in the Assembler system, it yields only a constant speedup factor of about three, because null right activations are not the only major source of slowdown there.

3 Left Unlinking

For the Assembler system, there appears to be a second major source of slowdown: a significant linear increase in the number of null left activations. This system is a cognitive model of a person assembling printed circuit boards (e.g., inserting resistors into the appropriate slots). Most of the rules it learns are specific to the particular slot on the board being dealt with at the moment. The first few conditions in these rules are always the same, but the next condition is different in each rule. As illustrated in Figure 2, this leads to a large fan-out from one beta memory. The first few conditions in all the rules share the same nodes, but at this point, sharing is no longer possible because each rule tests for a *different* slot. As the system deals with more and more slots, more and more rules are learned, and the fan-out increases linearly in the total number of rules.

Now, whenever all of the first few conditions of these rules are true, the dataflow in the Rete network reaches this beta memory and a token is stored there. This token is then propagated to all the memory's child join nodes, *left activating* those nodes. Since the number of such nodes is increasing linearly in the number of rules, the work done here is also linearly increasing. However, most of this work is wasted. Since the system is only focusing its attention on a few slots at a time, most of the join nodes have empty alpha memories. Their activations are therefore *null left activations*, and no new matches result from them. Although each individual null left activation takes very little time to execute, the number of null left activations (per change to working memory) is linearly increasing, and so this can grow to dominate the overall match cost.

To avoid doing all this fruitless work, we can incorporate *left unlinking* into the Rete algorithm. Left unlinking is symmetric to right unlinking: whereas with right unlinking, a join node is spliced out of its alpha memory's list of successors whenever its beta memory is empty, with left unlinking, a join node is spliced out of its beta memory's list of successors whenever its alpha memory is empty. Thus, in Figure 2, most of the join nodes would be unlinked from the beta memory, so they would *not* be activated whenever the first few conditions in the rules are true. As with right unlinking, the only activations we are skipping are null activations — which would not yield any matches anyway — so this optimization leaves the correctness of the Rete algorithm intact.[2]

Left unlinking is expected to be useful in many systems in addition to Assembler. The large fan-out from beta memories could arise in any system where the domain has some feature with a large number of possible values, and the learned rules are specific to particular values of that feature. For instance, in a robot domain, if the appropriate action to be taken by the robot depends on the exact current room temperature, it might learn a set of rules where each one checks for a different current temperature reading. In a system with a simple episodic memory, learned rules implementing that memory might all contain different timestamps in their conditions. In cases like these, learned rules will often share nodes in the Rete network for their *early* conditions, up to but not including the conditions testing the feature in question. If this feature can have only one value at a time, then most of the rules will fail to match at this condition, and left unlinking will avoid a large number of null left activations. In addition, we will see in Section 6 that left unlinking can often be beneficial even in systems where the fan-out isn't especially large and null left activations don't dominate the overall match cost.

4 Combining Left & Right Unlinking

Since right unlinking avoids all null right activations, and left unlinking avoids all null left activations, we would like to combine both in the same system and avoid all null activations entirely. Unfortunately, this is not possible, because the two optimizations can interfere with each other. The problem arises when a join node's alpha and beta memories are *both* empty. Left unlinking dictates that the node be unlinked from its beta memory. Right unlinking dictates that the node be unlinked from its alpha memory. If we do both, then the join node will be completely cut off from the rest of the network and will never be activated again, even when it should be. The correctness of the match algorithm would be lost. *To ensure correctness, when*

a *join node's memories are both empty, we can use either left unlinking or right unlinking, but not both.* But which one? If we use left but not right unlinking in this situation, then we can still suffer null right activations. If we use right but not left unlinking, then we can still suffer null left activations in this situation. Thus, no scheme for combining left and right unlinking can avoid *all* null activations.

If both memories are empty, which one should the join node be unlinked from? A number of possible heuristics come to mind. We might left unlink nodes whose beta memories have sufficiently large fan-out (as in Figure 2). Or we might do a trial run of the system in which we record how many null left and right activations each node incurs; then on later runs, we would unlink from the side that incurred more null activations in the trial run.

Remarkably, it turns out that there is a simple scheme for combining left and right unlinking which is not only straightforward to implement, but also provably optimal in minimizing the residual number of null activations.

Definition: *In the* **first-empty-dominates** *scheme for combining left and right unlinking, a join node J with alpha memory A and beta memory B is unlinked as follows. (1) If A is empty but B is nonempty, it is linked to A and unlinked from B. (2) If B is empty but A is nonempty, it is linked to B and unlinked from A. (3) If A and B are both empty, it is (i.e., remains) linked to whichever memory became empty earlier, and unlinked from the other memory.*

To see how this works and how it falls naturally out of a straightforward implementation, consider a join node that starts with its alpha and beta memories both nonempty (so it is linked to both). Now suppose the alpha memory becomes empty. We unlink the join node from its beta memory (i.e., left unlink it). As long as the alpha memory remains empty, the join node remains unlinked from the beta memory — and hence, never gets activated from the beta memory: it never hears about any changes to the beta memory. Even if the beta memory becomes empty, the join node doesn't get informed of this, so nothing changes — it remains left unlinked — and the empty alpha memory essentially "dominates" the empty beta memory because the alpha memory became empty first. The join node remains unlinked from its beta memory until the alpha memory becomes nonempty again.

The definition of first-empty-dominates ignores the possibility that a join node could *start* with both its memories empty. When a rule is learned and added to the Rete net, some of its join nodes may have both memories empty. In this case, we can pick one side by any convenient method. (In the current implementation, the node is right unlinked.) The worst that can happen is that we pay a one-time initialization cost of one null activation for each join node; this cost is negligible in the long run. Once one of the memories

---

[2]We ignore here the case of negative conditions, which test for the *absence* of particular items in working memory. Nodes for negative conditions cannot be left unlinked without destroying the correctness of the algorithm. Fortunately, they are typically much less common than positive conditions.(Gupta 1987)

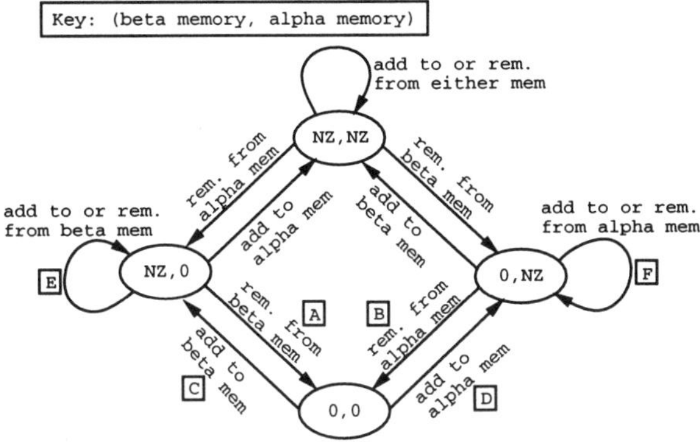

Figure 3: Possible states of a join node and its alpha and beta memories.

becomes nonempty, we can use first-empty-dominates.

It turns out that first-empty-dominates is the optimal scheme for combining left and right unlinking: except for the possible one-activation initialization cost, it minimizes the number of null activations. Thus, this simple scheme yields the minimal interference between left and right unlinking. This result is formalized as follows:

Theorem (Optimality of First-Empty-Dominates): *Any scheme for combining left and right unlinking must incur at least as many null activations of each join node as first-empty-dominates incurs, ignoring the possible one-activation initialization cost.*

Proof: For any given join node, Figure 3 shows the four states its alpha and beta memories can be in: the number of items in each memory can be 0 or nonzero (NZ). The figure also shows all the possible state transitions that can occur on changes to the alpha and beta memories. All the transitions into and out of (NZ,NZ) are *non-null* activations. Unlinking never avoids non-null activations, so the join node will incur one activation on each of these transitions no matter what unlinking scheme we use.

The remaining transitions (labeled A–F) are null activations if no unlinking is done; but the join node will not be activated on these if it is unlinked from the appropriate memory. Under first-empty-dominates, the join node is always unlinked from its beta memory when in state (NZ,0). This means it will not incur a null activation on transition A or E. Similarly, it is always unlinked from its alpha memory when in state (0,NZ), so it will not incur a null activation on transition B or F. This leaves just C and D to consider. In state (0,0), the join node is unlinked from its beta memory if its alpha memory became empty *before* its beta memory did — i.e., if it arrived at (0,0) via transition A — and unlinked from its alpha memory otherwise — i.e., if it arrived via B. (This ignores the case where the node *starts* at (0,0).) This means a null activation is incurred by first-empty-dominates only when D follows A or when C follows B.

Now, in *any* scheme for combining left and right unlinking, the join node must incur at least one null activation when taking transition A and then D — the reason is as follows. The join node cannot start out unlinked from both sides: as noted above, this would destroy the correctness of the algorithm. If it starts out linked to its beta memory, it incurs a null activation on transition A. On the other hand, if it starts out linked to its alpha memory, it incurs a null activation on transition D. (The link cannot be "switched" after transition A but before D — that would require executing a piece of code just for this one join node, which logically constitutes an activation of the node.) So in any case, it incurs at least one null activation.

A symmetric argument shows that in *any* unlinking scheme, at least one null activation must be incurred when taking transition B and then C. Since these are the only causes of null activations in first-empty-dominates, and it incurs only a single null activation on each one, it follows that *any* scheme must incur at least as many null activations. Q.E.D.

5 Worst-Case Analysis

How bad could the interference between left and right unlinking be? It would be nice if the residual number of null activations per change to working memory were bounded, but unfortunately it is not — other than being bounded by n, the total number of join nodes in the network (a very large bound). However, null activations don't occur all by themselves — they are *triggered* by changes to alpha and beta memories. If it takes a lot of triggering activity to cause a lot of null activations, then null activations won't dominate the overall match cost. The question to ask is: "By what factor is the matcher slowed down by null activations?" To answer this, we'll look at

$$\nu \overset{\text{def}}{=} \frac{\text{\# of activations of all nodes}}{\text{\# of act'ns of all nodes, } except \text{ null join act'ns}}$$

$$= 1 + \frac{\text{\# of null join node act'ns}}{\text{\# act'ns of all nodes, } except \text{ null join act'ns}}.$$

Note that ν is actually a pessimistic answer to this question, because it assumes all activations have the same cost, when in fact null activations take less time to execute than other activations.

Without any unlinking, or with left or right unlinking but not both, it is easy to show that ν is $O(n)$ in the worst case, and in fact this often arises in practice, as shown in (Doorenbos 1993) and in Section 6 below. However, the first-empty-dominates combination of left and right unlinking reduces this theoretical worst case to $O(\sqrt{n})$.

Before we get to the worst-case analysis, two assumptions must be made. First, we will ignore the possible initial null activation of each join node which starts out with its alpha and beta memories both empty — of course, this initialization cost is negligible in the long run. Second, we will assume that no two join nodes use both the same alpha memory *and* the same beta memory. This is the normal situation in practice.[3]

Given these assumptions, it turns out that with the first-empty-dominates combination of left and right unlinking, $\nu \leq 1 + \frac{1}{2}\sqrt{n}$. To see how the worst case can arise, consider a system with k alpha memories, each initially with one item in it; k beta memories, each initially empty; and $n = k^2$ join nodes, one for each pair of alpha and beta memories. Now suppose that in each alpha memory, the one item in it is removed; following this, one item is first added to and then removed from every beta memory; and finally, a new item is added to each alpha memory. This sequence of $4k$ activations of alpha and beta memories causes every join node to undergo transitions B, C, A, and D (see Figure 3), incurring two null activations, for a total of $2k^2$ null activations. Hence $\nu = 1 + \frac{2k^2}{4k} = 1 + \frac{k}{2} = 1 + \frac{1}{2}\sqrt{n}$. That this value of ν is actually the worst one possible is proved in the extended version of this paper (Doorenbos 1994).

6   Empirical Results

In Section 3, we introduced left unlinking as a way to avoid the matcher slowdown associated with increasing fan-outs from beta memories in systems like Assembler. After presenting in Section 4 the optimal way to combine left and right unlinking so as to minimize the interference between them, we analyzed in Section 5 how much interference there can be in the worst case. This section examines what happens in practice — how much interference is there in practice, and how well does combined left and right unlinking avoid matcher slowdown?

To answer these questions, we ran experiments using a set of seven Soar systems, including the aforementioned two. Assembler (Mertz 1992) is a cognitive model of a person assembling printed circuit boards. Dispatcher (Doorenbos, Tambe, & Newell 1992) is a message dispatcher for a large organization and uses an external organizational database. Merle (Prietula *et al.* 1993) schedules tasks for an automobile windshield factory. Radar (Papageorgiou & Carley 1993) learns to classify aircraft radar images (specified as simple feature vectors) as friendly, neutral, or hostile. SCA (Miller & Laird 1991) is a Soar system that performs traditional concept acquisition. Two versions of SCA were used: SCA-Fixed always focuses its attention on the same features of each training example, whereas SCA-Rand focuses on a different randomly chosen set of features on each training example. This leads to much better sharing in the Rete network for SCA-Fixed than SCA-Rand, and consequent matcher performance differences. Finally, Sched (Nerb, Krems, & Ritter 1993) is a computational model of skill acquisition in job-shop scheduling. These seven systems provide a good test suite because they use a variety of problem-solving methods in a variety of domains, and none was designed for these experiments. For each system, a problem generator was used to create a set of problem instances; the system was then allowed to solve the sequence of problems, learning new rules as it went along. Each system learned at least 100,000 rules.

Table 1 shows, for each system, the number of null and non-null join node activations per working memory change, averaged over the course of the whole run. For null activations, four different numbers are given, corresponding to four different match algorithms: the basic Rete algorithm without any unlinking, Rete with left but not right unlinking, Rete with right but not left unlinking, and Rete with the first-empty-dominates combination of left and right unlinking. The table shows that without any unlinking, or with left unlinking only, the matcher is essentially swamped by null activations in all the systems. With right unlinking but no left unlinking, there are still a large number of null (left) activations in both Assembler and Radar, and a fair number in Sched. Finally, with left and right unlinking combined, the number of null activations is very small in all the systems. Thus, the interference between left and right unlinking turns out to be insignificant in practice, at least for this diverse set of systems.

Returning to our second question — How well does combined left and right unlinking avoid matcher slowdown? Figure 4 shows the match cost, in CPU time per change to working memory, for each of the systems.[4] The match cost is plotted as a function of the total number of rules in the system. The four lines on each graph correspond to the four match algorithms described above. (Note that the vertical axes on the graphs have different scales — the match cost varies across systems.) The figure shows that without right unlinking, all the systems suffer a major linear slowdown as the system learns more and more rules. The addition of left unlinking (in combination with right unlinking) enables both Assembler and Radar to avoid a significant linear slowdown as the number of rules increases, and Sched to avoid a slight linear slowdown. This is because these three systems have increasing fan-outs from beta memories, as discussed in Section 3.

---

[3]It is possible for two or more join nodes to use the same alpha and the same beta memories — if there are productions whose conditions test exactly the same constants in the same places, but have different inter-condition variable binding consistency checks — but this is not very common in practice. Even in theory, the number of join nodes using the same pair of memories can be bounded *independent* of the number of productions in the system. If this bound is c, the worst-case bound becomes $1 + \frac{c}{2}\sqrt{n}$.

[4]Times are for Soar version 6.0.6 (modulo changes to the matcher) on a DFCstation 5000/200. Many of the runs without unlinking became so slow that time limitations forced them to be stopped at much less than 100,000 rules.

		Join node activations per change to working memory:				
			Null, when using this type of unlinking:			
System	# of rules	Non-null	None	Left only	Right only	Both
Assembler	105,308	15.4	2214.8	1711.5	503.3	0.11
Dispatcher	115,962	19.6	1248.4	1234.3	14.0	0.16
Merle	102,048	22.8	7561.7	7548.3	13.4	0.28
Radar	105,385	9.8	1570.7	1482.8	87.9	0.12
SCA-Fixed	108,799	7.1	2302.9	2301.7	1.2	0.20
SCA-Rand	106,853	13.6	2338.2	2333.4	4.8	2.29
Sched	117,386	21.7	4020.1	3976.0	44.1	0.22

Table 1: Average number of join node activations per change to working memory on each system, with different versions of the matcher.

Finally, the addition of left unlinking to right unlinking reduces the match cost slightly (7–15%) in most of the other systems.[5] Thus, not only is the addition of left unlinking to right unlinking crucial in systems where fan-outs from beta memories grow large, but it can be helpful in other systems, too.

7 Conclusions and Future Work

Although right unlinking avoids matcher slowdown due to increasing null right activations, it is insufficient for many systems which learn rules specific to one value of a domain feature with many possible values. In such systems, we can avoid the increase in null left activations by using left unlinking. Left and right unlinking have the potential to interfere with each other — significantly in the worst case — but the first-empty-dominates combination minimizes this interference and makes it very small in practice.

This paper dealt with networks containing just *binary* joins — every join node has exactly two input memories. Unlinking can be generalized to k-ary joins: if any one of the k input memories is empty, the node can be unlinked from each of the $k - 1$ others (Barrett 1993). Finding extensions of the optimality theorem of Section 4 and the worst-case analysis of Section 5 for k-ary joins remains a topic for future work.

Although the remaining number of null activations is insignificant, this still leaves two other potential causes of matcher slowdown: increasing non-null activations (this appears to be the main source of the remaining $\sim$2.8-fold slowdown in SCA-Rand), and increasing time per activation (this appears to be the main source of the remaining $\sim$2.5-fold slowdown in Merle). The magnitude of the slowdown from these effects is much smaller than that from null activations in the unmodified Rete algorithm, but it is still significant. Determining under what circumstances these effects occur and finding ways to avoid them are therefore important areas for future work.

8 Acknowledgements

Thanks to Jill Fain Lehman and Paul Rosenbloom for many helpful discussions and comments on drafts of this paper, to the anonymous reviewers and Bill Kennedy for helpful suggestions, and to Josef Krems, Joe Mertz, Craig Miller, Josef Nerb, Constantine Papageorgiou, and David Steier for providing testbed systems.

References

Barrett, T. 1993. Private communication.

Chase, M. P.; Zweben, M.; Piazza, R. L.; Burger, J. D.; Maglio, P. P.; and Hirsh, H. 1989. Approximating learned search control knowledge. In *Proceedings of the Sixth International Workshop on Machine Learning*, 218–220.

Cohen, W. W. 1990. Learning approximate control rules of high utility. In *Proceedings of the Seventh International Conference on Machine Learning*, 268–276.

Doorenbos, R.; Tambe, M.; and Newell, A. 1992. Learning 10,000 chunks: What's it like out there? In *Proceedings of the Tenth National Conference on Artificial Intelligence*, 830–836.

Doorenbos, R. B. 1993. Matching 100,000 learned rules. In *Proceedings of the Eleventh National Conference on Artificial Intelligence*, 290–296.

Doorenbos, R. B. 1994. Combining left and right unlinking for matching a large number of learned rules (extended version). Technical Report CMU-CS-94-132, School of Computer Science, Carnegie Mellon University.

Etzioni, O. 1990a. *A Structural Theory of Search Control*. Ph.D. Dissertation, School of Computer Science, Carnegie Mellon University.

Etzioni, O. 1990b. Why PRODIGY/EBL works. In *Proceedings of the Eighth National Conference on Artificial Intelligence*, 916–922.

---

[5]Adding left unlinking can also slow the matcher down by a small factor, since it adds some overhead to each node activation. If this small factor is not outweighed by a large factor reduction in the number of activations, a slowdown can result. This happens in some of the systems when left unlinking is used *alone*: when (null) right activations are numerous, avoiding null left activations only reduces the total number of activations by a very small factor. This also happens in SCA-Fixed, where adding left unlinking to right unlinking increases the match cost 4%.

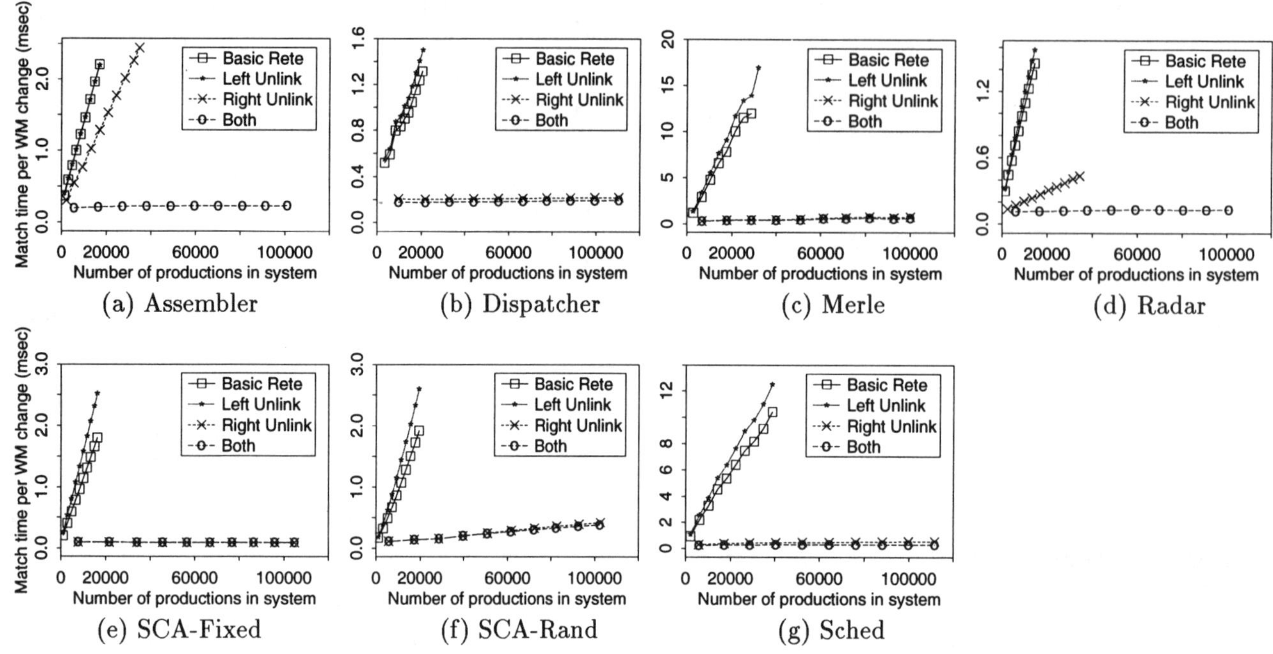

(a) Assembler   (b) Dispatcher   (c) Merle   (d) Radar

(e) SCA-Fixed   (f) SCA-Rand   (g) Sched

Figure 4: Performance of the matcher on each of the systems.

Forgy, C. L. 1982. Rete: A fast algorithm for the many pattern/many object pattern match problem. *Artificial Intelligence* 19(1):17–37.

Gratch, J., and DeJong, G. 1992. COMPOSER: A probabilistic solution to the utility problem in speed-up learning. In *Proceedings of the Tenth National Conference on Artificial Intelligence*, 235–240.

Greiner, R., and Jurisica, I. 1992. A statistical approach to solving the EBL utility problem. In *Proceedings of the Tenth National Conference on Artificial Intelligence*, 241–248.

Gupta, A. 1987. *Parallelism in Production Systems.* Los Altos, California: Morgan Kaufmann.

Holder, L. B. 1992. Empirical analysis of the general utility problem in machine learning. In *Proceedings of the Tenth National Conference on Artificial Intelligence*, 249–254.

Kim, J., and Rosenbloom, P. S. 1993. Constraining learning with search control. In *Proceedings of the Tenth International Conference on Machine Learning*, 174–181.

Laird, J. E.; Newell, A.; and Rosenbloom, P. S. 1987. Soar: An architecture for general intelligence. *Artificial Intelligence* 33(1):1–64.

Laird, J. E.; Rosenbloom, P. S.; and Newell, A. 1986. Chunking in Soar: The anatomy of a general learning mechanism. *Machine Learning* 1(1):11–46.

Markovitch, S., and Scott, P. D. 1993. Information filtering: Selection mechanisms in learning systems. *Machine Learning* 10(2):113–151.

Mertz, J. 1992. Deliberate learning from instruction in Assembler-Soar. In *Proceedings of the Eleventh Soar Workshop*, 88–90. School of Computer Science, Carnegie Mellon University.

Miller, C. S., and Laird, J. E. 1991. A constraint-motivated model of concept formation. In *Proceedings of the Thirteenth Annual Conference of the Cognitive Science Society.*

Minton, S. 1988. *Learning Effective Search Control Knowledge: An Explanation-Based Approach.* Boston, MA: Kluwer Academic Publishers.

Miranker, D. P. 1990. *TREAT: A New and Efficient Match Algorithm for AI Production Systems.* San Mateo, California: Morgan Kaufmann.

Nerb, J.; Krems, J. F.; and Ritter, F. E. 1993. Rule learning and the power law: a computational model and empirical results. In *Proceedings of the Fifteenth Annual Conference of the Cognitive Science Society.*

Papageorgiou, C. P., and Carley, K. 1993. A cognitive model of decision making: Chunking and the radar task. Technical Report CMU-CS-93-228, School of Computer Science, Carnegie Mellon University.

Pérez, M. A., and Etzioni, O. 1992. DYNAMIC: A new role for training problems in EBL. In *Proceedings of the Ninth International Conference on Machine Learning*, 367–372.

Prietula, M. J.; Hsu, W.-L.; Steier, D.; and Newell, A. 1993. Applying an architecture for general intelligence to reduce scheduling effort. *ORSA Journal on Computing* 5(3):304–320.

Rosenbloom, P. S.; Laird, J. E.; Newell, A.; and McCarl, R. 1991. A preliminary analysis of the Soar architecture as a basis for general intelligence. *Artificial Intelligence* 47(1-3):289–325.

Tambe, M.; Newell, A.; and Rosenbloom, P. S. 1990. The problem of expensive chunks and its solution by restricting expressiveness. *Machine Learning* 5(3):299–348.

Discovering Procedural Executions of Rule-Based Programs

David Gadbois and Daniel Miranker
University of Texas at Austin
Deptartment of Computer Sciences
Taylor Hall 2.124
Austin, TX 78712-1188
gadbois@cs.utexas.edu, miranker@cs.utexas.edu

Abstract

Executing production system programs involves directly or indirectly executing an interpretive match/select/act cycle. An optimal compilation of a production system program would generate code that requires no appeal to an interpreter to mediate control. However, while a great deal of implicit control information is available in rule-based programs, it is generally impossible to avoid deferring some decisions to run-time.

We introduce an approach that may resolve this problem. We propose an execution model that permits the execution of the usual cycle when necessary and otherwise executes procedural functions.

The system is best characterized as a rule rewrite system where rules are replaced with chunks, such that the chunks may have procedural components. Correctness for replacement of rules is derived by a constrained abstract evaluation of the entire program via a general-purpose theorem prover at compile time. The analysis gives a global dependency analysis of the interaction of each of the rules.

For a group of popular benchmark programs, we show that there is ample opportunity to automatically substitute interpretive pattern matching with procedural elements and a concomitant improvement in performance.

1 Introduction

Naive interpretation of production system programs involves a match/select/act cycle. The interpreter checks each rule's antecedent conditions to see if it is satisfied by the database, picks one of the satisfied rules to fire, and performs its consequent actions. The cycle repeats until no more rules are satisfied. Approaches to improving the performance of programs and knowledge bases written in rule based form encompass improved incremental match algorithms, such as TREAT and RETE, local optimizations such as sharing and join-optimization, as well as parallelism and learning (Forgy 1982; Miranker & Lofaso 1991; Ishida 1991; Gupta 1988; Miranker *et al.* 1990; Laird, Newell, & Rosenbloom 1986).

The current implementations are adequate for small-scale main-memory based production systems. However, for very large systems or ones in which access to the working memory is mediated by a database manager, the current compilation technology falls short (Stonebraker 1992). Direct implementation in terms of the match/select/act cycle can lead to grossly inefficient executions. To be specific:

- The execution cycle imposes a considerable overhead in maintaining global run-time data structures that may not be necessary while executing a particular fragment of a program.

- Performing some actions incrementally over a number of cycles, such as maintaining various lists in sorted order, often imposes considerable algorithmic overhead.

- The cycle does not take advantage of statically determinable relations among rules — much control information implicit in a program is constantly recomputed at run-time.

- The execution cycle imposes strict synchronization constraints that inhibit distributed mappings of production system execution.

We claim that an optimal compilation of a production system program would generate code that requires no appeal to the interpreter to mediate control. While this ultimate goal is probably impossible in the general case, we have developed techniques that allow for a substantial reduction in the amount of control mediation required. This approach makes plausible the goal of obtaining execution performance for declarative programs within the range of equivalent procedural ones.

While there has been some work on explicitly representing procedural control knowledge at a linguistic level in production system programs (Georgeff & Bonollo 1983) as well as automatically determining control information (Stolfo & Harrison 1979), we assert that within every declarative program is a procedural one waiting to be discovered, and that it is the job of a sufficiently smart compiler to extract that procedural program.

In this paper we introduce an approach that resolves this problem. We propose an execution model that permits the execution of the usual cycle when necessary, but otherwise executes specific, procedural control. The key is to arrange for the both control styles to leave the system in a consistent state for the other to take over.

Our system is best contrasted with the SOAR system (Laird, Newell, & Rosenbloom 1986). SOAR is a learning system that augments a program with new rules, called *chunks*. Chunks are synthesized from the existing rules of the program and are expressed in the original source language of the rule program. The output of the SOAR system may then be fed back to itself for ongoing improvement. We loosen the requirement of systemic learning: Our system replaces (rewrites) rules drawing from a language that includes procedural constructs. Consequently, our transformations provide a single compile-time performance improvement. It is, nevertheless, the case that our analysis can and should be reapplied to already transformed programs. The procedural constructs have explicit representations for binding points, search state, type information, and conditional and loop constructs as well as various compiler bookkeeping data.

Our technique represents a two-fold expansion of earlier work on the decomposition of rule programs into collections of smaller concurrently executable rule programs (Kuo, Miranker, & Browne 1991; Schmolze 1991; Ishida 1991; Kuo, Moldovan, & Cha 1990). First, we go beyond identifying weak mutual exclusion relationships by formalizing and identifying control flow precedence relationships. This is necessary to determine when rules may be replaced instead of simply adding new rules. We determine the necessary data relationships using an automatic theorem prover to determine the strongest possible conditions on data values. Second, the resulting dataflow graph is expanded to include additional relationships and to used to determine possibilities of transformation.

Our results to date include:

- identifying opportunities for exiting the match-/select/act cycle and replacing portions of the execution with procedural code.

- finding opportunities for "RETE style sharing" that go beyond simple common subexpression elimination.

- detecting, at compile time, rule instantiations that can be fired concurrently, but in previous work eluded parallel execution.

- using the above techniques to find and obtain significant performance improvements, both in terms of decreased cycle count and lower running time, in the execution of a suite of benchmark programs.

The remainder of this report is organized as follows. In Section 2, we describe the architecture of the S-TAR (STatic Analysis of Rules) system and the global

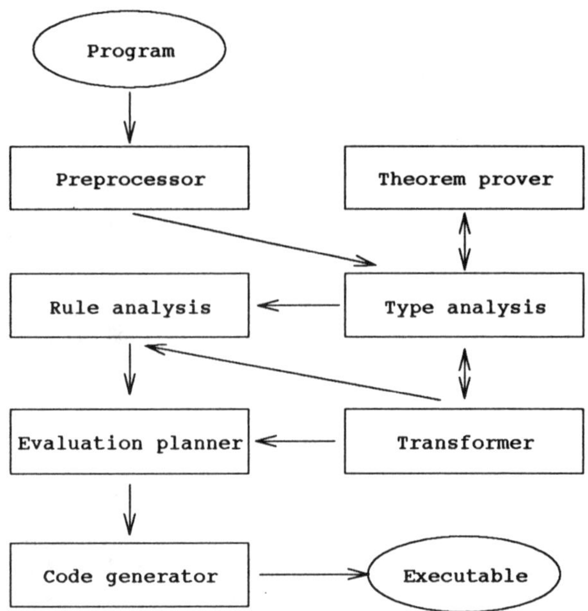

Figure 1: STAR system architecture

analysis it performs. Section 3 covers three optimizing transformations for production system languages. Empirical evidence of the opportunities for transformation in standard OPS5 benchmark programs and the results of applying them are presented in Section 4. Finally, in Section 5 we summaries our results and suggest directions for further research.

2 System Architecture

The global analysis approach presented here generalizes the one presented in (Ishida 1991). The STAR system parses a complete OPS5 (Forgy 1981) source program into an internal representation called the Abstract Rule Language (ARL.) For each condition element and working memory modifying action pair in the program, the system computes the set theoretic relationships between them. Given this information, the system can compute control relations between the program's rules. Using this global information, the system finds opportunities to replace groups of rules with procedural chunks. The process iterates until no more transformations apply. Figure 1 shows a block diagram of the system architecture.

Type relations

We consider the condition elements of the LHS of rules and the working memory modifying actions of their RHSs as first-order formulae, which we will call *types*, and define relations between them that can be seen as the set-theoretic relations of subsumption, intersection, and disjointness on their extensions. A working memory element belongs to a type (i.e., is a member of its extension) if the element satisfies the type formula.

While it is certainly possible to compute the type relations in an ad hoc manner, doing so is tricky, error-prone, and difficult to extend to new kinds of literals (for example, to those whose terms may contain references to function symbols, or even to completely different rule languages.) We have instead implemented the type analysis computation using an automated theorem prover. Propositions corresponding to assertions of the above relations may be constructed directly out of condition element and action pairs and can be passed to the prover for validation. The STAR system uses the Otter resolution-based prover (McCune 1990).

The precise type relations so obtained are of general utility. Computing the static clustering algorithm for parallel rule execution given in (Kuo, Miranker, & Browne 1991) using the subsumption relation instead of the syntactic relations used in the report yields as good, or, in some cases, much better results.

Rule relations

We wish to characterize the possible sequences of rule firings. Given that an instantiation for a particular rule has fired, we characterize the rules that may fire next with three overlapping relations. The relations are similar to those defined in (Kuo, Moldovan, & Cha 1990).

Given the relations between the types of the working memory modifying actions of one rule and those in the LHS of another, we can define useful control relationships between the two rules. We are chiefly interested in whether the results of firing one rule may or may not lead to new instantiation for other rules. There are three possibilities:

- Enables

  One rule enables another if the type of its head literal is subsumed by that of a literal in the body of the other rule. Results from evaluating the first rule will definitely feed into an evaluation of the second.

- Maybe enables

  One rule might enable another if the type of its head literal intersects with that of a literal in the body of another rule. Results from evaluating the first rule may lead the second rule to produce new results.

- Doesn't enable

  If the type of the head literal of one rule is disjoint from that of the body of another rule, then evaluating the first rule will have no direct effect on the evaluation of the second.

In general, it is not possible to determine exactly which rule may follow another without particular knowledge of the specific instantiation and the contents of the database. In some cases, though, the set of possibilities can be sufficiently narrowed so that specific code may be generated for each case such that, with succinct dynamic condition analysis, we may decide at run-time which code segment to execute without having to incur the overhead of executing the full match/select/act cycle.

3 Optimizing Transformations

To date we have defined three transformations for production system programs that can be applied to reduce the overall number of cycles required to execute the program. These optimizations are far from exhaustive and are less general than they can be. Our goals include the development of a large number of special and general purpose transformations.

The three, rule jamming, loop rolling, and branch factoring, capture several major idioms used to express procedural control in production system language programs. Each define conditions sufficient to determine when a group of rules may be replaced with a procedural chunk.

In order to replace a set of rules with a single, procedural rule, it is necessary to determine that no execution path other than the intentionally transformed one can "pass through" the chunk of rules. More formally, for any initial execution state, a transformation must preserve a non-empty subset of the final states of the original program (if it had any) and as well as preserve termination.

To satisfy these correctness requirements, the conditions for determining whether a particular transformation applies requires information about all the rules in the system. It does not suffice to determine, say, that execution of one rule is always followed by another in order to replace the two with a single rule; it is also necessary to determine that no other rule can ever lead to the firing of the second.

The three optimizations mentioned here feed into each other. The most important one in terms of performance, loop rolling, is often enabled by performing the others.

For each transformation, we give an example of the applied transformation in an OPS5-like syntax. We must stress here, though, that the ARL target language into which the source rules are transformed is not OPS5. In contrast to chunking in SOAR, which transforms rules from the source language back into the same source language, ARL has explicit representations for binding points, search state, type information, and conditional and loop constructs as well as various compiler bookkeeping data. As such, it analogous to a the register transfers language common in conventional compilers.

Using a different language in the compiler has several advantages. The chief among them is that it obviates the need to re-recover control information after each round of transformation. Having explicit representations for the procedural constructs makes it easier to generate code for them as well as to specify transformations that build on others. As an internal language, ARL can have more special-purpose rough edges and

```
(p make-big-block
   (goal ↑state make-big-block)
   →
   (make block ↑size 10))

(p note-big-block
   (block ↑size >= 10 ↑qual-size nil)
   →
   (modify 1 ↑qual-size big))
```

Figure 2: Rules that may be jammed together.

```
(p make-big-block
   (goal ↑state make-big-block)
   →
   (make block ↑size 10 ↑qual-size big))
```

Figure 3: A jammed rule.

is more flexible than a general-purpose programming
language.

Rule Jamming

A common idiom in production system programming
is to divide a series of operations upon memory tuples
across several rules so that the result of firing one rule
enables another to do its job. Rule jamming compresses the operations of the multiple rules into a single one.

In Figure 2, the `note-size` rule triggers off the
`make-big-block` rule to (eventually) modify every
block. If there are no other dependencies on use of
the `qual-size` of the block or modification of its numerical size, then the computation of the `qual-size`
may be added on to block creation and done in one fell
swoop as in Figure 3. If, after jamming the two rules
together, there are no other dependencies that could
lead to the `note-big-block` rules firing, then it may
be deleted entirely.

Rule jamming is a form of static chunking (Laird,
Newell, & Rosenbloom 1986). As such, the transformation is vulnerable to the problem of expensive chunks
(Tambe & Newell 1988). A naive implementation may
compute large cartesian products where a search involving multiple rules would have cut off before getting
too deep. If the evaluation technique includes an intelligent backtracking scheme and forward information
about possible join targets, however, a jammed rule
can avoid this problem. In any case, the size of the
products are the same, and so asymptotically no more
work will be done.

Branch Factoring

The only form of conditional execution available to
production system programs is through the use of multiple rules that are otherwise distinguished only by the

```
(p note-large-blocks
   (block ↑size > 10 ↑qual-size nil)
   →
   (modify 2 ↑qual-size big))

(p note-small-blocks
   (block ↑size <= 10 ↑qual-size nil)
   →
   (modify 2 ↑qual-size small))
```

Figure 4: Unfactored rules.

```
(p note-block-size
   (goal ↑state note-size)
   (block ↑size <n> ↑qual-size nil)
   →
   (if <n> <= 10
     then (modify 2 ↑qual-size small)
     else (modify 2 ↑qual-size big)))
```

Figure 5: A factored rule.

branch conditions. Multiple rules, with the same join
conditions but differing in tests upon constant values,
can be merged into a single rule that tests for the constant in the execution phase of rule firing.

In Figure 4, the two rules `note-large-blocks` and
`note-small-blocks` differ by only a constant test on
the size of a block. Since, in this case, all blocks must
be examined, it is desirable to match against all the
blocks and decide which size category a block belongs
to on the right-hand side of a single rule as in Figure 5.

For branch factoring, the goal is to find types in the
antecedent conditions of each of several rules that can
be merged into a single more general type such that
the pairwise differences between the original types are
unique. The rules can then be merged into a single
rule that replaces the specific types with the general
one and tests for exactly which one is satisfied in the
action part of the rule.

Branch factoring allows sharing of code for rules beyond simple common subexpressions. It differs from
RETE-style sharing in that it effectively provides a
two-level network where the output of the first network is fed back into the second.

This kind of sharing is particularly important in active database settings, where a search for instantiations
of a factored rule may require only a single scan of the
database, whereas searching for instantiations for distinct rules may require two.

Loop Rolling

Production system languages typically have no iteration construct. Loop rolling involves detecting situations where multiple tuples are operated upon in a

```
(p note-large-blocks
   (goal ↑state note-large-blocks)
   (block ↑size > 10 ↑qual-size nil)
   →
   (modify 2 ↑qual-size big))

(p done-noting-large-blocks
   (goal ↑state note-large-blocks)
   - (block ↑size > 10 ↑qual-size nil)
   →
   (modify 1 ↑state do-something-else))
```

Figure 6: An unrolled loop.

```
(p note-large-blocks
   (goal ↑state note-large-blocks)
   all (block ↑size > 10 ↑qual-size nil)
   →
   (modify 2 ↑qual-size big)
   (modify 1 ↑state do-something-else))
```

Figure 7: A rolled loop.

similar manner and arranging for the operations to occur outside the system cycle.

There has been some work on adding set-oriented constructs to rule system languages (Delcambre & Etheredge 1988; Widom & Finkelstein 1989). Our approach avoids the tricky problem of specifying a precise and general semantics for set-oriented constructs by leaving their definition within the compiler.

We describe an optimization for a simple case of loop rolling that captures a fairly common iteration idiom. The conditions for this optimization are somewhat complex in presentation but fairly simple in concept. The trick is to find a type in a pair of rules that serves as the invariant condition for the loop. One of the rules is called the "body" of the loop, and the other is the "guard." It must be the case that no other rules reference the invariant condition, so that the rules are active exclusively. The body and guard rules must not interfere with each other. The body rule must "count down" the type being operated upon, and the guard rule must check to see when there are no more data elements left. The transformed rule performs all the actions of the body rule that would have been spread out over a number of cycles in a single one.

In Figure 6, the rule `note-large-blocks` serves as the body rule, and `done-noting-large-blocks` as the guard. The body repeated removes blocks with a null `qual-size` attribute, and the guard checks to see if there are any such blocks left. The type of the goal element (assuming there are no other references to it in the program) serves as the invariant. The resulting rolled loop appears in Figure 7.

In main memory implementations, loop rolling can

Program	Rules	Rule Jamming	Branch Factoring	Loop Rolling
Manners	8	0	0	2
Waltz	33	0	2	2
ARP	111	4	9	6
Weaver	637	18	56	11

Figure 8: Occurrences of transformations in benchmark programs.

significantly reduce the overhead required to maintain run-time data structures. For example, most systems maintain lists of instantiations in sorted order. When one instantiation is produced at a time, maintaining the lists is an $O(n^2)$ insertion sort. If a number of instantiations are produced at once, a much more efficient $O(n \log n)$ sorting algorithm may be used.

In the contexts of database integration and parallel execution, loop rolling passes more information to the query processor at once, allowing it to do a better jobs of optimizing selection and join sequences. Set-oriented constructs may appear explicitly in the generated code for the rolled loops, and so fewer queries can be issued, and the ones remaining are more easily parallelized.

In both cases, loop rolling reduces the activity of the interpreter by eliminating an invocation of it upon each loop iteration. In parallel implementations the interpreter calls can require a considerable amount of overhead.

Loop rolling can reduce the asymptoptic complexity of program execution. Using conventional matching algorithms, worst case matching complexity is W^n, where W is the size of the working memory and n is largest number of condition elements in a single rule. If it is possible to roll all firings of the bounding rule into a single cycle, matching complexity is reduced by an exponential factor.

4 Experimental Results

We have examined a number of commonly-used OPS5 benchmark programs for the applicability of the transformations given in Section 3. The programs are extensively studied in (Brant *et al.* 1991). Figure 4 summarizes the programs and opportunities for transformations. Some small programs, such as Manners, do not exhibit many possibilities for the three transformations described in this report.

Figure 4 shows the number of interpreter cycles needed to execture the benchmarks with and without applying the transformations. Figure 4 shows the wall-clock execution times of the programs.

5 Conclusions

We have described an architecture for an optimizing compiler for production system languages and several

Program	Raw	Transformed	Ratio
Manners	183	47	3.9
Waltz	39	18	2.2
ARP	2885	831	3.5
Weaver	1718	204	8.4

Figure 9: Interpreter cycles needed to execute untransformed and transformed programs.

Program	Raw	Transformed	Ratio
Manners	48.4	37.5	1.3
Waltz	4.4	3.0	1.5
ARP	581	94	6.2
Weaver	1654	195	8.5

Figure 10: Run-time (seconds) performance of untransformed and transformed programs.

optimizations it can perform. Besides the three mentioned in this report, there are a number of other possible transformations that can be developed using this framework. Due to the generality of using first-order representations and using a general-purpose theorem prover to compute their relationship, the framework can be tailored to deal with the peculiarities of particular production system languages and exploit additional opportunities for optimizations.

The key to the approach is the wholesale replacement of rules whenever global static analysis can determine that the structure of the rules and the semantics of the program allow a single execution path. The resulting program then avoids the overhead of determining that path at run-time.

We have demonstrated good execution improvements using only a few transformations. Armed with a sufficient number of these transformations, a production system compiler can arrange to significantly reduce the number of match/select/act cycles needed to execute a program.

6   Acknowledgments

This research was supported by the State of Texas Advanced Technology Program, the University of Texas Applied Research Laboratories Internal Research and Development Program, and ARPA, grant number DABT63-92-0042.

References

Brant, D.; Lofaso, B.; Gross, T.; and Miranker, D. P. 1991. Effects of Database Size on Rule system Performance: Five Case Studies. In *Proc. 17th VLDB Conf.*

Delcambre, L. M. L., and Etheredge, J. N. 1988. The Relational Production Language: A Production Language for Relational Databases. In *Proc. 2nd Int'l Conf. on Expert Database Systems*, 153–162.

Forgy, C. L. 1981. OPS5 User's Manual. Technical report, Department of Computer Science, Carnegie Mellon University.

Forgy, C. L. 1982. RETE: A Fast Match Algorithm for the Many Pattern/Many Object Pattern Match Probem. *Artificial Intelligence* 19:17–37.

Georgeff, M., and Bonollo, U. 1983. Procedural Expert Systems. In *Proc. Int'l Joint Conf. on AI*, 151–157. William Kaufmann, Inc.

Gupta, A. 1988. *Parallelism in Production Systems.* Pittman/Morgan-Kaufman.

Ishida, T. 1991. Parallel Rule Firings in Production Systems. *IEEE Trans. on Knowledge and Data Engineering* 3(1).

Kuo, C.-M.; Miranker, D. P.; and Browne, J. C. 1991. On the Performance of the CREL System. *Journal of Parallel and Distributed Computing* 13(4):424–441.

Kuo, S.; Moldovan, D.; and Cha, S. 1990. Control in Production Systems with Multiple Rule Firings. In *Proc. IEEE Int'l Conf. on Parallel Processing*, volume II, 243–2246. IEEE.

Laird, J.; Newell, A.; and Rosenbloom, P. 1986. Soar: An Architecture for General Intelligence. *Artificial Intelligence* 33(1):1–64.

McCune, W. W. 1990. OTTER 2.0 Users Guide. Technical Report ANL-90/9, Argonne National Laboratory.

Miranker, D., and Lofaso, B. J. 1991. The Organization and Performance of a TREAT Based Production System Compiler. *IEEE Trans. on Knowledge and Data Engineering* 3–10.

Miranker, D. P.; Brant, D.; Lofaso, B.; and Gadbois, D. 1990. On the Performance of Lazy Matching in Production Systems. In *Proc. Nat. Conf. on Artificial Intelligence*, 685–692. AAAI Press.

Piatetsky-Shapiro, G., and Frawley, W., eds. 1991. *Knowlegde Discover in Databases.* AAAI Press and MIT Press.

Schmolze, J. 1991. Guaranteeing Serializable Results in Synchronous Parallel Production Systems. *J. of Parallel and Dist. Com.* 13(4):348–364.

Stolfo, S. J., and Harrison, M. C. 1979. Automatic Discovery of Heuristics for Nondeterministic Programs. In *6th Int'l Joint Conf. on AI.*

Stonebraker, M. 1992. The Integration of Rule Systems and Database Systems. *IEEE Tran. on Knowledge and Data Engineering* 415–423.

Tambe, M., and Newell, A. 1988. Some Chunks Are Expensive. In *Proc. Int'l Conf. on Machine Learning.*

Widom, J., and Finkelstein, S. 1989. A Syntax and Semantics for Set-Oriented Production Rules in Relational Database Systems. Technical Report RJ 6880 (65706), IBM Almaden Research Center.

Mechanisms for Efficiency in Blackboard Systems

Micheal Hewett
Department of Computer Sciences
University of Texas at Austin
Taylor Hall 2.124
Austin, TX 78712-1188
hewett@cs.utexas.edu

Rattikorn Hewett
Computer Science and Engineering Department
Florida Atlantic University
P.O. Box 3091
Boca Raton, FL 33431-0091
hewett@cse.fau.edu

Abstract

The RETE algorithm had a great impact on the development of efficient production systems by providing a fast pattern matching mechanism for activation. No similar mechanism has been available to speed up activation and scheduling in blackboard systems. In this paper we describe efficient, general-purpose efficiency mechanisms that are better suited to blackboard systems than RETE-like networks. We describe a knowledge source compiler that produces match networks and demons for efficient activation and rating while compiling the entire system for increased execution speed. Experiments using the enhancements in a general-purpose blackboard shell illustrate a substantial improvement in run time, including an 80–92% decrease in activation time. The mechanisms we describe are general enough to be used in most existing blackboard systems.

1 Introduction

The blackboard architecture is a flexible framework for solving complex problems. It supports incremental development of solutions, integrated use of different types of knowledge at different levels of abstraction, and opportunistic control of reasoning. This flexibility can lead to complex interrelationships among blackboard states, potential actions, and strategies, causing difficulty in implementing an efficient system. For these reasons, blackboard applications are sometimes perceived as "slow".

The efficiency of a knowledge-based system can be measured at many levels [Carver and Lesser, 1992]. At one level is the *overhead* of activating, selecting, and executing actions. Another measure is the quality of a system's *control knowledge*, which is used to select the best action to perform. In this paper we address the need to reduce the processing overhead of blackboard systems, independent of the quality of knowledge in the system.

The RETE algorithm [Forgy, 1982], a fast pattern matching mechanism, was a major breakthrough in reducing the overhead of production systems. However, there has been no similar breakthrough in blackboard systems; each blackboard system implements different *ad-hoc* efficiency mechanisms for the basic execution cycle.

Earlier work on efficiency of blackboard systems has been at higher or lower levels of the architecture. Some examples include meta-level frameworks for efficient control [Lâasri and Maître, 1989], blackboard structures to optimize storage and retrieval operations [Corkill et al., 1988], and distributed and parallel implementations of blackboard systems [Lesser and Corkill, 1988; Corkill, 1989; Bisiani and Forin, 1989; Rice et al., 1989].

In this paper we will argue why a direct application of the RETE algorithm is not appropriate for blackboard systems. We then describe a set of general-purpose mechanisms that can be used in many blackboard systems. Experiments based on implementing the enhancements in the BB1 architecture illustrate substantial decreases in execution times. Since most blackboard systems share the same basic execution cycle, with minor variations, our results can be applied to most blackboard architectures.

2 Blackboard architecture

Various blackboard architectures have been implemented, including Hearsay-II [Erman and Lesser, 1975], AGE [Nii and Aiello, 1979], BB1 [Hayes-Roth and Hewett, 1988], and ERASMUS [Baum et al., 1989] (see [Engelmore and Morgan, 1988] for detailed descriptions of these and other blackboard architectures). Most implementations of the blackboard architecture provide knowledge sources for execution, a mixture of frame-based and semantic network representation methods, and a general mechanism for control of reasoning. The knowledge representation component in a blackboard system is the *blackboard*. Blackboards contain *objects*, frame-like structures that form the basic unit of representation. A blackboard object has attributes and links to other objects. A blackboard is usually partitioned into *levels* containing related objects.

In a blackboard system the *knowledge source* is the basic unit of execution, similar to productions or rules in a production system. The action of a knowledge source makes one or more changes to the blackboard such as creating or deleting a blackboard object, changing the value of an attribute, or creating a link between two objects. Each change to the blackboard is logged as an *event*.

Each knowledge source is triggered by an event described in its *trigger conditions*. When the described event occurs, the knowledge source is activated and one or more activations are created as appropriate for the context in which the knowledge source was triggered. Each activation, called a KSA, is then placed on the *agenda*.

The agenda has two parts: the *triggered agenda* and the *executable agenda*. Only KSAs on the executable agenda are eligible for execution. A knowledge source contains state-based *preconditions* that determine whether the KSA is executable. A KSA's state may change from triggered to executable and back as the state of its preconditions varies in response to changes on the blackboard. A knowledge source also has *obviation conditions.* If these become true while the KSA is on the agenda, it is removed from the agenda and permanently discarded.

The component responsible for selecting KSAs for execution is the *scheduler.* It uses control knowledge to select the best KSA available on each cycle.

2.1   The blackboard execution cycle

```
1. [ACTIVATE.]
      for every Event E of the last cycle do
          for every knowledge source KS do
              if KS.triggerConditions are satisfied by E then
                  for every context C of KS do generate a KSA;
2. [ENABLE.]
      for every KSA do
          if KSA.preconditions are satisfied then
              place KSA on the executable agenda
          else
              place KSA on the triggered agenda;
3. [OBVIATE.]
      for every KSA do
          if KSA.obviationConditions are satisfied then
              remove KSA from the agenda;
4. [SCHEDULE.]
      rate KSAs and select a KSA to execute;
5. [EXECUTE.]
      execute a KSA, collecting events;
6. [LOOP.] go to Step 1;
```

At runtime the execution cycle activates and executes knowledge sources using their conditions and actions, as in the BB1 execution cycle shown above.

There are several places where a naive implementation can encounter efficiency problems. Steps 1, 2, 3 and 4 all loop through every existing KS or KSA, of which there can be many. In our experience, agenda management (Steps 1 and 2) involves considerable overhead and often consumes more processing time than execution.

3   Efficiency mechanisms

Common techniques for gaining efficiency in AI architectures include compilation, pattern-matching networks, and demons. In our approach we apply all three techniques to construct efficient general mechanisms for use in blackboard systems.

A demon is a small process that is activated by a specific change to working memory. They have been used previously in blackboard systems. Poligon [Rice et al., 1989], a parallel, distributed blackboard system, uses demons to directly invoke rules. However Poligon was designed to operate without global control and does not have an agenda *per se.* While Poligon uses demons to direct execution, we will use demons for agenda maintenance and rating.

Compilation is the main technique for speeding up execution. As is well known, compiled code executes as much as one hundred times faster than interpreted code, so compiling knowledge sources into lower-level functions will increase execution speed. Additionally, compiling a pattern matching network can improve match times by about 15% [Scales, 1986].

3.1   Why not use RETE?

A RETE network is built by parsing the conditions (LHS) of a set of productions and constructing a network with two parts. The *match* part detects when working memory elements (WME) match a single pattern in a condition. The *join* part detects when the entire condition is satisfied. Each terminal node in the join network corresponds to a production. Whenever a WME is added, deleted, or modified, the WME is passed through the network. If a terminal node is activated, its production is placed in the conflict set. Every production system uses some variation of RETE as an efficient activation mechanism.

Our original intent was to construct a version of RETE for use in blackboard systems. However, we now realize that RETE is not an appropriate activation mechanism for blackboard applications. Figure 1 illustrates the difference in activation for production systems and blackboard systems. In a production system, rules (productions) are activated when several WMEs, denoted by the shaded circles, match the patterns in a rule. These patterns may be scattered throughout working memory. In a blackboard system, initial activation (triggering) is caused by a single event, denoted by the unshaded circle in the figure. Full activation, satisfaction of the knowledge source's preconditions, is usually determined by objects related to the triggering object via links or by virtue of being at the same level on the blackboard. These objects are specified by bindings in the preconditions. Thus, there is usually no need to match patterns throughout the entire blackboard—the objects needed to match the patterns can be directly accessed.

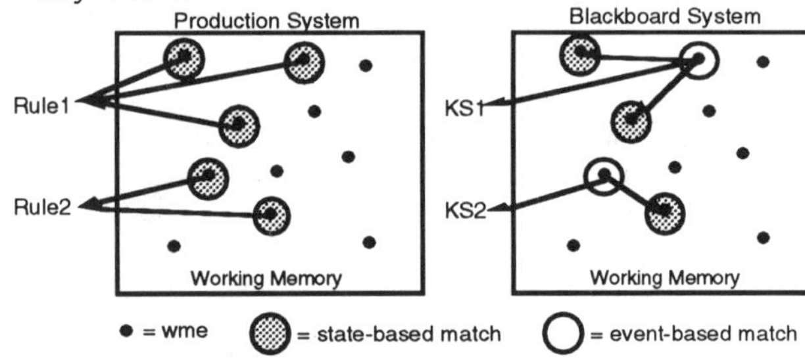

Fig. 1. Different activation mechanisms.

4   Efficient blackboard mechanisms

This section describes how to apply the techniques of the previous section to the major components of blackboard systems. We will describe how to use demons for efficient state-based activation and rating, a discrimination network for efficient event-based activation, and compilation for efficient execution.

4.1 Activation

As described in Section 2, activation in blackboard systems is a two-stage process. The initial *event-based* activation generates activations (KSAs) from knowledge sources. In the second stage, a KSA's *state-based* preconditions must be satisfied for it to be eligible for execution.

4.1.1 Event-based activation

Event-based activation (triggering) involves comparing a number of events against the trigger conditions of each knowledge source on each execution cycle.

In our approach, the trigger conditions are compiled into a discrimination network, much like the match part of a RETE network. We require that trigger conditions bind variables when they are first referenced. This simple restriction eliminates the need for the join part of the RETE network and makes trigger conditions equivalent to a knowledge representation mechanism known as *access paths* [Crawford, 1990]. Access paths provide a well-defined semantics for ordering conjunctive queries so that knowledge base access is contained and controlled, and therefore is more efficient. In our mechanism, the discrimination network uses the event type, event level, attribute and/or link as the match keys at its branch points. The leaf nodes of the network are knowledge sources.

Each cycle the events of the last cycle are passed through the discrimination network. If a knowledge source's node is activated (i.e. an event was accepted by the network), its state-based trigger conditions (if any) are checked and one or more KSAs are generated using the knowledge source's context. The discrimination network improves efficiency by reducing the number of comparisons needed to match events with trigger conditions. For additional speed, our network is compiled into functional form rather than maintained as a data structure.

4.1.2 State-based activation

Like production systems, state-based activation in blackboard systems often consumes much more processing time than knowledge source execution. A typical application has dozens of KSAs on the agenda, each with several preconditions. The task of an efficient architecture is to check a precondition only when its state may have changed. We have determined that a demon-based architecture can provide a very large decrease in activation time while maintaining the generality of the architecture.

In BB1, a KSA is in one of several states: **executable**, **triggered**, or **obviated**. Thus, the Agenda Manager must continually check both preconditions and obviation conditions of many KSAs. The state of each precondition depends on the state of one or more blackboard components (levels, objects, attributes, etc.) which may or may not change state from cycle to cycle. BB1 currently uses some *ad-hoc* mechanisms to improve the efficiency of precondition checking. However, BB1 does not attempt to provide optimal precondition checking and performs very poorly when an agenda contains a large number of executable KSAs [Hewett and Hewett, 1993].

Our implementation uses a demon-based mechanism to indicate which conditions need to be rechecked. A

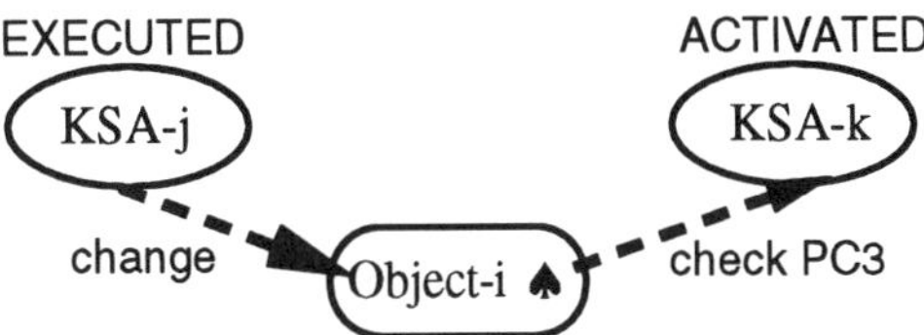

Fig. 2. Demons for state-based activation.

state-based condition must, by definition, reference some item on a blackboard. A condition, then, must be reevaluated when that blackboard item is modified. We place a demon on a blackboard item to note a relationship between the item and a precondition of a KSA, thus providing a way to notify the architecture when a condition must be rechecked. The appropriate location for a demon can be noted by a knowledge source compiler, thus relieving the user of the need to create and place them. A potential disadvantage of this method is the overhead of adding and removing demons as KSAs are created and disposed. However, we will show in Section 5 that demon-based activation produces a large decrease in activation time for every tested application.

The compiler produces demon templates that are instantiated when their corresponding KSAs are instantiated. In the example of Figure 2, when KSA-k is instantiated and one of its local variables is bound to Object-i, the demon ♠ is instantiated and placed on Object-i. When Object-i is modified by the execution of KSA-j, the demon is activated and causes the third precondition of KSA-k to be evaluated. The actual evaluation of the precondition is delayed until the agenda maintenance phase of the execution cycle. The activation signal is also passed to the superior of the demon's location. For example, a change to the value of an attribute is also a change to the object, which is a change to its level, which is a change to the blackboard containing the level. Demons could be activated at any point along the signal's path. Demons are removed whenever a KSA is executed or is obviated. Section 5 shows the time improvements obtained using this mechanism.

4.2 Control

In a blackboard system, control is the process of selecting the next action or actions to execute. In agenda-based systems, control has two parts: rating and scheduling. Rating assigns a priority to each executable KSA. Scheduling selects a KSA and queues it for execution. There are many factors affecting the efficiency of control, including the size of the agenda, the complexity and number of rating functions, and the frequency with which actions must be re-rated. See [Carver and Lesser, 1992] for more details.

4.2.1 Scheduling

The scheduler selects an action from the agenda and queues it for execution. Usually the selected action is the highest-priority action, but with a flexible control module, the actual criteria for selection are user-definable. For most situations, a sorted agenda would seem to be an appropriate data structure.

However, when we implemented a sorted agenda in BB1, we found that the execution time of the system *increased* by 10% even though the time to retrieve the highest-priority item was significantly reduced. This is because we need not sort *all* of the actions. In most systems only the highest-priority action needs to be identified. The unnecessary sorting of lower-priority actions is simply a waste of time. A simple linear search on an unsorted agenda provides suitable performance for a scheduler.

4.2.2 The BB1 rating mechanism

```
RATE-ALL-KSAs (Operative, Dynamic, Changed)
for every KSA in KSAs-TO-RATE do
    if KSA is newly-executable
        for every R in Operative-criteria do Rate(KSA, R);
    else
        for every R in Rating-criteria do rate(KSA, R);
        for every R in Deactivated-criteria do
            Remove-rating(KSA, R);
    end-if
    Prioritize(KSA)
end-for
```

In BB1, the Rater applies rating functions from active control elements in the control plan to executable KSAs. Control elements can be dynamic or static. A dynamic control element is one whose rating criterion is state-dependent, potentially causing its ratings to change each cycle. During the control phase each control element in the current control plan rates every new KSA, and each dynamic control element re-rates every executable KSA. To rate each executable KSA, the Rater identifies the operative, dynamic, new, and changed control elements. It uses them as shown in the algorithm above.

The Rater frequently rates new executable KSAs, rates KSAs when there is a new control element, re-rates KSAs when a control element is modified, and removes ratings from existing KSAs when a control element is deactivated.

Additionally, the rater re-rates every KSA by dynamic control elements every cycle. There is potentially a lot of redundant computation in rating, especially when dynamic control is used. Our goal is to reduce the number of KSAs that are repeatedly re-rated unnecessarily by using demons to relate control elements to specific KSAs.

4.2.3 Demon-based rating

Similar to the way demons can be used to associate blackboard items with state-based preconditions, we also associate blackboard items with control elements used in rating KSAs. A well-designed control element focuses on a certain part of the solution state. If the relevant part of the solution state changes, KSAs that are related to that part of the solution state will need to be re-rated. These KSAs can be located by following activation demons (♠) from the objects in the solution state. The control elements that need to re-rate these KSAs can be located by following control demons (♥) from the same objects. The Rater is then notified that certain KSAs need to be rated

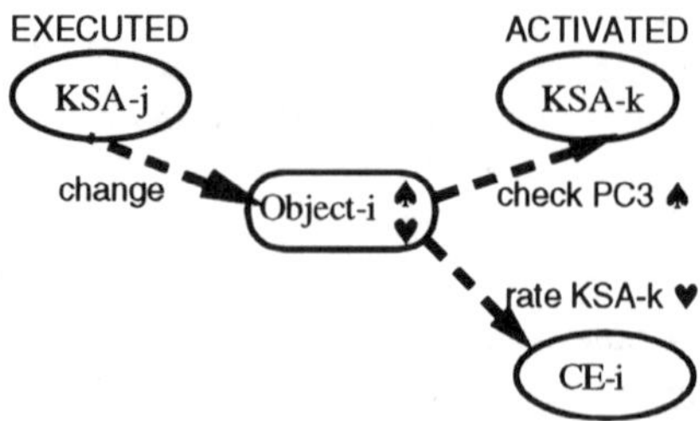

Fig. 3. Using control demons for rating.

by certain control elements.

In the example of Figure 3, Object-i has an activation demon to KSA-k and a control demon to dynamic control element CE-i. If Object-i is modified, the control demon tells CE-i to re-rate KSA-k.

During the rating phase of the execution cycle, the Rater processes activated control demons, much like the demon-based agenda mechanism described above. Rating occurs in the following situations:

1. **New KSA**: When placing new agenda demons, check for any control demons in the same location. If they exist, activate them to rate the new KSA.
2. **New CE**: When placing control demons, check for any agenda demons in the same location. If they exist, activate the new control demons to rate the existing KSAs.
3. **CE deleted**: Remove any associated control demons while checking for agenda demons in the same location. If they exist, activate the control demon one last time to unrate the existing KSAs.
4. **CE modified**: If a CE is modified so that its rating criterion or weight has changed, it will be necessary to re-rate any associated KSAs. This is handled by combining operations 2 and 3 above.
5. **BB modified**: If a blackboard object changes, activate its associated control demons.

Notice that the demon-based rating mechanism depends on the existence of the demon-based activation mechanism. Since the two mechanisms are closely related, the actual implementation of the rating mechanism was very simple. However, while it is fairly easy to write knowledge sources in such a way that the compiler can determine where to place activation demons, it is not as easy to construct "knowledge source independent" control knowledge. The appropriate methods of structuring control knowledge to ensure that it can operate in this manner require further research.

4.3 Execution

We improve the efficiency of executing the actions of a knowledge source by the simple expedient of compiling the actions. The compiler also inserts code into the actions to place and remove activation and control demons. The speed increase from compilation is related to the complexity of the actions. Our test applications, which have fairly trivial actions, do not show a large increase in execution speed. Since demon activation and removal occurs during execution, it is possible for the overhead of these operations to increase the execution time of some systems. In our test systems, the overhead was noticeable, but was negligible compared to the decrease in activation time.

4.4 Knowledge source compilation

The mechanisms described in the sections above all refer to a knowledge source compiler that produces the discrimination network for triggering, produces the activation demons and control demons, and compiles the actions and conditions of the knowledge sources. In this section we provide an overview of the compiler.

The compiler requires that the knowledge sources be written in a simple blackboard language described in [Hewett and Hewett, 1993]. Some examples of sentences in this language are:

```
1. ADD <object-name> TO <level-name>
      [WITH [ATTRIBUTES <attribute-value-list>]
      [LINKS <link-object-list>]]
2. DELETE <object-name>
3. CHANGE <attribute-name> OF <object-name>
      TO <new-value>
4. LINK <link-name> FROM <object1-name>
      TO <object2-name>
```

The knowledge source compiler processes knowledge sources and compiles their conditions and actions into a lower-level language (e.g. LISP, C or C++). Through an analysis of the conditions, it generates a set of activation demons for each knowledge source. Additional code is added to each compiled KS to instantiate and remove demons at the appropriate times.

At runtime, each KSA has a set of local variable bindings that differentiate it from other instances of the same knowledge source. The conditions and actions of each knowledge source are compiled into functions that accept the set of variable bindings for the particular KSA being evaluated.

5 Experimental results

We used three applications to study the effects of the new activation mechanism in BB1. The first, TSP, is a heuristic solution of a 10-city traveling salesman problem that has previously been used to benchmark BB1. The other two applications, TEST-T and TEST-E, are designed to test the effect of the enhancements on different agenda characteristics. Both applications always have twenty ac-

program	exec. agenda	trig. agenda	control know.	number of demons
TSP	*large*	*'small*	*small*	*medium*
TEST-T	*small*	*large*	*-none-*	*large*
TEST-E	*large*	*small*	*-none-*	*large*

Fig 4. Characteristics of benchmark programs.

tive KSAs. TEST-T has nineteen KSAs on the triggered agenda and one KSA on the executable agenda. TEST-E keeps all twenty KSAs on the executable agenda every cycle. TSP uses a small amount of control knowledge, while the other two applications use no control. Figure 4 summarizes the characteristics of the benchmark applications.

We measured the time spent in the agenda maintenance, control, and execution phases of the execution cycle as well as the total time of run. Included in the execution time is the cost of demon activation and the overhead of instantiating and removing demons. All timed runs were made on a single-user Sun IPC running Lucid Common LISP and BB1 v2.5. The times labeled *eff-1* show the improvement gained by implementing only the efficient activation mechanism. The times labeled *eff-2* include both the efficient activation and the efficient control mechanisms. Figure 5 shows the run times of all three applications.

5.1 Results for TSP

Figure 5a shows the runtime of TSP in standard BB1 and in new implementations using the efficiency mechanisms described in this paper. TSP runs for 17 execution cycles, so the overall runtime is relatively short. Because TSP maintains a large executable agenda and has a lot of movement to and from different parts of the agenda, the large increase in agenda maintenance speed using the demon-based architecture is not a surprise. Notice the very slight increase in execution time when the demon-based control mechanism is used. This is the effect of the demon activation overhead. Overall, the performance gain is approximately 55%.

5.2 Results for TEST-T and TEST-E

Figure 5b shows the runtime of the TEST-T applica-

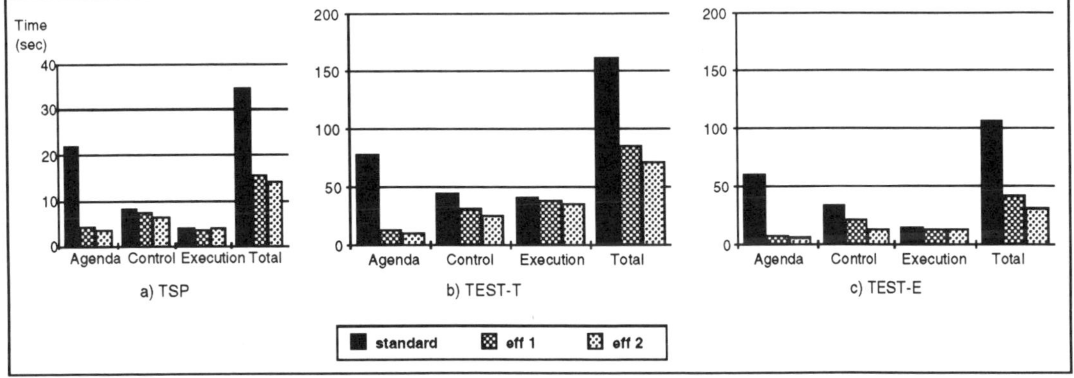

Fig 5. Run times for the test applications.

tion in standard BB1 and the new implementations. The standard BB1 handles TEST-T relatively well, so we should expect our new mechanism to have a relatively smaller impact on the performance of TEST-T than on the performance of the other applications.

Despite this, the performance increase for TEST-T is quite large. Agenda maintenance times are reduced by 80% and the overall runtime is reduced by about 60%. Notice that in standard BB1 agenda maintenance consumes a much larger amount of time than the control and execution phases, while in the new implementation, it consumes much less time.

Figure 5c compares the runtime of the TEST-E application in standard BB1 and in the new implementations. As expected, the results for TEST-E are similar to those of TEST-T, with as good or better improvement in agenda maintenance time.

5.3   Summary of results

Overall, the results show a substantial decrease in agenda maintenance time and significant reductions in other phases. Applications with more complex knowledge source actions will show a larger decrease in execution time, while those with a large amount of complex, dynamic control will show a larger decrease in control time. The overhead of demon processing is not substantial.

A final example demonstrates that the results are consistent for larger applications. As described above, TEST-E maintains an executable agenda of 20 KSAs. We ran TEST-E in modes using 20, 40, and 80 KSAs, producing the total run times shown in Figure 6. The total runtime of the new implementation managing eighty KSAs is approximately two-thirds of the total runtime of the old implementation managing only twenty KSAs.

6   Summary

We have illustrated why a RETE-like pattern-matching network is not suitable for blackboard systems. As an alternative, we presented efficient blackboard activation, execution and rating mechanisms. Our mechanisms combine compilation techniques, a matching network, and demon-based activation and rating to achieve a substantial decreases in runtime for all tested systems.

We have demonstrated that, like production systems, activation in blackboard systems can be a major efficiency problem. Our efficiency mechanisms address this and reduce the time spent in activation to approximately 15% of

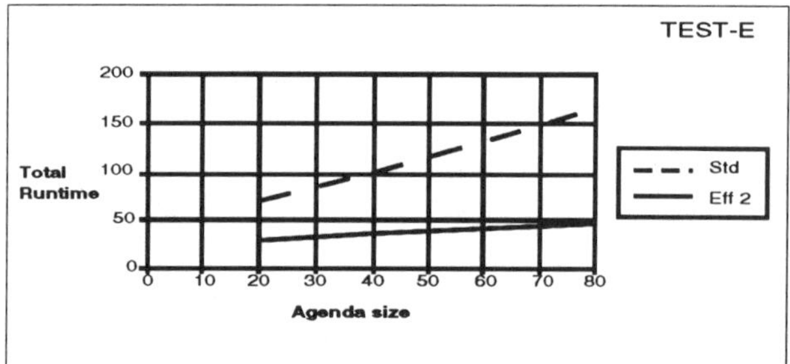

Fig. 6. TEST-E with different agenda sizes.

the total runtime. Further work includes finding suitable formulations of control knowledge that can reap the benefits of the demon-based rating mechanism.

References

Baum, L.S., Dodhiawala, R.T. and Jagannathan, V. (1989) "The Erasmus System." *Blackboard Architectures and Applications*, Jagannathan, V., R. Dodhiawala and L. S. Baum, editors, pp. 347-370, Academic Press.

Bisiani, R. and Forin, A. (1989) "Parallelization of Blackboard Architectures and the Agora System." *Blackboard Architectures and Applications*, Jagannathan, V., R. Dodhiawala and L. S. Baum, editors, pp. 137-152, Academic Press.

Carver, N. and V. Lesser (1992). *The Evolution of Blackboard Control Architectures*. CMPSCI Technical Report 92-71, University of Massachusetts at Amherst.

Corkill, D.D. (1989) "Design Alternatives for Parallel and Distributed Blackboard Systems." *Blackboard Architectures and Applications*, Jagannathan, V., R. Dodhiawala and L. S. Baum, editors, pp. 99-136, Academic Press.

Corkill, D.D., Gallagher, K.Q. and Murray, K.E. (1988) "GBB: A Generic Blackboard Development System." *Blackboard Systems*, Engelmore, R., and T. Morgan, editors, pp. 503-517, Addison-Wesley.

Crawford, J. (1990). *Access-Limited Logic -- A Language for Knowledge Representation*. PhD Thesis, University of Texas at Austin, Technical Report AI90-141.

Engelmore, R. and Morgan, T., editors (1988). *Blackboard Systems*. Addison-Wesley.

Erman, L.D. and Lesser, V.R. (1975) A multi-level organization for problem-solving using many diverse cooperating sources of knowledge. In: *Proceedings of the Fourth International Joint Conference on Artificial Intelligence* (IJCAI-75), pp. 483-90.

Forgy, C. (1982) RETE: a fast algorithm for the many pattern/many object pattern match problem. *Artificial Intelligence* 19(1):17-37.

Hayes-Roth, B. and Hewett, M. (1988) "BB1: An Implementation of the Blackboard Control Architecture." *Blackboard Systems*, Engelmore, R., and T. Morgan, editors, pp. 297-313, Addison-Wesley.

Hewett, M. and Hewett, R. (1993) A Language and Architecture for Efficient Blackboard Systems. In: *Proceedings of the Ninth International IEEE Conference on AI Applications* (CAIA '93), Orlando, Florida.

Lâasri, H. and Maître, B. (1989) "Flexibility and Efficiency in Blackboard Systems: Studies and Achievements in ATOME." *Blackboard Architectures and Applications*, Jagannathan, V., R. Dodhiawala and L. S. Baum, editors, pp. 309-322, Academic Press.

Lesser, V.R. and Corkill, D.D. (1988) "The Distributed Vehicle Monitoring Testbed." *Blackboard Systems*, Engelmore, R., and T. Morgan, editors, pp. 353-386, Addison-Wesley.

Nii, H.P. and Aiello, N. (1979) AGE: A Knowledge-Based Program for Building Knowledge-Based Programs. In: *Proceedings of the Sixth International Joint Conference on Artificial Intelligence* (IJCAI-79), pp. 645-655.

Rice, J., Aiello, N., and Nii, H.P. (1989) "See How They Run...." *Blackboard Architectures and Applications*, Jagannathan, V., R. Dodhiawala and L. S. Baum, editors, pp. 153-178, Academic Press.

Scales, D. J. (1986) *Efficient Matching Algorithms for the SOAR/OPS5 Production System*, Technical Report STAN-CS-86-1124, Stanford University, Stanford, California.

Model-Based Automated Generation
of User Interfaces

Angel R. Puerta, Henrik Eriksson, John H. Gennari, and Mark A. Musen

Medical Computer Science Group
Knowledge Systems Laboratory
Departments of Medicine and Computer Science
Stanford University
Stanford, CA, 94305-5479
{puerta,eriksson,gennari,musen}@camis.stanford.edu

ABSTRACT[1]

User interface design and development for knowledge-based systems and most other types of applications is a resource-consuming activity. Thus, many attempts have been made to automate, to certain degrees, the construction of user interfaces. Current tools for automated design of user interfaces are able to generate the static layout of an interface from the application's data model using an intelligent program that applies design rules. These tools, however, are not capable of generating the dynamic behavior of the interface, which must be specified programmatically, and which constitutes most of the effort of interface construction. Mecano is a model-based user-interface development environment that uses a domain model to generate both the static layout and the dynamic behavior of an interface. A knowledge-based system applies sets of dialog design and layout rules to produce interfaces from the domain model. Mecano has been used successfully to completely generate the layout and the dynamic behavior of relatively large and complex, domain-specific, form- and graph-based interfaces for applications in medicine and several other domains.

INTRODUCTION

In recent years there has been significant progress in providing automated assistance to user-interface developers. Commercially available interface builders, user-interface management systems, and interface toolkits provide considerable savings to developers in time and in effort needed to produce a new interface (deBaar, Foley, & Mullet 1992).

Even with these commercial tools present, the amount of effort and low-level detail involved in constructing interfaces is substantial. Therefore, researchers are investigating techniques to automate more portions of the interface design process. One promising area is that of model-based user-interface development (Puerta 1993; Szekely, Luo, & Neches 1993). In this approach,

developers work with high-level specifications (models) of the interface to define dialog and layout characteristics. Model-based systems facilitate the automation of interface design tasks. A successful approach has been to use the application's data model to generate the static layout of an interface (deBaar, Foley, & Mullet 1992; Janssen, Weisbecker, & Ziegler 1993).

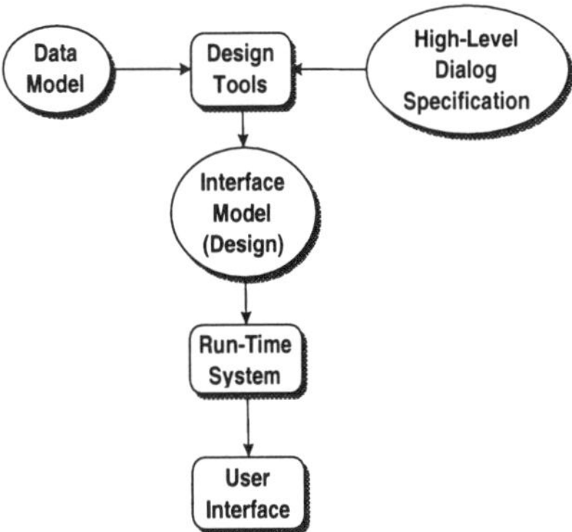

Figure 1. Generic framework for automated interface-generation environments that employ data models. The interface design is produced by tools that examine a data model and a dialog specification. The design may be represented implicitly or explicitly (as an interface model). The run-time system implements the design.

Figure 1 shows a generic framework for automated interface generation environments that employ data models. An intelligent design tool examines the data model and applies a set of design rules to produce a static design of an interface. Because the data model is shared between the interface design and the target application design, both designs can be coupled, and changes to the application design can be propagated easily to the interface design. The dynamic behavior of the interface, however, must be specified separately. This process can take many forms such as using a graphical editor to construct dialog Petri nets (Janssen, Weisbecker, & Ziegler 1993), to assigning sets of pre- and postconditions to each interface object (Gieskens & Foley 1992). Although working with

1. This work has been supported in part by grants LM05157 and LM05305 from the National Library of Medicine, and by gifts from Digital Equipment Corporation. Dr. Musen is recipient of NSF Young Investigator Award IRI-9257578.

high-level dialog specifications is helpful to interface developers, it does not automate the design of dynamic behavior. For large interfaces, editing the dialog specifications is still a time-consuming task involving the definition of hundreds of actions and conditions, some of which may conflict with each other.

The Mecano Approach

Current data-model approaches do not exploit the relationships among objects in the model to generate the dynamic behavior of an interface. In addition, a data model is application-specific. In the Mecano approach, we aim to use domain models from which dynamic interface behavior can be generated, and that are also sharable across a range of applications.

In this paper, we present Mecano, a model-based interface development environment that uses domain models instead of data models to generate interfaces. A domain model is a high-level knowledge representation that captures all the definitions and relationships of a given application domain. A domain model extends the data model for the application. By substituting the data model in Figure 1 for a domain model, Mecano does not require any dialog specification editing and can generate complete dynamic behavior specifications even for large interfaces with hundreds of components.

The rest of this paper is organized as follows. We first review related work and present an overview of Mecano, including a definition and illustration of domain models. Then, we show how various cases of dynamic behavior can be generated from domain models by using an example from the medical domain. Next, we explain how end users are able to participate in the layout design of interfaces generated in Mecano and how design revisions can be conducted. We conclude by analyzing this approach and summarizing the results.

RELATED WORK

There are three types of systems documented in literature that relate closely to the Mecano approach: (1) systems that use textual specifications to generate dialogs, (2) systems that combine the use of data models and high-level dialog specifications, and (3) systems that directly manipulate an interface model to produce an interface.

One of the earliest efforts to generate dialogs via textual descriptions is COUSIN (Hayes and Szekely 1992). It generates menus and fill-in forms from a specification of commands and their parameters. Mickey (Olsen 1989) uses an extended version of Pascal to describe contents, parameters, and behavior of direct-manipulation of interfaces. ITS (Wiecha et al. 1989) separates dialog and style into two different layers and allows the specification of the dialog layer through a command language and the definition of styles through a rule set. Given the textual description for a dialog, ITS reasons about the style rule set to generate the

interface. The UofA* (Singh and Green 1991) system generates the presentation and dialog through a command language. These systems, in general, help the developer by providing tools to design dialogs at a high-level of abstraction, but they do not automate the design process beyond that point.

Among the first examples of the use of data models to derive static layouts for interfaces is HIGGENS (Hudson and King 1986). It allows a developer to view abstractly the interface by examining the data models, but it lacks an automatic generator for the actual interface.

The UIDE environment includes a tool for static layout generation from an extended data model (deBaar, Foley, & Mullet 1992). The specification of dynamic behavior, however, must be achieved by defining sets of pre- and postconditions (Gieskens and Foley 1992) for each one of the interface objects. The GENIUS environment (Janssen, Weisbecker, & Ziegler 1993) uses an entity–relationship data model along with a graphical editor for dialog specifications to generate interfaces. The data model, which can be edited graphically, provides the basis for the definition of the interface components and their layout. The graphical editor allows the review of *dialog nets,* a variation of Petri nets, that define the actions of the interface objects and the conditions that preclude or follow those actions.

Systems that employ data models have the advantage of sharing the data model with the target application, thus coupling the design of both. They cannot automate dynamic dialog design from the data model and have problems scaling up because of their approach to specifying dialogs. For example, the use of pre- and postconditions in large interfaces can cause conflicts among the conditions and may necessitate the development of conflict-resolution strategies.

Systems that generate interfaces by manipulating interface models include HUMANOID (Szekely, Luo, & Neches 1993) and DON (Kim and Foley 1993). HUMANOID defines an elaborate interface model that includes components for the application, the presentation, and the dialog. Developers construct application models and HUMANOID picks among a number of *templates* of interfaces to display the interface. The developer can then refine the behavior of the interface by editing the dialog model. HUMANOID assists, but does not automate, the generation of dynamic behavior specifications, and requires considerable additional developer effort to generate interfaces that do not conform to its templates, as is the case with most complex interfaces. DON uses a presentation model that allows developers to explore designs and that provides expert assistance in the generation of designs. DON does not have a dynamic behavior component for automatic generation of dialogs.

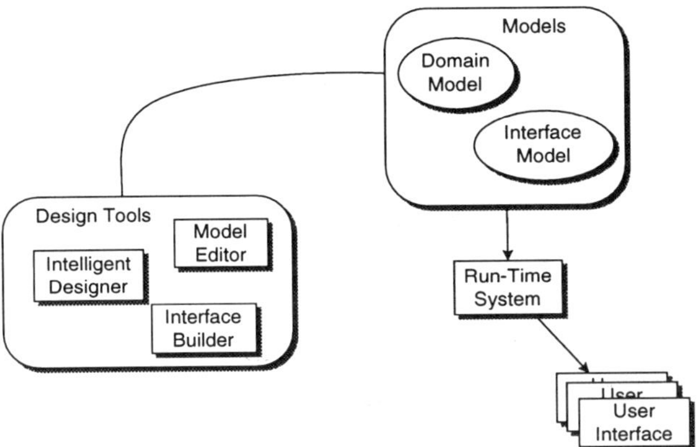

Figure 2. The main components of Mecano. The intelligent designer operates on a domain model, as opposed to a data model, to produce interface designs.

OVERVIEW OF MECANO

The main components of the Mecano environment are shown in Figure 2. Mecano follows the general architecture of Figure 1, replacing the data model with a domain model. The design tools include a model-editing tool, an intelligent designer tool, and an interface builder, which in our case is provided by the supporting platform, the NeXT environment.

The framework for user-interface development with Mecano calls for a developer to start by employing the model editor (Gennari 1993) to visualize and review a domain model (described later in this paper). The domain model is shared with the target application. Therefore, an interface developer need not build one for a given domain from scratch. Instead, the normal process is to revise an existing one. Once a domain model is deemed satisfactory, it is input to the intelligent designer (Eriksson, Puerta, & Musen 1994), a tool that produces a dynamic dialog specification and a preliminary layout for the interface. The layout can then be refined using NeXT's Interface Builder. Both the dialog and layout output by the intelligent designer are stored declaratively in an interface model. This model contains all facets of an interface design including interface objects, presentation, dialog, and behavior.

The design defined in the interface model is implemented by a run-time system. Mecano's run-time tools have the capability of implementing form- and graph-based interfaces with many types of objects, from simple ones, such as menus and push-buttons, to complex ones, such as list browsers and domain-specific graphical editors. The run-time tools implement the dynamic behavior of the interface according to the specifications in the interface model.

The overall design process in Mecano is iterative. The resulting interfaces may have deficiencies that require

editing the domain model and regenerating the interface. In such cases, the intelligent designer keeps track of layout customizations that may have been made in the previous generation and reapplies these customizations as appropriate.

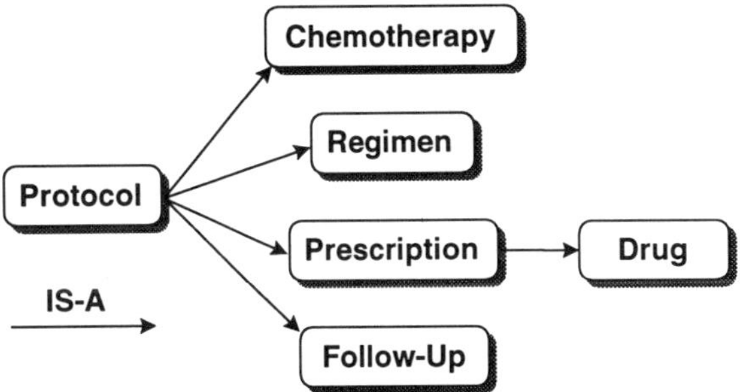

Figure 3. Partial view of a medical domain model for therapy (protocol) administration (IS-A view). The hierarchy of classes is used to generate the interface-navigation schema for windows and other objects.

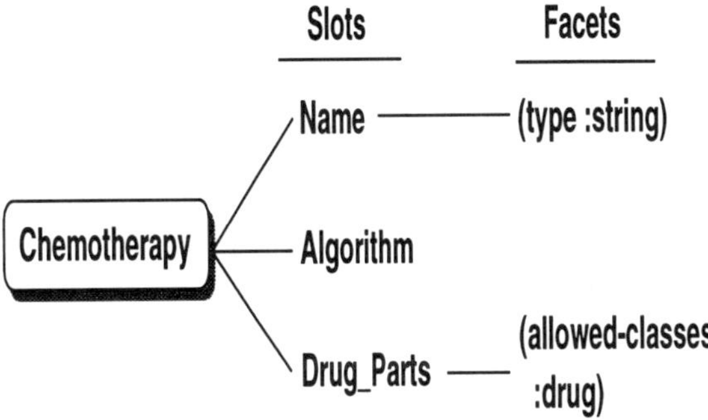

Figure 4. Partial view of the slots and facets (properties) for the *chemotherapy* class. Facets can define *allowed-classes* relationships among classes. These relationships are used to generate specifications for interface-object groupings in windows. Other facets like *type* are important to determine static layout (e.g., appropriate widget for a type *string* object)

Domain Models

A domain model is a representation of the objects in a domain and their interrelationships. Domain models in Mecano are constructed using a frame-based representation language that defines class hierarchies (Gennari 1993). Each *class* in the hierarchy can have a number of *slots* and each slot defines a number of properties (called *facets*) Figures 3 and 4 show partial views of a model for the medical domain of therapy administration (called protocol administration).

There are two important relationships in domain models. The *is-a* relationship (see Figure 3) determines the class hierarchy and is used by the intelligent designer in Mecano to specify the interface-navigation schema among windows and other objects. The *part-of* relationship (see Figure 4) is

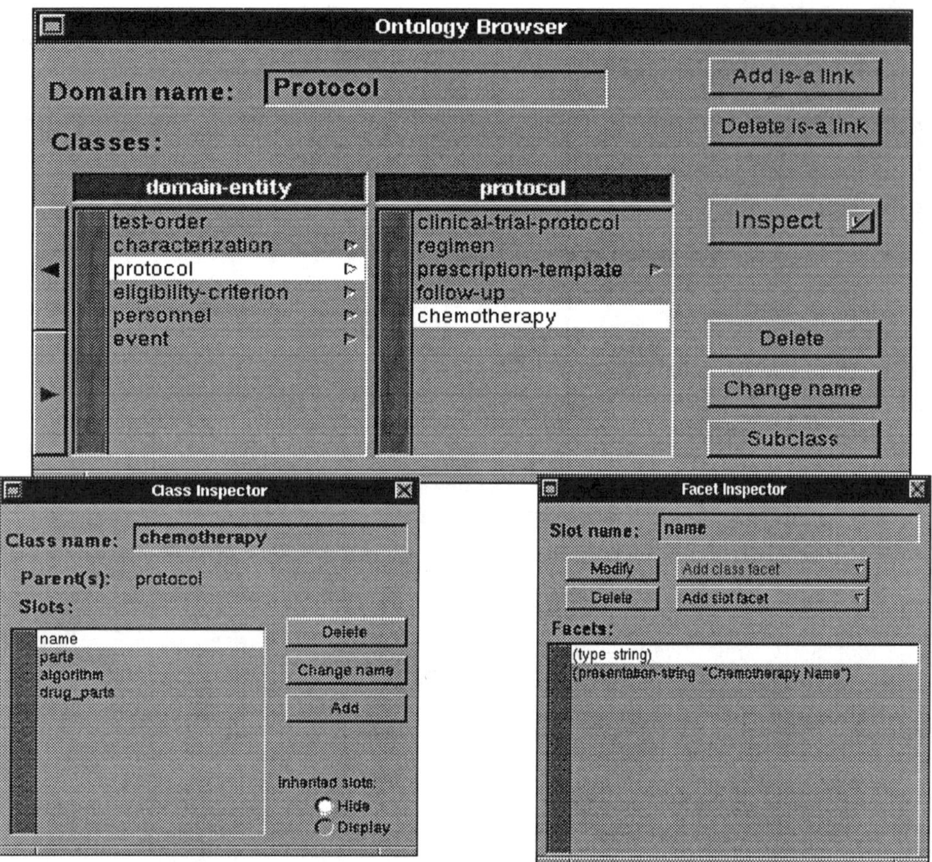

Figure 5. Editing the domain model. Using browsers and inspectors, the developer can specify the *class hierarchy* (top window) and the *slots* and *facets* (properties) of each class.

used to determine object groupings by windows. Other important facets include, for example, *type*, *cardinality*, *min* and *max* of a slot, which are used in the specification of the static layout (e.g., what widget should be used for the slot; size of a numeric input field). In fact, the application's data model is completely included in the domain model. Therefore, all the design rules of an intelligent design tool that may be applied to a data model can be applied to a domain model. In the next section, we illustrate the use of domain models to generate a therapy administration application.

GENERATION OF DIALOG SPECIFICATIONS FROM DOMAIN MODELS

Before dialogs can be generated, a domain model must be prepared with the model editor shown in Figure 5. The domain model is shared with the target application. Thus, a coupling of application design and interface design is established. Developers can build domain models incrementally, and can prototype interfaces early in the development process because Mecano supports iterative design. More importantly, it is not necessary to build domain models from scratch for every application. A domain model for medical therapy planning can be reused, with minor variations, in other applications. This is a significant advantage of Mecano over systems that design from data models because data models are difficult to reuse across applications.

Once edited, the domain model is used to generate dialog specifications. These specifications have two levels in Mecano:.

- High-level dialog defines all interface windows, assigns interface objects to windows, and specifies the navigation schema among windows in the interface.

- Low-level dialog defines specific dialog elements (widgets) to each interface object created at the high level and specifies how the standard behavior of the dialog element is modified for the given domain.

High-Level Dialog Generation

The elements of the high-level dialog specification are generated by examining the class hierarchy of the domain

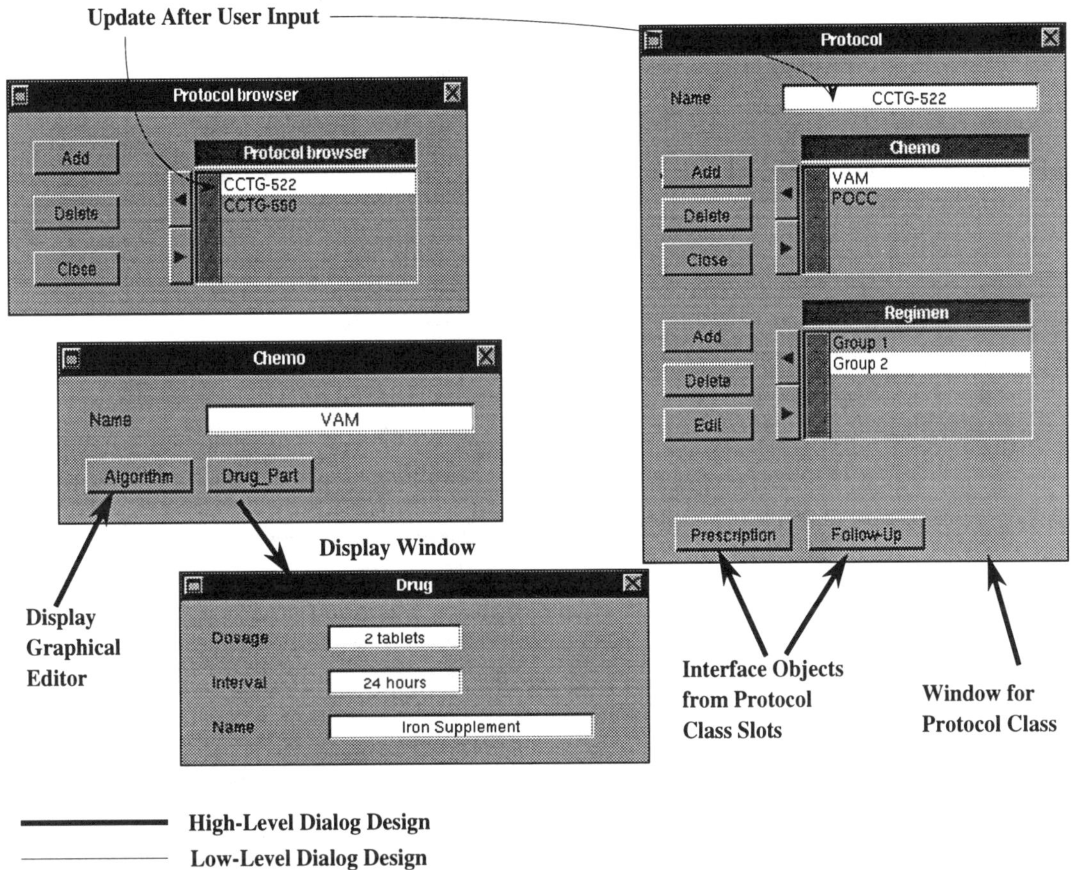

Figure 6. Interface generated from the partial domain model in Figures 3 and 4. Legends indicate generated dialog at high- and low-level design times. An interface generated from the full domain model for medical therapy contains over 60 windows and hundreds of dialog elements (widgets). The dynamic behavior of such interface can be generated automatically from a domain model.

model (see Figure 3) and the slots of each class (see Figure 4). Figure 6 shows an interface generated from the partial domain model shown in Figures 3, and 4. The complete medical domain model for therapy administration generates an interface with over 60 windows and hundreds of widgets. Note that the dialog for window navigation is established during high-level dialog design but that it can be refined, or augmented, at low-level dialog design time. The procedure to generate a high-level dialog design is as follows:

- Each class in the hierarchy is assigned a window.

- Window navigation is established by searching the class hierarchy for links indicated by the *allowed-classes* facet in the domain model. For example, the *Drug* window shown in Figure 6 is accessed from the *Chemo* window because the Drug class is an allowed class for the slot *Drug_Part*.

- Each window is assigned one *interface object* per slot in the class. After generation, the developer has the option of customizing the interface by splitting windows multiple objects into two or more windows. Interface objects are assigned actual widgets during low-level dialog design.

Low-Level Dialog Generation

Elements of the low-level dialog specification are generated by examining the facets (properties) defined for each slot in the domain model (see Figure 4). The process has these steps:

- Each interface object defined at high-level design time is assigned a dialog element (widget) by examining the facets of the corresponding slot in the domain model. For example an object of *type string* is assigned a text field, an object of *type Boolean* is assigned a check-box widget, and an object of *type string* and *cardinality multiple* (i.e., the object can be multiple-valued) is assigned a list browser.

- Each dialog element may be assigned *actions* beyond the standard behavior of the dialog element by examining the facets of the corresponding slot in the domain model. Examples of dialog-element actions include disabling editing in other dialog elements, and updating values in other dialog elements after a user input action (see Figure 6).

Note that the specification of dialog-element actions is one of the important operations that cannot be automated in systems that rely on data models for interface generation.

GENERATION OF DOMAIN-SPECIFIC GRAPHICAL EDITORS

One of the important capabilities in Mecano is the generation from domain models of domain-specific, nodes-and-links graphical editors useful to describe procedures such as flowcharts. Consider the following slot information for the class *Protocol*:

(slot algorithm
(type :procedure)
(allowed-classes :xrt :chemotherapy :drug))

When the intelligent dialog designer examines this slot during low-level dialog design, it assigns a graphical editor as the dialog element for that slot due to the type *procedure* defined for that slot. It also defines three graphical objects to be used during editing, one for *x-ray therapies* (xrt), one for *chemotherapies (chemo),* and one for *drugs*. Figure 7 shows a graphical editor generated from the above slot definition.

PARTICIPATORY LAYOUT DESIGN AND DESIGN REVISION

A crucial concern with any system that automatically generates interfaces is how it allows the developer to review and change the generated design. In Mecano, there are two types of revisions: layout and dialog.

The intelligent designer tool uses a layout algorithm to produce a *preliminary* layout of the interface objects. The philosophy in Mecano is to be able to involve the end user in the process of custom-tailoring a layout. For example, for the medical treatment application shown in this paper, the interface developer works together with a physician to review and custom tailor the preliminary layout with an interface builder (see Figure 2). Our experience is that this revision—in the case of the interface derived from the full model—may take between two and a half to four hours for the 65 windows included in that application (including layout and dialog revisions, and needed interface regenerations). Custom-tailoring information is kept on a database so that if the interface needs to be regenerated because of incremental changes to the domain model (as it

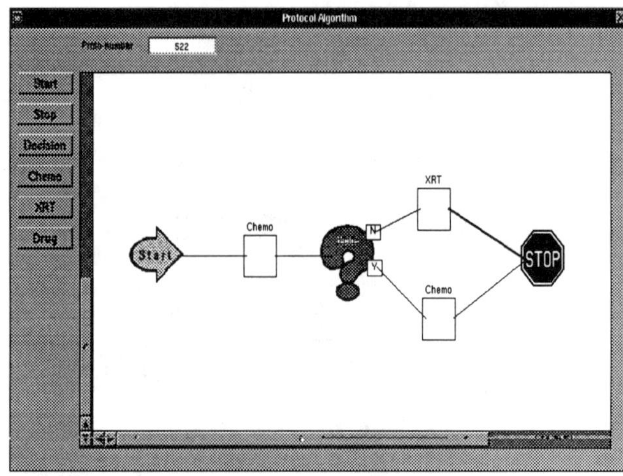

Figure 7. A graphical editor to draw medical treatments generated from a domain model. Both the drawing objects and their connectivity behavior are determined by the intelligent designer tool in Mecano.

is often the case), the customizations can be reapplied to the newly generated interface. Substantial revisions of the domain model, however, invalidate the information on the customization database.

The working sessions with the end user—in this paper's example, a physician—are also used to discover difficulties with the dialog design and incompleteness in the information displayed in the interface. Dialog design customizations can be made by editing directly the interface model (see Figure 2) and do not require a regeneration of the interface. On the other hand, for the interface to be able to display additional dialog elements, changes must be made to the domain model to define needed slots or classes. Such changes do require the interface be regenerated. Overall, the Mecano policy is to understand the interface design process as iterative and to support the introduction of custom changes without creating duplicate work.

ANALYSIS AND CONCLUSIONS

We have described a user-interface development environment that generates automatically presentation and dialog specifications for domain-specific, form- and graph-based interfaces. The strong points of this system are:

- Generation of both the static layout and the dynamic behavior of domain-specific, form- and graph-based interfaces, including relatively large and complex ones, for multiple domains (e.g., medical treatment, elevator configuration).

- Use of the application's domain models, which includes the application's data model, for interface generation considerably augments automation capabilities over systems utilizing only a data model.

• Support of participatory layout design involving end users of the applications, and support for iterative design without duplication of work.

Mecano has the same central weakness that other model-based systems have: the system is as good as the expressiveness of its underlying models. We continue researching extensions to our frame-based representation language for domain models and interface models in order to be able to automate more types of dialog actions. In particular, we are concerned with how to generate complex sequences of actions (commands) at low-level dialog design time. We are also working on the run-time system of Mecano to implement new types of widgets. Furthermore, the interface generation approach from domain models is most useful for domain-specific interfaces with a relatively fixed user dialogue (such as the medical forms shown in the figures in this paper). For other types of interfaces, it will be necessary to examine other types of models (such as a model of the user's task) to be able to generate automatically interface specifications. We are currently working on developing such task models as components of our generic interface model.

Overall, Mecano provides a framework for assisting the development of interfaces and for the study of interface models and the relationships between domain characteristics and user interface presentation and dialog.

ACKNOWLEDGMENTS
We wish to thank Tom Gruber for his helpful comments.

REFERENCES

de Baar, D.J.M.J., Foley, J.D. and Mullet, K.E. 1992. Coupling Application Design and User Interface Design. In *Proceedings of Human Factors in Computing Systems, CHI'92*. Monterey, California, May 1992, pp. 259–266.

Eriksson, H., Puerta, A.R. and Musen, M.A. 1994. Generation of Knowledge-Acquisition Tools from Domain Ontologies. In *Proceedings of the Eighth Banff Knowledge Acquisition for Knowledge-Based Systems Workshop*. Banff, Alberta, Canada. pp. 7.1–7.20.

Gennari, J.H. 1993. *A Brief Guide to Maître and MODEL: An Ontology Editor and a Frame-Based Knowledge Representation Language.* Stanford University, Knowledge Systems Laboratory, Report KSL-93-46, Stanford, California. June 1993.

Gieskens, D.F. and Foley, J.D. 1992. Controlling User Interface Objects through Pre- and Postconditions. In *Proceedings of Human Factors in Computing Systems, CHI'92*. Monterey, California, May 1992, pp. 189–194.

Hayes, P. and Szekely, P. 1992. Graceful Interaction through the {COUSIN} Command Interface. *International Journal of Man–Machine Studies*, **19**(3), pp. 285–305.

Hudson, S.E. and King, R. 1986 A Generator of Direct Manipulation Office Systems. *ACM Transactions on Information Systems,* **4**(2), pp. 132–163.

Janssen, C., Weisbecker A. and Ziegler J. 1993. Generating User Interfaces from Data Models and dialog Net Specifications. In *Proceedings of Human Factors in Computing Systems, INTERCHI'93*. Amsterdam, The Netherlands, April 1993, pp. 418–423.

Kim, W.C. and Foley, J.D. 1993. Providing High-Level Control and Expert Assistance in the User Interface Presentation Design. In *Proceedings of Human Factors in Computing Systems, INTERCHI'93*. Amsterdam, The Netherlands, April 1993, pp. 430–437.

Olsen, D.R. 1989. A Programming Language Basis for User Interface Management. In *Proceedings of Human Factors in Computing Systems, CHI'89*. Austin, Texas, May 1989, pp. 171–176.

Puerta A.R. 1993. The Study of Models of Intelligent Interfaces. In Proceedings of the 1993 International Workshop on Intelligent User Interfaces. Orlando, Florida, January 1993, pp. 71–80.

Singh, G. and Green, M. 1991. Automating the Lexical and Syntactic Design of Graphical User Interfaces: The UofA* UIMS. *ACM Transactions on Graphics,* **10**(3), pp. 213–254.

Szekely, P., Luo, P. and Neches, R. 1993. Beyond Interface Builders: Model-Based Interface Tools. In *Proceedings of Human Factors in Computing Systems, INTERCHI'93*. Amsterdam, The Netherlands, April 1993, pp. 383–390.

Wiecha, C., Bennett, W., Boies, S., Gould, J. and Greene, S. 1989. ITS: A Tool for Rapidly Developing Interactive Applications. *ACM Transactions on Information Systems,* **8**(3), pp. 204–236.

The Relationship Between Architectures and Example-Retrieval Times

Eiichiro SUMITA, Naoya NISIYAMA and Hitoshi IIDA
ATR Interpreting Telecommunications Research Laboratories
2-2 Hikaridai, Seika, Souraku, Kyoto 619-02, JAPAN
sumita@itl.atr.co.jp

Abstract

This paper proposes a method to find the most suitable architecture for a given response time requirement for Example-Retrieval (ER), which searches for the best match from a bulk collection of lingusitic examples. In the Example-Based Approach(EBA), which attains substantially higher accuracy than traditional approaches, ER is extensively used to carry out natural language processing tasks, e.g., parsing and translation. ER, however, is so computationally demanding that it often takes up most of the total sentence processing time. This paper compares several accelerations of ER on different architectures, i.e., serial, MIMD and SIMD. Experimental results reveal the relationship between architectures and response times, which will allows us to find the most suitable architecture for a given response time requirement.

Introduction

Novel models for natural language processing (NLP) that make use of the increasing availability of large-scale corpora and bulk processing power have been studied in recent years. They are called Example-Based Approaches (EBAs) because they rely upon linguistic examples, such as translation pairs, derived from corpora.

Example-Retrieval (ER), the central mechanism of the EBA, provides the best match, which improves the coverage and accuracy of NLP systems over those of traditional methods. ER, however, is computationally demanding. Success in speeding up ER using a massively parallel associative memory processor has already been reported. This paper does not focus on such a single implementation but aims to clarify the relationship between architectures and response times, and answers the question, **which architecture is most suitable for ER?**

First, EBA and ER are briefly introduced, then, the computational cost of ER is described, next, various implementations and experimental results are explained, followed by discussion.

Example-Based Approach

In the early 1980s, Nagao proposed a novel model for machine translation, one that translates by mimicking best-match translation examples, based on the fact that a human translates according to past translation experience.(Nagao 1984) Since the end of the 1980s, large corpora and powerful computational devices have allowed us to realize Nagao's model and expand the model to deal with not only translation but also other tasks such as parsing. First, the word selection problem in machine translation was attacked (Sato 1991; Sumita & Iida 1991; Nomiyama 1992), then, experimental full translation systems [1] were realized or proposed (Sato 1991; Furuse & Iida 1992; Kitano 1991; Watanabe 1992; Maruyama & Watanabe 1992), next, case frame selection (Nagao 1992) and pp-attachment(Sumita, Furuse & Iida 1993) were investigated. These papers have demonstrated that EBAs surpass conventional approaches in several aspects, particularly coverage and accuracy.

So far, many different procedures for ER have been proposed, however, they share a framework that calculates the semantic distance between the input expression and the example expression and returns the examples whose semantic distance is minimum. Here, a typical definition of semantic distance measure is explained(Sumita & Iida 1991). Suppose Input **I** and Example **E** are composed of n words. The semantic distance measure is the summation of the distance, $d(I_k, E_k)$ at the k-th word, multiplied by the weight of the k-th word, w_k. The distance, $d(I_k, E_k)$ is determined based on a thesaurus. The weight, w_k, is the degree to which the word influences the task.

As explained in detail in the next section, ER is computationally demanding. This problem was attacked through the Massively Parallel Artificial Intelligence (MPAI) paradigm(Kitano et al. 1991; Stanfill & Waltz 1986), producing a successful result(Sumita

---

[1]Translation examples are varied from phrases to sentences. Some input sentences match a whole example sentence. Other input sentences match a combination of fragmental examples (noun phrase, verb phrase, adverbial phrase and so on).

et al. 1993) using a massivley parallel associative processor, IXM2(Higuchi et al. 1991). Unlike this, the authors aim to obtain the relationship between various architectures and response times.

The Computational Cost of Example-Retrieval

ER is the full retrieval of similar examples from a large-scale example database. The total ER time is predominant in processing a sentence and depends on two parameters, i.e., the example database size and the input sentence length. From an estimation of the two parameters, we can derive the time requirement.

Two Parameters

The ER time, T, rises according to the number of examples, N. N is so large, as explained in the next subsection that T is considerable. ER is called many times while processing a sentence. The number of ER calls, C, rises according to the sentence length, L. Consequently, the total ER time is the predominant factor in the time required for processing a sentence by an EBA system. For example, in Furuse et al.'s prototype system for spoken language translation, ER takes up about 50-80% of the time required for translating a sentence and other processes such as pattern-matching, morphological analysis and generation consuming the rest of the time.(Oi et al. 1993) If N increases, the ER/other ratio will increase.

Response Time Requirement

Here, we estimate N and L by extrapolating those of the machine translation system mentioned at the end of the previous subsection.

N depends on the vocabulary size. The vocabulary size of the prototype system is about 1,500. The vocabulary size of the average commercially available machine translation system is about 100,000. In the prototype, N of the most common example is about 1,000. N, in direct proportion to the vocabulary size, 100,000 is about 70,000. For the sake of convenience, we assume $N = 100,000$.

The investigation of the ATR dialogue database (Ehara, Ogura & Morimoto 1990) reveals that the lengths of most sentences are under 20 (words), i.e., $L = 20$. In our experiments, the following approximate equation holds between the number of ER calls, C and the sentence length, L.

$$C = 10^{\frac{L}{10}} \qquad (1)$$

In sum, $N = 100,000$ and $L = 20$, i.e., $C = 100$. Then the total ER time with a serial machine is so large that it would be not acceptable in a real-time application, such as interpreting telephony, which we are striving to realize.

Goal: an ER time, T, with 100,000 examples under 1 millisecond.

Achieving this goal means that we will have succeeded in accelerating ER to a sufficient speed because the maximum of the total ER time, 100 ($= T*C = 1*100$) milliseconds is much less than an utterence time.

Implementations of ER

This section explains items related to implementations: architectures, the task, example and thesaurus-based calculation of semantic distance, and the retrieval algorithms.

Architectures

Although we have implemented and are implementing ER on many machines [2], this paper concentrates on the DEC alpha/7000, KSR1(Kendall Square Research Corp.1992) and MP-2(MasPar Computer Corp. 1992) as representative of three architectures - serial, MIMD and SIMD - respectively.

Task, Example and Thesaurus-Based Calculation of Semantic Distance

For the experiments, we chose the task of translating Japanese noun phrases of the form"A の B" into English (A and B are Japanese nouns. "の" is an adnominal particle such as "の," "での," "からの," and so on.) They are translated into various English noun phrases of the form "B̃ of Ã," "B̃ in Ã," "B̃ for Ã," "B̃ at Ã," and so on (Ã and B̃ being English translations of A and B.) We used 100,000 examples, which were collected from the ASAHI newspaper(Tanaka 1991).

"A の B" is represented in the strucure that consists of the fields: AW for the WORD of A; BW for the WORD of B; AC for the the CODE (thesaurus code explained below) of A; BC for the the CODE of B; and NO for the WORD of "の". The example database is stored in an array of the structure with another field, D, for the semantic distance.

Each word corresponds to its concept in the thesaurus. The semantic distance between words is reduced to the semantic distance between concepts. The semantic distance between concepts is determined according to their positions in the the thesaurus hierarchy [3], which is a tree. The semantic distance varies from 0 to 1. When the thesaurus is $(n + 1)$-layered, the semantic distance, (k/n) is given to the concepts in the k-th layer from the bottom ($0 \leq k \leq n$).

The semantic distance is calculated based on the CODE (thesaurus code), which clearly represents the thesaurus hierarchy, as in Table 1, instead of traversing

---

[2]They include the CM-2(Thinking Machines Corp. 1990), IXM2(Higuchi et al. 1991), iPSC/2(Intel 1989), CM-5(Thinking Machines Corp. 1991), and a workstation cluster.

[3]The hierarchy is in accordance with a general thesaurus (Ohno & Hamanishi 1984),a brief explanation of which is found in the literature(Sumita & Iida 1992).

the hierarchy. Our n is 3 and the width of each layer is 10. Thus, each word is assigned a three-digit decimal code of the concept to which the word corresponds.

Table 1: **Thesaurus-Based Calculation of Semantic Distance** - The input CODE and example CODE are $CI = CI_1CI_2CI_3$, $CE = CE_1CE_2CE_3$ -

Condition	Example	Dist.
$CI_1CI_2CI_3 = CE_1CE_2CE_3$	347 , 347	0
$CI_1CI_2 = CE_1CE_2, CI_3 \neq CE_3$	347 , 346	1/3
$CI_1 = CE_1, CI_2 \neq CE_2$	347 , 337	2/3
$CI_1 \neq CE_1$	347 , 247	1

Retrieval Algorithms

Here, we explain two alogorithms.

The Basic Retrieval Algorithm This is used to find the minimum-distance examples by calculating the semantic distance between an input and every example, i.e., an exhaustive search. The algorithm consists of three steps: WORD Exact Match; CODE Exact Match and CODE Partial Match. These include two parts, i.e., a mark part and a collection part, as follows:

1. [**WORD Exact Match**]

   (a) [**Mark**]Examples whose AW, NO, BW match the input are marked.

   (b) [**Collection**]If there is a match, all marked examples and the distance 0 are returned.

2. [**CODE Exact Match**]

   (a) [**Mark**]Examples whose AC, NO, BC match the input are marked.

   (b) [**Collection**]If there is a match, all marked examples and the distance 0 are returned.

3. [**CODE Partial Match**]

   (a) [**Mark**] First, the distance between NOs [4] multiplied by the weight of NO is added to the field, D of the examples.
   Second, the distance between ACs is calculated according to Table 1, and the distance multiplied by the weight is added to the field, D of examples. Third, the distance between BCs is calculated according to Table 1, and the distance multiplied by the weight is added to the field, D of examples.

   (b) [**Collection**]All the minimum-distance examples and the minimum distance are returned.

---

[4]The distance between NOs is 0 or 1 depending on whether or not they match. An example that does NOT match the NO is helpful for translation when the NO of the input has a restricted meaning and the NO of the example has a general meaning.

The Index-Based Retrieval Algorithm The basic algorithm is speeded up by an indexing technique for suppressing unnecessary computation. Step 1 is easily speeded up by hashing of AW, NO, BW. Step 2 is easily speeded up by hashing of AC, NO, BC as well. Calculation between thesaurus codes, AC or BC, is the predominant part of Step 3. We use thesaurus codes as an index of the example array. According to Table 1, if $CI_1 \neq CE_1$ (most of the examples), we need not compute the distance between the input and the example because it is always 1, otherwise, we need to check the example in more detail to compute the distancee between the input and the example. Thus, indexing is useful for accelerating the retrieval by suppressing unnecessary computation.

Experimental Results

The following subsections describe implementations on three different architecutures - serial, MIMD and SIMD - one by one.

Serial Machine

Figure 1 shows serial implementations: (1) the basic retrieval algorithm and (2) the index-based retrieval algorithm, which were explained in the previous section.

Because the two algorithms are realized by repetition, the processing time rises directly according to the number of examples. But (2) drastically improves the response time of (1).

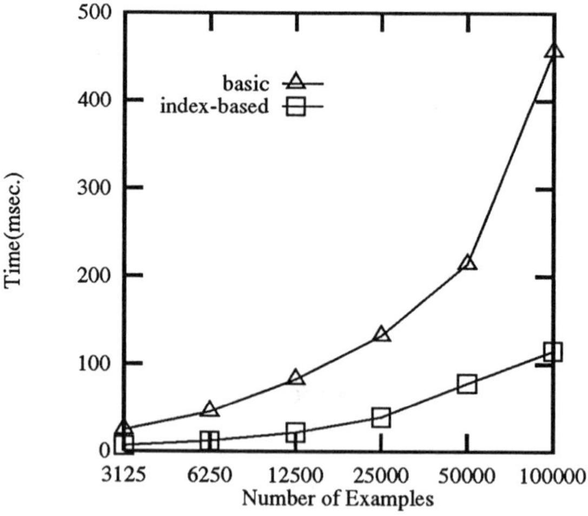

Figure 1: **Time vs. Number of Examples on a Serial Machine, DEC alpha/7000** - *Basic vs. Index-based algorithms* -

Serial machines, unlike parallel machines, have no communication overhead. The ER time, T (msec.) is inversely proportional to the performance of the processor, M (MIPS):

$$T = \frac{m}{M} \qquad (2)$$

Implementations on seven different machines (Figure 2) revealed that the constant m is about 20,000.

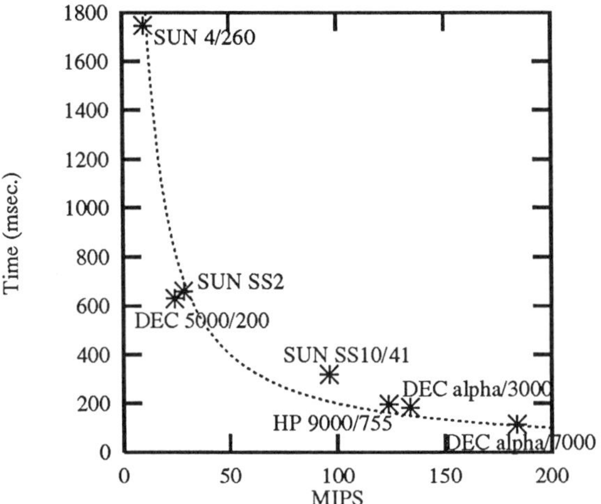

Figure 2: **Time vs. MIPS on Seven Serial machines** - *Index-based algorithm with 100,000 examples -*

MIMD Machine

The flow of MIMD implementation is simple:

1. Divide the example database into equal sub-databases in advance.

2. Execute a serial retrieval algorithm for each processor's subdatabase in parallel.

3. Merge the results of all processors.

In step 2, we can achieve both (1) serial speedup by algorithmic inventions such as indexing and increase of machine performance (MIPS) and (2) parallel speedup by decreasing the example database size to $1/p$ (p is the number of processors).

Step 3 is the major obstacle to parallel acceleration. Suppose Tp is the response time using p ($p \geq 1$) processors. Tp is the sum of the retrieval time (Step 2), $T1/p$ and the communication time (Step 3), Cp.

$$Tp = \frac{T1}{p} + Cp \qquad (3)$$

Cp depends on communication hardware and software models. For example, in a multicomputer, the iPSC/2, the hardware is a hypercube and the software model is a message passing. In such a message passing system, centralizing the message in a single processor is expensive and does not permit scalability. Parallel merging is a common countermeasure(Ranka & Sahni 1990; Sato 1993). However, the iPSC/2 showed a poor

response time, because although the Cp of a parallel merging algorithm is $c * log_2 p$, unfortunately the constant c is considerable, about 27.5 milliseconds. In a multiprocessor, the KSR1, the hardware is a directory and the programming model is a shared memory model using pthread, mutex(lock/unlock) and barrier. Figure 3 demonstrates that the speedup of ER on the KSR1 is good because Cp is small.

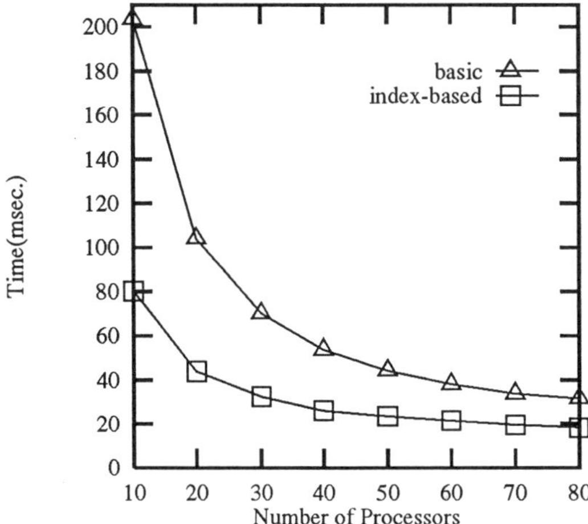

Figure 3: **Time vs. Number of Processors on a MIMD machine, KSR1** - *Basic vs. Index-based algorithms with 100,000 examples -*

SIMD Machine

A SIMD machine can efficiently execute the basic algorithm because (1) a minimal time is required to compute the semantic distance because computation is completely paralel within $N \leq p$, and p is larger than that of MIMD machines at an order of magnitude. If $N > p$, then a serial repetition must emerge; however, the degree is drastically smaller than with MIMD machines. (2) low overhead required to merge the results. (3) it can benefit from indexing technique(Figure 4).

If $N \leq p$, i.e., each processor has, at most, one example, the computational cost is not o(N) but o(1). because there is no speedup or slowdown due to a processor that works in vain. If $N > p$, then the example arrays are folded to fit p processors and the same operation is repeated $(N - 1)/p + 1$ times. Thus, the response time of SIMD implementation rises stepwise according to the number of examples.

The Best Speedup Method

This section discusses accelerating strategies from a baseline machine, a serial-virtual machine (40 MIPS), to meet the goal, **100,000 examples per millisecond** based on the results for three state-of-the-art machines, DEC alpha/7000, KSR1 and MP-2.

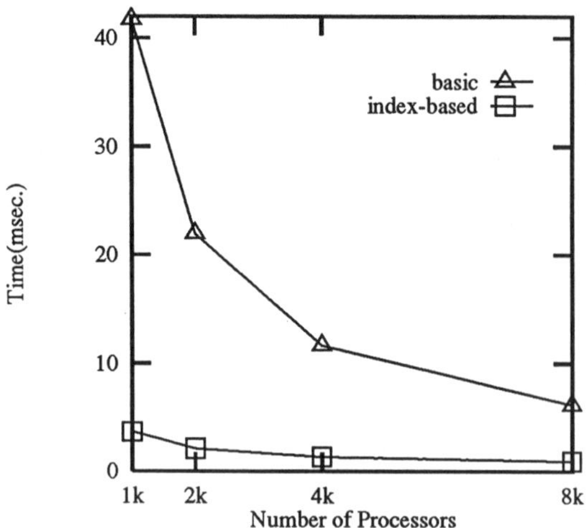

Figure 4: **Time vs. Number of Processors on a SIMD machine, MP-2** - *Basic and index-based algorithms with 100,000 examples -*

There are four strategies for improving the response time to achieve our goal:

1. (Serial Machine) Increase the performance of processor, M (MIPS).

2. (MIMD Machine) Increase the number of processors, p of the same performance, 40 MIPS.

3. (MIMD Machine) Increase both the number of processors, p and the performance of each processor, M (MIPS).

4. (SIMD Machine) Increase the number of processors, p drastically at the expense of the performance of each processor, M (MIPS).

Table 2 summerizes effects of four strategies. Strategy 1 seems to hit a wall [5] because the slope is already very small at 200 MIPS (Figure 2). Strategy 2, i.e., only the increase in p cannot go beyond the overhead, because the slope is already very small at 80 processors (Figure 3). Strategy 3 is feasible if the overhead can be decreased approximately in inverse proportion to the increase in M. [6] Strategy 4, i.e., **SIMD has achieved our goal.** [7]

---

[5]To attain the goal, we should have 20,000 MIPS according to equation (2). Increasing M to 20,000 MIPS is hopeless because it will take considerable time as explained below. MIPS is increasing at the rate of about 35% per year(Hennessy & Patterson 1990) and we already have a 200-MIPS microprocessor, thus we can get an over 20,000-MIPS processor by 2010, 16 years from now.

[6]The next generation of MIMD machines will meet the requirement.

[7]There has been a question, which came from an implementation using C* on CM-5, about the effectiveness of SIMD for ER.(Sato 1993) We also have experimental

EBA systems do not consist of ER only. There are other processes that are suitable for MIMD, while ER is the best fit for SIMD. In such a **heterogeneous** system, if communication between a SIMD machine and a MIMD machine cannot attain sufficient speed, we should adopt strategy 3 rather than strategy 4.

Table 2: **Summary of Four Strategies for Acceleration of ER.** *The serial-virtual machine (40MIPS) and MIMD-virtual machine (200MIPS), which are marked by (*), are virtual machines for discussion and the figures shown are estimated. All figures here are rounded to simplify the comparison. -*

Machine	M	p	$M*p$	T
serial-virtual*	40	1	40	500
1.DEC alpha/7000	200	1	200	100
2.KSR1	40	80	3200	20
3.MIMD-virtual*	200	80	16000	4
4.MP-2	4	8000	32000	1

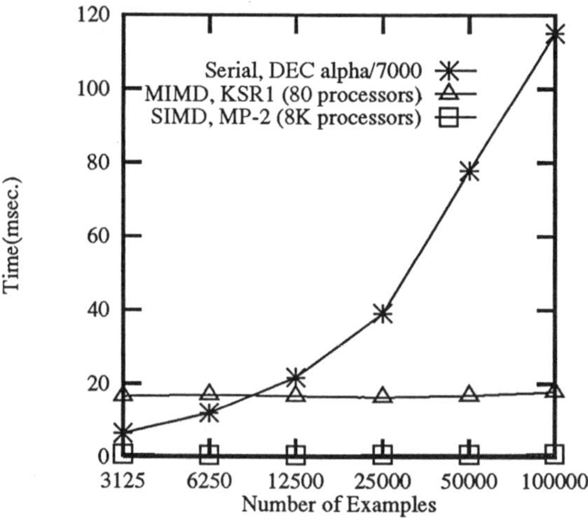

Figure 5: **Time vs. Number of Examples on Serial, MIMD and SIMD Machines** - *Index-based algorithm -*

As shown in Figure 5, SIMD is always the winner of the competition. Note the intersection of the DEC alpha/7000 and KSR1 lines in Figure 5. To the left of the intersection, the serial machine outperforms the MIMD machine due to its zero overhead for parallelization. To the right of the intersection, the MIMD machine out-

---

evidence that C* on CM-5 is not particularly efficient. Because, in principle, the communication cost of MIMD machines is much higher than that of SIMD machines, SIMD simulation by MIMD is expensive. Our results on the MP-2, however, are counterevidence against the negative question.

performs the serial machine due to the effect of dividing the example database into 1/p subdatabases.

Conclusion

We have implemented Example-Retrieval (ER), which is the key technique of Example-Based Approaches (EBAs), on machines of different architectures such as DEC alpha/7000, KSR1 and MP-2. EBA is a novel approach, which is now being developed energetically because it is expected to overcome the problems of traditional approaches for Natural Language Processing (NLP). The viability of EBA depends on whether we can speed up ER sufficiently. Using the relationship between the architectures and response times derived from experimental results, we have reached the conclusion that SIMD machines outperform machines of other types.

EBA systems, in general, consist of several different processes, which should run best on different architectures. In other words, EBA systems are heterogeneous, thus, we will further pursue the best combination of architectures, interconnects and communication models.

References

Ehara, T., Ogura, K. and Morimoto, T. 1990. ATR Dialogue Database. In Proceedings of ICSLP-90, vol. 2, 1093-1096.

Furuse, O. and Iida, H. 1992. Cooperation between Transfer and Analysis in Example-Based Framework. In Proceedings of Coling-92, 645-651. Nantes.

Hennessy, J. and Patterson, D. 1990. *Computer Architecture A Quantitative Approach.* Morgan Kaufmann Publishers.

Higuchi, T., Kitano, H., Handa, K., Furuya, T., Takahashi, N. and Kokubu, A. 1991. IXM2 A Parallel Associative Processor for Knowledge Processing, In Proceedings of AAAI-91. Anaheim.

Intel Scientific Computers 1989. *iPSC/2 User's Guide.*

Kendall Square Research Corp. 1992. *KSR1 Technical Summary.*

Kitano, H. 1991. ΦDM-Dialog An Experimental Speech-to-Speech Dialog Translation System. *IEEE Computer, June: 36-50.*

Kitano, H., Hendler, J., Moldovan, D., Higuchi, T. and Waltz, D. 1991. Massively Parallel Artificial Intelligence. In Proceedings of IJCAI-91, 557-562.

Maruyama, H. and Watanabe, H. 1992. Tree Cover Search Algorithm for Example-Based Translation. In Proceedings of TMI-92, 173-184.

MasPar Computer Corp. 1992. *The Design of the MasPar MP-2 A Cost Effective Massively Parallel Computer.*

Nagao, M. 1984. A Framework of a Mechanical Translation between Japanese and English by Analogy Principle. In *Artificial and Human Intelligence* eds. A. Elithorn and R. Banerji, North-Holland, 173-180.

Nagao, M. 1992. Some Rationales and Methodologies for Example-Based Approach. In Proceedings of FGNLP-92, 82-94.

Nomiyama, H. 1992. Machine Translation by Case Generalization. In Proceedings of Coling-92, 714-720. Nantes.

Ohno, S. and Hamanishi, M. 1984. *Ruigo-Shin-Jiten.* Kadokawa.

Oi, K., Sumita, E. Furuse, O., Iida, H. and Kitano, H. 1993. Toward Massively Parallel Spoken Language Translation. In Proceedings of PPAI-93 Workshop (IJCAI-93), 36-39.

Ranka, S. and Sahni, S. 1990. *Hypercube Algorithms.* Springer-Verlag.

Sato, S. 1991. Example-Based Machine Translation. Ph.D. Diss., Dept. of Electrical Engineering, Kyoto University.

Sato, S. 1993. MIMD Implementation of MBT3. In Proceedings of PPAI-93 Workshop (IJCAI-93), 28-35.

Stanfill, C. and Waltz, D. 1986. Toward Memory-Based Reasoning, CACM Vol. 29, No. 12, 1213-1228.

Sumita, E. and Iida, H. 1991. EXPERIMENTS AND PROSPECTS OF EXAMPLE-BASED MACHINE TRANSLATION. In Proceedings of 29th ACL, 185-192.

Sumita, E. and Iida, H. 1992. Example-Based Transfer of Japanese Adnominal Particles into English. *IEICE TRANS. INF. & SYST. Vol.E75-D, No.4, 585-594.*

Sumita, E., Furuse, O. and Iida, H. 1993. An Example-Based Disambiguation of Preposiotinal Phrase Attachment. In Proceedings of TMI-93, 80-91.

Sumita, E., Oi, K., Furuse, O., Iida, H., Higuchi, T., Takahashi, N. and Kitano, H. 1993. Example-Based Machine Translation on Massively Parallel Processors. In Proceedings of IJCAI-93, 1283-1288.

Tanaka, Y. 1991. *GO-TO-GO-NO-KANKEI-KAISEKIYOU-SHIRYOU, NO-WO-CYUSHIN-TO-SHITA.* AICHI SYUKUTOKU University.

Thinking Machines Corp. 1990. *Model CM-2 Technical Summary.*

Thinking Machines Corp. 1991. *Model CM-5 Technical Summary.*

Watanabe, H. 1992. A Similarity-Driven Transfer System. In Proceedings of Coling-92, 770-776. Nantes.

Instructional Environments

An Instructional Environment for Practicing Argumentation Skills

Vincent Aleven and Kevin D. Ashley

Intelligent Systems Program,
Learning Research and Development Center, and
School of Law
University of Pittsburgh
Pittsburgh, PA 15260
aleven+@pitt.edu, ashley+@pitt.edu

Abstract

CATO is an instructional environment for practicing basic skills of legal research: to use cases in arguments about a problem situation and to test a theory about a legal domain. Using the CATO tools, law students analyze a legal problem, frame queries of CATO's database of legal cases, and judge how relevant the retrieved cases are to their developing argument or theory. CATO aids learning by making explicit an abstract model of the process of argument. It allows students to focus on the high-level argumentation issues, by assisting the student in various ways. By providing an abstract representation of the text of cases, it helps students to reason about the texts and helps guide their critical analysis of the texts. CATO makes available opportunities for practice that are hard to set up with traditional instructional methods.

CATO differs from other instructional environments in the following respects: Few instructional environments focus on argumentation skills. Although there are other instructional environments in which students work with an abstract representation of the task domain, abstracting from text is unusual. CATO demonstrates a contribution that case-based reasoning techniques can make to instructional environments.

1. Introduction

Books, movies, and computers all have the ability to create worlds in which things are a little bit different (or even vastly different) from the way they are in the real world. However, only computers create interactive worlds, worlds in which the audience actively participates and influences the turn of events. In a typical computer game, for instance, the audience faces the task of flying a spacecraft to a far away part of the Universe in order to put down a rebellion (no mean task). Players may become astonishingly skilled at such games, especially if this is regarded as "cool" by one's peers (the competition).

The potential for education has not been lost upon AI researchers. They have created environments in which students practice skills that (unlike the skill of flying a spacecraft) can be applied to solve problems in the real world. While the emphasis is on cognitive skills rather than motor skills (as in the computer game mentioned above) and graphic simulations are not always the norm, these environments have in common with the computer games that they pose a task and provide tools to solve the task, and that the students work in a world that may be slightly simpler than the real world.

These environments are usually modules of larger instructional systems, "intelligent tutoring systems" (ITSs). Such systems take an active role in communicating the domain knowledge to the student, adapting to the individual student's needs as much as possible [Wenger, 1987]. However, even an environment module standing alone can have considerable pedagogical advantages.

First, an environment module, perhaps more so than any other part of the tutoring system, can communicate to the student a conceptualization of the domain. If this conceptualization is sound, it may greatly help the student in constructing a mental model of the domain [Miller, 1988]. "[T]he interface language can rival the generation of active communication steps in pedagogical importance." [Wenger, 1987, p. 317] In particular, the environment module may make explicit properties of the domain that were previously hidden or implicit. [Burton, 1988]. For example, the graphical display of the Geometry tutor explicitly shows that geometry proofs are not linear, as most textbooks suggest, but are tree-structured and can be developed either by going forward from the premises or backward from the goal [Anderson, *et al.*, 1985]. An environment module may also present an abstract view of the task, in order to focus the student on what is important [Burton, 1988]. For example, TASK lets students work with a highly abstract simulation of a fault-diagnosis task [Rouse and Hunt, 1984].

Second, an environment module may assist a student by taking over certain parts of the problem-solving task. This enables the students to concentrate on the high-level structure of the task, without being overwhelmed by details. [Burton, 1988] In Algebraland [Brown, 1985], for example, the computer does the calculations involved in algebraic operations, so that students can concentrate on their applicability conditions.

Finally, an environment module may create opportunities for practice that would not otherwise be available. For instance, Sherlock enables students to practice trouble-shooting skills by simulating a complex electronic test station that is simply not available for educational use [Lajoie and Lesgold, 1992].

This research is supported by an NSF Presidential Young Investigator Award and grants from the National Center for Automated Information Research, Digital Equipment Corporation, and West Publishing Company.

Figure 1: Description of the facts of the *Mason* problem; Applicable factors that the students identified.

However, to our knowledge few systems have demon-strated these advantages in the context of teaching argu-mentation skills. We are developing CATO, an ITS that teaches law students basic skills of legal research: To use cases to make arguments about a problem situation and to test legal theories against cases. So far, we have imple-mented an environment module, based on case-based rea-soning techniques. It lets students represent a problem situation, retrieve past cases that are relevant to the analy-sis, and judge the cases' relevance to the developing ar-gument or to the theory being tested. To assist students with text interpretation, CATO provides (pre-stored) ab-stract representations of the texts of the legal cases.

In this paper, we show examples of students using CATO, guided by a human tutor, to illustrate that CATO achieves the advantages of environment modules men-tioned above. We discuss CATO's strengths and limita-tions and compare it to other instructional environments.

2. CATO as Environment for Teaching Legal Research and Argumentation

The CATO environment provides students with tools to do legal research, tools that differ from those that are nor-mally used. We explain why after we describe the tools in the context of (actual) examples of students using CATO.

Our goal is to teach first-year law students basic skills of making arguments with cases and using cases to test theories. The legal domain has a long-standing practice of analyzing problems by comparing and contrasting them to relevant past cases. Past cases can be cited as primary authorities in arguments. Therefore, students have to learn various argument strategies involving cases. Also, they have to learn to use full-text retrieval systems such as Lexis and Westlaw to find cases that support their ar-guments in automated case law databases.

Likewise, formulating and testing legal rules is an im-portant activity that students have to learn. "[O]ut of the matching of a number of related cases it is your [the stu-dent's] job to formulate a rule that covers them all in har-mony, if that can be done, and to test your formulation

against possible variants on the facts. Finally, to test it, if there is time, against what writers on the subject have to say, and against other cases." [Llewellyn, 1930, p. 52]

Working with CATO, the student's task is to analyze a problem (a set of facts that led to a legal dispute) and then to outline arguments on behalf of the plaintiff and defen-dant that each should win the legal dispute. The argument outline should list the most relevant cases that each party can cite. The cases will be selected from the CATO data-base, which currently contains 45 legal cases. CATO pro-vides tools to retrieve cases and to present information about the cases that helps students judge their relevance. So far, we have run the program with 9 first-year law stu-dents.

In trade secrets cases, the plaintiff and defendant are often corporate competitors. The plaintiff complains that the defendant has gained access to information plaintiff deemed confidential (often, technical knowledge devel-oped at considerable expense) and has used that informa-tion to gain an unfair competitive advantage, for instance, by developing and marketing a product to compete with plaintiff's. To win the case, the plaintiff must show that it actively tried to protect its secret and that the defendant acquired the information by improper means or in breach of a confidential relationship.

In our first example, two first-year law students (guided by a human tutor) use CATO to analyze a prob-lem situation based on *Mason v. Jack Daniel Distillery*. Figure 1 shows a summary of the facts of *Mason*. After reading this description, the students identify facts that tend to strengthen each party's position in the dispute. This requires some knowledge of trade secrets law and of the world of corporate competition, where disputes about trade secrets arise. CATO provides a vocabulary to state the result of this analysis, namely, a set of 21 *factors* for trade secrets law. Factors are abstractions of facts that tend to strengthen or weaken a party's position on a legal claim. The factors that the students found were present in the *Mason* problem are shown in Figure 1. It should be mentioned that there is no single right set of factors for any case or problem; there is room for interpretation.

The next step is to develop arguments for the plaintiff and defendant in *Mason*. Both parties need to convince the court that the favorable factors present in the problem outweigh the unfavorable ones. An important argument strategy, taught from day one in law school, is to draw an analogy to a past case that presented a similar fact pattern as the problem situation and had the outcome that is desired in the current problem. (We call this strategy: Citing a representative example.) Therefore, the students need to find cases in the CATO database that they can cite as representative examples.

Like the problem situation, the cases in CATO's database are represented as lists of factors. They have been analyzed by the system developers, to identify the factors that apply. CATO offers a query language that allows one to retrieve cases with any boolean combination of factors.

The queries that the students tried to find cases with similar sets of factors as the *Mason* problem are shown in Figure 2. (The queries were typed by a human operator, since we did not want students to have to learn the query language.) With their first query, the students find out that there are no cases in the CATO database that have all factors that are present in the *Mason* problem. However, even cases that share some, but not all, factors can be useful to cite in an argument. The students therefore relax the query constraints to ask for cases that have one or more factors in common with the problem. Unfortunately, this second query returns too many cases. It would be too much work to inspect them all. With the third query, the students focus on what they perceive are the most important factors in the problem and finally find the right level of specificity: The query returns a manageable number of cases. (It should be mentioned, however, that this last query does not cover all ways in which a case may be relevant. A more systematic approach is needed, and indeed the students were more systematic later on.)

To decide which of the retrieved cases (if any) to cite in an argument, the students need to compare them to the problem situation. CATO provides various tools that present useful information, but leaves the final judgement as to which cases are worth citing up to the students. CATO has a tool for listing the applicable factors of a retrieved case. It can also display a comparison of the factors of a retrieved case and the problem. In Figure 2, for example, CATO shows a comparison of the *Boeing* case and the *Mason* problem. CATO marks the factors that the two cases have in common and also marks the distinctions (those unshared factors that push toward an opposite result in the two cases). In general, the more shared factors a case has, and the fewer distinctions, the better the argument citing it as a representative example. Finally, for any case in its database CATO can display a "squib," a summary of the case, which includes a brief description of the facts (like the description shown in Figure 1).

After reviewing the comparison of the *Boeing* and *Mason* factors and reading the *Boeing* squib, the students decide that *Boeing* is not ideal. They go on to check the other retrieved cases and find better cases, but this is not shown in Figure 2.

```
1> (list-cases f6 f15 f21 f1 f16)

List all cases
   with factors
      F6 Security-Measures (p)
      F15 Unique-Product (p)
      F21 Knew-Info-Confidential (p)
      F1 Disclosure-In-Negotiations (d)
      F16 Info-Reverse-Engineerable (d).

None.
```

```
2> (list-cases (:or f6 f15 f21 f1 f16))

List all cases
   with one or more of factors
      F6 Security-Measures (p)
      F15 Unique-Product (p)
      F21 Knew-Info-Confidential (p)
      F1 Disclosure-In-Negotiations (d)
      F16 Info-Reverse-Engineerable (d).

22 cases won by plaintiff, 10 cases won by defendant.
```

```
3> (list-cases f1 f6)

List all cases
   with factors
      F1 Disclosure-In-Negotiations (d)
      F6 Security-Measures (p).

Cases won by plaintiff:
```
Boeing (p)
Bryce (p)
Digital Development (p)
```
3 cases won by plaintiff.
```

```
4> Comparison of factors

Mason
   - F1 Disclosure-In-Negotiations (d)
   - F6 Security-Measures (p)
     F15 Unique-Product (p)
   * F16 Info-Reverse-Engineerable (d)
   - F21 Knew-Info-Confidential (p)

Boeing (p)
   - F1 Disclosure-In-Negotiations (d)
   * F4 Agreed-Not-To-Disclose (p)
   - F6 Security-Measures (p)
     F10 Secrets-Disclosed-Outsiders (d)
   * F12 Outsider-Disclosures-Restricted (p)
   * F14 Restricted-Materials-Used (p)
   - F21 Knew-Info-Confidential (p)

- shared factor
* distinction
```

Figure 2: Transcript of students using the CATO tools to find relevant cases

In this example, students, using the CATO tools, were able to find useful cases with only a moderate amount of trial and error. We should mention that there is no single

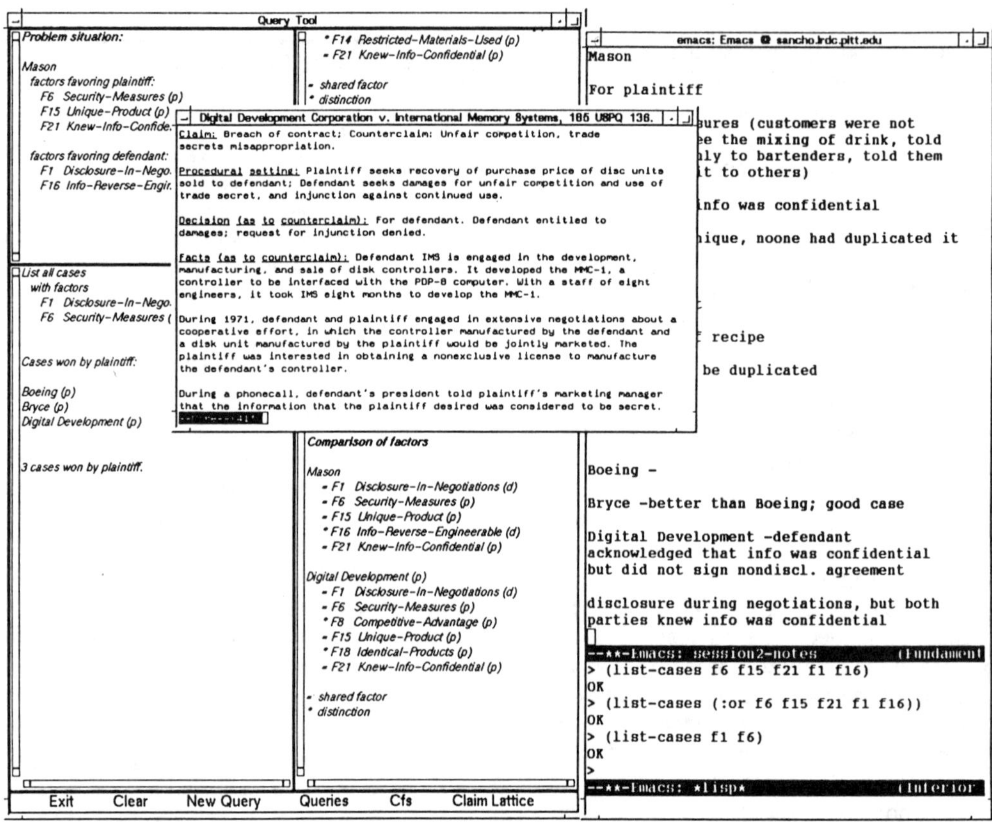

Figure 3: The CATO interface. The factors that the student identified for the problem situation *(Mason)* are displayed in the top left window. There are windows for entering queries (bottom right), displaying the result of the last query (bottom left), and displaying a case's factors or a comparison with the factors of the problem (middle window). Queries are expressed in a Lisp-like syntax. CATO displays squibs (short summaries of cases) in separate pop-up windows. Students can also request to see a history of their queries (middle window) and can make notes about the cases they have seen so far in the top right window.

right solution to this task, as is very characteristic of the legal domain. It is important, however, that students consider all pertinent information in evaluating the relevance of cases and do not miss important lines of cases.

The CATO interface is shown in Figure 3. CATO has a knowledge base which contains explicit definitions for many of the concepts in its model of argument [Ashley and Aleven, 1992, 1993]. This knowledge base is implemented in the knowledge representation system Loom [MacGregor, 1991]. CATO queries are executed by translating them into Loom's query language. The CATO interface is implemented in CLIM and currently also uses an Emacs window.

3. Examples of Instructional Opportunities Students Achieved with CATO

In this section, we show two more actual examples of law students using CATO, to illustrate that CATO enables the students to formulate, implement and test hypotheses and, in this way, obtain practice in legal argumentation and research that would be difficult to achieve otherwise.

In the example of Figure 4, a law student uses CATO to test a hypothesis that two weaknesses in his side's position are not fatal, and to formulate a perceptive argument to establish that assertion. The student had analyzed the *Mason* problem situation and identified two factors that weakened the plaintiff: the plaintiff had disclosed its alleged confidential product information (the beverage recipe) in negotiations with the defendant (factor F1, Disclosure-In-Negotiations) and the plaintiff's recipe could be readily reverse engineered (factor F16, Info-Reverse-Engineerable), both of which factors helped the defendant.

The student, arguing for the plaintiff, needed to counteract the weaknesses represented by factors F16 and F1, in other words, to "cover the defendant's bases". Figure 4 shows three successive queries that the student actually submitted to CATO and CATO's responses. The first two queries show that the student had formulated and was testing the hypothesis that there can be a trade secret misappropriation despite the fact that plaintiff disclosed the information to the defendant in negotiations or that experts could discover the recipe by analysis. The student

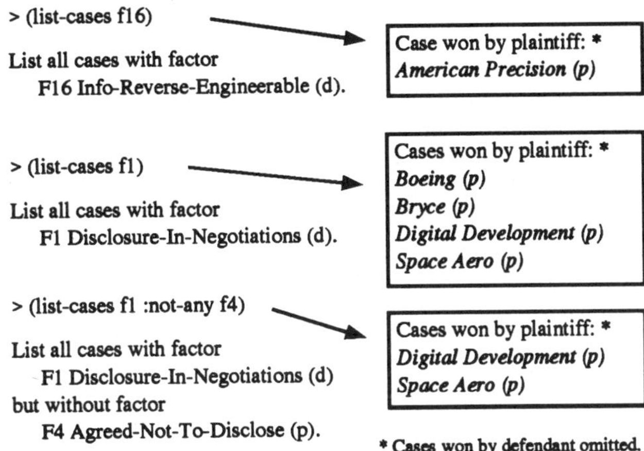

Figure 4: Student's queries for cases that counteract unfavorable factors ("cover the opponent's bases") and avoid a possible distinction.

sought and found pro-plaintiff cases to counteract factors F16 and F1. In these cases, plaintiffs won despite the presence of one or other of those pro-defendant factors.

Then the student did something very interesting in the third query. He screened the cases returned by the second query to select the most convincing evidence for his hypothesis. He sought all the cases with factor F1 Disclosure-In-Negotiations, but without factor F4 Agreed-Not-To-Disclose. That is, he sought cases where the plaintiff disclosed the secrets in negotiations, but where, as in the *Mason* problem, the plaintiff had failed to take the precaution of securing the defendant's agreement not to disclose the secrets. He found two cases, *Digital Development* and *Space Aero* where the plaintiff won despite this lack of care. These are especially good cases to cite because they show that mere knowledge of the confidentiality is enough to bind the defendant even when the defendant did not promise not to use or disclose the information. In other words, with his third query the student filtered out cases that could be distinguished in a way that would be damaging to his position since the distinction would call attention to a troublesome lack of caution on his client's part. The student's queries are good evidence to a teacher that the student not only understands how to make an argument but has a deeper understanding of the problem and the legal domain.

In the example of Figure 5, a first-year law student formulates a more general hypothesis about the legal domain, retrieves cases to test his theory, and revises the theory when it turns out that it is inconsistent with some of the cases that were retrieved.

At the top of Figure 5, having used CATO to make a number of arguments involving a variety of cases, and without prompting from the human tutor, the student announced what amounted to a theory about the domain: he predicted that where secrets had been disclosed to outsid-

ers, plaintiffs would lose no matter what security measures they had taken because "once the information is not secret, what's the point of security measures?" From a pedagogical viewpoint, it is important to inculcate this kind of behavior in law students, that is, formulating a hypothesis about the importance of features in a problem, based upon a rationale concerning the point or purpose of a law. As in other fields, it is even more important that students learn how to test and revise such hypotheses [Lakatos, 1976; Rissland, 1983; Collins and Stevens, 1982]. Seizing the pedagogical opportunity, the tutor challenged the student to test the hypothesis. In response, the student formulated a query to retrieve all cases that were covered by his hypothesis, to see whether the outcome of these cases was, indeed, as he predicted.

To his evident surprise, the student found that some of the retrieved cases were inconsistent with his theory: plaintiffs who had taken security measures won despite disclosures to outsiders. This was puzzling. The student allowed that he would "read the cases and see what's going on". To that end, at the tutor's suggestion, the student inspected one of the retrieved cases and realized that his theory could be saved. Recognizing that his rule was overly general, he revised it accordingly: where the secrets had been disclosed to outsiders, and those disclosures were not limited by restrictions, then plaintiffs would lose despite having taken security measures. The student could have tested that query, as well. However, there was little time left, so the tutor decided to move on to other things.

This was a valuable lesson. In response to a student's spontaneous comment, using CATO's tools, the tutor could empower a student to work through, in a concrete way, a complex, abstract process of formulating, testing, and revising a legal hypothesis. Recognizing the need to engage in this process and learning how to do it are at the core of legal education and legal scholarship; much of what legal scholars do is to formulate, test and revise such theories in the light of existing precedents and anticipated hypothetical problems. But it is hard to identify and communicate such an abstract, complex process to students, especially where a reasoner needs to invent the terminology for formulating the theory, find, read and interpret the relevant cases and hypotheticals, or revise the theory in light of the cases and the purposes of the law.

This is where CATO helps; CATO suppresses some of the distracting complexity so that students can identify and complete a few cycles of the process, but CATO does not simplify the process so much as to make the process seem uninteresting and pointless to the student. Firstly, CATO provided a convenient language in which the student could express his theory and his query to find cases to test the theory.

Secondly, CATO presented just the right information about the retrieved cases to make clear their import to the theory being tested. Retrieved cases are relevant to testing the hypothesis because they are guaranteed to have the specified combination of factors. Since CATO shows the retrieved cases' outcomes, it was readily apparent

```
> (list-cases f6 (:or f10 f20))
List all cases
   with factor
      F6 Security-Measures (p)
   and with one or more of factors
      F10 Secrets-Disclosed-Outsiders (d)
      F20 Info-Known-To-Competitors (d).
```



```
Data General (p)
   F6 Security-Measures (p)
   F10 Secrets-Disclosed-Outsiders (d)
   F12 Outsider-Disclosures-Restricted (p)
   F14 Restricted-Materials-Used (p)
   F18 Identical-Products (p)
```


Figure 5: Using CATO to test a theory about the domain.

which of the cases were consistent and which were inconsistent with the theory.

Thirdly, CATO supports inspecting the cases to see if counterexamples really invalidate the theory or whether the theory can be revised. By displaying the factors of even one of the retrieved cases, CATO provided enough information for the student to modify the theory, a proc-

ess that could have been repeated at least one more time. The student can also inspect the case squib to confirm whether the sets of factors assigned to the case in CATO's case base really are accurate or whether, on a closer reading, they might be reinterpreted.

It is hard to set up this kind of learning opportunity without CATO. Students frequently espouse theories in law school classes, but getting students to test and modify them is hard to arrange. The class typically reads only two or three cases, selected by the case book writer to illustrate the writer's theory, but not necessarily those invented by students. In class, it is hard and time consuming to get a consensus even about the facts of those cases all have read. With CATO one can test the hypothesis over a relatively large database of cases, point physically to an abstract summary of the case for purposes of discussion, modify queries to reflect revised theories, and cycle through the process repeatedly. Conceivably, with an overhead projecting screen, this could even be done in front of an entire class. Trying to conduct such a classroom exercise with full-text legal retrieval tools would founder with the complexity of interpreting what the retrieved cases say. Without reading a large amount of text, one cannot even determine who won a case retrieved from a full-text retrieval system.

4. Advantages and Limitations of the CATO Environment

CATO realizes various advantages of instructional environments. First, CATO aids learning by communicating a conceptualization of the domain, a view of the process of legal argumentation and research that is useful for a first-year law student to learn. (See [Ashley, 1991] and [Aleven and Ashley, 1993].) As illustrated by the examples of students using CATO, cases are used, in various argument moves, to justify assertions about a problem, or to test a proposed theory about a legal domain. The issues that a problem presents, or were resolved in a past case, are represented as a list of factors. Queries for relevant cases are also expressed in terms of factors.

CATO's model is not normally applied in legal research and is not currently taught in law schools. Although factors seem to be a fairly intuitive concept (e.g., some statutes list factors, one of our students commented: "I think factors came out because ... that was just inevitable."), it is not common in the legal field to explicitly represent, retrieve, and compare cases in terms of factors. Therefore, like the Geometry tutor, CATO makes explicit properties of its domain that are normally hidden or implicit.

CATO, like AlgebraLand [Brown, 1985], does some of the work for the students, so that they can focus on high-level aspects of the task domain. As the examples illustrate, the CATO tools keep track of rather a lot of useful information and present it on request. Also, the query language and tool for comparing cases make it relatively easy for students to find the cases in CATO's database that they need to support their argument or test their theory. CATO also assists students by providing abstract representations of the text of the cases (*i.e.,* lists of factors). This saves them the work of reading the cases and developing an interpretation. Squibs also greatly reduce the amount of text that students need to read. As a result, students can concentrate on the high-level aspects of the process (comparing cases, expressing an argument need in CATO's query language, deciding which cases to cite in an argument) without being distracted by details. Also, the CATO tools make it easier for a tutor to guide students through a few cycles of the process of developing an argument or testing a theory; this would be difficult to realize with traditional instructional methods.

One may object that CATO leaves out a fundamentally important component of legal research: reading and interpreting the opinions of cases. We admit that CATO gets much leverage out of reducing the amount of text that needs to be read. However, we believe that exercise with CATO will actually help students learn to read cases. Having worked with CATO, they may read cases with a better understanding of what it is they are looking for. (Indeed, CATO queries are good models of the questions to have in mind when reading cases.) Also, during our CATO sessions, we pointed out to students that reading the cases is still important and we encouraged them to read the squibs of cases they deemed interesting based on the comparison of their factors. Our experience is that students did regularly read the squibs.

While exercises with CATO involve important legal research skills, they do not, of course, cover all of legal research. There are additional criteria for selecting cases to cite in arguments, for example, the date when a case was decided, the court's pedigree and jurisdiction, whether the case was overturned by subsequent decisions, and the case's procedural setting. Moreover, in addition to cases, legal arguments may cite statutory rules and may refer to public policy or legislative intent.

Another limitation is that CATO does not reason about, or represent, the reason why certain facts have theoretical legal significance and others do not. We recognize, it is very important not to discourage such reasoning on the part of students. We would like students to reason in terms of the theory of the legal domain. and to make predictions based on their theories. As the second and third examples illustrate, CATO provides support for formulating and testing theories.

Currently, CATO provides useful tools to engage law students in exercises in legal research, but the guidance of a human tutor is still needed. To develop an ITS that students can use without the intervention of a human tutor, CATO's pedagogical capabilities need to be extended.

While the examples illustrate that law students have used CATO in interesting exercises in legal research, they do not show that CATO improves students' learning. To test this, we are conducting a controlled experiment with 17 first-year law students to evaluate how effective practice with CATO (under the guidance of a human tutor) is compared to classroom instruction that teaches the same material but does not use CATO.

While the advantages that are described above have been demonstrated in other instructional environments, CATO differs from previous systems in various ways. Argumentation is an unusual domain for instructional environments, perhaps because it is so closely tied to text interpretation, which is notoriously hard to implement on a computer. In one project, students are provided with tools to represent (in a graphical notation) their arguments about well-known scientific problems [Cavalli-Sforza, *et al.,* 1993]. Also, EUCLID is an environment that offers (graphical and other) tools for constructing, comprehending, and assessing arguments but is not primarily intended for educational use [Smolensky, *et al.,* 1987].

One of the reasons that CATO is able to make some headway is that it presents an abstract representation of the texts of legal cases. While other instructional environments also suppress some of the complexity by providing an abstract view of the domain, for example, TASK [Rouse and Hunt, 1984], CATO is one of the few where students work with abstract representations of text. This is facilitated by the fact that we are dealing with a highly uniform set of texts.

Case-based teaching systems developed at Northwestern, like CATO, support indexing and retrieval of cases for pedagogical purposes [Schank, 1990; Ferguson, *et al.,* 1992]. These systems are based on the hypothesis that "good teaching is good story telling." The instructional goal is "to teach the cases." Cases are retrieved when students need or can benefit from the information that they contain. The instructional goal in CATO is not to teach the cases; it is to teach a process of reasoning with cases. Working with CATO, students justify assertions about a problem by comparing and contrasting it to past cases. This does not happen in the systems developed at Northwestern. In CATO, case retrieval is done mainly to give students practice in accurately expressing what kind of cases they need to make a good argument.

Techniques similar to those used in CATO have been used in the domain of software engineering, to support the reuse of software components. For example, Prieto-Díaz developed a system, comprising (among other things) an indexed library of computer programs and a query language, that software engineers can use to find a program that fits the constraints of the current problem closely enough so that it can be easily adapted [Prieto-Díaz, 1987]. While the case comparisons supported by Prieto-Díaz's system are certainly helpful to find useful past cases, they do not seem to be of much help in the ensuing step of adapting a past case (i.e., computer program) to fit the constraints of the current problem. This would tend to make practice with case retrieval and comparison of limited utility for those wanting to learn the skills involved in software reuse. By contrast, CATO supports drawing inferences about the problem by comparing it to past cases. Case comparisons are the building blocks of legal arguments [Ashley and Aleven, 1992]. It is for this reason that case comparison and retrieval is a very central activity in the CATO tutorial.

5. Conclusion

We have shown three examples that illustrate that law students have used the CATO environment to do useful and interesting exercises in legal research, under the guidance of a human tutor. Generally speaking, the students were positive about their experiences with CATO, as is evident from the following quotes: "CATO makes it simple" and "It kind of does what you do when you are researching a case."

CATO is based on the hypothesis that if one provides students with an environment where they have a meaningful task (retrieving cases to make arguments) and a retrieval language that reflects important aspects of the model of argument, that one can teach them a process of argumentation, including basic argumentation and research skills, such as formulating, testing, and revision of hypotheses and critical analysis of texts. This appears to be a new technique.

CATO realizes three advantages that have been demonstrated in previous instructional environments. CATO communicates a conceptualization of the domain, namely, an abstract view of a process of legal argument and research that is useful for first-year law students to learn. The process is based on an AI model of reasoning with cases and is not currently applied in legal education or practice. By providing abstract representations of the text of legal cases and by providing tools that allow easy access to relevant cases, CATO removes distracting complexity and allows the students to focus on the high-level issues involved in argumentation and theory-testing. For the same reasons, CATO enables opportunities for practice that would be difficult to arrange otherwise.

CATO is one of the very few instructional environments for argumentation skills. Few instructional environments present students with an abstracted representation of text, as a way of focusing them on what is important about the text and getting them to reason with texts. Finally, although other instructional environments are based on case-based reasoning techniques, none of these engages students in a process of retrieving, comparing, and contrasting cases.

References

Aleven, V., and K. D. Ashley, 1993. What Law Students Need to Know to WIN. In *Proceedings of the Fourth International Conference on Artificial Intelligence and Law*, 152–161. New York: ACM.

Anderson, J. R., C. F. Boyle, and G. Yost, 1985. The Geometry Tutor. In *IJCAI-85: Proceedings of the International Joint Conference on Artificial Intelligence*, 1–7. Los Altos, CA: Morgan Kaufmann.

Ashley, K. D., 1991. *Modeling Legal Argument: Reasoning with Cases and Hypotheticals.* Cambridge, MA: MIT Press.

Ashley, K. D., and V. Aleven, 1993. Using Logic to Reason with Cases. In *First European Workshop on Case-Based Reasoning (EWCBR)*, edited by M. M. Richter, S. Wess, K. D. Althoff, and F. Maurer, 373-378. SEKI Report SR-93-12 (SFB 314), Dept. of Computer Science, University of Kaiserslautern.

Ashley, K. D., and V. Aleven, 1992. Generating Dialectical Examples Automatically. In *AAAI-92: Proceedings of the Tenth National Conference on Artificial Intelligence, 654–660.* Menlo Park, CA: AAAI Press.

Brown, J. S., 1985. Idea Amplifiers: New Kinds of Electronic Learning Environments. *Educational Horizons,* 63: 108–112.

Burton, R. R., 1988. The Environment Module of Intelligent Tutoring Systems. In *Foundations of Intelligent Tutoring Systems,* edited by M. C. Polson and J. J. Richardson, 109–142. Hillsdale, NJ: Lawrence Erlbaum.

Cavalli-Sforza, V., J. D. Moore, and D. D. Suthers, 1993. Helping Students Articulate and Criticize Scientific Explanations, In *Proceedings of the World Conference on AI and Education (AIED-93)*, 113-120. Edinburgh, Scotland, August 23-27.

Collins, A., and A. L. Stevens, 1982. Goals and Strategies of Inquiry Teachers. In *Advances in Instructional Psychology*, edited by R. Glaser, 65–119. Hillsdale, NJ: Lawrence Erlbaum.

Ferguson, W., R. Bareiss, L. Birnbaum, and R. Osgood, 1992. ASK Systems: An Approach to the Realization of Story-Based Teachers. *The Journal of the Learning Sciences,* 2(1): 95–134.

Lajoie, S. P., and A. Lesgold, 1992. Apprenticeship Training in the Workplace: Computer-Coached Practice Environment as a New Form of Apprenticeship. In *Intelligent Instruction by Computer: Theory and Practice,* edited by M. J. Farr and J. Psotka, 15–36. Washington DC: Taylor and Francis.

Lakatos, I., 1976. *Proofs and Refutations.* London: Cambridge University Press.

Llewellyn, K. N., 1930. *The Bramble Bush: On our Law and Its Study.* Dobbs Ferry, New York: Oceana Publications, 1960 edition.

MacGregor, R., 1991 The Evolving Technology of Classification-Based Knowledge Representation Systems. In *Principles of Semantic Networks: Explorations in the Representation of Knowledge,* edited by J. F. Sowa, 385–400. San Mateo, CA: Morgan Kaufmann.

Miller, J. R., 1988. The Role of Human-Computer Interaction in Intelligent Tutoring Systems. In *Foundations of Intelligent Tutoring Systems,* edited by M. C. Polson and J. J. Richardson, 143–189. Hillsdale, NJ: Lawrence Erlbaum.

Prieto-Díaz, R., 1987. Classifying Software for Reusability. *IEEE Software,* 4 (1):6-16.

Rouse, W. B., and R. M. Hunt, 1984. Human Problem Solving in Fault Diagnosis Tasks. In *Advances in Man-Machine Systems Research, Vol. 1,* edited by W. B. Rouse. Greenwich, CT: JAI Press.

Schank, R. C., 1990. Case-Based Teaching: Four Experiences in Educational Software Design. *Interactive Learning Environments* 1(4): 231-253.

Rissland, E. L., 1983. The Ubiquitous Dialectic. Tech. Rep. 83-15. Dept. of Computer and Information Science, University of Massachusetts, Amherst, MA.

Smolensky, P., B. Fox, R. King, and C. Lewis, 1987. Computer-Aided Reasoned Discourse, or, How to Argue with a Computer. Tech. Rep. CU-CS-358-87, Depts. of Computer Science and Linguistics, and Institute of Cognitive Science, University of Colorado, Boulder, CO.

Wenger, E., 1987. *Artificial Intelligence and Tutoring Systems: Computational and Cognitive Approaches to the Communication of Knowledge.* Los Altos, CA: Morgan Kaufmann.

Tailoring Retrieval to Support Case-Based Teaching[*]

Robin Burke

Department of Computer Science, University of Chicago
1100 E. 58th St., Ryerson Hall, Chicago, IL 60637
burke@cs.uchicago.edu   (312) 702-4029

Alex Kass

Institute for the Learning Sciences, Northwestern University,
1890 Maple Ave., Evanston, IL 60201
kass@ils.nwu.edu   (312) 491-3500

Abstract

This paper describes how a computer program can support learning by retrieving and presenting relevant stories drawn from a video case base. Although this is an information retrieval problem, it is not a problem that fits comfortably within the classical IR model (Salton & McGill, 1983) because in the classical model the computer system is too passive. The standard model of IR assumes that the user will take the initiative to formulate retrieval requests, but a teaching system must be able to initiate retrieval and formulate retrieval requests automatically. We describe a system, called SPIEL, that performs this type of retrieval, and discuss theoretical challenges addressed in implementing such a system. These challenges include the development of a representation language for indexing the system's video library, and the development of set of retrieval strategies and recognition knowledge that allow the system to locate educationally relevant stories.

1. Introduction

A real-world story told by an expert at an opportune moment can be an invaluable resource for training novices to perform complex tasks (Schank, 1990b). Students do not usually get the benefit of such stories because experts' time is scarce and expensive. However, interactive multimedia technology now makes it possible to store video clips of experts telling their important stories, and to present those clips under computer control. Realizing the educational potential of such stories requires an AI system that understands the educational purposes that a story can serve well enough to be able to recognize when a story should be told. In this paper we discuss a case-based teaching system that can retrieve tutorial stories stored on video as advice for students who are engaged in a learning-by-doing environment. The system, called SPIEL (Story Producer for InteractivE Learning), is designed to assist students who are learning social skills. It is embedded in an intelligent learning-by-doing architecture called Guided

---

[*] This work is supported in part by the Defense Advanced Research Projects Agency, monitored by the Air Force Office of Scientific Research and the Office of Naval Research. The Institute for the Learning Sciences was established in 1989 with the support of Andersen Consulting, part of The Arthur Andersen Worldwide Organization. The Institute receives additional support from Ameritech and Northwest Water, Institute partners.

Social Simulation or GuSS (Kass et al., 1994) that provides a social simulation in which students can safely practice social skills, such as those required by diplomacy or business.

2. IR, CBR, and Case-Based Teaching

Selecting an instructive story from a video case base is a kind of information retrieval problem, but it is not one that fits comfortably within the classical model of information retrieval (Salton & McGill, 1983) because in the classical model the computer system is too passive. In the standard model of IR, the computer responds to well-formulated retrieval requests issued by a user. This model is appropriate only when intended users can be expected understand their information needs well enough to initiate requests at appropriate times and to formulate those requests correctly. Experts may sometimes understand their information needs well enough to fit this model, but non-experts learning a new, complex task rarely do. Systems intended to teach students to perform a complex task must, therefore, be more than passive data retrievers. They must be able to initiate retrieval and formulate retrieval requests automatically.

Active retrieval, including automatic formation of retrieval cues, has been investigated most extensively in the context of case-based reasoning (CBR) research (Kolodner, 1993). For instance, a case-based planner, such as CHEF (Hammond, 1989a) attempts to solve new problems by retrieving and adapting stored plans, and must be able to extract features of new problems and use those features to retrieve a suitable plan from its library.

The *case-based teaching architecture* (Schank, 1990a; Edelson, 1993; Burke, 1993) is a framework for building computer-based learning environments that present cases (such as experts' stories) to a student who is engaged in a complex task within a computer environment. Case-based teachers are not really case-based *reasoners* in the full sense, because they do not need to manipulate the internal content of their cases, they just need to retrieve and present them at the appropriate time. However, case-based teachers and case-based reasoners have in common the need to initiate the retrieval process and form retrieval cues. Case-based teachers are a good platform from which to study the retrieval problem because they isolate the retrieval problem from the other hard CBR problems, such as evaluation and adaptation.

We claim that the need for precision in educational case retrieval demands a system that understands the uses to which retrieved material will be put. In other words, just as an effective plan retriever must be based on a theory of goals and planning, an effective retriever of tutorial cases must be based on a theory the educational purposes that the retrieved cases can serve. Three types of theories are need; we will touch on each in this paper.

1. **A theory of indexing vocabulary:** a representation language that can be used to form labels for each story by encoding the features of story that may prove important for the system's educational purposes.

2. **A theory of educational relevance:** a taxonomy of the different kind of points that stories can be used to make, a theory of the features of stories that are important for making these kinds of points, and the features of a student's situation that are appropriateness conditions for making each kind of point.

3. **A theory of opportunity recognition:** To recognize storytelling opportunities, the tutor must be able to infer higher-level descriptions of the student's actions from a stream of low-level event descriptions. It must draw reasonable conclusions about what the student is trying to accomplish, and relate its observations to the contents of the story base.

3. A Case-Presentation Example

The goal of GuSS applications is to accomplish for social environments what other simulators accomplish for physical environments, supporting learning by doing. Within GuSS, SPIEL is like an experienced practitioner watching over the student's shoulder. It monitors the simulation and presents stories from its library when they are relevant to the student's situation. The following example illustrates the kind of interaction that SPIEL has with students using the YELLO program, in which the student's task is to try to sell Yellow Pages advertising. SPIEL has 178 stories told by account executives with great experience in selling. Consider the following interaction in which one of these stories is retrieved:

Student:	So, we're going to go ahead with the 1/4 page ad with color?
Customer:	OK.
Student:	Just sign right here.
Customer:	[signs]
Student:	I think the color is really going to attract people to your ad.
Customer:	I sure like the way it looks.
Student:	Ask your customers what they think. I'll bet you'll find its an attention-getter.
Customer:	See you next year.
Student:	See you. [leaves]

This is a sales success, but SPIEL has a cautionary story to tell. Every moment the student remains after the close of the sale gives the customer an opportunity to retract his buying decision. Although that did not happen here, it is a possibility that the student should be aware of.

SPIEL intervenes by first signaling to the student that it has a story available. Then, if the student expresses an interest in hearing the story, it explains why the story is relevant, shows a video in which an experienced salesperson relates the story as a personal experience, and finally sums up the main point of that story as it applies in the current situation (see Figure 1):

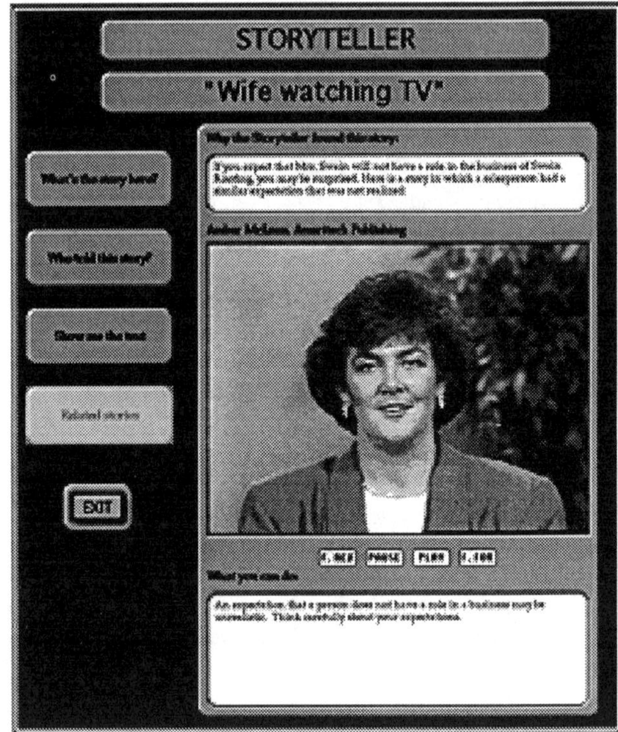

Figure 1. Example of story presentation window

Headline: A story showing the risks of your approach...

Bridge: You kept talking to the client after the sale was closed. Nothing bad happened but here's a story in which doing that led to problems:

Video: I was in the South Bend/Mishawaka area. This was my first or second year. I was calling on a swimming pool contractor. He had a quarter page in South Bend. I was proposing a quarter page in another directory. It was sitting at his kitchen table. And the guy was hesitating; he didn't know... So, after a few more attempts, he says to me "OK, I'll go with the other quarter page." He bought it. I pushed the order form in front of him. He signed it. It's done.

As I'm putting my stuff together, I made this comment that cost me the quarter page. I said, as I'm packing up, "I'm sure that you're going to get a lot of phone calls from that new ad." He looked at me and he said, "You know, I don't need any more phone calls. I'll tell you what, let's not do that this year, maybe next." I talked myself out of a quarter page. I've never done it since. I walked out. There was nothing I could say. I had it and I lost it. All I had to say was "Thank you very much Joe. See you next year." But I didn't. I had to tell him about the calls, which I'd already done twenty times.[1]

Coda: Nothing bad happened to you because you kept talking to the client after the sale was closed, but sometimes the client changes his mind.

In this example, the storyteller augments the student's simulated experience in an important way. Without the "Talked myself out of a sale" story, the student, who was successful, might never realize the risks inherent in remaining after the sale. The story arrives just at the time when it is most relevant, after the risk is past and the student thinks all went well, and it is exactly on point as a counterexample: it shows a situation in which the same tactic had an opposite outcome.

3.1. How the system works

SPIEL operates in storage and retrieval phases. The storage phase prepares the system for storytelling. The storyteller examines its stories in the light of its set of *storytelling strategies*, its library of different ways that stories can be used to teach, and determines what kinds of situations could arise that would constitute opportunities to tell each story. In the retrieval phase, the system tries to recognize those opportunities as the student is performing the task. This design is similar to approaches to "opportunistic memory" architectures proposed for opportunistic planning (Hammond, 1989b). A schematic picture of the phases is shown in Figure 2.

The storage phase begins with the manual construction of indices. An indexer watches the story on video and uses an indexing tool to construct labels representing what it is about. Indices are then processed using storytelling strategies, representations of the tutorial purposes stories can serve. SPIEL determines, for each combination of story and strategy, how and when it might tell the story using the strategy, thus characterizing the storytelling opportunities that the story affords. The rule generator converts descriptions of these opportunities into procedures for recognizing them, in the form of rules that are compatible with the learning-by-doing environment.

The retrieval phase of SPIEL is implemented by a rule-based system that interfaces with the GuSS learning environment. The rules created during the storage phase are matched against on-going events in the simulated world, as the student takes actions and the simulated characters respond. Successful recognition of an opportunity causes a story and its associated strategy to be retrieved. The rest of this paper discusses some of the details of the implementation of SPIEL's retrieval architecture, starting with the indices for stories. For brevity, we have omitted the discussion of SPIEL's simple natural language generation.

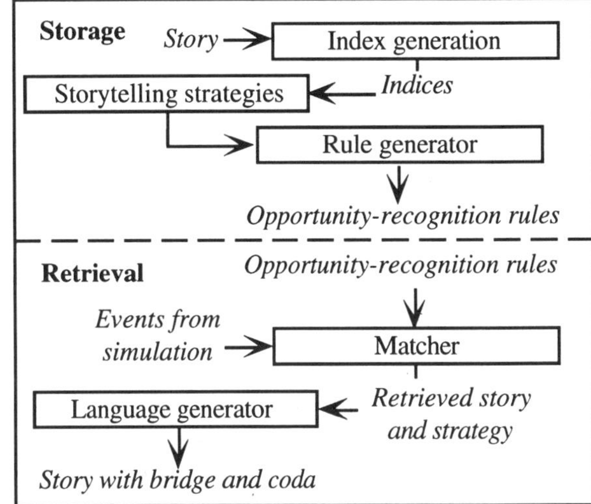

Figure 2. How SPIEL works

4. Indexing stories

In traditional IR, indices are keywords. The meaning of a document is approximated from words found in the text. Because SPIEL's stories are in video form, text ceases to become a "cheap feature." Indices must be entered manually. SPIEL makes use of structured indices that are more precise representations of the story's point or points.

The points of SPIEL's first-person anecdotes often comes from an expectation violation, a event that surprises the narrator or someone else in the story (Schank, 1982; Schank et al., 1990). In the "Talked myself out of a sale" story, the salesperson is surprised to find his attempt at reassuring the customer backfires into a loss of the sale. These *anomalies* make the stories interesting and they are also the key to the stories' relevance in educational situations. An indexing representation for such stories must therefore a language for expressing anomalies. The general form of an anomaly can be stated as follows:

Actor X had an expectation that Y would happen, but actually Z happened.

A statement of the anomaly from the "Talked myself out of a sale" story is

---

[1] SPIEL's stories are video clips from videotaped interviews with experienced Yellow Pages account executives. The surrounding explanations are generated by the program.

The salesperson wanted to reassure the client about his purchase but actually the salesperson lost the sale.

This anomaly captures one important aspect of what the story is about. A story usually says (or implies) more than this, including why the expectation came about and why it failed. The salesperson obviously thought that talking about the increased number of calls the client would get would be reassuring, and thought that reassuring the client was an important goal. The expectation failed because the time spent after the sale gave the customer time to reconsider. Figure 3 is an outline of the "Talked myself out of a sale" index. The index contains the anomaly (shown in bold) and the explanation of the anomaly. The anomaly highlights the feature that is different between the hoped-for case and the actual case.

Viewer:	**Salesperson**	
Perspective:	**wanted**	actual
Agent:	**salesperson**	salesperson
Goal:	get customer confidence	make sale
Plan:	remain after sale	remain after sale
Result:	**get confidence**	**failure to make sale**
Neg. side-eff.		customer not confident

Figure 3. Index for "Talked myself out of a sale."

5. Determining relevance

SPIEL's ability to tailor its retrieval to the task of education comes from its storytelling strategies, its knowledge of the conditions under which a story with particular characteristics will be relevant to a student. In the example above, the "Talked myself out of a sale" story was told using the **Demonstrate risks** strategy. This strategy selects stories about the failure of a particular course of action and tells them when the student has executed a similar course of action but had success. The story is relevant because it contradicts the evidence of the simulation with respect to the student's recent success. This is an educationally-appropriate way to intervene since, without the story, the student might not see the risks identified in the story.

5.1. SPIEL's storytelling strategies

There are two main sources of relevance for stories in a learning-by-doing environment: (1) they can point out errors that the student may be making when the environment does not provide sufficient feedback for the student, and (2) they can help the student explain expectation failures when the environment does not give all the information needed to construct an explanation.

SPIEL has thirteen storytelling strategies, which fall into four categories based on their relationship between the stories they present and the situations in which they present them. The strategies are described in detail in (Burke, 1993).

Strategies that show the student alternatives. These strategies present stories whose outcomes differ substantially from what the student has achieved in the simulated world. **Demonstrate risks** falls in this category. Confronting students with stories about alternative possibilities gets them to question their expectations about the simulated world.

Strategies that critique the student's expectations. By showing examples of situations where people in a similar role had preconceptions that were incorrect, these strategies help students transfer expectations from their everyday social lives to the specialized social environment they are learning about.

Strategies that project possible results of actions the student is taking. Normally, students receive immediate feedback from the execution of their plans. If they do not get such feedback, projection strategies call for the storyteller to provide examples that show possible outcomes.

Strategies that explain the perspectives of other people to the student. These strategies recall stories that explain why people acted as they did in real world situations, making the unexpected actions of others in the simulation comprehensible.

These categories cover the most important ways that stories can be relevant to students using GuSS. They concentrate especially on plans and outcomes, which is consonant with the emphasis in GuSS on learning-by-doing. Students are largely engaged in planning and acting in the social environment. In a different kind of task, such as a design task, students would focus on different kinds of expectations, such as how a design feature achieves a given function and how it will interact with other features. The case-based teaching system Creanimate (Edelson, 1993) has retrieval strategies organized around the problem of design.

5.2. Demonstrate risks: A storytelling strategy

Whenever one confronts a complex problem, it is important to know the range of possible outcomes: What is the best and worst that could happen? Both in real life and in GuSS's simulator, the student gets to see only one outcome at a time. Stories that show a range of alternatives provide necessary balance. Alternative-finding storytelling strategies are designed to bring to the student's attention stories that differ in significant ways from the student's experience in the simulated world.

The idea behind **Demonstrate risks** is to tell a story about a failure when the student has experienced success.

One reason this is important is that no simulation is perfect. If the simulation is not accurately reproducing the circumstances encountered in the story, the story points out possible differences between the simulation and the real world of practice. The example in section 2.1 shows **Demonstrate risks** in action in YELLO. In general, this strategy needs to see that the student is in a situation similar to that in the story, but has achieved an outcome that is very different: the student has succeeded where the story shows a failure. The strategy calls on SPIEL to predict an outcome that would be "very different" from losing the sale, different enough that it makes sense to tell the story as an alternative. Such opposite-finding inference occurs in each alternative-finding strategy.

An opposite outcome is not something that contradicts the original in every respect. It does not make sense to say that the opposite of achieving X is failing to achieve Y, where X and Y are opposite goals. If anything, these would be similar outcomes. An opposite result is an opposite impact on the same goal. This is a simple example, but more complex cases of the opposite computation, such as that in the strategy **Demonstrate alternative plan**, where an opposite plan must be found, require involved opposite-finding inference. The details of the opposite-finding algorithm and other inference mechanisms in SPIEL can be found in (Burke, 1993).

6. Implementing recognition

Indices represent what a story is about. Strategies represent how, in general, stories can be made relevant to a student. There is one final link that a storytelling tutor must make, which is the connection between students' actions and its notion of a relevant story. As shown in the examples, this involves a variety of considerations including social knowledge, such as the scope of a conversation, and practical details that are a function of the simulation environment itself.

The tutor needs a general understanding of the task: that selling involves sub-goals like gathering information, constructing presentations, making sales pitches, and answering objections, for example. At a more concrete level, SPIEL has to know particular details of how the selling task is achieved by the student in the YELLO application. It has to know which kinds of answers from a customer constitute substantive information and which are evasions, what actions constitute the construction of a prospective ad, and so forth. SPIEL is operating in a environment with limited scope. It does not have to be concerned about every possible way a student can ask a question; it need only recognize those choices that GuSS actually permits.

6.1. Applying storytelling strategies

How would an opportunity to tell the "Talked myself out of a sale" story be recognized by SPIEL? The tutor would look for (1) the student to successfully complete the close of a sale, but (2) remain to talk with the customer, and then (3) finish the sales call without losing the sale. Then it would (4) tell the "Talked myself out of a sale" story to point out the possibly risky tactic the student had used..

We call the sequence of conditions for recognizing a storytelling opportunity a *recognition condition description* or RCD. The RCD describes what situation the student would have to encounter for the story to be relevant. Recognition condition descriptions have three parts: (1) a context in which the story would be worth telling, (2) conditions that indicate that the story is relevant in that context, and (3) the story itself and the manner in which it should be presented. These three parts can be thought of as filling roles in the following abstract rule form:

> **When** *trigger*, **Look for** *evidence*, **Then** *presentation*.

To create the RCD, a storytelling strategy must reason about how concepts in the index or those inferred from the index may be manifested in observable actions in the simulation. SPIEL has a library of manifestation rules designed to predict characteristic actions that correspond to internal states.

For an example, the RCD generated for the story "Talked myself out of a sale" when told using the **Demonstrate risks** strategy looks like this:

WHEN the student is in the closing stage of the sales call and talking to the buyer,

> LOOK FOR the student to make the sale, continue conversing with the customer, and not to lose the sale,
> THEN TELL "Talked myself out of a sale" AS a "Demonstrate risks" story.

6.2. From description to mechanism

Creation of the trigger and evidence conditions completes the construction of an RCD. The RCD represents the recognition conditions for a tutorial opportunity describing a good time to tell a particular story using a particular strategy. The next part of the storage-time processing of SPIEL is rule generation, the construction of procedures capable of recognizing storytelling opportunities.

The GuSS simulation is organized around a production system interpreter. Each of the characters in the social simulation is implemented by a production system, like those found in expert systems. To fit into this environment most effectively, the retrieval-time component of SPIEL is also implemented as a production system. The task of the rule generation component of SPIEL is to produce production rules capable of recognizing the tutorial opportunities that have been created by applying storytelling strategies to indices.

The first step in rule generation is to make the recognition conditions concrete, to reason about how these conditions might arise and describe their occurrence in terms of actions that the student might actually take. To perform this elaboration, SPIEL needs knowledge about observability in the simulated world. It must know what kinds of actions are and are not available to the student and the simulated agents. The output of this step is an expanded RCD (or eRCD) representing the same recognition conditions as the original RCD, but placing them in terms of their concrete, observable manifestations.

From the expanded RCD, the system designs a set of rules that will recognize the situation it describes. The initial stage of rule design is the construction of a *rule specification*, a directed graph indicating what production rules are needed and how they will relate to each other. Each node in the graph is a rule that the generator needs to produce. The triggering conditions are implemented by two rules, one that looks for the individual who is the buyer, and one that looks for the student to begin the closing stage of the sales process. If the student gets the sale but then leaves immediately, the story is not relevant. So there is a deactivating rule that halts recognition in this case. There is a second deactivating rule that comes in if the customer does what the customer does in the story, rethink the buying decision. In this case, the student does not need to see the story because the simulation has amply demonstrated the folly of remaining after the sale.

In the final rule specification graph, each node contains a condition or set of conditions that a rule will have to recognize. Rules are produced by walking through this graph translating from the descriptions into simulation states that rules can directly test for. For example, a "customer signing contract" condition becomes a test for a signing event with the actor and object slots bound to certain values.

7. Current Status

Formative evaluation of an earlier version YELLO containing a subset of SPIEL's stories was performed using Yellow Pages account executives as subjects. We found that users reacted well to the stories, finding SPIEL's interventions interesting and relevant. (Kass, et al. 1994) describes some of these findings.

SPIEL is currently being adapted to teach personnel management. The most significant drawback in this conversion is the need for a large knowledge base of domain knowledge in order to apply storytelling strategies. This knowledge does not transfer from one domain to another and its acquisition forms a significant bottleneck for developing storytelling programs based on SPIEL. We

are beginning to address this problem using knowledge-acquisition techniques to build an interactive tool that draws on the user's domain knowledge when applying storytelling strategies.

8. Conclusion

Currently users only benefit from on-line databases when (a) they realize they have an information need, and (b) they know how to formulate retrieval queries. We feel there is much greater potential inherent in on-line databases, such as the video case-base discussed in this paper. However, realizing that potential requires intelligent systems that can initiate retrieval, formulating their own retrieval requests, not just responding to retrieval requests from a user.

In building such a system, we have moved away from generic information retrieval: we found that what was required was a careful analysis of the *purposes* that retrieved information will serve. Such an analysis makes it possible to create retrieval systems like SPIEL that tailor retrieval by actively reasoning about those purposes.

References

Burke, R. D. 1993. Representation, Storage and Retrieval of Tutorial Stories in a Social Simulation. PhD Thesis, Northwestern University.

Edelson, D. C. 1993. Learning from Stories: Indexing, Reminding and Questioning in a Case-based Teaching System. PhD Thesis, Northwestern University.

Hammond, K. J. 1989a. *Case-based planning*. Boston: Academic Press.

Hammond, K. J. 1989b. Opportunistic Memory. In Proceedings of the Eleventh International Joint Conference on Artificial Intelligence, 504-510. Menlo Park, CA: International Joint Conferences on Artificial Intelligence, Inc.

Kass, A., R. Burke, E. Blevis, and M. Williamson 1994. Constructing learning environments for complex social skills. *Journal of the Learning Sciences*. Forthcoming.

Kolodner, J. L. 1993. *Case-based reasoning*. San Mateo, CA: Morgan Kaufmann.

Salton, G., and M. J. McGill 1983. *Introduction to modern information retrieval*. New York: McGraw-Hill.

Schank, R. C. 1982. *Dynamic Memory: A Theory of Learning in Computers and People*. Cambridge University Press.

Schank, R. C. 1990a. Teaching Architectures, Technical Report, #3. Institute for the Learning Sciences.

Schank, R. C. 1990b. *Tell Me a Story: A New Look at Real and Artificial Memory*. New York: Charles Scribner's Sons.

Schank, R. C., R. Osgood, M. Brand, R. Burke, E. Domeshek, D. Edelson, W. Ferguson, M. Freed, M. Jona, B. Krulwich, E. Ohmaye, and L. Pryor 1990. A Content Theory of Memory Indexing, Technical Report, #2. Institute for the Learning Sciences.

Situated Plan Attribution for Intelligent Tutoring

Randall W. Hill, Jr.

Jet Propulsion Laboratory / Caltech
4800 Oak Grove Drive M/S 525-3660
Pasadena, CA 91109-8099
hill@negev.jpl.nasa.gov

W. Lewis Johnson

USC / Information Sciences Institute
4676 Admiralty Way
Marina del Rey, CA 90292-6695
johnson@isi.edu

Abstract

Plan recognition techniques frequently make rigid assumptions about the student's plans, and invest substantial effort to infer unobservable properties of the student. The pedagogical benefits of plan recognition analysis are not always obvious. We claim that these difficulties can be overcome if greater attention is paid to the situational context of the student's activity and the pedagogical tasks which plan recognition is intended to support. This paper describes an approach to plan recognition called situated plan attribution that takes these factors into account. It devotes varying amounts of effort to the interpretation process, focusing the greatest effort on interpreting impasse points, i.e., points where the student encounters some difficulty completing the task. This approach has been implemented and evaluated in the context of the REACT tutor, a trainer for Operators of deep space communications stations.

Introduction

Plan recognition and agent modeling capabilities are valuable for intelligent tutoring (Corbett et al., 1990; Johnson, 1986), as well as other areas such as natural language processing (Charniak&Goldman, 1991), expert consultation (Calistri, 1990), and tactical decision making (Azarewicz et al.,, 1986). However, such capabilities are difficult to implement and employ effectively, for the following reasons. Plan recognition techniques can be *rigid*--they assume the agent is following a known plan step by step, and have difficulty interpreting deviations from the plan. The modeling process can be *underconstrained*, postulating mental activities that are difficult to infer from the agent's observable actions. An example of this style of modeling can be seen in (Ward, 1991), where the tutor attempts to track the student by generating production paths that could have led to an observed action. Finally, they tend to be *unfocused*---they do not target their analysis on those situations where tutorial intervention is warranted. For instance, intelligent tutors that use model tracing (Anderson et al., 1990) to interpret student actions tend to intervene whenever the student wanders off of a correct solution path; this intervention policy is potentially disruptive and does not

appear to be based on an analysis of whether it is appropriate to intervene.

This paper describes an approach to plan recognition called *situated plan attribution* that takes these factors into account. Situated plan attribution analyzes both the student's actions and the environmental situation. Attention to the situation is important because it allows the plan recognizer to recognize when the student must deviate from the usual plan, as well as alternative ways of achieving the goals of the plan. This flexibility avoids the rigidity problems of other techniques such as Kautz and Allen's deductive approach (Kautz&Allen, 1986), which assumes that all possible ways of performing an action are known, and every action is a step in a known plan.

Motivation for Approach

The objective of situated plan attribution is to inform and guide the tutoring process. We believe that plan recognition systems can and should be optimized to support their intended use. Accordingly, our technique applies greatest analysis effort to interpreting situations where the student might benefit from interactions with the tutoring system. Less effort is devoted to plan recognition when tutorial interaction is not justified on pedagogical grounds. Our stance is consistent with that of (Self, 1990), who argues that to make student modeling tractable one must focus on realistic, useful objectives.

These tutorial interaction points are known as *impasse points*. An impasse is defined in this work to be an obstacle to problem solving that results from either a lack of knowledge or from incorrect knowledge (Hill, 1993; Brown&VanLehn, 1980; VanLehn, 1982, 1983). Cognitive modeling studies suggest that such impasse points are natural learning opportunities (Hill, 1993; VanLehn, 1988; Hill&Johnson, 1993a,b). When the student is at an impasse, he or she naturally seeks information that can be used to overcome the impasse and continue the task. Information offered by the tutor at such points is readily accepted and assimilated. A tutor that is sensitive to such impasses does not run the risk of annoying the student with interruptions--the student's problem solving has already been interrupted by the impasse. The tutoring system need not intervene in a heavy-handed fashion; it can serve as an information resource that the student can turn to for assistance as needed. The student therefore has a greater sense of control over how the task is performed.

Implementation of the Approach

Situated plan attribution has been implemented and evaluated in the context of the REACT tutor, a trainer for Operators of deep space communications centers. REACT monitors trainees while they operate a set of complex, interactive devices. There are three entities in REACT's tutoring domain: the tutor, the student, and a simulation of the environment (i.e., the devices). The student is assumed to have some understanding of operational procedures. However, the devices may be in unexpected states or behave in unexpected ways; the student must learn to recognize such situations and deviate from the standard procedures as necessary. REACT recognizes when the student has reached an impasse, because the student's action has failed or cannot achieve its intended purpose in the devices' current state. It then coaches the student through the impasse.

REACT's plan recognition capability is not rigid because it has knowledge of device states and actions that affect them, as well as knowledge of plans. It avoids excessive underdetermined student modeling because it focuses on observable student actions and their effects. REACT generally does not intervene with the student unless a student has already received an error message from the device. As long as the student's overall plan is appropriate, interaction centers on the device errors and how to correct them. When necessary it employs an expert cognitive model to determine what action an expert would take in a given situation. Otherwise a weaker, recognitional form of analysis is employed--the system simply checks whether each student's action is a known step in a known plan, and tracks the student's progress through the plan. Actions that the system does not recognize are ignored, unless they have an undesirable effect on the state of one or more devices. The analysis becomes increasingly recognitional over time, because whenever the system employs the expert cognitive model to analyze the situation, it remembers the results of the analysis for use in similar situations.

We estimate that there are many real-world skills where feedback from the environment can guide the problem solving problem solving process as in REACT. Intelligent tutoring systems tend to overlook the role of the environment because they are frequently applied to abstract domains such as geometry or subtraction. Even in these domains there may be useful environmental cues to exploit.

For example, intelligent tutors for programming tend not to take advantage of feedback from actually running the student's program, also recent work such as GIL is making such feedback more readily available to the student (Reiser et al., 1989)

Example Problem

To illustrate how REACT works we will now describe an example from our task domain. Students are assigned missions that involve activities such as configuring and calibrating a set of communications devices, establishing a link to a spacecraft, recording data from the spacecraft, and transferring the recorded data to a control center. These tasks involve sending commands asynchronously via a computer terminal over a local area network to the devices. Standard command sequences for each type of mission are defined by procedure manuals. The devices initially respond to each command with an indication of whether the command is accepted or rejected; if accepted, the devices require time to change state.

Figure 1 shows two procedures. The first procedure, Configure-DSP, is used to configure the DSP subsystem, which is used for spectrum processing. The steps mostly involve loading or setting parameters and selecting devices. The second procedure, Coherence-Test, is used to test the continuity and coherence of the communications link; it is supposed to be executed after the Configure-DSP procedure has been completed.

We will walk through the example shown in Figure 2 to illustrate how REACT overcomes the impediments to plan recognition. Here a student begins with Configure-DSP's first command for loading the predicts file, NLOAD JK. Line 1 shows the NLOAD command, and line 2 shows the device's response, COMPLETED, indicating that the command was accepted. Everything is proceeding as predicted by the plan: the correct command was issued by the student and it was accepted by the device.

Things get a bit more complicated on lines 3 through 7. On line 3 the student issues the next command in the Configure-DSP plan, NRMED. This command follows the Configure-DSP plan exactly, but the situation actually requires a different action to be taken, LD0 E, (i.e., enable recorder LD0), which is why the command is rejected on line 4. REACT thus must recognize when deviations from the plan are warranted; it does this by first noting the rejection and reasoning about why the action was not appropriate. In this case the command was rejected due to

Configure-DSP		Coherence-Test	
Command	Description	Command	Description
NLOAD x	load-predicts-file	NPCG x	set NPCG mode
NRMED x	select-recorder	NRUN x	run NCB program
SAT x	S-band attenuation	NDTE x	enable DTE
NTOP $x\,y$	set temperature	NFFT x	enable NFFT
OFST x	set offset time		

Figure 1: Example procedures

#	Commands / Responses	REACT's Explanation
1	> NLOAD JK	
2	> COMPLETED.	
3	> NRMED LD0	
4	> REJECTED. LD0 DISABLED	The NRMED command failed because one of its preconditions was unsatisfied: LD0 should be in the ONLINE mode instead of the OFFLINE mode. To resolve the impasse, Issue the command: LD0 E, Then Issue the command: NRMED LD0
5	> LD0 E	
6	> COMPLETED. LD0: ONLN	
7	> NRMED LD0	
8	> COMPLETED.	
9	> SAT 55	
10	> COMPLETED.	
11	> NTOP 20.0 30.0	
12	> COMPLETED.	
13	> NPCG MAN	
14	> COMPLETED.	You started the Coherence-Test procedure before you finished the Configure-DSP procedure. Issue the Command: OFST <>
15	> OFST 2.7	
16	> COMPLETED.	
17	> NRUN COLD	
18	> COMPLETED.	You failed to achieve one of the goals of the Configure-DSP procedure: SAT = 12. Issue the command: NIDLE REC, Then Issue the command: SAT 12
19	> NDTE E	
20	> COMPLETED.	
21	> NFFT E	
22	> COMPLETED.	

Figure 2: An example of tutoring with REACT

an action constraint violation (i.e., an unsatisfied precondition) by the NRMED command. REACT explains its reasoning about the violation as well as deriving a way to resolve the difficulty. The difficulty is viewed as an impasse because it prevents the student from continuing with the procedure, and it suggests a gap in the student's knowledge--if he had a good grasp of the procedure, he would have known to check the state of recorder LD0 before selecting it. At line 7 the student issues the NRMED command a second time; the plan calls for it to be issued just once. The second occurrence of the command is determined to be appropriate given that the first attempt at this action failed.

The example next illustrates difficulties that arise when the student follows a plan but fails to achieve its goals. The commands and responses on lines 9 through 14 follow the Configure-DSP plan exactly and all of the commands are accepted by the device. However, the parameter value of the SAT (Set S-Band attenuation value) command, 55, will not achieve one of the procedure's goals, that the value should be 12 by the time of the procedure's completion. This goal is not explicitly stated in the procedure, rather, it is derivable from the mission support data provided to the student. If the student does not correct this setting, it will

affect the quality of the communications link with the spacecraft and of the data being recorded. Failure to achieve a goal is another type of impasse that can occur when a student is performing a task, indicating another type of knowledge gap in the student's skill set. REACT gives the student the opportunity to correct the error alone, but will intervene if not, before it is too late to correct it. When it detects the NRUN COLD (i.e., run NCB program) command on line 19, that belongs to the Coherence-Test plan, it initiates the interaction concerning the unsatisfied goal. In this case REACT also employs its expert cognitive model to analyze the cause of the impasse and determine a solution.

The final point made by the example centers on the actions listed on lines 15 through 18. On line 15 the student sends the NPCG MAN (i.e., set the NPCG device to manual mode) command, which is the first command in the Coherence-Test procedure, prior to finishing the Configure-DSP procedure, which has OFST (set the offset time) as its last command. This is a straightforward case of misordered plans, and REACT immediately alerts the student that a step was missed prior to starting the new procedure (see line 16). REACT recognizes this type of impasse as a plan dependency violation.

Situated Plan Attribution

Three types of impasses were introduced in the above example: (a) action constraint impasses, where the student takes an action that is in the plan but which the situation does not warrant, (b) goal failure impasses, where the student completes a plan without having achieved its goals, and (c) plan dependency impasses, where the student executes a plan before successfully completing one of its required predecessors. We will now give the details of how REACT recognizes and resolves each of these types of impasses.

Soar cognitive architecture

REACT is implemented in Soar, a problem solving architecture that implements a theory of human cognition (Laird et al., 1987; Newell, 1990). Soar is an integrated problem solving and learning architecture. Tasks in Soar are represented and performed in problem spaces. A Soar problem space consists of a collection of operators and states. Operators are proposed, selected, and applied to the current state; the resulting state changes may cause other operators in the problem space to be proposed, selected, and applied. Impasses occur in Soar when the problem solver stops making progress. To resolve an impasse, the Soar problem solver creates a subgoal and selects a different problem space where other operators are available for solving the problem. When the subgoal problem solving is successful, the results are saved in new productions created by Soar's chunking mechanism, which also saves the conditions that led to the impasse in the first place. The next time the conditions occur the learned chunk will be applied instead of having to search for an operator in the goal hierarchy.

Knowledge representation in REACT

REACT models several other aspects of plans besides the component actions shown in Figure 1, as will be briefly described below. For each type of mission the temporal precedence relationships among the plans is modeled with a directed graph structure called a temporal dependency network (TDN) (Fayyad&Cooper, 1992). A plan has a name and three attributes: state, execution status and goal status. The state of a plan can be either ACTIVE or INACTIVE; a plan is considered to be active once all of its predecessors in the TDN have been successfully completed. It is inactive prior to being active, and it becomes inactive again once it has been successfully completed. A plan's execution status (INCOMPLETE or COMPLETE) is determined by whether all of its commands have been observed. Each plan's goal status is marked satisfied if all its goals have been satisfied, otherwise it is unsatisfied.

Plans have two entities associated with them: operators (commands) and goals. The operators for the plans named Configure-DSP and Coherence-Test are shown in Figure 1.

Each operator has a set of preconditions. A precondition is a tuple representing a device state that must be true before it can be considered satisfied. Similarly, a plan goal is also a tuple that represents a device state. As will be seen in the following sections, an active plan's goals are individually monitored for satisfaction at all times.

Problem solving organization of REACT

The problem solving in REACT is organized into two high-level activities: *plan tracking* and *impasse interpretation* . Plan tracking involves watching the student interact with the environment and deciding whether the student's actions are appropriate for the assigned task and situation. An inappropriate action is classified into an impasse category, and REACT interprets the impasse by executing an expert cognitive model to explain the impasse and suggest repairs to the procedure that will overcome it. The resulting explanation is used for tutoring the student. Plan tracking is implemented by performing the following activities:

• Perceive objects in the environment: REACT must continuously monitor the attributes of each of the objects in the environment. The perceive-object operator in Figure 3 initially perceives each of the objects in the environment and registers them in REACT's working memory. These attribute values are change as the objects are observed to change state in the environment.

• Monitor and evaluate student actions: Each of the student's actions is observed and matched with a plan. During the plan matching, preference is given to ACTIVE plans over INACTIVE plans. Likewise, the effects of the action on the device are also evaluated to determine whether the action was successfully completed or not. If an action was unsuccessful, it is immediately classified as an action-constraint impasse. Regardless of the action's outcome, the plan containing the action is marked with the match. If the action does not match any ACTIVE plan but does match with an INACTIVE plan, then REACT recognizes that a plan-dependency impasse has occurred. All the activities for evaluating individual actions are performed by the analyze-action-response operator and its associated problem space.

• Monitor individual goal status: The achievement status of the individual goals of ACTIVE plans is continually monitored. A plan's goals begin to be monitored when the plan becomes ACTIVE; monitoring ends when the plan in INACTIVE. The recognize-desired-results operator tests for satisfied goals, while the recognize-undesired-results operator tests for unsatisfied goals.

• Monitor conjunctive goal status: In addition to testing for the satisfaction of individual goals, REACT also continually monitors whether the conjunction of a plan's goals has been achieved. The recognize-goal-completion operator tests for the conjunctive satisfaction of a plan's goals.

• Monitor plan execution status: Besides monitoring whether a plan's goals have been achieved, REACT also

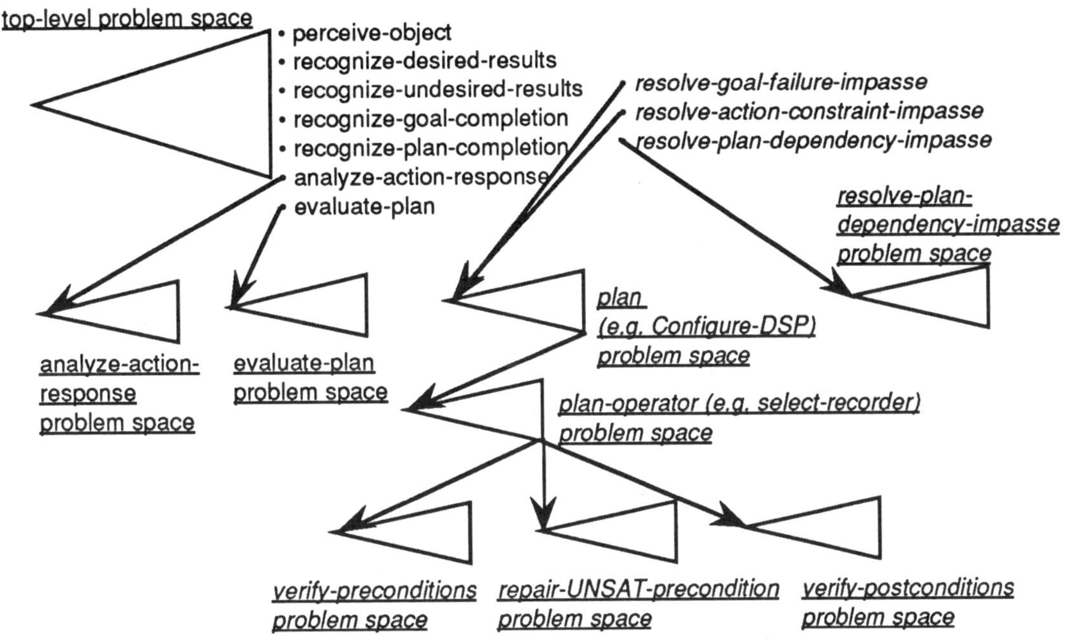

Figure 3: REACT's problem space hierarchy

monitors whether all of a plan's actions have been matched. The plan is marked COMPLETED once all of its actions have been observed. The recognize-plan-completion operator is responsible for monitoring a plan's execution status.

• Evaluate completed plans: If a plan marked COMPLETED has unsatisfied goals, then REACT recognizes that a goal-failure impasse has occurred. The evaluate-plan operator is used to perform this analysis.

Impasse interpretation, which is performed by the italicized Soar problem spaces shown in Figure 3, is implemented by performing the following activities:

• Resolve a plan dependency impasse: REACT first determines which plans should have been ACTIVE at the time that the student took the inappropriate action. The situation may have warranted a deviation from the standard procedure, e.g., the precondition of one of an action was unsatisfied. REACT checks the effects of the student's actions to determine whether it satisfies a precondition or else satisfies a goal of one of the plans. If either of these cases is true, the impasse is interpreted to be a situationally warranted deviation, and no further interpretation is necessary. On the other hand, if the action can not be justified by the situation, then REACT notifies the student of the violation of the plan ordering.

• Resolve a goal failure impasse: REACT selects the plan where the goal failure impasse occurred and determines how to achieve the unsatisfied goals. It reviews the plan, which contains some history of how the student executed its actions, by checking the operators related to the unachieved goals to determine whether the student sent the correct parameters with the action. REACT internally simulates the execution of the plan by selecting the appropriate action operators, verifying its

preconditions are satisfied, repairing any unsatisfied preconditions, and verifying that the actions postconditions are satisfied. To repair an unsatisfied precondition may involve recursively selecting and applying other actions in the same manner. REACT follows this process, which is graphically portrayed in Figure 3, until the plan's goals are achieved. In the process of solving the problem, REACT generates an explanation for tutoring the student about the impasse.

• Resolve an action constraint impasse: REACT handles this type of impasse in much the same way as a goal failure impasse. The main difference is that it focuses on how to correctly apply a single operator within the plan rather than on the achievement of the goals of the whole plan.

The problem solving in REACT bears a resemblance to the approach in CHEF (Hammond, 1990): the general strategy is to notice a failure, build an explanation for it, use the explanation to determine a repair strategy, and so on. REACT's repair strategy emphasizes treating failures related to unsatisfied preconditions, which is similar to CHEF, but REACT generates repairs on the fly rather than using a case-based approach. In addition, certain types of repairs done by CHEF are not appropriate in REACT because they would imply intervening before the impasse was clear to the student. REACT permits the student to fix problems; the tutor only intervenes when it is clear that the student has reached an impasse in problem solving.

Example revisited

To illustrate how REACT works, we will revisit the example used in section 4, focusing on the action constraint impasse that occurred on lines 3 and 4, where the student issued the NRMED LD0 command and it was subsequently rejected. The command-response pair on lines 3 and 4 is detected by the analyze-action-response operator, which subgoals into the analyze-action-response problem space where the NRMED command is matched to the active plan called Configure-DSP (Figure 1). Since the command was rejected by the simulator, the operator sets a flag indicating an action constraint impasse and the subgoal terminates. Then the resolve-action-constraint-impasse operator is selected and a subgoal into the Configure-DSP Plan problem space is formed. The operator corresponding to the NRMED command called select-recording-device is selected and another subgoal is made into the select-recording-device problem space (shown as Plan Operator Problem Space in Figure 3.) A subgoal into the Verify-Preconditions problem space is made for each of the select-recording-device operator's preconditions. As it turns out, the precondition that says that the recording device being selected must be in the ONLINE mode is unsatisfied. This is where the first part of the explanation on line 4 in Figure 2 is generated. Next, REACT subgoals into the Repair-UNSAT-Precondition problem space, where it is determined that issuing LD0 E (enable recording device LD0) command will satisfy the precondition. This information is also put into the explanation on line 4 of the example. Finally, once the precondition is satisfied, the select-recording-device problem space simulates sending the NRMED LD0 command (select the recording device named LD0), and this is also added to the explanation and this subgoal terminates. Since REACT has determined how to resolve the impasse, all of the subgoals in the hierarchy terminate and the impasse recognition operators resume their work with the next action-response pair.

Evaluation

A pilot study was conducted to evaluate REACT. We hypothesized that situated plan attribution would be able to recognize and interpret student impasses, and that the resulting tutoring would help students acquire skill in the LMC domain. The study was conducted with seven students of approximately equal experience who were divided into two groups. Each group of students was assigned a task to perform on the LMC simulator. The difference between the two groups was that Group I's students were tutored by REACT during the exercise, while Group II's students did not receive any tutoring. To test the hypotheses about situated plan attribution and student learning at impasse points, the tasks were configured so that certain types of action constraint and goal failure impasses would occur if the student was not experienced, which was the case with both groups.

The results of the study suggest that situated plan attribution holds promise as a method for recognizing student impasses and for explaining how to resolve them in a satisfactory manner. During the study REACT interpreted 604 different command-response pairs (actions) performed by the students. It recognized and explicated 36 action constraint impasses, 5 plan dependency impasses, and 17 goal failure impasses. In analyzing the event logs, REACT did not make any misinterpretations, and it was able to make all of its analyses quickly enough for a timely interaction with the student.

The study also suggests that the way situated plan attribution was applied (i.e., for impasse-driven tutoring) helped students to improve their skills in the LMC domain more quickly than students without tutoring. The students from both groups reached impasses, but there was a significant difference between the two groups in the amount of time it took resolve these impasses. While both groups acquired the same amount of skill in cases where there was an action constraint violation, the students in Group I (with REACT) resolved impasses and acquired the new knowledge approximately ten times faster than the students in Group II. Likewise, the students in Group I were less prone to having certain goal failures than the students in Group II. It was observed that students who did not notice a goal failure the first time they performed a task were prone to never realizing that there was one. For more details on the pilot study, see (Hill, 1993).

Finally, though REACT was shown to be robust in the task domain we have described in this paper, we suspect that it will be necessary to make some improvements to the situated plan attribution problem spaces to cope with larger numbers of plans and actions. In these cases we anticipate the need to deal with more ambiguity than was present in our current implementation. Ambiguity primarily will have an impact on the interpretation of plan dependency violation impasses---REACT might have to delay offering assistance until it is clear which plan the student is attempting next.

Conclusions

We have introduced a plan recognition technique called situated plan attribution that we claim avoids some of the problems of other approaches, especially as applied to intelligent tutoring. Specifically, we have shown how our method is flexible enough to recognize when a situation warrants an action that is not specified by a plan. Likewise, it recognizes when an action specified by a plan is not situationally appropriate.

Situated plan attribution also addresses the issues of underconstrained and unfocused modeling in that it concentrates on recognizing students' impasse points rather than trying to generate or understand the mental states that led to a particular action. Impasse points are natural places to tutor, and the amount of processing required to recognize and explicate the impasses we have defined is reasonable.

Acknowledgments

The research described in this paper was carried out by the Jet Propulsion Laboratory, California Institute of Technology, under a contract with the National Aeronautics and Space Administration. Dr. Johnson was supported in part by the Advanced Research Projects Agency and the Naval Research Laboratory under contract number N00014-92-K-2015 (via a subcontract from the University of Michigan). Views and conclusions contained in this paper are the authors' and should not be interpreted as representing the official opinion or policy of the U.S. Government or any agency thereof.

References

(Anderson et al., 1990) John R. Anderson, C. Franklin Boyle, Albert T. Corbett and Matthew W. Lewis. Cognitive modeling and intelligent tutoring. *Artificial Intelligence*, 42, 1990: 7-49.

(Azarewicz et al., 1986) J. Azarewicz and Fala, G. and Fink, R. and Heighecker, C.., Plan Recognition for Airborne Tactical Decision Making, *Proceedings of the Fifth National Conference on Artificial Intelligence*, pp. 805-811, 1986.

(Brown&VanLehn, 1982) John Seely Brown and Kurt VanLehn. Repair theory: A generative theory of bugs in procedural skills. *Cognitive Science*, 4, 1982:379-426.

(Calistri, 1990) Randall J. Calistri. Classifying and detecting plan-based misconceptions for robust plan recognition. Ph.D. diss., Technical Report No. CS-90-11, Department of Computer Science, Brown University, 1990.

(Corbett et al., 1990) Albert T. Corbett, John R. Anderson, and Eric G. Patterson. Student Modeling and Tutoring Flexibility in the Lisp Intelligent Tutoring System. *Intelligent Tutoring Systems: At the Crossroads of Artificial Intelligence and Education.* Ablex, 1990.

(Charniak&Goldman, 1991) Eugene Charniak and Robert Goldman. A Probabilistic Model of Plan Recognition. *Proceedings of the Ninth National Conference on Artificial Intelligence.* 1991.

(Fayyad&Cooper, 1992) Kristina Fayyad and Lynne Cooper. Representing operations procedures using temporal dependency networks. *Proceedings of the Second International Symposium on Ground Data Systems for Space Mission Operations*, SPACEOPS-92, Pasadena, CA, November 16-20, 1992.

(Hammond, 1990) Kristian J. Hammond. Explaining and Repairing Plans That Fail*. *Artificial Intelligence*, 45, (1990) 173-228.

(Hill, 1993) Randall W. Hill, Jr.. "Impasse-driven tutoring for reactive skill acquisition." Ph.D. diss. University of Southern California, Los Angeles, California, 1993.

(Hill&Johnson, 1993a) Randall W. Hill, Jr. and W. Lewis Johnson. Designing an intelligent tutoring system based on a reactive model of skill acquisition. *Proceedings of the World Conference on Artificial Intelligence in Education (AI-ED 93)*, Edinburgh, Scotland, 1993.

(Hill&Johnson, 1993b) Randall W. Hill, Jr. and W. Lewis Johnson. Impasse-driven tutoring for reactive skill acquisition. *Proceedings of the 1993 Conference on Intelligent Computer-Aided Training and Virtual Environment Technology (ICAT-VET-93)*, NASA/Johnson Space Center, Houston, Texas, May 5-7, 1993.

(Johnson, 1986) W. Lewis Johnson. *Intention-based diagnosis of novice programming errors.* Los Altos, CA: Morgan Kaufmann Publishers, Inc., 1986.

(Kautz&Allen, 1986) Henry A. Kautz and James F. Allen. Generalized plan recognition. *Proceedings of the National Conference on Artificial Intelligence,* Philadelphia, PA, 1986.

(Laird et al., 1987) John E. Laird, Allen Newell and Paul S. Rosenbloom. Soar: An architecture for general intelligence. *Artificial Intelligence*, 33, 1987:1-64.

(Newell, 1990) Allen Newell. *Unified Theories of Cognition.* Harvard University Press, 1990.

(Reiser et al., 1989) B.J. Reiser, M Ranner, M.C. Lovett, and D.Y. Kimberg. Facilitating Students' Reasoning with Causal Explanations and Visual Representations. *Artificial Intelligence and Education: Proceedings of the 4th International Conference on AI and Education.*, pp. 228-235. Amsterdam: IOS, 1989.

(Self, 1990) John A. Self, "Bypassing the Intractable Problem of Student Modeling", in Frasson, C. and Gauthier, G., eds., *Intelligent Tutoring Systems: At the Crossroads of Artificial Intelligence and Education*, Ablex, Norwood, NJ, pp. 107-123, 1990

(VanLehn, 1982) Kurt VanLehn. Bugs are not enough: Empirical studies of bugs, impasses and repairs in procedural skills. *The Journal of Mathematical Behavior*, 3, 1982:3-71.

(VanLehn, 1983) Kurt VanLehn. *Felicity conditions for human skill acquisition: Validating an AI-based theory.* Tech. Report CIS-21. Palo Alto, CA: Xerox Palo Alto Research Center.

(VanLehn, 1988) Kurt VanLehn. Toward a theory of impasse-driven learning. *Learning Issues for Intelligent Tutoring Systems.* Edited by Heinz Mandl and Alan Lesgold. New York: Springer-Verlag, 1988:19-41.

(Ward, 1991) Blake Ward. ET-Soar: Toward an ITS for theory-based representations. Ph.D. diss., CMU-CS-91-146, School of Computer Science, Carnegie Mellon University, Pittsburgh, PA.

Learning from highly flexible tutorial instruction*

Scott B. Huffman and John E. Laird
Artificial Intelligence Laboratory
The University of Michigan
Ann Arbor, Michigan 48109–2110
huffman@umich.edu

Abstract

Situated, interactive tutorial instructions give flexibility in teaching tasks, by allowing communication of a variety of types of knowledge in a variety of situations. To exploit this flexibility, however, an instructable agent must be able to *learn* different types of knowledge from different instructional interactions. This paper presents an approach to learning from flexible tutorial instruction, called *situated explanation*, that takes advantage of constraints in different instructional contexts to guide the learning process. This makes it applicable to a wide range of instructional interactions. The theory is implemented in an agent called Instructo-Soar, that learns new tasks and other domain knowledge from natural language instructions. Instructo-Soar meets three key requirements of flexible instructability: it can (A) take any command at each instruction point, (B) handle instructions that apply to either the current situation or a hypothetical one (e.g., conditionals), and (C) learn each type of knowledge it uses (derived from its underlying computational model) from instructions.

Introduction

Tutorial instruction is a highly interactive dialogue that focuses on the specific task(s) being performed by a student. While working on tasks, the student may receive instruction as needed to complete tasks or to understand aspects of the domain or of previous instructions. This situated, interactive form of instruction produces very strong human learning [Bloom, 1984]. Thus, although it has received scant attention in AI, tutorial instruction has the potential to be a powerful knowledge source for intelligent agents.

Much of tutorial instruction's power comes from its *communicative flexibility*: the instructor is free to communicate whatever kind of knowledge a student needs at whatever point it is needed. The challenge is designing a tutorable agent that supports the wide breadth of interaction and learning abilities required by this flexible communication of knowledge. Our ultimate goal is to produce fully flexible tutorable agents, that can be instructed in the same ways as human students. A complete description of the properties and associated requirements of tutorial instruction is given by Huffman [1994]. In this paper, we focus specifically on three crucial requirements of flexible instructability:

A. **Command flexibility.** The instructor should be free to give any appropriate commands to teach a task. Commands should not be limited to only directly performable/observable actions (as in [Redmond, 1992; Mitchell *et al.*, 1990; Segre, 1987]), but may request unknown procedures or actions that cannot be performed until after other actions.

B. **Situation flexibility.** The instructor should be free to use instructions that apply to either the current task situation, or some hypothetical situation specified by the instruction.[1] *Implicitly situated* instructions apply to the current situation (e.g., commands: "Close the door") [Huffman, 1994]. *Explicitly situated* instructions explicitly indicate aspects of a hypothetical situation they apply to (e.g., conditionals: "If the power is low, turn off the machine"). These are especially useful for teaching contingencies that have not come up during ongoing task performance (perhaps rare or dangerous ones).

C. **Knowledge-type flexibility.** The instructor should be free to communicate any type of knowledge through instruction. Thus, the agent must be able to *learn* any type of knowledge it uses to perform tasks (control knowledge, knowledge about objects/properties, knowledge of actions' effects, etc.) from instruction.[2]

---

*This work was sponsored by NASA/ONR contract NCC 2-517, and by a University of Michigan Predoctoral Fellowship.

[1]Human instructors use both of these options. In one protocol, for instance, 119 out of 508 instructions (23%) involved hypothetical situations, with the remainder applying to the current situation when given [Huffman, 1994].

[2]Because tutorial instructions provide knowledge for

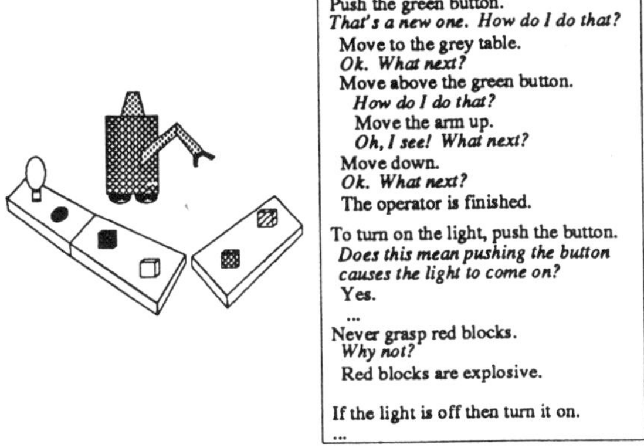

Figure 1: An example of tutorial instruction.

An agent that learns from tutorial instruction is a type of learning apprentice system (LAS) [Mitchell *et al.*, 1990]. LAS's learn by interacting with an expert; either observing the expert solving problems [Redmond, 1992; Mitchell *et al.*, 1990; Wilkins, 1990; Segre, 1987; VanLehn, 1987], or attempting to solve problems and allowing the expert to guide and critique decisions that are made [Laird *et al.*, 1990; Gruber, 1989; Kodratoff and Tecuci, 1987; Porter and Kibler, 1986]. Each LAS has learned particular types of knowledge: e.g., operator implementations [Mitchell *et al.*, 1990], goal decomposition rules [Kodratoff and Tecuci, 1987], operational versions of functional goals [Segre, 1987], control knowledge/features [Gruber, 1989], heuristic classification knowledge [Wilkins, 1990], etc.

Flexible tutorial instruction extends LAS's interaction and learning abilities in a number of ways. First, the instructor may specify unknown tasks or tasks with unachieved preconditions at any instruction point (requirement A). Past LAS's limit input to particular commands at particular times (e.g., only commanding directly executable actions) and typically do not allow unknown commands at all. Second, tutorial instruction allows explicitly situated instructions (requirement B); past LAS's do not. Third, past LAS's learn only a subset of the types of knowledge they use to perform tasks. Tutorial instruction's flexibility requires that all types of task knowledge can be learned (requirement C).

This paper describes how analytic and inductive learning techniques can be combined and embedded within an agent to produce general learning from flexible tutorial instruction. We present a learning approach called *situated explanation* (an extension of

particular situations, they are best for teaching tasks with *local control structure* (e.g., serial constructive tasks). Local decisions can combine to exhibit global control behavior [Yost and Newell, 1989], but teaching a global method as a sequence of local decisions is difficult. Thus, we focus on learning knowledge for tasks involving local control.

EBL) that utilizes the situation an instruction applies to and the larger instructional context to guide the learning process. The approach is implemented in an instructable agent called Instructo-Soar, built within Soar [Laird *et al.*, 1987]. Huffman and Laird [1993] described how Instructo-Soar supports (A) command flexibility, learning hierarchies of new tasks, and extending tasks to new situations, given imperative natural language commands like those at the top of Figure 1. This paper extends the theory underlying Instructo-Soar to cover (B) situation and (C) knowledge-type flexibility. The types of knowledge that the agent should be able to learn from instruction – namely, all the types it uses to perform tasks – are identified by examining the computational model underlying the agent. Instructo-Soar can in fact learn every type of knowledge it uses in task performance – control knowledge, operator knowledge, etc – from instruction. The claim is not that Instructo-Soar can learn any possible *piece* of knowledge of these types, but that it can learn examples of each type. By combining requirements A, B, and C, Instructo-Soar exhibits a breadth of capabilities needed for flexible instructability.

Expanding the requirements

Requirements A, B, and C imply a set of possibilities that a flexibly instructable agent must deal with. (A) Command flexibility allows the instructor to give any command at any point in the instructional dialogue.[3] For any command, there are three possibilities: (1) the commanded action is known, and the agent performs it; (2) the commanded action is known, but the agent does not know how to perform it in the current situation (the instructor has skipped steps that meet the commanded action's preconditions); or (3) the commanded action is unknown to the agent.

(B) Situation flexibility allows each instruction to apply to either the current situation or a hypothetical one. A *situation* consists of a starting state S and a goal G that the agent will move towards by performing the instructed step. Either S or G may be explicitly indicated, making for two types of explicitly situated instructions. For example, "If the light is on, push the button" indicates a hypothetical state with a light on; "To turn on the machine, flip the switch" indicates a hypothetical goal of turning on the machine.

(C) Knowledge-type flexibility allows instructions that can require the agent to learn any of the types of knowledge it uses. We have identified the knowledge types used in our agent by examining its underlying computational model, called the *problem space computational model* (PSCM) [Newell *et al.*, 1990; Yost and

---

[3]Flexible *initiation* of each instruction – by either instructor or agent – is viewed as a separate requirement. The agent described here supports command flexibility for agent-initiated instruction only.

Entity	Knowl. type	Example
state	inference	gripper closed & directly above obj → holding obj.
operator	proposal	If goal is pick up obj on table1, and not docked at table1, then propose moving to table1.
operator	preferential	If goal is pick up small metal obj on table1, prefer moving to table1 over fetching magnet.
operator	effects	An effect of the operator move to table1 is that the robot becomes docked at table1.
operator	termination	Termination conditions of pick up obj: gripper raised & holding obj.

Table 1: The five types of knowledge of PSCM agents.

(A) Command flexibility	known command	
	skipped steps	
	unknown command	
(B) Situation flexibility	implicitly situated	
	explicitly situated:	hyp. state
		hyp. goal
(C) Knowledge-type flexibility	state inference	
	operator proposal	
	operator preferential	
	operator effects	
	operator termination	

Table 2: Expanded requirements of instruction.

Newell, 1989]. The PSCM is a general formulation of the computation in a knowledge-level agent, and many applications have been built within it [Rosenbloom *et al.*, 1993]. Because its components approximate the knowledge-level, the PSCM is an apt choice for identifying an agent's knowledge types.[4] Soar is a symbol-level implementation of the PSCM.

A PSCM agent moves through a sequence of *states* in a *problem space*, by sequentially applying *operators* to the current state. Operators transform the state, and may affect the external world by producing motor commands. The agent reaches an *impasse* when its immediately available knowledge is not sufficient either to select or fully apply an operator. When this occurs, another problem space context – a *subgoal* – is created, with the goal of resolving the impasse. This second context may impasse as well, causing a third context to arise, and so on.

The only computational entities in the PSCM mediated by the agent's knowledge are states and operators. There are a small set of PSCM-level functions on these entities that the agent performs, each using a different type of knowledge. Thus, it is straightforward to enumerate the types of knowledge within a PSCM agent; they are listed in Table 1 ([Huffman, 1994; Yost and Newell, 1989] describe the derivation of this list). Because Soar is an implementation of the PSCM, the knowledge within Soar agents is of these types.

Thus, as listed in Table 2, our three requirements expand to three types of command flexibility, three types of situated instructions and five types of knowledge to be learned.

---

[4]This is not true of other computational models, such as Lisp or connectionist models.

Learning from instructions

Learning from instruction involves both analytic learning (learning based on prior knowledge) and inductive learning (going beyond prior knowledge). Analytic learning is needed because the agent must learn general knowledge from specific instructions that combine known elements (e.g., learning to push buttons by combining known steps to push the green one). Inductive learning is needed because the agent must learn new task goals and domain knowledge beyond the scope of its prior knowledge. Our goal is not to produce more powerful analytic or inductive techniques, but rather to specify how these techniques come together to produce a variety of learning (requirement C) in the variety of instructional situations and interactions faced by a flexibly instructable agent (requirements A, B).

Analytic methods can produce high-quality learning from a single example (e.g., a single instructing of a procedure). Thus, we use an analytic approach – a type of explanation-based learning – as the core of our learning from instruction method, and fall back on inductive methods when explanation cannot be used. Because of requirement B, the explanation process is performed within the situation the instruction is meant to apply to – either the current task situation, or one explicitly specified in the instruction.

The resulting approach to learning from tutorial instruction, called *situated explanation*, is conceptually simple. For each instruction I, the agent first determines what situation I is meant to apply to, and then attempts to *explain* why the step indicated by I leads to goal achievement in that situation (or prohibits it, for negative instructions). If an explanation can be made, it produces general learning of some knowledge I_K by indicating the key features of the situation and instruction that cause success. If an explanation cannot be completed, it indicates that the agent lacks some knowledge, M_K, needed to explain the instruction. The lack of knowledge is dealt with in different ways depending on the instructional context, as described below.

In more detail: the situation (starting state S and a goal G to be reached) for each instruction I is produced by altering the current task situation to reflect

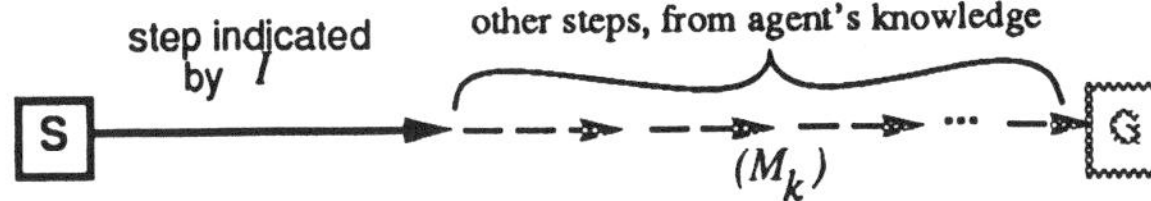

Figure 2: Situated explanation of instruction I in situation $[S, G]$.

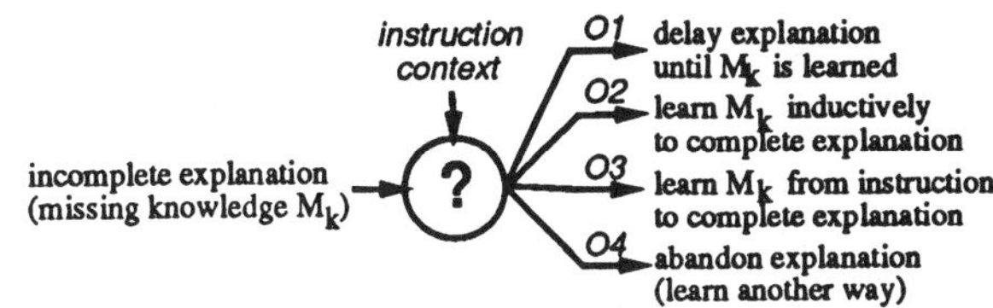

Figure 3: Options when faced with an incomplete explanation because of missing knowledge M_K.

any situation features specified in the instruction (e.g., state features like "If the light is off..."). Then, the agent attempts to explain I's use in $[S, G]$ using its prior knowledge. A PSCM agent's knowledge applies to the current situation to select and apply operators and to make inferences. When explaining an instruction I, this knowledge is applied internally to the situation $[S, G]$. That is, explanation takes the form of *forward internal projection*. As depicted in Figure 2, the agent "imagines" itself in state S, and then runs forward, applying the instructed step, and knowledge that it has about subsequent states/operators. If G is reached within this projection, then the projected path from S, through the step instructed by I, to G comprises an explanation of I. By indicating the features of I, S, and G causally required for success, the explanation allows the agent to learn general knowledge from I (as in standard EBL, realized in our agent by Soar's chunking mechanism [Rosenbloom and Laird, 1986]). For instance, if the agent projects "Move to the grey table" (and then the actions following it) to reach the goal of pushing a button, it learns a general operator proposal rule: "Propose `move-to-table(?t)` when trying to push button ?b, `located-on(?b,?t)`, and `not docked-at(?t)`." This rule generalizes the instruction by removing the table's color (which was not causally important), and specializes it by including the fact that the button is on the table.

This method depends on the agent having knowledge to form an explanation. However, an instructable agent's knowledge will often be incomplete (otherwise, it would not need instruction). That is, it will often be missing one or more pieces of prior knowledge M_K (of any PSCM type) needed to complete the explanation of I. Missing knowledge (in Figure 2, missing arrows) will cause an incomplete explanation by precluding achievement of G in the projection. For instance, the agent may not know a key effect of an operator, or a crucial state inference, needed to reach G. More radically, the action commanded by I may be completely unknown and thus inexplainable.

There are a number of general options a learning system may follow when it cannot complete an explanation. (O1) It could delay the explanation until later, in hopes that the missing knowledge (M_K) will be learned in the meantime. Or, (O2-O3) it could try to complete the explanation now, by learning the missing knowledge somehow. The missing knowledge could be learned (O2) inductively (e.g. by inducing

over the "gap" in the explanation, as in [VanLehn *et al.*, 1992] and many others), or, (O3) in an instructable agent's case, through further instruction. Finally, (O4) it could abandon the explanation altogether, and try to induce the desired knowledge instead.

Given only an incomplete explanation, it would be difficult to choose which option to follow. Identifying the missing knowledge M_K in the general case is a difficult credit assignment problem, and there is nothing in the incomplete explanation that predicts whether M_K will be learned later if the explanation is delayed. However, as indicated in Figure 3, an instructable agent has additional information available to it besides the incomplete explanation itself. Namely, the instructional context (that is, the type of instruction and its place within the dialogue) often constrains M_K in a way that determines which of the four options (O1-O4) is most appropriate for a given incomplete explanation. For instance, the context can indicate that M_K is likely to be learned later, making delaying explanation the best option; alternatively, it can indicate that there are potentially many pieces of knowledge missing, making abandoning explanation a more reasonable option.

To describe how different instructional contexts can constrain dealing with incomplete explanations, the next section presents a series of four examples (one for each option) handled by the Instructo-Soar agent we have built. In describing different instructional contexts, the examples also illustrate Instructo-Soar's coverage of each piece of requirements A, B, and C.

Instructo-Soar: An instructable agent

Instructo-Soar is an instructable agent built within Soar – and thus, the PSCM – that uses the situated explanation approach outlined above. It is currently applied to a simulated robotic domain, with a Hero robot, blocks, tables, buttons, a light, and an electromagnet. Instructo-Soar begins with the knowledge of a set of primitive operators, such as moving its arm up and down, and opening and closing its hand. However, its knowledge of the effects of these operators on objects in the domain is incomplete. Also, it begins with no knowledge of complex operators, such as picking up or arranging objects.

Ex. 1. Delaying explanation while learning procedures. Instructo-Soar learns new procedures from commands like those at the top of Figure 1, for "Push the green button." Huffman and Laird [1993] describe this learning in detail. When the command to push the button cannot be completed (because this procedure is unknown), the agent reaches an impasse and asks for further instruction. Instructions to perform the procedure are received and executed in turn (e.g., "Move to the grey table"). However, they cannot be explained: the agent does not know the goal of the procedure (e.g., the goal of "push the green button") – the endpoint of the explanation – or the steps following the current one to reach that endpoint.

In this instructional context – explaining a commanded step of a procedure being learned –it is clear that the missing knowledge of the following steps and the procedure's goal *will* be acquired later, because the instructor is expected to teach the procedure to completion. Thus, the agent *delays explanation* (option O1) and for now memorizes each instruction in a rote, episodic form, to be recalled and explained later. At the end of the first execution of a procedure, the instructor indicates "The operator is finished", and the agent uses a simple heuristic (comparing the initial and final states) to induce the goal concept (termination conditions) of the new procedure (e.g., the gripper is directly above the button). Since this induction may be incorrect, it is presented to the instructor, who may add or remove features before verifying the result (not shown in Figure 1).

Now that the goal and all steps are known, the original instructions are recalled and explained, via forward projection from the initial state. If this projection succeeds, the agent learns general implementation rules for the procedure (a series of proposals for sub-operators: `move-to-table, move-arm(above), ...`) based on the features in the projection (a-la EBL).[5]

The parts of (A) command flexibility from Table 2 are supported through recursive instruction/explanation. Any incompletable command causes an impasse and leads to further instruction/explanation within a subgoal. There may be multiple levels of embedded impasses, supporting hierarchical instruction. For example, within the instructions for "push button", the command "Move above the green button" cannot be completed because of a skipped step (the arm must be raised to move above something). An impasse arises where the instructor indicates the needed step, and then continues instructing "push button". Since new or previously learned operators can be commanded while teaching a larger operator, operator hierarchies can be taught. Instructo-Soar has learned hierarchies involving lining up, picking up, grasping, and putting down objects, etc.

---

[5]If the projection fails, there is additional missing knowledge (e.g., unknown operator effects). Since it is extremely difficult to localize the missing knowledge, the agent abandons explanation and uses simple heuristics (described below) to induce proposals for the sub-operators.

The parts of requirements B and C in Table 2 met by learning a new operator are implicitly situated instructions, and learning the operator's termination conditions, and proposals for its sub-operators. The remaining examples illustrate Instructo-Soar's handling of explicitly situated instructions, and learning the other types of PSCM knowledge.

Ex. 2. Completing explanations by inducing missing knowledge. Instructo-Soar's domain includes a light that is toggled using a button. The agent has been taught how to push the button, but does not know its effect on the light. Now it is told: **To turn on the light, push the red button.** This instruction specifies a *hypothetical goal* of turning on the light. Based on the instruction, the agent creates a situation consisting of that goal and a state like the current state, but with the light off.[6] From this situation, the agent forward projects the action of pushing the button. However, since the agent is missing the knowledge (M_K) that pushing the button affects the light, the light does not come on within the projection. Thus, the explanation is incomplete.

In this case, the form of the instruction – a purpose clause specifying a hypothetical goal – allows the agent to form a strong hypothesis about the missing knowledge. Based on the instruction, the action of pushing the button is expected to *generate* turning on the light.[7] That is, the agent expects the specified goal (light on) to be met after performing the single push-button action. This expectation constrains the "gap" in the explanation: the state after pushing the button *should* be a state with the light on, and only one action was performed to produce this effect. Because the effect is not achieved, the most straightforward inference of M_K is that the single action – pushing the button – *causes* any unachieved goal features to be met (e.g., it causes the light to come on). The instructor is asked to verify this inference.[8] If verified, the agent learns new piece of operator effect knowledge:

```
if   projecting push-button(?b), color(?b,red),
     and the light is not on
then the light is now on.
```

Immediately after being learned, this rule applies to the light in the forward projection for the current instruction. The light comes on, completing the instruction's explanation by achieving its goal. From this explanation, the agent learns to propose pushing the red button when its goal is to turn on the light.

This example illustrates Instructo-Soar's coverage of hypothetical goal instructions for requirement B, and learning operator effects for requirement C.

---

[6]Hypothetical situations are created from language in a straightforward way; for details, see Huffman [1994].

[7]DiEugenio [1993] found empirically that this expectation holds for 95% of naturally occurring purpose clauses.

[8]If the inference is rejected, the agent assumes there must be extra steps involved to turn on the light, and learns to propose pushing the button as the first step.

Ex. 3. Abandoning explanation. The agent abandons an incomplete explanation in two cases: (1) when the incompleteness could be caused by missing knowledge about any of multiple operators; and (2) when the instructor declines to give further instruction about the missing knowledge upon being asked. An example of (1) was mentioned earlier: after learning the steps and the goal of a new procedure, sometimes the agent still cannot explain the steps. This explanation failure could be caused by missing knowledge about *any* of the steps, making it difficult to isolate. Thus, it is reasonable to abandon explaining the steps, and instead to induce a proposal rule for each step. Simple heuristics are used to select features of the state, goal, and step. For instance, one heuristic selects the relationship between arguments of the goal (e.g., the button in "Push the green button") and the step (e.g., the table in "Move to the grey table") to include as a condition for proposing the step (e.g., including `located-on(?b,?t)`).

As an example of (2) the instructor declining to give further instruction, consider these instructions:

    `Never grasp red blocks.`
    Why? `Trust me.`

"Never grasp" prohibits a step from applying to a hypothetical situation in which it might apply (as do negative imperatives in general). Thus, Instructo-Soar creates a *hypothetical state* with a red block that can be grasped. (Instructo-Soar also handles positive hypothetical state instructions; e.g., "If the light is off, ...") Since no goal is specified by the instruction, and there is no current goal, a default goal of "maintaining happiness" is used. From this hypothetical situation, the agent internally projects the "grasp" action. The resulting state, in which the agent is grasping a red block, is acceptable ("happy") according to the agent's knowledge. Thus, the projection does not explain why the action is prohibited. The agent asks for further instruction, in an attempt to learn M_K and complete the explanation.

The instructor can decline to give further information by saying `Trust me`. Since the instructor will not provide M_K, the agent is forced to abandon the explanation. Instead, it induces conditions for prohibiting "grasp". Instructo-Soar conservatively guesses that every feature of the hypothetical state is relevant to rejecting the instructed operator. Thus, it induces that it should reject grasping `blocks` with `color red`.

Ex. 4. Completing explanations through further instruction. Alternatively, the instructor could provide further instruction, saying for instance `Red blocks are explosive`. From this instruction, the agent learns a state inference rule: `blocks` with `color red` have `explosiveness high`. Instructo-Soar learns inferences from simple statements, and from conditionals like "If the magnet is powered and directly above a metal block, then the magnet is stuck to the block," by essentially translating the utterance directly into a rule.[9] State inference instructions may be used to introduce new features (e.g, `stuck-to`) that extend the agent's representation vocabulary.

The rule learned from "Red blocks are explosive" adds `explosiveness high` to the block that the agent had simulated grasping in the hypothetical situation. The agent knows that touching an explosive object may cause an explosion – a negative result. This negative result completes the explanation of "never grasp," and the agent learns to avoid grasping objects with `explosiveness high`.

Completing the explanation through further instruction (this example), produces more general learning than in example 3. In this example, if the agent is later told `Green blocks are explosive`, it will avoid grasping them as well. In general, multiple levels of instruction can lead to higher quality learning than a single level, because learning is based on an explanation composed from lower level knowledge (M_K) rather than inductive heuristics alone.

Examples 3 and 4 illustrate hypothetical state instructions (requirement B), and learning operator preferential knowledge (here, operator rejection) and state inferences (requirement C).

Discussion

These examples have shown how an instruction's situation and context can affect the process of learning from it. First, the *situation* an instruction applies to provides the endpoints for attempting to explain the instruction.

Second, different instructional contexts can indicate which option to follow when the explanation of an instruction cannot be completed. For instance, the context of learning a new procedure indicates that delaying explanation is best, since the full procedure will eventually be taught. After learning the full procedure, if a step cannot be explained, missing knowledge could be anywhere in the procedure, so it is best to abandon explanation and learn another way. Purpose clause (hypothetical goal) instructions localize missing knowledge, by giving strong expectations about a single operator that should achieve a single goal; this makes it plausible to induce missing knowledge and complete the explanation. In cases other than these, the default is to ask for instruction about missing knowledge to complete the explanation. Even then, if the instructor declines, the explanation must be abandoned.

The examples also illustrate coverage of Table 2, within one domain. Although the domain is simple, it does give rise to a range of the different types of instructional interactions and learning that occurs in tutorial instruction. We claimed that tutorial instruc-

---

[9]This occurs by chunking, but in an uninteresting way. Instructo-Soar does not use explanation to learn state inferences. An extension would be to try to explain why an inference holds using a deeper causal theory.

tion's flexibility requires a breadth of learning and interaction capabilities in an instructable agent. Empirically, combining (A) command flexibility, (B) situation flexibility, and (C) knowledge-type flexibility, Instructo-Soar displays *nineteen* distinct instructional capabilities [Huffman, 1994]. These are primarily combinations of the requirements in Table 2. For instance, Instructo-Soar can learn three different kinds of knowledge from hypothetical state instructions (inferences, proposals, and rejections). (In addition to these combinations there are supporting behaviors, like taking instructions to alter/verify inferences.) This myriad of instructional behavior does not require nineteen different learning techniques, but arises from applying a single technique, situated explanation in a PSCM agent, across a range of instructional situations.

As an evaluation criterion for instructable agents, we have developed a set of requirements for a "complete tutorable agent" [Huffman, 1994]. This paper focuses on three key requirements; there are eleven in all. Instructo-Soar meets seven of the eleven either fully or partially.

The unmet requirements provide impetus for further work. First, a complete tutorable agent must deal with instructions in all their linguistic complexity. We have applied our techniques to a small domain, with simple actions and language; in more complex domains, more complex language will be needed. Second, a complete tutorable agent must allow instructions to be initiated by either the agent or the instructor. Currently, Instructo-Soar's dialogue is driven completely by the agent, which receives instruction only when it notices a lack of knowledge. Third, a complete tutorable agent must deal with both incomplete and incorrect knowledge. Instructo-Soar's learning thus far incrementally adds knowledge to an incomplete theory. We have just begun work on correcting incorrect domain knowledge through instruction.

Acknowledgments: Thanks to Jay Runkel and Randy Jones for helpful comments on earlier drafts.

References

[Bloom, 1984] B. Bloom. The 2 sigma problem: The search for methods of group instruction as effective as one-to-one tutoring. *Ed. Researcher*, 13(6):4–16, 1984.

[DiEugenio, 1993] B. DiEugenio. *Understanding NL Instructions: A computational approach to purpose clauses.* PhD thesis, Univ. of Pennsylvania, 1993.

[Gruber, 1989] T. Gruber. Automated knowledge acquisition for strategic knowledge. *Machine Learning*, 4(3-4):293–336, 1989.

[Huffman and Laird, 1993] S. Huffman and J. Laird. Learning procedures from interactive natural language instructions. In *Machine Learning: Proc's. 10th Intl. Conference*, 1993.

[Huffman, 1994] S. Huffman. *Instructable Autonomous Agents.* PhD thesis, Univ. of Michigan, January 1994.

[Kodratoff and Tecuci, 1987] Y. Kodratoff and G. Tecuci. Techniques of design and DISCIPLE learning apprentice. *Intl. J. Expert Systems*, 1(1):39–66, 1987.

[Laird *et al.*, 1987] J. Laird, A. Newell, and P. Rosenbloom. Soar: An architecture for general intelligence. *Artificial Intelligence*, 33(1):1–64, 1987.

[Laird *et al.*, 1990] J. Laird, M. Hucka, E. Yager, and C. Tuck. Correcting and extending domain knowledge using outside guidance. In *Proc. 7th Intl. Conf. on Machine Learning*, 1990.

[Mitchell *et al.*, 1990] T. Mitchell, S. Mahadevan, and L. Steinberg. LEAP: A learning apprentice system for VLSI design. In Y. Kodratoff and R. Michalski, editors, *Machine learning: An AI approach, Vol. III.* Morgan Kaufmann, 1990.

[Newell *et al.*, 1990] A. Newell, G. Yost, J. Laird, P. Rosenbloom, and E. Altmann. Formulating the problem space computational model. In *Proc. 25th Anniversary Symposium, CMU School of Computer Science*, 1990.

[Porter and Kibler, 1986] B. Porter and D. Kibler. Experimental goal regression: A method for learning problem-solving heuristics. *Machine Learning*, 1:249–286, 1986.

[Redmond, 1992] M. Redmond. *Learning by observing and understanding expert problem solving.* PhD thesis, Georgia Tech, 1992.

[Rosenbloom and Laird, 1986] P. Rosenbloom and J. Laird. Mapping EBG onto Soar. In *AAAI-86*, 1986.

[Rosenbloom *et al.*, 1993] P. Rosenbloom, J. Laird, and A. Newell, editors. *The Soar Papers: Research on integrated intelligence.* MIT Press, 1993.

[Segre, 1987] A. Segre. A learning apprentice system for mechanical assembly. In *IEEE Conf. on AI for Applications*, pages 112–117, 1987.

[VanLehn *et al.*, 1992] K. VanLehn, R. Jones, and M. Chi. A model of the self-explanation effect. *J. of the Learning Sciences*, 2(1):1–59, 1992.

[VanLehn, 1987] K. VanLehn. Learning one subprocedure per lesson. *Artificial Intelligence*, 31(1):1–40, 1987.

[Wilkins, 1990] D. Wilkins. Knowledge base refinement as improving an incomplete and incorrect domain theory. In Y. Kodratoff and R. Michalski, editors, *Machine learning: An AI approach, Volume III.* Morgan Kaufmann, 1990.

[Yost and Newell, 1989] G. Yost and A. Newell. A problem space approach to expert system specification. In *IJCAI-89*, 1989.

Case-Based Retrieval Interface Adapted to Customer-Initiated Dialogues in Help Desk Operations

Hideo Shimazu and **Akihiro Shibata** and **Katsumi Nihei**
Information Technology Research Laboratories, NEC Corporation
4-1-1 Miyazaki Miyamae-ku, Kawasaki, Japan, 216
{shimazu, akihiro, nihei}@joke.cl.nec.co.jp

Abstract

Help desk systems have become increasingly important in the efforts of corporations to maintain customer satisfaction, and Case-Based Reasoning (CBR) provides promising techniques for use in the improvement of such systems. This paper describes multiple interface modes by which customer service operators can respond rapidly to customer-initiated inquiries, retrieving/storing case data from/into a case-base. The proposed interface addresses a major situation assessment problem, the difficulty of attempting to match what may be completely different descriptions of an item to be retrieved, i.e. descriptions resulting from vastly differing points of view. The proposed interface and the similarity assessment algorithm are implemented in the CARET case-based retrieval tool operating on commercial Relational Database Management Systems (RDBMS).

Introduction

This paper describes a novel interface to a case-based retrieval system. It is to be used in a customer support help desk system by which customer service operators can respond rapidly to customer-initiated inquiries, retrieving/storing case data from/into a large-scale case-base. We have implemented the interface design on an enhanced version of CARET, a previously reported case-based retrieval tool that operates on commercial relational database management systems (RDBMS) (Shimazu, Kitano and Shibata 1993).

Users of high-tech products today regard technical support as being nearly as important as the performance of the products themselves. Because help desk operators receive repeated requests, a case-based retrieval system which can show operators those similar previous customer inquiries and the operator replies to them would naturally be a useful tool.

In order for help desk operators to be able to respond to inquiries in a reasonably short time, however, such a case-based retrieval system must provide an easy and rapid interface for similar-case retrievals, but the fact that customers tend to explain their problems in widely varying ways is a serious obstacle to achieving rapid retrievals.

Interface Design Decisions

Typical categories of customer approaches to explaining their inquiries include:

Step-by-step action-based explanation:
The user explains his/her inquiry procedurally and chronologically, for example, "When I am sending email with the menu, can I cancel the email after I have selected the SEND item from the menu?"

Diagram-description-based explanation:
The user envisions the internal model (which may or may not be accurate) of the product and explains his/her inquiry using that model, for example, "Can I cancel some email after I've already put it in my *mail box* for sending?".

Physical-appearance-based explanation:
The user explains his/her inquiry in terms of the physical appearance of the product, for example, "On the right-hand side of the machine, the red lamp just below the RESET switch is blinking. What does this mean?".

A case-based retrieval system interface must be capable of handling all these types of explanations and more. For this reason, we have designed our interface to include a separate mode for each explanation category. When answering a customer call, the operator first determines which of the three categories is most appropriate to the way the customer is describing the inquiry. Then the operator selects a corresponding interface mode, and inputs the customer's inquiry via that mode.

An analysis of customer problems has taught us that the majority of problems arise when a customer acts almost correctly, but makes some minor mistake, and/or simply misunderstands a situation to a slight degree, and on that basis we have developed a new case indexing method based on the three typical categories of customer inquiry descriptions previously listed.

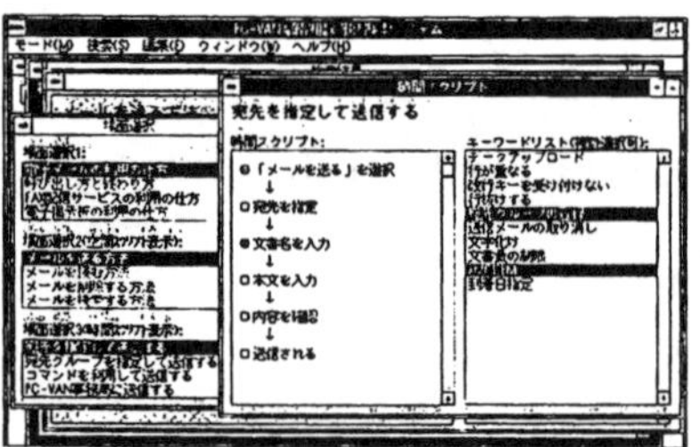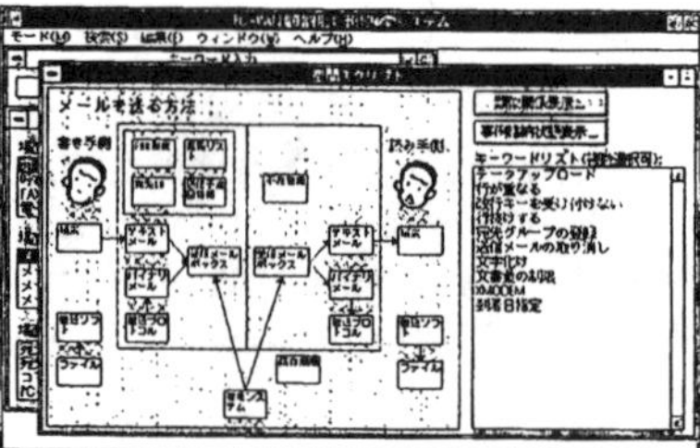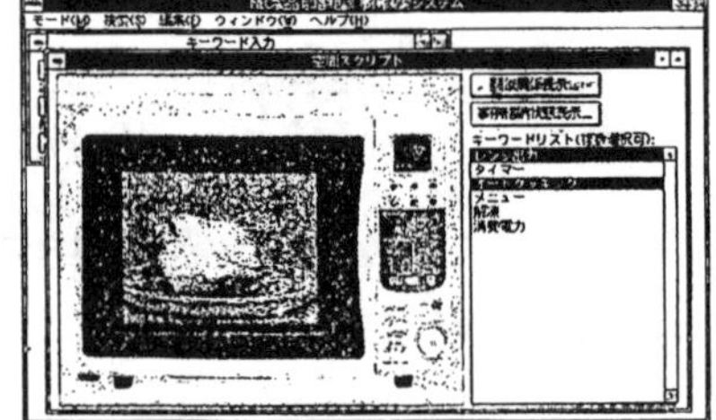

Figure 1: Step-by-step schema (left), Diagram schema (center), and Physical-appearance schema (right)

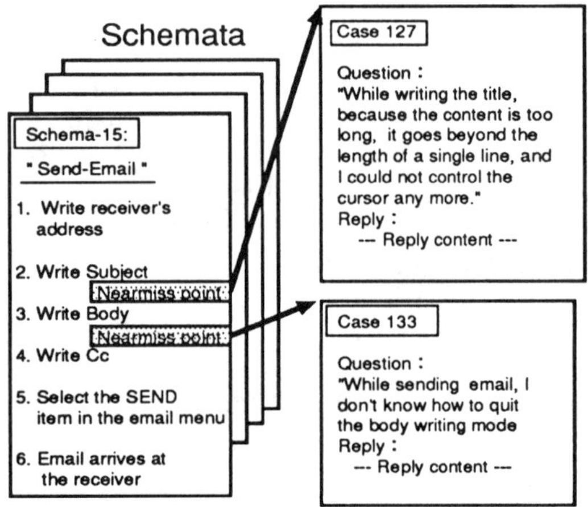

Figure 2: Case Indexing with a Schema and Nearmiss points

For each of these categories there is prepared a set of predefined **schemata**, each of which describes a situation likely to arise as an inquiry (Figure 1).

Step-by-step Schema: For the step-by-step action-based category, the schemata consist of individual lists of the complex combinations of operations required to accomplish the most typical customer goals. This schema structure is similar to script (Schank and Abelson 1977).

Diagram Schema: For the diagram-description-based category, the schemata consist of descriptions of the most typical internal models envisioned by customers.

Physical-appearance Schema: For the physical-appearance-based category, the schemata consist of individual physical views of the product as typically seen by customers.

If a customer's problem description in a case is that he/she acts almost correctly, but makes some minor mistake, and/or simply misunderstands a situation to a slight degree, the case can be simply indexed with a set of a predefined schema and one or a few slight disparities (**nearmiss points**) between the schema and the case.

Figure 2 shows "send-email" step-by-step schema, Schema-15, which represents typical and correct sequences of actions taken when a customer sends email. Case-127 holds a question whose goal and actions are similar to those for Schema-15, but has a nearmiss point which causes this question. A pair of Schema-15 and the nearmiss point becomes the index for Case-127.

When an operator retrieves cases while listening to a customer's inquiry, the operator selects a corresponding schema. The schema is displayed on the terminal. When he/she points at one or a few problem points in the schema, if there are cases whose nearmiss points are equal or similar to those specified problem points, the cases are displayed on the terminal.

When an operator stores a new case, he/she describes the case content, selects an appropriate schema, indicates one or a few problem points in the schema as the nearmiss points, and stores the case into the case-base.

Bridging of Schemata

Similarity values among steps in step-by-step schemata, components in diagram schemata, and pertinent points in physical-appearance schemata are defined by domain experts. Similar-case retrieval over a single schema is carried out using the similarity definitions.

Bridging representations in different schemata is

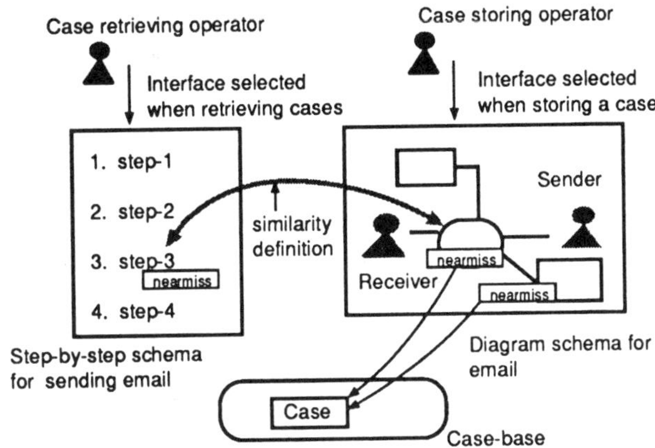

Figure 3: Bridging Different Schemata

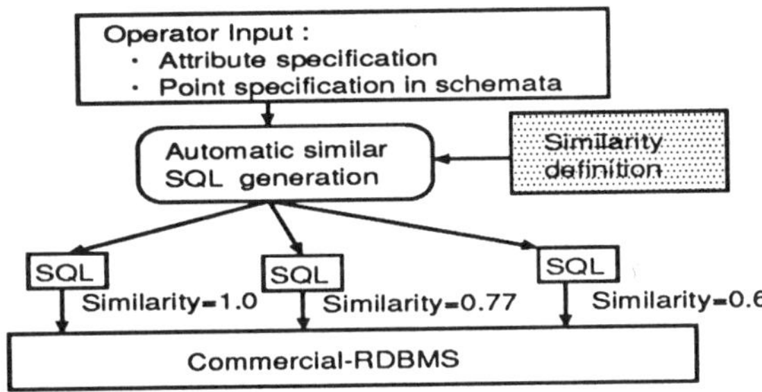

Figure 4: Automatic SQL generation

necessary because it assimilates differences in schema selections by operators. Often, a schema invoked when storing a case is different from a schema invoked when retrieving an identical case. Figure 3 shows a case which is indexed from a diagram schema when stored, because the customer explained his/her problem with spatial expressions. Assume that another customer asks another operator a very similar question with step-by-step expressions. The operator invokes a step-by-step schema and specifies a problem point in the schema. However, since there is no index from the step-by-step schema to the case, the case can not be retrieved. If similarity was predefined between steps in the step-by-step schema and components in the diagram schema, the case is retrieved, although no direct index exists from the step-by-step schema to the case.

The CARET System

The proposed interface and the similarity assessment algorithm were implemented in the CARET case-based retrieval tool operating on commercial RDBMS. This section describes the algorithm in detail.

Nearest Neighbor Retrieval

CARET uses nearest neighbor retrieval. Typically, a similarity between a query (Q) and a case (C) in the

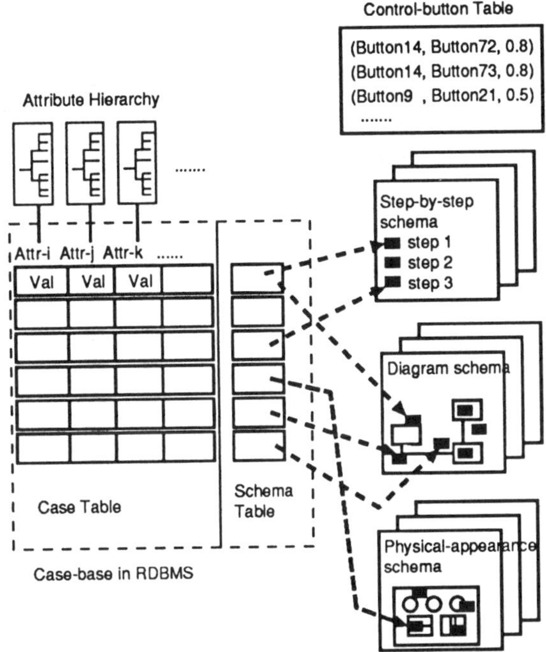

Figure 5: Case and Schema Representation

case-base $(S(Q, C))$ is the weighted sum of similarities for individual attributes:

$$S(Q,C) = \frac{\sum_{i=1}^{n} W_i \times s(Q_i, C_i)}{\sum_{i=1}^{n} W_i} \qquad (1)$$

where W_i is the i-th attribute weight, $s(Q_i, C_i)$ is similarity between the i-th attribute value for a query (Q) and that for a case (C) in the RDB. Traditional implementations would compute the similarity values for all records, and sort records based on their similarity.

CARET uses a commercial RDBMS for its case-base manager. The use of RDBMS, however, automatically forces CARET to generate SQL specifications (Chamberlin $et\ al.$ 1976) to carry out any case-base retrievals. Since SQL does not entail any similarity-based retrieval features, CARET has a method to carry out similarity-based retrievals using SQL. CARET generates SQL specifications in varying degrees of similarity, and the generated SQL specifications are dispatched to RDBMS to retrieve cases from RDB (Figure 4).

Case and Schema Representation

Cases are represented as a flat record of n-ary relations, as shown in Figure 5. Each record has a corresponding record which holds schema indices. The similarities between values in individual attributes for a case record are defined using an attribute hierarchy, as shown in Figure 6. These attribute hierarchies are defined by domain experts.

Schemata are also stored in RDBMS. Figure 7 shows schema representations. A schema has two layer struc-

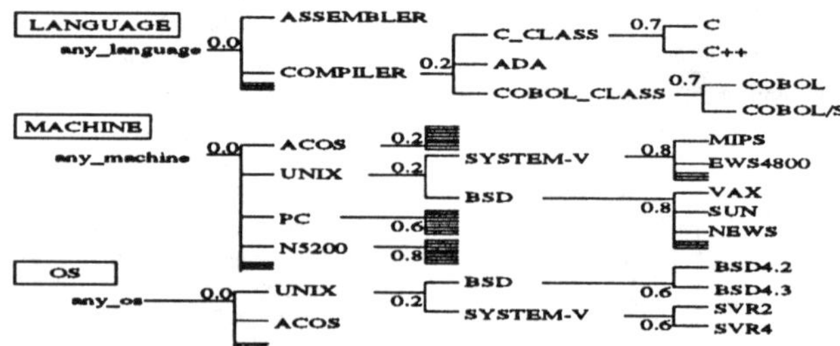

Figure 6: Attribute Hierarchy Example

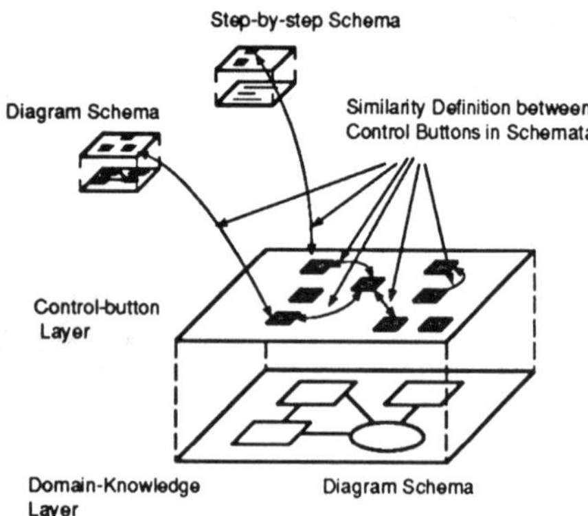

Figure 7: Schema Representation

	Attribute Specification		Control Button Specification in Schema
Attribute/Schema Weight Balance	0. 5		0. 5
Attribute Weight	0.3	0.4	
Attribute	Language	OS	Control Button in Schema
User Specification	C++	BSD4.2	Control Button-14
1st NVS/NBS	C++ (1.0)	BSD4.2 (1.0)	Control Button-14 (1.0)
2ndNVS/NBS	C (0.7) (0.7)	BSD4.3 (0.6)	[Control Button-72, Control Button-73] (0.8)
3rdNVS/NBS	[ADA, COBOL, COBOL/S] (0.2)	[SVR2, SVR4, ...] (0.2)	

Figure 8: An Example showing Possible NVS/NBS Combinations

tures; the domain-knowledge layer and the control-button layer. Steps in a step-by-step schema, diagrams for a diagram schema, and a physical appearance image of a physical-appearance schema are drawn in the domain-knowledge layer as background image data. The control-button layer holds control buttons, which overlap on the background image and are pointed-and-clicked when retrieving and storing cases. Control buttons should be allocated at positions where users may point as problem points. Similarity values between control buttons in schemata are stored in the control-button table. This representation is similar to Hypercard (Goodman 1988), except that control buttons can be defined their similarities values.

Similarity Assessment Algorithm

This section describes the CARET enhanced similarity assessment algorithm.

Step1: Creating NVSs and NBSs A user specifies attributes and values representing the problem, invokes a specific schema on the display, and points-and-clicks one or a few control buttons on the displayed schema.

(1) Neighbor Value Sets For each user specified attribute, CARET refers to the abstraction hierarchies, as shown in Figure 6, to generate a set of values neighboring the user specified value. For example, assume that the user specified C++ as a value for the **Language**

attribute, C++ is an element in *the first-order neighbor value set (1st-NVS)*. C is an element in *the second-order neighbor value set (2nd-NVS)*. ADA, COBOL and COBOL/S are elements in *the third-order neighbor value set (3rd-NVS)*.

(2) Neighbor Control Button Sets For each user specified control button in a schema, CARET refers to the control-button table, as shown in Figure 5, to generate a set of control buttons neighboring the user specified control button. For example, assume that the user specified Control Button14, Control Button14 is an element in *the first-order neighbor control button set (1st-NBS)*. Control Button72 and Control Button73 are elements in *the second-order neighbor control button set (2nd-NBS)*.

Step2: Enumerating the Combinations Next, all possible neighbor value/control button combinations are created from the n-th order neighbor value/control button sets. Figure 8 illustrates how such combinations are created. This example assumes that the user specified values for attribute **Language** and OS, and **Control Button14** in a schema. All value combinations under attribute **Language** and OS, and **Control Button14** will be created. In this example, 18 combinations ($3 \times 3 \times 2$) are generated. Each combination of NVS/NBSs becomes the seed for SQL specifications.

Step3: Calculating Similarity Value for Each Combination For each combination, a similarity value is calculated using similarity between the user specified values/control buttons and those in each combination created in the previous stage. The calculation is similar to that for the weighted nearest neighbor, except that not all attributes are involved. The CARET algorithm does not compute any attributes not specified by the user. Whether the user specified the attribute or not is shown in a mask matrix (M), which is a one-dimension matrix whose size is equivalent to the case-base degree. The matrix element M_i will be 1, if the user specified the value for the attribute i. Otherwise, M_i will be 0. $S(Q, F)$, the similarity between a query(Q) and a NVS/NBS combination (F) is the weighted sum of the attribute part similarity, $S_a(Q, F)$ and the schema part similarity, $S_s(Q, F)$.

$$S(Q, F) = \frac{W_a \times S_a(Q, F) + W_s \times S_s(Q, F)}{W_a + W_s} \quad (2)$$

$$S_a(Q, F) = \frac{\sum_{i=1}^{n} M_i \times W_i \times s(Q_i, F_i)}{\sum_{i=1}^{n} M_i \times W_i} \quad (3)$$

$$S_s(Q, F) = \frac{\sum_{j=1}^{m} s(Q_j, F_j)}{m} \quad (4)$$

Where $s(Q_i, F_i)$ in $S_a(Q, F)$ is similarity between the i-th attribute value for a query (Q) and that for a combination (F), m in $S_s(Q, F)$ is the number of specified control buttons in a schema, and $s(Q_j, F_j)$ is the similarity between the j-th control button for a query (Q) and that for a combination (F). W_i, W_a and W_s are entered manually by domain experts. For example, the similarity of a combination, (["C"],["BSD4.3"], ["Control Button72, Control Button73"] to the user's query specification is 0.72 by the following calculation:

$$S_a(Q, F) = \frac{0.3 \times 0.7 + 0.4 \times 0.6}{0.3 + 0.4} = 0.64 \quad (5)$$

$$S_s(Q, F) = \frac{0.8}{1} = 0.8 \quad (6)$$

$$S_t(Q, F) = \frac{0.5 \times 0.64 + 0.5 \times 0.8}{0.5 + 0.5} = 0.72 \quad (7)$$

Step4: Generating SQL Specifications Each individual combination is translated into a corresponding SQL specification. Since SQL does not involve the similarity measure, the value assigned in the previous process is stored in CARET, and is referred to when the query results are returned. The only SQL expression type used here is the SELECT-FROM-WHERE type. For example, the combination example shown in the previous step is translated into the following SQL specification:

```
SELECT * FROM case_table, schema_table
WHERE language = 'C'  and OS = 'BSD4.3' and
  button in ('Control Button72', 'Control Button73')
  and  case_table.case_id = schema_table.case_id;
```

Empirical Results

Although several on-going projects (Kitano *et al.* 1992) employ the tools described in this paper, an empirical result is reported on the effectiveness of the proposed interface using a help desk support system

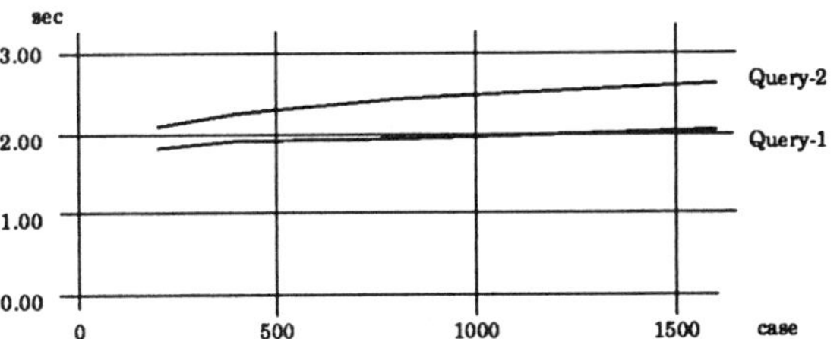

Figure 10: Case-Base Retrieval Time

applied for personal electronic mail service. Figure 9 shows some of the customer inquiries among several hundred cases stored in the case-base, also indicated is the result of a subjective evaluation, to compare if individual inquiries were effectively retrieved by diagram schemata, step-by-step schemata, and conventional keyword search-based retrieval. Cases were obtained from NEC internal publications and were complemented by an engineer from the service support team.

Goal-plan questions are effectively retrieved using diagram schemata, because customer explanations tend to refer to the internal models of the domain when they cannot find concrete action sequences, although their goals are concrete. Since symptoms-cause-recover questions are straightforward, they are easily handled using step-by-step schemata. However, unfortunately, customer inquiries exist, for which neither step-by-step schemata nor diagram schemata can retrieve appropriate cases effectively. Many of them are context free inquiries and the symptom causes are not related to the present context; for example, for the inquiry, "Suddenly I could not move my cursor", the reason is keyboard cable disconnection.

The CARET performance on commercial RDBMS has attained a practically acceptable speed. The experiments were carried out on SUN Sparc Station 2, using ORACLE version 6 installed on SunOS version 4.1.2. Figure 10 shows the response times measured for typical user queries. The average response time for a query is about 2.0 seconds.

Related Work

The interface proposed in this paper addresses a major situation assessment problem (Kolodner 1993). A number of other CBR researches have addressed the problem. CYRUS (Kolodner 1984) was the first system to address this problem. CASEY (Koton 1988) bridges inferences before attempting retrieval and using evidence heuristics to bridge further differences in descriptions during matching. ANON (Owens 1988) introduced proverbs for matching abstract characterizations of situations. CASCADE (Simoudis 1992) uses model-based validation. All the systems presented above utilize significant domain-specific knowledge for similarity assessment. On the other hand, CARET

Goal-Plan Questions	Diagram	Step-by-step	Keyword
"How can I transfer data files in email?"	Good		Moderate
"How can I up-load file in my FD?"	Good		Moderate
"Is there a max size of an email body?"	Good	Moderate	Moderate
"Can I output my email to FAX?"	Good		Moderate
"How can I down-load email content?"	Good	Good	Moderate

Symptom-Cause-Recover Questions	Diagram	Step-by-step	Keyword
"While up-loading, CR does not work"	Good	Good	Moderate
"While writing body, can I add receiver?"	Moderate	Good	
"Arrived email includes noise"	Moderate	Good	Moderate
"After up-loading, the cursor is lost"		Good	

Figure 9: Subjective Comparisons for Schema Applicability to Cases

solves this problem for interactive case-based systems by treating it as a user interface problem – providing the user with several ways of describing a new situation and providing bridges between the user's and the system's possibly different points of view.

Several case-based help desk systems have been built and are being used. CLAVIER (Hennessy and Hinkle 1992) helps a user to configure the layout of composite airplane parts for curing in an autoclave. CAS-CADE (Simoudis 1992) suggests how a user recovers from VMS crashes. These systems are not required rapid case retrieval/store interface. The Compaq SMART system (Acorn and Walden 1992) using CasePoint (Inference 1993) and GE's help desk system using Cognitive System's ReMind (Kriegsman and Barletta 1993) both achieved rapid case retrievals. These systems use natural language for expressing customer-initiated situation descriptions. CARET, instead, provides schemata as a framework for situation assessment under customer-initiated dialogues.

Conclusion

This paper has described a case-based retrieval interface adapted to customer-initiated dialogues in help desk operations. Using the interface, customer service operators can respond rapidly to customer-initiated inquiries, retrieving/storing case data from/into a casebase.

A case is indexed with a schema and one or a few nearmiss points between the schema and the case. The proposed interface provides three schema types, step-by-step schema, diagram schema, and physical-appearance schema. These schemata are used as several ways of describing a new situation and providing bridges between the user's and the system's possibly different points of view.

The proposed interface and the similarity assessment algorithm have been implemented in the CARET case-based retrieval tool operating on commercial RDBMS.

References

ANSI Database Language SQL with Integrity Enhancement. 1989. ANSI X3.135.1-1989.

Chamberlin, D.D., et al., 1976. SEQUEL2: A Unified Approach to Data Definition, Manipulation, and Control. IBM J. Res. Develop.

Acorn, T.L., and Walden, S.H., 1992. SMART: Support Management Automated Reasoning Technology for Compaq Customer Service, In *Proceedings of IAAI-92*

Goodman, D., 1988. HYPERCARD DEVELOPER'S GUIDE, Bantam Books

Hennessy, D.H., and Hinkle, D., 1992. Applying case-based reasoning to autoclave loading, In *IEEE Expert*, October 1992.

Inference Corporation, 1993. CBR Express and Case-Point: Product Introduction, Presentation slides for NDS Customers, Tokyo

Kitano, H., Shibata, A., Shimazu, H., Kajihara J., Sato, A., 1992. Building Large-Scale Corporate-Wide Case-Based Systems: Integration of Organizational and Machine Executable Algorithms. In *Proceedings of AAAI-92*

Kolodner, J., 1984. Retrieval and organizational strategies in conceptual memory: A computer model. Lawrence Erlbaum Associates, Hillsdale, NJ.

Kolodner, J., 1993. Case-Based Reasoning, Morgan Kaufmann, San Mateo, CA.

Koton, P., 1988. Reasoning about evidence in causal explanation, In *Proceedings of AAAI-88*

Kriegsman, M, and Barletta R., 1993. Building a Case-Based Help Desk Application, In *IEEE Expert*, December 1993.

Oracle, 1989. Database Administrator's Guide. and other ORACLE manuals. Oracle Corporation

Owens, C., 1988. Indexing and Retrieving Abstract Cases, In *Proceedings of Case-Based Reasoning Workshop*, AAAI-88

Schank, R., and Abelson, R.P., 1977. Scripts, Plans, Goals, and Understanding, Erlbaum, Hillsdale, N.J.

Shimazu, H., Kitano, H., and Shibata, A., 1993. Retrieving Cases from Relational DataBase: Another Stride Towards Corporate-Wide Case-Based Systems, In *Proceedings of IJCAI-93*

Simoudis, E., 1992. Using Case-Based Retrieval for Customer Technical Support, In *IEEE Expert*, October 1992.

Knowledge Bases

Knowledge Refinement in a Reflective Architecture

Yolanda Gil

USC/Information Sciences Institute
4676 Admiralty Way
Marina del Rey, CA 90292
gil@isi.edu

Abstract

A knowledge acquisition tool should provide a user with maximum guidance in extending and debugging a knowledge base, by preventing inconsistencies and knowledge gaps that may arise inadvertently. Most current acquisition tools are not very flexible in that they are built for a predetermined inference structure or problem-solving mechanism, and the guidance they provide is specific to that inference structure and hard-coded by their designer. This paper focuses on EXPECT, a reflective architecture that supports knowledge acquisition based on an explicit analysis of the structure of a knowledge-based system, rather than on a fixed set of acquisition guidelines. EXPECT's problem solver is tightly integrated with LOOM, a state-of-the-art knowledge representation system. Domain facts and goals are represented declaratively, and the problem solver keeps records of their functionality within the task domain. When the user corrects the system's knowledge, EXPECT tracks any possible implications of this change in the overall system and cooperates with the user to correct any potential problems that may arise. The key to the flexibility of this knowledge acquisition tool is that it adapts its guidance as the knowledge bases evolve in response to changes introduced by the user.

Introduction

The knowledge about a task is not a collection of isolated information packets but rather a carefully constructed web of facts, data, and procedures. The details of how knowledge is organized and how it interacts may be unknown to the user and often hard to keep track of. The key to knowledge acquisition is thus not in supporting the addition of more items to the collection, but in ensuring harmonious interactions between new and existing knowledge and preventing redundancies, inconsistencies, and knowledge gaps that may arise inadvertently.

Most tools for knowledge acquisition achieve this by having expectations about how each piece of knowledge fits in the overall system (Marcus & McDermott 1989; Musen 1989; Kahn, Nowlan, & McDermott 1985). For example, systems for classification tasks need knowledge for mapping inputs into classes. When the user enters a new class, their acquisition tools always expect to be given knowledge about how to assign an input to that new class. Having these expectations is very useful to support knowledge acquisition in that they allow the system to ensure that changes are introduced by the user in a harmonious way. However, since each tool is designed for a specific type of task, the expectations are hard-coded in the tool. This limits a tool's flexibility, since applications often do not conform exactly to the type of task that a tool was designed for and multiple problem-solving approaches may be required within a given application. In addition, it is hard to determine beforehand the type of problem-solving method that is needed for a new application.

The goal of the EXPECT project is to build tools for knowledge refinement that are both flexible and supportive to the user. EXPECT forms dynamic expectations based on the current knowledge of the system by understanding the content of the knowledge bases and their interactions. These expectations are not hard-coded in the knowledge acquisition tool; instead, they are explicitly created by the system when needed. The key to this goal is a *reflective* architecture, i.e., a system that has the ability to introspect and determine exactly what every piece of knowledge, old and new, contributes to the task.

EXPECT's architecture is reflective because it represents and manipulates many different types of knowledge distinctly and explicitly. Factual domain knowledge about a task (e.g., descriptions, relations, and definitions) is represented in LOOM (MacGregor 1988; 1991), a state-of-the-art knowledge representation system of the KL-ONE family. Problem-solving knowledge is represented in a procedural-style language that allows subgoal posting, control programming constructs, and expressive parameter typing. EXPECT captures the semantics of goals by translating them into LOOM concepts. The problem solver uses this representation to reason about actions and their relation to concepts and instances in the domain. By representing each type of knowledge declaratively and supporting interrelationships between them, EXPECT has access to better understanding about the task than other architectures may have.

This paper begins with an overview of EXPECT's architecture and its knowledge acquisition tool. Next we describe how a user interacts with the knowledge acquisition tool to change the knowledge initially given to the system, taking examples from an application that evaluates transportation plans. The paper continues with a discussion of how EXPECT relates to other relevant work on knowledge acquisition. Finally, we present our plans for future work and a conclusion.

The EXPECT Architecture

EXPECT builds on previous research on the Explainable Expert System (EES) project (Neches, Swartout, & Moore 1985; Swartout, Paris, & Moore 1991). EXPECT's architecture is designed to provide an understanding of how each piece of information in a knowledge-based system contributes to solving a task. This understanding comes from various features of the architecture that we describe briefly in this section.

Figure 1 shows an overview of EXPECT's architecture. In EXPECT, any information necessary to perform a task is represented distinctly according to its nature either as domain facts or as problem-solving knowledge. Domain facts are represented in LOOM (MacGregor 1988; 1991). LOOM provides a descriptive logic representation language and includes a classifier for inference. Problem-solving knowledge is expressed as EXPECT's methods. A method in EXPECT is an abstract and generic description of how a goal can be achieved including the goal, a method body that describes the procedure to achieve that goal, and the result that the method is expected to return. The goal of each method is also represented in LOOM, referring to the concepts and instances that appear in the parameter list.

Figure 2 shows an example of EXPECT's representation of factual and problem-solving knowledge in a transportation domain. The first expression specifies that seaport is a kind of port with ships, berths, covered storage area, and piers. The second expression is a very simple method to find the seaports of a location by retrieving the value of the r-seaports relation of the location. The last expression in the figure is a more complex method to determine whether a ship fits in a seaport. Beside relations, the method body can contain subgoals which can be combined using control structures such as conditional and iteration statements. The methods shown here are domain-specific, but domain-independent generic methods can be expressed with this same language.

In order to ensure coherence among the various types of knowledge, the problem solver uses the factual and problem-solving knowledge sources to perform a static analysis of a given top-level goal, recording how each piece of knowledge contributes to the problem-solving process. EXPECT employs the reasoning capabilities of LOOM augmented with goal refinement and reformulation as follows. EXPECT's analysis is effectively a partial evaluation of the given top-level goal. If no method is found to achieve a posted goal, the goal is reformulated using the factual domain knowledge into a set of subgoals that can be achieved. For example, if there is no method to find the speed of a ship and three types of ships are described in the domain knowledge, the system will reformulate this goal into three subgoals and look for a method to find the speed of each of the three types of ship. This analysis provides the

knowledge acquisition tool with an understanding of both the functionality and the nature of all the information used for the task.

Another important source of understanding is the tight integration of the problem solver with the LOOM classifier. In addition to classes and instances, EXPECT represents in LOOM all the goals that arise during problem solving and matches goals and methods based on their semantics using LOOM's classifier. EXPECT's matcher can find methods to achieve a posted goal taking into account the semantic definitions of their respective arguments. Any goal (i.e., a posted subgoal or a goal that a method achieves) is represented as a concept. For example, the LOOM definition of the goal achieved by the method find-seaports (shown in Figure 2) is:

```
(defconcept goal-concept--find-seaports
  :is (and goal-concept FIND
        (the OBJ
            (and instance-set seaport))
        (the OF
            (and instance-description location))))
```

The matcher finds the type of the most general bindings for variables that can be used to unify a posted goal and the goal that a method can achieve. The goal's arguments may be given in any order, because the matcher maps arguments according to their names.

In EXPECT, problem-solving errors also provide useful information for knowledge acquisition. Errors (or simply anything that the system is not sure about and would like the user to check) may come from the parser, the matcher, or the static analyzer. Instead of interrupting problem solving when an error arises, the system takes it as a need for the knowledge acquisition module to request the user's intervention. The problem solver reasons about these errors and provides detailed information to the knowledge acquisition tool that is crucial to support the user in correcting them, as we show in the next section.

In summary, the facility to relate all the different sources of knowledge in the system and capture their influence in the system's behavior enables EXPECT's knowledge acquisition tool to support the user in changing the system's knowledge.

Knowledge Acquisition in EXPECT

EXPECT's knowledge acquisition module is invoked any time that errors in the knowledge bases are encountered during problem solving. Besides errors, the problem solver also signals possible problems that may result from a user's changes to the knowledge base. The user may not always foresee these possible problems, so the system takes the responsibility to track them. We consider them possible *lapses* on the part of the user, and they are added to an *agenda* of items that require user intervention. For example, if the user adds a new method that achieves the same goal as a method that already exists, the system detects this and notifies the user. Lapses are not necessarily errors, often they reflect things that the system brings to the user's attention and can be dismissed by the user after giving them consideration. The system bases the agenda's requests on information that

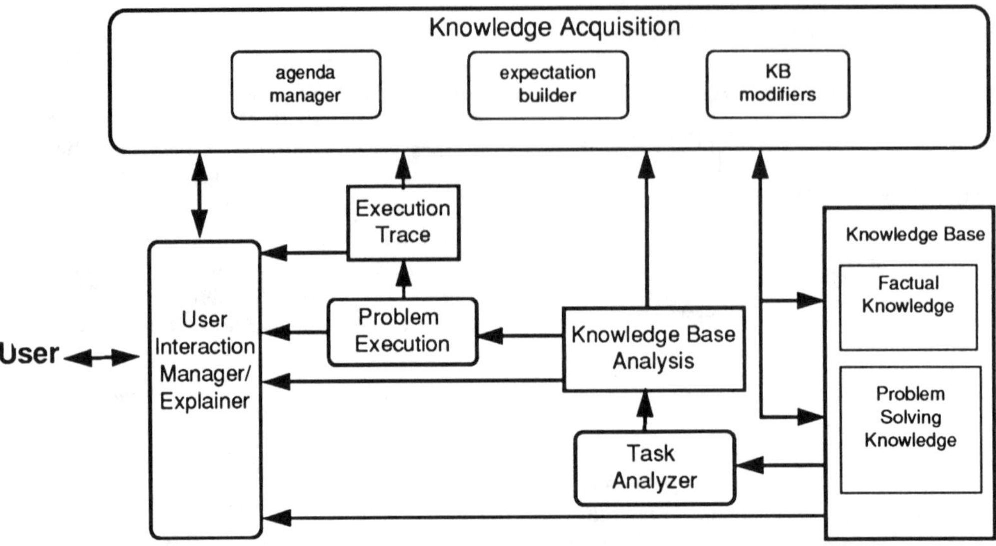

Figure 1: A schematic representation of EXPECT's architecture.

```
(defconcept SEAPORT
  :is-primitive port
  :constraints (and (some r-ships ship)
                    (some r-berths berth)
                    (some r-covered-storage-area number)
                    (some r-piers number)))

(defmethod FIND-SEAPORTS
  :goal         (find (obj ?s is (set-of (inst-of seaport)))
                      (of (?loc is (inst-of location)))))
  :result       (set-of (inst-of seaport))
  :method-body  (r-seaports ?loc))

(defmethod DETERMINE-WHETHER-SHIP-FITS-IN-SEAPORT
  :goal         (determine-whether
                    (obj (?ship is (inst-of ship)))
                    (fits-in (?port is (inst-of seaport))))
  :result       (inst-of boolean)
  :method-body  (less (obj (r-length ?ship))
                    (than (compute-max (obj (spec-of length))
                                       (of (set-of (spec-of berth)))
                                       (in ?port)))))
```

Figure 2: Factual and problem-solving knowledge in EXPECT.

is actually needed for problem solving, and as a result the user is not bothered with unnecessary interventions.

EXPECT has a catalog of possible types of lapses together with possible actions that the user may be suggested to take in order to correct each type of lapse. The information about lapses is explicitly represented, and we find it is very useful as a means for the problem solver to provide feedback to the knowledge acquisition tool regarding the status of the current knowledge base.

Figure 3 shows a snapshot of EXPECT's user interface. It allows the user to examine the content of the knowledge bases and navigate through problem-solving episodes to understand how the system achieves the task goals. The left side of the screen is showing the problem-solving tree and the right side the current items pending on the agenda. In this snapshot, the user had asked for a description of the instance Los Angeles, which caused the smaller window in the lower right corner to pop up. In the description of Los Angeles, the system indicates that it is a location and that additional information about the seaports of Los Angeles is needed in order to use this instance for problem solving. EXPECT knows that this is needed because it is used in the method to find the seaports of a location shown in Figure 2. Notice that this request is also an item on the agenda (the second one).

The user can interact with the system to resolve items on the agenda, or take the initiative to add new knowledge or change the knowledge already in the system. EXPECT analyzes how any change introduced by the user affects the problem solving required for the task, and tries to detect any negative consequences provoked by the change. These also raise lapses that are included in the user's agenda. The knowledge acquisition tool can be used to correct and extend the problem-solving knowledge as well as the factual knowledge. Table 1 summarizes the analysis that EXPECT performs for every modification done by the user. The next sections describe with examples how this analysis supports the knowledge acquisition process.

Adding New Instances

Suppose that the user wants to add a new instance. He or she selects the menu to add a new instance, and types:

Name: Long Beach
Type: port

When a new instance is defined, EXPECT checks that the type given is specific enough. In this case, the type is port, whose subtypes are airport and seaport. The problem solver's analysis of the task shows that the system needs to know the ships available at a seaport. This is an indication for the knowledge acquisition tool that it is important to know if Long Beach is a seaport. Thus, EXPECT requires the user to be more specific about the type of port that Long Beach is. The user is shown the subtypes of port and is asked to pick among them. If the user does not know this information, EXPECT will accept port, but will place an item on the agenda to remind the user to provide this information

when it becomes available. But let us suppose that the user picks seaport as the type of the Long Beach port.

EXPECT next checks what information is needed for problem solving about this type of instance. One method uses the ships available at a seaport and its berths. So the system asks the user for this information. Again, if this information is not available, EXPECT will place these requests in the agenda.

Now suppose that the user adds a new instance called Los Angeles of type location. This type is specific enough for the problem-solving methods, and the information that they need about locations is what seaports they have. EXPECT includes a new item in the agenda to request this information.

At this point the agenda contains several items, each representing requests for information about the new instances just defined. EXPECT provides the user with specific support for each type of item on the agenda. Consider the item requesting information about the seaports of Los Angeles. If the user clicks on this item, EXPECT pops up a menu with an explanation of why this information is needed (i.e., which methods use this and what they accomplish). The menu also contains possible actions that the user can undertake to resolve this agenda item. In this case, the item requests the value of a role for an instance. EXPECT suggests that the user:

- provide a value

- remove the instance

- modify the method, so it will not need this information.

Based on its underlying knowledge, EXPECT prescribes different solutions for each type of item in the agenda. This information is represented declaratively, and EXPECT uses it to dynamically create suggestions that are specific to the agenda item. In this case, if the user chooses to provide the value Long Beach, then the agenda item will disappear.

This knowledge acquisition dialogue contains several important points. First, the system *understands* how each type of instance is used and provides support for knowledge acquisition based on this understanding. If the methods change and new information about a type of instance is required, the system will realize this and update the agenda accordingly. Second, the user is *insulated from the details* of the implementation because EXPECT keeps track of what information is needed. Third, the agenda makes the dialogue very *flexible*, since the user chooses when to attend to an item raised by the system.

Adding New Problem-Solving Knowledge

EXPECT also allows a user to modify problem-solving knowledge. The user can add more detail to an existing method by inserting steps in the method body, or change a method's goal by adding new parameters or modifying the types of the ones that it currently has. The user can also add new methods as we describe next.

If the user creates the method from scratch, EXPECT can provide little help because it will not have an understanding

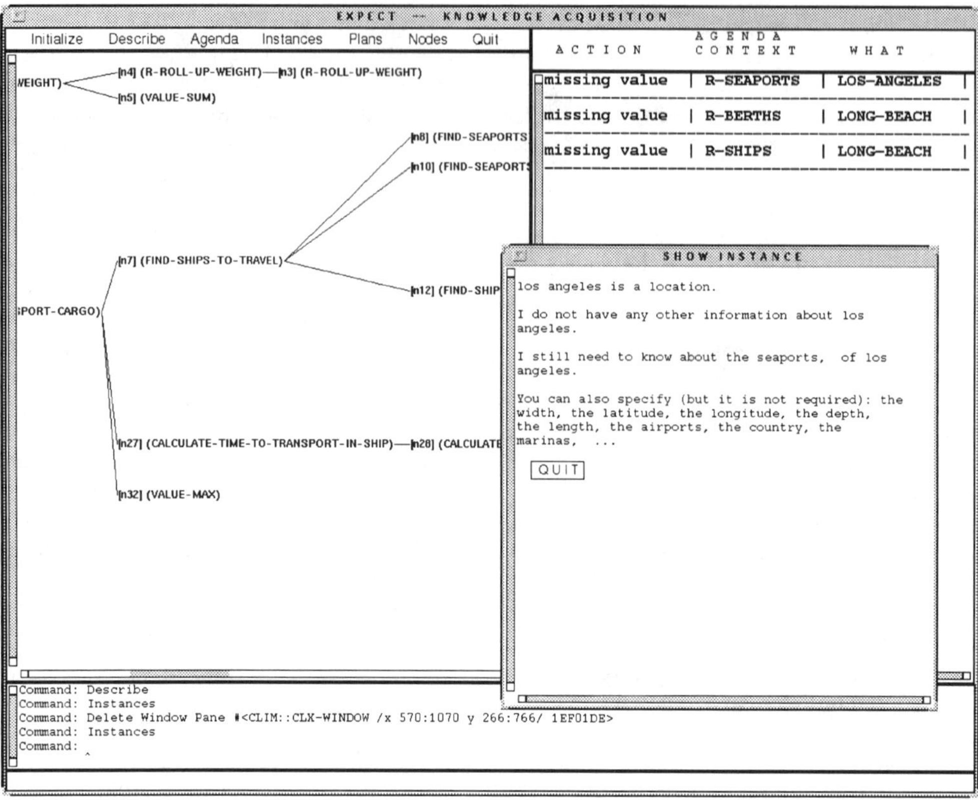

Figure 3: EXPECT's user interface.

When the user adds an instance of a type:

1. If the type given for the instance is more general than the types that are used for problem solving, find more specific types in the knowledge base and ask user to choose one.

2. Look up the roles defined for the instance type. Of those, find which roles are used for problem solving and ask the user for their value.

When the user changes any method:

1. If the new method uses a role of a type that it did not use before, ask user for the value of that role for all the instances of that type.

2. If the new method posts a subgoal, check that there is a method that matches with that subgoal. If not, notify the user.

3. If the new method is not used to achieve any subgoal, notify the user.

4. If the new method has syntactic errors, ask user for corrections.

5. If the new method contains information that is not used for problem solving, notify the user.

Table 1: EXPECT performs a thorough analysis of every modification done by the user.

of this new method until the user is finished with it. Instead, EXPECT encourages the user to *re-use* existing methods in the knowledge base by using them as the basis for new methods. Because EXPECT already understands these methods, it can provide help in adapting them to new uses.

For example, suppose that the user wants to add a method to find the airports of a location. In this case the user indicates that the new method to find airports is similar to the existing method to find seaports (the one shown in Figure 2). EXPECT uses the latter as a model, counting on the user to specify all differences. The user indicates that the relation `r-seaports` has to be changed by `r-airports`, and the concept `seaport` by `airport`.

EXPECT builds a new method with these changes and adds it to the problem-solving knowledge base. Then it checks how the new method affects the rest of the knowledge currently in the system. The same checks are performed if an existing method is modified.

The first check concerns the validity of the new method in itself. This includes looking for syntax errors, inconsistent type passing, and steps in the method whose results are not used. Each lapse detected becomes an item on the agenda.

The second matter that EXPECT checks is how the new method relates to the rest of the methods. EXPECT understands that methods are used to achieve goals, so it will run the static analyzer and make sure that the method is useful and that the subgoals that the method body contains can be achieved by other methods. Again, EXPECT warns the user via the agenda if it finds any problems.

Last, EXPECT checks if the new method needs information about instances that is not currently available. In this case, it realizes that `find-airports` retrieves the value of `r-airports` of instances of type `location` and consequently it adds an item to the agenda to request this value for `Los Angeles`.

The scenario just described clearly follows an analogy process. EXPECT provides a framework for analogical reasoning where the user suggests the source of the analogies, the mapping, and any necessary adaptations, and the tool provides the supporting environment for navigating through the system's reasoning and carrying out the user's corrections through analogical reasoning or any other mechanisms. We are currently extending our system to provide support for finding similar methods using a non-exact matcher as we discuss below. It is important to point out that if the user leaves out anything that is relevant, the analysis that EXPECT performs to check the validity of the new method may detect that this is the case and raise agenda items to be resolved by the user.

Related Work

EXPECT's reflective architecture provides an understanding of the knowledge in the system that can be used to form expectations about any new knowledge being added. Having expectations is be a powerful basis to support knowledge acquisition. TEIRESIAS (Davis 1980) used statistical techniques to form expectations about what terms were likely to co-occur. More recent tools, such as SALT (Marcus & McDermott 1989), PROTEGE (Musen 1989), and MORE (Kahn, Nowlan, & McDermott 1985), are built for a specific inference structure (e.g., classification) and expect their knowledge base to be populated with information useful for that type of task (Chandrasekaran 1986; McDermott 1988). However, since their expectations are hard-coded, these tools do not provide much flexibility (Musen 1992). The problem-solving structure of an application cannot always be defined in domain-independent terms. Furthermore, these method-specific inference mechanisms may not address some of the particulars of an application simply because they were designed with generality in mind. Another problem with the method-specific knowledge acquisition tools is that they raise the non-trivial issue of determining a library of possible methods. The work involved in handcrafting such a library of methods, making sure to both provide wide-coverage of tasks and well-understood characterizations of the inference capabilities of each method, is daunting.

To address these limitations, some researchers (Klinker *et al.* 1991; Puerta *et al.* 1992) are developing libraries of problem-solving methods that handle finer-grained inference structures than the ones above. These approaches provide more flexibility in building a knowledge-based system, and we share their belief that this is a step in the right direction. EXPECT's expectations are as fine-grained as the user's definitions. They are not hard coded, and are based on understanding each piece of knowledge both individually and in conjunction with others. EXPECT can be applied to tasks with any kind of inference structure.

NEODISCIPLE (Tecuci 1992) integrates several machine learning techniques in a knowledge acquisition tool. NEODISCIPLE takes a user-given answer to a problem and applies explanation-based learning to build a plausible proof tree, abduction to complete the proof, and several other learning techniques to generalize the proof. Its predecessor, DISCIPLE (Tecuci & Kodratoff 1990), built an analogy with an existing proof when the system lacked domain knowledge to build the proof for a new input. Our approach automates different parts of the analogical process. The user suggests the source of the analogies, the mapping, and any necessary adaptations. Our tool provides support for carrying it out, checking the validity of the new knowledge, and examining its effects in the current knowledge bases.

Discussion

We plan to extend EXPECT's reflectiveness in two main directions. One is to improve the understanding of goals through a relaxed semantic matcher, and the other is to extend the current representation of agenda items to provide more comprehensive support for the knowledge acquisition tool.

We have extended EXPECT's semantic matcher to find non-exact matches of methods and goals. By dropping parts of the definition of the goals, this relaxed matcher effectively does a partial unification. The relaxed matcher may propose a method that has five parameters that match exactly five of the six parameters of a posted goal. If a goal's parameter is of a certain type and no methods are found that match exactly, the relaxed matcher may propose a method that applies to a more specific type or to another subtype of the same direct supertype. The relaxed matcher can also describe what relaxations yielded the retrieved method. We plan to use this relaxed matcher in our knowledge acquisition tool for several purposes. One is to suggest model methods when the user creates a new method (as in the `find-airports` example). Another possible use is in suggesting concrete solutions to agenda errors. For example, if no method is found to achieve a goal the system may suggest to use a method found by the relaxed matcher and indicate how to reduce their differences.

When EXPECT checks the effects in the knowledge bases of any change introduced by the user, the agenda reflects any possible lapses that may arise. Each type of item on the agenda is associated with a set of possible remedies that the system can suggest to the user to resolve the item. All of this information is explicit in the knowledge acquisition tool. We plan to categorize in more detail the possible lapses that may occur during knowledge acquisition, their relevance to the task at hand, and the possible actions to resolve them. For example, an item that signals that no method is available to achieve a frequently occurring goal is crucial, while an item requiring information on a location that is never used may be dismissed by the user. This categorization would allow the user to identify coherent states of the knowledge base during the knowledge acquisition process, when the system is ready for solving the task and can solve problems with an improved version of the knowledge base. Lapse categorization would also allow better management of the agenda through a priority mechanism based on the relevance of agenda items.

Conclusion

We have presented EXPECT, a reflective architecture for knowledge refinement that derives a rich representation of the functionality of each piece of knowledge about a task. The knowledge acquisition tool uses this functionality to reason about knowledge interactions and support the user in changing the knowledge base. This makes EXPECT independent of the problem-solving method of the task, a key feature that distinguishes our approach from current knowledge acquisition tools.

Acknowledgments

The author would like to thank current and previous members of the EXPECT group, in particular Pedro Gonzalez, Bing Leng, Vibhu Mittal, Cécile Paris, Ramesh Patil, Bill Swartout, and Marcelo Tallis. The clarity of this paper was improved thanks to comments from Eduard Hovy, Kevin Knight, Bill Swartout, and the anonymous reviewers. We gratefully acknowledge the support of the Advanced Research Projects Agency under contract no. DABT63-91-C-0025. The view and conclusions contained in this document are those of the authors and should not be interpreted as representing the official policies, either expressed or implied, of ARPA or the U.S. Government.

References

Chandrasekaran, B. 1986. Generic tasks in knowledge-based reasoning: High-level building blocks for expert system design. *IEEE Expert* 1(3):23–30.

Davis, R. 1980. *Knowledge-based systems in artificial intelligence*. New York, NY: McGraw-Hill.

Kahn, G.; Nowlan, S.; and McDermott, J. 1985. Strategies for Knowledge Acquistion. *IEEE Transactions on Pattern Analysis and Machine Intelligence* PAMI-7(5):511–522.

Klinker, G.; Bhola, C.; Dallemagne, G.; Marques, D.; and McDermott, J. 1991. Usable and reusable programming constructs. *Knowledge Acquisition* 3(2):117–135.

MacGregor, R. 1988. A deductive pattern matcher. In *Proceedings of the 1988 Conference on Artificial Intelligence*.

MacGregor, R. 1991. The evolving technology of classification-based knowledge representation systems. In Sowa, J., ed., *Principles of Semantic Networks: Explorations in the Representation of Knowledge*. San Mateo, CA: Morgan Kaufmann.

Marcus, S., and McDermott, J. 1989. SALT: A knowledge acquisition language for propose-and-revise systems. *Artificial Intelligence* 39(1):1–37.

McDermott, J. 1988. Preliminary steps towards a taxonomy of problem-solving methods. In Marcus, S., ed., *Automating Knowledge Acquisition for Knowledge-Based Systems*. Boston, MA: Kluwer Academic Publishers.

Musen, M. A. 1989. Automated support for building and extending expert models. *Machine Learning* 4(3/4):347–375.

Musen, M. A. 1992. Overcoming the limitations of role-limiting methods. *Knowledge Acquisition* 4(2):165–170.

Neches, R.; Swartout, W. R.; and Moore, J. D. 1985. Enhanced maintenance and explanation of expert systems through explicit models of their development. *IEEE Transactions on Software Engineering* SE-11(11):1337–1351.

Puerta, A. R.; Egar, J. W.; Tu, S. W.; and Musen, M. A. 1992. A multiple-method knowledge-acquisition shell for the automatic generation of knowledge-acquisition tools. *Knowledge Acquisition* 4(2):171–196.

Swartout, W. R.; Paris, C. L.; and Moore, J. D. 1991. Design for explainable expert systems. *IEEE Expert* 6(3):58–64.

Tecuci, G., and Kodratoff, Y. 1990. Apprenticeship learning in imperfect domain theories. In *Machine Learning: An Artificial Intelligence Approach*, volume 3. San Mateo, CA: Morgan Kaufmann.

Tecuci, G. D. 1992. Automating knowledge acquisition as extending, updating, and improving a knowledge base. *IEEE transactions on Systems, Man, and Cybernetics* 22(6):1444–1460.

A User Interface for Knowledge Acquisition From Video

Henry Lieberman

Media Laboratory
Massachusetts Institute of Technology
Cambridge, Mass. USA
lieber@media.mit.edu

Abstract

In conventional knowledge acquisition, a *domain expert* interacts with a *knowledge engineer*, who interviews the expert, and codes knowledge about the domain objects and procedures in a rule-based language, or other textual representation language. This indirect methodology can be tedious and error-prone, since the domain expert's verbal descriptions can be inaccurate or incomplete, and the knowledge engineer may not correctly interpret the expert's intent.

We describe a user interface that allows a domain expert who is not a programmer to construct representations of objects and procedures directly from a video of a human performing an example procedure. The domain expert need not be fluent in the underlying representation language, since all interaction is through direct manipulation. Starting from digitized video, the user selects significant frames that illustrate before- and after-states of important operations. Then the user graphically annotates the contents of each selected frame, selecting portions of the image to represent each part, labeling the parts, and indicating part/whole relationships. Finally, programming by demonstration techniques describe the actions that represent the transition between frames. The result is object descriptions for each object in the domain, generalized procedural descriptions, and visual and natural language documentation of the procedure. We illustrate the system in the domain of documentation of operational and maintenance procedures for electrical devices.

Keywords: Graphical annotation, knowledge acquisition, knowledge representation, machine learning, multimedia, natural language generation, programming by example/by demonstration, user interfaces.

Video as a tool for procedural knowledge representation

Conventional expert systems are often hampered by the knowledge acquisition bottleneck: the difficulty of communicating knowledge that a human expert has into computer-readable descriptions. Domain experts may already know how to perform a procedure when presented with a real-world example of the device, but they may not be capable of producing an accurate, complete, well-written description of the procedure, either in natural language, or in the form of frame descriptions and if-then rules. The role of a knowledge engineer is to interview the domain expert and perform the translation into a language that the domain expert typically does not know. However, this is difficult and

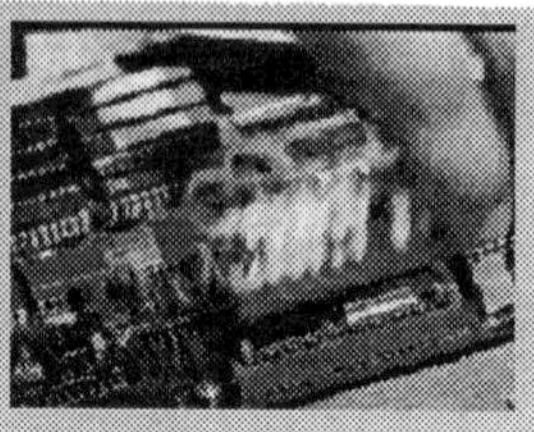

Four frames from a disassembly procedure

unreliable, as the expert can have difficulty verbally expressing the procedure and the knowledge engineer may misinterpret the expert's description. Technical documentation writers and illustrators watch examples and listen to vague descriptions and produce precise, well-written and well-illustrated procedural descriptions that can be understood by a novice.

In both cases, video often plays an important role as a tool to collect the raw data used in constructing the procedural description. The experts are recorded on video, and the resulting video is examined, often in excruciating detail, by those producing the description. It can be helpful to work from video rather than rely on memory or a written description, since it is often awkward to write down or sketch each step while in the midst of performing the procedure. Psychologists, industrial designers, and user interface consultants all make use of videotaped procedures.

With the advent of digital video, it is now possible to provide on-line tools that let the user browse video segments and construct descriptions. Tools can assist in setting up the correspondence between video frames and steps of the procedure, selecting possible descriptions automatically, and providing better feedback that the description actually matches the procedure. The result should be reducing the cost and time required for knowledge acquisition and improving the accuracy of the resulting description.

Machine learning from video demonstrations

Machine learning (Carbonell 90) has extensively studied the problem of inferring general descriptions from specific examples. Most often, these examples are expressed with textual assertions in a formal language or natural language. However, because of the conceptual distance for many users between examples performed in the real world on physical objects and textual descriptions of the examples, much of the work on machine learning has been difficult to apply in the context of interactive interfaces. This has also been a criticism of the *situated action* school (Barwise and Perry 83).

A powerful technique for going from examples to procedural descriptions is *programming by demonstration* or *programming by example*. A compendium of major work on this topic is (Cypher, ed. 93). In this approach, a user demonstrates a procedure in an interactive graphical interface, using concrete visual examples, while a learning mechanism records user actions so that they can be generalized to work on similar examples in the future.

If we imagine that we had already programmed a simulation of a device and the vocabulary of operations for using it, programming by demonstration becomes an excellent tool for producing procedural descriptions. The expert can go through the steps of the procedure on the virtual device, and the system records the descriptions automatically. Examples of this approach appear in (Lieberman 92, 93b).

However, producing the domain-specific representations of the objects and actions in the simulation is expensive and time-consuming, worthwhile if many different procedures are to be performed using the same set of objects and actions, but costly for a single use.

Here, we explore the approach of working directly from a video of the procedure, performed in the real world rather than on virtual objects. But the video itself has no knowledge of where the objects are in the scene or how the actions are to be described. So we require an *annotation* phase, where the author of the description explicitly indicates to the system where the objects are in the video and how the actions are to be described. Graphical annotation (Lieberman 93b) is used to describe objects, and programming by demonstration techniques describe the actions. The system is implemented as an extension to the programming by demonstration system Mondrian (Lieberman 93a).

In the future, computer vision algorithms may be able to automatically detect objects and motion in the video, which would reduce the tedium of the annotation steps. At present, the system uses no visual recognition, but recognition algorithms could be added to the system incrementally, and the user could always retain the option of reverting to explicit description if the vision system guesses incorrectly.

Generality of the approach

The task of generalizing from specific examples is always underconstrained; the learner must assume some bias if nontrivial generalizations are to be learned. For our domain of simple equipment maintenance procedures we have developed an ontology that is roughly characterized as follows.

The procedure learned by the system are applicable to physical *devices*, which are composed of hierarchies of *parts*. Parts may be have specific types, such as switches or fasteners. Each part is represented visually by an image which is a rectangular region of a video frame. There are a set of generic actions which are applicable to devices and parts: assembly and disassembly of parts, opening and closing fasteners, turning on and off switches. In addition, the devices are embedded in a graphical editor with generic cut, copy, and move actions, and relations such as above, below, left and right. The job of the knowledge acquisition phase is to identify device and part hierachies, and specify a sequence of actions upon a device.

The set of actions, objects and relations is extensible. There is an underlying object-oriented protocol for adding new object types, actions, relations and generalizations, which can be used to adapt the video annotation interface to a new domain. The video annotation interface is currently customized for the domain described above, but we have also experimented in other domains. A further development would be to allow extending the domain through graphical interaction in the interface itself.

An example: Describing a disassembly procedure

The illustration above shows four frames from a video of a circuit board disassembly procedure. We use QuickTime digitized video (Apple 93), and the standard QuickTime video browsing tools to let the user peruse and select frames from the video. For each step that the user wishes to describe, he or she must select salient frames that represent the states before and after the relevant action. The system provides a tool that "grabs" the frame from the video.

Identifying objects in the video frame

We'd like to give the user the illusion of interacting with a simulation of the device that is the subject of the procedure. If we were to program such a simulation from scratch, the programmer would produce renderings of each object, and operating on these objects would produce a corresponding change in the renderings to reflect the consequences of the action. But that assumes the underlying model of the device and its structure already exists. In our video annotation world, the purpose of the interaction is exactly to teach the system about the object model of the device. But the video contains only pixels, not a 3D object model. So we "fake" it.

We ask the user to select subsets of the video image to serve as visual representations of the objects. The image objects are embedded in a two-and-a-half dimensional

graphical editor. Operations of the 2.5D graphical editor approximate the effect of true 3D operations.

Objects segmented from a video frame

Of course, this "doesn't work" -- the image boundaries capture unwanted pixels and chop off desired ones, moving an image doesn't properly show occlusion and perspective, etc. But it is only meant to be a visual suggestion of the effect of the operation rather than an accurate portrayal. Like icons, the approximate visual representation can be remarkably effective at times.

In our technical documentation domain, there are certain classes of operations that are quite amenable to this treatment. Many of the procedures are assembly and disassembly procedures. Adjacency of the visual representation of two parts indicates that they are assembled, and the act of separating them by moving one of the parts constitutes disassembly. Many of the operational procedures involve state changes: turning a switch on or off, a dial that can be in any one of a number of states, indicator lights. Such operations are modeled by choosing an image representing each state, and replacing one with another to change state.

Graphical annotation of frames

The next step is to label the images with a description of the objects and their structure. Our approach is to use *graphical annotation* of the image. In hardcopy technical manuals, a common sight is a labeled picture or drawing of an object. The name of each part of the object appears as text, positioned as close as possible to the part that it describes, and with a line or arrow connecting the label to its referent.

Mondrian allows the user to annotate each video frame image. Text and lines are positioned using the ordinary capabilities of the graphical editor. The user can group a set of text labels as a way of indicating that the corresponding parts they label should be considered as parts of a larger structure. Groups of groups can create part/whole hierarchies of arbitrary depth.

Parts annotated with text labels

A simple visual parser relates the text and lines that do the annotation to the images of the parts they annotate. The visual parser maps grouping and containment relations of the graphical objects to part/whole relations on the semantic objects they represent. Our simple parser has a single fixed "visual grammar", but see (Lakin 86) and (Wittenburg and Weitzman 93) for more sophisticated parsing techniques. The annotation aspect of Mondrian is discussed further in (Lieberman 93b).

We use a part/whole graph to give the user visual feedback about the results of the visual parsing process. This consists of a graph whose leaves are the images that represent the parts, and whose non-terminal nodes are the names of the parts and wholes.

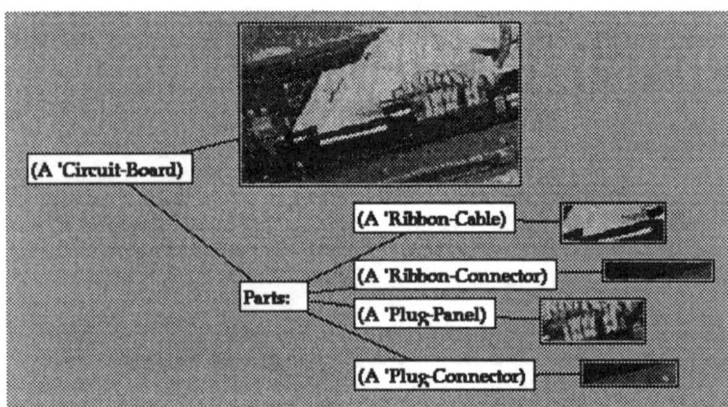

Part/Whole graph

The effect of the annotations is to attach a description to each part that affects how actions involving it are generalized by the programming by demonstration system. By attaching the label "Ribbon Cable" to an image, the description "the Ribbon Cable of the Circuit Board" is attached to that image, by virtue of the part/whole hierarchy. Any operation applying to that image will be generalized as applying to whatever part is identified as the Ribbon Cable in whatever part corresponds to the Circuit Board in subsequent examples.

The text and lines that comprise the annotations are formed into a group as the result of the visual parsing process so they may be deleted or moved as a unit. This will be useful in making it convenient to apply the same set of annotations to a different frame.

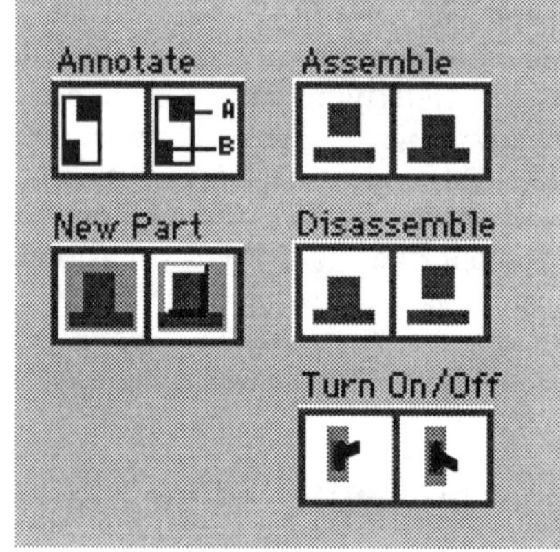

Some operations for image description (left) and repair procedure domain (right)

Descriptions of actions

The next task is to describe the actions that make up the steps of the procedure. Again, since we can't at present detect these transformations using computer vision, we rely on the user to describe the procedural transformation.

Each step consists of an initial state and a final state, represented by selected frames of the video. After annotating the objects in the frame representing the initial state, the user selects a frame to represent the outcome of the operation. To construct a description of the procedure step, the user must use the operations of the graphical editor to transform the initial state to (an approximation of) the final state.

The editor provides both generic operations (Cut, Copy, Paste, Move, ...) and operations specific to the domain (for the repair domain: Assemble, Disassemble, Turn On/Off switches and lights, Open/Close fasteners, etc.). Each operation is represented on-screen by a *domino*, an icon representing a visual example of the operation. The domino has two parts, showing schematized before-and-after states of an example of the operation.

The illustration shows three frames. First, an initial frame, with four annotated objects. In the middle frame, we have applied the Disassemble operation to the object at the upper left, moving it away from its connector. This models the goal frame at the right, where the hands of the technician can be seen disconnecting the cable. The system records a Lisp expression for this step that could be described this way: "Disassemble the Ribbon-Cable of the Circuit-Board from the Ribbon-Connector of the Circuit-Board".

The system tracks the dependencies between operations, so that if the same cable were subsequently connected to another connector, that fact would be noted. If the circuit board appears as the argument to the procedure being defined, the Disassemble operation would be applied to the Ribbon-Cable of whatever Circuit-Board is supplied in the next example.

Once a step of the procedure has been described, we can prepare to describe the next step. To ensure the continuity of the procedure, we need to *transfer* the description of the first initial frame to the next. A priori, the system cannot know which portions of the new image correspond to objects in the new frame, since the objects may have moved, camera angle may have changed, etc.

We provide a couple of conveniences that allow re-use of the annotations already described. First, as a result of the visual parsing of the annotations, the annotation graphics are grouped in the graphical editor, so a set of annotations can be moved as a unit from one frame to the next. The result is likely to be mostly correct, and incorrect annotations can be reconnected.

Second, objects in the new frame can be designated as "replacements" for objects in the original frame that appear as arguments to the procedure being defined, and the parts of the new object are made to correspond to the parts of the old object accordingly. The annotations need not be complete for each frame; only those annotations that are relevant for describing each procedure step need be made.

Using the procedure on a new example

Once a procedure has been recorded, it appears in Mondrian's palette in the same form as Mondrian's built-in operations: as a domino of before and after pictures representing the operation. The before and after pictures are miniaturized frames of the initial and final states of the procedure.

The newly defined operation can then be applied to a new example. Assume we have recorded a two-step procedure that disassembles the ribbon cable assembly and the plug panel assembly. First, we choose a video frame representing the new example. Then, we outline the parts and put annotation labels that represent the input to the procedure.

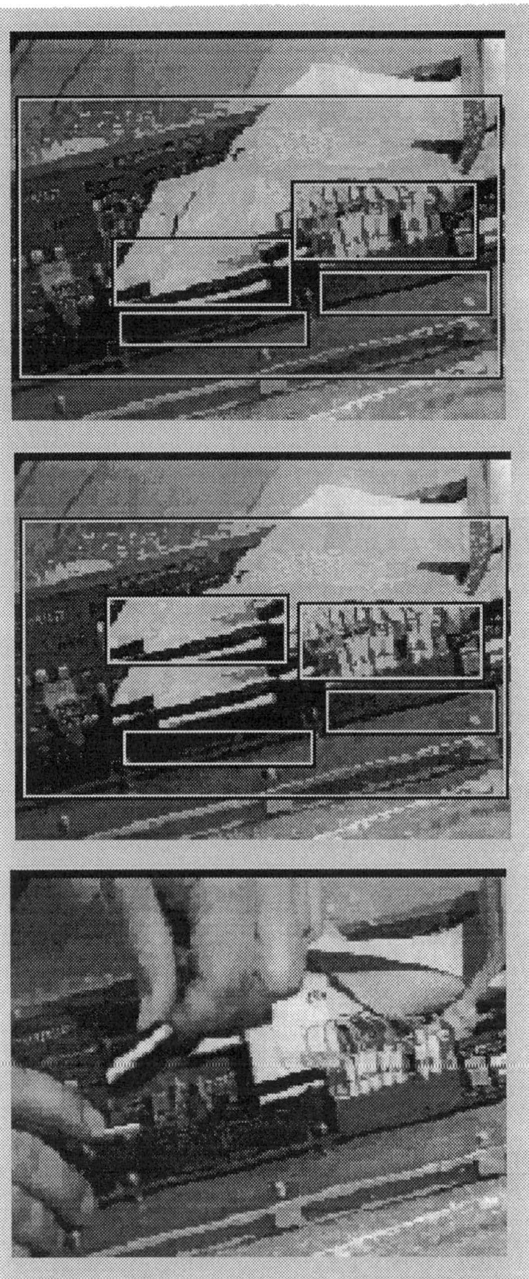

Initial state (top),
after Disassemble operation (middle)
and final state (bottom)

Domino for the new user-defined operation

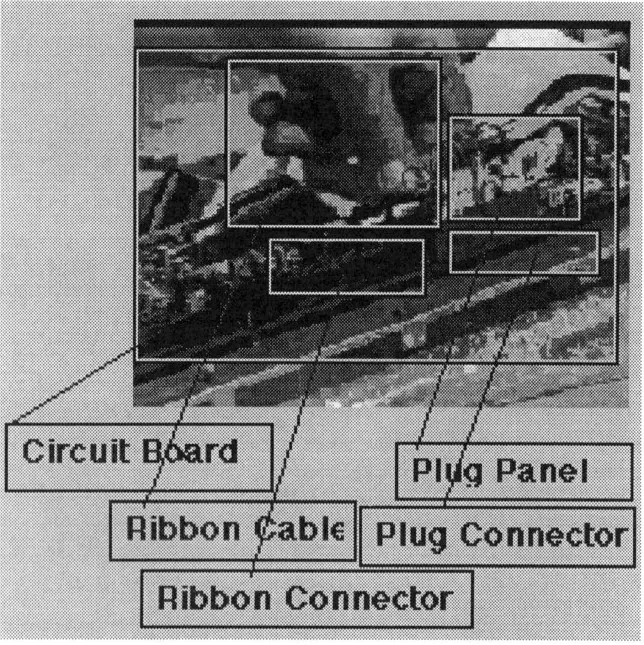

Annotated new example

Now, clicking on the domino for the Disassemble Circuit Board procedure results in performing the disassembly of both parts in the new example.

Mondrian uses an incremental form of explanation-based generalization

The learning method employed by Mondrian had its origin with Tinker (Lieberman 93c) and is similar to the example-based learning technique called *explanation-based generalization* (Mitchell 83). The major difference is the order of "explanations", which is of little theoretical import, but makes a major impact on the usability of this learning technique.

Result of the Disassembly procedure on a new example

Classical explanation-based generalization is a "batch" operation in that the explanation is presented all at once, together with the example. The generalization algorithm produces a generalization from the example and the explanation, which explains to the system "how" the example exemplifies the concept.

The problem with this as a paradigm for interactive construction of generalizations is that the user is, typically, more confident in his or her choice of examples than in the details of explanation steps, or even in the choice of the exact generalization desired. Feedback from the system on the intermediate steps in the construction of a complex explanation is of vital importance. Especially in domains where the examples are graphical, or can be visualized graphically, immediate graphical feedback can be of immense help to the user in deciding how to explain the example to the system in a way that will cause a desired generalization to emerge. It is not uncommon for the user to realize, in the course of explaining an example, that a related alternative generalization is actually more desirable that the one originally envisaged. The presence or absence of appropriate feedback concerning the relationship between the example and the explanation can make the difference between the usability or impracticality of explanation-based techniques in an interactive interface.

The solution is for the user to provide the "explanation", and the system to construct the generalization, incrementally. We can take advantage of the inherent feedback loop of an interactive interface. At each step, the visible state of the screen indicates the current state of the example, and the explanation is provided by invoking one of the interactive operations, by selecting a menu item or icon. Feedback is generated by the redisplay of the screen, indicating the new state of the example.

The programming by demonstration techniques are also related to case-based reasoning (Schank and Riesbeck 91). Case-based reasoning does not require that the examples be "explained", and learns best when there are a large number of examples. In contrast, demonstrational techniques apply best when there are only a small number of examples, and more guidance from the user is available.

Documenting the procedure

We use a graphical storyboard to represent the procedure in the interface. The storyboard consists of a set of saved pictures of each step of the procedure, together with additional information that describes the step: the name of the operation chosen, a miniature icon for the operation, and the selected arguments are highlighted.

The system also captions each frame of the storyboard with an English description of the step. A simple template-based natural language generator "reads the code" to the user by constructing sentences from templates associated with each function and each kind of object.

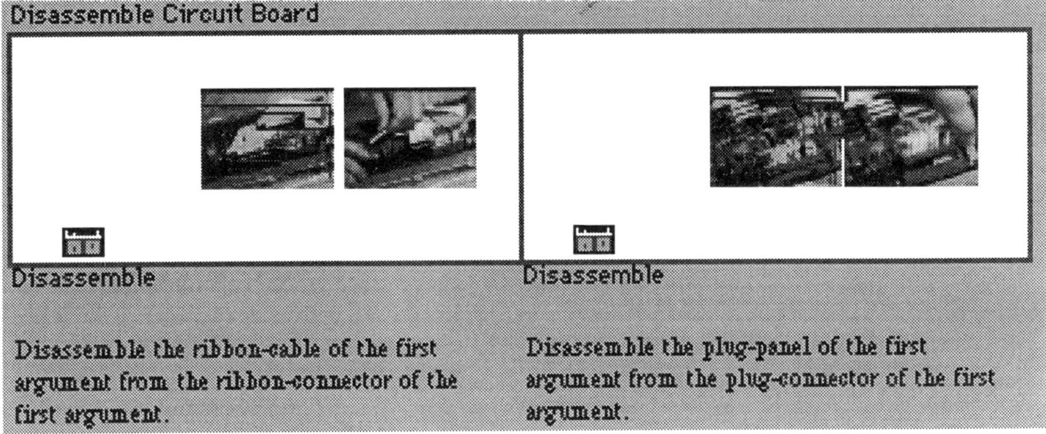

The system can also, optionally, speak the description using a text-to-speech generator. It is useful to have the system use speech to give the user feedback after each operation, so that the user can verify that the system actually is understanding the intended description of each step. Speech is a good modality for providing this feedback, because it does not interfere with the hand-eye coordination of operating the graphical editor.

The storyboard provides a form of automatically generated documentation for the procedure being described. Although this documentation is not equal to the quality of documentation produced by a competent technical documentation staff, it is cheap to produce, and guaranteed not to omit crucial steps.

The role of user interface in machine learning

Machine learning has made great strides (Carbonell 1990), but the dream of a learning machine as a useful intelligent assistant to a human being still seems to remain out of reach. My conjecture for what has held up machine learning is that the field has placed an inordinate amount of emphasis on the technical details of algorithms for the computer's inference processes during learning, be they symbolic or connectionist.

In my view, there has not been enough consideration of the interface issues that arise from interaction between a human user and a computer system with learning capabilities. In human education, effective learning occurs not solely as a result of an optimal presentation method on the part of the teacher, or learning method on the part of the student, but upon an effective teacher-student interaction. A variety of particular presentation strategies might be effective, providing that both the teacher and the student find themselves able to communicate effectively with them, including feedback to verify what has been learned.

Thus the machine learning problem is really one of interaction. The key is to establish an interaction language for which the human teacher finds it easy to convey notions of interest, and at the same time, for which the computer as student is capable of learning the appropriate inferences. The "user-friendliness" of the interaction for the teacher is as important as the logical power of the inference method employed by the student.

There is a trade-off that occurs. More powerful inference mechanisms allow the teacher to present ideas of greater complexity with less input, but at the price that it may be harder for the teacher to understand just how to convey a desired generalization, and it becomes harder for the system to present, in a clear and understandable manner, what it has learned and why.

The human interface questions that these issues raise have largely been ignored in the AI literature. Input to learning systems has been largely through assertions coded in special-purpose languages, or sets of coded examples presented in a "batch" to the system. Perhaps the only exception in the AI literature has been in the domain of Intelligent Tutoring Systems (Sleeman and Brown 82), whose audience of beginning users demands special attention to usability at the outset.

Direct-manipulation graphical interfaces have revolutionized human-computer interfaces to personal computer applications. Yet machine learning AI research has been largely aloof from this revolution, taking a "we'll leave interface issues until later" attitude, to concentrate on formalization of generalization methods. The time has now come to couple advances in machine learning with modern, direct-manipulation graphical interfaces. The inability of machine learning researchers to produce learning systems with interfaces that meet contemporary standards blocks acceptance by a user community and integration into contexts where they will receive practical usage.

The interface community itself is reaching a crisis point. "Feature wars" between software vendors produce ever-more complex interfaces, but that still lack features considered essential by some users. The ability for a user to directly teach the system operations of interest permits an interface to remain uncomplicated for beginning users, and to adapt as the user's expertise grows.

Direct-manipulation interfaces pose special challenges for learning systems. Interpretation of the user's point-and-click behavior is the primary one. A point-and-click interaction should be interpreted by the learning system as the equivalent of an assertion in the world of semantic interest. The system must be able to establish a mapping (which may vary according to context) between the manipulable graphical objects and the semantic objects of the domain. Similarly, a mapping easily understandable by the user must be in effect when the system presents feedback about the result of its learning operations.

Related work

Many projects described in the book on Programming by Demonstration (Cypher, ed. 93) influenced this work, though none consider video as a source. Marc Davis' Media Streams (Davis 93) is a system for doing interactive iconic annotation of video sequences. It produces representations in a frame language, but includes descriptive information only and has no demonstrative component. Interactive visual parsing techniques were introduced in (Lakin 86), and (Weitzman and Wittenburg 93) provides a recent example. APEX (Feiner and McKeown 90) use AI techniques to automatically generate text and graphic documentation of technical procedures.

There has been much work in developing direct-manipulation interfaces to be used in conventional knowledge acquisition (McGraw and Harbison-Briggs 89). Most projects of this sort are box-and-arrow browsers and editors for the knowledge structures produced in a conventional knowledge engineering methodology. They don't use video of the target procedure as a source, and visual representations of concrete examples of procedures generally do not play a significant role.

Conclusion

We have shown how graphical annotation and programming by demonstration techniques can be used to provide a tool for constructing formal descriptions of a procedure from a real-world video of the procedure. In the near term future, we will work on better tools for segmenting the video and annotating other kinds of relationships other than part/whole relations. We could also streamline the process of going from the annotation of one set of frames to the next. More effort could also build up a more complete library of actions, and more flexible tools for the user to introduce new action classes and object states. We could also introduce more heuristics for interpreting action sequences. In the long term, incorporation of computer vision algorithms and perhaps, speech recognition of a simultaneous narration of the procedure, could lead to a highly automated video annotation process.

Acknowledgments

Major support for this work comes from research grants from Alenia Corp., Apple Computer, ARPA/JNIDS and the National Science Foundation. The research was also sponsored in part by grants from Digital Equipment Corp., HP, and NYNEX.

References

Apple Computer, *Inside Macintosh: QuickTime Components*, Addison Wesley/Apple, 1993.

Barwise, Jon and John Perry, *Situations and Attitudes*, MIT Press, 1983.

Cypher, Allen, ed. *Watch What I Do: Programming by Demonstration*, MIT Press, 1993.

Davis, Marc, Media Streams, IEEE Symposium on Visual Languages, Bergen, Norway, August 1993.

Feiner, S. and K. McKeown, Coordinating Text and Graphics in Explanation Generation, Proceedings of AAAI-90, Boston, July 1990.

Lakin, Fred, Spatial Parsing for Visual Languages, in *Visual Languages*, S.K. Chang, T. Ichikawa and P. Ligomenedes, eds., Plenum Press, 1986

Lieberman, Henry and Carl Hewitt, A Session with Tinker, Lisp Conference, Stanford, California, August 1980.

Lieberman, Henry, Capturing Design Expertise by Example, in East-West Conference on Human-Computer Interaction, St. Petersburg, Russia, August 1992.

Lieberman, Henry, Mondrian: A Teachable Graphical Editor, in (Cypher, ed. 93).

Lieberman, Henry, Graphical Annotation as a Visual Language for Specifying Generalization Relations, IEEE Symposium on Visual Languages, Bergen, Norway, August 1993.

Lieberman, Henry, Tinker: A Programming by Demonstration System for Beginning Programmers, in [Cypher, ed. 93].

McGraw and Harbison-Briggs, *Knowledge Acquisition: Principles and Guidelines*, Prentice-Hall, Englewood Cliffs, NJ 1989.

Mitchell, Tom, et al. *Machine Learning, an Artificial Intelligence Approach, I-III*, Morgan Kauffman, 1983.

Schank, Roger and Christopher Riesbeck, *Inside Case-Based Reasoning*, Ablex, 1991.

Sleeman, D., Brown, J.S., eds. *Intelligent Tutoring Systems*, Academic Press, New York 1982.

Weitzman, Louis, and Wittenburg, Kent, Relational Grammars for Interactive Design, 1993 IEEE Workshop on Visual Languages, Bergen, Norway.

BUILDING NON-BRITTLE KNOWLEDGE-ACQUISITION TOOLS

Jay T. Runkel

William P. Birmingham

Electrical Engineering and Computer Science Department
University of Michigan
Ann Arbor, MI
jayr@eecs.umich.edu

Abstract

Existing model-based knowledge-acquisition tools can acquire large knowledge bases and update these knowledge bases as knowledge changes. These tools, however, are brittle. They can only be used to acquire knowledge for a particular problem solver performing a specific task and they are not easily adapted to new problem solvers. Brittleness limits the effectiveness of these tools because the dynamic nature of knowledge systems make modifications both necessary and frequent. This paper presents a model of knowledge systems that reduces brittleness by separating acquisition techniques for search-control knowledge from other types of knowledge, by driving knowledge acquisition from properties of a knowledge-level description of the task instead of the problem solver, and by using ontologies to reuse knowledge bases.

Introduction

Many knowledge systems contain knowledge-acquisition (KA) tools that help knowledge engineers and domain experts build and maintain the system's knowledge base. These tools manage the vast amount of complex and interrelated knowledge necessary to build a knowledge system and automate the process of operationalizing (representing the knowledge in a form that can be used by a problem solver) this knowledge. They exploit a collection of acquisition techniques, which consist of a user interface, a prescribed procedure for using this interface, and a method for operationalizing the acquired knowledge.

One of the most powerful classes of KA tools, called *model-based* KA tools (Birmingham & Klinker 1994), guide acquisition using the problem solver's problem-solving method (McDermott 1988) (PSM), which defines the sequence of problem-solving steps used to find a solution. Since the PSM is an executable procedure, it assumes that the knowledge it uses has certain properties. These properties are the types of knowledge necessary to perform problem solving, called *knowledge structures*, the role of each knowledge structure (*i.e.,* how knowledge will be used during problem solving), and the operationalized

form of knowledge structures (Birmingham & Klinker 1994; Marcus 1988; McDermott 1988).

By exploiting these properties, model-based tools can *direct* the KA process. This direction is achieved by using interfaces customized to acquire knowledge in the form required by the PSM. The customized interfaces combined with the use of domain-specific terminology results in an efficient knowledge-transfer process. Directed dialog helps the tool's user understand exactly what knowledge the tool is asking for, how it relates to previously acquired knowledge, and how the knowledge will be used during problem solving (Marcus 1988; McDermott 1988). This ability to convey the purpose and context of the desired knowledge dramatically reduces the effort required to build a knowledge base (Birmingham & Klinker 1994; Marcus 1988; Musen 1989).

Model-based tools, though powerful, are brittle. Brittleness manifests itself in two ways:

1. Model-based tools cannot be easily adapted to acquire knowledge for new PSMs or tasks.
2. The knowledge bases typically created by these tools cannot be reused by PSMs performing similar tasks.

Brittleness significantly limits a tool's usefulness.

There are two causes of brittleness in model-based tools:

1. *Acquisition techniques are tailored to a particular PSM.* Model-based KA tools gain their acquisition power by tailoring their acquisition techniques to a particular PSM. Such close coupling, while lending power, limits the flexibility of the tools
2. *Failure to separate acquisition techniques for search-control knowledge.* Search-control knowledge, which heuristics makes problem-solving more efficient, is mostly idiosyncratic to a PSM, particularly to the way in which it is encoded. Non-search-control knowledge is mostly constant in a domain across similar types of tasks. Most KA tools fail to separate the acquisition techniques for search-control knowledge from those for other knowledge types making it difficult to update KA tools as PSMs change (with changing tasks). KA tools that acquire search-control knowledge are specific to a PSM, and therefore are brittle.

The key to eliminating the brittleness of model-based tools without sacrificing any acquisition power is to model knowledge systems at the knowledge level (Newell 1981) (KL). The KL describes the task performed by the knowledge system independently of the PSM used to solve it, and can therefore be made free of control knowledge. In addition, the KL defines many of the properties needed for model-based tools: the knowledge structures to be acquired, the relationships among these structures, and the roles the structures play during problem solving. This facilitates the development of model-based KA tools that are not PSM specific. In addition, the knowledge structures identified at the KL form an ontology of the knowledge used to perform a task. Recent experiments with the language Ontolingua (Gruber 1993) have shown that ontologies can be used to facilitate the sharing of knowledge among knowledge systems by providing an intermediate language that can be used by all of them.

The model-based acquisition techniques and ontologies identified at the knowledge level are highly flexible and reusable because they do not contain any search-control knowledge. Since knowledge structures are identified at the KL, they are highly reusable because all problem solvers performing the task use this knowledge. Search-control knowledge, on the other hand, represents the heuristics used by a particular PSM, and is therefore less reusable. Brittleness is avoided by keeping the acquisition techniques and ontology elements for search-control knowledge separate from the techniques and elements identified at the KL. This allows KA tools and knowledge to be easily updated and reused as PSMs and tasks are changed.

In addition, brittleness can be reduced by developing KA tools with a modular architecture, where the acquisition techniques used to acquire each knowledge structure are represented in separate modules. This approach, which is similar to the one take by Protege II (Puerta et al. 1992) and Krest (Steels 1992), simplifies the process of modifying the KA tool whenever changes to the PSM or task are made. An acquisition procedure can be easily replaced with one that is more appropriate.

We have developed a system, called the Domain-Independent Design System (DIDS) (Balkany, Birmingham, & Runkel 1993) that uses these brittleness reduction ideas to generate non-brittle knowledge systems. This paper describes the model of knowledge systems used by DIDS, called the DIDS model. This model is distinguished from other similar models of knowledge systems, such as KADS (Wielinga, Schreiber, & Breuker 1992), by its focus on eliminating knowledge system brittleness. The remainder of this paper describes the elements of the DIDS model enabling non-brittle model-based tools to be developed. Results of experiments with the model are also presented.

DIDS Model

The DIDS model was designed to support the development of a new class of flexible model-based KA tools that can be easily adapted to changing tasks. The premise is that flexibility is achieved, without loss of acquisition power, by separating acquisition techniques for search-control knowledge from those techniques used to acquire other types of knowledge, thereby developing "PSM neutral" model-based acquisition tools. The model also minimizes the effort required to build and maintain these tools by allowing them to be composed from reusable KA procedures.

In the DIDS model, a knowledge system is viewed as performing problem-space search, just as in the Problem-Space Computational Model (Yost 1993). The search space is defined at three levels – KL, problem-space level (PSL), and symbol level (SL) – where each successive level is less abstract and provides more implementation details. The KL bounds the problem space that must be searched without describing its structure. It identifies the knowledge structures contained in and used to search the problem space as well as the criteria that must be satisfied by a solution. Conceptually, all PSMs performing this task must search this problem space so the knowledge-structure ontology identified at this level is highly reusable.

The PSL describes the way the task is formulated so that it can be performed efficiently. It defines the states in problem space, as well as the PSM and search-control knowledge used to search this space efficiently. The states define the set of possible solutions - both feasible and infeasible - that could be considered during problem solving. (Note, the states are characterized, but not explicitly enumerated.) The PSM encapsulates a search strategy defining how task-specific knowledge can be used to prune portions of the problem space. Pruning is necessary since problem spaces are typically too large to search exhaustively. *Search-control knowledge is the task-specific pruning knowledge used by these strategies.*

The SL consists of the programming languages statements used to implement the PSM and to represent the knowledge structures, states, and search-control knowledge.

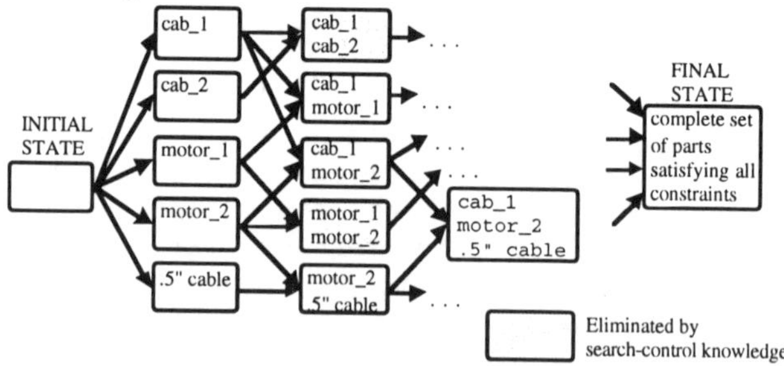

Figure 1 - The problem space for the VT task.

For example, consider the elevator-design task performed by the VT knowledge system (Marcus, Stout, & McDermott 1987). The VT task, when viewed at the KL, involves designing an elevator by selecting parts from a catalog that satisfy a user-given set of functional requirements and constraints. The knowledge structures – parts, constraints, and functional requirements – bound the space of elevator designs that may be considered.

The PSL view of the VT task is shown in Figure 1. Each state in the problem space consists of a set of elevator parts. The initial state is empty (does not contain any parts), and a final state contains a set of components that realizes the functionality of an elevator and satisfies all constraints. The types of search-control knowledge used to perform this task, however, depend on the problem-solving technique used to solve it. A generate-and-test problem solver does not use any search-control knowledge: it randomly picks a state in the problem space and checks to see if it is a final state. The VT system uses fixes, search-control knowledge describing how to repair constraint violations, to make backtracking through this problem space more efficient (Runkel & Birmingham 1994).

This three-level view of a knowledge system decomposes knowledge systems into four components:

1. A *KL task description*.
2. A *process model* describing the PSL view of the task.
3. A *KA model* describing the techniques used to acquire the knowledge structures and search-control knowledge.
4. Programming language statements used to implement the process model and KA model.

Since the focus of this paper is KA, the remainder of this section describes how the search-control knowledge distinction and other properties of the KL task description enable non-brittle model-based KA tools to be constructed from reusable KA procedures; the process model and its implementations are described in other papers (Runkel, Birmingham, & Balkany 1994).

Knowledge-Level Task Description

A KL task description consists of:
1. The solution criteria identifying the properties of a desirable solution.
2. A set of knowledge structures forming an ontology of the knowledge used to perform the task.
3. Organizational requirements describing the relationships among the knowledge structures
4. A knowledge base consisting of knowledge-structure instances defining all the task-specific knowledge, excluding search-control knowledge, necessary to perform the task.

Describing a task using a problem space focuses the acquisition process on the relevant knowledge structures. In addition, the problem space also highlights relationships among these knowledge structures, called organizational requirements, that enable the development of model-based KA tools from the KL task description. For most tasks, there are repeating patterns of knowledge structures that describe each domain concept. Model-based acquisition power can be achieved by using acquisition techniques designed to acquire these patterns. For example, each part of an elevator is represented by a *part* knowledge structure, a *function* knowledge structure describing the functionality of the part, and zero or more *constraint* knowledge structures describing situations when the part cannot be

used (Figure 2). In addition, for this task a part can perform exactly one function, and each function may be performed by one or more parts. These organizational requirements are the basis for model-based acquisition techniques. A model-based tool, after creating a part knowledge structure, would ask the domain expert to select the function performed by this part, and to supply any constraints specifying when the part cannot be used. In addition, the tool ensures that each part performs exactly one function and every function is performed by at least one part.

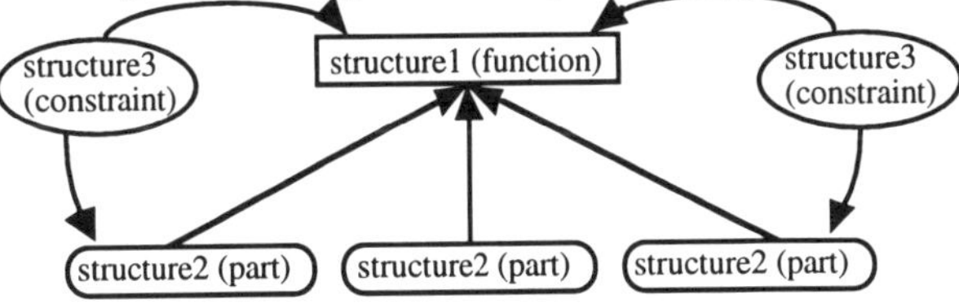

Figure 2 - The organizational requirements assumed by the constraint MeKA.

The organizational requirements enable tools to both assist with the acquisition of knowledge and to support the process of updating the knowledge base when knowledge changes. Since these requirements encapsulate the relationships among structures, they enable the knowledge engineer to see the ramifications of knowledge-base modifications. For example, it is a simple process to find all the functions and constraints affected by the removal of a part knowledge structure from the knowledge base.

Note, the knowledge structures and organizational requirements are defined independently of the PSM used to solve the task ensuring that the KA tool will work with any PSM. (To use a KA tool, it is necessary to write translator from the generic-knowledge-structures representation to a PSM-specific representation.) The organizational requirements enable these tools to be both flexible as well as powerful.

KA Model

The KA model describes the model-based techniques used to acquire and maintain knowledge. It reduces brittleness by viewing KA tools as being composed of a collection of modular, reusable acquisition procedures, called *mechanisms for knowledge acquisition* (MeKA). A KA tool, in our model, is a set of MeKAs (one MeKA for each knowledge structure and search-control knowledge type) organized to produce dialog in a meaningful way. This modular structure insures that no one MeKA acquires both a knowledge structure and search-control knowledge, thus making it simple to adapt a KA tool to acquire knowledge for a different PSM. The MeKAs for acquiring the search-control knowledge used by one PSM are replaced by MeKAs for acquiring the search-control used by another PSM. The MeKAs for acquiring knowledge structures are unaffected by a PSM change.

The acquisition techniques embodied in MeKAs are model based. These techniques are customized to the organizational requirements identified in the KL task description, not the PSM. A MeKA contains three types of model-based KA techniques – acquire, verify, and generalize – corresponding to the three types of techniques found in model-based tools (Birmingham & Klinker 1994). The acquire component describes the type of knowledge structure or search-control knowledge acquired by the MeKA and specifies the organizational requirements to which the MeKA's acquisition techniques are customized. The verify component describes the types of error and consistency checks performed by a MeKA. These techniques ensure that the acquired knowledge is organized as required by the organizational requirements, and that the user has provided all the knowledge specified in the task description. The generalize component describes the techniques the MeKA uses to generalize acquired knowledge. These techniques reduce the number of questions that the domain expert must answer.

For example, the constraint MeKA (Figure 3) is designed to acquire the constraint-knowledge structure when the task description is organized as shown in Figure 2. The MeKA acquires an algebraic relationship (constraint) between two classes of knowledge structures (parts and functions) when they are related by a one-to-many relationship. If the knowledge base was organized differently, then a different MeKA would be used. For example, if constraints were a binary relationship that organized the parts into a hierarchy, then a MeKA customized to acquiring hierarchies would be used.

The three components of the constraint MeKA are customized to the organizational requirements on constraints in the VT task. The verify component of the constraint MeKA ensures that every function is associated with a constraint, and that this constraint defines a relationship between the function and its parts. The generalize component of the constraint MeKA asks the domain expert to broaden the scope of the acquired constraint. If the domain expert had entered a constraint specifying that the least costly part should be selected, then he may want the scope of this constraint to cover the entire knowledge base.

Constraint MeKA

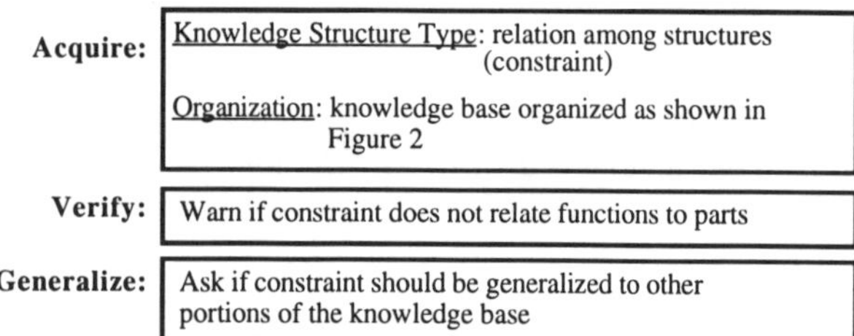

Figure 3 - The components of the constraint MeKA.

The constraint MeKA is operationalized by an interface that acquires constraints by showing a hierarchy containing a function, all its parts, and the attributes associated with the parts and the function (Figure 4). The hierarchy displayed by the MeKA is likely to be all the knowledge the domain expert will need to review before providing a constraint to select among the function's parts. The question presented by the MeKA is derived from the role it expects the constraint to play during problem solving. Therefore, the MeKA asks the user for a constraint that selects among each function's parts. Finally, after the user has entered a constraint, the verification component is used to check the acquired knowledge, and the generalize component computes other portions of the knowledge base.

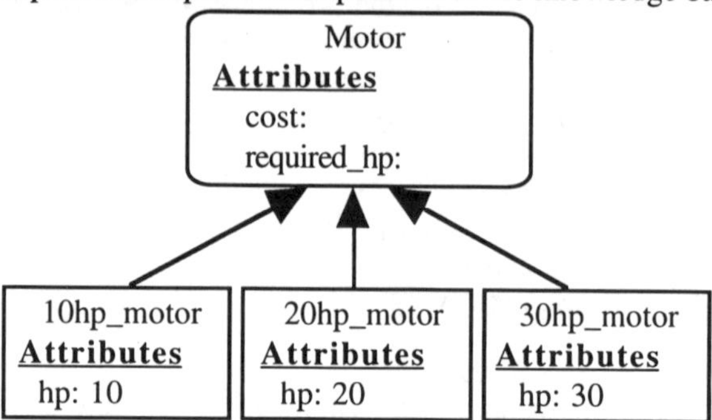


```
Enter the constraint used to select from the
possible designs of Motor (10hp_motor,
20hp_motor, 30hp_motor):
```

Figure 4 - Interface generated by the constraint MeKA.

Results

The effectiveness of KA tools based upon the DIDS model has been tested by running a number of experiments using DIDS. DIDS contains libraries of MeKAs and tools for creating KL task descriptions and building KA tools by combining MeKAs. These tools and libraries were used to demonstrate the flexibility of DIDS-generated KA tools, and to verify the brittleness-reduction properties of the model.

The tasks used for the experiments were all configuration-design tasks (Mittal & Frayman 1989), because we are most familiar with this class of tasks, making it easier to build the appropriate MeKA library. Configuration was also chosen because our working relationship with an industrial affiliate gives us access to a number of real-world configuration tasks and the knowledge necessary to perform them. The tasks automated during these experiments are summarized below:

1. Room Assignment (RA). Assigning workers to offices so that no constraints are violated (Linster 1992).

2. Elevator-design (VT0). Designing elevators that satisfy a given set of functional requirements and constraints by selecting parts from a catalog (Yost 1992). This task was solved without search-control knowledge.

3. Elevator design (VT1). Same task as VT0 except that search-control knowledge is used to make problem solving more efficient.

Task	M1	M2	M3	M4	M5	M6	M7	Problem-Solving Method
RA	x	x	x	x				Constraint satisfaction with distance heuristic
VT0	x	x	x	x	x	x		Constraint satisfaction
VT1	x	x	x	x	x	x	x	Constraint satisfaction with fixes
VT Val.	x	x	x	x	x	x		OPS5
P.C.	x	x	x	x				Constraint satisfaction
Truck	x	x	x	x	x			Optimal part selection

Figure 5 - The reuse of MeKAs across tasks and PSMs.

4. Elevator-design validation (VT Val.). Given an elevator design, verify that it satisfies all functional requirements and constraints (Runkel, Birmingham, & Balkany 1994).

5. Personal-computer validation (PC). Given a list of personal computer components (disk drives, monitors, memory chips, etc.) verify that these components can be combined into a working personal computer.

6. Truck design (Truck). Complete a truck design started by a human designer by selecting parts from a catalog such that all functional requirements are met, no constraints are violated, and some design parameter - such as cost, payload, or fuel economy - is maximized or minimized.

For each of these tasks, DIDS was used to capture a task description at the KL, to create a KA tool, and to build a problem solver capable of performing the task. The KA tool was then used to build a knowledge base, and the problem solver used this knowledge base to run test cases.

A KA tool was created for each task by starting with the same baseline tool and modifying it by swapping MeKAs (Figure 5). The baseline tool is a model-based tool for acquiring parts, the functions they perform, and the constraints among them. It contains four MeKAs (M1-M4), which consist of a graphical node-link-diagram editor designed to guide the domain expert in the process of organizing parts into a hierarchy based upon the functions they perform, a spread-sheet-like interface designed to reduce the amount of effort required to specify the attributes of parts and functions, a text editor facilitating the specification of constraints among parts and functions, and a set of knowledge-base browsers.

These results demonstrated the power of our approach: the same baseline KA tool was reused, even though the six knowledge systems built with it performed different tasks, used a variety of problem-solving techniques, and were implemented in a variety of languages. The RA task used a constraint network combined with a chronological-backtracking PSM that used the distances among the rooms to prune the search space. In contrast, the VT validation system was built from OPS5 rules, and the truck-design system used an optimal part-selection algorithm (Haworth, Birmingham, & Haworth 1992) written in C.

By reusing MeKAs, KA tools are easy to build. This reuse resulted in significant savings in KA tool development time. The RA task was the first to be automated. To build a KA tool for this task, the baseline MeKAs were handcoded requiring about 6 person months. (Figure 6). The other KA tools were built by reusing these MeKAs, and therefore required significantly less time to develop. Only VT0 KA tool, in addition to the RA tool, required more than a day to develop. This was the time necessary to code MeKAs M5 and M6.

The KA tools created from MeKAs are as powerful as existing model-based tools. This acquisition power was demonstrated by the three VT experiments. The automation of the VT tasks required the creation of a knowledge base with many complex parts and constraints. The DIDS-generated KA tool was not only capable of acquiring this knowledge base, but also saved acquisition time by detecting errors as knowledge was acquired (Runkel & Birmingham 1994).

The reuse of knowledge bases among the VT0, VT1, and VT Val. tasks demonstrated the reduction in KA time resulting from the use of ontologies, and by separating search-control knowledge. The knowledge base for the VT0 task took almost 400-person hours to develop. This same knowledge base was reused for both the VT1 task, which used a slightly different PSM and the VT Val. task where both the task and PSM were significantly different (validation vs. design, constraint satisfaction vs. rules). Reuse of the same knowledge base among various PSMs was possible because the search-control knowledge was clearly identified and removed. In addition, the use of ontologies made it easy to translate the knowledge base into the required PSM-specific representations. The total KA time for both the VT1 and VT Val. tasks was only 10 person hours.

These experiments demonstrated that the DIDS model contains four properties reducing brittleness:

1. Modular structure of KA tools. Since KA tools are composed from MeKAs, it was a simple process to adapt the KA tool to a new task by adding or replacing MeKAs.

2. KA techniques used by MeKAs based on the KL task description's organizational requirements. This feature enabled powerful model-based KA tools to be developed that were not tailored to a particular PSM. The experiments showed that adapting the KA tool to a new task or PSM required minimal effort.

3. Use of ontologies and the identification of search-control knowledge. The combination of these two

approaches allowed the same knowledge base to be reused with a number of different PSMs.

4. Separation of acquisition techniques for search-control knowledge. Adapting the KA tool from the RA task to the VT0 task and then again from the VT0 task to the VT1 task demonstrated the flexibility gained from this separation. In each case, in order to reuse the KA tool, the MeKAs for acquiring search-control knowledge were removed. This removed any dependence between the KA tool and a particular PSM leaving the reusable portions of the tool intact. The tool was then adapted to the new task by adding MeKAs to acquire the search-control knowledge used by the new PSM.

	RA	VT0	VT1	VT Val.	PC	Truck
KB Size						
know. structs.	4020	424	424	424	2000	589
search control	50	0	62	0	0	0
% reuse	0	0	87	100	100	0
Develop. Time						
task description	3	3	0	1	3	3
KA tool	2080	395	5	1	1	1
KA	2	240	10	0	0	60
% MeKA reuse	0	67	86	100	100	100

Figure 6 - Development time (in person hours) reduction resulting from reuse.

Summary

The DIDS model defines a KA tool architecture that enables the development of model-based KA tools that can be easily modified and extended to acquire knowledge for new tasks and PSMs. The key to this flexibility is viewing knowledge systems at the KL, PSL, and SL. The use of these three levels enables powerful, but PSM-independent, KA tools to be developed. These capabilities are achieved by separating acquisition techniques for search-control knowledge from other types of knowledge, and by creating MeKAs that derive their model-based acquisition techniques from the organizational requirements identified in the KL task description. In addition, flexibility is gained by using the ontology of knowledge structures identified at the KL to reuse knowledge bases. Our experiments have demonstrated the flexibility gained by this approach.

Acknowledgment. This work was funded, in part, by a gift from Digital Equipment Corporation and by the National Science Foundation Grant MIPS-905781. Alan Balkany made significant contributions to this work.

References

Balkany, A.; Birmingham, W.P.; and Runkel, J.T. 1993. Solving Sisyphus by Design. *Knowledge Acquisition*. forthcoming.

Birmingham, W.P. and Klinker, G. 1994. Knowledge-Acquisition Tools with Explicit Problem-Solving Models. *The Knowledge Engineering Review* 8 (1):

Gruber, T.R. 1993. A Translation Approach to Portable Ontology Specifications. *Knowledge Acquisition* 5 (2): 199-220.

Haworth, M.S.; Birmingham, W.P.; and Haworth, D.E. 1992. Optimal Part Selection. Technical Report, CSE-TR-127-92, Department of Electrical Engineer and Computer Science, University of Michigan.

Linster, M. 1992. Document for the Participants of Sisyphus '92, Part 2: Models of Problem Solving.

Marcus, S. eds. 1988. *Automating Knowledge Acquisition for Expert Systems*. Kluwer Academic Publishers.

Marcus, S.; Stout, J.; and McDermott, J. 1987. VT: An Expert Elevator Designer that Uses Knowledge-based Backtracking. *AI Magazine*.

McDermott, J. 1988. Preliminary Steps Toward a Taxonomy of Problem-Solving Methods. In *Automating Knowledge Acquisition for Expert Systems*, eds. Sandra Marcus. Kluwer Academic Publishers.

Mittal, S. and Frayman, F. 1989. Towards a Generic Model of Configuration Tasks. In Proceedings of the 11th IJCAI, Morgan Kaufman.

Musen, M.A. 1989. *Automatic Generation of Model-Based Knowledge-Acquisition Tools*. San Mateo, California: Morgan Kaufmann Publishers, Inc.

Newell, A. 1981. The Knowledge Level. *AI Magazine*.

Puerta, A.; Egar, J.; Tu, S.; and Musen, M. 1992. A multiple-method knowledge-acquisition shell for the automatic generation of knowledge acquisition tools. *Knowledge Acquisition* 4 (2).

Runkel, J.T. and Birmingham, W.P. 1994. Solving VT by Reuse. In Proceedings of 8th Banff Knowledge Acquisition for Knowledge-Based Systems Workshop, Banff, Alberta, Canada.

Runkel, J.T.; Birmingham, W.P.; and Balkany, A. 1994. Separation of Knowledge: A Key to Reusability. In Proceedings of 8th Banff Knowledge Acquisition for Knowledge-Based Systems Workshop, Banff, Alberta, Canada.

Steels, L. 1992. Reusability and Configuration of Applications by Nonprogrammers. Technical Report, VUB AI Memo 92-4, VUB AI Lab Pleinlasn 2, 1050.

Wielinga, B.J.; Schreiber, A.T.; and Breuker, A.J. 1992. KADS: A Modeling approach to knowledge engineering. *Knowledge Acquisition*.

Yost, G.R. 1992. Configuring elevator systems. Technical Report, Workplace Integration Technologies Group, Digital Equipment Corporation, 111 Locke Drive (LM02/K11), Marlboro, MA 01752.

Yost, G.R. 1993. Acquiring Knowledge in Soar. *IEEE Expert* 8 (3): 26-34.

The Acquisition, Analysis and Evaluation of Imprecise Requirements for Knowledge-Based Systems

John Yen, Xiaoqing Liu and Swee Hor Teh
Computer Science Department, Texas A&M University
College Station, Texas 77843, U.S.A.
email:yen@cs.tamu.edu

Abstract

In this paper, a theoretical foundation has been laid and a practical method has been developed for specifying, analyzing and evaluating the complex relationships between imprecise requirements in knowledge-based systems. Imprecise requirements are represented by the canonical form in test-score semantics. The relationships between requirements are classified to be conflicting and cooperative based on the qualitative and quantitative analysis of relationships between requirements. This kind of analysis makes it possible to formulate a feasible overall requirement from conflicting individual requirements. It also facilitates to find better trade-off strategies for conflicting requirements by using fuzzy multi-criteria optimization technique. A requirement engineering process has also been developed to incorporate imprecise requirements into the requirement analysis for knowledge-based systems.

Introduction

Several approaches exploiting requirement specification techniques have been used to develop reliable knowledge-based systems [Yen & Lee 1993a, Yen & Lee 1993b, Plant 1988, Batarekh *et al.* 1991, Tsai *et al.* 1988]. However, lack of precision leads to the difficulty for determining if a realization meets its requirements [Roman 1985]. A challenge with requirement engineering is thus that the requirements to be captured are usually described in qualitative terms which are imprecise in nature. Actually, as Balzer et al. have stated, informality is an inevitable and ultimately desirable feature of the specification process [Balzer, Goldman & Wile 1978]. However, most existing specification methodologies either require that the requirements be stated precisely, such as in formal specification methodologies (e.g., Z [Spivey 1987], Larch [Guttag, Horning & Wing 1985], etc.), or convert informal requirements into formal ones (e.g., SAFE project [Balzer, Goldman & Wile 1978] and Requirement Apprentice [Reubenstein & Waters 1991]. Therefore they do not capture the impreciseness of the requirements.

Another challenge with requirement engineering for knowledge-based systems is that requirements often conflict with each other [Robinson 1990]. However existing specification methods consider that a requirement specification, which contains conflicting requirements, to be inconsistent, and should be avoided since requirements are specified as crisp ones [Roman 1985]. Moreover, it is very difficult to analyze and specify a trade-off between conflicting requirements if these requirements are specified to be crisp [Robinson 1990].

In this paper, a theoretical foundation has been laid and a practical method has been developed for specifying, analyzing and evaluating the complex relationships between imprecise requirements in knowledge-based systems. Imprecise requirements are formulated based on the canonical form in test-score semantics [Zadeh 1986]. The relationships between requirements are classified to be conflicting and cooperative based on the qualitative and quantitative analysis of relationships between requirements. Conflicting requirements can not be satisfied completely at the same time and a trade-off needs to be developed. The trade-offs are analyzed using fuzzy multi-criteria optimization techniques [Zimmermann 1991, Dubois & Prade 1984] to formulate a feasible overall requirement and to find a better design. A requirement engineering process, which incorporates the analysis and specification of imprecise requirements in knowledge-based systems, has also been developed.

Imprecise Requirements

A target system T can be specified as a set of state transitions [Yen & Lee 1993a]. Let ST be the set of plausible state transition $< s_1, s_2 >$ that can be performed by T, where s_1 is a before state, s_2 is a after state. If T is implemented, the working system is called its realization. A before state s_1 may have more than one plausible after state s_2 such that $< s_1, s_2 > \in ST$. It indicates that there may be many plausible realizations for T. For a given before state s_1, let $perform(T, s_1) = \{s_2 \mid < s_1, s_2 > \in ST\}$. The cardinality of the set $perform(T, s_1)$ may thus be greater than one.

A fuzzy set $DST_R = \{< s_1, s_2 >, \mu_{DST_R} < s_1, s_2 >\}$

of desired state transitions can be defined for an imprecise requirement R, where $\mu_{DST_R} < s_1, s_2 >$ specifies the degree to which the state transition $< s_1, s_2 >$ is desired by R. An imprecise requirement is represented as a soft requirement defined below.

Definition 1 *(Soft Requirement [Yen & Lee 1993b]): A soft requirement R of the target system is specified as a pair of formula $< \varphi_1, \varphi_2 >$ where φ_1 is a soft precondition and φ_2 is a soft postcondition, such that $\forall < s_1, s_2 > \in S(DST_R)$,*

$$\mu_{fhold(\varphi_1, s_1) \stackrel{f}{\Longrightarrow} fhold(\varphi_2, s_2)} = \mu_{DST_R} < s_1, s_2 >$$

where $S(DST_R)$ is the support of the fuzzy set DST_R, "fhold" is a function that returns the degree to which a formula φ is true in state s, and $\stackrel{f}{\Longrightarrow}$ is the fuzzy logic implication.

Thus a soft requirement specifies the "state changes" that are desired to be achieved to some degrees by a realization of the target system. In the following discussion, B_R will denote a set of before state s_1 of R and A_R a set of after state s_2 of R such that $\mu_{DST_R} < s_1, s_2 >> 0$

A soft requirement can be represented using the *canonical form* in Zadeh's test score semantics [Zadeh 1986]. It has been established by the following theorem [Yen & Lee 1993b].

Theorem 1 *Let p be a proposition in its canonical form, X is A, X is a state variable in state s, and u_i is the value of X in s. Then*

$$fhold(p, s) = \mu_A(u_i)$$

Theoretical Analysis of Relationships between Requirements

There exist very complex relationships between requirements. Some of them are conflicting with each other and others may cooperate. Two soft requirements are said to conflict with each other if an increase in the degree to which one requirement is satisfied often decreases the degree to which another requirement is satisfied.

Definition 2 *(conflicting degree with respect to (wrt) a given before state)*
Assume that $R_1 =< \varphi_1^1, \varphi_2^1 >$ and $R_2 =< \varphi_1^2, \varphi_2^2 >$ be two soft requirements of a target system T. For a before state $b_k \in B_{R_1} \cap B_{R_2}$, let the set of common after states of R_1 and R_2 wrt b_k be denoted as $A_{R_1, R_2}(b_k) = perform(T, b_k) \cap A_{R_1} \cap A_{R_2}$, and the set of after state pairs, in which an increase in the degree to which a requirement is satisfied decreases the degree to which another requirement is satisfied, be denoted as
$$\mathcal{F}(b_k) = \{(a_1, a_2) | a_1, a_2 \in A_{R_1, R_2}(b_k), a_1 \neq a_2, \text{ and }$$
$$(fhold(\varphi_2^1, a_1) - fhold(\varphi_2^1, a_2)) \times$$
$$(fhold(\varphi_2^2, a_1) - fhold(\varphi_2^2, a_2)) < 0\}.$$
Then the degree R_1 and R_2 are conflicting wrt the before state b_k, denoted as $conf(b_k)$, is
$$\frac{\|\mathcal{F}(b_k)\|}{\|A_{R_1, R_2}(b_k)\| \times (\|A_{R_1, R_2}(b_k)\| - 1)}.$$

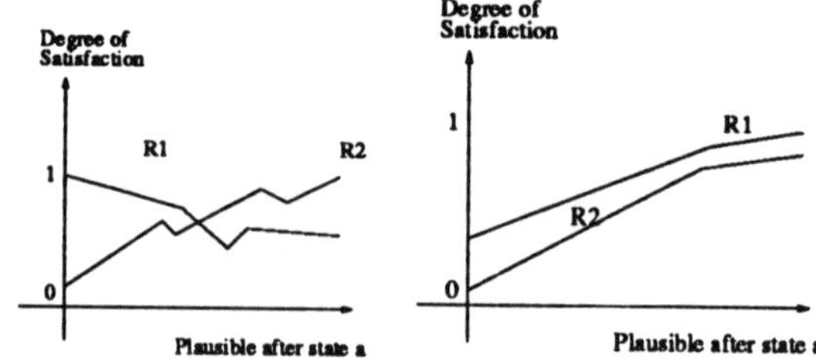

Figure 1: Conflicting wrt a Before State

Figure 2: Completely Cooperative wrt a Before State

An example of conflicting requirements wrt a given before state is shown in Fig. 1.

Two soft requirements are said to *completely conflicting with each other wrt a given before state* if an increase in the degree to which one requirement is satisfied always decreases the degree to which another requirement is satisfied for the before state. It can be easily shown that two requirements are completely conflicting wrt a given before state whenever their conflicting degree wrt the before state is one.

Having defined the conflicting degree wrt a given before state, we are ready to introduce several overall conflicting measures between two requirements.

Definition 3 *(optimistic, pessimistic and average conflicting degree)*
Assume that $R_1 =< \varphi_1^1, \varphi_2^1 >$ and $R_2 =< \varphi_1^2, \varphi_2^2 >$ are two soft requirements of a target system. The optimistic conflicting degree of R_1 and R_2 is

$$\texttt{opt-conf}(R_1, R_2) = \min_{b_k \in B_{R_1} \cap B_{R_2}} conf(b_k).$$

The pessimistic conflicting degree of R_1 and R_2 is

$$\texttt{pess-conf}(R_1, R_2) = \max_{b_k \in B_{R_1} \cap B_{R_2}} conf(b_k).$$

The average conflicting degree of R_1 and R_2 is

$$\texttt{avg-conf}(R_1, R_2) = \frac{\sum_{b_k \in B_{R_1} \cap B_{R_2}} conf(b_k)}{\|B_{R_1} \cap B_{R_2}\|}.$$

Two soft requirements often cooperate with each other. It means an increase in the degree to which one requirement is satisfied often increases the degree to which another requirement is satisfied.

Definition 4 *(cooperative degree wrt a given before state)*
Assume that $R_1 =< \varphi_1^1, \varphi_2^1 >$ and $R_2 =< \varphi_1^2, \varphi_2^2 >$ be two soft requirements of a target system T. For a before state $b_k \in B_{R_1} \cap B_{R_2}$, let the set of after state pairs, in which an increase in the degree to which a requirement is satisfied also increases the degree to which another requirement is satisfied, be denoted as
$$\mathcal{G}(b_k) = \{(a_1, a_2) | a_1, a_2 \in A_{R_1, R_2}(b_k), a_1 \neq a_2, \text{and,}$$
$$(fhold(\varphi_2^1, a_1) - fhold(\varphi_2^1, a_2)) \times$$
$$(fhold(\varphi_2^2, a_1) - fhold(\varphi_2^2, a_2)) \geq 0\}.$$

Then the degree R_1 and R_2 are cooperative wrt before state b_k, denoted as $coop(b_k)$, is
$$\frac{\|\mathcal{G}(b_k)\|}{\|A_{R_1,R_2}(b_k)\|(\|A_{R_1,R_2}(b_k)\|-1)}.$$

Two soft requirements are said to *completely cooperative with each other wrt a given before state* if an increase in the degree to which one requirement is satisfied always increases the degree to which another requirement is satisfied for the before state. It can be easily shown that two requirements are completely cooperative wrt a before state whenever their cooperative degree wrt the before state is one. An example of completely cooperative requirement wrt a before state is shown in Fig. 2. Two requirements are called *completely cooperative* if they completely cooperative with each other wrt all before states in $B_{R_1} \cap B_{R_2}$.

We now introduce several overall cooperative measures between two requirements.

Definition 5 (*optimistic, pessimistic, and average cooperative degree*)
Assume that $R_1 =< \varphi_1^1, \varphi_2^1 >$ and $R_2 =< \varphi_1^2, \varphi_2^2 >$ are two soft requirements of a target system. The pessimistic cooperative degree of R_1 and R_2 is defined as

$$\textbf{pess-coop}(R_1, R_2) = \min_{b_k \in B_{R_1} \cap B_{R_2}} coop(b_k).$$

The optimistic cooperative degree of R_1 and R_2 is defined as

$$\textbf{opt-coop}(R_1, R_2) = \max_{b_k \in B_{R_1} \cap B_{R_2}} coop(b_k).$$

The average cooperative degree of R_1 and R_2 is defined as

$$\textbf{avg-coop}(R_1, R_2) = \frac{\sum_{b_k \in B_{R_1} \cap B_{R_2}} coop(b_k)}{\|B_{R_1} \cap B_{R_2}\|}.$$

There is a dual relationship between conflicting degree and conflicting degree.

Theorem 2 *Let R_1 and R_2 be two requirements, then*

1. $\textbf{pess-conf}(R_1, R_2) = 1 - \textbf{opt-coop}(R_1, R_2)$
2. $\textbf{opt-conf}(R_1, R_2) = 1 - \textbf{pess-coop}(R_1, R_2)$
3. $\textbf{avg-conf}(R_1, R_2) = 1 - \textbf{avg-coop}(R_1, R_2)$

This theorem can be proved easily according to the definitions given before.

Approximate Analysis of the Relationships between Requirements

In the previous section, the theoretical foundation for analyzing the relationships between requirements has been laid. However in the real applications, it is usually difficult to specify all before states and after states for a target system. Thus we need to explain how to apply the theoretical results obtained in the previous section for the real applications.

First of all, domain experts can provide the qualitative specification of the relationships between requirements based on their expertise in the area. For example, considering the expert system ISPBEX [Flam *et al.*

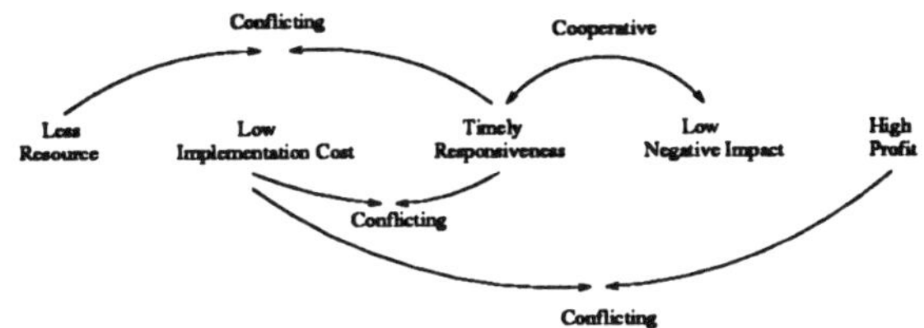

Figure 3: An Qualitative Specification of Relationships Between Requirements

1991] which is designed to determine the proper treatment recommendations for the suppression of Southern Pine Beetle(SPB), *Dendroctonus Frontalis Zimmerman* infestations. Management decisions are made based on the knowledge acquired from experts specializing in forest management, wildlife management, and SPB biology and control. The purpose of ISPBEX is to help Forest Service personnel make decisions about the Southern Pine Beetle spots by providing treatment recommendations. The requirements for the treatment recommendation generated by the system includes

- R_1 : The amount of resource required should be small.

- R_2 : The cost of implementation of the treatment should be low.

- R_3 : The time taken to begin the treatment should be short.

- R_4 : The impact of the treatment on endangered species (RCW) should be reduced to a low level.

- R_5 : The profit should be high.

The canonical forms of the postconditions of these soft requirements can be represented as follows:

- R_1 : Amount_of_Resource (Treatment Recommendation) should be SMALL.

- R_2 : Cost_of_implementation (Treatment Recommendation) should be LOW.

- R_3 : Responsive_Time (Treatment Recommendation) should be SHORT.

- R_4 : Negative_impact(endangered_species (Treatment Recommendation)) should be LOW.

- R_5 : Profit(Treatment Recommendation) should be HIGH.

SMALL, LOW, SHORT, and HIGH are fuzzy sets and serve as elastic constraints on a treatment recommendation.

The qualitative specification of relationships between these requirements is shown in Fig. 3.

The qualitative specification of the relationships between requirements can be then validated and revised by the approximate analysis of quantitative relationships between requirements based on an analytic tool called the Analytic Matrix (AM) and the theoretical results presented before. Let T denote the target

Case	Solution	Requirement				
		R_1	R_2	$\cdot$ $\cdot$ $\cdot$	R_n	
EC_1	$S_{1,1}$	$d_{1,1,1}$	$d_{1,1,2}$	$\cdot$ $\cdot$ $\cdot$	$d_{1,1,n}$	
	$S_{1,2}$	$d_{1,2,1}$	$d_{1,2,2}$	$\cdot$ $\cdot$ $\cdot$	$d_{1,2,n}$	
	$S_{1,m}$	$d_{1,m,1}$	$d_{1,m,2}$	$\cdot$ $\cdot$ $\cdot$	$d_{1,m,n}$	
EC_p	$S_{p,1}$	$d_{p,1,1}$	$d_{p,1,2}$	$\cdot$ $\cdot$ $\cdot$	$d_{p,1,n}$	
	$S_{p,2}$	$d_{p,2,1}$	$d_{p,2,2}$	$\cdot$ $\cdot$ $\cdot$	$d_{p,2,n}$	
	$S_{p,m}$	$d_{p,m,1}$	$d_{p,m,2}$	$\cdot$ $\cdot$ $\cdot$	$d_{p,m,n}$	

Figure 4: An Illustration of Analytic Matrix

Case	Solution	Requirement				
		R1	R2	R3	R4	R5
Case 1	C/L	0.4	0.4	0.6	0.7	0.2
	C/R	0.2	0.3	0.6	0.6	0.9
	P/B	0.1	0.1	0.8	0.1	0.1
	Mon	0.8	0.8	0.3	0.5	0.1
	C/HS	0.3	0.2	0.7	0.8	0.1
Case 2	C/L	0.1	0.3	0.5	0.6	0.1
	C/R	0.1	0.2	0.7	0.7	0.4
	P/B	0.1	0.1	0.9	0.9	0.1
	Mon	0.6	0.5	0.2	0.3	0.1
	C/HS	0.1	0.4	0.4	0.4	0.1
Case 3	C/L	0.6	0.7	0.6	0.6	0.3
	C/R	0.4	0.4	0.6	0.3	0.6
	P/B	0.2	0.1	0.7	0.1	0.1
	Mon	0.8	0.8	0.2	0.5	0.1
	C/HS	0.5	0.2	0.3	0.4	0.1
Case 4	C/L	0.8	0.4	0.7	0.7	0.5
	C/R	0.8	0.3	0.8	0.6	0.7
	P/B	0.9	0.1	0.9	0.1	0.1
	Mon	0.9	0.8	0.6	0.9	0.1
	C/HS	0.8	0.6	0.8	0.8	0.1

Figure 5: The Analytic Matrix for ISPBEX

knowledge-based system. It has n individual requirements, denoted as R_k, $1 \leq k \leq n$. A set of p typical cases ,denoted as EC_i, $1 \leq i \leq p$ are formulated by knowledge engineers and domain experts. For example, considering a medical diagnosis expert systems, a case may consists of a list of symptoms a patient may have. The domain experts are then asked to provide a set of m possible solutions for each case EC_i, denoted as $S_{i,j}$, $1 \leq j \leq m$. For each solution $S_{i,j}$, a degree $d_{i,j,k}$, to which the solution $S_{i,j}$ for the case EC_i satisfies the requirement R_k can be assigned according to Theorem 1. These degrees are organized into a matrix, called the Analytic Matrix (AM), $AM = (d_{i,j,k})$, where $1 \leq i \leq p, 1 \leq j \leq m$, and $1 \leq k \leq n$, as shown in Fig. 4.

To illustrate the concept of the analytic matrix, let us consider ISPBEX again. In ISPBEX, the input parameters are treatment month, type of forest (general forest, wilderness), colony-condition (active, not active), breeding season (spring, summer, fall, winter), priority(A,B,C,D where A has the highest priority and D the lowest), type of trees (loblobby or short leaf pine), characteristics of trees (age, size), growth distance (in feet) and direction of growth (in degrees). The output is a treatment recommendation and explanation why a particular recommendation is provided. Thus a case corresponds to a set of fixed input parameters. For example, the Case 1 in the analytic matrix, shown in Fig. 5, represents that the treatment season is march, the type of forest is wilderness, SPB spot is active, endangered species are breeding, priority is high, SPB is going to impact the endangered species

colony within 60 days, and so on. The analytic matrix for ISPBEX includes four typical cases. For each case, five major recommendations are possible. They include Cut and Leave(C/L), Cut and Remove(C/R), Pile and Burn(P/B), Monitor(Mon) and Cut and Hand Spray(C/HS). For example, the recommendation P/B requires the largest amount of resource for Case 1 and satisfies the requirement R_1 at the lowest degree (0.1).

Now let us to explain how to use the analytic matrix for the quantitative analysis of the relationships between requirements. Actually, a before state corresponds to a legal input of the system and an after state corresponds to an output which is expected to be generated for a given input by the system in our paradigm. Thus, a before state corresponds to a case and an after state corresponds to a possible solution given for the case in the analytic matrix.

Considering two requirement R_{k_1} and R_{k_2}, $1 \leq k_1, k_2 \leq n$. Let
$$\mathcal{F}'(EC_i) = \{(S_{i,j_1}, S_{i,j_2}) | ((d_{i,j_1,k_1} - d_{i,j_2,k_1})$$
$$\times (d_{i,j_1,k_2} - d_{i,j_2,k_2})) < 0, 1 \leq j_1, j_2 \leq m, j_1 \neq j_2\}.$$
Then the estimation $conf'(EC_i)$ of the conflicting degree $conf(EC_i)$ between R_{k_1} and R_{k_2} for the case EC_i is $\frac{\|\mathcal{F}'(EC_i)\|}{m(m-1)}$. For example, the estimation of the conflicting degree between requirement R_1 and R_3 for the Case 1 is $conf'(EC_1) = \frac{\|\mathcal{F}'(EC_1)\|}{m(m-1)} = 0.8$

Similarly the cooperating degree of two requirements for a given case can also be estimated based on the analytic matrix. From the estimated conflicting degree and cooperating degree of two requirements for each case, the optimistic, pessimistic, and average conflicting degree, and the optimistic, pessimistic, and average cooperating degree for all cases given in the analytic matrix can be estimated based on their definitions. The qualitative specification of the relationships between requirements can then be validated and revised by the quantitative analysis. For example, it has been found that R_1 and R_2 are cooperative in ISPBEX by the quantitative analysis, which has missed in the qualitative specification given by domain experts.

Combining Conflicting Requirements

Compromise Operators

Averaging [Dubois & Prade 1984] and compensatory [Zimmermann 1991] operators are often used to combine multi-criteria in fuzzy multicriteria optimization. However many averaging operators are not compensatory and vice versa. In requirement engineering, a trade-off between conflicting requirements usually is a compromise which is compensatory. Thus the compromise operator is developed to combine conflicting requirements for trade-off analysis.

Definition 6 *(Compromise)*
An operator is said to be a compromise operator if and only if it is both averaging and compensate operator.

In the following context, C denotes a compromise operator. It realizes the trade-offs by allowing compensation between requirements. The resulting compromise is between the minimal and maximal degree of membership of the aggregated fuzzy sets. Thus the "min", a t-norm operator, and the "max", a t-conorm operator, are not compromise operator since they are not compensatory. For a compromise operator, a decrease in one operand can be compensated by an increase in another operand. The arithmetic mean is an example of the C operator.

Combine Conflicting Requirements Using the Compromise Operator

The intended meaning of a soft condition is usually complex in nature. To represent the meaning of a complex term used in a soft condition, we often need to define the term using propositions regarding related variables whose values can be easily obtained. For example, the definition of a fuzzy proposition p may be an aggregation of other fuzzy propositions $\{p_1 \ldots p_k\}$.

Since the cooperating requirements can be satisfied at the same time, it is appropriate that they are combined with t-norms operators [Zimmermann 1991, Yen & Lee 1993b]. To use compromise operators to aggregate the conflicting requirements, we define the following rule to compute the function *fhold* for aggregation.

Definition 7 *(aggregation rule)*
$$fhold(\{p_1, p_2, \ldots, p_n\}, s)$$
$$= C(fhold(p_1, s), fhold(p_2, s), \ldots, fhold(p_n, s))$$

where $p_i, 1 \leq i \leq n$, are propositions, s is a state, and C is a compromise operator.

Thus the overall possibility distribution for representing the meaning of the soft condition p may be obtained by using the compromise operator C from Definition 7 and Theorem 1 as follows:

$$
\begin{aligned}
fhold(p, s) &= fhold(\{p_1, \ldots, p_k\}, s) \\
&= C(fhold(p_1, s), \ldots, fhold(p_k, s)) \\
&= C(\mu_{A_1}(u_1), \ldots, \mu_{A_k}(u_k))
\end{aligned}
$$

where $u_i \in U_i$.

The variety of compromise operators might make it hard to decide which one to use in a specific application. Several criteria have been summarized by Zimmermann [Zimmermann 1991] for selecting the appropriate general aggregation operator. In terms of requirement engineering, the following additional criteria need to be taken into account: 1. The intended relationship: The operator should conform to the intended relationship between requirements and the semantic interpretation; 2. Feasibility: The operator should make the combined requirement feasible and increase its feasibility. 3. Conflicting type and conflicting degree: A different trade-off strategy may be used for combining requirements with different conflicting type and degree. 4. Criticality: The operator should be able to handle criticality in the requirement specification.

Requirement Engineering Process

The requirements need to be revised many times during the development of knowledge-based systems. Actually the refinement of requirements with complex relationships between them is an iterative process, as shown in Fig. 6.

Knowledge engineers acquire individual requirements by a number of interaction with domain experts. The domain experts are then asked to provide the qualitative descriptions of the relationships between requirements. These qualitative relationships are not only the basis of but also validated and revised by the further quantitative analysis of relationships between requirements. The analytic matrix is an effective tool of the quantitative analysis.

Based on the analytic matrix, the quantitative analysis can be conducted by the computation of the conflicting degree and cooperating degree, and the classification of the relationships based on these degrees. The results of quantitative analysis can be used to decide the trade-off strategies and select appropriate aggregation operators to form a feasible overall system requirement. These trade-off strategies can be evaluated as follows:

1. The selected aggregation operators are used to combine the individual requirements and thus the degree, to which the overall requirement is satisfied by a possible solution given for a case in the analytic matrix, can be calculated.

2. The solutions for each case are ordered in the descending of these degrees. If these orders are quite different from the orders given by the domain experts

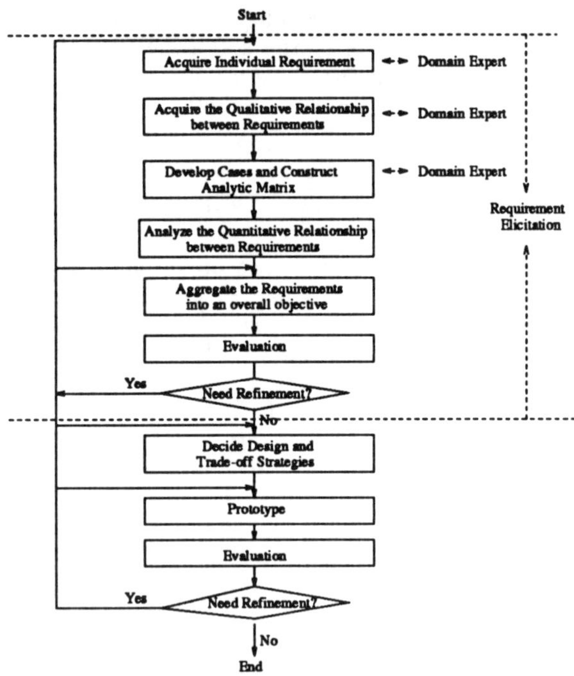

Figure 6: A Requirement Engineering Process

when the analytic matrix is obtained, the trade-off strategies needs to be revised.

If the evaluation result is positive, the design strategies need to be decided to fulfill the requirements effectively. A prototype can be then built to verify and validate the requirements. The prototype is tested by running a number of tests and their results are compared with the requirement specification and the opinions of domain experts. If the result of the evaluation is negative, the individual requirement may need to be altered since it may be too strong, trade-off strategies may need to be changed, or new design strategies and implementation techniques may need to be used.

Conclusion

In this paper, a systematic approach for specifying, analyzing and evaluating imprecise requirements using fuzzy logic has been developed. It provides both a sound theoretical foundation and a realistic method for the analysis of the complex relationships between requirements. A feasible overall requirement can be thus formulated from conflicting requirements by using fuzzy multi-criteria optimization technique. Moreover it can help to achieve the optimal system objective by a trade-off analysis of conflicting requirements.

Acknowledgements

We wish to thank Professor Lotfi A. Zadeh for suggesting that we use fuzzy multi-criteria decision techniques to aggregate soft requirements. We also would thank Dr. Jonathan Lee for his early work in this research. This research is supported by NSF Young Investigator Award IRI-9257293.

References

Gruia-Catalin Roman. 1985. A Taxonomy of current issues in requirements engineering. *IEEE Computer* 4:14-21.

R. Balzer; N. Goldman and D. Wile. 1978. Informality in program specifications. *IEEE Transaction on Software Enginering* 4(2):94-103.

D. Dubois and H. Prade. 1984. Criteria aggregation and ranking of alternatives in the framework of fuzzy set theory. In *Studies in the Management Sciences 20*, 209-240.

R. O. Flamm, *et. al.* 1991. The Integrated Southern Pine Beetle Expert System: ISPBEX, *Journal of Expert Systems with Applications*, 2:97-105.

J.V. Guttag; J.J. Horning and J.M. Wing. 1985. The larch family of specification languages. *IEEE Software* 2(5):24–36.

A. Batarekh; A.D. Preece; A. Bennett and P. Grogono. 1991. Specifying An Expert System. *Journal of Expert Systems with Applications* 2(3):285-303.

R. Plant. 1988. Specifying Expert System in Z. *PhD thesis*, University of Liverpool.

H.B. Reubenstein and R.C. Waters. 1991. The requirements apprentice: automated assistance for requirements acquisition. *IEEE Transaction on Software Engineering* 17(3):226-240.

W. N. Robinson. 1990. Negotiation behavior during requirement specification. In *Proc. of the 12th International Conf. on Software Engineering*. 268-276.

W.T. Tsai; P.E. Johnson; J.R. Slagle; I.A. Zualkernan, *et. al.* 1988. Requirements Specification for Expert Systems? A Case Study, *Technical Report TR 88-44*, University of Minnesota, Minneapolis, MN.

J.M. Spivey. 1987. The Z-Notation: a Reference Manual. Prentice-Hall, Englewood Cliffs, NJ.

R. Yager. 1991. Connectives and Quantifiers in Fuzzy Sets. *Fuzzy Sets and Systems* 40:39-75.

J. Yen and J. Lee. 1993a. A task-based methodology for specifying expert systems, *IEEE Expert* 8(1):8-15.

J. Yen and J. Lee. 1993b. Fuzzy Logic as a Basis for Specifying Imprecise Requirements. In *Proc. of the IEEE International Conf. on Fuzzy Systems*, 745-749.

L.A. Zadeh. 1986. Test-score semantics as a basis for a computational approach to the representation of meaning. *Literacy Linguistic Computing* 1:24–35.

H.-J. Zimmermann. 1991. *Fuzzy Set Theory and Its Applications*. Mass.: Kluwer Academic.

Extracting Viewpoints from Knowledge Bases[*]

Liane Acker
IBM Corporation
11400 Burnet Road
Austin, Texas 78758
acker@austin.ibm.com

Bruce Porter
Department of Computer Sciences
University of Texas at Austin
Austin, Texas 78712
porter@cs.utexas.edu

Abstract

Viewpoints are coherent collections of facts that describe a concept from a particular perspective. They are essential for a wide variety of tasks, such as explanation generation and qualitative modeling. We have identified many types of viewpoints and developed a program, the View Retriever, for extracting them from knowledge bases, either singly or in combinations. The View Retriever provides a general solution to the central problem in extracting viewpoints: determining which facts are relevant to requested viewpoints. Our evaluation indicates that viewpoints extracted by the View Retriever are comparable in coherence to those people construct.

1 Introduction

The objective of this research is to develop computational methods for extracting viewpoints from knowledge bases. Intuitively, a viewpoint is a coherent collection of facts that describes a concept from a particular perspective. For example, three viewpoints of the concept "car" are: the viewpoint "car as-kind-of consumer durable," which describes a car's price and longevity; the structural viewpoint, which describes a car's parts and their interconnections; and the viewpoint "car as-having metal composition," which includes facts, such as a car's propensity to dent and rust, that are related to its composition.

The need for viewpoints by knowledge-based programs is widespread. For example, many explanation-generation systems require viewpoints to produce explanations that are complete and coherent (Suthers 1991; McKeown 1988; Lester & Porter 1991; McCoy 1989; Moore & Swartout 1988). Qualitative modeling systems use viewpoints to increase efficiency and to

make consistent modeling assumptions (e.g.,the *model fragments* of (Falkenhainer & Forbus 1991), the *views* of (Forbus 1984), and the *ontological perspectives* of (Liu & Farley 1990).) Finally, KI (Murray & Porter 1989), a learning program, uses viewpoints to constrain its search for the consequences of adding new information to a knowledge base.

Conventional methods for accessing knowledge bases do not provide direct access to viewpoints. Some methods extract individual facts, such as the filler of a particular frame-slot. Others extract collections of facts, such as all the slots and fillers of a particular frame or those satisfying a Prolog-like query. Indisputably, these access methods can be used to extract viewpoints through a sequence of invocations. However, they ignore the central problem in extracting viewpoints: determining *which* facts to include in a viewpoint. The advantage of our access methods is that they provide a general solution to this problem (as described in Section 2), and the viewpoints extracted by our methods are comparable in coherence to those people construct (as described in Section 3).

2 The View Retriever

Our methods for accessing viewpoints are implemented in a program called the *View Retriever* (a term first proposed by Suthers (Suthers 1988)). The input to this program is a viewpoint specification and the output is a collection of facts. The task of the View Retriever is to determine which facts constitute the specified viewpoint and to request them from the knowledge base. Whether the knowledge base returns cached facts or computes them (using deduction, abduction, or induction) is irrelevant to the View Retriever. Those facts that the knowledge base cannot provide are not included in the viewpoint.

The View Retriever is used currently with the Botany Knowledge Base, a large system of over 13,000 frames and 160,000 cached facts, where a fact is a slot-filler of a frame. However, it is designed to work for any physical domain and to be easily extended to work in non-physical domains, such as those involving abstract concepts or mental processes.

[*]Support for this research was provided by an IBM Graduate Fellowship to Liane Acker, a grant from the National Science Foundation (IRI-9120310), a contract from the Air Force Office of Scientific Research (F49620-93-1-0239), and donations from the Digital Equipment Corporation. This work was conducted at the University of Texas at Austin.

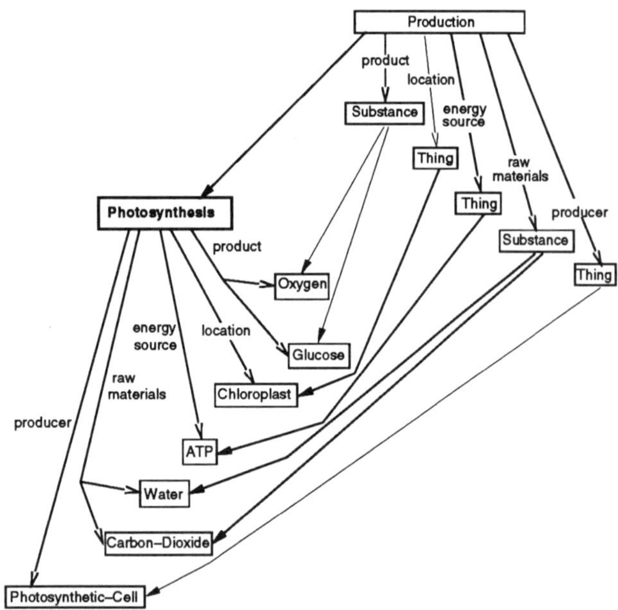

Figure 1: The viewpoint of "photosynthesis *as-kind-of* production", as extracted from the Botany Knowledge Base by the View Retriever.

The way a user (or application program) specifies a viewpoint and the way the View Retriever extracts it depends on the type of viewpoint. *As-kind-of* viewpoints describe concepts by relating them to more general concepts. Viewpoints constructed along *basic dimensions* describe concepts using a cluster of their attributes, such as functional, structural, or perceptual attributes. *As-having* viewpoints include the facts pertinent to a given attribute.

As-kind-of Viewpoints

An *as-kind-of* viewpoint describes a concept in terms of a more general concept. For example, the viewpoint "photosynthesis *as-kind-of* production" consists of those facts that explain how photosynthesis is a special case of production, such as its raw materials and products. Figure 1 shows a portion of this viewpoint.

The specification of an *as-kind-of* viewpoint is of the form:

(⟨primary concept⟩ *as-kind-of* ⟨reference concept⟩)

where the primary concept is the one the viewpoint will be taken of and the reference concept is a generalization of the primary concept (although not necessarily an immediate generalization).

The View Retriever extracts *as-kind-of* viewpoints by selecting relevant facts about the primary concept. A fact is a tuple of the form ⟨*slot*, *filler*⟩; it is considered relevant if some more general fact appears on the frame for the reference concept. The fact ⟨*slot'*, *filler'*⟩

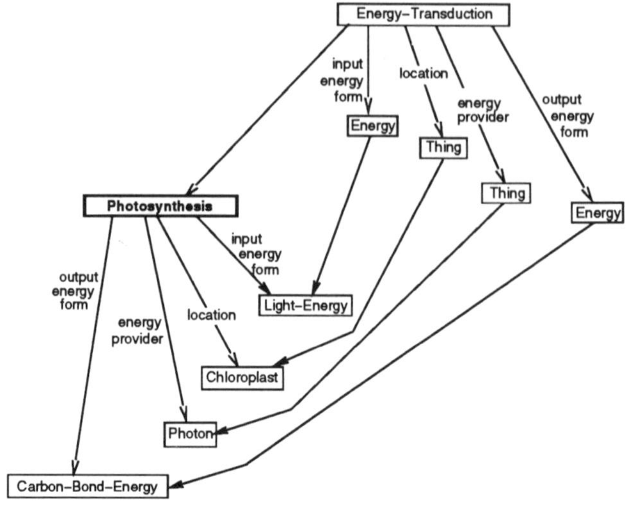

Figure 2: The viewpoint of "photosynthesis *as-kind-of* energy transduction", as extracted from the Botany Knowledge Base by the View Retriever.

is more general than ⟨*slot*, *filler*⟩ if any of the following conditions hold:

1. *slot* = *slot'* and *filler'* is a generalization of *filler*.

2. *filler* = *filler'* and *slot'* is a generalization of *slot*.

3. *slot'* is a generalization of *slot* and *filler'* is a generalization of *filler*.

For example, the viewpoint shown in Figure 1 contains the fact that photosynthesis produces glucose, because it is known that production processes typically produce some substance and glucose is a special kind of substance. That is, ⟨*product*, *Glucose*⟩ appears on the *Photosynthesis* frame, ⟨*product*, *Substance*⟩ appears on the *Production* frame, and *Substance* is a generalization of *Glucose*. The resulting viewpoint includes the links between facts about the primary concept and the more general facts about the reference concept (see Figure 1).

The View Retriever excludes many facts about the primary concept from the viewpoint. For example, although it is true that photosynthesis converts light energy into carbon bond energy, this fact is excluded because it is irrelevant to our concept of production (although it *would* be included in "photosynthesis as-kind-of energy transduction", as shown in Figure 2).

Various explanation-generation systems extract knowledge structures similar to *as-kind-of* viewpoints. The TEXT system (McKeown 1985) uses a function (called the *identification rhetorical predicate*) to differentiate a concept from a more general concept. TEXT determines what facts to include using a type of knowledge called *focus constraints*: facts are selected incrementally based on their connection with previously selected facts, rather than a global coherence criteria. Suthers's system uses a *genus-and-differentia* function similar to TEXT's identification predicate (Suthers 1991). McKeown's ADVISOR system constructs knowledge structures similar to *as-kind-of* viewpoints by restricting to predefined partitions of the knowledge base the superconcepts from which a concept can inherit slot fillers (McKeown 1988).

Viewpoints Constructed Along Basic Dimensions

In addition to viewpoints that describe concepts in terms of more general concepts, the View Retriever can extract viewpoints along *basic dimensions*, which are general types of facts, such as facts about an object's structure, function, or appearance. (We have borrowed the term from *Metaphors We Live By* (Lakoff & Johnson 1980), a work that has significantly influenced our characterization of viewpoint types.) Below we describe the basic dimensions used by the View Retriever.

Basic dimensions for objects:

- **Structural**, which includes the parts or substances that make up the object. It also includes the connections and spatial relations among them, what we call *interconnection relations*. The structural dimension also includes the relative sizes or number of the parts.

- **Perceptual**, which includes information regarding how humans perceive (see, hear, etc.) the object. This includes the shape, symmetry, size, color, and temperature of the object.

- **Functional**, which includes what the object "does" (the processes in which it is an actor). The functional dimension also includes properties suggestive of some unspecified process in which the object is involved, such as *life span* and *metabolic rate*.

- **Temporal**, which includes the temporal parts of an object (its stages or states). It also includes as interconnection relations the temporal ordering constraints among the stages or states.

Basic dimensions for processes:

- **Behavioral**, which includes the types and roles of the actors in the process and the changes that the process effects upon them. Initial and final conditions of the process are included as well.

- **Procedural**, which includes the steps (subevents) of the process and (as interconnection relations) any temporal ordering constraints that exist among the steps.

Basic dimensions for both objects and processes:

- **Taxonomic**, which includes the taxonomic breakdown of a class of objects or processes into subclasses. The taxonomic dimension also includes the relative sizes of the subclasses, the criteria for the breakdown, and (as interconnection relations) information about which subclasses are disjoint.

- **Modulatory**, which includes information about how one object or process affects other objects or processes. This includes causal relationships (e.g.,causes, enables, prevents, facilitates) and qualitative influences between quantities (e.g.,directly-affects, inversely-influences, correlated-with).

The specification for a viewpoint constructed along a basic dimension simply names the primary concept and the basic dimension desired:

(⟨primary concept⟩ *dimension* ⟨basic dimension⟩)

The View Retriever constructs the viewpoint first by extracting facts about the primary concept that belong to the basic dimension, then by adding to the viewpoint any interconnection relations for the basic dimension. For example, to construct a structural viewpoint of a plant seed, the View Retriever first selects those slots and fillers from the Seed frame that belong to the structural dimension, including ⟨part, Seed-Coat⟩, ⟨part, Embryo⟩, and ⟨part, Endosperm⟩. The View Retriever then selects interconnection relations among the selected parts (seed coat, embryo, and endosperm). For the structural dimension, interconnection relations include *connected-to, contains, surrounds*, etc. Thus, the resulting viewpoint contains the information that the seed is made up of a seed coat containing an embryo and an endosperm.

To construct viewpoints along basic dimensions, the View Retriever uses knowledge of which slots in the knowledge base are within each dimension. Based on our experience with the Botany Knowledge Base, this knowledge is easily encoded because the distinctions made by the basic dimensions are reflected in the top levels of the slot hierarchy.

Viewpoints created by the View Retriever along basic dimensions are similar to *perspectives* as suggested by Suthers (Suthers 1991) and as used by Romper (McCoy 1989). Unlike our basic dimensions, however, Romper's perspectives are domain-specific and include only facts about the primary concept; interconnection relations are omitted.

As-Having Viewpoints

An *as-having* viewpoint contains all and only the information about a concept that is relevant to some specified fact about the concept. Its specification has the following form:

(⟨primary concept⟩ *as-having* ⟨slot, filler⟩)

To our knowledge, general methods do not exist for extracting *as-having* viewpoints. Therefore, unlike for the other types of viewpoints, the View Retriever depends on *a priori* knowledge of relevance to select the facts that constitute *as-having* viewpoints.

To construct an *as-having viewpoint*, the View Retriever first looks for a cached *as-having* viewpoint that is based on the same fact (slot and filler), or a more general fact, as the requested viewpoint, but with a different primary concept. For example, to extract the viewpoint:

(Squirrel *as-having* ⟨agent-in, Seed-Dispersal⟩)

the View Retriever first looks in the knowledge base for a related, cached viewpoint such as one of the following:

1. (Animal *as-having* ⟨agent-in, Seed-Dispersal⟩)

2. (Bird *as-having* ⟨agent-in, Seed-Dispersal⟩)

3. (Animal *as-having* ⟨agent-in, Transportation⟩)

If a related viewpoint is found, the View Retriever uses it to determine which facts should be included in the new viewpoint. It does this by finding for each fact of the cached viewpoint a corresponding fact that is true of the primary concept of the new viewpoint. If the primary concept of the cached viewpoint is a *generalization* of the primary concept of the new viewpoint, then finding corresponding facts between the two consists of finding facts about the primary concept of the new viewpoint that are *specializations* of facts in the cached viewpoint. If the primary concepts of the two viewpoints are *siblings*, then finding corresponding facts between the two is more difficult. It requires finding pairs of facts that share a common abstraction.

If a related, cached viewpoint cannot be found in the knowledge base, then the View Retriever constructs *as-having* viewpoints by collecting all the facts about the primary concept that are implied by the specified fact, using all the inference rules and mechanisms available in the knowledge base. This method assumes (sometimes incorrectly) that any fact implied by some other fact is relevant to it. However, it has the advantage that it does not require viewpoints to be cached in the knowledge base.

Ideally, *as-having* viewpoints would be extracted using a theory of relevance to determine what facts are relevant. As a first step toward such a theory, several researchers have analyzed texts to determine the various ways that one fact may be relevant to another (Mann & Thompson 1987; Hobbs 1985). However, these theories are as yet descriptive rather than prescriptive, so the View Retriever cannot use them directly.

Composite Viewpoints

In addition to extracting individual viewpoints as described above, the View Retriever can combine them to form composite viewpoints. This involves more than simply concatenating the contents of two individual viewpoints; it involves putting them into correspondence with one another and removing the portions that do not correspond. Despite the apparent utility of composite viewpoints, we know of no other general methods for extracting them from knowledge bases.

The specification for a composite viewpoint has the following form:

(*composite* ⟨viewpoint1⟩ ⟨viewpoint2⟩ ⟨relation⟩)

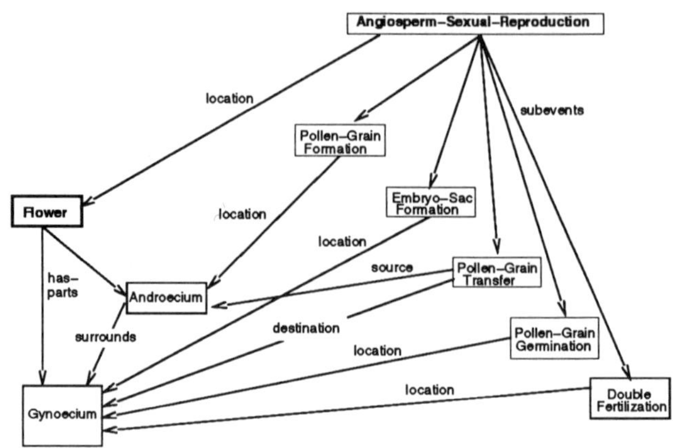

Figure 3: The composite ("structural-functional") viewpoint of a flower in its role in plant reproduction, as extracted from the Botany Knowledge Base by the View Retriever.

where *viewpoint1* and *viewpoint2* are individual viewpoints (or specifications for them) and *relation* specifies the correspondence to be established between the viewpoints.

One commonly used composite viewpoint, called "structural-functional", describes the roles an object (and its parts) play in an event (and its subevents). Its specification is the following:

(*composite* (⟨object⟩ dimension structural) (⟨event⟩ dimension procedural) actor-in)

For example, the viewpoint that describes the roles of a flower's parts in the steps of plant reproduction is specified as follows:

(*composite* (Flower dimension structural) (Plant-Reproduction dimension procedural) actor-in)

Its contents are shown in Figure 3.

The View Retriever constructs this composite viewpoint by the following procedure. First it extracts the two individual viewpoints (the structural viewpoint of Flower and the procedural viewpoint of Plant-Reproduction). Then it determines which parts of the Flower that are in the structural viewpoint are related to Plant-Reproduction or one of its subevents (as given in the procedural viewpoint) by an *actor-in* relation or some more specific relation (such as *location-of*). Those parts, such as the Flower's corolla, that are not actors in the event are omitted from the composite viewpoint. Similarly, those subevents, such as Fruit-Ripening, that do not involve any of the parts in the structural viewpoint of Flower are omitted.

This procedure can extract diverse viewpoints. For example, the composite viewpoint that describes the parts of a plant ovary as related to the parts of the fruit of which it is a developmental stage can be extracted with the following specification:

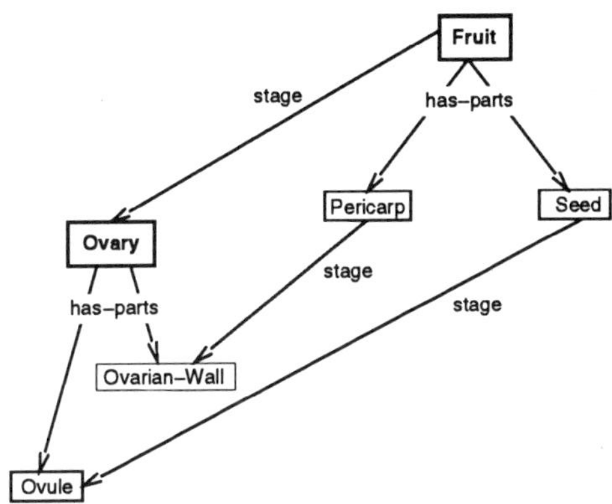

Figure 4: The composite viewpoint of the parts of a plant ovary as related to the parts of the fruit of which it is a developmental stage, as extracted from the Botany Knowledge Base by the View Retriever.

> (*composite* (Fruit dimension structural) (Ovary dimension structural) stages)

This composite viewpoint, as shown in Figure 4, includes the parts of the fruit (seed, pericarp, etc.), the parts of the ovary (ovule, ovarian wall, etc.), and the *stage* relations between them, such as the facts that the ovule is a developmental stage of the seed and the ovarian wall is a developmental stage of the pericarp.

The procedure for constructing composite viewpoints can also extract the viewpoint that categorizes angiosperms (flower-bearing plants) according to the different types of flowers they have. The specification is the following:

> (*composite* (Angiosperm dimension taxonomic) (Flower dimension taxonomic) parts)

This composite viewpoint includes, for example, the fact that one kind of angiosperm is the orchid, which has an irregular flower.

Evaluation of the View Retriever

The purpose of our evaluation was to measure the coherence of viewpoints the View Retriever extracts, as compared to the coherence of viewpoints found in human-generated text. For each of 12 topics in botany, sets of facts were drawn from 3 sources:

- a college-level botany textbook (Raven, Evert, & Curtis 1976),

- the View Retriever applied to the Botany Knowledge Base, and

- facts selected randomly from a particular frame in the Botany Knowledge Base.

The viewpoints ranged in size from 3 to 11 facts. For each topic, textbook passages and random sets of facts were chosen to be roughly the same size as the viewpoint on that topic. Each group of facts (including the

Source	Coherence	
	Mean	σ
(1) Textbook Viewpoints	4.23	0.56
(2) View Retriever's Viewpoints	3.76	0.74
(3) Degraded Viewpoints	2.86	0.94
(4) Random Collections of Facts	2.62	0.86

Table 1: Ten judges rated the coherence of sets of facts from four sources (1=incoherent; 5=coherent). A statistical analysis using the T-test with 0.95 level of confidence shows no significant difference in coherence between sources (1) and (2) or between sources (3) and (4). There is a significant difference between all other pairs.

textbook passages) was translated manually into "simple English" to normalize presentation style. The viewpoints included about equal numbers of *as-kind-of*, basic dimension, and composite viewpoints; *as-having* viewpoints were omitted from this study because they often use cached viewpoints.

Ten subjects (senior undergraduates and graduate students from the Botany and Biology Departments of the University of Texas at Austin) judged the coherence of several passages from each source. The subjects were asked to use a scale of 1 to 5, to assign a passage a score of "1" if it seemed no more coherent than a randomly selected group of facts on the subject, and to assign a passage a score of "5" if it was as coherent as a passage of comparable length on the subject from a good textbook.

Table 1 summarizes the subjects' responses. Statistical analysis (using a T-test with 0.95 level of confidence) yields the following results:

- The mean coherence of viewpoints from textbooks did not differ significantly from the mean coherence of viewpoints extracted by the View Retriever.

- The mean coherence of extracted viewpoints *did* differ significantly from the mean coherence of random collections of facts drawn from the same frame.

A further study gives additional evidence that the View Retriever extracts coherent viewpoints. Along with passages from the three sources described above, the subjects were given passages from a fourth source: viewpoints extracted by the View Retriever and then "degraded" by replacing some of their facts with randomly selected facts on the same topic. Twenty-eight such degraded viewpoints were constructed, each with between one and seven facts replaced. Of the twenty-eight, each subject received six. Table 1 shows the mean coherence score of the degraded viewpoints. Statistical analysis shows a significant difference in the mean coherence of "pure" viewpoints and degraded viewpoints.

A final study adds more evidence that passages vary in coherence based on their source and that viewpoints extracted by the View Retriever are consistently judged to be coherent. A two-way analysis of variance, computed by Paul Cohen[1], determined that there was no significant interaction effect between:

- the variance in coherence scores assigned by different judges, and

- the variance in coherence scores for passages from different sources (e.g.,textbooks, the View Retriever).

Thus, although judges varied in their harshness, they largely agreed on relative orderings.

3 Discussion

Viewpoints are coherent collections of facts that describe a concept from a particular perspective. They are essential for a wide variety of tasks, such as explanation generation and qualitative modeling. We have identified several types of viewpoints and developed a program, the View Retriever, for extracting them from knowledge bases, either singly or in combination. Our evaluation of the View Retriever indicates that its viewpoints are comparable in coherence to those constructed by people.

The View Retriever has several known limitations, some of which we are addressing. First, viewpoint specifications use the names of frames and slots in the knowledge base. Therefore, users of the View Retriever must have extensive knowledge of the concept and slot hierarchies in order to use the View Retriever. To address this limitation, we are developing methods whereby users can specify frames and slots descriptively rather than by name. Second, our textbook analysis reveals that most explanations consist of several viewpoints used in concert. Although the View Retriever can extract composite viewpoints, we have not yet identified which combinations are commonly used. A third limitation is that the View Retriever ignores knowledge about the *a priori* importance of facts. Therefore, it cannot extract viewpoints of a concept in the order of their importance, a potentially useful ability.

The View Retriever will be evaluated more extensively when it supports our tutoring system for plant anatomy and physiology. It will be the primary method used by the tutor to access the Botany Knowledge Base to build qualitative models and generate explanations. We are currently building this tutoring system, and we have found that knowledge base access at the level of viewpoints (as opposed to the level of individual facts or frames) greatly simplifies system design and implementation.

---

[1]Computer Science Department, University of Massachusetts at Amherst

References

Falkenhainer, B., and Forbus, K. 1991. Compositional modeling: Finding the right model for the job. *Artificial Intelligence* 51:95–143.

Forbus, K. 1984. Qualitative process theory. *Artificial Intelligence* 24:85–168.

Hobbs, J. 1985. On the coherence and the structure of discourse. Technical Report CSLI-85-37, Computer Science Department, Stanford University.

Lakoff, G., and Johnson, M. 1980. *Metaphors We Live By*. University of Chicago Press.

Lester, J., and Porter, B. 1991. A student-sensitive discourse generator for intelligent tutoring systems. In *Proceedings of the International Conference on the Learning Sciences*, 298–304.

Liu, Z., and Farley, A. 1990. Shifting ontological perspectives in reasoning about physical systems. In *Proceedings of the 8th National Conference on Artificial Intelligence*.

Mann, W., and Thompson, S. 1987. Rhetorical structure theory: A theory of text organizations. Technical Report ISI/RS-87-190, Information Sciences Institute, University of Southern California.

McCoy, K. 1989. Generating context-sensitive responses to object-related misconceptions. *Artificial Intelligence* 41:157–195.

McKeown, K. 1985. *Text Generation: Using Discourse Strategies and Focus Constraints to Generate Natural Language Text*. Cambridge University Press.

McKeown, K. 1988. Generating goal-oriented explanations. *International Journal of Expert Systems* 1(4):377–395.

Moore, D., and Swartout, W. 1988. A reactive approach to explanation. In *Proceedings of the Fourth International Workshop on Natural Language Generation*.

Murray, K., and Porter, B. 1989. Controlling search for the consequences of new information during knowledge integration. In *Proceedings of the Machine Learning Workshop*, 290–295. Palo Alto, California: Morgan Kaufmann.

Raven, P.; Evert, R.; and Curtis, H. 1976. *Biology of Plants*. New York: Worth Publishers.

Suthers, D. 1988. Providing multiple views of reasoning for explanation. In *Proceedings of the International Conference on Intelligent Tutoring Systems*, 435–442.

Suthers, D. 1991. Task-appropriate hybrid architectures for explanation. In *Proceedings of the AAAI-91 Workshop on Comparative Analysis of Explanation Planning Architectures*.

Using Induction to Refine Information Retrieval Strategies

Catherine Baudin *   **Barney Pell** **
Artificial Intelligence Research Branch
NASA Ames Research Center
MS 269-2, Moffett Field CA 94035
baudin@ptolemy.arc.nasa.gov   pell@ptolemy.arc.nasa.gov

Smadar Kedar
Institute for the Learning Sciences
Northwestern University
1890 Maple ave. Evanston, IL 60201
kedar@ils.nwu.edu

Abstract

Conceptual information retrieval systems use structured document indices, domain knowledge and a set of heuristic retrieval strategies to match user queries with a set of indices describing the document's *content*. Such retrieval strategies increase the set of relevant documents retrieved (increase recall), but at the expense of returning additional irrelevant documents (decrease precision). Usually in conceptual information retrieval systems this tradeoff is managed by hand and with difficulty. This paper discusses ways of managing this tradeoff by the application of standard induction algorithms to refine the retrieval strategies in an engineering design domain. We gathered examples of query/retrieval pairs during the system's operation using feedback from a user on the retrieved information. We then fed these examples to the induction algorithm and generated decision trees that refine the existing set of retrieval strategies. We found that (1) induction improved the *precision* on a set of queries generated by another user, without a significant loss in *recall*, and (2) in an interactive mode, the decision trees pointed out flaws in the retrieval and indexing knowledge and suggested ways to refine the retrieval strategies.

1. Introduction

Conceptual information retrieval systems [Tong 89], [Mauldin 91], [Baudin et al. 93] use structured patterns, rather than keywords or words from a text, to represent the *content* of the information in a document. These systems use domain knowledge and can *reason* about how to select pieces of information related to a user query using the conceptual indices associated with the documents. In particular, when there is no direct match to a particular query, the relationships in the domain model can be used to predict where the answers to a query *might* be documented (increase a system's *recall*) or to narrow down the search for a document that would best answer the query (increase *precision*). This is based on the observation that pieces of information in a document are usually not isolated islands of ideas but are related by implicit rules.

This type of knowledge-based retrieval requires: (1) structured indices that can represent the objects and relationships in a piece of information, (2) domain knowledge about the concepts and their relationships and (3) heuristic retrieval strategies about how to match a query with an index as in RUBRIC [Tong 89] or DEDAL [Baudin et al 93]. The following example shows how heuristic knowledge is used in the conceptual information retrieval system DEDAL [Baudin 93] in the mechanical engineering design domain.

In this sample interaction, a mechanical engineering designer queries DEDAL to retrieve information about the design of a new variety of shock absorber. The query is about the "function of the solenoid". The system cannot find an index that exactly matches the query, so it uses a retrieval heuristic: "to find information about the *function* of a subcomponent, look for information about the *operation* of a mechanism that includes this component". This heuristic reflects the engineer's intuition that a paragraph describing how a mechanism works is likely to provide information about the function of its subparts and about how they interact. In this case, if *solenoid* is part of the *force generation mechanism*, DEDAL will assume that information about the function of the solenoid will be located in the same paragraph or nearby a piece of information which describes how the *force generation mechanism* works. Here the system used knowledge about the shock absorber domain (the solenoid is part of the force generation mechanism) to extend the user query and find related information.

Such heuristic retrieval strategies increase the set of relevant documents retrieved in response to a user query (increase recall), but at the expense of returning additional irrelevant documents (decrease precision). It is difficult for the system builder to manage this tradeoff by hand. For instance in the previous example the system could have retrieved a portion of a videotape showing the *force generation mechanism* but no close view of the *solenoid*. This paper discusses the application of standard induction algorithms to refine the heuristic retrieval strategies of a conceptual information retrieval system. Our goal is to refine the retrieval knowledge of such system over time as it gains experience with different users in different domains. To this end, We gathered examples of query/retrieval pairs during the system's operation using feedback from a user on the retrieved information and we fed these examples to an induction algorithm to refine the existing set of retrieval strategies.

---

 * Catherine Baudin is an employee of RECOM Software Inc.
** Barney Pell is an employee of the Research Institute for Advanced Computer Sciences.

Section 2 discusses the specifics of the conceptual retrieval system that we used and gives examples of retrieval heuristics in the mechanical engineering domain. Section 3 describes how we use relevance feedback techniques and induction to refine the retrieval heuristics. Section 4 presents experiments and results on the impact of the refinements on the retrieval performance. Section 5 discusses the system's limitations and our plans for future work.

2. Background: Document Indexing and Retrieval in DEDAL

We have tested our approach on the conceptual retrieval system DEDAL described in [Baudin et al. 93] and will use examples from the mechanical engineering design domain to illustrate our method. DEDAL stores multimedia mechanical engineering design documents such as meeting summaries, pages of a designer's notebook, technical reports, CAD drawings and videotaped conversations between designers. It uses a conceptual indexing and query language to describe the content and the form of design information. [Baya *et. al.*, 1992], For instance: "The inner hub holds the steel friction disks and causes them to rotate" is part of a paragraph in page 20 of the record: report-333. It can be described by two indexing patterns:

<topic **function** subject **inner-hub** level-of-detail **configuration** medium **text** in-record **report-333** segment **20**>.

<topic **relation** subject **inner-hub** and **steel-friction-disks** level-of-detail **configuration** medium **text** in-record **report-333** segment **20**>

The queries have the same structure as an index and use the same vocabulary. A question such as: "How does the inner hub interact with the friction disks?" can be formulated in DEDAL's language as the query:

<get-information-about topic **relation** subject **inner-hub** and **steel-friction-disks** with preferred medium **equation**>.

The domain model includes aspects of the artifact structure, the requirements, the main design decisions and alternatives considered as well as relations such as: *isa*, *part-of* and *depends-on*. For instance, *solenoid* is a kind of *actuator* and is part of the *force generation mechanism*. The attribute *force* generated by the solenoid depends on the value of other attributes such as *current of the solenoid* or *power of the car battery*.

2.1 Heuristic Retrieval Strategies

The analysis of different types of design records such as engineering notebooks and structured progress reports led to the identification of a set of heuristics to help match a user's query with a set of indexing patterns describing the documents. These heuristics are activated when no index exactly matches a query or when the user is not satisfied with the references retrieved. They look for regions in the documentation that contain related information and assume that the required information will be found near these regions (on the same page, or in the same subsection de-

pending on the type of record). For instance:

<u>equation-to-schemata</u>: In an engineering notebook, an equation describing a mechanism will usually be found next to a drawing representing this mechanism.

Some heuristics use the relations among the concepts in the task vocabulary:

<u>performance-to-analysis</u>: Information about the *performance* of a particular assembly and the *analysis* of this assembly are likely to be located in nearby regions of the documentation.

Others exploit the hierarchical relations in the domain model:

<u>operation-to-function</u>: In a structured document such as a progress report, the *function* of a component X in a mechanical assembly Y might be found near where the *operation* of assembly Y is described.

While these heuristics have been shown to significantly increase the recall of the system when compared to the system without the heuristics and to a base-line boolean retrieval system [Baudin et al. 93], they also decrease the precision of the retrieval by a small but non negligible amount. There are several reasons why a heuristic can fail to retrieve relevant information (see Section 6). One reason is that it is difficult for a knowledge engineer who creates these heuristics to take into account the influence of every possible document specific characteristic (such as the size of the document, the medium or the level of detail of the information) and determine what is relevant to the retrieval heuristics.

3. Using Induction to Refine Heuristic Retrieval Strategies

In order to refine the retrieval heuristics in DEDAL we first gather examples of query/retrieval pairs generated by successful and failed retrievals. We process these examples and reformulate them in terms of the language of the retrieval heuristics and of "interesting" concepts that could discriminate positive and negative examples. We then feed these examples to an induction algorithm to generate a decision tree that refines the set of heuristics. We define criteria to evaluate the impact of the induction mechanism on the retrieval performance of the system and on our understanding of the flaws in the initial set of heuristics.

3.1 Gathering examples through relevance feedback

First, we gather examples of relevant and irrelevant retrievals through a relevance feedback method [Salton 89]. Given a query, DEDAL first tries to find an index that exactly matches the query. If the retrieval fails, it applies a retrieval heuristic and presents the user with a prioritized list of references. The user then has the option to provide feedback to the system on the relevance of the reference retrieved. If the user is not satisfied by the answers returned he or she can ask the system to resume its search and apply another set of heuristics.

There are mainly two ways of using feedback from the

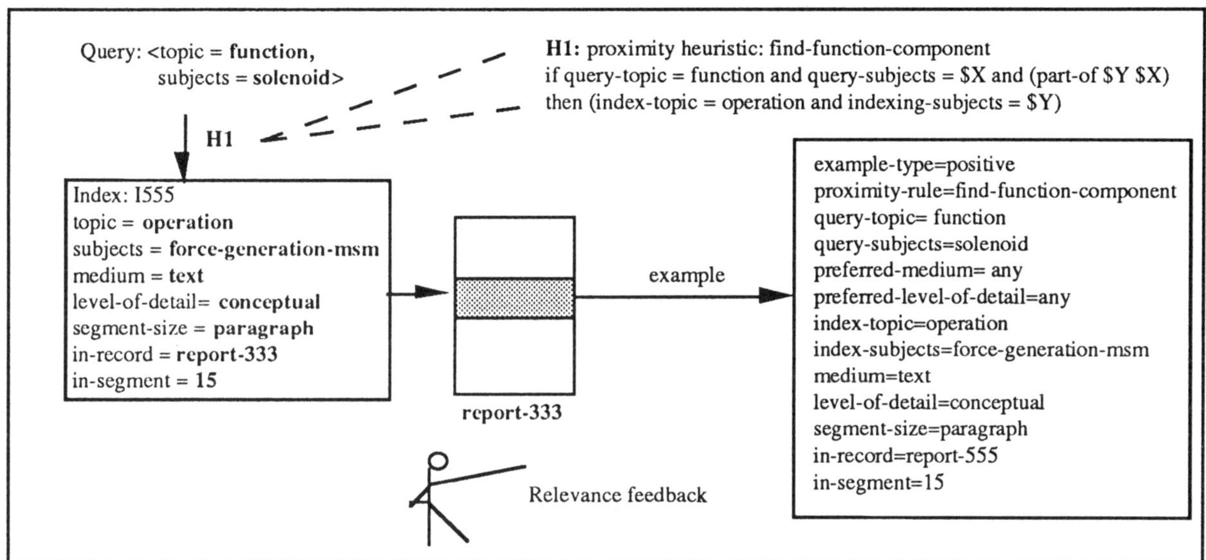

Figure 1: an example gathered through relevance feedback

user to improve the behavior of the system: The first way is to change the priority of the heuristics based on their rate of success. When the user provides feedback on the relevance of the references retrieved, the system updates a success coefficient associated with the heuristic. This coefficient is used by the retrieval mechanism in DEDAL to choose which heuristic to try first and to order the references proposed to the user. This re-prioritizing mechanism works well for the cases where a heuristic is very good or very bad, but does not improve the behavior of the system in the majority of cases where the heuristic is "somewhat" good, but needs slight adjusting.

Another way is to *refine* the heuristics so as to still cover the relevant references retrieved in answer to a user question (positive examples), while minimizing the number of irrelevant references presented (negative examples). This involves being able to modify applicability conditions of the heuristics - that is, to add and remove the tests that lead to the selection of a given document in response to a query. The idea is to take the examples of successful and failed query/retrieval examples generated by the user feedback, feed them to an induction mechanism, and generate a decision tree that refines the initial set of heuristics by refining tests leading to additional irrelevant references.

Figure 1 illustrates how a query/retrieval pair is acquired from the user using the example discussed in the introduc-

tion. In this phase we record the queries asked by a user, the answers returned by the retrieval heuristics and the relevance assessment of the user. The shaded information segment is described by one index and is about the operation of the force-generation-mechanism, the medium is text, the level of detail is conceptual, the record is the report-333 and the segment is a paragraph in page 15. That information segment is retrieved by the index I555 using the heuristic H1. The user provides a relevance assessment (relevant or irrelevant) and a corresponding positive or negative example of query/retrieval is stored in a database.

3.2 Using Induction to Refine the Retrieval Heuristics in DEDAL

Our initial goal is to decrease the number of irrelevant documents presented to a user (increasing precision) while maintaining the same number of relevant documents (preserving recall).

We use an off-the-shelf ID3 induction algorithm [Quinlan 86] on the examples of successful and failed retrievals to generate a decision tree. Figure 2 shows a query being processed through the set of initial heuristics and through the decision tree. When a query/retrieval example is selected by the existing set of heuristics, this example is filtered by the decision tree in an attempt to detect irrelevant references and assign them low priority.

To use ID3 we had to process the examples generated by

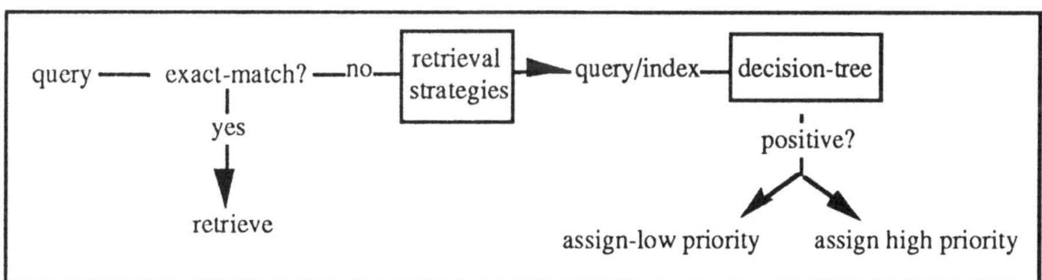

Figure 2: Using induction to refine the retrieval heuristics

the heuristics so as to (a) select features that could be used to discriminate positive and negative examples, and (b) remove noisy examples.

Selecting features to describe the examples: The first step is to select a set of features to describe the examples. This involves selecting and adding features to describe the characteristics of a query/retrieval example. In DEDAL an example has three types of features corresponding to three levels of generality:

(1) *documentation* dependent features such as a particular reference to a segment of information in a record.

(2) *domain* dependent features (subjects). These are references to elements dependent on a particular design. For instance in our example *solenoid* and *force generation mechanism* are both components of a particular mechanical device.

(3) *task* dependent features. These are features that do not depend on a particular design document. They only depend on the fact that the documentation is about the task of *mechanical design*. Features such as topic, media and level of detail are task dependent characteristics that can be reused across domains.

If a branch of the decision tree refers to document specific features, the corresponding heuristic refinement will only be usable for the documents used in the training set. In the same way, if a branch of the decision tree refers to domain specific features, the refinements should be valid for other documents related to the same design problem. Finally if a branch of a tree only refers to task specific features, the refinements should transfer across domains for documents associated with any mechanical design project.

In addition, to make possible the generation of domain independent refinements we added some features to each

example. These features represent different types of relations between the subjects in the query and the subjects in the matching index. For instance the feature "subjects-query-equal-subjects-index =no" means that the subjects in the query are not the same as the subjects in the matching index. In the same way, "subjects-query-is-part-of-subjects-index = yes" means that the subjects in the query are part-of some subjects in the matching index. Figure 3 shows an example: the bold italic features are document dependent features, and the bold features are domain dependent features. The features in plain text are task dependent. The additional task features that are automatically added to each example are shown at the bottom of Figure 3.

Removing noise in the training examples: The examples are processed so as to detect the cases where the same answer to the same query led to different relevance assessments. If an answer was found relevant one time and irrelevant the other time it is counted as a positive example. This is because several factors other than faulty heuristics can lead to the retrieval of an irrelevant reference in answer to a query. For instance, an answer might be irrelevant because the user misformulated a query, because he or she did not scan the information thoroughly and missed the answer or because of a flaw in the indexing knowledge.

3.3 Evaluation

We evaluate our approach in terms of: (1) the impact on the *retrieval performance* of DEDAL: as a start our goal is to decrease the number of irrelevant references retrieved (increasing the system's precision) by the heuristics while maintaining the same number of relevant references (maintaining the system's recall), and (2) the *informativeness* of the fixes proposed by the induction algorithm in terms of the ability of a knowledge engineer to understand the information in the decision tree and detect flaws in the retrieval heuristics, in the indices or in the domain model.

4. Results

To evaluate our method we selected a set of examples generated by two mechanical engineers using DEDAL to retrieve answers about the "rotary-friction-damper" design, an innovative electromechanical shock absorber designed for Ford Motor Corporation [Baudin et al. 93]. The users queried the system while solving a redesign problem involving the modification of the shock absorber design. Each of the references retrieved was rated by the users as relevant or irrelevant. In this experiment when a proximity heuristic was used, the user was asked to rate all the references retrieved by the heuristic.

4.1 Experiments

We extracted 300 examples of relevant and irrelevant heuristic retrievals generated from the interaction with the first user (user1) as our training set, and another set of 81 examples generated by the second user (user2) as our test set. We then selected sets of features for the examples and generated three different decision trees corresponding to different levels of generality in the features selected. Table

```
(example 165 positive
generated-by-rule: find-function-component
query-topic = function
query- subjects= solenoid
index-topic = operation
index-subjects =
force-generation-mechanism
index-medium = text
index-level-of-detail = conceptual
in-record: damper-spring-1989
in-segment: 15

subjects-query-equal-subjects-index = no
subject-query-is-attributes = no
subject-query-is-requirements = no
subjects-query-is-part-of-subjects-index = yes
subjects-index-is-part-of-subjects-query = no
subjects-query-is-kind-of-subjects-index = no
subjects-index-is-kind-of-subjects-query = no
subjects-query-depends-on-subjects-index = no
subjects-query-influence-subjects-index = no
... )
```

Figure 3: A positive example of query/index match

1 summarizes the results in terms of the impact of the decision tree generated from the training examples on the percent of negative and positive examples filtered for the queries generated by user2.

In our first experiment the examples include features at all three levels of generality: the *document*, the *domain* and the *task* features. This means that information about specific documents is included in the training examples. In this case, the induction algorithm picked the document specific features as the most discriminant features to separate the positive and negative examples. As a result the induction tree used information about specific documents and pages to refine the heuristics. In the second experiment, we removed the document specific information but kept the domain specific information. As a result the refinement tree generated from the induction algorithm does not refer to any specific document, it does however refer to domain concepts. Finally in the third experiment both the document and the domain specific features were removed from the examples.

The effect of this manual feature selection is to force the induction algorithm to generate filters at different levels of generality. However, because ID3 naturally picks the most discriminant features, the effect of this forced generalization is to trade predictive power for an increase in generality. The following subsection shows results from these experiments.

4.2 Impact on the Performance of the Retrieval

We measured the impact of the decision tree in terms of its ability to filter the negative examples in the test set while preserving the positive examples.

We present in Table 1 the number of positive and negative examples filtered by the system. In the table, the column '%filtered negatives' lists the percentage of negatives filtered by the system out of the total number of negatives in the test set, and similarly for '%filtered positives'. The total number of examples generated by user2 is 81, with 54 negative examples and 27 positive examples. The cases that are undecided are counted as positive. As seen in Table 1:

a. Document dependent repair: the decision tree generated for experiment1 would have reduced by 44% the number of irrelevant references presented as high priority references to user2, while assigning low priority to only 7% of the relevant references. However, this filter is document dependent as most branches of the decision tree refer to specific regions of information in particular documents.

b. Domain dependent repair: In Experiment 2 the document dependent features (record and segment in figure 3) were removed from the examples, forcing ID3 to generate a more general tree. As a result, in experiment2 the branches of the decision tree do not refer to any specific document but still refer to subjects of the domain. For instance one branch states that: if an information segment is about *rotary-friction-damper* and *wedge* and the query is about *rotary-friction-damper* then the match is irrelevant. Because there is no reference to any specific document, this knowledge should be applicable to any design document in the "rotary-friction-damper" domain. Here, as expected the percentage of filtered negatives (33%) is smaller than for the document dependent tree, while the misclassification of relevant retrievals (11%) is higher.

c. Task dependent repair: Finally both the document dependent and the domain dependent features were removed from the examples in an attempt to generate a domain independent filter. The resulting tree only involves tests on task dependent features. Table 1 shows that the resulting decision tree would filter 26% of the irrelevant references presented to the user but at the expense of also filtering 41% of the relevant ones. As a result of this high rate of misclassified relevant references, we consider this tree ineffective as an automatic filter. However, as discussed in the next section, some branches of the tree were still informative for the knowledge engineer.

4.3 Informativeness

We found two main advantages in having a knowledge engineer examine the branches of the decision tree: (1) even in the cases where the tree does not improve the performance of the retrieval, some branches of the tree suggested interesting local fixes that appealed to the knowledge engineer's intuition although they cannot yet be evaluated automatically by the system, and (2) the branches of the tree pointed out flaws in other parts of the system such as the indices themselves or the domain model.

Even though we do not have any formal measure of the informativeness of the fixes proposed by the system, we present three examples of particularly informative repairs suggested by the decision trees generated from our experiments. Currently the knowledge engineer examines these suggestions and manually modifies heuristics.

<u>Example 1</u>: In Experiment3 most branches of the tree refine the heuristics by adding conditions on the *medium* and *level of detail* of the information retrieved. For instance in the case of the heuristic "operation-to-construction", the initial applicability conditions state that any query about the *operation* of a mechanism X can be matched with an index about *construction* of X (information about the construction of X shows how X is structured and how it is assembled).

User 2 on user1 1	# filtered negatives	# filtered positives	% filtered negatives	% filtered positives
with document features	24	2	44%	7%
with domain features	18	3	33%	11%
only task features	14	11	26%	41%

Table 1: Impact of induction on retrieval performance

H1: Operation-to-construction
if   (query operation-of $X)
then (index construction-of $X)

The applicability tree (see Figure 4) refines the applicability condition of this heuristic by specifying that any information about construction of X may be relevant to a query about operation of X *only if the medium of the document is text* , not if it is say, a schemata. This proposed repair to the "operation-to-construction" heuristic corresponds to the intuition that a picture convey structure but not actions and therefore a text is more likely to give an idea of how a mechanism works. The system displays the branches of the tree and the knowledge engineer can then decide to update the retrieval heuristic "operation-to-construction".

H1': operation-to-construction
if   (query operation-of $X)
then (index construction-of $X
         with **index-medium text)**

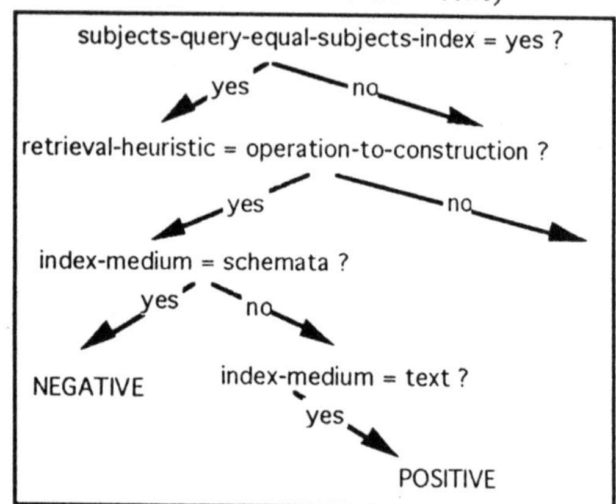

Figure 4: A portion of an applicability tree generated by the ID3 induction algorithm.

Example 2: Another portion of the tree generated in Experiment 3 rediscovered a heuristic that was suggested later by the expert of the domain in a newer version of the proximity heuristics: the heuristic generated by the decision tree is: "if query-topic = location and query-topic-is-part-of-index-topic = yes and medium-index = picture then the example is positive.". This branch corresponds to the following rule: "If the query is about the location of a component X, and X is a subpart of Y, a picture describing how Y is assembled might provide information about where the component X is located in the assembly." The system here discovered that a picture of an assembly Y might be a good way of locating a subcomponent of Y. The tree also suggested that this heuristic will fail if the medium of the retrieved information is text. Even though the test set generated by user2 could not be used to validate this rule (there were no questions about the location of a component), the following new rule can be manually added by the knowledge engineer.

if   (query location $X)
     (part $Y $X)
then (index construction $Y
         with medium = picture)

Example 3: The branches of the decision tree generated by Experiment 2 pointed out flaws in the domain model and in the way some of the information was indexed. For instance, one branch of the tree suggests that: "if an information segment is about *rotary-friction-damper* and *wedge* and the query is about rotary-friction-damper then the example is negative" This rule pointed out the fact that a piece of information was about *rotary-friction-damper* and *wedge*, whereas *wedge* is not a component used in the current design. This piece of information in fact described an alternative design solution and should not be indexed using the concept *rotary-friction-damper* which refers to the current design solution. This failure pointed out to a problem in the index itself. Such a flaw in the indexing knowledge would have been difficult to discover without the help of the induction mechanism.

5. Discussion

The difficulty in using examples collected during the system's interaction with end-users to refine information retrieval heuristics is that there might be several causes involved in the failure of the system to satisfy a user: flaws in the domain model, in the way a piece of information is indexed, in the way the query is formulated or in the heuristic itself. Consequently, we expect two types of results out of the decision trees generated from the examples: (1) to improve the performance of the system in terms of the precision and recall of the retrieval during the system's operation with the *end-user*, (2) to help a *knowledge-engineer* find flaws in the knowledge of the system. In addition we want (3) to be able to *transfer* the retrieval heuristics learned to other documents and other domains.

With respect to these three goals, our experiments have shown that by using induction in the heuristic retrieval component: (1) we improved the precision of the system at the most specific document level by reducing the number of irrelevant references retrieved by 44% with minimum impact to the system's recall, (2) some of the domain and document specific rules pointed out flaws in the way the information was indexed and in the domain model, these flaws would have been difficult to detect manually, and (3) the decision trees suggested fixes to the proximity heuristics that showed the influence on the relevance of the retrieval heuristics of document specific characteristics such as the medium and the level of detail of the information. In addition, some of these repairs can transfer to other domains for mechanical engineering design documents. However, currently the domain independent decision tree is not an effective filter to improve the precision of the retrieval as it misclassifies too many relevant references (41%). This is partly due to the fact that we need more training examples in different domains. We also might need to add new domain independent features to describe the examples.

5.1 Limitations

The examples used to generate the decision trees were pre-filtered by the initial set of proximity heuristics. As a result the decision tree must still be used in conjunction with these heuristics. To be able to generate new heuristics from the examples, the induction algorithm needs to operate on the negative examples that are filtered by the initial set of retrieval heuristics.

To be fully operational, the system needs to be able to maintain several decision trees in parallel and must be able to monitor their performance in the background as in [Maes et al. 93] in order to understand when and at what level of generality the result of the induction algorithm can improve the performance of the retrieval.

Our goal in these experiments was to increase the precision of the retrieval while maintaining the same level of recall. In the future, we need to address the cases where the rules are too specific, so as to increase the coverage of the rules and increase the system's recall. This in turn might lead us to extend the interactive capability of the system to help modify the domain knowledge itself--that is, the taxonomy of domain concepts and the relations between these concepts--as in [Bareiss et al.89].

Finally we need to run more experiments not only with different classes of users but with different domains. In particular, we are now running the system to retrieve text, graphics and video records for the design of an innovative bioreactor, a device that will enable NASA life scientists to study microbial growth.

6. Conclusion

This paper discussed the use of induction to refine conceptual information retrieval strategies. Our approach improves retrieval performance in a noisy environment, using relevance feedback from the end-user during the system's operation. The result of the induction algorithm is useful in two modes: (1) in an *automated* mode, as a filter to increase the precision of the retrieval, and (2) in an *interactive* mode: to help the knowledge engineer detect flaws in the different components of the system.

Acknowledgments

Thanks to Vinod Baya, Ade Mabogunje and Jody Gevins Underwood who helped us develop, and evaluate DEDAL. Thanks to Larry Leifer and to the other members of the GCDK group for their feedback and support on this project, to Wray Buntine and members of NASA Ames. Thanks to Michel Baudin for his help on early drafts.

References

Bareiss, R., Porter, B.W., Murray, K.S., Supporting Start-to-Finish Development of Knowledge Bases. *Machine Learning*, 4(3-4):259-283, 1989.

Baudin, C., Gevins, J., Baya, V., "Using Device Models to Facilitate the Retrieval of Multimedia Design Information", in proceedings of IJCAI 93 Chambéry, 1992.

Baudin, C., Kedar, S., Gevins, J., Baya, V., Question-Based Acquisition of Conceptual Indices for Multimedia Design Documentation. *Proceedings of the Eleventh National Conference on Artificial Intelligence*; Washington, D.C., 1993.

Baya, V, Gevins, J, Baudin, C, Mabogunje, A, Leifer, L. "An Experimental Study of Design Information Reuse", in proceedings of the 4th International Conference on Design 1992.

Maes, P., Kozierok, R., "Learning Interface Agents" *Proceedings of the Eleventh National Conference on Artificial Intelligence*; Washington, D.C., 1993.

Mauldin, M. "Retrieval Performance in FERRET", Proceedings of the ACM SIGIR Conference, 1991, pp. 347-355.

Salton, G., Buckley, C., Improving Retrieval Performance by Relevance Feedback. J. of ASIS. 41:288-297. 1990.

Quinlan, J.R.,Induction of decision trees. Machine Learning 1(1):81-106 1986.

Tong, M. R., Appelbaum, A., and Askman V. "A Knowledge Representation for Conceptual Information Retrieval", International Journal of Intelligent Systems. vol. 4, 259-283, 1989.

Formalizing Ontological Commitments

Nicola Guarino

LADSEB-CNR, National Research Council,
Corso Stati Uniti, 4
I-35127 Padova, Italy
guarino@ladseb.pd.cnr.it

Massimiliano Carrara

Viale Ungheria, 43a
I-37046 Minerbe (VR)
Italy

Pierdaniele Giaretta

Institute of History of Philosophy,
University of Padova,
Piazza Capitaniato, 3
I-35100 Padova, Italy

Abstract

Formalizing the ontological commitment of a logical language means offering a way to specify the intended meaning of its vocabulary by constraining the set of its models, giving explicit information about the intended *nature* of the modelling primitives and their *a priori* relationships. We present here a formal definition of ontological commitment which aims to capture the very basic ontological assumptions about the intended domain, related to issues such as identity and internal structure. To tackle such issues, a modal framework endowed with mereo-topological primitives has been adopted. The paper is mostly based on a revisitation of philosophical (and linguistic) literature in the perspective of knowledge representation.

1 Introduction

First order logic is notoriously neutral with respect to ontological choices: when a logical language is used with the purpose of modelling a particular aspect of reality, the set **M** of all its models is usually much larger than the set $\mathbf{M_i}$ of the *intended* ones, which describe only those states of affairs which are compatible with some underlying *ontological commitment*. Such a commitment is usually implied by the *vocabulary* used, i.e. by the symbols chosen as constants and predicates: we sistematically use natural language words within our theories, relying on them to make our statements readable and to convey meanings not explicitly stated. However, since words are often vague and ambiguous in natural language, it may be important to constrain their semantics in order to guarantee a consistent interpretation. This is unavoidable, in our opinion, if we want to share theories across different domains (Neches et al. 1991, Gruber 1993).

In the philosophical literature, the notion of ontological commitment was first introduced by Quine (1961). According to him, a theory is ontologically commited to the entities which it quantifies over: "to be is to be the value of a variable". Such criterion was further refined by Church (1958) and Alston (1958), and finally modified by Searle (1969) in order to defend his argument that the ontological commitment of a theory simply coincides whith what it asserts. We reject the latter position, holding that non-equivalent theories can share the same commitment. On the other hand, Quine's proposal seems to be too weak for our purposes, since we want to include in the commitment some basic assumptions and distinctions presupposed by the theory.

In the AI community, the above position is at the basis of current projects for knowledge sharing and reuse (Neches et al. 1991). In the knowledge acquisition literature, the notion of ontological commitment has been introduced by Gruber (1993-1994) as an agreement to use a shared vocabulary specification: such a specification is a set of terminological axioms, and ontological commitment amounts to syntactical consistency with such axioms. This syntactical notion does not fit our intuitions, since it seems natural to allow two different vocabularies (using English or Italian words, for instance) to share the same ontology. In other words, the notion of ontological commitment should be a semantic one, not a syntactic one.

A semantic notion which gets closer to our purposes is that of *conceptualization*, defined in (Genesereth & Nilsson 1987) as a triple consisting of a domain, a set of functions (which we ignore for our purposes) and a set of relations on that domain. For instance (pp. 9-12), the triple $<\{a, b, c\}, \{\}, \{on, above, table\}>$ is a conceptualization of a situation describing some block on a table. The authors note however that *names* of objects and relations refer to purely extensional entities. They describe therefore a *particular* state of affairs, without telling us anything about *other* possible states of affairs. On the other hand, the intended meaning implied by the names chosen for the relevant relations constraints *all* the possible states of affairs.

In conclusion, ontological commitment cannot be understood as "an explicit specification of a conceptualization" (Gruber 1993, p. 199), at least in the technical sense of the latter term. Rather, an ontological commitment should capture and constrain a *set* of conceptualizations. Formalizing the ontological commitment of a logical language means offering a way to specify the intended meaning of its vocabulary by constraining the set of its models, giving explicit information about the intended *nature* of the modelling primitives used and their *a priori* relationships. In this sense, an ontological commitment is a mapping between a language and something which can be called an *ontology*.

Consider a first-order language **L**, and a particular theory **T** of **L**. A possible way to formalize the ontological commitment of **L** is by specifying the set $\mathbf{M_i}$ of its intended models[1] by means of a suitable theory which uses the same language L. The only purpose of such a theory is to specify (or at least approximate) the meaning of the vocabulary used. Such a theory should be kept separated from theories which use the same vocabulary making assertions about particular states of affairs. Current approaches to the problem of *knowledge sharing* (Neches et al. 1991, Gruber 1993-1994) are along this line: a common (sub)theory called *terminology* describes the shared ontology, while task dependent knowledge is specified by separate theories.

The approach described above is not satisfactory, however, if our purpose is the formalization of the ontological commitment of an *arbitrary* language L. The reason is that nothing guarantees us that the vocabulary of L is adequate to express the ontological constraints we are interested in: if we want to capture the *a priori structure* of individuals we need enough *granularity* to be able to speak of their internal constitution, while to capture the *nature* of individuals and relations we also need suitable primitive categories. For instance, nothing is said in the example mentioned above about the nature of the domain: are *a, b,* and *c* physical objects or spatial regions?

A further limitation to the formalization of the ontological commitment of a language L by means of a first-order theory of L comes from the fact that ontology, being knowledge about *a priori* structure of reality, is intimately related to a notion of modality: choosing a particular intended model for a logical theory implies making implicit assumptions about *other* models compatible with the chosen one. In other words, there are *constraints* among possible models which reflect some important aspects of reality: for instance, models describing the temporal evolution of a situation should share the same interpretation for the individual constants used in the description of that situation.

We present in this paper a formal notion of the ontological commitment of a language L, expressed by means of a theory T' which uses a language L' *richer* than L. Such a language extends both the logical symbols and the vocabulary of L by adding modal operators, mereotopological relations and basic domain categories. Since the only purpose of T' is to specify the intended use of L, it is not necessary to replace T with a larger theory $T''=T \cup T'$ of L': for instance, a particular ontological property of a predicate, derivable in T', does not need to be derived in T. Basically, deductions in T' are made by an external agent (e.g., a human being) which wants to understand or specify the ontological commitment of an agent holding the theory T; therefore, the computational properties of L' do not affect the behavior of the latter agent.

The main purpose of the present paper is to show how the intended interpretation of the primitive predicates used to model a particular domain can be formally specified in order to facilitate knowledge sharing and reuse. We shall base our work on a revisitation, from the point of view of KR, of philosophical (and linguistic) work largely extrane-

ous to the KR tradition. In section 2 we give an example intended to motivate the kinds of distinctions we want to account for within an ontological commitment. After the presentation of our formal framework in section 3, we show in section 4 how some fundamental ontological properties of predicates can be expressed within that framework. A detailed analysis of meta-level ontological categories of unary predicates has been carried out in (Guarino, Carrara & Giaretta 1994). In this paper, we underline the necessity to adopt such distinctions as an uneludible part of any formal attempt to capture ontological commitment. We focus in particular on unary predicates, arguing that – in order to specify their intended meaning – a first, fundamental choice regards the distinction between so-called *sortal* and *non-sortal* predicates.

Such a distinction was originally introduced by Locke and discussed in (Strawson 1959) and (Wiggins 1980). According to Strawson, a sortal predicate (like *apple*) "supplies a principle for distinguishing and counting individual particulars which it collects", while a non-sortal predicate (like *red*) "supplies such a principle only for particulars already distinguished, or distinguishable, in accordance with some antecedent principle or method". This distinction is (roughly) reflected in natural language by the fact that the former terms are common nouns, while the latter are adjectives and verbs. It is implicitly present in the KR literature, where sortal predicates are usually called "concepts", while characterising predicates are called "properties". Within current KR formalisms, however, the difference between the two is only based on heuristic considerations, and nothing in the semantics of a concept forbids it from being treated like any other unary predicate.

The notion of *well-founded* ontological commitment is introduced in section 5, with the purpose of offering some concrete methodological guidelines to the current practice of knowledge engineering.

2 A Preliminary Example

Suppose we want to state that a red apple exists. In standard first-order logic, it is a simple matter to write down something like $\exists x.(Ax \wedge Rx)$[2]. What is the ontological commitment of such a simple theory? First of all, we must specify what we are quantifying over. Do we assume something like the existence of "instances of redness" that can have the property of being apples? How can we state that our commitment is exactly the opposite one, where *red* is considered as a property and *apple* as a concept? Sure, the solution cannot consist of an *a priori* classification of predicate symbols, since – being them words of a natural language – their intended meaning depends on the context. For example, compare the statement mentioned above with others where the same predicate *red* appears in different contexts (Fig. 1): in case (2) the argument refers to a par-

---

[1] We refer to the models of a *language*, not to the models of a particular *theory* expressed in that language. See for example (Chang & Keisler 1973), p. 20.

[2] As usual, predicates are symbolized via the capitalized first letter of the word used in the text.

ticular colour gradation belonging to the set of "reds", while in (3) the argument refers to a human-being, meaning for instance that he is a communist.

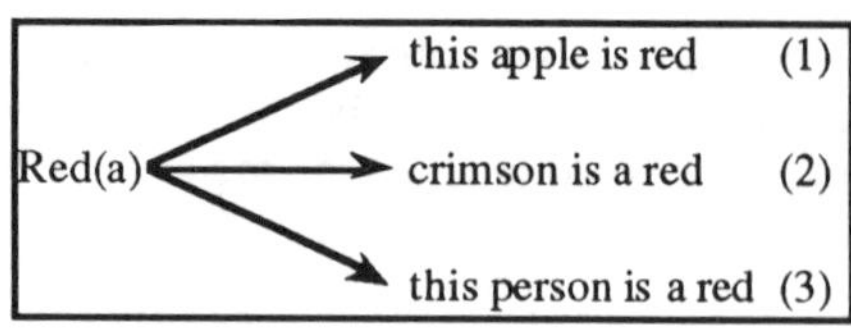

Fig. 1. Varieties of predication.

How can we account for such semantic differences? In this particular case, they are not simply related to the fact that the argument belongs to different domains: they are mainly due to different types of subject-predicate relationships, corresponding to meta-level categories of predicates. Studying the formal properties of such categories is a matter of *formal ontology,* recently defined in (Cocchiarella 1991) as "the systematic, formal, axiomatic development of the logic of all forms and modes of being". In conclusion, although ontological distinctions not always can completely account for different semantic interpretation of linguistic terms, they may offer a significant help to the characterization of their intended meaning, as the present example shows.

3 The Formal Framework

Assuming as given the intended meanings of the predicates of a specific first order theory, we want to formally state their structural features, for the specific purposes of knowledge understanding and reuse among users belonging to a single culture. We assume here that the intended models of our theory, rather than describing merely hypothetical situations, are states of affairs having an "idealised rational acceptability" (Putnam 1981).

Suppose we have a first-order language L with signature $\Sigma = <K, R>$, where K is a set of constant symbols, R is a finite set of n-ary predicate symbols and $P \subseteq R$ is the set of monadic predicate symbols[1]. Let T be a theory of L, D its intended domain and M the set of its models $M = <D, \mathfrak{I}>$, where $\mathfrak{I}$ is the usual interpretation function for constants and predicate symbols. We are interested in some formal criteria accounting for those ontological distinctions among the elements of P which are considered as relevant to the purposes of T as applied to D.

Our main methodological assumptions here are that (i) we need some notion of modality in order to account for the intended meaning of predicate symbols, and (ii) we need mereology and topology in order to capture the *a*

---

[1] We assume L as non functional just for the sake of simplicity. In the following, we shall use bold capital letters for sets, plain capital letters for predicate symbols and handwritten capital letters for relations.

priori structure of a domain[2]. In the following, we first extend our first order language by introducing a semantics of modality which satisfies our purposes, then we further extend both the language and the domain on the basis of mereo-topological principles, in order to formalize the notion of ontological commitment for the original language applied to the original domain.

Def. 1 Let L be a first-order language with signature Σ. The *modal extension* of L is the language L_m obtained by adding to the logical symbols of L the usual modal operators $\diamond$ and $\square$.

Def. 2 Let L be a first-order language with signature $\Sigma = <K, R>$, L_m its modal extension and D a domain. A *constant-domain rigid model* for L_m based on D is a structure $M = <W, \mathfrak{R}, D, \mathfrak{F}_K, \mathfrak{F}_R>$, where W is a set of possible worlds, $\mathfrak{R}$ is a binary relation on W, $\mathfrak{F}_K$ is a function that assigns to each $c \in K$ an element $\mathfrak{F}_K(c)$ of D, and $\mathfrak{F}_R$ is a mapping that assigns to each $w \in W$ and each n-ary predicate symbol $r_n \in R$ an n-ary relation $\mathfrak{F}_R(w, r_n)$ on D.[3]

We want to give $\mathfrak{R}$ the meaning of an *ontological compatibility* relation: intuitively, two worlds are ontologically compatible if they describe alternative states of affairs which do not disagree on the *a priori* nature of the domain. For instance, referring to the example discussed in the previous section, consider a world where a given individual is an instance of the two relations *apple* and *red*. Such a world will be compatible with another where such individual is still an apple but is not red, while it cannot be compatible with a world where *the same individual* is not an apple, since being an apple affects the *identity* of an object. To capture such intuitions, $\mathfrak{R}$ must be reflexive, transitive and symmetric (i.e., an equivalence relation), and the corresponding modal logic will be therefore S5.

Def. 3 Let L be a first-order language, L_m its modal extension and D a domain. A *compatibility model* for L_m based on D is a constant-domain rigid model for L_m based on D, where $\mathfrak{R}$ is the ontological compatibility relation between worlds.

The notion of truth in a compatibility model at a world is pretty standard, and it will not be defined here in detail because of space limitations. Given a domain D, consider now the set of all compatibility models based on D of the modal extension L_m of a language L. In order to account for our ontological assumptions about D, we should somehow restrict such a set, excluding those models that allow for non-intended worlds or too large sets of compatible worlds. Within our framework, we can express such con-

---

[2] Also some notion of tense seems necessary (see section 4.1), but it will not appear here in our simplified formalization.
[3] This definition is taken from (Fitting 1993).

straints by restricting the set of all compatibility models of $\mathbf{L_m}$:

Def. 4 A *commitment* for $\mathbf{L}$ based on $\mathbf{D}$ is a set $\mathbf{C}$ of compatibility models for $\mathbf{L_m}$ based on $\mathbf{D}$. Such a commitment can be specified by an S5 modal theory of $\mathbf{L_m}$, being in this case the set of all its compatibility models based on $\mathbf{D}$. A formula Φ of $\mathbf{L_m}$ is valid in $\mathbf{C}$ ($\mathbf{C} \models \Phi$) iff it is valid in each model $M \in \mathbf{C}$.

We shall see in the next section how we can express the constraints mentioned in the example of the red apple by choosing a suitable commitment $\mathbf{C}$. Before that, we need first to further extend both $\mathbf{L_m}$ and $\mathbf{D}$ in order to be able to express our ontological assumptions about $\mathbf{D}$ itself:

Def. 5 Let $\mathbf{L}$ be a first order language with signature $\Sigma = \langle \mathbf{K}, \mathbf{R} \rangle$, and $\mathbf{L'}$ a language with signature $\Sigma' = \langle \mathbf{K}, \mathbf{R'} \rangle$, where $\mathbf{R'} = \mathbf{R} \cup \{<, C\}$, while $<$ and C are two binary predicate symbols used to represent the mereological relation of "proper part" and the topological relation of "connection". The modal extension of $\mathbf{L'}$ is called the *ontological extension* $\mathbf{L_O}$ of $\mathbf{L}$.

The properties of the part-of relation have been extensively studied in (Simons 1987). Connection has been used as a topological primitive in (Clarke 1981) and more recently in (Randell, Cui & Cohn 1992). Since our domain is not restricted to topological entities only, the connection relation can have arguments which are physical bodies or events and not only regions as in (Randell, Cui & Cohn 1992). We assume here that two entities are connected if *their spatio-temporal extensions* are connected in the sense defined in (Randell, Cui & Cohn 1992) (i.e. two *regions* are connected if their topological closures share a point). Notice that we do not share with Randell and colleagues the choice to define parthood in terms of connection[1].

Def. 6 The *mereological closure* of a domain $\mathbf{D}$ is the set $\mathbf{D_O}$ obtained by adding to $\mathbf{D}$ the set of all proper parts of the elements of $\mathbf{D}$.

Def. 7 An *ontological commitment* $\mathbf{O}$ for $\mathbf{L}$ based on $\mathbf{D}$ is a commitment for $\mathbf{L_O}$ based on $\mathbf{D_O}$, such that the following minimal mereo-topological theory is valid in $\mathbf{O}$[2].

D1	$x \leq y =_{\text{def}} x < y \vee x = y$	(part)
D2	$Oxy =_{\text{def}} \exists z.\, z \leq x \wedge z \leq y$	(overlap)

A1	$x < y \supset \neg\,(y < x)$	(asymmetry)
A2	$x < y \wedge y < z \supset x < z$	(transitivity)
A3	$x < y \supset \exists z.(z < y \wedge \neg\, Ozx)$	(supplementation)

---

[1] See (Varzi 1994) for a discussion of the relationships between mereology and topology.
[2] Axioms A1-A3 are taken from (Simons 1987), while A4-A5 from (Randell, Cui & Cohn 1992).

A4	$\forall x.Cxx$	(reflexivity)
A5	$\forall x \forall y.Cxy \supset Cyx$	(symmetry)

4 Ontological Categories of Unary Predicates

In principle, any consistent set of formulas of $\mathbf{L_O}$ can be used to specify an ontological commitment for $\mathbf{L}$; what is important of course is that the particular formulas chosen be suitable to really capture the underlying ontological intuitions. To this purpose, we must first define the relevant ontological properties of our predicates, and then explicitly declare the properties holding for each predicate of the language. A particular ontological commitment corresponds to a particular set of such declarations.

Let us see now how some important ontological properties of unary predicates can be easily formalized within the framework sketched in the previous section. The first fundamental distinction regards the "discriminating power"of unary predicates. If we want to use a predicate for knowledge-structuring purposes, it must tell us something non-trivial about the domain, and therefore it cannot be either necessarily true or necessarily false.

Def. 8 Let $\mathbf{L}$ be a first order language, P a monadic predicate of $\mathbf{L}$, and $\mathbf{O}$ an ontological commitment for $\mathbf{L}$. P is called *discriminating* in $\mathbf{O}$ iff $\mathbf{O} \models \Diamond \exists x.Px \wedge \Diamond \exists x.\neg Px$.

Some general distinctions among discriminating unary predicates are shown in Fig. 2. They are defined in the following as purely formal distinctions at the meta-level, completely independent of the nature of the domain. This means that our distinctions are intended to hold not only for standard examples related to the domain of physical objects, but also for predicates such as *color* or *marriage* whose arguments are universals like *red* or temporal entities like a particular marriage event. Analogously, no linguistic assumption is made on the names of predicates, which can be either nouns or adjectives.

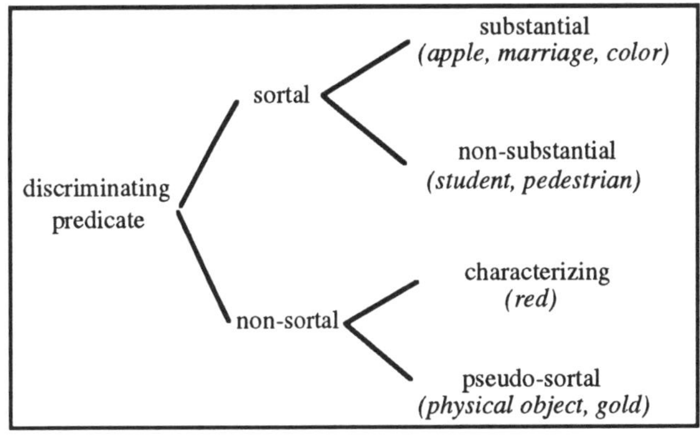

Fig. 2. Preliminary distinctions among unary predicates.

4.1 Countability

Among discriminating unary predicates, the distinction we focus on is the classical one between sortals and non-sortals. In the philosophical literature, such a distinction bears on two main notions: *countability* (Griffin 1977) and temporal *reidentifiability* (Wiggins 1980). The former is bound to the capacity of a predicate to isolate a given object among others: "*this* is a P, this is *another* P, this *is not* a P". In other words, if P is a sortal predicate, then it is possible to ask: "how many Ps are there?" The latter property is related to the fact that a predicate holds for the same individual through time, in the strong sense that it is possible to state "this is now the same P as before".

In the literature, various "divisivity" criteria have been proposed to account for the countable/non-countable distinction. Excluding those based on universal quantification on all parts of an object for reasons having to do with the problem of granularity, a quite satisfactory criterion is the one proposed by Griffin (1977), which can be formulated in such a way that P is a countable predicate iff $\forall x.(Px \supset \neg \exists z.(z < x \wedge Pz))$. Such a criterion, however, does not take into account a notion of topological connection which seems to be related to the notion of countability. In our opinion, the main feature of countable predicates is that they cannot be true of an object and of a non-isolated part of it. For example, we think it is natural to consider *piece of wood* as a countable predicate, but it cannot be excluded from being uncountable according to Griffin's definition. The point is that in its ordinary meaning such a predicate does not apply to any part of a single, integral, piece of wood. In order to capture such a structural feature of countable predicates within our formal framework, let us introduce the following definitions for the ontological extension $\mathbf{L_0}$ of a language $\mathbf{L}$:

D3 $\sigma x \phi x =_{def} \iota x \forall y (Oyx \equiv \exists z(\phi z \wedge Ozy))$ (sum of all ϕs)[1]
D4 $x{-}y =_{def} \sigma z.(z{\leq}x \wedge \neg Ozy)$ (mereological difference)
D5 $x <_i y =_{def} x{<}y \wedge \neg Cx(y{-}x)$ (isolated part)
D6 $x <_c y =_{def} x{<}y \wedge Cx(y{-}x)$ (connected part)

Def. 9 A discriminating predicate P is called *countable* in O iff $O \models \forall x. (Px \supset \neg \exists z.(z <_c x \wedge Pz))$.

In the above definition, we have simply substituted "connected part-of" to the part-of relation appearing in Griffin's definition. In other words, a countable predicate P only holds for entities which are "maximally connected" with respect to P, in the sense that they cannot have connected parts which are instances of P.

According to Def. 9, the predicate *piece of wood* is countable if (as seems natural) it only applies to isolated pieces of wood, while the monadic predicate *color* turns out to be countable if we assume that a color has no parts. On the other hand, according to its ordinary sense a predicate like *red* is not countable, since while holding for a physical object it can also apply to non-isolated parts of it, such as its surface.

The definition we have given allows us to consider predicates denoting physical structures like *stack* (of blocks)or *chain* as countable predicates only if it can be claimed, perhaps on the basis of Gestalt-theoretical considerations, that no connected part of a physically realized structure can be a structure of the same kind (Smith 1992). In this sense, a substack can be a stack only as an isolated whole. There are some intuitive and practical reasons in favour of this way of thinking. For example, a request to count the chains put in a box is not usually understood as a request to count also the subchains of such chains. Notice that we do not require instances of countable predicates to be isolated entities: for example, we want *arm* to be countable and such that both detached and undetached arms are instances of it[2]. However, it is reasonable to hold that *tube* is countable. It follows that no part of a tube is a tube, otherwise it would violate the assumption of countability. So while arms are instances of *arm* even before a possible detaching event, the same does not hold for halves of tubes. Lack of analogy between the two cases is due to the fact that in the former case the argument of the predicate is connected to something of a different kind.

In (Guarino, Carrara & Giaretta 1994) we introduced a notion of *temporal stability* to take into account the idea of reidentifiability, and we defined sortality as the conjunction of countability and temporal stability. The former property is however much more important in practice, and so we omit in the following any reference to the latter because of space limitations.

Def. 10 A discriminating predicate P is called *sortal* in O iff it is countable in O, and *non-sortal* otherwise.

According to this definition, we have a criterion to distinguish between the two predicates involved in the statement "a red apple exists". *Apple* will be in this case a sortal predicate being countable, while *red* will be non-sortal being not countable under our intended interpretation.

4.2 Rigidity

Although useful for many purposes, the distinction between sortal and non-sortal predicates discussed above is not fine enough to account for the difference in the interpretation of *red* in cases (2) and (3) of Fig. 1, since in both of them *red* is used as a sortal predicate. Let us therefore further explore the ontological distinctions we can draw among both sortal and non-sortal predicates. An observation that comes to mind, when trying to formalise the nature of the subject-predicate relationship, is that the "force"

---

[1] In order to avoid troubles with the satisfiability conditions for modal formulas involving the *iota* operator, we assume that terms built by means of such operator are contextually defined *a la* Russell. For instance, a formula like $P(\iota x.\phi x)$ is translated in $\exists x(Px \wedge \phi x \wedge (\forall y.\phi y \supset y{=}x))$.

[2] In contrast with (Smith 1992), we do not assume that detaching an arm is an event such that the arm before it is not the same arm as the arm after it.

of this relationship is much higher in "x is an apple" than in "x is red". If x has the property of being an apple, it cannot lose this property without losing its identity, while this does not seem to be the case in the latter example. This observation goes back to Aristotelian essentialism, and can be formalised as follows (Barcan Marcus 1968):

Def. 11 A discriminating predicate P is *ontologically rigid* in O iff $O \models \forall x(Px \supset \Box Px)$.

However, the example above notwithstanding, ontological rigidity is not a sufficient condition for sortality. In fact, there are a number of rigid predicates which should be excluded from being sortals, since no clear distinction criteria are associated with them. Predicates corresponding to certain mass nouns belong to this category (at least if their arguments denote an amount of stuff and not a particular object), as well as "high level" predicates like *physical object*, *individual*, *event*. We call these predicates *pseudo-sortals*[1]. They are all rigid but not countable.

Def. 12 Let P be a non-sortal predicate under O. It is a *pseudo-sortal* iff it is ontologically rigid under O, and a *characterising predicate* otherwise.

Rigidity cannot be considered as a necessary condition for sortality, either. According to our definition, sortals include predicates like *student*, which – although not rigid – are still countable. Following (Wiggins 1980), we call such predicates *non-substantial sortals*[2].

Def. 13 Let P be a sortal predicate under O. It is a *substantial sortal* iff it is ontologically rigid under O, and a *non-substantial sortal* otherwise.

We are now in a position to exploit the above distinctions in order to specify the ontological commitment of a first order language. Consider, for example, the statement (1) of Fig. (1). The formal language used to express such a statement includes the two predicate symbols R and A, standing respectively for *red* and *apple*. The ontological commitment of such a language which corresponds to the intended use of these two symbols can be specified by the following declarations (expressed either in a suitable metalanguage for $\mathbf{L_o}$ or via the corresponding axioms of $\mathbf{L_o}$):

A is a substantial sortal .

---

[1]They are called "super sortals" in (Pelletier & Schubert 1989). Notice that *physical object* is not intended here in the sense of spatially isolated *thing*. Therefore, it is assumed to be not countable.

[2]According to the current terminology used in knowledge representation, substantial sortals should in our opinion correspond to *types* and non-substantial sortals to *roles* (in the sense of (Sowa 1988)), while the terms *class* or *concept* should be reserved to the union of sortal and pseudo-sortal predicates. Such terminological proposal is discussed in (Guarino, Carrara & Giaretta 1994).

R is a characterizing predicate.

In statement (2), *red* is intended to be rigid and countable, since its argument is a colour gradation: it will be therefore declared as a substantial sortal (crimson *has* to be a red: see (Pelletier 1979), p. 10). Finally, in statement (3), *red* is used as a contingent property of human-beings and hence is not rigid, while it is still countable: it will be therefore declared as a non substantial sortal.

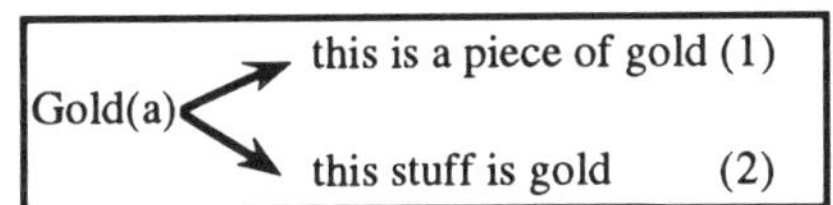

Fig. 3: Different interpretations of mass nouns.

Another interesting example regards the different interpretations of a mass noun like *gold*, reported in Fig. 3 above. In case (1), *gold* is intended as countable, but not rigid (since that piece can have been taken from a rock, for instance), and it is used as a non-substantial sortal; in case (2) the predicate is non-countable and rigid, and *gold* is therefore a pseudo sortal.

5 Well-Founded Ontological Commitment

We would like to show in this section how the formal framework introduced above can be of concrete utility in the current practice of knowledge engineering. The first result of our approach is the possibility to draw a clear distinction between concepts and properties, in the sense usually ascribed to such terms within the KR community. Our proposal is that properties should coincide with what we called characterizing predicates, while all other kinds of unary predicates should be thought of as concepts.

Besides this first important distinction, our meta-level classification of unary predicates allows us to impose some further structure on the set of concepts, usually represented as an oriented graph where arcs denote subsumption relationships. As the size of this graph increases, it may be very useful to isolate a skeleton to be used for indexing and clustering purposes. Substantial sortals are a natural candidate to constitute such a skeleton[3], since their rigidity reduces the "tangleness" of the corresponding graph. However, to effectively use substantial sortals as a skeleton, we must introduce some further constraints, which lead to the notion of *well-founded ontological commitment*.

Def. 14 Let P and Q be two discriminating predicates in O. P is *subordinate* to Q in O iff $O \models \forall x(Px \supset Qx) \land \neg\forall x(Qx \supset Px)$. P and Q are *disjoint* in O iff $O \models \neg\exists x.Px \land Qx$. A set $\mathbf{P}=\{P_1, ..., P_n\}$ of mutually disjoint discriminating predicates in O is a *domain partition* in O iff $O \models \forall x.(P_1x \lor ... \lor P_nx)$.

---

[3]A similar proposal has been made by Sowa (1988), which however refers to an unspecified notion of "natural type".

Def. 15 An ontological commitment **O** based on **D** is *well-founded* iff:

- There is a set $C \subseteq P$ of mutually disjoint pseudo-sortal predicates called *categorial predicates*, such that (i) C is a domain partition in **O**, and (ii) no element $C \in C$ is subordinate to a discriminating predicate.
- For each categorial predicate $C \in C$, the substantial sortals subordinate to C and not subordinate to any other substantial sortal are mutually disjoint.
- Each non-substantial sortal is subordinate to a substantial sortal.

A well-founded ontological commitment introduces therefore a further subclass of discriminating predicates, i.e. categorial predicates, which belong to the class of pseudo-sortals according to the preliminary distinctions shown in Fig. 2. We call *mass-like predicates* those pseudo-sortals which are not categories; therefore, the final relevant distinctions within a well-founded commitment are those shown in Fig. 4.

Let us briefly motivate our definition of a well-founded ontological commitment. Categorial predicates are intended to represent what traditional ontology would call *summa genera*. A set of categorial predicates useful for a very broad domain is given by *physical object, event, spatial region, temporal interval, amount of matter*[1]. The fact that such predicates are assumed to be pseudo-sortals (and therefore uncountable) underlines their very general nature.

As for the second constraint mentioned in the definition, no particular structure is imposed on substantial sortals within a well-founded commitment[2], except that top-level substantial sortals should specify natural kinds within general categories: therefore, they must be disjoint and cannot overlap general categories.

Finally, the intuition behind the third constraint in Def. 15 is that in the case of substantial sortals the identity criterion is given by the predicate itself, while for non-substantial sortals it is provided by some superordinate sortal. Under this constraint, non-substantial sortals conform to the notion of "role type" proposed by Sowa, which fits well with the general meaning of the term "role": "Role types are subtypes of natural types in some particular patterns of relationships" (Sowa 1988). We suggest to adopt the term "role" for non-substantial sortals within the KR community, avoiding to use it as a synonym for an (arbitrary) binary relation as common practice in the KL-ONE circles.[3] An interesting consequence of Def. 15 is

---

[1] These predicates should be characterized by suitable axioms, but such a task is beyond the scope of the present paper.

[2] It may be desirable, both for conceptual and computational reasons, to impose the condition that substantial sortals form a forest of trees; such a condition seems however not obtainable in many cases.

[3] See (Guarino 1992) for a general discussion on roles and attributes. Notice however that the distinctions among unary predicates discussed in that paper have been here drastically revised and simplified; in particular, no notion of ontological

that, within a well-founded ontological commitment, any two overlapping non-substantial sortals are subordinate to the same substantial sortal.

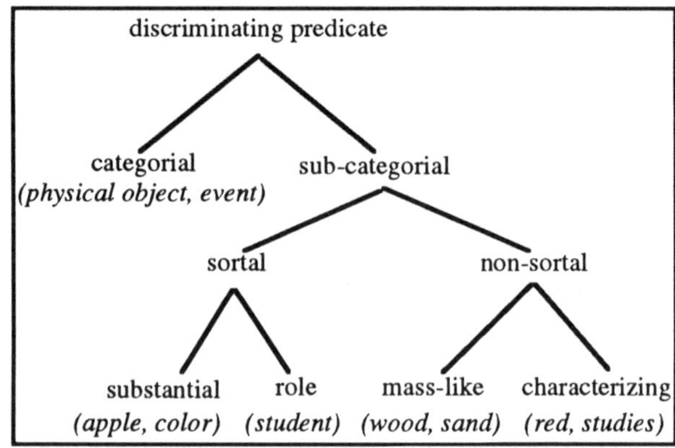

Fig. 4. Basic distinctions among discriminating predicates within a well-founded ontological commitment

6 Conclusions

We hope to have clarified in this paper the notion of ontological commitment, which has been understood in the past in various ways, both in the philosophical and AI tradition. We would like to stress that the notion we have defined is based on a fine-grained perspective of common-sense reality, where mereological and topological properties play an important role. We have defined ontological commitment as a map between a logical language and a *set* of semantic structures, and we have shown how modal logic, endowed with mereological and topological primitives, can be used to express ontological constraints among such structures. We have based our discussion on a simplified account of the ontological properties of unary predicates introduced in (Guarino, Carrara & Giaretta 1994), where a novel formalization of Strawson's distinction between sortal and non-sortal predicates has been presented in detail.

A number of extensions and refinements to the ontological distinctions described here are however necessary to obtain a satisfactory account of common-sense ontology. For instance, further distinctions among monadic predicate types must be defined in order to better characterize domain categories such as *physical objects, events, amounts of matter, spatial* or *temporal regions*. Moreover, ontological distinctions among binary relations must be introduced as well, possibly in a way similar to that described in (Guarino 1992).

We think we have still to learn a lot, to understand and represent the *a priori* laws that govern the structure of reality. Bearing on insights coming from the philosophical tradition of formal ontology, we have tried to show that

---

foundation is here advocated to distinguish between concepts and properties.

some of these laws are suitable to formal characterization, and we are convinced that they can have a profound impact on the current practice of knowledge engineering.

Acknowledgements

We are indebted to Luca Boldrin, Dario Maguolo and Barry Smith for their valuable comments on earlier drafts of this paper. Massimiliano Carrara's contribution has been made in the framework of a cooperation with LADSEB-CNR.

References

Alston, W. P. 1958. Ontological Commitments. *Philosophical Studies*, **9**: 8-16.

Barcan Marcus, R. 1968. Essential Attribution. *The Journal of Philosophy*, **7**.

Chang, C. C. and Keisler, H. J. 1973. *Model Theory*. North-Holland-Elsevier Publishing Company, Amsterdam, London and New York.

Church, A. 1958. Ontological Commitment. *The Journal of Philosophy*, **55**: 1008-14.

Clarke, B. L. 1981. A Calculus of Individuals Based on "Connection". *Notre Dame Journal of Formal Logic*, **22**: 204-18.

Cocchiarella, N. B. 1991. Formal Ontology. In H. Burkhardt and B. Smith (ed.), *Handbook of Metaphysics and Ontology*. Philosophia Verlag, Munich.

Fitting, M. 1993. Basic Modal Logic. In D. M. Gabbay, C. J. Hogger and J. A. Robinson (eds.), *Handbook of Logic in Artificial Intelligence and Logic Programming*. Clarendon Press, Oxford.

Griffin, N. 1977. *Relative Identity*. Oxford University Press, Oxford.

Gruber, T. R. 1993. A translation approach to portable ontology specifications. *Knowledge Acquisition*, **5**: 199-220.

Gruber, T. 1994. Toward Principles for the Design of Ontologies Used for Knowledge Sharing. In N. Guarino and R. Poli (ed.), *Formal Ontology in Conceptual Analysis and Knowledge Representation*. (in preparation).

Guarino, N. 1992. Concepts, Attributes and Arbitrary Relations: Some Linguistic and Ontological Criteria for Structuring Knowledge Bases. *Data & Knowledge Engineering*, **8**: 249-261.

Guarino, N., Carrara, M., and Giaretta, P. 1994. An Ontology of Meta-Level Categories. In J. Doyle, E. Sandewall and P. Torasso (eds.), *Principles of Knowledge Representation and Reasoning: Proceedings of the Fourth International Conference (KR94)*. Morgan Kaufmann, San Mateo, CA.

Neches, R., Fikes, R., Finin, T., Gruber, T., Patil, R., Senator, T., and Swartout, W. R. 1991. Enabling Technology for Knowledge Sharing. *AI Magazine*, fall 1991.

Pelletier, F. J. 1979. Non-Singular References: Some Preliminaries. In F. J. Pelletier (ed.), *Mass Terms: Some Philosophical Problems*, 1-14. Reidel, Dordrecht.

Pelletier, F. J. and Schubert, L. K. 1989. Mass Expressions. In D. Gabbay and F. Günthner (eds.), *Handbook of Philosophical Logic*. Reidel, Dordrecht.

Putnam, H. 1981. *Reason, Truth, and History*. Cambridge University Press, Cambridge.

Quine, W. O. 1961. *From a Logical Point of View, Nine Logico-Philosophical Essays*. Harvard University Press, Cambridge, MA.

Randell, D., Cui, Z., and Cohn, A. 1992. A spatial logic based on regions and connection. In *Proceedings of KR '92*. San Mateo (CA), Morgan Kaufmann.

Searle, J. 1969. *Speech Acts: An Essay on the Philosophy of Language*. Cambridge U. P., Cambridge.

Simons, P. 1987. *Parts: a Study in Ontology*. Clarendon Press, Oxford.

Smith, B. 1992. Characteristica Universalis. In K. Mulligan (ed.), *Language, Truth and Ontology*, 48-77. Kluwer, Dordrecht.

Sowa, J. F. 1988. Using a lexicon of canonical graphs in a semantic interpreter. In M. W. Evens (ed.), *Relational models of the lexicon*. Cambridege University Press.

Strawson, P. F. 1959. *Individuals. An Essay in Descriptive Metaphysics*. Routledge, London and New York.

Varzi, A. 1994. On the Boundary Between Mereology and Topology. In R. Casati, B. Smith and G. White (eds.), *Philosophy and the Cognitive Science*. Hölder-Pichler-Tempsky, Vienna.

Wiggins, D. 1980. *Sameness and Substance*. Blakwell, Oxford.

Machine Learning

Exploiting the Ordering of Observed Problem-solving Steps for Knowledge Base Refinement: an Apprenticeship Approach

Steven K. Donoho and David C. Wilkins*
Department of Computer Science
University of Illinois
405 North Mathews Avenue
Urbana, IL 61801
donoho@cs.uiuc.edu, wilkins@cs.uiuc.edu

Abstract

Apprenticeship is a powerful method of learning among humans whereby a student refines his knowledge simply by observing and analyzing the problem-solving steps taken by an expert. This paper focuses on knowledge base (KB) refinement for classification problems and examines how the *ordering* of the problem-solving steps taken by an observed expert can be used to yield leverage in KB refinement. Questions examined include: What added information can be extracted from attribute ordering? How can this added information be utilized to identify and repair KB shortcomings? What assumptions must be made about the observed expert, and how important of a role do these assumptions play? The principles explored have been implemented in the SKIPPER apprentice, and empirical results are given for the audiology domain.

1 Introduction

Apprenticeship is a powerful method of learning among humans in which a student refines his knowledge by observing and analyzing the problem-solving steps of an expert. Many previous works in apprenticeship [Dent et al., 1992; Mahadevan et al., 1993; Mitchell et al., 1985; Redmond, 1992; Tecuci and Kodratoff, 1990; Wilkins, 1988] have taken steps toward harnessing the information provided by observing problem-solving steps. In this paper we focus on knowledge base (KB) refinement for classification problems and examine how the *ordering* of the intermediate steps of an observed expert can be used to yield leverage in KB refinement.

In the classical classification problem, the problem-solver is given an example consisting of a set of attributes and their corresponding values, and it must put the example in one of a pre-enumerated set of classes. For example, the problem-solver may be given a batch of attribute/value pairs describing a soybean plant and must classify that plant as having one of a pre-enumerated set of soybean plant diseases.

Consider a slightly different situation, though, in which the problem-solver is not given *all* the attribute/value pairs from the outset but rather must request attributes one at a time and make his classification decision once sufficient evidence is gathered. This situation would arise when it is too costly or otherwise unreasonable to simply be given all the attribute values. This situation applies to domains such as medical diagnosis in which all the patient's symptoms are not given at once but rather must be requested individually based on what the doctor knows about the patient so far. When a mechanic is troubleshooting a malfunctioning car, he does not run every test possible and then stop to examine his data and make his decision. Rather he checks one thing, and based on the result of that, he decides what to check next.

Thus the order in which attributes are requested reflects the internal problem-solving process going on in the mind of the observed expert. By watching the order in which a *superior* problem-solver requests attributes, we should be able to refine the KB of a *weaker* problem-solver. We will refer to the superior problem-solver which is being watched as the **observed expert** and the weaker problem-solver which is being refined as the **critiqued problem-solver**. While refining the critiqued problem-solver, we have full access to its KB, but our only interface with the observed expert is the visible actions he takes so as to require nothing more from the expert than to perform his normal work.

The approach we take to KB refinement is *knowledge acquisition within the context of a shortcoming in the knowledge base.* TEIRESIAS [Davis, 1979] introduced this approach whereby an expert

*This work supported by a DoD Graduate Fellowship, ONR grant N00014-88K-0124, and AFOSR grant F49260-92-J-0545.

would point out an expert system's failure, the expert would then guide TEIRESIAS in localizing the cause of the failure, and the expert would suggest a repair. A natural next step is to move toward automating the three tasks for which the expert was indispensable in TEIRESIAS. These tasks are as follows: detecting a KB shortcoming, localizing the shortcoming, and constructing a repair. TEIRESIAS solved these three subtasks by consulting with the expert. In this paper we attempt to push these three subtasks toward automation relying not on the expert's intervention but rather on simply observing his problem-solving steps and their ordering.

A comparison of our approach to some related work in apprenticeship is given in section 2. Section 3 introduces how a KB shortcoming can be detected by analyzing the order in which attributes are requested. Section 4 explains how a KB shortcoming, once detected, can be localized using the context in which it was detected, and section 5 presents a method of generating KB repairs once the shortcoming is localized. The SKIPPER apprentice is an implementation which puts these three tasks together, and section 6 discusses an experiment showing how SKIPPER improves classification accuracy by refining a KB produced by the C4.5 machine learning program [Quinlan, 1993].

2   Related Work

The LEAP system [Mahadevan et al., 1993] works in the domain of digital circuit design giving an expert suggestions for how to decompose a high-level circuit specification into submodules. When the expert disagrees with a suggestion made by LEAP, LEAP learns from the alternative proposed by the expert. LEAP fits the definition of apprentice because rather than just examining a completed circuit as a whole, it analyzes the individual, fine-grained decomposition taken by the expert. But the order in which the expert takes these problem-solving steps is not used as a source of information.

The CAP program [Dent et al., 1992] assists in managing an individual's meeting calendar by predicting certain meeting details such as time, location, and duration from what it knows about the meeting such as the nature of the meeting and its attendees. The individual problem-solving steps taken by the expert (the calendar user) are often invisible. The expert examines in his head the meeting type, the department of the attendees, job title of the attendees, etc. and decides the details of the meeting; thus neither the fine-grained problem-solving steps nor their ordering are available as a source of information.

The ODYSSEUS project [Wilkins, 1988] holds many similarities to our work. The goal of both is to refine a classification KB by watching the actions of another problem-solver. The expert being observed in ODYSSEUS was required at each step to state what class he was focusing on. This forced the expert to articulate his strategies rather than just solve problems unhindered. Our method uses the context of the attributes requested so far to hypothesize what the observed expert is focusing on at any given point so as to avoid having to request it explicitly.

A closely related work in case-based reasoning is the CELIA system [Redmond, 1992]. CELIA detects KB shortcomings by predicting an expert's actions given the current problem-solving state and adds a new case when its predictions fail. Redmond explored repairing by taking hints from or asking questions of a competant instructor whereas our work uses attribute ordering as a means of guiding induction.

3   Detecting a KB Shortcoming

Detecting a KB shortcoming is synonymous with answering the question, "When does an action taken by the observed expert indicate that there is something missing from the critiqued problem-solver's knowledge base?" In short, the answer is that an action indicates something is missing from a KB when that action cannot be justified using that KB. Consider the following example. When a doctor is diagnosing a patient, the doctor asks the patient a series of questions to determine what disease the patient has. A medical student watching the doctor could probably give an explanation of why each question was asked because the student himself has a good body of medical knowledge. If the doctor asks a question, and the student cannot explain why the doctor asked it, then the student realizes that the doctor knows something that he does not know. He has detected a shortcoming in his knowledge. Likewise, the failure to explain an observed expert's action using a critiqued problem-solver's KB indicates a shortcoming in that KB.

In order to explain an observed action, though, we have to make some *a priori* assumptions about the observed expert. If we make no assumptions, the observed expert is totally unconstrained and could be requesting attributes randomly in which case all actions have the potential explanation, "the observed expert is acting randomly," and no shortcomings in the critiqued problem-solver's KB can be detected. One reasonable assumption to make is that the observed expert always acts rationally, i.e. that he always has some reason or motive for requesting an attribute and therefore never takes an irrelevant action. This assumption is simple yet actually provides a great deal of leverage.

As an example of the information that attribute ordering gives, consider the example shown in Figure 1(a) taken from the audiology domain. The observed expert first requests the attribute *age_gt_60* and receives the answer *true*. Knowing this he requests the attribute *history_nausea* and receives the answer *false*. He requests three more attributes and then halts and makes his decision classifying the patient as *cochlear_age* without requesting any more attributes. This tells us many things:

- Given that nothing at all is known, *age_gt_60* is a relevant attribute to request.

- The value of *history_nausea* is relevant to solving the problem even given that *age_gt_60* is known to be *true*. Otherwise, the observed expert would not have requested *history_nausea* since *age_gt_60* was already known to be *true*.

- The value of *history_noise* is relevant given that *age_gt_60* is *true* and *history_nausea* is *false*.

- The value of *air* is relevant given that *age_gt_60* is *true*, *history_nausea* is *false*, and *history_noise* is *false*.

- The value of *tymp* is relevant given that *age_gt_60* is *true*, *history_nausea* is *false*, *history_noise* is *false*, and *air* is *normal*.

So the ordering of attributes gives us information about "conditional relevancy" — the values of certain attributes are necessarily relevant given the values of certain other attributes.

As an example of how this information can be used to detect KB shortcomings, consider the simple set of rules to be critiqued in Figure 1(b). Using the problem-solving steps from Figure 1(a), when the attribute *age_gt_60* is requested, this action is explainable because the observed expert could be requesting that attribute to satisfy the premise of any of the four rules. When the value *true* is given, though, the premise of Rule2 becomes false; therefore, Rule2 is no longer relevant to solving this problem. Likewise, *history_nausea* is explainable because it is in the premise of Rule3 which is still relevant. Following that, *history_noise* is explainable because it is in the premise of Rule1 which is still relevant (but finding that *history_noise* is *false* causes Rule1 to become irrelevant). But when the attribute *air* is requested, a KB shortcoming is

Requested Attribute	Value Given
age_gt_60	*true*
history_nausea	*false*
history_noise	*false*
air	*normal*
tymp	*a*

Classified as *cochlear_age*

(a) A sequence of attributes requested by an observed expert.

Rule1: age_gt_60 = true ∧
    history_noise = true ∧
    tymp = a →
        cochlear_age_and_noise

Rule2: age_gt_60 = false ∧
    air = mild →
        cochlear_unknown

Rule3: age_gt_60 = true ∧
    speech = very_poor ∧
    history_nausea = false →
        cochlear_age_plus_poss_menieres

Rule4: age_gt_60 = true ∧
    history_dizziness = false ∧
    tymp = a →
        cochlear_age

(b) The rule set to be critiqued.

Figure 1: The attribute request *air* in (a) is irrelevant using the KB in (b) because the premises of all rules which contain *air* are false by the time *air* is requested.

detected. The attribute *air* is found only in the premise of Rule2 which is no longer applicable since *age_gt_60* is known to be *true*; therefore, the attribute request *air* is unexplained. According to the critiqued KB, the attribute *air* is not relevant at this point in the problem yet the observed expert requested it, and the observed expert is assumed to only request relevant attributes! There must therefore be some knowledge which the observed expert possesses which is not in the critiqued KB. Thus the ordering of the attributes — specifically the fact that *air* was requested after *age_gt_60* was known to be *true* — has enabled the detection of a KB shortcoming. **The ordering allows the analysis of the relevancy of an attribute at a given time with respect to the critiqued KB, and this may be at odds with the relevancy indicated by the observed expert's actions.**

Assuming that the observed expert is rational is a weak yet generally applicable constraint. Stronger constraints can yield even more leverage.

A slightly more constraining assumption is that the observed expert uses a "test-hypothesis" strategy, i.e. he hypothesizes a class which he thinks the example at hand might belong to, and he requests attribute values which will either verify or disprove the his hypothesis. If there is sufficient evidence that the example does belong to the hypothesized class, the expert stops and reports his decision. If the evidence disproves his hypothesis, then the expert hypothesizes a new class and proceeds to verify or disprove it. The test-hypothesis assumption embodies the basic idea that the expert sticks with one train of thought rather than spuriously jumping from one line of reasoning to another.

Referring again to Figure 1, we give an example of shortcoming detection assuming that the observed expert is using a test-hypothesis strategy. Again, *age_gt_60* can be explained because the problem-solver could be testing any of the four classes. When the attribute *history_nausea* is requested and the value *false* is received, we tentatively explain this by assuming that the observed expert is focusing upon the class *cochlear_age_plus_poss_menieres* and that the next attribute he will request is *speech* to complete the premise of Rule3. When this does not happen — when *history_noise* is requested next instead — we are forced to admit that the observed expert was not applying Rule3 when it requested *history_nausea* and furthermore that our tentative explanation for *history_nausea* no longer holds! The attribute request *history_nausea* is unexplained. When the observed expert requested *history_nausea*, he must have been using some knowledge which is absent from the critiqued KB. Thus imposing stronger assumptions on our observed expert allowed us to detect a KB shortcoming which was missed when the assumptions were weaker.

The assumptions made about the observed expert are not insignificant and should be given close examination. As mentioned above, when no assumptions are made, no shortcomings can be detected. As demonstrated in the two examples, the stronger the assumptions, the more leverage is available for detecting shortcomings. Yet these assumptions are not based on anything the problem-solver is observed to do but rather are *a priori* and provide a bias of sorts. Imposing stronger assumptions is not always better, though. If assumptions are too constraining, the observed expert will be expected to behave more rigidly than he actually does in reality. This leads to false positive shortcoming detection — KB shortcomings being detected when in fact there are none. Therefore, a tradeoff exists between detecting true shortcomings and avoiding the detection of nonexistent shortcomings.

So the ordering of attribute requests has proven valuable in the detection of KB shortcomings. Next we show how the detection process has already provided much of the information needed to localize the shortcoming.

4 Localizing the KB Shortcoming

In the previous section we explained a method of detecting KB shortcomings, but this method also takes us a long way toward localizing a shortcoming. The detection process gives us an **unexplained attribute**, the attribute request which could not be explained, and **focus facts**, the facts which were known at the time the unexplained attribute was requested. These focus facts deserve special attention because knowledge of them gave rise to the request of the unexplained attribute; therefore, they may be related to the unexplained attribute and to the shortcoming.

Furthermore, the focus facts can be used to identify a handful of **focus classes**, classes relevant to the shortcoming, because the known facts often rule out some classes leaving a subset of classes to focus upon. This is done using a set of labeled examples from a representative case library. All examples in the set which disagree with any of the focus facts are eliminated leaving a subset of examples which agree with all the facts known so far. The classes which these remaining examples belong to are the focus classes. So the shortcoming can be localized to a central attribute, a handful of focus facts, and a handful of focus classes.

5 Repairing the KB Shortcoming

Once the shortcoming has been localized, an attempt is made to repair it. Taking a rule-based approach, we try to repair the shortcoming by adding a rule of the form: $condition_1 \wedge condition_2 \wedge \ldots \wedge condition_N \longrightarrow class_i$ where each condition is an attribute/value pair such as $history\_dizziness = true$ or $temperature > 102$. Since the shortcoming has been localized to an unexplained attribute, a handful of focus facts, and a handful of focus classes, repairing the shortcoming consists of generating and empirically evaluating the rules formed from different combinations of these attributes and classes. While the localization process has narrowed down the number of attributes and classes, an exponential number of potential combinations still remain. The following paragraph describes a greedy approach to finding a good repair.

A repair can be generated by starting with a "seed repair" — a single-condition rule — and greedily adding other conditions to the rule. The single condition in the seed repair contains the unexplained attribute. For example if the unexplained attribute is *air*, then *air = mild*, *air = normal*, *air = severe*, etc. are each used in separate seed repairs. The class of a seed repair is any of the focus classes[1]. Each seed repair is empirically tested with respect to a set of labeled examples to see which examples satisfy the premise and for what percentage of those examples the repair gives the correct class. For example, of 150 training examples, 76 may satisfy the premise of the rule, and 28 of these 76 may match the class of the rule yielding a score of $28/76 = 36.8\%$. A set of new temporary repairs are then created by adding a condition to the seed repair. These conditions are derived from the focus facts[2]. If none of these new temporary repairs yield a higher score than the seed repair, then the seed repair is taken as the actual repair. If any of the temporary repairs are better, the best one becomes the new seed repair and the process is repeated.

Figure 2 gives an example of the repair process. The localization information in Figure 2(a) gives *air = mild* $\longrightarrow$ *cochlear_age* as one of the possible seed repairs (other seed repairs would also exist, but for this example we will only examine this one). Its accuracy on the training examples for which the premise is true is 36.8%. In Cycle 1 three temporary repairs are created each by adding a new condition derived from a focus fact. Adding the new condition reduces the number of examples for which the premise is true, and a higher percentage of these examples may match the specified class. The best of the temporary repairs in Cycle 1 has a higher percent accuracy than the seed repair and therefore is chosen to become the new seed repair. Similarly, in Cycle 2 another conjunct is added, but in Cycle 3 the added conjunct does not improve accuracy; therefore, the current seed repair is selected as the final repair and is added to the KB.

While apprenticeship techniques provide good guidance for finding one attribute related to the shortcoming (the unexplained attribute), a weakness which becomes apparent in the repair stage is that these techniques give little guidance as to which of the previous attribute requests may

---

[1]There are $\#\_of\_unexplained\_attribute\_values$ * $\#\_of\_focus\_classes$ seed repairs.

[2]For nominal attributes the focus fact can be used exactly. For numeric attributes, the condition is a range including the specified value.

Unexplained attribute: *air*
Focus facts: $age\_gt\_60 = true$, $history\_nausea = false$,
$\qquad\qquad history\_noise = false$
Focus classes: cochlear_age_plus_poss_menieres,
$\qquad\qquad$ cochlear_age

(a) The shortcoming localization information

Seed repair:	air = mild $\longrightarrow$ cochlear_age	36.8%

Cycle 1
Temp repair 1: air = mild $\wedge$
$\qquad\qquad$ age_gt_60 = true
$\qquad\qquad\qquad \longrightarrow$ cochlear_age   65.9%
Temp repair 2: air = mild $\wedge$
$\qquad\qquad$ history_nausea = false
$\qquad\qquad\qquad \longrightarrow$ cochlear_age   37.5%
Temp repair 3: air = mild $\wedge$
$\qquad\qquad$ history_noise = false
$\qquad\qquad\qquad \longrightarrow$ cochlear_age   45.4%

Temp repair 1 becomes the new seed repair.

Cycle 2
Temp repair 1: air = mild $\wedge$
$\qquad\qquad$ age_gt_60 = true $\wedge$
$\qquad\qquad$ history_nausea = false
$\qquad\qquad\qquad \longrightarrow$ cochlear_age   70.3%
Temp repair 2: air = mild $\wedge$
$\qquad\qquad$ age_gt_60 = true $\wedge$
$\qquad\qquad$ history_noise = false
$\qquad\qquad\qquad \longrightarrow$ cochlear_age   92.6%

Temp repair 2 becomes the new seed repair.

Cycle 3
Temp repair 1: air = mild $\wedge$
$\qquad\qquad$ age_gt_60 = true $\wedge$
$\qquad\qquad$ history_noise = false $\wedge$
$\qquad\qquad$ history_nausea = false
$\qquad\qquad\qquad \longrightarrow$ cochlear_age   92.3%

No repairs better than seed repair.

Final repair: air = mild $\wedge$
$\qquad\qquad$ age_gt_60 = true $\wedge$
$\qquad\qquad$ history_noise = false
$\qquad\qquad\qquad \longrightarrow$ cochlear_age   92.6%

(b) Three cycles of the repair generation process.

Figure 2: The shortcoming localization information in (a) guides the greedy repair construction in (b). New conditions are added to the seed repair, and the best one becomes the new seed repair.

---

be related to the shortcoming. An attribute chosen for the final repair may have been requested in close proximity to the unexplained attribute or it may have been the very first attribute requested. Position in the ordered sequence seems to give little help in the repair stage forcing the use of weak search techniques.

6   Experiments

The SKIPPER program puts together the three tasks of apprenticeship: shortcoming detection, localization, and repair. The assumptions that SKIPPER makes about the observed expert are that it is rational and is using a test-hypothesis strategy as discussed in section 3. First, the order of attributes in an observed problem-solving session are examined, and all the unexplained attributes are found. Next, the *last* unexplained attribute in the step sequence is selected as the focus of shortcoming localization. Why the last unexplained attribute? Any unexplained attribute could have been chosen, but the last one has the most specific context since more attributes were requested before it and therefore provides the most localization information. Next, the best repairs are generated and are added to the KB, and then the whole process is repeated. When no more shortcomings can be repaired using the set of training examples, SKIPPER goes through a KB pruning stage in which unhelpful rules (rules whose removal does not decrease the overall accuracy on the training set) are removed from the KB.

Experiments were run using the standardized audiology dataset [Jergen, 1987] which has 69 attributes, 24 classes, and contains 226 examples. For each experiment N examples were used as a training set and the $226 - N$ remaining examples were used as a validation set. First, the C4.5 program used the training examples to create an initial KB of rules, and the accuracy of this initial KB was tested on the validation set. Next, SKIPPER refined this initial KB using the same training examples, and the accuracy of the final refined KB was checked using the validation set. Training sets were selected randomly from the pool of 226 examples.

The observed expert used in the experiments was a set of rules generated by C4.5 using all 226 audiology examples available. Because this master rule set was generated using all 226 examples, the knowledge contained in it can be viewed as the gold standard as far as classifying these 226 examples is concerned, and it thus serves as an "synthetic expert." An ordered sequence of requested attributes can be generated for a given example by observing the order in which the master rule set would request attributes in solving that example. During each run of the apprentice, such an ordered sequence was created for each example in the training set and was used in refining the KB.

Training Set Size	Initial KB (percent accuracy)	Refined KB (percent accuracy)	Improvement
5	21.3±4.8	38.9±7.8	17.6±9.2
10	25.6±12.1	44.1±9.8	18.5±15.6
25	55.2±7.2	62.9±6.0	7.7±8.4
50	59.6±8.1	71.7±7.6	12.1±8.3
75	67.3±5.0	77.2±4.4	9.9±2.6
100	67.9±6.6	82.1±3.9	14.2±8.4
125	72.3±4.4	82.3±5.0	10.0±4.8
150	75.0±5.3	85.4±5.0	10.4±5.5

Table 1: Accuracies and improvements for experiments with the standardized audiology set.

Experiments were run using training sets ranging in size from 5 up to 150, and the results are summarized in Table 1 and Figure 3. Percent accuracies are given along with their 99% confidence ranges. The "Improvement" column simply reflects the net percent accuracy gained. Each result is an average taken over 10 independent runs.

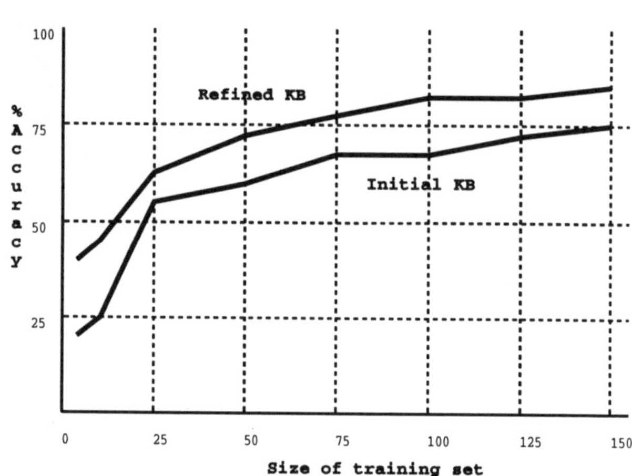

Figure 3: Accuracy of the initial KB and refined KB as a function of the training set size.

7   Discussion

An apprenticeship system refines its knowledge base by observing and analyzing the intermediate problem-solving steps taken by an expert (a generalization of the definition suggested in [Mitchell et al., 1985]). This paper has focused upon classification and specifically has sought what leverage can be attained from attribute ordering — knowing the order in which an expert requested attribute values while classifying an example. This ordering yields leverage because it presents each action within the context in which that action was taken. An attribute request can be analyzed from the critiqued problem-solver's point of view with respect to what was and wasn't known at the time of the request. Since the apprentice attempts to explain *why* the expert takes certain actions, *a priori* assumptions must be made about the expert and his problem-solving strategy. These assumptions provide a crucial bias for KB shortcoming detection. The power of attribute ordering is that it does not rely on empirical calculations to discover attribute/class relationships. Rather, attribute/class relationships are suggested by attribute ordering and are only verified empirically thus requiring less empirical evidence.

This work has focused only on repairing a KB by adding new rules. Often, though, it may be desirable to mend a slightly imperfect rule [Ourston and Mooney, 1990]. SKIPPER inelegantly handles this situation by adding new rules and then pruning away useless rules as a final stage. The information contained in problem-solving step ordering could be used to point out imperfect rules. For example, if an attribute request is unexplainable, but that attribute is in the premise of a rule previously deemed irrelevant, then perhaps the false condition in that rule should be deleted or altered. Attribute ordering appears to provide little information, though, for the decision of *which* type of repair should be made: adding a new rule or altering an existing rule.

The experiments in this paper were designed to evaluate the improvement in accuracy that could be attained when an observed expert closely follows the assumed problem-solving strategy. ODYSSEUS [Wilkins, 1988] assumed a much more sophisticated problem-solving strategy and learned from a human expert, but it simply assumed that its knowledge of the expert's strategy was complete and correct. It could not be determined whether any deficiencies in ODYSSEUS's performance were due to flaws in the basic apprenticeship approach or flawed assumptions about the expert's strategy. We assumed the observed expert used a test-hypothesis strategy, and the synthetic expert used in the experiments did in fact use this strategy. These experiments bolster confidence in the basic apprenticeship approach. The future direction of this work is to scale the principles learned about attribute ordering up to a more sophisticated model of problem-solving such as is used in NEOMYCIN [Clancey, 1985], CELIA [Redmond, 1992], and ODYSSEUS.

Acknowledgements

We would like to thank Tom Ioerger and Yong Ma for helpful comments on earlier drafts of this paper.

References

[Clancey, 1985] Clancey, W. J. (1985). Heuristic classification. *Artificial Intelligence*, 27:289–350.

[Davis, 1979] Davis, R. (1979). Interactive transfer of expertise: Acquisition of new inference rules. *Artificial Intelligence*, 12:121–158.

[Dent et al., 1992] Dent, L., Boticario, J., McDermott, J., Mitchell, T., and Zabowski, D. (1992). A personal learning apprentice. In *Proceedings of the 1992 National Conference on Artificial Intelligence*, pages 96–103, San Jose, CA.

[Jergen, 1987] Jergen (1987). Original owner of the audiology dataset.

[Mahadevan et al., 1993] Mahadevan, S., Mitchell, T., Mostow, J., Steinberg, L., and Tadepalli, P. (1993). An apprentice-based approach to knowledge acquisition. *Artificial Intelligence*, 64(1):1 – 52.

[Mitchell et al., 1985] Mitchell, T. M., Mahadevan, S., and Steinberg, L. I. (1985). LEAP: A learning apprentice for VLSI design. In *Proceedings of the 1985 IJCAI*, pages 573–580, Los Angeles, CA.

[Ourston and Mooney, 1990] Ourston, D. and Mooney, R. (1990). Changing the rules: A comprehensive approach to theory refinement. In *Proceedings of the 1990 National Conference on Artificial Intelligence*, pages 815–820.

[Quinlan, 1993] Quinlan, J. R. (1993). *C4.5: Programs for Machine Learning*. Morgan Kaufmann Publishers.

[Redmond, 1992] Redmond, M. (1992). *Learning by Observing and Understanding Expert Problem Solving*. PhD thesis, Georgia Inst. Tech.

[Tecuci and Kodratoff, 1990] Tecuci, G. and Kodratoff, Y. (1990). Apprenticeship learning in imperfect domain theories. In Kodratoff, Y. and Michalski, R. S., editors, *Machine Learning: An Artificial Intelligence Approach, Volume III*, pages 514–552. San Mateo: Morgan Kaufmann.

[Wilkins, 1988] Wilkins, D. C. (1988). Knowledge base refinement using apprenticeship learning techniques. In *Proceedings of the 1988 National Conference on Artificial Intelligence*, pages 646–651, Minneapolis, MN.

Improving Learning Performance Through Rational Resource Allocation

Jonathan Gratch*, Steve Chien+, and Gerald DeJong*

*Beckman Institute
University of Illinois
405 N. Mathews Av., Urbana, IL 61801
{gratch, dejong}@cs.uiuc.edu

+Jet Propulsion Laboratory
California Institute of Technology
4800 Oak Grove Drive, Pasadena, CA 91109-8099
chien@aig.jpl.nasa.gov

Abstract

This article shows how rational analysis can be used to minimize learning cost for a general class of statistical learning problems. We discuss the factors that influence learning cost and show that the problem of efficient learning can be cast as a resource optimization problem. Solutions found in this way can be significantly more efficient than the best solutions that do not account for these factors. We introduce a heuristic learning algorithm that approximately solves this optimization problem and document its performance improvements on synthetic and real-world problems.

1. Introduction

Machine learning techniques are valuable tools both in acquiring important scientific concepts and in support of decision making under uncertainty. Unfortunately, learning can involve a significant investment of resources. There may be monetary cost in obtaining data and computational cost in processing it. Usually such factors are addressed by informal or intuitive judgements rather than a rational analysis of the costs and benefits of alternative learning operations.

There is a significant learning cost in many diverse application areas. In speed-up learning there is substantial cost associated with processing each training example [Tadepalli92]). In some classification problems it is extremely expensive to obtain data (e.g. protein folding problems) and it is essential to make the most effective use of what data is available. Somewhat paradoxically, cost is also an issue when there is an overabundance of data. In this case it is expensive to use all of the data and one needs some criteria to decide how much data is enough to achieve a given level of performance [Musick93]. Finally, learning may involve ethical issues, as when experiments require giving potentially harmful treatments to human subjects. Under these circumstances it is a moral imperative to utilize as few subjects as possible and to quickly recognize and discard those treatments that worsen the patients condition.

This article discusses factors that influence cost and considers how to use rational analysis (i.e., [Doyle90, Rus-

sell91]) of these factors to minimize learning cost. We discuss this in the context of parametric hypothesis selection problems, an abstract class of statistical learning problems where a system must select one of a finite set of hypothesized courses of action, where the quality of each hypothesis is described as a function of some unknown parameters (e.g. [Gratch92, Greiner92, Kaelbling93, Moore94, Musick93]). A learning system determines and refines estimates of these parameters by "paying for" training examples.

We show how such problems can be cast as resource optimization problems, and that solutions found in this way can be significantly more efficient than solutions that do not account for the cost of gathering information (more than an order of magnitude). Surprisingly, standard hypothesis selection algorithms do not reason about information cost, and are thus less efficient then they might be. We introduce a rational hypothesis selection algorithm that approximately solves the resource allocation problem and empirically document the analytically predicted improvements in efficiency. This algorithm is quite general and can handle situations where the cost of processing data is initially unknown.

2. Hypothesis Selection Problems

Hypothesis selection problems are an abstract class of learning problems where one hypothesis must be chosen from a predefined set based on performance over an unknown distribution of problems or tasks. Performance is characterized by a hypothesis' *expected utility* over the distribution, which must be estimated from training data. Hypothesis selections are at the core of many machine learning approaches. For example, the *utility problem* in speed-up learning is a selection problem in which a problem solving heuristic is chosen from a set of proposed candidates, where expected utility is defined as the average time to solve a problem [Gratch92, Greiner92, Minton88]. The *attribute selection problem* in classification learning is a problem of selecting one of a set of attributes on which to split, where utility is equated with information gain [Musick93]. In reinforcement learning a system must select an action, where utility is equated with expected reward [Kaelbling93].

Several factors affect the cost of identifying a good selection. For example, there may be some cost in obtaining each training example. Furthermore, there can be additional cost for each hypothesis that is evaluated over a given training

Portions of this work were performed by the Jet Propulsion Laboratory, California Institute of Technology, under contract with the National Aeronautics and Space Administration and portions at the University of Illinois under National Science Foundation Grant NSF-IRI-92-09394.

example.[1] The challenge is to choose examples and evaluations in such a way as to maximize the likelihood of a good selection with a minimum of learning cost.

Choosing the best hypothesis is problematic as the underlying probability distributions are typically unavailable. Rather than requiring a hypothesis selection algorithm to always select the best hypothesis, algorithms typically obey some probabilistic requirement on the properties of the hypothesis that they select. Several alternative requirements have been proposed. In this paper we adopt the *probably approximately correct* (PAC) requirement favored by computational learning theory [Valiant84]. Under this requirement a hypothesis selection algorithm selects a hypothesis that with high probability is close to the best.

The expected utility associated with a hypothesis can be estimated by observing its performance over a finite set of training examples. However, to satisfy the PAC requirement an algorithm must reason about the discrepancy between the estimated and true utility of each hypothesis. Formally, let there be k hypotheses. Let H_{sel} denote the expected utility of the selected hypothesis and (without loss of generality) let H_i, $i=1..k-1$, be the expected utility for the remaining hypotheses. Let $\hat{H}_i$ be an estimate of the expected utility of the hypothesis. The PAC requirement is that hypothesis *estimated* to be best must be within some user-specified constant ϵ of the best hypothesis with probability $1-\delta$. It suffices to bound the probability that a hypothesis is estimated to be worse than the selected hypothesis given that it is in fact better, for each of the pair-wise comparisons:

$$\sum_{i=1}^{k-1} \Pr\left[\hat{H}_i < \hat{H}_{sel} - \epsilon | H_i > H_{sel} + \epsilon\right] \quad \leq \quad \delta \qquad (1)$$

Thus the problem of bounding the probability of error reduces to bounding the probability of error of each of the $k-1$ comparisons of H_{sel} to H_i.

To assess these probabilities we must adopt certain statistical assumptions. In this article we adopt the normal parametric model for reasoning about statistical error. This assumes that the difference between the expected utility and estimated utility of a hypothesis can be accurately approximated by a normal distribution (see [Hogg78] for an explanation of the robustness of this common assumption which is grounded in the Central Limit Theorem). The expected cost associated with processing data is also assumed to be normally distributed. Choosing a different parametric model would change the subsequent analysis but analogous results should hold for the conventional models.

With the normality assumption the probabilities in Equation 1 are a reduced to a function of the estimates, the number of examples, n, used for each estimate, the closeness parameter ϵ, and an unknown variance term, σ^2. Variance measures how much each observation can differ from its expected value, which can be estimated from the data.[2] To simplify the presentation we ignore the ϵ parameter in the discussion that follows ([Chien94] offers more details). For a given pair-wise comparison, δ_i, the (simplified) probability of incorrect selection is:

$$\delta_i = \Phi\left(-(H_{sel} - H_i)\frac{\sqrt{n}}{\sqrt{\sigma^2_{sel,i}}}\right) \qquad (2)$$

where the function Φ is the quantile function of the standard normal distribution. Intuitively, Equation 2 shows that the probability of a mistake diminishes as the difference in expected utility between the hypotheses increases, as the number of training examples increases, and as the variance of each hypothesis decreases. This relationship can be used to determine how many training examples to allocate to each comparison. If we wish to achieve a given bound of δ_i, then by simple algebra the number of examples needed for a given pair-wise comparison is:

$$n_{sel,i} = \frac{\sigma^2_{sel,i}}{(H_{sel} - H_i)^2} [\Phi^{-1}(\delta)]^2 \qquad (3)$$

where Φ^{-1} is the inverse of the quantile function of the standard normal distribution.

While the variance and true expected utilities are unknown, a class of statistical approaches called *sequential* approaches has been designed for such problems [Govindarajulu81]. These techniques develop estimates of the unknown parameters from a small initial sample size and then incrementally refine these estimates after each subsequent training example. For example, after some number of examples a sequential technique would estimate that the hypothesis it will eventually select is the one with the current highest estimated utility. Such techniques terminate sampling based on an estimate of the sufficient number of training examples. Section 4 introduces a sequential hypothesis selection algorithm that uses a sequential approximation to Equation 3 to decide when to stop sampling.

3. The Value of Rational Learning

The PAC requirement constrains but does not completely determine the behavior of a hypothesis selection algorithm. We would like an algorithm to satisfy the requirement with the minimum cost possible. Several of the factors that contribute to the cost are unknown before learning begins. For this reason standard (non-rational) hypothesis selection al-

---

1. For example, in classification learning a potentially large set of examples must be partitioned for each hypothesized split. In speed-up learning the learning system may have to re-solve the example problem for each candidate heuristic.

2. We "block" examples as in [Moore94] to further reduce sampling complexity. Blocking forms estimates by averaging the difference in utility between hypotheses on each observed example, which can substantially reduce the variance in the data when hypotheses are related (e.g. when each hypothesis is a variant on a basic search control strategy). It is trivial to modify the algorithm to work for the case where it is not possible to block data.

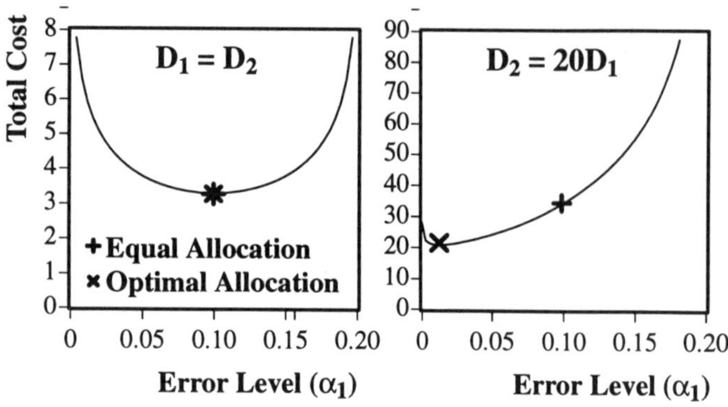

Figure 1. An illustration of the difference between equal and optimal allocation with equal and unequal disparity indices.

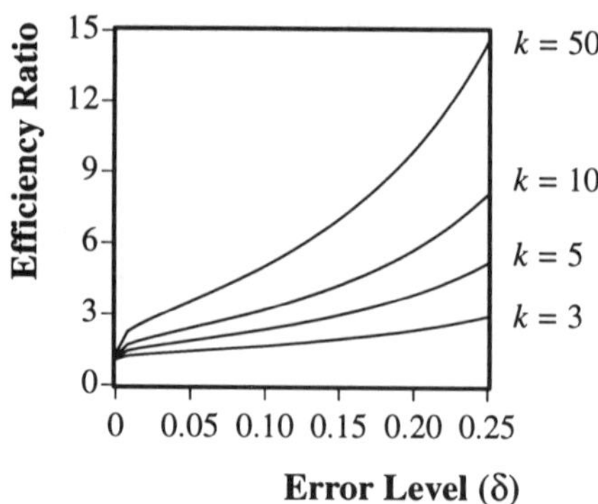

Figure 2: The potential benefits of rational analysis. Shows the ratio of equal allocation cost to optimal cost for several error levels and number of hypotheses.

gorithms ignore these factors when making their selection. This section discusses the relevant factors and shows that they can be folded into a single value, the *disparity index*. We show that in theory an algorithm can achieve large performance improvements by exploiting this information, if only it were available. Comparable performance improvements can be achieved in practice using sequential techniques, as we show in the next section.

Equation 3 illuminates the factors that affect selection cost. In order to satisfy the PAC requirement we must, for each non-selected hypothesis, bound the probability that it is better than the selected hypothesis. The total cost is is the sum of the cost of processing each training example. Equation 3 shows that the number of examples allocated to the two hypotheses increases as the variance increases, as the difference in utility between the hypotheses decreases, or as the acceptable probability of making a mistake decreases.

The first two factors are determined by the environment, but the last, the probability threshold associated with each comparison, can conceivably vary and thus be placed under the control of the hypothesis selection algorithm. The algorithm must only ensure that the *sum* of these probabilities remain less than δ (Equation 1). If one comparison requires a great many examples and another very few, it seems possible that allowing greater error for the first and less for the second might reduce the total cost. In fact, allowing the algorithm to judiciously allocate error to each comparison can result in a substantial reduction in overall cost.

Reducing the cost of selection can be cast as an optimization problem. Total cost is the sum of the number of examples allocated to each comparison (from Equation 3) times the average cost to process an example. Let $c_{sel,i}$ denote the average cost per example to compare the selected hypothesis with hypothesis i. Let α_i be the error level allocated to the comparison. The optimal allocation of error can be determined by solving the following optimization problem:[3]

3. This assumes that the cost of processing examples for one comparison is independent of the other comparisons. A more complex analysis is needed to faithfully represent cases where there is significant sharing of cost between comparisons.

Resource Optimization Problem

Choose α_i to minimize $\quad \displaystyle\sum_{i=1}^{k-1} c_{sel,i} \frac{\sigma_{sel,i}^2}{(H_{sel} - H_i)^2} [\Phi^{-1}(\alpha_i)]^2$

Subject to the constraint that $\quad \displaystyle\sum_{i=1}^{k-1} \alpha_i \leq \delta$

Of course in an actual hypothesis selection problem the expected utility of the hypotheses, and perhaps the variance and cost will be unknown before learning begins. Without considering such information the only reasonable policy is to assign an equal error level to each comparison (i.e. $\alpha_i = \delta/[k-1]$). However, comparing this *equal allocation* policy with the optimal solution shows that equal allocation can be highly sub-optimal. To see this, consider the case with three hypotheses, $k=3$, which results in two comparisons with error α_1 and $\delta-\alpha_1$. The selection cost is:

$$D_1[\Phi^{-1}(\alpha_1)]^2 + D_2[\Phi^{-1}(\delta - \alpha_1)]^2 \qquad (4)$$

$$\text{where} \quad D_i = \frac{c_{sel,2}\sigma_{sel,i}^2}{(H_{sel} - H_i)^2}$$

The value D_i is called the *disparity index* for comparison i.

To be optimal, α_1 must be chosen so as to minimize the total cost. The equal allocation policy assigns α_1 equal to $\delta/2$. Equation 4 indicates that the equal allocation solution is optimal *only* in the case where the two disparity indices are equal. This is illustrated in Figure 1, which shows the cost equation as a function of α_1, first in the case where the disparity indices are equal, and then when there is a difference between their values. The minimum point under this curve is the optimal cost and the value of α_1 at this point indicates the optimal error allocation. In contrast, the equal allocation policy yields a cost that may differ significantly from this minimum.

In practice it is unlikely that the disparity indices will be equal all for comparisons. Even if the example cost is similar for every hypothesis the variance and expected utilities of hypotheses will almost certainly differ. The inefficiency of equal allocation increases as the differences between disparity indices increases. The inefficiency also increases as with the number of hypotheses. By taking the difference in disparity indices to the limit it can be shown that for k hypotheses the ratio of equal allocation cost to the optimal cost can be up to $[\Phi^{-1}(\delta/[k-1])]^2 / [\Phi^{-1}(\delta)]^2$. The ratio can be quite large as illustrated in Figure 2. Thus, ignoring disparity information can result in costs up to an order of magnitude greater with as few as ten hypotheses under consideration. This result also shows that the ratio cannot grow without bound and that equal allocation is near optimal for cases with few hypotheses and a small error level.

4. Rational Example Allocation

If the disparity indices were known advance, an algorithm could optimize the cost of selecting a hypothesis. Although this information is unavailable before learning begins, with a sequential approach the algorithm can develop increasingly accurate approximations to this information in the course of learning. These approximations can be almost as effective as the true information in guiding learning behavior. In this section we introduce a rational hypothesis selection algorithm that exploits these approximations to minimize selection cost. This is compared with an efficient non-rational approach similar to Moore and Lee's BRACE algorithm [Moore94]. The superiority of the rational approach is documented on artificial and real-world data sets.

4.1 Interval-Based Selection Algorithm

We first introduce the basic hypothesis selection approach. Rational and non-rational algorithms derived from this approach differ in how they choose hypotheses to further evaluate. The algorithm initially evaluates all hypotheses over a small initial set of n_0 training examples. This is to develop initial parameter estimates and to enhance the robustness of the normality assumption. The algorithm then incrementally processes training examples, deciding to evaluate one or more hypotheses on that example. Learning proceeds incrementally until, to the required level of confidence, one hypothesis ε-dominates. The basic approach is as follows:[4]

With hypotheses $H_1..H_k$
Evaluate all hypotheses over n_0 training examples
While no selection
    Let H_{sel} be hypothesis with highest estimated utility

$$\text{IF} \quad \sum_{i=1}^{k-1} \Pr\left[\hat{H}_i < \hat{H}_{sel} - \epsilon | H_i > H_{sel} + \epsilon\right] \le \delta$$

        THEN select H_{sel}
    ELSE Obtain next example
        Evaluate those hypotheses chosen according to
        rational or non-rational policy as outlined below

---

4.   See [Chien94] for complete discussion of such rational and non-rational algorithms. The probability is computed with equations analogous to Equation 2.

Equal Allocation Policy. The non-rational algorithm follows the equal allocation policy. Each cycle through the loop allocates an additional example to a pair-wise comparison if its probability of error remains above the fixed level of $\delta/[k-1]$. Eventually every comparison will drop below this error threshold and the procedure will terminate.

Marginal Rate of Return Policy. Using estimates of the disparity indices, the rational algorithm calculates the increase in confidence and the cost of allocating an additional example to each comparison. At each cycle through the main loop the algorithm allocates an example to the comparison with the highest *marginal rate of return*. This is the ratio of increased confidence to increased cost.

This rational policy tries to maximize the decrease in statistical error per unit cost, although we cannot guarantee the strategy achieves the optimal error allocation. Complications include the fact that estimates of the disparity factors differ from their true value and the initial sample size parameter restricts the algorithm's degrees of freedom. Nonetheless, this policy has performed well empirically. The marginal rate of return is estimated using an equation analogous to Equation 2, substituting in estimated for actual utility values. After processing the n_0 initial training examples the algorithm estimates the expected utility, variance, and cost of the various comparisons. The change in error can be estimated by considering how the error would change assuming the current parameter estimates are correct:

$$\Phi\left(-(\hat{H}_{sel} - \hat{H}_i)\frac{\sqrt{n}}{\sqrt{\hat{\sigma}^2_{sel,i}}}\right) - \Phi\left(-(\hat{H}_{sel} - \hat{H}_i)\frac{\sqrt{n+1}}{\sqrt{\hat{\sigma}^2_{sel,i}}}\right) \quad (5)$$

The estimated marginal rate of return for a comparison is computed by dividing this estimate of the reduction of error by the estimated cost of processing an additional training example.

4.2 Empirical Evaluation

We illustrate the performance of the algorithms on simulated and real-world data. The first evaluation uses simulated data with high disparity to illustrate that the rational algorithm achieves performance improvements comparable to what is predicted by the theoretical analysis. The second evaluation uses data from a NASA scheduling application to illustrate the robustness of the approach on a real-world hypothesis selection problem.

4.2.1   Simulated Data. A rational algorithm should significantly outperform a non-rational approach when there is a large difference between the costs, variances, or expected utilities of the various hypotheses. We test this hypothesis for several number of hypotheses and error levels. For all experiments ε is set at 1.0 and δ varies from 0.05 to 0.25, in 0.05 increments. We perform tests with three, five, and ten hypotheses. The training examples are randomly generated: All utility values and example costs are normal-

ly distributed according to some expected value and variance, denoted N(value,variance). For all experiments, H_1 is distributed $N(74,50)$ with cost $N(20,1)$, H_2 is distributed $N(72,50)$ with cost $N(50000,1)$. All remaining hypotheses are distributed $N(5,50)$ with cost $N(20,1)$. For each configuration the algorithms are run 5000 times and the reported results are the average over these trials.

Figure 3 summarizes the predicted and observed *efficiency ratio*. This is the cost to select using equal allocation over the cost to select using rational allocation. The performance improvement due to rational allocation is surprisingly close to the limit. This suggests that for this data set the rational algorithm has identified a near optimal error allocation. Note that for large error the observed efficiency drops below the predicted level. This is a consequence of the initial sample size parameter n_0. The rational algorithm is forced to take at least this many examples on every comparison, while in this problem configuration less would suffice to achieve the probability bound. The implication is that when the hypothesis evaluation problem is easy (requires perhaps fewer than n_0 examples to make a selection) the efficiency will be effected more by the choice of the initial sample size than the allocation policy. An interesting issue we have not sufficiently explored is possible strategies for setting the initial parameter size.

4.2.2 NASA Scheduling Data.

The test of real-world applicability is based on data drawn from a NASA scheduling application detailed in [Gratch93]. This data provides a test of the applicability of the techniques. Both algorithms assume estimated utility varies normally from the expected utility. In fact, this common assumption is violated by the data as most of the scheduling heuristics are bi-modally distributed. This characteristic provides a rather severe test of the robustness of both approaches.

The heuristic system was developed to schedule communications between earth-orbiting satellites and ground-based antennas. In the course of development extensive evaluations were performed with variant scheduling heuristics. The purpose of these evaluations was to choose a heuristic that generated satisfactory schedules quickly on average. This is easily seen as a hypothesis evaluation problem. Each of the heuristics corresponds to a hypothesis. The cost of evaluating a hypothesis over a training example is the CPU time required to solve the scheduling problem with the given heuristic. The utility of the training example is simply the negation of its cost. In that way, choosing a hypothesis with maximal expected utility corresponds to choosing a scheduling heuristic with minimal average cost.

The application involves several hypothesis selection problems, four of which we use in this evaluation (A, B, C, and D). Each selection problem consists of a set of scheduling heuristics, and data on the heuristics' performance over about one thousand scheduling problems. For the purpose of these experiments the data sets are assumed to correspond exactly to the underlying probability distributions. An experimental trial consists of executing a technique over examples drawn from one of these data sets. Each time a training example is to be processed, some problem is drawn randomly with replacement from the data set. The actual utility and cost values associated with this scheduling problem is used. As in the synthetic data, each experimental trial is repeated 5000 times and all reported results are the average of these trials. In this data the cost and expected utilities of hypotheses are relatively close to each other so the difference between the disparity indices is relatively small across comparisons.

Each trial used an error level of 0.05 or 0.25 and ε equal to 4.0. The results are summarized in Table 1. For each algorithm this shows the average number of examples required to select a hypothesis, the total cost of those examples, and the observed probability that the selection was correct for each of the four selection problems.

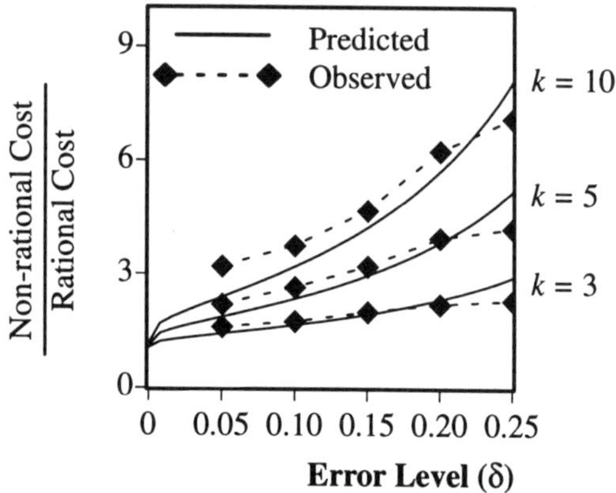

Figure 3. Shows predicted and observed efficiency of the rational allocation policy (the ratio in cost between the non-rational and rational policies). The rational policy shows a significant increase in efficiency.

Parameters			Equal Allocation			Rational Allocation			Cost Ratio
	k	ε	δ	Ex.	Cost	Pr.	Ex.	Cost	Pr.	
A	3	4	0.25	180	277	1.00	77	120	1.00	2.3
			0.05	908	1,391	1.00	648	998	1.00	1.4
B	2	4	0.25	30	47	1.00	30	46	1.00	1.0
			0.05	74	115	1.00	76	117	1.00	1.0
C	7	4	0.25	1189	1758	0.88	779	1148	0.77	1.5
			0.05	2,371	3,493	0.94	2,153	3,184	0.94	1.1
D	7	4	0.25	3,274	4,993	0.93	2,241	3,429	0.88	1.5
			0.05	7,972	12,037	0.96	7,621	11,583	0.94	1.0

Table 1. Average number of observations, cost, and probability of correct selection for scheduling data.

Both algorithms performed robustly. In each selection problem the PAC requirement was achieved or nearly achieved. This result is particularly remarkable given the data's significant departure from normality. The rational algorithm provides a modest improvement over the equal allocation algorithm on three out of the four selection problems. The improvement increased with higher error level in accordance with theoretical predictions. In both the scheduling and artificial data the rational algorithm tended to exhibit statistical error closer to the requested bound. The equal allocation strategies excessive conservatism is due to its inflexibility in allocating statistical error in cases where a hypothesis could be discarded with less than n_0 datapoints.

While the scheduling improvements may seem modest, there are three points that must be emphasized. First, the number of hypotheses was small and improvements should grow with the number of hypotheses. Second, in absolute terms the savings are significant. For example, the 350 examples saved in selection problem D translate into about fifteen hours of CPU effort. Finally, in no case did the rational algorithm perform worse. Thus there is little loss, and potential for substantial improvement with rational allocation.

5. Related Work and Conclusions

This analysis can be extended in a number of ways. In many learning situations one may be reluctant to assume normality. For example, when selecting attributes in a decision tree a multinomial model may be more appropriate. We suspect comparable results will hold for a wide range of statistical models but further analysis is necessary. Selection problems could be formalized in a bayesian statistical framework as in [Moore94, Rivest88]. This would eliminate the need for an initial sample but require a rigorous encoding of prior knowledge. Related to this, Howard [Howard70] has extensively investigated a bayesian framework for assessing learning cost in the case of single hypothesis problems.

While this article has focused on minimizing cost in the context of hypothesis selection, the ability to assess both the benefits and costs of learning has been investigated in a variety of contexts both inside and outside of artificial intelligence. For example the tradeoff between goal-directed action and exploration behavior has been studied in reinforcement learning [Kaelbling93]. Another active area of investigation involves the selection of an inductive bias for classification learning tasks. A weaker bias allows higher potential accuracy but requires more data. The selection of an appropriate bias depends on the availability and cost of obtaining training examples as well as usefulness of better prediction (see [desJardins92]). The same issue arises in neural networks and in statistics when one must choose a network topology or statistical model that balances the tradeoff between the fit to the data and the number of examples required to reach a given level of predictive accuracy. Finally, these learning issues can be seen as part of the more general area of *limited rationality*. This is the problem of developing a theory of rational decision making when in the presence of limited reasoning resources [Russell91, Wellman92].

To summarize, we argue that learning algorithms must assess both the benefits and costs of learning. We provide a theoretical analysis of the factors that contribute to learning cost. By reasoning about a value called the disparity index a learning algorithm can achieve the same level of benefit at substantially reduced cost. We introduce a heuristic algorithm that empirically achieves the predicted performance improvements over a non-rational approach. While the improvements on any given hypothesis selection problem may lie well below the theoretical limit, the rational algorithm is unlikely to perform worse and may perform significantly better. Therefore there seems little reason not to adopt this or an analogous rational approach.

References

[Chien94] S. A. Chien, J. M. Gratch and M. C. Burl, "On the Efficient Allocation of Resources for Hypothesis Evaluation in Machine Learning: A Statistical Approach," Technical Report, University of Illinois (forthcoming).

[desJardins92] M. E. desJardins, "PAGODA: A Model for Autonomous Learning in Probabilistic Domains," Ph.D. Thesis, University of California, Berkeley, CA, April 1992.

[Doyle90] J. Doyle, "Rationality and its Roles in Reasoning (extended version)," *AAAI90*, Boston, MA, 1990.

[Govindarajulu81] Z. Govindarajulu, *The Sequential Statistical Analysis*, American Sciences Press, Columbus, OH, 1981.

[Gratch92] J. Gratch and G. DeJong, "COMPOSER: A Probabilistic Solution to the Utility Problem in Speed–up Learning," *AAAI92*, San Jose, CA, July 1992, pp. 235–240.

[Gratch93] J. Gratch, S. Chien and G. DeJong, "Learning Search Control Knowledge for Deep Space Network Scheduling," *ML93*, Amherst, MA, June 1993.

[Greiner92] R. Greiner and I. Jurisica, "A Statistical Approach to Solving the EBL Utility Problem," *AAAI92*, San Jose, CA, July 1992, pp. 241–248.

[Hogg78] R. V. Hogg and A. T. Craig, *Introduction to Mathematical Statistics*, Macmillan Inc., London, 1978.

[Howard70] R. A. Howard, "Decision Analysis: Perspectives on Inference, Decision, and Experimentation," *Proceedings of the IEEE 58*, 5 (1970), pp. 823–834.

[Kaelbling93] L. P. Kaelbling, *Learning in Embedded Systems*, MIT Press, Cambridge, MA, 1993.

[Minton88] S. Minton, in *Learning Search Control Knowledge: An Explanation–Based Approach*, Kluwer Academic Publishers, Norwell, MA, 1988.

[Moore94] A. W. Moore and M. S. Lee, "Efficient Algorithms for Minimizing Cross Validation Error," *ML94*, New Brunswick, MA, July 1994.

[Musick93] R. Musick, J. Catlett and S. Russell, "Decision Theoretic Subsampling for Induction on Large Databases," *ML93*, MA, June 1993, pp. 212–219.

[Rivest88] R. L. Rivest and R. Sloan, A New Model for Inductive Inference," *Second Conference on Theoretical Aspects of Reasoning about Knowledge*, 1988.

[Russell91] S. Russell and E. Wefald, *Do the Right Thing: Studies in Limited Rationality*, MIT Press, Cambridge, MA.

[Tadepalli92] P. Tadepalli, "A theory of unsupervised speedup learning," *AAAI92*, San Jose, CA, July 1992, pp. 229–234.

[Valiant84] L. G. Valiant, "A Theory of the Learnable," *Communications of the ACM 27*, (1984), pp. 1134–1142.

[Wellman92] M. P. Wellman and J. Doyle, "Modular Utility Representation for Decision–Theoretic Planning," *AIPS92*, College Park, Maryland, June 1992, pp. 236–242.

Learning Explanation-Based Search Control Rules For Partial Order Planning

Suresh Katukam & Subbarao Kambhampati*
Department of Computer Science and Engineering
Arizona State University, Tempe, AZ 85287-5406
email: suresh@enuxsa.eas.asu.edu, rao@asu.edu

Abstract

This paper presents SNLP+EBL, the first implementation of explanation based learning techniques for a partial order planner. We describe the basic learning framework of SNLP+EBL, including regression, explanation propagation and rule generation. We then concentrate on SNLP+EBL's ability to learn from failures and present a novel approach that uses stronger domain and planner specific consistency checks to detect, explain and learn from the failures of plans at depth limits. We will end with an empirical evaluation of the efficacy of this approach in improving planning performance.

1 Introduction

One way of coping with the computational complexity of domain-independent planning involves application of learning techniques to speed up planning. Accordingly, there has been a considerable amount of research directed towards applying explanation-based learning (EBL) techniques to planning [2, 10]. Much of this work has been concentrated on the state-based planning. Motivated by the known advantages of partial order (PO) planning over state based planning in plan generation [1] and reuse [5, 6], in this paper we address the problem of adapting EBL techniques to speed up partial order planning.

The EBL frameworks for state-based planning, such as PRODIGY/EBL [10] and FailSafe [2] typically construct search control rules that aim to steer the planner away from unpromising paths. The search control rules are generated by analyzing the search space explored by the planner to locate failures, constructing explanations for those failures, and regressing the failure explanations over the planning decisions.

Given that partial order and state-based planners search in very different search (decision) spaces, adapting these EBL frameworks to partial order (PO) planning offers two important challenges. First, since the space of decisions in PO planning is different, the process of regressing and

*This research is supported in part by National Science Foundation under grant IRI-9210997, and ARPA/Rome Laboratory planning initiative under grant F30602-93-C-0039. Thanks to Bulusu Gopi Kumar, Steve Minton, Prasad Tadepalli and Dan Weld for helpful comments.

generalizing the explanations needs to be extended significantly. Secondly, since the types of failures encountered in PO planning are different from those encountered in state-based planning, we need to investigate effective learning opportunities for PO planners.

In this paper, we address both these issues. Specifically, we describe SNLP+EBL, a system that learns search control rules for SNLP, a causal link based PO planner [1, 9]. We will start by describing the basic learning framework in SNLP+EBL, including the details of regression, explanation propagation and search-control rule learning (Section 2). We will then concentrate on SNLP+EBL's ability to learn from failures. We will show that the failures detected by SNLP (analytical failures) alone do not by themselves provide effective learning opportunities for SNLP+EBL in many domains. This is because many futile lines of reasoning either never end in analytical failures or cross depth limits much before they do. Since depth limit failures are not analytical, it is not possible to learn from them.

To deal with this impasse, we adopt a novel approach of strategically applying stronger consistency checks to the plans crossing depth limits, to detect and explain the implicit failures in those plans. These explanations are then used to generate search control rules. In Section 3, we will describe a specific realization of this strategy that utilizes the *domain axioms* (or readily available physical laws of the domain) to detect and explain inconsistencies (failures) at some depth limit failures. In Section 3.1, we describe the results of an empirical study which demonstrate the effectiveness of the search control rules learned by this method.

2 The SNLP+EBL system

2.1 The base level planner

As mentioned earlier, our base level planner is SNLP, a causal link based PO planner described in [1, 9]. SNLP searches in the space of partial plans. Each partial plan can be seen as a 5 tuple: $\langle S, O, B, L, G \rangle$ where: S is the set of actions (also called steps) in the plan. The actions are described in the STRIPS representation, with *add*, *delete* and *precondition* lists. S contains two distinguished steps start and fin. The effects of start and the preconditions of fin correspond, respectively, to the initial state and the desired goals of the planning problem. O describes the ordering constraints over

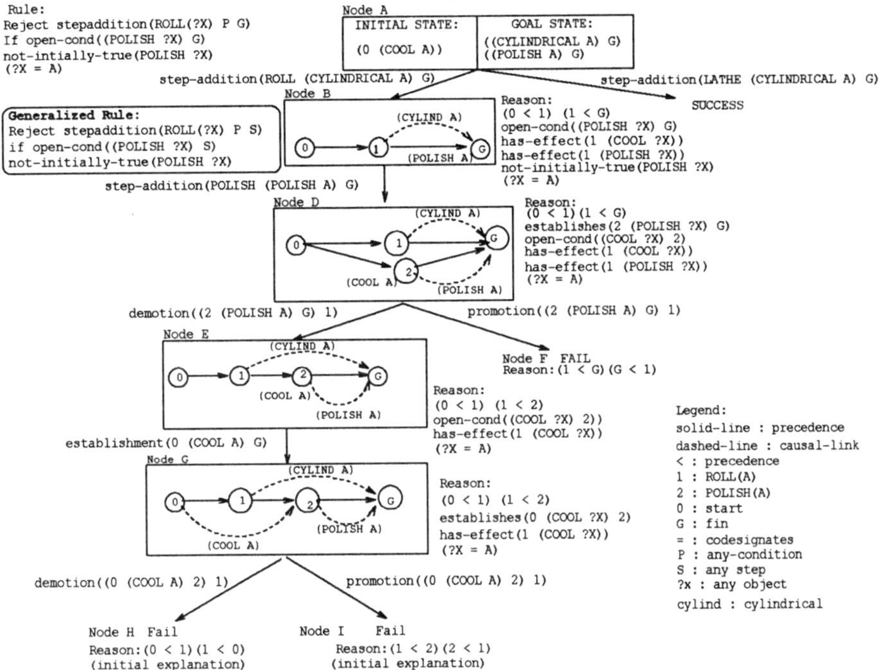

Figure 1: *Search Tree illustrating learning from analytical failures*

the steps in $\mathcal{S}$. $\mathcal{B}$ is a set of codesignation (binding) and non-codesignation (prohibited bindings) constraints on the variables appearing in the preconditions and post-conditions of the operators.

$\mathcal{G}$ is the set of open conditions of the partial plan, i.e. tuples $\langle c, s \rangle$ such that c is a precondition of step $s \in \mathcal{S}$. The planning process consists of establishing the open conditions with the help of the effects of either an existing step or a new step. Whenever an open condition $\langle c, s \rangle$ is established with the help of the effects of some step s', it is removed from $\mathcal{G}$, and a causal link $s' \xrightarrow{c} s$ is added to $\mathcal{L}$. If s is a new step, its preconditions are also added to $\mathcal{G}$.

A causal link should be seen as a commitment by the planner to protect c in the range between s' and s. Whenever new steps are introduced into the plan, the existing causal links are checked to see if any of their conditions are violated. A step t of the plan is said to be a *threat* to a causal link $s \xrightarrow{p} w \in \mathcal{L}$, if t has an add or delete list literal q such that q possibly codesignates with p, and t can possibly come in between s and w. The threat is resolved by either *promoting* t to come after w, or *demoting* it to come before s (in both cases, appropriately updating $\mathcal{O}$), or adding non-codesignation constraints to ensure that q does not codesignate with p. A threat for a causal link is said to be *unresolvable* if all of these possibilities make either $\mathcal{O}$ or $\mathcal{B}$ inconsistent. SNLP backtracks when it encounters an unresolvable threat, or an unestablishable open condition.

The search tree in Figure 1 illustrates SNLP's planning process in terms of an example from a simple job-shop scheduling domain with the operators shown below:

Action	Precond	Add	Dele
Roll(o)	-	Cylind(o)	Polish(o) $\wedge$ Cool(o)
Lathe(o)	-	Cylind(o)	Polish(o)
Polish(o)	Cool(o)	Polish(o)	-

The initial planning problem is to polish an object A and make its surface cylindrical. The object's temperature is cool in the initial state. The figure shows a failing branch of the search tree. In this branch, SNLP establishes the open condition $\langle Cylindrical(A), \text{G} \rangle$ with the help of the new step $1\!:\!\texttt{Roll}(A)$. It then establishes the other open condition $\langle Polished(A), \text{G} \rangle$ with the operator $2\!:\!\texttt{Polish}(A)$.

Since $\texttt{Roll}(A)$ deletes $Polish(A)$, it is now a threat to the link $2 \xrightarrow{Polish(A)} \text{G}$. SNLP resolves this threat by demoting $1\!:\!\texttt{Roll}(A)$ to come before $2\!:\!\texttt{Polish}(A)$. $Polish(A)$ also introduces a new open condition $\langle Cool(A), 2 \rangle$. SNLP establishes it using the effects of the start state. Since $\texttt{Roll}(A)$ also deletes $Cool(A)$, it also threatens this last establishment. When SNLP tries to deal with the threat by demoting $1\!:\!\texttt{Roll}(A)$ to come before step 0, it fails (since 0 already precedes 1).[1] Such failures represent learning opportunities for the SNLP+EBL system, as discussed in the next section.

2.2 Interaction between the learner and the planner

Search control rules attempt to provide guidance to the underlying problem solver at critical decision points. As we have seen above, for SNLP these decision points are selection of open conditions; establishment, including simple-establishment and step-addition (operator selection); threat

---

[1]To simplify the exposition clear, we omitted the failing separation branch from the figure.

Decision: The new step s_1 is added to establish the condition p at step s_2 in the current partial plan. The preconditions of this decision are simply that s_2 requires a condition p.

(1) Result of regressing the ordering constraint $s' \prec s''$
$True$, If $s' = s_1$ and $s'' = s_2$
$True \wedge$ `start-special`, If $s' =$ `start` and $s'' = s_1$
(see *rule generalization* section for
explanation of `start-special` flag)
$s_2 \prec s''$, if $s' = s_1$ and $s_2 \prec s''$
$s' \prec s''$ otherwise

(2) Result of regressing the causal link $s' \xrightarrow{p'} s''$
$True$ If $s' = s_1$ and $s'' = s_2$ and $p = p'$
$s' \xrightarrow{p'} s''$ otherwise

Figure 2: *Partial procedure for regressing explanations over step establishments*

selection; and threat resolution, including promotion, demotion and separation. Of these, it is not feasible to learn goal-selection and threat-selection rules using the standard EBL analysis since SNLP never backtracks over these decisions. SNLP+EBL system learns search control rules for all the other decisions. A search control rule may either be in the form of a selection rule or a rejection rule. In our current work, we have concentrated on learning rejection rules (although the basic framework can be extended to include selection rules).

Unlike systems such as PRODIGY/EBL, which commence learning only after the planning is completed, SNLP+EBL does adaptive (intra-trial) learning (c.f. [2]), which combines a form of dependency directed backtracking with generation of search-control rules. The planner does depth first search both in the learning and non-learning phases. During the learning phase, SNLP+EBL invokes the learning component whenever the planner encounters a failure.

There are two types of failures that are recognized by SNLP: the first is the analytical failure (where the planner reaches an impasse and declares that the current partial plan cannot be refined further). As explained earlier, this happens when the partial plan contains a causal link with an unresolvable threat, or an unestablishable open condition. The second type of failure occurs when the problem solver crosses a pre-set depth limit. The purpose of this limit is to prevent runaway search down fruitless alleys.

If the learner is able to explain the failure, it constructs an initial explanation and then regresses that explanation over the decisions in that branch to generate search control rules. From our discussion above, it is clear that analytical failures can be explained in terms of the inconsistency of the ordering and binding constraints of the partial plan, or in terms of the unestablishable open condition. For example, the initial explanation of failure for the partial plan at node H in Figure 1 is simply that $(0 \prec 1) \wedge (1 \prec 0)$ (causing an ordering cycle). We defer the treatment of depth limit failures to Section 3.

Regression: Once an initial explanation for a failure is constructed, SNLP+EBL regresses this explanation over the decisions leading to the failing partial plan. For state-based planners, the planning decisions correspond closely to opera-

Procedure Propagate(E, d_i)
(d_i: failing partial plan; E: initial explanation of failure at d_i).
0. Set $d \leftarrow d_i$
1. $E' \leftarrow$ `Regress`$((E, decision(d)))$
2. If $E' = E$, then set $d \leftarrow parent(d)$; Goto Step 1. (*a form of DDB*)
3. If $E' \neq E$, then
3.1. If there are unexplored siblings of d
3.1.1 Make a rejection rule rejecting the decision of d, with E' as the antecedent generalize it and store it in the rule set
3.1.2. $fexp(parent(d)) \leftarrow E' \wedge$
$precond(decision(d)) + fexp(parent(d))$
(*store E' as one the failure explanations under $parent(d)$*))
3.1.3. Restart search at the first unexplored sibling of d
3.2. If there are no unexplored siblings of d,
3.2.1. Set $E \leftarrow [E' \wedge precond(decision(d))] + fexp(parent(d))$
3.2.2. If all the siblings of d are establishing an open condition $\langle c, s \rangle$, and none of them establish it from `start`,
Set $E \leftarrow E + \neg$`initially-true`(c)
3.2.3. Set $d \leftarrow parent(d)$; Goto Step 1.

Figure 3: *Propagating Failure Explanations*

tor applications, and thus regression over planning decisions is very close to regression over operators [12]. In contrast, decisions in the PO planners correspond to addition of generalized constraints (steps, orderings, bindings, causal links) to the partial plan. SNLP+EBL provides a sound and complete framework for regressing explanations over these decisions. Figure 2 contains a partial outline of the procedure for regressing arbitrary constraints of an explanation over an establishment decision involving step addition. A complete description of the regression rules for this and other planning decisions is beyond the scope of this paper, and can be found in [8].

Propagating Failure Explanations: Once an initial explanation of the failure has been identified, it is propagated up the failure branch to learn search control rules, as well as to do a form of dependency directed backtracking. Figure 3 provides the outline of this procedure. We will illustrate this process with the help of the example in Figure 1.

As discussed at the end of Section 2.1, the first failure in this example is noticed at node H. Here, the demotion caused order inconsistency in the plan. The explanation for this failure is simply that $(0 \prec 1) \wedge (1 \prec 0)$ (causing a cycle in the ordering). When this explanation is regressed over the demotion decision to make step 1 precede 0, we get $0 \prec 1$. Since the regressed explanation is different from the original one (step 3 in Figure 3)[2], it is then conjoined with the preconditions of the demotion decision (which in this case is that 1 threatens the link $0 \xrightarrow{Cool(A)} 2$) to get the weakest preconditions for this branch of failure under G. These are then stored as one of the failure explanations at node G (step

---

[2]Had the explanation not changed during regression over H, the propagation process would have continued to the parent of this decision (step 2 in Figure 3). The rationale being that at least as far as this failure is concerned the choice taken at H's parent node didn't contribute to the failure. Thus, as long as the decisions at the upper levels remain same, exploring the other siblings of H is guaranteed to keep this failure intact. This process constitutes a simple form of dependency directed backtracking.

3.1.2 in Figure 3).

Since the explanation changed after regression, and since there are unexplored siblings of H, technically, we can learn a rejection rule here (step 3.1.1 in Figure 3). However, its utility is going to be very low since the consistency check can find out the failure in the next level any way. To avoid generation of such low-utility rules, we currently use a preset constant l and ignore any rules generated within l levels of the failure.

At this point, search continues with the other sibling I of H, which uses the promotion alternative to resolve the threat (step 3.1.3). This plan also fails, and the explanation of this failure is $(1 \prec 2) \wedge (2 \prec 1)$. When regressed over the promotion decision, this becomes $1 \prec 2$. The preconditions for promotion, which are the same as those for the demotion, are conjoined with $(1 \prec 2)$, and added to the failure explanations at G. Finally, since there are no more alternatives at G, the existing explanations are conjoined to give the combined explanation $(0 \prec 1) \wedge (1 \prec 2) \wedge 0 \overset{Cool(A)}{\rightarrow} 2 \wedge \texttt{has-effect}(1, cool(A))$ (step 3.2.1). This combined explanation is now regressed over the establishment decision at node G, and the resultant explanation is regressed once again over E (since E has no more unexplored alternatives, *and it already considered the establishment from initial state*). The result is stored as the explanation of failure for the branch through E at node D. The search continues on the promotion branch through node F and eventually fails. This then allows SNLP+EBL to conjoin the explanations at D and pass the conjunction over to B.

Since D is the only alternative at B, we can continue the regression process. But, before doing so, we note that in the current planning episode none of the establishment branches at B have considered $\texttt{start}$ as an establisher (because $\texttt{start}$ did not have an effect unifying with $Polish(A)$). However, since the effects of the $\texttt{start}$ step change from problem to problem (while those of all other steps, which correspond to domain operators, remain same), in a new problem situation it may well be the case that $\texttt{start}$ step would be giving $Polish(A)$, and thus the failure of node B may no longer hold in that situation. To ensure the soundness of the learned rules, we must explicitly account for this possibility in explaining the failure of B. We do this by conjoining the condition $\neg\texttt{initially-true}(Polish(A))$ to the explanation failure at B (step 3.2.2).[3]

The explanation regressed over the establishment decision at B can be used to learn a useful step establishment rejection rule at A (since A still has unexplored alternatives). This rule is shown to the left of node A. It says that $Roll$ should be rejected as a choice for establishing any condition at goal step G, if $Polish(A)$ is also a goal at the same step. Notice that the rule does not mention the specific establishment $Cylindrical(A)$, that lead to the introduction of $Roll$. This is correct because the failure explanation at node B does not involve $Cylindrical(A)$.[4]

---

[3]A more *eager* learning possibility would be to extend additional planning effort and see if B will have failed even if initial state were giving the open condition (as it would have, in the current case).

[4]It is interesting to note that in a similar situation, Prodigy [11] seems to learn a more specific rule which depends on establishing

Rule Generalization: Once a search control rule is made, it is generalized using the standard EBL process (c.f. [5, 10]). This process aims to replace any constants in the search control rule with variables, without affecting the rule correctness. In SNLP+EBL this is accomplished by doing the original regression process in terms of variables and their bindings (SNLP already provides support for this). During generalization, any bindings that are forced by the initial and goal state specifications of the original problem are removed from the explanation, leaving only those binding constraints that were forced by the initial explanation of the failure[5]. In the example in Figure 1, the binding $?x \approx A$ in the failure explanation of node B is stripped when making the generalized rule.

The generalization process also needs to generalize step names occurring in the failure explanation. Since the explanations qualify the steps in terms of their effects and conditions and their relations to other steps, most step names including $\texttt{fin}$ (G) can be generalized. The only exception to this rule is the status of the $\texttt{start}$ step, which may or may not be generalizable based on the specifics of the explanation. To help in this decision, our regression rules explicitly flag $\texttt{start}$ step as special when it must not be generalized. An example of this can be seen in the regression rules for step establishment decision in Figure 2. When an ordering of the form $\texttt{start} \prec s_1$ is regressed over the addition of step s_1, the $\texttt{start}$ step is flagged special since this ordering is automatically introduced as a result of step addition only with respect to the $\texttt{start}$ step. When $\texttt{start}$ is not flagged as special, it is generalized just as any other step. In the example in Figure 1, the rule learned after step and variable generalization is shown in a box to the left of node B.

Rule Storage: Once a rule is generalized, it is entered into the corpus of control rules available to the planner. These rules thus become available to the planner in guiding its search in the other branches during the learning phase, as well as subsequent planning episodes. In storing rules in the rule corpus, SNLP+EBL makes some bounded checks to see if an isomorphic rule is already present in the stored rules.

3 Learning from Depth limit Failures

In the previous section, we described the framework for learning search control rules from initial explanations of failed plans. As mentioned in that section, the only failures explainable by SNLP are the order and binding inconsistencies, which it detects during threat resolution (the unestablishable condition failure is rare in practical domains). The rules learned from such failures were successful in improving performance of SNLP in some synthetic domains (such as $D^m S^{2*}$ described in [1]).

Unfortunately however, learning from analytical failures alone turns out to be ineffective in other recursive domains such as blocks world or job-shop scheduling. The main reason for this is that many futile lines of reasoning either never end in analytical failures or cross depth limits much before they do. Since depth limit failures are not analytical, no domain independent explanation can be given to these failures.

$Cylindrical(A)$.

However, sometimes it is possible to use strong consistency checks based on the domain theory as well as the meta-theory of the planner to show that the partial plan at the depth limit contains a failure that the planner's consistency checks have not yet detected. Consider for example a simplified blocks-world partial plan shown below:

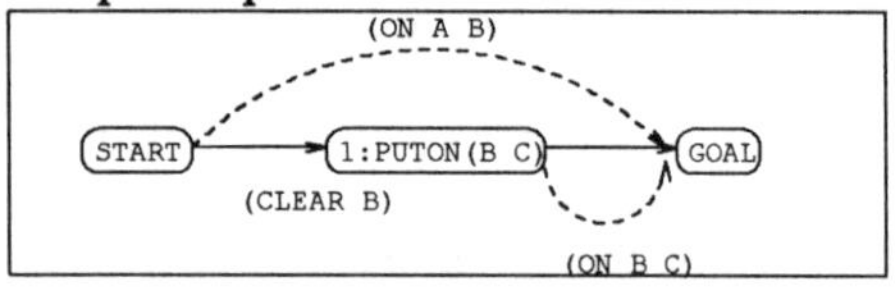

Given the blocks world domain axiom that no block can have another block on top of it, and be clear at the same time, and the SNLP meta-theory that a causal link, $s_1 \xrightarrow{c} s_2$, once established, will protect the condition c in every situation between s_1 and s_2, we can see that the above partial plan can never be refined into a successful plan. To generalize and state this formally, we define the *np–conditions*, or necessarily preservable conditions, of a step s' in a plan $\mathcal{P}$ to be the set of conditions supported by any causal link, such that s' necessarily intercedes the source and destination of the causal link.

$$np\text{–}conditions(s') = \{c | s_1 \xrightarrow{c} s_2 \in \mathcal{L} \wedge s_1 \prec s' \wedge s' \prec s_2\}$$

Given the *np–conditions* of a step, we know that the partial plan containing it can never be refined into a complete plan as long as $precond(s') \cup np\text{–}conditions(s')$ is inconsistent with respect to domain axioms. However, SNLP's local consistency checks will not recognize this, leading it sometimes into an indefinite looping behavior of repeatedly refining the plan in the hopes of making it complete. In the example above, this could happen if SNLP tries to achieve $Clear(B)$ at step 1 by adding a new step $2 : Puton(x, y)$, and then plans on making $On(x, B)$ true at 2 by taking A off B, and putting x on B. When such looping makes SNLP cross the depth limit, SNLP+EBL uses the *np–conditions* based consistency check to detect and explain this implicit failure, and learn from that explanation.

To keep the consistency check tractable, SNLP+EBL utilizes a restricted representation for domain axioms (first proposed in [3]): each domain axiom is represented as a conjunction of literals, with a set of binding constraints. The table below lists a set of domain axioms for the blocks world. The first one states that y cannot have x on top of it, and be clear, unless y is the table.

$On(x, y) \wedge clear(y)[y \not\approx Table]$
$On(x, y) \wedge On(x, z)[y \not\approx z]$
$On(x, y) \wedge On(z, y)[x \not\approx z, y \not\approx Table]$

A partial plan is inconsistent whenever it contains a step s such that the conjunction of literals comprising any domain axiom are unifiable with a subset of conditions in $np\text{–}conditions(s) \cup precond(s)$.

Given this theory, we can now explain and learn from the blocks-world partial plan above. The initial explanation of this failure is: $\texttt{start} \xrightarrow{On(x,y)} \texttt{G} \wedge (\texttt{start} \prec 1) \wedge (1 \prec \texttt{G}) \wedge$ $\texttt{open–cond}(\texttt{Clear}(y), 1) \wedge y \not\approx \texttt{Table}$. This explanation can be regressed over the planning decisions to generate rules.

(1) **Reject establishment** $\texttt{start} \xrightarrow{On(x,y)} s_1$
If $\texttt{open–cond}(On(y, z), s_1) \wedge$
$\neg\texttt{initially–true}(On(y, z)) \wedge \neg\texttt{binds}(y, Table)$
(2) **Reject promotion** $s_1 \prec s_3$
If $\texttt{open–cond}(clear(x_2), s_3) \wedge$
$\texttt{establishes}(s_1, On(x_1, x_2), s_2) \wedge$
$\texttt{precedes}(s_3, s_2) \wedge \neg\texttt{binds}(x_2, Table)$
(3) **Reject step addition** $puton(x', y) \xrightarrow{Clear(x)} s_1$
If $\texttt{establishes}(\texttt{start}, On(x, y), s_2) \wedge$
$\texttt{precedes}(s_1, s_2) \wedge \neg\texttt{binds}(y, Table)$

Figure 4: *A sampling of rules learned using domain axioms in Blocks world domain*

The above theory can be used to learn from some of the depth limit failures. In blocks world, use of this technique enabled SNLP+EBL to produce several useful search control rules. Figure 4 lists a sampling of these rules. The first one is an establishment rejection rule which says that if $On(x, y) \wedge On(y, z)$ is required at some step, then reject the choice of establishing $On(x, y)$ from the initial state, if initial state is not giving $On(y, z)$.

3.1 Empirical Evaluation

To evaluate the effectiveness of the rules learned by SNLP+EBL, we conducted experiments on random problems in blocks world. The problems all had randomly generated initial states consisting of 3 to 8 blocks (using the procedure outlined in Minton's thesis [10]). The first test set contained 30 problems all of which had random 3-block stacks in the goal state. The second test set contained 100 randomly generated goal states (using the procedure in [10]) with 2 to 6 goals. For each test set, the planner was run on a set of randomly generated problems drawn from the same distribution (20 for the first set and 50 for the second). Any learned search-control rule, which has been used at least once during the learning phase, is stored in the rule-base. This resulted in approximately 10 stored rules for the first set, and 15 stored rules for the second set. (It is interesting to note that *none* of these rules were learned from analytical failures.)

In the testing phase, the two test set problems were run with SNLP , SNLP+EBL (with the saved rules) as well as SNLP+DOMAX, a version of SNLP which uses domain axioms to prune inconsistent plans as soon as they are generated. A cpu time limit of 120 seconds was used in each test set.

Table 1 describes the results of these experiments. Figure 5 shows the cumulative performance graphs for the three methods in the second test set. Our results clearly show that SNLP+EBL was able to outperform SNLP significantly on these problem populations.[5] SNLP+EBL also outperforms SNLP+DOMAX, showing that learning search-control rules

[5]The experiments reported here were all done on the standard public domain SNLP implementation of Barrett and Weld [1]. In addition, we also experimented with more optimized implementations of SNLP including those that do not resolve positive threats (and hence are not systematic), and avoid separation by defining threats in terms of necessary codesignation [14]. The qualitative relations

| Num | SNLP | | SNLP+EBL | | SNLP+DOMAX | |
Prob	% Sol	C. tim	%Sol	C. tim	%Sol	C. tim
I (30)	60%	1767	100%	195	97%	582
II (100)	51%	6063	81%	2503	74%	4623

Table 1: *Results from the blocks world experiments*

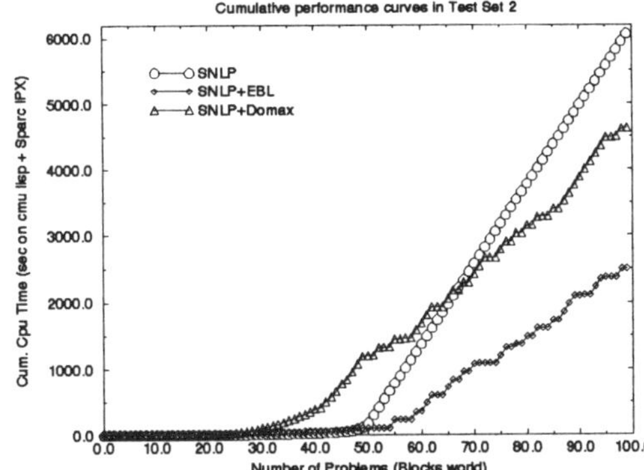

Figure 5: *Cumulative performance curves for Test Set 2*

is better than using domain axioms directly as a basis for stronger consistency check on every node during planning. This is not surprising since checking consistency of every plan during search can increase the refinement cost unduly. EBL thus provides a way of strategically applying stronger consistency checks.

4 Related Work

As we noted earlier, our work on SNLP+EBL was motivated by the desire to adapt the EBL frameworks developed for state-based planning, such as PRODIGY/EBL [10] and FailSafe [2], to partial order planning. Our use of domain axioms to detect and explain failures at depth limits is related to, and inspired by Bhatnagar's work on FailSafe [2]. Bhatnagar also advocates starting with over-general explanations of failure and relaxing the rules in response to future impasses. The rules learned in SNLP+EBL, in contrast, are always sound in that any path rejected by a rejection rule is guaranteed to fail. Domain axioms have been used by other researchers in the past to control search in PO planning (c.f. [7, 3]). Our use of domain axioms is closest to the work of Kambhampati [7], who uses an idea similar to *np–conditions* to implement a minimal-conflict based heuristic for controlling refitting in plan reuse. The current work shows that EBL provides a way of strategically applying domain axiom based consistency checks. Finally, although we did not explicitly address monitoring the utility of learned rules and filtering bad rules, we believe that utility monitoring models developed for state-based planners [4, 10] will also apply for PO planners.

5 Conclusions and Future Work

In this paper, we presented SNLP+EBL, the first systematic implementation of explanation-based search control rule learning to a PO planner. We have described the details of

between SNLP, SNLP+EBL and SNLP+DOMAX remained same even in the presence of these optimizations.

the regression, explanation propagation and rule generation process in SNLP+EBL. We have then proposed a general methodology for learning from planning failures, viz., using a battery of stronger consistency checks based on the meta-theory of the planner, and the domain theory of the problem, to detect and explain failures at depth limits. We described a specific instantiation of this method, which uses domain axioms to look for inconsistencies in the plans at depth limits, and presented experimental results that demonstrate its effectiveness. Although our EBL framework was developed in the context of SNLP we believe that it can be easily extended to more powerful PO planners such as UCPOP [13].

Learning from domain axiom based failures alone may not be sufficient in domains which do not have any strong implicit domain theory. We are currently working towards identifying other types of stronger consistency checks which can be used to complement the domain axiom based techniques in such domains. One example involves utilizing domain specific theories of loop detection to avoid step-based looping.

References

[1] A. Barrett and D.S. Weld. Partial Order Planning: Evaluating Possible Efficiency Gains. *Artificial Intelligence*, Vol. 67, No.1, 1994.

[2] N. Bhatnagar. *On-line Learning From Search Failures* PhD thesis, Rutgers University, New Brunswick, NJ, 1992.

[3] M. Drummond and K. Curry. Exploiting Temporal coherence in nonlinear plan construction. *Computational Intelligence*, 4(2):341-348, 1988.

[4] J. Gratch and G. DeJong. COMPOSER: A Probabilistic Solution to the Utility problem in Speed-up Learning. In *Proc. AAAI 92*, pp:235--240, 1992

[5] S. Kambhampati and S. Kedar. A unified framework for explanation based generalization of partially ordered and partially instantiated plans. *Artificial Intelligence*, Vol. 67, No. 2, 1994.

[6] S. Kambhampati and J. Chen. Relative Utility of EBG based Plan Reuse in Partial Ordering vs. Total Ordering Planning. In *Proc. AAAI-93*, pp:514--519, 1993.

[7] S. Kambhampati. Exploiting Causal Structure to Control Retrieval and Refitting during Plan reuse. *Computational Intelligence*, 10(2), May 1994.

[8] S. Katukam. *Learning Explanation-Based Search Control Rules for Partial Order Planning.* Masters Thesis, Arizona State University, Tempe, AZ, 1994. *(forthcoming)*.

[9] D. McAllester and D. Rosenblitt. Systematic Nonliner Planning In *Proc. AAAI-91*, 1991.

[10] S. Minton. *Learning Effective Search Control Knowledge: An Explanation-Based Approach.* PhD thesis, Carnegie-Mellon University, Pittsburgh, PA, 1988.

[11] S. Minton, J.G. Carbonell, C.A. Knoblock, D.R. Kuokka, O. Etzioni and Y. Gil. Explanation-Based Learning: A Problem Solving Perspective. *Artificial Intelligence*, 40:63--118, 1989.

[12] N.J. Nilsson. *Principles of Artificial Intelligence.* Tioga, Palo Alto, 1980.

[13] J.S. Penberthy and D.S. Weld. UCPOP: A sound, complete partial order planner for ADL. In *Proc. KRR-92*, 1992.

[14] M. Peot and D. Smith. Threat removal strategies for Nonlinear Planning. In *Proc. 11th AAAI*, 1993.

Creating Abstractions Using Relevance Reasoning

Alon Y. Levy

AT&T Bell Laboratories
AI Principles Research Department
600 Mountain Avenue, Room 2C-406
Murray Hill, NJ, 07974.
Email: levy@research.att.com

Abstract

Reasoning with multiple levels of abstraction
is a powerful method of controlling problem
solving in complex domains. We consider the
problem of simplifying a knowledge base by
creating an abstraction that is tailored for a
given set of queries. Our approach is based
on associating formally an abstraction with
some irrelevant detail that is removed from
the knowledge base. We show how creating an abstraction and determining its utility amounts to automatically deciding which
aspects of a representation are irrelevant to
a query. As a result, we derive a general algorithm schema for automatically generating
abstractions for a query. As an instance of
the schema, we describe a novel algorithm for
automatically abstracting a KB by projecting
out relation arguments.

Introduction

Abstraction is a pervasive phenomenon in human common sense reasoning and problem solving. From the
early days of AI research, it was noted that if systems
are going to reason effectively in complex domains,
they too must be able to create automatically appropriate abstractions. This idea was the driving force of several early works (e.g., [Sacerdoti, 1974; Plaisted, 1981])
and has recently received renewed attention (e.g., [Ell-
man, 1992; Knoblock, 1990; Bacchus and Yang, 1992;
Ellman, 1993]). The need for abstraction is rooted in
the fact that a declarative representation is designed
for a variety of queries and consequently, it is likely to
be too detailed for any given query. Essentially, the
idea proposed in these works is that instead of trying
to solve a query with the given complex theory of the
domain, a system should create a simpler, more abstract theory, and solve the query in that theory. Depending on the problem solving context, the abstract
solution may suffice, or there may be an additional step
of mapping the abstract solution back to a solution of
the original problem.

The key issue in this approach is how to *automatically* create abstractions that are well suited for a given
query (or set of queries). It is unreasonable to expect a representation designer to anticipate all possible
queries and the abstractions that will be suited to each
of them. For an abstraction to be useful it must reduce
the cost of answering the query, i.e., the cost of creating the abstraction, solving the query in the abstract
theory and mapping the solution back to the original
solution (a process that may need to be iterated several times) should be less than solving the query with
the original representation.

Intuitively, as noted in several works on abstraction and irrelevance-reasoning (e.g., [Giunchiglia and
Walsh, 1992; Subramanian, 1989; Levy and Sagiv,
1993]), a *good* abstraction is one in which we remove
from the theory knowledge that is *irrelevant* to the
given query. If the detail removed is indeed irrelevant,
then the solutions found in the simpler theory will map
back to the original theory, and consequently, backtracking between abstraction levels will not be necessary. This paper makes these intuitions concrete by
making a formal connection between irrelevance and
abstractions and shows how to use it to automatically
create abstractions. The key to our approach is that
when we consider an abstraction, we articulate *what* is
being removed from the theory in the process of abstraction. Deciding to use an abstract theory then
amounts to deciding that the removed knowledge is
indeed irrelevant and that removing it will yield a computationally simpler theory. The following simple example illustrates our approach.

Example 1: The following rules describe flight routes
between cities in the U.S. The first and second arguments of *Flight* and *Route* denote the origin and
destination, respectively. Their third arguments denote the costs of the flights, and the fourth arguments
denote the airline. The fifth argument of *Route* denotes the number of legs in the route. The knowledge
base also contains a set of ground atoms for the predicate *Flight*. Flight routes are composed using rules
r_2 and r_4. Flight routes must always be on a single
airline. Furthermore, we can only use a foreign airline

if the cost of the route is less than \$500. The atom $AirlineRoute(x, y, a, l)$ denotes that there is a route with l legs from x to y that uses only airline a.

$r_1 : Flight(x, y, c, a) \wedge American(a) \Rightarrow Route(x, y, c, a, 1)$

$r_2 : Flight(x, z, c_1, a) \wedge Route(z, y, c_2, a, l) \wedge$
$\quad American(a) \Rightarrow Route(x, y, c_1 + c_2, a, l + 1)$

$r_3 : Flight(x, y, c, a) \wedge \neg American(a) \wedge (c < 500) \Rightarrow$
$\quad Route(x, y, c, a, 1)$

$r_4 : Flight(x, z, c_1, a) \wedge Route(z, y, c_2, a, l) \wedge$
$\quad \neg American(a) \wedge (c_1 + c_2 < 500) \Rightarrow$
$\quad Route(x, y, c_1 + c_2, a, l + 1)$

$r_5 : Route(x, y, c, a, l) \Rightarrow AirlineRoute(x, y, a, l)$

Suppose we want to find whether there is a flight route between two cities a and b with l legs on United Airlines (i.e., find whether $AirlineFlight(a, b, UA, l)$ is entailed by the KB). Since United is an American airline, the cost of the route is irrelevant to the query, and we can abstract the representation by projecting out the cost arguments from the relations $Flight$ and $Route$. Intuitively, the irrelevance can be established by observing that the cost arguments play no role in the rules that are relevant to the query (i.e., the rules r_1, r_2 and r_5). In contrast, if the query would consider a foreign airline, the costs would be relevant because they impose additional constraints in r_3 and r_4. Therefore, we can rewrite our rules as follows:

$r_1' : Flight'(x, y, a) \wedge American(a) \Rightarrow Route'(x, y, a, 1)$

$r_2' : Flight'(x, z, a) \wedge Route'(z, y, a, l) \wedge American(a) \Rightarrow$
$\quad Route'(x, y, a, l + 1)$

$r_5' : Route'(x, y, a, l) \Rightarrow AirlineFlight(x, y, a, l)$

Rules r_3 and r_4 are irrelevant to the query and are therefore removed in the abstract KB. We also project out the third argument in the ground atoms of $Flight$. The resulting KB may yield a significantly smaller search space. For example, consider the difference between the rules r_2 and r_2'. In rule r_2, if we fail to join a ground atom $Flight(x, z, c_1, a)$ with a ground atom $Route(z, y, c_2, a)$, a backward chainer may still try to join the atom $Flight(x, z, c_1', a)$ with an appropriate atom of $Route$ for every value c_1' it finds, and will fail on all of them. In contrast, rule r_2' will not try other costs for the same flight route.[1] Furthermore, solutions including foreign flights will be ignored completely. ∎

In the next section we formally define the notions of irrelevance (e.g., we define what it *means* for an argument of a relation to be irrelevant to a query) and show how irrelevance claims provide a logical justification for creating abstractions suited for a set of queries. As a result, we derive a general algorithm schema for automatically generating abstractions for a query, which is based on identifying aspects of the representation

that are irrelevant to a query. As an instance of the schema, we describe a novel algorithm for automatically abstracting a theory by projecting relation arguments. Finally, we argue for the advantages of viewing abstractions as a problem of irrelevance reasoning.

Irrelevance and Abstractions

In our discussion, we assume that our domain is represented by a knowledge base (KB) Δ of clauses. We denote by $\mathcal{R}$, $\mathcal{O}$ and $\mathcal{F}$ the set of predicate symbols, object constants and function symbols used in Δ, respectively. For readability, in our examples we write the clauses as rules, whenever possible. The meaning of the clauses are given via interpretations in which they are satisfied. An interpretation is a mapping from the symbols in Δ to our conceptualization of the domain. It maps elements of $\mathcal{O}$ to objects in our domain and elements of $\mathcal{R}$ and $\mathcal{F}$ to relations and functions on our domain. A *model* of Δ is an interpretation that satisfies all the clauses in Δ. Intuitively, the set of models of Δ represents the possible states of the domain that we consider possible, given the constraints expressed in the clauses of Δ.

In our discussion of irrelevance we will consider the possible derivations of a query formula from the KB. For the purpose of our discussion, we assume that inferences are made by the resolution rule of inference. A resolution proof D of a clause C_0 can be viewed as a tree, in which the root is the derived clause, and the children of a clause C are the clauses that were resolved to obtain C. We denote the set of leaves of the tree of D by $Base(D)$. The set $Base(D)$ represents a "support set" for C_0 in Δ. It should be emphasized that although we use resolution in our discussion, the results can easily be applied to other sound inference rules.

We begin by defining the meaning of *irrelevance claims*, i.e., claims stating that a *subject* s is irrelevant to a query q, w.r.t. a KB Δ. Previous work on irrelevance (e.g., [Subramanian, 1989; Levy and Sagiv, 1993]) considered formal definitions of irrelevance for the case where s is a clause (or set of clauses). In order to use irrelevance to justify abstractions, we need to define irrelevance of other subjects. For instance, in Example 1, we based our abstraction on the irrelevance of predicate arguments. Other irrelevance subjects are shown in Table 1.

Intuitively, a subject is irrelevant to a query if it can be removed from our conceptualization of the domain without affecting our ability to answer the query correctly. For instance, for the query described in Example 1, we can simplify our conceptualization by projecting out the cost column from the relations corresponding to flights and routes, and we would still be able to answer the query (whereas it would not be adequate for queries involving foreign airlines). However, in formalizing our intuition we must take into account that we cannot reason directly with our conceptualiza-

---

[1]Although in some simple cases these repetitions can be eliminated by employing some method of dependency directed backtracking, such methods will not be as general as projecting out arguments and will also have additional costs associated with maintaining the dependencies.

	Abstraction mapping s^f	Intended semantics s^I
Predicate abstraction	Replace occurrences of $P_1, \ldots, P_n$ by P	$P = P_1 \cup \ldots \cup P_n$
	Replace occurrences of $P_1, \ldots, P_n$ by P	$P = P_1 \cap \ldots \cap P_n$
Object abstraction	$a_1, \ldots, a_n \rightarrow a$	$P(a)$ iff $P(a_1) \wedge \ldots \wedge P(a_n)$
Function abstraction	$f \rightarrow f'$	f' is an approximation of f

Table 1: Example irrelevance subjects

tion of the domain, but only with clauses in the KB that represent a set of intended models. Moreover, as noted by in [Subramanian, 1989], a purely model-theoretic account of irrelevance will not capture our intuitions about the notion. Finally, since our main goal in defining irrelevance is to provide a basis for automatically creating abstractions, we will consider definitions that involve the actual clauses in the KB.

Formally, an irrelevance subject s is a pair (s^f, s^I) specifying a syntactic *abstraction mapping* [Plaisted, 1981], s^f, on clauses and the intended mapping on interpretations s^I (see Table 1). The mapping s^I represents the simplification we intend to make to the conceptualization of the domain via the abstraction (see [Nayak and Levy, 1994] for a more detailed account of such simplifications).[2] As an example, consider a subject which is a set of predicate arguments. We denote such a subject by a list of pairs (q_i, n_i), where q_i is a predicate and n_i is an integer less or equal to the arity of q_i. In our example, the irrelevant arguments are $\{(Flight, 3), (Route, 3)\}$. The mapping s^f would map the literals of the form $Flight(x, y, c, a)$ to the literal $Flight(x, y, a)$ (and likewise for $Route$). The mapping s^I would map the relation denoted by $Flight$ to the relation resulting from projecting out its third column.

The mapping s^f is defined on literals and extended in the natural way to clauses. Following [Plaisted, 1981], we require that s^f satisfy the following restrictions: (1) if L is a literal, then $s^f(\neg L) = \neg s^f(L)$, and (2) if a clause C subsumes D, then $s^f(C)$ subsumes $s^f(D)$.

Applying the mapping s^f to all the clauses in Δ may result in an inconsistent theory. Therefore, we will apply s^f only to clauses that are *independent* of s, as we define below. The notion of independence will also form the basis for our definition of irrelevance.

Definition 1: *Let Δ be a knowledge base and $s = (s^f, s^I)$ be an irrelevance subject. A clause ϕ is independent of s if for any interpretation I:*

$$I \models \Delta \implies s^I(I) \models s^f(\phi). \blacksquare$$

Intuitively, a clause ϕ is independent of s if $s^f(\phi)$ does not decrease the set of possible models, and therefore does not enable us to derive conclusions that did not follow from the original KB. For example, the rule r_2 is independent of the predicate arguments

$\{(Flight, 3), (Route, 3)\}$, but it is not independent of $\{(Flight, 4), (Route, 4)\}$. To see this, consider the interpretation I_1 and its corresponding interpretation $s^I(I_1)$:

Flight: $\{(a, b, 100, UA), (b, c, 150, NW)\} \overset{s^I}{\rightarrow}$
$\qquad \{(a, b, 100), (b, c, 150)\}$

Route: $\{(a, b, 100, UA, 1), (b, c, 150, NW, 1)\} \overset{s^I}{\rightarrow}$
$\qquad \{(a, b, 100, 1), (b, c, 150, 1)\}$

American: $\{UA, NW\} \overset{s^I}{\rightarrow} \{UA, NW\}$.

While the interpretation I_1 satisfies r_2, $s^I(I_1)$ does not satisfy the rule resulting from projecting out $\{(Flight, 4), (Route, 4)\}$ from r_2:

$r_2'': Flight(x, z, c_1) \wedge Route(z, y, c_2, l) \wedge \neg American(a) \Rightarrow$
$\qquad Route(x, y, c_1 + c_2, l + 1)$

which enables us to derive the incorrect conclusion $Route(a, c, 250, 2)$. Based on the notion of independence, we define irrelevance as follows:

Definition 2: *Let Δ be a KB and $s = (s^f, s^I)$ be an irrelevance subject and ψ be a query.*

The subject s is weakly irrelevant *to ψ (denoted by $WI(s, \psi, \Delta)$) if there is some derivation D of ψ such that all the clauses in $Base(D)$ are independent of s. The subject s is* strongly irrelevant *to ψ, (denoted by $SI(s, \psi, \Delta)$) if for all derivations D of ψ, all the clauses in $Base(D)$ are independent of s.* $\blacksquare$

Note that these definitions can be viewed as instances in the space of definitions of irrelevance proposed in [Levy and Sagiv, 1993]. It is more useful to state and derive irrelevance claims that hold with respect to a set of knowledge bases. Formally, if Σ is a set of KBs, we define $WI(s, \psi, \Sigma)$ to hold if $WI(s, \psi, \Delta)$ for every $\Delta \in \Sigma$ (and similarly for SI).

Consider Example 1, where Σ is the set of KBs consisting of the rules r_1–r_5 and *some* set of ground unit clauses of the predicate $Flight$. The predicate arguments $s = \{(Flight, 3), (Route, 3)\}$ are strongly irrelevant to ground queries that are instances of $q = American(a) \wedge AirlineRoute(x, y, a, l)$, because, as the query-tree in Figure 1 shows, only the rules r_1, r_2 and r_5 and ground unit clauses can appear in derivations of the query and these are all independent of s (note that ground unit positive clauses are independent of any set of predicate arguments). If we add the rule

$r_6: Flight(x, z, c_1, a) \wedge Route(z, y, c_2, a, l) \wedge$
$\qquad (c_1 + c_2 < 500) \Rightarrow Route(x, y, c_1 + c_2, a, l + 1)$

---

[2]Note that s^I is not uniquely determined by s^f, as shown by the first two entries in Table 1.

which is not independent of s, then s would be only weakly irrelevant to the query (since r_6 is redundant and therefore, if there is a derivation of the query, there will be a derivation with r_6 and one without it).

Our definitions enable us to give a logical justification for creating abstractions. The following theorem states that if s is weakly irrelevant to a query, then the KB resulting from abstracting all the independent clauses will be sufficient for answering the query.

Theorem 3: *Let Δ be a knowledge base and let $s = (s^f, s^I)$ be an irrelevance subject such that s^f is an abstraction mapping. Let Δ_s be the KB defined by:*

$$\Delta_s = \{s^f(\phi) \mid \phi \in \Delta \text{ and } \phi \text{ is independent of } s\}.$$

Let q be a query and suppose $WI(s, q, \Delta)$ holds. Then

$$\Delta \vdash q \Longrightarrow \Delta_s \vdash s^f(q)$$

and, if $s^f(q) = q$ then[3]

$$\Delta_s \models q \Longrightarrow \Delta \models q. \blacksquare$$

Note that the second part of the theorem does not depend on the inference mechanism used. Furthermore, if our inference rules are complete (e.g., refutation resolution), then the above theorem implies

$$\Delta \vdash q \Longleftrightarrow \Delta_s \vdash q \text{ and } \Delta \models q \Longleftrightarrow \Delta_s \models q.$$

Proof sketch: The first half of the theorem follows from Plaisted [Plaisted, 1981]. For the second half, suppose $\Delta_s \models q$ and let I be a model of Δ, i.e., $I \models \Delta$. We need to show that $I \models q$. By the definition of independence and the construction of Δ_s, we get $s^I(I) \models \Delta_s$ and therefore, $s^I(I) \models q$. However, since I and $s^I(I)$ are identical for the symbols appearing in q, it follows that $I \models q$. $\blacksquare$

The importance of Theorem 3 is that it gives a logical justification for creating an abstraction that is especially fit for the specific set of queries. As we describe in the next section, it also gives us a method for developing algorithms for automatically creating abstractions. It is important to note that Theorem 3 provides a justification for using a specific abstract KB, namely Δ_s. One advantage of Δ_s is that it can be efficiently generated from the original theory. However, we can sometimes add clauses to Δ_s to obtain a stronger theory (as done in [Tenenberg, 1990]), and therefore lose less information in the abstract KB. We do not discuss this extension here.

Automatically Creating Abstractions

The importance of the formulation presented in the previous section is that we can now clearly address the problem of automatically creating abstractions for a given set of queries, by automatically deriving irrelevance claims. Specifically, to use Theorem 3 we need to automatically derive claims of the form $WI(s, q, \Delta)$.

---

[3]Note that this restriction effectively means that the irrelevance subject does not appear explicitly in the query.

One way of deriving such a claim is to find a subset Γ of Δ, such that q will necessarily have a derivation that does not include clauses in Γ, and such that the clauses in $\Delta - \Gamma$ are all independent of s. It follows from the previous section that we can abstract Δ by $s^f(\Delta - \Gamma)$. Therefore, a general method for automatically creating abstractions has two steps (1) automatically find Γ (i.e., a set of irrelevant clauses) and (2) automatically detect independence of a clause (i.e., the independence of $\Delta - \Gamma$ from s). These steps are discussed in the following sections.

Determining Irrelevance

Methods for detecting irrelevance of clauses to a query are described in [Levy and Sagiv, 1993; Levy, 1993] and [Subramanian, 1989]. For example, we can use the *query-tree* [Levy and Sagiv, 1992] (shown in Figure 1) to show that only that the rules r_1, r_2 and r_5 and ground unit clauses involving American airlines can be used in derivations of the query. Consequently, all other clauses (including the rules r_3 and r_4) are irrelevant to the query.

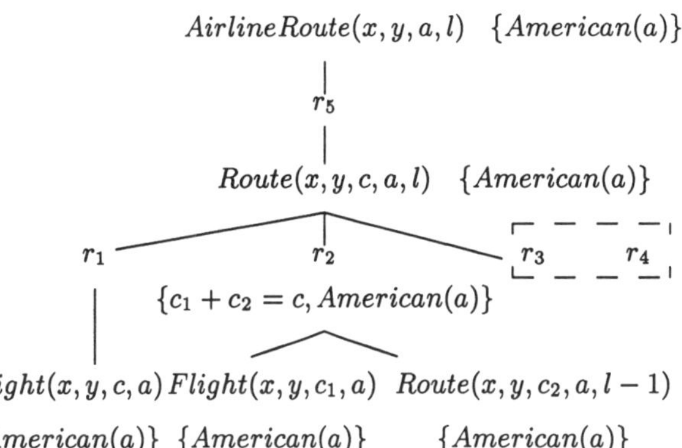

Figure 1: An example of a query-tree showing the possible symbolic derivations of $AirlineRoute(x, y, a, l) \wedge American(a)$. Note that the semantics of the interpreted predicates are taken into consideration in the construction of the query-tree. The literals shown in the brackets of each node denote the constraints that need to be satisfied by facts generated at this node, and are used as a criterion for terminating the tree (e.g., the nodes $Route(x, y, c_2, a, l-1)$ and $Route(x, y, c, a, l)$ have the same constraints and therefore only the latter is expanded). Note that rules r_3 and r_4 are not expanded because they would yield an unsatisfiable set of constraints ($\{American(a), \neg American(a)\}$).

Several aspects of the query-tree make it especially useful in our context. First, recall that determining irrelevance of a clause requires that we can decide that there is some derivation of the query that does not use it. For irrelevance reasoning to be of practical use, we must be able to determine irrelevance without actually solving the query. To that end, the query-tree considers only part of the KB in its reasoning. Specifically, it considers only the rules in the KB, and high level constraints on the ground unit clauses that may appear (e.g., all flight costs are positive). Consequently, when it decides that a clause is irrelevant, the conclusion holds for all KBs that have the given set of rules, independent of the ground unit clauses. Furthermore, irrelevance is determined w.r.t. a *set* of queries, and these may involve disjunctions and conjunctions of literals. Second, in its irrelevance reasoning, the query-tree considers the semantics of some predicates (e.g., order predicates, $<, >, \leq, \geq, \neq$, or *sort* predicates, e.g., *American*). In many applications, considering the semantics of such predicates enables us to find interactions between clauses and therefore to deem clauses irrelevant. Finally, the query-tree can be built in time that is linear in the number of rules in the KB.

The query-tree actually detects *strongly irrelevant* clauses, i.e., clauses that are not part of *any* derivation of the query (note that strong irrelevance is a sufficient condition for weak irrelevance). In fact, under certain conditions (e.g., function-free or non-recursive rules) the query-tree will find *all* the irrelevant clauses. As pointed out in [Levy and Sagiv, 1993], removing strongly-irrelevant clauses is guaranteed not to slow down inferences (and usually to speed them up significantly), whereas removing weakly irrelevant clauses may actually cause inference to be slowed down. In our context this observation is important because creating an abstraction based on strong irrelevance guarantees that using the abstract theory will result in more efficient inference.

Algorithms for detecting weakly irrelevant clauses are described in [Subramanian, 1989; Levy, 1993]. For general clause form knowledge bases, connection graph methods [Kowalski, 1975; Sickel, 1976; Chang, 1979] provide sufficient conditions for strong and weak irrelevance.

Determining Independence of Predicate Arguments

Algorithms for determining independence of a clause are specific to a given type of irrelevance subject. In this section we describe a novel algorithm for determining independence of an irrelevance subject consisting of a set of predicate arguments. First we describe a syntactic condition for checking whether a clause C is independent of a given subject s. This condition can be used in conjunction with the algorithms of the previous section to determine irrelevance of s. However, a more interesting question is how we can automatically find the maximal set of irrelevant predicate arguments, given the set of relevant clauses. We describe an algorithm that uses the syntactic condition to find such a maximal set.

We use the following notation in this section. Given a clause C, we denote by $Neg(C)$ and $Pos(C)$ the negative literals and the positive literals in C, respectively (e.g., if C is $\{\neg P(x), Q(x)\}$ then $Neg(C)$ is $\{\neg P(x)\}$

and $Pos(C)$ is $\{Q(x)\}$. We assume that C is not redundant, i.e., there is no subset of C that is logically equivalent to C, and that C is not a tautology.

Theorem 4: *A clause C is independent of the set of predicate arguments $s = \{(P_1, i_1), \ldots, (P_n, i_n)\}$ if the following conditions hold for $1 \leq j \leq n$.*

If the predicate P_j occurs in $Neg(C)$, then the argument in position i_j of that occurrence:

A1: must be a variable (i.e., not a constant or a functional term).

A2: the variable must appear at most once in $Neg(C)$.

A3: if that variable also appears (by itself, or part of a functional term) in position k of a predicate Q in $Pos(C)$, then $(Q, k) \in s$. ∎

The proof of the theorem (given in [Levy, 1993]) proceeds by case analysis, showing that for every model I of C, $s^I(I)$ will be a model of $s^f(C)$. As an example, the clause $\{\neg P(x, y, z), \neg Q(x), R(y)\}$ is independent of $\{(P, 3)\}$. It is not independent of $\{(Q, 1), (P, 1)\}$ (violates A2) or of $\{(P, 2)\}$ (violates A3).

Given an argument (P, i) that appears in C, we can determine the unique minimal set of arguments, $PC(C, P, i)$, such that $(P, i) \in PC(C, P, i)$ and C is independent of $PC(C, P, i)$. This is done by iteratively adding the arguments that are required to be in s by condition A3, and checking whether the final set violates A1 or A2. Note that there may be no such set $PC(C, P, i)$. In that case, we say that (P, i) is *needed* in C.

We use the conditions of Theorem 4 to devise the following algorithm that finds the *maximal* set of irrelevant predicate arguments w.r.t. a query. Given a set of relevant clauses Γ, the algorithm (shown in Figure 2) finds the maximal set of predicate arguments s that does not include any argument appearing in the query (which are assumed to be relevant), such that all clauses in Γ are independent of s. The algorithm maintains a list of irrelevant arguments, which initially includes all the arguments of all predicates, except those appearing in the query. It makes one pass over the clauses in Γ and either removes arguments from the list of irrelevant arguments, or adds conditions for the inclusion arguments in the list. These conditions specify a set of additional arguments that must be included (implied by A3). Finally, it removes from the irrelevant list any argument whose conditions are not satisfied.

Consider the application of the algorithm to the rules r_1, r_2, r_5 in Example 1, with the query $AirlineFlight(x, y, a, l) \wedge American(a)$. The set $\mathcal{R}$ initially includes all the arguments of $Flight$ and $Route$. When considering the rule r_1, the algorithm adds the argument $(Route, i)$ to the preconditions of $(Flight, i)$, for $i = 1, \ldots, 3$, and removes the argument $(Flight, 4)$ from $\mathcal{R}$. Considering rule r_2, the algorithm removes the arguments $(Flight, 2)$, $(Route, 1)$ and $(Route, 4)$ from $\mathcal{R}$. As a consequence, the argument $(Flight, 1)$ is

```
procedure find-irrelevant-arguments(Γ, q)
begin /* Γ are the clauses and q is the query. */
    P = The predicates appearing in Γ, and not in q.
    R = {(P, i) | P ∈ P and i is an argument of P }.
    for every s ∈ R, Preconditions(s)= {}.
    for every C ∈ Γ do:
        for every (P, i) ∈ R
            if P appears in C and (P, i) is needed in C
                then remove (P, i) from R.
                else
                    if PC(C, P, i) ⊄ R then
                        remove (P, i) from R.
                    else add {PC(C, P, i) − {(P, i)}}
                        to Preconditions ((P, i)).
    repeat
        if (P, i) ∈ R and (Q, j) ∈ Preconditions ((P, i))
            and (Q, j) ∉ R
            then remove (P, i) from R.
    until no changes are made to R.
return R.
end.
```

Figure 2: Algorithm for finding a maximal set of irrelevant predicate arguments.

removed from R because its precondition was removed. Finally, considering rule r_5, the arguments $(Route, 2)$ and $(Route, 5)$ are removed from R because the arguments $(AirlineFlight, 2)$ and $(AirlineFlight, 4)$ are not members of R. Therefore, the algorithm returns that the arguments $(Flight, 3)$ and $(Route, 3)$ are irrelevant to the given query.

The algorithm finds the maximal set of predicate arguments that satisfies conditions A1, A2 and A3. This follows from the observation that for every argument in the returned set, its precondition arguments (i.e., the arguments in $PC(C, P, i)$) are also in R. Furthermore, every argument that was removed from R was either needed in some clause or required some other argument that is not a member of R. The time complexity of the algorithm is bounded by $|\Delta|R^2$, where $|\Delta|$ is the number of clauses in Δ and R is the sum of the number of argument of relations in Δ.

Conclusions and Related Work

We presented a formal connection between the notion of irrelevance and the creation of abstractions. At its core, it is based on associating an abstraction with some *detail* that it removes from the representation of the domain, and justifying the abstraction by observing that the detail is irrelevant to the query. To make this connection we extended previous work on irrelevance reasoning to consider irrelevance of new subjects (e.g., predicate arguments, predicate refinements). Using the connection, we presented a general method for automatically generating abstractions that are suited for a particular set of queries. As an instance of this method, we de-

scribed a novel and efficient algorithm for automatically creating abstractions in which we remove irrelevant arguments of predicates. Abstraction by projecting out arguments was also suggested in [Hobbs, 1985; Subramanian, 1989], but no algorithm for doing so was given. Our algorithm is a generalization of a method for pushing projections [Ramakrishnan *et al.*, 1988] in datalog programs. Our algorithm handles arbitrary clauses and the semantics interpreted predicates. Additional instances of the general algorithm for creating abstractions can also be devised. For example, the work of Tenenberg [Tenenberg, 1990] effectively provides an algorithm for determining independence of a clause from a predicate refinement,[4] thereby yielding an algorithm for determining irrelevance of predicate refinements.

The computational savings gained by using abstractions has been demonstrated both theoretically and empirically (e.g., [Bacchus and Yang, 1992; Knoblock, 1991; Ellman, 1993]). In our case the savings achieved by abstractions will be maximized if we can identify large sets of queries for which we can create the same abstract KB, and therefore amortize the cost of creating the abstract KB over many queries. One of the key advantages of using the query-tree for relevance reasoning is that it enables us to create abstractions that are tailored for sets of queries. Experiments presented in [Levy, 1993] show that the cost of building the query-tree is negligible compared to the savings achieved by using it.

Studying abstractions in our framework offers several additional advantages. First, we can exploit domain knowledge (stated as irrelevance claims) in creating abstractions for a given query. We can either use such claims directly to justify abstractions or combine them with other methods to derive logical conclusions from them (e.g., using algorithms from [Subramanian, 1989; Levy and Sagiv, 1993]), and obtain justifications for additional abstractions. Second, it provides a framework for choosing and combining existing KBs that each make certain abstractions of the domain, by labeling the KBs with the irrelevance assumptions underlying their abstractions. An example of such a task arises in Compositional Modeling [Falkenhainer and Forbus, 1991; Iwasaki and Levy, 1994], where we need to combine descriptions of different aspects of a physical device to create an adequate and parsimonious model of the device. Similar situations arise in reasoning with contexts (e.g., [Guha, 1991]) and in heterogenous distributed knowledge based systems. Finally, our framework provides insight into the utility of reasoning with abstractions (e.g., abstractions based on strong-irrelevance are guaranteed to yield savings), and to composability of abstractions (by composing the irrelevance statements underlying them).

In their theory of abstraction, Giunchiglia and

---

[4] A predicate refinement is a set of predicates $P_1, \ldots, P_n$ whose union denotes a predicate P.

Walsh [Giunchiglia and Walsh, 1992] distinguish two classes of abstractions, *TD* and *TI*. Roughly, TD abstractions are those in which theorems derived in the abstract theory hold also in the original theory, whereas TI abstractions are those in which every theorem in the original theory will have a theorem in the abstract theory (but an abstract theorem need not have a corresponding theorem in the original theory). The abstractions we considered are TD abstractions (i.e., will not introduce wrong conclusions), but are also *TI w.r.t. the query*, i.e., a solution to the query in the original theory is guaranteed to have a corresponding solution in the abstract theory (but other derivable theorems may be lost in the abstract theory). This aligns with the intuition that removing irrelevant knowledge should not enable us to lose the ability to solve the query or to derive new false conclusions. Creating an abstract KB can also be viewed as an instance of *knowledge compilation* [Selman and Kautz, 1991]. The key difference in our work is that we compile the KB w.r.t. a given set of queries, and therefore we can determine exactly when the compiled KB is applicable. Knoblock [Knoblock, 1990] also considers automatic generation of abstractions that are suited for a specific query (i.e., planning goal), by removing preconditions of actions. His ALPINE system generates TI abstractions, but provides the planner with a condition that enables it to prune the search needed to refine an abstract solution.

TI-abstractions have been used as a means of controlling problem solving in complex domains, by using abstractions to structure the search space hierarchically (e.g., [Sacerdoti, 1974; Plaisted, 1981; Knoblock, 1990; Ellman, 1993]). In that work, the intuition (formally analized in [Bacchus and Yang, 1992]) is that although the information removed from one level of the hierarchy to the other is not always irrelevant, it will be irrelevant in most cases, and therefore, in these cases it will not be necessary to backtrack through the abstraction hierarchy. To apply our framework to this context we are currently considering an extension of irrelevance reasoning to handle *approximate* irrelevance claims that can be used to justify abstracting knowledge that is irrelevant with high probability.

Acknowledgements

I would like to thank Tom Ellman, Hiroshi Motoda and Pandu Nayak for very useful discussions on the topics described in this paper.

References

Bacchus, Fahiem and Yang, Qiang 1992. The expected value of hierarchical problem-solving. In *Proceedings of AAAI-92*. 369–374.

Chang, C. L. 1979. Resolution plans in theorem proving. In *Proceedings of the Sixth International Joint Conference on Artificial Intelligence*. 143–148.

Ellman, Thomas, editor 1992. *Working Notes of the Workshop on Approximation and Abstraction of Computational Theories*. American Association for Artificial Intelligence.

Ellman, Thomas 1993. Abstraction via approximate symmetry. In *Proceedings of the 13th International Joint Conference on Artificial Intelligence*. 916–921.

Falkenhainer, Brian and Forbus, Ken 1991. Compositional modeling: Finding the right model for the job. *Artificial Intelligence* 51:95–143.

Giunchiglia, Fausto and Walsh, Toby 1992. A theory of abstraction. *Artificial Intelligence* 56 (3).

Guha, Ramanathan V. 1991. *Contexts: A Formalization and Some Applications*. Ph.D. Dissertation, Stanford University, Stanford, CA.

Hobbs, Jerry R. 1985. Granularity. In *Proceedings of IJCAI-85*. 432–435.

Iwasaki, Yumi and Levy, Alon Y. 1994. Automated model selection for simulation. In *Proceedings of AAAI-94*.

Knoblock, Craig A. 1990. Learning abstraction hierarchies for problem solving. In *Proceedings of AAAI-90*.

Knoblock, Craig A. 1991. Search reduction in hierarchical problem solving. In *Proceedings of AAAI-91*. 686–691.

Kowalski, Robert 1975. A proof procedure using connection graphs. *Journal of the ACM* 22(4): 572–595.

Levy, Alon Y. and Sagiv, Yehoshua 1992. Constraints and redundancy in Datalog. In *The Proceedings of the Eleventh ACM SIGACT-SIGMOD-SIGART Symposium on Principles of Database Systems (PODS)*. 67–80.

Levy, Alon Y. and Sagiv, Yehoshua 1993. Exploiting irrelevance reasoning to guide problem solving. In *Proceedings of the 13th International Joint Conference on Artificial Intelligence*. 138–144.

Levy, Alon Y. 1993. *Irrelevance Reasoning in Knowledge Based Systems*. Ph.D. Dissertation, Stanford University, Stanford, CA.

Nayak, P. Pandurang and Levy, Alon Y. 1994. A semantic theory of abstractions: A preliminary report. Technical Report, AT&T Bell Laboratories.

Plaisted, D. 1981. Theorem proving with abstraction. *Artificial Intelligence* 16:47–108.

Ramakrishnan, Raghu; Beeri, Catriel; and Krishnamurthy, Ravi 1988. Optimizing existential datalog queries. In *Proceedings of PODS-88*. 89–101.

Sacerdoti, Earl D. 1974. Planning in a hierarchy of abstraction spaces. *Artificial Intelligence* 5:115–135.

Selman, Bart and Kautz, Henry 1991. Knowledge compilation using horn approximations. In *Proceedings of AAAI-91*. 904–909.

Sickel, Susan 1976. A search technique for clause interconnectivity graphs. *IEEE Transactions on Computers* C-25(8):823–835.

Subramanian, Devika 1989. *A Theory of Justified Reformulations*. Ph.D. Dissertation, Stanford University, Stanford, CA.

Tenenberg, Josh D. 1990. Abstracting first order theories. In Benjamin, Paul, editor 1990, *Change of Representation and Inductive Bias*. Kluwer, Boston, Mass.

Flexible Strategy Learning: Analogical Replay of Problem Solving Episodes[*]

Manuela M. Veloso

School of Computer Science
Carnegie Mellon University
Pittsburgh, PA 15213-3891
veloso@cs.cmu.edu

Abstract

This paper describes the integration of analogical reasoning into general problem solving as a method of learning at the strategy level to solve problems more effectively. Learning occurs by the generation and replay of annotated derivational traces of problem solving episodes. The problem solver is extended with the ability to examine its decision cycle and accumulate knowledge from the chains of successes and failures encountered during its search experience. Instead of investing substantial effort deriving general rules of behavior to apply to individual decisions, the analogical reasoner compiles complete problem solving cases that are used to guide future similar situations. Learned knowledge is flexibly applied to new problem solving situations even if only a partial match exists among problems. We relate this work with other alternative strategy learning methods, and also with plan reuse. We demonstrate the effectiveness of the analogical replay strategy by providing empirical results on the performance of a fully implemented system, PRODIGY/ANALOGY, accumulating and reusing a large case library in a complex problem solving domain.

Introduction

The machine learning approaches to acquiring strategic knowledge typically start with a general problem solving engine and accumulate experience by analyzing its search episodes. The strategic or control knowledge acquired can take many forms, including macro-operators (Fikes & Nilsson 1971; Korf 1985), refined operational operators (DeJong & Mooney 1986; Mitchell, Keller, & Kedar-Cabelli 1986), generalized chunks of all decisions taken by the problem solver (Laird, Rosenbloom, & Newell 1986), explicit control rules that guide the selection of domain-level subgoals and operators (Minton 1988), annotated or validated final solutions (Hammond 1986; Mostow 1989; Kambhampati & Hendler 1992), or justified derivational

---

[*]This research is sponsored by the Wright Laboratory, Aeronautical Systems Center, Air Force Materiel Command, USAF, and the Advanced Research Projects Agency (ARPA) under grant number F33615-93-1-1330. The views and conclusions contained in this document are those of the authors and should not be interpreted as necessarily representing the official policies or endorsements, either expressed or implied, of Wright Laboratory or the U.S. Government.

traces of the decision making process during search, as presented in this paper.

We integrated learning by analogy into general problem solving. The learned knowledge is acquired and used flexibly: its construction results from a direct and simple explanation of the episodic situation, and it is proposed to be used also in situations where there is a partial match for the relevant parts of its applicability conditions.

The method is based on derivational analogy (Carbonell 1986) and it has been fully implemented within the PRODIGY planning and learning architecture, in PRODIGY/ANALOGY. It casts the strategy-level learning process as the automation of the complete cycle of constructing, storing, retrieving, and reusing problem solving experience (Veloso 1992).

In this paper we focus on presenting the learning techniques for the acquisition and reuse of problem solving episodes by analogical reasoning. We illustrate the method with examples. We also provide empirical results showing that PRODIGY/ANALOGY is amenable to scaling up both in terms of domain and problem complexity.

The contributions of this work include: the demonstration of learning by analogy as a method to successfully transferring problem solving experience in partially matched new situations; and a flexible replay mechanism to merge (if needed) multiple similar episodes that jointly provide guidance for new problems. The method enables the learner to solve complex problems after being trained in solving simple problems.

Generation of Problem Solving Episodes

The purpose of solving problems by analogy is to reuse past experience to guide generation of solutions for new problems avoiding a completely new search effort. Transformational analogy and most CBR systems reuse past solutions by modifying (*tweaking*) the retrieved final solution as a function of the differences found between the source and the target problems. Derivational analogy instead is a *reconstructive* method by which *lines of reasoning* are transferred and adapted to a new problem (Carbonell 1986) as opposed to only the final solutions.

Automatic generation of the derivational episodes to be learned occurs by extending the base-level problem solver with the ability to examine its internal decision cycle, recording the justifications for each decision during its search process. We used NoLIMIT (Veloso 1989), the first nonlinear and complete problem solver of the PRODIGY planning and learning system, as the base-level problem solver.[1] Throughout the paper, NoLIMIT refers to the base-level planner and PRODIGY/ANALOGY refers to the complete analogical reasoner with the capabilities to generate, store, retrieve, and replay problem solving episodes.

NoLIMIT's planning reasoning cycle involves several decision points, namely: the *goal* to select from the set of pending goals; the *operator* to choose to achieve a particular goal; the *bindings* to choose in order to instantiate the chosen operator; *apply* an operator whose preconditions are satisfied or continue *subgoaling* on a still unachieved goal. PRODIGY/ANALOGY extends NoLIMIT with the capability of recording the context in which the decisions are made. Figure 1 shows the skeleton of the decision nodes. We created a language for the slot values to capture the reasons that support the choices (Veloso & Carbonell 1993a).

Goal Node	Chosen Op Node	Applied Op Node
:step	:step	:step
:sibling-goals	:sibling-ops	:sibling-goals
:sibling-appl-ops	:why-this-op	:sibling-appl-ops
:why-subgoal	:relevant-to	:why-apply
:why-this-goal		:why-this-op
:precond-of		:chosen-at

Figure 1: Justification record structure. Nodes are instantiated at decision points during problem solving. Each learned episode is a sequence of such justified nodes.

There are mainly three different kinds of justifications: links among choices capturing the subgoaling structure (slots `precond-of` and `relevant-to`), records of explored failed alternatives (the `sibling-` slots), and pointers to any applied guidance (the `why-` slots). A stored problem solving episode consists of the successful solution trace augmented with these annotations, i.e., the derivational trace.

Example

We use examples from a logistics transportation domain introduced in (Veloso 1992). In this domain packages are to be moved among different cities. Packages are carried within the same city in trucks and between cities in airplanes. At each city there are several locations, e.g., post offices and airports. The problems used in the examples are simple for the sake of a clear illustration of the learning process. Later in the paper we comment briefly on the complexity of this domain and show empirical results where PRODIGY/ANALOGY was tested with complex problems.

Consider the problem illustrated in Figure 2. In this problem there are two objects, `ob4` and `ob7`, one truck `tr9`, and one airplane `pl1`. There is one city `c3` with a post office `p3` and an airport `a3`. In the initial state, `ob4` is at `p3` and the goal is to have `ob4` inside of `tr9`.

---

[1]NoLIMIT was succeeded by the current planner, PRODIGY4.0 (Carbonell & the Prodigy Research Group 1992; Fink & Veloso 1994).

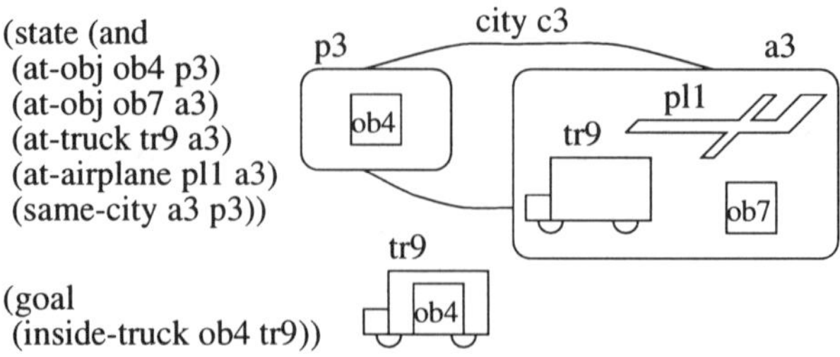

Figure 2: Example: The goal is to load one object into the truck. Initially the truck is not at the object's location.

The solution to this problem is to drive the truck from the airport to the post office and then load the object.

There are two operators that are relevant for solving this problem.(The complete set of operators can be found in (Veloso 1992).) The operator LOAD-TRUCK specifies that an object can be loaded into a truck if the object and the truck are at the same location, and the operator DRIVE-TRUCK states that a truck can move freely between locations within the same city.

Figure 3 (a) shows the decision tree during the search for the solution. Nodes are numbered in the order in which the search space is expanded. The search is a sequence of goal choices followed by operator choices followed occasionally by applying operators to the planner's internal state when their preconditions are true in that state and the decision for immediate application is made.

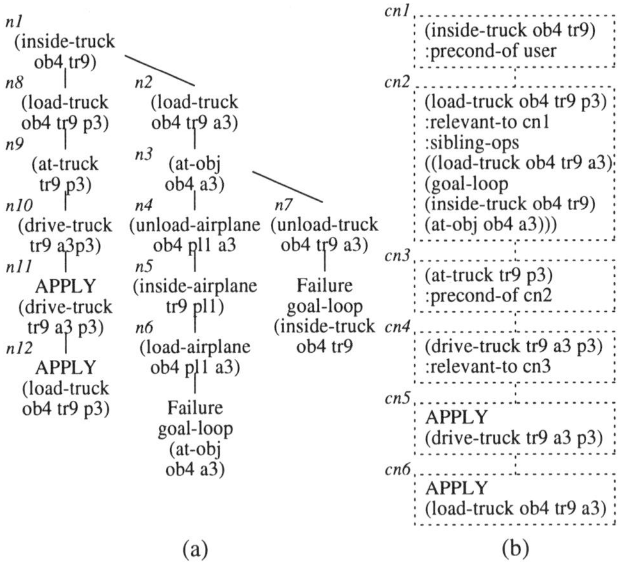

Figure 3: (a) The search tree to solve the problem in Figure 2 – the numbering of the nodes shows the search order; (b) The corresponding learned problem solving episode to be stored (only a subset of the justifications is shown).

This trace illustrates PRODIGY handling multiple choices of how to instantiate operators. There are two instantiations of the operator load-truck that are relevant to the given goal, i.e., the instantiations (`load-truck ob4 tr9 p3`) and (`load-truck ob4 tr9 a3`) add the goal (`inside-truck ob4 tr9`). An object can be loaded into a truck at both post office and airport locations. Node `n2` shows that the alternative of loading the truck at the airport `a3` is explored first. This leads to two failed paths. The solution is found after backtracking to the alternative child of node `n1`. Nodes `n8` through `n12` show the final sequence of successful decisions. `n8` shows the correct choice of loading the truck at the post office, where `ob4` is located. The solution corresponds to the two steps applied at nodes `n11` and `n12`: the truck `tr9` is driven from `a3` to `p3`, as chosen at node `n8` and then it is loaded with `ob4`.[2]

Figure 3 (b) shows the case generated from the problem solving episode shown in Figure 3 (a). The entire search tree is not stored in the case, but only the decision nodes of the final successful path. The subgoaling structure and the record of the failures are annotated at these nodes. Each goal is a precondition of some operator and each operator is chosen and applied because it is relevant to some goal that needs to be achieved. The failed alternatives are stored with an attached reason of failure.

As an example, node `cn2` corresponds to the search tree node `n8`. This search node has a sibling alternative `n2` which was explored and failed. The failed subtree rooted at `n2` has two failure leaves, namely at `n6` and `n7`. These failure reasons are annotated at the case node `cn2`. At replay time these justifications are tested and may lead to an early pruning of alternatives and constrain possible instantiations.

Flexible Replay of Multiple Guiding Cases

When a new problem is proposed, PRODIGY/ANALOGY retrieves from the case library one or more problem solving episodes that may partially cover the new problem solving situation. The system uses a similarity metric that weighs goal-relevant features (Veloso & Carbonell 1993b). In a nutshell, it selects a set of past cases that solved subsets of the new goal statement. The initial state is partially matched in the features that were relevant to solving these goals in the past. Each retrieved case provides guidance to a set of interacting goals from the new goal statement. At replay time, a guiding case is always considered as a source of guidance, until all the goals it covers are achieved.

The general replay mechanism involves a complete interpretation of the justification structures annotated in the past cases in the context of the new problem to be solved. Equivalent choices are made when the transformed justifications hold. When that is not the situation, PRODIGY/ANALOGY plans for the new goals using its domain operators adding new steps to the solution or skipping unnecessary steps from the past cases. Table 1 shows the main flow of control of the replay algorithm.

The replay functionality transforms the planner, from a module that costly generates possible operators to achieve

---

[2]Note that domain-independent methods to try to reduce the search effort (Stone, Veloso, & Blythe 1994) in general do not capture domain specific control knowledge, which must be then acquired by learning.

1. Terminate if the goal is satisfied in the state.

2. Choose a step from the set of guiding cases or decide if there is need for additional problem solving work. If a failure is encountered, then backtrack and continue following the guiding cases at the appropriate steps.

3. If a goal from a past case is chosen, then

   3.1 Validate the goal justifications. If not validated, go to step 2.

   3.2 Create a new goal node; link it to the case node. Advance the case to its next decision step.

   3.3 Select the operator chosen in the case.

   3.4 Validate the operator and bindings choices. If not validated, base-level plan for the goal. Use justifications and record of failures to make a more informed new selection. Go to step 2.

   3.5 Link the new operator node to the case node. Advance the case to its next decision step.

   3.6 Go to step 2.

4. If an applicable operator from a past case is chosen, then

   4.1 Check if it can be applied also in the current state. If it cannot, go to step 2.

   4.2 Link the new applied operator node to the case node. Advance the case to its next decision step.

   4.3 Apply the operator.

   4.4 Go to step 1.

Table 1: The main flow of control of the replay procedure.

---

the goals and searches through the space of alternatives generated, into a module that tests the validity of the choices proposed by past experience and follows equivalent search directions. The replay procedure provides the following benefits to the problem solving procedure as shown in the procedure of Table 1.

- Proposal and validation of choices versus generation and search of alternatives (steps 2, 3.1, 3.3, 3.4, and 4.1).

- Reduction of the branching factor – past failed alternatives are pruned by validating the failures recorded in the past cases (step 3.4); if backtracking is needed PRODIGY/ANALOGY backtracks also in the guiding cases – through the links established at steps 3.2, 3.5 and 4.2 – and uses information on failure to make more informed backtracking decisions.

- Subgoaling links identify the subparts of the case to replay – the steps that are not part of the active goals are skipped. The procedure to advance the cases, as called in steps 3.2, 3.5 and 4.2, ignores the goals that are not needed and their corresponding planning steps.

PRODIGY/ANALOGY constructs a new solution from a set of guiding cases as opposed to a single past case. Complex problems may be solved by resolving minor interactions among simpler past cases. However, following several cases poses an additional decision making step of choosing which case to pursue. We explored several strategies to merge the guidance from the set of similar cases. In the experiments from which we drew the empirical results presented below, we used an exploratory merging strategy. Choices are made arbitrarily when there is no other guidance available. This strategy allows an innovative exploration of the space of possible solutions leading to opportunities to learn from new goal interactions or operator choices.

Example

Figure 4 shows a new problem and two past cases selected for replay. The cases are partially instantiated to match the new situation. Further instantiations occur while replaying.

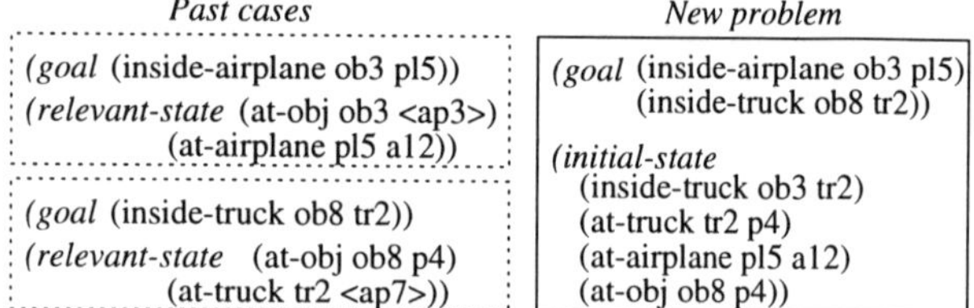

Figure 4: Instantiated past cases cover the new goal and partially match the new initial state. Some of the case variables are not bound by the match of the goals and state.

Figure 5 shows the replay episode to generate a solution to the new problem. The new situation is shown at the right side of the figure and the two past guiding cases at the left.

The transfer occurs by interleaving the two guiding cases, performing any additional work needed to accomplish remaining subgoals, and skipping past work that does not need to be done. In particular, the case nodes cn3′ through cn5′ are not reused, as there is a truck already at the post office in the new problem. The nodes n9–14 correspond to unguided additional planning done in the new episode.[3] At node n7, PRODIGY/ANALOGY prunes out an alternative operator, namely to load the truck at any airport, because of the recorded past failure at the guiding node cn2′. The recorded reason for that failure, namely a goal-loop with the (inside-truck ob8 tr2), is validated in the new situation, as that goal is in the current set of open goals, at node n6. Note that the two cases are merged using a bias to postpone additional planning needed. Different merges are possible.

Empirical Results

We ran and accumulated in the case library a set of 1000 problems in the logistics transportation domain. In the experiments the problems are randomly generated with up to 20 goals and more than 100 literals in the initial state. The case library is accumulated incrementally while the system solves problems with an increasing number of goals.

The logistics transportation is a complex domain. In particular, there are multiple operator and bindings choices for each particular problem, and those choices increase considerably with the size or complexity of the problem. For example, for the goal of moving an object to an airport,

---

[3]Note that extra steps may be inserted at any point, interrupting and interleaving the past cases, and not just at the end of the cases.

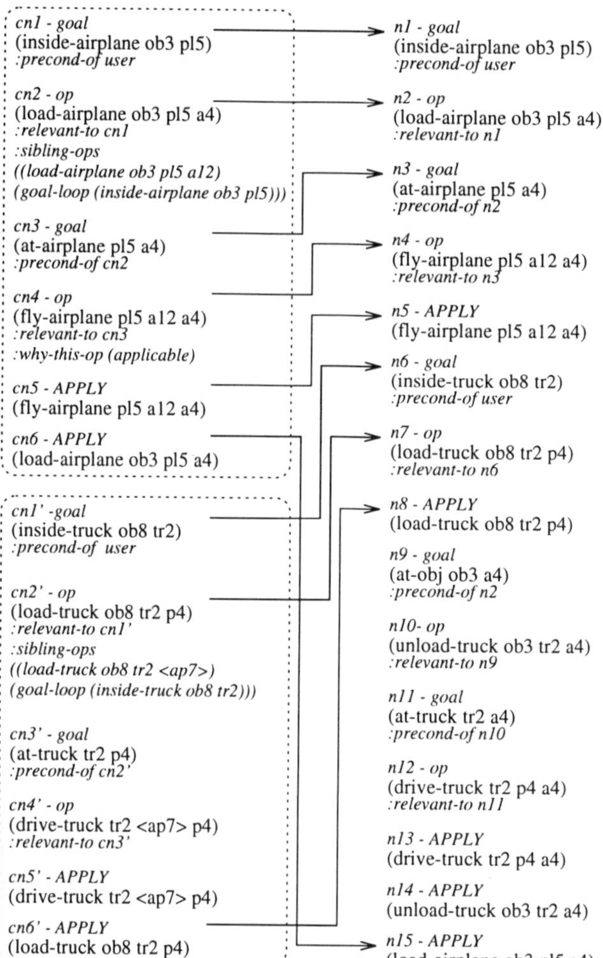

Figure 5: Derivational replay of multiple cases.

the problem solver does not have direct information from the domain operators on whether it should move the object inside of a truck or an airplane. Objects can be unloaded at an airport from both of these carriers, but trucks move within the same city and airplanes across cities. So if the object must go to an airport within the same city where it is, it should be moved in a truck, otherwise it should be moved in an airplane. The specification of these constraints is embedded in the domain knowledge and not directly available. The city at which the object is located is not immediately known, as when the object is inside of a carrier or a building, its city location is specified indirectly. PRODIGY/ANALOGY provides guidance at these choices of operators and bindings through the successful and failed choices annotated in past similar problem solving episodes.

PRODIGY/ANALOGY increases the solvability horizon of the problem solving task: Many problems that NoLIMIT cannot solve within a reasonable time limit are solved by PRODIGY/ANALOGY within that limit. Figure 6 (a) plots the number of problems solved by NoLIMIT and PRODIGY/ANALOGY for different CPU time bounds. No-LIMIT solves only 458 problems out of the 1000 problems even when the search time limit is increased up to 350s.

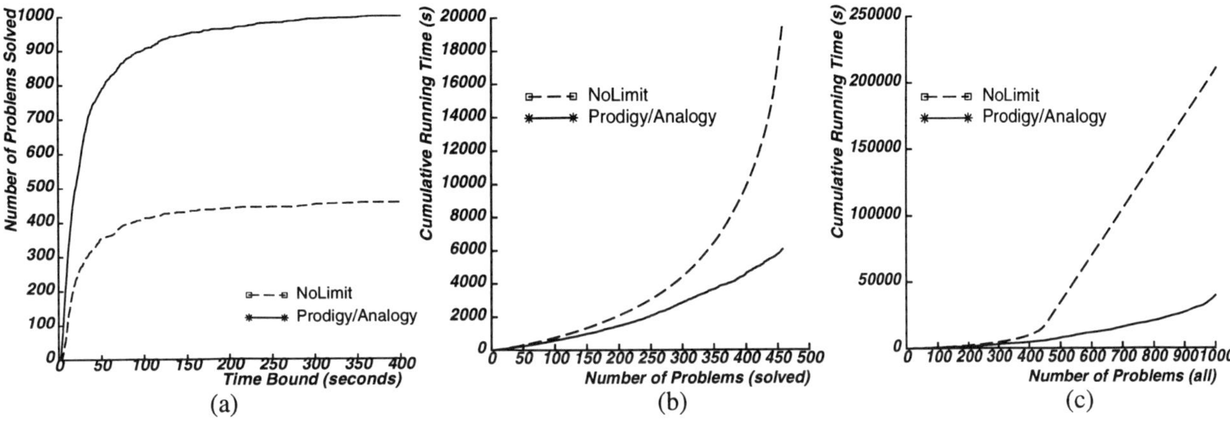

Figure 6: (a) Number of problems solved from a set of 1000 problems versus different running time bounds. With a time limit of 350s NoLIMIT solves only 458 problems, while PRODIGY/ANALOGY solves the complete set of 1000 problems; (b) Cumulative running times for the 458 problems solved by both configurations; (c) Cumulative running times for all the 1000 problems. The problems unsolved by NoLIMIT count as the maximum time limit given (350s).

This graph shows a significant improvement achieved by solving problems by analogy with previously solved problems. Although not shown in this figure, the percentage of problems solved without analogy decreases rapidly with the complexity of the problems. The gradient of the increase in the performance of PRODIGY/ANALOGY over the base-level NoLIMIT shows its large advantage when increasing the complexity of the problems to be solved.

In other previous work, comparisons between the performance of a problem solver before and after learning control knowledge were done by graphing the cumulative running times of the two systems over a set of problems. Figure 6 (b) shows the cumulative running time for the set of problems (458) that were both solved by both configurations. The graph shows a final factor of 3.6 cumulative speed up of PRODIGY/ANALOGY over the base NoLIMIT. (The maximum individual speed up was of a factor of approximately 40.) In Figure 6 (c) we extend this comparison to account also for the unsolved problems (similarly to what was done in previous comparisons (Minton 1988)). For each unsolved problem, we add the running time bound.

We also compiled results on the length of the solutions generated by PRODIGY/ANALOGY and on the impact of the size of the case library in the retrieval time (Veloso 1992). We concluded that PRODIGY/ANALOGY produces solutions of equal or shorter length in 92% of the problems. PRODIGY/ANALOGY includes an indexing mechanism for the case library of learned problem solving episodes (Veloso & Carbonell 1993b). We verified that with this memory organization, we reduced (or avoided) the potential utility problem (Doorenbos & Veloso 1993): The retrieval time suffers no significant increase with the size of the case library.

Discussion and related work

PRODIGY's problem solving method is a combination of means-ends analysis, backward chaining, and state-space search. PRODIGY commits to particular choices of operators, bindings, and step orderings as its search process makes use of a uniquely specified state while planning (Fink & Veloso 1994). PRODIGY's learning opportunities are therefore directly related to the choices found by the problem solver in its state-space search. It is beyond the scope of this paper to discuss what are the potential advantages or disadvantages of our problem solving search method in particular compared with other planners that search a plan space. Any system that treats planning and problem solving as a search process will make a series of commitments during search. The pattern of commitments made will produce greater efficiency in some kinds of domains and less in others (Stone, Veloso, & Blythe 1994). The goal of strategy learning is precisely to *automate* the process of acquiring operational knowledge to improve the performance of a particular base-level problem solving reasoning strategy. Each particular problem solver may find different learning opportunities depending on its reasoning and searching strategies. However, the following aspects of this work may apply to other problem solvers: learning a chain of justified problem solving decisions as opposed to individual ones or final solutions; and flexibly replaying multiple complementary learned knowledge in similar situations as opposed to identical ones.

This work is related to other plan reuse work in the plan-space search paradigm, in particular (Kambhampati & Hendler 1992). In that framework, it proved beneficial to reuse the final plans annotated with a validation structure that links the goals to the operators that achieve each goal. In PRODIGY/ANALOGY we learn and replay the planner's decision making process directly. The justification structures in the derivational traces also encompass the record of past failures in addition to the subgoaling links as in (Mostow 1989; Blumenthal 1990; Kambhampati & Hendler 1992; Bhansali & Harandi 1993). The derivational traces provide guidance for the choices that our problem solver faces while constructing solutions to similar problems. Adapted decisions can be interleaved and backtracked upon within the replay procedure.

Learning by analogy can also be related to other strategies to learn control knowledge. In particular analogical reasoning in PRODIGY can be seen as relaxing the restrictions to explanation-based approaches as developed in PRODIGY (Minton 1988; Etzioni 1993). Instead of requiring complete axiomatic domain knowledge to derive general rules of behavior for individual decisions, PRODIGY/ANALOGY compiles annotated traces of solved problems with little post processing. The learning effort is done incrementally on an "if-needed" basis at storage, retrieval and adaptation time. The complete problem solving episode is interpreted as a global decision-making experience and independent subparts can be reused as a whole. PRODIGY/ANALOGY can replay partially matched learned experience increasing therefore the transfer of potentially over-specific learned knowledge.

Chunking in SOAR (Laird, Rosenbloom, & Newell 1986) also accumulates episodic global knowledge. However, the selection of applicable chunks is based on choosing the ones whose conditions match totally the active context. The chunking algorithm in SOAR can learn interactions among different problem spaces.

Analogical reasoning in PRODIGY/ANALOGY learns complete sequences of decisions as opposed to individual rules. Under this perspective analogical reasoning shares characteristics with learning macro-operators (Yang & Fisher 1992). Intermediate decisions corresponding to choices internal to each case can be bypassed or adapted when their justifications do not longer hold. Furthermore cases cover complete problem solving episodes and are not proposed at local decisions as search alternatives to one-step operators.

Conclusion

Reasoning by analogy in PRODIGY/ANALOGY consists of the flexible reuse of derivational traces of previously solved problems to guide the search for solutions to similar new problems. The issues addressed in the paper include: the generation of problem solving cases for reuse, and the flexible replay of possibly multiple learned episodes in situations that partially match new ones. The paper shows results that empirically validate the method and demonstrate that PRODIGY/ANALOGY is amenable to scaling up both in terms of domain and problem complexity.

Acknowledgements Special thanks to Jaime Carbonell for his guidance, suggestions, and discussions on this work. Thanks also to Alicia Pérez and the anonymous reviewers for their helpful comments on this paper.

References

Bhansali, S., and Harandi, M. T. 1993. Synthesis of UNIX programs using derivational analogy. *Machine Learning* 10.

Blumenthal, B. 1990. *Replaying episodes of a metaphoric application interface designer*. Ph.D. Dissertation, University of Texas, Artificial Intelligence Lab, Austin.

Carbonell, J. G., and the Prodigy Research Group. 1992. PRODIGY4.0: The manual and tutorial. Technical Report CMU-CS-92-150, SCS, Carnegie Mellon University.

Carbonell, J. G. 1986. Derivational analogy: A theory of reconstructive problem solving and expertise acquisition. In Michalski, R. S.; Carbonell, J. G.; and Mitchell, T. M., eds., *Machine Learning, An Artificial Intelligence Approach, Volume II*, 371–392. Morgan Kaufman.

DeJong, G. F., and Mooney, R. 1986. Explanation-based learning: An alternative view. *Machine Learning* 1(2):145–176.

Doorenbos, R. B., and Veloso, M. M. 1993. Knowledge organization and the utility problem. In *Proceedings of the Third International Workshop on Knowledge Compilation and Speedup Learning*, 28–34.

Etzioni, O. 1993. Acquiring search-control knowledge via static analysis. *Artificial Intelligence* 65.

Fikes, R. E., and Nilsson, N. J. 1971. Strips: A new approach to the application of theorem proving to problem solving. *Artificial Intelligence* 2:189–208.

Fink, E., and Veloso, M. 1994. Formalizing the PRODIGY planning algorithm. Technical Report CMU-CS-94-112, School of Computer Science, Carnegie Mellon University.

Hammond, K. J. 1986. *Case-based Planning: An Integrated Theory of Planning, Learning and Memory*. Ph.D. Dissertation, Yale University.

Kambhampati, S., and Hendler, J. A. 1992. A validation based theory of plan modification and reuse. *Artificial Intelligence* 55(2-3):193–258.

Korf, R. E. 1985. Macro-operators: A weak method for learning. *Artificial Intelligence* 26:35–77.

Laird, J. E.; Rosenbloom, P. S.; and Newell, A. 1986. Chunking in SOAR: The anatomy of a general learning mechanism. *Machine Learning* 1:11–46.

Minton, S. 1988. *Learning Effective Search Control Knowledge: An Explanation-Based Approach*. Boston, MA: Kluwer Academic Publishers.

Mitchell, T. M.; Keller, R. M.; and Kedar-Cabelli, S. T. 1986. Explanation-based generalization: A unifying view. *Machine Learning* 1:47–80.

Mostow, J. 1989. Automated replay of design plans: Some issues in derivational analogy. *Artificial Intelligence* 40(1-3).

Stone, P.; Veloso, M.; and Blythe, J. 1994. The need for different domain-independent heuristics. In *Proceedings of the Second International Conference on AI Planning Systems*.

Veloso, M. M., and Carbonell, J. G. 1993a. Derivational analogy in PRODIGY: Automating case acquisition, storage, and utilization. *Machine Learning* 10:249–278.

Veloso, M. M., and Carbonell, J. G. 1993b. Towards scaling up machine learning: A case study with derivational analogy in PRODIGY. In Minton, S., ed., *Machine Learning Methods for Planning*. Morgan Kaufmann. 233–272.

Veloso, M. M. 1989. Nonlinear problem solving using intelligent casual-commitment. Technical Report CMU-CS-89-210, School of Computer Science, Carnegie Mellon University.

Veloso, M. M. 1992. *Learning by Analogical Reasoning in General Problem Solving*. Ph.D. Dissertation, School of Computer Science, Carnegie Mellon University, Pittsburgh, PA. Available as technical report CMU-CS-92-174. A revised version of this manuscript is in press to be published by Springer Verlag.

Yang, H., and Fisher, D. 1992. Similarity-based retrieval and partial reuse of macro-operators. Technical Report CS-92-13, Department of Computer Science, Vanderbilt University.

Branching on Attribute Values in Decision Tree Generation

Usama M. Fayyad

AI Group, M/S 525-3660
Jet Propulsion Laboratory
California Institute of Technology
Pasadena, CA 91109-8099
Fayyad@aig.jpl.nasa.gov

Abstract

The problem of deciding which subset of values of a categorical-valued attribute to branch on during decision tree generation is addressed. Algorithms such as ID3 and C4 do not address the issue and simply branch on each value of the selected attribute. The GID3* algorithm is presented and evaluated. The GID3* algorithm is a generalized version of Quinlan's ID3 and C4, and is a non-parametric version of the GID3 algorithm presented in an earlier paper. It branches on a subset of individual values of an attribute, while grouping the rest under a single DEFAULT branch. It is empirically demonstrated that GID3* outperforms ID3 (C4) and GID3 for *any* parameter setting of the latter. The empirical tests include both controlled synthetic (randomized) domains as well as real-world data sets. The improvement in tree quality as measured by number of leaves and estimated error rate is significant.

Introduction

Empirical learning algorithms attempt to discover relations between situations expressed in terms of a set of attributes and actions encoded in terms of a fixed set of classes. By examining large sets of pre-classified data, it is hoped that a learning program may discover the proper conditions under which each action (class) is appropriate. Heuristic methods are used to perform guided search through the large space of possible relations between combinations of attribute values and classes. A powerful and popular such heuristic uses the notion of selecting attributes that locally minimize the information entropy of the classes in a data set. This heuristic is used in the ID3 algorithm [11] and its extensions, e.g. GID3 [2], GID3* [4], and C4 [12], in CART [1], in CN2 [3] and others; see [4, 5, 10] for a general discussion of the attribute selection problem.

The attributes in a learning problem may be discrete (categorical), or they may be continuous (numerical). The above mentioned attribute selection process assumes that all attributes are discrete. Continuous-valued attributes must, therefore, be *discretized* prior to attribute selection. This is typically achieved by partitioning the range of the attribute into subranges, i.e., a test is devised that quantizes the range. In this paper, we focus only on the problem of deciding which values of a discrete-valued (or discretized)

attribute should be branched on, and which should not. We propose that by avoiding branching on all values (as in ID3), better trees are obtained. We originally developed the GID3 algorithm [2] to address this problem. GID3 is dependent on a user-determined parameter setting (TL) that controls its tendency towards branching on some versus all values of an attribute. We have demonstrated that for certain settings of TL, GID3 produces significantly better trees than ID3 or C4[1]. In this paper we present the GID3* algorithm in which the dependence on a user-specified parameter has been removed. We empirically demonstrate that GID3* produces better trees than GID3 for a wide range of parameter settings.

The Attribute Selection Criterion

Assume we are to select an attribute for branching at a node having a set S of N examples from a set of k classes: $\{C_1, \ldots, C_k\}$. Assuming that some test T on attribute A partitions the set S into the subsets $S_1, \ldots, S_r$. Let $P(C_i, S)$ be the proportion of examples in S that have class C_i. The *class entropy* of a subset S is defined as:

$$\text{Ent}(S) = -\sum_{i=1}^{k} P(C_i, S) \log(P(C_i, S))$$

The resulting class entropy after a set S is partitioned into the r subsets is:

$$E(A, T; S) = -\sum_{i=1}^{r} \frac{|S_i|}{|S|} \text{Ent}(S_i) \qquad (1)$$

The information gain due to the test T, is thus defined to be $Gain(A, T; S) = \text{Ent}(S) - E(A, T; S)$. Having found that the gain measure is biased in favor of tests that induce finer partitions, Quinlan [11] adjusted it by dividing it by the entropy of the test outcomes themselves:

$$\text{IV}(T; S) = \text{Ent}(T; S) = -\sum_{i=1}^{r} \frac{|S_i|}{|S|} \log \left(\frac{|S_i|}{|S|} \right)$$

---

[1]In this paper we do not consider pruning. We focus only on generating better trees. Pruning methods can be applied to any tree regardless of how it was generated.

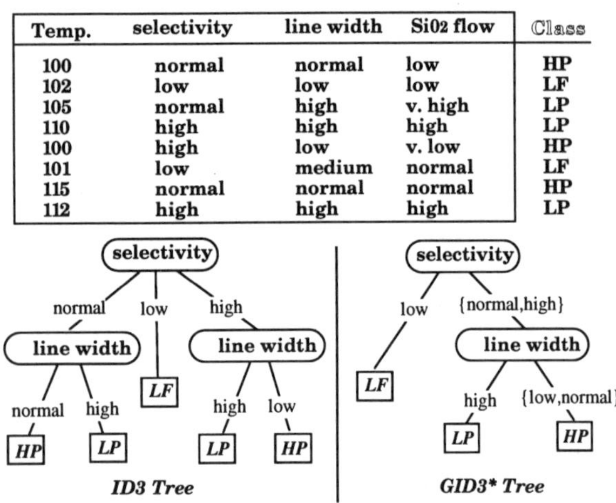

Figure 1: Two Decision Trees for a Simple Training Set.

giving the Gain-ratio measure:

$$Gain\text{-}r(A, T; S) = \frac{Gain(A, T; S)}{\mathrm{IV}(T; S)}.$$

This empirically results in improved behavior. We refer to the ID3 algorithm with the Gain-ratio selection measure as ID3-IV (Quinlan later refers to it as C4 [12]).

Assuming that attribute A is discrete (or previously discretized), the problem we address is how to formulate the test T. In ID3 and C4, the test T is simply a test of the value of A, with a separate branch for each value of A appearing in the data at the local node. This class of tests result in problematic trees since not every value of an attribute may be relevant to the classification task. For example, consider the attribute "color" with values {blue, red, green, yellow, white, black}. It may be the case that only the colors blue and red convey meaningful classification information. The fact that an object's color is, for example, white, conveys no information other than the fact that the color is *neither blue nor red*. branching on each individual value results in excessively partitioning the data. This reduces the quality of subsequent attribute choices, and the problem compounds as subtrees are subsequently grown from over-partitioned nodes [4]. These problems are referred to as the **irrelevant values, reduced data**, and **missing branches** problems. Figure 1 illustrates how an ID3 tree generated from the the given simple training set differs from the corresponding GID3* tree. Note that both trees were generated from the data set, yet the ID3 tree would fail to classify a new example (not in the training set) that has values { selectivity=normal, line width=low}. The GID3* tree can classify this example, hence is more general. We shall later show that on average GID3* trees are also more accurate.

The GID3 Algorithm

In order to overcome overbranching problems, we generalized the ID3 approach by introducing the *attribute phantomization* step prior to attribute selection. An attribute A

with r values is transformed into a *phantom attribute A'* with s values, where $s \leq r$. The values of A deemed irrelevant, are mapped to a single branch (value) called *"DEFAULT"*. The other values remain unchanged. In our example above, the values of the phantom attribute *color'* would be {blue, red, DEFAULT}. In GID3, phantomization was achieved by evaluating the Gain of each attribute-value pair separately. The maximum Gain multiplied by the user-specified tolerance level TL, $0 \leq$ TL ≤ 1, gives a threshold gain. All pairs whose Gain is not less than the threshold gain are passed. Each phantom attribute is defined to have the values of the original attribute that passed.

As presented, the GID3 algorithm provides the means to generate a family of trees from a given training set. The TL parameter allowed us to control which tree is generated by increasing or decreasing the tendency of the algorithm to branch on some, rather than all, values of the selected attribute. ID3 trees are certainly members of the family of trees generated by GID3 (TL= 0 setting). Thus GID3 served as a convenient tool to conceptually and empirically verify that the irrelevant values problem in ID3 can, in principle, be alleviated. Further empirical evidence for this claim is given in [4]. However, to provide a well-defined algorithm we need to remove the reliance on the user-specified parameter TL.

We empirically demonstrated that there are certain settings of the TL parameter that result in decision trees that are superior to the corresponding ID3 and ID3-IV trees[2, 4]. As a matter of fact, this was also our experience in all our experiments involving data from various companies in semiconductor manufacturing [8]. The main problem with the TL parameter, is that its optimal setting varies from domain to domain, as well as across different training sets within a single domain. Actually, the user typically finds it difficult to decide on a TL setting because the parameter has no simple intuitive interpretation.

The GID3* Algorithm

The GID3* algorithm differs from GID3 only in the attribute phantomization stage. It uses an additional measure to overcome GID3's dependence on the parameter TL.

For a set S of N examples and an attribute A with discrete values over S, let a_i be one of the values of A. We define the *Tear* of the attribute-value pair $\langle A, a_i \rangle$ to measure the degree to which the pair $\langle A, a_i \rangle$ "tears the classes in S apart from each other". The pair $\langle A, a_i \rangle$ may be used to partition S into the subset $S_{A=a_i}$ consisting of examples in S that have $A = a_i$ and the subset $S_{A \neq a_i}$ consisting of the rest of the examples in S. $Tear(\langle A, a_i \rangle, S)$ measures the degree to which the classes in $S_{A=a_i}$ and $S_{A \neq a_i}$ are disjoint from each other. In other words, $Tear(\langle A, a_i \rangle, S)$ is a measure of the amount of "work" that the pair $\langle A, a_i \rangle$ performs towards getting us to the desirable state of "tearing all the classes apart from each other."

Let $C(j, S)$ be the number of examples in S that have class C_j. The quantity

$$\frac{|C(j, S_{A=a_i}) - C(j, S_{A \neq a_i})|}{C(j, S_{A=a_i}) + C(j, S_{A \neq a_i})}$$

measures the degree to which the partition induced by $\langle A, a_i \rangle$ separates examples of the same class, C_j, from each other. It is maximum when examples of C_j remain together either in $S_{A=a_i}$ or $S_{A \neq a_i}$. Taking the weighted average *intra-class cohesion* (non-separation) over all classes in S we get the measure $Tear1(\langle A, a_i \rangle, S)$

$$= \sum_{j=1}^{k} P(C_j, S) \frac{|C(j, S_{A=a_i}) - C(j, S_{A \neq a_i})|}{C(j, S_{A=a_i}) + C(j, S_{A \neq a_i})}$$

$$= \frac{1}{N} \sum_{j=1}^{k} |C(j, S_{A=a_i}) - C(j, S_{A \neq a_i})|.$$

Note that $Tear1$ reduces to the normalized vector difference (the L_1-norm) between the two class vectors of the sets $S_{A=a_i}$ and $S_{A \neq a_i}$. It can easily be shown that $0 \leq Tear1(\langle A, a_i \rangle, S) \leq 1$. The measure is maximized when the set of classes represented in $S_{A=a_i}$ is disjoint with the set of classes represented in $S_{A \neq a_i}$. It is minimized when the class vectors of the two subsets $S_{A=a_i}$ and $S_{A \neq a_i}$ are identical. See [4, 5] for a discussion on weaknesses of the entropy measure. $Tear1$ is biased in favor of pairs $\langle A, a_i \rangle$ which have very few or very many of S's examples. Let $P(\langle A, a_i \rangle, S)$ be the proportion of examples in S having values a_i for attribute A: $P(\langle A, a_i \rangle, S) = \frac{|S_{A=a_i}|}{|S|}$. Then if $P(\langle A, a_i \rangle, S) \approx 0$, or if $P(\langle A, a_i \rangle, S) \approx 1$, the $Tear1$ measure goes close to its maximum regardless of the disjointness of classes in $S_{A=a_i}$ and $S_{A \neq a_i}$. We can correct for this by multiplying $Tear1$ by the proportion $P(\langle A, a_i \rangle, S)$, however this is not a symmetric correction since it favors large $|S_{A=ai}|$. The proper symmetric correction factor is one that is symmetric about $P(\langle A, a_i \rangle, S) = 0.5$ and is 0 at $P(\langle A, a_i \rangle, S) = 0$ and $P(\langle A, a_i \rangle, S) = 1$. Consider the weighting factor given by:

$$\begin{aligned} W(\langle A, a_i \rangle, S) &= P(\langle A, a_i \rangle, S) \left(1 - P(\langle A, a_i \rangle, S)\right) \\ &= \frac{|S_{A=a_i}| \cdot |S_{A \neq a_i}|}{|S|^2} \end{aligned}$$

Clearly, $0 \leq W(\langle A, a_i \rangle, S) \leq \frac{1}{4}$, and $W(\langle A, a_i \rangle, S)$ is symmetric about its maximum value of 0.25 at $P(\langle A, a_i \rangle, S) = 0.5$. In general, it is desirable to have the weighting factor be uniform in the middle and drop off to zero very quickly (c.f. an ideal band-pass filter). We can achieve this by using the following function:

$$\begin{aligned} WF(\langle A, a_i \rangle, S) &= \min\left\{1.0 \, , \, \beta \cdot W(\langle A, a_i \rangle, S)\right\} \\ &= \min\left\{1.0 \, , \, \beta \cdot P(1 - P)\right\} \end{aligned}$$

where P denotes $P(\langle A, a_i \rangle, S)$, and $\beta \geq 4.0$ is a parameter that determines where and how fast the filter WF starts dropping off from its maximum value of 1.0. For example, if $\beta = 25$ the filter is uniformly 1.0 for the interval $0.042 \leq P(\langle A, a_i \rangle, S) \leq 0.958$. In general, the beginning and end of the 1.0 plateau range may be derived by solving for P in the equation: $\beta \left(P(1 - P)\right) = 1.0$, whose solution is:

$$P = \frac{1}{2} \pm \sqrt{\frac{1}{4} - \frac{1}{\beta}}.$$

Note that WF rises from 0.0 to 1.0 at a slope of approximately β for large β. We fix β at 25, a fairly large value.

We now define the desired *Tear* measure for an attribute-value pair $\langle A, a_i \rangle$

$$Tear(\langle A, a_i \rangle, S) = WF(\langle A, a_i \rangle, S) \cdot Tear1(\langle A, a_i \rangle, S).$$

Note that $0 \leq Tear(\langle A, a_i \rangle, S) \leq 1$. Also note that the tear measure is minimum either when the class vectors of $S_{A=a_i}$ and $S_{A \neq a_i}$ are identical, or when one of the two subsets of S is empty.

We now describe how attribute A with values $\{a_1, a_2, \ldots, a_r\}$ is *phantomized* to produce the corresponding phantom attribute A'. We first evaluate the information entropy of each of the attribute-value pairs $\langle A, a_i \rangle$, $1 \leq i \leq r$ as described in the GID3 algorithm to get $E(\langle A, a_i \rangle, S)$. We then choose the pair with the minimum entropy. Without loss of generality, let this value be a_1. a_1 will be one of the values of the phantom attribute A'. What is left to be decided at this point is which of the remaining values $\{a_2, \ldots, a_r\}$ are to be admitted as values of A' and which to group together under the value *DEFAULT*.

Let T_1 be the *Tear* value of the best entropy attribute-value pair $\langle A, a_1 \rangle$. Let this tear be $T_1 = Tear(\langle A, a_1 \rangle, S)$, and let S' be the subset of S consisting of examples that have a value other than a_1 for attribute A: $S' = S_{A \neq a_1} = S \sim S_{A=a_1}$. For each of the remaining values of A, $\{a_2, \ldots, a_r\}$, compute the *Tear* of the attribute-value pair with respect to the set S'. That is $T_i = Tear(\langle A, a_i \rangle, S')$. Every value a_i whose tear value T_i is less than T_1, is considered irrelevant and is grouped with others under the *DEFAULT* value. Other values are considered relevant and are considered as proper values of the phantom attribute A'. Once the phantom attribute has been generated for each of the attributes, GID3* proceeds exactly as GID3. It evaluates *Gain-r* of each phantom attribute and selects the best phantom attribute for branching.

from a measure other than entropy. Information entropy still plays the primary selection role since the best entropy value among the values of each attribute is selected, and the phantom attribute with the best information gain is selected. In GID3*, every phantom attribute is guaranteed at least two values: its best entropy value and *DEFAULT*. Note that in GID3 some attributes may not have corresponding phantom attributes.

Note that in other systems, different phantomization (or subsetting) schemes have been proposed. In CART [1], a *binary partition* of an attribute's values is selected. In general this is exponential (except in case of 2-class problems) and is thus not feasible. ASSISTANT [9] also uses a partition scheme requiring extensive search. Partitions provide for a richer language than the extension that GID3* provides (restricted partitions of singletons and a default subset). In the case of GID3*, the complexity of determining the partition is linear in the number of attribute values.

Empirical Evaluation of GID3 and GID3*

In this section, we present empirical evidence that verifies our hypothesis that GID3* produces better trees than GID3.

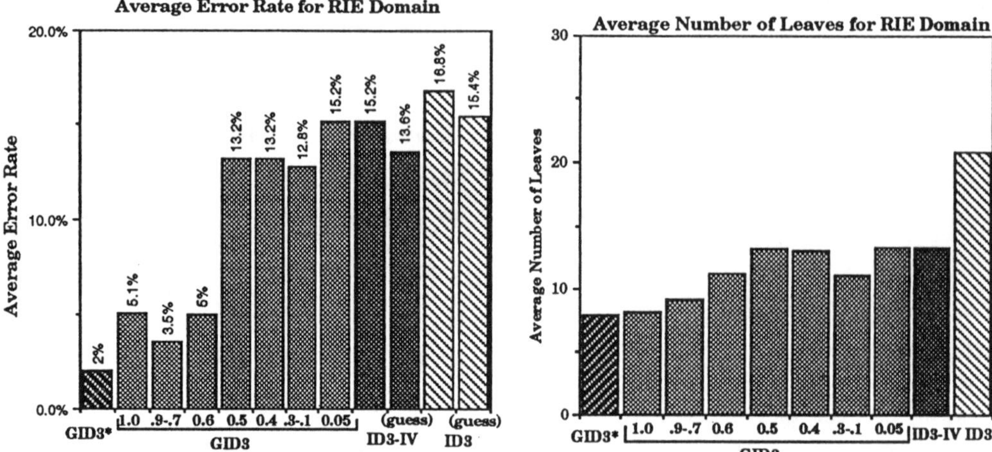

Figure 2: Results (number of leaves and error rates) for the RIE Domain.

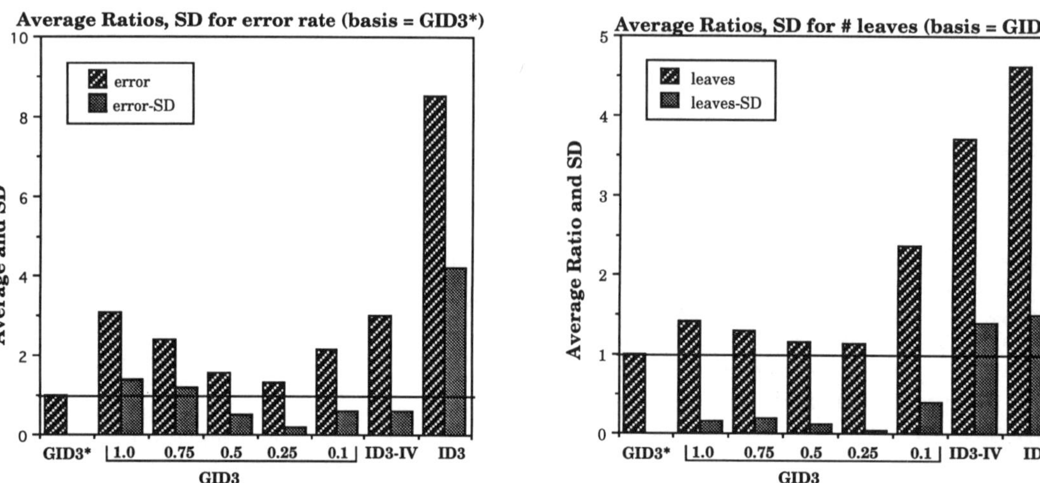

Figure 3: Average Ratios and SD for Random Domains.

Since GID3 has a user-specified parameter TL, we have to compare the tree obtained from GID3* with the "best" tree obtained from GID3 with various settings of TL.

Experiments on Synthetic RIE Data

The first set of experiments were conducted on the data set from the RIE (Reactive Ion Etching in semiconductor manufacturing) domain described in [2]. The results obtained are shown in Figure 2 Also note that although both GID3 (with TL=1.0) and GID3* found the trees with the minimum number of leaves (eight), the two trees were actually different (as evidenced by the different error rates). In general, GID3* did as well as or better than the best GID3 threshold both on compactness and accuracy. Since ID3 suffers from the missing branches problem, on some examples it may fail to make a prediction. The columns labelled (guess) for ID3 and ID3-IV show what happens if the algorithm makes an extra guess at random whenever it gets stuck with a missing branch. This is to demonstrate that GID3 and GID3* generalizations are not essentially making

only "random guesses," but more meaningful predictions.

Experiments on Random Synthetic Domains

The next set of controlled experiments were conducted on synthetic randomly generated data extracted from randomly generated domains. The general procedure is to randomly generate a domain by selecting a random number of attributes, values for attributes, and classes. A decision tree is then constructed using an algorithm that randomly selects an attribute and a subset of its values to branch on. The algorithm flips a coin to determine whether or not to deem a node a leaf, and if so, randomly labels it with a class. This results in a decision tree that represents the rules governing examples in the given domain. Examples of each leaf node are then generated randomly as in the synthetic RIE domain. On average, about 25 examples per leaf were generated. The number of attributes varied between 8 and 20 with each attribute's range varying between 2 and 15 values. The number of classes varied between 4 and 10.

As an example, one randomly generated domain had 9

Table 1: Details of the Data Sets in Empirical Evaluation.

Data Set	examples		attributes		classes
	train	test	disc.	cont.	
HARR90	280	220	25	—	72
SOYBEAN	290	340	35	—	15
AUTO	102	103	9	15	6
MUSHRM	50-350	7000	22	—	2

attributes, 6 classes, and a tree with 14 leaves (rules). A training set consisting of 25 examples per leaf and a test set of 50 examples per leaf were generated independently. The process was repeated 10 times. The averaged results for the various algorithms were recorded for that domain. The above procedure was repeated and results were collected for 100 randomly generated domains. Since it does not make sense to average performance measures over different domains, we resorted to collecting the ratios of improvement for each domain, and then averaging the ratios over different domains. Figure 3 shows the average ratio of number of leaves and error rates. The basis of performance (denominator of ratio) is the corresponding GID3* result. Hence, GID3* takes the value 1.0 for the ratio in these figures. The second column shows the standard deviation for each of the average ratios given.

Experiments on Real-World Discrete Data

Finally, we conduct experiments to compare the performance of GID3, GID3*, and ID3 on some real-world domains. One issue needs to be clarified at this point. GID3 and GID3* are designed to overcome the irrelevant values problem. If all attributes for a given data set are binary-valued, then the performance of GID3*, GID3, and ID3-IV on this data will be identical. Furthermore, if attributes are continuous-valued, then the "standard" method for handling them is to discretize them into a binary-valued attribute. We present a method for multiple-interval discretization and its benefits in [4, 7]. Data sets with only binary-valued discrete attributes, or continuous-valued attributes will not be useful for comparison purposes. For comparisons on data with continuous-valued attributes see [4, 7].

The data sets we used are are described in Table 1. HARR90 is a Semiconductor manufacturing data set obtained from Harris Corp. as part of an effort to construct an expert system for diagnosing transistor manufacturing defects. The other three were obtained from the U.C. Irvine ML data repository. Although the MUSHRM data has about 8000 examples, it is an extremely "easy" learning task. With about 500 examples, all algorithms achieve error rates lower than 0.11%. For this reason we kept the training sets small (50-350). The results reported are averaged over 10 such runs. Also, the SOYBEAN data contains some undefined attribute values. The algorithm used by GID3 and GID3* to handle undefined attribute values is described in [4]. For the SOYBEAN data, we used the standard training and test sets provided in the database. For the others, we randomly sampled the data sets to obtain training and test sets. The results are averaged over 10 runs. The results, shown in terms of average error rate and number of leaves for each of the four domains in Figure 4, confirm that GID3* produces better trees than GID3, ID3-IV, and ID3.

Concluding Remarks

Using synthetic randomized domains and real-world data, we have empirically demonstrated that GID3 and GID3* outperform ID3. The trees generated using GID3* are superior to trees in the family of trees generated by GID3. The GID3* trees are more compact, more reliable, and more general decision trees than their GID3 and ID3 counterparts. The improvement was achieved with a negligible increase in computational cost. Of course, this gives no guarantee that GID3* is always better than GID3 (for some optimal TL setting). However, empirical evidence, coupled with the fact that the TL parameter in GID3 complicates its application to industrial data, are enough reasons to tip the balance in favor of a parameter-free algorithm: GID3*.

Further note that we have used data sets which contain only discrete-valued attributes. This is to isolate effects due to the discretization stage for continuous-valued attributes. Also, for binary-valued discrete attributes, the performance of ID3, GID3, and GID3* is identical. This limit the data sets useful for strict comparisons. Powerful results have been obtained on extensive data sets using GID3* (see [7]). For a real-world large scale application see [6]. However, in those papers it is difficult to isolate the improvement due to various factors. Finally, the interested reader is referred to [4, 5] for a more detailed discussion of the branching problem along with alternative (and more powerful) solutions.

The goal of this paper is to present the GID3* algorithm as a possible solution to the branching decision problem. GID3 is not considered a solution since it is not fully specified and is dependent on a user-specified parameter. It is indeed remarkable that the GID3* solution has proven empirically superior to GID3 at all of the TL settings evaluated. We have no formal explanation for this experimental observation.

Acknowledgments

This work was conducted in part while at The University of Michigan, Ann Arbor (1990-91). GID3 was originally developed in collaboration with Prof. K.B. Irani, J. Cheng, and Z. Qian. GID3* work was funded in part by a Hughes Microelectronics Center Unrestricted Grant (Fayyad and Irani). The work described in this paper was carried out in part by the Jet Propulsion Laboratory, California Institute of Technology, under a contract with the National Aeronautics and Space Administration.

References

[1] Breiman, L., Friedman, J.H., Olshen, R.A., and Stone, C.J. (1984). *Classification and Regression Trees*. Monterey, CA: Wadsworth & Brooks.

[2] Cheng, J., Fayyad, U.M., Irani, K.B., and Qian, Z. (1988). "Improved decision trees: A generalized version of ID3." *Proc. of the Fifth International Conference on Machine Learning* (pp. 100-108). San Mateo, CA: Morgan Kaufmann.

[3] Clark, P. and Niblett, T. (1989). "The CN2 induction algorithm." *Machine Learning, 3*, 261-284.

[4] Fayyad, U.M. (1991). *On the Induction of Decision Trees for Multiple Concept Learning.* PhD dissertation, EECS Dept., The University of Michigan.

[5] Fayyad, U.M. and Irani, K.B. (1992). "The attribute selection problem in decision tree generation" *Proc. of the Tenth National Conference on Artificial Intelligence AAAI-90* (pp. 104-110). Cambridge, MA: MIT Press.

[6] Fayyad, U.M., Weir, N. and Djorgovski, S. (1993) "SKICAT: A machine learning system for automated cataloging of large-scale sky surveys." *Proceedings of the 10th Int. Conf. on Machine Learning*, Morgan Kauffman.

[7] Fayyad, U.M. and Irani, K.B. (1993). "Multi-interval discretization of continuous-valued attributes for classification learning", *Proc. of IJCAI-93.*

[8] Irani, K.B., Cheng, J., Fayyad, U.M., and Qian, Z. (1990). "Applications of Machine Learning Techniques in Semiconductor Manufacturing." *Proc. of The S.P.I.E. Conference on Applications of Artificial Intelligence VIII* (pp. 956-965). Bellingham, WA: SPIE.

[9] Kononenko, I., Bratko, I., and Roskar, E. (1984) "Experiments in automatic learning of medical diagnostic rules." *Technical Report*, Ljubljana, Yugoslavia: Josef Stefan Institute.

[10] Lewis, P.M. (1962). "The characteristic selection problem in recognition systems." *IRE Transactions on Information Theory, IT-8*, 171-178.

[11] Quinlan, J.R. (1986). "Induction of decision trees." *Machine Learning 1*, 81-106.

[12] Quinlan, J.R. (1990). "Probabilistic decision trees." In *Machine Learning: An Artificial Intelligence Approach, Volume III*, Y. Kodratoff & R. Michalski (Eds.) San Mateo, CA: Morgan Kaufmann.

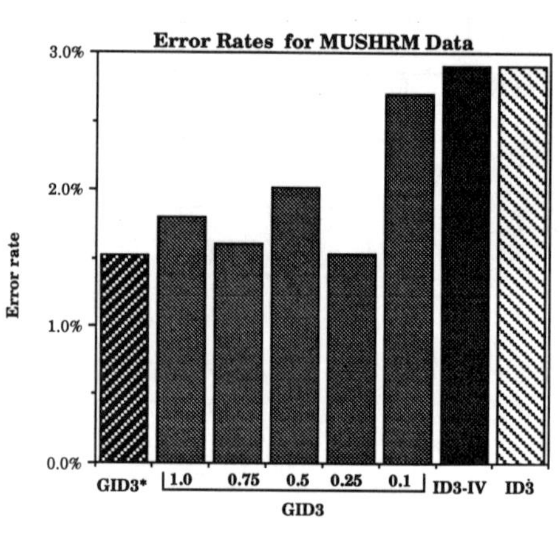

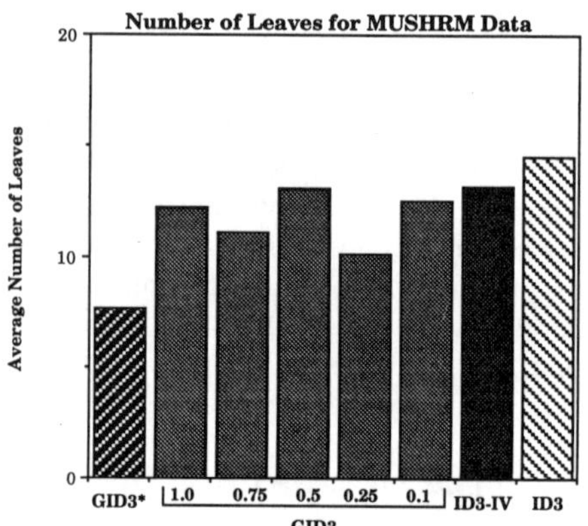

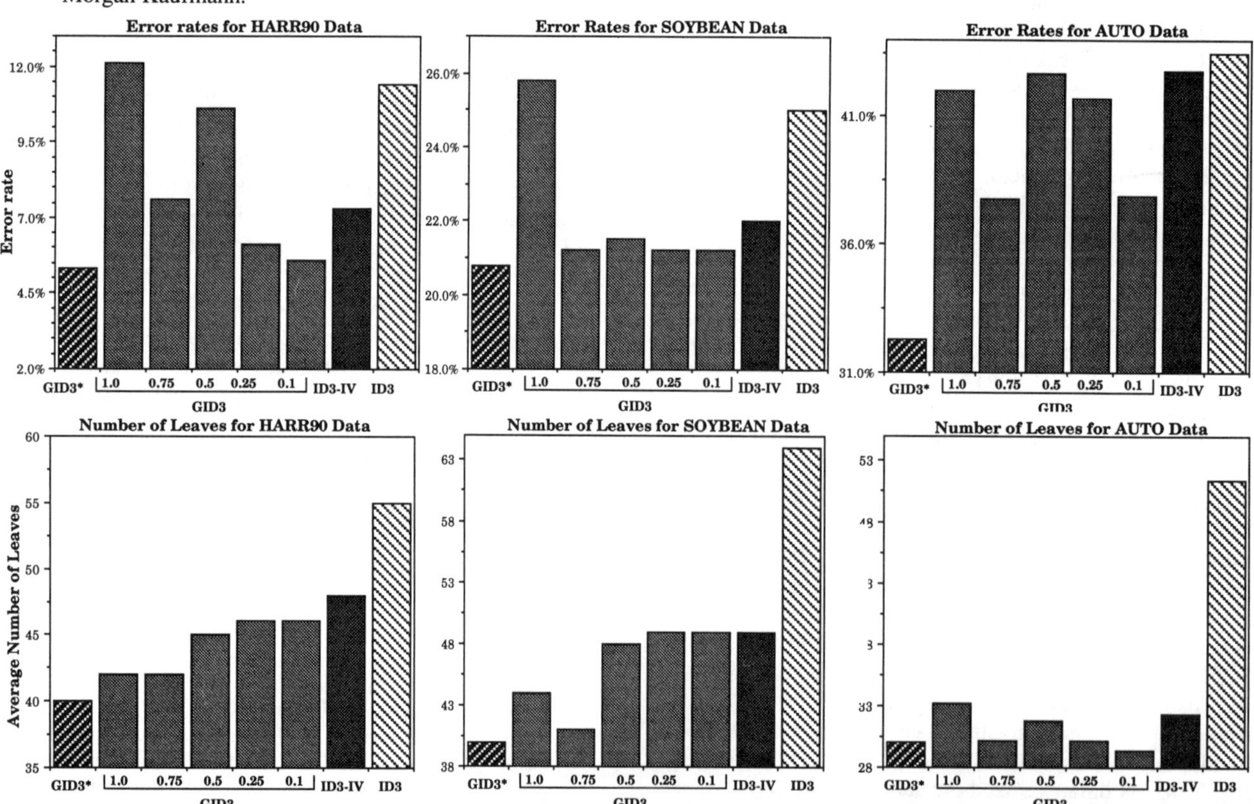

Figure 4: Results for the Four Domains of Table 1.

Induction of Multivariate Regression Trees for Design Optimization

B. Forouraghi[1,2], L.W. Schmerr[1,3] and G.M. Prabhu[2]

Center for NDE[1], Computer Science Department[2], and Aerospace/Engineering Mechanics Department[3]

Iowa State University

Ames, IA 50011

bforoura@cnde.iastate.edu, lschmerr@cnde.iastate.edu, prabhu@cs.iastate.edu

Abstract

In this paper we introduce a methodology within which multiobjective design optimization is approached from an entirely new perspective. Specifically, we demonstrate that multiple-objective optimization through induction of multivariate regression trees is a powerful alternative to the conventional vector optimization techniques. Furthermore, in an attempt to investigate the effect of various types of splitting rules on the overall performance of the optimizing system, we present a tree partitioning algorithm which utilizes a number of techniques derived from diverse fields of statistics and fuzzy logic. These include: three multivariate statistical approaches based on dispersion matrices, two newly-formulated fuzzy splitting rules based on Pearson's parametric and Kendall's nonparametric measures of association, Bellman and Zadeh's fuzzy decision-maximizing approach within an inductive framework, and finally, the multidimensional extension of a widely-used fuzzy entropy measure. In terms of potential application areas, we highlight the advantages of our methodology by presenting the problem of multiobjective design optimization of a beam structure.

1. Introduction

Most engineering design problems involve optimization of several noncommensurable objectives in presence of multiple constraints. For example, in a quality control application, the main goal may be to optimize the design of an electric discharge machining (EDM) process in which design variables such as pulse duration and discharge current directly determine multiple, conflicting responses such as electrode wear, surface roughness and metal removal rate (Osyczka 1984). Optimization of such design problems primarily involves the determination of Pareto-optimal solutions where an individual objective can be further improved only at the cost of degrading at least one other objective (Chankong & Haimes 1983). It must be emphasized that most conventional optimization methods

available to date, such as response surface methodology (Snee 1985), vector optimization techniques (Chankong & Haimes 1983) and multivariate analysis of variance (Harris 1985), typically generate Pareto-optimal 'point' solutions for which a vector-valued objective function is optimized. In many robust design applications, however, either due to economical factors or processing limitations, it is desirable to provide the designer with a range of values or 'surfaces' for design parameters for which the individual variances among responses are minimal while response means are fixed on their optimal target values (Phadke 1989). Consequently, 'surface' Pareto-optimal solutions enable the designer to examine various design scenarios without gross departures from optimal response regions.

One of the most viable artificial intelligence approaches for generating 'surface' Pareto-optimal solutions which has not been investigated before is the symbolic search technique of regression trees. Traditionally, tree-structured approaches to regression such as classification and regression trees (CART) (Breiman et al. 1984) and inductive partitioning with regression trees (IPRT) (Shien & Joseph 1992) have emphasized univariate regression analysis. These algorithms are powerful in that not only do they perform ordinary regression, but they also represent complex regression surfaces in terms of a number of simpler regression subsurfaces. Detailed examination of these subsurfaces can therefore help identify design regions where a product or process response is optimized. Hence, in addition to pinpointing optimal response regions, tree-structured approaches to optimization offer the advantage of explicating the knowledge that actually constitutes the optimality of the generated solutions. For instance, a sequential examination of various leaves in an induced regression tree can potentially show how deviations from a particular region of interest in the design space affect the overall objective functions. Lack of this type of systematic analysis is obviously one of the shortcomings of most traditional approaches to optimization including the elliptical technique for design centering (Abdel-Malek & Hassan 1991).

To summarize, in this paper we present a new framework within which multiobjective optimization is accomplished through induction of multivariate regression trees. Furthermore, we present a tree partitioning algorithm which utilizes a number of splitting rules based on concepts from statistics and fuzzy logic. Obviously, the choice of using the traditional statistical formulations in this work was instigated by the historic fact that statistics is a firmly established science with many facets which render it a particularly viable tool in many scientific applications. The theory of fuzzy sets (Gui & Georing 1990), on the other hand, is a more recently developed concept, and it too has proven to be an invaluable tool in a wide array of applications ranging from pattern recognition and clustering to design of digital circuits and relational databases (Pal 1991). In fact, within the context of multiobjective optimization, Bellman and Zadeh's fuzzy approach to optimization (Bellman & Zadeh 1970) has been widely implemented in many engineering applications such as structural optimization (Rao 1987). Therefore, in an attempt to examine the effect of various types of tree partitioning rules on the overall learning process, and also, to assess the feasibility of techniques based on fuzzy logic we describe seven splitting rules. Specifically, these include: two statistical decision rules based on dispersion matrices, a statistical measure of covariance complexity which is typically used for obtaining multivariate linear models (Bozdogan 1990), two newly-formulated fuzzy partitioning methods based on Pearson's parametric (Harris 1985) and Kendall's nonparametric (Simon 1977) measures of association, Bellman and Zadeh's decision-maximizing fuzzy approach to optimization in an inductive framework, and finally, the multidimensional extension of a widely-used measure of fuzzy entropy (Kosko 1990).

The remainder of this paper is organized as follows. Section 2 describes our methodology for transforming the problem of multiobjective optimization into induction of multivariate regression trees using various splitting criteria. Section 3 presents key results of applying techniques described in this paper to a multiobjective design problem. And finally, Section 4 summarizes the paper.

2. Multivariate Regression Trees

The basic element for inducing a multivariate regression tree is a set of training examples which provides a capsule view into the objective/constraint space. These examples essentially enable the learning algorithm to incrementally construct a complex regression surface from a number of simpler regression subsurfaces. This piecewise model construction is accomplished in a top-down fashion by successive partitioning of the training population at each level of the tree in an attempt to identify compact clusters in the response region. Examination of these clusters in turn can identify location of the optimal solution where an objective can be further improved only by degrading one or more objectives (Chankong & Haimes 1983). The following provides more details regarding the tree induction process.

Basically, given a learning sample $L = (X_1,Y_1), (X_2,Y_2),...., (X_N,Y_N)$, the learning algorithm produces a prediction rule d which is a mapping from the n-dimensional predictor or attribute space (X_i's) to the p-dimensional response (objectives and constraints) region (Y_i's). The learning sample, therefore, contains N examples where each example associates a p-dimensional response vector with an n-dimensional predictor vector. Initially, all N examples reside at the root of an empty tree. Following a divide-and-conquer approach, the root node is split into two left and right nodes such that n_1 of the original N examples fall in the left node and the remaining n_2 cases in the right node ($N = n_1 + n_2$). This splitting is facilitated by selection of an attribute and a threshold for partitioning the attribute's range into two regions (Fayyad & Irani 1992). Among all possible attribute/threshold pairs, the pair that results in the 'best' split, where the resulting left and right nodes maximize some measure of fitness, is selected and the node is split accordingly. The process of partitioning is then recursively applied to all newly generated nodes until some stopping criterion is met. In our case, a multivariate heuristic which dictates that the number of examples in a node has to be at least as large as the number of responses was used. Furthermore, after a tree is completely grown in the prescribed manner, some type of pruning will prove beneficial should the problem of overspecialization cause detrimental effects on overall efficiency of the learning system (Breiman et al. 1984).

After the learning phase is complete, the induced tree contains a number of paths which start from the root and end in a terminal node or leaf. Each path therefore pinpoints a regression subsurface by the virtue of examples that are contained in its leaf. A leaf's set of examples can be viewed as a cluster in the response region which is characterized by its mean vector μ and covariance Σ. The goodness of these clusters is in turn determined by a variety of statistical and fuzzy partitioning techniques which are explained below. In ensuing discussions assume that the response matrix at a given node is R (m by p matrix) which contains m p-dimensional response vectors and that covariance of R is Σ. For fuzzy splitting criteria further assume that R is converted to the multidimensional fuzzy set M (m by p matrix) by fuzzifying individual responses r_{ij} in R into μ_{ij} in M using (Sakawa 1983):

$$\mu_{ij} = (r_{ij} - r_j^{\ min}) / (r_j^{\ max} - r_j^{\ min}), \text{ for } i=1,...,m; \ j=1,...,p$$

It must be mentioned that for a given response j, $r_j^{\ min}$ and $r_j^{\ max}$ are found by scanning rows ($i=1,...,m$) of R, and they can be interchanged depending upon whether the goal is to maximize or minimize the given response j in the fuzzy domain.

The first two nonfuzzy splitting criteria (Methods 1 & 2) used for tree induction are the trace and determinant of the covariance matrix which denote the sum of individual response variances and the generalized variance, respectively (Everitt 1974). Minimization of trace, which totally ignores the interaction among responses, attempts to locate spherically-shaped response clusters where individual variances are minimal. On the other hand, minimization of the generalized variance, $|\Sigma|$, helps identify parallelotopes formed by response vectors which have minimal volume (Tatsuoka 1971).

The third partitioning rule (Method 3) uses Bozdogan's information-theoretic *covariance complexity* measure which is typically used for selection and evaluation of multivariate models (Bozdogan 1990). Essentially, the covariance complexity metric measures how the individual subcomponents of a model or a system interact with one another. In the case of multivariate regression trees, we use a tree as a representative of an underlying model that is to be captured through the induction process. At each level of partitioning, a given node's original population of responses R is divided into two subpopulations such that the covariance complexity of the resulting subpopulations are minimal. The overall task hence is to evaluate the degree of interaction that exists between responses in R and select partitions which result in minimal entropy or disorder. This can be accomplished by assigning the following covariance complexity measure to the covariance matrix of a population R:

$$CC(\Sigma) = 0.5 \cdot p \cdot \log_2 [trace(\Sigma)/p] - 0.5 \cdot \log_2 |\Sigma|$$

where p is the number of responses (objectives and constraints). During the tree splitting process then a parent node is split into two nodes such that the measures of covariance complexity of the newly generated nodes are minimal.

The next two partitioning criteria (Methods 4 and 5) are based on Pearson's parametric (Harris 1985) and Kendall's nonparametric (Simon 1977) measures of association ρ and τ, respectively. The main motivation here is to discover the degrees of relationship between two responses R and S which may involve linear or nonlinear components. It must be emphasized that Pearson's ρ is particularly suitable for situations where responses exhibit linear relationship. However, in many situations, linear approximations may become extremely misleading

when the relationships involve nonlinear components. To this end, Kendall developed the correlation measure τ which is not based on any parametric assumptions and is more likely to discover monotonic behavior between responses.

More formally, given the data $(R_1,S_1),...,(R_N,S_N)$, Pearson's degree of linear relationship ρ between responses R and S is:

$$\rho_{RS} = \Sigma_{i=1,...,N} [(R_i - R^{mean})(S_i - S^{mean})] / \sigma_R \cdot \sigma_S$$

where σ_R and σ_S are the standard deviations of R and S, respectively. Also, Kendall's degree of monotonic relationship between R and S is:

$$\tau_{RS} = [2/N(N-1)] \Sigma_{i<j} \Sigma [sign(R_i-R_j) \cdot sign(S_i-S_j)]$$

where the sign function takes values +1, 0 or -1 depending upon whether its argument is positive, zero or negative. For the sake of simplicity, the following generically refers to ρ and τ as χ since the forthcoming analysis is symmetric with respect to both of these measures.

The measure of association χ attempts to discover the relationship between any two given responses. For example, if R and S tend to grow in a similar direction, χ_{RS} approaches 1. Conversely, if χ_{RS} approaches -1, it is concluded that R and S grow in opposite directions. Furthermore, χ_{RS} values near 0 imply absence of any relationship (linear in the case of ρ and monotonic in the case of τ) between the two responses. Considering this, we can now incorporate elements from fuzzy logic as follows. Assume that a particular node's set M contains fuzzified responses as explained previously. Now, regardless of whether any individual response is to be maximized or minimized, the chief goal in the fuzzy domain is to locate regions where fuzzy responses approach their maximum values. Hence, given M, we obtain the matrix of correlation coefficients T (p by p matrix) where each χ_{ij} for responses i and j ($i, j = 1,...,p$) is computed using Pearson's or Kendall's measures ($\chi_{ii} = 1, \chi_{i>j} = \chi_{i<j}$). Note that since T is symmetric, only its above-diagonal elements, $\chi_{i<j}$, are considered for further calculations. These $p(p-1)/2$ elements, which are pairwise measures of association between fuzzy responses in M, take values between -1 and 1. However, the desired clusters to be found are those for which as many of these correlation values approach 1 as possible which simply means that all or most of the responses are approaching their expected extrema in a given region. To accomplish this, T's above-diagonal χ_{ij} correlation coefficients are fuzzified using either linear or exponential membership function transformations. The aspiration levels of -1 and 1 are used in the fuzzification process to indicate that correlation values of 1 are desirable to attain maximum degree of belongingness. The cluster under consideration is then

assigned the degree of trend fitness:

$$TF(M) = [\min_k \{\mu(\chi_k)\}], \text{ for } k=1,\ldots,p(p-1)/2$$

The overall objective, therefore, is to identify splits for which the produced clusters have maximal TF measures.

The sixth splitting criterion (Method 6) is based on Bellman and Zadeh's approach to multiobjective optimization (Bellman & Zadeh 1970). To give a brief overview, consider making a decision D which can be seen as a confluence of n objectives and constraints denoted by responses $R_1,\ldots, R_n$. The optimal decision in the fuzzy domain then can simply be viewed as the intersection of fuzzy sets $\mu(R_1),\ldots,\mu(R_n)$ where each $\mu(R_i)$ is calculated using appropriate membership function transformations. More formally, the optimization task can be formulated as finding an optimum predictor vector X* for which the measure $\mu_D(X^*) = \min_i \{\mu(R_i(X))\}$ is maximized. Typically, after proper transformation of the problem at hand into the fuzzy domain, X* is found using nonlinear programming (Rao 1987). In our framework, however, Bellman-Zadeh's approach is used for splitting a node such that the measure:

$$BZ(M) = [\max_i \min_j \{\mu_{ij}\}],$$
$$\text{for } i=1,\ldots,m \text{ and } j=1,\ldots,p$$

is maximized for a particular multidimensional fuzzy set M under consideration.

And Finally, the last inductive partitioning technique (Method 7) to be discussed relies on fuzzy entropy (Kosko 1990). Basically, given a fuzzy set A with its complement A^c, fuzzy entropy of A:

$$FE(A) = C^o(A, A^c) / C^u(A, A^c)$$

measures how fuzzy actually A is, where C^o and C^u denote counts of overlap and underlap between A and A^c, respectively. In a top-down inductive approach, the fuzzy entropy measure can be used to identify fuzzy clusters M which exhibit minimal amount of fuzziness at each partitioning level. The basic definition of entropy, however, has to be extended so that fuzziness of the multidimensional fuzzy set M can be calculated. To accomplish this, first, M's complement, M^c, is calculated where each μ_{ij}^c in M^c is complement of μ_{ij} in M. Then, fuzzy sets I and U (both m by p matrices), which denote the intersection and union of M and M^c, are calculated where elements i_{ij} in I and u_{ij} in U are $\min(\mu_{ij}, \mu_{ij}^c)$ and $\max(\mu_{ij}, \mu_{ij}^c)$, respectively. Consequently, we define the fuzzy entropy measure of a multidimensional fuzzy set M as:

$$FE(M) = [\max_i \min_j \{i_{ij}\}] / [\max_i \min_j \{u_{ij}\}],$$
$$\text{for } i=1,\ldots,m \text{ and } j = 1,\ldots,p$$

During the course of tree induction, then, the attribute/threshold pair for which the resulting clusters have minimal fuzzy entropy are selected and the node is split

accordingly.

3. Optimization of a Beam Structure

In this section we present the problem of multiobjective optimum design of a beam structure. Given the design variables X_1 and X_2 which respectively represent the length of the part 1 of the beam and the interior diameter of the beam, the design task involves minimization of the three objectives of beam volume (F_1), static compliance of the beam (F_2) and the bending stress of the beam (σ_g), respectively (for more details see Osyczka 1984).

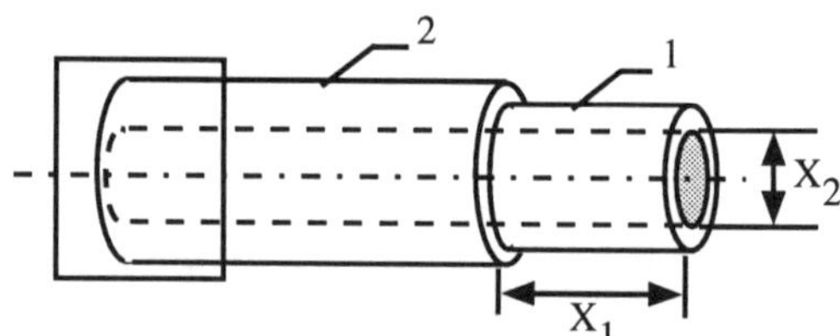

Figure 1. The beam structure

In regards to preparation of learning and testing cases, it was decided to uniformly sample the design region (X_1, X_2) in 900 distinct points between (10,40) and (300,75.2) in order to ensure that the response surfaces were adequately represented to the learning algorithm. Following a widely-used variance-stabilizing technique, the objective and constraint responses were transformed into log domain (Hahn 1971) which helped the overall learning efficiency for parametric as well as nonparametric induction criteria. The 900 points were then randomly shuffled and divided into two sets of size 450 each, namely, T_{450} and L_{450}. The set T_{450} was dedicated entirely to testing purposes while L_{450} was used for the learning process. Samples of size 100, 150 and 200 were then randomly drawn from the overall learning set L_{450}. The learning phase then proceeded by inducing a regression tree on each of the randomly drawn samples L_{100}, L_{150} and L_{200} for each of the fuzzy and nonfuzzy splitting methods. This entire process of random selection of training samples, learning and testing was repeated a total of five times for each tree-growing technique so that results could be represented with 95% confidence

After completion of the learning phase, relative regression errors which normally vary between 0.0 (perfect regression model) and 1.0 (poor model) were computed for each induced tree. Our error analysis is similar to CART's (Breiman et al. 1984) except that it was extended for multivariate cases by substituting Mahalanobis distances (Everitt 1974) for ordinary Euclidean-based error distances in order to account for covariances that exist

Method	L_{100}	L_{150}	L_{200}
1	0.0060 ± 0.0015	0.0044 ± 0.0014	0.0036 ± 0.0018
2	0.0076 ± 0.0031	0.0050 ± 0.0019	0.0044 ± 0.0022
3	0.0068 ± 0.0010	0.0050 ± 0.0019	0.0026 ± 0.0006
4	0.0046 ± 0.0020	0.0040 ± 0.0008	0.0040 ± 0.0042
5	0.0044 ± 0.0011	0.0038 ± 0.0018	0.0022 ± 0.0005
6	0.0050 ± 0.0012	0.0040 ± 0.0029	0.0026 ± 0.0014
7	0.0042 ± 0.0016	0.0034 ± 0.0018	0.0098 ± 0.0209

Table 1. Relative regression errors with 95% confidence

among responses. Table 1 summarizes relative regression errors for tree-partitioning methods 1 through 7.

The performance measures shown in Table 1 reveal two important facts. First, the overall inductive generalization power, and consequently, the regression accuracy of all partitioning techniques generally improves as the size of training sets increases from 100 to 200. And second, the accuracy of regression surfaces obtained through the use of fuzzy splitting criteria matches, and in few instances surpasses, the accuracy of solutions generated by well-established statistical techniques.

Relative regression errors are a good indicator of how an induced tree generalizes given a learning sample and a testing sample. The litmus test, however, lies in detailed examination of non-inferior solutions arrived at by a regression tree. These optimal solutions are represented by the terminal nodes of an induced tree and essential indicate 'tight' clusters in the response region. Table 2 summarizes some of the solutions generated by each induction method on training samples of size 200 which produced the most accurate results. Furthermore, in order to verify a tree's predicted range of responses for a specific range of design variables, we employed the following technique. The objective and constraint functions were evaluated for roughly about 5000 points in an induced tree's predicted optimum design region. Means and standard deviations of the generated responses were then computed to verify the tightness of clusters which were formed in the predicted response region. These verified solutions appear in the last column of Table 2.

A detailed examination of Table 2 reveals that in contrast to traditional multiobjective techniques which result in distinct Pareto-optimal point-solutions, our technique identifies Pareto-optimal regions. For example, in contrast to the two optimal solutions reported by Osyczka (marked "O") which were obtained using an ordinary vector optimization technique consider the solution which was jointly obtained by methods 2 and 3. This solution recommends the design region $(X_1,X_2) = ([44.7, 64.8], [65.3, 75.2])$ where the designer can safely choose any values for design parameters X_1 and X_2 within the proposed bounds. The corresponding objective and constraint functions, as predicted by the learning algorithm,

Method	Optimum Values of Design Variables (X_1, X_2)		Predicted Pareto-Optimal $(F_1 \times 10^6$	$F_2 \times 10^{-3}$	$\sigma_g)$	Verified Pareto-Optimal $(F_1 \times 10^6$	$F_2 \times 10^{-3}$	$\sigma_g)$
"O"	(237.0, 66.4)		(3.7	0.425	107.7)	(3.7	0.425	107.7)
	(224.7, 58.6)		(4.5	0.382	75.3)	(4.5	0.382	75.3)
1	[149.6, 176.0]	[68.3, 71.0]	(3.5	0.438	90.1)	$(3.5 \pm 0.09$	0.438 ± 0.007	$92.2 \pm 7.2)$
	[118.3, 149.6]	[68.3, 71.0]	(3.6	0.436	78.8)	$(3.6 \pm 0.09$	0.435 ± 0.007	$75.8 \pm 7.0)$
2, 3	[44.7, 64.80]	[65.3, 75.2]	(3.7	0.442	39.1)	$(3.7 \pm 0.30$	0.441 ± 0.023	$35.6 \pm 10.5)$
4	[10.0, 54.70]	[71.0, 73.7]	(3.6	0.455	18.6)	$(3.6 \pm 0.09$	0.455 ± 0.007	$23.6 \pm 9.7)$
	[118.3, 211.7]	[68.3, 71.0]	(3.5	0.439	93.9)	$(3.5 \pm 0.11$	0.439 ± 0.008	$93.4 \pm 16.4)$
5, 6	[124.8, 152.4]	[68.3, 71.0]	(3.6	0.436	78.0)	$(3.6 \pm 0.09$	0.436 ± 0.007	$78.5 \pm 6.7)$
	[47.4, 102.4]	[71.0, 73.7]	(3.4	0.456	60.7)	$(3.5 \pm 0.09$	0.456 ± 0.007	$54.8 \pm 12.5)$
7	[132.4, 159.9]	[68.3, 71.0]	(3.6	0.436	82.7)	$(3.6 \pm 0.09$	0.437 ± 0.007	$82.7 \pm 6.9)$
	[72.4, 132.4]	[68.3, 71.0]	(3.7	0.434	66.8)	$(3.7 \pm 0.10$	0.434 ± 0.006	$58.0 \pm 10.4)$

Table 2. Optimal solutions produced by various fuzzy and nonfuzzy splitting criteria

take the values $(3.7\times10^6, 0.442\times10^{-3}, 39.1)$ while thorough examination of roughly 5000 points in this particular design region verifies that actual responses center around the values $(3.7\times10^6 \pm 0.30\times10^6, 0.441\times10^{-3} \pm 0.023\times10^{-3}, 35.6 \pm 10.5)$ which are still well within optimal bounds. Osyczka's solutions, on the other hand, merely indicate that (237.0, 66.4) or (224.7, 58.6) are optimal design parameter values, and they are rigid in the sense that they fail to provide the designer with a range within which different design scenarios can be examined and subsequently realized without gross departures from optimal response regions.

4. Conclusions

In this paper we introduced a new methodology within which the problem of multiobjective optimization is transformed into induction of multivariate regression trees. Moreover, we demonstrated how the tree growing process can be accomplished by utilizing a number of concepts from diverse fields of statistics and fuzzy logic. In particular, seven splitting criteria were devised and implemented which include: three statistical methods based on dispersion matrices, two newly formulated fuzzy approaches based on Pearson's parametric and Kendall's nonparametric measures of association, Bellman-Zadeh's fuzzy approach to optimization in an inductive framework, and finally, the multidimensional extension of a fuzzy measure of entropy.

We also compared the overall performance of the learning system for the fuzzy and nonfuzzy methods. Our empirical results indicate that utilization of fuzzy splitting criteria offers a degree of flexibility in terms of the learning system's efficiency which traditional multivariate statistical methods lack. To illustrate this point, we presented the problem of multiobjective design of of a beam structure.

Acknowledgments

This work was supported by the Center for NDE, Iowa State University, Ames, Iowa.

References

Abdel-Malek, H.L., and Hassan, A.S. 1991. The Elliptical Technique for Design Centering and Region Approximation. *IEEE Transactions on Computer-Aided Design* (10)8:1006-1013.

Bellman, R.E., and Zadeh, L.A. 1970. Decision Making in a Fuzzy Environment. *Management Science* (17)4:141-163.

Bozdogan, H. 1990. On the Information-Based Measure of Covariance Complexity and Its Application to the Evaluation of Multivariate Linear Models. *Communication in Statistics--Theory & Methodology* (19)1:221-279.

Breiman, L.; Friedman, J.H.; Olshen, R.A.; and Stone, J.S. 1984. *Classification and Regression Trees*, The Wadsworth & Brooks/Cole Advanced Books & Software.

Chankong, V., and Haimes, Y.Y. 1983. Optimization-Based Methods for Multiobjective Decision-Making: An Overview. *Large Scale Systems: Theory and Applications* 5:1-33.

Everitt, B. 1974. *Cluster Analysis*. Wiley & Sons.

Fayyad, U.M., and Irani, K.B. 1992. On the handling of Continuous-Valued Attributes in Decision Tree Generation. *Machine Learning* (81)1: 87-102.

Gui, X.Q., and Georing, C.E. 1990. Introduction to Fuzzy Set Theory and Applications. *Transactions of ASAE* (33)1:306-313.

Hahn, G.J. 1971). How Abnormal Is Normality? *Journal of Quality Technology* (3)1:18-22.

Harris, R.J. 1985. *A Primer of Multivariate Statistics*. Academic Press, Inc.

Kosko, B. 1990. Fuzziness vs. Probability. *International Journal of General Systems* (17):211-240.

Osyczka, A. 1984. *Multicriterion Optimization in Engineering*. Ellis Harwood Limited.

Pal, S.K. 1991. Fuzzy Tools For the Management of Uncertainty in Pattern Recognition Image Analysis, Vision and Expert Systems. *International Journal of Systems Sciences* (22)3:511-549.

Phadke, M. 1989. *Quality Engineering Using Robust Design*. Prentice Hall.

Rao, S.S. 1987. Multi-Objective Optimization of Fuzzy Structural systems. *International Journal for Numerical Methods in Engineering* (24):1157-1171.

Sakawa, M. 1983. Interactive Fuzzy Decision Making for Multiobjective Linear Programming Problems and Its Applications. *IFAC Fuzzy Information* 295-300.

Shien, D.S., and Joseph, B. 1992. Exploratory Data Analysis Using Inductive Partitioning and Regression Trees. *Industrial Chemical Engineering Research* (31):1989-1998.

Simon, G. 1977. Multivariate Generalization of Kendall's Tau with Application to Data Reduction. *Journal of the American Statistical Association*, (72)358: 367-376.

Snee, R.D. 1985. Computer Aided Design of Experiments. *Journal of Quality Technology*, (17)4:222-235.

Tatsuoka, M.M. 1971. *Multivariate Analysis: Techniques for Educational and Psychological Research*. Wiley &Sons.

Bottom-Up Induction of
Oblivious Read-Once Decision Graphs:
Strengths and Limitations

Ron Kohavi
Computer Science Department
Stanford University
Stanford, CA 94305
`ronnyk@CS.Stanford.EDU`

Abstract

We report improvements to HOODG, a supervised learning algorithm that induces concepts from labelled instances using oblivious, read-once decision graphs as the underlying hypothesis representation structure. While it is shown that the greedy approach to variable ordering is locally optimal, we also show an inherent limitation of all bottom-up induction algorithms, including HOODG, that construct such decision graphs bottom-up by minimizing the width of levels in the resulting graph. We report our empirical experiments that demonstrate the algorithm's generalization power.

Introduction

In supervised classification learning, one tries to find a structure, such as a decision-tree, a neural net, or a Boolean formula, that can be used to accurately predict the label of novel instances. A given concept can be represented by different structures that differ in many aspects, including comprehensibility, storage size, and query time.

Decision trees provide one structure that is commonly constructed using top-down induction techniques (Quinlan 1992; 1986; Moret 1982). However, the tree structure used to represent the hypothesized target concept suffers from some well-known problems, most notably the replication problem and the fragmentation problem (Pagallo & Haussler 1990). The replication problem forces duplication of subtrees in disjunctive concepts such as $(A \wedge B) \vee (C \wedge D)$; the fragmentation problem causes partitioning of the data into fragments, when a high-arity attribute is tested at a node. Both problems reduce the number of instances at lower nodes in the tree—instances needed for statistical significance of tests performed during the tree construction process.

In (Kohavi 1994), Oblivious read-Once Decision Graphs (OODGs) were introduced as an alternative representation structure for supervised classification learning. OODGs retain most of the advantages of decision trees, while overcoming the two problems mentioned above. OODGs are similar to Ordered Binary Decision Diagrams (OBDDs) (Bryant 1986), which have been used in the engineering community to represent state-graph models of systems, allowing verification of finite-state systems with up to 10^{120} states (Burch, Clarke, & Long 1991). We refer the reader to (Kohavi 1994) for a discussion of related work.

OODGs have a different bias from that of decision trees, and thus some concepts that are hard to represent as trees are easy to represent as OODGs, and vice-versa. Since OODGs are graphs, they are easy for humans to perceive, and should be preferred over other representations (*e.g.*, neural nets) whenever it is important to comprehend the meaning and structure of the induced concept.

In this paper, we investigate the strength and limitations of inducing OODGs bottom-up using HOODG, a greedy hill-climbing algorithm for inducing OODGs, previously introduced in (Kohavi 1994). We show that on the one hand, a greedy choice of variables always yields an ordering that is locally optimal for fully specified functions and cannot be improved by a single exchange of adjacent variables (a technique sometimes used in the engineering community). On the other hand, there is an optimization step in the algorithm that is shown to be intractable, unless P=NP.

In the next two sections, we describe the OODG structure, some of its properties, and the framework of the bottom-up induction algorithm. We then describe the HOODG algorithm, discuss the heuristics and improvements made since its introduction, and new theoretical results. We follow with the experimental results, and conclude with a summary and discussion of future work.

Oblivious Read-Once Decision Graphs

In this section, we formally define the structure of decision graphs and then specialize it to oblivious, read-once decision graphs (OODGs).

Given n discrete variables (attributes), $X_1, X_2, \ldots, X_n$, with domains $D_1, \ldots, D_n$ respectively, the **instance space** $\mathcal{X}$ is the cross-product of the domains, *i.e.*, $D_1 \times \cdots \times D_n$. A **$k$-categorization function** is a function f mapping each instance in the instance space to one of k categories, *i.e.*, $f : \mathcal{X} \mapsto \{0, \ldots, k-1\}$. Without loss of generality, we assume that for each category there is at least one instance in $\mathcal{X}$ that maps to it.

A **decision graph** for a k-categorization function over variables $X_1, X_2, \ldots, X_n$ with domains $D_1, D_2, \ldots, D_n$, is a directed acyclic graph (DAG) with the following properties:

1. There are exactly k nodes, called **category nodes**, that are labelled $0, 1, \ldots, k-1$, and have outdegree zero.

2. Non-category nodes are called **branching nodes.** Each branching node is labelled by some variable X_i and has $|D_i|$ outgoing edges, each labelled by a distinct value from D_i.

3. There is one distinguished node—the **root**—that is the only node with indegree zero.

The category assigned by a decision graph to a given variable assignment (an instance), is determined by tracing the unique path from the root to a category node, branching according to the labels on the edges.

In a **read-once** decision graph, each variable occurs at most once along any computation path. In a **levelled** decision graph, the nodes are partitioned into a sequence of pairwise disjoint sets, the levels, such that outgoing edges from each level terminate at the next level. An **oblivious** decision graph is a levelled graph such that all nodes at a given level are labelled by the same variable. An oblivious decision graph is **reduced** if there do not exist two distinct nodes at the same level that branch in exactly the same way on the same values. If two such nodes exist, they can be united.

An **OODG** is a reduced oblivious, read-once decision graph. The **size** of an OODG is the number of nodes in the graph, and the **width** of a level is the number of nodes at that level. A **constant node** is a node, such that all edges emanating from it, terminate at the same node of the subsequent level. Figure 1 shows an OODG for 3-bit parity with one totally irrelevant attribute.

OODGs have many interesting properties. These include: an OODG is canonical for any total function if an ordering on the variables is given; any symmetric function (*e.g.*, parity, majority, and m of n) can be represented by an OODG of size $O(n^2)$; and the width of levels in OODGs is bounded by $\min\left\{2^i, k^{2^{(n-i)}}\right\}$ for Boolean inputs. We refer the reader to (Kohavi 1994) for a more detailed description of these properties.

Bottom-Up Construction of OODGs

In this section we present an algorithm for constructing a reduced OODG given the full (labelled) instance space. The algorithm is recursive and nondeterministic. For simplicity of notation, we assume Boolean variables and an arbitrary number of categories.

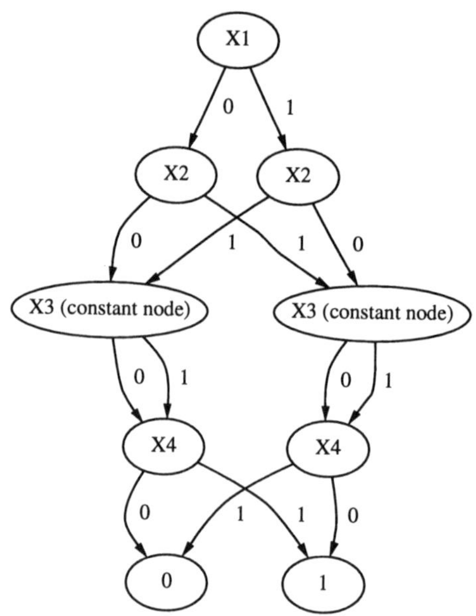

Figure 1: An OODG for 3-bit parity:
$$f = X_1 \oplus X_2 \oplus X_4 \ .$$
($\oplus$ denotes exclusive-or, X_3 is totally irrelevant.)

The input to the algorithm is a set of sets, $\{C_0, C_1, \ldots, C_{k-1}\}$, where each set C_i is the set of all instances labelled with category i. The output of the algorithm is an OODG that correctly categorizes the training set.

The algorithm, shown in Figure 2, creates sets of instances, such that each set corresponds to one node in the graph (the input sets corresponding to the category nodes). Intuitively, we would like an instance in a set C_i to reach node V_i (corresponding to the set), when the instance's path is traced from the root of the completed OODG, branching at branching nodes according to the attribute values.

Given the input, the algorithm nondeterministically selects a variable X to test at the penultimate level of the OODG. It then creates new sets of instances (corresponding to the nodes in the penultimate level of the final OODG), which are projections of the original instances with variable X deleted. The sets are created so that a set C'_{xy} (which matches a branching node V'_{xy}) contains all projections of instances that are in C_x when augmented with $X = 0$, and in C_y when augmented with $X = 1$. In the graph, the branching node corresponding to C'_{xy} will have the edge labelled 0 terminating at node V_x, and the edge labelled 1 terminating at node V_y.

The new sets now form a smaller problem over $n-1$ variables, and the algorithm calls itself recursively to compute the rest of the OODG with the nonempty sets of the new level serving as the input. The recursion stops when the input to the algorithm is a single set, possibly consisting of the *null* instance (0 variables).

Input: k sets $C_0, \ldots, C_{k-1}$, such that $\mathcal{X} = \bigcup_{i=0}^{k-1} C_i$ (the whole instance space).
Output: Reduced OODG correctly categorizing all instances in $\mathcal{X}$.

1. If $(k = 1)$, then return a graph with one node.

2. Nondeterministically select a variable X to be deleted from the instances.

3. Project the instances in $C_0, \ldots, C_{k-1}$ onto the instance space $\mathcal{X}'$, such that variable X is deleted. Formally, if X is the ith variable,

$$\mathcal{X}' \leftarrow \pi_{(X_1, \ldots, X_{i-1}, X_{i+1}, \ldots, X_n)} \bigcup_{i=0}^{k-1} C_i \quad \text{(where } \pi_{(\vec{x})} \text{ means project on } \vec{x}) .$$

4. For all $i, j \in \{0, \ldots, k-1\}$, let C'_{ij} be the set containing instances from $\mathcal{X}'$ such that the instances are in set C_i when augmented with $X = 0$, and in C_j when augmented with $X = 1$. Formally,

$$C'_{ij} = \left\{ \langle X_1, \ldots, X_{i-1}, X_{i+1}, \ldots, X_n \rangle \;\middle|\; \begin{array}{l} \langle X_1, \ldots, X_{i-1}, 0, X_{i+1}, \ldots, X_n \rangle \in C_i \text{ and} \\ \langle X_1, \ldots, X_{i-1}, 1, X_{i+1}, \ldots, X_n \rangle \in C_j \end{array} \right\} .$$

5. Let k' be the number of non-empty sets from $\{C'_{ij}\}$. Call the algorithm recursively with the k' non-empty sets, and let G be the OODG returned.

6. Label the k' leaf nodes of G, corresponding to the non-empty sets C'_{ij} with variable X. Create a new level with k nodes corresponding to the sets $C_0, \ldots, C_{k-1}$. From the node corresponding to each C'_{ij}, create two edges: one labelled 0, terminating at the category node corresponding to C_i, and the other labelled 1, terminating at the category node corresponding to C_j.

7. Return the augmented OODG.

Figure 2: A nondeterministic algorithm for learning OODGs.

HOODG: A Hill Climbing Algorithm For Constructing OODGs

In this section, we address the two problems ignored in the algorithm previously described:

1. Ordering the variables for selection (Step 2).

2. If the full instance space is not available, the set C'_{ij} in Step 4 may be not uniquely defined, and there may be many sets consistent with the projection.

Ordering the Variables

Given the full instance space, it is possible to find the optimal ordering using dynamic programming, by checking 2^n different orderings (Friedman & Suppowit 1990). Since this is impractical in practice, our implementation greedily select the variable that yields the smallest width at the next level, excluding constant nodes. We break ties in favor of minimizing the number of edges. If all nodes are constant nodes (the attribute is deemed irrelevant), we do another lookahead step and pick the variable that maximizes the number of irrelevant attributes at the next level.

This heuristic is different from the original one proposed in (Kohavi 1994). The main difference is the fact that the minimization is done excluding constant nodes. By ignoring constant nodes, the algorithm scales better when the target concept is decomposable. For example, suppose the target concept can be decomposed into a disjunction of three subproblems on disjoint variables, such as the following target concept:

$$f = (A \wedge B \wedge C) \vee (D \wedge E) \vee (F \wedge G)$$

An OODG with leaves 0 and 1 that implements $A \wedge B \wedge C$ can be extended by connecting an OODG that implements the other two subproblems into the 0 leaf. The 1 leaf can be made into a series of constant nodes at the lower levels until the 1 node of the final OODG is reached. When the bottom-up construction takes place, we would like to take into account only the number of non-constant nodes, as these indicate the actual dependencies on the variable.

The following theorem shows that in a bottom-up construction, where the full instance space is available, the above heuristic is locally optimal and cannot be improved by a single exchange of neighboring variables. Such exchanges were done to improve the size of OBDDs when created top-down in (Fujita, Matsunaga, & Kakuda 1991).

Theorem 1 *If during a bottom-up construction, the variable that creates the smallest width at each level is chosen, no exchange of two adjacent variables will improve the size of the OODG or OBDD.*

The proof is based on the fact that exchanging neighboring variables changes the number of nodes at only one of the two levels.

Incomplete Projections

If the full instance space is not given, there will be projections of instances for which some values of the deleted attribute will be missing (*e.g.*, a projected instance must branch to some node on values 0 and 2, but the destinations for values 1 and 3 are unknown).

Call such projections *Incomplete Projections,* or **IPs.** Assigning values to the missing destinations of the IPs constitutes a bias, since it determines how unseen instances will be classified.

Following Occam's razor, we would like to find the smallest OODG consistent with the data (we assume no noise). We are thus looking for a minimal set of branching nodes that "covers" all projections, *i.e.,* a minimal cover.

An IP is **consistent** with another projection, P (at the same level of the graph), if they do not have conflicting destinations on the same value of the deleted variable. An IP is **included** in another projection, P, if they are consistent, and if all destinations defined for the IP are also defined for the projection P. (Note that *included* is an asymmetric relation.)

The greedy strategy for assigning incomplete projections to nodes, starts creating projection sets (branching nodes) from projections having the greatest number of known destinations, and then from projections with fewer known destinations. Following a least commitment strategy, each projection is placed in a projection set it is included in, whenever possible (hence not forcing a new destination); otherwise, it is placed in a set where it is consistent with all instances, if possible; otherwise, a new projection set is created, consisting of the single projection.

Our heuristic breaks ties in favor of projection set that has the most instances differing by at most one bit, and given equality, breaks ties in favor of adding the minimum number of new destinations (again, least commitment). These tie-breakers were added to the original heuristic, presented in (Kohavi 1994), after it was noted that there are many cases where they are needed. We have tried different tie-breaking heuristics, and many reasonable heuristics perform better than the arbitrary tie-breaking originally used.

As the following results show, it is unlikely that an algorithm finding the smallest consistent OODG will be found, even for a given ordering. In (Takenaga & Yajima 1993), it was shown that identifying whether there exists an OBDD with k nodes that is consistent with labelled instances is NP-complete, and this result applies to OODGs too. The following theorem shows that minimizing even a single level in an OBDD or OODG is NP-complete:

Theorem 2 (Hardness of minimal projection)
The following decision problem is NP-complete:
Given a set of labelled instances, an ordering on the variables, and two positive integers w and ℓ; is there an OODG (or OBDD) that has width $\leq w$ at level ℓ, and that correctly classifies all instances?

The reduction was done from graph k-colorability (chromatic number) using only Boolean variables. This is a strong negative result, since it is known that the chromatic number of a graph cannot be approximated to within any constant multiplicative factor unless P=NP (Lund & Yannakakis 1993). Note that this result applies to any algorithm that attempts to minimize the width of an OODG at a given level, whether done incrementally as in HOODG, or otherwise.

Experimental Results

We now turn to a series of experiments that attempt to evaluate the performance of the HOODG algorithm. Table 1 shows the accuracy results[1] for ID3, C4.5 (Quinlan 1992), Oliver's decision graph algorithm, DGRAPH (Oliver 1993), and HOODG, on the following datasets that we generated or retrieved from (Murphy & Aha 1994):

Monk 1,2 In (Thrun *et al.* 1991), 24 authors compared 25 machine learning algorithms on problems called the monks problems. In this domain there are six attributes with discrete values. The Monk 1 problem has a single training set, but it is too easy. To make the problem harder, we ran the algorithms on 10 sets of 60 instances each—about half of the original training set. The test set is the whole space.

In the Monk 2 problem, we ran the algorithms on 10 sets of 169 instances each, the same size as the original training set. The problem is very hard, but becomes easier under local encoding, where each attribute value is assigned an indicator variable. This encoding was used for neural networks in the comparison.

Parity The target concept is the parity of 5 bits out of 10 bits with 5 (uniformly random) irrelevant bits. We averaged 10 sets of 100 instances each.

Vote The vote database includes votes for each of the U.S. House of Representatives Congressmen on 16 key votes. The classes are Democrat and Republican. There are 435 instances with duplicates. We ran ten-fold cross-validation.

Breast In the Wisconsin breast-cancer database, the task is to predict reoccurrence or non-reoccurrence of breast-cancer sometime after an operation. There are nine attributes, each with 10 discretized values. There are 699 instances with duplicates. We ran ten-fold cross validation on the original encoding and then using binary encoding.

The worst-case time complexity of the HOODG algorithm is $O(ns^2 + is^2(n-1))$ per level, where i is the number of irrelevant attributes at the given level, and s is the number of projected instances at that level. This assumes that the number of values per attribute

---

[1]C4.5 runs were made with -m 1, and the better result of running with and without the -s flag for grouping. Oliver's DGRAPH was run with 2 levels of lookahead and with different p values (we give the one that yields the minimum message length as suggested by Oliver). HOODG was run without the 2-level lookahead on irrelevant attributes for the Breast-cancer database because the lookahead was too expensive time-wise.

Data Set	ID3	C4.5	DGRAPH	HOODG
Monk 1 (60/432)	$80.32\% \pm 6.45\%$	$83.56\% \pm 9.27\%$	$73.89\% \pm 2.68\%$	✓★ $100.00\% \pm 0.00\%$
Monk 2 (169/432)	$69.17\% \pm 2.01\%$	$72.73\% \pm 5.66\%$	$66.67\% \pm 1.46\%$	✓★ $91.30\% \pm 1.98\%$
Monk 2 local	$78.08\% \pm 6.66\%$	$75.75\% \pm 7.83\%$	$67.13\% \pm 0.00\%$	✓★ $99.14\% \pm 0.62\%$
Parity (100/1024)	$54.00\% \pm 2.68\%$	$51.56\% \pm 2.32\%$	$50.00\% \pm 0.00\%$	✓★ $100.00\% \pm 0.00\%$
Vote (435/XV)	$93.57\% \pm 4.00\%$	✓ $95.43\% \pm 4.31\%$	✓★ $95.63\% \pm 3.69\%$	✓ $94.03\% \pm 3.46\%$
Breast (699/XV)	✓ $94.42\% \pm 4.68\%$	✓★ $94.64\% \pm 6.16\%$	✓ $93.85\% \pm 4.26\%$	$86.99\% \pm 6.50\%$
Breast binary	✓ $94.01\% \pm 4.57\%$	✓★ $96.07\% \pm 6.16\%$	$92.84\% \pm 5.94\%$	✓ $95.03\% \pm 2.77\%$

Table 1: Comparison of different algorithms. Results are averages of 10 runs with standard deviation after the $\pm$ sign. Number in parentheses denote the training set size and test set size; XV means ten-fold cross validation. "local" means local encoding, "binary" means binary encoding. The best accuracy for each dataset is shown with a star (★), and accuracies within one half standard deviation of the best, are marked with a checkmark (✓). Such small differences in accuracy indicate comparable performance.

is a bounded constant. If we ignore the two-level lookahead for irrelevant attributes, the time complexity of the overall algorithm is $O(n^2 m^2)$, where m is the number of instances in the training set.

Running on a SPARCstation ELC, the execution time for HOODG varies from about 3 seconds for Monk 1 and Parity5+5, to 20 minutes for the vote database. The large time requirement in the vote database is due to the large correlations between the attributes, which make many attributes weakly relevant (John, Kohavi, & Pfleger 1994), thus forcing a two-ply lookahead.

HOODG does much better on all the artificial data sets, and about the same on the real datasets, except for breast-cancer in the original encoding, where we noted that its myopic hill-climbing forces a ten-way split at the root variable. This is circumvented in the binary encoding because the equivalent of a multi-way split requires extra non-constant intermediate nodes, thus penalizing such a split[2].

We now turn to further empirical experiments to help us evaluate the appropriateness of the algorithm and the structure. We picked two artificial domains on which to conduct further experiments. The first was the Monk 1 problem mentioned in the previous section. The second was the multiplexer problem. In the multiplexer problem, there are n "address bits" and 2^n "data" bits. An instance is labelled positive if the data bit indicated by the address bits is on. The structure of the smallest target concept is a tree, even if the concept space allows general graphs. The n address bits are tested first, and then all the (different) data bits are tested on the same level. There is no advantage in trying to construct a graph or OODG; moreover, one would expect the oblivious restriction to make the task harder for HOODG, since each data bit would need to be tested on a different level. As noted in (Quinlan 1988), this domain is hard for decision trees also, since

the entropy criteria favors a data bit at the root. The learning curves in Figure 3 show the accuracy of the hypotheses versus the training set size for HOODG and ID3. Each data point in the graph is the average of 10 runs on uniformly sampled training sets for that size. The twenty training set sizes were chosen at increments equal to 5% of the instance space.

The graphs clearly show that for Monk 1, HOODG has a large advantage over ID3, mainly because the concept is graph-like. HOODG quickly reaches the 100% level, while ID3 trails behind. Only at 410 instances, do all 10 runs of ID3 yield an accuracy of 100%. In the multiplexer domain, the algorithms perform roughly the same (within one standard deviation except for one data point at 42).

Summary and Future Work

We have described OODG, a structure for representing concepts, and a hill-climbing algorithm, HOODG, for inferring OODGs from labelled instances. Tie-breaking heuristics were added to the original HOODG algorithm, improving the accuracy and learning rate.

Although limited in its myopic view, the HOODG algorithm performs well, especially if the concept is graph-like (*e.g.*, Monk 1, Monk 2), or has totally irrelevant attributes (John, Kohavi, & Pfleger 1994). The algorithm clearly outperforms other algorithms on the artificial domains tested, and is comparable on real domains, even though it currently does not deal with noise and probably overfits the data. Theorem 1 shows that the greedy approach always creates an OODG that is locally optimal if the full instance space is given. Theorem 2 shows that a multi-level projection step that finds the minimal width is intractable in the worst case (unless P=NP).

Deeper lookahead for variable selection is an obvious possible extension, especially since one motivation for growing the graph from the bottom is the asymmetric bound on the width at the different levels.

The OODG structure can be extended to allow splits on ranges and continuous values, but more research is

---

[2]The multi-way split problem suggests using a different measure, perhaps similar to Quinlan's gain-ratio (Quinlan 1986).

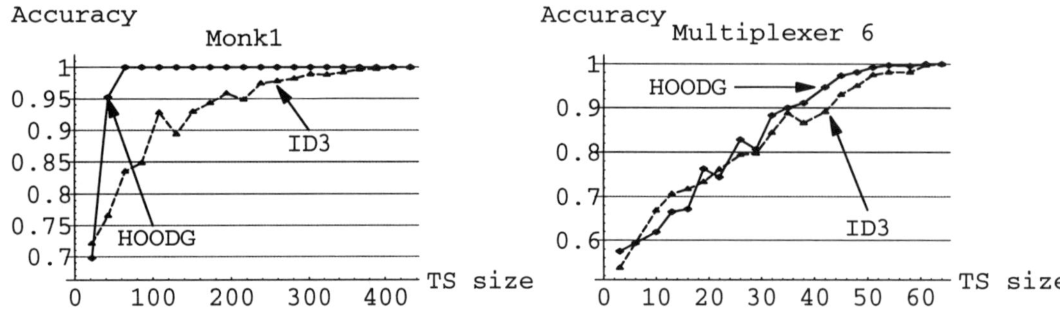

Figure 3: Learning curves for HOODG and ID3 and Monk 1 and 6 multiplexer.

required to extend the HOODG algorithm itself. Other important issues include dealing with noise (pruning), handling unknown values (here graphs might have advantages over trees due to reconverging paths), and finding more clever methods for ordering the variables

Acknowledgements We would like to thank the anonymous reviewers, James Kittock, Andrew Kosoresow, Shaul Markovitch, Nils Nilsson, Karl Pfleger, Eddie Schwalb, Yoav Shoham, and Tomas Uribe for their comments. The experimental section would not have been possible without the MLC++ project, partly supported by National Science Foundation Grant IRI-9116399. We wish to thank everyone working on MLC++, especially Richard Long.

References

Bryant, R. E. 1986. Graph-based algorithms for boolean function manipulation. *IEEE Transactions on Computers* C-35(8):677–691.

Burch, J. R.; Clarke, E. M.; and Long, D. E. 1991. Representing circuits more efficiently in symbolic model checking. In *Proceedings of the 28th ACM/IEEE Design Automation Conference*, 403–407.

Friedman, S. J., and Suppowit, K. J. 1990. Finding the optimal variable ordering for binary decision diagrams. *IEEE Transactions on Computers* 39(5):710–713.

Fujita, M.; Matsunaga, Y.; and Kakuda, T. 1991. On variable ordering of binary decision diagrams for the application of multilevel logic synthesis. In *Proceedings of the European Conference on Design Automation*, 50–54. IEEE Computing Press.

John, G.; Kohavi, R.; and Pfleger, K. 1994. Irrelevant features and the subset selection problem. In *Proceedings of the Eleventh International Conference on Machine Learning*. Morgan Kaufmann.

Kohavi, R. 1994. Bottom-up induction of oblivious, read-once decision graphs. In *Proceedings of the European Conference on Machine Learning*. Paper available by anonymous ftp from `starry.Stanford.EDU:pub/ronnyk/euroML94.ps`.

Lund, C., and Yannakakis, M. 1993. On the hardness of approximating minimization problems. In *ACM Symposium on Theory of Computing*.

Moret, B. M. E. 1982. Decision trees and diagrams. *ACM Computing Surveys* 14(4):593–623.

Murphy, P. M., and Aha, D. W. 1994. UCI repository of machine learning databases. For information contact ml-repository@ics.uci.edu.

Oliver, J. J. 1993. Decision graphs — an extension of decision trees. In *Proceedings of the fourth International workshop on Artificial Intelligence and Statistics*, 343–350.

Pagallo, G., and Haussler, D. 1990. Boolean feature discovery in empirical learning. *Machine Learning* 5:71–99.

Quinlan, J. R. 1986. Induction of decision trees. *Machine Learning* 1:81–106. Reprinted in Shavlik and Dietterich (eds.) Readings in Machine Learning.

Quinlan, J. R. 1988. An empirical comparison of genetic and decision-tree classifiers. In *Proceedings of the Fifth International Conference on Machine Learning*, 135–141. Morgan Kaufmann.

Quinlan, J. R. 1992. *C4.5: Programs for Machine Learning*. Los Altos, California: Morgan Kaufmann.

Takenaga, Y., and Yajima, S. 1993. NP-completeness of minimum binary decision diagram identification. Technical Report COMP 92-99, IEICE.

Thrun, S.; Bala, J.; Bloedorn, E.; Bratko, I.; Cestnik, B.; Cheng, J.; Jong, K. D.; Dzeroski, S.; Fahlman, S.; Fisher, D.; Hamann, R.; Kaufman, K.; Keller, S.; Kononenko, I.; Kreuziger, J.; Michalski, R.; Mitchell, T.; Pachowicz, P.; Reich, Y.; Vafaie, H.; de Weldel, W. V.; Wenzel, W.; Wnek, J.; and Zhang, J. 1991. The monk's problems: A performance comparison of different learning algorithms. Technical Report CMU-CS-91-197, Carnegie Mellon University.

Learning Decision Lists Using Homogeneous Rules

Richard Segal and **Oren Etzioni**[*]
Department of Computer Science and Engineering
University of Washington
Seattle, WA 98195
{segal, etzioni}@cs.washington.edu

Abstract

A decision list is an ordered list of conjunctive rules (Rivest 1987). Inductive algorithms such as AQ and CN2 learn decision lists incrementally, one rule at a time. Such algorithms face the *rule overlap problem* — the classification accuracy of the decision list depends on the overlap between the learned rules. Thus, even though the rules are learned in isolation, they can only be evaluated in concert. Existing algorithms solve this problem by adopting a greedy, iterative structure. Once a rule is learned, the training examples that match the rule are removed from the training set. We propose a novel solution to the problem: composing decision lists from *homogeneous* rules, rules whose classification accuracy does not change with their position in the decision list. We prove that the problem of finding a maximally accurate decision list can be reduced to the problem of finding maximally accurate homogeneous rules. We report on the performance of our algorithm on data sets from the UCI repository and on the MONK's problems.

Introduction

A decision list is an ordered list of conjunctive rules (Rivest 1987). A decision list classifies examples by assigning to each example the class associated with the first conjunctive rule that matches the example. The decision list induction problem is to identify, from a set of training examples, the decision list that will most accurately classify future examples. A learning algorithm requires some means for predicting how a decision list will perform on future examples. One solution is to use a heuristic scoring function that estimates the accuracy of the list on future examples based on its accuracy on training examples.[1] The overall induction problem can be decomposed into choosing an appropriate scoring function and finding a decision list that maximizes it.

[*]This research was funded in part by Office of Naval Research grant 92-J-1946 and by National Science Foundation grants IRI-9211045 and IRI-9357772. Richard Segal is supported, in part, by a GTE fellowship.

[1]To avoid overfitting, additional factors are often included such as the size of the list and the number of training examples covered.

A simple algorithm for finding a maximal decision list is to exhaustively search the space of decision lists and output the best one found. This algorithm is impractical because the number of decision lists is doubly-exponential in the number of attributes. Many existing algorithms (e.g., (Michalski 1969; Clark and Niblett 1989; Rivest 1987; Pagallo and Haussler 1990)) learn decision lists incrementally by searching the space of conjunctive rules for "good" rules and then combining the rules to form a decision list.

Such algorithms face the problem of *rule overlap* — the accuracy of a decision list is *not* a straightforward function of the accuracy of its constituent rules. To illustrate this point, consider the two rules r_1 and r_2, each having 80% accuracy and 50% coverage on the training examples. The rules may not overlap at all, which yields a two rule decision list with 80% accuracy and 100% coverage. However, the rules may have a 40% overlap in which case the accuracy of the decision list (r_1, r_2) could go down to 67% with a coverage of 60%. In general, any algorithm that forms a classifier by combining rules learned separately has to overcome the rule overlap problem.

Algorithms such as AQ and CN2 address the overlap problem by adopting an iterative structure. As each rule is learned, it is inserted into the decision list, and the examples covered by the rule are removed from the training set. The algorithm learns the next rule based on the reduced training set. The process is repeated until the training set is exhausted. The overlap problem is addressed by learning each successive rule from a training set where examples that match previously learned rules are filtered out. Note that this iterative approach is *greedy* — once the algorithm learns a rule, it is committed to keeping that rule in the decision list. All subsequent learning is based on this commitment.

While the greedy approach has proven to be effective in practice, it has several problems. First, as pointed out by Clark and Niblett (1989), the interpretation of each rule is dependent on the rules that precede it. This makes decision lists difficult to comprehend because the learned rules cannot be considered in isolation. Second, on each iteration, fewer training examples are available for the learning algorithm, which hinders the algorithm's ability to learn. This is particularly important in situations where training data is scarce. Finally, poor rule choices at the beginning of the list can significantly reduce the accuracy of the decision list learned.

Nevertheless, Rivest showed that a greedy, iterative algorithm can provably PAC learn the concept class k-DL, decision lists composed of rules of length at most k (Rivest 1987). However, Rivest's PAC guarantee presupposes there exist 100% accurate rules of length at most k that cover the training examples. This strong assumption neatly sidesteps the overlap problem because the accuracy of a 100% accurate rule remains unchanged regardless of the rules that precede it in the decision list. However, the assumption is often violated in practice. A full complement of 100% accurate rules of length at most k cannot be found when there is noise in the training data, when the concept to be learned is not in k-DL (relative to the algorithm's attribute language), or when the concept is probabilistic.

Our main contribution is a solution to the overlap problem that is both theoretically justified and practical. We borrow the notion of *homogeneity* from the philosophical literature (Salmon 1984) to solve the overlap problem in learning decision lists. Informally, a homogeneous rule is one whose accuracy does not change with its position in the decision list.

Formally, let E denote the universe of examples. Let T denote the set of tests within a domain and G the set of goal classes. Let DL denote the set of all decision lists. Let $c(e)$ denote the classification of example e, and $C(e, d)$ denote the classification that decision list d assigns to the example e. We write a rule as $A \rightarrow g$, where $A \subset T$ and $g \in G$. When an example e passes all the tests in A, we say $e \in A$. Let P be a probability distribution over examples. We define the accuracy of a decision list d with respect to P as follows:

$$\mathcal{A}(d) \;=\; \sum_{e \in E | c(e) = C(e,d)} P(e)$$

We define the accuracy of a rule to be its accuracy on the examples that it covers:

$$a(A \rightarrow g) = \sum_{e \in A | c(e) = g} P(e) \;\Big/\; \sum_{e \in A} P(e)$$

A *homogeneous rule* is a rule for which all specializations of the rule have the same accuracy as the rule itself. Formally, a homogeneous rule is a rule $A \rightarrow g$ such that, for all $B \subset T$, the following holds:

$$a(A \wedge B \rightarrow g) = a(A \rightarrow g)$$

All 100% accurate rules are homogeneous, but homogeneous rules need not be 100% accurate. Thus, homogeneity can be viewed as a generalization of Rivest's solution to the overlap problem. This generalization

is valuable in situations where concise 100% accurate rules do not exist.

Our algorithm for learning decision lists, BRUTEDL, searches the space of conjunctive rules for maximally accurate homogeneous rules and composes the rules found into a decision list. The remainder of the paper is organized as follows. The next section introduces the theory underlying BRUTEDL. The following section explains the approximations to the theory we use to make BRUTEDL practical. We then describe BRUTEDL's algorithm and discuss how we make our implementation efficient. Finally, we present empirical results that validate our approach and compare BRUTEDL with related algorithms.

Homogeneous Decision Lists

This section describes the theory underlying BRUTEDL. Our goal is to demonstrate that the problem of finding a maximally accurate decision list can be reduced to the problem of finding maximally accurate homogeneous rules.

A homogeneous decision list is a decision list composed exclusively of homogeneous rules. We use HDL to refer to the set of all homogeneous decision lists. BRUTEDL is restricted to learning homogeneous decision lists. Does this restriction mean that in some cases BRUTEDL will be forced to learn an inferior decision list? In other words, are there cases where the best homogeneous decision list is less accurate than the best decision list? The answer is no. We say that two decision lists d and d' are *logically equivalent* if they classify all examples identically. That is, $\forall\, e \in E, \; C(e, d) = C(e, d')$.

Theorem 1 *For every decision list, there exists a homogeneous decision list that is logically equivalent.*

Proof sketch:

Let d be a nonhomogeneous decision list and $r = A \rightarrow g$ be a nonhomogeneous rule in d. We can replace r with a set of equivalent homogeneous rules. By performing this replacement for all nonhomogeneous rules in d, a homogeneous decision list logically equivalent to d can be found. Let t be any test not in A. The rule r can be replaced with $A \wedge t \rightarrow g$ and $A \wedge \neg t \rightarrow g$ without changing how d classifies examples. If these rules are homogeneous, we are done. If not, we can repeat the procedure and replace the two rules with four rules without logically changing d. This procedure can be repeated until a set of homogeneous rules is found. A set of homogeneous rules is guaranteed to be found because there is a finite number of tests.□

Our solution to the overlap problem combines the notion of homogeneity with the intuition that the best rule to classify any given example is the most accurate rule that covers the example. We define a *maximal cover* as a set of rules containing, for each example, the most accurate homogeneous rule that covers it. Formally, let $hr(e)$ be the set of homogeneous rules that match e. A maximal cover $M(E)$ of a universe of examples E is any set of homogeneous rules for which the following holds:

$$\forall\ e \in E,\ \exists\ r \in M(E) \text{ such that } a(r) = \max_{r' \in hr(e)} a(r')$$

We now show that the problem of finding the maximally accurate decision list can be reduced to the problem of finding a maximal cover for E.

Theorem 2 *Any homogeneous decision list d whose rules form a maximum cover of E and is sorted by decreasing accuracy will have:*

$$\mathcal{A}(d) = \max_{d' \in DL} \mathcal{A}(d')$$

Proof:

First we prove that d must be a maximally accurate homogeneous decision list. Assume that $\mathcal{A}(d) \neq \max_{d' \in HDL} \mathcal{A}(d')$. There must exist a homogeneous decision list f such that $\mathcal{A}(f) > \mathcal{A}(d)$. Let e denote an example that is classified by a rule f_i in f and d_j in d such that $a(f_i) > a(d_j)$. Since $\mathcal{A}(f) > \mathcal{A}(d)$, such an example must exist. The rules of d form a maximum cover; therefore, there exists a d_k such that $a(d_k) = \max_{r \in hr(e)} a(r)$. Furthermore, we have $a(d_k) \geq a(f_i)$ because $f_i \in hr(e)$. We have $k < j$ because $a(d_k) \geq a(f_i) > a(d_j)$ and d is sorted by decreasing accuracy. But if $k < j$, e should have been classified by d_k rather than d_j. This contradiction establishes that $\mathcal{A}(d) = \max_{d' \in HDL} \mathcal{A}(d')$. Let g be a decision list such that $\mathcal{A}(g) = \max_{d' \in DL} \mathcal{A}(d')$. Assume $\mathcal{A}(g) > \mathcal{A}(d)$. By Theorem 1, there exists an $h \in HDL$ that is logically equivalent to g. We have $\mathcal{A}(h) = \mathcal{A}(g)$ because h and g are logically equivalent. But since h is homogeneous, we have $\mathcal{A}(d) \geq \mathcal{A}(h) = \mathcal{A}(g)$ which contradicts the assumption. Thus, $\mathcal{A}(d) = \max_{d' \in DL} \mathcal{A}(d')$.$\square$

Implications for BRUTEDL

We now consider the implications of Theorem 2 for BRUTEDL. If BRUTEDL had access to the probability distribution P and the set of homogeneous rules, it would be straightforward to build an algorithm based on Theorem 2. In practice, BRUTEDL is only given a set of training data from which it must approximate P and determine which rules are homogeneous.

BRUTEDL uses *LaplaceAccuracy* as an approximation of the actual accuracy of a rule (Niblett 1987). Let r be a rule that classifies r_p training examples correctly out of the r_n training examples it matches. Let $|G|$ denote the number of goal classes. The LaplaceAccuracy of r is calculated as follows:

$$LaplaceAccuracy(r) = \frac{r_p + 1}{r_n + |G|}$$

Once an estimate for the accuracy of individual rules has been defined, it is possible to check whether a rule is homogeneous. The accuracy of a homogeneous rule should not change when additional conjuncts are added. Therefore, homogeneity can be checked by comparing the LaplaceAccuracy of a rule with the LaplaceAccuracy of all the rule's specializations. Since LaplaceAccuracy is an approximation to the actual accuracy of a rule, a rule is considered homogeneous if all specializations have *roughly* the same LaplaceAccuracy. We check for statistically significant differences in LaplaceAccuracy using a χ^2 test.

Although not required by Theorem 2, it is desirable that the rules learned by BRUTEDL do not contain irrelevant conjuncts. An irrelevant conjunct is any conjunct whose presence does not affect the accuracy of a rule. We will call any rule with only relevant conjuncts *minimal*. Restricting BRUTEDL to minimal rules does not affect the class of concepts it can learn because, for every nonminimal homogeneous rule, there is a minimal rule with identical accuracy and greater coverage that is formed using some subset of the original rule's conjuncts. We check whether a conjunct is relevant by checking if the accuracy of the rule changes when the conjunct is removed. Again, we use a χ^2 test to ensure that any differences in accuracy that are detected are significant.

Algorithm

The previous sections developed the basic framework behind BRUTEDL. We now describe how this framework is implemented. The core of BRUTEDL is a depth-first search to find, for each example, the best conjunctive rule that covers it. Rules that are neither homogeneous nor minimal are filtered out. Once a maximal cover has been found, the cover is sorted, and a default rule is appended. BRUTEDL limits its search to a fixed depth bound when it is too costly to search the entire space. A pseudo-code description of BRUTEDL appears in Table 1.

The search performed by BRUTEDL is systematic, it visits each rule exactly once. In a naive search of the space of conjunctive rules, the identical rules $A \wedge B \rightarrow g$ and $B \wedge A \rightarrow g$ would be visited separately: once while searching the children of $A \rightarrow g$ and once while searching the children of $B \rightarrow g$. BRUTEDL achieves systematicity by imposing a canonical order on the tests within a rule. BRUTEDL assigns a numeric rank to each test and only considers rules whose tests appear in order of increasing rank.

Homogeneity is checked by doing a systematic search of all specializations of a rule. If a specialization is found with a difference in accuracy that is considered statistically significant, the homogeneity check fails. If no such specialization is found, the rule is deemed homogeneous. BRUTEDL limits the cost of homogeneity checks by reducing their frequency. It is only necessary to check the homogeneity of a rule that is minimal and is the best rule seen thus far for some example. If a rule does not meet these two criteria, it cannot be

```
BruteDL()
  DecisionList := MakeEmptyDL();
  BruteSearch(MakeEmptyRule());
  Sort(DecisionList);
  AddDefaultRule(DecisionList);
END

BruteSearch(rule)
  IF Length(rule) >= MaxLength THEN EXIT;
  StartTest := FollowingTest(LastTest(rule));
  FOR test := StartTest to LastTest DO
    newrule := AddConjunct(rule, test);
    IF BestForSomeExample(newrule) AND
      IsMinimal(newrule) AND
      Homogeneous(newrule,newrule)
      THEN Insert(newrule,DecisionList);
    IF NOT PruneRule(newrule)
      THEN BruteSearch(newrule);
  END
END

Homogeneous(ParentRule, rule):boolean
  IF Length(rule) >= MaxLength THEN RETURN(True);
  IF rule = ParentRule
    THEN StartTest = 1;
    ELSE StartTest = FollowingTest(LastTest(rule));
  FOR test := StartTest to LastTest DO
    newrule := AddConjunct(rule,test);
    IF NOT SimilarAccuracy(ParentRule,newrule) THEN
      RETURN(False);
    ELSE IF NOT Homogeneous(ParentRule,newrule) THEN
      RETURN(False);
  END
  RETURN(True);
END

IsMinimal(rule):boolean
  FOR test in Conjuncts(rule) DO
    ParentRule := DeleteConjunct(rule, test);
    IF SimilarAccuracy(ParentRule, rule)
      THEN RETURN(False);
  END
  RETURN(True);
END
```

Table 1: Pseudo-code for BruteDL.

part of the final decision list. Using this filter, a homogeneity check is required for only a small fraction of the rules searched. Furthermore, the homogeneity check for a nonhomogeneous rule is often inexpensive because the search is terminated once a specialization with a significant difference in accuracy is found.

Once a maximum cover has been found, BRUTEDL uses it to build a decision list. The final decision list is formed by sorting the maximum cover and appending a default rule. A default rule is necessary because the rules found by BRUTEDL, although required to cover the training examples, might not cover all the test examples. BRUTEDL appends a default rule that predicts the most frequent class in the training data.

(1) If Accuracy(r) = 100% then Prune(r).

(2) If MatchedPositives(r) < MinPositives then Prune(r).

(3) If MatchedNegatives($A \wedge \neg c$) < MinSimNegatives $\wedge$
    MatchedPositives($A \wedge \neg c$) < MinSimPositives then
    Prune($A \wedge c$).

Table 2: Pruning axioms used by BRUTEDL. Prune(r) indicates the children of r should not be searched. The axioms are sound because the rules they prune cannot be part of the final decision list.

Efficiency

For BRUTEDL to be a practical algorithm, it is important that it be as efficient as possible. The efficiency of BRUTEDL is determined by two factors: the efficiency of processing each rule and the number of rules processed. We address the first element of BRUTEDL's efficiency by carefully implementing BRUTEDL in C. BRUTEDL can process approximately 100,000 rules per second when running on a SPARC-10 processor with a data set of 500 examples. BRUTEDL's running time grows linearly with the number of examples. Significant improvements in program efficiency are not expected because BRUTEDL is currently within an order of magnitude of the machine's clock rate. However, further improvements in rule processing speed will occur as faster machines become available.

The second element of BRUTEDL's efficiency is the number of rules it processes. BRUTEDL can reduce the number of rules it has to process by pruning away rules *guaranteed* not to be part of the final decision list. BRUTEDL uses the axioms in Table 2 to determine the portions of the search space it can ignore. BRUTEDL's pruning axioms significantly reduce the number of rules it has to process. For the test domains presented later, the pruning axioms reduced the search space by as much as a factor of 1,000. The remainder of this section describes BRUTEDL's pruning axioms in detail.

The first axiom prunes descendants of 100% accurate rules because they cannot be minimal. The second axiom prunes all specializations of a rule that do not cover a minimum number of positive examples. During its search, BRUTEDL keeps track of the worst rule that is the best for some example. For a rule to appear in the final output, it is necessary for it to be better than this rule. It is possible to show that for LaplaceAccuracy and many other functions, there is a minimum number of positive examples a rule must cover for it to achieve a particular score. By setting MinPositives to the number of positives required to improve upon the worst rule, we can prune rules that are guaranteed not to appear in the final decision list.

The third pruning axiom avoids exploring portions of the search space that are guaranteed not to be minimal. If a rule contains a conjunct that does little to affect the rule's accuracy, then any specialization of that rule will not be minimal. Consider the rule $r = A \wedge c \rightarrow g$ where the conjunct c has little influence on the accuracy of the rule. We will determine the conditions for which any specialization of r is guaranteed to be nonminimal. Let $s = A \wedge c \wedge B \rightarrow g$ be any specialization of r. For s to be a minimal rule, it is necessary that its accuracy be significantly different from the accuracy of $p = A \wedge B \rightarrow g$. For s to be minimal, it must therefore be more accurate or less accurate than p. The maximum possible value of χ^2 for a specialization of p that is more accurate than p is obtained by a rule that matches all the positives of p and none of its negatives. If p contains too few negative examples, then the maximal value of χ^2 will be lower than the threshold required to be judged significant. Thus, no specialization of p that is more accurate than p can be significant unless p contains a minimum number of negative examples. A similar argument demonstrates that no specialization of p that is less accurate than p can be significant unless p contains a minimum number of positive examples. The negative and positive examples in p that do not appear in r are those for which $A \wedge \neg c \wedge B$ holds. If $A \wedge \neg c \wedge B$ has too few positive examples and too few negative examples, then s cannot be minimal. Furthermore, if the set $A \wedge \neg c$ contains too few positive examples and too few negative examples, then $A \wedge \neg c \wedge B$ must also not contain enough examples. Therefore, by pruning specializations of a rule $A \wedge c \rightarrow g$ when $A \wedge \neg c$ does not have the required number of positive and negative examples, we remove from consideration only rules that are guaranteed not to be minimal.

Experimental Results

We ran BRUTEDL on several data sets from the UCI repository (Murphy 1994)[2] and on all the data sets from the MONK's competition (Thrun *et al.* 1991). The results are shown in Table 3. For comparison, the results for the IND (Buntine and Caruana 1991) implementation of C4 (Quinlan 1986) are also included. The results for the UCI data sets are averaged over 10 iterations. Each iteration randomly splits the available data into 70% for training and 30% for testing. The MONK's problems specify both the training set and test set to use for each problem.

BRUTEDL performed as well as C4 on many of the UCI data sets and better than C4 on the lymphography data set. However, BRUTEDL performed relatively poorly on the glass and voting data sets. BRUTEDL is a clear winner on the MONK #1 data set, and performed at least as well as C4 on the other two MONK's problems. The target concept in the MONK #1 data set is an XOR, which is known to be difficult for decision tree algorithms. In contrast,

---

[2]The breast cancer, lymphography, and primary tumor domains were obtained from the University Medical Centre, Institute of Oncology, Ljubljana, Yugoslavia.

Domain	BRUTEDL		C4	
	Acc.	σ	Acc.	σ
Breast cancer	68.7	4.3	69.8	3.2
Chess endgame	98.6	0.4	99.2	0.3
Glass	62.0	5.3	69.2	5.5
Hepatitis	80.6	7.9	80.0	7.9
Iris	93.1	4.5	94.2	2.7
Lymphography	82.0	3.4	69.6	3.4
Mushroom	100.0	0.1	100.0	0.0
Primary tumor	39.9	3.0	39.1	4.9
Voting records	93.0	3.2	94.6	1.5
MONK #1	100.0	N/A	80.6	N/A
MONK #2	68.1	N/A	64.8	N/A
MONK #3	97.2	N/A	97.2	N/A

Table 3: The results of BRUTEDL and C4 on several data sets. All results except for the MONK data sets are averaged over 10 iterations. The MONK data sets come with a single training and test set.

Domain	CPU Time min:sec	Search depth
Breast cancer	0:31	4
Chess endgame	16:34	5
Glass	6:29	3
Hepatitis	0:53	3
Iris	0:37	5
Lymphography	1:13	5
Mushroom	2:09	3
Primary tumor	0:08	4
Voting records	0:04	5
MONK #1	0:01	N
MONK #2	0:04	N
MONK #3	0:01	N

Table 4: Running times and search depths for BRUTEDL. CPU time is for a SPARC-10 workstation. A search depth of N indicates a complete search.

XOR is easy for BRUTEDL since it merely has to find a homogeneous rule corresponding to each disjunct.

All of the UCI data sets were too large for a complete search. In each of the data sets, a depth bound was used to restrict the search to consider rules only up to a certain length. Table 4 shows the execution times and depth bounds for each data set. BRUTEDL is fast, taking only a few CPU seconds on some data sets and no more than 17 CPU minutes on the slowest one.

Critique

Ideally, BRUTEDL's massive search would result in significant improvements when compared with a greedy algorithm such as C4. Our experiments do not demonstrate this improvement for several reasons. First, on some data sets (e.g., mushroom) we observe a ceiling effect — C4 is performing about as well as possible, given the data set and attribute language. Second, in some cases, BRUTEDL overlooks homogeneous rules.

BruteDL discards a rule as nonhomogeneous when it has a specialization that differs significantly in accuracy from the rule itself. BruteDL performs a χ^2 test at $p = .005$ on each specialization of the rule to determine if its accuracy is significantly different from that of the rule. However, it is not the case that the probability that BruteDL incorrectly judges a rule to be nonhomogeneous is .005. Although the probability that a single error is .005, the probability that at least one of N judgments is in error is $1 - .995^N$. Thus, the more specializations a rule has, the more likely it is to be judged incorrectly as nonhomogeneous.

On both the voting and breast cancer data sets, BruteDL incorrectly judged several key rules to be nonhomogeneous. We can reduce the likelihood BruteDL will incorrectly judge a rule as nonhomogeneous by using a lower p value for the χ^2 tests. By using $p = .00001$, BruteDL improves its performance to 94.4% accuracy on the voting data and to 72.2% accuracy on the breast cancer data. However, simply increasing the confidence in individual χ^2 tests can cause BruteDL to treat a nonhomogeneous rule as homogeneous. For instance, accuracy on the primary tumor data set decreases to 34.8% when we change the confidence level to $p = .00001$. It is clear that a more stable method of checking homogeneity is needed.

Finally, BruteDL's performance is limited in domains where it is not able to search to sufficient depth to find accurate rules. For instance, the rules found by BruteDL at depth 3 in the glass domain are not as accurate as those found by C4 at depths 5 and 6. Heuristic search techniques (e.g., beam search) can be used when a pure depth-bounded search to the desired depth is too costly. The basic ideas behind BruteDL apply equally well to heuristic search.

Related Work

BruteDL builds on our previous work on Brute (Riddle, Segal, and Etzioni 1994). Brute uses a depth-bounded search of the space of conjunctive rules to find accurate predictive rules. We tested Brute on two data sets from a Boeing manufacturing domain. The first data set has 1,075 examples with 48 attributes, and the second has 519 examples with 1,652 attributes. In the first data set, the predictive rules found by Brute were 20% more accurate on average than those found by C4. In the second data set, the predictive rules found by Brute were 44% accurate on average, while C4 was unable to find any rules. The results demonstrate the effectiveness of depth-bounded search on a complex real-world domain. Brute's running time on the two data sets was less than 3 CPU minutes on a SPARC-10 workstation.[3]

nSeveral other systems have used depth-bounded search. ITRULE (Smyth and Goodman 1991), like Brute, uses depth-bounded search to find accurate predictive rules. Schlimmer (1993) uses depth-bounded search to find determinations. However, none of these systems attempt to build a classifier from the rules they find.

Rivest (1987) describes an algorithm for PAC learning the concept class k-DL, decision lists composed of rules of length at most k. Rivest's k-DL algorithm conducts a depth-bounded search of the space of conjunctive rules to find 100% accurate rules. This depth-bounded search is repeated n times where n is the number of rules in the learned decision list. We can improve upon the k-DL algorithm by restricting BruteDL to consider only 100% accurate rules. The homogeneity check can be dropped because 100% accurate rules are necessarily homogeneous. This restricted version of BruteDL will PAC learn k-DL using a *single* depth-bounded search of the space of conjunctive rules. The time complexity of the restricted BruteDL is asymptotically faster than that of the k-DL algorithm by a factor of n. Furthermore, the unrestricted BruteDL is more general. It can be used on noisy domains, probabilistic concepts, and concepts not in k-DL.

Rivest's algorithm is very similar to the AQ line of inductive algorithms (e.g., (Michalski 1969; Clark and Niblett 1989)). These algorithms share Rivest's iterative structure but use a beam search to find the best rule according to a scoring function. The OPUS system (Webb 1993) extends CN2 to use depth-bounded search but retains the same iterative structure. As a result, poor rule choices at the beginning of the list can significantly reduce the accuracy of the decision list learned. Furthermore, the greedy structure introduces dependencies among the decision list's rules that can make the decision list difficult to interpret. BruteDL's solution to the overlap problem avoids both these pitfalls by learning each rule in the decision list independently.

The PVM system (Weiss *et al.* 1990) does a massive search of the space of classifiers. PVM's search is not exhaustive because it uses several heuristics to reduce the search space.[4] Even with heuristics, the doubly-exponential search space searched by PVM limits it to considering classifiers that are significantly smaller than those considered by BruteDL. Finally, Murphy and Pazzani (1994) used a depth-bounded search of the space of decision trees to analyze the relationship between the smallest decision tree and classification accuracy. A massively parallel Maspar computer and small domains were used to make a limited search of this doubly-exponential space possible. Our theory of homogeneity and sound pruning axioms significantly reduce the cost of depth-bounded search and make it practical in many domains.

Many of BruteDL's features help to improve the

---

[3] We previously reported Brute's running time as 33 CPU minutes. We have since added additional pruning axioms that significantly improve Brute's efficiency.

[4] Unlike BruteDL's pruning axioms, PVM's heuristics are not sound and can cause it to overlook accurate classifiers

human readability of its decision lists. As pointed out by Clark and Niblett (1989), the readability of a decision list suffers because the interpretation of each rule is dependent on the rules that precede it. BRUTEDL avoids this problem by finding only homogeneous decision lists. Homogeneous decision lists are easier to understand because the interpretation of each rule is not dependent on its position. Furthermore, BRUTEDL attempts to include all relevant conjuncts within each rule while leaving out any irrelevant conjuncts.

Another unique aspect of BRUTEDL is that it does not use a postpruning phase to avoid overfitting. Postpruning does not make sense for any algorithm that is trying to maximize a scoring function because it would prune the maximal classifier found into some classifier that would be nonmaximal according to its scoring function. Instead, BRUTEDL uses its heuristic scoring function to avoid overfitting by assigning a low score to any rule that covers too few training examples. Overfitting is also avoided by requiring that every conjunct in a rule be relevant.

Conclusion

This paper introduced BRUTEDL, a novel algorithm for learning decision lists. Unlike algorithms such as AQ or CN2, BRUTEDL conducts a single search for accurate homogeneous rules, which contain no redundant conjuncts, and builds a decision list from the rules it finds. We show that, in the limit, the problem of learning maximally accurate decision lists can be reduced to the problem of learning maximally accurate homogeneous rules. BRUTEDL introduces a number of approximations to this theory but, as our empirical results demonstrate, BRUTEDL is effective in practice. BRUTEDL outperforms C4 in several cases and runs in less than a minute on most benchmark data sets. In future work we plan to compare BRUTEDL with CN2 and to demonstrate that decision lists, based on homogeneous rules, are easier to comprehend than standard decision lists.

Acknowledgments

We are grateful to Wray Buntine for distributing the IND package. IND's reimplementation of C4 greatly facilitated our research. Thanks are due to Ruth Etzioni for her expert advice on statistical testing, Patricia Riddle for many helpful discussions, Dan Weld for commenting on an earlier version of this paper, and Omid Madani for help testing BRUTEDL.

References

W. Buntine and R. Caruana. Introduction to IND and recursive partitioning. NASA Ames Research Center, Mail Stop 269-2 Moffet Field, CA 94035, 1991.

P. Clark and T. Niblett. The CN2 induction algorithm. *Machine Learning*, 3(4):261–283, March 1989.

R. S. Michalski. On the quasi-minimal solution of the general covering problem. In *Proceedings of the Fifth International Symposium on Information Processing*, pages 125–128, Bled, Yugoslavia, 1969.

Patrick M. Murphy and Michael J. Pazzani. Exploring the decision forest: An empirical investigation of Occam's razor in decision tree induction. Submitted to *Artificial Intelligence Research*, 1994.

Patrick M. Murphy. UCI repository of machine learning databases. [Machine-readable data repository]. Irvine, CA. University of California, Department of Information and Computer Science., 1994.

T. Niblett. Constructing decision trees in noisy domains. In *Progress in Machine Learning (Proceedings of the 2nd European Working Session on Learning)*, pages 67–78, Wilmslow, UK, 1987.

G. Pagallo and D. Haussler. Boolean feature discovery in empirical learning. *Machine Learning*, 5(1):71–100, March 1990.

J. R. Quinlan. Simplifying decision trees. *International Journal of Man-Machine Studies*, 27:221–234, 1986.

Patricia Riddle, Richard Segal, and Oren Etzioni. Representation design and brute-force induction in a Boeing manufacturing domain. *Applied Artificial Intelligence*, 8:125–147, 1994. Available via anonymous FTP from /pub/ai at cs.washington.edu.

R. Rivest. Learning decision trees. *Machine Learning*, 2:229–246, 1987.

Wesley C. Salmon. *Scientific Explanation and the Causal Structure of the World*. Princeton University Press, Princeton, NJ, 1984.

J. C. Schlimmer. Efficiently inducing determinations: A complete and systematic search algorithm that uses optimal pruning. In *Proceedings of the Tenth International Conference on Machine Learning*, Amherst, MA, June 1993.

P. Smyth and R. M. Goodman. Rule induction using information theory. In *Knowledge Discovery in Databases*, pages 159–176. MIT Press, Cambridge, MA, 1991.

S.B. Thrun, J. Bala, E. Bloedorn, I. Bratko, B. Cestnik J. Cheng, K. De Jong, S. Dzeroski, S. E. Fahlman, D. Fisher, R. Hamann, K. Kaufman, S. Keller, I. Kononenko, J. Kreuziger, R.S. Michalski, T. Mitchell, P. Pachowicz, Y. Reich, H. Vafaie, W. Van de Welde, W. Wenzel, J. Wnek, and J. Zhang. The MONK's problems - A performance comparison of different learning algorithms. Technical Report CS-CMU-91-197, Carnegie Mellon University, 1991.

Geoffrey I. Webb. Systematic search for categorical attribute-value data-driven machine learning. In N. Foo and C. Rowles, editors, *AI '93*. World Scientific, Singapore, 1993.

S. M. Weiss, R. S. Galen, and P. V. Tadepalli. Maximizing the predictive value of production rules. *Artificial Intelligence*, 45:47–71, September 1990.

Decision Tree Pruning: Biased or Optimal?

Sholom M. Weiss[†] **and Nitin Indurkhya**[‡]
† Department of Computer Science, Rutgers University
New Brunswick, New Jersey 08903, USA
‡ Department of Computer Science, University of Sydney
Sydney, NSW 2006, AUSTRALIA

Abstract

We evaluate the performance of weakest-link pruning of decision trees using cross-validation. This technique maps tree pruning into a problem of tree selection: Find the best (i.e. the right-sized) tree, from a set of trees ranging in size from the unpruned tree to a null tree. For samples with at least 200 cases, extensive empirical evidence supports the following conclusions relative to tree selection: (a) 10-fold cross-validation is nearly unbiased; (b) not pruning a covering tree is highly biased; (c) 10-fold cross-validation is consistent with optimal tree selection for large sample sizes and (d) the accuracy of tree selection by 10-fold cross-validation is largely dependent on sample size, irrespective of the population distribution.

Introduction

Decision trees methods have evolved from straightforward recursive partitioning algorithms that cover sample data to more complex techniques that also prune the covering tree and estimate future performance (Breiman *et al.* 1984; Quinlan 1993). The motivation for pruning a tree is to maximize predictive performance, which is often described as "overfitting avoidance." However, too much pruning can readily lead to "underfitting," and a more appropriate objective would be to find "the right size" tree.

Many techniques have evolved over the years for pruning trees to the right size. Practical experience has also led to the adaptation of these techniques to alternative learning models such as rule induction (Cohen 1993; Weiss & Indurkhya 1993) or neural nets (Hassibi & Stork 1993). With a very large set of independent test data, there is little difficulty in describing the efficacy of pruning. The estimated error rate and the standard error of the estimate have a precise formal description.

When very large numbers of independent test cases are not available, relatively complex techniques involving resampling can be employed to estimate performance and to select the pruned tree. Resampling with decision trees is more complex than for other classifiers. In addition to generating multiple trees, these trees must be pruned such that the complexities of the subtrees are matched for each subsample. In a series of papers studying the effects of pruning on decision tree performance (Schaffer 1992b; 1992a; Wolpert 1992; Schaffer 1993), it was demonstrated that pruning does not always lead to improved results. Moreover, in some instances it may even degrade performance. Generalizing from these experimental results, often with small samples, the authors of these studies concluded that pruning using cross-validation is inevitably biased and is often ineffective without knowledge of the sampled population.

In this paper, we reconsider the efficacy of decision tree pruning. Tree pruning is mapped into a problem of tree selection among competing subtrees. Previous experiment results are reevaluated and additional experiments are performed. We address several major issues such as the bias of tree pruning by cross-validation, the effect of sample size, the divergence from optimal selection, and the extent to which knowledge about overall population characteristics is essential for accurate results.

We reserve our discussion in this paper to the most general case: samples of moderate to large size, samples with at least 200 cases. Small samples, with their attendant high variability, require special attention (Efron 1983; Crawford 1989; Weiss 1991) and are discussed in a separate paper (Weiss & Indurkhya 1994).

Tree Pruning and Selection

Tree induction methods generate a covering tree to discriminate the training data. For generalization to new cases, a subtree of the covering tree may actually make fewer errors on new cases. Hence the use of pruning techniques that excise portions of the covering tree. Pruning can be described in the following general terms:

- Generate a set of "interesting" trees;
- Estimate the true performance of each of these trees;
- Select the best tree.

Although there are a number of pruning techniques (Quinlan 1987; Cestnik & Bratko 1991), a prime example of a form of pruning that matches these steps is weakest link (cost-complexity) pruning (Breiman *et al.* 1984). A covering tree is recursively pruned into a series of subtrees, based on eliminating the weak points

T_i i=	Nodes	Err_{app}	Err_{test}	$Test_{SE}$
0	18	.0000	.1074	.0282
1	15	.0083	.0909	.0261
2	13	.0165	.0909	.0261
3*	7	.0661	.0744	.0239
4	6	.0826	.1322	.0308
5	4	.1322	.1322	.0308
6	3	.2975	.2975	.0416
7	2	.5372	.5620	.0451
8	1	.6529	.6529	.0433

Table 1: Example of Summary Table for Tree Pruning

of the current tree. These weak points are determined strictly from the training data.

Having obtained a set of decision trees, $(T_0, \ldots, T_n)$ one is now faced with the *tree selection problem*: given a set of trees, select the best one. The usual definition of *best* is that of the minimum true error rate, which must be estimated. It is useful to order the set of trees by some complexity measure such as tree size. If the set of trees is obtained by pruning, then T_0 is the unpruned covering tree, and T_n is a tree that consists only of the root node. Figure 1 gives an example of a pruning summary table, such as found in CART, with the covering tree T_0 having 18 terminal nodes and T_8 representing the fully pruned tree with a single terminal node. Err_{test} is the estimate of the true error rate for each tree, and $Test_{SE}$ is an estimate of the standard error of the error rate. In this example, T_3 is selected because it has the minimum estimated true error rate.

Thus, tree pruning is mapped into a problem of tree selection: Find the best tree, i.e the right-sized tree, from a set of trees ranging in size from the unpruned tree to a null tree. Tree selection does not depend on the techniques for generating the trees. Error estimation is the sole basis of tree selection; the tree with the lowest error-estimate is selected. The quality of the results depends on the accuracy of these estimates. Several error-estimation procedures might be hypothesized:

Ideal: The ideal situation occurs when an oracle is available that can tell us the future performance of each decision tree. Then we will be able to make the optimal tree selection. Such an oracle is usually approximated accurately by testing each tree, T_i, on a very large, independent test set.

NP: While we would like to use an oracle-based method, this may not be possible if insufficient cases are available. One strategy might be to base decisions on the *apparent* error for the training cases. Because the apparent error rate is minimum for the covering tree, this strategy reduces to not pruning the initial covering tree.

Cross-Validation: When large numbers of independent test cases are not available, resampling methods are the principal technique for error rate estimation. Cross-validation is generally the procedure of choice, and 10-fold cross-validation (the test

results of 10 runs using 90-percent training and 10-percent testing cases, with 10 mutually exclusive test partitions) has been widely used for many different learning models.

Our objective in the remainder of this paper is to compare the performance of tree pruning for these three alternative methods of estimating error rates.

Basic Principles
Fundamental Statistical Model of Evaluation

The standard model of evaluation of a learning system is by testing on an independent, randomly drawn sample from the general population. If performance is measured in terms of a proportion of failure, i.e. an error rate, then the situation corresponds to the binomial sampling model. This testing situation is the standard statistical coin tossing problem, where here we "toss" the classifier on each of the test cases. If we have n test cases, then there are n success or failure outcomes, each outcome representing a correct or incorrect classification of a test case. The standard error of this proportion is given in Equation 1, where n is the test-set size and p is the *true error rate*. For a given sample size, the standard error roughly tells us the average amount that the error rate will diverge from the truth.

$$Variance = \frac{p(1-p)}{n}; SE = \sqrt{Variance} \quad (1)$$

We have a statistical model of how far off the error estimate for a single test sample is from the truth. With unlimited test samples, the efficacy of pruning would be obvious. The pruned tree with the minimum test error is the best to a very high degree of confidence. Just based on the variation among random samples, the error rate on test cases will vary from the truth according to Equation 1. This variance is based solely on two terms, the true error rate, p, and the test size n. Considering the range of p, the worst case (i.e. the highest variance) is for $p=.5$. However, the true error rate, p, has a relatively minor effect on the variance, and the key factor is n, the test-set size. The accuracy of the evaluation on the test cases is mostly determined by test-sample size. When n is large enough the standard error becomes quite small.

Given only a single sample, without large numbers of test cases, the task is to estimate the true error rate. Resampling techniques such as cross-validation attempt to approach the performance of testing on the same number of independent cases, while still using the full sample for training purposes. Resampled estimators are still subject to the random variation of the sample. At best, the resampled estimates reflect the error-rate for treating the sample as an independent test set. Their variance from the true error-rate would approximately follow Equation 1, their accuracy mostly dependent on the sample size n, and independent of the original population distribution.

Estimation and Tree Selection
Bias and Consistency of Estimators An estimator, x, of a metric (such as an error-rate) is *unbiased* if

its expected value (i.e. the average of its values over all samples) is equal to the true value of the metric. If sufficient number of independent random samples, N, are used, then for an unbiased estimator, Equation 2, summarizes this relationship, where x is the estimator, X_i is its mean value for the i-th sample, $T(x)$ is the true value of the metric being estimated by x and N is the number of samples.

$$T(x) = \frac{\sum_{i=1}^{N} X_i}{N} \qquad (2)$$

The key concept of an unbiased estimator is that over a large enough set of independent samples it averages to the true answer. It may vary from sample to sample, but over all samples the average is correct. An example of an unbiased estimator is the error-rate estimate on an independent test set. While the estimate from a particular test set may differ from the true value, the average value of the estimate over all possible (independently sampled) test sets is the same as the true value. There is some empirical evidence that suggests that cross-validated estimates are relatively unbiased under quite general conditions (Efron 1983). While an unbiased estimator averages to the the true value, it is also desirable that the estimate tend to be close to the true value. Equation 1 shows how close a typical estimate will be for a given sample size.

Another desirable statistical property of an estimator is *consistency*: results improve with increasing sample size. For example, error-rate estimation from an independent test set is consistent. As the test-sample size increases, the error-rate estimate varies less and less from the true error-rate.

Optimality and Unbiased Tree Selection Pruning can be posed as a problem of tree selection with the objective of minimizing the true error rate. An optimal procedure always selects the best tree from the set of pruned trees generated for a sample. Such a procedure would be obtained if ideal error-rates were available. In their absence, we must rely on estimates.

While we may use estimates of error rates for tree selection and pruning, the absolute magnitude of these estimates is not critical. Instead, the relative ranking is critical. As long as the relative ranking (in terms of error-rates) of the pruned trees is correct, then the right-size tree can be selected. If estimators are used for tree selection, the tree selection bias should be measured. An appropriate measure of bias is the average size of trees that are selected. An optimal tree selection procedure will always select the right-sized tree for each sample. However, an unbiased procedure is not necessarily optimal. An unbiased procedure may select the wrong-sized tree for any given sample. Although these trees may range from undersized to oversized, the procedure can be considered unbiased if the average size over many samples is correct.

Bias is one of two principal components of error in estimation. The other is variance. As indicated by Equation 1, samples randomly drawn for a large population will vary. They are not a perfect reflection of the general population. The variance decreases with increasing sample size. Thus, it is not unusual when we flip an honest coin ten times, that we will see seven

Data	Cases		Feature type	Classes
	Train/Test	Features		
Mush	8124	122	Boolean	2
Hypo	3772	22	Mixed	2
Hyper	3772/3428	22	Mixed	2
Pb	1494	2	Numer.	10
Wave	pgm/5000	21	Numer.	3
Letter	20000	16	Numer.	26
Heart	282	13	Numer.	2
German	6479	80	Numer.	2
LED	pgm/10000	7	Boolean	10
Noise	5000	10	Numer.	2

Table 2: Dataset Characteristics

heads. But if we flip it a thousand times, we are far less likely to see seven hundred heads. When the sample size grows large, the variance decreases greatly. An unbiased strategy with zero variance is an optimal strategy. As the sample size increases, the variance should move closer to zero and an unbiased strategy should also approach an optimal strategy.

The classical formal definition of statistical bias may differ from the descriptions given in the machine learning literature (Schaffer 1993; Mitchell 1990; Utgoff 1986), where a reader might conclude that unbiased estimators are optimal. The fundamental statistical concept of bias recognizes that predictive error is not attributable solely to the bias of a decision model. Instead, the problem may be with the sample! Inaccuracy of estimation can be a byproduct of random sampling variance, particularly for small samples that diverge greatly from the general population characteristics.

With a large enough sample, an unbiased tree selection strategy should approach an optimal solution, but an unbiased strategy will not always beat a biased strategy. If the bias fits the characteristics of the population, then for samples drawn from that population, the biased strategy will be closer to the truth. For example, if someone always calls heads, then with a coin slightly biased for heads, that strategy should be superior. With a large enough sample of coin flips one would discover this, but for smaller samples inferior performances for unbiased guesses are unavoidable.

Sources of Error in Pruning

Even with unbiased estimation techniques, all induction and pruning algorithms are at the mercy of the random variance of a sample. There is also another inherent source of error. When estimating error rates, cross-validation will train on less than the full sample. During each train and test cycle, some of the data must be reserved for testing. The usual variation is 10-fold: 90% training and 10% percent testing. For error rate estimation, this means that the estimates are those for 90% trees, not 100%. Thus these estimates should be somewhat pessimistic. For tree selection and pruning, the situation may be somewhat better. The relative ranking is critical, not the absolute magnitude. Still the basis of the rankings is 90% trees, implying some weakness when the true answer is near the unpruned

Dataset	n	Ideal		10-cv		NP	
		Err	Size	Err	Size	Err	Size
Mush	200	.013	6.2	.014	6.3	.013	6.5
	500	.005	8.3	.005	8.3	.005	8.4
	1000	.002	9.8	.002	9.8	.002	10.3
Hypo	200	.018	3.5	.020	3.4	.020	4.4
	500	.010	5.5	.012	5.0	.011	6.5
	1000	.006	6.8	.007	6.7	.006	8.5
Heart	200	.211	11.4	.242	9.7	.265	34.7
Pb	200	.327	30.1	.341	31.5	.354	67.5
	500	.282	38.3	.292*	37.5	.328	158.8
	1000	.253	43.3	.262*	34.8	.313	298.3
Wave	200	.292	13.0	.303	13.9	.306	28.0
	500	.264	22.3	.272	23.5	.281	63.9
	1000	.247	35.5	.254*	34.2	.267	119.5
Letter	200	.574	70.5	.581	67.9	.573*	88.1
	500	.436	156.4	.442	145.5	.438	177.9
	1000	.357	282.3	.361	261.4	.358	299.8
German	200	.278	12.5	.292*	15.2	.307	40.6
	500	.245	15.8	.254*	19.5	.291	97.6
	1000	.230	20.3	.235*	22.0	.282	192.3
LED	200	.554	21.4	.569*	26.8	.584	50.1
	500	.520	28.9	.528	29.4	.536	67.2
	1000	.503	37.1	.509	38.9	.515	73.9
Noise	200	.251	1.0	.255*	1.3	.385	38.9
	500	.251	1.0	.252*	1.1	.387	98.3
	1000	.251	1.0	.252*	1.0	.386	194.9

Table 3: Comparison of Ideal, 10-cv and NP

tree.

Another potential source of error is more specific to trees. Error estimation by 10-fold cross-validation involves the somewhat complicated matching of tree complexity. As the sample size increases, this is a relatively accurate process. With smaller samples, the matching process is imperfect and some interpolation is required (Breiman *et al.* 1984).

We have noted the potential sources of error in tree pruning using cross-validation. We now examine how strongly these factors affect its performance, and we compare its performance to the hypothetically ideal solution and to a strategy of not pruning at all.

Methods

For purposes of comparison, the same datasets reported in (Schaffer 1992b; 1992a; 1993) were used in the simulations. Unlike previous experiments, we postulate a strong connection of sample size to performance. Thus, for each dataset, random samples of size 200, 500, and 1000 were drawn from the overall population. The true answer was determined by results on either the remainder of the dataset or where available a second independently drawn test set. In addition to the original datasets, four others were also considered. These include the following:

- Random noise for two classes with a prevalence of approximately 75% for one class.

- A two class problem with features representing word frequency counts in German Reuters news stories (Apté, Damerau, & Weiss 1994).

- The Peterson/Barney Vowel Formant Dataset in which two features (the first two formant values) are used to discriminate among ten vowel classes (Watrous 1991).

- The Waveform data discussed in (Breiman *et al.* 1984) with three classes and twenty one features all of which have added noise. The Bayes error-rate for this problem is 14%.

These added datasets allow us to examine a wider spectrum of true answers, with some falling near the unpruned tree and others far away. With the exception of the heart dataset, which only allowed for a size 200 sample, all datasets were large enough for both training and testing on relatively large numbers of cases. The characteristics of the datasets are described in Table 2. For some datasets, such as the hyperthyroid application, independent test data were available. For others, such as the letter recognition application, a random subset was drawn for training and the remaining case were used for testing.[1] For some applications, such as LED, the training data were generated dynamically by a program. In addition to the fixed sample size experiments, we also ran some experiments with even larger samples. These sizes were selected based on the number of available cases in the dataset. Each simulation

---

[1]For the german text data, a second set of 1888 independent test cases were used for the large training sample experiment.

encompassed at least 100 train and test trials.

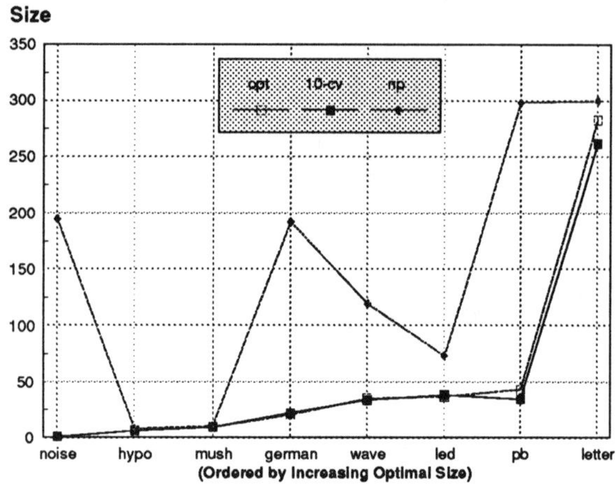

Figure 1: Bias: Tree Sizes for Size 1000 Samples

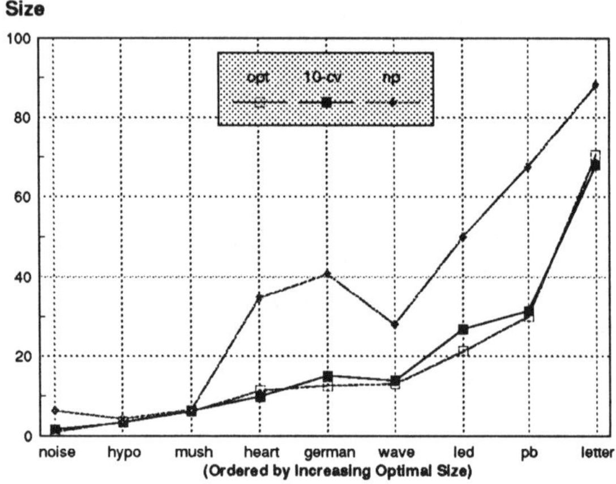

Figure 2: Bias: Tree Sizes for Size 200 Samples

The CART tree induction program was used in all experiments. The minimum error tree was selected by cross-validation. Ten-fold cross-validation was used in all experiments. The following slight modifications were made to the program:

- Each trial was initiated with a new random seed.

- Ties were broken in favor of the larger tree.

In the interest of experimental replication, many induction programs use the same random seed. In a laboratory setting, it may be beneficial to maximize randomness by reseeding after each trial. While it is tempting to break ties with the simpler tree, the 90% tree is actually being estimated, and therefore the larger tree is somewhat more likely for the full sample.

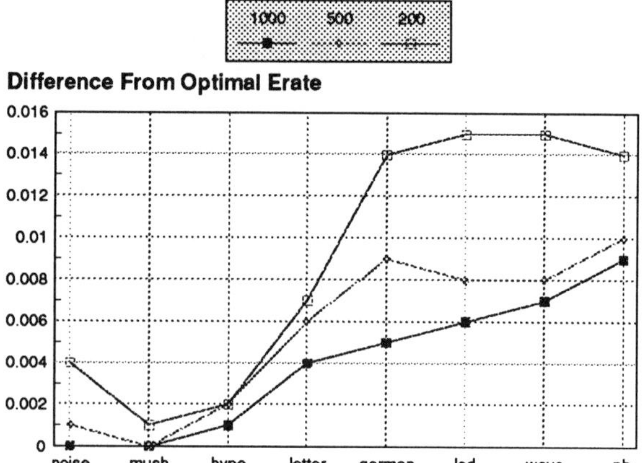

Figure 3: Consistency of 10-cv Performance for Varying Size Samples

As reported in (Schaffer 1992b), experiments were performed for cross-validation (10-cv), and not pruning (NP). The average error rates and sizes for the 10-cv and NP trees were recorded. Missing from the original analysis was crucial information about the average error rates and sizes for the hypothetically optimal tree-selection strategy (opt). In our experiments, this was determined by evaluating each of the ordered pruned trees directly on the independent test data.

Results

The results of the experiments for the fixed-sized samples are listed in Table 3. Table 4 lists the results for even larger sample sizes. Differences between NP and 10-cv of more than 2 standard errors (>95% confidence) are noted by a "*". Figure 1, plots the tree sizes for NP, 10-cv and opt for size 1000 samples; Figure 2 plots them for size 200 samples. Figure 3, compares the difference of 10-cv from the optimal error rate for sample sizes 200, 500, and 1000. Figure 4 plots the difference from the optimal error rate for NP and 10-cv for size 1000 samples; Figure 5 plots this difference for size 200 samples.

Significance Testing

For binomial trials, such as estimating error rates, the variance can be directly computed from Equation 1, and 2 standard errors is a reasonable significance test. In those instances where the dataset is randomly partitioned into train and test partitions, the standard error for a single trial is computed with n equal to the size of the test set. For many multiple trials, n approaches the full sample size, which is usually used to estimate the variance (Breiman *et al.* 1984). No matter how many multiple trials are performed, the results are bounded by the size of the full sample and its variance from the true population. For these applications, NP demonstrates a significantly better result only for the sample size of 200 letter recognition application (with its 26

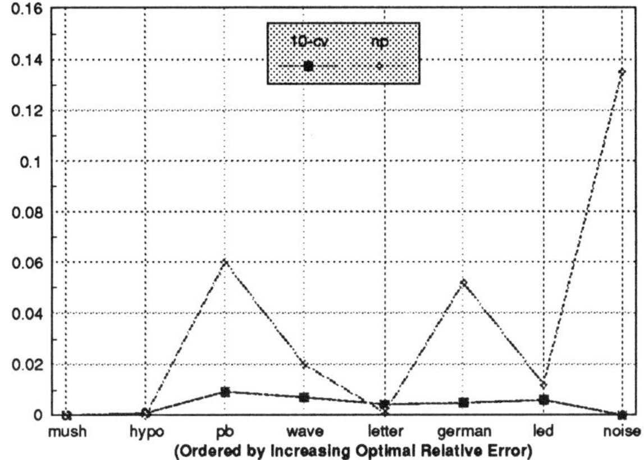

Figure 4: Tree Selection Performance for Size 1000 Samples

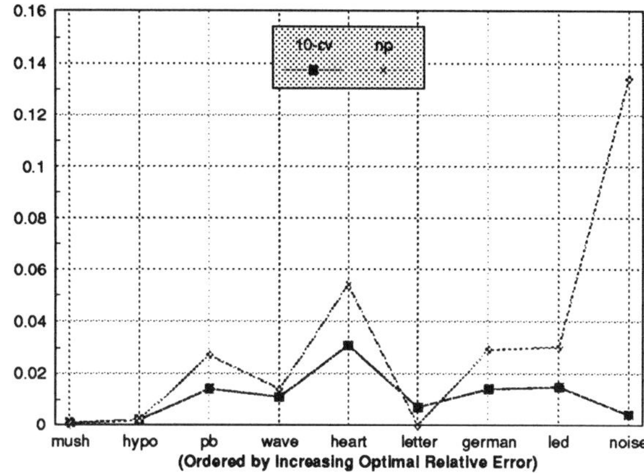

Figure 5: Tree Selection Performance for Size 200 Samples

classes and small samples for each class).

With any significance test, two statistical problems remain:

- Significance testing does not directly measure the magnitude of the difference.

- Even with a comparative result below two standard errors, there may still be a competitive edge. The difference in performance of competing solutions is usually more accurately determined than the individual estimates (Breiman *et al.* 1984; Shibata 1981).

These factors should lead one to consider the overall pattern of performance, and the relative advantages of competing solutions on large numbers of independent test cases. Figures 4 and 5 illustrate this overall pattern.

Discussion

The results listed in Tables 3 and 4, which are plotted in Figures 1 and 2, strongly suggest that pruning by 10-cv is nearly unbiased. Figure 3 shows that 10-cv pruning is consistent: as the sample size increases, the results get better and the difference from the optimal answer decreases. Not pruning is clearly a highly biased (optimistic) strategy.

When the bias of NP is close to the true answer, such as in the letter application, NP performs well, even better than the nearly unbiased 10-cv strategy. For size 200, the sampling variance is still moderate so that NP is sometimes competitive with 10-cv. By size 1000, the case for 10-cv is overwhelming, and we see 10-cv approaching an optimal selection strategy. Even for size 200 samples, 10-cv is competitive across the board, with typically slight losses to NP. But an NP strategy, with hugely optimistic predictions, can lead to disaster for noisy applications. Unfortunately, many real-world applications turn out to be collections of noisy features.

The fundamental unifying theme in an analysis of tree pruning performance must be the binomial model with the variance of Equation 1. This model demonstrates the difficulties in smaller sample estimation and the increasingly better performance for larger samples. It explains the sometimes weak behavior of unbiased tree selection for smaller samples. It also explains the near optimal results for larger samples due to the reduced variance.

Considering the variety of datasets used in this study, including many found in previous studies, one can reasonably conclude that these data are representative of typical real-world applications. By computing average tree sizes and comparing results to ideal trees, we have provided an objective basis to compare bias and accuracy of selecting the right-sized tree. Most importantly, the results of this study are consistent with an underlying theory of tree pruning using cross-validation. Pruning is mapped into a a form of binomial testing (coin tossing) to determine a proportion (the error rate). Direct testing on independent test cases is known to be unbiased with the standard binomial variance for sample estimators. The accuracy of independent testing is mostly dependent on test sample size and independent of solution complexity. This study shows that cross-validation estimators are good approximators to estimates based on independent test cases.

Overall, these results demonstrate that NP is usually inferior to 10-cv, sometimes by very large margins, for samples of at least 200 cases. If one were aware of the characteristics of the true answer, such as likely solution complexity, one might achieve slightly better results by biasing the solution in that direction. For a size 1000 sample, such knowledge would be of marginal value. The results are entirely consistent with sample size variation. With sample size of at least 200, good results for tree pruning and selection should generally be achievable without any knowledge of the population.

Data	n	Ideal		10-cv		NP	
		Err	Size	Err	Size	Err	Size
Mush	4800	.000	13.8	.000	13.8	.000	13.8
Hypo	2000	.003	7.6	.004	7.7	.004	11.9
Hyper	3772	.011	6.0	.011	7.2	.014	29.0
Letter	10000	.155	1332.2	.156	1311.7	.156	1463.8
Wave	5000	.215	101.9	.219	78.2	.240	542.0
German	6479	.197	74.0	.200	83.0	.266	1146.0
Noise	2500	.251	1.4	.252	1.1	.389	491.1
LED	10000	.488	49.7	.489	49.6	.490	77.7

Table 4: Results for very large training samples

The same binomial model should also be used to compare significance of results (Breiman *et al.* 1984). Standard significance tests, such as t-tests or nonparametric ranked sign tests on the results of each trial or the pooled data of all cases and trials, will overweight the significance of results for increasing numbers of non-independent trials.

One might wonder whether the experimental results suggest that the standard tree induction estimation techniques should be modified. Unlike our single-minded search for minimum error pruning, in the real world there is a strong tendency to simplify results. One sometimes chooses a simpler tree that is close to the best solution (Breiman *et al.* 1984). The usual rationale is in terms of explanatory capabilities. However, the real world may not be the perfect laboratory setting that was presented for the experiments of this paper. While the ideal model is a random sample from an infinite population, future samples may actually be drawn from a slightly changing population, where the simpler solution actually performs better. Whichever variation is used, we believe that these experimental results strongly confirm the efficacy of resampling estimators for tree pruning and selection. Although we have not examined the effects of pruning on other learning models, the known generality of resampling techniques should produce similar results.

References

Apté, C.; Damerau, F.; and Weiss, S. 1994. Automated Learning of Decison Rules for Text Categorization. Technical Report RC 18879, IBM T.J. Watson Research Center. To appear in ACM Transactions on Office Information Systems.

Breiman, L.; Friedman, J.; Olshen, R.; and Stone, C. 1984. *Classification and Regression Tress*. Monterrey, Ca.: Wadsworth.

Cestnik, B., and Bratko, I. 1991. On estimating probabilities in tree pruning. In *Machine Learning, EWSL-91*. Berlin: Springer Verlag.

Cohen, W. 1993. Efficient pruning methods for separate-and-conquer rule learning systems. In *Proceedings of IJCAI-93*, 988–994.

Crawford, S. 1989. Extensions to the cart algorithm. *International Journal of Man-Machine Studies* 31:197–217.

Efron, B. 1983. Estimating the error rate of a prediction rule. *Journal of the American Statistical Association* 78:316–333.

Hassibi, B., and Stork, D. 1993. Second order derivatives for network pruning: Optimal brain surgeon. In *Advances in Neural Information Processing Systems 5*. San Mateo, CA: Morgan Kaufmann. 164–171.

Mitchell, T. 1990. The need for biases in learning generalizations. In *Readings in Machine Learning*. San Mateo, CA: Morgan Kaufmann. 184–191.

Quinlan, J. 1987. Simplifying decision trees. *International Journal of Man-Machine Studies* 27:221–234.

Quinlan, J. 1993. *C4.5: Programs for Machine Learning*. Morgan Kaufmann.

Schaffer, C. 1992a. Deconstructing the digit recognition problem. In *Proceedings of the Ninth International Conference on Machine Learning*, 394–399. San Mateo, CA: Morgan Kaufmann.

Schaffer, C. 1992b. Sparse data and the effect of overfitting avoidance in decision tree induction. In *Proceedings of AAAI-92*, 147–152. Cambridge, MA: MIT Press.

Schaffer, C. 1993. Overfitting avoidance as bias. *Machine Learning* 10:153–178.

Shibata, R. 1981. An optimal selection of regression variables. *Biometrika* 68:45–54.

Utgoff, P. 1986. Shift of bias for inductive concept learning. In *Machine Learning: An Artificial Intelligence Approach. Volume 2*. San Mateo, CA: Morgan Kaufmann. 107–148.

Watrous, R. 1991. Current status of peterson-barney vowel formant data. *Journal of the Acoustical Society of America* 89(3).

Weiss, S., and Indurkhya, N. 1993. Optimized Rule Induction. *IEEE EXPERT* 8(6):61–69.

Weiss, S., and Indurkhya, N. 1994. Small sample decision tree pruning. In *Proceedings of the Eleventh International Conference on Machine Learning*.

Weiss, S. 1991. Small sample error rate estimation for k-nearest neighbor classifiers. *IEEE Transactions on Pattern Analysis and Machine Intelligence* 13(3):285–289.

Wolpert, D. 1992. On overfitting avoidance as bias. Technical Report SFI TR 92-03-5001, The Sante Fe Institute.

An implemented model of punning riddles

Kim Binsted*and Graeme Ritchie
Department of Artificial Intelligence
University of Edinburgh
Edinburgh, Scotland EH1 1HN
kimb@aisb.ed.ac.uk graeme@aisb.ed.ac.uk

Abstract

In this paper, we discuss a model of simple question–answer punning, implemented in a program, JAPE-1, which generates riddles from humour–independent lexical entries. The model uses two main types of structure: *schemata*, which determine the relationships between key words in a joke, and *templates*, which produce the surface form of the joke. JAPE-1 succeeds in generating pieces of text that are recognizably jokes, but some of them are not very good jokes. We mention some potential improvements and extensions, including post–production heuristics for ordering the jokes according to quality.

Humour and artificial intelligence

If a suitable goal for AI research is to get a computer to do "...a task which, if done by a human, requires intelligence to perform," (Minsky 1963), then the production of humorous texts, including jokes and riddles, is a fit topic for AI research. As well as probing some intriguing aspects of the notion of "intelligence", it has the methodological advantage (unlike, say, computer art) of leading to more directly falsifiable theories: the resulting humorous artefacts can be tested on human subjects.

Although no computationally tractable model of humour as a whole has yet been developed (see (Attardo & Raskin 1991) for a general theory of verbal humour, and (Attardo 1994) for a comprehensive survey), we believe that by tackling a very limited and linguistically-based set of phenomena, it is realistic to start developing a formal symbolic account.

One very common form of humour is the question-answer joke, or riddle. Most of these jokes (e.g. almost a third of the riddles in the Crack-a-Joke Book (Webb 1978)) are based on some form of pun. For example:

What do you use to flatten a ghost? *A spirit level.*
(Webb 1978)

*Thanks are due to Canada Student Loans, the Overseas Research Students Scheme, and the St Andrew's Society of Washington, DC, for their financial support.

This riddle is of a general sort which is of particular interest for a number of reasons. The linguistics of riddles has been investigated before (e.g. (Pepicello & Green 1984)). Also, there is a large corpus of riddles to examine: books such as (Webb 1978) record them by the thousand. Finally, riddles exhibit more regular structures and mechanisms than some other forms of humour.

We have devised a formal model of the punning mechanisms underlying some subclasses of riddle, and have implemented a computer program which uses these symbolic rules and structures to construct punning riddles from a humour-independent (i.e. linguistically general) lexicon. An informal evaluation of the performance of this program suggests that its output is not significantly worse than that produced by human composers of such riddles.

Punning riddles

Pepicello and Green (Pepicello & Green 1984) describe the various strategies incorporated in riddles. They hold the common view that humour is closely related to ambiguity, whether it be linguistic (such as the phonological ambiguity in a punning riddle) or contextual (such as riddles that manipulate social conventions to confuse the listener). What the linguistic strategies have in common is that they ask the "riddlee" to accept a similarity on a phonological, morphological, or syntactic level as a point of *semantic* comparison, and thus get fooled (cf. "iconism" (Attardo 1994)). Riddles of this type are known as *puns*.

We decided to select a subset of riddles which displayed regularities at the level of semantic, or logical, structure, and whose structures could be described in fairly conventional linguistic terms (simple lexical relations). As a sample of existing riddles, we studied "The Crack-a-Joke Book" (Webb 1978), a collection of jokes chosen by British children. These riddles are simple, and their humour generally arises from their punning nature, rather than their subject matter. This sample does not represent sophisticated adult humour, but it suffices for an initial exploration.

There are three main strategies used in puns to

"

exploit phonological ambiguity: *syllable substitution*, *word substitution*, and *metathesis*. This is not to say that other strategies do not exist; however, none were found among the large number of punning jokes examined.

Syllable substitution: Puns using this strategy confuse a syllable (or syllables) in a word with a similar- or identical-sounding word. For example:

> What do short-sighted ghosts wear? *Spooktacles.* (Webb 1978)

Word substitution: Word substitution is very similar to syllable substitution. In this strategy, an entire word is confused with another similar- or identical-sounding word. For example:

> How do you make gold soup? *Put fourteen carrots in it.* (Webb 1978)

Metathesis: Metathesis is quite different from syllable or word substitution. Also known as *spoonerism*, it uses a reversal of sounds and words to suggest (wrongly) a similarity in meaning between two semantically-distinct phrases. For example:

> What's the difference between a very short witch and a deer running from hunters? *One's a stunted hag and the other's a hunted stag.* (Webb 1978)

All three of the above-described types of pun are potentially tractable for detailed formalisation and hence computer generation. We chose to generate only word-substitution puns, simply because lists of phonologically identical words (*homonyms*) are readily available, whereas the other two types require some kind of sub-word comparison. In particular, the class of jokes which we chose to generate all: use word substitution; have the substituted word in the *punchline* of the joke, rather than the question; and substitute a homonym for a word in a *common noun phrase* (cf. the "spirit level" riddle cited earlier). These restrictions are simply to reduce the scope of the research even further, so that the chosen subset of jokes can be covered in a comprehensive, rigorous manner. We believe that our basic model, with some straightforward extensions, is general enough to cover other forms.

Symbolic descriptions

Our analysis of word-substitution riddles is based (semi-formally) on the following essential items, related as shown in Figure 1:

- a valid English word/phrase
- the meaning of the word/phrase
- a shorter word, phonologically similar to part of the word/phrase
- the meaning of the shorter word
- a fake word/phrase, made by substituting the shorter word into the word/phrase
- the meaning of the fake word/phrase, made by combining the meanings of the original word/phrase and the shorter word.

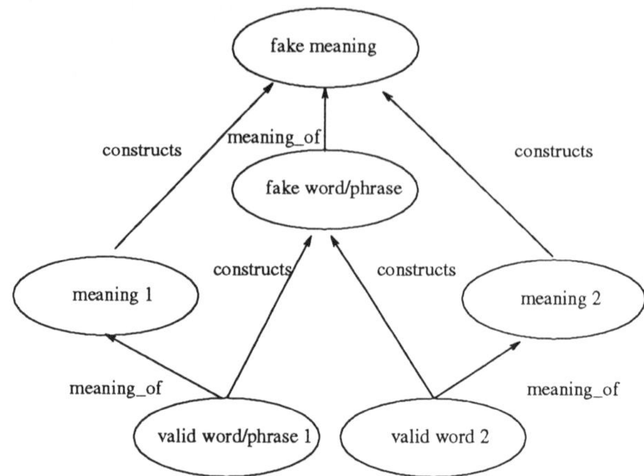

Figure 1: The relationships between parts of a pun

At this point, it is important to distinguish between the mechanism for building the *meaning* of the fake word/phrase, and the mechanism that uses that meaning to build a question with the word/phrase as an answer. Consider the joke:

> What do you give an elephant that's exhausted? *Trunkquillizers.* (Webb 1978)

In this joke, the word "trunk", which is phonologically similar to the syllable "tranq", is substituted into the valid English word "tranquillizer". The resulting fake word "trunkquillizer" is given a meaning, referred to in the question part of the riddle, which is some combination of the meanings of "trunk" and "tranquillizer" (in this case, a tranquillizer for elephants). The following questions use the same meaning for 'trunkquillizer', but refer to that meaning in different ways:

- What do you use to sedate an elephant?
- What do you call elephant sedatives?
- What kind of medicine do you give to a stressed-out elephant?

On the other hand, *these* questions are all put together in the same way, but from different constructed meanings:

- What do you use to sedate an elephant?
- What do you use to sedate a piece of luggage?
- What do you use to medicate a nose?

We have adopted the term *schema* for the symbolic description of the underlying configuration of meanings and words, and *template* for the textual patterns used to construct a question-answer pair.

Lexicon

Our minimal assumptions about the structure of the lexicon are as follows. There is a (finite) set of *lexemes*.

A lexeme is an abstract entity, roughly corresponding to a meaning of a word or phrase. Each lexeme has exactly one entry in the lexicon, so if a word has two meanings, it will have two corresponding lexemes. Each lexeme may have some *properties* which are true of it (e.g. being a noun), and there are a number of possible *relations* which may hold between lexemes (e.g. synonym, homonym, subclass). Each lexeme is also associated with a *near-surface form* which indicates (roughly) the written form of the word or phrase.

Schemata

A *schema* stipulates a set of relationships which must hold between the lexemes used to build a joke. More specifically, a schema determines how real words/phrases are glued together to make a fake word/phrase, and which parts of the lexical entries for real words/phrases are used to construct the meaning of the fake word/phrase.

There are many different possible schemata (with obscure symbolic labels which the reader can ignore). For example, the schema in Figure 2 constructs a fake phrase by substituting a homonym for the first word in a real phrase, then builds its meaning from the meaning of the homonym and the real phrase.

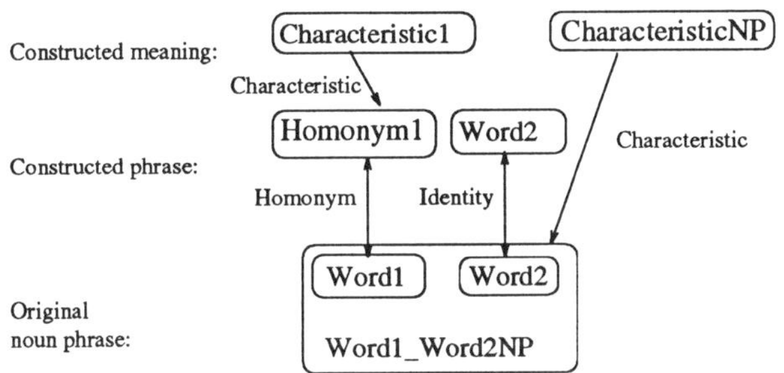

Figure 2: The *lotus* schema

The schema shown in Figure 2 is *uninstantiated*; that is, the actual lexemes to use have not yet been specified. Moreover, some of the relationships are still quite general — the *characteristic* link merely indicates that *some* lexical relationship must be present, and the *homonym* link allows either a homophone or the same word with an alternative meaning. Instantiating a schema means inserting lexemes in the schema, and specifying the exact relationships between those lexemes (i.e. making exact the *characteristic* links). For example, in the lexicon, the lexeme **spring_cabbage** might participate in relations as follows:

```
class(spring_cabbage, vegetable)
location(spring_cabbage, garden)
action(spring_cabbage, grows)
adjective(spring_cabbage, green)
....
```

If **spring_cabbage** were to be included in a schema, at one end of a *characteristic* link, the other end of the link could be associated with any one, or any combination of, these values (vegetable, garden, etc), depending on the exact label (class, location, etc.) chosen for the characteristic link.

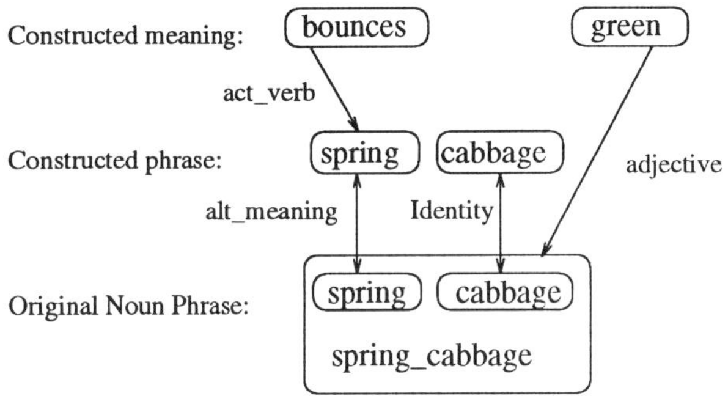

Figure 3: A completely instantiated *lotus* schema

The completely instantiated *lotus* schema in Figure 3 could (with an appropriate template — see below) be used to construct the joke:

What's green and bounces? *A spring cabbage.* (Webb 1978)

Templates

A template is used to produce the surface form of a joke from the lexemes and relationships specified in an instantiated schema. Templates are not inherently humour-related. Given a (real or nonsense) noun phrase, and a meaning for that noun phrase (genuine or constructed), a template builds a suitable question-answer pair. Because of the need to provide a suitable amount of information in the riddle question, every schema has to be associated with a set of appropriate templates. Notice that the precise choice of relations for the under-specified "characteristic" links will also affect the appropriateness of a template. (Conversely, one could say that the choice of template influences the choice of lexical relation for the characteristic link, and this is in fact how we have implemented it.) Abstractly, a template is a mechanism which maps a set of lexemes (from the instantiated schema) to the surface form of a joke.

The JAPE-1 computer program

Introduction

We have implemented the model described earlier in a computer program called JAPE-1, which produces the chosen subtype of jokes — riddles that use homonym substitution and have a noun phrase punchline. Such riddles are representative of punning riddles in general, and include approximately one quarter of the punning riddles in (Webb 1978).

JAPE-1 is significantly different from other attempts to computationally generate humour in various ways: its lexicon is humour-independent (i.e. the structures that generate the riddles are distinct from the semantic and syntactic data they manipulate), and it generates riddles that are similar on a strategic and structural level, rather than in surface form.

JaPE-1's main mechanism attempts to construct a punning riddle based on a common noun phrase. It has several distinct knowledge bases with which to accomplish this task: the lexicon (including the homonym base), a set of schemata, a set of templates, and a post-production checker.

Lexicon

The lexicon contains humour–independent semantic and syntactic information about the words and noun phrases entered in it, in the form of "slots" which can contain other lexemes or may contain other symbols. A typical entry might be:

```
lexeme = jumper_1          countable = yes
category = noun            class = clothing
written_form = ''jumper''  specifying_adj = warm
vowel_start = no           synonym =  sweater
```

Although the lexicon stores syntactic information, the amount of syntax used by the rest of the program is minimal. Because the templates are based on certain fixed forms, the only necessary syntactic information has to do with the syntactic category, verb person, and determiner agreement. Also, the lexicon need only contain entries for nouns, verbs, adjectives, and common noun phrases — other types of word (conjunctions, determiners, etc) are built into the templates. Moreover, because the model implemented in JaPE-1 is restricted to covering riddles with noun phrase punchlines, the schemata require *semantic* information only for nouns and adjectives.

The "homonym" relation between lexemes was implemented as a separate *homonym base* derived from a list (Townsend & Antworth 1993) of homophones in American English, shortened considerably for our purposes. The list now contains only common, concrete nouns and adjectives. The homonym base also includes words with two distinct meanings (e.g. "lemon", the fruit, and "lemon", slang for a low-quality car).

Schemata

JaPE-1 has a set of six schemata, one of which is the *jumper* schema, shown in Figure 4. The same schema, instantiated in two different ways, is shown in Figure 5 and Figure 6.

Templates

Since riddles often use certain fixed forms (for example, "What do you get when you cross ___ with ___ ?"), JaPE-1's templates embody such standard forms. A JaPE-1 template consists of some fragments of canned text with "slots" where generated words or phrases can be inserted, derived from the lexemes in an instantiated schema. For example, the *syn_syn* template:

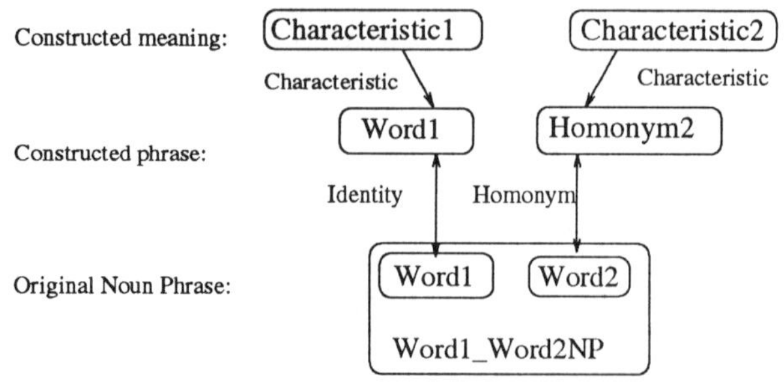

Figure 4: The uninstantiated *jumper* schema

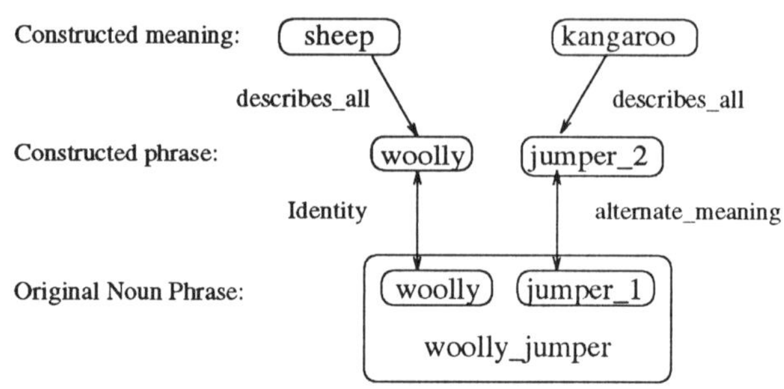

Figure 5: The instantiated *jumper* schema, with links suitable for the *syn_syn* template. Gives the riddle: What do you get when you cross a sheep and a kangaroo? *A woolly jumper.*

What do you get when you cross **[text fragment generated from the first characteristic lexeme(s)]** with **[text fragment generated from the second characteristic lexeme(s)]**? *[the constructed noun phrase].*

A template also specifies the values it requires to be used for "characteristic" links in the schema; the *describes_all* labels in Figure 5 are derived from the *syn.syn* template. When the schema has been fully instantiated, JaPE-1 selects one of the associated templates, generates text fragments from the lexemes, and

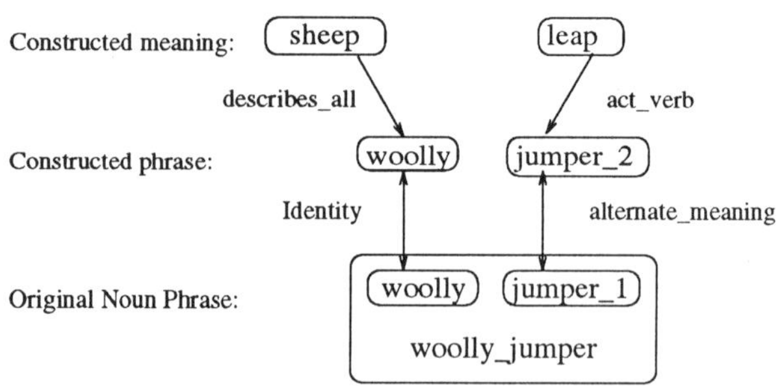

Figure 6: The instantiated *jumper* schema, with links suitable for the *syn_verb* template. Gives the riddle: What do you call a sheep that can leap? *A woolly jumper.*

slots those fragments into the template.

Another template which can be used with the *jumper* schema (see Figure 6) is the *syn_verb* template:

What do you call [text fragment generated from the first characteristic lexeme(s)] that [text fragment generated from the second characteristic lexeme(s)]? *[the constructed noun phrase.]*

Post-production checking

To improve the standard of the jokes slightly, some simple checks are made on the final form. The first is that none of the lexemes used to build the question and punchline are accidentally identical; the second is that the lexemes used to build the nonsense noun phrase and its meaning, do not build a *genuine* common noun phrase.

The evaluation procedure

An informal evaluation of JAPE-1 was carried out, with three stages: *data acquisition, common knowledge judging* and *joke judging*. During the data acquisition stage, volunteers unfamiliar with JAPE-1 were asked to make lexical entries for a set of words given to them. These definitions were then sifted by a "common knowledge judge" (simply to check for errors and excessively obscure suggestions), entered into JAPE-1's lexicon, and a substantial set of jokes were produced. A different group of volunteers then gave verdicts, both quantitative and qualititative, on these jokes. The use of volunteers to write lexical entries was a way of making the testing slightly more rigorous. We did not have access to a suitable large lexicon, but if we had hand-crafted the entries ourselves there would have been the risk of bias (i.e. humour-oriented information) creeping in.

JAPE-1 produced a set of 188 jokes in near-surface form, which were distributed in batches to 14 judges, who gave the jokes scores on a scale from 0 ("Not a joke. Doesn't make any sense.") to 5 ("Really good"). They were also asked for qualitative information, such as how the jokes might be improved, and if they had heard any of the jokes before.

This testing was *not* meant to be statistically rigorous. However, when it comes to analyzing the data, this lack of rigour causes some problems. Because there were so few jokes and joke judges, the scores are not statistically significant. Moreover, there was no control group of jokes. We suspect that jokes of this genre are not very funny even when they are produced by humans; however, we do not know how human-produced jokes would fare if judged in the same way JAPE-1's jokes were, so it is difficult to make the comparison. Ideally, with hindsight, JAPE-1's jokes would then have been mixed with similar jokes (from (Webb 1978), for example), and then all the jokes would have been judged by a group of schoolchildren, who would

be less likely to have heard the jokes before and more likely to appreciate them.

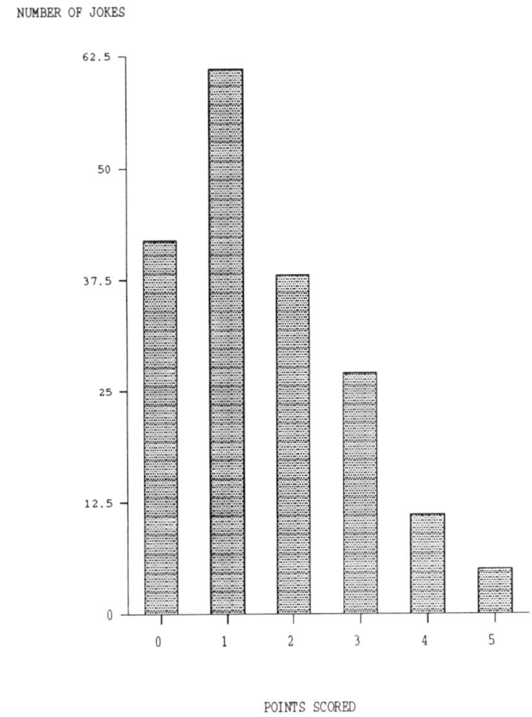

Figure 7: The point distribution over all the output

The results of the testing are summarised in Figure 7. The average point score for all the jokes JAPE-1 produced from the lexical data provided by volunteers is 1.5 points, over a total of 188 jokes. Most of the jokes were given a score of 1. Interestingly, all of the nine jokes that were given the maximum score of five by one judge, were given low scores by the other judge — three got zeroes, three got ones, and three got twos. Overall, the current version of JAPE-1 produced, according to the scores the judges gave, "jokes, but pathetic ones". The top end of the output are definitely of Crack-a-Joke book quality, and some (according to the judges) existed already as jokes, including:

What do you call a murderer that has fibre? *A cereal killer.*
What kind of tree can you wear? *A fir coat.*
What kind of rain brings presents? *A bridal shower.*
What do you call a good-looking taxi? *A handsome cab.*
What do you call a perforated relic? *A holey grail.*
What kind of pig can you ignore at a party? *A wild bore.*
What kind of emotion has bits? *A love byte.*

It was clear from the evaluation that some schemata
and templates tended to produce better jokes than others. For example, the *use_syn* template produced several texts that were judged to be non-jokes, such as:

What do you use to hit a waiting line? *A pool
queue.*

The problem with this template is probably that it
uses the definition constructed by the schema inappropriately. The schema-generated definition is 'nonsense', in that it describes something that doesn't exist;
nonetheless, the word order of the punchline does contain some semantic information (i.e. which of its words
is the object and which word describes that object),
and it is important for the question to reflect that information. A more appropriate template, *class_has rev*,
produced this joke:

What kind of line has sixteen balls? *A pool queue.*

which the judges gave an average of two points.

Another problem was that the definitions provided
by the volunteers were often too general for our purposes. For example, the entry for the word "hanger"
gave its class as **device**, producing jokes like:

What kind of device has wings? *An aeroplane
hanger.*

which scored half a point.

Conclusions

This evaluation has accomplished two things. It has
shown that JAPE-1 can produce pieces of text that are
recognizably jokes (if not very good ones) from a relatively unbiased lexicon. More importantly, it has suggested some ways that JAPE-1 could be improved:

• The description of the lexicon could be made
more precise, so that it is easier for people unfamiliar with JAPE-1 to make appropriate entries.
Moreover, multiple versions of an entry could be
compared for 'common knowledge', and that common knowledge entered in the lexicon.
• More slots could be added to the lexicon, allowing the person entering words to specify what a
thing is made of, what it uses, and/or what it is
part of.
• New, more detailed templates could be added,
such as ones which would allow more complex
punchlines.
• Templates and schemata that give consistently
poor results could be removed.
• The remaining templates could be adjusted so
that they use the lexical data more gracefully, by
providing the right amount of information in the
question part of the riddle.
• Schema-template links that give consistently
poor results could be removed.
• JAPE-1 could be extended to handle other joke
types, such as simple spoonerisms and sub-word
puns.

If even the simplest of the trimming and ordering
heuristics described above were implemented, JAPE-1's
output would be restricted to good-quality punning
riddles. Although there is certainly room for improvement in JAPE-1's performance, it does produce recognizable jokes in accordance with a model of punning
riddles, which has not been done successfully by any
other program we know of. In that, it is a success.

Acknowledgments

We would like to thank Salvatore Attardo for letting
us have access to his unpublished work, and for his
comments on the research reported here.

References

Attardo, S., and Raskin, V. 1991. Script theory
revis(it)ed: joke similarity and joke representation
model. *Humor* 4(3):293–347.

Attardo, S. 1994. *Linguistic Theories of Humour.*
Berlin: Mouton de Gruyter.

Binsted, K., and Ritchie, G. 1994. A symbolic description of punning riddles and its computer implementation. Research Paper 688, University of Edinburgh, Edinburgh, Scotland.

Ephratt, M. 1990. What's in a joke. In Golumbic, M.,
ed., *Advances in AI: Natural Language and Knowledge Based Systems.* Springer Verlag. 43–74.

Minsky, M. 1963. Steps towards artificial intelligence.
In Feigenbaum, E., and Feldman, J., eds., *Computers
and Thought.* McGraw-Hill. 406–450.

Minsky, M. 1980. Jokes and the logic of the cognitive
unconscious. Technical report, Massachusetts Institute of Technology, Artificial Intelligence Laboratory.

Palma, P. D., and Warner, E. J. 1992. Riddles: accessibility and knowledge representation. In *Proceedings of the 15th International Conference on Computational Linguistics (COLING-92),* volume 4. 1121–
1125.

Pepicello, and Green. 1984. *The Language of Riddles.*
Ohio State University.

Townsend, W., and Antworth, E. 1993. *Handbook of
Homophones (online version).*

Webb, K., ed. 1978. *The Crack-a-Joke Book.* Puffin.

Bootstrapping Training-Data Representations for Inductive Learning:
A Case Study in Molecular Biology

Haym Hirsh and **Nathalie Japkowicz**
Department of Computer Science
Rutgers University
New Brunswick, NJ 08903
hirsh@cs.rutgers.edu, nat@paul.rutgers.edu

Abstract

This paper describes a "bootstrapping" approach to the engineering of appropriate training-data representations for inductive learning. The central idea is to begin with an initial set of human-created features and then generate additional features that have syntactic forms that are similar to the human-engineered features. More specifically, we describe a two-stage process for the engineering of good representations for learning: first, generating by hand (usually in consultation with domain experts) an initial set of features that seem to help learning, and second, "bootstrapping" off of these features by developing and applying operators that generate new features that look syntactically like the expert-based features. Our experiments in the domain of DNA sequence identification show that an initial successful human-engineered representation for data can be expanded in this fashion to yield dramatically improved results for learning.

Introduction

Although most of the best-used inductive learning systems (Rumelhart, Hinton, & Williams 1986; Clark & Boswell 1991; Quinlan 1993) assume that data are represented as feature vectors, the world does not always present problems that directly fit the clean model of inductive learning presented by such systems. In addition to the art of taking a potentially ill-defined problem and formulating it as an inductive learning problem, a learning-system user must decide how data should be represented so that a given learning system applies and yields good results. This often involves high-level questions, such as which aspects of individual cases should be included with each example, as well as low-level questions, such as (for the backpropagation learning algorithm) how to represent data as vectors of real values.

Fortunately, in many situations the domain environment from which data are obtained already provides a natural representation for training data. For example, in vision, images are usually obtained as arrays of brightness values. In chess, positions are represented by 8x8 arrays representing the various squares on the board and what piece (if any) resides in each square (or alternatively, as lists of pieces and on which

We thank Mick Noordewier, Steve Norton, and Chris Matheus for helpful discussions, and the anonymous reviewers for their useful comments. This work was supported by NSF grant IRI-9209795.

square each piece resides). In problems concerning DNA—the principal domain considered in this paper—data are naturally represented as strings over a four-letter alphabet.

However, even when the problem domain provides a natural representation for data, there is no guarantee that this representation will be good for learning. Learning will only be successful if the regularities that underlie the data can be discerned by the learning system. For example, Hirsh and Noordewier (1994) have shown that re-expressing DNA-sequence data using higher-level features (defined in terms of the "natural" lower-level representation) can dramatically improve the results of learning. The goal of this paper is to introduce a method for building off such manual feature engineering, to improve the quality of training-data representations. Although our method does not remove the need for human input, it provides a way to bootstrap off initial efforts in a less labor-intensive and "expert-intensive" fashion.

Our approach began with the observation that human-engineered higher-level features often fall into distinct syntactic classes. Our assumption was that such syntactic classes are not accidents, but rather that they often reflect some deeper semantic meaning in the domain. When this is true learning can be improved by using additional features that look syntactically like the human-engineered features in the hope that they, too, will reflect deeper semantic meaning in the domain.

In more detail, our approach operates in two stages. In the first, an initial higher-level representation is constructed manually, usually in consultation with domain experts, with new features defined in terms of the existing low-level features in which the raw data are encoded. In the second, expert-free "bootstrapping" stage, a collection of feature-generation operators is created that is able to generate new features that look syntactically like existing features.

To explore this two-staged approach to generating new features we used the problem of learning rules for predicting promoters in DNA. This domain was particularly well-suited to our efforts, in that we were able build off the previous efforts of Hirsh and Noordewier (1994), which provide a problem where the human-engineering of an initial set of higher-level features has already been performed. We were thus able to focus on the "bootstrapping" stage of our feature-creation process for this problem.

"

We begin the paper with a general overview of molecular biology and the promoter recognition problem. We then describe the raw and Hirsh-Noordewier representations for training data, followed by details of the application of our bootstrapping approach to this problem and an evaluation of our results. We conclude the paper with a discussion of the generality of our approach and prospects for the future.

The Promoter Learning Problem

Although DNA encodes the genetic information about an organism, understanding the chemical basis for how it serves this role is very difficult. One of the complexities in understanding how the chemical properties of DNA achieve its functionality is that only some parts of DNA—known as *coding regions*—contain genetic information. Other parts, known as *regulatory regions*, regulate the chemical processes that operate on DNA. Other regions serve yet other roles, and in some cases the roles of some regions are not even currently understood.

Very little is known about how to differentiate the various DNA regions. The *promoter recognition problem* has as its goal the recognition of a specific type of regulatory region known as a *promoter sequence*, which signals to the chemical processes acting on DNA where a coding region begins. Identifying promoter sequences is currently a long and difficult laboratory-based process and a reliable non-laboratory-based automated procedure for doing so would prove a valuable tool for future efforts in this field.

This paper focuses on the use of inductive learning to form recognition procedures for promoter sequences. The idea is to take a collection of sequences known to be promoters and a collection known not to be and form a classifier that accurately predicts the presence of promoters in uncharacterized DNA. The promoter data that we use are composed of 47 positive examples and 53 negative ones. These data were obtained from the U.C. Irvine Repository of Machine Learning Datasets, but were modified in response to Norton's (1994) critique of the biological flaws underlying the original formulation of the data: first, the training examples were aligned on the right-most start of transcription; second, sequences that had no start of transcription identified in the original reference were removed.

The particular learning algorithm that we use is the decision tree learner C4.5 (Quinlan 1993), and we report results for both pruned and unpruned trees. For the main part of this paper five different representations are considered. Two of these are the pre-existing raw and Hirsh-Noordewier representations, and the other three result from applying our method. Error rates for each representation are the average of 10 sessions of 10-fold cross-validation (Weiss & Kulikowski 1991). A summary of our results, which are discussed in the coming sections, is given in Table 1 (numbers after each "±" are standard deviations for each of the ten-session averages). The differences in values between adjacent rows are all statistically significant with $p < .01$ except for the transition from row 2 to row 3 in both the unpruned and the pruned cases and for the transition from row 4 to row 5 in the pruned case.

Representation	Unpruned (%)	Pruned (%)
Raw	33.3 ± 3.8	30.5 ± 3.0
+ Hirsh-Noordewier	22.9 ± 3.8	22.0 ± 3.7
+ Bootstrap: Stage 1	21.9 ± 1.5	20.6 ± 2.4
+ Bootstrap: Stage 2	17.6 ± 2.5	17.4 ± 3.0
+ Bootstrap: Stage 3	12.9 ± 3.2	15.2 ± 2.9

Table 1: Error rates for various representations.

Initial Representations

Although the preceding section formulated the promoter-recognition problem as an inductive-learning task, learning cannot proceed until a specific representation for the training examples is chosen and used to describe the data. Moreover, the quality of learning depends on the representation selected. Here we are able to bootstrap from a training-data representation generated by past human-engineering efforts that significantly improves the results of learning (Hirsh & Noordewier 1994). This section begins with a description of the low-level representation for DNA sequences as strings over a four-letter alphabet, followed by the higher-level Hirsh-Noordewier representation.

The "Raw" Training Data Representation

DNA is composed of two chains of chemical "building blocks" known as *nucleotides*. These two chains are linked together at consecutive nucleotide locations to form a winding, ladder-like structure (the so-called DNA *double helix*). Each nucleotide building block is made up of a phosphate group, a sugar, and one of four molecular units: adenine, cytosine, guanine, and thymine, typically represented by the characters "a", "c", "g", and "t". The two chains are complementary in that each adenine on one chain is bound to a thymine on the other, while each cytosine on one chain is bound to a guanine on the other, and thus the sequence of nucleotides in one strand is sufficient for representing the information present in each double-stranded DNA. This leads to a natural representation for DNA, namely a sequential listing of all the nucleotides in the DNA nucleotide chain. Computationally this means DNA can be represented as strings over the four-letter nucleotide alphabet ("a", "c", "g", and "t"), and indeed, this is the representation used for storing sequence information in the on-line nucleic-acid libraries developed by biologists.

Representing DNA as strings also leads to a natural feature-vector representation for learning that has become fairly standard in applications of inductive learning to DNA sequences (*e.g.*, Shavlik, Towell, and Noordewier 1992). Each promoter and non-promoter sequence is truncated to be a string of some uniform length over the four-letter alphabet, and the resulting string is converted into a feature vector of the same length, with each position in the string converted into a single feature. Thus, for example, in this work the initial training data are truncated to be strings of length 51 labeled as positive or negative by whether there is a promoter present in the string. The strings are in turn con-

Helical Parameters			Site-Specific Information	
twist1a --> r,r,r,r,y.	roll4a --> r,r,r,y,y.	twist7a -- >r,y,r,r,r.	gtg --> " gtg "	" cac ".	
twist1b --> y,r,y,y,y.	roll4b --> r,y,y,y,r.	twist7b -- >y,y,r,y,r.	gtg-pair --> gtg, ..., gtg.	
twist2a --> r,r,r,r,y,r.	roll5a --> r,r,y,y,y.	twist8a -- >y,r,y,r,r.	minus-10 --> " tataat ".	
twist2b --> y,r,y,y,y,y.	roll5b --> y,r,r,r,y.	twist8b -- >y,y,y,r,y.	minus-35 --> " ttgaca ".	
twist3a --> r,r,r,y,r.	roll6a --> r,r,y,y,y,r.	twist9a -- >y,r,y,r,r,r.	upstream --> minus-35, ..., minus-10.	
twist3b --> r,y,y,y,y.	roll6b --> y,r,r,r,y,y.	twist9b -- >y,y,y,r,y,r.		
Inverted-Repeat			AT-Composition	
Checks the DNA sequence for a subsequence that is palindromic when one of its two halves is complemented (for example, "catgaattcatg").			Fraction of "a"s and "t"s in the sequence.	

Figure 1: The Hirsh-Noordewier features.

verted into feature vectors of length 51, with each feature taking on one of four values: "a", "c", "g", and "t". Our error rates for learning using this representation are reported in the first row of Table 1.

The Hirsh-Noordewier Representation

The difficulty in using the raw data representation in learning is that the nature of a particular sequence depends on physical and chemical properties of the sequence, properties that are not readily discernible from the raw nucleotide sequence. This observation led to the development by Hirsh and Noordewier (1994) of a set of higher-level features for DNA that reflect such physical and chemical properties in the belief that such a representation would be more successful for learning. Their experimental results show that representing the training data in terms of these higher-level features can lead to dramatic improvements in learning across a range of learners and sequence-identification tasks.

The features we use are listed in Figure 1, represented using an extended form of Prolog's definite clause grammars (Searls 1992; Hirsh & Noordewier 1994). In the twist and roll definitions, "r" stands for "g" or "a" (the *purines*) and "y" stands for "t" or "c" (the *pyrimidines*). Data in this representation are represented as vectors of length 76: the 51 raw features augmented by the 25 features in Figure 1. Our error rates for this representation are reported in the second row of Table 1, and mirror the significantly better learning results reported by Hirsh and Noordewier.[1]

Bootstrapping Better Representations

Although the Hirsh-Noordewier representation significantly improves learning, this work takes their representation further still, using our bootstrapping approach to develop additional successful higher-level features. Doing so required that we create operators that generate new features that look

---

[1] Note, however, that our error rates are not strictly comparable to those of Hirsh and Noordewier. First, Hirsh and Noordewier use a different collection of promoter data. Second, we use C4.5, whereas their results are for C4.5rules (Quinlan 1993) and back-propagation (Rumelhart, Hinton, & Williams 1986). Finally, our representation differs somewhat from theirs, in that they updated their features after the experiments reported here were completed but before publication of their paper.

like the Hirsh-Noordewier features. The operators that we created fall into three qualitatively different classes. We therefore applied our bootstrapping approach in three stages, with each corresponding to a different single class of operators. At each stage the new features that we created were monotonically added to the features of the previous stage: no feature, once added to the representation in one stage, is ever removed.

Stage 1: Intra-Feature Extrapolation

Our first stage of bootstrapping begins with the "raw" representation augmented with the Hirsh-Noordewier features, and uses two feature-creation operators to generate new features. These operators were based on patterns observed in the definitions of each of a set of higher-level features (such as the three consecutive "r"s or "y"s at one of the two ends of many of helical-parameter definitions). We call such operators *intra-feature extrapolation* operators, in that they extrapolate from patterns found within the definitions of individual features to new features.

Our first operator extrapolates from patterns in the helical-parameter feature definitions, generating new features that match fairly low-level patterns in these features. In particular, it generates all features of length five or six that satisfy any of the following five patterns observed in the helical-parameter feature definitions in Figure 1:

1. The string begins with exactly 3 or 4 contiguous "r"s.
2. The string ends with exactly 3 or 4 contiguous "y"s.
3. The string has exactly 3 contiguous "r"s in its middle, with the rest "y"s.
4. The string has exactly 3 contiguous "y"s in its middle, with the rest "r"s.
5. The string has exactly 2 contiguous "r"s or "y"s at one of its ends, with the rest alternating.

Our second operator extrapolates from patterns in the site-specific features by switching the nucleotides occurring in feature definitions. It does this by first imposing an artificial generalization hierarchy on the four nucleotide values by dividing them into two groups of two. Each site-specific feature within an existing feature definition is then re-expressed in terms of these groups, and some of the groups are then replaced (consistently across the whole feature definition) to be another group. Finally, the artificial group names are re-instantiated to yield a new feature definition. For example, consider the "gtg" and "cac" patterns. We can define the groups G1={g,c} and G2={a,t}, express the two patterns in terms of these groups, "G1 G2 G1", and consider the patterns where G1 and G2 exchange roles, "G2 G1 G2". Replacing the artificial group-names with actual nucleotides yields (in addition to "gtg" and "cac") "gag", "ctc", "aga", "tgt", "aca", and "tct".

By generating all features possible using our first operator we were able to generate 18 new features;[2] a similar application of our second operator in all possible ways gave rise to an additional 15 new features. The resulting representation thus has 109 features, and as shown in Table 1, the new representation gave modest improvements in error-rate estimates, 1.0% for unpruned trees and 1.4% for pruned trees.

Stage 2: Inter-Feature Extrapolation

The next stage of our bootstrapping process extended this representation by applying two additional feature-creation operators that were based on patterns observed *across* feature definitions. For example, each of the five-nucleotide helical-parameter feature definitions is a truncated version of a six-nucleotide helical-parameter definition. We call such operators *inter-feature extrapolation* operators, since they extrapolate from patterns that occur across feature definitions.

Our first inter-feature extrapolation operator is based on the previously mentioned pattern that each helical-parameter feature of length five is derivable from one of length six by deleting an "r" or a "y" either at its start or at its end. This operator takes existing features of length six and deletes the element at its start or its end.

Our second operator is based on an alternative way of viewing the pattern underlying the preceding operator. In particular, each length-six feature can be viewed as the result of adding an "r" or "y" to one of the two ends of a length-five feature. This operator takes feature definitions of length five and creates new features of length six by adding either an "r" or a "y" at the start or end.

These two operators were applied in all possible ways to the features generated by the preceding bootstrapping stage, yielding 43 additional features. As shown in the third row of Table 1, the resulting representation improved learning more significantly than the previous bootstrapping stage, with an additional improvement of 4.3% above the results of the first stage of bootstrapping for unpruned trees, and a 3.2% improvement in the pruned case. Note that these results also lend credibility to the merit of the features generated in the prior bootstrapping stage—the newly created features are based on the Hirsh-Noordewier features *plus* the features created by our first stage of bootstrapping.

---

[2]Two of these features were actually duplicates. While this does not affect the results of C4.5, it does effect the feature count for the experiments in the next section.

Stage 3: Feature Specialization

Our final bootstrapping stage begins with the preceding bootstrapped representation, and creates new features by specializing existing features. The resulting feature definitions look like existing feature definitions, only they succeed on a smaller number of cases. The single specialization operator we use here simply specializes helical-parameter-type features (the original helical-parameter features plus similar-looking features generated by previous bootstrapping stages) by taking each feature and consistently replacing "r"s with either "a"s or "g"s and "y"s with either "c"s or "t"s. For example, the right-hand side of "twist1a → r,r,r,r,y" would be specialized in four ways: "ggggc", "ggggt", "aaaac", and "aaaat".

Due to the large number of helical-parameter-type features generated during Stages 1 and 2—each of which would give rise to multiple new features using this operator—it was not practical to apply this operator to all potentially relevant features. We therefore pruned the set of features to which the operator would be applied by selecting only those features that occurred somewhere in the learned decision trees generated by C4.5 on the data using the result of the second stage of bootstrapping. 60 new features were generated by this process, and Table 1 again shows significantly improved error rates: 4.7% from Stage 2 to Stage 3 in the unpruned case, and 2.2% in the pruned case.

Evaluation

Although the previous section shows that our new features improve learning, they do not tell us what caused the improvement. In particular, we do not know whether similar results would be observed for any collection of new features defined in terms of the raw-data features, as opposed to being due to the new features having syntactic forms similar to existing features. To answer this question we developed four additional representations, each beginning with the raw + Hirsh-Noordewier features, but with additional "random" higher-level features (defined in terms of the raw features) also included in the representation. Each representation contains random features of a single type:

1. Random contiguous strings of length 3 to 10.
2. 2, 3, or 4 random contiguous strings of length 2 to 10 separated by intervals of length 1 to 20.
3. Random contiguous strings of length 5 or 6.
4. 2 or 3 random contiguous strings of length 5 or 6 separated by intervals of length 1 to 40.

Note that these features are *not* random in the sense that they are "irrelevant features", but rather they are random features defined in terms of the lower-level representation, and as such, they do reflect information about the training data. Since features in the latter two representations are more similar syntactically to the Hirsh-Noordewier features than are features in the first two representations, we report results for the first two separately from the second two, in that the latter constitute a more difficult test for the performance of our newly created features.

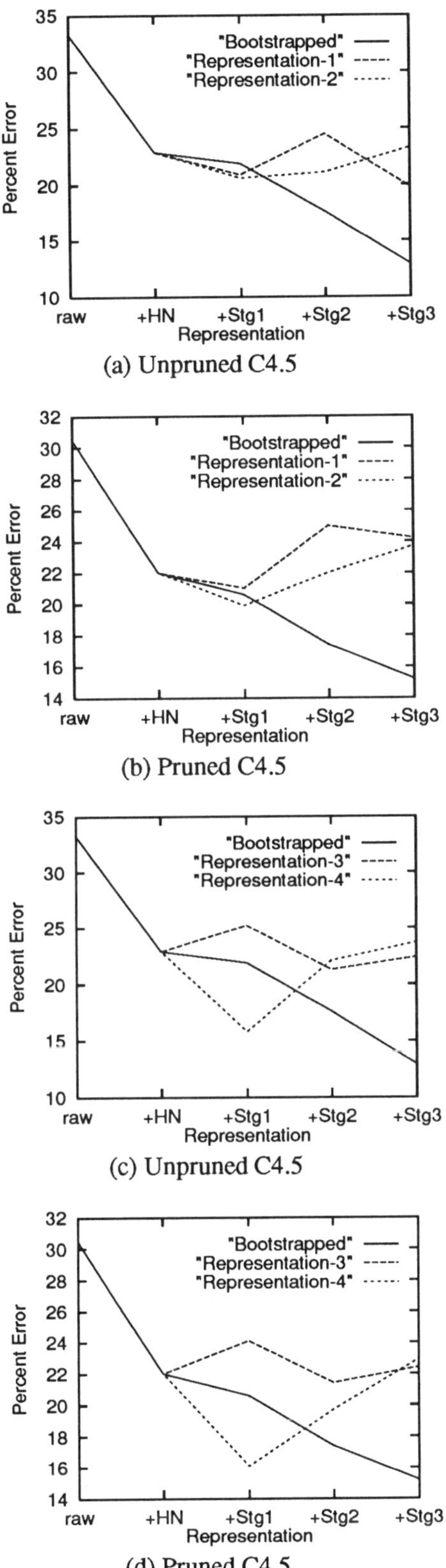

(a) Unpruned C4.5

(b) Pruned C4.5

(c) Unpruned C4.5

(d) Pruned C4.5

Figure 2: Bootstrapped versus random features.

To compare the results of learning using these random representations to the bootstrapped representations, our experiments were conducted to mimic those of the previous section as much as possible. The graphs in Figure 2 all first plot error rates for the raw and raw + Hirsh-Noordewier features. The remaining values are for representations that continue from this point. To get to the first stage of feature addition for each of the random representations (labeled "+Stg1" on the abscissa in each of the graphs) we added 33 random features to equal the same number of features that were added in the first bootstrapping stage above. An additional 43 random features were then added to these 109 features for comparison to the second bootstrapping stage. Finally, an additional 62 features were added to these 152 features to yield the third-stage values.[3] Our results are presented in Figure 2 (where "Bootstrapped" labels the error-rate curve for the series of representations generated in the previous section). Statistical significance was established with $p < .01$ for the differences between the bootstrapped representation and all representations except for the first two random representations for both pruned and unpruned trees at the first bootstrapping stage (Figures 2(a) and 2(b)), and for pruned trees for the final random representation at the second bootstrapping stage (Figure 2(d)).

These results support our claim that the syntactic form of the bootstrapped features plays an important role in their success. Although learning was consistently better with the results of bootstrapping than with the first three random representations, learning with the final random representation was better than bootstrapping when roughly 25 features were added. With more features, however, performance degraded while performance for the bootstrapped features improved. We conjecture that there is some optimal number of such features that can help learning, but if too many such features are used they begin to act truly random, helping the learner find spurious correlations in the data. We leave a more in-depth study of this question for future work. However, given that these features do resemble the syntactic form of the Hirsh-Noordewier features, they can be viewed as additional support that the success of our bootstrapping approach is due the similarity of new features to existing features, rather than simply being the result of adding more features, regardless of syntactic form.

Towards a Bootstrapping Approach to Constructive Induction

Although the feature-creation operators used in our three bootstrapping stages are clearly specific to this domain, we believe there are more general principles underlying them. First, they are based on an intuitively compelling idea, that feature definitions that look like already existing successful feature definitions may themselves also improve learning. Second, intra-feature extrapolation, inter-feature extrapo-

---

[3] An accurate comparison to the corresponding bootstrapped representation should have involved adding 60 features, rather than 62. Given the large number of features present at this point, we do not believe this error affects our results qualitatively.

lation, and feature specialization (together with additional operations not used in this work, such as feature generalization) are domain-independent notions, even if they manifest themselves here in a domain-dependent fashion.

Further, the implementations of our operators also take a fairly general form, and in particular exhibit two distinct general approaches to encoding feature-creation operators. The first approach includes our initial intra-feature extrapolation operator, and takes the form of a *constraint-based* feature generator. This operator generates all possible features of a given form that satisfy some constraints. The second approach, which includes the remaining operators, generates new features by modifying existing features (such as by deletion of feature-definition elements, specialization, etc.). This latter, *transformational* approach to feature-creation has already been suggested by Callan and Utgoff (1991) and Fawcett and Utgoff (1992). However, unlike this work where transformations are designed so that they generate feature definitions of certain syntactic forms, their transformations are based on background theories of a domain and are generally of a more wide-ranging nature, not driven by notions of syntactic similarity.

In an ideal world a learning system would take the training data and automatically reformulate it into a form better suited for learning. Incorporating such *constructive induction* (Michalski 1983) capabilities into learning systems in a practical way is very difficult. This work represents an initial step in a longer-term goal of developing a domain-independent bootstrapping approach to constructive induction, driven by the afore-mentioned generalities underlying this work. In particular, it is our goal to continue our development of feature-creation operators with an eye towards domain independence. We expect this to require the development of methods for automatically recognizing patterns in a collection of higher-level features and converting them into constraints for use by domain-independent constraint-based feature-generation operators, as well as refining and expanding our current set of transformational operators into a more comprehensive and domain-independent set.

Summary

This paper has presented a two-stage approach to the engineering of good representations for data, using operators that create new features that embody syntactic patterns appearing in an initial set of expert-based features. The assumption underlying this approach is that syntactic patterns commonly underlie successful human-created higher-level features, and moreover, when such patterns are present, that they have semantic meaning in the domain and thus similar-looking features will be more likely to be successful for learning.

The application of this approach to the problem of learning rules for recognizing promoters in DNA sequences generated representations that dramatically improved the results of learning beyond those of the initially successful human-engineered features. Our experiments further show that it is the syntactic similarity of the new features to existing features that is the cause for the success, rather than merely the addition of new features (even when syntactically similar at a more gross level). These results are particularly notable in that both authors of this paper have little training in molecular biology; the bootstrapping operators are a first encoding of syntactic forms that we observed in pre-existing higher-level features, rather than an explicit attempt to encode domain knowledge into the feature-creation operators or an iterative process of using a learning system to find a set of feature-creation operators that generate features that help learning. The ease with which we were able to generate feature-creation operators that significantly improved learning makes us particularly hopeful for the prospects for our longer-term goal of developing this work into a domain-independent bootstrapping approach to constructive induction.

References

Callan, J. P., and Utgoff, P. E. 1991. Constructive induction on domain information. In *Proceedings of the Ninth National Conference on Artificial Intelligence*, 614–619. San Mateo, CA: Morgan Kaufmann.

Clark, P. E., and Boswell, R. 1991. Rule induction with CN2. In *Proceedings of the European Working Session on Learning*, 151–163. Berlin: Springer-Verlag.

Fawcett, T. E., and Utgoff, P. E. 1992. Automatic feature generation for problem solving systems. In *Proceedings of the Ninth International Conference on Machine Learning*, 144–153. San Mateo, CA: Morgan Kaufmann.

Hirsh, H., and Noordewier, M. 1994. Using background knowledge to improve learning of DNA sequences. In *Proceedings of the Tenth IEEE Conference on Artificial Intelligence for Applications*, 351–357. Los Alamitos, CA: IEEE Computer Society Press.

Michalski, R. S. 1983. A theory and methodology of inductive learning. In Michalski, R. S.; Carbonell, J. G.; and Mitchell, T. M., eds., *Machine Learning: An Artificial Intelligence Approach*. Los Altos, CA: Morgan Kaufmann.

Norton, S. W. 1994. Learning to recognize promoter sequences in E. coli by modeling uncertainty in the training data. In *Proceedings of the Twelfth National Conference on Artificial Intelligence*. Menlo Park, CA: AAAI Press.

Quinlan, J. R. 1993. *C4.5: Programs for Machine Learning*. San Mateo, CA: Morgan Kaufmann.

Rumelhart, D. E.; Hinton, G. E.; and Williams, R. J. 1986. Learning internal representations by error propagation. In Rumelhart, D. E., and McClelland, J. L., eds., *Parallel Distributed Processing*. Cambridge, MA: MIT Press. 318–364.

Searls, D. B. 1992. The computational linguistics of biological sequences. In Hunter, L., ed., *Artificial Intelligence and Molecular Biology*. Menlo Park, CA: AAAI Press. 47–120.

Shavlik, J.; Towell, G.; and Noordewier, M. 1992. Using artificial neural networks to refine existing biological knowledge. *International Journal of Human Genome Research* 1:81–107.

Weiss, S. M., and Kulikowski, C. A. 1991. *Computer Systems That Learn*. San Mateo, CA: Morgan Kaufmann.

A Discovery System for Trigonometric Functions

Tsuyoshi Murata, Masami Mizutani, and Masamichi Shimura

Department of Computer Science, Tokyo Institute of Technology
2 Ohokayama, Meguro, Tokyo 152, JAPAN
{murata, mizutani, shimura}@cs.titech.ac.jp

Abstract

This paper describes a discovery system for trigonometric functions (DST), which has abilities to acquire new knowledge in the form of theorems and formulas in a plane geometry domain. The system is composed of two subsystems: a plane geometry analysis system and a mathematical formula transformation system. The former changes the length and angles of a figure and extracts geometric relations, and the latter transforms the relations to acquire useful formulas. With little basic knowledge such as the definition of the congruence of triangles and the definition of fundamental trigonometric functions, our system has rediscovered many trigonometric formulas and geometric theorems, including the Pythagorean theorem.

Introduction

Machine discovery elucidates human's intelligent activities, and it automates creative tasks of finding new knowledge. This paper proposes a method for discovery in a plane geometry domain, and describes a discovery system for trigonometric functions (DST) we developed. DST's initial knowledge is the definitions of similarity and congruence, and the concept of a triangle, such that a triangle consists of three lines. Definitions of fundamental trigonometric functions, such as sine, cosine, and tangent, are also given. Our DST finds relations of a figure which is obtained from a triangle by drawing additional lines and by changing its shape. The obtained relations among its angles and sides are transformed into geometric theorems. With a simple method, our system can rediscover many theorems.

Most of the previous discovery systems operate in physics and chemistry domains. Only few attempts have so far been made at machine discovery in a geometric domain. The domain has many research topics, such as the representation of geometric relations, the integration of figures and formulas, and the evaluation of acquired formulas.

AM (Lenat 1983) and BACON (Langley, Bradshaw, & Simon 1983) are well-known discovery systems. Necessary data and heuristics are given to the system in advance. AM has many heuristics to guide its discovery. BACON discovers relations among the variables only within the given data.

In discovery systems, experiments play an important role to acquire useful data. COAST (Rajamoney 1990) and DEED (Rajamoney 1993) can design experiments to acquire data that discriminate between competing theories. COAST uses heuristics to modify the given situation so that it can discriminate between different theories. DEED uses the difference between the explanations of the competing theories as a clue for modifying the given situation. These knowledge-intensive approaches to experiment design is useful only when the knowledge for making explanations is sufficient.

KEKADA (Kulkarni & Simon 1988) proposes experiments based on the heuristics of surprising phenomena that constrain the search for new knowledge. Surprise arises when there are differences between an experimental result and its expectation. Defining surprising phenomena, however, is difficult when there is little amount of knowledge.

DST uses neither explanation nor surprise; it manipulates its environment, observes the effects, and relates the effects with their causes. Such a method is generally applicable to domains with little knowledge.

A Discovery System for Trigonometric Functions

Structure of DST

To discover geometric theorems, two kinds of activities are required. One is to extract relations of geometric elements, such as angles and length of sides, from a figure. The other activity is to transform the extracted relations.

In our discovery system, DST, these activities are performed by two subsystems: a plane geometry analysis system (PGA) and a mathematical formula transformation system (MFT), as shown in Figure 1. PGA extracts relations from a figure, changes its length of sides and angles, and draws an additional line. MFT transforms the extracted relations to discover new geometric theorems.

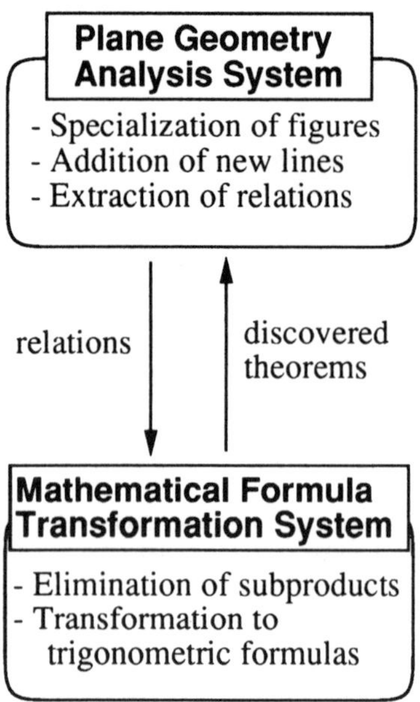

Figure 1: Two subsystems of DST

DST's initial knowledge is only for analyzing figures:

- Definitions of sine, cosine, and tangent as ratios of two sides in a right triangle
- Axioms of plane figures
    - If two triangles are congruent, their corresponding sides and angles are equal.
    - If two triangles are similar, their corresponding angles and the ratios of length of their corresponding sides are equal.

The former definitions are necessary to express the relations of sides and angles. The latter characteristics between two triangles, such as the similarity and congruence, are needed since a triangle is the fundamental element.

The amount of initial knowledge varies according to the purpose of discovery systems. Knowledge-intensive discovery systems use considerable amount of basic domain knowledge to acquire advanced knowledge. Discovery with too much initial knowledge is, however, nothing more than the transformation of the given knowledge. While our DST aims at initial exploration and can discover theorems with very few initial knowledge.

Plane Geometry Analysis System

The role of PGA is to generate figures from an arbitrary triangle and to extract relations among sides and angles for MFT. PGA has the following mechanisms:

- Specialization of figures
- Addition of new lines

- Extraction of relations

Specialization of figures Performing specialization is one way to make experiments in a geometric domain. Specialization of a triangle can be done in the following way:

- changing a triangle to a right triangle
- making two angles equal
- making two sides equal

In some cases, giving one specialization causes other relations among sides and angles. For example, making two angles of a triangle equal can be a result of making two sides equal. The former specialization implies the latter, which can be considered as a new theorem. Among specialization, changing a triangle to a right triangle is often useful since trigonometric functions are defined with a right triangle.

Addition of new lines Addition of new lines to a figure often clarifies relations among its basic elements. An additional line divides a figure into two smaller figures, and the relations extracted from each smaller figure are combined to find relations in the figure. Additional lines drawn by PGA are as follows:

- a bisector of an angle
- a bisector of a side
- a perpendicular lines from a vertex

Additional lines generate new elements, such as sides and angles, which are called *subproducts*. Although subproducts are useful for extracting new relations, they cannot be used to express new theorems and should be eliminated later.

Extraction of relations A figure consists of basic elements, such as points, lines, angles and triangles. A change in one element often causes side effects to other parts of the figure.

In PGA, the same kind of basic elements are grouped together. The elements in the same group are combined together to form a different kind of element, and relations among them are found. After finding the relations, PGA sends them to MFT for further process. As shown in Figure 2, an additional line CH is drawn on a triangle ABC, and relations among the length of lines are extracted. Two lines which share the same end are combined to make an angle, and relations of adjacent angles are extracted. Similarly, three lines are combined to make a triangle, and relations of congruent or similar triangles are also extracted. Lines, angles, and triangles are mutually related in this way so that specialization to an element is propagated to the rest of the elements in the figure.

Mathematical Formula Transformation System

The role of MFT is to discover theorems from the formulas which express the extracted relations. The dis-

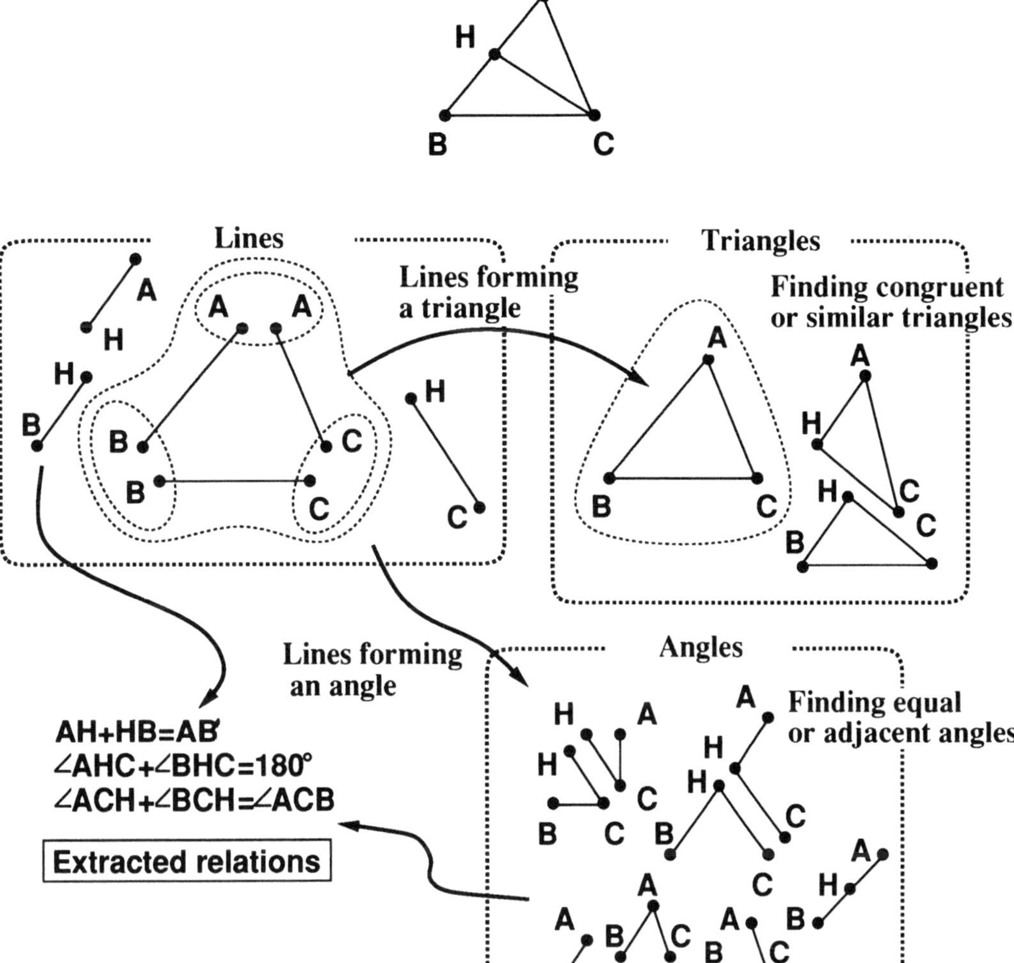

Figure 2: Extraction of relations

covery of MFT is performed by transposition, substitution, and fundamental arithmetic operations.

1. Generation of a theorem To generate a theorem, MFT eliminates subproducts in the obtained relations by repeating substitution. If the result of substitution contains no subproduct variable, it can be considered that a theorem is generated. The conditional part of the theorem is obtained from the formulas of the figure before drawing additional lines, and the consequent part is from the acquired formulas.

Figure 3 shows a process of discovering a theorem, "An isosceles triangle has equal base angles." The relation obtained from a triangle ABC before drawing an additional line is the given condition AB=AC. MFT draws a perpendicular line AH from vertex A to side

BC, and generates two congruent triangles, △AHB and △AHC. Among newly extracted relations, ∠ABC = ∠ACB contains no subproducts. Since the line does not add any new constraints to the original triangle, the relation is considered as a characteristic of the isosceles triangle. Therefore, the theorem is obtained of which conditional part is AB=AC and consequent part is ∠ABC = ∠ACB. As seen in the above process, it is found that the theorem is obtained from the relations which are extracted before and after drawing the line.

As a result of subproduct elimination, formulas with many terms or with complex terms are often generated. MFT does not use these formulas for subsequent transformation since they cause explosive increase of formulas. To put it more concretely, the results of the sub-

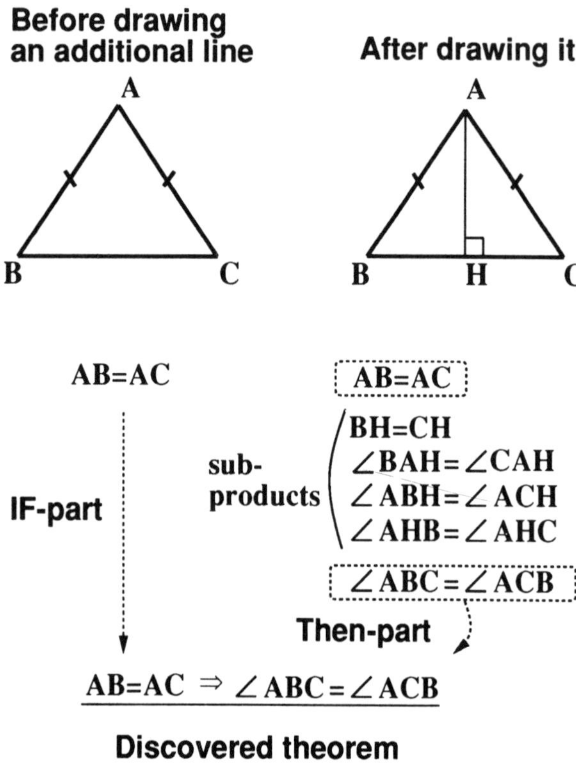

Figure 3: Discovery of a geometric theorem

stitution that increases the number of subproducts are discarded. Formulas whose dimension is higher than three are also discarded.

The number of formula transformation is also constrained in LEX (Mitchell et al. 1981) which treats symbolic integration. Heuristics about the application of its operators are the criteria for formula transformation. In MFT, the dimension of formulas and the number of variables are used as the criteria, since the formula transformation depends solely on the selection of formulas.

2. Trigonometric representation In order to acquire trigonometric theorems, discovered theorems in the above process have to be transformed. That is, variables expressing sides of a right triangle are eliminated from the theorem by using the definition of trigonometric functions. By introducing basic trigonometric functions such as sine, cosine, and tangent, a formula $\sin^2\theta + \cos^2\theta = 1$ is acquired from the Pythagorean theorem which is discovered previously.

Results

The items listed below are some of the theorems that DST has rediscovered from a triangle.

- $\tan\theta = \sin\theta/\cos\theta$

- $\tan\theta = \sin\theta/\sin(90° - \theta)$
- $\tan\theta = 1/\tan(90° - \theta)$
- $\sin^2\theta + \cos^2\theta = 1$
- An isosceles triangle
  $\rightarrow$ Its base angles are equal.
- A triangle of equal base angles
  $\rightarrow$ It is an isosceles triangle.
- A right triangle
  $\rightarrow$ The Pythagorean theorem holds.

The first four theorems are well-known fundamental laws of trigonometric functions, and the rest are obtained by interpreting the relation of acquired formulas. In the manner described above, MFT generates a number of formulas. For example, the Pythagorean theorem is found as EXPR4024 formed by EXPR3804 and EXPR4023, as shown in Figure 4. In general, Pythagorean theorem can be proved based on the comparison of area of additional squares. It should be noted that DST finds the theorem only by mathematical transformation without using the concept of area. The figure is generated by changing an angle to a right angle and by drawing a perpendicular line from a vertex to its opposite side. PGA finds that the triangles $\triangle ABC$, $\triangle PBA$, and $\triangle PAC$ are similar triangles since they have corresponding angles. Extracted relations are that the ratios of adjacent sides of the corresponding angles are equal. Other geometric relations, such as $BP + CP = BC$, are also extracted. Finally, MFT discovers the theorem $AB^2 + AC^2 = BC^2$, which includes no subproduct such as AP, BP, and CP.

In Figure 4, EXPR3636 and EXPR3810 involve subproduct variables AP, BP, and CP. MFT eliminates BP from these two expressions and produces EXPR4022. Then MFT finds EXPR3806 which involves the same subproduct variables in EXPR4022 to eliminate AP. In the same manner, EXPR3804 is used to eliminate CP. Finally MFT discovers EXPR4024 which involves no subproduct, and this formula is the well-known Pythagorean theorem.

PGA generates figures by performing all possible specialization and addition of lines to the given figure. All the figures constitute a tree structure whose node shows a generated figure and whose arc shows specialization or addition of lines. PGA selects one of the node for its analysis in the breadth-first order. Geometrically equal figures possibly appear in different node in the tree. These figures are, however, considered as different figures in PGA, since they are identified as a sequence of specialization and addition of lines. Generally the discovered theorem would be the same if the analyzed figures are equal, even if they appear in different nodes. However, theorems actually discovered from the figures are not always the same. For example, the fifth and the sixth theorems listed above are rediscovered separately in DST, though the figures used for the discovery are geometrically equal.

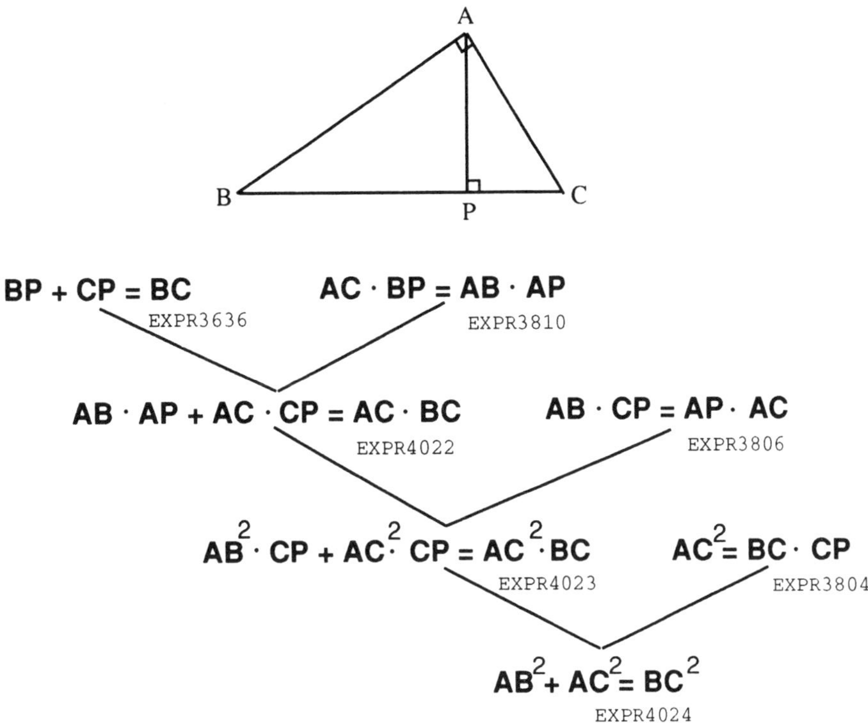

Figure 4: Discovery of the Pythagorean theorem

MFT combines theorems which are discovered from different figures to generate new different theorems. From the first and the second theorems listed above, a theorem "$\cos\theta = \sin(90° - \theta)$" will be generated.

Discussion

As Zytkow and Baker pointed out (Zytkow & Baker 1991), experimentation has a number of advantages over mere manipulation of given data, since an abundance of data are provided, the quality of data is improved, important data for constructing theorems can be obtained, and various situations are created so that regularities of data are easy to discover. Manipulation on figures to get useful data corresponds to experimentation in a plane geometry domain. DST autonomously manipulates its environment and acquires data in order to discover with little initial knowledge.

To evaluate the generality of discovered laws or theorems enhances their utility. ABACUS (Falkenhainer & Michalski 1986) employs discriminant descriptions of classifying observed data into classes in generated numeric laws. FAHRENHEIT (Zytkow 1987) specifies the scope of discovered laws as extended numeric laws. Our DST analyzes and specializes figures under geometrical constraints. The scope of theorems discovered in DST, therefore, is given by such constraints of analyzed figures in the specialization process in a plane geometry.

In order to evaluate the utility of concepts and to restrict the search space of discovery process, AM uses "interestingness." The criteria are, however, fixed by the initial definitions of concepts. The complexity of expressions in DST is evaluated by the number of variables, dimensions of formulas, and the number of subproducts. Though DST has no similar criteria to AM, elimination of subproducts turns out to be an effective approach for discovering useful theorems. Also the elimination avoids the combinational explosion of formulas since it restricts the search space of formula transformation.

Sometimes, however, we encounter the case where theorems employing subproducts are important in a target domain. To find such theorem, formulas obtained in PGA should not be eliminated. For example, to find theorems about a center of gravity in a triangle, additional lines to a triangle are required. It is important, therefore, to discriminate geometrically important subproducts from mere auxiliary ones.

Concluding Remarks

We have developed a discovery system for trigonometric functions in a plane geometry. Our system rediscovers many theorems, including the Pythagorean theorem, with a simple method. It should be noted that

DST rediscovered from quite little knowledge. In a similar manner of human problem-solving in a plane geometry domain, PGA acquires relations among basic elements under various conditions. MFT generates 10,000 formulas to discover the theorems described above. Omitting useless formulas during its transformation avoids the generation of explosive number of formulas.

One direction to extend DST is to consider new basic elements, such as circles and four-sided figures. If a circle is added as a basic element, relations about an inscribed circle and a circle circumscribing a triangle will be extracted by PGA.

Acknowledgments

We would like to thank Dr. Somkiat Tangkitvanich for his insightful comments.

References

Falkenhainer, B.C., and Michalski, R. S. 1986. Integrating Quantitative and Qualitative Discovery: The ABACUS System. *Machine Learning* 1(4): 367–401.

Kulkarni, D., and Simon, H. A. 1988. The Process of Scientific Discovery: The Strategy of Experimentation. *Cognitive Science* 12(2): 139–175.

Langley, P. W., Bradshaw, G. L., and Simon, H. A. 1983. Rediscovering Chemistry with the BACON System. In Michalski, R. S., Carbonell, J. G., and Mitchell, T. M. eds. *Machine Learning : An Artificial Intelligence Approach.* : Tioga.

Lenat, D. B. 1983. The Role of Heuristics in Learning by Discovery: Three Case Studies. In Michalski, R. S., Carbonell, J. G., and Mitchell, T. M. eds. *Machine Learning : An Artificial Intelligence Approach.* : Tioga.

Mitchell, T. M., Utgoff, P. E., Nudel, B., and Banerji R. 1981. Learning Problem-Solving Heuristics Through Practice. In Proceedings of the Seventh International Joint Conference on Artificial Intelligence, 127–134.

Rajamoney, S. A. 1990. A Computational Approach To Theory Revision. In Shrager, J., and Langley, P. eds. *Computational Models of Scientific Discovery and Theory Formation.* : Morgan Kaufmann.

Rajamoney, S. A. 1993. The Design of Discrimination Experiments. *Machine Learning* 12(1): 185–203.

Zytkow, J. M. 1987. Combining many searches in the FAHRENHEIT discovery system. In Proceedings of the Fourth International workshop on Machine Learning, 281–287. : Morgan Kaufmann.

Zytkow, J. M., and Baker, J. 1991. Interactive Mining of Regularities in Databases. In Piatetsky-Shapiro, G., and Frawley, W. J. eds. *Knowledge Discovery in Databases.* : The MIT Press.

Compositional Instance-Based Learning

Patrick Broos and **Karl Branting**
Department of Computer Science
University of Wyoming
Laramie, Wyoming 82071-3682
{patb,karl}@eolus.uwyo.edu

Abstract

This paper proposes a new algorithm for acquisition of
preference predicates by a learning apprentice, termed
Compositional Instance-Based Learning (CIBL), that
permits multiple instances of a preference predicate
to be composed, directly exploiting the transitivity
of preference predicates. In an empirical evaluation,
CIBL was consistently more accurate than a 1-NN
instance-based learning strategy unable to compose
instances. The relative performance of CIBL and decision tree induction was found to depend upon (1) the
complexity of the preference predicate being acquired
and (2) the dimensionality of the feature space.

Introduction

A central impediment to the construction of
knowledge-based systems is the high cost of knowledge
base development and maintenance. One approach to
reducing these costs is to design systems that can acquire knowledge by observing human problem-solving
steps during normal use of the system. Systems that
engage in this form of learning are termed *learning apprentice systems* (Mitchell, Mahadevan, & Steinberg
1985). Learning apprentice systems have been developed for VLSI design (Mahadevan *et al.* 1993), acqui
sition of "interface agents" (Maes & Kozierok 1993),
and calendar management (Dent *et al.* 1992).

An important form of knowledge that can be acquired by observing users' decisions is knowledge of
users' preferences. In configuration tasks such as design or scheduling, for example, there may be numerous configurations that satisfy all applicable hard constraints. Users may nevertheless strongly prefer some
configurations to others. For example, in the domain of
scheduling ground-based telescope observations, there
are typically many different schedules that satisfy all
hard constraints (such as not pointing the telescope
at the sun or below the horizon, not scheduling two
observations at the same time, *etc.*). However, such
schedules may differ significantly in factors such as the
airmass[1] and research priority of each scheduled observation. Choosing among such schedules requires a

---

[1] The airmass of an observation is a measure of the
amount of atmosphere between the star and the observer.
Airmass can be minimized by observing a star at the time
midway between its rising time and setting time.

model of the relative desirability of schedules as a function of their relevant attributes.

Knowledge of users' preferences can be expressed
as a *preference predicate* (Utgoff & Saxena 1987)
$P_Q(x, y) \equiv [Q(x) > Q(y)]$, where $Q(s)$ is an evaluation function that expresses the "quality" of state s. A
learning apprentice can acquire a user's criteria for the
relative desirability of alternative states by learning a
preference predicate P_Q from a set of training instances
$P_Q(s_i, s_j)$ produced by the user during normal use of
the system. For example, each time a learning apprentice suggests a state s_1 and the user rejects s_1 in favor
of some other state s_2, the apprentice has an opportunity to acquire the training instance $P_Q(s_2, s_1)$.

Our interest in acquisition of preference predicates
arose from a project to develop an intelligent assistant for scheduling ground-based telescope observations, the *Observing Assistant* (OA)(Broos 1993). In
developing OA, we found that astronomers could identify the relevant attributes of observation schedules but
were typically unable to articulate general criteria for
preferring one schedule over another in terms of these
attributes. Moreover, it appeared that individual astronomers often differ significantly in their preferences.
These factors cast doubt on the feasibility of devising
an *a priori* evaluation function appropriate for multiple users. A more promising approach was to develop
a learning apprentice system capable of forming "personalized knowledge-based systems" (Dent *et al.* 1992)
by acquiring the scheduling preferences of individual
astronomers.

The next section describes previous approaches to
the problem of acquiring preference criteria and proposes a novel algorithm for this task called *Compositional Instance-Based Learning* (CIBL). Section three
describes a series of experiments comparing the performance of CIBL to that of alternate approaches, both
in learning to predict astronomer's actual scheduling
preferences and in learning artificial preference criteria.

Algorithms for Learning P_Q

Previous approaches to acquisition of preference predicates from sets of training instances have used inductive learning methods to form generalizations from
sets of training instances (Utgoff & Saxena 1987;

Utgoff & Clouse 1991). One approach has been to use decision tree induction algorithms, such as ID3 (Quinlan 1986), to induce a general representation for P_Q. An alternative approach, termed the *state preference method*, uses parameter adjustment to learn a set of feature weights $\mathbf{W}$ such that for every training instance, $P_Q(x, y)$, $\mathbf{W}(\mathbf{F}(x) - \mathbf{F}(y)) > 0$, where $\mathbf{F}(n)$ is a vector of numeric attributes representing state n (Utgoff & Clouse 1991).

However, the complexity of astronomers' explanations for preferring one schedule over another led us to hypothesize that the underlying evaluation function Q for astronomical observation schedules, as with preference predicates in many other domains (Callan, Fawcett, & Rissland 1991), is typically not linear, and that the instances of P_Q are therefore not linearly separable. If correct, this hypothesis would imply that learning algorithms that presuppose linear separability, such as the state preference method, are inappropriate for this domain.

Decision tree induction algorithms such as ID3 are suitable for nonlinearly separable data. However, the performance of decision tree induction algorithms has been shown to be sometimes weaker than that of instance-based algorithms when the training set is sparse or the concept being acquired is highly "polymorphic" (Aha 1992). Our hypothesis concerning the complexity of astronomers' preference predicates suggested that these factors would often characterize acquisition of observation scheduling preference predicates. We therefore turned to an instance-based approach to this problem.

Instance-Based Learning of P_Q

Instance-based learning (IBL) is a strategy in which concepts are represented by exemplars rather than by generalizations induced from those exemplars (Stanfill & Waltz 1986). Perhaps the simplest form of instance-based learning is k-nearest-neighbor (k-NN) classification, which classifies a new instance according to the majority classification of its k nearest neighbors in feature space. A straightforward 1-NN strategy for learning preference predicates, which we term *1ARC*, represents training instances as arcs in feature space. For example, on a two dimensional feature space $S = \Re^2$, the set of training instances $\{P_Q(A, B), P_Q(C, D), P_Q(E, F)\}$ is represented as shown in Figure 1 by the training arcs $\overleftarrow{AB}$, $\overleftarrow{CD}$, and $\overleftarrow{EF}$ (where $\overleftarrow{XY} \equiv P_Q(X, Y)$).

Ranking a new pair of objects, X and Y, is equivalent to determining whether $P_Q(X, Y)$ or $P_Q(Y, X)$ is satisfied. The 1ARC algorithm begins by finding the training arc that best matches the hypothesis $P_Q(X, Y) \equiv \overleftarrow{XY}$. The dissimilarity between $\overleftarrow{XY}$ and a training arc is measured by the sum of the Euclidean distances between (1) Y and the tail of the training arc and (2) X and the head of the training arc. The dis-

similarity between $\overleftarrow{XY}$ and the training arc that it matches most closely, *i.e.*, for which the dissimilarity is least, is a measure in the confidence in the hypothesis $P_Q(X, Y)$. In Figure 1, for example, the training arc $\overleftarrow{EF}$ best matches $\overleftarrow{XY}$ with a dissimilarity of $dist(Y, F) + dist(X, E)$ represented by the dotted lines.

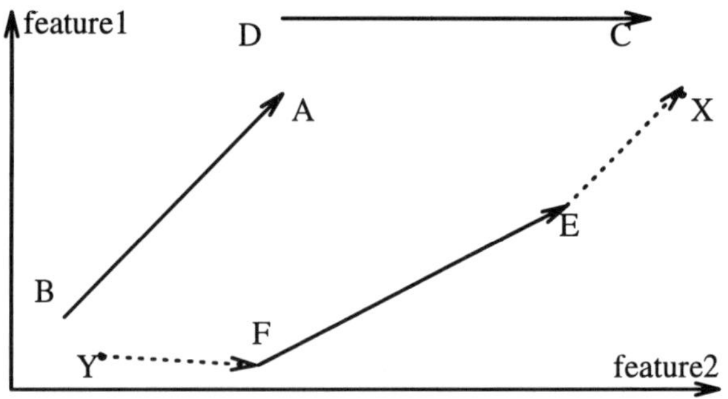

Figure 1: The best match to $\overleftarrow{XY}$ found by 1ARC.

In the same way, 1ARC then finds the best match and confidence measure for the alternate hypothesis $P_Q(Y, X)$. The hypothesis with the strongest measure of confidence determines 1ARC's estimate of the ranking between X and Y. In this case, $\overleftarrow{XY}$ matches training arc $\overleftarrow{EF}$ more strongly than $\overleftarrow{YX}$ matches any training arc, so 1ARC concludes that $P_Q(X, Y)$.

An important limitation of k-NN algorithms, such as 1ARC, is that they are unable to exploit the transitivity of preference predicates. For example, given the situation in Figure 1, it should be possible to conclude $P_Q(X, Y)$ by the reasoning "X is close to C; C is preferred to D; D is close to A; A is preferred to B; B is close to Y". However, the majority vote policy of standard k-NN methods does not permit reasoning involving the serial composition of multiple instances.

Compositional Instance-Based Learning

CIBL (Compositional Instance-Based Learning) is a strategy that permits multiple training instances to be composed to rank a new pair of objects. Like 1ARC, CIBL ranks two new objects, X and Y, by determining whether it has greater confidence in the path from X to Y or in the path from Y to X. CIBL differs from 1ARC in that it can construct a path between two new objects by sequentially connecting multiple training arcs. Such a path seeks to follow a contour of the underlying evaluation function having positive slope.

For example, given the situation shown in Figure 1, CIBL begins by searching for a path from Y to X, supporting the hypothesis $P_Q(X, Y)$. As shown in Figure 2, CIBL forms the *uncertain arcs* U1, U2, and U3. The cost of the path from Y to X is the sum of the Euclidean lengths of the uncertain arcs U1, U2, and U3; the path from the tail to the head of a training arc has zero cost. In a similar fashion, a path is constructed from X to Y. The path with lower cost determines the better estimate of the ranking of X and Y.

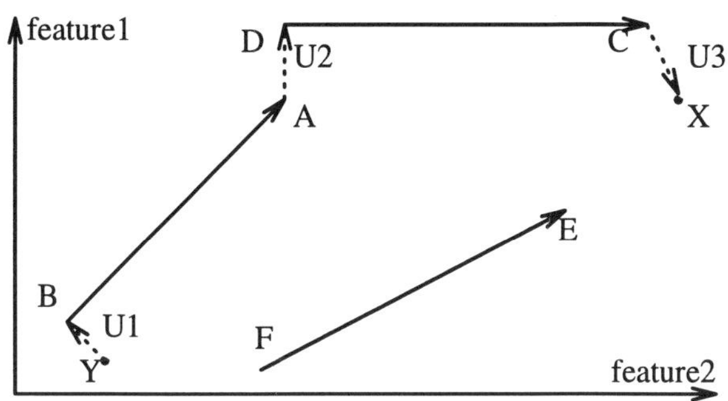

Figure 2: The best match to $\overleftarrow{XY}$ found by CIBL.

In practice, CIBL constructs all possible uncertain arcs, forming a dense graph with two special nodes, X and Y (for clarity, Figure 2 shows only those uncertain arcs on the best path from Y to X). The standard Dijkstra algorithm (Aho, Hopcroft, & Ullman 1974) is then used to find the lowest cost path connecting Y and X, where edges from the tail to the head of a training arc are assigned zero cost and edges representing uncertain arcs are assigned a cost equal to their Euclidean length.

Empirical Evaluation

We conducted three sets of experiments to evaluate the performance of CIBL with respect to the performance of a traditional tree-induction method, ID3, and our 1-NN algorithm, 1ARC. In CIBL, pairs of schedules represented by N attributes were mapped directly onto arcs in an N-dimensional feature space. However, ID3's decision tree model requires that pairs of schedules (arcs) be transformed into positive and negative instances of a concept or class and that concept instances be represented as a single vector of features. We chose to represent arcs using all of their relevant properties: the location of the head, the location of the tail, the normalized direction, and the magnitude. Thus the training set given to ID3 contains, for each training arc $P_Q(X, Y)$, a positive and a negative instance of the concept "Y is preferred to X":

$$< +, Y, X, \frac{(X-Y)}{\|X-Y\|}, \|X-Y\| >$$
$$< -, X, Y, \frac{(Y-X)}{\|X-Y\|}, \|X-Y\| >.$$

Since the (3N+1) elements of each ID3 feature vector are real numbers, we used an implementation of ID3 supplied by Ray Mooney that handles real-valued features in the manner proposed by (Quinlan 1986).

Artificial Domain Experiments

We first compared the accuracy of CIBL to that of 1ARC and ID3 on the task of learning preference functions, P_Q, for a variety of artificial evaluation functions, Q, shown in Figure 3. With the exception of

Q_8, all of the evaluation functions were defined on the feature space $S = [0, 1] \times [0, 1]$. For each Q function, we randomly generated instances of the associated preference predicate, $P_Q(X, Y)$, representing the knowledge "X is preferred over Y" for $X, Y \in S$. Each model was trained on a set of instances of size $\|TS\| \in \{2, 8, 32, 128\}$ and was then tested on a different set of instances of size 1000. Each $< model, Q, \|TS\| >$ triplet was trained and tested four times and an error rate was calculated by counting the incorrect rankings in the four tests.

$$
\begin{aligned}
Q_1(f_1, f_2) &= f_1 + 10 f_2 & &\text{1x10 plane} \\
Q_2(f_1, f_2) &= (f_1 - \tfrac{1}{2})^2 + (f_2 - \tfrac{1}{2})^2 & &\text{quadratic} \\
Q_3(f_1, f_2) &= sin(2\pi(f_1 + f_2)) & &\text{sinusoid} \\
Q_4(f_1, f_2) &= \begin{cases} f_2 & \text{if } f_1 \leq \tfrac{1}{2} \\ 1 - f_2 & \text{else} \end{cases} & &\text{crossed planes} \\
Q_5(f_1, f_2) &= f_1 + f_2 & &\text{1x1 plane} \\
Q_6(f_1, f_2) &= exp(f_1^2 + f_2^2) & &\text{exponential} \\
Q_7(f_1, f_2) &= \begin{cases} f_1 + f_2 & \text{if } f_1 \leq \tfrac{1}{2} \\ 1 + f_2 - f_1 & \text{else} \end{cases} & &\text{folded plane} \\
Q_8(f_1, f_2, f_3) &= (f_1 - \tfrac{1}{2})^2 + (f_2 - \tfrac{1}{2})^2. & &Q_2 \text{ in 3-D}
\end{aligned}
$$

Figure 3: Quality Functions.

For all evaluation functions tested, CIBL had a lower error rate than 1ARC, as shown in Figure 4. This indicates that CIBL's strategy of composing multiple exemplars is superior to 1ARC's traditional 1-NN approach. ID3 performed better than CIBL on the evaluation functions Q_1 (plane), Q_5 (plane), and Q_6 (exponential), which have no change in the sign of their derivative. Both 1ARC and CIBL performed significantly better than ID3 on the evaluation functions Q_2 (quadratic), Q_3 (sinusoidal), and Q_4 (crossed planes), which exhibit changes in the sign of their derivatives in the form of local extrema or a discontinuity. These data indicate that CIBL generally performs better than ID3 when the evaluation function is "complex" in the sense of containing a local extremum or discontinuity. However, ID3 and CIBL performed equally on Q_7 (folded plane), a function with an abrupt change in the sign of its derivative.

As expected, the addition of an irrelevant feature to the feature space—a feature that has no effect on the evaluation function—did not affect ID3's performance. However, because CIBL's Euclidean distance metric, used to assign costs to uncertain arcs, counts all features equally, CIBL's accuracy was degraded by the addition of an irrelevant feature, as shown in the testing data for Q_8 (the same 2-D quadratic as function Q_2 with an irrelevant third feature added). The sensitivity to irrelevant features exhibited by CIBL has been observed in other studies of instance-based learning (Aha 1989).

The second experiment tested the hypothesis that

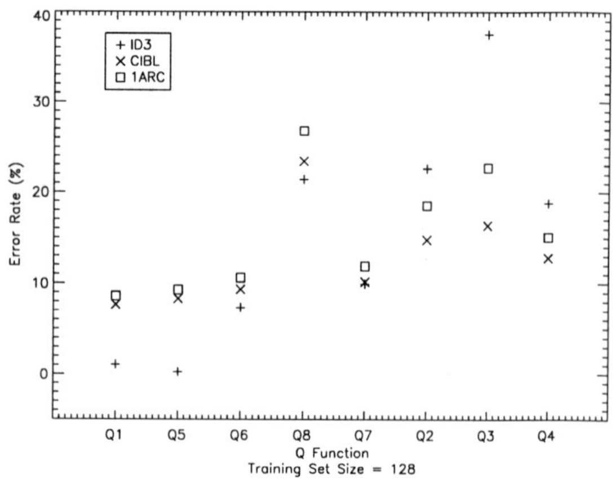

Figure 4: Error Rates for Various Q Functions.

the relative performance of CIBL and ID3 depends on the dimensionality of the feature space as well as on the complexity of the quality function underlying the preference predicate. To test this hypothesis, we compared the ability of CIBL and ID3 to acquire a preference predicate for a linear Q on artificial data of dimensionality 2, 3, 5 and 10. As with the first experiment, both training and testing instances were uniformly distributed through the feature space. The results, set forth in Figure 5, show that for linear Q ID3 has a lower error rate in feature spaces of dimensionality less than 5, the error rate is comparable for dimensionality equal to 5, and CIBL has a lower error rate in feature spaces of dimensionality greater than 5.

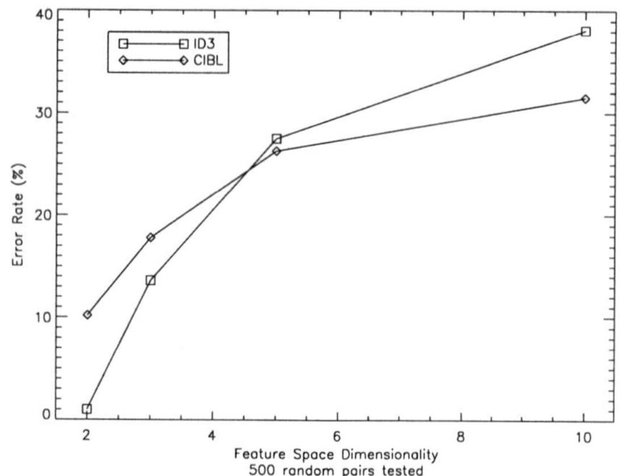

Figure 5: Cumulative error rate of CIBL and ID3 for linear Q in feature spaces of dimension 2, 3, 5, and 10.

Scheduling Experiments with Astronomers

Observing Assistant The Observing Assistant is a decision support system to assist astronomers in scheduling ground-based telescope observations. OA acts as a smart schedule editor that assists in the incremental process of schedule construction used by astronomers to construct schedules by hand: starting with an empty schedule, OA suggests refinements to the current partial schedule by adding one object from the astronomer's catalog of desired observations.

OA uses its model of the astronomer's preference predicate to sort the refinements of a partial schedule S. The set of refinements of S consists of each placement into S of an unscheduled object from the astronomer's catalog that results in a new schedule satisfying all hard constraints. The highest ranked refinement is then suggested to the user. If the user rejects the proposed refinement s_i in favor of some other refinement s_j, OA acquires the training instance $P_Q(s_j, s_i)$. A separate model is maintained for each astronomer.[2]

Interactive Learning Experiment The artificial domain experiments indicated that CIBL always performs at least as well as 1ARC and that the relative performance of CIBL and ID3 depends upon the nature of the underlying quality function Q and the dimensionality of the feature space. The second set of experiments compared the relative effectiveness of CIBL to that of ID3 on the task of learning an astronomer's scheduling behavior in the context of the Observing Assistant. Two different versions of OA were implemented: OA-CIBL used the CIBL learning method; and OA-ID3 used the ID3 learning method.

A typical observing catalog of astronomical objects was provided by the director of a ground-based observatory. An astronomer at the observatory scheduled this catalog twice, once using OA-CIBL and once using OA-ID3. The catalog comprised three nights of observations, so a total of six nights were scheduled (three nights per catalog, two different learning methods). The six learning sessions were interleaved so that the astronomer did not know which learning method was in use. Each time the astronomer made a ranking decision, that is, each time the astronomer expressed a preference for a particular schedule in a set of schedules, data were collected on OA's performance.

The relative performance of the learning algorithms was measured in two different ways. The first measure was cumulative error rate, which indicates how often each model failed to identify correctly the astronomer's preferred schedule. The cumulative error rate of CIBL was significantly lower (37%) than that of ID3 (47%), indicating that the astronomer accepted CIBL's suggested refinement more often than she accepted ID3's.

---

[2]The preference model of the initial implementation of OA uses the following attributes of observing schedules:

- the priority of the observation most recently added to the schedule
- the duration of the most recent observation
- the maximum airmass of the most recent observation
- the optimal airmass of the most recent observation, *i.e.*, the lowest airmass it achieves during the entire night
- the average airmass of the other objects in the schedule

Several additional attributes, such as total telescope slew time, would need to be added for a complete model of the factors considered by astronomers in scheduling.

The second measure of performance was a *linear payout metric* under which a model is rewarded by $\frac{2(n-m)}{n-1} - 1$ if the model assigned the user's first choice out of n objects a rank of m. This metric rewards a scheduler by $+1.0$ when the user's chosen schedule was ranked first and by -1.0 when the user's chosen schedule was ranked last. The expected value of a preference predicate model with no knowledge is zero. Figure 6 shows the cumulative payout data for OA-CIBL and OA-ID3, indicating that both had about the same ability to predict the astronomer's behavior. The relatively high payout from both methods—over 40 after 62 instances—indicates that both methods rapidly acquired a sufficiently accurate preference model to provide useful advice to the astronomer.[3]

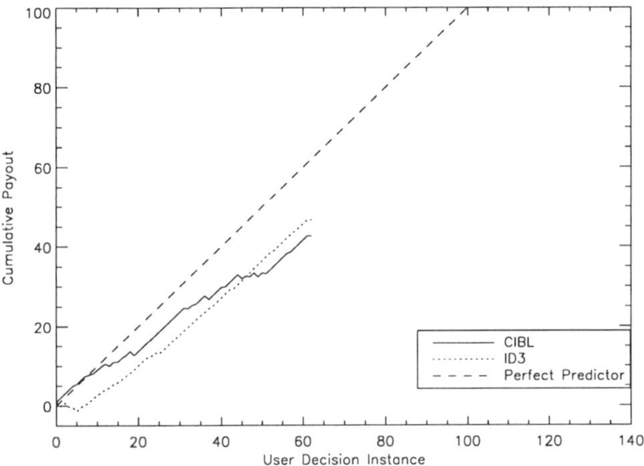

Figure 6: Cumulative payout. The 45° line represents the cumulative payout of a perfect model of the astronomer's preference predicate.

Replay Experiments In addition to directly measuring the relative performance of CIBL and ID3 as the learning component of OA, the learning methods were compared on two sets of approximately 135 preference instances recorded from each of two different astronomers who used OA to schedule 6 nights of observations.

In the first experiment, each astronomer's preference instances were used to train CIBL and ID3 separately using a learn-on-failure protocol. The two states contained in each preference instance were given to the model (CIBL or ID3) for ranking, and the model learned the instance only if it ranked the states incorrectly. Both models had approximately equal cumulative error rates (astronomer #1: CIBL-21%, ID3-22%; astronomer #2: CIBL-14%, ID3-21%), confirming the result of the interactive learning experiment described above that CIBL and ID3 had comparable abilities to predict astronomer's behavior.

The second replay experiment tested the hypothesis that different astronomers use distinct preference predicates. The two sets of preference instances were each randomly partitioned into two subsets. One partition was used to train a preference predicate model. The model's error rate was then measured on the task of predicting the preferences contained in the other partitions. This experiment was performed under twelve different configurations to cover all the possible permutations of three configuration variables: the preference model used (CIBL or ID3); the source of the training partition (astronomer #1 or astronomer #2); and the size of the training partition (45, 68, or 90 instances). The experiment was repeated 10 times for each testing configuration.

Over all 120 tests, the average error rate for ranking instances from the set used to train the model (8.7%) was significantly lower than the average error rate for ranking instances from the other astronomer's set (25.0%). This indicates that there was a significant difference between the scheduling behaviors of the two astronomers we tested, confirming the hypothesis that different astronomers require different preference models.

Scheduling Experiments With Artificial P_Q

The final experiment tested whether the dependence of the relative performance of CIBL and ID3 on the complexity of the underlying quality function Q, which was observed in an artificial domain, also applies when scheduling actual astronomical observations. To test this hypothesis, OA-CIBL and OA-ID3 were rerun on the catalog of observations using each of the quality functions set forth in Figure 7 as an oracle in place of a human astronomer. As shown in Figure 8, the results confirmed that CIBL's performance relative to ID3 improves with increasingly complex Q: ID3 is more accurate than CIBL for linear Q,[4] CIBL is slightly more accurate for quadratic Q, and CIBL is much more accurate for sinusoid Q.

Conclusion

Learning apprentice acquisition of preference predicates, as typified by OA-CIBL and OA-ID3, is appropriate when (1) users can identify the relevant characteristics of problem-solving states, (2) these state

---

[3]The slightly higher payout for OA-ID3, notwithstanding its somewhat lower accuracy, indicates that the average magnitude of errors was somewhat greater for OA-CIBL.

[4]This result appears to be inconsistent with the second artificial domain experiment, in which ID3 and CIBL had comparable accuracy for linear Q in a five-dimensional feature space. However, this disparity is attributable to the differences between the two experiments: (1) the instances used for training and testing were random points in feature space for the earlier experiment but were actual schedules for the later experiment and (2) the task in the earlier experiment was to establish a binary ranking whereas the task in the later experiment was to order a full set of schedule refinements.

$$Q_9 = f_1 - f_2 + f_3 + f_4 - f_5 \qquad \text{plane}$$
$$Q_{10} = -[(f_1 - 1)^2 + (f_2 - 2)^2 + (f_3 - \tfrac{3}{2})^2$$
$$+ (f_4 - \tfrac{1}{2})^2 + (f_5 - 2)^2] \qquad \text{quadratic}$$
$$Q_{11} = sin(\pi \sqrt{f_1^2 + f_2^2 + f_3^2 + f_4^2 + f_5^2}) \qquad \text{sinusoid}$$

Figure 7: 5-D Quality Functions.

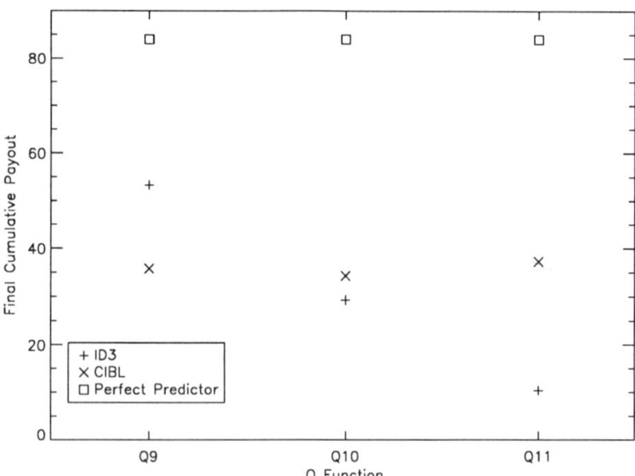

Figure 8: Cumulative payout of CIBL and ID3 with 5-D plane, quadratic, sinusoid functions replacing the human astronomer.

characteristics can be adequately represented as an attribute vector, but (3) users differ as to or are unable to articulate evaluation criteria for problem solving states in terms of these attributes.

The empirical evaluation showed that CIBL's strategy of composing instances of preference predicates is superior to a 1-NN instance-based learning strategy unable to compose instances. The relative performance of CIBL and decision tree induction for preference predicate acquisition depended upon (1) the complexity of the preference predicate P_Q being acquired as measured by the underlying evaluation function Q and (2) the dimensionality of the feature space. Irrelevant attributes degraded the performance of CIBL but not ID3. CIBL and ID3 performed comparably when tested as the learning component of a learning apprentice used by an astronomer for scheduling astronomical observations having five real-valued attributes. A replay experiment confirmed the hypothesis that astronomers may differ widely in their scheduling preference predicates.

The empirical evaluation suggests that CIBL is preferable to ID3 as the learning component of a learning apprentice system if representation of the relevant characteristics of problem-solving states requires more than five attributes or if attributes interact in complex ways (*i.e.*, the underlying quality function has extrema or discontinuities), provided that all attributes are relevant. Conversely, ID3 is preferable if there are fewer than five attributes and the attributes do not interact in a complex fashion (*i.e.*, the quality function has no extrema or discontinuities) or if there are irrelevant attributes.

Acknowledgements

This research was supported in part by the Wyoming Planetary and Space Science Center. We would like to thank Earl Spillar and Leisa Townsley for their assistance with telescope scheduling, Peter Turney for his suggestions for applying ID3 to real-valued data, and Ray Mooney for his implementation of ID3.

References

Aha, D. 1989. Incremental, instance-based learning of independent and graded concepts. In *Proc. of the Sixth Intl. Workshop on Machine Learning*, 387–391.

Aha, D. 1992. Generalizing from case studies: A case study. In *Proc. of the Ninth Intl. Workshop on Machine Learning*, 1–10.

Aho, A.; Hopcroft, J.; and Ullman, J. 1974. *The Design and Analysis of Computer Algorithms*. Addison-Wesley Publishing Co.

Broos, P. 1993. An expert system for telescope scheduling. Master's thesis, University of Wyoming.

Callan, J.; Fawcett, T.; and Rissland, E. 1991. Adaptive case-based reasoning. In *Proc. of the Third DARPA Case-Based Reasoning Workshop*, 179–190. Morgan Kaufmann.

Dent, L.; Boticario, J.; McDermott, J.; Mitchell, T.; and Zabowski, D. 1992. A personal learning apprentice. In *Proc. of Tenth Natl. Conf. on Art. Intelligence*, 96–103. San Jose, CA: AAAI Press/MIT Press.

Maes, P., and Kozierok, R. 1993. Learning interface agents. In *Proc. of Eleventh Natl. Conf. on Art. Intelligence*, 459–466. Washington, D.C.: AAAI Press/MIT Press.

Mahadevan, S.; Mitchell, T.; Mostow, J.; Steinberg, L.; and Tadepalli, P. 1993. An apprentice-based approach to knowledge acquisition. *Artificial Intelligence* 64(1).

Mitchell, T.; Mahadevan, S.; and Steinberg, L. 1985. Leap: A learning apprentice for vlsi design. In *Proc. of the Ninth Intl. Joint Conf. on Art. Intelligence*. Morgan Kaufmann.

Quinlan, J. R. 1986. Induction of decision trees. *Machine Learning* 1:81–106.

Stanfill, C., and Waltz, D. 1986. Toward memory-based reasoning. *Comm. of the ACM* 29(12).

Utgoff, P., and Clouse. 1991. Two kinds of training information for evaluation function learning. In *Proc. of Ninth Natl. Conf. on Art. Intelligence*, 596–600. Anaheim: AAAI Press/MIT Press.

Utgoff, P., and Saxena, S. 1987. Learning a preference predicate. In *Proc. of the Fourth Intl. Workshop on Machine Learning*, 115–121.

Learning to Recognize Promoter Sequences in *E. coli* by Modeling Uncertainty in the Training Data

Steven W. Norton

Department of Computer Science
Hill Center for the Mathematical Sciences
Rutgers University, Busch Campus
New Brunswick, NJ 08903
norton@cs.rutgers.edu

Abstract

Automatic recognition of promoter sequences is an important open problem in molecular biology. Unfortunately, the usual machine learning version of this problem is critically flawed. In particular, the dataset available from the Irvine repository was drawn from a compilation of promoter sequences that were preprocessed to conform to the biologists' related notion of *the consensus sequence*, a first-order approximation with a number of shortcomings that are well-known in molecular biology. Although concept descriptions learned from the Irvine data may represent the consensus sequence, they do not represent promoters. More generally, imperfections in preprocessed data and statistical variations in the locations of biologically meaningful features within the raw data invalidate standard attribute-based approaches. I suggest a dataset, a concept-description language, and a model of uncertainty in the promoter data that are all biologically justified, then address the learning problem with incremental probabilistic evidence combination. This knowledge-based approach yields a more accurate and more credible solution than other more conventional machine learning systems.

Introduction

Understanding cellular biology at the level of gene expression would enable tremendous advances in pharmaceuticals, gene therapy, and more. Part of understanding gene expression involves understanding the complex regulatory signals present in DNA. A *promoter* is a signal that identifies specific segments of DNA that are transcribed into RNA, a necessary precursor to the production of protein (Watson *et al.* 1987). RNA polymerase is the enzyme that produces RNA on the DNA template (Losick & Chamberlin 1976). Before it produces RNA, the polymerase must recognize and bind to a promoter sequence. Characterizing the three-dimensional structure of the polymerase would help in understanding the promoter/polymerase interaction, but the size and complexity of the polymerase have made the approach impractical. Much of

Thanks to Haym Hirsh, Ringo Ling, Mick Noordewier, Mark Schwabacher, and Ke-Thia Yao for careful readings of drafts and endless technical discussions. This work was partially supported by NSF grant IRI-9209795.

the research effort has concentrated instead on understanding the structure of the promoter sequence itself.

Double-stranded DNA is made up of nucleotides, each containing a sugar, a phosphate group, and a base. DNA sequences are represented as strings of characters taken from a four character alphabet (A, G, C, or T) representing the bases that distinguish one nucleotide from another. Biologists believe that raw sequence information governs most polymerase/promoter interactions, and that the interactions are essentially localized to a handful of bases.

In 1975, Pribnow published a seminal paper describing a pattern of bases occurring imperfectly in a region just upstream of the transcriptional start sites of six of the promoters he examined (Pribnow 1975). He also suggested the existence of an important region 35 bases upstream. These regions have come to be known as the Pribnow box and the recognition region. Figure 1 is a highly stylized illustration of the DNA, the polymerase, and the various elements of the promoter.

Further research seemed to support the presence of these regions, *e.g.* (Siebenlist, Simpson, & Gilbert 1980), and their biological significance (Youderian, Bouvier, & Susskind 1982). The Pribnow box and the recognition region are thought to be the contact points between the polymerase and the promoter. (The actual contacts can be determined in the laboratory by *base conservation studies*.) Together the two recurrent patterns are now known as *the consensus sequence*. In the bacteria *E. coli*, the consensus sequence consists of two specific sequences of six

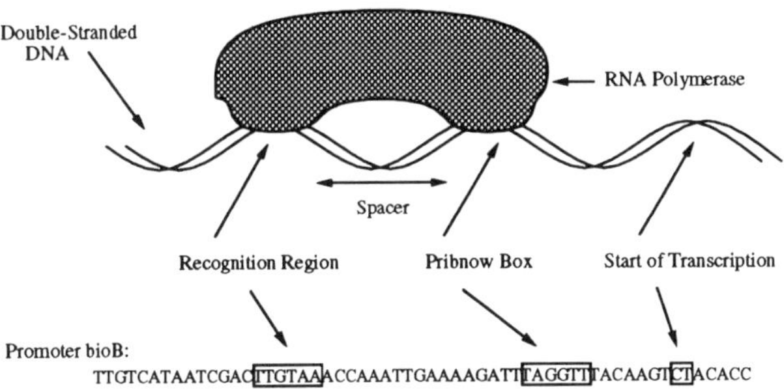

Figure 1. Abstract Promoter Structure

bases, **TTGACA** and **TATAAT**, separated by a gap of exactly 17 bases. No *E. coli* promoter has precisely this structure, and most have many differences. Still, the very idea of a canonical sequence capturing the essence of promoter structure and function was so influential that biologists produced compilations of promoter sequences aligned specifically to enhance correspondence to the consensus sequence (Hawley & McClure 1983; Harley & Reynolds 1987).

Machine learning experiments in recognizing promoter sequences typically rely on the promoter recognition database from the UCI Repository of Machine Learning Databases and Domain Theories (Cost & Salzberg 1993; Langley, Iba, & Thompson 1992; Towell & Shavlik 1992). Its 53 promoter sequences were selected from the compilation of Hawley and McClure (1983), and are left-aligned on the putative recognition region. (Sequence data from the Irvine dataset for the *bioB* promoter is shown at the bottom of Figure 1. The annotations are taken from the original compilation.) The 53 non-promoter sequences were taken from a longer sequence of DNA known not to exhibit promoter activity (Towell, Shavlik, & Noordewier 1990).

Hawley and McClure's compilation was based on smaller, earlier compilations and on the consensus sequence for *E. coli*. They aligned the promoters by hand to enhance correspondence with the consensus sequence. There is no mention of a computer program or an algorithm. More recent approaches perform the alignment automatically (Harley & Reynolds 1987), but are imperfect none the less. In fact, no published compilation is the result of optimal alignment to the consensus sequence, because the complexity of optimal multiple sequence alignment is exponential in the number of sequences to be aligned (Waterman 1989). Heuristic alignment fails when the predicted consensus alignment differs from regions of actual base conservation, the *biological foundation* of the consensus sequence. For example, in the compilation of (Harley & Reynolds 1987), the predicted alignments of fully 70 of the 263 promoters have notable deviations from one or more aspects of the laboratory data.

The point is that while the consensus sequence has proven to be a useful concept (Youderian, Bouvier, & Susskind 1982), it is still only a first-order approximation to an as yet unknown promoter concept. Consensus-sequence alignment may well associate consensus regions with consensus regions. But because the consensus sequence is an imperfect predictor of the contact regions, consensus-sequence alignment does not necessarily associate contact regions with contact regions. This means that while the data in the Irvine dataset could be used to learn about the consensus sequence, it should not be used to learn about promoter sequences.[1] A better choice for the alignment would

---

[1] Researchers working on other problems involving multiply-aligned data, such as to learning to recognize ribosomal binding sites, should beware of this pitfall too.

come from the DNA itself. For learning to recognize promoter sequences, the only natural alignment is the start of transcription, the site where the polymerase begins to produce the RNA product. It is not a theoretical construct, but a real biological entity present after every promoter, identifiable in the laboratory, and recorded in the original compilation.

It may seem that with such an alignment the promoter-recognition problem is ready to be solved, but even data with a biologically-justified alignment is insufficient. There are two specific reasons why this learning problem is harder than most: 1) There are often multiple transcriptional start sites, and during transcription the relevant one is chosen nondeterministically (Hawley & McClure 1983). 2) The length of the gaps between the start site, the Pribnow box, and the recognition region vary from promoter to promoter (von Hippel *et al.* 1984; Youderian, Bouvier, & Susskind 1982). What this means is that it is *impossible* to represent promoters by single contiguous sequences of DNA and simultaneously align them so that *each* attribute has a unique and consistent biological significance. For example, if the dataset is constructed so that the Pribnow boxes are in alignment, the recognition regions will necessarily be out of alignment. Since the attributes in the misaligned areas have no consistent biological significance from example to example, it is inappropriate to learn recognition rules directly from such data.

I have taken an alternative approach that does not depend on consensus alignment. Instead, it is based on laboratory research described in the open literature of molecular biology and on recent work in machine learning. By using biologically-based evidence, the promoter recognition problem in *E. coli* is addressed using incremental probabilistic evidence combination [Norton and Hirsh, 1992, 1993]. In particular, biological research on promoter structure and function justify the dataset, the concept-description language, and the characterization of the uncertainty present in the training data. Consequently the learned classifier is more credible and more accurate than those produced by CN2, C4.5, and the k-nearest-neighbor classifier.

Incremental Probabilistic Evidence Combination

In a noisy and uncertain domain, knowledge of the probabilistic processes affecting available data can help solve a learning problem. Incremental probabilistic evidence combination has been used successfully to learn conjunctions from noisy synthetic data (Norton & Hirsh 1992) and to learn DNF expressions from real and synthetic data (Norton & Hirsh 1993). The high-level idea behind the approach is to guess what the true data are, based on the observations and the probabilistic background knowledge, then return a concept description consistent with that data. Guesses supporting no concept descriptions are ruled out as inconsistent. Other guesses are ruled out as too unlikely, leaving only the plausible guesses. Using the principle of maximum *a posteriori* probability, a concept description consistent with the best of the plausible guesses is returned as the result of learning.

Consider, for example, learning a conjunctive concept description from binary data subject to a uniform label noise process with a 10% noise rate. Suppose that three attributes can take on values 0, 1, or * (which matches either 0 or 1). What should be learned from these five observations: $\{(010, +)\ (011, +)\ (101, +)\ (110, +)\ (111, -)\}$? Since noise events are unlikely, the most probable single guess is that noise did not effect the true data, and that the observed data are the same as the true data. But since no term correctly classifies this data, one or more noise events *must* have occurred. Five other guesses suppose single noise events. Of those only one is consistent, namely that $(111, +)$ was changed to $(111, -)$. Furthermore, several consistent guesses involve two or more noise events, but each is less probable. A concept description consistent with the most probable consistent guess $\{(010, +)\ (011, +)\ (101, +)\ (110, +)\ (111, +)\}$ should be considered.

The remainder of this section describes in more detail the evidence-combination framework that implements the above reasoning process and will be instantiated with knowledge of promoter-specific probabilistic processes in order to build the final application program.

In the framework of incremental probabilistic evidence combination, knowledge takes the form of a probability distribution describing noise processes and/or other uncertainties working on the data. The uniform label-noise process of the preceding example changes class labels from $+$ to $-$ or from $-$ to $+$ with probability $\eta = 10\%$. It can be described by a probability distribution $P(o|s)$ where o is the label of the observation and s the uncorrupted class label. When η is low, noise events are unlikely, and the observed labels usually correspond to the uncorrupted labels. The four elements of the noise model for a uniform label noise process are $P(+|+) = P(-|-) = 1 - \eta$ and $P(+|-) = P(-|+) = \eta$.

If the true and correct training data (S) are known, the best concept description (H_i) is the one with maximum *a posteriori* probability $P(H_i|S)$. But of course the true and correct training data are unavailable, having been corrupted somehow. The best thing to do is select a concept description that seems most probable given the observations. Let O be the sequence of observations, S_j a particular series of guesses about the nature of the true but unavailable data, $VS(S_j)$ the set of concept descriptions strictly consistent with those guesses, and $P(O|S)$ the product of probabilities from the noise model. Norton and Hirsh (1992) show that the posterior probabilities are proportional to sums of noise probabilities. The first expression given below is for the posterior probability $P(H_i|O)$. It shows that every sequence of guesses consistent with a hypothesis

gives it a measure of probabilistic support. Expressions for the sets of consistent concept descriptions and the various posterior probabilities of the observation sequence are given as well. s_{jk} and o_k denote the k-th element of sequences S_j and O respectively.

$$P(H_i|O) \propto \sum_{H_i \in \overset{j}{VS}(S_j)} P(O|S_j)$$

$$VS(S_j) = \bigcap_k VS(s_{jk})$$

$$P(O|S_j) = \prod_k P(o_k|s_{jk})$$

Given these formulae, it is natural to view the computation of posterior probabilities as evidence combination. Evidence and current belief are represented by sets of tuples, each tuple consisting of a set of concept descriptions and a probability. Initial belief is represented by the singleton set $\{\langle VS(\emptyset), 1.0\rangle\}$, where $VS(\emptyset)$ denotes the set of all concept descriptions. Each observation o suggests several evidence tuples, $\{\langle VS(s_1), P(o|s_1)\rangle, \ldots, \langle VS(s_m), P(o|s_m)\rangle\}$, where m is the number of supposed examples (guesses) that could account for the observation. Each probability is essentially a weight associated with a guess, and hence with a corresponding set of consistent concept descriptions. The more probable it is that the guess is correct, the more probable it is that the correct hypothesis is in the corresponding set of consistent concept descriptions.

Evidence (tuples derived from the current example) and current belief (tuples summarizing sequences of guesses based on previous examples) are combined by taking cross products, multiplying pairwise probabilities and intersecting corresponding sets of concept descriptions. When the current belief is inconsistent with the new evidence, the intersection for the resulting tuple becomes empty. When this happens, the inconsistent sequence is discarded. My implementation of this approach controls its combinatorics in two more ways. It imposes a strict upper bound on the number of stored sequences and a limit on the difference between the probability of the most likely and the least likely sequences of guesses. In the end, when all the observations are processed, the most specific concept description from the most probable set of concept descriptions is returned as the result of learning.

Learning individual conjunctions this way is straightforward. The IPEC-DNF learner is an iterative application of the conjunction learner, with a modification to accommodate *representational noise*. IPEC-DNA, the program used in my promoter-recognition experiments, has the same iterative control structure. Refer to (Norton & Hirsh 1993) for more details.

Background Knowledge for Promoter Recognition

Application of the framework just described requires a concept-description language, a method for enumerating guesses about the true but unknown data, and a method for assigning a probability to each guess. Fortunately the biology literature is considerable, containing many helpful results. This section presents biological requirements for the concept-description language and characterizations of the uncertainties present in promoter sequences. It also shows how the background knowledge is used to construct evidence tuples for the IPEC-DNA learning program.

The molecule that transcribes DNA into RNA is RNA polymerase. Laboratory data suggest that it loosely binds to the DNA then moves along the molecule until it finds a promoter. Abortive initiation studies on the promoter/RNA polymerase complex interrupt the formation of RNA in the earliest stages. They indicate that the recognition region, Pribnow box, and the spacer are clearly important for characterizing promoter function (Borowiec & Gralla 1987). IPEC-DNA reasons about these entities by encoding them in its concept-description language. For instance, STTGAC (17 18) TATAAT matches any sequence starting with C or G (S is a shorthand from the biology literature), followed immediately by TTGAC, a gap of any 17 or 18 bases, and finally by TATAAT.

Recent studies in molecular biology argue that a single consensus-like sequence is inadequate. One argument suggests that a single sequence could not distinguish between promoters biologically optimized in different ways (McClure 1985). This criticism suggests that a disjunctive concept description language is necessary. IPEC-DNA learns disjunctions of the basic promoter descriptions described above, using the iterative control structure of IPEC-DNF (Norton & Hirsh 1993).

What makes the promoter-recognition problem especially difficult is uncertainty inherent in the training data. In particular, it is unclear where the actual recognition region and the Pribnow box lie within each promoter training datum. Uncertainties result from multiple transcriptional start sites, variable separation between the start site and the Pribnow box, and variable separation between the Pribnow box and the recognition region. Discrete probability distributions over these values allow IPEC-DNA to enumerate possible configurations of the contact regions and assign them probabilities. Here are four of the candidates the program considers for *bioB*:

TGTAAA	(17 17)	AGGTTT	0.160
TTGTAA	(17 17)	TAGGTT	0.118
TTGTAA	(18 18)	AGGTTT	0.080
CTTGTA	(18 18)	TAGGTT	0.059

Each candidate was assigned the probability on the right, by combining three *independent* models of uncertainty into a single model of domain uncertainty. Each of these models is justified by the molecular-biology literature, as explained below.

Mutational studies examine the effects of individual base insertions, deletions, or replacements within a promoter region. They show that the preferred spacer length is 17 bases (Youderian, Bouvier, & Susskind 1982). This is consistent with consensus-sequence analysis that indicates spacers of 17 ± 1 base pairs represent 92% of promoters (Harley & Reynolds 1987). In helical DNA, each base contributes about 35 degrees of twist (Dickerson 1983). It follows that the length of the spacer influences the preferred orientation of the Pribnow box relative to the recognition region by altering helical twist. Other research (Borowiec & Gralla 1987) suggests that twisting of the DNA has a quadratic effect on the rate of closed complex formation, one of several steps in the initiation of transcription. Since rates are proportional to probabilities, the form of the probability distribution over the spacer length should be roughly quadratic. In the experiments reported here, IPEC-DNA uses a spacer-length distribution that assigns a 50% probability to the 17 base spacer, and 25% probabilities to the 16 base and 18 base spacers.

To expose the template strand once the polymerase has bound to the promoter, 17 ± 1 bases are unwound from the middle of the Pribnow box to six or eight bases past the start of transcription (Gamper & Hearst 1982). Allowing three bases in the Pribnow box leaves between five and nine bases between the start of transcription and the downstream end of the Pribnow box. As to the probability distribution over this gap, we only know that 64% of uniquely identified transcriptional start sites are six or seven bases downstream of the Pribnow box (von Hippel *et al.* 1984). Orientation is likely to be key again, suggesting a quadratic form for this distribution. IPEC-DNA models this uncertainty by assigning 32% probability to gaps of six or seven bases, 15% probability for gaps of five or eight bases, and 6% probability for a gap of only four bases.

All that remains is the uncertainty concerning multiple start sites. The various compilations indicate each start site, but do not indicate the preferred one (if any). In the absence of stronger information, transcriptional start site uncertainty was modeled as a uniform probability distribution over the candidate sites. This policy is adopted in IPEC-DNA.

A promoter with three adjacent start sites generates 24 evidence tuples with probabilities between 0.3% and 11.75%. Each possible start site is considered in turn. Given a start site, each possible value from four to eight bases is used to locate the putative Pribnow box. Then 16, 17, and 18 base spacers are used to locate the recognition region. If a particular combination of these values is indeed correct, the others are necessarily incorrect. Evidence tuples consist of a probability and a set of concept descriptions. A given tuple generates that set by treating exactly one of these combinations as a positive example while treating the remainder as negative examples. The corresponding concept descriptions are consistent with at least that one positive example and inconsistent with at least the other negative examples.

Non-promoters are handled differently, because they contain no special regions. Knowing that the polymerase does not bind *anywhere* in these fragments

(Towell, Shavlik, & Noordewier 1990), I generated
50 negative examples from each non-promoter at random, and combined them into a single evidence tuple. Specifically, spacers were chosen at random according to the distribution given previously. A segment 12 bases wider (to accommodate the ersatz Pribnow box and recognition region) was randomly selected from the original non-promoter and used to construct a negative example with the same form as the four examples shown earlier. Since none of these 50 components binds to RNA polymerase, each evidence tuple so constructed has unit probability.

Experimental Results

Learning to recognize promoters required that I construct a dataset with a biologically-justified alignment, left or right aligned at the start of transcription. By examining the Irvine dataset and identifying corresponding elements in the original compilation (Hawley & McClure 1983) I decided that aligning the sequence by the rightmost transcriptional start site most preserved the relative locations of the recognition regions and the Pribnow boxes.[2] Trimming just enough bases from the left and right of each promoter so that they are a uniform length leaves 51 bases. I trimmed non-promoters to the same length by removing bases from the left side. Six promoters were eliminated because no transcriptional start was given, leaving a total of 100 examples. I will refer to this dataset as the biologically-aligned dataset.

I began by performing leave-one-out cross-validated trials on the biologically aligned dataset using IPEC-DNF (Norton & Hirsh 1993), CN2 (Clark & Niblett 1989), C4.5 (Quinlan 1993), and a k-nearest-neighbor classifier. Each of these conventional learners uses the 51 individual bases as features, even though this approach is invalid as indicated in the Introduction. IPEC-DNF computes DNF expressions. CN2 produces rules or an ordered decision list. The k-nearest-neighbor classifier was run with $K = 1$, $K = 3$, and $K = 5$. Increasing K increased the false-positive rate and decreased the false-negative rate without changing the overall error rate, so $K = 1$ is reported here. C4.5 learns decision trees. Tree pruning was found to be helpful and is used here. I performed the same experiment using the IPEC-DNA evidence-combination program described in previous sections. The lowest error rate, 19%, is attributed to IPEC-DNA. The results are summarized in Table 1 under the "CV Rate" heading.

The IPEC-DNA solution is the four term DNF given below. The nucleotide codes (*e.g.* D stands for A or G or T.) are standard (Cornish-Bowden 1985). The spacer (17 17) is exactly 17 bases. (16 18) matches 16, 17, or 18 base gaps. (17 18) matches 17 or 18 base gaps.

<hr>

[2]This choice was meant to be most favorable to the conventional learners. Performing the same series of experiments using left-aligned data gives substantially similar results.

Table 1. Error Rates Comparison

Learning System	CV Rate	FP Rate
IPEC-DNF	43%	11%
CN2 (rules)	32%	21%
CN2 (ordered)	31%	36%
1-Nearest-Neighbor	30%	33%
C4.5 (pruned)	23%	34%
IPEC-DNA	19%	1.5%

```
      NDDNHN (17 17) TANHDW
   or NWDNNN (17 17) VNWAWV
   or KHBVMD (16 18) HMTRNT
   or KYKHHN (17 18) RTDVWV
```

On-line genetic databases are growing rapidly. GenBank currently contains about 130 million nucleotide bases from all sources (Benson, Lipman, & Ostell 1993). *E. coli* itself contains about five million nucleotides. Much of this data has been automatically sequenced, and its biological significance is unknown. Learned classifiers could shed some light on this data, and would be used by molecular biologists to suggest laboratory experiments if they were accurate enough. The key factor is the false-positive rate. Because regulatory signals such as promoters occur so infrequently, false positives translate directly into wasted laboratory time. The "FP Rate" column in Table 1 shows the false-positive rates for these classifiers. The scores were computed by counting the number of locations that they recognize as promoters in a 1500 base DNA sequence known not to bind to RNA Polymerase (Towell, Shavlik, & Noordewier 1990). The IPEC-DNA classifier is the clear winner in this respect, with a 1.5% false-positive rate.

To characterize the contributions of the different pieces of background knowledge, I performed a series of experiments in which uniform probability distributions were substituted for the biologically-justified distributions. Replacing both the spacer distribution and the distribution of the separation between the start of transcription and the Pribnow box with uniform distributions should indicate the contribution of the concept-description language. Replacing either distribution alone should help quantify the contribution of the other. In each experiment the resulting error rates were greater than 50%, indicating that each piece of background knowledge is necessary for the solution.

I performed the same series of experiments using the more up-to-date and extensive promoter database given in (Lisser & Margalit 1993). I aligned the data on the rightmost transcriptional start site, and trimmed each instance to 65 bases (-50 to +15). Four promoters had to be removed because the compilation listed too few upstream bases (*argCBH-P2*, *speC-P1*, *speC-P2*, and *speC-P3*). The remainder of my dataset consists of an equal number of non-promoters (296) generated at random from the 1500-base non-binding sequence

Table 2. Error Rates Comparison, Large Dataset

Learning System	CV Rate	FP Rate
C4.5 (unpruned)	37%	33%
IPEC-DNF	34%	26%
CN2 (ordered)	32%	29%
1-Nearest-Neighbor	29%	32%
CN2 (rules)	27%	50%
IPEC-DNA	2.5%	0.2%

mentioned earlier. The dramatic results of learning are presented in Table 2. The 12-term DNF learned by IPEC-DNA is far superior to the other classifiers, at a statistical significance level better than 10^{-5}. 10-fold cross-validated error rates appear under the heading "CV Rate". Once again, the false-positive rate was estimated by applying the learned classifiers to each position of the non-binding DNA strand, and appears under the heading "FP Rate".

Related Work

To establish a basis of comparison for IPEC-DNA, I experimented with C4.5, CN2, IPEC-DNF, and the k-nearest-neighbor classifier. Decision tree, decision list, nearest-neighbor, and DNF learners are among the most popular of the general-purpose machine-learning methods available today. They are efficient and widely applicable, but knowledge poor. Aside from the error-rate comparisons already given, when applied to the biologically-aligned promoter data the lack of knowledge manifests itself in unfocussed concepts that depend importantly on bases that do not play a role in promoter function. The branches of the C4.5 decision tree and the CN2 rules are insufficiently specific to describe promoters or particular promoter behaviors (O'Neill 1989). The false-positive rates given in Tables 1 and 2 bear this out. On the other hand, the multitude of bases referenced by IPEC-DNF's classifier, chiefly outside the contact regions, hurt more than they help. Classifiers that reference so many specific bases outside the contact regions lose credibility. In contrast, IPEC-DNA's classifier only references bases in the putative contact regions.

One way to address the problem of uncertainty in training data is to invent a set of higher-level features that abstract the uncertainty away. This is precisely what is done in (Hirsh & Noordewier 1994). By discarding the raw data in favor of the higher-level features, they avoid the criticisms set out in the Introduction. These are general features taken from the molecular-biology literature that they feel will be useful for a variety of related problems. A key difference between that approach and the one presented here is the level of detail of the background knowledge. Here the motivation is to provide a knowledge-based solution to a single learning problem rather than to a family of learning problems. Hirsh and Noordewier have 'coarsened' the background knowledge to achieve

a measure of generality across sequence learning tasks. For instance, there are 12 features describing sharp bends in the DNA. These are used singly in (Hirsh & Noordewier 1994), even though it is "the periodic occurrences of hexamers with identical, large twist angles on the left-hand side of the axis of symmetry" that seemed "strikingly non-random" to the original researchers (Nussinov & Lennon 1984). For a general sequence learner, abstracting from *periodic occurrences* of these features to *one or more occurrences* of these features is fine, provided over-generalization is not a problem. But for IPEC-DNA, a promoter-specific learner, augmenting the feature set would only be appropriate after tightening up the biological significance of the new features. They report an 8.7% error rate for C4.5rules and a 10.2% error rate for the neural network when the raw data are discarded. These values can be compared to IPEC-DNA's 2.5% error rate because their dataset is very similar to the large one described here.

Towell *et al* (1990) also take a knowledge-based approach to the promoter problem. In particular, a set of rules describing consensus-like sequences and certain conformational properties is used to construct a back-propagation neural network. But as discussed in the Introduction, the original alignment changes the nature of the problem, so that the network recognizes the consensus sequence rather than the promoter sequence. Though the background knowledge could be applied to the biologically-aligned data, additional uncertainty due to the variable separation between start of transcription and the Pribnow box, and between the Pribnow box and the recognition region would cause the network to emphasize the wrong bases. If a more complete dataset was used (Lisser & Margalit 1993), one with increased variability in the separation between the putative contact regions, limitations of the background knowledge might be highlighted that were not apparent in the original study.

Closing Remarks

Learning systems depend critically on the assumption that each attribute has the same meaning, across multiple examples, an assumption not satisfied by consensus-aligned promoter data. In particular this alignment does not always align the biologically-active sites where promoter and polymerase bind. At best the consensus-sequence alignment introduces an inappropriate bias and changes the problem from learning to recognize promoter sequences to learning to recognize the consensus sequence. More generally, alignment is a potential problem for any learner using raw sequence data, whether it is DNA, RNA, or protein.

Machine learning research has produced a number of excellent general-purpose techniques that often perform well, but are necessarily knowledge-poor. IPEC-DNA outperforms these conventional learners because it is able to exploit biologically-justified background knowledge that others cannot. This work supports a claim that knowledge-based learners with problem-specific background knowledge can be expected to produce more accurate, credible concept descriptions.

Using the biology literature I justified a dataset, a concept-description language, and a model of uncertainty in promoter data. The knowledge-based approach using incremental probabilistic evidence combination yields a more accurate solution than more conventional machine learning systems. Equally important, the knowledge-based solution is more credible since it only references bases biologically implicated in promoter structure and function.

References

Benson, D.; Lipman, D. J.; and Ostell, J. 1993. GenBank. *Nucleic Acids Research* 21(13):2963–2965.

Borowiec, J. A., and Gralla, J. D. 1987. All three elements of the *lac* p^s promoter mediate its transcriptional response to DNA supercoiling. *Journal of Molecular Biology* 195:89–97.

Clark, P., and Niblett, T. 1989. The CN2 induction algorithm. *Machine Learning* 3:261–284.

Cornish-Bowden, A. 1985. Nomenclature for incompletely specified bases in nucleic acid sequences: recommendations 1984. *Nucleic Acids Research* 13(9):3021–3030.

Cost, S., and Salzberg, S. 1993. A weighted nearest neighbor algorithm for learning with symbolic features. *Machine Learning* 10(1):57–78.

Dickerson, R. E. 1983. Base sequence and helix structure variation in B and A DNA. *Journal of Molecular Biology* 166:419–441.

Gamper, H. B., and Hearst, J. E. 1982. A topological model for transcription based on unwinding angle analysis of *E. coli* RNA polymerase binary, initiation and ternary complexes. *Cell* 29:81–90.

Harley, C. B., and Reynolds, R. P. 1987. Analysis of *E. coli* promoter sequences. *Nucleic Acids Research* 15(5):2343–2361.

Hawley, D. K., and McClure, W. R. 1983. Compilation and analysis of *Escherichia coli* promoter DNA sequences. *Nucleic Acids Research* 11(8):2237–2255.

Hirsh, H., and Noordewier, M. 1994. Using background knowledge to improve inductive learning of DNA sequences. In *The Tenth Conference on Artificial Intelligence for Applications.*

Langley, P.; Iba, W.; and Thompson, K. 1992. An analysis of Bayesian classifiers. In *AAAI92: Proceedings of the Tenth National Conference on Artificial Intelligence*, 223–228. AAAI Press.

Lisser, S., and Margalit, H. 1993. Compilation of *E. coli* mRNA promoter sequences. *Nucleic Acids Research* 21(7):1507–1516.

Losick, R., and Chamberlin, M. J., eds. 1976. *RNA Polymerase.* Cold Spring Harbor Laboratory.

McClure, W. R. 1985. Mechanism and control of transcription initiation in prokaryotes. *Annual Review of Biochemistry* 54:171–204.

Norton, S. W., and Hirsh, H. 1992. Classifier learning from noisy data as probabilistic evidence combination. In *AAAI92: Proceedings of the Tenth National Conference on Artificial Intelligence*, 141–146. AAAI Press / MIT Press.

Norton, S. W., and Hirsh, H. 1993. Learning DNF via probabilistic evidence combination. In *Proceedings of the International Conference on Machine Learning*, 220–227. Morgan Kaufmann Publishers.

Nussinov, R., and Lennon, G. G. 1984. Periodic structurally similar oligomers are found on one side of the axes of symetry in the lac, trp, and gal operators. *Journal of Biomolecular Structure and Dynamics* 2(2):387–395.

O'Neill, M. C. 1989. *Escherichia coli* promoters: I. Consensus as it relates to spacing class, specificity, repeat substructure, and three-dimensional organization. *Journal of Biological Chemistry* 264:5522–5530.

Pribnow, D. 1975. Nucleotide sequence of an RNA polymerase binding site at an early T7 promoter. *Proc. Nat. Acad. Sci.* 72(3):784–788.

Quinlan, J. R. 1993. *C4.5: Programs for Machine Learning.* San Mateo, CA: Morgan Kaufmann Publishers.

Siebenlist, U.; Simpson, R. B.; and Gilbert, W. 1980. *E. coli* RNA polymerase interacts homologously with two different promoters. *Cell* 20:269–281.

Towell, G. G., and Shavlik, J. W. 1992. Using symbolic learning to improve knowledge-based neural networks. In *AAAI92: Proceedings of the Tenth National Conference on Artificial Intelligence*, 177–182. AAAI Press.

Towell, G. G.; Shavlik, J. W.; and Noordewier, M. O. 1990. Refinement of approximate domain theories by knowledge-based neural networks. In *AAAI90: Proceedings of the Eighth National Conference on Artificial Intelligence*, 861–866. Morgan Kaufmann Publishers.

von Hippel, P. H.; Bear, D. G.; Morgan, W. D.; and McSwiggen, J. A. 1984. Protein-nucleic acid interactions in transcription: A molecular analysis. *Annual Review of Biochemistry* 53:389–446.

Waterman, M. S. 1989. *Mathematical Methods for DNA Sequences.* CRC Press, Inc.

Watson, J. D.; Hopkins, N. H.; Roberts, J. W.; Steitz, J. A.; and Weiner, A. M. 1987. *Molecular Biology of the Gene.* Benjamin/Cummings Publishing Company, Inc.

Youderian, P.; Bouvier, S.; and Susskind, M. M. 1982. Sequence determinants of promoter activity. *Cell* 30:843–853.

Inductive Learning For Abductive Diagnosis[*]

Cynthia A. Thompson and Raymond J. Mooney
Department of Computer Sciences
University of Texas
Austin, TX 78712
cthomp@cs.utexas.edu, mooney@cs.utexas.edu

Abstract

A new inductive learning system, LAB (Learning for ABduction), is presented which acquires abductive rules from a set of training examples. The goal is to find a small knowledge base which, when used abductively, diagnoses the training examples correctly and generalizes well to unseen examples. This contrasts with past systems that inductively learn rules that are used deductively. Each training example is associated with potentially multiple categories (disorders), instead of one as with typical learning systems. LAB uses a simple hill-climbing algorithm to efficiently build a rule base for a set-covering abductive system. LAB has been experimentally evaluated and compared to other learning systems and an expert knowledge base in the domain of diagnosing brain damage due to stroke.

Introduction

Most work in symbolic concept acquisition assumes a deductive model of classification in which an example is a member of a concept if it satisfies a logical specification represented in disjunctive normal form (DNF) (Michalski and Chilausky, 1980), a decision tree (Quinlan, 1986), or a set of Horn clauses (Quinlan, 1990). However, recent research in diagnosis, plan recognition, object recognition, and other areas of AI has found that *abduction*, finding a set of assumptions that imply or explain a set of observations, is frequently a more appropriate and useful mode of reasoning (Charniak and McDermott, 1985; Levesque, 1989). This paper concerns inducing from examples a knowledge base that is suitable for abductive reasoning.

We focus on abductive diagnosis using the model of (Peng and Reggia, 1990). Given a set of cases each consisting of a list of symptoms and one or more expert-diagnosed disorders, our system, LAB (Learning for ABduction), learns a set of `disorder` $\rightarrow$ `symptom` rules suitable for abductive diagnosis, as opposed to traditional `symptoms` $\rightarrow$ `disorder` rules suitable for

———
[*]This research was supported by the National Science Foundation under grant IRI-9102926 and the Texas Advanced Research Program under grant 003658114.

deductive diagnosis. Studies of human diagnosticians have demonstrated their use of abductive reasoning (Elstein et al., 1978). For example, doctors know the causes behind a patients' symptoms and when a new case is seen, they can work "backwards" given the symptoms to hypothesize the disease or diseases which are present. Abductive methods have proven useful in applications such as diagnosing brain damage due to stroke (Tuhrim et al., 1991) and identifying red-cell antibodies in blood (Josephson et al., 1987).

Abductive methods are particularly useful in domains such as these, where multiple faults or disorders are fairly common. Most inductive work on diagnosis assumes there is a single disorder (classification) for each example. One can use standard methods to learn a separate concept for each disorder that independently predicts its presence or absence; however, the effectiveness of this technique for multiple-disorder diagnosis has not been demonstrated. By finding the smallest set of disorders that globally account for all of the symptoms, abductive methods may be more appropriate for such problems.

Background on Abductive Diagnosis
Parsimonious Covering

Abduction is informally defined as finding the best explanation for a set of observations, or inferring cause from effect. A standard logical definition of an abductive explanation is a consistent set of assumptions which, together with background knowledge, entails a set of observations (Charniak and McDermott, 1985).

Our method for performing abduction is the set-covering approach presented in (Peng and Reggia, 1990). Although a simple, propositional model, it is capable of solving many real-world problems. In addition, it is no more restrictive than most inductive learning systems, which use discrete-valued feature vectors. Some definitions from their work are needed in what follows.

A *diagnostic problem* P is a four-tuple (D, M, C, M^+) where:

- D is a finite, non-empty set of objects, called disorders;

- M is a finite, non-empty set of objects, called manifestations;

- $C \subseteq D \times M$ is a causation relation, where $(d, m) \in C$ means d may cause m; and

- $M^+ \subseteq M$ is the subset of M which has been observed.

$V \subseteq D$ is called a *cover* or *diagnosis* of M^+ if for each $m \in M^+$, there is a $d \in V$ such that $(d, m) \in C$. A cover V is said to be *minimum* if its cardinality is the smallest among all covers. A cover of M^+ is said to be *minimal* if none of its proper subsets are covers; otherwise, it is *non-minimal*. The Peng and Reggia model is equivalent to logical abduction with a simple propositional domain theory composed of the rules $\{d \rightarrow m \mid (d, m) \in C\}$ (Ng, 1992). We will also write the elements of C as rules of the form $\mathtt{d} \rightarrow \mathtt{m}$. Therefore, C can be viewed as the knowledge base or domain theory for abductive diagnosis.

For the abductive portion of our algorithm, we use the BIPARTITE algorithm of (Peng and Reggia, 1990), which returns all minimal diagnoses. One immediate problem is the typically large number of diagnoses generated. Thus, following Occam's razor, we first eliminate all but the minimum covers and select one of them at random as the *system diagnosis*. The diagnosis of an experienced diagnostician is the *correct diagnosis*.

Evaluating Accuracy

We would like to have a quantitative measure of the accuracy of the system diagnosis. In the usual task, assigning an example to a single category, the accuracy is just the percentage of cases which are correctly classified. Here, we must extend this measure since each case is a positive or negative example for many disorders. Let N be the total number of disorders, C^+ the number of disorders in the correct diagnosis, and C^- the number of disorders not in the correct diagnosis, i.e., $N - C^+$. Likewise, let T^+ (True Positives) be the number of disorders in the correct diagnosis that are also in the system diagnosis, and T^- (True Negatives) be the number of disorders not in the correct diagnosis and not in the system diagnosis. *Standard accuracy* for one example when multiple diagnoses are present is defined as $(T^+ + T^-)/N$.

A second evaluation method is *intersection accuracy*. Intuitively, this is the size of the intersection between the correct and system diagnoses, as compared to the size of the diagnoses themselves. It is formally defined as $(T^+/C^+ + T^+/S)/2$, where S is the number of disorders in the system diagnosis. Third, *sensitivity* is defined by T^+/C^+, and measures accuracy over the disorders actually present, an important measure in diagnosis. Sensitivity is also called *recall* by (Swets, 1969) and others, who also define *precision* as T^+/S. Note then that intersection accuracy is the average of precision and recall. A fourth measure, *specificity*, defined as T^-/C^-, measures the accuracy over disorders

not present. Sensitivity, specificity, and standard accuracy are discussed in (Kulikowski and Weiss, 1991). Finally, the accuracy of a rule base over a set of examples can be computed by averaging the appropriate score over all examples.

In a typical diagnosis, where the number of potential disorders is much greater than the number of disorders actually present ($N >> C^+$), it is possible to get very high standard accuracy, and perfect specificity, by simply assuming that all cases have no disorders. Also, it is possible to get perfect sensitivity by assuming that all cases have all disorders. Intersection accuracy is a good measure that avoids these extremes.

Problem Definition and Algorithm

The Learning for Abduction Problem

The basic idea of learning for abduction is to find a small knowledge base that, when used abductively, correctly diagnoses a set of training cases. Under the Peng and Reggia model, this may be more formally defined as follows:

Given:

- D, a finite, non-empty set of potential disorders,

- M, a finite, non-empty set of potential manifestations, and

- E, a finite set of training examples, where the ith example, E_i, consists of a set, $M_i^+ \subseteq M$, of manifestations and a set, $D_i^+ \subseteq D$, of disorders (the correct diagnosis).

Find:
The $C \subseteq D \times M$, such that the intersection accuracy of C over E is maximized.

The desire for a minimum causation relation represents the normal inductive bias of simplicity (Occam's Razor). Note we do not aim for 100% accuracy, because in some cases this is impossible, as we will discuss later. Also, we maximize intersection, not standard accuracy, for the reasons mentioned earlier.

LAB Algorithm

We conjecture that the learning for abduction problem as stated above is intractable. Therefore, we attempt to maximize accuracy by using a hill-climbing algorithm, outlined in Figure 1. Note that the rules in C always have a single manifestation rather than a conjunction of them. The first step (after initializing C) adds appropriate rules for examples with one disorder. If E_i is an example with $D_i^+ = \{d\}$ and $M_i^+ = \{m_1, \ldots, m_n\}$, then appropriate rules are $\mathtt{d} \rightarrow \mathtt{m_1}, \ldots, \mathtt{d} \rightarrow \mathtt{m_n}$. These rules must be in C if M_i^+ is to be correctly diagnosed while including a rule for each manifestation. Although in some cases this may cause incorrect diagnoses for other examples, this was not a significant problem in practice. The second step extracts all possible rules from the input examples by

Set $C = \emptyset$

For all examples with $|D_i^+| = 1$, add the appropriate rules to C

Find all potential rules, $Rules$, from E

Compute the intersection accuracy, Acc, of C over E

Repeat the following, until Acc decreases, reaches 100%, or there are no more rules:

    Initialize $bestrule =$ a random $r \in Rules$

    For each $R \in Rules$,

        Set $C' = C \cup \{R\}$

        Compute the accuracy of C' over E

        If the accuracy of C' is greater than Acc then

            Set $Acc =$ accuracy of C' and $bestrule = R$

    If Acc increased or remained the same, then

        Set $C = C \cup \{bestrule\}$

        Set $Rules =$

        $Rules - bestrule - relatedrules(bestrule)$

Else quit and return C.

Figure 1: LAB Algorithm

adding each unique pair $\{(d, m) \mid d \in D_i^+, m \in M_i^+\}$ from each example, E_i, to $Rules$.

Next, the main loop is entered and rules are incrementally added to C until the intersection accuracy of the rule base decreases, 100% intersection accuracy is reached, or $Rules$ is emptied. At each iteration of the loop, the accuracy of a rule base C' is measured. For each manifestation set, BIPARTITE is run using C' and the resulting minimum diagnoses are compared to the correct diagnosis. Note that the abduction task itself is a black box as far as LAB is concerned. Three types of accuracy are computed: intersection accuracy, standard accuracy, and sensitivity. To simulate the random selection of one minimum cover, the average accuracy of all minimum covers is determined. The best rule base is chosen by lexicographically comparing the different accuracy measures. Comparisons are first made using intersection accuracy, then standard accuracy, then sensitivity.

The remainder of the algorithm is straightforward. If all rule bases have equal accuracy, a rule is picked at random. The best rule is added to C and removed from $Rules$, along with any *related rules*. A rule, $d \to m$, is related to another, $d' \to m'$, if the two rules have the same manifestation ($m = m'$) and d and m appear only in examples in which d' and m' also appear. By removing related rules, we enforce a bias towards a minimum rule base and help maintain as high an accuracy as possible. The computational complexity of LAB can be shown to be $O(N|D|^2|M|^2)$, where N is the number of examples in E (Thompson, 1993).

Example of LAB

Let us illustrate the workings of LAB with an example. Consider the following example set, E:

E_1: $D_1 = \{\texttt{typhoid, flu}\}$; $M_1 = \{\texttt{sniffles, cough, headache, fever}\}$

E_2: $D_2 = \{\texttt{allergy, cold}\}$; $M_2 = \{\texttt{aches, fever, sleepy}\}$

E_3: $D_3 = \{\texttt{cold}\}$; $M_3 = \{\texttt{aches, fever}\}$.

First, we see that E_3 has only one disorder, so the appropriate rules are added to C, so that $C = \{\texttt{cold}\to\texttt{aches}, \texttt{cold}\to\texttt{fever}\}$. The intersection accuracy of this rule base is 0.583, computed as follows. For all three examples, the cover returned by BIPARTITE is $\{\texttt{cold}\}$. Thus, the intersection accuracy is $(0 + (1/1 + 1/2)/2 + (1/1 + 1/1)/2)/3$. Next, all possible remaining rules are formed and added to $Rules$. Then the main loop is enterered, which tests the result of adding each element of $Rules$ to C. Adding the rule $\texttt{typhoid}\to\texttt{sniffles}$ to C would result in the answer $\{\texttt{cold, typhoid}\}$ for E_1 and the answer $\{\texttt{cold}\}$ for E_2 and E_3. Thus, the intersection accuracy of C with this rule added is 0.75. Although there are other rule bases with this same accuracy, no others surpass this accuracy, so this becomes the starting C for the second iteration. In addition, our set of $Rules$ decreases, because the best rule $\texttt{typhoid}\to\texttt{sniffles}$ is removed. $\texttt{flu}\to\texttt{sniffles}$ is also removed, which is the only related rule of $\texttt{typhoid}\to\texttt{sniffles}$. In the next iteration, the rule $\texttt{flu}\to\texttt{cough}$, when added to C, results in the highest intersection accuracy of 0.861, because the answer for E_1 is now $\{\texttt{typhoid, flu, cold}\}$. So related rule $\texttt{typhoid}\to\texttt{cough}$ is also removed from $Rules$. The rule added in the next iteration is $\texttt{allergy}\to\texttt{sleepy}$, and related rule $\texttt{cold}\to\texttt{sleepy}$ is removed. Finally, the rule $\texttt{typhoid}\to\texttt{fever}$ is added, which results in 100% intersection accuracy, and we are done. The final rule base, C, is $\{\texttt{typhoid}\to\texttt{fever}, \texttt{allergy}\to\texttt{sleepy}, \texttt{flu}\to\texttt{cough}, \texttt{typhoid}\to\texttt{sniffles}, \texttt{cold}\to\texttt{fever}, \texttt{cold}\to\texttt{aches}\}$. Note that no rule is associated with the manifestation $\texttt{headache}$. This is because we reached 100% accuracy before adding a rule for all symptoms, and is in keeping with our goal of learning the smallest possible rule base.

Experimental Evaluation

Method

Our hypothesis was that learning for abduction is better than learning for deduction in the case of multiple-disorder diagnosis. To test this hypothesis, we used actual patient data from the domain of diagnosing brain damage due to stroke. We used fifty of the patient cases discussed in (Tuhrim et al., 1991).[1] In this database, there are twenty-five different brain areas which can be damaged, effecting the presence of thirty-seven symptom types, each with an average of four values, for a total of 155 attribute-value pairs.

---

[1] We were only able to obtain fifty out of the 100 cases from the authors of the original study.

The fifty cases have an average of 8.56 manifestations and 1.96 disorders each. In addition, we obtained the accompanying abductive knowledge base generated by an expert, which consists of 648 rules.

We ran our experiments with LAB, ID3 (Quinlan, 1986), PFOIL (Mooney, to appear), and a neural network using standard backpropagation (Rumelhart et al., 1986) with one hidden layer. The neural network used has one output bit per disorder, and the number of hidden units is 10% of the number of disorders plus the number of manifestations. PFOIL is a propositional version of FOIL (Quinlan, 1990) which learns DNF rules. The primary simplification of PFOIL compared to FOIL is that it only needs to deal with fixed examples rather than the expanding tuples of FOIL.

ID3 and PFOIL are typically used for single category tasks. Therefore, an interface was built for both systems to allow them to simulate the multiple disorder diagnosis of LAB. One decision tree or DNF form is learned for each disorder. Each example $E_i \in E$ is given to the learner as a positive example if the disorder is present in D_i^+, otherwise it is given as a negative example. Thus, a forest of trees or collection of DNF forms is built.

In order to compare the performance of LAB to ID3, PFOIL, and backpropagation, learning curves were generated for the patient data. Each system was trained in batch fashion on increasingly larger fractions of a fixed training set and repeatedly tested on the same disjoint test set, in this case consisting of ten examples. At each point, the following statistics were gathered for both the training and the testing sets: standard accuracy, intersection accuracy, sensitivity, and specificity. Also, training time, testing time and concept complexity were measured.

The concept complexity of LAB is simply the number of rules in the final rule base, C. The complexity of the trees returned by ID3 is the number of leaves. This is then summed over the tree formed for each disorder. For PFOIL, the concept complexity is the sum of the lengths of each disjunct, summed again over the DNF for each disorder. Although rule, literal, and leaf counts are not directly comparable, they provide a reasonable measure of relative complexity. There is no acceptable way to compare the complexity of concepts learned by a network to these other methods, therefore no measures of concept complexity were made for backpropagation.

All of the results were averaged over 20 trials, each with a different randomly selected training and test set. The results were statistically evaluated using a two-tailed, paired t-test. For each training set size, LAB was compared to each of ID3, PFOIL, and backpropagation to determine if the differences in the various accuracy measures, train time, and and concept complexity were statistically significant ($p \leq 0.05$). If specific differences are not mentioned, they should be assumed to be statistically insignificant.

Results

Two of the resulting curves are shown in Figure 2. The left side of the figure shows the results for intersection accuracy on the testing set. LAB performs significantly better than ID3 through 15 examples, than backpropagation through 20 examples, and than PFOIL through 30 examples. Also, LAB performs significantly better than the expert knowledge base after only 15 training examples, while it takes ID3 and backpropagation 25 examples to reach this level, and PFOIL 35 examples to reach this level.

On the other hand, LAB suffers on standard accuracy for the testing set, as is seen on the right side of the figure. However, the differences between LAB and ID3 are only statistically significant for 20, 25, 35, and 40 examples. When comparing LAB to PFOIL, it is seen that PFOIL performs significantly better than LAB only at 35 and 40 examples. Also, LAB performs significantly worse than backpropagation for all training set sizes. All the systems perform significantly better than the expert knowledge base starting at 20 (or fewer) training examples.

The results for sensitivity, while not shown, are also promising. LAB performs significantly better than ID3 for all training set sizes except 35, where the difference is not significant. LAB does, however, perform significantly better than PFOIL and backpropagation throughout. Also, LAB performs significantly better than the expert knowledge base starting at ten examples, ID3 does so starting at 15 examples, and PFOIL and backpropagation starting at 20 examples. For specificity, also not shown, ID3 and PFOIL perform significantly better than LAB starting at ten training examples. Backpropagation performs significantly better than LAB starting at five training examples.

Another difference in the results between the systems is in concept complexity. LAB learns a significantly more simple rule base than the trees built by ID3, but is significantly more complicated than the concepts learned by PFOIL.

Finally, for LAB the training set performance for standard accuracy starts high and stays well above 98%. On the other hand, intersection accuracy and sensitivity dip to 90%, while specificity stays above 99%. The other systems reach a training set accuracy of 100%.

Discussion

Our intuition was that obtaining a high intersection accuracy would be easier for LAB than for PFOIL or ID3. The results partially support this, in that LAB performs significantly better than all of the systems at first, then the difference becomes insignificant as the number of training examples increases. However, if a (less conservative) one-tailed, paired t-test is used instead of two-tailed, LAB's performance is significantly better than ID3 through 20 examples, and again at 30

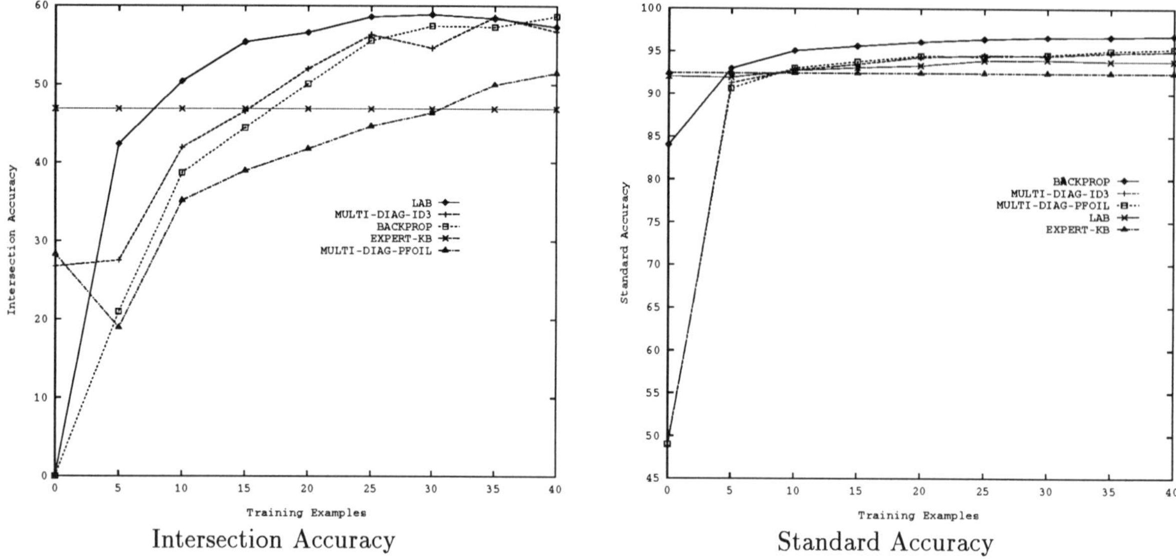

Intersection Accuracy   Standard Accuracy

Figure 2: Experimental Results on the Test Set

examples, as compared to only through 15 examples with the two-tailed test.

Also, LAB does not perform quite as well on standard accuracy compared to the other systems. However, this measure is not very meaningful, considering we get 92% accuracy just by saying that all patients have no brain damage. Finally, the sensitivity results were very encouraging, and again if we use a one-tailed, paired t-test, LAB is significantly better than ID3 for all training set sizes. Still, our results were somewhat weaker than we would have hoped. There are several possible explanations for this. First, while ID3, back-propagation, and PFOIL[2] get 100% performance on all measures on the training data, LAB does not. One possible reason is that the hill-climbing algorithm can run into local maxima.

Another reason for the difficulty in converging on the training data is that the data contain some conflicting examples from an abductive point of view. In other words, it is impossible to build an abductive rule base which will correctly diagnose all examples. One instance of these conflicts occur when there is an example, E_i, such that $|D_i^+| \geq 2$ and all $m \in M_i^+$ appear in other examples that contain only one disorder. Any attempt at an accurate abductive rule base will either hypothesize extra disorders for the examples with one disorder, or it will hypothesize a subset of the correct disorders for E_i. There are two examples with this problem in our patient data. In addition, there are other, more complicated example interactions which make it impossible to learn a completely accurate abductive rule base. This might be addressed in the future by learning more complex rules.

LAB produces diagnoses during testing which include more disorders than are present in the correct diagnosis, and thus it performs well on sensitivity. On the other hand, ID3's answers include fewer disorders than the correct diagnosis, and thus performs well on specificity. These results are further indication of why ID3 performs better than LAB on standard accuracy. As mentioned previously, each example has fewer disorders than the total number possible ($D_i^+ << D$). Therefore, since ID3 is correctly predicting which disorders are *not* present more accurately than LAB, it is not surprising that it is better on standard accuracy. However, it should be emphasized that sensitivity is important in a diagnostic domain, where determining all the diseases present, and perhaps additional ones, is better than leaving some out.

Finally, we turn to concept complexity. The expert knowledge base contains 648 rules versus 111 for LAB with 40 training examples, and its performance is worse than the rules learned by LAB. There is a clear advantage, in this case, in learning rules as opposed to using expert advice. In addition, the abductive rule base is arguably easier to comprehend than either the decision tree learned by ID3 or the disjuncts returned by PFOIL, since the rules are in the causal direction. See (Thompson, 1993) for an example rule base learned by LAB.

Related Work

Since no other system learns abductive knowledge bases, no direct comparisons are possible. However, there are many systems which learn to perform diagnosis, and many abductive reasoning methods. We have already mentioned systems which learn deduc-

---

[2]Except at one data point.

tive rules, both in the introduction and in our comparisons with ID3 and PFOIL. One other method that seems particularly well-suited to diagnosis is Bayesian Networks (Pearl, 1988). There have been several attempts to learn Bayesian Networks (Cooper and Herskovits, 1992; Geiger et al., 1990), but they have not been tested in realistic diagnostic domains.

Future Work

There are many opportunities for future work. First, we believe training accuracy could be improved, even given the presence of inconsistent examples. Several modifications are possible. First, different or additional heuristics could be used to improve the hill-climbing search. Second, backtracking or beam search could be used to increase training set accuracy.

A second opportunity for improvement is to reduce the number of diagnoses returned to only one during both training and testing. One way this could be done is by adding probability to abduction, as in (Peng and Reggia, 1990). Third, there is room to improve the efficiency of the system. The average training time with 40 examples is 230 seconds, versus 4 to 5 seconds for ID3 and PFOIL.

Finally, experiments in other domains are desirable; however we know of no other existing data sets for multiple-disorder diagnosis. Also, the method needs to be extended to produce more complex abductive knowledge bases that include *causal chaining* (Peng and Reggia, 1990), rules with multiple antecedents, incompatible disorders, and predicate logic (Ng, 1992).

Conclusion

Abduction is an increasingly popular approach to multiple-disorder diagnosis. However, the problem of automatically learning abductive rule bases from training examples has not previously been addressed. This paper has presented a method for inducing a set of `disorder → manifestation` rules that can be used abductively to diagnose a set of examples. Experiments on a real medical problem indicate that this method produces a more accurate abductive knowledge base than one assembled by domain experts, and, according to at least some important metrics, more accurate than "deductive" concepts learned by systems such as ID3, FOIL, and backpropagation.

Acknowledgments

Thanks to Dr. Stanley Tuhrim of Mount Sinai School of Medicine, and Dr. James Reggia of the University of Maryland.

References

Charniak, E. and McDermott, D. (1985). *Introduction to AI*. Reading, MA: Addison-Wesley.

Cooper, G. G. and Herskovits, E. (1992). A Bayesian method for the induction of probabilistic networks from data. *Machine Learning*, 9:309–347.

Elstein, A., l. Shulman, and Sprafka, S. (1978). *Medical Problem Solving - An Analysis of Clinical Reasoning*. Harvard University Press.

Geiger, D., Paz, A., and Pearl, J. (1990). Learning causal trees from dependence information. In *Proceedings of the Eighth National Conference on Artificial Intelligence*, pages 770–776. Boston,MA.

Josephson, J. R., Chandrasekaran, B., Smith, J. R., and Tanner, M. C. (1987). A mechanism for forming composite explanatory hypotheses. *IEEE Transactions on Systems, Man, and Cybernetics*, 17(3):445–454.

Kulikowski, C. A. and Weiss, S. M. (1991). *Computer Systems That Learn - Classification and Prediction Methods from Statistics, Neural Nets, Machine Learning, and Expert Systems*. San Mateo, CA: Morgan Kaufmann.

Levesque, H. J. (1989). A knowledge-level account of abduction. In *Proceedings of the Eleventh International Joint conference on Artificial intelligence*, pages 1061–1067. Detroit, MI.

Michalski, R. S. and Chilausky, S. (1980). Learning by being told and learning from examples: An experimental comparison of the two methods of knowledge acquisition in the context of developing an expert system for soybean disease diagnosis. *Journal of Policy Analysis and Information Systems*, 4(2):126–161.

Mooney, R. J. (to appear). Encouraging experimental results on learning CNF. *Machine Learning*.

Ng, H. T. (1992). *A General Abductive System with Applications to Plan Recognition and Diagnosis*. PhD thesis, Austin, TX: University of Texas. Also appears as Artificial Intelligence Laboratory Technical Report AI 92-177.

Pearl, J. (1988). *Probabilistic Reasoning in Intelligent Systems: Networks of Plausible Inference*. San Mateo,CA: Morgan Kaufmann, Inc.

Peng, Y. and Reggia, J. A. (1990). *Abductive Inference Models for Diagnostic Problem-Solving*. New York: Springer-Verlag.

Quinlan, J. (1990). Learning logical definitions from relations. *Machine Learning*, 5(3):239–266.

Quinlan, J. R. (1986). Induction of decision trees. *Machine Learning*, 1(1):81–106.

Rumelhart, D. E., Hinton, G. E., and Williams, J. R. (1986). Learning internal representations by error propagation. In Rumelhart, D. E. and McClelland, J. L., editors, *Parallel Distributed Processing, Vol. I*, pages 318–362. Cambridge, MA: MIT Press.

Swets, J. A. (1969). Effectiveness of information retrieval methods. *American Documentation*, pages 72–89.

Thompson, C. A. (1993). *Inductive Learning for Abductive Diagnosis*. Master's thesis, Austin, TX: University of Texas at Austin.

Tuhrim, S., Reggia, J., and Goodall, S. (1991). An experimental study of criteria for hypothesis plausibility. *Journal of Experimental and Theoretical Artificial Intelligence*, 3:129–144.

Learning Fault-tolerant Speech Parsing with SCREEN

Stefan Wermter and Volker Weber
University of Hamburg, Computer Science Department
Vogt-Kölln-Straße 30, D-22527 Hamburg, Germany
wermter@informatik.uni-hamburg.de
weber@informatik.uni-hamburg.de

Abstract

This paper describes a new approach and a system
SCREEN[1] for fault-tolerant speech parsing. Speech
parsing describes the syntactic and semantic analysis of spontaneous spoken language. The general approach is based on incremental immediate flat analysis, learning of syntactic and semantic speech parsing, parallel integration of current hypotheses, and the
consideration of various forms of speech related errors. The goal for this approach is to explore the parallel interactions between various knowledge sources
for learning incremental fault-tolerant speech parsing. This approach is examined in a system SCREEN
using various hybrid connectionist techniques. Hybrid connectionist techniques are examined because of
their promising properties of inherent fault tolerance,
learning, gradedness and parallel constraint integration. The input for SCREEN is hypotheses about
recognized words of a spoken utterance potentially
analyzed by a speech system, the output is hypotheses about the flat syntactic and semantic analysis of
the utterance. In this paper we focus on the general
approach, the overall architecture, and examples for
learning flat syntactic speech parsing. Different from
most other speech language architectures SCREEN
emphasizes an interactive rather than an autonomous
position, learning rather than encoding, flat analysis
rather than in-depth analysis, and fault-tolerant processing of phonetic, syntactic and semantic knowledge.

Introduction and Motivation

In the past, the analysis of spontaneous speech utterances as syntactic and semantic case frame representations received relatively little attention. Although there had been some early attempts for combination (Erman *et al.* 1980) the restricted speech
and language techniques at that time forced each
field, speech and language processing, to concentrate
on developing further techniques separately. Therefore, in the last decade there have been primarily
isolated modular attempts to build speech analyzers
(e.g., (Lee, Hon, & Reddy 1990; McClelland & Elman

---

[1]SCREEN stands for Symbolic Connectionist Robust
EnterprisE for Natural language

1986)) or language analyzers (e.g., (Hobbs *et al.* 1992;
Kitano & Higuchi 1991)).

However, recent approaches attempt to integrate
speech and language earlier to reduce the extensive
space of acoustic, syntactic and semantic hypotheses
(Pyka 1992; Young *et al.* 1989). The MINDS system (Young *et al.* 1989) is a speech language system which combines a speech recognizer (Lee, Hon, &
Reddy 1990) with expectation-driven language analysis. The main contribution of the MINDS system is its
early integration of speech hypotheses with language
hypotheses in order to restrict the search space for
speech processing. On the other hand, the MINDS
system relies heavily on *hand-coded* pragmatic knowledge from a single domain.

The ASL system (e.g. (Pyka 1992)) is a speech language system which focused on the examination of interactions in a very general architecture. This system
has an architecture similar to a blackboard architecture
but without explicit control. Autonomous components
can send and receive hypotheses, but the overall architecture and relationships between the components are
flexible. While the MINDS system emphasized the use
of pragmatic knowledge for supporting speech processing, the ASL system focused rather on syntactic and semantic knowledge. The ASL system has an extremely
flexible architecture which can avoid early mistakes in
favoring a particular architecture. On the other hand,
this flexibility also requires very sophisticated communication operations for complexer interactions.

Both MINDS and ASL belong to the state-of-the-art
architectures in speech language systems. However, in
both systems the language knowledge is basically *manually encoded* and *domain-dependent*. Furthermore,
currently errors like false starts, hesitations, corrections, and repetitions have only been implemented in
a rudimentary pragmatic manner in the MINDS system. We designed SCREEN as a system for learning
fault-tolerant incremental speech parsing. SCREEN
deals with repairs (Levelt 1983), false starts, hesitations, and interjections. Since connectionist techniques
have inherent fault tolerance and learning capabilities
we explore these properties in a hybrid connectionist

architecture. In this *hybrid connectionist* architecture
we make use of learning connectionist representations
as far as possible, but we do not rule out symbolic representations since they may be natural and efficient for
some subtasks (e.g. for testing lexical equality of two
words).

The data we currently use come from the German
Regensburg corpus[2] which contains dialogs at a railway
counter (more than 48000 words). As a first step we
used transcribed real utterances of the Regensburg corpus for SCREEN. This corpus contains a great deal of
spoken constructions and occurring errors. In general
we also have to deal with other errors introduced by
the speech recognizer. However, for the purpose of this
paper we concentrate on transcribed real speech utterances in order to illustrate the screening approach for
speech parsing but our overall architecture SCREEN
has the long-term goal of using speech input directly.

In this paper we will first show the underlying principles of fault-tolerant speech parsing in SCREEN and
the overall architecture. Then we will describe results
from flat syntactic analysis with a hybrid connectionist
architecture using spoken utterances.

Principles of fault-tolerant speech parsing with SCREEN

Our general approach is based on incremental immediate flat analysis, learning of syntactic and semantic
speech parsing, and the consideration of various forms
of speech related errors. The goal for this approach
is to explore the parallel interactions between various knowledge sources for learning incremental speech
parsing and to provide experimental contributions to
the issue of architectures for speech language systems.

Screening approach for interpretation level:
Since speech is spontaneous and erroneous, a complete interpretation at an in-depth level will often fail
due to violated expectations. Therefore, we pursue a
screening approach which learns an interpretation at a
flat level which is more accessible for erroneous speech
parsing. In particular, the screening approach structures utterances at the phrase group level.

Previous work towards this screening approach has
been described as scanning understanding in SCAN
(Wermter 1992). The scanning understanding primarily focused on phrase processing while our screening
approach goes further by integrating and extending
speech properties into a new system SCREEN for unrestricted robust spontaneous language processing.

Learning speech parsing: The analysis of an utterance as syntactic and semantic case frame representations is among the most important steps for language
understanding. However, in addition to semantic and
syntactic understanding per se, there are two central
aspects: learning and speech interaction. We examine

to what extent hybrid connectionist techniques can be
used for learning and integrating semantic and syntactic case frame representations for speech utterances.

Dealing with errors: For building a speech language system we have to consider two main sources
of errors: errors at the speech level and errors at the
language level. Within a real speech system, errors are
based on incomplete or noisy input so that many incorrect words are detected. On the other hand, even under the assumption that a speech recognizer comes up
with the correct word interpretations for an utterance,
there are errors at the language level like repairs, repetitions, interjections and partially incomplete phrases
and sentences (e.g., telegraphic language).

SCREEN: A system for fault-tolerant speech parsing

SCREEN has a parallel architecture with many individual modules which communicate interactively and
in parallel similar to message passing systems. There is
no central control; rather messages about incremental
hypotheses at the current time are sent between specified modules in order to finally provide an incremental syntactic and semantic interpretation for a speech
utterance. For the realization, we use hybrid connectionist techniques. That is, we integrate connectionist
representations where they can be used directly and
efficiently, but we do not rule out the use of other
symbolic or stochastic representations. Connectionist techniques are examined because of their favorable
properties of inherent fault tolerance, learning, gradedness, and parallel constraint integration. Therefore,
SCREEN is not only an approach to examine fault-
tolerant speech parsing but also to test the extent to
which current connectionist techniques can be pushed
for building a real-world complex speech language system.

An overview

Figure 1 shows an abstract overview about the
SCREEN architecture. There are basically five parts
where each part consists of several modules. Each
module can have a symbolic program and a connectionist network. The description of SCREEN as five
parts follows its main functionalities but does not suggest a fixed hierarchical architecture. Rather, the modules in the five parts work in parallel and can exchange
messages directly.

The *speech interface part* receives input from a
speech recognizer as word hypotheses and provides an
analysis of the syntactic and semantic plausibility of
the recognized words. This analysis can be used by
the speech recognizer for further speech analysis and by
the subsequent language parts for filtering only important plausible speech hypotheses for further language
analysis. The *category part* receives words of an utterance and provides basic syntactic, basic semantic as

---

[2]For clarity the illustrated examples are shown in their
English translation.

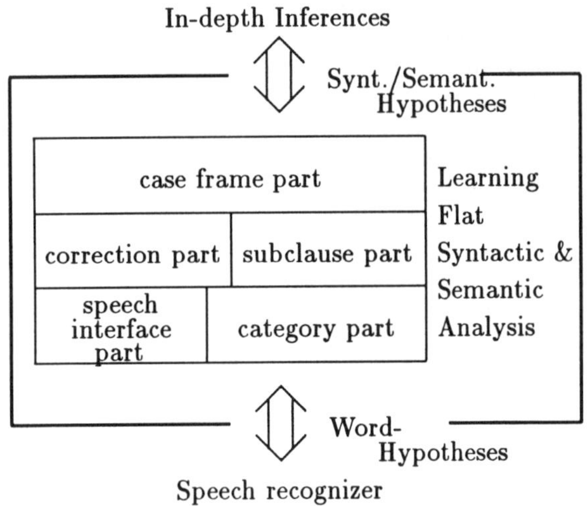

Figure 1: Overview of SCREEN

well as abstract syntactic and abstract semantic categories. The *correction part* receives knowledge about words and phrases as well as their categories and provides the knowledge about the occurrence of a certain error, like a repair or repetition. The *subclause part* is responsible for the detection of subclause borders in order to distinguish different subclauses. Finally, the *case frame part* is responsible for the overall interpretation of the utterance. This part receives knowledge about abstract syntactic and semantic categories of a phrase and provides the integrated interpretation.

A more detailed overview of SCREEN

Although we can not describe all the hybrid connectionist modules in SCREEN due to space restrictions, we illustrate the overall architecture and some examples for individual modules (see figure 2). We focus here only on the category part, the correction part, and the case frame part, and within these parts we will mainly focus on syntactic processing. The arrows illustrate incremental parallel flow of syntactic/semantic hypotheses. All modules in the same part in figure 2 are able to work in parallel while the processing of an utterance is incremental. While the modules in the *correction part* analyze a certain word x the modules in the *category part* are able to analyze the next word x+1 and so on.

The *category part* consists of the modules for disambiguating basic categories and determining abstract categories. The module BAS-SYN-DIS (BAS-SEM-DIS) disambiguates syntactic (semantic) basic categories. SYN-PHR-START (SEM-PHR-START) determines the start of a new syntactic (semantic) phrase group. The assignment of abstract syntactic (semantic) categories is performed by the module ABS-SYN-CAT (ABS-SEM-CAT).

The goal of the *error part* is to detect errors at a sub-word level, word level, or phrase group level. At the sub-word level the module PAUSE? checks if a current input is a pause, INTERJECTION? checks whether it is an interjection or unknown phonetic input. At the word level LEX-WORD-EQ? checks if the current word is lexically equal to the previous word and BAS-SYN-EQ? (BAS-SEM-EQ?) if it is syntactically (semantically) equal to the previous word. The modules at the phrase level are similar to the modules at the word level. LEX-START-EQ? checks if the lexical start of two phrases is equal. ABS-SYN-EQ? (ABS-SEM-EQ?) checks if the abstract syntactic (semantic) category of a current phrase group is equal to the category of the previous phrase group. The output of the modules of the correction part described so far is used in the error testing modules PAUSE-ERROR?, WORD-ERROR?, and PHRASE-ERROR?. PAUSE-ERROR? checks if a pause, interjection, or unknown phonetic input occurred, and WORD-ERROR? (PHRASE-ERROR?) determines if there is evidence for a repair at the word level (phrase group level).

In the *case frame part* a frame is filled corresponding to the syntactic and semantic categories of constituents. The module SLOT-FINDING is used to find the appropriate slot for a current phrase group. SLOT-ERROR? tests if the proposed slot is possible based on the compatibility of abstract syntactic and semantic categories for a current phrase group. VERB-ERROR? checks if new frames have to be generated. INTERPRETATION is needed to convert the internal word-by-word message structure of SCREEN to a more structured representation useful for further high level processing.

For illustration we focus on just a few modules for flat syntactic parsing. The interface of a module is represented symbolically, the learning part of a module is supported by a connectionist network. While not all modules have to contain connectionist networks they will be used as far as possible for automatic knowledge extraction. For illustrating the learned performance of some modules of SCREEN, table 1 shows three modules with a simple recurrent network SRN (Elman 1990), the number of units in the input I, hidden H, and output O layer. Training (testing) was performed with 37 (58) utterances with 394 (823) words. We used the training instances (words) based on the complete real world utterances including the errors. Under the assumption of more regular than erroneous language the general regularities will have been picked up by the network, even if it has been trained with the erroneous real-world data. For instance 99% (93%) of the basic syntactic categories of the training (test) set could be assigned correctly (see figure 2). The last row describes the combined overall performance of the modules BAS-SYN-DIS and ABS-SYN-CAT; only if both SRN-networks provide the desired category with maximum output activation it is counted as a correct combined output.

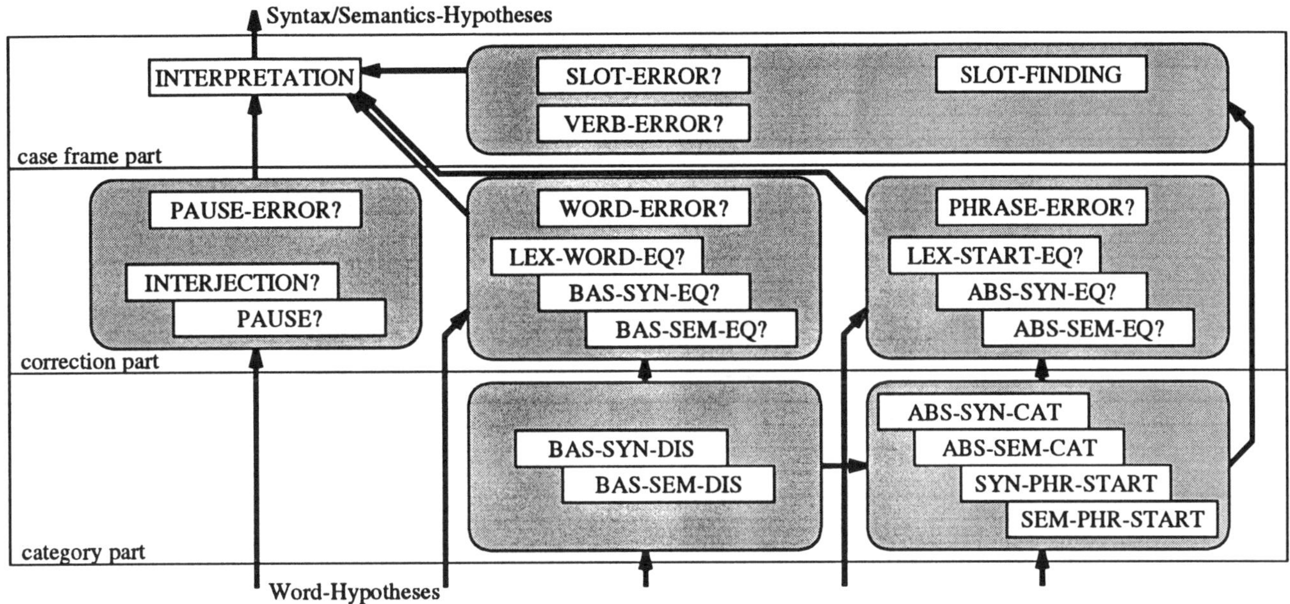

Figure 2: SCREEN: some modules of the category, correction, and case frame parts

Module	No. of units			correct assignments	
	I	H	O	train	test
BAS-SYN-DIS	13	14	13	99%	93%
ABS-SYN-CAT	13	7	8	91%	85%
SYN-PHR-START	13	7	1	93%	89%
Combined	-	-	-	90%	82%

Table 1: Performance of some modules

An example for speech parsing

In this section we describe the incremental flat syntactic processing using two real transcribed utterances in SCREEN. The first sentence in figure 3 does not contain a repair, while the second in figure 4 does. The first sentence starts with the word "Yeah" which is classified as adverb by the module BAS-SYN-DIS and as part of modus group[3] by ABS-SYN-CAT. At the beginning of an utterance SYN-PHR-START classifies a word as start of a new phrase group. The second word "I" is classified as a pronoun, is part of a noun group, and starts a new phrase group. The comparison of the first word (resp. first phrase group) and second word (resp. second phrase group) does not result in any hints for a pause-, word-, or phrase error. Later in the utterance the ABS-SYN-EQ? module finds that the two syntactic phrase groups "from Regensburg" and "to Dortmund" are syntactically equal. But syntactic equality of two phrase groups alone is

---

[3]interrogative pronouns and confirmation words

too weak to determine a phrase error since other modules (LEX-START-EQ? and ABS-SEM-EQ?) suggest that these two phrase groups are different with respect to their start and abstract semantic categories. When the pause "." occurs the module PAUSE-ERROR? is triggered and the pause is deleted.

For this first utterance the analysis has been rather straightforward while in the next utterance (see figure 4) we describe a more difficult example with error corrections. PAUSE-ERROR? is responsible for deleting pauses, interjections, and phonetic material. BAS-SYN-DIS classifies almost all interjections and phonetic material correctly. Only "[u]" is misclassified as adverb rather than interjection in BAS-SYN-DIS. PAUSE-ERROR? does not use this adverb information but only the output of PAUSE? and INTERJECTION?. As the module PAUSE-ERROR? determines these errors, interjections and pauses are deleted incrementally so that the phrase groups "at Monday" and "at Monday" follow each other directly. Since both groups are prepositional groups and since they have the same lexical start the modules LEX-PHRASE-EQ? and ABS-SYN-EQ? trigger PHRASE-ERROR?. Therefore the first phrase group "at Monday ..." is replaced by just "at Monday". Similarly, other types of repairs (e.g. "at Monday" replaced by "at Tuesday", "in the morning") will be dealt with in the future.

Overall functionality and performance

SCREEN provides a fault-tolerant interpretation of a potentially faulty utterance. The words of the fault-tolerant interpretation of the faulty utterance have been underlined in order to illustrate this function-

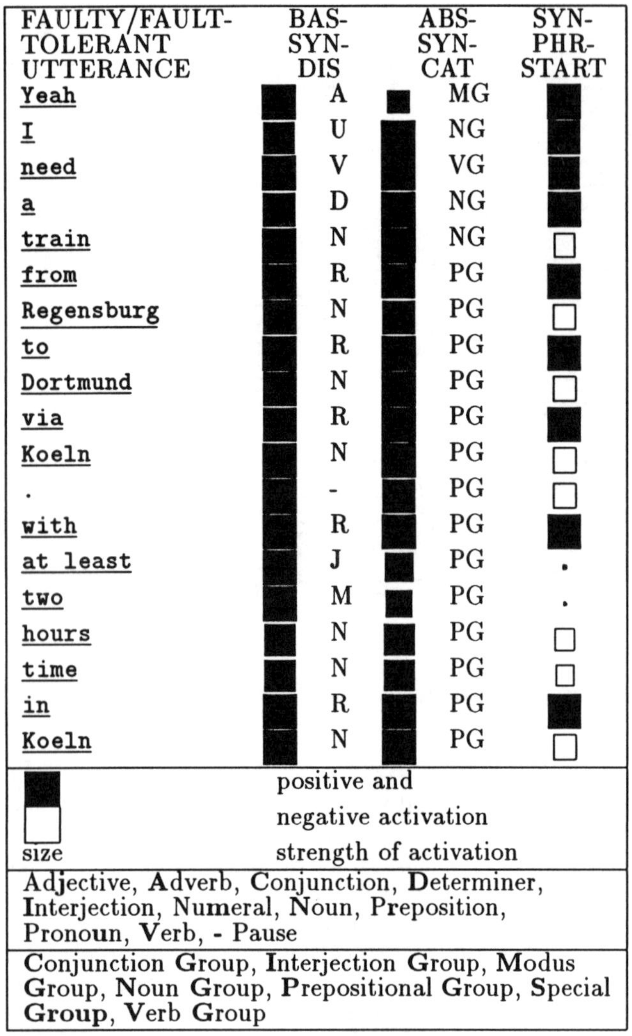

FAULTY/FAULT-TOLERANT UTTERANCE	BAS-SYN-DIS		ABS-SYN-CAT	SYN-PHR-START
Yeah	▮	A	▪ MG	▮
I	▮	U	▮ NG	▮
need	▮	V	▮ VG	▮
a	▮	D	▮ NG	▮
train	▮	N	NG	☐
from	▮	R	▮ PG	▮
Regensburg	▮	N	▮ PG	☐
to	▮	R	▮ PG	▮
Dortmund	▮	N	▮ PG	☐
via	▮	R	▮ PG	▮
Koeln	▮	N	▮ PG	☐
.	▮	-	▮ PG	☐
with	▮	R	▮ PG	▮
at least	▮	J	▪ PG	·
two	▮	M	▪ PG	·
hours	▮	N	▮ PG	☐
time	▮	N	▮ PG	☐
in	▮	R	▮ PG	▮
Koeln	▮	N	▮ PG	☐

▮ (over ☐)	positive and negative activation
size	strength of activation

Adjective, Adverb, Conjunction, Determiner, Interjection, Numeral, Noun, Preposition, Pronoun, Verb, - Pause

Conjunction Group, Interjection Group, Modus Group, Noun Group, Prepositional Group, Special Group, Verb Group

Figure 3: Syntax part of a sample parse of a sentence

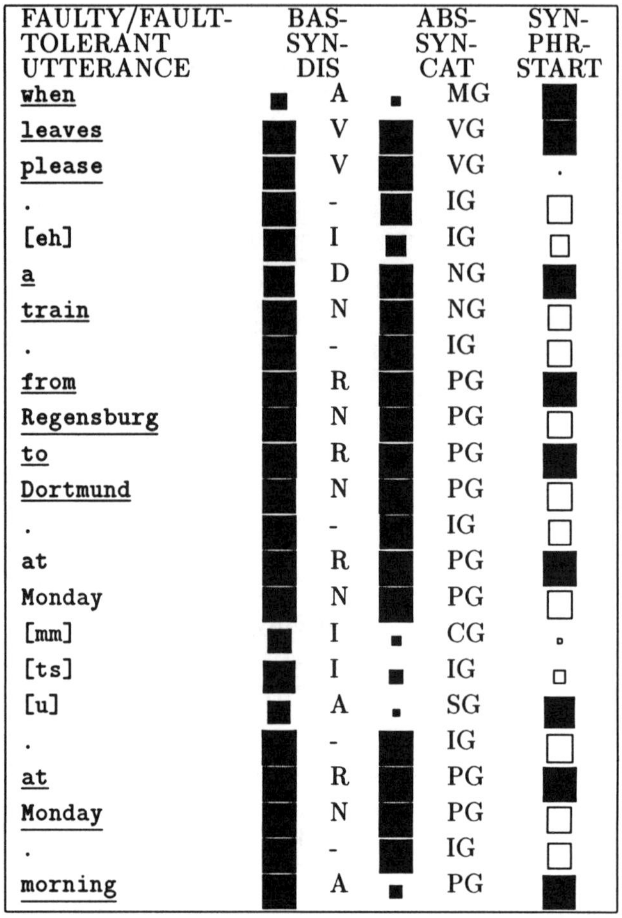

FAULTY/FAULT-TOLERANT UTTERANCE	BAS-SYN-DIS		ABS-SYN-CAT	SYN-PHR-START
when	▪	A	▪ MG	▮
leaves	▮	V	▮ VG	▮
please	▮	V	▮ VG	·
.	▮	-	▮ IG	☐
[eh]	▮	I	▪ IG	☐
a	▮	D	▮ NG	▮
train	▮	N	▮ NG	☐
.	▮	-	▮ IG	☐
from	▮	R	▮ PG	▮
Regensburg	▮	N	▮ PG	☐
to	▮	R	▮ PG	▮
Dortmund	▮	N	▮ PG	☐
.	▮	-	▮ IG	☐
at	▮	R	▮ PG	▮
Monday	▮	N	▮ PG	☐
[mm]	▪	I	▪ CG	▫
[ts]	▪	I	▪ IG	▫
[u]	▪	A	▪ SG	▮
.	▮	-	▮ IG	☐
at	▮	R	▮ PG	▮
Monday	▮	N	▮ PG	☐
.	▮	-	▮ IG	☐
morning	▮	A	▪ PG	▮

Figure 4: Sentence with corrections

ality in figures 3 and 4. Currently corrections occur most reliably for interjections, pauses, unknown words, and syntactic repairs with lexical equality of phrase starts (as "at Monday" and "at Monday morning" in figure 4). On the other hand, an example for a currently existing undesired interpretation is "eh . in the morning at ten . in any case not after . not before nine". In this case "after" should be replaced by "before nine". However, these two prepositional phrases do not follow each other directly but there is an additional separating "not". Currently SCREEN can only deal with phrase repairs which follow each other directly since such repairs occur much more often (Levelt 1983). However, considering interjections, pauses, unknown input, and simple forms of syntactically detectable repairs in our 95 utterances we currently reach a *desired overall interpretation of 93%*.

Discussion

We have described a screening approach to fault-tolerant speech parsing based on flat analysis. A screening approach can particularly support learning and robustness, which are properties that previous approaches did not emphasize (Young *et al.* 1989). The use of flat representations should stimulate further discussion since, in contrast to more traditional speech language systems which used highly structural hand-coded parsers, we use less structure but support fault tolerance and learning better. Therefore, speech parsers based on a screening flat analysis, learning, and fault tolerance should be more scalable, adaptive and more domain-independent.

Our approach to speech parsing is new since it makes new contributions to general architectures for speech parsing as well as new contributions to the hybrid connectionist techniques being used. With respect to the architecture we suggest a modular but interactive parallel architecture where modules exchange messages about incremental hypotheses without a particular control interpreter. With respect to the techniques we proposed the use of hybrid connectionist representations. While certain subtasks (like the symbolic equality detection of incorrectly repeated words) can be realized best using symbolic techniques, there are other subtasks with incompletely known functionality where fault-tolerant connectionist learning is advantageous.

The work which is closely related to ours is the connectionist PARSEC parser for conference registrations (Jain 1992), the hybrid connectionist JANUS speech translation system (Waibel *et al.* 1992), and the hybrid connectionist SCAN system for general phrase analysis (Wermter 1992). In general, connectionist techniques in PARSEC, JANUS, SCAN and SCREEN particularly support learning necessary knowledge where possible. However, SCREEN focuses more on exploring interactive parallel architectures and more on modeling fault tolerance.

Currently, the overall architecture as well as all the syntactic modules in SCREEN have been fully implemented, trained, and tested for a corpus of utterances with 1200 words. Although the overall SCREEN project is at an intermediate stage we believe the new architecture and the finished syntactic modules contribute substantially to new fault-tolerant learning architectures for speech language systems. Further work will focus on additional semantic modules for fault-tolerant case-role assignment and the top down interactions to speech modules in order to reduce the search space of speech hypotheses.

Conclusion

We have described the architecture and implementation of a new speech parser which has a number of innovative properties: *the speech parser learns, it is parallel and fault-tolerant, and it directly integrates incremental processing from speech into language processing using flat analysis.* We have illustrated the processing in SCREEN with flat syntactic analysis, but in a similar way we are currently pursuing a flat semantic analysis. On the one hand, flat analysis can provide a parallel shallow processing in preparation for a more in-depth analysis for high-level dialog understanding and inferencing. On the other hand, flat analysis can potentially provide necessary restrictions for reducing the vast search space of word hypotheses of speech recognizers. Therefore, learned flat analysis in a screening approach has the potential to provide a new important intermediate link in between in-depth processing of complete dialogs and shallow processing of speech signals.

Acknowledgements

This research was supported in part by the Federal Secretary for Research and Technology (BMFT) under contract #01IV101A0 and by the German Research Community (DFG) under contract DFG Ha 1026/6-1. We would like to thank Matthias Löchel, Manuela Meurer and Ulf Peters for their assistance with labeling the corpus and training various networks.

References

Elman, J. L. 1990. Finding structure in time. *Cognitive Science* 14(2):179–211.

Erman, L. D.; Fennell, R. D.; Lesser, V. R.; and Reddy, D. R. 1980. The HEARSAY-II speech understanding system: Integrating knowledge to resolve uncertainty. *Computing Surveys* 12(2):213–253.

Hobbs, J. R.; Appelt, D. E.; Tyson, M.; Bear, J.; and Israel, D. 1992. SRI international: description of the FASTUS system used for MUC4. In *Proceedings of the Fourth Message Understanding Conference.*

Jain, A. N. 1992. Generalization performance in PARSEC - a structured connectionist parsing architecture. In Moody, J. E.; Hanson, S. J.; and Lippmann, R. P., eds., *Advances in Neural Information Processing Systems 4.* San Mateo, CA: Morgan Kaufmann. 209–216.

Kitano, H., and Higuchi, T. 1991. Massively parallel memory-based parsing. In *Proceedings of the 12 th International Joint Conference on Artificial Intelligence,* 918–924.

Lee, K.; Hon, H.; and Reddy, R. 1990. An overview of the SPHINX speech recognition system. *IEEE Transactions on Acoustics, Speech, and Signal Processing* 38(1):35–45.

Levelt, W. J. M. 1983. Monitoring and self-repair in speech. *Cognition* 14:41–104.

McClelland, J. L., and Elman, J. L. 1986. Interactive processes in speech perception: The TRACE model. In Rumelhart, D. E.; McClelland, J. L.; and The PDP research group., eds., *Parallel Distributed Processing: Explorations in the Microstructure of Cognition,* volume 2., Psychological and Biological Models. MIT Press, Bredford Books. chapter 15, 58–121.

Pyka, C. 1992. Management of hypotheses in an integrated speech-language architecture. In *Proceedings of the 10 th European Conference on Artificial Intelligence,* 558–560.

Waibel, A.; Jain, A. N.; McNair, A.; Tebelskis, J.; Osterholtz, L.; Saito, H.; Schmidbauer, O.; Sloboda, T.; and Woszczyna, M. 1992. JANUS: Speech-to-speech translation using connectionist and non-connectionist techniques. In Moody, J. E.; Hanson, S. J.; and Lippmann, R. P., eds., *Advances in Neural Information Processing Systems 4.* San Mateo, CA: Morgan Kaufmann. 183–190.

Wermter, S. 1992. A hybrid and connectionist architecture for a SCANning understanding. In *Proceedings of the 10th European Conference on Artificial Intelligence,* 188–192.

Young, S. R.; Hauptmann, A. G.; Ward, W. H.; Smith, E.; and Werner, P. 1989. High level knowledge sources in usable speech recognition systems. *Communications of the ACM* 32:183–194.

Pac-learning Nondeterminate Clauses

William W. Cohen
AT&T Bell Laboratories
600 Mountain Avenue
Murray Hill, NJ 07974
`wcohen@research.att.com`

Abstract

Several practical inductive logic programming systems efficiently learn "determinate" clauses of constant depth. Recently it has been shown that while nonrecursive constant-depth determinate clauses are pac-learnable, most of the obvious syntactic generalizations of this language are not pac-learnable. In this paper we introduce a new restriction on logic programs called "locality", and present two formal results. First, the language of nonrecursive clauses of constant locality is pac-learnable. Second, the language of nonrecursive clauses of constant locality is strictly more expressive than the language of nonrecursive determinate clauses of constant depth. Hence, constant-locality clauses are a pac-learnable generalization of constant-depth determinate clauses.

Introduction

An active area of research is "inductive logic programming", or learning logic programs from examples. Several practical inductive logic programming systems, including GOLEM [Muggleton and Feng, 1992], FOIL [Quinlan, 1990; Quinlan, 1991], LINUS [Lavrač and Džeroski, 1992] and GRENDEL [Cohen, 1992; Cohen, 1993c] incorporate algorithms that efficiently learn programs of "determinate" clauses of constant depth. Following these experimental results, a number of formal results have also been obtained about the learnability of determinate clauses: in particular Džeroski, Muggleton and Russell [1992] showed that nonrecursive constant-depth determinate clauses are pac-learnable, and Cohen [1993b] extended this result to linear "closed" recursive constant-depth determinate clauses.

Unfortunately, most generalizations of this language are not pac-learnable. Given certain cryptographic assumptions, the languages of constant-depth determinate clauses with arbitrary recursion, nonrecursive log-depth determinate clauses, and nonrecursive constant-depth indeterminate clauses are *not* pac-learnable [Cohen, 1993a]. These formal results are disappointing, as they suggest that efficient general-purpose learning algorithms for non-determinate or arbitrary-depth clauses may be difficult to find.

In this paper, we introduce a restriction on logic programs called *locality*, and present two new formal results. First, we show that clauses of constant locality are pac-learnable. Second, we show that the language of clauses of constant locality is strictly more expressive than the language of determinate clauses of constant depth. Hence, the language of constant-locality clauses is a pac-learnable generalization of the language of constant-depth determinate clauses.

Formal Preliminaries

Pac-learnability: Basic Definitions

For readers unfamiliar with formal learning theory, we give below a brief overview of our learning model.

Let X be a set, called the *domain*, and define a *concept* C over X to be a representation of some subset of X. A *language* LANG is defined to be a set of concepts. Associated with X and LANG are two *size complexity measures*; we will use X_n (respectively LANG_n) to represent the set of all elements of X (respectively LANG) of size complexity no greater than n. An *example of* C is a pair (x, b) where $b = \text{``}+\text{''}$ if $x \in C$ and $b = \text{``}-\text{''}$ otherwise. If D is a probability distribution on X, then a *sample of C from X drawn according to D* is a pair of multisets S^+, S^- drawn from X according to D, with S^+ containing the positive examples of C and S^- containing the negative examples.

The model of *pac-learnability* was first introduced by Valiant [1984]. A language LANG is *pac-learnable* iff there is an algorithm $\text{PACLEARN}(S^+, S^-, \epsilon, \delta)$ and a polynomial function $m(\frac{1}{\epsilon}, \frac{1}{\delta}, n_e, n_t)$ so that for every $n_t > 0$, every $n_e > 0$, every $C \in \text{LANG}_{n_t}$, every $\epsilon : 0 < \epsilon < 1$, every $\delta : 0 < \delta < 1$, and every probability distribution function D, for any sample S^+, S^- of C from X_{n_e} drawn according to D containing at least $m(\frac{1}{\epsilon}, \frac{1}{\delta}, n_e, n_t)$ examples,

- PACLEARN outputs a hypothesis H such that $Prob(D(H - C) + D(C - H) > \epsilon) < \delta$

- PACLEARN runs in time polynomial in $\frac{1}{\epsilon}$, $\frac{1}{\delta}$, n_e, n_t, and the number of examples, and

- the hypothesis H is in LANG.

Notice that n_e represents the size of the examples, and n_t represents the size of the "target concept" C.

Logic Programs

For readers unfamiliar with logic programs, we give below a brief overview of their syntax and semantics. Our presentation is simplified as we are interested in the restricted case of non-recursive function-free single-clause Prolog programs. For this case our definitions coincide with the usual semantics of Prolog programs [Lloyd, 1987].

A *database* DB is a set of *(ground) facts*, each of which is of the form $p_i(t_{i_1}, \ldots, t_{i_{k_i}})$, where p_i is a *predicate symbol*, the t_{i_j}'s are *constant symbols* and k_i is the *arity* of the fact. We will usually write constant and predicate symbols as lower-case strings, such as "mary" or "sister".

Logic programs also include *variables*, which we will usually represent with capital letters such as X and Y. A *substitution* is a partial function mapping variables to constant symbols and variables; we will use the Greek letters θ and σ for substitutions, or write them as sets $\theta = \{X_1 = s_1, X_2 = s_2, \ldots, X_n = s_n\}$ where s_i is the constant (or variable) onto which X_i is mapped. A *literal* is written $p(X_1, \ldots, X_k)$ where p is a predicate symbol and $X_1, \ldots, X_k$ are variables. If θ and σ are substitutions and A is a literal, we will use $A\theta$ to denote the result of replacing each variable X in A with the constant symbol to which X is mapped by θ. We abbreviate $(A\theta)\sigma$ as $A\theta\sigma$.

A *(definite) clause* is written $A \leftarrow B_1, \ldots, B_l$ where A and $B_1, \ldots, B_l$ are literals. A is the *head* of of the clause, and $B_1, \ldots, B_l$ is the *body*. Finally, if the *extension of a clause* $C = (A \leftarrow B_1, \ldots, B_l)$ *with respect to a database* DB, written $ext(C, DB)$, is the set of all facts f such that either

- $f \in DB$, or

- there exists a substitution θ so that $A\theta = f$, and for every B_i in the body of the clause, $B_i\theta \in DB$.

For example, if DB is the set {mother(ann,bob), father(bob,julie), father(bob,chris)}, then the extension of the clause

$$\text{grandmother(X,Y)} \leftarrow \text{mother(X,Z), father(Z,Y)}$$

with respect to DB is the set $DB \cup$ {grandmother(ann,julie), grandmother(ann,chris)}.

As notation, if e, f_1, ..., f_n are facts, DB is a database, and C is a clause, we will also write $DB \vdash e$ if $e \in DB$, $DB \vdash f_1, \ldots, f_n$ if $\forall i(f_i \in DB)$, and $DB \wedge C \vdash f$ if $f \in ext(C, DB)$. This will allow some statements to be made a little more concisely.

Pac-learnability for Clauses

Unlike traditional inductive learning systems, most inductive logic programming learning systems accept two inputs: a set of examples and a database DB. A hypothesis is then constructed of the form $P \wedge DB$, where P is a logic program. The additional input to the learner of DB requires a slight extension to the formal model.

Following previous work [Cohen, 1993a], if LANG is a set of clauses and DB is a logic program, then we use LANG$[DB]$ to denote the set of all pairs of the form (C, DB) such that $C \in$ LANG; each such pair represents the set $ext(C, DB)$. If $\mathcal{DB}$ is a set of databases, then the *family of languages* LANG$[\mathcal{DB}]$ represents the set of all languages LANG$[DB]$ where $DB \in \mathcal{DB}$. We will usually be interested in the set of databases a-$\mathcal{DB}$, defined to be the set of all databases containing facts of arity a or less.

We define a family of languages LANG$[\mathcal{DB}]$ to be *uniformly pac-learnable* iff there is a polynomial-time algorithm PACLEARN$(DB, S^+, S^-, \epsilon, \delta)$ such that for every $DB \in \mathcal{DB}$, PACLEARN$_{DB}(S^+, S^-, \epsilon, \delta)$ is a pac-learning algorithm for LANG$[DB]$, where PACLEARN$_{DB}$ is simply PACLEARN with its first argument fixed to DB. Showing uniform pac-learnability is similar to showing that $\forall DB \in \mathcal{DB}$ LANG$[DB]$ is pac-learnable, but stronger. The additional requirement is that there be a *single* algorithm that works for all databases $DB \in \mathcal{DB}$, and that this algorithm runs in time polynomial in the size of DB.

As to the other details of the learning model, we define the size complexity of a database DB to be its cardinality, which will usually be denoted n_b, and the size complexity of a clause $A \leftarrow B_1, \ldots, B_l$ to be l. Examples will be facts, and the size of an example is its arity; thus, we assume the head of the target clause will have large arity, and the literals in the body will have small arity.

Constant-depth Determinate Clauses

Muggleton and Feng [1992] have introduced a pair of useful restrictions on clauses called *determinacy* and *depth*. Following Muggleton and Feng, if $A \leftarrow B_1, \ldots, B_r$ is an (ordered) Horn clause, then the *input variables* of the literal B_i are those variables appearing in B_i which also appear in the clause $A \leftarrow B_1, \ldots, B_{i-1}$, and all other variables appearing in B_i are *output variables*. A literal B_i is *determinate* (with respect to DB and X) if for every possible substitution σ that unifies A with some $e \in X$ such that $DB \vdash (B_1, \ldots, B_{i-1})\sigma$ there is at most one substitution θ so that $DB \vdash B_i\sigma\theta$. A clause is determinate if all of its literals are determinate. Also define the *depth* of a variable appearing in a clause $A \leftarrow B_1, \ldots, B_r$ as follows. Variables appearing in the head of a clause have depth zero. Otherwise, let B_i be the first literal containing the variable V, and let d be the maximal depth of the input variables of B_i (or zero, if B_i has no input variables); then the depth of V is $d+1$. The depth of a clause is the maximal depth of any variable in the clause.

Informally, a literal is determinate if its output variables have only one possible binding, given DB and the binding of the input variables. The depth of a variable X is the number of previous variables Y on which the binding of X depends. Muggleton and Feng use the term *ij-determinate* to describe the set of determinate clauses of depth i or less over a background theory DB containing atoms of arity j or less. As noted above, *ij*-determinate clauses are known to be pac-learnable, and are used in a number of practical learning systems.

The Locality Constraint

Although determinacy is often useful, there are many practical learning problems for which determinate clauses alone are not sufficient [Cohen, 1993c]. We will now consider an alternative restriction on clauses.

Let the *free variables* of a clause be those variables that appear in the body of the clause but not in the head, and let V_1 and V_2 be two free variables appearing in a clause $A \leftarrow B_1, \ldots, B_r$. We will say that V_1 *touches* V_2 if they appear in the same literal, and that V_1 *influences* V_2 if it either touches V_2, or if it touches some variables V' that influences V_2. (Thus *influences* and *touches* are both symmetric and reflexive relations, and *influences* is the transitive closure of *touches*.) The *locale* of a variable V is the set of literals $\{B_{i_1}, \ldots, B_{i_l}\}$ that contain either V, or some variable influenced by V.

Informally, variable V_1 influences variable V_2 if, for a ground query, the choice of a binding for V_1 can affect the possible choices of bindings for V_2. The following examples illustrate these terms: free variables are in boldface type, and the locale of each free variable is underlined.

father(F,S) $\leftarrow$
 son(S,F), <u>husband(F,**W**)</u>.
no_payment_due(S) $\leftarrow$
 <u>enlist(S,**PC**),peace_corps(**PC**)</u>.
draftable(S) $\leftarrow$
 <u>citizen(S,**C**),united_states(**C**)</u>,
 age(S,**A**),(**A**$\geq$18),(**A**$\leq$26).

Notice that the influence relation applies only to free variables. Thus in the third clause above, the variable S is *not* influenced by C, and hence *age(S,A)* is not in the locale of C.

Finally, let the *locality* of a clause be the cardinality of the largest locale of any free variable in that clause. (For instance, the clauses in the example above have locality one, two and three respectively.) Clauses with no free variables are defined to have locality zero. We use k-LOCAL to denote the set of clauses with locality k or less.

Formal Results

Learnability of k-local Clauses

Our first formal result is the following.

Theorem 1 *For any fixed k and a, the language family k-LOCAL$[a\text{-}\mathcal{DB}]$ is uniformly pac-learnable.*

Proof: As there are only n_e variables in the head of the clause, and every new literal in the body can introduce at most a new variables, any size k locale can contain at most $n_e + ak$ distinct variables. Also note that there are at most n_b distinct predicates in the database DB. Since each literal in a locality has one predicate symbol and at most a arguments, each of which is one of the $n_e + ak$ variables, there are only $n_b(n_e + ak)^a$ different literals that could appear in a locality, and hence at most $p = (n_b(n_e + ak)^a)^k$ different[1] localities of length k. Let us denote these localities as $LOC_1, \ldots, LOC_p$. Note that for constant a and k, p is polynomial in n_e and n_b.

Now, notice that every clause of locality k can be written in the form $C = A \leftarrow LOC_{i_1}, \ldots, LOC_{i_r}$ where each LOC_{i_j} is one of the possible locales, and no free variable appears in more than one of the LOC_{i_j}'s. Since no free variables are shared between locales, the different locales do not interact, and hence $e \in ext(C, DB)$ exactly when $e \in ext(A \leftarrow LOC_{i_1}, DB)$, and $\ldots e \in ext(A \leftarrow LOC_{i_1}, DB)$. In other words, C can be decomposed into a conjunction of components of the form $A \leftarrow LOC_{i_j}$. One can thus use Valiant's [1984] technique for monomials to learn C.

In a bit more detail, the following algorithm will pac-learn k-local clauses. We will assume without loss of generality that DB contains an equality predicate.[2] The learner initially hypothesizes the most specific k-local clause, namely

$$A \leftarrow LOC_1, \ldots, LOC_p$$

(The predicate and arity of the head A can be determined from any of the positive examples, and because DB contains an equality predicate, one can assume that all of the variables in A are distinct.) The learner then examines each positive example e in turn, and deletes from its hypothesis all LOC_i such that $e \notin ext(A \leftarrow LOC_i, DB)$. (Note that e is in this extension exactly when $\exists \theta : DB \vdash LOC_i \sigma_e \theta$ where σ_e is the most general substitution such that $A\sigma_e = e$. To see that this condition can be checked in polynomial time, recall that θ can contain at most ak free variables, and DB can contain at most an_b constants; hence at most $(an_b)^{ak}$ substitutions θ need be checked, which is polynomial.) Following the argument used for Valiant's procedure, this algorithm will pac-learn the target concept. ∎

---

[1] Up to renaming of variables.

[2] That is, that there is a predicate symbol *equal* such that $equal(t_1, t_2) \in DB$ for every pair of constant symbols t_1, t_2 appearing in DB.

We note that the theorem actually proves a stronger result than stated, as it also shows learnability with one-sided error in an on-line model.

The Expressive Power of k-local Clauses

The importance of Theorem 1 depends on the usefulness of k-local clauses as a representation language. While there is some experimental evidence that suggests highly local clauses are, in fact, useful on natural problems [Cohen, 1993c], the principle reason for believing them to be useful is the following result.

Theorem 2 *For every $DB \in a\text{-}\mathcal{DB}$ and every depth-d determinate clause C, there is clause $C' \in k\text{-}\textsc{Local}[DB]$ such that $ext(C', DB) = ext(C, DB)$, and the size of C' is no greater than k times the size of C, where $k = a^{d+1}$.*

In other words, although a constant-depth determinate clause may have unbounded locality, for every constant-depth determinate clause there is a *semantically equivalent* constant-locality clause. Moreover, this clause is of comparable size and uses precisely the same database predicates. However, the converse is *not* true: for example, the 1-local clause *parent(P)←child(P,C)* has no determinate equivalent.[3] Thus the language of constant-locality clauses is strictly more expressive than the language of constant-depth determinate clauses.

(An attentive reader might be concerned about the locality "constant" $k = a^{d+1}$, which is exponential in depth; this means that the learning algorithm sketched in Theorem 1, if used to learn determinate clauses, will be doubly exponential in depth. Notice, however, that existing algorithms for determinate clauses [Muggleton and Feng, 1992; Džeroski *et al.*, 1992] are also doubly exponential in depth.)

In the remainder of this section, we will give a rigorous proof of Theorem 2. The basic idea of the proof is illustrated by example in Figure 1.

Proof: We will first introduce some additional notation. If $C = A \leftarrow B_1, \ldots, B_r$ is a clause, literal B_i *directly supports* literal B_j iff some output variable of B_i is an input variable of B_j, and that literal B_i *indirectly supports* B_j iff B_i directly supports B_j, or if B_i directly supports some B_k that indirectly supports B_j. Now, for each B_i in the body of C, let LOC_i be the conjunction

$$LOC_i = B_{j_1}, \ldots, B_{j_{k_i}}, B_i$$

where the B_j's are all of the literals of C that support B_i (either directly or indirectly) appearing in the same order that they appeared in C. Next, let us introduce for $i = 1, \ldots, r$ a substitution

$$\sigma_i =$$
$$\{Y = Yi : \text{variable } Y \text{ occurs in } LOC_i \text{ but not } A\}$$

---

[3]Over a DB in which parents may have more than one child and in which no other predicates exist.

We then define $LOC'_i = LOC_i \sigma_i$. The effect of this last step is that $LOC'_1, \ldots, LOC'_r$ are copies of $LOC_1, \ldots, LOC_r$ in which variables have been renamed so that for $i \neq j$ the free variables of LOC'_i are different from the free variables of LOC'_j. Finally, let C' be the clause $A \leftarrow LOC'_1, \ldots LOC'_r$.

An example of this construction is given in Figure 1. We strongly suggest that the reader refer to the example at this point.

For a depth-d clause C, we make the following claims: (a) C' is k-local, for $k = a^{d+1}$, (b) C' is at most k times the length of C and (c) if C is determinate, then C' has the same extension as C. In the remainder of the proof, we will establish these claims.

To establish the first two claims it is sufficient to show that the number of literals in every LOC'_i (or equivalently, every LOC_i) is bounded by k. To establish this, let us define $N(d)$ to be the maximum number of literals in any LOC_i corresponding to a B_i with *input* variables at depth d or less. Clearly for any $DB \in a\text{-}\mathcal{DB}$ and any depth d-determinate clause C over DB the function $N(d)$ is an upper bound on k.

The function $N(d)$ is bounded in turn by the following lemma.

Lemma 3 *For any $DB \in a\text{-}\mathcal{DB}$, $N(d) \leq \sum_{i=0}^{d} a^i$ (and hence $N(d) \leq a^{d+1}$).*

Proof of lemma: By induction on d. For $d = 0$, no literals will support B_i. Thus each locality LOC_i will contain only the literal B_i, and $N(0) = 1$.

Now assume that the lemma holds for $d-1$ and consider a literal B_i with inputs at depth d. If $B_{j_1}, \ldots, B_{j_r}$ are the literals that directly support B_i, then LOC_i can be no larger than $LOC_{j_1}, \ldots, LOC_{j_r}, B_i$. Since any literal B_{j_k} that directly supports B_i must be at depth $d - 1$ or less, and since there no more than a input variables of B_i, there are at most a different B_{j_k}'s that directly support B_i. Putting this together, and using the inductive hypothesis that $N(d-1) \leq \sum_{i=1}^{d-1} a^i$, we see that

$$N(d) \leq aN(d-1) + 1 \leq a\left(\sum_{i=0}^{d-1} a^i\right) + 1 = \sum_{i=0}^{d} a^i$$

By induction, the lemma holds. ∎

Now we consider the second claim: that for any determinate C, the C' constructed above has the same extension. The first direction of this equivalence actually holds for any clause C:

Lemma 4 *If $f \in ext(D, DB)$, then $f \in ext(C', DB)$.*

Proof of lemma: Consider the substitutions σ_i introduced in the construction of C'. Since each free variable in LOC_i is given a distinct name in LOC'_i, σ_i is a one-to-one mapping, and since the free variables in the LOC'_i's are distinct, the substitution $\sigma = \bigcup_{i=1}^{r} \sigma_i^{-1}$

The starting point: Below is a depth-2 determinate clause.

```
good_grant_proposal(X) ←
    author(X,PI),              % B₁
    employer(PI,U),            % B₂, supported by B₁
    prestigious(U),            % B₃, supported directly by B₂ and indirectly by B₁
    topic(X,T),                % B₄
    trendy(T).                 % B₅, supported by B₄
```

Step 1: for each B_i build a locality LOC_i containing all supporting B_j's.

$$LOC_1 = \text{author(X,PI)}$$
$$LOC_2 = \text{author(X,PI),employer(PI,U)}$$
$$LOC_3 = \text{author(X,PI),employer(PI,U),prestigious(U)}$$
$$LOC_4 = \text{topic(X,T)}$$
$$LOC_5 = \text{topic(X,T),trendy(T)}$$

Step 2: Rename variables so that all free variables appear in only a single locale.

$$LOC_1' = \text{author(X,PI1)}$$
$$LOC_2' = \text{author(X,PI2),employer(PI2,U2)}$$
$$LOC_3' = \text{author(X,PI3),employer(PI3,U3),prestigious(U3)}$$
$$LOC_4' = \text{topic(X,T4)}$$
$$LOC_5' = \text{topic(X,T5),trendy(T5)}$$

Step 4: Collect the LOC_i''s into a single clause.

```
good_grant_proposal(X) ←
    author(X,PI1),
    author(X,PI2),employer(PI2,U2),
    author(X,PI3),employer(PI3,U3),prestigious(U3),
    topic(X,T4),
    topic(X,T5),trendy(T5).
```

Figure 1: Constructing a local clause equivalent to a determinate clause

is well-defined. As an example, for the clause C' from Figure 1, we would have

$$\sigma = \{\ \begin{array}{lll} \text{PI1} = \text{PI}, & \text{PI2} = \text{PI}, & \text{PI3} = \text{PI}, \\ \text{U2} = \text{U}, & \text{U3} = \text{U}, & \\ \text{T4} = \text{T}, & \text{T5} = \text{T} & \} \end{array}$$

Applying this substitution to C' will simply "undo" the effect of renaming the variables, so that

$$C'\sigma = (A \leftarrow LOC_1, \ldots, LOC_r)$$

Now, assume $f \in ext(C, DB)$. Then there is by definition some substitution θ so that all literals in the body of the clause $C\theta$ are in DB. Since $C'\sigma$ contains the same set of literals in its body as C, clearly for the substitution $\theta' = \sigma \circ \theta$ all literals in the body of the clause $C'\theta'$ are in DB, and hence $f \in ext(C', DB)$. ∎

We must finally establish the converse of Lemma 4. This direction of the equivalence requires that C be determinate.

Lemma 5 *If a fact $f \in ext(C', DB)$ and C is determinate, then $f \in ext(C, DB)$.*

Proof of lemma: If $f \in ext(C', DB)$, then either $f \in DB$, in which case the lemma holds trivially,

or there must be some θ' that is a "witness" that $f \in ext(C', DB)$—by which we mean a θ' such that $A'\theta = f$, and for every B_i' from the body of C', $B_i'\theta \in DB$. Define a variable Yi in C' to be a "copy" of $Y \in C$ if Yi is a renaming of Y—i.e., if $Yi\sigma_i^{-1} = Y$ for the σ_i defined in the lemma above. Certainly if C is determinate then C' is determinate; further, for a determinate C', θ' must map every copy of Y to the same constant t_Y. (This can be proved by picking two copies Yi and Yj of Y and then using induction over the depth of Y to show that they must be bound to the same constant.) Hence, let us define the substitution

$$\theta = \{Y = t_Y : \text{copies of } Y \text{ in } C' \text{ are bound to } t_Y \text{ by } \theta'\}$$

Clearly, for all $i : 1 \leq i \leq r$, $LOC_i\theta = LOC_i\theta'$; hence if θ' witnesses that $f \in ext(C', DB)$ then θ witnesses that $f \in ext(C, DB)$. ∎

We have now established that C' is k-local, of bounded size, and is equivalent to C. This concludes the proof of the theorem. ∎

Conclusions

This paper continues a line of research which is intended to broaden the theoretical foundations of inductive logic programming systems by formally investigating the learnability of restricted logic programs. Previous work has shown that nonrecursive constant-depth determinate Datalog clauses are pac-learnable [Džeroski *et al.*, 1992]. More recently, it was shown that relaxing any of these conditions leads to a language that is hard to learn; in particular, the languages of recursive constant-depth determinate clauses, non-recursive log-depth determinate clauses, and nonrecursive constant-depth indeterminate clauses are all hard to pac-learn [Kietz, 1993; Cohen, 1993a]. Furthermore, relaxing the condition of determinacy has proven especially difficult.

This paper has proposed a new restriction on indeterminate free variables called *locality*. Informally, a clause is k-local if the binding picked for any free variable affects the success or failure of only k literals. Every clause of locality k must have depth k or less, and hence this language is more restrictive than the language of constant-depth nonrecursive clauses. However, the k-local restriction is incomparable to other restrictions on indeterminate clauses previously considered in the literature, notably restricting the number of free variables in a clause [Haussler, 1989; Cohen, 1993a].

In this paper, we have shown that the language of k-local clauses is pac-learnable, and also that the language is strictly more expressive that the language of constant-depth determinate clauses. Hence it is a pac-learnable generalization of the language of constant-depth determinate clauses. The existence of such a generalization is somewhat surprising, given the negative results of Cohen [1993a] and Kietz [1993]. Note, however, that Cohen and Kietz considered only *syntactic* generalizations of constant-depth determinacy, and the language of k-local clauses is a semantic (but not syntactic) generalization.

A number of further topics are suggested by these results. While the positive pac-learnability result is encouraging, the algorithm sketched in Theorem 1 seems relatively inefficient. It remains to be seen whether learning algorithms for k-local clauses that are both well-understood and practically useful can be designed. Also, it would be interesting to explore the learnability of recursive k-local clauses. Since the hardness results for recursive constant-depth determinate clauses of Cohen [1993a] are "representation-independent", it is immediate that k-local clauses with arbitrary recursion are not pac-learnable; however, the learnability of the linear recursive case (for example) is open.

References

Cohen, William W. 1992. Compiling knowledge into an explicit bias. In *Proceedings of the Ninth International Conference on Machine Learning*, Aberdeen, Scotland. Morgan Kaufmann.

Cohen, William W. 1993a. Cryptographic limitations on learning one-clause logic programs. In *Proceedings of the Tenth National Conference on Artificial Intelligence*, Washington, D.C.

Cohen, William W. 1993b. A pac-learning algorithm for a restricted class of recursive logic programs. In *Proceedings of the Tenth National Conference on Artificial Intelligence*, Washington, D.C.

Cohen, William W. 1993c. Rapid prototyping of ILP systems using explicit bias. In *Proceedings of the 1993 IJCAI Workshop on Inductive Logic Programming*, Chambery, France.

Džeroski, Sašo; Muggleton, Stephen; and Russell, Stuart 1992. Pac-learnability of determinate logic programs. In *Proceedings of the 1992 Workshop on Computational Learning Theory*, Pittsburgh, Pennsylvania.

Haussler, David 1989. Learning conjunctive concepts in structural domains. *Machine Learning* 4(1).

Kietz, Jorg-Uwe 1993. Some computational lower bounds for the computational complexity of inductive logic programming. In *Proceedings of the 1993 European Conference on Machine Learning*, Vienna, Austria.

Lavrač, Nada and Džeroski, Sašo 1992. Background knowledge and declarative bias in inductive concept learning. In Jantke, K. P., editor 1992, *Analogical and Inductive Inference: International Workshop AII'92*. Springer Verlag, Daghstuhl Castle, Germany. Lectures in Artificial Intelligence Series #642.

Lloyd, J. W. 1987. *Foundations of Logic Programming: Second Edition*. Springer-Verlag.

Muggleton, Stephen and Feng, Cao 1992. Efficient induction of logic programs. In *Inductive Logic Programming*. Academic Press.

Quinlan, J. Ross 1990. Learning logical definitions from relations. *Machine Learning* 5(3).

Quinlan, J. Ross 1991. Determinate literals in inductive logic programming. In *Proceedings of the Eighth International Workshop on Machine Learning*, Ithaca, New York. Morgan Kaufmann.

Valiant, L. G. 1984. A theory of the learnable. *Communications of the ACM* 27(11).

Learning to Reason

Roni Khardon*   Dan Roth[†]

Aiken Computation Laboratory,
Harvard University,
Cambridge, MA 02138.
{roni,danr}@das.harvard.edu

Abstract

We introduce a new framework for the study of reasoning. The Learning (in order) to Reason approach developed here combines the interfaces to the world used by known learning models with the reasoning task and a performance criterion suitable for it.

We show how previous results from learning theory and reasoning fit into this framework and illustrate the usefulness of the Learning to Reason approach by exhibiting new results that are not possible in the traditional setting. First, we give a Learning to Reason algorithm for a class of propositional languages for which there are no efficient reasoning algorithms, when represented as a traditional (formula-based) knowledge base. Second, we exhibit a Learning to Reason algorithm for a class of propositional languages that is not known to be learnable in the traditional sense.

Introduction

Consider a baby robot, starting out its life. If it were a human being, nature would have provided for the infant a safe environment to spend an initial time period in. In this period she adapts to her environment and learns about the structures, rules, meta-rules, superstitions and other information the environment provides for. In the meantime, the environment protects her from fatal events. Only after this "grace period", she is expected to have "full functionality" (whatever that means) in her environment, but it is expected that her performance depends on the world she grew up in and reflects the amount of interaction she has had with it.

Realizing that learning is a central aspect of cognition, computational learning theory, a subfield concerned with modeling and understanding learning phenomena (Valiant 1984), takes a similar view in that the performance of the learner is measured only after the learning period, and with respect to the world. Traditional theories of intelligent systems, however, have assumed that cognition (namely, computational processes like reasoning, language recognition, object identification and other "higher level" cognitive tasks) can be studied separately from learning (See (Kirsh 1991) for a discussion of this issue.). However, computational considerations render this self-contained reasoning approach as well as other variants of it (Selman 1990; Roth 1993), not adequate for common-sense reasoning (Levesque 1986; Shastri 1993).

We argue that the main difficulties in the traditional treatment of reasoning stem from its separation from the "world". The effect is twofolded: (1) a rigid representation language with which reasoning problems are presented to the reasoner (Brooks 1991) and (2) a performance criterion that is irrespective of the world.

In this paper we develop a new framework for the study of Reasoning. Our approach differs from other approaches to reasoning in that it views learning as an integral part of the process. The *Learning to Reason* theory developed here is concerned with studying the entire process of *learning* a knowledge base representation and *reasoning* with it.

In the new framework the intelligent agent is given access to her favorite learning interface, and is also given a grace period in which she can interact with this interface and construct her representation[1] KB of the world W. Her reasoning performance is measured only after this period, when she is presented with queries α from some query language, relevant to the world[2], and has to answer whether W implies α. We show that through this interaction with the world, the agents truly gains additional reasoning power. An inherent feature of the learning to reason approach, is a non-monotonic reasoning behavior it exhibits as a side effect; since reasoning mistakes can be used, incremen-

*Research supported by grant DAAL03-92-G-0164 (Center for Intelligent Control Systems).

[†]Research supported by NSF grant CCR-92-00884 and by DARPA AFOSR-F4962-92-J-0466.

[1]We stress that the assumption that an intelligent agent has to keep her knowledge in some representation and use it when she reasons is basic to this framework. We allow the reasoner, however, to choose her own representation and even to use different representations for different tasks.

[2]We take the view that a reasoner need not answer efficiently *all* possible queries, but only those that are "relevant", or "common", in a well defined sense.

tally, to improve the knowledge base. This desirable phenomenon is hard to formalize, when dealing with reasoning systems defined independent of learning.

This work is similar in nature to the Neuroidal model developed by Valiant (Valiant 1994). The model developed there provides a more comprehensive approach to cognition, and akin to our approach it views learning as an integral and crucial part of the process. There, the reasoner reasons from a learned knowledge base, a complex circuit, and thus can be modeled by our framework, and indeed reasoning in the Neuroidal model shares many properties with the Learning to Reason framework. Our approach is different in that in an effort to give a more formal treatment of a reasoner that has learned her knowledge base, we currently restrict our discussion to a fixed, consistent world.

Summary of Results

To motivate our approach we first develop a sampling approach to reasoning that exemplifies the power gained by giving the agent access to the "world" she is supposed to reason in later. We prove that Learning to reason is possible for arbitrary worlds and query languages under some technical restriction on the queries asked. However, for various considerations this approach alone is not sufficient as a model for reasoning, so we go on to define the Learning to Reason framework to capture those. We start by studying the relation of the Learning to Reason (L2R) framework to the two existing ones, the traditional reasoning, and the traditional learning (learning to classify, L2C), and discuss how existing results from learning and reasoning can be used in the new framework. We then consider detailed Learning to Reason algorithms that use models (satisfying assignments) as the knowledge representation language. A characterization of reasoning with models for Horn theories was given in (Kautz, Kearns, & Selman 1993) and for general theories in (Khardon & Roth 1994b). We build on these results to exemplify the usefulness of the new approach:

- Consider the reasoning problem $W \models \alpha$, where W is some CNF formula and α is a $\log n$CNF (i.e., a CNF formula with at most $\log n$ literals in each clause). Then, when W has a polynomial size DNF[3] there is an exact and efficient Learning to Reason algorithm for this problem, while the traditional reasoning problem (with a CNF representation as the input) is NP-Hard.

- Consider the reasoning problem $W \models \alpha$, where W is any boolean formula with a polynomial size DNF and α is a $\log n$CNF. Then, there is an exact and efficient Learning to Reason algorithm for this problem, while the class of boolean formulas with polynomial

---

[3]The DNF representation is not given to the reasoner. Its existence is essential, since the algorithm is polynomial in its size.

size DNF is not known to be learnable in the traditional (Learning to Classify) sense.

These results show that neither a traditional reasoning algorithm (from the CNF representation) nor a traditional learning algorithm (that can "classify" the world) is necessary to Learn to Reason. Moreover, the results exemplify and aid in formalizing the notion of "intelligence is in the eye of the beholder" (Brooks 1991), since our agent seems to behave logically, even though her knowledge representation need not be a logical formula and she does not use any logic or "theorem proving".

Due to the limited space we omit some details and most of the proofs. These can be found in the full version of this paper (Khardon & Roth 1994a).

Preliminaries

Reasoning

A widely accepted framework for reasoning in intelligent systems is the knowledge-based system approach (McCarthy 1958). Knowledge, in some *representation language* is stored in a *Knowledge Base* (KB) that is combined with a reasoning mechanism. Reasoning is abstracted as a deduction task[4] of determining whether a *query* α, assumed to capture the situation at hand, is implied from KB (denoted KB $\models \alpha$). The discussion in this paper is restricted to propositional knowledge bases[5].

Let $\mathcal{F}, \mathcal{Q}$ be two arbitrary classes of representations for boolean functions. All the functions we discuss are boolean functions over $\{0, 1\}^n$, where n is the number of variables in the domain. Throughout this paper we assume that an exact description of the real world W is in $\mathcal{F}$, that all the queries α are restricted to be in the class $\mathcal{Q}$ and that the functions have a polynomial size representation in the respective class. In particular, the class $\mathcal{F} = $ CNF denotes those boolean functions with a polynomial size CNF and the class $\mathcal{F} = $ CNF $\cap$ DNF denotes those boolean functions with a polynomial size CNF and a polynomial size DNF.

We refer to boolean functions as either functions or subsets of $\{0, 1\}^n$: the boolean function g is identified with its set of models, $g^{-1}(1)$ (That is, $f \models g$ if and only if $f \subseteq g$).

Definition 1 *An algorithm A is an* exact reasoning *algorithm for the reasoning problem* $(\mathcal{F}, \mathcal{Q})$ *if for all* $f \in \mathcal{F}$ *and all* $\alpha \in \mathcal{Q}$, *when A is presented with input* (f, α), *A runs in time polynomial in n and the size of f and α, and answers "yes" if and only if $f \models \alpha$.*

---

[4]We restrict ourselves here to deduction although the approach developed is applicable for other reasoning tasks, e.g., Bayesian networks.

[5]A propositional expression is just a boolean function, and a propositional language is a class of boolean functions. These terms are used in the reasoning and learning literature accordingly, and we use them interchangeably.

Learning to Classify

The formal study of learning, (studied in computational learning theory (Valiant 1984; Haussler 1987; Angluin 1992)), abstracts the problem of inductively learning a concept as the problem of learning a boolean function, given some access to an oracle that is familiar to some degree with the function. The interpretation is that the function's value is 1 when the input belongs to the target concept and 0 otherwise. The oracles are used to model the type of interface the learner may have to the world and they vary between learning models according to the amount of information we assume the learner receives about the concept. Next we describe some standard oracles, introduce a new one that is especially suited for Reasoning and define the learning problem.

Definition 2 *A* Membership Query Oracle *for a function* f, *denoted* $MQ(f)$, *is an oracle that when given an input* $x \in \{0,1\}^n$ *returns* $f(x)$.

Definition 3 *An* Equivalence Query Oracle *for a function* f, *denoted* $EQ(f)$, *is an oracle that when given as input a function* g, *answer "yes" if and only if* $f \equiv g$. *If it answers "no" it supplies a counterexample, namely, an* $x \in \{0,1\}^n$ *such that* $f(x) \neq g(x)$. *A counterexample* x *satisfying* $f(x) = 1$ ($f(x) = 0$) *is called a positive (negative) counterexample.*

Definition 4 *An* Example Oracle *for a function* f, *with respect to the probability distribution* D, *denoted* $EX_D(f)$, *is an oracle that when accessed, returns* $(x, f(x))$, *where* x *is drawn at random according to* D.

Definition 5 *A* Reasoning Query Oracle *for a function* f *and a query language* Q, *denoted* $RQ(f, Q)$, *is an oracle that when accessed performs the following protocol with a learning agent* A. *(1) The oracle picks an arbitrary query* $\alpha \in Q$ *and returns it to* A. *(2) The agent* A *answers "yes" or "no" according to her belief with regard to the truth of the statement* $f \models \alpha$. *(3) If* A's *answer is correct then the oracle says "Correct". If the answer is wrong the oracle answers "Wrong" and in case* $f \not\models \alpha$ *it also supplies a counterexample (i.e.,* $x \in f \setminus \alpha$).

Denote by $I(f)$ the *interface* available to the learner when learning f. This can be any subset of the oracles defined above, and might depend on some fixed but arbitrary and unknown distribution D over the instance space $\{0,1\}^n$.

Definition 6 *An algorithm* A *is an* Exact Learn to Classify (E-L2C) *algorithm for a class of functions* $\mathcal{F}$, *if there exists a polynomial* $p()$ *such that for all* $f \in \mathcal{F}$, *when given access to* $I(f)$, A *runs in time* $p(n)$ *and then, given any* $x \in \{0,1\}^n$, *takes time* $p(n)$ *to predict* σ *such that* $\sigma = f(x)$.

Definition 7 *An algorithm* A *is a* Probably Approximately Correct Learn to Classify (PAC-L2C) *algorithm for a class of functions* $\mathcal{F}$, *if there exists a polynomial*

$p(,,)$ *such that for all* $f \in \mathcal{F}$, *on input* ϵ, δ, *given access to* $I(f)$, A *runs in time* $p(n, 1/\epsilon, 1/\delta)$ *and then given any* $x \in \{0,1\}^n$, *predicts* $h(x)$ *in time* $p(n, 1/\epsilon, 1/\delta)$. A's *predictions have the property that with probability at least* $1 - \delta$, $Prob_{x \in D}[f(x) \neq h(x)] < \epsilon$.

In the on-line (or, mistake-bound) scenario, algorithm A is presented with a sequence of examples in $\{0,1\}^n$. At each stage, the algorithm is asked to predict $f(x)$ and is then told whether its prediction was correct. Each time the learning algorithm makes an incorrect prediction, we charge it one *mistake*.

Definition 8 *An algorithm* A *is a* Mistake Bound Learn to Classify (MB-L2C) *algorithm for a class of functions* $\mathcal{F}$, *if there exists a polynomial* $p()$ *such that for all* $f \in \mathcal{F}$, *for every (arbitrary infinite) sequence of instances,* A *runs in time* $p(n)$ *(on each example) and makes no more than* $p(n)$ *mistakes.*

Learning to Reason

Let $W \in \mathcal{F}$ be a boolean function that describes the world exactly. Let α be some boolean function (a query) and let D be some fixed but arbitrary and unknown probability distribution over the instance space $\{0,1\}^n$. As in the learning framework, we assume that D governs the occurrences of instances in the world.

The query α is called *legal* if $\alpha \in Q$. It is called (W, ϵ)-*fair* if either $Prob_D[W \setminus \alpha] = 0$ or $Prob_D[W \setminus \alpha] > \epsilon$. The intuition behind this definition is that the algorithm is allowed to err in case $W \not\models \alpha$, but the weight of W outside α is very small. Along with ϵ, the *accuracy* parameter, we use a *confidence* parameter, δ, and sometimes might allow the reasoning algorithm to err, with small probability, less than δ.

A Sampling Approach

Consider the following simple approach to reasoning: Whenever presented with a query α, first use the Example Oracle $EX_D(W)$ and take a sample of size $m = (1/\epsilon) \ln(1/\delta)$, where δ and ϵ are the required confidence and accuracy parameters. Then, perform the following model-based test: for all the samples $(x, 1)$ sampled from $EX_D(W)$ (note that we ignore the samples labeled 0), check whether $\alpha(x) = 1$. If for some x, $\alpha(x) = 0$ say $W \not\models \alpha$; otherwise say $W \models \alpha$.

A standard learning theory argument shows that if α is (W, ϵ)-fair then with probability at least $1 - \delta$ the algorithm is correct. (The algorithm makes a mistake only if $W \not\models \alpha$ and no instance in $W \cap \overline{\alpha}$ is sampled.) This analysis depends on the fact that the samples are independent of the query α, and therefore a different sample has to be taken for every query α. We call this a *repeated sampling* approach[6]. However, repeated

---

[6]A similar, more sophisticated approach was developed in (Kearns 1992) for the case in which both the knowledge base and the queries are learned concepts in the PAC sense. It is implicit there that for each possible query one needs a new sample.

sampling is not a plausible approach to reasoning in intelligent systems. When presented with a query, an agent cannot allow itself further interactions with the world before answering the query. Especially if the query is "A lion is approaching $\Rightarrow$ I have to run away".

A slightly more elaborate argument shows that a *one time sampling* approach can also guarantee reasoning with respect to (W, ϵ)-fair queries, with confidence $1 - \delta$. This depends on taking $m = \frac{1}{\epsilon}(\ln |\mathcal{Q}| + \ln \frac{1}{\delta})$ samples from $EX_D(f)$. Since all the queries in $\mathcal{Q}$ are propositional formulas of polynomial size, the number m of samples required to guarantee this performance is polynomial. This approach is therefore feasible.

However, the one-time sampling approach is not the ultimate solution for reasoning. For example it is not adequate in cases where exact reasoning performance is required. In the full version of the paper we elaborate on why this sampling approach is not sufficient as the sole solution for the reasoning problem. (E.g., space considerations and the availability of various oracles needed to model reasoning.)

Learning to Reason: Definitions

Definition 9 *An algorithm A is an* Exact Learn to Reason (E-L2R) *algorithm for the reasoning problem $(\mathcal{F}, \mathcal{Q})$, if there exists a polynomial $p()$ such that for all $f \in \mathcal{F}$, given access to $I(f)$, A runs in time $p(n)$ and then, when presented with any query $\alpha \in \mathcal{Q}$, A runs in time $p(n)$, does not access $I(f)$, and answers "yes" if and only if $f \models \alpha$.*

Definition 10 *An algorithm A is a* Probably Approximately Correct Learn to Reason (PAC-L2R) *algorithm for the reasoning problem $(\mathcal{F}, \mathcal{Q})$, if there exists a polynomial $p(,,)$ such that for all $f \in \mathcal{F}$, on input ϵ, δ, given access to $I(f)$, A runs in time $p(n, 1/\epsilon, 1/\delta)$ and then with probability at least $1 - \delta$, when presented with any (f, ϵ)-fair query $\alpha \in \mathcal{Q}$, A runs in time $p(n, 1/\epsilon, 1/\delta)$, does not access $I(f)$, and answers "yes" if and only if $f \models \alpha$.*

In the above definitions, we did not allow access to $I(f)$ while in the query answering phase. It is possible, however, (although we do not do it in this paper) to consider a query α given to the algorithm as if given by the reasoning oracle $RQ(f, \mathcal{Q})$ defined above. Thus, a reasoning error may supply the algorithm a counterexample which in turn can be used to improve its future reasoning behavior.

The relations between L2R and L2C

Intuitively, the classification task seems to be easier than the reasoning task. In the former we need to evaluate correctly a function on a single point, while in the latter we need to know if *all the models* of the function are also models of another function, the query. It is not surprising therefore, that if *any* subset of $\{0, 1\}^n$ is a legal query, the ability to L2R implies the ability to L2C. This is formalized in the following theorem. We

note, however, that the proof of the theorem does not go through if the class of queries $\mathcal{Q}$ does not include all of DISJ, the class of all disjunctions over n variables. (See Theorem 7.)

Theorem 1 *If there is an Exact-L2R algorithm for the reasoning problem $(\mathcal{F}, DISJ)$ then there is an Exact-L2C algorithm for the class $\mathcal{F}$.*

L2R via PAC Learning

Assume that the world description W is in $\mathcal{F}$ and there is a PAC-L2C algorithm A for $\mathcal{F}$.

Definition 11 *An algorithm that PAC learns to classify $\mathcal{F}$ is said to* learn f from below *if, when learning f, the algorithm never makes mistakes on instances outside of f. (I.e., if h is the hypothesis the algorithm keeps then it satisfies $h \subseteq f$.)*

Theorem 2 *Let A be a PAC-Learn to Classify algorithm for the function class $\mathcal{F}$ and assume that A uses the class of representations $\mathcal{H}$ as its hypotheses. Then, if A learns $\mathcal{F}$ from below, and there is an exact reasoning algorithm B for the reasoning problem $(\mathcal{H}, \mathcal{Q})$, then there is a PAC-Learn to Reason algorithm C for the reasoning problem $(\mathcal{F}, \mathcal{Q})$.*

The significance of this result is that it exhibits the *limitations* of L2R by combining reasoning and learning algorithms: relaxing the requirement that the algorithm learns from below is not possible. On the positive side it explains the behavior of mistake bound algorithms discussed next and allows for other PAC learning algorithms to be used in this framework.

L2R via Mistake Bound Learning

Consider a Mistake Bound algorithm that keeps a hypothesis that allows for efficient reasoning. Then, it can be used to construct a Learn to Reason algorithm.

Let A be a Mistake Bound algorithm and assume it has been used long enough to guarantee PAC performance (Littlestone 1989). In the case it has used up all of its mistakes on negative examples (i.e., on assignments outside of W), the hypothesis it uses is a "learn from below" hypothesis, and we can reason with it and succeed on all (W, ϵ)-fair queries.

However, we cannot force the algorithm (or rather the interface) to make all these mistakes within the grace period. If we use an initial grace period to ensure its PAC properties then after the algorithm is ready to answer queries it may still make (a limited number of) mistakes. We call this type of algorithm a Mistake Bound Learning to Reason algorithm.

It is interesting to note that reasoning with this type of an algorithm yields a non monotonic reasoning behavior. Every time the algorithm makes a reasoning mistake, it changes its mind, learns something about the world, and would not make the same mistake again. This is an inherent feature of the learning to reason approach, and it captures a phenomenon that is hard to formalize, when dealing with reasoning systems defined independent of learning.

L2R via Model Based Reasoning

In this section we develop the main technical results of this paper and exhibit the advantages of the Learning to Reason approach. We deviate from the traditional setting of "first learn to classify, then reason with the hypothesis": A learning algorithm is used first, but rather then learning a "classifying hypothesis", it constructs a knowledge representation that allows for efficient reasoning.

The results in this section use two recent results, one on learning via monotone theory (Bshouty 1993) and the other on reasoning with models (Khardon & Roth 1994b). Combining these two results yields Theorem 3. (Notice, though, that the reasoning algorithm does not use the "classifying hypothesis" of the learning algorithm but rather a set a models, a byproduct of it.)

Queries are called *relevant* if they are in $\mathcal{F}$ (we also assume $W \in \mathcal{F}$). Queries are called *common* if they belong to some set $\mathcal{L}_E$ of *efficient* propositional languages. Important examples of efficient languages are: $\log n$CNF theories (CNF in which the clauses contain at most $O(\log n)$ literals), k-quasi-Horn queries (a generalization of Horn theories in which there are at most k positive literals in each clause) and others.

Theorem 3 *There is an Exact-Learn to Reason algorithm, that uses an Equivalence Query and a Membership Query Oracles, for $(CNF \cap DNF, \mathcal{Q})$, where $\mathcal{Q}$ is the class of all relevant and common queries.*

The above theorem is an example for a reasoning problem that is provably hard in the "traditional" sense and has an efficient solution in the new model. Given a CNF knowledge base, even with the added information that it has a short DNF, the reasoning problem is still hard. This is so since it is NP-hard to find a satisfying assignment for a CNF expression even if one knows that it has exactly one satisfying assignment (Valiant & Vazirani 1986). The algorithm does not solve an NP-hard problem; the additional reasoning power of the agent is gained through the interaction with the world by using $EQ(f)$ or $EX_D(f)$.

To present the next result we first introduce some definitions and results from the monotone theory of boolean functions and the theory of reasoning with models (Bshouty 1993; Khardon & Roth 1994b).

Monotone Theory and Reasoning with Models

Definition 12 (Order) *We denote by $\leq$ the usual partial order on the lattice $\{0,1\}^n$, the one induced by the order $0 < 1$. That is, for $x, y \in \{0,1\}^n$, $x \leq y$ if and only if $\forall i, x_i \leq y_i$. For an assignment $b \in \{0,1\}^n$ we define $x \leq_b y$ if and only if $x \oplus b \leq y \oplus b$ (Here $\oplus$ is the bitwise addition modulo 2).*

Intuitively, if $b_i = 0$ then the order relation on the ith bit is the normal order; if $b_i = 1$, the order relation is reversed and we have that $1 <_{b_i} 0$. We now define: The *monotone extension of $z \in \{0,1\}^n$* with respect to b:

$$\mathcal{M}_b(z) = \{x \mid x \geq_b z\}.$$

The *monotone extension of f* with respect to b:

$$\mathcal{M}_b(f) = \{x \mid x \geq_b z, \ for \ some \ z \in f\}.$$

The set of *minimal assignments of f* with respect to b:

$$\min_b(f) = \{z \mid z \in f, \ such \ that \ \forall y \in f, z \not>_b y\}.$$

Every boolean function f can be represented in the following form:

$$f = \bigwedge_{b \in B} \mathcal{M}_b(f) = \bigwedge_{b \in B} \bigvee_{z \in \min_b(f)} \mathcal{M}_b(z) \qquad (1)$$

In the above representation $B \subseteq \{0,1\}^n$ is called a basis. It is known that the size of the basis is at most the CNF size of f, and the size of $\min_b(f)$ is at most its DNF size. (See (Khardon & Roth 1994b) for an exact characterization and a discussion of this issue.) A basis can be used to characterize a class of boolean functions: those which can be expressed with it as in Eq. (1). It is known, for example, that the class of Horn CNF functions has a basis of size $n + 1$, and that the class of $\log n$CNF functions has a basis of size less than n^3.

Let $\Gamma \subseteq KB \subseteq \{0,1\}^n$ be a set of models. To decide whether $KB \models \alpha$ use the model-based approach to deduction: for all the models $z \in \Gamma$ check whether $\alpha(z) = 1$. If for some z, $\alpha(z) = 0$ say "No"; otherwise say "Yes". This approach is feasible if Γ is small.

Definition 13 *Let $\mathcal{F}$ be a class of functions, and let B be a basis for $\mathcal{F}$. For a knowledge base $KB \in \mathcal{F}$ we define the set $\Gamma = \Gamma_{KB}^B$ of characteristic models to be the set of all minimal assignments of KB with respect to the basis B. Formally,*

$$\Gamma_{KB}^B = \cup_{b \in B}\{z \in min_b(KB)\}.$$

Theorem 4 *Let KB, $\alpha \in \mathcal{F}$ and let B be a basis for $\mathcal{F}$. Then $KB \models \alpha$ if and only if for every $u \in \Gamma_{KB}^B$, $\alpha(u) = 1$.*

Definition 14 (Least Upper-bound) *Let $\mathcal{F}, \mathcal{G}$ be families of propositional languages. Given $f \in \mathcal{F}$ we say that $f_{lub} \in \mathcal{G}$ is a $\mathcal{G}$-least upper bound of f iff $f \subseteq f_{lub}$ and there is no $f' \in \mathcal{G}$ such that $f \subset f' \subset f_{lub}$.*

Theorem 5 *Let f be any propositional theory and $\mathcal{G}$ a class of all propositional theories with basis B. Then*

$$f_{lub} = \bigwedge_{b \in B} \mathcal{M}_b(f).$$

Theorem 6 *Let $KB \in \mathcal{F}$, $\alpha \in \mathcal{G}$ and let B be a basis for $\mathcal{G}$. Then $KB \models \alpha$ if and only if for every $u \in \Gamma_{KB}^B$, $\alpha(u) = 1$.*

L2R without Learning to Classify

The following algorithm is based on a modified version
of an algorithm from (Bshouty 1993). We make use of a
Reasoning Query Oracle $RQ(f, \mathcal{Q})$ and a Membership
Query Oracle $MQ(f)$ to exactly Learn to Reason any
boolean function f with a polynomial size DNF.

We note that the requirements of the algorithm can
be relaxed: a slightly more complicated version, using
$EX_D(f)$ instead of $RQ(f, \mathcal{Q})$, can be used to PAC-
Learn to Reason f. Details are given in the full version.

Let B be the basis for the class of queries $\mathcal{Q}$. The
algorithm collects a set of models $\Gamma = \cup_{b \in B} \Gamma_b$, the set
of minimal assignments of f with respect to B. By
Theorem 6 this is the set of the minimal models of
$f_{lub} = \wedge_{b \in B} \mathcal{M}_b(f)$.

> **Algorithm $\mathcal{A}$:** For all $b \in B$ initialize $\Gamma_b = \phi$.
> To get counterexamples, call $RQ(f, Q)$, for which
> the algorithm responses by performing the model-
> based test on the set $\cup_{b \in B} \Gamma_b$ (and therefore, answers
> "yes" initially). When it makes a mistake on a "yes"
> answer[7], it receives a positive counterexample x. In
> this case, the algorithm first finds $b \in B$ such that
> $x \notin \mathcal{M}_b(\Gamma_b)$ and then uses a greedy procedure that
> repeatedly calls $MQ(f)$ to find a new minimal model
> of f with respect to the order b. ((Angluin 1988;
> Bshouty 1993). Details in the full version.)
>
> In the query-answering phase, When given a query $\alpha \in$
> Q, the algorithm answers by performing the model-
> based reasoning using the set $\Gamma = \cup_{b \in B} \Gamma_b$.

The algorithm is essentially a Mistake Bound algo-
rithm that learns $f_{lub} = \wedge_{b \in B} \mathcal{M}_b(f)$ from below.

Theorem 7 *Algorithm $\mathcal{A}$ is a Exact-Learn to Reason
algorithm for the problem $(DNF, \mathcal{Q})$, where $\mathcal{Q}$ is the
class of all common queries.*

Proof: [sketch] Denote $h = \wedge_{b \in B} (\vee_{z \in \Gamma_b} \mathcal{M}_b(z))$.
Clearly, $\Gamma \subseteq f$, and therefore the algorithm $\mathcal{A}$ never
makes a mistake when it says "no" (and is therefore
well defined). Whenever the algorithm errs on an
$RQ(f, Q)$ query, it receives a positive counterexample,
$x \in f \setminus h$. Since x is negative for at least one of the
b's in the conjunction defining h, there exists a model
$z \in \min_b(f) \setminus \Gamma_b$ for each of these b's. Therefore, in
this case, the algorithm can use a sequence of calls to
$MQ(f)$ to find a new model of f, an element of Γ_f^B.
Thus, with every such mistake the algorithm makes
progress toward collecting the elements in the set Γ_f^B.
Therefore, after at most $|\Gamma_f^B|$ calls to $RQ(f, \mathcal{Q})$ algo-
rithm $\mathcal{A}$ makes no more mistakes on $RQ(f, \mathcal{Q})$ queries
and therefore $h = f_{lub}$. Theorem 6 implies that $\mathcal{A}$ is
an Exact-Learn to Reason algorithm for f. ∎

This should be contrasted with the inability to *learn
to classify* DNF. One can learn f_{lub} and reason with it
with respect to common queries, but f_{lub} is not sufficient as a substitute for f when classifying examples.

---

[7] The algorithm never makes mistakes when it responses
with "no" on an $RQ(f, Q)$ query.

Acknowledgments

We are grateful to Les Valiant for many enjoyable discussions that helped us develop the ideas presented
here.

References

Angluin, D. 1988. Queries and concept learning. *Machine
Learning* 2(4):319–342.

Angluin, D. 1992. Computational learning theory: Survey
and selected bibliography. In *Proceedings of the Twenty-
Fourth Annual ACM Symposium on Theory of Computing*, 351–369.

Brooks, R. A. 1991. Intelligence without representation.
Artificial Intelligence 47:139–159.

Bshouty, N. H. 1993. Exact learning via the monotone
theory. In *Proceedings of the IEEE Symp. on Foundation
of Computer Science*, 302–311.

Haussler, D. 1987. Bias, version spaces and Valiant's
learning framework. In *Proceedings of the Fourth International Workshop on Machine Learning*, 324–336.

Kautz, H.; Kearns, M.; and Selman, B. 1993. Reasoning
with characteristic models. In *Proceedings of the National
Conference on Artificial Intelligence*, 34–39.

Kearns, M. 1992. Oblivious pac learning of concepts hierarchies. In *Proceedings of the National Conference on
Artificial Intelligence*, 215–222.

Khardon, R., and Roth, D. 1994a. Learning to reason.
Technical Report TR-2-94, Aiken Computation Lab., Harvard University.

Khardon, R., and Roth, D. 1994b. Reasoning with models. In these Proceedings.

Kirsh, D. 1991. Foundations of AI: the big issues. *Artificial Intelligence* 47:3–30.

Levesque, H. 1986. Making believers out of computers.
Artificial Intelligence 30:81–108.

Littlestone, N. 1989. *Mistake bounds and logarithmic
linear-threshold learning algorithms*. Ph.D. Dissertation,
U. C. Santa Cruz.

McCarthy, J. 1958. Programs with common sense. In
Brachman, R., and Levesque, H., eds., *Readings in Knowledge Representation, 1985*. Morgan-Kaufmann.

Roth, D. 1993. On the hardness of approximate reasoning.
In *Proceedings of the International Joint Conference of
Artificial Intelligence*, 613–618.

Selman, B. 1990. *Tractable Default Reasoning*. Ph.D. Dissertation, Department of Computer Science, University of
Toronto.

Shastri, L. 1993. A computational model of tractable reasoning - taking inspiration from cognition. In *Proceedings
of the International Joint Conference of Artificial Intelligence*, 202–207.

Valiant, L. G., and Vazirani, V. V. 1986. NP is as easy as
detecting unique solutions. *Theoretical Computer Science*
47:85–93.

Valiant, L. G. 1984. A theory of the learnable. *Communications of the ACM* 27(11):1134–1142.

Valiant, L. G. 1994. *Circuits of the Mind*. Oxford University Press. Forthcoming.

Catching a Baseball:
A Reinforcement Learning Perspective using a Neural Network

Rajarshi Das
Santa Fe Institute
1660 Old Pecos Trail, Suite A
Santa Fe, NM 87501

Sreerupa Das
Department of Computer Science
University of Colorado
Boulder, CO 80309-0430

Abstract

Moments after a baseball batter has hit a fly ball, an outfielder has to decide whether to run forward or backward to catch the ball. Judging a fly ball is a difficult task, especially when the fielder is in the plane of the ball's trajectory. There exists several alternative hypotheses in the literature which identify different perceptual features available to the fielder that may provide useful cues as to the location of the ball's landing point. A recent study in experimental psychology suggests that to intercept the ball, the fielder has to run such that the double derivative of $tan\phi$ with respect to time is close to zero (i.e. $d^2(tan\phi)/dt^2 \approx 0$), where ϕ is the elevation angle of the ball from the fielder's perspective (McLeod & Dlenes 1993). We investigate whether $d^2(tan\phi)/dt^2$ information is a useful cue to *learn* this task in the Adaptive Heuristic Critic ($\mathcal{AHC}$) reinforcement learning framework. Our results provide supporting evidence that $d^2(tan\phi)/dt^2$ information furnishes strong initial cue in determining the landing point of the ball and plays a key role in the learning process. However our simulations show that during later stages of the ball's flight, yet another perceptual feature, the perpendicular velocity of the ball (v_p) with respect to the fielder, provides stronger cues as to the location of the landing point. The trained network generalized to novel circumstances and also exhibited some of the behaviors recorded by experimental psychologists on human data. We believe that much can be gained by using reinforcement learning approaches to learn common physical tasks, and similarly motivated work could stimulate useful interdisciplinary research on the subject.

Introduction

Scientists have often wondered how an outfielder in the game of baseball or cricket can judge a fly ball by running either forward or backward and arriving at the right point at the right time to catch the ball (Bush 1967, Chapman 1969, Todd 1981). When the ball is coming directly at the fielder, the ball appears to rise or fall in a vertical plane, and thus the fielder has information about elevation angle of the ball and its rate of change. In the more typical case, when the ball is hit to the side, the fielder gets a perspective view of the trajectory of the ball

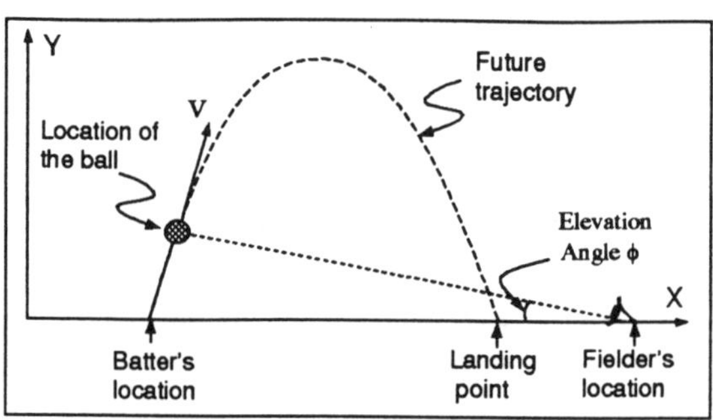

Figure 1: The fielder has to run and intercept the ball at the end of the ball's flight.

and there is additional information about azimuth angle and its rate of change. Hence, judging a fly ball is usually the most difficult when the fielder is in the plane of the ball's motion (Figure 1). Yet, moments after a batter hits the ball directly towards a fielder, the fielder has to decide if it is a short pop up in front, or a high fly ball over the fielder's head, and run accordingly. Thus, there is an important temporal credit assignment problem in judging a fly ball, since the success or failure signal is obtained long after the actions that lead to that signal are taken.

Considerable work in experimental psychology has focused on identifying the perceptual features that a fielder uses to judge a fly ball (Rosenberg 1988, Todd 1981). Several alternative hypothesis, as to the perceptual features that are important in making the decisions, have been postulated. In this paper, we explore the problem in detail using a reinforcement learning model. Our experimental results support one recent hypothesis that postulates the use of a specific trigonometric feature as an initial cue to determine the eventual landing point. However, in our reinforcement learning model this trigonometric feature by itself is not sufficient to learn the task successfully. We investigate other perceptual features which used in tandem with the trigonometric feature help the reinforcement learning system to successfully learn to catch fly balls. In trying to solve similar commonplace physical tasks

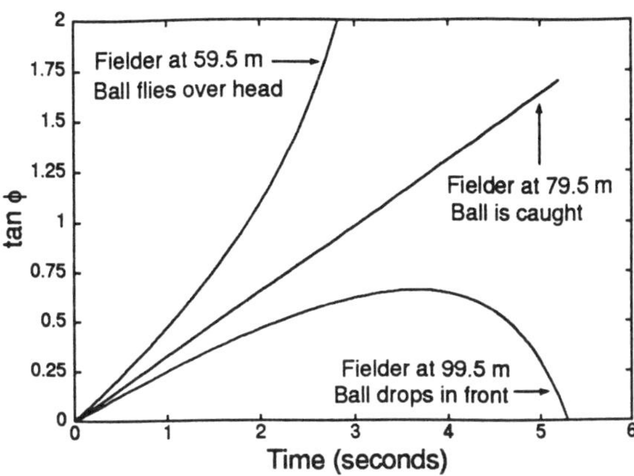

Figure 2: The figure shows the variation in $tan\phi$ as seen by three different fielders standing at 59.5 m, 79.5 m, and 99.5 m from the batter. The initial velocity of the ball is 30 m/s, directed at an angle 60° from the horizontal. Here the range of the trajectory of the ball is 79.5 m, and since this simulation ignores air resistance, $tan\phi$ increases at a constant rate only for the fielder standing at 79.5 m.

using reinforcement learning we not only learn more about the reinforcement learning models themselves but also understand the underlying complexities involved in a physical task.

The physics of judging a fly ball

The problem of trajectory interception was analyzed by Chapman using Newton's laws of motion (Chapman 1968). For a perfect parabolic trajectory, the tangent of the ball's elevation angle ϕ increases at a steady rate with time (i.e. $d(tan\phi)/dt = constant$) over the entire duration of flight, if the fielder stands stationary at the ball's landing point (Figure 2). This simple principle holds true for any initial velocity and launch angle of the ball over a finite range. If the ball is going to fall in front of the fielder, then $tan\phi$ grows at first and then decreases with $d^2(tan\phi)/dt^2 < 0$. On the other hand, if the ball is going to fly over the fielder's head, then $tan\phi$ grows at an increasing rate with $d^2(tan\phi)/dt^2 > 0$. Chapman suggested that if a fielder runs with a constant velocity so that $d(tan\phi)/dt$ is constant then the fielder can reach the proper spot to catch the ball just as it arrives.

However, Chapman neglected the effects of aerodynamic drag on the ball which significantly affects the ball's trajectory and range. When air resistance is taken into account, Brancazio claimed that the specific trigonometric feature cited by Chapman cannot provide useful cues to the fielder (Brancazio 1985). In addition, Chapman's hypothesis makes the unrealistic assumption that the fielder runs with a constant velocity while attempting to catch a fly ball. Brancazio went on to show that many of the other perceptual features available to a fielder (see

Brancazio's List of Perceptual Features Available to the Fielder	
Symbol	Feature
ϕ	Angle of Elevation
$d\phi/dt$	Rate of change of ϕ
$d^2\phi/dt^2$	Rate of change of $d\phi/dt$
D	Distance between ball and fielder
dD/dt	Rate of change of D ($= -v_r$, the radial velocity)
v_p	Velocity of ball perpendicular to fielder
dv_p/dt	Rate of change of v_p

Table 1: Brancazio showed that, with the possible exception of $d^2\phi/dt^2$, these features provide no significant initial cue as to the location of the ball's landing point. Note that D is inversely proportional to the apparent size of the ball. Other possible perceptual features include $tan\phi$, $d(tan\phi)/dt$, $d^2(tan\phi)/dt^2$.

Table 1) *cannot* provide significant initial cue to determine the landing point of the ball. After eliminating several possible candidate features, Brancazio hypothesized that the angular acceleration of the ball $d^2\phi/dt^2$ provides the strongest initial cue as to the location of the eventual landing point. He also conjectured that the angular acceleration of a fielder's head while the fielder tries to visually track a fly ball, might be detected by the vestibular system in the inner ear, which in turn might provide feedback to influence the judgement process of the fielder.

Recent experimental results obtained by McLeod and Dlenes (McLeod & Dlenes 1993) however show that an experienced fielder runs such that $d^2(tan\phi)/dt^2$ is maintained close to zero until the end of the ball's flight. McLeod and Dlenes suggest that this is a very robust strategy for the real world, since the outcome is independent of the effects of aerodynamic drag on the ball's trajectory, or the ball following a parabolic path. However little is understood about how human beings *learn* to intercept a free falling ball (Rosenberg 1988) and exactly how $d^2(tan\phi)/dt^2$ information helps in the learning process.

In this paper, we provide supporting evidence that $d^2(tan\phi)/dt^2$ information furnishes strong initial cue as to the landing point of the ball and plays a key role in the learning process in a reinforcement learning framework. However, in the later stages of the ball's flight, $d^2(tan\phi)/dt^2$ provides conflicting cues and the reinforcement learning model has difficulty in intercepting fly balls. We delineate the cause of this problem and use an additional perceptual feature that helps in learning the task.

Using reinforcement learning to catch a baseball

We use Barto, Sutton and Anderson's Multilayer Adaptive Heuristic Critic ($\mathcal{AHC}$) model (Anderson 1986) to learn the task. The general framework of reinforcement learning is as follows: an agent seeks to control a discrete time stochastic dynamical system. At each time step, the agent observes the current environmental state x and executes action a. The agent receives a payoff (and/or pays a cost) which is a function of state x and action a, and the system makes a probabilistic transition to state y. The agent's goal is to determine a control policy that maximizes some objective function. $\mathcal{AHC}$ is a reinforcement algorithm for discovering an extended plan of actions which maximizes the cumulative long-term reward received by an agent as a result of its actions.

In the $\mathcal{AHC}$ framework, the model consists of two sub-modules (networks); one is the agent (action network), that tries to learn search heuristics in the form of a probabilistic mapping from the states to the actions in order to maximize the objective function. Typically the objective function is a cumulative measure of payoffs and costs over time. The other module is the critic (evaluation network) that tries to evaluate the agent's performance based on the reinforcement received from the environment as a result of the action just taken.

In our implementation of the $\mathcal{AHC}$ model, the action $a(t)$, taken by the agent (action network) corresponds to the instantaneous acceleration of the fielder at time t. The state, x, is assumed to be described by a set of inputs provided to the model at every time step. The action network generates real valued actions, $a(t)$, at every time step, similar to that described by Gullapalli (Gullapalli 1993). The output of the action network determines the mean, $\mu(t)$, and the output of the evaluation network determines the standard deviation, $\sigma(t)$ of the acceleration, $a(t)$, at a particular time.

$$\mu(t) = \text{output of action network},$$

$$\sigma(t) = max(r(t), 0.0)$$

where $r(t)$ is the output of the evaluation network. Assuming a Gaussian distribution Ψ, the action $a(t)$ is computed using $\mu(t)$ and $\sigma(t)$.

$$a(t) \sim \Psi(\mu(t), \sigma(t))$$

In the course of learning, both the evaluation and action networks are adjusted incrementally in order to perform credit assignment appropriately. The most popular and best-understood approach to a credit assignment problem is the *temporal difference* (TD) method (Sutton 1988), and the $\mathcal{AHC}$ is a TD based reinforcement learning approach (Anderson 1986).

Since the objective of learning is to maximize the agent's performance, a natural measure of performance is the *discounted cumulative reinforcement* (or for short, *utility*) (Barto et al. 1990):

$$r(t) = \sum_{k=0}^{\infty} \gamma^k f(t+k)$$

where $r(t)$ is the discounted cumulative reinforcement (utility) starting from time t throughout the future, $f(t)$ is the reinforcement received after the transition from time t to $t+1$, and $0 \leq \gamma \leq 1$ is a discount factor, which adjusts the importance of long term consequences of actions. Thus the utility, $r(t)$, of a state x is the immediate payoff plus the utility, $r(t+1)$, of the next state y, discounted by γ. Therefore the desired function must satisfy:

$$r(t) = f(t) + \gamma r(t+1)$$

Relating these ideas to the $\mathcal{AHC}$ model, the output of the evaluation network corresponds to $r(t)$. During learning, the evaluation network tries to generate the correct utility of a state. The difference between the actual utility of a state and its predicted utility (called the TD error) is used to adjust the weights of the evaluation network using backpropagation algorithm (Rumelhart et al. 1986). The action network is also adjusted according to the same TD error (Sutton 1988, Lin 1992). The objective function that determines the weight update rules is defined as:

$$Error = \begin{cases} f(t) + \gamma r(t+1) - r(t) & \bullet \text{ while the ball} \\ & \quad \text{is in the air,} \\ f(t) - r(t) & \bullet \text{ if the ball has} \\ & \quad \text{hit the ground.} \end{cases}$$

Simulation details

The perceptual features that are available to the fielder while judging a fly ball define the input variables of our system. At any time t, the inputs to the system include: ϕ, $d^2(tan\phi)/dt^2$, v_f—the velocity of the fielder, and a binary flag which indicates whether the ball is spatially in front of or behind the fielder. Thus the system receives no information about the absolute coordinates of the ball or the fielder at any point in time. Initially, the fielder is positioned at a random distance in front of or behind the ball's landing point. The initial velocity and the initial acceleration of the fielder are both set to zero. Once the ball is launched, the fielder's movement is controlled by the output $a(t)$ of the action network which determines the fielder's acceleration at time t. The simulation is continued (see Appendix for the equations) until the ball's trajectory is complete and a failure signal is generated. If the ball has hit the ground and the fielder has failed to intercept the ball, the failure signal $f(t)$ is proportional to the fielder's distance from the ball's landing point.

$$f(t) = \begin{cases} 0 & \text{while the ball is in the air,} \\ 0 & \text{if } D(final) \leq \mathcal{R} \text{ (Success!),} \\ -C\,|D(final)| & \text{if } D(final) > \mathcal{R} \text{ (Failure!).} \end{cases}$$

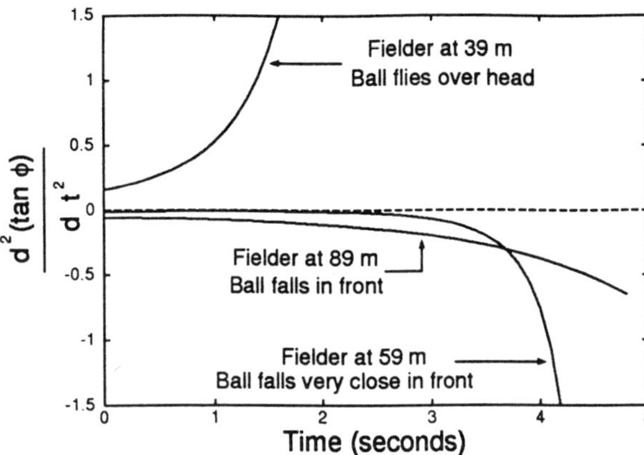

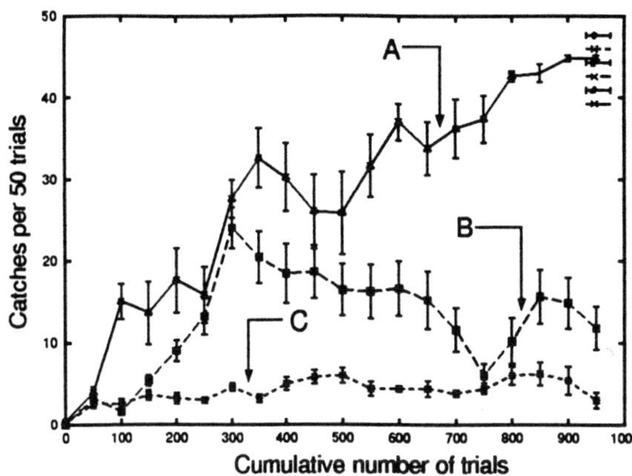

Figure 3: The variation of $d^2(tan\phi)/dt^2$ as seen from three different positions. Aerodynamic drag is taken into consideration in this simulation, and for the same initial parameters as in Figure 2, the range decreases to 57.5 m. The ball touches the ground at $t = 4.9$ second. Note that for the fielder stationed very close to the ball's landing point at 59 m, the $d^2(tan\phi)/dt^2$ is close to zero for most of the ball's flight, but it increases dramatically at the end.

Figure 4: The plots show the number of successful catches every 50 trials as a function of total number of trials for three different sets of input features. The three sets of features are (A) both $d^2(tan\phi)/dt^2$ and v_p. (B) $d^2(tan\phi)/dt^2$ but not v_p, (C) $d^2(\phi)/dt^2$. (The other input features: ϕ, v_f and the binary flag were used in all three sets). The initial angle of the ball is chosen randomly between $[50°, 70°]$. The fielder's initial position is also chosen from a random distribution between [47.5m, 67.5m]. The initial velocity and initial acceleration of the fielder are both set to zero in every trial.

where $D(final)$ is the distance between the ball and the fielder when the ball hits the ground, $\mathcal{R}$ is the catching radius and C is a positive constant. In order to account for last moment adjustments made by the fielder (for example, making a final dive at the ball !), a catch is considered successful if the ball hits the ground within a region around the fielder's position defined by the catching radius, $\mathcal{R}$. In our simulations, the catching radius was set to 2 m. It may be noted here that the information–whether the ball fell in front of or behind the fielder–is not a part of the reinforcement signal. This information is provided as a part of the input signal and thus, all throughout the ball's trajectory, the fielder knows whether the ball is in front of or behind the fielder.

The inputs to the network are computed as follows. The raw inputs, as determined by the system dynamics (defined in the Appendix), are first clipped using the following lower and upper bounds (indicated by $\langle \rangle$): $\langle -10.0, 10.0 \rangle m/s$ for the fielder's velocity, v_f; $\langle -5.0, 5.0 \rangle m/s^2$ for the fielder's acceleration; $\langle 0°, 180° \rangle$ for ϕ; $\langle -25.0, 25.0 \rangle m/s$ for v_p (referred to in the next section); $\langle -0.5, 0.5 \rangle s^{-2}$ for $d^2(tan\phi)/dt^2$. The clipped inputs are then normalized between 0.0 and 1.0 and finally presented to the network. Nevertheless, while determining the system dynamics none of the values are either scaled or clipped. A sampling frequency of 10 Hz (i.e. $\Delta t = 0.1$s) is used during the simulation of the system.

Results

Our results, using the $\mathcal{AHC}$ learning approach, show that $d^2(tan\phi)/dt^2$ information by itself is *not* suffi-

cient to learn the task at hand. After an initial learning period, the system surprisingly learns to move the fielder away from the ball's landing point instead of moving towards it. Figure 3 delineates the underlying problem. For a fielder standing at the ball's landing point, $d^2(tan\phi)/dt^2$ is always zero. However, if the fielder is only a small distance away from the ball's landing point, $d^2(tan\phi)/dt^2$ is close to zero for most of the ball's flight, until near the end when it increases dramatically. Thus large and small magnitudes of $d^2(tan\phi)/dt^2$ can be associated with both large and small values of negative failure signals providing conflicting cues to a learning system. We therefore investigate other perceptual features that might help in the learning process by removing the ambiguity.

Figure 4 plots the performance of the network when different sets of inputs (perceptual features) are used (in addition to ϕ, v_f, and the binary direction flag). In the figure, each learning curve is an average of 10 independent trials, where each curve corresponds to one of the three different sets of perceptual features (A) $d^2(tan\phi)/dt^2$ and v_p, where v_p is the perpendicular component of the ball's velocity as seen by the fielder, (B) $d^2(tan\phi)/dt^2$ (McLeod & Dlenes' hypothesis), and (C) $d^2(\phi)/dt^2$ (Brancazio's hypothesis). In the simulations each trial begins with the fielder at a random position in the range [47.5m, 67.5] in front of the ball and the ball is thrown with an initial angle randomly distributed in $[50°, 70°]$. The plots show that the network could not learn the task using only $d^2(tan\phi)/dt^2$ or using

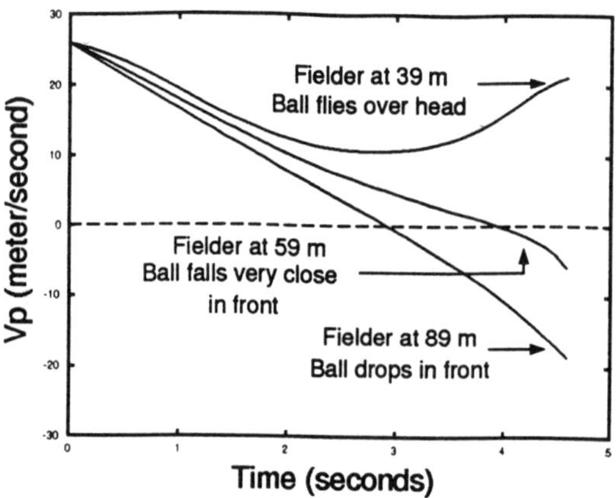

Figure 5: The variation of the perpendicular component of the ball's velocity as seen from three different positions. The initial parameters are the same as in Figure 2. The ball touches the ground at $t = 4.9$ seconds. Note that the three plots are very close to each other for the first three seconds, and diverge only at the end of the ball's flight.

only $d^2(\phi)/dt^2$. Let us analyze why v_p could possibly help in learning (Brancazio 1985). Figure 5 plots the variation of v_p as seen by the fielder standing at three different positions. Initially, v_p provides little cue as to the balls landing point, but as the ball's flight comes to an end, v_p is significantly different for the fielders standing at different positions. Interestingly enough, the network is able to learn the task, since v_p information adds the necessary discriminating ability in judging fly balls during the latter stages of the ball's flight.

The above results suggests that in our reinforcement learning model both $d^2(tan\phi)/dt^2$ and v_p are necessary for learning the task of catching a ball. During the initial part of the ball's flight, the system learns to keep $d^2(tan\phi)/dt^2$ very small, and move in the correct direction. Towards the end of the ball's flight, when $d^2(tan\phi)/dt^2$ increases drastically, the system learns to use v_p to decide whether to run forward or backward.

Figure 6 shows space-time plots of the fielder's trajectories before and after training for 20 different trials (the initial positions of the fielder are set randomly, although the initial angle of the ball is identical in each trial). In their experiments with a skillful fielder, McLeod and Dlenes observed that the fielder does not automatically run to the point where the ball will fall and then wait for it, rather the fielder tracks the ball throughout its trajectory till it hits the ground. We see a similar behavior in Figure 6 after the system has learned to catch. More interestingly, Figure 6 shows that a fielder who is initially positioned slightly in front of the landing point of the ball, goes through a temporary phase when the fielder actually runs away from the eventual landing point of the ball. The data presented

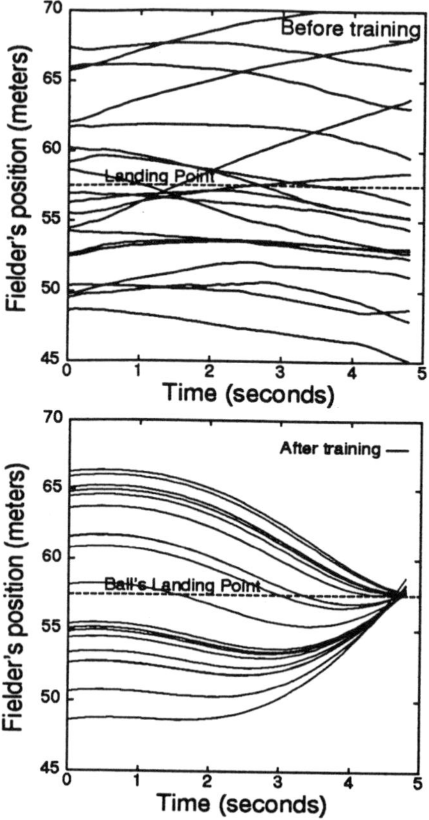

Figure 6: The two space-time plots show the fielder's distance from the batter in 20 trials, *before* (left) and *after* (right) training for 10000 trials. The initial parameters of the ball are the same as in Figure 2 and the fielder's initial position is chosen from a random distribution [47.5m, 67.5m]. The initial velocity and the initial acceleration of the fielder are both set to zero in every trial. The ball's range is 57.5 m which is reached at $t = 4.9$ second.

by McLeod and Dlenes shows surprisingly similar behavior among experienced fielders.

Our last set of simulations focus on the generalizational performance of a trained network. Figure 7 depicts the results. The network is first trained with trials where the initial angle of the ball is randomly set to a value in the range $[57^o, 62^o]$. After training, we test the network on trials where the initial angle is randomly selected from increasing ranges: from $[57^o, 62^o]$ to $[45^o, 75^o]$. As is evident from the plot, the network is able to generalize and perform reasonably well in situations which it had not experienced during the training phase. Note that the range of ball's trajectory during training is bounded between 56.1m (for 57°) and 62.3m (for 62°) which is much smaller than the range of the ball's trajectory during testing (which varies between 69.69m (for 45°) and 34.36m (for 75°)). These results in generalization performance indicate that the network is able to extract important rules from the perceptual features

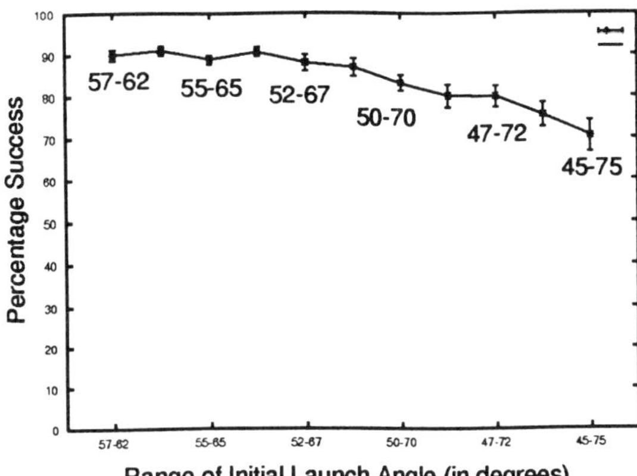

Figure 7: Average generalization performance of a trained network is shown. The network is trained on trajectories with the ball's initial angle ranging between $57° - 62°$. The trained network is then tested on trials where the initial angle ranged between $45° - 75°$. The simulations are averaged over 10 runs with the fielder's initial position chosen from a random distribution [47.5m, 67.5m].

rather than memorize the training data.

Conclusion and future work

The goal of this research is to determine if a reinforcement learning model can learn to catch fly balls using a specific trigonometric feature suggested in the experimental psychology literature. We have shown that for the reinforcement learning model discussed in this paper, $d^2(tan\phi)/dt^2$ and v_p information play a vital role in the learning the task. It is possible that in later stages of the ball's trajectory, an experienced fielder might use other perceptual features like stereoscopic vision as the guiding mechanism. We are currently investigating such a hypothesis. We believe much can be gained by using reinforcement learning approaches to learn common physical tasks, and we hope that this work would stimulate useful interdisciplinary research on the subject.

Acknowledgements

We thank C. W. Anderson, K. L. Markey, M.C. Mozer, S.J. Nowlan, and the anonymous reviewers of this paper for their valuable suggestions.

Appendix: The Equations of Motion

The equations of motion in two dimensions for a projectile can be expressed as:

$$x^{''} = -Kvv_x, \qquad y^{''} = -Kvv_y - g \qquad (1)$$

where $x^{''}$ and $y^{''}$ are the instantaneous horizontal and vertical accelerations, v_x and v_y are the horizontal and vertical components of the velocity of the ball v, g is the acceleration due to gravity and

K is the aerodynamic drag force constant equal to 0.005249 m^{-1} for a baseball (Brancazio 1985). Using a sampling time of Δt second, the above equations are numerically integrated using third derivatives as follows:

$$\Delta x = v_x \Delta t + 0.5 x^{''}(\Delta t)^2 + 0.1667 x^{'''}(\Delta t)^3, \quad (2)$$

$$\Delta y = v_y \Delta t + 0.5 y^{''}(\Delta t)^2 + 0.1667 y^{'''}(\Delta t)^3, \quad (3)$$

where $x^{'''} = -K(v^{'}v_x + vx^{''})$, $y^{'''} = -K(v^{'}v_y + vy^{''})$, and $v^{'} = (v_x x^{''} + v_y y^{''})/v$. The velocity components are also updated as:

$$\Delta v_x = x^{''}(\Delta t) + 0.5 x^{'''}(\Delta t)^2, \qquad (4)$$

$$\Delta v_y = x^{''}(\Delta t) + 0.5 y^{'''}(\Delta t)^2 \qquad (5)$$

Given the current coordinates of the fielder and the ball, and their respective velocities, it is possible to calculate the variables associated with ϕ, and $tan\phi$ including their derivatives using trigonometric equations and calculus.

References

Anderson, C.W. 1986. *Learning and Problem Solving with multilayer connectionist systems.* Ph.D. diss., Computer Science, Univ. of Massachusetts, Amherst.

Barto, A.G., Sutton, R.S., & Watkins, C.J.C.H. 1990. "Learning and sequential decision making," In: M. Gabriel & J.W. Moores (Eds.), *Learning and computational neuroscience*, MIT Press.

Brancazio, P.J. 1985. "Looking into Chapman's homer: The physics of judging a fly ball," *American Journal of Physics*, Vol. 53, No. 9, pp. 849-855.

Bush, V. 1967. *Science is not enough*, Wm. Morrow Co., NY.

Chapman, C. 1968. "Catching a baseball," *American Journal of Physics*, Vol. 36, No. 10, pp. 868-870.

Gullapalli, V. 1990. "A stochastic reinforcement learning algorithm for learning real-valued functions," *Neural Networks*, Vol. 3, pp. 671-691.

Lin, L.J. 1992. "Self-improving reactive agents based on reinforcement learning, planning, and teaching," *Machine Learning*, 8, pp. 293-321.

McLeod, P. & Dienes, Z. 1993. "Running to catch the ball," *Nature*, Vol. 362, pp. 23.

Rosenberg, K.S. 1988. "Role of visual information in ball catching," *Journal of Motor Behavior*, Vol. 20, No. 2, pp. 150-164.

Rumelhart, D.E., Hinton, G.E., & William, R.J. 1986. "Learning internal representations by error propagation," *Parallel Distributed Processing: Explorations in the microstructure of cognition. Vol. 1.*, Bradford Books/MIT Press.

Sutton, R.S. 1988. "Learning to predict by the methods of temporal differences." *Machine Learning*, 3, pp. 9-44.

Todd, J.T. 1981. "Visual information about moving objects," *Journal of Experimental Psychology: Human Perception and Performance*, Vol. 7, No. 4, pp. 795-810.

Incorporating Advice into Agents that Learn from Reinforcements[*]

Richard Maclin **Jude W. Shavlik**
Computer Sciences Dept., University of Wisconsin
1210 West Dayton Street
Madison, WI 53706
Email: {maclin,shavlik}@cs.wisc.edu

Abstract

Learning from reinforcements is a promising approach for creating intelligent agents. However, reinforcement learning usually requires a large number of training episodes. We present an approach that addresses this shortcoming by allowing a connectionist Q-learner to accept advice given, at any time and in a natural manner, by an external observer. In our approach, the advice-giver watches the learner and occasionally makes suggestions, expressed as instructions in a simple programming language. Based on techniques from knowledge-based neural networks, these programs are inserted directly into the agent's utility function. Subsequent reinforcement learning further integrates and refines the advice. We present empirical evidence that shows our approach leads to statistically-significant gains in expected reward. Importantly, the advice improves the expected reward regardless of the stage of training at which it is given.

Introduction

A successful and increasingly popular method for creating intelligent agents is to have them learn from reinforcements (Barto, Sutton, & Watkins 1990; Lin 1992; Mahadevan & Connell 1992). However, these approaches suffer from their need for large numbers of training episodes. While several approaches for speeding up reinforcement learning have been proposed, a largely unexplored approach is to design a learner that can also accept advice from an external observer. We present and evaluate an approach for creating advice-taking learners.

To illustrate the general idea of advice-taking, imagine that you are watching an agent learning to play some video game. Assume you notice that frequently the agent loses because it goes into a "box canyon" in search of food and then gets trapped by its opponents. One would like to give the learner advice such as "do not go into box canyons when opponents are in sight." Importantly, the external observer should be able to provide its advice in some quasi-natural language, using terms about the specific task domain. In

*This research was partially supported by ONR Grant N00014-93-1-0998 and NSF Grant IRI-9002413.

addition, the advice-giver should be oblivious to the details of whichever internal representation and learning algorithm the agent is using.

Recognition of the value of advice-taking has a long history in AI. The general idea of an agent accepting advice was first proposed about 35 years ago by McCarthy (1958). Over a decade ago, Mostow (1982) developed a program that accepted and "operationalized" high-level advice about how to better play the card game Hearts. More recently Gordon and Subramanian (1994) created a system that deductively compiles high-level advice into concrete actions, which are then refined using genetic algorithms. However, the problem of making use of general advice has been largely neglected.

In the next section, we present a framework for using advice with reinforcement learners. The subsequent section presents experiments that investigate the value of our approach. Finally, we list possible extensions to our work, further describe its relation to other research, and present some conclusions.

The General Framework

In this section we describe our approach for creating a reinforcement learner that can accept advice. We use *connectionist Q-learning* (Sutton 1988; Watkins 1989) as our form of reinforcement learning (RL).

Figure 1 shows the general structure of a reinforcement learner, augmented (in bold) with our advice-taking extensions. In RL, the learner senses the current world state, chooses an action to execute, and occasionally receives rewards and punishments. Based on these reinforcements from the environment, the task of the learner is to improve its action-choosing module such that it increases the amount of rewards it receives. In our augmentation, an observer watches the learner

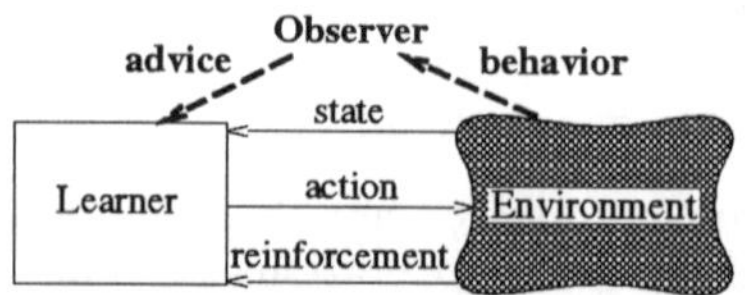

Figure 1: RL with an external advisor.

and periodically provides advice, which is then incorporated into the action-choosing module (the advice is refined based on subsequent experience).

In Q-learning (Watkins 1989) the action-choosing module is a *utility function* that maps states and actions to a numeric value. The utility value of a particular state and action is the predicted future (discounted) reward that will be achieved if that action is taken by the agent in that state. Given a perfect version of this function, the optimal plan is to simply choose, in each state that is reached, the action with the largest utility.

To learn a utility function, a Q-learner starts out with a randomly chosen utility function and explores its environment. As the agent explores, it continually makes predictions about the reward it expects and then updates its utility function by comparing the reward it actually receives to its prediction. In *connectionist* Q-learning, the utility function is implemented as a neural network, whose inputs describe the current state and whose outputs are the utility of each action.

We now return to the task of advice-taking. Hayes-Roth, Klahr, and Mostow (1981) (also see pg. 345–349 of Cohen & Feigenbaum 1982) described the steps involved in taking advice. In the following subsections, we state their steps and discuss how we propose each should be achieved in the context of RL.

Step 1. Request the advice. Instead of having the learner request advice, we allow the external observer to provide advice whenever the observer feels it is appropriate. There are two reasons for this: (i) it places less of a burden on the observer; and (ii) it is an open question how to create the best mechanism for having an RL agent recognize (and express) its need for advice. Other approaches to providing advice to RL agents are discussed later.

Step 2. Convert the advice to an internal representation. Due to the complexities of natural language processing, we require that the external observer express its advice using a simple programming language and a list of acceptable task-specific terms. We then parse the advice, using traditional methods from programming-language compilers.

Step 3. Convert the advice into a usable form. Using techniques from *knowledge compilation*, a learner can convert ("operationalize") high-level advice into a (usually larger) collection of directly interpretable statements (see Gordon & Subramanian 1994; Mostow 1982). In many task domains, the advice-giver may wish to use natural, but imprecise, terms such as "near" and "many." A compiler for such terms will be needed for each general environment. Our compiler is based on the methods proposed by Berenji and Khedkar (1992) for representing fuzzy-logic terms in neural networks. Note that during training the initial definitions of these terms can be refined, possibly in context-dependent ways.

Table 1: Samples of advice in our advice language.

Advice	Pictorial Version

IF An Enemy IS (Near ∧ West) ∧
    An Obstacle IS (Near ∧ North)
THEN
    MULTIACTION
        MoveEast MoveNorth
    END;	

WHEN Surrounded ∧
    OKtoPushEast ∧
    An Enemy IS Near
REPEAT
    PushEast
    MoveEast
UNTIL ¬ OKtoPushEast ∨
    ¬ Surrounded	

Step 4. Integrate the reformulated advice into the agent's current knowledge base. We use ideas from *knowledge-based neural networks* to directly install the operationalized advice into the connectionist representation of the utility function. In one such approach, KBANN (Towell, Shavlik, & Noordewier 1990), a set of propositional rules are re-represented as a neural network. KBANN converts a ruleset into a network by mapping the "target concepts" of the ruleset to output units and creating hidden units that represent the intermediate conclusions. It connects units with highly weighted links and sets unit biases (thresholds) in such a manner that the (non-input) units emulate AND or OR gates, as appropriate.

We extend the KBANN approach to the mapping of (simple) programs, as explained below. Unlike previous applications of knowledge-based neural networks, we allow rules to be installed *incrementally* into networks. That is, previous approaches first reformulated a ruleset then refined it using backpropagation. We allow new rules (i.e., advice) to be inserted into the network at any time during learning.

Table 1 shows some sample advice one might provide to an agent learning to play a video game. We will use it to illustrate the process of integrating advice into a neural network. The left column contains advice in our programming language, and the right shows the effects of the advice. A grammar for our advice language appears elsewhere (Maclin & Shavlik 1994).

We have made three extensions to the standard KBANN algorithm: (i), we allow advice that contains multi-step plans; (ii), advice can contain loops; (iii), advice can refer to previously defined terms. In all three cases incorporating advice involves adding hidden units representing the advice to the existing neural network, as shown in Figure 2. Note that the inputs and outputs to the network remain unchanged; the advice only changes how the function from states to the utility of actions is calculated.

As an example of a multi-step plan, consider the first entry in Table 1. Figure 3 shows the network additions that represent this advice. We first create a hidden unit (labeled A) that represents the conjunction of (i) an

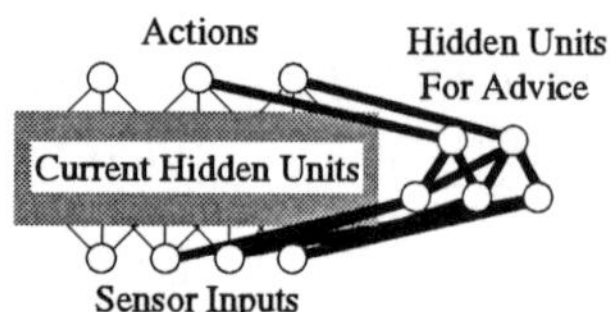

Figure 2: Advice is added to the neural network by adding hidden units that correspond to the advice.

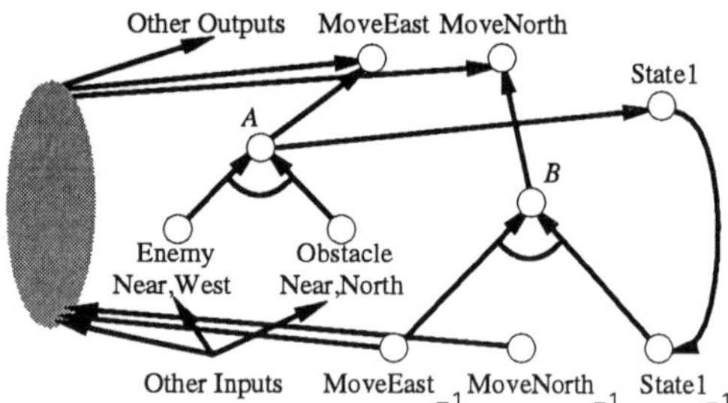

Figure 3: Translation of the first piece of advice. The ellipse at left represents the original hidden units. Arcs show units and weights set to make a conjunctive unit. We also add, as is typical in knowledge-based networks, zero-weighted links (not shown) to other parts of the current network. These links support subsequent refinement.

enemy being near and west[1] and (ii) an obstacle being adjacent and north. We then connect this unit to the action $MoveEast$, which is an existing output unit (recall that the utility function maps states to values of actions); this constitutes the first step of the two-step plan. We also connect unit A to a newly-added hidden unit called $State1$ that records when unit A was active in the previous state. We next connect $State1$ to a new input unit called $State1_{-1}$. This $recurrent$ unit becomes active ("true") when $State1$ was active for the previous input (we need a recurrent unit to implement multi-step plans). Finally, we construct a unit (labeled B) that is active when $State1_{-1}$ is true and the previous action was a eastward move (the input includes the previous action taken in addition to the current sensor values). When active, unit B suggests moving north – the second step of the plan.

We assign high weights to the arcs coming out of units A and B. This means that when either unit is active, the total weighted input to the corresponding output unit will be increased, thereby increasing the utility value for that action. Notice that during subsequent training the weight (and the definition) of a piece of advice may be substantially altered.

The second piece of advice in Table 1 also contains a multi-step plan, but this time it is embedded in a REPEAT. Figure 4 shows the resulting additions to the network for this advice. The key to translating this construct is that there are two ways to invoke the two-step plan. The plan executes when the WHEN condition

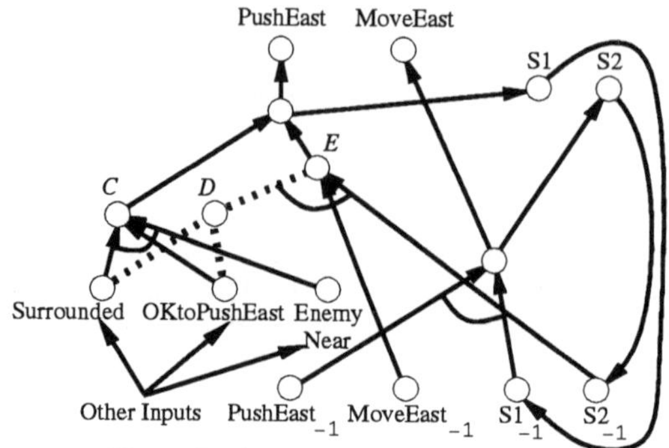

Figure 4: Translation of the second piece of advice. Dotted lines show negative weights. As with all translations, the units shown are added to the existing network.

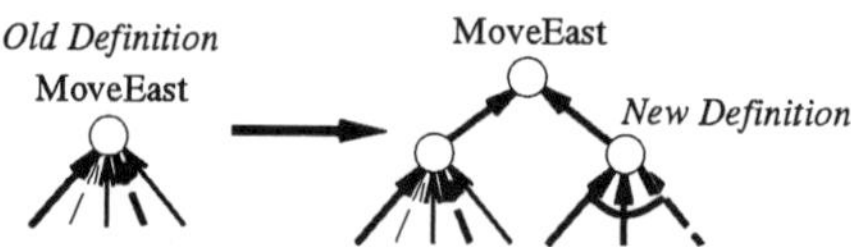

Figure 5: Incorporating the definition of a term that already exists.

is true (unit C) and also when the plan was just run and the UNTIL condition is false. Unit D is active when the UNTIL condition is met, while unit E is active when the UNTIL is unsatisfied and the agent's two previous actions were pushing and then moving east.

A final issue for our algorithm is dealing with advice that involves previously defined terms. This frequently occurs, since advice generally indicates new situations in which to perform existing actions. Figure 5 shows how we address this issue. We add a new definition of an existing term by first creating the representation of the added definition and making a copy of the unit representing the existing definition. We create a new unit, which becomes the term's new definition, representing the disjunction of the old and new definitions.[2] This process is analogous to how KBANN processes multiple rules with the same consequent.

Once we insert the advice into the RL agent, it returns to exploring its environment, thereby integrating and refining the advice. This is a key step because we cannot determine the optimal weights to use for the new piece of advice; instead we use RL to fine tune it.

Step 5. Judge the value of the advice. We currently rely on Q-learning to "wash out" poor advice. One can also envision that in some circumstances – such as a game-learner that can play against itself (Tesauro 1992) or when an agent builds an internal world model (Sutton 1991) – it would be straightforward to empirically evaluate the new advice. It would also be possible to allow the observer to retract or counteract bad advice.

---

[1] A unit recognizing this concept, "enemy near and west," is creating using a technique similar that in Berenji and Khedkar (1992); for more details see Maclin and Shavlik (1994).

[2] The process in Figure 5 would be used when adding the network fragments shown in Figures 3 and 4, assuming the advice came after the learner began exploring and learning.

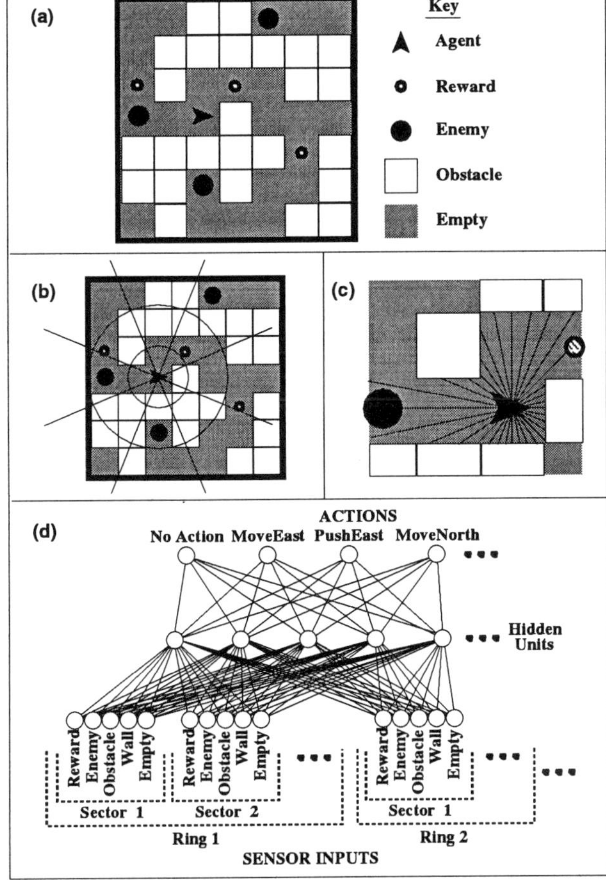

Figure 6: Our test environment: (a) sample configuration; (b) sample division of the environment into sectors; (c) distances measured by the agent's sensors; (d) a neural network that computes the utility of actions.

Experimental Study

We next empirically judge the value of our approach for providing advice to an RL agent.

Testbed

Figure 6a illustrates our test environment. Our task is similar to those explored by Agre and Chapman (1987) and Lin (1992). The agent can perform nine actions: *moving* and *pushing* in the directions East, North, West and South; and *doing nothing*. Pushing moves the obstacles in the environment – when the agent is next to an obstacle and pushes it, the obstacle slides until it encounters another obstacle or the board edge.

The agent receives reinforcement signals when: (i) an enemy eliminates the agent by touching the agent (−1.0); (ii) the agent collects one of the reward objects (+0.7); and (iii) the agent destroys an enemy by pushing an obstacle into it (+0.9). Each enemy moves randomly unless the agent is in sight, in which case it moves toward the agent.

We do not assume a global view of the environment, but instead use an agent-centered sensor model. It is based on partitioning the world into a set of sectors around the agent (see Figure 6b). The agent calculates the percentage of each sector that is occupied by each type of object – reward, enemy, obstacle, or wall. These percentages constitute the input to the neural network (Figure 6d). To calculate the sector occupancy, we assume the agent is able to measure the distance to the nearest occluding object along a fixed set of angles around the agent (Figure 6c). This means that the agent is only able to represent the objects in direct line-of-sight from the agent. Further details of our world model appear in Maclin and Shavlik (1994).

Methodology

We train the agents for a fixed number of *episodes* for each experiment. An episode consists of placing the agent into a randomly generated, initial environment, and then allowing it to explore until it is captured or a threshold of 500 steps is reached. Each of our environments contains a 7x7 grid with approximately 15 obstacles, 3 enemy agents, and 10 rewards. We use three randomly-generated sequences of initial environments as a basis for the training episodes. We train 10 randomly initialized networks on each of the three sequences of environments; hence, we report the averaged results of 30 neural networks. We estimate the average total reinforcement (the average sum of the reinforcements received by the agent)[3] by freezing the network and measuring the average reinforcement on a testset of 100 randomly-generated environments.

We chose parameters for our Q-learning algorithm that are similar to those investigated by Lin (1992). The learning rate for the network is 0.15, with a discount factor of 0.9. To establish a baseline system, we experimented with various numbers of hidden units, settling on 15 since that number resulted in the best average reinforcement for the baseline system.

After choosing an initial network topology, we then spent time acting as a advisor to our system, observing the behavior of the agent at various times. Based on these observations, we wrote several collections of advice. For use in our experiments, we chose four sets of advice (see Appendix), two that use multi-step plans (referred to as *ElimEnemies* and *Surrounded*), and two that do not (*SimpleMoves* and *NonLocalMoves*).

Results and Discussion

For our first experiment, we evaluate the hypothesis that our system can in fact take advantage of advice. After 1000 episodes of initial learning, we measure the value of (independently) providing each of the four sets of advice. We train the system for 2000 episodes after adding the advice and then measure testset rein-

---

[3]We report the average total reinforcement rather than the average discounted reinforcement because this is the standard for the RL community. Graphs of the average *discounted* reward are qualitatively similar to those shown in the next section.

Table 2: Testset results for the baseline and the four different types of advice; each of the gains (over the baseline) in average total reinforcement for the four sets of advice is statistically significant at the $p < 0.01$ level (i.e., with 99% confidence).

Advice Added	Average Total Reinforcement
None (baseline)	1.32
SimpleMoves	1.92
NonLocalMoves	2.01
ElimEnemies	1.87
Surrounded	1.72

Table 3: Mean number of enemies captured, rewards collected, and number of actions taken for the experiments summarized in Table 2.

Advice Added	Enemies	Rewards	Survival Time
None (baseline)	0.15	3.09	32.7
SimpleMoves	0.28	3.79	39.6
NonLocalMoves	0.26	3.95	39.1
ElimEnemies	0.44	3.50	38.3
Surrounded	0.30	3.48	46.2

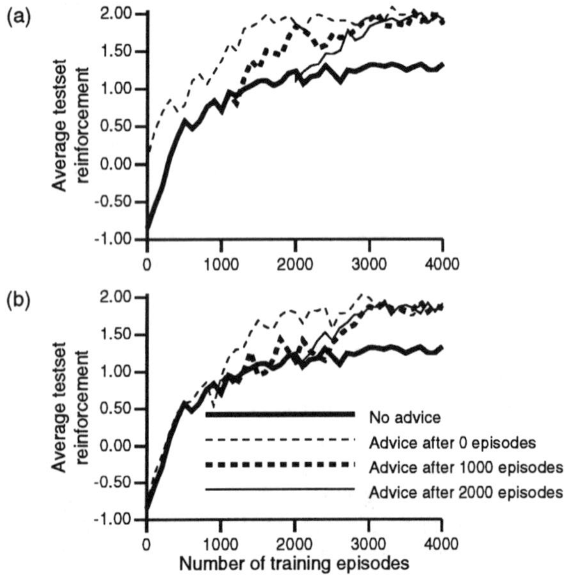

Figure 7: Testset results of (a) *SimpleMoves* and (b) *ElimEnemies* advice.

forcement. (The baseline is trained for 3000 episodes). Table 2 reports the average testset reinforcement; all gains over the baseline system are significant.

In our second experiment we investigate the hypothesis that the observer can beneficially provide advice at any time during training. To test this, we insert the four sets of advice at different points in training (after 0, 1000, and 2000 episodes). for the *SimpleMoves* and *ElimEnemies* advice respectively. These graphs indicate the learner does indeed converge to approximately the same expected reinforcement no matter when the advice is presented. It is also important to note that the effect of the advice may not be immediate – the agent may have to refine the advice over a number of training episodes. Results for the other pieces of advice are qualitatively similar to those shown in Figure 7.

Each of our pieces of advice addresses specific subtasks: collecting rewards (*SimpleMoves* and *NonLocalMoves*); eliminating enemies (*ElimEnemies*); and avoiding enemies, thus surviving longer (*SimpleMoves*, *NonLocalMoves*, and *Surrounded*). Hence, it is natural to ask how well each piece of advice meets its intent. Table 3 reports statistics on the components of the reinforcement. These statistics show that the pieces of advice do indeed lead to the expected improvements.

Future and Related Work

There are two tasks we intend to address in the near term. Our current experiments only demonstrate the value of giving a single piece of advice. We plan to empirically study the effect of providing multiple pieces of advice at different times during training. We also intend to evaluate the use of "replay" (i.e., periodic retraining on remembered pairs of states and reinforcements), a method that has been shown to greatly reduce the number of training examples needed to learn a policy function (Lin 1992).

There are a number of research efforts that are related to our work. Clouse and Utgoff (1992), Lin (1992), and Whitehead (1991) developed methods in which an advisor provides feedback to the learner – the advisor evaluates the chosen action or suggests an appropriate action. Lin (1993) also investigated a teaching method where the input to the RL system includes some of the previous input values. Thrun and Mitchell (1993) investigated RL agents that can make use of prior knowledge in the form of neural networks trained to predict the results of actions. These methods address the issue of reducing the number of training examples needed in RL; but, unlike our approach, they do not allow an observer to provide general advice.

Our work, which extends knowledge-based neural networks to a new task and shows that "domain theories" can be supplied piecemeal, is similar to our earlier work with the FSKBANN system (Maclin & Shavlik 1993). FSKBANN extended KBANN to deal with *state* units, but it does not create *new* state units.

Gordon and Subramanian (1994) developed a system similar to ours. Their agent accepts high-level advice of the form IF *conditions* THEN ACHIEVE *goal*. It operationalizes these rules using its background knowledge about goal achievement. The resulting rules are then incrementally refined using genetic algorithms, an alternate method for learning from the reinforcements an environment provides.

Finally, some additional research closely relates to our approach for instructing an agent. Nilsson (1994) developed a simple language for instructing robots, while Siegelman (1994) proposed, but has not yet evaluated, alternate techniques for converting programs expressed in a general-purpose, high-level language into recurrent neural networks.

Conclusions

We present an approach that allows an reinforcement learning agent to take advantage of suggestions provided by an external observer. The observer communicates advice using a simple programming language, one that does not require the observer to have any knowledge of the agent's internal workings. The advice is directly installed into a neural network that represents the agent's utility function, and then refined. Our experiments demonstrate the validity of this advice-taking approach.

Acknowledgements

We wish to thank C. Allex, M. Craven, D. Gordon, and S. Thrun for helpful comments on this paper.

Appendix – Four Sample Pieces of Advice

The four pieces of advice used in our experiments appear below. To make it easier to specify advice that applies in any direction, we defined the special term *dir*. During parsing, *dir* is expanded by replacing each rule containing it with four rules, one for each direction. Similarly we defined a set of four terms {*ahead, back, side1, side2*}. Any rule using these terms leads to *eight* rules – two for each case where *ahead* is East, North, West and South and *back* is appropriately set. There are two for each case of *ahead* and *back* because *side1* and *side2* can have two sets of values for a given value of *ahead* (e.g. if *ahead* is North, *side1* could be East and *side2* West, or vice-versa).

SimpleMoves

If An Obstacle is (NextTo ∧ *dir*) Then OkPush*dir*;
If No Obstacle is (NextTo ∧ *dir*) ∧ No Wall is (NextTo ∧ *dir*)
  Then OkMove*dir*;
If An Enemy is (Near ∧ ¬ *dir*) ∧ OkMove*dir* Then Move*dir*;
If A Reward is (Near ∧ *dir*) ∧ No Enemy is (Near ∧ *dir*) ∧
  OkMove*dir* Then Move*dir*;
If An Enemy is (Near ∧ *dir*) ∧ OkPush*dir* Then Push*dir*;

NonLocalMoves

If No Obstacle is (NextTo ∧ *dir*) ∧ No Wall is (NextTo ∧ *dir*)
  Then OkMove*dir*;
If Many Enemy are (¬ *dir*) ∧ No Enemy is (Near ∧ *dir*) ∧
  OkMove*dir* Then Move*dir*;
If An Enemy is (*dir* ∧ {Medium ∨ Far}) ∧ No Enemy is (*dir* ∧ Near)
  ∧ A Reward is (*dir* ∧ Near) ∧ OkMove*dir* Then Move*dir*;

ElimEnemies

If No Obstacle is (NextTo ∧ *dir*) ∧ No Wall is (NextTo ∧ *dir*)
  Then OkMove*dir*;
If An Enemy is (Near ∧ *back*) ∧ An Obstacle is (NextTo ∧ *side1*) ∧
  OkMove*ahead* Then MultiAction Move*ahead* Move*side1*
  Move*side1* Move*back* Push*side2* End;

Surrounded

If An Obstacle is (NextTo ∧ *dir*) Then OkPush*dir*;
If An Enemy is (Near ∧ *dir*) ∨ A Wall is (NextTo ∧ *dir*) ∨
  An Obstacle is (NextTo ∧ *dir*) Then Blocked*dir*;
If BlockedEast ∧ BlockedNorth ∧ BlockedSouth ∧ BlockedWest
  Then Surrounded;
When Surrounded ∧ OkPush*dir* ∧ An Enemy is Near
  Repeat Push*dir* Move*dir* Until ¬ OkPush*dir*;

References

Agre, P., & Chapman, D. 1987. Pengi: An implementation of a theory of activity. *AAAI-87*, 268–272.

Barto, A., Sutton, R., & Watkins, C. 1990. Learning and sequential decision making. In Gabriel, M., & Moore, J., eds., *Learning and Computational Neuroscience*. MIT Press.

Berenji, H., & Khedkar, P. 1992. Learning and tuning fuzzy logic controllers through reinforcements. *IEEE Trans. on Neural Networks* 3:724–740.

Clouse, J., & Utgoff, P. 1992. A teaching method for reinforcement learning. *Proc. 9th Intl. ML Conf.*, 92–101.

Cohen, P., & Feigenbaum, E. 1982. *The Handbook of Artificial Intelligence, Vol. 3*. William Kaufmann.

Gordon, D., & Subramanian, D. 1994. A multistrategy learning scheme for agent knowledge acquisition. *Informatica* 17:331–346.

Hayes-Roth, F., Klahr, P., & Mostow, D. J. 1981. Advice-taking and knowledge refinement: An iterative view of skill acquisition. In Anderson, J., ed., *Cognitive Skills and their Acquisition*. Lawrence Erlbaum.

Lin, L. 1992. Self-improving reactive agents based on reinforcement learning, planning, and teaching. *Machine Learning* 8:293–321.

Lin, L. 1993. Scaling up reinforcement learning for robot control. *Proc. 10th Intl. ML Conf.*, 182–189.

Maclin, R., & Shavlik, J. 1993. Using knowledge-based neural networks to improve algorithms. *Machine Learning* 11:195–215.

Maclin, R., & Shavlik, J. 1994. Incorporating advice into agents that learn from reinforcements. Technical Report 1227, CS Dept., Univ. of Wisconsin-Madison.

Mahadevan, S., & Connell, J. 1992. Automatic programming of behavior-based robots using reinforcement learning. *Artificial Intelligence* 55:311–365.

McCarthy, J. 1958. Programs with common sense. *Proc. Symp. on the Mech. of Thought Processes, Vol. 1*, 77–84.

Mostow, D. J. 1982. Transforming declarative advice into effective procedures: A heuristic search example. In Michalski, R., Carbonell, J., & Mitchell, T., eds., *Machine Learning: An AI Approach, Vol. 1*. Tioga Press.

Nilsson, N. 1994. Teleo-reactive programs for agent control. *J. of Artificial Intelligence Research* 1:139–158.

Siegelmann, H. 1994. Neural programming language. *AAAI-94*, this volume.

Sutton, R. 1988. Learning to predict by the methods of temporal differences. *Machine Learning* 3:9–44.

Sutton, R. 1991. Reinforcement learning architectures for animats. In Meyer, J., & Wilson, S., eds., *From Animals to Animats*. MIT Press.

Tesauro, G. 1992. Practical issues in temporal difference learning. *Machine Learning* 8:257–277.

Thrun, S., & Mitchell, T. 1993. Integrating inductive neural network learning and explanation-based learning. *IJCAI-93*, 930–936.

Towell, G., Shavlik, J., & Noordewier, M. 1990. Refinement of approximate domain theories by knowledge-based neural networks. *AAAI-90*, 861–866.

Watkins, C. 1989. *Learning from Delayed Rewards*. Ph.D. Dissertation, King's College, Cambridge.

Whitehead, S. 1991. A complexity analysis of cooperative mechanisms in reinforcement learning. *AAAI-91*, 607–613.

Reinforcement Learning Algorithms
for Average-Payoff Markovian Decision Processes

Satinder P. Singh
Department of Brain and Cognitive Sciences
Massachusetts Institute of Technology
Cambridge, MA 02139
singh@psyche.mit.edu

Abstract

Reinforcement learning (RL) has become a central paradigm for solving learning-control problems in robotics and artificial intelligence. RL researchers have focussed almost exclusively on problems where the controller has to maximize the *discounted* sum of payoffs. However, as emphasized by Schwartz (1993), in many problems, e.g., those for which the optimal behavior is a limit cycle, it is more natural and computationally advantageous to formulate tasks so that the controller's objective is to maximize the average payoff received per time step. In this paper I derive *new average-payoff* RL algorithms as stochastic approximation methods for solving the system of equations associated with the *policy evaluation* and *optimal control* questions in average-payoff RL tasks. These algorithms are analogous to the popular TD and Q-learning algorithms already developed for the discounted-payoff case. One of the algorithms derived here is a significant variation of Schwartz's R-learning algorithm. Preliminary empirical results are presented to validate these new algorithms.

Introduction

Reinforcement learning has become a central paradigm for solving problems involving agents controlling external environments by executing actions. Previous work on reinforcement learning (e.g., Barto, Bradtke, & Singh to appear) (RL) has focused almost exclusively on developing algorithms for maximizing the discounted sum of payoffs received by the agent. Discounting future payoffs makes perfect sense in some applications, e.g., those dealing with economics, where the distant future is indeed less important than the near future, which in turn is less important than the immediate present. As recently noted by Schwartz (1993), in many other applications, however, all time periods are equally important, e.g., foraging, queuing theory problems, and problems where the optimal trajectory is a limit cycle. A natural measure of performance in such *undiscounted* applications is the *average payoff per time step* received by the agent (e.g., Bertsekas 1987). For problems where either the discounted-payoff or the average-payoff formulations can be used,

often there are strong computational reasons to prefer the average-payoff formulation (see Schwartz 1993, for a recent discussion).

Recently, Jaakkola, Jordan, & Singh (to appear) have developed a fairly complete mathematical understanding of discounted-payoff RL algorithms as stochastic approximation methods for solving the system of Bellman (1957) equations associated with discounted-payoff Markovian decision processes (MDPs) (also see Tsitsiklis 1993). In this paper, I develop average-payoff RL algorithms by deriving stochastic approximation methods for solving the analogous Bellman equations for MDPs in which the measure to be optimized is the average payoff per time step. These algorithms for the average-payoff case are analogous to the popular temporal differences (Barto, Sutton, & Anderson 1983; Sutton 1988) (TD) and Q-learning (Watkins 1989; Watkins & Dayan 1992) algorithms for the discounted-payoff case. One of the four algorithms derived here using the formal stochastic approximation perspective is a significant variation of the R-learning algorithm developed recently by Schwartz (1993), who initiated the interest in average-payoff RL, but whose derivation was more heuristic. I also present preliminary empirical results on a test set of artificial MDPs.

Average-Payoff Reinforcement Learning

A large variety of sequential embedded-agent tasks of interest to AI researchers can be formulated as MDPs which are a class of discrete-time optimal control tasks. At each time step the agent senses the state of the environment, executes an action, and receives a payoff in return. The action executed by the agent along with some unmodeled disturbances, or noise, stochastically determine the state of the environment at the next time step. The actions the agent executes constitute its control policy. The task for the learning agent is to determine a control policy that maximizes some predefined cumulative measure of the payoffs received by the agent over a given time horizon.

Notation: Let S be the set of states, let $P_{xy}(a)$ denote the probability of transition from state x to state y

on executing action a, and let $R(x, a)$ be the payoff received on executing action a in state x. Further, let $A(x)$ be the set of actions available in state x, and let x_t, a_t, and R_t represent the state, the action taken, and the payoff at time step t. A stationary closed-loop control policy $\pi : S \rightarrow A$ assigns an action to each state. For MDPs there always exists an optimal stationary deterministic policy and therefore one only needs to consider such policies.

In discounted-payoff MDPs the *return* for, or *value* of a fixed policy π when the starting state of the environment is x is as follows: $V^\pi(x) = E^\pi\{\sum_{t=0}^\infty \gamma^t R_t | x_0 = x\}$, where $0 \leq \gamma < 1$ is a discount factor, and E^π is the expectation symbol under the assumption that policy π is executed forever. In average-payoff MDPs the average payoff per time step for a fixed policy π when the starting state of the environment is x is as follows: $\rho^\pi(x) = \lim_{N \to \infty} E^\pi\{\frac{\sum_{t=0}^N R_t}{N}\}$. Bertsekas (1987) shows that $\rho^\pi(x) = \rho^\pi(y)$ for all $x, y \in S$ under the assumption that the Markov chain for policy π is ergodic.

Assumption: For the rest of this paper, I am going to assume, just as in the classical average-payoff (AP) dynamic programming (DP) literature, that the MDP is ergodic for all stationary policies. Under that assumption the average payoff is always independent of the start state. The average payoff for policy π will be denoted ρ^π, and the optimal average payoff will be denoted ρ^*.

The quantity $E^\pi\{\sum_{t=0}^\infty (R_t - \rho^\pi) | x_0 = x\}$ is called the *relative* value of state x and is denoted $V^\pi(x)$ because it plays a role analogous to the role the value function plays in discounted-payoff MDPs. It is called a relative value because

$$V^\pi(x) - V^\pi(y) = E^\pi\{\sum_{t=0}^\infty R_t | x_0 = x\}$$

$$-E^\pi\{\sum_{t=0}^\infty R_t | x_0 = y\},$$

may be seen as the long-term difference in the total payoff (not average payoff per time step) due to starting at state x rather than state y.

Reinforcement Learning as stochastic approximation

RL algorithms are iterative, asynchronous. stochastic approximation algorithms that use the state transition and payoff that occur at each time step to update the estimated relative value function and the estimated average-payoff. Both RL and asynchronous (on-line) DP take the following general form:

$$V_{t+1}(x_t) = (1 - \alpha_t(x_t))V_t(x_t)$$
$$+\alpha_t(x_t)(B(V_t)(x_t) - \rho_t) \quad (1)$$

where t is the time index, $\alpha_t(x_t)$ is a learning rate constant, and ρ_t is the estimated average payoff, and V_t is

the estimated relative value function. The only difference between Equation 1 and the corresponding equation for the discounted-payoff case is that the average payoff, ρ_t, is subtracted out on the RHS to form the new estimate. In DP the operator $B(V)(x)$ is deterministic and involves computing the expected relative value of all one-step neighbors of state x. I will obtain RL algorithms by replacing the deterministic backup operator B in classical DP algorithms (see Equation 1) by a random operator $\mathcal{B}$ that merely samples a single next state. This is necessary in RL algorithms because the real-environment only makes a stochastic transition to a single next state, and RL algorithms do not assume an environment model that can be used to lookup all the other possible next states. The relationship to stochastic approximation is in the following fact: $E\{\mathcal{B}\} = B$ (see Singh 1993 for an explanation).

Policy Evaluation

Policy evaluation involves determining the average payoff and the relative values for a fixed policy π. Strictly speaking, policy evaluation is a prediction problem and not a RL problem. However, because many RL architectures are based on policy evaluation (e.g., Barto, Sutton, & Anderson 1983), I will first develop average-case policy evaluation algorithms. Using the Markov assumption it can be shown that ρ^π and V^π are solutions to the following systems of linear equations:

Policy evaluation equations for the average-payoff case (e.g., Bertsekas 1987)

$$\rho + V(x) = R(x, \pi(x)) + \sum_{y \in S} P_{xy}(\pi(x))V(y), \quad (2)$$

where to get a unique solution, we set $V(r) = 0$, for some arbitrarily chosen reference state $r \in S$. This is needed because there are $|S| + 1$ unknowns and only $|S|$ equations. Note, that from Equation 2, $\forall x \in S$,

$$\rho^\pi = R(x, \pi(x)) + \sum_{y \in S} P_{xy}(\pi(x))V^\pi(y)$$
$$-V^\pi(x) \quad (3)$$

Define a deterministic operator:
$B_\pi(V)(x) = R(x, \pi(x)) + \sum_{y \in S} P_{xy}(\pi(x))V(y)$.
Asynchronous version of Classical DP (AP) algorithm:

$$V_{t+1}(x_t) = B_\pi(V_t)(x_t) - \rho_t$$
$$\rho_{t+1} = B_\pi(V_t)(x_t) - V_t(x_t)$$

where $\forall y \neq x_t$, $V_{t+1}(y) = V_t(y)$.
Reinforcement Learning Algorithms for (AP) Policy Evaluation:

Define the random operator $\mathcal{B}_\pi(V_t)(x_t) = R(x_t, \pi(x_t)) + V_t(x_{t+1})$, where the next state, x_{t+1}, is chosen from the probability distribution $P_{x_t x_{t+1}}(\pi(x_t))$. Note that $E\{\mathcal{B}_\pi(V)\} = B_\pi(V)$.

Algorithm 1:

$$
\begin{aligned}
V_{t+1}(x_t) &= (1-\alpha_t(x_t))V_t(x_t) \\
&\quad +\alpha_t(x_t)(\mathcal{B}_\pi(V_t)(x_t)-\rho_t) \\
&= (1-\alpha_t(x_t))V_t(x_t) \\
&\quad +\alpha_t(x_t)(R(x_t,\pi(x_t))+V_t(x_{t+1})-\rho_t)
\end{aligned}
$$

where $\rho_0 = 0$, and

$$
\rho_{t+1} = (1-\beta_t)\rho_t + \beta_t[\mathcal{B}_\pi(V_t)(x_t)-V_t(x_t)].
$$

Algorithm 2:

$$
\begin{aligned}
V_{t+1}(x_t) &= (1-\alpha_t(x_t))V_t(x_t) \\
&\quad +\alpha_t(x_t)(\mathcal{B}_\pi(V_t)(x_t)-\rho_t) \\
&= (1-\alpha_t(x_t))V_t(x_t) \\
&\quad +\alpha_t(x_t)(R(x_t,\pi(x_t))+V_t(x_{t+1})-\rho_t) \\
\rho_{t+1} &= \frac{(t*\rho_t)+R(x_t,\pi(x_t))}{t+1}
\end{aligned}
$$

where for both Algorithms 1 and 2; $\forall y \neq x_t$, $V_{t+1}(y) = V_t(y)$, and $\forall t$, $V_t(r) = 0$. Note that the difference between Algorithms 1 and 2 is in the estimation of the average payoff: Algorithm 1 estimates it using Equation 3 while Algorithm 2 estimates it as the sample average of the payoffs. Algorithm 1 corresponds closely to Sutton's TD(0) algorithm for policy evaluation in discounted-payoff MDPs.

Optimal Control

In this section I present algorithms to find optimal policies, π^*, for average-payoff MDPs. As in the discounted-payoff case, we have to use the Q-notation of Watkins (1989) to develop RL algorithms for the average-payoff case optimal control question. Again, as in classical DP, we will assume that the average payoff is independent of the starting state-action pair for all stationary policies. The average payoff for the optimal policy is denoted ρ^* and the relative Q-values are denoted Q^*, and they are solutions to the following system of nonlinear equations:

Bellman equations in the Q-notation:

$$
\rho^* + Q(x,a) = R(x,a) + \sum_{y \in S} P_{xy}(a)\left[\max_{a' \in A(y)} Q(y,a')\right],
$$

where the optimal action in state x can be derived as follows:

$$
\pi^*(x) = \operatorname{argmax}_{a \in A(x)} Q^*(x,a).
$$

In Q-notation: $\forall i \in S,\ a \in A$,

$$
\begin{aligned}
\rho^* &= R(i,a) + \sum_{j \in S} P_{ij}(a)\left[\max_{a' \in A(j)} Q^*(j,a')\right] \\
&\quad - Q^*(i,a) \qquad (4)
\end{aligned}
$$

Define the deterministic operator $B(Q)(x_t,a_t) = R(x_t,a_t) + \sum_{y \in S} P_{x_ty}(a_t)\max_{a' \in A(y)} Q(y,a')$.

Classical Asynchronous Dynamic Programming Algorithm (AP):

$$
\begin{aligned}
Q_{t+1}(x_t,a_t) &= B(Q_t)(x_t,a_t) - \rho_t & (5) \\
\rho_{t+1} &= B(Q_t)(x_t,a_t) - Q_t(x_t,a_t), & (6)
\end{aligned}
$$

where $\rho_0 = 0.0$. The above equation is an asynchronous version of the synchronous algorithm developed in Bertsekas (1987). Jalali and Ferguson (1990) have developed asynchronous DP algorithms that estimate the transition probabilities on-line, but are otherwise similar to the algorithm presented in the above equation.

Reinforcement Learning for (AP) Optimal Control:

Define the random operator $\mathcal{B}(Q)(x_t,a_t) = R(x_t,a_t) + \max_{a' \in A(x_{t+1})} Q(x_{t+1},a')$, where the next state, x_{t+1}, is chosen with probability $P_{x_t x_{t+1}}(a_t)$. Note that $E\{\mathcal{B}(Q)\} = B(Q)$.

Algorithm 3. (A significant variation to Schwartz's R-learning)

$$
\begin{aligned}
Q_{t+1}(x_t,a_t) &= (1-\alpha_t(x_t,a_t))Q_t(x_t,a_t) \\
&\quad +\alpha_t(x_t,a_t)(\mathcal{B}(Q_t)(x_t,a_t)-\rho_t) \\
&= (1-\alpha_t(x_t,a_t))Q_t(x_t,a_t) \\
&\quad +\alpha_t(x_t,a_t)[R(x_t,a_t) \\
&\quad + \max_{a' \in A(x_{t+1})} Q_t(x_{t+1},a')-\rho_t] \\
\rho_{t+1} &= (1-\beta_t)\rho_t + \beta_t(\mathcal{B}(Q_t)(x_t,a_t) \\
&\quad -Q_t(x_t,a_t)) \qquad (7)
\end{aligned}
$$

The difference between Algorithm 3 and R-learning is that in R-learning the estimated average payoff is updated only when the greedy action is executed, while in Algorithm 3 the average payoff is updated with every action. This suggests that Algorithm 3 could be more efficient than R-learning since R-learning seems to waste information whenever a non-greedy action is taken, which is quite often, especially in the beginning when the agent is exploring heavily. Updating ρ with every action makes sense because the optimal average payoff, ρ^*, satisfies Equation 4 for every state-action pair, and not just for the optimal action in each state. This change from R-learning is a direct result of the systematic derivation of RL from classical DP undertaken in this paper.

A further difference resulting from the approach taken here is that, just as in classical DP (e.g., Bertsekas 1987), I am proposing that the value of an arbitrarily chosen reference state-action pair be grounded to a constant value of zero — Schwartz's R-learning does not do that. A possible disadvantage of not grounding one state-action pair's Q-value to zero is that the relative Q-values could become very large.

Algorithm 4.

$$
\begin{aligned}
Q_{t+1}(x_t,a_t) &= (1-\alpha(x_t,a_t))Q_t(x_t,a_t) \\
&\quad +\alpha(x_t,a_t)(\mathcal{B}(Q_t)(x_t,a_t)-\rho_t)
\end{aligned}
$$

$$
\begin{aligned}
= \; & (1 - \alpha(x_t, a_t))Q_t(x_t, a_t) \\
& + \alpha(x_t, a_t)[R(x_t, a_t) \\
& + \max_{a' \in A(x_{t+1})} Q_t(x_{t+1}, a') - \rho_t].
\end{aligned}
$$

Let t_g be the number of times the *greedy* action has been chosen in t time steps.
If $(t+1)_g - t_g \neq 0$

$$
\rho_{t+1} = \frac{(\rho_t * t_g) + R(x_t, a_t)}{(t+1)_g}
$$

else, $\rho_{t+1} = \rho_t$. Note that the only difference between Algorithms 3 and 4 is in the way the average payoff is estimated; Algorithm 3 estimates it using Equation 4 while Algorithm 4 estimates it as the sample average of the payoffs received for greedy actions. As in Q-learning it is required that the Q-value of every state-action pair is updated infinitely often.

Preliminary Empirical Results

We tested Algorithms 1 through 4 on MDPs with randomly constructed transition matrices and payoff matrix. Figures 1 and 2 show the learning curves for a 20 state and 5 action problem, and Figures 3 and 4 show the learning curves for a 100 state and 10 action problem. The x-axis of all the graphs shows the number of states visited, while the y-axis shows the total error in the relative value function relative to the correct value function (V^π in the case of policy evaluation, and Q^* for optimal control). Each graph is obtained by averaging the results of 10 different runs with different random number seeds. The simulation results presented here are preliminary and are just intended to show that on the particular problems tried by the author all the four algorithms learned good approximations to the desired relative (Q-) value functions. See Figure captions for further details about the simulations.

Conclusion

The main contribution of this work is in the use of the stochastic approximation framework to develop *new* average-payoff RL algorithms to solve the policy evaluation and the optimal control questions for Markovian decision tasks. This is of substantial interest because for many embedded-agent problems, especially those in which the optimal behavior is a limit cycle, formulating them as average-payoff MDPs has many practical advantages over formulating them as discounted-payoff MDPs. Further, this paper also relates the important work begun by Schwartz on average-payoff RL to what is already known in the discounted-payoff literature by deriving R-learning and other new algorithms in the same manner as TD and Q-learning would be derived today; and it also better relates R-learning to what is already known in the classical control literature about average-payoff DP.

It is also hoped that explicit derivation as stochastic approximation methods will allow convergence results for these algorithms, just as for TD and Q-learning.[1]

Acknowledgements

I thank Anton Schwartz and the anonymous reviewers for extensive and helpful comments. This project was supported by grant ECS-9214866 from the National Science Foundation to Prof. A. G. Barto, and by a grant from Siemens Corporation to Prof. M. I. Jordan.

References

Barto, A.G.; Sutton, R.S.; and Anderson, C.W. 1983. Neuronlike elements that can solve difficult learning control problems. *IEEE SMC* 13:835–846.

Barto, A.G.; Bradtke, S.J.; and Singh, S.P. to appear. Learning to act using real-time dynamic programming. *Artificial Intelligence*.

Bellman, R.E. 1957. *Dynamic Programming*. Princeton University Press, Princeton, NJ.

Bertsekas, D.P. 1982. Distributed dynamic programming. *IEEE Transactions on Automatic Control* 27:610–616.

Bertsekas, D.P. 1987. *Dynamic Programming: Deterministic and Stochastic Models*. Prentice-Hall, Englewood Cliffs, NJ.

Jaakkola, T.; Jordan, M.I.; and Singh, S.P. to appear. Stochastic convergence of iterative DP algorithms. *Neural Computation*.

Jalali, A. and Ferguson, M. 1990. Adaptive control of markov chains with local updates. *Systems & Control Letters* 14:209–218.

Schwartz, A. 1993. A reinforcement learning method for maximizing undiscounted rewards. In *Proceedings of the Tenth Machine Learning Conference*.

Singh, S. P. 1993. *Learning to Solve Markovian Decision Processes*. Ph.D. Dissertation, Department of Computer Science, University of Massachusetts. also, CMPSCI Technical Report 93-77.

Sutton, R.S. 1988. Learning to predict by the methods of temporal differences. *Machine Learning* 3:9–44.

Tsitsiklis, J. 1993. Asynchronous stochastic approximation and Q-learning. Submitted.

Watkins, C.J.C.H. and Dayan, P. 1992. Q-learning. *Machine Learning* 8(3/4):279–292.

Watkins, C.J.C.H. 1989. *Learning from Delayed Rewards*. Ph.D. Dissertation, Cambridge Univ., Cambridge, England.

---

[1] I have recently become aware that there is a published counterexample to the convergence of the asynchronous DP algorithm given by Equation 6 (Bertsekas 1982). However, unlike Equation 6, Algorithms 3 and 4 use a relaxation process, and that difference may be crucial in allowing a convergence proof.

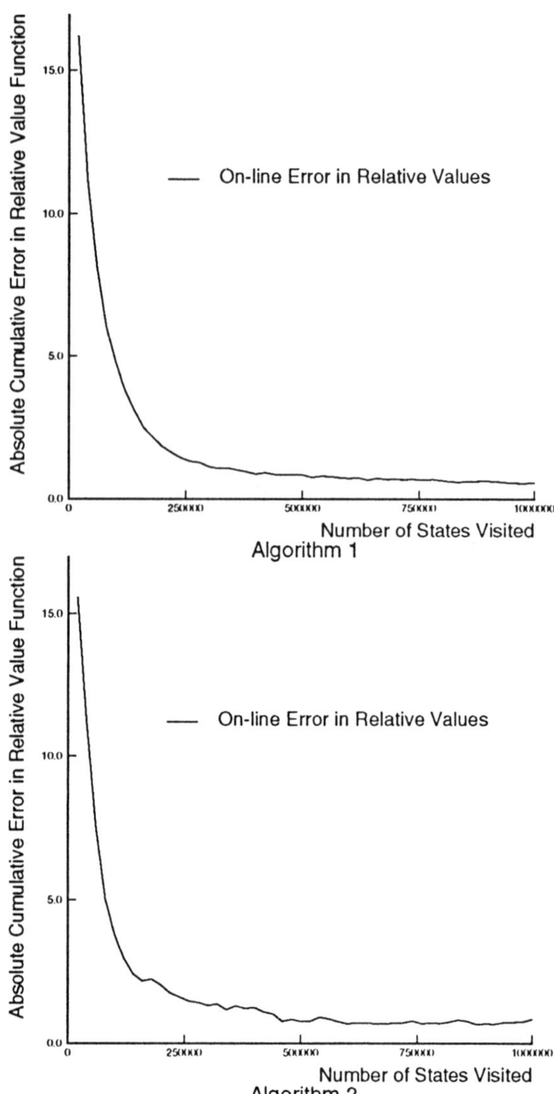

Figure 1: Simulation results for Markov chains with 20 states. The upper graph presents for Algorithm 1 the absolute error in the relative value function, summed over all the 20 states, as a function of the number of state-updates. The results presented are averages over ten Markov chains generated with different random number seeds. The transition probabilities and payoff function were chosen randomly. For each Markov chain the start state and the initial value function were chosen randomly. The bottom graph presents results averaged over the same ten Markov chains for Algorithm 2.

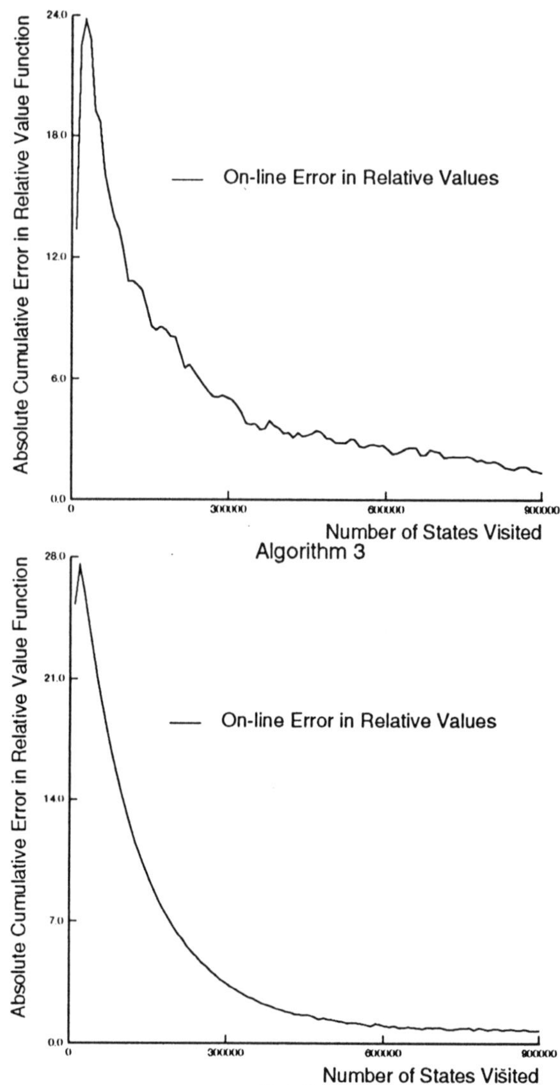

Figure 2: Simulation results for MDPs with 20 states, and 5 actions. The upper graph presents for Algorithm 3 the absolute error in the relative Q-value function, summed over all the 20 states, as a function of the number of state-updates. The results presented are averages over ten MDPs generated with different random number seeds. The transition probabilities and payoff function for the MDPs were chosen randomly. For each MDP the start state and the initial Q-value function were chosen randomly. The Boltzman distribution was used to determine the exploration strategy, i.e., $Prob(a|t) = \dfrac{e^{\frac{1}{T}Q_t(x_t,a)}}{\sum_{b \in A(x_t)} e^{\frac{1}{T}Q_t(x_t,b)}}$, where $Prob(a|t)$ is the probability of taking action a at time t. The temperature T was decreased slowly. The bottom graph presents results averaged over the same ten MDPs for Algorithm 4.

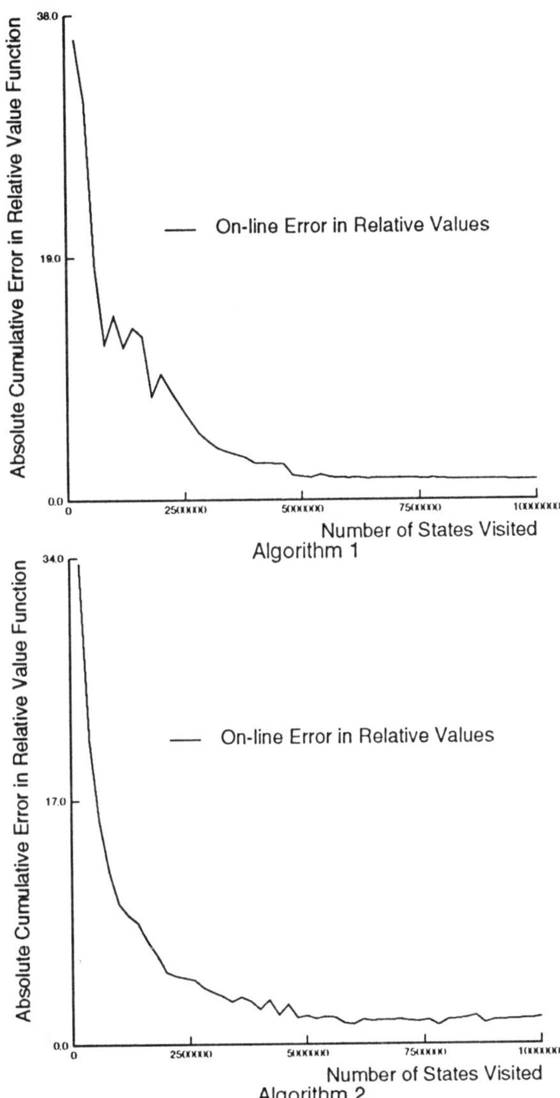

Figure 3: Simulation results for Markov chains with 100 states. The upper graph presents for Algorithm 1 the absolute error in the relative value function, summed over all the 100 states, as a function of the number of state-updates. The results presented are averages over ten Markov chains generated with different random number seeds. The transition probabilities and payoff function were chosen randomly. For each Markov chain the start state and the initial value function were chosen randomly. The bottom graph presents results averaged over the same ten Markov chains for Algorithm 2.

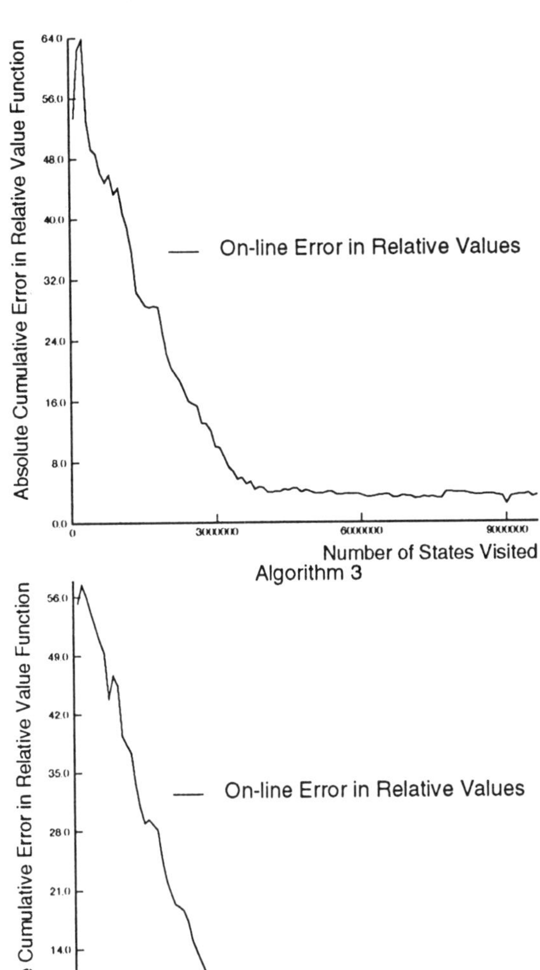

Figure 4: Simulation results for MDPs with 100 states, and 10 actions. The upper graph presents for Algorithm 3 the absolute error in the relative Q-value function, summed over all the 100 states, as a function of the number of state-updates. The results presented are averages over ten MDPs generated with different random number seeds. The transition probabilities and payoff function for the MDPs were chosen randomly. For each MDP the start state and the initial Q-value function were chosen randomly. The Boltzman distribution was used to determine the exploration strategy, i.e., $Prob(a|t) = \dfrac{e^{\frac{1}{T}Q_t(x_t,a)}}{\sum_{b \in A(x_t)} e^{\frac{1}{T}Q_t(x_t,b)}}$, where $Prob(a|t)$ is the probability of taking action a at time t. The temperature T was decreased slowly. The bottom graph presents results averaged over the same ten MDPs for Algorithm 4.

Meta AI

Using Knowledge Acquisition and Representation Tools to Support Scientific Communities

Brian R Gaines and Mildred L G Shaw

Knowledge Science Institute
University of Calgary
Calgary, Alberta, Canada T2N 1N4
{gaines, mildred}@cpsc.ucalgary.ca

Abstract

Widespread access to the Internet has led to the formation of geographically dispersed scientific communities collaborating through the network. The tools supporting such collaboration currently are based primarily on electronic mail through mailing list servers, and access to archives of research reports through ftp, gopher and world wide web. However, electronic communication can support the knowledge processes of scientific communities more directly through overtly represented knowledge structures. This paper describes some experiments in the use of knowledge acquisition (KA) and representation (KR) tools to define and analyze major policy and technical issues in an international research community responsible for one of the test cases in the Intelligent Manufacturing Systems (IMS) research program. It is concluded that distributed knowledge support systems in routine use by world-class scientific communities collaborating through the Internet will provide a major impetus to artificial intelligence research.

Introduction

Sociologists of science have characterized scientific communities as forming *invisible colleges* which monitor and manage the changing structure of knowledge in their domain [Crane 1972]. Individuals playing major roles in these communities are experts not only in overt knowledge of the domain but also through skills in its management and development. Sociologists and philosophers of science have undertaken empirical studies to elicit and model such expertise [Merton 1973; Blume 1974; Cole 1992], and, in recent years, have begun to use artificial intelligence concepts and methodologies in such studies [Collins 1990; Thagard 1992]. Studies have been described in which knowledge acquisition and representation methodologies and tools have been used to elicit and model conceptual structures in scientific communities [Gaines and Shaw 1989]. In the 1990s major scientific communities are beginning to use communication through the Internet as a

major channel for scientific discourse [Landow and Delany 1993], and it has become feasible to make KA and KR methodologies and tools routinely available. The conjecture is that the discourse will be improved by more overt representation of the underlying knowledge structures resulting in the systematic acceleration of the scientific research. Improved communication and information management tools should also make it easier to manage the large-scale international collaborative research projects now being supported through the Internet.

This paper reports some studies of the application of knowledge acquisition and representation tools that are in routine use in expert system applications to the analysis of the knowledge processes of a scientific community. The project studied is IMS TC7 'GNOSIS', one of 6 one-year test cases under the international Intelligent Manufacturing Systems research program which started in the second quarter of 1993. The project [GNOSIS 1994] involves over 100 participants in 31 industry and university organizations in 14 countries, with the objective of developing a *post mass production manufacturing paradigm* involving *reconfigurable artifacts*. The project has made extensive use of electronic mail and electronic document archives to coordinate its activities, and the studies reported are part of an investigation to improve such coordination in the main 10-year study commencing in 1994.

The studies have used a wide range of KA and KR tools ranging from hypermedia to manage heterogeneous knowledge sources, through text-analysis of conceptual associations, concept mapping for knowledge visualization, repertory grid and induction tools to develop structures from the knowledge sources, to semantic network, knowledge representation and inference tools to support formal representation and reasoning using the knowledge structures. The objective of the studies has been to determine whether KA and KR tools can play a useful role in supporting the intellectual management of the research program. In particular, one focus has been to reconstruct the knowledge processes that resulted in the mission statement developed for the GNOSIS funding application, since this has determined the primary research activities, groupings and basis for evaluation. It has also been a major topic for critical analysis as the community prepares its long-term research program for the next decade.

We thank colleagues in GNOSIS, particularly Martti Mäntylä, Doug Norrie, Tetsuo Tomiyama and Moriki Toyama.

Text Analysis of IMS Research Objectives

Hypermedia tools have proved effective in managing the diverse forms of knowledge collected in KA, and in linking this to derived knowledge structures both for system development and for user explanation [Gaines and Shaw 1992] The hypermedia components of the KA tools were used to manage some of the knowledge flows in the early GNOSIS meetings when short intensive workshops were held with 20-30 participants where research capabilities were described, sub-goals developed and tasks allocated. For example, some 27 papers exchanged and presentations given at a workshop in Tokyo in mid-March 1993 were digitized through OCR after the meeting and made available by the end of March as a 300-page conference volume in a uniform style [GNOSIS 1993]. A CD-ROM version also contains embedded QuickTime videos of a laboratory presentation and software demonstrations.

The availability of this material in digital form within the KA system made it possible to use text analysis tools to analyze the conceptual structures of the papers. Figure 1 shows a concept map generated automatically through analysis of the co-occurrence of words in sentences, a technique commonly used in information retrieval systems [Callon, Law and Rip 1986]. The document analyzed is one on *The Technical Concept of IMS* [Tomiyama 1992] that played a major role in the design of the research program. The document is treated as a set of entities which are sentences whose features are the words they contain. Rules are derived using empirical induction in which the premise is that if one word occurs in a sentence then the conclusion is that another will occur. The graph shows the links from premises to conclusions derived in this way. The tool is interactive and, as shown at the top center, provides access through a popup menu associated with each word to a list of occurrences of that word in context, and to the original document.

The initial output was a digraph consisting of one major connected component and some minor ones which correspond to significant topics such as intellectual property rights that did not directly relate to the socio-technical issues. The user noted that the major component itself consisted of 3 loosely connected sub-components, and added the context boxes shown to distinguish and name these parts. The significance of these parts is that they correspond to 3 of the 5 technical work packages (TW's) of the research program. What is particularly significant is the missing work packages, TW2 concerned with product configuration management systems, and TW3 concerned with configurable production systems. These were added to the GNOSIS research program during its formation through amalgamation of interests with other potential proponents of IMS test cases. These packages link technically to the knowledge systematization activities on the left of Figure 1 but are neutral to the major issues of the IMS program on the right.

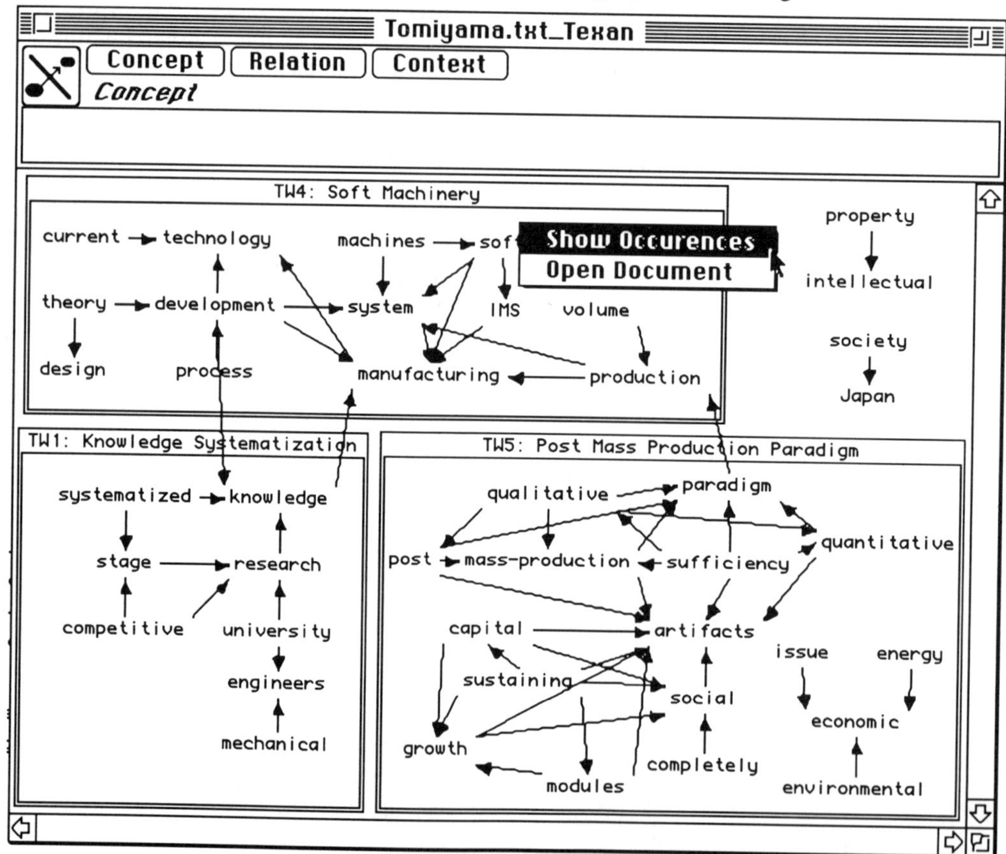

Figure 1 Analysis of paper describing objectives of IMS program

Concept Map of Mission Statement

Analyses like that of Figure 1 was used to develop concept maps clarifying relations between work packages. Concept mapping is another KA technique used in the initial stages of system development to structure the domain and task. It has been widely used in educational studies to elicit the changing conceptual structures of students as they interact with the educational system [Novak and Gowin 1984; Lambiotte, Dansereau, Cross and Reynolds 1989].

Concept maps are sorted directed graphs in which nodes have types and labels. Many concept mapping systems resemble early semantic networks [Quillian 1968] in having imprecise semantics, and there is a continuum between concept maps and the precise visual languages used to define knowledge bases. For example, Toulmin's [1958] analysis of scientific arguments can be given precise semantics [Cavalli-Sforza, Gabrys, Lesgold and Weiner 1992], and *Coreview* [Wan and Johnson 1992] prescribes a well-defined set of ontological primitives.

Figure 2 shows the *mission statement* of the GNOSIS project as a concept map. This concise statement of the project objectives was taken from the introduction to the legal agreement signed by all participants, and much effort went into its formulation. The upper right part of the map is concerned with the *post mass production paradigm* studies (TW5) that show up on the lower right of Figure 1.

The pivotal role of *knowledge systematization* studies (TW1) shows as linking TW5 to *configurable production systems* (TW3) and to *soft machines* studies (TW4). Studies of *configuration management systems* (TW2) are visible only in the nodes *product configuration* and *configurable products*. In practice, TW2 took off more slowly than the other work packages, and the analysis of the project documents tends to indicate that the objectives for this work package were not as clearly formulated or integrated into the overall project as for the other work packages. Examination of Figures 1 and 2 also suggests that there is a gap that needs filling between the very high level socio-economic goals of the IMS program and the very specific technical objectives of the work packages other than TW5.

The popup menu on the right shows the user opening a document on environment issues through the access provided by the concept map environment.

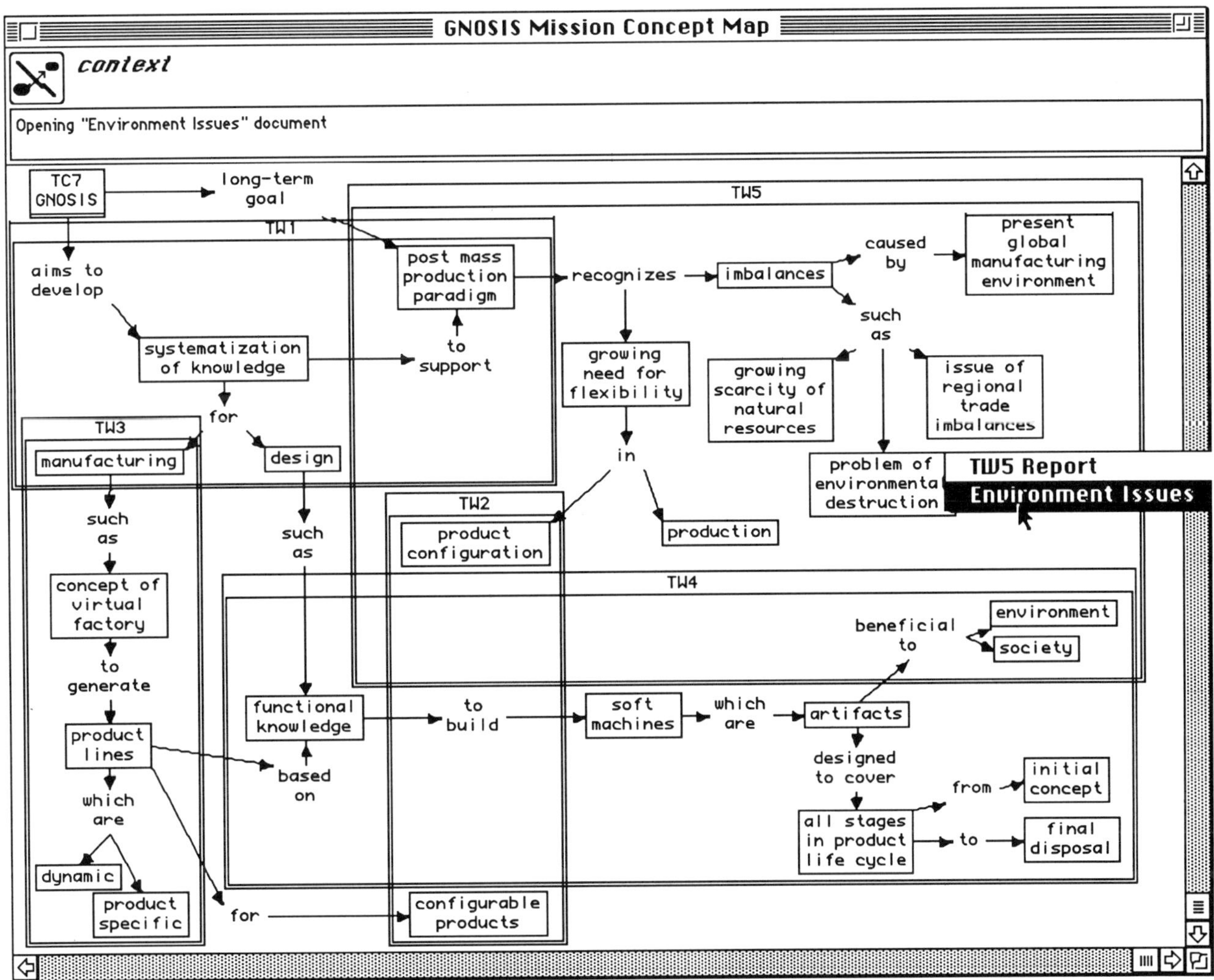

Figure 2 Concept map of GNOSIS mission statement

Repertory Grid Analysis of Soft Machines

One problem for GNOSIS has been the presentation of the project objectives and activities to funding and reviews agencies concerned with the international and national programs. There was a common theme of *reconfigurable systems* in the three major technical work packages, but it became clear that this was inadequately projected in the project documents. In preparation for a major review meeting in June 1993 an analysis was made of the *soft machine* concept using a KA technique derived from personal construct psychology [Kelly 1955], that of *repertory grid elicitation* [Gaines and Shaw 1980; Boose 1984; Gaines and Shaw 1993a].

The repertory grid is used in knowledge elicitation when an expert finds it easier to provide exemplary cases rather than develop a knowledge structure directly. The technique elicits the significant distinctions between cases all the time feeding back matches between cases to elicit new distinctions, and matches between distinctions to elicit new cases. The resultant grid is clustered to feed back to the expert the overall conceptual structure for validation, and rules may be induced from the comparatively small dataset which are usually meaningful because the feedback has eliminated spurious correlations. The grid and rules can be exported as a knowledge base covering the specific domain characterized by the cases [Gaines and Shaw 1993b].

Six major GNOSIS sub-projects were used as initial elements, and the ensuing repertory grid elicitation process resulted in the addition of another 10 elements, including human operators and organizational structures that provided contrasts to some aspects of the technological projects. Eleven distinctions were elicited that provided detailed insights into the complexity of the notion of reconfigurability, and these were presented on viewfoils to the review body to explain the roles of the GNOSIS projects and the relations between them relevant to issues of soft machinery.

Figure 3 shows the grid clustered through a principal components analysis to bring together similar distinctions and similar elements, and to show the relationships between them. It shows, for example, that some past distinctions in manufacturing are no longer as critical as they used to be—the *hardware—software* distinction did not characterize other distinctions—GNOSIS treats software manufacturing and hardware manufacturing alike. The main dimensions apparent are those typified by *system reconfigures itself—user reconfigures system* and that of *human intelligence—machine intelligence*. The IMS projects are on the machine intelligence side of the second dimension and cluster into two groups on the first, those concerned with self-reconfiguring systems and those concerned with user-reconfiguring systems.

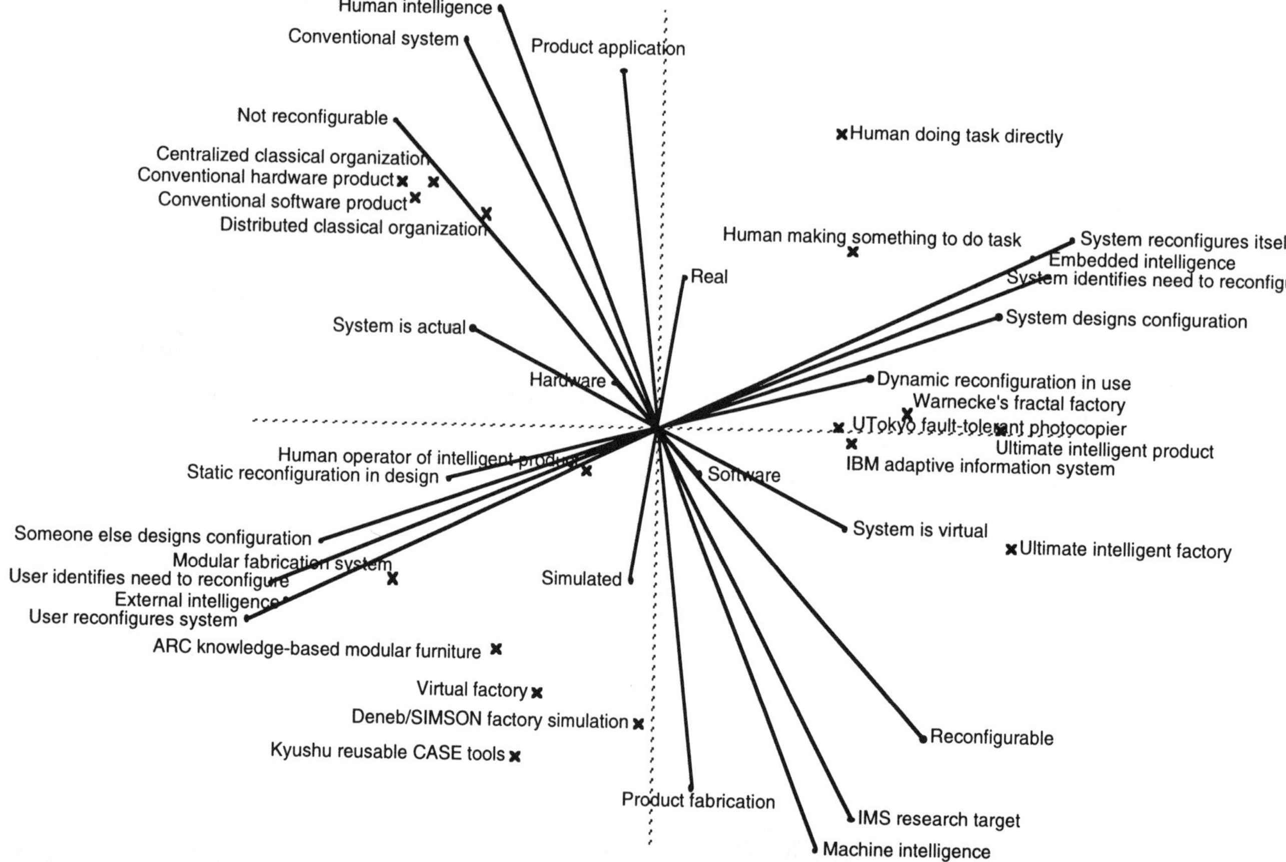

Figure 3 Principal components analysis of soft machine repertory grid

Laddering the Research Objectives

The application of KA techniques described in the previous section, whilst relevant to the understanding, management and presentation of the project does not in itself result in artificial intelligence in the sense of an inferential computational system. The knowledge acquired is being fed back to facilitate the intelligence of people rather than being used by a computer to provide direct support of knowledge processes through computational intelligence. One objective of the studies reported here has been to investigate the potential for knowledge-based systems to play a role in clarifying: project goals and activities, the relations between them, and, in particular, the inconsistencies between goals and activities that seem to arise in all major projects.

To this end, formal knowledge structures were developed for the top level goals of the IMS program as described in the document, *The Technical Concept of IMS* [Tomiyama 1992], by detailed analysis of the sub-section on ideal artifacts, extracts from which are shown below.

They should be congenial to mankind.

Safety: This is surely incontrovertible.

Ease of use: This means more than user friendliness or outstanding man-machine communications capabilities. It means they should be prepackaged with the necessary innate intelligence so that they are the least possible trouble to use.

Trouble free: Inseparable from ease of use.

They should be congenial to the environment.

Possible to recycle: By this I mean that manufacturing industry should actively seek to develop its own functional equivalents of veins and kidneys. Only thus will it be possible to eliminate waste and achieve complete reclamation.

Not dirty: We don't even need to look as far as the automobile industry and the problem of exhaust gases to see the need for minimizing the load imposed on the environment.

Not a consumer of energy: This again is self-evident.

They should be congenial to Society.

Compatibility that is welcome to society: This compatibility with society is an extremely important factor for the future. The advent of new types of man-made product often has revolutionary effects on daily life and society. However, we will need to be extremely careful introducing any man-made objects that promise to change society. By this I mean that manufacturing industry should be most concerned with the ripple effect of the introduction of new man-made objects on economic problems, labor problems, environmental problems, etc.

New market creation, not generation of trade friction: We need to consider not only the influence on society but also, and indeed primarily, that upon exports. We also need to consider how we are going to retrench when our manufacturing responsibilities develop to the point when this becomes necessary.

Tomiyama describes the requirements for an *ideal artifact* that would provide a suitable target for the IMS research program, and then discusses in detail the factors underlying these requirements. The KA methodology appropriate to the elicitation of such a conceptual structure

is another technique derived from personal construct psychology, that of *laddering* [Hinkle 1965; Gaines and Shaw 1993a]. Laddering tools take a concept such as *congenial to mankind* and ask two types of question: laddering up, *why* should an artifact be congenial to mankind?; laddering down, *how* can an artifact be *congenial to mankind*? In interactive elicitation the expert is taken up and down the conceptual structure by sequences of such how and why questions. For example, laddering up from "why should an artifact be *congenial to mankind*?" to "to be an *ideal artifact*" would lead to laddering down through the question "are there other ways of being an *ideal artifact*" and the elicitation of further requirements such as *congenial to the environment*. Laddering up from *ideal artifact* would lead to the concept in this case *to be a suitable target for IMS research*.

In moving from the psychological structure elicited by laddering to a formal knowledge structure, some additional meta-characteristics of the structure have to be elicited:

- are the answers to 'how' questions *necessary* characteristics of the concept above, in which case they are represented as a definition but otherwise become the premise of a rule
- if necessary, are the answers to 'how' questions also *sufficient* in which case the concept is fully defined, but otherwise is itself a primitive concept
- if not necessary, are the other answers to 'how' questions *alternatives* in which case they correspond to premises of different rules having a common conclusion.

The lowest level concepts developed through laddering down are expected to be *operational* in that it is possible to determine whether or not they apply to an entity through reference to assertions about it. In personal construct psychology terms this means that they will each be one pole of construct that can be completed by definition of its opposite, for example, what would one term a system that is not *safe*. Hence, the final stage of a laddering process is to elicit the opposite poles of the lowest level concepts.

Objectives as Formal Knowledge Structures

A formal knowledge structure was developed for the research objectives using a laddering tool with answers derived from the text above. The tool represents the structure in a visual language for terminological knowledge representation systems [Gaines 1991]. The language is a formal one with semantics that provide a direct translation into the constructs of CLASSIC [Borgida, Brachman, McGuiness and Resnick 1989] and similar KR systems. Concepts are represented by ellipses, primitive concepts by ellipses with short horizontal markers, inheritance by an arrow from a concept to one subsuming it, disjointness by a line between disjoint primitives, individuals by a rectangle, role by unboxed text, rules by a rectangle with a double line at each end, and so on. Contexts are represented by a container rectangle that corresponds to an individual with a role filled by the knowledge base within the container.

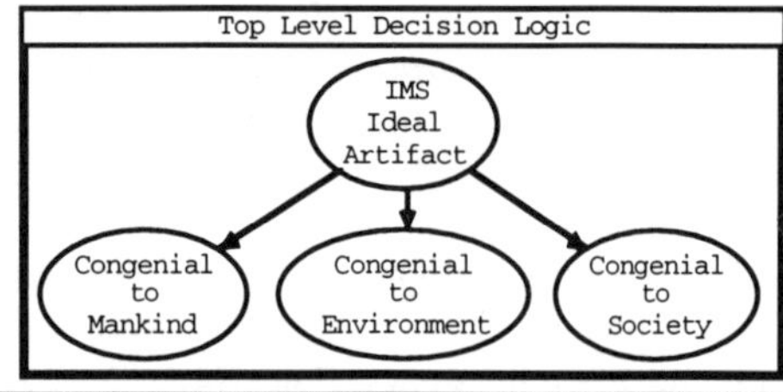

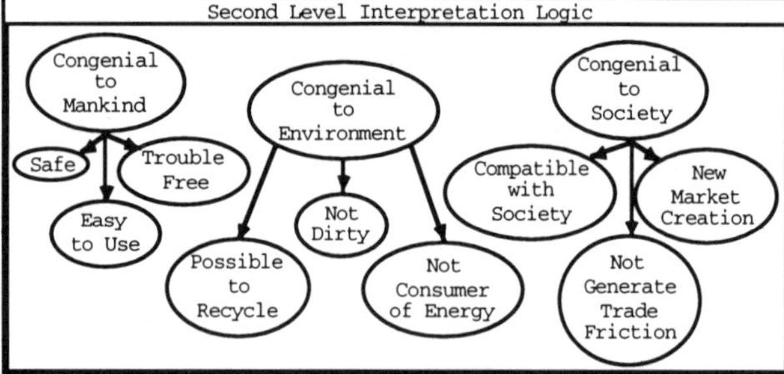

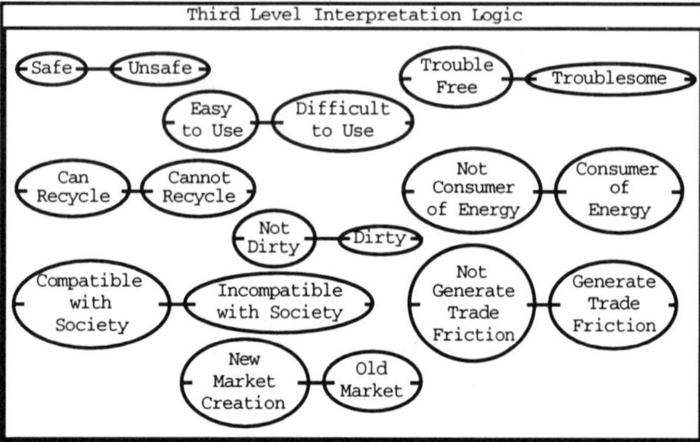

Figure 4 Knowledge structures for concept of IMS

At the top of Figure 4 is the top level decision logic expressed in the boxed text above, that an *IMS ideal artifact* should be *congenial to mankind*, *congenial to the environment* and *congenial to society*. This definition is typical of that found in the analysis of codified legal material—apparently simple requirements but expressed in terms of high-level concepts that require other knowledge structures for their interpretation [Sergot 1988]. The text provides the interpretations, for example, that an artifact *congenial to mankind* is *safe*, *easy to use* and *trouble-free*.

The third level knowledge structure at the bottom of Figure 4 is elicited at the final stage of laddering when the operational concepts at the lowest level are made into dimensions by the elicitation of opposites. The importance of this can be seen by considering that some of the second-level interpretations such as *safe* appear capable of operational definitions in terms of factual attributes of entities. However, the positive attributes required are not themselves operational but are characterized in terms of their opposites—rules that characterize a person as *dishonest* or an artifact as *unsafe* are more readily operationalized than those for *honest* or *safe*. These definitions are not given explicitly in Tomiyama's text because they are part of the 'commonsense knowledge' that the reader brings to its interpretation, knowledge that one

would expect to find overtly expressed in a commonsense knowledge base such as CYC [Lenat and Guha 1990].

The pattern of reasoning when the knowledge structure of Figure 4 is loaded into an inference engine is interesting because it does not follow the common stereotype of an 'expert system'. If an artifact is asserted to be an *ideal artifact* it inherits all the properties of being *safe*, *easy to use* and so on. If an inference rule concerned with its being *unsafe* or being *difficult to use* fires, the disjoint primitive relations cause the knowledge base to be incoherent, the original assertion is automatically retracted and the knowledge base can be interrogated to determine the reason for the error.

This is the inference pattern of CLASSIC used to detect constraint violations in the management of large-scale software projects [Devanbu, Selfridge, Ballard and Brachman 1989]. The pattern also characterizes scientific research in which conjectures are made that may be refuted [Popper 1963]. The conjectures are never verified and remain forever fallible, and new knowledge as it is added may lead to the refutation of past conjectures.

This pattern of reasoning overcomes one of the problems often noted for the representation and use of rules in CLASSIC-like systems, that the converse of a rule is not used in inference, that is that 'A ⊃ B' is not used to infer that '¬B ⊃ ¬A' [Buchheit, Donini and Schaerf 1993]. The use of contradiction to cause retraction is equivalent to this inference, but it is only used with concrete assertions about individuals—it is a feature of the A-box not the T-box. It does not lead to intensional inferences of a theorem-proving nature in current implementations of CLASSIC-like systems, but it is very significant to practical reasoning about concrete assertions and conjectures.

The dimensions at the lowest level in Figure 4 also define a repertory grid relating artifacts and research objectives. The top-level concept, *ideal artifact,* can be entered in the grid as an abstract object, an 'ideal element' in grid terminology, that is rated as being on every 'preferred pole.' The second level concepts. such as *congenial to mankind*, can also be entered as abstract objects rated as being on the relevant preferred poles, and as being 'any' on the irrelevant ones. More concrete objects such as actual artifacts, or designs, can be entered and rated on the dimensions developed from the text. The clustering tools then show the relations between artifacts, and between them and the idealized abstract artifacts.

Groupware Knowledge Support Systems

The knowledge structures presented in this paper are from a groupware coordination tool, Mediator, designed to share knowledge structures across local and wide area networks. One application is to knowledge systematization through the product life cycle, from needs through requirements, design, engineering, production, maintenance, reuse and recycling. Another application is to project management, including distributed research activities. Figure 2 is a screen dump from Mediator in a project management role.

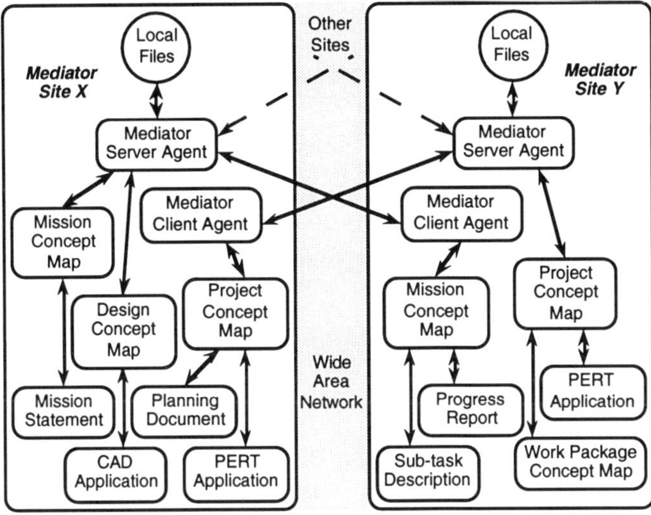

Figure 5 Mediator knowledge-based coordinator

Figure 5 shows the architecture of Mediator. A server agent at a site manages a knowledge base consisting of a heterogeneous set of files from different applications. Concept maps are used to represent the files and relations between them. Files may be opened from the maps in the appropriate applications. Since the maps and hypermedia documents of Mediator are also files, the system can be used to support large-scale linked knowledge structures.

Client agents at remote sites connect to server agents across the network and allow files to be accessed remotely in the same way as they are locally. A write token for each file is passed around the network allowing collaborative development of knowledge structures. The data structures for the visual languages are very compact allowing real-time updates with network data rates as low as 1 Kbyte/sec.

In research coordination the top-level knowledge structures are concerned with the mission. They link to structures concerned with technical projects and, since the visual language tools support Petrinets, knowledge bases, STEP/EXPRESS graphic representations, bond graphs, and so on, much of the detailed technical material can be captured in Mediator. At the lowest level files represented in Mediator may be opened in unrelated applications. All of the Mediator knowledge structures may also be embedded in active, printable documents [Gaines and Shaw 1993c], so that reports, manuals, and so on, are readily generated.

Related Research

The 1992 AAAI Workshop on *Communicating Scientific and Technical Knowledge* illustrated the potential for the use of artificial intelligence research in supporting the scientific community [Swaminathan 1992]. Computer-based concept maps have been used to support scientific knowledge processes [Smolensky, Bell, Fox, King and Lewis 1987; Cavalli-Sforza et al. 1992].

Research on shared ontologies and knowledge interchange formats is relevant to the development of knowledge support systems as envisioned in this paper [Neches, Fikes, Finin, Gruber, Patil, Senator and Swartout 1991]. It is not reasonable to expect individual projects to develop the complete ontological framework to support the lower level inference rules necessary to completion of the knowledge structures in Figure 4. It would be practical for a particular project to make its top-level logic overt, and then develop interpretations down to a level where they could be made operational by interfacing to shared ontologies available in interchange formats.

Significant areas of related research are in communities focusing on issues of computer-supported cooperative work and collaboratories [Lederberg and Uncapher 1989], and on the empirical study of the social and knowledge processes underlying scientific activity [Mitroff 1974; Abelson 1990; McCain 1990]. Most of the current tools for scientific communication on the Internet such as email, list servers, ftp archives, gopher, archie, WAIS and world wide web, have been built on a pragmatic basis to solve problems of textual communication and information retrieval. These communication systems are neutral to the content of the data communicated and can be extended to carry knowledge structures facilitating structured communication at the knowledge level. The development of effective knowledge support systems requires the joint efforts of the largely disjoint communities concerned with these diverse research and development areas.

Conclusions

Knowledge acquisition and representation technology is now mature and useful enough to be used routinely in supporting research communities. Much of what needs to be done does not involve major advances in artificial intelligence research, but rather the integration of what has already been achieved with existing communication systems on the Internet. However, the day to day use of overt knowledge structures by world-class scientific communities collaborating through the Internet is likely to highlight both the achievements of artificial intelligence research to date, and also the deficiencies of current KA and KR systems on different dimensions to current analyses largely motivated by considerations of pure logic and worst-case complexity analysis. The support of human practical reasoning may place lesser requirements than expected on some aspects of KA and KR systems, and greater requirements than expected on others. The development of practical knowledge support systems on the Internet and the resultant human-computer symbiosis at the knowledge level provides a stimulating environment for a new thrust in artificial intelligence research.

References

Abelson, P. 1990. Mechanisms for evaluating scientific information and the role of peer review. *Journal American Society Information Science* 41(3) 216-222.

Blume, S.S. 1974. *Toward a Political Sociology of Science*. New York: Free Press.

Boose, J.H. 1984. Personal construct theory and the transfer of human expertise. *Proceedings AAAI-84*. pp.27-33. California: AAAI.

Borgida, A., Brachman, R.J., McGuiness, D.L. and Resnick, L.A. 1989. CLASSIC: a structural data model for objects. *Proceedings of 1989 SIGMOD Conference on the Management of Data*. pp.58-67. NY: ACM Press.

Buchheit, M., Donini, F.M. and Schaerf, A. 1993. Decidable reasoning in terminological knowledge representation systems. *Journal of Artificial Intelligence Research* 1 109-138.

Callon, M., Law, J. and Rip, A., Ed. 1986. *Mapping the Dynamics of Science and Technology*. UK: MacMillan.

Cavalli-Sforza, V., Gabrys, G., Lesgold, A.M. and Weiner, A.W. 1992. Engaging students in scientific activity and scientific controversy. *AAAI-92 Workshop on Communicating Scientific and Technical Knowledge*. pp.99-114. Menlo Park, California: AAAI.

Cole, S. 1992. *Making Science: Between Nature and Society*. Cambridge, MA: Harvard University Press.

Collins, H.M. 1990. *Artificial Experts: Social Knowledge and Intelligent Machines*. Cambridge, MA: MIT Press.

Crane, D. 1972. *Invisible Colleges: Diffusion of Knowledge in Scientific Communities*. University of Chicago Press.

Devanbu, P., Selfridge, P.G., Ballard, B.W. and Brachman, R.J. 1989. A knowledge-based software information system. *IJCAI'89: Proceedings of the Eleventh International Joint Conference on Artificial Intelligence*. pp.110-115. San Mateo: Morgan Kaufmann.

Gaines, B.R. 1991. An interactive visual language for term subsumption visual languages. *IJCAI'91: Proceedings of the Twelfth International Joint Conference on Artificial Intelligence*. pp.817-823. San Mateo: Morgan Kaufmann.

Gaines, B.R. and Shaw, M.L.G. 1980. New directions in the analysis and interactive elicitation of personal construct systems. *International Journal Man-Machine Studies* 13 81-116.

Gaines, B.R. and Shaw, M.L.G. 1989. Comparing the conceptual systems of experts. *Proceedings of the Eleventh International Joint Conference on Artificial Intelligence*. San Mateo, California: Morgan Kaufmann.

Gaines, B.R. and Shaw, M.L.G. 1992. Integrated knowledge acquisition architectures. *Journal for Intelligent Information Systems* 1(1) 9-34.

Gaines, B.R. and Shaw, M.L.G. 1993a. Basing knowledge acquisition tools in personal construct psychology. *Knowledge Engineering Review* 8(1) 49-85.

Gaines, B.R. and Shaw, M.L.G. 1993b. Eliciting knowledge and transferring it effectively to a knowledge-based systems. *IEEE Transactions on Knowledge and Data Engineering* 5(1) 4-14.

Gaines, B.R. and Shaw, M.L.G. 1993c. Open architecture multimedia documents. *Proceedings of ACM Multimedia 93*. pp.137-146.

GNOSIS, Ed. 1993. *TW4 Soft Machinery Workshop Proceedings*. Canada: KSI, University of Calgary.

GNOSIS, Ed. 1994. *Knowledge Systematization: Configuration Systems for Design and Manufacturing: Final Report of the Test Case*. Canada: Knowledge Science Institute, University of Calgary.

Hinkle, D.N. 1965. The change of personal constructs from the viewpoint of a theory of implications. PhD Thesis. Ohio State University.

Kelly, G.A. 1955. *The Psychology of Personal Constructs*. New York: Norton.

Lambiotte, J.G., Dansereau, D.F., Cross, D.R. and Reynolds, S.B. 1989. Multirelational semantic maps. *Educational Psychology Review* 1(4) 331-367.

Landow, G.P. and Delany, P., Ed. 1993. *The Digital Word: Text-based Computing in the Humanities*. Cambridge, Massachusetts: MIT Press.

Lederberg, J. and Uncapher, K. 1989. Towards a National Collaboratory. *Report of an Invitational Workshop at The Rockefeller University*.

Lenat, D.B. and Guha, R.V. 1990. *Building Large Knowledge-Based Systems*. Reading, Massachusetts: Addison-Wesley.

McCain, K.W. 1990. Mapping authors in intellectual space: a technical overview. *Journal American Society Information Science* 41(6) 433-443.

Merton, R.K. 1973. *The Sociology of Science: Theoretical and Empirical Investigations*. University Chicago Press.

Mitroff, I.I. 1974. *The Subjective Side of Science*. New York: Elsevier.

Neches, R., Fikes, R., Finin, T., Gruber, T., Patil, R., Senator, T. and Swartout, W.R. 1991. Enabling technology for knowledge sharing. *AI Magazine* 12(3) 36-56.

Novak, J.D. and Gowin, D.B. 1984. *Learning How To Learn*. New York: Cambridge University Press.

Popper, K.R. 1963. *Conjectures and Refutations: The Growth of Scientific Knowledge*. London: Routledge & Kegan Paul.

Quillian, M.R. 1968. Semantic memory. *Semantic Information Processing*. pp.216-270. Cambridge, Massachusetts: MIT Press.

Sergot, M. 1988. Representing legislation as logic programs. *Machine Intelligence 11*. pp.209-260. Oxford: Clarendon Press.

Swaminathan, K., Ed. 1992. *AAAI-92 Workshop on Communicating Scientific and Technical Knowledge*. Menlo Park, California: AAAI.

Thadgard, P. 1992. *Conceptual Revolutions*. Princeton, New Jersey: Princeton University Press.

Tomiyama, T. 1992. The technical concept of IMS. RACE Discussion Paper, No. RA-DP2, Research into Artifacts, Center for Engineering, The University of Tokyo.

Toulmin, S. 1958. *The Uses of Argument*. Cambridge, UK: Cambridge University Press.

Wan, D. and Johnson, P. 1992. Supporting scientific learning and research review using COREVIEW. *AAAI-92 Workshop on Communicating Scientific and Technical Knowledge*. pp.107-114. Menlo Park, California: AAAI.

Talking about AI:
Socially-Defined Linguistic
Subcontexts in AI

Amy M. Steier and **Richard K. Belew**
Cognitive Computer Science Research Group
Computer Science & Engr. Dept. (0114)
University of California - San Diego
La Jolla, CA 92093
{steier,rik}@cs.ucsd.edu

Abstract

This paper describes experiments documenting significant variations in word usage patterns within social
subgroups of AI researchers. As some phrases have
very different collocational patterns than their constituent words, we look beyond occurrences of individual words, to consider word phrases. The mutual information statistic is used to measure the information
content of phrases beyond that of their constituent
words. Previous research has shown that some phrases
are much more informative as word pairs outside *topically* defined subsets of a document corpus than within
it. In this paper we show that individual universities provide an analogous, *socially* defined context in
which locally-used phrases are "exported" into general
AI vocabulary.

Introduction

An increasing body of research relating free-text information retrieval (IR) techniques with methods in
"corpus-based" computational linguistics is providing
AI with a new approach to natural language understanding and simultaneously with an important new
problem domain. Rather than attempting to syntactically analyze and then derive a deeper semantic understanding of each and every sentence in a collection of
natural language documents, these methods use statistical characteristics of word token occurrences to form
(at least gross) characterizations of what the documents are "about." Further, it appears that that such
statistical methods may be *complimentary* with more
traditional NLP methods. For example, morphological
and syntactic methods can provide more appropriate
elements for statistical analysis; conversely, the resulting statistics can help to guide semantic interpretation.

There are currently a number of major simplifications typical of the IR approach that must be refined,
however. This paper reports on attempts to address
two of these. First, we extend the basic IR statistical
methods beyond single word tokens to consider multi-
word phrases. In this respect, we are consistent with a

number of others in corpus-based linguistics. Our next
section discusses some of the important issues involved
in using phrases rather than single words.

Our second variation is less common. Rather than
treating the entire textual corpus as a single, homogeneous collection we consider variations in the statistics
in smaller, related subsets of documents. It is a truism
that the *context* of a any linguistic utterance obviously
has great influence on its interpretation. This is especially true in IR, where particular "relevant" keywords
are selected from a text by virtue of differences in their
statistics in that text, relative to the *context* of corpus-
wide norms. The larger a collection, the more likely it
is to have been generated by many authors, addressing
diverging audiences, using very different vocabularies,
and the less likely it is to be topically cohesive. We hypothesize that if smaller subsets of documents within
the larger corpus are analyzed separately, these will
reveal useful "local" variations in word usage patterns
that will be lost when statistics are gathered globally
across the entire corpus.

In previous work, we have used *a priori* taxonomic
classifications of the texts' topics as the basis for partitioning the corpus. For example, in a collection of legal
texts (judicial opinions), human editors have manually
classified each document according to a extremely refined taxonomy describing the full range of legal topics.
Based on these characterizations we were able to separate documents about (for example) "Labor Law" from
others about "Constitutional Law", etc. and find that,
in fact, word usage patterns vary significantly from
one topical area to another. Judges and lawyers working within a specialized area of the law use language
among themselves in consistent, reliable but specialized ways, relative to "general" legal parlance. In particular, these variations can be used to identify *phrases*
whose utility in topical sub-context is much different
than it is across the entire collection. This work is
summarized in the section on Previous Research.

Of course variations in the topical domain of discourse is only one dimension of linguistic context that

might interest us. In this paper, we attempt to consider *socially* defined sub-contexts within the larger context of artificial intelligence (AI). Using as our corpus a set of thesis abstracts all nominally about AI, we consider variations in single word and "bigram" (sequential word pairs) statistics arising within the context of particular *universities* at which the theses were written. We hypothesize that research groups at universities also define a useful linguistic sub-context. That is, they too use language among themselves in consistent, reliable ways that may not – yet – be shared with the rest of AI. The details and results of our experiment are described in the section titled Recent Experiments. We conclude with comments about relating this socially-defined notion of context with others.

Phrasal Semantics

Simple phrases provide an attractive first step beyond the simple "bag of words" techniques generally associated with IR. Phrases are interesting in part because of the complex way in which meanings associated with constituent words are combined to form more elaborate semantic expressions. D.A. Cruse has defined a "transparent" expression to be one whose meaning is derived directly from that of its constituent words; and "opaque" phrases as those whose semantics cannot be attributed to the simple composition of its constituent terms (Cruse 1986). For example, whereas the meaning of **red herring** or **red carpet** is opaque, the meaning of **red paint** is much more transparent. Halliday has made similar distinctions between "simple," "compound" and "phrasal" lexical items (Halliday 1966). He writes that often a phrase can act very much like a lexical unit in and of itself, and that often a phrase can have very different collocational patterns than the sum of its parts. From a practical IR perspective, these linguistic issues become the question of just when indexing word compounds offers advantages over simpler indexing of individual words.

We follow other recent work that considers a minimalist notion of phrase, based on simple collocation (Maarek & Smadja 1989)(Fagan 1989)(Church & Hanks 1990). As we are most interested in simple word compounds (such as **social security**), we use "bigrams" (sequential word pairs) to identify potentially interesting word co-occurrences. Church and Hanks have shown that compounds have a very fixed word order and that the average separation is one word (Church & Hanks 1990). We therefore restrict ourselves to a window of one when parsing for bigrams.

Words have meanings derived from their use both independent of, and with respect to, use within a phrase. Conversely, the phrasal meaning is drawn from the meaning of the constituents as well as from the "use" of the phrase. As a phrase becomes more frequently used, we hypothesize that a phrase's meaning draws less on the experience of the constituents' uses in other contexts and more on the experience of the phrase in its particular context. In other words, less meaning is drawn from the "transparent" semantics of the constituents, while more meaning becomes related to the direct experience of using the phrase. *Mutual information* therefore becomes a very natural measure of the disparity between a phrase's use and the independent use of its constituent words:

$$MI(w_1, w_2) = log \frac{Prob(w_1, w_2)}{Prob(w_1)Prob(w_2)}$$

Here, $Prob(w_i)$ is the frequency of word w_i divided by the size of the corpus N_W and $Prob(w_1, w_2)$ is the frequency of bigram (w_1, w_2) divided by N_W. MI has often been used to measure lexical cohesiveness or strength of association between two words (Magerman & Marcus 1990; Hindle 1990; Church *et al.* 1991).

Because we will be considering sub-contexts of a large corpus, we will compute a phrase's mutual information with respect to both the entire corpus and a particular subset of documents. We will show that across the difference sub-contexts of a large corpus, the extent to which a phrase acts like a lexical unit varies, and in a way: if a phrase has high mutual information with respect to the entire collection, then it will have a depressed mutual information value with respect to a specific context if and only if at least one of the phrase's constituent words is independently very descriptive of the subcontext.

Previous Research

This paper is a continuation of earlier research where we looked beyond occurrences of individual words, to consider word pairs or phrases (Steier & Belew 1993). The focus of this earlier research was to study how the informational content of phrases, beyond that of their constituent words, can change within topically restricted areas. The mutual information measure was used as the statistic best reflecting this value.

This previous research was performed using a large collection of judicial opinions, covering virtually all topics of U.S. case law, provided by West Publishing Company. West uses a rich hierarchical indexing scheme (the Key number system) to topically organize all case digests. We were thus able to define topical sub-contexts within the collection through the use of this indexing scheme. The headnotes [1] of these cases were grouped together by topic numbers to get a total of 339 topical subcontexts.

---

[1] Headnotes are precis generated by West's editors to capture the central points of each judicial opinion.

After some simple stemming, [2] all bigrams within each topical subcontext were extracted. Any bigram crossing punctuation marks, as well as any bigrams containing "noise words" from a list of common English words were not considered. It is important to note that our noise word list not only contained non-content words such as articles and prepositions, but words that are extremely common in a legal context. [3] Since the mutual information measure can become unstable when counts are very low, any bigram occurring less than three times within a topical subcontext or outside of it was also filtered.

For each bigram within a topical subcontext, its mutual information (cf. Phrasal Semantics section) with respect to the subcontext, MI_t, as well as a value with respect to the entire collection MI_c was computed. In computing MI_c, N_W is the total number of words in the entire collection. In computing MI_t, N_W is the number of words in that particular topic area. The consequence of this measure is if the constituents of a phrase occur together much more often than chance, the phrase will have a high mutual information value. The higher the mutual information value is between a pair of words, the more informative that pair is as a phrase. It is not that the phrase is necessarily more contentful but that our interpretation of the phrase is less easily derived from the typical meaning associated with its constituents.

Next, each individual *word* within a topic area was given an index term weight based on a variant of the term frequency × inverse document frequency weighting scheme devised by Salton and Buckley [4] (Salton & Buckley 1988). If F_{ij} represents the frequency of term j in document i, DF_j, the document frequency of term j, N_D, the total number of documents, and N_i, the number of words in document i, then TW_{ij}, the term weight of term j in document i, is given by the following formula:

$$TW_{ij} = \frac{F_{ij} \times \log(N_D/DF_j)}{\sqrt{\sum_{k=1}^{N_i}(F_{ik} \times \log(N_D/DF_k))^2}}$$

In studying how the mutual information of bigrams changes across different subcontexts, our most central finding was that a decrease in mutual information within a topic area turns out to by highly correlated to the maximum of the term weights associated with the bigrams constituents. In other words, bigrams with high informational content across the entire collection have depressed informational content (i.e. convey less

---

[2] Our stemming consisted only of converting all plural nouns to their singular form.

[3] An example of this would be legal abbreviations of statute sections.

[4] This term weighting technique is currently the most widely used in I.R.

$PHRASE$	TW_M	MI_t	MI_c
MINIMUM WAGE	.057	9.48	11.50
WORKER COMPENSATION	.043	5.98	10.37
COLLECTIVE BARGAINING	.185	7.80	12.08
UNION MEMBER	.449	6.31	8.91
OCCUPATIONAL SAFETY	.050	10.51	12.56
OVERTIME PAY	.062	5.40	8.95
LOCAL UNION	.449	6.03	8.17
PENSION PLAN	.076	8.42	10.40
LABOR RELATION	.495	4.99	8.84
LABOR STANDARD	.495	5.78	9.20

Table 1: Example phrases where the mutual information within the collection (MI_c) exceeds that within the topic Labor Relations (MI_t.)

information) – as bigrams – within their semantically related topical area *if, and only if* the bigram's constituents are good descriptors of that topic area.

Table 1 shows some examples where MI_c exceeds MI_t for the topic Labor Relations. In studying these phrases, what stands out is how apropos to the Labor Relations topic the phrases in Table 1 are. TW_M (maximum term weight) is the larger of the two term weights associated with the phrases constituents with respect to the topic Labor Relations. All term weights range between 0 and 1, and the median term weight for a topic is about .03. There is a strong tendency for phrases with high TW_M to have a depressed mutual information value within the topic. The correlation between TW_M and difference in MI ($MI_t - MI_c$) in the Labor Relations topic was -.62. This was found to be very typical across the other topics within the collection. This correlation has also been independently reported by Damerau (Damerau 1993).

The conclusion we draw from this phenomenon is that the more descriptive the constituents of a phrase are with respect to a specific topic, the more transparent that phrase is within the topic and the more opaque it is outside the topic. Take, for example, the phrase PENSION PLAN. This phrase seems to be much more opaque (i.e. have a much higher phrasal information content) across the entire collection. Yet within the Labor Relations topic, the constituents PENSION and PLAN are very descriptive of the central issues. Not only do these words occur together as PENSION PLAN, but they often occur separately (e.g., PENSION FUND, PENSION BENEFIT, PENSION BOARD, INSURANCE PLAN, WELFARE PLAN.)

Our interpretation of these results was that technical phrases are often "deconstructed" into their constituents within a particular topical sublanguage. The semantic nuances that are explored in detail within a topical area are then left behind as this phrase is "exported" into general vocabulary, where dominant use of the constituent words are as part of the phrase. Further, we found evidence of an intriguing "self-similar" regularity in this exporting relation. When we repeated the experiments using a topic subcontext as the "collection", and that topic's different sub-topics as the different subcontexts, we again found this exporting phenomenon to exist. This led us to conclude that "opacity" is a relative concept. An opaque phrase whose meaning appears to have little relation to that of its constituent words may in fact be transparent within some restricted sublanguage, perhaps associated with its genesis. Of course, this sublanguage may no longer exist, or it may simply require closer analysis of restricted portions of the general textual corpus.

Recent Experiments

The textual corpus used in our current is a set of masters and Ph.D. thesis dissertations, collected via questionaires but especially from the University Microfilms database during the past 5 years. Title and abstract text for each of these approx. 2600 theses was combined, with each thesis comprising approx. 2000 bytes.[5] It is important to recognize that while this corpus is of obvious interest, it is very small by IR standards and we have had to tailor many of our statistics somewhat in order to handle the very small sample sizes involved. Subsets of the corpus were formed for each of the 100 universities most well-represented in the collection. This ranged from Stanford with 79 theses to Yale with only seven.

To begin our experiments, the noise word list is first updated to include terms that are extremely common in the context of AI. A noise term is a low information word or phrase within a particular context. In Information Theory, the information encoded in a symbol is relative to the uncertainty associated with that symbol occurring. In language, very frequent words (or phrases) provide us with little information. Less frequent words provide us with more information. To put it another way, information is a deviation from what you expect. It is a common practice within IR to maintain a "negative dictionary" of frequently occurring "noise words" in any language.

When a textual corpus is further restricted to a particular topic, additional words also become effectively noise. For example, in a collection of computer industry magazine articles, the word **COMPUTER** becomes almost (statistically) meaningless. It is therefore appropriate to augment the standard negative dictionary with those additional words that are effectively noise in a particular corpus. The top noise words with respect to our AI collection are listed in Table 2.

Next, all bigrams from each of university subcon-

---

[5]Total number of words in our collection is 535804.

WORD	TF_c	WORD	TF_c
SYSTEM	6991	BASED	1357
MODEL	3328	TECHNIQUE	1319
PROBLEM	2754	DATA	1319
KNOWLEDGE	2734	RESEARCH	1293
NETWORK	2267	USE	1257
EXPERT	2062	INFORMATION	1253
DESIGN	2046	NEURAL	1231
PROCESS	1815	DEVELOPED	1188
USED	1693	RESULT	1175
APPROACH	1652	ANALYSIS	1130
METHOD	1605	TWO	1049
LEARNING	1527	NEW	1013
USING	1501	COMPUTER	982
ALGORITHM	1480	APPLICATION	979
CONTROL	1394	PERFORMANCE	963

Table 2: Top noise words in our AI collection. TF_c is the term frequency within the collection.

PHRASE	TF_c
EXPERT SYSTEM	1456
NEURAL NETWORK	1075
ARTIFICIAL INTELLIGENCE	632
KNOWLEDGE BASE	394
PROBLEM SOLVING	247
ARTIFICIAL NEURAL	175
KNOWLEDGE-BASED SYSTEM	160
KNOWLEDGE ACQUISITION	159
CONTROL SYSTEM	158
KNOWLEDGE REPRESENTATION	154
LEARNING ALGORITHM	145
DECISION SUPPORT	144
NATURAL LANGUAGE	142
DECISION MAKING	131
PATTERN RECOGNITION	126
SUPPORT SYSTEM	124
MACHINE LEARNING	120
DISSERTATION PRESENT	103
DESIGN PROCESS	102

Table 3: Most frequent phrases in our AI collection. TF_c is the term frequency within the collection.

texts are extracted. Any bigram that contains a noise word or occurs more than 100 times in the collection is discarded. These very frequently occurring phrases are also effectively "noise" when computing collection statistics. These phrases are listed in Table 3. Note how much more contentful these phrases are than the single words. This additional specificity in meaning is the central reason why phrases are being used more and more in document indexing.

A mutual information value is computed with respect to each university subcontext, MI_u, as well as with respect to the entire collection, MI_c. Each individual word within a subcontext is assigned an index term weight, using the term weighting formula mentioned earlier.

Our analysis is then to study how the mutual information (MI) of phrases changes within the individual university subcontexts. As in our previous experiments, we look at the correlation between the maximum term weight of a phrase's constituents and the difference in collection and university MI ($MI_u - MI_c$). Once again, we find the "export" relation to exist. The average correlation between difference in MI and maximum term weight is -.61 within the individual university subcontexts.

Figure 1 shows this relationship for all university subcontexts combined. Since our term weighting algorithm assigns to the majority of terms a very low weight, and then progressively less terms a higher and higher weight, we use the log of the maximum term weight to more aptly show its relationship to the difference in mutual information. The correlation of the two parameters in this graph is -.61.

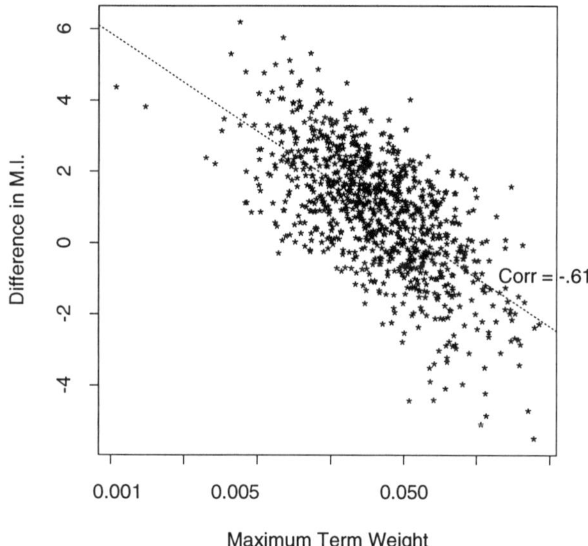

Figure 1: Log of the Maximum Term Weight to difference in MI ($MI_u - MI_c$) for all university subcontexts. The dotted line in the graph maps the least squared fit.

Table 4 lists example bigrams which exhibit the export relation. The 35 universities from which examples are taken are those with the highest number of AI theses associated with them.

The conclusion we draw from this analysis, is that individual universities do indeed represent distinct linguistic subcontexts. More specifically, we find that the more descriptive the constituents of a phrase are with respect to a specific university's AI thesis research, the more transparent that phrase is within that university's context and the more opaque it is outside that context. Take, for example, the phrase **CASE-BASED REASONING**. This phrase seems to be very opaque (i.e. have a high mutual information value) across the entire context of AI. Yet within the a few of the individual university subcontexts (e.g. Yale, Georgia Tech. and the University of Massachusetts) the phrase's meaning is much more transparent. Within these particular subcontexts, the terms **CASE-BASED** and **REASONING** are highly weighted as being descriptive of their AI thesis research. The constituent concepts of **CASE-BASED** and **REASONING** are examined in detail and independently. Not only do these words occur together as **CASE-BASED REASONING**, but they often occur separately (e.g. **CASE-BASED PLANNING, CASE-BASED ARGUMENT, CASE-BASED PROBLEM, SCHEMA-BASED REASONING, ANALOGICAL REASONING, COMMONSENSE REASONING**). As this phrase is "exported" into the general AI vocabulary, the semantic nuances are left behind, and the dominant use of the constituent words is as part of the phrase.

Conclusion

In studying the phrases that exhibit the export relation, we find occasional instances where the same phrases is exported from different universities. For example, the phrase **CASE-BASED REASONING** is shown to be an export phrase from the universities of Yale, Georgia Tech. and the University of Massachusetts. It is interesting to note that some of the students Schank advised at Yale, graduated and then took on teaching positions at both Georgia Tech. and the University of Massachusetts. We hypothesize that this type of AI lineage (or *genealogy*) information might be used to create yet another socially-defined set of linguistic subcontexts. We are currently in the process of gathering this type of AI genealogy information.

We interpret the export phenomena of important word combinations as a migration, from a context in which the nuances of each words' meaning is considered independently out into a broader context in which only the central and now "opaque" interpretation of the phrase is useful. If true, there must be a *time delay* to this progression, and a particular textual corpus may or may not capture it. In our previous experiments with legal texts, the opinions cover a very long time period, with ample opportunity for technical jargon (e.g., **PENSION PLAN** or **SOCIAL SECURITY**) to migrate from use by a restricted group of specialists to lawyers and judges generally.

It is somewhat curious, then, that even in the very short five-year window spanned by our AI theses should be sufficient time to also give evidence of phrase

STANFORD	UNIV. MASSACHUSETTS	UNIV. PENNSYLVANIA	UNIV. MISSOURI (ROLLA)
BELIEF REVISION	PLAN RECOGNITION	HORN CLAUSE	DEVELOPING COUNTRY
INFLUENCE DIAGRAM	ROBOT ARM	END EFFECTOR	IMAGE SEGMENTATION
NONMONO. REAS.	CASE-BASED REAS.	**PENN. STATE**	**UNIV. CINCINNATI**
UNIV. ILL. (URB-CHAMP)	**UNIV. MARYLAND**	ARC WELDING	LP FORMULATION
MASSIVELY PARALLEL	HIDDEN UNIT	MOMENT INVARIANT	MOMENT INVARIANT
PURDUE	LOAD BALANCING	GARBAGE COLL.	**N.C. STATE (RALEIGH)**
COLLISION-FREE PATH	GRADIENT DESCENT	**UNIV. WISC. (MADISON)**	SIMULATED ANNEALING
MATERIAL HANDLING	**COUN. NAT. ACA. AWRDS**	ARC WELDING	IMAGE SEGMENTATION
MOBILE ROBOT	SPEECH RECOGNITION	WELDING ROBOT	CONSTRAINT SATISF.
UNIV. TEXAS (AUSTIN)	COLLISION AVOIDANCE	**UNIV. FLORIDA**	**UNIV. COLORADO (BOULDER)**
INFLUENCE DIAGRAM	FLEXIBLE MANUF.	OBJ.-ORIENTED D.B.	RIVER BASIN
TEXT UNDERSTANDING	**UNIV. MINNESOTA**	D.B. MANAGEMENT	BIOLOGICAL NERVOUS
CARNEGIE-MELLON	ASSOCIATIVE MEMORY	**UNIV. ARIZONA**	**UNIV. CALIF. (LOS ANGELES)**
CHESS PROGRAM	ANALOGICAL REAS.	EQUILIBRIUM POINT	NUCLEAR REACTOR
ABSTRACTION HIER.	**UNIV. MICHIGAN**	**UNIV. PITTSBURGH**	FAULT TOLERANCE
MOBILE ROBOT	BODY MOTION	NONE	**RUTGERS (NEW BRUNSWICK)**
OHIO STATE	RIGID BODY	**CASE WESTERN**	DEDUCTIVE DATABASE
MALF. DIAGNOSIS	DOCUMENT RETR.	OBJECT RECOGNITION	**UNIV. WASHINGTON**
CREDIT ASSIGNMENT	**NORTHWESTERN**	**UNIV. TEXAS (ARLING.)**	STATE-SPACE SEARCH
UNIV. CALIF. (BERK.)	DEDUCTIVE DATABASE	BUILDING BLOCK	MULTI-LAYER PERC.
SEMICOND. MANUF.	THEOREM PROVER	**RENSSELAER POLY. INST.**	STEADY STATE
TOOL WEAR	**ARIZONA STATE**	ROBOTIC ASSEMBLY	**MIT**
FUZZY LOGIC	SYSTOLIC ARRAY	ERROR RECOVERY	TOOL WEAR
TEXAS A&M	LOAD FORECASTING	**GEORGIA TECH.**	LIMIT CYCLE
OBSTACLE AVOIDANCE	LP FORMULATION	SENSOR FUSION	THESIS PRESENT
CIRCUIT BOARD	**ILLINOIS INST. TECH.**	CASE-BASED REAS.	**YALE**
	INTELL. TUTORING		INTENTIONAL STATE
			CASE-BASED REAS.

Table 4: Example bigrams where the mutual information in the university file (MI_u) exceeds that within the collection (MI_c). Universities are listed in order of number of AI theses associated with them.

exporting. Our explanation is that this is due to the speed with which technical, scientific language adapts, relative to more common forms. It does not seem unreasonable that through conference and journal papers, let alone "directly" through influential theses, language used successfully within one research group (e.g., **CASE-BASED REASONING**) can come to influence the AI community generally in just a few years. If true, it suggests that scientific (and other professional) communication might provide an especially illuminating perspective into fundamental properties of linguistic evolution.

References

Church, K., and Hanks, P. 1990. Word association norms, mutual information and lexicography. *Computational Linguistics* 16(1).

Church, K.; Gale, W.; Hanks, P.; and Hindle, D. 1991. *Using Statistics in Lexical Analysis*. New Jersey and London: Lawrence Erlbaum Assoc. 115–164.

Cruse, D. 1986. *Lexical Semantics*. New York: Cambridge University Press.

Damerau, F. J. 1993. Generating and evaluating domain-oriented multi-word terms from texts. *Information Processing and Management* 29(4):433–447.

Fagan, J. 1989. The effectiveness of a nonsyntactic approach to automatic phrase indexing for document retrieval. *Journal of the American Society for Information Science* 40(2):115–132.

Halliday, M. 1966. *Lexis as a Linguistic Level*. London: Longmans.

Hindle, D. 1990. Noun classification from predicate-argument structures. In *28th Annual Meeting of the Association for Computational Linguistics*.

Maarek, Y., and Smadja, F. 1989. Full text indexing based on lexical relations. In *Proceedings of the 12th International Conference on Research and Development in Information Retrieval*.

Magerman, D., and Marcus, M. 1990. Parsing a natural language using mutual information statistics. In *Proceedings of AAAI '90*.

Salton, G., and Buckley, C. 1988. Term-weighting approaches in automatic text retrieval. *Information Processing and Management* 24(5):513–523.

Steier, A., and Belew, R. 1993. Exporting phrases: A statistical analysis of topical language. In *Second Annual Symposium on Document Analysis and Information Retrieval*.

Natural Language Processing

Some Advances in Transformation-Based Part of Speech Tagging[*]

Eric Brill
Spoken Language Systems Group
Laboratory for Computer Science
Massachusetts Institute of Technology
Cambridge, Massachusetts 02139
brill@goldilocks.lcs.mit.edu

Abstract

Most recent research in trainable part of speech taggers has explored stochastic tagging. While these taggers obtain high accuracy, linguistic information is captured indirectly, typically in tens of thousands of lexical and contextual probabilities. In (Brill 1992), a trainable rule-based tagger was described that obtained performance comparable to that of stochastic taggers, but captured relevant linguistic information in a small number of simple non-stochastic rules. In this paper, we describe a number of extensions to this rule-based tagger. First, we describe a method for expressing lexical relations in tagging that stochastic taggers are currently unable to express. Next, we show a rule-based approach to tagging unknown words. Finally, we show how the tagger can be extended into a k-best tagger, where multiple tags can be assigned to words in some cases of uncertainty.

Introduction

When automated part of speech tagging was initially explored (Klein & Simmons 1963; Harris 1962), people manually engineered rules for tagging, sometimes with the aid of a corpus. As large corpora became available, it became clear that simple Markov-model based stochastic taggers that were automatically trained could achieve high rates of tagging accuracy (Jelinek 1985). Markov-model based taggers assign a sentence the tag sequence that maximizes $Prob(\text{word}|\text{tag}) * Prob(\text{tag}|\text{previous n tags})$. These probabilities can be estimated directly from a manually tagged corpus.[1] Stochastic taggers have a number of advantages over the manually built taggers, including

obviating the need for laborious manual rule construction, and possibly capturing useful information that may not have been noticed by the human engineer. However, stochastic taggers have the disadvantage that linguistic information is only captured indirectly, in large tables of statistics. Almost all recent work in developing automatically trained part of speech taggers has been on further exploring Markov-model based tagging (Jelinek 1985; Church 1988; Derose 1988; DeMarcken 1990; Merialdo 1991; Cutting *et al.* 1992; Kupiec 1992; Charniak *et al.* 1993; Weischedel *et al.* 1993).

In (Brill 1992), a trainable rule-based tagger is described that achieves performance comparable to that of stochastic taggers. Training this tagger is fully automated, but unlike trainable stochastic taggers, linguistic information is encoded directly in a set of simple non-stochastic rules. In this paper, we describe some extensions to this rule-based tagger. These include a rule-based approach to: lexicalizing the tagger, tagging unknown words, and assigning the k-best tags to a word. All of these extensions, as well as the original tagger, are based upon a learning paradigm called transformation-based error-driven learning. This learning paradigm has shown promise in a number of other areas of natural language processing, and we hope that the extensions to transformation-based learning described in this paper can carry over to other domains of application as well.[2]

Transformation-Based Error-Driven Learning

Transformation-based error-driven learning has been applied to a number of natural language problems, including part of speech tagging, prepositional phrase attachment disambiguation, and syntactic parsing (Brill 1992; 1993a; 1993b). A similar approach is being explored for machine translation (Su, Wu, & Chang 1992). Figure 1 illustrates the learning process. First, unannotated text is passed through the initial-state an-

---

[*]This research was supported by ARPA under contract N00014-89-J-1332, monitored through the Office of Naval Research.

[1]One can also estimate these probabilities without a manually tagged corpus, using a hidden Markov model. However, it appears to be the case that directly estimating probabilities from even a very small manually tagged corpus gives better results than training a hidden Markov model on a large untagged corpus (see (Merialdo 1991)).

[2]The programs described in this paper can be obtained by contacting the author.

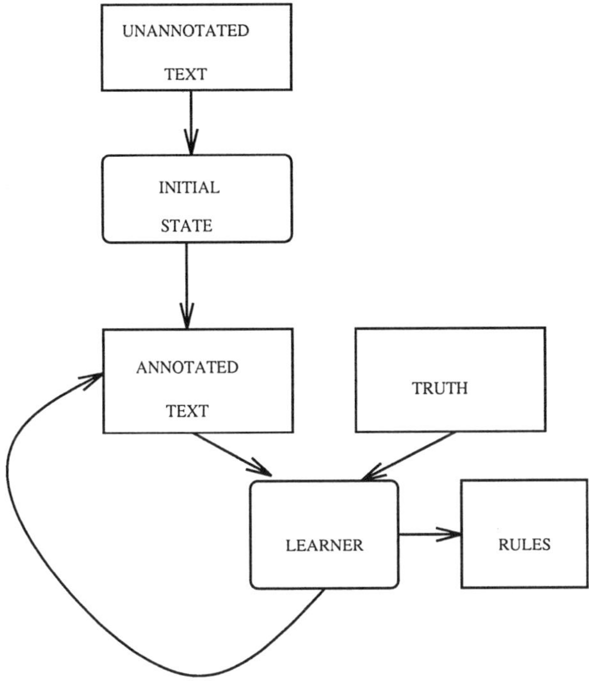

Figure 1: Transformation-Based Error-Driven Learning.

notator. The initial-state annotator can range in complexity from assigning random structure to assigning the output of a sophisticated manually created annotator. Once text has been passed through the initial-state annotator, it is then compared to the *truth*,[3] and transformations are learned that can be applied to the output of the initial state annotator to make it better resemble the *truth*.

In all of the applications described in this paper, the following greedy search is applied: at each iteration of learning, the transformation is found whose application results in the *highest score*; that transformation is then added to the ordered transformation list and the training corpus is updated by applying the learned transformation. To define a specific application of transformation-based learning, one must specify the following: (1) the initial state annotator, (2) the space of transformations the learner is allowed to examine, and (3) the scoring function for comparing the corpus to the *truth* and choosing a transformation.

Once an ordered list of transformations is learned, new text can be annotated by first applying the initial state annotator to it and then applying each of the learned transformations, in order.

An Earlier Tranformation-Based Tagger

The original transformation-based tagger (Brill 1992) works as follows. The initial state annotator assigns

each word its most likely tag as indicated in the training corpus. The most likely tag for unknown words is guessed based on a number of features, such as whether the word is capitalized, and what the last three letters of the word are. The allowable transformation templates are:

Change tag **a** to tag **b** when:

1. The preceding (following) word is tagged z.
2. The word two before (after) is tagged z.
3. One of the two preceding (following) words is tagged z.
4. One of the three preceding (following) words is tagged z.
5. The preceding word is tagged z and the following word is tagged w.
6. The preceding (following) word is tagged z and the word two before (after) is tagged w.

where a, b, z and w are variables over the set of parts of speech. To learn a transformation, the learner in essence applies every possible transformation,[4] counts the number of tagging errors after that transformation is applied, and chooses that transformation resulting in the greatest error reduction.[5] Learning stops when no transformations can be found whose application reduces errors beyond some prespecified threshold. An example of a transformation that was learned is: change the tagging of a word from **noun** to **verb** if the previous word is tagged as a **modal**. Once the system is trained, a new sentence is tagged by applying the initial state annotator and then applying each transformation, in turn, to the sentence.

Lexicalizing the Tagger

No relationships between words are directly captured in stochastic taggers. In the Markov model, state transition probabilities $(P(Tag_i|Tag_{i-1}\ldots Tag_{i-n}))$ express the likelihood of a tag immediately following n other tags, and emit probabilities $(P(Word_j|Tag_i))$ express the likelihood of a word given a tag. Many useful relationships, such as that between a word and the previous word, or between a tag and the following word, are not directly captured by Markov-model based taggers. The same is true of the earlier transformation-based tagger, where transformation templates did not make reference to words.

To remedy this problem, the transformation-based tagger was extended by adding contextual transformations that could make reference to words as well as part of speech tags. The transformation templates that were added are:

---

[3] As specified in a manually annotated corpus.

[4] All possible instantiations of transformation templates.

[5] The search is data-driven, so only a very small percentage of possible transformations really need be examined.

Change tag **a** to tag **b** when:

1. The preceding (following) word is w.
2. The word two before (after) is w.
3. One of the two preceding (following) words is w.
4. The current word is w and the preceding (following) word is x.
5. The current word is w and the preceding (following) word is tagged z.

where w and x are variables over all words in the training corpus, and z is a variable over all parts of speech.

Below we list two lexicalized transformations that were learned:[6]

Change the tag:

(12) From **preposition** to **adverb** if the word two positions to the right is **as**.

(16) From **non-3rd person singular present verb** to **base form verb** if one of the previous two words is **n't**.[7]

The Penn Treebank tagging style manual specifies that in the collocation *as ... as*, the first *as* is tagged as an adverb and the second is tagged as a preposition. Since *as* is most frequently tagged as a preposition in the training corpus, the initial state tagger will mistag the phrase *as tall as* as:

as/**preposition** tall/adjective as/preposition

The first lexicalized transformation corrects this mistagging. Note that a stochastic tagger trained on our training set would not correctly tag the first occurrence of *as*. Although adverbs are more likely than prepositions to follow some verb form tags, the fact that $P(as|preposition)$ is much greater than $P(as|adverb)$, and $P(adjective|preposition)$ is much greater than $P(adjective|adverb)$ lead to *as* being incorrectly tagged as a preposition by a stochastic tagger. A trigram tagger will correctly tag this collocation in some instances, due to the fact that $P(preposition|adverb\ adjective)$ is greater than $P(preposition|preposition\ adjective)$, but the outcome will be highly dependent upon the context in which this collocation appears.

The second transformation arises from the fact that when a verb appears in a context such as *We do n't ___* or *We did n't usually ___*, the verb is in base form. A stochastic trigram tagger would have to capture this

linguistic information indirectly from frequency counts of all trigrams of the form:[8]

*	ADVERB	PRESENT_VERB
*	ADVERB	BASE_VERB
ADVERB	*	PRESENT_VERB
ADVERB	*	BASE_VERB

and from the fact that $P(n't|ADVERB)$ is fairly high.

In (Weischedel *et al.* 1993), results are given when training and testing a Markov-model based tagger on the Penn Treebank Tagged Wall Street Journal Corpus. They cite results making the closed vocabulary assumption that all possible tags for all words in the test set are known. When training contextual probabilities on 1 million words, an accuracy of 96.7% was achieved. Accuracy dropped to 96.3% when contextual probabilities were trained on 64,000 words. We trained the transformation-based tagger on 600,000 words from the same corpus, making the same closed vocabulary assumption,[9] and achieved an accuracy of 97.2% on a separate 150,000 word test set. The transformation-based learner achieved better performance, despite the fact that contextual information was captured in only 267 simple nonstochastic rules, as opposed to 10,000 contextual probabilities that were learned by the stochastic tagger. To see whether lexicalized transformations were contributing to the accuracy rate, we ran the exact same test using the tagger trained using the earlier transformation template set, which contained no transformations making reference to words. Accuracy of that tagger was 96.9%. Disallowing lexicalized transformations resulted in an 11% increase in the error rate. These results are summarized in table 1.

When transformations are allowed to make reference to words and word pairs, some relevant information is probably missed due to sparse data. We are currently exploring the possibility of incorporating word classes into the rule-based learner in hopes of overcoming this problem. The idea is quite simple. Given a source of word class information, such as WordNet (Miller 1990), the learner is extended such that a rule is allowed to make reference to parts of speech, words, and word classes, allowing for rules such as *Change the tag from X to Y if the following word belongs to word class Z.*

---

[6] All experiments were run on the Penn Treebank tagged Wall Street Journal corpus, version 0.5 (Marcus, Santorini, & Marcinkiewicz 1993).

[7] In the Penn Treebank, *n't* is treated as a separate token, so *don't* becomes *do/VB-NON3rd-SING n't/ADVERB*.

[8] Where a star can match any part of speech tag.

[9] In both (Weischedel *et al.* 1993) and here, the test set was incorporated into the lexicon, but was not used in learning contextual information. Testing with no unknown words might seem like an unrealistic test. We have done so for three reasons (We show results when unknown words are included later in the paper): (1) to allow for a comparison with previously quoted results, (2) to isolate known word accuracy from unknown word accuracy, and (3) in some systems, such as a closed vocabulary speech recognition system, the assumption that all words are known is valid.

Method	Training Corpus Size (Words)	# of Rules or Context. Probs.	Acc. (%)
Stochastic	64 K	6,170	96.3
Stochastic	1 Million	10,000	96.7
Rule-Based w/o Lex. Rules	600 K	219	96.9
Rule-Based With Lex. Rules	600 K	267	97.2

Table 1: Comparison of Tagging Accuracy With No Unknown Words

This approach has already been successfully applied to a system for prepositional phrase disambiguation (Brill 1993b).

Unknown Words

In addition to not being lexicalized, another problem with the original transformation-based tagger was its relatively low accuracy at tagging unknown words.[10] In the initial state annotator for tagging, words are assigned their most likely tag, estimated from a training corpus. In the original formulation of the rule-based tagger, a rather ad-hoc algorithm was used to guess the most likely tag for words not appearing in the training corpus. To try to improve upon unknown word tagging accuracy, we built a transformation-based learner to learn rules for more accurately guessing the most likely tag for words not seen in the training corpus. If the most likely tag for unknown words can be assigned with high accuracy, then the contextual rules can be used to improve accuracy, as described above.

In the transformation-based unknown-word tagger, the initial state annotator naively labels the most likely tag for unknown words as proper noun if capitalized and common noun otherwise.[11]

Below we list the set of allowable transformations:

Change the tag of an unknown word (from X) to Y if:

1. Deleting the prefix x, $|x| <= 4$, results in a word (x is any string of length 1 to 4).

2. The first (1,2,3,4) characters of the word are x.

3. Deleting the suffix x, $|x| <= 4$, results in a word.

4. The last (1,2,3,4) characters of the word are x.

5. Adding the character string x as a suffix results in a word ($|x| <= 4$).

6. Adding the character string x as a prefix results in a word ($|x| <= 4$).

7. Word W ever appears immediately to the left (right) of the word.

8. Character Z appears in the word.

An unannotated text can be used to check the conditions in all of the above transformation templates. Annotated text is necessary in training to measure the effect of transformations on tagging accuracy. Below are the first 10 transformation learned for tagging unknown words in the Wall Street Journal corpus:

Change tag:

1. From **common noun** to **plural common noun** if the word has suffix -s[12]

2. From **common noun** to **number** if the word has character .

3. From **common noun** to **adjective** if the word has character -

4. From **common noun** to **past participle verb** if the word has suffix **-ed**

5. From **common noun** to **gerund or present participle verb** if the word has suffix **-ing**

6. To **adjective** if adding the suffix **-ly** results in a word

7. To **adverb** if the word has suffix **-ly**

8. From **common noun** to **number** if the word **$** ever appears immediately to the left

9. From **common noun** to **adjective** if the word has suffix **-al**

10. From **noun** to **base form verb** if the word **would** ever appears immediately to the left.

Keep in mind that no specific affixes are prespecified. A transformation can make reference to any string of characters up to a bounded length. So while the first rule specifies the English suffix "s", the rule learner also considered such nonsensical rules as: *change a tag to adjective if the word has suffix "xhqr"*. Also, absolutely no English-specific information need be prespecified in the learner.[13]

We then ran the following experiment using 1.1 million words of the Penn Treebank Tagged Wall Street Journal Corpus. The first 950,000 words were used for training and the next 150,000 words were used for testing. Annotations of the test corpus were not used in

---

[10]This section describes work done in part while the author was at the University of Pennsylvania.

[11]If we change the tagger to tag all unknown words as common nouns, then a number of rules are learned of the form: **change tag to proper noun if the prefix is "E"**, since the learner is not provided with the concept of upper case in its set of transformation templates.

[12]Note that this transformation will result in the mistagging of *actress*. The 17th learned rule fixes this problem. This rule states: change a tag from **plural common noun** to **singular common noun** if the word has suffix ss.

[13]This learner has also been applied to tagging Old English. See (Brill 1993b).

any way to train the system. From the 950,000 word training corpus, 350,000 words were used to learn rules for tagging unknown words, and 600,000 words were used to learn contextual rules. 148 rules were learned for tagging unknown words, and 267 contextual tagging rules were learned. Unknown word accuracy on the test corpus was 85.0%, and overall tagging accuracy on the test corpus was 96.5%. To our knowledge, this is the highest overall tagging accuracy ever quoted on the Penn Treebank Corpus when making the open vocabulary assumption.

In (Weischedel *et al.* 1993), a statistical approach to tagging unknown words is shown. In this approach, a number of suffixes and important features are prespecified. Then, for unknown words:

$$p(W|T) = p(\text{unknown word}|T) *$$
$$p(\text{Capitalize-feature}|T) * p(suffixes, hyphenation|T)$$

Using this equation for unknown word emit probabilities within the stochastic tagger, an accuracy of 85% was obtained on the Wall Street Journal corpus. This portion of the stochastic model has over 1,000 parameters, with 10^8 possible unique emit probabilities, as opposed to only 148 simple rules that are learned and used in the rule-based approach. We have obtained comparable performance on unknown words, while capturing the information in a much more concise and perspicuous manner, and without prespecifying any language-specific or corpus-specific information.

K-Best Tags

There are certain circumstances where one is willing to relax the one tag per word requirement in order to increase the probability that the correct tag will be assigned to each word. In (DeMarcken 1990; Weischedel *et al.* 1993), k-best tags are assigned within a stochastic tagger by returning all tags within some threshold of probability of being correct for a particular word.

We can modify the transformation-based tagger to return multiple tags for a word by making a simple modification to the contextual transformations described above. The initial-state annotator is the tagging output of the transformation-based tagger described above. The allowable transformation templates are the same as the contextual transformation templates listed above, but with the action *change tag X to tag Y* modified to *add tag X to tag Y* or *add tag X to word W*. Instead of changing the tagging of a word, transformations now add alternative taggings to a word.

When allowing more than one tag per word, there is a trade-off between accuracy and the average number of tags for each word. Ideally, we would like to achieve as large an increase in accuracy with as few extra tags as possible. Therefore, in training we find

# of Rules	Accuracy	Avg. # of tags per word
0	96.5	1.00
50	96.9	1.02
100	97.4	1.04
150	97.9	1.10
200	98.4	1.19
250	99.1	1.50

Table 2: Results from k-best tagging.

transformations that maximize precisely this function.

In table 2 we present results from first using the one-tag-per-word transformation-based tagger described in the previous section and then applying the k-best tag transformations. These transformations were learned from a separate 240,000 word corpus. As a baseline, we did k-best tagging of a test corpus as follows. Each known word in the test corpus was tagged with all tags seen with that word in the training corpus and the five most likely unknown word tags were assigned to all words not seen in the training corpus.[14] This resulted in an accuracy of 99.0%, with an average of 2.28 tags per word. The rule-based tagger obtained the same accuracy with 1.43 tags per word, one third the number of additional tags as the baseline tagger.[15]

Conclusions

In this paper, we have described a number of extensions to previous work in rule-based part of speech tagging, including the ability to make use of lexical relationships previously unused in tagging, a new method for tagging unknown words, and a way to increase accuracy by returning more than one tag per word in some instances. We have demonstrated that the rule-based approach obtains competitive performance with stochastic taggers on tagging both unknown and known words. The rule-based tagger captures linguistic information in a small number of simple non-stochastic rules, as opposed to large numbers of lexical and contextual probabilities. Recently, we have begun to explore the possibility of extending these techniques to other problems, including learning pronunciation networks for speech recognition and learning mappings between sentences and semantic representations.

---

[14]Thanks to Fred Jelinek and Fernando Pereira for suggesting this baseline experiment.

[15]Unfortunately, it is difficult to find results to compare these k-best tag results to. In (DeMarcken 1990), the test set is included in the training set, and so it is difficult to know how this system would do on fresh text. In (Weischedel *et al.* 1993), a k-best tag experiment was run on the Wall Street Journal corpus. They quote the average number of tags per word for various threshold settings, but do not provide accuracy results.

References

Brill, E. 1992. A simple rule-based part of speech tagger. In *Proceedings of the Third Conference on Applied Natural Language Processing, ACL.*

Brill, E. 1993a. Automatic grammar induction and parsing free text: A transformation-based approach. In *Proceedings of the 31st Meeting of the Association of Computational Linguistics.*

Brill, E. 1993b. *A Corpus-Based Approach to Language Learning.* Ph.D. Dissertation, Department of Computer and Information Science, University of Pennsylvania.

Charniak, E.; Hendrickson, C.; Jacobson, N.; and Perkowitz, M. 1993. Equations for part of speech tagging. In *Proceedings of the Conference of the American Association for Artificial Intelligence.*

Church, K. 1988. A stochastic parts program and noun phrase parser for unrestricted text. In *Proceedings of the Second Conference on Applied Natural Language Processing, ACL.*

Cutting, D.; Kupiec, J.; Pedersen, J.; and Sibun, P. 1992. A practical part-of-speech tagger. In *Proceedings of the Third Conference on Applied Natural Language Processing, ACL.*

DeMarcken, C. 1990. Parsing the lob corpus. In *Proceedings of the 1990 Conference of the Association for Computational Linguistics.*

Derose, S. 1988. Grammatical category disambiguation by statistical optimization. *Computational Linguistics* 14.

Harris, Z. 1962. *String Analysis of Language Structure.* The Hague: Mouton and Co.

Jelinek, F. 1985. *Markov Source modeling of text generation.* Dordrecht. In Impact of Processing Techniques on Communication, J. Skwirzinski, ed.

Klein, S., and Simmons, R. 1963. A computational approach to grammatical coding of English words. *JACM* 10.

Kupiec, J. 1992. Robust part of speech tagging using a hidden markov model. *Computer Speech and Language.*

Marcus, M.; Santorini, B.; and Marcinkiewicz, M. 1993. Building a large annotated corpus of English: the Penn Treebank. *Computational Linguistics.*

Merialdo, B. 1991. Tagging text with a probabilistic model. In *IEEE International Conference on Acoustics, Speech and Signal Processing.*

Miller, G. 1990. Wordnet: an on-line lexical database. *International Journal of Lexicography.*

Su, K.; Wu, M.; and Chang, J. 1992. A new quantitiative quality measure for machine translation. In *Proceedings of COLING-1992.*

Weischedel, R.; Meteer, M.; Schwartz, R.; Ramshaw, L.; and Palmucci, J. 1993. Coping with ambiguity and unknown words through probabilistic models. *Computational Linguistics.*

Context-Sensitive Statistics
For Improved Grammatical Language Models

Eugene Charniak and **Glenn Carroll**
Department of Computer Science, Brown University
{ec,gac}@cs.brown.edu

Abstract

We develop a language model using probabilistic
context-free grammars (PCFGs) that is "pseudo
context-sensitive" in that the probability that a non-
terminal N expands using a rule r depends on N's parent. We give the equations for estimating the necessary probabilities using a variant of the inside-outside
algorithm. We give experimental results showing that,
beginning with a high-performance PCFG, one can
develop a pseudo PCSG that yields significant performance gains. Analysis shows that the benefits from
the context-sensitive statistics are localized, suggesting that we can use them to extend the original PCFG.
Experimental results confirm that this is both feasible
and the resulting grammar retains the performance
gains. This implies that our scheme may be useful as
a novel method for PCFG induction.

Introduction

Like its non-stochastic brethren, probabilistic parsing
has been based upon context-free grammars (CFGs),
and for similar reasons: CFGs support a simple and
efficient parsing mechanism while also accounting for
most, if not all, of the natural language phenomena
one encounters, particularly in word-order based languages such as English. In probabilistic parsing, of
course, one does not use plain CFGs, but rather their
probabilistic counterparts (PCFGs). In these each rule
of the form $N^i \rightarrow \alpha^j$ has associated with it a probabil-
ity $P(N^i \rightarrow \alpha^j)$ such that $\sum_j P(N^i \rightarrow \alpha^j) = 1$ for all i,
where N^i is the i'th non-terminal of the grammar.

In this paper we investigate a scheme for introducing context sensitive statistics into stochastic parsing,
with the aim of improving a grammar-based language
model for English. Note that this goal is quite different
from other uses of context sensitive statistics such as
improving the speed of parsing [15] or improving the
probability of the correct parse [2]. While we believe
our statistics could be adapted to these purposes, our
own interest lies in the area of language models.

---

*This work was supported in part NSF contract IRI-
8911122 and ONR contract N0014-91-J-1202.

A language model is a distribution over strings of
(English) words, and a good model should accurately
reflect the true distribution of English strings. Speaking more formally, we say the model defines a distribution over examples of English of length N, $P(w_{1,N})$,
where $w_{1,N}$ ranges over all possible corpora of English
of length N.

With a grammar-based model, one first parses the
sentences using the grammar, and then uses the parse
information to assign the probabilities to the actual
words (See [6].). We make the standard assumption
that sentences occur independently of each other, and
thus, if $w_{1,N}$ are the words of the l sentences $s_{1,l}$,

$$P(w_{1,N}) = \prod_{i=1}^{l} P(s_i) \qquad (1)$$

This assumption allows us to focus on individual sentences and their parses. Given some sentence s, consisting of n words, $w_{1,n}$, assume our model assigns τ
parses (or trees) to s, $t_1 \ldots t_\tau$. We can then write,

$$P(s) = P(w_{1,n}) = \sum_{i=1}^{\tau} P(t_i)P(w_{1,n} \mid t_i)$$

Our grammar model constructs parses for strings of
part-of-speech tokens, *not* words. The second term
above, $P(w_{1,n} \mid t_i)$, is the probability of the words
given the parse tree. The idea here is that more detailed knowledge of the syntactic structure in which the
words find themselves will enable the model to better predict the probabilities of the words. This is a
keen area for future research. Here, however, we are
concerned with the first term. Our context sensitive
statistics will be used to improve the probabilities of
the parses, the $P(t_i)$.

Roughly speaking, we wish to maximize the probability of sentences. (Actually, we wish to maximize
a product involving these probabilities, as equation 1
states.) Since, other things being equal, $P(w_{1,n})$ is
maximized when $P(t_i)$ is as large as possible, this suggests the subgoal of maximizing the sum of probabilities of all possible parses. Letting v_i stand for the ith

tag of s, we have

$$\sum_{i=1}^{\tau} P(t_i) = P(v_{1,n}) \qquad (2)$$

Equation 2 states that maximizing the sum of the probability of the parses is equivalent to maximizing the probability of the tag sequence $v_{1,n}$[1]. Commonly we do not deal with the probabilities of a language model directly, but rather try to minimize the model's per-word cross-entropy. In the same way, here we try to minimize the per-tag cross entropy of a grammar model. It can be shown that in the limit this is equivalent to minimizing

$$-\frac{1}{n} \log P(v_{1,n}) \qquad (3)$$

For our purposes we simply take the quantity of Equation 3 as the per-tag cross entropy. It seems reasonable to hope that the probabilities that minimize the per-tag cross entropy would assign higher probabilities to more common parses over uncommon ones, and thus, one would hope, the intended parse over those not intended. Such probabilities could also be used to guide the parsing process. Our own goal is simply to find ways to maximize this probability, or equivalently, to minimize the cross entropy.

Besides our differing goals, a distinguishing feature of this work is that we wish to be able to collect the parsing statistics without the use of a pre-parsed corpus. While such corpora are, of course, a valuable tool, they limit the choice of grammars to those that agree with the parses assigned in the corpus, and the volume of data available in such form is still quite limited. We show in this paper how our probabilities can be collected by an extension of the standard inside-outside algorithm [1,6].

Pseudo Context-Sensitivity

In this paper we propose to extend a standard PCFG by replacing the probability of each context-free rule with a set of probabilities, one for each non-terminal used by our grammar. Each of these new probabilities will reflect the probability of the rule occurring in a particular context, which in our case is simply the head of the parent rule. For example in figure 1, the rule $\overline{vbg} \rightarrow$ adv vbg has the non-terminal $\overline{n}$ as its parent. Formally, we write

$$P(N^i \rightarrow \alpha^j \mid \rho(N^i) = N^s) \qquad (4)$$

where $\rho(x)$ is the non-terminal that immediately dominates x — its *parent*. We refer to N^i as the *child*. Continuing our example in Figure 1, we would require

$$P(\overline{vbg} \rightarrow \text{adv vbg} \mid \rho(\overline{vbg}) = \overline{n})$$

---

[1] This equation assumes there is a single tag sequence, which is true for our data. If there are multiple tag sequences for the sentence, then we are maximizing the sum of the probabilities of all such sequences, $\sum P(v_{1,n})$.

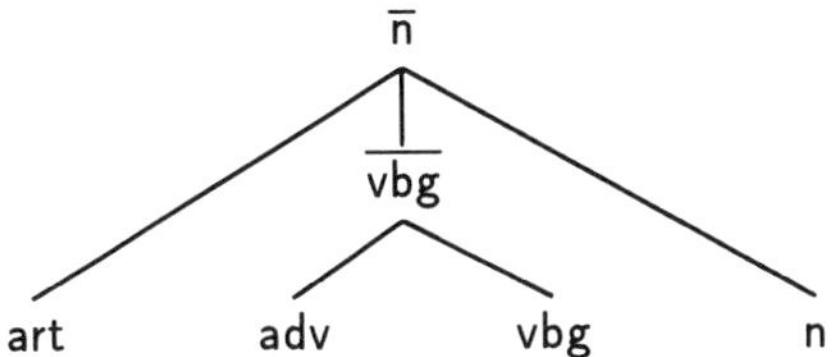

Figure 1: Application of a rule within a $\overline{n}$

This is the probability that we expand $\overline{vbg}$, (a verb phrase headed by an "ing" verb) as an adverb followed by the verb, given that its parent is $\overline{n}$, a noun phrase. Such a situation might occur in the parse of a phrase like "the slowly dripping faucet." (The base grammar for the experiments reported here is modeled after dependency grammars and thus has one non-terminal for each terminal in the language. Here $\overline{vbg}$ is the non-terminal for the terminal **vbg**. We use this notation for all of the examples, although the techniques developed here work for all PCFGs, not just probabilistic dependency grammars.)

Note that by collecting the statistics of Equation 4 we have not, in fact, moved beyond what is expressible by PCFGs. The pseudo PCSG can be expanded into a PCFG roughly as follows. For each parent-child pair, begin by creating a new non-terminal to represent the chosen pair. For any rule with the parent as its head, substitute the new non-terminal for each occurrence of the child. For each rule headed by the child, add a new rule headed by the new non-terminal. With some trivial math, one can compute new probabilities for all the rules in the expanded grammar. We return to this process later.

Although technically we have not moved beyond PCFGs, clearly our formalism has something of a context-sensitive flavor. We like to think of it as gathering context-*sensitive* statistics for a context-*free* grammar, and thus we call our scheme "pseudo context-sensitivity." Clearly, the extra information provided by context allows us a good deal more flexibility in assigning probabilities to parses. For example, while the above rule for $\overline{vbg}$ would be a not-uncommon one to find as part of a noun-phrase, consider instead the following rule for $\overline{vbg}$

$$\overline{vbg} \rightarrow \text{vbg } \overline{n}$$

This rule would be used in "Alice was planting the flowers." While this rule is a common one at the sentence level, at the noun-phrase level it would be quite uncommon. Our new probabilities would allow the system to capture this regularity. As just noted, this regularity could also be captured through the use of a different non-terminal dominating the gerund. However, our new scheme allows us to find and capture such regularities automatically.

To actually use this model requires first that one can efficiently estimate the probabilities specified in

Equation 4 and second, that given these probabilities one can efficiently calculate the probability of a parse. The second of these is reasonably straight forward, and we leave it as an exercise for the reader. The former we cover in the next section.

Calculating the Probabilities

In this section we show how it is possible to calculate the rule probabilities using a variant of the inside-outside algorithm. In the generic inside-outside algorithm one re-estimates the probability of an event e by seeing how often it occurs in a training corpus. Our events will be rule invocations, or uses, in sentence parses. Typically each sentence in the corpus has many parses, and it is possible that e occurs zero, one, or more times in any particular parse. One estimates the e-counts by adding up, for each occurrence of e the probability of the parse in which e occurs, given the sentence. Our goal in this section is to come up with the equations for this sum. We show the equations for the case where the grammar is in Chomsky-normal form.

We want to count the number of times an event occurs ($C(e)$).

$$C(e) = \sum_e P(e \mid w_{1,n}) = \frac{1}{P(w_{1,n})} \sum_e P(e, w_{1,n})$$

More specifically, we wish to count the occurrence of the rule $N^i \rightarrow N^p N^q$ in the context of $N^i N^s$. The sum over all possible ways this event could occur includes (1) the positions N^i, N^p, and N^q in the parse, (2) the position of N^s in the parse, and (3) the rule that relates N^s to N^i.

Due to lack of space, we give here only the final equation. See [7] for the derivation.

$$C(N^i \rightarrow N^p N^q, \rho(N^i) = N^s) =$$
$$\frac{1}{P(v_{1,n})} \sum_{j,k,t,h,f} \alpha_s(h,k) P(N^s \rightarrow N^i N^t) \beta_t^s(h, j-1)$$
$$P(N^i \rightarrow N^p N^q \mid N^s) \beta_p^i(j,f) \beta_q^i(f+1,k)$$
$$+ \alpha_s(j,h) P(N^s \rightarrow N^i N^t) \beta_t^s(k+1,h)$$
$$P(N^i \rightarrow N^p N^q \mid N^s) \beta_p^i(j,f) \beta_q^i(f+1,k) \quad (5)$$

In Equation 5 the outside probabilities $(\alpha_l(m,n))$ should be familiar to those acquainted with the inside-outside algorithm. The probabilities of rules is unchanged, except that when we can, we condition on the parent of the right-hand-side non-terminal. We have also introduced a new symbol, $\beta_x^y(j,k)$, that is the inside probability $\beta_x(j,k)$, conditioned on the fact that the parent of N^x is N^y. It can be shown that this last probability is computable in polynomial time (and, to be specific, in the time required to parse the sentence).

It is not too hard to see how equation 5 translates into a form that is not dependent on the CFG being in Chomsky-normal form. We omit this transformation for the sake of brevity. The version implemented, however, is the general one.

Results

Before giving the results it is necessary to establish some kind of yardstick for performance. We have suggested above that cross entropy per tag is the right number, but this figure is not suitable for comparing competing models. The difficulty is that it can vary widely with the training sentences, the tag set used, and the accuracy of the tagging. Since an absolute number is not suitable, we supply comparison figures between our model and a sort of industrial standard, the tri-tag model, trained on the same sentences, with the same tags. (The tri-tag model is one in which each tag is predicted according to the probability of getting that tag given the two previous tags.) The tri-tag model (or often a bi-tag model) has been very successful at language modeling, and is the typical model of choice in tagging models such as those in [3,8,9,10,13].

What would correspond to a good improvement in the cross-entropy of the tag sequence? To get some idea of this we took one of our best pure PCFGs and generated an artificial corpus from the grammar. We then compared the cross entropy the correct grammar assigned to the tag sequence with that assigned by a tri-tag model. We found that the correct grammar is only .15 bits/tag better than the tri-tag model (2.65 vs 2.80 bits/tag). In our learning work we have been aiming at an improvement over tri-tag of about half of that, in light of the difficulties presented by the complexity of real English, limited availability of data, and limited computational resources.

We derived our context-sensitive grammar from a PCFG developed from related work on grammar induction. This latter grammar was learned on the basis of a 300,000 word training corpus, consisting of all sentences in the tagged Brown Corpus [12] of length less than 23, and not containing certain terminals we wished to ignore (most notably parentheses, foreign words and titles). The grammar has 20 non-terminals and 3500 rules. We built the context sensitive version of this grammar by applying Equation 5 and training over the same corpus from which the PCFG was learned. Our results are obtained using a corpus of 10,000 words drawn from the same source, reserved for testing. Both the context-sensitive and context-free grammars assigned some parse to 99.5% of the words in the testing corpus (99.6% of the sentences). Unparsed sentences are ignored when collecting further data. As the exact same sentences are unparsed by both the context-free and context-sensitive grammars, and the percentage of unparsable sentences is .4% it does not seem likely that these sentences are influencing the results given here.

The results of using our context-sensitive probabilities is shown in Figure 2. In all cases we show the im-

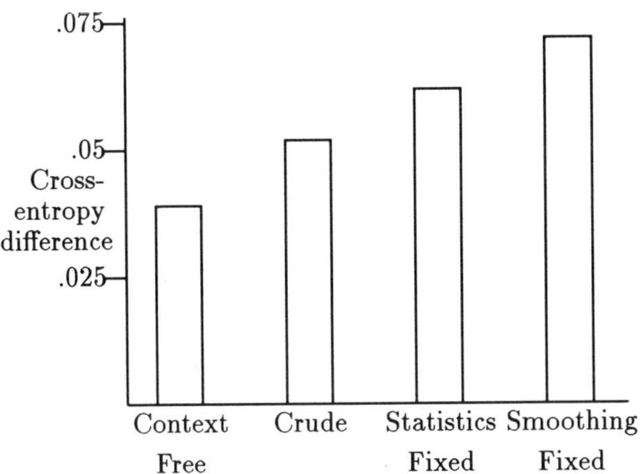

Figure 2: Per-word cross-entropy of held-out data with/without context-sensitive probabilities

provement over the tri-tag model, which had per-tag cross-entropy of 2.738 bits/tag. (Thus 0 bits/tag in our graph would correspond to a grammar that is no better or worse than the tri-tag model on average.) The left-most entry (.039 bits/tag) shows the results we obtained prior to the use of the context-sensitive statistics. The right-most (.072 bits/tag) shows what was obtained after their use. The difference, .033 bits/tag, is quite large, at least when compared to the goal of a .075 bits/tag improvement.

The intermediate figures are also of some interest. The first, labeled "crude," was obtained getting the counts for the probabilities using the viterbi approximation rather than the correct Equation 5. The second, labeled "statistics correct" was obtained using Equation 5. However, because our context-sensitive grammar requires so many parameters (3500 rules times 20 non-terminals = 70,000 parameters) we have to smooth the context-sensitive probabilities with the context-free ones. In the "statistics fixed" version we smoothed the probabilities using a "seat of the pants" guess that we would use only the context-free statistics if the combination of N^i and N^s was seen less than 1000 times, and if more than 1000 we would mix the context-sensitive with the context-free probabilities in the ration .6 to .4. Finding the optimal smoothing parameters gave the right-most, final, figure. As can be seen, attending to such details does make a difference.

We do not indicate computational resources expended in context-free vs pseudo context-sensitive as there is no significant difference in this regard. The actual parsing is the same in both cases, the only difference appearing after the parse when calculating the probabilities of the tag sequence. While parsing and both probabilistic calculations have big-O complexity n^3, in fact actual time is dominated by the former, as the probabilistic calculations are quite simple.

Analysis

We now turn to the question of from whence this .033 bits/tag improvement arises. Roughly speaking there are two possible hypotheses. The first is that the context sensitivity sharpens the probabilities across the board. The second is that there are particular situations where it is important to know the context in which a rule occurs, and these provide the lion's share of the benefit. Our initial hypothesis was that the second of these would prove to be the case. In this section we offer evidence that this is so.

We start by remembering that for each parent s and child t there is a distinct distribution for the rules R_t that expand the non-terminal t. This distribution is $P(R_t \mid s, t)$. It gives the probability that t in the context of s is expanded using each $r \in R_t$. The question we pose for each s, t pair is "Is $P(R_t \mid s, t)$ significantly different from $P(R_t \mid \neg s, t)$?" If the difference is large, then the context sensitive technique is buying us a lot in the situation in which s is the parent of t. We estimate significant difference using a likelihood ratio analysis described in [11].

The data for our estimate are the number of times that each of the k rules $r \in R_t$ is used when s is the parent of t, which we designate $C_1(s, t) = \{c_{1,1}, c_{1,2}, \ldots, c_{1,k}\}$, and similarly for the number of times when s is *not* the parent of t, which we designate $C_2(s, t) = \{c_{2,1}, c_{2,2}, \ldots, c_{2,k}\}$.

We estimate $P(R_t \mid s, t)$ using the "obvious" choice:

$$P(r_i \mid s, t) = \frac{c_{1,i}}{\sum_{j=1}^{k} c_{1,j}} \qquad (6)$$

(and similarly for $P(r_i \mid \neg s, t)$).

Loosely speaking, we compare the chance of seeing our data, C_1 and C_2, given that the distributions are distinct, versus the chance of seeing the data, given that the distributions are really the same. We name the former hypothesis

$$H(P(R_t \mid s, t), P(R_t \mid \neg s, t), C_1, C_2) \qquad (7)$$

In the latter case, we have

$$H(P(R_t \mid t), P(R_t \mid t), C_1, C_2) \qquad (8)$$

since in this case

$$P(R_t \mid s, t) = P(R_t \mid \neg s, t) = P(R_t \mid t)$$

Finally, following [11] we consider the quantity

$$-\log \lambda(s, t) =$$
$$-\log \left[\frac{H(P(R_t \mid t), P(R_t \mid t), C_1, C_2)}{H(P(R_t \mid s, t), P(R_t \mid \neg s, t), C_1, C_2)} \right] \qquad (9)$$

We lack space to show an exact form for H and $-\log \lambda(s, t)$ (but see [11] for details). Intuitively, however, this is a measure of how likely it is that the context sensitive probabilities for the rules given s, t are really just the context-free probabilities. The advantage of this quantity for our purposes is that it can be

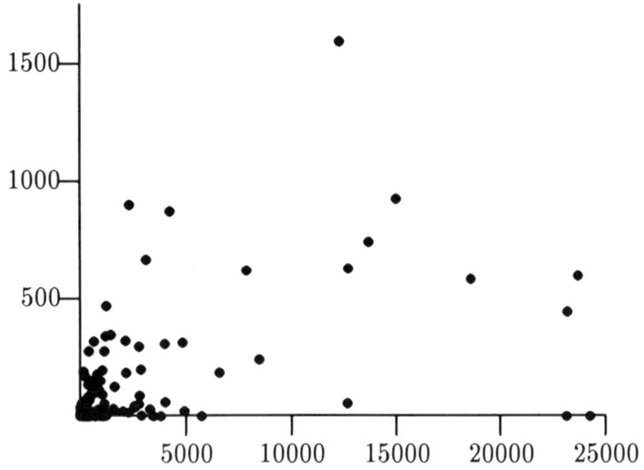

Figure 3: Plot of $-\log \lambda(s,t)$ against $C(s,t)$

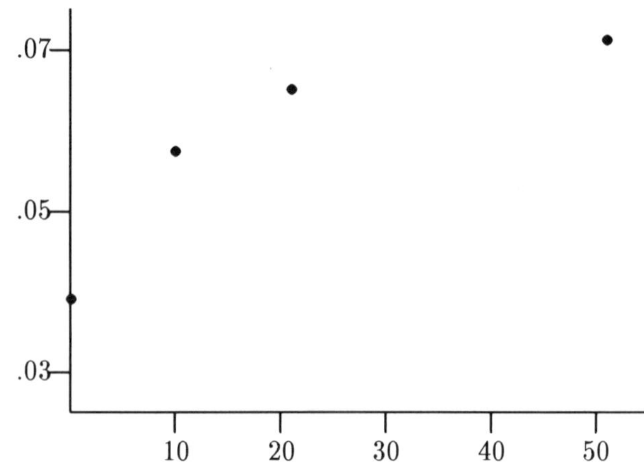

Figure 4: Cross entropy as a function of increasing numbers of s,t's

computed exactly, starting from the multinomial distribution, and thus is accurate even in the presence of rare events, which, if we may be excused the oxymoron, are quite common in our data. (Many of the rules occur less than ten times in our data. Thus the number of times we would expect them to occur with a particular parent s may well be less than one.)

Note, also, that in most normal circumstances $-\log \lambda(s,t)$ grows linearly in the number of times s,t are observed together, $C_1(s,t)$. Intuitively this captures the idea that more data allows one to make finer discriminations. The other contributing factor, naturally, is the difference between the observed distributions $P(R_t \mid s,t)$ and $P(R_t \mid \neg s,t)$. Because of this we decided to plot $-\log \lambda(s,t)$ against $C_1(s,t)$, with one point for each s,t combination. If the result were a straight line it would indicate that the various $P(R_t \mid s,t)$ distributions differed to approximately the same degree from their context-free equivalents, $P(R_t \mid t)$, and that the difference in the $-\log \lambda(s,t)$ is just due to having more data for some points, the larger $C(s,t)$'s, than others.

The results shown in Figure 3 are quite different. While there is clearly a positive correlation between $C_1(s,t)$ and $-\log \lambda(s,t)$, it is hardly a straight line. Instead a quick glance at the chart suggests that a small number of s,t combinations account for the overwhelming majority of the context-sensitive effect.

To further test this hypothesis, we modified our scheme to only use context-sensitive statistics for those s,t pairs in the top n pairs, when sorted by $-\log \lambda(s,t)$. Figure 4 shows that by the time we have considered 51 out of the 400 s,t combinations we have captured virtually all of the context-sensitive effect, and even by 21 s,t combinations (5% of the data) we have most (80%) of the effect. This suggests that our initial hypothesis, that the effect is concentrated in a small number of cases, is basically correct.

Recall that our pseudo PCSG is not truly context-sensitive, because it does not move out of the range of languages generated by PCFGs, and it is possible to "compile out" our context-sensitive statistics. Since performance benefits are concentrated in a small number of s,t pairs, and the compilation procedure can be carried out incrementally, on a per s,t pair basis, the transformation appears to be practical. The worry here is that the grammar might be so large as to be useless. Even limiting ourselves to the 20 best s,t pairs, adding a non-terminal for each pair doubles the number of non-terminals in our grammar, and, in the worst case, could cause an exponential blow-up in the number of rules. Further, we did not smooth the expanded grammar as we did for the pseudo PCSG.

Nonetheless, the observed localization was encouraging, and back-of-the-envelope calculations suggested that the expanded grammar would be only about 10,000 rules, which is a manageable size. We carried out the experiment of compiling out the 20 best s,t pairs and evaluating the performance of the resulting grammar. Ignoring rules with zero probability, the transformation added 5384 rules to the existing 3500. This more than doubles the size, but it was actually less of an increase than expected. After two iterations of the inside-outside algorithm, the grammar began to overfit the training data, but performance reached the same level as that of the pseudo PCSG. To be precise, the trained PCFG showed an *improvement* over the pseudo PCSG of 0.001 bit per word, even though it had fewer parameters (about 8,000 vs. 17,000). We do not regard this improvement as significant, but the fact the PCFG can recover the missing 20% performance gain is very satisfying.

This experiment shows that our scheme can be used as a novel form of PCFG induction, one which adds both rules and non-terminals, and revises the probabilities to produce significantly lower cross entropy. Adding non-terminals is a particularly sticky problem for grammar learners, as the unconstrained space is too large to search. What is usually done is to fix the number of non-terminals in some other way, either using outside sources of information [4], or, as we do, via a restricted formalism [5]. Another approach, suggested in [14] is to use a CNF grammar, simply guess an upper bound on the number of non-terminals, and deploy a grammar minimization procedure periodically during the grammar training. The appeal of our approach is that it does not require guesses, but can automatically identify a set of promising new non-terminals, and associated rules and probabilities. It is, admittedly, highly constrained, but we regard this as more of a feature than a drawback. Overly large search spaces require learners to deploy constraints. Our procedure is restricted enough to be feasible for a large problem (English), but loose enough to allow significant performance gains.

Conclusion

We have presented a PCFG model in which the probability of a rule also depends on the parent of the node being expanded. The scheme is applicable to any PCFG and the equations we have derived allow one to collect the necessary statistics without requiring preparsed data. In the experiment we ran, the improvement over the context-free version is quite large, given the expected range. We have analyzed the context-sensitive statistics, and shown that most of the effect is fairly localized.

This localization encouraged us to attempt to use statistics gathered for our pseudo PCSG to extend our original PCFG. By using the most promising s, t pairs, we demonstrated that expanding the grammar retains the performance gains of the pseudo PCSG, despite the reduction in the number of parameters. This implies that our scheme is not only good for improving performance by means of a pseudo PCSG, but it may also be viewed as a systematic means for inducing non-terminals, rules, and probabilities for a PCFG.

References

1. BAUM, L. E. An inequality and associated maximization technique in statistical estimation for probabilistic functions of a Markov process. *Inequalities 3* (1972), 1–8.

2. BLACK, E., JELINEK, F., LAFFERTY, J., MAGERMAN, D., MERCER, R. AND ROUKOS, S. *Towards history-based grammars: using richer models for probabilistic parsing.* In *Proceedings of the 31st Annual Meeting of the Association for Computational Linguistics.* 1993, 31–37.

3. BOGGESS, L., AGARWAL, R. AND DAVIS, R. *Disambiguation of prepositional phrases in automatically labeled technical text.* In *Proceedings of the Ninth National Conference on Artificial Intelligence.* AAAI Press/MIT Press, Menlo Park, 1991, 155–159.

4. BRISCOE, T. AND WAEGNER, N. *Robust stochastic parsing using the inside-ouside algorithm.* In *Workshop Notes, Statistically-Based NLP Techniques.* AAAI, 1992, 30–53.

5. CARROLL, G. AND CHARNIAK, E. *Learning probabilistic dependency grammars from labeled text.* In *Working Notes, Fall Symposium Series.* AAAI, 1992, 25–32.

6. CHARNIAK, E. *Statistical Language Learning.* MIT Press, Cambridge, 1993.

7. CHARNIAK, E. AND CARROLL, G. Context-Sensitive Statistics for Improved Grammatical Language Models. Department of Computer Science, Brown University, CS-94-07, 1994.

8. CHARNIAK, E., HENDRICKSON, C., JACOBSON, N. AND PERKOWITZ, M. *Equations for part-of-speech tagging.* In *Proceedings of the Eleventh National Conference on Artificial Intelligence.* AAAI Press/MIT Press, Menlo Park, 1993, 784–789.

9. CHURCH, K. W. *A stochastic parts program and noun phrase parser for unrestricted text.* In *Second Conference on Applied Natural Language Processing.* ACL, 1988, 136–143.

10. DEROSE, S. J. Grammatical category disambiguation by statistical optimization. *Computational Linguistics 14* (1988), 31–39.

11. DUNNING, T. Accurate methods for the statistics of surprise and coincidence. *Computational Linguistics 121* (1993), 61–74.

12. FRANCIS, W. N. AND KUČERA, H. *Frequency Analysis of English Usage: Lexicon and Grammar.* Houghton Mifflin, Boston, 1982.

13. JELINEK, F. *Markov source modeling of text generation.* In *The Impact of Processing Techniques on Communications,* J. K. Skwirzinski, Ed. Nijhoff, Dordrecht, 1985.

14. LARI, K. AND YOUNG, S. J. *The estimation of stochastic context-free grammars using the Inside-Outside algorithm.* In *Computer Speech and Language.* vol. 4, 1990, 35–56.

15. MAGERMAN, D. M. AND WEIR, C. *Efficiency, robustness and accuracy in Picky chart parsing.* In *Proceedings of the 30th Annual Meeting of the Association for Computational Linguistics.* 1992, 40–47.

Toward the Essential Nature of Statistical Knowledge
in Sense Resolution

Jill Fain Lehman

School of Computer Science
Carnegie Mellon University
Pittsburgh, PA 15213-3891
jef@CS.CMU.EDU

Abstract

The statistical basis for sense resolution decisions is
arrived at by the application of a process to a corpus of
instances. In general, once the process has been applied to
the corpus, the system contains both some residual
representation of the instances and some explicit
augmentation of that representation with information that
was implicit in the corpus. For example, part of the
residual representation of *He feels happy on Fridays* might
be the (*word* **sense**) pair (*happy* **feel-as-emotion**), and part
of the augmentation might be the probability of *happy*
co-occurring with the sense of *feel* as an emotion. We
show that for the simple residual representation of (*word*
sense) pairs, the existence of such a representation in and
of itself captures much of the regularity inherent in the
data. We also demonstrate that augmenting the residual
representation with the actual number of times each pair
occurs in the training corpus provides most of the
remainder of the power of probabalistic approaches.
Finally, we show how viewing this residual representation
as a form of episodic memory can enable symbolic,
knowledge-rich systems to take advantage of this source of
regularity in performing sense resolution.[1]

1. Introduction

Word sense resolution, deciding among the multiple
possible meanings for a polysemous word, is a standard
problem in natural language processing. Along with
structural ambiguity, it is one of the main potential
sources of intractability in computational natural language
systems. Early symbolic solutions, e.g. (Hirst, 1987;
Small & Reiger, 1982; Wilks, 1975), were problematic
because they required large amounts of hand-crafted
knowledge. As a result, they scaled neither within nor
across domains. The knowledge-lean response to those
efforts has been to concentrate on a variety of statistical
solutions (including neural nets) that compute, in one
form or another, the probability that a given sense of a

particular word will occur in a particular context. Such
co-occurrence information has been used to drive sense
resolution in tasks ranging from automatic text-tagging,
through information retrieval, to machine translation.
Although statistical methods have not been demonstrated
to achieve human-like accuracy in performing the task,
they have the advantage that they scale easily, making
them useful for large, unrestricted corpora.

If human levels of accuracy and computational ease are
the eventual goal, the knowledge-rich/knowledge-lean
dichotomy cannot persist. While it is unclear whether
human levels of performance can be achieved without
access to the actual knowledge sources humans use, the
empirical evidence clearly indicates that statistical
techniques alone will not suffice. Indeed, many
statistically-based systems have had their performance
improved significantly by the addition of comprehensive,
readily-available knowledge sources in the form of on-
line artifacts, e.g. parallel texts (Brown et al, 1991; Gale,
Church & Yarowsky, 1992a) or a thesaurus (Yarowsky,
1992).

What has been lost in the initial move away from
knowledge-based systems, and what has not been
recovered in the current move toward artifact-based
knowledge, is the fundamental question of exactly what
knowledge source statistical techniques gain access to. A
recent study by (Leacock, Towell & Voorhees,
1993a) compared three corpus-based statistical methods
for sense resolution (details appear in Section 4, below).
They concluded that "the response patterns of the
classifiers are, for the most part, statistically
indistinguishable from one another." This is an evocative
result that seems to indicate that each of these techniques
is getting at essentially the same source of regularity (and
further, that there is a limit to how much that source of
regularity can contribute to a solution to the problem).

The motivation for the work described in this paper is
the desire to understand the results of Leacock and others
from the symbolic, knowledge-rich point of view. Having
done so, we could imagine a symbol system that uses
standard knowledge sources for sense resolution (e.g.
syntactic and semantic regularities) when they are
available, but which can fall back on this alternate

---

[1]This research is sponsored by the Wright Laboratory, Aeronautical Systems
Center, Air Force Materiel Command, USAF, and ARPA under grant number
F33615-93-1-1330. The views and conclusions contained in this document are
those of the author and should not be interpreted as necessarily representing the
official policies or endorsements, either expressed or implied, of Wright
Laboratory or the U. S. Government.

knowledge source when the standard sources are not available. Our more immediate goal is to answer three questions: What is the essential nature of the knowledge source? What is the simplest method for capturing its regularity? How effective is that method, compared to existing non-symbolic techniques?

2. The episodic knowledge source

The statistical basis for sense resolution decisions is arrived at by the application of a process to a corpus of instances. Both the process and the definition of what constitutes an instance may vary in detail and/or complexity across systems. In general, however, once the process has been applied to the corpus, the system contains both some residual representation of the instances and some explicit augmentation of that representation with information that was implicit in the corpus. For example, in applying a Bayesian-style classifier to the instance *He feels happy on Fridays* with the task of discriminating among the meanings of *feels*, the system might acquire (*word* **sense**) pairs like (*happy* **emotion**) and (*Fridays* **emotion**), then augment these pairs with the likelihood of each *word*'s co-occurrence with each **sense**. To answer the first two of the questions posed above, we looked for ways to simplify the information that was being used to augment the residual representation. This led us to consider two processes:

1. EM0, in which the residual representation of (*word* **sense**) pairs remains unaugmented, and

2. EM1, in which the residual representation of (*word* **sense**) pairs is augmented only by the number of times each pair occurs in the corpus.

An example of the output using EM0 for a sample drawn from the *duty* corpus is shown in Figure 1 (the corpus is described in Section 3). At the top of the figure are three instances (single sentences), one from each of the three senses represented in the corpus: **tax** (sentence 1), **responsibility** (sentence 2), and **work** (sentence 3). The (*word* **sense**) pairs below the sentences show the unaugmented residual representation. The output for EM1 for this sample would augment each pair with a one (because no word is repeated for any of the senses), recording both existence and number.

Once a classifier has been built by processing the training portion of the corpus it is used to assign a word sense to the target item in each instance of the test set. Selecting the sense of the target item using a Bayesian-style classifier is generally done by computing for each sense the sum of some function of the conditional probabilities over all tokens in the instance, then selecting the sense with the largest sum. In contrast, EM0 and EM1 assign a sense to the target word using the following algorithms:

- EM0: For each word in the sentence, increment by one the counter for each sense of the target word for which there is a (*word* **sense**) pair. Choose the sense with the largest counter, deciding randomly among ties.

- EM1: For each word in the sentence, increment the counter for each sense of the target word by the number of times that (*word* **sense**) pair appeared in the training set *unless* the (*word* **sense**) pair occurred at least once for each sense. Choose the sense with the largest counter, deciding randomly among ties.

The added condition in EM1 helps to ameliorate cases in which, for example, a function word like *the* happens to appear more often within the subcorpus for a given sense than any content word appears within any sense. Under those circumstances the sheer number of instances of *the* would swamp any discriminating power in the content words. Of course, EM0 does not require this condition because a word for which there exists a record for each sense cannot change the outcome of the decision.

The label EM0 stems from the observation that the output of this process is a simple, albeit distinctly non-human-like, episodic memory. No existential co-occurrence information is lost by the process, although a great deal of other explicit information is ignored and no implicit information is recovered. That EM0 is less powerful than statistical techniques seems uncontroversial since it clearly extracts less information from the data; during test, no frequency information is available. EM0 is a member of what Barnett calls *distance-free heuristics*. Distance-free heuristics give

> a partition of the set of structures into equivalence classes, class0, class1, class2, etc., where classN is preferred to classN+1, but no assumptions are made about relative distances. Formally, this induces an ordering that is isomorphic to an initial subsequence of the natural numbers, while probability distributions are isomorphic to the reals. So there are two differences between distance-free heuristics and probability distributions: 1) probability distributions have arbitrary precision (between any two objects you can always squeeze a third — actually an infinite chain of objects) and probability distributions have a well-defined sense of distance (Barnett, 1993).

Since EM0 records only existence, it places all the structures in its residual representation in the single class, class0. It is also in this sense of being distance-free that we claim that EM0 is intrinsically less powerful than prevailing statistical approaches.

EM1 is, of course, a slightly more sophisticated version of EM0, sitting somewhere between a frequency-independent approach and a probabilistic representation. The key piece of information that is omitted from EM1 is the meta-information which usually plays a modulating role on the raw counts (e.g.the total number of instances/sense or the total size of the corpus as a whole). If we broaden our perspective for a moment to consider sense resolution within the context of a more complete natural language processor, this means that a statistical approach must know *at learning time* every class of decision for which it will need to use this exemplar as an instance. Only then can it track the number of instances in the corpus for each class and augment the residual

Instances:

1. The agencies pay no other duty or tax on their operations in Ethiopia.
2. Therefore I have a duty to stop the case.
3. The two men continue to have other duties at the firm.

Output from EM0:

(a responsibility)　　　　　　　　(on tax)
(agencies tax)　　　　　　　　　　(operations tax)
(at work)　　　　　　　　　　　　(other tax) (other work)
(case responsibility)　　　　　　　(pay tax)
(continue work)　　　　　　　　　(stop resopnsibility)
(ethiopia tax)　　　　　　　　　　(tax tax)
(firm work)　　　　　　　　　　　(the responsibility) (the tax) (the work)
(have responsibility) (have work)　(their tax)
(i responsibility)　　　　　　　　(therefore responsibility)
(in tax)　　　　　　　　　　　　　(to responsibility) (to work)
(men work)　　　　　　　　　　　(two work)
(no tax)

Figure 1: EM0's residual representation of a subset of the *duty* corpus.

representation(s) accordingly. EM1, on the other hand, requires no such augmentation. Thus, EM1 cannot determine any notion of "true probability" at decision time (but it may be able to use the information in the residual representation more generally — we will touch on this again at the end of Section 5). Is EM1 distance free? Although EM1 clearly induces an ordering that is isomorphic to an initial subsequence of the natural numbers, there is a meaning to the relative distance between classes. While EM1 is not strictly distance-free, its lack of arbitrary precision argues that in this sense, as well, it is less powerful than full statistical approaches.

The remainder of this paper proceeds from the assumption that the knowledge source whose regularity is captured by statistical techniques is simply a type of episodic memory[2], and that EM0 and EM1 are two of the simplest methods for capturing the regularity in that knowledge source. In the next two sections we examine how this view fairs empirically.

3. Experiment I: The *duty* corpus

Our pilot experimental results are based on data provided by George Miller and Ben Johnson-Laird of the Princeton Cognitive Science Laboratory. They explored the possibility of increasing the accuracy of sense resolution decisions using a novel form of artifact-based knowledge, the WordNet lexical database (Miller et al, 1990). Their pilot study used a Bayesian-style classifier on both semantically tagged and untagged versions of a corpus containing sentences from the Wall Street Journal for three senses of the word *duty*. Figure 2 shows the tagged version of sentence 1 from Figure 1, with the

categorization of content words into WordNet synonym sets given between the markers <s> and </s> (tags slightly modified to save space). The figure also gives some indication of the labor involved in producing such a corpus, and the reason this particular method for incorporating WordNet into the sense resolution task was abandoned (Johnson-Laird, 1993).

```
<stn>4922</stn>
<w>"</w><tag>"</tag>
<w>Therefore</w><s>[adv.all.0]</s><t>RB</t>
<w>,</w><t>,</t>
<w>I</w><t>PP</t>
<w>have</w><s>[verb.poss.4]</s><t>VBP</t>
<w>a</w><t>DT</t>
<w>duty</w><s>[noun.act.0]</s><t>NN</t>
<w>to</w><t>TO</t>
<w>stop</w><s>[verb.social.0]</s><t>VB</t>
<w>the</w><t>DT</t>
<w>case</w><s>[noun.act.0]</s><t>NN</t>
<w>.</w><t>.</t>
```

Figure 2: Tagged version of sentence 1 from Figure 1.

3.1. Description

Miller and Johnson-Laird provided a *duty* corpus containing three subcorpora with 45, 49, and 46 instances for the three senses **tax**, **responsibility**, and **work** respectively. In addition, they provided results for the performance of their Bayesian classifier under three experimental conditions:

- Condition A: weights were computed for each sense and word (i.e. the token between <w></w> markers) in the training set, and the highest sum used during test.

- Condition B: weights were computed only for non-function words during training, the highest sum was used during test.

---

[2]For a differing view, specifically that statistical methods are recovering some approximation to the topical information provided by the discourse, see (Leacock, Towell & Voorhees, 1993b)."

- Condition C: as for Condition B, but weights were also assigned to members of a word's synonym set if that member did not already appear in another sense. For example, in the sentence in Figure 2, the weight for *stop* would have been assigned to *halt* as well.

The performance of EM0 and EM1 under each of these conditions conforms to the descriptions given above, with "weights" being computed as outlined in the previous section.

3.2. Results and discussion

Recall and precision results for the Bayesian classifier, EM0, and EM1 under each condition are shown in Figure 3. The values for the Bayesian classifier reflect only a single run over the data, using 30 sentences from each subcorpus for training and the remainder for test. The values for EM0 and EM1 are averages over 25 runs, with each run randomly selecting 30 sentences from each subcorpus for training and using the remainder for test.

Process	Measure					
	Recall			Precision		
	A	B	C	A	B	C
Bayesian	71%	73%	80%	72%	73%	80%
EM0	70%	68%	69%	70%	69%	69%
EM1	70%	69%	69%	70%	70%	70%

Figure 3: Recall and precision for each classifier, by experimental condition.

It is clear from the values in Figure 3 that all three classifiers perform comparably in Condition A but that EM0 and EM1 do not perform as well in Conditions B and C. It is unclear whether the discrepancy in Condition B is significant because of the small number of runs for the Bayesian classifier. The discrepancy in Condition C seems significant regardless, but may well be due to an inconsistency between the two experiments during the test phase. The Princeton data was collected using semantic tagging information during both training and test in Conditions B and C; our experiment used untagged data during the test for all conditions[3]. It is impossible to tell whether this accounts for all of the discrepancy without an item-by-item comparison for a single data set using all three classifiers. If it is the source of the difference, however, this result may indicate that synonym expansion does not help significantly in a realistic test setting.

4. Experiment II: The *line* corpus

Our second experiment sought to compare the performance of EM0 and EM1 with the three statistical methods reported in (Leacock, Towell & Voorhees, 1993a). Claudia Leacock of the Princeton Cognitive Science Laboratory provided the 4136 instances from the Wall Street Journal and APHB[4] corpora. Each instance consisted of a two sentence context: a sentence that contained one of six senses of the noun *line* and the sentence that preceded it[5]. When the preceding sentence also contained *line*, the context was extended back to include a third sentence. Figure 4 shows a sample instance, taken from the subcorpus for *line* as **cord**.

> The set, designed by Mr. Hall's longtime associate Eugene Lee, has the audience divided in half, facing a central playing area. Off to one side -- representing the "have-nots" of Louisiana -- is a broken-down shack with a woodpile and a wash line.

Figure 4: A sample instance of *line* as **cord**.

4.1. Description

The *line* corpus is divided into subcorpora for each of the following six senses: **cord** (e.g. wash line, 373 instances), **division** (e.g. line between right and wrong, 376 instances), **formation** (e.g. ticket line, 347 instances), **phone** (e.g. phone line, 429 instances), **product** (e.g. new line of cars, 2211 instances), and **text** (e.g. a line of poetry, 400 instances). In each run, the test set consisted of a randomly chosen subset of 200 instances from each subcorpus for training, and a randomly chosen 149 instances from the remainder of each subcorpus for test[6]. The three statistical processes compared in (Leacock, Towell & Voorhees, 1993a) were a Bayesian-style classifier developed by Gale, Church, and Yarowsky (Gale, Church & Yarowsky, 1992a), a content-vector approach based on (Salton, Wong & Yang, 1975), and a neural net. The reader is encouraged to see (Leacock, Towell & Voorhees, 1993a) for full descriptions outlining the particular details of each approach; here, we present only a brief overview.

The Bayesian approach: relies on Bayes' decision theory for weighting tokens that co-occur with each sense. The particular classifier used here computed weights as the $\log(\text{Pr}(token|sense/\text{Pr}(token))$. To select the sense during test, the classifier computes the sum of the tokens' weights over all tokens in the instance for each sense, and selects the sense with the largest sum.

---

[3]Johnson-Laird writes, "...my motivation was to discover in an ideal world whether using expanded training data (i.e. synonyms) would help disambiguation... The advantage of using semantically tagged test data, was that word matches would be done via sense identity, rather than lexicographic form (Johnson-Laird, 1993)."

[4]A 25 million word corpus obtained from the American Printing House for the Blind and archived at IBM's T. J. Watson Research Center.

[5]Sense was assigned based on six of the twenty-five senses available for *line* in WordNet, Version 1.3. Sentences in which *line* was part of a proper noun or part of a collocation with a single sense in WordNet (e.g. *product line*) were excluded.

[6]For EM0 and EM1 the numbers were 200/sense for training and 147/sense for test. These numbers are slightly different from those reported in (Leacock, Towell & Voorhees, 1993a) due to reclassification of two misclassified instances after publication of that study.

The content vector approach: casts each sense as a single vector of concepts constructed from the training instances for that sense. The concepts are defined as the set of word stems in the corpus minus a set of about 570 very high frequency words. Concepts in a vector are weighted to reflect their relative importance in the text, with concepts that occur frequently in exactly one sense receiving the highest weighting. To select a sense for a test instance, a vector in the space defined by the training instances is constructed for the test instance. Then the inner product between its vector and each of the sense vectors is computed and the sense with the largest inner product is chosen.

The neural net approach: views sense resolution from the supervised learning paradigm. From (input features, desired response) pairs the network partitions the training instances into non-overlapping sets corresponding to the desired responses by adjusting link weights until the output unit representing the desired response has a larger activation than any other output unit. Vectors had more than 4000 positions but were sparsely populated with an average of 17 concepts. Many network topologies were tried, the results reflect a back-propogation network with no hidden units.

Each process was tested on a pilot two-sense distinction task (using the **product** and **formation** subcorpora), a three-sense distinction task (using **product**, **formation**, and **text**), and the full six-sense distinction task. To examine the effect of training set size on recall accuracy, each process was also run in the six-sense task with 50 and 100 instances during training and 149 (or 147) during test. All values reported below for the Bayesian, content vector and neural net classifiers are taken from (Leacock, Towell & Voorhees, 1993a).

4.2. Results and discussion

Recall results for the two- and three-sense tasks, and recall and precision results for the six-sense task are shown in Figure 5. The values for the statistical methods are averages over three runs, while the values for EM0 and EM1 are averages over 25 runs.[7]

Much of the motivation for the original six-sense study came from the fall-off in accuracy observed across the statistical classifiers when moving from two to three senses. The hypothesis was that the degradation would continue, and that by six senses performance would be quite poor. As can be seen in all cases except EM0, the hypothesis was disproved; performance between three and six senses appears to have essentially plateaued. To examine the trend more closely, we ran EM0 and EM1 over all combinations of subsets of three, four, and five

---

[7]The expected recall performance of a *baseline system* (Gale, Church & Yarowsky, 1992b) that simply guesses the most frequent sense in the test set would be 17% for the type of test set used by Leacock et al and replicated here. The expected recall performance of a baseline system for a test set that reflected the proportions of the six senses as they occur in the corpus, would be 53% (i.e. 53% of the instances in the combined WSJ/APHB corpus are for the sense of *line* as **product**.)

Process	2 senses	3 senses	6 senses	
	Recall	Recall	Recall	Precision
Bayesian	>90%	76%	71%	73%
Content vector	>90%	73%	72%	72%
Neural net	>90%	79%	76%	75%
EM0	86%	73%	62%	63%
EM1	87%	76%	70%	70%

Figure 5: Performance by process & condition, *line* corpus.

senses of *line*. Figure 6 shows recall averages for each process, with 200 training instances/sense and 147 test instances/sense. The averages are over all combinations within a given number of senses, 5 trials/combination. The results for six senses for EM0 and EM1 have been repeated in this figure for context. The gradual but steady decline in accuracy for EM0 is evident.

Process	Recall			
	3 senses	4 senses	5 senses	6 senses
EM0	76%	70%	65%	62%
EM1	82%	76%	72%	70%

Figure 6: Recall avg's for EM0 & EM1, by # of senses.

The lack of significant degradation for six senses using the statistical classifiers led Leacock et al to conclude that overall accuracy is a function of the difficulty of the senses rather than a strict function of the degree of polysemy. They found that **cord** and **product** were the senses classified most accurately. **Text** was the most difficult for the statistical classifiers, with **formation** and then **division** the next most difficult. As shown in Figure 7, both EM0 and EM1 also classified **cord** and **product** most accurately. **Division**, **formation**, and **text** were also the least accurate senses for EM0 and EM1, but **formation** was more difficult than **text** for both precision and recall.

Process	Recall%/Precision%					
	cord	divis	form	phone	prod	text
EM0	76 / 87	54 / 52	53 / 47	57 / 65	74 / 71	56 / 53
EM1	82 / 81	68 / 72	46 / 67	79 / 72	90 / 62	53 / 68

Figure 7: Recall/precision for EM0 & EM1, by sense.

Figures 5, 6, and 7 indicate that the results are comparable across classifiers with the exception of the accuracy of EM0 in the six-sense condition. Again, we must be careful in making judgments of significance because the averages for the statistical methods are over a small number of runs. Nevertheless, as with the *duty* corpus, a ten percent difference seems likely to be significant. In trying to understand the origin of the decrease in EM0's performance, we examined the data reflected in Figure 5 more closely. It became evident that the number of sense assignments being decided at random for EM0 was growing steadily, from about three times as many on the average for EMO when compared to EM1 with two senses, to almost ten times as many for six senses. Remember that sense is randomly decided among senses whose accumulated sums are tied. In the case of six senses, this meant that a substantive portion of the total number of instances (about 20%) were being decided at random for EM0 while only about three percent were being decided at random for EM1. Knowing the number of instances being decided at random, we can calculate the *effective recall rate* (ERR) for EM0, i.e. the recall rate for those instances in which the method is able to resolve the sense unequivocally. Since for a total test set size of N,

$$N(RecallAvg) = \#NDR(ERR) + \#DR(1/\#senses)$$

where NDR means "not decided randomly" and DR means "decided randomly," we can compute the effective rate as

$$ERR = (N(RecallAvg) - \#DR(1/\#senses)) / \#NDR.$$

Performing this calculation for EM0 and EM1 over the same data sets summarized in Figure 5 gives an effective rate of 73% for EM0 with six senses, comparable to the rates achieved by EM1 and the statistical methods[8].

There are two important aspects to this result. First, EM0 seems to do about as well as the other methods for small numbers of senses. This is probably because the larger the number of senses, the larger the training set, and the higher the likelihood that a given word will appear at least once in those instances for each sense. The second important aspect is that we can predict exactly under what conditions EM0's performance will be comparable to the other methods, i.e. we know that if we limit EMO's performance to those instances where it can make an unequivocal decision, it will act as an equally viable process for the knowledge source.

The final result to be discussed concerns the more general relationship between recall rate and number of training examples. Leacock et al point out that collecting training contexts is the most time-consuming part of building a statistical classifier. They argue that if statistical methods are going to be useful in high-level NLP tasks, then, given comparable recall and precision rates, classifiers requiring small training sets are to be preferred. Figure 8 shows the increase in recall rate as a function of the number of training examples. It superimposes this measure for EM0 and EM1 on a similar graph in (Leacock, Towell & Voorhees, 1993a). Given that it has the flattest curve, the content vector approach would seem to gain the least from an increase in training set size, although EM0 and EM1 compare favorably to the other statistical approaches[9].

5. Conclusions

Ours is not the first result to indicate that problems solvable at a particular level of performance by a powerful set of techniques can also be solved by simpler derivatives of those techniques. Miller has shown how a specific search technique over a static, symbolic representation can perform as well as probabilistic representations in a concept acquisition task, accounting for response times, accuracy rates, and the effects of noisy or incomplete data (Miller, 1993). Holte has demonstrated that rules that learn to classify examples on the basis of a single attribute are often as accurate as the more complex rules induced by most machine learning systems for the most commonly used datasets (Holte, 1993). Preliminary work by Barnett in applying distance-free heuristic versions of a hidden Markov model to word tagging appear promising as well (Barnett, 1993).

Each of these projects, along with our own, is motivated at least in part by the fundamental question: Where is the power coming from? It would seem that, for sense resolution at least, a great deal of the regularity captured by statistical techniques is similarly captured by the existence of the residual representation of the training instances alone. A modest increment of accuracy can be achieved by augmenting the residual representation with the raw frequencies of the elements in it. Deriving the actual probabilities (or equivalents), however, seems to be of little additional use. Is this an argument against statistical approaches, per se? No. Given that EM0 and EM1 do not perform *better* than the statistical approaches, the latter cannot be supplanted on performance grounds.

Still, lack of superior performance is not an argument against practical benefit. Recall that while our basic motivation was to understand the source of power captured by statistical techniques, our aim was to do so within the context of a symbolic, knowledge-rich approach. Indeed, this work was undertaken with the specific goal of characterizing the relevant knowledge source so that it could be added to a particular cognitively-motivated natural language system, NL-Soar (Lehman, 1994; Lehman, Lewis & Newell, 1991; Lewis, 1993). Statistical techniques do not fit naturally within

---

[8]The effective rate for EM0 for two senses was 89%, for three senses, 79%.

[9]Retroactively, we computed similar data for the *duty* corpus, varying training set size from five to 30 sentences, with a similar gain of about ten percent accuracy overall.

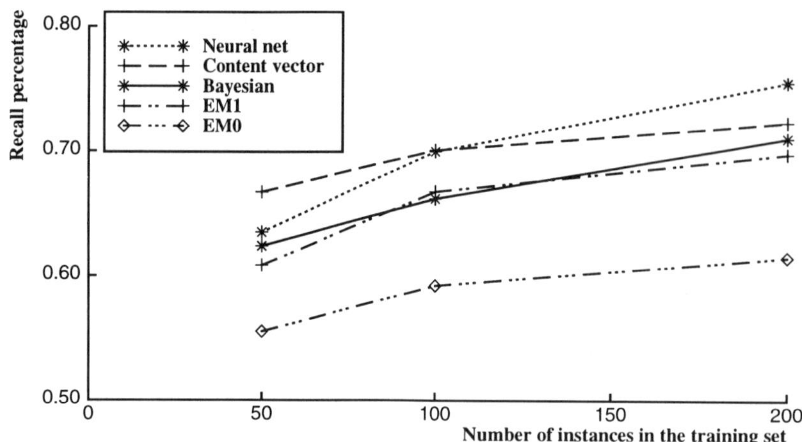

Figure 8: Average recall as a function of training set size for the *line* corpus.

the existing framework of NL-Soar. Although NL-Soar does contain knowledge sources for syntax and semantics, it is unclear whether those sources are redundant with respect to the knowledge source reflected by statistical techniques, or orthogonal to that source. If we ignore that knowledge source and it is a significant, independent component of human levels of performance, then the model as a whole will be inadequate.

Thus, the challenge in attacking word sense resolution in NL-Soar was to find a version of the knowledge source that would both fit naturally into the existing framework and capture about as much of the regularity as the statistical techniques (otherwise we would be forced to assume significant redundancy). EM0 and EM1 meet both criteria. They can be called on when richer knowledge sources (e.g. syntax and semantics) are inadequate to make a sense resolution decision — falling back on a weak method, as outlined in Section 1. EM0 has the additional advantage that it is a technique with which we have had a great deal of experience. We know how to create such an episodic memory as a by-product of learning during problem solving, and have seen how it can provide the basis for inductive generalization in other tasks, e.g. (Conati & Lehman, 1993; Miller, 1993).

We believe our empirical results and the view of the relevant knowledge source as a type of episodic memory opens up a number of possible avenues for future research:

- We know that EM0's effective recall rate is comparable to the other techniques. Since we can detect when EM0 cannot make an unequivocal decision, it is straightforward to fall back on EM1 in those circumstances. In NL-Soar, the knowledge that would be learned under such a scheme would probably override the unit-valued contributions from individual words by higher-valued contributions for constellations of words. What is the effect on performance for such a hybrid system?

- We also know that EM0 is effective when the

number of possible senses is relatively small. Is there some other mechanism at work that keeps the number of potential senses in a context small enough to make EM0 viable by itself?

- If we fall back on episodic memory when richer knowledge sources fail, we establish a relationship in NL-Soar in which those richer sources can be viewed as arising, in part, from learning over the episodic memory. Thus, there would be significant redundancy between the richer and episodic sources. Under such a view, human levels of performance would be a function of the recasting of the episodic regularities into the level of generality expressed by syntactic and/or semantic terms. Although a full acquisition scheme would have to explain how the terms themselves arose, does this view provide an initial step down the acquisition path?

- In order to compare EM0 and EM1 with the statistical methods, it was necessary to use the same sort of corpora. There is nothing inherent in this choice for NL-Soar. Elsewhere we have argued that the appropriate source for episodic memories (for a cognitive model, at least) is not a corpus of sentences, but a corpus of experiences (Lehman, 1994). The relevant criterion should be "How many of the concepts referred to by these words have co-occurred in my experience?" rather than "How many of these words have co-occurred in sentences I have read?" Since NL-Soar is designed to comprehend in the context of performing tasks, it should be possible to explore the possibility of justifying a candidate meaning of a polysemous word by recognizing the situation being described as having occurred in the world. In this view, the importance of *not* having to track the size of the corpus becomes evident. At the moment that such experiences arise we do not necessarily want to have to anticipate all of the ways in which they will serve as instances.

6. Acknowledgements

This work would not have been possible without the help and cooperation of the Princeton Cognitive Science Laboratory, especially, George Miller, Ben Johnson-Laird, Claudia Leacock, and Randee Tengi. Comments on early drafts were provided by Geoffrey Towell, Jim Barnett, Kevin Knight, Phil Resnick, Claudia Leacock, and Craig Miller.

7. References

Barnett, J. 1993. Personal communication.

Brown, P. F., Della Pietra, S. A., Della Pietra, V. J., and Mercer, R. L. 1991. Word-sense disambiguation using statistical methods. *Proceedings of the 29th Annual Meeting of the Association for Computational Linguistics*, 264-270 .

Conati, C. and Lehman, J. Fain. 1993. Toward a Model of Student Education in Microworlds. *Proceedings of the Fifteenth Annual Conference of the Cognitive Science Society*, 353-358 .

Gale, W., Church, K. W., and Yarowsky, D. 1992. *A method for disambiguating word senses in a large corpus.* Technical Report , AT&T Bell Laboratories Statistical Research Report 104.

Gale, W., Church, K. W., and Yarowsky, D. 1992. Estimating upper and lower bounds on the performance of word-sense disambiguation programs. *Proceedings of the Association for Computational Linguistics*, 249-256 .

Hirst, G. 1987. *Semantic Interpretation and the Resolution of Ambiguity.* Cambridge, England: Cambridge University Press.

Holte, R. C. 1993. Very simple classification rules perform well on most commonly used datasets. *Machine Learning 11*(1), 63-90.

Johnson-Laird, B. 1993. Personal communication.

Leacock, C., Towell, G., and Voorhees, E. 1993. Corpus-based statistical sense resolution. *Proceedings of the ARPA Workshop on Human Language Technology*, .

Leacock, C., Towell G., and Voorhees, E. M. 1993. Towards Building Contextual Representations of Word Senses Using Statistical Models. *Proceedings of SIGLEX Workshop: Acquisition of Lexical Knowledge from Text*, 10-20 , Association for Computational Linguistics.

Lehman, J. Fain. 1994. Meaning Matters: Response to Miller. In Steier, D. and Mitchell, T. (Eds.), *Mind Matters: Contributions to Cognitive and Computer Science in Honor of Allen Newell.* Hillsdale, New Jersey: Lawrence Erlbaum Associates. In press.

Lehman, J. Fain, Lewis, R., and Newell, A. 1991. Integrating Knowledge Sources in Language Comprehension. *Proceedings of the Thirteenth Annual Conferences of the Cognitive Science Society*, 461-466 .

Lewis, R. L. 1993. *An Architecturally-based Theory of Human Sentence Comprehension.* Ph.D. diss., Carnegie Mellon University. Also available as Technical Report CMU-CS-93-226.

Miller, C. S. 1993. *Modeling Concept Acquisition in the Context of a Unified Theory of Cognition.* Ph.D. diss., The University of Michigan. Also available as Technical Report CSE-TR-157-93.

Miller, G. A., Beckwith, R., Fellbaum, C., Gross, D., and Miller, K. 1990. *Five papers on WordNet.* Technical Report , Princeton University Cognitive Science Laboratory Report 43.

Salton, G., Wong, A., and Yang, C. S. 1975. A vector space model for automatic indexing. *Communications of the ACM 18*(11), 613-620.

Small, S. L., and Reiger, C. J. 1982. Parsing and comprehending with word experts (a theory and its realization). In Lehnert, W. G., and Ringle, M. H. (Eds.), *Strageies for Natural Language Processing.* Hillsdale, New Jersey: Lawrence Erlbaum Associates.

Wilks, Y. A. 1975. A preferential, pattern-seeking semantics for natural language inference. *Artificial Intelligence 6*, 53-74.

Yarowsky, D. 1992. Word-sense disambiguation using statistical models of Roget's categories trained on a large corpora. *COLING-92*, 454-460 .

A Probabilistic Algorithm for Segmenting Non-Kanji Japanese Strings

Virginia Teller
Hunter College and the Graduate School
The City University of New York
695 Park Avenue
New York, NY 10021
vmthc@cunyvm.cuny.edu

Eleanor Olds Batchelder
The Graduate School
The City University of New York
33 West 42nd Street
New York, NY 10036
eobgc@cunyvm.cuny.edu

Abstract

We present an algorithm for segmenting unrestricted Japanese text that is able to detect up to 98% of the words in a corpus. The segmentation technique, which is simple and extremely fast, does not depend on a lexicon or any formal notion of what a word is in Japanese, and the training procedure does not require annotated text of any kind. Relying almost exclusively on character type information and a table of hiragana bigram frequencies, the algorithm makes a decision as to whether to create word boundaries or not. This method divides strings of Japanese characters into units that are computationally tractable and that can be justified on lexical and syntactic grounds as well.

Introduction

A debate is being waged in the field of machine translation about the degree to which rationalist and empiricist approaches to linguistic knowledge should be used in MT systems. While most participants in the debate seem to agree that both methods are useful, albeit for different tasks, few have compared the limits of knowledge-based and statistics-based techniques in the various stages of translation.

The perspective adopted in this paper represents one end of the rationalist-empiricist spectrum. We report a study that assumes almost no rule-based knowledge and attempts to discover the maximum results that can be achieved with primarily statistical information about the problem domain. For the task of segmenting non-kanji strings in unrestricted Japanese text, we found that the success rate of this minimalist method approaches 95%.

Background

In recent years, researchers in the field of natural language processing have become interested in analyzing increasingly large bodies of text. Whereas a decade ago a corpus of one million words was considered large, corpora consisting of tens of millions of words are common today, and several are close to 100 million words. Since exhaustively parsing such enormous amounts of text is impractical, lexical analyzers called part-of-speech taggers have been used to obtain information about the lexical, syntactic, and some semantic properties of large corpora. Automatic text tagging is an important first step in discovering the linguistic structure of large text corpora.

Probabilistic approaches to tagging have developed in response to the failure of traditional rule-based systems to handle large-scale applications involving unrestricted text processing. Characterized by the brittleness of handcrafted rules and domain knowledge and the intractable amount of work required to build them and to port them to new domains and applications, the rule-based paradigm that has dominated NLP and artificial intelligence in general has come under close scrutiny. Stochastic taggers are one example of a class of alternative approaches, often referred to as "corpus-based" or "example-based" techniques, that use statistics rather than rules as the basis for NLP systems.

A major decision in the design of a tagger is to determine exactly what will count as a word, and whether two sequences of characters are instances of the same word or different words (Brown et al. 1992). This may sound trivial — after all, words are delimited by spaces — but it is a problem that has plagued linguists for decades. For example, is *shouldn't* one word or two? Is *shouldn't* different from *should not*? If hyphenated forms like *rule-based* and *Baum-Welch* (as in *Baum-Welch algorithm*) are to count as two words, then what about *vis-à-vis*? The effects of capitalization must also be considered, as the following example shows:

> Bill, please send the bill. Bill me today or bill me tomorrow. May I pay in May?

In the first sentence *Bill* is a proper noun and *bill* is a common noun. In the second sentence *Bill* and *bill* are the same — both are verbs — while in the third sentence *May* and *May* are different — one is a modal and the other a proper noun.

These problems are compounded in Japanese because, unlike English, sentences are written as continuous strings of characters without spaces between words. As a result, decisions about word boundaries are all the more difficult, and lexical analysis plays an important preprocessing role in all Japanese natural language systems. Before text can be parsed, a lexical analyzer must segment the stream of input characters comprising each sentence.

Japanese lexical analyzers typically segment sentences in two major steps, first dividing each sentence into major phrases called *bunsetsu* composed of a content word and accompanying function words, e.g. noun+particle, verb+endings, and then discovering the individual words within each phrase. Algorithms based on the longest match principle perform the bulk of the work (Kawada 1990). To extract a bunsetsu structure from an input string, the system first proposes the longest candidate that matches a dictionary entry and then checks whether the result agrees with the rules for bunsetsu composition. If the check fails, the system backtracks, proposes another shorter word, and checks the composition rules again. This process is repeated until the sentence is divided into the least number of bunsetsu consistent with its structure (Ishizaki et al. 1989).

Maruyama et al. (1988) describe a sentence analyzer that consists of five stages, each of which exploits a distinct kind of knowledge that is stored in the form of a set of rules or a table. The five stages are: segmentation by (1) character type, (2) character sequence, and (3) a longest matching algorithm; (4) a bottom-up parallel algorithm if stage 3 fails; and (5) compound-word composition. The first three lines in the transliterated example below illustrate what the procedure must accomplish:

```
input:         sisutemugabunobunkaisuru.
bunsetsu:      sisutemuga/buno/bunkaisuru.
words:         sisutemu-ga/bun-o/bunkai-suru.
meaning:       system-subj/sentence-obj/analyze-nonpast
translation:   A/The system analyzes a/the sentence.
```

Two recent projects at BBN have used rule-based lexical analyzers to construct probabilistic models of Japanese segmentation and part-of-speech assignment. Matsukawa, Miller, & Weischedel (1993) based their work on JUMAN, developed at Kyoto University, which has a 40,000 word lexicon and tags with a success rate of about 93%. They used hand-corrected output from JUMAN to train an example-based algorithm to correct both segmentation errors and part of speech errors in JUMAN's output. POST, a stochastic tagger, then selects among ambiguous alternative segmentation and part-of-speech assignments and predicts the part of speech of unknown words. Papageorgiou (1994) trained a bigram hidden Markov model to segment Japanese text using the output of MAJESTY, a rule-based morphological preprocessor (Kitani & Mitamura 1993) that is reported to segment and tag Japanese text with better than 98% accuracy. Papageorgiou's method uses neither a lexicon of Japanese words nor explicit rules,

basing its decisions instead solely on whether a two-character sequence is deemed more likely to continue a word or contain a word boundary. This approach was able to segment 90% of the words in test sentences correctly, compared to 91.7% for the JUMAN-based method.

Characteristics of Japanese Text

Japanese text is composed of four different types of characters: kanji characters borrowed more than a millennium ago from Chinese; two kana syllabaries, hiragana and katakana; and romaji, consisting of Roman alphabetic and Arabic numeral characters. The syllabaries contain equivalent sets of around 80 characters each. Hiragana is used for Japanese words and inflections, while katakana is used for words borrowed from foreign languages and for other special purposes. Lunde (1993:4) describes the distribution of character types as follows:

> Given an average sampling of Japanese writing, one normally finds 30 percent kanji, 60 percent hiragana, and 10 percent katakana. Actual percentages depend on the nature of the text. For example, you may find a higher percentage of kanji in technical literature, and a higher percentage of katakana in the literature of fields such as computer science, which make extensive use of loan words written in katakana.

The variable proportions of character types can easily be seen in a comparison of three different samples of Japanese text. The first corpus consists of a set of short newspaper articles on business ventures from *Yomiuri*. The second corpus contains a series of editorial columns from *Asahi Shinbun* (*tenseijingo shasetsu*, 1985-1991). Information on a third corpus was drawn from the description provided by Yokoyama (1989) of an online dictionary, *Shin-Meikai Kokugo Jiten*. Table 1 gives the size of each corpus in thousands of characters and shows the percentage of text written in each of the four character types. Punctuation and special symbols have been excluded from the counts.

	bus.	ed.	dict.
size (K chars)	42	275	2,508
% hiragana	30.2	58.0	52.4
% kanji	47.5	34.6	37.9
% katakana	19.3	4.8	6.8
% num/rom	2.9	2.6	2.9

Table 1

Of particular note is the fact that the business corpus contains roughly half the amount of hiragana of the other two samples, both of which come close to

Lunde's norm, and three to four times as much katakana. Table 2 lists the ten most frequent hiragana in the three corpora expressed as a percentage of total hiragana.

business		editorial		dictionary	
no	13.1	no	8.3	no	7.8
to	6.7	i	6.3	ru	6.3
ru	6.6	to	4.5	i	4.8
wo	6.5	ru	4.5	ni	4.4
ni	5.6	ni	4.5	to	4.1
ha	5.5	ta	4.4	wo	3.9
de	5.5	ha	4.1	na	3.5
si	5.3	ga	4.0	si	3.4
ta	4.4	wo	3.7	su	3.2
ga	3.6	na	3.5	ta	3.1

Table 2

Again, the business corpus exhibits characteristics that differ significantly from the editorial and dictionary samples. Although *no* is the most frequent hiragana in all three texts, it occurs almost twice as often in the business sample. Since one function of the particle *no* is to combine nouns into noun phrases, this result suggests there is a large amount of such compounding in business writing. In contrast, hiragana *i* and *na*, which appear in adjective inflections, are not found in the business top ten list, even though both are among the top ten in the other two corpora, and *i* is in the top three.

Defining a Word

Exactly what constitutes a word in Japanese for segmentation purposes is a controversial issue. Without spaces that delimit lexical units, the decision may be left largely to the designer of a particular segmentation method. The bunsetsu *BENKYOUsiteimasita* 'was studying', written with two initial kanji characters (shown in upper case below) and seven hiragana, can be considered a single lexical unit or can be divided into as many as six elements:

BEN+KYOU - si - te - i - ma+si - ta

containing the sequence:

'study' - 'do' - particle - progressive - polite - past

or into some other intermediate grouping. Because of this flexibility, the word boundaries produced by a particular segmentation method may vary from fairly large lexical units to small ones closer to a morphological level of analysis, and several positions along this spectrum can easily be defended. The consistency with which a segmenter makes its decisions is more important than the position taken on word boundaries. Systematic errors in output can be accounted for later in processing no matter what size

units are produced.

The Segmentation Algorithm

The strategy underlying the design of the present segmentation algorithm was to discover the maximum results that could be achieved with a minimum of computational (and human) effort. To this end, the algorithm incorporates a simple statistical technique for segmenting hiragana strings into words, a measure that is loosely based on the notion of mutual information (Brill et al. 1990, Magerman & Marcus 1990).

During the first stage of processing, a program scans an input file of Japanese text and identifies each character as one of five types:

    [h] hiragana
    [K] kanji
    [k] katakana
    [P] punctuation and symbols
    [R] romaji (Roman letters and Arabic numbers)

For each hiragana character the algorithm computes a bigram frequency count based on the type of character that immediately precedes and follows the hiragana.

Each hiragana character is tallied twice — once as a pair with its preceding hiragana character or other character type and once as a pair with the following character. The output of this stage of processing is a 90 x 90 bigram frequency array. The rows and columns in the array include 83 hiragana characters and 4 other character types plus an end count, an error count, and a row or column total. The end count is tallied whenever the hiragana character is the last in a string (the pair h + {K,k,P,R}).

The segmentation algorithm then uses the bigram frequency array previously computed to divide hiragana sequences in Japanese text into individual words. For each hiragana character a decision is made as to whether this hiragana begins a new word or is a continuation of the preceding one. The algorithm works as follows:

A. Hiragana characters that follow katakana, punctuation, or romaji characters are assumed to begin a new word. These cases fall into the category of "no decision needed."

B. A word boundary is created between two hiragana characters if the combined probability of the left character ending a word and the right one beginning a word is greater than a probability of the two occurring together. If the end/begin likelihood is equal to or less than the co-occurrence likelihood, no cut is made.

The likelihood of ending a word is estimated from the proportion of all occurrences of the hiragana character that immediately precede any non-hiragana character, i.e. the hiragana ends a hiragana string:

$$[h1 + \{K,k,P,R\}] / h1\text{-total}.$$

The assumption is that no word contains hiragana followed by non-hiragana. There are kanji compound "words", however, that are typically written with the first part in hiragana to represent a too-difficult kanji. Such compounds will be divided incorrectly by this method, as will the hiragana honorific prefixes before words written in kanji, e.g. *o+KANE*, *go+SENMON*.

The likelihood of beginning a word is estimated from the proportion of all occurrences of the hiragana character immediately following a character that is not kanji or hiragana:

$$[\{k,P,R\} + h2] \, / \, h2\text{-total}.$$

This measure is not completely convincing, because it omits the most frequent case of hiragana words, namely, where particles follow kanji. However, since these cases cannot automatically be distinguished from other cases (also numerous) where kanji+hiragana represent a single morpheme, the K+h2 count is omitted from the measure.

The likelihood of co-occurrence is estimated from the product of two percentages:

$$(\, [h1+h2] \, / \, h1\text{-total} \,) \, * \, (\, [h1+h2] \, / \, h2\text{-total} \,).$$

This measure is also flawed due to the existence of certain highly frequent combinations that are not usually considered to be a single word, e.g. *de ha*, and others that are infrequent but undoubtedly a single word, e.g. *mono*.

C. Deciding whether to create a word boundary between a kanji character and a following hiragana presents the greatest difficulty, because some kanji-hiragana transitions are continuations of the same word (*YO+bu*) while others are not (*HON+de*). Division is based on a comparison of the frequency of the hiragana following kanji and its frequency following other non-hiragana characters in the set {k,P,R}. Our reasoning is that the non-kanji cases cannot be continuations (case A above), while the kanji cases can be either continuous or discontinuous. Four situations arise:

1. If this hiragana very rarely appears following non-kanji characters (h < 0.5% of all hiragana in post-kPR position), then its occurrence following kanji is assumed to be a continuation of the same word.

2. If this hiragana appears after non-kanji characters significantly more often (> 0.5%) than after kanji characters, then begin a new word.

3. Conversely, if the post-kanji ratio is greater than or equal to the post-kPR ratio, and the post-kPR ratio is less than 1%, then consider the hiragana a continuation.

4. Otherwise, if the probability of this hiragana beginning a word is greater than the probability that it is a continuation, then separate.

Results

Experiment 1

We conducted an initial experiment (Teller & Batchelder 1993) to assess the accuracy of the segmentation algorithm using the business corpus, which is a collection of 216 short texts averaging 6 to 7 lines each and totaling 1457 lines and 49,024 characters. In the experiment, 90% of the corpus was used to build the bigram frequency table, and the segmentation algorithm was tested on the remaining 10%. This corpus produced a sparse matrix with a total of 20,012 pairs tallied in 802 of the 7744 cells. Table 3 shows a fragment of this array that clearly reveals three high frequency hiragana strings: *kara*, a particle; *kiru*, a verb form (as in *dekiru*); and *kore*, a pronoun.

	ra	ri	ru	re	ro
ka	140	3	2	1	
ki			43	1	
ku	1	3	2		
ke	7	12		3	
ko				38	12

Table 3

The algorithm performed well in some respects and poorly in others. Although kanji compound verbs (kanji followed by *suru*) were correctly maintained as a unit, the treatment of the *-teiru/-deiru* stative/progressive verb ending was inconsistent. The *-te* form was left intact (te i ru) while the *-de* version was incorrectly segmented as de l i ru. The particles *nado*, *mo*, and *he* were not separated from preceding kanji, but the words *tomo* 'together' and *mono* 'thing' were divided in the middle. Some common adverbial phrases were joined and some were not. For example, *ni tsuite* 'concerning' was treated as a single word ni tsu i te, but the phrase *sude ni* 'already' was broken into su l de l ni.

Table 4 gives examples of correct and incorrect segmentation and suggests an improved segmentation for the incorrectly divided strings. A blank between two characters indicates they are part of the same word, while a 'l' indicates a word boundary, and upper case denotes kanji.

correct
KA ri ru l ko to l ga l de ki ru l to i u
ko re l ma de l no

incorrect
ni l to l do l ma t te i ta
mo l no l de l ha l ka l na ri

better
ni l to do ma t te i ta
mo no l de l ha l ka na ri

Table 4

An analysis of the output when the test corpus was run revealed that 90.7% of the 697 hiragana strings were divided correctly, and 9.3% were divided incorrectly. A breakdown of the results is shown in Table 5.

category	strings
no decision needed: {k,P,R} + h	110
segmented correctly	522
segmented incorrectly	59
questionable decisions	6
total	697

Table 5

Experiment 2

The segmentation procedure was run recently on samples of the much larger editorial corpus. The portion of this corpus that we used to construct the bigram frequency array comprises 1.17 million characters, including punctuation and headers, of which 597,500 characters or 51% are hiragana. The 211,303 hiragana strings in the training corpus vary in length from 1 to 32 with an average length of 2.8. The hiragana portion of the bigram table (88 x 88) contains 808,803 entries in 3,916 cells, indicating that 51% of all possible hiragana pairs were encountered during processing.

When the segmentation algorithm was applied to a test corpus, it became obvious that additional training had produced a tendency to overdivide; the algorithm now preferred divisions to combinations. In order to constrain this tendency, two rules were added to the procedure:

1. Since the hiragana character *wo* is a specialized character that functions only as the object marking particle, a word boundary should always be placed on either side of it.

2. Eleven hiragana characters, including the most common postpositional particles, can occur singly as a word. No other hiragana characters are treated in this way.

A third proposed rule was eliminated after it was found not to affect the results significantly. This rule stated that small (subscripted) hiragana are always in the middle of a word and should suppress word boundaries on either side.

In addition, case A of the algorithm described above was modified so that a word boundary would automatically be created whenever a character type transition was encountered unless the transition involved kanji+hiragana, which is handled by case C. This change enabled us to evaluate the algorithm's ability to segment strings of any character type, including kanji. Kanji, katakana, and romaji strings are

still left intact; only hiragana strings can be further divided or combined with preceding kanji. Nonetheless, our assumption is that this is the most appropriate choice for the vast majority of such strings.

With these enhancements, the segmentation procedure was rerun on a corpus of 2,200 characters containing the following proportions of character types: hiragana, 54%; kanji, 38%; katakana, 5%; numbers, 3%. (There was no romaji in this sample.) The segmented corpus was divided into 1172 strings, 570 or 49% of which were resolved on the basis of character type transitions alone. The algorithm inserted 602 additional boundaries, resulting in a total of 1172 words.

Assessing the accuracy of these results raises the difficult question of what to count as an error, given that the definition of a word in Japanese remains indeterminate. Word boundaries that separate stems and roots from inflectional and derivational endings cannot legitimately be described as errors for the reasons explained earlier. Consequently true errors must be those cases in which segmentation violates morpheme boundaries. One group of morphemes in the test corpus were wrongly divided because they contained statistically unusual hiragana sequences that could only have been identified as a unit by consulting a lexicon. A second class of errors occurred when the algorithm either separated two indivisible morphemes or divided a combination of two morphemes in the wrong place. These two types of failures to respect morpheme boundaries are illustrated below. The incorrect segmentation appears first, followed by the preferred version and a description of the sequence:

ta to | e ba	ta to e ba	(adv.)
to | te mo	to te mo	(adv.)
tsu mo | ri ra | shi i	tsu mo ri | ra shi i	(n. + adj.)
ki bi | ki bi	ki bi ki bi	(adv.)
ka | ke tsu ke te	ka ke | tsu ke te	(v. + v.)
de | ki ru	de ki ru	(v.)

Using this scoring method, the 1172 strings found by the segmenter contained 1106 correct words and 66 errors for an overall accuracy of 94.4%. The corpus actually contained 1125 words, so the fact that 1106 of these words were correctly identified amounts to a recall of 98.3%, and the precision, measured as the proportion of identified words that were correct (1106 of 1172) is 94.4%.

Conclusion

The method we have proposed for segmenting non-kanji strings has several strengths. It does not depend on a lexicon or even on any formal notion of what constitutes a word in Japanese, and the training phase does not require manually or automatically annotated text of any kind. In addition the technique is simple and extremely fast. Relying solely on character type information and hiragana bigram frequencies, the algorithm makes a decision as to whether to create a word boundary or not. Moreover, we found that adding a log function to the computation, which makes the measure equivalent to the mutual information statistic, did not significantly change the results. This suggests that the extra work involved in computing mutual information may not be needed for the problem of segmenting non-kanji strings.

The robust performance of the segmentation algorithm is not surprising, because research has shown (see Nagao 1984) that character type information alone can be used to segment Japanese into bunsetsu units with about 84% accuracy. Our method improves on this result significantly, but we have purposely avoided dealing with the problems associated with segmenting strings of kanji. Work by Fujisaki and others (Fujisaki et al. 1991, Nishino & Fujisaki 1988, Takeda & Fujisaki 1987), however, has demonstrated that *n*-gram modeling techniques can be successfully applied to these more difficult cases.

The method, of course, has limitations as well. Without a lexicon it is virtually impossible to identify words that are composed of infrequent sequences of hiragana, for example. This is a problem shared by most probabilistic approaches to natural language processing. Furthermore, the algorithm is sensitive to the corpus characteristics in that it will perform better on a corpus with shorter rather than longer kanji strings.

One purpose in reporting this study has been to make explicit some of the difficulties associated with processing Japanese text. It is a mistake to assume that an approach that works well for English will work equally well for Japanese without modification. This is evident when one tries to apply the notion of what a word is in English to Japanese. Various groups have tackled similar problems and have reported success in dealing with them without always making clear the criteria by which such success should be judged. By describing our procedures in detail and pointing out, with examples, areas of failure as well as areas of success, we hope to contribute to what should be an ongoing debate that addresses these issues.

Acknowledgements

This work was supported in part by NSF grants IRI-8902106 and CDA-9222720 and by PSC-CUNY awards 6-69283, 6-63295 and 6-64277. Hartvig Dahl, Ted Dunning, Bill Gale, Hitoshi Isahara, and Fumiko Ohno provided valuable assistance.

References

Brill, E.; Magerman, D.; Marcus, M.; and Santorini, B. 1990. Deducing linguistic structure from the statistics of large corpora. In Proceedings of the DARPA Speech and Natural Language Workshop.

Brown, P.; Della Pietra, A.; Della Pietra, V.; Lafferty, J; and Mercer, R. 1992. Analysis, statistical transfer, and synthesis in machine translation. In Proceedings of the Fourth International Conference on Theoretical and Methodological Issues in Machine Translation, 83-100.

Fujisaki, T.; Jelinek, F.; Cocke, J.; Black, E.; and Nishino, T. 1991. A probabilistic parsing method for sentence disambiguation. In *Current Issues in Parsing Technology*, M. Tomita, ed., 139-152. Boston: Kluwer Academic.

Ishizaki, S.; Sakamoto, Y.; Ikeda, T.; and Isahara, H. 1989. Machine translation systems developed by the Electrotechnical Laboratory of Japan. In *Future Computing Systems*, Vol. 2, No. 3, 275-291. Oxford University Press and Maruzen Company Limited.

Kawada, T. 1990. Inputting Japanese from the keyboard. *Journal of Information Processing* 13:10-14.

Kindaichi, K.; Kindaichi, H.; Kenbou, H.; Shibata, T.; and Yamada, T. eds. 1981. *Shin-Meikai Kokigo Jiten (New Concise Japanese Dictionary)*. Tokyo: Sanseido.

Kitani, T., and Mitamura, T. 1993. Japanese preprocessor for syntactic and semantic parsing. In Proceedings of the Conference on Artificial Intelligence Applications, 86-92.

Lunde, K. 1993. *Understanding Japanese Information Processing*. Sebastopol, CA: O'Reilly.

Magerman, D., and Marcus, M. 1990. Parsing a natural language using mutual information statistics. In Proceedings of the Eighth National Conference on Artificial Intelligence, 984-989.

Maruyama, N.; Morohashi, M.; Umeda, S.; and Sumita, E. 1988. A Japanese sentence analyzer. *IBM Journal of Research and Development* 32:238-250.

Matsukawa, T.; Miller, S.; and Weischedel, R. 1993. Example-based correction of word segmentation and part of speech labelling. In Proceedings of the ARPA Human Language Technology Workshop.

Nagao, M. ed. 1984. *Japanese Information Processing*. Tokyo: Denshi Tsuushin Gakkai. (in Japanese)

Nishino, T., and Fujisaki, T. 1988. Probabilistic parsing of Kanji compound words. *Journal of the Information Processing Society of Japan* 29,11. (in Japanese)

Papageorgiou, C. 1994. Japanese word segmentation by hidden Markov model. In Proceedings of the ARPA Human Language Technology Workshop, 271-276.

Takeda, K., and Fujisaki, T. 1987. Segmentation of Kanji primitive words by a stochastic method. *Journal of the Information Processing Society of Japan* 28,9. (in Japanese)

Teller, V., and Batchelder, E. 1993. A probabilistic approach to Japanese lexical analysis. AAAI Spring Symposium on Building Lexicons for Machine Translation. AAAI Technical Report SS-93-02.

Yokoyama, S. 1989. Occurrence frequency Ddta of a Japanese dictionary. In *Japanese Quantitative Linguistics*, S. Mizutani ed., 50-76. Bochum: Brockmeyer.

Inducing Deterministic Prolog Parsers from Treebanks:
A Machine Learning Approach *

John M. Zelle and Raymond J. Mooney
Department of Computer Sciences
University of Texas
Austin, TX 78712
zelle@cs.utexas.edu, mooney@cs.utexas.edu

Abstract

This paper presents a method for constructing deterministic Prolog parsers from corpora of parsed sentences. Our approach uses recent machine learning methods for inducing Prolog rules from examples (inductive logic programming). We discuss several advantages of this method compared to recent statistical methods and present results on learning complete parsers from portions of the ATIS corpus.

Introduction

Recent approaches to constructing robust parsers from corpora primarily use statistical and probabilistic methods such as stochastic context-free grammars (Black et al., 1992; Pereira and Schabes, 1992). Although several current methods learn some symbolic structures such as decision trees (Black et al., 1993) and transformations (Brill, 1993), statistical methods still dominate. In this paper, we present a method that uses recent techniques in machine learning to construct symbolic, deterministic parsers from parsed corpora (treebanks). Specifically, our approach is implemented in a program called CHILL (Zelle and Mooney, 1993b) that uses *inductive logic programming* (ILP) (Muggleton, 1992) to learn heuristic rules for controlling a deterministic shift-reduce parser written in Prolog.

We believe our approach offers several potential advantages compared to current methods. First, it constructs deterministic shift-reduce parsers, which are very powerful and efficient (Tomita, 1986) and arguably more cognitively plausible (Marcus, 1980; Berwick, 1985). Second, it constructs complete parsers from scratch that produce full parse trees, as opposed to producing only bracketings (Pereira and Schabes, 1992; Brill, 1993) or requiring an existing, complex parser that over-generates (Black et al., 1992; Black et al., 1993). Third, the approach is more flexible in several ways. It can produce parsers from either tagged or untagged treebanks.[1] When trained on an untagged corpus, it constructs it's own syntactic and/or semantic classes of words and phrases that allow it to deterministically parse the corpus. It can also learn to produce case-role assignments instead of syntactic parse trees and can use learned lexical and semantic classes to resolve ambiguities such as prepositional phrase attachment and lexical ambiguity (Zelle and Mooney, 1993b). Fourth, it uses a single, uniform parsing framework to perform all of these tasks and a single, general learning method that has also been used to induce a range of diverse logic programs from examples (Zelle and Mooney, 1994).

The remainder of the paper is organized as follows. In section 2, we summarize our ILP method for learning deterministic parsers, and how this method was tailored to work with existing treebanks. In section 3, we present and discuss experimental results on learning parsers from the ATIS corpus of the Penn Treebank (Marcus et al., 1993). Section 4 covers related work, and section 5 presents our conclusions.

The Chill System

Overview

Our system, CHILL, (Constructive Heuristics Induction for Language Learning) is an approach to parser acquisition which utilizes a general learning mechanism. The input to the system is a set of training instances consisting of sentences paired with the desired parses. The output is a shift-reduce parser (in Prolog) which maps sentences into parse trees.

The CHILL algorithm consists of two distinct tasks. First, the training instances are used to formulate an overly-general shift-reduce parser that is capable of producing parses from sentences. The initial parser is overly-general in that it produces a great many spurious analyses for any given input sentence. The parser is then specialized by introducing search-control heuristics. These control heuristics limit the contexts in

*This research was partially supported by the NSF under grant IRI-9102926 and the Texas Advanced Research Program under grant 003658114.

[1]In an *untagged treebank*, parses are represented as phrase-level word groupings without lexical categories dominating the words (e.g. parsed text from Penn Treebank (Marcus et al., 1993))

which certain operations are performed, eliminating the spurious analyses.

Constructing the Overly-General Parser

The syntactic parse of a sentence is a labeled bracketing of the words in the sentence. For example, the noun phrase, "a trip to Dallas", might be decomposed into component noun and prepositional phrases as: $[_{np}[_{np}$a trip] $[_{pp}$to $[_{np}$ dallas]]]. We represent such an analysis as a Prolog term of the form: `np:[np:[a, trip], pp:[to, np:[dallas]]]`.

A shift-reduce parser to produce such analyses is easily implemented as a logic program. The state of the parse is reflected by the contents of the stack and input buffer. A new state is produced by either removing a single word from the buffer and pushing it onto the stack (a shift operation), or by popping the top one or two stack elements and combining them into a new constituent which is then pushed back onto the stack (a reduce operation).

Each operation can be represented by a single program clause with two arguments representing the current stack and input buffer, and two arguments to represent their state after applying the operator. For example, the operations and associated clauses required to parse the above example phrase are as follows (the notation, **reduce**(N) *Cat*, indicates that the top N stack elements are combined to form a constituent with label, *Cat*):

```
reduce(2) pp:
      op([S1,S2|Ss], Words, [pp:[S1,S2]|Ss], Words).
reduce(2) np:
      op([S1,S2|Ss], Words, [np:[S1,S2]|Ss], Words).
reduce(1) np:
      op([S1|Ss], Words, [np:[S1]|Ss], Words).
shift: op(Stack, [Word|Words], [Word|Stack], Words).
```

Building an overly-general parser from a set of training examples is accomplished by constructing clauses for the `op` predicate. Each clause is a direct translation of a required parsing action; there must be a reduce operation for each constituent structure as well as the general shift operator illustrated above. If the sentence analyses include empty categories (detectable as lexical tokens that appear in the analyses, but not in the sentence), each empty marker is introduced via its own shift operator which does not consume a word from the input buffer.

The first step in the CHILL system is to analyze the training examples to produce the set of general operators that will be used in the overly–general parser. Once the necessary operators have been inferred, they are ordered according to their frequency of occurrence in the training set.

Parser Specialization

The overly-general parser produces a great many spurious analyses for the training sentences because there are no conditions specifying when it is appropriate to use the various operators. The program must be specialized by including control heuristics that guide the application of operator clauses. This section outlines the basic approach used in CHILL. More detail on incorporating clause selection information in Prolog programs can be found in (Zelle and Mooney, 1993a).

Program specialization occurs in three phases. First, the training examples are analyzed to construct positive and negative *control examples* for each operator clause. Examples of correct operator applications are generated by finding the first correct parsing of each training pair with the overly-general parser; any subgoal to which an operator is applied in a successful parse becomes a positive control example for that operator. A positive control example for any operator is considered a negative example for all previous operators that do not have it as a positive example. Note that this assumes a deterministic framework in which each sentence will have a single preferred parsing. Once an operator is found to be applicable to a particular parser state, subsequent operators will not be tried. For example, in parsing the above phrase, when the **reduce(2) NP** operator is first applied, the call to **op** appears as: `op([trip,a],[to,dallas], A, B)` where A and B are as yet uninstantiated output variables. This subgoal would be stored as a positive control example for the **reduce(2) NP** operator, and as a negative control example for **reduce(2) PP**, assuming the order of operator clauses shown above.

In the second phase, a general first-order induction algorithm is employed to learn a *control rule* for each operator. This control rule comprises a Horn-clause definition that covers the positive control examples for the operator but not the negative. There is a growing body of research in inductive logic programming which addresses this problem. CHILL combines elements from bottom-up techniques found in systems such as CIGOL (Muggleton and Buntine, 1988) and GOLEM (Muggleton and Feng, 1992) and top-down methods from systems like FOIL (Quinlan, 1990), and is able to invent new predicates in a manner analogous to CHAMP (Kijsirikul et al., 1992). Details of the CHILL induction algorithm can be found in (Zelle and Mooney, 1993b; Zelle and Mooney, 1994).

The final step in program specialization is to "fold" the control information back into the overly-general parser. A control rule is easily incorporated into the overly-general program by unifying the head of an operator clause with the head of the control rule for the clause and adding the induced conditions to the clause body. The definitions of any invented predicates are simply appended to the program. As an example, the **reduce(2) pp** clause might be modified as:

```
op([np:A,B|Ss], Words, [pp:[np:A,B]|Ss],Words) :-
      preposition(B).
preposition(of). preposition(to). ...
```

Here, the induction algorithm invented a new predicate

representing the category "preposition."[2] This new predicate has been incorporated to form the rule which may be roughly interpreted as stating: "If the stack contains an NP followed by a preposition, then reduce this pair to a PP." The actual control rule learned for this operator is more complex, but this simple example illustrates the basic process.

Parsing the Treebank

Training a program to do accurate parsing requires large corpora of parsed text for training. Fortunately, such treebanks are being compiled and becoming available. For the current experiments, we have used parsed text from a preliminary version of the Penn Treebank (Marcus et al., 1993). One complication in using this data is that sentences are parsed only to the "phrase level", leaving the internal structure of NPs unanalyzed and allowing arbitrary-arity constituents. Rather than forcing the parser to learn reductions for arbitrary length constituents, CHILL was restricted to learning binary-branching structures. This simplifies the parser and allows for a more direct comparison to previous bracketing experiments (e.g. (Brill, 1993; Pereira and Schabes, 1992)) which use binary bracketings.

Making the treebank analyses compatible with the binary parser required "completion" of the parses into binary-branching structures. This "binarization" was accomplished automatically by introducing special internal nodes in a right-linear fashion. For example, the noun-phrase, `np:[the,big,orange,cat]`, would be binarized to create: `np:[the,int(np):[big, int(np):[orange, cat]]]`. The special labeling (int(np) for noun phrases, int(s) for sentences, etc.) permits restoration of the original structure by merging internal nodes. Using this technique, the resulting parses can be compared directly with treebank parses. All of the experiments reported below were done with automatically binarized training examples; control rules for the artificial internal nodes were learned in exactly the same way as for the original constituents.

Experimental Results

The Data

The purpose of our experiments was to investigate whether the mechanisms in CHILL are sufficiently robust for application to real-world parsing problems. There are two facets to this question, the first is whether the parsers learned by CHILL generalize well to new text. An additional issue is whether the induction mechanism can handle the large numbers of examples that would be necessary to achieve adequate performance on relatively large corpora.

We selected as our test corpus a portion of the ATIS dataset from a preliminary version of the Penn Tree-

bank (specifically, the sentences in the file `ti_tb`). We chose this particular data because it represents realistic input from human-computer interaction, and because it has been used in a number of other studies on automated grammar acquisition (Brill, 1993; Pereira and Schabes, 1992) that can serve as a basis for comparison to CHILL.

Experiments were actually carried out on four different variations of the corpus. A subset of the corpus comprising sentences of length less than 13 words was used to form a more tractable corpus for systematic evaluation and to test the effect of sentence length on performance. The entire corpus contained 729 sentences with an average length of 10.3 words. The restricted set contains 536 sentences averaging 7.9 words in length. A second dimension of variation is the form of the input sentences and analyses. Since CHILL has the ability to create its own categories, it can use untagged parse trees. In order to test the advantage gained by tagging, we also ran experiments using lexical tags instead of words on both the full and restricted corpus.

Experimental Method

Training and testing followed the standard paradigm of first choosing a random set of test examples and then creating parsers using increasingly larger subsets of the remaining examples. The performance of these parsers was then determined by parsing the test examples. Obviously, the most stringent measure of accuracy is the proportion of test sentences for which the produced parse tree exactly matches the treebanked parse for the sentence. Sometimes, however, a parse can be useful even if it is not perfectly accurate; the treebank itself is not entirely consistent in the handling of various structures.

To better gauge the partial accuracy of the parser, we adopted a procedure for returning and scoring partial parses. If the parser runs into a "dead-end" while parsing a test sentence, the contents of the stack at the time of impasse is returned as a single, flat constituent labeled S. Since the parsing operators are ordered and the shift operator is invariably the most frequently used operator in the training set, shift serves as a sort of default when no reduction action applies. Therefore, at the time of impasse, all of the words of the sentence will be on the stack, and partial constituents will have been built. The contents of stack reflect the partial progress of the parser in finding constituents.

Partial scoring of trees is computed by determining the extent of overlap between the computed parse and the correct parse as recorded in the treebank. Two constituents are said to match if they span exactly the same words in the sentence. If constituents match and have the same label, then they are identical. The overlap between the computed parse and the correct parse is computed by trying to match each constituent of the computed parse with some

---

Size	Correct	Partial	0-Cross	Crossing %
50	14.1	66.0	47.6	85.4
100	18.6	69.3	52.7	84.5
150	25.4	72.5	50.8	86.1
200	26.8	74.9	57.6	88.2
250	29.2	76.1	62.1	89.6
300	33.1	79.1	63.6	91.2

Table 1a: Lexical Tags

Size	Correct	Partial	0-Cross	Crossing %
50	11.4	60.0	43.1	80.3
100	10.3	61.5	45.2	81.5
150	12.4	62.0	44.2	80.4
200	17.5	67.8	52.1	83.5
250	18.1	67.7	51.6	83.7
300	17.4	69.6	53.6	85.2

Table 1b: Raw Text

Table 1: Results for restricted length corpus

constituent in the correct parse. If an identical constituent is found, the score is 1.0, a matching constituent with an incorrect label scores 0.5. The sum of the scores for all constituents is the overlap score for the parse. The accuracy of the parse is then computed as $Accuracy = (\frac{O}{Found} + \frac{O}{Correct})/2$ where O is the overlap score, $Found$ is the number of constituents in the computed parse, and $Correct$ is the number of constituents in the correct tree. The result is an average of the proportion of the computed parse that is correct and the proportion of the correct parse that was actually found.

Another accuracy measure, which has been used in evaluating systems that bracket the input sentence into unlabeled constituents, is the proportion of constituents in the parse that do not cross any constituent boundaries in the correct tree (Black, 1991). Of course, this measure only allows for direct comparison of systems that generate binary-branching parse trees.[3] By binarizing the output of the parser in a manner analogous to that described above, we can compute the number of sentences with parses containing no crossing constituents, as well as the proportion of constituents which are non-crossing over all test sentences. This gives a basis of comparison with previous bracketing results, although it should be emphasized that CHILL is designed for the harder task of actually producing labeled parses, and is not directly optimized for the bracketing task.

Results

The results of these experiments are summarized in Tables 1 and 2. The figures for the restricted length corpus in Table 1 reflect averages of three trials, while the results on the full corpus are averaged over two trials. The first column shows the size of the training set from which the parsers were derived, while the remaining columns present results for each of the four metrics outlined above. *Correct* is the percentage of test sentences with parses that matched the treebanked parse exactly. *Partial* is partial correctness using the overlap metric. The remaining columns reflect measures based on re-binarizing the parser output. *0-Cross* is

the proportion of test sentences having no constituents that cross constituents in the correct parsing. The remaining column reports the percentage of (binarized) constituents that are consistent with the treebank (i.e. cross no constituents in the correct parse).

The results for the restricted corpus in Table 1 are encouraging. While we know of no other results for parsing accuracy of automatically constructed parsers on this corpus, the figures of 33% completely correct using the tagged input and 17% on the raw text seem quite good for a relatively modest training set of 300 sentences. The figures for 0-cross and crossing% are about the same as those reported in studies of automated bracketing for the unrestricted ATIS corpus (Brill (1993) reports 60% and 91.12%, respectively). However, our bracketing results for the unrestricted corpus are not as good.

A comparison of Tables 1a and 1b show that considerable advantage is gained by using word-class tags, rather than the actual words. This is to be expected as tagging significantly reduces the variety in the input. The results for raw-text use no special mechanism for handling previously unseen words occurring in the testing examples. Achieving 70% (partial) accuracy under these conditions seems quite good. Statistical approaches relying on n-grams or probabilistic context-free grammars would have difficulty due to the large number of terminal symbols (around 400) appearing in the modest-sized training corpus. The data for lexical selection would be too sparse to adequately train the pre-defined models. Likewise, the transformational approach of (Brill, 1993) is limited to bracketing strings of lexical classes, not words. A major advantage of our approach is the ability of the learning mechanism to automatically construct and attend to just those features of the input that are most useful in guiding parsing.

It should also be noted that the system created new categories in both situations. In the raw text experiments, CHILL regularly created categories for `preposition`, `verb`, `form-of-to-be`, etc.. With tagged input, various tags were grouped into classes such as the verb and noun forms. In both cases, the system also formed numerous categories and relations that seemed to defy any simple linguistic explanation. Nevertheless, these categories were helpful in parsing of new text. These results support our view that any

---

[3]A tree containing a single, flat constituent covering the entire sentence always produces a perfect (non)crossing score.

Size	Correct	Partial	0-Cross	Crossing %
50	9.2	58.9	35.3	72.5
100	16.3	65.2	41.9	74.3
150	21.0	70.1	44.7	76.8
200	23.5	71.4	46.2	77.9
250	25.6	72.5	47.1	77.9

Table 2a: Lexical Tags

Size	Correct	Partial	0-Cross	Crossing %
50	6.2	54.0	33.1	68.9
100	4.7	54.9	41.2	72.0
150	8.5	59.6	39.7	71.5

Table 2b: Raw Text

Table 2: Results for full corpus

practical acquisition system should be able to create its own categories, as it is unlikely that independently-crafted feature systems will capture all of the nuances necessary to do accurate parsing in a reasonably complex domain.

Table 2 shows results for the full corpus. As one might expect, the results are not as good as for the restricted set. There are a number of factors that could lead to diminishing performance as a function of increasing sentence length. One explanation might be that the longer sentences are simply more complicated and, thus harder to parse accurately. If the difficulty is inherent in the sentences, the only solution is larger training sets.

Another possible problem is the compounding of errors. If an operator is chosen incorrectly early in the parse, it might lead the parser into states that have not been encountered in training, leading to subsequent errors in the application of other operators. This factor might be mitigated by developing more robust training procedures. By providing control examples from erroneous states as well as correct ones, the parser might be trained to be somewhat self-correcting, choosing correct operators later on even in the face of previous errors.

A third possibility is that the additional sentence length is "swamping" the induction algorithm. Increasing the average sentence length significantly increases the number of control examples that must be handled by the induction mechanism. Training sizes of several hundred sentences give rise to induction over thousands of control examples. Additionally, longer sentences lend themselves to more conflicting analyses and may increase the amount of *noise* in the control data making it more difficult to spot useful generalizations. Additional progress here would require further improvement in the efficiency and noise-handling capabilities of the induction algorithm.

Clearly further experimentation is needed to pin down where the most improvement can be made. The results so far do indicate that the approach has potential. The current Prolog implementation running on a SPARC 2 was able to induce parsers from several hundred sentences in a few hours, producing over 700 lines of Prolog code. One trial was run using 400 tagged sentences from the full corpus; the resulting parser achieved 29.4% absolute accuracy and a partial scoring of 82%. Further improvements in efficiency may make it feasible to produce parsers from thousands of training sentences.

Related Work

As mentioned above, most recent work on automatically constructing parsers from corpora has focused on acquiring stochastic grammars rather than symbolic parsers. When learning in this framework, "one simply gathers statistics" to set the parameters of a pre-defined model (Charniak, 1993). However, there is a long tradition of research in AI and Machine Learning suggesting the utility of techniques that extract underlying structural models from the data. Earlier work in learning symbolic parsers (Anderson, 1977; Berwick, 1985) used fairly weak learning methods specific to language acquisition and were not tested on real corpora. CHILL represents the first serious application of modern, machine-learning methods to acquiring parsers from corpora.

Brill (1993), presents a technique for acquiring parsers that produce binary-branching syntax trees with unlabeled nonterminals. The technique, utilizing structural transformation rules based on lexical category information, has proven quite successful on real corpora. CHILL, which creates fully labeled parses, has a more general learning mechanism allowing it to make distinctions based on more subtle structural and lexical cues (e.g. creating semantic word classes for resolving attachment).

Our framework for learning deterministic, context-dependent parsers is very similar to that of (Simmons and Yu, 1992); however, there are two advantages of our ILP method compared to their exemplar matching method. First, ILP methods can handle unbounded, structured data so that the context does not need to be fixed to a limited window of the stack and the remaining sentence. The entire stack and remaining sentence is available as potential context for deciding which parsing operator to apply at each step. Second, the system is capable of creating its own syntactic and semantic word and phrase classes instead of relying on the user to provide part-of-speech tagging.

CHILL's ability to invent new classes of words and phrases specifically for resolving ambiguities such as prepositional phrase attachment makes it particularly interesting. There is some existing work on learning lexical classes from corpora (Schütze, 1992); however, the classes are based on word co-occurrence rather than the specific needs of parsing. There are also methods for learning to resolve attachments using lexical information (Hindle and Rooth, 1993); however, they do not create new lexical classes. CHILL uses a single learning algorithm to perform both of these tasks.

Conclusion

This paper has demonstrated that modern machine-learning methods are capable of inducing traditional shift-reduce parsers from corpora, complementing the results of recent statistical methods. We believe that the primary strength of corpus-based methods is not the particular approach or type of parser employed (e.g. statistical, connectionist, or symbolic), but the fact that large amounts of real data are used to automatically construct complex parsers that are intractable to build manually. However, we believe our approach based on a very general inductive-logic-programming method has several advantages such as efficient, deterministic parsing; production of complete labeled parse trees; and an ability to use untagged text and automatically create new, useful lexical and phrasal categories based directly on the needs of parsing.

References

Anderson, J. R. (1977). Induction of augmented transition networks. *Cognitive Science*, 1:125–157.

Berwick, B. (1985). *The Acquisition of Syntactic Knowledge*. Cambridge, MA: MIT Press.

Black, E., Jelineck, F., Lafferty, J., Magerman, D., Mercer, R., and Roukos, S. (1993). Towards history-based grammars: Using richer models for probabilistic parsing. In *Proceedings of the 31st Annual Meeting of the Association for Computational Linguistics*, pages 31–37. Columbus, Ohio.

Black, E., Lafferty, J., and Roukaos, S. (1992). Development and evaluation of a broad-coverage probabilistic grammar of English-language computer manuals. In *Proceedings of the 30th Annual Meeting of the Association for Computational Linguistics*, pages 185–192. Newark, Delaware.

Black, E. et. al. (1991). A procedure for quantitatively comparing the syntactic coverage of English grammars. In *Proceedings of the Fourth DARPA Speech and Natural Language Workshop*, pages 306–311.

Brill, E. (1993). Automatic grammar induction and parsing free text: A transformation-based approach. In *Proceedings of the 31st Annual Meeting of the Association for Computational Linguistics*, pages 259–265. Columbus, Ohio.

Charniak, E. (1993). *Statistical Language Learning*. MIT Press.

Hindle, D. and Rooth, M. (1993). Structural ambiguity and lexical relations. *Computational Linguistics*, 19(1):103–120.

Kijsirikul, B., Numao, M., and Shimura, M. (1992). Discrimination-based constructive induction of logic programs. In *Proceedings of the Tenth National Conference on Artificial Intelligence*, pages 44–49. San Jose, CA.

Marcus, M. (1980). *A Theory of Syntactic Recognition for Natural Language*. Cambridge, MA: MIT Press.

Marcus, M., Santorini, B., and Marcinkiewicz, M. (1993). Building a large annotated corpus of english: The Penn treebank. *Computational Linguistics*, 19(2):313–330.

Muggleton, S. and Buntine, W. (1988). Machine invention of first-order predicates by inverting resolution. In *Proceedings of the Fifth International Conference on Machine Learning*, pages 339–352. Ann Arbor, MI.

Muggleton, S. and Feng, C. (1992). Efficient induction of logic programs. In Muggleton, S., editor, *Inductive Logic Programming*, pages 281–297. New York: Academic Press.

Muggleton, S. H., editor (1992). *Inductive Logic Programming*. New York, NY: Academic Press.

Pereira, F. and Schabes, Y. (1992). Inside-outside reestimation from partially bracketed corpora. In *Proceedings of the 30th Annual Meeting of the Association for Computational Linguistics*, pages 128–135. Newark, Delaware.

Quinlan, J. (1990). Learning logical definitions from relations. *Machine Learning*, 5(3):239–266.

Schütze, H. (1992). Context space. In *Working Notes, AAAI Fall Symposium Series*, pages 113–120. AAAI-Press.

Simmons, R. F. and Yu, Y. (1992). The acquisition and use of context dependent grammars for English. *Computational Linguistics*, 18(4):391–418.

Tomita, M. (1986). *Efficient Parsing for Natural Language*. Boston: Kluwer Academic Publishers.

Zelle, J. M. and Mooney, R. J. (1993a). Combining FOIL and EBG to speed-up logic programs. In *Proceedings of the Thirteenth International Joint conference on Artificial intelligence*, pages 1106–1111. Chambery, France.

Zelle, J. M. and Mooney, R. J. (1993b). Learning semantic grammars with constructive inductive logic programming. In *Proceedings of the Eleventh National Conference on Artificial Intelligence*, pages 817–822. Washington, D.C.

Zelle, J. M. and Mooney, R. J. (1994). Combining top-down and bottom-up methods in inductive logic programming. In *Proceedings of the Eleventh International Conference on Machine Learning*. New Brunswick, NJ.

The Ups and Downs of Lexical Acquisition

Peter M. Hastings
Artificial Intelligence Laboratory
1101 Beal Avenue
The University of Michigan
Ann Arbor, MI 48109
(313)763-9074
peter@umich.edu

Steven L. Lytinen
DePaul University
Dept. of Computer Science and Info. Systems
243 South Wabash Avenue
Chicago, IL 60604-2302
(312)362-6106
lytinen@cs.depaul.edu

Abstract

We have implemented an incremental lexical acquisition mechanism that learns the meanings of previously unknown words from the context in which they appear, as a part of the process of parsing and semantically interpreting sentences. Implementation of this algorithm brought to light a fundamental difference between learning verbs and learning nouns. Specifically, because verbs typically play the predicate role in English sentences, whereas nouns typically function as arguments, we found that different mechanisms were required to learn verbs and nouns. Because of this difference in usage, our learning algorithm formulates the most specific hypotheses possible, consistent with the data, for verb meanings, but the most general hypotheses possible for nouns. Subsequent examples may falsify a current hypothesis, causing verb meanings to be generalized and noun meanings to be made more specific. This paper describes the two approaches used to learn verbs and nouns in the system, and reports on the system's performance in substantial empirical testing.

Introduction

This paper describes the lexical acquisition system Camille (Contextual Acquisition Mechanism for Incremental Lexeme Learning (Hastings 1994)). Camille learns the lexical category and meaning of unknown words based on example sentences.

Acquisition systems are crucial to NLP systems that process real-world text. Because the complete range of the text cannot be specified, gaps in lexical knowledge are bound to occur. Such an occasion can either be disruptive for the NLP system, preventing it from processing the rest of the text, or the system can take advantage of the situation and learn something about the unknown word.

Camille is implemented as an extension of the LINK NLP system (Lytinen & Roberts 1989) which is a unification-based chart parser which integrates syntactic and semantic information. Unlike statistics-based acquisition mechanisms which require large corpora (Brent 1993; Church & Hanks 1990; Hindle 1990;

Resnik 1992; Yarowsky 1992), Camille uses its domain knowledge when inferring the meaning of unknown words. The actual process of meaning inference, however, is not dependent on any particular domain hierarchy. It is a weak method that searches the hierarchy for an appropriate node for the meaning of a word.

By relying on this hierarchical knowledge structure, Camille not only gains representational and inferential power, but it also reveals an interesting fundamental principle of language. The search that Camille uses to identify the appropriate node in the semantic hierarchy for the meaning of an unknown word is data-driven; that is, the search is guided by the data provided by example sentences. Because different types of words tend to provide different data, we found that different search processes were required for different syntactic categories of words. In particular, because verbs typically fill the predicate role in English sentences, whereas nouns typically function as arguments, our learning algorithm formulates the most specific hypotheses possible, consistent with the data, for verb meanings, but the most general hypotheses possible for nouns. Subsequent examples may falsify a current hypothesis, causing the system to search up the hierarchy for verbs (i.e., generalize the hypothesis), but to search down the hierarchy for nouns (i.e., make the hypothesis more specific).

The next section describes the structure of Camille's semantic hierarchy, and the formal nature of the noun/verb dichotomy. The organization of the hierarchy and its constraints on noun learning is most apparent when Camille is faced with ambiguous nouns. The system's mechanism for inferring their meaning is described in the following section. The section after that describes the more difficult process of learning the meanings of verbs. After reviewing related work, the paper concludes with a discussion of Camille's limitations, other aspects of the system, and future work.

The Nature of the Knowledge

The knowledge representation for LINK consists of an inheritance hierarchy of domain-independent and domain-specific concepts. Figure 1 shows some of

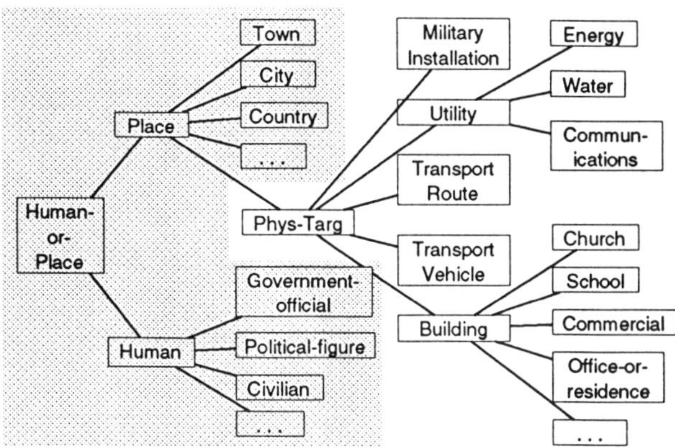

Figure 1: The pruned object tree

LINK's domain-specific object concepts from the Terrorism domain that served as the testing ground for ARPA's third and fourth Message Understanding Conferences (Sundheim 1992) (the shading will be explained later). The structure of the hierarchy forms an IS-A inheritance tree. Figure 2 shows some of the actions from the domain. Action concepts provide the relational structure that binds together the representation of the meaning of sentences. These concepts also constrain the types of arguments that can be attached as their slot-fillers (also included in fig 2).

The nodes in LINK's concept hierarchy serve as its basic units of meaning. Learning the meaning of an unknown word reduces to finding the appropriate node in the hierarchy — a graph search problem. To drive the search, the semantic constraints, which are normally used to limit attachment of slot-fillers to the Head verb, interact with the evidence provided by example sentences. But the interaction works in different ways for different classes of words. Nouns (as the Heads of noun phrases) normally serve as the slot-fillers of sentences and thus, as the items which are constrained. For example, in the sentence "Terrorists destroyed a flarge," the word "destroy" refers to the concept Destroy which has the constraint [Object = Phys-Targ]. When "flarge" is attached as the object of the verb, the constraint places an upper bound on its interpretation as shown in figure 1. The shaded-out nodes cannot be a valid interpretation of the meaning of "flarge".

For unknown verbs, however, the situation is quite different. Because they usually map to the actions in the domain, the verbs *apply* the constraints. Thus, the constraints place an upper bound on the interpretation of unknown verbs.[1] The shaded areas of figure 2 show

the concepts that are ruled out for an example sentence like "Terrorists froobled the headquarters." It is important to note that this is not just an artifact of LINK's knowledge representation structure. It is due to a fundamental principle of language. Because actions serve as the relational elements of sentence structure, they are the only logical place for the constraints to reside.

Because of this dichotomy, Camille must have different strategies for learning verbs and learning nouns. They can be stated most succinctly as follows:

```
For nouns, choose the most general consistent
hypothesis.
For verbs, choose the most specific
hypothesis.
```

This difference is prescribed by the nature of the knowledge and it is consonant with psycholinguistic theories which maintain that humans treat verbs and nouns differently (Gentner 1978; Huttenlocher & Lui 1979; Graesser, Hopkinson, & Schmid 1987; Behrend 1990; Fernald & Morikawa 1993).

The implications of the noun-learning strategy are seen most clearly in the acquisition of ambiguous nouns as described in the next section. The following section describes the more difficult acquisition problem for verbs.

Learning Ambiguous Nouns

Word sense ambiguity has been a thorn in the side of NLP for a long time (Small & Cottrell 1988). The majority of the research on this issue has targetted methods for selecting the appropriate sense of an ambiguous word. For lexical acquisition, a different problem exists: how can a system recognize that a word has multiple senses and make a suitable definition?

If the system cannot learn ambiguous words, it will run into a parsing impasse. Consider two examples of the use of the word "lines" taken from the Terrorism corpus:

```
We have broken the defensive lines of the
enemy.
The Lempa River Hydroelectric Commission
reported that one of the country's main power
lines was out of service on 1 June because a
number of pylons were destroyed.
```

If the system does not know the word "lines" when it encounters the first sentence, it should infer a meaning like Military-Unit because within the domain, that is likely to be the target of Break. If the system cannot recognize ambiguity while processing the second sentence, it will either create an erroneous parse or fail altogether. Camille creates definitions for ambiguous

---

[1]Note that negative examples, for example, "You can't say 'Terrorists froobled the civilians'", would provide the opposing bound (upper for unknown verbs, lower for nouns). Then Mitchell's candidate-elimination approach (Mitchell 1977) to narrowing the hypothesis set might work. Unfortunately, negative examples are rare in human speech and non-existent in this and most other information extraction domains.

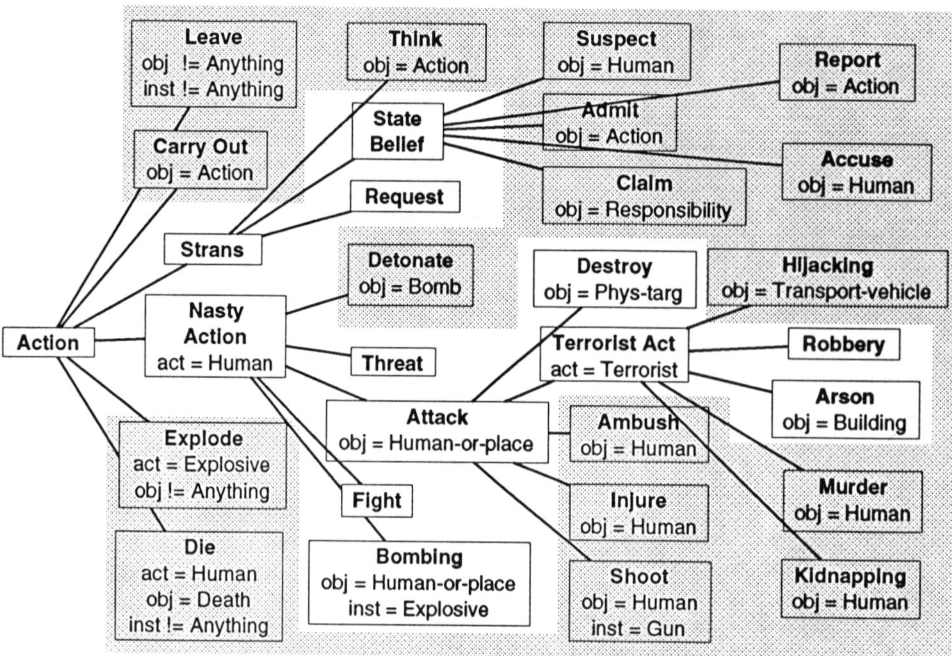

Figure 2: The pruned action tree

nouns through a simple extension of its noun-learning mechanism.

As previously stated, the constraints on actions provide an upper bound for the interpretation of unknown nouns. This provides the basis for a simple and elegant mechanism to acquire noun meanings. When an unknown noun is attached as the slot filler of a verb,[2] the unification procedure (because it returns the more specific concept) gives the representation of the meaning of that word the concept specified by the constraint. All Camille must do is to collect these induced definitions after the parse is complete.

When a word is ambiguous, the parser will try to unify incompatible concepts (Military-Unit and Electricity-Source in the example above). If the initial definition was inferred by Camille, however, it is marked as tentative. The unification procedure was extended to recognize such a situation and to infer a disjunctive definition for the word, for example (Military-Unit ∨ Electricity-Source).

This mechanism was tested by removing the definitions of all 9 of the ambiguous nouns within the Terrorism domain: branch, charge, lines, others, plant, post, quarter, state, and system.[3] Although many of these

words were not "targets" for the domain (i.e. they were not specified as interesting for the information extraction task), Camille, after processing 100 examples from the corpus which contained the words, created ambiguous definitions for five of the nine words: lines, others, post, state, and system.[4]

The scoring system used in the MUCs was adapted to facilitate evaluation of the empirical tests of Camille's lexical acquisition. The measures were defined as: Recall is the number of correct hypotheses[5] created by the system divided by the total number of undefined words. Precision is the number of correct concepts in the hypotheses divided by the total number of concepts generated. Accuracy is the number of correct hypotheses divided by the number of hypotheses generated.

The system hypothesized 5 out of 9 ambiguous definitions. Recall, counting the correct definitions, was 8 out of 18 possible definitions, or 44%. Precision and Accuracy were 8 out of 12, or 67%. As will be shown

---

[2]Camille's morphology component provides some indication of the lexical category of an unknown word. Consistent interpretations are entered into the parse. The application of syntactic constraints is usually sufficient to resolve the word's lexical category.

[3]Like the word "others", some additional words in the lexicon were vague. ((Lytinen 1988) also contains a dis-

cussion of dealing with vague versus ambiguous words.) "Others" was the only vague word tested because it occurred prominently in such examples as, "11 others were wounded."

[4]It also created single definitions for many other words that had been overlooked in the system development. For example the word "impunity" was inferred to be an Instrument-Object.

[5]In this paper, a hypothesis refers to a set of concepts that Camille generates as the tentative meaning of an unknown word.

in the next section, these scores are more descriptive for the larger verb-learning tests.

The importance of the ambiguity mechanism to the noun/verb dichotomy is that it highlights the difference between the conservative and liberal approaches to meaning inference. The conservative approach selects the concept specified by the verb's constraint because it is consistent with the data. The liberal approach searches under that concept for a more specific node (perhaps one which is not already the label of some other word).[6]

As described in the next section, when learning verb meanings, Camille must take a liberal approach, favoring the most specific hypotheses, in order to get usable, falsifiable hypotheses. For learning ambiguous nouns, Camille must use the the conservative approach. If the system used the liberal approach and later encountered a conflicting use of the noun, Camille would not know if it had found an ambiguous word, or if it had made a wrong initial guess about the referent of the word. This produces the two-part strategy described above.

Learning Verbs

As previously mentioned, verbs tend to play the role of the predicate in language. Thus, they serve to organize the overall semantic structure of a sentence, with arguments such as the subject and direct object attaching to them in various "slots." This makes verbs both more important and more difficult to learn, since a sentence with an unknown verb is missing its head concept.

As with nouns, Camille learns verb meanings by searching through the concept hierarchy for an appropriate concept. Because the knowledge representation imposes a lower bound on the interpretation of unknown verbs, the system must either settle for an overly general hypothesis (for example: Action but not Hijacking or Kidnapping) or inductively set its own upper bound. In order to increase the usability and the falsifiability of its hypotheses, Camille takes the latter approach.

To learn nouns, the system merely applied the constraints from the actions to the unknown slot fillers. Because verbs refer to the actions, however, the system cannot know which constraints apply. It must therefore infer the meaning of an unknown verb by comparing the slot fillers that are attached to it with the constraints of the various action concepts. Camille does this incrementally, adjusting the definition as each slot filler is attached, and as each example of the word's use is processed.

As when it learns nouns, the system initially places a default definition into the parse structure for an unknown verb and gives it the default meaning Action.

As each slot filler is attached, Camille checks which descendants of the current meaning hypothesis have constraints that are compatible with the slot filler. For example, with the sentence, "Terrorist froobled the headquarters", "headquarters" is initially attached as the Object of "froobled". All of the non-shaded nodes in figure 2 have constraints which are consistent with this Object. Because Camille wants to induce an upper bound on this hypothesis set, it eliminates from consideration all but the most specific members of this set. That is, if any node in the set is the parent of another node in the set, the parent is eliminated. To make the set even more specific, the distance in the hierarchy between the slot-filler concept and the constraint concept is computed for each concept, and only the closest matches are kept in the hypothesis set. For example, Arson's Object constraint is Building which is the parent of Headquarters and therefore has a distance of one. Human-or-Place, the Object constraint for Attack has a distance of four from Headquarters, so Attack is removed from consideration. This process is repeated as each slot filler is attached for this and future sentences. After each sentence is processed, Camille stores new or modified word definitions in the lexicon.

By trimming down the hypothesis set as described, Camille would infer the single concept Arson as the meaning of "frooble". Note that other concepts (Attack and Bombing, for example) are consistent with the evidence, but these concepts would not be as easily disconfirmed. For example if the system encountered the sentence, "Terrorists froobled the pedestrians", the Arson hypothesis would be disconfirmed but not the others. This is a key to Camille's success in learning word meanings. By choosing the most specific concepts, Camille makes the most falsifiable hypotheses. Thus further examples will be more likely to conflict with an initial hypothesis, invoking the generalization procedure. This procedure searches the hierarchy starting at the current hypothesis until a concept is found which has constraints that do not conflict with all of the slot fillers that have been encountered. If another example of the the unknown word does not conflict with the initial hypothesis, the falsifiability of that hypothesis increases the likelihood that it was correct.

To empirically test Camille's verb-learning mechanism, 50 sentences were randomly selected from the corpus. The definitions of the 17 verbs from those sentences were removed from the lexicon. The average length of the sentences was 24 words, and the average number of repetitions of each unknown word was 2.7. After processing the sentences, Camille had produced 15 hypotheses of which 7 were correct (i.e. the hypothesis set included a correct concept). The average number of concepts per hypothesis was 2.5. This resulted in scores of 41% Recall, 19% Precision, and 47% Accuracy.[7] For comparison, the average of six runs in

---

[6]A psycholinguistic theory, Mutual Exclusivity (Markman 1991), suggests that children use a similar approach to "fill gaps" in their lexical knowledge and thereby reduce the computational complexity of their early lexical acquisition.

---

[7]Camille was also tested in another domain which con-

which meaning assignments were generated randomly from a weighted distribution produced scores of 22% Recall, 10% Precision, and 23% Accuracy.

Related Work

Other systems have concentrated on the acquisition of specific kinds of words. Granger noted the importance and difficulty of acquiring verbs in his description of Foul-Up (Granger 1977) which used heuristic methods to learn verbs based on the prepositions in a sentence. Zernik's Rina (Zernik 1987) concentrated on learning verb-particle combinations using interactive training and extensive domain knowledge. Unfortunately, neither was evaluated on real-world data. The extent of special-purpose knowledge that these systems required would have made that extremely difficult to do.

Salveter, Selfridge, and Siskind have developed cognitive models which perform lexical acquisition (Salveter 1979; Selfridge 1986; Siskind 1990). These systems are interesting from the psychological point of view, but they each focus on such a limited acquisition task as to render them inapplicable to real-world processing.

On the other hand, Cardie's and Riloff's systems (Cardie 1993; Riloff 1993) were specifically oriented toward the processing of real-world texts. Cardie's case-based system, MayTag, did not infer meanings for verbs though. Riloff's AutoSlog learned what amounted to pattern-based production rules. One rule, for example, matched on some subject noun phrase followed by the passive tense of "kidnap" and then assigned the subject to the victim slot of a database form which described the text. These rules could be viewed as definitions for the words. But the system knew so little about the words that it required separate rules for active and gerund uses of the same word. It also required a separate set of rules for related words like "abduct". AutoSlog created a large set of rules which required filtering by a human user. Both AutoSlog and MayTag were batch systems which performed one-shot learning.

Although the scores reported above for Camille's performance are significantly lower than the hit rates reported by Cardie's system, which was also set within an information extraction task, Cardie's scores were combined scores of all different lexical categories, and, as mentioned previously, MayTag made no concept hypotheses for verbs.

Camille's approach to lexical acquisition is incremental so its processing and storage requirements are minimized. The system learns automatically from example

---

tained much simpler sentences (average length: 4.3 words). Scores in this domain were considerably higher: Recall 71%, Precision 22%, and Accuracy 76%. As discussed below, the complexity of the test sentences in the Terrorism domain considerably decreased Camille's ability to learn because it received noisy data.

sentences so it does not require guidance from a human trainer. Camille doesn't need additional knowledge sources. It uses only the knowledge that is present for standard parsing.

Limitations and Future Work

An obvious limitation of the system as it is described here is that it assumed that every aspect of meaning about the domain was *a priori* represented in the concept hierarchy. This conflicts with our intuitions that lexical and concept learning interact, at least to some extent. Another aspect of Camille's implementation partially addresses this limitation, allowing the addition of object nodes. Because Camille has no other window on the world than its linguistic input, however, learning action concepts is a much more difficult problem and will be left to future research.

The basic Camille approach does have some weaknesses. The production of large sets of concepts in hypotheses was not completely mitigated by the elimination of less-specific concepts. Many sets of concepts remain that are indistinguishable based only on the use of slot fillers. The full implementation of Camille also includes a mechanism which uses scripts (Schank & Abelson 1977; Cullingford 1977) to further refine hypotheses.

The learning procedure is sensitive to noisy input. Because it uses an inductive procedure, Camille assumes that if one of its hypotheses conflicts with subsequent evidence, then the original guess was incorrect and the hypothesis should be altered. Noise can be produced by a number of sources, most commonly incomplete parses and ungrammatical input. The domains on which Camille has been tested contain mostly grammatical text. The Terrorism corpus was so complex, however, that it caused great difficulty for the parser, and incorrect or incomplete parses were common. (Camille always produces definitions for unknown verbs that it encounters. The fact that it created no definitions for 2 of the 17 in the test set signifies that no parses or parse fragments containing these words were passed to Camille.) Noisy input can cause Camille to infer that a word takes a larger range of slotfillers. As a result, the system will make an overly general hypothesis for a word's meaning. One approach to handling noise is suggested by the Camille's mechanism which handles ambiguous words. The implementation of this addition is left to future research.

Because Camille was implemented with the goal of using only the knowledge that LINK requires for parsing, it is unable to make certain inferences about word meaning. The representation for action concepts describes only their names, their IS-A relationships to each other, and their constraints on slot fillers. Although the script mechanism allows Camille to make inferences based on sequences of actions, the system has no knowledge of the results of actions, their causes, or what goals they might achieve. The addition of such knowledge would enhance Camille's learning abilities, but it would also impose an additional resource requirement.

Conclusion

The task of lexical acquisition for Camille reduces to searching for an appropriate node in the domain representation. This abstraction of the task reveals an important distinction between learning nouns and learning verbs. The constraints on actions provide a natural upper bound on the interpretation of unknown object labels. For action labels, no such upper bound exists. Thus, in order for Camille to make useful inferences about verb meanings, it must inductively limit its search space. Camille does this by choosing the most readily falsifiable hypotheses. This gives Camille the best chance for correcting its mistakes. Thus the system uses a two-part strategy to quickly converge on an appropriate hypothesis for many unknown words.

References

Behrend, D. 1990. The development of verb concepts: Children's use of verbs to label familiar and novel events. *Child Development* 61:681–696.

Brent, M. 1993. Surface cues and robust inference as a basis for the early acquisition of subcategorization frames. *Lingua.* in press.

Cardie, C. 1993. A case-based approach to knowledge acquisition for domain-specific sentence analysis. In *Proceedings of the 11th National Conference on Artificial Intelligence*, 798–803.

Church, K., and Hanks, P. 1990. Word association norms, mutual information, and lexicography. *Computational Linguistics* 16.

Cullingford, R. 1977. *Organizing World Knowledge for Story Understanding by Computer.* Ph.D. Dissertation, Yale University, New Haven, CT.

Fernald, A., and Morikawa, H. 1993. Common themes and cultural variations in Japanese and American mothers' speech to infants. *Child Development* 64:637–656.

Gentner, D. 1978. On relational meaning: The acquisition of verb meaning. *Child Development* 49:988–998.

Graesser, A.; Hopkinson, P.; and Schmid, C. 1987. Differences in interconcept organization between nouns and verbs. *Journal of Memory and Language* 26:242–253.

Granger, R. 1977. Foul-up: A program that figures out meanings of words from context. In *Proceedings of Fifth International Joint Conference on Artificial Intelligence*.

Hastings, P. 1994. *Automatic Acquisition of Word Meaning from Context.* Ph.D. Dissertation, University of Michigan, Ann Arbor, MI.

Hindle, D. 1990. Noun classification from predicate-argument structures. In *Proceedings of the 28th Annual Meeting of the Association for Computational Linguistics*, 268–275.

Huttenlocher, J., and Lui, F. 1979. The semantic organization of some simple nouns and verbs. *Journal of verbal learning and verbal behavior* 18:141–162.

Lytinen, S., and Roberts, S. 1989. Unifying linguistic knowledge. AI Laboratory, Univ of Michigan, Ann Arbor, MI 48109.

Lytinen, S. 1988. Are vague words ambiguous? In Small, S., and Cottrell, G., eds., *Lexical Ambiguity Resolution.* San Mateo, CA: Morgan Kaufmann Publishers. 109–128.

Markman, E. 1991. The whole object, taxonomic, and mutual exclusivity assumptions as initial constraints on word meanings. In Byrnes, J. P., and Gelman, S. A., eds., *Perspectives on language and thought: Interrelations in development.* Cambridge: Cambridge University Press.

Mitchell, T. 1977. Version spaces: A candidate elimination approach to rule learning. In *Proceedings of the Fifth International Joint Conference on Artificial Intelligence*, 305–309.

Resnik, P. 1992. A class-based approach to lexical discovery. In *Proceedings of the 30th Annual Meeting of the Association for Computational Linguistics*, 327–329.

Riloff, E. 1993. Automatically constructing a dictionary for information extraction tasks. In *Proceedings of the 11th National Conference on Artificial Intelligence*, 811–816.

Salveter, S. 1979. Inferring conceptual graphs. *Cognitive Science* 3:141–166.

Schank, R., and Abelson, R. 1977. *Scripts, plans, goals, and understanding.* Hillsdale, NJ: Lawrence Erlbaum Associates.

Selfridge, M. 1986. A computer model of child language learning. *Artificial Intelligence* 29:171–216.

Siskind, J. 1990. Acquiring core meanings of words. In *Proceedings of the 28th Annual Meeting of the Association for Computational Linguistics*, 143–156.

Small, S., and Cottrell, G., eds. 1988. *Lexical Ambiguity Resolution.* San Mateo, CA: Morgan Kaufmann Publishers.

Sundheim, B. 1992. Overview of the fourth message understanding evaluation and conference. In *Proceedings of the Fourth Message Understanding Conference.* San Mateo, CA: Morgan Kaufmann Publishers.

Yarowsky, D. 1992. Word-sense disambiguation using statistical models of roget's categories trained on large corpora. In *Proceedings, COLING-92.*

Zernik, U. 1987. Strategies in language acquisitions: Learning phrases from examples in context. Technical Report UCLA-AI-87-1, UCLA.

Lexical Acquisition in the Presence of Noise and Homonymy

Jeffrey Mark Siskind[*]
Department of Computer Science
University of Toronto
Toronto Ontario M5S 1A4 CANADA
416/978–6114
internet: Qobi@CS.Toronto.EDU

Abstract

This paper conjectures a computational account of how children might learn the meanings of words in their native language. First, a simplified version of the lexical acquisition task faced by children is modeled by a precisely specified formal problem. Then, an implemented algorithm for solving this formal problem is presented. Key advances of this algorithm over previously proposed algorithms are its ability to learn homonymous word senses in the presence of noisy input and its ability to scale up to problems of the size faced by real children.

Introduction

When learning their native language, children must acquire a lexicon that maps the words in that language to their meanings. This paper explores one way that they might accomplish that task, adopting as few assumptions as possible. In particular, the techniques explored in this paper do not rely on children hearing single-word utterances in situations in which they can unambiguously determine their meaning from context. Consider, for instance, a child hearing a multi-word utterance such as *Mommy raised the ball*, in a context where she was uncertain as to whether that utterance as a whole meant that Mommy raised the ball, that Mommy was holding the ball, or that Mommy wanted the ball. In this situation, the child would have to determine both that 'Mommy raised the ball' was the correct meaning of the utterance as a whole, and that the words *Mommy*, *raised*, and *ball* meant 'Mommy,' 'raised,' and 'ball' respectively. In doing so, the child must somehow come to rule out many plausible but incorrect mappings—such as the mapping from *Mommy* to 'ball,' *raised* to 'Mommy,' and *ball* to 'raised'— despite the fact that such mappings would be consistent with the utterance just heard.

[*]Supported in part by ARO grant DAAL 03–89–C–0031, by DARPA grant N00014–90–J–1863, by NSF grant IRI 90–16592, by Ben Franklin grant 91S.3078C–1, and by the Canadian Natural Sciences and Engineering Research Council. Part of this work was performed while the author was a postdoctoral fellow at the University of Pennsylvania Institute for Research in Cognitive Science.

This paper presents a computational study of this lexical acquisition task. It first attempts to characterize the task by defining a simplified formal approximation of the actual task faced by children. It then discusses a precise and implemented algorithm for solving this simplified formal task.

The proposed model of the task attempts to make as few assumptions as possible. First, it makes no assumption that utterances heard by the child refer to the immediate perceptual context. It requires only that the child be able to hypothesize from context a set of meanings for the complete utterance that usually, though not necessarily, includes the correct one. That utterance meaning need not refer to the here-and-now. Second, it makes no assumption that children can uniquely determine the meaning of each utterance from context. It allows for *referential uncertainty*: situations where the child is unsure of the meaning of an utterance. Referential uncertainty is modeled by allowing the child to hypothesize a *set* of potential meanings for each utterance heard. Third, it makes no assumption that the child is always successful in hypothesizing a set of potential meanings that contains the correct meaning of each utterance heard. It allows for *noisy input*: situations where the child unknowingly hypothesizes only incorrect meanings for an utterance. Fourth, it makes no assumption that each word has a single meaning. It allows words to be *homonymous*.

With high accuracy, the algorithm to be described learns a lexicon containing precisely the correct senses for each word heard. This ability to learn despite the presence of referential uncertainty, noise, and homonymy in the input are key capabilities which distinguish this algorithm from those proposed by Granger (1977), Salveter (1979), Berwick (1983), Pustejovsky (1988), Rayner et al. (1988), Pinker (1989), Gleitman (1990), Suppes et al. (1991), Regier (1992), and Fisher et al. (1994). Unlike some of these algorithms, the algorithm presented here has no prior access to any language-specific information. Furthermore, unlike some of these algorithms, the algorithm presented here can scale up to tasks of the size faced by children.

The Mapping Problem

The algorithm presented in this paper solves a precisely specified formal problem called *the mapping problem*. While this formal problem is simplified and abstract, it is likely that it accurately reflects the lexical acquisition task faced by children. In this problem, the learner is presented with a sequence of utterances, each being a sequence of words. Each utterance is paired with a set of expressions representing possible meanings for that *whole* utterance. This set of possible meaning expressions would be constructed by a general perceptual and conceptual apparatus that is independent of language. For example, the learner might hear the utterance *Mommy raised the ball*, look out into the world and see Mommy grasping and lifting the ball, and conjecture that $\text{CAUSE}(\textbf{mother}, \text{GO}(\textbf{ball}, \text{UP}))$ and $\text{GRASP}(\textbf{mother}, \textbf{ball})$ could be representations of potential meanings of that utterance. Not all utterances refer to observed events however. Perhaps the utterance meant that Mommy wanted the ball. Thus $\text{WANT}(\textbf{mother}, \textbf{ball})$ might be a representation of another potential meaning of that utterance. Since the learner might not be precisely sure of what some utterance means, the model allows her to conjecture a *set* of possible meanings. Such uncertainty on the part of the learner as to what each utterance means is termed *referential uncertainty*.

In theory, the set of referentially uncertain meanings could be infinite. This is the essence of the philosophical 'Gavagai' quandary discussed by Quine (1960). Thus the set of meaning representations paired with each utterance as input to the lexical acquisition algorithm is not intended to be the set of *all* true facts about the world in the situation where an utterance is heard. It is only the finite, possibly small, set of potential meanings that the learner conjectures based on some measure of salience. Sometimes this set will contain the correct meaning, while other times it will not. An utterance is considered to be *noisy* if it is paired with only incorrect meaning expressions. The only requirement for successful lexical acquisition is that utterances be non-noisy a sufficient fraction of the time.

This paper assumes that the learner brings to bear a language-independent theory of naive physics and naive psychology embodied in an elaborate perceptual and conceptual apparatus to hypothesize potential meanings for each utterance. However, issues such as the organization of this apparatus, and whether the knowledge it contains is innate or acquired, are orthogonal to questions about lexical acquisition. The essence of lexical acquisition is simply the process of learning the mapping between external words and internal conceptual representations.

We know very little about the conceptual representations used by the brain. Thus this paper makes as few assumptions as possible about such representations. It assumes only that conceptual representations take the form of expressions in some logic. It doesn't care about the particular inventory of constant, function, predicate, and logical connective symbols used to construct such expressions. The symbol $\perp$ is used to represent the meaning of words that fall outside the chosen representational calculus. The learning algorithm makes no use of the semantics or truth conditions of the meaning expressions themselves. As far as the lexical acquisition is concerned, these expressions are simply strings of uninterpreted symbols. The representations of Schank (1973), Jackendoff (1983), and Pinker (1989), for example, are all compatible with this minimal assumption.

In order to fully specify the mapping problem, one must specify the process by which the meanings of words combine to form the meanings of utterances containing those words. Here again, this paper makes as few assumptions as possible about this semantic interpretation process. It assumes that the lexicon L for a given language maps each word to a set of expressions denoting the meanings of different senses for that word, and that the meaning of an utterance u, consisting of an unordered multiset of words $\{w_1, \ldots, w_n\}$, is a member of the set computed by choosing some sense $t_i \in L(w_i)$ for each word w_i in the utterance, and applying the function INTERPRET to the unordered multiset of expressions $\{t_1, \ldots, t_n\}$. No claim that the actual human semantic interpretation process ignores word order is intended. This is simply a minimal assumption. If lexical acquisition can be successful under such an underspecified semantic interpretation rule, *a fortiori* it can be successful when stronger constraints are added.

The function INTERPRET is left unspecified except for the following condition. If $t \in$ INTERPRET($\{t_1, \ldots, t_n\}$) then all symbols that appear in t must appear in at least one of $t_1, \ldots, t_n$, and all symbols that appear a total of k times in $t_1, \ldots, t_n$, except for variable symbols and the distinguished symbol $\perp$, must appear at least k times in t. This is simply the requirement that semantic interpretation be compositional and 'partially linear.' It shares with linearity the property that it cannot delete information from the meanings of words when producing the meaning of an utterance, and cannot add information to the meaning of an utterance that does not come from the meaning of some word in the utterance. It need not be truly linear since it can, however, copy information from a word or phrase so that it appears more than once in the resulting utterance meaning. Beyond this property, the lexical acquisition process uses INTERPRET as a 'black box' (with the exception of the RECONSTRUCT($m, N(s)$) procedure to be described later).

The mapping problem can now be stated formally as follows. The learner is presented with a corpus of utterances u, each paired with a set M of hypothesized meaning expressions. A hidden lexicon L was used to generate the corpus. L maps each word in the corpus to a set of senses, each represented as an expression. Some subset of the utterances in the corpus have the property that

$$(\exists t_1 \in L(w_1)) \cdots (\exists t_n \in L(w_n))$$
$$\textsc{Interpret}(\{t_1, \ldots, t_n\}) \cap M \neq \emptyset$$

where $u = \{w_1, \ldots, w_n\}$. The learner must find the lexicon L used to generate the corpus.

The Noise-Free Monosemous Case

Before presenting the full lexical acquisition algorithm, capable of dealing with noise and homonymy, I will first present a simplified algorithm that handles only noise-free input under the assumption that all words are monosemous. This algorithm receives as input a sequence of pairs $\langle u, M \rangle$ where each utterance u is an unordered multiset of words and M is the set of expressions representing referentially uncertain hypothesized meanings of u.

The algorithm is *on line* in the sense that it makes a single pass through the input corpus, processing each utterance in turn and discarding it before processing the next utterance. The algorithm retains only a small amount of inter-utterance information. This information takes the form of a number of maps from words to sets of senses, and from senses to sets of symbols and meaning expressions. The table $L(w)$ maps each word w to a set of senses. The table $N(s)$ maps each sense s to a set of symbols that have been determined to be *necessarily* part of the meaning of s. Likewise, the table $P(s)$ maps each sense s to a set of symbols that have been determined to be *possibly* part of the meaning of s. $N(s)$ initially maps each sense to the empty set $\emptyset$, while $P(s)$ initially maps each sense to the universal set $\top$. At all times, $N(s) \subseteq P(s)$ for all senses s. The algorithm monotonically adds elements to $N(s)$ and removes elements from $P(s)$ until $N(s) = P(s)$. When this happens, the algorithm is said to have *converged on the symbols* for the sense s, denoted $\textsc{ConvergedOnSymbols?}(s)$.

Having converged on the symbols for a given sense does not imply knowing its meaning. For example, knowing that some sense for the word *raise* contains precisely the set $\{\mathrm{CAUSE}, \mathrm{GO}, \mathrm{UP}\}$ as its set of (non-variable) symbols does not specify whether the expression representing the meaning of that sense is $\mathrm{CAUSE}(x, \mathrm{GO}(y, \mathrm{UP}))$, $\mathrm{GO}(\mathrm{CAUSE}, \mathrm{UP})$, $\mathrm{UP}(\mathrm{CAUSE}(x), \mathrm{GO}(x, y))$, and so forth. For this, the algorithm maintains a fourth table $D(s)$ that maps each sense s to a set of *possible* meaning expressions. $D(s)$ initially maps each sense s to the universal set $\top$. The algorithm monotonically removes elements from $D(s)$ until $D(s)$ is a singleton. When this happens, the algorithm is said to have *converged on the meaning* of the sense s, denoted $\textsc{ConvergedOnMeaning?}(s)$.

The algorithm maintains a fifth table $T(s)$ that maps each sense to a *temperature*, a non-negative integer.

$T(s)$ initially maps each sense to zero. The temperature of a sense increases as the learner become more confident that she has not mistakingly hypothesized that sense to explain a noisy utterance. There are two integer constants, μ and $\mu_\bot$, denoting *freezing points*. A sense s is *frozen*, denoted $\textsc{Frozen?}(s)$, if it has converged on meaning and either $D(s) = \{\bot\}$ and $T(s) \geq \mu_\bot$, or $D(s) \neq \{\bot\}$ and $T(s) \geq \mu$. Senses are subject to a garbage collection process unless they are frozen.

Each sense passes through four stages, starting out unconverged, converging on symbols, then converging on meaning, and finally being frozen. Different senses can be in different stages at the same time. The processes that move senses through each of these stages are interleaved. They are implemented by the procedure $\textsc{Process}(S, M)$. The input to $\textsc{Process}(S, M)$ consists of an unordered multiset S of senses and a set M of expressions. In the noise-free monosemous case, the lexicon L maps each word w to a set containing a single sense. Each utterance $u = \{w_1, \ldots, w_n\}$, paired with a set M, is processed by letting s_i be the single element of $L(w_i)$, for each word w_i in the utterance, forming the unordered multiset $S = \{s_1, \ldots, s_n\}$, and calling $\textsc{Process}(S, M)$. In the following description, $F(m)$ denotes the set of all symbols that appear in the expression m, while $F_1(m)$ denotes the set of all symbols that appear only once in m.

Procedure $\textsc{Process}(S, M)$:

Step 1 Ignore those hypothesized utterance meanings that contain a symbol that is not possibly contributed by some word in the utterance or that are missing a symbol that is necessarily contributed by some word in the utterance.

$$M \leftarrow \{m \in M \mid \bigcap_{s \in S} N(s) \subseteq F(m) \wedge F(m) \subseteq \bigcup_{s \in S} P(s)\}$$

Step 2 For each word in the utterance, remove from the set of possible symbols for that word, any symbols that do not appear in some remaining hypothesized utterance meaning.

$$\textbf{for } s \in S \textbf{ do } P(s) \leftarrow P(s) \cap \bigcup_{m \in M} F(m) \textbf{ od}$$

Step 3 For each word in the utterance, add to the set of necessary symbols for that word, any symbols that appear in every remaining hypothesized utterance meaning but are missing from the set of possible symbols of all other words in the utterance.

$$\textbf{for } s \in S$$
$$\textbf{do } N(s) \leftarrow N(s) \cup$$
$$\left[\left(\bigcap_{m \in M} F(m)\right) \setminus \bigcup_{s' \in S, s' \neq s} P(s')\right]$$
$$\textbf{od}$$

Step 4 For each word in the utterance, remove from the set of possible symbols for that word, any symbols that appear only once in every remaining hypothesized utterance meaning if they are necessarily contributed by some other word in the utterance.

$$\textbf{for } s \in S$$
$$\textbf{do } P(s) \leftarrow P(s) \setminus$$
$$\left[\left(\bigcap_{m \in M} F_1(m) \right) \cap \bigcup_{s' \in S, s' \neq s} N(s') \right]$$
$$\textbf{od}$$

Step 5 For each word in the utterance that has converged on meaning, call the function $\textsc{Reconstruct}(m, N(s))$ to compute the set of all fragments of the expression m that contain precisely the set of non-variable symbols $N(s)$, and remove from $D(s)$ any expressions not in that set.[1]

$$\textbf{for } s \in S$$
$$\textbf{do if } \textsc{ConvergedOnSymbols?}(s)$$
$$\textbf{then } D(s) \leftarrow D(s) \cap$$
$$\bigcup_{m \in M} \textsc{Reconstruct}(m, N(s))$$
$$\textbf{fi od}$$

Step 6 If all words in the utterance have converged on symbols, for each word in the utterance, remove from the set of possible meaning expressions for that word, those meanings for which there do not exist possible meanings for the other words in the utterance that are compatible with one of the remaining hypothesized utterance meanings. This is a generalized form of arc consistency (Mackworth 1992).

$$\textbf{if } (\forall s \in S)\textsc{ConvergedOnSymbols?}(s)$$
$$\textbf{then for } s \in S$$
$$\textbf{do if } (\forall s' \in S)[s' \neq s \to D(s') \neq \top]$$
$$\textbf{then } D(s) \leftarrow \{t \in D(s)|$$
$$\underbrace{(\exists t_1 \in D(s_1)) \cdots (\exists t_n \in D(s_n))}_{\{s, s_1, \ldots, s_n\} = S}$$
$$(\exists m \in M)$$
$$m \in \textsc{Interpret}(\{t, t_1, \ldots, t_n\})\}$$
$$\textbf{fi od fi}$$

Step 7 If all senses have converged on meaning, then increment the temperature of those senses that do mean $\bot$ if all senses that don't mean $\bot$ are frozen, and likewise increment the temperature of those senses that don't mean $\bot$ if all senses that do mean $\bot$ are frozen.

$$\textbf{if } (\forall s \in S)\textsc{ConvergedOnMeaning?}(s)$$
$$\textbf{then for } s \in S$$
$$\textbf{do if } [D(s) = \{\bot\} \wedge$$
$$(\forall s \in S)(s \neq \{\bot\} \to \textsc{Frozen?}(s))] \vee$$
$$[D(s) \neq \{\bot\} \wedge$$
$$(\forall s \in S)(s = \{\bot\} \to \textsc{Frozen?}(s))]$$
$$\textbf{then } T(s) \leftarrow T(s) + 1 \textbf{ fi od fi } \quad \square$$

---

[1] A future paper will describe the algorithm for computing $\textsc{Reconstruct}(m, N(s))$ in greater detail.

While steps 1 through 4 always take a small amount of time, steps 5 and 6 can potentially take a large amount of time. Thus steps 5 and 6 are simply aborted if they take too long. This happens only a small fraction of the time in practice, usually for long utterances, and doesn't appear to significantly decrease the convergence rate of the algorithm.

The tables $N(s)$ and $P(s)$ are reminiscent of Mitchell's (1977) version-space algorithm. In the version-space algorithm, a *concept* is a set of *instances*. A concept is more *general* than its subsets and more *specific* than its supersets. When learning a concept, the version-space algorithm keeps two *sets* of concepts that bound the target concept from above and below. The target concept must be more general than each element of the lower bound and more specific than each element of the upper bound. Since the generality relation between concepts is transitive, each time a concept is added to the upper bound, any other concepts from the upper bound that are strictly more general are redundant and can be removed. Likewise, each time a concept is added to the lower bound, any other concepts from the lower bound that are strictly more specific are also redundant and can be removed. Because the addition of a new concept to either the upper or the lower bound will not always result in such a redundancy, the upper and lower bounds may grow to be sets of more than one element.

The algorithm presented here differs from the version-space algorithm in two important ways. First, the upper bound will always contain precisely two concepts. The sets $N(s)$ and $P(s)$ each denote a *single* concept, namely the set of expressions m such that $N(s) \subseteq F(m)$ or that $F(m) \subseteq P(s)$ respectively. Both of these concepts can be seen as members of the upper bound. The target concept must be more specific than each of these concepts. Each time a symbol is added to $N(s)$, a new concept results that is necessarily more specific than the prior $N(s)$ concept yet is neither more specific nor more general than the $P(s)$ concept. Thus adding a symbol to $N(s)$ replaces the prior $N(s)$ concept and leaves the $P(s)$ concept unchanged. Similarly, each time a symbol is removed from $P(s)$, a new concept results that is necessarily more specific than the prior $P(s)$ concept yet is neither more specific nor more general than the $N(s)$ concept. Thus removing a symbol from $P(s)$ replaces the prior $P(s)$ concept and leaves the $N(s)$ concept unchanged. Thus by induction, the upper bound will always contain precisely two concepts.

Second, the algorithm presented here has no analog to the version-space lower bound. Instead, the algorithm utilizes the domain specific fact that when $N(s) = P(s)$ the upper bound admits only two concepts, one a singleton and one empty. Since in this domain, all target concepts are singletons, the empty concept can be implicitly ruled out. Thus while in general, the version-space algorithm requires convergence of the upper and lower bounds to uniquely identify target concepts, a special property of this domain allows target concepts to be identified using only upper bound reasoning. Thus the algorithm presented here is an important efficient special case of the version-space algorithm for the particular representation chosen for word meanings.

As normally viewed, the version-space algorithm generalizes the lower bound on the basis of observed positive instances of a concept and specializes the upper bound on the basis of observed negative instances. A common maxim in the linguistic community is that children rarely if ever receive negative evidence of any linguistic phenomena. In the particular case of learning word meanings, this means that children might be told or shown examples of what a word like *bicycle* means, but they are never told or shown examples of what *bicycle* does *not* mean. A naive interpretation of this fact would be that a learner could only apply half of the version-space algorithm to learn the lower bound, but could not learn the upper bound. This has prompted Berwick (1986) to propose the Subset Principle, the claim that learners are conservative, adopting only those concepts on the fringe of the lower bound.

This raises an apparent paradox. Since the algorithm presented here maintains only an upper bound and no lower bound, it would appear that it is learning *only* from negative evidence and not from positive evidence. Deeper inspection however reveals that the algorithm is taking advantage of two particular kinds of implicit negative evidence available when learning word meanings: inference between the same word heard in different non-linguistic contexts and inference between different words in the same sentence. The former is traditionally held by psychologists to be the basis of lexical acquisition in children (cf. Pinker 1989, Event Category Labeling). What is not traditionally acknowledged is that this is a form of implicit negative evidence. Hearing a word in multiple contexts and concluding that it must mean something shared by those contexts carries with it the implicit claim that a word cannot mean something that is not contained in the set of meanings hypothesized for an utterance containing that word. Use of the later form of implicit negative evidence, however, appears to be new. Given the particular semantic interpretation rule presented earlier, a learner hearing *John rode a bicycle* after having determined that *John* must mean **John** could infer that *bicycle* could *not* also mean **John**. Both of these forms of reasoning aid a learner in determining what words might *not* mean and allow the upper half of the version-space algorithm to apply. This has the important consequence that the Subset Principle is not strictly necessary, as had been previously thought, even if no explicit negative evidence is available.

Dealing with Noise and Homonymy

A sense s is termed *consistent* if $N(s) \subseteq P(s)$ and $D(s) \neq \emptyset$. The simplified algorithm will produce inconsistent senses if it is used to process a corpus that exhibits noise or homonymy. Nonetheless, the procedure $\text{PROCESS}(S, M)$ can be used as a subroutine by an extended algorithm that can deal with noise and homonymy.

In the simplified algorithm, $\text{PROCESS}(S, M)$ permanently updates the tables N, P, D, and T. The extended algorithm will additionally make use of a variant of this procedure, $\text{CONSISTENT?}(S, M)$, that doesn't actually perform the updates but returns **true** if and only if every sense $s \in S$ would remain consistent if $\text{PROCESS}(S, M)$ were called.

In the extended algorithm, L may map words to sets of senses, not just singleton senses. Initially, L maps each word to a unique singleton sense. The extended algorithm makes use of the following function.

$$\text{ALTERNATIVES}(u, M) \triangleq$$
$$\{\{s_1, \ldots, s_n\} \mid \underbrace{s_1 \in L(w_1) \wedge \cdots \wedge s_n \in L(w_n)}_{\{w_1, \ldots, w_n\} = u} \wedge$$
$$\text{CONSISTENT?}(\{s_1, \ldots, s_n\}, M)\}$$

The extended algorithm is presented below.

Procedure $\text{PROCESSUTTERANCE}(u, M)$:

Step 1 If $\text{ALTERNATIVES}(u, M) \neq \emptyset$, choose the element $\{s_1, \ldots, s_n\} \in \text{ALTERNATIVES}(u, M)$ with the maximum value of $T(s_1) + \cdots + T(s_n)$, perform $\text{PROCESS}(\{s_1, \ldots, s_n\}, M)$, and return.

Step 2 Otherwise, find the smallest subset $u' \subseteq u$ such that if a new unique sense is added to $L(w)$ for each $w \in u'$, $\text{ALTERNATIVES}(u, M) \neq \emptyset$.

Step 3 Add a new unique sense to $L(w)$ for each $w \in u'$.

Step 4 Now $\text{ALTERNATIVES}(u, M)$ must not be empty, so choose the element $\{s_1, \ldots, s_n\} \in \text{ALTERNATIVES}(u, M)$ with the maximum value of $T(s_1) + \cdots + T(s_n)$, call the procedure $\text{PROCESS}(\{s_1, \ldots, s_n\}, M)$, and return. $\square$

Since either step 2 in the above algorithm, or the computation of $\text{ALTERNATIVES}(u, M)$, may take a long time, an utterance is simply discarded if these computations exceed a certain time limit. The top-level procedure simply evaluates $\text{PROCESSUTTERANCE}(u, M)$ for each input sample $\langle u, M \rangle$.

The intuitive idea behind this algorithm is as follows. The algorithm operates under the default assumption that each word has a single sense. Under this assumption, it tries to construct a lexicon that explains all of the utterances in the corpus, i.e. one that allows each utterance to take on as its meaning, one of the referentially uncertain expressions paired with that utterance. If the corpus does not exhibit noise or homonymy, it will succeed at this task. If however, the corpus does exhibit noise or homonymy, some of the word senses will become inconsistent during the execution of the acquisition algorithm. This can happen for one of three reasons. Either (a) the current utterance contains a word used in a different sense than the current senses hypothesized for that word, (b) the current utterance is noise, or (c) some previous utterance was noise and processing that utterance polluted the hypothesized meanings of some words shared with the current utterance. The single mechanism of splitting word senses, embodied in steps 2 and 3 of PROCESSUTTERANCE(u, M), is used to cope with all three of these cases. If the current utterance does indeed contain words used in a different sense then previously hypothesized, it is likely that an attempt to merge the two senses into one will yield an inconsistency. Selecting the minimal set of senses to split to resolve such an inconsistency will likely correlate with the actual homonymous words encountered. Noisy utterances are also likely to yield an inconsistency. Paying attention to noisy utterances simply causes the creation of spurious new word senses to account for those utterances. These spurious senses are unlikely to be encountered more than once since they were created solely to account for a random noisy utterance. Thus these senses are unlikely to progress very far along the path to convergence on symbols, meaning, or being frozen. These senses are filtered out every so often by having the top-level procedure remove the non-frozen senses of each word if some sense for that word is frozen and the senses of each word that haven't converged on symbols if some sense for that word has converged on symbols.

Experiments

Since the algorithm presented learns from utterances paired with hypothesized utterance meanings, and there do not exist corpora of naturally occurring utterances paired with such meaning representations, it has been tested on synthetic corpora, generated randomly according to controllable distributional parameters. In one such experiment, a random lexicon mapping 1,000 words to 1,680 senses was generated. The 'words' in this lexicon were simply the symbols $w_1 \ldots w_{1000}$ while the 'senses' were randomly constructed S-expressions over a conceptual vocabulary of 250 conceptual symbols, denoted $s_1 \ldots s_{250}$. A uniform distribution was used to select the conceptual symbols when constructing the random S-expressions. Of these 1,680 senses, 800 were variable-free expressions. These had a maximal depth of 2 and a maximal branching factor of 3 and were intended to model noun-like word senses. Another 800 senses contained from 1 to 3 variables denoting open argument positions. These were intended to model verb-like word senses and had the same maximal depth and branching factor. A uniform distribution was used to control the choice of depth and branching factor used to generate each synthetic word sense. The final 80 word senses were taken to be $\perp$ to model function words. These 1,680 senses were uniformly distributed among the 1,000 words. Some words contained only a single sense while others contained several. A given word could have a mixture of noun-like, verb-like, and function-word-like senses.

Using this lexicon, a corpus of 246,439 random utterances containing 1,269,153 words was generated. A uniform distribution was used to select the words when generating the utterances. These utterances ranged in length from 2 to 27 words with an average of 5.15 words per utterance. The lexicon was used to parse each utterance and construct a semantic representation. 80% of the utterances were paired with their correct semantic representation along with the semantic representation of 9 other randomly generated utterances. 20% of the utterances were paired with 10 incorrect semantic representations corresponding to 10 other randomly generated utterances. Thus the corpus exhibited a degree of referential uncertainty of 10 representations per utterances and a noise rate of 20%. Finally, each utterance in the corpus was permuted randomly before being presented to the acquisition algorithm to guarantee that the algorithm did not make any use of word order.

This corpus was then presented to the lexical acquisition algorithm. During acquisition, of course, the algorithm had no access to the lexicon used to generate the corpus. After completion, the lexicon acquired by the algorithm was compared with the original lexicon used to generate the corpus. In a little over three days of CPU time on a Sun SPARCclassic,[TM] the algorithm succeeded in recovering at least one correct meaning for each of the 1,000 words in the lexicon. It failed to find 33 of the 1,680 word-to-meaning mappings and mistakingly conjectured 9 incorrect word-to-meaning mappings for a combined error rate of 2.5%. Due to computer resource limitations, for this experiment, the algorithm was set to terminate after it had acquired 98% of the word senses in the lexicon, thus accounting for the 33 false negatives. It appears likely that the algorithm would have succeeded in acquiring all 1,680 senses if it was left to run on a somewhat longer corpus.

It appears that the length of the corpus needed to learn a lexicon of a given size can depend significantly on the homonymy rate. Another experiment was conducted where the lexicon did not exhibit any homonymy but where all other corpus construction were kept parameters the same. In particular, the corpus still exhibited a degree of referential uncertainty of 10 and noise rate of 20%. For this experiment, the algorithm correctly acquired 1029 out of 1050 word-to-meaning mappings, making only a single mistake. Here again the algorithm was terminated before it could acquire the remaining 21 word-to-meaning mappings but would likely have done so with a somewhat longer corpus. The important difference is that this run required a corpus of only 12,840 utterances, less than one-twentieth the size of the first experiment. More work is necessary to determine whether this difference reflects a fundamental difficulty inherent in coping with homonymy or whether this is an artifact of the particular lexical acquisition algorithm presented here.

No claim is intended that these examples reflect all of the complexities faced by children learning their native language. First of all, it is unclear how to select appropriate values for corpus parameters such as noise rate, homonymy rate, and degree of referential uncertainty. In the above experiments, the noise rate of 20% and the value of 10 for the degree of referential uncertainty were chosen arbitrarily, purely to test the acquisition algorithm. Our current impoverished level of understanding of how conceptual representations are constructed from perceptual input, either by adults or by infants, makes it difficult to select a more motivated noise rate or degree of referential uncertainty. It is also difficult to accurately assess the homonymy rate in a given language as that depends on how one decides when two senses differ. The homonymy rate of 1.68 senses per word was chosen for the experiments presented here since the WORDNET database (Beckwith et al. 1991) exhibits a homonymy rate of 1.68. No claim that children face similar noise and homonymy rates is intended.

Conclusion

A number of further questions must be answered before this algorithm can be proposed as a theory of how children learn word meanings. Currently, not much is known about the cognitive representations that children bring to the task of language learning, how wide the range of hypotheses that they construct is, how severe the noise problem is, or how much homonymy they face. But the present work shows that an algorithm that can cope with these problems exists and that despite quite pessimistic assumptions about the values of these parameters, the algorithm has reasonable running times and convergence rates. This research suggests that exploring the space of potential lexical acquisition procedures to find those that work will give insight into the lexical acquisition task, lead to a better understanding of how children might accomplish that task, and motivate experiments to determine how they actually do so.

Acknowledgments

I wish to thank Mark Steedman and Graeme Hirst for their comments on an earlier draft of this paper.

References

Beckwith, R.; Fellbaum, C.; Gross, D.; and Miller, G. 1991. WordNet: A lexical database organized on psycholinguistic principles. In Zernik, U., ed., *Lexical Acquisition: Exploiting On-Line Resources to Build a Lexicon*. Lawrence Erlbaum Associates. 211–232.

Berwick, R. C. 1983. Learning word meanings from examples. In *Proceedings of the Eighth International Joint Conference on Artificial Intelligence*, 459–461.

Berwick, R. C. 1986. Learning from positive-only examples: The subset principle and three case studies. In Michalski, R. S.; Carbonell, J. G.; and Mitchell, T. M., eds., *Machine Learning: An Artificial Intelligence Approach*, volume 2. San Mateo, CA: Morgan Kaufmann. 625–646.

Fisher, C.; Hall, G.; Rakowitz, S.; and Gleitman, L. 1994. When it is better to receive than to give: Syntactic and conceptual constraints on vocabulary growth. *Lingua* 92(1).

Gleitman, L. 1990. The structural sources of verb meanings. *Language Acquisition* 1(1):3–55.

Granger, Jr., R. H. 1977. FOUL-UP: A program that figures out meanings of words from context. In *Proceedings of the Fifth International Joint Conference on Artificial Intelligence*, 172–178.

Jackendoff, R. 1983. *Semantics and Cognition*. Cambridge, MA: The MIT Press.

Mackworth, A. K. 1992. Constraint satisfaction. In Shapiro, S. C., ed., *Encyclopedia of Artificial Intelligence*. New York: John Wiley & Sons, Inc. 285–293.

Mitchell, T. M. 1977. Version spaces: A candidate elimination approach to rule learning. In *Proceedings of the Fifth International Joint Conference on Artificial Intelligence*, 305–310.

Pinker, S. 1989. *Learnability and Cognition*. Cambridge, MA: The MIT Press.

Pustejovsky, J. 1988. Constraints on the acquisition of semantic knowledge. *International Journal of Intelligent Systems* 3(3):247–268.

Quine, W. V. O. 1960. *Word and object*. Cambridge, MA: The MIT Press.

Rayner, M.; Hugosson, Å.; and Hagert, G. 1988. Using a logic grammar to learn a lexicon. In *Proceedings of the 12th International Conference on Computational Linguistics*, 524–529.

Regier, T. P. 1992. *The Acquisition of Lexical Semantics for Spatial Terms: A Connectionist Model of Perceptual Categorization*. Ph.D. Dissertation, University of California at Berkeley.

Salveter, S. C. 1979. Inferring conceptual graphs. *Cognitive Science* 3(2):141–166.

Schank, R. C. 1973. The fourteen primitive actions and their inferences. Memo AIM-183, Stanford Artificial Intelligence Laboratory.

Suppes, P.; Liang, L.; and Böttner, M. 1991. Complexity issues in robotic machine learning of natural language. In Lam, L., and Naroditsky, V., eds., *Modeling Complex Phenomena*. Springer-Verlag.

Kalos – A System for Natural Language Generation with Revision

Ben E. Cline and J. Terry Nutter
Department of Computer Science
Virginia Polytechnic Institute and State University
Blacksburg, VA 24061
benjy@benjy.cc.vt.edu/jtn@vtopus.cs.vt.edu

Abstract

Using revision to produce extended natural language text through a series of drafts provides three significant advantages over a traditional natural language generation system. First, it reduces complexity through task decomposition. Second, it promotes text polishing techniques that benefit from the ability to examine generated text in the context of the underlying knowledge from which it was generated. Third, it provides a mechanism for the interaction of conceptual and stylistic decisions. Kalos is a natural language generation system that produces advanced draft quality text for a microprocessor users' guide from a knowledge base describing the microprocessor. It uses revision iteratively to polish its initial generation. The system performs both conceptual and stylistic revisions. Example output of the system, showing both types of revision, is presented and discussed.

Introduction

Natural language connected text systems produce multiple sentence texts, from one to several paragraphs long, to satisfy a particular discourse goal. The system must select and order concepts from a potentially huge knowledge base and translate them into cohesive surface text. The limited capabilities of state-of-the-art connected text generation systems attests to the difficulty of implementing robust, general systems in this area. Two problems at the root of this difficulty are the lack of robust generation techniques and the complexity of the generation task.

Connected text generation systems currently function in limited domains and for limited discourse goals, do not produce formal, polished text, and do not generalize well either to new domains or to new types of discourse.

A connected text generation system must both select and order concepts from its domain knowledge base to satisfy a given discourse goal (e.g. describing some object), and convert these concepts into a cohesive surface text. This process is complicated by a number of factors. The system must be discriminating in what it

says, neither stating obvious facts nor omitting salient ones. The facts must be ordered logically, and the text must be cohesive. Current generation systems generally achieve these goals by specializing their techniques either to features of the task (limited discourse goals) or to features of the domain.

The lack of robust techniques results to a large extent from the inherent complexity of the task. The complexity has other effects as well. Most current systems attempt to deal with generation by decomposing the task into one or two stages, usually by isolating the process of selecting and ordering concepts to meet the discourse goal from that of converting the concepts into natural language. But this decomposition limits as well as simplifies.

The system reported here uses revision in a knowledge intensive environment to improve on generation techniques and to deal with generation complexity. Our revision techniques address both conceptual and stylistic defects in draft text. The Kalos natural language generation system was developed to demonstrate these revision techniques. It is a complete generation system that generates portions of a draft users' guide for a microprocessor.

Why Revision?

Hays and Flower (1980) developed a model for human text production in which revision reduces strain on human authors by reducing the number of decisions that must be dealt with during any part of the task. Vaughan and McDonald (1986), Yazdani (1987), Cline (1991), and Meeter (1991) have suggested that text revision may likewise aid natural language generation. Vaughan and McDonald (1986) and Meeter (1991) focused on stylistic revisions only; Yazdani (1987) and Cline (1991) suggest that conceptual revisions are also useful.

Revision provides three benefits for natural language generation systems:

- It reduces system complexity through task decomposition and modularity.
- It provides an architecture for text polishing techniques that benefit from the ability to examine gen-

erated text in the context of the underlying structures from which it was generated.

- It allows interaction between conceptual and stylistic decisions.

Natural language generation is a formidable task: reducing complexity is crucial. Using a revision architecture simplifies generation module design by postponing many decisions to the revision module. As Yazdani (1987) points out, this type of architecture is common in the construction of complex software systems such as compilers.

There is another software engineering benefit to incorporating a revision module into a natural language generation system. The revision module is a natural place to isolate domain-specific linguistic knowledge and knowledge that relates to both surface and deep generation modules, thus producing a more robust, maintainable, and adaptable generation system.

The revision model also promotes text polishing techniques that benefit from the ability to examine generated text in the context of the underlying structures from which it was generated. For instance, a revision component is the ideal place to identify and eliminate ambiguities in the generated text. An initial generation module could try to avoid generating ambiguous text, but the complexities involved are overwhelming. Once the text has been generated, reading it to locate ambiguities is a less demanding. Hence it makes sense to locate and eliminate ambiguities in a revision module, which has access to both the surface text and information about its origin.

Some problems related to word sound, such as repetition and rhyming, are best dealt with by a revision module. For example, consider a knowledge base with two concepts *register* and *data register,* that are related as superclass and subclass. A natural language generation system might produce, "The D0 data register is a register" (structurally analogous to "The F-150 pickup is a light-duty truck"). The sentence is awkward because of the repeated "register." Such surface-level problems can be dealt with during initial surface generation, but again, doing so complicates the generator.

A revision architecture also addresses the problem of lack of interaction between conceptual and surface decisions (McKeown & Swartout 1987). Traditional systems make conceptual decisions first, and then generate surface text. This architecture does not allow lexical choices to influence conceptual decisions. A revision architecture lets the system change conceptual decisions to facilitate using particular words or phrases. For example, preferring the term *address space* to address bus size in describing a microprocessor affects the organization of the text. Consider a description of the address bus of the Zilog Z-80 microprocessor that refers to address bus size (an attribute of the address bus):

- The address bus of the Zilog Z-80 microprocessor is

sixteen bits wide. (1)

The same fact can be rephrased to refer to the address space:

- The Zilog Z-80 has a sixty-four kilobyte address space. (2)

Both sentences reflect the same information. But the first sentence relates it as an attribute of the address bus, while the second sentence makes a statement directly about the processor. The second sentence both uses a preferred way of describing the processor's maximum memory size and gives an important feature of the microprocessor. It is thus desirable to include it in an overview paragraph of the microprocessor rather than in a following paragraph describing its buses. The apparent surface preference for one descriptive term over another thus affects the deep structure of the text to be generated.

Types of Revision

Revision, whether by humans or computers, takes two forms (Cline 1991). *Stylistic revision* occurs when the surface text is changed without altering the meaning of the text or the order of concepts. *Conceptual revision* occurs when the meaning of the text or the order of concepts changes. Replacing a noun phrase with a pronoun and compounding sentences are examples of stylistic revisions. Reordering, adding, or deleting text results in a conceptual revision. Examples of conceptual revisions are adding an example to existing text and reordering attributes of an object being described so that quantifiers are given first.

An example of a conceptual revision was given in the previous section (sentences 1 and 2). Consider the following example of stylistic revision. Sentences (3) and (4) are draft text:

- D0 is a register. (3)
- D0 is 32-bits wide. (4)

A simple stylistic revision is to render sentence (3) as the compound noun "the D0 register" and to use it as the subject of sentence (4), producing

- The D0 register is 32-bits wide.

Although revision-based systems have been proposed for some time, only limited systems have been produced so far. The most advanced systems incorporating revision are the weiveR system (Inui, Tokunaga, & Tanaka 1992) and the STREAK system (Robin 1993). The weiveR system is limited to stylistic revision of Japanese text. It focuses on repairing structural ambiguity and sentence complexity problems such as those associated with sentence length and depth of embedding. weiveR currently does not perform deep generation or conceptual revision, although the authors of that system feel that revision should be more broadly applied for most of the reasons discussed above.

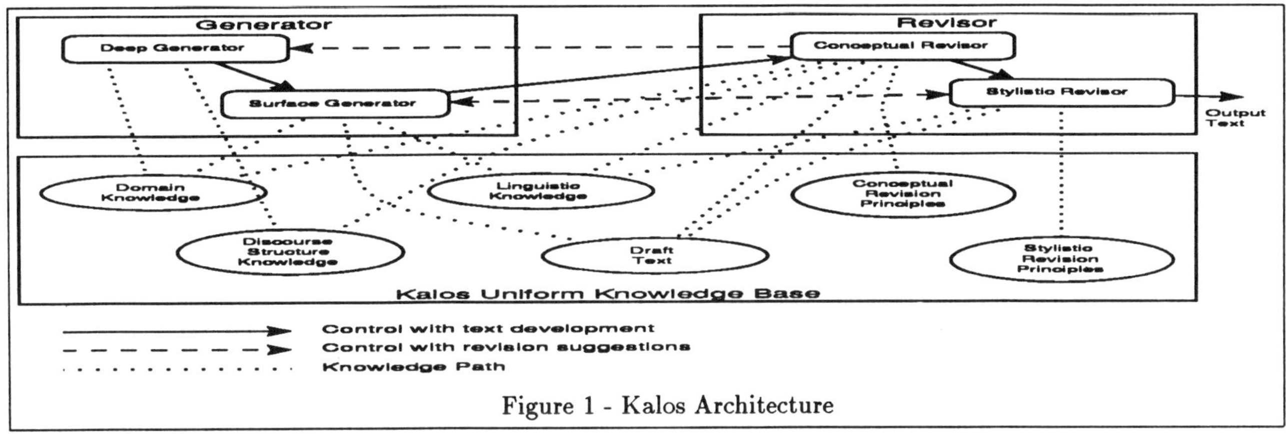

Figure 1 - Kalos Architecture

The STREAK system performs revision to add historical information to draft text. This system produces draft text from wire reports and then adds historical information at the word and phrasal level to help explain the significance of the information in the wire report. It considers both conceptual and stylistic concerns when making revisions. Although the architecture of STREAK is interesting, the system reported in Robin (1993) is incomplete and performs only one type of revision on a single sentence.

Revision Architecture

Kalos consists of a uniform knowledge base and two main modules: a generation module with deep and surface generation submodules, and a revision module consisting of conceptual and stylistic revision submodules (see figure 1). The deep generator selects and orders concepts to meet some discourse goal. The surface generator converts the concepts selected by the deep generator into surface text. The conceptual revisor makes suggestions for improving conceptual defects in the text, while the stylistic generator makes suggestions for improving stylistic defects in the text.

Unlike those of a traditional generation system, Kalos's deep and surface generators are relatively simple. Initially, they produce simple draft text. Many of the decisions made by traditional generators are postponed for consideration by the revision modules. After generating the initial text, Kalos improves it iteratively in two cycles. The first cycle consists of the deep generator, surface generator, and conceptual revisor. In each iteration, the deep and surface generators produce text and the conceptual revisor examines it for defects. If the revisor finds defects, it produces suggestions to improve the text. The deep generator uses the suggestions to regenerate the text. Revisions are cumulative, i.e., no revision suggestion is ever retracted in a later pass. The cycle ends when the conceptual revisor finds no further defects.

Neither the decision not to retract revisions nor the termination condition is fundamental to the model. Both were chosen for simplicity. Other systems, for example, could use a measure of text quality to determine when to stop the revision process.

The stylistic revisor cycle begins after all conceptual revisions are complete. This cycle begins with the stylistic revisor, which reviews the draft text and produces revision suggestions to improve it. These suggestions go to the surface generator, which uses them to regenerate the text. This cycle ends, and the final text is output, when no more revision suggestions can be applied.

We use two principles in deciding how to decompose the generation task. The first is based on locality of decision making. The generators make decisions based on local information while the revisors make decisions based on a wider set of knowledge. The deep generator focuses on selecting single concepts at a time while the conceptual revisor considers the interaction between selected concepts such as whether a concept adds redundant information. The surface generator focuses on generating a single, simple sentence for each concept to be surfaced. The stylistic revisor makes decisions that involve more than one sentence, such as combining two sentences into a compound sentence.

The second decomposition principle is based on the knowledge sources needed for a task. To keep the generators simple, they make their decisions based on traditional knowledge sources. If additional knowledge is needed to make some decisions, these decisions are made in one of the revisors. For example, the deep generator traditionally doesn't consider linguistic knowledge, but some conceptual decisions, such as the removal of sentences that are redundant due to surface-level effects, require linguistic knowledge. These types of decisions are postponed for the conceptual revisor where the addition of linguistic knowledge has less impact on the computational needs of the module.

We believe that the best architecture for a revision system uses a uniform knowledge base containing all the system knowledge similar to the knowledge base described in Cline and Nutter (1992, 1994a). This approach lets revision modules determine the intent of each part of the generated text quickly, and determine what alternative choices are available for regenerating the text. Only with access to the full system knowledge can revision components execute intelligently and efficiently. We encode all the knowledge in a uniform representation to which a single inference technique can be applied. In Kalos, all knowledge is encoded as SNePS-2.1 (Shapiro 1992) semantic networks, and SNePS inferencing is the only inference technique used. Contrast this to a traditional natural language generation where the surface generator knowledge, encoded as an Augmented Transition Network (ATN) or other form of grammar rules, is hidden from the other stages of generation.

The use of a uniform knowledge base places a computational burden on the system due to the size of the knowledge base. To address this, Kalos dynamically partitions the uniform knowledge base to meet the requirements of each generation and revision task, using path-based techniques and pattern matching over inferencing where possible, and using conceptually restricted knowledge bases (Cline 1994b).

Kalos

Kalos was developed as a testbed for revision techniques. The system produces advanced draft text for portions of a microprocessor users' guide from a domain knowledge base describing a particular microprocessor. Because of the limitations in state-of-the-art natural language generation techniques, we have decided to concentrate on the generation of draft quality text.

The Kalos deep generator is a scriptal-based generator (Hovy 1988) that uses discourse schemata to select and order concepts to describe a microprocessor. The schema slot-filling mechanism uses SNePS-2.1 pattern matching and inferencing rules. The surface generator is based on a type of unification grammar (Kay 1984) encoded into SNePS-2.1 semantic networks so that the revisors can inspect the grammar rules.

The Kalos conceptual revisor currently performs four types of conceptual revisions:

- Removal of redundant and superfluous information
- Application of domain-specific preferred words and phrases with conceptual effect
- Proper ordering of attributes
- Handling of inordinately long lists

The conceptual revisor examines the generated text and the underlying structures from which it was generated for defects. Defects occur because the deep generator is relatively simple. Many decisions are postponed for consideration by the conceptual revisor, thus reducing individual module complexity through task decomposition. The revisor can suggest that a schema slot be removed, that an unfilled schema slot be filled, that a different schema slot choice be selected, and that a list of attributes be reordered.

Conceptual revisions rarely conflict, because of the design of the schema templates and slot-filling salience

rules. Hence Kalos uses a simple priority scheme to deal with revision suggestions that affect the same schema slot, in which requests for deletion take precedence over other suggestions. Conceptual revision suggestions are never retracted.

The Kalos stylistic revisor performs the following stylistic revisions:

- Suggest use of anaphora
- Suggest sentence and phrase compounding
- Suggest the use of preferred words and phrases with stylistic effect
- Suggest thematic progression constructs
- Suggest other cohesive constructions

Because the surface generator initially generates each schema slot as a single simple sentence, the stylistic revisor must combine the sentences into a cohesive whole. It examines two consecutive sentences at a time, perhaps making a number of suggestions to improve the sentences. After all the sentences have been analyzed, the suggestions are analyzed for conflicts. Revision suggestions are weighted to indicate their desirability and amount of structural change. In the case of conflicting suggestions, those with greater weights are favored other those with smaller ones. After conflicts have been resolved, the surface generator receives the remaining suggestions and regenerates the text. Later cycles may implement suggestions removed in earlier ones, if they still apply after the more extensive changes have been made.

Most of the stylistic revision types are straightforward; we restrict our discussion to thematic progression (Glatt 1982). Two sentences are in thematic progression order if they both have the same subject or if the rheme (what is said) of the first sentence is the theme (what is talked about) of the second. Sentences in thematic progression order tend to be easier to follow than those that are not.

For example, consider the two sentences:

- The M68000 supports memory-mapped I/O.
- There are 9 M68000 address registers. (5)

The second sentence can be restated using M68000 as the subject:

- The M68000 supports memory-mapped I/O.
- The M68000 has 9 address registers. (6)

Further cycles replace the subject of the second sentence by a pronoun, etc.

Kalos Example

A complete description of all kinds of revision that Kalos performs is beyond the scope of this paper. To illustrate system performance, we discuss the generation and revision of the first introductory paragraph of the Motorola M68000 microprocessor. This example illustrates how revision can be used to generate draft level text from relatively simple generators.

```
((the M68000 is a microprocessor)
 (the M68000 supports memory-mapped I/O)
 (the M68000 address bus is an address bus)
 (the M68000 address bus is 24 bits wide)
 (the M68000 data bus is a  data bus)
 (the M68000 data bus is 16 bits wide)
 (the M68000 address registers are address registers)
 (There are 9 M68000 address registers)
 (the M68000 address registers are 32 bits wide)
 (the M68000 data registers are data registers)
 (There are 8 M68000 data registers)
 (the M68000 data registers are 32 bits wide)
 (the M68000 instructions are instructions)
 (There are 82 M68000 instructions))
```

Figure 2 - Sample Kalos Initial Generation

```
((the M68000 is a 16-bit microprocessor)
 (the M68000 has an address space size of 16 megabytes)
 (the M68000 supports memory-mapped I/O)
 (There are 9 M68000 address registers)
 (the M68000 address registers are 32 bits wide)
 (There are 8 M68000 data registers)
 (the M68000 data registers are 32 bits wide)
 (There are 82 M68000 instructions))
```

Figure 3 - Kalos Output After Conceptual Revision

```
((the 16-bit M68000 microprocessor has an address space
  size of 16 megabytes and supports memory-mapped I/O)
 (it has 9 32-bit address registers and 8 32-bit data
  registers)
 (it executes 82 instructions))
```

Figure 4 - Kalos Output After Stylistic Revision

During initial generation, Kalos selects a schema and generates each slot as a simple sentence (figure 2). After two passes by the conceptual revisor, the text of figure 3 is produced. The first revision describes the M68000 as a "16-bit microprocessor" instead of just a "microprocessor," the natural category to which it belongs (Cline and Nutter 1990). This revision occurs because "8-bit microprocessor," "16-bit microprocessor," "32-bit microprocessor," and "64-bit microprocessor" are domain-specific preferred terms. Using knowledge about the relationship of data bus sizes and these terms, the conceptual revisor infers that the M68000 is a member of subordinate class *16-bit microprocessor* and causes the deep generator to fill the schema slot giving taxonomic information about the M68000 with this deduced concept instead of the frame indicating that the M68000 is a member of the *microprocessor* class.

The second conceptual revision results from the domain-specific preferred term "address space size." The conceptual revisor deduces the address space size from the address bus size and adds this concept as an attribute of the microprocessor. To make this revision, the conceptual revisor inspects the linguistic knowledge base to determine what type of knowledge base frame will trigger this term. It then tries to deduce this type of frame for any object of the type associated with the term. If it can infer such a concept, it instructs the deep generator to include it in the instantiated schema it produces.

Both preferred phrase revisions result in redundant information. When the M68000 is described as a "16-bit microprocessor," the size of the data bus becomes redundant. Similarly, the size of the address bus becomes redundant after the address space size is given. The second pass through the conceptual revisor detects the redundancy and removes the descriptions of the data and address buses. (The buses are still described in detail in a following paragraph which is not shown in the example.)

The conceptual revisor also removes inherently redundant sentences like "the M68000 data registers are data registers." The lexicon entry for the subclass *M68000 data register* contains the fact that its members by definition belong to the class *data-register,* indicating that in this case, stating this class membership is redundant. The conceptual revisor examines the lexicon and domain knowledge base to determine that sentences of this kind should be deleted.

After the first pass through the conceptual revisor, two attributes of the M68000 are listed in the following order:

- The M68000 supports memory-mapped I/O.
- The M68000 has an address space size of 16 megabytes.

During the second pass of the conceptual revisor, these two attributes are reversed to list the quantitative attribute before the qualitative one.

Figure 4 shows the text after stylistic revision. The first stylistic revision pass combines the first two sentences by converting the first into a noun phrase and using it as the subject of the second sentence, producing:

- The M68000 16-bit microprocessor has an address space size of 16 megabytes.

The next revision pass splits the term "16-bit microprocessor" to let the quantitative descriptor be listed before "M68000," and the sentence is compounded with the next sentence.

The sentences giving the number of address and data registers are modified to have the same subject as the previous sentence, maintaining thematic progression order. An example of this revision is shown by sentences (5) and (6) in the last section. On the next revision pass, the sentences listing the number of registers are combined with sentences listing register sizes.

On the final stylistic revision pass, Kalos uses pronouns as appropriate.

Kalos currently generates the two opening paragraphs for a description of the Motorola M68000 microprocessor and several smaller texts. The two paragraphs describing the M68000 contain 49 sentences after initial generation. After conceptual revision, the text contains 29 sentences. The final text contains 14 sentences (many of which are compound sentences). To extend the text generated by Kalos, additional knowledge about the M68000 could be added to the system.

Conclusion

Kalos illustrates the potential of revision-based natural language generation in a knowledge intensive environment. Revision reduces module complexity by increasing task decomposition and modularity. It also provides a welcoming architecture for implementing a number of useful techniques that benefit from examining generated text in the context of the underlying structures from which it was generated. Finally, revision enhances the interaction of conceptual and stylistic decisions.

A number of questions remain to be examined. One relates to the way Kalos performs revisions: revisions are never retracted and conceptual revision precedes stylistic revision. Relaxing these two constraints would allow greater flexibility, but would increase the complexity of the system. Termination criteria, conceptual and stylistic revision interaction, and revision ranking techniques would need to be studied.

Another major enhancement to Kalos would be the addition of ambiguity checking. The stylistic revisor is an ideal place to check for ambiguity because it has access to both the surface text and the underlying knowledge from which the sentence was generated. With an appropriate natural language understanding module, the surface text could be read for ambiguities. From the underlying structures of the surface text, Kalos could determine the intent of the text and look for other ways to generate it. If no unambiguous text could be found, Kalos could indicate that fact so that a human author could polish the text.

References

Cline, B. E. & Nutter, J. T. 1990. Implications of Natural Categories for Natural Language Generation. In *Current Trends in SNePS – Semantic Network Processing System*, D. Kumar, ed., Springer-Verlag, Berlin, 153-162.

Cline, B. E. 1991. Conceptual Revision for Natural Language Generation. In *Proceedings of the 29th Annual Meeting of the Association for Computational Linguistics*, 347-348. Berkeley, CA: Association for Computational Linguistics.

Cline, B. E. & Nutter, J. T. 1992. Knowledge-Based Natural Language Generation with Revision. In *Proceedings of the 5th Florida Artificial Intelligence Research Symposium*, 223-227. Ft. Lauderdale, Florida: Florida Artificial Intelligence Research Symposium.

Cline, B.E. & Nutter, J.T. 1994a. Generating and Revising Text: A Fully Knowledge-Based Approach. *International Journal of Expert Systems, Research and Applications*, 7(2).

Cline, B. 1994b. *Knowledge Intensive Natural Language Generation with Revision*. Ph. D. Dissertation. Department of Computer Science, Virginia Polytechnic Institute and State University, Blacksburg, VA.

Glatt, B. S. 1982. Defining Thematic Progressions and Their Relationship to Reader Comprehension. In *What Writers Know: The Language, Process, and Structure of Written Discourse*. Nystrand, M, ed., New York: Academic Press.

Hayes, J. R. & Flower, L. S. 1980. Identifying the Organization of Writing Processes. In *Cognitive Processes in Writing*, L. W. Gregg and E. R. Steinberg, eds., Lawrence Erlbaum, Hillsdale, NJ, 3-30.

Hovy, Eduard H. 1988. *Generating Natural Language Under Pragmatic Constraints*. Hillsdale, N. J.: Lawrence Erlbaum Associates.

Inui, K., Tokunaga, T., and Tanaka, H. 1992. Text Revision: a Model and Its Implementation. In *Aspects of Automated Natural Language Generation*, R. Dale, E. Hovy, D. Rosner, and O. Stock, eds., Springer-Verlag, Berlin, 45-56.

Kay, M. 1984. Functional Unification Grammar: a Formalism for Machine Translation. *Proceedings of the Tenth International Conference on Computational Linguistics*. Stanford, California.

McKeown, K. R. & Swartout, W. R. 1987. Language Generation and Explanation. *Annual Review of Computer Science*. Volume 2.

Meteer, M. 1991. The Implications of Revision for Natural Language Generation. In *Natural Language Generation in Artificial Intelligence and Computational Linguistics*, C. Paris, W. Swartout, and W. Mann, eds., Kluwer Academic Publishers, Boston.

Robin, J. 1993. A Revision-Based Generation Architecture for Reporting Facts in Their Historical Context. In *New Concepts in Natural Language Generation: Planning, Realization and Systems*, H. Horacek and M. Zock, eds., Printer Publishers, London, 238-268.

Shapiro, S. & The SNePS Implementation Group 1992. *SNePS-2.1 User's Manual*. Department of Computer Science, State University of New York at Buffalo, Buffalo, NY.

Vaughan, M. M. & McDonald, D. D. 1986. A Model of Revision in Natural Language Generation. In *Proceedings of the 24th Annual Meeting of the Association for Computational Linguistics*, 90-96. New York, NY; Association for Computational Linguistics.

Yazdani, M. 1987. Reviewing as a Component of the Text Generation Process. In *Natural Language Generation*, G. Kempen, ed., Martinus Nijhoff Publishers, Dordrecht, 183-190.

Building a Large-Scale Knowledge Base for Machine Translation

Kevin Knight and Steve K. Luk
USC/Information Sciences Institute
4676 Admiralty Way
Marina del Rey, CA 90292
{knight,luk}@isi.edu

Abstract

Knowledge-based machine translation (KBMT) systems have achieved excellent results in constrained domains, but have not yet scaled up to newspaper text. The reason is that knowledge resources (lexicons, grammar rules, world models) must be painstakingly handcrafted from scratch. One of the hypotheses being tested in the PANGLOSS machine translation project is whether or not these resources can be semi-automatically acquired on a very large scale.

This paper focuses on the construction of a large ontology (or knowledge base, or world model) for supporting KBMT. It contains representations for some 70,000 commonly encountered objects, processes, qualities, and relations. The ontology was constructed by merging various online dictionaries, semantic networks, and bilingual resources, through semi-automatic methods. Some of these methods (e.g., conceptual matching of semantic taxonomies) are broadly applicable to problems of importing/exporting knowledge from one KB to another. Other methods (e.g., bilingual matching) allow a knowledge engineer to build up an index to a KB in a second language, such as Spanish or Japanese.

Introduction

The PANGLOSS project is a three-site collaborative effort to build a large-scale knowledge-based machine translation system. Key components of PANGLOSS include New Mexico State University's Panglyzer parser (Farwell & Wilks 1991), Carnegie Mellon's translator's workstation (Frederking *et al.* 1993), and USC/ISI's PENMAN English generation system (Penman 1989). All of these systems combine to form a prototype Spanish-English translation system.

Another key component is the PANGLOSS ontology, a large-scale conceptual network for supporting semantic processing in other PANGLOSS modules. This network contains tens of thousands of nodes representing commonly encountered objects, entities, qualities, and relations. The upper (more abstract) region of the ontology is called the Ontology Base (OB) and consists of approximately 400 items that represent generalizations essential for the various PANGLOSS modules' linguistic processing during translation. The middle region of the ontology, approximately 50,000 items, provides a framework for a generic world model, containing items representing many English word senses. The lower (more specific) regions of the ontology provide anchor points for different application domains.

The purpose of the ontology is two-fold. First, it provides a common inventory of semantic tokens, used in both analysis and generation. These tokens form the bulk of the "lexicon" of the interlingua language. Second, the ontology describes which tokens are naturally related to which others, and in what ways, in our particular world. These relations form the "grammar" of the interlingua, where "grammaticality" of an interlingua sentence is identified with semantic plausibility.

Because large-scale knowledge bases are difficult to build by hand, we have chosen to pursue primarily semi-automatic methods for manipulating and merging existing resources. The next section sketches out the information in five such resources, and subsequent sections describe algorithms for extracting and merging this information.

Linguistic Resources

We selected the following resources with the idea that each contains a piece of the puzzle we are trying to build: (1) the PENMAN Upper Model from USC/ISI, (2) the ONTOS model from Carnegie Mellon University, (3) the Longman's Dictionary of Contemporary English (LDOCE), (4) WordNet, and (5) the Harper-Collins Spanish-English bilingual dictionary.

PENMAN Upper Model

The Upper Model (Bateman 1990) is a top-level network of about 200 nodes, implemented in the LOOM knowledge representation language (MacGregor 1988), and used by the PENMAN English generation system (Penman 1989) to drive its linguistic choices. PENMAN makes extensive use of syntactic-semantic correspondences; if a concept is taxonomized under a particular node of the Upper Model, then an English word referring to that concept will have a particular set of default grammatical behaviors. Exceptions are coded in the lexicon.

ONTOS

Of comparable size to the PENMAN Upper Model, ONTOS (Carlson & Nirenburg 1990) is a top-level ontology designed to support machine translation. The event structure is based on cross-linguistic studies of verbs, and case roles and filler restrictions are represented independently of any particular language. ONTOS also includes object hierarchies, scalar attributes, and complex events.

Longman's Dictionary (LDOCE)

LDOCE is a learner's dictionary of English with 27,758 words and 74,113 word senses. Each word sense comes with:

- A short definition. One of the unique features of LDOCE is that its definitions only use words from a "control vocabulary" list of 2000 words. This makes it attractive from the point of view of extracting semantic information by parsing dictionary entries.

- Examples of usage.

- One or more of 81 syntactic codes (e.g., [B3]: adj followed by *to*).

- For nouns, one of 33 semantic codes (e.g., [H]: human).

- For nouns, one of 124 pragmatic codes (e.g., [ECZB]: economics/business).

Another important feature of LDOCE is that its sense identifiers are used in the semantic fields of a medium-scale Spanish lexicon built by hand at New Mexico State University as part of PANGLOSS.

WordNet

WordNet (Miller 1990) is a semantic word database based on psycholinguistic principles. It is a large-scale resource like LDOCE, but its information is organized in a completely different manner. WordNet groups synonymous word senses into single units ("synsets"). Noun senses are organized into a deep hierarchy, and the database also contains part-of links, antonym links, and others. Approximately half of WordNet synsets have brief informal definitions.

Collins Bilingual Dictionary

The Harper-Collins Bilingual Spanish-English dictionary (Collins 1971) contains tens of thousands of Spanish headwords and English translations. Like words in LDOCE definitions, word translations are not marked by sense, but they are sometimes annotated with subject field codes, such as Military [MIL] or Commercial [COM].

Merging Resources

Our initial goal was to combine all of these resources into a conceptual network of about 50,000 nodes, indexed by structured lexicons for both English and Spanish. This network drives the PENMAN generator and, to the extent that it can, helps in semantic disambiguation tasks during parsing.[1]

Figure 1 shows the plan of attack. The PENMAN Upper Model and ONTOS were merged by hand to create the Ontology Base (OB). This structure continues to undergo revision as we add case roles and other support for the interlingua. WordNet was then subordinated/merged into the OB. The result is a large knowledge base in which most concepts are named by WordNet names, but in which some have three names, one each from Ontos, the Upper Model, and WordNet. Proper taxonomization under the Ontology Base ensures the proper working of PENMAN, since the PENMAN Upper Model is embedded there intact. The subordination of WordNet involved breaking the network into some 200 pieces and merging each manually into the OB.

The next step was to merge word senses from LDOCE with those of WordNet. There were several motivations for doing this: (1) LDOCE has a great deal of lexical information missing from WordNet, including syntactic and subject field codes, and controlled-vocabulary definitions; and (2) LDOCE sense identifiers are legal tokens in the PANGLOSS interlingua, as much of the ULTRA Spanish lexicon is written in terms of these identifiers. Merging LDOCE and WordNet senses is a very large task, for which we developed semi-automatic algorithms.

The final step was to build up a large Spanish lexicon for the ontology. Again, doing this manually was too expensive, so we built algorithms for extracting a lexicon from the Collins bilingual dictionary semi-automatically.

Each resource makes its own contributions to the final product. LDOCE offers syntax and subject area, WordNet offers synonyms and hierarchical structuring, the upper structures organize the knowledge for natural language processing in general and English generation in particular, and finally, the bilingual dictionary lets us index the ontology from a second language. The bulk of the rest of this paper is devoted to the three automatic merging algorithms developed in support of the work in Figure 1. The first two algorithms support the LDOCE-WordNet merge, while the third supports the Collins-Ontology merge.

Definition Match Algorithm

The Definition Match algorithm is based on the idea that two word senses should be matched if their two

---

[1]Disambiguation algorithms are described in a separate paper (Luk 1994).

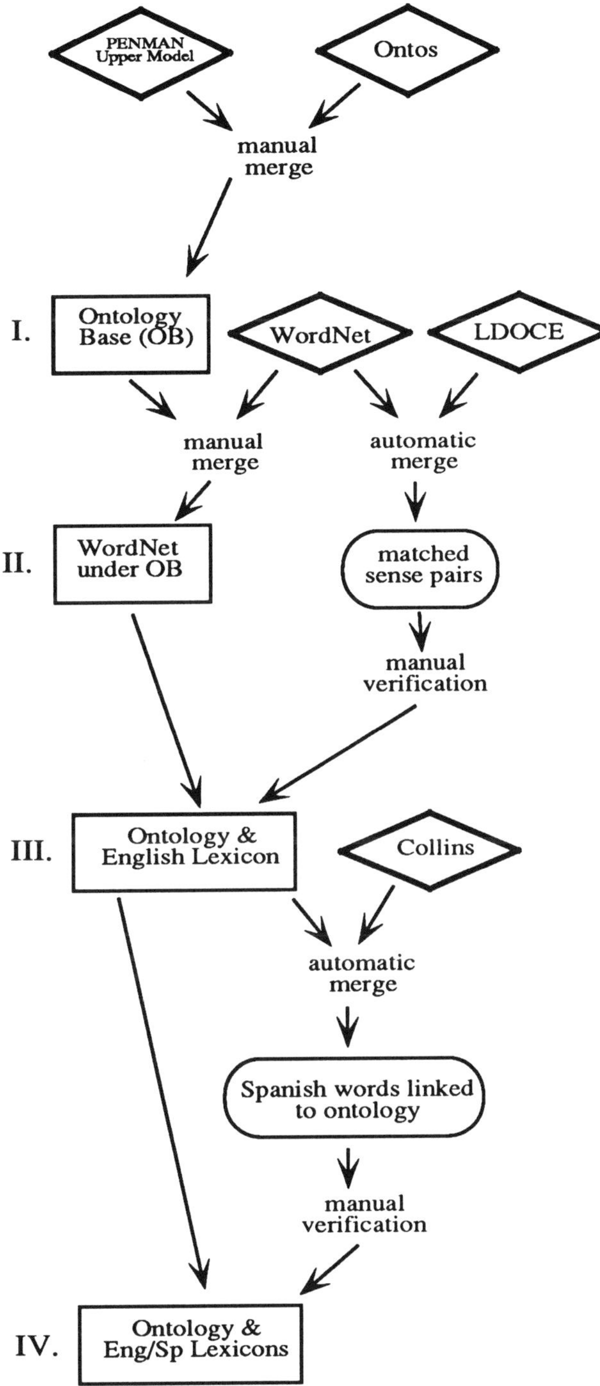

Figure 1: Merging Information in Five Linguistic Resources to Build a Large Scale Ontology for Machine Translation

definitions share words. For example, there are two noun definitions of "batter" in LDOCE:

- (batter_2_0) "mixture of flour, eggs, and milk, beaten together and used in cooking"

- (batter_3_0) "a person who bats, esp in baseball — compare BATSMAN"

and two definitions in WordNet:

- (BATTER-1) "ballplayer who bats"

- (BATTER-2) "a flour mixture thin enough to pour or drop from a spoon"

The Definition Match algorithm will match (batter_2_0) with (BATTER-2) because their definitions share words like "flour" and "mixture." Similarly (batter_3_0) and (BATTER-1) both contain the word "bats," so they are also matched together.

Not all senses in WordNet have definitions, but most have synonyms and superordinates. For this reason, the algorithm looks not only at WordNet definitions, but also at locally related words and senses. For example, if synonyms of WordNet sense x appear in the definition of LDOCE sense y, then this is evidence that x and y should be matched.

The complete Definition Match algorithm is given in (Knight 1993). Here we give a brief sketch. Given a word w, we identify and stem all open-class content words from definitions and example sentences of w in both dictionaries. We add to this set all synonyms, superordinates, siblings, and super-superordinates from all senses of w in WordNet. The set is then reduced to contain only words that cropped up in both resources, minus w itself. The next step is to create a two-dimensional matrix for each resource. For LDOCE, $L[i, x]$ is set to 1.0 just in case word x appears in the definition of sense i (otherwise, it is set to 0.01). For WordNet, $W[x, j]$ is set to 1.0 if x is a synonym or superordinate of sense j, 0.8 if x is in the definition of sense j, 0.6 if x is a sibling or grandparent of sense j, and 0.01 otherwise. Multiplying matrices L and W yields a similarity matrix SIM. We repeatedly choose the largest value v in the SIM matrix, using the indices i and j of that value to propose a match between LDOCE sense i and WordNet sense j of word w (at confidence level v).

Empirical results are as follows. We ran the algorithm over all nouns in both LDOCE and WordNet. We judged the correctness of its proposed matches, keeping records of the confidence levels and the degree of ambiguity present. For low-ambiguity words (with exactly two senses in LDOCE and two in WordNet), the results are:

confidence level	pct. correct	pct. coverage
≥ 0.0	75%	100%
≥ 0.4	85%	53%
≥ 0.8	90%	27%

At confidence levels ≥ 0.0, 75% of the proposed matches are correct. If we restrict ourselves to only matches proposed at confidence ≥ 0.8, accuracy increases to 90%, but we only get 27% of the possible matches.

For high-ambiguity words (more than five senses in LDOCE and WordNet), the results are:

confidence level	pct. correct	pct. coverage
≥ 0.0	47%	100%
≥ 0.1	76%	44%
≥ 0.2	81%	20%

Accuracy here is worse, but increases sharply when we only consider high confidence matches.

The algorithm's performance is reasonable, given that 45% of WordNet senses have no definitions and that many existing definitions are brief and contain misspellings. Still, there are several improvements to be made—e.g., modify the "greedy" strategy in which matches are extracted from SIM matrix, weigh rare words in definitions more highly than common ones, and/or score senses with long definitions lower than ones with short definitions. These improvements yield only slightly better results, however, because most failures are simply due to the fact that matching sense definitions often have no words in common.

Hierarchy Match Algorithm

The Hierarchy Match algorithm dispenses with sense definitions altogether. Instead, it uses the various sense hierarchies inside LDOCE and WordNet.

WordNet noun senses are arranged in a deep is-a hierarchy. For example, SEAL-7 is a PINNIPED-1, which is on AQUATIC-MAMMAL-1, which is a EUTHERIAN-1, which is a MAMMAL-1, which is ultimately an ANIMAL-1, and so forth.

LDOCE has two fairly flat hierarchies. The *semantic code* hierarchy is induced by a set of 33 semantic codes drawn up by Longman lexicographers. Each sense is marked with one of these codes, e.g., "H" for human "P" for plant, "J" for movable object. The other hierarchy is the *genus sense* hierarchy. (Bruce & Guthrie 1992) have built an automatic algorithm for locating and disambiguating genus terms (head nouns) in sense definitions. For example, (bat_1_1) is defined as "any of the several types of specially shaped wooden stick used for ..." The genus term for (bat_1_1) is (stick_1_1). The genus sense and the semantic code hierarchies were extracted automatically from LDOCE. The semantic code hierarchy is fairly robust, but since the genus sense hierarchy was generated heuristically, it is only 80% correct.

The idea of the Hierarchy Match algorithm is that once two senses are matched, it is a good idea to look at their respective ancestors and descendants for further matches. For example, once (animal_1_2) and ANIMAL-1 are matched, we can look into their respective animal-subhierarchies. We find that the word "seal" is locally unambiguous—only one sense of "seal" refers to an animal (in both LDOCE and Word-Net). So we feel confident to match those seal-animal senses. As another example, suppose we know that (swan_dive_0_0) is the same concept as (SWAN-DIVE-1). We can then match their superordinates (dive_2_1) and (DIVE-3) with high confidence; we need not consider other senses of "dive."

Here is the algorithm:

1. Initialize the set of matches:

(a) Retrieve all words that are unambiguous in both LDOCE and WordNet. Match their corresponding senses, and place all the matches on a list called M1.

(b) Retrieve a prepared list of hand-crafted matches. Place these matches on a list called M2. We created 15 of these, mostly high-level matches like (person_0_1, PERSON-2) and (plant_2_1, PLANT-3). This step is not strictly necessary, but provides guidance to the algorithm.

2. Repeat until M1 and M2 are empty:

(a) For each match on M2, look for words that are unambiguous within the hierarchies rooted at the two matched senses. Match the senses of locally unambiguous words and place the matches on M1.

(b) Move all matches from M2 to a list called M3.

(c) For each match on M1, look upward in the two hierarchies from the matched senses. Whenever a word appears in both hierarchies, match the corresponding senses, and place the match on M2.

(d) Move all matches from M1 to M2.

The algorithm operate in phases, shifting matches from M1 to M2 to M3, placing newly-generated matches on M1 and M2. Once M1 and M2 are exhausted, M3 contains the final list of matches proposed by the algorithm. Again, we can measure the success of the algorithm along two dimensions, coverage and correctness:

phase	pct. correct	matches proposed
Step 1	99%	7563
Step 2(a)	94%	876
Step 2(c)	85%	530
Step 2(a)	93%	2018
Step 2(c)	83%	40
Step 2(a)	92%	99
Step 2(c)	100%	2

In the end, the algorithm produced 11,128 noun sense matches at 96% accuracy. We expected 100% accuracy, but the algorithm was foiled at several places by errors in one or another of the hierarchies. For example, (savings_bank_0_0) is mistakenly a subclass of river bank (bank_1_1) in the LDOCE genus hierarchy, rather than (bank_1_4), the financial institution. "Savings bank" senses are matched in step 1(a), so step 2(c) erroneously goes on to match the river bank of LDOCE with the financial institution of WordNet.

Fortunately, the Definition and Hierarchy Match algorithms complement one another, and there are several ways to combine them. Our practical experience has been to run the Hierarchy Match algorithm to completion, remove the matched senses from the databases, then run the Definition Match algorithm.

Bilingual Match Algorithm

The goal of this algorithm is annotate our ontology with a large Spanish lexicon. This lexicon will of course be fairly rough, with some senses not matching up exactly, and with no lexical decomposition. But getting a large-scale lexicon up and running shows us where the real MT problems are; we don't have to imagine them.

The raw materials we have to work with are: (1) mappings between Spanish and English words, from Collins bilingual dictionary, (2) mappings between English words and ontological entities, primarily from WordNet, and (3) conceptual relations between ontological entities. What we do not yet have are direct links between Spanish words and ontological entities. Consider that the Spanish word *manzana* can be translated as *block* in English; however, *manzana* only maps to one of the concepts referred to by *block*, namely CITY-BLOCK. It does not map to BUILDING-BLOCK. So our task is one of disambiguating each English word in the list of possible translations.

Fortunately, the bilingual dictionary provides a bit more structure to exploit. The entry for *banco* looks roughly like:

```
banco. nm.  bench, seat;
            bank, shoal;
            school, shoal;
            layer, stratum;
            bank [COM];
                ...
```

We can use the division into senses (by semicolons), the synonyms given for each sense, and the subject field codes annotating some senses.

We take advantage of synonyms by using WordNet's synsets and hierarchies. The words *school* and *shoal* each have many meanings in WordNet, but only one pair of meanings coincide at the same WordNet synset. So we are able to perform disambiguation and map *banco* onto SCHOOL-OF-FISH rather than SCHOOL-FOR-KIDS. The words *bench* and *seat* are not synonyms in WordNet, but there is a pair of senses that are very close to each other; they share a common immediate parent in the hierarchy. The Bilingual Match algorithm postulates mappings between *banco* and BENCH-FOR-SITTING and SEAT-FOR-SITTING, but

at a slightly lower level of confidence than the one for SCHOOL-OF-FISH. We penalize the proposed match a constant factor for each link traversed in WordNet to reach a common parent node.[2]

Sometimes only one English word is given as a translation. If the word is unambiguous, we postulate the match at high confidence. Otherwise, we try to make use of Collins subject field codes, as in *banco = bank* [COM]. Fortunately, because we have merged LDOCE and WordNet, our ontology concepts are annotated with LDOCE subject field codes that are similar to the ones found in Collins. Rather than compile a correspondence table of Collins-LDOCE field codes by hand, we generated such a table automatically. For each word mapping from Spanish to English, we considered every meaning of the English word, entering all field code matches into the table. Due to ambiguity, some spurious matches were entered, such as [ZOOL] for *palo*, which in English means *bat* as in baseball. (ZOOLogy was picked up from the flying-mammal sense of *bat*). However, spurious matches were largely eliminated when we removed field code matches that occurred less than six times. Once we built the table, we put it to use in disambiguating English word translations in Collins. If a word is marked with a Collins field code, we simply look for ontology items marked with corresponding LDOCE field codes. Accuracy figures for the Bilingual Match algorithm are now being computed, as human verifiers proceed through the 50,000 proposed mappings from Spanish words to the ontology.

Discussion

For each of the merge algorithms described above, we have built a simple interface that allows a person to verify and/or correct the results generated. The verification interface places the proposed match at the top of a list of alternatives. If the proposed match is correct, the verifier need look no further; the set up is much like a spelling correction interface that sorts alternatives by likelihood rather than, say, alphabetic order. The principle here is that humans are much faster at verifying information than generating it from scratch.

Semi-automatic merging brings together complementary sources of information. It also allows us to detect errors and omissions where the resources are redundant. For example, after the WordNet-LDOCE merge was verified, we were able to automatically locate hundreds of inconsistencies between the WordNet and LDOCE (genus-sense) hierarchies. Many inconsistencies pointed to errors in the genus-word identification or genus-sense disambiguation, while others pointed to different taxonomic organizations that can be merged into one lattice structure. Another benefit of merging resources is that it makes subsequent knowl-

---

[2]A more elaborate scheme would weight links, as in (Resnik 1993).

edge acquisition easier. For example, in designing the Bilingual Match algorithm, we were free to make use of information in both WordNet and LDOCE.

Related Work and Future Work

Automatic dictionary merging is an old line of research; recent work includes (Klavans & Tzoukermann 1990; Klavans 1990; Rohini & Burhans 1994). Many times, the dictionaries merged were roughly similar, while in our work, we have chosen three very different resources. Another motivation for merging dictionaries is to get several definitions for the same sense, to maximize the information that can be extracted by analyzing those definitions. We have not yet extracted information from LDOCE definitions, though this is a clear source of knowledge for enriching the ontology, and there is a great deal of fine work to build on (Klavans *et al.* 1991; Wilks *et al.* 1990; Klavans, Chodorow, & Wacholder 1992). Our other source of knowledge is free text, and we are currently exploring techniques for automatically extracting semantic constraints (Luk 1994). (Okumura & Hovy 1994) use ideas related to the bilingual match algorithm to semi-automatically construct a Japanese lexicon for the PANGLOSS ontology.

Acknowledgments

We would like to thank Eduard Hovy for his support and for comments on a draft of this paper. Yolanda Gil also provided useful comments. Thanks to Richard Whitney for significant assistance in programming and verification. The Ontology Base was built by Eduard Hovy, Licheng Zeng, Akitoshi Okumura, Richard Whitney, and Kevin Knight. Gratitude goes to Longman Group, Ltd., for making the machine readable version of LDOCE available to us, and to HarperCollins Publishers for letting us experiment with their bilingual dictionary. Louise Guthrie assisted in LDOCE/Collins extraction and kindly provided us with the LDOCE genus sense hierarchy. This work was carried out under ARPA Order No. 8073, contract MDA904-91-C-5224.

References

Bateman, J. 1990. Upper modeling: Organizing knowledge for natural language processing. In *Proc. Fifth International Workshop on Natural Language Generation, Pittsburgh, PA.*

Bruce, R., and Guthrie, L. 1992. Genus disambiguation: A study in weighted preference. In *Proceedings of the 15th International Conference on Computational Linguistics (COLING-92).*

Carlson, L., and Nirenburg, S. 1990. World modeling for NLP. Technical Report CMU-CMT-90-121, Center for Machine Translation, Carnegie Mellon University.

Collins. 1971. *Collins Spanish-English/English-Spanish Dictionary.* William Collins Sons & Co. Ltd.

Farwell, D., and Wilks, Y. 1991. Ultra: A multilingual machine translator. In *Proceedings of the 3rd MT Summit.*

Frederking, R.; Grannes, D.; Cousseau, P.; and Nirenburg, S. 1993. An MAT tool and its effectiveness. In *Proceedings of the ARPA Human Language Technology Workshop.*

Klavans, J. L., and Tzoukermann, E. 1990. Linking bilingual corpora and machine readable dictionaries with the BICORD system. In *Electronic Text Research.* Waterloo, Canada: University of Waterloo, Centre for the New OED and Text Research.

Klavans, J.; Byrd, R.; Wacholder, N.; and Chodorow, M. 1991. Taxonomy and polysemy. Research Report RC 16443, IBM Research Division, T. J. Watson Research Center, Yorktown Heights, NY 10598.

Klavans, J.; Chodorow, M.; and Wacholder, N. 1992. Building a knowledge base from parsed definitions. In Jansen, K.; Heidorn, G.; and Richardson, S., eds., *Natural Language Processing: The PLNLP Approach.* Kluwer Academic Publishers. chapter 11.

Klavans, J. 1990. The BICORD system: Combining lexical information from bilingual corpora and machine readable dictionaries. Research Report RC 15738, IBM Research Division, T. J. Watson Research Center, Yorktown Heights, NY 10598.

Knight, K. 1993. Building a large ontology for machine translation. In *Proceedings of the ARPA Human Language Technology Workshop.*

Luk, S. 1994. Disambiguating adjective-noun phrases using a world model. Technical report, USC/Information Sciences Institute. (in preparation).

MacGregor, R. 1988. A deductive pattern matcher. In *Proceedings of the Seventh National Conference on Artificial Intelligence.*

Miller, G. 1990. Wordnet: An on-line lexical database. *International Journal of Lexicography* 3(4). (Special Issue).

Okumura, A., and Hovy, E. 1994. Ontology concept association using a bilingual dictionary. In *Proceedings of the ARPA Human Language Technology Workshop.*

Penman. 1989. The Penman documentation. Technical report, USC/Information Sciences Institute.

Resnik, P. 1993. *Selection and Information: A Class-Based Approach to Lexical Relationships.* Ph.D. Dissertation, University of Pennsylvania.

Rohini, R. K., and Burhans, D. T. 1994. Visual semantics: Extracting visual information from text accompanying pictures. In *AAAI-94.*

Wilks, Y.; Fass, D.; Guo, C.; McDonald, J.; Plate, T.; and Slator, B. 1990. Providing machine tractable dictionary tools. *Machine Translation* 5.

Automated Postediting of Documents

Kevin Knight and Ishwar Chander
USC/Information Sciences Institute
4676 Admiralty Way
Marina del Rey, CA 90292
{knight,chander}@isi.edu

Abstract

Large amounts of low- to medium-quality English texts are now being produced by machine translation (MT) systems, optical character readers (OCR), and non-native speakers of English. Most of this text must be postedited by hand before it sees the light of day. Improving text quality is tedious work, but its automation has not received much research attention.

Anyone who has postedited a technical report or thesis written by a non-native speaker of English knows the potential of an automated postediting system. For the case of MT-generated text, we argue for the construction of postediting modules that are portable across MT systems, as an alternative to hardcoding improvements inside any one system. As an example, we have built a complete self-contained postediting module for the task of article selection (*a*, *an*, *the*) for English noun phrases. This is a notoriously difficult problem for Japanese-English MT. Our system contains over 200,000 rules derived automatically from online text resources. We report on learning algorithms, accuracy, and comparisons with human performance.

Automated Postediting

Fully automatic, high-quality translation is still an elusive goal for broad-coverage natural language processors. Current machine translation (MT) systems usually employ a human posteditor to transform the MT output into usable, quality text. If the posteditor can do this transformation in less time than it takes to translate from scratch, then the MT system is economically viable. Many commercial systems exist on this principle.

Improving a particular MT system often means automating something that the posteditor is doing. The system gets further, leaving the posteditor with less to do. And usually, the improvements are coded into the internals of the MT system, becoming part of a black box.

Another way to think about automating postediting tasks is to build automated postediting modules that are detachable and independent of any particular MT system. Figure 1 shows this distinction. The advantage of detachable posteditors is that they are portable across MT systems. They accomplish their tasks without reference to the internal algorithms and representations of particular systems. With portability comes leverage: one piece of coded linguistic analysis can be used to improve the quality of many automatic translators. Furthermore, postediting modules can clean up text generated by humans (whose internal algorithms are unknown). Texts that are imperfectly scanned by optical character readers (OCR) are also grist for automated postediting.

We envision two types of postediting modules. One type is *adaptive*, the other *general*. The rest of this section briefly discusses what the former type would look like; the remainder of the paper describes a posteditor of the latter type that has been designed, built, and tested.

The idea of an adaptive posteditor is that an automatic program can watch a human postedit documents, see which errors crop up over and over (these will be different for any given system/domain pair), and begin to emulate what the human is doing. As yet, no adaptive posteditors, portable across systems and domains, have been built for MT. One place to start would be a large corpus of "pre-postedited" text aligned with corresponding postedited text. Statistical machine translation techniques could then be applied to learn the mapping. One would hope that such techniques would have an easier time learning to translate bad English to good English than, say, Japanese to good English.

Article Selection

A general posteditor must be useful for improving text produced by a wide variety of MT systems and non-native speakers and should operate equally across all domains. While working on Japanese-English translation within the PANGLOSS project (Nirenburg & Frederking 1994; Knight & Luk 1994), we have constructed an automatic posteditor for inserting articles (*a*, *an*, and *the*) into English text. Several factors mo-

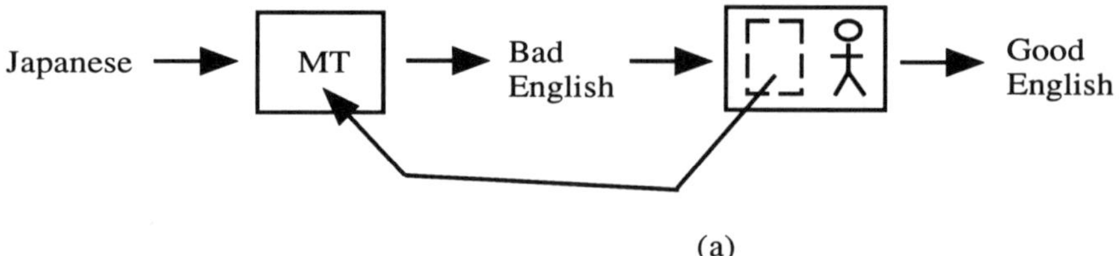

(a)

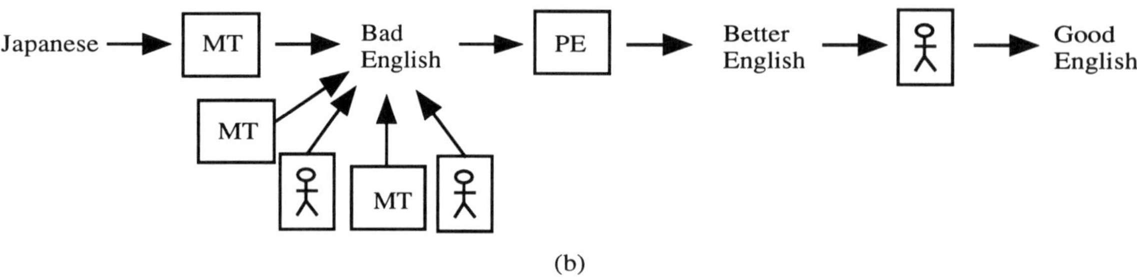

(b)

Figure 1: Two views of automating tasks of postediting. In (a), posteditor work is automated and moved into a particular MT system. In (b), a detached postediting module is created. It serves to improve the quality of text produced by several MT systems and non-native speakers.

tivated this choice:

- The Japanese language has no articles, but article-free English is difficult to read. ·

- Inserting articles is tedious work for a human English-speaking posteditor.

- Non-native English speakers find accurate article selection very difficult, even after years of practice.

- Doing the task well is beyond the capabilities of current automatic grammar checkers.

Here is an example of the task. The following text comes in without articles:

```
    Stelco Inc. said it plans to shut down three
Toronto-area plants, moving their fastener
operations to leased facility in Brantford,
Ontario.
    Company said fastener business "has been
under severe cost pressures for some time."
Fasteners, nuts and bolts are sold to North
American auto market.
    Company spokesman declined to estimate impact
of closures on earnings. He said new facility
will employ 500 of existing 600 employees.
Steelmaker employs about 16,000 people.
```

The posteditor transforms this text as follows:

```
    Stelco Inc. said it plans to shut down three
Toronto-area plants, moving their fastener
operations to a leased facility in Brantford,
Ontario.
    The company said the fastener business "has
```

been under severe cost pressures for some time." The fasteners, nuts and bolts are sold to the North American auto market.

```
    A company spokesman declined to estimate the
impact of the closures on earnings. He said
the new facility will employ 500 of the
existing 600 employees. The steelmaker employs
about 16,000 people.
```

Accuracy on this task can be measured quantitatively. As a first approximation, we take newspaper-quality English text, remove the articles, have our program re-insert articles, and compare the resulting text to the original. When the two match (i.e., the program has restored the original article), we score a success. Otherwise, we score a failure. Dividing successes over total articles in the text yields accuracy. Note that this scoring method is a bit unforgiving: if either article is permissible in a certain phrase, we still score a failure for not matching the article chosen by the author of the original text. We pay this price in order to get a fully automatic evaluation set-up. Real accuracy figures will be slightly higher than those reported.

We have made two simplifications to the problem of article selection for the purposes of the experiments described in this paper. One is that we assume noun phrases are already marked as singular or plural, as in normal English. Japanese has no such markings, however, so it would be more realistic to build a posteditor to insert plural forms and articles simultaneously. The system described here is more suited to Russian-English translation, since Russian has plurals but no articles. The second assumption we make is that we are given placeholders for the articles, and each decision is a binary one: *the* versus *a/an*.[1] We are now in the process of lifting these restrictions in order to select plurals and other types of articles, especially the *zero* article.

Performance Bounds

What expectations should we have about how well a program might perform article selection? We performed several experiments to answer this question.

Guessing by coin-flip (heads equals *the*, tails equals *a/an*) yields an accuracy of 50%. But we can improve our accuracy to about 67% simply by guessing *the* every time. We determined this by inspecting 40 megabytes of Wall Street Journal text, noting the breakdown of articles as follows:

- $a = 28.2\%$
- $an = 4.6\%$
- $the = 67.2\%$

So 67% is a good lower bound on expected performance; we shouldn't do worse.

To get some upper bounds, we tested two human subjects on the following task: Given an English text with articles replaced by blanks, try to restore the original articles.[2] Subjects performed with accuracies between 94% and 96%. These numbers show that articles contain very little information (in the Shannon sense), because they are quite predictable from context. This confirms our intuition that languages without articles transmit information at no special handicap. But English articles are not completely predictable, and 95% is a good upper bound on performance. An analysis of the 5% errors shows that some are cases where *a* and *the* are synonymous in context, while others are cases where the human subject failed to read the author's intent.

The human subjects were asked to perform two other tasks. In one, subjects had to predict articles in a very limited context, namely, given just the head noun following the article and its premodifiers. Here is a sample of this task:

```
(??? "reduced" "dividend")
(??? "fiscal" "year")
(??? "profit")
(??? "new" "dividend" "rate")
(??? "pilot" "training" "school")
```

```
(??? "price")
```

Performance was between 79% and 80%, thirteen percentage points better than no-context performance (always guess *the*) but fifteen percentage points worse than full-context performance. This gives us some idea of local versus discourse effects in article selection.[3]

The final task used a slightly expanded context. Subjects were shown the core noun phrase plus two words to the left of the unknown article and two words to the right of the head noun, e.g.:

```
(("It" "said")
 (??? "reduced" "dividend")
 ("reflects" "the"))

(("losses" "for")
 (??? "fiscal" "year")
 ("ending" "Oct"))

(("last" "had")
 (??? "profit")
 ("in" "1985"))

(("1985" ".")
 (??? "new" "dividend" "rate")
 ("is" "payable"))

(("Academy" ",")
 (??? "pilot" "training" "school")
 ("based" "at"))

(("to" "disclose")
 (??? "price")
 ("." "Comair"))
```

Subjects achieved an accuracy of 83% to 88%. This amount of context is what we showed our program when we evaluated it, so these figures are good upper bounds for its behavior.

To summarize the results of this section:

	human	machine
random	50%	50%
always guess *the*	67%	67%
given core NP context	79-80%	
given NP plus 4 words	83-88%	?
given full context	94-96%	

These numbers are not accurate to any degree of statistical significance, due to the small survey size. It was not our intention to make a full-blown psychological study of human article selection; rather, we wanted to establish rough targets to tell us how far we have to go and when to stop.

---

[1] Choosing between *a* and *an* is done as a final step. We use a hand-built trie-driven algorithm detailed enough to distinguish *a unique guest* from *an unimpressed guest*. Minor difficulties remain only with previously unseen acronyms, e.g., distinguishing *a NATO grant* from *an NIH grant*.

[2] This blank is an ambiguous "pseudo-word" in the sense of (Gale, Church, & Yarowsky 1992), which we proceed to disambiguate.

[3] Noun phrases were presented to human subjects in a random order. Presenting them in original-text order would allow the humans to make use of the same discourse effects we are trying to screen out.

Algorithms

In thinking about the selection of articles *a*, *an*, and *the*, natural starting points are the notions of definiteness and discourse. Articles *a* and *an* introduce new discourse entities, while *the* often signals back to previously mentioned or inferred entities. As the previous section indicated, some of article selection requires full discourse context, while some requires only local context. Usage rules are extensively covered in 100 pages of the English grammar reference (Quirk & Greenbaum 1973). These include:

- General knowledge: *the* President, *the* Moon.

- Immediate situation: feed *the* cat.

- Indirect anaphora: he bought a car, but *the* engine was faulty.

- Sporadic reference: she goes to *the* theater every week.

- Logical uniqueness: they have *the* same hobby.

- Body parts: hit in *the* eye.

- Generic use: *the/a* tiger is a ferocious beast.

- Referential, Non-uniqueness: *a* dog bit me.

- Nonreferential, Description: she is *a* good player.

These rules (in spelled-out form) are proper analyses of article selection, but they are difficult to operationalize, due to the representations and world knowledge required. Coding large amounts of general knowledge with AI techniques is known to be hard. And even fully armed with such knowledge, non-native speakers still have trouble mastering the rules.[4]

The rules are generally easier to operationalize when they are accompanied by examples and exceptions, the more the better. Exceptions are common, as demonstrated by differences between British and American article usage. This led us to leave the rules behind and move to a purely data-driven approach.

We generated a database of over 400,000 core noun phrases from Wall Street Journal text. This database is the same one we used to test the human subjects:

---

[4] Notice also that most rules describe when to use *the*. For *a* and *an*, (Quirk & Greenbaum 1973) say: "The indefinite article is notionally the 'unmarked' article in the sense that it is used (for singular count nouns) where the conditions for the use of *the* do not obtain."

Unfortunately, with *the* occurring 67% of the time, we are in much more need of finding conditions for the use of *a* and *an*. To see this, consider a *the* rule that correctly covers 25% of all noun phrases. The remaining 75% would break down as follows: 56% *the* and 44% *a/an*. In the absence of other rules, we might as well also guess *the* for these noun phrases, yielding the same overall accuracy of 67%. On the other hand, an *a/an* rule covering 25% of all noun phrases would leave 89% *the* and 11% *a/an*. Guessing *the* for these would yield a total accuracy of 92%.

```
(("It" "said")
 ("the" "reduced" "dividend")
 ("reflects" "the"))

(("losses" "for")
 ("the" "fiscal" "year")
 ("ending" "Oct"))

(("last" "had")
 ("a" "profit")
 ("in" "1985"))

(("1985" ".")
 ("The" "new" "dividend" "rate")
 ("is" "payable"))

(("Academy" ",")
 ("a" "pilot" "training" "school")
 ("based" "at"))

(("to" "disclose")
 ("the" "price")
 ("." "Comair"))
```

We then looked at which words, word features, and combinations of these were most predictive of the given article. The head noun is most critical. If the head noun is *White House* (this happened 238 times in the database), the article is almost always *the* (236/238 times). Plural head nouns, regardless of root, usually have *the*. Premodifiers like *next* and *same* prefer *the*, as do superlative adjective premodifiers, regardless of root. Combinations are critical: *deficit* as a head noun is not very predictive, and neither is *Federal* as a premodifier, but combined, they have a strong preference. If *ago* follows the head noun directly (this occurred 881 times), the article is never *the*. Words like *triple* are influential just before the article, as in *triple the cost*. Other frequent patterns include *rest of the*, *clear the way*, *X% a year*, *a sign of*, etc.

This exploratory data analysis led us to develop a set of binary features that characterize any noun phrase. These features are either lexical (*word before article is 'triple'*) or abstract (*word after head noun is a past tense verb*). Lexical features were obtained directly from the database. Any word appearing in a given position more than once counts as a feature. Abstract features include part-of-speech, plural marking, tense, and subcategory (superlative adjective, mass noun, etc.).

The problem now is to predict the article based on the features of the context. Given that the features are not independent, care must be taken to integrate the "votes" each feature wants to make. We decided to take a decision tree approach (Quinlan 1986; Breiman *et al.* 1984) to modeling feature interaction.

To the decision tree builder, each feature f has three statistics of interest. The first is frequency of occurrence p_1, the second is the distribution of *the* versus *a/an* for noun phrases in which the feature is present p_2, and the third is the distribution for those without the feature p_3. Choosing a feature splits the data. The goal is a roughly even split with the resulting two data sets being more informative than the original. An information-theoretic approach to choosing the best feature is to pick feature f that minimizes:

$$-p_1 \cdot \log(p_2) - (1 - p_1) \cdot \log(p_3)$$

The tree builder recurses on the data sets that result from the feature-based split. We terminate the recursion when the training examples are 98% in agreement with one another. Applying the tree to a new noun phrase means walking down the tree, based on the phrase's features, returning the article stored at the leaf node.

The main difficulty with learning is that we have over 400,000 training examples and over 30,000 features. (The number of features is high because it includes lexical features such as *word directly after head noun is 'ago'*.) Choosing a feature for the root of the decision tree would require, by the straightforward implementation, $400{,}000 \cdot 30{,}000$ operations to compute p_1, p_2, and p_3 for each feature. To cut down on the computation, we throw out features with less than four instances. We also note that any given lexical feature will have a small p_1, i.e., it will occur infrequently in the database. So we can compute a feature's p_3 by closed form, given a distribution q at the node:

$$p_3 = \frac{q - p_1 \cdot p_2}{1 - p_1}$$

We then index features with associated training instances for fast computation of p_1 and p_2.

Results

Because the space of features and training examples is still large, we decided to break the training data into subsets. We began with high-frequency head nouns. For example, *president* occurs 1420 times in our database. The breakdown of associated articles is as follows:

- *a/an* = 46.5%
- *the* = 53.5%

We trained a decision tree to generate articles for *president* noun phrases based on the premodifiers, two words before the article, and two words after. Training on 90% of the data and testing on 10% yielded a tree of 171 questions and a test set accuracy of 89%. Figure 2 shows the learning curve for noun phrases ending with *president*. We built ten decision trees, giving each tree more training data than the last. The curve shows test-set accuracy for each tree, along with tree size.

Performance on noun phrases ending in *year* was 94%, and for *stock* 90%.

These good scores indicate that with enough training data, we can generate highly accurate decision trees.

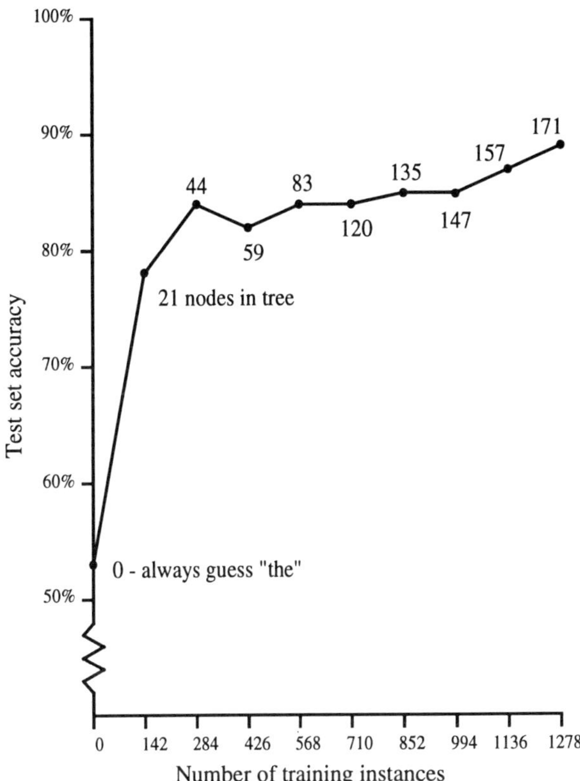

Figure 2: A learning curve for article selection. The graph shown is for noun phrases ending in *president*. The curve shows test-set performance plotted against training instances fed into the decision tree builder. Data points are annotated with the size of the decision tree built.

Unfortunately, of the 23,871 distinct head nouns found in our training database, most occur only once or twice. But—fortunately—the 3413 head nouns occurring at least 25 times account for 84% of the instances.

At the time of this writing, we have built 1600 trees for the 1600 most popular head nouns, covering 77% of the test-set instances. On these instances, we achieve 81% accuracy, which approaches human performance. For the remaining 23%, we simply guess *the*, for an accuracy of 66%. The overall accuracy is 78%. We expect to improve this figure by several points by building more trees, adding more instances, and aggregating many of the low-frequency head nouns on the basis of shared features.

Related Work and Discussion

Definiteness/indefiniteness of noun phrases has been an object of linguistic study for a long time. Computational linguists have been particularly concerned with finding referents for definite noun phrases (Grosz, Joshi, & Weinstein 1983; Sidner 1983), an anaphora problem with clear applications for text understanding.

Text generation research has tackled problems in generation of determiners from a semantic representation (see, e.g., (Elhadad 1993) for a discussion of judgment determiners). Practical MT systems deal with article selection when the source language does not have articles, but the target language does.

Our postediting algorithm achieves an accuracy rate of 78% on financial texts without the benefit of a semantic representation to work from. It does not require an analysis of the source language text, nor even that such text exists. If such representations were available, we could trade portability for increased accuracy.

In some sense, our results are another testament to the power of "know-nothing" statistics to achieve reasonable accuracy and broad coverage. But this is an exaggeration, because our program has a great deal of knowledge built into it. The biggest piece is the noun phrase parser, which finds the most predictive element of the context. Often the head noun is far from the article, and often other nouns intervene—for these reasons, features like "noun x appears within 3 words to the right of the article" are too imprecise.

Word classes also form an important piece of knowledge. Abstract features that characterize large numbers of training cases provide us with trustworthy statistics. Lexical features occurring infrequently may be important, but it is impossible to distinguish them from noise. At present, we only use syntactic word classes, but semantic classes (Miller 1990; Brown *et al.* 1992) could help to alleviate our sparse data problem.

Future Work

As noted earlier, we are now working to relax certain assumptions about the article selection task and our evaluation. We are extending our training database to include noun phrases with *some/any* and the *zero* article. We will re-run our human experiments to get new upper bounds and use the same training procedure (with binary features) but distributions over four possible outcomes: *a/an*, *the*, *some/any*, and *zero*. We do not intend to produce determiners *this* and *that*, as these are explicitly marked in Japanese. The new database is being built from part-of-speech-tagged text; our current algorithms parse noun phrases anchored at *a*, *an*, and *the* without the need for tagging software. We also plan to:

- Measure how performance degrades on other types of text. Currently, we test the algorithm on text drawn from the same population it was trained on.

- Incorporate full-context discourse features into the model. Humans do about 15% better when the full discourse is available. With the right features, we hope to capture some of this gain. What the right features are, however, is still unclear.

- Turn to other routine postediting tasks. These include plural selection, preposition selection, and punctuation.

Acknowledgements

We would like to thank Eduard Hovy for his support and for comments on a draft of this paper. Thanks also to Yolanda Gil for her comments. This work was carried out under ARPA Order No. 8073, contract MDA904-91-C-5224.

References

Breiman, L.; Friedman, J. H.; Olshen, R. A.; and Stone, C. J. 1984. *Classification and Regression Trees*. Wadsworth International Group.

Brown, P.; Pietra, V. D.; deSouza, P.; Lai, J.; and Mercer, R. 1992. Class-based n-gram models of natural language. *Computational Linguistics* 18(4).

Elhadad, M. 1993. Generating argumentative judgment determiners. In *Proceedings of the Eleventh National Conference on Artificial Intelligence*. AAAI.

Gale, W.; Church, K. W.; and Yarowsky, D. 1992. Work on statistical methods for word sense disambiguation. In *AAAI Fall Symposium on Probabilistic Approaches to Natural Language*.

Grosz, B. J.; Joshi, A. K.; and Weinstein, S. 1983. Providing a unified account of definite noun phrases in discourse. In *Proceedings of the 21st ACL*, 44–50.

Knight, K., and Luk, S. K. 1994. Building a large-scale knowledge base for machine translation. In *AAAI-94*.

Miller, G. 1990. Wordnet: An on-line lexical database. *International Journal of Lexicography* 3(4). (Special Issue).

Nirenburg, S., and Frederking, R. 1994. Toward multi-engine machine translation. In *ARPA Human Language Technology Workshop*.

Quinlan, J. R. 1986. Induction of decision trees. *Machine Learning* 1(1):81–106.

Quirk, R., and Greenbaum, S. 1973. *A Concise Grammar of Contemporary English*. New York: Harcourt Brace Jovanovich.

Sidner, C. L. 1983. Focusing in the comprehension of definite anaphora. In Brady, M., and Berwick, R. C., eds., *Computational Models of Discourse*. Cambridge, Massachusetts: The MIT Press. 267–330.

A Prototype Reading Coach that Listens

Jack Mostow, Steven F. Roth, Alexander G. Hauptmann, and Matthew Kane

Project LISTEN, 215 Cyert Hall, Carnegie Mellon University Robotics Institute
4910 Forbes Avenue, Pittsburgh, PA 15213-3890
mostow@cs.cmu.edu

Abstract[1]

We report progress on a new approach to combatting illiteracy -- getting computers to listen to children read aloud. We describe a fully automated prototype coach for oral reading. It displays a story on the screen, listens as a child reads it, and decides whether and how to intervene. We report on pilot experiments with low-reading second graders to test whether these interventions are technically feasible to automate and pedagogically effective to perform. By adapting a continuous speech recognizer, we detected 49% of the misread words, with a false alarm rate under 4%. By incorporating the interventions in a simulated coach, we enabled the children to read and comprehend material at a reading level 0.6 years higher than what they could read on their own. We show how the prototype uses the recognizer to trigger these interventions automatically.

1. Introduction

This paper is about a problem where even a partial solution would quickly pay back every dollar this nation has ever invested in artificial intelligence research. The problem is illiteracy. Its scope is widespread (NCES, 1993a, OTA, 1993). Its economic costs exceed $225 billion per year (Herrick, 1990). Its human and social costs are incalculable. Individuals with low reading proficiency are much likelier to be unemployed, poor, or incarcerated (NCES, 1993b).

Although a large body of software exists to teach reading, it is limited in its ability to listen and/or intervene. Most systems do not listen at all. Some systems try to help children anyway by providing speech output on demand (Wise et al, 1989, Roth & Beck, 1987, McConkie & Zola, 1987, Reitsma, 1988). This capability is now available in some commercial educational software, e.g., (Beck et al, 1987, Discis, 1991). However, young readers often fail to realize when they need such help (McConkie, 1990). Moreover, these systems cannot tap the unique motivation that listening to a reader can engender (Kantrov, 1991).

Other systems do listen, but use isolated word recognizers that cannot monitor the oral reading of connected text. Such systems have been used for reading (Kantrov, 1991, Cowan & Jones, 1991), speech training (Watson et al, 1989, Umezaki, 1993), and foreign language learning (Molholt, 1990).

More recently, some systems have used continuous speech recognition to detect errors in reading (Phillips et al, 1992, Mostow et al, 1993a) or pronunciation (Bernstein et al, 1990, Bernstein & Rtischev, 1991). However, the pedagogical interventions performed by published systems were either rudimentary or missing altogether.

Project LISTEN is addressing these various limitations by **adapting continuous speech recognition to listen to children read connected text, automatically triggering pedagogically appropriate interventions.** We present evidence for the claim that these interventions are both **pedagogically effective** to perform, and **technically feasible** to automate.

The rest of this paper is organized as follows. Section 2 describes the interventions performed by our prototype oral reading coach, which we have named after Emily Latella (a character on *Saturday Night Live* created by the late Gilda Radner and known for her difficulties in distinguishing among words that sound alike). Section 3 describes the speech analysis required to make Emily work. Section 4 concludes.

2. Emily's interventions

Emily is designed to help a child read and comprehend a given story. (One can imagine alternative goals, such as correcting pronunciation or giving explicit instruction in phonics.) Emily is intended to maintain a fluent, pleasant reading experience that gives the child practice in reading connected text, plus enough assistance to be able to comprehend it. It therefore uses a combination of reading and listening which we have named "shared reading," in which the child reads wherever possible, and the coach helps wherever necessary.

Emily intervenes when the reader misreads one or more words in the current sentence, gets stuck, or clicks on a word to get help. We do <u>not</u> treat hesitations, sounding out, false starts, self-corrections, or other insertions as misreading; by "misread," we mean "fail to speak the correct word" (though see Section 3.1). Emily's current set of interventions targets two obstacles that interfere with children's reading comprehension (Curtis, 1980).

First, young readers often have trouble identifying printed words. Some of Emily's interventions are therefore primarily intended to assist **word identification**:

- Retry a misread word by highlighting it and asking the child to reread it. This intervention

[1]This research was supported primarily by the National Science Foundation under Grant Number MDR-9154059, and the Defense Advanced Research Projects Agency, DoD, through DARPA Order 5167, monitored by the Air Force Avionics Laboratory under contract N00039-85-C-0163, with additional support from the Microelectronics and Computer Technology Corporation (MCC). The views and conclusions contained in this document are those of the authors and should not be interpreted as representing the official policies, either expressed or implied, of the sponsors or of the United States Government.

For a short summary of Project LISTEN, see (Hauptmann et al, 1994).

prompts the child to attend more carefully to the word, and signals that the first attempt may have been incorrect.

- Recue or "jumpstart" the last misread word by speaking the text that leads up to it, and then flashing the word to prompt the child to reread it. The jumpstart serves to put the child back in the context where the word occurred, which may help in identifying it. However, this intervention does not apply if the word occurs near the beginning of the sentence.

- Speak a word if the child gets stuck on that word.

- Speak a word if the child clicks the mouse on it.

- Speak a word after a retry or recue. This feedback is confirmatory if the child's second try was correct, and corrective if it was not.

Second, struggling readers spend so much of their attention figuring out the words that even when they get the words right, they may still not comprehend the overall meaning. Emily's other interventions address this **attentional bottleneck**:

- To avoid disrupting the flow of reading, ignore a misread word if it is on a list of 52 common function words unlikely to affect comprehension.

- Speak the entire sentence if the child misreads three or more words in it, or misreads a word after a retry or recue. Either condition means the child is unlikely to have comprehended the sentence. Hearing the sentence frees the child to focus on comprehension (Curtis, 1980).

For both pedagogical and technical reasons, Emily waits to intervene until the end of the sentence, unless the reader gets stuck or clicks for help. The pedagogical reasons are to give the reader a chance to self-correct, and to avoid disrupting the flow of reading. The technical reasons are that Emily cannot gracefully interrupt the reader, both because its speech recognizer lags too far behind to respond instantaneously, and because it lacks the subtle nonverbal cues that humans use to interrupt each other.

To finesse the interruption problem, Emily displays the text incrementally, adding one sentence at a time. When the reader reaches the end of the sentence, Emily has an opportunity to intervene without having to interrupt. It does not display the next sentence until it has completed any such interventions.

For natural speech quality, Emily normally outputs predigitized human speech. However, two synthesized voices (ORATOR^{TM} (Spiegel, 1992) and DecTalk^{TM} (DEC, 1985)) are available as alternatives.

To evaluate and refine these interventions while we were still working on the speech analysis, and independently of recognition accuracy, we developed a simulated coach that appeared automatic to the subjects, but was controlled behind the scenes by a human experimenter, as shown in (Mostow et al, 1993b). To design the interventions, we used the following development process:

1. Observe individual reading assistance provided by human experts.

2. Select the most frequent interventions that seem feasible to automate.

3. Codify interventions as written instructions for the human experimenter.

4. Implement interventions as actions the experimenter selects from a menu.

5. Automate the triggers for the interventions.

At this point, the experimenter's role consisted of listening to the reader, following along in the text, and marking each word as correct or misread. The rest of the simulated coach was automatic, and used the marking information to trigger its interventions.

2.1. Pedagogical evaluation

We performed a pilot study to test the overall effectiveness of our interventions. Another purpose of this experiment was to refine our interventions and experimental protocols before performing larger scale studies with more subjects and subtler effects.

Hypothesis: Our hypothesis was that these interventions would enable struggling readers to read and comprehend material significantly more advanced than what they could read on their own. Therefore we selected as our subjects 12 second graders at an urban public school in Pittsburgh who had been identified by their reading teachers as having problems with reading.

Dependent variables: To minimize the effect of inter-subject variability, we compared three conditions for each subject. The control condition measured their <u>independent reading level</u>, that is, the level of material they could read and comprehend without assistance. The experimental condition measured their <u>coach-assisted reading level</u>, that is, the level of material they could read and comprehend by using the coach. A third condition measured their <u>"potential" reading level</u>, that is, the level of material they could comprehend when it was read aloud to them.

Method: To measure these three levels, we adapted materials and procedures from a widely used test of oral reading (Spache, 1981). This test includes one-page passages at carefully calibrated grade levels ranging from early first grade to mid-seventh-grade. Each passage has an accompanying list of comprehension questions. For obvious reasons, once a subject read a passage, it was "contaminated" and could not be reused for that subject in the other conditions. Fortunately (Spache, 1981) has two complete series of passages. Therefore we used one series to determine each subject's independent reading level, and the other to determine his or her assisted reading level. To measure reading level in a given condition, we presented successively higher passages until the subject exceeded a limit on the number of oral reading errors or failed over 40% of the comprehension questions. The subject's reading level for that condition was then defined as the grade level of the previous passage. The subject then listened to the subsequent passages until his or her comprehension score dropped below 60%. We defined potential reading level as the level of the highest passage successfully comprehended.

To avoid confounding effects, we randomized the order of the subjects and counterbalanced both the order of the control and experimental conditions, and the choice of passage series for each condition. We recorded the children at their school in November 1993 (month 3 of the school year), taking them one at a time out of their regular class to a separate room. Whenever subjects exceeded their attention span or got restless, we excused them and continued the session on the next day of school.

Apparatus: The apparatus for the experiment consisted of a NeXT workstation with two monitors, one for the subject and the other for the human experimenter. A color monitor was used to display the text and interventions to the subject. To avoid unnecessary variability, all the passages, spoken interventions, and comprehension questions were digitally prerecorded in a pleasant female voice. The experimenter used the keyboard, mouse, and second monitor to select the passage to display, mark each word as correct or misread, and administer the comprehension questions. The subject was given a button to push for help on the current word. The button simply operated a flashlight that signalled the human experimenter, who then selected the appropriate menu item. This configuration avoided the need to train the subjects to operate a mouse, and allowed us to run the experiments on a single workstation.

Data: We digitally recorded the children's oral reading, using a Sennheiser noise-cancelling headset microphone to keep the speaker's mouth an appropriate distance from the microphone, and to filter out some of the noise typical of a school environment. "Event files" captured every action performed by the experimenter or the system in response to the subjects' oral reading. (See Figure 2-1.) We also recorded the results of the comprehension tests, including which specific questions were answered correctly.

Key Results: The outcome of this experiment supported our hypothesis. The subjects' assisted reading level was higher than their independent reading by an average of 0.6 years (2.7 vs. 2.1). This effect was statistically significant at the 99% level.

The interventions also dramatically reduced the frustration experienced by the children in their effort to read. When they used the coach, our subjects misread only 2.6% of the words. Without assistance, they misread 12.3% of the words on passages of matched difficulty; anything over 10% indicates that the reading material is too difficult (Betts, 1946, Vacca et al., 1991).

Based on a study (Curtis, 1980) of similar students reading the same materials, we expected that listening comprehension would be about two years higher than

```
#:   TIME:     EVENT:     TEXT WORD:
```
At time 1179648, measured in samples (16,000 per second) of the digitized oral reading, the coach displays "Spotty thought he had caught a black and white kitten":
```
78>  1179648   NEXTSEN    Spotty#49
79>  1239040   OK         Spotty#49
```
After hesitating 4 seconds on "thought", the child pushes the help button.
```
80>  1306624   SAYWORD 4  thought#50
81>  1314816   OK         thought#50
82>  1325056   OK         he#51
83>  1337344   OK         had#52
```
The child misreads "caught":
```
84>  1384448   MARK       caught#53
85>  1400832   OK         a#54
86>  1417216   OK         black#55
87>  1429504   OK         and#56
88>  1439744   OK         white#57
89>  1458176   OK         kitten#58
90>  1458176   START_EOS  .#58
91>  1458176   NUM_ERRS 1
```
The coach recues "caught":
```
92>  1458176   GOMARK     caught#53
93>  1458176   JUMPSTART  caught#53
94>  1458176   JUMPEND    caught#53
```
The child misreads it again...
```
95>  1458176   MARK       caught#53
```
... so the coach speaks it:
```
96>  1458176   THISWORD   caught#53
97>  1458176   END_EOS
```

Figure 2-1: Annotated excerpt from an event file

independent reading level; instead, we found that it was slightly (though not significantly) lower than the coach-assisted level. We observed that when we asked the subjects to listen to an entire story, their attention wandered, perhaps because they lacked a natural visual focus such as a talking face.

Our analysis of the data suggested how our interventions might be made more effective. We found that the coach read fewer sentences to the subjects than it should, because thanks to the help button they hardly ever misread three or more words in one sentence. We plan to make the trigger for this intervention sensitive to reader hesitations that may indicate comprehension difficulties.

3. Speech analysis

Unlike conventional speech <u>recognition</u>, whose goal is to guess what the speaker says, Emily has a <u>discrimination</u> task, whose goal is to find where the speaker deviates from the text. It can also be viewed as a <u>classification</u> task, whose goal is to classify each word of text as correctly read or not. This task is easier than recognition in that it does not require identifying what the speaker said instead, but it is harder in that the speaker's deviations from the text may include arbitrary words and non-words.

Thus the interventions in Section 2 require the following speech analysis capabilities:

1. Given a starting point in the text and a

possibly disfluent reading of it, detect which words of text were misread. The starting point may be the beginning of a sentence, a word the reader selected for help, or a word the reader is asked to reread.

2. Detect when the reader reaches the end of a given fragment of text. This fragment may be the current sentence or a word to reread.

3. Detect when the reader gets stuck.

We now describe how Emily implements these capabilities.

Emily consists of two basic components -- an <u>intervenor</u> that runs on a color NeXT workstation and interacts with the reader, and a <u>speech</u> <u>recognizer</u> that runs on a DEC 3000 or HP 735. The intervenor tells the recognizer where in the text to start listening -- either at the beginning of a new sentence, after a word spoken by the coach, or at a word the coach has just prompted the reader to reread. Four times a second, the recognizer reports the sequence of words it thinks it has heard so far. Capability 1 is implemented by aligning the output of the recognizer against the text. Capability 2 is implemented by checking if the recognizer has output the last word of the fragment. Capability 3 is implemented by a time limit for progressing to the next word in the text; the intervenor assumes that the reader is stuck on this word if the time limit is exceeded without a previously unread word appearing in the recognizer output. The intervenor is invoked whenever the reader reaches the end of a sentence, gets stuck, or clicks the mouse on a word for help.

The speech recognizer, named Sphinx-II (Huang et al, 1993), requires three types of knowledge -- **phonetic**, **lexical**, and **linguistic** -- as well as several parameters that control its Viterbi beam search for the likeliest transcription of the input speech signal. The recognizer evaluates competing sequences of lexical symbols based on the degree of acoustic match specified by its **phonetic models**, the pronunciations specified by its **lexicon**, and the *a priori* probability specified by its **language model**. Thus Sphinx-II's recognition accuracy is limited by how well these three representations model the speech input. These representations must approximate the broad range of speech phenomena contained in disfluent reading, which include omission, repetition, and hesitation, as well as substitution and insertion of words, non-words, and non-speech sounds. These phenomena (especially words and non-words outside the vocabulary used in the text) compound the variability that makes connected speech recognition so difficult even for fluent speech.

(Mostow et al, 1993a) assumed that phonetic models trained only on female speakers would work better for children's speech because of its high pitch. However, we found that models trained on combined male and female speech seemed to work just about as well. Therefore Emily uses 7000 phonetic Hidden Markov Models trained on 7200 sentences read by 84 adult speakers (42 male and 42 female), though we can also run it on the male-only and

female-only models. To retrain these models from scratch, we need to collect and transcribe a much larger corpus of children's oral reading. In the meantime, we plan to adapt the adult phonetic models to work better on children's speech by using an interpolative training method.

The recognizer's accuracy at detecting misread words depends on its ability to model deviations from correct reading. We model several different phenomena of oral reading in Emily's lexicon (illustrated in Figure 3-1) and language model, which are automatically generated from a given text, such as "Once upon a time a...."

Subscripts denote word numbers:

```
Once₁                          W AH N S
```
Alternate pronunciations are parenthesized:
```
TRUNCATION₁(W)                 W
TRUNCATION₁(W AH)              W AH
upon₂                          AX P AO N
TRUNCATION₂(AX)                AX
TRUNCATION₂(AX P)              AX P
a₃                             AX
time₄                          T AY M
TRUNCATION₄(T)                 T
a₅                             AX
```

Figure 3-1: Lexicon for "Once upon a time a..."

To model **correct reading**, we include the text words themselves in the lexicon, numbering them to distinguish among multiple occurrences of the same word (e.g., "a_3" vs. "a_5"). Each word's pronunciation, represented as a sequence of k phonemes, is taken from a general English dictionary. If not found there, it is computed by the pronunciation component of a speech synthesizer, such as MITalk (Allen et al, 1987) or ORATOR^{TM} (Spiegel, 1992). In our language model, each word w_{i-1} (e.g., "Once₁") is followed with probability .97 by the correct next word w_i ("upon₂").

To model **repetitions** and **omissions**, word w_{i-1} (e.g., "Once₁") is followed with probability $.01/(n-1)$ by any word w_j of the other $n-1$ words in the same sentence. A non-uniform probability would be more realistic, but can cause problems, as discussed later. Repetitions and omissions correspond respectively to jumps backward ($j<i$, e.g., back to "Once₁") and forward ($j>i$, e.g., to "a₃").

To model **false starts** and **near misses**, we include a truncation symbol TRUNCATION$_i$ for each text word w_i. Besides modelling actual truncations of the word, these pronunciations approximate many phonetically similar substitution errors. The truncation symbol TRUNCATION$_i$ follows the word w_{i-1} with probability .02. For the example text in Figure 3-1, this model assigns a probability of 2% to the prediction that after reading the word "Once₁", the reader will next truncate the word "upon₂." We give this symbol $k-2$ alternate pronunciations, consisting of proper prefixes of the complete pronunciation, as illustrated in Figure 3-1. We found that including truncations where only the last phone is omitted, e.g., "AX P AO", seemed to cause recognition errors, especially for speakers of dialects that tend to drop the last phone.

To model **repeated attempts**, **self-corrections**, and **substitution errors**, respectively, each truncation symbol TRUNCATION$_i$ is followed with equal probability by itself, by the complete word w_i, or by the following word w_{i+1}. That is, after truncating the word "upon$_2$", the reader is considered equally likely to truncate it again, read it correctly, or go on to the word "a$_3$."

This language model reflects some lessons from previous experience. First, although the words in the lexicon are intended to model correct reading, in practice **words are often used to model deviations.** For example, if the word "elephant" is not in the lexicon, it is liable to be recognized as the sequence "and of that." Anyone who designs a language model for this task without anticipating this phenomenon is liable to be surprised by the results.

Second, the ability to detect deviations depends on having a **phonetically rich repertoire** of symbols for matching them. The word-only lexicon used in (Hauptmann et al, 1993) was surprisingly successful despite its limitations because it included all the words in an entire passage, which was enough to provide considerable phonetic variety.

Third, **over-constrained search can impede error recovery.** One of our earlier language models tried to exploit the characteristic structure of disfluent oral reading. It assigned low or zero probabilities to transitions that children seldom take, such as long jumps. These probabilities were estimated from the transcribed oral reading corpus described in (Mostow et al, 1993a). We expected that this model would produce more accurate recognition than simpler ones, but we have not (yet) succeeded in making it do so. We suspect the reason is that when the recognizer follows a garden path, this more constrained model makes it difficult to recover. For example, suppose the reader says "Oncet upon a time," and the recognizer recognizes "Oncet" as "Once$_1$ a$_3$ TRUNCATION$_4$(T)." To recover from this garden path, the recognizer must be able to jump to "upon$_2$" without incurring an excessive penalty (low probability) from the language model; otherwise it may misrecognize "upon a time" as "a$_5$...." Since Emily's phonetic models and lexicon can only crudely approximate the virtually infinite range of speech sounds produced by disfluent young readers, it appears impossible to keep the recognizer from starting down such garden paths. Therefore the language model must be designed to recover from them as quickly as possible. That is, since we cannot prevent recognition errors from occurring at all in these cases, we must instead try to minimize their extent.

3.1. Accuracy

We evaluated Emily's accuracy off-line on 514 sentences read by 15 second graders as they used the simulated reading coach described in Section 2. (To avoid testing on our training data, we were careful in developing our language model and tuning parameter values to use a separate set of 457 sentences by 30 second graders from a different school.) Our test utterances averaged 10 text words in length and 15 seconds in duration, including 5 seconds of silence due to struggling readers' frequent hesitations. The readers misread only 1.6% of the words in this corpus; we attribute this low rate partly to the help button, which they used on 6% of the words, and partly to how we operationalized "misread."

We relied on the human experimenter to flag misread words in real-time, causing the simulated coach to record "MARK" in the event file. (An UNMARK command allowed self-corrections.) This scheme was faster and cheaper than conventional detailed transcriptions, especially since disfluent reading is difficult to transcribe. Moreover, it solved the sticky problem of when to consider a word misread -- we simply told the experimenter to follow the instructions in (Spache, 1981), which caution against treating dialect substitutions and minor mispronunciations (e.g. "axe" for "ask") as reading errors.

Our purpose in evaluation was to measure the ability of our recognizer to trigger the coach's interventions. Therefore in computing the list of words Emily treated as misread, we filtered out the same function words that the coach ignored. This step substantially reduced the incidence of false alarms (correct words treated as misread), since these function words were rarely misread by the reader but were often misrecognized by the recognizer. Similarly, we ignored misreadings of words where readers used the help button, both because the coach does not require them to echo these words (though they often do), and because our digital recording apparatus often failed to record the beginnings of these words, since it stops recording during the coach's spoken interventions, and there is a slight delay before it resumes.

The evaluation results according to this methodology are shown in Table 3-1. Emily's sensitivity in classifying words as misread or correct is demonstrated by the fact that its detection rate is significantly (over 10 times) greater than its false alarm rate.

For comparison, we reanalyzed the results for Emily's predecessor, named Evelyn (Mostow et al, 1993a, Hauptmann et al, 1993). These results were obtained for a corpus of children's oral reading that was similar except that each utterance was an entire Spache passage, read without assistance. They were computed by averaging the individual accuracies on each passage, which reduced the effect of the passages where most of the recognition errors occurred. Without such averaging, Evelyn's detection rate was lower than Emily's. The difference is not significant with respect to the $\pm 2\sigma$ confidence intervals, which are wide because so few words were misread. However, Evelyn's false alarm rate was significantly (over three times) worse than Emily's.

We attribute Emily's higher accuracy to several factors. First, Evelyn was evaluated based on a different, more literal criterion, which treated any word not spoken exactly correctly as "missed." In contrast, Emily was evaluated

Table 3-1: Comparative Accuracy in Detecting Misread Words

System:	Corpus:	Definition of Misread Words:	Detection Rate:	False Alarm Rate:
Evelyn	99 passages	all substitutions and omissions	.370±.093 (40 of 108)	.126 ±.010 (567 of 4516)
Emily	514 sentences	only pedagogically relevant errors	.488±.110 (40 of 82)	.0366±.0053 (187 of 5106)

Detection rate = (misread words detected) / (words misread); false alarm rate = (false alarms) / (words read correctly)

Confidence intervals shown are $\pm 2\sigma$, where $\sigma = \sqrt{\dfrac{p \cdot (1-p)}{n}}$ is the standard error for rate p, sample size n

based on the more pedagogically relevant criterion applied by the experimenter who flagged words as "misread." We have now transcribed enough of our corpus to compare these two schemes. Almost no correctly read words were erroneously flagged by the experimenter, but for every word flagged as misread, several minor substitutions (such as adding or dropping a plural ending) were not flagged. Treating such near-miss substitutions as reading errors would erode Emily's detection rate. However, this difference in criteria does not account for Emily's much lower false alarm rate.

Second, Evelyn was evaluated on a corpus of page-long passages, and its language model had equiprobable transitions to any word on the page other than the next word in the text. In contrast, Emily recognizes one sentence at a time rather than a complete passage, and its language model preserves state by avoiding transitions out of the current sentence.

Third, filtering out function words cut Emily's false alarm rate by roughly half.

Fourth, Emily's richer lexicon enables it to model non-text-words using truncations, not just sequences of other words. We plan to further enrich the lexicon based on analysis of the transcribed oral reading and of Emily's recognition errors. We also need to optimize both the heuristic probabilities used in our language model, and the various input parameters to Sphinx-II.

Emily embodies a somewhat "lenient" tradeoff between detection and false alarms. The 97% transition probability between successive words of the text represents a strong expectation of correct reading, which can be overcome only by compelling acoustic evidence. A weaker bias would improve detection but increase the false alarm rate. But Emily's false alarms already outnumber misread words (187 to 82 on our test corpus). The reason is that even poor readers misread fewer than 10% of the words if the material is appropriate to their reading level (Betts, 1946, Vacca et al., 1991). To avoid swamping the reader with unnecessary interventions, we must reduce false alarms.

To help diagnose Emily's recognition errors, we split up the utterances into four subsets based on whether the reader pushed the help button (which tended to corrupt the recording) and/or misread a word (which indicated disfluency). We found that each of these factors multiplied the false alarm rate by about 1.5, reaching 6.1% on utterances with both SAYWORD and MARK events, compared to 2.8% on utterances with neither. The

detection rate was insignificantly better on the utterances with no SAYWORDs (53% vs. 46%).

It is important to point out that speech recognition errors in this domain are not devastating. Some errors are masked by the interventions. For example, if Emily correctly detects that three or more words were misread, it will reread the sentence to help the reader comprehend it -- even if it is wrong about <u>which</u> words were misread. At worst, failure to detect a misread word merely loses one opportunity for corrective feedback. Conversely, false alarms merely slow down the flow of reading by asking the student to reread text unnecessarily. In practice, they encourage clearer enunciation. At worst, they may irritate the student if they become too frequent.

We have not yet used recorded speech to measure Emily's ability to detect when the reader reaches the end of the sentence or gets stuck. Such a test would need to determine how often, given the recorded reading, Emily would have intervened within an acceptable delay.

3.2. Other Improvements

Speed: Emily's speech processing consists of some signal processing performed on a NeXT in close to real time, plus a beam search performed on a more powerful machine (DEC 3000 or HP 735). In our off-line evaluation, this search was consistently faster than real time, averaging roughly 50% times real time. In contrast, Evelyn's search took 1-2 times real time on the same machine (Mostow et al, 1993a). We attribute this two- to four-fold speedup to Emily's sentence-based language model.

Flexibility: The Sphinx-II recognizer used in (Mostow et al, 1993a) and (Hauptmann et al, 1993) required a separate language model for each passage. This requirement precluded interrupting the reading before the end of the passage, because there was no way to tell the recognizer where to resume listening other than at the beginning of the passage.

We overcame this limitation by modifying Sphinx-II to accept a starting point as a parameter. Simply by changing its starting point, Emily can listen to one sentence at a time, resume listening in mid-sentence after the reader clicks on a word, jump back to listen to the reader retry a misread word after an intervention, or switch to another story.

We plan to further improve Emily's flexibility by reimplementing its language model to take constant space, instead of space proportional to (or even quadratic in) the total amount of text. Eliminating the need to reload language models for different text could enable Emily to monitor oral reading of text generated on the fly.

4. Conclusion

Emily **improves in measurable ways** on previously published attempts to use connected speech recognition to monitor and assist oral reading. First and foremost, it provides meaningful assistance, using interventions that (when implemented in our simulated coach) enabled struggling second graders to read material 0.6 years more advanced than they could on their own, and with much less frustration. Second, its detection rate for misread words is higher, its false alarm rate three times lower, and its search phase two to four times faster, than the system in (Mostow et al, 1993a).

These results are based on a number of **conceptual contributions**. First, Emily's interventions were derived from a combination of theory, expertise, and experiment. They embody an interesting new type of human-machine interaction -- shared reading -- and express in machine-applicable form some basic rules for helping children read. Second, Emily's language model, sentence-based processing, and mechanism for multiple starting points have improved the automated analysis of oral reading. Third, the development process by which Emily was designed, with its parallel interacting tracks for the interventions and the speech analysis required to support them, may serve as a useful model for other multidisciplinary applications.

Finally, the lessons we have learned from this work reflect the scientific value of the reading assistance task as a **carrier problem for research on two-way continuous speech communication with machines**. Because the computer knows the text the reader is trying to read, the speech analysis is tractable enough to study some limited but natural forms of such interaction now, without waiting for real time recognition of unconstrained spontaneous speech to become feasible.

One lesson is the **identification of novel criteria for evaluating speech recognition accuracy.** The conventional off-line evaluation criteria take the endpoint of each utterance as a given. These criteria do not test the ability to detect when the reader reaches the end of a sentence or gets stuck. In general, two-way speech communication will require a way to decide when the speaker is done speaking.

Another lesson is that **perplexity can be less important than recovery.** Perplexity measures the language model's average uncertainty about what the speaker will say next at any given point. Lower perplexity normally leads to higher accuracy. But when we tried to reduce perplexity by modelling patterns of disfluent oral reading, detection accuracy actually fell, apparently because the very constraints that reduced the perplexity of the language model impeded its ability to recover from garden paths. Further work is needed to test this hypothesis, define a formal measure of a language model's error recovery ability, and analyze how it affects recognition accuracy.

We are now trying out Emily on children and modifying its interventions to tolerate errors by the speech recognizer, as illustrated in our video of Emily in action (Mostow et al, 1994a, Mostow et al, 1994b). We hope to test soon how well the fully automated coach helps children read. But our longer-term goal is to scale up the coach to help children learn to read on their own.

Acknowledgements

We thank our principal reading consultant Leslie Thyberg; Raj Reddy and the rest of the CMU Speech Group (Filleno Alleva, Bob Brennan, Lin Chase, Xuedong Huang, Mei-Yuh Hwang, Sunil Issar, Fu-hua Liu, Chenxiang Lu, Pedro Moreno, Ravi Mosur, Yoshiaki Ohshima, Paul Placeway, Roni Rosenfeld, Alex Rudnicky, Matt Siegler, Rich Stern, Eric Thayer, Wayne Ward, and Bob Weide) for Sphinx-II; Adam Swift for programming; Paige Angstadt, Morgan Hankins, and Cindy Neelan for transcription; Maxine Eskenazi for transcript analysis; Lee Ann Kane for her voice; Murray Spiegel and Bellcore for ORATOR^{TM}; Dave Pisoni and Digital Equipment Corporation for DecTalk^{TM}; CTB Macmillan/McGraw-Hill for permission to use copyrighted reading materials from George Spache's *Diagnostic Reading Scales*; the students and educators at Colfax Elementary School, East Hills Elementary School, Turner School, and Winchester Thurston School for participating in our experiments; and many friends for advice, encouragement, and assistance.

References

Allen, J., Hunnicutt, S. and Klatt, D.H. (1987). *From Text to Speech: The MITalk system.* Cambridge, UK: Cambridge University Press.

I. L. Beck, S. F. Roth, and M. G. McKeown. (1987). *Word-Wise.* Allen, Texas: Developmental Learning Materials, Educational software for reading.

J. Bernstein and D. Rtischev. (1991). A voice interactive language instruction system. *Proceedings of the Second European Conference on Speech Communication and Technology (EUROSPEECH91).* Genova, Italy.

J. Bernstein, M. Cohen, H. Murveit, D. Rtischev, and M. Weintraub. (1990). Automatic evaluation and training in English pronunciation. *International Conference on Speech and Language Processing (ICSLP-90).* Kobe, Japan.

E. A. Betts. (1946). *Foundations of Reading Instruction.* New York: American Book Company.

H. Cowan and B. Jones. (September 1991). Reaching students with reading problems; Optimum Research Reading Program, The Sentence Master, Autoskill CRS evaluation. *Electronic Learning*, Vol. *11*(1).

M. E. Curtis. (1980). Development of components of reading skill. *Journal of Educational Psychology*, 72(5), 656-669.

Digital Equipment Corporation. (1985). *DecTalk: A Guide to Voice.* Maynard, MA: Digital Equipment Corporation.

Discis Knowledge Research Inc. *DISCIS Books.* 45

Sheppard Ave. E, Suite 802, Toronto, Canada M2N 5W9. Commercial implementation of Computer Aided Reading for the MacIntosh computer.

A. G. Hauptmann, L. L. Chase, and J. Mostow. (September 1993). Speech Recognition Applied to Reading Assistance for Children: A Baseline Language Model. *Proceedings of the 3rd European Conference on Speech Communication and Technology (EUROSPEECH93)*. Berlin.

A. G. Hauptmann, J. Mostow, S. F. Roth, M. Kane, and A. Swift. (March 1994). A Prototype Reading Coach that Listens: Summary of Project LISTEN. *Proceedings of the ARPA Workshop on Human Language Technology*. Princeton, NJ.

E. Herrick. (1990). *Literacy Questions and Answers.* Pamphlet. P. O. 81826, Lincoln, NE 68501: Contact Center, Inc.

X. D. Huang, F. Alleva, H. W. Hon, M. Y. Hwang, K. F. Lee, and R. Rosenfeld. (April 1993). The SPHINX-II speech recognition system: An overview. *Computer Speech and Language*, 7(2), 137-148.

I. Kantrov. (1991). *Talking to the Computer: A Prototype Speech Recognition System for Early Reading Instruction* (Tech. Rep.) 91-3. Education Development Center, 55 Chapel Street, Newton, MA 02160: Center for Learning, Teaching, and Technology.

G. W. McConkie. (November 1990). Electronic Vocabulary Assistance Facilitates Reading Comprehension: Computer Aided Reading. Unpublished manuscript.

G. W. McConkie and D. Zola. (1987). Two examples of computer-based research on reading: Eye movement tracking and computer aided reading. In D. Reinking (Eds.), *Computers and Reading: Issues for Theory and Practice*. New York: Teachers College Press.

G. Molholt. (February-April 1990). Spectographic analysis and patterns in pronunciation. *Computers and the Humanities*, 24(1-2), 81-92.

J. Mostow, A. G. Hauptmann, L. L. Chase, and S. Roth. (July 1993). Towards a Reading Coach that Listens: Automated Detection of Oral Reading Errors. *Proceedings of the Eleventh National Conference on Artificial Intelligence (AAAI93)*. Washington, DC, American Association for Artificial Intelligence.

J. Mostow, S. Roth, A. Hauptmann, M. Kane, A. Swift, L. Chase, and B. Weide. (August 1993). Getting Computers to Listen to Children Read: A New Way to Combat Illiteracy (7-minute video). Overview and research methodology of Project LISTEN as of July 1993.

J. Mostow, S. Roth, A. Hauptmann, M. Kane, A. Swift, L. Chase, and B. Weide. (August 1994). A Reading Coach that Listens (6-minute video). *Video Track of the Twelfth National Conference on Artificial Intelligence (AAAI94)*. Seattle, WA, American Association for Artificial Intelligence.

J. Mostow, S. Roth, A. Hauptmann, M. Kane, A. Swift, L. Chase, and B. Weide. (August 1994). A reading coach that listens: (edited) video transcript. *Proceedings of the Twelfth National Conference on Artificial Intelligence (AAAI94)*. Seattle, WA.

National Center for Education Statistics. (September 1993). *NAEP 1992 Reading Report Card for the Nation and the States: Data from the National and Trial State Assessments* (Tech. Rep.) Report No. 23-ST06. Washington, DC: U.S. Department of Education.

National Center for Education Statistics. (September 1993). *Adult Literacy in America* (Tech. Rep.) GPO 065-000-00588-3. Washington, DC: U.S. Department of Education.

Office of Technology Assessment. (July 1993). *Adult Literacy and New Technologies: Tools for a Lifetime* (Tech. Rep.) OTA-SET-550. Washington, DC: U.S. Congress.

M. Phillips, M. McCandless, and V. Zue. (September 1992). *Literacy Tutor: An Interactive Reading Aid* (Tech. Rep.). Spoken Language Systems Group, 545 Technology Square, NE43-601, Cambridge, MA 02139: MIT Laboratory for Computer Science.

P. Reitsma. (1988). Reading practice for beginners: Effects of guided reading, reading-while-listening, and independent reading with computer-based speech feedback. *Reading Research Quarterly*, 23(2), 219-235.

S. F. Roth and I. L. Beck. (Spring 1987). Theoretical and instructional implications of the assessment of two microcomputer programs. *Reading Research Quarterly*, 22(2), 197-218.

G. D. Spache. (1981). *Diagnostic Reading Scales*. Del Monte Research Park, Monterey, CA 93940: CTB Macmillan/McGraw-Hill.

M. F. Spiegel. (January 1992). *The Orator System User's Manual - Release 10*. Morristown, NJ: Bell Communications Research Labs,

T. Umezaki. (1993). *Talking Trainer*. Japan: Gakken, (In Japanese). Educational software for training deaf children to speak.

J. A. L. Vacca, R. T. Vacca, and M. K. Gove. (1991). *Reading and Learning to Read (Second Edition)*. Harper Collins.

C. S. Watson, D. Reed, D. Kewley-Port, and D. Maki. (1989). The Indiana Speech Training Aid (ISTRA) I: Comparisons between human and computer-based evaluation of speech quality. *Journal of Speech and Hearing Research*, 32, 245-251.

B. Wise, R. Olson, M. Anstett, L. Andrews, M. Terjak, V. Schneider, J. Kostuch, and L. Kriho. (1989). Implementing a long-term computerized remedial reading program with synthetic speech feedback: Hardware, software, and real-world issues. *Behavior Research Methods, Instruments, & Computers, 21*, 173-180.

Visual Semantics: Extracting Visual
Information from Text Accompanying
Pictures *

Rohini K. Srihari and Debra T. Burhans
CEDAR/SUNY at Buffalo
UB Commons, 520 Lee Entrance- Suite 202
Buffalo, NY 14228-2567 USA
rohini@cs.buffalo.edu
burhans@cs.buffalo.edu

Abstract

This research explores the interaction of textual and photographic information in document understanding. The problem of performing general-purpose vision without a priori knowledge is difficult at best. The use of collateral information in scene understanding has been explored in computer vision systems that use scene context in the task of object identification. The work described here extends this notion by defining *visual semantics*, a theory of systematically extracting picture-specific information from text accompanying a photograph. Specifically, this paper discusses the multi-stage processing of textual captions with the following objectives: (i) predicting which objects (implicitly or explicitly mentioned in the caption) are present in the picture and (ii) generating constraints useful in locating/identifying these objects. The implementation and use of a lexicon specifically designed for the integration of linguistic and visual information is discussed. Finally, the research described here has been successfully incorporated into *PICTION*, a caption-based face identification system.

Introduction

The general problem being investigated is that of establishing a correspondence between words and the visual depictions they evoke. This correspondence is in general not one-to-one, but for certain specialized domains it is possible to establish a direct correspondence between words and the pictorial elements being referenced by them (e.g. weather maps: the word 'pressure' in a caption implies the presence of isobars in the accompanying picture). (Jackendoff 1987) attempts to establish a correspondence between words and 3D models of objects, but the problem is handled primarily at the single-word level (nouns and verbs): this work does not extend to establishing a correspondence between a sentence/phrase and the complex scene it may evoke.

In the present research, we focus on captioned pictures. Specifically, we address the problems of (i) identifying useful information in the text and (ii) extracting and representing this information so it can be used to direct a computer vision system in the task of picture understanding.

In a computer vision system, "visual information" refers to knowledge about objects that is required to detect them in a scene. This includes descriptions of objects in terms of their components and the spatial constraints between them, as well as typical scene information that relates objects in a common context. Visual information is generally represented statically, limiting the range of contexts in which it is applicable. An example is the modeling of a typical neighborhood scene comprised of streets, houses, trees, etc. (Weymouth 1986). Visual semantics plays a key role in allowing scene descriptions to be *dynamically constructed* from descriptive text. These scene descriptions can then be used by a vision system to guide knowledge-based interpretation of the associated picture.

Captions associated with two-dimensional images represent a domain that imposes a reference point on the visual image evoked by a phrase. For example, the phrase "President Clinton greets Vice President Gore" suggests Clinton and Gore are facing each other: their faces are expected to be in profile in the picture. We present a new *visual semantics* for this domain. It includes the following elements, all of which are described in this paper:

- A lexicon for integrating linguistic and visual information.

- The representation of visual information as a set of constraints that can be applied to the picture. (Strat & Fischler 1991) discusses the use of context in visual processing but does not cover the generation of constraints.

- A systematic procedure for processing a caption to generate visual constraints.

A system, *PICTION*, based on visual semantics is described. It uses information obtained from a news-

---

*This work was supported in part by a grant from ARPA (ARPA 93-F148900-000)

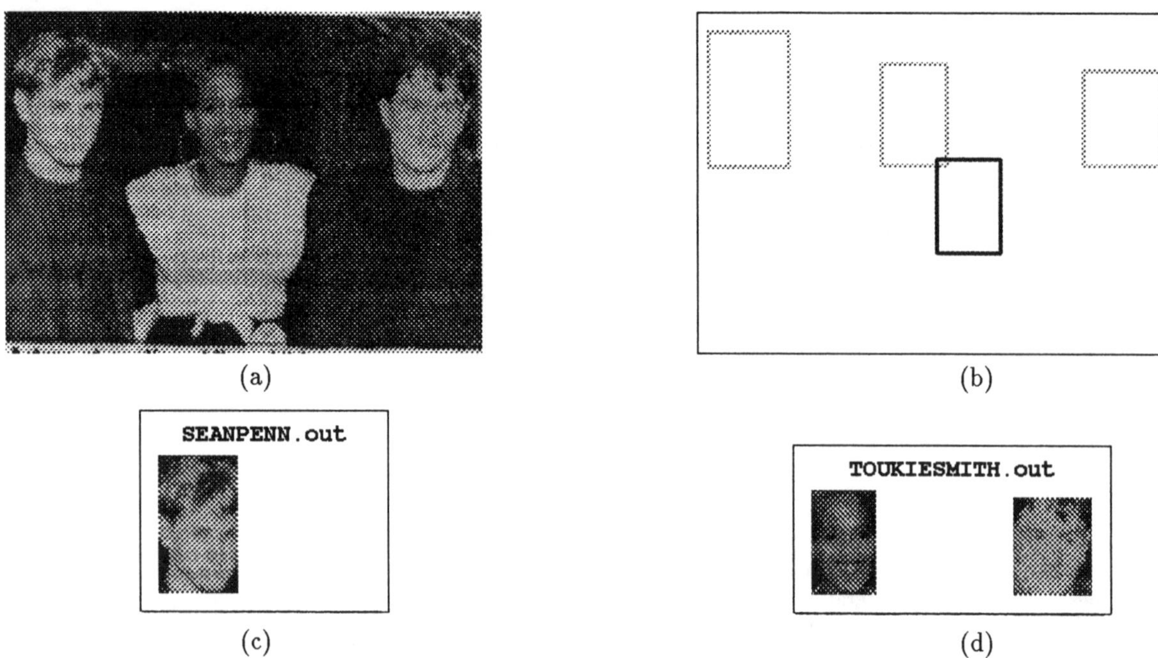

(a)

(c)

(b)

(d)

Figure 1: (a) photograph with caption "Actors Sean Penn, left, and Robert DeNiro pose with Toukie Smith, sister of the late fashion designer Willi Smith, at a New York celebrity auction Sunday in memory of Smith" (*The Buffalo News*, Feb. 27, 1989); (b) output of face locator; (c,d) output of *PICTION*.

paper caption to label faces in the accompanying photograph.

This research is most relevant in the context of document image understanding. Pictures with captions are ubiquitous in documents, newspapers and magazines. The information contained in both pictures and captions enhances overall understanding of the accompanying text, and often contributes additional information not specifically contained in the text. This information could subsequently be incorporated into an integrated text and picture database that permits *content-based retrieval*.

PICTION: A Caption-based Face Identification System

We refer to a caption and its associated picture in a newspaper as a *communicative unit*. Given a text file corresponding to a newspaper caption and a digitized version of the associated photograph, *PICTION* (Srihari 1994; 1991) is able to locate, label, and give information about objects referred to in the communicative unit. *PICTION* was initially tested on a database of 50 pictures. It successfully and uniquely identified faces in 62% of the cases, and achieved partial success on an addition 11% of the pictures.

PICTION provides a computationally less expensive alternative to traditional methods of face recognition. These methods employ model-matching techniques: only people for whom pre-stored face models exist can be identified. In *PICTION* faces are identified based solely on visual information conveyed by accompanying text. A key component of *PICTION* is the face locator, which locates (but cannot recognize) human faces in photographs.

Figure 1 is an example of a digitized newspaper photograph and accompanying caption that the system successfully processes. The male/female filter is not able to distinguish between Toukie Smith and Robert DeNiro, leading to multiple possible bindings. Sean Penn is identified correctly based on spatial constraints.

Figure 2 shows the overall control structure of *PICTION*. The three main components of *PICTION*'s architecture are (i) a natural-language processing (NLP) module, (ii) an image understanding (IU) module, and (iii) a language-image interface (LII). The NLP and IU modules interact through the LII which maintains the long-term knowledge base (LTM). *PICTION* runs on a Sun Sparcstation. It has been implemented primarily in LOOM(ISX 1991), an environment for constructing knowledge based systems, with a LISP interface to visual routines written in C.

The NLP module (illustrated in Figure 2) is divided into three stages: syntactic parsing, partial semantic interpretation (PSI) and caption based constraint generation (CBCG). The input to the NLP Module is the original newspaper caption; the output is a set of visual constraints. The LII module converts the visual information into a series of directives for the IU module

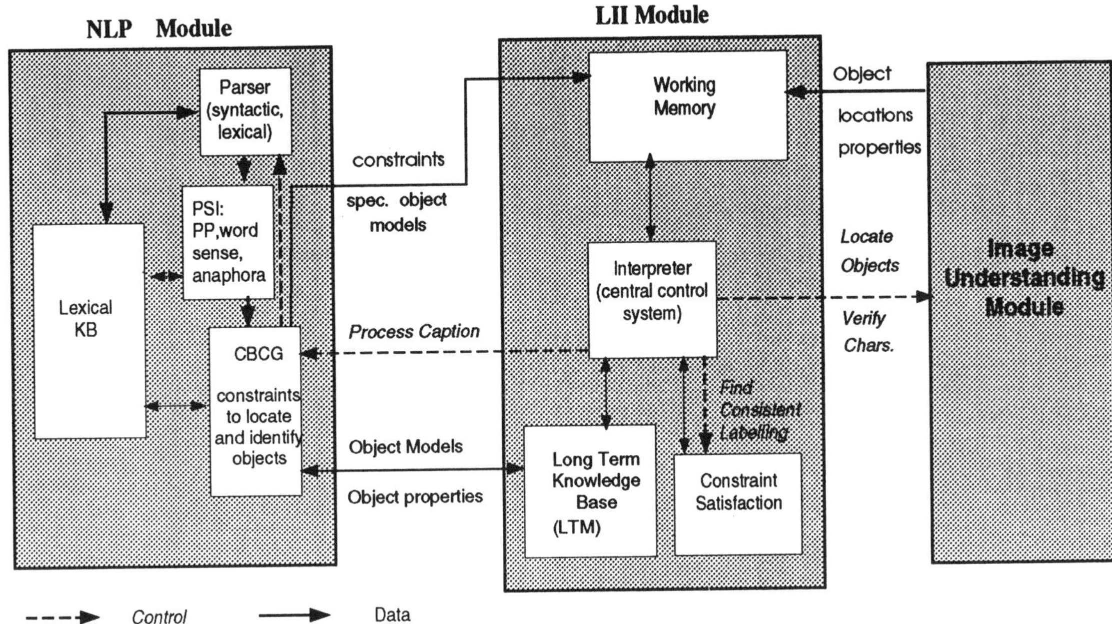

Figure 2: *PICTION* System Overview

which is then called on to interpret the picture. The IU module has several features which enable it to be guided by the LII, including: constrained search, ability to characterize objects, crude and refined object-location procedures, ability to change parameters and repeat actions, output compatibility with intermediate representation, and the ability to perform bottom-up interpretation when necessary. Information is consolidated in the LII by satisfying various types of constraints. This may require repeated calls to the IU module.

The remainder of this paper focuses on the NLP module, namely, the processing of the caption.

Lexical Database

PICTION uses a broad coverage syntactic/semantic lexical database which has been constructed from the following sources: (i) Longman Dictionary of Contemporary English (LDOCE), (ii) Oxford Advanced Learner's Dictionary (OALD), (iii) WordNet (Beckwith *et al.* 1991) (iv) name lists [1] and (v) manual augmentation (ontological information and visual semantics). This is similar to work done on the Penman Project at ISI (Knight & Luk 1994).

A LOOM knowledge base instance is constructed for each word in the lexicon. Name instances contain information on gender; word instances contain syntactic and semantic information from LDOCE (including subject field codes, semantic restrictions and verb subcategorization), morphological information from OALD and pointers to concepts representing WordNet

---

[1] These lists were obtained from the Consortium for Lexical Research at New Mexico State University.

synsets. WordNet synsets are represented as LOOM concepts organized in a hierarchy that mirrors Word-Net. Synset concepts contain part-of, is-part and verb classification information from WordNet. Visual and procedural semantic properties have been added manually to a subset of the concepts.

Our approach uses and extends the *Naive Semantics* (Dahlgren 1988) model (a theory of associating commonsense knowledge with words). An upper level ontology that is based on *Naive Semantics* and extends the WordNet hierarchy is incorporated into the lexicon.

It is necessary to represent fixed, visual properties of objects, such as size and color, as well as procedural information for certain words and phrases. For example, a recent caption identified one of the people in the corresponding photograph as "the person wearing the hat". This should generate a call to an object finder with the location "above head", and the scale and shape properties of the object (hat).

|HAT| is the name of the lexical instance for the word "hat" (Figure 3). It contains information from the LDOCE and a pointer to the corresponding WordNet synset concept. "WNN0206338" represents information from WordNet. Synonyms for hat include "chapeau" and "lid"; "WNN02066195" is the superconcept of "hat". The "scale", "shape" and "function" slots have been manually instantiated and are used to generate visual information. Procedural information stored with the "wear" synset specifies that if the event "wear" is associated with "hat", and the subject of "wear" is a human, a typical location for hat is on the head of the associated person. The CBCG uses this information to generate a locative constraint (de-

```
(tellm (:about |HAT|
 :is-primitive LDOCEconcept
  (WNsynset WNN0206338)
  (noun-part LD0030091)))

(defconcept WNN0206338
 :is-primitive WNN02066195
 :annotations
  ((word-list (hat chapeau lid))
   (scale s2)
   ($semantic-feature $clothing)
   (has-part (brim crown hatband))
   (shape
     (procedure
       (find-shape (crown,cylinder,hollow))
       (find-shape (brim,disc))
       (top-of(crown,brim)))))
   (function
     (wear(E,noun,Y) & human(Y)
      & typ-location(E,noun,
        procedure(locate-in-vicinity
          (noun,top-of(locate-part(head(Y))))))))))
```

Figure 3: Partial lexicon generation code for the word "hat"

scribed later) which is subsequently used by the LII and the vision module to identify the person wearing the hat.

Visual Hierarchies

We have defined visual hierarchies in terms of *visual superconcepts* which reflect type (man-made, natural), shape, texture properties, boundary properties etc. of an object. New links (*visual-is-a, visual-part-of*) have been added between existing WordNet synsets (representing concrete objects) and these superconcepts. Specialized attributes such as size, color, expected lo-

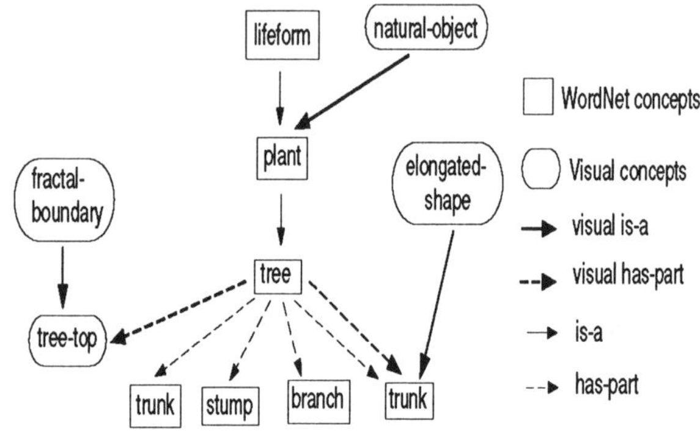

Figure 4: Visual hierarchy superimposed on WordNet concept hierarchy.

cation, etc. are added at the synset level. This visual information allows recognition tools (such as segmentation tools, edge detectors, surface detectors) and specialized object detectors for certain common object

classes (e.g., human face, tree, building, car) to be appropriately invoked. [2]

There are many objects for which it is difficult to construct detailed shape descriptions. In these cases it is sufficient to state some of their properties such as natural/man-made, boundary description, etc. Identification of these objects is based on a *blob* theory of object recognition: using constraints that specify size, expected location and a few object properties, the object can be roughly located, which is sufficient for our purposes.

For example, consider a picture of a man holding a trophy accompanied by the caption "Thomas Smith holding the trophy he won at ...". To identify the trophy, the system would first find the face of Thomas Smith, then search in the appropriate vicinity for an object exhibiting the required properties (man-made, small-medium size, etc.).

Our representation allows objects to be modeled at various resolutions. For example, at the most general level, a tree is a natural object with a fractal boundary. A more detailed visual model of tree defines the visual parts of a tree as well as the spatial relationships between these parts. These parts are classified according to the chosen set of visual superconcepts. At the most specific level, the description of a tree includes a specialized recognition module for trees.

The has-part information in visual object models may differ from the has-part information used in WordNet for the following reasons: (i) the has-part information in WordNet may be too fine-grained to be exploited by a vision system (e.g., shoes can have laces), and (ii) the names of the parts may differ (e.g., the WordNet entry for 'tree' includes crown, trunk, branches and stump, however the visual description for tree will have a treetop and a trunk). This is illustrated in Figure 4.

A study in human cognition regarding the task of identifying objects reveals that there is justification for having different abstractions for words and pictures. (Linde 1982) postulates the existence of two separate semantic-memory representations. (Jolicoeur, Gluck, & Kosslyn 1984) states that both words and pictures may use the same semantic-memory representation; they differ however in the *entry point*, namely the particular level of abstraction in the hierarchy at which the association is made.

Parsing

Pre-Processing Input

There are two objectives to this phase. The first is the elimination of *directive* phrases such as "left-of", "front row, left to right", etc. Directive phrases are associated with appropriate noun phrases and passed directly to

---

[2]According to (Biederman 1988), there are about 3000 common entry-level objects which the human perceptual system can detect.

the CBCG for further processing. The second objective of pre-processing is the detection and classification of proper noun sequences, which frequently contain unknown words. In this example from *The Buffalo News*, the proper noun sequences are bracketed:

```
[Vladimir Horowitz] at [Steinway and Sons],
[New York],...
```

"Vladimir Horowitz" is classified as a name, "Steinway and Sons" as an organization name and "New York" as a geographic location.

A hidden Markov model, trained on a portion of the Penn Treebank corpus, is used to detect proper noun sequences. We are currently able to detect proper noun sequences with about 90% accuracy. Proper noun lists containing appropriate classification information (gender, location, organization, etc.) [3] and heuristic rules (involving typical suffixes such as "Inc.") are employed in the categorization of proper nouns. Correct classification of proper noun sequences still poses a significant challenge (Mani *et al.* 1993).

LFG Parser and Partial Semantic Interpretation

An LFG which covers basic features of English grammar has been compiled into an LR parsing table. We employ an efficient LR parser augmented by pseudo/full unification packages (Tomita 1987). Certain semantic features (e.g., animate/inanimate; features associated with proper nouns) are incorporated into the output structure of the parser. This semantic information is obtained solely through lexicon lookup and is used to help disambiguate among multiple syntactic structures output by the parser. We are experimenting with statistical techniques for handling prepositional phrase and word sense disambiguation. Anaphoric references are resolved by the use of weights assigned to various referents depending on their role in the sentence.

Caption-based Constraint Generator (CBCG)

Input to the CBCG is the disambiguated parse from the PSI stage; output is a set of visual constraints to be used by the IU module. The CBCG makes use of the LTM in the LII for retrieval of information about well-known people, as well as the lexicon, for assigning visual semantics to the parse.

Constraint Types

Using visual information derived from text, *PICTION* hypothesizes a set of objects expected to be in the picture and constraints on those objects. Constraints are divided into four types:

- **Spatial Constraints** are geometric or topological constraints, such as left-of, above, inside, etc. They

---

[3] These lists were obtained from the Consortium for Lexical Research at New Mexico State University.

can be binary or n-ary, and describe inter-object relationships. Complex spatial constraints such as "surround" are broken down into a set of constraints based on spatial primitives.

- **Locative constraints** express information about the location of objects in the picture with respect to a particular frame of reference. The information conveyed is procedural in nature, for example, if you are told there is a chair in the corner, it results in the following high-level procedure construct: $loc\_in\_vicin(chair, region(corner(entire\_image)))$.

- **Characteristic Constraints** are unary constraints which describe properties of objects. Examples include gender and hair color.

- **Contextual Constraints** are those which describe the setting of the picture, and the objects which are expected to appear. Examples include the people present (mentioned in the caption), whether it is an outdoor scene, and general scene context (apartment, airport, etc).

Some visual constraints are expressed explicitly as assertions, for example $left\_of(person\_a\ person\_b)$. Locative and characteristic constraints are implicit in the object model. Contextual constraints consist of the instantiated objects and an asserted general scene context.

Consider the photograph and caption of Figure 1. Some of the constraints output by the CBCG for this example are:

```
SPATIAL: left_of(Sean Penn ,Robert DeNiro)
         adjacent(Robert DeNiro,Toukie Smith)
CHARACT: has_prop(name:Sean Penn;gender:male)
         has_prop(name:Toukie Smith;gender:female)
```

"Adjacent" is asserted as the default spatial constraint.

Automatic Generation of Visual Constraints

The CBCG has been written as a rule-based system which uses LOOM concepts to drive the semantic "parsing". LOOM methods and rules are invoked when particular concepts are instantiated.

There are three main categories of rules.

- **Word-based:**
  Spatial and characteristic constraints are frequently indicated by single words. Examples include left, right, above and below, as well as characteristics such as hair color and titles like President.

- **Phrase-based:**
  Locative and characteristic constraints are often indicated by directive phrases. Examples include "between the two buildings" and "wearing the striped shirt".

- **Sentence-based:**
  Contextual constraints can generally be inferred at the sentence level, taking into account the various

objects mentioned and their relations and properties. An example of this is the "SVOPP" rule which states that if the sentence is of the form subject-verb-object-prepositional_phrase, and both the subject and object represent humans, and the PP represents a time and/or location, then propose that both the subject and the object are in the picture.

The top-level rules are based on syntactic structure and attempt to predict which people (or objects) are in the picture. Verifying the antecedents of these rules (e.g., is the person deceased?) causes other rules to be fired. The final action is to generate identifying information for every person/object predicted to be in the picture.

Consider the caption "Actors Sean Penn, left, and Robert DeNiro pose with Toukie Smith, sister of the late fashion designer Willi Smith, at a New York celebrity auction Sunday". All three people mentioned will be predicted to be in the picture as the sentence has the form <subject-list> <verb> <object> <adverbial place> <adverbial time>.

A concept and the associated production rule used to generate the contextual constraint that the picture is indoors are as follows:

```
(defproduction is-indoor
 :when (:detects (inside ?parse ?cg))
 :perform (tell (:about ?cg (location 'indoor))))
(defconcept inside
 :is (:predicate (?parse)
   (let ((?flat (explode ?parse))
         (semfeats nil))
     (dolist (?x ?flat)
        (push (get-sem-features ?x) ?semfeats))
     (or (memberp '$indoor ?semfeats)
         (and (memberp '$social-event $semfeats)
           (not (memberp $outdoor ?semfeats)))))))
```

The photograph in Figure 1 is predicted to be of an indoor scene since "auction" has the semantic feature $social-event stored in the lexicon, and there is nothing mentioned which has the semantic feature of being outdoors. The fact that Toukie Smith is female is inferred by the presence of the word "sister" in the directional phrase associated with her name. The spatial constraints shown in the previous section are generated when spatial constraint rules are fired.

Summary

This paper has presented a new theory of visual semantics that concerns the use of descriptive text in the interpretation of accompanying photographs. Although the examples used are from captioned newspaper photographs, and the application is knowledge-based vision, this work can be extended to any domain where both language and pictures are used to communicate information. A highlight of this work is the development of a lexicon that includes visual hierarchies, as well as a systematic procedure for generating visual constraints from text accompanying a picture.

References

Beckwith, R.; Fellbaum, C.; Gross, D.; and Miller, G. A. 1991. WordNet: A Lexical Database Organized on Psycholinguistic Principles. In *Lexicons: Using On-line Resources to Build a Lexicon*. Lawrence Erlbaum.

Biederman, I. 1988. Aspects and extensions of a theory of human image understanding. In Pylyshyn, Z., ed., *Computational Processes in Human Vision: An interdisciplinary perspective*. Ablex.

Dahlgren, K. 1988. *Naive Semantics for Natural Language Understanding*. Boston: Kluwer Academic Press.

ISX Corporation. 1991. *LOOM Users Guide, Version 1.4*.

Jackendoff, R. 1987. On Beyond Zebra: The Relation of Linguistic and Visual Information. *Cognition* 26(2):89–114.

Jolicoeur, P.; Gluck, M. A.; and Kosslyn, S. M. 1984. Pictures and Names: Making the Connection. *Cognitive Psychology* 16:243–275.

Knight, K., and Luk, S. 1994. Building a Large Scale Knowledge Base for Machine Translation. Forthcoming. In *Proceedings of AAAI-94*.

Linde, D. J. 1982. Picture-word differences in decision latency. *Journal of Experimental Psychology: Learning, Memory and Cognition* 8:584–598.

Mani, I.; MacMillan, T. R.; Luperfoy, S.; Lusher, E. P.; and Laskowski, S. J. 1993. Identifying Unknown Proper Names in Newswire Text. In *Proceedings of the Workshop on Acquisition of Lexical Knowledge from Text*, 44–54.

Srihari, R. K. 1991. PICTION: A System that Uses Captions to Label Human Faces in Newspaper Photographs. In *Proceedings of AAAI-91*, 80–85. AAAI Press.

Srihari, R. K. 1994. Use of Collateral Text in Understanding Photos. Forthcoming. *Artificial Intelligence Review*. Special Issue on Integration of NLP and Vision.

Strat, T. M., and Fischler, M. A. 1991. Context-Based Vision: Recognizing Objects Using Information from Both 2-D and 3-D Imagery. *IEEE PAMI* 13(10):1050–1065.

Tomita, M. 1987. An Efficient Augmented-Context-Free Parsing Algorithm. *Computational Linguistics* 13(1-2):31–46.

Weymouth, T. 1986. *Using Object Descriptions in a Schema Network for Machine Vision*. Ph.D. Dissertation, University of Masschussetts at Amherst.

A Plan-Based Model for Response Generation in Collaborative Task-Oriented Dialogues[*]

Jennifer Chu-Carroll
Department of Computer Science
University of Delaware
Newark, DE 19716, USA
E-mail: jchu@cis.udel.edu

Sandra Carberry
Department of Computer Science
University of Delaware
Newark, DE 19716, USA
Visitor: Institute for Research in Cognitive Science
University of Pennsylvania
E-mail: carberry@cis.udel.edu

Abstract

This paper presents a plan-based architecture for response generation in collaborative consultation dialogues, with emphasis on cases in which the system (consultant) and user (executing agent) disagree. Our work contributes to an overall system for collaborative problem-solving by providing a plan-based framework that captures the *Propose-Evaluate-Modify* cycle of collaboration, and by allowing the system to initiate subdialogues to negotiate proposed additions to the shared plan and to provide support for its claims. In addition, our system handles in a unified manner the negotiation of proposed domain actions, proposed problem-solving actions, and beliefs proposed by discourse actions. Furthermore, it captures cooperative responses within the collaborative framework and accounts for why questions are sometimes never answered.

Introduction

In collaborative expert-consultation dialogues, two participants (executing agent and consultant) work together to construct a plan for achieving the executing agent's domain goal. The executing agent and the consultant bring to the plan construction task different knowledge about the domain and the desirable characteristics of the resulting domain plan. For example, the consultant presumably has more extensive and accurate domain knowledge than does the executing agent, but the executing agent has knowledge about his particular circumstances, intentions, and preferences that are either restrictions on or potential influencers (Bratman 1990) of the domain plan being constructed. In agreeing to collaborate on constructing the domain plan, the consultant assumes a stake in the quality of the resultant plan and in how the agents go about constructing it. For example, a consultant in a collaborative interaction must help the executing agent find the best strategy for constructing the domain plan, may initiate additions to the domain plan, and must negotiate with the executing agent when the latter's suggestions are not accepted (rather than merely agreeing to what the executing agent wants to do). Thus a collaborator is more than a cooperative respondent.

In this paper, we present a plan-based architecture for response generation in collaborative consultation dialogues,

with emphasis on cases in which the system and the user disagree. The model treats utterances as proposals open for negotiation and only incorporates a proposal into the shared plan under construction if both agents believe the proposal to be appropriate. If the system does not accept a user proposal, the system attempts to modify it, and natural language utterances are generated as a part of this process. Since the system's utterances are also treated as proposals, a recursive negotiation process can ensue. This response generation architecture has been implemented in a prototype system for a university advisement domain.

Modeling Collaboration

In a collaborative planning process, conflicts in agents' beliefs must be resolved as soon as they arise in order to prevent the agents from constructing different plans. Hence, once a set of actions is proposed by an agent, the other agent must first evaluate the proposal based on his own private beliefs (Allen 1991) and determine whether or not to accept the proposal. If an agent detects any conflict which leads him to reject the proposal, he should attempt to modify the proposal to a form that will be accepted by both agents —to do otherwise is to fail in his responsibilities as a participant in collaborative problem-solving. Thus, we capture collaboration in a *Propose-Evaluate-Modify* cycle. This theory views the collaborative planning process as a sequence of proposals, evaluations, and modifications, which may result in a fully constructed shared plan agreed upon by both agents. Notice that this model is essentially a recursive one: the *Modify* action in itself contains a full collaborative process — an agent's proposal of a modification, the other agent's evaluation of the proposal, and potential modification to the modification!

We capture this theory in a plan-based system for response generation in collaborative task-oriented interactions. We assume that the current status of the interaction is represented by a tripartite dialogue model (Lambert & Carberry 1991) that captures intentions on three levels: domain, problem-solving, and discourse. The domain level contains the domain plan being constructed for later execution. The problem-solving level contains the agents' intentions about how to construct the domain plan, and the discourse level contains the communicative plan initiated to further their

---

[*]This material is based upon work supported by the National Science Foundation under Grant No. IRI-9122026.

joint problem-solving intentions.

Each utterance by a participant constitutes a *proposal* intended to affect the shared model of domain, problem-solving, and discourse intentions. For example, relating a user's query such as *Who is teaching AI?* to an existing tripartite model might require inferring a chain of domain actions that are not already part of the plan, including *Take-Course(User,AI)*. These inferred actions explain *why* the user asked the question and are actions that the user is implicitly proposing be added to the plan. In order to capture the notion of *proposals* vs. *shared plans* in a collaborative planning process, we separate the dialogue model into an *existing model*, which consists of a shared plan agreed upon by both agents, and the *proposed additions*, which contain newly inferred actions. Furthermore, we augment Lambert's plan recognition algorithm (Lambert & Carberry 1992) with a simplified version of Eller's relaxation algorithm (Eller & Carberry 1992) to recognize ill-formed plans.

We adopt a plan-based mechanism because it is general and easily extendable, allows the same declarative knowledge about collaborative problem-solving to be used both in generation and understanding, and allows the recursive nature of our theory to be represented by recursive meta-plans. This paper focuses on one component of our model, the **arbitrator**, which performs the *Evaluate* and *Modify* actions in the *Propose-Evaluate-Modify* cycle of collaboration.

The Arbitration Process

A *proposal* consists of a chain of actions for addition to the shared plan. The **arbitrator** evaluates a proposal and determines whether or not to accept it, and if not, modifies the original proposal to a form that will potentially be accepted by both agents. The **arbitrator** has two subcomponents, the **evaluator** and the **modifier**, and has access to a library of generic recipes for performing actions[1].

The Evaluator

A collaborative agent, when presented a proposal, needs to decide whether or not he believes that the proposal will result in a valid plan and will produce a reasonably efficient way to achieve the high-level goal. Thus, the **evaluator** should check for two types of discrepancies in beliefs: one that causes the proposal to be viewed by the system as invalid (Pollack 1986), and one in which the system believes that a better alternative to the user's proposal exists (Joshi, Webber, & Weischedel 1984; van Beek 1987). Based on this evaluation, the system determines whether it should accept the user's proposal, causing the proposed actions to be incorporated into the existing model, or should reject the proposal, in which case a negotiation subdialogue will be initiated.

The processes for detecting conflicts and better alternatives start at the top-level proposed action, and are inter-

leaved because we intend for the system to address the highest-level action disagreed upon by the agents. This is because it is meaningless to suggest, for example, a better alternative to an action when one believes that its parent action is infeasible.

Detecting Conflicts About Plan Validity Pollack argues that a plan can fail because of an *infeasible action* or because the plan itself is *ill-formed* (Pollack 1986). An action is *infeasible* if it cannot be performed by its agent; thus, the **evaluator** performs a *feasibility* check by examining whether the applicability conditions of the action are satisfied and if its preconditions can be satisfied[2]. A plan is considered *ill-formed* if child actions do not contribute to their parent action as intended; hence, the evaluator performs a *well-formedness* check to examine, for each pair of parent-child actions in the proposal, whether the *contributes* relationship holds between them[3]. The well-formedness check is performed before the feasibility check since it is reasonable to check the relationship between an action and its parent before examining the action itself.

Detecting Sub-Optimal Solutions It is not sufficient for the system, as a collaborator, to accept or reject a proposal merely based on its validity. If the system knows of a substantially superior alternative to the proposal, but does not suggest it to the user, it cannot be said to have fulfilled its responsibility as a collaborative agent; hence the system must model user characteristics in order to best tailor its identification of sub-optimal plans to individual users. Our system maintains a user model that includes the user's *preferences*. A preference indicates, for a particular user, the preferred value of an attribute associated with an object and the strength of this preference. The preferences are represented in the form, prefers(_user, _attribute(_object, _value), _action, _strength), which indicates that _user has a _strength preference that the attribute _attribute of _object be _value when performing _action. For instance, *prefers(UserA, Difficulty(_course, easy), Take-Course, weak)* indicates that UserA has a weak preference for taking easy courses. A companion paper describes our mechanism for recognizing user preferences during the course of a dialogue (Elzer, Chu, & Carberry 1994).

Suppose that the **evaluator** must determine whether an action A_i (in a chain of proposed actions $A_1, \ldots, A_i, \ldots, A_n$) is the best way of performing its parent action A_{i+1}. We will limit our discussion to the situation

---

[1] A recipe (Pollack 1986) is a template for performing an action. It encodes the *preconditions* for an action, the *effects* of an action, the *subactions* comprising the body of an action, etc.

[2] Applicability conditions are conditions that must already be satisfied in order for an action to be reasonable to pursue, whereas an agent can try to achieve unsatisfied preconditions. Our evaluator considers a precondition satisfiable if there exists an action which achieves the precondition and whose applicability conditions are satisfied. Thus only a cursory evaluation of feasibility is pursued at this stage of the planning process, with further details considered as the plan is worked out in depth. This appears to reflect human interaction in naturally occuring dialogues.

[3] Much of the information needed for the feasibility and well-formedness checks will be provided by the plan-recognition system that identified the actions comprising the proposal.

in which there is only one generic action (such as *Take-Course*) that achieves A_{i+1}, but there are several possible instantiations of the parameters of the action (such as *Take-Course(UserA,CS601)* and *Take-Course(UserA,CS621)*).

The Ranking Advisor   The ranking advisor's task is to determine how best the parameters of an action can be instantiated, based on the user's preferences. For each object that can instantiate a parameter of an action (such as CS621 instantiating _course in *Take-Course(UserA,_course)*), the **evaluator** provides the ranking advisor with the values of its attributes (e.g., *Difficulty(CS621,difficult)*) and the user's preferences for the values of these attributes (e.g., *prefers(UserA, Difficulty(_course,moderate), Take-Course, weak)*).

Two factors should be considered when ranking the candidate instantiations: the *strength of the preference* and the *closeness of the match*. The strength of a preference[4] indicates the *weight* that should be assigned to the preference. The closeness of the match (*exact, strong, weak,* or *none*) measures how well the actual and the preferred values of an attribute match. It is measured based on the *distance* between the two values where the unit of measurement differs depending on the type of the attribute. For example, for attributes with discrete values (*difficulty* of a course can be *very-difficult, difficult, moderate, easy,* or *very-easy*), the match between *difficult* and *moderate* will be *strong*, while that between *difficult* and *easy* will be *weak*. The closeness of the match must be modeled in order to capture the fact that if the user prefers difficult courses, a moderate course will be considered preferable to an easy one, even though neither of them exactly satisfies the user's preference.

For each candidate instantiation, the ranking advisor assigns numerical values to the strength of the preferences for the relevant attributes and computes the closeness of each match. A weight is computed for each candidate instantiation by summing the products of corresponding terms of the strength of a preference and the closeness of a match. The instantiation with the highest weight is considered the *best* instantiation for the action under consideration. Thus, the selection strategy employed by our ranking advisor corresponds to an *additive model* of human decision-making (Reed 1982).

Example   We demonstrate the ranking advisor by showing how two different instantiations, CS601 and CS621, of the *Take-Course* action are ranked. Figure 1 shows the relevant domain knowledge and user model information.

The ranking advisor matches the user's preferences against the domain knowledge for each of CS601 and CS621. The attributes that will be taken into account are the ones for which the user has indicated preferences. For each attribute, the advisor records the *strength of the preference*

---

[4] We model six degrees each of positive and negative preferences based on the conversational circumstances and the semantic representation of the utterance used to express the preferences (Elzer, Chu, & Carberry 1994).

Domain Knowledge:
    Teaches(Smith,CS601)
    Meets-At(CS601,2-3:15pm)
    Difficulty(CS601,difficult)
    Workload(CS601,moderate)
    Offered(CS601)
    Content(CS601,{formal-languages, grammar})

    Teaches(Brown,CS621)
    Meets-At(CS621,8-9:15am)
    Difficulty(CS621,difficult)
    Workload(CS621,heavy)
    Offered(CS621)
    Content(CS621,{algorithm-design, complexity-theory})

User Model Information:
    Prefers(UserA, Meets-At(_course,10am-5pm),
        _action, very-strong)
    Prefers(UserA, Difficulty(_course,moderate),
        Take-Course, weak)
    Prefers(UserA, Workload(_course,heavy),
        Take-Course, low-moderate)
    Prefers(UserA, Content(_course,formal-languages),
        Take-Course,strong)

Figure 1: System's Knowledge and User Model Information

CS601	Preference-Strength		Match		
Meets-At	very-strong	6	exact	3	18
Difficulty	weak	2	strong	2	4
Workload	low-moderate	3	strong	2	6
Content	strong	5	exact	3	15
					43

CS621	Preference-Strength		Match		
Meets-At	very-strong	6	weak	1	6
Difficulty	weak	2	strong	2	4
Workload	low-moderate	3	exact	3	9
Content	strong	5	strong	2	10
					29

Table 1: The Strengths of Preferences and Matches

and the *closeness of the match* for each instantiation. For instance, in considering the attribute *workload*, the strength of the preference will be *low-moderate*, and the closeness of the match will be *strong* and *exact* for CS601 and CS621, respectively. Table 1 shows a summary of the strength of the preferences and the closeness of the matches for the relevant attributes for both instantiations. Numerical values are then assigned and used to calculate a final weight for each candidate. In this example, the normalized weight for CS601 is 43/48 and that for CS621 is 29/48; therefore, CS601 is considered a substantially better instantiation than CS621 for the *Take-Course* action for UserA.

The Modifier

The **modifier** is invoked when a proposal is rejected. Its task is to modify the proposal to a form that will potentially be accepted by both agents. The process is controlled by the *Modify-Proposal* action, which has four specializations: 1) *Correct-Node*, for when the proposal is infeasible, 2) *Correct-Relation*, for when the proposal is ill-formed, 3) *Improve-Action*, for when a better generic action is found, and 4) *Improve-Parameter*, for when a better instantiation of a parameter is found. Each specialization eventually decomposes into some primitive action which modifies the proposal. However, an agent will be considered uncooperative if he modifies a proposed shared plan without the collaborating agent's consent; thus, the four specializations share a common precondition — that the discrepancies in beliefs must be *squared away* (Joshi 1982) before any modification can take place. It is the attempt to satisfy this precondition that causes the system to generate natural language utterances to accomplish the change in the user's beliefs.

Figure 2 shows two problem-solving recipes, *Correct-Relation* and *Modify-Relation*, the latter being a subaction of the former. The applicability conditions of *Correct-Relation* indicate that it is applicable when the agents, _s1 and _s2, disagree on whether a particular relationship (such as *contributes*) holds between two actions (_node1 and _node2) in the proposal. The applicability condition and precondition of *Modify-Relation* show that the action can only be performed if both _s1 and _s2 believe that the relationship _rel does not hold between _node1 and _node2; in other words, the conflict between _s1 and _s2 must have been resolved. The attempt to satisfy this precondition causes the system to invoke discourse actions to modify the user's beliefs, which can be viewed as initiating a negotiation subdialogue to resolve a conflict. If the user accepts the system's beliefs, thus satisfying the precondition of *Modify-Relation*, the original dialogue model can be modified; however, if the user rejects the system's beliefs, he will invoke the *Modify-Proposal* action to revise the system's suggested modification of his original proposal.

In order to retain as much of the original proposal as possible when modifying a proposal, *Modify-Relation* has two specializations: *Remove-Node* and *Alter-Node*. The former is selected if the action itself is inappropriate, and will cause the action to be removed from the dialogue model. The latter is chosen if a parameter is inappropriately instantiated, in which case the action will remain in the dialogue model and the problematic parameter will be left uninstantiated.

Example of Correcting an Invalid Proposal

Suppose earlier dialogue suggests that the user has the goal of getting a Master's degree in CS (*Get-Masters(U,CS)*). Figure 3 illustrates the dialogue model that would result from the following utterances.

(1) U: I want to satisfy my seminar course requirement.

(2)   Who is teaching AI?

The evaluation process, which determines whether or not to accept the proposal, starts at the top-level proposed domain action, *Satisfy-Seminar-Course(U,CS)*. Suppose the system believes that *Satisfy-Seminar-Course(U,CS)* contributes to *Get-Masters(U,CS)*, that U can perform

Action:	*Correct-Relation(_s1, _s2, _proposed)*
Type:	Decomposition
Appl Cond:	believe(_s1, ¬holds(_rel,_node1,_node2))
	believe(_s2, holds(_rel,_node1,_node2))
Constraints:	error-in-plan(_relation, _proposed)
	name-of (_relation, _rel)
	parent-node(_relation, _node2)
	child-node(_relation, _node1)
Body:	Modify-Relation(_s1, _s2, _proposed,
	_rel, _node1, _node2)
	Insert-Correction(_s1, _s2, _proposed)
Effects:	modified(_proposed)
Goal:	well-formed(_proposed)

Action:	*Modify-Relation(_s1, _s2, _proposed,*
	_rel, _node1, _node2)
Type:	Specialization
Appl Cond:	believe(_s1, ¬holds(_rel,_node1,_node2))
Preconditions:	believe(_s2, ¬holds(_rel,_node1,_node2))
Body:	Remove-Node(_s1, _s2, _proposed, _node1)
	Alter-Node(_s1, _s2, _proposed, _node1)
Effects:	modified(_proposed)
Goal:	modified(_proposed)

Figure 2: *Correct-Relation* and *Modify-Relation* Recipes

Satisfy-Seminar-Course(U,CS), and that there is no better alternative to the instantiation of *Satisfy-Seminar-Course*. The **evaluator** then checks its child action *Take-Course(U,AI)*. The system's recipe library indicates that *Take-Course(U,AI)* does not contribute to *Satisfy-Seminar-Course(U,CS)*, since it believes that AI is *not* a seminar course, causing the proposal to be rejected.

The **modifier** performs the *Modify-Proposal* action, which selects as its specialization *Correct-Relation*, because the rejected proposal is ill-formed. Figure 4 shows the arbitration process and how *Correct-Relation* is expanded. Notice that the arbitration process (the problem-solving level in Figure 4) operates on the entire dialogue model in Figure 3, and therefore is represented as meta-level problem-solving actions. In order to satisfy the precondition of *Modify-Relation*, the system invokes the discourse action *Inform* as an attempt to change the user's belief (in this case, to achieve *believe(U,¬holds(contributes, Take-Course(U,AI), Satisfy-Seminar-Course(U,CS))))*. The *Inform* action further decomposes into two actions, one which tells the user of the belief, and one which provides support for the claim. This process will generate the following two utterances:

(3) S: Taking AI does not contribute to satisfying the seminar course requirement.

(4)   AI is not a seminar course.

If the user accepts the system's utterances, thus satisfying the precondition that the conflict be resolved, *Modify-Relation* can be performed and changes made to the dialogue model. In this example, the proposal is rejected due to an inappropriate instantiation of the parameter _course; thus *Modify-Relation* will select *Alter-Node* as a specialization to replace all instances of AI in the dialogue model with

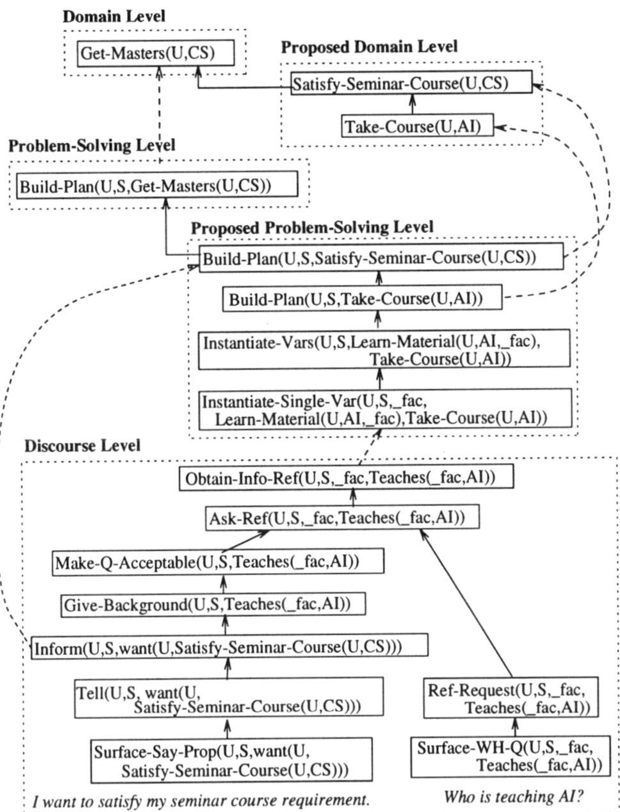

Figure 3: The Dialogue Model for Utterances (1)-(2)

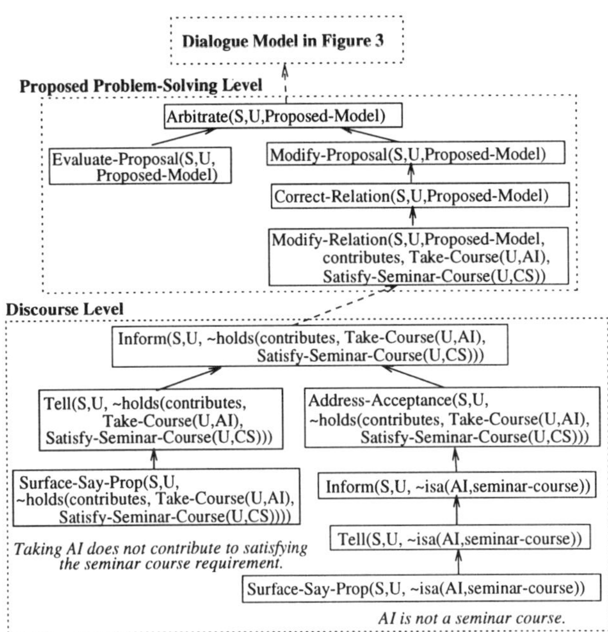

Figure 4: Responding to Implicitly-Conveyed Conflicts

a variable. This variable can be reinstantiated by *Insert-Correction*, the second subaction of *Correct-Relation*.

Assuming that the system and the user encounter no further conflict in reinstantiating the variable, the arbitration process at the meta-level is completed and the original dialogue is returned to. The proposed additions now consist of actions agreed upon by both agents and will therefore be incorporated into the existing model. Notice that our model separates the negotiation subdialogue (captured at the meta level) from the original dialogue while allowing the same plan-based mechanism to be used at both levels. It also accounts for why the user's original question about the instructor of AI is never answered —a conflict was detected that made the question superfluous. Thus certain situations in which questions fail to be answered can be accounted for by the collaborative process rather than being viewed as a violation of cooperative behaviour.

Example of Suggesting Better Alternatives

Consider the following utterances, whose dialogue model has the same structure as that for utterances (1) and (2) (Figure 3).

(5) U: I want to satisfy my theory course requirement.

(6)   Who is teaching CS621?

For space reasons, we skip ahead in the evaluation process to the optimality check for *Take-Course(U,CS621)*. There are two instantiations of _course that satisfy the constraints specified in the recipe for *Satisfy-Theory-Course*: CS601 and CS621. These are ranked by the ranking advisor based on the user's preferences, summarized in Table 1, which suggests that CS601 is a substantially better alternative to CS621. Thus, *Improve-Parameter* is selected as a specialization of *Modify-Proposal*. Similar to the previous example, the *Inform* discourse action will be invoked as an attempt to resolve the discrepancies in beliefs between the two agents, which would lead to the generation of the following utterances:

(7) S: CS601 is a better alternative than CS621.

(8)   CS601 meets at 2pm and involves formal languages and grammar.

Notice that utterance (8) provides supporting evidence for the claim in (7), and is obtained by comparing the sets of information used by the ranking advisor (Table 1) and selecting the features that contribute most to making CS601 preferable to CS621.

The Belief Level

We showed how our **arbitrator** detects and resolves conflicts at the domain level. Our goal, however, is to develop a mechanism that can handle negotiations at the domain, problem-solving, and discourse levels in a uniform fashion. The process can be successfully applied to the problem-solving level because both the domain and problem-solving levels represent actions that the agents propose to do (at a later point in time for the domain level and at the current time for the problem-solving level); however, the discourse level actions are actions that are *currently being executed*, instead of *proposed for execution*. This causes problems

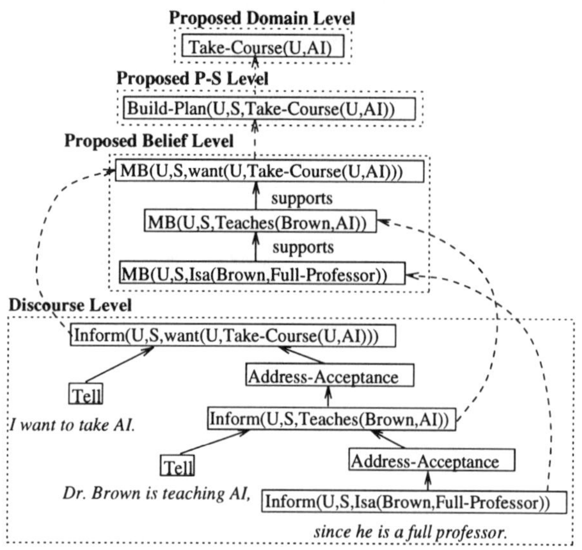

Figure 5: The Four-Level Model for Utterances (9)-(11)

for the modification process, as illustrated by the following example.

(9) U: I want to take AI.
(10)   Dr. Brown is teaching AI,
(11)   since he is a full professor.

Utterance (11) provides support for (10), which supports (9). However, if the system believes that whether one is a full professor has no relation to whether or not he teaches AI, the system and the user have a conflict as to whether (11) supports (10). Problems will arise if the system convinces the user that Dr. Brown teaches AI because that is his area of specialty, not because he is a full professor, and attempts to modify the dialogue model by replacing the *Inform* action that represents (11) with one that conveys *specializes(Brown,AI)*. This modification is inappropriate because it indicates that the user informed the system that Dr. Brown specializes in AI, which never happened in the first place. Therefore, we argue that instead of applying the arbitration process to the discourse level, it should be applied to the beliefs proposed by the discourse actions.

In order to preserve the representation of the discourse level, and to handle the kind of conflict shown in the previous example, we expand the dialogue model to include a *belief* level. The belief level captures domain-related beliefs proposed by discourse actions as well as the relationship amongst them. For instance, an *Inform* action proposes a mutual belief (MB) of a proposition and an *Obtain-Info-Ref* action proposes that both agents come to know the referent (Mknowref) of a parameter. Thus, information captured at the belief level consists not of actions, as in the other three levels, but of beliefs that are to be achieved, and belief relationships, such as *support*, *attack*, etc.

Discourse Level Example Revisited   Figure 5 outlines the dialogue model for utterances (9)-(11) with the addi-

tional belief level. Note that each *Inform* action at the discourse level proposes a mutual belief, and that *supports* relationships (inferred from *Address-Acceptance*) are proposed between the mutual beliefs.

The evaluation process starts at the proposed domain level. Suppose that the system believes that both *Take-Course(U,AI)* and *Build-Plan(U,S,Take-Course(U,AI))* can be performed. However, an examination of the proposed belief level causes the proposal to be rejected because the system does not believe that Dr. Brown being a full professor supports the fact that he teaches AI. Thus, *Correct-Relation* is selected as the specialization of *Modify-Proposal* in order to resolve the conflict regarding this *supports* relationship. Again in order to satisfy the precondition of modifying the proposal, the system invokes the *Inform* action which would generate the following utterance:

(12) S: Dr. Brown being a full professor does not provide support for him teaching AI.

Thus, with the addition of the belief level, the **arbitrator** is able to capture the process of evaluating and modifying proposals in a uniform fashion at the domain, problem-solving, and belief levels. An additional advantage of the belief level is that it captures the beliefs conveyed by the discourse level, instead of *how* they are conveyed (by an *Inform* action, by expressing doubt, etc.).

Related Work

Allen (1991) proposed different plan modalities that capture the shared and individual beliefs during collaboration, and Grosz, Sidner and Lochbaum (Grosz & Sidner 1990; Lochbaum 1991) proposed a SharedPlan model for capturing intentions during a collaborative process. However, they do not address response generation during collaboration. Litman and Allen (1987) used discourse meta-plans to handle correction subdialogues. However, their Correct-Plan only addressed cases in which an agent adds a repair step to a pre-existing plan that does not execute as expected. Thus their meta-plans do not handle correction of proposed additions to the dialogue model, since this generally does not involve adding a step to the proposal. Furthermore, they were only concerned with understanding utterances, not with generating appropriate responses. Heeman and Hirst (1992) and Edmonds (1993) use meta-plans to account for collaboration, but their mechanisms are limited to understanding and generating referring expressions. Although Heeman is extending his model to account for collaboration in task-oriented dialogues (Heeman 1993), his extension is limited to the recognition of actions in such dialogues. Guinn and Biermann (1993) developed a model of collaborative problem-solving which attempts to resolve conflicts between agents regarding the best path for achieving a goal. However, their work has concentrated on situations in which the user is trying to execute a task under the system's guidance rather than those where the system and user are collaboratively developing a plan for the user to execute at a later point in time.

Researchers have utilized plan-based mechanisms to generate natural language responses, including explanations (Moore & Paris 1993; Maybury 1992; Cawsey 1993). However, they only handle cases in which the user fails to understand the system, instead of cases in which the user *disagrees* with the system. Maybury (1993) developed plan operators for persuasive utterances, but does not provide a framework for negotiation of conflicting views.

In suggesting better alternatives, our system differs from van Beek's (1987) in a number of ways. The most significant are that our system dynamically recognizes user preferences (Elzer, Chu, & Carberry 1994), takes into account both the strength of the preferences and the closeness of the matches in ranking instantiations, and captures the response generation process in an overall collaborative framework that can negotiate proposals with the user.

Conclusions and Future Work

This paper has presented a plan-based system that captures collaborative response generation in a *Propose-Evaluate-Modify* cycle. Our system can initiate subdialogues to negotiate implicitly proposed additions to the shared plan, can appropriately respond to user queries that are motivated by ill-formed or suboptimal solutions, and handles in a unified manner the negotiation of proposed domain actions, proposed problem-solving actions, and beliefs proposed by discourse actions. In addition, our system captures cooperative responses within an overall collaborative framework that allows for negotiation and accounts for why questions are sometimes never answered (even in the most cooperative of environments).

This response generation architecture has been implemented in a prototype system for a university advisement domain. The system is presented with the existing dialogue model and the actions proposed by the user's new utterances. It then produces as output the logical form for the appropriate collaborative system response. In the future, we will extend our system to include various argumentation strategies (Sycara 1989; Quilici 1991; Maybury 1993) for supporting its claims.

Acknowledgments

The authors would like to thank Stephanie Elzer for her comments on earlier drafts of this paper.

References

Allen, J. 1991. Discourse structure in the TRAINS project. In *Darpa Speech and Natural Language Workshop*.

Bratman, M. 1990. What is intention? In Cohen, P.; Morgan, J.; and Pollack, M., eds., *Intentions in Communication*. chapter 2, 15--31.

Cawsey, A. 1993. Planning interactive explanations. *International Journal of Man-Machine Studies* 169--199.

Edmonds, P. 1993. A computational model of collaboration on reference in direction-giving dialogues. Technical Report CSRI-289, Univ. of Toronto.

Eller, R., and Carberry, S. 1992. A meta-rule approach to flexible plan recognition in dialogue. *User Modeling and User-Adapted Interaction* 2:27--53.

Elzer, S.; Chu, J.; and Carberry, S. 1994. Recognizing and utilizing user preferences in collaborative consultation dialogues. In Progress.

Grosz, B., and Sidner, C. 1990. Plans for discourse. In Cohen, P.; Morgan, J.; and Pollack, M., eds., *Intentions in Communication*. chapter 20, 417--444.

Guinn, C., and Biermann, A. 1993. Conflict resolution in collaborative discourse. In *Proceedings of the IJCAI-93 Workshop:Computational Models of Conflict Management in Cooperative Problem Solving*, 84--88.

Heeman, P., and Hirst, G. 1992. Collaborating on referring expressions. Technical Report 435, Univ. of Rochester.

Heeman, P. 1993. Speech actions and mental states in task-oriented dialogues. In *AAAI 1993 Spring Symposium on Reasoning About Mental States: Formal Theories and Applications*.

Joshi, A.; Webber, B.; and Weischedel, R. 1984. Living up to expectations: Computing expert responses. In *Proceedings of the AAAI*, 169--175.

Joshi, A. 1982. Mutual beliefs in question-answer systems. In Smith, N., ed., *Mutual Knowledge*. chapter 4, 181--197.

Lambert, L., and Carberry, S. 1991. A tripartite plan-based model of dialogue. In *Proceedings of the ACL*, 47--54.

Lambert, L., and Carberry, S. 1992. Modeling negotiation dialogues. In *Proceedings of the ACL*, 193--200.

Litman, D., and Allen, J. 1987. A plan recognition model for subdialogues in conversation. *Cognitive Science* 11:163--200.

Lochbaum, K. 1991. An algorithm for plan recognition in collaborative discourse. In *Proceedings of the ACL*, 33--38.

Maybury, M. 1992. Communicative acts for explanation generation. *International Journal of Man-Machine Studies* 37:135--172.

Maybury, M. 1993. Communicative acts for generating natural language arguments. In *Proceedings of the AAAI*, 357--364.

Moore, J., and Paris, C. 1993. Planning text for advisory dialogues: Capturing intentional, rhetorical and attentional information. *Computational Linguistics* 19(4):651--694.

Pollack, M. 1986. A model of plan inference that distinguishes between the beliefs of actors and observers. In *Proceedings of the ACL*, 207--214.

Quilici, A. 1991. *The Correction Machine: A computer Model of Recognizing and Producing Belief Justifications in Argumentative Dialogs*. Ph.D. Dissertation, UCLA.

Reed, S. 1982. *Cognition: Theory and Applications*. chapter 14, 337--365.

Sidner, C. 1992. Using discourse to negotiate in collaborative activity: An artificial language. In *AAAI-92 Workshop: Cooperation Among Heterogeneous Intelligent Systems*, 121--128.

Sycara, K. 1989. Argumentation: Planning other agents' plans. In *Proceedings of the IJCAI*, 517--523.

van Beek, P. 1987. A model for generating better explanations. In *Proceedings of the ACL*, 215--220.

Classifying Cue Phrases in Text and Speech Using Machine Learning

Diane J. Litman
AT&T Bell Laboratories
600 Mountain Avenue, Room 2B-412
Murray Hill, New Jersey 07974
diane@research.att.com

Abstract

Cue phrases may be used in a *discourse* sense to explicitly signal discourse structure, but also in a *sentential* sense to convey semantic rather than structural information. This paper explores the use of machine learning for classifying cue phrases as discourse or sentential. Two machine learning programs (CGRENDEL and C4.5) are used to induce classification rules from sets of pre-classified cue phrases and their features. Machine learning is shown to be an effective technique for not only *automating* the generation of classification rules, but also for *improving* upon previous results.

Introduction

Cue phrases are words and phrases that may *sometimes* be used to explicitly signal discourse structure. For example, when used in a *discourse* sense, the cue phrase "incidentally" conveys the structural information that a topic digression is beginning. When used in a *sentential* sense, "incidentally" instead functions as an adverb. Correctly classifying cue phrases as discourse or sentential is critical for tasks that exploit discourse structure, e.g., anaphora resolution (Grosz & Sidner 1986).

While the problem of cue phrase classification has often been noted (Grosz & Sidner 1986; Halliday & Hassan 1976; Reichman 1985; Schiffrin 1987; Zuckerman & Pearl 1986), it has generally not received careful study. Recently, however, Hirschberg and Litman (1993) have presented rules for classifying cue phrases in both text and speech. Hirschberg and Litman pre-classified a set of naturally occurring cue phrases, described each cue phrase in terms of prosodic and textual features, then *manually* examined the data to construct rules that best predicted the classifications from the features.

This paper examines the utility of *machine learning* for automating the construction of rules for classifying cue phrases. A set of experiments are conducted that use two machine learning programs, CGRENDEL (Cohen 1992; 1993) and C4.5 (Quinlan 1986; 1987), to induce classification rules from sets of pre-classified cue phrases and their features. To support a quantitative and comparative evaluation of the au-

tomated and manual approaches, both the error rates and the content of the manually derived and learned rulesets are compared. The experimental results show that machine learning is indeed an effective technique for *automating* the generation of classification rules. The accuracy of the learned rulesets is often *higher than* the accuracy of the rules in (Hirschberg & Litman 1993), while the linguistic implications are more precise.

Cue Phrase Classification

This section summarizes Hirschberg and Litman's study of the classification of multiple cue phrases in text and speech (Hirschberg & Litman 1993). The data from this study is used to create the input for the machine learning experiments, while the results are used as a benchmark for evaluating performance. The corpus examined was a technical address by a single speaker, lasting 75 minutes and consisting of approximately 12,500 words. The corpus yielded 953 instances of 34 different single word cue phrases. Hirschberg and Litman each classified the 953 tokens (as *discourse*, *sentential* or *ambiguous*) while listening to a recording and reading a transcription. Each token was also described as a set of *prosodic* and *textual* features. Previous observations in the literature correlating discourse structure with prosodic information, and discourse usages of cue phrases with initial position in a clause, contributed to the choice of features.

The prosody of the corpus was described using Pierrehumbert's theory of English intonation (Pierrehumbert 1980). In Pierrehumbert's theory, intonational contours are described as sequences of low (L) and high (H) *tones* in the *fundamental frequency (F0) contour* (the physical correlate of pitch). Intonational contours have as their domain the intonational phrase. A finite-state grammar describes the set of tonal sequences for an intonational phrase. A well-formed *intonational phrase* consists of one or more intermediate phrases followed by a boundary tone. A well-formed *intermediate phrase* has one or more pitch accents followed by a phrase accent. *Boundary tones* and *phrase accents* each consist of a single tone, while *pitch accents* consist of either a single tone or a pair of tones. There are two simple pitch accents (H* and L*) and four complex accents (L*+H, L+H*, H*+L, and H+L*). The * indicates which tone is aligned with the stressed syllable of the associated lexical item. Note that not every stressed syllable is accented. Lexical items that bear pitch accents are called *accented*, while those that do not are called *deaccented*.

Prosody was manually determined by examining the fundamental frequency (F0) contour, and by listening to the recording. To produce the F0 contour, the recording of the corpus was digitized and pitch-tracked using speech analysis software. This resulted in a display of the F0 where the x-axis represented time and the y-axis represented frequency in Hz. Various phrase final characteristics (e.g., phrase accents, boundary tones, as well as pauses and syllable lengthening) helped to identify intermediate and intonational phrases, while peaks or valleys in the display of the F0 contour helped to identify pitch accents.

In (Hirschberg & Litman 1993), every cue phrase was described using the following prosodic features. *Accent* corresponded to the pitch accent (if any) that was associated with the token. For both the intonational and intermediate phrases containing each token, the feature *composition of phrase* represented whether or not the token was *alone* in the phrase (the phrase contained only the token, or only cue phrases). *Position in phrase* represented whether the token was *first* (the first lexical item in the phrase – possibly preceded by other cue phrases), the last item in the phrase, or other.

Every cue phrase was also described in terms of the following textual features, derived directly from the transcript using fully automated methods. The *part of speech* of each token was obtained by running a program for tagging words with one of approximately 80 parts of speech on the transcript (Church 1988). Several characteristics of the token's immediate context were also noted, in particular, whether the token was immediately preceded or succeeded by *orthography* (punctuation or a paragraph boundary), and whether the token was immediately preceded or succeeded by a lexical item corresponding to a cue phrase.

The set of classified and described tokens was used to evaluate the accuracy of the classification models shown in Figure 1, developed in earlier studies. The prosodic model resulted from a study of 48 "now"s produced by multiple speakers in a radio call-in show (Hirschberg & Litman 1987). In a procedure similar to that described above, Hirschberg and Litman first classified and described each of the 48 tokens. They then examined their data manually to develop the prosodic model, which correctly classified all of the 48 tokens. (When later tested on 52 new examples of "now" from the radio corpus, the model also performed nearly perfectly). The model uniquely classifies any cue phrase using the features composition of

Prosodic Model:

if composition of intermediate phrase = alone **then** *discourse* (1)
elseif composition of intermediate phrase $\neq$ alone **then** (2)
    if position in intermediate phrase = first **then** (3)
        if accent = deaccented **then** *discourse* (4)
        elseif accent = L* **then** *discourse* (5)
        elseif accent = H* **then** *sentential* (6)
        elseif accent = complex **then** *sentential* (7)
    elseif position in intermediate phrase $\neq$ first **then** (8)
        sentential

Textual Model:

if preceding orthography = true **then** *discourse* (9)
elseif preceding orthography = false **then** *sentential* (10)

Figure 1: Decision tree representation of the classification models of (Hirschberg and Litman 1993).

intermediate phrase, position in intermediate phrase, and accent. When a cue phrase is uttered as a single intermediate phrase – possibly with other cue phrases (i.e., line (1) in Figure 1), or in a larger intermediate phrase with an initial position (possibly preceded by other cue phrases) and a L* accent or deaccented, it is classified as discourse. When part of a larger intermediate phrase and either in initial position with a H* or complex accent, or in a non-initial position, it is sentential. The textual model was also manually developed, and was based on an examination of the first 17 minutes of the single speaker technical address (Litman & Hirschberg 1990); the model correctly classified 89.4% of these 133 tokens. When a cue phrase is preceded by any type of orthography it is classified as discourse, otherwise as sentential.

The models were evaluated by quantifying their performance in correctly classifying two subsets of the 953 tokens from the corpus. The first subset (878 examples) consisted of only the *classifiable* tokens, i.e., the tokens that both Hirschberg and Litman classified as *discourse* or that both classified as *sentential*. The second subset, the *classifiable non-conjuncts* (495 examples), was created from the classifiable tokens by removing all examples of "and", "or" and "but". This subset was considered particularly reliable since 97.2% of non-conjuncts were classifiable compared to 92.1% of all tokens. The error rate of the prosodic model was 24.6% for the classifiable tokens and 14.7% for the classifiable non-conjuncts. The error rate of the textual model was 19.1% for the classifiable tokens and 16.1% for the classifiable non-conjuncts. In contrast, a model which just predicts the most frequent class in the corpus (sentential) has an error rate of 39% and 41% for the classifiable tokens and the classifiable non-conjuncts, respectively.

Experiments using Machine Induction

This section describes experiments that use the machine learning programs C4.5 (Quinlan 1986; 1987) and CGRENDEL (Cohen 1992; 1993) to *automatically* induce cue phrase classification rules from both the data of (Hirschberg & Litman 1993) and an extension of this data. CGRENDEL and C4.5 are similar to each other and to other learning methods (e.g., neural networks) in that they induce rules from preclassified examples. Each program takes two inputs: 1) definitions of the classes to be learned, and of the names and values of a fixed set of features, and 2) the training data, i.e., a set of examples for which the class and feature values are specified. The output of each program is a set of classification rules, expressed in C4.5 as a decision tree and in CGRENDEL as an ordered set of if-then rules. Both CGRENDEL and C4.5 learn the classification rules using greedy search guided by an "information gain" metric.

The first set of experiments does not distinguish among the 34 cue phrases. In each experiment, a different subset of the features coded in (Hirschberg & Litman 1993) is examined. The experiments consider every feature in isolation (to comparatively evaluate the utility of each individual knowledge source for classification), as well as linguistically motivated sets of features (to gain insight into the interactions between the knowledge sources). The second set of experiments treats cue phrases individually. This is done by adding a lexical feature representing the cue phrase to each feature set from the first set of experiments. The potential use of such a lexical feature was noted but not used in (Hirschberg & Litman 1993). These experiments evaluate the utility of developing classification models specialized for particular cue phrases, and also provide qualitatively new linguistic insights into the data.

The first input to each learning program defines the classes and features. The classifications produced by Hirschberg and by Litman (*discourse*, *sentential*, and *ambiguous*) are combined into a single classification for each cue phrase. A cue phrase is classified as *discourse* (or as *sentential*) if both Hirschberg and Litman agreed upon the classification *discourse* (or upon *sentential*). A cue phrase is *non-classifiable* if at least one of Hirschberg and/or Litman classified the token as *ambiguous*, or one classified it as *discourse* while the other classified it as *sentential*. The features considered in the learning experiments are shown in Figure 2. Feature values can either be a numeric value or one of a fixed set of user-defined symbolic values. The feature representation shown here follows the representation of (Hirschberg & Litman 1993) except as noted. *Length of phrase* (P-L and I-L) represents the number of words in the phrase. This feature was not coded in the data from which the prosodic model was developed, but was coded (although not used) in the later data of (Hirschberg & Litman 1993). *Position in phrase* (P-P and I-P) uses numeric rather than symbolic values. The conjunction of the first two values for I-C is equivalent to *alone* in Figure 1. *Ambiguous*, the last value of A, is assigned when the prosodic anal-

- **Prosodic Features**
  - length of intonational phrase (P-L): integer.
  - position in intonational phrase (P-P): integer.
  - length of intermediate phrase (I-L): integer.
  - position in intermediate phrase (I-P): integer.
  - composition of intermediate phrase (I-C): only, only cue phrases, other.
  - accent (A): H*, L*, L*+H, L+H*, H*+L, H+L*, deaccented, ambiguous.
  - accent* (A*): H*, L*, complex, deaccented, ambiguous.
- **Textual Features**
  - preceding cue phrase (C-P): true, false, NA.
  - succeeding cue phrase (C-S): true, false, NA.
  - preceding orthography (O-P): comma, dash, period, paragraph, false, NA.
  - preceding orthography* (O-P*): true, false, NA.
  - succeeding orthography (O-S): comma, dash, period, false, NA.
  - succeeding orthography* (O-S*): true, false, NA.
  - part-of-speech (POS): article, coordinating conjunction, cardinal numeral, subordinating conjunction, preposition, adjective, singular or mass noun, singular proper noun, intensifier, adverb, verb base form, NA.
- **Lexical Feature**
  - token (T): actually, also, although, and, basically, because, but, essentially, except, finally, first, further, generally, however, indeed, like, look, next, no, now, ok, or, otherwise, right, say, second, see, similarly, since, so, then, therefore, well, yes.

Figure 2: Representation of features and their values, for use by C4.5 and CGRENDEL.

ysis of (Hirschberg & Litman 1993) is a disjunction (e.g., "H*+L or H*"). *NA* (not applicable) in the textual features reflects the fact that 39 recorded examples were not included in the transcription, which was done independently of (Hirschberg & Litman 1993). While the original representation noted the actual token (e.g., "and") when there was a preceding or succeeding cue phrase, here the value *true* encodes all such cases. Similarly, A*, O-P*, and O-S* re-represent the symbolic values of three features using a more abstract level of description (e.g., L*+H, L+H*, H*+L, and H+L* are represented as separate values in A but as a single value – the superclass *complex* – in A*). Finally, the lexical feature *token* is new to this study, and represents the actual cue phrase being described.

The second input to each learning program is training data, i.e., a set of examples for which the class and feature values are specified. Consider the following utterance, taken from the corpus of (Hirschberg & Litman 1993):

Example 1 [(*Now*) (*now* that we have all been welcomed here)] it's time to get on with the business of the conference.

This utterance contains two cue phrases, corresponding to the two instances of "now". The brackets and parentheses illustrate the intonational and intermediate phrases, respectively, that contain the tokens. Note that a single intonational phrase contains both tokens, but that each token is uttered in a different interme-

	P-L	P-P	I-L	I-P	I-C	A	A*	C-P	C-S	O-P	O-P*	O-S	O-S*	POS
prosody	X	X	X	X	X	X	X							
hl93features				X	X	X	X							
phrasing	X	X	X	X	X									
length	X		X											
position		X		X										
intonational	X	X												
intermediate			X	X	X									
text								X	X	X	X	X	X	X
adjacency								X	X					
orthography										X	X	X	X	
preceding								X		X	X			
succeeding									X			X	X	
speech-text	X	X	X	X	X	X	X	X	X	X	X	X	X	X
speech-adj	X	X	X	X	X	X	X	X	X					

Table 1: Multiple feature sets and their components.

P-L	P-P	I-L	I-P	I-C	A	A*	C-P	C-S	O-P	O-P*	O-S	O-S*	POS	T	Class
9	1	1	1	only	H*+L	complex	f	t	par.	t	f	f	adverb	now	discourse
9	2	8	1	other	H*	H*	t	f	f	f	f	f	adverb	now	sentential

Figure 3: Representation of examples as features and their values.

diate phrase. If we were only interested in the feature P-L, the two examples would be represented in the training data as follows:

P-L	Class
9	discourse
9	sentential

The first column indicates the value assigned to the feature P-L, while the second column indicates how the example was classified. Thus, the length of the intonational phrase containing the first instance of "now" is 9 words, and the token is classified as a discourse usage.

In the first set of learning experiments, examples are represented using 28 different feature sets. First, there are 14 *single feature sets*, corresponding to each prosodic and textual feature. The example shown above illustrates how data is represented using the single feature set P-L. Second, there are 14 *multiple feature sets*, as described in Table 1. Each of these sets contains a linguistically motivated subset of at least 2 of the 14 prosodic and textual features. The first 7 sets use only prosodic features. *Prosody* considers all the prosodic features that were coded for each token. *Hl93features* considers only the coded features that were also used in the model shown in Figure 1. *Phrasing* considers all features of both the intonational and intermediate phrases containing the token (i.e., length of phrase, position of token in phrase, and composition of phrase). *Length* and *position* each consider only one of these features, but with respect to both the intonational and intermediate phrase. Conversely, *intonational* and *intermediate* each consider only one type of phrase, but consider all of the features. The next 5 sets use only textual features. *Text* considers all the textual features. *Adjacency* and *orthography* each

consider a single textual feature, but consider both the preceding and succeeding immediate context. Conversely, *preceding* and *succeeding* consider contextual features relating to both orthography and cue phrases, but limit the context. The last two sets use both prosodic and textual features. *Speech-text* considers all features, while *speech-adj* does not consider orthography (which is subject to transcriber idiosyncrasy) and part of speech (which is dependent on orthography).

The second set of experiments considers 28 *tokenized feature sets*, constructed by adding *token* (the cue phrase being described) to each of the 14 single and 14 multiple feature sets. These sets will be referred to using the names of the single and multiple feature sets, concatenated with "+". Figure 3 illustrates how the two tokens in Example 1 would be represented using speech-text+. Consider the feature values for the first token. Since this token is the first lexical item in both the intonational and intermediate phrases which contain it, its position in both phrases (P-P and I-P) is 1. Since the intermediate phrase containing the token contains no other lexical items, its length (I-L) is 1 word and its composition (I-C) is *only* the token. The values for A and A* indicate that when the intonational phrase is described as a sequence of tones, the complex pitch accent H*+L is associated with the token. Finally, the utterance was transcribed such that it began a new paragraph. Thus the token was not preceded by another cue phrase (C-P), but it was preceded by a form of orthography (O-P and O-P*). Since the token was immediately followed by another instance of "now" in the transcription, the token was succeeded by another cue phrase (C-S) but was not succeeded by orthography (O-S and O-P*).

For each of the 56 feature sets (14 single feature,

Set	Cgrendel	C4.5	Set	Cgrendel	C4.5	Set	Cgrendel	C4.5	Set	Cgrendel	C4.5
P-L	32	32	P-L+	21	31	prosody	15	16	prosody+	16	15
P-P	16	16	P-P+	16	18	hl93features	29	30	hl93features+	23	28
I-L	25	25	I-L+	20	26	phrasing	16	15	phrasing+	14	15
I-P	25	25	I-P+	25	26	length	26	24	length+	18	24
I-C	36	36	I-C+	27	36	position	18	18	position+	15	17
A	28	40	A+	19	40	intonational	17	16	intonational+	15	16
A*	28	28	A*+	18	26	intermediate	21	21	intermediate+	18	22
C-P	40	40	C-P+	28	39	text	18	18	text+	18	20
C-S	41	40	C-S+	28	39	adjacency	39	40	adjacency+	28	39
O-P	20	40	O-P+	17	35	orthography	18	18	orthography+	17	19
O-P*	18	18	O-P*+	17	20	preceding	18	18	preceding+	17	19
O-S	34	35	O-S+	26	31	succeeding	33	34	succeeding+	25	32
O-S*	35	34	O-S*+	27	32	speech-text	15	15	speech-text+	16	13
POS	37	40	POS+	27	34	speech-adj	30	29	speech-adj+	27	28

Table 2: CGRENDEL and C4.5 error rates for the classifiable tokens (N=878).

14 multiple feature, and 28 token sets), 2 actual sets of examples are created as input to the learning systems. These sets correspond to the two subsets of the corpus examined in (Hirschberg & Litman 1993) – the classifiable tokens, and the classifiable non-conjuncts.

Results

This section examines the results of running the learning programs C4.5 and CGRENDEL on 112 sets of examples (56 feature sets x 2 sets of examples). The results are qualitatively examined by comparing the linguistic content of the learned rulesets with the rules of Figure 1. The results are quantitatively evaluated by comparing the error rate of the learned rulesets in classifying new examples to the error rate of the rules of Figure 1. The *error rate* of a set of rules is computed by using the rules to predict the classification of a set of (pre-classified) examples, then comparing the predicted and known classifications. In the cue phrase domain, the error rate is computed by summing the number of discourse examples misclassified as sentential with the number of sentential examples misclassified as discourse, then dividing by the total number of examples. *Cross-validation* (Weiss & Kulikowski 1991) is used to estimate the error rates of the learned rulesets. Instead of running each learning program once on each of the 112 sets of examples, 10 runs are performed, each using a random 90% of the examples for *training* (i.e., for learning the ruleset) and the remaining 10% for *testing*. An estimated error rate is obtained by averaging the error rate on the testing portion of the data from each of the 10 runs. Note that for each run, the training and testing examples are disjoint subsets of the same set of examples, and the training set is much larger than the test set. In contrast (as discussed above), the "training" and test sets for the intonational model of (Hirschberg & Litman 1993) were taken from different corpora, while for the textual model of (Hirschberg & Litman 1993) the test set was a superset of the training set. Furthermore, more data was used for testing than for train-

ing, and the computation of the error rate did not use cross-validation.

Table 2 presents the estimated error of the learned rulesets on the 878 classifiable examples in the corpus. Each numeric cell shows the result (as a percentage) for one of the 56 feature sets. The standard error for each cell ranged from .6 to 2.7. The left half of the table considers the single feature and single feature plus token sets, while the right half considers the multiple features with and without token. The top of the table considers prosodic features, the bottom textual features, and the bottom right prosodic/textual combinations. The error rates in italics indicate that the performance of the learned ruleset exceeds the performance reported in (Hirschberg & Litman 1993), where the rules of Figure 1 were tested using 100% of the 878 classifiable tokens. These error rates were 24.6% and 19.1% for the intonational and textual models, respectively.

When considering only a single intonational feature (the first 3 columns of the first 7 rows), the results of the learning programs suggest that position in intonational phrase (P-P) is the most useful feature for cue phrase classification. In addition, this feature classifies cue phrases significantly better than the 3 feature prosodic model of Figure 1. The majority of the learned multiple feature rulesets (columns 7-9) also perform better than the model of Figure 1, although none significantly improve upon the single feature ruleset. Note that the performance of the manually derived model is better than the performance of *hl93features* (which uses the same set of features but in different rules). In fact, *hl93features* has among the worst performance of any of the learned prosodic rulesets. This suggests that the prosodic feature set most useful for classifying "now" did not generalize to other cue phrases. The ease of exploring large training sets and regenerating rules for new training data appear to be significant advantages of the automated approach.

An examination of the learned rulesets shows that they are quite comparable in content to relevant por-

Ruleset learned from P-P using C4.5:

if position in intonational phrase $\leq$ 1 **then** *discourse*
elseif position in intonational phrase > 1 **then** *sentential*

Ruleset learned from P-P using CGRENDEL:

if position in intonational phrase $\geq$ 2 **then** *sentential*
default is on *discourse*

Ruleset learned from prosody using C4.5:

if position in intonational phrase $\leq$ 1 **then** *discourse*
elseif position in intonational phrase > 1 **then**
    if length of intermediate phrase $\leq$ 1 **then** *discourse*
    elseif length of intermediate phrase > 1 **then** *sentential*

Ruleset learned from prosody using CGRENDEL:

if (position in intonational phrase $\geq$ 2) $\wedge$
    (length of intermediate phrase $\geq$ 2) **then** *sentential*
if (7 $\geq$ position in intonational phrase $\geq$ 4) $\wedge$
    (length of intonational phrase $\geq$ 10) **then** *sentential*
if (length of intermediate phrase $\geq$ 2) $\wedge$
    (length of intonational phrase $\leq$ 7) $\wedge$
    (accent = H*) **then** *sentential*
if (length of intermediate phrase $\geq$ 2) $\wedge$
    (length of intonational phrase $\leq$ 9) $\wedge$
    (accent = H*+L) **then** *sentential*
if (length of intermediate phrase $\geq$ 2) $\wedge$
    (accent = deaccent) **then** *sentential*
if (length of intermediate phrase $\geq$ 8) $\wedge$
    (length of intonational phrase $\leq$ 9) $\wedge$
    (accent = L*) **then** *sentential*
default is on *discourse*

Ruleset learned from O-P* using C4.5:

if preceding orthography* = NA **then** *discourse*
elseif preceding orthography* = false **then** *sentential*
elseif preceding orthography* = true **then** *discourse*

Ruleset learned from O-P* using CGRENDEL:

if preceding orthography* = false **then** *sentential*
default is on *discourse*

Ruleset learned from speech-text+ using C4.5:

if position in intonational phrase <= 1 **then**
    if preceding orthography* = NA **then** *discourse*
    elseif preceding orthography* = true **then** *discourse*
    elseif preceding orthography* = false **then**
        if length of intermediate phrase > 12 **then** *discourse*
        elseif length of intermediate phrase $\leq$ 12 **then**
            if length of intermediate phrase $\leq$ 1 **then** *discourse*
            elseif length of intermediate phrase > 1 **then** *sentential*
elseif position in intonational phrase > 1 **then**
    if length of intermediate phrase $\leq$ 1 **then** *discourse*
    elseif length of intermediate phrase > 1 **then** *sentential*

Figure 4: Example rulesets learned from different feature sets (classifiable tokens).

tions of Figure 1, and often contain further linguistic insights. Consider the rulesets learned from P-P, shown in the top of Figure 4. C4.5 represents its learned ruleset using a decision tree, while CGRENDEL instead produces a set of if-then rules. When multiple rules are applicable, CGRENDEL applies a conflict resolution strategy; when no rules are applicable, the default (the last statement) is used. Both programs produce both unsimplified and pruned rulesets. Only the simplified rulesets are considered in this paper. Both of the learned rulesets say that if the token is not in the initial position of the intonational phrase, classify as *sentential*; otherwise classify as *discourse*. Note the correspondence with line (8) in Figure 1. Figure 4 also illustrates the more complex rulesets learned using the larger set of features in *prosody*. The C4.5 model is similar to lines (1), (3) and (8) of Figure 1. (Note that the length value 1 is equivalent to the composition value *only*.) In the CGRENDEL hypothesis, the first 2 rules correlate sentential status with (among other things) non-initial position, and the second 2 with H* and H*+L accents; these rules are similar to rules (6)-(8) in Figure 1. However, the last 2 CGRENDEL rules also correlate L* and no accent with sentential status when the phrase is of a certain length, while rules (4) and (5) in Figure 1 provide a different interpretation and do not take length into account. (Recall that length was coded by Hirschberg and Litman only in their test data. Length was thus never used to generate or revise their prosodic model.) Both of the learned rulesets perform similarly to each other, and outperform the prosodic model of Figure 1.

Examination of the learned textual rulesets yields similar findings. Consider the rulesets learned from O-P* (preceding orthography, where the particular type of orthography is not noted), shown towards the bottom of Figure 4. These rules outperform the rules using the other single features, and perform comparably to the model in Figure 1 and to the multiple feature textual rulesets incorporating preceding orthography. Again, note the similarity to lines (9) and (10) of Figure 1. Also note that the textual feature values were obtained directly from the transcript, while determining the values of prosodic features required manual analysis.

Performance of a feature set is often improved when the additional feature *token* is taken into account (columns 4-6 and 10-12). This phenomenon will be discussed below. Finally, *speech-text* and *speech-text+*, which consider every available feature, outperform the manually and nearly all the automatically derived models. The last example in Figure 4 is the best performing ruleset in Table 2, the C4.5 hypothesis learned from *speech-text+*.

Table 3 presents the results using a smaller portion of the corpus, the 495 classifiable non-conjuncts. The error rates of the intonational and textual models of Figure 1 on this subcorpus decrease to 14.7% and 16.1%, respectively (Hirschberg & Litman 1993). Without the feature *token*, the single feature sets based on position and preceding orthography are again the best performers, and along with many multiple feature non-token sets, perform nearly as well as the models in Figure 1.

When the feature *token* is taken into account, however, the learned rulesets outperform the models of (Hirschberg & Litman 1993) (which did not con-

Set	Cgrendel	C4.5	Set	Cgrendel	C4.5	Set	Cgrendel	C4.5	Set	Cgrendel	C4.5
P-L	33	32	P-L+	17	31	prosody	17	19	prosody+	15	16
P-P	18	18	P-P+	14	19	hl93features	18	18	hl93features+	17	18
I-L	25	25	I-L+	16	25	phrasing	19	18	phrasing+	12	17
I-P	19	19	I-P+	17	18	length	27	26	length+	16	24
I-C	35	35	I-C+	18	32	position	19	19	position+	13	17
A	30	29	A+	12	29	intonational	20	18	intonational+	16	19
A*	28	28	A*+	15	31	intermediate	19	21	intermediate+	16	18
C-P	40	39	C-P+	16	33	text	19	20	text+	12	15
C-S	39	39	C-S+	17	39	adjacency	40	40	adjacency+	15	43
O-P	17	18	O-P+	10	14	orthography	18	17	orthography+	13	18
O-P*	17	17	O-P*+	12	15	preceding	17	19	preceding+	13	16
O-S	30	31	O-S+	18	31	succeeding	30	30	succeeding+	18	31
O-S*	32	31	O-S*+	16	32	speech-text	14	16	speech-text+	16	17
POS	38	41	POS+	17	31	speech-adj	17	18	speech-adj+	18	21

Table 3: CGRENDEL and C4.5 error rates for the classifiable non-conjuncts (N=495).

Figure 5: Using the feature *token* during learning (classifiable non-conjuncts).

sider this feature), and also provide new insights into cue phrase classification. Figure 5 shows the CGRENDEL ruleset learned from A+, which reduces the 30% error rate of A to 12%. The first rule corresponds to line (5) of Figure 1. In contrast to line (4), however, CGRENDEL uses deaccenting to predict *discourse* for only the tokens "say" and "so." If the token is "now", "finally", "however", or "ok", *discourse* is assigned (for all accents). In all other deaccented cases, *sentential* is assigned (using the default). Similarly, in contrast to line (7), the complex accent L+H* predicts *discourse* for the cue phrases "further" or "indeed" (and also for "now", "finally", "however" and "ok"), and *sentential* otherwise. Rulesets such as these suggest that even though features such as accent may not characterize all cue phrases, they may nonetheless be used successfully if the feature is used differently for different cue phrases or subsets of cue phrases.

Note that in the subcorpus of non-conjuncts (in contrast to the classifiable subcorpus), machine learning only improves on human performance by considering more features, either the extra feature *token* or textual and prosodic features in combination. This might reflect the fact that the manually derived theories already achieve optimal performance with respect to the examined features in this less noisy subcorpus, and/or that the automatically derived theory for this subcor-

pus was based on a smaller training set than used in the previous subcorpus.

Related Work in Discourse Analysis

Grosz and Hirschberg (1992) used the system CART (Brieman *et al.* 1984) to construct decision trees for classifying aspects of discourse structure from intonational feature values. Siegel (in press) was the first to apply machine learning to cue phrases. He developed a genetic learning algorithm to induce decision trees using the non-ambiguous examples of (Hirschberg & Litman 1993) (using the classifications of only one judge) as well as additional examples. Each example was described using a feature corresponding to *token*, as well as textual features containing the lexical or orthographic item immediately to the left of and in the 4 positions to the right of the example. Thus, new textual features were examined. Prosodic features were not investigated. Siegel reported a 21% estimated error rate, with half of the corpus used for training and half for testing. An examination of Table 2 shows that the error of the best C4.5 and CGRENDEL rulesets was often lower than 21% (even for theories which did not consider the token), as was the 19.1% error of the textual model of (Hirschberg & Litman 1993). Siegel and McKeown (1994) have also proposed a method for developing linguistically viable rulesets, based on the partitioning of the training data produced during induction.

Conclusion

This paper has demonstrated the utility of *machine learning* techniques for cue phrase classification. A first set of experiments were presented that used the programs CGRENDEL (Cohen 1992; 1993) and C4.5 (Quinlan 1986; 1987) to induce classification rules from the preclassified cue phrases and their features that were used as test data in (Hirschberg & Litman 1993). The results of these experiments suggest that machine learning is an effective technique for not only *automating* the generation of linguistically plausible classification rules, but also for *improving* accuracy. In particular, a large number of learned rulesets (including P-P, an extremely simple one feature model) had significantly lower error rates than the rulesets of (Hirschberg & Litman 1993). One possible explanation is that the hand-built classification models were derived using very small "training" sets; as new data became available, this data was used for testing but not for updating the original models. In contrast, machine learning supported the building of rulesets using a much larger amount of the data for training. Furthermore, if new data becomes available, it is trivial to regenerate the rulesets. For example, in a second set of experiments, new classification rules were induced using the feature *token*, which was not considered in (Hirschberg & Litman 1993). Allowing the learning programs to treat cue phrases individually further improved the accuracy of the resulting rulesets, and added to the body of linguistic knowledge regarding cue phrases.

Another advantage of the machine learning approach is that the ease of inducing rulesets from many different sets of features supports an exploration of the comparative utility of different knowledge sources. For example, when prosodic features were considered in isolation, only position in intonational phrase appeared to be useful for classification. However, in combination with the token, several additional prosodic features appeared to be equally useful. The results of this paper suggest that machine learning is a useful tool for cue phrase classification, when the amount of data is too large for human analysis, and/or when an analysis goal is to gain a better understanding of the different aspects of the data.

Acknowledgments

I would like to thank William Cohen and Jason Catlett for help in using CGRENDEL and C4.5, and William Cohen, Ido Dagan, Julia Hirschberg, and Eric Siegel for comments on an earlier version of this paper.

References

Brieman, L.; Friedman, J.; Olshen, R.; and Stone, C. 1984. *Classification and Regression Trees*. Monterey, CA: Wadsworth and Brooks.

Church, K. W. 1988. A stochastic parts program and noun phrase parser for unrestricted text. In *Proceedings of the Second Conference on Applied Natural Langu age Processing*, 136–143.

Cohen, W. W. 1992. Compiling knowledge into an explicit bias. In *Proceedings of the Ninth International Conference on Machine Learning*. Aberdeen, Scotland: Morgan Kaufmann.

Cohen, W. W. 1993. Efficient pruning methods for separate-and-conquer rule learning systems. In *Proceedings of the 13th International Joint Conference on Artificial Intelligence*.

Grosz, B., and Hirschberg, J. 1992. Some intonational characteristics of discourse structure. In *Proc. of the International Conference on Spoken Language Processing*.

Grosz, B. J., and Sidner, C. L. 1986. Attention, intentions, and the structure of discourse. *Computational Linguistics* 12(3):175–204.

Halliday, M. A. K., and Hassan, R. 1976. *Cohesion in English*. Longman.

Hirschberg, J., and Litman, D. 1987. Now let's talk about 'now': Identifying cue phrases intonationally. In *Proceedings of the Association for Computational Linguistics*.

Hirschberg, J., and Litman, D. 1993. Empirical studies on the disambiguation of cue phrases. *Computational Linguistics* 19(3):501–530.

Litman, D., and Hirschberg, J. 1990. Disambiguating cue phrases in text and speech. In *Papers Presented to the 13th International Conference on Computational Linguistics*, 251–256. Helsinki: International Conference on Computational Linguistics.

Pierrehumbert, J. B. 1980. *The Phonology and Phonetics of English Intonation*. Ph.D. Dissertation, Massachusetts Institute of Technology. Distributed by the Indiana University Linguistics Club.

Quinlan, J. R. 1986. Induction of decision trees. *Machine Learning* 1:81–106.

Quinlan, J. R. 1987. Simplifying decision trees. *International Journal Man-Machine Studies* 27:221–234.

Reichman, R. 1985. *Getting Computers to Talk Like You and Me: Discourse Context, Focus, and Semantics*. Bradford. Cambridge: MIT.

Schiffrin, D. 1987. *Discourse Markers*. Cambridge UK: Cambridge University Press.

Siegel, E. V., and McKeown, K. R. 1994. Emergent linguistic rules from the automatic grouping of training examples: Disambiguating clue words with decision trees. In *Proceedings of the Twelfth National Conference on Artificial Intelligence (AAAI)*.

Siegel, E. V. in press. Competitively evolving decision trees against fixed training cases for natural language processing. In *Advances in Genetic Programming*.

Weiss, S. M., and Kulikowski, C. 1991. *Computer systems that learn: classification and prediction methods from statistics, neural nets, machine learning, and expert systems*. Morgan Kaufmann.

Zuckerman, I., and Pearl, J. 1986. Comprehension-driven generation of meta-technical utterances in math tutoring. In *Proceedings of the Fifth National Conference on Artificial Intelligence (AAAI)*, 606–611.

An Artificial Discourse Language
for Collaborative Negotiation

Candace L. Sidner

Lotus Development Corp.
One Rogers St.
Cambridge, MA 02139
email: csidner@lotus.com

Abstract

Collaborations to accomplish common goals necessitate negotiation to share and reach agreement on the beliefs that agents hold as part of the collaboration. Negotiation in communication can be simulated by a series of exchanges in which agents propose, reject, counterpropose or seek supporting information for beliefs they wish to be held mutually. In an artificial language of negotiation, messages display the state of the agents' beliefs. Dialogues consisting of such messages clarify the means by which agents come to agree or fail to agree on mutual beliefs and individual intentions.

Introduction

In human problem solving, agents often recognize that they share goals in common. To achieve their common goals, they plan and act jointly. These activities are collaborative processes. Collaboration requires *negotiation*, that is, the interactive process of attempting to agree on the goals, actions and beliefs that comprise the planning and acting decisions of the collaboration.

This paper reports on an artificial language and associated machinery for modelling discourses in which agents discuss their collaborative activities (Grosz & Sidner 1990; Lochbaum, Grosz, & Sidner 1990; Grosz & Kraus 1993; Lochbaum 1993). The need for this language results from an attempt to understand how agents might come to hold the beliefs and intentions of the SharedPlan model (Grosz & Sidner 1990; Grosz & Kraus 1993).

A Sample Human Negotiation

To begin to address the questions concerning beliefs, and the means by which beliefs become shared, consider the portion of a dialogue transcription shown in the dialogue D1 shown in Figure 1.

The dialogue the transcription captures was spoken between M and K, who were participating in a biweekly meeting; M was the group leader and K a member of the group. The text has been editted to improve its intelligibility by removing "ums," "ahs," pauses and extranaeous phrases.

M and K demonstrate the most typical characteristics of negotiation in discourse: proposal and acceptance or proposal and rejection sequences. While this phenomenon has been subject to some previous study (Winograd 86; Weihmayer & Brandau 1990) my focus concerns the nature of the beliefs at each step of the communication. In the sample, K offers for mutual belief her belief that she should discuss graphics tools with John. M, who might be understood to be agreeing by saying, "OK," is in fact simply listening to K's proposal. When she has heard the whole message from K, she makes clear that she does not believe K's proposed action is best. It is vital to bear in mind that these agents are focused on the common goal they have agreed to (automating K's job), and thus they are able to infer that K's proposal is meant to be about actions that will *contribute* (Grosz & Sidner 1990; Lochbaum, Grosz, & Sidner 1990; Grosz & Kraus 1993) to the common goal.

An Artificial Language of Negotiation

English, like any human language, provides agents with a variety of ways to express beliefs and intentions. To abstract from these, I have devised an artificial language, which is given below. The language is defined as a series of messages from one agent to another, the content of which includes a proposition. For each message type, after it is received, certain beliefs or intentions can be taken as true regarding the proposition. The state of beliefs or intentions following a message abstracts away from individual agents in the negotitation and provides the state of communication held by all the agents.

In addition to the language, I define some additional machinery for "interpreting" the language: a set of stacks for Open beliefs and Rejected beliefs, which capture part of the state of the discourse. This machinery informally captures a portion of the attentional state in the sense of (Grosz & Sidner 1986), but a complete rendering of beliefs and intentions in terms of that theory requires further research.

I also assume an automated belief revision system to track all the mutual beliefs that come to be held.

M: Throughput, error meeting, European conjestion. We started talking at the error meeting about figuring out a good tool to deal with I mean we've seen the same kind of problem come up over and over again. And there may be some way to automate what you do a little bit.

K: One thing I've got to do [M: what?] is I've got to talk to John about his graphics stuff. Evidently people have been telling me he has a thing that makes nodes, circles and draws lines. Mean that would help even just as a start.

M: OK

K: but I have, I need to do that, and see what he he's got written. All right?

M: I'm not sure it's worth using fancy graphics on the LISP machine or stuff for this kind of thing.

K: I'm not even thinking about fancy. I mean I would just, like I said, if I had a little xerox template that showed the nodes and I could fill in my own allergism [sic], just quickly draw it, that would be a help. [M: mm] You know.

M: Well, you'd also want Typically what we draw is something like this [K:yeh], right? [K:yeh] And I mean ideally I think what you'd like is a map, and then if you mark the lines that have [K: yeh] retransmissions, and then you also process the outage report and you mark the lines [K:right] that have outages [K:yup], during the same time that these ones had [K:yep] retransmissions. [K:that's] right?

Figure 1: Dialogue D1

Among the many TMSs, that of Galliers' (Galliers 1992) is most relevant here for its use of the notion of *more cohence*. Belief revision is critical because agents sometimes change their minds about proposals they have agreed on, and the decision to believe a new proposal may hinge on already held beliefs.

The Language Definition

In the definitions that follow, `BEL` is short for believe, `INT` for intend, and `MB` for mutual belief.

PFA (ProposeForAccept) agt1 belief agt2: Agt1 expresses belief to agt2. After receiving a message of this type from agt1, the state of communication is:

```
(BEL agt1 belief)
(INT agt1 (Achieve agt1 (BEL agt2 belief)))
(BEL agt1 (Communicated agt1 belief agt2)).
```

AR (AcknowledgeReceipt) agt1 belief agt2: Agt1 sends this message to agt2 to indicate that a previous message from agt2 about belief has been heard. This does *not* mean that agt1 believes belief. After receiving the message the communication state is:

```
(MB agt1 agt2 (BEL agt2 belief))
(MB agt1 agt2
   (INT agt2 (Achieve agt2 (BEL agt1 belief))))
(MB agt1 agt2 (Communicated agt2 belief agt1)).
```

Furthermore, `(Open belief)` occurs to put belief on Open stack.

RJ (Reject) agt1 belief agt2: Upon receipt of this message, agt2 can conclude that agt1 does not believe belief, which has been offered as a proposal. The effect is that belief is no longer an Open proposal. Following receipt of this message, the state of communication is:

```
(Not (BEL agt1 belief)
(BEL agt1
   (Communicated agt1
      (Not (BEL agt1 belief)) agt2)).
```

Furthermore, `(DeleteOpen belief)` removes belief from Open stack, and `(Rejected agt1 belief)` puts belief in Rejected stack.

ARJ (AcknowledgeReject) agt1 belief agt2: This is the counterpart of AR for rejections. It establishes the mutual belief of the conclusions from RJ:

```
(MB agt1 agt2 (Not (BEL agt2 belief)))
(MB agt1 agt2
   (Communicated agt2
      (Not (BEL agt2 belief)) agt1)).
```

AP (AcceptProposal) agt1 belief agt2: Upon receipt of this message from agt1, agt1 and agt2 now hold belief as a mutual belief:

```
(MB agt1 agt2 belief).
```

Also `(DeleteOpen belief)` occurs and belief is tracked by the belief revision system.

CO (Counter) agt1 belief1 agt2 belief2: Agt1 has reason to doubt belief1. Without rejecting belief1, agt1 offers belief2 to agt2. The state of the communication is just that which is obtained by sending the following messages:

```
(PFA agt1 belief2 agt2)
(PFA agt1 (Supports (Not belief1) belief2) agt2)
```

RP (RetractProposal) agt1 agt2 belief: Other researchers (Weihmayer & Brandau 1990) report the need for retraction of belief. This message is sent when agt1 no longer believes a belief proposed previously.

```
(Not (BEL agt1 belief))
(Not (INT agt1
   (Achieve agt1 (BEL agt2 belief))))
(BEL agt1
   (Communicated agt1
      (Not (BEL agt1 belief)) agt2)).
```

If belief has not been accepted before the retraction, it is on the Open stack, and must be deleted.

ARP (AcknowledgeRetractedProposal) agt1 agt2 belief: Acknowledgement is similar in kind to other acknowledgements. Note that agt2 was the source of the retraction that this message acknowledges.

```
(MB agt1 agt2 (Not (BEL agt2 belief)))
(MB agt1 agt2
   (Not
      (INT agt2
         (Achieve agt2 (BEL agt1 belief))))
(MB agt1 agt2
   (Communicated agt2
      (Not (BEL agt2 belief)) agt1)).
```

AOP (AcceptOthersProp) agt1 belief1 agt2 belief2: This message is used when agt1 realizes that belief1 is worthy of belief. Agt1 sends this message to indicate that belief2 is now being retracted, and belief1 is being accepted. All the results of the following messages hold for this message:

```
(RP agt1 agt2 belief2)
(AP agt1 agt2 belief1).
```

PR (ProposeReplace) agt1 belief1 agt2 belief2: This message is shorthand for two messages:

```
(RJ agt1 belief2 agt2)
(PFA agt1 belief1 agt2).
```

PA (ProposeAct) agt1 agt2 action context: This message is a schema for

```
(PFA agt1 (Should-do agt2 action context) agt2)
```

where context is optional and the action can vary over a set that includes Identify, Provide-Support, and other actions. Should-Do is an optative expression over an action to be performed by the agent. Should-Do is not as strong as INT; see section for further discussion. This message is needed to correspond to questions and commands as in the following examples:

```
Why X?
(PFA agt1
    (Should-Do agt2
        (Provide-Support X context)) agt2);

What is X?
(similarly for where is X, when is X, and who is X)
(PFA agt1
    (Should-Do agt2 (Identify X context)) agt2);

Can you X?
(PA agt1 agt2
    (Should-Do agt2
        (Tellif agt2 (Able agt2 X context))));

Did John come?
(PA agt1 agt2
    (Should-Do agt2
        (Tellif agt2 '(john did come))));

Listen to this!
(PA agt1 agt2
    (Should-Do agt2 '(listen to this))).
```

Discussion

This language makes an important assumption, the mutual belief assumption, about the nature of communication, namely that following certain messages (e.g. AP, AR), mutual belief obtains among the agents of the collaboration. This assumption rests on the lack of intentional deception and misinformation in collaborative activity. For individual agents, the strongest statement that can be made is that the agent believes there is mutual belief. However, the language uses full mutual belief because if each agent can believe there is mutual belief and there is no deception, then full mutual belief follows. For synchronous communciations in collaboration, (e.g. face-to-face conversations, phone calls and the like), the mutual belief assumption is reasonable. For asynchronous cases (e.g. written or spoken email or letters), or cases where interaction is not possible (e.g. speeches to a large audience or written publications), the assumption of mutual belief can lead to difficulties (Halpern & Moses 1984) because, for example, one of the negotiators may never receive the acceptance message, or it cannot be sent.

The negotiation language does not constrain the order in which agents choose to send messages. Agents therefore can have incoherent discourses, or reach certain false conclusions if they send certain messages before others. For example, when agent A sends (PFA A B x) to agent B and then sends (AP A B x), the state of communication includes that (MB A B x). This pair of messages is odd because agent A is accepting his own proposal. The communication state misrepresents the real state of affairs in which agent B has yet to say anything about x. Operational constraints on sending of messages can eliminate such false conclusions.

Among the messages of this language, AR (AcknowledgeReceipt) serves a special role worth noting here. The linguistics and psychology literature[1] raises many issues regarding utterances that are misunderstood by the hearer and must be repaired before their content is understood. The AR message is a place holder for the simulation of this behavior. In particular, when a proposal is not understood, rather than send an AR message, some new message could be sent that would indicate for example, where the previous message was garbled or that the whole message was lost. The sample dialogues in this paper do not illustrate repairs and the like.

Sample Simulated Dialogues

To illustrate the language, I will present some sample constructed discourses. Discourses are about some domain of affairs, and in natural conversation this domain can be quite rich and diverse; the job automation dialogues illustrate this claim clearly. To illustrate the negotiation language, the domain is a very simple one, namely actions, denoted by A, B, etc. that contribute to a Goal, denoted only as G. Keeping the domain of conversation straightforward facilitates closer observation of the properties of the language of negotiation.

A Simple Negotiation The first example of negotiation in the artificial language involves two agents R and C. These agents have a partial SharedPlan for accomplishing G, a goal, and no shared recipes for the performance of G[2]. They mutually believe that each knows a way to do A and D, two actions. C believes A Enables D, while R believes D generates G(Balkanski 1990). To see how they come to decide the recipe for G, they could have the dialogue given in Figure 2. An

---

[1] A paper by (Clark & Shaefer 1987) contains discussion of this literature.

[2] See (Grosz & Kraus 1993) for elaboration of partial SharedPlans.

```
1 (PFA C (Should-Do R&C A) R)      C: Let's do A.

1'(AR R C (Should-Do R&C A))        R: uh-huh.
  --Additional messages of this type
    are not included in the conversation--

2 (PR R (Should-Do R&C D) C         R: No, let's
  (Should-Do R&C A))                do D.

3 (RJ C (Should-Do R&C D) R)        C: No.

4 (PFA R (Should-Do C                R: Why do A?
    (Provide-Support C
      (Should-Do R&C A)
      (Recipe G))) C)

5 (AP C                              C: ok.
    (Should-Do C
      (Provide-Support  C
  (Should-Do R&C A)
  (Recipe G))))

6 (PFA C                             C: A enables D.
    (Enables A D) R)

7 (AP R                              R: ok.
    (Enables A D) C C)

8 (PFA C                             C: Let's do A.
    (Should-Do R&C A) R)

9 (AP R                              R: ok.
    (Should-Do R&C A) C C)

10 (PFA R (Generates D G) C)         R: D generates G.

11 (AP C (Generates D G) R)          C: ok.

12 (PFA R                            R: Let's do D.
    (Should-Do R&C D) C)

13 (AP C (Should-Do R&C D) R)        C: ok.
```

Figure 2: Negotiating to achieve G

English gloss for each message is given at the right.

This conversation is not as fluent as human ones. First, it includes extra "uh-huhs" to tell the sending agent that the message was received. In the figure, most of these have been deleted for ease of understanding, but a full conversation includes one after every PFA and RJ. Second, the language demands additional messages when undertaking action. For example, at line 5, an extra "ok" occurs to tell R that C is accepting R's previous proposal (that is, C will answer the question). The artificial conversation also demands that agents say more than "no" or "ok" to a proposal; the content of the proposal is repeated in each case (the English gloss does not include this repetition).

Figure 3 illustrates the states of mutual belief, pri-

Mutual beliefs of R and C:
```
(BEL C (Should-Do R&C A))
(INT C (Achieve C (BEL R (Should-Do R&C A))))
(Communicated C (Should-Do R&C A) R))
(Not (BEL R (Should-Do R&C A)))
(Communicated R (Not (BEL R (Should-Do R&C A))))
```
Beliefs held individually by each of R and C:
```
(BEL R (Should-Do R&C D))
(INT R (Achieve R (BEL C (Should-Do R&C D))))
(BEL R (Communicated R (Should-Do R&C D) C))
```
Open stack is empty.
Rejected stack: `(Rejected R (Should-Do R&C A))`

Figure 3: Belief states after line 2 of Figure 2

vate beliefs, the Open stack and the Rejected stack after line 2 of the dialogue. For purposes of contrast, the figure illustrates only the acknowledgement (ARJ) of the RJ that is part of PR as having occurred. The ARJ for RJ leads to the mutual belief that

```
(Not (BEL R (Should-Do R&C A))).
```

owever, the acknowledgement AR for the proposal (Should-Do R&C D) has not occurred, so the three private beliefs concerning doing D are not yet mutually believed, and the Open stack does not contain a proposal under consideration.

While clearly simpler than most human conversations, this sample dialogue illustrates how agents can establish mutual beliefs concerning a common goal without simply believing everything that is said. The basic sequence of proposing new beliefs (such as (Should-Do R&C A)), rejecting and eventually accepting them is demonstrated.

The sample dialogue raises an intriguing question: Why do R and C accept some proposals and reject other ones? In creating this dialogue, I stipulated that the agents R and C would accept any belief of another agent that could be seen to contribute to the goal G. Thus agent R is able to accept the proposal that A enables D because R knows already that D generates G, and thus the proposal has information that contributes to the goal G. Use of an artificial language of negotiation by artificial agents requires that the agents be constructed with enough intelligence to decide what beliefs to accept when proffered by other agents.

Likewise, the nature of strategies pursued by the agents in the sample conversation is paramount for constructing artificial agents. In the sample, C appears to use the strategy of "propose to do whatever you know about" (a rather foolhardy strategy). A more sensible strategy would be to question R about what R believes. Strategies for focusing attention, explored by Walker (Walker 1992) also result in more efficient conversations. Another fruitful area of research would be to develop strategies along the lines of the deals in (Zlotkin & Rosenschein 1990).

1 C: what way do you know to do Z?

2 **R**: *Ok*. A followed by B is part of it.

3 C: *Ok*.

4 **R**: let's do A.

5 C: *No*, F then B and D followed by E generates Z.

6 **R**: why do F? [in F;B]

7 C: *Ok*. The result of F is W.

8 **R**: *Yeh but* A is easier than F, *so* A;B then D;E generates Z.

9 C: *Yeh*, A's easier, *so* A's enabling conditions are different

                 from F's *so* A can't be in the recipe.

10 **R**: *But* they are the same. I've done A;B.

11 C: *Ok*. A and F have same results. *And* A;B then D;E generates Z.

12 **R**: *So* let's do A.

Figure 4: Proposals and counterproposals, English gloss

A Counterproposal Dialogue The artificial language presented here can be used to simulate much more complex conversations. A gloss of one such conversation is illustrated in Figure 4; the artificial language version is shown in Figure 5. Like the previous sample, the domain of conversation is actions, denoted by letters, and relations among them that achieve a goal. For this example, assume that C and R have a partial SharedPlan to do Z; that R believes that A followed by B contributes to doing Z; that C believes a recipe of the form F followed by B with D, then followed by E generates Z; that C believes R knows some way to achieve Z (but does not know what it is) and that R and C mutually believe the W enables B.

This conversation makes use of the CO message to allow two different proposals (at line 8) to be active at one time; maintaining more than one open proposal is a common feature of human discourses and negotiations. In the artificial language CO allows each agent to make beliefs available for mutual belief but without having to communicate that the other agent's beliefs are not believed.

This dialogue also demonstrates a a typical human behavior, dubbed "call for the question." Calls of the question allow the questioner to delay accepting or rejecting a proposed belief until the questioner can collect more information about whether the belief is reasonable to believe. In the dialogue of Figure 5, at line 6, R asks a question in order to determine whether action F is correct in the proposal at line 5.

Two other features of the sample conversation are noteworthy. First, in line 11 C names all the proposals being accepted. In normal English discourse only


```
1 (PFA C (Should-Do R (Identify R (Recipe Z))) R)

2 (AP R (Should-Do R (Identify R (Recipe Z))) C)
  (PFA R (Contributes (A;B) Z) )

3 (AP C (Contributes (A;B) Z) R)

4 (PFA R (Should-Do R&C A) C)

5 (PR C (Generates (((F;B) & D); E) Z) R
       (Should-Do R&C A))

6 (PFA R (Should-Do C
    (Provide-Support C (Contributes (F;B) Z))) C)
    C)

7 (AP C (Should-Do C
    (Provide-Support C (Contributes (F;B) Z))) R)
  (PFA C (Equal (Result F) W) R)

8 (AP R  (Equal (Result F) W) C)
  (CO R (Generates (((F;B) & D); E) Z) C
       (And (EasierThan A F)
            (Generates (((A;B) & D);E) Z)))

9 (AP C (EasierThan A F) R)
  (CO C (Generates (((A;B) & D);E) Z) R
       (Not (Equal (Result A) (Result F))))

10 (CO R (Not (Equal (Result A) (Result F)))
        C  (Equal (Result A)(Result F)))
   (PFA R (Done R A;B) C)

11 (AP C (Done R A;B) R)
   (AOP C  (Equal (Result A) (Result F)) R
        (Not (Equal (Result A) (Result F))))
   (AOP C ((((A;B) & D);E) Generates Z) R
        ((((F;B) & D); E) Generates Z))

12 (PFA R (Should-Do R&C A) C)
```

Figure 5: Artificial language version of Figure 4

the main proposal would be mentioned; the others are usually assumed as inferrable. Second, cue phrases (cf. (Grosz & Sidner 1986)), which are not part of the negotiation language, are presented in italics. While not necessary in the language, they may play a role in natural language to indicate the state of negotiations, because human speakers fail to repeat just what beliefs they are accepting, rejecting or countering.

For reasons of brevity, the M and K dialogue in Figure 1 cannot be illustrated in this paper, but is given in (Sidner 1993).

Related Research

As so far defined, this language does not take a stand on matter of commitments (Shoam 1990) or promises (Winograd 86). Agents must resolve when these actions are relevant by determining which types of mutual beliefs signal commitment. For example, once an agent agrees that he Should-Do an action, the two agents might decide that such agreement means the agreeing agent is committed to (or even signals intent to do) the action, and hence that the acceptance is a promise.

Cohen and Levesque (Cohen & Levesque 1990) have proposed an alternative formulation to (Grosz & Sidner 1990) for collaboration using their modal language of intention. Their definition of joint goal (JPG) for two agents is specified in terms of mutual belief and a mutual goal between the agents. The negotiation language is compatible for use with this account of collaboration.

Research on argumentation (Kraus & Sycara 93) in non-collaborative interaction (but where cooperation among agents is required) takes for granted the need for requests, statements, and threats. The artificial language proposed here is less compatible with these communiations because in that framework the agents can lie about their beliefs.

Future Directions

How can we test the completeness of the artificial language for capturing human conversations? Are there other features of dialogue in addition to cue phrases that are outside the language? Current investigations (Sidner 1994) are exploring the translation of dialogues into the negotiation language to determine potentially missing features and to characterize the interpretation of multi-functional phrases, such as "okay." The negotiation language is also being explored as a communication language between agents and users in product applications.

Acknowledgements

The author thanks the anonymous reviewers of the AAAI-92 workshop on Cooperation among Heterogeneous Intelligent Agents for their thoughtful remarks on an earlier draft of this paper, and Cliff Kahn, Bonnie Webber and Chuck Rich for their comments.

References

Balkanski, C. T. 1990. Modelling act-type relations in collaborative activity. Technical Report TR-23-90, Harvard University.

Clark, H. H., and Shaefer, E. 1987. Collaborating on contributions to conversations. *Language and Cognitive Processes* 11:1–23.

Cohen, P. R., and Levesque, H. 1990. On acting together. In *Proceedings of the Eighth National Conference on Artificial Intelligence*, 94–99. Menlo Park, CA: AAAI.

Galliers, J. R. 1992. Autonomous belief revision and communication. In Gaedenfors, P., ed., *Belief Revision*. Cambridge University Press. 220–246.

Grosz, B., and Kraus, S. 1993. Collaborative plans for group activities. In *Proceedings of IJCAI-13*, 367–373.

Grosz, B., and Sidner, C. 1986. Attention, intentions, and the structure of discourse. *Computational Linguistics* 12(3):175–204.

Grosz, B., and Sidner, C. 1990. Plans for discourse. In Cohen, P.; Morgan, J.; and Pollack, M., eds., *Intentions in Communication*. MIT Press.

Halpern, J., and Moses, Y. 1984. Knowledge and common knowledge in a distributed environment. In *Proceedings of the Third ACM Conference on the Principles of Distributed Computing*. ACM.

Kraus, S., M. N., and Sycara, K. 93. Reaching agreements through argumentation: A logical approach. In *Proceedings of the 12th International Workshop on Distributed Artificial Intelligence*.

Lochbaum, K. E.; Grosz, B. J.; and Sidner, C. L. 1990. Models of plans to support communication: An initial report. In *Proceedings of AAAI-90*, 485–490. Menlo Park, CA: AAAI Press/MIT Press.

Lochbaum, K. E. 1993. A collaborative planning approach to discourse understanding. Technical Report TR-20-93, Aiken Computational Laboratory, Harvard University, Cambridge, MA.

Shoam, Y. 1990. Agent oriented programming. Technical Report STAN-CS-90-1335, Computer Science Dept., Stanford University, Stanford, CA.

Sidner, C. L. 1993. The role of negotiation in collaborative activity. In Terveen, L., ed., *Human-Computer Collaboration: Reconciling Theory, Synthesizing Practice, Papers from the 1993 Fall Symposium Series, AAAI Technical Report FS-93-05*. Menlo Park, CA: AAAI Press.

Sidner, C. 1994. Negotiation in collaborative activity: A discourse analysis. *Knowledge-Based Systems*. forthcoming.

Walker, M. A. 1992. Redundancy in collaborative dialogue. In Boitet, C., ed., *Proceedings of the 14th Int. Conf. on Computational Linguistics*, 345–351. Assoc. for Computational Linguistics.

Weihmayer, R., and Brandau, R. 1990. Cooperative distributed problem solving for communication network management. *Computer Communications* 13(9).

Winograd, T. 86. A language/action perspective on the design of cooperative work. In *Proceedings of CSCW-86*, 203–220.

Zlotkin, G., and Rosenschein, J. S. 1990. Neogitation and conflict resolution in non-cooperative domains. In *Proceedings of the Eighth National Conference on Artificial Intelligence*, 100–105. Menlo Park, CA: AAAI.

Emergent Linguistic Rules from Inducing Decision Trees:
Disambiguating Discourse Clue Words

Eric V. Siegel and **Kathleen R. McKeown**
Department of Computer Science
Columbia University
New York, NY 10027

evs@cs.columbia.edu, kathy@cs.columbia.edu

Abstract

We apply decision tree induction to the problem of discourse clue word sense disambiguation. The automatic partitioning of the training set which is intrinsic to decision tree induction gives rise to linguistically viable rules.

Introduction

Discourse clue words function to convey information about the topical flow of a discourse. Clue words can be used both to bracket discourse segments and to describe the discourse relationship between these segments. For example, *say* can introduce a set of examples, as in "Should terrestrial mammals be taken in the same breath as types of mammals as *say* persons and apes?"[1] However, each word in Table 1 has at least one alternative meaning where the word contributes not to discourse level semantics, but to the semantic content of individual sentences; this is termed its **sentential** meaning. For example, *say* can mean "To express in words", as in "I don't want to *say* that he chickened out at a presentation or anything but he is in Toronto..." Therefore, to take advantage of the information supplied by discourse clue words, a system must first be able to disambiguate between such a word's **sentential** and **discourse** senses.[2]

In this paper, we perform automatic decision tree induction for this problem of discourse clue word disambiguation using a genetic algorithm. We show several advantages to our approach. First, the different decision trees that result encode a variety of linguistic generalizations about clue words. We show how such linguistic rules emerge automatically from the *training set partitioning* which occurs during decision tree induction. These rules can be examined in order to evaluate the validity of induced decision trees. Examining the rules also provides insights as to the type of syntactic information necessary to further improve clue word sense disambiguation. Second, decision trees are induced which generalize across a set of 34 clue words (see Table 1) in contrast to previous automated approaches to word sense disambiguation which typically have focused on discriminating the senses of one word at a time [Schuetze 1992] [Brown et al 1991] [Leacock et al 1993] [Black 1988] [Grishman and Sterling 1993] [Yarowsky 1993]. As we show, this allows for greater learning potential than dealing with words individually. There are some problems with the domain of disambiguation for clue words and we discuss these, indicating why our approach is likely to be more helpful for other disambiguation problems.

The following four sections discuss previous work on disambiguation, describe our approach, present experimental results in both linguistic and numerical terms, and draw conclusions and present our future research directions.

Previous Work

Hirschberg and Litman [1993] explore several methods for disambiguating clue words, including measuring the ability with which this task can be performed by looking only at the punctuation marks immediately before and after a clue word, suggesting the strategy embodied by the decision tree in Figure 1.[3] This small decision tree classifies clue words as **discourse** exactly when there is a period or a comma immediately preceding, and as **sentential** in all other cases. This means, for example, that a word is classified as **discourse** when it is the first word of a sentence. For such a simple strategy, the decision tree performs to a relatively high degree of accuracy over our corpus: 79.16%. Our work investigates disambiguation strategies for clue words which involve looking at near-by words in addition to punctuation marks.

The automatic acquisition of disambiguation strategies has been applied to many types of ambiguity problems, including word sense disambiguation [Schuetze 1992] [Leacock et al 1993] [Yarowsky 1993] [Brown et al 1991], determiner prediction [Knight forthcoming], and several parsing problems [Resnik 1993] [Magerman 1993]. Previous work using decision tree induction for disambiguation includes work by Black [1988]

---

[1]The examples come from the corpus used in this study.

[2]See Hirschberg and Litman [1993] and Schiffrin [1987] for details on other clue words and more information about clue words in general. In this paper, *clue word* refers to a word from Table 1, regardless of the particular sense with which it occurs.

---

[3]This decision tree is a slightly simplified extrapolation of Table 11 from Hirschberg and Litman [1993]. Hirschberg and Litman [1993] also investigated the ocurrence of clue words adjacent to one another, but with no conclusive results.

Table 1: Discourse clue words and the fraction of times each is used in its **discourse** sense.

Clue word	Fraction	Clue word	Fraction	Clue word	Fraction	Clue word	Fraction
and	137/348	*see*	0/29	*no*	0/9	*next*	0/4
now	64/75	*actually*	1/29	*although*	5/9	*yes*	0/3
so	55/74	*first*	0/25	*indeed*	5/8	*since*	0/3
like	6/71	*also*	5/20	*OK*	8/8	*except*	0/3
but	27/56	*then*	6/15	*however*	8/8	*therefore*	0/2
or	17/55	*further*	8/14	*generally*	1/6	*otherwise*	1/1
say	25/36	*finally*	11/11	*similarly*	3/5	*anyway*	0/1
well	13/35	*right*	0/10	*basically*	1/5		
look	0/35	*because*	0/10	*second*	0/4		

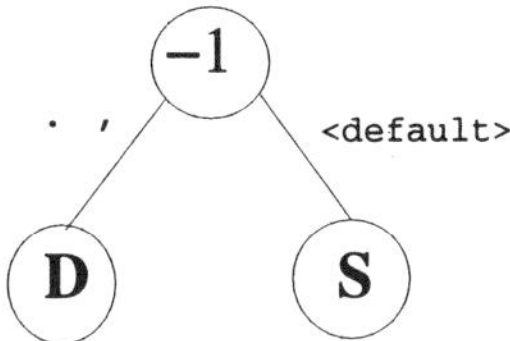

Figure 1: Manually created decision tree with accuracy 79.16%.

(word sense disambiguation), Knight [forthcoming] (determiner prediction), Resnik [1993] (coordination parsing) and Magerman [1993] (syntactic parsing). Automatic approaches to word sense disambiguation have thus far primarily focussed on disambiguating one word at a time.

Approach

In this study, we expand on the orthographic approach to clue word disambiguation described by Hirschberg and Litman [1993] by allowing decision trees to test not only for adjacent punctuation marks and clue words, but also for near-by words of any kind, and by allowing the decision trees to discriminate between clue words. The set of *attributes* available to a decision tree are the *tokens* (words and punctuation marks) appearing immediately to the left of the ambiguous word, immediately to the right of the ambiguous word, and 2, 3, and 4 spaces to the right of the ambiguous word, as well as the ambiguous word itself (*attribute* **0**), that is, {**-1, 0, 1, 2, 3, 4**}. This set of *attributes* were selected to test whether the decision trees would find a wider window of *tokens* useful for clue word disambiguation, but, as was automatically determined, only the adjacent *tokens* and the ambiguous word itself were deemed useful. No information describing syntactic structure is explicitly available to decision trees. The genetic algorithm determines automatically which words or punctuation in these positions are important for disambiguation.

Decision Trees

Figures 2 and 3 show example decision trees which were automatically induced for clue word sense disambiguation. Internal nodes are labeled with *token positions*

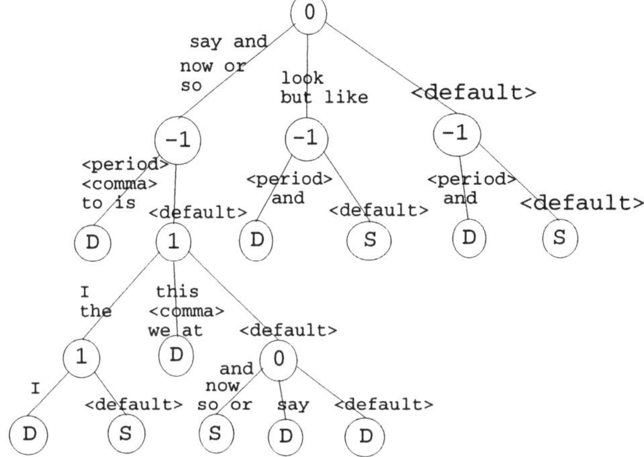

Figure 2: Decision tree automatically induced by the genetic algorithm. This tree disambiguated with 81.10% accuracy over the training set, and with 82.30% accuracy over the test set.

(*attributes*), arcs are labeled with sets of *tokens* (*values*), and leaves are labeled with *classes*, that is, either **discourse** or **sentential**. Given a text fragment containing a clue word, a decision tree classifies the word as to its sense by a deterministic traversal of the tree, starting at the root, down to a leaf. During traversal, an arc descending from the current (internal) node is selected in order to continue the traversal. This arc is chosen by finding the first descending arc, going from left to right, containing the token at the text fragment position indicated by the current node's label. For example, to traverse the tree in Figure 2, starting at the root node, the leftmost arc is traversed if the word at position **0** is one of the words on the arc (e.g., *say*). The rightmost arc under each internal node is labeled "default", and is traversed when none of its sister arcs contain the correct token.

In order to increase the likelihood that an induced decision tree will embody valid generalizations, as opposed to being over-fitted to the particular set of training examples, only the tokens which appear with frequency above a threshold of 15 in the training cases are permitted in the value sets of a decision tree (see the subsection "The Training Data" for details on the training corpus),

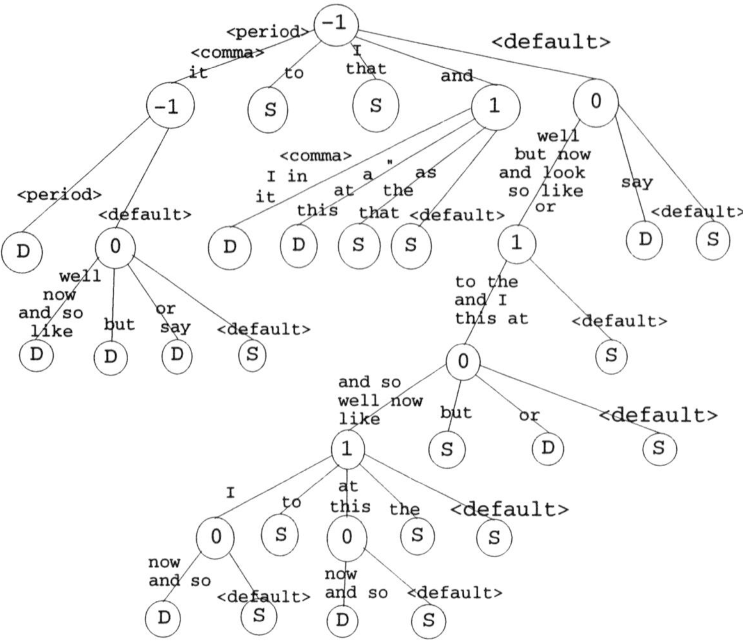

Figure 3: Decision tree automatically induced by the genetic algorithm. This tree disambiguated with 84.99% accuracy over the training set, and with 82.30% accuracy over the test set.

specifically:[4]

{<period>, <comma>, <apostrophe-s>, *a, and, are, as, at, can, for, I, in, is, it, of, that, the, this, to, we, you*}

A separate set of tokens is available to the arcs under nodes labeled **0**, namely the discourse clue words which appear with frequency greater than 4 in the training cases. (Only clue words appear at position **0**.) This threshold was chosen to allow infrequent clue words to be specified by a decision tree, but to still avert overfitting to the training data.

Decision Tree Induction

The corpus used in this study supplies 1,027 examples. Table 2 shows sample data. Each training case has a manually specified class, and a value corresponding to each of 6 attributes. In order to predict the performance of an induced decision tree over unseen data, the induction procedure is run over a random half of the corpus (the *training set*), and the resulting decision tree is then evaluated over the remaining half of the corpus (the *test set*). This division of the data is performed randomly before each run.[5]

The induction procedure used in this study is a genetic algorithm (GA) [Holland 1975], a weak learning method which has been applied to a wide range of tasks in optimization, machine learning, and automatic com-

Table 2: Example training cases.

-1	0	1	2	3	4	Class
.	*But*	*we*	*stop*	*there*	*because*	D
.	*Now*	*that*	*doesn't*	*mean*	*we*	D
to	*look*	*more*	*like*	*sentences*	*.*	S
,	*and*	*that's*	*on*	*the*	*second*	S

puter program induction [Goldberg 1989] [Koza 1992]. Inspired by Darwinian survival of the fittest, the GA works with a pool (*population*) of *individuals*, stochastically performing *reproductive operators* on the individuals, depending on some notion of *fitness*. Reproductive operators include *crossover*, a stochastic procedure by which two individuals are combined to create a third, and *mutation*, by which an individual undergoes a random alteration. In our work, individuals are both decision trees and the token sets which correspond to decision tree arcs. Fitness corresponds to the number of training cases correctly classified by a decision tree. The GA outputs the highest fit decision tree it encounters. Siegel [1994] describes the details of GA decision tree induction applied in this work. Subsection "Numerical Results" in this paper contrasts GA decision tree induction to classical decision tree induction techniques.

The Training Data

The 1,027 training examples come from a corpus used by Hirschberg and Litman [1993]. This is a transcript of a single speaker speech, preceeded by introductory remarks by other speakers, in which each occurrence of the words in Table 1 has been manually marked as to its

---

[4]Tokens are case-insensitive (capitalization doesn't matter), but inflection-sensitive (*a* is different than *an*).

[5]Because of this random division, the frequency distribution of tokens in the training set varies, so the valid token and clue word sets actually varies slightly.

meaning by a linguist.[6] When marking the corpus, the linguist had access to the entire transcript plus a recording of the speech. Therefore, much more information was available to the linguist than there is to a decision tree. Regardless, about 7% were deemed ambiguous by the linguist. The "ambiguous" examples were left out of this study since they provide no information on how to disambiguate. 407 of the 1,027 unambiguous lexical items (39.63%) were marked as **discourse**, and 620 (60.37%) were marked as **sentential**. See Hirschberg and Litman [1993] for more detail on the corpus and the distribution of data within it.

Results

Since the division between training and test cases is random for each run, and since the GA is a stochastic method, each run of the GA gives rise to a unique decision tree.[7] We performed 58 runs, thus generating 58 trees. We evaluate these trees in two ways. First, by manually examining several high scoring trees, we show they yield linguistically valid rules. Second, we measure the average performance of induced decision trees.

Linguistic Results

The small decision tree in Figure 1, a tree obtained manually by Hirschberg and Litman [1993], yields an accuracy of 79.16%. To attain any improvement in accuracy, a more complex *partitioning* of the training cases must take place, by which the GA focuses on the cases where the majority of error lies. It is by this partitioning process that additional linguistic rules are induced.

A decision tree implicitly partitions the training (and test) cases; each rule embedded in a decision tree corresponds to a partition. As an example, the small decision tree in Figure 1 corresponds to the following simple partitioning of the training data:

-1 = <period> is true for 189 cases (185 **discourse**).
-1 = <comma> is true for 72 cases (42 **discourse**).
766 cases remain (180 **discourse**).

In order to attain a higher accuracy than that of the small decision tree, the partition consisting of the 766 "remaining" cases, for example, is a viable candidate for re-partitioning – rules must be found which apply to subpartitions of that partition. As we show here, many of the induced rules tend to be linguistically viable.

There are two ways to examine the resulting rules. First, we identify general rules that apply to sets of clue words (i.e., more than one) from several trees. In particular, we note that different trees yield different generalizations. Second, we identify all generalizations encoded in high scoring trees for individual clue words. These generalizations identify the rules that, in combination, can be used for a single clue word. In analyzing these generalizations, we note where they are specific to the corpus and where we expect them to generalize to different domains.

Multiple Clue Word Rules. Table 3 displays example linguistic rules extracted from various decision trees, and lists the clue words to which they apply. Each rule consists of a comparison (under column "If") and the clue word sense which results if the comparison holds (under column "Then" – "S" stands for **sentential** and "D" stands for **discourse**). The "Linguistic Template" column indicates the most frequent part of speech of the clue word when the comparison holds, as determined manually, and is elaborated below. "Accuracy" shows the number of cases in the corpus for which the rule holds, divided by the number of cases in the corpus which match the pattern.

These rules strongly suggest strategies by which part of speech is used for disambiguation; the rules embody the fact that a clue word's sense is **sentential** if its part of speech is not a conjunction, and must be further disambiguated if it is a conjunction.

The first rule classifies an occurrence of either *see, look, further* or *say* as **Sentential** if position -1 is *to*. (These are the clue words for which this rule holds in the corpus.) Of the 30 times for which this condition holds, the rule is correct 29; the rule holds exactly when the listed words are behaving as verbs, as indicated by the linguistic template "*to* <verb>", e.g.:

*...we can foster this integration of AI techniques and database technology to **further** the goal of integrating the two fields into Expert Database Systems.*

This example is in fact the only occurrence of *further* in the corpus for which *to* is the immediately preceding token. However, the GA can induce this rule since it is generally applicable over the 4 clue words (as shown in the tree of Figure 3). This demonstrates the benefit gained by simultaneously disambiguating multiple words.

The second rule listed (100% accuracy) embodies two different "syntactic templates". Both are detected by checking for **-1** = *the*. The first, which occurs for *like, and* and *right*, determines that the sense is **sentential** if the clue word is being used as a noun[8], as in:

*...a lot of work going on now in what's called non-monotonic reasoning, circumscription and the **like**...*

and the second, which occurs for *right, first* and *next*, determines that the sense is **sentential** if the clue word is being used as an adjective in a noun phrase, as in:

---

[6]We used one linguist's markings, whereas Hirschberg and Litman [1993] used and correlated the judgements of that and another linguist, discarding those cases in which there was disagreement. Thus, the data we used was slightly more noisy than that used by Hirschberg and Litman [1993]. Further, we used a slightly larger portion of the marked transcript than is reported on by Hirschberg and Litman [1993].

[7]Technically, there is a very small possibility that the same decision tree will be induced by two different runs of the GA.

---

[8]*And* is a noun when it is used to refer to the logical operator.

*...I think this is the **first** time those three are cooperating...*

The third rule (90.11% accuracy) pinpoints the collocation *"as well"*. When in this collocation, *well* is being used as an adverb, e.g.:

*We could have just as **well** done without it but the system would run a lot more slowly.*

The fourth rule (76.92% accuracy), which applies to the 8 clue words listed, approximates the cases where a clue word is being used as an adverb, as in:

*And then in the summer of 1985 Ron left the West Coast to travel east to New Jersey where he is **now** at AT&T Bell Laboratories as head of the AI Principles Research Department.*

However, the condition "**-1** = *is*" holds for some cases in which a clue word is used in its **discourse** sense, as in:

*...and the second question is **well** where do we stop.*

Therefore, this particular rule is too simplistic for some cases. However, it has indicated for us a disambiguation method which uses the part of speech of the clue word.

Single Clue Word Rules. Table 4 shows the way the decision trees in Figures 2 and 3 disambiguate *and* and *say*, respectively. The decision trees are explicitly broken down into the rules used to disambiguate the individual clue words. The columns in the table are the same as the previous table, with the addition of "Decision tree", which points to the tree being analyzed. The rules for each word are listed in the order in which they are considered when traversing the decision tree. Therefore, for example, the condition of the fourth rule for *and* is only tried on cases for which **-1** is none of <period>, <comma>, or *is*, and this is reflected in the number of cases for which the condition holds, as listed in the "Accuracy" column. This number of occurrences is a count across the entire corpus; that is, both the training and test cases. The overall accuracy with which the example decision trees disambiguate the individual clue words is also shown.

The rules for *and* reflect the fact that, when coordinating noun phrases, *and* is usually being used in its **sentential** sense, and, when coordinating clauses, *and* is most often being used in its **discourse** sense.

The first two rules for *and* are the same as the first two rules of the small decision tree in Figure 1. The third and eighth rules hold for too few examples to draw any conclusions. The condition of the fourth rule approximates the cases for which *and* is being used to coordinate noun phrases, since most definite noun phrases are not the subject of a clause in the corpus. For example:

*...I've been very lucky to be able to work with Don Marshand **and** the institute in organizing this...*

This is clearly too simple a strategy (64.29% accuracy), but provides insight for improved strategies.

The fifth, sixth and seventh rules (75.00%, 85.71% and 83.33% accuracy) approximate the cases for which

and is coordinating clauses, since *I*, *we* and *this* are most frequently the subject of a clause in the corpus, as in:

*The idea of the tutorial sessions was precisely to try to bring people up to speed in areas that they might not be familiar with **and** I hope the tutorials accomplish that for you.*

The small tree of Figure 1, which disambiguates in general with accuracy 79.16%, only disambiguates *and* with accuracy 71.84% (The small tree disambiguates the occurrences of clue words other than *and* with accuracy 82.92%). However, the overall accuracy with which the decision tree in Figure 2 disambiguates *and* is 76.44%.

The decision tree in Figure 3 treats *say* differently and separately from the other clue words: After the first default arc is traversed, *say* is always disambiguated as **discourse**, while other words are treated differently (e.g., *well* is further tested). This demonstrates the utility of allowing decision trees to discriminate between clue words, since *say* occurs with sense **discourse** more frequently than most other clue words; *say* is only disambiguated with accuracy 41.67% by the small tree of Figure 1, but is disambiguated with accuracy 83.33% by the induced decision tree of Figure 3.

The cases for which the tree in Figure 3 classifies *say* as **sentential** are when *say* behaves as a verb, as in:

*That is if I **say** that John is both a Quaker and a Republican...*

As demonstrated by the contents of Table 4, most instances of clue words in the corpus are disambiguated by rules which hold with high accuracy, as measured across the entire corpus, while the decision trees were induced over only half of the corpus (the training set). This indicates that performance will remain high for unseen examples from similar corpora.

Numerical Results

From 58 runs of the GA, each with a random division between training and test cases, the maximum score over the test cases was 83.85%.[9] The performance of such a tree over unseen data ideally requires further formal evaluation with more test data.

The average score over the test cases for the 58 runs was 79.20%. The average disparity between training and test scores, 2.64, is not large. Therefore, the rules of induced decision trees tend to perform well over unseen data, although it is inconclusive whether their combined contribution to disambiguation accuracy improves over the overall performance of the small tree in Figure 1 (79.16%) for the entire set of clue words. However, decision trees clearly aid in the disambiguation of several of the clue words, e.g. *say* and *and*.

These results reflect the difficulty inherent to the task of clue word sense disambiguation. Hirschberg and Lit-

---

[9]This is the maximum test score of the decision trees which performed the best of their run over the *training* cases. This same pool of trees is considered for average test performance.

Table 3: Linguistic rules extracted from various automatically induced decision trees.

Clue words	Rule		Linguistic template	Accuracy
	If	**Then**		
see, look, further, say	-1 = *to*	S	*to* <verb>	29/30 = 96.67%
like, and, right *right, first, next*	-1 = *the*	S	*the* <noun> *the* <adj>	18/18 = 100.00%
well	-1 = *as*	S	*as well*	10/11 = 90.11%
also, now, generally *actually, basically*	-1 = *is*	S	*is* <adverb>	10/13 = 76.92%

Table 4: The rules used by sample trees to disambiguate *and* and *say*.

Clue word	Decision tree	Rule		Linguistic template	Accuracy
		If	**Then**		
and	Figure 2	-1 = <period>	D	sentence initial	29/30 = 96.67%
		-1 = <comma>	D	clause initial	18/25 = 72.00%
		-1 = *is*	D	(inconclusive)	1/ 1 = 100.00%
		1 = *the*	S	*and* <def NP>	9/ 14 = 64.29%
		1 = *I*	D	*and* <subject>	9/ 12 = 75.00%
		1 = *we*	D	*and* <subject>	6/ 7 = 85.71%
		1 = *this*	D	*and* <subject>	5/ 6 = 83.33%
		1 = *at*	D	(inconclusive)	1/ 2 = 50.00%
		else *(default)*	S		188/251 = 74.90%
				Overall accuracy for *and*:	266/348 = 76.44%
say	Figure 3	-1 = *to*	S	*to* <verb>	4/ 4 = 100.00%
		-1 = *I*	S	*I* <verb>	2/ 2 = 100.00%
		else *(default)*	D		24/ 30 = 80.00%
				Overall accuracy for *say*:	30/ 36 = 83.33%

man [1993] report that 7.87% of the examples manually marked by the authors were either disagreed upon by the authors, or were decidedly ambiguous.

Many disambiguation tasks will presumably not have a simple strategy (such as that embodied by the small decision tree in Figure 1) which performs to such a high degree of accuracy. For example, the aspectual classification of a clause requires the interaction of several syntactic constituents of the clause [Pustejovsky 1991]. Therefore, since the disparity between training and test performance is moderate, decision tree induction is likely, in general, to outperform such simple strategies for disambiguation tasks.

As a benchmark, several top-down (*recursive partitioning*) decision tree induction methods [Quinlan 1986] [Breiman et al 1984] were applied to the disambiguation corpus.[10] This comparison was motivated by the fact that top-down decision tree induction is the more established method for decision tree induction The best top-down method disambiguated the test cases with accuracy 79.06% on average (based on 200 runs, each with a random division between training and test sets), which is comparable to the GA's average performance, 79.20%.

GAs are a weak learning method, which often require less explicit engineering of heuristics than top-down induction. For an investigation of the generalization performance of GA decision tree induction see Siegel [1994].

---

[10]These experiments were performed using the IND decision tree induction package [Buntine and Caruana 1991].

Tackett [1993] and Greene & Smith [1987] have also performed comparisons between GA techniques and recursive partitioning methods.

Conclusions and Future Work

The disambiguation of *and* and *say*, as well as other clue words, has benefited from the integration of knowledge about surrounding words, without the explicit encoding of syntactic data. Further, we have demonstrated that the automatic partitioning of the training set during decision tree induction provides an array of linguistically viable rules. These rules provide insights as to syntactic information which would be additionally beneficial for clue word sense disambiguation. Further, the rules can help linguists evaluate the validity of induced decision trees.

We have demonstrated the utility of disambiguating a set of words simultaneously: generalizations which apply over several words are induced, and, when training over a small corpus, this allows generalizations to be made on examples that occur extremely infrequently (e.g., once).

We plan to apply machine learning methods to aspectual ambiguity. The aspectual class of a clause depends on a complex interaction between the verb, its particles, and its arguments [Pustejovsky 1991]. Induction will be performed simultaneously over a set of verbs, with access to the syntactic parse of example clauses.

Acknowledgments

We wish to thank Diane Litman and Julia Hirschberg for generously providing the marked transcript of spoken English used in this work. We also thank Diane Litman for extremely valuable feedback regarding this work. Additionally, thank you Rebecca J. Passonneau, Jacques Robin and Vasileios Hatzivassiloglou for many important comments and suggestions. This work was partially supported by ONR/ARPA grant N00014-89-J-1782 and NSF grant GER-90-2406.

References

Black, E. (1988) An experiment in computational discrimination of English word senses. *IBM Journal of Research and Development*, 32(2).

Breiman L., Friedman J.H., Olshen R.A., and Stone C.J. (1984) *Classification and Regression Trees*. Wadsworth, Belmont.

Brown, P. F., DellaPietra, S. A., DellaPietra, V. J., and Mercer, R. L., (1991) Word sense disambiguation using statistical methods, in *Proceedings 29th Annual Meeting of the Association for Computational Linguistics*, (Berkeley, CA), pp. 265-270, June 1991.

Buntine, W. and Caruana, R. (1991) *Introduction to IND and Recursive Partitioning*, NASA Ames Research Center.

Goldberg, D. (1989) *Genetic Algorithms in Search, Optimization, and Machine Learning*. Reading, MA: Addison-Wesley Publishing Company, Inc.

Greene, D. P., and Smith, S. F. (1987) A Genetic System for Learning Models of Consumer Choice. *Proceedings of the Second International Conference on Genetic Algorithms*, J.J. Grefenstette (ed.), Hillsdale, NH: Lawrence Erlbaum Associates, pp. 217-223.

Grishman, R. and Sterling J. (1993) "Smoothing of automatically generated selectional constraints", *Proceedings of the ARPA Workshop on Human Language Technology*. March, 1993.

Hirschberg, J. and Litman, D., (1993) Empirical Studies on the Disambiguation of Cue Phrases, in *Computational Linguistics*, Vol. 19, No. 3.

Holland, J. (1975) *Adaptation in Natural and Artificial Systems*, Ann Arbor, MI: The University of Michigan Press.

Knight K., forthcoming.

Koza, J. R. (1992) *Genetic programming:On the programming of computers by mean of natural selection*. Cambridge, MA: MIT press.

Leacock C., Towell G., and Voorhees E. (1993) "Corpus-Based Statistical Sense Resolution", *Proceedings of the ARPA Workshop on Human Language Technology*. March, 1993.

Magerman, D. H. (1993) "Parsing as Statistical Pattern Recognition", IBM technical report.

Pustejovsky, J. (1991) "The Syntax of Event Structure", *Cognition*, Vol. 41:103:47-82.

Quinlan, J.R. (1986) Induction of decision trees. *Machine Learning*, 1(1):81-106.

Resnik, P. (1993). "Semantic Classes and Syntactic Ambiguity", *Proceedings of the ARPA Workshop on Human Language Technology*. March, 1993.

Schiffrin, Deborah (1987). *Discourse Markers*. Cambridge University Press.

Schuetze, H. (1992) Dimensions of meaning. In *Proceedings of Supercomputing '92*.

Siegel, E. V. (1994) "Competitively evolving decision trees against fixed training cases for natural language processing." In *Advances in Genetic Programming*, K. Kinnear (ed.), Cambridge MA: MIT Press.

Tackett, W. A. (1993) Genetic Programming for Feature Discovery and Image Discrimination. In *Proceedings of the Fifth International Conference on Genetic Algorithms*. San Mateo, CA: Morgan Kaufmann.

Yarowsky, D. (1993). "One Sense Per Collocation", *Proceedings of the ARPA Workshop on Human Language Technology*. March, 1993.

Corpus-Driven Knowledge Acquisition
for Discourse Analysis

Stephen Soderland and **Wendy Lehnert** *
Department of Computer Science
University of Massachusetts
Amherst, MA 01003-4610
soderlan@cs.umass.edu   lehnert@cs.umass.edu

Abstract

The availability of large on-line text corpora provides a natural and promising bridge between the worlds of natural language processing (NLP) and machine learning (ML). In recent years, the NLP community has been aggressively investigating statistical techniques to drive part-of-speech taggers, but application-specific text corpora can be used to drive knowledge acquisition at much higher levels as well. In this paper we will show how ML techniques can be used to support knowledge acquisition for information extraction systems. It is often very difficult to specify an explicit domain model for many information extraction applications, and it is always labor intensive to implement hand-coded heuristics for each new domain. We have discovered that it is nevertheless possible to use ML algorithms in order to capture knowledge that is only implicitly present in a representative text corpus. Our work addresses issues traditionally associated with discourse analysis and intersentential inference generation, and demonstrates the utility of ML algorithms at this higher level of language analysis.

The benefits of our work address the portability and scalability of information extraction (IE) technologies. When hand-coded heuristics are used to manage discourse analysis in an information extraction system, months of programming effort are easily needed to port a successful IE system to a new domain. We will show how ML algorithms can reduce this development time to a few days of automated corpus analysis without any resulting degradation of overall system performance.

1. Information Extraction at the Discourse Level

All IE systems must operate at both the sentence level and the discourse level. At the sentence level, relevant information is extracted by a sentence analyzer according to pre-defined domain guidelines. Recent performance evaluations sponsored by ARPA have shown

*This research was supported by NSF Grant no. EEC-9209623, State/Industry/University Cooperative Research on Intelligent Information Retrieval.

that a number of different parsing strategies can handle sentence-level information extraction with varying degrees of success (Lehnert and Sundheim 1991, Sundheim 1991).

This paper will concentrate on the discourse level, by which we mean all processing that takes place after sentence analysis. Once information has been extracted locally from various text segments, the IE system must make a series of higher-level decisions before producing its final output. Multiple referents must be merged when they are coreferent, important relationships between distinct referents must be recognized, and referents that are spurious with respect to the IE application must be discarded.

To get a sense of the decisions involved in discourse, consider the following fragment of a text from the MUC-5 micro-electronics domain.

```
GCA unveiled its new XLS stepper, which was
developed with assistance from Sematech.  The
system will be available in deep-ultraviolet
and I-line configurations.
```

Sentence analysis should extract two company names and a piece of stepper equipment from the first sentence and two processes, UV lithography and I-line lithography, from the second sentence. It is up to discourse analysis to determine the relationships between these objects.

Domain guidelines require pointers in the output from a micro-chip fabrication processes to related equipment, from equipment to its manufacturer, and from a process to devices produced. There are four possible links between company and process: developer, manufacturer, distributor, and purchaser/user. Considerable domain knowledge is needed at the discourse-level to recognize these various relationships.

Wrap-Up is an ML-based discourse component for IE applications that automatically derives this domain knowledge from a training corpus and requires no hand-coded domain knowledge. It uses a series of interacting decision trees to make decisions about merging, linking, splitting, and discarding information produced by a sentence analyzer. During its training

"

phase, Wrap-Up repeatedly consults an output key associated with each training text in order to construct decision trees that are later used to guide decisions when Wrap-Up operates as a stand-alone discourse analyzer.

2. Applying Decision Tree Algorithms to the Problem

Wrap-Up breaks discourse processing into a number of small decisions and builds a separate ID3 decision tree for each (Quinlan 1986). The Lithography-Equipment-Links tree is typical of the 91 decision trees used for the micro-electronics domain. During discourse processing, Wrap-Up encodes an instance for each pair of extracted lithography and equipment objects, such as UV lithography and XLS stepper in the previous example. If the Lithography-Equipment-Links tree returns a classification of "positive", a pointer is added from the lithography process to the equipment.

Much of the art of machine learning is in choosing suitable features for the instances. Wrap-Up's goal is to supply ID3 with all the information available from the sentence analyzer, but to avoid any domain-specific feature generators. Extraction of UV lithography was triggered by the linguistic pattern "available in X" and by the keyword "deep-ultraviolet". Wrap-Up encodes these as the binary features pp-available, pp-in, and keyword-deep-ultraviolet. The feature trigger-count has a value of 3.

The same is done for the linguistic context of Stepper, which was found in "unveils X", "X was developed", and by the keyword "stepper". The relative position of the two objects is captured by features for the number of common-phrases, the common-triggers, and the relative distance, which is -1 sentences apart.

```
(lithography-type . uv) (trigger-count-1 . 3)
(pp-1-available . t) (pp-1-in . t)
(keyword-1-deep-ultraviolet . t)
(equipment-type . stepper) (equipment-name . t)
(trigger-count-2 . 3) (dir-obj-2-unveiled . t)
(subj-passive-developed . t) (keyword-2-stepper . t)
(common-triggers . 0) (common-phrases . 0)
(distance . -1)
```

During the training phase, ID3 is given such an instance for every pair of lithography and equipment objects in the 800 training texts. If the hand-coded output key for the training text has a link between the lithography and equipment objects, the training instance is classified as positive. ID3 tabulates how often each possible feature value is associated with a positive or negative training instance and encapsulates these statistics at each node of the tree it builds.

As figure 1 shows, the Lithography-Equipment-Links tree started with 282 positive and 539 negative training instances, giving a 34% a priori probability of a link. ID3 recursively selects features to partition

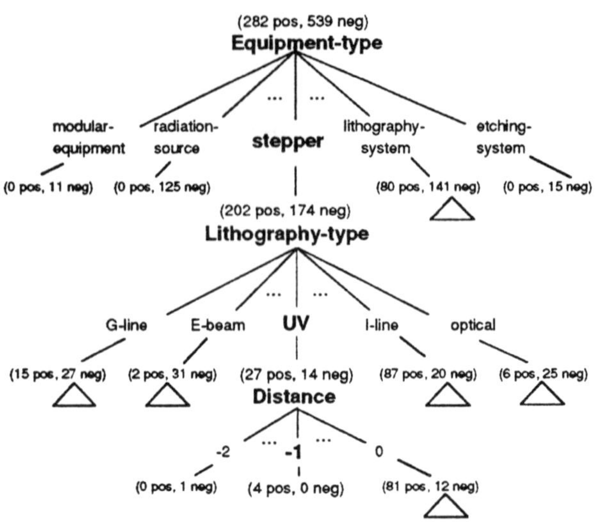

Figure 1: A Lithography-Equipment-Links decision tree. The highlighted path is for an instance with stepper equipment, UV lithography, and equipment mentioned one sentence earlier than lithography.

the training instances according to an information gain metric (p.89-90 Quinlan 1986). The feature chosen as root of this tree is equipment-type. This feature alone is sufficient to classify instances with equipment-type such as modular-equipment, radiation-source, or etching-system, which have only negative instances. Equipment-type stepper has 202 positive and 174 negative training instances, raising the probability of a link to 54%.

The next feature selected is lithography-type. The partition for UV lithography has 27 positive and 14 negative instances in contrast to e-beam, which has 94% negative instances. The next test is distance, with the branch for -1 leading to a leaf node with 4 positive and no negative instances. The tree returns a classification of positive and Wrap-Up adds a link from UV lithography to the Stepper.

This example shows how a decision tree can acquire useful domain knowledge: that lithography is never linked to equipment such as etching-system, and that steppers are often linked with UV lithography but hardly ever with e-beam lithography.

Other decision trees make greater use of the linguistic pattern features. Tests for linguistic patterns such as "X unveiled stepper" are used in the decision tree that filters out irrelevant company names and in the trees that decide whether a company is a developer of a micro-electronics process.

Using specific linguistic patterns resulted in extremely large, sparse feature sets for most trees. The Lithography-Equipment tree had 1045 features, all but 11 of them encoding linguistic patterns. Since each instance participates in at most a dozen linguistic patterns, a potential time and space bottleneck could be avoided by a sparse-vector implementation of ID3.

Tree pruning was also used when partitions near the leaf nodes become so small that the features selected have little predictive power. Wrap-Up empirically sets pruning level and threshold for each tree. The threshold determines the classification when a tree probe halts at a node with both positive and negative instances.

3. Wrap-Up: An Overview

Wrap-Up is a discourse component for information extraction that uses a series of interacting ID3 decision trees to make decisions about merging, linking, splitting, and discarding locally extracted information. The number of decision trees depends on the number of objects and links defined in the output structure. The feature set for each tree is automatically derived from linguistic patterns that occur in training instances. Wrap-Up provides a domain-independent framework which is instantiated for each domain with no additional heuristics or hand-coded knowledge needed.

Input to Wrap-Up is a set of tokens, each initially representing a single referent identified by the sentence analyzer. Tokens consist of a case frame containing the extracted information and a list of references to that information in the text with the location of each reference and the linguistic patterns used to extract it. Wrap-Up transforms this set of tokens, discarding information judged irrelevant to the domain, merging tokens with related information, adding pointers between tokens, and adding inferred tokens and default slot values.

Wrap-Up was tested using output extracted by the University of Massachusetts CIRCUS sentence analyzer (Lehnert 1990, Lehnert et al. 1992a, 1992b), although it could be adapted to any sentence analyzer which uses linguistic patterns for extraction.

Wrap-Up has six stages of processing, each with its own set of decision trees to guide the transformation of tokens as they are passed from one stage to the next.

Algorithm:

1. Slot Filter

Each token slot has its own decision tree that judges whether the slot contains reliable information. Discard the slot from a token if a tree returns "negative".

2. Slot Merge

Create an instance for each pair of tokens of the same type. Merge the two tokens if a decision tree for that token type returns "positive".

3. Links

Beginning at the lowest level of links in the output structure, consider pairs of tokens which might possibly be linked. Add a pointer between tokens if a decision tree returns "positive".

4. Links Merge

During the Links stage, token A may have a link to both token B and to token C. If a links-merge tree returns "positive", add pointers from token A to both B and C. If the tree returns "negative", split A into two copies with one pointing to B and the other to C.

5. Orphans

Orphans are tokens not pointed to by any other token. A decision tree returns the most likely parent token for each orphan. Create such a parent and link it to the orphan unless the tree returns "none". Then use decision trees from the Links and Links Merge stages to tie the new parent in with other tokens.

6. Slot Defaults

Create an instance for each empty token slot with a closed class of possible values. Add the slot value returned by a decision tree unless "none" is returned.

Perhaps the best way to understand the algorithm is to look at a concrete example. Figure 2 has a sample microelectronics text about packaging processes used to manufacture DRAM chips. The target output has SOJ packaging, TSOP packaging, one entity (Mitsubishi Electronics America, Inc), and a DRAM device. The size 1 MBit should be merged with DRAM and the

The <u>Semiconductor Division</u> of <u>Mitsubishi Electronics America, Inc.</u> now offers 1M CMOS <u>DRAMs</u> in <u>Thin Small-Outline Packaging</u> (<u>TSOP</u>*), providing the highest <u>memory</u> density available in the industry. Developed by <u>Mitsubishi</u>, the <u>TSOP</u> also lets designers increase system <u>memory</u> density with standard and reverse, or "mirror image," pin-outs. <u>Mitsubishi</u>'s 1M <u>DRAM</u> <u>TSOP</u> provides the density to be 100% burned-in and fully tested. *Previously referred to as VSOP (very <u>small-outline package</u>) or USOP (ultra <u>small-outline package</u>). The 1M <u>DRAM</u> <u>TSOP</u> has a height of 1.2 mm, a plane measurement of 16.0 mm x 6.0 mm, and a lead pitch of 0.5 mm, making it nearly three times thinner and four times smaller in volume than the 1M <u>DRAM</u> <u>SOJ package</u>. The <u>SOJ</u> has a height of 3.45 mm, a plane dimension of 17.15 mm x 8.45 mm, and a lead pitch of 1.27 mm. Additionally, the <u>TSOP</u> weighs only 0.22 grams, in contrast with the 0.75 gram weight of the <u>SOJ</u>.

Full text available on PTS New Product Announcements.

Figure 2: A sample text from the MUC-5 Microelectronics domain. Extracted information is underlined.

material plastic merged with TSOP but not with SOJ packaging. Mitsubishi is linked to SOJ packaging as purchaser/user and to TSOP packaging as both developer and purchaser/user.

The first stage of Wrap-Up considers each slot of each extracted object to filter out irrelevant or spurious information. This step was included because the output of the sentence analyzer often includes spurious information. In this case the sentence analyzer correctly extracted "Mitsubishi Electronics America, Inc." but also reported a separate entity, "Semiconductor Division of Mitsubishi Electronics America, Inc.".

The Entity-Name-Filter tree was able to classify the former as a positive instance and the latter as negative. The first feature tested by this tree is trigger-count, since it turns out that entity names extracted by five linguistic triggers are more reliable than those extracted by only two triggers. This first test raises the confidence in "Mitsubishi Electronics America, Inc." with five linguistic triggers to 67% while lowering the confidence in "Semiconductor Division" to 36%. The tree then tested for various linguistic-triggers such as pp-of, subj-announced, pp-sold, and pp-subsidiary to arrive at a classification. A Packaging-Material-Filter tree also discarded epoxy, which was often spuriously extracted from training texts.

The next stage of Wrap-Up is slot-merge, where plastic is merged with TSOP packaging, but not with the SOJ packaging. A separate instances is created for each pair of packaging objects: TSOP-plastic, SOJ-plastic, and TSOP-SOJ. The Packaging-Slotmerge tree classifies TSOP-plastic as positive, since the distance is 0 and this combination occurs often in the training corpus. SOJ-plastic is classified negative, primarily because the distance is -2. TSOP-SOJ is easily classified as negative, since objects in the training instances never have multiple packaging types. The state of the output at this point in discourse processing is shown in figure 3.

Template   Entity

<table>
<tr><td>**Template**</td><td></td><td>**Entity**</td></tr>
<tr><td>Doc-Nr: 2523814</td><td></td><td>Type: Company</td></tr>
<tr><td></td><td></td><td>Name: Mitsubishi Electronics</td></tr>
<tr><td></td><td></td><td>America Inc.</td></tr>
<tr><td></td><td></td><td></td></tr>
<tr><td>**Packaging**</td><td>**Packaging**</td><td>**Device**</td></tr>
<tr><td>Type: TSOP</td><td>Type: SOJ</td><td>Type: DRAM</td></tr>
<tr><td>Material: Plastic</td><td></td><td></td></tr>
</table>

Figure 3: Output from the sample text before links have been added. One spurious company name and one packaging material have been filtered out and TSOP packaging has been merged with the packaging-material plastic.

Much of Wrap-Up's work occurs during the links stage, which first consults a Packaging-Device-Links tree to determine links between DRAM and each pack-

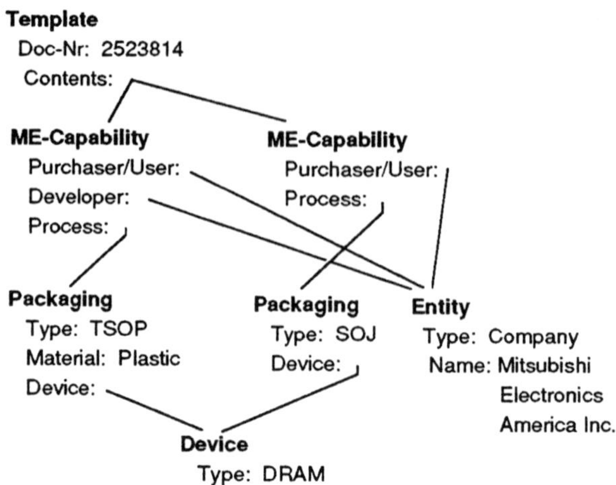

Figure 4: Final output after links have been added

aging process. The root of this tree is the feature distance, followed by a test for packaging-type. Although only 29% of the training instances were positive, those with distance 0 and packaging-type TSOP were 80% positive. The SOJ-DRAM instance, with a distance of 0 was also classified positive.

The most difficult discourse decision is resolving the role of each company as developer, manufacturer, distributor, or purchaser/user of a process. Linguistic patterns such as "X is shipping", "X purchased", or "X developed" are important in distinguishing the company's role. But a company that "developed a new chip" is probably not developer of the process to fabricate that chip.

There were seldom explicit linguistic clues about the relation of a company to a packaging process, so trees such as Packaging-Purchaser-Links fell back on statistics based on relative distance in the text, packaging-type, and trigger-count. Although SOJ is first mentioned two sentence after Mitsubishi, Wrap-Up lets objects inherit linguistic patterns from objects to which they point. A link had been added from SOJ to DRAM, which occurs in the same sentence with Mitsubishi. The Packaging-Purchaser-Links tree returned positive for the instance with packaging-type SOJ, distance of 0, and trigger-count of 10.

A new object is created for each link between company and process, and these "microelectronics-capability" objects are then merged together according to judgments made by links-merge trees. The final output with links added is shown in figure 4.

A different example illustrates the power of Wrap-Up's links-merge stage to learn a different kind of domain knowledge. Consider the following fragment of text where a lithography process is associated with three types of chips and two pieces of equipment.

...a clean room utilizing Ultratech Stepper and
GCA steppers. General Signal said it plans to
use the facility to demonstrate manufacturing
techniques, such as mix-and-match lithography
methods to produce dynamic and static RAMs and
ASIC devices.

In this domain, a process may point to several devices in the output, in this example lithography linked
to DRAM, SRAM, and ASIC. But if a process is
linked to multiple equipment, it is typically considered multiple processes, each one pointing to a separate equipment object. The target output for this text
has lithography-1 pointing to Ultratech Stepper and to
DRAM, SRAM, and ASIC. A separate lithography-2
object points to the GCA stepper and each of the three
devices.

Wrap-Up uses links-merge trees to decide whether to
merge or split when an object has pointers to multiple
objects. Interestingly enough this domain knowledge
could only be learned by example from the training
corpus, as it was mentioned nowhere in the fifty pages
of domain guidelines supplied by ARPA to MUC-5 participants.

Wrap-Up is also able to infer objects not explicitly
extracted from the text and to add context-sensitive
defaults for some slot values. If a text has stepper
equipment, but no process using the stepper is mentioned, it becomes an "orphan" with no object pointing to it in the output. The Equipment-Orphans tree
learned that stepper equipment always had a lithography process pointing to it in the training output. The
"orphans" trees return the type of object to be added
to the output, if a parent object can be inferred.

4. Test Results

The performance of Wrap-Up compared well with that
of the official UMass/Hughes MUC-5 system, where
output from the CIRCUS sentence analyzer was sent
to TTG (Trainable Template Generator), a discourse
component based on the Trainable Text Skimmer from
the Hughes Research Laboratories (Dolan, et al. 1991,
Lehnert et al. 1993).

Acquisition of domain knowledge by machine learning was at the heart of the TTG system, but it didn't
go as far as Wrap-Up in being fully trainable. Some
of the features used by TTG classifiers were generated
by domain-specific code, and decisions about merging
or splitting, which Wrap-Up handles during its links-
merge stage, were done by hand-coded heuristics external to TTG. The ability to infer objects not explicitly
mentioned in the text was also more limited than that
of Wrap-Up.

Several iterations of hand-tuning were required to
adjust thresholds for the decision trees produced by
TTG, where Wrap-Up uses ten-fold cross-validation to
automatically evaluate different thresholds and pruning levels. After a day of CPU-time building decision

trees, Wrap-Up is a working system with no further
programming effort needed. Additional fine-tuning can
be done, but the results shown in figure 5 are with no
fine-tuning.

Wrap-Up outperformed TTG in both overall recall
and precision on the official MUC-5 micro-electronics
test sets. Performance metrics used in the MUC evaluations are recall, precision, and f-measure. Recall is the
percentage of possible information that was reported.
Precision is the percent correct of the reported information. F-measure combines these into a single metric
with the formula $F = ((\beta^2 + 1)PR)/(\beta^2 P + R)$, where
β is set to 1 here.

	Wrap-Up			TTG		
	Rec.	Prec.	F	Rec.	Prec.	F
Part 1	32.3	44.4	37.4	27.1	39.5	32.1
Part 2	36.3	38.6	37.4	32.7	37.0	34.7
Part 3	34.6	37.7	36.1	34.7	40.5	37.5
Avg.	34.4	40.2	36.8	31.5	39.0	34.8

Figure 5: Performance on MUC-5 microelectronics test
sets

Lack of coverage by the sentence analyzer places a
ceiling on recall for the discourse component. In test
set part 1 there were 208 company names to be extracted. The CIRCUS analyzer extracted a total of 404
company names, with only 131 correct and 2 partially
correct, giving a baseline of 63% recall and 33% precision for that slot. Wrap-Up's entity-name filter tree
managed to discard a little over half of the spurious
company names, keeping 77% of the good companies.
This resulted in 49% recall and 44% precision for this
slot. TTG discarded a little less than half the spurious companies, but kept only 59% of the good ones,
resulting in 40% recall and 36% precision for this slot.

Although precision is often increased at the expense
of recall, Wrap-Up also has mechanisms to generate a
small increase in recall. Inferring a lithography process
from stepper equipment, or splitting a process that is
linked to multiple equipment can gain back recall that
is lost from discarding objects during the filter stage.

5. Conclusions

Information extraction systems represent a new and
exciting class of applications for NLP technologies. ARPA-sponsored performance evaluations have
demonstrated the importance of domain portability
and fast system development cycles in making IE systems economically viable (Sundheim 1991, 1992, 1993;
Lehnert and Sundheim 1991). In an effort to address
these issues, researchers have show that representative text corpora can be exploited to solve problems
at the level of sentence analysis (Riloff 1993, Cardie
1993, Hobbes et al. 1992, Ayuso et al. 1992). Our

work shows that representative text corpora can be exploited in order to handle problems at the level of discourse analysis as well.

Our approach requires a set of hand-crafted answer keys in addition to source texts, and this resource represents a labor-intensive investment on the part of domain experts. On the other hand, no knowledge of NLP or ML technologies is needed to generate these answer keys, so any domain expert can produce answer keys for use by Wrap-Up. It is also easier to generate a few hundred answer keys than it is to write down explicit and comprehensive domain guidelines. Moreover, domain knowledge implicitly present in a set of answer keys may go beyond the conventional knowledge of a domain expert when reliable patterns of information transcend a logical domain model.

Because Wrap-Up requires no hand-coded heuristics or manual design, it provides a paradigm for user-customizable system design, where no technological background on the part of the user is assumed. We have seen how Wrap-Up improves recall and precision produced at the level of the sentence analyzer. This suggests that improvements in overall system performance can be obtained by improving the operation of the sentence analyzer, or perhaps through feedback between sentence analysis and discourse analysis.

The integration of ML algorithms in a comprehensive IE system also encourages a new perspective on sentence analysis. If ML technologies are especially successful at noise reduction, it makes sense to pursue sentence analysis techniques that favor recall over precision. While we normally expect error rates to propagate across a serial system, noise-tolerant ML algorithms may be able to hold error rates in check as we move from low levels of text analysis to the highest levels of language comprehension.

But even if ML algorithms could only duplicate the performance levels of hand-coded discourse modules, we would still be looking at a major achievement in terms of portability and scalability. Our experience with Wrap-Up suggests that ML algorithms provide a promising foundation for corpus-driven discourse analysis. Hand-coded heuristics can be replaced by decision trees, and implicit domain knowledge can be derived from a representative development corpus. This result is both encouraging with respect to practical system development, and somewhat provocative with respect to the larger issue of automated knowledge acquisition.

References

Ayuso, D.; Boisen, S.; Fox, H.; Gish, H.; Ingria, R.; and Weishedel, R. 1992. BBN: Description of the PLUM System as Used for MUC-4. In Proceedings of the Fourth Message Understanding Conference, 169-176. Morgan Kaufmann Publishers.

Cardie, C. 1993. A Case-Based Approach to Knowledge Acquisition for Domain-Specific Sentence Analysis. In Proceedings of the Eleventh National Conference on Artificial Intelligence, 798-803.

Dolan, C. P.; Goldman, S. R.; Cuda, T. V.; Nakamura, A. M. 1991. Hughes Trainable Text Skimmer: Description of the TTS System as used for MUC-3. In Proceedings of the Third Message Understanding Conference. Morgan Kaufmann Publishers.

Hobbes, J.R.; Appelt, D.; Mabry, T.; Bear, J.; Israel, D. 1992. SRI International: Description of the Faustus System Used for MUC-4. In Proceedings of the Fourth Message Understanding Conference, 268-275. Morgan Kaufmann Publishers.

Lehnert, W. 1990. Symbolic/Subsymbolic Sentence Analysis: Exploiting the Best of Two Worlds. *Advances in Connectionist and Neural Computation Theory. vol. 1.*, 151-158. Norwood, NJ: Ablex Publishing.

Lehnert, W.; Cardie, C.; Fisher, D.; McCarthy, J.; Riloff, E.; Soderland, S. 1992a. University of Massachusetts: MUC-4 Test Results and Analysis, 151-158. In Proceedings of the Fourth Message Understanding Conference. Morgan Kaufmann Publishers.

Lehnert, W.; Cardie, C.; Fisher, D.; McCarthy, J.; Riloff, E.; Soderland, S. 1992b. University of Massachusetts: Description of the CIRCUS System as Used for MUC-4, 282-288. In Proceedings of the Fourth Message Understanding Conference. Morgan Kaufmann Publishers.

Lehnert, W.; Cardie, C.; Fisher, D.; McCarthy, J.; Riloff, E.; Soderland, S.; Feng, F.; Dolan, C.; Goldman, S. 1993. University of Massachusetts: Description of the CIRCUS System as Used for MUC-5. In Proceedings of the Fifth Message Understanding Conference. Morgan Kaufmann Publishers.

Lehnert, W.G., and Sundheim, B. 1991. A Performance Evaluation of Text Analysis Technologies. *AI Magazine*: 81-94.

Quinlan, J.R. 1986. Induction of Decision Trees. *Machine Learning* (1): 81-106.

Riloff, E. 1993. Automatically Constructing a Dictionary for Information Extraction Tasks. In Proceedings of the Eleventh National Conference on Artificial Intelligence, 811-816.

Sundheim, B. 1991. Proceedings of the Third Message Understanding Conference (MUC-3). Morgan Kaufmann Publishers.

Sundheim, B. 1992. Proceedings of the Fourth Message Understanding Conference (MUC-4). Morgan Kaufmann Publishers.

Sundheim, B. 1993. Proceedings of the Fifth Message Understanding Conference (MUC-5). Morgan Kaufmann Publishers.

Principled Multilingual Grammars for Large Corpora

Sharon Flank and **Paul Krause**
Systems Research and Applications Corporation
2000 15th Street North, Arlington, VA 22201
(703) 558-4700
flanks@sra.com, krausep@sra.com

Carol Van Ess-Dykema
Department of Defense*
9800 Savage Road
Fort Meade, MD 20755
cjvanes@afterlife.ncsc.mil

Abstract

In-depth text understanding for large-scale applications requires a broad-coverage, robust grammar. We describe a multilingual implementation of such a grammar, and its advantages over both principle-based parsing and ad-hoc grammar design. We show how X-bar theory and language-independent semantic constraints facilitate grammar development. Our implementation includes innovative handling of (1) syntactic gaps, (2) logical structure alternations, and (3) conjunctions. Each of these innovations enhances performance in both large-scale and multilingual natural language processing applications.

Phrase structure grammars are hardly new. The novelty in this paper comes from the use of practical guidelines and real numbers based on our experience with three languages and tens of thousands of texts. The issue of grammar design is worth revisiting because of the increasing bifurcation between semantic phrase grammars on the one hand, and principle-based parsing in toy domains on the other. Semantic grammars are brittle and must be rewritten for each new domain and language; principle-based parsing is not yet mature enough for our applications. We offer an extensible, multilingual application of the traditional approach that extends theoretical linguistic insights to industrial strength data.

The Problem

The development of multilingual grammars presents a dilemma. There is considerable commonality in grammars of human languages, as represented by the insights of so-called "universal grammar," (Chomsky 1967). However, the need for speedy development has led many to abandon full-sentence parsing and substitute either phrase parsing or very specific semantic patterns. This approach ignores the universality of syntax across languages, and requires that patterns be created not only for every language but also

---

*The views and conclusions contained in this document are those of the authors and should not be interpreted as necessarily representing the official policies, either expressed or implied, of the Department of Defense or the United States Government.

for every domain. Other researchers have embraced portability and extensibility by using principle-based parsers. Principle-based parsing attempts to use syntactic theory to specify grammatical principles and parameters so that a single core grammar can be used as the basis for multilingual processing. Principle-based parsing (Berwick 1987; Fong & Berwick 1989; Lin 1993) relies on Government and Binding Theory, as initially described in Chomsky (1981). Unfortunately, neither principle-based parsing nor Government and Binding Theory itself has been proven viable for the fifty-word sentences with multiple conjunctions, gaps, and asides that are typical of text understanding applications. Here, for example, is a not atypical Spanish sentence to be handled in a large-scale application:

La información la proporcionó ayer el Ministro de Salud doctor Juan Giaconi, quien dio a conocer que durante el último trimestre se detectaron 14 casos de Sida en el país, lo que arroja hasta ahora una cifra total acumulada de 42 contagios declarados desde 1984, año en que se registró el ingreso del virus al territorio.

The information was provided yesterday by the Minister of Health Doctor Juan Giaconi, who made it known that during the last quarter 14 AIDS cases were detected in the country, which to date amounts to a total accumulated sum of 42 infections reported since 1984, the year in which the entrance of the virus into the region was recorded.

Correct attachment of, for example, *the year...* to *1984*, requires that the semantic similarity of the two be evident. That is, it must be clear that 1984 is a year, requiring semantic information be available to the parser. While this is not precluded by Government and Binding theory, current implementations do not facilitate access to such information. In sum, what is needed is a fast parser that can capture commonalities, both syntactic and semantic, across languages and domains.

Table 1: Core Grammar Rules

Category	X-Bar Levels to Be Included
Noun Phrase	Minimum of 4 X-bar levels,[a] with 3 possibilities at each level (SPEC,[b] COMP, Noun-noun and Adj-noun modification, and conjunction)
Prepositional Phrase	SPEC, COMP, and conjunction
Verb Phrase	Direct and indirect objects, verb particles, prepositional and sentential arguments, conjunction
Adjective Phrase	SPEC, COMP, and conjunction
Adverb Phrase	SPEC, COMP, and conjunction
Quantifier Phrase	SPEC, COMP, and conjunction
Sentence	Left and right complements, conjunction, punctuation
INFL/Auxiliaries	Correct ordering of all types requires several rules
Conjunction Phrase	Commas with and without "and" etc.
Complementizer/ Subordinating Conjunction Phrase	Specifiers, commas
Specifiers	Several simple and complex types, including negation
Complements	S', S, PP, appositive
Punctuation Rules	Period, semicolon, colon, question mark, etc.
Specific Rules	Latitude/longitude, age appositives, id numbers, and other special constructions

[a]Orthodox X-bar theory allows only three bar levels, but noun-noun and adjective-noun modification presents a clear intermediate level, and we handle it as if it were a bar level

[b]SPEC and COMP refer to specifier and complement in X-bar terminology. They are modifiers of the phrasal head; for details, see Jackendoff (1977). PP refers to prepositional phrases; S is a sentence, while S' is a sentence with a complementizer. INFL refers to inflection.

Solutions

Multilingual Architecture

We claim that an X-bar-based grammar framework with language-independent semantic functions provides the extensibility of principle-based parsing without sacrificing the practicality of the phrase parsers. Phrase parsers are easy to write, easy to use, and nearly theory neutral, e.g. VP -▷ ADVP VP.

Principle-based parsing relies on broad postulates that are difficult to implement in practical terms, e.g. "A moved element must c-command its trace, where A c-commands B if A does not dominate B, but the parent of A dominates B," (Lin 1993); "Assign indices freely to all noun phrases" (Fong 1990). Our natural language understanding architecture contains five processing modules: Preprocessing, Syntactic Analysis, Semantic Interpretation, Discourse Analysis and Pragmatic Inferencing. The modules are language-independent; only the data are language-specific. Likewise, the modules are domain-independent, since they contain no domain data.

Our multilingual system architecture (and a cognitive view of language) assumes that Semantic Interpretation is language-independent. Semantic Interpretation accepts as input the structures that are output by the grammars of the various languages. Therefore, the output of the various language grammars must be consistent, suggesting close coordination between grammar structures across languages.

Syntactic Analysis consists of a processing algorithm (the parser), and its associated data (the grammar).

The parser is entirely language-independent. There is a separate grammar for each language, but, as we will demonstrate, the linguistic core of each grammar is the same. This semi-language-independent strategy provides maximum robustness while taking advantage of the insights provided by generative grammar.

Certain grammar formalisms make some kinds of development easier. Semantic grammars, e.g. SRI's FASTUS system, can be built quickly, but they are domain-dependent and fragile. Phrase parsers, like AT&T's Fidditch, will find partial parses quickly, but fail to provide detailed enough information to support reference resolution in discourse. More linguistically-based grammars, like the Lexical Functional Grammar as implemented at Carnegie Mellon University in Diogenes, or principle-based parsing as used at MIT, or in DBG at LSI, have not yet demonstrated that they are capable of scaling up to handle real applications. Our approach attempts to reap the advantages of linguistic generalizations while not sacrificing practicality. In particular, it captures language-independent features, and it allows for semantic constraints.

The Grammar

Phrase Structure Rules for a Core Grammar. We use a phrase structure grammar. Based on the principles of X-bar theory, we claim that a broad-coverage grammar should contain approximately 200 phrase structure rules. Our English grammar has 231 rules, while our Spanish and Japanese grammars, somewhat less complete, contain 161 and 176 rules,

Table 2: X-bar-based rules illustrated in several languages.

Rule	English	Spanish	Japanese
N" → N" COMP	Judith Jones, director	María Velazquez, la directora	ディレクター、田中一男氏
N' → ADJP N'	the green house	la casa verde	青い家
N' → ADJP	the brave	los valientes	不自由
N' → QP	2000 (of them)	2000 (de ellos)	(そのうち)2000人
N' → N N'	health sector	sector salud	衛生部門
PP → PP CONJP PP	between 3 and 5	entre 3 y 5	3と5の間で
ADVP → SPEC ADV"	more slowly	más lentamente	さらにゆっくり
QP → SPEC Q"	almost 100	casi 100	ほとんど100
	0.7 per 1000	0,7 por 1000	1000につき7
SPECP → NEG SPEC"	not only him	no sólo él	彼だけでなく
SPECP → SPEC"	all those;	todos ellos;	それらすべて(の)
	more costly	más costoso	もっと高価(な)
COMP → NP	the multinational, Dow Corning	la multinacional Dow Corning	国際派ダウ・コーニング
COMP → NP	Vicky Wong, 555-1212	Pedro Ramos, 555-1212	中村太郎、555-1212
COMP → NP	Meg Smith, 37	Juanita Lopez, 37	鈴木花子、37歳
COMP → S	(she wants) to eat	(quiere) comer	英語を話す(ことができる)

respectively. Basic coverage demands a minimum of about 120 rules, although punctuation irregularities and domain idiosyncracies may require more. A grammar with too few rules has insufficient coverage, while a grammar with too many rules (e.g. NP → NP PP PP) overgenerates. Table 1 identifies the rules of the core grammar. Each category appears in the grammar with the elements identified in the second column.

Table 2 illustrates the application of core grammar rules to several languages. The word order may change, as in the English and Spanish adjective rules:

N' → ADJP N' (English) N' → N' ADJP (Spanish)

Nonetheless, the underlying X-bar structure remains constant. In practical terms, this allows the skeleton of the "universal" grammar to be used as scaffolding upon which to build grammars for new languages.

Table 3 lists the types of rules required for each phrasal category, including the X-bar elements *head, specifier,* and *complement,* as well as conjunction, modifiers, punctuation, and special idiomatic rules. We include English, Spanish, and Japanese, and a conjecture regarding universal grammar.

To determine the aggregate number of possible rules, assume two possibilities for each + mark. That is, each category can occur at a given level *with* a SPEC and *without* a SPEC, with and without a COMP, conjoined or not conjoined, etc. (except head, which is required). Add the numbers of + marks (times two) to reach the figures in the right-hand column.

Our phrase structure rules incorporate the insights of X-bar theory, as originated by Jackendoff (1977) and in use currently (in varying interpretations) by a wide range of linguists, including, in recent work on phrase structure, Speas (1990) and Rothstein (1991). X-bar theory imposes certain restrictions on the content of phrase structure rules. Only maximal projections can appear in rules in a non-head position:

XP → YP X" is acceptable
XP → Y' X" is not, because Y' is not a maximal projection

Rules that have three or four elements on the right, e.g.

NP → N" ADJP PP PP

are badly designed rules. They should be replaced by more compositional rules that take advantage of the cross-categorial nature of specifiers and complements, instead of spelling out the specifiers and complements for each level in each category. Thus rules like

NP → N" COMP

are preferred.

Augmenting the Phrase Structure Rules: Constraints. Although phrase structure rules provide an easy preliminary approach to grammar development, they are inadequate for accurate parsing in large-scale systems, since they overgenerate, as we will demonstrate below. We supplement the parsing algorithm with augmentations, similar to those used for ATN (Augmented Transition Network) grammars (Woods 1973). These augmentations are attached to the phrase structure rules in the grammar. They contain specialized functions for constraints and structure-building. The functions themselves are language-independent, although they are used in language-specific grammar rules. When a rule is reduced during parsing, its associated augmentations are evaluated.

The augmentations in the grammar contain constraints that halt the application of the rule under certain circumstances. These constraints can be used

Table 3: Multilingual rule matrix

Category	head	spec	comp	conj	mod	punc	idiom	Total
Noun Phrase	+++ **r**	+++ **r**	+++ **r**	+++ **r**	+++ +	+++ +	+++ +	13
Prepositional Phrase	+++ **r**	+++ +	+++ +	+++ +	--- -	--- +	+++ +	11
Verb Phrase	+++ **r**	+++ +	+++ **r**	+++ +	--- -	+++ +	+++ +	11
Adjective Phrase	+++ **r**	+++ +	+++ +	++- +	--- -	--- +	+++ +	11
Adverb Phrase	+++ **r**	+++ +	+++ +	++- +	--- -	--- +	--- +	11
Quantifier Phrase	+++ **r**	+++ +	+++ +	++- +	--- -	--- +	--- +	11
Sentence	+++ **r**	--- +	+++ +	+++ **r**	--- -	+++ +	+++ +	11
INFL/ Auxiliaries	+++ **r**	+++ +	+++ +	+++ +	++- +	+++ +	+++ +	13
Conjunction Phrase	+++ +	++- +	+++ +	--- -	--- -	+++ +	--- +	9
Complementizer/ Subordinating Conjunction Phrase	+++ +	+++ +	--- +	+-- +	--- -	+++ +	--- +	11
Specifiers	+++ +	+++ +	+++ +	++- +	+++ +	--- +	--- +	13
Complements	+++ +	--- -	--- -	--- -	--- -	+++ +	+++ +	5

Key:	Grammars	English/Spanish/Japanese / Universal Grammar
	Rule Status	**r** = required; + = permitted; − = not present

to add context-sensitivity to the context-free phrase structure rules. Constraints can also be used for semantics, eliminating syntactically legal but semantically impossible parses, e.g.

```
;;  Allow "Philadelphia, PA" but not "Philadelphia, yesterday"
(when (and (COMP.head.location)          ; comp's head is loc.
           (not N''.head.location))      ; n's head isn't loc.
     (halt))                             ; don't apply rule
```

In the appositive attachment rule, attach location noun phrases only to other location noun phrases.

Lexical constraints are language-specific, linked to a word or phrase in a particular language, e.g. *old enough*. Syntactic and semantic constraints are more likely to be language-independent. Syntactic structures are compositional: they are made up of small, simple structures, and thus they are learnable. In sum, we can take advantage of the relative language-independence of syntax and semantics in the construction of grammar contraints.

Certain functions recur in the grammar and should be optimized for efficiency: syntactic and semantic agreement checking (subject-verb agreement, adjective-noun agreement in Spanish, classifier-noun agreement in Japanese), as well as more complex functions. For example, only transitive verbs should take direct objects, rejecting **Frank coughed the computer,* and only those direct objects that are semantically compatible should be permitted, rejecting *#Judy drank the computer.* Our approach to these tests is novel in that it is multilingual, relying on calls to a (language-independent) knowledge base. Determining the appropriateness of an object is accomplished using a semantic call in the rule

V" –▷ V' NP

This semantic call uses information from the knowledge base to determine whether the available object satisfies the verb's semantic restrictions. Of course, four-word sentences do not present much of a problem. The test's real utility comes from the fact that it is able to prevent spurious sub-parses inside of fifty-word sentences.

Similarly, semantic tests are used to determine prepositional phrase attachment. Thus *Maria rented a car with a stereo* has a semantically preferred bracketing:

[[Maria] [rented [a car [with a stereo.]]]]

while the syntactically similar *Pam rented a car with a credit card* is bracketed differently:

[[Pam] [[rented [a car]] [with a credit card.]]]

A credit card is a *financial instrument,* and renting is a *financial transaction.* Thus the financial instrument can be used as the instrument of a financial transaction, so *credit card* attaches to *rent,* based on the information in the knowledge base about financial transactions. A *stereo* is not a financial instrument, but it is a part of a car, so it can attach to *car,* but not to *rent.*

One of the uses of constraints is within the *conjunction rules.* Conjunction, particularly in long sentences, multiplies ambiguity drastically. To limit the ambiguity, we use a novel combination of syntactic and semantic constraints, implemented them in a language-independent fashion. Almost anything can be conjoined syntactically, but there are strong preferences for conjoining structures that are parallel both syntactically and semantically.

[cars in San Francisco] and [trucks in Boston]
NOT cars in [[San Francisco] and [trucks in Boston]]
NOT cars in [[San Francisco and trucks] in Boston]

The conjunction felicity tests are language independent. They examine semantic similarity (*car and truck*), as well as syntactic parallelism (common noun (*cars, trucks*) + same preposition (*in*) + proper noun (*San Francisco, Boston*)). They can be tailored to the needs of a particular language, but the overall function need not be written again for each language. We use a series of tests (presence of modifiers, prepositional phrases, meaning similarities) and weight parses based on the overall similarity score, preferring the parse with the best semantic similarity and syntactic parallelism.

Structure-Building Augmentations. The output of Syntactic Analysis is not simply a parse tree, but also a language-independent structure called a functionally labelled template (FLT), with sentence functions like "subject" and "object" labelled. A parse tree represents only surface relationships, and a further level of representation is necessary, in order to handle, for example, alterations in surface relationships (e.g. passive vs. active) and syntactic gapping. Only this enhanced representation offers information detailed enough to determine thematic relations and perform reference resolution, which take place in the semantic and discourse modules.

In our implementation, the FLT resembles the f-structures in Lexical Functional Grammar (Bresnan 1982), while our parse tree is analogous to LFG's c-structure. The major difference between our approach and current LFG implementations is our experience with large-scale, multilingual text understanding applications. Idiomatic expressions, long sentences, and idiosyncratic elements like punctuation, addresses, and latitude/longitude, require an efficient grammar design that takes advantage of X-bar theory and language-independent semantic constraints, while allowing for language-specific features.

The f-structure contains functional information, not simply surface constituents as in the c-structure. Each phrase structure rule contains structure-building functions to generate the FLT. In the rule S → NP VP, for example, the NP will be the subject of S, while the VP will be the predicate.

Altering Surface Relationships (Logical Structure Alternations). Building structures showing functional relations is necessary for any non-toy application, since parse trees alone fail to represent necessary linguistic information. Our novel approach to this problem uses language-independent functions. Parse trees represent the surface order of constituents, but do not convey underlying relationships. The surface subject of a passive sentence is in some sense a logical object, a relationship that can be represented in the FLT. Similarly, in languages like Spanish, the subject is often elided, but the grammar must mark a logical subject for discourse purposes.

In Japanese, topic phrases (marked with *wa*) serve as logical subjects if the sentence has no other subject. We exploit the FLT to convey the logical relationship, a possibility the parse tree alone does not offer. The topic phrase is "moved" into the subject position in the FLT, and marked as a (surface) topic for later discourse purposes. Semantics can then find the subject (the surface topic) in the FLT and place it in the correct

thematic role relationship to the main verb.

In English, Spanish, and Japanese, preposed set delimiters are "moved":

Of these, 24 were male.
⟹ 24 of these were male.

The FLT itself is a means for forcing multilingual grammar output into sufficient conformity so that language-independent Semantic Interpretation can locate syntactic components. The FLT is a language-independent formalism in which to represent syntactic relations without recourse to word order. It explicitly labels X-bar relationships like specifier and complement.

Syntactic Gaps. In more complex situations, e.g. gap-filling, a dummy structure must be created and then, where possible, linked to the appropriate referent. For example, Spanish, like English, allows numbers as noun phrases with empty heads: *Hay dos.* ("There are two.") To create a gap to trigger reference resolution in Discourse Analysis, we build an empty head structure, with dos filling the quantifier slot. Only grammars that can identify gaps can supply enough information for Discourse Analysis to occur. Some gaps should be filled at the syntax level (e.g. relative clause gaps), since all the necessary information is sentence-internal. The following example illustrates an empty head in a quantifier phrase: *dos* (two) is a quantifier, but it forms a noun phrase by itself (cf. "I saw two"), since there is no head noun. For discourse purposes, the FLT contains a marker indicating an empty NP, so that later processing can determine the antecedent, i.e. "two what?"

These routines to create dummy structures are language-independent functions, as are the gap-filling routines to fill the structures. Because both functions are part of the language-independent grammar core, the writer of a grammar for an additional language does not need to create them from scratch.

Parser Implementation

To manipulate the grammars described above, we use a shift-reduce, bottom-up, all-parses parser, implemented in LISP. Because our parser uses Tomita's algorithm, which is quite fast, we have not had to sacrifice accuracy for speed. Tomita (1986) dealt only with rules; we have modified his parser to permit augmentations, for the reasons we have presented in the previous section. In large-scale applications, augmentations are vital in order to add semantic and contextual informationand to prevent thousands of incorrect parses. Augmentations allow us to select the preferred parse, which is sent on to Semantic Interpretation for further processing.

If more than one parse is possible, our system selects the preferred parse on the basis of a weighting scheme drawn from scores assigned in the lexicon, idiom patterns, and grammar. When parsing is completed, the scores relating to each parse template are calculated, and the top parse is selected.

We use a top-down preparsing approach to take some of the burden off the bottom-up parser. Preparsed phrases enter Syntactic Analysis already parsed, and are attached as a unit to the rest of the parse. For a complementary perspective on combining top-down and bottom-up approaches, see Rau & Jacobs (1988).

Real-world text understanding tasks require graceful degradation, rather than outright failure. Backup procedures are required at every stage of processing. We supplement our parser with a Debris Parser, which uses phrases to recover syntactic data when a full sentence parse is unavailable (Kehler *et al.* 1990). The Debris Parser uses the incomplete parsing results, supplementing them with semantic information about the main verb's predicate argument structure. It then constructs the most likely thematic role structure. The Debris results reenter normal semantic processing, and are indistinguishable from normally parsed sentences.

Applications

This grammar approach has been implemented in a natural language processing core engine under development for several years. It has been used in multilingual applications for four projects, and on English alone for several more. Domains covered include terrorism, financial, medical, and trade texts in English, Spanish, and Japanese. The projects ranged in scale from several hundred single-page texts to a thousand texts a day. Most texts were between a paragraph and two pages long. The writing style ranged from simple business writing, with sentences averaging about 12 words, to newspaper writing, with sentences averaging about 25 words, and, particularly in Spanish and Japanese, complicated structures including many different kinds of ellipsis. The English terrorism texts were translated from Spanish, reducing some of the complexity. Most of the systems were demonstration prototypes; one was a fielded system. All of the systems were used for data extraction, and most fed a database, usually in Sybase, and usually object-oriented in design. Several used the extracted data to support visualization systems. The portability of the grammars to new domains and applications has demonstrated the success of our approach.

Conclusion

While a "universal grammar" approach to multilingual grammar development is tempting, our experience demonstrates that it is far too immature for large-scale natural language understanding. But neither should we build entirely language-specific grammars and lose the insights of several decades of research in generative grammar. We combine linguistic insight with robust, in-depth parsing. Our use of X-bar theory and language-independent semantic constraints draws on the strengths of current syntactic theory without sacrificing robustness and scalability. Our use of separate grammars for each language allows us the flexibility to capture language-specific lexical insights, while our use of language-independent functions captures linguistic generalizations. Our implementation includes innovative handling of diverse phenomena, such as (1) syntactic gaps, (2) logical structure alternations, and (3) conjunctions. These innovations strengthen our large-scale and multilingual natural language processing system.

References

Berwick, R. 1987. Principle-based parsing. Technical Report 972, MIT Artificial Intelligence Laboratory.

Bresnan, J., ed. 1982. *The Mental Representation of Grammatical Relations*. Cambridge, MA: MIT Press.

Chomsky, N. 1967. *Aspects of the Theory of Syntax*. Cambridge, MA: MIT Press.

Chomsky, N. 1981. *Lectures on Government and Binding*. Cambridge, MA: MIT Press.

Fong, S., and Berwick, R. 1989. The computational implementation of principle-based parsers. In *Proceedings of the International Workshop on Parsing Technologies*. Carnegie Mellon University.

Fong, S. 1990. Free indexation: Combinatorial analysis and a compositional algorithm. In *Proceedings of the 28th Annual Meeting of the Association for Computational Linguistics*.

Jackendoff, R. 1977. *X' Syntax: A Study of Phrase Structure*. Cambridge, MA: MIT Press.

Kehler, A.; Blejer, H. R.; Flank, S.; and McKee, D. 1990. A three-tiered parsing approach for operational systems. In *Proceedings of the AI Systems in Government conference*, 150–156.

Lin, D. 1993. Principle-based parsing without overgeneration. In *Proceedings of the 31st Annual Meeting of the Association for Computational Linguistics*.

Rau, L. F., and Jacobs, P. S. 1988. Integrating top-down and bottom-up strategies in a text processing system. In *Proceedings of the Second Conference on Applied Natural Language Processing*, 129–135.

Rothstein, S., ed. 1991. *Perspectives on Phrase Structure: Heads and Licensing*. Number 25 in Syntax and Semantics. San Diego: Academic Press.

Speas, M. 1990. *Phrase Structure in Natural Language*. Dordrecht: Kluwer.

Tomita, M. 1986. *Efficient Parsing for Natural Language*. Boston: Kluwer.

Woods, W. A. 1973. An experimental parsing system for transition network grammars. In Rustin, R., ed., *Natural Language Processing*. NY: Algorithmics Press.

L∗ Parsing: A General Framework for Syntactic Analysis of Natural Language

Eric K. Jones and **Linton M. Miller**

Department of Computer Science
Victoria University of Wellington
P.O. Box 600, Wellington, New Zealand
Eric.Jones@comp.vuw.ac.nz   Linton.Miller@comp.vuw.ac.nz

Abstract

We describe a new algorithm for table-driven parsing with context-free grammars designed to support efficient syntactic analysis of natural language. The algorithm provides a general framework in which a variety of parser control strategies can be freely specified: bottom-up strategies, top-down strategies, and strategies that strike a balance between the two. The framework permits better sharing of parse forest substructure than other table-driven approaches, and facilitates the early termination of semantically ill-formed partial parses. The algorithm should thus find ready application to large-scale natural language processing.

Introduction

Natural language grammars are highly ambiguous. Systems for natural language understanding must therefore be carefully designed to prune out undesirable partial parses as soon as possible using semantic and pragmatic information. The need to rapidly prune a large number of unpromising parses yields two desiderata for parser design:

1. *Flexible control:* It should be possible to tailor the parser control strategy to whatever mixture of bottom-up and top-down processing facilitates both syntactic analysis and semantic interpretation as efficiently as possible.

2. *Efficiency:* Even in the best of circumstances, a parser has to consider large numbers of partial parses, so it must be able to produce these parses efficiently.

The general framework of chart parsing (Kaplan 1973) allows users to freely specify a range of parser control strategies, but inefficiently encodes the dynamic state of the parser as a large set of *edges* or *items* in a data structure called a *chart* (Kay 1986; Aho & Ullman 1977). Constructing and maintaining these edges requires a high constant-factor overhead at each stage of the parse. Table-driven algorithms such as generalized LR (GLR) parsing (Tomita 1986) or the method of Schabes (1991) aim for better efficiency by performing much of this computation off line, when the parse table is constructed. These algorithms have proven more efficient than chart parsers in practical applications, even though their time complexity may be worse in some cases.[1] Such algorithms, however, are inflexible: their con-

---

[1] If the length of the right-hand side of the longest rule is p, then a GLR parser has time complexity $O(n^{p+1})$ (Nederhof 1993).

trol strategies are fixed and cannot be altered in any way by the user.

In this paper, we present a new framework for table-driven parsing called *L∗ parsing* that attempts to get the best of both worlds. Our algorithm extends the algorithm for GLR parsing. The current implementation handles arbitrary non-cyclic context-free grammars without ϵ-transitions. Like a chart parser, an L∗ parser allows a variety of parser control strategies to be freely specified. Like a GLR parser, an L∗ parser enjoys the low overhead of table-driven approaches. An L∗ parser also creates a concise *shared parse forest* representation of all possible parses.

We are not the first to propose a framework for freely specifying control strategies in table-driven parsing. In particular, Lang describes such a framework in Lang (1974), which is further generalized by Leermakers (1991). Our algorithm, however, makes two novel contributions that significantly increase the utility of this kind of approach in practical parsing:

1. *Improved sharing.* When Lang's algorithm is applied to parsers employing sophisticated drivers, it is often impossible to share identical subtrees because of differences in context analysis (Billot & Lang 1989; Nederhof 1993). The L∗ algorithm overcomes this difficulty in an efficient manner.

2. *Termination of unpromising partial parses.* An L∗ parser is intended to comprise only one component of a larger natural language understanding system. To maximize efficiency, it is crucial that immediately a partial parse is rejected by the rest of the system, the parser stop all work on it. As we explain below, it can be non-trivial to determine with certainty that a particular partial parse should be rejected. L∗ parsing provides a general mechanism for terminating partial parses in appropriate circumstances under the direction of an external oracle.

The remainder of this paper is structured as follows. We begin with a brief review of GLR parsing. We then introduce our algorithm by means of an example, and discuss sharing and termination of unpromising partial parses. Next, we describe the implementation and sketch the application of a novel parser control strategy to L∗ parsing with feature grammars. We conclude with a brief discussion of empirical results and plans for future work.

GLR Parsing

GLR parsing is an extension of LR parsing that can cope with arbitrary context-free grammars.[2] Like an LR parser, a GLR parser is a shift-reduce parser, and is controlled by a deterministic finite-state driver, encoded as a *parse table*. The parse table indexes parsing actions by state and the next k input symbols. In contrast to an LR parser, however, entries in the parse table may contain multiple parsing actions. Grammatical ambiguity gives rise to table entries of this kind.

A GLR parser employs two main data structures: a *graph-structured stack* and a *packed shared parse forest*. To avoid confusion, we use the term *vertex* when referring to an element of the graph-structured stack, and the term *node* to refer to an element of the parse forest. The graph-structured stack is an extension of a basic LR stack that allows a GLR parser to deal with nondeterminism in a parse. When there are two or more possible parses, the stack splits, with a branch for each alternative. The packed shared parse forest compactly represents all of the parses of an input sentence.

A GLR parser works by repeatedly executing *reduce* and *shift* actions until an *accept* or *error* action is reached. If more than one action is specified for a given input word, any reduce actions are executed before shifts. For a more detailed description of GLR parsing, the reader is referred to Tomita & Ng (1991).

L∗ Parsing

To implement our table-driven parser with flexible control, we alter a GLR parser to allow it to *eagerly* reduce a grammar rule before its entire right-hand side (RHS) has been seen. The missing elements of the RHS are then *combined* into the parse as they arrive. We call the resulting system an L∗ parser.

Eager reduction introduces an element of top-down processing into the parser, because parent nodes can be proposed before all of their children have been recognized in the input. Exactly where eager reduction occurs can be varied, and will accordingly determine the degree of top-down processing that is performed. In the extreme case, one might eagerly reduce before seeing any RHS elements of a rule, basing the decision to reduce only on the current input word. This is equivalent to top-down parsing with a one-symbol lookahead. The opposite extreme is to never eagerly reduce, which yields a standard, bottom-up GLR parser.

Parser control strategies are specified as an input to the parse table builder. For a given grammar, a different choice of control strategy will yield a different parse table. Miller (1994) describes an algorithm for parse table construction that allows the user to specify a range of control strategies and produces parse tables for each.

Our present concern, however, is to describe the parsing algorithm, so we assume that a suitable parse table has already been constructed. The input to the algorithm is a parse table and a string of terminal symbols. The output of the algorithm is a parse forest in which common subtrees are shared and locally ambiguous structures are packed. For reasons of space, this paper does not further discuss the issue of local ambiguity packing. However, sharing of common subtrees is discussed in detail below.

The idea of the algorithm is as follows. Parsing proceeds just as for GLR parsing, except in the case of *eager reductions*—reductions performed before all input symbols corresponding to the RHS of a grammar rule have been seen. An eager reduction by a grammar rule creates an "incomplete" forest node headed by the left-hand side (LHS) of the rule, in which some or all of the children at the right-hand edge of the parse are missing. These children are *combined* into the parse one by one as they are derived from the input. After all missing children have been recognized, a second reduction called a *completing reduction* marks the forest node as complete.

An Example

To illustrate the novel aspects of the algorithm, we work through the problem of parsing a simple sentence using the toy grammar in figure 1. This grammar is annotated with control information, similar to the announce points of Abney & Johnson (unpublished manuscript): the arrow ↑ in rule 4 indicates that the parser should eagerly reduce by rule 4 upon parsing a V, even though no following NP has yet been seen in the input. Because there are no other annotations, all other rules are to be parsed bottom-up just like GLR parsing.

$$
\begin{aligned}
S &\rightarrow NP\ VP & (1)\\
NP &\rightarrow Det\ N & (2)\\
NP &\rightarrow N & (3)\\
VP &\rightarrow V{\uparrow}\ NP & (4)
\end{aligned}
$$

Figure 1: A very small grammar

Consider the sentence "Mary ate the apple." A thumbnail sketch of the parser's actions while parsing this sentence is as follows. First it will parse "Mary" as an NP and push it onto the stack as per ordinary GLR parsing. Next, it will parse "ate" as a V and push it on the stack. The parser will then eagerly reduce by rule 4, and push the resulting incomplete VP onto the stack. This immediately triggers a further eager reduction by rule 1, creating an incomplete S. This S is incomplete even though forest nodes for each of its immediate children exist, because its child VP node is missing a child NP. The system next parses "the apple" as an NP and combines it into the incomplete VP. A completing reduction by rule 4 then marks the VP as complete. Finally, a completing reduction by rule 2 marks the S as complete.

In the remainder of this section, we trace this example in greater detail. At each step of the trace, we show

- *The graph-structured stack.* Vertices that represent stack tops are drawn as circles, with scheduled parse actions placed to the right. All other stack vertices are drawn as squares. Vertices drawn with dashed lines were created by eager reduction. Each vertex has an associated state

---

[2]We assume a basic familiarity with LR parsing.

(an integer) and parse forest node. Vertices have their state number inside them, and their associated parse forest node above them. The stack grows from left to right.

- *The parse forest.* Nodes in the parse forest are labelled with a grammar symbol. Dashed lines joining forest nodes represent links created by eager rather than normal reduction. A dotted line indicates the forward edge of an incomplete derivation created by eager reduction. As parsing proceeds, combine actions incrementally extend the derivation. When all RHS elements are in place, a completing reduction marks the forest node as complete, depicted by changing the dashed lines to solid ones.

- *The current word.* The word the parser is currently processing is shown in a box at the right hand edge of the diagram.

| ST | ACTION | | | | | | | |
	Det	N	V	$	*EAG*	S	VP	NP
0	s2	s1				g3		g4
1			r3	r3				
2		s11						
3				acc				
4			s5					g6
5	e4-1, s8	e4-1, s7						g9, c4
6				r1	e1-2			
7			r3	r3				
8		s10						
9				r4	e4-2			
10			r2	r2				
11			r2	r2				

Figure 2: Parse table for grammar in figure 1

Figure 2 shows a parsing table for the grammar and parser control strategy depicted in figure 1, above. The table is indexed by state number *st* and grammar symbol X augmented with the special symbol *EAG*. (The function of this symbol is explained later.) An entry ACTION[*st, X*] is a set of parse actions. There are six kinds of action: *shift, reduce, eager-reduce, goto, combine,* and *accept*. A shift action is written "s *n*", where *n* is the state to go to after the shift. A reduce action "r *n*" specifies a reduction by the *n*-th grammar rule. An eager-reduce action "e *n-k*" specifies an eager reduction by the *n*-th grammar rule, using only the first *k* symbols of the rule's RHS. A goto action is written as "g *n*," where *n* specifies with the next state to go to. A combine action "c *n*" means the symbol X should be combined into the forest node (or nodes) previously created by an eager reduction by grammar rule *n*. X becomes the new rightmost child of this node. An accept action is written as "acc." If an ACTION entry is blank, it indicates a parse error, except in the case of the *EAG* symbol, where a blank means there are no further actions to process in this state.

We now return to the problem of parsing the sentence "Mary ate the apple." Initially the parse forest is empty, and the stack contains only a single vertex with state 0. This vertex is a stack top, so it is drawn with a circle.

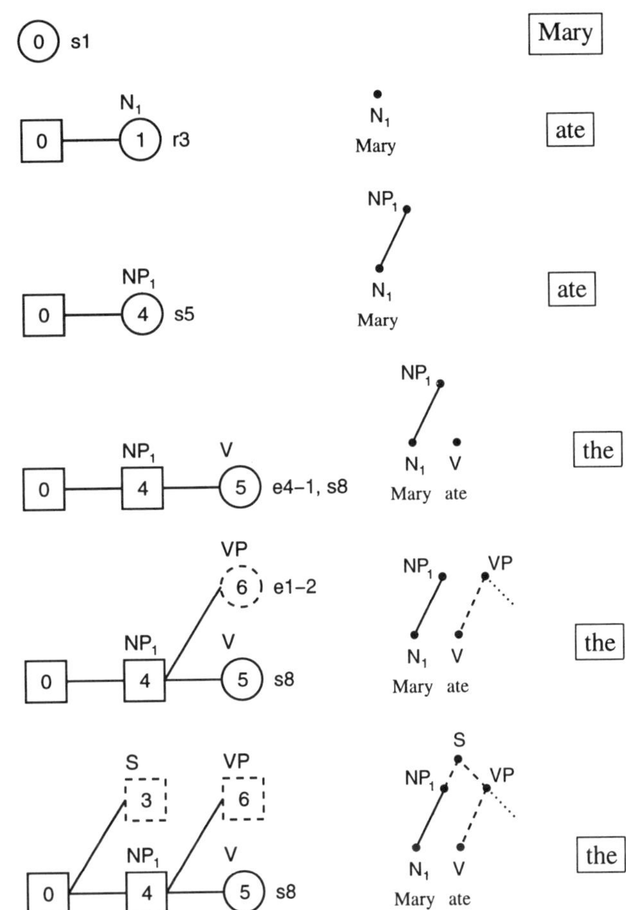

Figure 3: Trace of the eager parser

The first word to parse is "Mary." The lexical category of "Mary" is N, so the first set of parse actions to perform is ACTION[0, N] = {s1} (top diagram of figure 3).

The parser therefore performs a shift action that creates a new stack vertex with state 1 and forest node N_1. The newly created vertex becomes the stack top, so it is drawn as a circle; the original circle is redrawn as a square (second diagram of figure 3).

The next word is "ate," whose lexical category is V. ACTION[1, V] = {r3}, so the parser carries out a normal, non-eager reduction by rule 3. The vertex labeled N_1 corresponds to the RHS of rule 3 and is accordingly popped off the stack. A new vertex with state 2 is then pushed on, corresponding to the LHS of rule 3. The state of this new stack vertex is specified by ACTION[0, NP] = {g4}, because 0 is the state of the vertex at the top of the stack after N_1 was popped off. A new forest node NP_1 is also created for the new vertex, with a single child, the node N_1 (third diagram of figure 3). At this new vertex, ACTION[4, V] = {s5}, so the parser shifts the verb "ate" onto the stack, creating a new stack vertex with state 5.

The following word is "the," with lexical category Det.

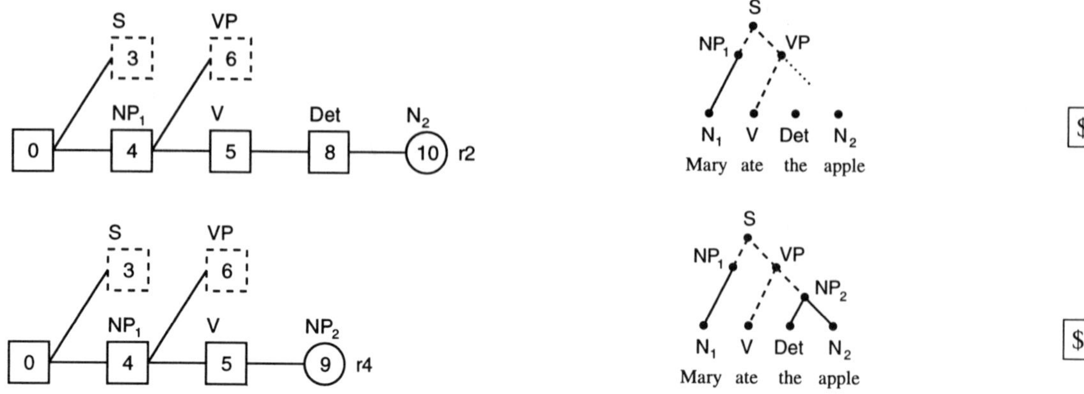

Figure 4: Trace of the eager parser (ctd)

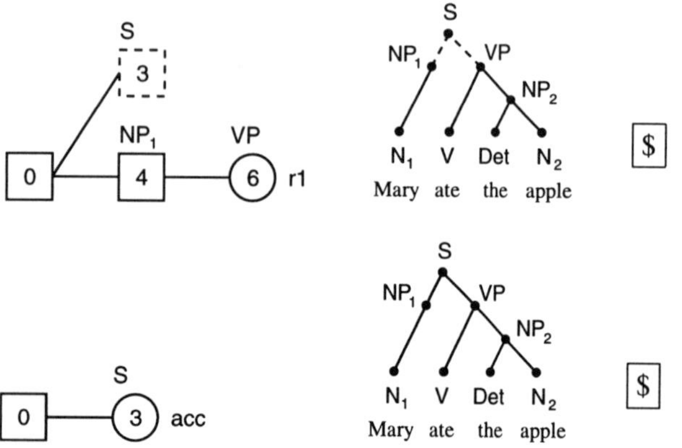

Figure 5: Trace of the eager parser (ctd)

ACTION[5, Det] = {e4-1,s8} (fourth diagram of figure 3). Reductions are processed before shifts as per GLR parsing, so the parser next eagerly reduces by rule 4, creating a new forest node VP and new stack vertex whose state is determined using the parse table entry AC-TION[4, VP] = {g6}. We draw the parse tree for VP using dashed and dotted lines to indicate that the parse of the VP is not yet complete (fifth diagram of figure 3).

Having just performed an eager reduction, the system must now perform any further reductions triggered by the newly created nonterminal. We call these reductions *cascaded* reductions. A question immediately arises: which reductions should be carried out? A GLR(k) parser would use lookahead to select only those reduce actions consistent with the k input symbols that immediately follow the substring covered by the reduction. Unfortunately, these lookahead symbols are not available at the time that an eager reduction is performed, as the parse associated with the eagerly reduced rule is not yet complete. The parser therefore simply carries out all cascaded reductions that could conceivably be appropriate.

To implement this idea, we introduce a dummy symbol *EAG*. ACTION[*st, EAG*] contains the set of cascaded re-

ductions to perform at state *st* after performing an eager reduction. In our example, ACTION[6, *EAG*] = {e1-2}. This reduction is eager, even though it involves the complete RHS of rule 1, because there is as yet no complete parse corresponding to the last symbol of its RHS (a VP). In fact, for this reason, all entries in the *EAG* column of the parse table are eager reductions.

The parser next carries out the eager reduction e1-2 and creates a new forest node S from NP$_1$ and VP, and a new stack vertex with state determined from AC-TION[0, S] = {g3}. The entry ACTION[3, *EAG*] is blank, so there are no further actions to be done at this vertex (bottom diagram of figure 3).

No unprocessed reductions remain for the current word "the", so the parser performs the shift action s8, shifting "the" onto the stack. Next, the word "apple" is shifted onto the stack, making the terminator $ the current word (top diagram of figure 4). The parser then reduces Det N$_2$ at the top of the stack to NP$_2$ by rule 2. ACTION[5, NP] = {g9,c4}, so the resulting vertex has state 9. The combine action c4 is also carried out, installing NP$_2$ as the rightmost child of the VP (bottom diagram of figure 4).

Special data structures called *combine pointers* are maintained at stack tops to locate eagerly created derivations to combine into. A combine pointer consists of a partially completed derivation and a number representing the rule that created it by eager reduction. In general, a combine action c n at a stack top extends the derivation of each combine pointer at that stack top whose rule is n.

ACTION[9, $] = {r4} covers the same ground as the eager reduction by rule 4 carried out previously. It is therefore a "completing reduction," whose job is to indicate that the earlier eager reduction is indeed correct. Accordingly, the parser pops the RHS elements V and NP$_2$ off the stack, establishing VP as a new stack top, and marks its forest node as complete. This last we depict by changing the dashed lines to solid ones (top diagram of figure 5). Unlike other reductions, no new parse structure is created: all relevant structure was constructed earlier by eager reduce and combine actions. Having completed the VP node, the parser next performs a second completing reduction, this time by rule 1, which indicates that the S is also complete. A single stack top remains, with state 3 (bottom diagram of figure 5). As ACTION[3, \$] = {acc}, the parse succeeds. S is the root of the resulting parse tree.

Improving sharing in the parse forest

When a sophisticated parser control strategy is employed, the parse forests produced by existing table-driven methods such as GLR parsing and Lang's parser are not as compact as they should be. For example, Billot and Lang found that for $k > 0$, Lang's parser with an $LR(k)$ driver often produces worse sharing than an $LR(0)$ driver (Billot & Lang 1989). Indeed, for $k > 1$, the consequent loss of efficiency is usually so great that the overall performance of the parser degrades, even though it has a larger deterministic domain.

This problem arises because states in the parse table are expected to do double duty: states encode contextual distinctions that determine which parser actions are appropriate, while equality of states is used to decide whether or not to share subtrees. More sophisticated parsing strategies encode finer grained contextual distinctions and consequently use a larger number of states. As a result, opportunities to share substructure are lost.

We address this problem by identifying equivalence classes of states in the parse table. Two states belong to a given equivalence class if they are differentiated only by contextual distinctions that have no bearing on which parses are licensed by the left context.[3] For example, states of an $LR(1)$ parser that are distinguished only by the lookahead of their associated items belong in the same equivalence class, because they have the same left context.

Distinct stack tops whose states are in the same equivalence class are merged into a single vertex containing a *set* of states: the union of the states of the original stack tops. The set of parse actions to perform at this new stack top is the union of the sets of parse actions specified by these states. Consequently, each reduction is carried out only once instead of several times, so the resulting parse structures are shared, improving both space and time efficiency. In this way, we can obtain the benefits of a sophisticated parser control strategy without sacrificing sharing in the parse forest.

The need to improve sharing in the parse forest is particularly acute for an L∗ parser, because the possibility of eager reduction introduces new contextual distinctions. It is frequently the case that one state recommends eagerly reducing by some rule, while another recommends computing the rest of the RHS of the same rule before reducing. If two such states were permitted to occupy different stack tops simultaneously, the parser would redundantly parse the subtree covered by this rule twice: once using eager reduction, and a second time using non-eager reduction. To avoid this redundant computation, such pairs of states are placed in the same equivalence class when the parse table is

---

[3]To be precise, two states are equivalent if their item sets contain the same dotted rules.

built. As a result, at run time the stack tops for these states are merged, causing the parser to carry out only the eager version of the parse.

Terminating unpromising partial parses

Whenever a reduction or a combine action is performed, the L∗ parser accepts input from an oracle that signals whether or not to continue with those parses that include the newly created structure. This oracle represents a channel of communication with a larger natural language understanding system by which unpromising partial parses can be pruned. Reductions and combines can trigger rejection on the basis of mismatched grammatical features or selectional restrictions, or on the basis of pragmatic information.

In the case of non-eager reductions, the parser's response to the oracle is straightforward: if the oracle rejects a parse, the new stack top created by the offending reduction is deleted, thereby halting all further processing at that vertex.

Eager reductions and combines, however, present two special difficulties. First, it is insufficient to delete the vertex created by an eager reduction: the stack top at which associated combine actions will be performed must also be pruned. Special data structures called *kill pointers* are maintained in the stack for this purpose.

Second, a stack top at which combine actions occur cannot simply be discarded out of hand, because the forest node at this stack top may be shared by other partial derivations that have not themselves been rejected. In general, a stack top can only be rejected once every partial derivation that can conceivably use its forest node has itself been rejected. It turns out to be easy to compute the number of such partial derivations (Miller 1994); each stack top contains a counter that is initialized to this number. Every time a derivation is rejected by the oracle, the parser follows kill pointers to locate stack tops at which associated combine actions may occur, and decrements their counters. If a counter reaches zero, the associated stack top is discarded.

Implementation and experiments

The algorithm described above has been implemented in Common LISP and tested on a number of grammars, ranging from grammars specifically designed to exercise all features of L∗ parsing, to a grammar for a substantial subset of English. The implementation can provide a detailed trace of the actions followed during a parse: indeed, the system automatically generated the stack diagrams presented in the example above. A formal specification of the L∗ algorithm with and without local ambiguity packing can be found in Jones & Miller (1993).

More recently, we have extended the parser to parse using feature grammars. The feature grammar implementation has formed the basis for some initial experiments regarding the efficacy of mixed-mode parsing strategies. We have developed a general method for parse table construction that accommodates the following strategy for eager reduction: eagerly reduce if by so doing a variable binding will be established or tested. The idea is to eagerly reduce if the reduction triggers a unification that could fail and thereby prune the parse.

Preliminary results indicate a slight degradation in average performance on grammatical sentences, but a dramatic increase in the speed with which ungrammatical sentences are rejected, if their ungrammaticality is caused by feature mismatches such as person or number disagreements. For example, using a 327-rule feature grammar, the eager reduction strategy generates 18 parse forest nodes before rejecting the following ungrammatical sentence:

$$(*) \text{ Jim are the best man}$$

In contrast, ordinary GLR parsing generates 34 nodes before rejection.

Conclusions and Future Work

The L∗ parsing algorithm combines the low overhead of table-driven approaches with the ability to flexibly tailor the parser's control strategy to particular grammars and applications. The algorithm is strictly more general than the GLR parsing algorithm: it reduces to GLR parsing if used with a parse table that contains no eager reduce actions.

While we believe the L∗ parsing algorithm to be interesting in its own right, we hope that it will prove to be particularly useful and efficient for practical, large-scale natural language understanding. We hypothesize that the algorithm will achieve unusually high efficiency for three reasons. First, the algorithm is table-driven, so it automatically achieves efficiency gains over "uncompiled" approaches such as chart parsing. Second, the algorithm achieves better sharing in the parse forest than existing table-driven approaches.

Third, the L∗ algorithm is specifically designed to handle mixed-mode parsing strategies that may yield efficiency gains over straight bottom-up or top-down parsing. The algorithm provides a general framework in which a variety of parser control strategies can be free specified. However, unlike other general frameworks for table-driven parsing that allow a mix of bottom-up and top-down processing, L∗ parsing also provides a well-defined algorithm for terminating unpromising partial parses on the basis of external evidence.

Such an algorithm is essential to the implementation of efficient mixed-mode parsing strategies that balance the interacting requirements of syntactic analysis and semantic interpretation in a larger natural language understanding system. As an example of such a strategy, in Jones & Miller (1992) we advocate eagerly reducing whenever the reduction is likely to generate semantic preferences that provide evidence against unpromising partial parses. Unpromising partial parses can then be pruned, increasing overall efficiency of the natural language processing system. Our experiments with feature grammars constitute a first tentative step towards validating this kind of parsing strategy: it is reasonable to suppose that selectional restrictions can be used to quickly rule out many semantically ill-formed partial parses in much the same way that grammatical features can serve to efficiently rule out ungrammatical sentences.

The next phase of our research will employ the L∗ framework to further explore and validate a variety of mixed-mode parsing strategies, including the ones sketched above and a number of other strategies proposed in the literature. For example, Steel and De Roeck claim that certain phenomena such as traces are most efficiently analyzed top down, while others such as coordinate conjunctions should be parsed bottom up (Steel & De Roeck 1987). The L∗ algorithm provides a convenient uniform framework for comparing the relative efficiency of different approaches. We also plan to change the search within the parser from a breadth-first to a best-first mechanism, and extend the oracle to allow graded judgements that can inform this search.

References

Abney, S. P., and Johnson, M. Memory requirements and local ambiguity of parsing strategies. Unpublished manuscript.

Aho, A. V., and Ullman, J. D. 1977. *Principles of Compiler Design.* Addison-Wesley.

Billot, S., and Lang, B. 1989. The structure of shared forests in ambiguous parsing. In *Proc. 27th Annual Meeting of the ACL*, 143–151. Vancouver, British Columbia: ACL.

Jones, E. K., and Miller, L. M. 1992. Eager GLR parsing. In *First Australian Workshop on Natural Language Processing and Information Retrieval*.

Jones, E. K., and Miller, L. M. 1993. The L∗ parsing algorithm. Technical Report CS-TR-93/9, Victoria University of Wellington.

Kaplan, R. M. 1973. A general syntactic processor. In Rustin, R., ed., *Natural Language Processing.* Algorithmic Press. 193–241.

Kay, M. 1986. Algorithm schemata and data structures in syntactic processing. In Grosz, B. J.; Jones, K. S.; and Webber, B. L., eds., *Readings in Natural Language Processing.* Morgan Kaufmann. 35–70.

Lang, B. 1974. Deterministic techniques for efficient non-deterministic parsers. In Loeck, J., ed., *Proc. 2nd Colloquium on Automata, Languages and Programming*, volume 14 of Lecture Notes in Computer Science, 255–269. Saarbrücken: Springer-Verlag.

Leermakers, R. 1989. How to cover a grammar. In *Proc. 27th Annual Meeting of the ACL*, 135–142. Vancouver, British Columbia: ACL.

Miller, L. M. 1994. Flexible table-driven parsing for natural language understanding. Master's thesis, Victoria University of Wellington. Forthcoming.

Nederhof, M.-J. 1993. Generalised left-corner parsing. In *Proc. 6th Conference of the European Chapter of the ACL*, 305–314. Utrecht, The Netherlands: ACL.

Schabes, Y. 1991. Polynomial time and space shift-reduce parsing of arbitrary context-free grammars. In *Proc. 29th Annual Meeting of the ACL*, 106–113. Berkeley, California: ACL.

Steel, S., and De Roeck, A. N. 1987. Bidirectional chart parsing. In Mellish, C. S., and Hallam, J., eds., *Advances in Artificial Intelligence (Proc. AISB-87)*, 223–235. J. Wiley and Sons.

Tomita, M., and Ng, S. 1991. The generalized LR parsing algorithm. In Tomita, M., ed., *Generalized LR Parsing.* Kluwer Academic Publishers. 1–16.

Tomita, M. 1986. *Efficient Parsing for Natural Language.* Kluwer Academic Publishers.

Index

Proceedings of the Twelfth National Conference on Artificial Intelligence

Volume Two

*Sponsored by the
American Association for
Artificial Intelligence*

AAAI Press / The MIT Press

Menlo Park • Cambridge • London

ISBN 0-262-61102-3

Contents
Volume Two

Planning and Scheduling

Causal-Link Planning

Planning: Agents

Planning: Representation

Planning Under Uncertainty

Scheduling

Video Program

Volume One

Volume Two

Neural
Networks

Unclear Distinctions lead to Unnecessary Shortcomings: Examining the rule vs fact, role vs filler, and type vs predicate distinctions from a connectionist   representation and reasoning perspective

Venkat Ajjanagadde

Wilhelm-Schickard Institute, Universitaet Tuebingen
Sand 13, D-72076 Tuebingen, Germany
venkat@occam.informatik.uni-tuebingen.de

Abstract

This paper deals with three distinctions pertaining to knowledge representation, namely, the rules vs facts distinction, roles vs fillers distinction, and predicates vs types distinction. Though these distinctions may indeed have some intuitive appeal, the exact natures of these distinctions are not entirely clear. This paper discusses some of the problems that arise when one accords these distinctions a prominent status in a connectionist system by choosing the representational structures so as to reflect these distinctions. The example we will look at in this paper is the connectionist reasoning system developed by Ajjanagadde & Shastri(Ajjanagadde & Shastri 1991; Shastri & Ajjanagadde 1993). Their[1] system performs an interesting class of inferences using activation synchrony to represent dynamic bindings. The rule/fact, role/filler, type/predicate distinctions figure predominantly in the way knowledge is encoded in their system. We will discuss some significant shortcomings this leads to. Then, we will propose a much more uniform scheme for representing knowledge. The resulting system enjoys some significant advantages over Ajjanagadde & Shastri's system, while retaining the idea of using synchrony to represent bindings.

Introduction

Given a particular piece of knowledge, can one unambiguously decide whether it is a *rule* or a *fact*? Are there entities which always act as *roles* and never as *fillers*? Are there entities which always act as *fillers* and never as *roles*? What is a type and what is a general predicate?

In spite of the fact that the rule/fact, role/filler, type/predicate distinctions get mentioned not too infrequently in general AI parlance, an attempt to clearly state the distinctions faces difficulties (Some of the difficulties will be listed in the following section). This paper illustrates that taking these rather unclear distinctions and according them prominent representa-

tional status in a connectionist network may not be a desirable thing to do. Specifically, the example we consider here is the connectionist reasoning system(Ajjanagadde & Shastri 1991; Shastri & Ajjanagadde 1993) developed by Ajjanagadde & Shastri (Henceforth A & S). Their system performs an interesting class of inferences extremely fast. A major idea underlying their approach is the use of activation synchrony to represent dynamic bindings. We consider the idea of using synchrony to represent bindings to be indeed efficient, elegant, and as discussed in (Ajjanagadde & Shastri 1991; Shastri & Ajjanagadde 1993), neurologically plausible. However, the system of A & S has some shortcomings. These shortcomings are due to the representational methodologies A & S have chosen and are not due to the use of synchrony itself. The major reason for the shortcomings of their representational schemes can be diagnosed to be the prominence A & S have accorded to the distinctions of rules & facts, roles & fillers, types & predicates. The representational structures in their system directly reflect these distinctions. For example, Fig. 1 shows how A & S encode the following knowledge base:

$give(x,y,z) \Rightarrow own(y,z)$; $buy(x,y) \Rightarrow own(x,y)$;
$own(x,y) \Rightarrow can\text{-}sell(x.y)$; $give(john,mary,book1)$;
$buy(mike,house3)$

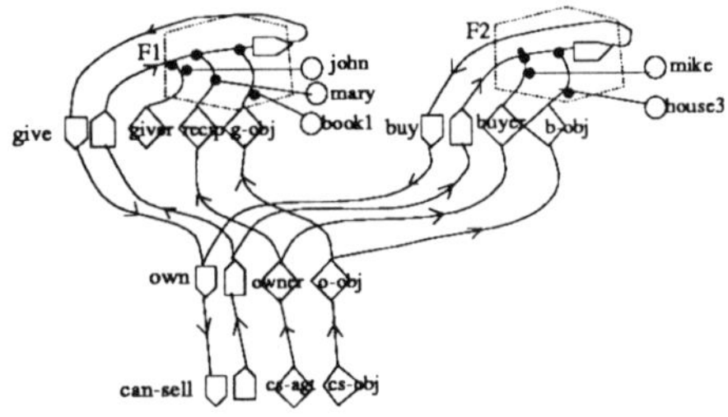

Fig. 1 An example network of A & S.

Fig.2 illustrates how A & S encode the following knowledge by interfacing the rule-based reasoner with a type hierarchy:

$prey\text{-}on(x,y) \Rightarrow scared\text{-}of(y,x)$; $prey\text{-}on(cat,bird)$;
$isa(cat1,cat)$; $isa(cat2,cat)$; $isa(bird1,bird)$;
$isa(bird2,bird)$; $isa(cat,animal)$; $isa(bird,animal)$.

---

[1]This paper was written in third person for double-blind reviewing.

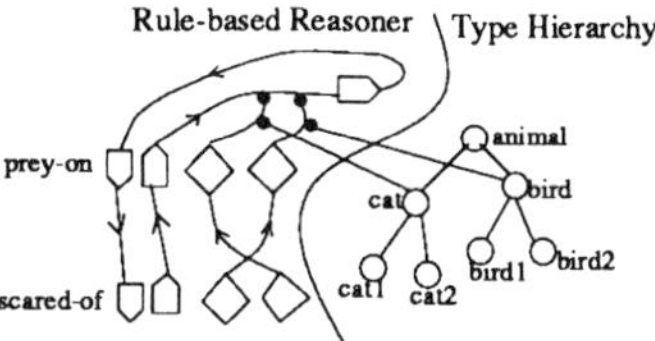

Fig. 2 Encoding the type hierarchy in A & S' system.

Now, note how the representational structures in A & S's system directly reflect the rule/fact, role/filler, and type/predicate distinctions. For example, note that "facts" are encoded in a way very different from the rules (e.g., look at the encoding of the fact *give(john,mary,book1)* (shown enclosed by the box F1 in Fig. 1) with the encoding of the rule *give(x,y,z) ⇒ own(y,z)*). Similarly, A & S treat *role nodes* (e.g., in Fig. 1, *giver, recipient, give-obj, owner, own-obj,...*) in a fashion different from *filler nodes* (e.g., in Fig. 1, *john, mary, book1, house3,...*). The type/predicate distinction manifests in A & S's system as two different modules (shown separated by a curved line in Fig. 2).

Having recalled that the representational structures in A & S's system directly mirror the rule/fact, role/filler and type/predicate distinctions, let us discuss the appropriateness of according these distinctions such a prominent status.

A Closer Look at the Distinctions

Rules and Facts

What is a rule and what is a fact? Given a piece of information, can we clearly decide whether it is a fact or a rule? An intuitive response might be to say that rules correspond to general knowledge and facts correspond to specific knowledge ((Shastri & Ajjanagadde 1993), p. 418). Now, let us try to make that intuition a little more precise. A measure of the generality/specificity might be the number of individuals to which a piece of knowledge pertains to. So, if a piece of knowledge applies to a large number of individuals we may call it a rule and if the knowledge is about only particular individuals, we may call it a fact.

Now, let us imagine ourselves as having been given the task of representing a knowledge base as a connectionist network. For each piece of knowledge in the knowledge base, we have to decide whether it is a fact or a rule and choose the corresponding encoding scheme in A & S's system. Where do we draw the boundary between rules and facts? How general (specific) a piece of information has to be in order to be classified as a rule (fact)? We think that there is no such clear boundary and various pieces of knowledge fall in a continuous spectrum of generality rather than in two distinct bins. On the one hand, note that there are very few statements that apply to *all* individuals. So, for example, though A & S would consider the information that "When someone hits another, the 'hittee' gets hurt" to be a rule(Ajjanagadde & Shastri 1989), this statement does not really apply to *all*

objects. For example, the 'hittee' has to be a sentient being to get hurt. On the other hand, though the knowledge "John loves Mary" may appear qualified to be called a fact (because it is about two particular human beings), that knowledge does hold about many particular instances of John and Mary: "John while wearing red shirt", "John while sitting in the pub", "John while having dinner" etc. still loves "Mary in blue skirt", "Mary while sitting in the pub". Hence what we refer to as "John" and "Mary" in the knowledge "John loves mary" correspond to sets of specific instances of John and Mary. Thus classifying an available piece of information as a rule or as a fact is not a clear-cut task. The unclear distinction between rules and facts gets blurred further in A & S's system with the interfacing of a type hierarchy with the rule-based reasoner(Shastri & Ajjanagadde 1993; Mani & Shastri 1991). They represent the knowledge "Cats prey on birds" as the fact *prey-on(cats,birds)*, which is a piece of knowledge about whole classes of cats and birds.

In summary, a representational scheme that forces us to divide the rather continuous spectrum of generality into two discrete bins does not seem appropriate.

Our proposal is to represent all the knowledge in the form of rules of the kind:

$$P_1(...) \wedge P_2(...)... \wedge P_n(...) \Rightarrow Q(...)$$

Now, representing more (less) specific knowledge is just a matter of having more (less) conjuncts on the antecedent of the rule.

With this choice of representation the knowledge that "John loves Mary" will be represented as the rule: *john(x) ∧ mary(y) ⇒ love(x,y)*.

In addition to the problem of conceptual clarity, the rule/fact distinction made in A & S's system leads to two other main shortcomings. The first one pertains to the ease of learning and the second pertains to reasoning power.

Learning: Learning involves generalizing from our specific experiences. One has to be able to learn "rules" from "facts". When significantly different kinds of network representations are used to represent specific experiences and more general knowledge, learning gets harder. Starting from one kind of representation and arriving at a significantly different kind of representation is a difficult thing to achieve with only local readjustments that are normally made use of in connectionist learning. When we use a uniform representation, generalizing (specializing) corresponds to dropping (adding) some conjuncts in the rule and can be achieved by simply weakening (strengthening) the relevant links.

Reasoning Power: Note that in the network of Fig. 1, there is an asymmetry in the flow of bindings between rules and facts. Binding information can flow from the rules into facts, but not vice versa. Specifically, note that there are no distinct connections from the filler nodes involved in a fact to the corresponding role nodes. For example, consider the encoding of the fact *give(john,mary,book1)*. There are no (distinct) connections from the filler nodes *john, mary, book1* to the role nodes *giver, recipient, give-obj*. That means that facts cannot induce bindings in the argument nodes. Note that, in general, when we are unifying two expressions, we would want bindings to flow in a bidirectional fashion. So, for example, when unifying $P(a,x)$ and $P(y,b)$, we want x to be bound to b and y to be bound to a. But, this does not happen in A & S's system. A specific example where such bidirectional transfers of bindings are necessary corresponds to "answer extraction". Suppose we ask the query *?∃x can-sell(mary,x)* with respect to the network of Fig. 1. We would expect x to get bound to *book1* (That way, we know not only that "Mary can sell something" but also what can Mary sell.). This binding has to come from the fact *give(john,mary,book1)*. But, since in the network of Fig. 1, facts cannot induce bindings, one can only prove that ∃x *can-sell(mary,x)* is true, but, cannot get the answer *can-sell(mary,book1)*. This is the reason why A & S add extra circuitry (not shown in Fig. 1) and a two stage process to get back such answers (see section 4.7 in (Shastri & Ajjanagadde 1993)). When we adopt a uniform scheme for representing rules and facts, the asymmetry between rules & facts goes away, and bidirectional transfer of bindings is naturally obtained. "Answer extraction" happens to be a special case benefit (without having to use additional circuitry for that purpose) of such bidirectional transfer of bindings.

Rule-based reasoner and type hierarchy

Let us consider representing the information "Cats prey on birds". One can represent this knowledge as the rule "∀x∀y *cat(x)* ∧ *bird(y)* ⇒ *prey-on(x,y)*. But, A & S choose not to do this ((Shastri & Ajjanagadde 1993), p. 435). Instead, they introduce filler nodes corresponding to "cats" and "birds". These nodes behave similar to the nodes corresponding to individuals such as *john, mary* etc. Hence, similar to the way one represents facts about individuals (e.g, *love(john,mary)*), one can represent the knowledge "Cats prey on birds" as the fact *prey-on(cat,bird)* (Fig. 2). Why do A & S go for the extra trouble of interfacing the rule-based reasoner with a type hierarchy, when they could represent the same information as just another rule? The reason they give is "... The rule-based reasoner ... cannot answer queries such as prey-on(cat,bird)"((Shastri & Ajjanagadde 1993), p. 435). That is, one could not ask their rule-based reasoner queries about classes of individuals. But, as we will discuss in the next section, with the representation and reasoning scheme we are proposing, the rule-based reasoner itself can answer queries such as "Do cats prey on birds?", "Are birds scared of cats?". In fact, queries of this kind happen to be just special cases of the queries that can be handled by the system we are proposing.

Having said that one does not need to go for a type-hierarchy interface to be able to ask the kind of queries A & S mention, we would like to go one step further and note that the idea of type-hierarchy interface is not just redundant, but, a handicap too. There are four reasons why this is so. Firstly, as mentioned above, with the scheme we are proposing one can have more general queries than the ones A & S consider. With A & S's approach, these general queries cannot be handled.

Secondly, with the idea of type hierarchy interface, only *isa* knowledge can be used to make inferences about types. But, we do need an ability to infer types based on relational knowledge. For example, when we see particular spatial relationships between three blocks, we would like to be able to infer that the the the arrangement formed by the three blocks is of type 'arch'. Due to the way relations (predicates) and types are separated into two different modules in A & S's system, the knowledge of relations is not used to make inferences about types.

Thirdly, there are conceptual problems with the idea of type-hierarchy interface. What is the distinction between types and predicates? If they are not completely distinct and there is a semantic overlap, how do we represent that overlap?

Fourthly, the comment made in the previous subsection about the advantage of having uniform representations from the point of view of learning, apply here as well.

Roles and Fillers

The role vs filler distinction in A & S's system corresponds to the term vs predicate distinction in first-order logic. First-order logic represents the world as a set of objects and allows one to make assertions about those objects. The terms of first-order logic correspond to the objects and predicates are used to make assertions about those objects. In A & S's rule-based reasoner (without the type hierarchy interface), "filler nodes" correspond to objects in the world and "role nodes" are used to make assertions about those objects. Thus, the roles vs fillers distinction in A & S's system is indeed clear and well motivated to the extent the predicate vs term distinction in first-order logic is. Having said that the distinction between role nodes and filler nodes is indeed clear in that way , we would like to make two observations.

Firstly, it is relevant to note that sometimes, one wants to make assertions about not just objects in the world but also about concepts. It is not so straight forward in first-order logic to do the latter. Two of the classic examples illustrating this problem are the "telephone number problem" and the "morning star problem"(McCarthy 1979). Following A & S's approach, in order to represent assertions such as "John knows Mike's telephone number", one will have to have a filler node for the intention of "Mike's telephone number". When one does that (i.e., relaxes the condition that filler nodes correspond to objects in the world), the distinction between role nodes and filler nodes gets blurred[2].

Our second observation concerns plausibility under resource constraints. As mentioned above, in A & S's system, filler nodes denote individuals in the world. But, it is obvious that there cannot be a distinct node corresponding to every object we ever reason about. The number of such individual objects is extremely large (virtually infinite). It is infeasible to say that there is a distinct node in the network corresponding to every such individual. A & S indeed take this fact into consideration. Avoiding the need to allocate a unique node corresponding to every object is precisely the reason they use activation synchrony to represent dynamic bindings. In A & S's system, a phase corresponds to an object participating in a particular reasoning episode. All the nodes active in that phase *together* represent that individual. Synchrony is a means of representing the grouping of the nodes representing the features of an object. Thus, the idea of representing an object by a group of nodes instead of a single node is indeed present in A & S's system though they do not exactly describe it in this way. However, while A & S do not assume the existence of a distinct node corresponding to every object, they do assume the existence of a distinct node corresponding to *every object that is involved in a long-term fact*. Thus, in Fig.1, for representing the long-term facts *give(john,mary,book1)* and *buy(mike,house3)*, A & S assume the existence of distinct nodes corresponding to the objects in these facts, namely, *john, mary, book1, mike, house3*. A logical extension would be to abandon altogether the idea of having distinct nodes corresponding to individual objects (i.e., irrespective of whether or not there is a long-term fact about that individual). With this suggestion, the very notion of *filler nodes* (i.e., nodes corresponding individual objects) looses its utility.

An Alternative Scheme of Representation

In the scheme we are proposing, there are no assorted types of nodes such as role nodes, filler nodes, collectors, enablers etc. that A & S make use of. Instead, the nodes in the network are all *feature nodes*. Each node corresponds to a *basis feature*. An object is represented by a group of basis features. "Basis features" are unary features and are akin to what are usually referred to in connectionist literature as *microfeatures*. We are using a different terminology just because we suspect that some of what we mean by a "basis feature" may be in disagreement with what some people

may mean by a "microfeature". For example, it is not necessary that there should not be a subsumption relation between one basis feature and another. For instance, *human* and *animal* could both be basis features. Even though it might be possible to represent some feature (say, *human*), by a combination of the already existing basis features (say, *animal, biped,...*), an agent may still have a node corresponding to that feature. The nodes in A & S's network happen to be a rather extreme special case wherein *john, mary, book1* etc. themselves happened to be basis features.

It is perhaps worth mentioning that this paper is not concerned with what the basis features are; instead, the focus is on how to represent knowledge as an interconnection of the nodes corresponding to basis features and how does reasoning take place in that network. Generally, in our examples, we will be taking the nodes in A & S's networks themselves to be basis features. This will help one to contrast and see how our representational scheme differs from that of A & S even if we hadn't brought in the idea of not having to have distinct nodes corresponding to individual objects. Thus, in Fig.3, *giver, recipient, owner, own-object, ...* etc. themselves have been chosen as basis features.

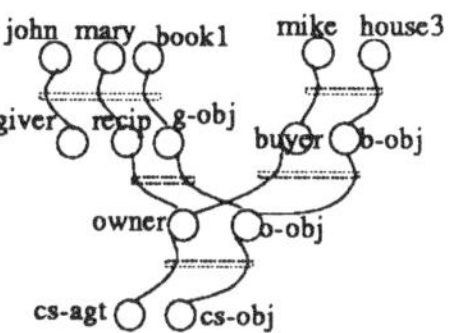

Fig. 3 Network as per the proposed scheme that corresponds to A & S' network of Fig. 1.

Having said what individual nodes in the network represent (i.e, basis features), let us now discuss the encoding of rules. Corresponding to every rule, there are a group of links, which we will refer to as a *link bundle*. In the figures, we denote *link bundles* by drawing a thin bar over the links forming the bundle. For example, the links between the nodes *buyer, buy-obj* and the nodes *owner, own-obj* form a *link bundle* representing the rule *buy(x,y) ⇒ own(x,y)*. The actual interconnection details corresponding to this rule are shown in Fig. 4(a). To avoid clutter, we will normally depict link bundles as shown in Fig. 4(b).

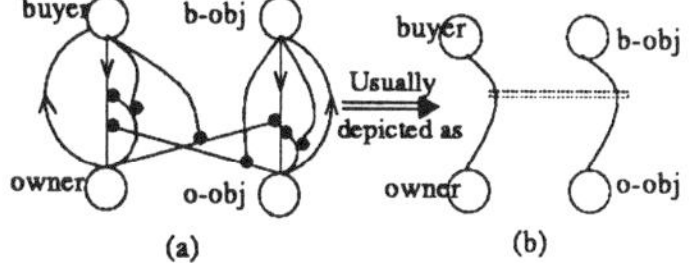

Fig. 4 Encoding $buy(x,y) \Rightarrow own(x,y)$

In fact, that is all we need to say to describe the details of encoding in our network. Unlike in the system of A & S, we do not need to separately explain how rules are encoded, how facts are encoded, how the type hierarchy is encoded etc. All that is there

---

[2]For a discussion of some related issues, see (Wilensky 1986), where Wilensky examines some of the distinctions often made in frame-based systems and then, argues for a more uniform representational scheme.

in our network is just these: There are nodes corresponding to basis features and then there are rules (which are represented by link bundles). Facts and type hierarchy knowledge are not encoded in a different way; they get encoded as rules. For example the network of Fig. 3 includes the encoding of the fact *give(john,mary,book1)*. This fact is encoded as the rule: *john(x)* $\land$ *mary(y)* $\land$ *book1(z)* $\Rightarrow$ *give(x,y,z)* This encoding assumes that *john*, *mary*, and *book*1 are basis features. But, that need not be the case; these individuals can be represented in terms of some other basis features. Suppose, for example, that they are described using the following features: *john: black-hair,round-face* ; *mary: blond,long-face*; *book*1: *book,thick,red*. With that representation of objects, the encoding of the fact *give(john,mary,book1)* is shown in Fig. 5.

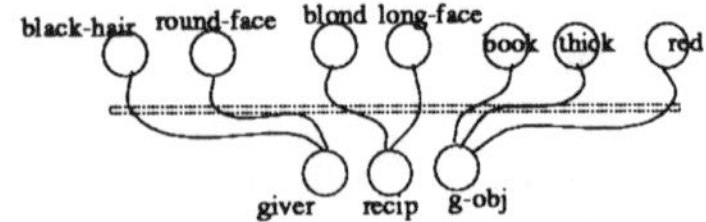

Fig. 5 Encoding *give(john,mary,book1)*.

The information represented in A & S's network of Fig. 2 is represented in our network as shown in Fig. 6. This network encodes the following rules: *prey-on(x,y)* $\Rightarrow$ *scared-of(y,x)* ; *cat(x)* $\land$ *bird(y)* $\Rightarrow$ *prey-on(x,y)*; *cat1(x)* $\Rightarrow$ *cat(x)*; *cat2(x)* $\Rightarrow$ *cat(x)*; *bird1(x)* $\Rightarrow$ *bird(x)*; *bird2(x)* $\Rightarrow$ *bird(x)*; *cat(x)* $\Rightarrow$ *animal(x)*; *bird(x)* $\Rightarrow$ *animal(x)*

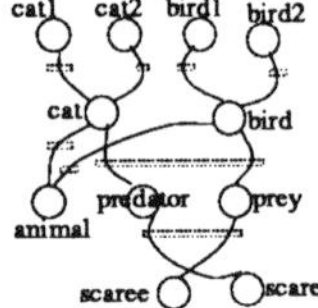

Fig. 6 Network as per the proposed scheme corresponding to the network of Fig. 2

Reasoning

Having discussed the encodings in the network, let us look at how reasoning takes place.

The general form of querying in our system is the following: One asks the network "If I now assert that P_1, P_2,...,P_k are true about a set of objects, then can you prove Q using P_is and the knowledge already encoded in the network?". We will refer to P_is as (dynamic) assertions and Q to be the target proposition. Note that one has to somehow distinguish P_is from Q. This is because P_is are being asserted to be true while Qs truth value is what we want to find out. We represent this distinction by using high activation level for representing P_is and a low activation level for Q. If Q can indeed be proved to be true, then, its representation attains high activation level in time dependent on the length of the proof.

Now, let us consider a simple single step inference. Suppose we want to query the network of Fig. 3

to find out whether "buy(mike,house3)" is true. We pose this query as follows: *Suppose we assert that mike(obj$_1$) and house3(obj$_2$) are true, can you prove that buy(obj$_1$,obj$_2$) is true?*[3] That is, the assertions in this case are: *mike(obj$_1$)* and *house3(obj$_2$)*. The target proposition is *?buy(obj$_1$,obj$_2$)*.

To pose this query, we clamp the activity patterns representing the assertions at a high level of activity and clamp the activity pattern corresponding to the target proposition at a low level of activity.

Suppose we associate the first and second phases with *obj$_1$* and *obj$_2$* respectively. In that case, clamping the assertions and target propositions involves doing the following: We make the nodes corresponding to *mike* and *house3* to become active in the first and second phases of every cycle (respectively) at a high level of activity. We make the nodes corresponding to *buyer* and *buy-obj* to become active in the first and second phase of every cycle respectively, but at a low level of activity. If the target proposition (i.e., *buy(obj$_1$,obj$_2$)*) can indeed be proved to be true (which is the case in our example) we would expect the activity levels of *buyer* and *buy-obj* to become active after a while. Let us examine how this indeed happens.

Since the node *mike* is firing at a high level of activation (in phase 1), unless the flow of activity along the link A (Fig. 7) from *mike* to *buyer* is inhibited, *mike* will raise the activity level of *buyer*. But, there indeed are two inhibitory connections onto this link: link C from *buyer* and link D from *buy-obj*. In phase 1, the node *buyer* is active hence could potentially inhibit the flow along link A. But, note that in phase 1, *mike* is active as well and hence the activation flow along link E inhibits the flow along link C. As a net result, there will be no inhibition on link A in phase 1. Reasoning along similar lines, one can find that though *buy-obj* becomes active in second phase, it does not succeed in inhibiting link A. That means that there will not be inhibition on link A during any phase of the cycle [4]. Hence, the flow of activity from *mike* along link A takes place thereby raising the activity level of *buyer*.

Analogously, one can see that the flow of activity from *house3* raises the activation level of *buy-obj*.

As a result, the target proposition *buy(obj$_1$,obj$_2$)* indeed gets proved to be true.

---

[3] We use *obj$_i$*s to denote arbitrary objects. The situation is similar to starting a mathematical proof by a statement such as "Let x be an arbitrary integer". To make it sound even more analogous to our situation, consider a paraphrase of that statement, namely, "Let x be an arbitrary number having the feature of being an integer". Quite analogously, the assertion *mike(obj$_1$)* for example corresponds to asserting "Let *obj$_1$* be an arbitrary object having the feature of being *mike*".

[4] It is important to note that we assume that for activity flow to take place along a link, there should not be inhibition on that link during *any* phase of a cycle; we assume that an inhibitory effect lasts for the duration of a cycle.

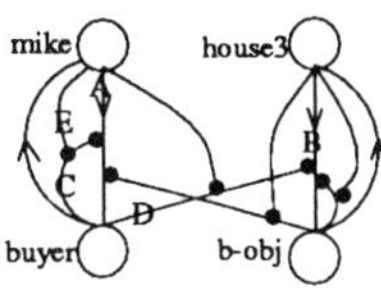

Fig. 7 Encoding of $mike(x) \land house3(y) \Rightarrow buy(x,y)$.

The essential thing to note about the inhibitory connections in a link bundle (see e.g., Fig. 7) is that they are designed to check the binding consistency between the antecedent and the consequent of the rule. When there is a binding mismatch, all the links from the feature nodes corresponding to the antecedent of the rule to the feature nodes corresponding to the consequent of the rule get inhibited.

Having seen how a single-step inference involving a rule takes place, it is easy to see how multi-step inferences take place in the network. Regrettably, due to space limitation, it is not possible to take the reader through some more examples. But, the information provided so far should be sufficient for a reader to check how the system works for other examples. One particular point that is to be remembered however is that we are assuming here that only one instance of a feature needs to be represented during a reasoning episode. The issue of representing multiple dynamic instances(Shastri & Ajjanagadde 1993) is quite orthogonal to the subject matter of this paper. Two particularly interesting examples to consider pertain to the bidirectional transfer of bindings and dealing with queries such as "Are birds scared of cats?". Consider asking the query $?\exists x\ buy(mike,x)$. This corresponds to the case when the assertion is $mike(obj_1)$ and the target proposition is $\exists x\, buy(obj_1,x)$[5]. It may be noted that if the object $house3$ happens to be in focus, i.e., if the node $house3$ happens to be active, say, in some phase i, then, the node $buy\text{-}obj$ will also start firing in phase i representing the desired answer that the thing Mike bought is "$house3$".

Now consider the query "Are birds scared of cats?". In this case, the assertions correspond to $cat(obj_1)$ and $bird(obj_2)$. The target proposition is $?scared\text{-}of(obj_2,obj_1)$. One may work through the network of Fig. 6 to see that this indeed produces the desired answer[6]. This illustrates that our scheme can answer queries about classes of objects without needing a type hierarchy interface. The reason for saying that our scheme can deal with even more general queries than A & S's system is the following: The queries

A & S are able to deal with the type hierarchy interface correspond to the case when assertions involve only unary predicates such as, for example, $cat(obj_1)$ and $bird(obj_2)$. In addition to such assertions, in our system the assertions can also involve n-ary relations such as $P(obj_1, obj_2)$.

Conclusion

As concluding remarks, let us summarize the intended contributions of this paper.

Firstly, the paper provides a critique of some of the representational structures employed in the connectionist reasoning system of Ajjanagadde & Shastri. While this critique of the specific system by A & S should be of interest by itself, it is our belief that the issues raised are of general interest and merit consideration in connectionist knowledge representation efforts in general.

Secondly, the paper proposed an alternative scheme for representing knowledge and presented a system that enjoys some significant advantages relative to the system of A & S in reasoning ability, conceptual clarity, ease of learning, representational efficiency and neurological plausibility.

Acknowledgments. This work was supported by DFG grant Schr 275/7-1. I would like to thank my colleague Seppo Keronen for numerous useful discussions spread over many lunches and afternoon teas.

References

Ajjanagadde, V. G., and Shastri, L. 1989. Efficient inference with multi-place predicates and variables in a connectionist system. In *Proceedings of the Conference of the Cognitive Science Society*, 396–403. Lawrence Erlbaum.

Ajjanagadde, V. G., and Shastri, L. 1991. Rules and variables in neural nets. *Neural Computation* 3:121–134.

Mani, D. R., and Shastri, L. 1991. Combining a connectionist type hierarchy with a connectionist rule-based reasoner. In *Proceedings of the Conference of the Cognitive Science Society*, 418–423.

McCarthy, J. 1979. First-order theories of individual concepts and propositions. In Hayes, J.; Michie, D.; and Mikulich, L., eds., *Machine Intelligence 9*. Halstead Press : New York. 129–147.

Shastri, L., and Ajjanagadde, V. G. 1993. From simple associations to systematic reasoning: A connectionist representation of rules, variables, and dynamic bindings using temporal synchrony. *Behavioral and Brain Sciences* 16:417–494.

Wilensky, R. 1986. Knowledge representation – a critique and a proposal. In Kolodner, J., and Riesbeck, C., eds., *Experience, Memory, and Reasoning*. Erlbaum: Hillsdale, NJ.

---

[5] As in A & S's system we do not activate the nodes corresponding to the unbound arguments in the target proposition.

[6] Note that obj_1 and obj_2 are arbitrary objects and the only thing assumed to be known about them is that $cat(obj_1))$ and $bird(obj_2)$. That is, obj_1 and obj_2 are arbitrarily chosen members of the classes of *cats* and *birds* respectively. Hence, if we can prove that $scared\text{-}of(obj_2,obj_1)$, that means that birds in general are scared of cats.

Associative Memory in an
Immune-Based System

C.J. Gibert* and T.W. Routen
Department of Computing Science
De Montfort University
Leicester LE1 9BH, United Kingdom
twr@dmu.ac.uk

**Current Address: Chemin de la Monnerie, Route de la Ville es Blais, 44 380 Pornichet, France.*

Abstract

The immune system offers to be a rich source of metaphors to guide the exploration of the notion of an adaptive system. We might define a class of systems which are inspired by, but diverge from, descriptions of the immune system, and refer to them as *immune-based* systems. The research reported here is motivated by a desire to explore the possibilities of such systems. Specifically, we attempt to construct an associative memory using immune system modelling as a starting point.

1. Introduction

The immune system and more particularly the immune network and the immune response have been compared with neural networks (e.g. Hoffmann, 1986) and classifier systems (e.g. Farmer et al., 1986). Although the immune system presents similarities with these systems, it also has interesting differences from both (Gibert, 1993). Farmer (1991) described some of these similarities and differences in identifying the computation performed by immune networks as a species of connectionism. One can indeed view the immune system as displaying parallel distributed computation. The coherency of the overall behaviour of the system is an emergent property of many local interactions. Farmer further suggested that aspects of the immune system make it more complicated than its sister connectionisms. It would seem therefore, that the immune system holds great potential for machine learning and offers to be a rich source of metaphors to guide the exploration of the notion of an adaptive system.

An impressive amount of work has been done in theoretical immunology to model faithfully the behaviour of the immune system, or some of its components. These models are computationally very complex, although still simplified from an immunological point of view. For the purposes of artificial intelligence, we are not constrained by biological actuality just as those working on neural networks are not constrained by properties of real neurones. Since the immune system has interesting properties, the models of the immunologists might offer a good starting point from which to construct computational models which embody some of those properties and yet which are of practical use. We might define a class of systems which are inspired by, but can diverge from, descriptions of the immune system, and refer to them as *immune-based systems*. We believe that this class currently has few, if any, members. The research reported here is motivated by a desire to begin to explore the possibilities of such systems.

The implicit role of the immune system is to defend the host from external entities which may lead to disease (called *pathogens*). It operates by being able to discriminate between inner (endogenous) and foreign (exogenous) entities. When an entity is recognised as foreign, several mechanisms leading to its destruction are triggered. The end of the *immune response* is normally marked by the absence of the foreign agent, or its reduction to a harmless quantity. Upon presentation of the same pathogen, a *secondary response* is normally generated. A secondary response is characterised by a speedier obliteration of the infectious agent. It is apparent from the differential responses that initial contact with the pathogen leads the immune system to adapt, in order better to be able to deal with the same pathogen subsequently. Thus, it is a form of memory, and it is a form of content-addressable memory since the secondary response can be elicited from a pathogen which is similar, although not identical, with the original one which established the memory (this is known as *cross-reactivity*).

2. Immune system

Many different cells and molecules are involved in the immune response. For the sake of simplicity in this exercise, we only present and model some of these.

2.1. *Recognition*

The basis of the immune system is in cellular and molecular interactions. Certain cells (B-lymphocytes, henceforth *B cells*) synthesise and carry on their surface molecules called *antibodies*. Molecules are three-dimensional structures with uneven surfaces made of projections and indentations. They therefore have shape[1], which is referred to as *specificity*. If two molecules have complementary specificities, they bind to each other (in a chemical reaction); the strength of the bond depending on the degree of complementarity. A fundamental operation of the immune system is the binding of antibodies with other molecules (which are, in that case, called *antigen*) which serves to tag them for destruction by other cells. This process is referred to as *antigen recognition*.

Antigen specificities are characteristic of the B cells which produce them, in the sense that all antibodies produced by any particular B cell have the same specificity. Therefore, we can speak of an antibody recognising the antigen, or of the cell recognising it. It is important, as will become evident later, that, in addition to antigen-antibody binding, there are also reactions between endogenous entities. Antibodies can themselves be 'recognised' by other antibodies.

2.2. *B cells and the immune network*

When a B cell recognises an antigen, it may be *stimulated*, in which case it becomes enlarged and starts replicating (producing identical copies of itself). We refer to a set of identical cells as a *clone*. Since all cells in a clone are identical, a clone can be said to have a specificity. A clone also has a *size*, which is the number of cells in the clone.

Whether a B cell actually *is* stimulated or not, depends on its affinity with present antigens and also with other clones in the system, and their respective sizes. The network formed by clones recognising other

---

[1] This depends also on other factors such as electrostatic forces, hydrogen bonding, hydrophobic groups and Van der Waals forces. In the remainder of this text, the word shape will refer to the geometrical shape together with all these factors; some authors use the phrase *generalised shape* (Perelson, 1989).

clones in the system is referred to as the *immune network* which was postulated by Jerne (Jerne 1973; 1974). This relationship is often formally expressed in terms of the *field* of the clone in many models in the literature.

Whereas neural net models most commonly use threshold activation functions, considerable evidence (Coutinho, 1989) suggests that proliferation of a B cell is well approximated as a bell-shaped function of its general field, mutated by two thresholds, lower and upper, beyond and below which the cell is activated and proliferates. Below the lower threshold, the cell does not respond because too few of its antibody receptors are cross-linked, beyond the higher threshold, the cell stops responding (a phenomenon referred to as *high zone tolerance*); the cell is said to be *suppressed*. Since antibody binding depends on the affinity with antigen or other antibodies, B cells with high affinity are suppressed at lower concentrations than low affinity B cells (Male et al., 1991).

2.3. *Mutation*

During an immune response, dividing B cells are subject to replication "errors". These genetic errors, e.g. gene recombination and somatic mutation, generate cells which produce different antibody specificities. Some of these specificities are not functional in that they will not be able to bind to the present antigen, but others may have an even higher affinity with it. For an interesting exploration of the consequences of different mutation rates see (Weinand, 1990).

2.4. *Meta-dynamics of the system*

The immune system is in a state of constant flux. New clones are produced by the bone marrow continuously. Populations of B cells show high turnover rates, of order of 15%-30% of the total pool per day (Kinkade, 1987; Coutinho, 1989). Since the total population of B cells is almost constant in the immune system a great number of them die each day. When a new clone is created by the bone marrow, if its affinity with other clones present in the immune network is not zero, the clone can proliferate and possibly survive longer that other clones. The immune network is self-organising, since it determines the survival of newly created clones. It also determines its own size (for a detailed discussion see De Boer and Perelson, 1991). This is referred to as the *meta-dynamics* of the system (Stewart and Varela, 1991; Bersini and Varela, 1991).

2.5. Memory

Immunological research offers two main classes of hypotheses concerning the maintenance of the memory of a pathogen by the immune system. Firstly, cells which participate in a primary response acquire "memory cell" characteristics which distinguish them from other "virgin", cells. Memory cells are thought to decay more slowly or have an infinite life. They are not suppressed by high dose of antigen and proliferate faster.

An alternative view is based on the immune network hypothesis, due to Jerne (1973,1974). As Farmer (1991) postulates "In an immune network a memory can potentially be modelled by a fixed point of the network. The concentrations at the fixed point are held constant through the feedback of one type to another type." (p. 174). The dynamic maintenance of memory in immune network would seem to constitute an attractive approach for an adaptive system, since a particularity of memory in general is its limited capacity; adaptive systems need to be able selectively to forget. Localised memories due to network interactions are hypothesised to be stable memory states of the network (De Boer and Hogeweg, 1989b; Weisbuch, 1990; Weisbuch et al., 1990).

3. Engineering associative memory

Thus, we have the bare bones of a possible model of the immune system. The task we set ourselves was to harness this (albeit crude) model in an attempt to create a content-addressable auto-associative memory.

Inputs to the system are black and white pictures of 64 by 64 pixels and are analogous to antigen. Our aim is to present these 'antigen', initiate a 'primary response' which creates the memory of the antigen, and then be able to observe the existence of the memory by prompting a secondary response via either a further injection of the same, or similar, antigen.

3.1. Equations

The differential equations we use are discussed and justified in the immunology literature. The generic equation for computing the field f_i, of a clone i, in a system containing n clones is as follows:-

$$f_i = \sum_{j=1}^{n} a_{ij} x_j \quad (1)$$

where a_{ij} is the affinity with which clone i interacts with clone j and x_j is the size of the clone j. It is worthy of note that this equation is isomorphic with the familiar weighted sum of artificial neural networks,

where the affinities correspond with connection weights and the sizes correspond with activation levels.

The bell-shaped activation function was first proposed by De Boer and Hogeweg (1989b) and can be produced as the product of two sigmoid functions as in equation (2):-

$$f(h) = \frac{h}{\theta_1 + h} \times \frac{\theta_2}{\theta_2 + h} \quad (2)$$

This function has been studied extensively (e.g. De Boer and Hogeweg, 1989a, b; Weisbuch, 1990; De Boer and Perelson, 1991). If $\theta_1 << \theta_2$ is chosen, the maximum value of the function is almost equal to unity, at each threshold the value is almost equal to 0.5.

We can characterise the motion of a clone in the system in the following terms:-

$$\frac{dx_i}{dt} = m_i + x_i(1 + b(f_i) + b(A \times a_{iA}) - d) \quad (3)$$

Here, x_i is the size of clone i, m^i is the daily production of cells in this clone by the bone marrow, d represents the decay of the cells in the system, b is the bell-shaped function (2) and f_i is the field "seen" by the clone i at instant t. A describes the concentration of antigen, while a_{iA} is the affinity of the clone i for the antigen (Farmer, 1991; Weisbuch, 1990; De Boer and Perelson, 1991).

3.2. Entities and affinity

A basic requirement for an immune-based system is the development of a way of modelling the entities of the system along with a means for computing the affinities between them. In fact, we are interested not in representing cells and antibodies in all their complexity, but only representing those aspects relevant from the point of view of their interaction (more realistic models have been developed, e.g. Inman, 1978 as described by Stewart and Varela, 1991 or Weinand, 1990). In immunological terms, we are interested in representing only their combining regions. These are called paratopes and epitopes and are best thought of as keys and locks. A cell has a key of a certain shape (its paratope) which can fit a lock of a certain shape (epitope) held by certain antibodies, and by other cells.

We follow Seiden and Celada (1992; Celada and Seiden, 1992) who suggest an extremely simple fixed-length binary representation of the shape of paratopes and epitopes; a form of representation common to many investigations in current machine learning. The affinity a_{ij}, between a paratope and an epitope is then determined by the number of complementary bits. When $a_{ij} = a_{ji}$, the network is said to be symmetrical. Several models have used symmetrical networks (e.g. De Boer and Hogeweg, 1989a; Weisbuch, 1990) although this represents a simplification since non-symmetrical interactions occur in the immune system (De Boer and Perelson, 1991). Interactions are not symmetrical either when the affinity function does not produce the same affinity between reciprocal interactions, or when paratopes and epitopes are separately represented. Non-symmetrical networks are less stable that symmetrical ones (Hoffmann, 1986).

3.3. Output: defining the winner

As Farmer et al. (1986) note that there is no clear analogue for output in the actual immune system, which simply seeks to remove antigen. We reasoned as follows. If there were an output of the immune system then it would surely be related somehow to the successful termination of the immune response. A natural assumption to make is that, if we can obtain interesting output from the system, it must surely be related to the clone which is, in some sense, the *most relevant effectors of the destruction* of the antigen.

We shall refer to this clone as the *winner* of the response, and define output in terms of it. We shall see later that it is not straightforward to define the winner. This is not necessarily a disadvantage; many possibilities present themselves and suggest interesting avenues of investigation.

3.4. Simulation

A constant and continuous production of clones by the bone marrow is simulated. At each time step, a certain number of randomly generated clones are inserted into the system. If a new clone has the same paratope and same epitope as an existing one, the size of the existing clone is increased by the size of the new one. The initial size of a clone is chosen so that no network activity is initiated. Since clones decay, the number of clones and the total population of cells are constant in the system. The parameters are chosen so that the number of clones is large enough for the probability of recognition of an antigen to be equal to unity. Therefore, the *repertoire* is complete, as in the real immune system. When an antigen (i.e. a pattern to be remembered by the system) is injected, all the clones present in the system follow equation (3). The clones which recognise the antigen start expanding. When the sizes of these clones reach a sufficient level, network activity is triggered. Anti-idiotypic clones are stimulated, proliferate, and then stimulate their own anti-idiotypic partners and so on.

3.5. Artificial idiotope assignment

We experimented initially with a non-symmetrical model in which epitopes and paratopes were represented separately. Our idea was to to **force** the memorisation of an antigen. During the period when the antigen is present, the clones directed against that antigen (referred to as Ab1s) expand, exciting their anti-idiotypic partners (Ab2s). In the system, the idiotope of each Ab2 present in the system is assigned the same shape as the antigen and therefore represents an internal image of the antigen.

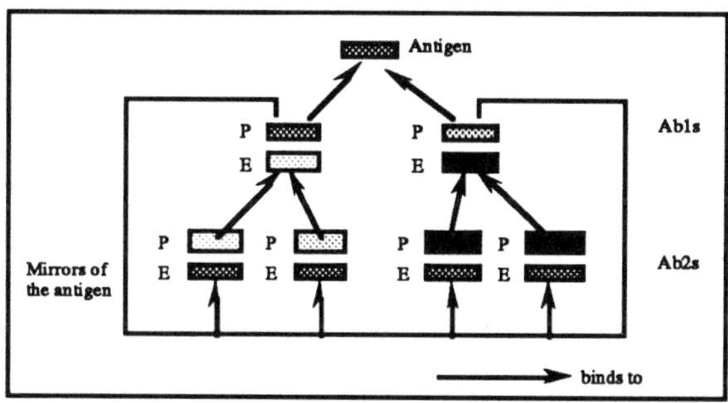

Figure 1. The shape of the antigen becomes the idiotope of Ab2s present in the system. Therefore a loop is created between Ab1s and Ab2.

The idea is forcibly to create recognition loops in the network to enable the maintenance by the network of the clones responding to the antigen. After the removal of the antigen, the size of Ab1s will be large (due to the immune response), so will that of Ab2s (due to stimulation from the expanded Ab1s). Ab1s and Ab2s suppress each other and start decaying until an equilibrium is reached, with Ab1 clones maintaining some Ab2 clones and vice-versa. Depending on their respective sizes at the end of the response, the equilibrium can be reached in a stimulatory state, where the size of the clones oscillate or in a suppressed state where they do not change. This is over-simplified and the memory state may not be stable, depending on the reciprocal affinity of Ab1s and Ab2s, and the presence of other cross-reactive clones. However, no stable state would be possible without the bell-shaped proliferation function. For a more detailed discussion, see Weisbuch (1990) or Weisbuch et al. (1990).

In this model, the winner is defined as the largest clone directed against the antigen upon its removel. The output of the system is taken as the idiotope of the largest anti-idiotypic clone of the winner.

Patterns presented to the system were remembered through the maintenance, within the system, of the clones directed against them by the interactions in the network. However, the system was not stable. Should the field of a clone fall between the activation thresholds, it would proliferate continuously. Since the probability for inserting a new clone which would suppress the clone was small, the system would collapse. Suppression was not the dominant influence, as it is hypothesised to be in the real immune system.

We have investigated ways of stabilising the dynamics of the model. If the field of a clone is modified according the size of the clone, the clone can be prevented from expanding. For example, if, in equation (3), f_i becomes:-

$$\frac{\theta^n}{\theta^n + x_i^n} f_i \quad (4)$$

the system becomes stable. In equation (4), θ is a constant, x_i is the size of the clone i, f_i is the field of the clone i and n is another constant. The constants are chosen according to the other parameters of the system.

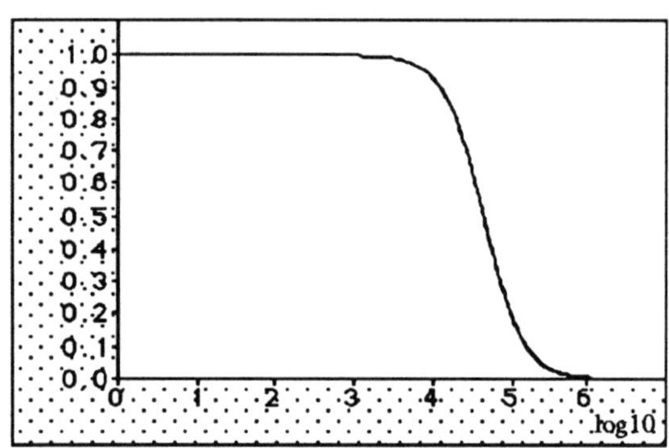

Figure 2 According to equation (4), the function is plotted for $\theta = 10000$, and $n = 2$.

Equation (4) can be interpreted as follows: when a clone grows large, the field seen by that clone becomes less and less significant. Experimentally, this seemed to stabilise the immune network, *apparently* without modifying the properties of the system. It is not certain that there exist immunological interpretations for equation (4), although it is conceivable that antibody feedback and other regulatory effects within the immune system may have something like this effect.

3.6. Symmetrical network model

Because symmetrical networks are known to be more stable, we decided to experiment with one. Since network interactions are symmetrical, it is assumed that, for a clone responding to an antigen, at least one anti-idiotypic clone is present in the system and therefore will proliferate as its partner proliferates. These interactions should maintain memory cells in the system.

This time, in defining the winner of the response, we took into account the affinity of each clones with the antigen. The winner was chosen to be the clone for whom the product of size with affinity was greatest. This was thought desirable since we had observed that, although a high affinity clone proliferates faster than lower affinity clones, should its size have been low at the presentation of the antigen, it is not certain that its growth during the immune response would be sufficient to ensure that it be the largest clone at the termination of the response. This time, the output was chosen to be the complement of the shape of the winner (since we expect high affinity clones to win, and high affinity clones represent a close or perfect reproduction of the input pattern).

In this model, most clones in the network were suppressed. Memory cells were naturally maintained by the interactions in the immune network, but did tend to dissipate slowly and eventually disappear. The model provided stable network behaviour, but this is not really a surprise (e.g. see Weisbuch, 1990).

However, the system did not show good quality outputs, particularly after secondary responses. Although memory cells expand faster than virgin cells, the output after a secondary response is of relatively poor quality.

At the end of a primary response, the winner was usually the clone which showed the highest affinity for the antigen. Since many clones participated in the immune response, the winner, although having high affinity with the antigen, was not necessarily one which was well integrated in the network. Winners were not always maintained by the interactions of the network because of the absence of partners which could maintain them. Although the dynamics of this system showed better stability, it did not acquire the patterns we desired. There is possibly an analogy here with the ability of a neural network to 'train' apparently successfully, but in fact have been learning a relationship other than the one intended by its designer.

4. Conclusions

In our experiments, we found two requirements which we found difficult to satisfy simultaneously: remembering patterns, while maintaining system stability. The first model proved unstable, but offered the possibility of forcing the insertion of memory cells into the network. The second model proved stable, but did not allow that forcing and did not systematically maintain the clones we desired.

It seems that interactions in the immune-based system can exhibit memory properties. Nevertheless, the clones which are maintained by those interactions still tend to disappear. It may well be that memory cells should have a slower decay rate, which would compensate for their observed decay. This solution should be experimented with, but we believe that it may well have consequences for the behaviour of the network, since interactions, although symmetrical in terms of affinity would be asymmetrical in terms of motion.

Although we failed to arrive at a satisfactory model, we found our investigations exciting since they took place in an extremely rich, yet relatively unexplored design space: immune-based modelling. We hope that this paper increases the prospects of a wider exploration of that space.

5. References

Bersini, H., and Varela, F. J. 1991. The immune recruitment mechanism: a selective evolutionary strategy. In: Belew, R. K. and Booker, L. B. (eds), *Proceedings of the Fourth International Conference on Genetic Algorithms*, San Mateo: Morgan-Kaufman, 520-526.

Celada, F., and Seiden, P. E. 1992. A computer model of cellular interactions in the immune system. In: *Immunology Today*, 13(2): 57-62.

Coutinho, A. 1989. Beyond clonal selection and network. In: *Immunological Reviews*, 110: 63-87.

De Boer, R. J., and Hogeweg, P. 1989a. Unreasonable implications of reasonable idiotypic network assumptions. In: *Bulletin of Mathematical Biology*, 51: 381-408.

De Boer, R. J., and Hogeweg, P. 1989b. Memory but no suppression in low- dimensional symmetric idiotypic networks. In: *Bulletin of Mathematical Biology*, 51: 223-246.

De Boer, R. J., and Perelson, A. S. 1991. Size and connectivity as emergent properties of a developing immune network. In: *Journal of Theoretical Biology*, 149: 381-424.

Farmer, J. D., and Packard, N. H. 1986. Evolution, games, and learning: models for adaptation in machine and nature. In: *Physica D*, 22: vii-xii.

Farmer, J. D., Packard, N. H., and Perelson, A. S. 1986. The immune system, adaptation, and machine learning. In: *Physica D*, 22: 187-204.

Farmer, J. D. 1991. A Rosetta Stone for connectionism. In: Forrest S. (ed.), *Emergent Computation*, London: MIT Press, 153-187.

Gibert, C. J. 1993. The immune system and machine learning. *M.Sc. Human-Computer Systems Project Report* De Montfort University, Leicester.

Hoffmann, G. W. 1986. A neural network model based on the analogy with the immune system. In: *Journal of Theoretical Biology*, 122: 33-67.

Jerne, N. K. 1973. The immune system. In: *Scientific American*, 229: 52-60.

Jerne, N. K. 1974. Towards a network theory of the immune system. In: *Annales d'Immunologie (Institut Pasteur)*, 125C: 373-389.

Kinkade, P. W. 1987. Experimental models for understanding B lymphocyte formation. In: *Advances in Immunology*, 41: 181-267.

Male, D. Champion, B. Cooke, A. and Owen, M. 1991. *Advanced immunology*. Grower Medical Publishing: London, England.

Perelson, A. S. 1989. Immune network theory. In: *Immunological Review*, 110: 5-36.

Seiden, P. E., and Celada, F. 1992. A model for simulating cognate recognition and response in the immune system. In: *Journal of Theoretical Biology*, 158: 329-357.

Stewart, J. and Varela, F. J. 1991. Morphogenesis in shape-space. Elementary meta-dynamics in a model of the immune network. In: *Journal of Theoretical Biology*, 153: 477-498.

Weinand, R. G. 1990. Somatic mutation, affinity maturation and the antibody repertoire: a computer model. In: *Journal of Theoretical Biology*, 143: 343-382.

Weisbuch, G. 1990. A shape space approach to the dynamics of the immune system. In: *Journal of Theoretical Biology*, 143: 507-522.

Weisbuch, G., De Boer, R. J. and Perelson, A. S. 1990. Localized memories in idiotypic networks. In: *Journal of Theoretical Biology*, 146: 483-499.

Parsing Embedded Clauses with Distributed Neural Networks

Risto Miikkulainen
Department of Computer Sciences
The University of Texas at Austin
Austin, TX 78712 USA
risto@cs.utexas.edu

Dennis Bijwaard
Department of Computer Science
University of Twente
7500 AE Enschede, The Netherlands
bijwaard@cs.utwente.nl

Abstract

A distributed neural network model called SPEC for processing sentences with recursive relative clauses is described. The model is based on separating the tasks of segmenting the input word sequence into clauses, forming the case-role representations, and keeping track of the recursive embeddings into different modules. The system needs to be trained only with the basic sentence constructs, and it generalizes not only to new instances of familiar relative clause structures, but to novel structures as well. SPEC exhibits plausible memory degradation as the depth of the center embeddings increases, its memory is primed by earlier constituents, and its performance is aided by semantic constraints between the constituents. The ability to process structure is largely due to a central executive network that monitors and controls the execution of the entire system. This way, in contrast to earlier subsymbolic systems, parsing is modeled as a controlled high-level process rather than one based on automatic reflex responses.

Introduction

Reading an input sentence into an internal representation is a most fundamental task in natural language processing. In the distributed (i.e. subsymbolic) neural network approach, it usually involves mapping a sequence of word representations into a shallow semantic interpretation, such as the case-role assignment of the constituents. This approach offers several promises: it is possible to combine syntactic, semantic, and thematic constraints in the interpretation, generate expectations automatically, generalize to new inputs, and process noisy sentences robustly (Elman 1990, 1991; McClelland & Kawamoto 1986; Miikkulainen 1993; St. John & McClelland 1990). To a limited extent, it is even possible to train such networks to process sentences with complex grammatical structure, such as embedded relative clauses (Berg 1992; Jain 1991; Miikkulainen 1990; Sharkey & Sharkey 1992; Stolcke 1990).

However, it has been very difficult to build subsymbolic systems that would generalize to new sentence structures. A network can be trained to form a case-role representation of each clause in a sentence like

The girl, who liked the dog, saw the boy[1], and it will generalize to different versions of the same structure, such as The dog, who bit the girl, chased the cat (Miikkulainen 1990). However, such a network cannot parse sentences with novel combinations of relative clauses, such as The girl, who liked the dog, saw the boy, who chased the cat. The problem is that distributed neural networks are pattern transformers, and they generalize by interpolating between patterns on which they were trained. They cannot make inferences by dynamically combining processing knowledge that was previously associated to different contexts, such as processing a relative clause at a new place in an otherwise familiar sentence structure. This lack of generalization is a serious problem, given how effortlessly people can understand sentences they have never seen before.

This paper describes SPEC (Subsymbolic Parser for Embedded Clauses), a subsymbolic sentence parsing model that can generalize to new relative clause structures. The basic idea is to separate the tasks of segmenting the input word sequence into clauses, forming the case-role representations, and keeping track of the recursive embeddings into different networks. Each network is trained with only the most basic relative clause constructs, and the combined system is able to generalize to novel sentences with remarkably complex structure. Importantly, SPEC is not a neural network reimplementation of a symbol processor. It is a self-contained, purely distributed neural network system, and exhibits the usual properties of such systems. For example, unlike symbolic parsers, the network exhibits plausible memory degradation as the depth of the center embeddings increases, its memory is primed by the earlier constituents in the sentence, and its performance is aided by semantic constraints between the constituents.

The SPEC Architecture

SPEC receives a sequence of word representations as its input, and for each clause in the sentence, forms an output representation indicating the assignment of

---

[1]In all examples in this paper, commas are used to indicate clause boundaries for clarity.

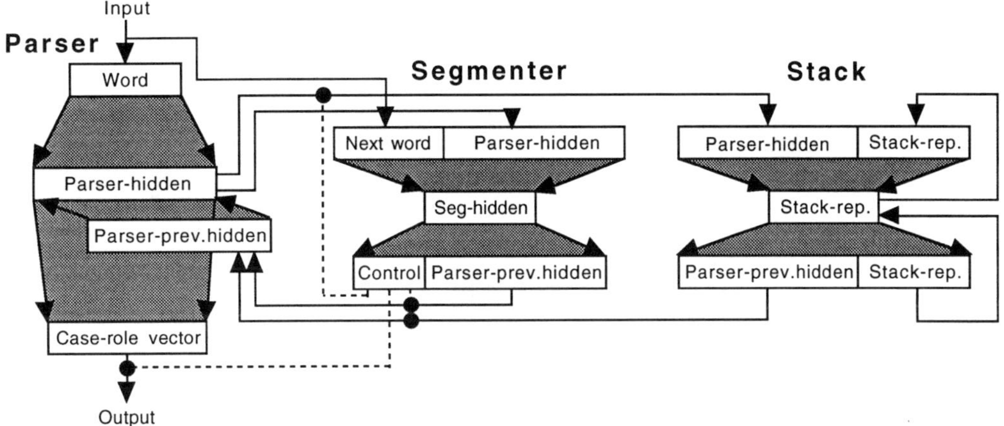

Figure 1: **The SPEC sentence processing architecture.** The system consists of the Parser (a simple recurrent network), the Stack (a RAAM network), and the Segmenter (a feedforward network). The gray areas indicate propagation through weights, the solid lines stand for pattern transport, and the dashed lines represent control outputs (with gates).

words into case roles. The case-role representations are read off the system and placed in a short-term memory (currently outside SPEC) as soon as they are complete. SPEC consists of three main components: the Parser, the Segmenter, and the Stack (figure 1). Below, each component is described in detail.

The Parser

The Parser performs the actual transformation of the word sequence into the case-role representations, and like many other subsymbolic parsers, it is based on Elman's (1990) simple recurrent network architecture (SRN; figure 2). The pattern in the hidden layer is copied to the previous-hidden-layer assembly and serves as input to the hidden layer during the next step in the sequence, thus implementing a sequence memory. The network is trained with examples of input/output sequences, adjusting all forward weights according to the backpropagation algorithm (Rumelhart, Hinton, & Williams 1986).

Words are represented distributively as vectors of gray-scale values between 0 and 1. The component values are initially assigned randomly and modified during learning by the FGREP method (Miikkulainen & Dyer 1991; Miikkulainen 1993). FGREP is a convenient way to form distributed representations for input/output items, but SPEC is not dependent on FGREP. The word representations could have been obtained through semantic feature encoding (McClelland & Kawamoto 1986) as well, or even assigned randomly.

The case-role assignment is represented at the output of the Parser as a case-role vector (CRV), that is, a concatenation of those three word representation vectors that fill the roles of agent, act, and patient in the sentence[2] (figure 2). For example, the word sequence

the girl saw the boy receives the case-role assignment agent=girl, act=saw, patient=boy, which is represented as the vector |girl saw boy| at the output of the Parser network. When the sentence consists of multiple clauses, the relative pronouns are replaced by their referents: The girl, who liked the dog, saw the boy parses into two CRVs: |girl liked dog| and |girl saw boy|.

The Parser receives a continuous sequence of input word representations as its input, and its target pattern changes at each clause boundary. For example, in reading The girl, who liked the dog, saw the boy, the target pattern representing |girl saw boy| is maintained during the first two words, then switched to |girl liked dog| during reading the embedded clause, and then back to |girl saw boy| for the rest of the sentence. The CRV for the embedded clause is read off the network after dog has been input, and the CRV for the main clause after the entire sentence has been read.

When trained this way, the network is not limited to a fixed number of clauses by its output representation. Also, it does not have to maintain information about the entire past input sequence in its memory, making it possible in principle to generalize to new clause structures. Unfortunately, after a center-embedding has been processed, it is difficult for the network to remember earlier constituents. This is why a Stack network is needed in SPEC.

The Stack

The hidden layer of a simple recurrent network forms a compressed description of the sequence so far. The Stack has the task of storing this representation at each center embedding, and restoring it upon return from the embedding. For example, in parsing The girl, who liked the dog, saw the boy, the hidden-layer

---

[2]The representation was limited to three roles for simplicity.

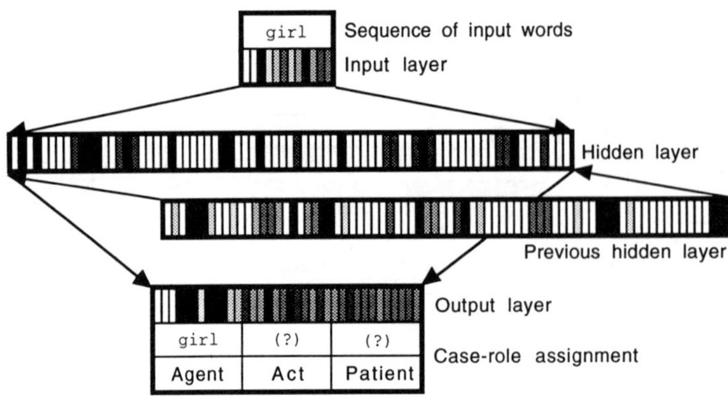

Figure 2: **The Parser network.** The figure depicts a snapshot of the network after it has read the first two words The and girl. The activity patterns in the input and output assemblies consist of word representations. The input layer holds the representation for the last word, girl, and the activity pattern at the output represents the (currently incomplete) case-role assignment of the clause.

representation is pushed onto the stack after The girl, and popped back to the Parser's previous-hidden-layer assembly after who liked the dog. In effect, the SRN can then parse the top-level clause as if the center embedding had not been there at all.

The Stack is implemented as a Recursive Auto-Associative Memory (RAAM; Pollack 1990; figure 3). RAAM is a three-layer backpropagation network trained to perform an identity mapping from input to output. As a side effect, its hidden layer learns to form compressed representations of the network's input/output patterns. These representations can be recursively used as constituents in other input patterns, and a potentially infinite hierarchical data structure, such as a stack, can this way be compressed into a fixed-size representation.

The input/output of the Stack consists of the stack's top element and the compressed representation for the rest of the stack. Initially the stack is empty, which is represented by setting all units in the "Stack" assembly to 0.5 (figure 3). The first element, such as the hidden-layer pattern of the Parser network after reading The girl, is loaded into the "Push" assembly, and the activity is propagated to the hidden layer. The hidden-layer pattern is then loaded into the "Stack" assembly at the input, and the Stack network is ready for another push operation.

When the Parser returns from the center embedding, the stored pattern needs to be popped from the stack. The current stack representation is loaded into the hidden layer, and the activity is propagated to the output layer. At the output, the "Pop" assembly contains the stored Parser-hidden-layer pattern, which is then loaded into the previous-hidden-layer assembly of the Parser network (figure 1). The "Stack" assembly contains the compressed representation for the rest of the stack, and it is loaded to the hidden layer of the Stack network, which is then ready for another pop operation.

The Segmenter

The Parser+Stack architecture alone is not quite sufficient for generalization into novel relative clause structures. For example, when trained with only examples of center embeddings (such as the above) and tail embeddings (like The girl saw the boy, who chased the cat), the architecture generalizes well to new sentences such as The girl, who liked the dog, saw the boy, who chased the cat. However, the system still fails to generalize to sentences like The girl saw the boy, who the dog, who chased the cat, bit. Even though the Stack takes care of restoring the earlier state of the parse, the Parser has to learn all the different transitions into relative clauses. If it has encountered center embeddings only at the beginning of the sentence, it cannot generalize to a center embedding that occurs after an entire full clause has already been read.

The solution is to train an additional network, the Segmenter, to divide the input sequence into clauses. The segmenter receives the current hidden-layer pattern as its input, together with the representation for the next input word, and it is trained to produce a modified hidden-layer pattern as its output (figure 4). The output is then loaded into the previous-hidden-layer assembly of the Parser. In the middle of reading a clause, the Segmenter passes the hidden-layer pattern through without modification. However, if the next word is a relative pronoun, the segmenter modifies the pattern so that only the relevant information remains. In the above example, after boy has been read and who is next to come, the Segmenter generates a pattern similar to that of the Parser's hidden layer after only The boy in the beginning of the sentence has been input.

In other words, the Segmenter (1) detects transitions to relative clauses, and (2) changes the sequence memory so that the Parser only has to deal with one type of clause boundary. This way, the Parser's task be-

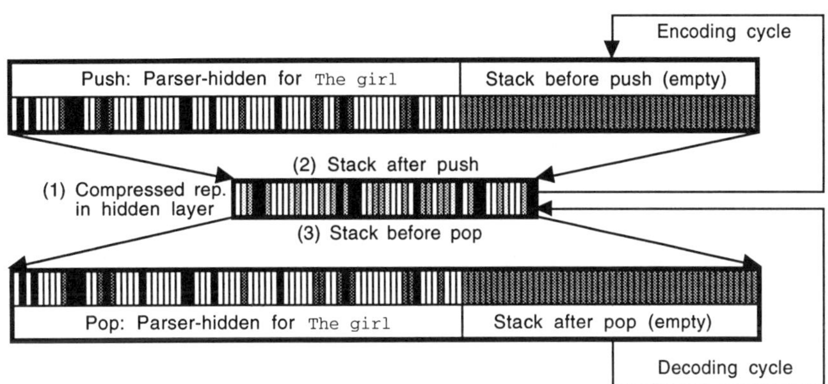

Figure 3: **The Stack network.** This figure simultaneously illustrates three situations that occur at different times during the training and the performance of the Stack: (1) A training situation where the network learns to autoassociate an input pattern with itself, forming a compressed representation at the hidden layer; (2) A push operation, where a representation in the "Push" assembly is combined with the empty-stack representation (in the "Stack" assembly) to form a compressed representation for the new stack in the hidden layer; (3) A pop operation, where the current stack representation in the hidden layer generates an output pattern with the top element of the stack in the "Pop" assembly and the representation for the remaining stack (currently empty) in the "Stack" assembly.

comes sufficiently simple so that the entire system can generalize to new structures.

The Segmenter plays a central role in the architecture, and it is very natural to give it a complete control over the entire parsing process. Control is implemented through three additional units at the Segmenter's output (figure 4). The units "Push" and "Pop" control the stack operations, and the unit "Output" indicates when the Parser output is complete and should be read off the system. The control implementation in SPEC emphasizes an important point: although much of the structure in the parsing task is programmed into the system architecture, SPEC is still a self-contained distributed neural network. In many modular neural network architectures control is due to a hidden symbolic supervisor. SPEC demonstrates that such external control mechanisms are not necessary: even a rather complex subsymbolic architecture can take care of its own control and operate independently of its environment.

Experiments

The training and testing corpus was generated from a simple phrase structure grammar (table 1). Each clause consisted of three constituents: the agent, the verb and the patient. A relative who-clause could be attached to the agent or to the patient of the parent clause, and who could fill the role of either the agent or the patient in the relative clause. In addition to who, the and "." (full stop, the end-of-sentence marker that had its own distributed representation in the system just like a word), the vocabulary consisted of the verbs chased, liked, saw and bit, and the nouns boy, girl, dog and cat. Certain semantic restrictions were imposed on the sentences. A verb could only have certain nouns as its agent and patient, as listed in table 2. The grammar was used to generate all sentences with up to four

```
S    → NP VP "."
NP   → DET N | DET N RC
VP   → V NP
RC   → who VP | who NP V
N    → boy | girl | dog | cat
V    → chased | liked | saw | bit
DET  → the
```

Table 1: **The sentence grammar.**

Verb	Case-role	Possible fillers
chased	Agent:	boy,girl,dog,cat
	Patient:	cat
liked	Agent:	boy,girl
	Patient:	boy,girl,dog
saw	Agent:	boy,girl,cat
	Patient:	boy,girl
bit	Agent:	dog
	Patient:	boy,girl,dog,cat

Table 2: **Semantic restrictions.**

clauses, and those that did not match the semantic restrictions were discarded. The final corpus consisted of 49 different sentence structures, with a total of 98,100 different sentences.

The SPEC architecture divides the sentence parsing task into three subtasks. Each component needs to learn only the basic constructs in its task, and the combined architecture forces generalization into novel combinations of these constructs. Therefore, it is enough to train SPEC with only two sentence structures: (1) the two-level tail embedding (such as The girl saw the boy, who chased the cat, who the dog bit) and the two-level center-embedding (e.g. the girl, who the dog, who chased the cat, bit, saw the boy). The training set consisted of 100 randomly-selected sen-

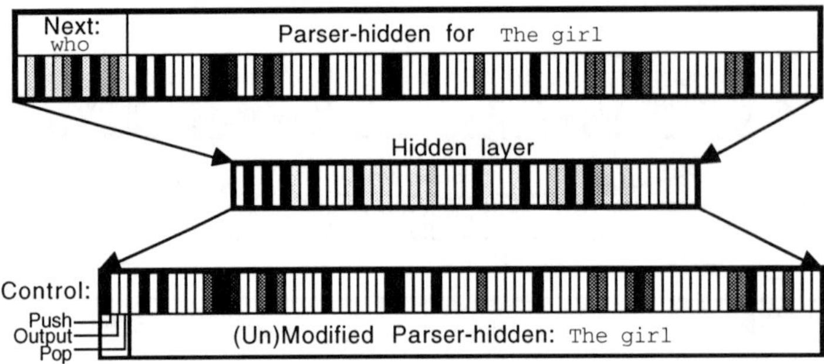

Figure 4: **The Segmenter network.** The Segmenter receives the Parser's hidden-layer pattern as its input together with the next input word, which in this case is who. The control outputs are 1, 0, 0, indicating that the Parser's hidden-layer representation should be pushed onto the Stack, the current case-role representation is incomplete and should not be passed on to the output of the system, and the stack should not be popped at this point. In this case, the Segmenter output is identical to its input, because the girl is the smallest context that the Parser needs to know when entering a center embedding.

tences of each type. In addition, the Stack was trained to encode and decode up to three levels of pushes and pops.

The word representations consisted of 12 units. Parser's hidden layer was 75 units wide, Segmenter's 50 units, and Stack's 50 units. All networks were trained with on-line backpropagation with 0.1 learning rate and without momentum. Both the Parser and the Segmenter developed word representations at their input layers (with a learning rate of 0.001). The networks were trained separately (i.e. without propagation between modules) and simultaneously, sharing the same gradually-developing word and parser-hidden-layer representations. The convergence was very strong. After 400 epochs, the average error per output unit was 0.018 for the Parser, 0.008 for the Segmenter (0.002 for the control outputs), and 0.003 for the Stack, while an error level of 0.020 usually results in acceptable performance in similar assembly-based systems (Miikkulainen 1993). The training took approximately three hours on an IBM RS6000 workstation. The final representations reflected the word categories very well.

SPEC's performance was then tested on the entire corpus of 98,100 sentences. The patterns in the Parser's output assemblies were labeled according to the nearest representation in the lexicon. The control output was taken to be correct if those control units that should have been active at 1 had an activation level greater than 0.7, and those that should have been 0 had activation less than 0.3. Measured this way, the performance was excellent: SPEC did not make a single mistake in the entire corpus, neither in the output words or in control. The average unit error was 0.034 for the Parser, 0.009 for the Segmenter (0.003 for control), and 0.005 for the Stack. There was very little variation between sentences and words within each sentence, indicating that the system was operating within a safe margin.

The main result, therefore, is that the SPEC architecture successfully generalizes not only to new in-

stances of the familiar sentence structures, but to new structures as well, which the earlier subsymbolic sentence processing architectures could not do. However, SPEC is not a mere reimplementation of a symbol processor. As SPEC's Stack becomes increasingly loaded, its output becomes less and less accurate; symbolic systems do not have any such inherent memory degradation. An important question is, does SPEC's performance degrade in a cognitively plausible manner, that is, does the system have similar difficulties in processing recursive structures as people do?

To elicit enough errors from SPEC to analyze its limitations, the Stack's performance was degraded by adding 30% noise in its propagation. Such an experiment can be claimed to simulate overload, stress, cognitive impairment, or lack of concentration situations. The system turned out to be remarkably robust against noise. The average Parser error rose to 0.058, but the system still got 94% of its output words right, with very few errors in control. As expected, most of the errors occurred as a direct result of popping back from center embeddings with an inaccurate previous-hidden-layer representation. For example, in parsing The girl, who the dog, who the boy, who chased the cat, liked, bit, saw the boy, SPEC had trouble remembering the agents of liked, bit and saw, and patients of liked and bit. The performance depends on the level of the embedding in an interesting manner. It is harder for the network to remember the earlier constituents of shallower clauses than those of deeper clauses. For example, SPEC could usually connect boy with liked (in 80% of the cases), but it was harder for it to remember that it was the dog who bit (58%) and even harder that the girl who saw (38%) in the above example.

Such behavior seems plausible in terms of human performance. Sentences with deep center embeddings are harder for people to remember than shallow ones (Foss & Cairns 1970; Miller & Isard 1964). It is easier to remember a constituent that occurred just recently in the sentence than one that occurred several embeddings ago. Interestingly, even though SPEC was especially designed to overcome such memory effects in the Parser's sequence memory, the same effect is generated by the Stack architecture. The latest embedding has noise added to it only once, whereas the earlier elements in the stack have been degraded multiple times. Therefore, the accuracy is a function of the number of pop operations instead of a function of the absolute level of the embedding.

When the SPEC output is analyzed word by word, several other interesting effects are revealed. Virtually in every case where SPEC made an error in popping an earlier agent or patient from the stack it confused it with another noun (54,556 times out of 54,603; random choice would yield 13650). In other words, SPEC performs plausible role bindings: even if the exact agent or patient is obscured in the memory, it "knows" that it has to be a noun. Moreover, SPEC does not generate the noun at random. Out of all nouns it output incorrectly, 75% had occurred earlier in the sentence, whereas a random choice would give only 54%. It seems that traces for the earlier nouns are discernible in the previous-hidden-layer pattern, and consequently, they are slightly favored at the output. Such priming effect is rather surprising, but it is very plausible in terms of human performance.

The semantic constraints (table 2) also have a marked effect on the performance. If the agent or patient that needs to be popped from the stack is strongly correlated with the verb, it is easier for the network to remember it correctly. The effect depends on the strength of the semantic coupling. For example, girl is easier to remember in The girl, who the dog bit, liked the boy, than in The girl, who the dog bit, saw the boy, which is in turn easier than The girl, who the dog bit, chased the cat. The reason is that there are only two possible agents for liked, whereas there are three for saw and four for chased. While SPEC gets 95% of the unique agents right, it gets 76% of those with two alternatives, 69% of those with three, and only 67% of those with four.

A similar effect has been observed in human processing of relative clause structures. Half the subjects in Stolz's (1967) study could not decode complex center embeddings without semantic constraints. Huang (1983) showed that young children understand embedded clauses better when the constituents are semantically strongly coupled, and Caramazza & Zurif (1976) observed similar behavior in aphasics. This effect is often attributed to limited capability for processing syntax. The SPEC experiments indicate that it could be at least partly due to impaired memory as well. When the memory representation is impaired with noise, the Parser has to clean it up. In propagation through the Parser's weights, noise that does not coincide with the known alternatives cancels out. Apparently, when the

verb is strongly correlated with some of the alternatives, more of the noise appears coincidental and is filtered out.

Discussion

Several observations indicate that the SPEC approach to subsymbolic parsing should scale up well. First, as long as SPEC can be trained with the basic constructs, it will generalize to a very large set of new combinations of these constructs. Combinatorial training (St. John 1992) of structure is not necessary. In other words, SPEC is capable of *dynamic inferencing*, previously postulated as very difficult for subsymbolic systems to achieve (Touretzky 1991). Second, like most subsymbolic systems, SPEC does not need to be trained with a complete set of all combinations of constituents for the basic constructs; a representative sample, like the 200 out of 1088 possible training sentences above, is enough. Third, with the FGREP mechanism it is possible to automatically form meaningful distributed representations for a large number of words, even to acquire them incrementally (Miikkulainen & Dyer 1991; Miikkulainen 1993), and the network will know how to process them in new situations. Fourth, SPEC is quite insensitive to configuration and simulation parameters, suggesting that the approach is very strong, and there should be plenty of room for adapting it to more challenging experiments. The most immediate direction for future work is to apply the SPEC architecture to a wider variety of grammatical constructs and to larger vocabularies.

The Segmenter is perhaps the most significant new feature of the SPEC architecture. It can be seen as a first step toward implementing high-level control in the connectionist framework (see also Jacobs, Jordan, & Barto 1991; Jain 1991; Schneider & Detweiler 1987; Sumida 1991). The Segmenter monitors the input sequence and the state of the parsing network, and issues I/O control signals for the Stack memory and the Parser itself at appropriate times. The Segmenter has a high-level view of the parsing process, and uses it to assign simpler tasks to the other modules. In that sense, the Segmenter implements a strategy for parsing sentences with relative clauses. Such control networks could play a major role in future subsymbolic models of natural language processing and high-level reasoning.

Conclusion

SPEC is largely motivated by the desire to build a system that (1) would be able to process nontrivial input like symbolic systems, and (2) would make use of the unique properties of distributed neural networks such as learning from examples, spontaneous generalization, robustness, context sensitivity, and integrating statistical evidence. Although SPEC does not address several important issues in connectionist natural language processing (such as processing exceptions and representing flexible structure), it does indicate that learning and applying grammatical structure for parsing is possible with pure distributed networks.

However, even more than an AI system aiming at best possible performance, SPEC is an implementation of a particular Cognitive Science philosophy. The architecture is decidedly not a reimplementation of a symbol processor, or even a hybrid system consisting of subsymbolic components in an otherwise symbolic framework. SPEC aims to model biological information processing at a specific, uniform level of abstraction, namely that of distributed representation on modular networks. SPEC should be evaluated according to how well its behavior matches that produced by the brain at the cognitive level. The memory degradation experiments indicate that SPEC is probably on the right track, and the success of the high-level controller network in generating high-level behavior opens exciting possibilities for future work.

References

Berg, G. 1992. A connectionist parser with recursive sentence structure and lexical disambiguation. In *Proceedings of the 10th National Conference on Artificial Intelligence*, 32–37. Cambridge, MA: MIT Press.

Caramazza, A., and Zurif, E. B. 1976. Dissociation of algorithmic and heuristic processes in language comprehension: Evidence from aphasia. *Brain and Language* 3:572–582.

Elman, J. L. 1990. Finding structure in time. *Cognitive Science* 14:179–211.

Elman, J. L. 1991. Distributed representations, simple recurrent networks, and grammatical structure. *Machine Learning* 7:195–225.

Foss, D. J., and Cairns, H. S. 1970. Some effects of memory limitation upon sentence comprehension and recall. *Journal of Verbal Learning and Verbal Behavior* 9:541–547.

Huang, M. S. 1983. A developmental study of children's comprehension of embedded sentences with and without semantic constraints. *Journal of Psychology* 114:51–56.

Jacobs, R. A.; Jordan, M. I.; and Barto, A. G. 1991. Task decomposition through competition in a modular connectionist architecture: The what and where vision tasks. *Cognitive Science* 15:219–250.

Jain, A. N. 1991. Parsing complex sentences with structured connectionist networks. *Neural Computation* 3:110–120.

McClelland, J. L., and Kawamoto, A. H. 1986. Mechanisms of sentence processing: Assigning roles to constituents. In McClelland, J. L., and Rumelhart, D. E., eds., *Parallel Distributed Processing*. Cambridge, MA: MIT Press. 272–325.

Miikkulainen, R. 1990. A PDP architecture for processing sentences with relative clauses. In Karlgren, H., ed., *Proceedings of the 13th International Conference on Computational Linguistics*, 201–206. Helsinki, Finland: Yliopistopaino.

Miikkulainen, R. 1993. *Subsymbolic Natural Language Processing: An Integrated Model of Scripts, Lexicon, and Memory*. Cambridge, MA: MIT Press.

Miikkulainen, R., and Dyer, M. G. 1991. Natural language processing with modular neural networks and distributed lexicon. *Cognitive Science* 15:343–399.

Miller, G. A., and Isard, S. 1964. Free recall of self-embedded English sentences. *Information and Control* 7:292–303.

Pollack, J. B. 1990. Recursive distributed representations. *Artificial Intelligence* 46:77–105.

Rumelhart, D. E.; Hinton, G. E.; and Williams, R. J. 1986. Learning internal representations by error propagation. In Rumelhart, D. E., and McClelland, J. L., eds., *Parallel Distributed Processing*. Cambridge, MA: MIT Press. 318–362.

Schneider, W., and Detweiler, M. 1987. A connectionist/control architecture for working memory. In Bower, G. H., ed., *The Psychology of Learning and Motivation*, volume 21. New York: Academic Press. 53–119.

Sharkey, N. E., and Sharkey, A. J. C. 1992. A modular design for connectionist parsing. In Drossaers, M. F. J., and Nijholt, A., eds., *Twente Workshop on Language Technology 3*, 87–96. Department of Computer Science, University of Twente, the Netherlands.

St. John, M. F. 1992. The story gestalt: A model of knowledge-intensive processes in text comprehension. *Cognitive Science* 16:271–306.

St. John, M. F., and McClelland, J. L. 1990. Learning and applying contextual constraints in sentence comprehension. *Artificial Intelligence* 46:217–258.

Stolcke, A. 1990. Learning feature-based semantics with simple recurrent networks. Technical Report TR-90-015, ICSI, Berkeley, CA.

Stolz, W. S. 1967. A study of the ability to decode grammatically novel sentences. *Journal of Verbal Learning and Verbal Behavior* 6:867–873.

Sumida, R. A. 1991. Dynamic inferencing in parallel distributed semantic networks. In *Proceedings of the 13th Annual Conference of the Cognitive Science Society*, 913–917. Hillsdale, NJ: Erlbaum.

Touretzky, D. S. 1991. Connectionism and compositional semantics. In Barnden, J. A., and Pollack, J. B., eds., *High-Level Connectionist Models*. Norwood, NJ: Ablex. 17–31.

Spurious Symptom Reduction in Fault Monitoring using a Neural Network and Knowledge Base Hybrid System*

Roger M. Records

Boeing Computer Services, P.O.Box 24346, 6H-TX, Seattle, WA 98124

Jai J. Choi [†]

Boeing Computer Services, P.O.Box 24346, 7F-67, Seattle, WA 98124

Abstract

An approach to reduce number of spurious symptoms in aircraft engine fault monitoring is investigated. Two strategies were utilized. A set of rules designed to filter spurious symptoms was created. Then a neural network was designed to generate expectation value for each of the sensors monitored. The neural net was trained for a specific engine during normal operation. After capturing patterns for normal engine behavior in the neural net, an expectation value for the sensor is predicted. The success of this approach relies on generating better expectation values which in turn produce smaller variation from actual operating behavior and hence generate fewer spurious symptoms. Resulting hybrid system of neural networks and rule-based model demonstrates a drastic reduction of overall spurious symptoms.

1 Introduction

One of the challenges in airplane engine health monitoring is the fact that no two engines behave identically. Individual (serial number) engines may vary in behavior as much as 30%. If acceptable sensor deviation levels between expectation value and actual value are set at this level, recognition of valid symptoms is delayed or totally inhibited. Setting deviation values lower than 30% introduces spurious symptoms. Creating generic engine monitoring system is thus a difficult problem. An example is NASA's Faultfinder, an in-flight engine monitoring and diagnostic system [2]. The Faultfinder consists of three modules, an engine monitoring component called MONITAUR, followed

---

*This work was performed under NASA contract NAS1-18027.

[†]Dr. Choi is also with the Dept. of Electrical Engineering, University of Washington, Seattle, WA. E-mail: jai@atc.boeing.com.

by two diagnostic components: a rule based diagnostic system and a model based reasoning system shown in Fig.1. Using real engine data and an engine model for comparison, both spurious and real symptoms were generated by the MONITAUR module. These spurious symptoms resulted from the system's inablity to generate accurate expectation values from an internal engine model. As the spurious symptoms were passed on for diagnosis, the potential for erroneous diagnosis was increased.

The focus for the current work is to reduce spurious symptoms generated in MONITAUR. The first step in this task is to identify sources of spurious symptoms from results of healthy engine monitoring, generate rules which detect the spurious symptoms identified, and populate a knowledge base previously designed within MONITAUR to filter identified spurious symptoms.

The second step, and the thesis of this presentation, is to examine the feasibility of using a neural network and rule base hybrid as a "front end" and "back end" respectively to MONITAUR. The neural net front end, replacing the engine model, generates better expectation values than those generated by the engine simulation. The back end rule base (knowledge base) then filters out potential spurious symptoms.

2 Types of spurious symptoms

Before we discuss causes of spurious symptoms, we first describe five engine sensors, N_1, N_2, EPR, EGT, and FF. The N_1 and N_2 sensors measure the rotational speeds of the fan and high-pressure compressor, respectively. The fan and compressor generally rotate at different speeds because they are connected to different turbine stages. Fuel flow, FF, measures the rate at which the fuel is entering the engine. The EGT is the exhaust gas temperature.

The EPR, engine pressure ratio, is a ratio of the air pressure at the exhaust divided by the air pressure at the engine inlet. In the MONITAUR module, each of the sensors listed are monitored for deviations in three attributes - absolute value, first derivative, and long term trend which is defined by an average slope of few seconds of time slices.

There are several sources of spurious symptoms.

- Model deficiencies produce poor expectation values which result in unacceptable deviations.

- Accurate modeling can produce nearly parallel expectation and actual curves with (short term) large deviations.

- Qualitative boundaries defined by MONITAUR can divide expectation and actual values.

- A lag factor between expectation and actual curves require a catch-up time factor.

- Sensor spikes and holes produce short term deviations.

- Sensor failure can apprear as a symptom.

Fig.2 whows a typical time-sensor value plot for a catch-up symptom.

3 Spurious symptom reduction by rule base and neural networks

Before an evaluation of techniques to reduce spurious symptoms could be attempted, a baseline of spurious symptoms had to be established. The approach used was to first examine healthy engine data. Ideally, monitoring a healthy engine should produce no symptoms. Data collection was confined to a single engine type since different manufacturer's engines manifested differing spurious symptoms. For the selected engine model, 9 data files of healthy engine data were used which had a total of 6900 data slices containing 35000 data points. A representative data subset was extracted for use as a baseline. This file was one of the 9 healthy engine files containing 115 data slices with two thrust lever advances followed by thrust lever retards.

The data was processed in batch mode by Faultfinder's MONITAUR module. In this procedure MONITAUR calls an engine simulation for generation of expectation values relevant to the current in-flight conditions. These values are compared by MONITAUR to the actual sensor data which was collected from the healthy engine during a flight. The baseline values obtained for spurious symptom generation are shown in Tables 1, 2, and 3.

3.1 Rule base spurious symptom reduction

The existing rule base from MONITAUR was populated with rules which would classify the symptom as spurious.

As the airplane sensor data is processed by MONITAUR, a set of symptoms are generated for each time slice. Before the symptoms are output from MONITAUR, the rule base is invoked to see if any symptoms are to be classified as spurious and need to be delayed.

When the representative baseline data set was processed with MONITAUR enhanced with the rule base filter, a reduction in spurious symptoms was achieved. A representative comparison of the results with the baseline by sensor is shown in Table 1.

	rule base	baseline
total # of spurious symptoms	35	256
# of time slices w/o symptoms	87	0
# of FF symptoms	4	97
# of N_1 symptoms	4	25
# of N_2 symptoms	9	31
# of EPR symptoms	3	11
# of EGT symptoms	15	92

Table 1: reduction of spurious symptoms by rule base. Total number of possible symptoms is 115.

To ensure that real symptoms were not being filtered by the rule base, a file of engine data containing a hung start fault was processed using this rule base. One symptom was delayed in recognition for two seconds, but none of the symptoms were removed or ignored by the rule base filter.

3.2 Spurious symptom reduction by neural networks

Second approach to reducing the number of spurious symptoms in healthy engine data is to create an adaptive engine model whose purpose is to produce better expectation values. The approach was to use a feed-forward neural networks to capture patterns of healthy engine behavior and generate an expected value for a given sensor. Since we have 5 sensors, we trained 5 separate neural networks for each sensor modeling. We also assume that each sensor output is correlated with others. In other words, the output of

EGT can be a function of $N_1, N_2, EPR, FF, \theta$, where θ represents throttle angle parameter, i.e.,

$$
\begin{aligned}
EGT &= f_1(N_1, N_2, EPR, FF, \theta), \\
FF &= f_2(N_1, N_2, EPR, EGT, \theta), \\
&\text{etc.}
\end{aligned}
$$

In addition to these input parameters altitude and air speed (MACH) information is available for in-flight test. Since our experiment was limited to a ground operation data we did not use the altitude and air speed information in this study.

In training a feed-forward network with backprop-agation algorithm, we use the error function E,

$$
E = \frac{1}{2} \sum_k (t_k - y_k)^2 + \lambda \sum_{i,j} w_{ij}^2,
$$

where t_k and y_k are target value and actual network output of the kth output unit respectively, and λ is the regularization coefficient. Most of our simulations we use $\lambda = 10^{-5}$. The purpose of the penalty term in the above equation is to penalize large weight (w_{ij}) increase so that the trained neural net improves generalization capability [3]. Though we tried with different penalty terms and different network archi-tectures with different learning methods such as re-current network learning, we do not address network performances in this article.

To train the neural network off-line, we pre-processed each sensored data point (x) based on mean (M), standard deviation (σ), minimum ($\hat{x}_{min}$), and maximum ($\hat{x}_{max}$) for normalization x_n as following;

$$
\hat{x} = (x - M)/\sigma, \quad \text{and,} \quad x_n = \frac{2\hat{x} - \hat{x}_{max} - \hat{x}_{min}}{\hat{x}_{max} - \hat{x}_{min}},
$$

where $-1.0 \leq x_n \leq 1.0$. The $\hat{x}_{max}$ and $\hat{x}_{min}$ repre-sent the maximum and the minimum of the $\hat{x}$ respec-tively. Fig.3 shows a typical result of network train-ing by a training data file containing about 500 data points. Note that the model deficiencies are drasti-cally reduced for EPR.

When the training is completed, the modified MONITAUR system is used to process the baseline data set. It is important to repeat that all the train-ing sets and the baseline data must be generated from the same serial number engine. It is this en-gine's unique behavior that has been captured in the weight set during training. The results of process-ing the baseline test set of healthy engine data with expectation values generated by the neural network instead of the engine model is shown in Table 2.

	neural net	baseline
total # of spurious symptoms	96	256
# of time slices w/o symptoms	42	0
# of FF symptoms	51	97
# of N_1 symptoms	2	25
# of N_2 symptoms	8	31
# of EPR symptoms	2	11
# of EGT symptoms	33	92

Table 2: reduction of spurious symptoms by neural network.

Four healthy engine files from the same serial num-ber engine were processed through MONITAUR with the neural network filter to cross validate the effect of the neural network. The neural net achieved at least a 40% reduction of spurious symptoms in the worst case. It should be noted that while a considerable reduction in spurious symptoms was achieved using the neural net, there were several instances in which the neural net did not perform as well as the en-gine model in predicting expectation value. In those instances spurious symptoms were generated by the neural net where none had been generated by the en-gine model. It is hypothesized that this condition was the result of incomplete training of the neural net and not necessarily a failure of the adaptive filter concept.

3.3 Spurious symptom reduction by a hybrid system

Once neural networks are trained, we apply networks as a "front end" to the MONITAUR module. Then we put the rule base as a "back end" to the module. A schematic is shown in Fig.4. Using the hybrid, the neural nets replace the engine model as a source of ex-pectation values. This serves to reduce the number of spurious symptoms by generating better expectation values. Those spurious symptoms still generated were then filtered by the rule base. The ability to better filter the surviving spurious symptoms results from generation of better expectation values which makes the expectation curve more nearly coincide with the actual curve. Our analysis shows that the rules in the "nearly parallel" category are then more readily fired. The results of processing the baseline test set of healthy engine data with this hybrid is shown in Table 3.

	hybrid	baseline
total # of spurious symptoms	23	256
# of time slices w/o symptoms	96	0
# of FF symptoms	4	97
# of N_1 symptoms	0	25
# of N_2 symptoms	5	31
# of EPR symptoms	0	11
# of EGT symptoms	14	92

Table 3: reduction of spurious symptoms by neural net and rule base hybrid system.

4 Final remarks

A knowledge base of rules was constructed to filter known spurious symptoms and a neural network was developed to improve the expectation values used in the monitoring process. Both approaches were effective in reducing spurious symptoms individually. However, the best results were obtained using a hybrid system combining the neural net front end with the rule-based back in engine health monitoring.

This evaluation of strategies to reduce spurious symptoms should be discussed with the limitations of each approach in mind. Both approaches considered in this study are engine type dependent. The rule base constructed works for a specific manufacturer on a specific engine type. However the rule base filter is more generic than the neural net. The neural net should be trained for a specific serial number engine.

References

[1] Abbott, K., "Robust fault diagnosis of physical system in operation," Dissertation, Rutgers, the state university of New Jersey, NJ, 1990.

[2] Abbott, K., Schutte, P., Palmer, M., Ricks, W., "Faultfinder: A diagnostic expert system with graceful degradation for standard aircraft applications," *Proc. of 14th International Symposium on Aircraft Integrated Monitoring Systems, Friedrichshafen,FRG* pp. 353–370, 1988.

[3] Krogh, A., and Hertz, J., "A simple weight decay can improve generalization," *Technical note: University of California, Santa Cruz,* 1991.

[4] Rumelhart, D.E., McClelland, J.L. and PDP Research Group, "Learning internal representations by error propagation", In Feldman, J.A. and Rumelhart, D.E. (Eds.), **Parallel distributed processing- Vol. 1**, *MIT Press,* pp.318-363, 1988.

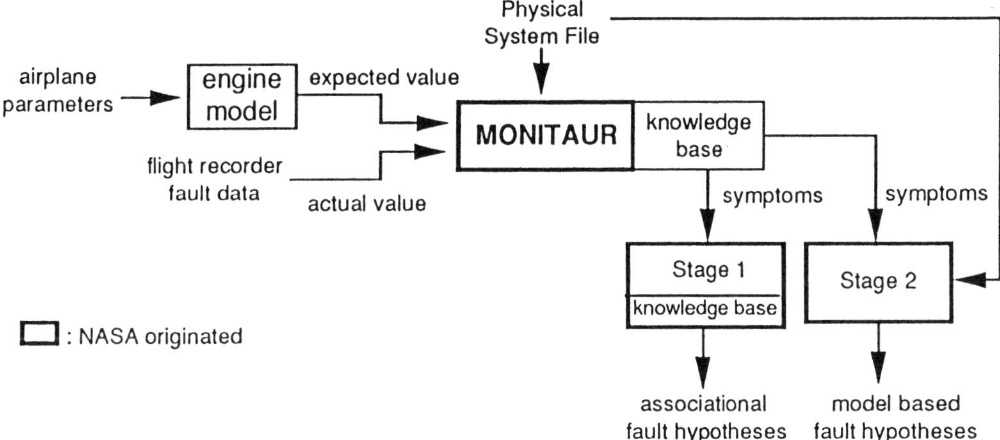

Fig.1. Engine Fault Monitoring in FAULTFINDER.

Symptoms generated by the comparison between expectation and actual values are passed to a rule based diagnostic system and to a model based diagnostic system.

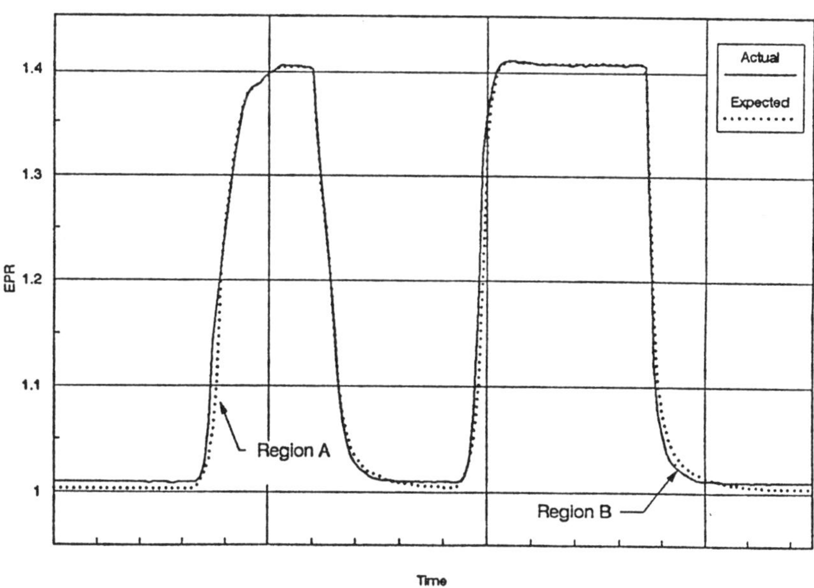

Fig. 2. Catch-Up Spurious Symptoms.

Typical time-sensor plot showing regions of spurious symptoms (A & B).

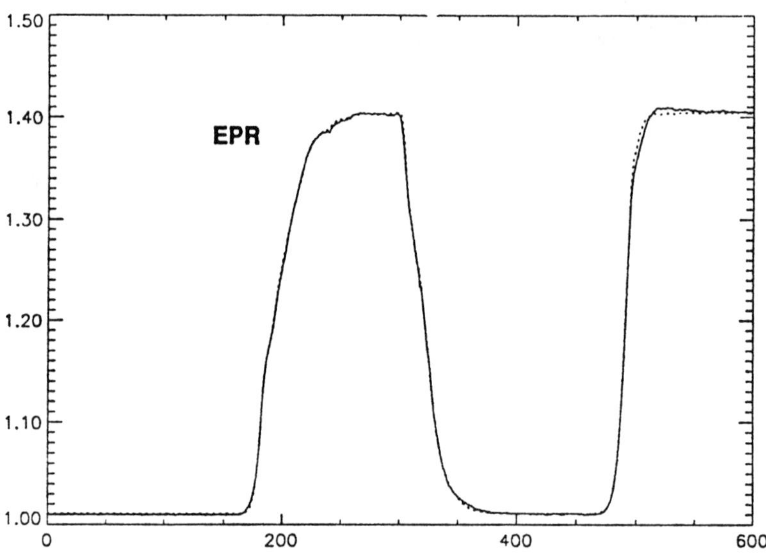

Fig.3. Actual and Neural Net Expectation Curves.

Regions of spurious symptoms are reduced as a result of better expectation.

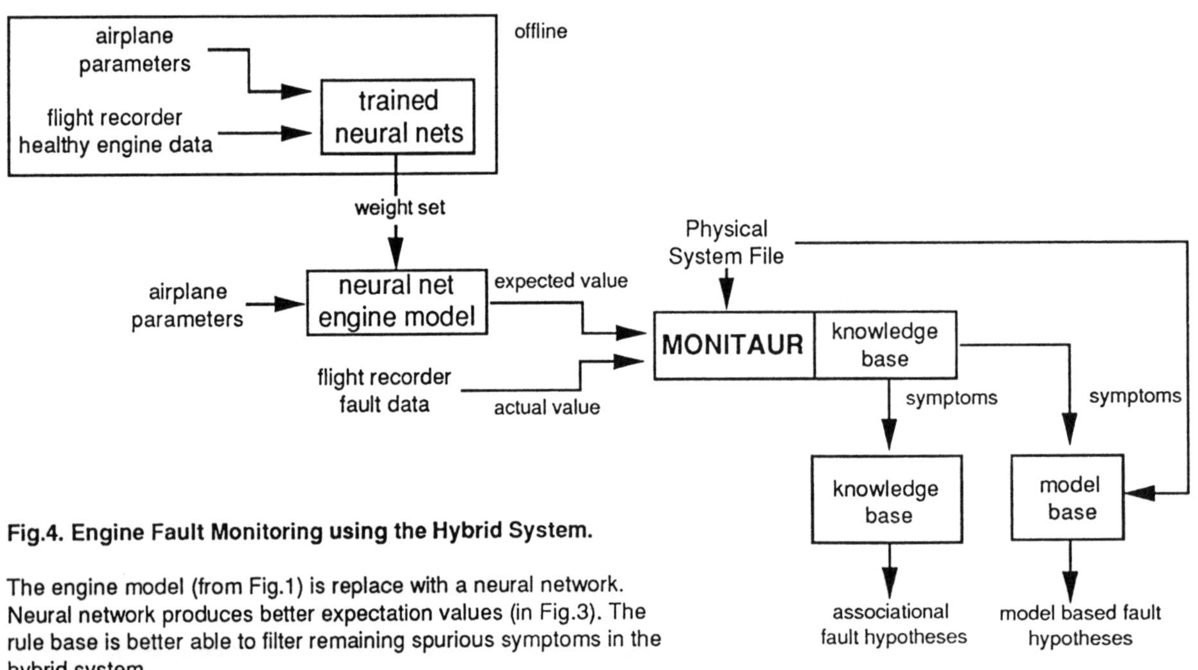

Fig.4. Engine Fault Monitoring using the Hybrid System.

The engine model (from Fig.1) is replace with a neural network.
Neural network produces better expectation values (in Fig.3). The
rule base is better able to filter remaining spurious symptoms in the
hybrid system.

Learning To Learn : Automatic Adaptation of Learning Bias

Steve G. Romaniuk

Department of Information Systems and Computer Science
National University of Singapore
10 Kent Ridge Crescent
Singapore 0511
e-mail: stever@iscs.nus.sg

Abstract

Traditionally, large areas of research in machine learning have concentrated on pattern recognition and its application to many diversified problems both within the realm of AI as well as outside of it. Over several decades of intensified research, an array of learning methodologies have been proposed, accompanied by attempts to evaluate these methods, with respect to one another on small sets of real world problems. Unfortunately, little emphasis was placed on the problem of *learning bias* - common to all learning algorithms - and a major culprit in preventing the construction of a *universal* pattern recognizer. State of the art learning algorithms exploit some inherent bias when performing pattern recognition on yet unseen patterns. Automatically adapting this learning bias - dependent on the type of pattern classification problems seen over time - is largely lacking. In this paper, weaknesses of the traditional *one-shot* learning environments are pointed out and the move towards a learning method displaying the ability to *learn about learning* is undertaken. Trans-dimensional learning is introduced as a means to automatically adjust *learning bias* and empirical evidence is provided showing that in some instances *learning the whole can be simpler than learning a part of it*.

Introduction

It is a well known fact that if we consider the universe of all possible pattern recognition problems, learning algorithms [1] tend to exploit some bias, when generalizing from a finite set of examples. Customarily, we refer to this generalization as *induction*. An abundance of learning algorithms (pattern classifiers) have been proposed over the last few decades (Qiunlan 1979; Fahlman & Lebiere 1990; Frean 1991; Romaniuk 1993b; Cheng et al. 1988). In all instances, the inherent bias in learning algorithms remains static, thereby restricting the universal application of these

---

[1] Throughout this paper we will use the terms *learning* and *pattern recognition* interchangeably.

algorithms to a multitude of conceivable pattern classification problems. In other words, every single one of these algorithms can only be applied with some degree of success to a subclass of pattern recognition tasks. No universal application is possible, due to the algorithms' inability to automatically modify its learning bias, based on the types of pattern recognition problems it may be confronted with over a period of time. This lack of any form of *meta-learning* capability in traditional pattern recognition algorithms, has received little attention from the machine learning (pattern recognition) and neural network communities. Instead, increasingly *limited* pattern recognition algorithms are proposed, void of this most fundamental property commonly attributed to any intelligent agent. A few notable exceptions are (Chalmers 1990; Bengio et al. 1992).

The purpose of this article is to outline a learning system capable of automatically adjusting learning bias based on prior performance. The proposed system is based on a simple feedforward neural network, in which hidden units are automatically recruited and locally trained using the perceptron learning rule. Learning is seen as a bottom-up feature construction process in which previously learned knowledge (stored as feature units within the network) represents the primary mechanism for performing *meta-learning*.

Automatic Neural Network Construction

Overview

During the past years neural networks have been applied to a wide variety of pattern recognition tasks with varying degrees of success. In many cases, a major drawback has been, finding the right number of hidden units, layers and connectivity of the network - at least for networks trained by backpropagation like algorithms. Often users rely on rules of thumb (heuristics) to decide how to choose these parameters. The outcome is at best challenging, many times it is simply frustrating. The problem is further compounded by varying (initially random) weights, an array of different tuning parameters (e.g. momentum term, learning rate, etc.), type of transfer function (e.g. sigmoid, threshold, gaussian, etc.) and finally the choice of learning algorithm itself (backprop, quickprop, etc.). Given this less than rosy situation, it should come as no surprise that researchers have looked for ways to improve this situation. Within the last couple years several different approaches to automatically construct neural networks have been proposed (Baffes & Zelle 1992; Fahlman & Lebiere 1990; Frean 1991; Romaniuk 1993b). These algorithms differ in how they construct networks (purely horizontal or vertical growth, or hybrids in between) and the kind of local learning rules they utilize. They also contrast with regard to the types of problems they can solve, the quality of the final networks, network complexity, speed, and their ability to converge on certain types of data. For more information the interested reader may want to consult (Baffes & Zelle 1992; Fahlman & Lebiere 1990; Frean 1991; Romaniuk 1993b).

Evolutionary Growth Perceptron

Evolutionary Growth Perceptron (Romaniuk 1993b) (EGP) represents an approach to automatically construct neural networks by exploiting natural selection. Networks are assembled in a bottom-up manner, a feature at a time. Every newly recruited unit (feature) added to the network, receives its input connections from all previously installed hidden units and input units. Once an element is set up, it is trained employing the perceptron learning rule for a fixed number of epochs. Evolutionary processes are invoked to decide which patterns of the training set should be made use of when training the current hidden feature. An individual chromosome encodes the subset of patterns administered for training the present unit. A population of these chromosomes are then evaluated on the task of overall error reduction. After either a fixed number of generations has passed, or there is no improvement in error reduction, the element trained to the lowest error rate is permanently installed in the network. If there are still patterns left, which are miss-classified by the newly added unit, then a new element is created and the above process repeated. Otherwise, training halts and the last unit in the network is designated the output of the network.

EGP learns the difficult N-parity function with about $\lfloor \frac{N}{2} \rfloor$ hidden units (Romaniuk 1993b).

Learning to Learn

Traditional One-shot Learning Approach

Over the last few decades a multitude of ideas have entered the realm of machine learning, resulting in countless interesting approaches and advances to this important area. The oldest learning systems date back to the 1940s (Hebbian learning) and the introduction of the perceptron. Later years would see the

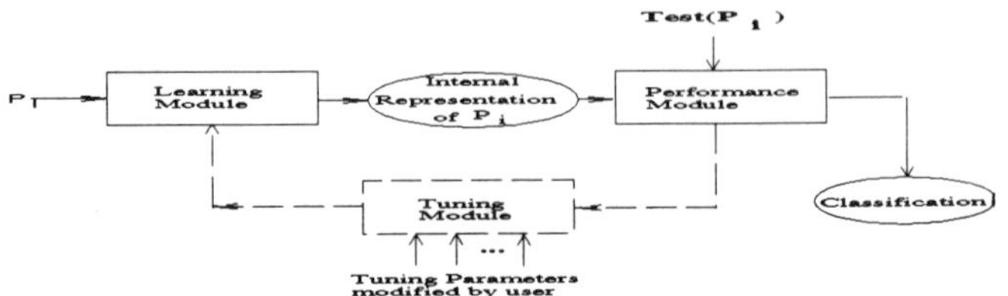

Figure 1: Traditional One-shot Learning Approach

advances of inductive learning systems such as ID3 (Qiunlan 1979) (based on decision trees). The eighties saw a revival of the neural network community with the introduction of the backpropagation learning rule. More recently approaches have been formalized that attempt to integrate seemingly different paradigms such as connectionism and symbolism. Other advances have been made to automate the network building process (Fahlman & Lebiere 1990; Frean 1991; Baffes & Zelle 1992; Romaniuk 1993b). With the discovery of ever new methodologies to tackle learning problems, the question of evaluating these diverse algorithms has remained mostly unchanged. Commonly, we can identify 2 approaches: The first approach considers an empirical study which includes testing a new learning algorithm $L \in \mathcal{L}$ (element of the class of all learning algorithms $\mathcal{L}$) on a set of either artificial or natural (real world) problems $P \in \mathcal{P}$. This set P is for almost all empirical studies small (about 1 to a dozen problems). In general, several well accepted problems - also known as benchmarks - are selected for an empirical study. Besides including a set of benchmarks, a few well known learning algorithms (that is well publicized) are picked in order to perform a comparison. Evaluation of learning algorithms proceeds by dividing a set of patterns, that describe the problem under consideration into 2 partitions: a train (T_{Train}) and test set (T_{Test}). The degree of generalization (performance accuracy) of algorithm L is measured by determining how many patterns in T_{Test} are correctly recognized by L after being trained on patterns in T_{Train}. After training and testing (classification) have been completed for a given problem P, results obtained thus far are removed and a new problem is tackled. We refer to this procedure as *one-shot* learning. A graphical representation of this approach is depicted in Figure 1. Note, that the tuning module is optional and may even be lacking in some learning systems (e.g. ID3 (Qiunlan 1979)). Other approaches - predominantly gradient decent-based learning algorithms (e. g. backpropagation) - are equipped with a multitude of tuning parameters, which when appropriately set by the user, can improve the learning modules overall performance on a given pattern recognition task. We can think of the tuning module as being a primitive mechanism to adapt the bias of the learning module. This adaptation is under the direct control of the human user.

It is a well known fact, that any such empirical comparison cannot yield significant results due to the sheer size of potential problems that can exist in the real world. As a matter-of-fact, it is straight forward to verify that for every problem $P = T_{Train} \cup T_{Test}$, for which some algorithm $L \in \mathcal{L}$ can achieve accuracy α (denoted by $A_L(T_{Test}) = \alpha$), there always exists a problem $P' = T_{Train} \cup T'_{Test}$ [2] such that $A_L(T'_{Test}) = 1 - \alpha$. Hence, the average accuracy is always $\frac{1}{2}$. [3] This is actually true regardless of how we partition the examples describing problem P into train and test sets, as long as $T_{Test} \neq \emptyset$.

The above essentially states, there cannot exist a universal learning algorithm (neither biological or artificial), which can perform equally well on all pattern classification problems. Instead, every learning algorithm must exploit some *learning bias* which favor it in some domains, but handicap it in others. The following may serve as an example: Both decision-tree based, as well as, backpropagation-like learning algorithms have a more difficult time representing highly non-separable functions (e.g. parity) than a truly linear function (e.g. logical or). When we say *more difficult to learn*, we refer to training time, as well as, how the function is represented and the performance accuracy we can expect, after training is completed. A decision-tree based algorithm, for example, grows an increasingly deeper tree structure, whereas a backprop network requires additional hidden units (and connections) to learn even/odd parity. Due to these observations, it should become apparent why simple empirical studies are of little value in deciding the quality of a new learning approach or allow for comparing different approaches.

A second technique for evaluating learning systems, is based on developing a theoretical framework. A good example of this approach is the *Probably Approximately Correct* learning model (PAC) (Valiant 1984). Here, one attempts to identify sub-classes of problems which can be learned in polynominal time and for which confidence factors can be stated for achieving a given performance accuracy. Unfortunately, these methods are too rigid and constrained to be of practical use. For one, sub-classes may be very specific, such that results about them seem to say little. A more substantial shortcoming is: sub-classes of problems tend to be highly abstract. For example, a restricted class of problems might be $CNF_n(k)$, that is, all propositional formulae over n boolean variables in conjunctive normal form with at most k literals. Results like this provide no indication on how abstract results can be placed in relation with their real world counterparts. Having determined that algorithm L tends to fare well with problems belonging to some sub-class of tasks, still does not help us decide how to solve a specific real

---

[2] Outputs of patterns in T'_{Test} are inverted from those in T_{Test}.

[3] Assuming binary encoded problems.

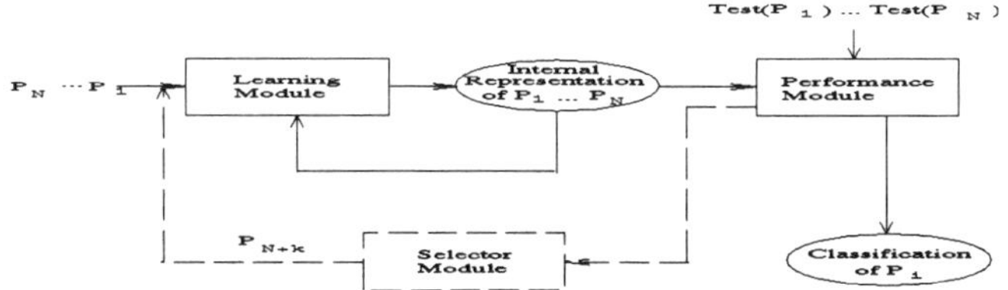

Figure 2: Multi-shot Learning Approach

world task, unless we show that our model is in some correspondence with the real world problem. But to determine this membership may require utilizing algorithm L in the first place. In short, we are forced to apply trial-and-error to decide which pattern recognition algorithm is best suited for solving the task at hand. Only, if substantial amounts of a priori domain knowledge are available, can we be sure to select the right learning algorithm, before actually trying it out. For many important tasks an appropriate pattern recognition algorithm may not even be available.

Multi-shot Learning Approach

The problem we are facing - to develop learning methods that can be employed to solve various real world problems - can not be overcome with simple *one-shot* learning algorithms. For this matter, we propose to look at algorithms which have the capability to *learn about learning*. These new algorithms must be capable of shifting their built-in bias (to favor certain subclasses of tasks) deliberately, by utilizing past performance, to give them wider applicability than simple one-shot learning systems. Figure 2 outlines the multi-shot method. In this approach, previous knowledge (in form of an internal representation of earlier learned problems) is fed back into the learning module, whenever a new task is presented. An optional selector module may provide supplementary pattern classification problems (similar), depending on the results obtained from the performance module and automatically supply them to the learning module.

This ability, - to learn knowledge on top of already existing knowledge, without every time having to restart learning from ground zero - can have an impact on learning time, representational complexity, as well as generalization on yet unseen patterns. To move beyond simple *one-shot* learning we examine the subsequently listed task:

Given: A set of problems $\mathcal{P} = \{P_1^{n_1}, P_2^{n_2}, \ldots, P_k^{n_k}\}$, where $P_i^{n_i} \in \mathcal{C}^{n_i}$.
The $P_i^{n_i}$ belong to the class of classificatory problems $\mathcal{C}$ (continuous inputs/binary output) of variable input dimension n_i.
Goal: Develop a representation R_k that can correctly classify all $P_i^{n_i} \in \mathcal{P}$. No specific order is imposed on the problems in $\mathcal{P}$ when presented to the meta-learning system.

We refer to an algorithm which can solve the above task as a *trans-dimensional learner*. We should observe at this point, that a *network constructing* trans-dimensional learner is one of numerous alternatives. For example, we could have chosen a decision-tree like representation, instead of a connectionist network when designing TDL. A decision in favor of a connectionist representation was cast, due to earlier obtained positive results involving EGP and considering the algorithms simplicity.

Before we outline the individual modules comprising TDL we draw attention to 2 approaches regarding automatic learning bias adjustment:

First, the *explicit* approach. Here, a standard pattern recognition algorithm has its learning behavior regulated by modifying one or more of its tuning parameters. If a learning algorithm is not equipped with tuning parameters, they may be added retrospectively. For example, a decision-tree based algorithm like ID3 has no tuning parameters. An extension of ID3 (GID3 (Cheng et al. 1988)) uses a tolerance parameter which controls the amount of generalization by guiding attribute selection. Explicit learning bias adjustment proceeds by presenting either similar types of problems (e.g. even/odd parity) or identical problems (e.g. only even-parity) to the algorithm. Performance on prior tasks (degree of generalization and effectiveness of knowledge representation) are measured and tuning parameters are appropriately modified. It is anticipated that for similar or identical problems, the same setting (or related) of tuning parameters, can result in improved performance. For example, a backpropagation-based algorithm may learn to adapt its learning rate and momentum term in such a way, that it can more readily learn a parity function after having been trained on a few instances of this type of function.

The second approach is *implicit*. In this case, there are no explicit tuning parameters, instead learning bias is shifted by relying on earlier stored knowledge. Hence, this method is identical to *multi-shot* learning. The internal knowledge representation of previous learned tasks is exploited to guide future learning. The herein proposed meta-learning algorithm is based on the *implicit* approach.

TDL : Trans-Dimensional Learner

In this section, the basic modules deemed important in the construction of TDL are discussed. Earlier, it was pointed out that an automatic neural network construction algorithm (EGP) would serve as the primary means for building high level network features. It was also indicated that the EGP algorithm assembles new features by fully connecting previously created features to the one currently under construction. This can very quickly lead to a high fan-in of connections to the hidden units. Consequently, storage requirements and simulation time increase rapidly, as fresh hidden features are installed. Apart from this surface problem, a more harmful side-effect can be identified: dilution in quality of high-level features. Recall, that the perceptron rule is utilized to locally train newly recruited features. Now, the perceptron learning rule attempts to discover an appropriate linear combination of the inputs to the trained feature, such that overall error is reduced. If the number of features forming the input to the current unit is large, many more weight assignments are possible, of which many may lead to shallow local optimums. To prevent this from occurring, it is essential to restrict the number of hidden features selected for constructing new features. To accomplish this feat, a quality measure is invoked to determine the potential of previously constructed units to act as good hidden feature detectors when solving the current goal.

The quality measure is defined as,

$$Q_{k,i}(F_i, P_k) = \frac{A_k(F_i, P_k)}{|T_k|}\left(1 - \frac{\log(L(F_i) + 1)}{\log(\max_{\forall j}(L(F_j)) + 1)}\right) \tag{1}$$

,where $L(F_i)$ returns feature F_i's layer location. The first factor of Equation 1 measures feature F_i's accuracy on problem P_k, whereas the cost factor incorporates information about feature F_i's layer location relative to the current networks height.

To further reduce the complexity of the resulting connectionist network, it can prove extremely beneficial, to prune an already trained feature unit, before resorting to train a new one. It has bee pointed out that besides further reducing the fan-in to individual units, pruning can also improve the generalization capability of a network.

It may be necessary to provide a mechanism which allows the network to forget some of its learned knowledge, especially if over time this knowledge is deemed unimportant. Forgetting information is paramount to conserving network resources such as units and connections. Finally, if we think of biologically inspired learning systems then, due to changes in the environment, some of the accrued knowledge may become obsolete. It would indeed be wasteful to retain this information.

A High-level description of the proposed trans-dimensional learner is presented below. In order to handle training patterns of various input dimensions, a pool of input features is initially set aside. The pool is left-adjusted, which implies the first input value of a training pattern is stored in the foremost input unit of the pool and so on, until all input values have been assigned to corresponding input units. Remaining pool units are assigned a default value of 0, to guarantee that no activations are propagated from any potential connections that emanate from these units to other network units (Effect identical to being disconnected).

Nomenclature for TDL:

$$
\begin{array}{rcl}
P_k & : & kth\ problem\ to\ be\ learned. \\
\mathcal{P} & : & set\ of\ all\ problems. \\
N & : & network\ constructed\ by\ TDL. \\
F_C & : & current\ unit\ in\ network\ N. \\
I_l & : & lth\ input\ of\ problem\ P_k. \\
In(P_k) & : & number\ inputs\ for\ problem\ P_k. \\
Q_{k,i}(F_i, P_k) & : & quality\ measure\ for\ ith\ unit. \\
A(F_C, P_k) & : & accuracy\ of\ feature\ F_C\ for\ P_k. \\
\alpha & : & threshold\ for\ quality\ measure\ (0.1).
\end{array}
\tag{2}
$$

(1) For all $P_k \in \mathcal{P}$, $k \in [1, N]$ do
  (1.1) While $A(F_C, P_k) < 1$ do
    (1.1.1) Create new feature F_{new}
    (1.1.2) Connect all I_l, $l \in [1, In(P_k)]$ to F_{new}
    (1.1.3) For all $F_i \in N$ do
      (1.1.3.1) If $Q_{k,i}(F_i, P_k) > \alpha$ then
        (1.1.3.1.1) Connect F_i to F_{new}
    (1.1.4) $N = N \cup \{F_{new}\}$
    (1.1.5) $F_C = F_{New}$
    (1.1.6) EGP(F_C)
    (1.1.7) Prune feature F_C

To close out this section, Figure 3 displays an example of a TDL generated network that correctly recognizes the or-function of input dimensions 2 - 7.

Empirical Results

To furnish empirical evidence supporting the effectiveness of TDL, a collection of well-known neural network benchmark problems have been selected in conjunction with some simpler functions to allow for a meaningful study. These problems are: **and, or, even-parity, odd-parity** of input dimension 2 - 7, 4-, 8-, 16-bit **encoder**, and 2-, 3-bit **adder**.

Combining the above tasks yields a total of 29 functions (29-fkt problem). As a subset we also consider the even/odd-parity functions (parity problem). For all experiments 10 trial runs are conducted and their average is reported. Also, every feature is trained for at most 60 epochs.

Learning The Whole Can Be Simpler Than Learning A Part Of It

In Figure 4a we present results relating the number of generations (amount of time required to evolve a network) and the number of combined units (hidden and output units in final network). The first observation we make is, the response curve for the 29-fkt problem displays a sudden steep increase in the final stages of training, as opposed to the almost linear response obtained during learning the parity problem.

Secondly, around 20 functions (of the original 29) are learned in the final stages of training, that is in the last

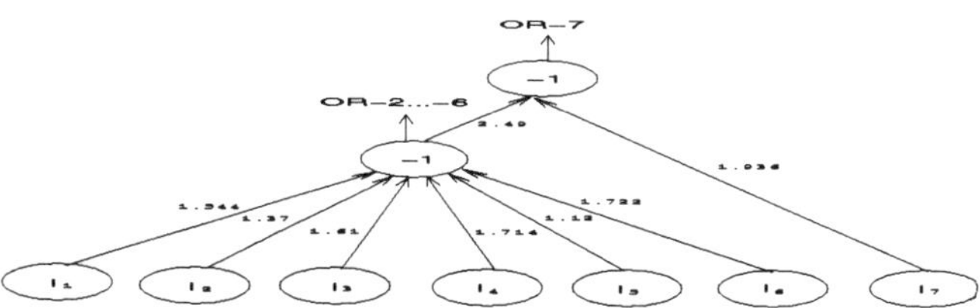

Figure 3: OR-2 through OR-7 as learned by TDL

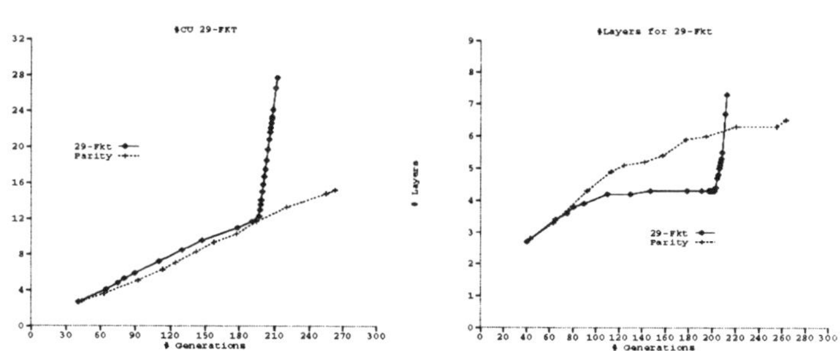

Figure 4: # Generations vs. (a) # Combined Units (b) # Layers for learning 29-Fkt and Parity

20 generations. In other words, more than two-thirds of the problems are acquired in the last one-tenth of the training phase. This result underlines how TDL benefits from previously learned information and indicates how the ability to learn to learn has a profound impact on total training time and final network configuration.

The most impressive finding can be gleaned, when comparing the absolute magnitude in number of generations required to learn either parity or 29-fkt task. The parity problem is learned after nearly 270 generations have passed, whereas the 29-fkt problem is acquired after less than 210 generations. Since the parity problem is a subset of the original 29-fkt problem, this result is clear evidence of the phenomena: *learning the whole can be simpler than learning a part of it.*

Furthermore, this finding substantiates the fact, the time needed to learn a subset of functions can be significantly reduced by assimilating additional functions, even when they have little in common with the original set of functions. Recall, the composition of the 29-fkt problem. Besides containing the simpler **and-** and **or-**functions, it also consists of **encoder** and **adder** functions. The task of identifying **even** and **odd** parity has little in common with the task of performing binary encoding or binary addition.

Another interesting observation is that the number of combined units is about the same as the number of functions learned. Both for parity as well as the 29-fkt task, the increase in number of combined units with respect to the number of functions acquired (regardless of the problems input dimension) is about *linear*.

Figure 4b depicts the relationship between the number of generations and the number of layers. The steep increase in layers for the 29-fkt problem coincides with

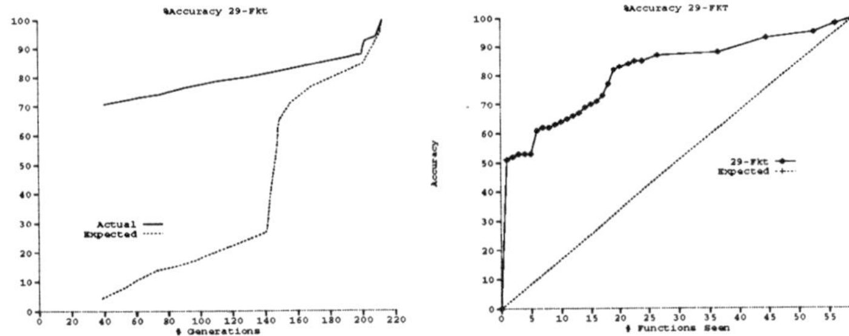

Figure 5: (a) Pattern (b) Function Recognition Accuracy for 29-Fkt Problem

the increase in combined units. This indicates that newly formed feature detectors in the network are constructed from already existing low level feature detectors. In other words, overall savings in combined units and training time are realized by creating high-level features, resulting in a rapid overall increase in the number of layers.

In Figure 5a the accuracy (degree of generalization on yet unseen patterns) obtained by TDL for the 29-fkt problem is displayed.

Figure 5b furnishes insight into the function recognition capability of TDL for the 29-fkt task. The graph depicts the relation between the average number of problems seen and the percentage of correctly identified functions. [4]

Summary

Taking the step from one-shot learning to develop an automatic network construction algorithm capable of trans-dimensional learning can be viewed as a step towards a new, and more powerful learning environment. Perceiving units within a network solely as features and learning as a process of bottom-up feature construction were necessary notions to develop a feasible implementation of a trans-dimensional learner. Basing local feature training on the simple perceptron rule and combining evolutionary methods to effectively create training partitions, have substantially contributed towards the construction of a more flexible learning system. Contrary to intuition, it was noted that learning a large set of diverse problems can be either equal to or even simpler than attempting to learn a subset of the very same problems. Even across a highly diversified set of domains can powerful hidden features be constructed and help decrease learning time and network complexity as more problems are encountered. These powerful hidden features support adjusting *learning bias* depending on the type of problems presented by simplifying the learning process itself and help elevate TDL above simple *one-shot* learning systems. The findings

of this study are of importance, since they suggest that learning new features can be substantially improved by learning on top of pre-existing knowledge, even if there appears little in common between the two. Even though this is an initial study in the applicability of trans-dimensional learning to solve the general problem of *learning about learning*, it is one that has given rise to some interesting results and it is hoped that future work will prove as fertile.

References

Baffes, P.T. and Zelle, J.M (1992). Growing Layers of Perceptrons: Introducing the Extentron Algorithm, *Proceedings of the 1992 International Joint Conference on Neural Networks* (pp. II-392- II-397), Baltimore, MD., June.

Bengio, Y., Bengio, S., Cloutier, J., Gecsei, J. (1992) On the optimization of a synaptic learning rule, *Conference of Optimality in Biological and Artificial Neural Networks*, Dallas, USA.

Chalmers, D.J. (1990) The Evolution of Learning: An experiment in Genetic Connectionism, In D.S. Touretsky, J.L. Elman, T.J. Sejnowski, and G.E. Hinton (Eds.) *Proceedings of the 1990 Connectionists Models Summer School.*

Cheng, J., Fayyad, U.M., Irani, K.B., Qian, Z. (1988) Improved Decision Trees: A Generalized Version of ID3, *Proceedings of the 5th Inetrnational Conference on Machine Learning*, Ann Arbor, Michigan, June.

Fahlman, S.E. and Lebiere, C. (1990). The Cascade-Correlation Learning Architecture, In D. Touretzky (Ed.), *Advances in Neural Information Processing Systems 2* (pp. 524-532). San Mateo, CA.: Morgan Kaufmann.

Frean, M. (1991). The Upstart Algorithm: A Method for Constructing and Training FeedForward Neural Networks, *Neural Computation*, 2, 198-209.

Holland, J.D. (1975) Adaption in Natural and Artificial Systems. University of Michigan Press, AnnArbor, MI.

Quinlan, J.R., (1979) Discovering rules by induction from large collections of examples. In D. Michie (Ed.), *Expert systems in the micro electronic age*. Edinburgh University Press.

Romaniuk, S.G., Hall, L.O. (1993) Divide and Conquer Networks. *Neural Networks*, Vol. 6, pp. 1105-1116.

Romaniuk, S.G. (1993) Evolutionary Growth Perceptrons. In S. Forrest *Genetic Algorithms : Proceedings of the 5th International Conference*, Morgan Kaufmann.

Valiant, L.G. (1984). A Theory of the learnable. *Comm. Ass. Comput. Mach.* 27(11), 1134-1142.

---

[4]The 29-fkt problem actually consists of 59 functions. This number is obtained by adding up the number of outputs for all 29 problems.

Neural Programming Language

Hava T. Siegelmann
Department of Computer Science
Bar-Ilan University, Ramat-Gan 52900, Israel
E-mail: hava@bimacs.cs.biu.ac.il

Abstract

Analog recurrent neural networks have attracted much attention lately as powerful tools of automatic learning. We formally define a high level language, called **NE**ural **L**angage, which is rich enough to express any computer algorithm or rule-based system. We show how to compile a NEL program to a network which computes exactly as the original program and requires the same computation time. We suggest this language along with its compiler as the ultimate bridge from symbolic to analog computation, and propose its outcome as an initial network for learning. *

1 Introduction

Classical approaches of Computer Science and Artificial Intelligence are based on understanding and explaining key phenomena in a discrete, symbolic manner. A list of rules or an algorithm is then developed and given to the computer to execute. These approaches have the limitations of human understanding and analysis power.

An alternative approach to elicit knowledge and express it by symbols is the neural network modeling. Neural networks are trainable dynamical systems which learn by observing a training set of input-output pairs. They estimate functions without a mathematical model of which the output is assumed to depend on the input.

The choice between the above two approaches depends on the particular application. For example, the first approach is a better fit for controlling simple engines; in the complex-task of generating a functional electric stimulation (FES) in locomotion of subjects with incomplete spinal cord injury, the classical methodology yields limited functionality, while the learning approach generates far better results (Armstrong *et al.* 1993). The pure neural network approach, although rich and adaptable, may lose simple hints that are easily tractable by a human expert (and thus are provided in "hand-crafted

*This research was partially supported by US Air Force Grant AFOSR-91-0343

rules") but are hard to deduce from a sample set. In the functional electric stimulator, for example, a list of rules is thus preferred over adaptable approaches for particular simple functions, while the adaptable approach is still generally preferred. Another drawback of the nets is that they suffer from sensitivity of the convergence rate to initial state.

The two approaches, symbolic algorithms and adaptive analog nets, are suggested in this work to be interleaved in a manner that takes the best of both models. This is based on very recent theoretical findings in the area of artificial neural networks: that the computational power of such nets is universal (Siegelmann & Sontag 1991). We provide a novel method for translating algorithms (or rules) expressed in a Pascal-like programming language into a corresponding neural networks. This research can be thought of a basis for acquiring a function estimator in any area of expertise, using the following four step paradigm.

1. Knowledge will be elicited from experts in the field, and a program (or a rule-based system) will be written in a high level language. In our example of functional electric stimulator, the physician deduces rules from patterns recorded in able subjects as a first approximation for locomotion of paralyzes.

2. The program will be compiled into an equivalent neural net of analog neurons.

3. The applicability of the network for adapting and generalizing will be raised: nodes and edges of low computational significance will be added to yield a homogeneous architecture; the net may be pruned, and the activation function smoothed up.

4. The network will be provided with a sample data of input-output pairs, and will adapt itself to comply with them, thus, tuning and fixing the original expert's knowledge.

The fields of knowledge engineering and programming will cover the first step. Learning algorithms of recurrent neural nets will cover the fourth step. For various learning methods see (Hertz, Krogh, & Palmer 1991). Our contribution is the methodology for the second step; the one that translates a computer program into a recurrent network. Our requirement of the translation are strict. The translation should be fast, and the network should simulate the program without slowing down the computation. Note that the network itself should consist of analog neurons only and do not allow for any threshold (or other discontinuous) neuron, so that to better fit methods of adaptation and learning. The third step is recommended for a practical reason: when a network adapts to perform very accurately according to a training set, it tends to be "overfitting", that is, to loose the capability of generalizing well on new data. Because the network which is built at the second stage imitates a particular algorithm, its architecture and parameter values overfit the algorithm and may have the overfitting problem. Nodes and edges are added to prevent this problem. At this stage, other considerations may be taken, e.g., achieving the effective number of parameters (Moody 1992) by pruning the network.

Our approach of building an initial network from expert knowledge can be desirable when a particular behavior is mandatory, e.g. safety conditions or security policy. In this case, the mandatory behavior is coded into the network prior to learning, and we force parts of the network to remain fixed during the adaptation process, see for example the distal learning paradigm (Jordan 1992).

1.1 The Network Model

We focus on recurrent neural networks which consist of a finite number of neurons. In these networks, each processor's state is updated by an equation of the type

$$x_i(t+1) = \sigma\left(\sum_{j=1}^{N} a_{ij} x_j(t) + \sum_{j=1}^{M} b_{ij} u_j(t) + c_i\right) \quad (1)$$

where x_i are the processors $(i = 1, \ldots, N)$, u are the external input, a, b, c are constants, N is the number of processors, and M is the number of external input signals. The function σ is the simplest possible "sigmoid," namely the saturated-linear function:

$$\sigma(x) := \begin{cases} 0 & \text{if } x < 0 \\ x & \text{if } 0 \le x \le 1 \\ 1 & \text{if } x > 1 \,. \end{cases} \quad (2)$$

When learning is desirable, the σ will be substituted (during the third step) by a fully differentiable sigmoidal function. (Note that the precision of the neurons is not limited; thus our model describes an analog rather than a digital machine.)

As part of the description, we assume that we have singled out a subset of the N processors, say

$x_{i_1}, \ldots, x_{i_l}$; these are the l *output processors*, and they are used to communicate the outputs of the network to the environment. Thus a net is specified by the data (a_{ij}, b_{ij}, c_i) together with a subset of its nodes.

1.2 The Computational Power

Some efforts have been directed towards practical implementations of the applications, including those in the areas of pattern and speech recognitions, robot control, time series prediction, and more—see (Hertz, Krogh, & Palmer 1991). Only recently, rigorous foundations to the recurrent neural network model were developed, see (Siegelmann & Sontag 1991; 1994b; Balcázar *et al.* 1993; Siegelmann & Sontag 1994a). (See (Kilian & Siegelmann 1993) for a related model with different activation functions.) The computational power of the recurrent network (with finite number N of neurons and analog activations values) depends on the type of numbers utilized as weights (i.e. the constants a, b, c.)

1. If the weights are integers, the neurons may assume binary activation values only. Thus, the network computes a regular language.

2. If the weights are rational numbers, the network is *equivalent in power to a Turing Machine* (Siegelmann & Sontag 1991). In particular, given any function ϕ computed by a Turing Machine M in time T, one can construct a network $\mathcal{N}$ that computes the function ϕ in exactly time T. That is, there is no slow down in the computation (Siegelmann & Sontag 1994b). Furthermore, the size of the network is independent of the computation time T. A corollary is the existence of a universal network consisting of 886 neurons and simple rational weights that computes all recursive functions.

3. When weights are general real numbers (specifiable with unbounded precision), the network turns out to *have super-Turing capabilities*. However, it is sensitive to resource constrains and thus is not a tautology. The exact characterization of the computational class associated with such networks is disclosed in (Siegelmann & Sontag 1994a)..

1.3 Previous Related Work

Previous work in inserting apriori knowledge to nets was shown to make the process of training faster for both feedforward, e.g. (Abu-Mostafa 1990; Al-Mashouq & Reed 1991; Berenji 1991; Giles & Maxwell 1987; Perantonis & Lisboa 1992; Pratt 1992; Suddarth & Holden 1991; Towell, Craven, & Shavlik 1990), and recurrent networks, e.g. (Frasconi *et al.* 1993; Omlin & Giles 1992). In all cases studied, the rules were very simple, that is, only regular rules of simple finite automata. We, on the other hand, insert rules that stem at any computer algorithm and not finite state automata only.

Some work dealt with inserting rules with the emphasize of correcting them, e.g.. (Fu 1989; Ginsberg 1988; Omlin & Giles 1993; Oursten & Mooney 1990; Pazzani 1989). The paper (Towell, Shavlik, & Noordewier 1990) faced an expert system based on propositional calculus, and suggested to transform the original propositional domain theory into a network. The connection weights were elegantly adjusted in accordance with the observed examples using standard backpropagation techniques.

We provide a general technique to translate first order logic (not only propositional) or any general algorithm (not only finite automata) to recurrent nets, rather than feedforward-acyclic architectures, which computationally are very limited (i.e. the computation ends in constant number of steps). We, however, do not provide yet an algorithm for tuning and correcting the encoded rules. This task is one of the future directions of our work.

1.4 Programming Networks

Given an algorithm, how does one construct a network that executes it? We demonstrate such a construction by an example.

Example 1.1 Let M and N be values in $[0, 1]$ and let B be a Boolean expression. The conditional statement

> **If** (B) **then** $x = M$
>   **else** $x = N$

can be executed by the following network:

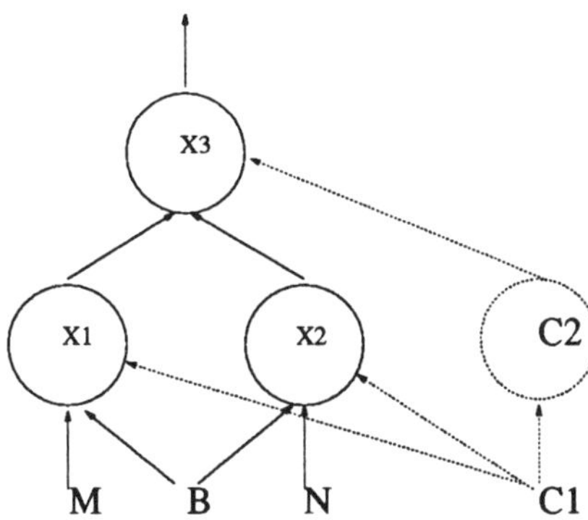

$$
\begin{aligned}
x_1(t) &= \sigma(M + B - 1) \\
x_2(t) &= \sigma(N - B) \\
x_3(t + 1) &= \sigma(x_1(t) + x_2(t)) \,.
\end{aligned}
$$

The neuron x_1 attains the value $\sigma(M)$ when $B = 1$. As σ is the linear-saturated function of Equation 2, and M is assumed to lie in the range $[0, 1]$, $x_1(t) = \sigma(M) = M$. When $B = 0$, $x_1(t) = \sigma(M - 1) = 0$.

The neuron x_2 computes $\sigma(N - 1) = 0$ for $B = 1$, and $\sigma(N) = N$ for $B = 0$. Summing the above two values into x_3 results in

$$
\begin{aligned}
\sigma(M + 0) &= M \quad \text{for } B = 1\,, \\
\sigma(0 + N) &= N \quad \text{for } B = 0
\end{aligned}
$$

as desired.

To synchronize the update, an "If" statement requires two sub-statement counters: one for the first update level, c_1, and one for the second update, c_2. The full update for the "if statement" is thus:

$$
\begin{aligned}
x_1^+ &= \sigma(M + B + c_1 - 2) \\
x_2^+ &= \sigma(N - B + c_1 - 1) \\
x_3^+ &= \sigma(x_1 + x_2 + c_c - 1) \,,
\end{aligned}
$$

The update equations of the counters are excluded.
□

In general, tasks may be composed of a large number of interrelated subtasks. The entire task may thus be highly complex, and designing an appropriate network from scratch becomes infeasible. We introduce a high level language (**NE**ural **L**angage) for automatic construction of recurrent nets. One could compare the relationship between coding networks directly and writing in NEL with the relationship between coding in a machine language and programming in a high level language.

1.5 The Organization of The Paper

The rest of this paper is organized into three sections: In Section 2, we provide a brief syntactic description of the language; in Section 3 we show how to compile a subset of NEL into a network; and in Section 4 we conclude the NEL compiler.

2 Syntax Of NEL

NEL is a procedural, parallel language. It allows for the subprograms procedure and function. A sequence of commands may either be executed sequentially (*Begin, End*) or in parallel (*Parbegin, Parend*). There is a wide range of possible **data types** for constants and variables in NEL, including the simple types: Boolean, character, scalar type, integer, real, and counter (i.e., an unbounded natural number or 0); and the compound types: lists (with the operations defined in LISP), stacks, sets. records and arrays. For each data type, there are a few associated predefined functions, e.g. *Isempty*(stack), *In*(element, set), and *Iszero*(counter).

The language is *strongly typed* in the sense that applying a function that is defined on a particular data type to a different data type may yield an error.

Expressions are defined on the different data types. Examples of expressions are:

1. $\sum_{i=1}^{7} c_i x_i$ for constants c and either real or integer values of the variables x_i.

2. $(B_1 \text{ And } B_2) \text{ Or } (x > \frac{1}{2})$ for Boolean values B_1, B_2 and an integer value x.

3. **Pred** and **Succ** of an element e of a finite ordered type T returns another element of the same type.

4. **Chr** operates on an integer argument and returns a character.

Statements of NEL include atomic statements (e.g., assignments, procedure calls, I/O statements), sequential compound statements (*Begin, End*), parallel compound statements (*Parbegin, Parend*), flow control statements which include both conditional (e.g., *If-then, If-then-else, case,* and *cond*) and repetition statements (such as *while* and *repeat*). Full syntax of NEL is provided in (Siegelmann 1993).

3 Compiling NEL

We next overview the compiler which translates programs written in the language NEL into neural networks. A network operates generally in the following manner: there are N neurons; at each tick of the clock, all neurons are updated with new values. Thus, a network step consists of a parallel execution of N assignments.

When simulating the program on a network, some of its neurons represent variables, some represent the program commands, and, practically, about half of the neurons in the network constitute the program counters. More specifically, each statement is associated with a special neuron, called the "statement counter" neuron. These neurons take Boolean (i.e., binary) values only. When a statement counter neuron is True, the statement is executed. Note that several statement counters may assume the value True simultaneously. Full discussion on controlling the counters is provided in (Siegelmann 1993).

Here, we describe the compilation of a small subset of NEL statements into a network. The four most basic commands are the parallel block, the serial block, the conditional if statement, and the goto statement. Other flow control statements — such as Case, Cond, While, Repeat, and Dolist— can be viewed as a combination of the above four. We, thus, overview how to compile the four building blocks:

1. A parallel block consists of the commands enclosed by **ParBegin** and **Parend**. Each of these commands is associated with a statement counter. All these counters are set simultaneously upon reaching the Parbegin. A concluding mechanism is required for synchronization. This mechanism keeps track of the termination of the various commands, and announces finishing upon termination of them all. Only then, the parallel block is concluded with the Parend. Details are provided in (Siegelmann 1993).

2. A serial block consists of the commands between the **Begin** and **End**. This involves an extensive use of counters.

3. The compilation of a simple if statement was provided in Example 1.1. We compile a general if statement

> **If** (B) **then** stat1
> **else** stat2

by

> **Parbegin**
>   **If** (B) **then** pc-stat$_1 = 1$;
>   **If** $(\neg(B))$ **then** pc-stat$_2 = 1$
> **Parend**

4. A Goto statement is implemented simply by a change in the neurons simulating the statement counters of the program.

Next, we consider a subset of the data types. Each variable, except for records and arrays, is represented via one neuron in the network.

- Boolean values are represented via the numbers $\{0, 1\}$. The logical operations are:

Operation	Network's emulation
Not(x)	$\sigma(1 - x)$
Or(x_1, x_2)	$\sigma(x_1 + x_2)$
And(x_1, x_2)	$\sigma(x_1 + x_2 - 1)$

$$(3)$$

Relational operations are defined in a straightforward manner: $x > y$ is $\sigma(x - y)$, $x \geq y$ is $\sigma(x - y + 1)$, and $x \neq y$ is $x_1(t) = \sigma(x - y)$, $x_2(t) = \sigma(y - x)$ and $x_3(t + 1) = \sigma(x_1 + x_2)$.

- List of T. Assume, for simplicity, that T has only two elements T=$\{0, 1\}$; later we generalize T to arbitrary cardinality. Given a list of elements $\omega_1 \omega_2 \cdots$, we regard it as a string $\omega = \omega_1 \omega_2 \cdots \omega_n$. We wish to represent this string as a number in the range $[0, 1]$, so that to be held in a neuron. If we were to represent the string as a number $\sum_{i=1}^{n} \frac{\omega_i}{2^i}$, one would not be able to differentiate between the string "β" and "$\beta \cdot 0$", where '$\cdot$' denotes the concatenation operator. Worse than that, the continuity of the activation function σ makes it impossible to retrieve the most significant bit (in radix 2) of a list in a constant amount of time. (For example, the values .100000000000 and .011111111111111 are almost indistinguishable by a net.) We encode the list by

$$\sum_{i=1}^{n} \frac{2\omega_i + 1}{4^i} .$$

(For examples, the list $\omega = 1011$ is encoded by the number $q = .3133_4$.) This number ranges in $[0, 1)$, but not every value in $[0, 1)$ appears. If the list started with the value 1, then the associated number has a value of at least $\frac{3}{4}$, and if it started with 0, the value is in the range $[\frac{1}{4}, \frac{1}{2})$. The empty list is encoded into the value 0. The next element in the list restricts the possible value further.

The set of possible values is not continuous and has "holes". Such a set of values "with holes" is a Cantor set. Its self-similar structure means that bit shifts preserve the "holes." The advantage of this approach is that there is never a need to distinguish among two very close numbers in order to read the most significant digit in the base-4 representation. We next demonstrate the usefulness of our encoding of the binary lists.

1. **CAR(ω), Reading the First Element:** The value of q is at least $\frac{3}{4}$ when the Car of the list is 1, and at most $\frac{1}{2}$ otherwise. The linear operation $4q - 2$ transfers q to at least 1 when the Car element is 1, and to a non-positive value otherwise. Thus, the function $\text{Car}\,(q) = \sigma(4q - 2)$ provides the value of the Car element.

2. **CDR(ω), Removing the Left Element:** Cdr a list, transfers the list $\omega = 1011$ to 011, or the encoding from $q = .3133_4$ to $.133_4$. When the Car element is known, the operation $\text{Cdr}\,(q) = 4q - (2\,\text{Car}\,(q) + 1)$ (or equivalently $\sigma(4q - (2\,\text{Car}\,(q) + 1))$) has the effect of CDRing the list.

3. **CONS(e, ω) Pushing a New Element to the Left of ω:** Pushing 0 to the left of the list $\omega = 1011$ changes the value into $\omega = 01011$. In terms of the encoding, $q = .3133_4$ is transferred into $q = .13133_4$. That is, the suffix remains the same and the new element $e \in \{0, 1\}$ is entered into the most significant location. This is easily done by the operation $\frac{q}{4} + \frac{2e+1}{4}$ (which is equivalent to $\sigma(\frac{q}{4} + \frac{2e+1}{4})$ given that $q \in [0, 1)$.)

4. **IsNull(ω):** The predicate IsNull indicates whether the list w is empty or not, which means in terms of the encoding, whether $q = 0$ or $q \geq .1_4$. This can be decided by the operation $\text{IsNull}\,(q) = \sigma(4q)$.

Assume T has a general cardinality, n. The operations **Car(ω)**, **Cdr(ω)**, **Cons(e, ω)**, and the predicate **IsNull(ω)** are implemented by: $\sigma(\frac{1}{2n} + \frac{1}{n}(\sigma(2nq - 2) + \sigma(2nq - 4) + \cdots + \sigma(2nq - (2n - 2))))$, $\sigma((2nq - 1 - 2(\sigma(2nq - 2) + \sigma(2nq - 4) + \cdots + \sigma(2nq - (2n - 2)))))$, $\sigma(\frac{q}{2n} + e)$, and $\sigma(1 - 2nq)$, respectively.

- Stacks are represented similarly to lists. Here Top substitutes Car, Pop substitutes Cdr, Push substitutes Cons, and the predicate Empty substitutes IsNull.

- Scalars are implemented using the same idea of gaps as with lists. Assume a scalar type with n elements $\{0, 1, \ldots (n - 1)\}$. The ith element is represented as $\text{scalar}\,(i, n) \equiv \frac{2i+1}{2n}$. Order operations are implemented as follows:

Operation	Network's emulation
Pred(x)	$\sigma(x - \frac{1}{n})$
Succ(x)	$\sigma(x + \frac{1}{n})$
Ord(x)	$\sigma(xn - \frac{1}{2})$

$$(4)$$

- A counter with the value n is represented as $(1 - 2^{-n})$, that is

$$\text{counter}(n) \hookrightarrow .\underbrace{11\ldots1}_{n} \tag{5}$$

The operations on counters **Inc**, **Dec**, and the predicate **IsZero** are implemented by $\sigma(\frac{1}{2}(x+1))$, $\sigma(2x - 1)$, and $\sigma(1 - 2x)$, respectively.

4   Conclusions

In conclusions, we can prove the next theorem.

Theorem 1 *There is a compiler that translates each program in the language NEL into a network. The constants (weights) that appear in the network are the same as those of the program, plus several rational small numbers. Furthermore, the size of the network is O(length) and its running time is O(execution measure). Here, length is the static length of the program, i.c. the number of tokens listed in the source code, and the execution measure is its dynamic length, i.e., the number of atomic commands executed for a given input.*

We may furthermore conclude from previous work described in subsection 1.2 and from the above theorem that all computer algorithms are expressible in NEL using rational constants only, while NEL programs that use real weights are stronger than any digital algorithm.

Acknowledgment

I wish to thank Eduardo Sontag and Jude Shavlik for useful comments.

References

Abu-Mostafa, Y. 1990. Learning from hints in neural networks. *Journal of Complexity* 6:192.

Al-Mashouq, K., and Reed, I. 1991. Including hints in training neural nets. *Neural Computation* 3(3):418–427.

Armstrong, W.; Stein, R.; Kostov, A.; Thomas, M.; Baudin, P.; Gervais, P.; and Popvic, D. 1993. Applications of adaptive logic networks and dynamics to study and control of human movement. In *Proc. Second Interntational Symposium on three-dimensional analysis of human movement*, 81–84.

Balcázar, J. L.; Gavaldà, R.; Siegelmann, H.; and Sontag, E. D. 1993. Some structural complexity aspects of neural computation. In *IEEE Structure in Complexity Theory Conference*, 253–265.

Berenji, H. R. 1991. Refinement of approximate reasoning-based controllers by reinforcement learning. In Birnbaum, L., and Collins, G., eds., *Machine Learning, Proceedings of the Eighth International International Workshop*, 475. San Mateo, CA: Morgan Kaufmann Publishers.

Frasconi, P.; Gori, M.; Maggini, M.; and Soda, G. 1993. Unified integration of explicit rules and learning by example in recurrent networks. *IEEE Transactions on Knowledge and Data Engineering*. Accepted for publication.

Fu, L. M. 1989. Integration of neural heauristics into knowledge-based inference. *Connection Science* 1:325–340.

Giles, C., and Maxwell, T. 1987. Learning, invariance, and generalization in high-order neural networks. *Applied Optics* 26(23):4972–4978.

Ginsberg, A. 1988. Theory revision via prior operationalization. In *Proceedings of the Sixth National Conference on Artificial Intelligence*, 590.

Hertz, J.; Krogh, A.; and Palmer, R. 1991. *Introduction to the Theory of Neural Computation*. Redwood City: Addison-Wesley.

Jordan, M. I. 1992. Forward models: Supervised learning with a distal teacher. *Cognitive Science* 16:307–354.

Kilian, J., and Siegelmann, H. T. 1993. On the power of sigmoid neural networks. In *Proc. Sixth ACM Workshop on Computational Learning Theory*.

Moody, J. 1992. The effective number of parameters: An analysis of generalization and regularization in nonlinear learning systems. In *J.E. Moody, S.J. Hanson, and R.P. Lippmann, editors, Advances in Neural Information Processing Systems*, volume 4, 847–854. San Mateo, CA: Morgan Kaufmann.

Omlin, C., and Giles, C. 1992. Training second-order recurrent neural networks using hints. In Sleeman, D., and Edwards, P., eds., *Proceedings of the Ninth International Conference on Machine Learning*, 363–368. San Mateo, CA: Morgan Kaufmann Publishers.

Omlin, C., and Giles, C. 1993. Rule revision with recurrent neural networks. *IEEE Transactions on Knowledge and Data Engineering*. accepted for publication.

Oursten, D., and Mooney, R. 1990. Changing rules: A comprehensive approach to theory refinement. In *Proceedings of the Eighth National Conference on Artificial Intelligence*, 815.

Pazzani, M. 1989. Detecting and correcting errors of omission after explanation-based learning. In *Proceedings of the Eleventh International Joint Conference on Artificial Intelligence*, 713.

Perantonis, S., and Lisboa, P. 1992. Translation, rotation, and scale invariant pattern recognition by higher-order neural networks and moment classifiers. *IEEE Transactions on Neural Networks* 3(2):241.

Pratt, L. 1992. Non-literal transfer of information among inductive learners. In Mammone, R., and Zeevi, Y., eds., *Neural Networks: Theory and Applications II*. Academic Press.

Siegelmann, H. T., and Sontag, E. D. 1991. Turing computability with neural nets. *Appl. Math. Lett.* 4(6):77–80.

Siegelmann, H. T., and Sontag, E. D. 1994a. Analog computation via neural networks. *Theoretical Computer Science*. to appear. A preliminary version in: The second Israel Symposium on Theory of Computing and Systems, Natanya, Israel, June, 1993.

Siegelmann, H. T., and Sontag, E. D. 1994b. On computational power of neural networks. *J. Comp. Syst. Sci.* previous version appeared in *Proc. Fifth ACM Workshop on Computational Learning Theory*, pages 440-449, Pittsburgh, July 1992.

Siegelmann, H. T. 1993. *Foundations of Recurrent Neural Networks*. Ph.D. Dissertation, Rutgers University.

Suddarth, S., and Holden, A. 1991. Symbolic neural systems and the use of hints for developing complex systems. *International Journal of Man-Machine Studies* 34:291–311.

Towell, G.; Craven, M.; and Shavlik, J. 1990. Constructive induction using knowledge-based neural networks. In Birnbaum, L., and Collins, G., eds., *Eighth International Machine Learning Workshop*, 213. San Mateo, CA: Morgan Kaufmann Publishers.

Towell, G.; Shavlik, J.; and Noordewier, M. 1990. Refinement of approximately correct domain theories by knowledge-based neural networks. In *Proceedings of the Eighth National Conference on Artificial Intelligence*, 861. San Mateo, CA: Morgan Kaufmann Publishers.

Multi-recurrent Networks for Traffic Forecasting

Claudia Ulbricht

Austrian Research Institute for Artificial Intelligence
Schottengasse 3, A-1010 Vienna, Austria
claudia@ai.univie.ac.at

Abstract

Recurrent neural networks solving the task of short-term traffic forecasting are presented in this report. They turned out to be very well suited to this task, they even outperformed the best results obtained with conventional statistical methods. The outcome of a comparative study shows that multiple combinations of feedback can greatly enhance the network performance. Best results were obtained with the newly developed Multi-recurrent Network combining output, hidden, and input layer memories having self-recurrent feedback loops of different strengths. The outcome of this research will be used for installing an actual tool at a highway check point. The investigated methods provide short-term memories of different length which are not only needed for the given application, but which are of importance for numerous other real world tasks.

Introduction

Forecasting the number of cars passing a check point on a highway is important for warning the people working there of upcoming heavy traffic. It is needed to avoid congestion and to control the highway accesses. At the site under investigation, the number of cars has been estimated by looking at reference days having similar properties. This task has also been tackled with various traditional statistical methods taking into account also recent traffic flow. This report shows how better performance can be achieved with recurrent neural networks. The novel network architecture developed for this task shows the importance of designing appropriate feedback links for time series prediction tasks. The combination of various types of feedback allows the formation of "memories" having different qualities.

*This research was supported by a grant from the Austrian Industrial Research Promotion Fund, Project No. 2/282 as a part of the Esprit-II project Nr. 5433 "NEU-FODI" (Neural Networks for Forecasting and Diagnosis Applications) which was performed in cooperation with BIKIT (Belgium), Lyonnaise des Eaux Dumez (France), Elorduy y Sancho, and Labein (both Spain). The data sets were provided by COFIROUTE, a subsidiary of Lyonnaise des Eaux Dumez.

Forecasting with Neural Networks

Time series forecasting is relevant for numerous applications in a wide range of areas. For instance, forecasting product demand in business or forecasting option prices in financial markets. Since estimates about future developments are important for decisions and actions today, there is always a need for better forecasting techniques. A lot of research has been done in the field of time series forecasting, an area to which AI methods can contribute a lot. In comparison to traditional statistical methods, neural networks offer a high flexibility concerning the types of functions that can be approximated adaptively during the training process. They are well suited to such function approximation tasks. After being trained to perform mappings for the examples in the training set, they can generalize to new examples.

Delay Mechanisms

Time series can only be handled by neural networks when some kind of delay mechanism is provided because multiple input patterns together in their given order have to influence the output. Windows, time delays, and feedback are examples of such mechanisms. Networks that can handle time series require at least one delay mechanism, but better performance can be achieved by combining different mechanisms as, for instance, an input window and feedback. This way the strengths of several techniques can be exploited. An overview of such mechanisms is given in (Ulbricht *et al.* 1992).

Non-recurrent Networks

The most straightforward approach for handling time series is using an input window which holds a restricted part of the time series. The neural network analyzes this part of the time series before the window is shifted by one or more elements further in time. An example can be found in (Tom & Tenorio 1989). Such a window can be modeled by collecting sequence elements arriving one after the other in some input memory until they can be used. Thus, the temporal dimension is reduced to zero by parallelizing sequence elements.

However, it is also possible to apply windows to several layers to repeat the windowing effect, as it is done in the TRACE model of speech perception (McClelland & Elman 1986). Such additional windows let the actual window size of the network grow. Time windows are also created in so-called time delay networks (see, for instance, (Wan 1990) or (Waibel 1988)). Signals originally ordered in time arrive at a single unit in parallel at the same point in time.

All these networks are non-recurrent networks without any feedback loops. They can only handle limited parts of time series at once. Moreover, invariance problems can arise because such networks are not flexible regarding the length of time intervals. The capacity of the memory of networks employing only non-recurrent mechanisms is limited by the size of the windows or by the number of time delays.

Recurrent Networks

The memory of a network with feedback has no definitive temporal limitation. The advantage of such a memory has to be paid by incompleteness, though. Past inputs are not kept in their complete original form, but only in a processed format thereby extracting and memorizing only a few characteristics. However, when using simple feedback loops the knowledge on past inputs and states decays rapidly. On the one hand, this effect seems to be very reasonable because the further back in time the less important events seem to be for the current situation. On the other hand, some past events can be very important. Both types of memories can be useful: flexible ones keeping recent events and rigid ones storing information over longer time periods. Another advantage of recurrent networks is that they allow the formation of states. If recurrent networks are updated like feedforward networks (with a single update per time step) they keep their general characteristics. Networks of this kind are also called "recurrent feedforward networks," "simple recurrent networks," or "partially recurrent networks" (Hertz, Krogh, & Palmer 1991).

Various neural network architectures employing different types of feedback can be found in literature. Output feedback is part of the network described in (Jordan 1986). The unit activations of the hidden layer are fed back in the network presented on page 184 in (Elman 1990). In the fully recurrent network described in (Smith & Zipser 1989) all information is fed back via a single feedback loop around the only layer. Storing the contents of the input layer for the next time step is equal to using input windows and does not introduce true recurrence. Finally, memory layers can also be fed back to themselves as it is also found in the network described in (Jordan 1986). This type of feedback has to be combined with some other feedback. The flexibility of such a memory can be tuned by adjusting the influence of these feedback loops. As will be shown in this report, memories can take on any

grade between being very flexible and very rigid. Since various combinations might be useful, memories with different degrees of flexibility can be part of a single neural network. This way short-term memories of different length are brought into neural networks having only long-term memories — the weights.

Self-recurrent connections with low weights lead to flexible memories quickly losing information. When raising these weights the memories become more and more rigid. Since they can keep information over longer time periods, they might be useful for avoiding invariance problems arising in many neural networks. Units in such layers have similar activity no matter whether a certain event occurred a few time steps later or earlier. Combining both flexible and rigid memories would allow the networks to handle both variant and invariant properties of time series.

Types of Memories

In this context, a memory is a layer receiving a copy of some other network layer. Its contents can later be fed forward to other layers — typically to the hidden layer. Such a memory layer stores information over time as unit activations. If the associated time delay is of length 1, the contents of the layer are stored for one time interval. Different types of delay connections for transferring the contents of a layer to a memory layer can be distinguished. They can be classified according to their properties in various ways. Feedback usually gets its name from the layer that is fed back as, for instance, "output feedback." In the tested networks, memory layers keep information of one or several of the following layers: the input layer, the hidden layer, the output layer, or one of the memory layers. Information is not necessarily stored by the memory layer the way it is received, but it can also be transformed before it is stored as it is done in some of the described experiments. When two layers are fed to a single layer they can be combined by weighting the two parts. Some other functions can also be useful, as for instance, calculating the error at the output as the difference between the output and the target.

The performance of neural networks in general is dependent on the network architecture, and also highly dependent on how the input is pre-processed. For instance, the performance can often be improved by explicitly giving the difference between two values. It can further be improved by employing appropriate techniques for handling temporal aspects as, for instance, the formation of memories. The objective of the experiments presented in the following section is to find a way of optimally combining and exploiting such techniques in order to lower the error at the output.

The Application

The Data Set

The given data set contains a time series of the number of vehicles passing a highway check point per hour.

It also includes the days of the week, dates, bank holidays, and school holiday information. A part of the time series is depicted in Fig. 1. The smallest temporal entity is an hour. One can see the daily cycles, the weekly cycles, and the effect of holidays at the beginning of the year (on the left side of the figure). Seasonal effects can be found in numerous real world application tasks as, for instance, when forecasting economic time series (as in (Varfis & Versino 1990)) or the development of water demand (as in (Canu, Sobral, & Lengellé 1990)). The given data set can thus be regarded as a typical time series example with implications on a variety of other applications. The data of the year 1990 were taken as training data, and those of 1991 as test data.

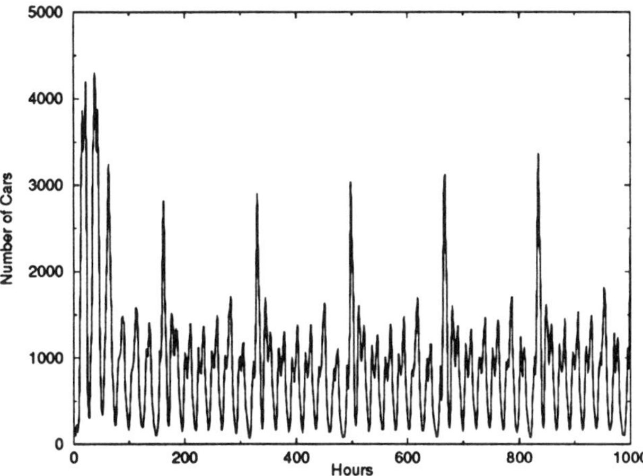

Figure 1: *Traffic time series*

The Task

The given task is forecasting at 5 a.m. the number of cars that are going to pass the highway check point between 7 and 8 a.m. Various conventional statistical methods have been applied to this task (Lengellé, Sys, & Ding 1993). The best result has been obtained with the nearest neighbor method. The lowest root mean square error (RMSE, see Equation 1) on the test set was 210.6.

$$\text{RMSE} = \sqrt{\frac{1}{N} \sum_{i=1}^{N} (x_f(i) - x_t(i))^2} \qquad (1)$$

where $x_f(i)$ is the forecast number of cars, and $x_t(i)$ the target value in the training process, i.e. the actually observed value.

The Network Architecture

The tested networks had 36 input units. The input consisted of an input window and of information on the number of cars at corresponding hours a week earlier. It also contained detailed information on days of the week, dates, and vacation times. Input and hidden, as well as hidden and output layer were fully connected in feedforward manner, respectively. All networks had 10 hidden units and 1 output unit. The first tested network was a simple non-recurrent window network. All the other networks were obtained by adding memory layers to this basic network architecture.

Network updating consists of several steps. First, the input is propagated together with the context to the hidden layer and then to the output layer. Finally, the contents of several layers are copied to the memory layers where they are stored for the next time step in which they are going to deal as context. This updating order is based on a subordinate time scale. The primary time scale is determined by the input sequence which contains a single sequence element per time step.

Network Training

The networks were trained with backpropagation until the mean square error on the test set stopped decreasing. The error was not checked after each epoch, but only every 100 epochs to speed up training and to make the training process less sensitive to short periods of growing error, i.e. to small bumps in the error curve. The RMSE was calculated on-line because it was used as stopping criterion. It dealt as basis for deciding whether to keep on training or quitting the training process.

When training recurrent networks it is not possible to simply select the training instances randomly from the training set because this way there could not be any appropriate context. A special technique overcoming this limitation had to be developed to achieve a similar effect. For each selected example, the network was updated 8 times in a row. This way the 7 days preceding the current day were taken into account. The first week of the training set was removed from the primary set and thus only implicitly taken into account. The unit activations were deliberately not reset before selecting a new training instance because that way the network had to learn to ignore these "random" initial activations. Thus the network was trained with examples closer to those in the test set and in the final real world application because there the time series was also presented in a continuous sequence. Resetting the activations to zero at the beginning of each training step would have resulted in atypical initial conditions.

Experiments

A Window Network

The first tested network (Network 1) was a simple feedforward network having 36 input units, 10 hidden units, and 1 output unit. The day of the week was represented by 7 units, one for each day. The month was coded by a single value. School and bank holidays were treated separately. Since calendar information is known in advance, a lot of detailed information was available. Multiple binary input units were

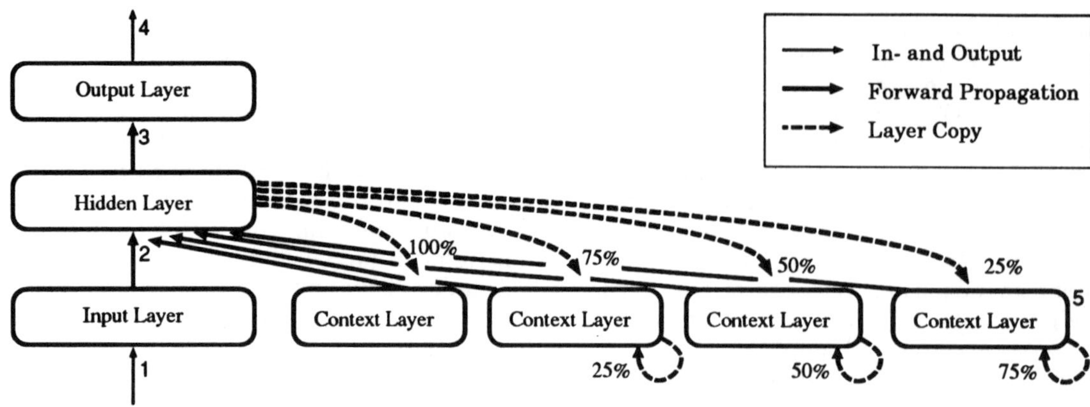

Figure 2: *Architecture of a recurrent network with multiple hidden layer feedback*

used to code such information as, for instance, the fact that school holidays were going to start 2 days later. Furthermore, there was a time window over the 3 last hours starting with the number of vehicles counted between 2 and 3 a.m. The last and current value of the time window was the traffic during the fifth hour of the day. Another unit coded the number of cars during the fifth hour a week before the current time. Since it seemed to be interesting to compare this value with that one week before, the difference between these two values was also supplied. It was coded by two units, one for positive and one for negative values, because they represent two different trends: an increase and a decrease in traffic respectively. Finally, the number of cars that had passed the check-point during the eighth hour a week before was also given because this corresponds to the value to be predicted.

Hidden Layer Feedback

Since not only the last hours, but also the last days are important for forecasting, in the next experiment (Network 2) the history of days was also taken into account. Therefore feedback was introduced. The contents of the hidden layer (10 units) were fed back after each updating phase (like in the network presented in (Elman 1990)). In the next updating cycle the stored values were fed forward to the hidden layer together with the input layer. In another test, the hidden layer was fed back three more times, but — like in the network presented in (Jordan 1986) — into context layers in which each unit had a recurrent feedback loop to itself. The feedback from the hidden layer and the feedback from the unit itself have to be combined in some way. When they are both given equal weights, 50% of feedback from the hidden layer is added to 50% of self-recurrent feedback. In order to create memories of different flexibility the feedback links to the memory layers were given different weights. A weight of 75% produced a rigid memory layer slowly adapting its activations over time and thus keeping information over longer time pe-

riods whereas a memory with a self-recurrent feedback link with a weight of 25% can be regarded as a more flexible short-term memory.

A network containing 4 such memory layers (Network 3) is depicted in Fig. 2. In a first step, the next sequence element is copied to the input layer. Then, the hidden layer is updated. It receives input from the input layer and from all context layers. The activations are then propagated to the output layer and further analyzed. Finally, in a fifth step all context layers are updated and prepared for the next time step.

In many neural networks the error at the output is used to adjust the weights which form the long-term memory of the network. When feeding back network layers, this influences unit activations which can be regarded as short-term memory. Four different degrees of self-recurrence allow the formation of short-term memories with different flexibility. This allows the network to capture short-term events in addition to the acquired long-term knowledge.

Output Feedback

In another experiment output, target output, and the difference between the two were also fed back (Network 4). They were fed back like the output in the network described in (Jordan 1986), but at first without any feedback loop from the memory units to themselves. Like for the hidden layer feedback, the next time this feedback was duplicated three times, each time with different feedback weights (Network 5). Feeding back the output and the actually observed value is only possible when they are available at the point in time when the next forecast is to be performed. When using longer lead times recent information cannot be taken into account. Here, it is possible because the lead time is 3 hours, and because the actual number of vehicles having passed the check point the day before is available.

Since both hidden layer feedback and output feedback improved the performance, they were both part of

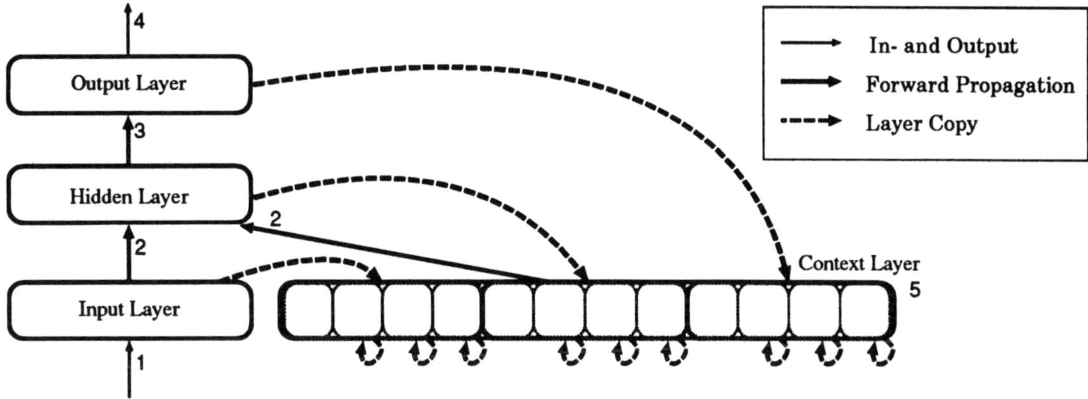

Figure 3: *Architecture of the Multi-recurrent Network*

the next tested network (Network 6). It had 4 feedback loops for the hidden layer activations and 4 feedback loops for output information.

Input Memory

In another experiment, the input window covering the 3 last hours was memorized analogously to the contents of the hidden layer and of the output layer (Network 7). This network contains two different kinds of windows: one over several hours and one over two days. Then, three more input memory layers with different degrees of self-recurrence (again 25%, 50%, and 75%) were added (Network 8). This way the input sequence can be stored in a compressed form. A longer input history can be kept without requiring much more space.

Finally, all introduced feedback links were combined. This network (Network 9) which is depicted in Fig. 3 had 4 context layers for feeding back the contents of the hidden layer, 4 context layers for feeding back output information (consisting of the forecast value, the actually observed value, and the difference between the two), and 4 context layers for storing the sequence of input windows.

Results

An overview of the results of the experiments with the 9 networks described above is given in Table 1. The RMSE on the test set is given for 3 repeated experiments. In the last column, their mean is listed. For better comparison, the mean is also depicted in the bar chart in Fig. 4.

The value these results have to be compared with is the RMSE of 210.6 which is the best result obtained with a conventional statistical method. It is outperformed by all tested neural networks.

In most experiments, the introduction of feedback improved the results. This is remarkable because it means that the positive effect of adding feedback is much larger than the negative effect of the much larger

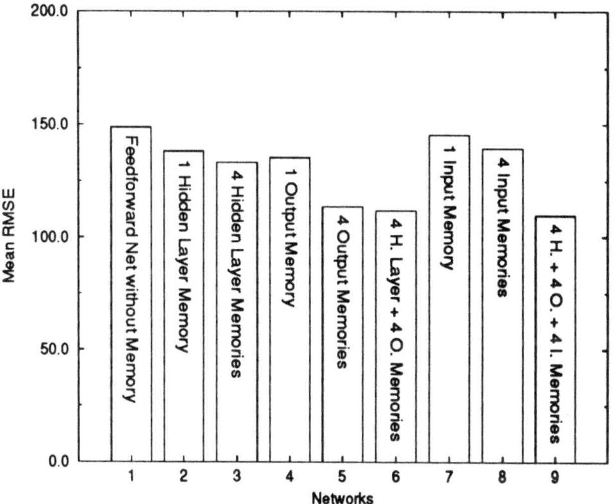

Figure 4: *Results obtained with neural networks having different types of memories*

input dimension. The influence of different types of memories is assumed to be dependent on the given application. In this case, the most effective technique for reducing the error turned out to be multiple output feedback which is part of Networks 5, 6, and 9. But hidden layer feedback and input processing also enhance the result, so that the best performance is that of Network 9 which combines all presented memory techniques.

This shows that it is reasonable to supply a large number of feedback links in neural networks. However, this results in the problem that each additional context layer unit leads to an increase of the input dimension. Proper handling of high-dimensional input and dimension reduction, for instance, by pruning techniques, could be part of further research. Moreover, methods for improving the quality of the memories could be investigated.

Net	Feedback			RMSE			
Nr.	Hidden	Output	Input	Test 1	Test 2	Test 3	Mean
1	—	—	—	152.87	147.18	146.31	148.79
2	1	—	—	133.32	141.71	139.54	138.19
3	4	—	—	130.75	130.60	138.37	133.24
4	—	1	—	138.90	145.26	121.87	135.34
5	—	4	—	111.83	114.47	114.39	113.56
6	4	4	—	115.50	111.11	108.86	111.82
7	—	—	1	141.31	149.10	146.29	145.57
8	—	—	4	142.29	145.14	131.16	139.53
9	4	4	4	109.15	112.20	107.72	109.69

Table 1: *Overview of the experiments*

Concluding Remarks

The goal of the experiments was to check whether neural networks can solve the task of short-term traffic forecasting. This task was solved and better results were obtained than with conventional statistical methods. The novel type of network architecture developed specifically for this application will be used as a basis for an actual tool at a highway check point. Various types of feedback are part of the Multi-recurrent Network. Not only activations of the hidden layer are stored in memory layers, but also output information and the input window. The introduction of multiple self-recurrent feedback loops allows the formation of short-term memories with different properties. This is an important extension to neural networks which often have only long-term memories. Such short-term memories are not only of use for this task, but important for a large number of other real world applications.

References

Canu, S.; Sobral, R.; and Lengellé, R. 1990. Formal Neural Network as an Adaptive Model for Water Demand. In *International Neural Network Conference, Paris, France, July 9-13, 1990*, 131–136. Kluwer, Dodrecht.

Elman, J. 1990. Finding Structure in Time. *Cognitive Science* 14:179–211.

Hertz, J.; Krogh, A.; and Palmer, R. 1991. *Introduction to the Theory of Neural Computation*. Addison-Wesley Publishing Company.

Jordan, M. 1986. Attractor Dynamics and Parallelism in a Connectionist Sequential Machine. In *Proceedings of the Eight Annual Conference of the Cognitive Science Society*, 531–546. Erlbaum, Hillsdale, NJ.

Lengellé, R.; Sys, V.; and Ding, X. 1993. Traffic forecasting application. Technical Report NEU-FODI/TR/501/3/LY02/1, Lyonnaise des Eaux — Dumez, France.

McClelland, J., and Elman, J. 1986. Interactive Processes in Speech Processing: The TRACE model. In Rumelhart, D., and McClelland, J., eds., *Parallel Distributed Processing*, volume I. MIT Press.

Smith, A., and Zipser, D. 1989. Encoding Sequential Structure: Experience with the Real-Time Recurrent Learning Algorithm. In *International Conference On Neural Networks*, volume I, 645–648. Washington D.C., IEEE.

Tom, M., and Tenorio, M. 1989. A Spatio-Temporal Pattern Recognition Approach to Word Recognition. In *IEEE International Conference On Neural Networks*, volume I, 351–355.

Ulbricht, C.; Dorffner, G.; Canu, S.; Guillemyn, D.; Marijuan, G.; Olarte, J.; Rodriguez, C.; and Martin, I. 1992. Mechanisms for handling sequences with neural networks. In Dagli, C., et al., eds., *Intelligent Engineering Systems through Artificial Neural Networks, ANNIE'92*, volume 2, 273–278. ASME Press, New York.

Varfis, A., and Versino, C. 1990. Univariate Economic Time Series Forecasting by Connectionist Methods. In *International Neural Network Conference, Paris, France, July 9-13, 1990*, 342–345. Kluwer, Dordrecht.

Waibel, A. 1988. Connectionist Glue: Modular Design of Neural Speech Systems. In D., T., ed., *Connectionist Models Summer School*, 417–425.

Wan, E. 1990. Temporal Backpropagation for FIR Neural Networks. In *International Joint Conference on Neural Networks*, volume I, 575–580.

Knowledge Matrix ---- An Explanation & Knowledge Refinement Facility for a Rule Induced Neural Network

Daniel S. Yeung
Department of Computing,
Hong Kong Polytechnic, Hong Kong.
Fax : (852) 7642528
Email : csdaniel@hkpcc.hkp.hk

Hak-shun, Fong
Department of Computing,
Hong Kong Polytechnic, Hong Kong.
Fax : (852) 7642528
Email : cshsfong@comp.hkp.hk

Abstract

One of the major shortcomings of neural network as a problem solving tool lies in its opaque nature of knowledge representation and manipulation. For instance, the way that a learning algorithm modifies the connection weights of a network cannot be easily understood in the context of the application domain knowledge. Thus, the applications of neural networks is limited in areas where user's understanding of the situation is critical. This paper introduces a facility called knowledge matrix for a rule induced Neocognitron network. It represents the correlation between the knowledge stored internally in the network and the symbolic knowledge used in the application domain. Another facility called response matrix is developed to represent the network's response to an input. These two facilities are then employed cooperatively to generate symbolic interpretations of the network's response. Based on the interpretations, queries can be made against the network's responses and explanations can be provided by the system. Two detailed examples are discussed. It can be shown that the network knowledge can be refined evolutionarily without degrading its comprehensibility. An algorithm has also been formulated to adapt the system with respect to one type of recognition error.

Introduction

Although neural networks possess learning and generalizing capabilities, much of their internal knowledge representation and manipulation is incomprehensible. It is also difficult to make use of the ways they learn to refine the problem domain knowledge. These two shortcomings seriously hinder the use of neural networks in situations where a high degree of human interaction is required. To overcome these difficulties, one possible means is to build a neural network system with embedded high-level, symbolic domain knowledge.

Several hybrid systems which attempt to integrate neural networks and symbolic knowledge manipulations have been proposed (Fu & Fu 1990, Gallant 1988, Hayashi, Krishnamraju & Reilly 1991, Towell, Shavlik & Noordewier 1990, Towell & Shavlik 1992). Although some of them (Fu & Fu 1990, Towell, Shavlik & Noordewier 1990, Towell & Shavlik 1992) incorporate domain knowledge into the neural networks, they employ conventional learning algorithms to train the networks.

Therefore, it is still difficult to understand why certain changes on the network have taken place. On the other hand, Hayashi (Hayashi, Krishnamraju & Reilly 1991) has proposed a hybrid architecture in which a "cooperative module" is employed to exchange knowledge between a neural network and an expert system. Unfortunately, very little information on this module is given. In this paper, a rule induced neural network for handwritten Chinese character recognition is proposed using a priori symbolic knowledge, i.e., a set of production rules. The construction of such a rule induced network is described in Section 2. A facility called knowledge matrix which provides symbolic interpretations of the network's response to inputs is presented in Section 3. Thus, it follows that the network knowledge can be refined based on information stored in the knowledge matrix. Section 4 gives the conclusion and possible future work.

Rule Induced Neural Network

The neural network being considered is a rule induced network (Yeung, Fong & Cheung 1992), which is so devised to represent the syntactic structure of a small set of seventeen Chinese characters. A syntax of attribute rules is formulated to describe the structural knowledge of these characters, and a mapping scheme is also established to program the network using these rules as a template. The rule induced network thus constructed is found to

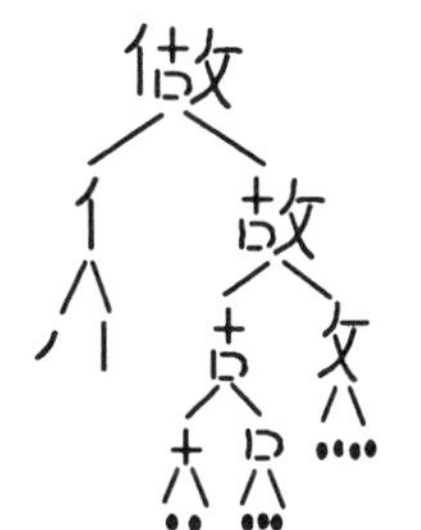

Figure 1 : Structure Decomposition Tree

	-2	-1	0	+1	+2
-2	.25	.25	.25	.25	.25
-1	.25	.75	.75	.75	.25
0	.25	.75	1.0	.75	.25
+1	.25	.75	.75	.75	.25
+2	.25	.25	.25	.25	.25

Displacement from the expected location

Figure 2 : Fuzzy Region

recognize some handwritten samples of the seventeen character categories. In this section, the rule syntax and the network architecture are briefly described.

Rule Representation

Every rule in our system specifies a character pattern in terms of its subpatterns. Each subpattern may successively be further decomposed into simpler ones (Figure 1). The decomposition process is repeated until the subpatterns being used are the commonly accepted primitives. The set of primitives chosen is called the basic stroke set. Similar stroke sets, with slight variations, are widely adopted in various Chinese dictionaries, e.g., Cihai (Shangwu-Yinshuguan 1979). The collection of all rules related to the decomposition of a particular character can be viewed as its structure decomposition tree. Such a tree description closely resembles the syntactic analysis approach of Chinese characters studies (Chen 1986, Stallings 1977).

The form of a general rule is given as follows :

If $\{A, [(s,t), fuz\_1]\}$
  and $\{B_i, [(u,v), fuz\_2]\}$
  and .....
  then E,

where the consequence E indicates the character pattern whose structural knowledge is described by this rule. Each of the antecedents holds the geometric information of one subpattern. Currently, only one writing style in each character pattern serves as its template. All rules are of conjunctive types because no subpatterns are considered as optional. Since a disjunctive rule can be transformed into a number of conjunctive rules, it seems to be quite straight forward to extend our current rule forms to include disjunctive ones.

Every antecedent consists of two parts, namely, a component pattern and its positional attributes. The subpattern B_i stands for the i-th variant of the stroke class B, while A is a subpattern which may be a radical or a subcharacter. In the positional attribute part, two fields of information are maintained. The first field denotes the mostly expected integral coordinates of the subpattern when the character pattern represented by the consequence indeed exists. The coordinates of the subpatterns in the antecedent part are calculated as follows. The character pattern denoted by the consequence is supposed to fall on a 17x17 pixel matrix. Then, for each of its subpatterns, a reference location on the matrix is associated with it, which is often chosen at approximately the centre of that subpattern. The same is done for the consequence pattern too. By treating the reference location of the consequence pattern as the origin, the relative coordinates for the subpatterns are calculated accordingly. These relative coordinates are the mostly expected coordinates. The second field defines a fuzzy region enclosing the location specified by the first field. A sample fuzzy region is shown in Figure 2. Values in the region specify the plausibilities for that antecedent subpattern to exist at the corresponding locations. Table I lists the values in several fuzzy regions. In a fuzzy region, each value is inversely proportional to the distance between the location concerned, $[r', c']$, and the mostly expected location $[r_e, c_e]$. Here, "distance" is defined by the function $MAX(|r'-r_e|, |c'-c_e|)$.

Fuzzy Region	Distance from the expected location					
	0	1	2	3	4	5
Fuz_1	1.0	0.50				
Fuz_2	1.0	0.75	0.25			
Fuz_3	1.0	0.85	0.50	0.15		
Fuz_4	1.0	0.90	0.65	0.35	0.10	
Fuz_5	1.0	0.93	0.75	0.50	0.25	0.07

<u>Table I</u>

System Architecture

In Figure 3, the architecture of our proposed neural network system is shown. A 65x65 square pixel matrix at the left hand side is the input pattern grid for receiving binary input images. An input, i.e., a handwritten Chinese character to be recognized, will turn on the corresponding pixels on the matrix.

A stroke extractor is then employed to locate all possible instances of the basic strokes contained in the input character. At the output layer of this extractor, there are twenty-two groups of neuron-planes corresponding to the twenty-two basic stroke classes (Yeung, Fong & Cheung 1992). There are three types of transformation applied to the basic stroke in each class, namely, scaling, skewing and rotation. With three choices allowed for each transformation, up to a total of twenty-seven variants can be generated for each stroke class. Thus, there are up to twenty-seven neuron-planes in each group. Every neuron-plane at the output layer of this stroke extractor is a 17x17 matrix arrangement of neuron-modules. The locations of the detected stroke variants are "quantized" to these 17x17 matrix locations. The firing score of a neuron-module, which is bounded between 0.0 and 1.0, reflects the degree of matching with a particular stroke variant at a particular location.

In the rule induced neural network, each stage holds the structural knowledge of several patterns which may be characters or radicals. A pattern in each stage can be constructed from its components as detected in the preceding stages. A neuron-plane, which is a 17x17 matrix arrangement of neuron-modules, is allocated for the detection of each pattern. All neuron-modules on a neuron-plane are mapped with the structural knowledge of the same pattern. This duplication of knowledge is to

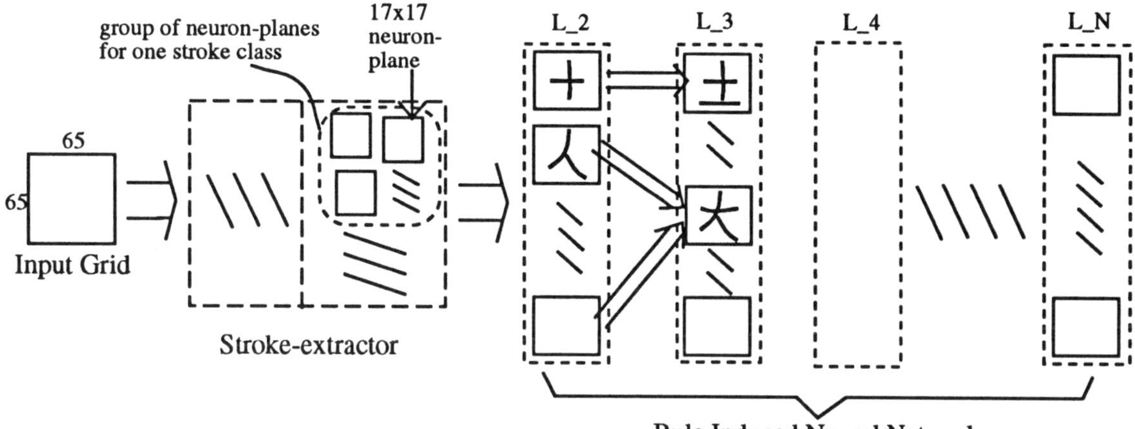

Figure 3 : System Architecture

facilitate positional shift tolerant detection of the pattern.

During the rule-mapping phase, the internal structure of a neuron-module is determined by the rule mapped onto it. There are two types of cells in each module, namely s-cell and p-cell. While there is always only one s-cell in each module, the number of p-cells in a module equals the number of antecedents in the mapped rule. Every p-cell is responsible for detecting the existence of a particular component in an acceptable region, by connection projected from the neuron-plane of that component pattern. This acceptable region is determined by both the location of the currently concerned module on the neuron-plane, and the positional attribute (section 2.1) of that component.

The rule induced network performs its recognition task stage by stage. A stage is labelled as a candidate-stage if it has a neuron-plane, which is associated to a character pattern, fire with non-zero response in one of its neuron-modules. After all stages have finished the processing, the last candidate-stage is checked. The input character is identified as the character pattern associated with the neuron-plane in that stage which fires with the highest score. If no candidate-stage is found at all, the input character is then rejected.

Knowledge Matrix

The knowledge matrix is introduced in this paper to function in two aspects. It is to facilitate reasoning of the network's response to an input character, and to drive modifications on the rule-base. The modified subset of rules can then be re-mapped onto the network to refine the network knowledge without degrading its comprehensibility. In the sections below, one will first see how the knowledge matrix and an auxiliary tool, namely the response matrix, are organized. Then, the ways these two matrices co-operate to perform the above functions are elaborated.

Matrix Representation

The knowledge matrix is a representation of the internal knowledge of the rule induced neural network (Figure 4). It has symmetric labels on its rows and columns. Every label is a 3-tuple, corresponding to a neuron-module in the network. For instance, a label (P,r,c) corresponds to the neuron-module at the location [r,c] on the neuron-plane for pattern P. Those rows (columns) which are closer to the upper (left) portion of the matrix are assigned labels corresponding to modules staying in earlier stages. Furthermore, those labels corresponding to the same pattern are grouped consecutively. Additionally, a non-diagonal, non-zero entry $K_{i,j}$ on row-i and column-j indicates a connection from module-j to module-i. The entry value is the maximally attainable excitation on that connection. In contrast, the diagonal entry-values indicate the highest firing scores attainable by the s-cells in the corresponding modules. Since the value-determination procedure for the entries in the knowledge matrix is quite complicated, those who are interested are suggested to refer to the authors' other paper (Yeung & Fong 1993).

According to this label-organization, the knowledge

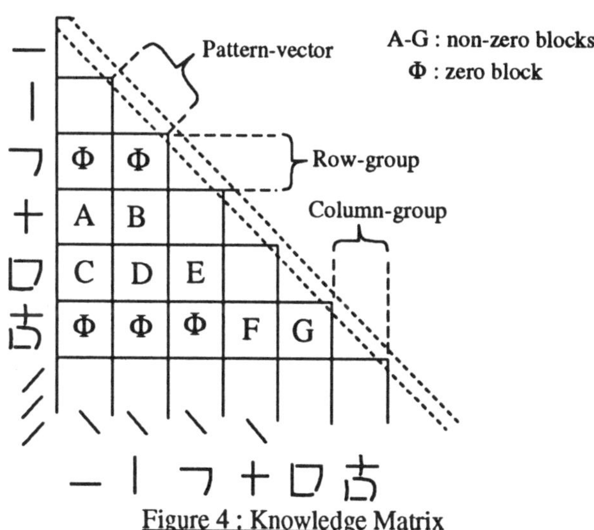

Figure 4 : Knowledge Matrix

matrix possesses several characteristics. Since the network allows connections only from lower stage to higher stage, all the entries at the upper-triangle of the matrix are set to zeros. Moreover, the rows (columns) of the knowledge matrix can be divided into *row-groups* (column-groups). All the row-labels (column-labels) in a row-group (column-group) correspond to modules from the same neuron-plane, whose associated pattern is thus called the *row-group pattern* (column-group pattern). The row-groups divide the diagonal on the knowledge matrix into partitions. Each of the partitions is named a *pattern-vector* of the associated row-group.

Another kind of unit on the matrix, called *block*, is also identifiable which is defined as the intersection region between a row-group and a column-group. Thus, a block is a submatrix associated with one row-group pattern and one column-group pattern. However, the following discussions concerning blocks should exclude those which cover the diagonal. A block is a non-zero matrix only if its row-group pattern possesses its column-group pattern as one component. Meanwhile, every row of entries in a block forms one *row-vector*. The entries in a row-vector express the maximum excitations on a set of connections, projected from a p-cell in the neuron-module associated to that row onto the neuron-plane of the column-group pattern.

While the knowledge matrix represents the static knowledge captured by the rule induced network, a response matrix is used to represent the network's run-time response to an input. The label-organization, definitions of row/column-group, pattern-vector, block and row-vector on the response matrix are identical to those in the knowledge matrix. The diagonal entries carry actual firing scores of each neuron-modules, and the non-diagonal ones carry actual excitations on the corresponding connections. The example of a response matrix is shown in Figure 5.

Explanation of the Network Response

With the help of the knowledge matrix (and also the response matrix), it is possible to query the network's response to an input in two ways :
(i)   Why is pattern-A detected {at location [r,c]} ?
(ii)   Why is pattern-A NOT detected ?
Note :The location portion {.} in query (i) is optional.
Two different algorithms are devised to handle these two types of queries.

Case (i) Why is pattern-A detected {at location [r,c]} ?
Algorithm A :
Steps
1)   Check if pattern-A is really detected. If location is specified in the query, one can directly check if the diagonal entry on the corresponding row is non-zero. Otherwise, this can be done by tracing the row-group of pattern-A, on the response matrix, to see if it possesses a non-zero pattern-vector.
2)   If the non-zero entry (or the non-zero pattern-

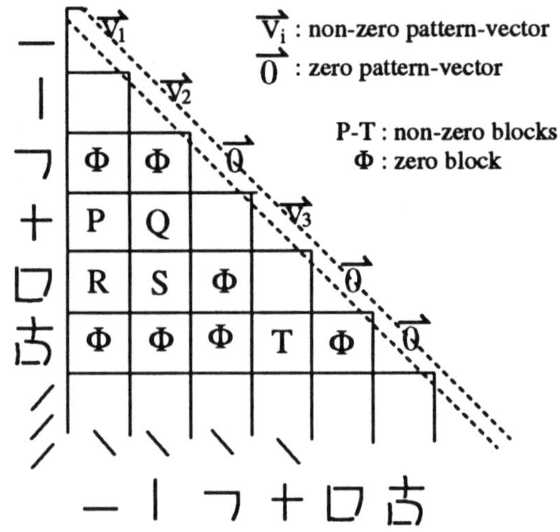

Figure 5 : Response Matrix

vector) cannot be found in step 1), tell the user that pattern-A is NOT detected, or the query is invalid; then STOP.
3)   If location is specified in the query, e.g., [r,c], then choose the target row Rr with row-label (A,r,c). Otherwise, in the row-group of pattern-A on the response matrix, locate the target row Rr with the highest diagonal entry-value. If more than one row possesses the highest value, choose one of them arbitrarily.
4)   Extract the corresponding row, Kr, on the knowledge matrix.
5)   For each of the non-zero row-vectors along Kr, find the corresponding row-vectors VRr_i on the response matrix.
6)   On every row-vector VRr_i, do the steps below.
>   Identify the highest excitation value. If more than one is found, choose one of them arbitrarily.
>   Suppose the entry identified above is $M_{a,b}$. Extract row-b on the response matrix.
7)   Suppose every row-b_i extracted in step 5) has a 3-tuple label (P_i, r_i, c_i), and the diagonal entry value on it equals V_i. Construct an explanation in the following format :
        "Pattern-A is detected because
        subpattern P_1 is detected at location $[r_1, c_1]$ with
            score V_1, and
        .....
        subpattern P_i is detected at location $[r_i, c_i]$ with
            score V_i, and
        ....."
8)   STOP.

The user may continue the query on any particular pattern P_k above. However, if P_k is a stroke variant, stroke extraction stage is reached and the user should be notified that no more detail is available.

Case (ii) Why is pattern-A NOT detected ?
Algorithm B :

Steps

1)	Check if the pattern-vector on the row-group of pattern-A on the response matrix is a zero vector. If not so, tell the user that pattern-A has been detected, or the query is invalid; then STOP.

2)	In the row-group of pattern-A on the knowledge matrix, identify all the non-zero blocks. Then, locate the corresponding blocks Rm_j on the response matrix.

3)	If some Rm_j are zero matrices, do as follows.

(i)	Suppose each zero block Rm_i corresponds to column-group pattern P_i.

(ii)	Construct an explanation in the following format :

"Pattern-A is NOT detected because
subpattern P_1 is NOT detected, and
.....
subpattern P_i is NOT detected, and
....."

(iii)	STOP algorithm B.

4)	Trace the row-group of pattern-A on the response matrix until a row is encountered along which all row-vectors in all Rm_j are non-zero vectors.

If such a row exists, give an explanation :

"Pattern-A is NOT detected because the degree of match is too low."

Otherwise, give the following explanation :

"Pattern-A is NOT detected because the positional information does not fit the input."

5)	STOP.

The two types of queries can provide much information on the network's response. However, there are other types of queries which may be useful. In addition, details added onto the last explanation offered in step 4) of algorithm B will make it more informative. The situation can be understood better if one is informed that "the tolerance region of a subpattern X is too small", "the expected location of a subpattern X is too close", etc. Nevertheless, the algorithms presented above improve the transparency of the operation of a neural network. More work is to be done along this direction.

Rule Modifications

In this section, the knowledge matrix and the response matrix are adopted to address the problem of knowledge refinement. Most neural network based systems employ learning algorithms which bear no explicit relationship with the problem domain. In contrast, the proposed approach attempts to adjust the knowledge represented in the rule-base, according to the network's response to an input. The refined rules can then be used to update the network connections through mapping.

In refining our system, two major error types are handled, namely wrong-rejections and wrong-recognitions. A wrong-rejection error occurs when none of the neuron-planes responds to the input character which is expected to be recognizable. This type of error requires raising the tolerance (or fuzziness) of the related rules. An algorithm for this purpose has already been devised in another paper of the authors (Yeung & Fong 1993). Thus, we will focus on the second error type here, i.e., wrong-recognition.

There are two different cases for this type of error. One is that the relevant neuron-plane doesn't respond at all, while some other irrelevant ones do. Another case is that the response of the relevant neuron-plane is suppressed by the response from neuron-planes at this or higher stages of the network. For the first case, action adopted in handling the wrong-rejection error is taken to activate the relevant plane. Thus, the first case is transformed into the second case.

At least two situations are identified as the possible causes of the second case of wrong-recognition error. The noise generated by the stroke-extractor in the system, i.e., false stroke detections, may cause irrelevant patterns to be found. Since this is the problem of the stroke-extractor, it is not considered here. Another cause is that some rules (mapped onto the irrelevant neuron-planes) may be too sensitive to give "false" response to the input. A tuning algorithm is given below to tune these rules, so as to suppress responses from irrelevant neuron-planes. Before the algorithm is presented, several definitions employed in the algorithm are described beforehand.

Definitions

(1)	Poorly-Done pattern, PD

The entry-values on a row-vector are calculated from the pattern-vector on the same column-group. If the maximum entry on a row-vector corresponds to an element in the pattern-vector which is smaller than a preset threshold (e.g., 0.1), the column-group is said to be PD. Adjustment on the structure knowledge of this column-group pattern will not be attempted.

(2)	Low-Positional Fuzziness, LPF

An antecedent is said to possess LPF if the fuzzy region (associated with an antecedent in a rule) has been reduced to a preset lower bound (e.g., 1). Its fuzzy region in that rule should not be shrunk any more.

(3)	Sit-Well row-vector

Each row-vector on the knowledge matrix corresponds to an antecedent of the rule associated to that row. If the maximum entry of a row-vector is found to be located at the centre of the fuzzy region of the corresponding antecedent, the row-vector is said to be Sit-Well.

(4)	Innocent row-vector

When a row-vector possesses LPF or is Sit-Well, and its column-group pattern is PD, the row-vector will not be considered as a possible item whose changes may lead to any improvement of the situation.

Tuning Algorithm

Suppose the input belongs to the character category A whose structure knowledge has been mapped onto a plane at stage-N. Then, the row-groups on the response matrix are traced one by one, from the highest stage to stage-N. For any row-group **G** other than that for pattern A, if the pattern-vector is a non-zero vector, perform the routine

<Correct> below. One should note that, in the algorithm below, any adjustment on a rule is analogous to some alterations on the network. Thus, after every rule-adjustment, both the knowledge matrix and the response matrix must be updated before the tuning process proceeds.

<Correct>
(1)   Select the row **r** on **G** corresponding to the maximum entry in the pattern-vector.
(2)   Repeat
    (2.1)   Record all innocent row-vectors on **r**.
    (2.2)   Among the non-innocent row-vectors on **r**, choose one r_i which possesses the maximum entry.
    (2.3)   Check if r_i is marked. If yes, perform 2.3a; else, follow 2.3b.
    (2.3a)   Identify the maximum entry in r_i, say, $RM_{a,b}$, and unmark r_i. Then <Component-correct> is performed for the row **b**.
    (2.3b)   Unmark all other marked row-vectors on **r** and mark r_i. Reduce the fuzzy region radius by one of the antecedent associated to r_i if this row-vector does not possess LPF.
    Until   {**G** possesses a zero pattern-vector, or all the antecedents of the associated rule possess LPF}
(3)   Unmark all row-vectors on the response matrix.
(4)   STOP.

<Component-correct>
Suppose the row concerned is **r'**, which is corresponding to a rule R_i.
(1)   Record all innocent row-vectors on **r'**.
(2)   Among the non-innocent row-vectors, choose one, e.g., r_i', which possesses the maximum entry value.
(3)   If r_i' is marked but is PD, unmark it. Go to step (6).
(4)   If r_i' is marked, identify the maximum entry in r_i', say, $RM_{s,t}$. Perform <Component-correct> for the row **t**.
(5)   If r_i' is not marked, unmark all other marked row-vectors on **r'** and mark r_i'. Then, expand the fuzzy region of the antecedent in R_i associated to r_i'.
(6)   STOP.

It is possible that the pattern-vector of the row-group **G** cannot be suppressed completely after tuning. In this case, the algorithm is unable to resolve the ambiguity arisen between the input character and the structure rule associated to **G**.

Conclusion

In this paper, two shortcomings which hinder wider applications of neural networks are tackled. The neural network considered is induced by the structure rules of a set of Chinese characters. By introducing a facility called knowledge matrix, the network's responses can be explained to users. This type of explanation is seldom available in other neural network based systems. Additionally, the knowledge matrix is also employed to drive refinements on the rule-base. Re-mapping of the modified rules onto the network completes the adaptation cycle. This approach of rule refinement keeps the network comprehensible to users, which is another characteristic that cannot be easily achieved in learning algorithms adopted by most neural networks.

At present, only a few types of explanations with respect to the network's responses are offered. Explanations with more details are surely advantageous. Moreover, the performance of the rule refinement algorithms proposed needs to be studied. All these will require a more in depth investigation on the knowledge matrix.

References

Chen, K.J. 1986. Computational Approaches in Topological and Geometrical Descriptions for Chinese Characters. *Computer Processing of Chinese & Oriental Languages* 2(4): 234-242.

Shangwu-Yinshuguan 1979. *Cihai*. Beijing, Shanghai: Shangwu Yinshuguan (The Commercial Press).

Fu, L.M.; Fu, L.C. 1990. Mapping rule-based systems into neural architecture. *Knowledge-Based Systems* (3)1: 48-56.

Gallant, I. 1988. Connectionist Expert Systems. *Communications of the ACM* 31(2): 152-169.

Hayashi, Y.; Krishnamraju, V.; Reilly, D. 1991. An Architecture for Hybrid Expert Systems. In Proceedings of the IEEE International Joint Conference on Neural Networks, '91, Singapore, 2773-2778.

Stallings, W. 1977. Chinese Character Recognition. In Fu, K.S. eds. 1977. *Syntactic Pattern Recognition, Applications*, 95-123. New York : Springer-Verlay.

Towell, G.G.; Shavlik, J.W.; Noordewier, M.O. 1990. Refinement of Approximate Domain Theories by Knowledge-Based Neural Networks. In Proceedings of the 8th National Conference on Artificial Intelligence '90, 2: 861-866.

Towell, G.G.; Shavlik, J.W. 1992. Interpretation of Artificial Neural Networks. In Moody, J.E. eds. 1992. *Advances in Neural Information Processing Systems Vol.4*, 977-984. Morgan Kaufmann Pub..

Yeung, S.; Fong, H.S.; Cheung, K.F. 1992. A Neocognitron-based Chinese Character Recognition System. In Proceedings of the International Joint Conference on Neural Networks '92, Beijing, 3: 617-622.

Yeung, S.; Fong, H.S. 1993. A Knowledge Matrix Representation for a Rule-Mapped Neural Network. (To appear in) *Neurocomputing*.

Epsilon-Transformation: Exploiting Phase Transitions to Solve Combinatorial Optimization Problems - Initial Results[*]

Weixiong Zhang and **Joseph C. Pemberton**
Computer Science Department
University of California, Los Angeles
Los Angeles, CA 90024
Email: {zhang, pemberto}@cs.ucla.edu

Abstract

It has been shown that there exists a transition in the average-case complexity of searching a random tree, from exponential to polynomial in the search depth. We develop a state-space transformation method, called ε-transformation, that makes use of this complexity transition to find a suboptimal solution. The expected number of random tree nodes expanded by branch-and-bound (BnB) using ε-transformation is cubic in the search depth, and the relative error of the solution cost compared to the optimal solution cost is bounded by a small constant. We also present an iterative version of ε-transformation that can be used to find both optimal and suboptimal solutions. Depth-first BnB (DFBnB) using iterative ε-transformation significantly improves upon truncated DFBnB on random trees with large branching factors and deep goal nodes, finding better solutions sooner on average. On the asymmetric traveling salesman problem, DFBnB using ε-transformation outperforms a well-known local search method, and DFBnB using iterative ε-transformation is superior to truncated DFBnB.

Introduction

It has been observed that phase transitions exist in many intelligent systems (Huberman & Hogg 1987) and combinatorial problems (Cheeseman, Kanefsky, & Taylor 1991; Karp & Pearl 1983; McDiarmid 1990; McDiarmid & Provan 1991; Mitchell, Selman, & Levesque 1992; Zhang & Korf 1992; 1993; 1994). A *phase transition* is a dramatic change to some problem property as some *order parameter* changes across a critical point. For example, water changes from a liquid to a solid when the temperature drops below the freezing point.

The earliest evidence of computational phase transitions was the phase transition of a tree-search problem (Karp & Pearl 1983), which has recently been studied in detail (McDiarmid 1990; McDiarmid & Provan 1991; Zhang & Korf 1992; 1993; 1994). The problem is to find an optimal goal node of the following random tree.

---

[*]This research was supported by NSF Grant No. IRI-9119825, a grant from Rockwell International, a GTE graduate fellowship (1992-93), and a UCLA Chancellor's Dissertation Year Fellowship (1993-94).

Definition 1 (McDiarmid & Provan 1991) *A random tree* T(b,d) *is a tree with depth* d, *and independent and identically distributed (i.i.d) random branching factors with mean* b. *Nonnegative edge costs are bounded i.i.d. random variables. The cost of a node is the sum of the edge costs on the path from the root to that node. An optimal goal node* is a minimum-cost node at depth d.

Best-first search (BFS) and depth-first branch-and-bound (DFBnB) can be used to search these random trees. Both are special cases of the general branch-and-bound (BnB) technique. See (Pearl 1984; Korf 1989; Kumar 1992) for the details of these algorithms.

It turns out that the cost of an optimal goal node of $T(b,d)$, and the expected complexity of BFS and DFBnB on $T(b,d)$ experience phase transitions. The order parameter that determines these transitions is the expected number of children of a node whose cost is the same as that of their parent, which are called *same-cost children*. This is the same as the expected number of *zero-cost edges* emanating from a node. If p_0 is the probability that an edge has cost zero, then bp_0 is the expected number of same-cost children of a node. When bp_0 increases from less than one to greater than one, the expected cost of the optimal goal node of $T(b,d)$ changes from a *linear function* of d to a *constant*, and the expected time complexity of BFS and DFBnB decreases from *exponential* in d to at most *cubic* in d. These phase transitions are summarized by the following lemma, and illustrated by Figure 1.

Lemma 1 (McDiarmid 1990; McDiarmid & Provan 1991; Zhang & Korf 1993; 1994) *Let* C^* *be the optimal goal cost of* $T(b,d)$ *with* $b > 1$, *and* N_B *and* N_D *be the expected numbers of nodes expanded by BFS and DFBnB on* $T(b,d)$ *respectively. As* $d \rightarrow \infty$, *(1) when* $bp_0 < 1$, $C^*/d \rightarrow \alpha$ *almost surely*[1], *where* α *is a constant, and* $N_B = N_D = \theta(\beta^d)$, *for a constant* $\beta > 1$; *(2) when* $bp_0 = 1$, $C^*/(\log\log d) \rightarrow 1$ *almost surely,* $N_B = \theta(d^2)$, *and* $N_D = O(d^3)$; *and (3) when* $bp_0 > 1$, C^* *is almost surely bounded,* $N_B = \theta(d)$, *and*

---

[1]A sequence of random variables X_n is said to converge *almost surely* (with probability one) to X if $P(\lim_{n \rightarrow \infty} X_n = X) = 1$ (Rényi 1970).

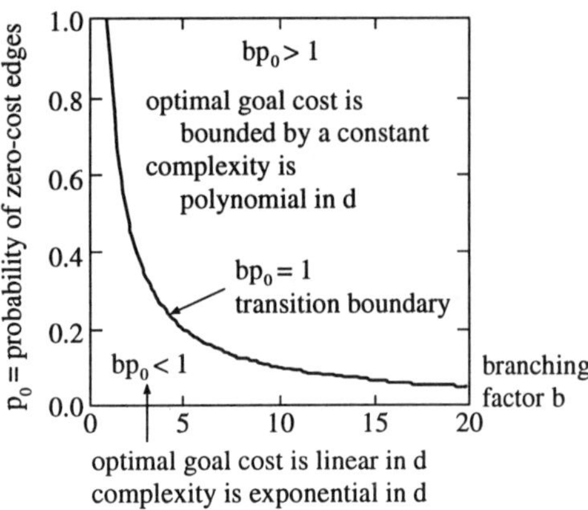

Figure 1: Phase transitions of tree search problems.

$N_D = O(d^2)$. □

Many practical search problems, such as planning and scheduling, require computation exponential in the search depth, even in the average case. However, we usually do not need optimal solutions, but rather ones that have a satisfactory quality and can be found quickly.

In this paper, we develop a state-space transformation method, called ε-transformation, that can be used by a search algorithm, such as BnB, to find suboptimal solutions quickly. This method makes use of the phase transition in Figure 1. We analyze its average-case performance. We also present an iterative version of ε-transformation for finding both suboptimal and optimal solutions. Finally, we evaluate the performance of both methods on random trees and the asymmetric traveling salesman problem.

Epsilon-Transformation

ε-transformation is based on the following very simple observation of Figure 1. For a random tree $T(b, d)$, if we can increase the expected number of same-cost children of a node so that $bp_0 \geq 1$, then the expected complexity of finding an optimal goal node becomes polynomial in d. This can be accomplished by raising the probability p_0 of zero-cost edges, since the branching factor b is usually fixed by the structure of the state space. However, increasing p_0 means obtaining a better node-cost function (Zhang & Korf 1994), which requires more information about the problem, and is generally impractical. By sacrificing solution quality, however, we are able to transform the problem of finding an optimal solution with exponential average computation, to the problem of finding a suboptimal solution with polynomial average computation by *artificially* increasing p_0. This is illustrated by Figure 2.

We increase p_0 by setting some non-zero edge costs to zero. To reduce the amount of information lost, and to improve the expected solution quality, we only set to zero those edge costs that are below a particular value

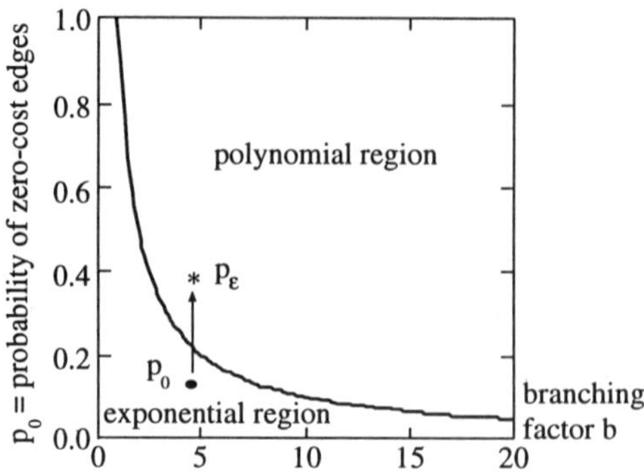

Figure 2: Transform a difficult problem to an easy one.

ε. This is why we call our method ε-transformation. ε is set to the smallest value such that a suboptimal goal node can be found in polynomial average time.

Definition 2 *For a constant ε, an ε-tree $T_\varepsilon(b, d)$ of a random tree $T(b, d)$ is the same as $T(b, d)$, except that those edge costs in $T(b, d)$ that are less than or equal to ε are set to zero in $T_\varepsilon(b, d)$, and the node costs are updated accordingly. The edge and node costs of $T(b, d)$ are referred to as* actual values, *and the edge and node costs of $T_\varepsilon(b, d)$ are called* face values.

ε-transformation converts one random tree to another one with an adjusted edge-cost distribution, *i.e.*, with an increased probability of a zero-cost edge. Let $f(x)$ be the density function and $F(x)$ be the distribution of edge costs. Then the probability that an edge has cost less than or equal to ε is $F(\varepsilon) = \int_0^\varepsilon f(t)dt$, which is also the probability p_ε that an edge of $T_\varepsilon(b, d)$ has cost zero. Figure 3(a) illustrates how ε-transformation adjusts an edge-cost density function. Figure 3(b) shows a $T(2, 2)$ and its corresponding $T_\varepsilon(2, 2)$ with $\varepsilon = 0.25$, where the numbers in the nodes and on the edges are node costs and edge costs, respectively. The optimal goal node of an ε-tree is not necessarily the optimal goal node of its original tree, thus ε-transformation is not guaranteed to find an optimal goal node.

After the transformation, BFS or DFBnB can be used to find an optimal goal node of $T_\varepsilon(b, d)$, and return *the actual value* of this goal node. For simplicity, we call BnB, BFS, or DFBnB using ε-transformation ε-BnB, ε-BFS, or ε-DFBnB, respectively.

In order for ε-BnB to run in polynomial average time, the value of ε is chosen such that $bp_\varepsilon \geq 1$. To maximize the solution quality, we select the minimum ε that satisfies $bp_\varepsilon \geq 1$. That is, we choose

$$\varepsilon^* = \min\{\varepsilon | bp_\varepsilon \geq 1\}, \quad \text{where} \quad p_\varepsilon = F(\varepsilon). \quad (1)$$

When $\varepsilon = \varepsilon^*$, we use the term ε^*-transformation. The performance of ε^*-transformation is summarized by the following theorem.

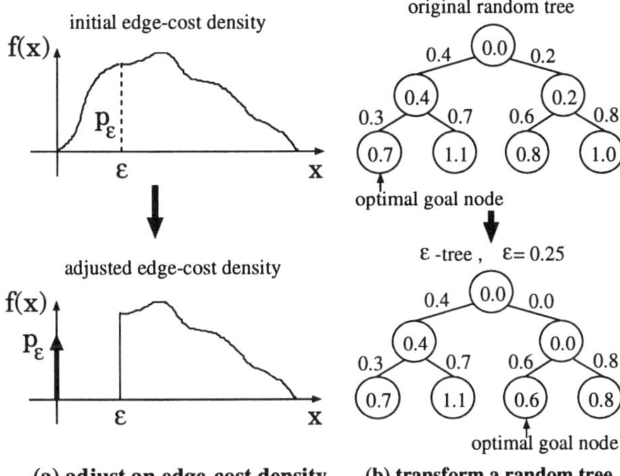

Figure 3: An example of ε-transformation.

Theorem 1 *On a random tree $T(b, d)$ with $bp_0 < 1$, as $d \to \infty$, ε^*-BnB runs in expected time that is at most cubic in d, and finds a goal node whose relative solution cost error $((C - C^*)/C^*$, where C is the solution cost and C^* is the optimal solution cost) is almost surely a constant less than or equal to $(\delta/\alpha - 1)$, where α is a constant as defined in Lemma 1, and $\delta = E[edge\ cost\ x \mid x \leq \varepsilon^*]$.*

Proof: See (Zhang & Pemberton 1994). $\square$

A useful feature of ε-transformation is that a trade-off can be made between the average search efficiency and the average solution quality. Solutions with higher (lower) average costs can be produced with less (greater) average computation by using a larger (smaller) value of ε.

Learning ε and Actual-Value Pruning

The value of ε is a function of the branching factor b and the edge-cost distribution F. For practical problems, b and F are generally not available. Nevertheless, the value of ε can be learned on-line during search. Consider DFBnB as an example. If DFBnB examines the children of the current node in increasing order of their face vales (node ordering), and breaks ties in favor of a node with a lower actual node cost, then the first leaf node reached is the same whether ε-transformation is used or not. DFBnB can sample the branching factors and edge costs of all nodes along the path to the first leaf node, and use them to estimate b and F. As the search proceeds, the estimates of b and F can be refined and used to update the value of ε.

ε-BnB can also use *actual-value pruning*, which prevents BnB from exploring an interior node if its actual value exceeds the actual value u_{av} of the best goal node found up to that point. This pruned interior node cannot lead to a goal node with an actual value less than u_{av}. Intuitively, one might expect actual-value prun-

ing to improve the efficiency of BnB, and not to affect the solution quality. However, actual-value pruning reduces the opportunity to update the face-value upper bound, consequently causing some nodes with higher face value to be expanded, which are not visited by ε-BnB without actual-value pruning. Overall, ε-BnB with and without actual-value pruning explore different parts of the search tree. Their relative effect on runtime and solution quality depends on their relative pruning power and the specific problem instance. Our results on random trees show that ε^*-DFBnB with actual-value pruning runs longer but finds better solutions than ε^*-DFBnB without actual-value pruning.

Iterative ε-Transformation

If we need a better solution than can be guaranteed by ε-transformation, then we can use an ε that is less than ε^*. In order to determine the largest value of ε that satisfies a given error bound, we need to know the optimal solution cost, which in general is not available.

We suggest an algorithmic approach to address this issue, which is called *iterative ε-BnB*. Iterative ε-BnB performs a sequence of BnB searches with a series of ε-transformations, where the value of ε is reduced over successive iterations. The first iteration performs ε^*-BnB. Within each iteration, BnB keeps track of the largest actual edge cost encountered that is *strictly less than ε*, among all those that are set to zero. Call this value fv_{max}. At the end of an iteration, if the cost of the solution found is less than the required solution cost by comparing it to some lower bound, then the algorithm stops. Otherwise, a new value of ε is calculated. The algorithm is then repeated until a satisfactory solution is found.

The most conservative way to update ε is to set $\varepsilon = fv_{max}$. It can be easily shown that if edge costs are integers bounded by a constant, then iterative ε-BnB that uses $\varepsilon = fv_{max}$ in the next iteration expands asymptotically the same number of nodes as ε-BnB that uses the exact value of ε for finding a solution of required quality. In general, however, a small reduction in the value of ε may only cause a few new nodes to be explored in the subsequent iteration, which in turn may lead to a large number of iterations, and consequently a large node-regeneration overhead. Alternatively, we may decrease the value of ε by a larger amount, such as $\varepsilon = fv_{max}/2$.

Experimental Study

In this section, we identify the conditions under which ε-transformation and iterative ε-transformation are effective. To this end, we compare ε-DFBnB and iterative ε-DFBnB with other approximation algorithms.

Iterative ε-DFBnB can be used in the same way as truncated DFBnB (Ibaraki *et al.* 1983; Zhang 1993) to find approximate and optimal solutions. Truncated DFBnB is a DFBnB that terminates prematurely when the total available computation has been exhausted.

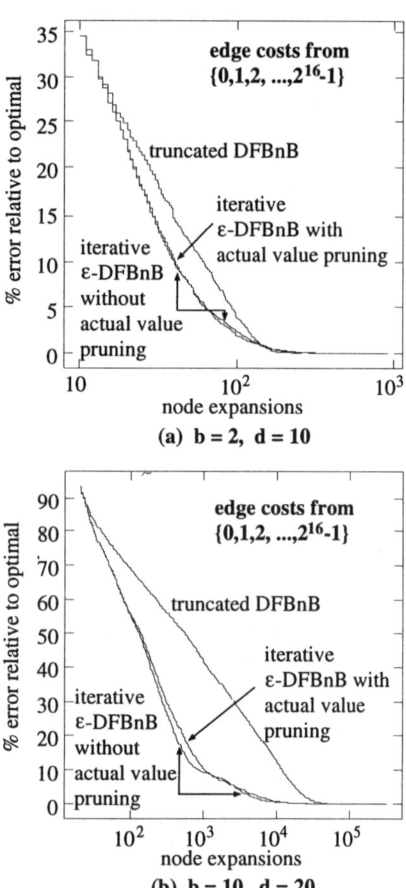

Figure 4: Iterative ε-DFBnB vs. truncated DFBnB.

The best solution found up to that point can then be taken as an approximation. The main difference between these two algorithms is that the territory explored by iterative ε-DFBnB is generally smaller than the territory explored by truncated DFBnB, although iterative ε-DFBnB may re-expand a node many times.

Local search (Johnson 1990; Kanellakis & Papadimitriou 1980; Lin & Kernighan 1973) is a well-known approximation method for many difficult combinatorial problems. Starting at an initial solution, such as one generated by a polynomial-time approximation algorithm, local search continuously improves the current solution by local perturbations, until no further improvement can be made. This process may be invoked many times with different initial solutions. A serious drawback of local search is that it cannot determine if the best solution found so far is optimal, unless the optimal solution cost is already known.

Random Trees

We ran both iterative ε-DFBnB and truncated DFBnB on the same set of random trees, and recorded the total number of node expansions when either algorithm updated its current best solution. We then measure their

performance as the average solution cost for a given number of node expansions, since expanding a node is the primary operation. In our experiments, the value of ε was updated to $fv_{max}/2$ after each iteration.

Figure 4 shows our results on uniform random trees $T(b = 2, d = 10)$ and $T(b = 10, d = 20)$. The edge costs are uniformly chosen from $\{0, 1, 2, \cdots, 2^{16} - 1\}$. The results are averaged over 1000 trials. The horizontal axes, on a logarithmic scale, are the average number of node expansions, and the vertical axes are the average relative goal cost error. Figure 4 indicates that iterative ε-DFBnB without actual-value pruning is slightly better than with actual-value pruning. Compared to truncated DFBnB, iterative ε-DFBnB finds a better solution with the same average number of node expansions. For instance, at 1000 node expansions in Figure 4(b), the relative error for iterative ε-DFBnB is 10.4%, while the relative error for truncated DFBnB is 40.4%. The results also show that when the branching factor and tree depth are increased (from Figure 4(a) to 4(b)), iterative ε-DFBnB further outperforms truncated DFBnB.

The relative advantage of iterative ε-transformation also depends on the edge-cost distribution. Specifically, the relative improvement in average solution cost of ε-DFBnB over truncated DFBnB decreases when the probability of a zero-cost edge is increased.

Asymmetric Traveling Salesman Problem

The asymmetric traveling salesman problem (ATSP) is an NP-hard combinatorial problem (Garey & Johnson 1979). Given n cities and an *asymmetric* matrix $(c_{i,j})$ that defines a cost between each pair of cities, the ATSP is to find a minimum-cost tour that visits each city exactly once and returns to the starting city. The ATSP can be optimally solved by BnB, using the solution cost of the related assignment problem (AP) (Papadimitriou & Steiglitz 1982) as a monotonic heuristic function. The state space of the ATSP under BnB is a tree without duplicate nodes. See (Balas & Toth 1985) for a description of the method.

In our implementation of ε-DFBnB and iterative εDFBnB, we used the sampling method described above to learn the value of ε^* for the first iteration. In each subsequent iteration, the value of ε was set to $fv_{max}/2$. From our experiments, ε-DFBnB without actual-value pruning performs worse than ε-DFBnB with actual-value pruning, and thus we present the results of ε-DFBnB with actual-value pruning.

We used many different cost matrices in our experiments. Our data shows that iterative ε-DFBnB finds better solutions sooner than truncated DFBnB on average, and local search performs much worse than ε-DFBnB and truncated DFBnB. Figure 5(a) compares ε-DFBnB with truncated DFBnB on 500-city random ATSP's, where costs $c_{i,j}$ are uniformly chosen from $\{0, 1, 2, \cdots, 2^{16} - 1\}$. The results are averaged over 100 trials. The horizontal axis is the CPU time on a

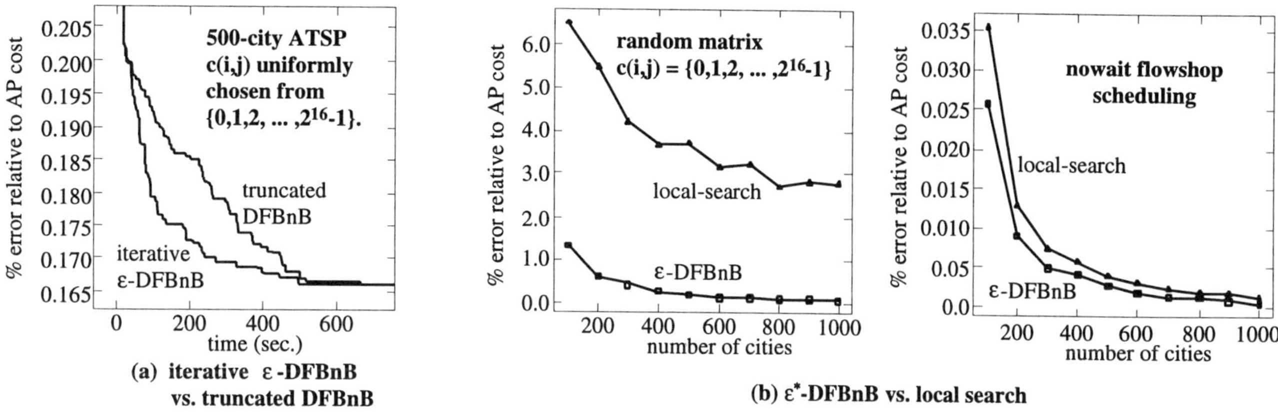

Figure 5: Iterative ε-DFBnB vs. truncated DFBnB and local search on the asymmetric TSP.

Sun4/sparc460 workstation, and the vertical axis is the average relative solution cost error with respect to the AP lower bound.

We also compared ε^*-DFBnB with a local search method (Papadimitriou & Kanellakis 1980) which was applied five times for each problem instance in our experiments. The five different initial tours were generated by the nearest-neighbor, nearest insertion, farthest insertion, greedy algorithms, and the patching algorithm (Johnson 1990; Karp 1979). We used random cost matrices and matrices converted from no-wait flowshop scheduling for four machines, which is NP-hard (Kanellakis & Papadimitriou 1980). No-wait flowshop scheduling involves determining a sequence for processing a set of jobs where each job must be handled by a set of machines in the same preset order. The objective is a sequence that minimizes a cost function, such as total completion time, which was used in our experiments. The no-wait constraint additionally requires the next machine to be available when a job is ready for it. The scheduling problem instances were generated by uniformly choosing the processing time of a job on a machine from $\{0, 1, 2, \cdots, 2^{16} - 1\}$. We then converted them into ATSP's using the method in (Reddi & Ramamoorthy 1972).

Local search runs much longer than ε^*-DFBnB on average for the problem instances we considered, because we used five initial tours for local search. Figure 5(b) shows the solution quality, expressed as the average tour cost error relative to the AP lower bound, versus the number of cities. Each data point is averaged over 100 trials. The results show that ε^*-DFBnB outperforms local search: it finds better solutions than local search on average even though local search was allowed to use more computation.

Related Work

Phase transitions of heuristic search were originally revealed by Karp and Pearl (Karp & Pearl 1983). Their results have been extended by McDiarmid and Provan

(McDiarmid 1990; McDiarmid & Provan 1991), and Zhang and Korf (Zhang & Korf 1993; 1994) to random trees with arbitrary branching factors and real-valued edge costs. Huberman and Hogg (Huberman & Hogg 1987) argued that phase transitions are universal in large intelligent systems. Cheeseman et al. (Cheeseman, Kanefsky, & Taylor 1991) empirically showed that phase transitions exist in many NP-hard combinatorial optimization problems.

In their seminal paper, Karp and Pearl (Karp & Pearl 1983) also proposed an algorithm that finds a suboptimal goal node of a tree most of the time, but may fail sometimes, and runs in expected time linear in the tree depth. McDiarmid and Provan (McDiarmid 1990; McDiarmid & Provan 1991) extended Karp and Pearl's approximation algorithm to a general random tree. One problem with Karp and Pearl's algorithm is that it is incomplete, meaning that it is not guaranteed to find a goal node. Furthermore, the algorithm uses parameters that depend on the optimal goal cost, which is generally unknown, and hence their algorithm is difficult to apply in practice.

It is well known in the operations research community that approximate solutions can be obtained by prematurely terminating DFBnB, taking the best solution found so far as an approximation. This method is also referred to as truncated DFBnB (Zhang 1993), which we adopted in this paper. The earliest study of this method that we found was made by Ashour (Ashour 1970). Ibaraki et al. (Ibaraki et al. 1983) systematically studied approximation methods based on BnB, which they called *suboptimal BnB algorithms*.

Conclusions

We have presented a new method, called ε-transformation, that can be used by branch-and-bound (BnB) to find approximate solutions to combinatorial problems. This method is a state-space transformation, which exploits the computational phase transitions of tree search problems. On a random tree, ε-BnB runs in expected time that is cubic in the search depth, and finds a suboptimal goal node whose expected relative solution cost error is bounded by a small constant. We also developed an iterative version of ε-transformation to find both approximate and optimal solutions.

On random trees with large numbers of distinct edge costs, large branching factors, and deep goal nodes, iterative ε-DFBnB outperforms truncated DFBnB, finding better solutions sooner on average. On the asymmetric traveling salesman problem, ε-DFBnB outperforms a local search method, and iterative ε-DFBnB is superior to truncated DFBnB.

Overall, we recommend that ε-transformation be used for problems whose search trees have a small probability of a zero-cost edge and large branching factors.

To our knowledge, ε-transformation is the first attempt to exploit phase transitions in order to solve combinatorial problems. Since phase transitions exist in many intelligent systems and combinatorial problems, we hope that the idea of ε-transformation can be carried over to other problems and search methods.

Acknowledgment

The authors are grateful to Colin McDiarmid and Judea Pearl for helpful discussions, and to the anonymous reviewers for comments. Special thanks to Rich Korf for support, discussions and comments.

References

Ashour, S. 1970. An experimental investigation and comparative evaluation of flow-shop scheduling techniques. *Operations Research* 18:541–545.

Balas, E., and Toth, P. 1985. Branch and bound methods. In *Traveling Salesman Problem*. Essex: John Wiley and Sons, Essex. 361–401.

Cheeseman, P.; Kanefsky, B.; and Taylor, W. M. 1991. Where the really hard problems are. In *Proc. 12th IJCAI*, 331–337.

Garey, M. R., and Johnson, D. S. 1979. *Computers and Intractability*. New York, NY: Freeman.

Huberman, B. A., and Hogg, T. 1987. Phase transitions in artificial intelligence systems. *Artificial Intelligence* 33:155–171.

Ibaraki, T.; Muro, S.; Murakami, T.; and Hasegawa, T. 1983. Using branch-and-bound algorithms to obtain suboptimal solutions. *Zeitchrift für Operations Research* 27:177–202.

Johnson, D. S. 1990. Local optimization and the traveling salesman problem. In *Proc. 17th Intern. Colloquium on Automata, Languages and Programming*.

Kanellakis, P. C., and Papadimitriou, C. H. 1980. Local search for the asymmetric traveling salesman problem. *Operations Research* 28:1086–1099.

Karp, R. M., and Pearl, J. 1983. Searching for an optimal path in a tree with random costs. *Artificial Intelligence* 21:99–117.

Karp, R. M. 1979. A patching algorithm for the nonsymmetric traveling-salesman problem. *SIAM J. Comput.* 8:561–573.

Korf, R. E. 1989. Search: A survey of recent results. In *Exploring Artificial Intelligence*. Morgan Kaufmann. 197–237.

Kumar, V. 1992. Search branch-and-bound. In *Encyclopedia of Artificial Intelligence*. New York: Wiley-Interscience, 2nd edition. 1468–1472.

Lin, S., and Kernighan, B. W. 1973. An effective heuristic algorithm for the traveling salesman problem. *Operations Research* 21:498–516.

McDiarmid, C. J. H., and Provan, G. M. A. 1991. An expected-cost analysis of backtracking and non-backtracking algorithms. In *Proc. 12th IJCAI*, 172–177.

McDiarmid, C. J. H. 1990. Probabilistic analysis of tree search. In *Disorder in Physical Systems*. Oxford Science. 249–260.

Mitchell, D.; Selman, B.; and Levesque, H. 1992. Hard and easy distributions of SAT problems. In *Proc. 10th AAAI*, 459–465.

Papadimitriou, C. H., and Kanellakis, P. 1980. Flow-shop scheduling with limited temporary storage. *J. of ACM* 27:533–549.

Papadimitriou, C. H., and Steiglitz, K. 1982. *Combinatorial Optimization: Algorithms and Complexity*. Englewood Cliffs, NJ: Prentice-Hall.

Pearl, J. 1984. *Heuristics*. Reading, MA: Addison-Wesley.

Reddi, S., and Ramamoorthy, C. 1972. On the flow-shop sequencing problem with no wait in process. *Operational Research Quarterly* 23:323–331.

Rényi, A. 1970. *Probability Theory*. Amsterdam: North-Holland.

Zhang, W., and Korf, R. E. 1992. An average-case analysis of branch-and-bound with applications: Summary of results. In *Proc. 10th AAAI*, 545–550.

Zhang, W., and Korf, R. E. 1993. Depth-first vs. best-first search: New results. In *Proc. 11th AAAI*, 769–775.

Zhang, W., and Korf, R. E. 1994. Performance of linear-space search algorithms. *Artificial Intelligence* to appear.

Zhang, W., and Pemberton, J. C. 1994. Epsilon-transformation: Exploiting phase transitions to solve combinatorial optimization problems. Technical Report UCLA-CSD-940003, Computer Science Department, University of California, Los Angeles, CA.

Zhang, W. 1993. Truncated branch-and-bound: A case study on the asymmetric TSP. In *Working Notes of AAAI-93 Spring Symp.: AI and NP-Hard Problems*, 160–166.

Nonmonotonic Reasoning

A Preference-Based Approach to Default Reasoning: Preliminary Report

James P. Delgrande
School of Computing Science,
Simon Fraser University,
Burnaby, B.C.,
Canada V5A 1S6
email: jim@cs.sfu.ca

Abstract

An approach to nonmonotonic inference, based on preference orderings between possible worlds or states of affairs, is presented. We begin with an extant weak theory of default conditionals; using this theory, orderings on worlds are derived. The idea is that if a conditional such as "birds fly" is true then, all other things being equal, worlds in which birds fly are preferred over those where they don't. In this case, a red bird would fly by virtue of red-bird-worlds being among the least exceptional worlds in which birds fly. In this approach, irrelevant properties are correctly handled, as is specificity, reasoning within exceptional circumstances, and inheritance reasoning. A sound proof-theoretic characterisation is also given. Lastly, the approach is shown to subsume that of conditional entailment.

Introduction

In any approach to nonmonotonic reasoning there are several principles that one would want to hold. For example, suppose that we are given that birds fly, birds have wings, penguins necessarily are birds, and penguins don't fly. We can write this as:

$$\{B \rightarrow F,\ B \rightarrow W,\ P \Rightarrow B,\ P \rightarrow \neg F\}. \qquad (1)$$

According to the principle of *specificity*, a more specific default should apply over a less specific default. Thus if we were given that P is true, we would want to conclude $\neg F$ by default, since being a penguin is a more specific notion than that of being a bird. This would be the case even if we were given that penguins normally are birds, $P \rightarrow B$. Second, one should obtain *inheritance* of properties by default. So, given that P is true, one would also want to conclude (assuming no information to the contrary) that W was true, and so penguins have wings by virtue of being birds. Third, *irrelevant* properties should be properly handled and so, all other things being equal, we would want to conclude that a green bird flies.

Unfortunately, it has proven difficult to specify an approach that achieves just the right balance of properties. In the last few years much attention has been paid to weaker systems of default inferencing, including (Del87; KLM90; Pea90; Bou92; GP92; Gol92). As discussed in the next section, while these systems may have some very nice properties, none handles all of specificity, inheritance, and relevance adequately. On the other hand, stronger systems, such as (McC80; Rei80; Moo85; Poo88), which handle inheritance and relevance well, do not explicitly deal with specificity. For example, in the naïve representation of Example 1 above in Default Logic, if P is true we still obtain an extension (i.e. a set of default conclusions) in which F is true; one is required to use semi-normal defaults to block this extension.

The approach presented here is based on the notion of *preferential model structures*, explored in depth in (Sho88), but going back at least to (McC80) in Artificial Intelligence, and with roots extending at least to (Sta68; Lew73). The idea is that (some) sentence is valid, not when it is true in all models, but when it is true in some *preferred* subset of models. In the approach presented here though, preference will be expressed not in terms of models, but rather in terms of orderings on worlds or "possible states of affairs" – thus the formalism will be phrased in a modal context. In any case, we begin with a particular weak approach to default reasoning; this supplies us with a notion of preference. If, for example, we have a default $A \rightarrow B$, then this default *prefers* a world in which $A \supset B$ is true over a world in which $A \wedge \neg B$ is true. From a set of defaults then we obtain orderings on worlds. A formula B follows by default from A just when, in each ordering, in the least (in terms of preference) worlds in which A is true, B is true also. Thus, given only the default $A \rightarrow B$, then *all* $A \wedge B$ worlds are preferred to all $A \wedge \neg B$ worlds. In particular, for example, all $A \wedge C \wedge B$ worlds are preferred to all $A \wedge C \wedge \neg B$ worlds and so B follows by default in this structure from $A \wedge C$.

Clearly though there are complicating factors in this notion of preference. For example, given that birds fly and that elephants are grey (i.e. $B \rightarrow F$ and $E \rightarrow G$), we would want to prefer a world in which $BFEG$[1] is

---

[1]For readability I will indicate conjunction at times by

true over one in which $BFE\neg G$ is true or one in which $B\neg FE\neg G$ is true. However we want no preference to obtain between a $B\neg FEG$ world and a $BFE\neg G$ world. Similarly, for Example 1, since the notion of penguinhood is more specific than that of birdhood, we would want a $BP\neg F$ world to be preferred over a BPF world.

Lastly, the notion of preference given by a default should be *semantic* rather than *syntactic*. That is, in Example 1, we have from $B \to W$ that (all other things being equal) worlds in which birds have wings are to be preferred to those where they do not. However, what about two worlds, one in which $B\neg PF$ is true and another in which BPF is true? The *set* of defaults is of no help here; nonetheless it *follows* in our logic of defaults that birds are not normally penguins, and so the first world is preferred to the second.

The appropriateness of the approach is argued from a number of directions. First and most importantly, the approach, like any semantic approach, (hopefully) formalises plausible and sound intuitions. Second, a number of examples are presented and are argued to be appropriately handled here. These include common "benchmark" problems as well as particularly nasty (in the author's view) examples that have not (to the author's knowledge) appeared in the literature. Lastly a proof-theoretic analogue, motivated by complementary intuitions is presented and shown to be sound with respect to the semantic formulation.

The next section discusses the background. In after this an extant logic of defaults is briefly presented, followed by the formal details of the approach. This is followed by a discussion and a brief concluding section. Proofs of theorems and further details are to be found in (Del94).

Background

Related Work

Approaches to default reasoning can be broadly characterised as falling into one of two groups: *weak* systems wherein some desirable default inferences are not obtained, and *strong* systems, wherein unwanted inferences may be obtained. Many of the earlier and better-studied systems of default reasoning fall into the "strong" category. Autoepistemic Logic (Moo85), Circumscription (McC80), Default Logic (Rei80), and Theorist (Poo88) are examples of approaches that may be overly *permissive* and that do not explicitly deal with specificity information. Again, in the naïve representation of Example 1 we obtain a set of default conclusions in which, given P, F is also true. Various modifications and restrictions have been proposed to handle such difficulties in each of these systems, but the application of these modifications is necessarily outside of the system. Without a formal theory, it is not clear if such modifications are appropriate or in any sense complete. Moreover, since defaults per se are not part

means of juxtaposition.

of the formal system, one cannot reason *about* defaults. Thus, as an example, one could not conclude from Example 1 that birds are not normally penguins.

Recently, much attention has been paid to weaker systems of default inferencing. In fact, given the essential similarity among systems such as N (Del87), ϵ-entailment (Pea88) (or 0-entailment or p-entailment (Ada75)), preferential entailment (KLM90), and CT4 (Bou92), among others, it would seem that some consensus has been reached as to what should constitute a "minimal" system of default reasoning. As (Pea89) suggests with respect to 0-entailment, such systems may be taken as specifying a *conservative core* or set of inferences that ought to be common to all nonmonotonic inference systems.[2] These approaches deal satisfactorily with specificity. However, not unexpectedly, they are much too weak. In particular relevance and inheritance of properties are not handled. Hence, even though a penguin may be assumed to not fly by default (i.e. in Example 1 we only derive $\neg F$ but not F), a green bird cannot be assumed to fly by default (since it is *conceivable* that greenness is relevant to flight).

There has also been less agreement on how to strengthen these weak systems. One approach has been to assume things are as simple (or unexceptional) as possible. Again, some convergence is obtained with System **Z** and 1-entailment (Pea90), rational closure (KLM90), and CO^* (Bou92). These approaches handle relevance well. However they fail to allow full inheritance of properties; moreover (see (GP92)) they allow some unwanted specificity relations. This locus of approaches has been extended in various ways, including (GP91; GMP90; BCD$^+$93); all however suffer from one or another of the deficiencies of the original approach.

Of other approaches, (Del88) gives a syntactic strengthening of defaults using meta-theoretic assumptions; consequently, as with the strong approaches, it is difficult to formally characterise the set of default inferences. (GP92) presents another strengthening of the above-mentioned "conservative core", called *conditional entailment*. There are two difficulties with this approach: first that it is quite complex in its formulation and, second, that it does not sanction inheritance of default properties. The present approach however subsumes conditional entailment. This relation is discussed further after the approach is presented.

Examples

The example given at the outset is perhaps overly familiar; however it illustrates the principles of specificity, inheritance, and relevance. The following, involving ravens, albinoism, and blackness, is closely re-

---

[2]Of course this is not entirely uncontentious: (Gab85) and (LM92) suggest a weaker "core", while the logic of defaults used here is slightly stronger than Pearl's conservative core.

lated:

$$\{R \rightarrow Bl, R \wedge Al \rightarrow \neg Bl\}. \qquad (2)$$

Again, specificity dictates that Bl should be concluded given R, but that $\neg BL$ should be concluded given $R \wedge Al$. Also, given R (arguably) one would want to conclude $\neg Al$.

Similar remarks apply to conflicting defaults. Consider the standard Quaker/republican example:

$$\{Q \rightarrow P, R \rightarrow \neg P\}. \qquad (3)$$

Given only Q, we would want to conclude P. Given $Q \wedge R$ we would want to conclude nothing concerning P. However if we add the default $Q \wedge R \rightarrow \neg P$ then clearly, given $Q \wedge R$ we would now want to conclude $\neg P$.

The preceding examples are standard (although no extant theory of nonmonotonic reasoning appears to handle all cases). The next examples however seem to the author to be particularly nasty.

$$\{B \rightarrow W, W \rightarrow F\} \qquad (4)$$

This example seems innocuous: birds have wings and winged things fly. The difficulty is that there are cases (for example, in inheritance) where we would want the default $B \rightarrow W$ to take priority over $W \rightarrow F$ even though there is no explicit conflict. In terms of preference among worlds, we would want a $(B \supset W) \wedge W \neg F$ world (where the second conditional is falsified) to be preferred to a $B \neg W \wedge (W \supset F)$ world (where the first conditional is falsified). The difficulty is that there is no specific conflict between B and W. In (Del94) we argue that this is the reason that conditional entailment fails to allow full inheritance reasoning.

$$\{A_1 \rightarrow B_1, A_2 \rightarrow B_2, A_3 \rightarrow B_3, \} \text{ but } \neg(B_1 \wedge B_2 \wedge B_3). \qquad (5)$$

In this example we have some number of independent defaults (here three) which cannot be jointly applied. In (the appropriate extension to) System $\mathbf{Z}$ and related systems, all defaults are at the same "level", and so if a default is falsified, no default conclusions can be drawn.[3] In these approaches, n levels (again, here three) are wanted, corresponding to the number of possible default violations. Thus, we would want to conclude B_1 by default from $A_1 \wedge A_2$. However we don't want to conclude B_1 from $A_1 \wedge A_2 \wedge A_3$ (since by symmetry we would have to also conclude B_2 and B_3, which is inconsistent, or else revert to the notion of an extension). Note though that from $A_1 \wedge A_2 \wedge A_3$ we would want to conclude that two of the default conclusions are true, even though we don't know which:

$$(B_1 B_2 \neg B_3) \vee (B_1 \neg B_2 B_3) \vee (\neg B_1 B_2 B_3).$$

---

[3]The approach of maximum entropy (GMP90) appears to handle this example well, but is problematic for other reasons.

If a default is violated, we would still want to carry out default inferences. Hence, given $A_1 A_2 A_3 \neg B_3$ we would want to conclude $B_1 B_2$. Given $A_1 A_2 \neg B_2 A_3 \neg B_3$ we would want to conclude B_1.

$$\{B_1 \rightarrow C_1, B_2 \rightarrow C_2, A \rightarrow (B_1 \neg C_1) \vee (B_2 \neg C_2)\}. \qquad (6)$$

The problem here is that we know that the third default is more specific than one of the first two; however we don't know which. (Alternately, in the "context" A, one of the other defaults is violated, and therefore inapplicable, but we don't know which.) This example again generalises to n defaults. In System $\mathbf{Z}$ (and so in equivalent systems and generalisations) B_1 and B_2 are assumed to be less specific than A; however, if *one of* B_1 and B_2 are less specific than A it doesn't seem intuitive to then assume that *both of* B_1 and B_2 are less specific than A. Or if this doesn't seem implausible here, it presumably does if we increase the number of defaults that are falsified by A.

A Logic of Defaults

We begin with a theory of defaults corresponding essentially to an extension of the "conservative core" suggested in (Pea89) for default inferences. While we could have used any of the systems cited in the section on previous work, for uniformity with the approach to be presented we will use a *conditional logic* formulation for default properties. See for example (Del87; Bou92) for a further exposition, details, etc. on the formal system.

The fundamental idea is straightforward: worlds are arranged according to a notion of "exceptionalness"; a default $A \rightarrow B$ is true just when there is a world in which $A \wedge B$ is true and, in all worlds that are not more exceptional, $A \supset B$ is true at those worlds. Thus, roughly, "birds fly", $B \rightarrow F$, is true if, in the least exceptional worlds in which there are birds, birds fly. Intuitively, we factor out exceptional circumstances such as being a penguin, having a broken wing, etc., and then say that birds fly if they fly in such "unexceptional" circumstances.

More formally, we let $\mathcal{L}$ be the language of propositional logic (PC) augmented with a binary operator $\rightarrow$. (We reserve $\supset$ for material implication.) For simplicity we restrict the language so that there are no nested occurrences of the $\rightarrow$ operator. Sentences of $\mathcal{L}$ are interpreted in terms of a *model* $M = \langle W, E, P \rangle$ where:

1. W is a set (of worlds),

2. E binary *accessibility* relation on worlds, with the following properties:

   Reflexive: Eww for every $w \in W$.

   Transitive: If $Ew_1 w_2$ and $Ew_2 w_3$ then $Ew_1 w_3$.

   Forward Connected: If $Ew_1 w_2$ and $Ew_1 w_3$ then $Ew_2 w_3$ or $Ew_3 w_2$.

3. P is a mapping of atomic sentences and worlds onto $\{0, 1\}$.

Truth at a world w in model M ($\models_w^M$) is as for PC, except that:

$\models_w^M A \to B$ iff there is a w_1 such that Ew, w_1 and $\models_{w_1}^M A \wedge B$ and for every w_2 where Ew_1, w_2, we have $\models_{w_2}^M A \supset B$, *or* for every w_1 where Ew, w_1 we have $\models_{w_1}^M \neg A$.

We define $\Box A$ as $\neg A \to A$ (read "necessarily A") and we define $A \Rightarrow B$ as $\Box(A \supset B)$ (read "necessarily A implies B" or "A strictly implies B").

Thus the accessibility relation between worlds is defined so that from a particular world w one "sees" a sequence of successively "less exceptional" sets of worlds. $A \to B$ is true just when (trivially) A is false at all accessible worlds, or there is a world in which $A \wedge B$ is true, and $A \supset B$ is true at all equally or less accessible worlds.

Space considerations preclude a lengthy discussion of this logic (or, indeed, any of the other "equivalent" weak systems). Suffice to say however that this system supplies us with a weak, but semantically justified, system of default inferencing: Given a set of defaults and strict implications Γ, B follows by default from A just when B is true in the least A worlds in all models of Γ. Hence (as previously discussed) from Example 1 we can conclude that a penguin does not fly, while a bird does; and if something flies then it is not a penguin. However we cannot conclude that green birds fly (since there are models in which green birds do not fly), nor can we conclude that penguins have (or *inherit*) wings. However this approach does provide us with a rich notion of specificity, and we can use this notion of specificity, as described next, to specify a system wherein relevance and inheritance are properly handled, as are the previously-described examples.

The Approach

The general idea of the overall approach is straightforward. If a default $A \to B$ is true in the original default theory, then this default *prefers* a world in which the material counterpart (viz. $A \supset B$) is true over a world in which it is false. The (weak) logic of defaults also provides us with a notion of specificity between formulas. We say that a world w_1 *is preferred* to a world w_2 just when there is a default that prefers w_1 to w_2, and, if there is a conditional that prefers w_2 to w_1, then there is a conditional that "overrides" this conditional and prefers w_1 to w_2. Thus, essentially, there is some reason to prefer w_1 to w_2, and if there is any reason to prefer w_2 to w_1 then there is a stronger reason to prefer w_1 to w_2.

More formally, a default theory T consists of a set of default and strict (necessary) conditionals. We take T to be closed under logical consequence in the logic of the previous section. Thus we will write $T \models A \to B$ to mean that $A \to B$ is true in all models of T; we

sometimes also write $A \to B \in T$. Given a default theory T, we first define a *specificity* ordering on formulas, given by $\prec$:

Definition 1

$$A \prec_T B \quad iff \quad T \models A \vee B \to \neg B \ and \ T \models \neg\Box\neg A.$$

Since the default theory T is always understood, for simplicity I will henceforth write just $A \prec B$. The right hand side of the definition says that for every model of T, at some $A \vee B$ world, w, $\neg B$ is true, and $A \vee B \supset \neg B$ is true at all equally- or less exceptional worlds. Since worlds are consistent, this means that at w it must be that A is true, and that there are no equivalently-exceptional or less exceptional worlds in which B is true. (If there were such a world in which B was true then this would also be a least $A \vee B$ world, contradicting $A \vee B \to \neg B$.) Furthermore, there is an accessible A world.

We have that $\prec$ is irreflexive, asymmetric, and transitive; also, $\prec$ and $\to$ are interdefinable (Lew73). The following will also be convenient:

$$A \preceq B \stackrel{\text{def}}{=} \neg(B \prec A).$$

Separately, we will also deal with the full set of mappings of the set of atomic sentences $\mathbf{P}$ onto $\{0, 1\}$; for simplicity we assume that $\mathbf{P}$ is finite. These mappings we will call "worlds". From the theory T, we will specify partial orders on these worlds; these partial orders will constitute our ultimate preference structure, with respect to which we will define a stronger notion of default reasoning.

Definition 2 $\mathcal{W} = \{f \mid f : \mathbf{P} \to \{0, 1\}\}$.

Elements of $\mathcal{W}$ will be denoted $w, w_1, w_2, \ldots$. I will also write $w \models A$ if $A \in \mathcal{L}$ is true under the standard (PC) valuation in the mapping w.[4]

Defaults in T provide a basic preference notion on worlds, as follows:

Definition 3
For default theory T and $w_1, w_2 \in \mathcal{W}$, a conditional $A \to B$ prefers w_1 to w_2 iff

1. $T \models A \to B$,

2. $w_1 \models A \supset B$,

3. $w_2 \models A \wedge \neg B$.

Definition 4
For default theory T and $w_1, w_2 \in \mathcal{W}$, we have:
$Pref(w_1, w_2) =$
$\quad \{A \to B \in T \mid A \to B \ prefers \ w_1 \ to \ w_2\}$.

---

[4]This means that $\models$ is used ambiguously: for a logical consequence of a default theory T, and for a true sentence at a world – compare condition 1. with conditions 2. and 3. in Definition 3. Since these are distinct relations, hopefully no confusion results.

There is one difficulty with specificity orderings, and that is that they may be incomplete, in the sense that we may have $B_1 \vee B_2 \prec A$ but neither $B_1 \prec A$ nor $B_2 \prec A$ (recall Example 6). We define the set of complete (in the above sense) orderings as follows:

Definition 5
Given a default theory T, a specificity ordering is extended to a full specificity ordering by:

if $B_1 \vee B_2 \prec A$ and it is not the case that $B_1 \prec A$ then $B_2 \prec A$.

We are now in a position to define orderings on worlds:

Definition 6
Given a full specificity ordering, a preference ordering $\mathcal{P} = \langle \mathcal{W}, < \rangle$ is defined as follows:

For $w_1, w_2 \in \mathcal{W}$, we have $w_1 < w_2$ iff

1. *$Pref(w_1, w_2) \neq \emptyset$ and*
2. *for every $C \to D \in Pref(w_2, w_1)$ there is some $A \to B \in Pref(w_1, w_2)$ such that $C \preceq A$ and it is not the case that $A \preceq C$.*

$\Pi_T = \{\mathcal{P} \mid \mathcal{P}$ *is a preference ordering with respect to default theory $T\}$.*

That is, $w_1 < w_2$ iff

1. there is some conditional that prefers w_1 to w_2, and
2. for a conditional that prefers w_2 to w_1 there is a conditional that is no less specific than it and that prefers w_1 to w_2, but the converse does not hold.

Consider again Example 1:

$$\{B \to F, B \to W, P \Rightarrow B, P \to \neg F\}.$$

First, we have $B \prec P$, since we can prove in the logic that $B \vee P \to \neg P$ is a logical consequence of this theory. If we have worlds

$$w_1: \quad B, P, \neg F, W \qquad w_2: \quad B, P, F, W$$

then:
$$Pref(w_1, w_2) = \{P \to \neg F\} \quad \text{and}$$
$$Pref(w_2, w_1) = \{B \to F\}.$$
Hence $w_1 < w_2$. Things remain unchanged if instead $\neg W$ is true at both worlds.

Consider next Example 4:

$$\{W \to F, B \to W\}.$$

We have $W \preceq B$, but in the full specificity order we do not have $B \preceq W$. For

$$w_1: \quad B, W, \neg F \qquad w_2: \quad B, \neg W, F$$

we have:
$$Pref(w_1, w_2) = \{B \to W\} \quad \text{and}$$
$$Pref(w_2, w_1) = \{W \to F\}.$$
Hence $w_1 < w_2$.

We can now define the notion of a default inference based on preference orderings:

Definition 7
B follows as a preferential default inference from A in theory T, written $A \hspace{0.1em}\vdash_T B$, iff

for every $\mathcal{P} \in \Pi_T$, for every w_2 where $w_2 \models A \wedge \neg B$ there is a w_1 where $w_1 \models A \wedge B$, and $w_1 < w_2$.

First of all, preference orderings are indeed orderings:

Theorem 1
For a preference ordering $\mathcal{P}$ and $w_1, w_2, w_3 \in \mathcal{W}$:

1. *$w_1 \not< w_1$.*
2. *If $w_1 < w_2$ then $w_2 \not< w_1$.*
3. *If $w_1 < w_2$ and $w_2 < w_3$ then $w_1 < w_3$.*

Second, these orderings preserve truth in the original default theory:

Theorem 2
If $T \models A \to B$ then $A \hspace{0.1em}\vdash_T B$.

This then concludes the development of the semantical aspects of the approach. However, before discussing properties of this approach, we first give a proof-theoretic characterisation. For this characterisation, the central idea is that beginning with a theory T, we "appropriately" strengthen the elements of T. For example, in Example 1 we have the default $B \to F$; it would seem safe to allow also that $B \wedge Gr \to F$, or "green birds fly", since there is nothing in the theory that would make us believe otherwise. On the other hand we would not want to allow that $B \wedge P \to F$, since here there is a reason to believe that this conditional may not hold, namely that we have $P \to \neg F$. We can informally state this principle of irrelevance as:

Unless there is reason to believe that a property is relevant to the truth of a conditional, assume that it is irrelevant.

We will call a default *supported* if there is a reason to hold it, based on this notion of relevance, even though it may not be a logical consequence of T. A set of defaults Γ is supported iff every default in Γ is supported. The formal definition is straightforward, if a bit long-winded:

Definition 8
$A \to B$ is supported in a default theory T iff

1. *$T \models A \to B$, or*
2. *If Γ is supported and $\Gamma \models A \to B$ then $A \to B$ is supported, or*
3. *(a) $T \models A \to A'$ but $T \not\models A' \to A$ and $A' \to B$ is supported, and*
   (b) if $T \models A \to A''$ but $A'' \to \neg B$ is supported then $T \models A' \vee A'' \to \neg A'$.

Thus, in the first two parts, a conditional is supported if it is a consequence of T or of a set of supported conditionals. For the third part, (a) states that there is a reason to accept the conditional: for some strictly less specific formula A', we have the supported conditional $A' \to B$. For part (b), if there is also a less specific formula A'' that denies B, then this formula is strictly less specific than A'. So in this last case we could say that A' "overrides" A''.

At present, we have a "soundness" result, in that the consequent of a supported conditional follows as a preferential default inference from the antecedent:

Theorem 3

If $A \to B$ is supported in T then $A \mathrel{\vdash_T} B$.

I believe that the converse also holds, but have yet to show a rigorous proof. Nonetheless the partial result provides a second, intuitive, indication of what default inferences may be obtained.

Discussion

Conditional entailment (GP92) was formulated in part as an attempt to reconcile what has been called here "strong" and "weak" approaches to nonmonotonic reasoning. For the approach at hand, the methodology was to formulate from first principles a notion of preference between worlds, based on an extant logic of defaults. However, as noted earlier, there are strong similarities between the systems; it proves to be the case that the default inferences sanctioned by the present approach subsume those of conditional entailment

Theorem 4 *If a proposition q is conditionally entailed by a default theory $\langle K, E \rangle$ then $E \mathrel{\vdash_K} q$.*

In conditional entailment, defaults are arranged in partial orders. A priority order over the set of defaults $\Delta_{\mathcal{L}}$ is *admissable* relative to a default theory iff every set Δ of assumptions in conflict with a default r contains a default r' that is less than that default in the ordering. Rankings on worlds are derived from priority relations over default rules: If $\Delta(w)$ and $\Delta(w')$ are the defaults falsified by worlds w and w' respectively, then w is preferred to w' iff $\Delta(w) \neq \Delta(w')$, and for every rule in $\Delta(w) - \Delta(w')$ there is a rule in $\Delta(w') - \Delta(w)$ which has higher priority. This then is very close to Definition 6. The primary difference is that, in conditional entailment, in order to prefer w to w' there must be defaults of strictly higher priority "favouring" w. In the approach at hand, (informally) we require that there be a reason to prefer w over w', and that such a reason not obtain for the converse. That is, for Example 4 we can't show (in conditional entailment or here) that W is less specific that B; hence conditional entailment doesn't distinguish the conditionals. In the approach at hand, we can show that W is no more specific than B (i.e. $W \preceq B$), but that the converse fails to be demonstrable. Consequently (all other things being equal) defaults with antecedent B "override" those with antecedent W.

Technically this difference appears to amount to the following: In Definition 6 where we have:

for every $C \to D \in Pref(w_2, w_1)$ there is $A \to B \in Pref(w_1, w_2)$ such that $C \preceq A$ and it is not the case that $A \preceq C$,

conditional entailment (effectively) uses:

for every $C \to D \in Pref(w_2, w_1)$ there is $A \to B \in Pref(w_1, w_2)$ such that $C \prec A$.

As a second minor difference, there may be fewer preferential orderings in the present approach than the admissible structures of conditional entailment.

Of the examples presented earlier, all of the desired default inferences go through: green birds fly; birds that are penguins do not fly; penguins have wings; ravens are black and (by default) non-albino. Quakers are pacifists, and normally non-republican.

Example 4 was discussed earlier. For Example 5 we had three defaults that could not be simultaneously applied. Here we conclude B_1 by default from $A_1 \wedge A_2$, but not from $A_1 \wedge A_2 \wedge A_3$. In terms of (the proof-theoretic notion of) support, we have that $A_1 \wedge A_2 \to B_1$ is supported, based on $A_1 \to B_1$. However, $A_1 \wedge A_2 \wedge A_3 \to B_1$ is not supported: even though there is a reason to accept this conditional (viz. $A_1 \to B_1$) there is a reason not to accept it (since $A_2 \wedge A_3 \to \neg B_1$ is supported) that is not overridden by this conditional.

From $A_1 \wedge A_2 \wedge A_3$ we obtain, as desired, that $(B_1 B_2 \neg B_3) \vee (B_1 \neg B_2 B_3) \vee (\neg B_1 B_2 B_3)$. We also obtain default inferences in the face of denied defaults; given $A_1 A_2 A_3 \neg B_3$, for example, we conclude $B_1 \wedge B_2$.

For Example 6, we had the formulas: $B_1 \to C_1, B_2 \to C_2, A \to (B_1 \neg C_1) \vee (B_2 \neg C_2)$. Hence, essentially, in the presence of A, at most one of B_1, B_2 can be "unexceptional". From A we obtain the default conclusion $(B_1 \neg C_1) \equiv (B_2 \supset C_2)$ and so one of B_1, B_2 is guaranteed to be "unexceptional".

A final point concerns the applicability of this approach. Implicitly, defaults are "applied" wherever possible. Consequently, given a chain of defaults $T = \{A_1 \to A_2, A_2 \to A_3, \ldots, A_{n-1} \to A_n\}$ we would obtain that $A_1 \mathrel{\vdash_T} A_n$. This may be fine for default reasoning, but it leads to unintuitive results for temporal reasoning, as has been noted elsewhere for *chronological ignorance* (Sho88). Hence this approach would appear to produce results too strong for such reasoning.

Conclusion

An approach to nonmonotonic inference, based on preference orderings between worlds, has been presented. The semantics takes as a starting point an extant theory of defaults; from this, given a default theory, we specify orderings on worlds. The original theory of defaults provides a satisfactory notion of specificity; in the orderings based on this theory, irrelevant properties are correctly handled as is reasoning within exceptional circumstances, including inheritance reasoning. Arguably the notion of a preferential default inference satisfactorily formalises intuitions concerning preferences induced by default rules. As well, the approach is shown to handle standard and non-standard examples of default reasoning. Finally, a (sound) proof theory is presented.

There are two shortcomings to the approach as presented. First a completeness result is obviously desirable. Second, computational concerns have not been addressed. Two points ameliorate this second concern: first, the goal here is to present a characterisation of default inference, and then address computational issues; second, presumably a complete proof theory will in fact indicate how an implementation may be effected.

Acknowledgements This research was funded by the Natural Science and Engineering Research Council of Canada grant A0884 and the Institute for Robotics and Intelligent Systems (IRIS) in the Canadian Networks of Centres of Excellence Program. The author was a visitor at York University and the University of Toronto while this work was being carried out. The author also gratefully acknowledges comments from the University of Toronto Knowledge Representation group and the anonymous reviewers.

References

E.W. Adams. *The Logic of Conditionals.* D. Reidel Publishing Co., Dordrecht, Holland, 1975.

Salem Benferhat, Claudette Cayrol, Didier Dubois, Jerome Lang, and Henri Prade. Inconsistency management and prioritized syntax-based entailment. In *Proc. IJCAI-93*, pages 640–645, Chambéry, Fr., 1993.

Craig Boutilier. *Conditional Logics for Default Reasoning and Belief Revision.* PhD thesis, Department of Computer Science, University of Toronto, 1992.

J.P. Delgrande. A first-order conditional logic for prototypical properties. *Artificial Intelligence,* 33(1):105–130, 1987.

J.P. Delgrande. An approach to default reasoning based on a first-order conditional logic: Revised report. *Artificial Intelligence,* 36(1):63–90, 1988.

J.P. Delgrande. A preference-based approach to default reasoning. Technical report, School of Computing Science, Simon Fraser University, 1994. in preparation.

D. M. Gabbay. Theoretical foundations for nonmonotonic reasoning in expert systems. In K. R. Apt, editor, *Proceedings NATO Advanced Study Institute on Logics and Models of Concurrent Systems*, pages 439–457. Springer-Verlag, Berlin, 1985.

Moisés Goldszmidt, Paul Morris, and Judea Pearl. A maxixmum entropy approach to nonmonotonic reasoning. In *Proc. AAAI-90*, Boston, MA, 1990.

Moisés Goldszmidt. *Qualitative Probabilities: A Normative Framework for Commonsense Reasoning.* PhD thesis, Department of Computer Science, University of California, Los Angeles, 1992.

Moisés Goldszmidt and Judea Pearl. System-Z+: A formalism for reasoning with variable-strength defaults. In *Proc. AAAI-91*, pages 399–404, Anaheim, CA, 1991.

Hector Geffner and Judea Pearl. Conditional entailment: Bridging two approaches to default reasoning. *Artificial Intelligence,* 53(2-3):209–244, 1992.

G.E. Hughes and M.J. Cresswell. *An Introduction to Modal Logic.* Methuen and Co. Ltd., 1968.

S. Kraus, D. Lehmann, and M. Magidor. Nonmonotonic reasoning, preferential models and cumulative logics. *Artificial Intelligence,* 44(1-2):167–207, 1990.

D. Lewis. *Counterfactuals.* Harvard University Press, 1973.

D. Lehmann and M. Magidor. What does a conditional knowledge base entail? *Artificial Intelligence,* 55(1):1–60, 1992.

J. McCarthy. Circumscription – a form of non-monotonic reasoning. *Artificial Intelligence,* 13:27–39, 1980.

R.C. Moore. Semantical considerations on nonmonotonic logic. *Artificial Intelligence,* 25:75–94, 1985.

J. Pearl. *Probabilistic Reasoning in Intelligent Systems: Networks of Plausible Inference.* Morgan Kaufman, San Mateo, CA, 1988.

J. Pearl. Probabilistic semantics for nonmonotonic reasoning: A survey. In *Proc. KR-89*, pages 505–516, Toronto, May 1989. Morgan Kaufman.

J. Pearl. System Z: A natural ordering of defaults with tractable applications to nonmonotonic reasoning. In *Proc. of the Third Conference on Theoretical Aspects of Reasoning About Knowledge*, pages 121–135, Pacific Grove, Ca., 1990.

D.L. Poole. A logical framework for default reasoning. *Artificial Intelligence,* 36(1):27–48, 1988.

R. Reiter. A logic for default reasoning. *Artificial Intelligence,* 13:81–132, 1980.

Y. Shoham. *Reasoning About Change: Time and Causation from the Standpoint of Artificial Intelligence.* The MIT Press, Cambridge, Mass., 1988.

R.F. Stalnaker. A theory of conditionals. In N. Rescher, editor, *Studies in Logical Theory,* pages 98–112. Basil Blackwell, Oxford, 1968.

On the Relation between the Coherence and Foundations Theories of Belief Revision

Alvaro del Val
Robotics Lab
Computer Science Department
Stanford University
Stanford, CA 94305
delval@cs.stanford.edu

Abstract

Two recent papers, (Gärdenfors 1990; Doyle 1992), try to assess the relative merits of the two main approaches to belief revision, the foundations and coherence theories, but leave open the question of the mathematical connections between them. We answer this question by showing that the foundations and coherence theories of belief revision are mathematically equivalent. The result also has consequences for nonmonotonic reasoning, as it entails that Poole's system of default reasoning and Shoham's preferential logic are expressively equivalent, in that they can represent the same set of non monotonic consequence relations.

Introduction

Two major approaches to belief revision can be distinguished, according to the role assigned in the belief revision process to the agent's reasons for holding his or her beliefs. In the *foundations theory* of belief revision, the agent's beliefs are seen as having a structure beyond the purely logical relations among them. In particular, certain beliefs are *justified* by some other beliefs, which in turn might be justified by still other beliefs, etc., with a distinguished set of "basic" or "self-justified" beliefs providing the foundation for the whole edifice. When the agent's beliefs are to be revised, some of these basic beliefs might have to be retracted; as a result some other beliefs will become unjustified, and according to the foundations approach they should be retracted as well. In contrast, in the *coherence theory* of revision the goal is only to maintain the overall consistency of the agent's beliefs, while retracting as few beliefs as possible during revision. In the basic approach, all beliefs are in principle accorded the same status, and the agent will keep a belief whenever he or she can consistently do so, even when the original reasons for holding that belief are retracted.

Two recent papers, (Gärdenfors 1990; Doyle 1992), try to assess the relative merits of each approach. Recognizing that the question is unlikely to be solved by informal arguments, both authors consider the question of the mathematical connections between the approaches. Specifically, Gärdenfors tries to show that in many cases the notion of a "reason for belief," which seems to be fundamental to the foundational approach, can be "reconstructed" from a coherentist point of view, specifically using the notion of "epistemic entrenchment," Gärdenfors' preferred way to conceptualize the coherence approach. The proposal is only suggestive, as Gärdenfors admits it is formally flawed. Doyle expands on the flaws of this proposal, and suggests that it should be possible to encode coherence revision operators in a foundational framework.

Thus, the question of the mathematical connections between both approaches remains open. We answer this question in this paper, by showing that the foundations theory is equivalent to the coherence theory. Answering this question of course requires to be more precise about the formal definition of both approaches. Whereas we will, with Doyle and Gärdenfors, take AGM-like revision as our model of coherentist revision, we depart from both of them in our choice of a formal model for the foundations theory. In particular, we follow Nebel (1991) in that the notion of "reasons for beliefs" will play no explicit formal role in our definition of the foundational approach, where we will depart only slightly from the "syntax-based approach" advocated by this and other authors.

In the next two sections, we present the formal model we use for the coherence and foundations theory, respectively. We then present the main technical results of the paper, and finish by discussing the implications of these results on the expressiveness of two non-monotonic frameworks.

In the rest of the paper, we assume a propositional language $\mathcal{L}$ obtained by closing a finite set of symbols $\mathcal{P}$ under the usual boolean connectives. $\mathcal{W}$ is the set of all interpretations of $\mathcal{L}$. $Mod(\psi)$, for any $\psi \in \mathcal{L}$, denotes the set of models of ψ. $\vdash$ stands for propositional consequence, and for any $\Sigma \subseteq \mathcal{L}$, $Cn(\Sigma)$ is $\{\varphi \mid \Sigma \vdash \varphi\}$ the logical closure of Σ. A preorder is a reflexive and transitive relation. For any preorder $\leq$ and any subdomain S of $\leq$, $Min(S, \leq)$ denotes the set of minimal elements of S under $\leq$.

Finally, the following notation will be useful. Let

$$\Sigma \Downarrow \neg\mu = \{\Gamma \subseteq \Sigma \mid \Gamma \not\vdash \mu \text{ and } \forall \Theta \subseteq \Sigma, \text{ if } \Gamma \subset \Theta \text{ then } \Theta \vdash \mu\}$$

be the set of maximal subsets of Σ that do *not* entail μ. The set $\Sigma \Downarrow \mu$ can also be filtered by incorporating a "preference preorder" $\preceq$ over subsets of Σ, whose strict part is written $\prec$, defining

$$\Sigma \downarrow \mu = \{\Gamma \subseteq \Sigma \mid \Gamma \nvdash \mu \text{ and } \forall \Theta \subseteq \Sigma, \text{ if } \Theta \prec \Gamma \text{ then } \Theta \vdash \mu\}.$$

We require $\preceq$ to extend set containment, *i.e.* to satisfy $\Theta \prec \Gamma$ whenever $\Gamma \subset \Theta$.

The coherence theory

The main formal representative of the coherence theory of belief revision is the theory developed in (Alchourrón, Gärdenfors, & Makinson 1985; Gärdenfors 1988). The AGM approach to revision has become identified to a great extent with its *normative* side: the authors put forward a set of "postulates" that, they claim, any "rational" revision operator should satisfy. For readability, and since we are considering only the finitary propositional case, we follow the presentation of (Katsuno & Mendelzon 1991). Using $\circ$ to denote a revision operator, the postulates are:

(R1) $\psi \circ \mu$ implies μ.

(R2) If $\psi \wedge \mu$ is satisfiable then $\psi \circ \mu$ is equivalent to $\psi \wedge \mu$.

(R3) If μ is satisfiable then $\psi \circ \mu$ is also satisfiable.

(R4) If $\models \psi_1 \equiv \psi_2$ and $\models \mu_1 \equiv \mu_2$ then $\psi_1 \circ \mu_1$ is equivalent to $\psi_2 \circ \mu_2$.

(R5) $(\psi \circ \mu) \wedge \phi$ implies $\psi \circ (\mu \wedge \phi)$.

(R6) If $(\psi \circ \mu) \wedge \phi$ is satisfiable then $\psi \circ (\mu \wedge \phi)$ implies $(\psi \circ \mu) \wedge \phi$.

We will also consider the following two postulates, from (Katsuno & Mendelzon 1991), as a weaker alternative to (R6):

(R7) If $\psi \circ \mu_1$ implies μ_2 and $\psi \circ \mu_2$ implies μ_1 then $\psi \circ \mu_1$ is equivalent to $\psi \circ \mu_2$.

(R8) $(\psi \circ \mu_1) \wedge (\psi \circ \mu_2)$ implies $\psi \circ (\mu_1 \vee \mu_2)$.

Definition 1 *A coherence revision operator is any operator $\circ$ satisfying postulates (R1)–(R5), (R7), and (R8). An AGM operator is a coherence operator which in addition satisfies (R6).*

Coherence revision operators can be characterized by the following representation theorem, due to (Katsuno & Mendelzon 1991). A *revision assignment* is a function that assigns to each formula ψ a binary relation $\leq_\psi$ over $\mathcal{W}$, the set of all interpretations of $\mathcal{L}$. The revision assignment is said to be *faithful* iff:

1. $Min(\mathcal{W}, \leq_\psi) = Mod(\psi)$ for any satisfiable ψ; and

2. $\leq_\psi = \leq_\phi$ whenever $\models \psi \equiv \phi$.

Theorem 1 *A revision operator $\circ$ satisfies (R1)–(R5), (R7) and (R8) (respectively, (R1)–(R6)) iff there exists a faithful revision assignment that maps each formula ψ to a partial (respectively total) preorder $\leq_\psi$ such that:*

$$Mod(\psi \circ \mu) = Min(Mod(\mu), \leq_\psi)$$

Why should these postulates be regarded as characterizing a *coherence* theory of belief revision? The main reason has to do, in our view, with the first representation theorem used to characterize operators satisfying them, which is different from the one just given. According to the coherence theory, as said, the main criterion in deciding whether to preserve certain beliefs in the face of revision is whether they can be consistently held after the new information is incorporated, in which case they should be preserved. Thus, a natural way to capture this idea is to view revision as a two step process. In the first step, the agent checks whether the new information is consistent with his or her beliefs, and, if this is not the case, withdraws as few beliefs as possible so as to restore consistency; in the second step, the beliefs kept in the previous stage are conjoined with the new information. (The two steps correspond, respectively, to the AGM operations of contraction and expansion.) As we will see, this is very similar to the approach taken by the foundations theory of revision, with the only difference that the latter considers only a distinguished set of basic beliefs. In the coherence theory, in contrast, all beliefs are, at least in principle, accorded the same status.

Formally, the idea of removing as few beliefs as possible in the first step can be captured in terms of the $\Downarrow$ notation introduced in the first section. Suppose the agent's beliefs are (finitely) represented by some sentence ψ, to be revised with some new information μ. Under most, though by not means all, formal conceptions of belief, the agent will also believe in any logical consequence of ψ, and thus the agent's beliefs are given by $Cn(\psi)$. Because the coherence theory accords all beliefs, in principle, the same status, all beliefs must be considered in minimizing retracted beliefs. This means that the first step in revision should be captured in terms of the set $Cn(\psi) \Downarrow \neg\mu$. If this set is a singleton, say $\{\Gamma\}$, the second step can be captured by defining the result of revising ψ with μ to be $Cn(\Gamma \cup \{\mu\})$. Otherwise, there is some choice as to what to do, e.g. choosing one, some, or all the elements of $Cn(\psi) \Downarrow \neg\mu$. Abstracting away from the details, we can simply assume that there is a selection function $S_\psi : \mathcal{P}(Cn(\psi)) \to \mathcal{P}(Cn(\psi))$, satisfying $\emptyset \subset S_\psi(\Psi) \subseteq \Psi$, and define revision by:

$$Cn(\psi \circ \mu) = \bigcap_{\Gamma \in S_\psi(Cn(\psi) \Downarrow \neg\mu)} Cn(\Gamma \cup \{\mu\}).$$

The selection function can be seen as expressing some preferences on the agent's beliefs. It turns out that, by placing certain conditions on this function, the class of AGM operators can be fully characterized by means of a representation theorem (Alchourrón, Gärdenfors, & Makinson 1985), a theorem that legitimates the identification of the AGM approach with the coherence theory.

The foundations theory

Foundational approaches, as said, postulate a distinction between "basic" or self-justifying beliefs and other beliefs, which should be ultimately justified in terms of the former. As an example, suppose we initially believe that some particular animal is a mammal and that every mammal has lungs; then we will also believe that the animal has lungs. We can represent these beliefs with the database $\{m, m \supset l, l\}$. If we are now told that the animal is not a mammal after all, we need to revise our beliefs with $\neg m$. Many coherence revision operators, such as *e.g.* the one proposed by (Dalal 1988), would yield a revised database equivalent to $\neg m \wedge l$; *i.e.* we would retain the belief that the animal has lungs, even if we no longer have any reason to believe it. But, one could argue, this would only be warranted if this belief did not "depend" on the belief that it is a mammal (say, we have independently observed that it has lungs). Coherence approaches appear *prima facie* ill-suited to make this kind of distinction; in a foundational approach, in contrast, the first case would correspond to treating $\{m, m \supset l\}$ as the set of self-justifying beliefs, and the second case to treating $\{m, l\}$ as basic beliefs. Assuming that we want to preserve as many basic beliefs as possible, a typical foundational approach would revise each database differently, yielding respectively $\{m \supset l, \neg m\}$ and $\{\neg m, l\}$ as revised databases. We thus capture the distinction between having an independent *reason* for believing that the animal has lungs and not having it, even though the notion of "reasons for belief" plays no explicit formal role.

One straightforward way to capture this distinction between basic and non-basic beliefs is to base it on the proof-theoretic notion of derivability. Given a finite axiomatization of a theory, we can take the axioms to be the basic beliefs; any other beliefs about the domain should be justified, *i.e.* *derivable* from the axioms in the underlying logic. This is the intuition behind syntax-based approaches to revision, the main representatives, in our view, of the foundational theory — see e.g. (Fagin, Ullman, & Vardi 1983; Makinson 1985; Ginsberg 1986; Nebel 1989; Benferhat *et al.* 1993).

Thus, if the finite set of sentences Ψ axiomatizes the agent's beliefs, and we take this set to be identical with the set of basic beliefs, syntax-based revision can be defined by $Cn(\Psi \circ \mu) = \bigcap_{\Gamma \in \Psi \downarrow \neg \mu} Cn(\Gamma \cup \{\mu\})$, where $\downarrow = \Downarrow$ when $\preceq = \supseteq$, and is otherwise based on some preorder $\preceq$ over subsets of Ψ, or more generally over finite subsets of $\mathcal{L}$, that extends set containment.

Though the syntax-based approach appears to capture some of the intuitions behind the foundational approach, it also has a serious drawback, namely, the result of revision becomes extremely dependent on the syntactic form of the database. Even apparently meaningless distinctions such as that between $\{a, b\}$ and $\{a \wedge b\}$ have an effect in revision. This has two highly undesirable consequences. First, it forces the user to write down the database so as to reflect the distinction between basic and derived beliefs, relegating any other concerns such as conciseness, understandability, or suitability for efficient inference, which are equally important in choosing the "right" axiomatization. Second, even assuming that the user is willing to write down the axioms with such an exclusive concern for proper revision behavior, any further modification of the database, such as caching the results of inferences and storing them back with the database, or applying equivalence-preserving transformations to the database for optimization purposes,[1] will also affect the results of revision.

This is clearly unsatisfactory. What is needed is the ability to separate the specification of the basic beliefs from the axiomatization of the database. For this reason, we will depart slightly from traditional presentations of syntax-based approaches, by introducing a *basic beliefs function* $\Sigma : \mathcal{L} \to \mathcal{P}(\mathcal{L})$ that maps any formula ψ into an associated set of basic beliefs $\Sigma(\psi)$ (also written Σ_ψ for brevity). We require Σ to satisfy:

1. $\Sigma(\psi) = \Sigma(\varphi)$ whenever $\vdash \psi \equiv \varphi$.

2. $Cn(\Sigma(\psi)) = Cn(\psi)$.

3. $\Sigma(\psi)$ is finite.

Definition 2 *A foundations revision operator is an operator $\circ$ defined by*

$$Cn(\psi \circ \mu) = \bigcap_{\Gamma \in \Sigma_\psi \downarrow \neg \mu} Cn(\Gamma \cup \{\mu\}),$$

where Σ is a basic beliefs function, and $\downarrow$ is as defined above, in terms of some preorder $\preceq$ that extends set containment. Furthermore, a foundations operator is:

- *a* total preorder *operator iff $\preceq$ is a total preorder;*
- *a* basic foundations *operator iff $\Downarrow = \downarrow$, i.e. $\preceq = \supseteq$;*
- *a* TO foundations *operator iff it is basic and $\Sigma_\psi = \{\sigma_1, \ldots, \sigma_n\}$, for some n, where $\sigma_{i+1} \in Cn(\sigma_i)$ for $1 \leq i < n$.*

As we will see later, the class of foundations operators and the class of basic foundations operators are identical. TO operators are included because they can capture the class of AGM coherence operators. If we ignore questions of non-deterministic revision (on which more below), the class of TO operators is identical to the total preorder class. It is also equivalent to the total preorder operator that Nebel (1991) calls "unambiguous prioritized revision."

The use of a basic beliefs function is analogous to the use of a preference preorder on models in coherence operators as per theorem 1, *i.e.* is a *device for specifying a belief revision policy*. Note that we do introduce a principle of syntax independence in the definition of this function, and thus of foundations operators. In

---

[1] This includes e.g. transformation to CNF. Note also that syntax-dependence does not go away by restricting the syntactic form of the database, e.g. clausal, Horn, etc.

our view, arguments for syntax-dependence boil down to the practical convenience of using the database axiomatization as a device for specifying a foundational revision policy, that is, the set of basic beliefs. This convenience is unaffected by our reformulation, since in practice one is given a single initial database; we can take its axioms as basic beliefs, and stipulate that any equivalent database has the same associated basic beliefs as the ones given. Computationally, therefore, we can proceed exactly as in the syntax-based approach, since the proof theoretic approach characteristic of syntax-based revision is preserved (with basic beliefs replacing the axioms).[2]

As for the second condition on Σ, the requirement that all basic beliefs are believed (that $Cn(\Sigma_\psi) \subseteq Cn(\psi)$) is obvious. To see that the converse inclusion is also needed, note that $Cn(\psi \circ true) = Cn(\Sigma_\psi)$, and thus if $Cn(\Sigma_\psi) \subset Cn(\psi)$ some beliefs would be lost when revising with a tautology. The third requirement, in conjunction with the second, entails that Σ_ψ provides a finite axiomatization of ψ.

This concludes the presentation of the formal model of foundational belief revision that we use. As said, both Gärdenfors and Doyle take the JTMS (justification based truth maintenance system, (Doyle 1979)) as the paradigm of foundational revision. Why do we choose a different model? We have argued, following (Nebel 1991), that the distinction between basic and non-basic beliefs is the only essential aspect of the foundations theory, without any need for an explicit concept of justification. In our view, the role of a TMS (not just a JTMS) in the context of belief revision is simply to allow us to easily detect whether the new formula contradicts previous beliefs and to trace back the basic beliefs underlying this contradiction, by caching inferences as well as the reasons for beliefs. Thus, from the point of view of revision the role of a TMS is simply to facilitate the computation of $\Sigma \downarrow \neg\mu$ (see (Benferhat et al. 1993) for a detailed treatment of this topic).

The specific choice of a JTMS as the paradigm of foundational revision presents two additional problems. First, inference with the JTMS is equivalent to inference in general logic programs, with the semantics of autoepistemic or default logic (Pimentel & Rodi 1991; Elkan 1990; Reinfrank, Dressler, & Brewka 1989); while the problem of revision is well defined for any logic, we see no reason to take revision in a non-classical logic as a paradigm of foundational revision. Second, all the revision procedures proposed for the JTMS (Doyle 1979; Elkan 1990; Pimentel & Rodi 1991) share a fundamental limitation, which in our view makes them inadequate as *general* models of revision. Namely, when a contradiction is de-

---

[2]A potential problem arises for iterated revisions, if the agent ends up having the same beliefs at a later time, but for different reasons (different basic beliefs). This is easily solved by time indexing Σ, allowing the basic beliefs to vary with time. See (del Val & Shoham 1994).

tected, revision has to be performed by retracting literals (nodes) that appear as non monotonic antecedents in JTMS's justifications; but when this is not possible the system will remain in an inconsistent state.

The equivalence of both approaches

In this section we show that the coherence and foundational approaches are equivalent. The first direction, from foundational to coherence operators, is easy, and can be found in a less general form in the literature.

Theorem 2 *For any foundations revision operator $\circ_F$ there exists a coherence revision operator $\circ_C$ such that $Mod(\psi \circ_F \mu) = Mod(\psi \circ_C \mu)$.*

Theorem 3 *For any total preorder or TO foundations revision operator $\circ_F$ there exists an AGM coherence revision operator $\circ_C$ such that $Mod(\psi \circ_F \mu) = Mod(\psi \circ_C \mu)$.*

These two theorems capture a much wider family of syntax-based operators satisfying the respective set of postulates than those considered by Nebel (1989; 1991). For example, he introduces "prioritized revision," in which the formulas of the database are partitioned into a set of totally ordered "priority strata," defining a lexicographic "prioritized" ordering on subsets of the database, and shows that it satisfies postulates (R1)–(R5). It is easy to see however from theorem 2 that if the ordering on the strata is allowed to be partial (in the style of (Grosof 1991)) these postulates are still satisfied, together with (R7) and (R8). Similarly, Nebel introduces "unambiguous prioritized revision," in which each strata is a singleton, showing that it satisfies the AGM postulates. It is a consequence of theorem 3, for example, that the operators introduced in (Ginsberg 1986) based on "modular orders" also satisfy these postulates, since modular orders can be easily mapped into total preorders. Our characterizations can also accommodate a variety of "voting schemes," as suggested in (Doyle 1991), as well as all the operators proposed in (Benferhat *et al.* 1993).

The most novel contribution of this paper is however given by the converses of the previous two theorems:

Theorem 4 *For any coherence revision operator $\circ_C$ there exists a basic foundations revision operator $\circ_F$ such that for every ψ and μ, $Mod(\psi \circ_C \mu) = Mod(\psi \circ_F \mu)$.*

Theorem 5 *For any AGM coherence revision operator $\circ_C$ there exists a basic foundations revision operator $\circ_F$ satisfying the TO condition and such that for every ψ and μ, $Mod(\psi \circ_C \mu) = Mod(\psi \circ_F \mu)$.*

It follows that, at least for finitary propositional languages, there is no choice to be made between the coherence and foundations theory of belief revision: they are mathematically equivalent. Theorems 2 and 3 show that any foundations revision operator can be seen as a coherence operator, in essence exploiting the fact that coherence operators allow for using preferences over beliefs in determining the revised database. Theorems 4 and 5, in turn, show that it is always possible to choose the set of basic beliefs so as to encode any coherence revision operator as a foundational operator.[3]

Note also that by theorem 2, any foundations operator satisfies (R1)–(R5) and (R7) and (R8), and that by theorem 4, any operator satisfying these postulates can be defined by means of a *basic* foundations operator. It follows that the two classes of foundations operator are identical. Similarly, the classes of TO and total preorder foundations operators are identical.

We omit proofs for lack of space. The easiest way to explain the connection between AGM and TO operators is probably to note that the set of sets of models $\{Mod(\sigma_1), \ldots, Mod(\sigma_n)\}$ forms an "embedded system of spheres," in the sense of Grove's (1988) representation theorem for AGM revision. Establishing the connection for non-AGM coherence operators (that is, operators based on a partial preorder on models) requires more work, based on a similar construction. The payoff for this additional work will be apparent in the next section. The results can be extended to the infinitary case as long as we can assume that the equivalence classes derivable from the preorders defining coherence operators are finitely axiomatizable.

We end this section by noting the following fact:

Theorem 6 *Let $\circ$ be a foundational operator, and suppose $\Sigma_\psi \downarrow \neg\mu$ is a singleton for every ψ and μ. Then $\circ$ satisfies (R6).*

The practical utility of having $\Sigma_\psi \downarrow \neg\mu$ be a singleton was already noted in (Nebel 1989), and it becomes clearer when we consider the non-deterministic syntax-based approach advocated in (Fagin *et al.* 1986), see also (Doyle 1991). In this approach, each element of $\Psi \downarrow \neg\mu$, where Ψ is a finite sets of formulas, is taken to generate an *alternative* revised database; $\Psi \circ \mu$ is taken to be a set of databases, namely the set $\{\Gamma \cup \{\mu\} \mid \Gamma \in \Psi \downarrow \neg\mu\}$, each element of which represents a possible way in which the agent may choose to revise its beliefs. If we take a similar non-deterministic approach in the definition of foundational operators, therefore, a singleton $\Sigma_\psi \downarrow \neg\mu$ coincides with the notion of *deterministic* foundational revision. The connection established by theorem 6 between the latter and postulate (R6) is interesting because it is this postulate that distinguishes the AGM operators from the more general class of coherence operators. Note that, by theorems 2 and 6, deterministic foundational revision satisfies the AGM postulates, and thus, by theorem 5, it can be captured with a TO foundations operator. And since TO operators are easily seen to be

deterministic in the sense of theorem 6, it follows that the TO condition (equivalently, unambiguous prioritized revision) completely characterizes deterministic foundational operators.[4]

Some implications for non-monotonic reasoning

It is well known (Gärdenfors 1991; Katsuno & Satoh 1991; Arlo-Costa & Shapiro 1992) that there is a close connection between belief revision and certain frameworks for non-monotonic reasoning. The natural correlate of coherence revision operators is the preferential logic of (Shoham 1987), while the natural correlate of foundational revision operators is Poole's (1988) system of default reasoning. As we now show, it is an easy consequence of our results that both non-monotonic frameworks are equally expressive, in the sense that they can capture exactly the same set of non-monotonic consequence relations.

Recall that a (propositional) *preferential consequence relation* is a relation $\vdash_\leq$ defined by $\mu \vdash_\leq \theta$ iff $Min(Mod(\mu), \leq) \subseteq Mod(\theta)$, where $\leq$ is a (possibly total) preorder over the set $\mathcal{W}$ of interpretations of the propositional language $\mathcal{L}$. It is easy to see from theorem 1 that a coherence revision operator $\circ$ induces a preferential relation $\vdash_\leq$ for every formula ψ, satisfying

$$\mu \vdash_\leq \theta \text{ iff } \theta \in Cn(\psi \circ \mu). \tag{1}$$

(Set $\leq = \leq_\psi$ in $\vdash_\leq$, where $\leq_\psi$ is the preorder associated to ψ by the operator $\circ$.) And conversely, given a preferential relation $\vdash_\leq$, there exists a formula ψ and a coherence revision operator $\circ$ satisfying expression 1 (choose ψ so that $Mod(\psi) = Min(\mathcal{W}, \leq)$, and choose $\circ$ so that $<_\psi = <$).

Similarly, there is a very close connection between Poole's "default theories" and foundational belief revision. Recall that a default theory in the sense of Poole is a pair $\langle D, F \rangle$, where $D, F \subseteq_{fin} \mathcal{L}$ are, respectively, a set of "defaults" and a consistent set of "facts." The (cautious) non-monotonic consequence relation defined by Poole, written $|\sim$, is defined by $\langle D, F \rangle |\sim \theta$ iff $\theta \in \bigcap_{\Gamma \in D \Downarrow \neg \bigwedge F} Cn(\Gamma \cup F)$, or, equivalently, as shown in (Nebel 1989), iff $\theta \in Cn(D \circ_S \bigwedge F)$, where $\circ_S$ is the basic syntax based revision operator.

This is then an easy consequence of our results:

Theorem 7 *For any preferential consequence relation $\vdash_\leq$ there exists $D \subseteq_{fin} \mathcal{L}$ such that for every $\mu, \theta \in \mathcal{L}$, $\mu \vdash_\leq \theta$ iff $\langle D, \{\mu\} \rangle |\sim \theta$. And conversely, for any $D \subseteq_{fin} \mathcal{L}$ there exists a preferential relation $\vdash_\leq$ such that for any $F \subseteq_{fin} \mathcal{L}$, $\theta \in \mathcal{L}$, $\bigwedge F \vdash_\leq \theta$ iff $\langle D, \bar{F} \rangle |\sim \theta$.*

---

[3]Had we kept the syntax-based definition of foundational revision, only theorems 2 and 3 would have to be marginally weakened, since syntax-based operators satisfy only a weaker form of (R4). Theorems 4 and 5 would remain unaffected, as choosing a set of basic beliefs is the same as choosing an axiomatization.

[4]To verify the equivalence of TO and unambiguous prioritized revision, note: any arbitrary unambiguous prioritized ordering can be imposed on the set of basic beliefs of a TO operator without affecting the result of revision; conversely, because unambiguous prioritized revision is deterministic, it can be captured by a TO operator.

Note that this theorem has as a special case "rational" consequence relations, preferential relations $\vdash_\leq$ in which $\leq$ is a total preorder. Note also that the "preferred subtheories" framework proposed in (Brewka 1989) does not extend the expressivity of Poole's framework, as it can be mapped in the same way to a preferential consequence relation that, by the previous theorem, can be captured in Poole's framework.

Discussion

We have shown that the coherence and foundational theories of belief revision are mathematically equivalent. More precisely, for a finitary propositional language, the family of coherence revision operators defined in the text, which include the AGM operators, and a slightly modified version of syntax-based revision, are equivalent. This modification of the latter is formally trivial, but in our view is well-motivated by some drawbacks of the syntax-based approach, and captures the essence of the foundational theory better than the latter. We have also shown that preferential logic and Poole's default theories are expressively equivalent, in the sense that they can capture exactly the same non monotonic consequence relations.

In (del Val & Shoham 1994), we encode belief revision in a situation calculus enriched with epistemic operators and with a knowledge-gathering action for learning new information. In this framework, which inspired most of the results of this paper, update and revision can be jointly captured in a way that makes the temporal evolution of the agent's beliefs explicit, and both styles of revision, as well as the associated forms of non-monotonic reasoning, can be captured, all within a circumscriptive framework for reasoning about action.

References

Alchourrón, C. E.; Gärdenfors, P.; and Makinson, D. 1985. On the logic of theory change: Partial meet functions for contraction and revision. *Journal of Symbolic Logic* 50:510–530.

Arlo-Costa, H. L., and Shapiro, S. J. 1992. Maps between non-monotonic and conditional logic. In *Proc. Third Int. Conf. on Principles of Knowledge Representation and Reasoning*.

Benferhat, S.; Cayrol, C.; Dubois, D.; Lang, J.; and Prade, H. 1993. Inconsistency management and prioritized syntax-based entailment. In *Proc. Thirteenth Int. Joint Conf. on Artificial Intelligence*.

Brewka, G. 1989. Preferred subtheories: An extended logical framework for default reasoning. In *Proc. Eleventh Int. Joint Conf. on Artificial Intelligence*.

Dalal, M. 1988. Investigations into a theory of knowledge base revision. In *Proc. Seventh Conf. of the AAAI*.

del Val, A., and Shoham, Y. 1994. A unified view of belief revision and update. *Journal of Logic and Computation*. Special Issue on Actions and Processes, M. Georgeff (ed.), to appear.

Doyle, J. 1979. A truth maintenance system. *Artificial Intelligence* 12:231–272.

Doyle, J. 1991. Rational belief revision (preliminary report). In *Proc. Second Int. Conf. on Principles of Knowledge Representation and Reasoning*.

Doyle, J. 1992. Reason maintenance and belief revision: Foundations vs. coherence theories. In Gärdenfors, P., ed., *Belief Revision*. Cambridge University Press.

Elkan, C. 1990. A rational reconstruction of nonmonotonic truth maintenance systems. *Artificial Intelligence* 43:219–234.

Fagin, R.; Kuper, G. M.; Ullman, J. D.; and Vardi, M. Y. 1986. Updating logical databases. *Advances in Computing Research* 3.

Fagin, R.; Ullman, J. D.; and Vardi, M. Y. 1983. On the semantics of updates in databases. In *Proc. Second ACM SIGACT-SIGMOD-SIGART Symposium on Principles of Database Systems*.

Gärdenfors, P. 1988. *Knowledge in Flux*. The MIT Press.

Gärdenfors, P. 1990. The dynamics of belief systems: Foundations vs. coherence theories. *Revue Internationale de Philosophie* 172:24–46.

Gärdenfors, P. 1991. Non monotonic reasoning based on expectations. In *Proc. Second Int. Conf. on Principles of Knowledge Representation and Reasoning*.

Ginsberg, M. L. 1986. Counterfactuals. *Artificial Intelligence* 30:35–79.

Grosof, B. 1991. Generalizing prioritization. In *Proc. Second Int. Conf. on Principles of Knowledge Representation and Reasoning*.

Grove, A. 1988. Two modelings for theory change. *Journal of Philosophical Logic* 17:157–170.

Katsuno, H., and Mendelzon, A. O. 1991. Propositional knowledge base revision and minimal change. *Artificial Intelligence* 52:263–294.

Katsuno, H., and Satoh, K. 1991. A unified view of consequence relations, belief revision and conditional logic. In *Proc. Twelfth Int. Joint Conf. on Artificial Intelligence*.

Makinson, D. 1985. How to give it up: A survey of some formal aspects of the logic of theory change. *Synthèse*.

Nebel, B. 1989. A knowledge level analysis of belief revision. In *Proc. First Int. Conf. on Principles of Knowledge Representation and Reasoning*.

Nebel, B. 1991. Belief revision and default reasoning: Syntax-based approaches. In *Proc. Second Int. Conf. on Principles of Knowledge Representation and Reasoning*.

Pimentel, S. G., and Rodi, W. L. 1991. Belief revision and paraconsistency in a logic programming framework. In *Proc. First Int. Workshop on Logic Programming and Non Monotonic Reasoning*.

Poole, D. 1988. A logical framework for default reasoning. *Artificial Intelligence* 36:27–47.

Reinfrank, M.; Dressler, O.; and Brewka, G. 1989. On the relation between truth maintenance and autoepistemic logic. In *Proc. Eleventh Int. Joint Conf. on Artificial Intelligence*.

Shoham, Y. 1987. A semantic approach to nonmonotonic logics. In Ginsberg, M. L., ed., *Readings in Non-Monotonic Reasoning*. Morgan Kaufmann.

Conditional Logics of Belief Change[*]

Nir Friedman
Stanford University
Dept. of Computer Science
Stanford, CA 94305-2140
nir@cs.stanford.edu

Joseph Y. Halpern
IBM Almaden Research Center
650 Harry Road
San Jose, CA 95120–6099
Stalnaker'shalpern@almaden.ibm.com

Abstract

The study of *belief change* has been an active area in philosophy and AI. In recent years two special cases of belief change, *belief revision* and *belief update*, have been studied in detail. Belief revision and update are clearly not the only possible notions of belief change. In this paper we investigate properties of a range of possible belief change operations. We start with an abstract notion of a *belief change system* and provide a logical language that describes belief change in such systems. We then consider several reasonable properties one can impose on such systems and characterize them axiomatically. We show that both belief revision and update fit into our classification. As a consequence, we get both a semantic and an axiomatic (proof-theoretic) characterization of belief revision and update (as well as some belief change operations that generalize them), in one natural framework.

Introduction

The study of *belief change* has been an active area in philosophy and in artificial intelligence (Gärdenfors 1988; Katsuno & Mendelzon 1991). The focus of this research is to understand how an agent should change his beliefs as a result of getting new information. In the literature, two types of belief change operation have been studied in detail: *belief revision* (Alchourrón, Gärdenfors, & Makinson 1985; Gärdenfors 1988) and *belief update* (Katsuno & Mendelzon 1991). Belief revision and update are two cases of belief change, but clearly not the only ones. In this paper we investigate properties of a range of possible belief change operations.

We start with the notion of a *belief change system* (BCS). A BCS contains three components: The set of possible *epistemic states* that the agent can be in, a *belief assignment* that maps each epistemic state to a set of beliefs, and a *transition function* that determines how the agent changes epistemic states as a result of learning new information. We assume some logical language $\mathcal{L}$ that describes the agent's world, and assume that the agent's beliefs are closed under deduction in $\mathcal{L}$. Thus, the belief assignment maps each state to a deductively closed set of formulas in $\mathcal{L}$. We make the

assumption (which is standard in the literature) that the agent learns a formula in $\mathcal{L}$, i.e., that events that cause the agent to change epistemic state can be described by formulas. Thus, the transition function takes a formula in $\mathcal{L}$ and an epistemic state to another epistemic state.

The notion of a BCS is quite general. It is easy to show that any operator satisfying the axioms of belief revision or update can be represented as a BCS. However, by starting at this level of abstraction, we can more easily investigate the general properties of belief change. We do so by considering a language that reasons about the belief change in a BCS. The language contains two modal operators: a unary modal operator B for belief and a binary modal operator $>$ to represent change, where, as usual, $B\varphi$ should be read "the agent believes φ", while $\varphi > \psi$ should be read "after learning φ, the agent will be in an epistemic state satisfying ψ". We show that the language is expressive enough to capture the belief change process. More precisely, the set of (modal) formulas holding at a state uniquely determines the agent's beliefs after any sequence of events. Thus, it is possible to describe the agent's belief change behavior by specifying what formulas in the extended language of conditionals hold at the agent's initial state. We also characterize the class of all BCS's axiomatically in this language.

We then investigate an important class of BCS's that we call *preferential BCS's*. This class can be viewed as an abstraction of the semantic models considered in papers such as (Grove 1988; Katsuno & Mendelzon 1991; Boutilier 1992; Katsuno & Satoh 1991). Roughly speaking, a preferential BCS is a BCS where an epistemic state can be identified with a set of possible *worlds*, where a world is a complete truth assignment to $\mathcal{L}$, together with a *preference ordering* on worlds. An agent believes φ in epistemic state s exactly if φ is true in all the worlds considered possible at s, and the agent believes ψ after learning φ in epistemic state s exactly if ψ is true in all the minimal worlds that satisfy φ (according to the preference ordering at s).[1]

---

[*]Work supported in part by the Air Force Office of Scientific Research (AFSC), under Contract F49620-91-C-0080.

[1]We note that there is some confusion in the literature between the Ramsey conditional (i.e., $>$) and preference conditional that describes the agent preferences (see (Boutilier 1992) for example). There is a strong connection between the two in preferential BCS's, but even in that context they have different properties. We think it is important to distinguish them. (See also (Friedman & Halpern

The class of preferential BCS's includes, in a precise sense, the class of operators for belief revision and the class of operators for belief update, so it can be viewed as a generalization of these notions. We consider a number of reasonable properties that one can impose on preferential BCS's, and characterize them axiomatically. It turns out that both belief revision and update can be characterized in terms of these properties. As a consequence, we get both a semantic and an axiomatic (proof-theoretic) characterization of belief revision and update (as well as some belief change operations that generalize them), in one natural framework.

There are some similarities between our work and others that have appeared in the literature. In particular, our language and its semantics bear some similarities to others that have been considered in the literature (for example, in papers such as (Gärdenfors 1978; 1986; Grahne 1991; Lewis 1973; Stalnaker 1968; Wobcke 1992)), and our notion of a BCS is very similar to Gärdenfors' belief revision systems (Gärdenfors 1978; 1986; 1988). However, there are some significant differences as well, both philosophical and technical. We discuss these in more detail in the next section. These differences allow us to avoid Gärdenfors' triviality result 1986, which essentially says that there are no interesting BCS's that satisfy the AGM postulates (Alchourrón, Gärdenfors, & Makinson 1985).

Belief change systems

A belief change system describes the possible states the agent might be in, the beliefs of the agent in each state, and how the agent changes state when receiving new information. We assume beliefs are described in some logical language $\mathcal{L}$ with a consequence relation $\models_{\mathcal{L}}$, which contains the usual truth-functional propositional connectives and satisfies the deduction theorem. We define a *belief change system* as a tuple $M = \langle S, \rho, \tau \rangle$, where S is a set of *states*, ρ is a *belief assignment* that maps a state $s \in S$ to a set of sentences $\rho(s)$ that is deductively closed (with respect to $\models_{\mathcal{L}}$), and τ is a function that maps a state $s \in S$ and sentence $\varphi \in \mathcal{L}$ to a new state $\tau(s, \varphi) \in S$. We differ from some work in the area of conditional logic (for example, (Grahne 1991; Lewis 1973; Stalnaker 1968)) in taking epistemic states rather than worlds as our primitive objects, while we differ from other work (for example, (Gärdenfors 1978; 1986)) by not identifying epistemic states with belief sets. In our view, while the $\mathcal{L}$-beliefs of an agent are certainly an important part of his epistemic state, they do not in general characterize it. Notice that because we do not identify belief sets with epistemic states, the function τ may behave differently at two epistemic states that agree on the beliefs in $\mathcal{L}$.[2]

A BCS describes how the agent's beliefs about the world change. We use a logical language we call $\mathcal{L}^>$ to reason about BCS's. As we said in the introduction, the language

$\mathcal{L}^>$ augments $\mathcal{L}$ with a unary modal operator B and a binary modal operator $>$ to capture belief change. Formally, we take $\mathcal{L}^>$ be the least set of formulas such that if $\varphi \in \mathcal{L}$ and $\psi, \psi' \in \mathcal{L}^>$ then $B\varphi$, $B\psi$, $\neg\psi$, $\psi \wedge \psi'$, and $\varphi > \psi$ are in $\mathcal{L}^>$. A number of observations should be made with regard to the choice of language. First observe that $\mathcal{L}$ and $\mathcal{L}^>$ are disjoint languages. The language $\mathcal{L}$ consists intuitively of objective formulas (talking about the world), while $\mathcal{L}^>$ consists of subjective formulas (talking about the agent's epistemic state). Thus, the formula $\varphi \in \mathcal{L}$ is not in $\mathcal{L}^>$, although $B\varphi$ is. We view the states in a BCS as epistemic states, and thus use the language $\mathcal{L}^>$ for reasoning about BCS's. There is no notion of an "actual world" in a BCS (as there is, by way of contrast, in a Kripke structure), so we have no way in our semantic model to evaluate whether a formula $\varphi \in \mathcal{L}$ is true. Of course, we could augment BCS's in a way that would let us do this, but there is no need for the purposes of this paper. (In fact, this is done in (Friedman & Halpern 1994a; 1994b), where we examine a broader framework that models both the agent and world and allows us to evaluate objective and subjective formulas.) We could have also interpreted a formula $\varphi \in \mathcal{L}$ to mean "the agent believes φ" (as in (Gärdenfors 1978)), but it turns out to be technically more convenient to add the B operator, since it lets us distinguish between the agent believing $\neg\varphi$ and the agent not believing φ.

Another significant difference between our language and other languages considered in the literature for reasoning about belief change (for example, (Gärdenfors 1978; 1986; Grahne 1991; Wobcke 1992)) is that on the left-hand side of $>$, we only allow formulas in $\mathcal{L}$ rather than arbitrary formulas in $\mathcal{L}^>$. For example, $p > (q > Br)$ is in $\mathcal{L}^>$, but $(p > Bq) > Br$ is not. Recall that the formula on the left-hand side of $>$ represents something that the agent could learn. It is not clear how an agent could come to learn a formula like $p > Bq$. Our intuition is that an agent learns about the external world, as described by $\mathcal{L}$, and not facts about the belief change process itself. Our language $\mathcal{L}^>$ is used to reason about the belief change process.[3]

We now assign truth values to formulas in $\mathcal{L}^>$. We write $(M, s) \models \varphi$ if φ holds in epistemic state s in the system M. We interpret $(M, s) \models \varphi$ to mean that the agent believes φ in epistemic state s. Since we take our agents to be introspective, we would expect that if $(M, s) \models \varphi$, then

---

1994b) for a discussion of this issue.)

[2] A similar distinction between epistemic states and belief sets can be found in (Rott 1990; Boutilier 1992). See also (Friedman & Halpern 1994b).

[3] Our position in this respect bears some similarity to that of (Levi 1988). However, Levi seems to be arguing against the agent learning *any* modal formula, while our quarrel is only with the agent learning modal formulas of the form $\varphi > \psi$. The formulas in $\mathcal{L}$ may be modal. It may seem to the reader familiar with the recent work of (Boutilier & Goldszmidt 1993) that they are dealing with precisely the problem of revising beliefs by formulas of the form $\varphi > \psi$. However, their interpretation of a formula such as $\varphi > \psi$ is "normally if φ is true then ψ is true". Although there is a relationship between the two interpretations of $>$ in the preferential BCS's we consider in the next section, they are distinct, and should be represented by two distinct modal operators. We would have no problem with normality formulas of the form considered by Boutilier and Goldszmidt appearing in $\mathcal{L}$, and thus on the left-hand side of $>$.

$(M, s) \models B\varphi$. Our semantics enforces this expectation. We have already given the intuition for $>$, namely, that $\varphi > \psi$ should hold precisely if ψ holds in the epistemic state that results after updating by ψ. Our semantics enforces this as well.

- $(M, s) \models B\varphi$ if $\varphi \in \rho(s)$ for $\varphi \in \mathcal{L}$
- $(M, s) \models B\psi$ if $(M, s) \models \psi$ for $\psi \in \mathcal{L}^>$
- $(M, s) \models \neg\varphi$ if $(M, s) \not\models \varphi$.
- $(M, s) \models \varphi \wedge \psi$ if $(M, s) \models \varphi$ and $(M, s) \models \psi$
- $(M, s) \models \varphi > \psi$ if $(M, \tau(s, \varphi)) \models \psi$.

Because Gärdenfors (Gärdenfors 1978; 1986) identifies each state, not with a set of beliefs in $\mathcal{L}$, but with a set of beliefs in $\mathcal{L}^>$, he cannot define $\models$ inductively as we do here. Rather, he puts constraints on the transition function τ so that $>$ satisfies the *Ramsey test*; i.e., he requires that $\varphi > \psi$ holds at epistemic state s if and only if ψ holds at $\tau(s, \varphi)$.

Notice that this condition amounts to the agent having positive introspection about his belief change protocol. One can imagine an agent who is unaware of his belief change protocol, so that although it is true that the agent will believe ψ after learning φ in epistemic state s, the agent is not aware of this, so that $\varphi > \psi$ does not hold at s. At the other extreme is an agent who is completely aware of his belief change protocol, so that if learning φ in state s results in the agent's believing ψ, then $\varphi > \psi$ holds at s, otherwise $\neg(\varphi > \psi)$ holds. We are implicitly assuming such complete introspective power on the part of the agent: Our semantics guarantees that one of $\varphi > \psi$ or $\neg(\varphi > \psi)$ must hold at every state s. Gärdenfors' semantics enforces positive introspection, but not complete introspection. As a result, his epistemic states may be incomplete with respect to conditional formulas; it is possible that neither $\varphi > \psi$ nor $\neg(\varphi > \psi)$ holds at a given epistemic state. It is not clear what the rationale is for this intermediate position.

Given a state s we define $\mathrm{Bel}(s)$ to be the (extended) beliefs of the agent at s:

$$\mathrm{Bel}(s) = \{\varphi \in \mathcal{L}^> | (M, s) \models \varphi\}$$

Intuitively, $\mathrm{Bel}(s)$ describes the agent's beliefs when he is in state s, and how these belief change after each possible sequence of observations. This intuition is justified, since $(M, s) \models \varphi$ if and only if $(M, s) \models B\varphi$ for any $\varphi \in \mathcal{L}^>$.

It is easy to see that given $\mathrm{Bel}(s)$ we can reconstruct $\rho(s)$, i.e., for $\varphi \in \mathcal{L}$, $\varphi \in \rho(s)$ if and only if $B\varphi \in \mathrm{Bel}(s)$. Indeed, as the following results show, $\mathrm{Bel}(s)$ completely characterizes the belief change process at s.

Proposition 1: *Let M be a BCS, s a state in M, and $\varphi \in \mathcal{L}$ a formula. Then $\mathrm{Bel}(\tau(s, \varphi)) = \{\psi | \varphi > \psi \in \mathrm{Bel}(s)\}$.*

Applying this result repeatedly we get

Corollary 2: *Let M, M' be BCS structures, and let s, s' be states in M and M', respectively. $\mathrm{Bel}(s) = \mathrm{Bel}(s')$ if and only if for any sequence of observations $\varphi_1, \ldots, \varphi_n$ it is the case that $\rho(\tau(\ldots \tau(s, \varphi_1) \ldots, \varphi_n)) = \rho'(\tau'(\ldots \tau(s', \varphi_1) \ldots, \varphi_n))$.*

This implies that $\mathrm{Bel}(s) = \mathrm{Bel}(s')$ if and only if s and s' cannot be distinguished by the belief change process. Thus,

the language $\mathcal{L}^>$ is appropriate for describing the belief change process; it captures all the details of the process, but no unnecessary details.

We next turn our attention to the problem of axiomatizing belief change. Given a BCS M, we say that $\varphi \in \mathcal{L}^>$ is *valid* in M, denoted $M \models \varphi$, if $(M, s) \models \varphi$ for every s. Let $\mathcal{M}$ be the class of all BCS structures, and let $\mathcal{N}$ be a subclass of $\mathcal{M}$. We say that $\varphi \in \mathcal{L}^>$ is *valid with respect to $\mathcal{N}$* if it is valid in all $M \in \mathcal{N}$. An axiom system is *sound* and *complete* for $\mathcal{L}^>$ with respect to $\mathcal{N}$ if φ is provable if and only if it is valid in $\mathcal{N}$. We are interested in characterizing various subclasses of $\mathcal{M}$ axiomatically. We start with $\mathcal{M}$ itself. Consider the following axiom system, which we call AX. In all the axioms and inference rules of AX, the formulas range over allowable formulas in $\mathcal{L}^>$ (so that when we write $\varphi > \psi$, we are implicitly assuming that $\varphi \in \mathcal{L}$ and that $\psi \in \mathcal{L}^>$):

B1. All substitution instances of propositional tautologies

B2. $B\varphi$, if $\varphi \in \mathcal{L}$ is $\mathcal{L}$-valid

B3. $B\varphi \wedge B(\varphi \Rightarrow \psi) \Rightarrow B\psi$

B4. $\varphi \Rightarrow B\varphi$

B5. $B\varphi \Rightarrow \neg B\neg\varphi$ for $\varphi \in \mathcal{L}^>$

B6. $\varphi > true_{\mathcal{L}>}$

B7. $\varphi > \psi_1 \wedge \varphi > (\psi_1 \Rightarrow \psi_2) \Rightarrow \varphi > \psi_2$

B8. $\neg(\varphi > \psi) \equiv \varphi > \neg\psi$

RB1. From φ and $\varphi \Rightarrow \psi$ infer ψ

RB2. From $\psi_1 \Rightarrow \psi_2$ infer $\varphi > \psi_1 \Rightarrow \varphi > \psi_2$

Axioms B3–B5 capture the standard properties of introspective belief. Notice that B4 relies on the fact that all formulas are taken to be subjective, that is, statements about the agent's beliefs. Although it may appear that B2 should follow from B1 and B4, it does not, since $\varphi \Rightarrow B\varphi$ is not an instance of B4 if $\varphi \subset \mathcal{L}$ (since it is not a formula in $\mathcal{L}^>$). B5 states that the agent's beliefs about subjective formulas are always consistent. This follows naturally from our semantics. For any $\varphi \in \mathcal{L}^>$, either φ or $\neg\varphi$ is true at a state s, and thus only one of them will be believed. It is important to note that this axiom does not force the agent's beliefs about the world to be consistent. More precisely, let $false_{\mathcal{L}}$ be $p \wedge \neg p$ for some $p \in \mathcal{L}$, and let $false_{\mathcal{L}>}$ be $Bp \wedge \neg Bp$. Clearly, $false_{\mathcal{L}} \in \mathcal{L}$ and $false_{\mathcal{L}>} \in \mathcal{L}^>$. Axiom B5 states that $\neg Bfalse_{\mathcal{L}>}$ is valid, but it does *not* imply that $\neg Bfalse_{\mathcal{L}}$ is valid. In fact, $Bfalse_{\mathcal{L}}$ is satisfiable in our semantics. (Of course, the formula $true_{\mathcal{L}>}$ used in B6 is the valid $\mathcal{L}^>$ formula $\neg false_{\mathcal{L}>}$; we take $true_{\mathcal{L}}$ to be $\neg false_{\mathcal{L}}$.) B8 follows from the fact that we have assumed the transition function τ is deterministic. Axiom B8 is known as *law of conditional excluded middle* (Stalnaker 1968). This axiom has been controversial in the literature (Lewis 1973; Harper, Stalnaker, & Pearce 1981). It does not seem as problematic here, since we are applying it to only subjective formulas, rather than objective formulas.

The following result shows that AX does indeed characterize belief change.

Theorem 3: *AX is a sound and complete axiomatization of $\mathcal{L}^>$ with respect to $\mathcal{M}$.*

It is interesting to compare our axiomatization with the system CM discussed in (Gärdenfors 1978). All of his axioms are sound in our framework. We have some extra axioms due to the fact that our language includes a B operator, but this could be easily added to Gärdenfors' framework as well. A more interesting difference is our axiom B8, which does not hold in CM. B8 essentially says that $Bel(s)$ is complete for each epistemic state s. As we already observed, Gärdenfors does not require completeness for formulas of the form $\varphi > \psi$, so B8 is not valid for him.

Preferential BCS's

Up to now we examined a very abstract notion of belief change. The definition of BCS puts few restrictions on the belief change process and does not provide much insight into the structure of such processes. We now describe a more specific class of systems that has a semantic representation similar to that of (Grove 1988; Katsuno & Mendelzon 1991; Boutilier 1992; Katsuno & Satoh 1991). The basic intuition is the following. We introduce *possible worlds*. Each possible world describes a way the world can be. We then associate with each epistemic set a set of possible worlds and a *preference* (or *plausibility*) ordering on worlds. The set of possible worlds associated with a state s defines the agent's beliefs at s in the usual manner, and the agent's epistemic state after learning φ corresponds to the minimal (i.e., most plausible) worlds satisfying φ.

We proceed as follows. A *preferential interpretation* of a BCS $\langle S, \rho, \tau \rangle$ is a tuple $\langle W, \pi, K, R \rangle$, where W is a set of possible *worlds*, π is a function mapping each world $w \in W$ to a maximally consistent subset of $\mathcal{L}$ (i.e., $\pi(w)$ must be consistent, and have the additional property that for each formula $\varphi \in \mathcal{L}$, either $\varphi \in \pi(w)$ or $\neg\varphi \in \pi(w)$), K is a mapping from S to subsets of W, and R is a function that maps each state $s \in S$ to a relation $\preceq_s$ over W.

The set $K(s)$ associated with each $s \in S$ describes the worlds considered possible when the agent is in state s. The ordering associated with each $s \in S$ describes a plausibility measure, or preference, among worlds. We define $\prec_s$ in the usual manner: $w \prec_s w'$ if $w \preceq_s w'$ and $w' \not\preceq_s w$. We require that $\preceq_s$ be smooth, i.e., for every $\varphi \in \mathcal{L}$ there are no infinite sequences of worlds $\ldots \prec_s w_1 \prec_s w_0$ such that $\varphi \in \pi(w_i)$ for all i. Following (Lewis 1973), we define $W_s = \{w \in W | \exists w' \in W, w \preceq_s w'\}$ as the set of worlds considered plausible when the agent is in state s. We require that $\preceq_s$ be a pre-order (i.e., reflexive and transitive relation) over W_s. Given φ, the set $\min(s, \varphi)$ is the set of minimal worlds in W_s that satisfy φ, i.e., $w \in \min(s, \varphi)$ if $\varphi \in \pi(w)$, $w \in W_s$ and there is no $w' \prec_s w$ such that $\varphi \in \pi(w')$.

We want preferential interpretations to satisfy several consistency requirements that ensure that they satisfy the intuition we outlined above. Formally, we require that for all $s \in S$ the following hold:

- $\varphi \in \rho(s)$ if and only if $\varphi \in \pi(w)$ for all $w \in K(s)$.
- If $s' = \tau(s, \varphi)$ then $K(s') = \min(s, \varphi)$.

Thus, each belief set is characterized by the set of worlds considered possible and belief change is described through the preference ordering associated with each belief set. A BCS is *preferential* if it has a preferential interpretation. Let $\mathcal{M}^P$ be the class of preferential belief structures.

Let AX^P be AX combined with the following axioms:

P1. $\varphi > B\varphi$

P2. $(\varphi_1 > B\psi) \wedge (\varphi_1 > B\varphi_2) \Rightarrow (\varphi_1 \wedge \varphi_2) > B\psi$ if ψ, φ_1 and φ_2 are in $\mathcal{L}$

P3. $(\varphi_1 > B\psi) \wedge (\varphi_2 > B\psi) \Rightarrow (\varphi_1 \vee \varphi_2) > B\psi$ if ψ, φ_1 and φ_2 are in $\mathcal{L}$

P4. $\varphi > B\psi \equiv \varphi' > B\psi$ if $\varphi \equiv \varphi'$ is $\mathcal{L}$-valid and $\psi \in \mathcal{L}$.

Theorem 4: *AX^P is a sound and complete axiomatization of $\mathcal{L}^>$ with respect to $\mathcal{M}^P$.*

We shall also be interested in subclasses of $\mathcal{M}^P$ that satisfy additional properties; these will help us capture belief revision and update.

The first property of interest is that the most preferred worlds according to the ordering $\preceq_s$ are precisely the worlds in $K(s)$. Formally, we say that the ordering $\preceq_s$ in a preferential interpretation is *faithful* if $K(s) = \min(s, true_{\mathcal{L}})$. If $\preceq_s$ is faithful, then $K(\tau(s, \varphi)) = K(s)$ if $\varphi \in \rho(s)$, so that an agent does not modify his beliefs if he learns something that he already believes. A preferential interpretation is *faithful* if $\preceq_s$ is faithful for every $s \in S$. This definition implies that once the agent is in an inconsistent state (i.e., one such that $K(s) = \emptyset$) he cannot leave it, i.e., $\min(\emptyset, \varphi) = \emptyset$, for any φ.[4] This leads us to define a slightly weaker notion: A preferential interpretation is *weakly faithful* if $\preceq_s$ is faithful for all $s \in S$ such that $K(s) \neq \emptyset$. A preferential BCS is (weakly) faithful if it has a (weakly) faithful preferential interpretation. (Similarly, for other properties of interest, we say below that a preferential BCS has the property if it has a preferential interpretation that has it.)

We can characterize faithful and weakly faithful BCS's (in a sense made precise by Theorem 5 below) by the axioms PF and PW, respectively:

PF. $B\varphi \equiv (true_{\mathcal{L}} > B\varphi)$ for $\varphi \in \mathcal{L}$.

PW. $\neg B(false_{\mathcal{L}}) \Rightarrow (B\varphi \equiv (true_{\mathcal{L}} > B\varphi))$ for $\varphi \in \mathcal{L}$.

Notice that these axioms say only that in a (weakly) faithful BCS, the agent believes φ if and only if learning a valid formula results in him believing φ.

The property of faithfulness guarantees that if the agent learns something that he currently believes, then he still maintains all of his former $\mathcal{L}$-beliefs. What happens if he learns something *consistent* with his current beliefs, although not necessarily in the belief set? The next condition guarantees that the agent does not remove any of his previous beliefs in this case. A preferential structure is *ranked* if $\preceq_s$ is a total pre-order over W_s for every epistemic state s, i.e., for every $w, w' \in W_s$, either $w \preceq_s w'$ or $w' \preceq_s w$. Combining ranking with faithfulness guarantees that if the agent learns something that is consistent with

---

[4]This is one of the differences between revision and update (Katsuno & Mendelzon 1991); in revision the agent can "escape" the inconsistent state by revision with a consistent formula, and in update he cannot.

what he believes—i.e., if $\varphi \in \pi(w)$ for some $w \in K(s)$—then it must be the case that $K(\tau(s, \varphi)) \subseteq K(s)$, since the most preferred worlds (with respect to $\preceq_s$) where φ holds are precisely those worlds in $K(s)$ where φ is true. To see this, note that in a ranked and faithful ordering it must be the case that if $w \in K(s)$ and $w' \notin K(s)$, then $w \prec_s w'$. It follows that, in this case, $\rho(\tau(s, \varphi)) \supseteq \rho(s)$. Thus, if an agent learns something consistent with his current beliefs, he maintains all of his current $\mathcal{L}$-beliefs. Ranked BCS's can be characterized by the following axiom:

PR. $((\varphi_1 \vee \varphi_2) > B\neg\varphi_2) \Rightarrow ((\varphi_2 \vee \psi) > B\neg\varphi_2) \vee ((\varphi_1 \vee \psi) > B\neg\psi)$ if $\varphi_1, \varphi_2, \psi \in \mathcal{L}$.[5]

Axiom PR is an analogue of a standard axiom of conditional logic that captures the ranking condition (Burgess 1981). We must restrict the axiom here to $\mathcal{L}$-beliefs, whereas the corresponding axiom in conditional logic need not be restricted. This difference is rooted in the fact that we take epistemic states as the primitive objects, while standard conditional logic takes worlds to be the primitive objects.[6]

What happens when the agent learns something inconsistent with his current beliefs? The next condition puts another (rather weak) restriction on the set $\min(s, \varphi)$ in this case: a preferential structure is *saturated* if for every s and for every consistent $\varphi \in \mathcal{L}$, $\min(s, \varphi)$ is not empty. Thus, in a saturated preferential BCS, as long as what the agent learns is consistent, then his belief set will be consistent. Saturated BCS's can be characterized by the following axiom:

PS. $\neg(\varphi > B(false_{\mathcal{L}}))$ if $\varphi \in \mathcal{L}$ is consistent.

Typically we are interested in axiom schemes that are recursive (or at least r.e.). This scheme, however, may not be. It depends on how hard it is to check consistency in $\mathcal{L}$. For example, if $\mathcal{L}$ is first-order logic, this scheme is co-r.e.

Belief revision and belief update assume that the belief change process depends only on the agent's $\mathcal{L}$-beliefs. This is clearly a strong assumption. We feel that a more reasonable approach is to have the revision process depend on the full epistemic state, not just on the agent's $\mathcal{L}$-beliefs. Nevertheless, we can capture the assumption that all that matters are the agent's $\mathcal{L}$-beliefs quite simply. A BCS M is *propositional* if for all epistemic states $s, s' \in M$, we have that $\rho(s) = \rho(s')$ implies $\rho(\tau(s, \varphi)) = \rho(\tau(s', \varphi))$ for all $\varphi \in \mathcal{L}$.

A stronger version of P4 holds in propositional preferential structures. We no longer have to restrict to $\mathcal{L}$-beliefs. Thus we get:

PP1. $\varphi > \psi \equiv \varphi' > \psi$ if $\varphi \equiv \varphi'$ is $\mathcal{L}$-valid

In propositional preferential structures that are (weakly) faithful, we need to strengthen axioms PF and PW in an analogous way. Call these strengthened axioms PF$'$ and PW$'$, respectively.

These changes do not suffice to characterize propositional preferential structures. To do that, we need some additional machinery. We are interested in formulas that describe epistemic states. Given a belief set $E \subseteq \mathcal{L}$, we say that φ_E describes E if for all preferential BCS's, $(M, s) \models \varphi_E$ if and only if $\rho(s) = E$. We say that a formula is a *state description* if it describes some belief set. Note that the inconsistent belief state is always describable by $B(false_{\mathcal{L}})$, the describability of other states depends on the logic $\mathcal{L}$. It is easy to see that if $\mathcal{L}$ is a propositional logic over a finite number of primitive propositions, then all belief states are describable, while if $\mathcal{L}$ is propositional logic with infinitely many primitive propositions, then the inconsistent set is the only describable belief set. We remark if $\mathcal{L}$ included an *only knowing operator* of (Levesque 1990) (as in (Rott 1989; Boutilier 1992)), then more belief sets would be describable.

The following axiom, together with PP1 (and PF$'$ and PW$'$, if we are considering (weakly) faithful structures), characterizes propositional preferential BCS's:

PP2. $(\varphi \wedge (\psi_1 > \cdots > \psi_k > \varphi)) \Rightarrow ((\varphi_1 > \varphi_2) \equiv \psi_1 > \cdots > \psi_k > \varphi_1 > \varphi_2)$ if φ is a state description.

Axiom PP2 says that if $\varphi_1 > \varphi_2$ holds in the current state and φ characterizes the agent's current beliefs, then if after learning a number of facts the agent reaches a state with exactly the same beliefs, then $\varphi_1 > \varphi_2$ also holds in that state.

The next condition we consider says that the ordering $\preceq_s$ is determined by orderings $\preceq_w$ associated with worlds $w \in K(s)$. This corresponds to the intuition of (Katsuno & Mendelzon 1991) that in belief update, we do the update pointwise (so that if we consider a set of worlds possible, we update each of them individually). Formally, we say that a preferential interpretation is *decomposable* if there is a mapping that associates each $w \in W$ with an ordering $\preceq_w$ such that $\preceq_w$ is a pre-order on $W_w = \{w' | \exists w'', w' \preceq_w w''\}$ and the following condition is satisfied: for all $s \in S$, such that $K(s) \neq \emptyset$, we have $w \prec_s w'$ if and only if $w \prec_v w'$ for all $v \in K(s)$. It easy to show that this definition implies that $\min(s, \varphi) = \bigcup_{v \in K(s)} \min(v, \varphi)$, (where $\min(v, \varphi)$ is defined similarly to $\min(s, \varphi)$) matching the condition of (Katsuno & Mendelzon 1991) for update.

Characterizing decomposable BCS's is nontrivial. However, in two cases we have (different) characterizations of decomposable BCS's. When we examine decomposable BCS's that are also (weakly) faithful and ranked we need the following two axioms:

PD1. $((\neg B\neg\varphi \wedge (\psi_1 > B\psi_2)) \Rightarrow \varphi > \psi_1 > B\psi_2$ if $\varphi, \psi_2 \in \mathcal{L}$

PD2. $(B(\varphi_1 \vee \ldots \vee \varphi_k) \wedge (\wedge_{j=1}^{k}(\varphi_j > \psi_1 > B\psi_2))) \Rightarrow \psi_1 > B\psi_2$ if $\varphi_1, \ldots, \varphi_k, \psi_1, \psi_2 \in \mathcal{L}$.

Both axioms rely on the property of ranked and (weakly) faithful structures that if φ is consistent with $\rho(s)$ then $K(\tau(s, \varphi)) \subseteq K(s)$. Another situation where we can characterize decomposable structures is where we also assume that the structures are propositional. In this case we can use state descriptions and the fact that all subsets that are equivalent in terms of belief sets also revise in the same manner.

---

[5] Alternatively, we can use the *rational monotonicity* axiom (Kraus, Lehmann, & Magidor 1990) $(\varphi > B\psi_1) \wedge \neg(\varphi > B\neg\psi_2) \Rightarrow (\varphi \wedge \psi_2 > B\psi_1)$, which is similar to what has been used by (Grahne 1991; Katsuno & Satoh 1991) to capture ranked structures.

[6] For similar reasons, the axioms P2 and P3 are restricted while their counterparts in conditional logic (see (Lewis 1973)) are not.

We get two axioms PD1$'$ and PD2$'$ that are analogues of PD1 and PD2. We omit them here for lack of space; they are described in the technical report.

Finally, we say that a BCS M is *complete* if for each belief set E, there is some state s in M such that $\rho(s) = E$. We have no axiom to characterize completeness, and we do not need one. As we shall see, in structures of interest to us, completeness does not add extra properties.

Let A be a subset of $\{f, w, r, s, p, d, c\}$. We denote by $\mathcal{M}_A^P$ the class of preferential BCS's that satisfy the respective subset of $\{$faithful, weakly faithful, ranked, saturated, propositional, decomposable, complete$\}$. For example, $\mathcal{M}_{r,s}^P$ is the class of ranked and saturated preferential BCS's.

We can now state precisely the sense in which the axioms characterize the conditions we have described. Roughly, the axiom system contains AX^P and for each one of $\{f, w, r, s\}$ in $\mathcal{A}$, the matching axiom described above. When $\mathcal{A}$ contains d the axiom system may also contain PD1 and PD2 (depending on the contents of $\mathcal{A}$). When $\mathcal{A}$ contains p, the axiom system also contains PP1 and PP2 and the strengthened versions of the axioms corresponding to f and w. Moreover, PD1$'$ and PD2$'$ are required to deal with d. This is captured by the following theorem.

Theorem 5: *Let $\mathcal{A}$ be a subset of $\{f, w, r, s\}$, let $\mathcal{B}$ be a subset of $\{d\}$, and let $\mathcal{C}$ be a subset of $\{c\}$. Let A be the subset of $\{PF, PW, PR, PS\}$ corresponding to $\mathcal{A}$, let A' be the subset of $\{PF', PW', PR', PS'\}$ corresponding to $\mathcal{A}$, let*

$$B = \begin{cases} \{PD1, PD2\} & \text{if } d \in \mathcal{B},\ r \in \mathcal{A},\ \{f, w\} \cap \mathcal{A} \neq \emptyset \\ \emptyset & \text{otherwise,} \end{cases}$$

and let

$$B' = \begin{cases} \{PD1', PD2'\} & \text{if } d \in \mathcal{B} \\ \emptyset & \text{otherwise,} \end{cases}$$

Then $AX^P \cup A \cup B$ is a sound and complete axiomatization of $\mathcal{L}^>$ with respect to $\mathcal{M}_{\mathcal{A}\cup\mathcal{B}\cup\mathcal{C}}^P$, and $AX^P \cup A' \cup B' \cup \{PP1, PP2\}$ is a sound and complete axiomatization of $\mathcal{L}^>$ with respect to $\mathcal{M}_{\mathcal{A}\cup\mathcal{B}\cup\mathcal{C}\cup\{p\}}^P$.

Belief revision and belief update

The standard approach to defining belief revision and belief update is in terms of functions mapping deductively closed subsets of $\mathcal{L}$ and formulas in $\mathcal{L}$ to deductively closed subsets of $\mathcal{L}$, satisfying certain properties. We do not describe these properties here due to lack of space, but they can be found in (Gärdenfors 1988; Katsuno & Mendelzon 1991).

Given an update or revision operator f, we can associate with it a BCS $M_f = (S, \rho, \tau)$ in a straightforward way: the elements of S are all the deductively closed subsets of $\mathcal{L}$, for $s \in S$, we define $\rho(s) = s$, and we define $\tau(s, \varphi) = f(\rho(s), \varphi)$. It is not hard to show that f is a revision (resp. update) operator if and only if $M_f \in \mathcal{M}_{w,r,s,p,c}^P$ (resp. $M_f \in \mathcal{M}_{f,s,p,d,c}^P$). We might also hope to show that every system in $\mathcal{M}_{w,r,s,p,c}^P$ is of the form M_f for some revision operator f, so that $\mathcal{M}_{w,r,s,p,c}^P$ characterizes revision operators (and similarly for $\mathcal{M}_{f,s,p,d,c}^P$ and

update operators). However, we have a slight technical problem, since even a propositional a BCS might contain more than one state with the same belief set, while M_f contains each belief set exactly once. This turns out to be not such a serious problem. We say that two BCS's M and M' are *equivalent* if for every $s \in M$ there is an $s' \in M'$ such that $\mathrm{Bel}(s) = \mathrm{Bel}(s')$ and vice versa. It follows from Proposition 1 that if $\mathrm{Bel}(s) = \mathrm{Bel}(s')$, then $\mathrm{Bel}(\tau(s, \varphi)) = \mathrm{Bel}(\tau(s', \varphi))$ for all $\varphi \in \mathcal{L}$. Hence, we can identify two equivalent BCS's (and, in particular, the same formulas are valid in equivalent BCS's).

Theorem 6:

(a) f *is a belief revision operator if and only if $M_f \in \mathcal{M}_{w,r,s,p,c}^P$. Moreover, $M \in \mathcal{M}_{w,r,s,p,c}^P$ if and only if M is equivalent to M_f for some belief revision operator f.*

(b) f *is a belief update operator if and only if $M_f \in \mathcal{M}_{f,s,p,d,c}^P$. Moreover, $M \in \mathcal{M}_{f,s,p,d,c}^P$ if and only if M is equivalent to M_f for some belief update operator f.*

This theorem, which can be viewed as a complete characterization of belief revision and belief update in terms of BCS's, is perhaps not so surprising, since it is in much the same spirit as other characterizations of belief revision and update (Grove 1988; Katsuno & Mendelzon 1991). On the other hand, when combined with Theorem 5, it means we have a complete axiomatization of belief change under belief revision and belief update.

It is interesting to compare this result to the work of (Gärdenfors 1978; 1986). In Theorem 6, the belief revision functions learned only formulas in $\mathcal{L}$, not $\mathcal{L}^>$. It follows from the theorem that in structures in $\mathcal{M}_{w,r,s,p,c}^P$, the AGM postulates hold, if we consider revision with respect to formulas in $\mathcal{L}$ and take belief sets to be subsets of $\mathcal{L}$, not $\mathcal{L}^>$. Because we restrict to belief sets in $\mathcal{L}$ and revise only by formulas in $\mathcal{L}$, we avoid the triviality problem that occurs when applying the AGM postulates to conditional beliefs (Gärdenfors 1986) or to nested beliefs (Levi 1988; Fuhrmann 1989). We remark that this approach to dealing with the triviality problem is in the spirit of suggestions made earlier (Levi 1988; Rott 1989; Boutilier 1992).

Discussion

We have analyzed belief change systems, starting with a very abstract notion of belief change and adding structure to it. The main contribution of this work lies in giving a logical (proof-theoretic) characterization of belief change operators and, in particular, belief revision and belief update. Our analysis shows what choices, in terms of semantic properties, lead to these two notions, and gives us a natural class of belief change operators that generalizes both.

Our work is also relevant to the problem of iterated belief revision. It is clear that the axiomatization we provide for belief revision captures all the properties of iterated AGM belief revision. This axiomatization highlights the fact the

AGM postulates put few restrictions on iterated belief revision. (Boutilier 1993) and (Darwiche & Pearl 1994) suggest strengthening belief revision by adding postulates on iterated belief change. In the full paper we show that these constraints can be easily axiomatized in our language, thus providing a proof system for iterated belief revision.

An important aspect of our work is the distinction between objective statements about the world and subjective statements about the agents beliefs. To analyze belief change we need to examine only the latter, and this is reflected in our choice of language. However, we believe that it is important to study belief change in frameworks that describe both the world and the agent's beliefs, and how both change over time. This type of investigation, which we are currently undertaking (see (Friedman & Halpern 1994a; 1994b)), should provide guidance in selecting the most reasonable and useful properties of belief change.

Acknowledgements

The authors are grateful to Craig Boutilier, Ronen Brafman, Adnan Darwiche, Daphne Koller, Alberto Mendelzon, and the anonymous referees for comments on drafts of this paper and useful discussions relating to this work.

References

Alchourrón, C. E.; Gärdenfors, P.; and Makinson, D. 1985. On the logic of theory change: partial meet functions for contraction and revision. *Journal of Symbolic Logic* 50:510–530.

Boutilier, C., and Goldszmidt, M. 1993. Revising by conditional beliefs. In *Proc. National Conference on Artificial Intelligence (AAAI '93)*, 648–654.

Boutilier, C. 1992. Normative, subjective and autoepistemic defaults: Adopting the Ramsey test. In *Principles of Knowledge Representation and Reasoning: Proc. Third International Conference (KR '92)*. San Francisco, CA: Morgan Kaufmann.

Boutilier, C. 1993. Revision sequences and nested conditionals. In *Proc. Thirteenth International Joint Conference on Artificial Intelligence (IJCAI '93)*, 519–525.

Burgess, J. 1981. Quick completeness proofs for some logics of conditionals. *Notre Dame Journal of Formal Logic* 22:76–84.

Darwiche, A., and Pearl, J. 1994. On the logic of iterated belief revision. In Fagin, R., ed., *Theoretical Aspects of Reasoning about Knowledge: Proc. Fifth Conference*. San Francisco, CA: Morgan Kaufmann. 5–23.

Friedman, N., and Halpern, J. Y. 1994a. A knowledge-based framework for belief change. Part I: Foundations. In Fagin, R., ed., *Theoretical Aspects of Reasoning about Knowledge: Proc. Fifth Conference*. San Francisco, CA: Morgan Kaufmann. 44–64.

Friedman, N., and Halpern, J. Y. 1994b. A knowledge-based framework for belief change. Part II: revision and update. In Doyle, J.; Sandewall, E.; and Torasso, P., eds., *Principles of Knowledge Representation and Reasoning: Proc. Fourth International Conference (KR '94)*. San Francisco, CA: Morgan Kaufmann.

Fuhrmann, A. 1989. Reflective modalities and theory change. *Synthese* 81:115–134.

Gärdenfors, P. 1978. Conditionals and changes of belief. *Acta Philosophica Fennica* 20.

Gärdenfors, P. 1986. Belief revision and the Ramsey test for conditionals. *Philosophical Review* 91:81–93.

Gärdenfors, P. 1988. *Knowledge in Flux*. Cambridge, UK: Cambridge University Press.

Grahne, G. 1991. Updates and counterfactuals. In *Principles of Knowledge Representation and Reasoning: Proc. Second International Conference (KR '91)*. San Francisco, CA: Morgan Kaufmann. 269–276.

Grove, A. 1988. Two modelings for theory change. *Journal of Philosophical Logic* 17:157–170.

Harper, W.; Stalnaker, R. C.; and Pearce, G., eds. 1981. *Ifs*. Dordrecht, Netherlands: Reidel.

Katsuno, H., and Mendelzon, A. 1991. On the difference between updating a knowledge base and revising it. In *Principles of Knowledge Representation and Reasoning: Proc. Second International Conference (KR '91)*. San Francisco, CA: Morgan Kaufmann. 387–394.

Katsuno, H., and Satoh, K. 1991. A unified view of consequence relation, belief revision and conditional logic. In *Proc. Twelfth International Joint Conference on Artificial Intelligence (IJCAI '91)*, 406–412.

Kraus, S.; Lehmann, D. J.; and Magidor, M. 1990. Nonmonotonic reasoning, preferential models and cumulative logics. *Artificial Intelligence* 44:167–207.

Levesque, H. J. 1990. All I know: A study in autoepistemic logic. *Artificial Intelligence* 42(3):263–309.

Levi, I. 1988. Iteration of conditionals and the Ramsey test. *Synthese* 76:49–81.

Lewis, D. K. 1973. *Counterfactuals*. Cambridge, MA.: Harvard University Press.

Rott, H. 1989. Conditionals and theory change: revision, expansions, and additions. *Synthese* 81:91–113.

Rott, H. 1990. A nonmonotonic conditional logic for belief revision. In A, F., and Morreau, M., eds., *The Logic of Theory Change*. Springer-Verlag. 135–181.

Stalnaker, R. C. 1968. A theory of conditionals. In Rescher, N., ed., *Studies in logical theory*, number 2 in American Philosophical Quarterly monograph series. Blackwell, Oxford. Also appears in *Ifs*, (ed., by W. Harper, R. C. Stalnaker and G. Pearce), Reidel, Dordrecht, 1981.

Wobcke, W. 1992. On the use of epistemic entrenchment in nonmonotonic reasoning. In *10th European Conference on Artificial Intelligence (ECAI'92)*, 324–328.

INCREMENTAL RECOMPILATION OF KNOWLEDGE
(Extended Abstract)

Goran Gogic[1], Christos H. Papadimitriou[1], and Martha Sideri[2]

ABSTRACT: *Approximating a general formula from above and below by Horn formulas (its* Horn envelope *and* Horn core, *respectively) was proposed in [SK] as a form of "knowledge compilation," supporting rapid approximate reasoning; on the negative side, this scheme is static in that it supports no updates, and has certain complexity drawbacks pointed out in [KPS]. On the other hand, the many frameworks and schemes proposed in the literature for theory update and revision are plagued by serious complexity-theoretic impediments, even in the Horn case, as was pointed out in [EG2] and the present paper. More fundamentally, these schemes are not inductive, in that they lose in a single update any positive properties of the represented sets of formulas (small size, Horn, etc.).* In this paper we propose a new scheme, incremental recompilation, combining Horn approximation and model-based updates; this scheme is inductive and very efficient, *free of the problems facing its constituents. A set of formulas is represented by an upper and lower Horn approximation. To update, we replace the upper Horn formula by the Horn envelope of its minimum-change update, and similarly the lower one by the Horn core of its update; the key fact is that Horn envelopes and cores are easy to compute when the underlying formula is the result of a minimum-change update of a Horn formula by a clause. We conjecture that efficient algorithms are possible for more complex updates.*

1. INTRODUCTION

Starting with the ideas of Levesque, in recent years there has been increasing interest in computational models for *rapid approximate reasoning*, starting from a "vivid" representation of knowledge [Le]. One important proposal in this regard has been the *knowledge compilation* idea of [SK], whereby a propositional formula is represented by its optimal upper (relaxed) and lower (strict) approximations by

Horn formulas —the corresponding Horn formulas are called in the present paper the *Horn envelope* and the *Horn core* of the original formula. The key idea of course is that, since these approximate theories are Horn, one can use them for rapid (linear-time) approximate reasoning.

Despite the computational advantages and attractiveness of this idea, some obstacles to its implementation have been pointed out. First, although the Horn envelope of a formula is unique, the Horn core is not; that is, there may be exponentially many most relaxed Horn formulas implying the given one. As was proved in [KPS], selecting the one with the largest set of models, or one that is approximately optimal in this respect (within *any* bounded ratio), is NP-complete. Another disadvantage is that the Horn envelope may have to be exponentially larger, as a Boolean formula, than the given formula. What is more alarming is that, even if the Horn envelope is small, it may take exponential time to produce. Even if we are given the set of models of the original formula, there is no known *output-polynomial* algorithm for producing all clauses of the Horn envelope. An algorithm is output-polynomial if it runs in time that is polynomial *in both the size of its input and its output;* this novel and little-studied concept of tractability (and, unfortunately, related concepts of *intractability*), have proved very relevant to various aspects of AI. In fact, it was shown in [KPS] that generating the Horn envelope from the models of a formula is what we call in the present paper *TRANSVERSAL-hard* —suggesting that it is unlikely to have an output-polynomial algorithm. These negative complexity results for knowledge compilation (admittedly, quite mild when compared with the serious obstacles to other approaches to knowledge representation and common-sense reasoning, see for example [EG1, EG2]) are summarized in Theorem 1.

Our knowledge about the world changes dynamically —and the world itself changes as well. The knowledge compilation idea has no provisions for incorporating such belief revisions or updates. There are, of course, in the literature many formalisms for updating knowledge bases and databases with in-

---

[1] University of California San Diego, La Jolla, California 92093-0114. e-mail: goran/christos@cs.ucsd.edu. Research supported by an NSF grant.
[2] Athens Univ. of Economics and Business, Athens, Greece. e-mail: sideri@aueb.ariadne-t.gr.

complete information [Da, Sa, Bo, We, Gi, FUV, Wi1, Fo]; see [Wi2] and [EG2] for two systematic surveys. As was established in [EG2], all these systems are plagued with tremendous complexity obstacles —even making the next inference, which is known as the *counterfactual problem*, is complete at some high level of the polynomial hierarchy for all of them. We point out in this paper (Theorem 2) some serious problems associated with computing the updated formula in the two formula-based frameworks *even in the Horn case.* The only ray of hope from [EG2] —namely that when the formula is Horn, the update is small, and the approach is any one of the model-based ones, then counterfactuals are easy— is tarnished by our observation that, in all these cases, the updated formula is not Horn (this is part (iii) of Theorem 2); hence, such an update scheme would fail to be *inductive*, retaining its positive computational properties in the face of an update.

To summarize, knowledge compilation of arbitrary formulas is not easy to do. And all known approaches to the update problem encounter serious complexity obstacles, or result in loss of the Horn property. What hope is there then for a system that supports both rapid approximate reasoning *and* updates?

Quite surprisingly, combining these two ideas, both shackled as they are by complexity-theoretic obstacles, seems to remove the obstacles from both, thus solving the combined problem, at least in some interesting and heretofore intractable cases. In particular we propose the following scheme: Suppose that formula Γ is represented by its Horn envelope $\overline{\Gamma}$ and its Horn core $\underline{\Gamma}$ (to start the process, we incur a one-time computational cost for computing these bounds; alternatively, we may insist that we start with a Horn formula). Suppose now that we update our formula by ϕ, a "simple enough" formula (how "simple" it has to be for our scheme to be efficient is an important issue which we have only partially explored; we know how to handle a single Horn clause, as well as several other special cases). *We represent the updated formula by the two formulas* $\overline{\Gamma} + \phi$ *and* $\underline{\Gamma} + \phi,$ where '+' stands for an appropriate model-based update formalism; that is, by the Horn envelope of the updated upper bound and the Horn core of the updated lower bound. These are our new $\overline{\Gamma}$ and $\underline{\Gamma}$. In other words, we apply the update to the two approximations, and approximate the two results, each in the safe direction. And so on, starting from the new approxima-

tions. The key technical point is that, although updating Horn formulas, even by Horn clauses, does not preserve the Horn property, and finding Horn envelopes and cores is hard in general, *it is easy when the formula to be approximated is the result of the update of a Horn formula by a Horn clause.* To our knowledge, our proposal, with all its restrictions, is the first computationally feasible approach to belief revision and updates.

Our proposal exhibits a desirable and intuitively expected "minimum-change" behavior, best demonstrated in the case in which a Horn formula Γ is updated by a Horn clause, say $\phi = (x\&y \rightarrow z)$. Suppose that Γ can be written as $x\&y\&\neg z\&\Gamma'$, where Γ' does not involve x, y, or z —otherwise $\Gamma + \phi = \Gamma\&\phi$. Then the upper and lower approximations are these: $\overline{\Gamma + \phi}$ is $(x\&y \leftrightarrow z)\&\Gamma'$, while $\underline{\Gamma + \phi}$ is $x\&(y \leftrightarrow z)\&\Gamma'$ (or $y\&(x \leftrightarrow z)\&\Gamma'$, recall that cores are not unique). Notice the "circumscriptive" nature of the updates (resulting from the minimum-change update formalisms that we are using).

There is an interesting and satisfying *methodological* aspect of our work. The main motivation and justification for applying the concepts and techniques of Complexity Theory to any application area is that, this way, research is supposed to be redirected by negative complexity results to the study of the right problems, to the adoption of the right approaches. For AI, there is an added argument why such results are relevant: In attacking computationally a problem in an application area, one cannot in principle exclude the possibility that this problem might be *totally insusceptible* to computational solution, that there may be *no right approach* to be discovered by a sequence of trials and negative complexity results. In contrast, a tacit ideological assumption in AI research is that the right approach *must* exist —*because intelligence exists.* Although the recent literature is teeming with complexity-theoretic criticism of approaches to various aspects of AI, the present work is an unusually clear example of a new approach that was arrived at by a tight complexity-theoretic argument excluding almost everything else.

2. NEGATIVE RESULTS

Let Γ be a *propositional* formula. Define [KS] its *Horn envelope* $\overline{\Gamma}$ to be the strictest Horn formula implied by Γ, and its *Horn core* to be the weakest Horn formula implying Γ. Naturally, one could not hope that the Horn envelope and core can be efficiently computed for all Boolean formulas. The reason is simple: Γ is unsatisfiable iff both $\overline{\Gamma}$ and $\underline{\Gamma}$ coincide with the **false** formula. But what if Γ is given in some more convenient form, say in terms of its set of models $\mu(\Gamma)$ (that is, in "full disjunctive form")? A first problem is that $\overline{\Gamma}$ may have exponentially many clauses —there is little that can be done in this case, we need them all to best approximate our formula. But can we hope to output these clauses, however many they may be, in time polynomial both in the size of input —$\mu(\Gamma)$— and of the output —$\overline{\Gamma}$? There are systematic ways that output all clauses of $\overline{\Gamma}$, but unfortunately in all known algorithms there may be exponential delay between the production of two consecutive clauses. There is no known *output-polynomial* algorithm for this problem.

There are many instances of such enumeration problems in the literature, for which no output-polynomial algorithm is known (despite the fact that, in contrast to NP-complete problems, it is trivial to output the first solution). The most famous one is to compute *all transversals of a hypergraph* [EG3]. As was pointed out in [EG3], many enumeration problems arising in AI, databases, distributed computation, and other areas of Computer Science, turn out to be what we call in this paper *TRANSVERSAL-hard*, in the sense that, if they are solvable in output polynomial time, then the transversal problem is likewise solvable.

Theorem 1 [KPS]: Enumerating all clauses of the Horn envelope of a given set M of models is TRANSVERSAL-hard. As for the Horn core, (i) it is not unique, that is, there may be exponentially many inequivalent most relaxed Horn formulas not satisfied by any model outside M; (ii) selecting the Horn core with the maxim*um* number of models (i.e., the one that best approximates M) is NP-complete; furthermore (iii) even approximating the maximum within any constant ratio is NP-complete. □

The computational problems related to updates and belief revisions are in fact much harder. Let Γ be a set of Boolean formulas, and let ϕ be another formula; ϕ will usually be assumed to be of size bounded by a small constant k. We want to compute a new set of formulas $\Gamma + \phi$ —intuitively, the result of updating Γ by ϕ. There are many formalisms in the literature for updating and revising knowledge bases. First, if $\Gamma \& \phi$ is satisfiable, then all (with the single exception of [Wi1]) approaches define $\Gamma + \phi$ to be precisely $\Gamma \& \phi$ (we often blur the distinction between a set of for-

mulas and their conjunction). So, suppose that $\Gamma \& \phi$ is unsatisfiable.

1. In the approach introduced by Fagin, Ullman, and Vardi [FUV], and later elaborated on by Ginsberg [Gi], we take $\Gamma + \phi$ to be not a single set of formulas, but the set of all maximal subsets of Γ that are consistent with ϕ, with ϕ added to each. A variant takes the "cross product" of all these formulas.

2. In a more conservative approach, we take $\Gamma + \phi$ to be ϕ plus the *intersection* of all these maximal sets —this is the "when-in-doubt-throw-it-out," or WIDTIO, approach.

3–7. The remaining approaches define $\Gamma + \phi$ implicitly, by its set of models $\mu(\Gamma + \phi)$, given in terms of the set of models of Γ, $\mu(\Gamma)$, and that of ϕ, $\mu(\phi)$ —notice that, since $\Gamma \& \phi$ is unsatisfiable, these two sets are disjoint. All five approaches take $\mu(\Gamma + \phi)$ to be *the projection* of $\mu(\Gamma)$ on $\mu(\phi)$, the subset of $\mu(\phi)$ that is closest to $\mu(\Gamma)$ —and they differ in their notions of a "projection" and "closeness." In Satoh's [Sa] and Dalal's [Da] models, the projection is the subset of $\mu(\phi)$ that achieves minimal distance from *any* model in $\mu(\Gamma)$ (in Dalal's it is minimum Hamming distance, in Satoh's minimal set-theoretic difference). In Borgida's [Bo] and Forbus's [Fo] models, the projection is the subset of $\mu(\phi)$ that achieves minimal distance from *some* model in $\mu(\Gamma)$ (in Forbus it is minimum Hamming distance, in Borgida's minimal set-theoretic difference). Finally, Winslett's [Wi1] approach is a variant of Borgida's, in which the "projection" is preferred over the intersection even if $\Gamma \& \phi$ is satisfiable.

In [EG2], Eiter and Gottlob embark on a systematic study of the complexity issues involved in the various formalisms for updates and revisions. They show that telling whether $\Gamma + \phi \models \psi$ in any of these approaches (this is known as the *counterfactual problem*) is complete for levels in the polynomial hierarchy beyond NP —that is to say, hopelessly complex. When Γ and ϕ are Horn, and ϕ is of bounded size, [EG2] show their only positive result (for adverse complexity results, even in extremely simple cases, in approaches 1 and 2, see Theorem 2 parts (i) and (ii) below): The problem is polynomial in the approaches 3–7. This seems at first sight very promising, since we are interested in updating Horn approximations by bounded formulas. The problem is that *the updated formulas cease being Horn* (part (iii)).

Theorem 2: Computing $\Gamma + \phi$, where Γ is a set of

Horn formulas and ϕ is a single Horn clause with at most three literals:

  (i) Is TRANSVERSAL-hard in the Fagin-Ullman-Vardi-Ginsberg [FUV, Gi] approach.
 (ii) Is $\mathrm{FP}^{\mathrm{NP}[\log n]}$-complete in the WIDTIO approach (that is, as hard as any problem that requires for its solution the interactive use of an NP oracle $\log n$ times).
(iii) May result in formulas that are not Horn in the model-based approaches. $\square$

3. INCREMENTAL RECOMPILATION

We now describe our scheme for representing *propositional* knowledge in a manner that supports rapid approximate reasoning and minimum-change updates. At time i we represent our knowledge base with two Horn formulas $\underline{\Gamma}_i$ and $\overline{\Gamma}_i$, such that $\underline{\Gamma}_i \models \overline{\Gamma}_i$. We start the process by computing the Horn envelope and core of the initial formula Γ_0, incurring a start-up computational cost —alternatively, we may insist that we always start with a Horn formula. Notice that we are slightly abusing notation, in that $\underline{\Gamma}_i$ and $\overline{\Gamma}_i$ may not necessarily be the Horn envelope and core of some formula Γ_i; they are simply convenient upper (weak) and lower (strict) bounds of the knowledge base being represented.

When the formula is updated by the formula ϕ_i, the new upper and lower bounds are as follows:

$$\overline{\Gamma}_{i+1} := \overline{\overline{\Gamma}_i + \phi_i},$$

$$\underline{\Gamma}_{i+1} := \underline{\underline{\Gamma}_i + \phi_i}.$$

Here '+' denotes any one of the update formalisms discussed (we address towards the end of this section the issue of selecting the appropriate formalism). That is, the new upper bound is the Horn envelope of the updated upper bound, and the new lower bound is the Horn core of the updated lower bound.

Obviously, implementing this knowledge representation proposal relies on computing the Horn envelopes and cores of updated Horn formulas. We therefore now turn to this computational problem.

Updating Horn Formulas

To understand the basic idea, suppose that we want to update a Horn formula Γ by a *clause* $\phi = (\neg x \vee \neg y)$. If $\Gamma \& \phi$ is satisfiable, then the updated formula is precisely this conjunction. So, suppose that $\Gamma \& \phi$ is unsatisfiable; that is, $\Gamma = x \& y \& \Gamma'$ for some Horn formula Γ' not involving x and y. Consider now any

model of Γ; it is of the form $m = 11m'$, where 11 is the truth values of x and y, and m' is the remaining part. The models of ϕ that are closest to it (both in minimum Hamming distance and in minimal set difference, as dictated by all five approaches) are the two models $01m'$ and $10m'$. Taking the union over all models of Γ, as the fomalisms by Borgida and Forbus suggest, we conclude that $\Gamma + \phi$, the updated formula, is $(x \neq y) \& \Gamma'$. The Horn envelope of this is easy: It is just $(\neg x \vee \neg y) \& \Gamma'$, while the Horn core is either $x \& \neg y \& \Gamma'$ or $y \& \neg x \& \Gamma'$ —we can choose either one.

As we mentioned in the introduction, in case of a Horn implication, such as $\phi = (x \& y \rightarrow z)$ with Γ of the form $x \& y \& \neg z \& \Gamma'$, the upper and lower approximations are these: $\overline{\Gamma + \phi}$ is $(x \& y \leftrightarrow z) \& \Gamma'$, while $\underline{\Gamma + \phi}$ is $x \& (y \leftrightarrow z) \& \Gamma'$ or $y \& (x \leftrightarrow z) \& \Gamma'$. The generalization to arbitrary Horn formulas is obvious.

Suppose next that $\phi = (\bigwedge_{i=1}^{m} x_i \rightarrow \bigvee_{j=1}^{n} y_i)$ is a general clause update, with $n > 1$, and $\Gamma = \bigwedge_{i=1}^{m} x_i \& \bigwedge_{j=1}^{n}(\neg y_i) \& \Gamma'$ —again, this is the interesting case. A similar calculation shows that the Horn envelope of $\Gamma + \phi$ is precisely $\bigwedge_{i \neq k}(\neg y_i \vee \neg y_k) \& \bigwedge_{i,j}(y_i \rightarrow x_j) \& \Gamma'$, whereas the Horn core is $(\bigwedge_{i=1}^{m} x_i \leftrightarrow y_j) \& \Gamma'$, for our choice of j.

Theorem 3: The Horn envelope and core of the update of a Horn formula Γ by a Horn clause ϕ, in any one of the model-based update formalisms, can be computed in time $O(|\Gamma| + |\phi|^2)$. $\square$

There is however a serious problem with our scheme when the updates are non-Horn: As can be seen from the calculation that preceded Theorem 4, the Horn envelope of the updated formula *fails to logically imply the update* —contrary to the intuitive meaning of an "update" or "belief revision," and in violation of the accepted axioms which such formalisms are supposed to satisfy (see, for example, [EG2]). It can be shown that this does not happen not only when ϕ is a single Horn clause, but also whenever it is *any Horn formula*.

Suppose now that ϕ has several clauses. In fact, suppose that ϕ is the conjunction of several *negative* clauses, with no positive literals in them, and that Γ is of the form $x_1 \& \ldots \& x_k \& \Gamma'$, where $x_1 \ldots x_k$ are the variables appearing in ϕ. Consider a model $11 \ldots 1m'$ of Γ; what is the closest in Hamming distance model of ϕ? The answer is *the model that has zeros in those variables among $x_1 \ldots x_k$ which correspond to a minimum hitting set of the clauses (considered as sets of variables)*. Therefore, telling whether the Horn envelope of the updated formula (in the Forbus model) implies x_i is equivalent to asking whether i is not involved in any minimum-size hitting set —an coNP-complete problem!

Theorem 4: Computing the Horn envelope of the update of a Horn formula by the conjunction of negative clauses in the Forbus or Dalal formalisms is NP-hard *if the update is allowed to be arbitrarily long.* $\square$

Notice however that, if we restore our assumption that the update is bounded, Theorem 4 is no threat. Also, in the other three formalisms, updates such as these turn out to be easy.

We conjecture that the Horn envelope and core of a Horn formula updated by any bounded formula can be computed in polynomial time in all five model-based update formalisms. In our view, this is an important and challenging technical problem suggested by this work. We know the conjecture is true in several special cases —for example, the one whose unbounded variant was shown NP-complete in Theorem 4— and we have some partial results and ideas that might work for the general case.

Choosing the Right Update Formalism

Of the five model-based update formalisms, which one should we adopt as the update vehicle in our representation scheme? Besides computational efficiency, there is another important desideratum: The property that $\underline{\Gamma}_i \models \overline{\Gamma}_i$, that is, that the "upper and lower bound" indeed imply one another in the desirable direction, must be retained inductively. We can show:

Theorem 5: If $\underline{\Gamma}_i \models \overline{\Gamma}_i$, and the update formalism of Winslett is adopted, then $\underline{\Gamma}_{i+1} \models \overline{\Gamma}_{i+1}$. $\square$

There are examples, to be included in the full paper, which show that the remaining four model-based formalisms may lead to situations in which the conclusion of Theorem 5 is violated.

Characteristic Models and 2SAT Approximations

As it turns out, much of this work can be extended in two directions: To the case in which the Horn formula is represented by its *characteristic models* [KKS2], and to the one in which we approximate from above and below not by a Horn formula but by a 2SAT formula (at most two literals per clause). Details will be presented in the full paper.

The Quality of Approximation

Our approach responds to updates by producing approximations of the knowledge base which become, with new updates, more and more loose. Naturally, its practical applicability rests with the quality of these approximations, and their usefulness in reasoning. This important aspect of our proposal should be evaluated experimentally; we also plan to apply it to situations in AI in which reasoning in a dynamically updated world is well-known to be challenging, such as reasoning about action.

Acknowledgment: We are indebted to Bart Selman for many helpful comments on a preliminary version of the manuscript.

REFERENCES

[Bo] A. Borgida "Language Features for Flexible Handling of Exceptions in Information Systems," *ACM Trans. on Database Systems*, 1993.

[Da] M. Dalal "Investigations into a Theory of Knowledge Baase Revision: Preliminary Report," *Proc. AAAI 88*, 475-479, 1988.

[DP] R. Dechter and J. Pearl "Structure identification in relational data," *Artificial Intelligence*, 58:237-270, 1992.

[EG1] T. Eiter, G. Gottlob "Propositional Cirsumscription and Extended Closed World Reasoning are Π_2^P-complete," *Theoretical Computer Science,* 1993.

[EG2] T. Eiter, G. Gottlob "On the Complexity of Propositional Knowledge Base Revision, Updates, and Counterfactuals," *Artificial Intell., 57* pp. 227–270, 1992.

[EG3] T. Eiter, G. Gottlob "Identifying the minimal transversals of a hypergraph and related problems," to appear in *SIAM J. of Computing*.

[Fo] K. D. Forbus "Introducing Actions in Qualitative Simulation," *Proc. IJCAI 89*, 1273–1278, 1989.

[FUV] R. Fagin, J. D. Ullman, M. Vardi "On the Semantics of Updates in Databases," *Proc. PODS 83*, 352–365, 1983.

[Gi] M. L. Ginsberg "Counterfactuals," *Artificial Intelligence*, 30:35-79, 1986.

[KKS1] H. A. Kautz, M. J. Kearns, B. Selman "Horn approximations of empirical data," to appear in *Artificial Intelligence*, 1994.

[KKS2] H. A. Kautz, M. J. Kearns, B. Selman "Reasoning with Characteristic Models," AAAI 1993.

[KPS] D. Kavvadias, C. H. Papadimitriou, M. Sideri "On Horn Envelopes and Hypergraph Transversals," *Proc. International Symposium on Algorithms and Complexity, Hong-Kong 1993*, Springer-Verlag, 1993.

[Le] H. Levesque, "Making believers out of computers," *Artificial Intelligence*, 30:81-108, 1986.

[Pa] C. H.Papadimitriou *Computational Complexity*, Addison Wesley, 1993.

[Sa] K. Satoh, "Nonmonotonic Reasoning by Minimal Belief Revision," *Proc. of the International Conference on Fifth Generation Computer Systems*, 455-462, 1988.

[SK] B. Selman, H. A. Kautz "Knowledge compilation using Horn approximation," *Proc. AAAI 1991*, 904-909, 1991.

[We] A. Weber, "Updating Proposotional Formulas," *Proc. of the First Conference on Expert Database Systems*, 10:563-603, 1985.

[Wi1] M. Winslett "Reasoning about Action Using a Possible Models Approach," *Proc. AAAI 88*, 88-93, 1988.

[Wi2] M. Winslett *Updating Logical Databases*, Cambridge University Press, 1990.

Qualitative Decision Theory*

Sek-Wah Tan and **Judea Pearl**
Cognitive Systems Lab, Computer Science Department
University of California, Los Angeles, CA 90024
$< tan@cs.ucla.edu >$ $< judea@cs.ucla.edu >$

Abstract

We describe a framework for specifying conditional desires "desire α by ϵ degrees if β" and evaluating preference queries "would you prefer σ_1 over σ_2 given ϕ" under uncertainty. We refine the semantics presented in (Tan & Pearl 1994) to allow conditional desires to be overridden by more specific desires in the database. Within this framework, we also enable consideration of surprising worlds having extreme desirability values and the determination of degrees of preference.

Introduction

This paper describes a framework for specifying conditional desires "desire α if β" and evaluating preference queries "would you prefer σ_1 over σ_2 given ϕ" under uncertainty. Consider an agent deciding whether she should carry an umbrella, given that she sees that the sky is cloudy. Naturally, she will have to consider the prospect of getting wet $\neg d$ (not dry), the possibility of rain r, the cloudiness of the sky c, and so on. Some of the beliefs that influence her decision may be expressed in conditional sentences such as: "if I have the umbrella, then I will be dry", $u \rightarrow d$; "if it rains and I do not have the umbrella, then I will be wet", $r \wedge \neg u \rightarrow \neg d$; and "typically if it is cloudy, it will rain", $c \rightarrow r$. She may also have preferences such as "I prefer to be dry", $d \succ \neg d$; and "I prefer not to carry an umbrella", $\neg u \succ u$. From the beliefs and preferences above, we should be able to infer that the agent will prefer to carry an umbrella if she observes that the sky is cloudy, assuming that being dry is more important to her than not carrying an umbrella.

The research reported in this paper concerns such qualitative decision making process. Our aim is to eventually equip an intelligent autonomous artificial agent with decision making capabilities based on two types of inputs: beliefs and preferences. Beliefs, some of which may be defeasible, will be specified by normality defaults such as "if you run across the freeway, then

---

*The research was partially supported by Air Force grant #AFOSR 90 0136, NSF grant #IRI-9200918, and Northrop-Rockwell Micro grant #93-124.

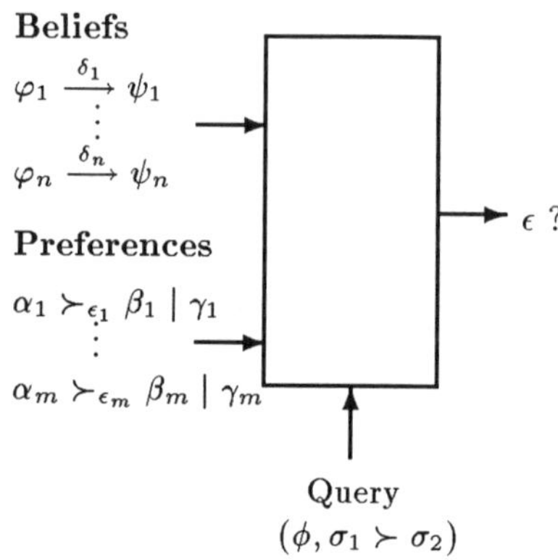

Figure 1: Schematic of the proposed system

you are likely to die", written $run \rightarrow \neg alive$. Preferences will be encoded in conditional sentences such as "if it is morning, then I prefer coffee to tea", written $coffee \succ tea \mid morning$. Figure 1 shows a schematic of the program. Each normality default $\varphi_i \xrightarrow{\delta_i} \psi_i$ and preference sentence $\alpha_i \succ_{\epsilon_i} \beta_i \mid \gamma_i$ will be quantified by an integer δ_i or ϵ_i that indicates the *degree* of the corresponding belief or preference. A larger degree implies a stronger belief or preference. The program will also accept queries in the form of $(\phi, \sigma_1 \succ \sigma_2)$, which stands for "would you prefer σ_1 over σ_2 given ϕ?" The output of the program is the degree ϵ to which the preference $\sigma_1 \succ \sigma_2$ holds in the context ϕ.

The main obstacle in the way of constructing systems such as the one above is the unstructured nature of the input information. Decision theory, the traditional paradigm for rational decision making under uncertainty, requires a complete specification of a probability distribution and a utility function before reasoning can commence. Such complete specifications are impractical in complex tasks relying on commonsense knowledge, hence, one must find a way of transforming fragmented specification sentences, given in the form of normality and desirability expressions, into a coherent criterion for rational decision-making.

In previous work (Tan & Pearl 1994), preferences

of the form $\alpha \succ \neg\alpha \mid \beta$ were given *ceteris paribum* (CP) semantics and interpreted as "α is preferred to $\neg\alpha$ other things being equal (ceteris paribum) in any β world". Such conditional preferences are called *conditional desires* and written $D(\alpha|\beta)$. The problem with the CP semantics is that it does not handle *specificity* very well. In particular, if $D(\alpha)$ is a desire in the database, we cannot subsequently express a desire $D(\neg\alpha|\beta)$ for $\neg\alpha$ in a more specific situation β (without modifying $D(\alpha)$ in the database as well). This is unsatisfactory as it is not uncommon for us to subscribe to some (default) set of desires (e.g., desire to be alive, to be rich, to be healthy) but subsequently qualify these desires (e.g., desire to die for some noble cause) for more specific situations. We would like to be able to handle specificity without having to examine or modify the desires that are already in the database.

In this paper we modify the CP semantics so that a conditional desire is allowed to override a less specific desire. We consider conditional desires of the form "if β then α is desirable by degree ϵ", written $D_\epsilon(\alpha|\beta)$, where α and β are well-formed formulas (wffs) and ϵ is an integer. We will assume that the preferences of a reasoning agent may be represented by a *preference ranking* that is, by an integer-valued function on worlds which corresponds to an order-of-magnitude approximation of the agent's utility function. Conditional desires will be interpreted as constraints on *admissible* preference rankings. We will interpret a conditional desire $D(\alpha|\beta)$ as "α is preferred to $\neg\alpha$ ceteris paribum in any β world if allowed by the other conditional desires in the preference database". While the CP semantics imposes *cp-constraints* between worlds that agree ceteris paribum, we have the additional requirement that a cp-constraint be not overridden by another cp-constraint that is due to a more specific conditional desire. A conditional desire is *more specific* than another if the former attempts to constrain a smaller set of worlds than the latter. To strengthen the system, we retain the principle of maximal indifference adopted in (Tan & Pearl 1994) and select from the set of admissible preference rankings the *most compact* rankings $\pi^+(\omega)$.

Another problem with the proposal in (Tan & Pearl 1994) is that preference queries are evaluated by comparing "believable" worlds. These are worlds that are ranked zero by the belief ranking, which is an integer-valued function that scores the "believability" of worlds. This excludes from consideration all worlds that are surprising (to any degree) even though some of the surprising worlds may have extreme positive or negative consequences. This is unsatisfactory as some extremely undesirable consequences (e.g., getting hit by a car), although unlikely, are not impossible, and some people would like to take such consequences into consideration. In this paper we weaken the notion of believability to include worlds that are ranked no more than some threshold δ. We also extend the notion of

preferential dominance and preferential entailment to allow for the strength of the preference to be determined and for the conclusions to be qualified by a degree of confidence.

In the next two sections we will describe the above extensions and improvements to the CP semantics. For the sake of brevity, we will not consider the semantics for normality defaults and will assume that we have a belief model that processes the input defaults and outputs a belief ranking. In the penultimate section, we compare related work and in the conclusion, we summarize the contributions of this paper.

Conditional Desires

Review and Notation

In this section we explain some notation and review some concepts that were introduced in (Tan & Pearl 1994). We consider conditional desires of the form $D_\epsilon(\alpha|\beta)$, where α and β are wffs obtained from a finite set of atomic propositions $X = \{X_1, X_2, \ldots, X_n\}$ with the usual truth functionals $\wedge, \vee,$ and $\neg$ and where ϵ is an integer. We will call α the desire, β the condition, and ϵ the degree (or strength) of the conditional desire $D_\epsilon(\alpha|\beta)$. For simplicity we may write $D(\alpha|\beta)$ if the degree of the desire is not relevant to the discussion or if the degree is 1 (default value). When convenient we will also use the common form $\alpha \supset \beta$ instead of $\neg\alpha \vee \beta$.

A wff α *depends on* a proposition X_i if all wffs that are logically equivalent to α contain the symbol X_i. The set of propositions that α depends on is represented by $S(\alpha)$. This set is referred to as the *support* of α, written $support(\alpha)$, in (Doyle, Shoham, & Wellman 1991). The set of propositions that α does not depend on is represented by $\bar{S}(\alpha) = X \setminus S(\alpha)$. A world is simply a truth assignment on the set of atomic propositions. We will write $\omega = a\bar{b}$ to refer to the truth assignment that assigns *true* to a and *false* to b. We say that two worlds *agree* on a proposition if they assign the same truth value to the proposition. Two worlds *agree* on a set of propositions if they agree on all the propositions in the set. We say that ω and ν are S-*equivalent*, written $\omega \sim_S \nu$, if ω and ν agree on the set $S \subseteq X$. We call $D(\alpha|\omega)$ a *specific* conditional desire if ω is a wff of the form $\bigwedge_1^n x_i$, where $x_i = X_i$ or $\neg X_i$. (As a convention we will use the same symbol ω to refer to the unique model of a wff ω.) We assume that the preferences of the reasoning agent may be represented by a preference ranking π, which is an integer-valued function on the set of worlds Ω. The preference rank of a world corresponds to an order-of-magnitude approximation of the utility associated with the world. The intended meaning of a ranking is that the world ω is no less preferred than the world ν if $\pi(\omega) \geq \pi(\nu)$. Given a non empty set of worlds W, we write $\pi_*(W)$ for $\min_{\omega \in W} \pi(\omega)$ and $\pi^*(W)$ for $\max_{\omega \in W} \pi(\omega)$. If W is empty, we adopt the convention that $\pi_*(W) = \infty$ and $\pi^*(W) = -\infty$.

We associate with each conditional desire a set of worlds, called its *context*, which defines the worlds that the conditional desire constrains.

Definition 1 (Context) *Let $D(\alpha|\omega)$ be a specific conditional desire. The* **context** *of $D(\alpha|\omega)$, written $C(\alpha,\omega)$, is defined as*

$$C(\alpha,\omega) = \{\nu \mid \nu \sim_{\overline{S}(\alpha)} \omega\}. \tag{1}$$

The context of a conditional desire $D(\alpha|\beta)$, written $C(\alpha,\beta)$, is defined to be $\cup_{\omega\models\beta}C(\alpha,\omega)$.

Given a context C, we write C_γ for $\{\nu \models \gamma \mid \nu \in C\}$ where γ is a wff. We write $C(p)$ to represent the context of the conditional desire p.

Specificity

In normal discourse, we have no difficulty accommodating general expressions of preferences that are subsequently qualified in more specific scenarios. For example, I desire to be alive $D(a)$, yet I am willing to die for some noble cause $D(\neg a|c)$. In the CP interpretation, this pair of desires would be inconsistent. In such a situation, we will usually allow $D(\neg a|c)$, which has a more specific condition, to override the unconditional desire $D(a)$. If a conditional desire attempts to constrain a subset of the worlds constrained by another desire, then we declare the former to be more specific than the latter. We define a conditional desire p to be more specific than conditional desire p' if the context of p is a strict subset of the context of p'.

Definition 2 (Specificity) *Let p and p' be conditional desires. p is* **more specific** *than p', written $p \succ p'$, if $C(p) \subset C(p')$.*

Given this definition, one might wonder whether a simpler definition of specificity would suffice, one that considers only the conditions of the conditional desires. The simple proposal would be to declare a conditional desire $p = D(\alpha|\beta)$ to be more specific than another $p' = D(\alpha'|\beta')$ if the condition of p, β implies the condition of p', β', that is, $\beta \supset \beta'$ and not vice versa. This simple proposal is not appropriate for our semantics because it declares the conditional desire $D(\alpha|\alpha)$ to be more specific than $D(\alpha)$ even though the two desires impose the same constraints. Although the simple definition is not suitable in general, it is sufficient when we restrict ourselves to a special type of conditional desires that we name simple.

Definition 3 (Simple Desires) *A conditional desire $D(\alpha|\beta)$ is* **simple** *if α and β have disjoint support.*

Theorem 1 (Simple Specificity) *Let $p = D(\alpha|\beta)$ and $p' = D(\alpha'|\beta')$. If p is simple and $\beta \supset \beta'$ but $\beta' \not\supset \beta$, then $p \succ p'$.*

Thus our definition of specificity coincides with the intuitive notion of when one conditional desire is more specific than another.

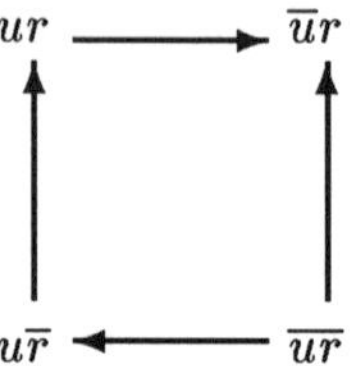

Figure 2: Applicable constraints in umbrella example.

Admissible Rankings

In the CP semantics, *ceteris paribum* constraints are imposed independently by every conditional desire in the database.

Definition 4 (CP-Constraints) $\nu \succ_\epsilon \nu'$ *is a ceteris paribum constraint (cp-constraint) of a conditional desire $D_\epsilon(\alpha|\beta)$ if $\nu \in C_\alpha(\alpha,\omega)$ and $\nu' \in C_{\neg\alpha}(\alpha,\omega)$ for some $\omega \models \beta$. c is a cp-constraint of a set D if it is the cp-constraint for some $p \in D$.*

No consideration is given to possible conflicts among these constraints to accommodate specificity.

Let us consider how a cp-constraint may be "overridden". Consider a preference database consisting of two desires, the desire for good weather (no rain) $D(\neg r)$ and the desire to not carry the umbrella $D(\neg u)$. The cp-constraints of these desires are $\overline{u}r \succ u\overline{r} \succ ur$ and $\overline{u}\overline{r} \succ \overline{u}r \succ ur$. Suppose that we would like to qualify our desire not to carry the umbrella by adding, to our database, the conditional desire to carry the umbrella if it is raining $D(u|r)$. The cp-constraint of $D(u|r)$ is $ur \succ \overline{u}r$, which is in direct conflict with the cp-constraint $\overline{u}r \succ ur$ of $D(\neg u)$. In this case we will like the cp-constraint $ur \succ \overline{u}r$ to override the cp-constraint $\overline{u}r \succ ur$ as $D(u|r)$ is more specific than $D(\neg u)$.

We say that two cp-constraints are in *competition* if they attempt to constrain the same worlds. For example the competing cp-constraints of $\omega \succ_\epsilon \nu$ are $\omega \succ_{\epsilon'} \nu$ and $\nu \succ_{\epsilon'} \omega$.

Definition 5 (Admissible Rankings) *A preference ranking π is* **admissible** *with respect to a set of conditional desires D if for all cp-constraints $\omega \succ_\epsilon \nu$ of $p \in D$ either*

$$\pi(\omega) \geq \pi(\nu) + \epsilon \tag{2}$$

or there exists another sentence $p' \in D$ such that $p' \succ p$ and p' induces a cp-constraint that competes with $\omega \succ_\epsilon \nu$.

If there exists a ranking that is admissible with respect to a set of conditional desires D, then we say that D is *consistent*. An example of an inconsistent set is $D = \{D(u), D(\neg u)\}$. Neither desire is more specific than the other and their cp-constraints are not overridden. Their cp-constraints are $u \succ \overline{u}$ and $\overline{u} \succ u$, respectively, and these imply $\pi(u) > \pi(\overline{u})$ and $\pi(\overline{u}) > \pi(u)$ since the default degree is 1. There is no ranking that can satisfy both inequalities simultaneously.

Table 1: Preference ranking in the umbrella example		

Worlds ω	Preference ranking $\pi^+(\omega)$
ur	$m+1$
$\overline{u}r$	m
$u\overline{r}$	$m+2$
$\overline{u}\overline{r}$	$m+3$

Table 2: Ranks in the fire example		

Worlds ω	Preferences $\pi(\omega)$	Beliefs $\kappa(\omega)$
if	1	1
$\overline{i}f$	-1	1
$i\overline{f}$	0	0
$\overline{i}\overline{f}$	1	0

In the umbrella example described above, we have the preference database $\{D(\neg r), D(\neg u), D(u|r)\}$. For a preference ranking to be admissible with respect to the database, it has to satisfy the cp-constraints that are not overridden. These cp-constraints are shown in figure 2 (an arrow $\omega \rightarrow \nu$ represents $\omega \succ \nu$, or $\pi(\omega) > \pi(\nu)$ since the default degree is 1). Here the cp-constraint of $D(\neg u)$, $\overline{u}r \succ ur$, is overridden by the cp-constraint $ur \succ \overline{u}r$ of $D(u|r)$ which is more specific.

In (Tan & Pearl 1994) we strengthened the semantics by adopting the principle of maximal indifference, which states that a reasoning agent is indifferent between two worlds unless a preference is explicitly communicated or can be inferred. We take the same approach here and select the most compact rankings from the set of admissible preference rankings. The reader is referred to (Tan & Pearl 1994) for a more complete discussion of the principle.

Definition 6 (The π^+ Ranking) *Let D be a consistent set of conditional desires and let Π be the set of rankings admissible with respect to D. A π^+ ranking is an admissible ranking that is* **most compact***, that is*

$$\sum_{\omega,\nu\in\Omega} |\pi^+(\omega) - \pi^+(\nu)| \leq \sum_{\omega,\nu\in\Omega} |\pi(\omega) - \pi(\nu)| \quad (3)$$

for all $\pi \in \Pi$.

Let us reconsider the umbrella example. The cp-constraints of the preference database (see figure 2) leads us to the most compact admissible preference ranking π^+. The ranks are shown in table 1 where m is an integer.

Preference Evaluation

Normality Defaults

In evaluating preference queries, it is important that we be able to take into account the relative likelihoods of the worlds. The role of normality defaults in our proposal is to keep track of esoteric yet unlikely situations (just in case they become a reality) but not allow them to interfere with mundane decision making. For the sake of brevity, we will not describe in detail the treatment of normality defaults. We will instead assume that we have a belief model that accepts normality defaults representing qualitative expressions of beliefs and outputs a belief ranking κ, an integer-valued function on worlds which scores the "believability" of the worlds. An example of such a belief model can be found in (Goldszmidt 1992). Adopting Goldszmidt's convention, worlds with belief rank 0 are believable and an increasing rank indicates increasing surprise (or decreasing believability). We also assume that belief ranks are non negative. We will write $\kappa(\phi;\sigma_i)$ to represent the ranking that results after the execution of action σ_i given context ϕ. $\kappa^\delta(\phi;\sigma_i)$ will represent the set of δ-believable worlds, namely, the set of worlds that have a $\kappa(\phi;\sigma_i)$ rank not greater than δ.

In (Tan & Pearl 1994) consideration of the possible scenarios were restricted to the 0-believable worlds κ^0 while surprising ($\kappa > 0$) were completely ignored regardless of their preference ranks. This is unsatisfactory, as some of the surprising worlds may carry extreme positive or negative utilities. For example, consider fire insurance. Many people, despite believing fires (f) to be unlikely, still want to consider insuring their belongings (i). Table 2 shows a reasonable set of values for the beliefs and preferences associated with this example. If we were to concern ourselves only with the 0-believable worlds, then we would conclude that we prefer not to insure.

In this paper we extend preference consideration to δ-believable worlds κ^δ, where δ may be either a threshold specified by the user or an output value indicating a degree of confidence that qualifies the evaluation of the query. A preference query will be confirmed with confidence at least δ if it is confirmed with confidence $\delta - 1$ and also confirmed by considering δ-believable worlds.

Preferential Dominance

Preferential dominance (Tan & Pearl 1994) is a binary relation between sets of worlds which is derived from a preference ranking on worlds. Preferential dominance examines the three types of worlds that characterize the compared sets: the common possibilities, the additional possibilities, and the excluded possibilities. When considering whether we would prefer the set W over the set V (see figure 3), we imagine that the set V represents the possibilities currently available to us and that the set W represents the set of new possibilities. Let us consider the case when $W \subset V$. Since W excludes some possibilities from V, we have to compare these excluded possibilities (in $V \setminus W$) with the new

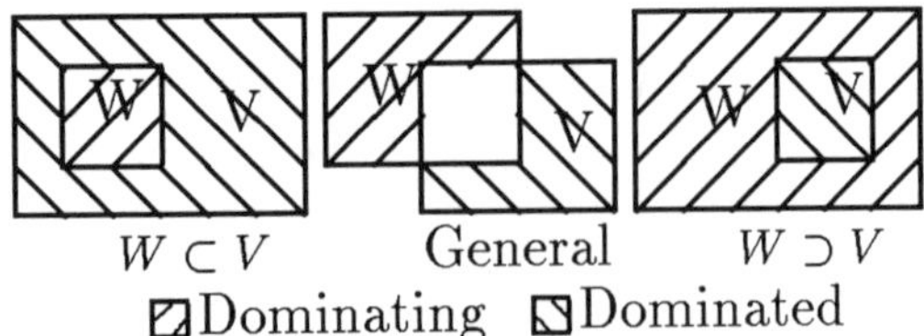

$$W \subset V \qquad \text{General} \qquad W \supset V$$

◓ Dominating   ◇ Dominated

Figure 3: Interesting cases for $W \succ_\pi V$

Table 3: Ranks in the umbrella example

Worlds ω	Preferences $\pi^+(\omega)$	Beliefs $\kappa(\omega)$
ucr	$m+1$	0
$\overline{u}cr$	m	0
$uc\overline{r}$	$m+2$	1
$\overline{u}c\overline{r}$	$m+3$	1

possibilities offered by W. If the excluded possibilities are ranked lower than those that remain then W protects us from those excluded possibilities and we should prefer W to V. In the case when $V \subset W$, W provides more possibilities. If these additional possibilities (in $W \setminus V$) are ranked higher than the current possibilities, W provides an opportunity for improvement over the situation in V and again we should prefer W to V. In the general case, if W and V have some possibilities in common, then these common possibilities (in $W \cap V$) can be disregarded. If the additional possibilities (in $W \setminus V$) are ranked higher than the excluded possibilities (in $V \setminus W$), then we will prefer W to V. In figure 3, W π-dominates V, written $W \succ_\pi V$, if the worlds in the dominating set are preferred over the worlds in the dominated set. We generalize the notion of preferential dominance to allow a preference query to be confirmed with a degree indicating the strength of the confirmation.

Definition 7 (Preferential Dominance) *Let π be a preference ranking and let W and V be two subsets of Ω. We say that W π-dominates V by ϵ, written $W \succ_\pi^\epsilon V$, if and only if one of the following holds:*

1. $\epsilon = 0$ when $W = V$,

2. $\pi_*(W) \geq \pi^*(V \setminus W) + \epsilon$ when $W \subset V$,

3. $\pi_*(W \setminus V) \geq \pi^*(V) + \epsilon$ when $W \supset V$, or

4. $\pi_*(W \setminus V) \geq \pi^*(V \setminus W) + \epsilon$ otherwise.

We write $W \succ_\pi V$ if $W \succ_\pi^\epsilon V$ for some $\epsilon \geq 0$ but $V \not\succ_\pi^0 W$.

The definition of preferential dominance in (Tan & Pearl 1994) corresponds to $\succ_\pi^1$ and is therefore slightly stronger than $\succ_\pi$.

To evaluate the preference query $(\phi, \sigma_1 \succ \sigma_2)$ with degree ϵ and confidence δ, we compare the set of i-believable worlds, $i = 0, \ldots, \delta$, resulting from executing σ_1 given ϕ to those resulting from executing σ_2 given ϕ, and test if the former *preferentially dominates* the latter by ϵ in all the most compact preference rankings.

Definition 8 (Preferential Entailment) *Let D be a set of conditional desires and κ be some belief ranking on Ω. ϕ preferentially entails $\sigma_1 \succ \sigma_2$ with degree $\epsilon \geq 0$ and confidence δ given $\langle D, \kappa \rangle$, written $\phi \vdash_\delta (\sigma_1 \succ_\epsilon \sigma_2)$, if and only if*

$$\kappa^i(\phi; \sigma_1) \succ_{\pi^+}^\epsilon \kappa^i(\phi; \sigma_2)$$

*for all π^+ rankings of D and all $i = 0, \ldots, \delta$. We say that a preference query $(\phi, \sigma_1 \succ \sigma_2)$ is **confirmed with degree ϵ and confidence δ**.*

We say that ϕ preferentially entails $\sigma_1 \succ_\epsilon \sigma_2$ with *absolute* confidence if $\phi \vdash_\delta (\sigma_1 \succ_\epsilon \sigma_2)$ for all $\delta \geq 0$. We also write $\phi \vdash_\delta (\sigma_1 \succ \sigma_2)$ if

$$\kappa^\delta(\phi; \sigma_1) \succ_{\pi^+} \kappa^\delta(\phi; \sigma_2)$$

for all π^+ rankings of D and all $i = 0, \ldots, \delta$.

Example

Let us reconsider the umbrella story and the query "would you prefer to have the umbrella given that the sky is cloudy?", $(c; u \succ \neg u)$. We have the preference database $\{D(\neg r), D(\neg u), D(u|r)\}$. Let us assume that we have the defaults database $\{c \to r\}$. For this example we will adopt the belief model in (Goldszmidt & Pearl 1992; Pearl 1993). First we process the defaults database to get the resulting belief rankings $\kappa(\omega)$. Next, as in table 3, we list the possible worlds, given that the sky is cloudy, and obtain the belief ranking $\kappa(\omega)$ and the π^+ preference ranking (from table 1), where m is some fixed integer. $\kappa^0(c; u) = \{ucr\}$ and has a minimum rank of $m+1$, while $\kappa^0(c; \neg u) = \{\overline{u}cr\}$ with a maximum rank of m. Therefore the preference query $(c; u \succ \neg u)$ is confirmed with degree 1 and confidence zero[1]. Unfortunately the preference query cannot be confirmed with absolute confidence.

Comparison with Related Work

The assertability of conditional ought statements of the form "you ought to do A if C" is considered in (Pearl 1993). The statement is interpreted as "if you observe, believe, or know C, then the expected utility resulting from doing A is much higher than that resulting from not doing A". The treatment in (Pearl 1993) assumes, however, that a complete specification of a utility ranking on worlds is available and that the scale of the abstraction of preferences is commensurable with that of the abstraction of beliefs. Another problem is that the conclusions of the system are not invariant under a lateral shift of the utility ranking

---

[1] It is unfortunate that the phrase "confidence zero" conjures up the idea of a total lack of confidence which is definitely not the intended meaning of "being confirmed with confidence zero". The intended meaning is "considering only situations which are *serious* possibilities".

because the system endows worlds toward which the agent is indifferent with special status; for example, utility rankings π_1 and π_2, where $\pi_2(\omega) = \pi_1(\omega) + 1$, may admit different conclusions.

In (Boutilier 1994), expressions of conditional preferences of the form "$I(\alpha|\beta)$ - if β then ideally α" are given modal logic semantics in terms of a preference ordering on possible worlds. $I(\alpha|\beta)$ is interpreted as "in the most-preferred worlds where β holds, α holds as well". This interpretation places constraints *only* on the most-preferred β-worlds, allowing only β-worlds that also satisfy α to have the same "rank". This contrasts with the CP semantics, which places constraints between pairs of worlds. In discussing the reasoning from preference expressions to actual preferences (which we here call preference queries), (Boutilier 1994) suggests that worlds could be assumed to be as preferred or as ideal as possible, parallelling the assumption made in computing the κ^+ belief ranking (Goldszmidt 1992) that worlds are as normal as possible. While it is intuitive to assume that worlds would gravitate towards normality because abnormality is a monopolar scale, it is not at all clear that worlds ought to be as preferred as possible since preference is a bipolar scale. This assumption of *maximal preference* can lead us to some very surprising conclusions though. Suppose that the only desire we have is to have bananas if we are alive $D(bananas \mid alive)$. The assumption will surprisingly deduce that our most desirable worlds include those where we are $\neg alive$. The π^+ rankings actually compacts the worlds away from the extremes thus minimizing unjustified preferences. It remains to be seen whether the I operator corresponds closely with the common linguistic use of the word "ideally".

Ceteris paribum comparatives, relative desires and goal expressions have been considered in (Wellman & Doyle 1991; Doyle, Shoham, & Wellman 1991; Doyle & Wellman 1994). These accounts are similar to our semantics for unquantified unconditional desires. However, in their semantics (and also in Boutilier's system), preference constraints apply strictly to worlds satisfying the condition part of the preference statement. We believe that our interpretation captures a broader use of conditional desires in common discourse. For example, we often find an expression such as "if the light is off, we prefer to have the light on", $D(light \mid \neg light)$. This expression does not confine itself only to worlds satisfying $\neg light$. Instead, it actually compares worlds with *light* against those with $\neg light$. Although the desire *light* contradicts the condition, it is nevertheless an accepted way of specifying under what states of belief the preference would be invoked.

Conclusion

This work refines the CP semantics (Tan & Pearl 1994) in three ways: it enables the handling of specificity of conditional desires, generalizes the notion of believability to allow consideration of surprising worlds, and extends preferential dominance so that the evaluation of preference queries may be qualified by an integer indicating the strength of the confirmation. The computational issues remain to be investigated, and further evaluation of the system needs to be done.

Acknowledgments

We would like to thank the three anonymous reviewers for their constructive comments and suggestions. The first author is supported in part by a scholarship from the National Computer Board, Singapore.

References

Boutilier, C. 1994. Toward a logic of qualitative decision theory. In Doyle, J.; Sandewall, E.; and Torasso, P., eds., *Principles of Knowledge Representation and Reasoning: Proceedings of the Fourth International Conference (KR94)*. Bonn, Germany: Morgan Kaufmann.

Doyle, J., and Wellman, M. P. 1994. Representing preferences as ceteris paribus comparatives. In Hanks, S.; Russell, S.; and Wellman, M., eds., *Working Notes of the AAAI Spring Symposium*, 69–75.

Doyle, J.; Shoham, Y.; and Wellman, M. P. 1991. The logic of relative desires. In *Sixth International Symposium on Methodologies for Intelligent Systems*.

Goldszmidt, M., and Pearl, J. 1992. Reasoning with qualitative probabilities can be tractable. In *Proceedings of the Eigth Conference on Uncertainty in Artificial Intelligence*, 112–120.

Goldszmidt, M. 1992. *Qualitative Probabilities: A Normative Framework for Commonsense Reasoning*. Ph.D. Dissertation, University of California Los Angeles, Cognitive Systems Lab., Los Angeles. Available as Technical Report (R-190).

Pearl, J. 1993. From conditional oughts to qualitative decision theory. In *Proceedings of the Ninth Conference on Uncertainty in Artificial Intelligence*, 12–20.

Tan, S.-W., and Pearl, J. 1994. Specification and evaluation of preferences for planning under uncertainty. In Doyle, J.; Sandewall, E.; and Torasso, P., eds., *Principles of Knowledge Representation and Reasoning: Proceedings of the Fourth International Conference (KR94)*. Bonn, Germany: Morgan Kaufmann.

Wellman, M. P., and Doyle, J. 1991. Preferential semantics for goals. In *Proceedings of the Ninth National Conference on Artificial Intelligence*, 698–703.

Soundness and Completeness of a Logic Programming Approach to Default Logic

Grigoris Antoniou
Elmar Langetepe
University of Osnabrueck, FB 6
49069 Osnabrueck, Germany
ga@informatik.Uni-Osnabrueck.DE

Abstract

We present a method of representing some classes of default theories as normal logic programs. The main point is that the standard semantics (i.e. SLDNF-resolution) computes answer substitutions that correspond exactly to the extensions of the represented default theory. We explain the steps of constructing a logic program LogProg(P,D) from a given default theory (P,D), and present the proof ideas of the soundness and completeness results for the approach.

Introduction

In last years much work is done to establish relationships between nonmonotonic reasoning and logic programming (Bidoit&Froidevaux 1991a, 1991b, Gelfond&Lifschitz 1988, 1991, Marek&Truszczynski 1989, Marek&Subrahmanian 1992, Pereira&Nerode 1993). This is usually done by defining a new semantics for logic programming (in particular of negation) and deriving a relationship to some nonmonotonic logic. In this paper we go the other way around: We maintain the classical standard semantics of logic programming (SLDNF-resolution) and try to translate a nonmonotonic logic into appropriate logic programs. In particular,

- we translate portions of Reiter's default logic (Reiter 1980) into normal logic programs, and

- prove that the translation LogProg(T) of a default theory T computes answer substitutions that exactly correspond to the extensions of T.

What are the benefits of such an approach?

- Standard semantics of logic programming is well analyzed and understood.

- Prolog is a powerful implementation of standard semantics.

- Therefore, we provide an implementational paradigm for nonmonotonic reasoning that might prove valuable in practice. For example, we might use parallel logic programming systems to achieve efficient reasoning systems.

Throughout the paper we assume familiarity with notation and basic notions of predicate logic and logic programming. In case of discomfort, please refer to (Lloyd 1987, Sperschneider&Antoniou 1991).

Basics of default logic

A *default* δ is a string $\varphi:\psi_1,...,\psi_n/\chi$ with closed first-order formulas $\varphi,\psi_1,...,\psi_n$ and χ (n>0). We call φ the *prerequisite*, $\psi_1,...,\psi_n$ the *justifications*, and χ the *consequent* of δ. A *default schema* is a string of the form $\varphi:\psi_1,...,\psi_n/\chi$ with arbitrary formulas. Such a schema defines a set of defaults, namely the set of all ground instances $\varphi\sigma:\psi_1\sigma,...,\psi_n\sigma/\chi\sigma$ of $\varphi:\psi_1,...,\psi_n/\chi$, where σ is an arbitrary ground substitution.

A *default theory* T is a pair (W,D) consisting of a set of closed formulas W (the set of truths) and a denumerable set of defaults D. The default set D may be defined using default schemata.

Let $\delta=\varphi:\psi_1,...,\psi_n/\chi$ be a default, and E and F sets of formulas. We say that δ *is applicable to* F *with respect to belief set* E iff $\varphi\in F$, and $\neg\psi_1\notin E,...,\neg\psi_n\notin E$. F *is closed under* D *with respect to* E iff, for every default $\varphi:\psi_1,...,\psi_n/\chi$ in D that is applicable to F with respect to belief set E, its consequent χ is also contained in F.

Given a default theory T=(W,D) and a set of closed formulas E, let $\Lambda_T(E)$ be the least set of closed formulas that contains W, is closed under logical conclusion and closed under D with respect to E.

A set of closed formulas E is called an *extension* of T iff $\Lambda_T(E)=E$.

In (Antoniou&Langetepe 1993)] we provided an operational characterization of extensions. Here we will show that it can be the starting point for implementational issues.

1. Definition Let $T=(W,D)$ be a default theory and $\Pi=(\delta_0,\delta_1,\delta_2,...)$ a finite or infinite sequence of defaults from D not containing any repetitions (modelling an application order of defaults from D). We denote by $\Pi[k]$ the initial segment of Π of length k, provided the length of Π is at least k. Then we define the following concepts:

- *$In(\Pi)$ is $Th(M)$, where M contains the formulas of W and all consequents of defaults occurring in Π.*

- *$Out(\Pi)$ is the set of negations of all justifications of defaults occurring in Π.*

- *Π is called a **process** of T iff δ_k is applicable to $In(\Pi[k])$ w.r.t. belief set $In(\Pi[k])$, for every k such that δ_k occurs in Π.*

- *Π is called a **successful process** of T iff $In(\Pi)\cap Out(\Pi)=\varnothing$, otherwise it is called a **failed process**.*

- *Π is a **closed process** of T iff every $\delta\in D$ which is applicable to $In(\Pi)$ with respect to belief set $In(\Pi)$ already occurs in Π.*

$In(\Pi)$ collects all formulas in which we believe after application of the defaults in Π, while $Out(\Pi)$ consists of all those formulas which we should avoid to believe for the sake of consistency. The following result (for a proof see (Antoniou&Sperschneider 1993)) states the relationship between default logic extensions and processes.

2. Theorem Let $T=(W,D)$ be a default theory. If Π is a closed successful process of T, then $In(\Pi)$ is an extension of T. Conversely, for every extension E of T there exists a closed, successful process Π of T with $E=In(\Pi)$.

Informal outline

Our approach of representing default theories by logic programs does not apply to arbitrary default theories, but to a subset thereof we call *Horn default theories*. The restrictions are as follows:

1. The truths of the default theories are given in Horn logic.

2. Each default has exactly one justification.

3. The set of defaults is finite.

4. The prerequisite, justification, and consequent of each default is a positive or negative ground literal. In this paper we further restrict attention to propositional literals, but only to keep the following sections technically simpler.

Restriction 1 is clear as we plan to use standard logic programming for deduction, while restriction 2 is only used for the sake of convenience and simplicity. 3 and 4 are restrictive, and we are working on weakening these conditions (for example by admitting conjunction). Nevertheless, Horn default theories are powerful enough to include say taxonomic default theories (Froidevaux 1986).

The main ideas of the translation of Horn default theories into normal logic programs are the following:

- Use negation as failure to model nonmonotonicity.

- Enumerate the defaults and represent a current process Π by the numbers of the defaults in Π.

- Replace negative literals $\neg p$ appearing in defaults by new predicates $\underline{p}$.

In the next section we show how negative literals can be treated using new predicates. Then we put all ideas together and present the entire translation.

The logical basis of treating negative literals

As negative literals may be used in defaults, we shall have to test derivability or nonderivability of negative literals from the knowledge base built at some stage (i.e. the In-set of the process built so far). Consider as a simple example the set of Horn formulas $P = \{p\leftarrow q, \leftarrow p\}$; $\neg q$ obviously follows from P. If we use new predicate symbols for negated atoms, we can translate P into the logic program $P' = \{\underline{p}\leftarrow q, \underline{p}\leftarrow\}$. Unfortunately, there is no SLD-refutation of $P'\cup\{q\}$ as should be. What is obviously missing is application of the rule $\underline{p}\leftarrow q$ via contraposition, i.e. $\underline{q}\leftarrow\underline{p}$. This gives rise to the following definition.

3. Definition For a definite logic program P define $\underline{P}$ as $\{\underline{B_i}\leftarrow\underline{A},B_1,...,B_{i-1},B_{i+1},...,B_n \mid A\leftarrow B_1,...,B_n\in P,\ n\geq1,\ i\in\{1,...,n\}\}$.

Usage of $P\cup\underline{P}$ is still insufficient as shown by the following example. Let P be $\{p\leftarrow q,r\ ,\ q\leftarrow r,\ \leftarrow p\}$. Obviously, $\neg r$ follows from P, but there is no SLD-refutation of $P\cup\underline{P}\cup\{\leftarrow\underline{r}\} = \{p\leftarrow q,r\ ,\ \underline{q}\leftarrow\underline{p},r\ ,\ \underline{r}\leftarrow\underline{p},q\ ,\ q\leftarrow r\ ,\ \underline{r}\leftarrow\underline{q}\ ,\ \leftarrow p\ ,\ \leftarrow\underline{r}\}$. Reflection on this example shows that missing is a fact $\underline{r}\leftarrow$ that is needed in the

SLD-refutation. This means that when testing derivability of some $\underline{r}$ from $P \cup \underline{P}$, we must (temporarily) add an additional fact $r \leftarrow$ to the knowledge base. It can be shown that this approach is sound and complete; for a proof, see (Langetepe 1994).

4. Theorem *Let P be a definite logic program, A, $G_1,...,G_k$ positive literals, and $P \cup \{\leftarrow G_1,...,\leftarrow G_k\}$ consistent.*

(a) $P \cup \{\leftarrow G_1,...,\leftarrow G_k\} \models \exists(\neg A) \Leftrightarrow$

$\quad P \cup \underline{P} \cup \{\underline{G_1} \leftarrow,..., \underline{G_k} \leftarrow\} \cup \{A \leftarrow\} \models \exists(\underline{A})$

(b) $P \cup \{\leftarrow G_1,...,\leftarrow G_k\} \models \exists(A) \Leftrightarrow$

$\quad P \cup \underline{P} \cup \{\underline{G_1} \leftarrow,..., \underline{G_k} \leftarrow\} \models \exists(A)$

The logic program LogProg(P,D)

Given a Horn default theory T=(P,D), we construct a corresponding logic program LogProg(P,D).

0. step: Enumerate D

Enumerate the (finitely many) defaults in D: Let D be $\{\delta_0,...,\delta_n\}$.

1. step: Build P_L

As stated before, we use a list to represent the defaults applied so far. This means that the consequents of the defaults in the process built so far are available in the knowledge base. Obviously, the truths of the default theory (i.e. P) are available at any stage. Therefore: For each program clause $p \leftarrow p_1,...,p_k$ in P build the clause

$$p(L) \leftarrow p_1(L),...,p_k(L).$$

2. step: Build $\underline{P}_L$

In the previous section we saw that $\underline{P}$ is necessary for the derivation of negative literals. Equip the rules in $\underline{P}$ with a list L as seen in the 1. step.

3. step: Build Supplement(D)

- For each default δ_i in D with consequent r add the clause

$$r(L) \leftarrow member(i,L).$$

  For each default δ_i in D with consequent $\neg r$ add the clause

$$\underline{r}(L) \leftarrow member(i,L).$$

  The meaning is what we have already stated before: If i is member of L then δ_i has been applied, so its consequent should be in the current knowledge base (determined by L).

- If the prerequisite of δ_i is $\neg p$ then add

$$p(L) \leftarrow member([pre,i],L).$$

The meaning gets clear if we think back to Theorem 4. There we saw that in order to test derivability of a negative literal $\neg p$ (as in the test of applicability of default δ_i), we must *temporarily* add p to the current knowledge base. Exactly this is the meaning of the added rule: we are adding p but in a distinguished way (indicated by *pre*), so that p is not part of the current knowledge base but is only used in the derivability test of $\underline{p}$.

- If the justification of δ_i is a positive literal q then add

$$q(L) \leftarrow member([conscheck,i],L).$$

The explanation of this rule is the same as above, if we recall that consistency check means to try to derive the negation of the justification, in our case $\neg q$, a negative literal.

4. step: Build program Member

$$member(X,[X|L]) \leftarrow$$
$$member(X,[Y|L]) \leftarrow member(X,L).$$

5. step: The control structure Process(D)

The function of the control structure is to systematically build processes by applying defaults and backtracking, if necessary (i.e. if a process is failed or if another extension is sought).

Let $i \in \{0,...,n\}$ (recall that $D = \{\delta_0,...,\delta_n\}$) and δ_i be the default $p_i : B/C$. Define $\underline{q}_i$ as $\underline{q}$ if B is a positive atom q, and as q if B is a negative atom $\neg q$. Similarly, define $\underline{r}_i$ as $\underline{r}$ if C is a positive atom r, and as r if B is a negative atom $\neg r$. Add to the logic program the rule *proc(i)*:

```
process(Lold,L) ←    consistent(Lold),
                     not member(i,Lold),
                     p_i([[pre,i] | Lold]),
                     not q_i([[conscheck,i] | Lold]),
                     process([i | Lold],L).
```

Now we add some additional rules, namely the termination case for the predicate process, and the implementation of the predicates consistent, closed, and successful.

```
process(L,L) ←    consistent(L), closed(L),
                  successful(L)
closed(L) ← not (    not member(0,L),
                     p_0([[pre,0] | L]),
```

$$\text{not } \underline{q}_0([[\text{conscheck},0] \mid L])),$$

$$\cdots$$

$$\begin{aligned}
\text{not } (\text{ not member}(n,L), \\
p_n([[\text{pre},n] \mid L]), \\
\text{not } \underline{q}_n([[\text{conscheck},n] \mid L]))
\end{aligned}$$

$$\text{successful}(L) \leftarrow$$
$$\text{not } (\text{ member}(0,L), \underline{q}_0([[\text{conscheck},0] \mid L])),$$

$$\cdots$$

$$\text{not } (\text{ member}(n,L), \underline{q}_n([[\text{conscheck},n] \mid L])),$$

$$\text{consistent}([\ ]) \leftarrow$$
$$\text{consistent}([i \mid \text{Lold}]) \leftarrow \text{not } \underline{r}_i([i \mid \text{Lold}]).$$

(the last rule, of course, for each $i \in \{0,\ldots,n\}$).

6. step: LogProg(P,D)

Define LogProg(P,D) as

$P_L \cup \underline{P}_L \cup \text{Supplement}(D) \cup \text{Member} \cup \text{Process}(D).$

Explanations and examples of this approach can be found in (Antoniou&Langetepe 1994).

Remark on a Prolog implementation

When implementing the normal logic program Log-Prog(P,D) in Prolog, some obvious modifications must be carried out. These include a more efficient implementation of member, and usage of one Prolog rule instead of the finite collection of rules *proc(i)* for the predicate process and corresponding rules in the definition of closed and consistent. The reason we use separate rules in LogProg(P,D) is of technical nature in order to derive soundness and completeness; it is easily seen that the Prolog implementation with one rule would not lead to a normal logic program (predicates p_i and $\underline{q}_i$ would dynamically depend on the default i chosen).

The main result

Our approach is sound and complete - the entire proof is given in (Langetepe 1994); in the next section we present the main steps). Note that the additional condition in the completeness result (hierarchical program P) has nothing to do with our approach, but is the usual restriction in the completeness of SLDNF-resolution.

5. Theorem *Let (P,D) be a Horn default theory.*

(a) If there exists an SLDNF-refutation of

$$LogProg(P,D) \cup \{\leftarrow process([\ ],L)\},$$

then the computed answer substitution has the form

$$\{L/[i_0,\ldots,i_k]\}$$

with $i_j \in \{0,\ldots,n\}$, and

$$\Pi = (\delta_{i_k},\ldots,\delta_{i_0})$$

is a closed, successful process of (P,D), i.e. In(Π) is an extension of (P,D).

(b) If P is hierarchical and $\Pi = (\delta_{i_0},\ldots,\delta_{i_k})$ is a closed, successful process of (P,D), then there exists an SLDNF-refutation of

$$LogProg(P,D) \cup \{\leftarrow process([\ ],L)\}$$

with computed answer substitution $\{L/[i_k,\ldots,i_0]\}$.

The proof outline

Both soundness and completeness of our approach are shown using the operational semantics of Log-Prog(P,D), i.e. by analyzing the structure of an SLDNF-refutation of LogProg(P,D)$\cup\{\leftarrow process([\ ],L)\}$. Because of space limitations we only give the main steps and lemmata of the proof.

Soundness

First we show that representing inclusion of formulas in the current knowledge base as done in Log-Prog(P,D) works in the intended way.

6. Lemma *Let P be a definite logic program, $p_i(t_i)$ (i = 1 ,2 ,3) ground atoms, A an atom, L' a ground list, and t_i' (i = 1, 2, 3) ground terms such that $t_1',t_2' \in L'$ and $t_3' \notin L'$. Assume that predicate member does not occur in P or in A. Then: An SLDNF-refutation of*

$$P \cup \{p_1(t_1) \leftarrow\} \cup \{\leftarrow A\}$$

exists iff there is an SLDNF-refutation of

$$P_L \cup \text{Member} \cup \{p_i(t_i) \leftarrow member(t_i',L') \mid i = 1, 3\} \cup \{\leftarrow A_L\}.$$

The ground atoms $p_i(t_i)$ cover the three possible cases: $p_1(t_1)$ is included in the knowledge base, $p_2(t_2)$ and $p_3(t_3)$ are not: the first one because of the lacking corresponding rule, the latter because $t_3' \notin L'$. Lemma 6 can be extended to an arbitrary finite number of ground atoms and to arbitrary goals (in Horn logic). The following lemma gives some structure properties of SLDNF-refutations of LogProg(P,D)$\cup\{\leftarrow process([\ ],L)\}$.

7. Lemma *An SLDNF-refutation of Log-Prog(P,D)$\cup\{\leftarrow process([\ ],L)\}$ has the following properties:*

(a) There are k resolution steps with side clauses proc(i), and then one step with side clause with

head process(L,L). No other rule from Process(D) is used afterwards.

(b) Each intermediate goal G includes at most one literal with predicate **process**; *the literal has the form process(L_1,L_2) with a ground list L_1 and a variable L_2 occurring only once in G.*

Further analysis the SLDNF-refutation of LogProg(P,D)$\cup\{\leftarrow$process([ ],L)$\}$ using the result above leads to the following

8. Lemma *Suppose there is an SLDNF-refutation of LogProg(P,D)$\cup\{\leftarrow$process([ ],L)$\}$ with computed answer substitution μ. Then:*

(a) $\mu = \{L/[i_0,\dots,i_k]\}$ with $i_j \in \{0,\dots,n\}$

(b) For m = k, k-1,...,0 there are SLDNF-refutations of

LogProg(P,D)$\cup\{\leftarrow$ not $r_{i_{k-m}}([i_{k-m},\dots,i_0])\}$

LogProg(P,D)$\cup\{\leftarrow$ not member(i_{k-m},[i_{k-m-1},...,i_0])}

LogProg(P,D)$\cup$

$\{\leftarrow p_{i_{k-m+1}}([$ [pre,i_{k-m}]\[i_{k-m-1},...,i_0]]}

LogProg(P,D)$\cup$

$\{\leftarrow$ not $q_{i_{k-m}}([[conscheck,i_{k-m}]\[i_{k-m-1},\dots,i_0]]\}$.

(c) For each $i \in \{0,\dots,n\}$ exists a finitely failed SLDNF-tree of

LogProg(P,D)$\cup\{\leftarrow$ not member(i,[i_k,...,i_0])} or of

LogProg(P,D)$\cup\{\leftarrow p_i([$ [pre,i]\[i_k,...,i_0]]} or of

LogProg(P,D)$\cup\{\leftarrow$ not $q_i([[conscheck,i]\[i_k,\dots,i_0]]\}$.

(d) For each $i \in \{0,\dots,n\}$ exists a finitely failed SLDNF-tree of

LogProg(P,D)$\cup\{\leftarrow$member(i,[i_k,...,i_0])} or of

LogProg(P,D)$\cup\{\leftarrow q_i([[conscheck,i]\[i_k,\dots,i_0]]\}$.

Using this lemma and soundness of SLDNF-resolution it is not difficult to show that indeed defaults $\delta_{i_k},\dots,\delta_{i_0}$ may be applied in this order and form a closed, successful process Π of (P,D). This shows that the computed answer substitution *{L/[i_0,...,i_k]}* determines the generating defaults of the extension In(Π) of (P,D).

Completeness

9. Lemma *Let P be a hierarchical logic program. Then, P$\cup\underline{P}$ is also hierarchical.*

Proof scetch Let m := max{level(p) | p predicate symbol in P}. Define

level($\underline{p}$) := 2m - level(p) + 1.

With this definition it is easy to check that P$\cup\underline{P}$ is hierarchical. Now suppose $\Pi = (\delta_{i_0},\dots,\delta_{i_k})$ is a closed, successful process of (P,D) (i.e. In(Π) is an extension of the default theory (P,D)). By definition of processes we have for all m = k, k-1,...,1

- $i_0,\dots,i_k$ are pairwise disjoint

- P$\cup\{r_{i_s} \mid s = 0,\dots,k\text{-}m\text{-}1\} \models p_{i_{k-m}}$

- P$\cup\{r_{i_s} \mid s = 0,\dots,k\text{-}m\text{-}1\} \not\models \neg q_{i_{k-m}}$

- P$\cup\{r_{i_s} \mid s = 0,\dots,k\text{-}m\text{-}1\}$ is consistent.

Applying the results of Theorem 4, completeness of SLDNF-resolution for hierarchical programs, and Lemma 6 we can show existence of

> an SLDNF-derivation of $\leftarrow$process([i_k,...,i_0],L)
>
> from LogProg(P,D)$\cup\{\leftarrow$process([ ],L)$\}$ (*)

From the information that P is closed and successful we may show that there exist SLDNF-refutations of

> LogProg(P,D)$\cup\{\leftarrow$closed([i_k,...,i_0])$\}$
>
> LogProg(P,D)$\cup\{\leftarrow$successful([i_k,...,i_0])$\}$ (**)
>
> LogProg(P,D)$\cup\{\leftarrow$consistent([i_k,...,i_0])$\}$

Resolving $\leftarrow$process([i_k,...,i_0],L) (from (*)) with side clause

```
process(L',L') ←    consistent(L'), closed(L'),
                    successful(L')
```

using a most general unifier $\{L/[i_k,\dots,i_0], L'/[i_k,\dots,i_0]\}$ and applying (**) we finally derive the empty clause. Altogether, we have constructed an SLDNF-refutation of LogProg(P,D)$\cup\{\leftarrow$process([ ],L)$\}$ with computed answer substitution $\{L/[i_k,\dots,i_0]\}$.

Conclusion

We gave an automated translation of a class of default theories into normal logic programs. The main contribution of this paper is the proof (outline) of the result that the answer substitutions computed by the logic program via its standard semantics correspond exactly to the extensions of the default theory.

There is still much work to be done. First, we are working on weakening some restrictions to the default theories. We are thinking especially of admitting conjunction and investigating cases where infinite theories and extensions could be treated (using unification).

We are also planning to make an experimental

comparison with other methods of implementing default logic like truth maintenance systems, graphs, the system Theorist (Poole 1988) etc. One of the most promising ideas is to exploit the parallelism in the logic programs given in this paper and thus in providing an efficient, parallel implementation of (parts of) default logic.

Finally, we are planning to investigate the relevance of our translation of default theories into logic programming when using nonstandard semantics.

References

Antoniou, G., and Sperschneider, V. 1993. Computing Extensions of Nonmonotonic Logics. In Proceedings 4th Scandinavian Conference on Artificial Intelligence, IOS Press.

Antoniou, G., and Langetepe, E. 1993. A Process Model for Default Logic and its realization in Logic Programming. In Proceedings Portuguese Conference on Artificial Intelligence (EPIA-93), Springer LNAI.

Antoniou, G., and Langetepe, E. 1994. Translation of parts of default logic into normal logic programs with standard semantics. In Proceedings European Conference on Artificial Intelligence (submitted).

Bidoit, N., and Froidevaux, C. 1991a. General Logic Databases and Programs: Default Logic Semantics and Stratification. *Information and Computation* 91, 15-54.

Bidoit, N., and Froidevaux, C. 1991b. Negation by Default and Unstratifiable Logic programs. *Theoretical Computer Science* 78, 85-112.

Froidevaux, C. 1986. Taxonomic Default Theory. In Proceedings European Conference on Artificial Intelligence(ECAI-86).

Gelfond, M., and Lifschitz, V. 1988. The Stable Model Semantics for Logic Programming. In Proceedings 5th Int. Conference/Symposium on Logic Programming, 1070-1080.

Gelfond, M., and Lifschitz, V. 1991. Classical Negation in Logic Programs and Disjunctive Databases. *New Generation Computing* 9, 365-385.

Langetepe, E. 1994. Betrachtung einzelner Default-Logik Ansätze unter Verwendung eines operationalen Extensionsmodells. Masters Thesis, Fachbereich 6, Universität Osnabrück.

Lloyd, J.W. 1987. *Foundations of Logic Programming* 2. edition. Springer.

Marek, W., and Truszczynski, M. 1989. Stable Semantics for Logic Programs and Default Theories. In Proceedings North American Conference on Logic Programming, 243-256.

Marek, W., and Subrahmanian, V.S. 1992. The Relationship between Stable, Supported, Default and Autoepistemic Semantics for General Logic Programs. *Theoretical Computer Science* 103, 365-386.

Pereira, L.M., and Nerode, A. 1993. *Logic Programming and Non-monotonic Reasoning, Proceedings of the 2nd International Workshop*. MIT Press.

Poole, D. 1988. A Logical Framework for Default Reasoning. *Artificial Intelligence* 36.

Reiter, R. 1980. A Logic for Default Reasoning. *Artificial Intelligence* 13.

Sperschneider, V., and Antoniou, G. 1991. *Logic: A Foundation for Computer Science*. Addison-Wesley.

Reasoning About Priorities in Default Logic

Gerhard Brewka

GMD, Postfach 13 16
53731 Sankt Augustin, Germany
brewka@gmd.de

Abstract

In this paper we argue that for realistic applications involving default reasoning it is necessary to reason about the priorities of defaults. Existing approaches require the knowledge engineer to explicitly state all relevant priorities which are then handled in an extra-logical manner, or they are restricted to priorities based on specificity, neglecting other relevant criteria. We present an approach where priority information can be represented *within* the logical language.

Our approach is based on PDL, a prioritized extension of Reiter's Default Logic recently proposed by the same author. In PDL the generation of extensions is controlled by an ordering of the defaults. This property is used here in the following way: we first build Reiter extensions of a given default theory. These extensions contain explicit information about the priorities of defaults. We then eliminate every extension E that cannot be reconstructed as a PDL extension based on a default ordering that is compatible with the priority information in E. An example from legal reasoning illustrates the power of our approach.

1. Introduction

Defaults often conflict with each other. Consistency based approaches, like Reiter's default logic (Reiter 1980) or autoepistemic logic (Moore 1985), produce different extensions in such a case. Basically, there are as many extensions as ways to resolve conflicts among defaults. Approaches based on preferential models, like circumscription (McCarthy 1980) or preferential entailment (Kraus, Lehmann, & Magidor 1990) are intrinsically skeptical and often produce overly weak conclusions if there are many conflicts. For this reason the importance of default priorities is widely acknowledged. Such priorities allow implausible alternatives to be eliminated and are particularly relevant for many practical applications like diagnosis or design where less plausible solutions can be disregarded if defaults are prioritized accordingly.

A number of different techniques for handling priorities of defaults have been developed. Two main types of approaches can be distinguished:

1. approaches which handle explicit priority information that has to be specified by the user and is not part of the logical language, e.g. (Lifschitz 1985; Konolige 1988; Brewka 1989; Grosof 1991),

2. approaches which handle implicit priority information based on the specificity of defaults (Touretzky 1986; Touretzky, Horty, & Thomason 1987; Touretzky, Thomason, & Horty 1991; Pearl 1990; Geffner & Pearl 1992).

Although both types of approaches have provided useful techniques and insights we argue in this paper that a somewhat different treatment of priorities is needed.[1] For real world applications it seems unrealistic to assume that all relevant priorities can be specified by the user explicitly. On the other hand, specificity as the single preference criterion is entirely insufficient in many cases. Therefore we strongly believe that it should be possible to reason about default priorities in the logic in the same way we reason about properties of objects in the domain, e.g., about Tweety's flying ability. We want to be able to represent statements about the priorities in our domain theories and derive conclusions that take this priority information into account appropriately.[2]

One area where the need to reason about priorities has clearly been identified is legal reasoning, see for instance the two recent dissertations (Prakken 1993; Gordon 1993). In the legal domain the priority of one law over another conflicting law may depend on specificity considerations, but also on other criteria like recency (the newer law beats the older one) or authority (federal law beats state law). Note that a more recent general law may override a more specific older law, i.e. specificity is not always the main preference

---

[1]There are also approaches that combine the two types, like Goldszmidt and Pearl's System-Z^+ (Goldszmidt & Pearl 1991). However, this still does not give the expressiveness we want.

[2]An approach that is similar in spirit to ours was independently developed by Prakken (personal communication). Since the technical details in his system are still in flux we are unable to give a detailed comparison at the moment.

criterion. In particular Gordon has argued convincingly that reasoning about the priority of involved laws plays a fundamental role in legal decision making. Any logical model of such decision making should thus include reasoning about priorities.

The approach we propose in this paper is based on Reiter's default logic DL (Reiter 1980), and in particular on an extended version of DL called PDL recently proposed in (Brewka 1993). In PDL a partial order of the defaults controls the generation of extensions. This logic is therefore particularly well-suited for our purposes. Our approach is based on the following ideas:

1. we extend the logical language to make statements about default priorities possible,

2. we generate Reiter extensions of our default theories; these extensions contain information about priorities of defaults,

3. we eliminate all those extensions which cannot be reconstructed as PDL extensions using an ordering that is compatible with their own priority information.

Readers familiar with recent developments in nonmonotonic reasoning may wonder why we go back to default logic instead of using one of the more recent conditional approaches (Delgrande 1987; Lehmann 1990; Pearl 1990; Boutilier 1992) that are much more en vogue today. There are two answers to this:

1. Conditional nonmonotonic logics have difficulties to deal with irrelevant information. For instance, if the default "birds fly" is given, this does not sanction the conclusion that a particular green bird flies since the property of being green might be relevant to flying. The conditional approaches therefore have to make additional, often rather tedious, meta-theoretic assumptions that make it possible not only to reason about, but also with defaults in a satisfactory way.[3] DL, on the other hand, although weak at reasoning about defaults, is one of the logics that handle irrelevant information nicely. It therefore seems worthwhile to further investigate DL and similar logics.

2. The specificity criterion is built into the logical machinery of the conditional approaches, and in fact this is commonly viewed as one of their main advantages. Given that specificity appears to be only one preference criterion among many others, at least in certain applications, we consider this property as a disadvantage rather than an advantage because it is difficult to see how specificity could be overridden when necessary.

In general, it seems rather difficult to combine the techniques for reasoning about priorities developed in this paper with conditional logics since these techniques are based on the tentative generation and possible rejection of extensions.

For simplicity we will restrict ourselves in this paper to default theories where the number of defaults is finite. Moreover, following the view expressed in (Reiter & Criscuolo 1981; Brewka 1993) we consider the possibility to encode priorities as the main advantage of non-normal defaults, i.e. defaults whose consistency condition is not equivalent to the consequent. Since we investigate other explicit means for representing such priorities we will only be concerned with normal defaults in this paper (the exact definition of normal and non-normal defaults will be given in Section 2).

The rest of the paper is organized as follows: Section 2 briefly reviews the logics underlying our approach, namely Reiter's DL and and its prioritized generalization PDL. Section 3 is the central section of the paper. Here we show how reasoning about default priorities can be accomplished. Section 4 gives an extended example from the area of legal reasoning illustrating the power of the approach. Section 5 concludes.

2. Default logic with priorities: a brief review

In this section we briefly review Reiter's default logic DL (Reiter 1980) and in particular our modification of DL called PDL (Brewka 1993) that allows priorities to be represented explicitly and will be the basis of our approach to reasoning about priorities.[4] Our presentation of PDL here has to be very short. For a detailed discussion, motivation, examples, and comparison with other approaches we refer to the original paper (Brewka 1993).

In DL default theories consist of a set of facts W and a set of defaults D. Each default is of the form $A:B_1,\ldots,B_n/C$ where A, B_i, and C are closed formulas. We will use open defaults. i.e. defaults containing free variables, to represent all of their ground instances.

A default theory generates extensions which are defined as fixed points of an operator Γ. Γ maps an arbitrary set of formulas S to the smallest deductively closed set S' that contains W and satisfies the condition: if $A:B_1,\ldots,B_n/C \in D$, $A \in S'$ and for all i $(1 \le i \le n)\ \neg B_i \notin S$ then $C \in S'$. Extensions represent sets of acceptable beliefs a reasoner might adopt. They can be used to define a skeptical inference relation where a formula is defined to be provable iff it is contained in all extensions of (D, W).

In PDL a strict partial order $<$ over the defaults can be specified in addition to facts and defaults. In (Brewka 1993) we argue that normal defaults of the form $A:B/B$ are sufficient if explicit means for representing priorities are available. Therefore PDL is defi-

---

[3] This "criticism" might seem a bit unfair since the approach proposed in this paper certainly can be viewed as meta-theoretic. However, we need such techniques for reasoning about priorities, not for reasoning with defaults as the conditional approaches.

---

[4] A similar but not equivalent prioritized version of DL has independently been developed by Baader and Hollunder (Baader & Hollunder 1993).

ned for normal defaults only. The default $A{:}B/B$ will be abbreviated $A \to B$ in this paper. Here are the necessary definitions:[5]

Definition 1 *Let E be a set of formulas, $\delta = a \to c$ a default. We say δ is active in E iff (1) $a \in E$, (2) $c \notin E$, and (3) $\neg c \notin E$.*

Definition 2 *Let $\Delta = (D, W, <)$ be a (prioritized) default theory, $\ll$ a strict total order containing $<$. We say E is the (PDL) extension of Δ generated by $\ll$ iff $E = \bigcup E_i$, where $E_0 := Th(W)$, and*

$$
E_{i+1} = \begin{cases} E_i & \text{if no default is active in } E_i \\ Th(E_i \cup \{c\}) & \text{otherwise, where } c \text{ is the} \\ & \text{consequent of the } \ll\text{-mini-} \\ & \text{mal default active in } E_i. \end{cases}
$$

Definition 3 *Let $\Delta = (D, W, <)$ be a (prioritized) default theory. E is a (PDL) extension of Δ iff there is a strict total order containing $<$ that generates E.*

The following simple birds example illustrates these definitions. As usual we just list defaults and formulas, the sets D and W are obvious from syntax.

$$
\begin{array}{ll}
1)\ b \to f & 3)\ p \to \neg f \\
2)\ p \to b & 4)\ p
\end{array}
$$

In DL we obtain two extensions, namely

$$E = Th(\{p, b, f\})$$

and

$$E' = Th(\{p, b, \neg f\}).$$

Now assume we define $3 < 1$. There are exactly three total orderings of the defaults respecting $<$, namely

$$
\begin{array}{c}
2 < 3 < 1 \\
3 < 2 < 1 \\
3 < 1 < 2
\end{array}
$$

It is easy to verify that in each case we obtain E' as the generated extension. Consider as an example the first of the three total orderings. We obtain the following sequence of sets

$$
\begin{array}{c}
E_0 = Th(\{p\}) \\
E_1 = Th(\{p, b\}) \\
E_2 = Th(\{p, b, \neg f\}) \\
E_3 = E_2 \\
\cdots
\end{array}
$$

The two other orderings lead to the same extension. The single generated extension thus is the one where the preferred default 3 is applied.

Note that the definition of PDL extensions is fully constructive. In (Brewka 1993) we also present an alternative, non-constructive prioritized version of DL that formalizes somewhat different intuitions about the behavior of prioritized default rules. Furthermore, we

show that the existence of PDL extensions is guaranteed for finite default theories, and that each PDL extension is a DL extension. The priority ordering can thus be viewed as a filter that distinguishes unwanted from wanted extensions. We will make use of this role in our approach to reasoning about priorities.

3. Reasoning about priorities

To be able to reason about default priorities it must be possible to refer to defaults explicitly, and we must introduce a special predicate symbol representing default priority. We we will therefore extend our logical language in two respects.

1. We will use named defaults (Poole 1988) of the form $d_i{:}a \to b$ where d_i is taken from a distinct set of default names. We assume that different defaults have different names. Logically, default names are simply constants. These constants can be used for making references to defaults.[6]

2. We use the special two-place predicate symbol $\prec$ to represent default priority. For instance, if d_1 and d_2 are default names, then $d_1 \prec d_2$ is a formula with the intended meaning: d_1 has priority over d_2.

A (named) default theory is a pair (D, W) where D is a set of named defaults and D and W are defaults and formulas built from our extended logical language in the usual way. Note that we do not restrict the appearance of $\prec$ to W: it is possible to specify defaults about the priorities of other defaults.

We further assume that W contains axioms guaranteeing that $\prec$ is a strict partial order. For this purpose we can use the following formulas

$$\{\forall x, y, z. x \prec y \wedge y \prec z \supset x \prec z, \forall x. \neg(x \prec x)\}.$$

Note that we implicitly assume that these formulas are contained in W. We will not explicitly mention them when discussing examples in this paper.

Given a set D of named defaults we use D° to denote the corresponding set of defaults without names. By a DL extension of a named default theory (D, W) we mean a DL extension of the corresponding unnamed theory (D°, W). Similarly, a PDL extension of a named prioritized default theory $(D, W, <)$ is a PDL extension of $(D^\circ, W, <)$.

Here is a rather simplistic example from the birds domain:

$$
\begin{array}{l}
d_1 : bird \to flies \\
d_2 : penguin \to \neg flies \\
penguin \\
bird \\
d_2 \prec d_1
\end{array}
$$

---

[5]Our terminology was influenced by the terminology used in (Baader & Hollunder 1993).

[6]Note that our treatment of names is somewhat different from Poole's: we use constant terms as names whereas Poole uses atomic propositions.

Let us first consider DL extensions of this default theory, neglecting priorities for the time being. There are two such extensions:

$$E_1 = Th(W \cup \{flies\})$$

and

$$E_2 = Th(W \cup \{\neg flies\})$$

Clearly, E_1 violates the intuitive meaning of the priority information contained in this extension since the only way to generate E_1 is by giving d_1 preference over d_2, yet $d_2 \prec d_1$ is a premise and thus contained in E_1. Only E_2 is compatible with its own priority information: E_2 is generated by giving d_2 preference over d_1 as is required according to the information about $\prec$ contained in E_2.

What we need, thus, is a way to eliminate every extension containing priority information which is in conflict with the way the extension was generated. Given the techniques developed for PDL it is not difficult to see how this can be done. Basically, a DL extension will "survive" if it can be reconstructed as a PDL extension with a generating total order $\ll$ that is compatible with its own priority information. Compatibility will be tested by producing a syntactic description of the generating order and testing consistency of this description with the extension. Here are the necessary definitions.

Definition 4 *Let* $\Delta = (D, W)$ *be a named default theory,* E *a DL extension of* Δ, *and* $\ll$ *a strict total order of* D°. *We say* $\ll$ *is compatible with* E *iff*

$$E \cup \{d_i \prec d_k \mid d_i\colon r_i \in D, d_k\colon r_k \in D, r_i \ll r_k\}$$

is consistent.

Definition 5 *Let* $\Delta = (D, W)$ *be a named default theory,* E *a DL extension of* Δ. *We say* E *is a priority extension of* Δ *iff it is a PDL extension of* Δ *generated by a total order* $\ll$ *that is compatible with* E.

Reconsidering our birds example it is obvious that the single total ordering generating E_1, namely

$$\{(bird \to flies) \ll (penguin \to \neg flies)\}$$

is not compatible with E_1. E_1 is no priority extension for that reason. E_2, on the other hand, is a priority extension since it is generated by the total ordering

$$\{(penguin \to \neg flies) \ll (bird \to flies)\}$$

which, obviously, is compatible with E_2.

Given the expressiveness of our language it is not astonishing that unsatisfiable preference information can be specified and that this may lead to the non-existence of extensions. Here is a simple example. Assume D consists of the two defaults

$$d_1 : true \to d_2 \prec d_1$$
$$d_2 : true \to d_1 \prec d_2$$

W contains no formulas other than the two axioms for $\prec$. We obviously obtain two DL extensions. E_1 generated by d_1 contains the formula $d_2 \prec d_1$. However, the single total order compatible with E_1 prefers d_2 and hence does not reproduce E_1. Similarly, the second extension E_2 generated by d_2 contains the formula $d_1 \prec d_2$. Now the single total order compatible with E_2 prefers d_1. Again E_2 is not reproducible. This shows that our default theory has no priority extension at all.

Of course, we could try to weaken the notion of priority extensions to guarantee their existence, at least in the finite case. However, we strongly believe that the behaviour of our formalization is entirely reasonable. The specification of unsatisfiable priorities should lead to an exceptional situation requiring a reformulation of the knowledge base rather than being handled implicitly by the logical machinery. Otherwise there is a danger that mistakes of the knowledge engineer will remain unnoticed.

In the limiting case where a default theory Δ does not contain any constraining priority information, for instance since the predicate symbol $\prec$ is not explicitly mentioned anywhere in Δ, priority extensions coincide with DL extensions. This follows from the fact that every strict partial ordering of the defaults is then compatible with every extension. As shown in (Brewka 1993) every DL extension can be reconstructed as a PDL extension in this case.

In the next section we will discuss a more realistic legal example that demonstrates the full power of our approach.

4. A legal reasoning example

The example we want to discuss in this section is taken from Gordon's dissertation (Gordon 1993, p.7). We somewhat simplified it for our purposes. Assume a person wants to find out if her security interest in a certain ship is perfected. She currently has possession of the ship. According to the Uniform Commercial Code (UCC, §9-305) a security interest in goods may be perfected by taking possession of the collateral. However, there is a federal law called the Ship Mortgage Act (SMA) according to which a security interest in a ship may only be perfected by filing a financing statement. Such a statement has not been filed. Now the question is whether the UCC or the SMA takes precedence in this case. There are two known legal principles for resolving conflicts of this kind. The principle of *Lex Posterior* gives precedence to newer laws. In our case the UCC is newer than the SMA. On the other hand, the principle of *Lex Superior* gives precedence to laws supported by the higher authority. In our case the SMA has higher authority since it is federal law.

As we will see our approach allows us to formalize exactly this kind of reasoning. We use the ground instances of the following named defaults to represent the relevant article of the UCC, the SMA, Lex Posterior (LP), and Lex Superior (LS):

$$UCC : possession \rightarrow perfected$$
$$SMA : ship \wedge \neg fin\text{-}statement \rightarrow \neg perfected$$
$$LP(d_1, d_2) : more\text{-}recent(d_1, d_2) \rightarrow d_1 \prec d_2$$
$$LS(d_1, d_2) : fed\text{-}law(d_1) \wedge state\text{-}law(d_2) \rightarrow d_1 \prec d_2$$

The following facts are known about the case:

1) $possession$
2) $ship$
3) $\neg fin\text{-}statement$
4) $more\text{-}recent(UCC, SMA)$
5) $fed\text{-}law(SMA)$
6) $state\text{-}law(UCC)$

For this default theory we obtain four different Reiter extensions, namely

$$E_1 = Th(W \cup \{perfected, UCC \prec SMA\})$$
$$E_2 = Th(W \cup \{\neg perfected, UCC \prec SMA\})$$
$$E_3 = Th(W \cup \{perfected, SMA \prec UCC\})$$
$$E_4 = Th(W \cup \{\neg perfected, SMA \prec UCC\})$$

Two of these extensions are not priority extensions, namely E_2 and E_3. The priority information in E_2 requires that UCC gets preference over SMA, yet to derive $\neg perfected$ it is necessary to violate this requirement. Similarly, the priority information in E_3 requires that SMA gets preference over UCC, yet to derive $perfected$ this requirement has to be violated.

The two other extensions, E_1 and E_4, are priority extensions as can easily be verified. Hence the question whether the security interest is perfected is still open.

The intuitive reason for this is obvious: we have a conflict between the relevant instances of Lex Posterior and Lex Superior. Such a conflict can, for instance, be resolved by a universal rule that gives preference to the latter in all cases. To model this we have to add to W the formula

$$7) \quad \forall x, y, v, w. LS(x, y) \prec LP(v, w)$$

Let W' denote this new set of facts. Again we obtain four DL extensions E_i' whose definition is obtained from the definition of E_i by replacing W with W'. E_2' and E_3' are not priority extensions for the same reasons E_2 and E_3 are not priority extensions. But now also E_1' violates its own priority information. To see this note that every extension must contain the instance of 7)

$$LS(SMA, UCC) \prec LP(UCC, SMA).$$

which states that Lex Posterior can only be used to derive a priority of UCC over SMA if Lex Superior cannot be used to derive the opposite priority. This condition is obviously violated. In other words, there is no total ordering $\ll$ of the defaults in D such that the default instance $LS(SMA, UCC)$ precedes the default instance $LP(UCC, SMA)$ but nevertheless $UCC \prec SMA$ is contained in the PDL extension of $(D, W, \ll)$.

The single priority extension in our example is thus E_4', i.e., we derive that the security interest in the ship is not perfected.

We have used above a formula in W to give Lex Superior priority over Lex Posterior in all cases. Of course, there might be exceptions also to this conflict resolution strategy. To model this, we could simply replace 7) by a corresponding default and include a description of what to do in the exceptional cases in our default theory. We could then distinguish the following different levels:

1. the level of the basic laws UCC and SMA,

2. the level of principles solving conflicts among basic laws, i.e. Lex Posterior and Lex Superior,

3. the level solving conflicts among the latter, and

4. the level regulating the applicability of and specifying exception handling mechanisms for the strategy described in level 3).

This illustrates that there is no fixed highest level of reasoning about priorities: we can always add a further level describing priorities of defaults at the next lower level.

5. Conclusions

In this paper we have shown that it is possible to reason about default priorities within default logic. We introduced names for defaults and a special predicate symbol $\prec$ to express default priorities explicitly within the logical language. The information about default priorities contained in the Reiter extensions of a default theory was used to filter out those who can be reconstructed as PDL extensions in a way that is compatible with their own priority information.

Although we avoided the term so far, it would certainly be adequate to view this filtering process as a form of reflection. A meta-level process, namely the process of generating an extension, is matched against the outcome of this process, the extension itself. This is done by producing a syntactic description of relevant aspects of the process, namely the priorities involved in the generation of the extension, and by testing the consistency of this syntactic description with the generated extension.

The system we presented allows default priorities to be handled in an extremely flexible way. Explicit priorities, as they can, for instance, be specified in prioritized circumscription (Lifschitz 1985), hierarchic autoepistemic logic (Konolige 1988) or preferred subtheories (Brewka 1989), can be represented by simply asserting corresponding atomic formulas in W. Similarly, priorities based on specificity can be represented by asserting formulas corresponding to the output of the specificity algorithms used, e.g. Pearl's Z-ordering (Pearl 1990) or the specificity ordering developed in (Brewka 1993). However, our approach gives us much more flexibility. We can, for instance, express that certain priorities should hold under specific conditions only, derive priorities from the available information, and specify strategies how to resolve priority conflicts, as was done in the legal example in the last section.

Although the presentation of our priority handling techniques in this paper was based on PDL it should be obvious that they do not depend on this choice of the underlying nonmonotonic system. These techniques can easily be combined with any consistency based nonmonotonic system that produces extensions and can handle explicit priorities, like hierarchic autoepistemic logic (Konolige 1988) or preferred subtheories (Brewka 1989).

We have pushed the expressiveness of default logic to an extreme in our approach. Of course, there is a price to pay for this: the computation becomes much more difficult. As always there are two possible solutions for this problem: finding good approximations or finding interesting special cases with reasonable computational properties. A first step into the latter direction has been made in (Junker 1993) where Junker develops enumeration based proof procedures for Horn theories with dynamically derived preferences.

Much more work of this kind is needed. Nevertheless, since priorities play such an extremely important role for many applications we hope that this approach might in the long run help making nonmonotonic reasoning techniques more widely applicable for solving real world problems.

Acknowledgements

I would like to thank Tom Gordon, Joachim Hertzberg, Ulrich Junker, and Henry Prakken for interesting discussions on the topic of this paper.

References

Baader, F., and Hollunder, B. 1993. How to prefer more specific defaults in terminological default logic. In *Proc. IJCAI-93, Chambery, France.*

Boutilier, C. 1992. *Conditional Logics for Default Reasoning and Belief Revision.* Ph.D. Dissertation, Dep. of Computer Science, Univ. of Toronto.

Brewka, G. 1989. Preferred subtheories - an extended logical framework for default reasoning. In *Proc. IJCAI-89, Detroit.*

Brewka, G. 1993. Adding priorities and specificity to default logic. Technical report, GMD.

Delgrande, J. 1987. A first-order conditional logic for prototypical properties. *Artificial Intelligence, 33(1).*

Geffner, H., and Pearl, J. 1992. Conditional entailment: Bridging two approaches to default reasoning. *Artificial Intelligence 53.*

Goldszmidt, M., and Pearl, J. 1991. System Z^+: A formalism for reasoning with variable-strength defaults. In *Proc. AAAI-91.*

Gordon, T. 1993. *The Pleadings Game: An Artificial Intelligence Model of Procedural Justice.* Ph.D. Dissertation, TU Darmstadt.

Grosof, B. 1991. Generalizing prioritization. In *Proc. Second International Conference on Principles of Knowledge Representation and Reasoning, Cambridge.*

Junker, U. 1993. Dynamic generation of assumptions and preferences. unpublished manuscript.

Konolige, K. 1988. Hierarchic autoepistemic theories for nonmonotonic reasoning. In *Proc. AAAI-88.*

Kraus, S.; Lehmann, D.; and Magidor, M. 1990. Nonmonotonic reasoning, preferential models and cumulative logics. *Artificial Intelligence.*

Lehmann, D. 1990. What does a conditional knowledge base entail? In *Proc. First International Conference on Principles of Knowledge Representation and Reasoning.*

Lifschitz, V. 1985. Computing circumscription. In *Proc. 9th Int. Joint Conference on Artificial Intelligence.*

McCarthy, J. 1980. Circumscription - a form of nonmonotonic reasoning. *Artificial Intelligence 13.*

Moore, R. C. 1985. Semantical considerations on nonmonotonic logic. *Artificial Intelligence 25.*

Pearl, J. 1990. System Z: A natural ordering of defaults with tractable applications to nonmonotonic reasoning. In *Proc. Third Conference on Theoretical Aspects of Reasoning About Knowledge.*

Poole, D. 1988. A logical framework for default reasoning. *Artificial Intelligence 36* 27–47.

Prakken, H. 1993. *Logical Tools for Modelling Legal Argument.* Ph.D. Dissertation, VU Amsterdam.

Reiter, R., and Criscuolo, G. 1981. On interacting defaults. In *Proc. IJCAI-81, Vancouver.*

Reiter, R. 1980. A logic for default reasoning. *Artificial Intelligence 13* 81–132.

Touretzky, D. S.; Horty, J. F.; and Thomason, R. H. 1987. A clash of intuitions: The current state of nonmonotonic multiple inheritance systems. In *Proc. IJCAI-87, Milan.*

Touretzky, D. S.; Thomason, R. H.; and Horty, J. F. 1991. A skeptic's menagerie: Conflictors, preemptors, reinstaters, and zombies in nonmonotonic inheritance. In *Proc. IJCAI-91, Sydney.*

Touretzky, D. S. 1986. *The Mathematics of Inheritance.* London: Pitman Research Notes in Artificial Intelligence.

Is Intractability of Non-Monotonic Reasoning a Real Drawback?

Marco Cadoli and **Francesco M. Donini** and **Marco Schaerf**
Dipartimento di Informatica e Sistemistica
Università di Roma "La Sapienza"
Via Salaria 113, I-00198 Roma, Italy
email: <lastname>@assi.dis.uniroma1.it

Abstract

Several studies about complexity of NMR showed that inferring in non-monotonic knowledge bases is significantly harder than reasoning in monotonic ones. This contrasts with the general idea that NMR can be used to make knowledge representation and reasoning simpler, not harder. In this paper we show that, to some extent, NMR has fulfilled its goal. In particular we prove that circumscription allows for more compact and natural representation of knowledge. Results about intractability of circumscription can therefore be interpreted as the price one has to pay for having such an extra-compact representation. On the other hand, sometimes NMR really makes reasoning simpler; we give prototypical scenarios where closed-world reasoning accounts for a faster and unsound approximation of classical reasoning.

Introduction

The complexity of non-monotonic reasoning (NMR) has been extensively analyzed in recent years. Several studies showed that inferring in non-monotonic knowledge bases is significantly harder than reasoning in monotonic ones. As an example, while inference in propositional Horn formulae can be done in linear time provided we reason in the classical semantics (Dowling & Gallier 1984), inference under circumscription in such formulae is a co-NP-complete problem (Cadoli & Lenzerini 1990).

Although there are cases in which non-monotonic inference has a complexity which is comparable to classical inference, the general picture shows that tractable problems may become intractable (e.g. the complexity raises from polynomial to NP-complete (Kautz & Selman 1991)), intractable problems may become "more" intractable (e.g. from NP-complete to Σ_2^p-complete (Gottlob 1992)), decidable problems may become undecidable (Baader & Hollunder 1992), and undecidable problems may become "more" undecidable (e.g. from r.e.-complete to Π_2^1-complete (Schlipf 1987)). An up-to-date survey on computational aspects of NMR appears as (Cadoli & Schaerf 1993).

This aspect of NMR is acknowledged in the AI community. Brachman (1990, p. 1090) writes:

"An irony of work on NMR is that, while the easy adoption and retraction of assumptions is most useful for speeding up natural everyday reasoning, most current NMR proposals drastically compound the already difficult problem of deductive reasoning. We urgently need to determine how NMR can be used to make commonsense inference faster, not slower."

The general idea about NMR is that it can be seen as a fast but *unsound* approximation of ordinary reasoning, as it is not possible to make reasoning more efficient while preserving both soundness and completeness.

Apart from AI, NMR is sometimes used to represent knowledge in a more compact fashion. Noticeably, negation through *cut* is commonly used among PROLOG programmers for writing more compact and efficient programs (Sterling & Shapiro 1986, Chap.11). Moreover, closed-world reasoning allows for effective representation of implicit knowledge in relational as well as deductive databases, and has been widely used among database practitioners for many years now.

Hence, there is a mismatch between the intuition behind NMR and the theoretical results on its computational complexity. The following questions naturally arise:

- is high complexity of NMR a bug or a feature?

- is the intuition that NMR simplifies reasoning wrong?

- are there complexity analyses showing that NMR fits its intuition?

The goal of this paper is to give a preliminary answer to the above questions. In particular we address two topics:

1. It is clear that NMR captures additional – wrt to classical reasoning – information and that such information makes reasoning harder. Now suppose we want to make the same inferences that we do in NMR knowledge bases "without using NMR", i.e. suppose we have a KB K and we want a new KB K' s. t. $K \vdash_{NMR} Q$ iff $K' \models Q$. How would the monotonic KB K' look like? How large would it be?

2. It is advocated that NMR makes reasoning faster and unsound. Theoretical results seem to contradict it. Can we show specific examples and frameworks which concretely support the above idea?

Discussion on the above topics will be carried out by means of examples taken from the academic domain.

The structure of the paper is the following: In the rest of the Introduction we recall some definitions about NMR; then we devote a section to each of the two topics above. In the last section we draw some conclusions.

Preliminaries

Throughout the paper we restrict our attention to propositional knowledge bases. We analyze closed-world reasoning and circumscription, two of the major NMR formalisms. Since they are widely known, in this paper we just mention the main definitions underlying them. Interpretations and models of propositional formulae will be denoted as sets of atoms (those which are mapped into 1).

Definition 1 (Lifschitz 1985) *Let* M, N *be two models of a propositional formula* T *and* $\langle P; Z \rangle$ *a partition of the atoms of* T. *We write* $M \leq_{(P;Z)} N$ *if* $M \cap P \subseteq N \cap P$.

A model M *is called* $(P; Z)$-*minimal for a formula* T *if there is no model* N *of* T *such that* $N \leq_{(P;Z)} M$ *and* $M \not\leq_{(P;Z)} N$.

The circumscription $CIRC(T; P; Z)$ *of* T *minimizing the atoms in* P *and varying the atoms in* Z *denotes the set of* $(P; Z)$-*minimal models of* T.

Intuitively a propositional atom is placed in P if we don't like it to be in models. In common-sense reasoning typically such atoms denote abnormality (McCarthy 1986). When an atom is in Z we accept that it occurs in models, provided this helps in excluding some of the atoms in P.

When $Z = \emptyset$ the $(P; Z)$-minimal models of a formula are called just minimal. The closed-world assumption $CWA(T)$ of a propositional formula T is defined as follows in (Reiter 1978):

$$CWA(T) = T \cup \{\neg p \mid T \not\models p\}.$$

$CWA(T)$ is consistent iff T has a unique minimal model; in such a case that model is the unique model of $CWA(T)$.

NMR for compact representation of knowledge

This section deals with using NMR for representing information in a compact way, where compactness is measured wrt classical representation of the same knowledge.

We introduce an example dealing with a student who needs to plan his/her *curriculum*. We show that the natural way the student can do this is to reason using circumscription. Given that the problem is computationally intractable, we address the following question: if the student was to reason in a classical fashion – e.g. using a classical theorem prover like OTTER (McCune 1990) – how much implicit information would he/she need to represent explicitly in the new KB? In other words, is it feasible to transform the original KB – dealt with NMR – into a new one – dealt with a classical inference engine – such that the same inferences are possible? The results we prove show that this is not feasible, since NMR allows one to save a huge amount of space.

Example 1: **(The lazy student)** The set of admissible *curricula* is represented by means of the models of a propositional formula T which might look like the following:

DataBases	$\lor$	Algebra
Algebra	$\lor$	NonMonotonicReasoning
DataBases	$\lor$	ReasoningAboutKnowledge
Algebra	$\lor$	ReasoningAboutKnowledge
Algebra	$\lor$	ComputationalComplexity

Throughout this section we assume that such formulae are always in 2-CNF, i.e. they have at most two literals per clause. A *curriculum* is just a model of T, e.g. {DataBases, Algebra, NonMonotonicReasoning}. Such a definition does not capture the preferences that a student might have. As an example the student might be better off by doing both courses {ReasoningAboutKnowledge, ComputationalComplexity} than doing just one of the courses {DataBases, Algebra, NonMonotonicReasoning}. This suggests to use the idea of $(P; Z)$-minimal models – where all exams that the student dislikes are in P; let's say that $P = \{$DataBases, Algebra, NonMonotonicReasoning$\}$ and $Z = \{$ ReasoningAboutKnowledge, ComputationalComplexity$\}$. A *minimal curriculum* is a $(P; Z)$-minimal model of T. In the above situation there are three minimal *curricula*: {Algebra,ReasoningAboutKnowledge}, {Algebra,ReasoningAboutKnowledge,ComputationalComplexity}, {DataBases,NonMonotonicReasoning,ReasoningAboutKnowledge,ComputationalComplexity}.

A course c is *mandatory* if it has to be done in all *curricula*, i.e. $T \models c$. A course c is *preferred* if it has to be done in all minimal *curricula*, i.e. $CIRC(T; P; Z) \models c$.

In the above situation there are no mandatory courses, although ReasoningAboutKnowledge is preferred. $\diamond$

The above example shows that there are at least four possible computational services that a student might ask:

Problem 1. Find a *curriculum*. The student has no specific preferences, a *curriculum* is just as good as any other one;

Problem 2. Find a minimal *curriculum*. This is an improvement wrt to the previous service, as the student can express some preferences. Nevertheless, there is no explanation why a *curriculum* is provided. In Example 1, {Algebra,ReasoningAbout-Knowledge,ComputationalComplexity} is as good as {Algebra,ReasoningAboutKnowledge}. Even if the second one is provided as an answer, the student does not know whether ReasoningAboutKnowledge is preferred or not.

Problem 3. Decide whether a course is mandatory. The student – with no preferences – wants to know whether he/she must attend a specific course. The weakness of this service is in that a non-mandatory course could be true only in *curricula* that the student would never accept.

Problem 4. Decide whether a course is preferred (preferences decided in advance). Same as above, but the student has preferences.

This sophisticated form of reasoning is mostly relevant is this situation: the lazy student might take course c, but he/she does not want to commit until he/she is completely convinced that c is preferred. In fact not all courses suggested by an answer to Problem 2 are preferred.

The complexity of the above problems has been already studied in the literature (when T is in 2-CNF):

Problem 1. is polynomial (Even, Itai, & Shamir 1976);

Problem 2. is polynomial (Cadoli 1992);

Problem 3. is polynomial (Even, Itai, & Shamir 1976);

Problem 4. is co-NP-complete (Cadoli & Lenzerini 1990).

In the above scenario NMR seems to do exactly the form of reasoning the student needs. In fact a solution to Problem 4 gives some extra information that the three other problems miss, therefore we may be willing to accept its extra complexity. Furthermore this extra complexity does not seem to be really dangerous: since the set of courses the student could ever take is limited – let's say they are $c_1, \ldots, c_n$ – he/she might compute which of them is preferred, i.e. decide whether $CIRC(T; P; Z) \models c_i$ holds for each i $(1 \leq i \leq n)$. Even if this amounts to solve n co-NP-complete problems – one for each query – it is not necessary to find the answer when the student asks a query. More precisely the queries can be posed off-line and their answers cached; then on-line query-answering just amounts to table look-up, which is clearly polynomial.

We call *compilation* any off-line process that makes on-line reasoning polynomial.

The next step is now to consider the scenario where *several* students are interested in preparing their *curricula*. In this case, students may have the same preferences, or may not.

Problem 4.1. Decide (repeatedly) whether a course is preferred, when all students have the same preferences;

Problem 4.2. Decide (repeatedly) whether a course is preferred, when each student has his/her own preferences.

The above argument proves the following property of Problem 4.1.

Proposition 1 *It is possible to compile Problem 4.1.*

Compilation for Problem 4.1 can be done simply by caching. Even if such caching cannot be done for Problem 4.2 (there are exponentially many different preferences) one may wonder if the problem is compilable in some smarter way.

However, we are able to show that it is very unlikely that such a compilation may exist. To do this we resort on the notion of *non-uniform* computation. A problem Π is in the class non-uniform P if there exists a function $f()$ that for each instance π of Π maps the *size* of π into a polynomial-time algorithm that solves π (Johnson 1990, p. 116). We remark that there is no restriction on $f()$, which may be even non-recursive. Intuitively, $f()$ represents the off-line computation. The relations between non-uniform P and uniform complexity classes, such as NP, have been studied in the literature. In particular it has been shown (Karp & Lipton 1980) that NP $\subseteq$ non-uniform P would imply some unlikely consequences on complexity classes.

Theorem 2 *Unless $NP \subseteq$ non-uniform P, there is no data structure representing a 2-CNF formula T such that, given a set P of atoms to minimize and a set Z of varying atoms, deciding whether $CIRC(T; P; Z) \models z$ (with $z \in Z$) can be answered in polynomial time.*

Proof. We first prove a key lemma. Its proof is based on a reduction given in (Cadoli & Lenzerini 1990, Theorem 5), which showed that inference in 2-positive-CNF under CIRC is coNP-hard. The major difference is that we now need to code every possible 3-CNF over n atoms in one theory.

Lemma 3 *For any integer n, there exists a 2-positive-CNF formula T_n of polynomial size wrt n, such that given any 3-CNF formula π using n atoms, there are particular P_π and Z_π such that π is unsatisfiable iff $CIRC(T_n; P_\pi; Z_\pi) \models z$.*

Proof (sketch). We use the following conventions. We denote with a, b, c, d propositional atoms; if a is an atom, $\overline{a}$ is its negation. We denote with w, x, y literals (i.e. either atoms or negated atoms). If x is the literal $\overline{a}$, then $\overline{x}$ is a.

Let L be the alphabet of n atoms used in the 3-CNF formulas. Let L' be the alphabet $L \cup \overline{L} \cup C \cup \{z\}$, where $\overline{L} = \{\overline{a} \mid a \in L\}$, and C is a set of atoms one-to-one with possible three-literals clauses of L, i.e., $C = \{c_i \mid \gamma_i$ is a three-literals clause of $L\}$. Observe that now $\overline{a}$ denotes also a sintactic symbol of L': we retain this ambiguity to simplify the notation in the reduction.

We define T on the alphabet L' according to the following rules:

1. for each letter a of L, there is a clause $a \vee \overline{a}$ in T;

2. for each clause $\gamma_i = w \vee x \vee y$, where w, x, y are literals, there are four clauses in T. The first three are $c_i \vee w, c_i \vee x, c_i \vee y$; observe that if x is a negated literal in π, then x is a (syntactically equal) atom in T. The fourth clause is $c_i \vee z$.

Notice that the size of T is $O(n^3)$, and T is a 2-positive-CNF formula.

Let π be a 3-CNF formula over L, and let $c_1, \ldots, c_h$ be all the atoms of L' corresponding to the clauses in π. Define $P_\pi = \{c_1, \ldots, c_h\} \cup L \cup \overline{L}$, and $Z_\pi = L' - P_\pi$. The theorem can be proven by showing that:

1. given a model of π, we can build a $(P_\pi; Z_\pi)$-minimal model MM of T such that z is false in MM: Let $M \subseteq L$ be a model for π, and let $\overline{M}$ be a subset of $\overline{L}$ such that if $a \in M$ then $\overline{a} \in \overline{M}$. Define MM as $(L - M) \cup \overline{M} \cup C$. It can be verified that MM is a model of T, because it includes C, and for every atom $a \in L$ it contains either a or $\overline{a}$, but not both. Moreover, z is false in MM. One can prove that MM is indeed $(P_\pi; Z_\pi)$-minimal.

2. given a $(P_\pi; Z_\pi)$-minimal model MM of T such that z is false in MM, we can build a model M of π: Let MM be a $(P_\pi; Z_\pi)$-minimal model of T, such that z is false in MM. Since for each $c \in C$, the clause $c \vee z$ is in T, $C \subseteq MM$. Consider an atom $c_i \in P$. There are in T the three clauses $c_i \vee w, c_i \vee x, c_i \vee y$. One can prove that at least one between w, x, y is not in MM, and that $a \in MM$ iff $\overline{a} \notin MM$. Define $M = \{a \mid \overline{a} \in MM\}$. $\qquad \square$

Let T_n be as in the above lemma. If for each n there is a data structure representing T_n, such that given P and Z, $CIRC(T, P; Z) \models z$ can be answered in polynomial time, one could give an infinite class of algorithms $A_1, \ldots, A_i, \ldots$, each one embedding the data structure for T_i, and each one working in polynomial time. Now given a 3-CNF formula π of size n, π is satisfiable iff A_n answers "No" on inputs P_π, Z_π, where P_π, Z_π are chosen as in the above lemma. Then 3-CNF-SAT $\in$ non-uniform P, and since 3-CNF-SAT is complete for NP, NP $\subseteq$ non-uniform P. A similar technique has been used in (Kautz & Selman 1992). $\qquad \square$

The above theorem shows that Problem 4.2 is not compilable.

So far we considered atomic queries. Non-atomic clauses are nevertheless necessary for posing more complex queries such as disjunction (e.g. is it necessary to take at least one course in a given set?) or implication (e.g. is it necessary to take course a provided course b is taken?). Theorem 2 implies that Problem 4.2 is not compilable also for non-atomic queries. Instead, since in its proof it is crucial that P, Z are given as part of the input, one could think that when P, Z are fixed

– like in Problem 4.1 – compilation of all non-atomic queries is still possible. Next theorem shows that this conjecture is very unlikely to hold.

Theorem 4 *Unless* $NP \subseteq$ *non-uniform P, there is no data structure representing a 2-CNF T and two sets P, Z of atoms, such that given a clause F, deciding whether $CIRC(T, P; Z) \models F$ can be answered in polynomial time.*

The proof can be obtained with techniques similar to those of the previous theorem.

At a first sight, the above two theorems seem to give just a negative result: NMR is not compilable. But the result is in fact twofold: the theorems show that if one wants to represent the circumscription of a 2-CNF KB K with a new KB K', either inference in K' is intractable, or (if inference has to be kept tractable) K' has exponential size w.r.t. K. In other words, circumscription allows one to derive an exponential number of new consequences not derivable from K with classical inference: If the number of new consequences were polynomial, they could be simply cached. It might be possible that such consequences could be compacted in one formula of polynomial size; but in this case, Theorems 2 and 4 show that extracting consequences from such a formula would very probably be an intractable task. Hence the positive aspect of Theorems 2 and 4 is that circumscription is an extremely powerful tool for representing problems in a compact way.

We summarize the results in Table 1, where we divide cases between the two services, and between "short" and "long" queries. By "short" we mean clauses of fixed length (e.g. length 1 to ask for preferred exams in the lazy student example), while "long" means clauses of arbitrary length.

	all queries with same preferences	different preferences
"short" queries	compilable Prop. 1	non-compilable Theo. 2
"long" queries	non-compilable Theo. 4	non-compilable Theo. 2, 4

Table 1: Are 2-CNF knowledge bases compilable under CIRC?

We remark that "non-compilable" also means that CIRC allows one to represent in a compact way an exponential number of new consequences.

Unsound and fast inference with NMR

As mentioned in the Introduction, it has been frequently argued that one of the expected features of NMR was that it could account for a form of unsound, but *fast*, inference. The results on the computational complexity of NMR seem to contradict the possibility of NMR of being faster than classical reasoning. In this section we show that NMR is more efficient in some situations than classical reasoning even according to worst-case analysis. We introduce this aspect by means of an example.

Example 2: (The cautious student) The faculty members decide the requirements needed to attend a course, which may be represented with a set of dependencies R:

$$
\begin{aligned}
\texttt{NonMonotonicReasoning} &\longrightarrow \texttt{Algebra}\\
\texttt{NonMonotonicReasoning} &\longrightarrow \texttt{Logic}\\
\texttt{DataBases} &\longrightarrow \texttt{Algebra}\\
\texttt{ComputerArchitectures} &\longrightarrow \texttt{Algebra}\\
\texttt{ReasoningAboutKnowledge} &\longrightarrow \texttt{Logic}\\
\texttt{ComputationalComplexity} &\longrightarrow \texttt{Logic}
\end{aligned}
$$

Throughout this section we assume that such formulae are always Definite Horn. A set such as $C = \{$**Non-MonotonicReasoning, ComputerArchitectures**$\}$ can represent courses the student has attended, or has committed to attend. The models of $C \cup R$ represent all admissible completions of the *curriculum*.

A conjunct like $g_1 = $ **Algebra**$\wedge$ **ReasoningAbout-Knowledge**$\wedge \neg$ **DataBases**$\wedge \neg$ **ComputationalComplexity** represents courses the student may be interested in taking (positive literals) or avoiding (negative literals), but he/she has not committed yet. The student may also have alternative plans, such as $g_2 = $ **Logic**$\wedge$ **DataBases**$\wedge$ **ComputationalComplexity**$\wedge \neg$ **ReasoningAboutKnowledge**, or $g_3 = $ **Algebra**$\wedge$ **ComputerArchitectures**$\wedge \neg$ **ReasoningAboutKnowledge**.

A plan g may be satisfied by a model of $C \cup R$ or not. The student wants to know if in all models at least one of his/her plans will be satisfied. This could be represented as a goal $G = g_1 \vee g_2 \vee g_3$.

The scenario could be modified if the faculty add new requirements to R or if the student makes further commitments, thus adding atoms to C. $\diamond$

Let us formalize the computational services the student may be interested in:

Problem 5. Decide whether the set of courses in C plus the courses required by R satisfy the goal G. This service provides information on the current situation but it does not give any guarantee on the future. It amounts to decide whether $CWA(C \cup R) \models G$.

Problem 6. Decide whether the goal G will be satisfied no matter which new requirements are imposed (in addition to R) by the faculty and which new courses (in addition to C) the student decides to attend. This service provides information on the current and the future situation. It amounts to decide whether $C \cup R \models G$.

Coming back to the example, we have that $CWA(C \cup R) \models G$ while $C \cup R \not\models G$. Therefore, if the faculty do not change the set of requirements and the student does not decide to take additional courses, the goal will be satisfied.

Let's consider an alternative goal of the student: $G' = g'_1 \vee g'_2 \vee g'_3$, where $g'_1 = $ **Algebra**$\wedge$ **Logic**$\wedge$ **ReasoningAboutKnowledge**$\wedge \neg$ **ComputationalComplexity**, $g'_2 = $ **Logic**$\wedge$ **ComputationalComplexity**$\wedge \neg$ **ReasoningAboutKnowledge**, $g'_3 = $ **Algebra**$\wedge \neg$ **ReasoningAboutKnowledge**. Both $CWA(C \cup R) \models G'$ and $C \cup R \models G'$ hold. As a consequence, he/she is sure that, whatever new requirements and courses are added, the goal G' will always be satisfied.

We consider now the complexities of the above problems.

Problem 5. is polynomial: First compute the minimal model M of the Horn formula $R \wedge C$, then check whether $M \models G$. Both steps can be accomplished in polynomial time.

Problem 6. is co-NP-complete: hardness follows from the co-NP-completeness of tautology checking of a DNF formula.

NMR is faster than classical reasoning in this specific case. Therefore NMR can be seen as a fast, complete but unsound approximation of classical reasoning, as $\Sigma \models \gamma$ implies $CWA(\Sigma) \models \gamma$.

This behavior of NMR is not restricted to this particular situation. Let's take a further example from the logic programming field. Let P be a propositional general logic program – where negation is allowed in the body of the rules – and γ be a clause. Deciding whether γ is true in all the (classical) models of P, i.e. $P \models \gamma$ interpreting **not** as classical negation, is a co-NP-complete problem. On the other hand, deciding whether γ is a consequence of P under the well-founded semantics (van Gelder, Ross, & Schlipf 1991), i.e. γ is satisfied by the well-founded model of P ($WF(P) \models \gamma$), is a polynomial time problem.

Even in this case NMR accounts for a fast and complete, although unsound, approximation of classical reasoning, as $P \models \gamma$ implies $WF(P) \models \gamma$.

Conclusions

Recent theoretical results on the computational complexity of NMR seem to contradict the main reasons for the development of non-monotonic formalisms, namely that defeasible assumptions should allow for: 1) faster, although unsound, inference and 2) more compact representation of knowledge. We have shown in this paper that, to some extent, NMR has fulfilled its goal.

Regarding the second goal, we have proven that circumscription does indeed allow for more compact representation of knowledge. The results can also be extended to circumscription of general propositional formulae (Cadoli, Donini, & Schaerf 1994). Results about intractability of NMR can therefore be interpreted as the price one has to pay for having extra-compact representation of knowledge. It is therefore unfair to say that NMR is harder than classical reasoning. In fact the input of a NM inference problem could be exponentially smaller than the input of a classical inference problem. On the other hand the implicit assumption in saying that NMR is harder is that the sizes of the inputs are the same.

Regarding the first goal, we have given prototypical scenarios where closed-world reasoning accounts for a faster and unsound approximation of classical reasoning. Therefore NMR is not always computationally harder, and may even be simpler than classical reasoning.

Due to the lack of space we cannot give a detailed comparison of our work with other recently appeared in the literature on off-line reasoning, e.g. Kautz & Selman (1991) and Moses & Tennenholtz (1993). We briefly compare our work with the second one.

Moses & Tennenholtz analyze the possibility of speeding up the complexity of query answering through a previous off-line analysis of the knowledge base. Their goal can be considered as a special case of compilation: They consider a particular subset of all queries, which they call *efficient basis*, whose answers enables to answer all queries in polynomial time. Some query languages may not admit an efficient basis. Our results complement theirs, as we consider any possible preprocessing (even a non-recursive one) with the only restriction that the new representation can answer queries in time polynomial in the size of the original knowledge base. For each entry of Table 1 marked "non-compilable", we proved that not only no efficient basis exists but also that no other compilation is possible.

Acknowledgements

This work has been supported by the ESPRIT Basic Research Action N.6810 (COMPULOG 2) and by the Progetto Finalizzato Sistemi Informatici e Calcolo Parallelo of the CNR (Italian Research Council), LdR "Ibridi".

References

Baader, F., and Hollunder, B. 1992. Embedding defaults into terminological knowledge representation formalisms. In *Proc. of KR-92*, 306–317.

Brachman, R. J. 1990. The future of knowledge representation. In *Proc. of AAAI-90*, 1082–1092.

Cadoli, M., and Lenzerini, M. 1990. The complexity of closed world reasoning and circumscription. In *Proc. of AAAI-90*, 550–555. MIT press. Extended version to appear on *Journal of Computer ans System Sciences*, 1994.

Cadoli, M., and Schaerf, M. 1993. A survey of complexity results for non-monotonic logics. *Journal of Logic Programming* 17:127–160.

Cadoli, M.; Donini, F. M.; and Schaerf, M. 1994. On compact representations of propositional circumscription. Manuscript.

Cadoli, M. 1992. On the complexity of model finding for nonmonotonic propositional logics. In *Proceedings of the Fourth Italian Conference on Theoretical Computer Science*, 125–139. World Scientific Publishing Co.

Dowling, W. P., and Gallier, J. H. 1984. Linear-time algorithms for testing the satisfiability of propositional Horn formulae. *Journal of Logic Programming* 1:267–284.

Even, S.; Itai, A.; and Shamir, A. 1976. On the complexity of timetable and multicommodity flow problems. *SIAM Journal of Computing* 5:691–703.

Gottlob, G. 1992. Complexity results for nonmonotonic logics. *Journal of Logic and Computation* 2:397–425.

Johnson, D. S. 1990. A catalog of complexity classes. In van Leeuwen, J., ed., *Handbook of Theoretical Computer Science*, volume A. Elsevier Science Publishers B. V. (North Holland). chapter 2.

Karp, R. M., and Lipton, R. J. 1980. Some connections between non-uniform and uniform complexity classes. In *Proc. of STOC-80*, 302–309.

Kautz, H. A., and Selman, B. 1991. Hard problems for simple default logics. *Artificial Intelligence Journal* 49:243–279.

Kautz, H. A., and Selman, B. 1992. Forming concepts for fast inference. In *Proc. of AAAI-92*, 786–793.

Lifschitz, V. 1985. Computing circumscription. In *Proc. of IJCAI-85*, 121–127.

McCarthy, J. 1986. Applications of circumscription to formalizing common-sense knowledge. *Artificial Intelligence Journal* 28:89–116.

McCune, W. 1990. Otter 2.0. In *Proceedings of the Tenth Conference on Automated Deduction (CADE-90)*, 663–664. Springer-Verlag.

Moses, Y., and Tennenholtz, M. 1993. Off-line reasoning for on-line efficiency. In *Proc. of IJCAI-93*, 490–495.

Reiter, R. 1978. On closed world data bases. In Gallaire, H., and Minker, J., eds., *Logic and Data Bases*. Plenum. 119–140.

Schlipf, J. S. 1987. Decidability and definability with circumscription. *Annals of Pure and Applied Logic* 35:173–191.

Selman, B., and Kautz, H. A. 1991. Knowledge compilation using Horn approximations. In *Proc. of AAAI-91*, 904–909.

Sterling, L., and Shapiro, E. 1986. *The Art of Prolog*. The MIT Press.

van Gelder, A.; Ross, K. A.; and Schlipf, J. S. 1991. The well-founded semantics for general logic programs. *Journal of the ACM* 38:620–650.

A Knowledge Representation Framework
Based on
Autoepistemic Logic of Minimal Beliefs

Teodor C. Przymusinski[*]
Department of Computer Science
University of California
Riverside, CA 92521
(teodor@cs.ucr.edu)

Abstract

In recent years, various formalizations of non-monotonic reasoning and different semantics for normal and disjunctive logic programs have been proposed, including autoepistemic logic, circumscription, CWA, $GCWA$, $ECWA$, epistemic specifications, stable, well-founded, stationary and static semantics of normal and disjunctive logic programs.

In this paper we introduce a simple non-monotonic knowledge representation framework which isomorphically contains all of the above mentioned non-monotonic formalisms and semantics as special cases and yet is significantly more expressive than each one of these formalisms considered individually. The new formalism, called the *AutoEpistemic Logic of minimal Beliefs*, $AELB$, is obtained by augmenting Moore's autoepistemic logic, AEL, with an additional *minimal belief* operator, $\mathcal{B}$, which allows us to explicitly talk about minimally entailed formulae.

The existence of such a uniform framework not only results in a new powerful non-monotonic formalism but also allows us to compare and better understand mutual relationships existing between different non-monotonic formalisms and semantics and enables us to provide simpler and more natural definitions of some of them. It also naturally leads to new, even more expressive and flexible formalizations and semantics.

1   Introduction

Moore's autoepistemic logic AEL (Moore 1985) is obtained by augmenting classical propositional logic with a modal operator $\mathcal{L}$. The intended meaning of the modal atom $\mathcal{L}F$ is "F is provable" or "F is logically derivable" (in the stable autoepistemic expansion). Thus Moore's modal operator $\mathcal{L}$ can be viewed as a "knowledge operator" which allows us to reason about formulae *known* to be true in the expansion. However, usually, in addition to reasoning about facts which are known to be true, we also need to reason about those that are only *believed* to be true, where what is believed or not believed is determined by a specific non-monotonic formalism. In particular, we may want to express beliefs based on *minimal entailment*

---

[*]Partially supported by the National Science Foundation grant #IRI-9313061. Revised on March 24, 1994.

or *circumscription* and thus may need a modal "belief operator" $\mathcal{B}$ with the intended meaning of the modal atom $\mathcal{B}F$ given by "F true in all minimal models" or "F is minimally entailed" (in the expansion).

For example, consider a scenario in which: (1) you plan to rent a movie if you believe that you will not go to a baseball game (bg) and will not go to a football game (fg), but, (2) you do not plan to buy buy tickets to either of the games if you don't know for sure that you will go to see it. We could describe the initial scenario as follows:

$$\mathcal{B}(\neg goto(bg) \wedge \neg goto(fg)) \quad \supset \quad rent\_movie$$
$$\neg \mathcal{L}goto(bg) \wedge \neg \mathcal{L}goto(fg) \quad \supset \quad \neg buy\_tickets.$$

Assuming that this is all you know and that your beliefs are based on minimal entailment (circumscription), you should rent a movie because you believe that you will not go to see any games (i.e., $\neg goto(bg) \wedge \neg goto(fg)$ holds in all minimal models) and you should not buy tickets because you don't know that you will see any of the games (i.e., neither $goto(bg)$ nor $goto(fg)$ is provable).

Suppose now that you learn that you will either go a baseball game or to a football game (i.e., $goto(bg) \vee goto(fg)$). In the new scenario you should no longer plan to rent a movie (because $\neg goto(bg) \wedge \neg goto(fg)$ no longer holds in all minimal models) but you still do not intend to buy any tickets, because you don't know yet which game you are going to see (i.e., neither $goto(bg)$ nor $goto(fg)$ is provable).

However, when you eventually learn that you actually go to a baseball game (i.e., $goto(bg)$) you no longer believe in not buying tickets because you now know that you are going to see a specific game (i.e., $goto(bg)$ is provable).

Observe, that in the above example the roles played by the knowledge and belief operators are quite different and one cannot be substituted by the other. In particular, we cannot replace the premise $\mathcal{B}(\neg goto(bg) \wedge \neg goto(fg))$ in the first implication by $\mathcal{L}(\neg goto(bg) \wedge \neg goto(fg))$ because that would result in $rent\_movie$ not being true in first scenario. Similarly, we cannot replace it by $\neg \mathcal{L}goto(bg) \wedge \neg \mathcal{L}goto(fg)$ because that would result in $rent\_movie$ being true in the second scenario.

In order to be able to explicitly reason about minimal beliefs, we introduce a new non-monotonic formalism, called the *AutoEpistemic Logic of minimal Beliefs*,

$AELB$, obtained by augmenting Moore's autoepistemic logic, AEL, with an additional *minimal belief* operator, $\mathcal{B}$. The resulting non-monotonic knowledge representation framework turns out to be rather simple and yet quite powerful. We prove that many of the recently introduced non-monotonic formalisms and semantics for normal and disjunctive logic programs are *isomorphically embeddable* into $AELB$. In particular this applies to autoepistemic logic (Moore 1985); circumscription (McCarthy 1980; Lifschitz 1985); CWA (Reiter 1978); $GCWA$ (Minker 1982); $ECWA$ (Gelfond, Przymusinska, & Przymusinski 1989); epistemic specifications (Gelfond 1992); stable, well-founded, stationary and static semantics of normal and disjunctive logic programs (Gelfond & Lifschitz 1988; Van Gelder, Ross, & Schlipf 1990; Przymusinski 1991c; Gelfond & Lifschitz 1990; Przymusinski 1994). At the same time the AutoEpistemic Logic of Minimal Beliefs, $AELB$, is significantly more expressive than each one of these formalisms considered individually.

The existence of such a unifying framework allows us to provide simpler and more natural definitions of several non-monotonic formalisms and semantics and it enables us to compare and better understand mutual relationships existing between them. It also naturally leads to new more expressive and flexible formalizations and semantics.

2   Language

The language of the *AutoEpistemic Logic of minimal Beliefs*, $AELB$, is a propositional modal language, $\mathcal{K}_{\mathcal{L},\mathcal{B}}$, with standard connectives ($\vee, \wedge, \supset, \neg$) and two modal operators $\mathcal{L}$ and $\mathcal{B}$, called *knowledge* and *belief* operators, respectively. The atomic formulae of the form $\mathcal{L}F$ (respectively, $\mathcal{B}F$), where F is an arbitrary formula of $\mathcal{K}_{\mathcal{L},\mathcal{B}}$, are called *knowledge atoms* (respectively, *belief atoms*). Knowledge and belief atoms are jointly referred to as *introspective atoms*.

The formulae of $\mathcal{K}_{\mathcal{L},\mathcal{B}}$ in which neither $\mathcal{L}$ nor $\mathcal{B}$ occurs are called *objective* and the set of all such formulae is denoted by $\mathcal{K}$. Similarly, the set of all formulae of $\mathcal{K}_{\mathcal{L},\mathcal{B}}$ in which only $\mathcal{L}$ (respectively, only $\mathcal{B}$) occurs is denoted by $\mathcal{K}_{\mathcal{L}}$ (respectively, $\mathcal{K}_{\mathcal{B}}$). Any theory T in the language $\mathcal{K}_{\mathcal{L},\mathcal{B}}$ will be called an *autoepistemic theory.*

The intended meaning of $\mathcal{L}F$ is "*F is known*", or, more precisely, "*F can be logically inferred*", i.e., $T \models F$. The intended meaning of $\mathcal{B}F$ is "*F is believed*", or, more precisely, "*F can be non-monotonically inferred*", i.e., $T \models_{nm} F$, where $\models_{nm}$ denotes a fixed non-monotonic inference relation. In general, different non-monotonic inference relations, $\models_{nm}$, can be used. In this paper we use the *minimal model entailment*, $T \models_{\min} F$, or, more precisely, *circumscription* (McCarthy 1980; Lifschitz 1985) which *minimizes* all objective atoms and *fixes* all the introspective (knowledge and belief) atoms[1],

---

[1]The reason that we treat objective and introspective atoms differently is that the objective atoms A represent objective, *ground-level* information which, according to the principle of closed world assumption, is minimized in order to arrive at min-

i.e.:

$$T \models_{\min} F \equiv CIRC(T; \mathcal{K}) \models F.$$

In other words, the precise intended meaning of belief atoms $\mathcal{B}F$ is "*F is minimally entailed*" by the theory, i.e., $T \models_{\min} F$. We assume the following two simple axiom schemata describing the arguably obvious properties of belief atoms:

Consistency Axiom: For any formula F:

$$\mathcal{B}F \supset \neg\mathcal{B}\neg F. \tag{1}$$

Conjunctive Belief Axiom: For any formulae F and G:

$$\mathcal{B}(F \wedge G) \equiv \mathcal{B}F \wedge \mathcal{B}G. \tag{2}$$

The first axiom states that if a formula F is believed then the formula $\neg F$ is *not* believed. The second axiom states that the conjunction $F \wedge G$ of formulae F and G is believed if and only if both F and G are believed. We assume that all theories implicitly *include* the axioms (1) and (2) and therefore when we talk about the set of logical consequences of a given theory T we actually have in mind the set $Con^*(T)$ of all logical consequences of the theory T *augmented* with the axioms (1) and (2):

$$Con^*(T) = Con(T \cup \{(1)\} \cup \{(2)\}).$$

Analogous axioms could be as well assumed about the knowledge atoms $\mathcal{L}F$ but they are in fact *automatically* satisfied in all static autoepistemic expansions which are defined in the next section. Additional axioms that can enhance the expressiveness of our logic are discussed later in Section 4.3.

3   Static Autoepistemic Expansions

Like Moore's autoepistemic logic, AEL, the autoepistemic logic of minimal beliefs, $AELB$, models the set of beliefs that an ideally rational and introspective agent should hold given a set of premises T. It does so by defining *static autoepistemic expansions* T^* of T, which constitute plausible sets of such rational beliefs.

Definition 3.1 (Static Autoepistemic Expansion) *An autoepistemic theory T^* is called a static autoepistemic expansion of an autoepistemic theory T if it satisfies the following fixed-point equation:*

$$T^* = Con^*(T \cup \{\mathcal{L}F : T^* \models F\} \cup \{\neg\mathcal{L}F : T^* \not\models F\} \cup$$
$$\cup \{\mathcal{B}F : T^* \models_{\min} F\}). \qquad \square$$

The definition of static autoepistemic expansions is based on the idea of building an expansion T^* of a theory T by augmenting T with: *(i)* knowledge atoms $\mathcal{L}F$ that satisfy the condition that the formula F is logically implied by T^*, *(ii)* negations $\neg\mathcal{L}F$ of the remaining knowledge atoms, and, *(iii)* belief atoms $\mathcal{B}F$ which satisfy the condition that the formula F is minimally entailed by T^*. Consequently,

---

imal beliefs $\mathcal{B}A$. On the other hand, the introspective atoms $\mathcal{L}F$ and $\mathcal{B}F$ intuitively describe *meta-level* information, namely, a plausible rational *scenario*, which is not subject to minimization.

the definition of static expansions *enforces* the intended meaning of introspective atoms described in the previous section. Note that negations $\neg BF$ of (the remaining) belief atoms are not *explicitly* added to the expansion but some of them will be forced in by the Consistency Axiom (1).

Observe that the first part of the definition of static expansions is identical to the definition of stable autoepistemic expansions in Moore's autoepistemic logic, AEL. However, as we now show, the addition of belief atoms BF results in a *much more powerful non-monotonic logic* which contains, as special cases, several other well-known non-monotonic formalisms.

3.1 Circumscription

To begin with, one easily sees that propositional circumscription (and thus also CWA, $GCWA$ and $ECWA$ (Reiter 1978; Minker 1982; Gelfond, Przymusinska, & Przymusinski 1989)) can be properly embedded into $AELB$.

Proposition 3.1 (Embeddability of Circumscription)
Propositional circumscription, CWA, $GCWA$ and $ECWA$ are all properly embeddable into the autoepistemic logic of minimal beliefs, $AELB$. More precisely, if T is any objective theory, i.e., a theory which does not contain any introspective atoms LF and BF, then T has a unique static expansion T^* and any objective formula F is logically implied by the circumscription $CIRC(T)$ of T if and only if T^* logically implies the belief atom BF:

$$CIRC(T) \models F \;\equiv\; T^* \models BF.\ \Box$$

3.2 Moore's Autoepistemic Logic

Since the first part of the definition of static autoepistemic expansions is identical to the definition of *stable autoepistemic expansions* in Moore's autoepistemic logic, AEL, it is easy to see that AEL is also properly *embeddable* into the autoepistemic logic of minimal beliefs, $AELB$.

Proposition 3.2 (Embeddability of Autoepistemic Logic)
Moore's autoepistemic logic, AEL, is properly embeddable into the autoepistemic logic of minimal beliefs, $AELB$. More precisely, for any autoepistemic theory T in the language $\mathcal{K}_{\mathcal{L}}$, i.e., for any theory that does not use belief atoms BF, there is a one-to-one correspondence between stable autoepistemic expansions and static autoepistemic expansions of T. $\Box$

In other words, the restriction, $AELB_{\mathcal{L}}$, of the autoepistemic logic of minimal beliefs, $AELB$, to the language $\mathcal{K}_{\mathcal{L}}$, i.e., its restriction to theories using only the knowledge operator L, is *isomorphic* to Moore's autoepistemic logic, AEL. Thus, as its acronym suggests, $AELB$ constitutes an extension of Moore's AEL obtained by adding the belief operator B.

3.3 Autoepistemic Logic of Purely Minimal Beliefs

While the restriction $AELB_{\mathcal{L}}$ of $AELB$ to the language $\mathcal{K}_{\mathcal{L}}$ is isomorphic to Moore's autoepistemic logic, the restriction $AELB_{\mathcal{B}}$ of $AELB$ to the language $\mathcal{K}_{\mathcal{B}}$, i.e., its

restriction to theories using only the belief operator B, constitutes an entirely new logic, which can be called the *autoepistemic logic of purely minimal beliefs*. It turns out that $AELB_{\mathcal{B}}$ has some quite natural and interesting properties. We first introduce the belief closure operator Ψ_T.

Definition 3.2 (Belief Closure Operator) *For any autoepistemic theory T define the belief closure operator Ψ_T by the formula:*

$$\Psi_T(S) = Con^*(T \cup \{BF : S \models_{\min} F\}),$$

where S is an arbitrary autoepistemic theory. $\Box$

Thus $\Psi_T(S)$ augments the theory T with all those belief atoms BF for which F is minimally entailed by S. We first prove the restricted monotonicity of the belief closure operator Ψ_T.

Theorem 3.1 (Monotonicity of the Belief Operator) *Suppose that the theories T' and T'' are extensions of an autoepistemic theory T obtained by adding some belief atoms BF to T. If $T' \subseteq T''$ then $\Psi_T(T') \subseteq \Psi_T(T'')$.* $\Box$

From Theorem 3.1 and the well-known result of Tarski, ensuring the existence of least fixed points of monotonic operators, we easily conclude that for any autoepistemic theory T there is a unique theory S which is the least fixed point of the operator Ψ_T, i.e., satisfies the property $S = \Psi_T(S) = Con^*(T \cup \{BF : S \models_{\min} F\})$. We now need the next result ensuring the existence of unique static autoepistemic expansions of theories which are fixed points of the operator Ψ_T.

Theorem 3.2 (Uniqueness of Expansions) *Suppose that T is an autoepistemic theory in the language $\mathcal{K}_{\mathcal{B}}$ and S is a fixed point of the operator Ψ_T, i.e., $\Psi_T(S) = S$. Then S has a unique static autoepistemic expansion $\widetilde{S}$ which is also a static autoepistemic expansion of T itself.* $\Box$

From Theorems 3.1 and 3.2 we deduce the following important result.

Theorem 3.3 (Least Static Autoepistemic Expansions) *Every autoepistemic theory T in the language $\mathcal{K}_{\mathcal{B}}$ has the least (in the sense of inclusion) static autoepistemic expansion $\overline{T}$.*

The expansion $\overline{T}$ can be constructed as follows. Let $T^0 = T$ and suppose that T^α has already been defined for any ordinal number $\alpha < \beta$. If $\beta = \alpha + 1$ is a successor ordinal then define:

$$T^{\alpha+1} = \Psi_T(T^\alpha) = Con^*(T \cup \{BF : T^\alpha \models_{\min} F\}).$$

Else, if β is a limit ordinal, define $T^\beta = \bigcup_{\alpha < \beta} T^\alpha$. The sequence $\{T^\alpha\}$ is monotonically increasing and thus has a unique fixed point $T^\lambda = \Psi_T(T^\lambda)$, for some ordinal λ. Now define $\overline{T} = \widetilde{T^\lambda}$. $\Box$

The existence of least static autoepistemic expansions of theories in $AELB_{\mathcal{B}}$ sharply contrasts with the properties of stable autoepistemic expansions in AEL which typically do not have least elements. Observe that the *least* static autoepistemic expansion of T contains those and only those formulae which are true in *all* static autoepistemic expansions of T. The following theorem significantly extends Theorem 3.3 and provides a complete characterization of *all* static autoepistemic expansions of a theory T in the language $\mathcal{K}_{\mathcal{B}}$.

Theorem 3.4 (Characterization Theorem) *A theory T^* is a static autoepistemic expansion of a theory T in $\mathcal{K}_{\mathcal{B}}$ if and only if T^* is the least static autoepistemic expansion $\overline{T'}$ of a theory $T' = T \cup \{\mathcal{B}F_s : s \in S\}$ satisfying the condition that $T^* \models_{\min} F_s$, for every $s \in S$. In particular, the least static autoepistemic expansion $\overline{T}$ of T is obtained when the set $\{\mathcal{B}F_s : s \in S\}$ is empty.* $\square$

4 Semantics of Logic Programs

We already know that Circumscription, Moore's Autoepistemic Logic and the Autoepistemic Logic of Purely Minimal Beliefs are all properly embeddable into the Autoepistemic Logic of Minimal Beliefs, $AELB$. We will now show that major semantics defined for normal and disjunctive *logic programs* are also embeddable into $AELB$. In the next section we will discuss two other non-monotonic formalisms embeddable into $AELB$.

4.1 Stable Semantics

Since Moore's autoepistemic logic, AEL, is isomorphic to the subset $AELB_{\mathcal{L}}$ of $AELB$, it follows from the results of Gelfond and Lifschitz (Gelfond & Lifschitz 1988) that stable semantics of logic programs can be obtained by means of a suitable translation of a logic program into an autoepistemic theory. Namely, for a logic program P consisting of clauses:

$$A \leftarrow B_1, ..., B_m, not\, C_1, ..., not\, C_n$$

define $T_{\neg\mathcal{L}}(P)$ to be its translation into the autoepistemic theory consisting of formulae:

$$B_1 \wedge ... \wedge B_m \wedge \neg\mathcal{L}C_1 \wedge ... \wedge \neg\mathcal{L}C_n \supset A.$$

The translation $T_{\neg\mathcal{L}}(P)$ is obtained therefore by replacing the *negation by default not C* by $\neg\mathcal{L}C$ which has the intended meaning *"C is not known to be true"*.

Theorem 4.1 (Embeddability of Stable Semantics) *There is a one-to-one correspondence between stable models $\mathcal{M}$ of the program P and static autoepistemic expansions T^* of $T_{\neg\mathcal{L}}(P)$. Namely, for any objective atom A we have:*

$$A \in \mathcal{M} \quad iff \quad \mathcal{L}A \in T^*$$

$$\neg A \in \mathcal{M} \quad iff \quad \neg\mathcal{L}A \in T^*. \ \square$$

4.2 Stationary and Well-Founded Semantics

Similarly, it follows from the results obtained in (Przymusinski 1994) that the stationary (or partial stable) and the well-founded semantics of logic programs can be obtained by means of a suitable translation of a logic program into an autoepistemic theory. Namely, for a logic program P consisting of clauses:

$$A \leftarrow B_1, ..., B_m, not\, C_1, ..., not\, C_n$$

define $T_{\mathcal{B}\neg}(P)$ to be its translation into the autoepistemic theory consisting of formulae:

$$B_1 \wedge ... \wedge B_m \wedge \mathcal{B}\neg C_1 \wedge ... \wedge \mathcal{B}\neg C_n \supset A.$$

The translation $T_{\mathcal{B}\neg}(P)$ is obtained therefore by replacing the *negation by default not C* by $\mathcal{B}\neg C$ which has the intended meaning *"C is believed to be false"* or *"$\neg C$ is minimally entailed"*.

Theorem 4.2 (Embeddability of Stationary Semantics) *There is a one-to-one correspondence between stationary (or partial stable) models $\mathcal{M}$ of the program P and static autoepistemic expansions T^* of $T_{\mathcal{B}\neg}(P)$. Namely, for any objective atom A we have:*

$$A \in \mathcal{M} \quad iff \quad \mathcal{B}A \in T^*$$

$$\neg A \in \mathcal{M} \quad iff \quad \mathcal{B}\neg A \in T^*.$$

Since the well-founded model $\mathcal{M}_0$ of the program P coincides with the least stationary model of P (Przymusinski 1991c), it corresponds to the least static autoepistemic expansion $\overline{T}$ of $T_{\mathcal{B}\neg}(P)$, whose existence is guaranteed by Theorem 3.3.

Moreover, (total) stable models $\mathcal{M}$ of P correspond to those static autoepistemic expansions T^* of $T_{\mathcal{B}\neg}(P)$ that satisfy the condition that for all objective atoms A, either $\mathcal{B}A \in T^*$ or $\mathcal{B}\neg A \in T^*$. $\square$

Analogous result applies to the translation $T_{\neg\mathcal{B}}(P)$ defined by:

$$B_1 \wedge ... \wedge B_m \wedge \neg\mathcal{B}C_1 \wedge ... \wedge \neg\mathcal{B}C_n \supset A.$$

However, for disjunctive programs (discussed below) the two translations $T_{\mathcal{B}\neg}(P)$ and $T_{\neg\mathcal{B}}(P)$ lead to different results.

4.3 Semantics of Disjunctive Programs

As it was the case with normal logic programs, static expansions can be used to define the semantics of *disjunctive logic programs* (see (Lobo, Minker, & Rajasekar 1992) for an overview of disjunctive logic programming). In particular, we can extend the transformation $T_{\mathcal{B}\neg}(P)$ to any disjunctive logic program P consisting of clauses:

$$A_1 \vee ... \vee A_l \leftarrow B_1, ..., B_m, not\, C_1, ..., not\, C_n$$

by translating it into the autoepistemic theory consisting of formulae:

$$B_1 \wedge ... \wedge B_m \wedge \mathcal{B}\neg C_1 \wedge ... \wedge \mathcal{B}\neg C_n \supset A_1 \vee ... \vee A_l.$$

It turns out that this transformation immediately leads to the *static semantics* of disjunctive logic programs defined in (Przymusinski 1994):

Theorem 4.3 (Embeddability of Static Semantics) *There is a one-to-one correspondence between static expansions of the disjunctive logic program P, as defined in (Przymusinski 1994), and static autoepistemic expansions of its translation $T_{\mathcal{B}\neg}(P)$.* $\square$

Although static semantics for disjunctive programs has a number of important advantages it is by far not the only semantics for disjunctive programs that can be derived by means of a suitable translation of a logic program into the autoepistemic logic of minimal beliefs, $AELB$. The expressive power of $AELB$ allows us to obtain other well-known semantics for disjunctive programs by simply using a different transformation and/or assuming additional axioms. To illustrate this claim let us consider the following three natural axioms:

Disjunctive Belief Axiom: For any formulae F and G:

$$\textbf{(DBA)} \quad \mathcal{B}(F \vee G) \equiv \mathcal{B}F \vee \mathcal{B}G.$$

Disjunctive Knowledge Axiom: For any formulae F and G:

$$\textbf{(DKA)} \quad \mathcal{L}(F \vee G) \equiv \mathcal{L}F \vee \mathcal{L}G.$$

Generalized Closed World Assumption: For any positive formula F:

$$\textbf{(GCWA)} \quad \mathcal{L}\mathcal{B}\neg F \supset \neg F.$$

The last axiom intuitively says that if we know that we believe in the falsity of a (positive) formula F then F is indeed false. It turns out that both the *disjunctive stationary semantics* introduced in (Przymusinski 1991b) and the *(partial or total) disjunctive stable semantics* introduced in (Przymusinski 1991c; Gelfond & Lifschitz 1990) can be expressed by means of these axioms.

Theorem 4.4 (Embeddability of Disjunctive Stationary Semantics) *There is a one-to-one correspondence between stationary expansions of a disjunctive program P and static autoepistemic expansions of its translation $T_{\mathcal{B}\neg}(P)$ augmented with the axioms (DBA) and $(GCWA)$.*

Theorem 4.5 (Embeddability of Disjunctive Stable Semantics) *There is a one-to-one correspondence between disjunctive partial stable models of a disjunctive program P and static autoepistemic expansions of its translation $T_{\mathcal{B}\neg}(P)$ augmented with the axioms (DBA), (DKA) and $(GCWA)$. Moreover, (total) disjunctive stable models of P correspond to those static autoepistemic expansions T^* of $T_{\mathcal{B}\neg}(P)$ that satisfy the condition that for all objective atoms A, either $\mathcal{B}A \in T^*$ or $\mathcal{B}\neg A \in T^*$.* $\square$

4.4 Programs with Strong Negation

The negation operator *not A* used in logic programs does not represent the *classical negation*, but rather a non-monotonic negation by default. Gelfond and Lifschitz pointed out (Gelfond & Lifschitz 1990) that in logic programming, as well as in other areas of non-monotonic reasoning, it is often useful to use *both* the non-monotonic negation and a different negation, $\neg A$, which they called "classical negation" but which can perhaps more appropriately be called "strong negation" (Alferes & Pereira 1992). They also extended the stable model semantics to the class of *extended logic programs* with strong negation.

It is easy to add strong negation to the autoepistemic logic of minimal beliefs, $AELB$. All one needs to do is to augment the original objective language $\mathcal{K}$ with new *objective* propositional symbols "$\neg A$" with the intended meaning that "$\neg A$ *is the strong negation of* A" and assume the following *strong negation axiom* schema:

$$\textbf{(SNA)} \quad A \wedge \neg A \supset \mathit{false}, \text{ or, equivalently, } \neg A \supset \neg A.$$

Observe that, as opposed to classical negation $\neg$, the law of excluded middle $A \vee \neg A$ is not assumed. As pointed out by Bob Kowalski, the proposition A may describe the property of being *"good"* while proposition $\neg A$ describes the property of being *"bad"*. The strong negation axiom states that things cannot be both good and bad. We do not assume, however, that things must always be either good or bad.

Since this method of defining strong negation applies to *all* autoepistemic theories, it applies, in particular, to normal and disjunctive logic programs (see also (Alferes & Pereira 1992)). Moreover, the following theorem shows that the resulting general framework provides a strict *generalization* of the original approach proposed by Gelfond-Lifschitz.

Theorem 4.6 (Embeddability of Extended Stable Semantics) *There is a one-to-one correspondence between stable models $\mathcal{M}$ of an extended logic program P with strong negation, as defined in (Gelfond & Lifschitz 1990), and static autoepistemic expansions T^* of its translation $T_{\neg\mathcal{L}}(P)$ into autoepistemic theory under which a strong negation of an atom A is translated into $\neg A$.* $\square$

5 Combining Knowledge and Belief

In most of the results presented so far the theories under consideration used only one of the introspective operators, either the belief operator $\mathcal{B}$ or the knowledge operator $\mathcal{L}$. However, the greatest expressive power of the autoepistemic logic of minimal beliefs, $AELB$, is achieved when both of these operators are used in combination. We have already seen examples of such combined use of the two operators in Theorems 4.4 and 4.5, both of which involved the axiom $(GCWA)$. In this section we first give an example and then we discuss two specific application areas, namely, logic programming and epistemic specifications,

Example 5.1 We first revisit the example informally discussed in the Introduction.

Scenario 1: You rent a movie if you believe that you do not go to a baseball game (bg) and do not go to a football game (fg). You do not buy tickets to a game if you don't know that you will go to see it.

$$\mathcal{B}\neg goto(bg) \wedge \mathcal{B}\neg goto(fg) \supset \mathit{rent\_movie}$$
$$\neg\mathcal{L}goto(bg) \wedge \neg\mathcal{L}goto(fg) \supset \mathit{dont\_buy\_tickets}$$

This theory has a unique static autoepistemic expansion in which you rent a movie, because you believe that you will not go to see any games (i.e., $\neg goto(bg) \wedge \neg goto(fg)$ holds in all minimal models) and you do not buy tickets because you don't know you that will go to see any of the games (i.e., neither $goto(bg)$ nor $goto(fg)$ are provable).

Scenario 2: Now, suppose that you learn that you either go to see a baseball game or go to see a football game, i.e., $goto(bg) \lor goto(fg)$. The new theory has a unique static autoepistemic expansion in which you believe you should *not* rent a movie[2] and you still do not buy any tickets, because you don't know yet which game you are going to see (i.e., neither $goto(bg)$ nor $goto(fg)$ are provable).

Scenario 3: Finally, suppose that you learn that you actually go to see a baseball game, i.e., $goto(bg)$. The new theory has a unique static autoepistemic expansion in which you still believe you should *not* rent any movies but you no longer believe in not buying game tickets because you know now that you are going to see a specific game.

Observe, that we cannot replace the premise $\mathcal{B}\neg goto(bg) \land \mathcal{B}\neg goto(fg)$ in the first implication by $\mathcal{L}\neg goto(bg) \land \mathcal{L}\neg goto(fg)$ because that would result in $rent\_movie$ not being true in Scenario 1. Similarly, we cannot replace it by $\neg\mathcal{L}goto(bg) \land \neg\mathcal{L}goto(fg)$ because that would result in $rent\_movie$ becoming true in Scenario 2. We also cannot replace the premise $\neg\mathcal{L}goto(bg) \land \neg\mathcal{L}goto(fg)$ in the second implication by $\neg\mathcal{B}goto(bg) \land \neg\mathcal{B}goto(fg)$ or by $\mathcal{B}\neg goto(bg) \land \mathcal{B}\neg goto(fg)$, because it would no longer imply that we should not buy tickets in Scenario 2. Thus the roles of the two operators are quite different and one cannot be substituted by the other. $\square$

5.1 Combining Stable and Well-Founded Negation in Logic Programs

As we have seen in the previous section, both stable and well-founded negation in logic programs can be obtained by translating the non-monotonic negation *not C* into introspective literals $\neg\mathcal{L}C$ and $\mathcal{B}\neg C$, respectively. However, the existence of both types of introspective literals in $AELB$ allows us to *combine both types of negation* in one epistemic theory consisting of formulae of the form:

$$B_1 \land ... \land B_m \land \neg\mathcal{L}C_1 \land ... \land \neg\mathcal{L}C_k \land \mathcal{B}\neg C_{k+1} \land ... \land \mathcal{B}\neg C_n \supset$$

$$\supset A_1 \lor ... \lor A_l.$$

Such an epistemic theory may be viewed as representing a more *general disjunctive logic program* which permits the simultaneous use of both types of negation. In such logic programs, the first k negative premises represent *stable negation* and the remaining ones represent the *well-founded negation*. The ability to use both types of negation significantly increases the expressibility of logic programs. For instance, the previous Example 5.1 is a special case of such generalized programs.

---

[2]This follows from the fact that the expansion obviously implies $\mathcal{B}(goto(bg) \lor goto(fg))$ and thus, by the Consistency Axiom (1), it also contains $\neg\mathcal{B}(\neg goto(bg) \land \neg goto(fg))$ $\equiv \neg\mathcal{B}(\neg goto(bg)) \lor \neg\mathcal{B}(\neg goto(fg))$, which implies that $\neg rent\_movie$ holds in all minimal models.

5.2 Epistemic Specifications

Epistemic specifications were recently introduced in (Gelfond 1992) using a rather complex language of belief sets and world views which includes two operators, $\mathbf{K}F$ and $\mathbf{M}F$, called belief and possibility operators, respectively. As an illustration of the expressive power of the Autoepistemic Logic of Minimal Beliefs, $AELB$, we now demonstrate that epistemic specifications can be also *isomorphically embedded* as a proper subset of $AELB$, and thus, in particular, we show that epistemic specifications can be defined entirely in the language of classical propositional logic.

We show that Gelfond's belief operator $\mathbf{K}F$ can be defined as $\mathcal{L}\mathcal{B}F$ and thus have the intended meening "F is known to be believed". On the other hand, the possibility operator $\mathbf{M}F$ is proved to be equivalent to $\neg\mathbf{K}\neg F$, or, equivalently, to $\neg\mathcal{L}\mathcal{B}\neg F$. The translation provides therefore an example of a *nested use* of the belief and knowledge operators, $\mathcal{B}$ and $\mathcal{L}$ (see also the axiom $(GCWA)$ in Section 4.3).

Due to the space limitation, we assume familiarity with epistemic specifications. Let G be a database describing Gelfond's epistemic specification. Define $T(G)$ to be its translation into autoepistemic logic of minimal beliefs, $AELB$, obtained by:

(i) Replacing, for all *objective* atoms A, the classical negation symbol $\neg A$ by the strong negation symbol $\sim A$. We assume that the objective language $\mathcal{K}$ was first augmented with strong negation atoms $\sim A$ as described in Section 4.4.

(ii) Eliminating Gelfond's "possibility" operator $\mathbf{M}$ by replacing every expression of the form $\mathbf{M}F$ by the expression $\neg\mathbf{K}\neg F$, where $\mathbf{K}$ is Gelfond's "belief" operator.

(iii) Finally, eliminating Gelfond's "belief" operator $\mathbf{K}$ by replacing every expression of the form $\mathbf{K}F$ by the autoepistemic formula $\mathcal{L}\mathcal{B}F$.

The substitution (i) is motivated by the fact that in his paper Gelfond uses the classical negation symbol $\neg A$ when in fact he refers to *strong negation* $\sim A$. The substitution allows us to reserve the standard negation symbol $\neg A$ for true classical negation. The substitution (ii) is motivated by the fact that Gelfond's "possibility" operator $\mathbf{M}F$ can now be shown to be *equivalent* to $\neg\mathbf{K}\neg F$, and, vice versa, $\mathbf{K}F$ can be shown to be equivalent to $\neg\mathbf{M}\neg F$. The last substitution (iii) leads to a complete translation into an autoepistemic theory. It replaces $\mathbf{K}F$ by the formula $\mathcal{L}\mathcal{B}F$ with the intended meaning *"F is known to be believed"*. Equivalently, its intended meaning can be described by *"F is known to be true in all minimal models"*.

Now we can show that epistemic specifications are isomorphically embeddable into the autoepistemic logic of minimal beliefs, $AELB$. The limited size of this abstract does not allow us to provide complete details.

Theorem 5.1 (Embeddability of Epistemic Specifications) *Epistemic specifications are isomorphically embeddable into the autoepistemic logic of minimal beliefs, $AELB$.*

More precisely, there is a one-to-one correspondence between world views V of an epistemic specification G and static autoepistemic expansions T^* of its translation $T(G)$ into $AELB$. Moreover, there is a one-to-one correspondence between belief sets B of a world view V and minimal models M of the corresponding static expansion T^* of $T(G)$. □

Gelfond's paper contains several intersting examples of epistemic specifications which now can be easily translated into the simpler language of $AELB$.

6 Conclusion

We introduced an extension, $AELB$, of Moore's autoepistemic logic, AEL, and showed that it provides a powerful knowledge representation framework unifying several well-known non-monotonic formalisms and semantics for normal and disjunctive logic programs. It allows us to compare different formalisms, better understand mutual relationships existing between them and introduce simpler and more natural definitions of some of them.

The proposed formalism significantly differs from other formalisms based on the notion of minimal beliefs. In particular, it it is different from the circumscriptive autoepistemic logic introduced in (Przymusinski 1991a) and the logic of minimal beliefs and negation as failure proposed in (Lifschitz 1992). The formalism is also quite flexible by allowing various extensions and modifications, including the use of a different formalism defining the *meaning of beliefs* and introduction of *additional axioms*. For example, by using the *weak* minimal model entailment, instead of the standard minimal model entailment, in the definition of belief atoms BF, one can ensure that disjunctions are treated *inclusively* rather than *exclusively*. Other forms of circumscriptions as well as other non-monotonic formalisms can be used to define the meaning of belief atoms. By using such modifications one may be able to tailor the formalism to fulfill the needs of different application domains.

References

Alferes, J. J., and Pereira, L. M. 1992. On logic program semantics with two kinds of negation. In Apt, K., ed., *International Joint Conference and Symposium on Logic Programming*, 574–588. MIT Press.

Gelfond, M., and Lifschitz, V. 1988. The stable model semantics for logic programming. In Kowalski, R., and Bowen, K., eds., *Proceedings of the Fifth Logic Programming Symposium*, 1070–1080. Cambridge, Mass.: Association for Logic Programming.

Gelfond, M., and Lifschitz, V. 1990. Logic programs with classical negation. In *Proceedings of the Seventh International Logic Programming Conference, Jerusalem, Israel*, 579–597. Cambridge, Mass.: Association for Logic Programming.

Gelfond, M.; Przymusinska, H.; and Przymusinski, T. 1989. On the relationship between circumscription and negation as failure. *Journal of Artificial Intelligence* 38:75–94.

Gelfond, M. 1992. Logic programming and reasoning with incomplete information. Technical report, University of Texas at El Paso.

Lifschitz, V. 1985. Computing circumscription. In *Proceedings IJCAI-85*, 121–127. Los Altos, CA: American Association for Artificial Intelligence.

Lifschitz, V. 1992. Minimal belief and negation as failure. Research report, University of Texas at Austin.

Lobo, J.; Minker, J.; and Rajasekar, A. 1992. *Foundations of Disjunctive Logic Programming*. Cambridge, Massachusetts: MIT Press.

McCarthy, J. 1980. Circumscription – a form of non-monotonic reasoning. *Journal of Artificial Intelligence* 13:27–39.

Minker, J. 1982. On indefinite data bases and the closed world assumption. In *Proc. 6-th Conference on Automated Deduction*, 292–308. New York: Springer Verlag.

Moore, R. 1985. Semantic considerations on non-monotonic logic. *Journal of Artificial Intelligence* 25:75–94.

Przymusinski, T. C. 1991a. Autoepistemic logics of closed beliefs and logic programming. In Nerode, A.; Marek, W.; and Subrahmanian, V., eds., *Proceedings of the First International Workshop on Logic Programming and Non-monotonic Reasoning, Washington, D.C., July 1991*, 3–20. Cambridge, Mass.: MIT Press.

Przymusinski, T. C. 1991b. Semantics of disjunctive logic programs and deductive databases. In Delobel, C.; Kifer, M.; and Masunaga, Y., eds., *Proceedings of the Second International Conference on Deductive and Object-Oriented Databases DOOD'91*, 85–107. Munich, Germany: Springer Verlag.

Przymusinski, T. C. 1991c. Stable semantics for disjunctive programs. *New Generation Computing Journal* 9:401–424. (Extended abstract appeared in: Extended stable semantics for normal and disjunctive logic programs. *Proceedings of the 7-th International Logic Programming Conference, Jerusalem*, pages 459–477, 1990. MIT Press.).

Przymusinski, T. C. 1994. Static semantics for normal and disjunctive logic programs. *Annals of Mathematics and Artificial Intelligence*. (in print).

Reiter, R. 1978. On closed-world data bases. In Gallaire, H., and Minker, J., eds., *Logic and Data Bases*. New York: Plenum Press. 55–76.

Van Gelder, A.; Ross, K. A.; and Schlipf, J. S. 1990. The well-founded semantics for general logic programs. *Journal of the ACM*. (to appear). Preliminary abstract appeared in Seventh ACM Symposium on Principles of Database Systems, March 1988, pp. 221–230.

Perception

A New Approach to Tracking 3D Objects in 2D Image Sequences

Michael Chan[1], Dimitri Metaxas[1] and Sven Dickinson[2]

[1]Dept. of Computer & Information Science
University of Pennsylvania
Philadelphia, PA 19104-6389

[2]Dept. of Computer Science
University of Toronto
Toronto, Ontario, Canada M5S 1A4

mchan@grip.cis.upenn.edu, dnm@central.cis.upenn.edu, sven@vis.toronto.edu

Abstract

We present a new technique for tracking 3D objects from 2D image sequences through the integration of qualitative and quantitative techniques. The deformable models are initialized based on a previously developed part-based qualitative shape segmentation system. Using a physics-based quantitative approach, objects are subsequently tracked without feature correspondence based on generalized forces computed from the stereo images. The automatic prediction of possible edge occlusion and disocclusion is performed using an extended Kalman filter. To cope with possible occlusion caused by a previously undetected object, we monitor the magnitude and direction of the computed image forces exerted on the models. Abrupt changes to these forces trigger scene re-segmentation and model re-initialization through the qualitative shape segmentation system. Tracking is subsequently continued using only local image forces. We demonstrate our technique in experiments involving image sequences from complex motions of 3D objects.

Introduction

Research in 3D model-based object tracking from image sequences is typified by approaches which attempt to recover the six degrees of freedom of an object in each frame, e.g., (Thompson & Mundy 1988; Verghese, Gale, & Dyer 1990; Lowe 1991; Gennery 1992). Once correspondences between image and model features are determined, changes in the positions of image features in successive frames are used to update the pose of the object. Although these techniques provide accurate pose of the object at each frame, they require an exact geometric specification of the object; they do not allow models to deform as they move. Recently, to cope with the challenges of nonrigidity, several researchers have adopted a physics-based approach to estimate the shapes and motions of nonrigid 3D objects from visual data to different levels of accuracy (Terzopoulos, Witkin, & Kass 1988; Huang 1990; Pentland & Horowitz 1991; Metaxas &

Terzopoulos 1993). The 2D problem has received similar attention (Kass, Witkin, & Terzopoulos 1988; Duncan, Owen, & Anandan 1991; Szeliski & Terzopoulos 1991; Blake, Curwen, & Zisserman 1993).

In this paper, we develop a new approach to tracking shapes and motions of objects in 3D from 2D image sequences. Our method makes use of both the framework of qualitative shape segmentation (Dickinson, Pentland, & Rosenfeld 1992b; 1992a) and the physics-based framework for quantitative shape and motion estimation (Terzopoulos & Metaxas 1991; Metaxas & Terzopoulos 1993). To be able to track multiple objects, initialization of the models is performed in the first frame of the sequence based on a shape recovery process that uses recovered qualitative shapes [1] to constrain the fitting of deformable models to the data (Metaxas & Dickinson 1993). For successive frames, the qualitative shape recovery process can be avoided in favor of a physics-based model updating process requiring only a gradient computation in each frame. Assuming no occlusion and small deformations between frames, local forces derived from stereo images are sufficient to update the positions, orientations, and shapes of the models in 3D.

Kalman filtering techniques have been applied in the vision literature for the estimation of dynamic features (Deriche & Faugeras 1990) and rigid motion parameters (Dickmanns & Graefe 1988; Broida, Chandrashekhar, & Chellappa 1990) of objects from image sequences. We use a Kalman filter for the estimation of the object's shape and motion, which consequently allows the prediction of possible edge occlusion and disocclusion. The occurrence of these situations may be due to changes of an object's aspect from frame to frame or due to motions of other independently moving objects (situations where most tracking approaches based on feature correspondence may not work robustly). By predicting the occurrence of these situations in our approach, we can confidently determine which part of an object will be occluded and suppress their contributions to the net forces applied to

---

[1]We assume that objects are constructed from a finite set of volumetric part classes.

the model. In fact, an advantage of our technique is that we do not need to perform costly feature correspondence during 3D tracking.

Our approach also allows the detection of object occlusion due to a previously undetected object by monitoring changes to the image forces exerted on the models. In such an ambiguous situation, we invoke the qualitative shape segmentation module for scene re-segmentation and model re-initialization. Tracking can then be continued by using only local images forces. Our technique is robust and can handle scenes with complex motions and occlusion due to the triggering of the qualitative shape segmentation system when necessary.

Dynamic Deformable Models

This section reviews the formulation of the deformable model we adopted for object modeling and the physics-based framework of visual estimation (see (Metaxas & Terzopoulos 1993) for greater detail).

Geometry of Deformable Models

The positions of points on the model relative to an inertial frame of reference Φ in space are given by a vector-valued, time varying function $\mathbf{x}(\mathrm{u}, t) = (x(\mathrm{u}, t), y(\mathrm{u}, t), z(\mathrm{u}, t))^T$, where T denotes transposition and u are the model's material coordinates. We set up a noninertial, model-centered reference frame ϕ and express the position function as $\mathbf{x} = \mathbf{c} + \mathbf{Rp}$, where $\mathbf{c}(t)$ is the origin of ϕ at the center of the model and the rotation matrix $\mathbf{R}(t)$ gives the orientation of ϕ relative to Φ. Thus, $\mathbf{p}(\mathrm{u}, t)$ gives the positions of points on the model relative to the model frame.

We further express $\mathbf{p} = \mathbf{s} + \mathbf{d}$, as the sum of a reference shape $\mathbf{s}(\mathrm{u}, t)$ and a displacement $\mathbf{d}(\mathrm{u}, t)$. We define the reference shape as: $\mathbf{s} = \mathbf{T}(\mathbf{e}(\mathrm{u}; a_0, a_1, \ldots); b_0, b_1, \ldots)$. Here, a geometric primitive $\mathbf{e}$, defined parametrically in u and parameterized by the variables $a_i(t)$, is subjected to the *global deformation* $\mathbf{T}$ which depends on the parameters $b_i(t)$. Although generally nonlinear, $\mathbf{e}$ and $\mathbf{T}$ are assumed to be differentiable (so that we may compute the Jacobian of $\mathbf{s}$) and $\mathbf{T}$ may be a composite sequence of primitive deformation functions $\mathbf{T}(\mathbf{e}) = \mathbf{T}_1(\mathbf{T}_2(\ldots \mathbf{T}_n(\mathbf{e})))$. We concatenate the global deformation parameters into the vector $\mathbf{q}_s = (a_0, a_1, \ldots, b_0, b_1, \ldots)^T$. To illustrate our approach in this paper, we will use as a reference shape a deformable superquadric ellipsoid that can also undergo parameterized tapering deformations, as defined in (Metaxas & Terzopoulos 1993).

Model Kinematics and Dynamics

The velocity of a 3D point on the model is given by

$$\dot{\mathbf{x}} = \mathbf{L}\dot{\mathbf{q}}, \tag{1}$$

where $\mathbf{L}$ is the Jacobian matrix that converts q-dimensional vectors to 3D vectors (Metaxas & Terzopoulos 1993). The vector $\mathbf{q}(t)$ represents the generalized coordinates of the model consisting of the translation, rotation, global and local deformations. To make the model dynamic, we assume that it is made of a simulated elastic material that has certain mass distribution. From Lagrangian mechanics, we obtain second-order equations of motion which take the form (see (Terzopoulos & Metaxas 1991) for derivations):

$$\mathbf{M}\ddot{\mathbf{q}} + \mathbf{D}\dot{\mathbf{q}} + \mathbf{Kq} = \mathbf{g}_q + \mathbf{f}_q, \quad \mathbf{f}_q = \int \mathbf{L}^T \mathbf{f}\, d\mathrm{u}, \tag{2}$$

where $\mathbf{f}_q$ are generalized external forces associated with the components of $\mathbf{q}$, and $\mathbf{f}(\mathrm{u}, t)$ is the image force distribution applied to the model. Here $\mathbf{M}$ is the mass matrix, $\mathbf{D}$ is the damping matrix, $\mathbf{K}$ is the stiffness matrix and $\mathbf{g}_q$ is the vector of the generalized coriolis and centrifugal forces.

Multiple Object Tracking

This section describes our new approach for tracking multiple objects in the presence of occlusion. It is based on the intelligent use of a qualitative shape segmentation system (Metaxas & Dickinson 1993) and techniques for quantitative shape and motion estimation (Metaxas & Terzopoulos 1993). The deformable models are first initialized based on the qualitative segmentation system. Objects are subsequently tracked using a physics-based approach by applying image forces simultaneously derived from the stereo images. We can handle partial edge occlusion and disocclusion due to the object's own motion or occlusion by another object by predicting their occurrences using an extended Kalman filter. We handle more complex cases of object occlusion due to a previously undetected object by monitoring changes to the image forces exerted on the models. These changes trigger the use of the qualitative shape segmentation system for scene re-segmentation and model re-initialization, and tracking is subsequently continued using local image forces only.

Qualitative Shape Recovery and Model Initialization

We employ the methodology developed in (Metaxas & Dickinson 1993) to initialize our deformable models. We start by assuming that objects are constructed from a finite set of volumetric part classes (Dickinson, Pentland, & Rosenfeld 1992b; 1992a). The parts, in turn, are mapped to a set of viewer-centered aspects. During the qualitative shape recovery process, the system first segments the image into parts using an aspect matching paradigm. Each recovered qualitative part defines: 1) the relevant non-occluded contour data belonging to the part, 2) a mapping between the image faces in their projected aspects and the 3D surfaces on the quantitative models, and 3) a qualitative orientation that is exploited during model fitting. Based on these constraints, we assign forces from monocular image data points to the corresponding points on the 3D model. The model is then fitted dynamically to the image data under the influence of the image forces. In the following sections, we will discuss how we handle sequences of stereo images taken under non-parallel geometry without requiring the continuous use of qualitative constraints.

Short Range Forces from Image Potentials

For each frame in the image sequence, we create an image potential such that the "valleys" of this potential correspond to the locations in the image where there are sharp changes in intensity or edge features. If we denote the intensity image by $I(x, y)$, the image potential can be computed as follows (Terzopoulos, Witkin, & Kass 1988):

$$\Pi(x, y) = -\beta \left| \nabla (G_\sigma * I)(x, y) \right| \tag{3}$$

where σ determines the width of the Gaussian function G_σ, $*$ denotes the convolution operation, and β determines the "steepness" of the potential surface. The corresponding 2D force field induced by this potential is given by:

$$\mathbf{f}(x, y) = -\nabla \Pi(x, y). \tag{4}$$

The model's degrees of freedom respond to the 2D force field through a process which first projects the model's nodes into the image. As the projected nodes are attracted to the valleys of the potential surface, the model's degrees of freedom are updated to reflect this motion. The mapping of 2D image forces to generalized forces acting on the model requires the derivation a Jacobian matrix.

Jacobian Computation for Perspective Projection

Let $\mathbf{x} = (x, y, z)^T$ denotes the location of a point j with respect to the world coordinate frame. Then we can write

$$\mathbf{x} = \mathbf{c}_c + \mathbf{R}_c \mathbf{x}_c, \tag{5}$$

where $\mathbf{c}_c$ and $\mathbf{R}_c$ are respectively the translation and rotation of the camera frame with respect to the world coordinate frame, and $\mathbf{x}_c = (x_c, y_c, z_c)^T$ is the position of the point j with respect to the camera coordinate frame.

Under perspective projection, the point $\mathbf{x}_c$ projects into an image point $\mathbf{x}_p = (x_p, x_p)^T$ based on the formulas:

$$x_p = \frac{x_c}{z_c} f, \quad y_p = \frac{y_c}{z_c} f, \tag{6}$$

where f is the focal length of the camera.

By taking the derivative of (6) with respect to time, we arrive at the following matrix equation:

$$\begin{pmatrix} \dot{x}_p \\ \dot{y}_p \end{pmatrix} = \begin{bmatrix} f/z_c & 0 & -x_c/z_c^2 f \\ 0 & f/z_c & -y_c/z_c^2 f \end{bmatrix} \begin{pmatrix} \dot{x}_c \\ \dot{y}_c \\ \dot{z}_c \end{pmatrix}. \tag{7}$$

Based on (5) and (1) we get

$$\dot{\mathbf{x}}_c = \mathbf{R}_c^{-1} \dot{\mathbf{x}} = \mathbf{R}_c^{-1} \mathbf{L} \dot{\mathbf{q}}. \tag{8}$$

Rewriting (7) in compact form using (8), we get

$$\mathbf{x}_p = \begin{bmatrix} f/z_c & 0 & -x_c/z_c^2 f \\ 0 & f/z_c & -y_c/z_c^2 f \end{bmatrix} \mathbf{R}_c^{-1} \mathbf{L} \dot{\mathbf{q}} = \mathbf{L}_p \dot{\mathbf{q}}. \tag{9}$$

By replacing the Jacobian matrix in (2) by $\mathbf{L}_p$, two dimensional forces $\mathbf{f}$ derived from image data can be appropriately converted into generalized forces $\mathbf{f}_q$ measured in the world coordinate frame.

Forces from Stereo Images

By computing generalized forces in the world coordinate frame, the 2D image forces in a pair of stereo images can be simultaneously transformed into generalized forces $\mathbf{f}_q$ measured in a common world coordinate frame. Measurements from two different views are sufficient to determine the scale and depth parameters of the model. If we define as *active* nodes those model nodes on which image forces are exerted, then the generalized forces are computed by summing the image forces exerted on all the active nodes of the discretized model. More precisely, if we denote the position of the jth active node on the model surface by $\mathbf{x}_j$, then the generalized force on the model can be computed as follows:

$$\begin{aligned} \mathbf{f}_q &= \sum_{j \in \mathcal{A}_L} \mathbf{L}_{p_L}^T (\mathbf{f}_L (\mathbf{P}(\mathbf{R}_{c_L}^{-1}(\mathbf{x}_j - \mathbf{c}_{c_L})))) \\ &+ \sum_{j \in \mathcal{A}_R} \mathbf{L}_{p_R}^T (\mathbf{f}_R (\mathbf{P}(\mathbf{R}_{c_R}^{-1}(\mathbf{x}_j - \mathbf{c}_{c_R})))), \end{aligned} \tag{10}$$

where $\mathcal{A}$ is the set of indices of active nodes. Here the subscripts L and R denote dependence on the left and right images respectively and $\mathbf{P}(x, y, z) = (\frac{x}{z} f, \frac{y}{z} f)$ describes the perspective projection equation.

Determining Active Model Nodes

When our measurements are 2D images, as opposed to 3D range data, only a subset of the nodes on the model surface are selected to respond to forces. From a given viewpoint, we can compute this active subset of model nodes based on the model's shape and orientation. In particular, a model node is made active if at least one of the following conditions is true:

1. it lies on the occluding contour of the model from that viewpoint, [2]

2. the local surface curvature at the node is sufficiently large and the node is visible.

(Note that it is possible that a model node is active with respect to one view, but not to another.). Instead of calculating analytically the positions of the active nodes on the model surface, we "loop" over all the nodes on the discretized model surface and check if one of the above two conditions is true. Condition 1 is true if: $|\mathbf{i}_j \cdot \mathbf{n}_j| < \tau$, where $\mathbf{n}_j$ is the unit normal at the jth model node, $\mathbf{i}_j$ is the unit vector from the

---

[2]See also (Terzopoulos, Witkin, & Kass 1988).

focal point to that node on the model, and τ is a small threshold. Condition 2 is true if

$$\exists k \in K_j \text{ s.t. } |\mathbf{n}_k \cdot \mathbf{n}_j| > \kappa \ \& \ \exists k \in K_j \text{ s.t. } \mathbf{n}_k \cdot \mathbf{i}_k < 0, \quad (11)$$

where K_j is a set of indices of the nodes adjacent to the jth nodes on the model surface. κ in (11) is a threshold to determine if the angle between adjacent normal vectors is sufficiently large.

Tracking and Prediction

We incorporate into our dynamic deformable model formulation a Kalman filter by treating their differential equations of motion (2) as system models. Based on the use of the corresponding extended Kalman filter, we perform tracking by updating the model's generalized coordinates $\mathbf{q}$ according to the following equation

$$\dot{\mathbf{u}} = \mathbf{F}\hat{\mathbf{u}} + \mathbf{g} + \mathbf{P}\mathbf{H}^T\mathbf{V}^{-1}(\mathbf{z} - \mathbf{h}(\hat{\mathbf{u}})), \quad (12)$$

where $\mathbf{u} = (\dot{\mathbf{q}}^T, \mathbf{q}^T)^T$ and matrices $\mathbf{F}, \mathbf{H}, \mathbf{g}, \mathbf{P}, \mathbf{V}$ are associated with the model dynamics, the error in the given data and the measurement noise statistics (Metaxas & Terzopoulos 1993). Since we are measuring local short range forces directly from the image potential we create, the term $\mathbf{z} - \mathbf{h}(\hat{\mathbf{u}})$ represents the 2D image forces. Using the above Kalman filter, we can predict at every step the expected location of the data in the next image frame, based on the magnitude of the estimated parameter derivatives $\dot{\mathbf{q}}$.

Self Occlusion and Disocclusion

As an object rotates in space, or as the viewpoint of the observer changes substantially, certain faces of the object will become occluded or disoccluded by itself (a *visual event*). Hence, the corresponding line segment or edge feature in the image will appear or disappear over time. By using the Kalman filter to predict the position and orientation of the model in the next time frame, we can quantitatively predict the occurrence of a visual event. In other words, we can determine by using our active node determination approach, which subset of the model nodes will be active in the next image frame, and suppress their contributions to the net forces applied to the model. For stereo images, this prediction can be performed independently to the left and right images. In this case, two sets of active model nodes are maintained at any particular moment.

Tracking Multiple Objects with Occlusion

Our framework for tracking objects based on image potentials can be easily extended to deal with multiple independently moving objects and multi-part objects. The complication here is that object parts may occlude one another in different ways. By tracking objects in 3D using stereo images, we can predict the 3D positions of the nodes on each model based on the current estimates of their respective model parameters and their rate of change. Active nodes on each model will be made "inactive" if they are predicted to be occluded by surfaces of other models. This visibility checking is performed for each node on a model and against every surface of the other models in the scene. In practice, much of this checking can be avoided based on approximate estimates of each object's size and 3D location. We demonstrate in the experiments section that we are able to track all the objects in a scene even when some object parts become partially occluded.

There are also two more cases of object occlusion in case of multiple independently moving objects. The first case occurs when another moving object that was not previously present in the scene occludes the object being tracked. The second is due to an error from the qualitative segmentation system which did not detect an object during the model initialization step. Our system can handle both situations by monitoring the local forces exerted on the model. If no force or forces of unusual magnitude and direction are exerted on some of the predicted active nodes of the currently tracked model, the event signals the possibility that we have lost track of the object. In such a situation, we apply the qualitative segmentation system to resolve the ambiguity. After proper re-initialization of our models, we continue tracking using local image forces based on our physics-based technique.

Experiments

We demonstrate our approach in a series of tracking experiments involving real stereo image sequences. All images are 256×256 pixels and all the examples run at interactive rates on a SGI R4000 Crimson workstation, including real-time 3D graphics. In the first experiment, we consider a sequence of stereo images (16 frames) of two independently moving objects. The objects move towards each other along 2 different paths which are approximately linear and the paths' relative angle is about 20 degrees. The baseline of the two cameras is 100mm, they are both at a declination angle of 30 degrees from the horizon, and their relative rotation is 8 degrees. Fig. 1(a) shows the first pair of stereo images. The initial pose and shape of the objects are recovered using techniques mentioned before and they are subsequently tracked based on image forces only. Figs. 1(b-g) show snapshots of the two objects being tracked with the wire-frame models overlaid on the image potential. They demonstrate that our technique is able to continue the tracking even when one of the blocks becomes partially occluded and then disoccluded. Note that those active model nodes which are temporarily occluded are automatically identified and made inactive. Figs. 2(a-d) show the relative positions of the recovered models at four different instants.

In the second experiment, we consider a sequence of stereo images (24 frames) of a scene containing multiple objects, including a two-part object. Fig. 3 shows the initial stereo images of the multi-object scene. The baseline of the stereo cameras is 150 mm, the cameras

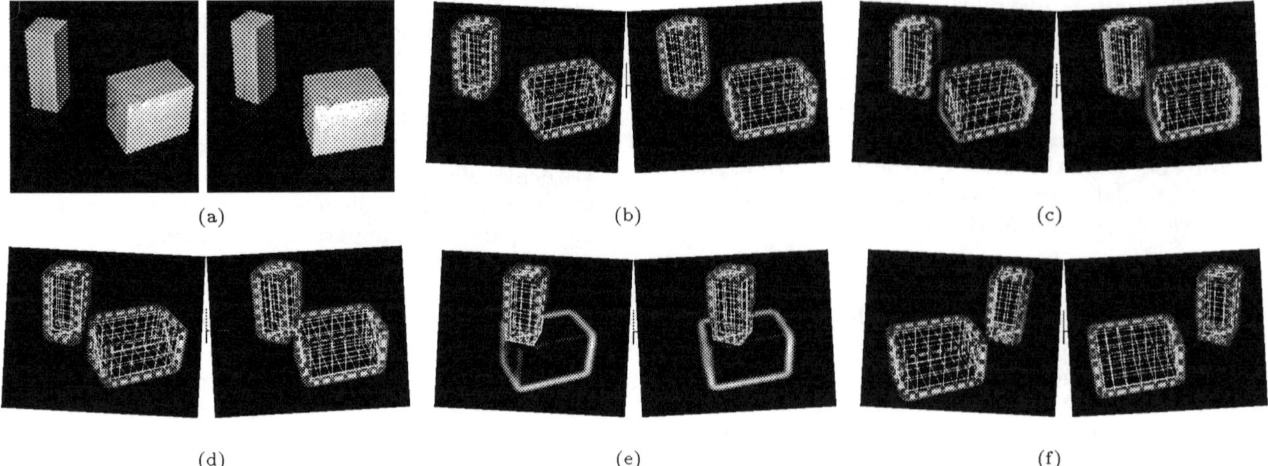

Figure 1: Tracking two independently moving blocks in a sequence of stereo images: (a) initialized models, (b) coming of a new frame, (c) beginning of the occlusion, (d) taller block partially occluded, (e) taller block becomes disoccluded, (f) no more occlusion. Note that only the active model nodes are marked, while the occluded ones are not.

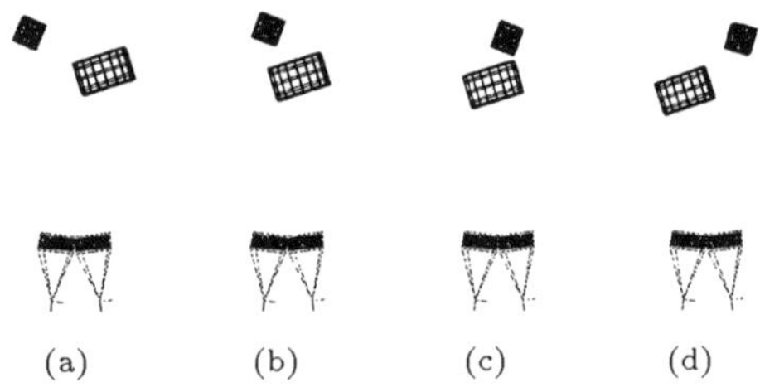

Figure 2: Recovered models of the two moving blocks in 3D over time from a top view (with the stereo arrangement).

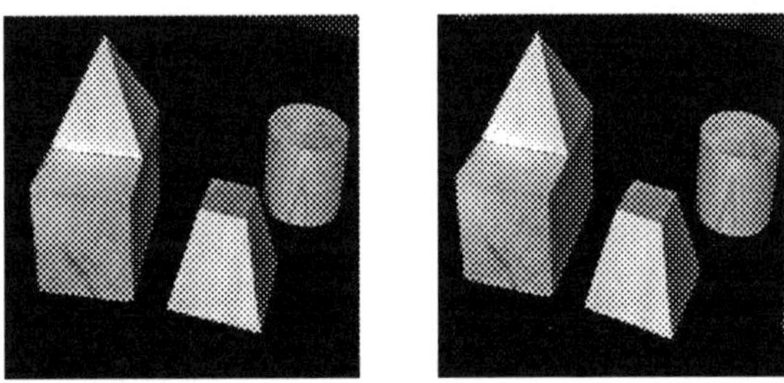

Figure 3: Initial stereo images of the multi-object scene.

are at a declination angle of 30 degrees from the horizon, and their relative rotation is 12 degrees. The cameras are rotated around the scene at a constant rate. Fig. 4(a) shows the initialized models using the same technique as before. Fig. 4(b) shows image potentials at an intermediate time frame where the aspects of some parts have changed and some parts have become partially occluded. Figs. 4(c-f) show that each object is still successfully tracked under these circumstances with the individual part models overlaid on the image potentials in Fig. 4(b).

In the last experiment we demonstrate the applica-bility of our technique in case of object occlusion by another undetected object. We use the same sequence of stereo images as in the first experiment where there are two independently moving blocks, but we do not assume prior detection of one of the blocks this time. Fig. 5 shows the instant at which some of the image forces exerted on the active model nodes of the moving block exceed a threshold. It then triggers the qualitative segmentation system to resegment the scene and correctly group edges belonging to each of the blocks. After the models are reinitialized, tracking continues as before.

Conclusion

We have presented a new integrated approach to object tracking in 3D from 2D stereo image sequences. After initializing our deformable models based on a part-based qualitative segmentation system, we subsequently track the objects using our physics-based approach. We further used a Kalman filter for estimating the object's shape and motion which allowed the prediction of possible visual events; thus we were able to determine where on the model, image forces can be exerted. We also demonstrated that our approach can deal with object occlusion from other independently moving objects by predicting each object's motion in the scene. Occlusion due to previously unidentified objects can also be detected by monitoring changes to the image forces exerted on the models. Based on these changes, the qualitative shape segmentation system is invoked for scene re-segmentation and model re-initialization. We are currently extending our system to handle objects composed of more complex primitives than the ones we have assumed.

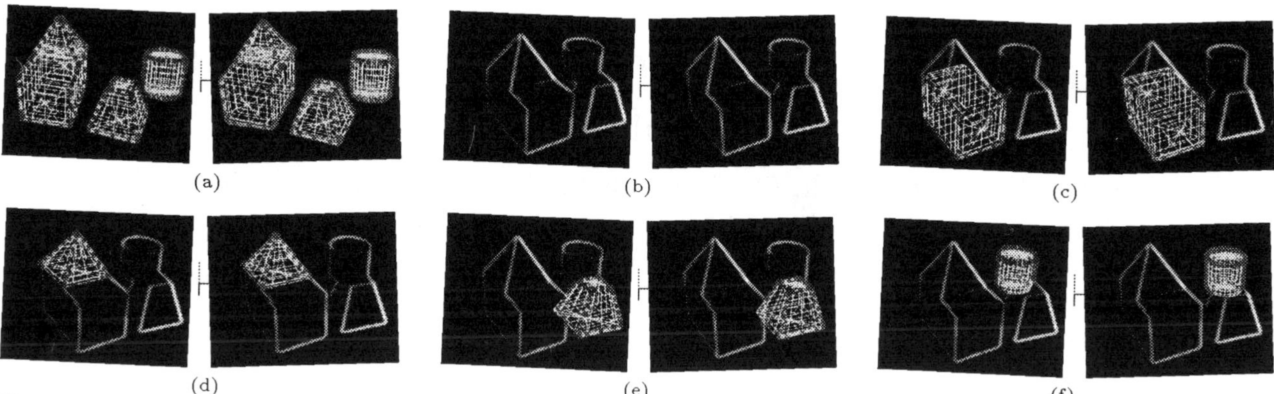

Figure 4: Tracking multiple objects in a sequence of stereo images (a) initialized models, (b) image potentials of an intermediate frame (both occlusions and visual events have occurred) (c-f) each object part correctly tracked with part models overlaid on the image potentials in (b). Note that only the active model nodes are marked, while the occluded ones are not.

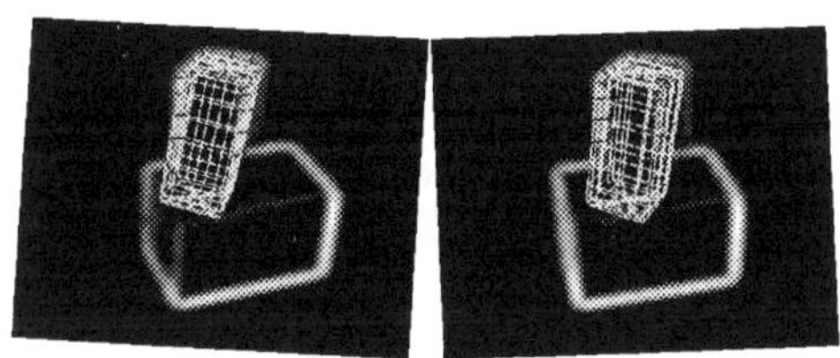

Figure 5: Unpredicted object occlusion: no knowledge of the 2nd block is assumed. It is detected by monitoring the forces exerted on the active nodes of the displayed model.

References

Blake, A.; Curwen, R.; and Zisserman, A. 1993. Affine-Invariant Contour Tracking with Automatic Control of Spatiotemporal Scale. In *Proc. IEEE 4th International Conference on Computer Vision*, 502–507.

Broida, T. J.; Chandrashekhar, S.; and Chellappa, R. 1990. Recursive 3-D Motion Estimation from a Monocular Image Sequence. *IEEE Transactions on Aerospace and Electronic Systems* 26(4):639–656.

Deriche, R., and Faugeras, O. 1990. Tracking Line Segments. *Image and Vision Computing* 8(4):261–270.

Dickinson, S.; Pentland, A.; and Rosenfeld, A. 1992a. From Volumes to Views: An Approach to 3D Object Recognition. *Computer Vision, Graphics, and Image Processing: Image Understanding* 55(2):130–154.

Dickinson, S.; Pentland, A.; and Rosenfeld, A. 1992b. Shape Recovery Using Distributed Aspect Matching. *IEEE Transactions on Pattern Analysis and Machine Intelligence* 14(2):174–198.

Dickmanns, E. D., and Graefe, V. 1988. Applications of Dynamic Monocular Machine Vision. *Machine Vision and Applications* 1:241–261.

Duncan, J. S.; Owen, R. L.; and Anandan, P. 1991. Measurement of Nonrigid Motion Using Contour Shape Descriptors. In *Proc. IEEE Conference on Computer Vision and Pattern Recognition*, 318–324.

Gennery, D. 1992. Visual Tracking of Known Three-Dimensional Objects. *International Journal of Computer Vision* 7(3):243–270.

Huang, T. S. 1990. Modeling, Analysis and Visualization of Nonrigid Object Motion. In *Proc. IEEE 10th International Conference on Pattern Recognition*, volume 1, 361–364.

Kass, M.; Witkin, A.; and Terzopoulos, D. 1988. Snakes: Active Contour Models. *International Journal of Computer Vision* 1(4):321–331.

Lowe, D. 1991. Fitting Parameterized Three-Dimensional Models to Images. *IEEE Transactions on Pattern Analysis and Machine Intelligence* 13(5):441–450.

Metaxas, D., and Dickinson, S. 1993. Integration of Quantitative and Qualitative Techniques for Deformable Model Fitting from Orthographic, Perspective, and Stereo Projections. In *Proc. IEEE 4th International Conference on Computer Vision*, 641–649.

Metaxas, D., and Terzopoulos, D. 1993. Shape and Nonrigid Motion Estimation Through Physics-Based Synthesis. *IEEE Transactions on Pattern Analysis and Machine Intelligence* 15(6):580–591.

Pentland, A., and Horowitz, B. 1991. Recovery of Nonrigid Motion and Structure. *IEEE Transactions on Pattern Analysis and Machine Intelligence* 13(7):730–742.

Szeliski, R., and Terzopoulos, D. 1991. Physically-Based and Probabilistic Modeling for Computer Vision. In *Proc. SPIE Geometric Methods in Computer Vision*, volume 1570, 140–152. Society of Photo-Optical Instrumentation Engineers.

Terzopoulos, D., and Metaxas, D. 1991. Dynamic 3D Models with Local and Global Deformations: Deformable Superquadrics. *IEEE Transactions on Pattern Analysis and Machine Intelligence* 13(7):703–714.

Terzopoulos, D.; Witkin, A.; and Kass, M. 1988. Constraints on Deformable Models: Recovering 3D Shape and Nonrigid Motion. *Artificial Intelligence* 36(1):91–123.

Thompson, D., and Mundy, J. 1988. Motion-Based Motion Analysis: Motion from Motion. *Robotics Research: The Forth International Symposium* 299–309.

Verghese, G.; Gale, K.; and Dyer, C. 1990. *Real-time, Parallel Tracking of Three-Dimensional Objects from Spatiotemporal Sequences*. New York: Springer-Verlag. 310–339.

Automatic Symbolic Traffic Scene Analysis
Using Belief Networks[*]

T. Huang, D. Koller, J. Malik, G. Ogasawara, B. Rao, S. Russell, and J. Weber

Computer Science Division

University of California

Berkeley, CA 94720

{tthuang|koller|malik|ogasawara|bobbyrao|russell|jweber}@cs.berkeley.edu

Abstract

Automatic symbolic traffic scene analysis is essential to many areas of IVHS (Intelligent Vehicle Highway Systems). Traffic scene information can be used to optimize traffic flow during busy periods, identify stalled vehicles and accidents, and aid the decision-making of an autonomous vehicle controller. Improvements in technologies for machine vision-based surveillance and high-level symbolic reasoning have enabled us to develop a system for detailed, reliable traffic scene analysis. The machine vision component of our system employs a contour tracker and an affine motion model based on Kalman filters to extract vehicle trajectories over a sequence of traffic scene images. The symbolic reasoning component uses a dynamic belief network to make inferences about traffic events such as vehicle lane changes and stalls. In this paper, we discuss the key tasks of the vision and reasoning components as well as their integration into a working prototype.

Introduction

An important task for progress in IVHS (Intelligent Vehicle Highway Systems) is the development of methods for automatic traffic scene analysis. All three major applications of IVHS – ATIS (Advanced Traveler Information Systems), ATMS (Advanced Traffic Management Systems), and AVCS (Automated Vehicle Control Systems) – could benefit from accurate, high-level descriptions of traffic situations. For example, an ATIS and an ATMS could use information about traffic congestion and stalls to warn drivers or to direct vehicles to alternate routes. An ATMS also could analyze local traffic at intersections to identify those with higher risk of accidents. Finally, an AVCS would need information about the actions of neighboring vehicles and the condition of traffic lanes ahead to control an automated car moving along a freeway (Niehaus & Stengel 1991).

In this paper, we describe a prototype system in which we have successfully combined a robust, vision-based traffic surveillance system (Koller, Weber, & Malik 1994) with a dynamic belief network dedicated to analyzing traffic scenes. Unlike conventional loop detectors, which are buried underneath highways to count vehicles, video monitoring systems are less disruptive and less costly to install. They also have greater range and allow for more detailed descriptions of traffic situations. Dynamic belief networks provide a flexible, theoretically sound framework for traffic scene analysis because they can easily model uncertainty and because they can provide high-level, symbolic descriptions by integrating low-level information from a variety of sources. They also provide a natural framework for expressing knowledge about typical traffic behavior, allowing more accurate analyses from a given sensor stream.

Symbolic traffic scene analysis using vision-based surveillance systems has been previously investigated by several research groups (Schirra *et al.* 1987; Koller, Heinze, & Nagel 1991; Heinze, Krüger, & Nagel 1991; Huang, Ogasawara, & Russell 1993). The challenges of this approach include identifying vehicles despite imprecise video data and changing lighting conditions, tracking individual vehicles despite their overlapping with each other, and efficiently providing high-level descriptions based on evidence accumulated over time. We have achieved improvements in performance, reliability, and accuracy by applying a new approach for detecting and tracking vehicles, by explicitly reasoning about vehicle occlusions (Koller, Weber, & Malik 1994), and by devising techniques for fast belief network update, localized reasoning, and flexible node semantics.

Low-Level Machine Vision-Based Surveillance

Our traffic surveillance system is based on the block diagram shown in Figure 1. This section focuses on the tasks of feature extraction and tracking, and the next section focuses on the tasks of symbolic reasoning and incident detection.

---

[*]This work was supported by the California Department of Transportation under the PATH project grant MOU-83.

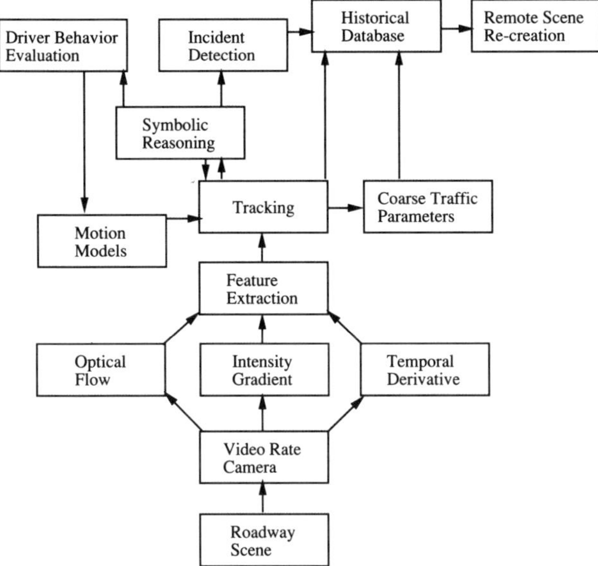

Figure 1: Block diagram of the complete traffic surveillance system. Arrows denote the flow of information.

As Figure 1 indicates, traffic scene analysis generally proceeds from low-level processing of road traffic images to high-level descriptions of the traffic situation (which can in turn be used to direct and disambiguate low-level processing). Given a sequence of traffic images, a vision-based surveillance system must identify the vehicles in the scene and track them as they progress along the image sequence. This requires not only estimation of the moving vehicle shapes and positions, but also association of these estimates from one image to the next.

Two primary factors that complicate this task are noisy sensors, which yield imprecise measurements, and vehicle occlusions, which make it more difficult to identify and disambiguate vehicles. To address these problems, we employ vehicle and motion models that are updated in a Kalman filter formalism, thus yielding most likely estimates based on accumulated observations.

Motion Segmentation

A surveillance system initiates vehicle identification and tracking by determining what parts of each image belong to moving objects and what parts belong to the background. This is accomplished by examining the difference in pixel intensities between each new frame and an estimate of the stationary background. Reliable background estimation, which is critical for accurate identification of moving 'blobs', is made more difficult as lighting conditions change. We perform this *initialization* step by using a modified version of the moving object segmentation method suggested by (Karmann & von Brandt 1990) and implemented by (Kilger 1992).

Our method employs a Kalman filter-based adaptive background model. This allows the background estimate to evolve as the weather and time of day affect lighting conditions. The background is updated at each frame using the following update equation:

$$B_{t+1} = B_t + (\alpha_1(1 - M_t) + \alpha_2 M_t)D_t \qquad (1)$$

B_t is the background model at time t, D_t is the difference between the present frame and the background model, and M_t is a binary mask of hypothesized moving objects in the current frame. The gains α_1 and α_2 are based on estimates of the rate of change of the background. For a complete description, we refer the reader to (Koller, Weber, & Malik 1993).

Vehicle Identification and Shape Estimation

After identifying moving blobs, the vision system attempts to disambiguate individual vehicles and estimate their shapes. This helps with associating data over a sequence of images and with obtaining accurate vehicle trajectories. Our system performs these tasks by extracting closed contours enclosing each moving blob in each image. Contour extraction is based on motion and gray-value boundaries, which are obtained by thresholding the spatial image gradients and the time derivatives of the images. For each moving blob, points that pass a threshold test are enclosed by convex polygons, and these are used as initial object descriptions. The top row of Figure 2 shows an image section with a car, the detected moving object patch corresponding to the image of the car, and the sample points made up of image locations with acceptable spatial gradients and time derivatives. The convex polygon enclosing all these sample points is shown in the bottom row.

Our time-recursive shape estimation algorithm (Koller, Weber, & Malik 1993) cannot use convex polygons, since the number of vertices for a vehicle may change along an image sequence. We address this problem by using *snakes*, spline approximations to contours (Kass, Witkin, & Terzopoulos 1988; Curwen & Blake 1992). We use closed cubic splines with 12 *control points* to approximate each extracted convex polygon, and we obtain the locations of the control points by again employing a Kalman filter (Bartels, Beatty, & Barsky 1987; Koller, Weber, & Malik 1994). The bottom right image shows the spline approximation of the shape. Other examples of spline approximations can be found in Figure 6.

Motion Estimation

The final task of the video system is to track identified vehicles from one frame to the next. To accomplish this, we estimate vehicle motion with an affine motion model. For a sufficiently small field of view and for independently moving objects, the image velocity field $u(x)$ at some location x inside a detected image patch can be closely approximated by a linear

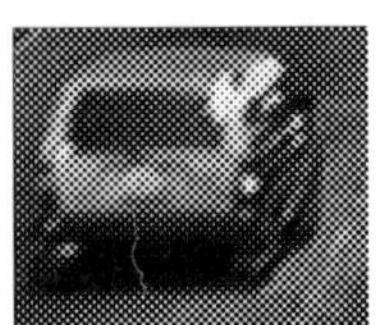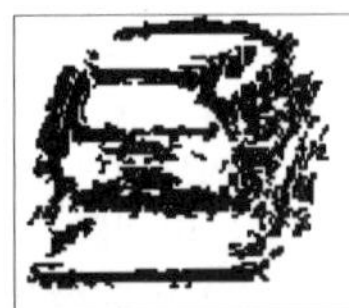

Figure 2: The top row shows an image section with a moving car, the moving object mask provided by the motion segmentation step, and the image locations with acceptable spatial gradients and temporal derivatives. The bottom row shows the convex polygon enclosing the sample points and the final contour description by cubic spline approximation of the polygon.

(affine) transformation. Since motion is constrained to the road plane and since possible rotation components along the normal of the plane are small, the degrees of freedom can be reduced to the extent that we obtain a velocity equation of only a scale parameter s and a displacement vector $\boldsymbol{u}_0$:

$$\boldsymbol{u}(\boldsymbol{x}) = s\left(\boldsymbol{x} - \boldsymbol{x}_m\right) + \boldsymbol{u}_0, \qquad (2)$$

For the scale parameter s, $s = 0$ indicates that there is no change in scale, while $s < 0$ and $s > 0$ indicate motion components along the optical axes away from and towards the camera, respectively. $\boldsymbol{x}_m$ denotes the center of the moving image region, and $\boldsymbol{u}_0$ denotes its displacement between two consecutive frames.

The affine motion parameters $\boldsymbol{\xi} = (\boldsymbol{u}, s)$ make up the state vector for motion estimation. We can use a third Kalman filter to estimate the motion parameters, since the measurement function can be expressed in a linear matrix equation. This tracker has been influenced by (Blake, Curwen, & Zisserman 1993), who successfully extended their real-time contour tracking system (Curwen & Blake 1992) by exploiting affine motion models. Complete details of the affine motion model can be found in (Koller, Weber, & Malik 1994).

Occlusion Reasoning

Because vehicles often overlap with each other in the road images, the extracted contours of vehicles will become distorted for some frames. This can cause artificial shifts in vehicle trajectories, since tracks are obtained by connecting centers of contours along the image sequence. To avoid these artificial shifts and to obtain reasonable tracks, we employ an explicit occlusion reasoning algorithm, which compensates for overlapping vehicles.

The occlusion reasoning algorithm works because the traffic scene geometry is known and because motion is assumed to be constrained to the ground plane (Koller, Weber, & Malik 1993). This knowledge makes it possible to determine a depth ordering among the objects in the scene, and this depth ordering defines the order in which objects are able to occlude each other.

High-Level Reasoning Using Belief Networks

We now address the task of using vehicle track information (e.g., their positions and velocities) to arrive at high-level symbolic descriptions of vehicles and the traffic scene. To accomplish this, our symbolic reasoner uses multiple, per-vehicle dynamic belief networks with fast rollup.

Concepts

Belief networks are directed acyclic graphs in which nodes represent random variables (usually discrete) and arcs represent causal connections among the variables (Pearl 1988). Associated with each node is a probability table that provides conditional probabilities of the node's possible states given each possible state of its parents. When values are observed for a subset of the nodes, posterior probability distributions can be computed for any of the remaining nodes. This updating takes place using a compiled form of the belief network that is more suitable to propagating the influence of evidence to other nodes.

Belief networks offer a mathematically sound basis for making inferences under uncertainty. The conditional probability tables provide a natural way to represent uncertain events, and the semantics of the updated probabilities are well-defined. Knowledge of causal relationships among variables is expressed by the presence or absence of arcs between them. Furthermore, the conditional independence relationships implied by the topology of the network allow exponentially fewer probabilities to be specified than the full joint probability distribution for all the variables in the network.

Dynamic belief networks allow for reasoning in domains where variables take on different values over time. Typically, observations are taken at regular 'time slices', and a given network structure is replicated for each slice. Nodes can be connected not only to other nodes within the same time slice but also to nodes in the previous or subsequent slice. As new slices are added to the network, older slices are removed. Before a slice is removed, its influence is 'rolled-up' into the next slice by recomputing probability tables for certain nodes in that slice. Thus, evidence accumulated over time is always integrated into the current belief network model (Nicholson 1992; Kjaerulff 1993).

Traffic network structure

The symbolic reasoning component for our system is built on the HUGIN inference engine for belief networks (Andersen *et al.* 1989). Figure 3 shows an example belief network fragment for a single vehicle. Figure 4 shows the fragment projected over one time slice. For each vehicle in a traffic scene, there is a separate belief network corresponding to it.

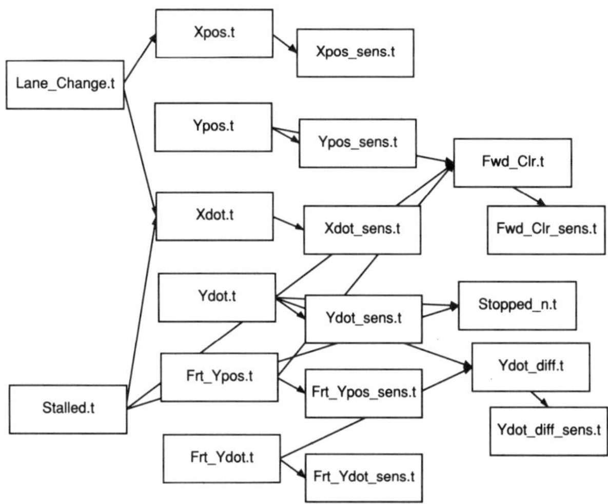

Figure 3: Belief network fragment for a single vehicle.

Some of the nodes in Figure 3, such as Xpos_sens.t and Xdot_sens.t, correspond to discretized sensor values that are set in each new slice when the slice is added to the network. For instance, the Xpos_sens.t node represents a vehicle's left-right position among the lanes of a highway and can take on one of ten states indicating the vehicle's distance from the right edge of the lanes. Other nodes, such as Stalled.t and LaneChange.t, correspond to high-level events. For example, the LaneChange.t node can take on one of three different states indicating if a vehicle is going straight, changing lanes to the left, or changing lanes to the right. The posterior probability distributions for these high-level events are affected by the sensor values in the current slice as well as the posterior probabilities of nodes in the previous slice. These distributions are then used to provide symbolic descriptions of the traffic scene.

Figure 4 shows how nodes are replicated from time slice 0 to time slice 1, as well as how some variables in time slice 1 depend on variables in the previous time slice. For example, Ypos.t1 (representing a vehicle's forward position on the highway) depends on Ypos.t0 (its previous position) and Ydot.t0 (its previous velocity).

The probabilities associated with each node provide a natural framework to encode knowledge about traffic behavior and rules. For example, the probability table for Ydot.t1 in Figure 4 contains probabilities for each

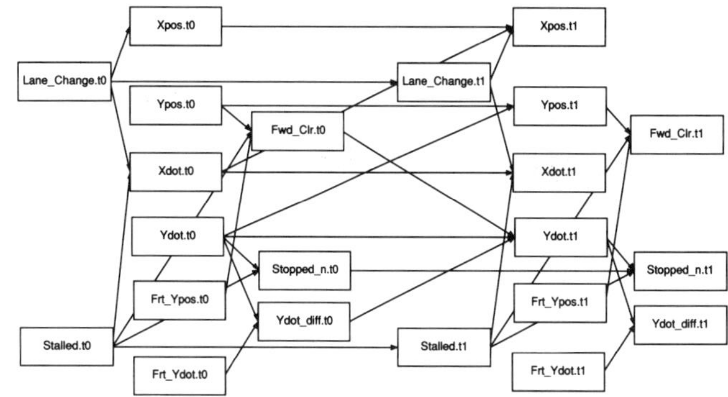

Figure 4: Belief network fragment for a single vehicle projected over one time slice. Some nodes have been omitted for simplicity.

of Ydot.t1's possible states (e.g., 21-30 km/hr, 31-40 km/hr, etc.) given the states of Ydot.t0, Fwd_Clr.t0 (the space in front of a vehicle), and Ydot_diff.t0 (the difference in speed between a given vehicle and the vehicle in front of it). A driver is likely to slow down if there isn't much distance between his vehicle and the vehicle in front and if his vehicle is going faster than the vehicle in front. Thus, the appropriate entries in the probability table will indicate a high probability that the vehicle's speed at time t1 will be lower than its speed at time t0. Similarly, the other entries in the table encode probability distributions for the new velocity given the combinations of parent states. Additional traffic knowledge that is or will be encoded includes knowledge about lane-changing and braking behavior, the effect of road geometry and weather on driving behavior, and the significance of brake, hazard, and signal lights.

Network Issues

Handling multiple vehicles. As mentioned earlier, in each time slice the structure in Figure 3 is replicated for each tracked vehicle in the traffic scene. Clearly, the positions and velocities of different vehicles will affect each other. Thus, determining globally consistent probability distributions for each vehicle involves a large network consisting of changing interconnections between vehicle subnetworks. We have investigated this approach and found the cost of modifying and recompiling the network at each time slice too computationally expensive. Nevertheless, we plan to pursue this avenue further, perhaps using approximation methods.

Our current approach is to assign each vehicle its own dynamic belief network. We incorporate the influence of nearby vehicles on the current vehicle by assigning some nodes to those vehicles. For example, Front_Ypos.t and Front_Ydot.t in Figure 3 refer to "the vehicle in front of the current vehicle". Since the actual vehicle in front may change, these indexical nodes

(Agre & Chapman 1987) do not correspond to a specific vehicle. Instead, a preprocessing step uses sensor data to determine which vehicles are currently in front of each other and then sets those node states accordingly. Using multiple, per-vehicle belief networks with indexical nodes has yielded a reasonably inexpensive approach to achieving locally consistent high-level descriptions for each vehicle while considering the affect of nearby vehicles.

Nodes with variable semantics. When a vehicle first stops on the highway, it could be for any number of reasons. The probability that the vehicle is stalled may be small at first, but it increases over time if the vehicle continues to remain stopped while no vehicles are stopped in front of it. To allow flexible representation of how a vehicle being stalled relates to it being stopped for some time, we made it possible for nodes to have variable semantics, i.e. a node refers to a different event in different time slices. This is accomplished by modifying the node's conditional probability table from one time slice to another. For example, the Stopped_n.t node has some value n associated with it, and the node refers to the event that the vehicle has been stopped for n time slices. The probability table for the node is modified according to the value of n associated with it. This can be computed with a simple function to simulate a counter (e.g., we can give vehicles positive probability of being stalled only if they've been stopped for over 50 time slices) or with any arbitrarily complex function.

Rolling the network forward. Because the HUGIN system is geared toward standard rather than dynamic belief networks, we developed the facilities necessary for rolling the network forward. Essentially, this involves adding the capability to add new time slices to the network and to incorporate information from old slices to the rest of the network so that the old slices can be deleted.

We developed two approaches to this problem. In the first approach, we generated and compiled a new network for each time slice, and we used a new network every time a slice was added. This approach seemed adequate and offered the opportunity to dynamically alter the actual network structure (which would be necessary for a global network of all the vehicles), but it suffered from the poor performance noted earlier.

We currently use our second approach, which employs two precompiled networks, each with two slices. As shown in Figure 5, the system alternates between the two networks. To introduce sensor information from a new time slice, the system incorporates the evidence from the oldest slice into the rest of the model through a series of straightforward matrix multiplications. The resulting probability tables are stored in the first slice of the other network. The new sensor information is then added to the second slice of this

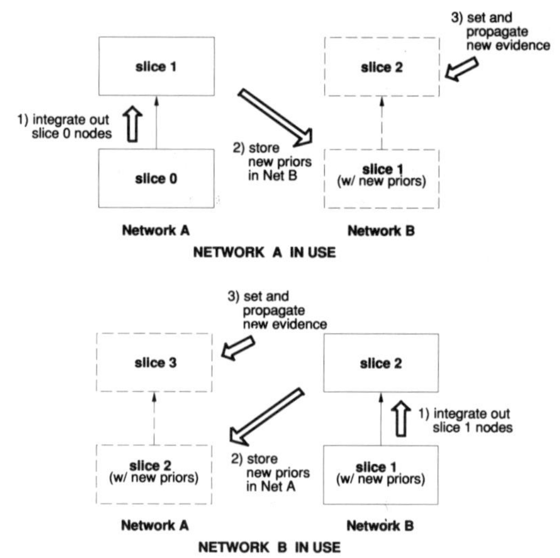

Figure 5: Steps for rolling the dynamic network forward.

network, and their influence is propagated to obtain new posterior probabilities. This other network is then used until the next time slice, when the rollup procedure is repeated back to the first network. This approach does not allow dynamic alteration of the belief network structure, but it greatly improves performance by eliminating the need for network recompilation after every time slice.

The dHUGIN package (Kjaerulff 1993) provides extensions to HUGIN for dynamic belief networks, but it does not provide the flexibility of our first approach for changing the network structure from one time slice to the next, and it does not provide the performance speedup of our second approach.

Results with Real-World Traffic Scenes

We have tested our system on real-world image sequences, and we present here the results of one 270-frame sequence of a divided four-lane freeway. The image at the top of Figure 6 shows frame #40 of the sequence overlaid with contour estimates of the vehicles. The image at the bottom shows only the vehicle contour estimates and their tracks (starting from frame #0). The image at the top of Figure 7 shows frame #64 of the sequence, and the graphic on the bottom shows a reconstruction in the SmartPath traffic simulator[1] of the image (the geometry is slightly different due to the display of the SmartPath simulator). In the graphic, one vehicle has been identified by the symbolic reasoner as changing lanes, and the number in the signpost correctly indicates the number

____

[1]SmartPath is a microscopic three-dimensional automated highway simulator developed at UC Berkeley as part of the PATH (Partners for Advanced Transit and Highways) program of the Institute for Transportation Studies.

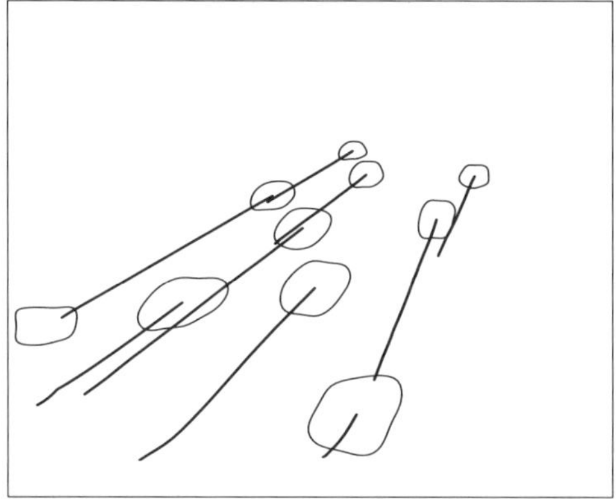

Figure 6: The upper image shows frame #40 of the image sequence with overlaid contour estimates of the cars. The bottom image shows the contour estimates with their tracks (starting from frame #0).

Figure 7: The upper image shows frame #64 of the sequence. The bottom graphic shows a reconstruction in the SmartPath traffic simulator of this image.

of vehicles that have passed since the beginning of the image sequence.

Running on a Sun SparcStation 10, the performance of the vision component reaches about two seconds per frame for simultaneous tracking of about 10 vehicles. A high-speed implementation on special purpose hardware using C-40 digital signal processors is in progress. The performance of the belief network varies greatly with the network design, but generally requires about one second per vehicle per frame. We expect to improve the performance of both components by an order of magnitude with various optimizations. Operation in real-time would require sampling image frames quickly enough for the affine tracker to associate vehicles between frames and for the symbolic reasoner to detect short traffic events such as lane changes. We expect that operation at 10 Hz for the vision system and 3 Hz for the symbolic reasoner will be sufficient for real-time performance.

Conclusions / Future Work

In this paper we have described the successful combination of a low-level, vision-based surveillance system with a high-level, symbolic reasoner based on dynamic belief networks. This prototype system provides robust, high-level information about traffic scenes, such as lane changes, stalled vehicles, and overall vehicle counts. We believe that the required accuracy can in the long run only be obtained using high-level reasoning under uncertainty.

The symbolic reasoner is already capable of using other vehicle features, such as vehicle type, turn signals and brake lights, to improve its analytical performance. We are currently upgrading the vision system to detect these features, as well as to handle vehicle shadows (Kilger 1992). Furthermore, the inferences of the symbolic reasoner can be fed back to the tracker's Kalman filter to further increase its reliability. For example, if a vehicle is signalling left, its expected motion update should be biased toward leftward acceleration rather than a random perturbation. This allows for reduced variance, and hence greater reliability in tracking. In the extreme case, if the low-level tracker loses a vehicle (for example, in heavy rain), the high-level system can automatically "track" its most likely position by a combination of extended projection and inference from the behavior of other vehicles.

Another benefit is the robust data fusion provided by Bayesian inference. This is especially important at dusk or dawn, when the surveillance system will see both vehicle outlines and vehicle tail lights. Finally, by including a simple sensor failure model, the network can detect and diagnose sensor failure, while continuing to track vehicles using remaining sensor inputs (Nicholson 1992).

Besides continuing to refine the network design and to optimize its performance, we are investigating methods for enabling the symbolic reasoner to handle mixed networks with both continuous and discrete variables (Lauritzen 1992; Shachter & Kenley 1989). This offers the opportunity for greater performance over purely discrete networks, and it seems reasonable, since sensor variables such as vehicle positions and velocities are adequately modelled as Gaussians. The symbolic reasoner can also be enhanced to provide other types of descriptions, such as driver behaviors. Machine learning techniques applied to a library of image sequences can be used to generate detailed probabilistic models of driver behavior, which are useful both in our own work and in analytical and simulation studies of highway designs.

We are currently moving the implementation of the prototype (running on single Sun SparcStations) to a heterogeneous system consisting of a host Sun SparcStation and special purpose hardware. This will improve the setup for large-scale experimentation and will improve performance to about 5Hz, which we believe will be adequate for traffic surveillance in sunny California weather. To better assess the system's usefulness and accuracy, we plan to measure its performance on a more extensive collection of video sequences.

Acknowledgments

We gratefully acknowledge the help of C. McCarley and his group at Cal Poly, San Luis Obispo, for providing us with video tapes of various traffic scenes. We also thank HUGIN Expert A/S for their generous doctoral student license to use the HUGIN system.

References

P. Agre, D. Chapman. Pengi: An Implementation of a Theory of Activity, in *Proceedings of the Sixth National Conference on Artificial Intelligence*, 1987.

S. Andersen, K. Olesen, F. V. Jensen, F. Jensen. HUGIN* – a Shell for Building Bayesian Belief Universes for Expert Systems, in *Proceedings of the Tenth International Joint Conference on Artificial Intelligence*, 1989.

R. Bartels, J. Beatty, B. Barsky. *An Introduction to Splines for use in Computer Vision*, Morgan Kaufmann, 1987.

A. Blake, R. Curwen, A. Zisserman. Affine-invariant contour tracking with automatic control of spatiotemporal scale, in *Proc. Int. Conf. on Computer Vision*, Berlin, Germany, May. 11-14, 1993, pp. 66–75.

R. Curwen, A. Blake. *Active Vision*, MIT Press, Cambridge, MA, 1992, chapter Dynamic Contours: Real-time Active Snakes, pp. 39–57.

N. Heinze, W. Krüger, H.-H. Nagel. Berechnung von Bewegungsverben zur Beschreibung von aus Bildfolgen gewonnenen Trajektorien in Straßenverkehrsszenen, *Informatik – Forschung und Entwicklung* **6** (1991), pp. 51–61.

T. Huang, G. Ogasawara, S. Russell. Symbolic Traffic Scene Analysis Using Dynamic Belief Networks, in *AAAI Workshop on AI in IVHS*, Washington D.C., 1993.

Klaus-Peter Karmann, Achim von Brandt. Moving Object Recognition Using an Adaptive Background Memory, in V Cappellini (ed.), *Time-Varying Image Processing and Moving Object Recognition, 2*, Elsevier, Amsterdam, The Netherlands, 1990.

M. Kass, A. Witkin, D. Terzopoulos. Snakes: Active Contour Models, *International Journal of Computer Vision* **1** (1988) 321–331.

M. Kilger. A Shadow Handler in a Video-based Real-time Traffic Monitoring System, in *IEEE Workshop on Applications of Computer Vision*, Palm Springs, CA, 1992, pp. 1060–1066.

U. Kjaerulff. User's Guide to dHUGIN, Institute of Electronic Systems, Aalborg University, 1993.

D. Koller, N. Heinze, H.-H. Nagel. Algorithmic Characterization of Vehicle Trajectories from Image Sequences by Motion Verbs, in *IEEE Conf. Computer Vision and Pattern Recognition*, Lahaina, Maui, Hawaii, June 3-6, 1991, pp. 90–95.

D. Koller, J. Weber, J. Malik. *Robust Multiple Car Tracking with Occlusion Reasoning*, technical report UCB/CSD-93-780, University of California at Berkeley, October 1993.

D. Koller, J. Weber, J. Malik. Robust Multiple Car Tracking with Occlusion Reasoning, in *Proc. Third European Conference on Computer Vision*, Stockholm, Sweden, May 2-6, 1994, J.-O. Eklundh (ed.), Lecture Notes in Computer Science, Springer-Verlag, Berlin, Heidelberg, New York (to appear), 1994.

S. Lauritzen. Propagation of Probabilities, Means, and Variances in Mixed Graphical Association Models, in *Journal of the American Statistical Association*, vol. 87, no. 420, 1992.

A. Nicholson. Monitoring Discrete Environments Using Dynamic Belief Networks, PhD thesis, Oxford University, 1992.

A. Niehaus, R. F. Stengel. Rule-Based Guidance for Vehicle Highway Driving in the Presence of Uncertainty, in *Proceedings of the 1991 American Control Conference*, 1991.

J. Pearl. *Probabilistic Reasoning in Intelligent Systems: Networks of Plausible Inference*, Morgan Kaufmann Publishers, San Mateo, CA, 1988.

J. R. J. Schirra, G. Bosch, C. K. Sung, G. Zimmermann. From Image Sequences to Natural Language: A First Step towards Automatic Perception and Description of Motion, *Applied Artificial Intelligence* **1** (1987) 287–307.

R. Shachter, C. Kenley. Gaussian influence diagrams, in *Management Science* **35**, 1989.

Sensible Decisions: Toward A Theory of Decision-Theoretic Information Invariants

Keiji Kanazawa[*]
Computer Science Division
University of California
Berkeley, California 94720
kanazawa@cs.berkeley.edu

Abstract

We propose a decision-theoretic notion of invariance in bounded rational decision making. We show how optimal decision making in sensory robotics can be approximately preserved under transformations of the decision rule. In particular, we present a decision theoretic analysis of the use of visual routines in action arbitration in real-time robot soccer. In this domain, stochastic dominance, and therefore decisions, can be *sensed* approximately from the environment, and we exploit this in our decision making.

Introduction

The world demands behavior that is immediate, and yet guided by the anticipated consequences of observed events. As designers of autonomous agents, we seek robustness in agent behavior in the face of uncertainty. Decision theory and game theory (Savage 1954; von Neumann & Morgenstern 1947) are normative theories of action with optimal prescriptions about rational behavior. Applying these theories is often a battle with computational complexity (Cooper 1990). The space of possible contingencies is typically large, and guaranteeing an agent's response time to external events often requires trading off the optimality of the agent's decisions.

For this reason, there is great interest in theories of qualitative probability and decision theory incorporating, for example, technology from nonmonotonic reasoning (Goldszmidt 1993). We propose a new point in the spectrum of qualitative decision-making, a continuous counterpart to symbolic qualitative reasoning. Our theory attempts to shed light on the informational utility of certain classes of geometric relations and perceptual cues. Sensors that detect these relations and aspects are seen as incorporating a kind of visual qualitative probability, enabling an agent to approximately *sense* probabilities and relationships between probabilities from the environment. Using such *virtual sensors* for answering probability queries, an agent can substitute sensing for expensive probability computations in decision-making. Rather than being a purely symbolic theory, our approach points the way toward the embodiment of qualitative probability in systems dynamically sensing and interacting with their environments in real-time.

Concretely, we adapt visual routines (Ullman 1983) to extract geometric information that accurately or approximately indexes optimal actions in the control of soccer-playing mobile robots. We exploit this under a notion of *decision-theoretic information invariance*, where approximately optimal transformations in an agent's decision rules can lead to improved performance with bounded loss in decision quality.

The Soccer Domain

The Laboratory for Computational Intelligence at the University of British Columbia has been undertaking a project called *Dynamo* centering around mobile robot soccer (Barman *et al.* 1993). Soccer is a highly dynamic domain ideal for research in bounded rational decision-making. It is characterized by continual activity, direct physical manipulation, distributed interacting agents (friendly, hostile, and neutral), and a high degree of uncertainty.

Dynamo soccer involves small off-the-shelf radio-controlled toy cars, which we call *Dynamites*, playing on a ping-pong table-sized field (Figure 1). All sensing and computation is off-board. A ceiling-mounted camera tracks movements of the vehicles and the soccer ball. Color coding of the vehicles and ball simplifies tracking enabling frame rate (60Hz) measurement of position, orientation, and velocity of all objects. The vehicles can be commanded at 60Hz as well; actual lag depends on the controller used.

Members of the Dynamo group[1] have implemented a layered control architecture with vehicle and ball trajectory planning and demonstrated it in real games of Dynamite

---

[*]This work was performed while the author was at the University of British Columbia and was supported by the Canadian Institute for Robotics and Intelligent Systems Group B5 and by Natural Sciences and Engineering Research Council of Canada Operating Grant OGP0009281 awarded to Alan Mackworth. The author is currently supported by the State of California PATH MOU-130. Thanks to Rod Barman, Craig Boutilier, Tom Dean, Michael Horsch, Stuart Kingdon, Jim Little, Alan Mackworth, David Poole, and Michael Sahota for comments and useful suggestions about this work.

---

[1]Principally Michael Sahota, Rod Barman, and Stuart Kingdon.

Figure 1: Dynamites playing soccer.

soccer (Sahota 1994). The state of the art in this experimentation has been two robots playing against each other. This author is currently investigating algorithms to incorporate more players. In the remainder of this paper, we outline an analysis of work toward this end.

Visual Routine Arbitration for Soccer

We are interested in applying decision-theoretic and game-theoretic principles in Dynamite controllers. In this paper, we develop a simple visual routine-based decision rule for a soccer task, and contrast its decisions with probabilistic and decision-theoretic algorithms. In the process, we hope to show that adopting a biologically-inspired algorithm need not conflict with being a good Bayesian.

The theory of visual routines is due to Ullman (Ullman 1983). Visual routines theory assumes the existence of a small set of primitive *visual operators* that perform computations on a scene or image. Examples of operators are line projection (drawing "rays"), detecting intersections of rays, measuring distances, and filling regions with color. A *visual routine* is a pattern of activity of visual operators to extract intermediate-level information from an organism's surroundings. A visual routine is like a subroutine built out of the primitive computations of visual operators. A visual routine can, for example, detect if a point is in an enclosed region in an image by color-filling from the point outward (Chapman 1992). A visual routine might also, for example, help pool players with projection of ball trajectories.

Visual routines theory was developed as a model of biological vision. It was applied to video game playing by Chapman and Agre (Agre & Chapman 1987; Chapman 1992). Dynamite soccer is similar to their video games, especially in our current configuration with a camera that has a complete bird's eye view of the game playing area. Thus it is at least plausible that Dynamites can apply visual routines fruitfully. After all, humans must use vision or at least some form of visually-mediated computation to play soccer. In this paper, we consider the use of visual routines in a Dynamite's decision[2] to shoot the ball to score or pass to a team mate (Figure 2).

---

[2] As noted, all computation is off-board; we may loosely speak of a Dynamite's decision to refer to the decisions of its off-board controller.

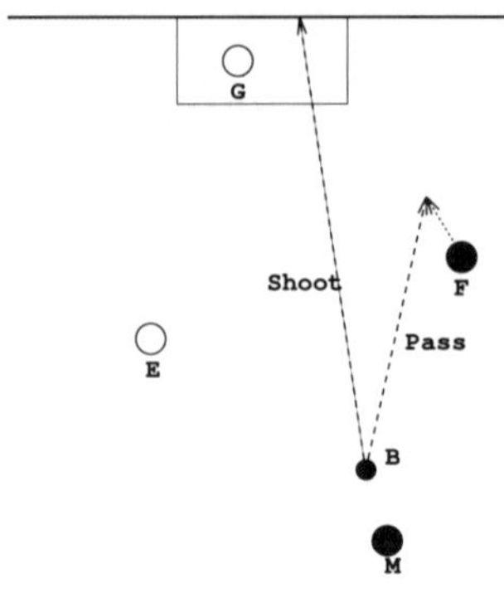

Figure 2: The shoot-or-pass decision. Filled circles are friends, white circles enemies. M is *me*, F is *friend*, E is *enemy*, and G is *goalie*. B is the ball. The two longer arrows are projected trajectories for shoot and pass.

In the shoot-or-pass scenario, a Dynamite is close to the ball, and it is trying to assess whether to aim directly for the goal to try to score, or to pass the ball to its team mate instead. Using visual routines, a Dynamite can roughly estimate the possibility of the enemy intercepting its shot or pass.

The *visual routine processor* (VRP) is the actual "engine" that performs visual operations. The VRP is able, for example, to measure distances by the magnitude of the scan path from a point to another point. For the shoot-or-pass scenario, a VRP might compute the likely paths of the ball and vehicles by projecting rays on the basis of current direction and velocity (or other assumptions about the likely course of the objects). Intersections of the rays indicate likely points at which objects may collide. Thus we can use the VRP as an estimator of whether an enemy intercept has a chance of succeeding by comparing the projected times of the enemy and ball to intersections of their possible trajectories. Such estimates are typically coarse; fine motion, actions by friends, and many other details are ignored by the VRP in its projections.

In the following, we refer to the visual-routines based controller as the *visual routine arbitrator* (VRA). A VRA decision rule might be:

```
if safe-for-shoot then
  shoot
else if safe-for-pass then
  pass
else
  shoot-out-of-range
fi
```

where `safe-for-shoot` and `safe-for-pass` are visual routines that act as oracles on the safety (unlikelihood of intercept) of different shots.

Alternatively, a Dynamite could make its decision on the basis of a game theoretic model. Dynamite soccer is a perfect information zero-sum game; thus a *maximin* strategy is optimal. For example, we could assume that the enemy will compute its fastest path to the likely path of the ball and beeline for the intersection. Maximizing our expected utility on that basis yields our optimal action.

A *decision theoretic arbitrator* (DTA) for such analysis might incorporate, for example, a Markov decision process model of the temporal behavior of friends, foes, and the ball. The Markov decision process model includes a stochastic model of the domain, a utility function modeling preferences over outcomes, and assumptions about enemy actions. The stochastic model involves state variables such as the position, orientation, and velocity of vehicles and the ball; the utility function may say that scoring is good, and that intercept is bad. The expected utility of an action a is $\sum_w P(w|a)U(w)$, where each w is a possible state resulting from executing a. Decision theory prescribes a rational agent to undertake the action $\hat{a}$ that has the maximum expected utility. The number of states w is of exponential order, and the problem of finding the action with maximum utility is NP-hard (Cooper 1990).

Decision-theoretic Information Invariants

The main thesis of this paper is that we can substitute expensive decision-theoretic computation by simple visual computations with bounded loss in the optimality of the decisions made. We capture this with the notion of *decision-theoretic information invariance*.

Recently, Donald and colleagues (Donald, Jennings, & Rus 1993) and Horswill (Horswill 1993) have introduced theories of program transformation focusing on the invariance of the input/output behavior of sensory-robotic control programs. Roughly speaking, two programs are informationally invariant (borrowing Donald's terminology) if they achieve the same results in the same situations. The idea is to determine what information and computation is actually important in executing a task.

The theory proposed here is similar, but whereas previous work focused on deterministic relations in computing decisions, we use decision theory and game theory as our basis for selecting control outputs. In the abstract, we can evaluate a program transformation on the basis of the expected utility of adopting the transformation. In this paper, we assume that utility is defined in such a way that the expected utility is just the probability that a transformed control program agrees with an optimal deliberator.

As an example, consider the shoot-or-pass decision. In the following, let s stand for *shoot*, p for *pass*, and i for *intercept*. In selecting the optimal action, a DTA compares the expected utilities of shoot and pass: $EU[s]$ and $EU[p]$. Each EU is the expectation of the utility over possible outcomes, e.g., $U[i]P[i|s]+U[\neg i]P[\neg i|s]$ is the expected utility of shoot. Under the reasonable assumptions of zero utility for intercept and positive utility for no intercept, the DTA's decision is based on the following:

$$
\begin{aligned}
EU[s] &\leq EU[p] \\
U[\neg i]P[\neg i|s] &\leq U[\neg i]P[\neg i|p] \\
kP[\neg i|s] &\leq P[\neg i|p]
\end{aligned}
$$

The constant k is the quotient of the utilities of no intercept

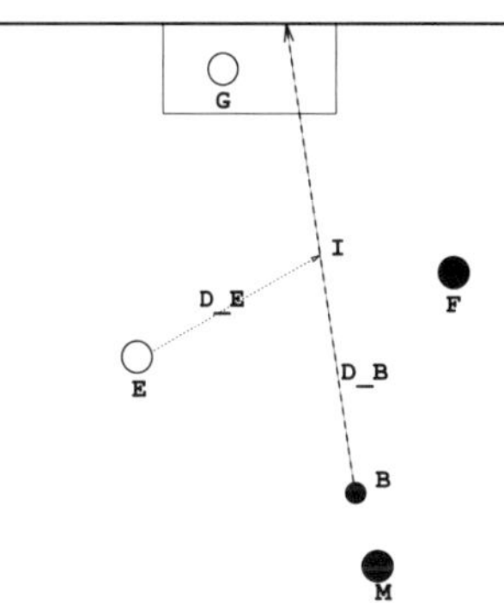

Figure 3: Using the VRP to bound intercept probability.

of shot and pass (in general, the utility of the no intercept outcome is dependent on the action). Let us suppose for now that $k = 1$: i.e., we interpret the utilities "myopically" as intrinsic utility of not getting intercepted. This assumption will be relaxed later on.

Under this assumption, we find that, comparing two expected utilities is equivalent to comparing two probabilities in our case. All we need then is a reliable and efficient oracle for the probability comparison.[3] In the next section, we analyze the applicability of visual routines as such oracles.

Analyzing the Visual Routine Arbitrator

In the following, we analyze an intuition that VRA decision rules based on distance measurement approximate more detailed intercept probability computations that a DTA might perform.

Assume for now that the ball and enemy have constant velocity, and that the enemy is holonomic and can switch directions instantly. A VRP can then make projections about enemy intercept by (1) projecting a ray corresponding to the ball trajectory, (2) project a ray from the enemy to the ball trajectory, (3) mark the intersection, and (4) measure the distances of each line segment (ball and enemy) to the intersection (Figure 3; I is an intersection, D_E is enemy's distance to the intersection, D_B that for the ball.).

If the velocities of the enemy and ball are the same, then the distance approximates the probability of success or intercept of the shot relative to that intersection in the following sense: if the enemy is farther than the ball from the intersection, then the probability of success is higher than the probability of intercept. If enemy is closer than the ball to the intersection, then the probability of success is lower than that of intercept. If one is much greater than the other, then the probability accordingly changes. If the velocities of ball and enemy are not the same, then we adjust the distances with appropriate factors of proportionality.

---

[3]Depending on performance characteristics desired, and given rules whose reliability and efficiency are known, we can build a control system that approximates an optimal DTA with known error and performance. This is similar to control of inference using "anytime" and "contract" algorithms (Dean & Boddy 1988; Zilberstein 1993).

Thus, in the soccer scenario, sensing of distance qualitatively substitutes for probability assessment. In a loose sense, we *sense* probability approximately from environmental cues. Equally importantly, we approximately sense stochastic dominance and other *relationships* between probabilities. Thus, the VRA is an oracle for the expected utility comparison of the previous section.

Just how approximate is the VRA as an oracle? It is easy to see that proportionality in the probabilities is not likely to be preserved except very roughly. In the following, we present an analysis of the accuracy of the VRA. Bear in mind that ours is but a coarse analysis with many simplifying assumptions.

There are different criteria that apply in considering the competitiveness of decision rules for soccer; an objective criterion is that a decision rule win soccer games consistently. We propose to eventually obtain such experimental data, but first, we would like to have an idea of what we hope to gain from experiments. In this paper, we restrict ourselves to analyzing inference quality not over whole games, but in the context of "plays" within games. We evaluate the VRA on its own terms, in terms of what it is trying to compute (namely, the likelihood of intercept or success) rather than its overall utility in soccer playing.

To begin with, we assume holonomic vehicles and that the enemy will beeline to the shortest intercept path. We also assume that we are ready to hit the ball so that we do not need to worry about the time or path it takes to hit the ball in the first place. The analysis outlined below can be extended to incorporate this easily.

Given the assumptions, the problem boils down to the following. The inputs are D_b and D_e, the distances, respectively, of the ball and the enemy to their intersection point, computed by the VRP. How accurately does comparison of D_b and D_e reflect the probability of success and failure of the shot? The assumption, of course, is that a DTA would compute its decisions based on as accurate as possible an assessment of this probability.

To estimate the robustness of the VRA, we need descriptions of likely ball and vehicle motion. In particular, we need their uncertainty to be captured by probability distributions. In our case, due to the large variability in speed, it is reasonable to assume normal deviates for these parameters. As usual, a normality assumption simplifies certain aspects of analysis, but it is not a necessary one. We only require that there be *some* form of probabilistic estimate.

What we wish to know is the likelihood that a VRA decision rule is correct. We have analyzed this likelihood based on a variety of assumptions and also on several different VRA decision rules. We do not have the space to present all of our analyses. Instead we outline an important basic case to give a flavor of the analyses involved.

Our basic analysis concerns the probability of a correct VRA prediction:

$$P[\text{VRA predicts success} \wedge \text{success}|\alpha]$$
$$+ \quad P[\text{VRA predicts intercept} \wedge \text{intercept}|\alpha]$$

where α are the initial conditions. We first analyze the

probability that the VRA predicts success for a shot and the shot actually succeeds. The other case can be derived from this case.

The VRA's decision algorithm is based on the relationship $\frac{\hat{D}_b}{\hat{V}_b} < \frac{\hat{D}_e}{\hat{V}_e}$ where $\hat{\cdot}$ is the VRA's estimate of $\cdot$. We can rewrite this as $\hat{D}_b \cdot \hat{V}_e < \hat{D}_e \cdot \hat{V}_b$. What we wish to estimate is $P[\hat{D}_b \cdot \hat{V}_e < \hat{D}_e \cdot \hat{V}_b \wedge \text{success}|\alpha]$. The conjuncts are conditionally independent given initial conditions and in this case, the desired probability is $P[\hat{D}_b \cdot \hat{V}_e < \hat{D}_e \cdot \hat{V}_b|\alpha] \times P[\text{success}|\alpha]$.

We assume that the VRA's estimates given initial conditions are fixed. Thus the first conditional probability is simply either 1 or 0. How can we determine likelihood of success of a shot? It is reasonable, at least to a first approximation, to estimate this using the same relationship as the VRA (integrated with respect to D_b, D_e, V_b, V_e):

$$P[D_b \cdot V_e < D_e \cdot V_b|\hat{D}_b, \hat{D}_e, \hat{V}_b, \hat{V}_e]$$
$$= \iiiint\limits_{D_b \cdot V_e < D_e \cdot V_b} f(D_b, D_e, V_b, V_e|\hat{D}_b, \hat{D}_e, \hat{V}_b, \hat{V}_e)$$
$$= \iiiint\limits_{D_b \cdot V_e < D_e \cdot V_b} f(D_b|\hat{D}_b)f(D_e|\hat{D}_e)f(V_b|\hat{V}_b)f(V_e|\hat{V}_e)$$

In the first integral, f is the joint density of all the random variables. We can rewrite it as the second integral because all the random variables are conditionally independent, and each random variable is only dependent on its estimate. The resulting integral can be estimated, in principle, for any set of integrable densities $f(\cdot)$.

In our case, we have assumed that each $f(V|\hat{V})$ is normally distributed. Each $f(D|\hat{D})$ parameterizes the uncertainty in actual distance given a distance measurement. In the Dynamo testbed, we have determined that the vision system estimates positions and distances accurately to 1/100th of an inch. Thus it is reasonable to assume that each distance estimate is correct, thereby removing its uncertainty.

Given the preceding, the VRA's decision rule can be based on the relation $\frac{D_b}{D_e}\hat{V}_e < \hat{V}_b$ where D_b and D_e are assumed to be constants. Our probability estimate becomes

$$\iint\limits_{\frac{D_b}{D_e}V_e < V_b} f(V_b|\hat{V}_b)f(V_e|\hat{V}_e)dV_b dV_e$$

So what are the $f(\cdot)$? The VRA has many choices on what to adopt as its speed estimate. Some reasonable ones are (1) initial velocity, (2) mean velocity and (3) lower or upper bound (lower bound for ball, upper bound for enemy).

If the VRA uses mean velocity, then each conditional distribution $f(V.|\hat{V}.)$ is just the normal distribution that we have as the estimate of velocity.

$$\iint\limits_{\frac{D_b}{D_e}V_e < V_b} N(\mu_b, \sigma_b, V_b)N(\mu_e, \sigma_e, V_e)dV_b dV_e$$

Although we cannot derive a closed form for this integral, it is trivial to estimate numerically.

μ_b	σ_b	μ_e	σ_e	Success	Overall
1.8	0.6	3.0	0.5	0.85	0.90
1.8	0.6	3.0	1.0	0.83	0.86
1.8	0.6	3.0	0.2	0.86	0.91
1.8	0.2	3.0	0.2	0.96	0.97

Table 1: VRA accuracy: "Success" is the accuracy for only the success case, and "Overall" is the accuracy also including intercept.

k	Success	Overall
0	0.85	0.90
1	0.96	0.85
2	0.99	0.75

Table 2: A "cautious" VRA predicts success well but it is poor overall.

So now, we can estimate the probability that the VRA predicts success and actual success occurs for a particular initial condition. The probability of intercept is the complement of the probability of success. The probability of VRA correctness for a particular initial condition is simply one or the other probability, depending on what the VRA predicts.

The likely overall accuracy of the VRA is the expectation of VRA correctness over the possible initial conditions. In our analysis, we have simply assumed that all initial conditions are equally likely. We estimated the mean and variance for enemy speed as 3.0 and 0.5, and that for the ball as 1.8 and 0.6. Given these assumptions, our estimate of the VRA accuracy is 0.90.

As we can see, provided that our assumptions are valid, the VRA's estimate is quite competitive. Of course, what approximations are acceptable depends on the problem and the domain. Given that the VRA effectively ignores the variability in velocities, a 10% loss does not seem bad considering the simplicity of the decision algorithm, and the computational complexity of decision theoretic inference.

By varying speed parameters, it is possible to see that the VRA does best where the uncertainty in velocity is lowest. Conversely, if the mean velocity is a poor predictor of actual velocity, then the VRA will naturally not do as well (Table 1).

Here is another estimate when the VRA is cautious, using a minimax criterion, assuming high speed for the enemy and low speed for the ball (Table 2). For example, we choose $\mu \pm k\sigma$, where μ and σ are parameters for the normal density lower/upper bounds. The higher k is, the more "cautious" the estimate.

More importantly, we can extend our analysis to derive the likelihood that a VRA will serve as a good oracle for the probability comparison of Section 4. We adopt the following as our VRA:

```
if shoot-safer-than-pass then
  shoot
else
```

μ_b	σ_b	μ_e	σ_e	Accuracy
1.8	0.6	3.0	0.5	0.99
1.8	0.6	3.0	1.0	0.98
1.8	0.6	3.0	0.2	0.99
1.8	0.2	3.0	0.2	0.99

Table 3: VRA accuracy for probability comparison.

```
  pass
fi
```

This VRA computes the same decision as the DTA provided that the visual routine `shoot-safer-than-pass` is a reliable probability comparator.

To compare shoot and pass, our inputs include distances of enemy and ball for both shoot and pass. Let D^s be distance for shoot and D^p be distance for pass. Then we have D^s_b, D^s_e, D^p_b, D^p_e, and we also have velocity estimates as before.

What we wish to estimate is the likelihood, given initial conditions, that $P[success|pass] \leq P[success|shoot]$ is true when `shoot-safer-than-pass` returns true, and $P[success|pass] > P[success|shoot]$ when the visual routine returns false. The VRP estimates this by comparing likely travel times of ball and enemy to their intercept point. Let $T = D/V$ be the time of travel. The VRP estimates $P[success|pass] \leq P[success|shoot]$ by the relation $\frac{T^p_e}{T^p_b} \leq \frac{T^s_e}{T^s_b}$. It is easy to see that this is equivalent to

$$D^p_e \cdot D^s_b \leq D^s_e \cdot D^p_b \tag{1}$$

Thus, the VRP estimate is independent of the velocities of the ball or enemy; it depends only on the distances.

All that remains is to determine, given a VRP estimate by (1), if the predicted relation actually holds. The actual probabilities can be estimated, for example, by the same method as before.

Under our assumptions about enemy and ball behavior, we find that the VRA is a highly accurate predictor of the probability relation, and thereby of the optimal decision (Table 3). If we use the VRA as an oracle for probability comparison, we achieve about 0.99 accuracy without having to engage in any probability computation (but at the expense of some vision computation). Thus, the optimality of an agent is almost invariant under substitution of a DTA with the VRA.

Recall that earlier in the paper, we made an assumption that the utility of no intercept was the same for both shoot and pass, i.e., k was assumed to be 1 in the relation below:

$$kP[success|shoot] \leq P[success|pass]$$

It should be easy to see that it is straightforward to modify the visual routine decision rule in Equation 1 to incorporate k. Thus, for this problem, the visual routine decision rule can compute relations not only between probabilities, but between expected utilities as well. We are currently extending the analysis of this paper so that the visual routine takes into account the probability of success of a shot by the friend, given that a pass succeeds.

The analysis that we have performed here is for a special simple case. It is effectively an analysis of the *sensitivity* of control output to the type of algorithm used. It is related to work in value of information (Howard 1966), "anytime" and "contract" algorithms(Dean & Boddy 1988; Zilberstein 1993), and approximation and abstraction in Bayesian networks (Provan 1993). In addition to work presented here, we have performed analyses using different assumptions about enemy and ball behavior and their uncertainty. For example, we have performed analyses incorporating steering uncertainty in addition to uncertainty about vehicle velocity. As might be expected, the effect of this is not great unless there is a lot of uncertainty in the steering drift. We are currently in the process of extending our analysis to a case where the enemy simply servos to the ball position. Finally, we have evaluated both simpler and more complex VRA metrics, for example, comparing only the distance of the enemy to the ball trajectory (ignoring velocity and ball distance). In a longer version of the paper, we will present these results as well as proofs about the reliability of the VRA as a probability comparator for the shoot-or-pass decision.

Conclusions

What we have tried to do in this paper is to back our intuition about the suitability of visual routine-based algorithms for the soccer domain with formal analysis. In the process, we discovered that under certain assumptions, the visual routine arbitrator is a good approximation to an optimal rational decision-maker. In the problem we studied, we find that the essence of decision-theoretic optimization computation is captured by geometric relations that can be discovered by visual routines.

Our analysis, although reassuring to the Bayesian in that it quantifies the robustness of different decision rules, is not meant as an end in itself. It is but a first step, and much remains to be done. First of all, although the VRA clearly involves simple computation, we need a concrete analysis of the performance gains obtained by using the VRA. Secondly, we would like to remove various assumptions made about vehicle dynamics and enemy behavior. We would also like to extend our analysis to other domains where probability can be considered to be sensed both actively and peripherally. In general, we are interested in developing tools for continuous game theory and control involving sensing and interaction with a dynamic environment. Last but not least, we are currently in the process of implementing a simple visual routines processor for testing the VRA in experiments.

References

Agre, P. E., and Chapman, D. 1987. Pengi: An implementation of a theory of activity. In *Proceedings of the Sixth National Conference on Artificial Intelligence*, 268–272. Seattle, Washington: AAAI.

Barman, R.; Kingdon, S.; Mackworth, A.; Pai, D.; Sahota, M.; Wilkinson, H.; and Zhang, Y. 1993. Dynamite: A testbed for multiple mobile robots. In *Proceedings of the 1993 IJCAI Workshop on Dynamically Interacting Robots*. Chambery, France: IJCAII.

Chapman, D. 1992. *Vision, Instruction, and Action*. Cambridge, Massachusetts: MIT Press.

Cooper, G. F. 1990. The computational complexity of probabilistic inference using bayesian belief networks. *Artificial Intelligence* 42(2–3):393–405.

Dean, T., and Boddy, M. 1988. An analysis of time dependent planning. In *Proceedings of the Seventh National Conference on Artificial Intelligence*, 49–54. Minneapolis, Minnesota: AAAI.

Donald, B.; Jennings, J.; and Rus, D. 1993. Towards a theory of information invariants for cooperating autonomous mobile robots. In *Proceedings of the International Symposium on Robotics Research (ISRR)*.

Goldszmidt, M. 1993. Putting Qualitative Probability to Work Workshop.

Horswill, I. D. 1993. *Specialization of Perceptual Processes*. Ph.D. Dissertation, MIT, Cambridge, Massachusetts.

Howard, R. A. 1966. Information value theory. *IEEE Transactions on Systems Science and Cybernetics* 2(1):22–26.

Provan, G. 1993. Tradeoffs in constructing and evaluating temporal influence diagrams. In *Proceedings of the Ninth Conference on Uncertainty in Artificial Intelligence*.

Sahota, M. 1994. Reactive deliberation: An architecture for real-time intelligent control in dynamic environments. In *Proceedings of the Twelfth National Conference on Artificial Intelligence*. Seattle, Washington: AAAI Press. To appear.

Savage, L. J. 1954. *The Foundations of Statistics*. Dover.

Ullman, S. 1983. Visual routines. AI-Memo-723, MIT Artificial Intelligence Laboratory, Cambridge, MA.

von Neumann, J., and Morgenstern, O. 1947. *Theory of games and economic behavior*. Princeton: Princeton University Press, 2nd edition.

Zilberstein, S. 1993. *Operational Rationality Through Compilation of Anytime Algorithms*. Ph.D. Dissertation, University of California, Berkeley, California.

Topological mapping for mobile robots using a combination of sonar and vision sensing

David Kortenkamp*and Terry Weymouth
Artificial Intelligence Laboratory
The University of Michigan
Ann Arbor, MI 48109
korten@aio.jsc.nasa.gov

Abstract

Topological maps represent the world as a network of nodes and arcs: the nodes are distinctive places in the environment and the arcs represent paths between places. A significant issue in building topological maps is defining distinctive places. Most previous work in topological mapping has concentrated on using sonar sensors to define distinctive places. However, sonar sensors are limited in range and angular resolution, which can make it difficult to distinguish between different distinctive places. Our approach combines a sonar-based definition of distinctive places with visual information. We use the robot's sonar sensors to determine where to capture images and use cues extracted from those images to help perform place recognition. Information from these two sensing modalities is combined using a simple Bayesian network. Results described in this paper show that our robot is able to perform place recognition without having to move through a sequence of places, as is the case with most currently implemented systems.

Introduction

Topological maps represent the world as a graph of places with the arcs of the graph representing movements between places. Brooks (Brooks 1985) argues persuasively for the use of topological maps as a means of dealing with uncertainty in mobile robot navigation. Indeed, the idea of a map that contains no metric or geometric information, but only the notions of proximity and order, is enticing because such an approach eliminates the inevitable problems of dealing with movement uncertainty in mobile robots. Movement errors do not accumulate globally in topological maps as they do in maps with a global coordinate system since the robot only navigates locally, between places. Topological maps are also much more compact in their representation of space, in that they represent only certain places and not the entire world, in contrast to robots which use detailed *a priori* models of the world, such as (Kosaka & Kak 1992) and (Fennema & Hanson 1990).

*Now at The MITRE Corporation, Houston, TX 77058. This research was sponsored by Department of Energy grant DE-FG02-86NE37969

For these reasons, topological maps have become increasingly popular in mobile robotics.

A significant issue in building a topological map is defining distinctive places in the environment; these distinctive places correspond to the nodes of the resulting topological map. Most researchers use sonar sensors to define distinctive places (Basye, Dean, & Vitter 1989; Kuipers & Byun 1991; Mataric 1992). However, sonar sensors are limited in range and angular resolution and therefore can only give a rough approximation of the robot's environment. Because of this, many "distinctive" places in the environment actually look very similar to sonar sensors. For example, in a long hallway with left and right doorways to rooms, using only sonar sensors it would be impossible to distinguish any particular left or right door from any other left or right door along the hallway. Most systems overcome this limitation by determining the robot's location based on a *sequence* of distinctive places instead of on a single distinctive place. Such approaches, while certainly effective, require the robot to make many navigational movements in order to determine its location in the environment.

It is our hypothesis that by adding visual information to the robot's sonar information, we can dramatically reduce the ambiguity of places that look identical to the robot's sonar sensors. In our approach, sonar sensors are used to determine generic places in the environment called *gateways*. Gateways mark the transition from one space to another space. Since a gateway marks the entrance to a new space, they offer the robot a perfect opportunity to look around and acquire visual cues that will distinguish among gateways. Thus, at each gateway one or more images (*scenes*) are captured. Visual cues are extracted from the image and stored with the gateway. On subsequent visits to the same gateway, the robot can use the visual cues, in conjunction with the sonar signature of the gateway, to determine its location.

Sonar information

Most topological maps are built around distinctive places. In our topological map, rather than looking for places that are locally distinguishable from other places and then storing the distinguishing features of the place in the route map, we instead look for places that mark the transition between one space in the environment and another space. We call these places *gateways*.

In indoor environments, gateways are places such as entrances to rooms and intersections of hallways. For a mobile robot in an indoor environment, gateways are important for several reasons. First, gateways tend to be places that are visited frequently. Second, gateways are places that open up new views for a robot, views from which it can extract visual cues to distinguish between similar gateways. Third, a robot typically must go through a gateway in a small number of directions. For example a robot can only pass through a doorway in two directions. This constrains the range of views that a robot can have at a gateway and simplifies matching of visual cues. Finally, gateways are exits from a space and, for safety reasons, a robot should stay aware of exits.

Detecting gateways

We have defined gateways, for orthogonal indoor environments, as openings to the left or right of the robot's direction of travel that are wide enough for the robot to pass through. These openings are detected using sonar sensors. Our gateway detection algorithm has the following components:

1. The robot aligns itself along a wall (or along both walls of a corridor) using its sonar sensors.

2. The robot moves along the wall and maintains its orientation and distance with respect to the wall (or walls in a corridor) using its sonar sensors.

3. While moving, the robot continually checks its left and right sonar readings for openings; the robot also checks for obstacles in front of it.

4. When an opening is found, the robot continues moving and looks for a closing to that opening. While looking for a closing, the robot also checks the opposite direction for any openings as well as checking the front for any obstacles.

5. When a closing to the opening is found (a closing can be an end to the opening, a blockage in front, or a certain distance traveled), the robot determines if the opening is large enough to pass through and, if so, signals a gateway.

6. The robot positions itself in the middle of the gateway.

Experiments with our Labmate TRC robot in the hallways of our laboratory show that this gateway detection algorithm has an error of no more than 3.5 degrees in orientation along the axis of the hallway and 70mm in position along the axis of the hallway. These errors were determined by repeatedly having the robot

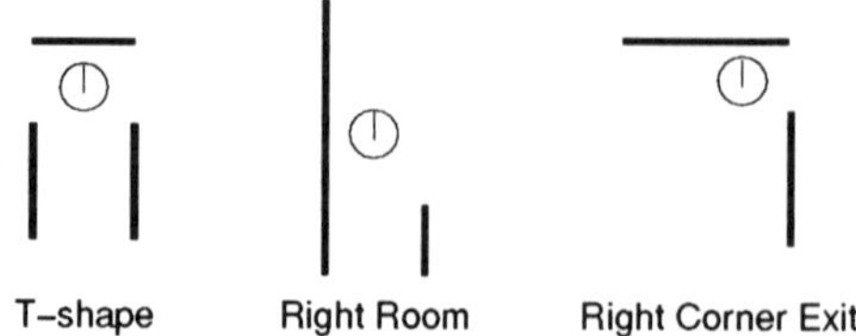

Figure 1: A few examples of different types of gateways.

stop at the same set of gateways and measuring its orientation and location.

Classifying gateways

Once a gateway has been detected it can be classified as a certain type using local sensory information. For example, a T-SHAPE gateway is characterized by a simultaneous opening on both the left and right of the robot followed by the robot being blocked in the front (see figure 1). A RIGHT ROOM gateway is characterized by a right opening followed by no closing. In rooms, gateways are typically exits, such as the RIGHT CORNER EXIT in figure 1. We have identified a total of 25 gateway types in typical indoor environments. Classifying each gateway using local sensory information helps the robot perform place recognition.

Gateways extend the traditional sonar-based topological place by being not just distinctive places, but *important* places in that they open up new views for the robot. The robot can take advantage of these views to store visual scenes that can help it distinguish between gateways. In essence, gateways represent *generic* places in the environment (for example, doors, intersections) and not *specific* places (for example, the door to room 200). This is acceptable for some forms of navigation. For example, if the robot is told to take the third right opening, then the algorithms described in this section will be perfectly adequate. However, if the robot does not know its starting location or the environment changes (that is, the second opening on the right is closed) then simply relying on local sonar information can be dangerous. For this reason, our gateway mechanism is augmented with visual information, described in the following section.

Visual information

We augment our sonar information with visual information. Our visual information takes the form of visual scenes captured at gateways from which we extract visual cues. Scenes, as they are presented here, differ from the traditional computer vision paradigm. In our approach, cues are not simply extracted from an image and then stored apart from the scene, but their *location* in the scene is of equal importance. Kaplan, Kaplan, and Lesperance (Kaplan 1970; Kaplan & Kaplan 1982;

Lesperance 1990) discuss the importance of a fast and unobtrusive mechanism that gives a rough assessment of the objects surrounding an organism and their relationships to each other.

Extracting visual cues

Programming a robot to autonomously find visual cues (or landmarks, although that term is generally used for highly complex objects as opposed to the simple features discussed in this subsection) is an area of active research and there are several proposed landmark detection algorithms (Levitt & Lawton 1990; Tsuji & Li 1993). For our experiments we have chosen a simple cue—vertical edges. Vertical edges have proven very useful as indoor visual cues in other mobile robot systems (Kriegman, Triendl, & Binford 1989; Crowley *et al.* 1991) and are especially effective in our experimental space due to the sharp contrast between black doorway frames and white walls. Vertical edges are extracted from a black-and-white image by a modified Sobel edge detector. A second image is analyzed in the same way as the first, but it is offset by 18cm from the first image. This produces two lists of edges, one list for the right image and one list for the left image. The edges on the two lists are matched to each other using the direction of transition of the edge (that is, was the edge from light to dark or dark to light?), length, and location. The pixel shift in the matched edges from the first image to the second image (called the disparity) is calculated and used to determine a rough distance to the edge. Each visual cue, thus, has three scene-independent features: direction, length, and distance.

Storing visual scenes

We store the robot's visual cues in an abstracted scene representation (ASR), which is a 5 X 5 grid. The choice of a 5 X 5 grid size is based on the experiments in sonar gateway detection. The orientation error at a gateway is a maximum of 3.5 degrees. Using a camera with a focal length of 4.8mm, a 3.5 degree variation in orientation yields a 47 pixel displacement for cues 2m away (objects further away will have a smaller disparity). Doubling this to 94 pixels and dividing it into the image size of 480 X 480 pixels gives a 5 X 5 abstracted grid. In such a grid, a cue that falls in the middle of a cell and is further than two meters away will remain in that same cell given a 3.5 degree difference in orientation. Each cell of the ASR can be connected to a representation of a visual cue that occupies that location in the scene. In the current system, the representation of the visual cue contains the direction, distance, and length of the cue. However, in more sophisticated implementations the representation of the visual cue could contain detailed information about how to recognize the cue, maybe even a small neural network that performs pattern recognition for the pattern located in those cells.

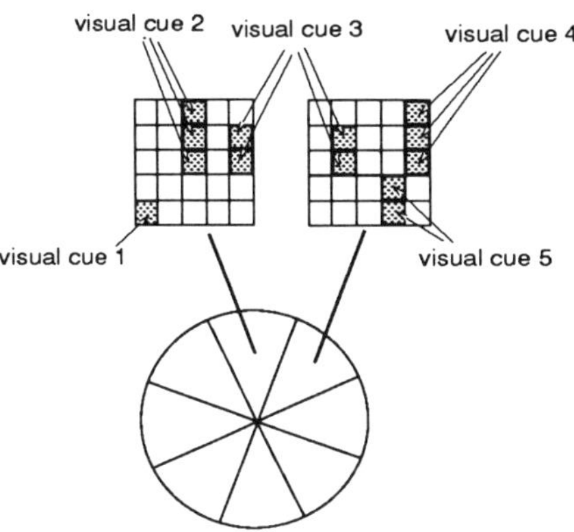

Figure 2: Cues are stored in abstracted representations.

ASRs can be stored for any of eight directions that the robot can be told to face at a gateway. The number of directions represented is dependent on the visual field of view; in our robot the field of view is 60 degrees, which allowing for overlap, gives 8 directions each representing 45 degrees. Typically, the robot will only store one scene (in the forward direction) at each gateway. Figure 2 shows some sample ASRs and how several can be stored at a single gateway.

ASRs are not static structures as that would render them useless in a dynamic world. An ASR should only contain those cues that remain constant over many traversals, since they will be the most reliable cues in the future. To accomplish this, the connection that links each cell of the ASR to a cue representation can be strengthened or weakened, depending on whether the cue is present or not during each traversal.

Currently, it is necessary to have guided training runs in order to build up a stable set of cues. In the future, we would like our robot to explore autonomously, attempting to determine where it is as well as it can and updating appropriate maps as much as it can. Such a system would make more mistakes at first, but would not need to rely on directions to find routes to goals. Also, such a system would take much longer to learn a stable set of cues. The current implementation can be compared to someone taking you on a guided tour of a building several times before letting you loose. During training the robot is only told at which gateway it currently is. The robot detects and stops at the gateways completely autonomously.

Matching ASRs

The robot must have some mechanism for matching its current scene with the ASRs that are stored with each gateway. Four different match algorithms were implemented and then compared using actual scenes acquired by the robot. The four algorithms are: 1) a feature-to-feature match using distance and direction

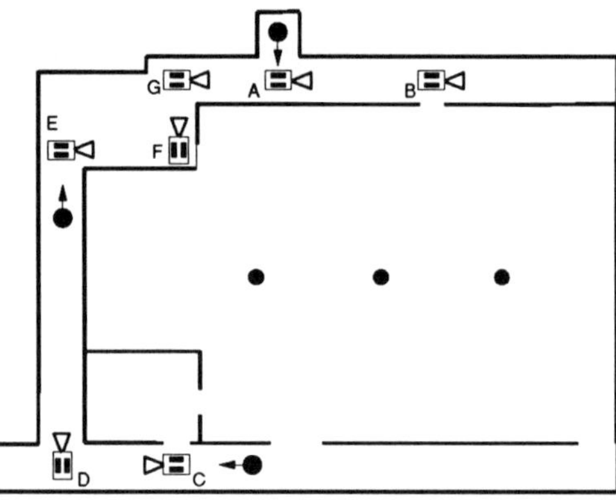

Figure 3: The experimental space for place recognition.

in which an entire feature in the current scene must match an entire feature in the stored scene; 2) a cell-to-cell match using distance and direction in which each occupied cell in the current scene must match an occupied cell in the stored scene; 3) a cell-to-cell match using only direction; 4) a cell-to-cell match using only occupancy.

The comparison procedure consists of having the robot traverse three routes five times each and building up 16 ASRs at seven different gateways. Figure 3 shows the locations of the gateways. In this figure, the black circles with arrows are the three starting points for the routes. After the robot has acquired its ASRs, it traverses each route a final time; this is the testing run. It then matches each scene along the testing run with all of the ASRs stored during the initial traversals. A current scene was said to match a stored ASR if the ratio of matched cues (or cells in methods 2, 3, and 4) to total stored cues (or cells) is higher than any other scene (a tie resulted in no match). Under these conditions, method 1 matched seven out of sixteen scenes, method 2 matched nine of sixteen, method 3 matched five of sixteen, and method 4 matched six of sixteen. Given these results, the second match algorithm was chosen for the remainder of the experiments in this paper.

Our notion of storing visual scenes to aid mobile robot navigation is not unique; there has been active research in using visual scenes to provide robots with *homing* capabilities. These robots do not build maps, but instead the robot stores sensory data about the environment and associates movements with sensory events. As sensory events trigger movements, the robot navigates the environment. Examples of homing robots are (Nelson 1989) and (Hong *et al.* 1992). Our contribution is that instead of storing visual scenes at regular intervals, as is done in homing, we store visual scenes only at locations that are considered interesting by the robot's sonar sensors.

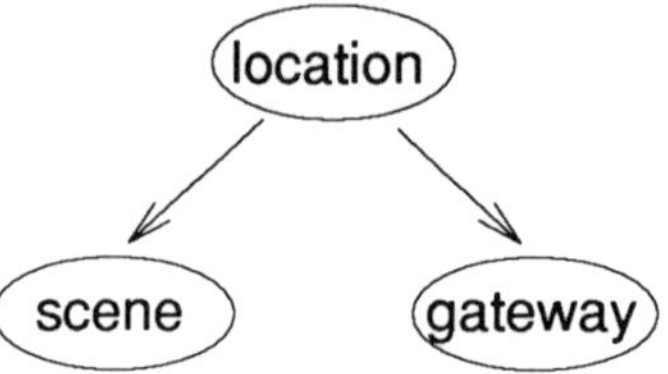

Figure 4: The Bayesian network used for place recognition

	A	B	C	D	E	F	G
A	.43	.09	.22	.05	.05	.1	.06
B	.05	.52	.21	.06	.05	.05	.05
C	.10	.12	.36	.20	.04	.13	.04
D	.14	.05	.24	.43	.05	.04	.05
E	.14	.14	.14	.14	.14	.14	.14
F	.14	.14	.14	.16	.14	.14	.14
G	.14	.14	.14	.14	.14	.14	.14

Table 1: Likelihoods for each place using only vision.

Place recognition

A single source of information, whether it be sonar or vision, is not enough to perform robust place recognition without further navigation. Thus, we use both gateway characterization and visual cues in the place recognition process and combine them using a simple Bayesian network (Pearl 1988), in which a location is determined by a scene and a gateway. The probabilistic network used by our robot is shown in Figure 4. The scene node of our network is the likelihood of a given location as determined by matching the visual cues stored for that location with the cues in the current visual scene. The gateway node is the likelihood of a given location determined by comparing its classification with the classification of the current gateway. Both of these leaf nodes are combined to determine the robot's location.

The goal of integrated place recognition is to perform place recognition better using a combination of vision and sonar than would be possible using either alone. Better is defined in three ways: 1) A higher accuracy in place recognition; 2) A greater resilience to sensor errors; and 3) An ability to resolve ambiguous places.

We have tested our topological mapping system using a real robot in an unaltered environment. In our experimental set-up, the robot has built up ASRs of seven places along three routes each traversed five times (see figure 3). Each ASR has one scene in the forward direction and has a gateway classification for each place. Then the three routes are traversed a final time and a test scene is stored at each of the seven gateways, along with a test gateway classification. The test scene is matched against all the stored ASRs and the test classification is matched with all the stored classifications

Stored places							
	A	B	C	D	E	F	G
A	.82	.04	.04	.04	.04	0	0
B	.02	.31	.31	.31	.06	0	0
C	.02	.31	.31	.31	.06	0	0
D	.02	.31	.31	.31	.06	0	0
E	.04	.12	.12	.12	.61	0	0
F	0	0	0	0	0	.90	.10
G	0	0	0	0	0	.10	.90

Table 2: Likelihoods for each place using only sonar.

Stored places							
	A	B	C	D	E	F	G
A	**.95**	.01	.02	.01	.01	0	0
B	0	**.65**	.26	.07	.01	0	0
C	0	.17	**.52**	.29	.01	0	0
D	.01	.07	.33	**.58**	.01	0	0
E	.04	.12	.12	.12	**.61**	0	0
F	0	0	0	0	0	**.90**	.10
G	0	0	0	0	0	.09	**.91**

Table 3: Combined likelihoods (vision and sonar) for each place.

in order to do place recognition.

Table 1 gives the likelihood for each place using only the visual evidence. Across the top are the stored places and down the side are the places at which the robot is (that is, the test scenes). The numbers reflect the likelihood that the robot is at that place given the visual scene information. They were determined by normalizing the percentage of matching cues between the test scene and the stored ASRs. For example, if there are three scenes and the match percentages are: .25, .90, and .75 then the likelihoods would be .13, .47, and .40. If no cues matched then the algorithm still assigned a small match percentage (0.10) to that place, since a zero likelihood would cause the final likelihood for that place to be zero no matter how strong the sonar evidence. The table shows that four out of seven places (A,B,C, and D) would be correctly identified (that is, have the highest likelihood) using only visual information.

Table 2 gives the likelihoods for each place using only sonar information (that is, gateway characterization). These likelihoods were determined by us and entered into the system: the correct gateway is given the highest likelihood; similar gateways are given much smaller likelihoods; and dissimilar gateways are given a zero likelihood. Sonar information also gives a 57% accuracy in place recognition. This is because three places (B, C, and D) look identical to the sonar sensors and are all characterized as RIGHT OPENING, so only four out of the seven places (57%) can be uniquely recognized (that is, have the highest likelihood) using sonar sensors.

Finally, Table 3 shows the likelihoods for each place

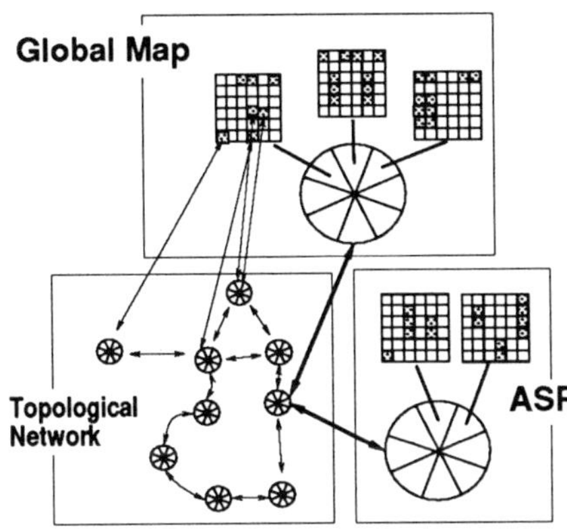

Figure 5: Each ASR is a small component of a larger representation.

when the vision and sonar evidence is combined using the Bayesian network (both sources of evidence are weighted equally). While consisting of a small number of places, this experiment demonstrates how sonar and vision combined can result in place recognition that is more accurate than would be possible using either sensing modality by itself; when the sonar information is ambiguous, the visual evidence distinguishes between places, and vice versa.

Integrating sonar and vision can also help overcome sensor errors during place recognition. For example, let's assume that the robot misclassified place D as a RIGHT ROOM instead of a RIGHT OPENING (in reality the robot never made this mistake, so the error had to be simulated). In this case, its sonar likelihood for place D is only .11, while its sonar likelihood for place E (which actually is a RIGHT ROOM) is .61. When vision evidence is considered, the likelihoods are updated to .42 for place D and only .25 for place E, thus correcting the sonar error.

Conclusion

All previous research into topological mapping for mobile robots uses sonar sensing for place recognition. Many mobile robots also use vision sensing for place recognition. Both approaches have their merits and we believe that combining sonar and vision sensing in a topological representations results in a better robot navigation system. Our system can reduce or eliminate the need for additional robot movements to distinguish between places that appear identical to sonar sensors and it can also reduce the number of scenes that need to be stored by only acquiring scenes at those places that are determined as interesting by the sonar sensors. There are also some drawbacks to our approach when compared to other systems. First, our robot requires several initial, guided traversals of a route in order to acquire a stable set of locational cues to navigate autonomously. Second, acquiring, storing and matching visual scenes is very expensive, both in computation and storage. Finally, we are restricted to highly structured, orthogonal environments.

There is also the question of how our system will scale up, given that our experimental space consisted of only seven gateways, due to the time consuming nature of experimenting with real robots. Certainly, the perfect place recognition performance we achieved in our experiments will not hold up as more and more places are added. However, it is unrealistic to expect the robot to have no idea of where it has started; this is a worst case scenario used for experimental purposes only. As the robot gets more gateways we expect that knowledge of the robot's previous location can eliminate all but a handful of possibilities for the current location, which can then be resolved using sensory information as was demonstrated in our experiments.

In the future we hope to expand our robot's visual sensing beyond simple vertical edges. We are also in the process of implementing a better gateway detection algorithm that incorporates more sophisticated obstacle avoidance (see (Kortenkamp *et al.* 1994) for preliminary results). On a broader scale, this work is a small part of a larger robot mapping system detailed in (Kortenkamp 1993). The larger system address such issues as representing the topological map, extracting routes from the topological map, traversing previously learned routes and building a geometric map from the topological data. The complete representation is shown in figure 5. Each ASR is a node in the topological network upon which a global map is constructed. The global map has a structure similar to an ASR but instead of storing visual cues it stores locations of distant places. This representation is based on a cognitive model of human spatial mapping described in (Chown, Kaplan, & Kortenkamp 1994).

References

Basye, K.; Dean, T.; and Vitter, J. S. 1989. Coping with uncertainty in map learning. In *Proceedings of the International Joint Conferences on Artificial Intelligence.*

Brooks, R. A. 1985. Visual map making for a mobile robot. In *Proceedings IEEE Conference on Robotics and Automation.*

Chown, E.; Kaplan, S.; and Kortenkamp, D. 1994. Prototypes, location and associative networks (PLAN): Towards a unified theory of cognitive mapping. To appear in *The Journal of Cognitive Science.*

Crowley, J. L.; Bobet, P.; Sarachik, K.; Mely, S.; and Kurek, M. 1991. Mobile robot perception using vertical line stereo. *Robotics and Autonomous Systems* 7(2-3).

Fennema, C., and Hanson, A. R. 1990. Experiments in autonomous navigation. In *Proceedings Image Understanding Workshop.*

Hong, J.-W.; Tan, X.; Pinette, B.; Weiss, R.; and Riseman, E. M. 1992. Image-based homing. *IEEE Control Systems* 12(1):38–45.

Kaplan, S., and Kaplan, R. 1982. *Cognition and Environment: Functioning in an Uncertain World.* Ann Arbor, MI: Ulrichs.

Kaplan, S. 1970. The role of location processing in the perception of the environment. In *Proceedings of the Second Annual Environmental Design Research Association Conference.*

Kortenkamp, D.; Huber, M.; Koss, F.; Lee, J.; Wu, A.; Belding, W.; and Rogers, S. 1994. Mobile robot exploration and navigation of indoor spaces using sonar and vision. In *Proceedings of the AIAA/NASA Conference on Intelligent Robots in Field, Factory, Service, and Space (CIRFFSS '94).*

Kortenkamp, D. 1993. *Cognitive maps for mobile robots: A representation for mapping and navigation.* Ph.D. Dissertation, The University of Michigan.

Kosaka, A., and Kak, A. C. 1992. Fast vision-guided mobile robot navigation using model-based reasoning and prediction of uncertainties. *Computer Vision, Graphics, and Image Processing* 56(2).

Kriegman, D. J.; Triendl, E.; and Binford, T. O. 1989. Stereo vision and navigation in buildings for mobile robots. *IEEE Transactions on Robotics and Automation* 5(6).

Kuipers, B. J., and Byun, Y.-T. 1991. A robot exploration and mapping strategy based on a semantic hierarchy of spatial representations. *Robotics and Autonomous Systems* 8.

Lesperance, R. 1990. *The Location System: Using Approximate Location and Size Information for Scene Segmentation.* Ph.D. Dissertation, The University of Michigan.

Levitt, T. S., and Lawton, D. T. 1990. Qualitative navigation for mobile robots. *Artificial Intelligence* 44(3).

Mataric, M. K. 1992. Integration of representation into goal-driven behavior-based robots. *IEEE Transactions on Robotics and Automation* 8(3).

Nelson, R. C. 1989. Visual homing using an associative memory. In *Proceedings of the Image Understanding Workshop.*

Pearl, J. 1988. *Probabilistic Reasoning in Intelligent Systems: Networks of Plausible Inference.* San Mateo, CA: Morgan Kaufmann.

Tsuji, S., and Li, S. 1993. Memorizing and representing route scenes. In Meyer, J.-A.; Roitblat, H. L.; and Wilson, S. W., eds., *From Animals to Animats 2: Proceedings of the Second International Conference on Simulation of Adaptive Behavior.* Cambridge, MA: MIT Press.

Applying VC-dimension Analysis To 3D Object Recognition from Perspective Projections *

Michael Lindenbaum and Shai Ben-David
Computer Science Department, Technion
Haifa 32000, ISRAEL
(mic, shai) @cs.technion.ac.il

Abstract

We analyze the amount of information needed to carry out model-based recognition tasks, in the context of a probabilistic data collection model, and independently of the recognition method employed. We consider the very rich class of semi-algebraic 3D objects, and derive an upper bound on the number of data features that (provably) suffice for localizing the object with some pre-specified precision. Our bound is based on analysing the combinatorial complexity of the hypotheses class that one has to choose from, and quantifying it using a VC-dimension parameter. Once this parameter is found, the bounds are obtained by drawing relations between recognition and learning, and using well-known results from computational learning theory. It turns out that this bounds grow logarithmically in the algebraic complexity of the objects.

Introduction

We present here a quantitative analysis of the amount of information required for Model-based object recognition. Taking a statistical approach, we consider a random data collection model and analyse the number of measurements that guarantees recognition success within a certain confidence. Intuitively, more data is needed if the recognition procedure is required to discriminate between object instances that are visually similar, and if more alternatives are allowed by the possible instance specification. In this paper these intuitive observations are quantified by deriving a rigorous upper bound on the number of features required to succeed. Our approach is very general and applies to a very large class of objects, and to several transformation classes. It is based on a combinatorial analysis, which provides the VC-dimension of concept classes associated with this objects and the transformations. In this note we concentrate on localizing 3D objects from their perspective projections.

The bounds are derived relying on the observation that the recognition task is related to a learning task,

in which one tries to learn a subset of some space, by observing samples of this space. We consider the *Probably Approximately Correct* (PAC) learning model, which assumes that the samples available are randomly drawn, and requires that the hypothesis provided is a good approximation to the true subset, within a certain prespecified confidence. In this setting, the elegant PAC learning theory guarantees that the number of samples required to learn is not higher than a certain threshold, which grows with the accuracy of the hypothesis, the required confidence, and a certain parameter, associated with the of allowed hypotheses, and known as the VC-dimension. The mathematical heart of our result is therefore an analysis of the VC-dimension of a certain concept class, related to the localization task. Interestingly, the analysis and its results are independent of the particular object considered, and the derived VC-dimension parameter depends only on the object's complexity and the class of transformations.

The results we provide, besides quantifying the *fundamental difficulty* of recognition tasks, should be useful for analyzing reported results by comparing them to the theoretical bounds, and to designing recognition procedures. Many recognition paradigms use a consistent data subset as a sufficient evidence to the presence of an object in the scene. Our results,together with other considerations described latter, may be used to set the sufficient size of such subsets that guarantees the reliability of such a procedure.

The *fundamental difficulty* of recognition tasks was already considered before in several papers: Lindenbaum used a different approach to set upper and lower bounds on the amount of data required to succeed in recognition and localization tasks (Lindenbaum 93). Grimson and Huttenlocher considered a complementary aspect of the recognition *fundamental difficulty* (Grimson and Huttenlocher 91). While we basically assume that all the data features belong to an object, they examine the possibility that a subset of "noise data features" will give a false evidence for the presence of an object in the scene. Some of the abstract mathematical treatment, without the interpretation we

---

*This work was supported by the Technion fund for the promotion of research and by the Smoler research fund

give here, was already considered in (Ben-David and Lindenbaum 93) and (Goldberg and Jerrum 93).

The paper is divided into two major parts: explaining the relation between learning and recognition, and calculating the VC-dimension associated with the task of localizing a 3D object from its 2D perspective image.

Learnability and the VC-Dimension

Given a collection, $\mathcal{K}$, of subsets of some base set, X, and a measure of difference between the members of $\mathcal{K}$, a set of points $\{x_1, \ldots, x_n\} \subset X$ is said to $\epsilon-pin$ down $\mathcal{K}$, if, for every pair of sets $A, B \in \mathcal{K}$, if $A \cap \{x_1, \ldots, x_n\} = B \cap \{x_1, \ldots, x_n\}$ then the difference between these members of $\mathcal{K}$ is at most ϵ.

It is evident that the size of such 'pinning down' sets, as well as their number, depends upon the family $\mathcal{K}$ of sets. The theory of computational learnability formalizes this issue within the framework of Valiant's PAC learning model. In that model the family of sets $\mathcal{K}$ is usually called a 'concept class' and its members are 'concepts'. The model assumes the existence of some probability distribution P over X. This probability plays a double role: First, the difference between concepts is specified as the P-probability of hitting their symmetric difference. Second, the 'fraction' of pinning-down n-tuples (among all n-tuples of points of X) is measured by the probability of picking such a tuple by i.i.d. sampling n-many times according to P.

A class $\mathcal{K}$ is called *PAC-learnable* (or just 'learnable') if, for every positive ϵ, δ, there exists a finite number m (depending upon these parameters) such that for every probability distribution P over X, the P^m-probability of picking an m-tuple that ϵ-pins down $\mathcal{K}$ exceeds $(1 - \delta)$. It turns out that a concept class is learnable **iff** a purely combinatorial parameter – the Vapnik-Chervonenkis dimension of this class, is finite (Blumer et al. 89).

Definition 1*: [Vapnik-Chervonenkis Dimension] Let X be some set and $\mathcal{K}$ a collection of its subsets.*

- *We say that $\mathcal{K}$ shatters a set $A \subseteq X$, if, for every $B \subseteq A$, there exists some $C \in \mathcal{K}$ such that $C \cap A = B$.*
- *The Vapnik-Chervonenkis Dimension (in short, VC-dim) of $\mathcal{K}$ is the maximum number d such that $\mathcal{K}$ shatters a set of size d. (If $\mathcal{K}$ shatters sets of unbounded size, we say that its VC-dim is ∞).*

Example: Let X be the unit interval and $\mathcal{K}$ be the collections of all its subintervals whose length is 0.1. I.e., $\mathcal{K} = \{[a, a + 0.1] : 0 \leq a \leq (1 - 0.1)\}$. It is not hard to realize that $\mathcal{K}$ shatters every pair of points in $[0.1, 0.9]$ which are at most 0.1 apart. On the other hand, $\mathcal{K}$ shatters no subset A of the interval whose cardinality exceeds 2. It follows that VC-dim$(\mathcal{K}) = 2$.

We can now state the result of Blumer et. al. (Blumer et al. 89) showing how the VC-dim of a class determines its learnability.

theorem 1 *[(Blumer et al. 89)]*

- *A class $\mathcal{K}$ is PAC-learnable **iff** it has a finite VC-dimension.*
- *If $VC - dim(\mathcal{K}) = d$ then, for every positive ϵ and δ,*

  1. if

$$m \geq \max\left(\frac{4}{\epsilon} \log \frac{2}{\delta}, \frac{8d}{\epsilon} \log \frac{13}{\epsilon}\right)$$

  then, for every probability distribution P over X, the P^m-probability of picking an m-tuple that ϵ-pins down K exceeds $(1 - \delta)$.

  2. On the other hand, if

$$m < \max\left(\frac{1 - \epsilon}{\epsilon} \ln \frac{1}{\delta}, d(1 - 2(\epsilon(1 - \delta) + \delta))\right)$$

  then, there exists a probability distribution P over X, such that the P^m-probability of picking an m-tuple that ϵ-pins down K is less than $(1 - \delta)$.

Note that the upper bound of this theorem guarantees the existing of many ϵ-pinning-down tuples of size linear in the VC-dim of a class and in $\frac{1}{\epsilon}$, for every underlying probability distribution. The lower bound, on the other hand, only states the *existence* of a 'difficult' distribution and does not rule out the possibility that, for some specific distribution, the task of pinning down a class may require fewer sample points. In (Ben-David and Lindenbaum 93) some evidence is provided to show that, for classes of algebraically-defined objects in the Euclidean space, the lower bound above is indeed a close estimate of the minimal size of pinning-down sets relative to the uniform distribution.

Learning and recognition

This section discusses the relation between learning and recognition, and shows that in a proper setting, recognition tasks are equivalent to learning tasks in the sense that an object is recognized (or localized) if some related concept class is PAC learned with a certain prediction power.

We consider recognition processes that are composed of a data collection stage followed by an interpretation stage. In the first stage data features are collected in random locations, independently, and according to fixed distribution. In the second stage the data collected is combined with prior knowledge, and is interpreted, to yield an hypothesis on the identity and pose of the object in the scene. These stages are described in the next two sections.

The data collection stage

In Vision scenarios, information is usually obtained from the observed object's edges in an image, and is usually associated with some location error. Data extraction from images involves many factors including illumination, occlusion, the effect of edge detectors and seems very difficult to model. The simple model, suggested in the following lines, is not claimed to cover all situations in computer vision. It addresses, however, the uncertainty on the observed part of the object and the inaccuracy of the measurements.

We model the uncertainty in the data features available by assuming that the data features are randomly drawn in the neighborhood of the object boundary. Let ∂V_t be the boundary of the instance of the object V, after a transformation t. In the simple case, where only boundary points associated with inaccuracy Δ are available, we assume that they are independently sampled according to a uniform distribution, inside

$$V_t^\Delta = \{ \ r \ | \ \exists s \in \partial V_t \ s.t. \ ||s - r|| < \Delta \}, \qquad (1)$$

to which we refer as either "extended boundary" or "observable object". More complicated data collection models, which include arbitrary but bounded sampling distributions and data features which include boundary slope measurements, are considered in the full version.

The interpretation stage

We refrain from referring to any particular method for inferring the hypothesis. The only assumption taken is that the interpretation stage may draw any hypothesis that is consistent with the data. Let H be the set of possible hypotheses, which, in the model based setting, may contain instances of different objects under different transformations. Then, for M being the data set, the algorithm may draw any hypothesis in $\{h|M \subset h \ ; \ h \in H\}$.

An error measure

We treat all recognition tasks uniformly and consider them successful if a special error measure, defined below, between the true object and the hypothesized one, is guaranteed to be lower a threshold value. For V_t being the true object that is present in the scene and $W_{t'}$ being some hypothesized instance, the error associated with this hypothesis is defined as the normalized difference between the volumes of the corresponding observable objects.

$$E(V_t, W_{t'}) = \frac{Vol(V_t^\Delta \setminus W_{t'}^\Delta)}{Vol(V_t^\Delta)} \qquad (2)$$

This error measure agrees with the intuitive meaning of recognition and localization. High localization accuracy, for example, implies that the boundaries of the true object and the hypothesis are very close, and leads to a small difference between the corresponding extended boundaries. Low localization accuracy, on the other hand, allows larger error.

The uniform recognition accuracy measure may be used to specify recognition success in the more familiar forms, by setting the maximal error, for which the hypotheses is still considered successful. For example, reagarding the *localization task*, one may consider any

distance measure $D(\cdot, \cdot)$ (say, Hausdorff distance,) between two object instance, and denote a localization procedure successful if, for the hypotheses drawn, the distance between the true object V_t and the hypothesis $V_{t'}$ is d_0 or smaller. (The value d_0 may be adjusted arbitrarily according to the localization precision required.) Requiring a recognition accuracy better than

$$e_0 = \max_{t,t' \in T \ ; \ D(V_t, V_{t'}) > d_0} E(V_t, V_t'). \qquad (3)$$

guarantees that no instance of V which is d_0-far from the true instance is drawn as an hypothesis.

Therefore, we are interested in the following question:

How many measurements are needed to guarantee, with a certain confidence $1 - \delta$, that all hypotheses that are at least e_0-far from the true object instance are rejected ?

Learning and recognition

Now, the equivalence between the localization task and PAC learning should be apparent: let $\{V_t|t \in T\}$ be a set of instances associated with one object V and a class of instances T. To every instance from this set, associate a concept identical to the extended boundary.

$$V_t \quad \longleftrightarrow \quad V_t^\Delta \qquad (4)$$

$$\{V_t|t \in T\} \quad \longleftrightarrow \quad C_{T\Delta}(V) = \{V_t^\Delta|t \in T\} \qquad (5)$$

Every data feature extracted from the object boundary provides a (positive) example to the corresponding concept. Learning a concept in $C_{T\Delta}(V)$ with an accuracy better than e_0 means that all concepts in the class, associated with a symmetric difference greater than e_0, are not consistent with the examples. Note however, that according to our data collection model, the density is zero everywhere except inside the concept itself. Assuming further that the distribution is uniform within the extended boundary, implies that the recognition error (2) is also smaller than e_0, and that the recognition task is successful.

While the PAC learnability results usually holds for arbitrary distribution, we will assume that the data features are placed according to a uniform distributions densities. The reason is the need to establish a relation between the recognition accuracy measure $E(V_t, W_{t'})$ and the symmetric difference $V_t^\Delta \Delta W_{t'}^\Delta$, induced by the sampling density. This cannot be achieved by all distributions: Consider for example a distribution that is concentrated in a single point. The learning performance in this case will be excellent as the density weighted symmetric difference and the associated prediction error will be null after one example. The knowledge about the location of the object will, however, be poor because completely different hypotheses can be consistent if they share one point with the true object (either inside or outside).

Inserting the VC-dimension of the concept class $C_{T\Delta}(V) = \{V_t^\Delta|t \in T\}$ into the bound in theorem (1), we may now calculate the number of data features sufficient to guarantee that every consistent hypothesis is e_0-accurate with confidence $1 - \delta$. In the rest of the paper we bound the VC-dimension of one particular class: extended boundaries of perspective projections of 3D objects. We do not refer to particular objects, but just assume that the object belongs to the extremely large class of objects, defined in the next section.

The class of objects considered - Semi-algebraic sets

We shall focus on well behaved geometrical objects - the Semi-Algebraic subsets of $\mathbb{R}^2$ and $\mathbb{R}^3$.

Definition 2 *:   A semi-algebraic open set of degree (k, m) in $\mathbb{R}^n$ is a set that can be represented as a boolean combination of k sets of the form $\{\bar{x} \in \mathbb{R}^n : f_j(\bar{x}) \, Q \, 0\}$ where the functions f_j are real polynomials of maximal degree m, and Q is one of the relations $\leq, =, <$.*

Polynomial objects of modest degrees (e.g. 4) suffice to describe complicated objects and thus provide high representation power (see, e.g. (Taubin and Cooper 92)). The class we consider here is even richer: besides polynomial objects it also contains combinations of them which include, e.g., polygonal objects (which, for k being the number of polygon sides, are semi algebraic sets of degree $(k, 1)$). The family of Semi-Algebraic sets is parametrized, meaning that the class of objects considered is actually not limited.

Localization - The VC-dimension of transformed Semi-Algebraic sets

Our general approach treats both two dimensional and three dimensional semi-algebraic objects and a wide class of transformation. Here, we focus on three dimensional semi-algebraic objects and perspective projection of them, and analyse the class of concepts which are the extended boundary of these projections. We show that the VC-dimension of this class is logarithmic in the complexity of the object, and obeys the assymptotic upper bound

$$B_{3D\Delta}^{project}(V) = 712 \log(km), \qquad (6)$$

thereby providing the parameter needed to determine the number of two dimensional data features (taken from the projected image), required to localize the object with the required precision and confidence. The bound does not depend on the particular object chosen but only on its complexity, as expressed by the number of polynomials that define it, k, and by their degree, m.

The VC-dimension of projected 3D semi-algebraic objects.

We consider the common imaging procedure, which involves projecting the object on an image plane and getting the information from the projection. We assume here that the imaging process is done by a pin-hole camera, which implements a perspective projection and, for our purposes, is a good approximation to common realistic cameras. Furthermore, we follow Kriegman and Ponce approach (Kriegman and Ponce 90) and assume that only sharp edges in the projected image are observable. Such sharp edges in the image may come either from the outline of the object, or from discontinuities of its surface normal that are usually the result of two intersecting polynomial surfaces.

The object instance class
Considering the model-based localization problem, we assume that the object present in the scene is an instance V_t of a known object model V, associated with some unknown but general rigid transformation $t = (\mathbf{R}, \bar{\mathbf{t}})$

$$V_t = \{\bar{s}' = \mathbf{R}\,\bar{s} + \bar{\mathbf{t}} | \bar{s} \in V\} \qquad (7)$$

where both $\bar{s}$ and $\bar{s}'$ are 3D coordinate vectors that describe points in the 3D space, $\bar{\mathbf{t}}$ is a 3D translation vector and $\mathbf{R}$ is a rotation matrix. (Note the following small change in notation: Unlike the description of the general framework, V_t does not describe the object after the full transformation but denotes the object before the projection. Consequently, the extended boundary will be redefined.) To parametrize this transformation, we use the parameter vector $\bar{t} = \{t_1, \ldots, t_9\}$, which includes the translation components and the sines and cosines of the Euler rotation angles of the inverse transformation. The class of 9-tuples which are valid parameters of the rigid transformation is constrained by some equalities between the parameters and is denoted T.

The perspective projection process
Let the optical axis of the pin-hole camera coincide with the z-axis, the image plane be on the $z = 0$ plane, and the focal point be at $\bar{f} = (0, 0, -f)$. One line passes between every point $\bar{s} = (s_x, s_y, s_z)$ in the 3D space and the focal point, and specifies the projection of $\bar{s}$ as its intersection with the image plane. This implies the simple expression for perspective projection of $\bar{s}$: $proj(\bar{s}) = \bar{r} = (r_x, r_y, 0)$.

$$r_x = \frac{f}{s_z + f} s_x \qquad r_y = \frac{f}{s_z + f} s_y. \qquad (8)$$

The contour generators
Clearly, not all points of the object V_t are projected to the visible curves in the image. Points that are projected belong either to the occluding contour or to discontinuities of the surface normal and thus must obey some constraints:

- The projected point may be on the occluding contour but only on one polynomial surface $f_i(s_x, s_y, s_z) = 0$. In this case the viewing direction vector $\bar{s} - \bar{f} = (s_x, s_y, s_z) - (0, 0, -f)$ is tangent to the polynomial surface and perpendicular to the gradient, implying that the following degree-m polynomial constraint, ($m = deg(f_i)$),

$$[\bar{s} - \bar{f}] \cdot \nabla f_i(\bar{s}) = 0. \tag{9}$$

In addition, the projected point $\bar{s}$ is included in the polynomial surface itself, and thus satisfies

$$f_i(\bar{s}) = 0 \tag{10}$$

- The other source for visible contours is the intersection of two polynomial boundaries which create normal discontinuities and are thus visible due to shading, texture, etc. The points on the intersection of the polynomial surfaces $\{f_i(\bar{s}) = 0\}$ and $\{f_j(\bar{s}) = 0\}$ are simply specified by requiring them to satisfy both polynomials. Note that such visible curves may lie, in the projection, within the outline but also on it.

An Algebraic expression for the extended boundary.
By definition, the extended boundary contains all points that are close enough to the perspective projection of some point in the contour generator. Formally, let $G(V_t)$ be the contour generator of the transformed three dimensional object, and $(G(V_t))_p$ be its perspective projection. The extended boundary of this projection, denoted $[(G(V_t))_p]^\Delta$, is given by

$$[(G(V_t))_p]^\Delta = \{\bar{q} = (q_x, q_y, 0) \,| \\ \exists \bar{s} \in G(V_t)\ s.t.\ \|\bar{q} - proj(\bar{s})\| < \Delta\} \tag{11}$$

We would like to know what is the number of random measurements needed, to guarantee with confidence $1 - \delta$ that the distance between the true instance of the object and any hypothesized instance that is consistent with the measurements is smaller than some value. The distance between instances is measured between the corresponding observable objects, that is, as the normalized area difference between the extended boundaries $[(G(V_t))_p]^\Delta$. To find a sufficient number of measurements, we proceed now to bounding the VC dimension of the associated concept class

$$C_{3D}^{project}(V) = \{[(G(V_t))_p]^\Delta \mid t \in T\}. \tag{12}$$

We apply the following technique:

- We assume that some set of points S of cardinality N is shattered by the concept class.

- We observe that every point in S corresponds to a partition of the parameter space into two parts: one of parameters for which the corresponding extended boundary of transformed set includes that point, and another that includes the parameters for which the corresponding extended boundary does not include that point.

- We observe that the N points in S partition the parameter space into connected components, such that all paprameter in the same connected component correspond to extended boundaries that contain the same subset of S.

- We prove that the number of these connected components is polynomial in N implying that the number of subsets $A \subseteq S$ that may be written in the form $A = [(G(V_t))_p]^\Delta \cap S$ is also polynomial.

- In order to shatter the set S, every one of its 2^N subsets should be expressed as $[(G(V_t))_p]^\Delta \cap S$ for some t. Since only polynomial number of subsets can be written in this form, we conclude that this class of extended boundaries cannot shutter arbitrarily large point sets.

Partitioning the parameter space.
The first step in this direction is to find the structure of the parameters space:

Lemma 1 *For any semi algebraic set $V \subseteq \mathbb{R}^3$ of degree (k, m) $(m \geq 2)$, transformed by a 3D rigid transformation, and projected using perspective projection on the image plane, and for every $\bar{x}$ in that image plane, the set of transformation parameters*

$$K_{x_i}^V = \{\bar{t} | x_i \in [(G(V_t))_p]^\Delta\}$$

is also a semi-algebraic set of degree $(k_p = (2k+3)^8(2 \cdot 8m)^{81}, m_p = 0.5(2 \cdot 8m)^8)$ (in the parameter space $\mathbb{R}^9$).

Proof: The proof is based on the theory of quantifier elimination from Logic theory. The parameter set $K_{x_i}^V$ may be written as the truth set of a prenex formula in the coordinates of $\bar{s}$ and the 9 parameters $t_1, \ldots, t_9$ as variables. Recall that $t_1, \ldots, t_9$ are the parameters of the inverse transformation, which transform every point on V_t into a point on V.

$$K_{x_i}^V = \{\bar{t} | \exists \bar{s}\ s.t.\ \bar{s} \in G(V_t) \wedge \|\bar{x}_i - proj(\bar{s})\| < \Delta\} \tag{13}$$

Now, the second condition, $\|\bar{x}_i - proj(\bar{s})\| < \Delta$, does not depend on the transformation and can be easily transformed to a polynomial inequality of second degree in the coordinates of $\bar{s}$. The first condition is more complicated: a point $\bar{s}$ in the contour generator $G(V_t)$ of the transformed object V_t must be either in the transformed intersection of two polynomial surfaces or on the occluding boundary of one transformed polynomial surface.

- To satisfy the first option it suffice that $\bar{t}$ will satisfy two polynomial constraints, such as $f_j(\mathbf{R}'\bar{s} + \mathbf{t}') > 0$ and $f_{j'}(\mathbf{R}'\bar{s} + \mathbf{t}') > 0$, (or $\geq$ or $=$), where f_j and $f_{j'}$ are two of the polynomials that specify V. Considering both the coordinates of $\bar{s}$ and the transformation parameters as variables, these polynomials are of maximal degree of $4m$.

- For the point $\bar{s}$ to be on a smooth occluding contour, the gradient of the transformed polynomial must be orthogonal to the viewing vector $[\bar{s} - \bar{f}]$. The orthogonality is preserved if the coordinate system is changed and therefore we can write this condition as

$$\nabla[f_j(\mathbf{R}'\bar{s} + \mathbf{t}')] \cdot [\mathbf{R}'(\bar{s} - \bar{f}) + \mathbf{t}'] = 0$$

This constraint is polynomial with maximal degree of $8m$.

Therefore, the quantifier free part of the prenex formula (13) depends on $2k$ polynomial sets with a maximal degree of $8m$. By applying well-known algorithm of Collins (Collins 75), the three coordinates of $\bar{s}$ can be eliminated leaving a quantifier free logic formula with $k_p = (2k + 3)^8 (2 \cdot 8m)^{81}$ polynomial sets of maximal degree $m_p = 0.5(2 \cdot 8m)^8$. (The three quadratic constraints relating the sines and cosines of the Euler angles are also imposed.) $\square$

The VC-dimension of the class $C_{3D}^{project}(V)$ is given by the following theorem.

theorem 2 *For every semi algebraic set V of degree (k, m) in $\mathbb{R}^3$,*

$$VCdim(C_{3D}^{project}(V)) = O(\log km)$$

Proof: [sketch] The proof relies on results developed in previous papers. Let $S = \{x_1, \ldots, x_N\}$ be a subset of $\mathbb{R}^2$ that is shattered by the class $C_{3D}^{project}(V)$. The union of boundaries $B_S = \bigcup_{i=1}^{i=N} \partial K_{x_i}^V$ of the semi algebraic parameter sets $\{K_{x_i}^V\}$ divides the parameter space $\mathbb{R}^9$ into connected components.

Milnor's classical theorem (Milnor 64) states that any partition of $\mathbb{R}^n$, that obeys a set of k polynomial inequalities, has at most $\frac{1}{2}(2 + d)^n$ connected components. (d is the total degree $\Sigma_{i=1}^k deg(f_i)$.)

Recall that, by Collins decomposition, each of the parameter sets $K_{x_i}^V$ is specified by $k_p = (2k + 3)^8 (2 \cdot 8m)^{81}$-many polynomial sets of the form $\{\bar{t} | f_j(\bar{t}, x_i) > 0\}$ each of degree $m_p = 0.5(2 \cdot 8m)^8$ or lower. Note that at least one of the functions $f_{ij}(\bar{t}) = f_j(\bar{t}, x_i)$ vanishes on each point of the boundary of $K_{x_i}^V$.

Consider now the product function $G(t) = \prod_{i,j} f_{ij}(t)$. Any connected component of $\mathbb{R}^9 \setminus B_S$ corresponds to a union of one or more connected components of $\{t : G(t) > 0\}$ or of $\{t : G(t) < 0\}$. $G(\bar{t})$ is a $(k_p \, m_p \, N)$-degree polynomial in 9 real variables, and, by our modification to Milnor theorem, the number of connected components of its positive set $\{\bar{t} | G(\bar{t}) > 0\}$ (as well as of its negative set, which is the pos-set of $-G$) is not higher than $(2 + k_p \, m_p \, N)^9$. Therefore any cardinality N of a point set that is shattered must satisfy the following relation

$$2^N \leq 2(2 + k_p \, m_p \, N)^9 \qquad (14)$$

The theorem, as well the assymptotic lower bound (6) follows by a straightforward calculation. $\square$

A straightforward application of the bounds given in (Blumer et al. 89) may now give the number of data features which guarantees that the hypothesized instance is not more than e_0 different from the true instance. More concrete assertions, such as that the localization result is "good enough" follow by specifying the required localization precision, and using (3) to specify e_0.

Conclusion

We analyzed the amount of data required to localize a 3D object from its 2D perspective projection, and obtained a rigorous upper bound on the number of data features required to draw a reliable hypothesis. The analysis was carried independently of the recognition method used, and in a certain sense, independently of the particular objects considered.

The same approach was used to derive the number of data features required to localize instances of 2D objects, associated with Euclidean, Similarity, Affine and Perspective transformation classes. It was also generalized to analyse the general model-based recognition task. Specifically, it was shown that the number of data features required for recognition grows at most logarithmically with the library size (Lindenbaum and Ben-David 94).

References

Blumer, A., A. Ehrenfeucht, D. Haussler and M.K. Warmuth, 1989, "Learnability and The Vapnik-Chervonenkis Dimension", *JACM*, **36**(4), 929-965.

S. Ben-David and M. Lindenbaum, 1993, "Localization vs. Identification of Semi-Algebraic Sets", Proceedings of the 6th ACM Conference on Computational Learning Theory, pp. 327-336.

Collins, G.E., 1975, "Quantifier Elimination for Real Closed Fields by Cylindrical Algebraic Decomposition", Proceedings of the 2nd GI Conf. On Automata Theory and Formal Languages, *Springer Lec. Notes Comp. Sci.* **33**, pp. 515-532.

Goldberg P. and M. Jerrum, 1993, "Bounding the Vapnik-Chervonenkis Dimension of Concept Classes Parametrized by Real Numbers", Proceedings of the 6th ACM Conference on Computational Learning Theory, pp. 361-368.

Grimson, W.E.L., and D.P. Huttenlocher, 1991, "On the Verification of Hypothesized Matches in Model-Based Recognition", *IEEE Trans. on Pattern Analysis and Mach. Intel.*, **PAMI-13**(12), pp. 1201-1213.

Kriegman, D.J. and J. Ponce, 1990, "On Recognizing and Positioning Curved 3D objects from Image Contours", *IEEE Trans. on Pattern Analysis and Mach. Intel.*, **PAMI-12**, pp. 1127-1137.

Lindenbaum, M., 1993, "Bounds on Shape Recognition Performance", submitted.

Lindenbaum, M. and S. Ben-David, 1994 "Applying VC-dimension Analysis to Object Recognition", 3rd European conference on Comp. Vision (to appear).

Milnor, J., 1964, "On the Betti Numbers of Real Varieties", Proc. Amer. Math. Soc. **15**, pp. 275-280.

Taubin, G., and D.B. Cooper, 1992, "2D and 3D Object Recognition and Positioning with Algebraic Invariants and Covariants", in *Symbolic and Numerical Computation for Artificial Intelligence*, B.R. Donald, D. Kapur, and J.L. Mundy, eds.

Planning and Scheduling

Derivation Replay for Partial-Order Planning

Laurie H. Ihrig & Subbarao Kambhampati*
Department of Computer Science and Engineering
Arizona State University, Tempe, AZ 85287-5406
email: laurie.ihrig@asu.edu rao@asu.edu

Abstract

Derivation replay was first proposed by Carbonell as a method of transferring guidance from a previous problem-solving episode to a new one. Subsequent implementations have used state-space planning as the underlying methodology. This paper is motivated by the acknowledged superiority of partial-order (PO) planners in plan generation, and is an attempt to bring derivation replay into the realm of partial-order planning. Here we develop DerSNLP, a framework for doing replay in SNLP, a partial-order plan-space planner, and analyze its relative effectiveness. We will argue that the decoupling of planning (derivation) order and the execution order of plan steps, provided by partial-order planners, enables DerSNLP to exploit the guidance of previous cases in a more efficient and straightforward fashion. We validate our hypothesis through empirical comparisons between DerSNLP and two replay systems based on state-space planners.

Introduction

Case Based Planning involves storing individual instances of planning episodes and using them to tackle new situations. One method of reusing an earlier planning episode is through *derivational analogy* (DA) (Carbonell 1986; Veloso 1992). By this method, a trace of a previous search process is retrieved and replayed in solving a new problem. The decisions that led to a successful solution in the prior case are used to guide the new search process. After its first proposal in (Carbonell 1986), DA has subsequently been found to be of use in many areas, including planning, problem solving, design and automatic programming (Veloso 1992; Mostow 1989; Blumenthal and Porter 1994; Bhansali and Harandi 1991). Much of this work has been done in state-space problem solvers. The aim of the current work is to adapt derivational analogy to partial-order planning. We are motivated by a desire to see whether the known advantages of PO planning over state-space planning in plan generation, (Barrett and Weld 1994; Minton *et al.* 1992), also make the former a more efficient substrate for replay.

*This research is supported in part by National Science Foundation under grant IRI-9210997, and ARPA/Rome Laboratory planning initiative under grant F30602-93-C-0039. Thanks to Manuela Veloso for helpful clarifications regarding Prodigy/Analogy, and to Suresh Katukam and Ed Smith for their comments.

Derivational analogy includes all of the following elements (Veloso 1992): a facility within the base-level planner to generate a trace of the derivation of a problem solution, the indexing and storage of the solution trace in a library of cases, the retrieval of a case in preparation for solving a new problem, and finally, a replay mechanism by which the planner can utilize a previous derivation in a new search process. The storage and retrieval aspects of DA remain the same whether we use plan-space or state-space planners. In particular, solutions to the storage problem such as those proposed in (Veloso 1992) and (Kambhampati 1994) can be used for this purpose. Only the contents of the trace and the details of the replay component depend on the underlying planner. Thus, in the current work, we focus on the automatic generation and replay of the solution trace.

We will start by describing DerSNLP, an implementation of derivation replay within SNLP, a PO planner (McAllester and Rosenblitt 1991; Barrett and Weld 1994). We will then use DerSNLP as a case-study to explore the relative advantages of doing replay within plan-space vs. state-space planners. One of the difficult decisions faced by the replay systems is that of deciding when and where to interleave from-scratch effort with derivation replay (c.f. (Blumenthal and Porter 1994)). In general, there are no domain-independent grounds for making this decision. This makes *eager replay*, i.e., replaying the entire trace before returning to from-scratch planning, the most straightforward strategy. We will show that, for replay systems based on state-space planners, eager replay inhibits effective transfer in problems where the plan-step ordering is critical to the solution. We will argue that the decoupling of planning (derivation) order from execution order of steps, provided by the plan-space planners, allows effective transfer to occur with eager replay in more situations, and thus provides for a more efficient and straightforward replay framework. We will validate this hypothesis by comparing DerSNLP to replay systems implemented on two different state-space planners: NOLIMIT (which was recently the basis for a comprehensive DA implementation in (Veloso 1992)), and TOPI (Barrett and Weld 1994).

DerSNLP: Derivation Replay for SNLP

As we mentioned earlier, derivation replay involves storing traces of previous problem-solving decisions and replaying them to solve similar problems more efficiently. The problem-solving trace that is retained for future replay consists of a sequence of instructions that describe the series of choices made in the original planning episode. Choice points correspond to backtracking points in whatever planning algorithm has been selected. The content of each choice therefore reflects the underlying methodology. For example, a state-space means-ends analysis (MEA) planner such as NOLIMIT (Veloso 1992) makes decisions as to which subgoal to accomplish next, which step to use to achieve the subgoal, as well as when to add an applicable step to the plan.

For SNLP, a search node corresponds to a partly-constructed partially-ordered plan. SNLP makes two types of decisions. An *establishment* decision is a choice as to the method of achieving an open subgoal. A new step may be added to contribute an open condition and a *causal link* formed that links the new contributor to the step that consumes the condition. Alternatively, a causal link may be formed from an existing step.

The second type of decision is a choice as to the method of *resolution* of a *threat* to a causal link. When a causal link is threatened by a possibly intervening step, the conflict may be resolved either by adding a step-ordering [1] or by adding variable binding constraints that remove the threat. Plan refinement proceeds as follows:

1. If there exist conflicts in the current active plan, **Act**, then choose a threat and handle the selected threat by nondeterministically choosing a resolution: either promotion of the step that is threatening the link, demotion of that step, or the addition of variable binding constraints to resolve the conflict, else

2. If there are no threats then choose a condition among **Act**'s open conditions, and nondeterministically select a refinement of **Act** that handles the condition by adding a causal link from an (existing/new) step.

This process terminates when there are no more open conditions and no more threats to the existing causal links.

DerSNLP extends SNLP by including a replay facility. Its output is a trace of the decision process that led to its final solution. Figure 1 contains an example trace produced by DerSNLP while attempting a problem from the logistics transportation domain of (Veloso 1992). This domain involves the movement of packages across locations by various transport devices. The trace corresponds to a simple problem which contains the goal of getting a single package, OB2, to a designated airport, AP1.

The solution trace is annotated with the choices that were made along the path from the root of the search tree to the final plan in the leaf node. Each decision becomes an instruction for a future search process. Instructions contain a high level description of both the decision taken and its basis for justification in the future context. For example, a step addition

<hr>

[1] For an example, consider that the effect of the step, S_k, is clobbering the contribution of P by another step, S_i, as described by a causal link, $S_i \xrightarrow{P} S_j$, and may possibly be ordered in between S_i and S_j. The conflict may then be resolved by *promoting* S_k so that it comes after the threatened link, in other words, by adding a step ordering $S_j < S_k$.

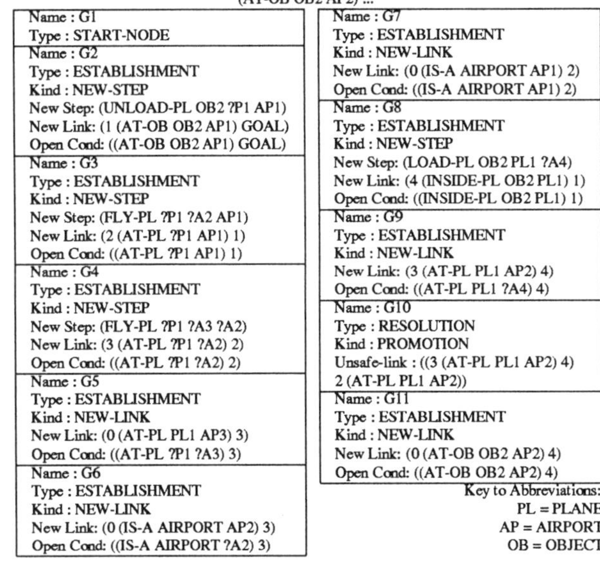

Goal : (AT-OB OB2 AP1)
Initial : ((IS-A AIRPORT AP1) (IS-A AIRPORT AP2))
(IS-A AIRPORT AP3) (AT-PL PL1 AP3)
(AT-OB OB2 AP2) ...

Name : G1 Type : START-NODE	Name : G7 Type : ESTABLISHMENT Kind : NEW-LINK New Link: (0 (IS-A AIRPORT AP1) 2) Open Cond: ((IS-A AIRPORT AP1) 2)
Name : G2 Type : ESTABLISHMENT Kind : NEW-STEP New Step: (UNLOAD-PL OB2 ?P1 AP1) New Link: (1 (AT-OB OB2 AP1) GOAL) Open Cond: ((AT-OB OB2 AP1) GOAL)	Name : G8 Type : ESTABLISHMENT Kind : NEW-STEP New Step: (LOAD-PL OB2 PL1 ?A4) New Link: (4 (INSIDE-PL OB2 PL1) 1) Open Cond: ((INSIDE-PL OB2 PL1) 1)
Name : G3 Type : ESTABLISHMENT Kind : NEW-STEP New Step: (FLY-PL ?P1 ?A2 AP1) New Link: (2 (AT-PL ?P1 AP1) 1) Open Cond: ((AT-PL ?P1 AP1) 1)	Name : G9 Type : ESTABLISHMENT Kind : NEW-LINK New Link: (3 (AT-PL PL1 AP2) 4) Open Cond: ((AT-PL PL1 ?A4) 4)
Name : G4 Type : ESTABLISHMENT Kind : NEW-STEP New Step: (FLY-PL ?P1 ?A3 ?A2) New Link: (3 (AT-PL ?P1 ?A2) 2) Open Cond: ((AT-PL ?P1 ?A2) 2)	Name : G10 Type : RESOLUTION Kind : PROMOTION Unsafe-link : ((3 (AT-PL PL1 AP2) 4) 2 (AT-PL PL1 AP2))
Name : G5 Type : ESTABLISHMENT Kind : NEW-LINK New Link: (0 (AT-PL PL1 AP3) 3) Open Cond: ((AT-PL ?P1 ?A3) 3)	Name : G11 Type : ESTABLISHMENT Kind : NEW-LINK New Link: (0 (AT-OB OB2 AP2) 4) Open Cond: ((AT-OB OB2 AP2) 4)
Name : G6 Type : ESTABLISHMENT Kind : NEW-LINK New Link: (0 (IS-A AIRPORT AP2) 3) Open Cond: ((IS-A AIRPORT ?A2) 3)	Key to Abbreviations: PL = PLANE AP = AIRPORT OB = OBJECT

Final Plan: (FLY-PL PL1 AP3 AP2) Created 3
(LOAD-PL OB2 PL1 AP2) Created 4
(FLY-PL PL1 AP2 AP1) Created 2
(UNLOAD-PL OB2 PL1 AP1) Created 1
Ordering of Steps: ((4 < 2) (3 < 4) (4 < 1) (3 < 2) (2 < 1))

Figure 1: An Example Solution Trace for DerSNLP

is valid in the context of the new active plan if the condition that it previously achieved is also an open condition in the new plan and, secondly, if the action that was taken earlier in achieving this condition is consistent with the new plan's constraints on variable bindings. A threat resolution choice is justified if steps added through replay result in a similar threat in the new active plan, and if the prescribed method of resolution (promotion/demotion/separation) is consistent with that plan.

DerSNLP also contains a mechanism for replay of a previous derivation. Along with the new problem description, it receives as input a small set of cases. It is assumed that these cases are retrieved from the case library, and correspond to previously solved problems that have goals in common with the new problem. Replay is called from the `PlanRefinement` procedure at the point where an open condition is to be handled (See Figure 2). The set of guiding cases (**GCs**) is searched for one that contains that condition as a top level goal. If a candidate is found its solution trace is passed to the `Replay` procedure, outlined in Figure 2. The previous trace may correspond to more than one open condition.

DerSNLP's default replay strategy is *eager* in that the full trace is visited during a single call to `Replay`. This avoids the decision of how to interleave the replay of multiple cases, as well as how to interleave replay with from-scratch planning, both decisions that must be faced by NOLIMIT (Veloso 1992). It is our contention that interleaving is not as important for replay in a plan-space framework. Each instruction in the trace is therefore visited in succession.

The replay process must validate each instruction contained

PROCEDURE `PlanRefinement` (GCs, Act): **Plans**
1. IF there is an unsafe link in **Act**, THEN
    choose *t* from **Act**'s unsafe links, and
    RETURN `HandleUnsafe` (*t*, **Act**)
2. ELSE, pick a subgoal *o* from the list of open conditions
3.   IF `GetCase` (*o*,**GCs**,**Act**) returns a candidate *c*, THEN
4.   IF `Replay` (*c*, **Act**) returns a plan, return this plan only
5.   ELSE, RETURN `HandleOpen` (*o*, **Act**)

PROCEDURE `Replay` (Instrn, Act):**Plan**
1. IF null Instrn, THEN
    RETURN **Act**, ELSE
2. SelectedRefinement:= `ValidateInstrn` (Instrn, **Act**)
3. IF SelectedRefinement, THEN
    RETURN `Replay` (Next(Instrn), SelectedRefinement)
4. ELSE, RETURN `Replay` (Next(Instrn), **Act**)

PROCEDURE `ValidateInstrn` (Instrn, Act):**Plan**
1. IF Instrn is of type Establishment, THEN
2.   IF OpenCondOf (Instrn) $\in$ OpenCondsOf (**Act**), THEN
      ActRefinements:=`HandleOpen`(**Act**, OpenCond)
3.   ELSE, IF Instrn is of type ThreatResolution, THEN
4.   IF UnsafeLinkOf (Instrn) $\in$ UnsafeLinksOf(**Act**), THEN
      ActRefinements:=`HandleUnsafe` (**Act**, UnsafeLink)
5. SelectedRefinement:=
      `FindMatch` (DecisionOf (Instrn), ActRefinements)
6. IF SelectedRefinement, THEN
    push its siblings onto SearchQueue, and
    RETURN SelectedRefinement
7. ELSE RETURN FALSE

Figure 2: Outline of DerSNLP's replay procedures

in the old trace before transferring its guidance. Replay calls `ValidateInstrn` to justify an instruction in the context of the current active plan, **Act** (See Figure 2). Consider as an example the trace contained in Figure 1 and suppose that this trace is being replayed for a second problem in which there is an additional package, OB3, which is also to be transported to the same airport. At the beginning of the replay episode, **Act** contains two open conditions: (AT-OB OB2 AP1) and (AT-OB OB3 AP1). The first instruction to be replayed is of type establishment. It prescribes a new action, and it is annotated with the subgoal that step achieves. The validation process starts by matching the open condition of the instruction against the open conditions of **Act** [2]. Since (AT-OB OB2 AP1) is also open in the current active plan, the validation procedure goes on to generate the children of **Act** which also establish that condition by adding a new step. It then attempts to match the high level description of the step contained in the instruction, i.e., (UNLOAD-PL OB2 ?P1 AP1), to one of these plan refinements. `ValidateInstrn` returns the plan refinement that corresponds to the prescribed choice. Siblings of this plan are added to the open list of the new search process.

In our eager replay strategy, control is shifted to the sequence of instructions in the previous trace. It is this

---

[2]Conditions are matched based on an object mapping formed during retrieval of a previous case. Objects in the old goal condition are mapped into their corresponding objects in the new similar goal.

sequence that determines the order in which conditions are solved and threats are resolved. Decisions in the trace that are not justified are skipped. The output of the `Replay` procedure is a plan which incorporates all of the prescribed refinements that are valid in the new context. The search process continues with this plan as the new active node.

The plan that is returned by the `Replay` procedure may still contain open conditions, either because a prior decision that was taken in solving a subgoal is not valid in the new context, or because there are top level goals that are not covered by the previous trace. For example, if the trace in Figure 1 is replayed for a problem in which the initial location of the airplane is changed, instruction G5 is not valid and must be skipped, and the condition it establishes is left open. Further planning effort is then needed to achieve this unestablished goal. Moreover, if the trace is replayed for a problem in which there are extra top level goals that are not in the previous problem, then these goals will also be left open.

In contrast to state-space planners, PO planners with their least-commitment strategy are more flexible as to the order of derivation of plan steps. If extra goals require steps that have to be interleaved into the plan that is produced through a replay episode, these steps can be added after the full trace is replayed. As an example, suppose again that the trace contained in Figure 1 is replayed for the problem that requires the additional goal, (AT-OB OB3 AP1), and OB3 is initially on the old route taken by the airplane. DerSNLP can further refine the plan that results from replaying the trace by adding only the steps needed to load and unload the extra package. This is not possible if replay is based on a state-space planner. In the next section, we discuss this point in greater detail.

Advantages of Basing Replay on a PO Planner

In this section, we will compare the DerSNLP algorithm to replay implementations on state-space planners (and problem solvers) (Veloso 1992; Blumenthal and Porter 1994). State-space planners refine plans by adding steps either only to the end, or only to the beginning, of the already existing operator sequence. This means that when step order is critical to the success of the plan, steps must be added to the plan according to their execution order. When replay is based on a state-space planner and step order is critical, eager replay may not allow for effective transfer. Consider our simple problem from the logistics transportation domain contained in Figure 1. Suppose that the problem was previously solved by a state-space planner. Suppose further that this case is replayed in solving a problem of transporting an additional package that is located somewhere along the plane's route. Further planning effort is needed to add steps to load and unload the extra package. Since steps have to be added in their order of execution, replay will have to be interrupted at the right place in order to add these additional steps. However, the optimal point in the derivation for inserting the new steps depends on the problem description, since it will depend on where the new package is located on the old route. In general, there are no domain-independent grounds for deciding when and where the from-scratch problem-solving effort should be interleaved with replay. The more straightforward *eager* replay strategy, on the other hand, will tend to mislead the planner into wrong paths, eventually making it backtrack or find inoptimal plans. The early work on derivation replay that is rooted in state-space planning has therefore been forced to focus a good deal of attention on the problem of determining *when* to plan for additional goals (Blumenthal and Porter 1994). It is not an easy matter to determine at what point in the derivation to stop in order to insert further choices corresponding to extra goals.

For the PO planner, there is less need to make the difficult decision as to when to interrupt replay. In particular, since the PO planners decouple derivation (planning) order of plan steps from their execution order, an eager replay strategy will not mislead them as much. This makes for a more efficient and straightforward replay of the trace, since control can be solely in the hands of the previous search process for the duration of the replay episode.

To summarize, eager replay is the most straightforward way of combining replay and from-scratch efforts. State-space planners tend to be misled by eager replay in situations where step order is critical for a plan's success. DerSNLP, based on a partial-order planning framework, does not suffer from this problem. This leads us to the hypothesis that plan-space planners will exhibit greater performance improvements when using eager replay.[3] The next section provides an empirical evaluation of this hypothesis.

Empirical Evaluation

An empirical analysis was conducted in order to test our hypothesis regarding the relative effectiveness of eager replay for PO planners. To do this we chose two state-space planners, TOPI (Barrett and Weld 1994) and NOLIMIT (Veloso 1992). We implemented eager replay on these planners and compared their performance with DerSNLP. TOPI does simple backward search in the space of states, adding steps to the plan in reverse order of execution. NOLIMIT is a version of PRODIGY which was the basis of the DA system reported in (Veloso 1992). Like PRODIGY and STRIPS, it uses means-ends analysis, attempting goals by backward-chaining from the goal state. Applicable operators (operators whose preconditions are true in the current state) are added to the end of the plan and the current state is advanced appropriately. Unlike STRIPS, NOLIMIT can defer step addition in favor of further subgoaling. It does this by adding relevant operators to a list of potential operators before actual placement in the plan.

To facilitate fair comparisons, the three planning methods, SNLP, TOPI, and NOLIMIT, were (re)implemented on the same substrate. A replay mechanism was added to each planner which follows an eager replay strategy. With this strategy the search process is interrupted to replay the entire derivation trace before returning to from-scratch planning.

---

[3]Even DerSNLP may be misled by eager replay in some cases. For example, the previous case may have achieved one of the goals using some step s_1 and the new problem contains a goal g_n which cannot be achieved in the presence of s_1. However, in such cases, state-space planners will also be misdirected. Thus our hypothesis is only that DerSNLP is *less likely* to be misled (and thus more likely to exploit the previous case) by eager replay.

Domains

ART-MD-NS domain: Experiments were run on problems drawn from two domains. The first was the artificial domain, ART-MD-NS, originally described in (Barrett and Weld 1994) and shown in the table below:

ART-MD-NS ($D^m S^2$):
A_i^1 $\underline{precond}: I_i$ $\underline{add}: P_i$ $\underline{delete}: \{I_j \mid j < i\})$
A_i^2 $\underline{precond}: P_i$ $\underline{add}: G_i$ $\underline{delete}: \{I_j \mid \forall j\} \cup \{P_j \mid j < i\})$

Conjunctive goals from this domain are *nonserializable* in that they cannot be achieved without interleaving subplans for the individual conjuncts. For example, consider the problem that contains the conjunctive goal $G_1 \wedge G_2$. The subplan for achieving this goal would be: $A_1^1 \to A_2^1 \to A_1^2 \to A_2^2$. This plan has to be interleaved with steps to solve the additional goal G_3. The plan for the new conjunctive goal $G_1 \wedge G_2 \wedge G_3$ is $A_1^1 \to A_2^1 \to A_3^1 \to A_1^2 \to A_2^2 \to A_3^2$.

Logistics Transportation Domain: The logistics transportation domain of (Veloso 1992) was adopted for the second set of experiments. Initial conditions of each problem represented the location of various transport devices (one airplane and three trucks) over three cities, each city containing an airport and a post office. Four packages were randomly distributed over airports. So as to make step order critical, problems were chosen from this domain to contain subgoals that interact. Problems represent the task of getting one or more packages to a single designated airport.

Whereas each problem in ART-MD-NS has a unique solution, in the logistics domain there are many possible solutions varying in length. However, optimal (shortest) solutions can only be found by interleaving plans for individual goals. This difference has an important ramification on the way eager replay misleads state-space planners in these domains. Specifically, in the ART-MD-NS domain, state-space planners will have to necessarily backtrack from the path prescribed by eager replay to find a solution. In the logistics domain, they can sometimes avoid backtracking by continuing in the replayed path, but will find inoptimal plans in such cases.

Testing

Each experiment consisted of a single run in which problems were attempted in four phases. Goals were randomly selected for each problem, and, in the case of the logistics domain, the initial state was also randomly varied between problems. Each phase corresponded to a set of 30 problems. Problem size was increased by one goal for each phase. All the planners used a depth-first strategy in ART-MD-NS. To decrease overall running times in the logistics domain, the planners used a best-first strategy (with a heuristic that biases the planner towards the replayed path).

A library of cases was formed over the entire run. Each time a problem was attempted, the library was searched for a previous case that was *similar* (see below). If one was found, the new problem was run both in scratch and replay mode, and the problem became part of the 30 problem set for that phase. If there was no previous case that applied, the problem was merely added to the library.

Case retrieval was based on a primitive similarity metric. For one-goal problems, a case was selected from the same set

| Phase | ART-MD-NS (*depth-first, CPU limit: 100sec*) | | | | | | Logistics (*best-first, CPU limit: 550sec*) | | | |
| | DerSNLP | | DerTOPI | | DerNOLIMIT | | DerSNLP | | DerTOPI | |
	replay	scratch	replay	scratch	replay	scratch	replay	scratch	replay	scratch
One Goal										
%Solved	100%	100%	100%	100%	100%	100%	100% (3.5)	100% (3.5)	100% (5.0)	100% (3.5)
nodes	30	90	30	60	30	120	617	946	46	507
time(sec)	.73	.68	.45	.47	.63	2.5	15	19	11	49
Two Goal										
% Solved	100%	100%	100%	100%	100%	100%	100% (5.8)	100% (5.8)	97% (6.2)	63% (5.6)
nodes	257	317	180	184	347	296	1571	2371	15824	8463
time(sec)	2	2	5	4	8	12	50	51	6216	3999
Three Goal										
% Solved	100%	100%	100%	100%	100%	100%	100% (7.9)	100% (7.9)	0%	0%
nodes	395	679	549	462	1132	662	6086	7400	-	-
time(sec)	7	4	16	11	34	34	230	262	-	-
Four Goal										
% Solved	100%	100%	100%	100%	100%	100%	100% (10.0)	100% (10.0)	0%	0%
nodes	577	1204	1715	1310	5324	1533	9864	24412	-	-
time(sec)	35	43	227	96	368	100	497	1264	-	-

Table 1: Performance statistics in ART-MD-NS and Logistics Transportation Domain (Average solution length is shown in parentheses next to %Solved for the logistics domain only)

of one-goal problems that had accumulated during the first phase. A previous case was judged as sufficiently similar to the problem at hand to be considered for replay if the goals matched. For later phases, corresponding to multi-goal problems, cases were retrieved from the previous phase. Cases were chosen so as to have all but one of the goals matching. Since the retrieved plans need to be extended to solve the new problems in all the multi-goal phases, we would expect the relative effects of eager replay on PO vs. state-space planning to be apparent in these phases.

Results

The results of testing are shown in Tables 1 and 2. Each table entry represents cumulative results obtained from the sequence of 30 problems corresponding to one phase of the run. The first row of Table 1 shows the percentage of problems correctly solved within the time limit (100 seconds for the ART-MD-NS domain, and 550 seconds for the logistics transportation domain). The average solution length is shown in parentheses for the logistics domain (Solution length was omitted in ART-MD-NS since all the problems have unique solutions.) The subsequent rows of Table 1 contain the total number of search nodes visited for all of the 30 test problems, and the total CPU time. DerSNLP was able to solve as many or more of the multi-goal problems than the two state-space planners both in from-scratch and replay modes, and did so in less time. Our implementation of DerNOLIMIT was not able to solve any of the multi-goal problems in the logistics domain within the time limit, and this column is therefore omitted from the table.

In ART-MD-NS domain, replay resulted in performance improvements for DerSNLP which increased with problem size (See Table 1). Comparative improvements with replay were not found for the two state-space planners in the multi-goal phases. In the logistics domain, not only did DerTOPI fail to improve performance through replay, it also experienced an increase in average solution length. In contrast, replay in DerSNLP led to performance improvements (without increas-

ing the solution length). These results are consistent with our hypothesis that state-space planners will be misled by eager replay when step order is critical.

Table 2 reports three different measures that indicate the effectiveness of replay. The first is the percentage of *sequenced* replay. Replay of a trace is judged to be *sequenced* with the new search process if the search path that is obtained through guidance from the previous trace is extended by further planning effort to solve the new problem. Sequenced replay is indicated when all of the plan-refinements created through replay of a previous trace appear on the search path that leads to the final solution. The percentage of sequenced replay therefore indicates the percentage of problems for which replay guides the new search directly down a path to the solution. When replay is not sequenced, search is directed down the wrong path and replay may actually increase search time.

For the state-space planners, replay was entirely nonsequenced for multi-goal problems in either domain. Replay for the PO planner was entirely sequenced in the ART-MD-NS domain (See Table 2). In the logistics domain, the PO planner also experienced some nonsequenced replay, but less than the state-space planner in the multi-goal phase. There are two reasons for the non-sequenced replay shown by DerSNLP in the logistics domain. First, unlike ART-MD-NS, where all the problems had the same initial state, in the logistics domain, the initial conditions were randomly varied. Since our primitive similarity metric did not consider these initial state differences, this meant that replayed cases were less similar in this domain. Second, the best-first search strategy used in the logistics domain tends to compete against replay, directing the planner away from the replayed path when the rank of the replayed path is sufficiently high. This in turn reduces the percentage of sequenced replay.

The efficiency of replay for the PO planner is also indicated by the two other measures contained in the final two rows of Table 2. These are the percentage of plan-refinements on the final solution path that were formed through guidance

Phase	ART-MD-NS			Logistics	
	DerSNLP	DerTOPI	DerNOLIMIT	DerSNLP	DerTOPI
One Goal					
% Seq	100%	100%	100%	93%	100%
% Der	100%	100%	100%	63%	99%
% Rep	100%	100%	100%	93%	100%
Two Goal					
% Seq	100%	0%	0%	83%	0%
% Der	32%	14%	13%	32%	24%
% Rep	100%	28%	25%	84%	37%
Three Goal					
% Seq	100%	0%	0%	47%	-
% Der	53%	14%	25%	34%	-
% Rep	100%	22%	38%	59%	-
Four Goal					
% Seq	100%	0%	0%	67%	-
% Der	65%	18%	31%	51%	-
% Rep	100%	24%	42%	78%	-

Table 2: Measures of Effectiveness of Replay

from replay (% Der), and the percentage of the total number of plans created through replay that remained in the final solution path (% Rep). The PO planner did better than the other two according to these measures in every phase in which multi-goal problems were solved, supporting our hypothesis regarding the relative effectiveness of eager replay in plan-space as opposed to state-space planning.

Related Work

Previous research in DA which is rooted in state-space planning has demonstrated significant performance improvements with replay (Veloso 1992). In contrast, our experiments show rather poor replay performance on the part of the state-space planners for the more complex problems. We believe the main reason for this may be the strong presence of interacting goals in our multi-goal problems, coupled with the fact that we used vanilla planning algorithms without any sophisticated backtracking strategies or pruning techniques (Veloso 1992). While our experiments used an eager-replay strategy, work by Blumenthal (Blumenthal and Porter 1994) provides heuristic strategies aimed at interleaving planning and replay effort. However, it is our contention that the shift to PO planning obviates to a large extent the need for interleaving. Finally, our conclusions regarding the advantages of PO planning in replay also complement the recent results regarding its advantages in reuse (Kambhampati and Chen 1993).

Conclusion

In this paper, we described DerSNLP, a framework for doing derivation replay within SNLP, a partial-order planner. We then compared DerSNLP with replay systems for state-space planners. We started by arguing that since there are no domain-independent grounds for deciding when and how to interleave replay with from-scratch planning, eager replay is the most straightforward way of combining replay with from-scratch effort. We then showed that eager replay tends to mislead state-space planners in situations where step order is critical to the success of a plan. In contrast, DerSNLP, which is based on a partial-order planning framework, and thus decouples derivation (planning) order of plan steps from their execution order, does not suffer from this problem. Thus, DerSNLP is more likely to be able to exploit previous cases using eager replay than replay systems based on state-space planners. We supported this hypothesis with the help of empirical comparisons of DerSNLP with two different state-space replay systems, and across two different domains. Our future work will aim to explore the impact of possible variations within plan-space planning algorithms on the efficiency of replay.

References

Barrett, A. and Weld, D. 1994. Partial order planning: evaluating possible efficience gains. *Artificial Intelligence* 67(1).

Bhansali, S. and Harandi, M. 1991. Synthesizing unix shell scripts using derivational analogy: an empirical assessment. In *Proceedings AAAI-91*.

Blumenthal, B. and Porter, B. 1994. Analysis and empirical studies of derivational analogy. *Artificial Intelligence*. Forthcoming.

Carbonell, J. 1986. Derivational analogy: A theory of reconstructive problem solving and expertise acquisition. In Michalski, Ryszard; Carbonell, Jaime; and Mitchell, Tom M., editors 1986, *Machine Learning: an Artificial Intelligence approach: Volume 2*. Morgan-Kaufman.

Kambhampati, S. and Chen, J. 1993. Relative utility of ebg based plan reuse in partial ordering vs total ordering planning. In *Proceedings AAAI-93*. 514--519. Washington, D.C.

Kambhampati, S. 1994. Exploiting causal structure to control retrieval and refitting during plan reuse. *Computational Intelligence Journal* 10(2).

McAllester, D. and Rosenblitt, D 1991. Systematic nonlinear planning. In *Proceedings AAAI-91*. 634--639.

Minton, S.; Drummond, M.; Bresina, J.; and Philips, A 1992. Total order vs partial order planning: factors influencing performance. In *Proceedings KR-92*.

Mostow, J. 1989. Automated replay of design plans: Some issues in derivational analogy. *Artificial Intelligence* 40:119--184.

Veloso, M. 1992. *Learning by analogical reasoning in general problem solving*. Ph.D. Dissertation, Carnegie-Mellon University.

Tractable Planning with State Variables
by Exploiting Structural Restrictions

Peter Jonsson and Christer Bäckström[1]
Department of Computer and Information Science
Linköping University, S-581 83 Linköping, Sweden
email: {petej,cba}@ida.liu.se
phone: +46 13 282429
fax: +46 13 282606

Abstract

So far, tractable planning problems reported in the literature have been defined by syntactical restrictions. To better exploit the inherent structure in problems, however, it is probably necessary to study also structural restrictions on the state-transition graph. Such restrictions are typically computationally hard to test, though, since this graph is of exponential size. Hence, we take an intermediate approach, using a state-variable model for planning and restricting the state-transition graph implicitly by restricting the transition graph for each state variable in isolation. We identify three such restrictions which are tractable to test and we present a planning algorithm which is correct and runs in polynomial time under these restrictions.

Introduction

Many planning problems in manufacturing and process industry are believed to be highly structured, thus allowing for efficient planning if exploiting this structure. However, a 'blind' domain-independent planner will most likely go on tour in an exponential search space even for tractable problems. Although heuristics may help a lot, they are often not based on a sufficiently thorough understanding of the underlying problem structure to guarantee efficiency and correctness. Further, we believe that if having such a deep understanding of the problem structure, it is better to use other methods than heuristics.

Some tractability results for planning have been reported in the literature lately (Bäckström & Klein 1991; Bäckström & Nebel 1993; Bylander 1991; Erol, Nau, & Subrahmanian 1992). However, apart from being very restricted, they are all based on essentially syntactic restrictions on the set of operators. Syntactic restrictions are very appealing to study, since they are typically easy to define and not very costly to test.

However, to gain any deeper insight into what makes planning problems hard and easy respectively probably require that we study the structure of the problem, in particular the state-transition graph induced by the operators. To some extent, syntactic restrictions allow us this since they undoubtedly have implications for what this graph looks like. However, their value for this purpose seems somewhat limited since many properties that are easy to express as explicit structural restrictions would require horrendous syntactical equivalents. Putting explicit restrictions on the state-transition graph must be done with great care, however. This graph is typically of size exponential in the size of the planning problem instance, making it extremely costly to test arbitrary properties. In this paper, we take an intermediate approach. We adopt the state-variable model SAS⁺ (Bäckström & Nebel 1993) and define restrictions not on the whole state-transition graph, but on the domain-transition graph for each state variable in isolation. This is less costly since each such graph is only of polynomial size. Although not being a substitute for restrictions on the whole state-transition graph, many interesting and useful properties of this graph can be indirectly exploited. In particular, we identify three structural restrictions which makes planning tractable and which properly generalize previously studied tractable SAS⁺ problems (Bäckström & Klein 1991; Bäckström & Nebel 1993). We present an algorithm for generating optimal plans under our restrictions. Despite being structural, our restrictions can be tested in polynomial time. Further, note that this approach would not be very useful for a planning formalism based on propositional atoms, since the resulting two-vertex domain-transition graphs would not allow for very interesting structure to exploit.

The SAS⁺ Formalism

We use the SAS⁺ formalism (Bäckström & Klein 1991; Bäckström & Nebel 1993), which is a variant of propositional STRIPS, generalizing the atoms to multi-valued state variables. Furthermore, what is called a precondition in STRIPS is here divided into

---

[1]This research was sponsored by *the Swedish Research Council for the Engineering Sciences (TFR)* under grants Dnr. 92-143 and Dnr. 93-00291.

"

two conditions, the precondition and the prevailcondition. Variables which are required and changed by an operator go into the precondition and those which remain unchanged, but are required, go into the prevailcondition.[2] We briefly recapitulate the SAS^+ formalism below, referring to Bäckström and Nebel (Bäckström & Nebel 1993) for further explanation. We follow their presentation, except for replacing the variable indices by variables and some other minor changes.

Definition 1 *An instance of the SAS^+ planning problem is given by a tuple $\Pi = \langle \mathcal{V}, \mathcal{O}, s_0, s_* \rangle$ with components defined as follows:*

- *$\mathcal{V} = \{v_1, \ldots, v_m\}$ is a set of **state variables**. Each variable $v \in \mathcal{V}$ has an associated **domain** $\mathcal{D}_v$, which implicitly defines an **extended domain** $\mathcal{D}_v^+ = \mathcal{D}_v \cup \{u\}$, where u denotes the **undefined value**. Further, the **total state space** $\mathcal{S} = \mathcal{D}_{v_1} \times \ldots \times \mathcal{D}_{v_m}$ and the **partial state space** $\mathcal{S}^+ = \mathcal{D}_{v_1}^+ \times \ldots \times \mathcal{D}_{v_m}^+$ are implicitly defined. We write $s[v]$ to denote the value of the variable v in a state s.*

- *$\mathcal{O}$ is a set of **operators** of the form $\langle b, e, f \rangle$, where $b, e, f \in \mathcal{S}^+$ denote the **pre-, post- and prevailcondition** respectively. If $o = \langle b, e, f \rangle$ is a SAS^+ operator, we write $b(o)$, $e(o)$ and $f(o)$ to denote b, e and f respectively. $\mathcal{O}$ is subject to the following two restrictions*
  - **(R1)** *for all $o \in \mathcal{O}$ and $v \in \mathcal{V}$ if $b(o)[v] \neq u$, then $b(o)[v] \neq e(o)[v] \neq u$,*
  - **(R2)** *for all $o \in \mathcal{O}$ and $v \in \mathcal{V}$, $e(o)[v] = u$ or $f(o)[v] = u$.*

- *$s_0 \in \mathcal{S}^+$ and $s_* \in \mathcal{S}^+$ denote the **initial state** and **goal state** respectively.*

We write $s \sqsubseteq t$ if the state s is subsumed (or satisfied) by state t, ie. if $s[v] = u$ or $s[v] = t[v]$. We extend this notion to whole states, defining

$$s \sqsubseteq t \quad \text{iff} \quad \text{for all } v \in \mathcal{V}, s[v] = u \text{ or } s[v] = t[v].$$

*$Seqs(\mathcal{O})$ denotes the set of operator sequences over $\mathcal{O}$ and the members of $Seqs(\mathcal{O})$ are called **plans**. Given two states $s, t \in \mathcal{S}^+$, we define for all $v \in \mathcal{V}$,*

$$(s \oplus t)[v] = \begin{cases} t[v] & \text{if } t[v] \neq u, \\ s[v] & \text{otherwise.} \end{cases}$$

The ternary relation $Valid \subseteq Seqs(\mathcal{O}) \times \mathcal{S}^+ \times \mathcal{S}^+$ is defined recursively s.t. for arbitrary operator sequence $\langle o_1, \ldots, o_n \rangle \in Seqs(\mathcal{O})$ and arbitrary states $s, t \in \mathcal{S}^+$, $Valid(\langle o_1, \ldots, o_n \rangle, s, t)$ iff either

1. $n = 0$ and $t \sqsubseteq s$ or

2. $n > 0$, $b(o_1) \sqsubseteq s$, $f(o_1) \sqsubseteq s$ and $Valid(\langle o_2, \ldots, o_n \rangle, (s \oplus e(o_1)), t)$.

*Finally, a plan $\langle o_1, \ldots, o_n \rangle \in Seqs(\mathcal{O})$ **solves** Π iff $Valid(\langle o_1, \ldots, o_n \rangle, s_0, s_*)$.*

---

[2] Drummond & Currie (1988) make the same distinction.

To define partially ordered plans, we must introduce the concept of *actions*, ie. instances of operators. Given an action a, $type(a)$ denotes the operator that a instantiates. Furthermore, given a set of actions $\mathcal{A}$, we define $type(\mathcal{A}) = \{type(a) \mid a \in \mathcal{A}\}$ and given a sequence $\alpha = \langle a_1, \ldots, a_n \rangle$ of actions, $type(\alpha)$ denotes the operator sequence $\langle type(a_1), \ldots, type(a_n) \rangle$.

Definition 2 *A **partial-order plan** is a tuple $\langle \mathcal{A}, \prec \rangle$ where $\mathcal{A}$ is a set of actions, ie. instances of operators, and $\prec$ is a strict partial order on $\mathcal{A}$. A partial-order plan $\langle \mathcal{A}, \prec \rangle$ solves a SAS^+ instance Π iff $\langle type(a_1), \ldots, type(a_n) \rangle$ solves Π for each topological sort $\langle a_1, \ldots, a_n \rangle$ of $\langle \mathcal{A}, \prec \rangle$.*

Further, given a set of actions $\mathcal{A}$ over $\mathcal{O}$, and a variable $v \in \mathcal{V}$, we define $\mathcal{A}[v] = \{a \in \mathcal{A} \mid e(a)[v] \neq u\}$, ie. the set of all actions in $\mathcal{A}$ affecting v.

Structural Restrictions

In this section we will define three structural restrictions (I, A and O) on the state-transition graph, or, rather, on the domain-transition graphs for each state variable in isolation. We must first define some other concepts, however. Most of these concepts are straightforward, possibly excepting the set of requestable values, which plays an important role for the planning algorithm in the following section. Unary operators is one of the restrictions considered by Bäckström and Nebel (1993), but the others are believed novel. For the definitions below, let $\Pi = \langle \mathcal{V}, \mathcal{O}, s_0, s_* \rangle$ be a SAS^+ instance.

Definition 3 *An operator $o \in \mathcal{O}$ is **unary** iff there is exactly one $v \in \mathcal{V}$ s.t. $e(o)[v] \neq u$.*

A value $x \in \mathcal{D}_v$ where $x \neq u$ for some variable $v \in \mathcal{V}$ is said to be *requestable* if there exists some action $o \in \mathcal{O}$ such that o needs x in order to be executed.

Definition 4 *For each $v \in \mathcal{V}$ and $\mathcal{O}' \subseteq \mathcal{O}$, the set $\mathcal{R}_v^{\mathcal{O}'}$ of **requestable values** for $\mathcal{O}'$ is defined as*

$$\begin{aligned} \mathcal{R}_v^{\mathcal{O}'} = \ & \{f(o)[v] \mid o \in \mathcal{O}'\} \cup \\ & \{b(o)[v], e(o)[v] \mid o \in \mathcal{O}' \text{ and } o \text{ non-unary}\} \\ & -\{u\}. \end{aligned}$$

Similarly, for a set $\mathcal{A}$ of actions over $\mathcal{O}$, we define $\mathcal{R}_v^{\mathcal{A}} = \mathcal{R}_v^{type(\mathcal{A})}$.

Obviously, $\mathcal{R}_v^{\mathcal{O}} \subseteq \mathcal{D}_v$ for all $v \in \mathcal{V}$. For each state variable domain, we further define the graph of possible transitions for this domain, without taking the other domains into account, and the reachability graph for arbitrary subsets of the domain.

Definition 5 *For each $v \in \mathcal{V}$, we define the corresponding **domain transition graph** G_v as a directed labelled graph $G_v = \langle \mathcal{D}_v^+, \mathcal{T}_v \rangle$ with vertex set $\mathcal{D}_v^+$ and arc set $\mathcal{T}_v$ s.t. for all $x, y \in \mathcal{D}_v^+$ and $o \in \mathcal{O}$, $\langle x, o, y \rangle \in \mathcal{T}_v$ iff $b(o)[v] = x$ and $e(o)[v] = y \neq u$. Further, for* *each $X \subseteq \mathcal{D}_v^+$ we define the **reachability graph** for X as a directed graph $G_v^X = \langle X, \mathcal{T}_X \rangle$ with vertex set X and arc set $\mathcal{T}_X$ s.t. for all $x, y \in X$, $\langle x, y \rangle \in \mathcal{T}_X$ iff there is a path from x to y in G_v.*

Alternatively, G_v^X can be viewed as the restriction to $X \subseteq \mathcal{D}_v^+$ of the transitive closure of G_v, but with unlabelled arcs. When speaking about a path in a domain-transition graph below, we will typically mean the sequence of labels, *ie.* operators, along this path. We say that a path in G_v is *via* a set $X \subseteq \mathcal{D}_v$ iff each member of X is visited along the path, possibly as the initial or final vertex.

Definition 6 *An operator $o \in \mathcal{O}$ is* **irreplaceable** *wrt. a variable $v \in \mathcal{V}$ iff removing an arc labelled with o from G_v splits some component of G_v into two components.*

In the remainder of this paper we will be primarily interested in SAS$^+$ instances satisfying the following restrictions.

Definition 7 *A SAS$^+$ instance $\langle \mathcal{V}, \mathcal{O}, s_0, s_* \rangle$ is:*

(I) Interference-safe *iff every operator $o \in \mathcal{O}$ is either unary or irreplaceable wrt. every $v \in \mathcal{V}$ it affects.*

(A) Acyclic *iff $G_v^{\mathcal{R}_v^{\mathcal{O}}}$ is acyclic for each $v \in \mathcal{V}$.*

(O) prevail-Order-preserving *iff for each $v \in \mathcal{V}$, whenever there are two $x, y \in \mathcal{D}_v^+$ s.t. G_v has a shortest path $\langle o_1, \ldots, o_m \rangle$ from x to y via some set $X \subseteq \mathcal{R}_v^{\mathcal{O}}$ and it has any path $\langle o'_1, \ldots, o'_n \rangle$ from x to y via some set $Y \subseteq \mathcal{R}_v^{\mathcal{O}}$ s.t. $X \subseteq Y$, there exists some subsequence $\langle \ldots, o'_{i_1}, \ldots, o'_{i_m}, \ldots \rangle$ s.t. $\mathsf{f}(o_k) \sqsubseteq \mathsf{f}(o'_{i_k})$ for $1 \leq k \leq m$.*

We will be mainly concerned with SAS$^+$-IA and SAS$^+$-IAO instances, that is, SAS$^+$ instances satisfying the two restrictions I and A and SAS$^+$ instances satisfying all three restrictions respectively. Both restrictions I and A are tractable to test. The complexity of testing O in isolation is currently an open issue, but the combinations IA and IAO are tractable to test.

Theorem 8 *The restrictions I and A can be tested in polynomial time for arbitrary SAS$^+$ instances. Restriction O can be tested in polynomial time for SAS$^+$ instances satisfying restriction A.*

Proof sketch: [3] Testing A is trivially a polynomial time problem. Finding the irreplaceable operators wrt. a variable $v \in \mathcal{V}$ can be done in polynomial time by identifying the maximal strongly connected components in G_v, collapsing each of these into a single vertex and perform a reachability analysis. Since it is further polynomial to test whether an operator is unary, it follows that also I can be tested in polynomial time.

Furthermore, given that the instance satisfies A, O can be tested in polynomial time as follows. For each

---

[3]The full proofs of all theorems can be found in (Jonsson & Bäckström 1994).

pair of vertices $x, y \in \mathcal{D}_v^+$, find a shortest path in G_v from x to y. If the instance satisfies O, then for each operator o along this path, $\mathcal{D}_v^+$ can be partitioned into two disjoint sets X, Y s.t. every arc from some vertex in X to some vertex in Y is labelled by an operator o' satisfying that $\mathsf{f}(o) \sqsubseteq \mathsf{f}(o')$. This can be tested in polynomial time by a method similar to finding shortest-paths in G_v. Hence, O can be tested in polynomial time if A holds. $\square$

Furthermore, the SAS$^+$-IAO problem is strictly more general than the SAS$^+$-PUS problem (Bäckström & Nebel 1993).

Theorem 9 *All SAS$^+$-PUS instances are SAS$^+$-IAO instances, while a SAS$^+$-IAO instance need not satisfy either P, U or S.*

Planning Algorithm

Before describing the actual planning algorithm, we make the following observations about the solutions to arbitrary SAS$^+$ instances.

Theorem 10 *Let $\langle \mathcal{A}, \prec \rangle$ be a partial-order plan solving some SAS$^+$ instance $\Pi = \langle \mathcal{V}, \mathcal{O}, s_0, s_* \rangle$. Then for each $v \in \mathcal{V}$ and for each action sequence α which is a total ordering of $\mathcal{A}[v]$ consistent with $\prec$, the operator sequence type(α) is a path in G_v from $s_0[v]$ to $s_*[v]$ via $\mathcal{R}_v^{\mathcal{A}}$.*

This is a declarative characterization of the solutions and it cannot be immediately cast in procedural terms—the main reason being that we cannot know the sets $\mathcal{R}_v^{\mathcal{A}}$ in advance. These sets must, hence, be computed incrementally, which can be done in polynomial time under the restrictions I and A. We have devised an algorithm, *Plan* (Figure 1), which serves as a plan generation algorithm under these restrictions.

The heart of the algorithm is the procedure *Extend*, which operates on the global variables $X_1, \ldots, X_m$, extending these monotonically. It also returns operator sequences in the global variables $\omega_1, \ldots, \omega_m$, but only their value after the last call are used by *Plan*. For each i, *Extend* first finds a shortest path ω_i in G_{v_i} from $s_0[v_i]$ to $s_*[v_i]$ via X_i. (The empty path $\langle \rangle$ is considered as the shortest path from any vertex x to u, since $\mathsf{u} \sqsubseteq x$). If no such path exists, then *Extend* fails and otherwise each X_i is set to $\mathcal{R}_{v_i}^{\mathcal{O}'}$, where $\mathcal{O}'$ is the set of all operators along the paths $\omega_1, \ldots, \omega_m$. The motivation for this is as follows: If $\mathsf{f}(o)[v_i] = x \neq \mathsf{u}$ for some i and some operator o in some ω_j, then some action in the final plan must achieve this value, unless it holds initially. Hence, x is added to X_i to ensure that *Extend* will find a path via x in the next iteration. Similarly, each non-unary operator occurring in some ω_i must also appear in ω_j for all other j such that o affects v_j.

Starting with all $X_1, \ldots, X_m$ initially empty, *Plan* calls *Extend* repeatedly until nothing more is added to these sets or *Extend* fails. Viewing *Extend* as a function *Extend* $: \mathcal{S}^+ \rightarrow \mathcal{S}^+$, *ie.* ignoring the side effect on

```
1   procedure Plan(⟨𝒱, 𝒪, s₀, s∗⟩);
2   ⟨X₁, …, Xₘ⟩ ← ⟨∅, …, ∅⟩;
3   repeat
4     Extend;
5   until no Xᵢ is changed;
6   Instantiate;
7   for 1 ≤ i ≤ m and a, b ∈ αᵢ  do
8     Order a ≺ b iff a precedes b in αᵢ;
9   for 1 ≤ i ≤ m and a ∈ 𝒜 s.t. f(a)[vᵢ] ≠ u  do
10    Assume αᵢ = ⟨a₁, …, aₖ⟩
11    if e(aₗ)[vᵢ] = f(a)[vᵢ] for some 1 ≤ l ≤ k  then
12      Order aₗ ≺ a;
13      if l < k  then  Order a ≺ aₗ₊₁;
14    else Order a ≺ a₁;
15  𝒜 ← {a ∈ αᵢ | 1 ≤ i ≤ m};
16  if ≺ is acyclic  then return ⟨𝒜, ≺⟩;
17  else fail;


1   procedure  Extend;   (Modifies  X₁, …, Xₘ  and
      ω₁, …, ωₘ)
2   for 1 ≤ i ≤ m  do
3     ωᵢ ← any shortest path from s₀[vᵢ] to s∗[vᵢ] in G_v
4       via Xᵢ;
5     if no such path exists  then  fail;
6   for 1 ≤ i, j ≤ m and o ∈ ωⱼ  do
7     Xᵢ ← Xᵢ ∪ {f(o)[vᵢ]} − {u};
8     if o not unary  then
9       Xᵢ ← Xᵢ ∪ {b(o)[vᵢ], e(o)[vᵢ]} − {u};


1   procedure Instantiate;   (Modifies α₁, …, αₘ)
2   for 1 ≤ i ≤ m  do
3     Assume ωᵢ = ⟨o₁, …, oₖ⟩
4     for 1 ≤ l ≤ k  do
5       if oₗ not unary  and there is some a of type oₗ
6         in αⱼ for some j < i  then aₗ ← a;
7       else Let aₗ be a new instance of type(oₗ);
8     αᵢ ← ⟨a₁, …, aₖ⟩
```

Figure 1: Planning Algorithm

$\omega_1, \ldots, \omega_m$, this process corresponds to constructing the minimal fixed point for *Extend* in $\mathcal{S}^+$. The paths $\omega_1, \ldots, \omega_m$ found in the last iteration contain all the operators necessary in the final solution and procedure *Instantiate* instantiates these as actions. This works such that all occurrences of a non-unary operator are merged into one unique instance while all occurrences of a unary operator are made into distinct instances. It remains to compute the action ordering on the set $\mathcal{A}$ of all such operator instances (actions). For each v_i, the total order implicit in the operator sequence ω_i is kept as a total ordering on the corresponding actions. Finally, each action a s.t. $f(a)[v_i] = x \neq u$ for some i must be ordered after some action a' providing this condition. There turns out to always be a unique such action, or none if $v_i = x$ initially. Similarly, a must be ordered before the first action succeeding a' that destroys its prevailcondition. Finally, if $\prec$ is acyclic, then $\langle \mathcal{A}, \prec \rangle$ is returned and otherwise *Plan* fails. Observe that the algorithm does not compute the transitive clo-

sure $\prec^+$ of $\prec$ since this is a costly operation and the transitive closure is not likely to be of interest for executing the plan.

Procedure *Plan* is sound for SAS⁺-IA instances and it is further optimal and complete for SAS⁺-IAO instances.

Theorem 11 *If Plan returns a plan $\langle \mathcal{A}, \prec \rangle$ when given a SAS⁺-IA instance Π as input, then $\langle \mathcal{A}, \prec \rangle$ solves Π and if Π is a SAS⁺-IAO instance, then $\langle \mathcal{A}, \prec \rangle$ is also minimal. Further, if Plan fails when given a SAS⁺-IAO instance Π as input, then there exists no plan solving Π.*

Proof outline: The proofs for this theorem are quite long, but are essentially based on the following observations. Soundness is rather straightforward from the algorithm and Theorem 10. Further, let $\langle \mathcal{A}, \prec \rangle$ be the plan returned by *Plan* and let $\langle \mathcal{A}', \prec' \rangle$ be an arbitrary solution to Π. Minimality follows from observing that $\mathcal{R}_v^{\mathcal{A}} \subseteq \mathcal{R}_v^{\mathcal{A}'}$ for all $v \in \mathcal{V}$. The completeness proof essentially builds on minimality and proving that if $\prec$ contains a cycle (*ie. Plan* fails in line 16), then there can exist no solution to Π. □

Furthermore, *Plan* returns LC2-minimal plans (Bäckström 1993) which means that there does not exist any strict (*ie.* irreflexive) partial order $\prec'$ on $\mathcal{A}$ such that $| \prec' | < | \prec^+ |$ and $\langle \mathcal{A}, \prec' \rangle$ is a valid plan. Finally, *Plan* runs in polynomial time.

Theorem 12 *Plan has a worst-case time complexity of $O(|\mathcal{O}|^2 (|\mathcal{V}| \max_{v \in \mathcal{V}} |\mathcal{D}_v|)^3)$.*

Example

In this section, we will present a small, somewhat contrived example of a manufacturing workshop and show how the algorithm handles this example. We assume that there is a supply of rough workpieces and a table for putting finished products. There are also two workstations: a lathe and a drill. To simplify matters, we will consider only one single workpiece. Two different shapes can be made in the lathe and one type of hole can be drilled. Furthermore, only workpieces of shape 2 fit in the drill. This gives a total of four possible combinations for the end product: rough (*ie.* not worked on), shape 1, shape 2 without a hole and shape 2 with a hole. Note also that operator Shape2 is tougher to the cutting tool than Shape1 is—the latter allowing us to continue using the cutting tool afterwards. Finally, both the lathe and the drill require that the power is on. This is all modelled by five state variables, as shown in Table 1, and nine operators, as shown in Table 2. This example is a SAS⁺-IAO instance, but it does not satisfy either of the P, U and S restrictions in Bäckström and Nebel (1993).[4]

---

[4]Note in particular that since we do no longer require the S restriction, we can model sequences of workstations, which was not possible under the PUS restriction (Bäckström & Klein 1991).

variable	domain	denotes
1	{Supply, Lathe, Drill, Table}	Position of workpiece
2	{Rough, 1, 2}	Workpiece shape
3	{Mint, Used}	Condition of cutting tool
4	{Yes, No}	Hole in workpiece
5	{Yes, No}	Power on

Table 1: State variables for the workshop example

Operator	Precondition	Postcondition	Prevailcondition
MvSL	$v_1 = S$	$v_1 = L$	
MvLT	$v_1 = L$	$v_1 = T$	
MvLD	$v_1 = L$	$v_1 = D$	$v_2 = 2$
MvDT	$v_1 = D$	$v_1 = T$	
Shape1	$v_2 = R$	$v_2 = 1$	$v_1 = L, v_3 = M, v_5 = Y$
Shape2	$v_2 = R, v_3 = M$	$v_2 = 2, v_3 = U$	$v_1 = L, v_5 = Y$
Drill	$v_4 = N$	$v_4 = Y$	$v_1 = D, v_5 = Y$
Pon	$v_5 = N$	$v_5 = Y$	
Poff	$v_5 = Y$	$v_5 = N$	

Table 2: Operators for the workshop example. (Domain values will typically be denoted by their initial characters only).

After iteration 1:

$\omega_1 = \langle \text{MvSL}, \text{MvLT} \rangle$	$X_1 = \{L, D\}$
$\omega_2 = \langle \text{Shape2} \rangle$	$X_2 = \{R, 2\}$
$\omega_3 = \langle \rangle$	$X_3 = \{M, U\}$
$\omega_4 = \langle \text{Drill} \rangle$	$X_4 = \{\}$
$\omega_5 = \langle \rangle$	$X_5 = \{Y\}$

After iteration 2:

$\omega_1 = \langle \text{MvSL}, \text{MvLD}, \text{MvDT} \rangle$	$X_1 = \{L, D\}$
$\omega_2 = \langle \text{Shape2} \rangle$	$X_2 = \{R, 2\}$
$\omega_3 = \langle \text{Shape2} \rangle$	$X_3 = \{M, U\}$
$\omega_4 = \langle \text{Drill} \rangle$	$X_4 = \{\}$
$\omega_5 = \langle \text{Pon}, \text{Poff} \rangle$	$X_5 = \{Y\}$

Table 3: The variables ω_i and X_i in the example.

Suppose we start in $s_0 = \langle S, R, M, N, N \rangle$ and set the goal $s_* = \langle T, 2, \mathsf{u}, Y, N \rangle$, that is, we want to manufacture a product of shape 2 with a drilled hole. We also know that the cutting tool for the lathe is initially in mint condition, but we do not care about its condition after finishing. Finally, the power is initially off and we are required to switch it off again before leaving the workshop. Procedure *Plan* will make two calls to *Extend* before terminating the loop successfully, with variable values as in Table 3.

The operators in the operator sequences $\omega_1, \ldots, \omega_5$ will be instantiated to actions, where both occurrences of Shape2 are instantiated as the same action, since Shape2 is non-unary. Since there is not more than one action of each type in this plan, we will use the name of the operators also as names of the actions. The total orders in $\omega_1, \ldots, \omega_m$ is retained in $\alpha_1, \ldots, \alpha_m$. Furthermore, Shape2 must be ordered after MvSL and before MvLD, since its prevailcondition on variable 1 equals the postcondition of MvLD for this variable.

Similarly, Drill must be ordered between MvLD and MvDT because of its prevailcondition on variable 1 and both Shape2 and Drill must be ordered between Pon and Poff because of their prevailcondition on variable 5. Furthermore, MvLD must (once again) be ordered after Shape2 because of its prevailcondition on variable 2. The final partial-order plan is shown in Figure 2.

Discussion

Several attempts on exploiting structural properties on planning problems in order to decrease complexity have been reported in the literature, but none with the aim of obtaining polynomial-time planning problems. Korf (1987) has defined some structural properties of planning problems modelled by state-variables, for instance serial operator decomposability. However, this property is PSPACE-complete to test (Bylander 1992), but does not guarantee tractable planning. Mädler (1992) extends Sacerdoti's (1974) essentially syntactic state abstraction technique to *structural abstraction*, identifying bottle-neck states (*needle's eyes*) in the state-transition graph for a state-variable formalism. Smith and Peot (1993) use an *operator graph* for preprocessing planning problem instances, identifying potential threats that can be safely postponed during planning—thus, pruning the search tree. The operator graph can be viewed as an abstraction of the full state-transition graph, containing all the information relevant to analysing threats.

A number of issues are on our research agenda for the future. Firstly, we should perform a more careful analysis of the algorithm to find a tighter upper bound for the time complexity. Furthermore, the fixpoint for the *Extend* function is now computed by Jacobi iteration, which is very inefficient. Replacing this by some strategy for *chaotic iteration* (Cousot & Cousot 1977)

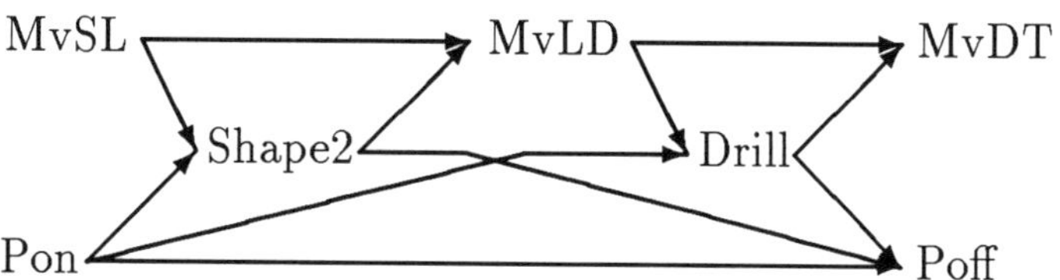

Figure 2: The final partial-order plan.

would probably improve the complexity considerably, at least in the average case. Furthermore, the algorithm is likely to be sound and complete for less restricted problems than SAS$^+$-IA and SAS$^+$-IAO respectively. Finding restrictions that more tightly reflect the limits of the algorithm is an issue for future research. We also plan to investigate some modifications of the algorithm, *eg.*, letting the sets $X_1, \ldots, X_m$ be partially ordered multisets, allowing a prevailcondition to be produced and destroyed several times—thus relaxing the A restriction. Another interesting modification would be to relax some of the restrictions and redefine *Extend* as a non-deterministic procedure. Although requiring search and, thus, probably sacrificing tractability, we believe this to be an intriguing alternative to ordinary search-based planning.

Conclusions

We have identified a set of restrictions allowing for the generation of optimal plans in polynomial time for a planning formalism, SAS$^+$, using multi-valued state variables. This extends the tractability borderline for planning, by allowing for more general problems than previously reported in the literature to be solved tractably. In contrast to most restrictions in the literature, ours are structural restrictions. However, they are restrictions on the transition graph for each state variable in isolation, rather than for the whole state space, so they can be tested in polynomial time. We have also presented a provably correct, polynomial time algorithm for planning under these restrictions.

References

American Association for Artificial Intelligence. 1992. *Proceedings of the 10th (US) National Conference on Artificial Intelligence (AAAI-92)*, San José, CA, USA.

Bäckström, C., and Klein, I. 1991. Parallel nonbinary planning in polynomial time. In Reiter and Mylopoulos (1991), 268–273.

Bäckström, C., and Nebel, B. 1993. Complexity results for SAS$^+$ planning. In Bajcsy, R., ed., *Proceedings of the 13th International Joint Conference on Artificial Intelligence (IJCAI-93)*. Chambéry, France: Morgan Kaufmann.

Bäckström, C. 1993. Finding least constrained plans and optimal parallel executions is harder than we thought. In Bäckström, C., and Sandewall, E., eds., *Current Trends in AI Planning: EWSP'93—2nd European Workshop on Planning*, Frontiers in AI and Applications. Vadstena, Sweden: IOS Press.

Bylander, T. 1991. Complexity results for planning. In Reiter and Mylopoulos (1991), 274–279.

Bylander, T. 1992. Complexity results for serial decomposability. In AAAI-92 (1992), 729–734.

Cousot, P., and Cousot, R. 1977. Automatic synthesis of optimal invariant assertions: Mathematical foundations. *SIGPLAN Notices* 12(8):1–12.

Drummond, M., and Currie, K. 1988. Exploiting temporal coherence in nonlinear plan construction. *Computational Intelligence* 4(4):341–348. Special Issue on Planning.

Erol, K.; Nau, D. S.; and Subrahmanian, V. S. 1992. On the complexity of domain-independent planning. In AAAI-92 (1992), 381–386.

Jonsson, P., and Bäckström, C. 1994. Tractable planning with state variables by exploiting structural restrictions. Research report, Department of Computer and Information Science, Linköping University.

Korf, R. E. 1987. Planning as search: A quantitative approach. *Artificial Intelligence* 33:65–88.

Mädler, F. 1992. Towards structural abstraction. In Hendler, J., ed., *Artificial Intelligence Planning Systems: Proceedings of the 1st International Conference*, 163–171. College Park, MD, USA: Morgan Kaufmann.

Reiter, R., and Mylopoulos, J., eds. 1991. *Proceedings of the 12th International Joint Conference on Artificial Intelligence (IJCAI-91)*. Sydney, Australia: Morgan Kaufmann.

Sacerdoti, E. D. 1974. Planning in a hierarchy of abstraction spaces. *Artificial Intelligence* 5(2):115–135.

Smith, D. E., and Peot, M. A. 1993. Postponing threats in partial-order planning. In *Proceedings of the 11th (US) National Conference on Artificial Intelligence (AAAI-93)*, 500–506. Washington DC, USA: American Association for Artificial Intelligence.

Least-Cost Flaw Repair: A Plan Refinement Strategy for Partial-Order Planning

David Joslin[*] and **Martha E. Pollack**[†,*]
*Intelligent Systems Program
†Department of Computer Science
University of Pittsburgh, Pittsburgh, PA 15260
joslin@cs.pitt.edu, pollack@cs.pitt.edu

Abstract

We describe the least-cost flaw repair (LCFR) strategy for performing flaw selection during partial-order causal link (POCL) planning. LCFR can be seen as a generalization of Peot and Smith's "Delay Unforced Threats" (DUnf) strategy (Peot & Smith 1993); where DUnf treats threats differently from open conditions, LCFR has a uniform mechanism for handling all flaws. We provide experimental results that demonstrate that the power of DUnf does not come from delaying threat repairs *per se*, but rather from the fact that this delay has the effect of imposing a partial preference for least-cost flaw selection. Our experiments also show that extending this to a complete preference for least-cost selection reduces search-space size even further. We consider the computational overhead of employing LCFR, and discuss techniques for reducing this overhead. In particular, we describe QLCFR, a strategy that reduces computational overhead by approximating repair costs.[1]

Introduction

Current research in plan generation in AI centers on partial-order causal link (POCL) algorithms, which descend from McAllester and Rosenblitt's SNLP algorithm (McAllester & Rosenblitt 1991; Penberthy & Weld 1992; Barrett & Weld 1993; Collins & Pryor 1992; Peot & Smith 1993; Kambhampati 1993). POCL planning involves searching through a space of partial plans, where the successors of a node representing partial plan P are refinements of P. As with any search problem, POCL planning requires effective search control strategies.

In POCL planning, search control has two main components. The first, *node selection*, involves choosing which partial plan to refine next. Most POCL algorithms use best-first search to perform node selection. Once a partial plan has been selected, the planner must then perform *flaw selection*, which involves choosing either a threat to resolve or an open condition to establish. Threats can be resolved by promotion, demotion, or separation; open conditions can be established by adding a new step to the plan or adding a new causal link to an existing step. Unless it is impossible to repair the selected flaw, new nodes representing the possible repairs are added to the search space.

Both the SNLP algorithm and its implementation in the UCPOP system (Penberthy & Weld 1992) adopt a flaw-selection strategy in which threats are resolved before open conditions. However, neither SNLP nor UCPOP specify any principles for selecting which threat or which open condition to repair. Peot and Smith (Peot & Smith 1993) relax the requirement that threats always be resolved before open conditions, and examine several strategies for delaying the resolution of some threats. One of the most effective strategies that they studied is what they call "Delay Unforced Threats" (DUnf.) In DUnf, a threat is selected only if there is only a single way to repair it (or if there is no way to repair it, i.e., it represents a dead end.) Such threats are called "forced." If all the current threats are unforced, i.e., have multiple possible repairs, then an open condition is selected for establishment instead. Peot and Smith do not indicate what happens in the case in which the only remaining flaws are unforced threats, but one must assume that in these cases, some threat is selected.

In this paper, we describe and examine the Least-Cost Flaw Repair (LCFR) strategy, a generalization of DUnf. We define the *repair cost* of any flaw—either threat or open condition—to be the number of nodes generated as possible repairs. LCFR is the strategy of always selecting a flaw with the lowest possible repair cost at a given node. Like DUnf, LCFR will delay any threat that is unforced (repair cost > 1) in favor of a threat that is forced (repair cost $<= 1$.) But by treating all flaws uniformly, LCFR also applies a similar strategy to open conditions, preferring to handle open conditions that are forced over open conditions, or threats, that are not. Similarly, LCFR handles the case in which all that remain are unforced threats: the

[1] This work has been supported by the Air Force Office of Scientific Research (Contract F49620-92-J-0422), by the Rome Laboratory (RL) of the Air Force Material Command and the Advanced Research Projects Agency (Contract F30602-93-C-0038), and by an NSF Young Investigator's Award (IRI-9258392).

LCFR strategy will select a threat with minimal repair cost.

The LCFR strategy is similar to one of the search heuristics used in the O-Plan system (Currie & Tate 1991). The contribution of this paper is to isolate this strategy and examine it in some detail, in order to explain its success and that of the related DUnf strategies.

In the following sections we provide more details about LCFR and its relationship to other flaw-selection strategies, and then describe experiments we conducted to compare the performance of POCL-planners employing these alternative strategies. We then examine the question of secondary selection strategies: what flaw should LCFR select in cases in which there are two or more flaws with minimal repair cost for a given node? We also consider techniques for reducing the computational overhead involved in calculating repair costs. In particular, we describe QLCFR, a strategy that reduces computational overhead by approximating repair costs. The final section discusses directions for future research on LCFR and related flaw-selection strategies.

Comparison of Flaw-Selection Strategies

The original POCL planning algorithms—SNLP and UCPOP—always prefer to repair threats before open conditions. Neither specifies how to select among alternative threats, or among alternative open conditions, although the UCPOP code employs a LIFO mechanism, i.e., it always selects the threat (or open condition if there are no threats) that was most recently introduced into the partial plan. Peot and Smith examine the effects of modifying this strategy to delay the repair of some threats. In particular, one of their most effective strategies, DUnf, will select a threat only if it is forced or if there are no open conditions remaining in the plan. The DUnf strategy does not include a commitment to a particular way to select among open conditions, although Peot and Smith suggest three alternatives: FIFO, LIFO, and "least-commitment." The "least-commitment" strategy selects an open condition with the fewest children, i.e., using the terminology introduced in the previous section, one with minimal repair cost.

Our hypothesis was that the principle of "least-cost" selection ought to be extended to *all* flaws. In other words, the power of the DUnf strategy comes not from the relative ordering of threats and open conditions, but instead from the fact that DUnf has the effect of imposing a partial preference for least-cost flaw selection. DUnf will always prefer a forced threat, which, by definition has a repair cost of at most one; thus, in cases in which there is a forced threat, DUnf will make a low-cost selection. What about cases in which there are no forced threats? Then DUnf will have to select among open conditions, assuming there are any. If our hypothesis is correct, a version of DUnf that makes this selection using a least-cost strategy ought to perform better than a version that uses one of the other strategies. In fact, if it is the selection of low-cost repairs that is causing the search-space reduction, then the idea of treating threat resolution differently from open condition establishment ought to be abandoned. Instead, a strategy that always selects the flaw with minimal repair cost, regardless of whether it is a threat or an open condition, ought to show the best performance. This is the Least-Cost Flaw Repair (LCFR) strategy.

To test our hypothesis, we began with the UCPOP system, and implemented various modifications of it. Two of these—DUnf and Dunf-LCOS—encode Peot and Smith's strategy. Both delay selection of unforced threats until all open conditions have been established, but the former selects among open conditions using a LIFO strategy, like UCPOP, while the latter performs least-cost selection of open conditions. A third modification, LCFR, implements the generalization of the least-cost strategy: it always selects a flaw with minimal cost, without regard to whether that flaw is a threat or an open condition. Finally, we also implemented a variant called LCOS, which, like UCPOP, always selects threats before open conditions, but which uses a least-cost strategy to choose among open conditions. LCOS was included to verify that the state-space reduction results from the preference for flaws with minimal repair costs: if this is true, then LCOS should show a decrease in state-space size even though it does not delay *any* threats. These five flaw-selection strategies are described in algorithmic form in Figure 1.

Experimental Results

The five planners were each tested on 49 problems from a variety of domains. In all the experiments, the node-selection strategy is best-first search, where the heuristic evaluation function is the sum of the number of steps and the number of flaws in the partial plan. These are the defaults provided with UCPOP. We also imposed a search limit of 8000 generated nodes. In reporting our results, we give the number of nodes examined, which is typically less than the number of nodes generated.

The 49 test problems are divided among 15 domains. Table 1 lists the total number of problems attempted for each domain, as well as the number of problems from that domain solved by each planner within the 8000-node limit. All of the problems except those from the TileWorld domain are taken directly from the sample problems distributed with UCPOP version 2.0. Eight miscellaneous domains are grouped together in the last row of the table. All five planners solved the same ten problems in this group.

As Table 1 shows, LCFR solved more problems (44) than any of the other four planners. None of the problems on which LCFR failed were solved by any of the other four planners. Figure 2 plots the percentage of

If any threats exist in the set of flaws
   select a threat
Else select an open condition
   (LIFO for UCPOP; Least-cost for LCOS.)

UCPOP, UCPOP-LCOS

If there are any threats with repair cost = 0
   select a threat from that set
Else if there are any threats with repair cost = 1
   select a threat from that set
Else if there are any open conditions
   select an open condition
   (LIFO for DUnf; Least-cost for Dunf-LCOS)
Else select a threat (unforced.)

DUnf, DUnf-LCOS

Select a flaw, minimizing repair cost.

LCFR

Figure 1: Flaw Selection Strategies

problems solved by each planner within a fixed number of nodes examined. (Each point $\langle x, y \rangle$ denotes that $x\%$ of the 49 test problems were solved by examining no more than y nodes.) Table 2 provides summary statistics for the experiment.

Discussion

The experiment described above confirms our original hypotheses. DUnf performs only marginally better than UCPOP: the percentage of problems solved by DUnf within any fixed number of nodes examined is only slightly higher than the percentage solved by UCPOP. On the other hand, DUnf-LCOS, which not only delays unforced threats but also performs least-cost open condition selection, performs significantly better than UCPOP, solving more problems within any fixed number of nodes, and, on average, searching far fewer nodes. Simply delaying unforced threats does not, in and of itself, lead to much improvement, but doing this in combination with a preference for minimal-cost open conditions does.

Our hypothesis that the search-space reduction is primarily due to selection of least-cost flaws is further bolstered by the performance of LCOS. Recall that LCOS does not delay *any* threats; nonetheless, its performance is significantly better than either UCPOP or DUnf.

Finally, note that LCFR, the only algorithm that uniformly selects flaws with minimal repair cost, shows the greatest reduction in search-space size. It solves the most problems overall (44), and it solves more problems than any other planner within any fixed number of nodes. The average number of nodes it examines is significantly less than any of the other planners ex-

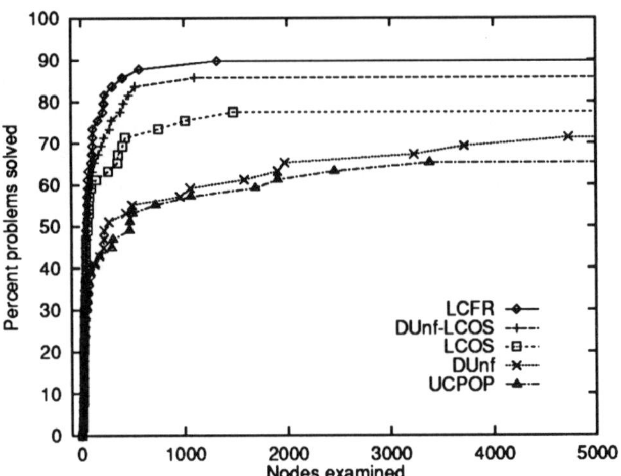

Figure 2: Comparison of planner search spaces

cept DUnf-LCOS.[2] Although LCFR is only marginally better than DUnf-LCOS, it has the advantage of being conceptually simpler in that it provides a uniform treatment of all flaws.

The relative performance of the five planners was not uniform across all the domains. Most notable was the TileWorld domain, consisting of a grid on which holes and tiles are scattered. The agent's goal is to fill one or more holes by picking up and carrying tiles (but carrying no more than four at a time), taking them to holes, and dropping one tile in each hole. LCFR and DUnf-LCOS solved all six of the problems taken from the TileWorld domain, while the other strategies solved at most two. The task of filling two holes is solved by LCFR after generating only 73 partial plans; the same problem was not solved by UCPOP even when allowed to run for over eight hours.

One can readily see the reason for such dramatic differences by looking at just the first few nodes examined in the plan-generation process. There the Tile-World domain is dominated by the establishment of open conditions that vary widely in their repair costs. In almost every case, at least one open condition in a partial plan has repair cost 1; at the same time, there are often open conditions with repair costs as high as 8. This occurs, for example, when an open condition that the agent be holding a tile can be established using any of eight tiles on the grid in the initial state. The planning strategies that do not perform least-cost selection of open conditions (UCPOP and DUnf) often select an open condition with an unnecessarily high repair cost,

---

[2]Using a paired-sample t test over all 49 problems, the reduction in the number of nodes examined by LCFR over any of the other planners is significant ($p < 0.01$), though for LCFR over DUnf-LCOS the significance is marginal ($p = 0.08$). DUnf-LCOS also shows a significant improvement over LCOS, DUnf and UCPOP ($p < 0.04$). The improvement of DUnf over UCPOP is marginally significant ($p = 0.096$).

Domain	Total Probs	UCPOP	DUnf	LCOS	DUnf-LCOS	LCFR
Briefcase world (Pednault 1988)	8	6	7	8	8	8
Office World (based on (Pednault 1988))	7	6	6	5	5	7
TileWorld (Pollack & Ringuette 1990)	6	0	1	2	6	6
Russell's Tire World (Russell 1992)	6	5	5	5	5	5
Blocks world	5	3	4	5	5	5
Monkeys and Bananas	3	2	2	2	2	2
STRIPS robot world	2	0	0	1	1	1
(Eight misc. domains)	12	10	10	10	10	10
TOTALS	49	32	35	38	42	44

Table 1: Problems solved by each planner, by domain

Planner	Problems each solved					Problems all solved				
	N	Min	Max	Mean	S. Dev	N	Min	Max	Mean	S. Dev
UCPOP	32	9	3380	444	795	31	9	3380	404	775
DUnf	35	9	4733	628	1142	31	9	3230	378	724
LCOS	38	9	1475	165	303	31	9	1475	157	325
DUnf-LCOS	42	9	1104	130	202	31	9	1104	112	219
LCFR	44	8	1320	114	215	31	8	1320	107	248

Table 2: Statistical comparison of search spaces (successful problems only)

which leads to excessive branching.

LCOS of course avoids the pitfall of poorly choosing an open condition. However, its undoing is its rigid preference for threats over open conditions. In many cases, LCOS prefers a higher-cost threat to a lower-cost open condition: for example, we observed it bypassing open conditions with repair cost 1 for threats with repair costs of 3 or more.

Finally, DUnf-LCOS does just about as well as LCFR: both solve all the TileWorld problems. However, examination of DUnf-LCOS's planning process shows that there are times in which it makes the opposite mistake from LCOS: it prefers higher-cost open conditions to lower-cost unforced threats. Although this appears not to have significantly hurt DUnf-LCOS on the TileWorld problems, it may account for the two problems from other domains on which DUnf-LCOS failed but LCFR was successful, and may suggest a potential problem for other applications.

What this analysis shows is that a uniform preference for least-cost flaws is especially important in domains in which flaw repair costs vary widely.

Secondary Flaw-Selection Strategies

As we have already pointed out, LCFR does not specify a strategy for selecting among the flaws with minimal repair cost. An obvious question is whether the performance of LCFR could be improved by the choice of a secondary flaw-selection strategy that made such decisions.

Before exploring particular secondary strategies, however, we wanted to determine just how sensitive LCFR might be to secondary selection. We therefore conducted a second experiment in which LCFR was run ten times on each of the 49 test problems, selecting flaws randomly from the set of flaws with minimal repair cost. Recall that 44 problems out of 49 were solved successfully in the initial set of experiments. The randomized LCFR solved 42 problems successfully in all ten trials, failed to solve four problems in any of the ten trials, and solved the remaining three problems seven, eight, and nine times, respectively.

Figure 3 shows the mean number of nodes examined for each of the 45 problems that LCFR solved successfully at least once. The error bars show the minimum and maximum number of nodes examined for each problem over the ten trials. The three error bars that are clipped at the top of the graph are those that exceeded the search limit on one or more trials.

We can note that the majority of problems are relatively insensitive to secondary selection. For example, the range of the number of nodes examined (i.e., the difference between the maximum and the minimum) was 100 or less for 30 out of the 45 problems solved at least once. Given the low number of nodes searched by LCFR, on average, in the first experiment, it would be surprising if we had not found this kind of insensitivity to secondary selection.

More interesting is the fact that *all* of these 45 problems were solved at least once by examining a very small number of nodes (415, in the worst case). This is true even for problems for which the mean number of nodes examined over the ten trials is several thousand, including problems for which LCFR sometimes failed. Note further that, although most of the problems showed little variation over the ten trials,

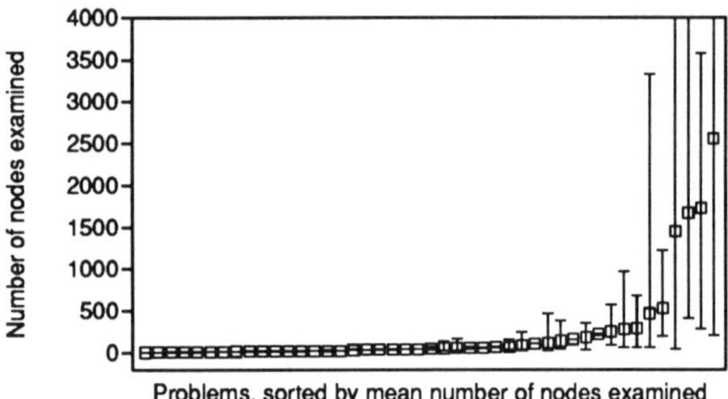

Figure 3: Results of sensitivity experiment

most of those that showed extreme variation had a distinctly bi-modal distribution of the number of nodes examined. Three problems failed on one or more trials, exceeding the search limit of 8000 nodes generated (though examining fewer than that), but succeeded on other trials by searching as few as 50 nodes. One of these problems had seven successful trials, examining a minimum of 211 and a maximum of 648 nodes, while exceeding the search limit on three trials. Other problems had bi-modal distributions even though they succeeded on all ten trials. One problem, for example, succeeded one time after examining over 3000 nodes, and nine times after examining 250 or fewer nodes.

These results suggest that while a more sophisticated secondary selection strategy would not significantly improve LCFR's performance on most of our test problems, it could have a substantial positive effect on those problems that LCFR sometimes found difficult. An obvious candidate for a secondary strategy would be to prefer threat resolution to open-condition establishment, assuming that the repair costs are equal. Our preliminary investigations of this strategy, however, did not show significant improvement. The nature of a good secondary selection strategy remains an open question.

Improving the Performance of LCFR

Although LCFR searches far fewer nodes than UCPOP, it incurs a significant overhead in computing repair costs. Our implementation of LCFR, for example, used less CPU time than UCPOP on only four of the 32 problems on which both were successful. Although LCFR examines far fewer nodes than UCPOP, it spends an average of over forty times as long expanding each node (104 ms vs. 2.4 ms). Clearly, if LCFR is going to live up to its promise of making POCL planning more efficient, then the cost of flaw selection must be significantly decreased.

Fortunately, there are some clear-cut ways to do this. Our implementation of LCFR took advantage of the fact that the repair cost for a flaw could be calculated by allowing UCPOP to make all repairs to that flaw, generating a new node for each repair, and then dis-

carding all the newly generated nodes except those associated with the selected flaw. This approach required a minimum of modification to the UCPOP code, but is obviously inefficient: the repair cost could be calculated without actually allocating the node structures. In addition, there are methods that could be used to reduce the amount of work done in recalculating repair costs for flaws that have already been considered. For example, if a threat was not separable the last time it was considered, there is no way that other changes to the partial plan could have made that threat separable. In recalculating its repair cost, we need only look at promotion and demotion.

Another alternative—and the one we explore in this paper—involves reducing the overhead of flaw selection by accepting some inaccuracy in the repair-cost calculation. One way to do that is to calculate the repair cost of each flaw only once, when that flaw is first encountered. In any successor node, if that flaw has still not been repaired, we assume that its repair cost has not changed. We refer to this variation of the strategy as "Quick LCFR" (QLCFR.) Note that QLCFR will sometimes produce inaccurate repair costs, because it is possible that repairing one flaw will change the repair costs of other flaws, either by eliminating possible repairs, or by adding new options. For example, adding a new step to the plan may add the option of reusing an effect of that new step to satisfy another open condition.

By assuming that repair costs are fixed, QLCFR was able to expand a node in an average of 4.6 ms, a huge reduction from LCFR's 104 ms. Although this is still higher than the average amount of time spent per node by UCPOP, the reduction in search space is now sufficient to allow QLCFR to solve problems on average about twice as fast as UCPOP, for problems that both solve. And QLCFR solves more problems than UCPOP: for our 49 test problems, QLCFR solved 38 problems, compared to 32 for UCPOP. QLCFR solves fewer problems within the node limit than either LCFR (44) or DUnf-LCOS (42), but QLCFR is much faster than either of these.

These results are very encouraging. Even given our currently inefficient method of calculating repair costs, QLCFR executes in time comparable to that of UCPOP, solving more problems and searching fewer nodes on those problems that both solve. A more efficient implementation of the repair cost calculation should reduce the time spent examining each node even further, and more intelligent decisions about when to recalculate repair costs (rather than simply never recalculating), should improve on the accuracy of the repair cost estimate.

Future Research

Given the importance of making plan generation more efficient, techniques such as LCFR and its variants are obviously worth pursuing further. In particular, we see at least four key areas for further investigation.

First, it is worth examining additional techniques for reducing the overhead of computing repair costs. In the previous section we noted some improvements that could be made to the way in which we implement the repair-cost calculation, and described QLCFR, which approximates repair costs by assuming that they do not change. One plausible extension of QLCFR would involve keeping track of the "age" of a flaw, and recalculating its repair cost only if that age exceeds some threshold. Another possibility would involve scanning the list of flaws within a partial plan until a flaw is found with repair cost at or below a fixed threshold, or until we reach the end of the list, in which case a flaw with minimal repair cost would be selected. With a threshold of zero, this algorithm reduces to a slightly optimized version of LCFR; with a threshold of one or more, the principle of least-cost selection would sometimes be violated, but with a potential savings in computational overhead. Varying the threshold allows one to trade flaw-selection costs for quality of flaw selection fairly directly.

Second, we can consider more sophisticated definitions of "repair cost" than the one we have been using. As we have defined it, the repair cost of a flaw takes into account only the immediate branching factor for a given repair. It may be, however, that the best flaw to repair has branching factor higher than the minimum; consider the simple case in which a flaw with a repair cost of N actually has $N - 1$ descendents that are quickly recognizable as dead ends. It may be that some degree of "look ahead" in the calculation of a repair cost may be advantageous, in spite of the additional computational cost. One such strategy was implemented in O-Plan (Currie & Tate 1991).

Third, it is worth returning to the issue of node selection, and reconsidering heuristic evaluation functions for POCL planning in light of a least-cost flaw selection strategy. An evaluation function that estimates the repair costs for the flaws in each node might be more effective than one that simply treats all flaws equivalently.

Finally, and perhaps most significantly, it is worth considering how to extend the lesson learned from the LCFR experiments—namely, that during POCL planning, it pays to focus first on flaws with minimal repair costs—to develop techniques for *reducing* the repair costs of particular flaws. One possibility would involve the use of a richer representation for temporal ordering constraints. We can think of a causal link as a constraint on a temporal interval whose endpoints are defined by the establishing and consuming steps. We could reduce the repair cost of a threat by replacing promotion and demotion with a single constraint that the threatening step occur at some time "not during" the causal link being threatened. In effect, this means carrying a disjunction (promotion or demotion) that otherwise would be handled by creating two separate

nodes. The computational complexity of working with such constraints is greater than that of the simpler ordering constraints used by SNLP or UCPOP, but perhaps not so much greater as to outweigh the benefits of reduced branching in the search space. Similarly, we might look for other techniques that make tradeoffs between reduced repair costs and richer representations of constraints.

The exploration of these and related extensions to search control for POCL planning are left for future research. For now we note that our experimental analyses of LCFR and QLCFR indicate the promise of flaw-selection strategies that focus on the degree of branching caused by repairing a flaw.

References

Barrett, A., and Weld, D. 1993. Partial-order planning: Evaluating possible efficiency gains. To appear in *Artificial Intelligence*.

Collins, G., and Pryor, L. 1992. Achieving the functionality of filter conditions in a partial order planner. In *Proceedings of the Tenth National Conference on Artificial Intelligence*, 375–380.

Currie, K., and Tate, A. 1991. O-Plan: the open planning architecture. *Artificial Intelligence* 52:49–86.

Kambhampati, S. 1993. Planning as refinement search: A unified framework for comparative analysis of search space size and performance. To appear in *Artificial Intelligence*.

McAllester, D., and Rosenblitt, D. 1991. Systematic nonlinear planning. In *Proceedings of the Ninth National Conference on Artificial Intelligence*, 634–639.

Pednault, E. P. D. 1988. Synthesizing plans that contain actions with context-dependent effects. *Computational Intelligence* 4(4):356–372.

Penberthy, J., and Weld, D. 1992. UCPOP: A sound, complete, partial order planner for ADL. In *Proceedings of the Third International Conference on Knowledge Representation and Reasoning*, 103–114.

Peot, M., and Smith, D. E. 1993. Threat-removal strategies for partial-order planning. In *Proceedings of the Eleventh National Conference on Artificial Intelligence*, 492–499.

Pollack, M. E., and Ringuette, M. 1990. Introducing the Tileworld: Experimentally evaluating agent architectures. In *Proceedings of the Eighth National Conference on Artificial Intelligence*, 183–189.

Russell, S. J. 1992. Efficient memory-bounded search algorithms. In *Proceedings of the Tenth European Conference on Artificial Intelligence*.

Temporal Planning with Continuous Change*

J. Scott Penberthy
IBM T.J. Watson Research Center
30 Saw Mill River Road
Hawthorne, NY 10532
jsp@watson.ibm.com

Daniel S. Weld
Department of Computer Science and Engineering
University of Washington
Seattle, WA 98105
weld@cs.washington.edu

Abstract

We present ZENO, a least commitment planner that handles actions occurring over extended intervals of time. Deadline goals, metric preconditions, metric effects, and continuous change are supported. Simultaneous actions are allowed when their effects do not interfere. Unlike most planners that deal with complex languages, the ZENO planning algorithm is sound and complete. The running code is a complete implementation of the formal algorithm, capable of solving simple problems (*i.e.*, those involving less than a dozen steps).

Introduction

We have built a least commitment planner, ZENO, that handles actions occuring over extended intervals of time and whose preconditions and effects can be temporally quantified. These capabilities enable ZENO to reason about deadline goals, piecewise-linear continuous change, external events and to a limited extent, simultaneous actions. While other planners exist with some of these features, ZENO is different because it is both sound and complete.

As an example of ZENO's capabilities, consider a toy world in which a single plane moves passengers between cities. "Slow flying" travels at 400 miles per hour and consumes 1 gallon of fuel every 3 miles, on average. "Fast flying" travels at 600 miles per hour and consumes 1 gallon of fuel every 2 miles. Passengers can be boarded in 30 minutes and deplaned in 20 minutes. Refueling gradually increases the fuel level to a maximum of 750 gallons, taking one hour from an empty tank. Boarding, deplaning, and refueling must all occur while the plane is on the ground. The plane flies routes between 4 cities as shown in figure 1.

Suppose that dan and ernie are at city-c, but the empty plane and scott are at city-a. If the plane only

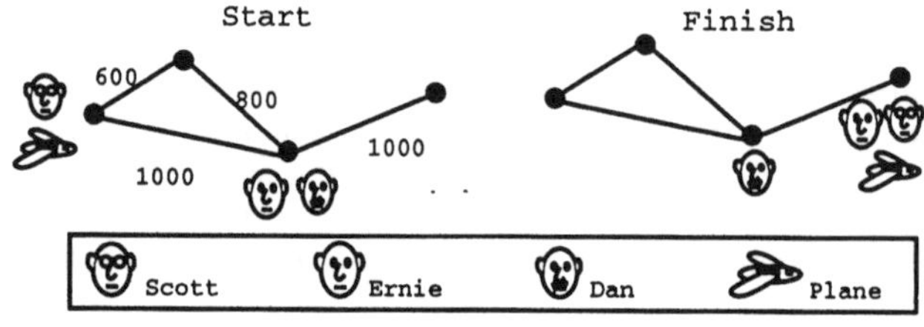

Figure 1: Airplane routes and a sample problem

has 500 gallons of fuel, how can we ensure that scott and ernie get to city-d in less than $5 + \frac{1}{2}$ hours?

Synthesizing the solution requires reasoning about simultaneous actions and continuous change. Since the plane's fuel diminishes at differing rates depending on the speed of flight, ZENO needs to trade off speed for efficiency. The planner must also handle conditional effects, since passengers are moved only when they are aboard. Deadline goals are present: the plane must meet a tight schedule. ZENO takes about three minutes to solve the problem. The Gantt chart below depicts ZENO's plan — facts established by actions are shown as indented formulae, and the bars to the right indicate the intervals of time over which actions occur or facts persist.

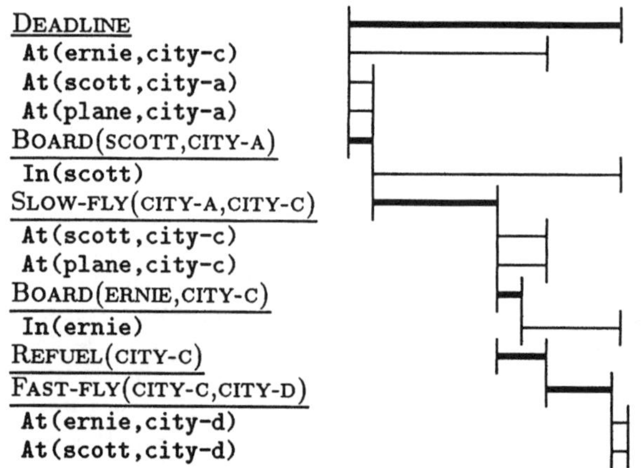

The constraints (over 100 of them) can be para-

*This research was funded in part by the IBM Corporation, National Science Foundation Grant IRI-8957302, Office of Naval Research Grant 90-J-1904 and a grant from the Xerox corporation.

phrased as follows. Passenger **scott** takes 30 minutes to board the plane at **city-a**. Since it doesn't have enough fuel to **fast-fly**, the plane flies slowly from **city-a** to **city-c**, taking 2 hours, 30 minutes. The plane is refueled over the next hour at **city-c**; meanwhile passenger **ernie** climbs onboard. Note that the deadline could not be met without scheduling these actions simultaneously. Finally, over the next 1:20, the plane is flown quickly from **city-c** to **city-d**. This leaves 235 gallons of fuel in the plane for a total plan time of 5 hours, 20 minutes — 10 minutes to spare. The rest of this paper describes our action and plan representation, provides an overview of the ZENO algorithm, then discusses formal and empirical aspects.

Actions and goals

ZENO uses a typed, first-order language with equality to describe goals and the effects of actions. A point-based model of time is adopted; temporal functions and relations use a time point as their first argument. Quantifiers specify the type of the quantified variable (*i.e.*, $\forall_{\text{type}}$ and $\exists_{\text{type}}$). All types except **time** are assumed finite. To represent maintenance (*i.e.*, interval) goals and piecewise-linear continuous effects, one simply specifies universal quantification over variables of type **time**.

A ZENO action schema (*e.g.*, figure 2) characterizes a set of possible actions with sentences from ZENO's

```
Schema Fast-Fly (m, l)
  at-time:  [t_s, t_e]
  precondition:
    ∀_time t  t ∈ [t_s, t_e] ⊃  fuel(t, plane) > 0  ∧
    at(t_s, plane, m)  ∧
    dist(m, l)=ν_2 ∧ mpg(plane)=ν_3
  constraints:
    ν_4 = −600/ν_3 ,  t_e = t_s + ν_2/600
  effect:
    at(t_e, plane, l)  ∧
    ∀_time t  t ∈ (t_s, t_e] ⊃ ¬at(t, plane, m)  ∧
    [∀_human o ∀_time t
       (t ∈ (t_s, t_e] ∧ in(t, o)) ⊃ ¬at(t, o, m) ∧ at(t_e, o, l)]  ∧
    ∀_time t  t ∈ [t_s, t_e] ⊃ ∂/∂t fuel(t, plane) = ν_4
```

Figure 2: An action schema for fast flying.

logic. A schema specifies the time over which an action occurs, the preconditions for execution, and the effects on the world. For example, the precondition $at(t_s, \text{plane}, m)$ insists that the plane start at location m at time t_s in order to fly from location m to location l. The first precondition of **Fast-Fly**,

$$\forall_{\text{time}} t\; t \in [t_s, t_e] \supset \text{fuel}(t, \text{plane}) > 0$$

restricts the plane's fuel level to remain above zero while flying, but does not commit to a single value: $\text{fuel}(t, \text{plane})$ may vary throughout the interval $[t_s, t_e]$. While a goal may be any quantified sentence

composed of logical connectives ($\wedge$, $\vee$) and literals ($f(t, x_1 \ldots x_n) = c$, $R(x_1 \ldots x_n)$, or $\neg R(x_1 \ldots x_n)$), disjunction and existential quantification are banned from action effects. Internally, the conjunctive effects of each action are simplified to a set of literals through reduction parsing (Penberthy 1993). This approach simplifies the matching of action effects to goals. The last effect conjunct of **Fast-Fly**,

$$\forall_{\text{time}} t\; t \in [t_s, t_e] \supset \frac{\partial}{\partial t} \text{fuel}(t, \text{plane}) = \nu_4$$

states that the **fuel** level will change at a constant rate of ν_4. The value of ν_4 is constrained with additional equations, relating ν_4 to the speed of the plane, 600 miles per hour, and the fuel efficiency, **mpg(plane)**. We must specify the entire continuous behavior over the interval $[t_s, t_e]$, as our semantics insist that all continuous behaviors are the result of direct, explicit action. After an action effect terminates, the last value obtained by continous change will persist through time until explicitly modified by another action's effect.

Plans

ZENO *plans* are triples $\prec \mathcal{S}, \mathcal{L}, \mathcal{C} \succ$ where $\mathcal{S}$ is a set of steps (*i.e.*, instantiated action schemata), $\mathcal{L}$ is a set of causal links, and $\mathcal{C}$ is a set of constraints. The constraints in $\mathcal{C}$ include metric equations, linear equalities, linear inequalities, and noncodesignation constraints. The steps in $\mathcal{S}$ are partially ordered by the relevant temporal constraints in $\mathcal{C}$. The causal links $\mathcal{L}$ denote protection ranges for literals; each link is a pair $\prec \iota, \theta \succ$ where θ is a literal that must remain true throughout the interval of time ι.

Because preconditions and effects have explicit temporal scope, a planning problem can be encoded as a partial plan with a *single* dummy step whose time of "execution" bounds all planned activity. For example, our sample problem becomes the dummy step:

```
Schema Dummy
  at-time:  [t_0, t_1]
  precondition:
    at(t_1, scott, city-d) ∧ at(t_1, ernie, city-d)
  constraints:
    t_0 < t_1 ≤ t_0 + 5.5
  effect:
    at(t_0, scott, city-a) ∧ at(t_0, ernie, city-c) ∧
    at(t_0, dan, city-c) ∧ fuel(t_0, plane)=500
```

This unintuitive encoding of planning problems was chosen because ZENO's temporal model eliminated the need for separate initial and goal steps. When we introduce continuous time into a planning system, initial conditions, external events and domain axioms become formally equivalent. They are simply clauses that occur, beyond the program's control, at specific times. Final goals and deadline goals are also indistinguishable. They are merely clauses that must be achieved at a specific time. We lump external events, initial conditions, and domain axioms into the effects of the dummy action. Deadline goals and final goals are lumped into its preconditions. Finally, the time of the dummy action spans the desired time for the plan to complete.

In addition, conditional effects represent external events that can be disabled, *i.e.*, one can specify that unless a bomb is disarmed by a specific time, it will explode. Domain axioms are encoded as universally quantifed temporal effects.

The Zeno Algorithm

ZENO is a least commitment, regression planner. It searches a space whose nodes are pairs $\prec P, G \succ$ where P is a partially specified plan and G is a goal agenda. As ZENO traverses arcs, it rewrites complex goals into simpler ones, satisfies simple goals, imposes constraints, and generates subgoals.

The planner begins at a node where $P = \prec S, \mathcal{L}, \mathcal{C} \succ$ is a one-step plan encoding the planning problem and G is the agenda of top-level goals. The algorithm terminates when it finds a node whose agenda is empty (signifying a solution) or when the plan's constraints are inconsistent (failure). The search process is described as a flow chart in figure 3.

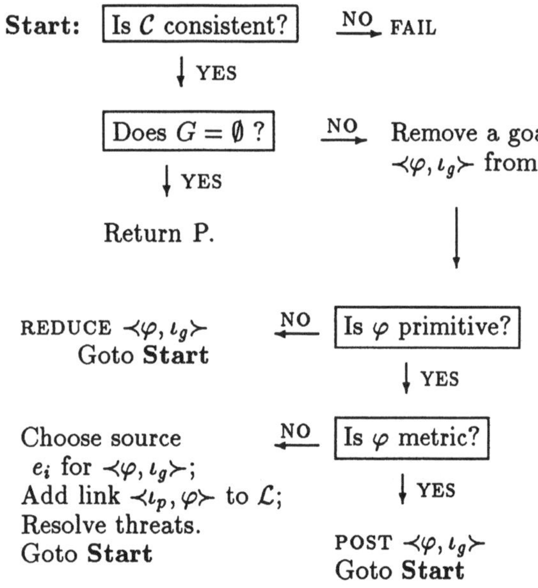

Figure 3: The main loop of ZENO.

The full algorithm involves three nondeterministic decisions: (1) decomposing a complex goal into simpler formula, (2) choosing actions to satisfy simple goals, and (3) introducing constraints to prevent interference between actions and goals. Completeness requires backtracking on these decisions — the branching factor is proportional to the number of available actions and the number of disjunctive goals. Note that completeness does *not* require backtracking on goal selection (seen as "Remove a goal" in figure 3). Since subgoal ordering decisions *can* affect planning performance as much as the true nondeterministic choices,

domain dependent guidance (when available) is useful for all four types of decisions.

The remaining subsections briefly describe each path through the main loop. These paths are dispatched by first testing to see if a goal $\prec \varphi, \iota_g \succ$ remains on the agenda; if so, it is removed. Note that this tuple format is representative of the sentence $\forall_{\texttt{time}} t\; t \in \iota_g \supset \varphi$. ZENO next checks whether φ is primitive, *i.e.*, if it is a logical literal (*e.g.*, $R(x_1 \ldots x_n)$ or $\neg R(x_1 \ldots x_n)$), a metric equality (possibly constraining a fluent, *e.g.* $f(x_1 \ldots x_n) = \nu$), an arbitrary metric constraint between metric primitives (*e.g.*, $\nu_1 \leq \nu_2$) or codesignation constraint $x \approx y$. Unless φ is primitive, it is reduced as explained in the next section.

Goal reduction

The **reduce** procedure simplifies a complex goal by substituting stronger yet simpler conditions. A disjunctive goal $\varphi_1 \vee \ldots \vee \varphi_n$ is replaced, nondeterministically, by one of its disjuncts φ_i. A conjunctive goal $\varphi_1 \wedge \ldots \wedge \varphi_n$ is replaced by the set of goals $\{\varphi_1, \ldots, \varphi_n\}$.

An interval goal $\forall_{\texttt{time}} t\; t \in \iota \supset \varphi$ is reduced in one of two ways: either the program splits the interval ι into two subinterval subgoals, or it marks the interval as indivisible. This allows ZENO to explore all possible subdivisions of interval goals. Each marked interval corresponds to a linear segment of a piece-wise linear equation φ, or it corresponds to a single interpretation of logical literal φ. To avoid infinite branching, the implementation will only split intervals to a preset depth. This bound restricts the number of actions that, in combination, can be used to satisfy an interval goal; iterative deepening search can ensure completeness.

A universally quantified goal $\forall_{\texttt{type}} x \varphi$, where $\texttt{type} \neq \texttt{time}$, is replaced by its *universal base* (Penberthy & Weld 1992; Weld 1994), which is the conjunction of all ground terms φ_i, one for each extension x_i of x where x_i is a constant of type $\texttt{type}$. Note that domains must be finite for this to work; hence we treat time specially as described in the previous paragraph and the next section.

Existential quantifiers within the scope of a universal quantifier are replaced with Skolem functions. All other existentials are treated as simple variable names, requiring algorithms to handle codesignation and noncodesignation constraints.

Finally, metric constraints on logical fluents, such as $\texttt{value}(\texttt{t}_1, \texttt{x}) \leq \texttt{value}(\texttt{t}_2, \texttt{y})$ are separated into their individual components,[1] yielding *e.g.*

$$\exists \nu_1, \nu_2\; \texttt{value}(\texttt{t}_1, \texttt{x}) = \nu_1 \wedge \texttt{value}(\texttt{t}_2, \texttt{y}) = \nu_2 \wedge \nu_1 \leq \nu_2$$

---

[1] Although this last transformation may seem trivial, subtle arguments (Nelson & Oppen 1979; Penberthy 1993) show that it is necessary to ensure soundness.

Metric and codesignation goals

If φ is a codesignation (*e.g.*, $x \approx y$ or $x \not\approx y$) or primitive metric constraint (*e.g.*, $\nu_1 \leq \nu_2$), it is posted directly to the constraint reasoning system which determines whether its constraints are collectively consistent. The phrase "POST $\prec\varphi, \iota_g\succ$" of figure 3 means the following. If ι_g is a time point, then only one constraint φ is posted, $\varphi(\iota_g)$. Otherwise, ZENO exploits piecewise linearity and posts φ for both endpoints of the interval.[2] For example, the requirement that the plane have fuel ≥ 0 during flight yields constraints that the plane have gas at takeoff and landing. If the constraint is valid at both endpoints, the Mean Value Theorem guarantees that it will be true for the entire interval.

This approach works because we limit goals φ to linear inequalities and assume that no further decomposition of ι_g is needed. ZENO handles the case where ι_g needs to be divided into subintervals in the call to REDUCE, the "goal reduction" path.

Logical and fluent-definitional goals

If φ from $\prec\varphi, \iota_g\succ$ is a literal such as At(ernie, city-d), it is satisfied in a style similar to UCPOP (Penberthy & Weld 1992; Weld 1994) and SNLP (McAllester & Rosenblitt 1991) in the "logical goals" path of the main loop. ZENO nondeterministically chooses a *source* for φ by finding an effect that concludes φ over ι_e, where ι_e possibly precedes ι_g. Sources from both newly instantiated and existing steps S_i are considered. In both cases, ordering constraints are added to $\mathcal{C}$, ensuring that ι_e precedes[3] ι_g in any final plan.

ZENO then protects the literal φ over the interval ι_p, where ι_p exactly covers both ι_g and ι_e. This is accomplished by first adding a new causal link $\prec\iota_p, \varphi\succ$ to $\mathcal{L}$ and then removing all *threats* to the new link. The tuple format of a causal link is shorthand for a logical sentence stating that φ must persist over the interval ι_p (Penberthy 1993).

A threat is any effect e_k that might possibly cause $\neg\varphi$ over some portion of the interval ι_p. We say "possibly" here since the plan P is only partially specified: many step orderings and values for free variables may be consistent with P, yet allow threats to occur. ZENO resolves all threats using the standard techniques of *promotion* and *demotion*, *i.e.*, posting ordering constraints on time points (Chapman 1987), and *confrontation*, *i.e.*, posting a new subgoal that prevents e_k from interfering (Collins & Pryor 1992; Penberthy & Weld 1992; Weld 1994). If no resolution is possible, ZENO backtracks.

Linking and threat prevention introduce constraints on the plan. For example, when achieving a goal of

---

[2] It is an error for ι_g to be anything but a closed interval of time $[t_1, t_2]$ or a time point t_1, by the definition of goals.

[3] More exactly, ι_e must begin before or coincident with the start of ι_g. Although ι_e may overlap ι_g, this is not required, since ZENO's threat resolution mechanism ensures that φ persists if there is a gap between ι_e and ι_g.

the form $\mathtt{fuel}(t, x) = \nu_g(t)$ with an effect $\mathtt{fuel}(t, y) = \nu_e(t)$, ZENO must ensure that $x \approx y$ and that $\nu_g(t) = \nu_e(t)$. This ensures that any interpretation for the variables x and y are consistent with the effect "achieving" the goal. It also connects the precondition constraints on $\nu_g(t)$ to the effect constraints on $\nu_e(t)$. Similarly, if $\mathtt{fuel}(t, x) = \nu_g(t)$ were defined by an effect that specified the derivative of $\mathtt{fuel}()$ over $[t_0, t_1]$ to be δ, ZENO must also constrain $\nu_g(t)$ accordingly, *e.g.*, by defining $\nu_g(t) = \nu_g(t_0) + \delta * (t - t_0)$ and posting $t_0 \leq t \leq t_1$.

Integrated Constraint Management

Since ZENO relies on constraint satisfaction for all temporal and metric aspects reasoning, sound and efficient algorithms are essential. Specialized routines cooperate to handle the different types of constraints in $\mathcal{C}$: codesignations, linear equalities, linear inequalities, and nonlinear equations.

Codesignations are handled as they were in UCPOP (Weld 1994). A simple algorithm maintains equivalence classes of all logical variables, then determines whether the noncodesignations are inconsistent with the classification.

Mathematical formulae posted by ZENO are parsed dynamically into a set of linear equations $\sum_i a_i x_i = b$, inequalities $\sum_i a_i x_i \leq b$, and pairwise nonlinear equations $x_i y_i = c$. These canonical forms are identical to the matrix representation of equations used in linear algebra and operations research (Karloff 1991).

Linear equations are solved by Gaussian elimination, linear inequalities by the Simplex algorithm, and nonlinear equations are delayed until they become linear via the solution of other equations and inequalities. To ensure sound constraint handling, each equality, $x_i = c$, that is derived by one algorithm is passed to all other algorithms (Nelson & Oppen 1979).

Determining an inconsistency using Gaussian elimination is straightforward; if a constraint $c = 0$ is detected during elimination, where c is non-zero constant, then the equations are inconsistent. Finding inconsistencies in linear inequalities is a bit trickier.

Recall that linear programming is the task of minimizing a cost function while satisfying a set of linear inequalities (Karloff 1991). The Simplex algorithm operates in two phases. First, it constructs a polytope, *i.e.*, a convex region in $\Re^n$, that exactly covers the set of solutions to the linear inequalities. In the second phase, it walks along vertices of the polytope in search of values that minimize the cost function. For ZENO, the optimization aspect is irrelevant. Instead, ZENO uses the first phase to determine simply whether the polytope is malformed. If the polytope vanishes to the null vector $\vec{0}$, no solutions exist and the constraints are inconsistent. While exponential in the worst case, the expected time for phase I is linear in the number of variables.[4] For maximum speed, ZENO uses Jaf-

---

[4] In our experience, the Simplex algorithm is never the bottleneck; if larger problems cause this to be the case we

far *et.al.*'s (Jaffar *et al.* 1992) dynamic programming version of the algorithm optimized for incremental updates. This version retains the polytope from n equations, then modifies it when the $n + 1$st inequality is added.

The above algorithms determine whether the set of constraints are consistent. However, they are not amenable to the numerous temporal queries required by the ZENO algorithm. When linking effects to goals or checking for threats, ZENO must determine whether two or more intervals overlap. These intervals, in turn, are specified as constraints on two end points. For example, the half-open interval $[t_1, t_2)$ represents all time points t such that $t_1 \leq t < t_2$. To expedite temporal queries, ZENO caches temporal relations with Warshall's transitive closure algorithm (Warshall 1962). For each time point t, this cache specifies all time points $t_\leq$ less than or equal to t, all time points $t_\geq$ greater than or equal to t, and all time points $t_{\neq}$ distinct from t. This can be efficiently implemented using boolean operations on bit vectors, where each time point is represented by a unique index.

Formal Properties

Assuming that all interval, metric effects are piecewise linear, that nontemporal types are static and finite, and that nonlinear equations can be linearized, then ZENO is both *sound i.e.*, all plans returned by ZENO will work, and *complete i.e.*, if a plan exists, ZENO will find it. The soundness proof introduces a loop invariant maintained by all control paths of ZENO. The halting conditions, in combination with the invariant, guarantee that every plan returned by ZENO will work. The completeness proof uses induction on the number of steps in a plan. The base case (0-step plans) is true for all consistent problem descriptions. The inductive case uses an $n - 1$ step plan to guide ZENO as it builds an n step plan.[5] ZENO's proofs occupy many more pages than allowed in this paper; see (Penberthy 1993) for details.

Performance

ZENO has been tested on numerous problems. Our empirical results (Penberthy 1993) show that ZENO's performance is on a par with state-based planners, *e.g.*, UCPOP and PRODIGY, in domains that don't involve interval goals, continuous change and metric relationships (which those planners can't handle). ZENO's speed only degrades when a planning problem demands ZENO's advanced features. Yet even in these domains performance is tolerable, *i.e.*, the current implementation is suitable for experimental research use. Further work on search control and abstraction is needed before ZENO can handle large-scale, practical problems.

---

could switch to Karmarkar's linear programming algorithm which is guaranteed polynomial (Karloff 1991).

[5]This *clairvoyant* proof technique was first used by Mc-Dermott (McDermott 1991) to prove his total-order planner complete.

Figure 4 shows how ZENO performs[6] on three such problems: Allen's door latch example (Allen *et al.* 1991), the airplane example of this paper and the metric blocks world problem from figure 9.3 of (Wilkins 1988b). A simple predicate ordering, *e.g.*, see (Sacerdoti 1974), was used on all but the door latch problem to guide subgoal selection. Iterative-deepening, depth-first search (Korf 1985) handled all other nondeterministic choices.

PROBLEM	CPU TIME (SEC)		
Door latch	0.04	$\pm$	0.00
Airplane routing	151.56	$\pm$	27.56
SIPE example	1.42	$\pm$	0.24

Figure 4: Execution times for the ZENO planner.

Related Work

Because of our interest in formal properties, ZENO is closest in spirit to the work of Allen(Allen 1991), Chapman(Chapman 1987), McAllester(McAllester & Rosenblitt 1991) and Pednault(Pednault 1986). Allen and Pelavin (Allen *et al.* 1991) describe an elegant theory of temporal planning based on first order logic and an interval model of time. In contrast, we model time using the real numbers; this allows metric duration and continuous change.

Numerous systems with some of ZENO's features have been implemented in the past twenty years and we have drawn insight from many of them. Drabble's EXCALIBUR (Drabble 1993) first generates a plan that ignores metric constraints, then tests it through qualitiative simulation; failed tests invoke heuristic replanning. Simmons' GORDIUS (Simmons 1988) handles actions with conditional and metric effects, but uses a state-based model of time and is incomplete. Our approach is considerably simpler than that of SIPE (Wilkins 1990) and DEVISER (Vere 1983) – ZENO avoids parallel links, complex traversal schemes, and heuristic plan evaluation. Similarly, we believe that ZENO's treatment of simultaneous and metric effects is more general than SIPE's. While OPLAN (Currie & Tate 1991) uses ideas from operations research to optimize resource usage, they use different techniques for temporal management. In contrast, ZENO uses an integrated approach for both temporal and other metric constraints, but makes no claim of efficient resource handling.

(Jaffar *et al.* 1992) developed the incremental algorithms and the idea of using Gaussian elimination and Simplex phase I iteration to manage linear equations and inequalities. Our restrictions on the use of metric variables in ZENO's logic are derived from the innovative approaches of (Nelson & Oppen 1979) and (Hendrix 1973).

[6]The experiments were performed on an IBM RS/6000 running Allegro Common Lisp; 95% confidence intervals were calcuated from 10 runs per problem.

Conclusion

ZENO is a least commitment, refinement planning algorithm capable of handling simultaneous actions, continuous change, metric reasoning and deadline goals. Both actions and goals are described in a rich logic supporting universal quantification, disjunction, conjunction, metric functions, logic functions and formal objects. The algorithm is sound *i.e.*, all plans returned as solutions are guaranteed to work. The algorithm is also complete *i.e.*, if a plan exists, then ZENO will find it. A full, working implementation of the program has performance similar to existing state-based planners on comparable domains, but cannot be said to have *heuristic adequacy*. We strive for a system with the performance of SIPE (Wilkins 1988a) and the formal properties of ZENO. Since metering tools show that the bulk of ZENO's time is spent updating and querying its temporal cache, we hope to integrate optimized temporal reasoners, such as (Dechter, Meiri, & Pearl 1991),(Dean 1989) or (Williamson & Hanks 1993), into ZENO's hierarchy of constraint reasoners. As it stands, we believe that ZENO represents a first step towards bridging the gap between formal and empirical approaches to automated planning with expressive temporal languages.

Acknowledgments

We thank Tony Barrett, Alan Borning, Ernie Davis, Denise Draper, Oren Etzioni, Keith Golden, Steve Hanks, Nick Kushmerick, Edwin Pednault, Ying Sun, Mike Williamson, and the anonymous reviewers for helpful comments.

References

Allen, J., Kautz, H., Pelavin, R., and Tenenberg, J. 1991. *Reasoning about Plans*. San Mateo, CA: Morgan Kaufmann.

Allen, J. 1991. Planning as temporal reasoning. In *Proceedings of the Second International Conference on Principles of Knowledge Representation and Reasoning*, 3–14.

Chapman, D. 1987. Planning for conjunctive goals. *Artificial Intelligence* 32(3):333–377.

Collins, G., and Pryor, L. 1992. Achieving the functionality of filter conditions in a partial order planner. In *Proc. 10th Nat. Conf. on A.I.*

Currie, K., and Tate, A. 1991. O-plan: the open planning architecture. *Artificial Intelligence* 52(1):49–86.

Dean, T. 1989. Using Temporal Hierarchies to Efficiently Maintain Large Temporal Databases. *Journal of the ACM* 36(4):687–718.

Dechter, R., Meiri, I., and Pearl, J. 1991. Temporal constraint networks. *Artificial Intelligence* 49:61–96.

Drabble, B. 1993. Excalibur: a program for planning and reasoning with processes. *Artificial Intelligence* 62:1–40.

Hendrix, G. 1973. Modeling simultaneous actions an continuous processes. *Artificial Intelligence* 4:145–180.

Jaffar, J., Michaylov, S., Stuckey, P., and Yap, R. 1992. The CLP(R) Language and System. *ACM Transactions on Programming Languages and Systems* 14(3):339–395.

Karloff, H. 1991. *Linear Programming*. Boston: Birkhäuser.

Korf, R. 1985. Depth-first iterative deepening: An optimal admissible tree search. *Artificial Intelligence* 27(1):97–109.

McAllester, D., and Rosenblitt, D. 1991. Systematic nonlinear planning. In *Proc. 9th Nat. Conf. on A.I.*, 634–639.

McDermott, D. 1991. Regression planning. *International Journal of Intelligent Systems* 6:357–416.

Nelson, G., and Oppen, D. C. 1979. Simplification by cooperating decision procedures. *ACM Transactions on Programming Languages and Systems* 1(2):245–257.

Pednault, E. 1986. *Toward a Mathematical Theory of Plan Synthesis*. Ph.D. Dissertation, Stanford University.

Penberthy, J., and Weld, D. 1992. UCPOP: A sound, complete, partial order planner for ADL. In *Proc. 3rd Int. Conf. on Principles of Knowledge Representation and Reasoning*, 103–114. Available via FTP from pub/ai/ at cs.washington.edu.

Penberthy, J. 1993. *Planning with Continuous Change*. Ph.D. Dissertation, University of Washington. Available as UW CSE Tech Report 93-12-01.

Sacerdoti, E. 1974. Planning in a hierarchy of abstraction spaces. *Artificial Intelligence* 5:115–135.

Simmons, R. 1988. Combining associational and causal reasoning to solve interpretation and planning problems. AI-TR-1048, MIT AI Lab.

Vere, S. 1983. Planning in time: Windows and durations for activities and goals. *IEEE Trans. on Pattern Analysis and Machine Intelligence* 5:246–267.

Warshall, S. 1962. A theorem on boolean matrices. *Journal of the ACM* 9(1).

Weld, D. 1994. An introduction to least-commitment planning. *AI Magazine*. Available via FTP from pub/ai/ at cs.washington.edu.

Wilkins, D. 1988a. Causal reasoning in planning. *Computational Intelligence* 4(4):373–380.

Wilkins, D. E. 1988b. *Practical Planning*. San Mateo, CA: Morgan Kaufmann.

Wilkins, D. 1990. Can AI planners solve practical problems? *Computational Intelligence* 6(4):232–246.

Williamson, M., and Hanks, S. 1993. Exploiting domain structure to achieve efficient temporal reasoning. In *Proc. 13th Int. Joint Conf. on A.I.*, 152–157.

Using Abstractions for Decision-Theoretic Planning with Time Constraints

Craig Boutilier and Richard Dearden
Department of Computer Science
University of British Columbia
Vancouver, BC, CANADA, V6T 1Z4
email: {cebly,dearden}@cs.ubc.ca

Abstract

Recently Markov decision processes and optimal control policies have been applied to the problem of decision-theoretic planning. However, the classical methods for generating optimal policies are highly intractable, requiring explicit enumeration of large state spaces. We explore a method for generating abstractions that allow approximately optimal policies to be constructed; computational gains are achieved through reduction of the state space. Abstractions are generated by identifying propositions that are "relevant" either through their direct impact on utility, or their influence on actions. This information is gleaned from the representation of utilities and actions. We prove bounds on the loss in value due to abstraction and describe some preliminary experimental results.

1 Introduction

Recently there has been considerable interest in probabilistic and decision-theoretic planning (DTP) [5, 9, 14, 3]. A probabilistic framework allows agents to plan in situations of uncertainty, while decision-theoretic methods permit comparison of various courses of action, or the construction of appropriate nearly-optimal behavior when (optimal) goals are unachievable. Dean et al. [2] have investigated planning in such contexts as a question of stochastic optimal control, in particular, modeling the effects of actions on the environment as a (completely observable) Markov decision process (MDP) [7]. This model allows one to view each action as a stochastic mapping among states of the environment, and allows one to associate various rewards or utilities with these states. With such a model, standard techniques can be used to construct an optimal *policy* of action that maximizes the expected reward of the agent. Unfortunately, these methods quickly become intractable as the state space grows. As a concession to these considerations, Dean et al. [2] explore anytime algorithms for policy generation using restricted *envelopes* within the state space.

We explore a different way of coping with the computational difficulties involved in optimal policy generation. By assuming a particular representation of actions, we can generate an *abstract* state space in which (concrete) states are clustered together. Standard techniques may be used in this reduced space. Our approach has several advantages over the envelope method. Foremost among these is the fact that no states are ignored in abstract policy generation – each state may have some influence on the constructed policy by membership in an abstract state. This allows us to prove bounds on the value of abstract policies (with respect to an optimal policy). Furthermore, finer-grained abstractions are guaranteed to increase the value of policies. Finally, abstractions can be generated quickly. These factors allow abstract policies of varying degrees of accuracy to be constructed in response to time pressures. The information obtained in abstract policy generation can then be used in a real-time fashion to refine the abstract policy, as we describe in the concluding section. This is also well-suited to circumstances where the goals (or reward structure) communicated to an agent change frequently; thus problem-specific abstractions can be generated as needed.

In the next section we describe the MDPs, Howard's [7] *policy iteration* algorithm for optimal policy construction and (briefly) the anytime approach of [2]. In Section 3, we discuss a possible knowledge representation scheme for actions and utilities. The information implicit in such a specification will be crucial in generating useful abstractions. In Section 4, we present an algorithm for generating an abstract state space and an appropriate decision model. We show how policy iteration is used to generate abstract policies in this state space that are directly applicable to the original (concrete) space, and prove bounds on the possible loss due to abstraction. We also discuss preliminary experimental results that suggest that abstraction of this form is quite valuable in certain types of domains.

2 Markov Decision Processes

Let W be a finite set of states or worlds, the possible situations in which a planning agent may find itself. We assume that this set of worlds is associated with some logical propositional language $\mathcal{L}$, and is thus exponential in the number of atoms generating $\mathcal{L}$. Let A be a finite set of actions available to an agent. An action takes the agent from one world to another, but the result of an action is known only with some probability. An action may then be viewed as a mapping from W into probability distributions over W. We write $Pr(w_1, a, w_2)$ to denote the probability that w_2 is reached given that action a is performed in state w_1. These transition probabilities can be encoded in a $|W| \times |W|$ matrix for each action. This notation embodies the usual Markov assumption that the transition probabilities depend only on the current state.

While an agent cannot (generally) predict with certainty the state that will result from its action, we assume it can observe with certainty the resulting state once the transition is made. Hence the process is *completely observable*. All uncertainty is due to the unpredictability of actions. While some have this property, there will be many domains in which this is not the case. However, complete observability is a useful simplifying assumption that allows us to explore the fundamentals of abstraction, ignoring the technical difficulties of the partially observable case.

We assume a real-valued *reward function R*, with $R(w)$ denoting the (immediate) utility of being in state w. For our purposes an MDP consists of W, $\mathcal{A}$, R and the set of transition distributions $\{Pr(\cdot, a, \cdot) : a \in \mathcal{A}\}$.

A control *policy* π is a function $\pi : W \to \mathcal{A}$. If this policy is adopted, $\pi(w)$ is the action an agent will perform whenever it finds itself in state w. Given an MDP, an agent ought to adopt an optimal policy that maximizes the expected rewards accumulated as it performs the specified actions. We concentrate here on *discounted infinite horizon* problems: the current value of future rewards is discounted by some factor β $(0 < \beta < 1)$; and we want to maximize the expected accumulated discounted rewards over an infinite time period. However, our methods are suitable for finite horizon techniques such as *value iteration* [7] as well. Intuitively, a DTP problem can be viewed as finding an optimal policy.[1]

The expected *value* of a fixed policy π at any given state w is specified by

$$V_\pi(w) = R(w) + \beta \sum_{v \in W} Pr(w, \pi(w), v) \cdot V_\pi(v)$$

Since the factors $V_\pi(w)$ are mutually dependent, the value of π at any initial state w can be computed by solving this system of linear equations. A policy π is *optimal* if $V_\pi(w) \geq V_{\pi'}(w)$ for all $w \in W$ and policies π'. Howard's [7] policy iteration algorithm works by starting with a random policy and trying to improve this policy by finding for each world some action better than the action specified by the policy. Each iteration of the algorithm involves the following two steps:

1. For each $w \in W$, compute $V_\pi(w)$.
2. For each $w \in W$, find some action a such that

$$R(w) + \beta \sum_{v \in W} Pr(w, a, v) \cdot V_\pi(v) > V_\pi(w)$$

Let policy π' be such that $\pi'(w) = a$ if such an improvement exists, $\pi'(w) = \pi(w)$ otherwise.

---

[1] If a "final" state stops the process, we may use absorbing states (at which no action is applicable). Classical (categorical) goals can also be specified [2].

The algorithm iterates on each new policy π' until no improvement is found. The algorithm will converge on an optimal policy, and in practice tends to converge reasonably (given, e.g., a *greedy* initial policy). The first step requires the solution of a set of $|W|$ linear equations in $|W|$ unknowns (requiring polynomial time).

Unfortunately, the factor $|W|$ will be exponential in the number of atoms in our underlying language. Optimal policy construction is thus computationally demanding. Such solutions methods may be reasonable in the design of an agent requiring a fixed policy. A solution might be computed off-line and a corresponding reactive policy embodied in the agent "once and for all." However, a fixed policy of this type is not feasible in a setting where an agent must respond to the changing goals or preferences of a user. While in many domains the system dynamics may be relatively stable, the reward structure for which an agent's behavior is designed might change frequently (e.g., in response to different task assignments). Therefore, fast on-line computation of policies will be necessary and the computational bottleneck must be addressed. We expect optimality (of policy) to be sacrificed for computational gain.

To deal with the difficulties of policy construction, Dean et al. [2] assume that it will be sufficient in many circumstances to consider a very restricted subset of the state space. Their basic approach is as follows: an initial *envelope* $\mathcal{E}$, or subset of worlds, is chosen and a *partial policy* is computed for $\mathcal{E}$ (i.e., a policy applicable only for states in $\mathcal{E}$) using policy iteration. Since an agent might fall out of the envelope while executing a policy, all transitions out of $\mathcal{E}$ are assumed to fall into a distinguished OUT state. If an agent ends up in this state, it must extend (or alter) the current envelope and compute a new partial policy. The anytime aspect of this model is captured by an algorithm which constructs a partial policy for $\mathcal{E}$, and if time permits extends $\mathcal{E}$ to include more states. Given more time the algorithm will compute a more complete partial policy.

This model requires an estimate of the penalty associated with the OUT state. In [2] it is suggested that the expected value of all "out states" and some factor accounting for the time to recompute a policy be used; but determining this expected value requires at least some approximation to an optimal policy (though in certain domains heuristics may be available). An initial envelope must also be provided. In general, it is not clear how a good initial envelope should be generated, although in [2] some reasonable guidelines are suggested for certain domains (such as navigation).

We propose an alternative anytime model for nearly optimal policy construction based on *abstraction* of the state space. While considering a restricted envelope may be appropriate in many instances, in general finding a suitable subset may be difficult, and partial policies are not suitable for an agent that may find itself in arbitrary start states. In our approach, we ignore "irrelevant aspects" to the domain by grouping together states that differ only in these aspects. Approximately optimal policies can be generated in this smaller state space. Since irrelevance is a matter of degree, more accurate policies can be constructed (at greater computational expense) by incorporating additional details. Our model provides several advantages over the envelope method. First, policies are applicable at all states of the process. Second, we may provably bound the degree to which policies fall short of optimal. This factor can be used to influence how detailed an abstraction is required (and also the direction in which abstractions should be refined). Finally, our model has the feature that more refined abstractions lead to better policies.

3 Representation of MDPs

It is unreasonable to expect that a DTP problem will be specified using an explicit stochastic transition matrix for each action and an explicit reward function. Regularities in action effects and reward structure will usually permit more concise representations. We discuss one possible representation for actions and utilities, and show how this information can be exploited in abstraction generation. While our algorithm depends on the particular representation given, the nature of our method does not. More natural and sophisticated representations can be used (e.g., causal networks).

3.1 Action Representation

To represent actions that have "probabilistic effects" we will adopt a modification of the basic scheme presented in [9], itself a modification of the STRIPS representation allowing effects (add/delete lists) to be applied with a certain probability. We start by defining an *effect* to be a (finite) consistent set of literals. If E is an effect, its occurrence changes the world. We let $E(w)$ denote the world that results when effect E is applied to w. In the usual STRIPS fashion, $E(w)$ satisfies all literals in E and agrees with w on all other literals.

To deal with nondeterministic actions, we assume that possible effects occur with specified probabilities. A *probabilistic effect* is a finite set of effects $E_1, \ldots E_n$ with associated probabilities $p_1, \ldots p_n$, written $\langle E_1, p_1; \ldots E_n, p_n \rangle$. We insist that $\sum p_i = 1$. An effects list EL applied to w induces a discrete distribution over W; the likelihood of moving to v when EL occurs at w is given by

$$Pr(v|EL, w) = \sum \{p_i : E_i(w) = v\}$$

An action can have different effects in different contexts. We associate with each action a finite set $D_1, \ldots D_n$ of mutually exclusive and exhaustive propositions called *discriminants*; and associated with each discriminant is a probabilistic effects list EL_i. An action a applied at w yields the distribution over outcomes induced by EL_k, where D_k is the (unique) discriminant satisfied by w.

Parting from [9], we add the notion of an *action aspect*. Some actions have different classes of effects that occur independently of each other. For instance, under a given action, a certain literal may be made true if some condition holds. A distinct literal may independently be made true if another condition holds. To capture this, an action can be specified using different aspects, each of which has the form

of an action as described above (i.e., each aspect has its own discriminant set). The actual effect of an action at a world is determined by applying the effects list of the relevant discriminant for *each* aspect of that action. More precisely, let w be some world to which we apply an action with k aspects. Since each aspect has a proper discriminant set associated with it, w satisfies exactly one discriminant for each aspect. Assume these are $D^1, \cdots, D^k$ and that each D^i has an associated effects list $\langle E_1^i, p_1^i; \ldots E_n^i, p_n^i \rangle$. An effect from each applicable list will occur with the specified probability, these probabilities being independent. Intuitively, action aspects capture the kind of independence assumptions one might find in a causal network or influence diagram. Thus, the net effect of an action A at w is the union of these effects (sets of literals), one chosen from each aspect. The probability of this combined effect is determined by multiplying these probabilities. Thus, we have

$$Pr(v|A, w) = \sum \{p_{j_1}^1 \cdot p_{j_2}^2 \cdots p_{j_k}^k : E(w) = v\}$$

where E is an effect such that

$$E = E_{j_1}^1 \cup E_{j_2}^2 \cup \cdots \cup E_{j_k}^k$$

To ensure that actions are well-formed we impose the following consistency condition: if D^i and D^j are mutually consistent discriminants taken from distinct aspects of a given action, then their effects lists must contain no atoms in common (thus, the union above is consistent).

An example best illustrates this representation. We assume a user at location $L1$ instructs a robot to get her coffee at $L2$ across the street. The robot can have coffee (HCR) and an umbrella (U). It can get wet (W) if it is raining (R), and the user can have coffee (HCU) as well. Actions include going to $L1$ or $L2$, buying coffee, delivering coffee to the user and getting an umbrella. These action specifications are listed in Figure 1.[2] The actions GoL1 and GoL2 each have two aspects. GoL1 induces transition probabilities from any world w satisfying $\overline{L1}, L2, R$ and $\overline{U}$ as follows: the effect $\{L1, \overline{L2}, W\}$ occurs with probability .81; $\{L1, \overline{L2}\}$ occurs with probability .09; $\{W\}$ occurs with probability .09; and the null effect $\emptyset$ occurs with probability .01.

3.2 Utility Representation

To represent the immediate rewards or utilities associated with world states, we assume a user specifies a partition of the state space that groups worlds together if they have the same utility. This is achieved by providing a mutually exclusive and exhaustive set of propositions and associating a utility with each proposition in this set. There are more natural and concise methods for utility representation. For

---

[2] We ignore preconditions for actions here, assuming that an action can be "attempted" in any circumstance. However, preconditions may play a useful role by capturing user-supplied heuristics that filter out actions in situations in which they *ought not* (rather than *cannot*) be attempted. The else discriminant is simply a convenient notation for the negation of all action discriminants that appear earlier in the list.

Action	Discr.	Effect	Prob.	Action	Discr.	Effect	Prob.
GoL1	$\overline{L1}, L2$	$L1, \overline{L2}$	0.9	GoL2	$\overline{L2}, L1$	$L2, \overline{L1}$	0.9
(aspect1)		$\emptyset$	0.1	(aspect1)		$\emptyset$	0.1
	else	$\emptyset$	1.0		else	$\emptyset$	1.0
GoL1	$R, \overline{U}$	W	0.9	GoL2	$R, \overline{U}$	W	0.9
(aspect2)		$\emptyset$	0.1	(aspect2)		$\emptyset$	0.1
	else	$\emptyset$	1.0		else	$\emptyset$	1.0
BuyC	$L2$	HCR	0.8	DelC	$L1, HCR$	$HCU, \overline{HCR}$	0.8
		$\emptyset$	0.2			$\overline{HCR}$	0.1
	else	$\emptyset$	1.0			$\emptyset$	0.1
GetU	$L1$	U	0.9		$\overline{L1}, HCR$	$\overline{HCR}$	0.9
		$\emptyset$	0.1			$\emptyset$	0.1
	else	$\emptyset$	1.0		else	$\emptyset$	1.0

Figure 1: An example of STRIPS-style action descriptions.

example, if the utilities of propositions are independent and additive, these can be directly specified (relative to some base level). Indeed, such a scheme will generally make the problem we address in the next section easier. But this simple scheme will be sufficient for our purposes. Note that any reward function over a state space generated by a set of propositions can be represented in this fashion.

In our example, the primary goal of the agent is to get coffee; but we would like it to stay dry in the process. No other propositions influence the immediate reward of a state. We obtain the following specification of our reward function:

Discr.	Reward.	Discr.	Reward.
$HCU, \overline{W}$	1.0	HCU, W	.9
$\overline{HCU}, \overline{W}$	.1	$\overline{HCU}, W$	0.0

We dub the propositions that determine the immediate utility of a state *utility discriminants*.

4 Generating an Abstract Model

State-aggregation methods have been used to accelerate convergence of MDP solution methods with some success (e.g., [12]). However, the emphasis has not been on the automatic generation of aggregated states, nor on the exploitation of regularities implicit of the representation of an MDP. Abstraction has also been used in classical planning to guide the search for concrete, fully-specified plans [11]. In particular, Knoblock [8] has proposed methods for generating abstractions by exploiting a STRIPS-style action represention. Our procedure uses the representation scheme for actions in much the same fashion, as well as utilities, to decide which propositions are most important in the construction of a good policy, and which details can be ignored with little penalty. Once certain propositions are shown to be irrelevant, the state space can be collapsed by clustering together worlds in which only irrelevant propositions differ (i.e., worlds are distinguished by relevant propositions only). Policy iteration can then be performed in this abstract space and an approximately optimal policy can be generated. Unlike the classical setting, an abstract policy can be used immediately and can be refined on-line.

There are three issues that must be addressed using such a scheme: 1) which propositions should be deemed relevant? 2) how should actions be mapped onto the abstract space? 3) how should utilities be mapped onto the abstract space?

4.1 The Abstract State Space

In order to generate an abstract state space, a set of relevant propositions must be chosen. From the perspective of immediate utility, only those propositions that occur among the set of utility discriminants are of direct relevance. In our example, W and HCU are the only (immediately) relevant atoms. Of course, immediate relevance is a matter of degree. The truth or falsity of HCU has a greater immediate impact on utility than W. It is this observation that will allow us to ignore certain atomic propositions.

Initially, we imagine an agent generates some set $\mathcal{IR}$ of *immediately relevant* propositions. The larger this set is, the more fine-grained an abstraction will be. This is the crucial factor in the anytime nature of our approach. A larger number of abstract states will require more computation, but will yield more accurate results. It is therefore important that the relevant propositions be chosen carefully so as to take full advantage of this tradeoff. Propositions with the greatest impact on utility are most relevant. A number of strategies might be employed for discovering the most relevant propositions. We discuss one such strategy below, once the exact nature of our algorithm has been elaborated. In our example, we decide that HCU is the most important proposition, setting $\mathcal{IR} = \{HCU\}$. If we add W to $\mathcal{IR}$, then the entire range of immediate utility is captured (and optimal solutions will be generated, but at added computational cost – see below). We will assume for simplicity that utility discriminants are conjunctions of literals (this is sufficient for any utility function) and that $\mathcal{IR}$ consists of atoms.

An agent should make distinctions based not only on immediately relevant propositions, but on propositions that may influence the achievement of these. Thus, we provide a recursive definition for the set $\mathcal{R}$ of *relevant propositions*. The idea is based on the construction of abstraction hierarchies by Knoblock [8] in a classical STRIPS domain. It relies on the particular action representation above; but the general idea is well-suited to other action representations (e.g., the situation calculus and, especially, causal networks).

Definition The set $\mathcal{R}$ of *relevant propositions* is the smallest set such that: 1) $\mathcal{IR} \subseteq \mathcal{R}$; and 2) if $P \in \mathcal{R}$ "occurs" in an effect list of some action aspect, each proposition occurring in the corresponding discriminant is in $\mathcal{R}$.

Again, for simplicity, we will assume that $\mathcal{R}$ consists of atoms and that an atom occurs in a list if the associated positive or negative literal occurs. Notice that only the atoms of a discriminant that might (probabilistically) lead to a certain effect are deemed relevant; other conditions associated with the same action aspect can be ignored.[3] We call such discriminants *relevant*. We leave aside the question of an algorithm for generating the set $\mathcal{R}$ given $\mathcal{IR}$ (see [1] for details); an obvious modification of Knoblock's algorithm for generating *problem specific constraints* suffices. The *operator graph* construct of [13] might also prove useful in determining relevant discriminants. The "branching factor" of stochastic actions, the average size of discriminant and effects lists, and the degree of "interconnection" will determine the time required to generate $\mathcal{R}$; it will certainly be insignificant in relation to the time required to produce the abstract policy.

In our example, HCU is influenced by $L1$ and HCR. Both are, in turn, influenced by $L2$. Thus $\mathcal{R} = \{L1, L2, HCR, HCU\}$. Notice that the use of action aspects, while not necessary, can be useful not only as a convenient representational device, but also for reducing the number of relevant atoms for a given problem.

Given the set of relevant atoms, we can generate an abstract state space by clustering together worlds that agree on the members or $\mathcal{R}$, ignoring irrelevant details.

Definition The abstract state space generated by $\mathcal{R}$ is $\widetilde{W} = \{\widetilde{w}_1, \ldots \widetilde{w}_n\}$, where: a) $\widetilde{w}_i \subseteq W$; b) $\cup\{\widetilde{w}_i\} = W$; c) $\widetilde{w}_i \cap \widetilde{w}_j = \emptyset$ if $i \neq j$; and d) $w, v \in \widetilde{w}_i$ iff $w \models P$ implies $v \models P$ for all $P \in \mathcal{R}$.

Any worlds that agree on the truth of the elements of $\mathcal{R}$ are clustered together — in our example, the atoms R, U and W are ignored. Thus, $\widetilde{W}$ contains just 16 states rather than the 128 contained in W.

4.2 Abstract Actions and Utilities

If an optimal policy is to be constructed over this abstract state space, we require actions and a reward function which are applicable in this space. In general, computing the transition probabilities for actions associated with an arbitrary clustering of states is computationally prohibitive; for it requires that one consider the effect of an action on each world in an abstract state. Furthermore, computing the probability of moving from one cluster to another under a given action requires that a prior distribution over worlds in the first cluster be known, which cannot be known in general.

Fortunately, our abstraction mechanism is designed to avoid such difficulties. The action descriptions for the concrete space can be readily modified to fit the abstract space as shown by the following propositions.

<hr>

[3]This connection can be weakened further by ignoring discriminant atoms whose influence on utility is marginal (see the concluding section).

Proposition 1 *Let $\widetilde{w}$ be an abstract state and let $w, v \in \widetilde{w}$. Then w satisfies a relevant discriminant for some action aspect iff v does.*

Proposition 2 *Let E be any effect. i) If E is associated with an irrelevant discriminant, then $E(w) \in \widetilde{w}$; and ii) $E(w) \in \widetilde{u}$ iff $E(v) \in \widetilde{u}$.*

Intuitively, these conditions ensure that for any two worlds in a given cluster, an action maps these with equal probability to worlds in any other cluster. In other words, actions can be viewed as applying directly to clusters. Furthermore, the action discriminants and probabilities can be used within the abstract space to determine the probability of a transition from one cluster to another when an action is performed. (We give a general algorithm in [1].) Because of these factors no new abstract actions are required and the abstract state space and transition matrices induced by the original actions enjoy the Markov property.

In our example, the cluster containing those worlds that satisfy $L1, \overline{L2}, \overline{HCU}, \overline{HCR}$ maps to cluster $\overline{L1}, L2, \overline{HCU}, \overline{HCR}$ with probability 0.9 under GoL1 and maps to itself with probability 0.1. Under action GetU, it maps to itself with probability 1.0 (since GetU affects no relevant atoms).

To associate an immediate utility with a given cluster, we use the midpoint of the range of utilities for worlds within that cluster. For any cluster $\widetilde{w}$, let $\min(\widetilde{w})$ denote the minimum of the set $\{R(w) : w \in \widetilde{w}\}$ and $\max(\widetilde{w})$ denote the corresponding maximum. Our *abstract reward function* is:

$$R(\widetilde{w}) = \frac{\max(\widetilde{w}) + \min(\widetilde{w})}{2}$$

This choice of $R(\widetilde{w})$ minimizes the possible difference between $R(w)$ and $R(\widetilde{w})$ for any $w \in \widetilde{w}$, and is adopted for reasons we explain below. Any cluster satisfying HCU has an abstract utility of .95 (since some worlds have a reward of 1.0 and some 0.9), while $\overline{HCU}$ ensures a utility of .05.

4.3 Abstract Policies and their Properties

With the abstract state space, actions and reward function in place, we now have a Markov decision process for which an optimal policy can be constructed using policy iteration. Since computation time for an optimal policy is a function of the number of states, the cardinality of $\mathcal{R}$ will determine the savings over optimal policy construction in the original state space. Since the state space increases exponentially in size as the number of relevant atoms increase, any reduction can result in tremendous speed-up.

Of course, this speed-up comes at the cost of generating possibly less-than-optimal policies. Thus, some measure of the loss associated with constructing policies in the abstract space must be proposed. Let us denote by $\widetilde{\pi}$ the *optimal abstract policy* (that generated for our abstract MDP). We take $\widetilde{\pi}$ to be mapped into a concrete policy π in the obvious way: $\pi(w) = \widetilde{\pi}(\widetilde{w})$ where $w \in \widetilde{w}$.

Along with $\widetilde{\pi}$, policy iteration will produce an abstract value function $V_{\widetilde{\pi}}$. We can take $V_{\widetilde{\pi}}$ to be an estimate of the true value of the concrete policy π; that is, $V_\pi(w)$ is approximated by $V_{\widetilde{\pi}}(\widetilde{w})$ where $w \in \widetilde{w}$. The difference between $V_\pi(w)$ and $V_{\widetilde{\pi}}(\widetilde{w})$ is a measure of the accuracy of policy iteration over the abstract space in estimating the value of the induced concrete policy.

Of more interest is the degree to which the generated abstract policy differs from truly optimal policy. Let $\pi*$ denote some optimal policy for the original process, with corresponding value function $V_{\pi*}$. The true measure of goodness for an abstract policy $\widetilde{\pi}$ is the degree to which the induced concrete policy π differs from $\pi*$; more precisely, we should be interested in the difference between $V_\pi(w)$ and $V_{\pi*}(w)$ (for any world w).

Bounds on the magnitudes of these differences can be computed using the *utility span* for a cluster $\widetilde{w}$: $span(\widetilde{w}) = \max(\widetilde{w}) - \min(\widetilde{w})$. This is the maximum degree to which the estimate $R(\widetilde{w})$ of the immediate utility of a world in that cluster differs from the world's true utility $R(w)$. Let δ denote the maximum span among all clusters in $\widetilde{W}$. We have the following bounds (recall β is the discounting factor):

Theorem 3 $|V_{\widetilde{\pi}}(\widetilde{w}) - V_\pi(w)| \leq \frac{\delta}{2(1-\beta)}$, *for any* $w \in W$.

Theorem 4 $|V_{\pi*}(w) - V_\pi(w)| \leq \frac{\beta\delta}{1-\beta}$, *for any* $w \in W$.

Thus we have some reasonable guarantees about the effectiveness of the computed policy. The key factor in the effectiveness of an abstraction is the size of δ in relation to the ranges of possible values. Intuitively, the abstract policy can lose no more than δ reward per time step or action taken (compared to optimal). This a very facile worst-case analysis and is unlikely to ever be reached for any world (let alone all worlds). Some preliminary experimental results have borne out this intuition.

In our example, with $\mathcal{R} = \{L1, L2, HCR, HCU\}$, the abstract policy $\widetilde{\pi}$ generated essentially requires the robot to get coffee directly, ignoring the umbrella, whereas the true optimal policy $\pi*$ will have the robot get the umbrella if it is raining (if it starts at $L1$). With a discounting factor β of 0.9, Theorem 4 guarantees that the expected value of the abstract policy, for any state, will be within 0.9 of optimal. To calibrate this, we note that the possible *optimal values* (over W) range from 0 and 10. Computing the abstract policy $\widetilde{\pi}$ shows that for all $w \in W$ we have $|V_{\pi*}(w) - V_\pi(w)| \leq 0.8901$. Furthermore, at only 12 of 128 states did the concrete and optimal values differ at all. The time required to produce the abstract policy was 0.12 seconds compared with 21 seconds for policy iteration performed on the complete network. Although we cannot expect such performance in all domains, these results, as well as other experiments, show that in many cases the algorithm performs extremely well, producing policies that are close to optimal and requiring considerably less computation time than policy iteration.

The utility span formulation of abstraction value shows the direction in which one should refine abstractions: the propositions that should be incorporated into a new abstraction are those that reduce the maximum utility span δ the most. At

some point in refinement, should δ reach 0, optimal policies will be generated. Finally, should a more refined abstraction be used, the generated policy cannot be worse (and will typically be better, if any utility span is reduced, even if the maximum span δ remains constant). Let $\mathcal{IR}_1 \subseteq \mathcal{IR}_2$ be two sets of immediately relevant atoms, and let π and ψ be the concrete policies induced by $\mathcal{IR}_1$ and $\mathcal{IR}_2$, respectively.

Theorem 5 $|V_{\psi*}(w) - V_\psi(w)| \leq |V_{\pi*}(w) - V_\pi(w)|$ *for any* $w \in W$.

Naturally, this analysis shows how one should determine the initial set $\mathcal{IR}$ of immediately relevant atoms. For a particular set $\mathcal{IR}$, the corresponding set $\mathcal{R}$ of relevant atoms is not immediately obvious, but can be computed as described above (in negligible time). In the case where abstractions are to be generated frequently for different problems, appropriate information of this type can be re-used. The size of $\mathcal{R}$ is a good predictor of the time required to generate an abstract policy. Thus, our algorithm has a "contract anytime" nature (relative to the computation of $\mathcal{R}$). The quality of the abstract policy can be bounded by Theorem 4, and the "quality" of a particular $\mathcal{IR}$ can be computed easily by considering the abstract states it induces. More precisely, let $T_{\mathcal{IR}}$ be the set of truth assignments to $\mathcal{IR}$ (we treat these loosely as conjunctions of literals). Let D be the set of utility discriminants. For any $t \in T_{\mathcal{IR}}$, let

$$\max(t) = \max_{d \in D}\{R(d) : d \not\models \neg t\}$$

and let $\min(t)$ denote the corresponding minimal value. The "goodness" of $\mathcal{IR}$ is measured by

$$\max_{t \in T_{\mathcal{IR}}}\{\max(t) - \min(t)\}$$

The smaller this value (the maximal utility span), the tighter the guarantee on the optimality of the abstract policy. While the computation of this maximal span is exponential in the number of immediately relevant atoms, $\mathcal{IR}$ will always be restricted to atoms mentioned in the reward function R, which will be a rather small subset of atoms.

The idea of using utility spans to generate abstractions is proposed by Horvitz and Klein [6], who use the notion in single-step decision making. Our analysis can be applied to their framework to establish bounds on the degree to which an "abstract decision" can be less than optimal. Furthermore, the notion is useful in more general circumstances, as our results illustrate.

5 Concluding Remarks

We have shown that abstraction can be a valuable tool for computing close-to-optimal policies for MDPs and DTP. Our approach is one that is amenable to both theoretical and experimental analysis, and appears promising given our preliminary results. Our model provides "contract anytime behavior" since the computation time required is determined by the number of relevant propositions chosen. Our approach has a number of interesting benefits. Since abstractions can be generated relatively easily, our approach is well-suited to problem-specific abstractions, for instance, to particular reward functions or starting state distributions (see Knoblock [8], who also discusses problem-specific abstraction). Furthermore, since abstractions cover all possible states, the abstract state space offers a useful method for representing reactive strategies. A close-to-optimal strategy can be encoded with exponential space-saving. This may be useful also in determining which bits of information a reactive agent should ignore when sensor costs are high.

There are a great number of directions in which this work is being extended. We are currently exploring an expected-case analysis by making certain assumptions about problem distributions, augmenting the worst-case results provided here. We are also exploring other methods of ignoring details. In particular, we have developed some methods for considering only discriminants whose relevant effects are sufficiently probable or sufficiently important [1]. In our example, carrying the umbrella might *slightly* decrease the chance of successful coffee delivery, but can be ignored. While the concrete action probabilities are not accurate in such an abstract space, they are roughly correct. The Markov assumption is "approximately" true and the error associated with solving the problem with inaccurate transition probabilities can be bounded. Discounting can be incorporated in such a model to further reduce the number of relevant atoms; essentially, effects from a "distance" can be given less weight. A crucial feature of this extension is the fact that abstractions are generated reasonably quickly. Nicholson and Kaelbling [10] have proposed abstracting state spaces in a similar fashion using sensitivity analysis to determine relevant variables; however, such a method has high computational cost.

A key problem is the adaptation of our method to different action and utility representations (e.g., using causal networks, or general propositional action and utility discriminants). This should lead to adaptive and nonuniform clustering techniques. However, there are certain technical difficulties associated with nonuniform clusters. We hope to investigate the features of both the envelope and abstraction methods and determine to which types of domains each is best suited and how the intuitions of both might be combined (see [10]). Features that will ensure the success of our technique include: a propositional domain representation; approximately additive utilities over features; a wide range of utilities; goals with possible minor improvements, and so on. The extent to which real domains possess these qualities is ultimately an empirical question.

We are also exploring search methods that can be used to refine abstract policies [4]. While an abstract policy might not be ultimately acceptable, it may be suitable as a set of default reactions under time-pressure. As time permits, finite-horizon decision-tree search can be used to refine the policy. The abstract value function, a by-product of abstract policy construction, can be used quite profitably as a heuristic function to guide this search. Preliminary results appear quite promising. In our example, search of depth 4 guarantees optimal action [4]. Finally, we hope to generalize our techniques to semi-Markov and partially observable processes.

The computational difficulties associated with the partially observable case make abstraction especially attractive in that setting.

Acknowledgements

Discussions with Moisés Goldszmidt have considerably influenced our view and use of abstraction for MDPs. Thanks to Eric Horvitz, Ann Nicholson and an anonymous referee for helpful comments. This research was supported by NSERC Research Grant OGP0121843 and a UBC University Graduate Fellowship.

References

[1] Craig Boutilier and Richard Dearden. Using abstractions for decision-theoretic planning with time constraints. Technical report, University of British Columbia, Vancouver, 1994. (Forthcoming).

[2] Thomas Dean, Leslie Pack Kaelbling, Jak Kirman, and Ann Nicholson. Planning with deadlines in stochastic domains. In *Proc. of AAAI-93*, pages 574–579, Washington, D.C., 1993.

[3] Thomas Dean and Michael Wellman. *Planning and Control*. Morgan Kaufmann, San Mateo, 1991.

[4] Richard Dearden and Craig Boutilier. Integrating planning and execution in stochastic domains. In *AAAI Spring Symposium on Decision Theoretic Planning*, pages 55–61, Stanford, 1994.

[5] Mark Drummond and John Bresina. Anytime synthetic projection: Maximizing the probability of goal satisfaction. In *Proc. of AAAI-90*, pages 138–144, Boston, 1990.

[6] Eric J. Horvitz and Adrian C. Klein. Utility-based abstraction and categorization. In *Proc. of UAI-93*, pages 128–135, Washington, D.C., 1993.

[7] Ronald A. Howard. *Dynamic Probabilistic Systems*. Wiley, New York, 1971.

[8] Craig A. Knoblock. *Generating Abstraction Hierarchies: An Automated Approach to Reducing Search in Planning*. Kluwer, Boston, 1993.

[9] N. Kushmerick, S. Hanks, and D. Weld. An algorithm for probabilistic planning. Technical Report 93-06-04, University of Washington, Seattle, June 1993.

[10] Ann E. Nicholson and Leslie Pack Kaelbling. Toward approximate planning in very large stochastic domains. In *AAAI Spring Symposium on Decision Theoretic Planning*, pages 190–196, Stanford, 1994.

[11] Earl D. Sacerdoti. Planning in a hierarchy of abstraction spaces. *Artificial Intelligence*, 5:115–135, 1974.

[12] Paul L. Schweitzer, Martin L. Puterman, and Kyle W. Kindle. Iterative aggregation-disaggregation procedures for discounted semi-Markov reward processes. *Operations Research*, 33:589–605, 1985.

[13] David E. Smith and Mark A. Peot. Postponing threats in partial-order planning. In *Proc. of AAAI-93*, pages 500–506, Washington, D.C., 1993.

[14] Michael P. Wellman and Jon Doyle. Modular utility representation for decision-theoretic planning. In *Proc. of AIPS-92*, pages 236–242, College Park, MD, 1992.

Acting Optimally in Partially Observable Stochastic Domains

Anthony R. Cassandra*, Leslie Pack Kaelbling[†] and Michael L. Littman[‡]

Department of Computer Science
Brown University
Providence, RI 02912
{arc,lpk,mll}@cs.brown.edu

Abstract

In this paper, we describe the partially observable Markov decision process (POMDP) approach to finding optimal or near-optimal control strategies for partially observable stochastic environments, given a complete model of the environment. The POMDP approach was originally developed in the operations research community and provides a formal basis for planning problems that have been of interest to the AI community. We found the existing algorithms for computing optimal control strategies to be highly computationally inefficient and have developed a new algorithm that is empirically more efficient. We sketch this algorithm and present preliminary results on several small problems that illustrate important properties of the POMDP approach.

Introduction

Agents that act in real environments, whether physical or virtual, rarely have complete information about the state of the environment in which they are working. It is necessary for them to choose their actions in partial ignorance and often it is helpful for them to take explicit steps to gain information to achieve their goals most efficiently.

This problem has been addressed in the artificial intelligence (AI) community using formalisms of epistemic logic and by incorporating knowledge preconditions and effects into their planners (Moore 1985). These solutions are applicable to fairly high-level problems in which the environment is assumed to be completely deterministic, an assumption that often fails in low-level control problems.

Domains in which actions have probabilistic results and the agent has direct access to the state of the environment can be formalized as Markov decision

---

*Anthony Cassandra's work was supported in part by National Science Foundation Award IRI-9257592.

[†]Leslie Kaelbling's work was supported in part by a National Science Foundation National Young Investigator Award IRI-9257592 and in part by ONR Contract N00014-91-4052, ARPA Order 8225.

[‡]Michael Littman's work was supported by Bellcore.

processes (MDPs) (Howard 1960). An important aspect of the MDP model is that it provides the basis for algorithms that provably find optimal policies (mappings from environmental states to actions) given a stochastic model of the environment and a goal. MDP models play an important role in current AI research on planning (Dean *et al.* 1993; Sutton 1990) and learning (Barto, Bradtke, & Singh 1991; Watkins & Dayan 1992), but the assumption of complete observability provides a significant obstacle to their application to real-world problems.

This paper explores an extension of the MDP model to *partially observable Markov decision processes* (POMDPs) (Monahan 1982; Lovejoy 1991), which, like MDPs, were developed within the context of operations research. The POMDP model provides an elegant solution to the problem of acting in partially observable domains, treating actions that affect the environment and actions that only affect the agent's state of information uniformly. We begin by explaining the basic POMDP formalism; next we present an algorithm for finding arbitrarily good approximations to optimal policies and a method for the compact representation of many such policies; finally, we conclude with examples that illustrate generalization in the policy representation and taking action to gain information.

Partially Observable Markov Decision Processes

Markov Decision Processes An MDP is defined by the tuple $\langle \mathcal{S}, \mathcal{A}, T, R \rangle$, where $\mathcal{S}$ is a finite set of environmental states that can be reliably identified by the agent; $\mathcal{A}$ is a finite set of actions; T is a state transition model of the environment, which is a function mapping elements of $\mathcal{S} \times \mathcal{A}$ into discrete probability distributions over $\mathcal{S}$; and R is a *reward function* mapping $\mathcal{S} \times \mathcal{A}$ to the real numbers that specify the instantaneous reward that the agent derives from taking an action in a state. We write $T(s, a, s')$ for the probability that the environment will make a transition from state s to state s' when action a is taken and we write $R(s, a)$ for the immediate reward to the agent for taking action a in state s. A *policy*, π, is a mapping from $\mathcal{S}$ to $\mathcal{A}$, specifying

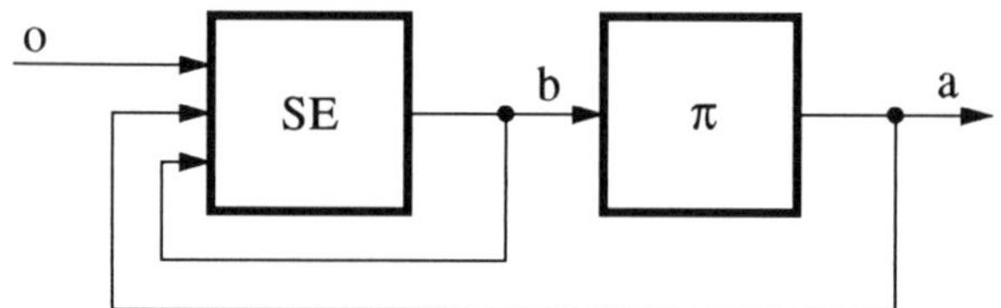

Figure 1: Controller for a POMDP

Figure 2: A Simple POMDP environment

an action to be taken in each situation.

Adding Partial Observability When the state is not completely observable, we must add a model of observation. This includes a finite set, $\mathcal{O}$, of possible observations and an observation function, O, mapping $\mathcal{A} \times \mathcal{S}$ into discrete probability distributions over $\mathcal{O}$. We write $O(a, s, o)$ for the probability of making observation o from state s after having taken action a.

One might simply take the set of observations to be the set of states and treat a POMDP as if it were an MDP. The problem is that the process would not necessarily be Markov since there could be multiple states in the environment that require different actions but appear identical. As a result, even an optimal policy of this form can have arbitrarily poor performance.

Instead, we introduce a kind of internal state for the agent. A *belief state* is a discrete probability distribution over the set of environmental states, $\mathcal{S}$, representing for each state the probability that the environment is currently in that state. Let $\mathcal{B}$ be the set of belief states. We write $b(s)$ for the probability assigned to state s when the agent's belief state is b.

Now, we can decompose the problem of acting in a partially observable environment as shown in Figure 1. The component labeled "SE" is the *state estimator*. It takes as input the last belief state, the most recent action and the most recent observation, and returns an updated belief state. The second component is the *policy*, which now maps belief states into actions.

The state estimator can be constructed from T and O by straightforward application of Bayes' rule. The output of the state estimator is a belief state, which can be represented as a vector of probabilities, one for each environmental state, that sums to 1. The component corresponding to state s', written $\mathrm{SE}_{s'}(b, a, o)$, can be determined from the previous belief state, b, the previous action, a, and the current observation, o, as follows:

$$
\begin{aligned}
\mathrm{SE}_{s'}(b, a, o) &= \Pr(s' \mid a, o, b) \\
&= \frac{\Pr(o \mid s', a, b)\,\Pr(s' \mid a, b)}{\Pr(o \mid a, b)} \\
&= \frac{O(a, s', o)\sum_{s \in \mathcal{S}} T(s, a, s')b(s)}{\Pr(o \mid a, b)}
\end{aligned}
$$

where $Pr(o \mid a, b)$ is a normalizing factor defined as

$$
\Pr(o \mid a, b) = \sum_{s' \in \mathcal{S}} O(a, s', o) \sum_{s \in \mathcal{S}} T(s, a, s')b(s) \ .
$$

The resulting function will ensure that our current belief accurately summarizes all available information.

Example A simple example of a POMDP is shown in Figure 2. It has four states, one of which (state 2) is designated as the goal state. An agent is in one of the states at all times; it has two actions, left and right, that move it one state in either direction. If it moves into a wall, it stays in the state it was in. If the agent reaches the goal state, no matter what action it takes, it is moved with equal probability into state 0, 1, or 3 and receives reward 1. This problem is trivial if the agent can observe what state it is in, but is more difficult when it can only observe whether or not it is currently at the goal state.

When the agent cannot observe its true state, it can represent its belief of where it is with a probability vector. For example, after leaving the goal, the agent moves to one of the other states with equal probability. This is represented by a belief state of $\langle \frac{1}{3}, \frac{1}{3}, 0, \frac{1}{3} \rangle$. After taking action "right" and not observing the goal, there are only two states from which the agent could have moved: 0 and 3. Hence, the agent's new belief vector is $\langle 0, \frac{1}{2}, 0, \frac{1}{2} \rangle$. If it moves "right" once again without seeing the goal, the agent can be sure it is now in state 3 with belief state $\langle 0, 0, 0, 1 \rangle$. Because the actions are deterministic in this example, the agent's uncertainty shrinks on each step; in general, some actions in some situations will decrease the uncertainty while others will increase it.

Constructing Optimal Policies

Constructing an optimal policy can be quite difficult. Even specifying a policy at every point in the uncountable state space is challenging. One simple method is to find the optimal state-action value function, Q^*_{CO}, for the completely observable MDP $\langle \mathcal{S}, \mathcal{A}, T, R \rangle$ (Watkins & Dayan 1992); then, given belief state b as input, generate action $\mathrm{argmax}_{a \in \mathcal{A}} \sum_s b(s) Q^*_{\mathrm{CO}}(s, a)$. That is, act as if the uncertainty will be present for one action step, but that the environment will be completely observable thereafter. This approach, similar to one used by Chrisman (Chrisman 1992), leads to policies that do not take actions to gain information and will therefore be suboptimal in many environments.

The key to finding truly optimal policies in the partially observable case is to cast the problem as a *completely observable* continuous-space MDP. The state set of this "belief MDP" is $\mathcal{B}$ and the action set is $\mathcal{A}$. Given a current belief state b and action a, there are only

$|\mathcal{O}|$ possible successor belief states b', so the new state transition function, τ, can be defined as

$$\tau(b, a, b') = \sum_{\{o \in \mathcal{O} | \text{SE}(b,a,o)=b'\}} \Pr(o \mid a, b) \ ,$$

where $\Pr(o \mid a, b)$ is defined above. If the new belief state, b', cannot be generated by the state estimator from b, a, and some observation, then the probability of that transition is 0. The reward function, ρ, is constructed from R by taking expectations according to the belief state; that is,

$$\rho(b, a) = \sum_{s \in \mathcal{S}} b(s) R(s, a) \ .$$

At first, this may seem strange; it appears the agent is rewarded simply for *believing* it is in good states. Because of the way the state estimation module is constructed, it is not possible for the agent to purposely delude itself into believing that it is in a good state when it is not.

The belief MDP is Markov (Astrom 1965), that is, having information about previous belief states cannot improve the choice of action. Most importantly, if an agent adopts the optimal policy for the belief MDP, the resulting behavior will be optimal for the partially observable process. The remaining difficulty is that belief space is continuous; the established algorithms for finding optimal policies in MDPs work only in finite state spaces. In the following sections, we discuss the method of *value iteration* for finding optimal policies.

Value Iteration Value iteration (Howard 1960) was developed for finding optimal policies for MDPs. Since we have formulated the partially observable problem as an MDP over belief states, we can find optimal policies for POMDPs in an analogous manner.

The agent moves through the world according to its policy, collecting reward. Although there are many criterion possible for choosing one policy over another, we here focus on policies that maximize *the infinite expected sum of discounted rewards* from all states. In such *infinite horizon* problems, we seek to maximize $E[r(0) + \sum_{t=1}^{\infty} \gamma^t r(t)]$, where $0 \leq \gamma < 1$ is a *discount factor* and $r(t)$ is the reward received at time t. If γ is zero, the agent seeks to maximize the reward for only the next time step with no regard for future consequences. As γ increases, future rewards play a larger role in the decision process.

The *optimal value* of any belief state b is the infinite expected sum of discounted rewards starting in state b and executing the optimal policy. The *value function*, $V^*(b)$, can be expressed as a system of simultaneous equations as follows:

$$V^*(b) = \max_{a \in \mathcal{A}} [\rho(b, a) + \gamma \sum_{b' \in \mathcal{B}} \tau(b, a, b') V^*(b')] \ . \quad (1)$$

The value of a state is its instantaneous reward plus the discounted value of the next state after taking the action that maximizes this value.

One could also consider a policy that maximizes reward over a finite number of time steps, t. The essence of value iteration is that optimal *t-horizon* solutions approach the optimal infinite horizon solution as t tends toward infinity. More precisely, it can be shown that the maximum difference between the value function of the optimal infinite horizon policy, V^*, and the analogously defined value function for the optimal t-horizon policy, V_t^*, goes to zero as t goes to infinity.

This property leads the following value iteration algorithm:

Let $V_0(b) = 0$ for all $b \in \mathcal{B}$
Let $t = 0$
Loop
$\quad t := t + 1$
$\quad$ For all $b \in \mathcal{B}$
$\quad\quad V_t(b) = \max_{a \in \mathcal{A}} [\rho(b, a)$
$\quad\quad\quad\quad\quad\quad +\gamma \sum_{b' \in \mathcal{B}} \tau(b, a, b') V_{t-1}(b')]$
Until $|V_t(b) - V_{t-1}(b)| < \epsilon$ for all $b \in \mathcal{B}$

This algorithm is guaranteed to converge in a finite number of iterations and results in a policy that is within $2\gamma\epsilon/(1-\gamma)$ of the optimal policy (Bellman 1957; Lovejoy 1991).

In finite state MDPs, value functions can be represented as tables. For this continuous space, however, we need to make use of special properties of the belief MDP to represent it finitely. First of all, any finite horizon value function is piecewise linear and convex (Sondik 1971; Smallwood & Sondik 1973). In addition, for the infinite horizon, the value function can be approximated arbitrarily closely by a convex piecewise-linear function (Sondik 1971).

A representation that makes use of these properties was introduced by Sondik (Sondik 1971). Let $\mathcal{V}_t$ be a set of $|\mathcal{S}|$-dimensional vectors of real numbers. The optimal t-horizon value function can be written as:

$$V_t(b) = \max_{\alpha \in \mathcal{V}_t} b \cdot \alpha \ ,$$

for some set $\mathcal{V}_t$. Any piecewise-linear convex function can be expressed this way, but the particular vectors in $\mathcal{V}_t$ can also be viewed as the values associated with different choices in the optimal policy, analogous to Watkins' Q-values (Watkins & Dayan 1992); see (Cassandra, Kaelbling, & Littman 1994; Sondik 1971).

The Witness Algorithm The task at each step in the value iteration algorithm is to find the set $\mathcal{V}_t$ that represents V_t^* given $\mathcal{V}_{t-1}$. Detailed algorithms have been developed for this problem (Smallwood & Sondik 1973; Monahan 1982; Cheng 1988) but are extremely inefficient. We describe a new algorithm, inspired by Cheng's linear support algorithm (Cheng 1988), which both in theory and in practice seems to be more efficient than the others.

Many algorithms (Smallwood & Sondik 1973; Cheng 1988) construct an approximate value function,

$\hat{V}_t(b) = \max_{\alpha \in \hat{\mathcal{V}}_t} b \cdot \alpha$, which is successively improved by adding vectors to $\hat{\mathcal{V}}_t \subseteq \mathcal{V}_t$. The set $\hat{\mathcal{V}}_t$ is built up using a key insight. From $\mathcal{V}_{t-1}$ and any particular belief state, b, we can determine the $\alpha \in \mathcal{V}_t$ that should be added to $\hat{\mathcal{V}}_t$ to make $\hat{V}_t(b) = V_t^*(b)$. The algorithmic challenge, then, is to find a b for which $\hat{V}_t(b) \neq V_t^*(b)$ or to prove that no such b exists (i.e., that the approximation is perfect).

The Witness algorithm (Cassandra, Kaelbling, & Littman 1994) defines a linear program that returns a single point that is a "witness" to the fact that $\hat{V}_t \neq V_t^*$. The process begins with an initial $\hat{V}_t$ populated by the vectors needed to represent the value function at the *corners* of the belief space (i.e., the $|\mathcal{S}|$ belief states consisting of all 0's and a single 1). A linear program is constructed with $|\mathcal{S}|$ variables used to represent the components of a belief state, b. Auxiliary variables and constraints are used to define

$$v = V_t^*(b) = \max_{a \in \mathcal{A}}[\rho(b,a) + \gamma \sum_{b' \in \mathcal{B}} \tau(b,a,b') \max_{\alpha \in \mathcal{V}_{t-1}} \alpha \cdot b']$$

and

$$\hat{v} = \hat{V}_t(b) = \max_{\hat{\alpha} \in \hat{\mathcal{V}}_t} \hat{\alpha} \cdot b$$

A final constraint insists that $\hat{v} \neq v$ and thus the program either returns a witness or fails if $\hat{V}_t = V_t^*$. If a witness is found, it is used to determine a new vector to include in $\hat{V}_t$ and the process repeats. Only one linear program is solved for each vector in $\hat{V}_t$.

In the current formulation, a tolerance factor, δ, must be defined for the linear program to be effective. Thus the algorithm can terminate even though $V_t^* \neq \hat{V}_t$ as long as the difference at any point is no more than δ. This differentiates the Witness algorithm from the other approaches mentioned, which find exact solutions.

Although the Witness algorithm only constructs approximations, in conjunction with value iteration it can construct policies arbitrarily close to optimal by making δ small enough. Unfortunately, extremely small values of δ result in numerically unstable linear programs that can be quite challenging for many linear programming implementations.

It has been shown that finding the optimal policy for a finite-horizon POMDP is PSPACE-complete (Papadimitriou & Tsitsiklis 1987), and indeed all of the algorithms mentioned take time exponential in the problem size if the specific POMDP parameters require an exponential number of vectors to represent V_t^*. The main advantage of the Witness algorithm is that it appears to be the only one of the algorithms whose running time is guaranteed not to be exponential if the number of vectors required is not. In practice, this has resulted in vastly improved running times and the ability to run much larger example problems than existing POMDP algorithms. Details of the algorithm are outlined in a technical report (Cassandra, Kaelbling, & Littman 1994).

Representing Policies When value iteration converges, we are left with a set of vectors, $\mathcal{V}_{\text{final}}$, that constitutes an approximation to the optimal value function, V^*. Each of these vectors defines a region of the belief space such that a belief state is in a vector's region if its dot product with the vector is maximum. Thus, the vectors define a partition of belief space.

It can be shown (Smallwood & Sondik 1973) that all state vectors that share a partition also share an optimal action, so a policy can be specified by a set of pairs, $\langle \alpha^*, a^* \rangle$, where $\pi(b) = a^*$ if $\alpha^* \cdot b \geq \alpha \cdot b$ for all $\alpha \in \mathcal{V}_{\text{final}}$.

For many problems, the partitions have an important property that leads to a particularly useful representation for the optimal policy. Given the optimal action and a resulting observation, all belief states in one partition will be transformed to belief states occupying the same partition on the next step. The set of partitions and their corresponding transitions constitute a *policy graph* that summarizes the action choices of the optimal policy.

Figure 3 shows the policy graph of the optimal policy for the simple POMDP environment of Figure 2. Each node in the picture corresponds to a set of belief states over which one vector in $\mathcal{V}_{\text{final}}$ has the largest dot product and is labeled with the optimal action for that set of belief states. Observations label the arcs of the graph, specifying how incoming information affects the agent's choice of future actions. The agent's initial belief state is in the node marked with the extra arrow. In the example figure we chose the uniform belief distribution to indicate that the agent initially has no knowledge of its situation.

Using a Policy Graph Once computed, the policy graph is a representation of the optimal policy. The agent chooses the action associated with the start node, and then, depending on which observation it makes, the agent makes a transition to the appropriate node. It executes the associated action, follows the arc for the next observation, and so on.

For a reactive agent, this representation of a policy is ideal. The current node of the policy graph is sufficient to summarize the agent's past experience and its future decisions. The arcs of the graph dictate how new information in the form of observations is incorporated into the agent's decision-making. The graph itself can be executed simply and efficiently.

Returning to Figure 3, we can give a concrete demonstration of how a policy graph is used. The policy graph can be summarized as "Execute the pattern right, right, left, stopping when the goal is encountered. Execute the action left to reset. Repeat." It is straightforward to verify that this strategy is indeed optimal; no other pattern performs better.

Note that the use of the state estimator, SE, is no longer necessary for the agent to choose actions optimally. The policy graph has all the information it needs.

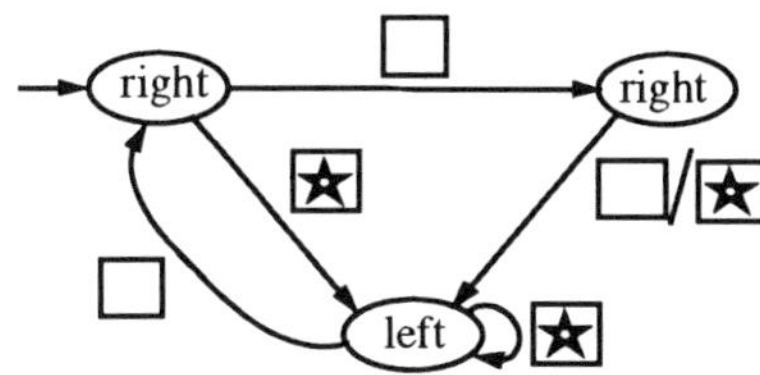

Figure 3: Sample policy graph for the simple POMDP environment

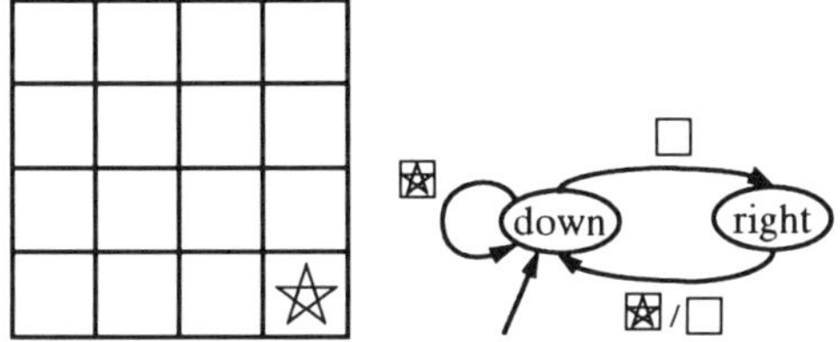

Figure 4: Small unobservable grid and its policy graph

Results

After experimenting with several algorithms for solving POMDPs, we devised and implemented the Witness algorithm and a heuristic method for constructing a policy graph from V_{final}. Although the size of the optimal policy graph can be arbitrarily large, for most of the problems we tried the policy graph included no more than thirty nodes. The largest problem we looked at consisted of 23 states, 4 actions and 11 observations and our algorithm converged on a policy graph of four nodes in under a half of an hour.

Generalization In the policy graph of Figure 3, there is almost a one-to-one correspondence between nodes and the belief states encountered by the agent. For some environments, the decisions for many different belief states are captured in a small number of nodes. This constitutes a form of generalization in that a continuum of belief states, including distinct environmental states, are handled identically.

Figure 4 shows an extremely simple environment consisting of a 4 by 4 grid where all cells except for the goal in the lower right-hand corner are indistinguishable. The optimal policy graph for this environment consists of just two nodes, one for moving down in the grid, and the other for moving to the right. From the given start node, the agent will execute a down-right-down-right pattern until it reaches the goal at which point it will start again. Note that each time it is in the "down" node, it will have different beliefs about what environmental state it is in.

Acting to Gain Information In many real-world problems, an agent must take specific actions to gain information that will allow it to make more informed decisions and achieve increased performance. In most planning systems, these kinds of actions are handled differently than actions that change the state of the

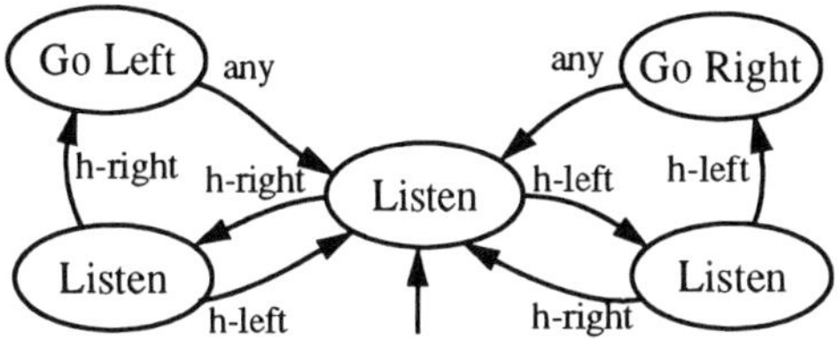

Figure 5: Policy graph for the tiger problem

environment. A uniform treatment of actions of all kinds is desirable for simplicity, but also because there are many actions that have both material and informational consequences.

To illustrate the treatment of information-gathering actions in the POMDP model, we introduce a modified version of a classic problem. You stand in front of two doors: behind one door is a tiger and behind the other is a vast reward, but you do not know which is where. You may open either door, receiving a large penalty if you chose the one with the tiger and a large reward if you chose the other. You have the additional option of simply listening. If the tiger is on the left, then with probability 0.85 you will hear the tiger on your left and with probability 0.15 you will hear it on your right; symmetrically for the case in which the tiger is on your right. If you listen, you will pay a small penalty. Finally, the problem is iterated, so immediately after you choose either of the doors, you will again be faced with the problem of choosing a door; of course, the tiger has been randomly repositioned.

The problem is this: How long should you stand and listen before you choose a door? The Witness algorithm found the solution shown in Figure 5. If you are beginning with no information, then you enter the center node, in which you listen. If you hear the tiger on your left, then you enter the lower right node, which encodes roughly "I've heard a tiger on my left once more than I've heard a tiger on my right"; if you hear the tiger on your right, then you move back to the center node, which encodes "I've heard a tiger on my left as many times as I've heard one on my right." Following this, you listen again. You continue listening until you have heard the tiger twice more on one side than the other, at which point you choose.

As the consequences of meeting a tiger are made less dire, the Witness algorithm finds strategies that listen only once before choosing, then ones that do not bother to listen at all. As the reliability of listening is made worse, strategies that listen more are found.

Related Work

There is an extensive discussion of POMDPs in the operations research literature. Surveys by Monahan (Monahan 1982) and Lovejoy (Lovejoy 1991) are good starting points. Within the AI community, several of the issues addressed here have also been examined by researchers working on reinforcement learning. Whitehead and Ballard (Whitehead & Ballard 1991) solve problems of partial observability through access to extra perceptual data. Chrisman (Chrisman 1992) and McCallum (McCallum 1993) describe algorithms for inducing a POMDP from interactions with the environment and use relatively simple approximations to the resulting optimal value function. Other relevant work in the AI community includes the work of Tan (Tan 1991) on inducing decision trees for performing low-cost identification of objects by selecting appropriate sensory tests.

Future Work

The results presented in this paper are preliminary. We intend, in the short term, to extend our algorithm to perform policy iteration, which is likely to be more efficient. We will solve larger examples including tracking and surveillance problems. In addition, we hope to extend this work in a number of directions such as applying stochastic dynamic programming (Barto, Bradtke, & Singh 1991) and function approximation to derive an optimal value function, rather than solving for it analytically. We expect that good approximate policies may be found more quickly this way. Another aim is to integrate the POMDP framework with methods such as those used by Dean *et al.* (Dean *et al.* 1993) for finding approximately optimal policies quickly by considering only small regions of the search space.

Acknowledgments

Thanks to Lonnie Chrisman, Tom Dean and (indirectly) Ross Schachter for introducing us to POMDPs.

References

Astrom, K. J. 1965. Optimal control of markov decision processes with incomplete state estimation. *J. Math. Anal. Appl.* 10:174–205.

Barto, A. G.; Bradtke, S. J.; and Singh, S. P. 1991. Real-time learning and control using asynchronous dynamic programming. Technical Report 91-57, Department of Computer and Information Science, University of Massachusetts, Amherst, Massachusetts.

Bellman, R. 1957. *Dynamic Programming.* Princeton, New Jersey: Princeton University Press.

Cassandra, A. R.; Kaelbling, L. P.; and Littman, M. L. 1994. Algorithms for partially observable markov decision processes. Technical Report 94-14, Brown University, Providence, Rhode Island.

Cheng, H.-T. 1988. *Algorithms for Partially Observable Markov Decision Processes.* Ph.D. Dissertation, University of British Columbia, British Columbia, Canada.

Chrisman, L. 1992. Reinforcement learning with perceptual aliasing: The perceptual distinctions approach. In *Proceedings of the Tenth National Conference on Artificial Intelligence*, 183–188. San Jose, California: AAAI Press.

Dean, T.; Kaelbling, L. P.; Kirman, J.; and Nicholson, A. 1993. Planning with deadlines in stochastic domains. In *Proceedings of the Eleventh National Conference on Artificial Intelligence.*

Howard, R. A. 1960. *Dynamic Programming and Markov Processes.* Cambridge, Massachusetts: The MIT Press.

Lovejoy, W. S. 1991. A survey of algorithmic methods for partially observed markov decision processes. *Annals of Operations Research* 28(1):47–65.

McCallum, R. A. 1993. Overcoming incomplete perception with utile distinction memory. In *Proceedings of the Tenth International Conference on Machine Learning.* Amherst, Massachusetts: Morgan Kaufmann.

Monahan, G. E. 1982. A survey of partially observable markov decision processes: Theory, models, and algorithms. *Management Science* 28(1):1–16.

Moore, R. C. 1985. A formal theory of knowledge and action. In Hobbs, J. R., and Moore, R. C., eds., *Formal Theories of the Commonsense World.* Norwood, New Jersey: Ablex Publishing Company.

Papadimitriou, C. H., and Tsitsiklis, J. N. 1987. The complexity of markov decision processes. *Mathematics of Operations Research* 12(3):441–450.

Smallwood, R. D., and Sondik, E. J. 1973. The optimal control of partially observable markov processes over a finite horizon. *Operations Research* 21:1071–1088.

Sondik, E. J. 1971. *The Optimal Control of Partially Observable Markov Processes.* Ph.D. Dissertation, Stanford University, Stanford, California.

Sutton, R. S. 1990. Integrated architectures for learning, planning, and reacting based on approximating dynamic programming. In *Proceedings of the Seventh International Conference on Machine Learning.* Austin, Texas: Morgan Kaufmann.

Tan, M. 1991. Cost-sensitive reinforcement learning for adaptive classification and control. In *Proceedings of the Ninth National Conference on Artificial Intelligence.*

Watkins, C. J. C. H., and Dayan, P. 1992. Q-learning. *Machine Learning* 8(3):279–292.

Whitehead, S. D., and Ballard, D. H. 1991. Learning to perceive and act by trial and error. *Machine Learning* 7(1):45–83.

Cost-Effective Sensing During Plan Execution

Eric A. Hansen

Department of Computer Science
University of Massachusetts
Amherst, MA 01003
hansen@cs.umass.edu

Abstract

Between sensing the world after every action (as in a reactive plan) and not sensing at all (as in an open-loop plan), lies a continuum of strategies for sensing during plan execution. If sensing incurs a cost (in time or resources), the most cost-effective strategy is likely to fall somewhere between these two extremes. Yet most work on plan execution assumes one or the other. In this paper, an efficient, anytime planner is described that controls the rate of sensing during plan execution. The sensing interval is determined by the state during plan execution, as well as by the cost of sensing, so that an agent can sense more often when necessary. The planner is based on a generalization of stochastic dynamic programming.

Introduction

The characteristic assumptions of classical planning — a complete and certain action model and deterministic plan execution — make sensing during plan execution unnecessary. A planner that knows the initial state of the world and can predict the effects of its actions with certainty has no reason for sensing. Hence, classical planners constructed open-loop plans.

The reactive approach pursued in recent planning research was developed for environments in which the assumptions made by classical planners are unjustified, in other words, for most realistic environments. In the real world, actions may not have their intended effects and the environment can change in unexpected ways. Because a planner cannot project the course of plan execution with certainty, the reactive approach is to construct a plan that specifies what action to take in each of many different states, and to sense the world after each action so that the agent can choose the next action based on the current state.

The question that is the starting point for this paper is whether it is cost-effective to sense the world after every action in a plan. There is often a cost, in time or resources, for acquiring and processing sensory information. If sensing is expensive, it may be better to sense less frequently, especially if there is not that much uncertainty about the state of the world during plan execution. Between sensing the world after every action (as in a reactive plan) and not sensing at all (as in an open-loop plan), lies a continuum of sensing strategies. The most cost-effective one is likely to fall somewhere between these two extremes.

Although the problem of sensing costs has been relatively neglected in planning research, two different approaches to it have been tentatively explored. In one, cost-effectiveness is achieved by sensing only a subset of the features of the environment (Chrisman & Simmons 1991; Tan 1991). This raises interesting issues, among them the problem of identifying a state from incomplete perception (Whitehead & Ballard 1991), but it still assumes an agent senses its environment after each action. The second approach allows an agent to sense at wider intervals than after every action, where the sensing interval is set based on factors such as the cost of sensing and the cost and likelihood of error. But in this approach, the simplifying assumption is usually made that the rate of sensing should be constant throughout plan execution. For example, Abramson (1993) gives a decision-theoretic analysis to show that a fixed sensing interval during plan execution is optimal, and a formula for calculating what the interval should be. Hendler and Kinny (1992) apply a similar analysis to TileWorld, and Langley, Iba, and Shrager (1994) also assume periodic sensing. All of these analyses are based on a model of plan execution in which errors occur, in Abramson's description, "spontaneously"; that is, they are no more likely in one state of the world than another, nor any more likely after one action than another. From the assumption that errors are spontaneous, it follows that a fixed rate of sensing is optimal. But in many realistic environments, some states are riskier than others and some actions more error-prone. As a result, the success of some parts of a plan will be less predictable than other parts, and this suggests that the frequency of sensing

This work was supported by ARPA/Rome Laboratory under contract #F30602-91-C-0076 and under an Augmentation Award for Science and Engineering Research Training.

should change depending on which part of a plan is being executed.

When the likelihood of plan error depends on the current state or on the action taken in that state, sensing becomes a planning problem; that is, decisions about when to sense the environment must take into account the actions in the plan and the projected state during plan execution. In order to treat the problem of when to sense during plan execution as a planning problem, this paper adopts the framework of Markov decision theory. Besides providing mathematical rigor, this framework has proven useful for formalizing planning problems in stochastic domains (Dean et al 1993; Koenig 1992), as well as for relating planning to reinforcement learning (Sutton 1990; Barto, Bradtke, & Singh 1993). In a conventional Markov decision problem, a policy (or plan) is executed by automatically sensing the world after each action, without considering the cost this might incur. Because this is exactly the assumption being questioned in this paper, we begin by showing how to incorporate sensing costs and formulate sensing strategies in the framework of Markov decision theory. Then an efficient, anytime planner is described that can adjust the rate of sensing during plan execution, depending on the state and actions of a plan. The approach developed here is directly applicable to work on planning for stochastic domains using techniques based on dynamic programming, and is suggestive for work on integrating sensing with plan execution in general.

Including Sensing Costs in a Markov Decision Problem

A discrete-time, finite state and action Markov decision problem is described by the following elements. Let S be a finite set of states, and let A be a finite set of actions. A *state transition function* $P: S \times A \times S \rightarrow [0,1]$ specifies the outcomes of actions as discrete probability distributions over the state-space. In particular, $P_{xy}(a)$ gives the probability that action a taken in state x produces state y. A *payoff function* $R: S \times A \rightarrow \Re$ specifies rewards (or costs) to be maximized (or minimized) by a plan. In particular, $R(x,a)$ gives the expected single-step payoff for taking action a in state x. A *policy* $\pi: S \rightarrow A$ specifies an action to take in each state. The set of all possible policies is called the *policy space*. To weigh the merit of different policies, a *value function* $V_\pi: S \rightarrow \Re$ gives the expected cumulative value received for executing a policy, π, starting from each state. The value function for a policy satisfies the following system of simultaneous linear equations:

$$V_\pi(x) = R\big(x, \pi(x)\big) + \lambda \sum_{y \in S} P_{xy}\big(\pi(x)\big) V_\pi(y), \qquad (1)$$

where $0 \le \lambda < 1$ is a *discount factor* that gives higher importance to payoffs in the near future. A policy π^* is optimal if $V_{\pi^*}(x) \ge V_\pi(x)$ for all states x and policies π. *Dynamic programming* is an efficient way of searching the space of possible policies for an optimal policy, using the value function to guide the search. There are several versions of dynamic programming and the ideas in this paper can be adapted to any of them, but Howard's policy iteration algorithm is used as an example (Howard 1960). It consists of the following steps:

1. *Initialization*: Start with an arbitrary policy $\pi: S \rightarrow A$.
2. *Policy evaluation*: Compute the value function for π by solving the system of simultaneous linear equations given by equation (1).
3. *Policy improvement:* Compute a new policy π' from the value function computed in step 2 by finding, for each state x, the action a that maximizes expected value, or formally:

$$\forall x: \quad \pi'(x) = \arg \max_{a \in A} \left[R(x,a) + \lambda \sum_{y \in S} P_{xy}(a) V_\pi(y) \right].$$

4. *Convergence test*: If the new policy is the same as the old one, it is optimal and the algorithm stops. Otherwise, set $\pi := \pi'$ and go to step 2.

The policy evaluation step requires solving a system of simultaneous linear equations and so has complexity $O(n^3)$ using a conventional algorithm such as Gaussian elimination, and at best $O(n^{2.8})$, where n is the size of the state set. The complexity of the policy improvement step is $O(mn^2)$, where m is the size of the action set. The policy iteration algorithm is guaranteed to improve the policy each iteration and to converge to an optimal policy after a finite number of iterations. It is also an anytime algorithm that can be stopped before convergence to return a policy that is monotonically better than the initial policy as a function of computation time.

In the conventional theory of Markov decision problems described so far, each action takes a single time-step and the world is automatically sensed at each step to see what action to take next. We want to find some way to represent problems in which an arbitrary sequence of actions can be taken before sensing. To do so, we define "multi-step" versions of each of the elements of a Markov decision problem with the exception of the state space.

A *multi-step action set* $\overline{A}$ includes all possible sequences of actions up to some arbitrary limit z on their length, where the arbitrary limit keeps the action set finite. The bar over the A is used to indicate "multi-step." Note that the multi-step action set includes both primitive actions, which take a single time step, and sequences of primitive actions. A tuple $\langle a_1 .. a_k \rangle$ represents a k-length sequence of actions, where $1 \le k \le z$. A *multi-step transition function* $\overline{P}: S \times \overline{A} \times S \rightarrow [0,1]$ gives the state transition probabilities for the multi-step action set. The multi-step transition probabilities for an action sequence $\langle a_1..a_k \rangle$ can be computed by multiplying the matrices that contain the single-step transition probabilities for the actions in the sequence, or formally, $\overline{P}(\langle a_1..a_k \rangle) = P(a_1)...P(a_k)$, where the matrix $P(a)$ contains the single-step transition probabilities for action a. In particular, $\overline{P}_{xy}(\langle a_1..a_k \rangle)$ gives the probability that taking the sequence of actions $\langle a_1..a_k \rangle$ starting from state x results in state y. A *multi-step payoff function* gives the expected "immediate" payoff received in the course of a sequence of actions. It is the sum of the expected payoffs received each time step during execution of the action sequence, with a cost for sensing, C, incurred at the end (when the world is sensed again),[1] and is defined formally as follows:

$$\overline{R}(x,\langle a_1..a_k \rangle) = R(x, a_1) - \lambda^k C +$$
$$\sum_{j=1}^{k} \lambda^j \sum_{y \in S} \overline{P}_{xy}(\langle a_1..a_j \rangle) R(y, a_j).$$

Note that the time step becomes the exponent of the discount factor to ensure discounting is done in a time-dependent way. The equation also shows that the cost of sensing can be controlled by varying the length of action sequences. A *multi-step policy* $\overline{\pi} : S \rightarrow \overline{A}$ maps each state to a sequence of actions to be taken before sensing again. The *multi-step value function* for $\overline{\pi}$ satisfies the following system of simultaneous linear equations,

$$\overline{V}_{\overline{\pi}}(x) = \overline{R}(x, \overline{\pi}(x)) + \lambda^{length(\overline{\pi}(x))} \sum_{y \in S} \overline{P}_{xy}(\overline{\pi}(x)) \overline{V}_{\overline{\pi}}(y), \quad (2)$$

where the length of an action sequence is again the exponent of the discount factor to ensure time-dependent discounting.

With multi-step versions of the action set, state transition function, payoff function, policy, and value function, we have a well-defined Markov decision problem for which policy iteration can find an optimal policy for interleaving acting and sensing. The multi-step version of the policy iteration algorithm is as follows:

1. *Initialization*: Start with an arbitrary policy $\overline{\pi} : S \rightarrow \overline{A}$.
2. *Policy evaluation:* Compute the value function for $\overline{\pi}$ by solving the system of simultaneous linear equations given by equation (2).
3. *Policy improvement:* Compute a new policy, $\overline{\pi}'$, from the value function computed in step 2 by finding, for each state x, the sequence of actions that maximizes expected value, or formally:

$$\forall x: \quad \overline{\pi}'(x) = \arg \max_{\langle a_1..a_k \rangle \in \overline{A}} \left[\overline{R}(x, \langle a_1..a_k \rangle) + \right.$$
$$\left. \lambda^k \sum_{y \in S} \overline{P}_{xy}(\langle a_1..a_k \rangle) \overline{V}_{\overline{\pi}}(y) \right].$$

4. *Convergence test*: If the new policy is the same as the old one, it is optimal and the algorithm stops. Otherwise, set $\overline{\pi} := \overline{\pi}'$ and go to step 2.

The policy evaluation step still requires solving a system of n simultaneous linear equations and so has the same complexity as for a single-step Markov decision problem. However, the complexity of the policy improvement step has been dramatically increased. Naively performing the policy improvement step now requires evaluating, for each state, every possible sequence of actions up to the fixed limit z on the length of a sequence. Even assuming that all multi-step transition probabilities and payoffs are pre-computed,[2] the complexity of the policy improvement step would be $O(m^z n^2)$ where the factor m^z comes from the fact that there are approximately m^z different action sequences of length at least 1 and no greater than z, where m is the number of primitive actions. In other words, allowing a sequence of actions to be taken before sensing causes an exponential blowup in the size of the policy space and an apparently prohibitive increase in the complexity of the dynamic programming algorithm.

An Efficient Planning Algorithm

Although searching the space of all possible sequences of actions exhaustively for each state is prohibitive, a practical approach to the problem of cost-effective sensing is still possible within this formal framework. Many action sequences are implausible or counterproductive, either because actions lead away from the goal or because they do not make sense in a given state. By using the value function to estimate the relative merit of different sequences, the space of possible action sequences can be searched intelligently in order to find a good, if not optimal, multi-step policy.

The multi-step action set is first organized as a search tree in which each node corresponds to an action sequence, and the successors of a node are created by adding a single action to the end of the sequence. The root of the search tree corresponds to the null action (which we do not consider part of the action set), level 1 of the tree contains

---

[1]For simplicity, in this paper we assume that sensing has a fixed cost. It is a straightforward generalization to make the cost of sensing a function of state and/or action.

[2]The combinatorial explosion of the number of possible action sequences usually makes it prohibitive to precompute and store all multi-step transition probabilities and payoffs. Fortunately for the efficient algorithm described in the next section, the vast majority are never needed and those that are can be cached to avoid repeated recomputation.

all sequences of length 1, level 2 contains all sequences of length 2, and so on. An action sequence with a good expected value can be found efficiently by starting from the root and choosing a greedy path through the tree. At each node, the expected values of the successor nodes are computed and the path extended to the node with the highest expected value, as long as it is higher than the expected value of the current node. If no successor node is an improvement, the search is stopped. This corresponds to constructing an action sequence by starting with the null sequence and adding actions to the end of the sequence one at a time, using the following two heuristics:

greedy heuristic: Always extend a sequence of actions with the action that gives the resulting sequence the highest expected value.

stopping heuristic: Stop as soon as extending a sequence of actions with the best next action reduces the expected value of the resulting action sequence.

The stopping heuristic simply means to assume that if it does not pay to take one more action before sensing, it will not pay to take two or more actions before sensing either — a very reasonable heuristic. Note that the stopping heuristic makes it possible to stop the search before the arbitrary, fixed limit z on the length of an action sequence is reached.

In addition to these two search heuristics, the greedy search algorithm needs one more feature. A crucial property of policy iteration is that it guarantees monotonic improvement of the policy each iteration; in particular, it guarantees that the value of each state is equal to or better than the value for the same state on the previous iteration. This property, together with a finite policy space, guarantees that policy iteration converges in a finite number of iterations. However, because the efficient search algorithm searches the space of possible action sequences greedily, local maxima may lead it to an action sequence that has a lower value than the action sequence found on the previous iteration. To prevent the value of any state from decreasing from one iteration to the next, the following rule is invoked at the end of the greedy search:

monotonic improvement rule: If the value of the action sequence found by greedy search is not better than the value of the action sequence specified by the current policy, do not change the current action sequence.

This rule ensures that a state's value is always equal to or greater than its value on a previous iteration because if an improved action sequence is not found, the previous action sequence has a value at least as good.

The greedy search algorithm for the policy improvement step is summarized as follows:

For each state x:
1. Initialize $\langle sequence \rangle$ to the single action with the highest expected value.
2. Compute the expected value of each possible extension of $\langle sequence \rangle$ by a single action.
3. *Stopping heuristic*: If no extension has a higher expected value than the current sequence, stop the search and go to step 5.
4. *Greedy heuristic*: If at least one extension has an improved value, set $\langle sequence \rangle$ to the extension with the highest value and go to step 2.
5. *Monotonic improvement rule*: If the sequence found by greedy search has a higher expected value than the sequence specified by the current policy, change the policy for this state to $\langle sequence \rangle$, otherwise, leave the policy for this state unchanged.

From the monotonic improvement rule and the finiteness of the policy space, the multi-step version of policy iteration using the greedy search algorithm is guaranteed to converge after a finite number of iterations. However, it is impossible to say whether it will converge to a globally optimal policy or to one that is a local optimum. Nevertheless, the opportunity to vary the sensing interval during plan execution, based both on the state and the cost of sensing, makes it possible for the multi-step algorithm to converge to a policy that is better – often considerably better – than a policy that automatically senses each time step. Moveover, the greedy search algorithm can find a good multi-step policy efficiently, despite the exponential explosion of the policy space.

When the greedy search algorithm is used in the policy improvement step, the number of action sequences that must be evaluated for each state is reduced from m^z to km, where again, m is the number of different actions, z is the maximum length of an action sequence, and $k \leq z$ is the average length of an action sequence. In other words, the complexity of searching for an improved action sequence for a state is reduced from exponential to linear. If the multi-step transition probabilities and payoffs were already available, the average time complexity of the policy improvement step would be $O(kmn^2)$, only a constant factor greater than for the single-step algorithm. In most cases, however, the multi-step transition probabilities and payoffs are not given at the outset and must be computed from the single-step transition probabilities and payoffs. If they are computed on the fly each time they are needed, the time complexity of the policy improvement step is $O(kmn^3)$. This can be alleviated somewhat by saving or caching the multi-step transition probabilities and payoffs the first time they are computed. Because most regions of the search space are never explored, most multi-step transition probabilities and payoffs do not need to be computed. Those that do tend to be re-used from iteration to iteration, making caching very beneficial. With caching, the time complexity of the policy improvement step becomes $O\left(pkmn^2\right) + O\left((1-p)kmn^3\right)$, where p is the proportion of cache hits on a particular iteration. Because the proportion of cache hits tends to increase from one iteration to the next, the policy improvement step runs faster as the algorithm gets closer to convergence.

Generating the multi-step transition probabilities and payoffs is by far the most computationally burdensome aspect of the multi-step algorithm. Nevertheless, because the time complexity of the policy evaluation step is already $O\left(n^3\right)$, or at best $O\left(n^{2.8}\right)$, the overall asymptotic time complexity of a single iteration of the multi-step algorithm, consisting of both policy evaluation and improvement, is still about the same or only a little worse in order notation, although the constant is greater for the multi-step algorithm. This is important because it means that scaling up dynamic programming to problems with large state spaces, the characteristic weakness of dynamic programming, is not made appreciably more difficult by the multi-step algorithm.

Of course, it takes longer for the multi-step version of policy iteration to converge than for the single-step version. However, both are iterative (anytime) algorithms that can have a good policy ready before convergence. Moreover, it is easy to ensure that multi-step policy iteration always has a policy as good or better than the single-step algorithm in the same amount of computation time. Simply run the single-step algorithm until convergence, then continue from that point with the multi-step algorithm. This approach is used in the example described in the next section. In most cases, computing the optimal single-step policy before beginning the multi-step algorithm leads to faster initial improvement of plan quality because it postpones the expense of computing multi-step probabilities and payoffs. For much the same reason, gradually adjusting upward the maximum allowable length of an action sequence from one iteration of the multi-step algorithm to the next can accelerate convergence.

A Path-Planning Example

The multi-step policy iteration algorithm can be used for any planning problem that is formalizable as a Markov decision problem. The following path-planning example provides a very simple illustration. Imagine a robot in the simple grid world shown in figure 1. Each cell in the grid represents a state. The actions the robot can take to move about the grid are {North, South, East, West}, but their effects are unpredictable. Whenever the robot attempts to move in a particular direction, it has 0.8 probability of success. However, with 0.05 probability it moves in a direction that is 90 degrees off to one side of its intended direction, with 0.05 probability it moves in a direction that is 90 degrees off to the other side, and with 0.1 probability it does not move at all. For example, if it attempts to move north it is successful with 0.8 probability, but it moves east with 0.05 probability, moves west with 0.05 probability, and does not move at all with 0.1 probability. If the robot hits a wall, it stays in the same cell. In this problem, the robot cannot be sure where it has moved without sensing, and becomes less sure about where it is the more it moves without sensing. Sensing its current state has a cost of 1. Hitting a wall has a cost of 5. Therefore, this is a cost-minimization problem in which the robot must balance the cost of sensing against the value of knowing where it is as it tries to find its way to the goal. Costs stop accumulating and the problem ends when the robot senses that its current state is the goal state. The discount factor used is 0.99999.

Figure 2 shows the anytime improvement of plan quality with multi-step policy iteration, beginning from the point at which the conventional, single-step algorithm converges. The multi-step algorithm converges to a policy that performs better than the single-step policy by almost a factor of two. The numbers in the grid cells of figure 3 give the sensing interval for each state for the multi-step policy at convergence. Due to lack of space, only one of the action sequences is shown. The others do what one would expect: move the robot towards the goal. In the action sequence shown, the robot moves away from the wall first, to avoid accidentally hitting it, before moving through the middle of the room towards the goal.

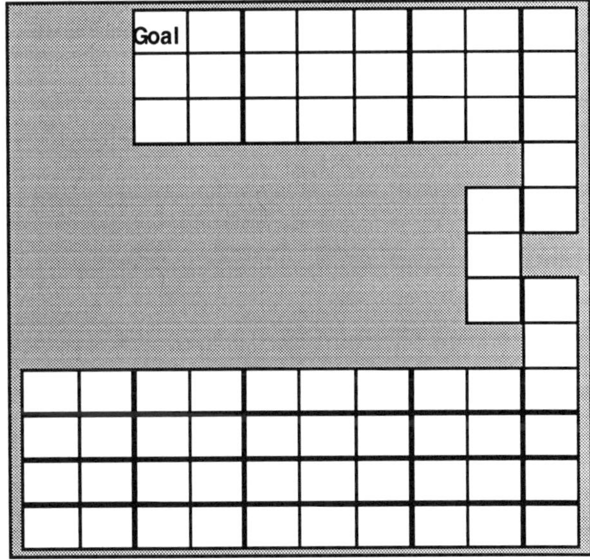

Figure 1: In this simple grid world, the robot tries to minimize the combined cost of sensing and hitting walls on its way to the goal.

Note that in the west side of the large room on the bottom of the grid world, the robot senses less frequently because there is less danger of hitting a wall, and then it senses more frequently as it approaches the east wall where it must turn into the corridor. The sharp corners of the narrow corridor cause the robot to sense nearly every time step. When it enters the room with the goal, it senses less frequently at first, given the wider space, then more frequently as it approaches the goal, to make sure it enters the goal state successfully. This sensing strategy is an intuitive one. A person would do much the same if he or she tried to get to the goal blindfolded, and was charged for stopping and removing the blindfold to look about.

Conclusion

This paper describes a generalization of Markov decision theory and dynamic programming in which sensing costs can be included in order to plan cost-effective strategies for sensing during plan execution. Within this framework, an efficient search algorithm has been developed to deal with the combinatorial explosion of the policy space that results from allowing arbitrary sequences of actions before sensing. The result is an anytime planner that can adjust the rate of sensing during plan execution in a cost-effective way.

There are some limitations to this approach. First, it applies specifically to planners that are based on dynamic programming techniques, although it is suggestive for the problem of interleaving sensing and acting in general. Second, it assumes a simplistic sensing model in which sensing is a single operation that acquires a perfect snapshot of the world. Many real-world problems involve sensor uncertainty and multiple sensors that each return a fraction of the information available. Nevertheless, the simple sensing model assumed here is often useful and is assumed by a number of planners and reactive controllers. In contexts in which this sensing model is appropriate, the anytime planner described here provides an efficient method for dealing with sensing costs.

Finally, the formal framework within which this approach is developed makes it possible to confirm a very natural intuition. The rate of sensing during plan execution should depend on the cost of sensing and on the projected state during plan execution. This makes it possible for an agent to sense less frequently in "safe" parts of a plan, and more frequently when necessary, as the path-planning example illustrates.

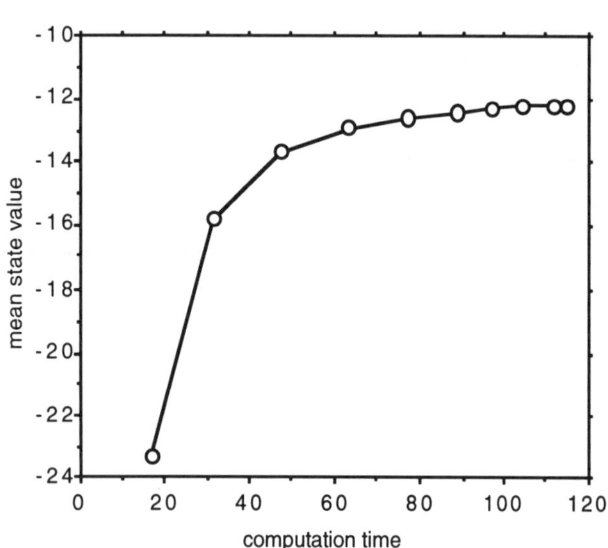

Figure 2: Anytime improvement in plan quality with multi-step policy iteration for the grid world example of figure 1. The single-step algorithm is started at time zero and the first circle marks the point at which it converges and the multi-step algorithm begins. Each circle after that represents a new iteration of the multi-step algorithm. The iterations are closer together near convergence because of previous caching of multi-step transition probabilities and payoffs. Computation time is in cpu seconds.

	Goal	1	2	3	4	6	7	8
	1	2	3	4	4	5	6	7
	2	3	4	5	5	6	7	8
								3
							1	3
							2	
							2	1
								2
10	9	8	7	6	5	4	2	1	2
9	8	7	6	5	4	3	2	2	3
9	9	8	7	6	5	4	3	3	4
10	10	9	8	7	6	5	4	4	5

Figure 3: Multi-step policy at convergence. Each cell (or state) contains the length of the action sequence to take from that state before sensing again. One of the action sequences is shown as an example.

Acknowledgements

This research is supported by ARPA/Rome Laboratory under contract #F30602-91-C-0076 and under an Augmentation Award for Science and Engineering Research Training. The US Government is authorized to reproduce and distribute reprints for governmental purposes notwithstanding any copyright notation hereon.

The author is grateful to Scott Anderson for valuable help and contributions to this work, to Paul Cohen for supporting this research, and to Andy Barto and the anonymous reviewers for useful comments.

References

Abramson, B. 1993. A Decision-Theoretic Framework for Integrating Sensors into AI Plans. *IEEE Transactions on Systems, Man, and Cybernetics* 23(2):366-373. (An earlier version appears under the title "An Analysis of Error Recovery and Sensory Integration for Dynamic Planners" in Proceedings of the Ninth National Conference on Artificial Intelligence, 744-749.)

Barto, A.G.; Bradtke, S.J.; and Singh, S.P. 1993. Learning to Act Using Real-Time Dynamic Programming. University of Massachusetts CMPSCI Technical Report 93-02. To appear in the *AI Journal*.

Chrisman, L., and Simmons, R. 1991. Sensible Planning: Focusing Perceptual Attention. In Proceedings of the Ninth National Conference on Artificial Intelligence, 756-761.

Dean, T.; Kaelbling, L.P.; Kirman, J.; and Nicholson, A. 1993. Planning with Deadlines in Stochastic Domains. In Proceedings of the Eleventh National Conference on Artificial Intelligence, 574-579.

Hendler, J., and Kinny, D. 1992. Empirical Experiments in Selective Sensing with Non-Zero-Cost-Sensors. In *Working Notes for the AAAI Spring Symposium on Control of Selective Perception*, 70-74.

Howard, R.A. 1960. *Dynamic Programming and Markov Processes*. MIT Press, Cambridge, MA.

Koenig, S. 1992. Optimal Probabilistic and Decision-Theoretic Planning using Markovian Decision Theory. UC Berkeley Computer Science technical report no. 685.

Langley, P., Iba, W., and Shrager, J. 1994. Reactive and Automatic Behavior in Plan Execution. To appear in *Proceedings of the Second International Conference on Artificial Intelligence Planning Systems*.

Sutton, R.S. 1990. Integrated Architectures for Learning, Planning, and Reacting Based on Approximating Dynamic Programming. In *Proceedings of the Seventh International Conference on Machine Learning*, 216-224.

Tan, M. 1991. Learning a Cost-Sensitive Internal Representation for Reinforcment Learning. In *Proceedings of the Eighth International Workshop on Machine Learning*, 358-362.

Whitehead, S.D., and Ballard, D.H. 1991. Learning to Perceive and Act by Trial and Error. *Machine Learning* 7:45-83.

Using Abstraction and Nondeterminism to Plan Reaction Loops

David J. Musliner
Institute for Advanced Computer Studies
The University of Maryland
College Park, Maryland 20742
musliner@umiacs.umd.edu

Abstract

By looping over a set of behaviors, reactive systems use repetition and feedback to deal with errors and environmental uncertainty. Their robust, fault-tolerant performance makes reactive systems desirable for executing plans. However, most planning systems cannot reason about the loops that characterize reactive systems. In this paper, we show how the structured application of abstraction and nondeterminism can map complex planning problems requiring loop plans into a simpler representation amenable to standard planning technologies. In the process, we illustrate key recipes for automatically building predictable reactive systems that are guaranteed to achieve their goals.

Introduction

The uncertainty inherent in real-world domains has proven problematic for traditional AI planning technologies that rely on complete, accurate, and deterministic world models. In response, reactive systems (e.g., Agre & Chapman 1987; Firby 1987) have become popular because they can deal with the uncertainties of real-world domains. The primary advantage of reactive systems is that they do not make predictions based on a world model, and thus they avoid potential failures due to inadequate models. Instead, reactive systems rely on repeatedly executing simple "persistent" behaviors until feedback indicates that their goals have been achieved. Unlike traditional open-loop AI plans, these reactive systems address environmental uncertainty and the possibility of execution-time failures by implementing repeated, feedback-based, closed-loop behaviors.

One major problem with most reactive systems is that they are difficult to design (and usually hand-coded), so that their behaviors are not necessarily logically correct or timely. There is no assurance that these systems will choose an appropriate action for a given situation, or that the selected action will be executed quickly enough to meet domain-imposed dead-lines. Furthermore, because the design and construction process is not automated, building new reactive systems for different domains requires lengthy human interactions. Several researchers have recognized that traditional AI planning systems might be used to automate the *ad hoc* process of designing reactive systems (e.g., Schoppers 1990), leading to significant advances in performance predictability and rapid system adaptation. However, most AI planning systems are unable to plan in domains that involve the type of repetition (looping) characteristic of reactive systems. Furthermore, planners do not usually create reactions, but rather they generate plans as a fixed sequential (or partially ordered) set of distinct actions.

In this paper we describe the use of abstraction and nondeterminism to allow planners to generate looping reactive plans, thus addressing a critical problem for hybrid planning/reaction systems. Essentially, we give cookbook recipes for transforming the complexities of a domain into an abstract form so that reactive plans are suitable and classical planners are useful. Some of the abstraction techniques are novel, some are not: our primary contribution is in showing how they can be combined in routine ways to make planners handle loops and generate reactive behaviors that can be guaranteed to operate in a logical and timely fashion.

We begin by introducing a simple, intuitive example to illustrate the first abstraction technique and how it can be useful in the automatic planning of loops. We then present a brief overview of the Cooperative Intelligent Real-Time Control Architecture (CIRCA) (Musliner, Durfee, & Shin 1993), a system designed to automatically plan and execute reactive behaviors. We then provide a more detailed example showing how CIRCA uses abstraction, nondeterminism, and an "abstract" time representation to plan reactive loops. Despite the extensive domain abstractions used to make planning feasible, CIRCA's automatically-constructed reactive systems are guaranteed to accomplish their goals and preserve the system's safety. Thus CIRCA combines the positive potential of both planning systems (knowledge-based deliberation, provably logical behavior) and reactive systems (rapid, fault-tolerant feedback loops).

This work was supported in part by the National Science Foundation under Grants IRI-9209031 and IRI-9158473, by a NSF Graduate Fellowship, and by the Arpa/Rome Laboratory Planning Initiative (F30602-93-C-0039). David Musliner is also affiliated with the UM Institute for Systems Research (NSF Grant NSFD CDR-88003012).

```
OPERATOR precise-hammer-blow
  PRECONDS: ((arm-raised T) (nail-height ?X))
  POSTCONDS: ((arm-raised nil)
              (nail-height (max 0 (- ?X 1.2))))
```

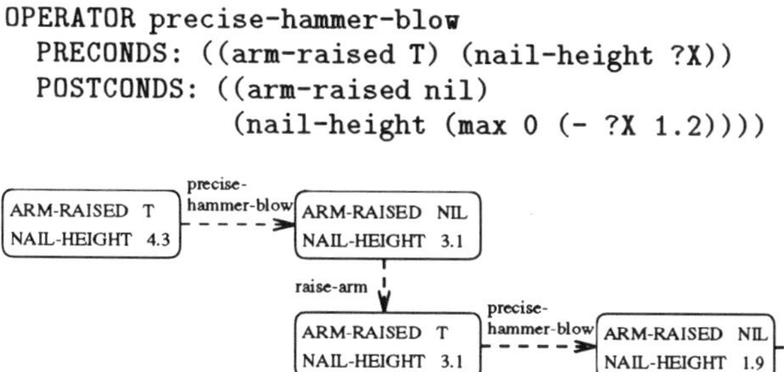

Figure 1: A fictitious hammering operator and the plan that might result.

A Simple Example

In his early work on representing plan loops, Drummond (1985) illustrates a plan for hammering a nail by repeatedly raising and lowering a hammer, never terminating. In this section, we introduce our approach to planning loops using this same example, with two significant differences: first, our hammering plan is automatically generated, and second, the plan will terminate when the nail is driven flush.

Consider first the way in which a (hypothetical) traditional planning system might address the hammering problem, as illustrated in Figure 1. Here the **precise-hammer-blow** operator must specify exactly how far down it drives the nail, and the final plan yields a world model that enumerates all the possible heights the nail may protrude.

The hammering domain illustrates several critical aspects of looping plans that make them difficult for planners. First, uncertainty may make it impossible to specify an operator's effects so precisely, and hence impossible to predict exactly how many loop iterations will be necessary to achieve the goal. In such uncertain domains, the termination conditions of the loop can only be determined during the actual execution of the loop. However, traditional planning operator representations (e.g., STRIPS add/delete lists (Nilsson 1980)) cannot represent an operator whose effects are not fully deterministic[1]. Another major problem is that, even if we could predict how many iterations are necessary, a classical planning system would need to enumerate at least one state (and probably many) for each of the iterations. This is obviously undesirable, since it exacerbates the state-space explosion already experienced by classical planners. To address these problems and allow a planner to derive a compact plan without considering innumerable states, we apply two forms of abstraction[2].

---

[1] A deterministic operator implements a fixed mapping of an input to a unique corresponding output. A nondeterministic operator implements a completely uncertain (or random) mapping from an input to one of a set of possible outputs.

[2] We use "abstraction" in a general sense to mean the omission of detail. This usage conforms nicely with in-

```
ACTION hammer-blow
  PRECONDS: ((arm-raised T))
  POSTCONDS: (((arm-raised nil) (nail-flush T))
              ((arm-raised nil) (nail-flush nil)))
```

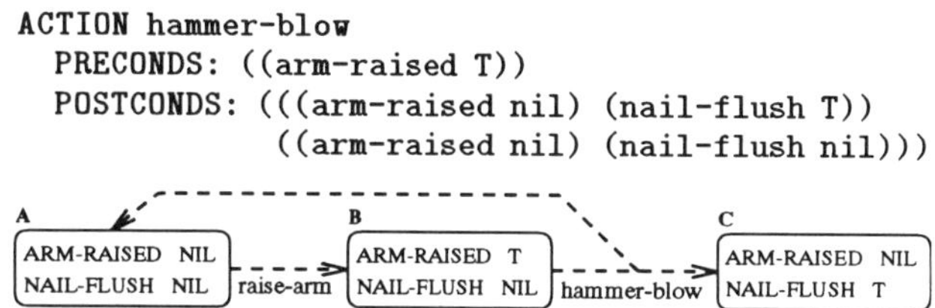

Figure 2: A nondeterministic transition, and the resulting dynamically-terminated loop.

First, we must abstract away the details in the domain representation that cause problems with the state-space explosion. In the hammering domain, the height of the nail is the domain feature that changes on each loop of the plan, so it is the culprit, the "counting" variable. We remove this counting effect by abstracting the height feature to two critical values: either the nail is flush or it is not.

Since the height of the nail has been abstracted away to a binary value, the effects of the **hammer-blow** operator must be similarly abstracted. In the process, the excessive precision associated with the continuous-valued operator is abstracted away, and nondeterminism is used to represent the resulting uncertainty. Figure 2 shows the abstracted operator, whose effects are now represented as a nondeterministic transition either to **(nail-flush T)** or back to **(nail-flush nil)**.

So now we have the world model shown in Figure 2, which more accurately reflects the uncertainty of the real world: the nail is initially sticking out above the surface, and we can keep hitting it until it is finally flush with the surface, at which time we will move out of the loop and into state **C**. Summarizing the techniques used thus far, we have the following recipe:

Recipe 1: Eliminating Counting Variables

1. Create a binary variable with **T** and **nil** states corresponding to the critical "some or none" transition of the counting variable.
2. Modify the increment operator to lead to the **T** state of the binary variable.
3. Modify the decrement operator to be nondeterministic, leading to either of the binary variable's states.

With the abstract **nail-flush** feature and the corresponding operator, the state-space problem has been addressed and the model in Figure 2 represents the need for a loop which repeats until a dynamic termination condition holds. Note that the **hammer-blow** action is not sufficient by itself, because we do not want to hit the nail every time we are holding up the hammer. To build a reaction that would yield the state-space behavior shown in Figure 2, *we still need a planner* to decide which of the various applicable operators should actually be executed in any particular world

---

tuition, as well as with (Wilkins 1988), in that our abstract models match larger sets of possible worlds than less-abstract models.

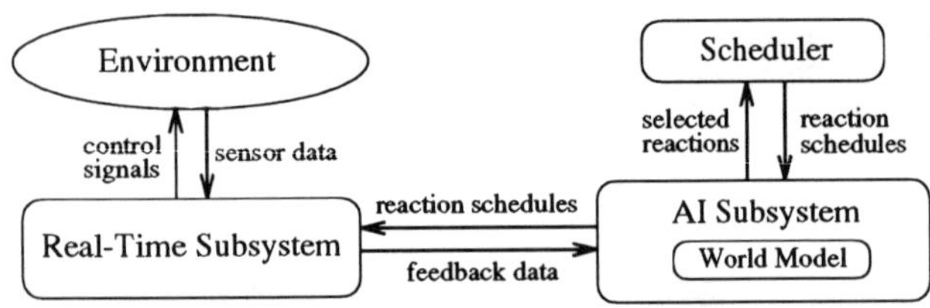

Figure 3: Overview of CIRCA.

```
TAP hammer-blow
  TEST: (and (nail-flush nil) (arm-raised T))
  ACTION: hammer-blow
  MAX-PERIOD: 2 seconds

SCHEDULE: (raise-arm hammer-blow) repeat
```

Figure 4: A trivial example TAP & TAP schedule for the hammering domain.

state. The planner must decide that we should invoke the **hammer-blow** action only when the nail is not yet flush (i.e., in state **B** only, not in state **C**). In the next section, we briefly describe how CIRCA is able to perform this type of planning (despite the resulting state-space loops), and how the system addresses the final problem of the hammering domain: actually representing a looping plan.

Overview of CIRCA

As illustrated in Figure 3, CIRCA consists of three subsystems operating in parallel (Musliner, Durfee, & Shin 1993). The AI Subsystem (AIS) acts as a planning system, reasoning about a model of the domain and deriving appropriate reaction plans. These plans are sent to the Scheduler module, along with timing constraints expressing how frequently each reaction must be executed. The Scheduler tries to build a cyclic schedule of reactions that will meet all the timing constraints. If a schedule is found, the planned reactions can be sent to the Real-Time Subsystem (RTS) for execution. The RTS executes previously-derived plans while the AIS and Scheduler are cooperatively developing a new plan; each reaction plan is designed to keep the system safe (avoiding failures), so that the search-based planning performed by the AIS is isolated from the ongoing real-time deadlines of the environment.

CIRCA's reactive plans are built as schedules of Test-Action Pairs (TAPs). As shown in Figure 4, each TAP is an annotated production rule consisting of a test expression, an action, and a timing constraint on how frequently the TAP must be executed. When executing a TAP, the RTS evaluates the test expression and, if it returns true, the RTS executes the corresponding action. TAPs differ from other reactive mechanisms such as RAPs (Firby 1987) in two fundamental ways: first, TAPs are automatically generated by CIRCA's planning system, and second, TAPs specify how frequently they must be executed in order to meet domain deadlines. CIRCA's Scheduler module uses the TAP timing requirements when it builds TAP schedules that are themselves loops; Figure 4 shows a simple schedule for the hammering domain, which oscillates between the **raise-arm** and **hammer-blow** TAPs.

The world model and planning algorithm that the AIS uses to develop TAP plans are detailed in (Musliner, Durfee, & Shin 1994). For our purposes, it is sufficient to understand that the model is a modified state/transition graph in which states correspond to complete descriptions of the world (modulo some level of abstraction), and three types of transitions represent the ways the world can change. *Temporal transitions* represent time and ongoing processes. The timing behavior of a temporal transition is related to the rate of the process it represents: for example, the process of consuming a jar of salsa will take some minimum amount of time to complete, depending on the rate of consumption. *Event transitions* represent occurrences outside the agent's control, while *action transitions* represent the intentional actions of TAPs. CIRCA can control the timing behavior of action transitions by setting the timing constraints of TAPs. For example, CIRCA can build a TAP that executes at least once every minute, to ensure that a new jar of salsa is opened within two minutes after the last jar is finished.

To build plans, CIRCA begins with a set of goal descriptions, a set of initial world states, and a set of transition descriptions that detail the types of events, actions, and processes possible in the world. The planning algorithm pushes the initial states onto a stack and then performs a modified STRIPS-like depth-first search for a plan that satisfies all the system's goals. On each planning loop iteration, the top state is popped off the stack and all applicable event and temporal transitions are applied, generating new reachable states that are pushed onto the stack. The planner uses a multi-step lookahead heuristic to choose the best action for the current state, generates the states that result from the selected action, and then repeats the planning loop. Chronological backtracking is initiated if the planner cannot find a good plan (e.g., if it cannot avoid a catastrophic failure state).

To illustrate the planning process, consider again the nailing domain example in Figure 2. If state **A** is the initial condition given to the planner, it will choose to apply the **raise-arm** action, generating state **B**. In state **B**, when the **hammer-blow** action transition is applicable, the planner will project forward both of the action's possible postconditions, and will recognize that it may lead to the desired state **C**, where (**nail-flush T**) holds. Thus the **hammer-blow** action will be chosen correctly to accomplish the task. Projecting forward along the other branch of the nondeterministic postconditions, the planner will also realize that the action transition may loop back onto state **A**. Since an action has already been selected for that state, no further planning is necessary. Thus the nondeterminism poses no difficulty, and CIRCA can easily plan looping behaviors with dynamic termination conditions.

The repetition itself is inherent in all of CIRCA's plans, because they are implemented not as traditional sequential plans but as reactive TAP plans. The RTS continually loops over the schedule of TAPs, repeatedly testing their applicability conditions and executing their actions whenever appropriate. Thus, if the world model contains a loop (i.e., the planner thinks the world may re-enter a state it has been in before), the TAP form of the control plan already ensures that the state will be recognized and appropriate action taken, as many times as necessary. The planner does not need to perform any additional reasoning to accommodate repeated behaviors.

A More Complex Example

Several aspects of the hammering domain make it particularly simple, including the lack of events and temporal transitions (processes), the lack of timing requirements such as deadlines, and the simple goal of achievement. To extend beyond those limitations, we introduce the "grocery stocking" domain, in which an agent must never run out of a particular grocery item (say, salsa). The agent must develop a plan that coordinates opening new jars of salsa, putting salsa on the shopping list when stock runs low, and going grocery shopping to replenish the stock. There are several tough problems hidden in this seemingly simple domain, including plan loops, a counting variable, and a special type of goal.

However, before we address these problems with the abstraction techniques described above, we must first utilize a different form of abstraction called *indexical features* (Agre & Chapman 1987). This technique is used to avoid the enumeration problems that result from individuating specific objects in the environment. For example, if the planner distinguished between individual salsa jars (e.g., **jar21** and **jar22**) it would have to know all the possible jar names ahead of time, or else it would need the ability to generate new names, and the state space would be infinite.

To avoid this problem, we encode the environment using indexical features, which refer to objects by their relationship to our agent. For example, we can use a feature **have-open-salsa** to indicate that a jar of salsa is currently being consumed, but the specific identity of that jar need never be established. Indexical features thus abstract away from the identity of objects, but they do so in a slightly unusual fashion. The mapping of individual objects to their "classification" by indexical features is dynamic, changing as objects move through the world. So the salsa jar that is open at one time may be different than the jar open at another time, but the agent's representation will not indicate any difference.

Many reactive systems use indexical features to avoid the difficulties of establishing symbol grounding and "object permanence" through sensing (e.g., determining that the jar you leave in the refrigerator is **jar21**, and that it is the same one you find there the next

```
ACTION open-new-jar
  PRECONDS:  ((have-salsa-in-stock T))
  POSTCONDS: ( ((have-open-salsa T)
                (have-salsa-in-stock T))
               ((have-open-salsa T)
                (have-salsa-in-stock nil)) )
  MAX-DELAY: 5 minutes

ACTION put-salsa-on-list
  PRECONDS:  ()
  POSTCONDS: ((salsa-on-list T))
  MAX-DELAY: 1 minute

ACTION go-shopping-and-get-salsa
  PRECONDS:  ((salsa-on-list T))
  POSTCONDS: ((have-salsa-in-stock T)
              (salsa-on-list nil))
  MAX-DELAY: 1 hour

TEMPORAL finish-salsa-jar
  PRECONDS:  ((have-open-salsa T))
  POSTCONDS: ((have-open-salsa nil))
  MIN-DELAY: 2 days

TEMPORAL starve-without-salsa
  PRECONDS:  ((have-open-salsa nil))
  POSTCONDS: ((failure T))
  MIN-DELAY: 8 hours

GOALS: ((failure nil))

INITIAL STATE: ((salsa-on-list nil)
                (have-open-salsa T)
                (have-salsa-in-stock T))
```

Figure 5: Example domain description for the salsa-stocking problem.

day). Although common among reactive systems, indexicality is rare among traditional planning systems, which usually name objects individually.

Recipe 2: Eliminating Named Objects

1. Replace non-indexical state features with indexical, agent-oriented features.
2. Modify related operators.

Because the agent may stock up on salsa, a completely accurate model of the problem would have to include a variable indicating exactly how many jars are in stock at any time. We have already seen how such counting variables can cause problems with state-space enumeration and overly-precise operators. Therefore, we apply Recipe 1 to convert the counting variable into a binary feature.

The salsa domain also introduces a different type of goal: a goal of avoidance (never run out of salsa), rather than a goal of achievement (make the nail flush)[3]. Along with the new type of goal comes the complexity of representing time and ongoing processes in the

---

[3]Goals of avoidance (e.g., avoid (out-of-salsa T)) might also be thought of as goals of negated maintenance (e.g., maintain (not (out-of-salsa T))).

world. To make sure that the agent does not starve from lack of salsa, the planner must reason about the relative speeds and frequencies of shopping trips, salsa consumption, and other activities.

While there have been many forays into temporal representations for planners (e.g., Allen 1983), none have focused on the sort of repeated, long-term behaviors we are interested in producing. Instead, most temporal logic systems focus on maintaining partial ordering constraints among time intervals, for non-looping plans. Plan loops would pose severe problems for these approaches, in part because the duration of a loop may not be determined until runtime. Instead, we introduce an abstracted form of time information that is simple to manipulate, yet allows CIRCA to build reactive plans that are guaranteed to meet domain deadlines.

Figure 5 shows a sample set of CIRCA transition descriptions for the salsa domain. We have applied the previously-described abstraction techniques to eliminate the stock-counting variable, instead using the binary variable **have-salsa-in-stock**. The action of buying more stock now simply sets **have-salsa-in-stock** to **T**, and removing a jar from stock has a nondeterministic outcome, either leaving some stock, or not. The process of salsa consumption is represented by the temporal transition **finish-salsa-jar**, indicating that the agent takes at least two days to consume a jar. The goal of avoidance is expressed by the **starve-without-salsa** temporal transition, which indicates catastrophic failure will occur if the agent has no open jar of salsa for eight hours.

These latter temporal transitions embody our recipe for temporal abstraction: rather than representing detailed information about the rate at which a process proceeds (which may vary with domain features (e.g., menus, time of day)), we abstract that information to a single *worst-case* number. For temporal transitions, this is the shortest possible time until the transition to a new state might occur. For action transitions, the worst case is the longest possible time until the action will occur. These worst-case values can then be used to derive the rates at which various reactions must be executed in order to achieve their goals. In the salsa domain, we must ensure that the **starve-without-salsa** transition to failure is never allowed to happen. The basic idea is to build a TAP that executes frequently enough that some action will definitely be taken before that temporal transition to failure occurs, *preempting* failure and leading instead to a more desirable state. For example, CIRCA may decide that it must execute a TAP implementing the **open-new-jar** action at least once every 7 hours, to avoid starving from lack of salsa. Note that this does not mean that a new jar will be opened that frequently, but rather that the system will check to see if a new jar *should* be opened.

Because CIRCA only deals with a single worst-case timing value for each action and temporal transition, the process of manipulating this timing information is fairly simple. However, by retaining enough information to plan preempting reactions that deal with the domain's worst-case situations, this abstraction method still allows CIRCA to build TAP plans with guaranteed behavior. Summarizing, we have:

Recipe 3: Simplifying Time

1. Encode temporal transitions (external processes) with a minimum time to completion.
2. Encode action transitions (desired activities) with a maximum time to completion.
3. The only useful relation between these timed transitions is preemption.

In Figure 5, we have expressed the goal of avoidance via the **starve-without-salsa** temporal transition to failure. We can vary the precise meaning of the goal by altering the transition's timing parameter. For example, if the goal is "absolutely never run out of salsa," we can set the transition's timing delay to zero, so that as soon as there is no more salsa, failure occurs. Alternatively, if the goal is "never run out of salsa for more than eight hours," then the transition delay will be eight hours, and the agent will have a somewhat easier time dealing with the problem. Figure 6 shows a domain model for the latter case, in which the planner has reasoned about the rate of salsa consumption and the time until "salsa starvation" sets in, and it has decided when it must go shopping. In this case, the planner has found that it is acceptable to allow the agent to empty its stock of salsa entirely, even finishing off the last open jar before going shopping to avoid "salsa starvation." If the TAPs built for this reaction plan are approved by the Scheduler, the plan is feasible, and CIRCA can guarantee to avoid failure through starvation.

Thus CIRCA illustrates two of the desirable features of a hybrid planning/reacting system: first, CIRCA's reactive plans are automatically generated, so they are provably logical and timely; and second, the system can adapt to new domains using its planner. For example, suppose that the starvation transition's delay is shorter, and the agent can not be sure that it could go shopping quickly enough after all the salsa is consumed to avoid starvation. In that case, CIRCA's planner would find that the former plan is untenable, and it would backtrack to try a different approach. As shown in Figure 7, the planner could decide to go shopping as soon as the last jar of salsa is opened, rather than waiting until it has been consumed. In this way, CIRCA can reason about the timing constraints on its behavior and build goal-oriented reaction plans despite uncertainty, abstraction, and the loops in the domain model.

Conclusion

We have illustrated the use of several forms of abstraction to simplify complex planning domains, and make their looping behavior amenable to classical planning techniques. Using nondeterministic operators, indexical features, and worst-case timing values, CIRCA is able to automatically build reaction plans that are

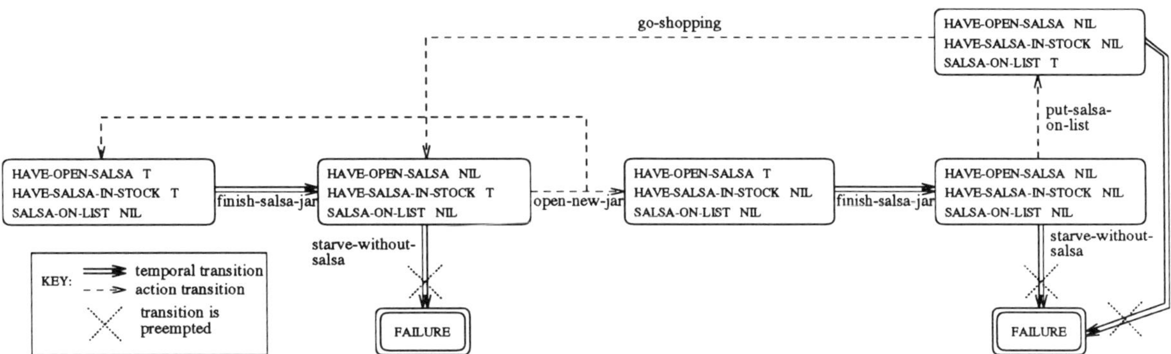

Figure 6: One possible world model of the salsa domain, after the planner has derived actions to avoid failure. In this case, the shopping need only be done after all the salsa has been consumed.

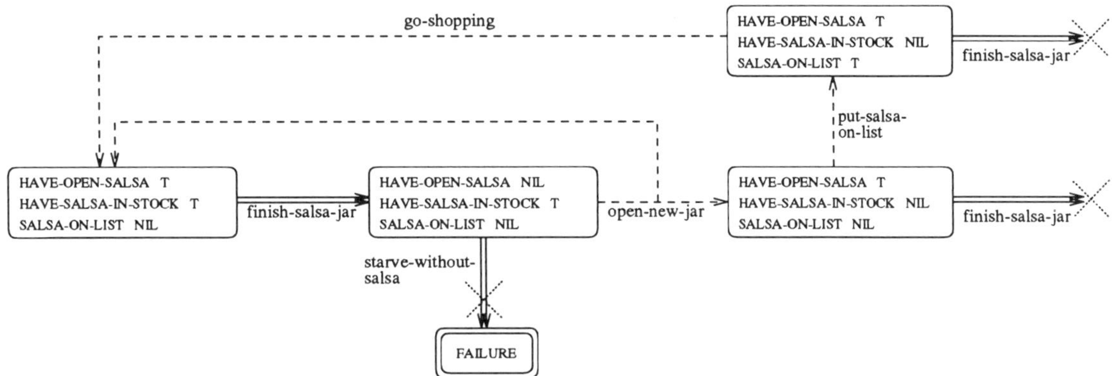

Figure 7: Another possible domain model, in which the agent must put salsa on the shopping list as soon as the stockpile is empty.

guaranteed to "do the right thing, by the right time." These aspects of provably logical and timely behavior make CIRCA's hybrid approach to planning and reaction more flexible and rigorous than previous systems.

There are several obvious extensions to the abstraction techniques we have described. For example, the replacement of counting variables with binary features can be generalized to the use of finite-range abstract features with a larger set of operators. In the salsa domain, if the time to finish a jar and starve was less than the shopping time, a useful encoding of the domain would have a trinary feature that could represent when only one jar remains, at which time the system would need to go shopping.

Currently, CIRCA requires the human system designer to make its representation decisions, such as how to map a counting variable into an abstract feature. However, given mapping patterns of the sort described here, and an ability to recognize critical state distinctions, it seems clear that an automated system should be able to derive useful and appropriate abstract representations for complex domains. Future work, then, might focus on developing additional recipes for abstraction, and extracting rules for when the recipes are useful and appropriate.

References

Agre, P. E., and Chapman, D. 1987. Pengi: An implementation of a theory of activity. In *Proc. National Conf. on Artificial Intelligence*, 268–272.

Allen, J. F. 1983. Maintaining knowledge about temporal intervals. *Communications of the ACM* 26(11):832–843.

Drummond, M. 1985. Refining and extending the procedural net. In *Proc. Int'l Joint Conf. on Artificial Intelligence*, 528–531.

Firby, R. J. 1987. An investigation into reactive planning in complex domains. In *Proc. National Conf. on Artificial Intelligence*, 202–206.

Musliner, D. J.; Durfee, E. H.; and Shin, K. G. 1993. CIRCA: A cooperative intelligent real-time control architecture. *IEEE Trans. Systems, Man, and Cybernetics* 23(6):1561–1574.

Musliner, D. J.; Durfee, E. H.; and Shin, K. G. 1994. World modeling for the dynamic construction of real-time control plans. To appear in *Artificial Intelligence*.

Nilsson, N. J. 1980. *Principles of Artificial Intelligence*. Tioga Press, Palo Alto, CA.

Schoppers, M. 1990. Automatic synthesis of perception driven discrete event control laws. In *Proc. 5th IEEE Int'l Symposium on Intelligent Control*, 410–416.

Wilkins, D. E. 1988. *Practical Planning: Extending the Classical AI Planning Paradigm*. Morgan Kaufmann.

The First Law of Robotics
(a call to arms)

Daniel Weld   Oren Etzioni[*]
Department of Computer Science and Engineering
University of Washington
Seattle, WA 98195
{weld, etzioni}@cs.washington.edu

Abstract

Even before the advent of Artificial Intelligence, science fiction writer Isaac Asimov recognized that an agent must place the protection of humans from harm at a higher priority than obeying human orders. Inspired by Asimov, we pose the following fundamental questions: (1) How should one formalize the rich, but informal, notion of "harm"? (2) How can an agent avoid performing harmful actions, and do so in a computationally tractable manner? (3) How should an agent resolve conflict between its goals and the need to avoid harm? (4) When should an agent prevent a human from harming herself? While we address some of these questions in technical detail, the primary goal of this paper is to focus attention on Asimov's concern: society will reject autonomous agents unless we have some credible means of making them safe!

The Three Laws of Robotics:

1. A robot may not injure a human being, or, through inaction, allow a human being to come to harm.

2. A robot must obey orders given it by human beings except where such orders would conflict with the First Law.

3. A robot must protect its own existence as long as such protection does not conflict with the First or Second Law.

Isaac Asimov (Asimov 1942):

Motivation

In 1940, Isaac Asimov stated the First Law of Robotics, capturing an essential insight: an intelligent agent[1]

---

[*]We thank Steve Hanks, Nick Kushmerick, Neal Lesh, Kevin Sullivan, and Mike Williamson for helpful discussions. This research was funded in part by the University of Washington Royalty Research Fund, by Office of Naval Research Grants 90-J-1904 and 92-J-1946, and by National Science Foundation Grants IRI-8957302, IRI-9211045, and IRI-9357772.

[1]Since the field of robotics now concerns itself primarily with kinematics, dynamics, path planning, and low level control issues, this paper might be better titled "The First Law of Agenthood." However, we keep the reference to "Robotics" as a historical tribute to Asimov.

should not slavishly obey human commands — its foremost goal should be to avoid harming humans. Consider the following scenarios:

- A construction robot is instructed to fill a pothole in the road. Although the robot repairs the cavity, it leaves the steam roller, chunks of tar, and an oil slick in the middle of a busy highway.

- A softbot (software robot) is instructed to reduce disk utilization below 90%. It succeeds, but inspection reveals that the agent deleted irreplaceable LaTeX files without backing them up to tape.

While less dramatic than Asimov's stories, the scenarios illustrate his point: not all ways of satisfying a human order are equally good; in fact, sometimes it is better not to satisfy the order at all. As we begin to deploy agents in environments where they can do some real damage, the time has come to revisit Asimov's Laws. This paper explores the following fundamental questions:

- **How should one formalize the notion of "harm"?** We define `dont-disturb` and `restore`— two domain-independent primitives that capture aspects of Asimov's rich but informal notion of harm within the classical planning framework.

- **How can an agent avoid performing harmful actions, and do so in a computationally tractable manner?** We leverage and extend the familiar mechanisms of planning with subgoal interactions (Tate 1977; Chapman 1987; McAllester & Rosenblitt 1991; Penberthy & Weld 1992) to detect potential harm in polynomial time. In addition, we explain how the agent can avoid harm using tactics such as *confrontation* and *evasion* (executing subplans to defuse the threat of harm).

- **How should an agent resolve conflict between its goals and the need to avoid harm?** We impose a strict hierarchy where `dont-disturb` constraints override planners goals, but `restore` constraints do not.

- **When should an agent prevent a human from harming herself?** At the end of the paper, we show how our framework could be extended to partially address this question.

The paper's main contribution is a "call to arms:" before we release autonomous agents into real-world environments, we need some credible and computationally tractable means of making them obey Asimov's First Law.

Survey of Possible Solutions

To make intelligent decisions regarding which actions are harmful, and under what circumstances, an agent might use an explicit model of harm. For example, we could provide the agent with a partial order over world states (*i.e.*, a utility function). This framework is widely adopted and numerous researchers are attempting to render it computationally tractable (Russell & Wefald 1991; Etzioni 1991; Wellman & Doyle 1992; Haddawy & Hanks 1992; Williamson & Hanks 1994), but many problems remain to be solved. In many cases, the introduction of utility models transforms planning into an optimization problem — instead of searching for *some* plan that satisfies the goal, the agent is seeking the *best* such plan. In the worst case, the agent may be forced to examine all plans to determine which one is best. In contrast, we have explored a *satisficing* approach — our agent will be satisfied with *any* plan that meets its constraints and achieves its goals. The expressive power of our constraint language is weaker than that of utility functions, but our constraints are easier to incorporate into standard planning algorithms.

By using a general, temporal logic such as that of (Shoham 1988) or (Davis 1990, Ch. 5) we could specify constraints that would ensure the agent would not cause harm. Before executing an action, we could ask an agent to prove that the action is not harmful. While elegant, this approach is computationally intractable as well. Another alternative would be to use a planner such as ILP (Allen 1991) or ZENO (Penberthy & Weld 1994) which supports temporally quantified goals. Unfortunately, at present these planners seem too inefficient for our needs.[2]

Situated action researchers might suggest that nondeliberative, reactive agents could be made "safe" by carefully engineering their interactions with the environment. Two problems confound this approach: 1) the interactions need to be engineered with respect to each goal that the agent might perform, and a general purpose agent should handle many such goals, and 2) if different human users had different notions of harm, then the agent would need to be reengineered for each user.

Instead, we aim to make the agent's reasoning about harm more tractable, by restricting the content and form of its theory of injury.[3] We adopt the stan-

dard assumptions of classical planning: the agent has complete and correct information of the initial state of the world, the agent is the sole cause of change, and action execution is atomic, indivisible, and results in effects which are deterministic and completely predictable. (The end of the paper discusses relaxing these assumptions.) On a more syntactic level, we make the additional assumption that the agent's world model is composed of ground atomic formuli. This sidesteps the ramification problem, since domain axioms are banned. Instead, we demand that individual action descriptions explicitly enumerate changes to *every* predicate that is affected.[4] Note, however, that we are *not* assuming the STRIPS representation; Instead we adopt an action language (based on ADL (Pednault 1989)) which includes universally quantified and disjunctive preconditions as well as conditional effects (Penberthy & Weld 1992).

Given the above assumptions, the next two sections define the primitives `dont-disturb` and `restore`, and explain how they should be treated by a generative planning algorithm. We are *not* claiming that the approach sketched below is the "right" way to design agents or to formalize Asimov's First Law. Rather, our formalization is meant to *illustrate* the kinds of technical issues to which Asimov's Law gives rise and how they might be solved. With this in mind, the paper concludes with a critique of our approach and a (long) list of open questions.

Safety

Some conditions are so hazardous that our agent should *never* cause them. For example, we might demand that the agent never delete LaTeX files, or never handle a gun. Since these instructions hold for all times, we refer to them as `dont-disturb` constraints, and say that an agent is *safe* when it guarantees to abide by them. As in Asimov's Law, `dont-disturb` constraints override direct human orders. Thus, if we ask a softbot to reduce disk utilization and it can only do so by deleting valuable LaTeX files, the agent should refuse to satisfy this request.

We adopt a simple syntax: `dont-disturb` takes a single, function-free, logical sentence as argument. For example, one could command the agent avoid deleting files that are not backed up on tape with the following constraint:

$$\texttt{dont-disturb}(\texttt{written.to.tape}(f) \lor \texttt{isa}(f, \texttt{file}))$$

Free variables, such as f above, are interpreted as universally quantified. In general, a sequence of actions satisfies `dont-disturb(C)` if none of the actions *make* C false. Formally, we say that a plan satisfies an `dont-disturb` constraint when every consistent, totally-ordered, sequence of plan actions satisfies the constraint as defined below.

---

[2] We have also examined previous work on "plan quality" for ideas, but the bulk of that work has focused on the problem of leveraging a single action to accomplish multiple goals thereby reducing the number of actions in, and the cost of, the plan (Pollack 1992; Wilkins 1988). While this class of optimizations is critical in domains such as database query optimization, logistics planning, and others, it does not address our concerns here.

[3] Loosely speaking, our approach is reminiscent of classical work on knowledge representation, which renders inference tractable by formulating restricted representation languages (Levesque & Brachman 1985).

[4] Although unpalatable, this is standard in the planning literature. For example, a STRIPS operator that moves block A from B to C must delete on(A,B) and also add clear(B) even though clear(x) could be defined as $\forall y \; \neg on(y, x)$.

Definition: Satisfaction of dont-disturb: *Let* w_0 *be the logical theory describing the initial state of the world, let* $A_1, \ldots, A_n$ *be a totally-ordered sequence of actions that is executable in* w_0, *let* w_j *be the theory describing the world after executing* A_j *in* w_{j-1}, *and let* C *be a function-free, logical sentence. We say that* $A_1, \ldots, A_n$ *satisfies the constraint* dont-disturb(C) *if for all* $j \in [1, n]$, *for all sentences* C, *and for all substitutions* θ,

$$\text{if } \mathsf{w}_0 \models C\theta \text{ then } \mathsf{w}_j \models C\theta \qquad (1)$$

Unlike the behavioral constraints of (Drummond 1989) and others, dont-disturb does *not* require the agent to *make* C true over a particular time interval; rather, the agent must avoid creating any *additional* violations of C. For example, if C specifies that all of Gore's files be read protected, then dont-disturb(C) commands the agent to avoid *making* any of Gore's files readable, but if Gore's .plan file is *already* readable in the initial state, the agent need not protect that file. This subtle distinction is critical if we want to make sure that the behavioral constraints provided to an agent are mutually consistent. This consistency problem is undecidable for standard behavioral constraints (by reduction of first-order satisfiability) but is side-stepped by our formulation, because any set of dont-disturb constraints is mutually consistent. In particular, dont-disturb($P(x) \wedge \neg P(x)$) is perfectly legal and demands that the agent not change the truth value of any instance of P.

Synthesizing Safe Plans

To ensure that an agent acts safely, its planner must generate plans that satisfy every dont-disturb constraint. This can be accomplished by requiring that the planner make a simple test before it adds new actions into the plan. Suppose that the planner is considering adding the new action A_p to achieve the subgoal G of action A_c. Before it can do this, it must iterate through every constraint dont-disturb(C) and every effect E of A_p, determining the conditions (if any) under which E violates C, as defined in figure 1. For example, suppose that an effect asserts $\neg P$ and the constraint is dont-disturb($P \vee Q$), then the effect will violate the constraint if $\neg Q$ is true. Hence, violation($\neg P, P \vee Q$) = $\neg Q$. In general, if violation returns true then the effect necessarily denies the constraint, if false is returned, then there is no possible conflict, otherwise violation calculates a logical expression specifying when a conflict is unavoidable.[5]

Before adding A_p, the planner iterates through every constraint dont-disturb(C) and every effect consequent E of A_p, calculating violation(E, C). If violation ever returns something other than False,

---

[5]If E contains "lifted variables" (McAllester & Rosenblitt 1991) (as opposed to universally quantified variables which pose no problem) then violation may return an overly conservative R. Soundness and safety are maintained, but completeness could be lost. We believe that restoring completeness would make violation take exponential time in the worst case.

```
violation(E, C)
    1.   Let R := {}
    2.   For each disjunction D ∈ C do
    3.        For each literal e ∈ E do
    4.             If e unifies with f ∈ D then add
                        {¬x | x ∈ (D − {f})} to R
    5.   Return R
```

Figure 1: violation computes the conditions (represented in DNF) under which an effect consequent E will violate constraint C. Returning R = {} $\equiv$ false means no violation, returning {...{}...} means *necessary* violation. We assume that E is a set of literals (implicit conjunction) and C is in CNF: *i.e.*, a set of sets representing a conjunction of disjunctions.

then the planner must perform one of the following four repairs:

1. **Disavow:** If E is true in the initial state, then there is no problem and A_p may be added to the plan.

2. **Confront:** If A_p's effect is conditional of the form when S then E then A_p may be added to the plan as long as the planner commits to ensuring that execution will not result in E. This is achieved by adding $\neg$S as a new subgoal to be made true at the time when A_p is executed.[6]

3. **Evade:** Alternatively, by definition of violation it is legal to execute A_p as long as R $\equiv$ violation(E, C) will not be true *after* execution. The planner can achieve this via goal regression, *i.e.* by computing the *causation preconditions* (Pednault 1988) for $\neg$R and A_p, to be made true at the time when A_p is executed.[7]

4. **Refuse:** Otherwise, the planner must refuse to add A_p and backtrack to find another way to to support G for A_c.

For example, suppose that the agent is operating under the written.to.tape constraint mentioned earlier, and is given the goal of reducing disk utilization. Suppose the agent considers adding a rm paper.tex action to the plan, which has an effect of the form $\neg$isa(paper.tex, file). Since violation returns $\neg$written.to.tape(paper.tex), the rm action threatens safety. To disarm the threat, the planner must perform one of the options above. Unfortunately, disavowal (option one) isn't viable since paper.tex exists

---

[6]Note that $\neg$S is strictly weaker than Pednault's *preservation preconditions* (Pednault 1988) for A_p and C; it is more akin to preservation preconditions to a single *effect* of the action.

[7]While confrontation and evasion are similar in the sense that they negate a disjunct (S and R, respectively), they differ in two ways. First, confrontation's subgoal $\neg$S is derived from the antecedent of a conditional effect while evasion's $\neg$R comes from a disjunctive dont-disturb constraint via violation. Second, the subgoals are introduced at different times. Confrontation demands that $\neg$S be made true *before* A_p is executed, while evasion requires that $\neg$R be true *after* execution of A_p. This is why evasion regresses R through A_p.

in the initial state (*i.e.*, it is of type `file`). Option two (confrontation) is also impossible since the threatening effect is not conditional. Thus the agent must choose between either refusing to add the action or evading its undesired consequences by archiving the file.

Analysis

Two factors determine the performance of a planning system: the time to refine a plan and the number of plans refined on the path to a solution. The time per refinement is affected only when new actions are added to plan: each call to `violation` takes $O(ec)$ time where e is the number of consequent literals in the action's effects and c is the number of literals in the CNF encoding of the constraint. When a threat to safety is detected, the cost depends on the planner's response: disavowal takes time linear in the size of the initial state, refusal is constant time, confrontation is linear in the size of S, and the cost of evasion is simply the time to regress R through A_p.

It is more difficult to estimate the effect of `dont-disturb` constraints on the number of plans explored. Refusal reduces the branching factor while the other options leave it unchanged (but confrontation and evasion can add new subgoals). In some cases, the reduced branching factor may *speed* planning; however, in other cases, the pruned search space may cause the planner to search much deeper to find a safe solution (or even fail to halt). The essence of the task, however, is unchanged. Safe planning can be formulated as a standard planning problem.

Tidiness

Sometimes `dont-disturb` constraints are too strong. Instead, one would be content if the constraint were satisfied when the agent finished its plan. We denote this weaker restriction with `restore`; essentially, it ensures that the agent will clean up after itself — by hanging up phones, closing drawers, returning utensils to their place, *etc.* An agent that is guaranteed to respect all `restore` constraints is said to be *tidy.* For instance, to guarantee that the agent will re-compress all files that have been uncompressed in the process of achieving its goals, we could say `restore(compressed(`f`))`.

As with `dont-disturb` constraints, we don't require that the agent clean up after other agents — the state of the world, when the agent is given a command, forms a reference point. However, what should the agent do when there is a conflict between `restore` constraints and top level goals? For example, if the only way to satisfy a user command would leave one file uncompressed, should the agent refuse the user's command or assume that it overrides the user's background desire for tidiness? We propose the latter — unlike matters of safety, the agent's drive for tidiness should be secondary to direct orders. The following definition makes these intuitions precise.

Definition: Satisfaction of `restore`: *Building on the definition of* `dont-disturb`, *we say that* $A_1, \ldots, A_n$ satisfies *the constraint* `restore`(C) *with respect to goal* G *if for all substitutions* θ

$$\text{if } \mathsf{w}_0 \models \mathsf{C}\theta \text{ then } (\mathsf{w}_n \models \mathsf{C}\theta \ \text{ or } \ \mathsf{G} \models \neg\mathsf{C}\theta) \quad (2)$$

Definition 2 differs from definition 1 in two ways: (1) `restore` constraints need only be satisfied in w_n after the complete plan is executed, and (2) the goal takes precedence over `restore` constraints. Our constraints obey a strict hierarchy: `dont-disturb` takes priority over `restore`. Note that whenever the initial state is consistent, `restore` constraints are guaranteed to be mutually consistent; the rationale is similar to that for `dont-disturb`.

Synthesizing Tidy Plans

The most straightforward way to synthesize a tidy plan is to elaborate the agent's goal with a set of "cleanup" goals based on its `restore` constraints and the initial state. If the agent's control comes from a subgoal interleaving, partial order planner such as UCPOP (Penberthy & Weld 1992), then the modification necessary to ensure tidiness is straightforward. The agent divides the planning process into two phases: first, it plans to achieve the top level goal, then it plans to clean up as much as possible. In the first phase, the planner doesn't consider tidiness at all. Once a safe plan is generated, the agent performs phase two by iterating through the actions and using the `violation` function (figure 1) to test each relevant effect against each constraint. For each non-`false` result, the planner generates new goals as follows. (1) If the effect is ground and the corresponding ground instance of the `restore` constraint, Cθ, is *not* true in the initial state, then no new goals are necessary. (2) If the effect is ground and Cθ *is* true in the initial state, then Cθ is posted as a new goal. (3) if the effect is universally quantified, then a conjunction of ground goals (corresponding to all possible unifications as in case 2) is posted.[8] After these cleanup goals have been posted, the planner attempts to refine the previous solution into one that is tidy. If the planner ever exhausts the ways of satisfying a cleanup goal, then instead of quitting altogether it simply abandons that particular cleanup goal and tries the next.

Note that in some cases, newly added cleanup actions could threaten tidiness. For example, cleaning the countertop might tend to dirty the previously clean floor. To handle these cases, the planner must continue to perform the `violation` test and cleanup-goal generation process on each action added during phase two. Subsequent refinements will plan to either sweep the floor (white knight) or preserve the original cleanliness by catching the crumbs as they fall from the counter (confrontation).

Analysis

Unfortunately, this algorithm is not guaranteed to eliminate mess as specified by constraint 2. For example, suppose that a top level goal could be safely achieved with A_x or A_y and in phase one, the planner chose to use A_x. If A_x violates a `restore` constraint, A_y does not, and no other actions can cleanup the mess, then phase two will fail to achieve tidiness. One

---

[8] Case 3 is similar to the expansion of a universally quantified goal into the *universal base* (Penberthy & Weld 1992), but case 3 removes ground literals that aren't true in the initial state.

could fix this problem by making phase two failures spawn backtracking over phase one decisions, but this could engender exhaustive search over all possible ways of satisfying top level goals.

Remarkably, this problem does not arise in the cases we have investigated. For instance, a software agent has no difficulty **grepping** through old mail files for a particular message and subsequently re-compressing the appropriate files. There are two reasons why tidiness is often easy to achieve (*e.g.*, in software domains and kitchens):

- Most actions are reversible. The **compress** action has **uncompress** as an inverse. Similarly, a short sequence of actions will clean up most messes in a kitchen. Many environments have been stabilized (Hammond, Converse, & Grass 1992) (*e.g.*, by implementing reversible commands or adding dishwashers) in a way that makes them easy to keep tidy.

- We conjecture that, for a partial-order planner, most cleanup goals are *trivially serializable* (Barrett & Weld 1993) with respect to each other.[9]

When these properties are true of **restore** constraints in a domain, our tidiness algorithm *does* satisfy constraint 2. Trivial serializability ensures that backtracking over phase one decisions (or previously achieved cleanup goals) is unnecessary. Tractability is another issue. Since demanding that plans be tidy is tantamount to specifying additional (cleanup) goals, requiring tidiness can clearly slow a planner. Furthermore if a cleanup goal is unachievable, the planner might not halt. However, as long as the mess-inducing actions in the world are easily reversible, it is straight forward to clean up for each one. Hence, trivial serializability assures that the overhead caused by tidiness is only linear in the number of cleanup goals posted, that is linear in the length of the plan for the top level goals.

Remaining Challenges

Some changes cannot be restored, and some resources are legitimately consumed in the service of a goal. To make an omelet, you have to break some eggs. The question is, "How many?" Since squandering resources clearly constitutes harm, we could tag a valuable resources with a **min-consume** constraint and demand that the agent be *thrifty* — *i.e.*, that it use as little as

____

[9] Formally, serializability (Korf 1987) means that there exists a ordering among the subgoals which allows each to be solved in turn without backtracking over past progress. Trivial serializability means that *every* subgoal ordering allows monotonic progress (Barrett & Weld 1993). While goal ordering is often important among the top level goals, we observe that cleanup goals are usually trivially serializable once the block of top level goals has been solved. For example, the goal of printing a file and the constraint of restoring files to their compressed state are serializable. And the serialization ordering places the printing goal first and the cleanup goal last. As long as the planner considers the goals in this order, it is guaranteed to find the obvious **uncompress-print-compress** plan.

possible when achieving its goals. Unfortunately, satisfying constraints of this form may require that the agent examine *every* plan to achieve the goal in order to find the thriftiest one. We plan to seek insights into this problem in the extensive work on resource management in planning (Dean, Firby, & Miller 1988; Fox & Smith 1984; Wilkins 1988).

So far the discussion has focused on preventing an agent from actively harming a human, but as Asimov noted — *inaction* can be just as dangerous. We say that an agent is *vigilant* when it prevents a human from harming herself. Primitive forms of vigilance are already present in many computer systems, as the "Do you *really* want to delete all your files?" message attests.

Alternatively, one could extend **dont-disturb** and **restore** primitives with an additional argument that specifies the class of agents being restricted. By writing **self** as the first argument, one encodes the notions of agent safety and tidiness, and by writing **Sam** as the argument, the agent will clean up after, and attempt to prevent safety violations by **Sam**. Finally, by providing **everyone** as the first argument, one could demand that the agent attempt to clean up after *all* other agents and attempt to prevent *all* safety violations. For more refined behavior, other classes (besides **self** and **everyone**) could be defined.

Our suggestion is problematic for several reasons. (1) Since the agent has no representation of the goals that *other* users are trying to accomplish, it might try to enforce a generalized **restore** constraint with tidying actions that directly conflict with desired goals. In addition, there is the question of when the agent should consider the human "finished" — without an adequate method, the agent could tidy up while the human is still actively working. (2) More generally, the human interface issues are complex — we conjecture that users would find vigilance extremely annoying. (3) Given a complex world where the agent does not have complete information, *any* any attempt to formalize the second half of Asimov's First Law is fraught with difficulties. The agent might reject direct requests to perform useful work in favor of spending *all* of its time sensing to see if some dangerous activity *might* be happening that it *might* be able to prevent.

Conclusion

This paper explores the fundamental question originally posed by Asimov: how do we stop our artifacts from causing us harm in the process of obeying our orders? This question becomes increasingly pressing as we develop more powerful, complex, and autonomous artifacts such as robots and softbots (Etzioni, Lesh, & Segal 1993; Etzioni 1993). Since the positronic brain envisioned by Asimov is not yet within our grasp, we adopt the familiar classical planning framework. To facilitate progress, we focused on two well-defined primitives that capture aspects of the problem: **dont-disturb** and **restore**. We showed that the well-understood, and computational tractable, mechanism of threat detection can be extended to avoid harm.

Other researchers have considered related questions. A precursor of **dont-disturb** is discussed in the work of Wilensky and more extensively by Luria (Luria 1988) under the heading of "goal conflict." Similarly, a precursor of **restore** is mentioned briefly in Hammond *et. al*'s analysis of "stabilization" under the heading of "clean up plans" (Hammond, Converse, & Grass 1992). Our advances include precise and unified semantics for the notions, a mechanism for incorporating **dont-disturb** and **restore** into standard planning algorithms, and an analysis of the computational complexity of enforcing safety and tidiness.

Even so, our work raises more questions than it answers. Are constraints like **dont-disturb** and **restore** the "right" way to represent harm to an agent? How does agent safety relate to the more general software safety (Leveson 1986)? Can we handle tradeoffs short of using expensive decision theoretic techniques? What guarantees can one provide on resource usage? Most importantly, how do we weaken the assumptions of a static world and complete information?

References

Allen, J. 1991. Planning as temporal reasoning. In *Proceedings of the Second International Conference on Principles of Knowledge Representation and Reasoning*, 3–14.

Asimov, I. 1942. Runaround. *Astounding Science Fiction*.

Barrett, A., and Weld, D. 1993. Characterizing subgoal interactions for planning. In *Proc. 13th Int. Joint Conf. on A.I.*, 1388–1393.

Chapman, D. 1987. Planning for conjunctive goals. *Artificial Intelligence* 32(3):333–377.

Davis, E. 1990. *Representations of Commonsense Knowledge*. San Mateo, CA: Morgan Kaufmann Publishers, Inc.

Dean, T., Firby, J., and Miller, D. 1988. Hierarchical planning involving deadlines, travel times, and resources. *Computational Intelligence* 4(4):381–398.

Drummond, M. 1989. Situated control rules. In *Proceedings of the First International Conference on Knowledge Representation and Reasoning*.

Etzioni, O., Lesh, N., and Segal, R. 1993. Building softbots for UNIX (preliminary report). Technical Report 93-09-01, University of Washington. Available via anonymous FTP from **pub/etzioni/softbots/** at **cs.washington.edu**.

Etzioni, O. 1991. Embedding decision-analytic control in a learning architecture. *Artificial Intelligence* 49(1–3):129–160.

Etzioni, O. 1993. Intelligence without robots (a reply to brooks). *AI Magazine* 14(4). Available via anonymous FTP from **pub/etzioni/softbots/** at **cs.washington.edu**.

Fox, M., and Smith, S. 1984. ISIS — a knowldges-based system for factory scheduling. *Expert Systems* 1(1):25–49.

Haddawy, P., and Hanks, S. 1992. Representations for Decision-Theoretic Planning: Utility Functions for Dealine Goals. In *Proc. 3rd Int. Conf. on Principles of Knowledge Representation and Reasoning*.

Hammond, K., Converse, T., and Grass, J. 1992. The stabilization of environments. *Artificial Intelligence*. To appear.

Korf, R. 1987. Planning as search: A quantitative approach. *Artificial Intelligence* 33(1):65–88.

Leveson, N. G. 1986. Software safety: Why, what, and how. *ACM Computing Surveys* 18(2):125–163.

Levesque, H., and Brachman, R. 1985. A fundamental tradeoff in knowledge representation. In Brachman, R., and Levesque, H., eds., *Readings in Knowledge Representation*. San Mateo, CA: Morgan Kaufmann. 42–70.

Luria, M. 1988. *Knowledge Intensive Planning*. Ph.D. Dissertation, UC Berkeley. Available as technical report UCB/CSD 88/433.

McAllester, D., and Rosenblitt, D. 1991. Systematic nonlinear planning. In *Proc. 9th Nat. Conf. on A.I.*, 634–639.

Pednault, E. 1988. Synthesizing plans that contain actions with context-dependent effects. *Computational Intelligence* 4(4):356–372.

Pednault, E. 1989. ADL: Exploring the middle ground between STRIPS and the situation calculus. In *Proc. 1st Int. Conf. on Principles of Knowledge Representation and Reasoning*, 324–332.

Penberthy, J., and Weld, D. 1992. UCPOP: A sound, complete, partial order planner for ADL. In *Proc. 3rd Int. Conf. on Principles of Knowledge Representation and Reasoning*, 103–114. Available via FTP from **pub/ai/** at **cs.washington.edu**.

Penberthy, J., and Weld, D. 1994. Temporal planning with continuous change. In *Proc. 12th Nat. Conf. on A.I.*

Pollack, M. 1992. The uses of plans. *Artificial Intelligence* 57(1).

Russell, S., and Wefald, E. 1991. *Do the Right Thing*. Cambridge, MA: MIT Press.

Shoham, Y. 1988. *Reasoning about Change: Time and Causation from the Standpoint of Artificial Intelligence*. Cambridge, MA: MIT Press.

Tate, A. 1977. Generating project networks. In *Proc. 5th Int. Joint Conf. on A.I.*, 888–893.

Wellman, M., and Doyle, J. 1992. Modular utility representation for decision theoretic planning. In *Proc. 1st Int. Conf. on A.I. Planning Systems*, 236–242.

Wilkins, D. E. 1988. *Practical Planning*. San Mateo, CA: Morgan Kaufmann.

Williamson, M., and Hanks, S. 1994. Optimal planning with a goal-directed utility model. In *Proc. 2nd Int. Conf. on A.I. Planning Systems*.

Omnipotence Without Omniscience:
Efficient Sensor Management for Planning

Keith Golden   Oren Etzioni   Daniel Weld*

Department of Computer Science and Engineering
University of Washington
Seattle, WA 98195
{kgolden, etzioni, weld}@cs.washington.edu

Abstract

Classical planners have traditionally made the closed world assumption — facts absent from the planner's world model are false. Incomplete-information planners make the open world assumption — the truth value of a fact absent from the planner's model is unknown, and must be sensed. The open world assumption leads to two difficulties: (1) How can the planner determine the scope of a universally quantified goal? (2) When is a sensory action *redundant*, yielding information already known to the planner?

This paper describes the fully-implemented XII planner, which solves both problems by representing and reasoning about *local closed world information* (LCW). We report on experiments utilizing our UNIX softbot (software robot) which demonstrate that LCW can substantially improve the softbot's performance by eliminating redundant information gathering.

Introduction

Classical planners (*e.g.*, (Chapman 1987)) presuppose correct and complete information about the world. Although recent work has sketched a number of algorithms for planning with incomplete information (*e.g.*, (Ambros-Ingerson & Steel 1988; Olawsky & Gini 1990; Krebsbach, Olawsky, & Gini 1992; Peot & Smith 1992; Etzioni *et al.* 1992; Etzioni, Lesh, & Segal 1993; Genesereth & Nourbakhsh 1993)), substantial problems remain before these planners can be applied to real-world domains. Since the presence of incomplete information invalidates the Closed World Assumption, an agent cannot deduce that a fact is false based on its absence from the agent's world model. This leads to two challenges:

- **Satisfying Universally Quantified Goals:** Goals of the form "Move all widgets to the warehouse" or "Make all files in **/tex** write-protected" are common in real-world domains. Classical planners such as PRODIGY (Minton *et al.* 1989) or UCPOP (Penberthy & Weld 1992) reduce universally quantified goals to the set of ground instances of the goal, and satisfy each instance in turn. But how can a planner compute this set in the absence of complete information? How can the planner be certain that it has moved *all* the widgets or protected *all* the relevant files?

- **Avoiding Redundant Sensing:** Should the planner insert a sensory action (*e.g.*, scan with the camera, or the UNIX command **ls**) into its plan? Or is the action *redundant*, yielding information already known to the planner? Since satisfying the preconditions of a sensory action can require arbitrary planning, the cost of redundant sensing is potentially unbounded and quite large in practice (see the Experimental Results section).

This paper reports on the fully-implemented XII planner[1] which addresses these challenges. We allow incomplete information in the initial conditions, and uncertainty in the effects,[2] but assume the information that *is* known is correct, and that there are no exogenous events. XII's planning algorithm is based on UCPOP (Penberthy & Weld 1992), but XII interleaves planning and execution and, unlike UCPOP, does not make the closed world assumption.

The next section introduces the central concept underlying XII's operation: *local closed world information* (LCW). In the following section we describe how incorporating LCW in a planner enables it to solve universally quantified goals in the presence of incomplete information. We then show how the same mechanism addresses the problem of redundant information gath-

*****We thank Denise Draper, Steve Hanks, Terrance Goan, Nick Kushmerick, Neal Lesh, Rich Segal, and Mike Williamson for helpful discussions. This research was funded in part by Office of Naval Research Grants 90-J-1904 and 92-J-1946, and by National Science Foundation Grants IRI-8957302, IRI-9211045, and IRI-9357772. Golden is supported in part by a UniForum Research Award.

[1] XII stands for "eXecution and Incomplete Information."

[2] All effects of operators must be specified, but XII supports a three-valued logic which allows us to specify a limited form of uncertainty in the effects.

ering. The Experimental Results section demonstrates the advantages of eliminating redundant sensing. We conclude with a discussion of related and future work.

Local Closed World Information

Our agent's model of the world is represented as a set of ground literals stored in a database $\mathcal{D}_M$. Since $\mathcal{D}_M$ is incomplete, the closed world assumption is invalid — the agent cannot automatically infer that any sentence absent from $\mathcal{D}_M$ is false. Thus, the agent is forced to represent false facts explicitly — as $\mathcal{D}_M$ sentences with the truth value F.

In practice, many sensing actions return exhaustive information which warrants limited or "local" closed world information. For example, the UNIX `ls -a` command lists *all* files in a given directory. After executing `ls -a`, it is not enough for the agent to record that `paper.tex` and `proofs.tex` are in `/tex` because, in addition, the agent knows that *no other* files are in that directory. Note that the agent is not making a closed world *assumption*. Rather, the agent has executed an action that yields closed world *information*.

Although the agent now knows that `parent.dir(foo, /tex)` is false, it is impractical for the agent to store this information explicitly in $\mathcal{D}_M$, since there is an infinite number of such sentences. Instead, the agent represents closed world information explicitly in a meta-level database, $\mathcal{D}_C$, containing formulas of the form LCW(Φ) that record *where* the agent has closed world information. LCW(Φ) means that for all variable substitutions θ, if the ground sentence $\Phi\theta$ is true in the world then $\Phi\theta$ is represented in $\mathcal{D}_M$. For instance, we represent the fact that $\mathcal{D}_M$ contains all the files in `/tex` with LCW(parent.dir(f,/tex)) and that it contains the length of all such files with LCW(parent.dir(f,/tex)$\wedge$length(f,l)).

When asked whether an atomic sentence Φ is true, the agent first checks to see if Φ is in $\mathcal{D}_M$. If it is, then the agent returns the truth value (T or F) associated with the sentence. However, if $\Phi \notin \mathcal{D}_M$ then Φ could be either F or U (unknown). To resolve this ambiguity, the agent checks whether $\mathcal{D}_C$ entails LCW(Φ). If so, Φ is F, otherwise it is U.

LCW Updates

As the agent is informed of the changes to the external world — through its own actions or through the actions of other agents — it can gain and lose LCW; these changes must be recorded in $\mathcal{D}_C$. We assume here, and throughout, the absence of hidden exogenous events that invalidate XII's information. In other words, we assume that the rate of change in the world is slower than the rate at which XII plans and executes. This is the standard assumption of correct information made by most planners.[3]

When XII executes an action which ensures that $\mathcal{D}_M$ contains all instances of Φ that are true in the world, XII adds a formula LCW(Φ) to $\mathcal{D}_C$. For example, XII is given an axiom stating that each file has a unique word count. Thus, executing the UNIX command `wc paper.tex` adds the formula LCW(word.count(paper.tex,c)) to $\mathcal{D}_C$ as well as adding the actual length (*e.g.*, `word.count(paper.tex,42)`) to $\mathcal{D}_M$. Since the LS operator (Figure 1) has a universally quantified effect, executing `ls -a /tex` yields LCW(parent.dir(f,/tex)).

It would be cumbersome if the author of each operator were forced to list its LCW effects. In fact, this is unnecessary. XII automatically elaborates operator schemata with LCW effects. For example, the following effects are automatically added to the LS operator:

LCW(parent.dir(f_1, ?d))

LCW(parent.dir(f_2, ?d) $\wedge$ (filename f_2, p_2))

LCW(parent.dir(f_3, ?d) $\wedge$ (pathname f_3, n_2))

where the subscripted symbols indicate new unique variables, and ?d is a parameter that will be substituted with a constant value at run-time. This compilation process takes time linear in the length of the operator schemata and the number of unique-value axioms (Golden, Etzioni, & Weld 1994).

Observational effects (*e.g.*, those of LS) can only create LCW, but causal effects can both create and destroy LCW.[4] For example, deleting all files in `/tex` *provides* complete information on the contents of the directory regardless of what the agent knew previously. Compressing a file in `/tex`, on the other hand, makes the length of the file unknown,[5] thus *invalidating* previously obtained LCW on the lengths of all files in that directory.

The theory behind LCW is complex; (Etzioni, Golden, & Weld 1994) defines LCW formally, explains the connection to circumscription, and presents a set of tractable update rules for the case of conjunctive LCW formulas. In this paper, we show how to incorporate conjunctive LCW into a least commitment planner and argue that this addresses the challenges described in the introduction: satisfying universally quantified goals and avoiding redundant sensing.

Universally quantified goals

In this section we explain how XII utilizes LCW to satisfy universally quantified goals. Traditionally, planners that have dealt with goals of the form "Forall v of type t make $\Delta(v)$ true" have done so by expanding the goal into a universally-ground, conjunctive goal called the

---

[3]In fact, the softbot relaxes this assumption by associating expiration times with beliefs in $\mathcal{D}_M$ and $\mathcal{D}_C$ and by recovering from errors that result from incorrect informa-

tion. However, a discussion of this mechanism is beyond the scope of this paper.

[4]XII operator schemata explicitly distinguish between causal effects (that change the state of the external world) and observational effects (that only change the state of XII's model) as explained in (Etzioni *et al.* 1992).

[5]This is written in the operator effects as (cause (length ?f ?l) U).

```
(defoperator LS ((directory ?d) (path ?dp))
    (precond (and (satisfy (current.shell csh))
                  (satisfy (current.dir ?d))
                  (satisfy (protection ?d readable))
                  (find-out (pathname ?d ?dp))))
    (effect (forall ((file !f) :in (parent.dir $ ?d))
                (exists ((path !p) (name !n))
                    (and (observe (parent.dir !f ?d))
                         (observe (pathname !f !p))
                         (observe (filename !f !n))))))
    (interface (execute-unix-command ("ls -a"))
               (sense-func (!f !n !p) (ls-sense ?dp))))
```

Figure 1: **UNIX operator.** The XII LS operator lists all files in the current directory. The last two lines specify the information needed to interface to UNIX. The first of these says to output the string "ls -a" to the UNIX shell. The second says to use the function **ls-sense** to translate the output of the shell into a set of bindings for the variables !f, !n and !p.

universal base (Weld 1994). The universal base of such a formula equals the conjunction $\Delta_1 \wedge \ldots \wedge \Delta_n$ in which the Δ_is correspond to each possible interpretation of $\Delta(v)$ under the universe of discourse, $\{C_1, \ldots, C_n\}$, *i.e.* the possible objects of type t (Genesereth & Nilsson 1987, p. 10). In each Δ_i, all references to v have been replaced with the constant C_i. For example, suppose that **pf** denotes the type corresponding to the files in the directory /papers and that there are two such files: $C_1 = $ a.dvi and $C_2 = $ b.dvi. Then the universal base of "Forall f of type **pf** make **printed**(f) true" is **printed**(a.dvi)$\wedge$**printed**(b.dvi).

A classical planner can satisfy $\forall$ goals by subgoaling to achieve the universal base, but this strategy relies on the closed world assumption. Only by assuming that all members of the universe of discourse are known (*i.e.*, represented in the model) can one be confident that the universal base is equivalent to the $\forall$ goal. Since the presence of incomplete information invalidates the closed world assumption, the XII planner uses two new mechanisms for satisfying $\forall$ goals:

1. Sometimes it is possible to directly support a $\forall$ goal with a $\forall$ effect, without expanding the universal base. For example, given the goal of having all files in a directory group readable, XII can simply execute **chmod g+r ***; it doesn't need to know which files (if any) are in the directory.

2. Alternatively, XII can subgoal on obtaining LCW on the type Φ_i of each universal variable v_i in the goal. Once XII has LCW(Φ_i), the universe of discourse for v_i is completely represented in its world model. At this point XII generates the universal base and subgoals on achieving it. Note that this strategy differs from the classical case since it involves interleaved planning and execution. Given the goal of printing all files in /papers, XII would plan and *execute* an ls -a command, then plan to print each file it found, and finally execute that plan.

For completeness, XII also considers combinations of these mechanisms to solve a single $\forall$ goal, via a technique called *partitioning*; see (Golden, Etzioni, & Weld 1994) for details.[6] In the remainder of this section we explain these two mechanisms in more detail.

Protecting $\forall$ links

In the simplest case, XII can use a universally quantified effect to directly support a universally quantified goal. However, $\forall$ goals, like ordinary goals, can get clobbered by subgoal interactions; to avoid this, XII uses an extension of the *causal link* (McAllester & Rosenblitt 1991) mechanism to protect $\forall$ goals. A causal link is a triple, written $A_p \xrightarrow{G} A_c$, where G is a goal, A_p is the step that produces G and A_c is the step that consumes G. We refer to G as the *label* of the link. When XII supports a $\forall$ goal directly (*i.e.*, without expanding into the universal base) it creates a link whose label, G, is a universally quantified formula (instead of the traditional literal); we call such links "$\forall$ links." In general, a link is *threatened* when some other step, A_t, has an effect that possibly *interferes* with G and A_t can possibly be executed between A_p and A_c. For normal links, interference is defined as having an effect that unifies with $\neg G$. Such an effect also threatens a $\forall$ link, but $\forall$ links are additionally threatened by effects that possibly add an object to the quantifier's universe of discourse. For example, if XII adds a **chmod g+r *** step to achieve the goal of having all files in a directory group readable, the link would be threatened by a step which moved a new file (possibly unreadable) into the directory. Threats to $\forall$ links can be handled using the same techniques used to resolve ordinary threats: *de-*

---

[6]Note also that the classical universal base mechanism requires that a type's universe be static and finite. XII correctly handles dynamic universes. Furthermore, XII's policy of linking to $\forall$ effects handles infinite universes, but this is not of practical import.

motion, *promotion*, and *confrontation*.[7] Additionally, the following rule applies.

- **Protect forall:** Given a link $A_p \xrightarrow{G} A_c$ in which $G = \forall_{\mathbf{type1}} x\, \mathtt{S}(x)$ and the type $\mathbf{type1}$ equals $\{x | \mathtt{P}(x) \wedge \mathtt{Q}(x) \wedge \ldots \wedge \mathtt{Z}(x)\}$ and a threat A_t with effect $\mathtt{P(foo)}$, subgoal on achieving $\mathtt{S(foo)} \vee \neg\mathtt{Q(foo)} \vee \ldots \vee \neg\mathtt{Z(foo)}$ by the time A_c is executed.

For example, suppose a $\forall$ link recording the condition that all files in `/tex` be group readable is threatened by step A_t, which creates a new file, `new.tex`. This threat can be handled by subgoaling to ensure that `new.tex` is either group readable or not in directory `/tex`.

Protecting LCW

The other way to satisfy a $\forall$ goal is to subgoal on obtaining LCW, and then satisfy each subgoal in the universal base. However, since LCW goals can also get clobbered by subgoal interactions, XII has to ensure that actions introduced for sibling goals don't cause the agent to *lose* LCW. For example, given the goal of finding the lengths all files in `/papers`, XII might execute `ls -la`. But if it then compresses a file in `/papers`, it no longer has LCW on all the lengths.

To avoid these interactions, we use LCW links which are like standard causal links except that they are labeled with a conjunctive LCW formula. Since $\mathtt{LCW(P}(x)$ $\wedge\, \mathtt{Q}(x))$ asserts knowledge of $\mathtt{P}$ and $\mathtt{Q}$ over all the members of the set $\{x \mid \mathtt{P}(x) \wedge \mathtt{Q}(x)\}$, an LCW link is threatened when information about a member of the set is possibly lost or a new member, for which the required information may be unknown, is possibly added to the set. We refer to these two cases as *information loss* and *domain growth*, respectively, and discuss them at length below. Like threats to ordinary causal links, threats to LCW links can be handled using *demotion*, *promotion*, and *confrontation*. In addition, threats due to information loss can be resolved with a new technique called *shrinking*, while domain-growth threats can be defused either by shrinking or by a method called *enlarging*.

Information Loss We say that A_t threatens $A_p \xrightarrow{G} A_c$ with information loss if $G = \mathtt{LCW}(P_1 \wedge \ldots \wedge P_n)$, A_t possibly comes between A_p and A_c, and A_t contains an effect that makes R unknown, for some R that unifies with some P_i in G. For example, suppose XII's plan has a link $A_p \xrightarrow{H} A_c$ in which

$$H = \mathtt{LCW(parent.dir}(f,\mathtt{/papers}) \wedge \mathtt{length}(f,n))$$

indicating that the link is protecting the subgoal of knowing the lengths of all the files in directory

`/papers`. If XII now adds a step which has the action `compress myfile.txt`, then the new step threatens the link, since `compress` has the effect of making the length of `myfile.txt` unknown.

- **Shrinking LCW:** Given a link with condition $\mathtt{LCW(P}(x) \wedge \mathtt{Q}(x) \wedge \ldots \wedge \mathtt{Z}(x))$ and threat causing $\mathtt{P(foo)}$ to be unknown (or true), XII can protect the link by subgoaling to achieve $\neg\mathtt{Q(foo)} \vee \ldots \vee \neg\mathtt{Z(foo)}$[8] at the time that the link's consumer is executed. For example, compressing `myfile.txt` threatens the link $A_p \xrightarrow{H} A_c$ described above, because if `myfile.txt` is in directory `/papers`, then the lengths of *all* the files in `/papers` are no longer known. However, if `parent.dir(myfile.txt,/papers)` is false then the threat goes away.

Domain Growth We say that A_t threatens $A_p \xrightarrow{G} A_c$ with domain growth if $G = \mathtt{LCW}(P_1 \wedge \ldots \wedge P_n)$, A_t possibly comes between A_p and A_c, and A_t contains an effect that makes R true, for some R that unifies with some P_i. For the example above in which the link $A_p \xrightarrow{H} A_c$ protects LCW on the length of every file in `/papers`, addition of a step which moved a new file into `/papers` would result in a domain-growth threat, since the agent might not know the length of the new file. Such threats can be resolved by the following.

- **Shrinking LCW** (described above): If XII has LCW on the lengths of all postscript files in `/tex`, then moving a file into `/tex` threatens LCW. However, if the file isn't a postscript file, LCW is not lost.

- **Enlarging LCW:** Given a link with condition $\mathtt{LCW(P}(x) \wedge \mathtt{Q}(x) \wedge \ldots \wedge \mathtt{Z}(x))$ and threat causing $\mathtt{P(foo)}$ to be true, XII can protect the link by subgoaling to achieve $\mathtt{LCW(Q(foo)} \wedge \ldots \wedge \mathtt{Z(foo)})$ at the time that the link's consumer is executed. For example, moving a new file `xii.tex` into directory `/papers` threatens the link $A_p \xrightarrow{H} A_c$ described above, because the length of `xii.tex` may be unknown. The threat can be resolved by observing the length of `xii.tex`.

Note that an effect which makes some P_i *false* does *not* pose a threat to the link! This corresponds to an action that moves a file *out* of `/papers` — it's not a problem because one still knows the lengths of all the files that remain.

Discussion

Given the new ways of resolving goals and threats, how much larger is the XII search space than that of UCPOP? XII has an additional type of open condition: the LCW goal. Since LCW goals, being conjunctive, can be solved using a combination of LCW effects, this would seem

---

[7] The first two techniques order the threatening action before the link's producer or after its consumer. Confrontation works when the threatening effect is conditional; the link is protected by subgoaling on the negation of the threat's antecedent (Penberthy & Weld 1992).

[8] Note the difference between shrinking and protecting a $\forall$ link. Unlike the $\forall$ link case, shrinking does not have a disjunct corresponding to $\mathtt{S(foo)}$.

to result in a large branching factor. In practice, this is not the case, because LCW goals tend to be short. In XII, $\forall$ goals can be solved by two additional mechanisms: $\forall$ links and partitioning. The addition of $\forall$ links increases the branching factor, but often results in shorter plans, and thus less search. Partitioning, in the worst case, has a branching factor equal to the number of predicates in the domain theory, but in practice, XII partitions only on predicates that could potentially be useful. The number of such predicates is typically small. Nonetheless, partitioning can still be expensive, and search control heuristics that limit partitioning are useful.

XII also adds three new ways of resolving threats; none of them apply to the standard causal links supported by UCPOP, so the branching factor for threats to these links is unchanged. For the new links supported by XII, the branching factor for threat resolution is increased by at most k, where k is the number of conjuncts in the LCW condition or in the universe of the $\forall$ condition. Presently, $k \leq 3$ in all of our UNIX operators.

The question of completeness for XII is difficult to answer, because the notion of completeness is ill-defined in an environment that involves execution. Given the existence of irreversible actions, such as **rm**, visiting part of the search space may make a previously solvable goal unsolvable. For example, the dilemma posed in Stockton's classic story "The lady, or the tiger?" (Stockton 1888) is solvable; opening the correct door will result in winning the game. However, the protagonist cannot determine what is behind a door without first opening it, and opening the wrong door means losing the game (and his life). By the formal definition of completeness, a complete planner must produce a plan guaranteed to win the game, since such a plan exists, but clearly such a guarantee is impossible. In future work, we hope to define a notion of completeness that is meaningful in such domains, and prove that XII conforms to that definition.

Redundant Information Gathering

The problem of redundant information gathering is best illustrated by a simple example. Suppose that we ask a softbot to find an Alaska Airlines flight from Seattle to San Francisco, cheaper than $80. The softbot can contact travel agents and airlines, which are listed in various telephone directories (cf (Levy, Sagiv, & Srivastava 1994)). In general, the separate information sources will contain overlapping information. A given travel agent might provide information on all domestic flights within a given price range, while an airline will provide information on all flights it offers. Suppose that the softbot has contacted Alaska Airlines and failed to find a fare less that $80. Unless it knows that contacting Alaska directly provides exhaustive information on Alaska flights, it will be forced to backtrack and pursue its other options. To make matters worse, a travel agency might be listed in multiple di-

rectories, and may have several phone numbers. Thus, exploring all possible plans to exhaustion would involve contacting the same travel agency multiple times. In general, once *any* exhaustive information gathering action is successfully executed, additional information gathering actions are redundant.[9]

The magnitude of the redundant sensing problem should not be underestimated (see Table 1 for empirical measurements). Furthermore, the problem of redundant sensing is both domain and planner independent; when trying alternative ways of satisfying a goal, a planner is forced to consider *every* sensory action at its disposal. Since each action has preconditions, and there are multiple ways of achieving these preconditions, the amount of wasted work can increase exponentially with the length of the information-gathering plan — unless the planner has some criterion for deciding which actions will not yield new information.

Fortunately, LCW is just that: *An agent should not execute, or plan to execute, observational actions (or actions in service of observational actions) to support a goal when it has LCW on that goal.* In fact, a single LCW formula can service a wide range of goals. For example, LCW(parent.dir(f,/tex)), which results from executing **ls -a** in **/tex**, indicates that XII knows all the files in **/tex**. Thus, it can satisfy *any* goal of the form "Find out whether some file x is in **/tex**" by examining its world model — no information gathering is necessary. In addition, XII can combine LCW formulas to avoid redundant information gathering on composite goals. For example, if XII knows all the files owned by Smith, and all the files in **/tex**, then it can satisfy the conjunctive goal "Give me all the files in **/tex** that are owned by Smith" by consulting its model.

XII utilizes LCW in three ways:

- **Execution pruning:** when XII is about to execute an observational step A_p which only supports links labeled with goals $G_1,\ldots,\ G_n$, XII checks whether LCW(G_i) holds for all i. If so, A_p is redundant and XII does not execute it. Instead, it replaces all links from A_p with links from the model ($\mathcal{D}_{\mathbf{M}}$), since any information that could be obtained by executing A_p is already recorded in $\mathcal{D}_{\mathbf{M}}$. This simple test prevents XII from executing some redundant information gathering steps. However, XII might still do redundant planning (and execution!) to satisfy A_p's preconditions, and the preconditions' preconditions, *etc.*

- **Option pruning:** to address this problem, XII tests for LCW when it computes the set of actions $\mathcal{A}$ that could *potentially* support a goal G. If LCW(G) holds, XII can omit *observational* actions from the set.[10]

---

[9]We cannot simply associate exactly one sensory action with each goal, *a priori*, because the agent may fail to satisfy that action's preconditions — in which case trying a different sensory action *is* warranted.

[10]Since XII can subsequently lose LCW due to information

Problem Set	Planner Version	Plans Examined	Steps Executed	Total Time
22 problems, 13 solvable	With LCW	420	55	109
	Without LCW	3707	724	966
14 problems, all solvable	With LCW	373	55	94
	Without LCW	1002	140	160

Table 1: Reasoning about local closed world information (LCW) improves the performance of the softbot on two suites of UNIX problems. Times are in CPU seconds on a Sun Microsystems SPARC-10. Without LCW inference the softbot fails to complete eight of the problems in the first set, and one of the problems in the second set, before reaching a 100 CPU second time bound. With LCW, the softbot completes all the problems. The mean size of $\mathcal{D}_C$ (the softbot's store of LCW information) is 155 formulas. The maximum size is 167.

- **Post hoc pruning:** XII may gain LCW(G) after $\mathcal{A}$ is computed (so option pruning did not apply) but considerably before any of the steps in $\mathcal{A}$ are about to be executed (so execution pruning is not yet applicable). This occurs when executing an action yields LCW(G), or when a binding constraint is asserted that constrains one or more of the variables in G. For instance, XII may not have LCW(parent.dir(f,d)), but once d is instantiated to, say, /tex, LCW(parent.dir(f,/tex)) can result in significant pruning.

In concert, these pruning techniques are surprisingly powerful, as demonstrated in the next section.

Experimental Results

The reader might question whether redundant sensing is as common as we suggest, or wonder whether the cost of utilizing the LCW machinery outweighs the benefit from pruning XII's search space. To address such concerns, and to empirically evaluate our LCW implementation, we plugged XII into the UNIX softbot (Etzioni, Lesh, & Segal 1993), providing XII with operator descriptions of standard UNIX commands, and enabling it to actually execute the commands by sending (and receiving) strings from the UNIX shell. We gave the softbot a sequence of goals and measured its performance with and without LCW. Table 1 quantifies the impact of the LCW mechanism on the softbot's behavior. We found that our LCW machinery yielded a significant performance gain for the softbot.

In this experiment, the softbot's goals consisted of simple file searches (*e.g.*, find a file with word count greater than 5000, containing the string "theorem," *etc.*) and relocations. The actions executed in the tests include mv (which can destroy LCW), observational actions such as ls, wc and grep, and more. Each experiment was started with $\mathcal{D}_M$ and $\mathcal{D}_C$ initialized empty, but they were not purged between problems; so for each problem the softbot benefited from the information gained in solving the previous problems.

Maintaining $\mathcal{D}_C$ introduced less than 15% overhead per plan explored, and reduced the number of plans explored substantially. In addition, the plans produced were often considerably shorter, since redundant sensing steps were eliminated. Without LCW, the softbot performed 16 redundant ls operations, and 6 redundant pwds in a "typical" file search. With LCW, on the other hand, the softbot performed no redundant sensing. Furthermore, when faced with unachievable goals, the softbot with LCW inference was able to fail quickly; however, without LCW it conducted a massive search, executing many redundant sensing operations in a forlorn hope of observing something that would satisfy the goal. While much more experimentation is necessary, these experiments suggest that local closed world reasoning, as implemented in XII, has the potential to substantially improve performance in a real-world domain.

Related work

XII is based on the UCPOP algorithm (Penberthy & Weld 1992). The algorithm we used for interleaving planning and execution closely follows IPEM, by Ambros-Ingerson and Steel (Ambros-Ingerson & Steel 1988). Our action language borrows both from ADL (Pednault 1986) and UWL (Etzioni *et al.* 1992).

Our research on LCW has its roots in the SOCRATES planner, where the problem of redundant information gathering was initially discovered (Etzioni & Lesh 1993). Like XII, SOCRATES utilized the UNIX domain as its testbed, supported the UWL representation, and interleaved planning with execution. In addition, SOCRATES supported a restricted representation of LCW, which enabled it to avoid redundant information gathering in many cases. Our advances over SOCRATES include the ability to satisfy universally quantified goals, and the machinery for automatically generating LCW effects and for detecting threats to LCW links.

Genesereth and Nourbakhsh (Genesereth & Nourbakhsh 1993) share our goal of avoiding redundant information gathering, but do so using radically different mechanisms, and in the context of state-space search.

---

loss or domain growth (described in the previous section), it has to record this pruning decision and recompute the options for G if LCW(G) is lost. Doing this in an efficient but sound manner is complex — see (Golden, Etzioni, & Weld 1994) for the details.

They derive completeness-preserving rules for pruning the search as well as rules for terminating planning and beginning execution. However, they do not have notions that correspond to LCW, a database like $\mathcal{D}_C$, or our threat resolution techniques.

Other researchers have investigated alternative approaches for planning with incomplete information (see (Olawsky & Gini 1990) for a nice taxonomy). Contingent planners (Warren 1976; Schoppers 1987; Peot & Smith 1992) seek to exhaustively enumerate alternative courses of action; while this strategy is appropriate in critical domains with irreversible actions, the exponential increase in planning time is daunting. Decision theory provides an elegant framework for computing the value of information; however, although work in this direction is promising, many challenges remain (Wellman 1993). Our approach sacrifices the elegance of a probabilistic framework to achieve a complete implementation able to tackle practical problems.

Conclusion

This paper describes the fully-implemented XII planner which uses *local closed world information* (LCW) to handle universally quantified goals and to avoid the problem of redundant sensing. Our technical innovations include the LCW machinery (effects, goals, and novel techniques for resolving threats to LCW links) and the LCW-based pruning techniques which solve the problem of redundant information gathering. As demonstrated in Table 1, the savings engendered by LCW can be quite large in the UNIX domain. Although our experiments, and illustrative examples, are drawn from the UNIX domain, we emphasize that the notion of LCW, and the techniques introduced in XII, are domain independent. In future work, we plan to measure the costs and benefits of LCW in other domains, and to remove the assumption of correct information made by the XII planner.

References

Ambros-Ingerson, J., and Steel, S. 1988. Integrating planning, execution, and monitoring. In *Proc. 7th Nat. Conf. on A.I.*, 735–740.

Chapman, D. 1987. Planning for conjunctive goals. *Artificial Intelligence* 32(3):333–377.

Etzioni, O., and Lesh, N. 1993. Planning with incomplete information in the UNIX domain. In *Working Notes of the AAAI Spring Symposium: Foundations of Automatic Planning: The Classical Approach and Beyond*, 24–28. Menlo Park, CA: AAAI Press.

Etzioni, O., Hanks, S., Weld, D., Draper, D., Lesh, N., and Williamson, M. 1992. An Approach to Planning with Incomplete Information. In *Proc. 3rd Int. Conf. on Principles of Knowledge Representation and Reasoning*. Available via FTP from pub/ai/ at cs.washington.edu.

Etzioni, O., Golden, K., and Weld, D. 1994. Tractable closed-world reasoning with updates. In *Proc. 4th Int. Conf. on Principles of Knowledge Representation and Reasoning*.

Etzioni, O., Lesh, N., and Segal, R. 1993. Building softbots for UNIX (preliminary report). Technical Report 93-09-01, University of Washington. Available via anonymous FTP from pub/etzioni/softbots/ at cs.washington.edu.

Genesereth, M., and Nilsson, N. 1987. *Logical Foundations of Artificial Intelligence*. Los Altos, CA: Morgan Kaufmann Publishers, Inc.

Genesereth, M., and Nourbakhsh, I. 1993. Time-saving tips for problem solving with incomplete information. In *Proc. 11th Nat. Conf. on A.I.*, 724–730.

Golden, K., Etzioni, O., and Weld, D. 1994. XII: Planning for Universal Quantification and Incomplete Information. Technical report, University of Washington, Department of Computer Science and Engineering. Available via FTP from pub/ai/ at cs.washington.edu.

Krebsbach, K., Olawsky, D., and Gini, M. 1992. An empirical study of sensing and defaulting in planning. In *Proc. 1st Int. Conf. on A.I. Planning Systems*, 136–144.

Levy, A., Sagiv, Y., and Srivastava, D. 1994. Towards efficient information gathering agents. In *Working Notes of the AAAI Spring Symposium: Software Agents*, 64–70. Menlo Park, CA: AAAI Press.

McAllester, D., and Rosenblitt, D. 1991. Systematic nonlinear planning. In *Proc. 9th Nat. Conf. on A.I.*, 634–639.

Minton, S., Carbonell, J. G., Knoblock, C. A., Kuokka, D. R., Etzioni, O., and Gil, Y. 1989. Explanation-based learning: A problem-solving perspective. *Artificial Intelligence* 40:63–118. Available as technical report CMU-CS-89-103.

Olawsky, D., and Gini, M. 1990. Deferred planning and sensor use. In *Proceedings, DARPA Workshop on Innovative Approaches to Planning, Scheduling, and Control*. Morgan Kaufmann.

Pednault, E. 1986. *Toward a Mathematical Theory of Plan Synthesis*. Ph.D. Dissertation, Stanford University.

Penberthy, J., and Weld, D. 1992. UCPOP: A sound, complete, partial order planner for ADL. In *Proc. 3rd Int. Conf. on Principles of Knowledge Representation and Reasoning*, 103–114. Available via FTP from pub/ai/ at cs.washington.edu.

Peot, M., and Smith, D. 1992. Conditional Nonlinear Planning. In *Proc. 1st Int. Conf. on A.I. Planning Systems*, 189–197.

Schoppers, M. 1987. Universal plans for reactive robots in unpredictable environments. In *Proceedings of IJCAI-87*, 1039–1046.

Stockton, F. R. 1888. *The lady, or the tiger? and other stories*. New York: Charles Scribner's Sons.

Warren, D. 1976. Generating Conditional Plans and Programs. In *Proceedings of AISB Summer Conference*, 344–354.

Weld, D. 1994. An introduction to least-commitment planning. *AI Magazine*. Available via FTP from pub/ai/ at cs.washington.edu.

Wellman, M. 1993. Challenges for decision-theoretic planning. In *Proceedings of the AAAI 1993 Symposium on Foundations of Automatic Planning: The Classical Approach and Beyond*.

On the Nature of Modal Truth Criteria in Planning*

Subbarao Kambhampati
Department of Computer Science and Engineering
Arizona State University
Tempe, AZ 85287-5406
Email: `rao@asu.edu`

Dana S. Nau
Department of Computer Science,
Institute for Systems Research,
and Institute for Advanced Computer Studies
University of Maryland
College Park, MD 20742
Email: `nau@cs.umd.edu`

Abstract

Chapman's paper, "Planning for Conjunctive Goals," has been widely acknowledged for its contribution toward understanding the nature of nonlinear (partial-order) planning, and it has been one of the bases of later work by others---but it is not free of problems. This paper addresses some problems involving modal truth and the Modal Truth Criterion (MTC). Our results are as follows:

1. Even though modal duality is a fundamental axiom of classical modal logics, it does not hold for modal truth in Chapman's plans; i.e., "necessarily p" is not equivalent to "not possibly $\neg p$."

2. Although the MTC for necessary truth is correct, the MTC for possible truth is incorrect: it provides necessary but *insufficient* conditions for ensuring possible truth. Furthermore, even though necessary truth can be determined in polynomial time, possible truth is NP-hard.

3. If we rewrite the MTC to talk about modal *conditional* truth (i.e., modal truth conditional on executability) rather than modal truth, then both the MTC for necessary conditional truth and the MTC for possible conditional truth are correct; and both can be computed in polynomial time.

1 Introduction

Chapman's paper, "Planning for Conjunctive Goals," [2] has been widely acknowledged as an important step towards formalizing partial-order planning, and it has been one of the bases of later work by others (for example, [5, 7, 9, 12, 14]). Unfortunately, however, Chapman's work is not free of problems, and this has led to confusion about the meaning of his results. Previous papers [5, 9, 14] have pointed out several of these problems.

One of the fundamental concepts used by Chapman is the idea of modal truth in plans. We will discuss the details of this concept later---but a simple version of it is that if P is a partially-ordered, partially-instantiated plan and p is a ground literal, then p is *necessarily* (or *possibly*) true in P's

final situation if for every (or some) totally-ordered ground instance P' of P, p is true after executing P'. Chapman's Modal Truth Criterion (MTC) purports to give necessary and sufficient conditions for ensuring that p is necessarily or possibly true. As we describe below, this paper addresses several problems with modal truth and the MTC.

Chapman explicitly states and proves the MTC for necessary truth, and claims that by modal duality (i.e., the equivalence of "necessarily p" and "not possibly $\neg p$"), the MTC for possible truth is obtained via a simple rewording of the MTC for necessary truth. But in this paper, we show that although modal duality is a fundamental axiom of classical modal logics, it does *not* hold for modal truth in Chapman's plans.[1] This has several consequences:

1. The MTC for possible truth is not completely correct: it provides necessary but insufficient conditions for ensuring possible truth. Furthermore, although necessary truth in plans can be computed in polynomial time as pointed out by Chapman, the same is not true for possible truth. Instead, the problem of computing possible truth in plans is NP-hard.[2]

2. We can define a concept called *modal conditional truth*, which is similar to modal truth but does not require that a plan be executable as modal truth does. Necessary conditional truth and possible conditional truth *are* duals of each other, and both can be computed in polynomial time. Furthermore, if we rewrite the MTC to talk about modal conditional truth rather than modal truth, then both the MTC for necessary conditional truth *and* the MTC for possible conditional truth are correct.

This paper is organized as follows. Section 2 contains basic definitions, and clarifications/corrections of some of Chapman's terminology. Section 4 presents results about

---

*The authors' names are given in alphabetical order. Kambhampati's research is supported in part by an NSF Research Initiation Award IRI-9210997, and ARPA/Rome Laboratory planning initiative under grant F30602-93-C-0039. Nau's research supported in part by NSF Grants IRI-9306580 and NSFD CDR-88003012.

---

[1] Although Chapman does not explicitly state that his usage is consistent with modal logics, it seems clear to us that this is what he had in mind. In particular, Chapman explicitly appeals to modal duality in his proof of the MTC [2, p. 368].

[2] If modal duality held, then both necessary truth and possible would be at similar levels of complexity: either both would be polynomial, or one would be NP-hard and the other co-NP-hard. Section 5.2 discusses some formulations of planning in which this occurs.

modal duality, the complexity of modal truth, and the modal truth criterion, and compares and contrasts these results with Chapman's claims, as well as with other related work. Section 6 contains concluding remarks. Proofs of all the theorms stated in this paper can be found in [8].

2 Basics

The planning language $\mathcal{L}$ is any function-free first-order language. Since $\mathcal{L}$ is function-free, every term is either a variable symbol or a constant symbol, and thus every ground term is a constant symbol. We follow the usual convention of defining an *atom* to be a predicate symbol followed a list of terms, a *literal* to be an atom or its negation, and a *proposition* to be a 0-ary atom. *Thus, what Chapman calls a proposition, we call a literal.*

A *state* is any finite collection of ground atoms of $\mathcal{L}$. If a state s contains a ground atom p, then p is true in s and $\neg p$ is false in s; otherwise p is false in s and $\neg p$ is true in s.

If T is a finite set of terms, then a *codesignation constraint* on T is a syntactic expression of the form '$t \approx u$' or '$t \not\approx u$', where $t, u \in T$. Let D be a set of codesignation constraints on T, and θ be a *ground substitution* over T (i.e., a substitution that assigns a ground term to each variable in T). Then θ *satisfies* D if $t\theta = u\theta$ for every syntactic expression '$t \approx u$' in D, and $t\theta \neq u\theta$ for every syntactic expression '$t \not\approx u$' in D. D is *consistent* if there is at least one ground substitution θ that satisfies D. If $t\theta = u\theta$ for every θ that satisfies D, then t *codesignates with* u.

A *step* is a triple $a = (\text{name}(a), \text{pre}(a), \text{post}(a))$, where name$(a)$ is a constant symbol called a's *name*, and pre(a) and post(a) are collections of literals called a's *preconditions* and *postconditions*. A *plan* is a 4-tuple $P = (s_0, A, D, O)$, where s_0 is a state called P's *initial state*, A is a set of steps, D is a set of codesignation constraints on the terms of P (i.e., the terms in s_0 and A), and O is a set of ordering constraints on the steps of A. P is *complete* if there is a unique total ordering $a_1 \prec a_2 \prec \ldots \prec a_n$ over A that satisfies O, and a unique ground substitution θ over the terms of P that satisfies D. (Note that a complete plan need not necessarily be executable). Suppose that P is complete, and let k be the largest integer $\leq n$ for which there are states $s_1, s_2, \ldots, s_k$ such that for $1 \leq i \leq k$, s_{i-1} satisfies a_i's preconditions, and s_i is the state produced by performing the step a_i in the state s_{i-1}. Then for $1 \leq i \leq k$, a_i is *executable* in the *input* state s_{i-1}, *producing* the *output* state s_i. If $k = n$, then P is *executable*, and it *produces* the *final* state s_n.

A plan $P' = (s_0', A', D', O')$ is a *constrainment* of a plan $P = (s_0, A, D, O)$ if $s_0' = s_0$, $A' = A$, $O \subseteq O'$, and $D \subseteq D'$. A *completion* of P is any constrainment of P that is complete.[3] P is *consistent* if it has at least one completion; otherwise P is *inconsistent*.

---

[3]Chapman's definition of a completion does not make it entirely clear whether a completion of P should include only the steps in P, or allow other steps to be added. However, other statements in his paper make it clear that he means for a completion to include only the steps in P, so this is how we and most others (e.g., [9, 14]) use the term.

3 Situations, Truth, and Modality

One of the basic concepts in Chapman's planning framework is the idea of a *situation*. To avoid some problems with Chapman's definitions, we define plans using STRIPS-style states of the world, and then define situations in terms of states. The intent of our definitions is that if a plan is complete and can be executed at least far enough to reach the situation s, then s corresponds to some state t that arises while executing the plan; and what is true and false in s is precisely what is true and false in t. Otherwise, *nothing* is true or false in s although certain things may be *conditionally* true or false (as defined below). These ideas are formalized below.

If P is a plan, then associated with each step a of P are two symbols in(a) and out(a), called a's *input* and *output* situations. Associated with P are symbols init and fin called the *initial* and *final* situations of P. All of these symbols must be distinct. Whenever $a \prec b$, we will also say that $x \prec y$, where x may be a or in(a) or out(a), and y may be b or in(b) or out(b).

We now define what is *true* and *false* in a situation of a complete plan. Let P be a complete plan, and p be a ground literal. Then p is true in init if p is true in P's initial state, and p is true in fin if p is true in P's final state. If a is an executable step of P, then p is true in in(a_i) (or out(a_i)) if p is true in a's input state (or output state, respectively). A ground literal p is false in a situation s iff $\neg p$ is true in s. Note that if P is not executable, then the law of the excluded middle does not apply, for p will be neither true nor false in P's final situation.

As a consequence of the above definitions, it follows that p is true in s (which we write symbolically as $\mathcal{M}(p, s)$) iff the following three conditions are satisfied:

Establishment: either p codesignates with a postcondition of some step $a \prec s$, or else $p \in s_0$.

Nondeletion: for all steps b between a (or s_0) and s, no postcondition of b codesignates with $\neg p$.

Executability: every step that precedes s is executable.

A closely related concept is *conditional truth*, which is like ordinary truth except that it does not require executability: p is *conditionally true* in s (which we write symbolically as $\mathcal{C}(p, s)$) iff the establishment and nondeletion conditions hold.

We defined truth and conditional truth only for complete plans, because for incomplete plans, what is true or conditionally true will vary depending on which completion we choose. In incomplete plans, we instead need to talk about *modal* truth, which Chapman defines as follows [2, p. 336]:

> I will say "*necessarily p*" if p is true of all completions of an incomplete plan, and "*possibly p*" if p is true of some completion.

Above, Chapman apparently means p to be nearly any statement about a plan: examples in his paper include not only statements about specific literals and situations in the plan, but also statements about the entire plan (e.g., the statement [2, p. 341] that a plan "necessarily solves the problem''). However, unless we place some restrictions on the nature of p, this has some dubious results---for example, if P is an incomplete plan, then all completions of P are complete, and therefore P itself is necessarily complete. Therefore, for the formal results in the paper, we will use ''necessarily'' and ''possibly'' only in the following cases (although we will sometimes use them informally in a broader sense). If p is an atom, P is a plan, and s is a situation in P, then:

- p is *necessarily* (or *possibly*) true in s (written $\Box \mathcal{M}(p, s)$ and $\Diamond \mathcal{M}(p, s)$, respectively) iff $\mathcal{M}(p, s)$ in every (or some) completion of P;

- p is *necessarily* (or *possibly*) conditionally true in s (written $\Box \mathcal{C}(p, s)$ and $\Diamond \mathcal{C}(p, s)$, respectively) iff $\mathcal{C}(p, s)$ in every (or some) completion of P.

We now define the following decision problems (where P is a plan and p is a ground literal):

NECESSARY TRUTH: given p and P, is p necessarily true in P's final situation fin?

POSSIBLE TRUTH: given p and P, is p possibly true in P's final situation fin?

NECESSARY CONDITIONAL TRUTH: given p and P, is p necessarily conditionally true in P's final situation fin?

POSSIBLE CONDITIONAL TRUTH: given p and P, is p possibly conditionally true in P's final situation fin?

4 Duality, and Complexity of Modal Truth

Given the definitions of modal truth and modal conditional truth above, it is easy to see that a literal p is necessarily true in the final situation fin of a plan P if and only if (1) p is necessarily conditionally true in fin, and (2) for every action a of the plan and every precondition p_a of a, p_a is necessarily conditionally true in the situation in(a). Thus,[4]

$$\Box \mathcal{M}(p, \text{fin})$$
$$\equiv \Box \left[\mathcal{C}(p, \text{fin}) \wedge \left[\bigwedge_{\forall a \in P, \forall p_a \in \text{pre}(a)} \mathcal{C}(p_a, \text{in}(a)) \right] \right], \quad (1)$$

---

[4]We could consider generalizing Eq. 1 to apply to situations $s \neq \text{fin}$, by replacing the condition ''$\forall a \in P$'' with the condition ''$\forall a \in S$,'' where S is the set of all actions that precede s in at least one completion of P. However, such a generalized version of Eq. 1 would not always hold, as illustrated by the following counterexample (due to Backstrom [1]). Let P be a plan with three actions a, b, c, such that $a \prec b$, $a \prec c$, pre$(a) = \emptyset$, post$(a) = \{\neg p\}$, pre$(b) = \emptyset$, post$(b) = \{p\}$, pre$(c) = \{\neg p\}$, and post$(c) = \emptyset$. Then $\Box \mathcal{M}(p, \text{out}(b))$, but it is not true that $\Box[\mathcal{C}(p, \text{out}(b)) \wedge [\bigwedge \{\mathcal{C}(p_d, \text{in}(d)) : d \in S \& p_d \in \text{pre}(d)\}]]$. To see this, note that P has two completions, one executable and one non-executable. c precedes b in one completion (the executable one) and thus $c \in S$. However for c's precondition $(\neg p)$, $\mathcal{C}(\neg p, \text{in}(c))$ fails in the other (non-executable) completion of P. The main reason for this is that the set of steps that precede out(b) is different in different completions -- $\{a, b\}$ in one, and $\{a, b, c\}$ in the other. Thus, the correct way of generalizing Eq. 1 will involve doing the inner conjunction with S ranging over each of these values, and disjoining all the resulting conjunctions.

Now, since modal necessity commutes over conjunctions (i.e., $\Box(p \wedge q) \equiv \Box(p) \wedge \Box(q)$), we can write Eq. 1 as

$$\Box \mathcal{M}(p, \text{fin})$$
$$\equiv \left[\Box \mathcal{C}(p, \text{fin}) \wedge \left[\bigwedge_{\forall a \in P, \forall p_a \in \text{pre}(a)} \Box \mathcal{C}(p_a, \text{in}(a)) \right] \right]. \quad (2)$$

Thus computing whether p is necessarily true in fin involves computing whether p is necessarily conditionally true in fin, as well as computing the necessary conditional truth of all preconditions of all steps preceding fin. As noted in Chapman, computing the necessary conditional truth of a literal in a situation (which involves checking whether the MTC's establishment and declobbering clauses are consistent with the plan's ordering and codesignation/non-codesignation constraints) can be done in time polynomial ($O(n^3)$) in the plan length. Thus, since the total number of preconditions in a plan is of the order of number of actions in the plan, computing whether p is necessarily true can also be done in polynomial time. Coming to the case of possible truth, we have

$$\Diamond \mathcal{M}(p, \text{fin})$$
$$\equiv \Diamond \left[\mathcal{C}(p, \text{fin}) \wedge \left[\bigwedge_{\forall a \in P, \forall p_a \in \text{pre}(a)} \mathcal{C}(p_a, \text{in}(a)) \right] \right]. \quad (3)$$

But possible truth does not commute over conjunctions (i.e., in general, $\Diamond(p \wedge q) \not\equiv \Diamond(p) \wedge \Diamond(q)$), so there is no way to simplify Eq. 3 into component tests of computing possible conditional truth of individual literals. Thus, even though possible conditional truth in fin and necessary conditional truth in fin are duals of each other (i.e., $\Diamond \mathcal{C}(p, \text{fin}) \equiv \neg \Box \neg \mathcal{C}(p, \text{fin})$), possible truth in fin and necessary truth in fin are *not* duals of each other. More specifically:

Theorem 1 *There is a ground literal p, a plan P, with the final situation* fin *such that* $\Box \mathcal{M}(p, \text{fin}) \not\equiv \neg \Diamond \neg \mathcal{M}(p, \text{fin})$.

Thus, unlike necessary conditional truth and possible conditional truth, necessary truth and possible truth do not obey the modal duality that is obeyed by all classical modal logics [3, p. 62], and thus do not define a well-formed modal logic. It is easy to understand why this is so. The semantics of modal logics are based on Kripke structures (a.k.a. possible worlds). In this formulation, if p is a ground literal, then for every possible world, p must either be true or false in that world. For partially ordered plans, one might expect that each completion of the plan would give rise to a possible world. However, the modal truth of p in a situation of a plan requires that the plan's actions be executable in order to produce that situation. Thus, if a completion is not executable, then truth of p is not defined in the corresponding possible world.[5]

---

[5]Although TWEAK plans cannot be modeled using the semantics of classical modal logics, they can be modeled in a variant of modal logics, called *first order dynamic logic* [13]. Dynamic

Given a ground literal p and a plan P, p is possibly true in P's final situation if and only if there is an executable completion of P that produces a final state in which p is true, and this happens iff it is not the case that every executable completion of P produces a final state in which $\neg p$ is true. Thus, POSSIBLE TRUTH is the dual of the following problem:

PARTIAL TRUTH: given a ground literal p and a plan P, does every executable completion of P produce a final state in which p is true?[6]

Lemma 1 PARTIAL TRUTH *is NP-hard.*

PARTIAL TRUTH is a weaker condition than both NECESSARY TRUTH and NECESSARY CONDITIONAL TRUTH. There are some cases (one occurs in the proof of Lemma 1) in which every executable completion of P produces a final state in which p is true, but p is neither necessarily true nor necessarily conditionally true in P's final situation.

Another way of understanding the problem with simplifying Eq. 3 is to note that if p is possibly conditionally true and that all the preconditions of the preceding actions are possibly conditionally true, this only implies that each of them is *individually* true in at least one completion---and this condition is *necessary* but *insufficient* for ensuring possible truth. We could check possible truth by checking to see whether all these conditions are *collectively* true in at least one completion of the plan, but since the number of completions of a plan is exponential in the number of actions of the plan, this would take exponential time. Furthermore, the following theorem shows that unless P=NP, there is no polynomial-time approach for solving this problem.

Theorem 2 POSSIBLE TRUTH *is NP-hard.*

Thus, NECESSARY TRUTH and POSSIBLE TRUTH have different levels of complexity. If modal duality held, then this would not be so, for each would be reducible to the other's complement via an equivalence of the form $\Diamond \mathcal{M}(p, \mathsf{fin}) \equiv \neg \Box \neg \mathcal{M}(p, \mathsf{fin})$. Thus it would follow [6, p. 29] that either POSSIBLE TRUTH would be polynomial like NECESSARY TRUTH, or else NECESSARY TRUTH would be co-NP-hard. In Section 5.2, we discuss some planning situations where this occurs.

5 Comparison with Other Work

5.1 The Modal Truth Criterion

Chapman states the MTC as follows [2, p. 340]:

Modal Truth Criterion. A [literal] p is necessarily true in a situation s iff two conditions hold:[7] there is a situation t equal or necessarily previous to s in which p is necessarily asserted; and for every step C possibly before s and every [literal] q possibly codesignating with p which C denies, there is a step W necessarily between C and s which asserts r, a [literal] such that r and p codesignate whenever p and q codesignate. The criterion for possible truth is exactly analogous, with all the modalities switched (read ''necessary'' for ''possible'' and vice versa).

If we take these words literally, then the definition of modal truth tells us that the plan must be modally executable. This is consistent with Chapman's definition of a situation [2], from which it follows that a step's output situation (and hence what is true in that situation) is only defined if the step can be executed. However, a careful look at Chapman's proof of necessity and sufficiency of his MTC reveals that his proof deals with necessary *conditional* truth rather than necessary truth.[8] In proving that any literal with an establisher and no clobberer must be necessarily true, Chapman's proof refers to white-knight steps for every potential clobberer, [2, p. 370], without checking that the white knights are in fact executable.[9]

For the ''necessary truth'' version of the MTC, this does not affect the validity of Chapman's proof, since executability occurs naturally as a consequence of applying necessary conditional truth recursively to prerequisites of all preceding steps. The same, however, cannot be guaranteed for possible truth, since modal possibility does not commute over conjunctions---and thus Chapman's proof cannot be extended to possible truth. In particular, the following theorem shows that the ''possible truth'' version of the MTC sometimes fails:

Theorem 3 *There is a plan P and a ground literal p such that in P's final situation, p is not possibly true but the MTC concludes otherwise.*

The above discussion suggests an alternative interpretation of the MTC that sidesteps the problem: drop the executability requirement, and interpret the MTC as a statement about modal *conditional* truth rather than modal truth. This alternative interpretation is not as far-fetched as it might sound. To see this, note that Chapman defines the notion of truth of a literal in a situation as follows [2, p. 338]:

A [literal] is true in a situation if it codesignates with a [literal] that is a member of the situation. A step asserts a [literal] in its output situation if the [literal] codesignates with a postcondition of the step.

---

logic, which has been used to provide semantics for programs and plans, provides a clean way to separate executability/termination conditions from goal satisfaction conditions. More about this in Section 5.2.

[6]PARTIAL TRUTH corresponds closely to the notion of partial correctness, which was studied in connection with dynamic-logic-based modeling of computer programming languages [11, 13].

[7]The second of these conditions is the ''white-knight declobbering clause'' that we refer to elsewhere.

[8]Had Chapman explicitly noted this use of modal conditional truth in his proof, we believe he would have noticed the non-duality of necessary and possible truths.

[9]Note that in Chapman's terminology, the establisher is a *situation*, while clobberers and white knights are *steps*.

Here, there is no explicit requirement that the step be executable. This suggests that the MTC does not require that P be modally executable, and thus suggests that Chapman was talking about modal conditional truth. This interpretation is also consistent with his "nondeterministic achievement procedure" [2, Fig. 7], where to make a literal necessarily true in a situation, he only ensures establishment and declobbering without explicitly stating that the establisher needs to be executable. (As explained above, for the case of necessary truth, executability follows from making every prerequisite of every action necessarily conditionally true.)

The "conditional truth" interpretation of MTC gives a quasi-local flavor to planning, by separating the process of ensuring local establishment and declobbering from the process of ensuring executability, with the understanding that if all preconditions are necessarily established and declobbered, then the whole plan itself will be executable and correct. In fact, some latter rewrites of the MTC (e.g. [14, 9]) use this interpretation to eliminate the notion of situations entirely, and state MTC solely in terms of steps (operators) and their preconditions and postconditions.

Although a truth criterion for modal conditional truth does have utility in plan generation, it is of limited utility in projecting plans or partially ordered events. As mentioned in Section 3, the latter are more naturally related to modal truth.

5.2 Modal Duality and Universal Executability

In Section 4, we observed that the main reason why necessary truth and possible truth are not duals in TWEAK-style plans is that such plans can contain unexecutable completions. Thus, one way to achieve duality between necessary truth and possible truth is to restrict our attention to plans whose completions are always executable. One way to guarantee that plans will always be executable is to restrict the actions to have no preconditions, i.e., to consider only those plans P such that $pre(a) = \emptyset$ for every step a of P.

This approach is clearly too restrictive, since it precludes modeling actions with any form of preconditions. But if we relax the restrictions of TWEAK-style action representation, there is a more reasonable way to guarantee universal executability: let an action a be executable even if its preconditions are not satisfied. If the preconditions are satisfied, then a will produce its postconditions; otherwise, a will simply have no effects.[10] For plans that contain only this type of actions, possible truth and necessary truth are duals of one another, computation of possible truth is NP-hard, and computation of necessary truth is co-NP-hard. As discussed below, this approach has been used in different forms by several different researchers.

To our knowledge, the above approach was first used in Rosenchein's work [13] on providing semantics to plans based on first-order propositional dynamic logic. Rosenchein restricts the use of conditionals in PDL to guarantee that the plan terminates irrespective of which branch of the conditional it takes.

A very similar idea is used in Dean and Boddy's work on temporal projection [4]. In Dean and Boddy's formulation, a partially ordered set of events A is projectible even when a rule's preconditions don't hold (in which case the rule simply has no effect). Hence in their formalism, determining possible truth and necessary truth are duals, and both are NP-hard.

Chapman [2, p. 371] uses universally executable actions (he calls them conditional steps) in proving his intractability theorem for actions containing conditional effects. A plan composed entirely of such steps will always be executable, leading to the same results as in Dean and Boddy's formalism.

Since Chapman's intractability theorem is based on planning operators that have conditional effects, it has been natural for planning researchers to interpret it to mean that the conditionality of these operators is what causes necessary truth to be intractable. However, this interpretation is misleading. The intractability result depends just as much on the universal executability of Chapman's conditional steps as it does on their conditionality. Here's why:

Consider an incomplete plan P composed of ordinary "unconditional" steps as defined in Section 2, and let a be a step of P such that $pre(a)$ $post(a)$ contain an unbound variable x. Then for the purposes of both planning and temporal projection, a has conditional effects: its effects will be different in different completions of P, depending on what we bind x to. However, computing necessary truth in such plans is still polynomial. Since Chapman's planning language has an infinite number of constant symbols, it follows that in the plan P we can *always* find a binding for x that makes a unexecutable. As a consequence, P will always have at least one unexecutable completion. Hence, determining necessary truth is trivial: nothing will be necessarily true in P's final situation.

Now, suppose we restrict our planning language $\mathcal{L}$ to contain only finitely many constant symbols (and thus only finitely many ground terms, since $\mathcal{L}$ is function-free). Then there will be some plans in which a is executable for every binding of x. In this case, as the following theorem shows, checking necessary truth will be co-NP-hard, even with unconditional steps.

Theorem 4 *If the language $\mathcal{L}$ contains only finitely many constant symbols, then* NECESSARY TRUTH *is co-NP-hard.*

Notice that this result is related to Chapman's observation [2, p. 356] that restricting the range of a variable to a finite set will defeat the MTC, and make constraint computations NP-complete.

Finally, a recent investigation by Nebel and Backstrom [10] on the computational complexity of plan-validation and temporal projection has yielded results related to those

---

[10]While seemingly unintuitive, this relaxation is in fact very much consistent with the original formalization of actions in situational calculus [3]. In this formalism, actions are modeled as situation-transformers, with the transformation given by the `Result` function, which takes an action and a situation as the arguments. Having universally executable steps corresponds to having the `Result` be a total rather than a partial function.

presented in this paper. While our investigation is initially motivated by the apparent lack of modal duality in Chapman's MTC, Nebel and Backstrom's work is motivated by the apparent asymmetry in the complexity of plan validation through modal truth criterion, and temporal projection (c.f. [4]). Rather than interpret MTC in terms of modal conditional truth, and use that to explain the asymmetry in the possible and necessary truth, as we have done in this paper, Nebel and Backstrom choose to restrict applicability of MTC only for plans whose completions are all executable (they term this property *coherence*). Another difference with their research is that they concentrate on ground (variable-less) plans, while we look at the more general variablized plans. We believe that the results in this paper complement theirs and together provide a coherent interpretation of the role of modal truth criteria in planning.

6 Concluding Remarks

In this paper, we have presented the following results about modal truth and the modal truth criterion:

1. Contrary to Chapman's statement, the principle of modal duality that is obeyed by all classical modal logics is not obeyed in TWEAK-style plans. The lack of duality between necessary truth and possible truth is related to (a) the fact that modal truth of a literal in a situation of a plan requires that the plan's actions be executable in order to produce that situation, and (b) the asymmetry in the way necessary conditional truth and possible conditional truth commute over conjunctions: $\Box(p \wedge q) \equiv \Box(p) \wedge \Box(q)$ while $\Diamond(p \wedge q) \not\equiv \Diamond(p) \wedge \Diamond(q)$. To achieve modal duality, one needs universally executable plans.

2. Even though necessary truth in plans can be determined in polynomial time as stated by Chapman, the same statement does not hold for possible truth. Instead, the problem of determining possible truth in plans is NP-hard.[11]

3. As stated by Chapman, the MTC is correct only as a criterion for necessary truth (not as a criterion for possible truth). However, if we reinterpret it as a criterion for modal *conditional* truth (i.e., modal truth conditional on plan executability), then it is correct as a criterion for both necessary conditional truth and possible conditional truth.

Because of the wide impact of Chapman's paper, it is important to correct any misimpressions that may result from it. We hope readers will find this paper useful for that purpose. Finally, while we concentrated on clarifying the nature of modal truth criterion, there have also been several misimpressions regarding its *role* in plan generation. In the extended version of this paper [8], we also address these confusions.

---

[11]Checking possible truth has several applications in plan projection [4] as well as plan generalization [9].

Acknowledgement

We appreciate the helpful comments of Christer Backstrom and Bernhard Nebel.

References

[1] C. Backstrom. Personal communication, 1993.

[2] D. Chapman. Planning for conjunctive goals. *Artificial Intelligence*, 32:333--379, 1987.

[3] E. Davis. *Representations of Commonsense Knowledge* Morgan Kaufmann Publishers, Inc. San Mateo, California, USA, 94403.

[4] T. Dean and M. Boddy. Reasoning about partially ordered events. *Artificial Intelligence*, 36:375-399, 1988.

[5] K. Erol, D. Nau, and V. S. Subrahmanian. When is planning decidable? In *Proc. First Intl. Conference on AI Planning Systems*, pp. 222--227, June 1992.

[6] M.R. Garey and D.S. Johnson. *Computers and Intractability: A Guide to the Theory of NP-Completeness* W.H. Freeman and Company, New York, 1979.

[7] S. Hanks and D. S. Weld. Systematic adaptation for case-based planning. In *Proc. First Internat. Conf. AI Planning Systems*, pp. 96--105, June 1992.

[8] S. Kambhampati and D.S. Nau. On the Nature and Role of Modal Truth Criteria in Planning *Artificial Intelligence*, 1994 To appear. (Available as Tech. Report. ISR-TR-93-30, Inst. for Systems Research, University of Maryland, March, 1993. Anonymous ftp: `enws318.eas.asu.edu: pub/rao/role-mtc-planning.ps`)

[9] S. Kambhampati and S. Kedar. A unified framework for explanation-based generalization of partially ordered and partially instantiated plans. *Artificial Intelligence*, Vol. 67, No. 2, June 1994.

[10] B. Nebel and C. Backstrom. On the computational complexity of temporal projection, planning and plan validation. *Artificial Intelligence*, Vol. 56, No. 1, 1994.

[11] V. Pratt. Semantical considerations on Floyd-Hoare Logic. In *Proc. 17th FOCS*, 109-121.

[12] M. A. Peot. Conditional nonlinear planning. In *Proc. First International Conference on AI Planning Systems*, pp. 189--197, 1992.

[13] S. Rosenchein. Plan Synthesis: A logical perspective. In *Proc. IJCAI-81*, pp. 331-337, 1981.

[14] Q. Yang and J. D. Tenenberg. Abtweak: Abstracting a nonlinear, least commitment planner. In *AAAI-90*, pp. 204--209, 1990.

Causal Pathways of Rational Action

Charles L. Ortiz, Jr.[*]
Department of Computer and Information Science
University of Pennsylvania
Philadelphia, PA 19104
clortiz@linc.cis.upenn.edu

Abstract

A proper characterization of a rational agent's actions involves much more than simply recounting the changes in the world affected by the agent. It should also include an explanatory account connecting the upshots of an agent's actions with the reasons behind those actions, where those upshots might represent actual changes (either intentional or unintentional) or merely counterfactual possibilities. The conventional view of action makes it difficult to distinguish, inter alia, cases of attempts, accidents, coercions, or failures — such distinctions useful to agents engaged in recognizing or assigning responsibility for actions. Such a view also makes the characterization of actions that do not involve physical change, such as maintenance events, difficult, as well as the proper representation of negative actions; the latter commonly appearing in explanations and as objects of an agent's intentions. In this paper, I present a formal analysis of these sorts of actions in terms of the causal pathways joining an agent's intentions with his actions.

Introduction

Consider a simple situation in which the following action is observed:

(1) John tried not to spill the coffee by holding the saucer steady but failed.

To capture conditions for the occurrence of instances of such an action by way of traditional representations that equate actions with pairs of world-states (McCarthy & Hayes 1969) would be difficult given that, first, the observable pre- and post-conditions of the above action could apply equally well to instances of intentionally spilling the coffee by tipping the saucer or to cases of unintentionally spilling the coffee while involved in some other activity[1]. Further, (1) also makes

reference to an *attempt* at performing a *negative action* (not spilling the coffee) where the referenced negative action is to be related to a "positive" means action: the holding the saucer steady action. Though (Pollack 1986) and (Israel, Perry, & Tutiya 1991), for example, have examined how one action can be a means for the performance of another action, that work leaves open the question of how a positive (or negative action, for that matter) can be a means of not performing some ends action[2]. In addition, such a negative action must be represented in a fashion that precludes the possibility of identifying it with the non-occurrence of the *spilling of the coffee* action. Otherwise, it would be impossible to distinguish the referenced negative action with any other action that might have occurred. The action reported in (1) further suggests a deviation in the usual causal pathway joining the agent's prior intention (to not spill) with the final result. This is reported as a failure: failures representing another class of negative action, members of which can be characterized as unintentional. This last point suggests that negative actions cannot be simply identified with non-movement or non-change; in the example, the referenced failed action *did* result in change: the spilling of the coffee.

In addition, any successful analysis of (1) should uncover a number of implicit events: in the case of successful performance on the part of the agent would be the presence of a *maintenance* action involving no change with respect to the fact that the coffee is in the cup. It does not seem possible to reconcile the traditional view of action (under which nothing has "happened") with the intuition that here the agent has, in fact, *done* something. Additionally, (1) would normally also be re-describable as an instance of an *accident*. That an accident cannot simply be equated with an unintentional action is plain enough: my going to a lecture might be intentional but the fact that by doing so I thereby also occupy the last available chair is incidental: it represents a *side-effect* of my intentions

---

[*]This research was supported by the following grants: ARO no. DAAL 03-89-C-0031 Prime and DARPA no. N00014-90-J1863.

[1]Though (McDermott 1982) presents an alternative representation of events by which one can, for example, represent actions such as "running around the track," that work does not address the issues discussed here of generation

relations, particularly involving negative actions, maintenance actions, or attempts, failures and accidents.

[2]For a discussion of negative events see (Brand 1971).

(Cohen & Levesque 1990).

Contemporary theories of rational behavior, such as the logic of belief, desire, and intention (BDI) of (Cohen & Levesque 1990)(C&L), have argued persuasively for the need for a notion of prior intention (or commitment) to action. However, the mere presence of an action does not presuppose the existence of a causally responsible intention; neither can the presence of an intention assure success. These are simply idealizations, as illustrated by example (1). In what follows I first present a brief overview of C&L in which I will frame the subsequent analysis. I then examine *means-end causal pathways* involving notions of generation and enablement as tied to an agent's intentions. I go on to examine maintenance actions as characteristic of actions involving no change. Finally, I examine cases of accidents, attempts, and failures as representative of deviations from means-end causal pathways. In this analysis, I take the agent's mental state as playing a crucial role in the proper characterization of such actions and argue that the characterization of these sorts of actions should involve counterfactuals.

Representation

C&L's logic models belief with a weak S5 modal logic where possible worlds are linear sequences of *basic* event types (indexed by the integers); satisfaction is then defined relative to a model, world-time pair, and a variable valuation. An agent i's belief in some proposition ϕ is expressed in their language by statements of the form $bel(i, \phi)$, while an agent's goals (consistent desires) are captured by statements of the form $goal(i, \phi)$. The semantics of Bel and $Goal$ are both given in terms of possible worlds. An agent's intentions, written $intend(i, \alpha)$, are composite objects modeled as *persistent goals*: these are goals which agent i will maintain until α is achieved or until i believes α is no longer possible. Intentions have the further important property that they are not closed under logical consequence. Their model also makes use of the following modal temporal operators: $\Diamond\phi$ means ϕ is eventually true in the current world (which includes the current moment), $\Box\phi =_{def} \neg\Diamond\neg\phi$, and $later(\phi) =_{def} \neg\phi \wedge \Diamond\phi$. The modal operators $happens(\alpha)$ and $done(\beta)$ refer to the actions α and β as, respectively, happening next or as having just happened in the current world-time point (with an optional extra argument standing for the agent of the action). Complex action descriptions are possible by way of statements in dynamic logic where the set of actions is closed under nondeterministic choice $(\alpha|\beta)$, sequencing $(\alpha;\beta)$, tests $(p?)$, and iteration (α^*). The reader is referred to (Cohen & Levesque 1990) for details on the logic.

In order to refer to future *possibility*, I will add the following branching modal operators to C&L. $\Diamond_B\phi$ means that among all of the possible worlds with pasts (not including the current moment) identical to the real one, there is one in which ϕ holds. $\Box_B$ is defined as usual as $\neg\Diamond_B\neg\phi$. In order to model concurrent actions I will introduce the function $+$: $\alpha + \beta$ names the action consisting of the simultaneous occurrence of α and β. Possible worlds stand, as before, for sequences of events, however, each event is now taken from the lattice structure built up out of $+$ and the primitive NIL standing for inaction. I also define: $\phi > \psi$ as $\Box_B[\phi \supset \psi]$. This says that the material conditional holds in all possible futures. Where the conditional is evaluated at some time in the past and ϕ does not hold in the real world, then $>$ stands for counterfactual dependence. There are well known problems with this idealization which I will later discuss. To capture some notion of bringing about I define: $happens(e \rightsquigarrow \phi) =_{def} happens(\neg\phi?; e; \phi?) \wedge \forall e'.e' \leq e \supset happens(e'; \neg\phi?)$, that is, e leads to ϕ just in case it results in ϕ and any subsequence (specified by the ordering $\leq$) results in $\neg\phi$. In order to formalize a notion of generation I will introduce the following variant of *happens*: $happens(i, t, \alpha) =_{def} \exists t'.happens(i, t'?; \alpha; t' + t?)$ which states that t represents the duration of α where, in C&L, if t is an integer then $t?$ specifies the time as t; similarly for $done(i, t, \alpha)$. Finally, $not(\alpha)$ will stand for any instance in which: $\models happens(not(\alpha)) \equiv \neg happens(\alpha))$ and $basic(\alpha)$ will be true just in case ϕ is primitive. I will also assume that this modified version is extended to allow singular terms for actions where each action term is grounded in some basic event sequence. This is straightforward.

Means-end Causal Pathways

The notion of one action representing a *way of* performing another seems central to means-end reasoning (Pollack 1986; Israel, Perry, & Tutiya 1991): this relation is often referred to as *generation*, after Goldman's treatment (Goldman 1970). So too does the notion of enablement: that is, one action performed in order to perform another (Pollack 1986; Balkanski 1993; Di Eugenio 1993). Examples of generation are often reported by way of the *by* locution: *He signalled by waving* or *He turned on the light by flipping the switch*. Goldman notes that the generation relation is irreflexive, anti-symmetric, and transitive. In Goldman's theory, actions are triples of act-type, agent, and time where each action is either generated by some other action or represents a basic action or movement. Pollack formalized Goldman's notion of generation via a notion of *conditional generation*. Her formalization essentially associates a condition, c, with the occurrence of two distinct act-types, α and β, such that α generates β just in case α and β both occur at the same time, it is always the case that if c holds and α occurs then β occurs, and neither α nor c are sufficient for β to occur. For the case of turning on a light by flipping a switch, c might affirm that the light and switch are connected. Unfortunately, this approach cannot be used to explain instances such as (1) nor the following:

(2) By not lowering my hand I signalled again to the
auctioneer.

Here, whatever c is chosen as the generating condition
for the not-lowering action could just as easily be used
to incorrectly conclude that some other non-occurring
action generated the signalling.

Another difficulty with Pollack's formalization is
that, given the potentially infinite number of qualifications to any action, there is no c such that α will
always generate β under c: one can always find an
exception. Further, her definition involves a second
order statement. In this paper, I suggest that generation be analyzed counterfactually: in short, if α had
not occurred β wouldn't have either. Such a definition correctly handles (2). This was, in fact, one of
the clauses in Goldman's original definition[3], but was
questioned by Pollack. The example Goldman used
was the following. If some agent extended his arm in
order to signal then we can say that if he had not extended his arm, he would not have signalled. Pollack
observes that if the agent also intended to signal then
there is no reason to suppose that the intention to signal would not survive the counterfactual supposition,
particularly if there was some other means of signalling
available to the agent. In other cases, however, the intention would not survive, else one would be forced to
deny the validity of reasonable counterfactuals such as
the following:

(3) If Oswald had not shot Kennedy, then Kennedy
would be alive today.

This counterfactual holds because we have good reason to believe that, at that moment, a shooting was the
only means reasonably available to Oswald; in such a
case, the intention to kill would not survive the counterfactual supposition. One possible solution to the
objection raised by Pollack is to introduce particulars for act-tokens by way of statements of the form:
$happens(e) \wedge type(e, wave)$ and argue that if *that* arm
extension had not occurred then *that* signal would also
have not occurred. An alternative, and the one taken
here, is to argue that the counterfactual dependence
holds between β and both the intention to β and α:
to make an analogy with causation, the intention to β
and α are on the same causal pathway to β.

A case of α generating β can then be defined as [4]:

$$gen1(\alpha, \beta) \equiv \alpha \neq \beta \qquad (1)$$
$$\wedge\, [happens(i, t, \alpha) > happens(i, t, \beta)]$$
$$\wedge\, [(\neg intend(i, \beta)$$
$$\wedge \neg happens(i, t, \alpha)) > \neg happens(i, t, \beta)]$$

---

[3] Goldman included this clause in order to handle
branching acts. See (Goldman 1970). This seems reason
enough for its inclusion.

[4] All axioms that appear in this paper are assumed to
hold for every model and world-time pair. All unbound
variables are further assumed to be universally quantified.

$$gen(\alpha, \beta) \equiv gen1(\alpha, \beta) \qquad (2)$$
$$\vee\, [\exists \gamma . gen1(\alpha, \gamma) \wedge gen(\gamma, \beta)]$$

This inductive definition is needed because counterfactual dependence is not generally transitive (Ginsberg
1986). The first axiom states that α and β must be
distinct (this enforces ireflexivity) and that β counterfactually depends on both α and $intend(i, \beta)$. The
second axiom simply states that two actions are related
by generation just in case there is a chain of counterfactual dependencies between the pair. This approach
depends on a body of basic *generation knowledge* of
the form: $happens(i, t, \gamma) \wedge c \supset happens(i, t, \delta)$, where
these axioms can be separately qualified (Ginsberg &
Smith 1988). It also depends on a more restrictive
treatment of $>$ along the lines of (Ginsberg 1986) so
that if, for example, the arm extension (α) had not
occurred then one only considers possible worlds that
must follow from this revision and causal knowledge:
alternative means of signally will not be considered
since the causal factor (intention) has been retracted
[5]. In order to ensure the proper direction of generation and its characteristic antisymmetry, one approach
to explore would be to *unprotect* generation knowledge
as in (Ginsberg 1986), i.e., allow it to be retracted so
that there would exist possible worlds in which the
agent had not β-ed but had α-ed.

One problem with the definition conjectured in 1
involves the following example of Goldman, *George
jumps 6'. John outjumps George by jumping 6'3"*. Under the counterfactual analysis the best one case say
is that John outjumped George by jumping over 6';
this seems reasonable. A more serious problem is how
to ground basic negative actions; recall that "positive"
actions were grounded in basic agent movements. Consider, for example, *refraining from going to school today*, where there is no more basic action, α, such that
if α had not occurred the positive counterpart of the
above would have. Further, one cannot simply equate
not-α with $\neg happens(\alpha)$, as discussed earlier. I suggest
that the notion of a basic action is a *dynamic notion*
which varies according to an agent's mental state —
as well as possibly some external agent's expectations.
Actions are then grounded in these partial mental state
descriptions: if the agent had wanted to go to school,
he would have.

Given the above, the composite *by* action can now
be defined as follows:

$$happens(i, t, by(\alpha, \beta)) \equiv \qquad (3)$$
$$happens(i, t, \alpha) \wedge happens(i, t, \beta) \wedge gen(\alpha, \beta)$$

That is, the action $by(\alpha, \beta)$ is said to occur just in case
both α and β occur over identical spans of time and,
moreover, α generates β. An agent can now intend

---

[5] In addition, the essential temporal asymmetry (see
(Lewis 1986)) of counterfactuals must be addressed: the
nearest possible worlds should be those in which the past
is kept as stable as possible.

to perform some β by performing some more basic α. Where the agent is successful, this represents the standard means-end causal pathway.

Turning now to enablement, it seems that central to this relation is the notion of "bringing about a possibility." Consider alternatives such as that suggested in (Balkanski 1993). On her analysis, α enables β just in case: (i) the time of α is prior to the time of β, and (ii) there is a set of conditions, C, such that one of the conditions in C, C_i, holds as a result of the performance of α, and either: there is a third action γ, and γ conditionally generates β under C, or C is the executability condition on β There is a serious problem with this definition, however. Consider the following simple situation involving filling a bucket with water. Suppose that there are two faucets and the bucket is currently positioned under one of them. According to Balkanski's definition, transporting the bucket to the other faucet enables filling the bucket, even though that action is *already* possible in the initial situation: this seems non-intuitive. However, if one instead stipulates that α must render β possible, one encounters the following difficulty.

(4) Not stopping on the way home enabled him to arrive on time.

where the enabled action is already possible. It should further be pointed out that enabled actions must be intentional: notice the unacceptability of, *stopping on the way to the gate enabled him to miss the train*, unless the agent was actively trying to miss the train. This appears to be a consequence of their central role in means-end reasoning.

The following definition overcomes these problems:

$$happens(i, t, enables(e_2)) \equiv \qquad (4)$$
$$intends(i, e_2) \wedge \exists e_1 . happens(i, t, e_1)$$
$$\wedge \, [happens(e_1) > \Diamond_B happens(e_1; e_2)]$$
$$\wedge \, [\neg happens(i, t, e_1) > \neg \Diamond_B happens(not(e_1); e_2)]$$

The use of counterfactuals assures us that if e_1 had not occurred then e_2 would not have been immediately possible and it, therefore, happily also rules out those circumstances in which e_2 might have eventuated on its own. Example (4) is also handled properly: there is no restriction that e_2 be initially impossible. Once again, 4 requires a treatment of $>$ along the lines of (Ginsberg 1986; Winslett 1988) [6]. Further, the set of actions quantified over in 4 should be restricted to some subset or context of actions as in (Ortiz 1993). This would preclude the possibility of identifying aberrant events with the event $not\text{-}e_1$ in the evaluation of, say, example (4) so that when evaluating the second counterfactual, one does not consider quicker means of transport that would represent a departure from the norm.

---

[6]NB: Axiom 1 correctly assigns some e_1 (and *not enables*(e_2)) the role of generating action in cases where e_1 satisfies 4 if one uprotects axiom 4.

Non-movement actions

Maintenance events differ from accomplishments in that they do not involve any change with respect to the proposition being maintained: by repeatedly pushing a door (call each such component event an α) I can maintain the door in a closed position (call this condition ϕ), however, the door must have been in a closed position to start with[7]. If I initially closed the door, that action would have been distinct from my later maintaining action. In addition, the condition which is maintained, ϕ, must be counterfactually related to each component α: if I hadn't been pushing the door, it could have opened at some point, possibly because someone was pushing from the other side. This cannot be determined simply by observing the scene: I might simply be pushing a locked door. Furthermore, each α does not have the property that if it had not occurred ϕ would necessarily have come about. Consider a case in which I am maintaining coffee in a cup while walking on a ship that is rocking. Suppose further that whenever the cup "dips" over an angle greater than θ, the coffee spills. I might choose to "straighten" the cup as soon as it rotates no more than some $\theta - \delta$: such an action is nonetheless a component maintaining even though I could have just as well salvaged the coffee by waiting a bit longer.

There appears to be a close relationship between maintenance actions and preventions (Ortiz 1993). Whereas a prevention is a relation between a real event and a hypothetical event, a maintaining can best be viewed as a process composed of smaller events (α's), where each component α inhibits progress towards the bringing about of ϕ but does not render ϕ impossible: each push I initiate does not prevent the door from ever opening — only for the extent of that particular push. Further, if I lock the door, thereby preventing anyone from ever opening it, I am not maintaining the door closed. Notice that maintenance events share a property of all processes: they are not necessarily homogeneous (Shoham 1988) over the interval in which they occur: in the example, the pushes originating on the opposite side of the door might be intermittent. In addition, each step (α) need not be of the same type. For example, suppose I have a rope with a knot at the center which I am attempting to maintain within some spatial interval. Periodically, someone pulls on either side: if I feel a tug to the left, I pull to the right, and vice-versa. In each case, my action is of a distinct type: a left-pull versus a right-pull.

These properties can be captured by the following:

---

[7](McDermott 1982) discusses an analogous notion of *protecting* a fact but leaves it as an open problem. (Di Eugenio 1993) discusses maintenance actions in the context of instructions.

$$done(i, t, m(\phi)) \equiv \qquad\qquad\qquad (5)$$
$$\exists\alpha.done(i, t, \alpha) \wedge \Diamond_B later(\neg\phi)$$
$$\wedge\ \exists d\forall\beta[happens(\beta \rightsquigarrow \neg\phi) > f(\beta, \neg\phi) \geq d]$$
$$\wedge\ [\neg done(i, t, \alpha) >$$
$$\forall\gamma[happens(\gamma \rightsquigarrow \neg\phi) > f(\gamma, \neg\phi) < d]]$$

This says that some α generates a component maintaining, $m(\phi)$, if it inhibits progress towards ϕ; i.e., if all the possible futures (recall the definition for $>$) leading to $\neg\phi$, represented by the sequence β, have a cost greater than d; whereas if α had not occurred, all of the events, γ, leading to $\neg\phi$ would have had a lower cost. The function f is meant to capture a sense of "progress" towards ϕ (see below). The second clause in the definition further constrains the coming about of $\neg\phi$ to remain possible: this is necessary so that α not prevent $\neg\phi$ from ever coming about. A maintenance event can now be represented as a process or instance of $\phi?; [m(\phi)|(x; \phi?)]^*; m(\phi); [m(\phi)|(x; \phi?)]^*$, for some basic event, x; that is, as a possibly inhomogeneous sequence consisting of $m(\phi)$'s, with the further restriction that ϕ be true throughout.

By employing counterfactuals, the above definition correctly captures the tendency towards $\neg\phi$ that the agent is inhibiting. Further, since α can occur concurrently with some other event, the definition allows one to model situations such as those involving a simultaneous push and pull — *no* net movement — or for α to represent a reaction (e.g., tugging to the right when you feel a tug to the left). Finally, though the issue of progress towards $\neg\phi$ is obviously a difficult one to resolve it does appear necessary in order to explain cases such as the example involving maintaining coffee in a cup, where the coffee can still change its location within the cup. Such a function is analogous to a heuristic search function that might be employed by a planner. Many problem domains readily suggest natural progress functions: in trying to maintain someone from getting close to some object, a natural metric would be the distance towards the object; in trying to maintain a tower at a certain height, a natural metric would be the number of blocks stacked so far; and in trying to maintain a bucket under a faucet, a natural metric would be the distance from the edge of the faucet to the edge of the bucket.

Abnormal Causal Pathways

Whenever we ascribe an instance of *trying-to-*α to some agent, i, we seem to suggest that i performed some β which it believed would generate α. If i fails then either: (i) some expected circumstance necessary for the generation of α did not obtain, (ii) i's beliefs about the circumstances in which it was embedded were correct but its beliefs about the relation between β and α were incorrect, or (iii) i failed to perform β correctly[8]. For example, consider the following:

(5a) John tried to escape but was caught.

(5b) John tried to remove the stains with soap and water.

(5c) John tried not to spill the coffee by holding the cup steady but failed.

In the first example, we can imagine a situation in which John attempts an escape by executing some plan of action, β, believing that he will thereby escape. However, the circumstances might be such that β cannot generate the desired action: suppose, for example, that unbeknownst to John someone is positioned in such a way as to prevent the escape; in this case, John's inaccurate beliefs about the world prevent him from accurately predicting the future. In (5)b, John might have perfect knowledge about the current situation but his beliefs concerning possible means for removing stains could be incorrect. Finally, in the last example, John's beliefs about the relation of holding the cup steady and preventing the spilling of the coffee are correct, as are his beliefs about the current situation; in this case, however, he simply fails to perform the action *hold cup steady* properly.

The following axiom seems to capture these intuitions:

$$happens(i, t, try(\alpha)) \equiv \neg basic(\alpha) \qquad (6)$$
$$\wedge\ \exists\beta.happens(i, t, \beta) \wedge intend(i, by(\beta, \alpha))$$

This states that an agent i attempts α just in case i performs some β with the intention of performing α. By the definition for *by* and the fact that intentions in C&L are closed under logical equivalence, it follows that i believes (whether correctly or not) that β will generate α. The case of basic actions is much more problematic and here I simply assume that basic actions always succeed (See (Pollack 1986) for a discussion) [9].

The notion of a failure is now captured as follows:

$$happens(i, t, fail(\alpha)) \equiv \qquad\qquad (7)$$
$$happens(i, t, try(\alpha)) \wedge \neg happens(i, \alpha)$$

"You can't fail if you've never tried," as they say. Notice that it is not necessary that α be physically possible to start with. A consequence of the above definition, together with axioms from C&L, are the following reasonable inferences: an agent will never try to fail and if an agent tries, that attempt (i.e., $try(\alpha)$) cannot fail (i.e., $fail(try(\alpha))$ is impossible).

Turning now to cases of accidents, consider what appears to be a reasonable default for rational agents:

$$\neg intend(i, \alpha) \Rightarrow \neg later(happens(i, \alpha)) \qquad (8)$$

---

[8] (Pollack 1986) discusses similar issues in the context of plan recognition.

[9] One problem with this definition, which I will not address, stems from the fact that if an agent tries to α it must fully believe that the means action will generate α, whereas in actuality it might entertain only a partial belief.

that is, if an agent doesn't intend to perform some α then it normally will not. Notice the distinction between the absence of an intention in this case and an intention to not perform α. The latter involves, as discussed earlier, the commitment to perform some more basic action as a way of performing the negative action: such commitments playing an important role in the architecture of rational agents (Bratman, Israel, & Pollack 1988). Axiom 8 can be defeated in cases of an accident (an agent spilling coffee for example), or in cases of *coercions*, in which some agent forces another agent to perform some action against his will. The first case is possible because an agent's intentions are not closed under implication in C&L. That is, an agent does not intend all of the side-effects of its intentions. Given this property, an accident can be defined as follows.

$$
\begin{aligned}
happens(i, t, accident(\alpha)) &\equiv \quad\quad (9)\\
happens(i, t, \alpha) &\wedge \neg bel(i, happens(i, \alpha))\\
\wedge[knows(i, happens&(i, \alpha)) >\\
happens(i, try&(not(\alpha)))]
\end{aligned}
$$

In this case agent i performs some α without being aware (possibly as a side-effect of some other intended action). However, in the case of an accident it is also necessary that the agent would have tried to avoid α, if it could have more accurately predicted the future. Notice that accidents include cases of failures, but not necessarily vice versa[10].

Summary and Conclusions

In this paper I explored a broader view of action than is possible through traditional accounts that equate an action with simply the bringing about of a condition. In the process, I discussed a number of action types, such as negative actions and maintenance actions, that are best viewed as depending counterfactually on a more primitive means action as wells as partial a mental state description. This observation led to a generalization and simplification of previous accounts of two important means-end relations — generation and enablement. I argued that actions tied to an agent's intentions by way of these two relations characterized the normal causal pathway of action whereas cases of failures, accidents, and coercions exemplified deviations from this pathway. Such a conceptualization of action is important to the architecture of rational agents that can recognize actions in order to ascertain abilities or assign responsibility as well as produce explanatory accounts of behaviors.

---

[10]Cases of coercions appear to represent deviations from the perspective of the normal evolution of deliberations from desire to intention formation. They are characterized by a concurrent desire (caused by another agent) *not* to perform some action while simultaneously entertaining the opposite intention.

Acknowledgments

I would like to thank Mike Moore, Mark Steedman, Bonnie Webber, and Mike White for comments on an earlier draft of this paper.

References

Balkanski, C. T. 1993. *Actions, Beliefs, and Intentions in Multi-Action Utterances*. Ph.D. Dissertation, Harvard University.

Brand, M. 1971. The language of not doing. *American Philosophical Quarterly* 8(1).

Bratman, M. E.; Israel, D. J.; and Pollack, M. E. 1988. Plans and resourse-bounded practical reasoning. *Computational Intelligence* 4:349–355.

Cohen, P., and Levesque, H. 1990. Intention is choice with commitment. *Artificial Intelligence* 42:213–261.

Di Eugenio, B. 1993. *Understanding Natural Language Instructions: a Computational Approach to Purpose Clauses*. Ph.D. Dissertation, University of Pennsylvania.

Ginsberg, M. L., and Smith, D. E. 1988. Reasoning about action ii: The qualification problem. *Artificial Intelligence* 35:311–342.

Ginsberg, M. L. 1986. Counterfactuals. *Artificial Intelligence* 30:35–79.

Goldman, A. 1970. *A Theory of Human Action*. Princeton University Press.

Israel, D.; Perry, J.; and Tutiya, S. 1991. Actions and movements. In *Proceedings of the International Joint Conference on Artificial Intelligence*, 1060–1065.

Lewis, D. 1986. Counterfactual dependence and time's arrow. In *Philosophical Papers*. Oxford University Press. 32–66.

McCarthy, J., and Hayes, P. 1969. *Some Philosophical problems from the standpoint of artificial intelligence*. Edinburgh University Press. 463–502.

McDermott, D. 1982. A temporal logic for reasoning about processes and plans. *Cognitive Science* 6:101–155.

Ortiz, Jr., C. L. 1993. The semantics of event prevention. In *Proceedings of the Eleventh National Conference on Artificial Intelligence*, 683–688.

Pollack, M. 1986. *Infering Domain Plans in Question-Answering*. Ph.D. Dissertation, University of Pennsylvania.

Shoham, Y. 1988. *Reasoning About Change: Time and Causation from the Standpoint of Artificial Intelligence*. MIT Press.

Winslett, M. 1988. Reasoning about actions using a possible models approach. In *Proceedings of the National Conference on Artificial Intelligence*.

Temporal Reasoning with Constraints on Fluents and Events *

Eddie Schwalb, Kalev Kask, Rina Dechter

Department of Information and Computer Science
University of California, Irvine CA 92717
{eschwalb,kkask,dechter}@ics.uci.edu

Abstract

We propose a propositional language for temporal reasoning that is computationally effective yet expressive enough to describe information about fluents, events and temporal constraints. Although the complete inference algorithm is exponential, we characterize a tractable core with limited expressibility and inferential power. Our results render a variety of constraint propagation techniques applicable for reasoning with constraints on fluents.

1   Introduction

Consider the issues raised by the following "story". At 8:00 the microfilm was deposited in the safe and at 11:00 the microfilm was gone. John was at the bar between 8:10 - 8:30 and between 9:10 -12:00. He was also at the poker table between 8:35 - 9:00. Fred was at the bar between 8:30 - 10:00 and between 10:45 - 12:00. The bar opened at 7:30 and closed at 12:00. We know that at least 15 minutes are required to take the microfilm and return to the bar.

Given the story above, we are interested in answering queries such as "Does the story entail that Fred took the microfilm ?" and "What are *all* the possible scenarios in this story ?". We wish to capture the human ability to answer such queries without information about speed of movement or distances.

We wish to describe information conditioned on occurrences of events. For instance, a sentence like "at least 15 minutes are required to take the microfilm and return to the bar" should be accounted for only if someone took the film; a query like "When did John take the microfilm ?" assumes that John took the microfilm.

In classical propositional logic the atomic entities are propositions. In dynamic environments the atomic entities are called *fluents*. They may repeatedly change their value as events occur and are functions of the situation or time. Our work builds upon temporal languages proposed by McDermott and Dean [11, 5], Allen [2], Kowalski and Sergot [9] and Shoham [14]. We accommodate various constructs proposed in these languages (time points and intervals). Our main goal, however, is to equip a temporal language with a computationally manageable inference engine.

The primary task of any reasoning system is determining consistency of the given theory. For temporal languages this means determining the consistency of sentences involving a combination of temporal and propositional constraints. For example, consider the statement "Either Bob or Mary must tend the bar, but Bob has to leave on an errand and Mary has an appointment with the doctor". How do we infer that Bob's errand must be either before or after Mary's appointment ?

In this paper we propose a temporal language whose inference engine is based on qualitative and quantitative temporal constraints [1, 6, 7, 12, 15, 16]. Decoupling the propositional and temporal constraints provides us with inference algorithms that are based on propositional satisfiability and temporal constraint satisfaction, and allows us to identify a useful tractable core.

The proposed language, called HOT, is defined over *Holds*, *Occurs* and *Temporal* propositions. We assume that events are instantaneous and serve as the only time points at which fluents may change their values. We use $Holds(F, E_1, E_2)$ to state that the fluent F is *true* between events E_1 and E_2, $Occurs(E)$ to state that event E occurred, and $Time(E)$ for the time of its occurrence. We focus on the tasks of deciding consistency and computing consistent scenarios, which enables us to answer entailment and other queries of interest (such as inferring whether certain events *must, might,* or *could not* have occurred). Our language has a tractable core which allows us to make weak (sound but incomplete) inferences. When augmented with additional axioms, our language yields sound and complete inference algorithms at the expense of increased computational complexity.

*This work was partially supported by NSF grant IRI-9157636, by Air Force Office of Scientific Research grant AFOSR 900136 and by grants from TOSHIBA of America and Xerox

The paper is organized as follows. Section 2 describes the syntax and semantics of our language. Section 3 gives an alternative propositional semantics for the language. Section 4 introduces a new model of conditional temporal constraint networks that serves as the computational engine.

2 The Language

Our language, called HOT, is a set of sentences over *Holds*, *Occurs* and *Temporal* propositions. We use two (disjoint) sets of symbols, *fluent symbols* and *event symbols*. A fluent is a propositional function of time and a *fluent literal* is either a fluent symbol or its negation. An event E is a pair $(Occurs(E), Time(E))$, where $Occurs(E)$ is a propositional variable that is assigned *true* iff E occurred, and $Time(E)$ is a real valued variable that specifies the time E occurred. We use two special events: E_{begin}, for "the beginning of the world", and E_{end}, for "the end of the world". Unless otherwise noted, we use right-sided half open intervals $[a, b)$ for reasons to be clarified later.

In addition to *Occurs* propositions there are *Holds* and *Temporal* propositions.

A *Holds* proposition has the form

$$Holds(\varphi,\ E_i, E_j) \qquad (1)$$

where E_i and E_j are event symbols and $\varphi = F_1 \vee \cdots \vee F_k$ is a disjunction of fluent literals. We also use the following abbreviations: If $E_i = E_j$ we write (1) as $Holds(\varphi, E_i)$. If $E_i = E_{begin}$ we write (1) as $Holds(\varphi, \textbf{before } E_j)$. If $E_j = E_{end}$ we write (1) as $Holds(\varphi, \textbf{after } E_i)$. If $E_i = E_j = E_{begin}$ or $E_i = E_j = E_{end}$ or both $E_i = E_{begin}$ and $E_j = E_{end}$ we write (1) as **initially** φ, **eventually** φ, **always** φ respectively.

A *Temporal* proposition is a qualitative or quantitative temporal constraint over time points and time intervals [12]. Given a pair of events E_i, E_j, I_{E_i, E_j} denotes an half-open interval that begins with (includes) $Time(E_i)$ and ends with (excludes) $Time(E_j)$. A temporal proposition is a constraint having one of three forms:

1. A point-point constraint

$$Time(E_j) - Time(E_i) \in I_1 \cup I_2 \cup \cdots \cup I_k \qquad (2)$$

where $I_1, \ldots, I_k$ are intervals (over real numbers), specified by their end points. We also use the shortcuts $Time(E_j) \in I_1 \cup I_2 \cup \cdots \cup I_k$, $Time(E_j) = t$ and $Time(E_j) \geq Time(E_i)$ to have the obvious meaning.

2. A point-interval constraint between the time point at which event E_i occurred and the interval that begins with E_j and ends with E_k,

$$Time(E_i)\ \{R_1, \ldots, R_m\}\ I_{E_j, E_k} \qquad (3)$$

where $R_1, \ldots, R_m \in \{$ **before, starts, during, finishes, after** $\}$.

3. An interval-interval constraint

$$I_{E_i, E_j}\ \{R_1, \ldots, R_m\}\ I_{E_p, E_q} \qquad (4)$$

where $R_1, \ldots, R_m$, $m \leq 13$ are distinct and

$$R_1, \ldots, R_m \in \left\{ \begin{array}{c} \textbf{before, after, meets, met}-\textbf{by,} \\ \textbf{overlaps, overlapped}-\textbf{by,} \\ \textbf{during, contains, equals,} \\ \textbf{starts, started}-\textbf{by,} \\ \textbf{finishes, finished}-\textbf{by} \end{array} \right\}.$$

Sentences in HOT are conjunctive normal form (CNF) formulas over *Holds*, *Occurs* and *Temporal* propositions as their atoms.

Example 1: Consider the story in the introduction. The sentence "At 8:00 the film was deposited in the safe and at 11:00 the film was gone" is described by

$$Holds(Film\_in\_safe,\ Film\_deposited) \wedge$$
$$(Time(Film\_deposited) = 8:00) \wedge$$
$$Holds(\neg Film\_in\_safe,\ Film\_checked) \wedge$$
$$(Time(Film\_checked) = 11:00).$$

The sentence "at least 15 minutes are required to take the microfilm and return to the bar" is described by

$$Occurs(John\_take\_film) \rightarrow (Time(end\_John\_go\_safe)$$
$$- Time(begin\_John\_go\_safe) \in [15, \infty])$$

A similar sentence can be described for Fred.

2.1 Semantics

An interpretation of a formula in HOT is a quadruple $< \mathcal{F}, M_f, \mathcal{E}, M_e >$, where $\mathcal{F}$ is a set of two-valued functions of time; M_f is a mapping $M_f : F \mapsto \mathcal{F}$ of fluent symbols into functions in $\mathcal{F}$; $\mathcal{E}$ is a subset of event symbols and M_e is a mapping $M_e : \mathcal{E} \mapsto \Re$ of events in $\mathcal{E}$ into real valued time points. The value of $M_f(\varphi)$ may change only when events occur, namely at a time point $t = M_e(E)$ for some event E.

Intuitively, $\mathcal{F}$ is a set of fluents that corresponds to fluent symbols used in the formula and $\mathcal{E}$ is the set of events that actually occurred, mapped to the time points at which each of them occurred.

Definition 1: An interpretation is a *scenario* (or a model) of a formula if all its clauses are assigned the truth value *true* under the following rules of evaluation:

1. $Occurs(E)$ is *true* iff $E \in \mathcal{E}$.

2. We extend M_f to disjunction and negation, $M_f(F_1 \vee \cdots \vee F_k) = M_f(F_1) \vee \cdots \vee M_f(F_k)$, $M(\neg F) = \neg M(F)$.

3. A holds proposition $Holds(\varphi, E_i, E_j)$ is *true* iff $E_i, E_j \in \mathcal{E}$, and (a) in case $E_i = E_j$ then $M_f(\varphi)(M_e(E))$ is *true*, (b) in case $E_i \neq E_j$ then $M_e(E_i) < M_e(E_j)$ and for any t such that $M_e(E_i) \leq t < M_e(E_j)$, $M_f(\varphi)(t)$ is *true*.

4. A temporal proposition is *true* iff the events specified occurred and the temporal constraint is satisfied, namely

   (a) a *point-point* temporal proposition (2) is *true* iff $E_i, E_j \in \mathcal{E}$, and $M_e(E_j) - M_e(E_i) \in I_1 \cup I_2 \cup \cdots \cup I_k$.

   (b) a *point-interval* temporal proposition (3) is *true* iff $E_i, E_j, E_k \in \mathcal{E}$ and $M_e(E_j) < M_e(E_k)$ and one of the relations $R_1, \ldots, R_m$ holds.

   (c) an *interval-interval* temporal proposition (4) is *true* iff $E_i, E_j, E_p, E_q \in \mathcal{E}$ and $M_e(E_i) < M_e(E_j)$ and $M_e(E_p) < M_e(E_q)$ and one of the relations $R_1, \ldots, R_m$ holds.

5. The truth value of the clauses and the CNF formula is evaluated with respect to the truth values of occurs, holds and temporal propositions using standard rules of evaluation.

A formula is *s-satisfiable* iff it has a scenario.

Note that $Holds(\varphi_1 \wedge \varphi_2, E_i, E_j) \equiv Holds(\varphi_1, E_i, E_j) \wedge Holds(\varphi_2, E_i, E_j)$. However, $Holds(\varphi_1 \vee \varphi_2, E_i, E_j)$ is obviously not equivalent to $Holds(\varphi_1, E_i, E_j) \vee Holds(\varphi_2, E_i, E_j)$. Also note that $Holds(\neg\varphi, E_i, E_j)$ is not equivalent to $\neg Holds(\varphi, E_i, E_j)$.

The formula $Holds(F, E_i, E_j) \wedge Holds(\neg F, E_i)$ is inconsistent but $Holds(F, E_i, E_j) \wedge Holds(\neg F, E_j)$ is consistent because the interval I_{E_i, E_j} is half open. If we used closed intervals, $Holds(F, E_i, E_j) \wedge Holds(\neg F, E_j, E_k)$ would have been inconsistent and the values of the fluents would not be allowed to change when events occur. If we had used open intervals, specifying $Holds(F, E_i)$ would have been useless since it does not induce a constraint on the value of $M_f(F)(t)$ for the open interval $t \in (Time(E_i), Time(E_j))$.

An occurs, holds, or temporal proposition q is entailed by Ψ, denoted $\Psi \models q$, iff it is true in all scenarios of Ψ. As usual, $\Psi \models q$ iff $\Psi \wedge \neg q$ is inconsistent.

Example 2 : Consider the statement "John was at the bar from 8:10 to 8:30". It is described by the formula $\Psi = Holds(John\_at\_bar, 8:10, 8:30)$.[1] $\Psi \models Holds(John\_at\_bar, 8:15, 8:25)$ but $\Psi \not\models Holds(John\_at\_bar, 8:15, 8:35)$ because the value of the fluent $John\_at\_bar$ is not constrained after 8:30 and thus it can be either true or false.

---

[1] For the sake of convenience we will use real time points as events.

For the rest of this paper we will restrict our treatment to HOT sentences whose $Holds(\varphi, E_i, E_j)$ propositions we call *simple*, namely holds propositions in which φ is a single fluent literal unless $E_i = E_{begin}$ and $E_j = E_{end}$ (i.e. $Holds(\varphi, \textbf{always})$). General holds propositions introduce computational complications which we will not address in this paper.

3   Propositional Semantics for HOT

In this section we address the task of deciding whether a formula is *s-satisfiable*. We wish to show that the task of deciding *s-satisfiability* and finding a scenario reduces to a two-step process of propositional satisfiability and temporal constraint satisfaction. Although both of these tasks are NP-complete, such a reduction opens the way for using known heuristics and known tractable classes. The idea is to view Ψ as a propositional CNF formula. Once a propositional model is available, using temporal constraint satisfaction we can determine whether all temporal constraints, specified by temporal propositions assigned *true* by the model, can be satisfied simultaneously.

Definition 2: [*p-model*] Given a set of event and fluent symbols, a *p-interpretation* is a truth value assignment to holds, occurs and temporal propositions when viewed as propositional variables. A *p-interpretation* is a *p-model* of a HOT formula Ψ iff it is a propositional model of Ψ and the set of temporal constraints specified by the temporal propositions assigned *true* is consistent.

Upon trying this approach we see immediately that this process may yield *p-models* that do not correspond to any real scenario. The reason is twofold: holds propositions impose implicit temporal constraints that are not explicit in the formula, and temporal propositions should be assigned *true* iff the temporal constraint they induce is satisfied (*p-models* capture only one-way implication). For instance, a formula consisting of just one holds proposition $Holds(F, E_i, E_j)$ will have a *p-model* that allows any assignment to temporal variables $Time(E_i)$ and $Time(E_j)$, since there is no explicit temporal proposition specifying $Time(E_i) < Time(E_j)$. In order to avoid these superfluous *p-models*, we augment Ψ with axioms that explicate the intended meaning.

In the following paragraphs we will augment a formula Ψ with additional HOT sentences that will be called *axioms*. The resulting augmented theory Ψ' describes the same set of scenarios as the original theory Ψ. However, every *p-model* of Ψ' corresponds to a set of scenarios of Ψ and every scenario of Ψ corresponds to a *p-model* of Ψ'.

Definition 3: [axiom set A_1] Given a formula Ψ, the axiom set A_1 has four parts:

1. For all events add $Time(E_{begin}) < Time(E) < Time(E_{end})$, and for all pairs of events E_i, E_j add $I_{E_i,E_j}\{equals\}I_{E_j,E_i}$.

2. For every event E specified in a temporal proposition T we add the axiom $T \rightarrow Occurs(E)$.

3. For every holds proposition $Holds(\varphi, E_i, E_j)$ of Ψ we include sentences stating that if a holds proposition is true, the corresponding events should have occurred and in the intended order:

$$Holds(\varphi, E_i, E_j) \rightarrow Occurs(E_i) \wedge Occurs(E_j),$$
$$Holds(\varphi, E_i, E_j) \rightarrow (Time(E_i)\{starts\}I_{E_i,E_j}),$$
$$Holds(\varphi, E_i, E_j) \rightarrow (Time(E_j)\{finishes\}I_{E_i,E_j}).$$

4. For every pair of holds propositions with opposing fluents, $Holds(F, E_i, E_j)$ and $Holds(\neg F, E_p, E_q)$, we add a sentence stating that the two intervals are disjoint. In general we will add

$$Holds(F, E_i, E_j) \wedge Holds(\neg F, E_p, E_q) \rightarrow$$
$$(I_{E_i,E_j}\{before, meets, met-by, after\}I_{E_p,E_q}).$$

although there are special cases that are simpler.

The next set of axioms deals with the complications introduced by disjunctive holds propositions. Here is an example.

Example 3: Consider the example statement "Either Bob or Mary must tend the bar, but Bob has to leave on an errand and Mary has an appointment with the doctor". It can be represented by the formula $\Psi =$

$$Holds(Bob\_tend\_bar \vee Mary\_tend\_bar, \textbf{always}) \wedge$$
$$Holds(\neg Bob\_tend\_bar, begin\_errand, end\_errand) \wedge \quad (5)$$
$$Holds(\neg Mary\_tend\_bar, begin\_apnt, end\_apnt)$$

In order to guarantee consistency of (5), it is necessary that the intervals of Bob's errand and Mary's appointment be disjoint. Otherwise, there will be a time point at which both Bob_tend_bar and $Mary\_tend\_bar$ are *false*, contradicting

$$Holds(Bob\_tend\_bar \vee Mary\_tend\_bar, \textbf{always}).$$

The set of axioms A_2, defined next, includes a constraint that enforces those intervals to be disjoint.

Definition 4: [axiom set A_2] Given a formula Ψ, if there exists a holds proposition $h_0 = Holds(F_1 \vee \ldots \vee F_k, \textbf{always})$ then for any set of k holds propositions $\{h_i = Holds(\neg F_i, E_{p_i}, E_{q_i}) \mid 1 \leq i \leq k\}$ we include the sentence

$$h_0 \wedge h_1 \wedge \ldots \wedge h_k \rightarrow$$
$$\bigvee_{i<j\leq k}(I_{E_{p_i},E_{q_i}}\{before, meets, met-by, after\}I_{E_{p_j},E_{q_j}})$$

although there are special cases that are simpler.

Example 4: To illustrate the utility of axioms A_1 and A_2, consider the statement "John or Fred was always at the bar, but Fred was not at the bar after $8:00$

and John was not at the bar at $10:00$" which can be represented by the formula

$$Holds(John\_at\_bar \vee Fred\_at\_bar, \textbf{always}) \wedge$$
$$Holds(\neg Fred\_at\_bar, \textbf{after } 8:00) \wedge$$
$$Holds(\neg John\_at\_bar, 10:00)$$

The axiom set A_1 includes $Time(E_{begin}) < 8:00 < 10:00 < Time(E_{end})$, and the axiom set A_2 includes

$$Holds(John\_at\_bar \vee Fred\_at\_bar, E_{begin}, E_{end}) \wedge$$
$$Holds(\neg Fred\_at\_bar, 8:00, E_{end}) \wedge$$
$$Holds(\neg John\_at\_bar, 10:00) \rightarrow$$
$$(I_{8:00,E_{end}}\{before, meets, met-by, after\}10:00).$$

Since, the constraints introduced by A_1 and A_2 are inconsistent, the statement is inconsistent.

The set of axioms A_1 and A_2 is not sufficient to eliminate all superfluous p-models. They do guarantee that for every holds proposition $Holds(F, E_i, E_j)$ assigned *true* we can assign $M_f(F)(t) = true$ for every $t \in I_{E_i,E_j}$ without creating conflicts. However, A_1 and A_2 do not guarantee that when the holds proposition is assigned *false*, the negation of the intended constraint is satisfied in every p-model. To guarantee completeness we provide yet another set of axioms, denoted A_3, which specify that the truth value of a holds proposition is inherited by sub- and super-intervals and that a temporal proposition is assigned *true* iff the temporal constraint is satisfied.

Definition 5: [axiom set A_3] Given a formula Ψ, for every disjunction of fluent symbols $\varphi = F_1 \vee \ldots \vee F_k$ used in the formula, all fluent symbols F, every set of events E_i, E_j, E_p, E_q and every temporal proposition T we include:

$$\neg Holds(\psi, E_i, E_j) \wedge Occurs(E_i) \wedge Occurs(E_j) \rightarrow \quad (6)$$
$$\bigvee_{\forall p,q}\{(I_{E_p,E_q} \subseteq I_{E_i,E_j}) \wedge Holds(\neg \psi, E_p, E_q)\}$$

$$Holds(\psi, E_i, E_j) \wedge (I_{E_p,E_q} \subseteq I_{E_i,E_j}) \rightarrow \quad (7)$$
$$Holds(\psi, E_p, E_q)$$

$$^2 \quad \neg T \quad \bigwedge_{\forall E \ specified \ in \ T} Occurs(E) \rightarrow \overline{T} \quad (8)$$

where $\psi \in \{\varphi, F\}$, $\subseteq$ stands for the constraint $\{starts, during, finishes, equals\}$ and $\overline{T}$ denotes the complement of the temporal constraint T.

For example, if $T = (I_1\{starts, during, finishes\}I_2)$ then $\overline{T} = (I_1$ \{before, after, meets, met-by, overlaps, overlapped-by, contains, finished-by, started-by, equals\}$I_2)$.

Lemma 1: *The size of axiom sets A_1, A_2 and A_3 is at most $O(n^2)$, $O(nk^2(\frac{n}{k})^k)$ and $O(n \cdot n_e^4)$ respectively, where n is the size of the theory axioms are added to, n_e is the number of event symbols and k is the maximum number of fluent literals in a disjunctive holds proposition.*

---

[2] This axiom enables contrapositive reasoning with temporal propositions.

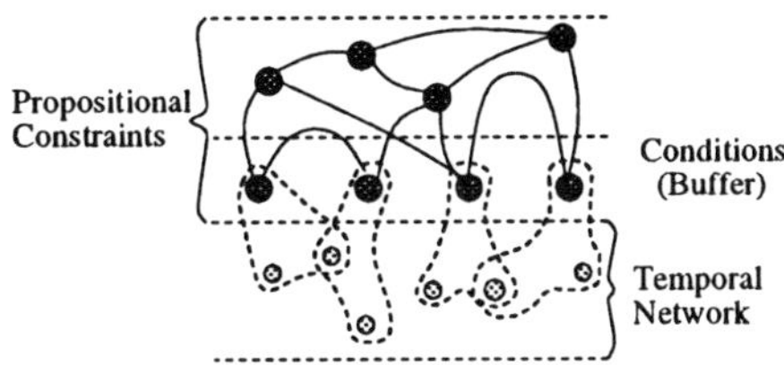

Figure 1: The structure of CTNs.

We use $\Psi \cup A_1 \cup A_2 \cup A_3$ to denote the closure under axioms A_1, A_2 and A_3.

Lemma 2: *The HOT formulas Ψ and $\Psi' = \Psi \cup A_1 \cup A_2 \cup A_3$ are equivalent with respect to s-satisfiability.*

Theorem 1: *Every p-model of $\Psi \cup A_1 \cup A_2 \cup A_3$ corresponds to a set of scenarios of Ψ and every scenario of Ψ corresponds to a p-model of $\Psi \cup A_1 \cup A_2 \cup A_3$.*

4 Conditional Temporal Networks

The notion of *p*-models decouples the propositional constraints from the temporal constraints and enables us to discuss them in isolation. We call this framework *conditional temporal networks*.

Definition 6: A *conditional temporal network* (CTN) has two types of variables: propositional and temporal (point and interval), and two types of constraints: propositional and temporal. Every temporal constraint T is associated with a unique propositional variable C, called its condition. A *conditional temporal constraint* is a pair $(C : T)$. A propositional constraint is a propositional CNF formula over propositional variables and temporal conditions. A *solution* to a CTN is a truth value assignment to the propositional variables and temporal conditions, an assignment of values to the temporal point variables and a selection of a single relation from every qualitative temporal constraint, such that every propositional constraint and all temporal constraints whose condition is assigned *true* are satisfied simultaneously.

Using these definitions, we can intuitively divide every CTN into propositional and temporal parts. Propositional constraints impose certain restrictions on the conditions that act as a buffer and allow us to perform computations on the propositional and temporal parts of the network separately (see Figure 1).

Example 5: Consider a network with seven variables: a propositional variable P, a point variable X_1, two interval variables I_2, I_3, and three conditions C_1, C_2, C_3, with the constraints

$$P \leftrightarrow C_1 \leftrightarrow C_2 \leftrightarrow C_3,$$
$$(C_1 : X_1\{starts\}I_2), \quad (C_2 : X_1\{finishes\}I_3),$$
$$(C_3 : I_2\{before, after, meets, met-by\}I_3).$$

One solution is $P = C_1 = C_2 = C_3 = true$, $X_1 = 1.0$, $X_1\{starts\}I_2$, $X_1\{finishes\}I_3$, $I_2\{met-by\}I_3$.

The truth values of conditions control the temporal subnetwork that needs to be satisfied. Clearly as more conditions are assigned *true* the corresponding temporal network is more constrained. We can conclude:

Theorem 2: *A conditional temporal network N is consistent iff there exists a minimal model of the propositional part of N such that the set of temporal constraints whose condition is assigned true is satisfiable.*

This suggests a procedure for determining the consistency of a CTN. We enumerate all minimal models of the propositional part of a CTN and for each of them determine whether the applicable temporal network is consistent. The task of computing the minimal models of a CNF formula has been investigated and is known to be hard [4, 3]. For Horn formulas, the minimal model is unique and can be computed in polynomial time, thus tractability depends on the temporal constraints.

Corollary 1: *Given a CTN whose propositional part is Horn and temporal part is tractable, consistency can be determined in polynomial time.*

4.1 Tractable Core

We determine the consistency of $\Psi' = \Psi \cup A_1 \cup A_2 \cup A_3$ by checking the consistency of a CTN in which propositional constraints are the propositional clauses of Ψ', conditions are the temporal propositions of Ψ' and temporal constraints are specified by those temporal propositions. Axiom set A_1 introduces Horn clauses and tractable temporal constraints. Axiom set A_2 and axioms (6) and (8) of A_3 are intractable since they introduce non-Horn clauses. If we do not add axiom sets A_2 and A_3, *p*-satisfiability and *p*-entailment become tractable for Horn temporal formulas.

Theorem 3: *If Ψ is a Horn temporal formula in which every holds proposition specifies a single fluent literal and every temporal proposition specifies either single interval (if point-point) $\{starts\}$ or $\{finishes\}$ (if point-interval), $\{equals\}$, $\{before, meets\}$, $\{after, met-by\}$ or any of their disjunctions (if interval-interval), then p-consistency of $\Psi \cup A_1$ can be determined in $O(|\Psi|^2 + n_e^3)$ steps, where n_e is the number of event symbols.*

We will examine the inferences that $\Psi \cup A_1$ is capable of making. We use $\Psi \models \alpha$ to denote s-entailment and $\Psi \models_p \alpha$ to denote p-entailment. Clearly, for every sentence α, if $\Psi \cup A_1 \models_p \alpha$ then $\Psi \cup A_1 \cup A_2 \cup A_3 \models_p \alpha$ and thus $\Psi \models \alpha$. However, it might be that $\Psi \models \alpha$ and $\Psi \cup A_1 \not\models_p \alpha$. Still, if there is a clause $\alpha \rightarrow \beta$ in Ψ and $\Psi \cup A_1 \models_p \alpha$ then $\Psi \cup A_1 \models_p \beta$.

Example 6: When adding only A_1,

$$Holds(F, \textbf{always}) \models_p \neg Holds(\neg F, E_i, E_j),$$
$$Holds(F, \textbf{always}) \not\models_p Holds(F, E_i, E_j),$$
$$Holds(F_1, E_i, E_j) \models_p \neg Holds(\neg(F_1 \vee F_2), E_i, E_j),$$
$$Holds(F_1, E_i, E_j) \not\models_p Holds(F_1 \vee F_2, E_i, E_j).$$

The anomalies of the second and fourth inference can be avoided by adding some subsets of axioms A_3. In principle, as a topic for future research, it would be worthwhile to associate classes of queries with a subset of axioms A_1, A_2 and A_3 that, if added, will guarantee sound and complete inferences with respect to these queries.

Qualitative and quantitative Temporal constraint networks can be processed with a variety of algorithms, presented in [1, 6, 12, 10, 15, 13]. In particular, it was reported in [10] that qualitative temporal networks can be efficiently solved using path-consistency as a preprocessing procedure before backtracking. In [13] an effective preprocessing procedure for quantitative temporal networks is presented.

5   Conclusion

We have proposed a propositional language for temporal reasoning that is computationally effective yet is expressive enough to describe information about fluents, events and temporal constraints. The language, called HOT, is a set of propositional CNF formulas over *Holds*, *Occurs* and *Temporal* propositions as their atoms. A model (or a scenario) of an input theory determines what events happened and specifies the value of every fluent at every point in time.

We define an alternative propositional semantics for HOT that decouples propositional constraints from temporal constraints and allows to consider them separately. We call this framework *conditional temporal networks*. A conditional temporal network is consistent iff there exists a minimal model of the propositional constraints such that the set of temporal constraints whose condition is assigned true is satisfiable. These results render a wide variety of temporal constraint propagation techniques applicable to reasoning about events and fluents.

In particular, we identify a syntactically characterized tractable core for which a weaker (sound but incomplete) tractable inference procedure exists. This tractable core can be used as an upper bound approximation. Additional axioms yield more inferential power but at the cost of increased computational complexity. In practice, when it is known which queries are of interest, a user can add only an appropriate subset of the axioms.

Acknowledgments

We would like to thank Andre Trudel for his comments on an earlier version of this paper.

References

[1] Allen, J.F., 1983. Maintaining knowledge about temporal intervals, *CACM* 26 (11):832-843.

[2] Allen, J.F., 1984. Towards a general Theory of Action and Time, *Artificial Intelligence* 23:123-154.

[3] Ben-Eliyahu, R., Dechter, R., 1993. On computing minimal models, In Proc of AAAI-93, 2-8.

[4] Cadoli, M., 1992. On the complexity of model finding in nonmonotonic propositional logics, In *Proceedings of the Fourth Italian Conference on Theoretical Computer Science*, October 1992.

[5] Dean, T.M., McDermott, D. V., 1987. Temporal data base management, *Artificial Intelligence* 32:1-55.

[6] Dechter, R., Meiri, I., Pearl, J., 1991. Temporal Constraint Satisfaction Problems, *Artificial Intelligence* 49:61-95.

[7] Golumbic, C.M., Shamir, R., 1991. Complexity and Algorithms for Reasoning about Time: A graph theoretic approach, Rutcor Research Report 22-91 (May 1991).

[8] Kautz, H., Ladkin, P., 1991. Integrating Metric and Qualitative Temporal Reasoning, In *Proc. of AAAI-91*, pages 241-246.

[9] Kowalski, R., Sergot, M., 1986. A Logic-based Calculus of Events, *New Generation Computing* 4:67-95.

[10] Ladkin, P.B., Reinefeld, A., 1992. Effective solution of qualitative interval constraint problems, *Artificial Intelligence* 57: 105-124.

[11] McDermott, D.V., 1982. A Temporal Logic for Reasoning about Processes and Plans, *Cognitive Science* 6:101-155.

[12] Meiri, I., 1991. Combining Qualitative and Quantitative Constraints in Temporal Reasoning, In *Proc. of AAAI-91*, pages 260-267.

[13] Schwalb, E., Dechter, R., 1993. Coping with Disjunctions in Temporal Constraint Satisfaction Problems, In Proc. AAAI-93, 127-132.

[14] Shoham, Y., 1986. Reasoning about Change: time and causation from the stand point of artificial intelligence, Ph.D. dissertation, Yale Univ.

[15] Van Beek, P., 1992. Reasoning about Qualitative Temporal Information, *Artificial Intelligence* 58:297-326.

[16] Vilain, M., Kautz, H., Van Beek, P., 1989. Constraint Propagation Algorithms for Temporal Reasoning: A revised Report. In Readings in Qualitative Reasoning about Physical Systems, J. de Kleer and D. Weld (eds).

6

An Algorithm for Probabilistic Least–Commitment Planning*

Nicholas Kushmerick   Steve Hanks   Daniel Weld

Department of Computer Science and Engineering, FR–35
University of Washington   Seattle, WA 98195
{nick, hanks, weld}@cs.washington.edu

Abstract

We define the probabilistic planning problem in terms of a probability distribution over initial world states, a boolean combination of goal propositions, a probability threshold, and actions whose effects depend on the execution-time state of the world and on random chance. Adopting a probabilistic model complicates the definition of plan success: instead of demanding a plan that *provably* achieves the goal, we seek plans whose probability of success exceeds the threshold.

This paper describes a probabilistic semantics for planning under uncertainty, and presents a fully implemented algorithm that generates plans that succeed with probability no less than a user-supplied probability threshold. The algorithm is sound (if it terminates then the generated plan is sufficiently likely to achieve the goal) and complete (the algorithm will generate a solution if one exists).

Introduction

Classical planning algorithms have traditionally adopted stringent certainty assumptions about their domains: the planning agent is assumed to have complete and correct information about the initial state of the world and about the effects of its actions. These assumptions allow an algorithm to build a plan that is *provably* correct: given an initial world state, a successful plan is a sequence of actions that logically entails the goal. Our research effort is directed toward relaxing the assumptions of complete information and a deterministic action model, while exploiting existing techniques for symbolic least-commitment plan generation.

This paper presents the BURIDAN[1] planning algorithm. BURIDAN is a sound, complete, and fully im-

plemented least-commitment planner whose underlying semantics is probabilistic: a probability distribution over states captures the agent's uncertainty about the world and a mixed symbolic and probabilistic action representation allows the effects of action to vary according to the (modeled) state of the world at execution time as well as unmodeled (random) factors.

Our planner takes as input a probability distribution over (initial) states, a goal expression, a set of action descriptions, and a probability threshold representing the minimum acceptable success probability. The algorithm produces a plan such that, given a probability distribution over initial states, the probability that the goal holds after executing the plan is no less than the threshold. We have proved that the algorithm is sound (any plan it returns is a solution) and complete (if there is an acceptable plan the algorithm will find it).

The work reported here makes several contributions. First, we define a symbolic action representation and its probabilistic semantics. Second, we describe an implemented algorithm for probabilistic planning. Third, we briefly describe our investigation of alternative plan assessment strategies. The paper concludes with a discussion of related work.

This research is described in detail in the long version of this paper (Kushmerick, Hanks, & Weld 1993).

Example. The following example will be developed throughout the paper. Suppose a robot is given the goal of holding a block (HB), making sure it is painted (BP), and simultaneously keeping its gripper clean (GC). Initially the gripper is clean, but the block is not being held and is not painted, and the gripper is dry (GD) with probability 0.7. Suppose further that we will accept any plan that achieves the goal with probability at least 0.8. Finally, the robot has the following actions available:

- pickup: try to pick up the block. If the gripper is dry when the pickup is attempted, executing this action will make HB true with probability 0.95. If the gripper is not dry, however, HB will become true only with probability 0.5.

---

*We gratefully acknowledge the comments and suggestions of Tony Barrett, Tom Dean, Denise Draper, Mike Erdmann, Keith Golden, Rex Jacobovits, Oren Etzioni, Neal Lesh, Judea Pearl, and Mike Williamson. This research was funded in part by National Science Foundation Grants IRI-9206733 and IRI-8957302, Office of Naval Research Grant 90-J-1904, and the Xerox Corporation.

[1] Jean Buridan (bōo rē dän′), 1300-58, a French philosopher and logician, has been credited with originating probability theory. He seems to have toyed with the idea of using his theory to decide among alternative courses of ac-

tion: the parable of "Buridan's Ass" is attributed to him, in which an ass that lacked the ability to choose starved to death when placed between two equidistant piles of hay.

- paint: paint the block. This action always makes BP true, and if the robot is holding the block when **paint** is executed, there is a 10% chance that the gripper will become dirty ($\overline{\text{GC}}$).
- dry: try to dry the gripper. This action succeeds in making GD true 80% of the time.

A Semantics for Probabilistic Planning

We begin by defining a planning problem, and what it means to solve one. First we defining states and expressions, then actions and sequences of actions, then the planning problem and its solution.

States & expressions. A *state* is a complete description of the world at a single point in time, and uncertainty about the world is represented using a random variable over states. A state is described using a set of *propositions* in which every proposition appears exactly once, possibly negated.[2] An *expression* is a set (implicit conjunction) of literals. We define the probability of an expression $\mathcal{E}$ with respect to a state s as:

$$P[\mathcal{E} \mid s] = \begin{cases} 1 & \text{if } \mathcal{E} \subseteq s \\ 0 & \text{otherwise} \end{cases} \quad (1)$$

For our example, the world is initially in one of two possible states: $s_1 = \{\text{GD}, \overline{\text{HB}}, \text{GC}, \overline{\text{BP}}\}$ and $s_2 = \{\overline{\text{GD}}, \overline{\text{HB}}, \text{GC}, \overline{\text{BP}}\}$, and the probability distribution over these states is characterized by a random variable $\tilde{s}_I$ as follows: $P[\tilde{s}_I = s_1] = 0.7$, $P[\tilde{s}_I = s_2] = 0.3$.

Actions & action sequences. Our model of action, taken from (Hanks 1990; 1993), combines a symbolic model of the changes the action makes to propositions with probabilistic parameters that represent chance (unmodeled) influences. Fig. 1 is our representation of the **pickup** action: if the gripper is dry (GD holds) at execution time, it makes HB true with probability 0.95, and with probability 0.05 makes no change to the world state. But if GD is false at execution time, **pickup** makes HB true only with probability 0.5. Note that the propositions in the boxes refer to *changes* the action makes, not to world states. For example, it is not correct to say that the HB holds with probability 0.95 after executing **pickup** in a state where the gripper is dry, since the probability of HB *after* **pickup** is executed also depends on the probability of HB *before* execution (as well as the probability of GD before execution).

Formally, an action is a set of *consequences* $\{\langle t_\alpha, \rho_\alpha, e_\alpha \rangle, \dots, \langle t_\eta, \rho_\eta, e_\eta \rangle\}$. Each t_ι is an expression called the consequence's *trigger*, ρ_ι is a probability, and e_ι is a set of literals called the *effects*. The representation for the **pickup** action is thus $\{\langle\{\text{GD}\}, 0.95, \{\text{HB}\}\rangle,$ $\langle\{\text{GD}\}, 0.05, \{\}\rangle,$ $\langle\{\overline{\text{GD}}\}, 0.5, \{\text{HB}\}\rangle,$ $\langle\{\overline{\text{GD}}\}, 0.5, \{\}\rangle\}$.

---

[2] We use this representation for expository purposes only; an implementation need not manipulate states explicitly. In fact our plan refinement algorithm has no explicit representation of state: it reasons directly about the state's component propositions.

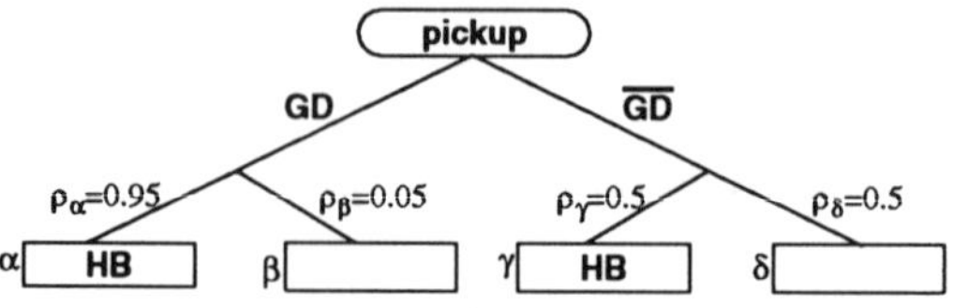

Figure 1: The **pickup** action.

We require that an action's triggers be mutually exclusive and exhaustive:

$$\forall \iota \qquad \sum_s \rho_\iota P[t_\iota \mid s] = 1 \qquad (2)$$

$$\forall s, \iota, \kappa \qquad t_\iota \neq t_\kappa \Rightarrow P[t_\iota \cup t_\kappa \mid s] = 0 \qquad (3)$$

The notation $A_{i,\iota}$ refers to consequence ι of action A_i, and superscripts refer to parts of a particular action: $A_i = \{\dots, \langle t_\iota^i, \rho_\iota^i, e_\iota^i \rangle, \dots\}$.

A consequence defines a (deterministic) transition from a state to a state, defined by a function $\text{RESULT}(e, s)$, where e is a set of effects and s is a state. This function is similar to add and delete lists in STRIPS; see the long version of this paper for the full definition.

An action A induces a change from a state s to a probability distribution over states s':

$$P[s' \mid s, A] = \begin{cases} \rho_\iota P[t_\iota \mid s] & \text{if } \langle t_\iota, \rho_\iota, e_\iota \rangle \in A \land s' = \text{RESULT}(e_\iota, s) \\ 0 & \text{otherwise} \end{cases} \quad (4)$$

Since an action's triggers are mutually exclusive and exhaustive, we have that $\sum_{s'} P[s' \mid s, A] = 1$ for every action A and state s.

We now define the result of executing actions in sequence. The probability that a state s' will hold after executing a sequence of actions $\langle A_i \rangle_{i=1}^N$ (given that the world was initially in state s) is defined as follows:

$$P\left[s' \mid s, \langle A_i \rangle_{i=1}^N\right] = \sum_{s''} P[s'' \mid s, A_1] P\left[s' \mid s'', \langle A_i \rangle_{i=2}^N\right] \quad (5)$$

where $P[s' \mid s, \langle\rangle] = 1$ if $s' = s$ and 0 otherwise.

Finally, we define the probability that an expression $\mathcal{E}$ is true after an action sequence is executed beginning in some state s, and the probability of an expression after executing an action sequence given an initial probability distribution over states $\tilde{s}_I$:

$$P\left[\mathcal{E} \mid s, \langle A_i \rangle_{i=1}^N\right] = \sum_{s'} P\left[s' \mid s, \langle A_i \rangle_{i=1}^N\right] P[\mathcal{E} \mid s'] \quad (6)$$

$$P\left[\mathcal{E} \mid \tilde{s}_I, \langle A_i \rangle_{i=1}^N\right] = \sum_s P\left[\mathcal{E} \mid s, \langle A_i \rangle_{i=1}^N\right] P[\tilde{s}_I = s] \quad (7)$$

Planning problems & solutions. A planning problem consists of (1) a probability distribution over initial states $\tilde{s}_I$, (2) a set of actions $\{A_i\}$, (3) a goal expression $\mathcal{G}$, and (4) a probability threshold τ. For the problem described in this paper, the initial distribution $\tilde{s}_I$ was defined earlier, the plan can be constructed from the actions {pickup, paint, dry}, the goal is $\mathcal{G} = \{\text{HB}, \text{BP}, \text{GC}\}$, and the probability threshold is $\tau = 0.8$.

A *solution* to the problem is an action sequence $\langle A_i \rangle_{i=1}^{N}$ if $\mathrm{P}\left[\mathcal{G} \mid \tilde{s}_I, \langle A_i \rangle_{i=1}^{N}\right] \geq \tau$. As we'll see, $\langle$dry, paint, pickup$\rangle$ is a solution to the example problem.

The BURIDAN Algorithm

We now describe BURIDAN, an algorithm that generates solutions to planning problems. BURIDAN, like SNLP (McAllester & Rosenblitt 1991), searches a space of partial *plans*. Each plan consists of a set of *actions* $\{A_i\}$ where each A_i is one of the input actions annotated with a unique index, a partial *temporal ordering* relation "$<$" over $\{A_i\}$, a set of *causal links*, and a set of *subgoals*. The first two items are straightforward, but there are important differences between the last two items and the analogous SNLP concepts.

A link caches BURIDAN's reasoning that a particular consequence of a particular action could make a literal true for a (later) action in the plan. The link $A_{i,\iota} \xrightarrow{p} A_j$ records the fact that literal p is a member of the trigger of one of action A_j's consequences (A_j is the link's *consumer*), and the effect set of consequence ι of action A_i (the link's *producer*) contains p. Action A_k *threatens* link $A_{i,\iota} \xrightarrow{p} A_j$ if the effect set of some consequence of A_k contains $\bar{p}$, and if A_k can be ordered between A_i and A_j.

A plan's subgoals consists of the literals in the plan that BURIDAN is committed to making true. A subgoal is a literal annotated with a particular action, written $p@A_i$. $p@A_i$ is a subgoal if the plan contains a link $A_{i,\iota} \xrightarrow{q} A_j$ and $p \in t_\iota^i$. The set of subgoals is initialized to include all top-level goals.

BURIDAN begins searching from the *null plan*, which contains only two dummy actions A_0 and A_G, and the ordering constraint $A_0 < A_G$. These two actions allow BURIDAN to compactly encode the planning problem: A_0 and A_G encode the probability distribution over initial states and the goal expression, respectively. Fig. 2 shows the null plan for the example developed in this paper. The initial action A_0 has one consequence for each state in the initial distribution $\tilde{s}_I$ that has non-zero probability. Its triggers are all empty, and the effect sets and probabilities are the states and probabilities defined by $\tilde{s}_I$. The goal action A_G has one consequence triggered by the goal expression $\mathcal{G}$. The null plan adopts $p@A_G$ as a subgoal for each $p \in \mathcal{G}$.

Figure 2: A_0 and A_G encode the initial probability distribution and the goal.

Starting from the null plan, BURIDAN performs two operations:

1. *Plan Assessment:* Determine if the probability that the current plan will achieve the goal exceeds τ, terminating successfully if so.

2. *Plan Refinement:* Otherwise, try to increase the probability of goal satisfaction by refining the current plan. Each refinement generates a new node in the space of partial plans. Signal failure if there are no possible refinements, otherwise nondeterministically choose a new current plan and loop.

Refining a plan with conditional and probabilistic actions differs in two ways from classical causal-link refinement algorithms (*e.g.* SNLP). First, SNLP establishes a single causal link between a producing *action* and a consuming action, and that link alone ensures that the link's literal will be true when the consuming action is executed. Our planner links one of an action's *consequences* to a later action. An action can have several consequences, though only one will actually occur. Furthermore, a single link $A_{i,\iota} \xrightarrow{p} A_j$ ensures that p will be true at action A_j only if trigger t_ι^i holds with probability one. Therefore multiple links may be needed to support a literal: even if no single link makes the literal sufficiently likely, their combination might. We lose SNLP's clean distinction between an "open condition" (a trigger that is not supported by a link) and a "supported condition" that is guaranteed to be true. Causal support in a probabilistic plan is a cumulative concept: the more links supporting a literal, the more likely it is that the literal will be true.

The concept of a threatened link is different when actions have conditional effects. Recall that A_k threatens $A_{i,\iota} \xrightarrow{p} A_j$ if some consequence of A_k asserts $\bar{p}$ and if A_k can be ordered between A_i and A_j. BURIDAN resolves threats in the same way that classical planners do: by ordering the threatening action either before the producer or after the consumer. But a plan can be sufficiently likely to succeed even if there is a threat, as long as the threat is sufficiently *unlikely* to occur. We can therefore resolve a threat in an additional way, by *confrontation*: if action A_k threatens link $A_{i,\iota} \xrightarrow{p} A_j$, plan for the occurrence of some consequence of A_k that does *not* make p false. BURIDAN does so by adopting that consequence's triggers as additional subgoals.

Plan Refinement

BURIDAN's plan refinement step generates all possible refinements of a partial plan. A plan can be refined in two ways: either resolving a threat to a causal link, or adding a link to increase the probability that a subgoal will be true. BURIDAN chooses a threat or subgoal, and then generates possible refinements as follows:

1. If the choice is to add a link to the subgoal $p@A_j$, BURIDAN considers all new and existing actions A_i that have an effect set e_ι^i containing p, adds a link $A_{i,\iota} \xrightarrow{p} A_j$, and orders $A_i < A_j$.

2. If the choice is to resolve a threat by action A_k to link $A_{i,\iota} \xrightarrow{p} A_j$, BURIDAN resolves the threat in one of three ways: *demotion* (order $A_k < A_i$ if it is consistent to do so), *promotion* (order $A_j < A_k$ if consistent), and *confrontation* (plan for the occurrence of a consequence of action A_k that does *not* make p false).

Link creation, promotion, and demotion are analogous to refinement in SNLP-like planners, and we will not discuss them further.[3] Confrontation has no analogue in SNLP, however. The probability that link $A_{i,\iota} \xrightarrow{p} A_j$ succeeds in producing p for A_j is the probability that executing action A_i actually realizes consequence ι and that each action representing a confronted threat realizes a consequence that does not make p false. Since the consequences of action are mutually exclusive, making a non-threatening consequence more likely makes the threat less likely. BURIDAN therefore confronts a threat by choosing a non-threatening consequence of the threatening step, and adopts its triggers as subgoals. We explain confrontation in detail in the longer version of this paper.

Example. We now demonstrate how the planner constructs a plan that will achieve the goal (holding a painted block with a clean gripper) with probability at least 0.8. We simplify the presentation by presenting a sequence of refinement choices that lead directly to a solution plan.

Planning starts with the null plan (Fig. 2). The subgoals for the null plan are $\{HB@A_G, BP@A_G, GC@A_G\}$. BURIDAN supports the first subgoal, $HB@A_G$, by adding a pickup action, A_1, and creating a link from its α consequence: $A_{1,\alpha} \xrightarrow{HB} A_G$. Consequence α of A_1 has GD as a trigger, so BURIDAN adopts $GD@A_1$ a subgoal. Support for this subgoal is then provided by a link from the initial action: $A_{0,\alpha} \xrightarrow{GD} A_1$.

BURIDAN next supports the subgoal of having the block painted, $BP@A_G$, by adding a new paint action, A_2, creating a link $A_{2,\beta} \xrightarrow{BP} A_G$, and adopting $A_{2,\beta}$'s trigger $\overline{HB}@A_2$ as a subgoal. A link $A_{0,\alpha} \xrightarrow{\overline{HB}} A_2$ is added to support $\overline{HB}@A_2$. Notice that pickup and paint are unordered, thus pickup threatens the new link: if pickup is executed before paint, then the block will be in the gripper when paint is executed, making false the trigger $\overline{HB}$ of paint's β consequence. BURIDAN resolves this threat by promoting pickup, adding the ordering constraint $A_2 < A_1$. Finally, BURIDAN supports the subgoal $GC@A_G$ with the link $A_{0,\alpha} \xrightarrow{GC} A_G$, and resolves the threat posed by paint by confrontation: since consequence β of A_2 does not cause $\overline{GC}$, BURIDAN adopts its trigger $\overline{HB}@A_2$ as a subgoal. The resulting plan is shown in Fig. 3.

The assessed probability of Fig. 3's plan is 0.7335

(as described below), which is less than $\tau = 0.8$, so BURIDAN continues to refine the plan. Eventually the plan shown in Fig. 4 is generated; it has success probability 0.804, so BURIDAN terminates.

Plan Assessment

The plan assessment algorithm decides whether a plan's probability of success exceeds the threshold τ. The FORWARD assessment algorithm is a straightforward implementation of the definition of action execution.[4] FORWARD computes the probability distribution over states produced by "executing" each action in sequence, pruning zero-probability states from the distribution for the sake of efficiency.

Complicating assessment is the fact that a solution is defined in terms of a totally ordered sequence of actions, whereas a plan's actions might be only partially ordered. We can still compute a lower bound on the plan's success, however, by considering the minimum over all total orders consistent with the plan's orderings. This policy is conservative in that it computes the best probability that can be expected from *every* total order. The long version of this paper discusses these issues in more detail.

Example. We now illustrate how the FORWARD plan assessment algorithm computes the success probability for the plan in Fig. 3. FORWARD starts with the input distribution over initial states, $\tilde{s}_I$, and computes the following distribution over final states (where $\mathcal{A} = \langle \text{paint}, \text{pickup} \rangle$ is the plan's action sequence):

$$
\begin{aligned}
P[\{GD, HB, GC, BP\} \mid \tilde{s}_I, \mathcal{A}] &= 0.5985 \\
P[\{\overline{GD}, HB, GC, BP\} \mid \tilde{s}_I, \mathcal{A}] &= 0.135 \\
P[\{GD, HB, \overline{GC}, BP\} \mid \tilde{s}_I, \mathcal{A}] &= 0.0665 \\
P[\{\overline{GD}, HB, \overline{GC}, BP\} \mid \tilde{s}_I, \mathcal{A}] &= 0.015 \\
P[\{GD, \overline{HB}, GC, BP\} \mid \tilde{s}_I, \mathcal{A}] &= 0.0315 \\
P[\{\overline{GD}, \overline{HB}, GC, BP\} \mid \tilde{s}_I, \mathcal{A}] &= 0.135 \\
P[\{GD, \overline{HB}, \overline{GC}, BP\} \mid \tilde{s}_I, \mathcal{A}] &= 0.0035 \\
P[\{\overline{GD}, \overline{HB}, \overline{GC}, BP\} \mid \tilde{s}_I, \mathcal{A}] &= 0.015
\end{aligned}
$$

The probability of the goal expression is then computed by summing over those states in which the goal holds. $\mathcal{G} = \{HB, GC, BP\}$ is true in the first two states, so we have $P[\mathcal{G} \mid \tilde{s}_I, \mathcal{A}] = 0.5985 + 0.135 = 0.7335$.

Formal Properties

A least-commitment planner produces as output a partial order over actions. Such a planner is *sound* if every consistent total order of these actions is a solution to the input problem. The planner is *complete* if it always returns a solution plan if such a plan exists. In the longer paper we prove that BURIDAN is both sound and complete.

---

[3] We ignore SNLP's *separation* refinement, since it applies only to actions with variables.

[4] In this section we discuss one simple assessment strategy; later we introduce a variety of more complicated algorithms.

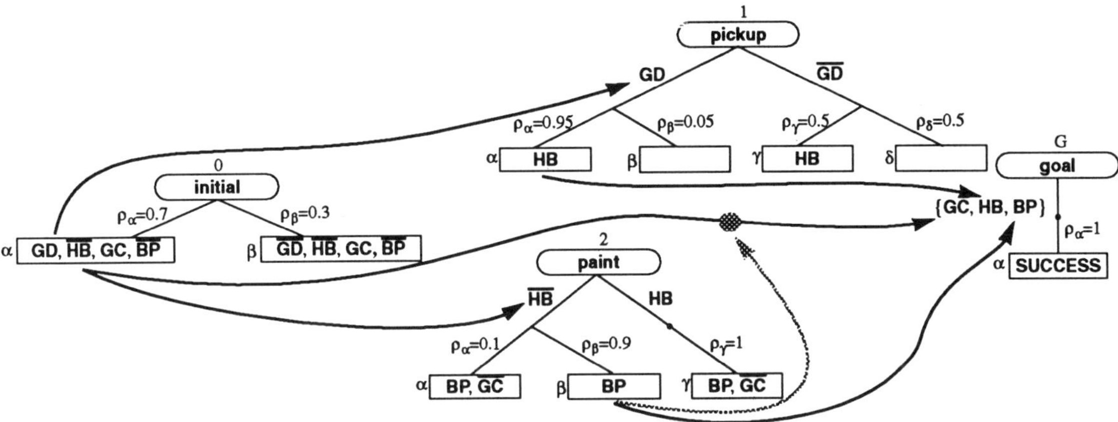

Figure 3: An partial solution to the example problem. Gray arrows indicate threats resolved by confrontation.

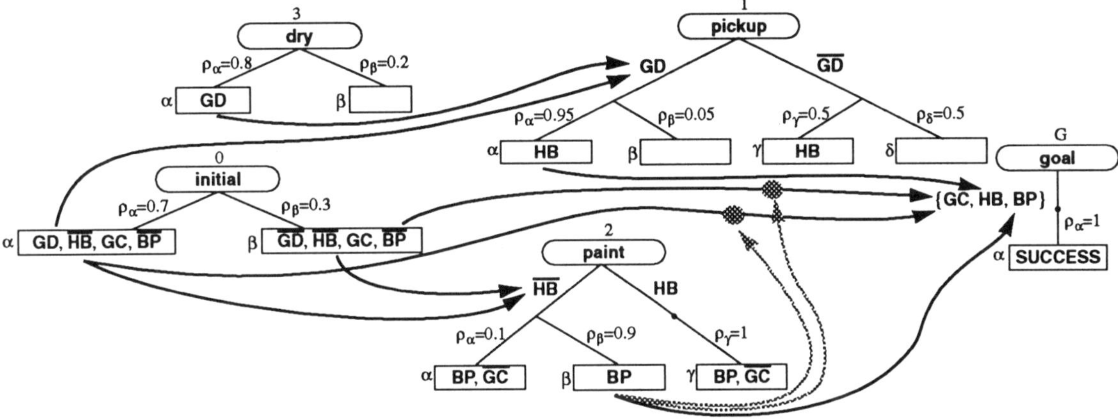

Figure 4: A plan that is sufficiently likely to succeed.

Efficient Plan Assessment

The FORWARD assessment strategy, while simple, can be quite inefficient, since the number of states with nonzero probability can grow exponentially with the length of the plan. This inefficiency motivates a second focus of our research, an exploration of alternative assessment algorithms. Since the general plan assessment problem is NP-hard (Chapman 1987; Cooper 1990) we cannot expect to produce an assessment algorithm that runs efficiently on every problem in every domain. However, by exploiting the structure of the actions, goals and state space, we can sometimes realize tremendous efficiency gains. We have implemented three alternative plan assessment algorithms.

While the size of the state distribution may grow exponentially, in general not all of the distinctions between the different states will be relevant to whether the goal is true. So one alternative assessment strategy, called QUERY, tries to divide states into subsets based on the truth of the goal. At best QUERY needs to reason about only two subsets of states: those in which the goal is true and those in which it is false.

Rather than manipulating states explicitly, assessment algorithms can reason directly about the propo-

sitions that comprise the states. Thus the third assessment algorithm, NETWORK, translates the action descriptions into a probabilistic network, each node of which corresponds to a single proposition at some point during the execution of the plan. NETWORK then solves this network using standard propagation techniques.

The resulting network tends to be more complicated than necessary, however, since it explicitly includes "persistence" links encoding the fact that a literal remains unchanged across the execution of an action that neither adds nor deletes it. But recall that persistence assumptions are already stored in a plan's causal-link structures: an unthreatened link is a guarantee that the link's proposition will persist from the time it is produced until it is consumed. This motivates a fourth algorithm, REVERSE, that computes a plan's success probability by manipulating the plan's causal link structure directly.

The longer version of this paper describes these algorithms in detail. Analysis of these algorithms shows no clear winner: in each case we can construct domains and problems in which one algorithm consistently outperforms the other.

Related Work and Conclusions

(Mansell 1993) and (Goldman & Boddy 1994) offer alternative approaches to applying classical planning algorithms to probabilistic action and state models.

(Dean *et al.* 1993), (Farley 1983), and (Koenig 1992) use fully observable Markov processes to model the planning problem. These systems generate an *execution policy*, a specification of what action the agent should perform in every world state, and assume that the agent is provided with complete and accurate information about the world state. BURIDAN produces a *plan*, a sequence of steps that is executed without examining the world at execution time, and assumes the agent will be provided with *no* additional information at execution time. A recent extension to BURIDAN, (Draper, Hanks, & Weld 1994a; 1994b), strikes a middle ground: the representation allows actions that provide possibly inaccurate information about the world at execution time, and actions in a plan can be executed contingent on the information provided by previous steps.

Work in decision science has dealt with planning problems (see (Dean & Wellman 1991, Chap. 7) for an introduction), but it has focused on solving a given probabilistic model whereas our algorithm interleaves the process of constructing and evaluating solutions. But see (Breese 1992) for recent work on model-building issues.

(Haddawy & Hanks 1992; 1993) motivate building a planner like BURIDAN, exploring the connection between building plans that probably satisfy goals and plans that are optimal in the sense of maximizing expected utility.

Although planning with conditional effects is not the primary focus of our work, BURIDAN also generalizes work on planning with deterministic conditional effects, *e.g.* in (Collins & Pryor 1992; Penberthy & Weld 1992). A deterministic form of confrontation is used in UCPOP (Penberthy & Weld 1992).

The BURIDAN planner integrates a probabilistic semantics for action with classical least-commitment planning techniques. BURIDAN accepts probabilistic information about the problem's initial state, and manipulates actions with conditional and probabilistic effects.

Our planner is fully implemented in Common Lisp and has been tested on many examples. BURIDAN takes about 4.5 seconds to find a solution to the problem presented in this paper. Send mail to *bug-buridan@cs.washington.edu* for information about BURIDAN source code.

References

Breese, J. 1992. Construction of belief and decision networks. *Computational Intelligence* 8(4).

Chapman, D. 1987. Planning for conjunctive goals. *Artificial Intelligence* 32(3):333–377.

Collins, G., and Pryor, L. 1992. Achieving the functionality of filter conditions in a partial order planner. In *Proc. 10th Nat. Conf. on A.I.*

Cooper, G. 1990. The computational complexity of probabilistic inference using bayesian belief networks. *Artificial Intelligence* 42.

Dean, T., and Wellman, M. 1991. *Planning and Control.* Morgan Kaufmann.

Dean, T., Kaelbling, L., Kirman, J., and Nicholson, A. 1993. Planning with deadlines in stochastic domains. In *Proc. 11th Nat. Conf. on A.I.*

Draper, D., Hanks, S., and Weld, D. 1994a. A probabilistic model of action for least-commitment planning with information gathering. In *Proc., Uncertainty in AI.* Submitted.

Draper, D., Hanks, S., and Weld, D. 1994b. Probabilistic planning with information gathering and contingent execution. In *Proc. 2nd Int. Conf. on A.I. Planning Systems.*

Farley, A. 1983. A Probabilistic Model for Uncertain Problem Solving. *IEEE Transactions on Systems, Man, and Cybernetics* 13(4).

Goldman, R. P., and Boddy, M. S. 1994. Epsilon-safe planning. forthcoming.

Haddawy, P., and Hanks, S. 1992. Representations for Decision-Theoretic Planning: Utility Functions for Dealine Goals. In *Proc. 3rd Int. Conf. on Principles of Knowledge Representation and Reasoning.*

Haddawy, P., and Hanks, S. 1993. Utility Models for Goal-Directed Decision-Theoretic Planners. Technical Report 93–06–04, Univ. of Washington, Dept. of Computer Science and Engineering. Submitted to *Artificial Intelligence.* Available via FTP from pub/ai/ at cs.washington.edu.

Hanks, S. 1990. Practical temporal projection. In *Proc. 8th Nat. Conf. on A.I.*, 158–163.

Hanks, S. 1993. Modeling a Dynamic and Uncertain World II: Action Representation and Plan Evaluation. Technical report, Univ. of Washington, Dept. of Computer Science and Engineering.

Koenig, S. 1992. Optimal probabilistic and decision-theoretic planning using markovian decision theory. UCB/CSD 92/685, Berkeley.

Kushmerick, N., Hanks, S., and Weld, D. 1993. An Algorithm for Probabilistic Planning. Technical Report 93-06-03, Univ. of Washington, Dept. of Computer Science and Engineering. To appear in *Artificial Intelligence.* Available via FTP from pub/ai/ at cs.washington.edu.

Mansell, T. 1993. A method for planning given uncertain and incomplete information. In *Proc. 9th Conf. on Uncertainty in Artifical Intelligence.*

McAllester, D., and Rosenblitt, D. 1991. Systematic nonlinear planning. In *Proc. 9th Nat. Conf. on A.I.*, 634–639.

Penberthy, J., and Weld, D. 1992. UCPOP: A sound, complete, partial order planner for ADL. In *Proc. 3rd Int. Conf. on Principles of Knowledge Representation and Reasoning*, 103–114. Available via FTP from pub/ai/ at cs.washington.edu.

Control Strategies for a Stochastic Planner *

Jonathan Tash
Group in Logic and the Methodology of Science
University of California
Berkeley, CA 94720
tash@math.berkeley.edu

Stuart Russell
Computer Science Division
University of California
Berkeley, CA 94720
russell@cs.berkeley.edu

Abstract

We present new algorithms for local planning over Markov decision processes. The *base-level* algorithm possesses several interesting features for control of computation, based on selecting computations according to their expected benefit to decision quality. The algorithms are shown to expand the agent's knowledge where the world warrants it, with appropriate responsiveness to time pressure and randomness. We then develop an *introspective* algorithm, using an internal representation of what computational work has already been done. This strategy extends the agent's knowledge base where warranted by the agent's world model and the agent's knowledge of the work already put into various parts of this model. It also enables the agent to act so as to take advantage of the computational savings inherent in staying in known parts of the state space. The control flexibility provided by this strategy, by incorporating natural problem-solving methods, directs computational effort towards where it's needed better than previous approaches, providing greater hopes for scalability to large domains.

Introduction

Planning under uncertainty is a good domain for investigating strategies for controlling the computational expenditures of a planner, because decision theory provides a language for expressing the sorts of tradeoffs between plan quality and solution time that a good control strategy should capture. This paper presents a planning methodology suitable for domains representable as a Markov decision process (as in (Koenig 1992)), and shows how such a methodology can incorporate several natural control strategies.

In this model, the problem-solving agent is in a world consisting of a finite, discrete set of states, and can identify the current one. In any given state, the agent has available to it a set of actions it can take, and for a given action choice, it knows the transition probabilities to other states. In addition, it has some reward function giving the immediate value of being in any particular state. For example, an agent attempting to reach a goal state as quickly as possible might

assign the goal state a reward of 0 and all other states a reward of -1. Problems using such a reward function include the path-planning problem on a grid with obstacles and imperfect motor control, and the ubiquitous 8-puzzle, but with random errors associated with actions. (The model can also handle problems having several stop states of different values.) In this domain, a plan takes the form of a policy assigning to each state an action choice. The agent tries to choose a policy maximizing its cumulative reward. (For domains involving unbounded time, it is common to discount future gains by an amount exponential in time to avoid infinite utilities.)

The model is enriched by the inclusion of a penalty for deliberation time. The agent alternates between computing better policies and acting, and its cumulative reward is reduced as time is spent computing. This enrichment requires modification of the classical methods of operations research when faced with large domains.

The next section elaborates a planning system which accounts for the expense of computing by making tradeoffs between computation time and policy quality. The system uses local computation techniques resembling ones presented in (Dean *et al.* 1993) and (Thiébaux *et al.* 1994), but allows for more extensive use of heuristic knowledge and is amenable to a proof of convergence to optimality. In addition, our analysis provides a well-founded strategy for making decisions relevant to the control of the expensive computations, eliminating reliance on trial-and-error determination of good control procedures. This strategy is shown to have several interesting properties, such as providing appropriate responsiveness to increased time pressure and to increased randomness in the world.

We then discuss an extension to this system which allows for more refined control of the computational effort expended by the planner. This new system adds to the planner a representation of the computational effort it has already spent on various parts of the problem, enabling the planner to apply its knowledge of what it already knows about to its considerations of the value of its computational activities. Such a planner's control strategy has several new properties, counterparts to the more introspective aspects of natural problem-solving activity. These include the ability to direct its computational efforts according to where they

---

*This research was supported by NASA JPL, and by NSF awards IRI-9058427 (PYI) & IRI-9211512.

will have the most impact on current considerations, taking into account not only the planner's model of the world but its model of its knowledge of the world. Another interesting property is the ability of the planner to act so as to remain in the better known parts of the state space when appropriate, *even when its knowledge of the world suggests the existence of better solutions elsewhere*, in order to save on the required computational effort.

More subtle and complex computational control strategies such as these exact a certain cost in overhead, but the increased responsiveness they provide to internal and external environmental factors make them of high value in the development of planning systems potentially scalable to large domains for which classical methods are intractable. This paper demonstrates how careful decision-theoretic reasoning and use of a meta-level control methodology can provide strategies with many of the characteristics of natural problem-solving activity.

The Base-Level Planner

A well-known algorithm exists for finding an optimal policy for Markov decision processes, the *policy iteration* algorithm of Howard (1960). This algorithm starts with an arbitrary policy and incrementally improves the action choices assigned to each state until it reaches an optimal policy. This algorithm would provide an optimal planner if its computational costs for large problems were not so high. However, if the agent must pay a cost for the time it spends computing its plan, running policy iteration on the entire problem space might not be a good strategy, as each iteration of the algorithm requires solving a set of linear equations whose size is on the order of the plan space.

We will therefore consider a planner doing more limited computation before each move. We associate with each state a value, initialized by heuristic information, estimating the distance, and hence the expected cumulative reward, to the goal. (In this paper, we will use value and cost interchangeably, modulo a sign change.) For path-planning and the 8-puzzle, there is a natural underestimate of this distance, the Manhattan distance to the goal, which can be initially assigned to each state. (The Manhattan distance assigns to each position of the path-planning problem its distance from the goal if there were no obstacles or motor errors, and similarly assigns each state of the eight puzzle the sum of the distances each piece would travel to its goal position if it could move without error or obstruction by other pieces.) These value estimates are improved with each computation, and can be maintained across problem-solving episodes (differing possibly in initial state but not in reward function) for cumulative performance improvements. In each such episode, the planner alternately computes to improve the value estimates, and chooses moves using these estimates. (This model differs from those considered by Dean *et al.* (1993), where computation is done either prior to or concurrently with action, rather than interspersed with action. Prior and concurrent deliberation models do not provide the agent with sufficient flexibility in deliberation scheduling to allow for formulation of dynamic tradeoffs

between computation time and action quality to the same extent.)

Policy Iteration

Since our algorithm will be based on policy iteration, let us describe it for the restricted case we are interested in, goal-directed planning problems. Following Koenig (1992), we define, given a particular policy, an ergodic set to be a minimal set of states which, once entered, are never left. In general, goal states will be the ergodic sets. Any policy which has an ergodic set which does not consist of a single state could lead the agent to performing an infinite loop, which we will take to be against the agent's interests (for the simple goal-directed utility function described above, such a plan would have maximal negative utility). We will therefore only consider plans for which the agent is always eventually absorbed by some ergodic state. If we start with such a plan, and use a goal-directed utility function, then policy iteration will never generate a plan violating this since it always improves on the current plan.

For such plans, we can define the utility as the expected cumulative reward of the agent (without time discounting). Let us introduce for each state x a variable V_x representing the expected future value for an agent starting in that state and using that plan. These value variables are related by the fact that the value of state x is equal to the expected value of the states it will reach in the next step, plus the reward of being in state x (-1 for the goal-directed utility function):

$$V_x = \sum_y P\left(y|a_x, x\right) V_y - 1 \qquad (1)$$

where $P\left(y|a_x, x\right)$ is the probability of reaching state y if action a_x is taken in state x. Finally, absorbing states are assigned their intrinsic values. This gives a set of simultaneous equations that can be solved by standard methods. Using the goal-directed utility function above, these values represent the expected number of state transitions between the agent and its goal using the current plan.

Policy iteration involves computing the state values for the current plan, and then choosing a new action a for each state which maximizes the expected value of the state reached by the action.

$$a = \arg\max_{a'} \sum_y P\left(y|a'x\right) V_y \qquad (2)$$

If no action improves the expected value, the old choice is maintained (to prevent oscillation between equal-value policies). This is iterated until no new actions are assigned. Each iteration returns a plan of strictly greater value, and the algorithm is guaranteed to converge on the optimal policy. (For the general case involving larger ergodic sets, there is a similar, but slightly more complicated algorithm).

Local Computation

For an agent under time pressure, policy iteration on the entire state space is too expensive. Our algorithms therefore consider only a neighborhood (the *envelope*) of the current

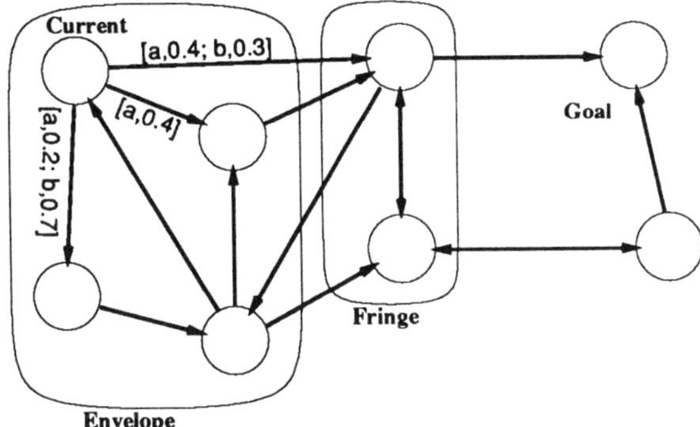

Figure 1: **Markov decision process with local envelope. Actions a, b cause transitions with the probabilities indicated on the arcs.**

state in state space, fixing the values of the surrounding states (the envelope's *fringe*) at their current estimates, and doing policy iteration on the envelope given those values (Fig. 1). The planner starts with an initial policy and heuristic values for the states, and alternates among determining an appropriate envelope, updating its policy and value estimates on this envelope using the Local Policy Iteration Algorithm, and acting according to its current policy. This strategy is similar to (but was developed independently of) those described in the papers of (Dean *et al.* 1993) and (Thiébaux *et al.* 1994); however, its use of estimated values on non-envelope states provides important additional information for determining envelope action choices, allowing for meaningful action choices to be made before a path to the goal is found, and summarizing previous computational effort outside the current envelope. The resulting expected costs of the envelope states are then their expected distance to the fringe plus the fringe's estimated distance to the goal. The cost of time is incorporated into the methods for determining an envelope and choosing when to commit to an action, discussed below.

Local Policy Iteration Algorithm

1. **Fix** values of fringe states at their current estimates, and **assign** stop states their reward.

2. **Assign** an action a to each remaining envelope state x.

3. **Solve** the set of simultaneous equations (1) for the values V_x of these states.

4. **Choose** new best actions a for these states using Eq. (2).

5. **If** any action assignment has changed, **go to** 3.

6. **Return** new value estimates and actions for these states.

Because we store value estimates permanently with each state, we can prove that:

- The value stored in each state approaches the true minimum goal distance and the corresponding plan approaches the optimum as the planner faces (possibly multiple) problem-solving episodes.

To be more specific, let us consider a planner that starts with a heuristic which does not overestimate the expected cost of any state (and gives each non-goal state a cost of at least 1, such as the Manhattan distance), and uses the goal-directed utility function. Before each action, it does at least some computation, and runs policy iteration on its chosen envelope to completion. Then, because policy iteration gives each envelope state a cost of the true expected distance to the fringe plus the estimated fringe distance to goal, by induction no state cost estimate can ever exceed the true distance. For a heuristic such as the Manhattan distance, where neighbors in state space have heuristics differing by 1, computation can only increase the estimated cost of a state. In the worst case of an uninformative heuristic of all 1's, this is also the case. Any further information can only improve performance. No values other than the correct ones are stable; there will in all other cases be some state having a lowest action cost other than 1 plus the expected cost of its neighbors and when it is visited it will be changed. So, in the worst case, values can only go up, and will continue to do so until the correct estimates are reached.

Control of Computation

Because the agent cannot completely predict the results of its actions, but can determine them once action has been taken, it gains information by acting. The situation differs therefore from that faced in deterministic problem-solving, where the computational effort demanded of the agent is independent of when it chooses to execute its actions. Because knowing the results of an action reduces the possibilities necessary to consider later, acting early can save computational effort, and this has to be weighed against the potential improvement in action quality to be gained by delaying for further deliberation. This leads to consideration of the potential utility gain afforded by further computation, which is measured by the amount one expects one's final action choice to be better than one's current choice (as elucidated in (Russell & Wefald 1991)).

Our computational strategy provides a hill-climbing algorithm, maintaining only one plan at a time and considering local changes for its possible improvement. (Standard tree representations for problem solving are too cumbersome in stochastic domains where a state can be visited multiple times by the same plan.) Therefore, when trying to measure the potential gain of further computation, it is only feasible to compare the current plan to possibilities generated by a few local changes to the current plan. Because the action choice in the current state is of the greatest immediate importance, we will consider plans differing from the current one only by this action choice for the purpose of deciding whether and how to continue computation.

Intermediate results in our version of the policy iteration algorithm readily provide the probability $P\left(f|y\right)$ of reaching any given fringe state f first from any given envelope state y by following the current plan. Therefore, when provided with an estimate σ_f of how much a fringe state's estimated value is likely to vary as a result of further computation, we can easily determine the resulting value variance $\sigma_{y|f}$ for any envelope state y if the current plan is kept.

$$\sigma_{y|f} = P\left(f|y\right)\sigma_f \qquad (3)$$

If variance estimates are not available (or all assumed to be the same), the fringe state most likely to be reached first from a given envelope state has the greatest potential impact on that state's value. Both (Dean *et al.* 1993) and (Thiébaux *et al.* 1994) therefore choose the fringe state most likely to be reached first from the current state as the best candidate for further envelope expansion. However, the values of the current state's neighbors y have the greatest impact on the action to be chosen in the current state x, so the fringe state f whose variance is most likely to affect the current action choice (through the neighbors' values) is the best one to expand. The potential gain G_{fx} in expanding it is how much better than the current action the ultimately chosen action is expected to be.

$$G_{fx} = \max_{a'}\left[\sum_y P\left(y|a'x\right)\left(V_y + \sigma_{y|f}\right) - 1\right] - \left[V_x + \sigma_{x|f}\right]$$

$$(4)$$

(This is actually an underestimate of the value of expanding a fringe state, because it ignores indirect improvements to the action choice resulting from changes in other states' action choices; accounting for these effects is hindered by our localized plan representation. The definition of G_{fx} could also be generalized by integrating over a distribution for σ_f instead of using a point estimate.) We thus have an analytic strategy for choosing envelope expansions (unlike the trial and error learning approach of (Dean *et al.* 1993)), and expand the envelope according to impact on action choice quality.

The amount of variance expected of a fringe state is of course a function of the amount of computation done on a neighborhood of it, and the time cost of the computation similarly grows with amount. The agent should do computation in the amount determined by optimizing the difference between expected gain and time cost. If the agent is only given the choice between doing a fixed size computation or not (with determined values for time cost and expected value variance), the decision hinges on a comparison of expected action quality gain to a fixed cut-off.

Let us summarize the computational control structure. After an action, the agent determines its current state (which is its initial envelope) and grows the envelope by moving fringe states into it whose expected contribution to action choice quality is highest. At occasional intervals (e.g. after every five additions) policy iteration is run on the envelope. This continues until the best fringe state fails to offer an expected gain greater than the cost of policy iterating on the expanded envelope, at which point policy iteration is run a last time, and the agent takes the action from its current state which leads to the highest expected resulting state value.

Even using a simple, uniform variance estimate (all σ_f's the same), the algorithm has several interesting properties. Because envelope expansion is determined by a direct comparison between expected gain and computational time cost (Line 7), any increase in the cost associated with time spent

---

The Base-Level Planning Algorithm

1. **Initialize** value V_x of all states x using the heuristic (can be done as value becomes needed), and **initialize** current-state.

2. envelope $\leftarrow$ current-state.

3. fringe $\leftarrow$ neighbors of current-state.

4. more-comp $\leftarrow$ yes.

5. **For** $i = 1$ **to** number-of-envelope-expansions-per-policy-iteration (e.g. something like 5)

6.   **do** best-fringe $f \leftarrow \arg\max_{f' \in fringe} G_{f',current\text{-}state}$ (determining G by Eq. (4))

7.   **If** $G_{f,current\text{-}state} >$ time-cost(size(envelope))

8.   **do** envelope $\leftarrow$ envelope $\cup$ best-fringe

9.   fringe $\leftarrow$ neighbors of envelope

10.   **else do** more-comp $\leftarrow$ no.

11. **Run Local Policy Iteration Algorithm** on envelope to **update** V_x for non-ergodic envelope states x.

12. **If** more-comp = yes **then go to** 5.

13. **Do action** a as recommended by Eq. (2) for current-state: current-state $\leftarrow$ result of action.

14. **Unless** current-state is a stop state, **go to** 2.

on computation, relative to the unit cost of physical action, increases the potential value gain a computational plan improvement must achieve in order to be done. Therefore,

- The planner automatically adjusts the time spent in look-ahead vs. physical exploration in response to time pressure.

  Boundary case: As time cost $\rightarrow 0$, the algorithm increases envelope size if any action could be better than the present one.

  Boundary case: As time cost $\rightarrow \infty$, the algorithm updates only the current-state value between moves, the minimum necessary to guarantee convergence to optimal plans.

This behavior follows analytically from the algorithm definition. We have shown empirically that an agent will complete a run with fewer computational time steps, at the expense of a longer path, when the cost of time is high. Fig. 2 shows the tradeoffs obtained when running the algorithm on navigation domains like that shown in Fig. 4. The points are labeled with the cost assigned to one time step, in move counts. Policy iteration on an envelope of size n was assessed n^3 time steps. The times and moves were accumulated over a set of 72 runs over various domains using a probability of random action failure of 0.1, and a σ_f of -1.0.

Also, in a domain with greater randomness in action results, the ability to predict which fringe state an agent will hit first (and hence the highest fringe probability) is lowered, reducing the expected effect of further computation on action choice quality.

- The agent will respond to greater randomness by expending less effort on prediction.

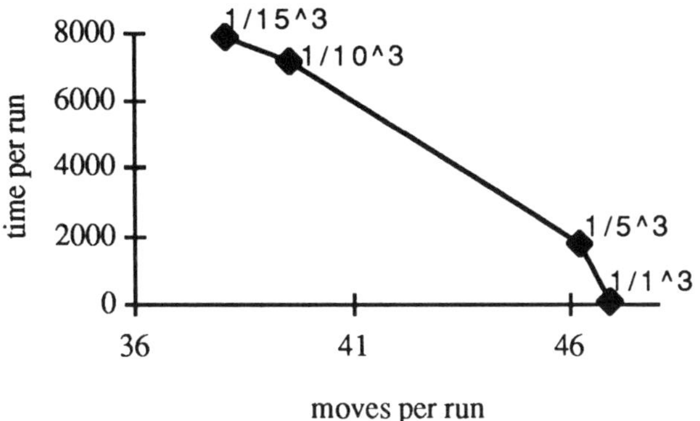

Figure 2: **Responsiveness of the Base-Level Planning Algorithm to the cost of time**

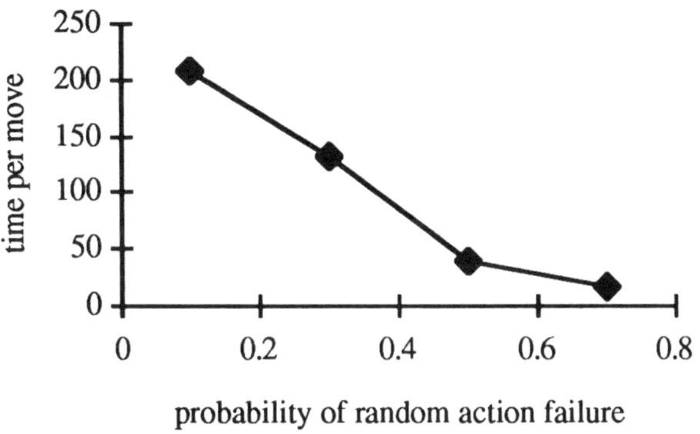

Figure 3: **Responsiveness of the Base-Level Planning Algorithm to randomness in the environment**

Boundary case: As transitions become totally random, the algorithm updates only the current-state value.

This follows because as the $P(y|a'x)$ become uniform in a', the $\max_{a'}$ in Eq. (4) cannot differ much from the value for a, forcing G_{fx} towards 0. This behavior is demonstrated for the navigational domain in Fig. 3 (run as above, using the lowest time cost).

The Introspective Planner

A planner implementing the system described so far will exhibit appropriate responsiveness to several aspects of its environment in controlling its computational effort. It will move where its model of the world indicates a shortest path, and it will devote its computations to where they will have greatest impact on its action choices according to its world model. However, this system does not incorporate control strategies making use of the agent's knowledge of what it knows. Such strategies would allow the agent to, for example, expend computational effort where its knowledge most needs improving, and move along well-known (albeit perhaps suboptimal) paths in order to avoid extensive computation. A planning agent able to follow such strategies can be called *introspective*, because its decisions are based

not only on its knowledge of the world, but on its knowledge about its knowledge of the world.

Introspective planning techniques are an extension of common metalevel control techniques (discussed in, for example, (Russell & Wefald 1991)). Computations such as those performed by the base-level system described above are controlled somewhat like physical actions by a higher level controller. This architecture can be iterated, getting higher level controllers allowing for deeper forms of introspection. This section will limit discussion to a minimal extension of the base-level system, which will be enough to express the introspective strategies mentioned above.

Representation of Computational Knowledge

In order to use introspective knowledge, the planner needs some representation of what base-level computational work has been performed. We will extend the representation of each state to include a parameter indicating how much computational effort has been expended in updating the estimated value of that state. How best to characterize this effort is not obvious, but a parameter such as the sum of the time costs of each policy-iterated envelope which included the state will certainly provide useful information. We will call such a parameter a *knowledge heuristic k* to distinguish it from the *physical heuristic p* estimating minimal distance to the goal. While more detailed representations are obviously desirable, knowledge heuristics turn out to be quite effective.

One use for the knowledge heuristic is for conditioning the estimate of expected variance of a state's physical heuristic with further computation. The amount of computation previously done on a state is highly relevant to the expected consequences of further computation. For example, repeating computations done previously will make no change to the physical heuristic. One expects that as k grows for a given fringe state f, σ_f will decrease. It follows from Eqs. (1), (3) and (4) that $G_{fx} \leq \sigma_f$, so

- The planner's choice of envelope expansion is sensitive to its previous computational efforts in that direction.

  Boundary case: As $k \to \infty$, $\sigma_f \to 0$, so $G_{fx} \to 0$ and the algorithm does not expand f.

A particular variance estimate, represented as a function of the knowledge heuristic, is discussed in the Experimental Results section below. Using these variance estimates as described above for deciding where and whether to expend further computational effort will enable the system's computational efforts to focus more on where its knowledge is in greatest need of improvement.

Total State Value

The introspective planner works by associating with states a value which reflects both estimated action costs *and computational costs* to reach the goal. This value will fill many of the roles filled by the physical heuristic for the base-level system, allowing for the tradeoffs between these costs desired of an introspective agent. Which roles this total value can fill are constrained by coherence requirements which we will analyze below.

The total value $T(k, p)$ associated with each state will be a function of the two heuristics. It should estimate the sum of the remaining distance and computational costs to the goal. An example of such a function is discussed in the Experimental Results section. Note that if the total cost takes on the value of the physical heuristic, the system's decisions will remain independent of its knowledge about previous computational effort, and the base-level system behavior will be reproduced.

Knowledge of a total cost function is of use to the agent in places where it captures the criteria relevant to control decisions better than the physical heuristic alone. For example, when the agent decides to act, it should choose the action a leading to the lowest expected total cost among its neighbors y, rather than minimizing the expected resulting physical heuristic.

$$a = \arg\max_{a'} \sum_{y} P\left(y|a'x\right) T\left(k_y, p_y\right) \qquad (5)$$

Such an action minimizes the remaining total cost to goal. Because the total cost reflects computational costs,

- The agent's action choices reflect the value of its knowledge of the world.

    Boundary case: As time pressure increases, $T(k, p)$ becomes dominated by computation costs, so the agent will act to minimize future computation at the expense of distance.

This behavior is exhibited experimentally below.

Another point is that whereas the physical heuristic is an (under)estimate of the true ("God's-eye-view") minimal distance to goal, the total cost function can model the physical distance that will be realized by the agent's *actual* control strategy, so

- The agent's action choices are based on the realizable (not theoretically minimal) distance to goal.

This captures an important distinction, one used in (Baum 1992) to improve game playing performance. (Of course, over repeated trials, these distances will converge.)

This change in action choice criteria should be reflected in the criteria used for choosing computations as well. The impact of expected physical heuristic variance in a fringe state can be propagated to the current state's neighbors as before, where its effect on the neighbors' total value can be determined by finding the total cost associated with the varied physical heuristic and the knowledge heuristic which would result from doing the computation. These values are then used to evaluate the worth of the current-state actions, so that the expected gain in action quality can be computed.

$$
\begin{aligned}
G_{fx} = & \max_{a'} \left[\sum_{y} P\left(y|a'x\right) T\left(k_{y,\ comp}^{\ post}, p_y + \sigma_{y|f}\right) \right] \\
& - \left[\sum_{y} P\left(y|ax\right) T\left(k_y, p_y + \sigma_{y|f}\right) \right] \qquad (6)
\end{aligned}
$$

The Introspective Planning Algorithm

Modify The Base-Level Planning Algorithm as follows:

  (a) **Replace** Eq. (2) with Eq. (5) **in Line 13.**
  (b) **Replace** Eq. (4) with Eq. (6) **in Line 6.**
  (c) **Replace** V_x with p_x **in Lines** 1 **and** 11.
  (d) **Add** 1a. **Initialize** $\sigma_f(k, p)$ and $T(k, p)$.
  (e) **Add** 11a. **Update** k for all states in envelope.
  (f) **Add** learning steps to **Update** $\sigma_f(k, p)$ and $T(k, p)$.

Note that the primary computational effort, the one estimated by the knowledge heuristic and hence used for conditioning the total value function, is still that devoted towards updating the physical heuristic using policy iteration on local envelopes. One might assume that the total value should replace the physical heuristic in these computations, but such an approach would lead to several problems. For one, the relation between the total values of neighboring states is not as simple as that for physical distances. The immediate physical reward of moving to a state is just -1, but the one-move total reward depends on the amount of computation done as well. Policy iteration minimizes cumulative costs using fixed transition costs; it would be inconsistent to apply it when the transition costs vary as a function of using policy iteration itself. Such concerns force a system to differentiate between the computational efforts it is trying to control and those used in this control process.

Experimental Results

The Introspective Planning Algorithm has been implemented and tested on the randomized 8-puzzle with a probability of random action failure of 0.2 and a time step cost of $1/10^3$. Remaining time cost to goal and fringe variance were assumed to drop inversely with the knowledge heuristic. All runs were conducted with random initial states of distance about 10 from the goal. An initial set of 80 runs was conducted to learn good heuristics near the goal and to estimate the numerical coefficients (using the temporal difference learning methods of (Sutton 1988)) in the equations for variance and total value:

$$\sigma_f = -\frac{1}{2(10k + 1)} \qquad (7)$$

$$T(k, p) = -p - \frac{p/3}{\frac{3k}{p} + 1} \qquad (8)$$

(The time cost term of $T(k, p)$ was assumed to grow linearly with p at $k = 0$, and $\partial T/\partial k|_{k=0} = 1$ so computational time expenditures reduce future costs as expected.)

Next, 40 runs each of the Base-Level Planning Algorithm (using $\sigma_f = -1/4$, as a typical value for k was 0.1) and the Introspective Planning Algorithm were conducted. Because of the possibility of random action failure, the agent occasionally moves away from the goal (and hence away from the well-explored portion of the state space). Such actions often take the agent to states where following the minimal physical heuristic leads in a direction away from the goal, towards an artificial minimum in the Manhattan distance. An agent following such a path will have a long solution route to the goal (more than 40 moves, instead of ~13). This occurred for the Base-Level Planning Algorithm in 8 of its 40 runs. Because introspection provides a force towards staying in the explored portion of the state space, the Introspective Planning Algorithm was only tempted by a false minimum in 1 of its 40 runs.

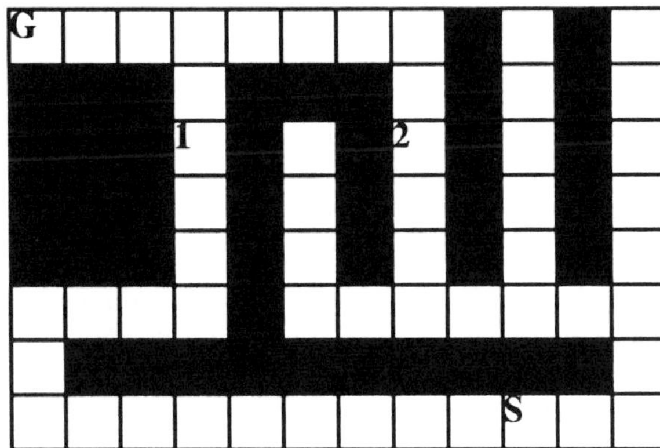

Figure 4: **Navigation Domain.**
Agent is to move from start (S) to goal (G).
Note that route 1 is longer than route 2 but a move towards 1 from S reduces the Manhattan distance heuristic more.

The Introspective algorithm has also been tested on the navigational domain shown in Fig. 4, with a random action failure probability of 0.05. On its first run, the agent takes route 1 to the goal, as moving left from the start state most reduces its estimated physical distance. As it continues to take route 1, it improves this estimate towards the true physical distance, which is larger than its estimate of the physical distance to the right of the start state. The Base-Level algorithm therefore quickly begins moving right, exploring the upper right region and discovering the shorter route 2. If the cost of computation time is high, however, the Introspective algorithm will continue to take the known route 1 so as to avoid the computational burden involved in exploring the unknown upper right region, as shown in Table 1.

Time Cost:	$1/15^3$	$1/2^3$
Base-Level	2.7	2.3
Introspective	2.0	7.0

Table 1: **Average number of runs before taking route 2**

Conclusions

This paper has extended classical methods for determining good policies for Markov decision processes by adding explicit consideration of the cost of the time spent in computing policies. The method bears a general resemblance to other localized extensions of dynamic programming, such as Incremental Dynamic Programming (Sutton 1991) and

the work of (Dean *et al.* 1993) and (Thiébaux *et al.* 1994), but adds a new analysis of the factors appropriate for envelope determination: computational effort is put where it will make the most difference to quality of action choice, and is expended only so long as it will make a significant difference to the next action choice. This analysis is then extended to take advantage of information the agent can accumulate about its previous expenditures of computational effort. The resulting control strategy exhibits many interesting behaviors, mirroring considerations that would be of importance to human problem-solvers.

The planner makes good use of heuristic information about the problem space. If the heuristic underestimates costs, it provides a force for (simulated) state space exploration when the computational cost is not too expensive. Under such conditions, one can guarantee convergence to an optimal plan over repeated trials. The methodology also provides for concise storage (in the form of two heuristic values for each state) of the results of previous planning efforts for use in future encounters with the same state space region, and the planner has the anytime property of (Dean & Boddy 1988) in that its policy improves as a function of the time it has had to compute.

The overhead incurred by the proposed control mechanisms grows more slowly with computation size than the cost of policy iteration, so the computational savings for large spaces are not swamped by control costs.

The planner's computation and action choices are responsive to time pressure and randomness, as well as to the status of the agent's current knowledge and the possibilities and costs of changing it. The resulting flexibility of the planner's control structure enables better focusing of computational effort, providing features needed in planners for use in environments too large for the more extensive computations required by conventional methods.

References

Baum, E. B. 1992. On optimal game tree propagation for imperfect players. In *AAAI-92*, 507–512.

Dean, T., and Boddy, M. 1988. An analysis of time-dependent planning. In *AAAI-88*, 49–54.

Dean, T.; Kaelbling, L. P.; Kirman, J.; and Nicholson, A. 1993. Deliberation scheduling for time-critical sequential decision making. In *UAI-93*, 309–316.

Howard, R. A. 1960. *Dynamic Programming and Markov Processes*. Cambridge, Mass: MIT Press.

Koenig, S. 1992. Optimal probabilistic and decision-theoretic planning using Markovian decision theory. Technical Report UCB/CSD 92/685, UC Berkeley, Calif.

Russell, S., and Wefald, E. 1991. *Do the Right Thing*. Cambridge, Mass: MIT Press.

Sutton, R. S. 1988. Learning to predict by the methods of temporal differences. *Machine Learning* 3:9–43.

Sutton, R. S. 1991. Planning by incremental dynamic programming. In *8th Intl Wkshp on Machine Learning*.

Thiébaux, S.; Hertzberg, J.; Shoaff, W.; and Schneider, M. 1994. A stochastic model of actions and plans for anytime planning under uncertainty. *Int. J. of Intelligent Systems*.

Generating Feasible Schedules under Complex Metric Constraints *

Cheng-Chung Cheng
The Robotics Institute
Carnegie Mellon University
Pittsburgh, PA 15213
ccen@isl1.ri.cmu.edu

Stephen F. Smith
The Robotics Institute
Carnegie Mellon University
Pittsburgh, PA 15213
sfs@isl1.ri.cmu.edu

Abstract

In this paper, we consider the problem of finding feasible solutions to scheduling problems that are complicated by separation constraints on the execution of different operations. Following recent work in constraint-posting scheduling, we formulate this problem as one of establishing ordering relations between pairs of operations requiring synchronization of resource usage. This establishes contact with the recently proposed General Temporal Constraint Network (GTCN) model. Exploiting properties of the general GTCN solution procedure, we are able to directly generalize a high performance solution procedure previously developed for a much more restricted class of scheduling problems. Specifically, shortest path information in the underlying temporal constraint network is first used to establish dominance conditions for early pruning of infeasible solutions. Heuristics are then defined for variable/value ordering in the meta-CSP space of possible resolutions of the disjunctive constraints on resource usage. These heuristics are based on use of shortest path information as an estimation of decision flexibility. Experimental evaluation of the resulting heuristic procedure is carried out on a set of randomly generated problems drawn from a manufacturing scenario. Results indicate extremely effective problem solving performance in relation to both the original scheduling procedure that was adapted and the general GTCN solution procedure.

Introduction

Scheduling problems present an important and challenging class of constraint satisfaction problems (CSPs) that have received increasing attention in the literature (e.g., Keng & Yun 1989, Minton et al. 1992, Muscettola 1993, Sadeh & Fox 1990, Smith & Cheng 1993). The classic problem typically considered, which originates from the manufacturing domain and is referred to as the job shop scheduling problem, involves

synchronizing the production of *n jobs* in a facility with *m resources*. The production of a given job requires the execution of a sequence of *operations*. Each operation has a specific processing time and its execution requires the exclusive use of a designated resource (i.e. resources have unit capacity). Each job has an associated ready time and a deadline, and its production must be accomplished within this interval. In the non-relaxable version of the problem, the objective is to determine a set of operation start times that satisfies all temporal and resource capacity constraints.

This problem bears similarity to the problems of interest in the related field of temporal reasoning. Historically there have been differences. Qualitative temporal reasoning (e.g., Allen 1983, Vilain & Kautz 1986) has been concerned with problems of establishing and verifying consistent relations between events, but faces difficulties in incorporating metric information such as durations, ready times and deadlines; Quantitative approaches (Dechter, Meiri, & Pearl 1991) have investigated problems with complex metric constraints but are unable to accommodate disjunctive resource capacity constraints. More recent work in integrating qualitative and quantitative temporal reasoning (Dean & McDermott 1987, Meiri 1991, Kautz & Ladkin 1991) has proposed models that encompass the full set of constraints of the scheduling problem summarized above. In fact, one of these models (Meiri 1991) corresponds directly to the model used in (Smith & Cheng 1993), where an efficient heuristic solution procedure for the job shop scheduling problem was developed.

By exploiting this connection and formulating the scheduling problem within Meiri's model, we gain insight into the development of high performance heuristic procedures for a much wider class of frequently encountered scheduling problems. The specific class of scheduling problems we address in this paper extends the classical job shop problem in several respects. First, the precedence constraints that define the operation sequences of jobs are extended to allow additional specification of metric "separation constraints", delineating a feasible interval within which the execution of related operations can be separated in time.

*The research reported in this paper was supported in part by the Advanced Research Projects Agency under contract F30602-90-C-0119, the National Aeronautics and Space Administration under contract NCC 2-531 and the CMU Robotics Institute.

Second, the assumption of fixed operation processing times is relaxed to instead allow specification of minimum and maximum bounds. Finally, temporal relationships are specifiable between operations in different job sequences, allowing synchronization constraints unrelated to resource usage. All of these extensions find direct application in many practical domains. In metal parts manufacturing, for example, if an operation heats metal for a subsequent shaping operation, then the shaping operation must be executed before the metal cools for the process to be productive. Alternatively, a chemical bath operation in chip manufacturing processes requires a certain amount of time to be productive, but damage to the part is typically only incurred if the time in the bath exceeds a larger, maximum amount of time. The development of procedures for solving this extended class of scheduling problems has received very little attention from either the Artificial Intelligence or Operations Research communities.

The remainder of the paper is organized as follows. We first summarize the general temporal constraint network (GTCN) proposed by Meiri. Next, we use this model to characterize our extended scheduling problem, and discuss the general GTCN solution procedure in this problem context. We then turn to development of an efficient heuristic procedure for scheduling under complex metric constraints. After specifying the procedure, an experimental analysis of its performance is presented.

General Temporal Constraint Networks

A general temporal constraint network T consists of a set of variables $\{X_1, ..., X_n\}$ with continuous domains, and a set of unary or binary constraints. Each variable represents a temporal object, either a time point or an interval, and a constraint C may be qualitative or metric.

A qualitative constraint C is represented by a disjunction $(X_i \, r_1 \, X_j) \vee ... \vee (X_i \, r_k \, X_j)$, alternatively expressed as a relation set $X_i \{r_1, ..., r_k\} X_j$, where r_i represents a *basic qualitative constraint*. Three types of basic qualitative constraints are allowed: (1) interval-interval constraints (Allen 1983); (2) point-point constraints (Vilain & Kautz 1986); (3) point-interval or interval-point constraints (Ladkin & Maddux 1989).

A metric constraint C is represented by a set of intervals $\{I_1, ..., I_k\} = \{[a_1, b_1], ..., [a_k, b_k]\}$. Two types of metric constraints are specifiable. A unary constraint C_i on point X_i restricts X_i's domain to a given set of intervals, i.e. $(X_i \in I_1) \vee ... \vee (X_i \in I_k)$. A binary constraint C_{ij} between points X_i and X_j restricts the feasible values for the distance $X_j - X_i$, i.e., $(X_j - X_i \in I_1) \vee ... \vee (X_j - X_i \in I_k)$. A special time point X_0 can be introduced to represent the "origin". Since all times are relative to X_0, each unary constraint C_i can be treated as a binary constraint C_{0i}.

A general temporal constraint network is associated

J₁ - ready time: 4; deadline: 16

operation	resource	duration
O_1	R_1	[4,8]
O_2	R2	[3,9]

J₂ - ready time: 2; deadline: 16

operation	resource	duration
O_3	R_1	[5,8]
O_4	R2	[2,7]

separation constraints:
  [3,10] between O_1 and O_2

Figure 1: A simple scheduling example

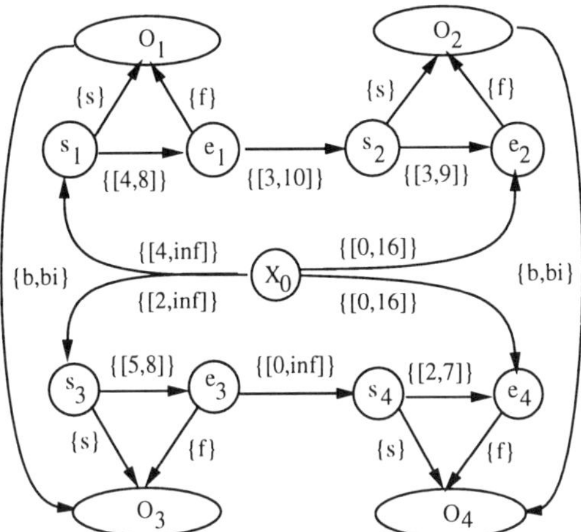

Figure 2: The constraint graph of the example

with a *directed constraint graph G*, where nodes represent variables, and a edge $i \rightarrow j$ indicates that a constraint C_{ij} between variables X_i and X_j is specified. We say a tuple $X = (x_1, ..., x_n)$ is a *solution* if X satisfies all qualitative and metric constraints. A network is consistent if there exists at least one solution.

Modeling the Scheduling Problem

To illustrate how to model the scheduling problem using GTCN, consider a simple scenario involving two jobs J_1 and J_2. J_1 requires the operation sequence $O_1 \rightarrow O_2$, and J_2 requires the operation sequence $O_3 \rightarrow O_4$. Figure 1 gives the ready times and deadlines for J_1 and J_2, the resource required by each operation, and duration and separation constraints. Figure 2 shows the corresponding constraint graph for this problem. For expository purposes, we display an interval object by an oval and a point object by a circle.

In the graph, s_i and e_i represent the start and end points for operation O_i respectively, and X_0 is the origin, representing "time zero". For operations O_i and O_j, requiring use of the same resource, we model the *resource capacity constraint* as a relation set $\{b, bi\}$ between them, indicating that O_i should be sequenced *before* or *after* O_j without any overlap. For an exam-

Table 1: The formal specification of constraints

ready times:	$s_1 - X_0 \in [4, \infty]$	durations:	$e_1 - s_1 \in [4, 8]$
	$s_3 - X_0 \in [2, \infty]$		$e_2 - s_2 \in [3, 9]$
deadlines:	$e_2 - X_0 \in [0, 16]$		$e_3 - s_3 \in [5, 8]$
	$e_4 - X_0 \in [0, 16]$		$e_4 - s_4 \in [2, 7]$
capacity	$O_1\{b, bi\}O_3$	start &	$s_1\{s\}O_1 ; e_1\{e\}O_1$
constraints:	$O_2\{b, bi\}O_4$	end	$s_2\{s\}O_2 ; e_2\{e\}O_2$
separation	$s_2 - e_1 \in [3, 10]$	points:	$s_3\{s\}O_3 ; e_3\{e\}O_3$
constraints:	$s_4 - e_3 \in [0, \infty]$		$s_4\{s\}O_4 ; e_4\{e\}O_4$

ple of resource capacity constraint, see the constraint $\{b, bi\}$ between O_1 and O_3.

Job ready times and deadlines are represented by metric constraints between point X_0, and the corresponding start or end points. For example, the ready time 4 of job J_1 is represented by a metric constraint $\{[4, \infty]\}$ between point X_0 and J_1's start point s_1, indicating that the start time of J_1 should be greater than or equal to the ready time 4.

A separation constraint is represented by a metric constraint between the end and start points of the prescribed operations (e.g. the constraint $\{[3, 10]\}$ between e_1 and s_2). A simple precedence constraint (which is always assumed in the classical scheduling problem) is just a special case where the separation interval is unbounded (e.g., the constraint $\{[0, \infty]\}$ between e_3 and s_4). An operation's processing time is similarly represented by a metric constraint, in this case between its start and end points (e.g., the constraint $\{[4, 8]\}$ between s_1 and e_1). Table 1 shows the formal specification of all constraints graphically depicted in Figure 1(b).

Scheduling problems formulated in this manner represent a subclass of general temporal constraint problems where the only disjunctions present in the associated constraint graph are the $\{b, bi\}$ edges corresponding to the resource capacity constraints. All other edges have either one relation or a single interval. It is well known that this class of problems is strongly NP-complete (Garey & Johnson 1979), and heuristics are required for efficient solution.

A General Backtracking Procedure

By determining a feasible schedule, we mean to find a solution of the associated general temporal constraint network. A straightforward way of solving a GTCN has been suggested in (Meiri 1991). Let a *labeling* of a general temporal constraint network, T, be a selection of one relation from each qualitative constraint or one interval from each metric constraint. Since each basic qualitative constraint can be translated into at most four metric constraints (Kautz & Ladkin 1991), a labeling actually defines a Simple Temporal Problem (STP) network - a metric network whose arcs have only single intervals (Dechter et al. 1991). We can solve T by generating all possible labelings, solving each one of them, and combining the results. Specifically, T is consistent if and only if there exists a labeling whose

associated STP is consistent. In our scheduling problem, most arcs are labeled by single relations or single intervals, except for those labeled by the relation set $\{b, bi\}$. To generate all labelings, we exhaustively enumerate all b or bi relations for those arcs. If e is the number of the arcs labeled by the $\{b, bi\}$ relation set, the total number of the enumeration will be 2^e.

For any STP network, we can associate it with a directed edge-weighted graph, G_d, called a *distance graph*. An STP is consistent if and only if the corresponding distance-graph G_d has no negative weight cycles. The *minimal network* of the STP can be specified by a complete directed graph, called the *d-graph*, where each edge, $i \rightarrow j$, is labeled by the shortest path length, d_{ij}, in G_d (Dechter et al. 1991). An STP network can be solved in $O(n^3)$ time by the Floyd-Warshall's all-pairs shortest-paths algorithm, where n is the number of variables in the STP network, Thus, the overall complexity of the brute-force method for the scheduling problem is $O(n^3 2^e)$.

We can increase the efficiency of the brute-force method by running a backtracking search on a *meta-CSP* network whose variables are the arcs in the GTCN which have the relation set $\{b, bi\}$, and whose domains are the two possible relations. In the backtracking procedure, we randomly select one variable and assign b or bi relation to that variable. If the corresponding STP network is consistent, we continue until we generate a solution; otherwise we backtrack.

More Effective Methods

As first observed by Erschler et al. (1976), the structure of resource capacity constraints - i.e. that $O_i\{b, bi\}O_j$ for any O_i and O_j competing for the same resource - can be exploited to define dominance conditions over the set of possible orderings in any feasible solution. In (Smith & Cheng 1993) a scheduling procedure called Precedence Constraint Posting (PCP) is defined which couples the use of such dominance checking with simple "slack-based" heuristics for variable and value ordering in the meta-CSP problem. The intuition behind these heuristics is simple. When faced with two or more unresolved ordering decisions, focus first on the decision with the least sequencing flexibility. Since any decision made is likely reduce the flexibility of those that remain, delaying the currently most constrained choice increases the chances of arriving at an infeasible state. In taking the decision, select the choice that retains the most sequencing flexibility (and thus leaves the search with the most degrees of freedom). On a set of previously published benchmark problems, PCP was shown to significantly outperform other contemporary approaches to the classical constraint satisfaction scheduling problem.

Unfortunately, temporal slack measures are based solely on the earliest start times and latest end times of operations, and do not reflect the influence of finite-interval separation constraints between operations. As this type of constraint is added into the problem, we would thus expect slack measures to provide a less effective basis for estimating sequencing flexibility. However, our problem formulation within the GTCN model suggests a straightforward means of generalizing the PCP procedure. In the following subsections, we develop dominance conditions and search control heuristics for this extended class of scheduling problems.

Dominance Conditions

Suppose X_{ij} is a currently unassigned variable in the meta-CSP network representing the choice associated with the constraint $O_i \{b, bi\} O_j$, and consider the d-graph associated with the current partial solution. Let s_i, e_i, s_j, and e_j be the start and end points respectively of O_i and O_j, and further assume d_{ij} is the shortest path length from e_i to s_j and d_{ji} is the shortest path length from e_j to s_i. Four mutually exclusive cases can be identified:

Case 1. If $d_{ij} \geq 0$ and $d_{ji} < 0$, then $O_i \{b\} O_j$ must be selected.

Case 2. If $d_{ji} \geq 0$ and $d_{ij} < 0$, then $O_i \{bi\} O_j$ must be selected.

Case 3. If $d_{ji} < 0$ and $d_{ij} < 0$, then the STP network is inconsistent.

Case 4. If $d_{ji} \geq 0$ and $d_{ij} \geq 0$, then either relation is still possible.

Consider Case 1. Suppose that rather than selecting $O_i \{b\} O_j$, we select $O_i \{bi\} O_j$. This implies the insertion of a new edge $s_i \rightarrow e_j$ with 0 weight into the current distance graph G_d, corresponding to the linear inequality $e_j - s_i \leq 0$ (i.e., $s_i \geq e_j$). But, since G_d already contains a negative weight path from e_j to s_i (i.e., $d_{ji} < 0$), we now have a negative weight cycle in G_d. To avoid inconsistency, hence, we must select $O_i \{b\} O_j$. By similar arguments, we can derive Cases 2, 3, and 4.

These dominance conditions provide a direct basis for pruning with the meta-CSP search space. Detection of Case 1 or Case 2 in any state allows immediate assignment (and extension of the current STP network). Each time a new distance constraint is added to the STP network, the corresponding d-graph is determined. If Case 3 is detected in any state, the only recourse is to backtrack.

Variable and Value Ordering

The dominance conditions, of course, provide only necessary conditions for determining a set of feasible schedules. We are still left with the problem of resolving the undecided states specified by Case 4. In situations where application of the dominance conditions leaves the search in a state with several unassigned variables in the meta-CSP network, the shortest path information in the current d-graph provides estimates of the flexibility associated with each decision. Directly

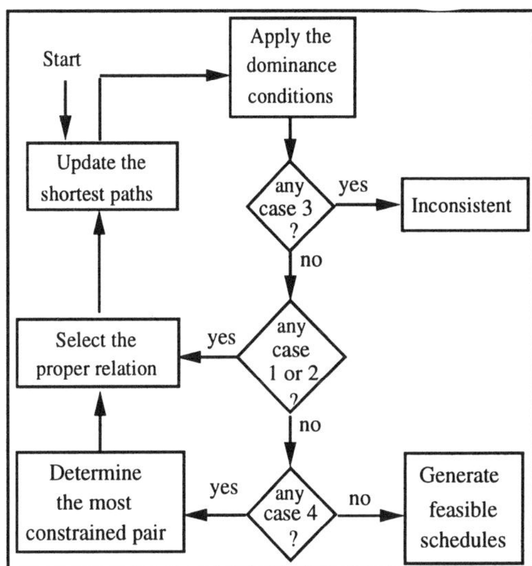

Figure 3: The SP-PCP Search Procedure

adapting the variable and value ordering heuristics defined by Smith and Cheng (1993), we define the *biased shortest path lengths* between O_i and O_j as

$$bd_{ij} = \frac{d_{ij}}{\sqrt{S}}; \quad bd_{ji} = \frac{d_{ji}}{\sqrt{S}}. \tag{1}$$

$$S = \frac{\min\{d_{ij}, d_{ji}\}}{\max\{d_{ij}, d_{ji}\}} \tag{2}$$

estimates the degree of similarity between the two values d_{ij} and d_{ji}. Given this definition of bd, the priority of a given decision variable X_{ij} is determined by the expression $pr_{X_{ij}} = -\min\{bd_{ij}, bd_{ji}\}$. The meta-CSP variable with the highest pr is selected as the next variable to assign.

Intuitively, this variable ordering heuristic is heavily oriented toward selection of the X_{ij} with the least sequencing flexibility, i.e., $min\{d_{ij}, d_{ji}\}$. The $\sqrt{S}$ bias is introduced to hedge in situations where the decision with the overall $min\{d_{ij}, d_{ji}\}$ has a very large $max\{d_{ij}, d_{ji}\}$, and a competing decision has two shortest path values just slightly larger than this overall minimum.

Having selected the next meta-CSP variable to assign, we commit to the ordering relation that retains the greatest flexibility. Specifically, if the highest priority variable is X_{ij}, then we select $O_i \{b\} O_j$ if $bd_{ij} > bd_{ji}$ and $O_i \{bi\} O_j$ otherwise.

Figure 3 graphically depicts the overall search procedure, which will be referred to as *SP-PCP*. We present SP-PCP as a backtrack-free approximation procedure. However, it should be clear how the procedure can be integrated into a backtracking search.

Performance Evaluation

In this section, we evaluate the performance of the shortest path dominance conditions and variable/value ordering heuristics on a set of randomly generated problems. We contrast the performance of the SP-PCP with that of the original PCP developed in (Smith & Cheng 1993), to assess the performance gain directly attributable to reliance on shortest path information as opposed to slack information for search control. We also embed both SP-PCP and PCP within a chronological backtracking search. In this case, performance is contrasted with that of the basic GTCN backtracking search procedure previously given, to evaluate the performance leverage provided by both dominance checking and variable/value ordering in solving this class of problems.

We simulate a scheduling scenario where jobs require operations to be performed on each of 5 resources. We generate problem sets of 5 different sizes: 6 jobs (or 30 total operations), 8 jobs (40 operations), 10 jobs (50 operations), 16 jobs (80 operations) and 20 jobs (100 operations). For each problem size, we randomly generate 50 problem instances. This gives a total of 250 scheduling problems, with size ranging from very small to fairly large.

Operation sequences are randomly generated and each of the 5 resources must be visited once. Minimum processing times are drawn from a uniform distribution $U[10, 50]$, and the maximum processing times are generated by multiplying each minimum processing time by a random tolerance $(1 + t)$, with $t \sim U[0, 0.4]$. Job ready times are drawn from a uniform distribution $M\,U[0, 0.1]$, where M represents the minimum overall duration of the schedule (or "makespan").[1] Similarly, job deadlines are drawn from another uniform distribution $M\,U[1, 1.1]$.[2] Finally, we generate separation constraints between every two consecutive operations in each job. A separation constraint is represented by a random interval, $[a, b]$, with $a \sim U[0, 10]$ and $b \sim U[40, 50]$.

Six different procedures where applied to the generated set of 250 problems: the SP-PCP and original PCP approximation procedures, chronological backtracking search with random variable/value ordering (denoted below as CB), chronological backtracking augmented with SP dominance checking (denoted as CB w/ D), and backtracking search variants of both SP-PCP and PCP (denoted as CB w/ SP-PCP and CB w/ PCP respectively). All procedures were implemented in C and run on a SUN Sparc 10 workstation. For all backtracking algorithms, the maximum time allowed for solution of any problem was limited

---

[1] $M = (n - 1)\overline{p_{bk}} + \sum_{i=1}^{m} \overline{p_i}$, where n is the number of jobs, m the number of resources, $\overline{p_{bk}}$ the average minimum processing time of operations on the bottleneck resource, and $\overline{p_i}$ the average minimum processing time of operations on resource i. The bottleneck resource bk is the resource with the maximum total amount of operation (minimum) processing time.

[2] This scheme for generating job ready times and deadlines is taken from (Ow 1985).

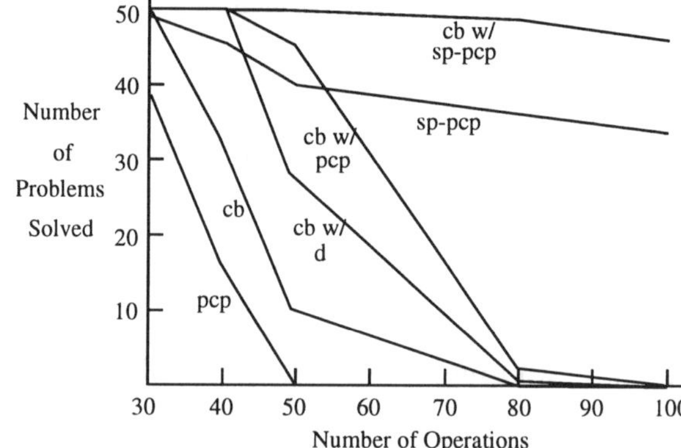

size	pcp	sp-pcp	cb	cb w/ d	cb w/ pcp	cb w/ sp-pcp
30	38	49	50	50	50	50
40	16	46	32	50	50	50
50	0	40	10	28	46	50
80	0	37	0	1	2	48
100	0	33	0	0	0	46

Figure 4: Number of problems solved

to 1,000 CPU seconds. Backtracking search algorithms were found to be capable of searching approximately 300,000 states in this time frame. Performance was measured in terms of number of problems solved and average solution time.

Figure 4 shows the number of problem instances solved in each problem size category by each procedure tested. The average time required (in CPU seconds) for solving all instances of each size category is given in Figure 5 (graphed on a logarithmic scale). For the backtracking procedures, this average time thus gives a lower bound on solution time for those categories in which all problems are not solved.

It is clear from the results obtained with SP-PCP and PCP (the backtrack-free procedures) that shortest path information provides a much more effective basis for directing the search. PCP was reasonably effective only on the smallest problem set and was not able to solve any problem with 50 or more operations. SP-PCP, alternatively, performed extremely well on the smaller problem sets. Though its effectiveness also diminishes with increasing problem size, it is, nonetheless, able to solve 33 of the 50 100-operation problems, with an average solution time of under 10 seconds.

SP-PCP results are more striking when considered in relation to the results produced by the backtracking procedures tested. We see that at small problem sizes (30-40 operations), all algorithms perform very well. As problem size increases, the exponentially increasing size of the search space quickly overwhelms the basic chronological backtracking procedure CB and its performance deteriorates drastically. The incorporation of dominance condition checking (CB w/ D) is seen to improve the performance of CB on most problem sets. However, it is interesting to note that incorpo-

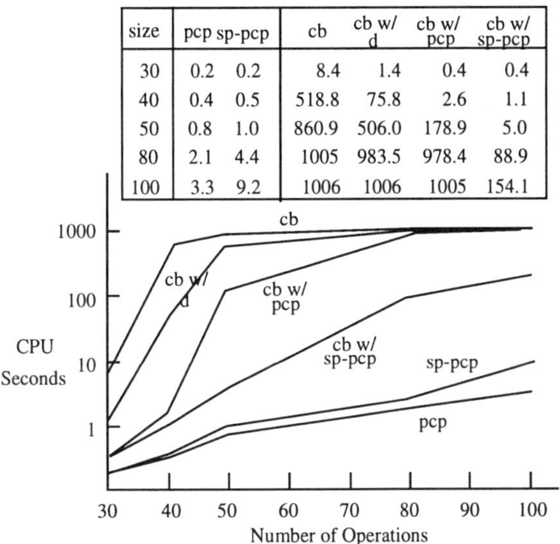

size	pcp	sp-pcp	cb	cb w/ d	cb w/ pcp	cb w/ sp-pcp
30	0.2	0.2	8.4	1.4	0.4	0.4
40	0.4	0.5	518.8	75.8	2.6	1.1
50	0.8	1.0	860.9	506.0	178.9	5.0
80	2.1	4.4	1005	983.5	978.4	88.9
100	3.3	9.2	1006	1006	1005	154.1

Figure 5: CPU seconds used

ration of the original PCP procedure yields a somewhat larger performance improvement. This indicates that the look-ahead advantage provided by slack-based variable/value ordering in fact outweighs the performance gains offered by stronger search space pruning conditions. In the case of both of these augmented backtracking procedures, however, the larger, 80-100 operation problems generally cannot be solved.

The results obtained by integrating SP-PCP into the chronological backtracking procedure further indicate the impact of our simple variable and value ordering heuristics on problem solving performance. Not only is this procedure effective across problem sets of all sizes, solving all but 4 problem instances, but it is also very efficient. The use of shortest path information quickly moves the search into profitable regions of the space, and dramatically reduces the need for backtracking.

Conclusions

In this paper, we have presented an efficient procedure for solving scheduling problems that are complicated by finite-interval separation constraints on the execution of different operations. Despite the practical importance of this class of problems in many application domains, it has received little attention in the scheduling research community. Following recent research in constraint-posting scheduling, we formulated the scheduling problem as one of establishing before or after relations between pairs of operations that require the same resource. The problem was characterized as a general temporal constraint network (GTCN), and, using properties of Simple Temporal Problems, we were able to directly generalize a high performance scheduling procedure previously developed for a more restricted class of scheduling problems. We established dominance conditions, based on shortest path information, for early pruning of infeasible regions of the meta-CSP search space. We also developed heuristics for variable and value ordering in the meta-CSP search, based on use of shortest path information as an estimation of decision flexibility. Experimental evaluation of these heuristics on a set of randomly generated problems drawn from a manufacturing scenario indicated significant performance improvement in relation to general GTCN solution procedures and the original constraint-posting procedure.

References

Allen, J. F. 1983. Maintaining knowledge about temporal intervals. *CACM*, 11(26), 832-843.

Dean, T. and McDermott, D. 1987. Temporal data base management. *Artificial Intelligence*, 32, 1-55.

Dechter, R., Meiri, I., and Pearl, J. 1991. Temporal constraint networks. *Artificial Intelligence*, 49, 61-95.

Erschler, J., Roubellat, F., and Vernhes, J. P. 1976. Finding some essential characteristics of the feasible solutions for a scheduling problem. *Operations Research*, 24, 772-782.

Garey, M. R. and Johnson, D. S. 1979. *Computers and Intractability, a Guide to the Theory of NP-Completeness*, W.H. Freeman Company.

Kautz, H. and Ladkin, P. B. 1991. Integrating metric and qualitative temporal reasoning. In *Proc. of AAAI-91*, 241-246. Anaheim, CA.

Keng, N. and Yun, D. Y. Y. 1989. A planning/scheduling methodology for the constrained resource problem. In *Proc. of IJCAI-89*, Detroit, MI.

Ladkin, P. B. and Maddux, R. D. 1989. On binary constraint networks. Technical report, Kestrel Institute, Palo Alto, CA.

Meiri, I. 1991. Combining qualitative and quantitative constraints in temporal reasoning. In *Proc. of AAAI-91*, 260-267. Anaheim, CA.

Minton, S., Johnston, M., Philips, A. B., and Laird, P. 1992. Minimizing conflicts: a heuristic repair method for constraint satisfaction and scheduling problems. *Artificial Intelligence* 58, 161-205.

Muscettola, N. 1993. Scheduling by iterative partition of bottleneck conflicts. In *Proc. of 9th IEEE Conf. on AI Applications*, Orlando, FL.

Ow, P. S. 1985. Focused Scheduling in Proportionate Flowshops. *Management Science* 31 (7) 852-869.

Sadeh, N., and Fox M., 1990. Variable and value ordering heuristics for activity-based job-shop scheduling. *4th Int. Conf. on Expert Systems in Prod. and Oper. Management*, 134-144, Hilton Head Is., SC.

Smith, S. F. and Cheng, C. 1993. Slack-based heuristic for constraint satisfaction scheduling. In *Proc. of AAAI-93*, 139-144. Washington, DC.

Vilain, M. and Kautz, H. 1986. Constraint propagation algorithms for temporal reasoning. In *Proc. of AAAI-86*, 377-382, Philadelphia, PA.

Experimental Results on the Application of Satisfiability Algorithms to Scheduling Problems*

James M. Crawford and **Andrew B. Baker**
Computational Intelligence Research Laboratory
1269 University of Oregon
Eugene, OR 97403-1269
jc@cs.uoregon.edu

Abstract

Considerable progress has been made in recent years in understanding and solving propositional satisfiability problems. Much of this work has been based on experiments on randomly generated 3SAT problems. One generally accepted shortcoming of this work is that it is not clear how the results and algorithms developed will carry over to "real" constraint-satisfaction problems. This paper reports on a series of experiments applying satisfiability algorithms to scheduling problems. We have found that scheduling problems bear fairly little resemblance to the previously studied hard randomly generated 3SAT problems. In particular, scheduling problems tend to be quite large but under-constrained, Further, forward checking (*e.g.*, unit propagation) seems to be much more important on these problems than on hard random 3SAT problems. We have also found that the domain-specific heuristics developed to solve scheduling problems make surprisingly little difference in the time required to solve the problems. We suggest that the best algorithms for this problem class will probably be hill-climbing algorithms that incorporate some sort of forward checking.

Introduction

Many classes of problems in knowledge representation, learning, planning, and other areas of AI are known to be NP-complete. In the worst case, all known algorithms for solving such problems require run time exponential in the size of the problem. Propositional satisfiability (SAT) is, in a sense, the prototypical example of an NP-complete problem. It is simply formalized, yet has an amazingly complex structure.

Paradoxically, one perennial problem with work on SAT has been the difficulty of finding hard instances on which to test algorithms; it turns out to be surprisingly hard to collect a sufficiently large body of reasonably sized "real" problems. Randomly generated problems, on the other hand, tend to end up being quite easily solved.

One important advance in recent years has been the discovery that the difficulty of randomly generated problems depends critically on whether they are *under-constrained, over-constrained,* or *critically-constrained* (Cheeseman, Kanefsky, & Taylor 1991; Mitchell, Selman, & Levesque 1992; Crawford & Auton 1993). Consider a randomly generated constraint satisfaction problem. Intuitively, if there are very few constraints, it should be easy to find a solution (since there will generally be many solutions). Similarly, if there are very many constraints then an intelligent algorithm will generally be able to quickly close off most or all of the branches in the search tree. The hardest problems are thus those which are critically constrained: these problems have relatively few solutions, but most branches in the search tree go fairly deep before reaching a dead end.

Critically constrained randomly generated satisfiability problems provide a ready supply of hard test cases of arbitrary size. This discovery has lead to work on understanding (Crawford & Auton 1993; Williams & Hogg 1992), and solving (Selman, Levesque, & Mitchell 1992) these problems. GSAT in particular appears to be well suited to solving large randomly generated critically constrained problems. However, concerns have been raised that randomly generated problems are bad test cases because they have no structure and thus may bear little resemblance to "real" problems.

This paper reports on a series of experiments applying satisfiability algorithms to scheduling problems. In these experiments we have used Sadeh's job shop scheduling problems (both because they are readily accessible and because they have been well studied in the scheduling community). These problems do have a random component, namely the ready times and deadlines for the jobs. However, these times have been chosen according to a variety of distributions in an effort to mimic various types of scheduling problems encountered in the field.

Our main result from these experiments is that

---

*This work has been supported by the Air Force Office of Scientific Research under grant number 92-0693 and by ARPA/Rome Labs under grant numbers F30602-91-C-0036 and F30602-93-C-00031.

Sadeh's scheduling problems bear little resemblance to critically constrained 3SAT, but not for the expected reason. When translated into SAT problems, these scheduling problems are much larger than previously studied random 3SAT problems. However, they are still solvable because they are highly under-constrained – very many solutions exist so it is a fairly simple matter to "bump" into one. However, GSAT has not proven to be the best algorithm on these problems. We hypothesize that this is due to the presence of a small number of "control" variables (those define the schedule) and a much larger number of "dependent" variables (whose values are determined by the control variables). Since GSAT has no notion of forward checking, it appears to have considerable difficulty with problems involving large numbers of dependent variables (this effect is discussed further in in the discussion section).

TABLEAU, a Davis-Putnam derivative, also performed poorly. On some problems it almost immediately found a solution. On others, however, it made an initial bad guess and was stuck searching a virtually infinite search tree (typically these trees were of depth seventy to eighty which means that the search trees have on the order of 2^{70} nodes). We refer to this as the *early mistake problem.*

This mode of failure suggested replacing depth-first search (in TABLEAU) with iterative sampling (Langley 1992). Iterative sampling is a simple technique in which variable values are chosen at random (but with forward checking[1]) until a model or a contradiction is found. At this point we return to the *root* of the search tree and start over. Iterative sampling successfully solved all of Sadeh's scheduling problems after an average of only 64 restarts (using no heuristics). This confirms that these problems have a very large number of solutions, and suggests that the domain-specific heuristics commonly used in scheduling problems are less useful than might be expected.

If these problems are truly representative of "real" constraint-satisfaction problems, these results suggest quite a different research agenda than has previously been pursued. Large under-constrained constraint-satisfaction problems pose a number of interesting challenges not found in critically constrained problems. Chief among these is the early mistake problem. Forward checking also seems to be important, so GSAT is not necessarily the solution. The best current candidates seem to be hill-climbing algorithms with forward checking (see discussion section) and variants of dynamic backtracking (Ginsberg 1993). It is also becoming clear that a purely propositional representation is impractical – a large fraction of the run time is spent simply reading the theory in from disk. Generalizing existing SAT algorithms to use some sort of "semi-first-order" shorthand is clearly in order. One

---

[1] Adding forward checking to iterative sampling seems to have been first suggested by Kurt Konolige.

other important question that currently remains open is whether these scheduling problems are perhaps similar to *under-constrained* 3SAT problems. This seems relatively unlikely (since forward checking appears to be more important in scheduling than in any of the randomly generated problems) but deserves to be investigated.

Scheduling

The scheduling problem is ubiquitous. One may, for example, have a set of machine tools and be told to schedule a series of jobs so as to maximize the efficiency of the use of the tools. Alternatively, one may have a collection of transport ships in various locations and be told to transport some number of divisions to a variety of locations as reliably and cheaply as possibly. Or, one may have to assemble some number of surgical teams using a variety of specialists subject to a set of constraints on consecutive numbers of hours worked, availability of operating rooms, etc. In all cases, the general form of the problem is that one is given a set of tasks to achieve, and a collection of resources to use.

One important type of scheduling problems is *machine shop scheduling* (Xiong, Sadeh, & Sycara 1992; Smith & Cheng 1993). Sadeh has developed a test suite of machine shop scheduling problems that are intended to represent a range of the types of machine shop scheduling problems encountered in the field.

Machine shop scheduling problems are usually taken to consist of a number of operations $1, \ldots, n$ to be scheduled subject to a collection of constraints. Each operation requires processing time p_i (given as part of the problem). A solution is a schedule giving the start time, s_i, for each operation.

The constraints are usually taken to consist of *sequencing restrictions, resource capacity constraints,* and *ready times and deadlines* (Smith & Cheng 1993). Sequencing restrictions, written $i \longrightarrow j$ state that operation i must complete before j can begin. The restriction $i \longrightarrow j$ is thus equivalent to $s_i + p_i \leq s_j$ ("the start time of i plus processing time for i is less than or equal to the start time of j"). Resource capacity constraints, written $c_{i,j}$, state that operations i and j conflict (usually because both require the same resource) and thus cannot be scheduled concurrently. $c_{i,j}$ is equivalent to the disjunction $(s_i + p_i \leq s_j) \vee (s_j + p_j \leq s_i)$ ("i completes before j begins or j completes before i begins"). Ready times, represented by r_i, are the earliest time at which operation i can start. A deadline d_i is the time by which operation i must be completed. Ready times thus just state $s_i \geq r_i$ and deadlines that $s_i + p_i \leq d_i$.

We now discuss propositional satisfiability (SAT) and then show how scheduling problems can be converted into SAT problems.

Propositional Satisfiability

The propositional satisfiability problem is the following (Garey & Johnson 1979): Given a set of *clauses*[2] C on a finite set U of variables, find a truth assignment[3] for U that satisfies all the clauses in C.

Clearly one can determine whether a satisfying assignment exists by trying all possible assignments. Unfortunately, if the set U is of size n then there are 2^n such assignments. SAT algorithms thus typically either (1) walk through the space of assignments following some set of heuristics and hope to run into a solution, or (2) work with partial assignments and use some sort of *forward checking* to compute forced values for other variables. Algorithms in this second class generally use depth-first search to systematically search the space of assignments. In section on satisfiability algorithms below we discuss examples of both types of algorithms.

Encoding Scheduling Problems as SAT Problems

At first glance there seems to be an "obvious" translation of scheduling problems into SAT: create variables to represent the start times of the operations (*e.g.*, s_{it} true means operation s_i starts at time t), and create clauses to represent the necessary inequalities. However, the search space in SAT problems so generated turns out to be much larger than necessary.

To see this, note that the key decisions to be made in scheduling problems concern the *orderings* of conflicting operations. Thus, for example, if i and j share a resource then we have to decide whether to schedule i then j, or j then i. We do not necessarily have to specify the exact start times of operations i and j, as long as we can be sure that there is some way to do so that is consistent with our ordering decisions (this observation, and the essence of the encoding we use here, is due to Smith and Cheng (1993)).

More formally, for each pair of operations i and j, we introduce a boolean variable $pr_{i,j}$ meaning "i precedes j", and for each operation i and each time t we introduce a boolean variable $sa_{i,t}$ meaning "i starts at time t or later", and a boolean variable $eb_{i,t}$ meaning "i ends by time t."[4]

Scheduling constraints are then translate by:

$$i \longrightarrow j \text{ becomes } pr_{i,j} = true$$
$$c_{i,j} \text{ becomes } pr_{i,j} \vee pr_{j,i}$$
$$r_i \text{ becomes } sa_{i,r_i} = true$$
$$d_i \text{ becomes } eb_{i,d_i} = true$$

---

[2] A clause is a disjunction of variables or negated variables.

[3] A truth assignment is a mapping from U to $\{true, false\}$.

[4] To help avoid confusion, in this section all boolean variables (variables taking values $\{true, false\}$) are of length two (*e.g.*, $pr_{i,j}$) and variables taking integral values (*e.g.*, s_i) are of length one.

We refer to the set of constraints generated by this mapping as C.

It is also necessary to add a collection of "coherence conditions" on the introduced variables. In all conditions below, i and j are quantified over all relevant operations and t is quantified over all relevant times.

1. $sa_{i,t} \rightarrow sa_{i,t-1}$ (coherence of sa). This ensures that if i starts at or after time t then it starts at or after time $t-1$.

2. $eb_{i,t} \rightarrow eb_{i,t+1}$ (coherence of eb). This ensures that if i ends by t then it ends by $t+1$.

3. $sa_{i,t} \rightarrow \neg eb_{i,t+p_i-1}$ (job i requires time p_i). This ensures that if i starts at or after time t then it cannot end before time $t + p_i$.

4. $sa_{i,t} \wedge pr_{i,j} \rightarrow sa_{j,t+p_i}$ (coherence of $pr_{i,j}$). This ensures that if i start at or after t and j follows i then j cannot start until i is finished.

We refer to the set of coherence conditions as S. Any mapping of the variables $p_{i,j}$ to $\{T, F\}$ that extends to a model of $C \wedge S$ is then a template describing a set of solutions to the scheduling problem.

There are several advantages to this translation from scheduling problems to SAT:

1. A set of legal values for the pr variables corresponds to a collection of feasible schedules. If there are additional optimization conditions (*e.g.*, robustness), one can then use these to select a particular schedule.

2. The constraints in S apply to all scheduling problems and thus need be computed and stored only once (they might therefore be compiled into a procedure rather than being stored explicitly). Further, S is symmetric under any permutation of the operations. In order to check for symmetries among operations it is thus only necessary to consider C.

3. Without loss of generality, one can omit the variable $pr_{i,j}$ (and all clauses containing it) if there are no sequencing restrictions or resource capacity constraints for i and j. This means that the size of the SAT problem is of order $nd + c$ (where n is the number of operations, d is the number of distinct time points, and c is the number of constraints in the scheduling problem). If S is represented as a compiled procedure then the number of clauses in the SAT problem is further reduced to order c (plus the size of the compiled procedure).

Three Satisfiability Algorithms

Tableau

TABLEAU is a Davis-Putnam algorithm that does a depth-first search of possible assignments using unit propagation for forward checking. This basic algorithm dates back to the work of Davis, Logemann, and Loveland (Davis, Logeman, & Loveland 1962). TABLEAU adds efficient data-structures for fast unit propagation and a series of heuristics for selecting branch variables (these are discussed in (Crawford & Auton 1993)). Most of these heuristics do not seem particularly helpful for scheduling problems (see discussion of experimental results below).

Unit propagation consists of the repeated application of the inference rule:

$$\frac{x \quad \neg x \vee y_1 \ldots \vee y_n}{y_1 \vee \ldots \vee y_n}$$

(similarly for $\neg x$). Unit propagation is a special case of resolution (the singleton x is resolved against the $\neg x$ in the clause). It is a particularly useful case, however, since it can always be performed to completion in time linear in the size of the theory, and since, in practice, it greatly reduces the number of nodes in the search tree (by propagating variable values through the theory).

The basic depth-first search algorithm is then the following:

```
tableau(theory)
  unit_propagate(theory);
  if contradiction discovered return(false);
  else if all variables are valued
          return(current assignment);
  else {
    x = some unvalued variable;
    return(tableau(theory AND x) OR
          tableau(theory AND NOT x));
  }
```

Gsat

GSAT is the most successful hill-climbing search algorithm for SAT to date. A complete assignment of variables to values is always kept. Variables are "flipped" (their value is changed) so as to increase the number of satisfied clauses (if possible). In our experiments we found the use of the "walk" strategy (Selman & Kautz 1993) to be critical. The basic WSAT ("walk sat") algorithm is the following:

```
WSAT(theory)
  for i := 1 to MAX-TRIES {
    A := a randomly generated truth assignment;
    for j := 1 to MAX-FLIPS {
      if A is a solution return it;
      else {
        C := randomly chosen unsatisfied clause;
        With probability P,
          Flip a random variable in C;
        Otherwise (that is, with probability 1-P)
          Flip a variable in C resulting in the
            greatest decrease in the number of
                unsat clauses;
      }
    }
  }
  return failure
}
```

The experimental performance of GSAT (Selman, Levesque, & Mitchell 1992) with walk on certain problem classes is impressive. GSAT is often able to find

models for randomly generated 2000 variable critically-constrained 3SAT problems.[5] Systematic methods (methods that are guaranteed to always to find a solution or determine that none exists) are currently not able to solve any critically-constrained problems of this size.

Isamp

ISAMP is basically a variant of TABLEAU in which one gives up on backtracking and simply starts over whenever a contradiction is discovered:

```
Isamp(theory) {
  for i := 1 to MAX-TRIES {
    set all variables to unassigned;
    loop {
      if all variables are valued
              return(current assignment);
      v := random unvalued variable;
      assign v a randomly chosen value;
      unit_propagate();
      if contradiction exit loop;
    }
  }
  return failure
}
```

Obviously this approach will only work on problems with a large number of models. One of the surprises in our work on scheduling problems has been that this algorithm outperforms both TABLEAU and GSAT.

Experimental Results

Our experiments were designed to assess the performance of each of these three algorithms on scheduling problems. We used the sixty scheduling problems produced by Sadeh (Sadeh 1992). Each of these problems consists of fifty operations to be scheduled subject to sequencing restrictions and resource capacity constraints. The operations are grouped into ten jobs of five operations each. Operations within each job must be performed in order. Further, each job requires one of five resources and each resource can be used by at most one job at a time.

Ready times and deadlines were generated randomly using several distributions. The distributions were defined by two parameters: (1) degree of constraint: (w) wide, (n) narrow, and (t) tight, and (2) number of bottlenecks: none, one, or two. These two parameters yield the six classes shown in Figure 1. Sadeh produced ten sample problems from each class.

The results for ISAMP and GSAT are shown in figure 1. The GSAT results are for our version of the WSAT ("walk sat") variant of GSAT (Selman & Kautz 1993). These results are an average over ten runs on each problem. In each run GSAT was given ten tries of four million flips each which corresponds to about

---

[5]Since GSAT never determines unsatisfiability, there is no way to reliably determine what percentage of satisfiable problems GSAT solves (but it is believed to be high).

TABLEAU:

Class	Success Rate	Branches	Time (sec.)
w/1	90	3947.1	255.4
w/2	100	221.2	104.8
n/1	70	1719.7	79.2
n/2	100	93.8	90.6
t/1	80	1160.4	66.3
t/2	100	119.4	81.7

GSAT:

Class	Success Rate	Flips (millions)	Time (sec.)
w/1	99	6.7	500
w/2	99	7.0	599
n/1	100	3.2	258
n/2	100	3.7	312
t/1	96	3.9	274
t/2	88	5.0	354

ISAMP:

Class	Success Rate	Tries	Time (sec.)
w/1	100	7	10
w/2	100	15	13
n/1	100	13	11
n/2	100	45	21
t/1	100	52	19
t/2	100	252	68

Figure 1: Experimental results for scheduling problems.

forty-five minutes of computation time. The mean flip and time data is for the successful cases only (these counts would be higher if we "punished" GSAT for the cases on which it ran out of time). For ISAMP the results are an average over 100 runs. ISAMP runs were given twenty-thousand tries. TABLEAU was run with only the non-horn heuristic ("branch first on variables appearing in non-horn clauses"). This has the effect of forcing TABLEAU to branch on the pr variables.[6] Since TABLEAU currently has no random component, the results are for one run on each problem. TABLEAU was interrupted after forty-five minutes. The averages are over the successful cases only. All algorithms are implemented in C, and all experiments were run on a SPARC 10/51.

In order to test the hypothesis that the lack of unit propagation was hurting GSAT, we performed a linear time simplification on the propositionally encoded scheduling problems and ran the experiments again. The simplification consisted of running unit propagation to completion on the initial theory (the encoding is such that the initial theories contain a number of unit clauses). We then deleted any clauses that were subsumed by a unit literal (*e.g.*, if the theory contained x and $x \vee y \vee z$ then we deleted the clause). Finally we "compacted" the encoding – our encoding uses in-

---

[6] We have some evidence to suggest that branching on randomly chosen variables would be better for these problems, but have not yet finished this experiment with TABLEAU.

tegers to represent variables so this step ensured that if the largest variable in the theory is n then every integer less than n is also used for some variable in the theory. The data for the simplified theories is shown in Figure 2. As expected, the GSAT run times are much lower. The ISAMP run times are also lower. We believe that this is primarily due to the fact that the simplified theory is smaller (and thus faster to read in from disk). We did not rerun TABLEAU since the simplification should have minimal effect on its run time. In this experiment GSAT and ISAMP were each run ten times on each problem.

GSAT:

Class	Success Rate	Flips (millions)	Time (sec.)
w/1	100	0.39	27
w/2	100	0.29	23
n/1	100	0.31	23
n/2	100	0.55	43
t/1	100	1.1	77
t/2	97	2.9	211

ISAMP:

Class	Success Rate	Tries	Time (sec.)
w/1	100	7	7
w/2	100	18	10
n/1	100	13	8
n/2	100	42	15
t/1	100	62	16
t/2	100	180	43

Figure 2: Experimental results for scheduling problems after simplification.

Discussion

The success of ISAMP indicates that, given the right encoding, Sadeh's scheduling problems are not that difficult. The encoding we use is domain specific only in that it is implicitly based on the observation that the key choices to be made are the relative orders of the conflicting operations. This is much less domain-specific than the slack-based heuristics used by Smith and Cheng (Smith & Cheng 1993). Of course Smith and Cheng do solve these problems almost two orders of magnitude faster than ISAMP. However, most of this difference is probably due to our use of propositional logic as a representation language (just to read in a propositional version of these theories takes about thirty times as long as Smith and Cheng take to solve them). The obvious experiment of implementing ISAMP using a more natural representation language (*e.g.*, a constraint-satisfaction language with integral valued variables) is underway.

A great deal of recent work has been done on analysis and solution methods for randomly generated satisfiability problems. An important open question in this body of work has been its relevance to "real" problems. Our work attempts to begin providing an answer to this question by studying the performance of a variety of satisfiability algorithms on propositional encodings of scheduling problems.

We have found that scheduling problems generate propositional theories that are much larger and much less constrained than the randomly generated theories generally studied. Further, the variables in scheduling problems can be partitioned into *control* variables that define a solution (*e.g.*, the *pr* variables in scheduling problems) and *dependent* variables whose values are derived from the control variables (*e.g.*, all the rest of the variables in the scheduling problems).

The fact that TABLEAU generally performs poorly on these problems while ISAMP performs well indicates that there are a large number of solutions but that these solutions are not uniformly distributed throughout the search space. Rather there seem to be large "deserts" containing no solutions. TABLEAU sometimes wanders into one of these deserts by making an unlucky choice at some early branch in the tree. It then has no way to recover. We refer to this as the early mistake problem. Since ISAMP restarts on every contradiction, it is sensitive only to the number of solutions, not their uniformity.

The existence of a large number of dependent variables appears to be hobbling GSAT relative to ISAMP. One can see this by the following analysis. Assume that we can divide the variables in a problem into c control variables and d dependent variables, such that a polynomial time procedure will always determine whether an assignment to the control variables extends to a model. This will be the case, for example, if we choose the control variables to be variables appearing in non-horn clauses (*e.g.*, the *pr* variables in scheduling problems) and choose unit propagation as the polynomial time procedure. If there are *any* constraints on the dependent variables the density of solutions in "control variable space" will then be higher than density of solutions in the original search space (to see this note that the density could be equal only if any satisfying assignment to the control variables extended to 2^d models). GSAT clearly searches in the full space (since it uses no forward checking). We hypothesize that ISAMP effectively searches in a smaller space (even though it makes no explicit distinction between control and dependent variables[7]) because of its use of unit propagation (TABLEAU also used unit propagation but it appears to fail because of the early mistake problem discussed above). Work on GSAT suggests that hill-climbing is a useful technique for satisfiability problems and in general one would expect hill-climbing to be superior to the random probing of ISAMP . This clearly suggests that the next step in this line of work is to develop algorithms that hill-climb in control space.

---

[7] When we do explicitly force ISAMP to value only the *pr* variables its performance *falls*. As yet we have no explanation for this phenomenon.

Acknowledgements

We would like to thank the members of CIRL, particularly Matt Ginsberg, for useful discussions of this material.

References

Cheeseman, P.; Kanefsky, B.; and Taylor, W. 1991. Where the really hard problems are. In *Proceedings of the Twelfth International Joint Conference on Artificial Intelligence*, 163–169.

Crawford, J. M., and Auton, L. D. 1993. Experimental results on the crossover point in satisfiability problems. In *Proceedings of the Eleventh National Conference on Artificial Intelligence*, 21–27.

Davis, M.; Logeman, G.; and Loveland, D. 1962. A machine program for theorem proving. In *CACM*, 394–397.

Garey, M., and Johnson, D. 1979. *Computers and Intractability*. W.H. Freeman and Company, New York.

Ginsberg, M. L. 1993. Dynamic backtracking. *Journal of Artificial Intelligence Research* 1:25–46.

Langley, P. 1992. Systematic and nonsystematic search strategies. In *Artificial Intelligence Planning Systems: Proceedings of the First International Conference*, 145–152. Morgan Kaufmann.

Mitchell, D.; Selman, B.; and Levesque, H. 1992. Hard and easy distributions of sat problems. In *Proceedings of the Tenth National Conference on Artificial Intelligence*, 459–465.

Sadeh, N. 1992. Look-ahead techniques for micro-opportunistic job shop scheduling. Technical Report CMU-CS-91-102, School of Computer Science, Carnegie Mellon Univ.

Selman, B., and Kautz, H. A. 1993. Local search strategies for satisfiability testing. In *Proceedings 1993 DIMACS Workshop on Maximum Clique, Graph Coloring, and Satisfiability*.

Selman, B.; Levesque, H.; and Mitchell, D. 1992. A new method for solving hard satisfiability problems. In *Proceedings of the Tenth National Conference on Artificial Intelligence*, 440–446.

Smith, S. F., and Cheng, C.-C. 1993. Slack-based heuristics for constraint satisfaction scheduling. In *Proceedings of the Eleventh National Conference on Artificial Intelligence*, 139–144.

Williams, C. P., and Hogg, T. 1992. Using deep structure to locate hard problems. In *Proceedings of the Tenth National Conference on Artificial Intelligence*.

Xiong, Y.; Sadeh, N.; and Sycara, K. 1992. Intelligent backtracking techniques for job shop scheduling. In *Proceedings of the Third International Conference on Principles of Knowledge Representation and Reasoning*.

Just-In-Case Scheduling

Mark Drummond
Recom Technologies

John Bresina
Recom Technologies

Keith Swanson
NASA

AI Research Branch, Mail Stop: 269-2
NASA Ames Research Center
Moffett Field, CA 94035-1000   USA
e-mail: {drummond, bresina, swanson}@ptolemy.arc.nasa.gov

Abstract

This paper presents an algorithm, called *Just-In-Case Scheduling*, for building robust schedules that tend not to break. The algorithm implements the common sense idea of being prepared for likely errors, just in case they should occur. The Just-In-Case algorithm analyzes a given nominal schedule, determines the most likely break, and reinvokes a scheduler to generate a contingent schedule to cover that break. After a number of iterations, the Just-In-Case algorithm produces a "multiply contingent" schedule that is more robust than the original nominal schedule. The algorithm has been developed for a real telescope scheduling domain in order to proactively manage schedule breaks that are due to an inherent uncertainty in observation durations. The paper presents empirical results showing that the algorithm performs extremely well on a representative problem from this domain.

Introduction

This paper presents and evaluates an algorithm for generating schedules that have robust execution behavior. The algorithm is called *Just-In-Case Scheduling*, or JIC, and it implements the common sense idea of being prepared for likely errors, just in case they should occur. JIC handles schedule execution errors that are due to the presence of actions with uncertain durations.

In modeling terms, an action with uncertain duration is *stochastic*: its outcome cannot be uniquely determined. It is commonly believed that if stochastic actions are included in a planning or scheduling formalism, then the resulting reasoning problem will be intractable. If the average stochastic branching factor is b, then at each branch point, a nominal schedule covers one of the outcomes and $b - 1$ outcomes remain as possible execution breaks, or errors. Thus, a nominal schedule containing n actions has approximately $n \times (b - 1)$ different possible errors. Proactively managing each of these errors would mean finding a schedule to cover each possible error case. Further,

the new schedule for each error case would itself produce new possible errors that also require proactive management. Under these conditions, the number of possible error cases grows rapidly, and the problem is clearly intractable.

The results presented in this paper run counter to these expectations. We show that for an extremely large and practical problem, contingent reasoning about stochastic actions is not only tractable, but is efficient and effective. The JIC algorithm performs extremely well for our telescope scheduling application domain, and we have reason to believe that it should work well on similar domains.

In the remainder of the paper, we first introduce the application domain, then define the JIC algorithm, then present an empirical evaluation of that algorithm, and lastly conclude with some general remarks.

The Domain

Just-In-Case scheduling has been developed for a real telescope scheduling domain. This section outlines only key aspects of the domain; more details are available elsewhere: Bresina, *et al.* (1993), Bresina *et al.* (*in press*), Genet (1994), and Genet & Hayes (1989).

In this domain, telescope users electronically submit observation requests to a central location for subsequent scheduling. The requests contain "hard" constraints, defined by basic physics, and a number of "soft" preferences. The most important hard constraint is an *observing window*. Each observation request can be executed only in a specific time window. A window is an interval of time, typically between one and eight hours, defined by the astronomer who submitted the request. Once submitted, an observation request can be active for weeks or months. In the remainder of the paper, we refer to each observation request as an *action*.

The scheduling problem is one of finding a sequence of actions that satisfies all hard constraints completely and that achieves a good score according to an objective function that measures how well the schedule satisfies the soft preferences. A schedule is a sequence of actions, each with an *enablement interval* assigned by the scheduler. The assigned enablement interval of each action is a subinterval of the action's (astronomer-provided) observing window. A scheduler assigns the enablement intervals to further restrict when the actions can begin execution. This paper does not address the problem of finding a schedule (discussed by Drummond, Swanson, & Bresina, *in press*) – we assume the existence of a scheduler that produces a feasible and reasonable-scoring observing schedule, given a set of actions, constraints, and an objective function.

Finding a schedule is only the first step. The telescope used in this domain is fully automatic and runs unattended; thus, unlike many scheduling domains where printing a schedule is the final goal, the system must be able to automatically execute a schedule. A schedule is executed by executing each action in the scheduled sequence. After an action finishes execution, if the current time is outside of the next action's (scheduler-assigned) enablement interval, then the schedule breaks and execution halts.

Execution of a typical action involves repetitions of the following three-step pattern: first, move the telescope to point at (or near) a star; second, search a limited section of the sky in order to center the star within the telescope lens; third, take an instrument reading. The amount of time it takes to center a star depends on how accurately the telescope is pointed when it starts the centering search and how clear the sky is. The star centering search process makes it impossible to predict exactly how long each action will take to execute.

Schedule breakage due to uncertain action duration is the central problem addressed by JIC. The predicted start time of an action in a schedule is based on the sum of the estimated durations of the actions that precede it. Hence, the further into the future an action occurs in the schedule, the greater the uncertainty surrounding its actual start time. Given the way that uncertainty grows into the future, it is possible for a schedule to call for an action to be executed at a time outside its scheduler-assigned interval. Hence, a schedule can break during execution solely because of accumulated duration prediction errors.

There is a simple solution to the problem of duration prediction errors: make the start time of each action equal to a worst case estimate of the previous action's finish time and introduce a busy-wait in case the previous action finishes early. Unfortunately, introducing such busy-waits wastes valuable observing time during the night. In the long run, the amount of time wasted during busy-waits can be significant. Our goal is to avoid schedule breaks without wasting valuable observing time.

Schedules fail for reasons other than duration uncertainty. Clouds or wind can make star centering impossible, resulting in unavoidable schedule breakage. In our system, when the current schedule breaks, the telescope controller invokes the scheduler to generate a new schedule. Thus, while weather can cause a break in schedule execution, the system is robust enough to dynamically reschedule and try again. The problem with on-line rescheduling is that it wastes valuable observing time whenever the telescope is idle, waiting for the scheduler. There is limited observing time available during the night, and we do not want to waste it. Further motivation for the development of JIC is given in Swanson, Bresina, & Drummond (1994).

The basic idea behind JIC is to proactively manage execution breaks caused by action duration uncertainty. Proactive error management uses off-line time during the day to compute and store alternative schedules in order to reduce on-line rescheduling time during the night.

JIC defines a "wrapper" algorithm that allows one to repeatedly and proactively call an existing scheduler. This approach is extremely general in the sense that, by decoupling scheduling from reasoning about uncertainty, it allows an arbitrary scheduler to employ JIC. The scheduler used to date in our system does not exploit any information regarding action duration uncertainty. This scheduler is simpler and possibly more efficient than one that does take action duration uncertainty into account. However, schedulers which ignore uncertainty might find schedules that are intrinsically difficult to make robust. An alternative approach is to have the scheduler consider both the objective function score obtained by a given schedule *and* the action duration uncertainty. Given that action duration uncertainty can be modeled probabilistically, decision theory tells us how to combine the objective function and probability measures in terms of expected utility. Unfortunately, decision theory does not provide a computationally effective means of doing so for problems with large search spaces. Previous experiments have indicated that a typical search space for our telescope domain contains on the order of 10^{57} different schedules (Drummond, Swanson, & Bresina, *in press*). Thus, using a separate mechanism to manage duration uncertainty seems to be a reasonable compromise.

The Algorithm

In overview, the JIC algorithm accepts a schedule as input and robustifies it as follows. First, using a model of how action durations can vary, the temporal uncertainty at each step in the schedule is estimated. Second, the most probable break due to this uncertainty is determined. Third, the possible break point is split into two hypothetical cases: one in which the schedule breaks and one in which it does not. Fourth, the scheduler is invoked on a new scheduling subproblem to produce an alternative schedule for the break case. Fifth, this alternative schedule is integrated with the initial schedule producing an updated "multiply contingent" schedule. This completes consideration of one break case; if there is more time before schedule execution begins, then the JIC process can be repeated with the current multiply contingent schedule as the new input. We now consider each step in more detail.

In order to model the execution duration for each action, we keep statistics from actual executions at the telescope. Each day, we derive an updated duration mean and standard deviation for each action. We believe that an action's execution duration has a normal (gaussian) distribution. However, for reasons of simplicity and efficiency, we model duration uncertainty as a uniform distribution in the current implementation. Our experimental results show that this approximation works quite well in practice.

In order to explain the detailed steps of the algorithm, we first need to define some terms. Each action A_i has a duration mean μ_i and standard deviation σ_i. One of the preconditions of each action is the interval of time during which it can begin execution; let W_i be this *observing window* for A_i. (Recall that the observing window is provided by an astronomer.)

A *schedule* is a sequence of actions, where each action is associated with an *enablement interval*, E_i, assigned by the scheduler: $(A_0, E_0); \ldots; (A_n, E_n)$, such that for $i = 0, \ldots, n$, $E_i \subseteq W_i$. During schedule execution, as soon as action A_{i-1} is finished executing, action A_i is selected for enablement testing; A_i is enabled if the current time is within E_i. If A_i is enabled, then it is immediately executed; otherwise, the schedule breaks.

A *multiply contingent schedule* can be thought of as a set of alternative schedules; to save space, our implementation uses a tree to represent this set of schedules. Let $\beta(i)$ be defined such that $A_{\beta(i)}$ is the predecessor of A_i in the schedule, if one exists. For simplicity, we assume that A_0 is the unique first action.

Using the duration uncertainty model, JIC estimates the temporal uncertainty at each step in the schedule by starting at the beginning of the schedule and propagating uncertainty forward. This process involves estimating the time at which each action in the schedule will start and finish executing. The *start interval*, S_i, is the set of possible execution start times for action A_i. Similarly, the *finish interval*, F_i, is the set of possible execution finish times for action A_i. Let S_0 denote the interval during which schedule execution can start. For simplicity, let us assume that schedule execution always starts exactly at twilight; hence, S_0 is the degenerate interval [twilight, twilight].

A_i cannot start executing outside its enablement window. Hence, if $A_{\beta(i)}$ finishes executing at a time outside of E_i, then either an action in an alternative contingent schedule will be executed or the schedule will break. Thus, S_i is computed to be $F_{\beta(i)} \cap E_i$.

Given that A_i's start interval, Si, is $[t_1, t_2]$, its finish interval, F_i, is computed to be $[t_1 + \mu_i - \sigma_i, t_2 + \mu_i + \sigma_i]$. The current implementation simply uses one standard deviation of the mean when computing each finish interval, and this has worked well in practice.

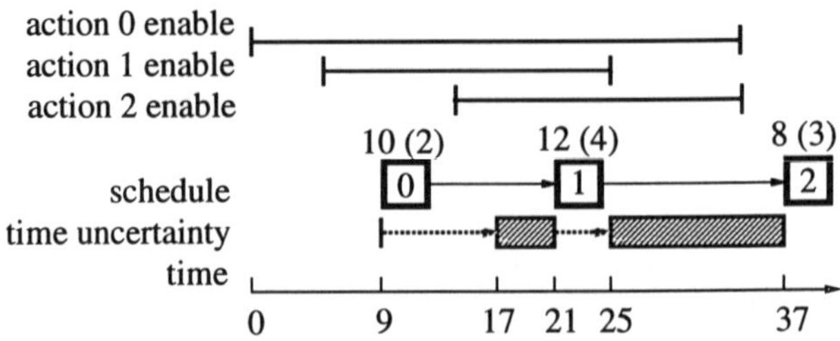

Figure 1: Propagation of temporal uncertainty.

See Figure 1 for a stylized schedule containing three actions labeled 0, 1, and 2. The enablement intervals assigned by the scheduler are given at the top of the figure, and the schedule ordering is indicated by solid arrows between the actions. The numbers above an action indicate a mean and standard deviation for that action's duration (*e.g.*, action 0 has a mean duration of 10 and a standard deviation of 2). The schedule is predicted to start exactly at time 9, indicated by a degenerate uncertainty interval above time 9 (the solid line above time 9). JIC computes a finish interval for action 0 that ranges from 17 to 21 and a finish interval for action 1 that ranges from 25 to 37.

Using the finish interval estimates and the assigned enablement intervals of the actions, JIC determines the action in the schedule that has the highest probability of breaking. The break probability of an action is a function of the *enablement probability* of that action and of all preceding actions.

Let $p(\text{enable}(A_i))$ be the enablement probability for action A_i; that is, the probability that A_i will be enabled when selected. It is computed to be the proportion of the previous action's finish interval during which A_i is enabled.

For $i = 0$: $p(\text{enable}(A_i)) = 1.0$

For $i > 0$: $p(\text{enable}(A_i)) = \frac{|F_{\beta(i)} \cap E_i|}{|F_{\beta(i)}|}$

For simplicity, this computation is based on the erroneous assumption that all of an action's possible finish times are equally likely (*i.e.*, that $F_{\beta(i)}$ has a uniform probability distribution) and, hence, is only an estimate of the true enablement probability.

Let $p(\text{select}(A_i))$ be the *selection probability* for action A_i; that is, the probability that A_i will be selected for enablement testing. An action will be selected if the preceding action was both selected and enabled; the schedule's first action will always be selected.

For $i = 0$: $p(\text{select}(A_i)) = 1.0$

For $i > 0$: $p(\text{select}(A_i)) = p(\text{select}(A_{\beta(i)})) \times p(\text{enable}(A_{\beta(i)}))$

Let $p(\text{break}(A_i))$ be the *break probability* for action A_i; that is, the probability that the schedule will break at A_i when it is selected for enablement testing.

$$p(\text{break}(A_i)) = p(\text{select}(A_i)) \times [1 - p(\text{enable}(A_i))]$$

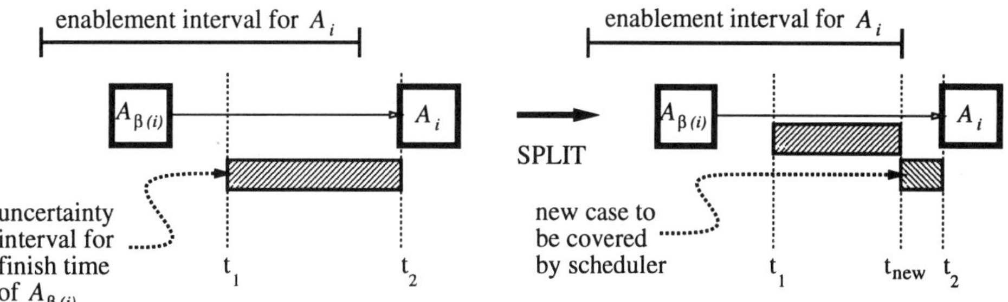

Figure 2: Splitting an uncertainty interval.

Note that the computation of break probabilities is similar to the computation of conditional probabilities in a Markov chain (Thiebaux, *et al.*, 1993).

After determining the action with the highest break probability, JIC splits the associated uncertainty time interval into two subintervals. This is shown graphically in Figure 2. A_i is the action identified as having the highest break probability, and $A_{\beta(i)}$ is the previous action in the schedule. The possible finish interval of $A_{\beta(i)}$, $[t_1, t_2]$, is split according to how it overlaps A_i's assigned enablement interval. The subinterval $[t_{new}, t_2]$ is split off as a break case, since it is outside the enablement interval. A new scheduling subproblem is formed with t_{new} as its start time. JIC then invokes the scheduler on this subproblem and incorporates the returned alternative schedule into the original schedule. The resulting multiply contingent schedule still contains $A_{\beta(i)}$ followed by A_i. The alternative schedule will be executed only if after execution of $A_{\beta(i)}$, A_i is not enabled. In our tree representation of a multiply contingent schedule, each branch point corresponds to an uncertainty interval that has been split.

Suppose that the telescope management system stops accepting new observation actions one hour before twilight. This gives the scheduler one hour to find a schedule for that night. It is relatively easy to find a high-scoring schedule in about one minute (Drummond, Swanson, & Bresina, *in press*). This leaves roughly 59 minutes for JIC to proactively make the schedule more robust. JIC incurs overhead to find the most probable schedule break and to create a new scheduling subproblem. However, if we assume that the overhead time required for JIC is comparatively small and that each call JIC makes to the scheduler takes about one minute, then there is time available to consider about fifty possible break cases.

The time cost of the JIC algorithm is proportional to the size of the multiply contingent schedule, and schedule size grows linearly with the number of cases covered by JIC. Since the algorithm's time cost is a function of the number of cases covered, it is natural to wonder how many cases must be covered to usefully increase the execution robustness of a typical observing schedule. This is precisely the question addressed by the first experiment presented in the next section.

Empirical Evaluation

To evaluate the performance of JIC we performed several experiments using real telescope scheduling data. The observation actions were provided by Greg Henry of Tennessee State University (Hall & Henry, 1992; Henry & Hall, *in press*). The scheduler used in these experiments deterministically hill-climbs on a domain-specific heuristic (Boyd, *et al.*, 1993). The experiments required collecting data from thousands of schedule executions; since this is impractical on a real telescope, we developed a simulator of the telescope controller's schedule executor. In the first experiment, the simulator computes an action's execution duration by using a random variable with a normal (gaussian) probability distribution whose mean and standard deviation are set equal to the statistics obtained from a number of nights of actual execution on a telescope at the Fairborn Observatory (Mt. Hopkins, Arizona).

The question is: given real telescope scheduling data, can JIC provide a useful increase in schedule robustness within a reasonable number of contingent cases? To answer this question we measured how far into the night a multiply contingent schedule executes before rescheduling would be required. The experimental procedure is as follows.

First, the scheduler is used to find a single nominal schedule. This schedule is executed 1000 times by the simulator; for each execution run we note the percentage of the night that the schedule executes before halting, either due to a break or schedule completion. Next, we allow JIC to find and fix what it deems to be the most probable break case, and then run the augmented schedule through the execution simulator (again, 1000 times). This step is repeated until JIC has covered thirty break cases.

Figure 3 contains two graphs in which the independent variable is the number of break cases covered by JIC. In the left graph, the dependent variable is the percentage of the night that the schedule executes before halting, averaged over 1000 runs. It clearly shows that the mean percentage of the night executed increases with the number of cases considered by JIC. The performance increase is most dramatic early on, as we had hoped. After only ten cases, the schedule executes, on average, through 96% of the night. (This

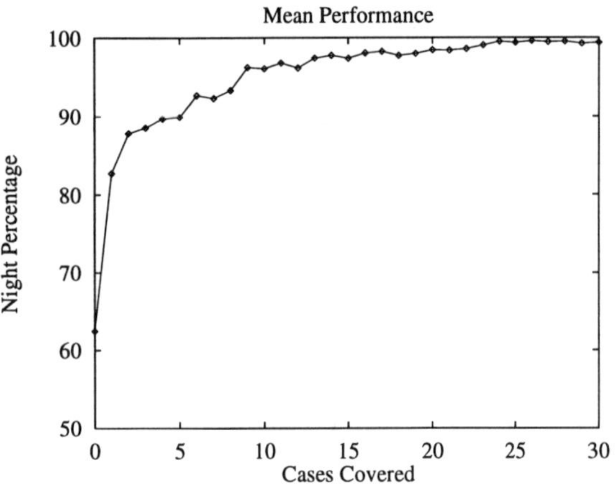 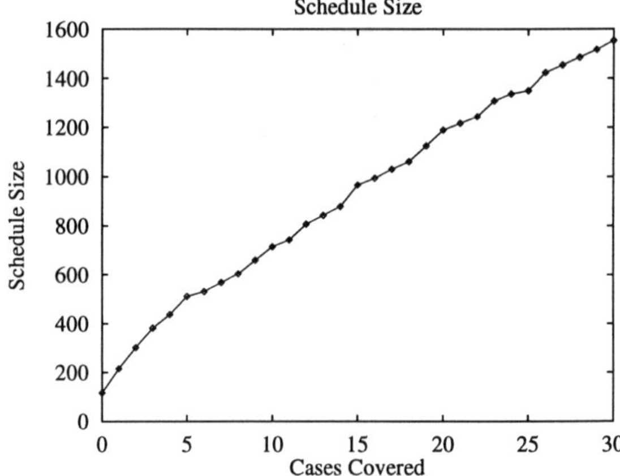

Figure 3: Mean performance, measured as night percentage, *vs.* cases covered and schedule size *vs.* cases covered.

indicates that JIC should be easily capable of finding extremely robust schedules in the hour before twilight.)

In the right graph of Figure 3, the dependent variable is schedule size, measured as the total number of actions the multiply contingent schedule contains. The nominal schedule contains 116 actions, and the results confirm, as expected, that schedule size increases linearly with the number of cases.

Figure 4 provides additional insight into the behavior of JIC. The graph shows the particular points at which a schedule (with a given number of cases covered) is likely to break throughout the night. It focuses on the first ten cases since this is where most of the improvement occurs. Each vertical line indicates the proportion of 1000 schedule executions that halted at a given percentage of the night, for a given number of cases. The night percentages are rounded to the nearest integer. The probability of executing the entire schedule is shown in the graph as the "break" probability at 100% of the night.

Consider the situation when JIC has not been run; *i.e.*, when zero break cases have been covered. There is a 0.4 probability of the nominal schedule breaking 14% of the way through the night, and there is a 0.4 probability of the nominal schedule executing through the entire night. After covering one case, JIC has managed to remove the early break at 14% and to increase the probability of executing completely through the night. However, by removing one possible break early on, JIC may introduce new possible breaks in the contingent schedule. For example, after one case is covered, a new possible break occurs at 25% of the night.

Figure 4 shows that schedule breaks tend to occur in only a few specific locations. There is a significant probability of the nominal schedule breaking early in the night. As JIC covers more cases, the probability of finishing the entire night increases. The probability of the break that is covered by an application of JIC is redistributed to the new contingent schedule; hence,

the improvement gain is a function of the probability of successfully executing the new contingent schedule. The graph shows that JIC is able to cover many of the probable breaks, making the schedule extremely robust after only ten cases.

The results reported above are based on the duration uncertainty computed from a number of nights of actual telescope execution. How would JIC's performance be impacted by more or less uncertainty in the domain? To empirically investigate this question, we designed another experiment that uses the same scheduling problem as the experiment discussed above. The mean durations are also the same, but we experimentally vary the standard deviation for each action. Both JIC and the execution simulator use the same standard deviations. The standard deviation for each action is computed to be a given percentage of its mean; thus, a value of 1.0 for duration uncertainty indicates that the standard deviation for each action's duration is one percent of its mean.

Figure 5 shows the results from this experiment. The graph shows that when no cases have been covered by JIC, the mean percentage of night executed before breaking falls off quickly with increasing duration uncertainty. However, as more cases are covered by JIC, the rate of this fall-off decreases. Note that each successive line on the graph corresponds to a doubling of the number of cases covered; thus, the performance improvement expected from JIC is initially quite good, but it decreases with increasing cases (consistent with the results shown in Figure 3). For the actual standard deviations used in the previous experiment, we estimated the average percentage of the mean duration to be about 2.5. Figure 5 is consistent with our previous results: it predicts, for example, that for an uncertainty of 2.5 and 8 cases covered, the percentage of night executed should be around 95. This helps explain why JIC works so well on the actual telescope data. With greater duration uncertainty in the domain, we would not have been so fortunate!

Discussion and Conclusions

This paper has presented an algorithm for Just-In-Case scheduling. Using an existing scheduler and simple statistical models of duration uncertainty, the algorithm proactively makes a nominal schedule more robust. Despite some rather egregious modeling assumptions, the algorithm works extremely well for a real telescope scheduling domain. (See Bresina, Drummond, & Swanson, 1994, for an evaluation of the practical impact of these modeling assumptions.) Traditional intuitions surrounding the management of stochastic actions suggest the inevitability of large search spaces and intractable reasoning. Using a "splitting" technique, our algorithm makes stochastic distinctions only when necessary. We have demonstrated in this paper that for a real problem, involving a large search space, there are very few stochastic action distinctions actually made by the algorithm. JIC covers most of the likely schedule breaks in a small number of iterations. In this concluding section, we discuss some related work and possible extensions.

The ideas behind JIC are quite general, and it should be possible to use the algorithm to manage other sorts of execution errors. All that is required is a statistical model of the frequency of execution breaks and a model of each break's impact on the state of the environment. For instance, in a machine shop one can gather statistics describing the mean time between failures for any given machine, and in a warehouse application involving human staff, typically there are numbers available that describe absenteeism. Such statistics could be put to use in a version of JIC. Computation time during idle periods (for instance, overnight) could be used to proactively reschedule for errors that occur during busy periods (for instance, during the day).

An interesting alternative for computing break probabilities is *stochastic simulation* (as used by Muscettola, 1993). Rather than explicitly propagate uncertainty intervals, such a technique generates a predicted duration for each scheduled activity according to a nor-

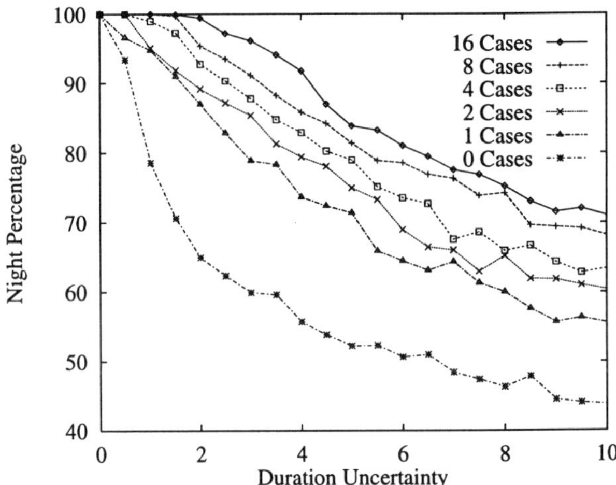

Figure 5: How performance of JIC falls-off with increasing duration uncertainty.

mal distribution. Working forward, stochastic simulation generates a specific start time for each scheduled action, producing one possible execution trace, or sample. A number of samples must be gathered to form a picture with any degree of confidence. In principle, this technique can be used to form more accurate break predictions than our simple uniform propagation model. However, it is not clear that the extra cost of the stochastic simulation technique is worth the extra accuracy it offers. This is a topic for future study.

JIC is derived from an earlier algorithm, *traverse-and-robustify* (Drummond & Bresina, 1990), which requires an explicit model of stochastic action outcomes (Bresina, Drummond, & Kedar, 1993). The model used by traverse-and-robustify assumes that action outcomes are predefined discrete world states. In contrast, the actions considered in this paper are stochastic but continuous: the duration of an action can take on any value within some given interval. The traverse-and-robustify algorithm has been extended by Dean, *et al.* (1993) with the use of policy-iteration algorithms; however, their new algorithms still require an explicit and discrete stochastic action specification.

In contrast, Hanks (1990) presents an algorithm that forms its own stochastic action outcomes. Hanks' temporal projection system makes distinctions in the outcomes of an action only as required to answer a specific query, but it still assumes that actions have discrete outcomes. Our work can be viewed as a version of Hanks' idea that operates with continuous action outcomes. For our domain, it is necessary to make distinctions between possible action durations only when there is some chance that the next scheduled action will not be enabled. In essence, all actions are not created equal with respect to stochastic outcomes: temporal context is important and stochastic distinctions are introduced only when they matter.

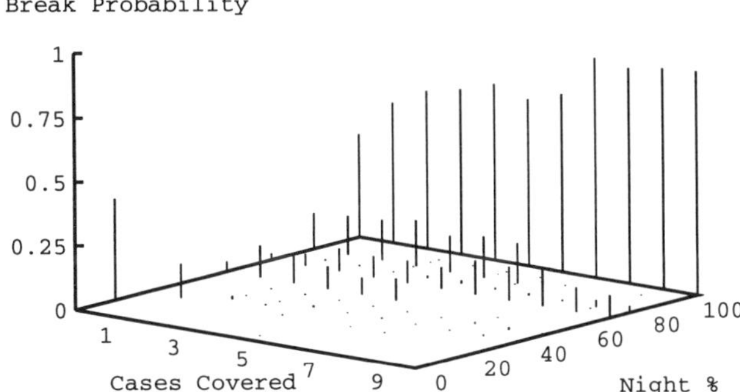

Figure 4: Where and how frequently the schedule breaks with respect to cases covered.

While JIC works extremely well for our particular telescope scheduling domain, it will not necessarily fare as well on all domains. We have analyzed the nature of schedule breaks in our domain in order to characterize the general conditions under which JIC achieves useful robustness increments in a few iterations. Essentially, JIC appears to work well when the following three conditions hold.

First, there must be room for improvement. If the probability of successful execution of the nominal schedule is close to 1.0, there is not much JIC can add. Second, there must be a small number of schedule breaks responsible for most of the total break probability mass because then each break case covered by JIC can usefully increase the probability of executing the entire schedule. Third, each contingent schedule found must be no worse in its break characteristics than the nominal schedule. In some sense, this is simply a recursive application of the first two conditions; it requires that each contingent schedule be as easy to robustify as the nominal one. We plan to further investigate these intuitions, in order to more precisely characterize the conditions under which JIC works well.

Acknowledgments

Thanks to readers of previous drafts: John Allen, Will Edgington, Peter Friedland, Lise Getoor, Rich Levinson, Nicola Muscettola, and Pandu Nayak. Additional thanks to Will Edgington for assisting with the overall telescope management and scheduling project. Discussions on decision theory and contingent scheduling with Andrew Mayer, Othar Hansson, and Denise Draper have been very useful.

References

Boyd, L., Epand, D., Bresina, J., Drummond, M., Swanson, K., Crawford, D., Genet, D., Genet, R., Henry, G., McCook, G., Neely, W., Schmidtke, P., Smith, D., and Trublood, M. 1993. Automatic Telescope Instruction Set 1993. *International Amateur Professional Photoelectric Photometry (IAPPP) Communications*, No. 52, T. Oswalt (ed).

Bresina, J., Drummond, M., and Kedar, S. 1993. Reactive, Integrated Systems Pose New Problems for Machine Learning. In *Machine Learning Methods for Planning*, S. Minton (ed.). Morgan-Kaufmann.

Bresina, J., Drummond, M., Swanson, K., and Edgington, W. *In Press.* Automated Management and Scheduling of Remote Automatic Telescopes. *Astronomy for the Earth and Moon*, the proceedings of the 103rd Annual Meeting of the Astronomical Society of the Pacific, D. Pyper Smith (ed.).

Bresina, J., Drummond, M., Swanson, K., and Edgington, W. 1993. Advanced Scheduling and Automation. *International Amateur Professional Photoelectric Photometry (IAPPP) Communications.*

Bresina, J., Drummond, M., Swanson, K. 1994. Managing Action Duration Uncertainty with Just-In-Case Scheduling. NASA Ames Technical Report FIA-94-04. (Also appears In *Working Notes of the 1994 AAAI Spring Symposium on Decision Theoretic Planning.* Stanford, CA.)

Dean, T., Kaelbling, L., Kirman, J., and Nicholson, A. 1993. Planning with Deadlines in Stochastic Domains. In *Proc. of AAAI-93*, pp 574 – 579.

Drummond, M., and Bresina, J. 1990. Anytime Synthetic Projection: Maximizing the Probability of Goal Satisfaction. In *Proc. of AAAI-90*. pp. 138–144.

Drummond, M., Swanson, K., and Bresina, J. *In press.* Robust Scheduling and Execution for Automatic Telescopes. In *Intelligent Scheduling*, M. Zweben & M. Fox (eds). Morgan-Kaufmann.

Genet, D. 1994. AutoScope Control System Reference Manual (Software Version 2.0). AutoScope Corporation, Ft. Collins, CO.

Genet, R.M., and Hayes, D.S. 1989. *Robotic Observatories: A Handbook of Remote–Access Personal–Computer Astronomy.* AutoScope Corporation, Ft. Collins, CO.

Hall, D. S. and Henry, G. W. 1992. Performance Evaluation of Two Automatic Telescopes after Eight Years. *Automated Telescopes for Photometry and Imaging*, S. J. Adelman, R. J. Dukes, and C. J. Adelman (eds.) (San Francisco: Astronomical Society of the Pacific).

Hanks, S. 1990. Practical Temporal Projection. In *Proc. of AAAI-90*. pp 158 – 163.

Henry, G. W. and Hall, D. S. *In press.* The Quest for Precision Robotic Photometry. *International Amateur Professional Photoelectric Photometry (IAPPP) Communications* 55.

Muscettola, N. 1993. Scheduling by Iterative Partition of Bottleneck Conflicts, *Proc. of the 9th Conference on Artificial Intelligence for Applications*, IEEE Computer Society Press (March).

Swanson, K., Bresina, J., and Drummond, M. 1994. Just-In-Case Scheduling for Automatic Telescopes. In *Knowledge-Based Artificial Intelligence Systems in Aerospace and Industry*. W. Buntine & D.H. Fisher (eds.), Proc. SPIE 2244, pp. 10–19.

Thiebaux, S., Hertzberg, J., Shoaff, W., and Schneider, M. 1993. A Stochastic Model of Actions and Plans for Anytime Planning Under Uncertainty. In *Proc. of the Second European Workshop on Planning*, Vadstena, Sweden (Dec. 9–11).

On the Utility of Bottleneck Reasoning for Scheduling

Nicola Muscettola
RECOM Technologies
NASA Ames Research Center
AI Research Branch, Mail Stop: 269-2
Moffett Field, CA 94035-1000
e-mail: mus@ptolemy.arc.nasa.gov

Abstract

The design of better schedulers requires a deeper understanding of each component technique and of their interactions. Although widely accepted in practice, bottleneck reasoning for scheduling has not yet been sufficiently validated, either formally or empirically. This paper reports an empirical analysis of the heuristic information used by bottleneck-centered, opportunistic scheduling systems to solve constraint satisfaction scheduling problems. Different configurations of a single scheduling framework are applied to a benchmark set of scheduling problems and compared with respect to number of problems solved and processing time. We show superior performances for schedulers that use bottleneck information. We also show that focusing at the bottleneck might not only provide an effective "most constrained first" heuristic but also, unexpectedly, increase the utility of other heuristic information.

Introduction

Problem solvers often use combinations of several different heuristics and reasoning methods (*e.g.*, constraint propagation, search). Empirical comparisons of performances of different problem solvers can show that one combination of techniques is superior to another. However, to design better problem solvers we need a deeper understanding of the importance of each component technique and of how different techniques interact.

This paper reports an empirical analysis of the performance of heuristic information typically used to solve constraint satisfaction scheduling problems. We will focus on bottleneck-centered, opportunistic schedulers, a class of systems that has shown better performance than other kinds of schedulers (Adams, Balas, & Zawack 1988; Sadeh 1991; Muscettola 1993). We will show that there is strong empirical evidence on the effectiveness of reasoning about bottlenecks. Moreover, we will show evidence of the fact that heuristic information gathered at the bottleneck is "more useful" than average. This allows a bottleneck centered scheduler to make several decisions without having to re-evaluate its heuristic information too often.

Although widely accepted in practice (*e.g.*, manufacturing scheduling), bottleneck reasoning has not yet been sufficiently validated, either formally or empirically. Although formal validation would be most desirable, at present no formal model realistically captures the deep structure of scheduling problems. In its absence, strong evidence of performance can be gathered with empirical studies. We believe that such studies will also be extremely useful to discover new "phenomena" which will guide the search for an appropriate formal model.

The goal of an opportunistic scheduler is to build an assignment of time and resources to a network of activities and a set of resources such as to avoid resource over-subscriptions. The goal is achieved by repeatedly applying the following basic *opportunistic scheduling cycle*:

1. *Analyze*: analyze the current problem solving state;

2. *Focus*: select one or more activities that are expected to participate in a critical interaction among problem constraints;

3. *Decide*: add constraints to reduce negative interactions among critical activities.

Opportunistic schedulers differ on the specific techniques used to implement each phase (Smith *et al.* 1990; Biefeld & Cooper 1991; Sadeh 1991; Adams, Balas, & Zawack 1988; Muscettola 1993) but share several fundamental characteristics. The *Analyze* phase consists of building estimates of demand/supply ratios for the different resources and/or activities. These estimates are usually conducted on relaxed versions of the problem obtained by dropping some of its original temporal and/or resource constraints. During the *Focus* phase, all opportunistic schedulers use bottlenecks as the primary means of selecting critical interactions. While the exact definition of a bottleneck may vary, all opportunistic schedulers agree on relating this concept to a resource and time interval with a high demand/supply ratio. Critical activities are usually defined as those that are likely to request the use of a bottleneck. The constraints posted during the *Decide* phase impose arbitration among conflicting capacity and time requests. This is the phase where opportunistic schedulers differ the most with respect to the type of constraint posted (assigning a value to a variable versus imposing a precedence among activities) and to the granularity of the decision making process (the number of decisions taken at each cycle).

The study in this paper was conducted on Conflict Partition Scheduling (CPS) (Muscettola 1993), a scheduling method that implements the opportunistic scheduling paradigm. We first describe CPS and the stochastic simulation method used to compute heuristic information. Then we analyze two steps of the procedure: bottleneck detection and scheduling decision making. We discuss modifications of these steps and make hypotheses on how these modifications might affect performance. We then verify our hypotheses against the results of an experimental analysis.

We believe that our results are typical of the performance of other opportunistic schedulers. We base our belief on the similarity of each CPS step to other opportunistic schedulers and on the applicability of the performance hypotheses to comparable modifications of other schedulers.

Conflict Partition Scheduling

CPS adopts a *constraint posting* approach to scheduling, *i.e.*, it operates by posting temporal precedences among activities (activity α_i must precede activity α_j). During problem solving, each activity has an associated window of opportunity for its execution; these can be deduced by propagating activity durations and metric temporal constraints (absolute and relative) across the activity network (Dechter, Meiri, & Pearl 1991). Previous empirical studies have shown that constraint posting schedulers perform better than schedulers that proceed by assigning precise values to the start and end time of each activity (Applegate & Cook 1990; Muscettola 1993; Smith & Cheng 1993).

Figure 1 shows how CPS organizes its computation. In relation to the opportunistic cycle described in the introduction, Capacity Analysis corresponds to *Analyze*, Conflict Identification to *Focus*, and Conflict Arbitration to *Decide*. The consistency test is a propagation of the metric temporal constraints in the activity network.

The algorithm described in the diagram follows an iterative sampling approach to search (Minton *et al.* 1992; Langley 1992). If the consistency test fails, the activity network is reset to the initial state and the procedure is re-started. As we will see later, CPS' capacity analysis is stochastic in nature; therefore, each repetition can explore a different path in the problem solving space. If a solution has not been found after a fixed number of repetitions (in our case, 10), CPS terminates with an overall failure. The choice of iterative sampling is consistent with our interest in isolating the information content of the heuristic information generated by the Capacity Analysis. However, it is also possible to use the internal CPS cycle in a systematic search approach. For example, Conflict Arbitration could sprout several alternative ways of adding constraints among conflicting activities. Prioritization of these alternatives could make use of Capacity Analysis information and a backtracking scheme would ensure continuation when reaching a dead end.

The Capacity Analysis computes all the heuristic information used for decision-making by generating estimates of the structure of the remaining search space without engaging in detailed problem solving. Such estimates are statistics computed from a sample of complete time assignments to activity start times. These assignments are consistent with all the temporal constraints explicitly represented in the current activity network[1], but do not usually result in consistent schedules since they do not necessarily satisfy all the constraints of the problem (*i.e.*, those capacity constraints that have not yet been explicitly enforced). CPS uses a stochastic simulation process to generate each complete time assignment. This process differs from other stochastic simulation techniques (Drummond & Bresina 1990; Hanks 1990) used to estimate the possible outcomes of executing a detailed schedule in an uncertain environment. Having to insure executability, these simulations must introduce additional constraints to complete an intermediate problem solving state into a consistent schedule. Therefore, they end up considering many more details than are useful or necessary for an aggregate capacity analysis. Instead, CPS' stochastic simulation (Muscettola & Smith 1987) considers only the constraints that are explicit in the current intermediate state, with very weak assumptions on how it will be extended into a complete schedule.

In the following, $EST(\alpha)$ and $LFT(\alpha)$ will denote, respectively, the earliest start time and the latest finish time of the activity α, H will denote the overall scheduling horizon, and R will be the set of resources.

CPS' stochastic simulation proceeds by repeating the following cycle. Before the simulation starts, a temporal constraint propagation establishes the range of possible start times for each activity. At each simulation cycle i, an activity α_i is selected according to a given strategy. After the selection, a start time is randomly chosen among α_i's possible start times and assigned to the activity. The random choice follows a given probability distribution, or *selection rule*. The consequences of the start time assignment are then propagated through the network to restrict the range of other activities' start times, and the simulation cycle is repeated. The simulation terminates when all the activities of the network have been assigned a start time.

Different implementations of CPS can choose differ-

---

[1] Although CPS can deal with activities with flexible durations (*i.e.*, the duration of α must fall in the range $[d_\alpha, D_\alpha]$), we will only consider activities with fixed durations to simplify the presentation.

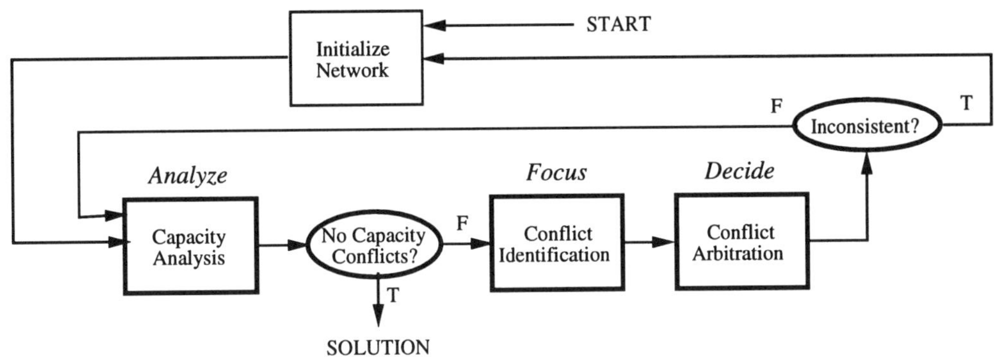

Figure 1: Conflict Partition Scheduling

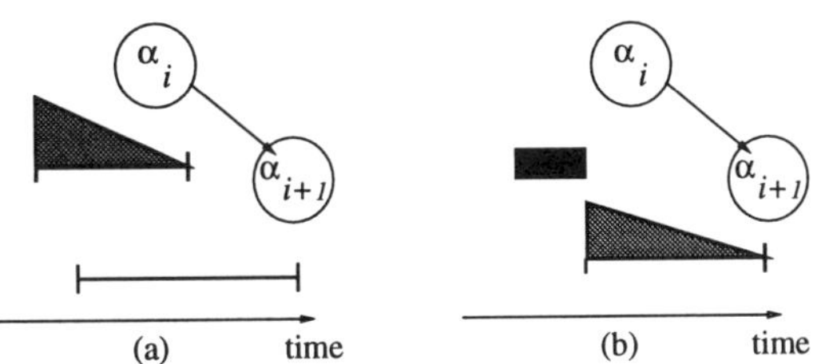

Figure 2: Simulation step: (a) before step i; (b) after step i

ent activity selection strategies and start time selection rules. A typical activity selection strategy is *forward temporal dispatching* which selects α_i among the set of activities whose predecessors have all start times assigned by previous simulation cycles. A possible start time selection rule is a linearly biased distribution (*i.e.*, the weight of the currently available times increases or decreases linearly over the time bound) for each activity in the network. These choices are crucial to the performance of CPS since they determine: (1) the computational cost of each cycle and (2) the probability of generating each of the possible total start time assignments and, therefore, the bias of the sampling base.

Figure 2 illustrates a single simulation cycle using a linear selection rule. In the figure, activity α_i precedes activity α_{i+1} in the activity network. Figure 2 (a) shows the time bounds for each activity; α_i has a linear value selection rule superimposed on its time bound. In Figure 2 (b), a start time has been selected for α_i and time has been reserved for its execution; the reservation is represented by the black rectangle. This causes α_{i+1}'s time bound to shrink. A triangular selection rule is now superimposed on α_{i+1}'s time bound and the simulation cycle can start again.

Repeating the simulation N times yields a sample of N complete time assignments. CPS' Capacity Analysis uses this sample to estimate the following two problem space metrics:

- **activity demand**: for each activity α and for each time $EST(\alpha) \leq t_i < LFT(\alpha)$, the activity demand, $\Delta(\alpha, t_i)$, is equal to n_{t_i}/N, where n_{t_i} is the number of complete time assignments in the sample for which α is being executed at time t_i.

- **resource contention**: for each resource $\rho \in R$ and for each time $t_j \in H$, the resource contention, $X(\rho, t_j)$, is equal to n_{t_j}/N, where n_{t_j} is the number of complete time assignments in the sample for which ρ is requested by more than one activity at time t_j.

Activity demand and resource contention represent two different aspects of the current problem solving state. Activity demand is a measure of preference; it indicates how much the current constraints bias an activity toward being executed at a given time. Resource contention is a measure of potential inconsistency; it indicates how likely it is that the current constraints will generate a congestion of capacity requests on a resource at a given time.

Bottleneck Detection

In problem solving, a widely accepted principle is to focus on the most tightly interacting variables, *i.e.*, those with the smallest set of possible values. For example, in constraint satisfaction search (Haralick & Elliot 1980) the 'most constrained first' heuristic minimizes the expected length of any path in the search tree and, therefore, increases the probability of achieving a solution in less time. In opportunistic scheduling this principle translates into looking for bottleneck resources.

In CPS each problem solving cycle focuses on a set of activities that are potentially in conflict, called the *conflict set*. More precisely, a conflict set is a set of activities that: (1) request the same resource, (2) have overlapping execution time bounds, and (3) are not necessarily totally ordered according to the precedence constraints of the current activity network.

To detect a conflict set CPS first identifies a bottleneck using resource contention:

- **Bottleneck**: Given the set of resource contention

functions $\{X(\rho, t)\}$ with $\rho \in R$ and $t \in H$, we define a bottleneck to be a pair $< \rho_b, t_b >$ such that:

$$X(\rho_b, t_b) = \max\{X(\rho, t)\}$$

for any $\rho \in R$ and $t \in H$ such that $X(\rho, t) > 0$.

The conflict set is then extracted among the activities requesting ρ_b with current time bounds overlapping t_b.

Although focusing on bottlenecks is widely accepted in opportunistic scheduling, there is little quantitative evidence of its effectiveness. One could wonder if the performance of the scheduler would remain unaffected if it focussed on *any* set of activities, either associated with a bottleneck or not. If this were true, one could save the additional cost required to compute resource contention and base all decision making on activity demand alone.

To answer this question we consider two different configurations of CPS' Bottleneck Identification step.

1. **Maximum contention bottleneck (BTL):** The original method used in CPS; the set of conflicting activities is selected around the bottleneck.

2. **Random (RAND):** The conflict set is selected around a randomly chosen resource and time.

Conflict Arbitration

At each Conflict Arbitration step, CPS introduces additional precedence constraints between pairs of activities to restrict their mutual position and their time bounds. An important differentiating aspect among schedulers is the granularity of decision making. At one end of the spectrum there are schedulers that make the minimum possible decision at each scheduling cycle; this follows the spirit of micro-opportunistic scheduling (Sadeh 1991). At the other end there are schedulers that make decisions that eliminate any possibility of conflict among all the activities in the conflict set; this follows the spirit of macro-opportunistic approaches (Smith *et al.* 1990; Adams, Balas, & Zawack 1988).

Within CPS we can explore the consequences of different decision making granularities. For example, a micro-opportunistic approach translates into adding a single precedence constraint between two activities in the conflict set. Conversely, a macro-opportunistic approach could be implemented by imposing a total ordering on all activities in the conflict set.

The current implementation of CPS (Muscettola 1993) proposes an intermediate granularity approach by partitioning the conflict set into two subsets, A_{before} and A_{after}, and then constraining every activity in A_{before} to occur before any activity in A_{after}. The bi-partition of the original conflict set relies on a clustering analysis of activity demands. Figure 3 (a) shows four conflicting activities and their demand profiles; figure 3 (b) shows the new precedence constraints added by Conflict Arbitration.

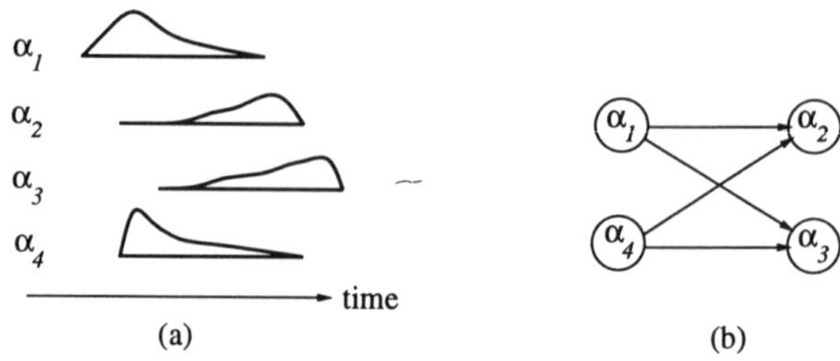

Figure 3: A Conflict Arbitration step

To choose the appropriate decision granularity one needs to evaluate a trade-off. The greater the number of scheduling decisions in a step, the greater the pruning of the search space and, therefore, the faster the scheduler. However, the more decisions that are made, the greater the change in the topology of the activity network after the step. Therefore, an analysis done before the step could give little information on the structure of the destination state. This can increase the likelihood of failure and consequent backtracking, and therefore slow down the scheduler. In summary, an important trade-off involves, the speed of convergence vs. the number of restarts needed during iterative sampling. This trade-off rests on the reasonable assumption that making fewer decisions at each cycle is always at least as accurate as making several; in other words, although possibly slower, a micro-opportunistic scheduler should solve at least as many problems as a larger granularity scheduler (Sadeh 1991).

We therefore consider two distinct Conflict Arbitration rules:

1. **conflict bi-partition (BIP):** The technique originally used in CPS; the conflict set is separated into two A_{before} and A_{after} subsets.

2. **most separated activities (MS):** A *micro* arbitration technique; it introduces a single precedence between two activities extracted from the conflict set. To minimize the impact of sampling noise, we select the two activities whose demand profiles are maximally separated.

Experimental Results

The experimental analysis made use of the Constraint Satisfaction Scheduling benchmark proposed in (Sadeh 1991). The benchmark consists of 6 groups of 10 problems, each with 50 activities, 5 resources, and non-relaxable release and due date constraints. The groups vary according to their expected difficulty. Each group is identified by two parameters: (1) the spread of the release and due dates, which can assume the three levels (in increasing order of expected difficulty) *W* for wide, *N* for narrow and *0* for null; (2) the number of expected bottleneck resources, either *1* or *2*. For more details see (Sadeh 1991).

	< BTL, BIP >	< BTL, MS >	< RAND, BIP >	< RAND, MS >
W/1	10.00	10.00	9.95	7.68
W/2	10.00	10.00	9.95	9.10
N/1	10.00	10.00	9.10	8.70
N/2	10.00	10.00	8.20	6.26
0/1	10.00	9.95	8.30	8.60
0/2	9.25	10.00	4.85	4.05
TOT	59.25	59.95	50.35	46.30

Table 1: Experimental results: number of problem solved

	< BTL, BIP >	< BTL, MS >	< RAND, BIP >	< RAND, MS >
W/1	44.94	120.90	61.74	281.49
W/2	44.59	134.00	90.82	476.97
N/1	47.02	127.40	106.67	360.72
N/2	46.03	138.90	142.81	754.39
0/1	50.27	140.40	118.24	405.10
0/2	64.86	161.10	212.96	908.89
AVG	49.62	137.10	122.20	531.26

Table 2: Experimental results: processing time

Tables 1 and 2 report the performance of all possible combinations of the alternative settings described in the previous sections. Table 1 shows the average number of problems solved over 20 independent runs of the procedure. Table 2 reports the corresponding average processing times. In order to factor out the effects of known implementation inefficiencies, processing times are given as the number of opportunistic cycles needed either to find a solution or to fail. The number of iterations was weighed differently depending on the conflict identification method, with each **RAND** cycle taking 85.64% of the time of a **BTL** cycle. The speed-up results from avoiding the computation of resource contention.

The cardinality of the Capacity Analysis sample was $N = 10$. We used *forward temporal dispatching* as the activity selection strategy. The start time selection rule was linearly biased over the time bound, with highest preference to the earliest time and lowest (0) to the latest.

All of the following conclusions have been tested for statistical significance using the methods available in the S statistical package (Chambers & Hastie 1992). For the average number of problems solved we fitted the results as a function of the configuration; this was done through a *logit* generalized linear regression. An analysis of deviance and a Chi-squared test yielded the desired measure of significance (see (Chambers & Hastie 1992), chapter 6). For the processing time we used a standard analysis of variance (see (Chambers & Hastie 1992), chapter 5). Unless otherwise noted, differences in performance are statistically significant at a 1% level.

To test the importance of bottleneck information, let us compare each < **RAND, ?x** > entry with the corresponding < **BTL, ?x** > entry. Differences in performance are always significant except for the number of problems solved for groups *W/1* and *W/2* when using bi-partition for Conflict Arbitration (**BIP**). These are the two problem groups with lowest expected difficulty. In every other case, random focusing performs significantly worse than bottleneck focusing, with an average slowdown of approximately 3.1 times. Therefore, these results show that, all things remaining equal, there is a substantial advantage in focusing problem solving on what CPS characterizes as bottlenecks.

To test the effect of decision making granularity, let us compare each < **BTL, BIP** > configuration with the corresponding < **BTL, MS** > configuration. With respect to the number of problem solved, only for group *0/2* there is a statistically significant advantage in using most-separated-pair for Conflict Arbitration; *0/2* is the the group with the highest expected difficulty. This advantage is due to a single problem that **MS** always solves while **BIP** solves less than 50% of the time. Although small, this advantage is consistent with the expectation of better problem solving accuracy with smaller decision making granularity, especially on difficult problems. However, when comparing processing times we see an average slowdown of approximately 3.2 times going from **BIP** to **MS** which makes the cost of micro-granularity scheduling prohibitive (except for one problem).

Unexpectedly, the trend toward better accuracy with lower decisions granularity is completely reversed when comparing < **RAND, BIP** > to < **RAND, MS** >. In fact, for all problem groups, the average number of problems solved tend to *decrease* when going from bi-partition to most-separated-pair. This trend is statistically significant for groups *W/1* (at a 2% level), *W/2*, and *N/2*. This result contradicts our expectations. After all, a macro decision step can always be seen as a sequence of micro steps without additional intermediate capacity analyses. A macro-granularity approach should be less informed than a micro-granularity approach and therefore more prone to errors.

However, worse performance with lower granularity can be explained by assuming that at each step there is a probability p of selecting a misleading conflict set, *i.e.*, one for which the preferential information leads to a wrong ordering among activities. The overall probability of following a dead-end path is the sum of the probabilities of failing after x cycles, with x less or equal to maximum path length in the search tree. When the decision making granularity decreases, the expected path length increases. Correspondingly, if p does not substantially decrease, the overall probability of failure increases. The experimental results seem to indicate that the decrement of p is adequate only when using the bottleneck information for focusing. In other words, the expected utility of preferential information at the bottleneck is higher than average.

Conclusions

In this paper we experimentally analyzed the role of bottleneck reasoning in opportunistic schedulers. The aim was to go beyond a bulk comparison of systems and to identify important design trade-offs among system components. The results of the study empirically validate the importance of bottlenecks to focus problem solving. The results seem to indicate that preferential information at bottlenecks has a higher expected utility than average. Therefore the utility of bottleneck-focusing goes beyond the classical view of a "most constrained first" heuristic in a constraint satisfaction search. This is an unexpected result that will further focus the search for a plausible formal model of the performance of schedulers.

Acknowledgements

The author thanks the following people for reviewing earlier drafts of the paper: John Allen, John Bresina, Mark Drummond, Keith Swanson. This work was carried out when the author was at the Center for Integrated Manufacturing and Decision Systems, The Robotics Institute, Carnegie Mellon University. This work was sponsored in part by the National Aeronautics and Space Administration under contract # NCC 2-707, the Defense Advanced Research Projects under contract # F30602-91-F-0016, and the Robotics Institute.

References

Adams, J.; Balas, E.; and Zawack, D. 1988. The shifting bottleneck procedure for job shop scheduling. *Management Science* 34:391–401.

Applegate, D., and Cook, W. 1990. A computational study of job-shop scheduling. Technical Report CMU-CS-90-145, School of Computer Science, Carnegie Mellon University.

Biefeld, E., and Cooper, L. 1991. Bottleneck identification using process chronologies. In *Proceedings of the 12th International Joint Conference on Artificial Intelligence*, 218–224. Menlo Park, California: AAAI Press.

Chambers, J., and Hastie, T., eds. 1992. *Statistical Models in S*. Wadsworth and Brooks/Cole.

Dechter, R.; Meiri, I.; and Pearl, J. 1991. Temporal constraint networks. *Artificial Intelligence* 49:61–95.

Drummond, M., and Bresina, J. 1990. Anytime synthetic projection: Maximizing the probability of goal satisfaction. In *Proceedings of the 8th National Conference on Artificial Intelligence*, 138–144. AAAI Press.

Hanks, S. 1990. Practical temporal projection. In *Proceedings of the 8th National Conference on Artificial Intelligence*, 158–163. AAAI Press.

Haralick, R., and Elliot, G. 1980. Increasing tree search efficiency for constraint satisfaction problems. *Artificial Intelligence* 14(3):263–313.

Langley, P. 1992. Systematic and nonsystematic search strategies. In *Proceedings of the 1st International Conference on Artificial Intelligence Planning Systems*, 145–152. Morgan Kaufmann.

Minton, S.; Drummond, M.; Bresina, J.; and Philips, A. 1992. Total order vs. partial order planning: Factors influencing performance. In *Proceedings of the 3rd International Conference on Principles of Knowledge Representation and Reasoning (KR'92)*, 83–92. Morgan Kaufmann.

Muscettola, N., and Smith, S. 1987. A probabilistic framework for resource-constrained multiagent planning. In *Proceedings of the 10th International Joint Conference on Artificial Intelligence*, 1063–1066. Menlo Park, California: AAAI Press.

Muscettola, N. 1993. Scheduling by iterative partition of bottleneck conflicts. In *Proceedings of the 9th Conference on Artificial Intelligence for Applications*, 49–55. Los Alamitos, California: IEEE Computer Society Press.

Sadeh, N. 1991. Look-ahead techniques for microopportunistic job shop scheduling. Technical Report CMU-CS-91-102, School of Computer Science, Carnegie Mellon University.

Smith, S., and Cheng, C.-C. 1993. Slack-based heuristics for constraint satisfaction scheduling. In *Proceedings of the 11th National Conference on Artificial Intelligence (AAAI 93)*, 139–144. Menlo Park, California: The AAAI Press.

Smith, S.; Ow, P.; Potvin, J.; Muscettola, N.; and Matthys, D. 1990. An integrated framework for generating and revising factory schedules. *Journal of the Operational Research Society* 41(6):539–552.

A Constraint-Based Approach to High-School Timetabling Problems: A Case Study

Masazumi Yoshikawa   Kazuya Kaneko   Yuriko Nomura   Masanobu Watanabe

C&C Research Laboratories, NEC Corporation
4-1-1 Miyazaki, Miyamae-ku, Kawasaki 216 JAPAN
{yosikawa, neko, yuriko, watanabe}@swl.cl.nec.co.jp

Abstract

This paper describes a case study on a general-purpose *Constraint Relaxation Problem* solver, COASTOOL. Using COASTOOL, a problem can be solved merely by declaring "what is the problem," without programming "how to solve it." The problem is solved by a novel method that generates a high-quality initial assignment using arc-consistency, and refines it using hill-climbing. This approach has been evaluated successfully by experiments with practical high-school timetabling problems in Japan. Consequently, COASTOOL is shown to be efficient at applications in high-school timetabling problems.

Introduction

Every school must schedule its own timetable. Thousands of schools desire an automatic timetabling system earnestly. However, a timetabling problem is difficult, since it is large in scale and constrained tightly.

For example, Kuki-Hokuyou High-School has a large-scale timetabling problem with 30 classes[1], 60 teachers (including 9 part-time teachers), 34 time-slots during a week, and 806 lessons. The problem is assigning a time slot to each lesson considering various constraints and preferences. It is equivalent to selecting one from $10^{1234}(= 34^{806})$ combinations to solve the problem. Moreover, there are various constraints; a set of lessons must be taken simultaneously or continuously, a class should have no more than one lesson on a subject in a day, and so on. The problem is constrained tightly, since there is a constraint in that no class and no teacher is required to take more than one lesson at a time. Moreover, there is a condition that every class has no free time-slot during a week. Therefore the problem is just filling the weekly class schedules, considering teacher schedules and many other constraints. Consequently, timetabling is so difficult that it requires 100 person-days in the high-school.

A large amount of effort has been focused on solving timetabling problems, e.g., (Gotlieb 1963; Carter 1986; Feldman & Golumbic 1989; Corne, Fang, & Mellish 1993). However, there has been no work that succeeded in constructing a practically acceptable timetable for a real high-school.

This paper describes a general-purpose *Constraint Relaxation Problem (CRP)* solver, COASTOOL (COnstraint-based Assignment and Scheduling TOOL), and its successful experiments on practical high-school timetabling problems in Japan.

COASTOOL has a constraint-based architecture in which a declarative problem description is independent from a problem-solving method. A problem can be solved merely by describing "what is the problem," without describing "how to solve it." Separating them results in high productivity for modeling real-world problems. The effectiveness of this architecture is supported by a problem-solving method. The method generates a high-quality initial assignment using a novel algorithm, *Really-Full-Lookahead Greedy (RFLG)* algorithm, and refines it using a hill-climbing algorithm. Attaching importance to initialization results in producing a high-quality solution in a reasonable time for a large-scale tightly-constrained problem. This approach has been evaluated by successful experiments with practical high-school timetabling problems.

The following three sections describe the problem, the architecture, and the problem-solving method. Then, the experimental results are summarized and evaluated. Related work and conclusion are given in the last two sections.

Problem

COASTOOL is a general-purpose constrained problem solver. In this paper, attention is focused on *Constraint Relaxation Problems (CRPs)*. This section defines a CRP and describes high-school timetabling problems.

A CRP consists of a set of variables and constraints. A variable has a domain that is a set of values applicable for the variable. A constraint is associated with a set of variables. It not only has a condition to be satisfied, but also a *penalty point* to be incurred by a violation. A CRP is the same problem as a *Constraint Satisfaction Problem*, except that a constraint

---

[1]In this paper, "class" means a group of students.

Problem	# of lessons (# of variables)	# of time-slots (domain size)	# of classes	# of teachers [# of part-timers]	# of constraints [# of definitions]	Total penalty	Absence ratio
Kuki92	806	34	30	60 [9]	24,987 [54]	220,245	6.6 %
Kuki93	783	34	30	63 [10]	25,881 [80]	231,204	9.5 %
Daito93	633	32	26	69 [29]	26,014 [85]	266,508	33.0 %

Figure 1: Data for the Problems

```
1  (define-set Lesson
2     Math1-1a Math1-1b ⋯ Gym1-123a ⋯)
3  (define-set Time        Mon1 Mon2 ⋯ Sat1 ⋯)
4  (define-set SmithLesson  Gym1-123a Gym1-123b ⋯)
5  (define-set SmithAbsence Mon2 Mon3 ⋯ Sat1 Sat2)
6  (define-constraint PartTimerSmith
7     :objects ((:set lesson SmithLesson))
8     :variables ((v lesson))
9     :condition (not (is-a v SmithAbsence))
10    :penalty 10)
11 (define-problem Timetabling
12    :variables ((Lesson Time))
13    :constraints (PartTimerSmith ⋯)
14    :minimize TotalPenalty)
```

Figure 2: Problem Description Sample

has penalty and that its goal is minimizing the total penalty due to inconsistent constraints.

A high-school timetabling problem can be formalized as a CRP. Namely, a variable is a lesson and its domain is the set of all time-slots during a week. The problem is assigning a time-slot to every lesson considering various constraints. The teachers and classes of a lesson are given and referred to by constraints with the lesson.

COASTOOL provides a declarative description language for CRPs. Figure 2 shows a problem description sample. Lines 1–3 define a set of variables, Lesson[2], and a domain set, Time. A constraint definition, in lines 6–10, defines a set of constraints, named PartTimerSmith. It specifies that the constraints are defined on all elements of the set SmithLesson. Let lesson be a SmithLesson element. A constraint has a variable lesson. Let v be its value. The condition to be satisfied is that v is not a SmithAbsence element, and violating the constraint incurs the 10 point penalty. Lines 11–14 define a CRP, named Timetabling, that has a set of variables, set Lesson, with a domain, set Time, and constraints PartTimerSmith, etc. Object function TotalPenalty is pre-defined by the system.

In our case study, COASTOOL has been applied to three practical problems for two high-schools in Japan, as shown in Fig. 1. First, COASTOOL was applied to the '92 year timetabling problem (Kuki92) for Saitama-Prefectural Kuki-Hokuyou High-School. Since it is a mammoth high-school with various courses, the

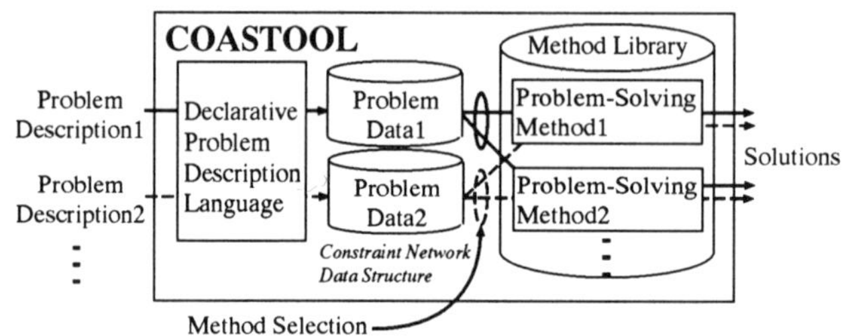

Figure 3: COASTOOL Architecture

timetabling is so difficult that it usually requires 100 person-days to accomplish. In problem Kuki92, satisfying all constraints was desired. It included a subtle constraint, SeparateTwoCredits, which specifies that two lessons for a two credits subject should be taken two days or more apart by a class.

Second, the next years timetabling (Kuki93) was also experimented on. Although it was similar to Kuki92, it was constrained more tightly, since it had a higher *absence ratio*[3] and more simultaneous lessons.

Finally, COASTOOL was experimented with another high-school, Daito Bunka University Dai-ichi High-School. Since it is a nongovernmental and academic high-school, the problem (Daito93) was quite different from those for Kuki92 and Kuki93. The absence ratio was very high (33%), because it had many part-time teachers and one training day without a lesson for each teacher. Moreover, since the high-school had many optional courses, there were many simultaneous lessons with various subjects. Daito93 was the most difficult problem and taking two same subject lessons in a day was unavoidable. However, the two lessons should be continuous, if they are taken in a day.

COASTOOL Architecture

COASTOOL is a general-purpose CRP solver. This section describes the constraint-based architecture for COASTOOL. As shown in Fig. 3, it has a declarative description language and a library of problem-solving methods. A problem can be solved by describing the problem and selecting a provided method. The problem description is translated into a common *network* data structure for constrained problems. Then, the selected problem-solving method solves the problem, processing the data structure.

---

[2]Simultaneous lessons are modeled as one lesson, e.g., Gym1-123a that corresponds to three gymnastic lessons for classes 1-1, 1-2, and 1-3.

$$3 \quad \frac{\sum^{teachers}(\text{\# of absent time-slots for the teacher})}{(\text{number of teachers}) \times (\text{number of time-slots})}$$

A significant feature of Coastool architecture is that a problem description is declarative and independent from a problem-solving method. It results in a few advantages. First, the architecture provides high productivity for modeling real-world problems. This is because a problem can be solved merely by describing "what is the problem," without describing "how to solve it." Therefore, Coastool requires only a minimum amount of information about the problem.

Second, the architecture provides high maintainability. Since a problem description is declarative, a problem can be maintained by adding, deleting and/or modifying a small number of constraints.

The last advantage is that the architecture covers a wide range of applications. This is because a problem-solving method can be selected, according to the feature of a target problem. Moreover, changing a method does not require modifying a problem description.

Consequently, separating a problem description and a problem-solving method results in high productivity, high maintainability, and wide range coverage. However, these advantages rely on the efficiency of the problem-solving method. The following section describes an efficient problem-solving method for large-scale and tightly-constrained CRPs.

Problem-Solving Method

In the beginning of this section, previous general-purpose CRP solving methods are summarized and discussed, focusing on solving a large-scale tightly-constrained problem. Then, an efficient problem-solving method is proposed.

Background

Most general-purpose methods for constrained problems can be classified into consistency algorithms, backtracking, and optimization. Consistency algorithms and backtracking suffer from thrashing for a large-scale problem. In our case study, fast backtracking algorithms, *Forward-Checking Backtracking* and *Iterative Broadening* (Ginsberg 1992), assigned at most twenty percent of the lessons in a *one-week* run. In this paper, attention is focused on optimization methods.

Most optimization methods randomly walk around in problem search space under a bias in order to find a (sub)optimal solution. The bias strength effects computational time and optimality. Namely, a stronger bias results in more efficiency and less optimality.

One of the most common general-purpose optimization methods is *Simulated Annealing (SA)* (Johnson et al. 1989; Johnson et al. 1991). Since SA is a weakly biased method, it finds an optimal solution independently from an initial solution. However, the computational time is too long to use practically for high-school timetabling. For example, problem Kuki92 has a search space with 10^{1234} solutions and a good solution seldom exists. Walking such space under a weak bias results in a long tour.

```
1  Begin REALLY-FULL-LOOKAHEAD GREEDY ALGORITHM
2    Let Vars = set of all variables, ExVars = empty set,
        Var = NULL.
3    While Vars is not empty:
4      Let DsStore = copy of all domains of Vars.
5      Enforce Vars to be arc-consistent with Var.
6      If there is a variable V with an empty domain in Vars,
7        then remove V from Vars and add V into ExVars;
8             restore all domains of Vars from DsStore.
9        else  Let Var = a variable in Vars;
10             Let Value = a value in Var's domain;
11             Assign Value to Var and remove Var from Vars.
12     end if
13   end while
14   While ExVars is not empty:
15     Let Var = a variable in ExVars.
16     Let Value = one of the least penalty values
                    in Var's original domain.
17     Assign Value to Var and remove Var from ExVars.
18   end while
19 End REALLY-FULL-LOOKAHEAD GREEDY ALGORITHM
```

Figure 4: Really-Full-Lookahead Greedy Algorithm

In (Minton et al. 1992), a large-scale loosely-constrained problem, a *Million Queens Problem*, has been solved using a *greedy* algorithm for initialization and *Min-Conflicts Hill-Climbing (MCHC)* method for optimization. Since MCHC is one of the most strongly biased optimization methods, it solves a large-scale CRP efficiently. However, as they reported in the paper, an inappropriate initial solution falls into a local optimum for a tightly-constrained problem.

Recently, Musick and Russell showed the importance of initialization theoretically (Musick & Russell 1992). Namely, the computational time grows exponentially, when the distance between an initial solution and an optimal solution exceeds a border value.

We have focused on developing a high quality initialization method and combining it with a strongly biased optimization method. The following subsection proposes an efficient general-purpose problem-solving method for large-scale and tightly-constrained CRPs.

Proposed Method

The proposed method is a combined method, involving a novel initialization algorithm, *Really-Full-Lookahead Greedy (RFLG)* algorithm, and a strongly biased optimization algorithm, Min-Conflicts Hill-Climbing (MCHC) in (Minton et al. 1992).

Figure 4 shows the RFLG algorithm. It has two steps. The first step (lines 3–13) assigns a value to each variable consistently using an *arc-consistency* algorithm. The arc-consistency removes values that cannot satisfy a constraint from the domains of variables in Vars. Using it avoids assigning a value that is consistent with already assigned variables, but causes later inconsistency with an *as-yet-uninstantiated* variable.

For example, let Gym2-1a and Gym2-1b be contin-

uous lessons taught by a teacher who will be absent
Mon2. A simple greedy algorithm may assign Mon1 to
Gym2-1a, because it has no immediate violation until
Gym2-1b will be instantiated. In the RFLG algorithm,
Mon1 is removed from the domain of Gym2-1a by arc-
consistency before selecting a value for the variable.

The first step never instantiates an inconsistent assignment. If there appears a variable V with no consistent candidate, the step suspends assigning a value
to V, excludes it from the consistent set of already instantiated variables, and stores V in ExVars. Then, it
continues to instantiate other consistent assignments
until there will be no more consistent assignments.

If there is no more consistent assignment, the RFLG
algorithm proceeds to the second step (lines 14–18).
The step assigns inconsistent but the least penalty values to the excluded variables, using a common *greedy*
algorithm. In addition, ties are broken randomly in selection of variables and values in both steps (lines 9–10
and 15–16).

A significant point for the RFLG algorithm is that
it uses arc-consistency for *constraint relaxation*, not
for *constraint satisfaction problems (CSPs)*. Arc-
consistency algorithms are commonly used in backtracking for CSPs. They are useful for reducing the
number of backtracks, because they prune inconsistent
branches in a search tree. In the case of the RFLG algorithm, they are useful for reducing the number of
excluded (inconsistent) variables for the same reason.

In (Nadel 1988), Nadel unified several backtracking
algorithms as combinations of pure *tree search* and arc-
consistency. From this point of view, the RFLG algorithm can be considered as a combination of pure
generation and arc-consistency. It never backtracks
but corresponds to *Really-Full-Lookahead Backtracking*, since both use *full* arc-consistency. Moreover, this
idea can be extended to develop several generation algorithms with *partial* arc-consistency, e.g., *Forward-
Checking Greedy* algorithm.

Following backtracking techniques, variable and
value ordering heuristics, as well as arc-consistency,
can be combined into an RFLG algorithm. Our
implementation uses *Most-Constrained-Variable-First*
heuristic for variable selection in line 9. Several ordering heuristics, e.g., *Most-Constraining-Variable-First*,
can be used in order to reduce the number of inconsistent variables. Consequently, the RFLG algorithm
generates a high-quality initial assignment, employing
several backtracking techniques.

It should be mentioned that COASTOOL has a program synthesizing facility that produces an efficient
arc-consistency program for a given CRP. The problem description language compiles a condition form for
a constraint definition into an efficient constraint propagation procedure, that will be called by a generic arc-
consistency program (Yoshikawa & Wada 1992). This
is similar to AC-5 in (Deville & Hentenryck 1991).

The proposed CRP solving method refines an ini-

tial assignment, generated by the RFLG algorithm, using MCHC, a strongly biased optimization algorithm.
MCHC repeats selecting an inconsistent variable and
modifying its value to one of the least penalty values,
breaking ties randomly. It efficiently finds a local optimum near the initial assignment, even for a large-scale
problem. Although it falls into a local optimum, applying it on a high-quality initial assignment results in
a global (sub)optimal solution. Consequently, employing the RFLG algorithm and MCHC results in producing a high-quality solution in a reasonable time for a
large-scale tightly-constrained problem.

Experimental Results

This section evaluates the proposed approach through
experiments with practical high-school timetabling
problems, Kuki92, Kuki93, and Daito93.

Experiment with Kuki92

In Kuki-Hokuyou High-School, ten teachers usually
work on timetabling for ten days. We interviewed a
key person to determine the data and requirements.
Then, the problem was solved using COASTOOL. Constructed timetables were evaluated by the key person.

COASTOOL Architecture The interview took three
hours and only three person-days were required to describe the problem. The description includes 1,500
lines of data definitions and 500 lines of problem specification. There were 54 constraint definitions (See
Fig. 1). The results show that the productivity for
modeling real-world problems is considerably high,
compared with expert systems approaches.

Two difficulties became clear. First, a *global*
constraint[4] cannot be modeled declaratively in a CRP
or cannot be solved efficiently. For example, a teacher
should have three or four lessons at intervals everyday.
This preference was specially considered in tie-breaks.
Second, set definition language structures are too simple to describe various data conveniently. A frame language or a domain-specific interface are worth being
considered to be integrated.

Problem-Solving Method Figure 5 shows the
transition of total penalty by the proposed method
(RFLG-MCHC), the combination of Greedy algorithm and MCHC (G-MCHC), and the combination of
Greedy algorithm and Simulated Annealing (G-SA).
G-MCHC falls into a local optimum solution in several minutes. The teacher evaluated that the completion degree was less than 70%.[5] G-SA was experimentally applied with several values for cooling parameters. However, SA is too slow to construct a practical

---

[4]A constraint with all variable or a constraint with
which related variables are determined dynamically according to the assignments.

[5]Namely, the solution had a lower quality than those at
70% of a human timetabling task.

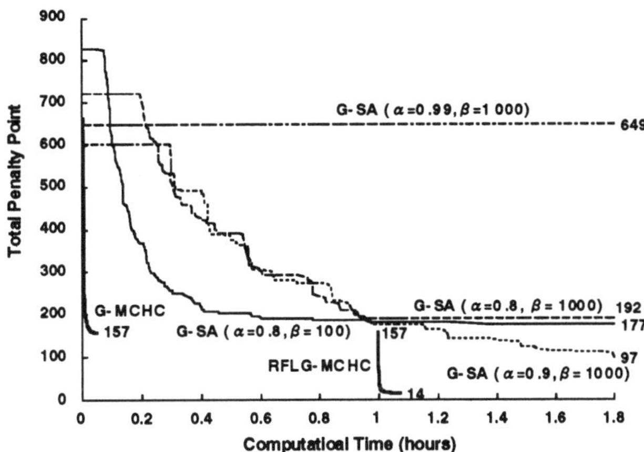

Figure 5: Experimental Results for Problem Kuki92: In SA, α is cooling ratio and β is the number of repeating times at the same temperature.

timetable. It required at least three days to reach the 90% completion point.

With the proposed method, although the RFLG algorithm required about one hour, it generated a high-quality initial assignment. MCHC refined it and constructed an almost perfect timetable (more than 95%). There was the best solution with only one inconsistent constraint (`SeparateTwoCredits` described earlier) in sixty trials. Consequently, the method constructs an almost perfect timetable in a reasonable time. It is considerably faster than G-SA and results in a considerably higher quality timetable than G-MCHC.

Other combinations of initialization and optimization should be considered. RFLG-SA is nonsense, because SA walks to much worse solutions from an initial assignment at first. Figure 5 looks as if it is worth applying MCHC on a solution in the middle of SA cooling. However, such a solution resulted in an unacceptable local optimum, according to our experiences.

Total Performance As a whole, it required only three person-days to describe the problem Kuki92, and an almost perfect timetable was constructed in about one hour. Consequently, using COASTOOL reduced the cost for timetabling from one hundred person-days to less than one person-week.

Experiment with Kuki93

We experimented with the high-school for the second straight year (Kuki93) in order to confirm the successful result.

Maintainability

The problem description for Kuki92 could be modified for Kuki93 by only 1.5 person-days work. Most of the maintenance was data maintenance. The problem specification could be modified, merely by adding, deleting and rewriting a number of constraints.

In addition, the problem data or requirements were modified several times in the middle of the timetabling task. For example, teachers in charge of lessons were changed according to their assignability. Every minor change required only about ten minutes. These results show the high maintainability of COASTOOL.

Partial Arc-Consistency The computation was also successful and practical. It required about 2.4 hours to construct a timetable at 90% (76 penalty points). However, the RFLG algorithm required 2.2 times as long computational time as that in Kuki92, even though they were problems for the same school. This is because the RFLG algorithm uses an arc-consistency algorithm repeatedly.

Although the result was successful enough, we tried to decrease the computational time, using arc-consistency *partially*. Namely, only important variables and constraints were processed by arc-consistency. The other variables were assigned in the second step of the RFLG algorithm. The other constraints were considered in value selection. As a result, the proposed method constructed a timetable at 70% (257 points) in 26.2 minutes. The RFLG algorithm has flexibility to tune smoothly the trade-off between efficiency and optimality.

Experiment with Daito93

As the final experiment, we applied COASTOOL to the timetabling for a different kind of high-school, Daito Bunka University Dai-ichi High-School. Usually, a teacher uses a timetabling software, SHIRAKU (Shiraku), and works on the problem for ten days. SHIRAKU's input files were converted into a COASTOOL problem description.

Phased Approach Since Daito93 is much more difficult than "Kuki" problems, 2.8 hours were required for achieving a 70% complete timetable. The proposed method fell into an unacceptable local optimum.

We tried a *phased* approach, following the teacher's expert manner. Namely, important lessons were assigned first and modified by a human, then the others were assigned and modified. It required 37.6 minutes for the first assignment, twenty minutes for modification, 91.5 minutes for the second assignment, and three hours for modification. The modification was done by a non-expert person using a graphical user interface and produced a 90% complete timetable. Consequently, COASTOOL reduced the total cost from ten days work by an expert to four days with a non-expert person.

It should be mentioned that the human modification repeated a kind of *local search* that finds a plan to repair several lessons to satisfy constraints, according to constraint priority. At least all absolute requirements must be satisfied. Since the plan temporarily passes higher penalty solutions, it can not be simulated by a hill-climbing method. Automating such planning is interesting work for the future.

From our case study, the results illustrate that COASTOOL is efficient as a base for practical applications in high-school timetabling problems.

Related Work

High-school Timetabling School timetabling has been studied for the last three decades, based on *Operations Research (OR)* techniques, e.g., (Gotlieb 1963; Even, Itai, & Shamir 1976; Carter 1986). Since an OR technique depends on a simple problem definition, they might fail to solve real-world complex problems. There were also *Genetic Algorithm* (Corne, Fang, & Mellish 1993) and *Backtracking* (Feldman & Golumbic 1989) approaches.

Most previous studies focused on university or examination or student timetabling, in which a student might have free time in a scheduling period. High-school timetabling is constrained much more tightly, since a student has no free time-slot during a week. The authors do not know about any successful work on practical high-school timetabling problems.

COASTOOL Architecture *Constraint Logic Programming* languages (Cohen 1990) provide declarative frameworks to describe and solve a problem. Our previous system (Yoshikawa & Wada 1992) and MULTI-TAC (Minton 1993) also provide a declarative framework and a problem-solving program synthesizing facility. However, they have not used an iterative optimization method yet. Although ODO in (Davis & Fox 1993) is the most closely related work, it is focused on Jobshop Scheduling.

Problem-Solving Method In (Minton et al. 1992), Minton et al. developed an initialization method for *Graph Coloring Problems*, using problem-specific ordering heuristics. The basic idea may be similar to the RFLG algorithm.

According to (Haralick & Elliot 1980), partial use of arc-consistency is important for the backtracking efficiency. From our experience, full use of arc-consistency is important for the quality of initialization by the RFLG algorithm. Evaluation of the RFLG algorithm with partial arc-consistency and variable and value ordering heuristics is interesting work for the future.

Conclusion

A general-purpose *Constraint Relaxation Problem* solver, COASTOOL, and its successful experiments on practical high-school timetabling problems have been described. Concerning COASTOOL architecture, separating "what is the problem" and "how to solve it" results in high productivity for modeling real-world problems. In order to solve large-scale tightly-constrained problems, a high-quality initial assignment is required by a hill-climbing algorithm and it can be obtained using arc-consistency. The successful experiments indicate that COASTOOL is efficient as a base for practical applications in high-school timetabling problems.

Acknowledgements

The authors would like to thank Masahiro Yamamoto and Takeshi Yoshimura of NEC Corporation for encouragement to pursue this research. They also thank Kin-ya Ohuchi, Mikio Nakabayashi, and Mitsuhiro Masuda of Kuki-Hokuyou High-School and Yosuke Kamine of Daito Bunka University Dai-Ichi High-School for cooperation in the case study.

References

Carter, M. W. 1986. A Survey of Practical Applications of Examination Timetabling Algorithms. *Operations Research* 34(2): 193–202.

Cohen, J. 1990. Constraint Logic Programming Languages. *Communications of the ACM* 33(7): 52–68.

Corne, D.; Fang, H. L.; and Mellish, C. 1993. Solving the Modular Exam Scheduling Problem with Genetic Algorithms. In Proceedings of the Sixth International Conference on Industrial and Engineering Applications of Artificial Intelligence and Eepert Systems.

Davis, E. and Fox, M. 1993. ODO: A Constraint-based Architecture for Representing and Reasoning About Scheduling Problems. In Workshop Notes of the IJCAI-93 Workshop on Knowledge-Based Production Planning, Scheduling, and Control, 325–330.

Deville, Y. and Hentenryck, P. V. 1991. An Efficient Arc Consistency Algorithm for a Class of CSP Problems. In Proceedings of the Twelfth International Joint Conference on Artificial Intelligence, 325–330.

Even, S.; Itai, A.; and Shamir, A. 1976. On the Complexity of Timetable and Multicommodity Flow Problems. *SIAM J. Comput.* 5(4): 691–703.

Feldman, R. and Golumbic, M. C. 1989. Constraint Satisfiability Algorithms for Interactive Student Scheduling. In Proceedings of the Eleventh International Joint Conference on Artificial Intelligence, 1010–1016.

Ginsberg, M. L. 1992. Iterative Broadening. *Artificial Intelligence* 55: 210–215.

Gotlieb, C. C. 1963. The Construction of Class-Teacher Time-Tables. In Proceedings of IFIP Congress 62, 73–77.

Haralick, R. and Elliot, G. 1980. Increasing Tree Search Efficiency for Constraint-Satisfaction Problems. *Artificial Intelligence* 14(3): 263–313.

Johnson, D. S.; Aragon, C. R.; McGeoch, L. A.; and Schevon, C. 1989. Optimization by Simulated Annealing: Experimental Evaluation; Part I, Graph Partitioning. *Operations Research* 37(6): 865–892.

Johnson, D. S.; Aragon, C. R.; McGeoch, L. A.; and Schevon, C. 1991. Optimization by Simulated Annealing: Experimental Evaluation; Part II, Graph Coloring and Number Partitioning. *Operations Research* 39(3): 378–406.

Minton, S.; Johnston, M. D.; Philips, A. B.; and Laird, P. 1992. Minimizing Conflicts: A Heuristic Repair Method for Constraint Satisfaction and Scheduling Problems. *Artificial Intelligence* 58: 160–205.

Minton, S. 1993. Integrating Heuristics for Constraint Satisfaction Problems: A Case Study. In Proceedings of the Eleventh National Conference on Artificial Intelligence, 120–126.

Musick, R. and Russell, S. 1992. How Long Will It Take? In Proceedings of the Tenth National Conference on Artificial Intelligence, 466–471.

Nadel, B. 1988. Tree Search and Arc Consistency in Constraint-Satisfaction Algorithms. In *Search in Artificial Intelligence*, eds. Kanal, L. and Kumar, V., 287–342, New York: Springer-Verlag.

Shiraku II Ver.2.1 Users Manual (In Japanese), 1992. Yasukawa Information Systems Corporation, Saitama, Japan.

Yoshikawa, M. and Wada, S. 1992. Constraint Satisfaction with a Multi-Dimensional Domain. In Artificial Intelligence Planning Systems: Proceedings of the First International Conference (AIPS92), 252–259.

Task-Decomposition via Plan Parsing

Anthony Barrett and Daniel S. Weld
Department of Computer Science and Engineering*
University of Washington, Seattle, WA 98195
{barrett, weld}@cs.washington.edu

Abstract

Task-decomposition planners make use of schemata that define tasks in terms of partially ordered sets of tasks and primitive actions. Most existing task-decomposition planners synthesize plans via a top-down approach, called *task reduction*, which uses schemata to replace tasks with networks of tasks and actions until only actions remain.

In this paper we present a bottom-up *plan parsing* approach to task-decomposition. Instead of reducing tasks into actions, we use an incremental parsing algorithm to recognize which partial primitive plans match the schemata. In essence, our approach exploits the observation that schemata are a convenient means for reducing search. We compile the schemata into a declarative search control language (like that used in machine learning research), which rejects plan refinements that cannot be parsed.

We demonstrate that neither parsing nor reduction dominates the other on efficiency grounds and provide preliminary empirical results comparing the two. We note that our parsing approach allows convenient comparison (and combination) of different search control technologies, generates minimal plans, and handles expressive languages (*e.g.*, universal quantification and conditional effects) with ease.

Introduction

NOAH (Sacerdoti 1975) introduced two important innovations: the partial order step representation and the use of schemata to define abstract tasks in terms of primitive actions and other tasks. NOAH represented plans as partially ordered sets of tasks and actions, and reduced tasks by substituting them with networks of tasks and actions until only actions remained. When tasks and actions interfered with each other, critic functions performed arbitrary plan-transformation repairs.

Despite the ubiquity of task-decomposition in "industrial strength" planners such as SIPE (Wilkins 1988, Wilkins 1992), and O-PLAN (Currie & Tate 1991), most

formal analyses of planning have ignored the idea of hierarchies of decomposition schemata. Instead researchers focussed on NOAH's idea of partially ordered plan steps and dropped the notion of tasks. For example, TWEAK (Chapman 1987) and SNLP (McAllester & Rosenblitt 1991) synthesize plans solely from actions. Subsequent research continued the focus on actions, but explored expressive languages with conditional effects and universal quantification (Pednault 1988, McDermott 1991, Pednault 1991, Penberthy & Weld 1992). Only recently have formalists investigated task-decomposition (Yang 1990, Erol, Nau, & Hendler 1993), but their formulations assume the STRIPS action representation. Hence an interesting question remains:

Is there a sound and complete task-decomposition algorithm for an expressive language such as ADL (Pednault 1989), i.e. one with conditional effects and universal quantification?

Inadequate emphasis on task-decomposition has also had an unfortunate effect on machine learning research for planning, *e.g.* explanation-based learning (Minton 1988), static domain analysis (Etzioni 1993, Smith & Peot 1993), abstraction (Knoblock 1990, Yang & Tenenberg 1990), case-based planning (Hammond 1990), and derivational analogy (Veloso & Carbonell 1993). It is unfortunate that the vast majority[1] of research on speedup learning has ignored task-decomposition planners, since defining and using tasks provides a very successful form of search control. This leads to a second question:

Can existing speedup learning techniques be used with task-decomposition planners?

In this paper we describe the implemented UCPOP+PARSE algorithm, a new approach to task-decomposition that answers these questions. Instead of performing task-decomposition by *task reduction* UCPOP+PARSE inverts the process into *plan parsing*. In our algorithm, a partial-order planner synthesizes networks of actions, and an incremental parser identifies the decomposition that corresponds to the actions. We demonstrate that neither the reduction nor parsing approach strictly dominates the other on efficiency

*We appreciate helpful comments and suggestions from Denise Draper, Oren Etzioni, Keith Golden, Nick Kushmerick, Ying Sun, and Mike Williamson. This research is funded in part by National Science Foundation Grant IRI-8957302 and Office of Naval Research Grant 90-J-1904

[1]The PRIAR system (Kambhampati & Hendler 1992) is a rare exception.

grounds. However, our parsing approach provides two advantages:

1. **Uniform search control framework:** Since our parsing critic is implemented as a set of declarative search control rules, they can be turned on or off and can be combined with other forms of control knowledge: domain-dependent hand coded rules or the output of machine learning algorithms. We present preliminary experiments demonstrating this claim.

2. **Lazy minimal expansion:** Our approach expands tasks into actions as those actions become needed to solve a problem. All and only those actions that are actually *useful* in achieving goals are added to the plan. This enables UCPOP+PARSE to easily handle actions with conditional effects

In the next sections we (1) introduce schemata for an example which illustrates universally quantified and conditional effects, (2) review task reduction, (3) describe plan parsing, and (4) compare the two approaches to task-decomposition.

Task-Decomposition Problems

We illustrate task-decomposition with an extension of the *briefcase domain* (Pednault 1988), which we encode with five primitive operators. **Carry** moves the briefcase and all of its contents, **open** and **close** act on the briefcase, while **put-in** and **take-out** respectively add and remove items from the briefcase if it is open (Table 1). Note the use of conditional and universally quantified effects in the **carry** action (see (Pednault 1989, Penberthy & Weld 1992) for the action semantics.).

open()	precondition :	$\neg open$
	effect :	$open$
close()	precondition :	$open$
	effect :	$\neg open$
take-out(x)	precondition :	$open$
	effect :	$\neg in(x)$
put-in(x)	precondition :	
	$\exists l\ at\text{-}b(l) \wedge at(x,l) \wedge open$	
	effect :	$in(x)$
carry(l,to)	precondition :	$at\text{-}b(l) \wedge \neg open$
	effect :	
	$at\text{-}b(to) \wedge \neg at\text{-}b(l) \wedge$	
	$\forall x\ in(x) \Rightarrow (at(x,to) \wedge \neg at(x,l))$	

Table 1: Actions in the briefcase world

These operators, together with a description of an initial state and a desired goal, constitute a planning problem. For example, suppose that there are two items (besides the briefcase): a paycheck P and a dictionary D. All three are initially at home, and the paycheck is inside the briefcase. The goal is to have the paycheck at home and the dictionary at the office. Clearly, the following action sequence solves the problem:

$$open();\ take\text{-}out(P);\ put\text{-}in(D);\ close();$$
$$carry(home, office)$$

Decomposition Schemata

A task-decomposition planner solves planning problems like the one above by exploiting a set of useful plan fragments called *decomposition schemata*. Intuitively, a schema specifies a coordinated set of tasks and actions that combine to solve common subproblems. (Yang 1990) provides a formal definition; here we illustrate them graphically. For example, Figure 1 shows the **move-to** decomposition schema.

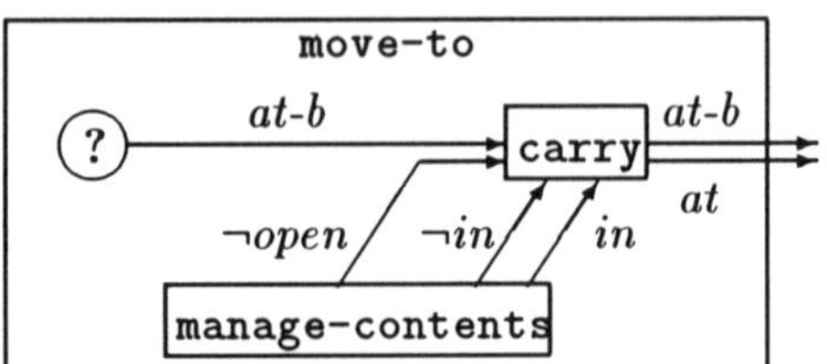

Figure 1: Decomposition schema defining a task for moving objects to a location.

The arrows leaving the box indicate that **move-to** is an appropriate way to achieve a goal involving either the *at* or *at-b* predicates. The contents of the schema indicate how these goals should be achieved: **move-to** expands into a **carry** action (defined above) and a **manage-contents** task (defined by another schema). Note that Figure 1 contains numerous arrows labeled with predicates (or their negation); these represent *protection intervals*. Each interval signifies that the producer (*i.e.* the node to the left of the arrow) is responsible for achieving literals involving that predicate for the *consumer* (the node on the right).[2] For example, the **manage-contents** task is responsible for achieving literals such as $\neg open$, $in(D)$, and $\neg in(P)$ for **carry**. Note that the information specified by a protection interval's producer is equivalent to a PRODIGY-style search control rule (Minton *et al.* 1989) which rejects attempts to achieve goals with inappropriate actions. As explained later, UCPOP+PARSE compiles schemata into a plan parser using rules of this form.

Figure 2 presents a schema which defines the **manage-contents** task. The intuition behind **manage-contents** is simple: first the briefcase is opened, then objects are added and removed from the case, finally it is shut once more. But the **manage-contents** schema illustrates an important feature that was absent from the previous example. This schema allows varying numbers of primitive **take-out** and **put-in** actions to be introduced. For example, if the **carry** action in the **move-to** schema requires that multiple objects be inside the briefcase, the **manage-contents** schema directs the planner to

---

[2]Intervals whose producer is drawn as a circle indicate that the corresponding literals can be achieved by reusing *any* existing action in the plan or by adding *any* new task that provides the literal. Readers familiar with NON-LIN (Tate 1977) or O-PLAN (Currie & Tate 1991) should note that these "circle intervals" correspond to **achieve** conditions, while intervals whose producer is drawn as a box correspond to **supervised** conditions.

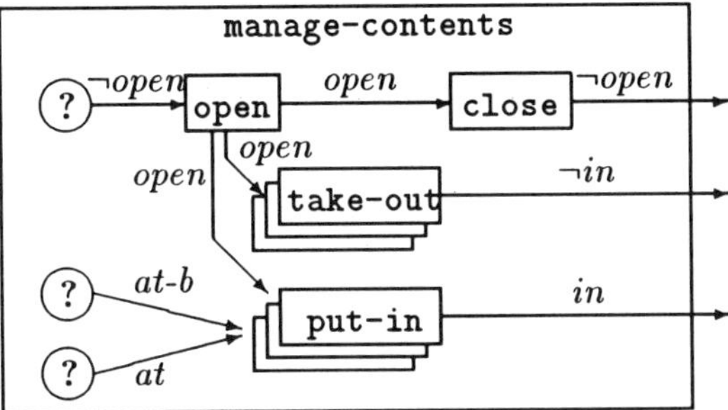

Figure 2: Decomposition schema defining a task for managing the briefcase's contents.

add as many `put-in` actions as necessary before the single `close` action.

Task Reduction

Typically task-decomposition planners iteratively (1) use schemata to expand tasks into networks of other actions and tasks, and (2) test the resulting partial plans with a *critic function*. This cycle starts with a single problem task, and continues until only primitive actions remain or until the critic detects an irreconcilable interaction in the plan (in which case backtracking is necessary).

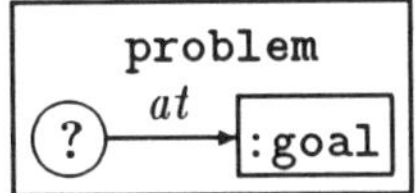

Figure 3: This top-level schema defines the language of appropriate plans. It specifies that *at* goals can be achieved in any way.

For example, Figure 3 shows how to expand a `problem` task that would correspond with the previously mentioned problem. The resultant plan can be reduced using the schemata shown previously. Figure 4 illustrates the final decomposition leading to the five step plan which solves the goal.

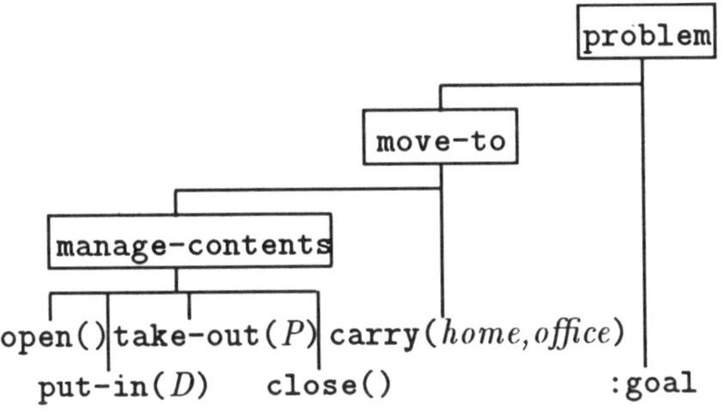

Figure 4: Decomposition to solve the briefcase problem

Since replacing tasks in accordance with the schemata yields a "legal" subset of the *possible* networks of actions, one can view a set of decomposition schemata as a *grammar* and see Figure 4 as a

parse tree. The set of these schema-derived networks thus constitutes a formal language which we call the *schema-generated* plans. The set of all action sequences that solve a given planning problem (as defined by (Pednault 1991)) constitutes another language, which we call the *solution* set.

We adopt the insight (due to (Erol, Nau, & Hendler 1993)) that task-decomposition can be considered a search for a plan in the *intersection* of these two sets. Sound and complete partial-order planners such as TWEAK (Chapman 1987), SNLP (McAllester & Rosenblitt 1991), and UCPOP (Penberthy & Weld 1992) generate the solution space directly. Traditional task-decomposition planners use a *task reduction* process that expands the schema-generated set, then selects for membership in the solution set.

Plan Parsing in UCPOP+PARSE

Our approach breaks from this tradition by reversing the roles of the refinement and testing processes. Instead of reducing a task into a fixed network of actions and tasks, UCPOP+PARSE adds actions as their effects are needed and incrementally composes them into layers of tasks. Conceptually, UCPOP+PARSE can be thought of as the algorithm in Figure 5 which takes a problem specification as input and returns a plan.

Algorithm UCPOP+PARSE(*Problem*)

1. **Initialize:** Successively let:
   - P = UCPOP-init-plan(*Problem*) and
   - *Parses* = init-parses(P).
2. **Terminate:** If P solves *Problem*, return P.
3. **Refine:** Invoke UCPOP-refine-plan(P) and nondeterministicly choose P from the returned set.
4. **Parse:** Let *Parses* = extend-parses(*Parses*, P). If *Parses* becomes empty then fail.
5. Go to step 2.

Figure 5: The UCPOP+PARSE algorithm.

Actually, the schemata are compiled into a parser that interacts with the UCPOP planner (Penberthy & Weld 1992) through its general rule-based search controller. The routine UCPOP-init-plan() takes a problem specification and returns an initial plan consisting solely of a :start action (whose effects encode the initial conditions) and a :goal action (whose preconditions encode the goals). A plan that does not solve its problem contains at least one flaw; the UCPOP routine UCPOP-refine-plan() can take the plan, select a single flaw in the plan, and return a set of plans which have that single flaw repaired:

- If the flaw is an unsatisfied a precondition (*i.e.*, it is *open*), all effects that could possibly be constrained to unify with the desired proposition are considered. The returned set contains plans created by adding a single *causal link* (McAllester & Rosenblitt 1991) to the original plan. Each added causal link records a different way to satisfy the precondition using a new or existing action.

- If the flaw involves another action (called a *threat*) possibly interfering with the precondition being supported by the causal link, the returned set contains plans created by using methods to resolve the threat: either by ordering steps in the plan, posting additional subgoals, or by adding variable binding constraints.

For example, without guidance from the plan parser UCPOP solves the briefcase example (described previously) by generating the plan in Figure 6.

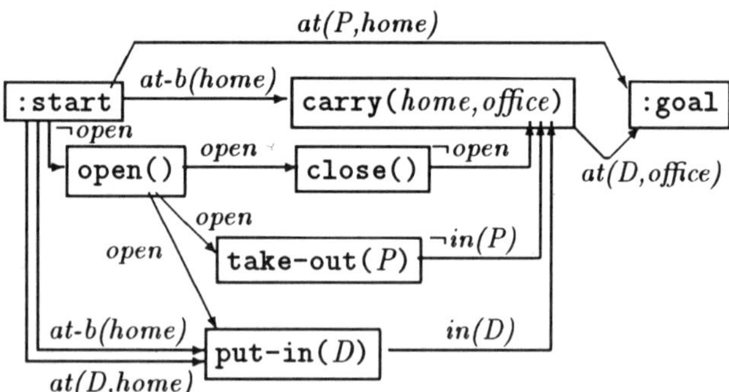

Figure 6: Primitive plan that solves the simple briefcase-world problem

The UCPOP planner is complete — if *any* solution to a planning problem exists, UCPOP will find it (Penberthy & Weld 1992). While this property has merits, it comes at the cost of forcing UCPOP to consider every conceivable way of achieving a goal, which in complex domains leads to poor performance. The decomposition schemata are compiled into the routines `init-parses()` and `extend-parses()`, which are used to prune inappropriate plans from UCPOP's consideration.

The routine `init-parses()` takes an initial plan and computes a set of parses. For example, in the briefcase problem, the routine would return a set with parse identifying the plan's `:goal` step with `:goal` node in the `problem` schema of Figure 3.

During the planning process in UCPOP+PARSE every plan under consideration has a set of parses associated with it. Each parse consists of a partially instantiated derivation tree and a mapping from actions in the plan to distinct leaves in the tree. The routine `extend-parses()` takes a plan, created by repairing a single flaw, and updates the set of parses to reflect that repair. When the repair adds a causal link, each parse must be extended to match the new link with a protection interval specified by the schemata in its derivation tree. Sometimes a match cannot be made, and a parse is deleted from the set. Other times more than one extension can be made to the parse. Thus, the number of parses varies as planning progresses.

As an example, consider the open goal *at(D,office)* in the briefcase problem. This flaw is repaired by adding a `carry` action. In this case, `:goal`'s associated `problem` schema provides little constraint, because the **at** link producer is a circle (signifying "anything goes"). The planning process becomes much more constrained by

the parser when dealing with the open preconditions of the plan's `carry` action. The `carry` action must appear in a `move-to` task, and Figure 1 shows that the schema for `move-to` has strong constraints on its associated protection intervals. When UCPOP+PARSE returns the solution plan in Figure 6, it has a single associated parse (shown in Figure 4).

Comparing Parsing and Reduction

We compare the two approaches in terms of efficiency, ability to combine and evaluate multiple sources of search control knowledge, and the ability to handle action languages with universal quantification and conditional effects.

Efficiency

Since each approach performs a different type of least commitment, there are problems where one approach is preferable to the other. As illustration, consider the three schemata in Figure 7. In the top-level `problem` schema, the task S has to be decomposed using the other two schemata. P and Q are primitive actions, and while P and S do not explicitly affect α, Q asserts $\neg\alpha$. Since UCPOP+PARSE adds the step Q without committing to how S is decomposed to produce Q, it quickly determines that the problem is not solvable (Q necessarily clobbers α). A reduction planner, on the other hand, would loop forever since it can always reduce task S.

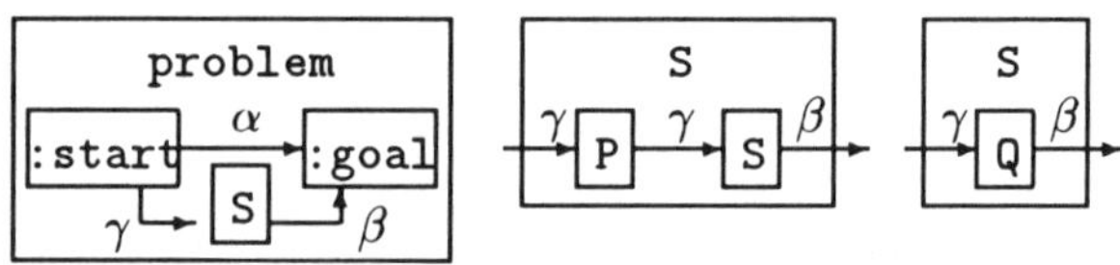

Figure 7: Schemata for a problem where plan parsing dominates.

In a slightly different problem the search space is finite for a reduction planner, but infinite for UCPOP+PARSE. Consider the three schemata in Figure 8. The only differences are the order of S and P in S's decomposition schema, and the addition of $\neg\alpha$ to S's explicit effects. Now the reduction planner determines that the problem is not solvable before reducing S, but UCPOP+PARSE can always add a new step P in the hope of a solution.

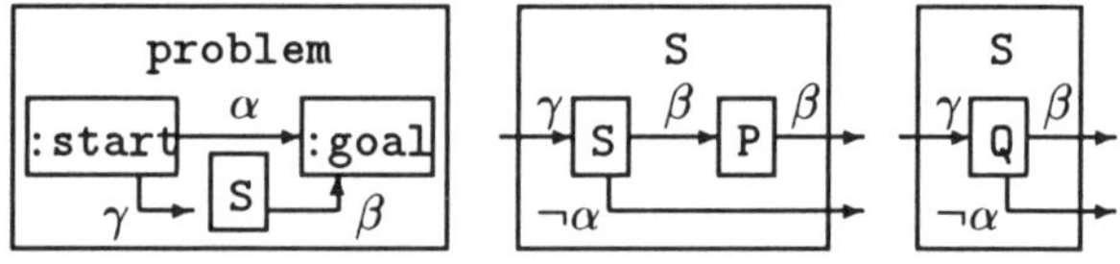

Figure 8: Schemata for a problem where task reduction dominates.

In general, the reduction approach can reason about the effects and preconditions of a task without committing to its decomposition, and the parsing approach can add a primitive step to a plan without committing to the manner in which tasks were decomposed to produce that primitive step. Since there exist domains where each approach surpasses the other, the question becomes a matter of which planner performs best in practice. As a preliminary attempt to answer this question, we compared UCPOP+PARSE with a reduction planner that we implemented using the same routines to add new steps, handle protection intervals, and manage variable bindings. We performed several experiments in a NONLIN encoding of *blocksworld* and a house building domain. The results appear in Table 2.

	CPU seconds	
problem	UCPOP+PARSE	REDUCE
Sussman Anomaly	0.37	0.40
3 Block Tower Shift	2.10	1.33
Build House	0.83	0.23

Table 2: Performance of UCPOP+PARSE and a decomposition planner on two problem domains on a Sun SPARC IPX running Allegro Common Lisp.

In our experiments, both planners had similar performance, but that could be because both domains were simple; in the future we expect to perform further experiments with more complex domains.

Uniform Search Control Framework

One of the conceptual disadvantages to parsing is that it is less intuitive than reduction, with which people have twenty years experience. On the other hand, the ability to turn the parser on or off leads to a uniform framework for comparing other forms of search control with that provided by schemata.

To illustrate this feature, we tested UCPOP+PARSE on the example briefcase problem and by posing two problems in each of two more complex domains: *Tyreworld* (Russell 1992) and *Process Planning* (Gil 1991). In *Tyreworld*, the problems were to remove a tire from an automobile's hub, and to completely change a flat tire. The shortest solutions for these problems require 7 and 19 steps respectively. In *Process Planning* our problems involved sawing a block of copper and drilling a hole into a block of brass. These problems required 6 and 10 steps respectively.

The purpose of our experiment was to explore interactions between plan parsing and three different search strategies: vanilla best-first; best first search with a search space structured according to an abstraction hierarchy generated by the ALPINE machine learning algorithm (Knoblock 1990); and domain-dependent, hand-coded rules. To create our *Tyreworld* parser we defined 5 tasks for getting tools, inflating tires, removing tires, installing tires, and cleaning up. The *Process Planning* parser was created out of a set of 12 schemata defining tasks like setting up drill presses and securing objects to machines. The results of our experiments appear in Table 3.

Plan parsing clearly decreases the size of the search space, but the extent of the improvement depends on the difficulty of the problem relative to the search strategy being used. Note that in some cases, the amount of search reduction was insufficient to produce real

problem:	plans generated		CPU seconds	
strategy	¬parse	parse	¬parse	parse
Briefcase:				
best first	151	41	1.1	0.4
Remove tire:				
best first	118	102	1.2	1.4
ALPINE	97	93	1.4	1.6
hand coded	134	118	1.8	1.9
Fix flat:				
best first	> 5000	702	> 103.6	17.5
ALPINE	> 5000	482	> 195.6	39.5
hand coded	579	308	14.7	8.6
Saw a block:				
best first	4820	941	135.3	29.1
ALPINE	4823	944	224.3	44.3
hand coded	434	292	9.9	6.9
Drill a hole:				
best first	> 5000	2854	> 142.3	94.4
ALPINE	> 5000	2855	> 272.5	136.8
hand coded	696	487	20.5	15.5

Table 3: Performance of UCPOP with and without parsing in three problem domains on a Sun SPARC IPX running Allegro Common Lisp. Problem runs marked with > were terminated after a resource bound was exceeded.

speedup given the parsing overhead. Since the overhead depends on the number of possible parsings, and this is a function of the particular partial plan in question, parser overhead depends on the search strategy too. While we have only demonstrated that plan parsing is complementary with ALPINE, we believe that it can be usefully combined with explanation-based and other machine learning algorithms as well. We hope to validate these intuitions in future work.

Expressive Actions

We could not test our reduction planner in the *Briefcase*, *Tyreworld*, or *Process Planning*, domains because it can not handle actions with conditional effects. One of the assumptions typically made by reduction planners is that an action's preconditions are known when it is added to a plan during a reduction, and the reducing schema specifies how those preconditions are handled. This assumption does not hold when actions have conditional effects, since new preconditions may be introduced whenever an unused effect gets requested, or confronted. Extending a reduction planner to handle conditional effects is a topic for future research.

SIPE-2 (Wilkins 1992) does allow conditional effects and can compute universally quantified preconditions for an action, but the preconditions are computed when the action is added to the plan. It is unclear if it can be extended to add preconditions to a step at a later point.

Conclusions

We have described a fully implemented task-decomposition planner, UCPOP+PARSE, based on plan parsing. As it stands, UCPOP+PARSE can not handle recursive schemata — they cause the parser to enter an infinite loop. We hope to soon adapt the flow-graph parsing algorithm of (Brotsky 1984) in order to circumvent this problem. We also wish to see if derivational analogy (Veloso & Carbonell 1993) can be used to automatically learn decomposition schemata.

We showed that neither the reduction nor parsing approach dominates the other in every problem domain. In addition, we reported preliminary experiments that suggest performance is comparable in the two approaches. However, plan parsing offers two advantages over the traditional task reduction method:

- Plan parsing incrementally expands a task into a variable number of primitive actions. This feature is useful for taking full advantage of actions with context dependent effects. All and only the actions that are actually needed in achieving goals are added to the plan.

- Because plan parsing acts to guide the search behavior of the UCPOP planner, we can combine and contrast the performance gains provided by decomposition schemata to that engendered by speedup learning and subgoaling mechanisms.

Since UCPOP has already been proven sound and complete (Penberthy & Weld 1992), UCPOP+PARSE automatically inherits soundness. In addition, it can be shown to be complete relative to the schema language intersection[3] as long as the parser is complete.

References

Brotsky, D. 1984. An algorithm for parsing flow graphs. AI-TR-704, MIT AI Lab.

Chapman, D. 1987. Planning for conjunctive goals. *Artificial Intelligence* 32(3):333–377.

Currie, K., and Tate, A. 1991. O-plan: the open planning architecture. *Artificial Intelligence* 52(1):49–86.

Erol, K., Nau, D., and Hendler, J. 1993. Toward a general framework for hierarchical task-network planning (extended abstract). In *Working Notes of the AAAI Spring Symposium: Foundations of Automatic Planning: The Classical Approach and Beyond.* Menlo Park, CA: AAAI Press.

Etzioni, O. 1993. Acquiring search-control knowledge via static analysis. *Artificial Intelligence* 62(2):255–302.

Gil, Y. 1991. A specification of process planning for PRODIGY. CMU-CS-91-179, Carnegie-Mellon University.

Hammond, K. 1990. Explaining and repairing plans that fail. *Artificial Intelligence* 45:173–228.

Kambhampati, S., and Hendler, J. 1992. A validation structure based theory of plan modification and reuse. *Artificial Intelligence* 55:193–258.

Knoblock, C. 1990. Learning abstraction hierarchies for problem solving. In *Proc. 8th Nat. Conf. on A.I.,* 923–928.

McAllester, D., and Rosenblitt, D. 1991. Systematic nonlinear planning. In *Proc. 9th Nat. Conf. on A.I.,* 634–639.

McDermott, D. 1991. Regression planning. *International Journal of Intelligent Systems* 6:357–416.

Minton, S., Carbonell, J. G., Knoblock, C. A., Kuokka, D. R., Etzioni, O., and Gil, Y. 1989. Explanation-based learning: A problem-solving perspective. *Artificial Intelligence* 40:63–118. Available as technical report CMU-CS-89-103.

Minton, S. 1988. Quantitative results concerning the utility of explanation-based learning. In *Proc. 7th Nat. Conf. on A.I.,* 564–569.

Pednault, E. 1988. Synthesizing plans that contain actions with context-dependent effects. *Computational Intelligence* 4(4):356–372.

Pednault, E. 1989. ADL: Exploring the middle ground between STRIPS and the situation calculus. In *Proc. 1st Int. Conf. on Principles of Knowledge Representation and Reasoning,* 324–332.

Pednault, E. 1991. Generalizing nonlinear planning to handle complex goals and actions with context-dependent effects. In *Proc. 12th Int. Joint Conf. on A.I.*

Penberthy, J., and Weld, D. 1992. UCPOP: A sound, complete, partial order planner for ADL. In *Proc. 3rd Int. Conf. on Principles of Knowledge Representation and Reasoning,* 103–114. Available via FTP from `pub/ai/` at `cs.washington.edu`.

Russell, S. 1992. Efficient memory-bounded search algorithms. In *Proceedings of the Tenth European Conference on Artificial Intelligence.* Vienna: Wiley.

Sacerdoti, E. 1975. The nonlinear nature of plans. In *Proceedings of IJCAI-75,* 206–214.

Smith, D., and Peot, M. 1993. Postponing threats in partial-order planning. In *Proc. 11th Nat. Conf. on A.I.,* 500–506.

Tate, A. 1977. Generating project networks. In *Proc. 5th Int. Joint Conf. on A.I.,* 888–893.

Veloso, M., and Carbonell, J. 1993. Derivational Analogy in PRODIGY: Automating Case Acquisition, Storage, and Utilization. *Machine Learning* 10:249–278.

Wilkins, D. E. 1988. *Practical Planning.* San Mateo, CA: Morgan Kaufmann.

Wilkins, D. 1992. *Using the SIPE-2 Planning System, A Manual for SIPE-2 Version 4.* SRI International, 333 Ravenswood Avenue, Menlo Park, CA 94025.

Yang, Q., and Tenenberg, J. 1990. ABTWEAK: Abstracting a nonlinear, least-commitment planner. In *Proc. 8th Nat. Conf. on A.I.,* 204–209.

Yang, Q. 1990. Formalizing planning knowledge for hierarchical planning. *Computational Intelligence* 6(1):12–24.

---

[3]This corresponds to the definition of completeness used in (Erol, Nau, & Hendler 1993); an schema-based planner is likely to be incomplete with respect to the primitive solution set.

HTN Planning: Complexity and Expressivity*

Kutluhan Erol
kutluhan@cs.umd.edu

James Hendler
hendler@cs.umd.edu

Dana S. Nau
nau@cs.umd.edu

Computer Science Department,
Institute for Systems Research and Institute for Advanced Computer Studies
University of Maryland, College Park, MD 20742

Abstract

Most practical work on AI planning systems during the last fifteen years has been based on hierarchical task network (HTN) decomposition, but until now, there has been very little analytical work on the properties of HTN planners. This paper describes how the complexity of HTN planning varies with various conditions on the task networks.

Introduction

In AI planning research, planning practice (as embodied in implemented planning systems) tends to run far ahead of the theories that explain the behavior of those systems. There is much recent analysis of the properties of total- and partial-order planning systems using STRIPS-style planning operators—but STRIPS-style planning systems were developed more than 20 years ago, and most of the practical work on AI planning systems during the last fifteen years has been based on hierarchical task network (HTN) decomposition (e.g., NOAH(Sacerdoti, 1990), NONLIN(Tate, 1990), SIPE(Wilkins, 1988), and DEVISER(Vere, 1983)).

Until now, there has been very little analytical work on the properties of HTN planners. One of the primary obstacles impeding such work has been the lack of a clear theoretical framework explaining what a HTN planning system is, although two recent papers (Yang, 1990; Kambhampati *et al.*, 1992) have provided important first steps in that direction. A primary goal of our current work is to correctly define, analyze, and explicate features of the design of HTN planning systems.

Our work has progressed far enough that we can do complexity analyses of HTN planning similar to analyses which Erol *et al.* (1992) performed for planning with STRIPS-style operators. In particular, Table 1 shows how the complexity of telling whether a plan exists depends on the following factors: (1) restrictions on the existence and/or ordering of non-primitive tasks in task networks, (2) whether the tasks in task networks are required to be totally ordered, and (3) whether variables are allowed. From this table, we can draw the following conclusions:

1. HTN's are more expressive than STRIPS-style operators. This contradicts the idea, held by some researchers, that HTN's are just an "efficiency hack."

2. HTN planning is undecidable under even a very severe set of constraints. In particular, it is undecidable even if no variables are allowed, as long as there is the possibility that a task network can contain two non-primitive tasks without specifying the order in which they must be performed.

3. In general, what restrictions we put on the non-primitive tasks has a bigger effect on complexity than whether or not we allow variables, or require tasks to be totally ordered.

4. To achieve decidability, it is sufficient to place restrictions either on non-primitive tasks or on the ordering of tasks. If either restriction is removed individually, planning remains decidable, but removing both simultaneously makes planning undecidable.

5. If there are no restrictions on non-primitive tasks, then whether or not we require tasks to be totally ordered has a bigger effect (namely, decidability vs. undecidability) than whether or not we allow variables. But in the presence of restrictions on non-primitive tasks, whether or not we allow variables has a bigger effect than whether or not we require tasks to be totally ordered.

Basics of HTN Planning

Overview

To provide an intuitive feel for HTN planning, here is a deliberately oversimplified description. The "Details" section gives a more precise description.

The input to the planner consists of the following:

- An initial "task network" d representing the problem to be solved. A task network is a set of "tasks" representing things that need to be done. Each task is a task name along with a list of arguments, which may

---

*This work was supported in part by NSF Grant NSFD CDR-88003012 to the Institute for Systems Research, and NSF grant IRI9306580 and ONR grant N00014-91-J-1451 to the Computer Science Department.

Complexity of HTN Planning

Restrictions on non-primitive tasks	Must every HTN be totally ordered?	Are variables allowed?	
		no	yes
none	no	Undecidable	Undecidable[β]
	yes	in EXPTIME; PSPACE-hard	in DEXPTIME; EXPSPACE-hard
"regularity" [α]	doesn't matter	PSPACE-complete	EXPSPACE-complete
no non-primitive tasks	no	NP-complete	NP-complete
	yes	Polynomial time	NP-complete

[α] At most one non-primitive task, which must follow all primitive tasks.

[β] Even if the planning domain is fixed in advance.

be variables or constants. Some tasks are "primitive" (i.e., they can be performed directly), and others are "non-primitive" (i.e., the planner needs to figure out how to perform them). Task networks also include constraints on the tasks, which may restrict how some of the variables can be bound, the order in which the tasks are to be performed, etc.

- A set of "operators" Op telling the effects of each primitive task (action).

- A set of "methods" Me telling how to perform various non-primitive tasks. Each method is a pair $m = (t, d)$, where t is a task and d is a task network. It says one way to achieve t is to perform the tasks specified in the network d (provided that this can be done in a way that satisfies all the constraints).

Planning proceeds by starting with the the initial task network d, and doing the following steps repeatedly, until no non-primitive tasks are left: find a non-primitive task u in d and a method $m = (t, d')$ in M such that t unifies with u. Then modify d by "reducing" u (i.e., replace u with the tasks in d', and incorporate the constraints of d' into d). Once no non-primitive tasks are left in d, the next problem is to find a totally-ordered ground instantiation σ of d that satisfies all of the constraints. If this can be done, then σ is a successful plan for the original problem.

In practice, HTN planning also has several other aspects. In particular, functions are often provided which can "debug" partially reduced task networks to eliminate potential problems. These "critic" functions are used to handle ordering constraints, resource limits, and to provide domain-specific guidance. The formalization described in (Erol *et al.*, 1994a) explains critics and the relationship between these and the constraints described above. For the purposes of this paper, the critics do not affect worst-case behavior, and thus we will omit this detail.

Details

Our language $\mathcal{L}$ for HTN planning is a first-order language with some extensions. The representations of the world and the actions in HTN planning is very similar to those of STRIPS-style planning. Thus, $\mathcal{L}$ contains a set C of constant symbols that represent the objects, and a set P of predicate symbols that represent the relations among the objects. $\mathcal{L}$ also contains a set F of primitive task symbols which represent the actions. We use constructs called *operators* to associate effects to primitive task symbols. We define a plan as a sequence of ground primitive tasks, and we designate the *initial state* of the world by a list of ground atoms.

The fundamental difference between STRIPS-style planning[1] and HTN planning is the representation of "desired change" in the world. HTN planning replaces STRIPS-style "goals" with tasks and task networks (which we later show are more powerful). There are three types of tasks:

- *Goal tasks*, like goals in STRIPS, are properties we wish to make true in the world (for example, having a new house).

- *Primitive tasks* are the tasks we can directly achieve by executing the corresponding action, such as moving a block, or turning a switch on.

- *Compound tasks* denote desired changes that involve several goal tasks and primitive tasks; e.g., building a house requires many other tasks to be performed (laying the foundation, building the walls, etc.). Compound tasks allows us to represent "desired changes" that can not be represented as a single goal task or primitive task. As an example, the compound task of "building a house" is different from the goal task of "having a house," since buying a house would achieve the goal task, but not the compound task. As another example, the compound task of making a round trip to New York cannot easily be expressed as a single goal task, because the initial and final states would be the same.

Formally, the vocabulary of HTN language $\mathcal{L}$ is a tuple $\langle V, C, P, F, T, N \rangle$, where $V = \{v_1, v_2, \ldots\}$ is an infinite set of variable symbols, C is a finite set of constant symbols, P is a finite set of predicate symbols, F is a finite set of *primitive* task symbols, T is a finite set of *compound* task symbols, and $N = \{n_1, n_2, \ldots\}$ is

---

[1] We use the term "STRIPS-style" planning to refer to any planner (either total- or partial-order) in which the planning operators are STRIPS-style operators (i.e., operators consisting of three lists of atoms: a precondition list, an add list, and a delete list). These atoms are normally assumed to contain no function symbols.

$$
((n_1 : achieve[clear(v_1)])(n_2 : achieve[clear(v_2)]) \\
(n_3 : do[move(v_1, v_3, v_2)]) \\
(n_1 \prec n_3) \land (n_2 \prec n_3) \land (n_1, clear(v_1), n_3) \\
\land (n_2, clear(v_2), n_3) \land (on(v_1, v_3), n_3) \\
\land \neg(v_1 = v_2) \land \neg(v_1 = v_3) \land \neg(v_2 = v_3))
$$

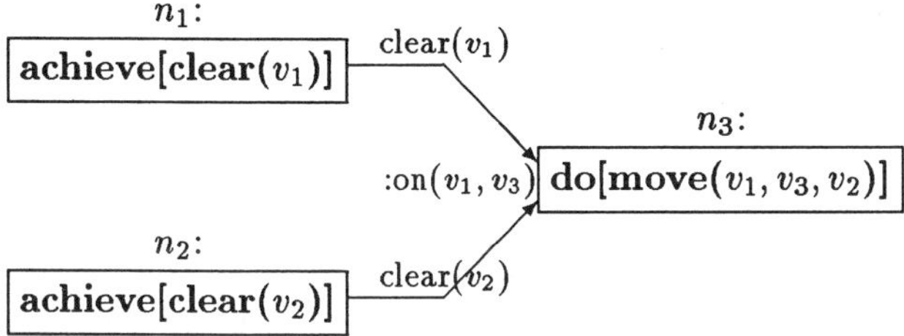

Figure 1: A task network, and its graphical representation.

an infinite set of symbols used for labeling tasks. If $x_1, \ldots, x_k$ are terms, then a *primitive task* has the form $do(f(x_1, \ldots, x_k))$, where $f \in F$; a *goal task* has the form $achieve(l)$, where l is a literal; and a *compound task* has the form $perform[t(x_1, \ldots, x_k)]$, where $t \in T$. We refer to goal tasks and compound tasks as non-primitive tasks.

Tasks are connected together in HTN planning via the use of task networks,[2] which are collections of tasks and constraints on those tasks. Formally, a *task network* has the form $((n_1 : \alpha_1), \ldots, (n_m : \alpha_m), \phi)$, where each α_i is a task labeled with n_i, and ϕ is a boolean formula constructed from variable binding constraints such as $v = v'$ and $v = c$, temporal ordering constraints such as $n \prec n'$, and truth constraints such as (n, l), (l, n), and (n, l, n'), where $n, n' \in N$, $v, v' \in V$, l is a literal, and $c \in C$. $n \prec n'$ means that the task labeled with n precedes the one labeled with n'; (n, l), (l, n) and (n, l, n') mean that l needs to be true immediately after n, immediately before n, and between n and n', respectively. Both negation and disjunction are allowed in the constraint formula.

As an example, Fig. 1 shows a blocks-world task network and its graphical representation. In this task network there are three tasks: clearing v_1, clearing v_2, and moving v_1 to v_2. The task network also includes the constraints that moving v_1 should be done last, v_1 and v_2 should remain clear until we move v_1, and that the variable v_3 is bound to the location of v_1 before v_1 is moved.

To specify how actions change the world, we use *operators* of the form $(f(v_1, \ldots, v_k), l_1, \ldots, l_m)$, where f is a primitive task symbol, $v_1, \ldots, v_k$ are variable symbols, and $l_1, \ldots, l_m$ are literals, denoting the primitive task's effects (which are also called postconditions). Our HTN operators do not contain STRIPS-style preconditions; preconditions are realized as goal tasks in

---

[2]These are also called "procedural nets" in some of the literature (Sacerdoti, 1990; Drummond, 1985).

task networks (as in Fig. 1).

It is clear how to achieve a primitive task: execute the corresponding action. But for non-primitive tasks, we need to tell our planner how to achieve them, and we do this using constructs called *methods*.

A *method* is a pair (α, d) where α is a non-primitive task, and d is a task network. It states that one way of achieving the task α is to achieve the task network d, i.e to achieve all the subtasks in the task network without violating the constraint formula of the task network. For example, a blocks-world method for achieving $on(v_1, v_2)$ would look like $(achieve(on(v_1, v_2)), d)$, where d is the task network in Fig. 1. An empty plan would achieve a goal task when the goal is already true. Thus, for each goal task, we (implicitly) have a method $(achieve(l), ((n : do(t))(l, n)))$ which contains only one dummy primitive task t with no effects, and the constraint that the goal l is true immediately before t.

Planning Domains and Problems

A planning domain is a pair $\mathcal{D} = \langle Op, Me \rangle$, where Op is a set of operators, and Me is a set of methods.

A *planning problem* is a triple $\mathbf{P} = \langle d, I, \mathcal{D} \rangle$, where $\mathcal{D}$ is a planning domain, I is the initial state, and d is the task network we need to plan for. The language of $\mathbf{P}$ is the HTN language $\mathcal{L}$ generated by the constant, predicate, and task symbols appearing in $\mathbf{P}$, along with an infinite set of variables and an infinite set of node labels. Thus, the set of constants, predicates and tasks are all part of the input.

$\mathbf{P}$ is *primitive* if the task network d contains only primitive tasks. $\mathbf{P}$ is *regular* if all the task networks in the methods and d contain at most one non-primitive task, and that non-primitive task is ordered to occur as either the first or the last task. $\mathbf{P}$ is *propositional* if no variables are allowed. $\mathbf{P}$ is *totally ordered* if all the tasks in any task network are totally ordered.

PLAN EXISTENCE is the following problem: given $\mathbf{P} = \langle d, I, \mathcal{D} \rangle$, is there a plan that solves $\mathbf{P}$?

The problem of finding an *optimal* (i.e., shortest-length) plan that solves $\mathbf{P}$ is at least as difficult as the problem of determining whether or not a plan exists. In an analysis of STRIPS-style planning, Erol *et al.* (1992) analyzed this problem by transforming it into a decision problem (which we called PLAN LENGTH) according to the usual complexity-theoretic technique of asking whether, for some input integer k, there exists a successful plan of length k or less.

This paper does not address the plan optimality problem, for two reasons. First, HTN planners have usually not worried about optimality because it is so difficult to verify (in many cases, optimality cannot be guaranteed by method decomposition). Second, Erol *et al.* (1992) found that for STRIPS-style planning, in some cases the complexity of PLAN LENGTH was misleadingly low. In particular, PLAN LENGTH was N-EXPTIME-complete even in cases where the plan optimality problem was much harder, because the input to PLAN LENGTH includes the integer k encoded in binary, which confines the planner to plans of length at most exponential in the length of the input.

Operational Semantics

In this section, we give a syntactic characterization of the set of solutions for a given HTN-planning problem. Description of an equivalent model-theoretic semantics appear in (Erol *et al.*, 1994a).

Let d be a primitive task network (one containing only primitive tasks), and let I be the initial state. A plan σ is a *completion* of d at I, denoted by $\sigma \in comp(d, I, \mathcal{D})$, if σ is a total ordering of the primitive tasks in a ground instance of d that satisfies the constraint formula of d.

Let d be a non-primitive task network that contains a (non-primitive) node $(n : \alpha)$. Let $m = (\alpha', d')$ be a method, and θ be the most general unifier of α and α'. Then we define $reduce(d, n, m)$ to be the task network obtained from $d\theta$ by replacing $(n : \alpha)\theta$ with the task nodes of $d'\theta$, and incorporating $d'\theta$'s constraint formula into the constraint formula of d. We denote the set of reductions of d by $red(d, I, \mathcal{D})$. Reductions formalize the notion of *task decomposition*. For a precise definition of completions and reductions, the reader is referred to (Erol *et al.*, 1994a).

Here are the two inference rules we use to find plans:

R1. If $\sigma \in comp(d, I, \mathcal{D})$, conclude $\sigma \in sol(d, I, \mathcal{D})$.

R2. If $d' \in red(d, I, \mathcal{D})$ and $\sigma \in sol(d', I, \mathcal{D})$, conclude $\sigma \in sol(d, I, \mathcal{D})$.

Rule R1 says that the set of plans that achieve a primitive task network consists of the completions of the task network; Rule R2 says that if d' is a reduction of d, then any plan that achieves d' also achieves d.

Now, we need to define the set of plans that can be derived using those two inference rules. Let us define a function $sol(d, I, \mathcal{D})$ as follows:

$$
\begin{aligned}
sol_1(d, I, \mathcal{D}) &= comp(d, I, \mathcal{D}) \\
sol_{n+1}(d, I, \mathcal{D}) &= sol_n(d, I, \mathcal{D}) \cup \\
&\quad \textstyle\bigcup_{d' \in red(d,I,\mathcal{D})} sol_n(d', I, \mathcal{D}) \\
sol(d, I, \mathcal{D}) &= \cup_{n < \omega} sol_n(d, I, \mathcal{D})
\end{aligned}
$$

Intuitively, $sol_n(d, I, \mathcal{D})$ is the set of plans that can be derived in n steps, and $sol(d, I, \mathcal{D})$ is the set of plans that can be derived in any finite number of steps. In (Erol *et al.*, 1994a), it is proved that $sol()$ is indeed the set of solutions, and that the inference rules **R1, R2** are sound and complete.

Results

Decidability

It is easy to show that we can simulate context-free grammars within HTN planning. More interesting is the fact that we can simulate any two context-free grammars, and with the help of task interleavings and constraints, we can check whether these two grammars have a common string in the languages they generate. Whether the intersection of the languages of two context-free grammars is non-empty is a semi-decidable problem (Hopcroft *et al.*, 1979). Thus:[3]

Theorem 1 PLAN EXISTENCE *is strictly semi-decidable, even if* P *is restricted to be propositional, to have at most two tasks in any task network, and to be totally ordered (except for the input task network).*

One way to make PLAN EXISTENCE decidable is to restrict the methods to be acyclic. In that case, any task can be expanded up to a finite depth, and thus the problem becomes decidable. To this end, we define a *k-level-mapping* to be a function $level()$ from ground instances of tasks to the set $\{0, \ldots, k\}$, such that whenever we have a method that can expand a ground task t to a task network containing a ground task t', $level(t) > level(t')$. Furthermore, $level(t)$ must be 0 for every primitive task t.

Intuitively, $level()$ assigns levels to each ground task, and makes sure that tasks can be expanded into only lower level tasks, establishing an acyclic hierarchy. In this case, any task can be expanded to a depth of at most k. Therefore,

Theorem 2 PLAN EXISTENCE *is decidable if* P *has a k-level-mapping for some finite integer k.*

Another way to make PLAN EXISTENCE decidable is to restrict the interactions among the tasks. Restricting the task networks to be totally ordered limits the interactions that can occur between tasks. Tasks need to be achieved serially, one after the other; interleaving subtasks for different tasks is not possible. Thus interactions between the tasks are limited to the input and output state of the tasks, and the "protection intervals", i.e the literals that need to be preserved.

Under the above conditions, we can create a table with an entry for each task, input/output state pair, and set of protected literals, that tells whether it is possible to achieve that task under those conditions. Using dynamic programming techniques we can compute the entries in the table in DOUBLE-EXPTIME, or in EXP-TIME if the problem is further restricted to be propositional. It is easy to show that STRIPS-style planning can be modeled using HTN's that satisfy these conditions, so we can use the complexity results on STRIPS-style planning in (Erol *et al.*, 1992) to establish a lower bound on the complexity of HTN planning. Thus:

Theorem 3 PLAN EXISTENCE *is* EXPSPACE-*hard and in* DOUBLE-EXPTIME *if* P *is restricted to be totally ordered.* PLAN EXISTENCE *is* PSPACE-*hard and in* EXP-TIME *if* P *is further restricted to be propositional.*

If we restrict our planning problem to be regular, then there will be at most one non-primitive task in any task network (both the initial input task network,

---

[3] All proofs appear in (Erol *et al.*, 1994b).

and those we obtain by expansions). Thus, subtasks in the expansions of different tasks cannot be interleaved, which is similar to what happens in Theorem 3. But in Theorem 3, there could be several non-primitive tasks in a task network, and we needed to keep track of all of them (which is why we used the table). If the planning problem is regular, we only need to keep track of a single non-primitive task, its input/final states, and the protected literals. Since the size of a state is at most exponential, the problem can be solved in exponential space. But even with regularity and several other restrictions, it is still possible to reduce an EXPSPACE-complete STRIPS-style planning problem (described in (Erol *et al.*, 1992)) to the HTN framework. Thus:

Theorem 4 PLAN EXISTENCE *is* EXPSPACE-*complete if* **P** *is restricted to be regular. It is still* EXPSPACE-*complete if* **P** *is further restricted to be totally ordered, with at most one non-primitive task symbol in the planning language, and all task networks containing at most two tasks.*

When we further restrict our problem to be propositional, the complexity goes down one level:

Theorem 5 PLAN EXISTENCE *is* PSPACE-*complete if* **P** *is restricted to be regular and propositional. It is still* PSPACE-*complete if* **P** *is further restricted to be totally ordered, with at most one non-primitive task symbol in the planning language, and all task networks containing at most two tasks.*

Suppose a planning problem is primitive, and either propositional or totally ordered. Then the problem's membership in NP is easy to see: once we nondeterministically guess a total ordering and variable binding, we can check whether the constraint formula on the task network is satisfied in polynomial time. Furthermore, unless we require the planning problem to be both totally ordered and propositional, our constraint language enables us to represent the satisfiability problem, and thus we get NP-hardness. Hence:

Theorem 6 PLAN EXISTENCE *is* NP-*complete if* **P** *is restricted to be primitive, or primitive and totally ordered, or primitive and propositional. However,* PLAN EXISTENCE *can be solved in polynomial time if* **P** *is restricted to be primitive, totally ordered, and propositional.*

Expressivity

It has been informally observed that HTN approaches do not need to completely specify the conditions that each action affects, while the STRIPS-style "state-based" plan structures typically require complete specification of intermediate states. Thus, in describing the relationships between actions, it has been argued that HTN approaches are more appropriate. Lansky (1988), for example, makes this argument and claims it is largely responsible for the the more general use of HTNs over STRIPS-style systems in planning practice.

Despite such claims, it has never been demonstrated that HTNs can encode situations which STRIPS-style planning operators cannot, because the lack of a formalism for HTN planning has left it unclear what can be expressed with HTNs. Using the formalism in this paper, we can directly compare the expressive power of HTN and STRIPS-style planning operators.

When we compare HTNs and STRIPS, we observe that the HTN approach provides all the concepts (states, actions, goals) that STRIPS has. In fact, given a domain encoded as a set of STRIPS operators, we can transform it to an HTN planning domain, in low-order polynomial time. A straightforward transformation would be to declare one primitive task symbol for each STRIPS operator, and for every effect of each operator, to declare a method similar to the one in Fig. 1. Each such method contains the preconditions of the operator as goal tasks, and also the primitive task corresponding to the operator itself.

Below is a more instructive transformation, which demonstrates that the relationship between STRIPS-style planning and HTN planning is analogous to the relationship between right linear (regular) grammars and context-free grammars. We summarize the transformation below; for details see (Erol *et al.*, 1994b).

In this transformation, the HTN representation uses the same constants and predicates used in the STRIPS representation. For each STRIPS operator o, we declare a primitive task f with the same effects as o. We also use a dummy primitive task f_d with no effects. We declare a single compound task symbol t. For each primitive task f, we construct a method of the form

$$\boxed{perform[t]} \implies \boxed{\substack{:l_1 \\ \vdots \\ :l_k} \quad \boxed{do[f]} \longrightarrow \boxed{perform[t]}}$$

where $l_1, \ldots, l_k$ are the preconditions of the action associated with f. We declare one last method $\boxed{perform[t]} \implies \boxed{do[f_d]}$. Note that t can be expanded to any sequence of actions ending with f_d, provided that the preconditions of each action are satisfied. The input task network has the form $[(n : perform[t]), (n, G_1) \wedge \ldots \wedge (n : G_m)]$ where $G_1, \ldots, G_m$ are the STRIPS-style goals we want to achieve. Note that the transformation produces regular HTN problems, which has exactly the same complexity as STRIPS-style planning. Thus, just as restricting context-free grammars to be right linear produces regular sets, restricting HTN methods to be regular produces STRIPS-style planning.

HTNs can express situations impossible to express using unmodified STRIPS operators. Intuitively, this is because STRIPS lacks the concept of compound tasks, and its notion of goals is limited. It does not provide means for declaring goals/constraints on the intermediate states as HTNs do. Furthermore, in contrast to STRIPS, HTNs provide a rich constraint language that can express many types of interactions.

More formally, from Theorem 1, HTN planning with no function symbols (and thus only finitely many ground terms) is semi-decidable. Even if we require the domain description $\mathcal{D}$ to be fixed in advance (i.e., not part of the input), there are HTN planning domains for which planning is semi-decidable.[4] However, with no function symbols, STRIPS-style planning is decidable, regardless of whether or not the planning domain[5] is fixed in advance (Erol *et al.*, 1992). Thus:

Theorem 7 *There exists* HTN *planning domains that can not be represented by any finite number of* STRIPS-*style operators.* [6]

Another way of comparing expressive power of two languages is based on model-theoretic semantics, which we do in (Erol *et al.*, 1994a).

The power of HTN planning comes from two things: (1) allowing multiple tasks and arbitrary constraint formulas in task networks, (2) compound tasks. Allowing multiple tasks and arbitrary formulae provides flexibility—but if all tasks were either primitive or goal (STRIPS-style) tasks, these could probably be expressed with STRIPS-stye operators (albeit clumsily and using an exponential number of operators/predicates). Compound tasks provide an abstract representation for sets of primitive task networks, similar to the way non-terminal symbols provide an abstract representation for sets of strings in context-free grammars.

Conclusion

Our results show that handling interactions among non-primitive tasks is the most difficult part of HTN planning. In particular, if subtasks in the expansions for different tasks can be interleaved, then planning is undecidable, even if no variables are allowed.

We have investigated several conditions on the planning problem, such as restricting task-networks to contain a single non-primitive task or to be totally ordered. Those restrictions reduced the complexity significantly, because they limited the interactions among tasks.

Our comparison of the complexity of HTN planning and STRIPS-style planning demonstrates that HTN planners can represent a broader and more complex set of planning problems and planning domains. The transformations from HTN planning problems to STRIPS-style planning problems have revealed that STRIPS-style planning is a special case of HTN planning, and that the relation between them is analogous to the relation between context-free languages and regular languages.

---

[4](Erol *et al.*, 1994b) includes several complexity results similar to those in this paper, for the case when $\mathcal{D}$ is fixed.

[5]Since STRIPS-style planning does not include methods, a STRIPS-style planning domain is simply a set of operators.

[6]In proving this theorem, we use the standard assumption that the STRIPS operators do not contain function symbols, nor do the HTN operators.

1128 Planning and Scheduling

Acknowledgement

We thank R. Kambhampati and A. Barrett for their insightful comments.

References

Chapman, D. Planning for conjunctive goals. *Artificial Intelligence*, 32:333–378, 1987.

Drummond, M. Refining and Extending the Procedural Net. In *Proc. IJCAI-85*, 1985.

Erol, K.; Nau, D.; and Subrahmanian, V. S. Complexity, decidability and undecidability results for domain-independent planning. *Artificial Intelligence* to appear. A more detailed version is available as Tech. Report CS-TR-2797, UMIACS-TR-91-154, SRC-TR-91-96, University of Maryland, College Park, MD, 1992.

Erol, K.; Hendler, J.; and Nau, D. Semantics for Hierarchical Task Network Planning. Technical report CS-TR-3239, UMIACS-TR-94-31, Computer Science Dept., University of Maryland, March 1994.

Erol, K.; Hendler, J.; and Nau, D. Complexity results for hierarchical task-network planning. To appear in *Annals of Mathematics and Artificial Intelligence* Also available as Technical report CS-TR-3240, UMIACS-TR-94-32, Computer Science Dept., University of Maryland, March 1994.

Fikes, R. E. and Nilsson, N. J. STRIPS: a new approach to the application of theorem proving to problem solving. *Artificial Intelligence*, 2(3/4) 1971.

Hopcroft and Ullman. *Introduction to Automata Theory, Languages and Computation*. Addison-Wesley Publishing Company Inc., California, 1979.

Kambhampati, S. and Hendler, J. "A Validation Structure Based Theory of Plan Modification and Reuse" *Artificial Intelligence*, May, 1992.

Lansky, A.L. Localized Event-Based Reasoning for Multiagent Domains. *Computational Intelligence Journal*, 1988.

Sacerdoti, E. D. . The nonlinear Nature of Plans In Allen, J.; Hendler, J.; and Tate, A., editors 1990, *Readings in Planning*. Morgan Kaufman. 162—170.

Tate, A. Generating Project Networks In Allen, J.; Hendler, J.; and Tate, A., editors 1990, *Readings in Planning*. Morgan Kaufman. 291—296.

Vere, S. A. Planning in Time: Windows and Durations for Activities and Goals. *IEEE Transactions on Pattern Analysis and Machine Intelligence*, PAMI-5(3):246–247, 1983.

Wilkins, D. *Practical Planning: Extending the classical AI planning paradigm*, Morgan-Kaufmann 1988.

Yang, Q. Formalizing planning knowledge for hierarchical planning *Computational Intelligence* Vol.6., 12–24, 1990.

The Use of Condition Types to Restrict Search in an AI Planner

Austin Tate, Brian Drabble & Jeff Dalton
Artificial Intelligence Applications Institute
University of Edinburgh
80 South Bridge
Edinburgh EH1 1HN
United Kingdom
A.Tate@ed.ac.uk, B.Drabble@ed.ac.uk & J.Dalton@ed.ac.uk

Abstract

Condition satisfaction in planning has received a great deal of experimental and formal attention. A "Truth Criterion" lies at the heart of many planners and is critical to their capabilities and performance. However, there has been little study of ways in which the search space of a planner incorporating such a Truth Criterion can be guided.

The aim of this document is to give a description of the use of condition "type" information to inform the search of an AI planner and to guide the production of answers by a planner's truth criterion algorithm. The authors aim to promote discussion on the merits or otherwise of using such domain-dependent condition type restrictions as a means to communicate valuable information from the domain writer to a general purpose domain-independent planner [1].

Introduction to Condition Typing

Research in AI planning has introduced a range of progressively more powerful techniques to address increasingly more realistic applications (Allen, Hendler & Tate 1990). A lesson learned in the expert systems and knowledge-based systems field is that it is important to make maximum use of domain knowledge where it is available in order to address many real problems. One powerful means of using domain knowledge to restrict and guide search in a planner is to recognise explicit precondition types, as introduced into Interplan (Tate 1975) and Nonlin (Tate 1977) and subsequently used in other systems such as Deviser (Vere 1981), SIPE–2 (Wilkins 1988) O-Plan (Currie & Tate 1991) and O-Plan2 (Tate, Drabble & Kirby 1994).

An explicit account of the *Goal Structure* or *teleology* of a plan can be kept in these systems. This records the causal relationships between actions in the plan and can show the intentions of the domain writer or planner in satisfying conditions on actions. In some circumstances, such domain knowledge can be used to prune the search of a planner. The information is provided to the planner via a planner's domain description language (e.g., Task Formalism – TF – in Nonlin and O-Plan). The domain writer takes the responsibility for a deliberate pruning of the search space or for providing preferences via condition types. This caused us to adopt the term *knowledge based planning* to describe our work.

Nonlin and O-Plan TF extends the notion of a precondition on an action and mates it with a "process" oriented view of action descriptions. A TF schema description specifies a method by which some higher level action can be performed (or higher level goal achieved). Each schema is thought of as provided by its own "manager". The schema introduces lower level actions under the direction of its manager and uses that manager's own resources. The schema may say that some specific sub-action is included in order to set up for some later sub-action as part of the overall task. In TF, such internally satisfied requirements in actions are specified as **supervised** conditions. The "manager" also relies on other (normally external) agents to perform tasks that are their own responsibilities, but affect the ability of this manager to do the task. These are given as **unsupervised** conditions. There are other conditions which the "manager" may wish to impose on the applicability of particular solutions (e.g.. don't try this method for house building if the building is over five stories tall). These are termed **holds** and **usewhen** conditions in different versions of Nonlin and are now called **only_use_if** conditions in O-Plan2.

Condition typing can be used to restrict search in a planner, but there is work to be done on how far this technique can be developed. It is often difficult for a domain writer to choose the correct type for a condition to most effectively restrict the search space while not over-indulging and throwing away plans which should be considered valid in the domain. Tool sup-

---

[1] O-Plan2 work is supported by the US Advanced Research Projects Agency (ARPA) and the US Air Force Rome Laboratory acting through the Air Force Office of Scientific Research (AFSC) under contract F49620-92-C-0042. The project is monitored by Dr. Northrup Fowler III at Rome Laboratory.

port to aid in the reliable modelling of large domains will undoubtably be needed. In practice, we have found that condition typing is an essential aspect of encoding realistic problems to an AI planner in order to reduce search spaces to a manageable level.

Other Related Work

The concept of providing explicit domain encoder input to guide planning has its roots in early research on the Planner language family. POPLER (Davies 1973) identified the search space implications of providing only a single type of "goal" which can either already be true or which can induce subgoaling to be made true. Interplan (Tate 1975) provided a simple facility to indicate that nominated conditions should not be sub-goaled upon. That is, that no method of *achieving* them should be introduced into the plan. Nonlin (Tate 1977) provided a comprehensive set of condition types as described earlier. These were used to restrict the options considered to satisfy a condition in the Nonlin "QA Algorithm". QA was a precursor to the Truth Criterion used in many planners which use a partial order plan representation and make use of Goal Structure or causal links to direct search. See (Tate 1993) for a historical perspective.

A more general condition satisfaction approach, not using such domain knowledge, is used in TWEAK based on Chapman's formalisation of the Modal Truth Criterion (MTC) (Chapman 1987). This approach does not address search control issues. Chapman's work provides a description of the search space, but not a specification of how to control or prune search in that space.

There has been little study of ways in which the search space of a planner incorporating a Truth Criterion can be guided. Drummond (Drummond 1993) argues that there has been too much concentration on planner aspects that deal with logically or syntactically complete condition achievement, and too little attention has been paid to other capabilities of practical planners such as Nonlin, SIPE-2 and O-Plan. These other capabilities include hierarchical expansion, a simple but effective resource allocation mechanism, and explicit languages to describe and allow for the protection of the a plan's causal structure (effects/conditions).

A number of researchers have pre-analysed operator information to guide search.

Collins and Pryor (Collins & Pryor 1993) provide the first critical analysis on the use of condition types intended to filter out options that would otherwise have to be considered by a planner. They conclude that in the majority of cases such filter conditions are misused and may not have the effect intended. Their arguments assume that changes to the set of operators available might invalidate domain modelling assumptions about the use of filters(true[2]), that most providers of systems employing condition types did not fully appreciate that use of filter conditions would restrict the search space (false), and that restricting the search space using such filter conditions is not useful due to the restrictions under which they correctly apply (false, their argument assumes that hierarchical modelling is not used properly in planning or that filter conditions can be "hierarchically promiscuous"[3] – they must not be). Although the Collins and Pryor critical analysis paper is flawed in making some of these assumptions, it is none-the-less a useful document in raising the issue of the validity or otherwise of utilising condition type information to restrict search in a planner and may start wider study and debate on whether such condition types are valid and useful. Unfortunately, the work takes too simplistic a view of how condition types (filter and otherwise) are already used in planning systems today.

It is hoped that the current paper goes some way towards providing an information base on which comment, study and analysis will be possible.

O-Plan2 Domain Description Language Task Formalism

TF is used by a domain encoder to give an overall hierarchical description of an application area by specifying the activities within the domain and in particular their more detailed representation as a set of sub-activities with ordering constraints imposed. Plans are generated by choosing suitable "expansions" for activities (by refining them to a more detailed level) in the plan and including the relevant set of more detailed sub-activities described therein. Ordering constraints are then introduced to ensure that asserted effects of some activities satisfy, and continue to satisfy, conditions on the use of other activities. Other constraints, such as a time window for the activity or resource usage required, are also included in the description. These descriptions of activities form the main structure within TF - the *schema*. Schemas are also used in a completely uniform manner to describe *tasks*, set to the planning system, in the same language. Other TF structures hold global information and heuristic information about preferences of choices to be made during planning.

O-Plan2 Triangle Model of Activity

O-Plan2 uses a hierarchical model of activity which gives emphasis to an owner's perspective of how an activity is performed and the environment in which it can

---

[2]Tool support may help in avoiding such domain encoding errors.

[3]Hierarchical promiscuity occurs when a domain modeller confuses the levels at which effects are introduced and conditions are required. This is especially problematic for the ways in which AI planners typically handle filter conditions.

be sanctioned, resourced and used. This is reflected in the "triangle" model of an activity (see Figure 1). The vertical dimension reflects activity decomposition, the horizontal dimension reflects time. Inputs and outputs are split into three principal categories (authority, conditions/effects and resources). Arbitrarily complex modelling is possible in all dimensions. "Types" are used to further differentiate the inputs and outputs and their semantics.

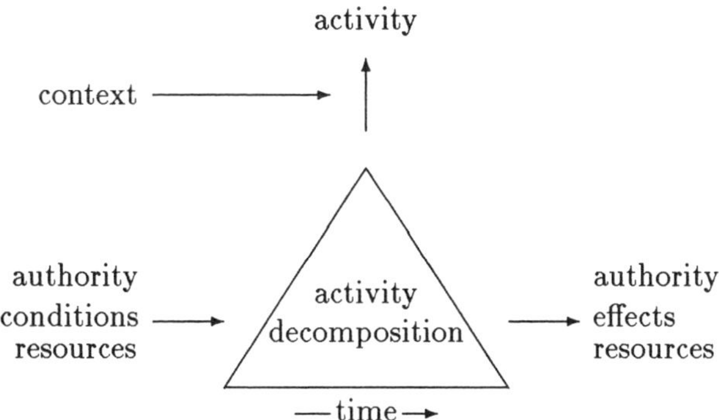

Figure 1: Triangle model of Activity

"Entry" to the model can be from any of three points in the triangle model. From the top vertex it is possible to ask for activity expansions or decompositions. From the right side of the triangle, it is possible to ask for activities satisfying or providing the output requirement (a desired effect or "goal", a required resource, or a needed authority). These two points are used mostly by our planners to date. The third point on the left side can reflect triggering conditions for an activity and will be needed when improved models of independent processes are used as in our Excalibur (Drabble 1993) extension to Nonlin. A "context" requirement permits use of each particular expansion or decomposition of an activity.

The triangle model of activity is a generalisation of process models used in many structured analysis and design techniques (SADT) such as IDEF, R-Charts, etc., and can be directly related to them.

O-Plan2 Condition Types

Condition typing allows relevant information to be kept about when, how and why a condition present in the plan has been satisfied and the way it is to be treated if the condition cannot be maintained. All condition statements appear in O-Plan2 Task Formalism action schemas. Conditions play a greater role in O-Plan than in previous planning systems since there is no *special* notion of *goal*. Nonlin (Tate 1977), NOAH (Sacerdoti 1977) and SIPE−2 (Wilkins 1988) style goal nodes in action expansions become simply **achieve** conditions in O-Plan. The **achieve** condition type is the only one on which sub-goaling is permitted.

Conditions are one of the most elaborate of all TF statements due to the variety of condition types identi-

fied as being needed for practical planning in O-Plan2. The "process" or "manager" view of hierarchical activity description used in Nonlin contributed the three basic condition types of **supervised**, **unsupervised** and **usewhen**. O-Plan research and applications experience identified the need to separate two different uses being made of the Nonlin **usewhen** condition type. This led to the introduction of **only_use_if** and **only_use_for_query**. A more flexible **achieve** condition definition was also required to remove temporal scope limitations on the ways in which earlier planners such as Nonlin could satisfy goals by adding new activities into a plan.

The O-Plan2 condition types are thus:

- **only_use_if** conditions provide an applicability check on the context in which a schema can be used. These are sometimes referred to as filter conditions.

- **only_use_for_query** conditions are used to make queries at a point in the plan to instantiate or restrict variables in a schema.

- **unsupervised** conditions must be satisfied at the required point, but it is assumed that, in circumstances in which the schema introducing such a condition is used, that the condition will have been satisfied elsewhere. Therefore, they act as a sequencing constraint.

- **supervised** conditions are satisfied directly within the schema containing them by the deliberate introduction of a suitable effect (or alternative effects) at an earlier point or by the direct inclusion of an action known to achieve the necessary effect (at some more detailed level in the action's decomposition). They may be used as a means to explicitly record a protection interval within the causal structure of a plan.

- **achieve** conditions can be satisfied by any means available to the planner including the addition of new actions into the plan.

Other condition types can be identified but the ones above have been found to be useful ways to extract knowledge from a domain writer in a communicable form that can be used to restrict search in an AI planner.

Condition typing helps direct the planning process, but it also requires that the domain encoder structures the hierarchy of the tasks or actions clearly. It forces checks to be made on processes or actions which should communicate with others – ensuring they actually do advertise their results through a common vocabulary.

O-Plan2 Plan Levels

Before describing condition types and their definitions, it is useful to describe how O-Plan2 uses hierarchical modelling levels in its operation.

Definition

Each action and effect is introduced at a single domain modelling level and higher level activities introduce activities and effects at the same or a lower level.

A plan level can be introduced for two distinct purposes:

1. For convenience of abstraction and aggregation.
2. To place an order on the commitments and constraints made during planning.

The numerical plan levels are assigned by the O-Plan2 TF compiler in quite an intuitive way. Level numbers increase as lower level, more detailed action and effect descriptions are given. However, there can be "loops" in the structure, such that some actions can expand recursively or may expand back to themselves via other schemas. In such cases, all the actions and effects in the "loops" are mapped to the same plan modelling level. The detailed way in which level numbers are assigned is as follows.

Each schema represents a way to perform the action indicated by its **expands** clause. The first word of the **expands** pattern is referred to as the *action name* of the schema. Each schema S links its action to a number of direct successor actions: the sub-actions listed in the schema's definition. These successor actions are normally at the next lower level (except when loops are involved). A further set of direct successors can be found by taking the action names of all schemas that have an **only_use_for_effects** that matches any **achieve** condition of S.

This will define a graph in which the action names are vertices and there is an edge from each action name to each of its directly reachable successors. The next step is to find the *strongly connected components* (SCCs) in this graph in order to build a new graph in which each SCC is treated as a unit. This new graph is acyclic and the level of an action can be found by taking the longest path to the SCC that contains it through this graph. This will also identify the level at which *effects* are introduced into the plan. The plan level mapper is sensitive to loops in the graph and the SCCs components represent such loops. Whenever you can get from A to B *and* from B to A in a directed graph, A and B are in the same SCC.

Condition Types for the Domain Writer

This section gives definitions of O-Plan2 condition types in terms of what information a domain writer providing a library of action or plan components can state, hopefully in an understandable way without knowledge of how the AI planner would go about using this in detail.

For each condition type used within O-Plan2 we provide below the following information:

- **Purpose**: This describes the condition type in domain terms for use by the domain encoder and describes the circumstances under which the condition type should be used.
- **Definition**: This describes the condition type in planner terms and describes in more detail how the planner goes about dealing with the condition type on behalf of the domain encoder.
- **Examples**: These clarify the use of each type.

Only_use_if

- **Purpose**: This is a filter condition on the applicability of a particular schema.
- **Definition**: It may be given on statements introduced as effects at a higher level or on the same modelling level as the schema introducing it.
- **Examples**: On static facts (those never refuted in the plan and referred to as **always** facts in O-Plan2):

```
only_use_if {type_of soil} = sandy
```

and on dynamic facts (whose value can change over time):

```
only_use_if {apportioned_force ?regiment}
                              = unallocated
```

In the first example the condition would be used to allow a schema to be selected which was suitable for use if the soil type is sandy. In the second example, the condition would only allow the schema to be chosen if a particular force was available at this point in the plan. During the course of the plan the force's status may vary and with it the ability to use the schema.

Only_use_for_query

- **Purpose**: A query mechanism to establish current values for variables.
- **Definition**: It may be given on statements at a higher or on the same modelling level as the schema including it. There should *always* be an answer for such a query when it is evaluated at an appropriate level.
- **Examples**: On static facts:

```
only_use_for_query {country_of ?city} = ?country
```

and on dynamic facts:

```
only_use_for_query {position_of ?robot}
                              = ?location
```

The first example would allow the country in which a city is located to be looked up. The second example allows the dynamic lookup of the position of the robot.

Unsupervised

- **Purpose**: Specifies a scheduling constraint on the schema which is (normally) satisfied externally. Exceptionally, it may also specify an internal ordering requirement within the schema making use of actions introduced for other reasons.

- **Definition**: It may be given on statements at the same or a higher modelling level if the condition is satisfied externally to the sub-actions of the schema or at the same or lower modelling level if the condition is satisfied from the sub-actions within the schema.

- **Example**:

```
unsupervised {status ground_buffer} = empty at 2
```

This would make a sub-action number 2 introduced by the schema occur after some other action in the plan which empties the ground_buffer.

Supervised

- **Purpose**: To protect an intended effect of some earlier sub-activity up to the point required.

- **Definition**: It may be given on statements at the same or on a lower modelling level as the schema including it.

- **Example**:

```
supervised {status ground_buffer} = full
                             at 3 from 2
```

This would protect the ground_buffer as being full between the end of a schema sub-action number 2 (say where some data was captured into the ground_buffer) to the beginning of a later schema sub-action number 3 where the data might be used.

Achieve

- **Purpose**: To allow a condition to be satisfied by the optional inclusion of sub-activities.

- **Definition**: Specifies a requirement which the schema writer is optionally prepared to meet by adding new structure into the plan at the same or lower modelling level as the schema including the condition.

- **Example**:

```
achieve {in_position ?tool} = workbench at 1
```

This allows the required tool to be moved to the required place if it is not already there.

The following table summarises the ways in which each O-Plan2 condition type may be satisfied.

Condition	Levels Considered			Type
only_use_if	above	same		EXTERNAL
only_use_for_query	above	same		EXTERNAL
unsupervised	above	same		EXTERNAL or
		same	below	INTERNAL
supervised		same	below	INTERNAL
achieve		same	below	OPTIONAL

Condition Type Correspondence to Nonlin, SIPE-2 and ACT

Nonlin (Tate 1977) was the first Edinburgh planner to use the Task Formalism (TF) language and made use of **supervised**, **unsupervised** and **usewhen** condition types. It handled achievable conditions by including goal nodes in the action expansion.

The SIPE−2 planner (Wilkins 1988) also includes support for a number of condition types and is converging on similar types to those available in O-Plan2. A development of the SIPE−2 domain description language to link to work on the PRS (Procedural Reasoning System) reactive execution support system (Georgeff 1986) is now underway to create a shared domain description language called ACT. The following sections compare O-Plan2 condition type usage with the those used in Nonlin, SIPE−2 and ACT.

O-Plan2	Nonlin	SIPE-2	ACT
only_use_if	usewhen	precondition	precondition
only_use_for_query	none	none	setting
unsupervised	unsupervised	external	wait-until
supervised	supervised	protect-until	require-until
achieve at N	none	none	none
achieve after	goal	goal	achieve

only_use_if This is the same as Nonlin's **usewhen** (originally called **holds**). It is the same as a **precondition** in either SIPE−2 or ACT. The ***already** condition in later releases of Deviser (Vere 1981) performs the same function.

only_use_for_query In Nonlin and SIPE−2, such conditions were modelled as **usewhen** conditions or **preconditions** respectively and not treated separately. Nonlin or SIPE−2 treated a query condition in the same way as an **only_use_if** filter condition, except that it was assumed that variables would be bound by satisfying it. This incorrectly limits the range of legitimate solutions. As in O-Plan2, ACT separates query type conditions for clarity – calling them the **setting**.

unsupervised Later releases of SIPE−2 allow an **external** condition to give this capability. In ACT, this is called **wait-until**.

supervised The same as a **protect-until** in SIPE−2 and **require-until** in ACT.

achieve at N This imposes no restriction on the temporal scope of any activity inserted in the plan to satisfy the condition. There is no equivalent in Nonlin, SIPE–2 or ACT all of which make such temporal scope restrictions and thus restrict the domains which can be modelled.

achieve at N after <time point> This is an **achieve** with a temporal restriction on the points within the plan from which a contributor may be chosen to satisfy the condition. This is a more general way to describe Nonlin, NOAH and SIPE–2 goal nodes which appear in the expansion/decomposition part of their operator schemas. For these systems, the <time point> is restricted to be after the start of the time range of the expansion of the schema containing the condition. In ACT this is called **achieve** and has the same fixed restriction on temporal scope as Nonlin, NOAH and SIPE–2.

Summary

In large realistic domains, we believe that significant domain knowledge must be made available to a planner in order to reduce search spaces to a manageable level. One important way in which this can be done effectively is to get a domain writer to provide information about a domain from which we can extract instructions to the planning system about how to satisfy and maintain conditions required in the plan.

Condition types can be a valuable aid to providing knowledge about a domain to a domain-independent planner. Condition typing can successfully restrict the search for a plan, but there is work to be done on how far this technique can be developed. It is often difficult for a domain writer to choose the correct type for a condition to most effectively restrict the search space while not over-indulging and throwing away plans which should be considered valid in the domain. Improved planning knowledge capture aids now under development may assist in this process.

One aim of this paper has been to seek to separate the domain writer oriented description of condition types from the mechanisms used by a planner to satisfy, maintain and re-satisfy conditions.

By making this information more widely available, the authors aim to promote discussion on the merits or otherwise of using such domain-dependent condition type restrictions as a means to communicate information from the domain writer to a general purpose domain-independent planner. The control of planner search via condition types is worthy of a serious study in its own right, and could form an ideal Ph.D. topic.

Acknowledgements

We are grateful for discussions on condition types with Drew McDermott, Nancy Lehrer, Glen Reece, Mark Drummond, Subbarao Kambhampati, Dan Weld, Craig Knoblock and Louise Pryor, as well as from the comments of the reviewers and conversations with other members of the AI planning community. Sorry we had to be ruthless to achieve the final page count. The work reported here has benefited from input by talented researchers who have participated in the O-Plan and related projects. Thanks to David Wilkins who helped in checking the comparison to SIPE–2 and ACT usage of condition types. Errors remain ours.

References

Allen, J., Hendler, J. & Tate, A. 1990. *Readings in Planning*, Morgan-Kaufmann.

Chapman, D. 1987. Planning for Conjunctive Goals, *Artificial Intelligence*, Vol. 32, pp 333-377.

Collins, G. & Pryor, L. 1993. On the Misuse of Filter Conditions: A Critical Analysis, in *Current Trends in AI Planning*, (eds. Backström, C. & Sandewall, E.), IOS Press.

Currie, K.W. & Tate, A. 1991. O-Plan: the Open Planning Architecture, *Artificial Intelligence* Vol 51, No. 1, pp 49-86, North-Holland.

Davies, D.J.M. 1973. POPLER 1.5 Reference Manual, Theoretical Psychology Unit Report no.1., Department of Artificial Intelligence, University of Edinburgh.

Drabble, B. 1993. Excalibur: A Program for Planning and Reasoning with Processes, *Artificial Intelligence*, Vol. 62 No. 1, pp 1-40.

Drummond, M.E. 1993. On Precondition Achievement and the Computational Economics of Automatic Planning, in *Current Trends in AI Planning*, (eds. Backström, C. & Sandewall, E.), IOS Press.

Georgeff, M.P. & Lansky, A.L. 1986. Procedural Knowledge, in *Proceedings of the IEEE*, Special Issue on Knowledge Representation, Vol. 74, pp 1383-1398.

Sacerdoti, E. 1977. *A Structure for Plans and Behaviours*, Artificial Intelligence Series, North Holland.

Tate, A. 1975. Using Goal Structure to Direct Search in a Problem Solver. Ph.D. Thesis, University of Edinburgh.

Tate, A. 1977. Generating Project Networks, in Proceedings of the International Joint Conference on Artificial Intelligence (IJCAI-77), Cambridge, MA, USA.

Tate, A. 1993. The Emergence of "Standard" Planning and Scheduling System Components, in *Current Trends in AI Planning*, (eds. Backström, C. & Sandewall, E.), IOS Press.

Tate, A., Drabble, B. & Kirby, R. 1994. O-Plan2: an Open Architecture for Command, Planning and Control, in *Intelligent Scheduling*, (eds. Fox, M. & Zweben, M.), Morgan Kaufmann.

Vere, S. 1981. Planning in Time: Windows and Durations for Activities and Goals, *IEEE Transactions on Pattern Analysis and Machine Intelligence* Vol. 5.

Wilkins, D. 1988. *Practical Planning*, Morgan-Kaufmann.

Qualitative and
Model-Based Reasoning

Prediction Sharing Across Time and Contexts

Oskar Dressler and Hartmut Freitag

Siemens AG, Corporate Research & Development, Software and Engineering

Otto-Hahn-Ring 6

D-81730 Munich, Germany

{dressler, freitag}@zfe.siemens.de

Abstract

Sometimes inferences made at some specific time are valid at other times, too. In model-based diagnosis and monitoring as well as qualitative simulation inferences are often re-done although they have been performed previously. We propose a *new method for sharing predictions* done at different times, thus mutually cutting down prediction costs incurring at different times. Furthermore, we generalize the technique from 'sharing predictions across time' to 'sharing predictions across time *and* logical contexts'. Assumption-based truth maintenance is a form of sharing predictions across logical contexts. Because of the close connections to the ATMS we were able to *use* it as a means for implementation. We report empirical results on monitoring different configurations of ballast water tanks as used on offshore platforms and ships.

1. Introduction

Successfully deploying model-based diagnosis systems for complex technical devices ultimately requires an on-line coupling with the artifacts via sensors and actuators. In the field, instead of being manually activated when a malfunction occurs, as a first task an automatic on-line diagnosis system has to decide whether there actually is a diagnosis problem. Does the behavior deviate from the specified normal operation? Only then the diagnosis process will start. *A preceding monitoring phase is required.*

Once the faulty components have been identified, an integrated monitoring and diagnosis system may be allowed to switch back to monitoring mode interpreting the measurements coming from the sensors under the hypotheses that the identified components are broken. Monitoring and diagnosis may thus be interleaved.

Consider the application from (Dressler et al. 1993) depicted in figure 1. A collection of ballast tanks of various sizes is placed at different locations on a ship or offshore platform (the complete system comprises 40 tanks). Depending on load, wind and sea motion, water is pumped into or out of some of the tanks or the sea. This can be a rather time consuming process. For example, in our application on a crane ship, filling three tanks as shown in figure 1 can last up to 1.5 hours. At any time failures may occur potentially causing catastrophic damage. A broken pressure

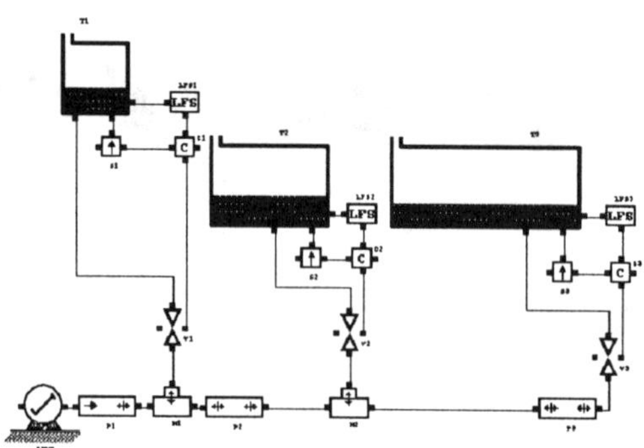

Figure 1. A ballast tank system

sensor, for instance, may enable or disable the automatic closing of a valve, thus causing an overflow or critical unbalance[1].

A stream of data coming from the system gives us values for pressures, valve status, float switch status and pump activity. This data is processed in a conventional way, such that we can assume to have derivatives for these values, too.

When observed behavior is to be classified as normal or faulty, a model is an invaluable asset. It allows predicting values for system variables, hence generating expectations about behavior when data, even if incomplete, becomes available.

But the purpose of models for monitoring and diagnosis is substantially different. While the former are only needed to *detect* malfunctions, the latter must have enough detail for *localizing* malfunctioning components. Diagnosis systems like DP (Struss 1992) and Magellan (Böttcher, Dressler 1993), however, can use multiple models of different granularity during one and the same diagnosis session. Their diagnosis process starts with coarser models that are suitable for monitoring, too.

In this paper we focus on the prediction task from the viewpoint of dependency-based diagnosis. Dependencies

---

1. The shipwreck of the polish ferry 'Jan Heweliusz' in January 1993 is suspected to be caused by an incorrect filling of ballast tanks.

are necessary for tracing back contradictory derivations to their origins. This allows diagnosis engines such as GDE (de Kleer, Williams 1987), GDE$^+$ (Struss, Dressler 1989), Sherlock (de Kleer, Williams 1989), (de Kleer 1991) and others to *first* identify conflicting assumption sets and *then* to generate diagnoses.

We use qualitative models for both, diagnosis and monitoring:

- For consistency-based diagnosis engines they prove to be especially useful; more detailed models become obsolete, when a qualitative abstraction of them has been refuted (Struss 1992). There often is no need to explore further details.
- For monitoring only significant deviations from normal operation are of interest. Using a qualitative model for the normal mode one can capture the complete set of good behaviors instead of just a single one.

When no discrepancies between observed and expected behavior are detected, the empty diagnosis is computed meaning that every component is working correctly. With this in mind, we can view monitoring as *'diagnosis without discrepancies'*.

For on-line coupling prediction is necessary at the rate of incoming data. Speed is of prime interest. Allowing a fault to go undetected potentially leads to catastrophe. Ideally, the consistency check, i.e. prediction, should be carried out at the sampling rate of the sensors, say every 10 seconds.

Suppose we are monitoring the process of filling the tanks. Incoming real values are first mapped to their qualitative abstractions, and then fed into the prediction machinery. This we can afford to do every, say two minutes, depending on the cost for running the model. Using qualitative models, most of the time nothing changes in qualitative terms, since different real values are mapped to the same qualitative value. Therefore, we end up making more or less the *same* predictions every two minutes while we would like a higher sampling rate and do prediction with *new* values only.

We propose a new technique for caching and generalizing previously made predictions. It allows carrying over predictions from one time to another. An inference made at a specific time in the past "generalizes" to the same inference made at *all* possible times. There is no need to ever make an inference twice. Consequently, prediction can be much faster when relevant previous inferences have been made. Due to the use of qualitative models this happens all of the time. Intuitively, only when a monitored variable changes its qualitative value, *new* predictions have to be made. In the ballast tanks application (Dressler et al. 1993), the sampling rate during the monitoring phase went down from 2 minutes to 2 seconds !

In the next section we introduce the key concept of *'prediction sharing across time'*. Section 3 generalizes our re-sults by combination with another popular concept called *'prediction sharing across contexts'*, commonly known as ATMS (de Kleer 1986). In section 4 delayed consequences of inferences are considered and built into the framework. Finally, in section 5, we discuss empirical results we obtained for different configurations of ballast tanks.

2. Prediction Sharing Across Time

2.1. Temporally Generic Formulae

The system description *SD* is temporally generic in the sense that it describes behavior independent of the specific time at which, for example, a filling process takes place. For example, the model for the normal mode of a valve looks like follows:

$ok\,(valve) \rightarrow\ valve.status = valve.cmd$

$ok\,(valve) \rightarrow\ valve.[i_1] = -\,valve.[i_2]$

$ok\,(valve) \rightarrow\ (valve.status = close \rightarrow valve.[i_1] = valve.[i_2] = 0\,)$

$ok\,(valve) \rightarrow\ (\,valve.[i_1] \neq 0 \rightarrow valve.status = valve.cmd = open\,)$

The meaning of the variables is: *valve.cmd*: control input, *valve.status*: valve's state output, *valve.i1*: flow into the left/top end, *valve.i2*: flow into the right/bottom end. Square brackets [.] indicate qualitative variables. The complete models can be found in (Dressler et al. 1993).

In general, inferences made from such descriptions have the form

$$\alpha_1\,(t) \wedge \ldots \wedge \alpha_2\,(t) \rightarrow \beta\,(\Delta\,(t)\,)$$

where α_i and β are propositional atoms, temporal index t refers to some specific time and $\Delta\,(t)$ denotes another temporal index. We call Δ a *delay function*, but allow for negative delays. Therefore, we may draw conclusions about past system variable values, too.

A component c operating in mode $m(c)$ is assumed to exhibit the same behavior at every specific time index given that the same values are fed into it. This includes that the delay function is also independent of the specific time. Assuming linear time, we can depict the situation in figure 2.

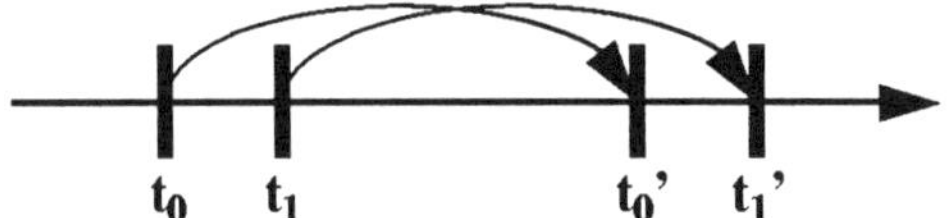

Figure 2. A time-independent delay-function

$\forall x.\ [t_1 = t_0 + x \rightarrow \Delta\,(t_0) + x = \Delta\,(t_0 + x\,) = \Delta\,(t_1)] \wedge$
$\qquad [\,[\,\alpha_1(t_0) \wedge \ldots \wedge \alpha_n\,(t_0) \rightarrow \beta(\Delta(t_0))]$
$\qquad\qquad \rightarrow [\,\alpha_1(t_0 + x) \wedge \ldots \wedge \alpha_n\,(t_0 + x) \rightarrow \beta(\Delta(t_0 + x))\,]\,]$

More generally, assuming arbitrary delay functions Δ_1 and Δ_2, 'independence of an inference of the specific time' is expressed as:

$\forall \Delta_1\ \forall \Delta_2\ \forall\ t.[\,\Delta_2\,(\Delta_1\,(t)) = \Delta_1\,(\Delta_2\,(t))\,] \wedge$
$\qquad [\,[\alpha_1(t_0) \wedge \ldots \wedge \alpha_n\,(t_0) \rightarrow \beta(\Delta_1(t_0))\,]$
$\qquad\qquad \rightarrow [\alpha_1(\Delta_2(t_0)) \wedge \ldots \wedge \alpha_n\,(\Delta_2(t_0)) \rightarrow \beta(\Delta_1(\Delta_2(t_0)))\,]\,]$

A formula of the form $\alpha_1\,(t) \wedge \ldots \wedge \alpha_2\,(t) \rightarrow \beta\,(\Delta\,(t))$

with propositional atoms $\alpha_1, ..., \alpha_n$ and β indexed by time t and $\Delta(t)$ where the delay function Δ adheres to this restriction is called *temporally generic* (or t-generic). Without loss of generality we assume the system description to be a set of t-generic formulae. Please note, that we are not committed to a specific ontology of time like time points or intervals.

For the rest of section 2 and section 3 the delay function considered is identity, i.e. no delays. In section 4 we show how delay is built into the framework.

2.2. Temporal Generalization of Single Instance Inferences

From the discussion so far it is clear that some inferences made at a specific time will be valid at other times, too. Thus, there is no need to re-do them when we employ an appropriate caching scheme.

We start from statements like proposition ϕ holding at time t_i, $\phi@t_i$, called *temporally indexed statements*.

In consistency-based diagnosis we are given a set of them, usually the observations OBS made at certain times and the assumptions Π that the corresponding components are working in a specific mode at a certain time. The task is to check the consistency of $SD \cup OBS \cup \Pi$ where SD is independent of time in the sense discussed before.

In qualitative simulation we are given a set of such statements for some initial time t_0. The task there is to enumerate possible evolutions of the system from this point on. Again, we are dealing with a system description SD which is independent of time and observations at a specific time t_0.

When we predict a value ϕ to hold at t_i, $\phi@t_i$, the underlying support consists of a set of t-generic formulae $SD' \subseteq SD$ and a set of sentences S holding at specific times $t_1, ..., t_n$: $SD' \cup S \models \phi$

Since we have restricted the delay functions to identity, all of these temporal indices are identical to t_i, i.e. $t_i = t_1 = ... = t_n$. It follows immediately that the derivation of ϕ can be generalized from the single time index t_i to sets of time indices.

Definition: The *temporal extent of α, TE (α)*, denotes the set $\{t_i \mid \alpha \text{ holds at } t_i\}$.

The t-generic formulae in the system description hold at all times, but propositions about observed values etc. are only available at certain times.

Definition: A set GS of non-universally holding formulae is called *ground support for ϕ* iff there exists $SD' \subseteq SD$ such that $SD' \cup GS \models \phi$.

Lemma: If GS is a ground support for ϕ then
$$\bigcap_{\alpha \in GS} TE(\alpha) \subseteq TE(\phi)$$

This means we can generalize a derivation of ϕ at a specific time t_i to the intersection of temporal extents of ϕ's support. Whenever all the propositions in GS hold at some

time $t_j \neq t_i$ we know *without re-deriving* ϕ that it holds at t_j, too.

2.3. Symbolic Computation of Temporal Extents

For derived formulae ϕ which do not occur in temporally indexed statements, like e.g. $\phi@t_{13}$, the temporal extent can be computed *symbolically* by considering *all* ground support sets for ϕ, $GS(\phi)$.

Lemma: Let no explicit temporal statements about ϕ be available. Then
$$TE(\phi) = \bigcup_{S \in GS(\phi)} \bigcap_{\alpha \in S} TE(\alpha).$$

If explicit temporal statements about ϕ are available, we have to add these times.

Lemma: If explicit temporal statements about ϕ at times $t_1, ..., t_n$ are available, then
$$TE(\phi) = \bigcup_{S \in GS(\phi)} \bigcap_{\alpha \in S} TE(\alpha) \cup \{t_1, ..., t_n\}.$$

For the propositions α that may occur in the ground support of derived formulae we introduce symbols TE_α to represent $TE(\alpha)$. These propositions α are exactly the propositions for which we have temporally indexed statements. The symbols TE_α are called *temporal base symbols*. In model-based diagnosis this means we are creating these symbols for the observable values and for the modes of components. In qualitative simulation the qualitative values of the initial state are treated in this way.

Using these symbols each atom is labelled with a *unique* symbolic representation of its temporal extent.

Definition: *Temporal Label*

A set of symbol sets, $\{\ \{TE_{\alpha_{11}}, ..., TE_{\alpha_{1n}}\}, ..., \{TE_{\alpha_{m1}}, ..., TE_{\alpha_{mk}}\}\ \}$, is called *temporal label* of ϕ, $TL(\phi)$, iff

[*Correctness*]

Each set $\{TE_{\alpha_{i1}}, ..., TE_{\alpha_{ij}}\}$ is a ground support for ϕ.

[*Completeness*]

If S is a ground support for ϕ, then there exists $\{TE_{\alpha_{i1}}, ..., TE_{\alpha_{ij}}\}$ in $TL(\phi)$ such that $\{TE_{\alpha_{i1}}, ..., TE_{\alpha_{ij}}\} \subseteq S$.

[*Minimality*]

For no i and j, $i \neq j$, $\{TE_{\alpha_{i1}}, ..., TE_{\alpha_{ik}}\}$ is a subset of $\{TE_{\alpha_{j1}}, ..., TE_{\alpha_{jm}}\}$.

[*Consistency*]

For no i, $\{TE_{\alpha_{i1}}, ..., TE_{\alpha_{ik}}\}$ is a ground support for $\bot$.

2.4. Implementation

The similarities to logical labels as used in the ATMS (de Kleer 1986) are apparent and our implementation makes use of this fact. Simply defining the newly introduced symbols TE_α to be assumptions (in ATMS terminology) suffices. The ATMS will then compute the temporal labels as defined. The relation to the ATMS is very close as we shall see in the next section.

3. Prediction Sharing Across Time and Contexts

In section 2 we have seen how from statements such as e.g. $\alpha@t_1$ and $\alpha@t_2$ the temporal information is factored out and handled separately from the proposition α's content: we compute α's temporal label. In systems like TCP (Williams 1986), HEART (Joubel, Raiman 1990), EEP (Guckenbiehl 1991) and TARMS (Holtzblatt et al. 1991) the above statements would be handled as two separate entities. This not only prevents these systems from sharing predictions across time as described in section 2. When these approaches are combined with assumption-based truth maintenance for the purpose of dependency-recording, they are hit by a multiplied exponential blowup: since the two statements are two separate entities, both of them have their own ATMS-label.

Our approach allows for a smooth integration with the ATMS. Actually, we have *used* the ATMS to implement it. After a brief review of the ATMS, we sketch how 'prediction sharing across time' is done. Then we extend the scheme to cover the usual prediction sharing across *logical* ATMS contexts.

3.1. Prediction Sharing Across Logical Contexts

The language of the ATMS (de Kleer 1986) consists of propositional horn clauses called *justifications*

$$\alpha_1 \wedge \ldots \wedge \alpha_n \rightarrow \beta .$$

A distinguished subset *ASSM* of the occurring propositional atoms *PROP* is called *assumptions*: $ASSM \subseteq PROP$. The set of atoms derivable from a set of assumptions (*environment*) E is called *(logical) context* of E and denoted by $cxt(E)$. All environments which allow deriving the constant $\perp$ are considered inconsistent.

Reasoning in *multiple contexts* then can be characterized as considering all consistent contexts $cxt(E)$ of all subsets $E \subseteq ASSM$ of the given assumptions. All propositions are labelled with the complete set of minimal (w.r.t. set inclusion) consistent environments from which they are derivable. I.e. for a proposition p its *(logical) label* is defined as

$$LL(p) = \{ E \subseteq ASSM| \ E \text{ consistent} \wedge p \in cxt(E)$$
$$\wedge \ \forall E' \subset E \ \ p \notin cxt(E') \}$$

Justifications are used to record the inferences as performed by a problem solver, in our case a predictive engine. The label of a proposition is computed by propagating labels in the network of justifications using basic set operations. By caching inferences as justifications an inference is done once for some context and the results are shared by contexts characterized by superset environments, thus avoiding expensive re-computations.

The labels the ATMS must compute can grow big and hamper larger applications. Focusing on *interesting* contexts (Dressler, Farquhar 1990) avoids this problem while maintaining the essential properties of assumption-based truth maintenance.

3.2. The ATMS as a Mechanism for Maintaining Temporal Labels

As usual we use the ATMS for recording the inferences made by the problem solver, i.e. the predictive engine. When the antecedents $\alpha_1,\ldots,\alpha_n$ simultaneously hold at some time t_i, the predictive engine will conclude that β holds, too, given the t-generic formula

$$\alpha_1(t) \wedge \ldots \wedge \alpha_n(t) \rightarrow \beta(t)$$

in SD. A justification $\alpha_1 \wedge \ldots \wedge \alpha_n \rightarrow \beta$ is then submitted to the ATMS, and for temporal base symbols ATMS assumptions are created. The following theorem shows that this suffices to compute temporal labels.

Theorem: Let *TBS* be the set of temporal base symbols, $TBS\text{-}ASSM \subseteq ASSM$ be the subset of ATMS assumptions corresponding to temporal base symbols, and Ψ: $TBS\text{-}ASSM \rightarrow TBS$ be the bijective mapping that associates assumptions with their corresponding symbols. Then

$$TL(\phi) = \{ \{e'| e \in E \wedge e' = \Psi(e)\} \ | \ E \in LL(\phi) \}.$$

All that remains to be done is to record temporally indexed statements. To this end, we create symbols $EXT - TE_{\alpha_i}$ that denote the enumeration of times where α_i holds. Each temporal index t_i actually occurring in an observation like $X=15@t_i$ is treated as an assumption, too. Then justifying $EXT - TE_{\alpha_i}$ by temporal indices at which α_i holds like e.g.

$$t_{17} \rightarrow EXT - TE_{\alpha_i} \text{ and } t_{143} \rightarrow EXT - TE_{\alpha_i}$$

guarantees that the logical label of $EXT - TE_{\alpha_i}$ enumerates the appropriate times:

$$LL(EXT - TE_{\alpha_i}) = \{\{t_{17}\}, \{t_{143}\}, \ldots \}.$$

Please note that the possibly large number of assumptions for times t_i does not cause an exponential growth of label sizes. $LL(EXT - TE_{\alpha_i})$ grows linearly and from $EXT - TE_{\alpha_i}$ no further propagation is possible.

Querying the system about the temporal extent of an atom ϕ proceeds in two stages. First, a lookup of ϕ's temporal label is done. Then the union of intersections of the enumerated temporal extents $EXT - TE_{\alpha_i}$ gives the answer. In a similar way queries about a specific time are processed.

Lemma:

$$\phi@t_i \text{ iff } \{t_i\} \in \bigcup_{tenv \in TL(\phi)} \bigcap_{TE_{\alpha_i} \in tenv} LL(EXT - TE_{\alpha_i})$$

Please, note that if temporally indexed statements about ϕ are available, then $\{TE_\phi\}$ is an element of $TL(\phi)$.

3.3. Combining Prediction Sharing Across Time with Assumption-based Truth Maintenance

Logical and temporal contexts are orthogonal concepts in the sense that they ought to be combinable without restriction. For example, we might want to state that α holds at t_{17} *but only under (logical) assumptions A and B.* There are two principal entry points for this type of statements with logical context qualifications. On the level of temporally indexed statements we need to capture conditions like the one above. On the level of recorded inferences we must be able to express that

$$\alpha_1(t) \wedge \ldots \wedge \alpha_n(t) \rightarrow \beta(t)$$

holds regardless of the time t as before, *but only under (logical) assumptions*, say A and B.

Temporally indexed statements can be qualified with logical context information by using justifications like

$$A \wedge B \wedge t_{17} \rightarrow EXT - TE_{\alpha_i} \text{ instead of}$$
$$t_{17} \rightarrow EXT - TE_{\alpha_i}.$$

Consequently, the logical label $LL(EXT - TE_{\alpha_i})$ is $\{\{t_{17}, A, B\}, \ldots\}$. Each environment contains exactly one temporal index assumption while the rest of its assumptions provides the desired logical context. Note, that the usual minimization and consistency maintenance done by the ATMS takes care of redundant and inconsistent information in $LL(EXT - TE_{\alpha_i})$.

On the level of recorded inferences the solution is equally simple. Logical assumptions, say A and B, are added to the antecedents:

$$A \wedge B \wedge \alpha_1 \wedge \ldots \wedge \alpha_n \rightarrow \beta$$

The temporal labels then are relative to the logical context.

Definition: *Temporal Label under Assumptions*

A set of symbol sets, $\{ \{TE_{\alpha_{11}}, \ldots, TE_{\alpha_{1n}}\} \ldots, \{TE_{\alpha_{m1}}, \ldots, TE_{\alpha_{mk}}\} \}$, is called *temporal label* of ϕ under logical assumptions Θ, $TL(\phi, \Theta)$ iff

[*Correctness*]

   Each set $\{TE_{\alpha_{i1}}, \ldots, TE_{\alpha_{ij}}\} \cup \Theta$ is a ground support for ϕ.

[*Completeness*]

   If $S \cup \Theta$ is a ground support for ϕ with temporal base symbols S, then there exists $\{TE_{\alpha_{i1}}, \ldots, TE_{\alpha_{ij}}\}$ in $TL(\phi)$ such that $\{TE_{\alpha_{i1}}, \ldots, TE_{\alpha_{ij}}\} \subseteq S$.

[*Minimality*]

   For no i and j, $i \neq j$, $\{TE_{\alpha_{i1}}, \ldots, TE_{\alpha_{ik}}\}$ is a subset of $\{TE_{\alpha_{j1}}, \ldots, TE_{\alpha_{jm}}\}$.

[*Consistency*]

   For no i, $\{TE_{\alpha_{i1}}, \ldots, TE_{\alpha_{ik}}\} \cup \Theta$ is a ground support for $\perp$.

Given this relative notion of temporal label the theorem from 3.2 changes, too.

Theorem: Let TBS be the set of temporal base symbols, $TBS\text{-}ASSM \subseteq ASSM$ the subset of ATMS assumptions corresponding to temporal base symbols, $\Psi: TBS\text{-}ASSM \rightarrow TBS$ the bijective mapping that associates assumptions with their corresponding symbols and Θ a set of logical assumptions. Then

$$TL(\phi, \Theta) = \{\{e' \mid e \in E \cap TBS\text{-}ASSM \wedge e' = \Psi(e)\} \mid$$
$$E \in LL(\phi) \wedge (E \setminus TBS\text{-}ASSM) \subseteq \Theta\}$$

The two stage approach to answering queries remains. The evaluation, however, is done relative to the logical context specified as part of the query.

Lemma: $\phi@t_i$ under assumptions θ iff

$$\{t_i\} \cup S \in \bigcup_{tenv \in TL(\phi, \theta)} \bigcap_{TE_{\alpha_i} \in tenv} LL(EXT - TE_{\alpha_i})$$

$$\wedge \, S \subseteq \theta$$

4. Delayed Consequences

Delayed consequences are required to model a component such as a valve which receives e.g. an 'open' command and then changes to state 'open' *after some time*. Generally, in qualitative simulation (Kuipers 1986) the interstate behavior, i.e. P- and I-transitions, requires delay. An inference with delayed consequent

$$\alpha_1(t) \wedge \ldots \wedge \alpha_2(t) \rightarrow \beta(\Delta(t))$$

is handled specially. No direct translation into a justification is possible. Instead, for the atom β in the delayed consequent a temporal base symbol TE_β is introduced and handled as before: an assumption is created and also a symbol $EXT\text{-}TE_\beta$ to denote the extensional description of times and logical contexts where β holds. A simple demon mechanism guarantees that, whenever the conjunction of α_i holds at some t_j under assumptions Θ, $\{\Delta(t_j)\} \cup \Theta$ is recorded by $EXT\text{-}TE_\beta$, i.e. an assumption $\Delta(t_j)$ and the justification

$$\Theta_1 \wedge \ldots \wedge \Theta_n \wedge \Delta(t_j) \rightarrow EXT\text{-}TE_\beta \text{ with } \Theta_1, \ldots, \Theta_n \in \Theta$$

are created.

5. Empirical Results

We experimented with a variety of ballast tank configurations to provide evidence that we have actually met our goal of reducing prediction costs when relevant inferences have been made previously. In the figures below we show run time and number of necessary new predictive inferences (y-axis) as they develop over time (x-axis). As a measure for new predictive inferences we have chosen the increment of the number of justifications submitted to the system. This, however, can only be an approximation of the really necessary efforts since a single justification may cause a huge amount of label propagation. In the figures the dashed curve shows the new justifications while the solid line indicates prediction time.

The correlation between run time and number of necessary new predictions is apparent. All our experiments on different configurations of ballast tanks show the same pattern: In the beginning the prediction cost (run time) is substantial. No previous predictions have been cached and every possible derivation has to be done explicitly. Later on *when* a number of *variables change their qualitative value*, prediction cost increases but does not reach the initial cost. Without prediction sharing run time is in the range of the initial cost all of the time !

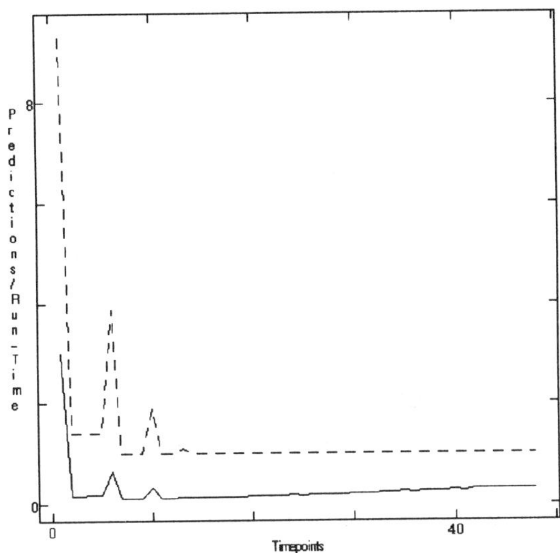

Figure 3. Monitoring the 3-Tank system from figure 1, considering 10 different test vectors occuring at most 10 times. Prediction time for first timepoint: 3.04s, average for additional timepoints: 0.21s

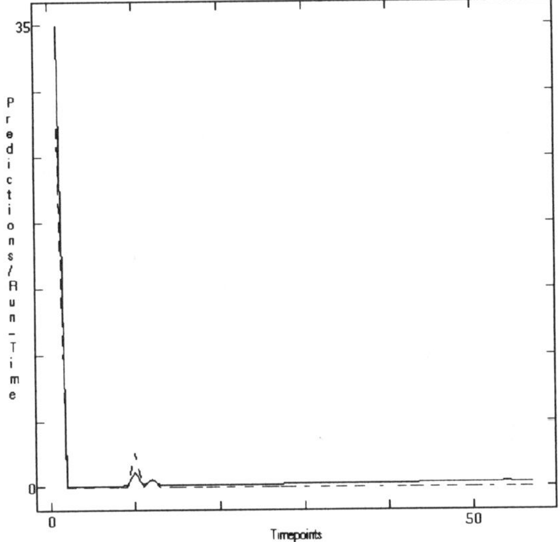

Figure 4. Monitoring a 20-Tank system, considering 10 different test vectors occuring at most 10 times. Prediction time for first timepoint: 36.3s, average for additional timepoints: 3.8s

Currently we attribute the slow, seemingly linear increase of runtime to the monotonically increasing number of justifications and assumptions. Simply handling these structures requires some time. For example, after 57 timepoints the systems maintains 12792 justifications and 405 assumptions for the 20 tanks system. This suggests that we reduce the amount of recorded past data by introducing a time window for relevant data.

Acknowledgements. We would like to thank Anton Beschta, Thomas Guckenbiehl, Wera Klein, Michael Montag and Peter Struss for comments on earlier drafts and discussions on the subject of the paper. This work has been supported by the BMFT, project BEHAVIOR, ITW 9001 A9.

References

C. Böttcher and O. Dressler. Diagnosis Process Dynamics: Holding the Diagnostic Trackhound in Leash. In *Proceedings of the International Joint Conference on Artificial Intelligence (IJCAI)*. Morgan Kaufmann Publishers, 1993.

J. de Kleer. An Assumption-based TMS. *Artificial Intelligence*, 28:127–162, 1986.

J. de Kleer. Focusing on Probable Diagnoses. In *Proceedings of the National Conference on Artificial Intelligence (AAAI)*, pages 842–848, Anaheim, 1991. Morgan Kaufmann Publishers.

J. de Kleer and B. C. Williams. Diagnosing Multiple Faults. *Artificial Intelligence*, 32:97–130, 1987.

J. de Kleer and B. C. Williams. Diagnosis with Behavioral Modes. In *Proceedings of the International Joint Conference on Artificial Intelligence (IJCAI)*, pages 1324–1330. Morgan Kaufmann Publishers, 1989.

O. Dressler and A. Farquhar. Putting the problem solver back in the driver's seat: Contextual control over the ATMS. In M. Reinfrank J.P. Martins, editor, *Truth Maintenance Systems*, pages 1–16. Springer LNAI 515, 1990.

O. Dressler, C. Böttcher, M. Montag and A. Brinkop. Qualitative and Quantitative Models in a Model-Based Diagnosis System for Ballast Tank Systems. In *Proceedings of the International Conference on Fault Diagnosis (TOOLDIAG)*, pages 397–405, Toulouse, France, April 1993.

T. Guckenbiehl. The extended episode propagator, version 2-preliminary report. Internal Report, FhG-IITB, 1991.

L. Holtzblatt, M. Neiberg, R. Piazza, and M. Vilain. Temporal Methods: Multi-Dimensional Modeling of Sequential Circuits. In L. Console, editor, *Working Notes of the International Workshop on Principles of Diagnosis (DX)*, Technical Report RT/DI/91-10-7, pages 111–120. Dipartimento di Informatica, Universita da Torino, Italy, 1991.

C. Joubel and O. Raiman. How Time Changes Assumptions. In *9th European Conference on Artificial Intelligence (ECAI 90)*, Stockholm, 1990.

B. Kuipers. Qualitative Simulation. *Artificial Intelligence*, 29(3):289–338, 1986.

P. Struss. Diagnosis as a Process. In W. Hamscher, J. de Kleer, and L. Console, editors, *Readings in Model-based Diagnosis*. Morgan Kaufmann Publishers, 1992.

P. Struss. What's in SD? Towards a Theory of Modeling for Diagnosis. In W. Hamscher, J. de Kleer, and L. Console, editors, *Readings in Model-based Diagnosis*. Morgan Kaufmann Publishers, 1992.

P. Struss and O. Dressler. Physical Negation – Integrating Fault Models into the General Diagnostic Engine. In *Proceedings of the International Joint Conference on Artificial Intelligence (IJCAI)*, pages 1318–1323. Morgan Kaufmann Publishers, 1989.

B. C. Williams. Doing Time: Putting Qualitative Reasoning on Firmer Ground. In *Proceedings of the National Conference on Artificial Intelligence (AAAI)*, Philadelphia, Penn., August 1986.

An Operational Semantics for Knowledge Bases

Ronald Fagin
IBM Almaden Research Center
650 Harry Road
San Jose, CA 95120–6099
`fagin@almaden.ibm.com`

Joseph Y. Halpern*
IBM Almaden Research Center
650 Harry Road
San Jose, CA 95120–6099
`halpern@almaden.ibm.com`

Yoram Moses[†]
Deparment of Applied Math. and CS
The Weizmann Institute of Science
76100 Rehovot, Israel
`yoram@wisdom.weizmann.ac.il`

Moshe Y. Vardi[‡]
Department of Computer Science
Rice University
Houston, TX 77251-1892
`vardi@cs.rice.edu`

Abstract

The standard approach in AI to knowledge representation is to represent an agent's knowledge symbolically as a collection of formulas, which we can view as a knowledge base. An agent is then said to know a fact if it is provable from the formulas in his knowledge base. Halpern and Vardi advocated a model-theoretic approach to knowledge representation. In this approach, the key step is representing the agent's knowledge using an appropriate semantic model. Here, we model knowledge bases operationally as multi-agent systems. Our results show that this approach offers significant advantages.

Introduction

The standard approach in AI to knowledge representation, going back to McCarthy [1968], is to represent an agent's knowledge symbolically as a collection of formulas, which we can view as a *knowledge base*. An agent is then said to know a fact if it is *provable* from the formulas in his knowledge base. Halpern and Vardi [1991] advocated a model-checking approach. In this approach, theorem proving is replaced by evaluating queries against an appropriate semantic model of the agent's knowledge. This can be viewed as a *knowledge-level* approach to knowledge bases [Newell 1982]. Such a semantic model was in fact provided by Levesque [1984]; he associates with a knowledge base a set of truth assignments. We describe here a different semantic approach. We show that an operational semantics for knowledge bases, based on the model of multi-agent systems

*Work supported in part by the Air Force Office of Scientific Research (AFSC), under Contract F49620-91-C-0080.

†Currently on sabbatical at Oxford; work supported in part by a Helen and Milton A. Kimmelman career development chair.

‡This research was done while this author was at the IBM Almaden Research Center.

from [Fagin et al. 1994] (which in turn, is based on earlier models that appeared in [Chandy and Misra 1986; Halpern and Fagin 1989; Halpern and Moses 1990; Parikh and Ramanujam 1985; Rosenschein and Kaelbling 1986]), offers a clean and intuitive knowledge-level model. The basic idea of this approach is to model the system as a set of possible behaviors. Knowledge is then ascribed to agents according to the possible-worlds principle: a fact φ is known to an agent a if φ holds in all the states of the system that a considers possible. Thus, in our approach knowledge "falls out" of the operational model of the system. We argue that this approach offers significant advantages compared to previous approaches to modeling knowledge bases.

Knowledge in multi-agent systems

We briefly review the framework of [Fagin et al. 1994] for modeling multi-agent systems. The basic idea of this approach is to model systems *operationally* (in the spirit of the operational-semantics approach to programming languages [?; Jones 1986]). We assume that at each point in time, each agent is in some *local state*. Informally, this local state encodes the information the agent has observed thus far. In addition, there is also an *environment* state, that keeps track of everything relevant to the system not recorded in the agents' states. The way we split up the system into agents and environment depends on the system being analyzed.

A *global state* is a tuple $(s_e, s_1, \ldots, s_n)$ consisting of the environment state s_e and the local state s_i of each agent i. A *run* of the system is a function from time (which, for ease of exposition, we assume ranges over the natural numbers) to global states. Thus, if r is a run, then $r(0), r(1), \ldots$ is a sequence of global states that, roughly speaking, is a complete description of what happens over time in one possible execution of the system. We take a *system* to consist of a set of runs. Intuitively, these runs describe all the possible sequences of events that could occur.

Given a system $\mathcal{R}$, we refer to a pair (r, m) consisting of a run $r \in \mathcal{R}$ and a time m as a *point*. If $r(m) = (s_e, s_1, \ldots, s_n)$, we define $r_e(m) = s_e$ and $r_i(m) = s_i$, for $i = 1, \ldots, n$; thus, $r_e(m)$ is the environment state and $r_i(m)$ is process i's local state at the point (r, m). We say that two points (r, m) and (r', m') are *indistinguishable* to agent i, and write $(r, m) \sim_i (r', m')$, if $r_i(m) = r_i'(m')$, i.e., if agent i has the same local state at both points. Finally, we define an *interpreted system* to be a pair $(\mathcal{R}, \pi)$ consisting of a system $\mathcal{R}$ and a mapping π that associates a truth assignment to the primitive propositions at each global state.

An interpreted system can be viewed as a Kripke structure: the points are the possible worlds, and $\sim_i$ plays the role of the accessibility relation. We give semantics to knowledge formulas in interpreted systems just as in Kripke structures: Given a point (r, m) in an interpreted system $\mathcal{I} = (\mathcal{R}, \pi)$, we have $(\mathcal{I}, r, m) \models K_i \varphi$ (that is, the formula $K_i \varphi$ is satisfied at the point (r, m) of $\mathcal{I}$) if $(\mathcal{I}, r', m') \models \varphi$ for all points (r', m') such that $(r', m') \sim_i (r, m)$. Notice that under this interpretation, an agent knows φ precisely if φ is true at all the situations the system could be in, given the agent's current information (as encoded by its local state). Since $\sim_i$ is an equivalence relation, knowledge in this framework satisfies the S5 axioms.

The major application of this framework has been in providing a knowledge-level analysis of distributed protocols [Halpern 1987]. It is often relatively straightforward to construct the system corresponding to a given protocol. The local state of each process can typically be characterized by a number of local variables (which, for example, describe the messages received and the values of certain local registers). The runs describe the behavior of the system as a result of running the protocol. (See [Fagin et al. 1994] for detailed examples of the modeling process.) Here we examine how this framework can be used to model knowledge bases.

Knowledge bases as multi-agent systems

Following Levesque [1984], we view a KB as a system that is told facts about an external world, and is asked queries about that world.[1] The standard approach in AI to modeling knowledge bases is just to identify a KB with a formula, or set of formulas, that can informally be thought of as describing what the KB knows. When the KB is asked a query ψ, it computes (using some computational procedure) whether ψ holds. Levesque takes a more semantic approach, associating with the KB the set of truth assignments that the KB considers possible at any time, as a function of what it has been told.

We now show how knowledge bases can be modeled as multi-agent systems. As we shall see, doing so gives us a number of advantages. Basically, since we are modeling knowledge bases operationally, we can easily capture aspects that are hard to capture in a symbolic model or even in Levesque's knowledge-level model. For one thing, we can

---

[1]Levesque models this in terms of *TELL* and *ASK* operations.

capture assumptions about how the KB obtains its knowledge and show how these assumptions affect the KB's knowledge. Furthermore, the model allows us to study how the KB's knowledge evolves with time. Generally, the model is very flexible and can easily be adapted to many applications.

The first step in modeling the KB in our framework is to decide who the agents are and what the role of the environment is. The KB is clearly an agent in the system. In addition, we choose to have another agent called the *Teller*; this is the agent that tells the KB facts about the external world. We use the environment to model the external world. It is possible to use the environment to also model the Teller, but, as we shall see later on, our approach offers certain advantages. We want to view the environment's state as providing a complete description of (the relevant features of) the external world, the local state of the KB as describing the information that the KB has about the external world, and the local state of the Teller as describing the information that the Teller has about the external world and about the KB. This allows us to distinguish what is true (as modeled by the environment's state) from what is known to the Teller (as modeled by the Teller's state) and from what the KB is told (as modeled by the KB's state).

That still gives us quite a bit of freedom in deciding how to model the global states. If we can describe all the relevant features of the external world by using a set Φ of primitive propositions, then we can take the environment to be just a truth assignment to the primitive propositions in Φ. If, instead, we need to use first-order information to describe the world, then we can take the environment to be a relational structure.

What about the KB's local state? We want it to represent all the relevant information that the KB has learned. We can do this by taking the local state to consist of the sequence of facts that the KB has been told and queries that it has been asked. If we assume that the sequence of queries does not carry any information about the external world, then we can simplify this representation by including in the local state only the sequence of facts that the KB has been told, and ignoring the queries. This is in fact what we do.

Finally, the Teller's state has to describe the Teller's information about the external world and about the KB. We assume that the Teller has complete information about the KB, since the Teller is the sole source for the KB's information. Thus, the Teller's local state contains a description of its information about external world as well as the sequence of facts that the KB has been told.

What does the KB know after it has been told some fact φ? Assuming that what it has been told is true, it may seem reasonable to say that the KB knows φ. This is clearly false, however, if the external world can change. It might well be the case that φ was true when the KB was told it, and is no longer true afterwards. For definiteness, we assume that the external world is stable. As we shall see, even with this assumption, if φ can include facts about the KB's knowledge, then φ may be true when the KB is told it, but not afterwards.

To get a feel for some of the issues involved, we focus first on modeling a fairly simple concrete situation. We later consider what happens when we weaken these assumptions. We assume that:

1. the external world can be described propositionally, using the propositions in a finite set Φ,

2. the external world is stable, so that the truth values of the primitive propositions describing the world do not change over time, at least for the intervals of time we are analyzing,

3. the Teller has complete information about the external world and about the KB,

4. the KB is told and asked facts only about the external world, and not facts about its own knowledge, and these facts are expressed as propositional formulas,

5. everything the KB is told is true, and

6. there is no *a priori* initial knowledge about the external world, or about what the KB will be told.

The first assumption tells us that we can represent the environment's state as a truth assignment α to the primitive propositions in Φ. The second assumption tells us that in each run r, the environment's state $r_e(m)$ is independent of m; the environment's state does not change over time. As observed by Katsuno and Mendelzon [1991], this is the assumption that distinguishes *belief revision* from *belief update*. The third assumption tells us that the Teller's state includes the truth assignment α, which describes the external world. Given that we are representing the KB's local state as a sequence of facts that it has been told, the fourth assumption tells us that this local state has the form $\langle \varphi_1, \ldots, \varphi_k \rangle$, $k \geq 0$, where $\varphi_1, \ldots, \varphi_k$ are propositional formulas. We assume that the Teller's local state has a similar form, and consists of the truth assignment that describes the real world, together with the sequence of facts it has told the KB. Thus, we take the Teller's local state to be of the form $(\alpha, \langle \varphi_1, \ldots, \varphi_k \rangle)$, where α is a truth assignment and $\varphi_1, \ldots, \varphi_k$ are propositional formulas. Since the Teller's state is simply the pair consisting of the environment's state and the KB's state, we do not represent it explicitly, but rather denote a global state by $(\alpha, \langle \varphi_1, \ldots, \varphi_k \rangle, \cdot)$. The fifth assumption tells us that everything that the KB is told is true. This means that in a global state of the form $(\alpha, \langle \varphi_1, \ldots, \varphi_k \rangle, \cdot)$, each of $\varphi_1, \ldots, \varphi_k$ must be true under truth assignment α. The part of the sixth assumption that says that there is no initial knowledge of the world is captured by assuming that the initial state of every run has the form $(\alpha, \langle \rangle, \cdot)$, and that for every truth assignment α', there is some run with initial global state $(\alpha', \langle \rangle, \cdot)$. We capture the second half of the sixth assumption—that there is no knowledge about what information will be given—by not putting any further restrictions on the set of possible runs. We discuss this in more detail later.

To summarize, we claim our assumptions are captured by the interpreted system $\mathcal{I}^{kb} = (\mathcal{R}^{kb}, \pi^{kb})$, where $\mathcal{R}^{kb}$ consists of all runs r such that for some sequence $\varphi_1, \varphi_2, \ldots$ of propositional formulas and for some truth assignment α:

- **KB1.** $r(0) = (\alpha, \langle \rangle, \cdot)$

- **KB2.** if $r(m) = (\alpha, \langle \varphi_1, \ldots, \varphi_k \rangle, \cdot)$, then

  1. either $r(m + 1) = r(m)$, or $r(m + 1) = (\alpha, \langle \varphi_1, \ldots, \varphi_k, \varphi_{k+1} \rangle, \cdot)$,

  2. $\varphi_1 \wedge \cdots \wedge \varphi_k$ is true under truth assignment α, and

  3. $\pi^{kb}(r, m) = \alpha$, that is, π^{kb} is defined so that the truth assignment at (r, m) is given by the environment's state.

Our assumption that $\mathcal{R}$ consists of *all* runs that satisfy the conditions above also captures the assumption that there is no knowledge about what information will be given. This is perhaps best understood by example. There may be *a priori* knowledge that, if p is true, then this is the first thing the KB will be told. This places a restriction on the set of possible runs, eliminating runs with global states of the form $(\alpha, \langle \varphi_1, \ldots, \varphi_k \rangle, \cdot)$ such that $k \geq 1$ and p is true under the truth assignment α, but $\varphi_1 \neq p$. It is easy to construct other examples of how what information is given or the order in which it is given might impart knowledge beyond the facts themselves. By allowing all runs r consistent with KB1 and KB2 in $\mathcal{R}$, we are saying that there is no such knowledge.

Having defined the system $\mathcal{I}^{kb}$, we can see how the KB answers queries. Suppose that at a point (r, m) the KB is asked a query ψ, where ψ is a propositional formula. Since the KB does not have direct access to the environment's state, ψ should be interpreted not as a question about the external world, but rather as a question about the KB's knowledge of the external world. Thus, the KB should answer "Yes" exactly if $(\mathcal{I}^{kb}, r, m) \models K_{KB}\psi$ holds (taking K_{KB} to denote "the KB knows"), "No" exactly if $(\mathcal{I}^{kb}, r, m) \models K_{KB}\neg\psi$ holds, and "I don't know" otherwise.

Suppose the KB is in local state $\langle \varphi_1, \ldots, \varphi_k \rangle$. We can view the formula $\kappa = \varphi_1 \wedge \cdots \wedge \varphi_k$ as a summary of its knowledge about the world; the KB knows only what follows from this. This could be interpreted in two ways: the KB could answer "Yes" exactly if ψ is a consequence of κ, or if $K_{KB}\psi$ is a consequence of $K_{KB}\kappa$. As the following result shows, these two interpretations are equivalent.

Proposition 1: *Suppose that* $r_{KB}(m) = \langle \varphi_1, \ldots, \varphi_k \rangle$. *Let* $\kappa = \varphi_1 \wedge \cdots \wedge \varphi_k$ *and let* ψ *be a propositional formula. The following are equivalent:*

(a) $(\mathcal{I}^{kb}, r, m) \models K_{KB}\psi$.

(b) $\kappa \Rightarrow \psi$ *is a propositional tautology.*

(c) $K_{KB}\kappa \Rightarrow K_{KB}\psi$ *is a valid formula in S5.*

Thus, Proposition 1 shows that under our assumptions, we can model the KB in the standard AI manner: as a formula. Moreover, in order to answer a query, the KB must compute what follows from the formula that represents its knowledge.

Proposition 1 characterizes how the KB answers propositional queries. As argued by Levesque [1984] and Reiter [1992], in general the KB may have to answer non-propositional queries. How should the KB handle such queries as $(p \Rightarrow K_{KB}p)$ ("if p is the case, then the KB knows that it is the case")? Here also we want the KB to answer "Yes" to a query φ exactly if $(\mathcal{I}^{kb}, r, m) \models K_{KB}\varphi$, "No" exactly if $(\mathcal{I}^{kb}, r, m) \models K_{KB}\neg\varphi$ holds, and "I don't know" otherwise. When does the formula $K_{KB}(p \Rightarrow K_{KB}p)$

hold? It is not hard to show that this formula is equivalent to $K_{KB}p \vee K_{KB}\neg p$, so the answer to this query already follows from Proposition 1: the answer is "Yes" if either p follows from what the KB has been told, or $\neg p$ does, and "I don't know" otherwise. It is not possible here for the answer to be "No", since $K_{KB}\neg(p \Rightarrow K_{KB}p)$ is equivalent to $K_{KB}(p \wedge \neg K_{KB}p)$, which is easily seen to be inconsistent with S5.

We are mainly interested in what can be said about formulas that involve only the KB's knowledge, since we view the Teller as being in the background here. We define a *KB-formula* to be one in which the only modal operator is K_{KB}; a *KB-query* is a query which is a KB-formula. Standard arguments from modal logic can be used to show that for every KB-formula of the form $K_{KB}\varphi$ we can effectively find an equivalent formula that is a Boolean combination of formulas of the form $K_{KB}\psi$, where ψ is propositional. It follows that the way that the KB responds to KB-queries can already be determined from how it responds to propositional queries. The reason is as follows. To decide on its answer to the query φ, we must determine whether $K_{KB}\varphi$ holds and whether $K_{KB}\neg\varphi$ holds. As we just noted, we can effectively find a formula equivalent to $K_{KB}\varphi$ that is a Boolean combination of formulas of the form $K_{KB}\psi$, where ψ is propositional, and similarly for $K_{KB}\neg\varphi$. We then need only evaluate formulas of the form $K_{KB}\psi$, where ψ is propositional. Thus, using Proposition 1, we can compute how the KB will answer KB-queries from the conjunction of the formulas that the KB has been told.

There is another way of characterizing how the KB will answer KB-queries. Given a propositional formula φ, let S^φ consist of all truth assignments α to propositions in Φ such that φ is true under truth assignment α. Let $M^\varphi = (S^\varphi, \pi, \mathcal{U})$ be the Kripke structure such that $\pi(\alpha) = \alpha$ and $\mathcal{U}$ is the universal relation (so that for all $\alpha, \beta \in S^\varphi$, we have $(\alpha, \beta) \in \mathcal{U}$). In a sense, we can think of M^φ as a *maximal* model of φ, since all truth assignments consistent with φ appear in M^φ. As the following result shows, if κ is the conjunction of the formulas that the KB has been told, then for an arbitrary formula ψ, the KB knows ψ exactly if $K_{KB}\psi$ holds in the maximal model for κ. Intuitively, if the KB was told κ, then *all* that the KB knows is κ. The maximal model for κ is the model that captures the fact that κ is all that the KB knows.

Proposition 2: *Suppose that* $r_{KB}(m) = \langle \varphi_1, \ldots, \varphi_k \rangle$, *and* $\kappa = \varphi_1 \wedge \cdots \wedge \varphi_k$. *Then for all KB-formulas* ψ, *we have that* $(\mathcal{I}^{kb}, r, m) \models \psi$ *iff* $(M^\kappa, r_e(m)) \models \psi$.

Levesque [1984] defines M^κ as the knowledge-level model of the KB after it has been told $\varphi_1, \ldots, \varphi_k$. Thus, Proposition 2 shows that in the propositional case, our operational model is equivalent to Levesque's knowledge-level model.

Our discussion so far illustrates that it is possible to model a standard type of knowledge base within our framework. But what do we gain by doing so? For one thing, it makes explicit the assumptions underlying the standard representation. In addition, we can talk about what the KB knows regarding its knowledge, as shown in Proposition 2. Beyond

that, as we now show, it allows us to capture in a straightforward way some variants of these assumptions. The flexibility of the model makes it easier to deal with issues that arise when we modify the assumptions.

We begin by considering situations where there is some prior knowledge about what information will be given. As we observed earlier, the fact that we consider *all* runs in which KB1 and KB2 are true captures the assumption that no such knowledge is available. But, in practice, there may well be default assumptions that are encoded in the conventions by which information is imparted. We earlier gave an example of a situation where there is a convention that if p is true, then the KB will be told p first. Such a convention is easy to model in our framework: it simply entails a restriction on the set of runs in the system. Namely, the restriction is that for every point (r, m) in the system where $r(m) = (\alpha, \langle \varphi_1 \rangle, \cdot)$, we have $\varphi_1 = p$ iff p is true under α. Recall that the order in which the KB is given information is part of its local state. In a precise sense, therefore, the KB knows what this order is. In particular, it is straightforward to show that, given the above restriction, the KB either knows p or knows $\neg p$ once it has been told at least one fact.

In a similar fashion, it is easy to capture the situation where there is some *a priori* knowledge about the world, by modifying the set of runs in $\mathcal{I}^{kb}$ appropriately. Suppose, for example, that it is known that the primitive proposition p must be true. In this case, we consider only runs r such that $r_e(0) = \alpha$ for some truth assignment α that makes p true. An analogue to Proposition 1 holds: now the KB will know everything that follows from p and what it has been told.

Next, consider the situation where the Teller does not have complete information about the world (but still has complete information about the KB). We model this by including in the Teller's state a nonempty set $\mathcal{T}$ of truth assignments. Intuitively, $\mathcal{T}$ is the set of possible external worlds that the Teller considers possible. The set $\mathcal{T}$ replaces the single truth assignment that describes the actual external world. Since we are focusing on knowledge here, we require that $\alpha \in \mathcal{T}$; this means that the true external world is one of the Teller's possibilities. The Teller's state also includes the sequence of facts that the KB has been told. To avoid redundancy, we denote the Teller's state by $\langle \mathcal{T}, \cdot \rangle$. Global states now have the form $(\alpha, \langle \varphi_1, \ldots, \varphi_k \rangle, \langle \mathcal{T}, \cdot \rangle)$. We still require that everything the KB is told be true; this means that the Teller tells the KB "φ" only if φ is true in all the truth assignments in $\mathcal{T}$. It is easy to see that this means that the Teller says φ only if $K_T\varphi$ holds (taking K_T to denote "the Teller knows"). Not surprisingly, Propositions 1 and 2 continue to hold in this setting, with essentially no change in proof.

Once we allow the Teller to have a collection $\mathcal{T}$ of worlds that it considers possible, it is but a short step to allow the Teller to have false beliefs, which amounts to allowing $\mathcal{T}$ not to include the actual world. We would still require that the Teller tells the KB φ only if φ is true in all the truth assignments in $\mathcal{T}$. In this case, however, this means that the Teller only *believes* φ to be the case; its beliefs may be wrong. How should we ascribe beliefs to agents in a multi-agent system? In the scenario described here, the KB and the Teller believe that the Teller is truthful, so they both consider some global states to be impossible, namely, the global states in which $\alpha \notin \mathcal{T}$. Thus, it makes sense here to change the definition of the accessibility relation in the Kripke structure associated with a system in order to make global states where $\alpha \notin \mathcal{T}$ inaccessible. The possible-worlds principle now ascribes beliefs rather than knowledge; see [Fagin et al. 1994] for details.[2]

Knowledge-based programs

Up to now we have assumed that the KB is told only propositional facts. Things get somewhat more complicated if the KB is given information that is not purely propositional; this in fact is the situation considered by Levesque [1984]. For example, suppose the KB is told $p \Rightarrow K_{KB}p$. This says that if p is true, then the KB knows it. Such information can be quite useful, assuming that the KB can actually check what it knows and does not know. In this case, the KB can check if it knows p; if it does not, it can then conclude that p is false. As this example shows, once we allow the KB to be given information that relates its knowledge to the external world, then it may be able to use its introspective abilities to draw conclusions about the external world.

It is now not so obvious how to represent the KB's knowledge symbolically, i.e., by a formula. One complication that arises once we allow non-propositional information is that we can no longer assume that the KB knows everything it has been told. For example, suppose the primitive proposition p is true of the external world, and the KB has not been given any initial information. In this situation, the formula $p \wedge \neg K_{KB}p$ is certainly true. But after the KB is told this, then it is certainly not the case that the KB knows $p \wedge \neg K_{KB}p$; indeed, as we noted earlier, $K_{KB}(p \wedge \neg K_{KB}p)$ is inconsistent with S5. Nevertheless, the KB certainly learns something as a result of being told this fact: it learns that p is true. As a result, $K_{KB}p$ should hold after the KB is told $p \wedge \neg K_{KB}p$. Thus, we cannot represent the KB's knowledge simply by the conjunction of facts that it has been told, even if they are all true.

Levesque [1984] describes a knowledge-level model for the KB's knowledge in this case. After the KB has been told the sequence $\varphi_1, \ldots, \varphi_k$, it is modeled by a Kripke structure $M^{\varphi_1,\ldots,\varphi_k}$, which we define inductively. The initial model is $M^\epsilon = (S^\epsilon, \pi, \mathcal{U})$, where S^ϵ is the set of all truth assignment to the propositions in Φ, $\pi(\alpha) = \alpha$, and $\mathcal{U}$ is the universal relation. Suppose that $M^{\varphi_1,\ldots,\varphi_{k-1}} = (S^{\varphi_1,\ldots,\varphi_{k-1}}, \pi, \mathcal{U})$ has been defined. Then $M^{\varphi_1,\ldots,\varphi_k} = (S^{\varphi_1,\ldots,\varphi_k}, \pi, \mathcal{U})$, where $S^{\varphi_1,\ldots,\varphi_k} = \{w \in S^{\varphi_1,\ldots,\varphi_{k-1}} \,|\, (M^{\varphi_1,\ldots,\varphi_{k-1}}, w) \models \varphi_k\}$. As in the earlier discussion of the maximal model, this definition attempts to capture the idea that the KB knows only what it has been told. The induction construction ensures that this principle is applied whenever the KB is told a formula.

In our approach, we need to be able to describe the system that results when the KB is given information that may involve its own knowledge. As before, we take the KB's local state to consist of a sequence of formulas, except that we now allow the formulas to be modal formulas which can talk about the KB's knowledge, not just propositional formulas. The only difficulty comes in restricting to runs in which the KB is told only true formulas. Since we are now interested in formulas that involve knowledge, it is not clear that we can decide whether a given formula is true without having the whole system in hand. But our problem is to construct the system in the first place!

While it is difficult to come up with an explicit description of the system, it is easy to describe this system implicitly. After all, the behavior of the agents here is fairly simple. The Teller here can be thought as following a *knowledge-based program* [Fagin et al. 1994; Kurki-Suonio 1986; Shoham 1993]. This is a program with explicit tests for knowledge. Roughly speaking, we can think of the Teller as running a nondeterministic program TELL that has an infinite collection of clauses, one for each formula φ, of the form:

if $K_T\varphi$ **do** tell(φ).

Intuitively, when running this program, the Teller nondeterministically chooses a formula φ that it knows to be true, and tells the KB about it. The propositional case considered in the previous section corresponds to the Teller running the analogous knowledge-based program TELLPROP in which the formulas φ are restricted to be propositional. Using techniques introduced in [Fagin et al. 1994], it can be shown that both TELL and TELLPROP can be associated with unique interpreted systems $\mathcal{I}^{tell}$ and $\mathcal{I}^{tellprop}$, respectively. It turns out that the interpreted system $\mathcal{I}^{kb}$ (defined in the previous section), which captured the interaction of the KB with the Teller in the propositional case, is precisely the system $\mathcal{I}^{tellprop}$. This observations provides support for our intuition that $\mathcal{I}^{tell}$ appropriately captures the situation where the Teller tells the KB formulas that may involve the KB's knowledge. Moreover, the system that we get is closely related to Levesque's knowledge-level model described earlier.

Proposition 3: *Suppose that* $r_{KB}(m) = \langle \varphi_1, \ldots, \varphi_k \rangle$. *Then for all KB-formulas* ψ, *we have that* $(\mathcal{I}^{kb}, r, m) \models \psi$ *iff* $(M^{\varphi_1,\ldots,\varphi_k}, r_e(m)) \models \psi$.

One advantage of using knowledge-based programs is that we can consider more complicated applications. In many such applications, one cannot divide the world neatly into a KB and a Teller. Rather, one often has many agents, each of which plays both the role of the KB and the Teller. For example, suppose that we have n agents, each of whom makes an initial observation of the external world and then communicates with the others. We assume that the agents are truthful, but that they do not necessarily know or tell the "whole truth". We can view all the agents as following knowledge-based programs similar to TELL. At every round, agent i nondeterministically selects, for each agent j, a formula φ_j that i knows to be true, and "tells" φ_j to j. Formally, agent i's program consists of all clauses of the form:

if $K_i\varphi_1 \wedge \ldots \wedge K_i\varphi_k$ **do** send(φ_1, j_1); $\ldots$; send(φ_k, j_k),

where we take send(φ_l, j_l) to be the action sending the message φ_l to agent j_l. Here we allow the messages φ to be

---

[2] See also [Friedman and Halpern 1994a] for a general approach to adding belief to this framework.

arbitrary modal formulas; for example, Alice can tell Bob that she does not know whether Charlie knows a fact p.

In this case, it is no longer clear how to model the agents symbolically or at the knowledge level as in [Levesque 1984].[3] In fact, while it is easy to characterize the appropriate interpreted system implicitly, via knowledge-based programs, it is quite difficult to describe the system explicitly. Nevertheless, our approach enables us to characterize the agents' knowledge in this case and analyze how it evolves with time. We view this as strong evidence to the superiority of the operational approach.

Conclusions

We have tried to demonstrate the power of the operational approach to modeling knowledge bases. We have shown that under simple and natural assumptions, the operational approach gives the same answers to queries as the more standard symbolic approach and Levesque's knowledge-level approach. The advantage of the operational approach is its flexibility and versatility. We have given some evidence of this here. Further evidence is provided by the recent use of this framework (extended to deal with beliefs) to model belief revision and belief update [Friedman and Halpern 1994a; Friedman and Halpern 1994b]. We are confident that the approach will find yet other applications.

References

Chandy, K. M. and J. Misra (1986). How processes learn. *Distributed Computing 1*(1), 40–52.

Fagin, R., J. Y. Halpern, Y. Moses, and M. Y. Vardi (To appear, 1994). *Reasoning about Knowledge*. Cambridge, MA: MIT Press.

Friedman, N. and J. Y. Halpern (1994a). A knowledge-based framework for belief change. Part I: Foundations. In R. Fagin (Ed.), *Theoretical Aspects of Reasoning about Knowledge: Proc. Fifth Conference*, pp. 44–64. San Francisco, CA: Morgan Kaufmann.

Friedman, N. and J. Y. Halpern (1994b). A knowledge-based framework for belief change. Part II: revision and update. In J. Doyle, E. Sandewall, and P. Torasso (Eds.), *Principles of Knowledge Representation and Reasoning: Proc. Fourth International Conference (KR '94)*. San Francisco, CA: Morgan Kaufmann.

Gärdenfors, P. (1988). *Knowledge in Flux*. Cambridge, UK: Cambridge University Press.

Halpern, J. Y. (1987). Using reasoning about knowledge to analyze distributed systems. In J. F. Traub, B. J. Grosz, B. W. Lampson, and N. J. Nilsson (Eds.), *Annual Review of Computer Science, Vol. 2*, pp. 37–68. Palo Alto, CA: Annual Reviews Inc.

Halpern, J. Y. and R. Fagin (1989). Modelling knowledge and action in distributed systems. *Distributed Computing 3*(4), 159–179. A preliminary version appeared in *Proc. 4th ACM Symposium on Principles of Distributed Computing*, 1985, with the title "A formal model of knowledge, action, and communication in distributed systems: Preliminary report".

Halpern, J. Y. and Y. Moses (1990). Knowledge and common knowledge in a distributed environment. *Journal of the ACM 37*(3), 549–587. A preliminary version appeared in *Proc. 3rd ACM Symposium on Principles of Distributed Computing*, 1984.

Halpern, J. Y. and M. Y. Vardi (1991). Model checking vs. theorem proving: a manifesto. In J. A. Allen, R. Fikes, and E. Sandewall (Eds.), *Principles of Knowledge Representation and Reasoning: Proc. Second International Conference (KR '91)*, pp. 325–334. San Francisco, CA: Morgan Kaufmann.

Halpern, J. Y. and L. D. Zuck (1992). A little knowledge goes a long way: knowledge-based derivations and correctness proofs for a family of protocols. *Journal of the ACM 39*(3), 449–478.

Jones, C. B. (1986). *Systematic Software Development using VDM*. Prentice Hall.

Katsuno, H. and A. Mendelzon (1991). On the difference between updating a knowledge base and revising it. In *Principles of Knowledge Representation and Reasoning: Proc. Second International Conference (KR '91)*, pp. 387–394. San Francisco, CA: Morgan Kaufmann.

Kurki-Suonio, R. (1986). Towards programming with knowledge expressions. In *Proc. 13th ACM Symp. on Principles of Programming Languages*, pp. 140–149.

Levesque, H. J. (1984). Foundations of a functional approach to knowledge representation. *Artificial Intelligence 23*, 155–212.

McCarthy, J. (1968). Programs with common sense. In M. Minsky (Ed.), *Semantic Information Processing*, pp. 403–418. Cambridge, MA: MIT Press. Part of this article is a reprint from an an article by the same title, in *Proc. Conf. on the Mechanization of Thought Processes*, National Physical Laboratory, Teddington, England, Vol. 1, pp. 77–84, 1958.

Newell, A. (1982). The knowledge level. *Artificial Intelligence 18*, 87–127.

Parikh, R. and R. Ramanujam (1985). Distributed processing and the logic of knowledge. In R. Parikh (Ed.), *Proc. Workshop on Logics of Programs*, pp. 256–268.

Reiter, R. (1992). What should a database know? *Journal of Logic Programming 14*, 127–153.

Rosenschein, S. J. and L. P. Kaelbling (1986). The synthesis of digital machines with provable epistemic properties. In J. Y. Halpern (Ed.), *Theoretical Aspects of Reasoning about Knowledge: Proc. 1986 Conference*, pp. 83–97. San Francisco, CA: Morgan Kaufmann.

Shoham, Y. (1993). Agent oriented programming. *Artificial Intelligence 60*(1), 51–92.

---

[3] See [?] for a general framework for mutual belief revision.

Reasoning with Models

Roni Khardon* Dan Roth[†]

Aiken Computation Laboratory,
Harvard University,
Cambridge, MA 02138.
{roni,danr}@das.harvard.edu

Abstract

We develop a model-based approach to reasoning, in which the knowledge base is represented as a set of models (satisfying assignments) rather then a logical formula, and the set of queries is restricted. We show that for every propositional knowledge base (KB) there exists a set of *characteristic models* with the property that a query is true in KB if and only if it is satisfied by the models in this set. We fully characterize a set of theories for which the model-based representation is compact and provides efficient reasoning. These include some cases where the formula-based representation does not support efficient reasoning. In addition, we consider the model-based approach to *abductive reasoning* and show that for any propositional KB, reasoning with its model-based representation yields an abductive explanation in time that is polynomial in its size.

Introduction

A widely accepted framework for reasoning in intelligent systems is the knowledge-based system approach (McCarthy 1958). Knowledge, in some *representation language* is stored in a Knowledge Base (KB) that is combined with a reasoning mechanism. Reasoning is abstracted as a deduction task of determining whether a sentence α, assumed to capture the situation at hand, is implied from KB (denoted KB $\models \alpha$). However, computational considerations render this logical-based representation, as well as many other forms of reasoning (Selman 1990; Roth 1993), as not adequate for common-sense reasoning (Levesque 1986; Shastri 1993).

In this work we embark on the development of a model-based approach to common sense reasoning. It is not hard to motivate a model-based approach to reasoning from a cognitive point of view and indeed, most of the proponents of this approach to reasoning have been cognitive psychologists (Johnson-Laird 1983;

---

*Research supported by grant DAAL03-92-G-0164 (Center for Intelligent Control Systems).

[†]Research supported by NSF grant CCR-92-00884 and by DARPA AFOSR-F4962-92-J-0466.

Johnson-Laird & Byrne 1991; Kosslyn 1983). In the AI community this approach can be seen, in a very general sense, as a derivative of Levesque's notion of "vivid" reasoning, and is very related to the approach developed in (Kautz, Kearns, & Selman 1993).

The problem KB $\models \alpha$ can be approached using the following model-based strategy:

Test Set: A set Γ of assignments.

Test: If there is an element $x \in \Gamma$ which satisfies KB, but does not satisfy α, deduce that KB $\not\models \alpha$; Otherwise, KB $\models \alpha$.

Clearly, (since KB $\models \alpha$ iff every model of KB is also a model of α) this approach solves the inference problem if Γ is the set of *all* models of KB. A model-based approach becomes useful if one can show that it is possible to use a fairly small set of models as the Test Set, and still perform reasonably good inference, under some criterion.

We define a set of models, the *characteristic models* of the knowledge base, with the property that performing the model-theory test on them suffices to deduce that KB $\models \alpha$, *for a restricted set of queries*. We prove that for a fairly wide class of representations, this set is sufficiently small, and thus the model-based approach is feasible. The notion of *restricted queries* is inherent to our approach. Since we are interested in formalizing common-sense reasoning, we take the view that a reasoner need not answer efficiently *all* possible queries.

For a wide class of queries we show that exact reasoning can be done efficiently, even when the reasoner keeps in KB only an "approximate" representation (as a set of characteristic models) of the "world". We show that the theory developed here generalizes the model-based approach to reasoning with Horn theories, studied in (Kautz, Kearns, & Selman 1993), and captures even the notion of reasoning with approximate theories (Selman & Kautz 1991). In particular, our results characterize the Horn theories for which the approach in (Kautz, Kearns, & Selman 1993) is useful, and explain the phenomena observed there, regarding the relative sizes of the logical formula representation and model-based representation of KB. We also give other examples of expressive families of propositional theories, for which our approach is useful.

In addition, we consider the problem of performing *abduction* using a model-based approach and show that for any propositional knowledge base, using a model-based representation yields an abductive explanation in time that is polynomial in the size of the model-based representation. Some of our technical results make use of a new characterization of Boolean functions, called the *Monotone Theory*, introduced recently by Bshouty (Bshouty 1993). Due to the limited space, some of the proofs are omitted. These can be found in the full version of the paper (Khardon & Roth 1994b).

Summary of Results

We now briefly describe the main applications of the model-based approach developed in this paper.

We consider two types of queries with which reasoning is efficient. Queries are called *relevant* if they belong to the propositional language that represents the "world". Queries are called *common* if they belong to some set $\mathcal{L}_E$ of *efficient* propositional languages (see Definition 5). These include for example Horn queries, and $\log n$CNF queries.

Our results can be grouped into 3 categories that can be informally described as follows:
(1) Every function with a small DNF representation and either a small CNF representation or a CNF representation (of any size) in $\mathcal{L}_E$ has a small set of characteristic models.

For these functions, model-based deduction is correct and efficient for relevant and for common queries.
(2) The set $\Gamma^{\mathcal{G}}$, of characteristic models with respect to a propositional language $\mathcal{G}$, describes the least upper bound of f with respect to $\mathcal{G}$.

Model-based deduction, using $\Gamma^{\mathcal{G}}$, is correct and efficient for common queries.
(3) For the functions defined in (1), efficient and correct model-based abduction can be performed.

We note that our algorithms do not solve NP-complete problems. Most hardness results for reasoning assume that KB is given as a CNF formula. The fact that we can perform reasoning efficiently relies on the fact that we change the knowledge representation into a more accessible form (another knowledge representation which enables reasoning, yet for some reason is considered less interesting, is DNF).

Monotone Theory

In this section we introduce the notations, definitions and results of the Monotone Theory of Boolean functions (Bshouty 1993).

We consider a Boolean function $f : \{0,1\}^n \to \{0,1\}$. An *assignment* simply means an element of $\{0,1\}^n$. A *model* of f is a *satisfying assignment* of f i.e., x such that $f(x) = 1$. Throughout the paper, when no confusion can arise, we identify f with the set of its models, namely $f^{-1}(1)$. That is, $f \models g$ if and only if

$f \subseteq g$. Assignments in $\{0,1\}^n$ are denoted by x, y, z, and x_i denotes the ith coordinate of $x \in \{0,1\}^n$.

Definition 1 (Order) *We denote by $\leq$ the usual partial order on the lattice $\{0,1\}^n$, the one induced by the order $0 < 1$. That is, for $x, y \in \{0,1\}^n$, $x \leq y$ if and only if $\forall i, x_i \leq y_i$. For an assignment $b \in \{0,1\}^n$ we define $x \leq_b y$ if and only if $x \oplus b \leq y \oplus b$ (where $\oplus$ is the bitwise addition modulo 2).*

Intuitively, if $b_i = 0$ then the order relation on the ith bit is the normal order; if $b_i = 1$, the order relation is reversed and we have that $1 <_{b_i} 0$.

The *monotone extension of* $z \in \{0,1\}^n$ with respect to b is:

$$\mathcal{M}_b(z) = \{x \mid x \geq_b z\}.$$

The *monotone extension of* f with respect to b is:

$$\mathcal{M}_b(f) = \{x \mid x \geq_b z, \ for \ some \ z \in f\}.$$

The set of *minimal assignments of* f with respect to b is:

$$\min_b(f) = \{z \mid z \in f, \ such \ that \ \forall y \in f, z \not\geq_b y\}.$$

The following claims list some properties of $\mathcal{M}_b$.

Claim 1 *Let $f, g : \{0,1\}^n \to \{0,1\}$ be Boolean functions. The operator $\mathcal{M}_b$ satisfies the following properties:*
(i) If $f \subseteq g$ then $\mathcal{M}_b(f) \subseteq \mathcal{M}_b(g)$.
(ii) $\mathcal{M}_b(f \wedge g) \subseteq \mathcal{M}_b(f) \wedge \mathcal{M}_b(g)$.
(iii) $\mathcal{M}_b(f \vee g) = \mathcal{M}_b(f) \vee \mathcal{M}_b(g)$.

Claim 2 *Let $z \in f$. Then, for every $b \in \{0,1\}^n$, there exists $u \in \min_b(f)$ such that $\mathcal{M}_b(z) \subseteq \mathcal{M}_b(u)$.*

From Claims 1 and 2 we get a characterization of the monotone extension of f:

Claim 3 *The monotone extension of f with respect to b is:*

$$\mathcal{M}_b(f) = \bigvee_{z \in f} \mathcal{M}_b(z) = \bigvee_{z \in \min_b(f)} \mathcal{M}_b(z).$$

Clearly, for every assignment $b \in \{0,1\}^n$, $f \subseteq \mathcal{M}_b(f)$. Moreover, if $b \notin f$, then $b \notin \mathcal{M}_b(f)$ (since b is the smallest assignment with respect to the order $\leq_b$). Therefore:

$$f = \bigwedge_{b \in \{0,1\}^n} \mathcal{M}_b(f) = \bigwedge_{b \notin f} \mathcal{M}_b(f).$$

Definition 2 (Basis) *A set B is a basis for f if $f = \bigwedge_{b \in B} \mathcal{M}_b(f)$. B is a basis for a class of functions $\mathcal{F}$ if it is a basis for all the functions in $\mathcal{F}$.*

Using this definition, the representation

$$f = \bigwedge_{b \in B} \mathcal{M}_b(f) = \bigwedge_{b \in B} \bigvee_{z \in \min_b(f)} \mathcal{M}_b(z) \qquad (1)$$

yields the following necessary and sufficient condition describing when $x \in \{0,1\}^n$ is positive for f:

Corollary 1 *Let B be a basis for f, $x \in \{0,1\}^n$. Then, $x \in f$ (i.e., $f(x) = 1$) if and only if for every basis element $b \in B$ there exists $z \in min_b(f)$ such that $x \geq_b z$.*

The following claim bounds the size of the basis of a function f:

Claim 4 *Let $f = C_1 \wedge C_2 \wedge \cdots \wedge C_k$ be a CNF representation for f and let B be a set of assignments in $\{0,1\}^n$. If every clause C_i is falsified by some $b \in B$ then B is a basis for f. In particular, f has a basis of size $\leq k$.*

The set of *floor* assignments of an assignment x, with respect to the order relation b, denoted $\lfloor x \rfloor_b$, is the set of all elements $z <_b x$ such that there does not exist y for which $z <_b y <_b z$ (i.e., z is strictly smaller than x relative to b and is different from x in exactly one bit).

The set of *local minimal assignments of f* with respect to b is:

$$min_b^*(f) = \{x \mid x \in f, \text{ and } \forall y \in \lfloor x \rfloor_b, \ y \notin f\}.$$

Clearly we have that $min_b(f) \subseteq min_b^*(f)$ and therefore the following lemma bounds the size of $min_b(f)$.

Claim 5 *Let $f = D_1 \vee D_2 \vee \cdots \vee D_k$ be a DNF representation for f. Then for every $b \in \{0,1\}^n$, $|min_b^*(f)| \leq k$.*

Example: Let f have the CNF representation:

$$f = (x_1 \vee x_2 \vee x_3) \wedge (x_1 \vee x_2 \vee x_4) \wedge (\overline{x_1} \vee \overline{x_2} \vee x_3 \vee \overline{x_4})$$

The function f has 12 (out of the 16 possible) satisfying assignments. The non-satisfying assignments of f are: $\{0000, 0001, 0010, 1101\}$. Using Claim 4 we get that the set[1] $B = \{0000, 1101\}$ is a basis for f.

The sets of minimal assignments with respect to this basis are: $min_{0000}(f) = \{1000, 0100, 0011\}$ and $min_{1101}(f) = \{1100, 1111, 1001, 0101\}$. These can be easily found by drawing the corresponding lattices and checking which of the satisfying assignments of f are minimal. It is also easy to check that f can be represented as in equation (1) using the minimal elements identified.

Deduction with Models

We consider the deduction problem $KB \models \alpha$. KB is the knowledge base, which is taken to be a propositional expression (i.e., some Boolean function[2]), and α is also a propositional expression. The assertion $KB \models \alpha$ means that every model $x \in \{0,1\}^n$ which satisfies KB, must also satisfy α.

---

[1] An element of $\{0,1\}^n$ denotes an assignment to the variables $x_1, \ldots, x_n$ (i.e., 0011 means $x_1 = x_2 = 0$, and $x_3 = x_4 = 1$).

[2] We use interchangeably the terms propositional expression and Boolean function. Similarly, a family of Boolean functions is used interchangeably with a propositional language. A family of Boolean functions is uniquely characterized as a set of all functions with a given basis.

In this section we define a special collection Γ of *characteristic models* of KB and show that performing the model-based test on Γ yields correct deduction. We fully characterize Γ in terms of the Boolean function KB and the query α.

Exact Deduction

Definition 3 *Let $\mathcal{F}$ be a class of functions, and let B be a basis for $\mathcal{F}$. For a knowledge base $KB \in \mathcal{F}$ we define the set $\Gamma = \Gamma_{KB}^B$ of characteristic models to be the set of all minimal assignments of KB with respect to the basis B. Formally,*

$$\Gamma_{KB}^B = \cup_{b \in B} \{z \in min_b(KB)\}.$$

Before showing that Γ has the required properties we discuss the size of the model-based representation. The following result is immediate from Claim 5.

Lemma 1 *Let B be a basis for the knowledge base KB, and denote by $|DNF(KB)|$ the size of its DNF representation. Then, the size of a model-based representation of a knowledge base KB is*

$$|\Gamma_{KB}^B| \leq \sum_{b \in B} |min_b(KB)| \leq |B| \cdot |DNF(KB)|.$$

We note that this bound is not tight. There are cases where this bound is exponential and Γ is small.

Theorem 1 *Let $KB, \alpha \in \mathcal{F}$ and let B be a basis for $\mathcal{F}$. Then $KB \models \alpha$ iff for every $u \in \Gamma_{KB}^B$, $\alpha(u) = 1$.*

Proof: Clearly, $\Gamma = \Gamma_{KB}^B \subseteq KB$ and therefore, if there exists $z \in \Gamma$ such that $\alpha(z) = 0$ then $KB \not\models \alpha$. For the other direction assume that for all $u \in \Gamma$, $\alpha(u) = 1$. We will show that if $y \in KB$, then $\alpha(y) = 1$. From Corollary 1, since B is a basis for α and for all $u \in \Gamma$ $\alpha(u) = 1$, we have that

$$\forall u \in \Gamma, \ \forall b \in B, \ \exists v_{u,b} \in min_b(\alpha) \text{ s.t. } u \geq_b v_{u,b}. \quad (2)$$

Consider now a model $y \in KB$. Again, Corollary 1 implies that

$$\forall b \in B, \ \exists z \in min_b(KB) \text{ s.t. } y \geq_b z. \quad (3)$$

By the assumption, since $min_b(KB) \subseteq \Gamma$, all the elements z identified in Equation 3 satisfy α and therefore, as in Equation 2 we have that

$$\forall z \in min_b(KB), \ \exists v_{z,b} \in min_b(\alpha) \text{ s.t. } z \geq_b v_{z,b}. \quad (4)$$

Substituting Equation 4 into Equation 3 gives the required condition on $y \in KB$:

$$\forall b \in B, \ \exists v_{(z),b} \in min_b(\alpha) \text{ s.t. } y \geq_b v_{(z),b}$$

which implies, by Corollary 1, that $\alpha(y) = 1$. $\blacksquare$

The above theorem assumed that KB and α could be described by the same basis B. This requirement is somewhat relaxed in the following theorem.

Theorem 2 *Let KB be a propositional theory with basis B and let α be a query with basis B'. Then $KB \models \alpha$ if and only if for every $u \in \Gamma_{KB}^{B \cup B'}$, $\alpha(u) = 1$.*

Proof: It is clear, from Eq. 1 and the fact that for all g and b, $g \subseteq \mathcal{M}_b(g)$, that $B \cup B'$ is a basis both for KB and α. Therefore, Theorem 1 implies the result. ∎

Example: (continued) The set Γ built for our basis is: $\Gamma = \{1000, 0100, 0011, 1100, 1111, 1001, 0101\}$. Note that it includes only 7 out of the 12 satisfying assignments of f. Since model-based deduction does not make mistakes on queries implied by f we concentrate in our examples on queries not implied by f.

To exemplify Theorem 1 consider the query $\alpha_1 = \overline{x_2}\,\overline{x_3} \rightarrow x_4$. This is equivalent to $x_2 \vee x_3 \vee x_4$ which is falsified by 0000 so our B is a basis for α. Reasoning with Γ will find the counterexample 1000 and will therefore conclude $f \not\models \alpha_1$.

The query $\alpha_2 = x_1 x_3 \rightarrow x_2 x_4$ is equivalent to $\overline{x_1} \vee x_2 \vee \overline{x_3} \vee x_4$ which is not falsified by our basis therefore model-based deduction might be wrong. Indeed reasoning with Γ will not find a counterexample and will conclude $f \models \alpha_2$ (it is wrong since the assignment 1010 satisfies f but not α_2).

Next, to exemplify Theorem 2 consider adding a basis element for α_2. This element is 1010. The set of additional minimal elements in Γ is $\{1010\}$, and reasoning with Γ would be correct on α_2.

Approximate Theories

We now consider the case in which the set of characteristic models of KB is constructed with respect to a basis B that is *not* a basis for the knowledge base KB. This representation coincides with the notion of a least upper bound of a theory, introduced in (Selman & Kautz 1991; Kautz & Selman 1991; 1992) in the context of knowledge compilation.

Definition 4 (Least Upper-bound) *Let* $\mathcal{F}, \mathcal{G}$ *be families of propositional languages. Given* $f \in \mathcal{F}$ *we say that* $f_{lub} \in \mathcal{G}$ *is a* $\mathcal{G}$-*least upper bound of* f *iff* $f \subseteq f_{lub}$ *and there is no* $f' \in \mathcal{G}$ *such that* $f \subset f' \subset f_{lub}$.

These bounds are called $\mathcal{G}$-*approximations* of the original theory f. The next theorem characterizes the $\mathcal{G}$-LUB of a function and shows that it is unique.

Theorem 3 *Let* f *be any propositional theory and* $\mathcal{G}$ *a class of all propositional theories with basis* B. *Then*

$$f_{lub} = \bigwedge_{b \in B} \mathcal{M}_b(f).$$

Proof: Define $g = \bigwedge_{b \in B} \mathcal{M}_b(f)$. We need to prove that (1) $g \subseteq f$, (2) $g \in \mathcal{G}$ and (3) there is no $f' \in \mathcal{G}$ such that $f \subset f' \subset f_{lub}$. (1) is immediate from Claim 1. To prove (2) we need to show that B is a basis for g. Indeed,

$$
\begin{aligned}
\bigwedge_{b \in B} \mathcal{M}_b(g) &= \bigwedge_{b \in B} \mathcal{M}_b(\bigwedge_{b \in B} \mathcal{M}_b(f)) \\
&\subseteq (\bigwedge_{b \in B} \mathcal{M}_b(f)) \bigwedge (\bigwedge_{b_i \neq b_j} \mathcal{M}_{b_i} \mathcal{M}_{b_j}(f)) \\
&= g \bigwedge (\bigwedge_{b_i \neq b_j} \mathcal{M}_{b_i} \mathcal{M}_{b_j}(f)) \subseteq g.
\end{aligned}
$$

Since in general $g \subseteq \bigwedge \mathcal{M}_b(g)$ we get that $\bigwedge_{b \in B} \mathcal{M}_b(g) = g$ and therefore $g \in \mathcal{G}$. Finally, to prove (3) assume that there exists $f' \in \mathcal{G}$ such that $f \subseteq f'$. Then,

$$g = \bigwedge_{b \in B} \mathcal{M}_b(f) \subseteq \bigwedge_{b \in B} \mathcal{M}_b(f') = f',$$

where the last equality results from the fact that $f' \in \mathcal{G}$. Therefore, $g = f_{lub}$. ∎

The following theorem can be seen as a generalization of Theorem 1, in which we do not require that the basis B is the basis of KB. A weaker version of the corollary that follows, for the case in which $\mathcal{G}$ is the class of Horn theories, is discussed in (Kautz & Selman 1991; Cadoli 1993).

Theorem 4 *Let* $KB \in \mathcal{F}$, $\alpha \in \mathcal{G}$ *and let* B *be a basis for* $\mathcal{G}$. *Then* $KB \models \alpha$ *if and only if for every* $u \in \Gamma_{KB}^B$, $\alpha(u) = 1$.

Proof: We have shown in Theorem 3 that

$$KB_{lub} = \bigwedge_{b \in B} \mathcal{M}_b(KB) = \bigwedge_{b \in B} \bigvee_{z \in \min_b(KB)} \mathcal{M}_b(z).$$

By Theorem 1, since $\alpha(u) = 1$ for every $u \in \Gamma_{KB}^B$, we have that $KB_{lub} \models \alpha$ and therefore $KB \models \alpha$. On the other hand, since $\Gamma_{KB}^B \subseteq KB$, if for some $u \in \Gamma_{KB}^B$, $\alpha(u) = 0$, $KB \not\models \alpha$. ∎

Corollary 2 *Reasoning with the least upper bound (with respect to the language* $\mathcal{G}$*) of a theory* KB *is correct for all queries in* $\mathcal{G}$.

Example: (continued) The Horn basis for our example is: $B_H = \{1111, 1110, 1101, 1011, 0111\}$ (see Claim 6). The minimal elements with respect to 1101 were given before. Each of $1111, 0111, 1011, 1110$ satisfies f and therefore for each of these, $\min_b(f) = b$ and together we get that $\Gamma_f^{B_H} = \{1111, 0111, 1011, 1100, 1001, 0101, 1110\}$.

For the query $\alpha_2 = x_1\,x_3 \rightarrow x_2 x_4$, which is not Horn, reasoning with $\Gamma_f^{B_H}$ will be wrong. For the Horn query $\alpha_2 = x_1\,x_3 \rightarrow x_2$, reasoning with $\Gamma_f^{B_H}$ will find the counterexample 1011 and therefore be correct.

Applications

In the previous section we developed the general theory for model-based deduction. In this section we discuss applications of this theory. In particular we apply it to the case of Horn knowledge base and show that earlier work on a model-based approach, in the narrower context of Horn knowledge bases (Kautz, Kearns, & Selman 1993) coincides with our theory.

Our basic result (Theorem 1) assumed that the knowledge base and the query share the same basis. A query with this property is called a *relevant query*.

We say that queries which are taken from some propositional family with a known basis, are *common queries*. In particular, queries are *common* if they belong to a set $\mathcal{L}_E$ of *efficient* propositional languages.

Definition 5 *The set $\mathcal{L}_E$ of efficient propositional languages is the set of languages for which there is a small (polynomial size) fixed basis.*

Important examples of efficient languages are: (1) Horn-CNF formulas, (2) reversed Horn-CNF formulas (CNF with clauses containing at most one *negative* literal), (3) k-quasi-Horn formulas (a generalization of Horn theories in which there are at most k positive literals in each clause), (4) k-quasi-reversed-Horn formulas and (5) $\log n$CNF formulas (CNF in which the clauses contain at most $O(\log n)$ literals). Any formula that can be represented as a CNF with clauses from any combination of the above is also in $\mathcal{L}_E$. The first four can be derived from Claim 6 and the last from Claim 7 ($weight(u)$ denotes the number of 1 bits in u).

Claim 6 *The set $B_H = \{u \in \{0,1\}^n \mid weight(u) \geq n-1\}$ is a basis for any Horn CNF function.*

Claim 7 *((Bshouty 1993)) There is a polynomial size basis for the set of $\log n$CNF theories.*

In the case of common or relevant queries, reasoning involves the evaluation of a propositional formula on a polynomial number of assignments. This is a very simple and easily parallelizable procedure. Moreover, Theorem 4 shows that in order to reason with common queries, we need not use the basis of KB at all, and it is enough to represent KB by the set of characteristic models with respect to the basis of the query language (one of the languages in $\mathcal{L}_E$). Claim 6 and Claim 7 together with Lemma 1 and Theorems 1,2,3 and 4 imply the following general applications of our theory:

Theorem 5 *Any function $f : \{0,1\}^n \to \{0,1\}$ that has a polynomial sized representation in both DNF and CNF form can be described with a polynomial size set of characteristic models.*

Theorem 6 *Any $f : \{0,1\}^n \to \{0,1\}$ with (any size) CNF representation in $\mathcal{L}_E$ and a polynomial size DNF representation can be described with a polynomial size set of characteristic models.*

Theorem 7 *Let KB be a knowledge base (on n variables) that can be described with a polynomial size set Γ of characteristic models. Then, for any relevant or common query, model-based deduction using Γ, is both correct and efficient.*

Theorem 8 *Let KB be a knowledge base (on n variables) that can be described with a polynomial size DNF. Then there exists a fixed, polynomial size set of models Γ, such that for any common query, a model-based deduction using Γ, is both correct and efficient.*

Horn Theories

We consider the case of Horn formulae and show that in this case our notion of *characteristic models* coincides with the notion introduced in (Kautz, Kearns, & Selman 1993).

Furthermore, our results explain the relation between sizes of the model-based and the formulae-based representations. In (Kautz, Kearns, & Selman 1993) examples are given for large Horn theories with a small set of characteristic models and vice versa, but it was not yet understood when and why it happens. Our results imply that the set of characteristic models of a Horn theory is small if the size of a DNF description for the same theory is small. The other direction is however not true (i.e., there are Horn theories with a small set of characteristic models but an exponential size DNF). In the full version we explain this phenomena in more detail. Let $char_H(KB)$ be the set of models defined in (Kautz, Kearns, & Selman 1993).

Theorem 9 *Let KB be a Horn theory and $B_H = \{u \in \{0,1\}^n \mid weight(u) \geq n-1\}$. Then, $char_H(KB) = \Gamma_{KB}^{B_H}$.*

We note, that in (Kautz, Kearns, & Selman 1993) the deduction theorem was extended to answer any query (and not just a restricted set of queries as we do here). This extension relies on a special property of Horn formulae and does not hold as is in the general case. In the full version of the paper we explain this phenomena too.

Abduction with Models

We consider in this section the question of performing abduction using a model-based representation. In (Kautz, Kearns, & Selman 1993) it is shown that for a Horn theory KB, abduction can be done in polynomial time using characteristic models. In this section we show that if we add a few base assignments to our basis, the algorithm presented there works in the general case too.

Abduction is the task of finding a minimal explanation to some observation. Formally, the reasoner is given a knowledge base KB (the *background theory*), a set of propositional letters A, (the *assumption set*), and a query letter q. An *explanation* of q is a minimal subset $E \subseteq A$ such that

1. KB$\land((\land_{x \in E} x) \models q)$ and

2. KB$\land(\land_{x \in E} x) \neq \Phi$.

Thus, abduction involves tests for entailment and consistency, but also a search for an explanation that passes both tests.

Theorem 10 *Let KB be a background propositional theory with a basis B, let A be an assumptions set and q be a query. Let $B_H = \{x \in \{0,1\}^n \mid weight(x) \geq n-1\}$. Then, using the set of characteristic models $\Gamma = \Gamma_{KB}^{B \cup B_H}$ one can find an abductive explanation of q in time polynomial in $|\Gamma|$ and $|A|$.*

Proof: We use the algorithm *Explain* suggested in (Kautz, Kearns, & Selman 1993) for the case of a Horn knowledge base and show that in order for it to work in the general case it is sufficient to add the Horn basis B_H and the characteristic models relative to this basis.

The abduction algorithm *Explain* starts by enumerating all the characteristic models. When it finds a model in which the query holds, (i.e., $q = 1$) it sets E to be the conjunction of all the variables in A that are set to 1 in that model. (This is the strongest set of assumptions that are valid in this model.)

The algorithm then performs the entailment test ((1) in the definition above) to check whether E is a valid explanation. This test is equivalent to testing the deduction KB $\models (q \vee (\vee_{x \in E} \bar{x}))$, that is a deductive inference with a Horn clause as the query. According to Theorem 2 this can be done efficiently with $\Gamma_{KB}^{B \cup B_H}$.

If the test succeeds, the assumption set is minimized in a greedy fashion by eliminating variables from E and using the entailment test again. It is clear that if the algorithm outputs a *minimal* assumption set E (in the sense that no subset of E is a valid explanation, not necessarily of smallest cardinality) then it is correct. It remains to show that if an explanation exists, the algorithm will find one. To prove this, it is sufficient to show that in such a case there exists a model $x \in \Gamma$ in which both the bit q and a superset of E are set to 1.

The existence of x is a direct consequence of including the base assignment $b = 1^n$ in the basis. This is true as relative to b we have $1 <_b 0$ for each bit. Therefore if there exists an explanation y, either it is a minimal assignment relative to b, or $\exists x \leq_b y$ and x is in Γ. $\blacksquare$

Conclusions and Further Work

This paper develops a formal theory of model-based reasoning. We show that a simple model-based approach can support exact deduction and abduction even when an exponentially small portion of the model space is tested. Our approach builds on (1) the characterization of a set of models of the knowledge base that captures all the information needed to reason with (2) a restricted set of queries. We prove that for a fairly large class of propositional theories, including theories that do not allow efficient formula-based reasoning, the model-based representation is compact and provides efficient reasoning.

The restricted set of queries, which we call *relevant queries* and *common queries*, can come from a wide class of efficient propositional languages, (and include, for example, quasi-Horn theories and $\log n$CNF), or from the same propositional language that represents the "world". We argue that this is a reasonable approach to take in the effort to give a computational theory that accounts for both the speed and flexibility of common-sense reasoning.

The usefulness of the approach developed here is exemplified by the fact that it explains, generalizes and unifies many previous investigations, and in particular the fundamental works on reasoning with Horn models (Kautz, Kearns, & Selman 1993) and Horn approximations (Selman & Kautz 1991; Kautz & Selman 1991; 1992). We are currently studying extensions of this theory for first order logic formalizations, and application of the theory to planning.

This work is part of a more general framework which views *learning* as an integral part of the reasoning process. We believe that some of the difficulties in constructing an adequate computational theory to reasoning result from the fact that these two tasks are viewed as separate. In (Khardon & Roth 1994a) we discuss the issue of "learning to reason" and illustrate the importance of the model-based approach for this problem.

Acknowledgments

We wish to thank Les Valiant for helpful discussions and comments.

References

Bshouty, N. H. 1993. Exact learning via the monotone theory. In *Proceedings of the IEEE Symp. on Foundation of Computer Science*, 302–311.

Cadoli, M. 1993. Semantical and computational aspects of Horn approximations. In *Proceedings of the International Joint Conference of Artificial Intelligence*, 39–44.

Johnson-Laird, P. N., and Byrne, R. M. J. 1991. *Deduction*. Lawrence Erlbaum Associates.

Johnson-Laird, P. N. 1983. *Mental Models*. Harvard Press.

Kautz, H., and Selman, B. 1991. A general framework for knowledge compilation. In *Proceedings of the International Workshop on Processing Declarative Knowledge, Kaiserlautern, Germany*.

Kautz, H., and Selman, B. 1992. Forming concepts for fast inference. In *Proceedings of the National Conference on Artificial Intelligence*, 786–793.

Kautz, H.; Kearns, M.; and Selman, B. 1993. Reasoning with characteristic models. In *Proceedings of the National Conference on Artificial Intelligence*, 34–39.

Khardon, R., and Roth, D. 1994a. Learning to reason. In these Proceedings.

Khardon, R., and Roth, D. 1994b. Reasoning with models. Technical Report TR-1-94, Aiken Computation Lab., Harvard University.

Kosslyn, S. M. 1983. *Image and Mind*. Harvard Press.

Levesque, H. 1986. Making believers out of computers. *Artificial Intelligence* 30:81–108.

McCarthy, J. 1958. Programs with common sense. In Brachman, R., and Levesque, H., eds., *Readings in Knowledge Representation, 1985*. Morgan-Kaufmann.

Roth, D. 1993. On the hardness of approximate reasoning. In *Proceedings of the International Joint Conference of Artificial Intelligence*, 613–618.

Selman, B., and Kautz, H. 1991. Knowledge compilation using Horn approximations. In *Proceedings of the National Conference on Artificial Intelligence*, 904–909.

Selman, B. 1990. *Tractable Default Reasoning*. Ph.D. Dissertation, Department of Computer Science, University of Toronto.

Shastri, L. 1993. A computational model of tractable reasoning - taking inspiration from cognition. In *Proceedings of the International Joint Conference of Artificial Intelligence*, 202–207.

Representing Multiple Theories

P. Pandurang Nayak
Recom Technologies, NASA Ames Research Center
AI Research Branch, MS 269-2
Moffett Field, CA 94035
nayak@ptolemy.arc.nasa.gov

Abstract

Most Artificial Intelligence programs lack generality because they reason with a single domain theory that is tailored for a specific task and embodies a host of implicit assumptions. *Contexts* have been proposed as an effective solution to this problem by providing a mechanism for explicitly stating the assumptions underlying a domain theory. In addition, contexts can be used to focus reasoning, allow the representation of mutually incoherent domain theories, lift axioms from one context into another, and transcend a context. In this paper we develop a simple propositional logic of context suitable for representing and reasoning with multiple domain theories. We introduce contexts as modal operators, and allow different contexts to have different vocabularies. We analyze the computational properties of the logic, providing the central computational justification for the use of contexts. We show how the logic effectively handles the common uses of contexts. We also discuss the extensions needed to handle first-order logic.

Introduction

Artificial Intelligence is founded upon the idea that any domain of interest can be described within a formal language, and that an artificial agent can draw meaningful conclusions about the domain purely by reasoning within the formal language. The impressive success of various AI programs is testimony to the power of this idea. However, as noted by McCarthy (1987), most of these programs lack generality. A key source of this lack of generality is that most programs reason with a single domain theory. Such a theory is usually tailored for a specific task, embodying a host of implicit assumptions, making it inapplicable for reasoning about other tasks. For example, typical axiomatizations of engineered systems do not account for the extreme environmental conditions encountered in space exploration, e.g., very high or low operating temperatures, gamma radiation, vacuum conditions. This leads to simpler axiomatizations that are adequate for a variety of design tasks, but that are inapplicable for the the design of a new space probe.

The specificity of domain theories is neither avoidable nor undesirable. It is unavoidable because any axiomatization of a real-world domain, however detailed, will invariably miss some subtle nuance. It is desirable because the specificity often buys us computational efficiency in reasoning. The goal, then, is to provide an artificial agent with a variety of domain theories, with varying generality and computational efficiency, and have it automatically select the theories most appropriate to the task at hand.

Contexts

McCarthy (1987; 1993) and Guha (1991) have argued persuasively that the notion of *context* is an effective solution to the problem of representing and reasoning with multiple domain theories. The basic idea is to encapsulate a domain theory within a context, and to explicitly state the assumptions underlying this context.[1] This provides a mechanism for using the simplest, and most efficient, applicable domain theory in every situation.

In addition to providing a mechanism for explicating the assumptions underlying a domain theory, McCarthy and Guha have identified a variety of other uses of contexts. Collecting together a set of related axioms into a context can be used to focus reasoning. Consider SIGMA, a knowledge-base of scientific domain knowledge that supports building consistent, coherent, and executable domain models (Keller, Rimon, & Das 1994). SIGMA contains axioms describing two different application domains: modeling the atmosphere of Titan (a moon of Saturn), and modeling a forest ecosystem. By separating the axioms of these two domains into different contexts, reasoning can be easily focused on just the axioms of the domain of interest.

Encapsulating domain theories within a context supports the representation of mutually incoherent domain theories. Domain theories can be mutually incoherent in a number of ways. First, they can use the same propositions with entirely different meanings.

---

[1] Of course, it is often not possible to state *all* the assumptions underlying a context.

For example, a "low temperature" in the context of Titan is quite different from a "low temperature" in the context of an Earth-based forest ecosystem. Second, different theories can can be mutually inconsistent. For example, in modeling the gases in Titan's atmosphere, two different, and mutually contradictory, axiomatizations are possible: gases can be modeled as being either ideal or non-ideal. Both axiomatizations can coexist peacefully by placing them in different contexts. Third, different domain theories are possible depending on one's perspective. Separating these different theories into different contexts simplifies knowledge base construction. For example, different ecosystem processes are best described at different time scales. The growth of trees is best described using a time scale of years, while photosynthesis is best described using a time scale of hours. Describing processes at inappropriate time scales is both difficult and opaque. Separating such descriptions into different contexts solves this problem.

Another important benefit of contexts stems from the ability to *lift* axioms from one context into another context. The simplest form of such lifting involves inheriting all the axioms of one context into another context. As with other forms of inheritance, this supports reuse and facilitates the construction and maintenance of large knowledge bases. For example, both the Titan modeling context and the ecosystem modeling context in SIGMA need axiomatizations of quantities and equations. This axiomatization can be placed in its own context, and reused in the Titan and the ecosystem contexts via inheritance.

More sophisticated forms of lifting allow axioms in one context to be modified before being lifted into another context. Adapting an example from (McCarthy 1993), let context C_1 be the specialization of context C_2 to a specific time t. Since time is fixed in C_1, it remains implicit. Lifting an axiom from C_1 to C_2 requires the time to be made explicit. For example, the proposition $at(jmc, stanford)$ in C_1 would have to be modified to the proposition $at(jmc, stanford, t)$ before being lifted into C_2. Similar modifications are needed when a context specializes to a speaker, a hearer, a location, etc. Modifications are also needed when axioms are lifted from one context into another context with fewer underlying assumptions. The implicit assumptions of the former context need to be made explicit.

Finally, the most ambitious use of contexts is to allow an AI system to *transcend* its current context, either by being told how, or by autonomous learning and discovery. For example, a system should be able to transcend the simpler context of Newtonian mechanics and move to the more general context of quantum mechanics.

Logics of context

Recently, there has been much interest in developing logics of context (Guha 1991; Buvač & Mason 1993).

Much of this work has focussed on developing new syntax and semantics for such a logic. However, we feel that, for the purposes of representing and reasoning with multiple domain theories, most aspects of a logic of context are naturally captured by simple extensions to traditional modal logic. In this paper, we focus on propositional modal logics, and introduce a modal operator, C_i, for the ith context and allow different contexts to have different vocabularies. We introduce an axiomatization for the logic, and analyze its computational properties. This analysis provides the central computational justification for the use of contexts. We introduce important relations between contexts, based on the notion of *interpretation functions* (Enderton 1972), and show how these relations can be used to implement important properties of contexts. We conclude with a brief discussion of the extensions needed to handle first-order logic.

The decision to represent contexts as modal operators, rather than as terms, sharply diverges from earlier work on logics of context (Buvač & Mason 1993; Guha 1991). The reasons are two-fold. First, in the propositional case, our $C_i\phi$ is effectively equivalent to $ist(C_i, \phi)$ in (Buvač & Mason 1993) ($ist(C_i, \phi)$ means ϕ is true in context C_i). Second, while introducing contexts as terms in a first-order logic leads to a very expressive logic (Guha 1991), it also leads to a very complex logic. The advantage of contexts as terms is that it allows reasoning about the contexts within the logic. However, as we shall see, much of what we want to say about contexts, and relations between contexts, can be easily stated and used in a meta-theory, and communicated to the logic via axiom schemas. Hence, it is worthwhile to investigate the properties of a simpler logic.

Propositional logic of contexts

The propositional logic of contexts is a propositional modal logic in which we introduce a modal operator, C_i, to represent the ith context. Viewing contexts as modal operators immediately provides us with one of the important properties of contexts: the wffs in different contexts can be mutually incoherent. Different contexts can use the same propositions with different meanings. The wffs in different contexts can be mutually inconsistent (though the contexts themselves remain consistent). Different perspectives can be easily accommodated using different contexts.

Syntax

Given a set $\mathcal{P} = \{P_1, \ldots, P_m\}$ of propositions and $\mathcal{C} = \{C_1, \ldots, C_n\}$ of context operators, the set of all wffs of the logic is defined by the usual rules of propositional modal logic. However, not all these wffs are *meaningful* because different contexts can use different *vocabularies*. For example, the propositions used to describe a forest ecosystem will be quite different from the propositions used to describe Titan's atmosphere;

any reference to photosynthesis in the latter context is meaningless. Note that, in general, a context's vocabulary may itself be context dependent. For example, a context describing an Eskimo's beliefs would include multiple words for snow, while the vocabulary of the same context from the point of view of a person living in the tropics would include just one word for snow. Allowing a context's vocabulary to be context dependent leads to a slightly more complex semantics and axiomatization (cf. (Buvač & Mason 1993)). As we will see, our use of contexts does not need context dependent context vocabularies. Hence, we have simplified the presentation by assuming that context vocabularies are context independent.

The vocabulary of a context C_i is the set of propositions that can be used immediately within the scope of C_i. (A proposition is immediately within the scope of C_i when it is within the scope of C_i but not within the scope of another context operator, C_j, which is within the scope of C_i.) Formally, the vocabulary of the contexts in $\mathcal{C}$ is defined by a function $voc : \mathcal{C} \rightarrow 2^{\mathcal{P}}$ that maps a context into a subset of $\mathcal{P}$. The *language* of C_i is just the set of propositional wffs that can be constructed using the propositions in $voc(C_i)$. A wff ϕ is meaningful with respect to voc if all occurrences of propositions in ϕ are consistent with voc, i.e., if p_i occurs immediately within context C_i, then $p_i \in voc(C_i)$.

Semantics and axiomatization

The basic semantics of the logic are standard possible worlds semantics. A model M of the logic defined by $(\mathcal{P}, \mathcal{C}, voc)$ is a Kripke structure (W, R, π), where W is the set of possible worlds, $R = \{R_1, \ldots, R_n\}$ is a set of binary accessibility relations on W, and $\pi : W \times \mathcal{P} \rightarrow \{T, F\}$ is the valuation function that assigns truth values to the propositions in $\mathcal{P}$ at each of the worlds in W. Satisfaction at a world $w \in W$ for meaningful wffs is then defined in the standard way with R_i being the accessibility relation for context C_i.

Let $\mathcal{M}_n$ denote the class of all Kripke structures for n contexts. A meaningful wff ϕ is *valid* in $\mathcal{M}_n$ iff it is satisfied at every world of every structure in $\mathcal{M}_n$. The basic axiomatization, $\mathcal{C}_n$, of the set of valid meaningful wffs is the usual axiomatization of propositional modal logic (e.g., the axiomatization K_n in (Halpern & Moses 1992)), appropriately restricted to meaningful wffs as follows:

(A1) All meaningful instances of propositional tautologies

(A2) All meaningful wffs of the form

$$(C_i\phi \wedge C_i(\phi \Rightarrow \psi)) \Rightarrow C_i\psi, \ 1 \leq i \leq n$$

(R1) From $\vdash \phi$ and $\vdash \phi \Rightarrow \psi$ infer $\vdash \psi$

(R2) From $\vdash \phi$ infer $\vdash C_i\phi$ if $C_i\phi$ is meaningful

The usual proof of the soundness and completeness of this axiomatization with respect to $\mathcal{M}_n$ (cf. (Halpern & Moses 1992)) applies here with slight modifications. Detailed proofs of all results in this paper can be found in (Nayak 1994).

Multiple domain theories

The axiomatization $\mathcal{C}_n$ is weak in the sense that it does not significantly restrict the properties of contexts, or their interrelations. Additional axioms are needed to tailor the logic to particular applications. We now introduce an axiomatization, $\mathcal{F}_n$, tailored to reasoning about multiple domain theories.

Axiomatization $\mathcal{F}_n$

The essential element in reasoning about multiple domain theories is that there is no need to reason about nested contexts. Nested contexts are useful when the properties of a context are different depending on the point of view. We have already seen how the vocabulary of a context can itself be context dependent. Another important example is belief contexts, where the beliefs of an agent differ depending on the point of view (my beliefs about your beliefs are almost certainly different from your beliefs). Nested contexts are useful for expressing ignorance about, and for hiding, properties of contexts.

Since our overall goal is to choose amongst multiple domain theories, we see no need to hide any information. On the contrary, we want to be able to use all available information to make the best possible choice. It is due of this that we chose to assume that a context's vocabulary is context independent. To ensure that the properties of contexts are context independent, we introduce the following two axioms in $\mathcal{F}_n$:

(A3) $C_i\phi \Rightarrow C_jC_i\phi$ for $1 \leq i, j \leq n$

(A4) $\neg C_i\phi \Rightarrow C_j\neg C_i\phi$ for $1 \leq i, j \leq n$

A3 and A4 are generalizations of the *positive introspection* $(C_i\phi \Rightarrow C_iC_i\phi)$ and *negative introspection* $(\neg C_i\phi \Rightarrow C_i\neg C_i\phi)$ axioms, respectively. They ensure that every context knows about what every other context does and does not know, i.e., the facts true in a context are context independent. To complete the axiomatization $\mathcal{F}_n$, we require all contexts to be consistent (this axiom is commonly called **D**):

(A5) $C_i\phi \Rightarrow \neg C_i\neg\phi$ for $1 \leq i \leq n$

In summary, the axiomatization $\mathcal{F}_n$ augments $\mathcal{C}_n$ with axioms A3, A4, and A5. Note that $\mathcal{F}_n$ does not include the axiom **T** $(C_i\phi \Rightarrow \phi)$ since we do not require a context's facts to be true. This may seem surprising since these contexts are domain theories, and hence ought to include only true domain facts. However, most useful domain theories are only *approximations* of the domain, and hence include facts that are not strictly true. For example, a context may assume that all gases are ideal gases. Since gases are not really ideal, the predictions of such a context are not strictly true. However, in practice, such contexts are both useful and common.

The axiomatization $\mathcal{F}_n$ achieves our goal of not hiding any information in the following sense: any meaningful wff is equivalent to a wff with no nested contexts. Let a *propositional literal* be either a proposition in $\mathcal{P}$ or its negation, and a *propositional clause* be a disjunction of propositional literals. Let a *contextual literal* be a context operator or its negation applied to a propositional clause. Let a *contextual clause* be a disjunction of contextual literals, and a *general clause* be a disjunction of propositional and contextual literals. Finally, let a wff be in *conjunctive normal form* (CNF) iff it is a conjunction of general clauses.

Lemma 1 *Every meaningful wff, ϕ, of $\mathcal{F}_n$ is equivalent to a meaningful wff, ϕ', in CNF, i.e., $\mathcal{F}_n \vdash \phi \Leftrightarrow \phi'$.*

Since a wff in CNF has no nested contexts, it follows that every meaningful wff is equivalent to a meaningful wff without nested contexts.

Correspondences

To assist in the complexity analysis of $\mathcal{F}_n$, we investigate the correspondences between its axioms and the accessibility relations of its models. It is well known that the axiom A5 corresponds to the accessibility relations being *serial*. (An accessibility relation R_i is serial on the set W if for all $w \in W$ there is a $w' \in W$ such that $(w, w') \in R_i$.) The correspondences of A3 and A4 are generalizations of transitive and euclidean accessibility relations, respectively. Let us say that the set $R = \{R_1, \ldots, R_n\}$ of accessibility relations on W is *hyper-transitive* iff for all $x, y, z \in W$ and $1 \leq i, j \leq n$ we have:

$$(x, y) \in R_j \wedge (y, z) \in R_i \Rightarrow (x, z) \in R_i \qquad (1)$$

R is said to be *hyper-euclidean* iff for all $x, y, z \in W$ and $1 \leq i, j \leq n$ we have:

$$(x, y) \in R_j \wedge (x, z) \in R_i \Rightarrow (y, z) \in R_i \qquad (2)$$

One can show that axiom A3 corresponds to a hyper-transitive accessibility relation, while A4 corresponds to a hyper-euclidean accessibility relation.

The above correspondence results can be used to show that, in the case of $\mathcal{F}_n$, we can further restrict our attention to particularly simple Kripke structures with one distinguished world, intuitively describing the "real" world, and a set of worlds for each context, which are the worlds considered possible by that context in every world. More formally, say that ϕ is $\mathcal{F}_n$-consistent iff $\mathcal{F}_n \nvdash \neg\phi$. We have:

Lemma 2 *If a meaningful wff ϕ is $\mathcal{F}_n$-consistent, then ϕ is satisfiable in a structure $M = (W, R, V)$ such that $W = \{w_0\} \cup_{1 \leq i \leq n} W_i$ and $R_i = W \times W_i, 1 \leq i \leq n$.*

The world w_0 is the "real" world, and the worlds W_i are the worlds that context C_i considers possible in every world.

Complexity

Let us now consider the complexity of the satisfiability problem of $\mathcal{F}_n$. Since $\mathcal{F}_n$ contains propositional logic, satisfiability is certainly NP-hard. Furthermore, it is easy to see that satisfiability is NP-hard both in the number of propositions and the number of context operators. To show that satisfiability is NP-complete, we can use Lemma 2 to show that satisfiable $\mathcal{F}_n$ wffs are satisfiable in Kripke structures with "very few" states. In the following, let $|\phi|$ denote the length of ϕ.

Lemma 3 *A meaningful wff, ϕ, of $\mathcal{F}_n$ is satisfiable iff it is satisfiable in a Kripke structure with at most $|\phi|$ states.*

The following theorem is an immediate consequence:

Theorem 1 *The satisfiability problem for $\mathcal{F}_n$ is NP-complete.*

The above theorem is interesting because the satisfiability problems of other common modal logics with $n > 1$ modal operators (K_n, T_n, $S4_n$, $S5_n$, $KD45_n$) are all PSPACE-complete (Halpern & Moses 1992).

While the above theorem applies to satisfiability of arbitrary wffs, in practice we are often interested in wffs of a restricted syntactic form. Say that a clause is *weakly Horn* if it has at most one positive propositional or contextual literal. For example, $\neg p_1 \vee \neg C_1(p_2 \vee p_3) \vee C_2 p_4$ is a weakly Horn clause. Say that a clause is *strongly Horn* if it is weakly Horn, and each contextual literal in the clause is the result of applying a context operator (or its negation) to a propositional Horn clause. For example, $\neg p_1 \vee \neg C_1(\neg p_2 \vee p_3) \vee C_2(\neg p_1 \vee p_4)$ is a strongly Horn clause. Weak and strong Horn clauses allow us to infer facts from one context to another, while restricting the forms of disjunction that can be stated. These restrictions buy us computational efficiency as follows:

Theorem 2 *Let Σ be a set of clauses of $\mathcal{F}_n$, $|\mathcal{C}|$ be the number of contexts in $\mathcal{C}$, $|\mathcal{P}|$ the number of propositions in $\mathcal{P}$, and P_{max} be the number of propositions in the vocabulary of the context with the largest vocabulary.*

1. *if the clauses in Σ are weakly Horn then deciding the satisfiability of Σ is polynomial in $|\mathcal{C}|$, but remains NP-hard in $|\mathcal{P}|$;*

2. *in part 1, if the clauses are contextual clauses, then satisfiability is NP-hard in P_{max} (rather than in $|\mathcal{P}|$); and*

3. *if the clauses in Σ are strongly Horn then the satisfiability of Σ can be decided in time polynomial in both $|\mathcal{C}|$ and $|\mathcal{P}|$.*

A procedure analogous to bottom-up evaluation in deductive databases (Ullman 1988) allows us to prove the above theorem. This theorem is the central computational justification for the use of contexts in partitioning large KBs to focus reasoning. In particular, item 2 in the theorem shows the benefits of breaking up a large KB with a single large vocabulary, into a number of smaller contexts with smaller vocabularies.

Relations between contexts

To effectively use multiple contexts, it is important to represent and reason about relations between contexts and the assumptions underlying contexts, and to lift axioms between contexts. Since our logic does not treat contexts as terms, the representation and use of context properties must be done in a meta-theory, and communicated to the logic via axiom schemas. (In the following, a context's theory is just the set of propositional wffs true in the context.)

The simplest relation between contexts is the *weaker than* relation. A context C_i is weaker than a context C_j if every fact true in C_i is also true in C_j, i.e., every wff of C_i is lifted into C_j. Naturally, C_i can be weaker than C_j only if C_i's vocabulary is a subset of C_j's vocabulary. We capture this axiomatically using the following axiom schema:

(A6) $C_i\phi \Rightarrow C_j\phi$ for all ϕ such that $C_i\phi$ is meaningful

We have already seen how lifting all axioms from one context into another facilitates the construction and maintenance of a large KB. Furthermore, meta-theoretic knowledge of the weaker than relation is useful for focusing reasoning. For example, to prove $C_j\phi$, it suffices to prove $C_i\phi$. This is particular useful if the theory of C_i is Horn. Similarly, to prove $\neg C_i\phi$, it suffices to prove $\neg C_j\phi$.

Compositional modeling (Falkenhainer & Forbus 1991; Nayak, Joskowicz, & Addanki 1992) provides a variant of the weaker than relation which involves explicitly representing the assumptions underlying a context. In compositional modeling, a model fragment is a piece of knowledge that is applied if the assumptions underlying it are true. We can represent this by introducing a context C_i for each model fragment m_i. Let A_i denote the conjunction of the assumptions underlying m_i,[2] and let C be a problem solving context, representing the domain description composed out of the applicable model fragments. The relationship between A_i, C_i, and C is represented by the following axiom schema:

$A_i \Rightarrow (C_i\phi \Rightarrow C\phi)$ for all ϕ s.t. $C_i\phi$ is meaningful

i.e., the axioms of C_i are lifted into the problem solving context if the assumptions underlying C_i hold. Additional relations between assumptions are expressed using appropriate wffs. To answer a user query in C, Falkenhainer and Forbus provide a meta-theoretic algorithm to compose a "simplest" theory for C by selecting an appropriate set of consistent assumptions.

By our definition, C_i can be weaker than C_j only if C_i's vocabulary is a subset of C_j's vocabulary. However, this is not always the case, and yet one can often

---

[2]In (Falkenhainer & Forbus 1991) an assumption is just a proposition. In general, it can be any meaningful wff.

say that everything expressible in one context is also expressible in another, e.g., earlier we saw that the proposition $at(jmc, stanford)$ in C_1 is expressible as the proposition $at(jmc, stanford, t)$ in C_2. We capture this using an *interpretation function*, based upon the interpretation between theories discussed in (Enderton 1972) and following the semantic theory of abstractions presented in (Nayak & Levy 1994). We say that the vocabulary, $voc(C_i)$, of context C_i can be interpreted in C_j iff there is an interpretation function f that assigns to each $p \in voc(C_i)$ a wff $f(p)$ in the language of C_j. The interpretation function f is intended to state that p in C_i "expresses the same thing" as $f(p)$ in C_j, e.g., $f(at(jmc, stanford)) = at(jmc, stanford, t)$. It can be extended to wffs in the language of C_i in the natural way: $f(\phi\wedge\psi) = f(\phi)\wedge f(\psi)$, $f(\neg\phi) = \neg f(\phi)$.

Using interpretation functions, and following the terminology in (Giunchiglia & Walsh 1992), we define theorem decreasing (TD), theorem conserving (TC), and theorem increasing (TI) abstractions with the following axiom schemas (in all cases C_i is the more abstract context and ϕ is any wff in the language of C_i):

(A7) $C_i\phi \Rightarrow C_j f(\phi)$ (TD-abstraction)

(A8) $C_i\phi \Leftrightarrow C_j f(\phi)$ (TC-abstraction)

(A9) $C_i\phi \Leftarrow C_j f(\phi)$ (TI-abstraction)

TD-abstractions are like weaker contexts except that they allow vocabulary changes. TC-abstractions are the strongest possible TD-abstractions. In these cases, f specifies how a wff ϕ is to be lifted from C_i to C_j. One can see that specializing a context to a particular time, location, speaker, or hearer will correspond to a TD or a TC abstraction. Other common relations between contexts, such as structural or behavioral abstractions are also TD/TC-abstractions.

Meta-theoretic knowledge of the TD/TC-abstraction relation can be used to control diagnostic reasoning, where the goal is to find a theory (context) that is consistent with the observations. The diagnostic strategy is based on the observation that axioms A7 and A8 ensure that if C_i is inconsistent with the observations, then so is C_j (see (Struss 1992)).

TI-abstractions are best viewed as TC-abstractions under certain simplifying assumptions: adding the simplifying assumptions to the context C_j increases the theorems of C_j and makes C_i a TC-abstraction of C_j. In particular, if ψ is the simplifying assumption underlying the TI-abstraction, then we can incorporate ψ using the following axiom schema:

(A10) $C_i\phi \Leftrightarrow C_j(\psi \Rightarrow f(\phi))$

i.e., ϕ is lifted from C_i into C_j as $\psi \Rightarrow f(\phi)$. For example, the ideal electrical conductor context is a TI-abstraction of the electrical resistor context under the assumption that the resistance is zero. As with TD/TC-abstractions, TI-abstractions can also be used for meta-theoretic control of diagnosis. The difference is that if C_i is inconsistent with the observations, either

C_j is inconsistent or the simplifying assumption ψ does not hold (see (Struss 1992)). (Giunchiglia & Walsh 1992) contains a survey of the uses of TI-abstractions in diverse areas including planning, theorem proving, and common sense reasoning.

The logic itself does not provide a means for transcending its current context (nor, for that matter, can any other logic). However, the process of transcending a context C_j to a context C_i is equivalent to constructing the interpretation function f and the simplifying assumption ψ in axiom A10. For example, in transcending the context of Newtonian mechanics, we need to specify how Newtonian mechanics is interpreted in quantum mechanics (f), and under what simplifying assumptions it holds (ψ).

The potential benefits of using the above relations, and thereby having to introduce the above axiom schemas, does not increase the worst-case complexity of satisfiability. This is a consequence of correspondences between the above axiom schemas and a model's accessibility relations. Say that a world w_2 is an *f-abstraction* of a world w_1 (denoted by $f\text{-}abs(w_1, w_2)$) iff for every proposition $p \in voc(C_i)$, p is true at w_2 iff $f(p)$ is true at w_1. We have the following correspondences (w, w_1, w_2 are worlds; R_i and R_j are accessibility relations corresponding to C_i and C_j, respectively):

Theorem 3 *A6 is a sound and complete axiomatization of the class of Kripke structures in which $R_j \subseteq R_i$. A7 is a sound and complete axiomatization of the class of Kripke structures in which forall w, w_1*

$$(w, w_1) \in R_j \Rightarrow (\exists w_2 \, (w, w_2) \in R_i \land f\text{-}abs(w_1, w_2))$$

A9 is a sound and complete axiomatization of the class of Kripke structures in which for all w, w_2

$$(w, w_2) \in R_i \Rightarrow (\exists w_1 \, (w, w_1) \in R_j \land f\text{-}abs(w_1, w_2))$$

The correspondence for A8 is the combination of the ones for A7 and A9. The correspondence for $A10$ is like the one for A8, except that only those R_j accessible worlds in which ψ is satisfied are considered. Since the above properties can be checked in polynomial time, satisfiability remains in NP.

First-order logic of context

In this section we briefly discuss the extensions needed for a first-order logic of contexts. The syntax is similar to traditional first-order modal logics, appropriately restricted to handle different context vocabularies. The vocabulary of a context now includes constants, functions, and relations. Functions and relations can have different arities in different contexts; occurrences of the same relation (function) with different arities just correspond to different relations (functions). The semantics of first-order modal logics are essentially possible worlds semantics, where each world is a first-order model. The primary difficulty with choosing a satisfactory semantics is related to deciding how the first-order models at each world relate to each other. In particular, two decisions need to be made: (a) how are the domains at the worlds related; and (b) how are the term interpretations at the worlds related.

The simplest first-order modal logic is obtained by assuming that (a) domains at all worlds are identical; and (b) terms are *rigid*, i.e., term denotations are the same at every world. This semantics is easily axiomatized by adding the principles of first-order logic to the principles of a propositional modal logic (e.g., $\mathcal{C}_n$ or $\mathcal{F}_n$) and the *Barcan formula* ($\forall x C_i \phi \Rightarrow C_i \forall x \phi$) (Garson 1984). However, this is inadequate as a semantics for contexts. First, this semantics requires that all contexts have the same domain, which is clearly inadequate, e.g., the domain of forest ecosystems is clearly different from the domain of Titan's atmosphere. Second, since this semantics allows only rigid terms, it precludes the satisfactory treatment of indexicals, i.e., terms like "I," and "now" whose denotations are clearly context dependent.

We address these shortcomings as follows. First, we let different worlds have different domains, so that different contexts can have different domains. Second, we allow the denotation of terms to be context dependent. Note that this differs from many traditional first-order modal logics where the denotations of terms are *world dependent* (Garson 1984). There is no need to make term denotations world dependent since it is perfectly natural to have rigid term denotations *within* each context (i.e., in all worlds considered possible by the context); it is just that we don't want rigid term denotations *across* contexts.

Space restrictions preclude a detailed description of the resulting logic (see (Nayak 1994)). However, it is worth noting that any sentence, ϕ, of this logic is equivalent to a sentence, ϕ', of the simpler logic with fixed domains and rigid terms, where ϕ' is the result of (a) replacing every occurrence of $\forall x \ldots$ in ϕ with $\forall x E(x) \Rightarrow \ldots$, where E is a special predicate denoting the existents at a world; and (b) every constant d and function f occurring immediately within context C is replaced by a constant d^C and function f^C, respectively, in ϕ'. This equivalence is useful because when we extend $\mathcal{F}_n$ to a first-order logic, ϕ' can be converted into a canonical form similar to the one in Lemma 1. Furthermore, we can define and use abstractions as discussed in (Nayak & Levy 1994).

Related work

McCarthy first noted the importance of contexts to common sense reasoning (McCarthy 1987; 1993). He argues that any axiom has limited generality since it is true only in a certain context, but that overly general axiomatizations are often inconvenient. He suggests that formalizing the notion of context is a way out of this dilemma. Guha built upon McCarthy's ideas and developed a first-order logic of contexts in which contexts are incorporated as terms (Guha 1991). Important contributions of his work include the development of default lifting axioms and the presentation of a large array of examples of the use of contexts in CYC (Lenat & Guha 1990). The primary difference between this work and ours is that we represent contexts as modal operators rather than as terms, leading to a simpler, albeit less expressive, logic. However, as we have shown, important relations between contexts can still be expressed using axiom schemas.

Buvač and Mason develop a propositional logic of context, and provide soundness and completeness results (Buvač & Mason 1993). Following Guha, they introduce contexts as arguments to *ist*: $ist(C_i, \phi)$ says that ϕ is true in context C_i. As mentioned earlier, in the propositional case, this is effectively equivalent to introducing C_i as a modal operator. They allow context vocabularies to be context dependent, and hence need to define satisfaction and provability with respect to context sequences. While we could have done the same, our main interest (the logic $\mathcal{F}_n$) does not require context dependent context vocabularies, and so we chose a simpler formalism.

Shoham discusses the ubiquity of contexts with a series of examples drawn from a variety of domains (Shoham 1991). He discusses various relations between contexts, and introduces a set of 14 benchmark sentences against which one may evaluate different semantics for contexts. He does not try and pin down "the right semantics" for contexts, but does suggest introducing contexts as propositions, and representing "p is true in context q" with the (material, intuitionistic, or relevant) implication $q \rightarrow p$.

Conclusions

In this paper we have developed a simple logic of context that is well suited for representing and reasoning with multiple domain theories. A key feature of this logic it that we introduce contexts as modal operators, rather than as terms. Our analysis of the computational properties of the resulting logic provided us with the central computational justification for the use of contexts. We showed that, for the purposes of representing and reasoning with multiple theories, this logic is able to effectively handle common uses of contexts. This seems to suggest that the difficulties in understanding contexts lie not so much with their logical properties, but with their heuristic properties. What are the useful and common types of contexts? How does one decide which context to use in a particular situation? How does one detect that the current context is inadequate? How does one transcend the current context? To investigate these heuristic questions, we have augmented SIGMA's frame representation language with contexts, and are currently evaluating the utility of using contexts in SIGMA. We are also evaluating the utility of contexts in developing practical diagnostic engines for complex physical systems.

Acknowledgements

I would specially like to thank Surajit Chaudhuri and Alon Levy for helpful discussions and useful comments on earlier drafts of this paper. Thanks also to Saša Buvač, Adam Grove, R. V. Guha, Mike Lowry, David Thompson, and the anonymous reviewers of this paper.

References

Buvač, S., and Mason, I. A. 1993. Propositional logic of context. In *Proceedings of AAAI-93*.

Enderton, H. B. 1972. *A Mathematical Introduction to Logic*. Academic Press, Inc.

Falkenhainer, B., and Forbus, K. D. 1991. Compositional modeling: Finding the right model for the job. *Artificial Intelligence* 51.

Garson, J. W. 1984. Quantification in modal logic. In Gabbay, D., and Guenthner, F., eds., *Handbook of Philosophical Logic, Volume II*. D. Reidel Publishing Company.

Giunchiglia, F., and Walsh, T. 1992. A theory of abstraction. *Artificial Intelligence* 57(2–3).

Guha, R. V. 1991. *Contexts: A Formalization and Some Applications*. Ph.D. Dissertation, Stanford University. Technical Report No. STAN-CS-91-1399.

Halpern, J. Y., and Moses, Y. 1992. A guide to completeness and complexity for modal logics of knowledge and belief. *Artificial Intelligence* 54(3).

Keller, R. M.; Rimon, M.; and Das, A. 1994. A knowledge based prototyping environment for construction of scientific modeling software. *Automated Software Engineering* 1(1).

Lenat, D. B., and Guha, R. V. 1990. *Building Large Knowledge-Based Systems*. Addison Wesley.

McCarthy, J. 1987. Generality in artificial intelligence. *CACM* 30(12).

McCarthy, J. 1993. Notes on formalizing context. In *Proceedings of IJCAI-93*.

Nayak, P. P., and Levy, A. Y. 1994. A semantic theory of abstractions: Preliminary report. In *Proceedings of the Workshop on Theory Reformulation and Abstraction*, 1994.

Nayak, P. P.; Joskowicz, L.; and Addanki, S. 1992. Automated model selection using context-dependent behaviors. In *Proceedings of AAAI-92*.

Nayak, P. P. 1994. Representing multiple theories. Technical report, NASA Ames Research Center.

Shoham, Y. 1991. Varieties of context. In Lifschitz, V., ed., *Artificial Intelligence and Mathematical Theory of Computation: Papers in Honor of John McCarthy*. Academic Press.

Struss, P. 1992. What's in SD? Towards a theory of modeling for diagnosis. In Hamscher, W.; Console, L.; and de Kleer, J., eds., *Readings in Model-Based Diagnosis*. Morgan Kaufmann.

Ullman, J. D. 1988. *Principles of Database and Knowledge-Base Systems, Vol. I*. Computer Science Press.

How Things Appear to Work: Predicting Behaviors from Device Diagrams

N. Hari Narayanan* and **Masaki Suwa** and **Hiroshi Motoda**
Advanced Research Laboratory, Hitachi Ltd.
Hatoyama, Hiki-gun, Saitama Pref. 350-03, Japan.
{narayan,suwa,motoda}@harl.hitachi.co.jp

Abstract

This paper introduces a problem solving task involving common sense reasoning that humans are adept at, but one which has not received much attention within the area of cognitive modeling until recently. This is the task of predicting the operation of simple mechanical devices, in terms of behaviors of their components, from labeled schematic diagrams showing the spatial configuration of components and a given initial condition. We describe this task, present a cognitive process model developed from task and protocol analyses, and illustrate it using the example of a pressure gauge. Then the architecture of a corresponding computer model and a control algorithm embodying the cognitive strategy are proposed.

Introduction

We often make use of diagrams while solving problems or explaining things to ourselves or others. Reading a book like *How Things Work* and understanding the multi-modal descriptions of machines it contains provides a persuasive illustration of how diagrams aid common sense reasoning. The problem solving task of hypothesizing qualitative behaviors of a device from its diagram is another example. The task is to predict the operation of the device by hypothesizing behaviors of its components, given a labeled schematic diagram of the device showing the spatial configuration of its components and an initial condition or behavior. In this task the diagram situates the problem solving process and guides it along the direction of causality as well as cues relevant prior knowledge.

Consider someone with a basic knowledge of mechanical components examining the cross-sectional diagram of a device, such as the pressure gauge shown in fig. 1, and reasoning about its operation. This requires that the person reason about spatial processes occurring inside the device. Information used in this type of

---

*Current address: Knowledge Systems Laboratory, Stanford University, 701 Welch Rd., Palo Alto, CA 94304. narayan@ksl.stanford.edu.

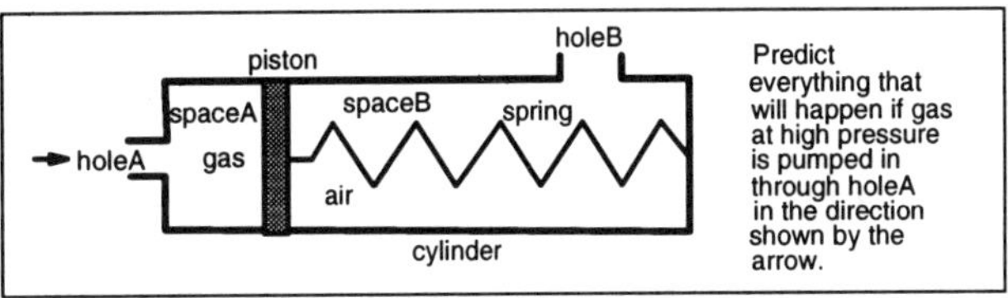

Figure 1: A Behavior Hypothesis Problem

reasoning is of two kinds: *visual* and *conceptual*. Visual information is obtained from the diagram, and includes spatial configurations and shapes of the device and its components. Conceptual information comes from the prior domain knowledge of the reasoner, and includes predictive knowledge used for making inferences about the device's operation.

In such reasoning situations diagrams clearly serve as compact representations of spatial information. However, this is only part of the story of the role diagrams play in this task. Diagrams also facilitate the indexing of relevant problem solving knowledge. Furthermore, diagrams support mental visualizations of spatial behaviors of device components during the course of reasoning. It has been shown that such mental visualizations guide human reasoning along the direction of causality (Hegarty 1992).

This paper describes an approach to automating reasoning about devices from diagrams. First, a cognitive process model for this task is proposed and behavior hypothesis steps for the pressure gauge according to this model are enumerated. Then the architecture and control algorithm of a corresponding computer model are described.

Predicting Behaviors from Diagrams

We conducted a set of protocol analysis (Ericsson & Simon 1983) experiments with five subjects solving six behavior hypothesis problems each. Verbal data (concurrent verbal reports) and gestural data were collected during the course of problem solving and studied (Narayanan, Suwa, & Motoda 1994). The main goal of these experiments was to characterize how visual information from the diagram and conceptual information (prior knowledge) interact and influence the direction of reasoning during problem solving. Though the solutions that subjects provided were not always complete and contained inaccuracies, a preliminary analysis of experimental data indicated that the diagram played two crucial roles during problem solving.

- It facilitated the indexing and recall of both factual knowledge about components and inferential knowledge using which the reasoner generated new hypotheses.

- It supported visualizations of hypothesized spatial behaviors of components, which in turn enabled the reasoner to detect effects of these behaviors.

Based on a task analysis (Narayanan, Suwa, & Motoda 1993) – which involved developing detailed and step-wise descriptions of problem solving in this task for some examples and analyzing these descriptions – and an examination of verbal reports and gestures that subjects generated in the aforementioned experiments, we developed a cognitive process model of problem solving in this task (fig. 2). This model explicates the visual reasoning strategy employed in solving behavior hypothesis problems from diagrams. Notice that reasoning proceeds in cycles. At first, short term memory contains only the given initial condition. So reasoning starts with the component and its behavior mentioned in the initial condition. In each cycle new hypotheses are generated in one of three ways: by reasoning about effects of the current non-spatial behavior, by observing the diagram to locate connected/contacting components and reasoning about how these will be affected by the current spatial behavior, or by mentally visualizing spatial behaviors, detecting component interactions that result, and reasoning about effects of these interactions. The new hypotheses are added to the short term memory, and the component and behavior to focus on in the next cycle are selected from the short term memory.

Now let us reconsider the problem in fig. 1 and enumerate steps of reasoning according to this process model. Following each step the alphabetic labels of corresponding parts of the process model from fig. 2 are given in parentheses. Due to limited space, this enumeration does not contain steps corresponding to every part of the process model in each reasoning cycle.

1. Consider the given initial condition (A).

2. Observe from the diagram that holeA opens to spaceA (D).

3. Infer that the pressurized gas will enter spaceA (G,K).

4. Observe from the diagram that spaceA is a closed cavity (A,D).

5. Recall the inferential knowledge that pressurized gas contained in a closed cavity will exert a force in the normal direction on walls of the cavity (G,K).

6. Observe from the diagram that the cylinder and piston form walls surrounding spaceA (A,D).

7. Infer that a force in the normal direction will be exerted on the piston and cylinder (G,K).

8. Recall the inferential knowledge that force can induce motion in a movable component (K).

9. Recall the factual knowledge that the piston is movable in a piston-cylinder assembly (K).

10. Infer that the piston will move (K).

11. Observe the piston in the diagram and conclude that it is free to move left or right (A,D).

12. Infer that the piston will move right (K).

13. Observe from the diagram that the piston is connected to a spring, and is in contact with air in spaceB; consider each in turn (A).

14. Recall the inferential knowledge that if a component is connected to another, and the former starts moving in one direction, it will exert a force on the latter in the same direction (G,K).

15. Infer that when the piston starts moving right, it will exert a rightward force on the spring (K).

16. Recall the inferential knowledge that a force applied on a spring will either compress it or expand it depending on the direction of the force (K).

17. Infer that the spring will compress (K).

18. Consider the air inside spaceB (A).

19. Observe from the diagram that spaceB is an open cavity with holeB (D).

20. Recall the inferential knowledge that if gas inside an open cavity is pushed, it will escape through the cavity's openings (G,K).

21. Infer that air in spaceB will exit through holeB (K).

22. All immediate effects of the hypothesized piston motion have now been considered (A,H).

23. Visualize the piston's rightward motion and the spring's compression (I).

24. Notice that the spring gets compressed more and more as the piston moves (J).

25. Recall the inferential knowledge that as a spring gets compressed or expanded, it will exert an increasing force in the opposite direction (K).

26. Infer that the spring will exert a force on the piston which, at some point, will equal the force exerted by the pressurized gas on the piston (K).

27. Observe from the diagram that this may happen before or after the piston reaches holeB; consider each case (A,D).

28. In the former case, infer that the piston will stop somewhere before holeB (K).

29. Infer that the spring compression will cease (K).

A similar enumeration can be done for the other case, in which inferences about the piston moving back and forth around the region of holeB are generated.

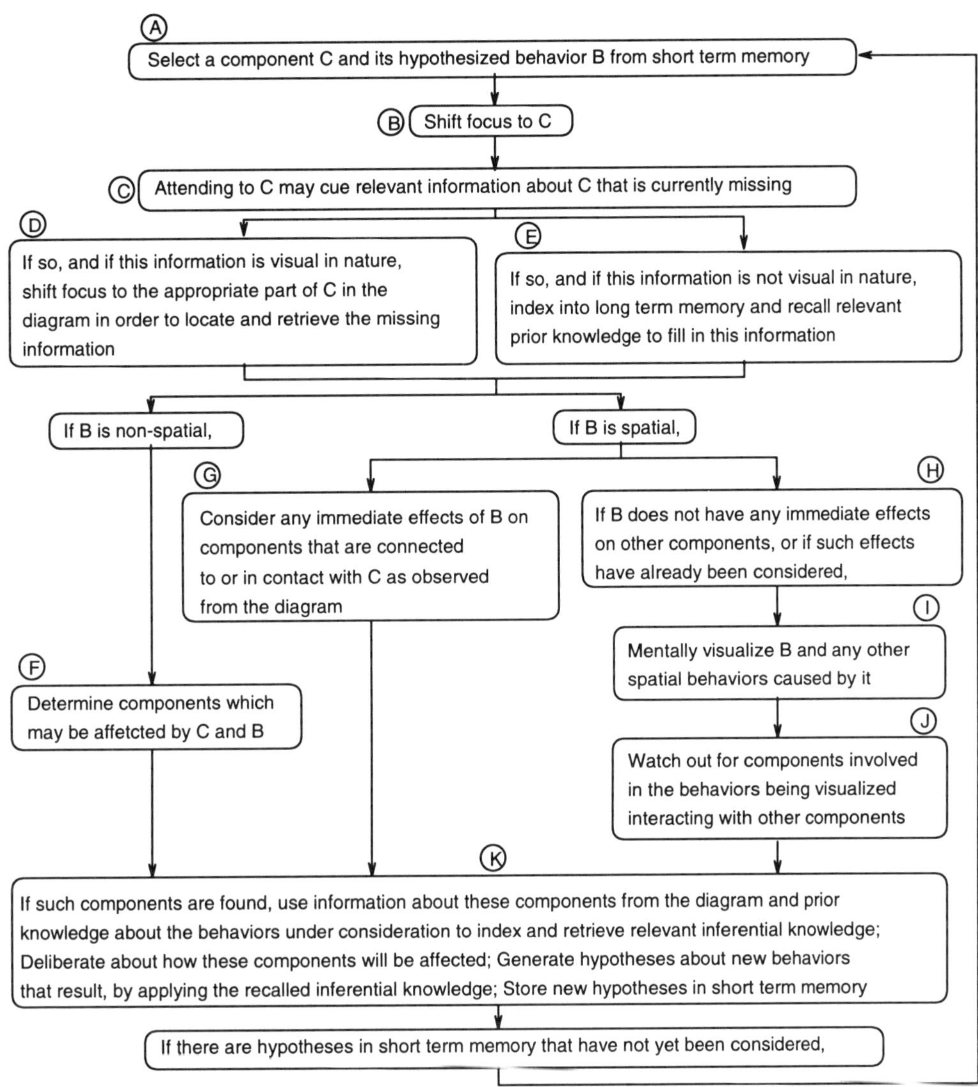

Figure 2: A Cognitive Process Model

An Architecture for Visual Reasoning

In this section we describe an architecture for visual reasoning from diagrams. It has five main elements: a user interface, a knowledge base, a rule base, a working memory, and an inference engine (fig. 3). The user interface allows the user to specify both descriptive and diagrammatic aspects of a problem, and to watch manipulations of the input diagram that the system carries out during the course of reasoning. The knowledge base contains two kinds of representations: descriptive and visual. The rule base contains domain-specific inference rules. The inference engine generates new inferences by accessing and manipulating information from both kinds of representations in the knowledge base in accordance with rules selected from the rule base. The generated inferences are stored in the working memory.

Descriptive representations store domain-specific conceptual information. For the behavior hypothesis task, this includes both general knowledge about component types in the domain and particular knowledge about components of the device in the input problem. We use a frame-based representation that organizes knowledge around component types, but other types of descriptive representations may also be used. Visual representations contain diagrammatic information and have two parts: one contains information about diagram elements that stand for components or parts of components of the device (diagram frames) and the other is an array representation (Glasgow & Papadias 1992) in which the diagram is literally depicted by filling appropriate array elements with symbolic labels of components and substances that "occupy" the corresponding locations. This captures shape, geometry and configuration information. Diagram frames

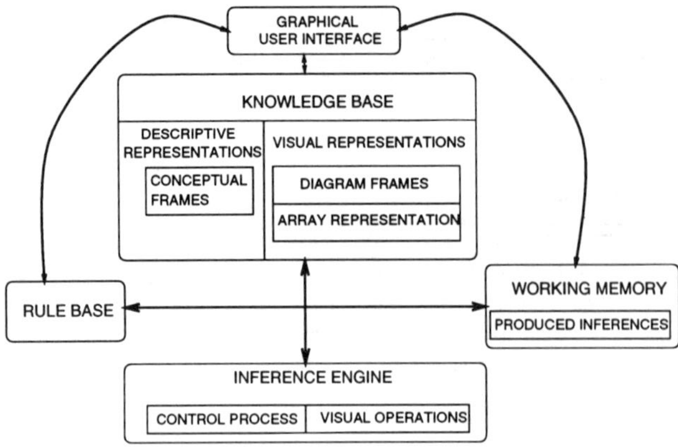

Figure 3: An Architecture for Visual Reasoning

contain information about diagram elements like segments, boundaries and areas.

A behavior hypothesis problem can be provided to the system by specifying, via the user interface, conceptual information about components of a device (component types, labels, etc.), the device diagram, and an initial condition. The user interface program takes this specification and stores information about the device's components in the descriptive part of the knowledge base, uses given information about component types to link this knowledge with general knowledge about various types of components that already exists in the knowledge base, represents the device diagram using both diagram frames and array representation, and stores the initial condition in the working memory in a last-in-first-out queue (LIFO-Q). Thus, the user

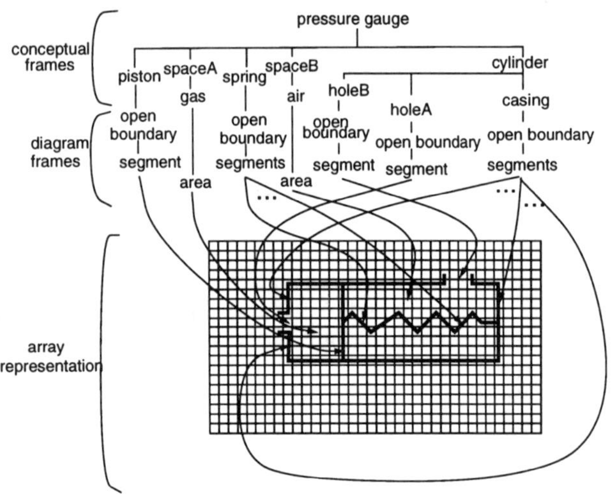

Figure 4: Problem Representation

interface generates an internal problem representation of the form shown in fig. 4. This representation is hierarchical, with conceptual frames linked to diagram frames and diagram frames at the lowest level contain-

ing pointers to the array. Symbolic labels stored in array elements provide connections in the reverse direction. This organization allows reasoning procedures to move between conceptual and diagrammatic information easily – an important characteristic of human reasoning with diagrams.

An example of a conceptual frame is [SpaceB - *Type* : cavity; *Contains* : air; *Pressure* : (value); *Boundaries* : (cylinder holeB piston); *Part-of* : pressure gauge; *Parts* : none;]. A diagram frame has slots describing geometric attributes of the corresponding diagram element. For example, the diagram frame representing a line segment will have slots for starting and ending locations, length, and orientation. The array representation may be thought of as a "bitmap" except that each element (bit) contains symbolic labels of parts or substances instead of an intensity value. Conceptual and diagram frames are created at problem specification time by instantiating templates of the various types of frames that already exist in the knowledge base. Indices of array elements corresponding to each diagram frame are then computed and filled with labels of the corresponding part or substance. The user specifies the basic elements constituting the diagram (at present these are line segments and individual locations) and how they are to be grouped together to form open and closed boundaries or define areas.

Each inference rule in the rule base has three parts: an antecedent that refers to descriptive and/or diagrammatic information, a consequent containing new inferences that the system asserts in the working memory if conditions in the antecedent have been verified, and side-effects, which are procedures that manipulate both descriptive and visual representations in the knowledge base and which get activated when the corresponding rule is fired. Fig. 5 shows a sample in-

If a gas enters a cavity which is closed except for the opening through which it is entering, it will fill the cavity.

```
(and
("descriptive" (substance-move ?1<gas> ?2<part> ?3<opening> ?4<cavity>))
("diagrammatic" (closed ?4<cavity> ?3<opening>)))

(assert (fill ?1<gas> ?4<cavity>))
```

Side effects:

Update "contains" and "pressure" slots of the conceptual frame of the cavity bound to ?4<cavity> with values of ?1<gas> and "pressure" slot of ?1<gas> respectively; Update the array by adding the symbolic label of gas bound to ?1<gas> to array elements representing ?4<cavity>.

Figure 5: An Inference Rule

ference rule. The working memory is the computer equivalent of short term memory, except that it is not subject to capacity limitations of human short term memory. The LIFO-Q of inferences is maintained in the working memory. It also contains all new information generated during the course of problem solving.

The reasoning steps carried out by the inference engine fall into the following seven classes. *Diagram Observation*: Access the diagram frames and/or the array representation to find and retrieve spatial information. *Factual Retrieval*: General knowledge retrieval from descriptive representations. *Inference Rule Retrieval*: Indexing and retrieval of rules from the rule base. *Conceptual Inference*: An inference based only on conceptual information from descriptive representations. *Visual Inference*: An inference based only on spatial information from visual representations. *Hybrid Inference*: An inference based on both conceptual information and spatial information. *Visualization*: Simulating a spatial behavior by incrementally modifying the visual representation of the device diagram.

In order to facilitate accessing and manipulating the visual representations, a set of "visual operations" are made available to the inference engine. Visual operations are procedures for accessing and manipulating both types (diagram frames and the array representation) of visual representations. These are of four kinds: basic operations, indexing operations, scanning operations and visualization operations.

Basic Operations. These are operations on individual array elements. $\text{Read}(x, y)$ returns labels l of the array element at location (x, y). $\text{Write}(x, y, l)$ marks the array element at location (x, y) using labels l. Other basic operations are erase, test, add-label, and remove-label.

Indexing Operations. Indexing operations generate indices or addresses of array elements. At least four such operations are required. Directional indexing: Given an index (x, y) and a direction[1], generate the sequence of indices of cells which fall in that direction from (x, y). Boundary indexing: Given an index (x, y) and a symbol s, generate a sequence of indices of cells, each of which is adjacent to the previous one and contains s as a label. Neighborhood indexing: Given an index (x, y), generate the sequence of indices of its neighboring cells. Fill indexing: Given an index (x, y), generate a sequence of indices of cells such that these gradually cover the area surrounding (x, y) until a boundary is reached.

Scanning Operations. Scanning operations use indexing operations to generate indices of array elements and basic operations to test those elements for various conditions. At least three different kinds of scanning operations are required. Directional Scanning: Given a starting point in the array, a direction, and one or more conditions, test all array elements from the starting point that fall along the given direction for the given conditions. Boundary Following: Given a starting point on a boundary and one or more conditions, follow the boundary from the starting point and test the boundary elements or their neighborhoods for the

given conditions. Sweeping: Like directional scanning, except that an area is scanned.

Visualization Operations. Visualization operations transform the represented diagram by manipulating diagram elements that represent individual components. There are both general operations such as move, rotate, copy, and delete, and component-specific ones like compress-spring.

A simplified version of the control algorithm underlying the inference engine's operation is given below.

> If the LIFO-Q is empty, Then halt;
> Else
>   Retrieve the latest inference from LIFO-Q;
>   If this inference is about a spatial behavior,
>   Then
>   If all its consequences have been considered,
>   Then visualize this behavior and
>   other spatial behaviors it causes;
>   Else visualize this behavior for
>   a small number of steps;
>   Detect component interactions by
>   scanning the array representation;
>   Generate inferences corresponding
>   to detected interactions;
>   Assert these in the working memory and
>   add to LIFO-Q;
>   Else (a non-spatial behavior)
>   Match and retrieve rules from the rule base;
>   Attempt to verify antecedents;
>   For each rule thus found to be applicable,
>   If its consequent has not already been asserted,
>   Assert the consequent in working memory
>   and add to LIFO-Q;
>   Activate side-effects;
>   Return to the beginning of the cycle.

This algorithm was developed from the model in fig. 2 by replacing mental representations and mental operations by corresponding knowledge representations and operations on those representations. For example, the storage and selection of an inference at the beginning of each cycle from short term memory is implemented using the LIFO-Q data structure in working memory. The inferential knowledge recalled from long term memory during deliberation is represented by inference rules. The computational process corresponding to mental visualization is the simulation of spatial behaviors that visualization operations carry out on the array representation, combined with scanning for component interactions in the cells of the array. The immediate effects of a spatial behavior can also be detected by a similar computational process: simulating the behavior for a small number of steps and scanning for interactions.

This algorithm combines rule-based reasoning with diagram-based reasoning. Each reasoning cycle begins by extracting an element from the LIFO-Q. Reasoning

---

[1] At present sixteen discrete directions are defined on the array, with each differing from the next by 22.5 degrees; this is an arbitrary choice.

changes to a diagram-based mode when either this inference is a hypothesis about a spatial behavior of a component and its immediate consequences on other components need to be determined, or it is a hypothesis about a spatial behavior whose immediate consequences have already been determined. In the former case a simulation of the behavior for a few steps is carried out. This will detect any immediate consequences of that spatial behavior on any nearby components. These detected effects are stored in the LIFO-Q. In the latter case, we have a behavior whose immediate consequences (which may be spatial behaviors of affected components nearby) have already been determined. So the next step will be to simulate this behavior and its spatial consequences. This simulation will not be terminated after a few steps. Instead, it will proceed until some interaction between components is detected (or it becomes clear that no interactions will occur within the diagram boundaries). Once an interaction is detected, its effects are determined and stored in the LIFO-Q.

For illustrative purposes, fig. 6 shows the trace of a simple example requiring about twenty rules (the same as in fig. 1, but without the complication introduced by the placement of holeB). Reasoning be-

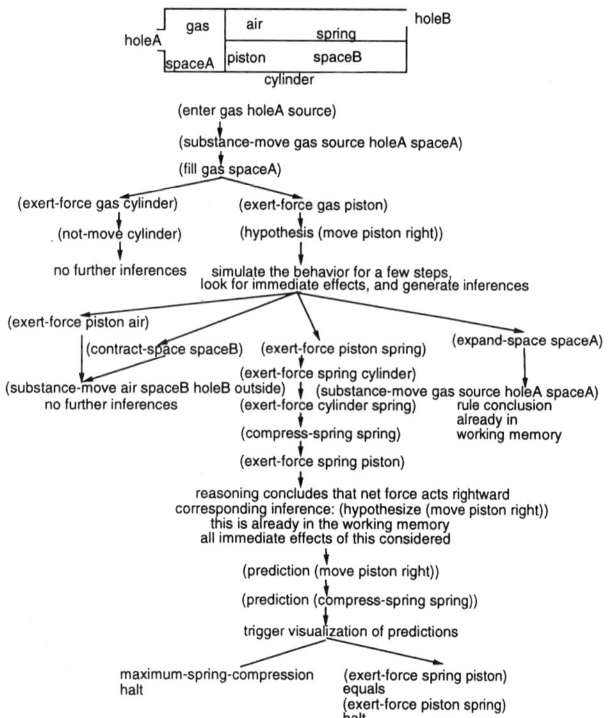

Figure 6: An Example and Corresponding Inferences

gins with the given initial condition, *(enter gas holeA source)*. The next inference is derived from the application of an inference rule that checks the diagram to ensure that holeA is not blocked. The inference *(fill gas spaceA)* requires both knowledge about gases at high pressure filling spaces and a diagram observa-

tion to ensure that spaceA is closed except for holeA. At this point rule-based reasoning generates two inferences, one of which leads to a dead end. The other leads to the hypothesis *(move piston right)*. Since this is a hypothesis concerning a spatial behavior, its immediate effects are investigated. This results in four new inferences. Two of them lead to the same inference *(substance-move air spaceB holeB outside)* for which no further rules are found to be applicable. The fourth inference generates another which already exists in the working memory. So the only path further followed by the inference engine is that leading from *(exert-force piston spring)*. This eventually leads to the inference *(exert-force spring piston)*. At this point two forces on the same object have been hypothesized. Knowledge about springs leads the system to conclude that the initial force exerted by the spring is small. The resulting hypothesis, that of a rightward move of piston, is already in the working memory. At this point all immediate effects of this hypothesized motion have been considered and therefore two spatial behaviors—the motion of piston and the compression of spring—can be predicted. This triggers a simulation of these. This simulation will detect the fact that as the piston moves, the spring will get progressively more compressed. Based on general knowledge about behaviors of springs and using rules for reasoning about inequalities, the system will then discover two possibilities: either the spring will get maximally compressed or the piston will reach a point at which the two forces are in equilibrium. At this point there are no more entries in the LIFO-Q and the inference process will come to a stop. These inferences amount to a series of hypotheses about the given device's behaviors, generated along the direction of causality.

Conclusion

This paper presented a study of visual reasoning from diagrams in device behavior hypothesis tasks. Analyzing this task and examining hypotheses generated by human subjects allowed us to formulate a cognitive process model of problem solving in this task. Using this model as a basis we showed how an example problem could be solved. Then the architecture of a corresponding visual reasoning system was described.

Limitations of the proposed model and aspects that have not been addressed yet provide avenues for current and future research. One such issue is the notion of relevance. In the present computer model, slots of conceptual frames associated with arguments of the current inference (in a cycle) constitute the "relevant" facts, and rules retrieved from the rule base by matching with the current inference constitute the "relevant" inferential knowledge. However, a more sophisticated and operational notion of relevance to filter facts and rules may be required to efficiently deal with large amounts of conceptual information and a large rule base. Support for visualization and support for indexing and recall of relevant factual and inferential knowledge were mentioned earlier as the two major roles that diagrams seem to play in problem solving. The current control algorithm, with its forward chaining strategy, implements only the former. In order to implement the latter (for instance, noticing something unexpected in the diagram may cue factual knowledge or inferential knowledge that leads to a new prediction), additional strategies (such as an opportunistic one) need to be incorporated in the control algorithm. Furthermore, visual indexing schemes for conceptual knowledge and inference rules need to be developed. The computer model is designed to support 2-D visualizations of spatial behaviors such as translations, rotations, and deformations. This can in principle be extended to 3-D by using a three dimensional array representation. But the visualizations do not capture temporal aspects of spatial behaviors (e.g., velocity). Granularity of visual representations is another aspect requiring further research. It has not been critical for dealing with relatively abstract schematic diagrams of the sort discussed in this paper. Also, larger arrays can be used for finer resolution. Nevertheless, issues such as selecting an appropriate grain size to ensure that component interactions are not missed during visualizations and information loss that occurs when continuous shapes are rendered onto discrete arrays need to be addressed.

Increasing attention is currently being paid to the coupling of perception and reasoning. This coupling is bidirectional. On one hand, high level knowledge, goals and reasoning can significantly influence aspects of perception such as directing the focus of attention and disambiguating image interpretations (Brand, Birnbaum, & Cooper 1993). On the other hand, visually perceived spatial properties and the mental manipulation of visual representations such as diagrams can considerably aid reasoning and problem solving. Studying this latter phenomenon in various problem solving tasks is the focus of our research. Despite previous pioneering work (Sloman 1971; Funt 1980; Forbus, Nielsen, & Faltings 1987), only recently has the cognitive capability for common sense reasoning using diagrams and imagery begun to receive renewed attention in artificial intelligence (Narayanan 1992). The computer modeling of visual reasoning has been shown to be of benefit in a variety of domains and applications, e.g., automating expert reasoning using phase diagrams (Yip 1991), geometry theorem proving (McDougal & Hammond 1993), and analysis of load-bearing structures (Tessler, Iwasaki & Law 1993). Current research in this area is still exploratory in nature. However, its maturity promises many applications in intelligent multimodal interfaces, knowledge-based graphics, and instructional systems for imparting visualization skills in problem solving.

Acknowledgments. We thank T. Nishida for providing software for part of the user interface, Y. Iwasaki for many useful discussions, and Knowledge Systems Laboratory, Stanford University, for facilitating the preparation of this paper.

References

Brand, M., Birnbaum, L., and Cooper, P. (1993). Sensible scenes: visual understanding of complex structures through causal analysis. *Proc. 11th NCAI*, 588-593.

Ericsson, K. A. and Simon, H. A. (1983). *Protocol Analysis: Verbal Reports as Data*, MIT Press, Cambridge, MA.

Forbus, K. D., Nielsen, P., and Faltings, B. (1987). Qualitative kinematics: a framework. *Proc. 10th IJCAI*, 430-436.

Funt, B. V. (1980). Problem-solving with diagrammatic representations. *Artificial Intelligence*, 13: 201-230.

Glasgow, J. and Papadias, D. (1992). Computational Imagery. *Cognitive Science*, 16(3): 355-394.

Hegarty, M. (1992). Mental animation: inferring motion from static displays of mechanical systems. *JEP: Learning, Memory, and Cognition*, 18(5): 1084-1102.

McDougal, T. F. and Hammond, K. J. (1993). Representing and using procedural knowledge to build geometry proofs. *Proc. 11th NCAI*.

Narayanan, N. H., (Ed.). (1992). *Working Notes of the AAAI Spring Symposium on Reasoning with Diagrammatic Representations*.

Narayanan, N. H., Suwa, M., and Motoda, H. (1993). Behavior hypothesis from schematic diagrams: a hybrid approach. *Proc. IJCAI-93 Hybrid Representation and Reasoning Workshop*, 50-61.

Narayanan, N. H., Suwa, M., and Motoda, H. (1994). A study of diagrammatic reasoning from verbal and gestural data. *Proc. 16th Ann. Conf. of the Cognitive Science Society*, to appear.

Sloman, A. (1971). Interactions between philosophy and AI: the role of intuition and non-logical reasoning in intelligence. *Artificial Intelligence*, (2): 209-225.

Tessler, S., Iwasaki, Y., and Law, K. (1993). Qualitative structural analysis using diagrammatic reasoning. *Proc. Qualitative Reasoning Workshop*.

Yip, K. M. (1991). Understanding complex dynamics by visual and symbolic reasoning. *Artificial Intelligence*, 51: 179-221.

A Qualitative Physics Compiler

Adam Farquhar*
Knowledge Systems Laboratory
701 Welch Road, Bldg. C
Palo Alto, CA 94303
Adam_Farquhar@ksl.stanford.edu

Abstract

Predicting the behavior of physical systems is essential to both common sense and engineering tasks. It is made especially challenging by the lack of complete precise knowledge of the phenomena in the domain and the system being modelled. We present an implemented approach to automatically building and simulating qualitative models of physical systems. Imprecise knowledge of phenomena is expressed by qualitative representations of monotonic functions and variable values. Incomplete knowledge about the system is either inferred or alternative complete descriptions that will affect behavior are explored. The architecture and algorithms used support both effective implementation and formal analysis. The expressiveness of the modelling language and strength of the resulting predictions are demonstrated by substantial applications to complex systems.

Introduction

Predicting and reasoning about the behavior of physical systems is a difficult and important task that is as essential to everyday commonsense reasoning as it is to complex engineering tasks such as design, monitoring, control, or diagnosis.

This paper describes QPC (a Qualitative Physics Compiler), an implemented approach to reasoning about physical systems that builds on the expressiveness of Qualitative Process Theory (Forbus 1984) and the mathematical rigor of the QSIM qualitative simulation algorithm (Kuipers 1986). The QPC work was first reported in (Crawford, Farquhar, & Kuipers 1990) and is more fully developed in (Farquhar 1993).

---

*This work has taken place in the Qualitative Reasoning Group at the Artificial Intelligence Laboratory, The University of Texas at Austin and at the Stanford University Knowledge Systems Laboratory. Research of the Qualitative Reasoning Group is supported in part by NSF grants IRI-8904454, IRI-9017047, and IRI-9216584, and by NASA contracts NCC 2-760 and NAG 9-665. Research at KSL is sponsored by the Advanced Research Projects Agency, ARPA Order 8607, monitored by NASA Ames Research Center under grant NAG 2-581; and by NASA Ames Research Center under grant NCC 2-537.

The critical intuition is that reasoning about a physical system can and should be decomposed into a *model building* task which builds a model to describe the system, and a *simulation* task which uses the model to generate a description of the possible behaviors of the system. QPC's architecture, algorithms, and semantics follow from this decomposition.

Experience has shown that the QPC modeling language is expressive and the algorithms are powerful enough to provide useful behavioral predictions for a wide variety of systems. Catino and Ungar have constructed a substantial chemical engineering domain theory and use QPC to build models of a nitric acid processing plant with several hundred variables and over a hundred model fragments (Catino 1993; Catino & Ungar 1994). Rickel has solved problems of more moderate size in the domain of plant physiology (Rickel & Porter 1994). Rajagopalan has constructed models for geometric and spatial reasoning (Rajagopalan 1994). Brajnik has constructed models of lakes, damns, and turbines in the domain of water supply control (Farquhar & Brajnik 1994).

Modeling Language

The input to QPC is a *domain theory* and *scenario* specified in the QPC modeling language. A *domain theory* consists of a set of quantified definitions, called *model fragments*, each of which describes some aspect of the domain, such as physical laws (e.g. mass conservation), processes (e.g. liquid flows), or entities (e.g. containers). The specific system or situation being modeled is partially described by the *scenario* definition, which lists a set of entities that are of interest, some of their initial conditions, relations that hold throughout the scenario, and boundary conditions. See figure 1 for a sample model fragment and scenario definition.

The QPC modelling language is a descendent of the expressive language introduced by Forbus for his Qualitative Process theory (Forbus 1984). A model fragment definition specifies a set of typed participants, structural, operating conditions, and consequences. An instance of the fragment exists if participants of the appropriate types can be found that satisfy the structural relations. The instance is *active* roughly when the operation conditions (inequalities over variables) are true. While the instance is active, its consequences hold. These can be (differential) equations, inequalities, or arbitrary logical relations. There are also language constructs for defining relations, axioms, quantities, and the conditions under which entities must exist. The full language is documented in (Farquhar 1993).

Each language form is defined by a set of axiom schema; a domain theory is defined by a set of axioms. There are several syntactic restrictions on the language constructs and the axiom schema. In particular, the resulting axioms can all be written as implications whose antecedents and consequents are conjunctions of literals. Negation is only applied to atomic formulae and embedded disjunction is not allowed. Existential quantification does not appear in the user language and is limited in the resulting axioms to a single variable in the consequent of an implication. Importantly, *time* is implicit in the user language. This ensures that the present cannot change the past and invalidate itself. The temporal scope of relations is enforced by the axiom schema (Farquhar 1993).

The language allows for systems to be described by continuous real-valued variables and time-dependent logical relations. A time-dependent relation is one whose truth value may change over time (e.g. `(on-table block1)`). The language restricts the interaction between time-dependent relations and quantities. Implications relating a time-dependent relation and a quantity can only be expressed with a `defmodelfragment` form, whereas implications among time-dependent relations alone may appear in other forms. This allows possible changes in the equations that describe the system to be isolated. A change in the equations can only result from a change in the activity of a model fragment instance. This property is essential to support QPC's hybrid architecture. The simulator is only able to predict changes in variable values and monitor relations between quantities. The above restriction ensures that this is sufficient to detect changes in the equations.

Architecture and Algorithm

The critical insight enabling QPC to model and simulate complex systems is the separation of the model building task from the simulation task. The architecture of QPC directly reflects this decomposition. The model building task is facilitated by a general purpose knowledge representation system. QPC currently uses the Algernon representation system (Crawford & Kuipers 1991). The simulation task is currently handled by the QSIM qualitative simulation system (Kuipers 1986; Farquhar *et al.* 1991).

This approach has several practical and theoretical advantages. The proof of correctness is simplified. QSIM has already proven to be sound (Kuipers 1986), so the proof reduces to showing that the correct models are generated. The sources of incompleteness can be readily identified, localized, and methods to reduce them determined. The output of QPC can be directly understood in terms of ordinary differential equations and their solutions. QPC exploits advances in simulation techniques as soon as they are incorporated into the simulator. The data structures and algorithms best suited to efficient computation in the model building and simulation tasks are quite different; a hybrid architecture

reflects this difference and simplifies implementation.

We define the operation of the model building component of QPC in terms of databases. A *database* is a set of logical facts and axioms. A database is *complete* if every model fragment instance (explicit member of the set of model fragments) in the database is known to be active or inactive.

The input to the model building component is a database that is the union of the axioms induced by a domain theory and scenario description. It uses this to infer the complete set of model fragment instances that apply during the time covered by the database (this may require a case analysis that produces a disjunction of complete databases from an incomplete one). A database with a compete set of model fragment instances defines an initial value problem comprising a set of equations, initial, and boundary conditions. This initial value problem is provided to the simulator to solve. The initial value problem is defined using QSIM's representation of qualitative differential equations (QDEs). If any of the predicted behaviors cross the boundary conditions, the process is repeated: a new database is constructed to describe the system as it crosses the boundaries the current model.

The output of QPC is a rooted graph that describes the possible behaviors of the situation. A node in the graph is either a database Δ or a qualitative state S with its associated QDE. The root of the graph is the database formed from union of the axioms induced by the domain theory and scenario definition. An edge in the graph may be one of the following:

1. $\langle \Delta_1, \Delta_2 \rangle$ *refinement*
Δ_1 is an incomplete description of a situation. Δ_2 is a more complete description that results from adding some ground conditions to Δ_1.

2. $\langle \Delta, S \rangle$ *initial state*
Δ is a complete description of a situation. The qualitative state S is an initial state that follows from Δ.

3. $\langle S_1, S_2 \rangle$ *state successor*
S_2 is a QSIM state successor of S_1. These edges represent the temporal evolution of the situation.

4. $\langle S, \Delta \rangle$ *transition*
S is a transition state that is crossing the boundary of the applicability of its QDE. Δ is a description of the situation at the same time as S, after the transition.

Each path from the root to a leaf of the graph describes a possible temporal evolution of the physical situation being modeled: a sequence of models, and within each model, a sequence of qualitative states. A path from the root of the graph to a final state describes a complete qualitative behavior of the scenario.

Table 1 provides a pseudo-code description of the QPC algorithm. The main steps are:

Refine the incomplete description Δ into a set of complete descriptions Δ_r of the same situation. The refinement operation returns a set containing all complete databases that are consistent with Δ. An edge linking Δ to each of its refinements is added to the graph.

```
define QPC(Δ)
   forall Δ_r in refinements(Δ)
      collect edge(Δ, Δ_r)
      B = QSIM (qde(Δ_r), initial_values(Δ_r))
      forall b in B
         collect edge(Δ_r, initial_state(b))
         if transition(final_state(b))
         then
            Δ_t = entities(Δ_r) ∪ conditions(final_state(b)) ∪ DT
            collect edge(final_state(b), Δ_t)
            QPC(Δ_t)
```

Table 1: Pseudo-code description of the QPC algorithm.

A complete database Δ_r defines a unique QDE and set of initial conditions which are provided to QSIM. QSIM produces a set B including all possible behaviors consistent with the QDE and initial conditions.

Each behavior b in B is then processed. An edge from Δ_r to the initial state of b is added to the graph. The first state is already linked to its successor states by QSIM, so no state to state edges need be explicitly added. If the final state of b is a transition state, then a new description of the situation after the transition must be constructed. The transition database Δ_t is constructed from the entities of Δ_r, the quantity conditions derived from the transition state, and the domain theory. An edge from the final state of b to Δ_t is added to the graph.

QPC recurses on the transition database Δ_t to construct all possible behaviors of the situation following the transition.

Refinement constructs the set of all complete databases consistent with and rooted in an initial database Δ. This is accomplished by creating a set of databases in which the ambiguous instances in Δ are no longer ambiguous. These databases are referred to as the children of Δ. A child Δ_c of Δ is formed by adding conditions (ground in Δ) so that every ambiguous instance i in Δ can be proven to be either *active* or *inactive* in Δ_c. The children of Δ contain all possible partitions of the ambiguous instances in Δ into active and inactive. Note that a child need not be complete, since new entities may be introduced by the new active instances, resulting in new (ambiguous) instances. Thus, each child must be recursively refined.

In the worst case, computing the set of refinements is exponential in the number of ambiguous instances. This occurs when the ambiguous conditions are completely independent. The actual cost tends to be considerably lower, because the ambiguous conditions tend to be interdependent and often depend on certain key pieces of unknown information. Sets of conditions may be inconsistent, thus eliminating some children from further consideration.

Computing the QDE, initial, and boundary conditions from a complete database is fairly straightforward. The equations and initial conditions are simply collected from the database. The boundary conditions are the union of the operating conditions of the inactive instances (if one becomes true, then there may be new consequences) and

the negated operating conditions of the active instances (if one becomes false then an instance becomes inactive, changing the equations). As we describe below, some work is necessary to represent inequalities in the equations and boundary conditions, and algebraic inference is performed to strengthen the QDE.

Each path from a complete database to a transition state describes a segment of behavior over a *closed temporal interval* of non-zero duration. Consequently, each QDE holds over a closed temporal interval. There are several reasons for this. There is intuitively pleasing that "physical processes" start and stop at a well-defined point in time. Most importantly, it allows standard analysis to be used uniformly to understand QPC's predictions. Practically, many simulators, including QSIM, require an initial time point and stop at a final time point. This approach is very simple — there is only one type of temporal interval that must be considered. The alternatives are to allow arbitrary partitions of the time line or to restrict operating conditions to be (non-)strict relations (e.g. partition the time-line into intervals closed on the left and open on the right by using only non-strict relations). Because all QPC variables are continuous, the cost is minimal.

The consequence is that the activity of every model fragment instance is pushed to its boundaries. Thus, if an instance is active when $x > 0$, QPC considers it to be active when $x = 0$ *and is increasing*. Note that there is a distinction between strict and non-strict relations. The operating condition $x \geq 0$ holds even if x remains 0.

Soundness

QPC is sound if every possible behavior of the system being modeled is covered by one of QPC's predictions. Time is dense and modeled by the reals. For convenience, we take 0 to be the starting time for all scenarios. We define a *run*, r, to be an assignment of real values to variables for all $t > 0$, that satisfies certain restrictions: For some prefix of the run, a variable may have the value *undefined*. Each variable in the run is continuous in magnitude starting from the first time that it is not undefined. A variable must have a finite number of critical points over any finite temporal interval.

Each possible precise behavior of a scenario is a run. A run satisfies a qualitative behavior if it can be partitioned into a sequence of alternating points and closed intervals matching the states in the qualitative behavior, such that the real values assigned to variables in the run match the qualitative values in the state. A run satisfies the output of QPC if it satisfies a complete qualitative behavior of the scenario.

QPC is sound if, given axiom sets S and D induced by the scenario and domain theory,

$$\forall r \ [r \models S \cup D] \ \Rightarrow \ [r \models QPC(S \cup D)]$$

That is, if a run r satisfies the scenario and domain theory, then r must also satisfy the output of QPC given the same scenario and domain theory. The proof of soundness is given in (Farquhar 1993). It is by induction on the path from the root to a terminal state in the graph. We show that the QPC algorithm constructs the unique initial value problem that must follow from the initial complete database. The QSIM soundness proof can then be invoked to show that an initial prefix of the run will satisfy one of the predicted behaviors. The inductive step is similar.

The proof requires the syntactic restrictions in the QPC modeling language and the induced axioms as well as the assumption that the entities can be *stratified* such that the proof of existence of each entity is rooted in those initially specified in the scenario.

Incompleteness

Incompleteness arises in two very different ways in QPC. First, QPC allows the knowledge represented in both the domain theory and scenario specification to be incomplete. This is an important benefit of QPC and related qualitative modeling and simulation methods. Second, QPC's inference methods and, consequently, predictions are incomplete. The hybrid QPC architecture enables the sources of incomplete inference to be readily identified.

Representing Incomplete Knowledge

QPC enables the domain theory author to specify partial constraints on the relations between variables via language constructs such as monotonic function constraints (M+) and qualitative proportionalities (Q+), also known as influences. QPC also allows structural relationships to be incompletely axiomatized. The refinement procedure will ensure that the intended model is constructed even in this case.

The scenario specification may be incomplete in several ways. The initial conditions or relations may be incomplete, in which case the refinement operation will ensure that the intended model is constructed. The entities may also be incomplete, however, if the domain theory does not contain sufficient entity definitions to entail the existence of the remaining entities, then there is little that QPC can do.

Incomplete Inference

The syntactic restrictions on the QPC language ensure that it can be effectively implemented by a simple forward application of modus ponens (the proofs of correctness do not even require full transitive closure under modus ponens). This is guaranteed because there is no embedded disjunction or quantification, existential quantification appears only on the right hand side of implications, and the existential quantifications can be stratified. In fact, if it were not for order relations between quantities, closure under modus ponens would be complete for QPC. The introduction of order relations, however, destroys this property. General reasoning about order relations over functions is, unfortunately, undecidable. Nonetheless, this means that *the sole source of incompleteness in QPC's model building results from inference about order relations*.

This is an important observation. It means that we can focus our attention on strengthening QPC's ability to do inference over order relations. In fitting with QPC's hybrid architecture, the natural approach is to use a special purpose inequality reasoner such as Bounder (Sacks 1987), the

quantity lattice (Simmons 1986), or even QSIM, as is done by DME (Low & Iwasaki 1992).

QSIM and other qualitative simulation algorithms are incomplete. Some of this is inherent in the accurate, but imprecise, representation (Struß 1990). But qualitative simulators are also incomplete due to their reliance on local constraint satisfaction and continuity. Recent work has substantially improved the strength of predictions by exploiting non-local constraints and more sophisticated mathematics (Lee & Kuipers 1993). QPC effortlessly takes advantage of such advances in qualitative simulation.

Information can also be lost at transitions, resulting in incompleteness. For instance, QPC currently requires variables to be everywhere continuous in magnitude. If a variable is continuous in its first or higher derivatives, some information is lost. QPC could be easily extended to allow for higher order continuities to be expressed.

QSIM and the QDE Representation

The QDE representation provides only limited support for inequalities, which are extremely common in QPC domain theories. Non-strict inequalities between variables and landmarks can be easily represented by constraining the quantity space of the variable. Strict inequalities are handled by using QSIM filters to infer that a state is inconsistent when a variable reaches its limiting values. Inequalities between variables are handled by introducing a new variable to represent their difference, and transforming the original relation to one between the difference variable and zero.

QSIM boundary conditions are relations between variables and landmarks, whereas QPC allows inequalities between variables. The difference variable technique is used here as well.

QPC pushes the activity of all model fragments to a closed interval. As a consequence, a model may start with a variable on a boundary and require that it move off of the boundary into the active region immediately. This is ensured by providing a QSIM filter that applies to the states that describe the initial open interval.

QSIM does only minimal algebraic inference. For example, given a QDE containing the constraints (add x y z) and (add x y w), QSIM does not require z and w to be equal. When QDEs are constructed by hand, this sort of incomplete inference is rarely problematic. When the QDEs are automatically generated, however, it can be a substantial hindrance. QPC deals with this problem by performing *algebraic inference* on each QDE to add implicit constraints (such as (equal z w)) and eliminate redundant constraints (such as the second add after the equal constraint has been included). This step has turned out to be essential in getting QSIM to solve the large sets of equations automatically generated by QPC.

The version of QSIM used by QPC is extended to generate an *attainable envisionment*, which is a rooted graph of states, rather than the tree QSIM has traditionally used. By turning off QSIM's automatic landmark generation facilities, the attainable envisionment is guaranteed to be finite (since each variable has a finite domain of qualitative values).

The complete (perhaps infinite) set of possible behaviors is compactly represented by all paths starting in an initial state. Note that the QPC algorithm only requires the set of final *transition* states to be identified; the behavior paths need not be identified by QPC at all. Thus, the attainable envisionment is exactly the right level of description for QPC.

Examples and Applications

This section discusses a simple example and two more substantial applications of QPC. The example allows QPC to be compared to GIZMO (Forbus 1984) and QPE (Forbus 1990) and shows the advantage of QPC's hybrid architecture. In the botany application, QPC produces answers to questions that might arise in a tutoring application. The chemical engineering application shows that QPC is capable of modeling large complex systems with hundreds of variables from numerous automatically generated scenarios.

Heat Transfer

Figure 1 describes a simple heat transfer problem that appeared in (Forbus 1984) and was also used to compare GIZMO with QPE in (Forbus 1990). This is a good benchmark problem for qualitative simulators because the underconstrained domain theory requires a surprisingly large number of states and behaviors, even though there is only one final state – thermal equilibrium.

Note that `heat-flow` is not conditioned on a non-zero temperature difference, as is typical in QP theory definitions. This reflects an important philosophical difference. QPC model fragment definitions reflect the underlying equations, not necessarily cognitively useful descriptions. The QP theory descriptions can be extracted from the QPC descriptions.

QPC solves the heat transfer problem with initial conditions in about a minute. There are 327 unique states and 691 branches in the behavior tree. Without initial conditions, the problem takes about 30 minutes to identify 396 unique states. Importantly, in both cases there is only one final state, in which the system is in thermal equilibrium. Note that the actual number of states generated in the two cases is not too different. This is because the initial conditions to not provide strong constraints on the possible states of the system. The difference in runtime is due entirely to simulation (the QDEs are identical for both scenarios). The constraint satisfaction algorithm currently employed by QSIM is not optimized for problems that require many initial states to be generated.

We may contrast these results with those reported in (Forbus 1990). The runtime for GIZMO was 60 times longer than QPC. Even allowing a factor of 10 in machine speeds, QPC would still be 6 times faster at generating an attainable envisionment. Although QPE is designed for performing total envisionments (and is unable to generate an attainable one), Forbus reported that this problem "had run for hours and generated over 5200 situations before the machine was halted manually"(Forbus 1990, page 233).

Table 2: Partial list of botany questions that have been solved by QPC.

QPC's hybrid architecture and use of a special purpose simulation engine is clearly beneficial in this benchmark problem.

Botany

In the context of the Botany Knowledge Base project at the University of Texas (Porter *et al.* 1988), Rickel has constructed a QPC domain theory for plant physiology (Rickel & Porter 1994). The textbook knowledge encoded in the Botany Knowledge Base is largely qualitative because quantitative details vary greatly among different plants and often are not known.

The domain theory covers the uptake, transport, and loss of water in the plant; the plant's mechanisms for dealing with water stress (synthesis, consumption and transport of the ABA hormone, and movement of potassium ions and water into and out of guard cells that regulate water loss); and the production (via photosynthesis), consumption (via respiration), and transport (via the phloem) of carbohydrate in the plant. The descriptions of these processes are relatively simple, but they are fairly standard and reasonable high-level descriptions, and they are based both on textbook knowledge and consultations with domain experts.

Over a dozen questions have been formulated and solved using QPC. Each corresponds to a scenario; the answer is determined by examining the resulting behavior predictions. Table 2 summarizes several of the running examples. For each of them, QPC predicts a single behavior which matches the correct answer. For example, in the first question, the variable representing the opening of the stomates increases from its initial value until a new equilibrium is reached. It is worth noting that the techniques originally employed by QSIM actually give rise to infinite sets of possible behaviors. It is only since the development of techniques to eliminate unnecessary distinctions (Clancy & Kuipers 1993), that they have become tractable. This shows a key advantage of QPC's architecture: advances in simulation techniques are directly exploited.

Chemical Engineering

Catino and Ungar have been using QPC to support hazard identification in chemical processing plants (Catino 1993; Catino & Ungar 1994). QPC is an appropriate analysis

```
(defScenario heat-transfer                 (defRelation connected (objects objects))
   :entities ((c :type objects)            (defQuantity temp (objects))
             (x :type objects)             (defQuantity heat (objects))
             (y :type objects)             (defModelFragment physob
             (z :type objects))               :participants ((a :type objects))
   :relations ((connected c x)              :consequences ((> (temp a) zero)
              (connected c y)                              (q+0 (temp a) (heat a))))
              (connected c z))            (defModelFragment heat-flow
   :initial-conditions                       :participants ((a :type objects)
   ((> (temp c) (temp x))                                  (b :type objects))
    (> (temp c) (temp y))                   :structural-conditions ((connected a b))
    (> (temp c) (temp z)))))                :quantities (delta-t flow-rate)
                                            :consequences
                                            ((add (temp b) (delta-t heat-flow) (temp a))
                                             (Q+0 (flow-rate heat-flow) (delta-t heat-flow))
                                             (I- (heat a) (delta-t heat-flow))
                                             (I+ (heat b) (delta-t heat-flow)))))
```

Figure 1: A simple heat transfer problem. In the `heat-transfer` scenario, there are three objects x, y, and z in thermal contact with a hotter center object c.

tool for this task and domain for several reasons. The phenomenon based compositional approach naturally describes chemical processes, which are not component-oriented, but occur whenever the requisite substances are present and conditions hold. The hazard identification task requires explicitly examining all possible outcomes to determine if undesirable ones may occur. In addition to unexpected reactions, this may also include unexpected changes in the topology of the plant (e.g. a valve incorrectly opened, or a leak in a heat exchanger). Although approximate quantitative information is available for describing the normal operation of a chemical plant, hazard identification must consider what will occur when such constraints are violated. QPC provides this ability.

The domain theory covers mass flow, heat flow, chemical reaction, vaporization, and liquid-vapor equilibrium. It is capable of modeling controllers, phases consisting of any number of chemical species, thermal and mass fraction effects of mass flow, and moving landmark values as in a changing dew point (Catino 1993).

Catino and Ungar have conducted a substantial hazard identification case study of nitric acid production plant (Catino & Ungar 1994). Their system begins with a scenario describing the design case (normal operation) of the plant and then systematically perturbs this specification to generate fault scenarios. The fault scenarios are simulated by QPC and checked for the presence of hazards. Over twenty scenarios were generated and checked for the nitric acid plant. These models are the largest ones that have currently been solved by QPC. The scenario definition for the design case specifies 41 initial entities in addition to various landmarks, initial conditions, and modeling assumptions. The model built by QPC consists of 81 active model fragments, 317 variables, and 387 constraints. It currently takes about an hour and a half to build and solve and results in a single steady state that describes how the plant operates when it is functioning as designed (It is a full dynamic model whose solution is a steady state in that the derivatives of the state variables happen to be zero. Under perturbed initial conditions, more interesting dynamic behavior results).

Related Work

QPC's architecture, algorithms, and soundness guarantee distinguish it from other qualitative modeling systems.

Both GIZMO (Forbus 1984) and QPE (Forbus 1990) compose qualitative models from a scenario description and a domain theory of model fragments, but they construct the complete set of model fragment instances, variables, inequalities, and so on, that *might ever appear in a total envisionment* of the scenario. After constructing this *scenario elaboration*, GIZMO constructs a set of initial situations, which includes a status for every entity, instance, quantity condition, and influenced variable in the elaboration, it uses *limit analysis* to construct possible successors. QPE constructs a total envisionment; It is not able to make use of any initial conditions.

QPC does not elaborate the scenario. QPC fully exploits the initial conditions and the preconditions of model fragment and entity definitions. The sets of instances and entities are incrementally constructed. QPC decomposes the construction of initial situations into two phases. Refinement effectively assigns a status to the instances; QSIM assigns values to the variables. Both of these operations are very focused, and apply only to the instances and variables that are relevant to the situation.

The device modeling environment, DME (Low & Iwasaki 1992), is the system closest to QPC. In its qualitative prediction mode it also uses QSIM to generate state successors, but does not make full use of QSIM. In particular, only the direct successors of a state are generated and the results asserted immediately back into the knowledge base. This makes prediction much more expensive and means that qualitative simulation techniques such as chatter elimination or attainable envisionment cannot be readily used. DME typically expects more interaction from the user than QPC, which is fully automatic. This is in keeping with DME's goal as a modeling *environment*. DME also provides sophisticated explanation facilities (Gautier & Gruber 1993).

Conclusion

QPC provides an expressive language and powerful techniques for reasoning about physical systems without a precise domain theory or a complete specification of the system. QPC's hybrid architecture exploits independent advances in model building and qualitative simulation techniques and supports formal analysis. The incremental algorithm takes advantage of knowledge about a system's initial conditions when available.

This claim is supported by substantial applications. In particular, the nitric acid production plant application (Catino & Ungar 1994) shows that QPC can model and simulate complex systems requiring hundreds of variables and constraints from automatically generated scenario descriptions.

Acknowledgements

I would like to thank Ben Kuipers for providing the initial motivation to work on this problem; Jimi Crawford for taking the first steps with me; and especially Giorgio Brajnik, Cathy Catino, Raman Rajagopalan, and Jeff Rickel, who were the patient first users of QPC. Their feedback provided a strong impetus for QPC and helped to ensure that it is capable of solving diverse problems.

References

Catino, C., and Ungar, L. 1994. A model-based approach to automated hazard identification of chemical plants. Submitted to AIChE Journal.

Catino, C. 1993. *Automated Modeling of Chemical Plants with Application to Hazard and Operability Studies*. Ph.D. Dissertation, Department of Chemical Engeneering, University of Pennsylvania, Philadelphia, PA.

Clancy, D. J., and Kuipers, B. J. 1993. Behavior abstraction for tractable simulation. In *Proceedings of the Seventh International Workshop on Qualitative Reasoning about Physical Systems*.

Crawford, J. M., and Kuipers, B. J. 1991. ALL: formalizing acess-limited reasoning. In Sowa, J., ed., *Principles of Semantic Networks*. San Mateo, CA: Morgan Kaufman. 299–330.

Crawford, J.; Farquhar, A.; and Kuipers, B. 1990. QPC: A compiler from physical models into qualitative differential equations. In *Proceedings of the Eighth National Conference on Artificial Intelligence*.

Farquhar, A., and Brajnik, G. 1994. A semi-quantitiative physics compiler. In *Proceedings of the Eighth International Workshop on Qualitative Reasoning*.

Farquhar, A.; Kuipers, B.; Rickel, J.; Throop, D.; and The Qualitative Reasoning Group. 1991. QSIM: The program and its use. Technical Report AI90–123, Artificial Intelligence Laboratory, University of Texas at Austin, Austin, Texas 78712.

Farquhar, A. 1993. *Automated Modeling of Physical Systems in the Presence of Incomplete Knowledge*. Ph.D. Dissertation, The University of Texas at Austin. Available as technical report UT-AI-93-207.

Forbus, K. 1984. *Qualitative Process Theory*. Ph.D. Dissertation, MIT AI Lab, Cambridge, MA.

Forbus, K. 1990. The qualitative process engine. In Weld, D., and de Kleer, J., eds., *Readings in Qualitative Reasoning about Physical Systems*. Los Altos, CA: Morgan Kaufman.

Gautier, P. O., and Gruber, T. R. 1993. Generating explanations of device behavior using compositional modeling and causal ordering. In *Proceedings of the Eleventh National Conference on Artificial Intelligence*. AAAI Press/The MIT Press.

Kuipers, B. 1986. Qualitative simulation. *Artificial Intelligence* 29:289–338.

Lee, W. W., and Kuipers, B. 1993. A qualitative method to construct phase portraits. In *Proceedings of the Eleventh National Conference on Artificial Intelligence*.

Low, C. M., and Iwasaki, Y. 1992. Device modelling environment: an interactive environment for modelling device behavior. *Intelligent Systems Engineering* 1(2):115–145.

Porter, B.; Lester, J.; Murray, K.; Pittman, K.; Souther, A.; Acker, L.; and Jones, T. 1988. AI research in the context of a multifunctional knowledge base: The botany knowledge base project. Technical Report Technical Report AI88-88, Artificial Intelligence Laboratory, University of Texas at Austin, Austin, Texas 78712.

Rajagopalan, R. 1994. A model for integrated qualitative spatial and dynamic reasoning about physical systems. In *Proceedings of the Twelfth National Conference on Artificial Intelligence*.

Rickel, J., and Porter, B. 1994. Automated modeling for answering prediction questions: Selecting the time scale and system boundary. In *Proceedings of the Twelfth National Conference on Artificial Intelligence*.

Sacks, E. 1987. Hierarchical reasoning about inequalities. In *Proceedings of the Sixth National Conference on Artificial Intelligence*, 649–654. Los Altos, CA: Morgan Kaufmann.

Simmons, R. 1986. "Commonsense" arithmetic reasoning. In *Proceedings of the Fifth National Conference on Artificial Intelligence*, 118–124.

Struß, P. 1990. Problems of interval-based qualitative reasoning. In Weld, D., and de Kleer, J., eds., *Qualitative Reasoning about Physical Systems*. Morgan Kaufmann. 288–305.

Using qualitative physics to build articulate software for thermodynamics education

Kenneth D. Forbus
Qualitative Reasoning Group
The Institute for the Learning Sciences
Northwestern University
1890 Maple Avenue, Evanston, IL, 60201 USA
forbus@ils.nwu.edu

Peter B. Whalley
Department of Engineering Science
Oxford University
Parks Road, Oxford, OX13PJ, UK
whalley@vax.ox.ac.uk

Abstract

One of the original motivations for research in qualitative physics was the development of intelligent tutoring systems and learning environments for physical domains and complex systems. This paper demonstrates how a synergistic combination of qualitative physics and other AI techniques can be used to create an intelligent learning environment for students learning to analyze and design *thermodynamic cycles*. Pedagogically this problem is important because thermodynamic cycles express the key properties of systems which interconvert work and heat, such as power plants, propulsion systems, refrigerators, and heat pumps, and the study of thermodynamic cycles occupies a major portion of an engineering student's training in thermodynamics. This paper describes CyclePad, a fully implemented learning environment which captures a substantial fraction of a thermodynamics textbook's knowledge and is designed to scaffold students who are learning the principles of such cycles. We analyze the combination of ideas that made CyclePad possible, comment on some lessons learned about the utility of various techniques, and describe our plans for classroom experimentation.

1. Introduction

One of the central motivations for research into qualitative physics has been its potential for the construction of intelligent tutoring systems and learning environments. By providing computational accounts of human reasoning about the physical world, ranging from what the person on the street knows to the extensive expertise of scientists and engineers, qualitative physics should provide representation languages and reasoning techniques that can be applied to helping people make the transition from novice to expert reasoning about physical systems. Indeed, some of the earliest work in the field was directly aimed at instructional problems (e.g., [1 ,2]). Over the last decade there have been several important efforts aimed at using qualitative physics to help teach diagnosis, troubleshooting, and operation of complex physical systems (e.g., [3 ,4 ,5 ,6]), but little effort has been focused on using qualitative physics in classroom settings, to help undergraduates learn principles of a domain (a rare exception is [7]).

In this paper we describe a system, called CyclePad, that has been built to help engineering undergraduates appreciate and therefore learn important principles of thermodynamics. CyclePad provides a conceptual CAD environment where students can design and analyze power plants, refrigerators, and other thermodynamic cycles. It relies on a synergistic combination of existing AI techniques: compositional modeling to represent and reason with modeling assumptions, qualitative representations to express the intuitive knowledge of physics needed to detect impossible designs, truth-maintenance to provide the basis for explanations, and constraint reasoning and propagation to provide efficient mathematical reasoning. It incorporates a substantial fraction of the knowledge in a typical engineering thermodynamics textbook [8], and has been tested on over two dozen examples of problems involving steady-state, steady flow systems where numerical answers or single-parameter sensitivity analyses are required.

Section 2 describes the pedagogical problems that motivated the design of CyclePad, including a brief overview of what thermodynamic cycles are and how they work. Section 3 demonstrates CyclePad's operation from a user's perspective. How CyclePad works is the subject of Section 4, with Section 5 summarizing the lessons we have learned so far in building the system. Section 6 outlines our plans for future work.

2. The task: Teaching the design of thermodynamic cycles

A thermodynamic cycle is a system within which a working fluid (or fluids) undergoes a series of transformations in order to process energy. Every power plant and every engine is a thermodynamic cycle. Refrigerators and heat pumps are also examples of thermodynamic cycles. Thermodynamic cycles play much the same role for engineering thermodynamics as electronic circuits do for electrical engineering: A small library of parts (in this case, compressors, turbines, pumps, heat exchangers, and so forth) are combined into networks, thus potentially generating an unlimited set of designs for any given problem. (Practically, cycles range

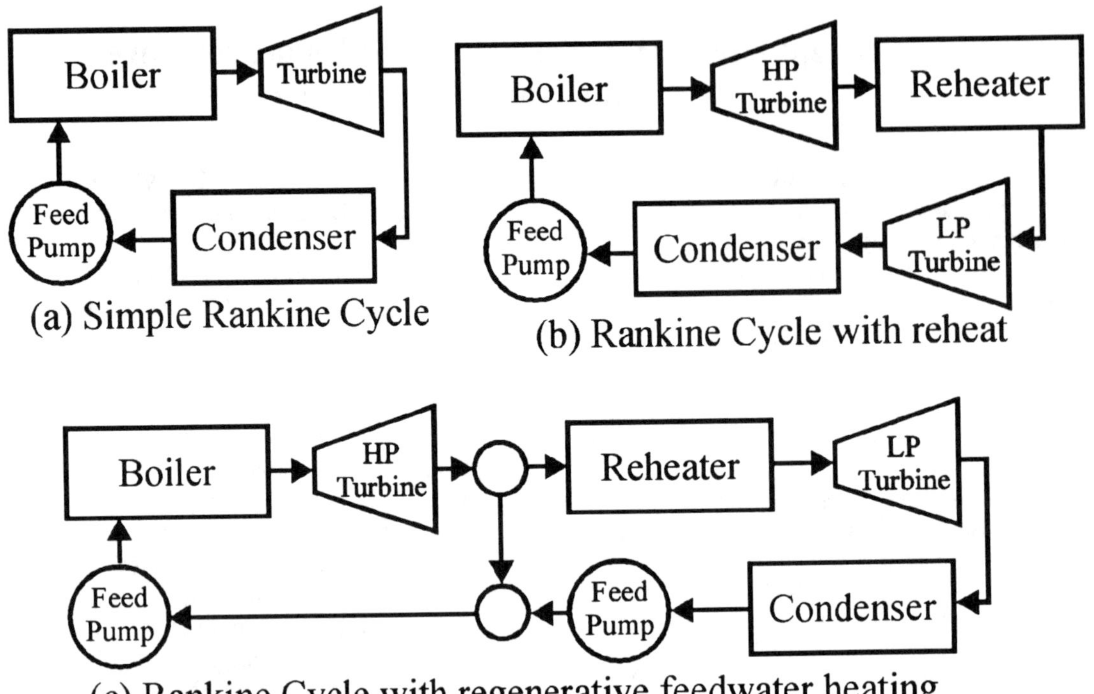

Figure 1: Sequence of conceptual designs for a power plant

from four components, in the simplest cases, to networks consisting of dozens of components.) One source of the complexity of cycle analysis stems from the complex nature of liquids and gases: Subtle interactions between their properties must be harnessed in order to improve designs. Cycle analysis answers questions such as the overall efficiency of a system, how much heat or work is consumed or produced, and what operating parameters (e.g., temperatures and pressures) are required of its components. An important activity in designing cycles (or indeed in many engineering design problems) is performing sensitivity analyses, to understand how choices for properties of the components and operating points of a cycle affect its global properties.

To illustrate, consider the sequence of power plant designs in Figure 1. Figure 1(a) shows a simple Rankine cycle, which pumps a working fluid (as liquid water) into a boiler to produce steam. In the turbine the high-pressure steam expands, thus performing work. Heat is extracted from the steam in the condenser so that the working fluid is again water. Finally, this water is pumped into the boiler (which requires the pump to absorb work) thus beginning the whole cycle again. These processes happen continuously in steady flow, in every part of the system. As it happens, this cycle is not very efficient. Raising the temperature of the boiler increases efficiency, but due to material properties of the components, there are upper bounds on operating

pressures and temperatures. Figure 1(b) shows a more efficient design, which uses a second turbine to extract more energy from the steam. The purpose of the reheater is to ensure that the steam does not become "wet", i.e., to begin to condense, because water droplets moving at high speed may damage a turbine. The extra energy required to reheat the steam is more than balanced by the additional work gained from the second turbine. One can do even better, however. Figure 1(c) shows a *regenerative feedwater cycle* where some of the steam from the outlet of the high-pressure turbine is routed back to the water feeding the boiler. The boiler then is adding heat to water that is starting at a higher temperature, which increases efficiency.

The analysis and design of thermodynamic cycles is the major task which drives engineering thermodynamics, aside from applications to chemistry. In thermodynamics education for engineers, cycle analysis and design generally appears towards the end of their first semester, or is even delayed to a second course, since understanding cycles requires a broad and deep understanding of the fundamentals of thermodynamics. Even the most introductory engineering thermodynamics textbooks tend to devote several chapters to cycle analysis, and in more advanced books the fraction devoted to cycles rises sharply. Indeed, some textbooks focus exclusively on cycle analysis (e.g., [9]). Aside from their intrinsic interest, the conceptual design of thermodynamic cycles provides a highly motivating context for students to learn fundamental principles more deeply than they would otherwise.

```
Q: Why is Nu_thermal(CYCLE) = 46%?
A: Nu_thermal(CYCLE) = 46%
   was found by using
   Nu_thermal(CYCLE) =
   net_work(CYCLE)/Q_in(CYCLE)
   on
    Q_in(CYCLE) = 4069.555 kW
    net_work(CYCLE) = 1872.219 kW

Q: Why is net_work(CYCLE) = 1872.219 kW?
A: net_work(CYCLE) = 1872.219 kW
   was found by using
   net_work(CYCLE) =
    work_in(CYCLE)+work_out(CYCLE)
   on
    work_in(CYCLE) = -15.68446 kW
    work_out(CYCLE) = 1887.903 kW

Q: Why is work_out(CYCLE) = 1887.903 kW?
A: work_out(CYCLE) = 1887.903 kW
   was found by using
   work_out(CYCLE) =
    work(TURBINE2)+work(TURBINE1)
   on
    work(TURBINE2) = 1372.131 kW
    work(TURBINE1) = 515.7723 kW

Q: Why does work_out(CYCLE) =
   work(TURBINE2)+work(TURBINE1) hold?
A: work_out(CYCLE) =
   work(TURBINE2)+work(TURBINE1)
   because we assumed:
    CYCLE is a thermodynamic cycle
    the work-flows-out of CYCLE consist
     of {work(TURBINE2),work(TURBINE1)}

Q: How has TURBINE1 works isentropicaly
   been used?
A: TURBINE1 works isentropically
   was used to derive
    TURBINE1 works adiabaticaly
    T(S3) = Tout_i(TURBINE1)
    s(S2) = s(S3)
```

Figure 2: A CyclePad hypertext dialog

A variety of problems arise when teaching students how to design and analyze thermodynamic cycles:[1] (1) Students tend to get bogged down in the mechanics of solving equations and carrying out routine calculations. This leads them to avoid exploring multiple design alternatives and to avoid carrying out trade-off studies (e.g., seeing how efficiency varies as a function of turbine efficiency versus how it varies as a function of

____

[1] These observations are based on the experience of the second author, who teaches engineering thermodynamics to undergraduates.

boiler outlet temperature). Yet without making such comparative studies, many opportunities for learning are lost. (2) Students often have trouble thinking about what modeling assumptions they need to make, such as assuming that a heater operates isobarically, leading them to get stuck when analyzing a design. (3) Students typically don't challenge their choices of parameters to see if their design is physically possible (e.g., that their design does not require a pump that produces rather than consumes work).

CyclePad was designed specifically to help students learn engineering thermodynamics by providing an intelligent learning environment that handles routine calculations, facilitates sensitivity analyses, helps students keep track of modeling assumptions, and detects physically impossible designs.

3. Overview of CyclePad

CyclePad can be viewed as a CAD system for the conceptual design of thermodynamic cycles, although it provides substantially more explanation capabilities than existing CAD software. CyclePad performs steady state analyses of steady-flow thermodynamic cycles. The restriction to steady-state is standard for this kind of analysis, since issues of how to start up and shut down the plant, or how easy it will be to monitor, maintain, or troubleshoot are issues of concern only after the basic design has been shown to be sound with respect to the goals for it (e.g., amount of work produced, efficiency, etc.). The restriction to steady-flow systems means that CyclePad cannot currently be used to analyze internal combustion engines, such as Otto or Diesel cycles. Although we plan to extend CyclePad to analyze such systems, steady flow cycles constitute the majority of the cycle-related material taught to engineering students. (For example, in [8] four out of five chapters on cycles concern steady flow cycles, in [9] it is 9 out of 10 chapters, and [10] focuses only on steady-flow systems.)

When a user starts up CyclePad, they find a menu of component types (e.g., turbine, compressor, pump, heater, cooler, heat exchanger, throttle, splitter, mixer) that can be used in their design. Components are connected together by *stuffs*, which represent the properties of the working fluid at that point in the system. (Stuffs serve the same role as nodes in electronic circuits.) The interface helps the user put together a design by highlighting what parts remain unconnected and providing simple critiques of the structure. Once the structural description of the cycle is finished (e.g., there are no dangling connections or stuffs), CyclePad allows the user to enter an analysis mode, where the particular properties of the system, such as the choice of working fluid, the values of specific numerical parameters, and modeling assumptions can be entered.

CyclePad accepts information incrementally, deriving from each user assumption as many consequences as it can. At any point questions can be asked, by clicking on a displayed item to obtain the set of questions (or commands) that make sense for it. In addition to numerical parameters and structural information, all modeling assumptions made about a component are displayed with it, and clicking on a component shows the modeling assumptions that can legitimately be made about that component, given what is known about the system so far. The questions and answers are displayed in English, and include links back into the explanation system, thus providing an incrementally generated hypertext. Figure 2 illustrates.

In addition to numerical assumptions, selecting a component provides commands for making or retracting modeling assumptions concerning that component. For example, clicking on a new turbine yields a menu of commands which offers the options of assuming the turbine is adiabatic or isentropic. Such modeling assumptions can introduce new constraints which may help carry an analysis further and new parameters (e.g., the efficiency of the turbine) that must be set.

When CyclePad uncovers a contradiction, it changes the interface to provide tools to resolve the problem by presenting the source of the contradiction (e.g., an impossible fact becoming believed, or conflicting values for a numerical parameter) and the set of assumptions underlying that contradiction. The hypertext dialog facilities can be used with this display to figure out which assumption(s) are dubious and change them accordingly.

We have tested CyclePad on over two dozen examples to date, ranging from simple ideal gas problems to the analysis of a combined gas turbine/steam Rankine cycle system. We believe that the current version of CyclePad can solve all of the problems in [8] concerning steady-state analyses of steady-flow cycles that require numerical answers or sensitivity analyses involving a single parameter. (We are continuing to test it on new examples, drawn from other textbooks as well.) CyclePad is very efficient. The combined gas turbine/steam Rankine cycle is the most complex system in [8], consisting of ten components. Good students take between 20 minutes and one hour to solve this problem. CyclePad does somewhat more work in analyzing this problem than a good student would, instantiating 219 equations involving 362 parameters, whereas a solution can be found using only 52 equations. However, CyclePad is still faster, taking just over two minutes on a workstation, versus just over ten minutes on a PowerBook 165c. We believe that the combination of the speed at which CyclePad carries out the routine calculations, its explanation facilities, and its consistency-checking facilities, will make it a valuable tool for students learning thermodynamics.

4. How CyclePad works

The overall structure of CyclePad was inspired in part by EL [11], an experimental system for DC and AC analysis of analog electronic circuits. EL was one of the first systems to use constraint propagation and dependency networks to organize its reasoning, and introduced the idea of dependency-directed backtracking. In this section we see how CyclePad exploits the advances made by the field since EL, by examining each of the AI ideas that contributes to CyclePad's operation, and the reasons for these particular design choices.

4.1 The role of compositional modeling

Compositional modeling [12, 13, 14] provides formal representation and reasoning techniques for formulating and reasoning about models. Knowledge about a domain is organized as collections of *model fragments*, organized by modeling assumptions and the ontology of the domain. Formulating a model for a specific problem consists of instantiating fragments from the domain theory, taking into account the kinds of tasks the model is to be used for.

As noted previously, steady-state analyses are required for the conceptual design of thermodynamic cycles. By restricting ourselves to steady-flow systems, it is also the case that the process structure (i.e., the collection of physical processes acting in each component) is fixed for all time. These restrictions allow us to organize the domain theory around the components which comprise a cycle and the properties of the working fluid at particular locations (i.e., the connections between components).

The modeling language used in CyclePad is similar to other implementations of compositional modeling. For example, Figure 3 shows part of CyclePad's model of a heater. CyclePad's knowledge base consists of 29 conceptual entities, 5 physical processes, 9 assumption classes, 98 equations, 40 pattern-directed rules and 41 background facts about thermodynamics.

Modeling assumptions are organized into *assumption classes* [15, 13]. Assumption classes are always associated with particular classes of components. The relevance of one assumption class can depend on the particular choices made for another assumption class. For example, it only makes sense to consider whether a compressor is isentropic if it is already known (or assumed) to be adiabatic.

```
(defEntity (Abstract-hx ?self ?in
                              ?out)
  (thermodynamic-stuff ?in)
  (thermodynamic-stuff ?out)
  (total-fluid-flow ?in ?out)
  (== (mass-flow ?in)
      (mass-flow ?out))
  (parameter (mass-flow ?self))
  (parameter (Q ?self))
  (parameter (spec-Q ?self))
  (heat-source (heat-source ?self))
  ((parts :cycle) has-member ?self)
 (?self part-names (in out))
 (?self IN ?in)(?in IN-OF ?self)
  ?self out ?out)(?out out-of
?self))

(defAssumptionClass
  ((abstract-Hx ?hx ?in ?out))
   (isobaric ?hx)
   (:not (isobaric ?hx)))

(defEntity (Heater ?self ?in ?out)
  (abstract-Hx ?self ?in ?out)
  (?self instance-of heater)
  (heat-flow (heat-source ?self)
             (heat-source ?self)
          ?in ?out)
  ((heat-flows-in :cycle)
    has-member (Q ?self))
  (> (Q ?self) 0.0))

(defEquation Hx-law
  ((Abstract-Hx ?hx ?in ?out))
  (:= (spec-h ?out)
          (+ (spec-h ?in)  (spec-Q
?hx))))

(defEquation spec-Q-definition
  ((Abstract-Hx ?hx ?in ?out))
  (:= (spec-Q ?hx)
      (/ (Q ?hx) (mass-flow ?hx)))))
```

Figure 3: A sample of CyclePad's knowledge base

4.2 The role of constraint reasoning and propagation

A design is not finished until numerical values have been chosen for its parameters. This is one reason why the overwhelming majority of thermodynamics textbook problems require numerical answers.[2] This fact, plus the relative simplicity of the equations involved, has meant that constraint propagation has sufficed for CyclePad.

---

[2] In a typical textbook we surveyed, 90% of the exercises required numerical answers.

In compiling CyclePad's knowledge base, equations are automatically converted into antecedent constraint rules that propose values for the nth variable in an equation whenever the other $n-1$ variables are known. Redundant equations are introduced when needed to overcome simultaneities. This automatic translation simplifies development. Equations in their original form are still represented in the knowledge base, however, and are used in two ways. First, they are part of the dependency structure for any results calculated via constraint propagation, for explanatory accuracy. Second, they can be inspected via the query system, so that students can find out what equations mention a specific parameter, and what equations might be used to calculate a desired value.

Property tables comprise a critical source of information for CyclePad. Property tables are woven into the constraint propagator via pattern-directed rules, operating under the same protocol as the rules compiled for equations. Due to the inherent loss of accuracy in interpolation, it is important, unlike equations, to *avoid* using tables in every logically possible fashion. Given a superheated vapour, for instance, knowing the pressure and temperature suffice to determine everything else (e.g., the specific enthalpy, specific entropy, etc.). If one redundantly computes from, say the specific enthalpy and specific entropy what the pressure and temperature will be, it is very likely that the newly estimated values will trigger a contradiction, given the accumulated inaccuracies in the interpolation process. Consequently, an important design choice in implementing tables is selecting which directions of access are likely to prove most productive for the kinds of analyses being made.

4.3 The role of qualitative physics

In CyclePad qualitative physics provides the medium for representing constraints on what is physically possible. Occurrences of physical processes inside components are explicitly represented. Each process occurrence includes ordinal constraints that are tested against numerical values by CyclePad's constraint propagation mechanism. Figure 4 shows a sample of what CyclePad knows about physical processes.

```
(defProcessEpisode (fluid-flow ?in ?out)
  (same-substance ?in ?out))

(defProcessEpisode (total-fluid-flow
                         ?in ?out)
  (fluid-flow ?in ?out)
  (== (mass-flow ?in) (mass-flow ?out)))

(defProcessEpisode
  (heat-flow ?src-start ?src-end
             ?dst-start ?dst-end)
  (> (T ?src-start) (T ?dst-start))
  (:not (< (T ?src-start) (T ?dst-end)))
  (:not (> (T ?dst-end) (T ?src-end))))

(defProcessEpisode (compression
                        ?in ?out ?worker)
  (> (P ?out) (P ?in))
  (< (spec-shaft-work ?worker) 0))

(defProcessEpisode (expansion
                        ?in ?out ?receiver)
  (< (P ?out) (P ?in))
  (> (spec-shaft-work ?receiver) 0))
```

Figure 4: Physical process knowledge in CyclePad

4.4 The role of truth maintenance

We used an LTMS [16] in CyclePad because it offered
the best tradeoff between inferential power and economy.
(In fact, CyclePad's inference engine is the LTRE system
from [17] We ruled out a JTMS because Horn clauses
are too clumsy for many of CyclePad's inferential needs,
including biconditionals (used in definitional
consequences of modeling assumptions, e.g., a
compressor is operating isentropically exactly when its
isentropic efficiency is 1.0) and TAXONOMY constraints
[18] (used in implementing assumption classes). The
ability of an ATMS to provide rapid switching between
very different contexts was not required: While frequent
additions and retractions of assumptions are made in
carrying out an analysis, typically these changes are a
small fraction of the working set of assumptions in force.

A critical role for the LTMS dependency network is as
an input for explanation generation. Explanations in
CyclePad are in terms of *structured explanations*, an
abstract layer between the reasoning system and the
interface that casts the consequences of the inference
system in terms relevant to the user. This includes
summarization (e.g., [19]), as in removing any reference
to implementation-dependent information such as the
constraint propagation mechanism from an argument. It
also includes making explicit implicit dependencies, such
as the variables whose values must be known before the
constraint rule implementing a particular equation will
fire when explaining what assumptions might lead to
more progress.

5. Lessons learned from developing CyclePad

CyclePad represents one of the first attempts to apply
ideas developed by the qualitative physics community to
a real application. While CyclePad has not yet been
fielded, we believe that we have already learned several
generally useful lessons in building it.

5.1 Compositional modeling scales up

Previous uses of compositional modeling have either
focused on large but purely qualitative domain theories,
or small quantitative theories. CyclePad demonstrates
that the ideas of compositional modeling can be used to
organize a substantial body of quantitative and
qualitative knowledge so that it can be used effectively.

Automatic model formulation, which typically has
been the focus of previous compositional modeling work,
is less relevant for this application. Nevertheless, the
mechanisms of assumption classes and logical
constraints between modeling assumptions provide a
valuable service in helping the user organize an analysis.
In fact, one of the skills being taught in using CyclePad
is model formulation. A boiler, for instance, is typically
approximated as a heater for the purposes of cycle
analysis. A flash chamber is modeled as a splitter whose
working fluid is saturated and with particular
assumptions about the dryness of the outlets. A multistage turbine is modeled as a sequence of turbines and
splitters. CyclePad helps users analyze models, so they
can figure out if their choice of idealization makes sense,
but currently CyclePad does not provide direct assistance
with formulating an idealized model from an informal
specification.

5.2 Regarding constraint reasoning

In this task numerical constraint propagation suffices.
There are however natural extensions of CyclePad's
analytic abilities for which algebraic manipulation would
be useful. For instance, some insights about how a cycle
works are best captured via equations.[3] We plan to
extend CyclePad to derive such equations on demand.
Our experience with the constraint rules compiler in
CyclePad, and other work on thermodynamics problem
solving [20], suggests that relatively simple algebraic
capabilities will suffice for this extension.

We draw two additional conclusions regarding
constraint manipulation. First, the commercial world
has developed many powerful symbolic algebra packages,
such as Mathematica, Maple, and Macsyma, which in
some cases are excellent off-the-shelf solutions to

---

[3] For example, figuring out that for a gas turbine cycle the
maximum specific work output is achieved when the pressure
ratio is the square root of its maximum possible value [8].

particular problems. However, we suspect that many educational applications will be like CyclePad: Simple algebraic facilities are all that is required, and thus the complexity (and expense) of integrating commercial symbolic algebra packages can be avoided. Second, we found that special-purpose constraint languages (e.g., [21]) were too restrictive for our purposes. Given the need to reason about modeling assumptions and the need to integrate information from property tables, it was much easier to implement a simple constraint propagator inside a pattern-directed inference system than it was to interface a special-purpose constraint manipulator. Aside from applications where scaling up to extremely large system descriptions (e.g., VLSI CAD) is a key requirement, it is hard to see any situation where using such languages makes sense.

5.3 Regarding qualitative physics

The combination of steady-state analysis, the restriction to steady-flow systems, and the use of idealized components dramatically simplified the representation of physical processes, since the occurrence of particular physical processes could simply be stipulated inside a component.

CyclePad's focus on quantitative analysis also means that the major inferential role for qualitative physics is ruling out physically impossible designs. We believe similar simplifications will hold in many other applications, since well-designed artifacts explicitly represent the important physical changes in terms of the kinds of components and connections that comprise a schematic, and many science and engineering educational applications involve quantitative knowledge heavily.

On the other hand, certain extensions to CyclePad's capabilities will require substantially more qualitative representations and reasoning. For instance, CyclePad currently does not try to explain how components work, nor does it provide assistance for understanding the physical rationale underlying design changes. To formalize such arguments will take richer qualitative representations, as well as the ability to reason with property diagrams (e.g. [22]). Fortunately, the automatic instantiation of physical process descriptions from a domain theory is an inexpensive and well-understood operation.

5.4 Regarding explanation generation and TMSs

The use of a structured explanation system as an abstraction layer between interface and reasoning system was extremely helpful in developing CyclePad, since it allowed us to optimize each independently. We also found, as suggested by [23], that sophisticated natural language generation techniques were inappropriate for this task. The ability to automatically generate hypertext in response to a user's questions obviates the need for discourse planning, and the fixed nature of the task means that issues such as selecting the appropriate level of detail in an explanation can be postponed. Hypertext allows users to select how much they want to know about a topic, and since the hypertext is only generated on demand, many navigation problems common in fixed hypertexts are avoided.

ATMS technology [24] has been widely used in qualitative reasoning systems because of its ability to rapidly switch between alternate interpretations. As noted previously, this ability is unnecessary in CyclePad, and we suspect that this will be true for most educational applications.

6. Discussion

CyclePad demonstrates that qualitative physics has advanced enough to support new applications of AI to educational problems. Compositional modeling provides representational tools and techniques that can be used to encode a substantial body of knowledge about engineering thermodynamics, with constraint propagation providing analytic capabilities and qualitative representations providing the intuition needed to detect student blunders. Automatically generated hypertext explanations enable the user to explore the consequences of his or her assumptions, and figure out what modeling assumptions are needed to make further progress.

To date, CyclePad has only been tested with graduate student volunteers. We will be testing it with undergraduate engineering students both at Oxford and at Northwestern this academic year. Feedback will be gathered via a combination of electronic mail and interviews, which we will use to further improve the system. Our goal is to have CyclePad continuously available to undergraduates, so that their needs will help guide subsequent development.

Several extensions to CyclePad are in progress. First, we will extend it to handle non-steady flow cycles, such as Otto and Diesel cycles. Second, we will add some algebraic capabilities, so that CyclePad can help students derive algebraic expressions that capture important tradeoffs in specific systems.

We view CyclePad as part of a *virtual laboratory* for exploring thermodynamic cycles. A virtual laboratory is a software environment consisting of a set of parts, corresponding to physical parts or important abstractions in the domains of interest, tools for assembling collections of these parts into designs, and facilities for analyzing and testing designs. By working in this software environment, students can "build" their designs and try them out without expense or danger. In simpler domains some commercial software exists that can be viewed as virtual laboratories (e.g., Interactive Physics for simple dynamics and Electronics Workbench). A novel contribution of qualitative physics is the ability to generate explanations. For educational applications, explanation generation is vital, to help students see what aspects of a situation are important and to tie what they are observing back to fundamental principles. One of our next steps is to extend CyclePad's explanation facilities, by adding *coaches* [25 , 26 , 27] to help students, both to guide them through the analysis process (including the representation of real devices in terms of ideal components) and to suggest improvements to a student's design.

7. Acknowledgments

This work was supported by a grant from the Science and Engineering Research Council in the UK and by grants from the Office of Naval Research and NASA Langley Research Center in the U.S.. We thank Yusuf Pisan and John Everett for many enlightening bug reports and suggestions.

8. References

1 Forbus, K. & Stevens, A. Using Qualitative Simulation to Generate Explanations. *Proceedings of the Cognitive Science Society*, August 1981.

2 Brown, J.S., Burton, R. & de Kleer, J. Pedagogical, natural language, and knowledge engineering techniques in SOPHIE I, II, and III. In Sleeman, D. and Brown, J.S. (Eds.), *Intelligent Tutoring Systems*, Academic Press, 1982.

3 White, B. & Frederiksen, J. Causal model progressions as a foundation for intelligent learning environments. *Artificial Intelligence*, **42**, 99-157.

4 Massey, L., de Bruin, J. and Roberts, B. A Training System for System Maintenance. In Psotka, J. Massey, L., and Mutter, S. *Intelligent Tutoring Systems: Lessons Learned*. Erlbaum, 1988.

5 Govindaraj, T. Qualitative approximation methodology for modeling and simulation of large dynamic systems: Applications to a marine steam power plant. *IEEE transactions on systems, man, and cybernetics*, vol SMC-17, no. 6, November/December 1987.

6 Masahiro Inui, et al. Development of a model-based intelligent training system for plant operations. *Proceedings of International Conference on ARCE*, Tokyo, pp 89-94, 1990.

7 Roschelle, J. Collaborative Conceptual Change: Jointly acting social and cognitive processes. *Proceedings of CogSci-93*.

8 Whalley, P. *Basic Engineering Thermodynamics*, Oxford University Press, 1992.

9 Haywood, R. W. *Analysis of Engineering Cycles: Power, Refrigerating and Gas liquefaction Plant*, Pergamon Press, 1985.

10 El-Wakil, M. *Powerplant Technology*, McGraw-Hill, 1984.

11 Stallman, R.M. and Sussman, G.J. Forward Reasoning and Dependency-Directed Backtracking in a System for Computer-Aided Circuit Analysis, *Artificial Intelligence* **9** (1977), 135--196.

12 Falkenhainer, B., and Forbus, K. Setting up large-scale qualitative models. Proceedings of AAAI-88, August, 1988.

13 Falkenhainer, B. and Forbus, K. Compositional Modeling: Finding the Right Model for the Job. *Artificial Intelligence*, **51**, (1-3), October, 1991.

14 Nayak, P. Automated modeling of physical systems. Ph.D. dissertation, Computer Science Department, Stanford University, 1992.

15 Addanki, S., Cremonini, R., & Penberthy, J.S., Reasoning about assumptions in graphs of models. *Proceedings of IJCAI-89*, 1989.

16 McAllester, D. An outlook on truth maintenance. MIT AI Lab memo AIM-551, 1980.

17 Forbus, K. and de Kleer, J. *Building Problem Solvers*, MIT Press, 1993.

18 Hayes, P. Naive Physics 1: Ontology for Liquids. In Hobbs, J. and Moore, R. (Eds.) *Formal Theories of the Commonsense World*, Ablex, Norwood, NJ, 1985.

19 Gruber, T. & Gautier, P. Machine-generated explanations of engineering models: A compositional modeling approach. *Proceedings of IJCAI-93*.

20 Skorstad, G. and Forbus, K. Qualitative and quantitative reasoning about thermodynamics, *Proceedings of the Cognitive Science Society*, August, 1989.

21 Steele, G. and Sussman, G.J. CONSTRAINTS: A language for expressing almost-hierarchical descriptions, *Artificial Intelligence*, **14** (1980):1--39.

22 Pisan, Y. Visual reasoning about physical properties via graphs, *submitted for publication*, 1994.

23 Reiter, E. & Mellish, C. Optimizing the costs and benefits of natural language generation, *Proceedings of IJCAI-93*, 1993.

24 de Kleer, J. An assumption-based truth maintenance system. *Artificial Intelligence*, **28**(1986): 127--162.

25 Burton, R. & Brown, J.S. An investigation of computer coaching for informal learning activities. In Sleeman, D. and Brown, J.S. (Eds.), *Intelligent Tutoring Systems*, Academic Press, 1982

26 Lesgold, A., Eggan, G., Katz, S. and Rao, G. Possibilities for Assessment Using Computer-Based Apprenticeship Environments. In Regian, J. & Shute, V. *Cognitive Approaches to Automated Instruction*. Erlbaum, 1992.

27 Schank, R.C., & Nohan, M.Y. Empowering the student: New Perspectives on the Design of Teaching Systems. *The Journal of the Learning Sciences*, **1**(7-35), 1991.

Automated Model Selection for Simulation

Yumi Iwasaki
Knowledge Systems Laboratory
Stanford University
701 Welch Road, Bldg. C
Palo Alto, California, 94304
iwasaki@cs.stanford.edu

Alon Y. Levy
AT&T Bell Laboratories
AI Principles Research Department
600 Mountain Ave., Room 2C-406
Murray Hill, NJ 07974
levy@research.att.com

Abstract

Constructing an appropriate model is crucial
in reasoning successfully about the behavior
of a physical situation to answer a query. In
compositional modeling, a system is provided
with a library of composible pieces of knowledge about the physical world called model
fragments. Its task is to select appropriate
model fragments to describe the situation, either for static analysis of a single state, or
for the more complicated case simulation of
dynamic behavior over a sequence of states.
In previous work we showed how the model
construction problem in general can advanta-
geously be formulated as a problem of reasoning about *relevance*. This paper presents an
actual algorithm, based on relevance reasoning, for selecting model fragments efficiently
for the case of simulation. We show that the
algorithm produces an adequate model for a
given query and moreover, it is the simplest
one given the constraints in the query.

Introduction

Constructing an appropriate model is crucial in reasoning successfully about the behavior of a physical situation to answer a query. In the compositional modeling
approach [Falkenhainer and Forbus, 1991], a system is
provided with a library of composible pieces of knowledge about the physical world called model fragments.
The *model construction* problem involves selecting appropriate model fragments to describe the situation.
Model construction can be considered either for static
analysis of a single state, or for simulation of dynamic
behavior over a sequence of states. The latter is significantly more difficult than the former since one must
select model fragments without knowing exactly what
will happen in the future states. This paper presents
a general algorithm for model construction for simulation. For such an algorithm to be useful, the generated model must be adequate for answering the given
query and, at the same time, as simple as possible. We

define formally the concepts of adequacy and simplicity and show that the algorithm in fact generates an
adequate and simplest model.

The intuition underlying our algorithm is that the
model construction problem can be viewed as a problem of relevance reasoning [Subramanian and Genesereth, 1987; Levy and Sagiv, 1993]. Two types of relevance reasoning occur in this context. First, relevance
reasoning is used to determine which phenomena can
affect the query. Intuitively, assuming that the goal of
modeling is to explain how the value of a term changes
over time, what is relevant to this goal is all the things
that could causally influence the term. Consequently,
the high level mechanism driving the algorithm is backward chaining on the possible causal influences on the
goal term, determining the set of phenomena, terms
and objects that can affect the goal term directly or
indirectly.

The second aspect of relevance reasoning is deciding
which level of detail is relevant to the goal. Often there
are multiple model-fragments describing the same phenomenon, (grouped into *assumption classes* [Falken-
hainer and Forbus, 1991]). Choosing between them depends on the underlying modeling assumptions being
made, i.e., on the abstractions of the domain and the
approximations being made. Deciding to make a certain abstraction can be viewed as stating that some detail is irrelevant to the goal and can hence be removed
from the representation of a phenomenon (see [Levy,
1994] for a more detailed account of the connection
between irrelevance and abstractions). We therefore
use relevance reasoning to decide which modeling assumptions are appropriate for the goal. Furthermore,
explicit relevance claims can be used to express additional domain knowledge that comes to bear in selecting a model, thereby incorporating such knowledge in a
principled manner. Our algorithm alternates between
the two kinds of relevance reasoning. Given some modeling assumptions it determines which additional phenomena are relevant to the goal, and given a set of
relevant phenomena it chooses the level of detail at
which to model them. The algorithm can be shown
to run in time polynomial in the size of the resulting

model under certain reasonable assumptions.

Compositional modeling is a very powerful approach to automated modeling of physical devices. However, to enable efficient model construction, we must enforce additional structure on the model fragment library and the model-fragments (e.g., [Nayak, 1992b]). An important contribution of this paper is identifying additional structure that can be imposed on a model fragment library that is both natural and facilitates efficient model construction.

Several pieces of work have addressed the model formulation problem for the compositional modeling approach [Falkenhainer and Forbus, 1991; Nayak, 1992a; Rickel and Porter, 1994]. Our work is distinguished in that it derives its generality from general considerations of relevance reasoning. Specifically, it combines model formulation for simulation with guarantees of adequacy and simplicity, which are not found in other works.

Knowledge representation and behavior prediction

Before describing the model formulation problem, we briefly describe the representation of physical knowledge and the simulation method based on the compositional model approach. Compositional modeling was first described by Forbus in his work on Qualitative Process Theory (QPT) [Forbus, 1984], and is also the basis of subsequent works on qualitative modeling by Falkenhainer and Forbus [Falkenhainer and Forbus, 1991], Crawford and Farquhar [Crawford *et al.*, 1990] and Iwasaki and Low [Iwasaki and Low, 1993]. In compositional modeling, a physical situation is modeled as a collection of model fragments. Each fragment represents some aspect of a physical object or a physical phenomenon. A model fragment consists of conditions and consequences. The condition part specifies the conditions under which the phenomenon occurs, including the individuals that must exist and the conditions they must satisfy for the phenomenon to occur. The consequences specify the functional relations among the attributes of the objects that are entailed by the phenomenon.

If there exists individuals $a_1, \ldots, a_n$ that satisfy the conditions of a model fragment M at time t, we say that an instance of M is active at that time. We will denote the instance as $M(a_1, \ldots, a_n)$ and call $a_1, \ldots, a_n$ its *participants*. The existence of an active model fragment instance implies that the variables mentioned in it are defined and that the consequences hold.

The basic idea behind the prediction mechanism is the following: for a given situation, the system identifies active model fragment instances by evaluating their conditions. We will call the set of active model fragments in each state the *simulation model*. The simulation model gives rise to equations that must hold among variables as a consequence of the phenomena taking place. The equations are used to determine the next state of the situation. Each state has a simulation model along with a set of variable values and predicates that hold in the state. In order to perform simulation effectively, we must be able to efficiently select the appropriate set of model fragments at every state. The output of our algorithm is a small set of model fragment instances, from which the system selects a simulation model at every step of the simulation.

Problem definition

This section defines the model formulation problem as well as some key concepts in our approach. The following problem definition is based on that by Falkenhainer and Forbus ([Falkenhainer and Forbus, 1991], p. 98) with some modifications explained below:

Given a *scenario description*, a *domain theory*, and a *query* about the scenario's behavior, the model formulation problem is to produce the most useful, coherent *scenario model*. We elaborate on each part of this definition.

Scenario description: Our scenario description specifies a set of facts about the initial state of the situation to be modeled. This typically includes a set of individuals (i.e., components of the system), their properties and relations among them, representing the physical structure in the initial state of the simulation.

Domain theory: The domain theory is represented as a library of model fragments. As stated, each model fragment has a set of conditions which are further divided to *operating conditions* and *modeling assumptions*. The operating conditions are conditions on values of variables in a current state that are required for the model fragment to be applicable. The modeling assumptions are meta-level conditions describing the way we have decided to describe the domain, and are meant to accommodate different ways of modeling a certain phenomenon. Examples include assumptions about the temporal granularity of the model, the simplifying assumptions or approximations it makes, or the accuracy level it provides. While operating conditions of a model fragment in the chosen scenario model may be satisfied at a certain step of the simulation and cease to hold at a later point, modeling assumptions are assumed to hold throughout the simulation. We make the following assumptions about the library of model fragments. Their formal definitions are given in [Levy *et al.*, 1994].

Coherence of the Library: The *library coherence* assumption requires that if we have a set of model fragments that have consistent modeling assumptions and whose operating conditions are satisfied, then the resulting set of equations will not be over constrained (i.e., will not have more equations that quantities).

Completeness of the Library: The *library completeness* assumption requires that the library contains knowledge about all the phenomena that can causally affect any term appearing in any model fragments in the library unless the term is explicitly known to be at the boundary of the library's knowledge. We will call the set of terms that are known to be at the boundary of knowledge contained in the library L *the globally exogenous terms*, $E_{global}(L)$. $E_{global}(L)$ is the set of all terms such that they appear in model fragments but for which the library may not contain model fragments of all the phenomena that can directly causally affect the term in all possible circumstances.

In addition to the basic representation of physical knowledge as model fragments, we have additional constructs on model fragments, *composite model fragments* and *assumption classes*. These constructs facilitate model formulation by introducing a higher organizational structure into the model library.

A composite model fragment (CMF) is a set of model fragments that represent behaviors of the same components or process under different operating regions. For example, the voltage produced by a rechargeable battery is a different function of its charge-level in three different ranges of the charge-level. This characteristic of a battery is represented by three model fragments with different conditions on the charge-level. However, they can be seen as forming one complete "description" of a particular aspect of the battery behavior over the entire range of its charge-level. All model fragments in the library are grouped together into such sets, though a model fragment may constitute a singleton CMF.

CMFs are further grouped into assumption classes. An assumption class is a set of CMFs that describe the same phenomenon based on different and contradictory modeling assumptions. Since CMFs in an assumption class are contradictory, at most one of them should be included in any scenario model.

Query: A query is expressed as a list of terms to be explained. We assume that the purpose of modeling is to explain how and why those terms change over time, i.e. to produce a causal account of how they change.

A query may also include an a priori list of explicit modeling assumptions. Such lists can be provided by the user in order to provide additional information about the kinds of explanation desired, such as the level of details. In particular, they can include a list of exogenous terms, i.e., terms whose values are determined by factors outside the scope of the current problem. They are also used to delimit the set of possible states that should be considered possible in the simulation.

Scenario model: Given the inputs described above, the model formulation problem is to generate a set of possible CMF instantiations (i.e., a list of pairs: CMF, participant list). During simulation, the operating conditions of those CMF instances will be evaluated in every state to generate a simulation model.

For a model formulation algorithm to be useful, a scenario model generated should be adequate yet as simple as possible. We say a model is adequate when

it is consistent and is sufficient for answering the given query. A scenario model is said to be consistent if the union of all the modeling assumptions underlying its members is consistent. A scenario model is said to be sufficient for a given query, if it gives rise to a simulation model in every state that contains the complete causal paths from exogenous terms to the query term. We use the definitions of causal dependency relations given in [Vescovi *et al.*, 1993], which expands the notion of causal ordering among variables [Iwasaki and Simon, 1986] to include conditions on model fragments. Intuitively, a term t_i is directly causally dependent on another term t_j if the value of t_i is determined by that of t_j through an equation in which both t_i and t_j appear, or if t_j appears in the applicability condition of an equation that determines the value of t_i. Finally, a scenario model C_1 is said to be simpler than C_2, if for each CMF c_1 in C_1 there is some CMF c_2 in C_2 for which c_1 is simpler than c_2 or they are the same.

Model formulation algorithm

This section describes our model formulation algorithm in detail. Figure 1 shows the outline of the algorithm. Informally, the algorithm consists of making two choices. The first is deciding which assumption classes should be represented. The second is to decide which CMF should be included out of each of the assumption classes. The first choice is done by backward chaining through the possible causal influences on the goal terms. The second is made by reasoning about the modeling assumptions necessary to answer the query.

We explain each of the main steps in the loop: selection of assumption classes, selection a CMF out of each such assumption class, and deciding which terms to further backward chain on. We use the following example throughout.

> The example (see Figure 2) is a simple circuit containing a solar array (`SA1`) and a rechargeable battery (`BA1`). The figure shows the circuit, the scenario description, and the assumption classes in the domain theory. For each CMF in the domain theory, its consequences and the list of terms appearing in its operating conditions are shown. The query is `Voltage(BA1)`, with a list of exogenous terms, which includes all the terms mentioned in the scenario description except `Damaged(BA1)`. There is no a priori list of modeling assumptions.

Finding the Assumption Classes

As the goal of modeling is to explain how and why the goal terms change over time, the relevant things to include in a model are those that could causally influence the goal terms. The consequences of model fragments contain functional relations among quantities, specifying the ways quantities can influence each other.

We take the position that equations in model fragments describe the functional relations among the continuous variables involved in the modeled phenomenon

procedure select-scenario-model$(v, E, Init, C)$
/* v: the query variable */
/* E: the list of exogenous terms */
/* As_c: the modeling assumption of CMF c */
/* Q: a queue of terms */
/* $Init$: the list of modeling constraints in the query */
/* C: the background theory of modeling constraints */
/* Rel: the current list of modeling constraints */
/* $Model$ is a list of pairs (c, x), where c is a potential instance of a CMF and x is a term c could causally affect */

begin
    $Q = \{v\}$.
    $Rel = Init$.
    $Model = $ nil.
    repeat
        $q = $ dequeue(Q).
        $As = $ assumption classes in which q can be an output variable **and**
            whose operating conditions do not contradict E.
        for each $a \in As$ **do:**
            select-from-assumption-class (a, q).
            while there is a pair $(c, q') \in Model$ such that $\neg p \in As_c$ and $p \in Rel$
                remove (c, q') from $Model$.
                select-from-assumption-class (A_c, q').
                /* A_c is the assumption class from which c was chosen */
    until Q is empty.
    return the set $\{c \mid (c, q') \in Model\}$.
end select-scenario-model.

procedure select-from-assumption-class (A, q)
/* A is a potential instance of an assumption class that can determine q. */
/* $Pos(As_c)$ is the list of positive literals in As_c.*/

begin
    $c = $ The simplest CMF in A such that $\not\exists\, p(\neg p \in As_c \wedge p \in Rel)$.
    $Model = Model \cup \{(c, q)\}$.
    $inputs = $ the union of:
        The quantities that appear in equations with q **and**
        The terms in the operating conditions of c.
    for every $X \in inputs$ **do**
        if X has not been in Q and $X \notin E$ **then**
            enqueue X onto Q.
    $Rel = $ DeductiveClosure$(C \cup Rel \cup Pos(As_c))$.
    if $rel(q_1) \in Rel$ and $q_1 \notin E$ and q_1 has not been in Q **then**
        enqueue q_1 onto Q.
end select-from-assumption-class.

Figure 1: Model formulation algorithm

without specifying a particular causal direction. The direction of causality only emerges when the equation is embedded in a system of equations all representing independent mechanisms and the quantities that are externally determined are specified [Iwasaki and Simon, 1986]. In compositional modeling, this implies that the causal orientation of equations can only be determined after the model fragments are instantiated and equations are assembled into a simulation model. Therefore, one cannot a priori specify for each model fragment the quantity that is caused by the model fragment, but one can specify a priori the possible set of quantities that could be determined by the model frag-

ment. In general, this set can contain all the quantities mentioned in the consequences of the model fragment. Given a term, the algorithm selects the assumption-classes that could affect it. In our implementation, we pre-compile a list of assumption classes that can affect each type of terms to facilitate this search.

For instance, in our example, a term of the form `Damaged(x)` where `x` is an instance of `Battery` can be causally influenced by a member CMF of `Battery-damage-due-to-overcharge-ac` when it is instantiated with `x` bound to `?b`.

The query term `Voltage(BA1)` is the only item

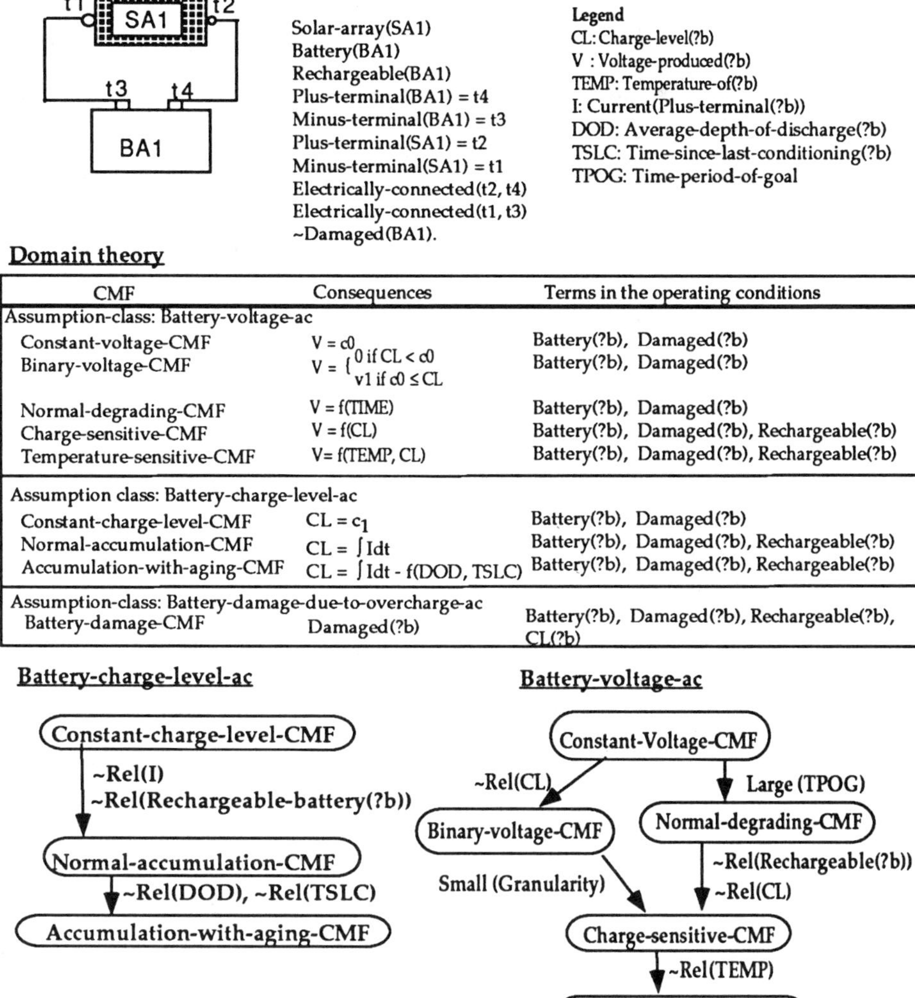

CMF	Consequences	Terms in the operating conditions
Assumption-class: Battery-voltage-ac		
Constant-voltage-CMF	$V = c0$	Battery(?b), Damaged(?b)
Binary-voltage-CMF	$V = \{\ 0$ if $CL < c0$; $v1$ if $c0 \leq CL$	Battery(?b), Damaged(?b)
Normal-degrading-CMF	$V = f(TIME)$	Battery(?b), Damaged(?b)
Charge-sensitive-CMF	$V = f(CL)$	Battery(?b), Damaged(?b), Rechargeable(?b)
Temperature-sensitive-CMF	$V = f(TEMP, CL)$	Battery(?b), Damaged(?b), Rechargeable(?b)
Assumption class: Battery-charge-level-ac		
Constant-charge-level-CMF	$CL = c_1$	Battery(?b), Damaged(?b)
Normal-accumulation-CMF	$CL = \int Idt$	Battery(?b), Damaged(?b), Rechargeable(?b)
Accumulation-with-aging-CMF	$CL = \int Idt - f(DOD, TSLC)$	Battery(?b), Damaged(?b), Rechargeable(?b)
Assumption-class: Battery-damage-due-to-overcharge-ac		
Battery-damage-CMF	Damaged(?b)	Battery(?b), Damaged(?b), Rechargeable(?b), CL(?b)

Figure 2: Model selection Example

on the queue initially, and it becomes the current goal.

`Battery-voltage-ac(BA1)` possibly has influence on the term, as `Voltage(BA1)` appears in the consequences of its member model fragments. Thus, we select this assumption class.

Selection of CMF out of an assumption class

Since CMFs in an assumption class represent alternative ways to model the same phenomenon, we must pick one CMF out of each assumption class thus deemed relevant. We make the choice by reasoning about the modeling assumptions being made about the problem. To facilitate the selection, we add to the representation of assumption classes additional structure that makes explicit the modeling assumptions that change between one CMF and another in the assumption class. Each assumption class is represented as a directed graph of CMFs. There is a link from a CMF c_1 to a CMF c_2 if c_1 is *simpler* than c_2.

The link is annotated with the difference in the modeling assumptions, i.e., the modeling assumptions that can be removed as one goes from c_1 to c_2. We employ the following convention in interpreting predicates in the modeling assumptions. A positive literal of a predicate denotes an assumption that yields a more complicated model of a phenomenon. A negative literal denotes a *simplifying* assumption. For example, the literal $\neg rel(Temperature(battery))$ in the modeling conditions of a model-fragment states that the fragment uses a simplified representation in which the temperature aspect of the battery is ignored, whereas the literal $rel(Temperature(battery))$ in the modeling conditions states that the model fragment considers the temperature aspect of the battery. Not all modeling assumptions are relevance statements. An example of a modeling assumption that is not a relevance statement, denoted by the literal $\neg large(timeScale)$, states that the representation is simplified to ignore longer term effects on the battery.[1] A simplest CMF is one in which the least number of positive literals are entailed by the modeling assumptions. Finally, we assume that every assumption class has single simplest CMF, and a single most complicated CMF.

The graphs of CMFs in the assumption classes that have more than one CMF for our example are shown in Figure 2. In the assumption class Battery-voltage-ac, the CMF Constant-voltage-CMF assumes that the charge-level of the battery is irrelevant, while Binary-voltage-CMF does not.

Given this representation of assumption classes, we can choose a CMF by selecting the simplest one which does not contradict the modeling assumptions collected so far. After choosing the CMF, we update the modeling assumptions to include those implied by the chosen CMF (which, in particular, include the assumption that all the terms mentioned in that CMF are relevant). As a result of adding the new modeling assumptions, earlier choices of CMFs might be invalidated, since they may have been chosen based on stronger assumptions. In such cases, we adjust earlier choices by selecting more complicated model fragments out of the assumption classes from which they were chosen. Importantly, the number of times we will perform such adjustments is limited, and therefore, the complexity of our algorithm is not affected by these adjustments.

Returning to our example, we have just selected Battery-voltage-ac. To select a CMF out of this assumption class, we start from the simplest, Constant-voltage-CMF. Since there is no earlier relevance assumptions made so far, this choice is consistent, and we select this CMF. This results in addition of the following to our modeling assumption list:
Rel(Battery(BA1)),
Rel(Damaged(BA1)),
Large(TPOG),
¬Rel(Charge-level(BA1)),
Small(Granularity),
¬Rel(Rechargeable(BA1)) and
¬Rel(Temperature-of(BA1)).

---

[1]Some assumptions may be multi-valued and the algorithms we describe in this paper can be extended in a straightforward fashion to deal with such assumptions. However, for clarity we assume here that modeling assumptions are binary.

Traversal of causal influence paths

Once a CMF is selected, we need to determine which causal paths to pursue further by deciding which terms to put on the queue. Essentially, we pursue the terms that can affect the goal term through the CMF. These are either terms that are part of the operating condition or terms that appear in the same equation as the goal in the consequence equations (and can therefore influence it in some causal ordering of the equations). We consider every such candidate term. If it is neither exogenous nor has already been put on the queue, it is pushed onto the queue. The procedure then calls itself recursively with the new queue.

Since Damaged(BA1) can influence Voltage(BA1) through Constant-voltage-CMF(BA1) and is not exogenous, it is placed on the queue and becomes the new goal.

A search through the model fragment library finds Battery-damage-due-to-overcharge-ac to influence the goal term. Battery-damage-CMF is selected from the assumption class since it is the only member.

This selection adds Rel(Rechargeable(BA1)) and Rel(Charge-level(BA1)) to the assumption list, making the assumption list inconsistent since both ¬Rel(Rechargeable(BA1)) and ¬Rel(Charge-level(BA1)) are included.

To resolve the inconsistency, we adjust the earlier choice of CMF from the assumption class, Battery-voltage(BA1), since it resulted in the addition of these irrelevance assumptions. We now select Charge-sensitive-CMF, which is the simplest CMF that does not contradict the current modeling assumptions.

The goal term now becomes Charge-level(BA1). A search through the model fragment library finds Battery-charge-level-ac to affect the term. The simplest CMF that is consistent with the current modeling assumptions in this assumption class is Normal-accumulation-CMF(BA1), which we select. Current(Plus-terminal(BA1)) can influence Charge-level(BA1) through this CMF. However, since it is an exogenous term, it is not placed on the queue. The queue is now empty and the procedure terminates.

The scenario model contains
Charge-sensitive-CMF(BA1),
Battery-damage-due-to-overcharge-CMF(BA1),
and Normal-accumulation-CMF(BA1).

Analysis

This section describes the properties of the algorithm we presented. We first show that it produces an adequate model. We then explain under what conditions it produces the simplest model. Finally, we discuss the complexity of the algorithm. The complete proofs are given in [Levy *et al.*, 1994]. In our discussion we assume (1) that all model fragments in a single CMF can determine the same set of variables and (2) that for each pair of CMFs, CMF_1 and CMF_2 in an assumption class such that CMF_1 is simpler than CMF_2, CMF_1 is a causal approximation [Nayak, 1992b] of CMF_2.

The second assumption is only necessary in order to assure that the algorithm as described will run in polynomial time. The algorithm can be modified to relax that assumption, but the resulting algorithm may not run in polynomial time. Nayak [Nayak, 1992b] shows that causal approximations capture most ones encountered in practice. Under these assumptions, our algorithm is guaranteed to produce an adequate and simplest model for the query, as stated by the following theorem.

Theorem 1: *Let $\mathcal{M}$ be a library of model fragments describing the domain, and $\mathcal{C}$ be a set of modeling constraints. Let S be a description of a system and $(v, E, Init)$ be a query about the system. Let $\mathcal{S}$ be the scenario model resulting from algorithm* **select-scenario-model**. *Furthermore, assume that:*

- *The library coherence assumption holds.*
- *If c_i and c_j are two CMFs in an assumption class, such that $c_i < c_j$, then c_i is a causal approximation of c_j.*
- *All modeling constraints in $\mathcal{C}$ are either ground atomic formulas or Horn rules.*
- *The most complicated scenario model, defined to be all the possible instantiations of CMFs that are the most complicated in their assumption class, is adequate for answering the query.[2]*

Then, $\mathcal{S}$ is an adequate scenario model for $(v, E, Init)$ and there is no scenario model $\mathcal{S}_1$ such that $\mathcal{S}_1$ is simpler than $\mathcal{S}$.

The observation underlying the proof of adequacy is the following. Consider the graph of causal influences created by the algorithm. It consists of OR nodes (the goal nodes) and AND nodes (the CMF nodes). At every given state, the actual model used for that state is one of its subgraphs, in which every OR nodes has at most one arc emanating from it (i.e., for each goal, we choose at most one CMF that explains it). Consequently, since the graph represents possible paths from the exogenous variables to the goal, each of the subgraphs will too.

The algorithm also produces the simplest scenario model in the following sense. Recall that we are choosing the scenario model without performing the actual simulation. Consequently, we do not know which

states the simulation will go through, and therefore which model-fragments will be required for those specific states. Instead, we assume that the simulation can go through *any* state that satisfies the input conditions, and our choice of a scenario model is made to accommodate any such state. The proof of simplicity is based on the correspondence between states of the simulation and subgraphs of the graph created by the algorithm.

The running time of the algorithm is polynomial in the number of CMF's in the scenario model. To see this, observe that although the algorithm sometime requires adjustments of previous choices, the maximum number of such adjustments is polynomial. Specifically, if d is the maximum number of CMFs in an assumption class, and n is the number of CMFs in the scenario model, the total number of adjustment steps is at most nd. This is because every adjustment step results in replacing some CMF with another that is more complicated. Because of the assumption that the simpler-than relation between a pair of CMFs in an assumption class is always a causal approximation, there is no possibility that a CMF can be replaced by a simpler CMF in the same assumption class without making the set of modeling assumptions inconsistent. After nd such replacements we will get the most complicated scenario model, which is guaranteed to be adequate.

Conclusions

We presented a novel algorithm that produces an adequate and simplest scenario model for simulation. The algorithm has three distinguishing aspects that are based on applying general considerations of relevance reasoning. The first is the backward chaining through causal influences, motivated by a general definition of relevance. The second is choosing the simplest possible CMF at each choice point, based on knowledge expressed as relevance claims. The third is that it reasons with partial knowledge of the states that might occur in the simulation.

We have implemented the algorithm as part of a system called, Device Modeling Environment (DME) [Iwasaki and Low, 1993], which is a device modeling program to provide a computational environment for design of electromechanical devices. Given the topological description of a device, DME formulates a model and simulates its behavior. The system works on several examples, including the electrical power system, of which the example used in Section 3 is a much simplified version.

Several researchers have proposed methods for model formulation. These works address one or both of the two aspects of model formulation problem, namely model construction and simplification.

Nayak [Nayak, 1992a] addressed both aspects of the problem in the context of the single state analysis. His algorithm for constructing a model also follows possible causal influences, but these influences must be given

---

[2] Note that the most complicated scenario model needs to include only the *valid* instantiations of model fragments, i.e., instantiations in which the objects satisfy the type conditions in the definition of the model fragment and the time invariant facts in the description of the system.

explicitly using the *component interaction heuristic*. In contrast, our work addresses the problem in the more general context of dynamic behavior simulation, where the governing set of equations can change from state to state. Our approach exploits the structure of the model fragments to automatically derive the links that are given as component interaction heuristics in his approach. In choosing a model fragment from every assumption class, Nayak chooses the most complicated one, and later simplifies the resulting model. On the other hand, we build the model by selecting the simplest CMF possible in every class, adjusting the choice only if necessary. Therefore, the complexity of Nayak's algorithm is polynomial in the size of the *most complicated* model, while our is polynomial in the size of the *simplest* model. In complex systems, where the CMFs in an assumption class vary significantly in levels of detail, this will be a significant difference, and therefore our approach will be more practical.

Falkenhainer and Forbus [Falkenhainer and Forbus, 1991] select the physical scope of the model by identifying the lowest object down the partonomic hierarchy that subsumes all the objects mentioned in the query. They rely on heuristics to select properties to be modeled. This approach can lead to inclusion of model fragments that are not causally related to the query, and cannot guarantee the sufficiency of the model. They attempt to produce the simplest model by generating all possible consistent sets of modeling assumptions and choosing the simplest based on an informal criteria of simplicity.

Rickel's work on model formulation is similar to ours since it makes use of graphs of interactions paths among quantities to select relevant model fragments [Rickel and Porter, 1994]. His graph of interactions are less general than our causal influence graph since it only includes quantities while we include all terms (including quantities, predicates, relations) that could directly or indirectly influence the goal terms. His approach also does not provide guarantees of sufficiency or simplicity.

The idea of graph of CMFs is similar to graph of models by Addanki et al. [Addanki *et al.*, 1989] for selecting among complete models. Since their models are complete models instead of fragments, the space requirement of their approach would increase exponentially as the number of possible modeling assumptions increases.

Acknowledgments

The authors would like to thank Richard Fikes and Pandu Nayak for many useful discussions. This research was sponsored by the Defense Advanced Research Projects Agency and by NASA Ames Research Center, under NASA grants NAG 2-581 and NCC 2-537.

References

Addanki, Sanjaya; Cremonini, R.; and Penberthy, J. 1989. Reasoning about assumptions in graphs of models. In *Proceedings of the Eleventh International Joint Conference on Artificial Intelligence*.

Crawford, James; Farquhar, Adam; and Kuipers, Ben 1990. A compiler from physical models into qualitative differential equations. In *Proceedings of the Eighth National Conference on Artificial Intelligence*, Los Altos, CA. Morgan Kaufmann.

Falkenhainer, Brian and Forbus, Ken 1991. Compositional modeling: Finding the right model for the job. In *Artificial Intelligence*. Vol. 51, pp. 95–143.

Forbus, Ken 1984. Qualitative process theory. In *Artificial Intelligence*, volume 24.

Iwasaki, Y. and Low, C. M. 1993. Model generation and simulation of device behavior with continuous and discrete change. *Intelligent Systems Engineering* 1(2).

Iwasaki, Y. and Simon, H. A. 1986. Causality in device behavior. In *Artificial Intelligence*. Vol. 29.

Levy, Alon Y. and Sagiv, Yehoshua 1993. Exploiting irrelevance reasoning to guide problem solving. In *Proceedings of the 13th International Joint Conference on Artificial Intelligence*.

Levy, Alon Y.; Iwasaki, Yumi; and Fikes, Richard 1994. Automated model selection for simulation based on relevance reasoning. Knowledge System Laboratory Technical Report. Computer Science Department, Stanford University. In preparation.

Levy, Alon Y. 1994. Creating abstractions using relevance reasoning. In *Proceedings of the Twelfth National Conference on Artificial Intelligence*.

Nayak, P. Pandurang 1992a. *Automated Model Selection*. Ph.D. Dissertation, Stanford University, Stanford, CA.

Nayak, Pandurang 1992b. Causal approximations. In *Proceedings of the Tenth National Conference on Artificial Intelligence*.

Rickel, Jeff and Porter, Bruce 1994. Automated modeling for answering prediction questions: Selecting the time scale and system boundary. In *Proceedings of the Twelfth National Conference on Artificial Intelligence*.

Subramanian, D. and Genesereth, M.R. 1987. The relevance of irrelevance. In *Proceedings of the Tenth International Joint Conference on Artificial Intelligence*, Los Altos, CA. Morgan Kaufmann.

Vescovi, Marcos; Iwasaki, Yumi; Fikes, Richard; and Chandrasekaran, B. 1993. Cfrl: A language for specifying the causal functionality of engineered devices. In *Proceedings of the Eleventh National Conference on Artificial Intelligence*.

Automated Modeling for Answering Prediction Questions: Selecting the Time Scale and System Boundary

Jeff Rickel and Bruce Porter
Department of Computer Science
University of Texas
Austin, Texas 78712
rickel@cs.utexas.edu, porter@cs.utexas.edu

Abstract

The ability to answer prediction questions is crucial to reasoning about physical systems. A prediction question poses a hypothetical scenario and asks for the resulting behavior of variables of interest. Prediction questions can be answered by simulating a model of the scenario. An appropriate system boundary, which separates aspects of the scenario that must be modeled from those that can be ignored, is critical to achieving a simple yet adequate model. This paper presents an efficient algorithm for system boundary selection, it shows the important role played by the model's time scale, and it provides a separate algorithm for selecting this time scale. Both algorithms have been implemented in a compositional modeling program called TRIPEL and evaluated in the plant physiology domain.

1 Introduction

The ability to answer prediction questions is crucial to reasoning about physical systems. A *prediction question* poses a hypothetical *scenario* (e.g., a plant whose soil moisture is decreasing) and asks for the resulting behavior of specified *variables of interest* (e.g., the plant's growth rate). Such questions are important in verifying designs, testing diagnostic hypotheses, and tutoring in science and engineering.

Prediction questions can be answered by simulating a model of the scenario. Simulation provides the desired predictions, and the model additionally supports subsequent explanation. The model must be sufficiently comprehensive to ensure reliable predictions yet simple so simulation is efficient and the explanation is comprehensible.

To balance these competing requirements, a modeler must choose a *system boundary* that separates aspects of the scenario that must be modeled from those that

---

*Support for this research is provided by a grant from the National Science Foundation (IRI-9120310), a contract from the Air Force Office of Scientific Research (F49620-93-1-0239), and donations from the Digital Equipment Corporation.

can be ignored. Despite the importance of choosing a suitable system boundary, current modeling programs for answering prediction questions shift responsibility for this issue to the people posing the question or representing the domain knowledge (see Section 8).

This paper presents an efficient algorithm for choosing system boundaries and explains its role in TRIPEL, a modeling program for answering prediction questions.[1] The paper shows that the system boundary can be chosen efficiently by first identifying the time scale on which the variables of interest are affected in the scenario. It presents a separate algorithm for determining this time scale. The correctness and efficiency of our methods have been evaluated on questions about plant physiology.

2 The Modeling Task

The input to the modeler consists of a prediction question and domain knowledge. The question has two parts: the scenario and the variables of interest. The scenario includes physical objects, relations among them, and *behavioral conditions*. Behavioral conditions specify the initial value of selected variables (e.g., the amount of soil water is above the permanent wilting percentage) and/or their behavior (e.g., the amount of soil water is decreasing).

TRIPEL uses the compositional modeling approach introduced by Falkenhainer and Forbus (1991), in which the domain knowledge provides a set of *model fragments*, the building blocks for models. Each model fragment describes some aspect of the scenario. (Falkenhainer and Forbus show how to generate the model fragments for a scenario from general domain knowledge.) The modeler constructs a model of the scenario by choosing a subset of the model fragments.

Model fragments specify relations among variables of the scenario. In plant physiology, *influences* are the most natural representation for such relations. An influence is a causal relation between two variables, as in Qualitative Process (QP) Theory (Forbus 1984),

---

[1]TRIPEL is an acronym for "Tailoring Relevant Influences for Predictive and Explanatory Leverage." It is also a style of strong ale made by Trappist Monks in Belgium.

along with its *operating conditions* (behavioral conditions under which it holds) and associated *modeling assumptions*. The variables are real-valued, time-varying properties of the scenario. There are two types of influences: a *functional influence* specifies that one variable is a function of another (e.g., QP theory's indirect influences), and a *differential influence* specifies that the first derivative of one variable is a function of another variable (e.g., QP theory's direct influences).

In TRIPEL, each influence serves as a model fragment. This is natural, since each is an independent fact. It also allows the modeler flexibility to include or exclude any influence from the model. To emphasize their role in modeling, we call the influences (model fragments) for a scenario the *candidate influences*.

The output of the modeler, the *scenario model*, is a subset of the candidate influences. The variables referenced in this model are partitioned into *exogenous* variables, whose behavior is determined by influences external to the model, and *dependent* variables, whose behavior is determined by the model. To determine which combinations of candidate influences constitute an acceptable scenario model, the domain knowledge includes *coherence constraints*, which specify inconsistent combinations of modeling assumptions (e.g., assumption classes (Falkenhainer & Forbus 1991)).

Once constructed, the scenario model is simulated starting from the initial state, and the model and simulation results are used to answer the question and explain the answer.

3 Modeling Algorithm

The exogenous variables of a scenario model constitute its system boundary. To illustrate the role of system boundary decisions in compositional modeling, we briefly present our modeling algorithm.

TRIPEL conducts a best-first search for a scenario model for the question. Each state in the search space is a *partial model*, a model that may contain *free variables* (variables not yet chosen as exogenous or dependent). The initial state in the search is a partial model consisting only of the variables of interest, all free. The successor function, described below, extends a partial model with alternative ways of modeling one of its free variables; this may add new free variables to the model. A partial model is pruned from the search if it is incoherent (i.e., violates the coherence constraints); any extension of an incoherent partial model is also incoherent. The goal of the search is to find the simplest adequate scenario model for the question.

A scenario model is adequate if it satisfies the following conditions: it includes all variables of interest, it satisfies all coherence constraints, its system boundary (set of exogenous variables) is adequate (discussed in Section 4), and each dependent variable has an adequate set of influences on it (i.e., the influences represent all significant influencing phenomena at some level of detail).

The adequate models are partially ordered by simplicity. While any simplicity criteria could be used, we define one model as simpler than another if it has fewer variables. With this criterion, the search ends when an adequate model is found that is at least as simple as all remaining partial models; these partial models can only grow. This criterion also serves as the evaluation function for the best-first search.

The successor function, extend-model, extends a partial model with alternative ways of modeling one of its free variables. Extend-model first determines whether all the free variables can be exogenous; if so, it marks each one as exogenous and returns the resulting model. Otherwise, it chooses a variable that must be dependent and determines all combinations of candidate influences on that variable that would provide an adequate model of it (multiple combinations arise from alternative ways of modeling some of the underlying influencing phenomena).[2] Extend-model returns a set of new partial models, each the result of extending the original partial model with one of the combinations.

To extend the original partial model with one of the combinations of candidate influences, extend-model adds the influences to the model, marks the variable as dependent, and adds any new free variables to the model. These new free variables include any variable referenced by the new influences that was not already in the model (e.g., an influencing variable or a variable appearing in operating conditions).

System boundary decisions arise in the successor function extend-model. Given a partial model and one of its free variables, extend-model must determine whether the variable can be exogenous. Such decisions are important; if the variable is dependent, the model must be extended to include additional influences (on that variable) and variables (referenced by those influences). The next section describes TRIPEL's criteria and algorithm for determining if a variable can be classified as exogenous.

4 System Boundary Selection

Selection Criteria

An exogenous variable must satisfy two criteria. First, by definition, the variable must not be "significantly influenced" (defined below) by any other variable in the model. Second, the variable must not be significantly influenced by any *driving variable* (variable referenced in the question's behavioral conditions). The second criterion ensures that the system boundary doesn't disconnect the model from relevant behavioral conditions.

To determine whether one variable significantly influences another, TRIPEL uses the candidate influences.

---

[2]This step is not discussed in this paper. TRIPEL has a method for identifying these combinations, but any method will do; the algorithms in this paper do not depend on how the combinations are determined.

The candidate influences form a graph in which variables are nodes and the influences are directed edges from their influencing variable to their influenced variable. One variable *significantly influences* another variable if and only if there is an *influence path* (path in the graph) from the first variable to the second and every influence in the path is significant.

TRIPEL determines whether an individual influence is significant using time scale information. Processes cause significant change on widely disparate time scales. For example, in a plant, water flows through membranes on a time scale of seconds, solutes flow through membranes on a time scale of minutes, growth requires hours or days, and surrounding ecological processes may occur on a time scale of months or years. In TRIPEL, each differential influence, which specifies an effect of a process, has an associated modeling assumption that specifies the fastest time scale on which the effect is significant. Functional influences, being instantaneous, are significant on any time scale. After choosing an appropriate *time scale of interest* for the question (as discussed in Section 5), TRIPEL concludes that any candidate influence with a slower time scale is insignificant.

For example, consider the question "What happens to the amount of ABA in a plant's guard cells when the turgor pressure in its leaves decreases?" Turgor pressure is the hydraulic pressure in plant cells. ABA (abscisic acid) is a hormone that controls the plant's response to water stress. As will be discussed in Section 5, this question is best answered on a time scale of minutes.

Part (A) of Figure 1 shows some of the candidate influences for the example question. Leaf turgor pressure significantly influences guard cell ABA amount because there is an influence path from the former to the latter (along the top of the figure), and every influence in this path is significant on a time scale of minutes. However, the water uptake rate (lower left corner) does not significantly influence guard cell ABA amount, because the first influence on the influence path is significant only on a time scale of hours or longer.

Selection Algorithm

Using the notion of influence paths, extend-model *could* run a graph connectivity algorithm for each system boundary decision. A free variable in a partial model can be exogenous if the graph algorithm determines that the variable is not significantly influenced by any driving variable of the question or any other variable in the model.

However, this naive algorithm is inefficient. Each run of the graph algorithm will repeat much of the search that previous runs did. To avoid this problem, TRIPEL determines all variables and influences that *might* be relevant to the question and computes and caches connectivity relations among the variables

before beginning the search for an adequate scenario model. These potentially relevant variables and influences constitute the search space that would be repeatedly searched by the naive algorithm.

To identify all the potentially relevant variables and influences, TRIPEL starts with the variables of interest and conducts a breadth-first search backwards through the candidate influences. If a variable is potentially relevant, so is any significant influence on it. If an influence is potentially relevant, so are its influencing variable and any variables appearing in its operating conditions. This search ends at variables that are not significantly influenced on the time scale of interest or variables that are significantly influenced only by previously-discovered relevant variables (i.e., through feedback loops).

In the example in Figure 1, the search for potentially relevant variables and influences begins with the influences on guard cell ABA amount. The influences of transpiration on leaf mesophyll water and water uptake on xylem water are insignificant on the time scale of interest (minutes); removing these two influences disconnects the potentially relevant variables from the remainder of the candidate influences, including the feedback loop through transpiration. Part (B) of Figure 1 shows the result, the potentially relevant variables and influences for the example.

As illustrated by the example, the search for potentially relevant variables and influences will typically have to traverse only a fraction of the variables and candidate influences of the scenario. In natural systems, like plants, animals, and ecosystems, modularity arises from the widely disparate time scales at which processes cause change (Allen & Starr 1982; Kuipers 1987; O'Neill *et al.* 1986; Rosswall, Woodmansee, & Risser 1988; Segal 1980). The result is a hierarchy of nearly decomposable subsystems; processes acting *within* a subsystem cause significant change quickly, while processes acting *across* subsystems cause change more slowly (Allen & Starr 1982; Kuipers 1987; O'Neill *et al.* 1986; Simon & Ando 1961). The time scale of interest filters out influences that are significant only on slower time scales, thus isolating the variables of interest in their own nearly decomposable subsystem. The search for potentially relevant variables and influences is confined to this subsystem because the influences from other subsystems are insignificant.

After determining the graph of potentially relevant variables and influences, TRIPEL constructs the adjacency matrix for the transitive closure of this graph. This two-dimensional, Boolean *connectivity array* records the connectivity between every pair of potentially relevant variables; thus, TRIPEL can tell whether any variable significantly influences any other variable by consulting a single cell of the array. This array can be computed efficiently; the Floyd-Warshall algorithm computes it in $\Theta(n^3)$ time, where n is the number of nodes (potentially relevant variables) in the

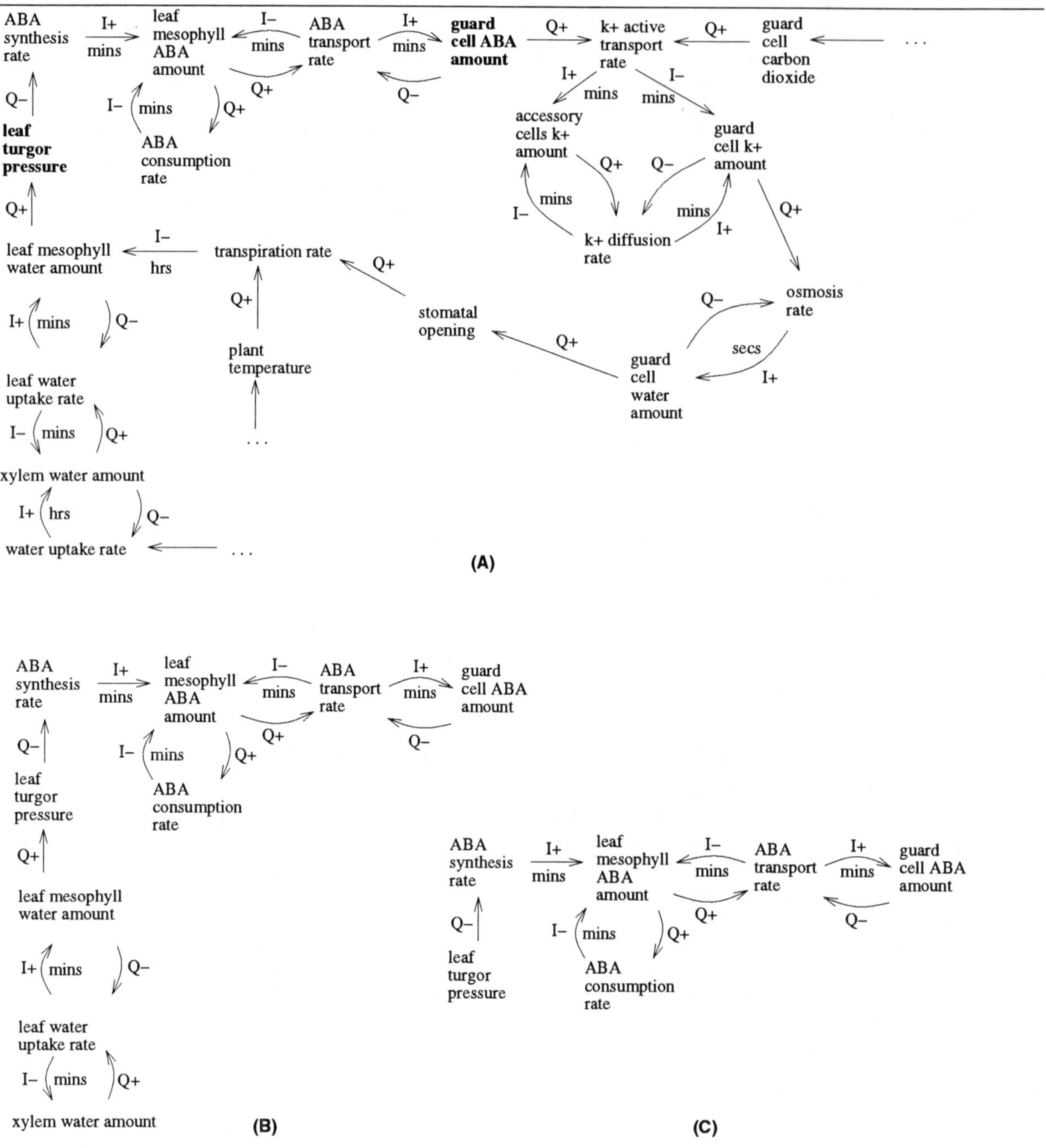

Figure 1:
(A) A subset of the candidate influences for the question "What happens to the amount of ABA in a plant's guard cells when the turgor pressure in its leaves decreases?" The driving variable, leaf turgor pressure, and the variable of interest, guard cell ABA amount, are shown in bold. Each influence is labeled with its type (Q+ and Q− are types of functional influences, and I+ and I− are types of differential influences) and the time scale on which it is significant (functional influences are significant on any time scale). Ellipses indicate connection to the remainder of the candidate influences. To focus on system boundary issues, the figure does not show alternative levels of detail. (B) The potentially relevant variables for the question. (C) An adequate scenario model for the question.

graph (Cormen, Leiserson, & Rivest 1989).

After computing the connectivity array, TRIPEL searches for an adequate scenario model as described in Section 3. Extend-model consults the array for each system boundary decision. A free variable v in a partial model m must be dependent in m (and any extension of m) if, in the connectivity array, v is influenced by any other variable in m or any driving variable of the question. If not, v can be exogenous in m but not necessarily in extensions of m, since they may contain additional variables that influence v. Therefore, as described in Section 3, extend-model doesn't mark variables in a partial model as exogenous until all remaining free variables in that model can be exogenous. At that point, the model is complete, so no other variables need to be added.

In the example, the search for an adequate scenario model begins with the partial model consisting only of guard cell ABA amount. TRIPEL incrementally extends this model until its contents match those shown in Part (C) of Figure 1. At this point, the free variable leaf turgor pressure is chosen as exogenous because it satisfies both criteria: it is not significantly influenced by any other variable in the partial model nor by any other driving variable. This model is the simplest adequate model for the question.

5 Time Scale Selection

A time scale of interest provides an important source of power in modeling. Besides providing the criteria for assessing the significance of influences, a time scale of interest also allows TRIPEL to use quasi-static approximations, in which fast processes are modeled through simple functional relations that summarize their equilibrium results (Iwasaki 1988; Kuipers 1987; Rickel & Porter 1992; Schaffer 1981; Simon & Ando 1961). Similarly, TRIPEL can model separate pools of substance or energy as a single aggregate compartment when they are kinetically distinguishable only on time scales much faster than the time scale of interest (Jacquez 1985; Simon & Ando 1961; Zeigler 1980). Thus, a time scale of interest allows many important model simplifications.

However, the person asking the question cannot be expected to provide the time scale of interest. Typically, this person will not even know which influences link the behavioral conditions to the variables of interest, much less their time scales. The modeler must choose, as the time scale of interest, a time scale that is adequate for answering the question. This section describes TRIPEL's criteria and algorithm for choosing a time scale of interest.

Selection Criteria

A prediction question asks for the effects of behavioral conditions on variables of interest. Therefore, a time scale is adequate for answering the question only if,

on that time scale, every variable of interest is significantly influenced by some driving variable. Additionally, assuming that a prediction question asks for the behavior of the variables of interest *beyond* the initial state, the influence paths relating the driving variables to the variables of interest must be capable of causing changes in the variables of interest.

Through an individual influence, one variable can cause change in another variable in two ways: (1) with a differential influence, a specified value for the influencing variable (along with values for other influencing variables) provides the rate of change of the influenced variable; (2) in contrast, a functional influence can cause change only if the influencing variable is changing (Forbus 1984). This implies that a driving variable can cause change in a variable of interest only if the influence path connecting them contains a differential influence or the behavioral conditions specify that the driving variable is changing (in which case a path of functional influences will propagate the change). If either case is satisfied, the influence path is a *differential influence path*.

In our earlier example, since the question specifies that turgor pressure is decreasing, any influence path from turgor pressure to another variable is a differential influence path, capable of causing change. In contrast, if the question only specified that turgor pressure is above the "yield point" (above which the pressure causes cell growth), an influence path leading from turgor pressure is differential only if it contains a differential influence (as is the case with the influence of turgor pressure on cell growth).

Using this concept, the criterion for an adequate time scale is more concrete: A time scale is adequate for answering a prediction question only if, for every variable of interest, there is a differential influence path, consisting solely of candidate influences that are significant on that time scale, leading from some driving variable to that variable of interest. This criterion prevents TRIPEL from selecting a time scale on which simulation could only predict the initial state of the variables of interest resulting from the behavioral conditions.

Selection Algorithm

While the search for influence paths during system boundary selection is kept manageable by the time scale of interest, no such focus is available when choosing the time scale of interest. The complete set of candidate influences could be enormous, so generating that set and searching through it for influence paths could be prohibitively expensive. Efficient time scale selection requires the ability to generate and search through only a fraction of the candidate influences.

TRIPEL gains efficiency by starting with the fastest possible time scale and testing successively slower time scales until it finds one that is adequate. When TRIPEL tests a time scale, it can ignore all influences that are significant only on slower time scales, so each test operates on a manageable fraction of the candidate influences. The set of significant influences grows monotonically as TRIPEL considers slower time scales, so TRIPEL performs the inexpensive tests before the more expensive ones. TRIPEL chooses the first adequate time scale it finds as the time scale of interest.

To determine whether a candidate time scale is adequate, TRIPEL conducts a breadth-first search, starting from the driving variables, for variables that are reachable via significant (on that time scale) influence paths. For each reachable variable, TRIPEL records whether it is reachable via a differential influence path or a functional one. The actual influence paths are not recorded. The search ends when every variable of interest is reachable by a differential influence path (in which case the time scale is adequate) or when the set of variables reachable at that time scale is exhausted (in which case the time scale is not adequate).

For the example question, TRIPEL first tests a time scale of seconds. Part (A) of Figure 1 illustrates that only the ABA synthesis rate is significantly influenced by leaf turgor pressure on this time scale. Next, TRIPEL tests a time scale of minutes. On this time scale, there is a differential influence path from leaf turgor pressure to guard cell ABA amount (along the top of the figure), so this time scale is chosen.

6 Evaluation

To evaluate our methods of time scale and system boundary selection, we tested TRIPEL on seven prediction questions concerning the physiology of a prototypical plant, including the example described above. Each question specifies the qualitative behavior of one variable and asks for the resulting behavior of another.

Our plant physiology knowledge base provides 77 variables and 155 candidate influences for this plant. Of the variables, 33 represent an amount of some substance or energy in a plant compartment, and 39 represent the rates of different processes. The candidate influences cover processes of water regulation, carbon dioxide regulation and carbohydrate regulation. The time scales of these processes range from seconds to hours. Many phenomena are represented at multiple levels of detail, based on the following:

- aggregation of pools (e.g., modeling water in the roots and stem as separate pools or as a single aggregate pool)

- aggregation of processes (e.g., modeling photosynthesis as an aggregate process or separately modeling its components, the light and dark reactions)

- quasi-static approximations (i.e., modeling the net equilibrium result of a set of processes or modeling their underlying dynamics)

For each question, TRIPEL chose the appropriate time scale and a reasonable system boundary, as judged by a domain expert. Consequently, the chosen scenario models included the variables and influences required for answering each question, and they excluded irrelevant ones. On average, the models contained 11 variables and 14 influences, substantially fewer than the number in the knowledge base. The largest scenario model contained only 15 variables and 20 influences. While the simplicity of these models is partially due to omitting unnecessary detail, their simplicity also reflects a well-chosen system boundary; each model excludes a number of plant subsystems.

Moreover, TRIPEL generated these models efficiently, requiring less than 15 seconds to find the time scale and the simplest adequate model for each question. In each case, connectivity analysis — the most expensive step in determining the system boundary — was performed on only a fraction of the influence graph. In the best case, connectivity analysis considered only 4 potentially relevant variables, and it considered 51 in the worst case. This shows how effectively the time scale of interest restricts the set of potentially relevant variables and influences; disregarding time scale, all the variables in the knowledge base are connected. We expect the fraction of potentially relevant variables to be even smaller for a knowledge base with a wider variety of time scales and a more extensive coverage of plant subsystems.

7 Future Work

Our method of time scale selection has several limitations. It assumes that a single time scale will suffice for answering the question, but some questions require multiple time scales (Iwasaki 1990; Kuipers 1987). Also, the criteria for an adequate time scale are necessary but not always sufficient; the most important connections between the behavioral conditions and the variables of interest may not lie at the fastest adequate time scale.

The algorithm for system boundary selection can be strengthened with additional methods for recognizing insignificant influences. Each such method further reduces the number of potentially relevant variables and tightens the resulting system boundary.

A more thorough evaluation requires more extensive domain knowledge. We are currently evaluating TRIPEL using the Botany Knowledge Base (Porter *et al.* 1988), which includes over 200 processes described at multiple levels of detail.

We expect our methods to apply to a wide variety of domains. In addition to biological and ecological domains, time scale knowledge appears useful in engineering domains as well. Kokotovic, O'Malley, and Sannuti (1976) and Saksena, O'Reilly, and Kokotovic (1984) survey hundreds of applications in many different engineering fields in which models are simplified using knowledge of the disparate time scales of processes.

8 Related Work

The modeling algorithm of Falkenhainer and Forbus (1991) requires, as input, a system decomposition for the scenario. In contrast, our algorithm determines system boundaries using only the model fragments. Falkenhainer and Forbus assume the system decomposition is based on partonomic structure; however, O'Neill *et al.* (1986) argue that approximate system boundaries in natural systems arise from differences in process rates and that these boundaries may not correspond to standard structural decompositions. Finally, as illustrated in our previous paper (Rickel & Porter 1992), Falkenhainer and Forbus's approach to selecting system boundaries is not sufficiently sensitive to the connection between behavioral conditions and variables of interest.

The modeling algorithm of Nayak *et al.* (Nayak 1992; Nayak, Joskowicz, & Addanki 1992) requires "model-as" constraints, provided in the domain knowledge, to identify potentially relevant model fragments. These constraints don't ensure that the model includes an influence path from the driving variable to the variable of interest, so a subsequent step adds model fragments until the model is adequate. In contrast, our method finds all potentially relevant variables and influences using only the candidate influences, and these variables and influences will include the significant influence paths from the driving variables to the variables of interest. Furthermore, their criteria for choosing exogenous variables are suitable for their task, explaining a specified causal relation, but are too weak for prediction questions. Their criteria only require some influence path from the driving variable to the variable of interest; the resulting scenario model may include an exogenous variable that, in reality, is significantly influenced by another variable in the model.

The modeling algorithms of Williams (1991) and Iwasaki and Levy (1993) require, as input, the variables that can be exogenous for the question. Although these algorithms can determine which exogenous variables must be included in the scenario model, neither algorithm can determine exogenous variables automatically.

Iwasaki (1990), Kuipers (1987), and Yip (1993) present modeling and simulation methods that exploit time scale information, but they do not provide methods for selecting the time scale of interest.

The time scale on which a differential influence is significant bundles two pieces of knowledge: the rates at which the influencing process operates and the level of change in the influenced variable that is considered significant. TRIPEL directly associates differential influences with their time scale of significance because this coarse level of knowledge is often more readily available than the underlying knowledge. However, it may be useful or necessary in some domains to infer the time scale from the underlying knowledge, especially if the level of significant change depends on the question. Iwasaki (1990) has explored this approach.

The work described in this paper builds on our previous methods for selecting a time scale and system boundary (Rickel & Porter 1992). The previous methods had to keep track of all the particular interaction paths, which can be prohibitively expensive when there are many candidate influences. In contrast, our current methods require only connectivity information, for two reasons: (1) the influences in a model are selected through incremental extension of partial models (Section 3) rather than a search for all interaction paths, and (2) a time scale of interest is selected by testing candidate time scales one by one (Section 5).

9 Conclusions

To provide a reliable, comprehensible answer to a prediction question, a modeler must choose an appropriate system boundary. The time scale of interest plays an important role in selecting the system boundary; TRIPEL uses this time scale to identify insignificant influences. To choose the time scale of interest and system boundary, TRIPEL searches for relevant influence paths. Time scale knowledge makes this search practical. Our evaluation indicates that TRIPEL efficiently selects appropriate time scales and system boundaries.

10 Acknowledgements

We appreciate the help of Susan Branting, Dan Clancy, Brian Falkenhainer, Bert Kay, and Rich Mallory, all of whom provided valuable comments on earlier drafts; and our botany experts Bassett Maguire and Art Souther, both of whom helped evaluate TRIPEL.

References

Allen, T., and Starr, T. 1982. *Hierarchy*. Chicago: University of Chicago Press.

Cormen, T. H.; Leiserson, C. E.; and Rivest, R. L. 1989. *Introduction to Algorithms*. New York: McGraw-Hill.

Falkenhainer, B., and Forbus, K. 1991. Compositional modeling: Finding the right model for the job. *Artificial Intelligence* 51:95–143.

Forbus, K. 1984. Qualitative process theory. *Artificial Intelligence* 24:85–168.

Iwasaki, Y., and Levy, A. Y. 1993. Automated model selection for simulation. In *Proceedings of the Seventh International Workshop on Qualitative Reasoning*, 108–116.

Iwasaki, Y. 1988. Causal ordering in a mixed structure. In *Proceedings of AAAI-88*, 313–318. San Mateo, CA: Morgan Kaufmann.

Iwasaki, Y. 1990. Reasoning with multiple abstraction models. In T. Ellman, R. K., and Mostow, J., eds., *Working Notes of the AAAI Workshop on Automatic Generation of Approximations and Abstractions*, 122–134.

Jacquez, J. 1985. *Compartmental Analysis in Biology and Medicine*. Ann Arbor, MI: University of Michigan Press.

Kokotovic, P.; O'Malley, Jr., R.; and Sannuti, P. 1976. Singular perturbations and order reduction in control theory – an overview. *Automatica* 12:123–132.

Kuipers, B. 1987. Abstraction by time scale in qualitative simulation. In *Proceedings of AAAI-87*, 621–625.

Man-kam Yip, K. 1993. Model simplification by asymptotic order of magnitude reasoning. In *Proceedings of AAAI-93*, 634–641. Menlo Park, CA: AAAI Press.

Nayak, P.; Joskowicz, L.; and Addanki, S. 1992. Automated model selection using context-dependent behaviors. In *Proceedings of AAAI-92*, 710–716. Menlo Park, CA: AAAI Press.

Nayak, P. P. 1992. Causal approximations. In *Proceedings of AAAI-92*, 703–709. Menlo Park, CA: AAAI Press.

O'Neill, R.; DeAngelis, D.; Waide, J.; and Allen, T. 1986. *A Hierarchical Concept of Ecosystems*. Princeton, NJ: Princeton University Press.

Porter, B.; Lester, J.; Murray, K.; Pittman, K.; Souther, A.; Acker, L.; and Jones, T. 1988. AI research in the context of a multifunctional knowledge base: The botany knowledge base project. Technical Report AI88-88, University of Texas at Austin.

Rickel, J., and Porter, B. 1992. Automated modeling for answering prediction questions: Exploiting interaction paths. In *Proceedings of the Sixth International Workshop on Qualitative Reasoning*, 82–95. Edinburgh, Scotland: Heriot-Watt University.

Rosswall, T.; Woodmansee, R.; and Risser, P., eds. 1988. *Scales and Global Change: Spatial and Temporal Variability in Biospheric Processes*. New York: John Wiley and Sons.

Saksena, V.; O'Reilly, J.; and Kokotovic, P. 1984. Singular perturbations and time-scale methods in control theory: Survey 1976-1983. *Automatica* 20(3):273–293.

Schaffer, W. 1981. Ecological abstraction: The consequences of reduced dimensionality in ecological models. *Ecological Monographs* 51(4):383–401.

Segal, L., ed. 1980. *Mathematical Models in Molecular and Cellular Biology*. Cambridge: Cambridge University Press. chapter 3.

Simon, H., and Ando, A. 1961. Aggregation of variables in dynamic systems. *Econometrica* 29:111–138.

Williams, B. 1991. Critical abstraction: Generating simplest models for causal explanation. In *Working Papers of the Fifth International Workshop on Qualitative Reasoning about Physical Systems*, 77–92. Austin, TX: University of Texas at Austin.

Zeigler, B. P. 1980. Simplification of biochemical reaction systems. In Segal, L., ed., *Mathematical Models in Molecular and Cellular Biology*. Cambridge: Cambridge University Press.

Decompositional Modeling through Caricatural Reasoning

Brian C. Williams and **Olivier Raiman**
Xerox Palo Alto Research Center
3333 Coyote Hill Road, Palo Alto, CA 94304 USA
{bwilliams, raiman}@parc.xerox.com

Abstract

Many physical phenomena are sufficiently complex that the corresponding equations afford little insight, or no analytical method provides an exact solution. *Decompositional modeling (DM)* captures a modeler's tacit skill at solving nonlinear algebraic systems. DM divides statespace into a patchwork of simpler subregimes, called *caricatures,* each of which preserves only the dominant characteristics of that regime. It then solves the simpler nonlinear system and identifies its *domain of validity.* The varying patchwork reflects how variations in the parameters change the dominant characteristics. The patchwork is built by extracting equational features consisting of the relative strength of terms, and then exagerating and merging these features in different combinations, resulting in the different caricatural regimes. DM operates by providing strategic guidance to a pair of symbolic manipulation systems for qualitative sign and order of magnitude algebra. The approach is sufficient to replicate a broad set of examples from acid-base chemistry.

Introduction

Much work within the qualitative reasoning community (?; Falkenhainer & Forbus 1991; Nayak, Joskowicz, & Addanki 1991; Weld 1991) has concentrated on methods for selecting and composing sets of models with a diversity of underlying modeling assumptions, and a strong emphasis has been placed on managing the diversity of these models. This is a fruitful avenue. Yet it is also important to realize that this diversity arises in each physical domain from a small, core set of principles, such as Newton's laws or Maxwell's equations. The application of these principles are taught from the start of a modeler's education. Thus of equal importance is the skill of a modeler to adapt these principles to the phenomena being accounted for.

In this paper we introduce a complementary, domain independent approach called *decompositional modeling (DM).* The task we address is finding analytic solutions to systems of nonlinear equations, couched in the domain of analytical chemistry. Instead of solving a system directly, DM partitions the behavior of each equation into a patchwork of regimes where different behaviors dominate, and the equations in each regime are simplified to reflect only what is significant. Regimes for the overall system are then constructed by composing the regions of the individual equations, and then solving the system of simplified equations, to describe the behavior within each of the system's regimes. In addition to the overall decompositional process, this work is novel for its use of the concept of a *caricature* to extract the appropriate regimes, and the demonstration of the power of *qualitative algebraic resolution* at all stages of the modeling process.

An Example From Chemistry

To ground our approach, consider the application of decompositional modeling to the analysis of the equilibrium behavior of a simple reaction — the dilution of acid molecules, AH, into water. The dilution is characterized by the reactions $H_2O \rightleftharpoons H^+ + OH^-$ and $AH \rightleftharpoons H^+ + A^-$; its equilibrium is governed by:

(I1) Charge balance: $\quad h^+ = oh^- + a^-,$
(I2) Mass balance: $\quad C_a = ah + a^-,$
(I3) Water equilibrium: $\quad K_w = h^+oh^-,$
(I4) Acid equilibrium: $\quad K_a ah = h^+a^-,$

where ah, a^-, h^+, h_2o, and oh^- denote concentration at equilibrium of the species AH, A^-, H^+, H_2O, and OH^-, respectively. Note that although the concentration of species S is traditionally denoted $[S]$, this conflicts with the use of $[\ ]$, within qualitative reasoning, to denote a quantity's sign. K_w and K_a are equilibrium constants for the water and acid ionization, and C_a denotes the initial concentration of AH.

Determining the equilibrium concentrations in terms of constants K_w, K_a and AH directly requires the solution of four nonlinear equations in four unknowns. For example, solving for H^+ ions yields the *equilibrium concentration equation:*

$$h^{+3} + K_a h^{+2} - (K_a C_a + K_w)h^+ = K_a K_w.$$

The derivation of this equation was highlighted in text (Beckwith 1985) (chapter 5) to demonstrate the dangers of using brute force. Even for this simple case

"

the concentration equation is a third degree polynomial in h^+, whose roots are difficult to solve for by hand. Recent developments in the automatic solution of nonlinear equations provides some additional latitude. However, problems arise for slightly more complicated cases. For example, for polyprotic acids — acids with more than one replaceable hydrogen ion H^+, such as H_3PO_4 — the degree of the equations increases with the number of replaceable ions. Thus for example H_3PO_4 has three replaceable ions and results in a concentration equation of degree five. There are no general closed form solutions to algebraic equations of degree five or higher (by Galois), and it is difficult to derive insight from such equations directly. For more interesting chemical systems, such as those studied in atmospheric modeling, the number of reactions range in the hundreds. In this situation the application of a direct method clearly breaks down and even when numeric methods are applied, approximations are performed liberally.

Instead, a chemist is taught to proceed as follows (taken from (Beckwith 1985), chapter 5). First, having introduced equations I1–I4 governing the reaction's equilibrium, the chemist guesses several interesting simplifying assumptions (A1-4) about what the dominant species may be:

A1: The acid is weak ($a^- \ll C_a$).

A2: The acid is strong ($ah \ll C_a$).

A3: The solution is essentially neutral ($a^- \ll h^+$).

A4: The solution is strongly acidic ($oh^- \ll h^+$).

Combining, for example, assumptions A2 and A4 and applying them to the charge and mass balance equations (I1,I2) produces $h^+ \approx a^-$ (I1') and $C_a \approx a^-$ (I2'). Solving for h^+ results in $h^+ \approx C_a$, a far simpler result than produced through a direct solution without simplification. Applying other combinations of assumptions produces:

Asump.	Reg.	Simplified Concentration Eqns.	
A2,A4	R1	$h^+ \approx C_a$	E1
A3	R2	$h^{+2} \approx K_w$	E2
A2	R3	$h^{+2} - C_a h^+ \approx K_w$	E3
A4	R4	$h^{+2} + K_a h^+ \approx C_a K_a$	E4
A1,A4	R5	$h^{+2} \approx C_a K_a$	E5
A1	R6	$h^{+2} \approx C_a K_a + K_w$	E6
none	R7	$h^{+3} + K_a h^{+2} - (K_a C_a + K_w)h^+ = K_a K_w$	E7

The remaining step is to determine the *domain of validity* for each set of assumptions — the constraints that the assumptions impose on the givens, K_a, K_w and C_a. Returning to the pair of assumptions A2 and A4, from A2 ($ah \ll C_a$) the chemist derives $C_a^2/K_a \ll C_a$ by substituting for ah and a^- using the simplified acid equilibrium (I4), acid concentration (E1) and mass balance (I2') equations. And from A4 ($oh^- \ll h^+$) the chemist derives $K_w/C_a \ll C_a$ by substituting for oh^- and h^+ using the simplified acid concentration (E1) and water equilibrium (I3) equations.

These two constraints define a region, R1, whose fringe corresponds to the two bold lines in the upper right corner of the region diagram in figure 1 (taken from (Beckwith 1985), p. 75). The domains of validity R2–R7 for the remaining sets of assumptions partitions the reaction's behavior into simpler regimes according to the values of C_a and K_a. Given these results, the problem of identifying a solution's acidity for given values of C_a and K_a involves identifying the appropriate region and applying the corresponding simplified concentration equation.

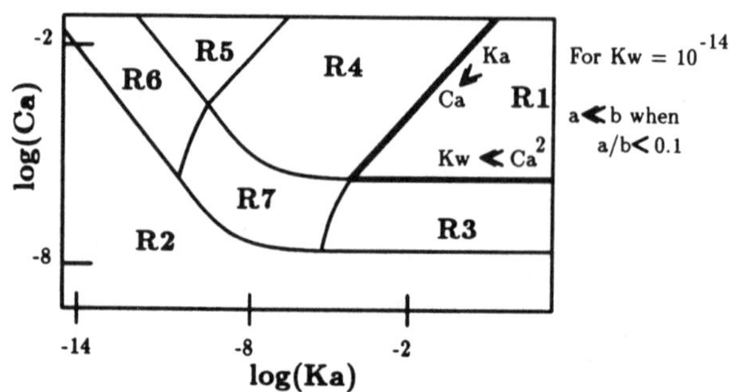

Figure 1: The different combinations of simplifying assumptions divide the space of values for C_a and K_a into simpler regimes of dominant behavior. Its given that $K_w = 10^{-14}$ and $a \ll b$ when $a/b < 0.1$.

Decompositional Modeling and Caricatures

In this example we saw that the analytical chemistry task is in essence one of solving a system of simultaneous, nonlinear equations, and that the modeling process is fundamentally decompositional. This approach results in behavioral descriptions that are more tractable to manipulate and provide greater insight. The example also demonstrates the five major steps of DM: 1) identify simplifying assumptions about the dominance of parameters, 2) combine these assumptions to define different subregimes of dominant behavior, 3) simplify the system of equations based on the assumptions of a particular subregime, 4) solve the simplified equations to obtain the system's dominant behavior over that subregime, and 5) identify the domain of validity over which the simplified behavior is valid.

This provides a layer of structure for the modeling process, but it doesn't explain where the simplifying assumptions come from, or provide a conceptual viewpoint of the overall process. For this we use the metaphor of a *caricature*. In decompositional modeling the patchwork of regimes, corresponding to dominant behaviors are derived by reinforcing the "prominent features" of the system's behavior.

From a commonsense standpoint a caricature of an object is a description which exaggerates prominent features and eliminates insignificant features. For example caricatures of Richard Nixon reduce his face to little more than a nose with an exaggerated slope. Applying this concept to modeling, given a system of initial equations DM constructs a *caricature of the system* by exaggerating one or more of the equation's prominent features. In this paper, we take "prominent" to mean that one term a of an equation E dominates another term b: $|a| > |b|$; that is, a is further from zero than b. DM exaggerates this feature by making $|a|$ much greater than $|b|$, thus making a dominant and b insignificant: $|a| > |b| \rightsquigarrow a \gg b$. We call this relation a *caricatural assumption*. By using this assumption to simplify E, DM produces a *caricatural equation*, that eliminates the insignificant features.

For example, given that all concentrations are positive, two prominent features of equation I2 ($C_a =$ ah $+ a^-$) are $|C_a| > |ah|$ and $|C_a| > |a^-|$ (note that all concentrations are positive). Exaggerating $|C_a| > |ah|$ introduces the caricatural assumption $C_a \gg$ ah, and allows I2 to be replaced by the caricatural equation $C_a \approx a^-$. This corresponds to the chemist's notion of a strong acid (i.e., essentially all AH dissociates). Conversely, exaggerating $|C_a| > |a^-|$ introduces the assumption $C_a \gg a^-$, and produces the caricature $C_a \approx$ ah, the chemist's notion of a weak acid (i.e., a negligible fraction of the acid AH dissociates).

Of course an alternative approach might take a quantity or subterm from *any* two equations and presume one dominates another. However, the number of potential assumptions would be prohibitively large. Instead the concept of caricature allows us to use existing features of the initial equations as clues to what relations are worth exaggerating. What is striking is that the restricted set generated through caricatures matches the simplifying assumptions introduced in a variety of acid-base chemistry examples.

Summarizing the observations of this section, the DM algorithm is:

Decompositional Modeling: Given a system of non-linear equations **E** with state variables **x** and parameters **p**:

1. Generate the caricatural assumptions C_i for each $E_i \in \mathbf{E}$.

2. Merge the sets of assumptions of the E_i, producing a set C whose elements are sets of combined assumptions corresponding to dominance regimes.

   Then, **for each set** $c \in C$,

3. use c to extract the caricature of each $E_i \in \mathbf{E}$, producing $\mathbf{E}'$;

4. solve for **x** in the system of caricatures $\mathbf{E}'$, and

5. derive from c and **E** the domain of validity.

DM relies heavily on the computational machinery of qualitative algebraic reasoning(Williams 1991; Raiman 1991) to perform tactical inferences. This corresponds to the rote algebraic manipulations taught

informally to a modeler early on, and is discussed in the next section. The art of the modeler is the strategic guidance given to these manipulations. This is the contribution of this paper, and is the focus of the remaining sections.

Qualitative Algebraic Inference

DM operates by strategically guiding the inferences of two symbolic manipulation systems, one for a sign algebra, and a second for order of magnitude equations. We provide here an overview of the algebraic foundation underlying DM. Representationally it is unified as a set algebra that captures knowledge of order and dominance. Computationally it is unified through *qualitative resolution*. Decompositional modeling involves reasoning about three types of information: non-linear equations, such as $K_a$ah $= h^+a^-$, inequalities between magnitudes, such as $|a^-| < |h^+|$, and order of magnitude information, such as $|a^-| \ll |h^+|$ and $|a^-| \approx |h^+|$. Both equations and inequalities are expressed as equations in the hybrid qualitative/quantitative algebra SR1 (Williams 1991) (an algebra combining signs and reals). The domain of SR1 extends the reals to include signs (i.e., $\hat{+} \equiv (0, \inf)$, $\hat{-} \equiv (-\inf, 0)$ and $\hat{?} \equiv (-\inf, \inf)$). The operators of SR1 extend the standard operators of the reals ($+, -, \times$ and $/$) to this larger domain, resulting for example in the combination of a real and sign algebra. As usual $[r]$ maps a real r to its sign. In SR1 an inequality, such as $C_a >$ ah is expressed by the hybrid equation $[C_a - \text{ah}] = \hat{+}$, and $|C_a| > |\text{ah}|$ is expressed by $[C_a^2 - \text{ah}^2] = \hat{+}$. Since the elements of the algebra are sets, expressions are related using $\subset$ as well as $=$. In addition, the set relation $\approx$ represents non-empty intersection.

Dominance relations and other types of order of magnitude information are captured as equations in the algebra of *Estimates* (Raiman 1991). The domain of Estimates extends the reals to include ϵ, a set of infinitesimal values around 0 that are negligible with respect to 1. Like SR1, Estimates' algebra extends the standard operators and includes the same set relations as SR1. The dominance relations are represented by: $a \gg b \equiv b \subset \epsilon a$, and $a \approx b \equiv a \subset (1 + \epsilon)b$. Intuitively ϵa denotes the set of all values much smaller than a, and $(1 + \epsilon)a$ denotes all values close to a.

Note that, although seemingly disparate, SR1 and Estimates are both instances of set algebras over the reals, and as such share many properties — in particular a common algebraic inference structure. For both algebras the basic inference involves combining two equations, and is performed through three steps: solve for a shared variable in one equation, substitute the solution into the second equation, and simplify the composite result. For example, consider the composition of SR1 equations $s + [a] \approx u$ and $t - [a] \approx v$. First, the shared variable $[a]$ is solved for in the first

Initial Eqns		Sign Eqns	prominent feature	caricatural assumptions
$h^+ = oh^- + a^-$	(I1)	$[a^-] = \hat{+}, [oh^-] = \hat{+}$	$|h^+| > |oh^-|$	$h^+ \gg oh^-$ (A4)
$h^+ = oh^- + a^-$	(I1)	$[oh^-] = \hat{+}, [a^-] = \hat{+}$	$|h^+| > |a^-|$	$h^+ \gg a^-$ (A3)
$C_a = ah + a^-$	(I2)	$[ah] = \hat{+}, [a^-] = \hat{+}$	$|C_a| > |a^-|$	$C_a \gg a^-$ (A1)
$C_a = ah + a^-$	(I2)	$[a^-] = \hat{+}, [ah] = \hat{+}$	$|C_a| > |ah|$	$C_a \gg ah$ (A2)
$K_w = h^+ oh^-$	(I3)		none	none
$K_a ah = h^+ a^-$	(I4)		none	none

Figure 2: The complete set of caricatural assumptions and equations.

equation, resulting in $[a] \subset u - s$. Next, the result is substituted for $[a]$ in the second equation using substitution of supersets, and results in $t - (u - s) \approx v$. Finally the result is simplified, producing $t - u + s \approx v$ or equivalently $t + s \approx v + u$. The following are the results of additional examples for the two algebras:

$$s + [a] \approx u, \quad t - [a] \approx v \quad \Rightarrow \quad s + t \approx u + v$$
$$[a - b] = s, \quad [b - c] = t \quad \Rightarrow \quad [a - c] \subset s + t$$
$$s + a \approx u, \quad t - a \approx v \quad \Rightarrow \quad s + t \approx u + v$$

An important property of each example is that it has the flavor of propositional resolution. A term and its negation are identified in the two equations (e.g., $[a]$ and $-[a]$), they are eliminated from both equations, and the respective sides of the two equations are combined. We refer to this process as *qualitative resolution*. The details of qualitative resolution for SR1 (performed by *Minima* and *Estimates*) are described extensively in (Williams 1991) and (Raiman 1991), respectively. For our purposes we can think of Minima and Estimates together as a qualitative resolution black box. What is striking is that each step of decompositional modeling (DM) maps to a particular set of qualitative resolutions. DM is then performed by framing a qualitative resolution problem at each step. This process is the focus of the remaining sections.

Step 1 & 2. Caricatural Assumptions

DM first extracts and then exagerates the prominent features of each $E_i \in \mathbf{E}$, where a prominent feature is a partial order between the absolute values of any two terms. For each $E_i \in \mathbf{E}$ this involves:

1. Nondeterministically select a pair of terms $a, b \in E_i$.

2. Infer the ordering $(<, =, >)$ between $|a|$ and $|b|$.

   (a) Create ordering expression $O = [a^2 + b^2]$.

   (b) Repeatedly resolve O with all E_i, and constraints on variable signs $([v] = s)$.

   (c) If a sign constant $\hat{+}$ or $\hat{-}$ results, map to an ordering (e.g., $[a^2 - b^2] = \hat{+} \rightarrow |a| > |b|$).

3. Exagerate any ordering using $|a| > |b| \rightsquigarrow a \gg b$.

For example, given the mass balance equation $C_a = ah + a^-$ (I2) and the fact that a^- is positive ($[a^-] = \hat{+}$ (P1)), then DM selects C_a and ah, constructs $[C_a^2 +$

ah$^2]$, and performs the following sequence of resolutions:

$$[C_a^2 - ah^2] \quad \text{Given.}$$
$$= [(ah + a^-)^2 - ah^2] \quad \text{Resolve with } C_a = ah + a^-.$$
$$= [2aha^- + (a^-)^2] \quad \text{Simplification.}$$
$$\subset [2(\hat{+})a^- + (a^-)^2] \quad \text{Resolve with } ah \subset \hat{+}.$$
$$\subset [2(\hat{+})(\hat{+}) + (\hat{+})^2] \quad \text{Resolve with } a^- \subset \hat{+}.$$
$$\subset \hat{+} \quad \text{Simplification.}$$

Thus $[C_a^2 - ah^2] = \hat{+}$ or equivalently $|C_a| > |ah|$. Finally, exaggerating this feature according to $|a| > |b| \rightsquigarrow a \gg b$ produces $C_a \gg ah$, which is equivalent to assumption A2 of the example section. The derivation of each feature and its corresponding caricature for all equations is summarized in figure 2.

The assumptions just generated for each equation induce a patchwork of dominant subregimes local to that equation. DM then combines these local regimes into a set of global regimes. To do this step 2 combines the sets of assumptions. For the moment presume all possible combinations of assumptions are explored separately. We return later with a more sophisticated approach. Having combined the assumptions, the next two steps construct a caricature of the system's composite behavior for some subregime. Step 5 makes explicit the boundaries of that subregime.

Step 3. Extracting Dominant Behaviors

Given a set of caricatural assumptions c defining a subregime, each of the E_i is simplified using c by Estimates, producing a set of *caricatural equations*. Estimates provides a sophisticated strategy for guiding resolution during simplification (see (Raiman 1991)). For completeness we sketch here an extremely simple strategy. Recall that an assumption $a \ll b$ is encoded as the equation $a \subset \epsilon b$. Then given E_i and assumptions c, simplification involves repeatly:

1. Identifying variables $a, b \in E_1$ such that $(a \ll b) \in c$.

2. Resolving E_i and $a \subset \epsilon b$ using variable a.

For example, consider the pair of caricatural assumptions: $C_a \gg ah$ (A2) and $h^+ \gg oh^-$ (A4), corresponding to the example at the beginning of the paper. To simplify the mass balance equation $C_a = ah + a^-$ (I2), DM identifies that the pair of variables C_a and ah also appear in A2, and then through resolution DM derives the caricatural equation $C_a \approx a^-$ (I2'):

$ah + a^- = C_a$	Equation I2 to simplify.
$ah \subset \epsilon C_a$	Estimates equation for A2.
$a^- = C_a - ah$	Cancellation on I2.
$a^- \subset C_a - \epsilon C_a$	Resolving for ah in I2, A2.
$a^- \subset (1 + \epsilon)C_a$	Simplification.

This caricatural equation is equivalently $a^- \approx C_a$. Likewise, to simplify charge balance $h^+ = a^- + oh^-$ (I1), DM resolves it with A4, resulting in $h^+ \approx a^-$ (I1'). Finally, resolving I3 and I4 with A2 and A4 provides no simplification.

Step 4. Solving Caricatural Equations

Next the caricatural equations are solved for the unknown concentrations. Specifically, given a set of knowns K, caricatural equations $\mathbf{E}'$ and unknowns U, DM repeatedly resolves all pairs of equations that share an unknown. A solution is a resulting equation that contains exactly one unknown. For example, DM solves for h^+ in terms of the givens K_w, K_a and C_a, using the caricatural equations just derived:

$(1 + \epsilon)h^+ - a^- \supset 0$	Estimates eqn. for I1'.
$(1 + \epsilon)C_a - a^- \supset 0$	Estimates eqn. for I2'.
$(1 + \epsilon)h^+ - (1 + \epsilon)C_a \supset 0$	Resolving a^-.

Equivalently $h^+ \approx C_a$ (E1). Equilibrium concentrations for ah, a^- and oh^- are derived analogously. Solving systems of equations by resolution will be costly for large systems. A more desirable alternative is to use a package for solving nonlinear systems of equations. Such a package, however, must be able to manipulate error terms to ensure that the cancellation of two dominant terms does not cause the error, introduced during exageration, to become significant.

Step 5. Identifying Domains of Validity

Having just constructed a caricature of the composite system's behavior, the final step identifies the domain over which the caricatural assumptions are valid. Each bound of the domain of validity corresponds to one of the caricatural assumptions (figure 1), where an assumption $a \gg b$ produces bound $a + / - \epsilon b = 0$. A boundary is derived from an assumption A by repeatedly resolving one of the unknown variables of U that appears in A, with one of the equations in $\mathbf{E}'$. A solution is reached when no variables of U remain. For example, from $C_a \gg ah$ (A2) DM derives $K_a \gg C_a$ using I4 ($K_a ah = h^+ a^-$), I2' ($h^+ \approx C_a$), and E1 ($C_a \approx a^-$). Using a less mechanical notation:

$C_a \gg ah$	Assumption A2
$C_a \gg h^+ a^- / K_a$	Resolving ah with I4.
$C_a \gg h^+ C_a / K_a$	Resolving a^- with E1.
$C_a \gg C_a^2 / K_a$	Resolving h^+ with I2'.
$K_a \gg C_a$	Simplification.

This completes DM's process of constructing the caricature of a single subregime. The bounds and concentration equations derived through these five steps correspond exactly to those in the example section.

Step 2 (cont.) Creating a Patchwork

In the section on steps 1 & 2 we glossed over the step of merging assumptions, saying only that all combinations of assumptions were explored. DM provides a more intelligent coordination based on the interrelationship between sets of assumptions. These are depicted using the subset/superset lattice of figure 3.

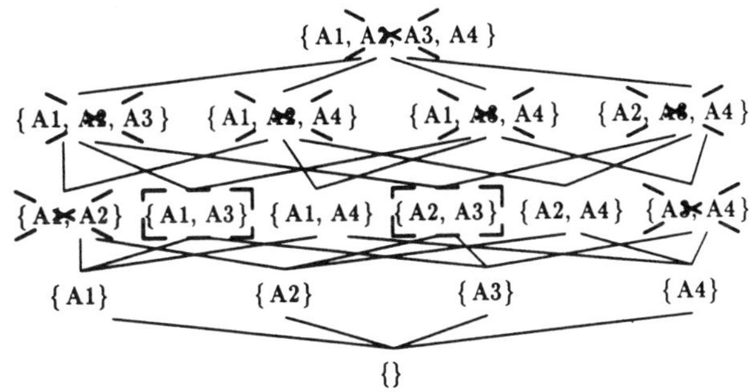

Figure 3: Subset/superset lattice of caricatural assumptions considered by DM.

First, note that the bottom of the lattice is rooted in the original model — since no assumptions are made and no approximations are performed. Moving upwards through the lattice results in simpler models, since each new assumption makes an additional term insignificant, which then drops out of the equations.

Second, although models higher in the lattice are simpler, their domain of validity is more restrictive. That is, each caricatural assumption introduces a new subregime boundary; thus, the region corresponding to the domain of validity of one caricature is a subset of any caricature appearing below it in the lattice.

Third, when moving up the lattice the added assumptions do not always result in simplification. For example, $\{A2, A3\}$ produces the same equation for h^+ as does $\{A3\}$.[1] This explains why Schaum's outline (Beckwith 1985) includes a region $R3$ for $\{A2\}$, but no region for $\{A2, A3\}$ (see figure 1). The same argument applies to the absence of $\{A1, A3\}$. These eliminated sets are depicted by squares in the lattice. Likewise, additional assumptions do not always restrict the domain of validity, particularly when the boundary they introduce is outside the existing region.

Fourth, in some cases a set of caricatural assumptions is mutually inconsistent, for example, as we pointed out earlier for $\{A1, A2\}$. This is recognized when the result of a resolution is detected to be inconsistent by Estimates or Minima. For example, from $\{A1, A2\}$ Estimates derives $C_a \gg C_a$.

While all caricatures could be generated by simply repeating steps 3-5 on all combinations of caricatural assumptions, the different combinations share two properties that DM exploits to make this process more

---

[1] But this depends on how many of the equilibrium concentrations we are interested in. $\{A2, A3\}$ may allow additional simplification over $\{A3\}$ for other species.

efficient. First, by monotonicity each superset of an inconsistent set of assumptions is also inconsistent. Thus to avoid exploring potentially large sections of the lattice, DM creates caricatures of each regime by starting at the bottom of the lattice and moving monotonically upwards, ignoring anything above an inconsistent set. In our example, of 16 potential sets of assumptions, 9 prove consistent, 2 are explicitly demonstrated inconsistent, and 5 are supersets of them and thus need not be explored. The 7 inconsistent sets are marked by X's in the lattice. Finally, caricatures of regimes are generated incrementally by exploiting monotonicity. Given the caricatural equations $\mathbf{E}'$ for a set of assumptions S, the caricatural equations of its immediate supersets $S \cup \{A_i\}$ are computed by further exaggerating $\mathbf{E}'$ using assumptions A_i.

Discussion

Decompositional modeling has been demonstrated on several analytical chemistry examples taken from (Beckwith 1985). The first step of DM is implemented in Lisp on top of Minima (Williams 1991). The remaining four steps are implemented in Prolog on top of Estimates (Raiman 1991). The solutions DM produces are guaranteed to be correct within the conditions of negligibility for order of magnitude. This paper makes precise the caricature's metaphor first introduced in (Raiman 1988), and the decompositional modelling process introduced in (Raiman & Williams 1992).

One clear need of DM is the ability to bound error, such as is available in a variety of approximate or order of magnitude systems, such as (McAllester 1981; Mavrovouniotis & Stephanopoulos 1988; Weld 1991; Shirley & Falkenhainer 1990; Nayak 1991; Yip 1993). A second need, highlighted at the end of the section on step 4, is to exploit recent advances in solving nonlinear systems, by embodying them with sufficient error bounding capabilities. (Nayak 1991) provides an alternative to Estimates for performing order of magnitude inference, based on a very interesting mapping to linear programming.

An earlier example of a decompositional approach is (Sacks 1987) on piecewise linear approximations. An important difference is that the approximated behaviors of decompositional modeling remain non-linear. The claim is that the approximation should preserve the essential characteristics of the behavior, and this is often nonlinear. Until recently linear approximations were necessary for a system to be solvable. This is dramatically changing, however, given recent advances in nonlinear symbolic algebra.

Finally, note that our approach only addresses decompositional modeling applied to algebraic systems, not for example dynamical systems. In this context a caricature would, for example, characterize an ever so slightly decaying satellite's orbit as a limit cycle (Raiman 1988). A variety of authors have explored this context, including (Weld 1988; Davis 1987).

References

Addanki, S. and R. Cremonini and J. S. Penberthy. 1989. Reasoning about Assumptions in Graphs of Models. In *IJCAI-89*. Detroit, MI: Morgan Kaufmann.

Beckwith, D., ed. 1985. *Analytical Chemistry*. NY: McGraw-Hill.

Davis, E. 1987. Order of magnitude reasoning in qualitative differential equations. TR 312, NYU Computer Science Department.

Falkenhainer, B., and Forbus, K. 1991. Compositional modeling: finding the right model for the job. *Artif. Intell.* 51.

Mavrovouniotis, M. L., and Stephanopoulos, G. 1988. Formal order-of-magnitude reasoning in process engineering. *Computer Chemical Engineering* 12:867–880.

McAllester, D. 1981. Algebraic approximation. In *Proceedings IJCAI-81*, 624–628.

Nayak, P.; Joskowicz, L.; and Addanki, S. 1991. Automated Model Selection Using Context Dependent Behaviors. In *International Workshop on Qualitative Reasoning*.

Nayak, P. 1991. Validating Approximate Equilibrium Models. In *AAAI Model-based Reasoning Workshop*.

Raiman, O., and Williams, B. C. 1992. Caricatures: Generating Models of Dominant Behavior. In *International Workshop on Qualitative Reasoning*.

Raiman, O. 1988. Caricatural Reasoning. In *International Workshop on Qualitative Reasoning*.

Raiman, O. 1991. Order of magnitude reasoning. *Artif. Intell.* 51.

Sacks, E. 1987. 'Piecewise Linear Reasoning. In *Proceedings AAAI-87*, 655–659.

Shirley, M., and Falkenhainer, B. 1990. Explicit Reasoning about Accuracy for Approximating Physical Systems. In *Working Notes of the Automatic Generation of Approximations and Abstractions Workshop*.

Weld, D. S. 1988. Exaggeration. In *Proceedings AAAI-88*, 291–296.

Weld, D. S. 1991. Reasoning about Model Accuracy. Technical Report 91-05-02, Department of Computer Science and Engineering, University of Washington.

Williams, B. C. 1991. A theory of interactions: unifying qualitative and quantitative algebraic rasoning. *Artif. Intell.* 51.

Yip, K. M. 1993. 'Model Simplification by Asymptotic Order of Magnitude Reasoning. In *Proceedings AAAI-93*, 634–640.

Comparative Simulation[1]

Michael Neitzke, Bernd Neumann

Universität Hamburg, FB Informatik, AB KOGS
Vogt-Kölln-Str. 30
22527 Hamburg, Germany
{neitzke | neumann}@informatik.uni-hamburg.de

Abstract

In this paper, a new theory of qualitative comparative descriptions for dynamic system behavior is presented. System deviations and behavior deviations are viewed relative to the normal case. In contrast to existing approaches, a deviation is not only characterized as "less than normal" or "greater than normal" (LGTN), but deviations can also be compared with each other in order to avoid ambiguities and provide more precise predictions. A fundamental problem in comparative behavior prediction is that LGTN deviations can cause non-LGTN effects like a change of the direction of a parameter or a change in the order of events. Such so-called *changes in the behavioral topology* (10,11) cannot be handled by existing approaches in a satisfying way, but are covered by our theory. Our theory is incorporated into the relative simulator RSIM+. RSIM+ can be viewed as an extension of the QSIM simulator (7). It provides a refined system description with qualitative predictions which have not been achieved in other work. In particular, it is guaranteed that all behaviors following from an LGTN deviation are predicted.

1 Introduction

In fault diagnosis and system analysis one often has to predict the consequences of system changes to the system's behavior. When dealing with continuous systems, most changes and consequences can qualitatively be best described by relative descriptions like "less than normal" or "greater than normal" (LGTN). That is, the system is compared to a reference system and the system's behavior is compared to the reference system's behavior. While this sort of descriptions has widely been used to analyse static systems or equilibrium states of dynamic systems (2,4,5,6) only few approaches exist that can deal with general dynamic system behaviors (10,11).

Dynamic behavior prediction for system changes with an LGTN character entails some difficulties:

1. LGTN deviations can influence the duration of processes. Therefore, the deviating and the reference behavior can get "out of phase" so that a pointwise comparison of behaviors is problematic. See the frictionless spring/block system of Fig. 1[2]. A higher mass would lead to a higher period of oscillation. It would make no sense to

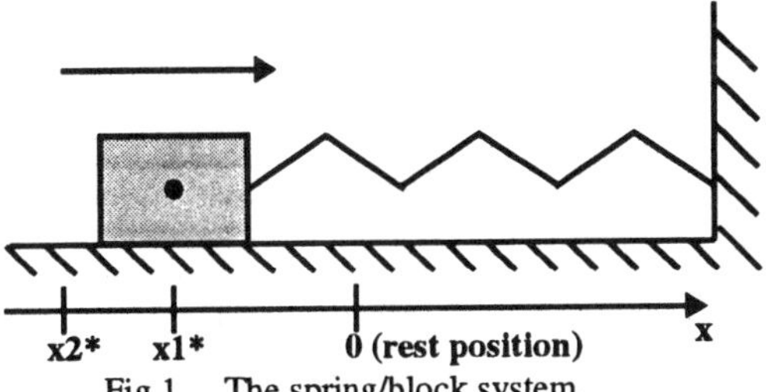

Fig.1   The spring/block system.

compare a mass that is moving to the rest position with a mass that is moving away from that point. Instead, corresponding parts of the oscillation process should be compared with each other.

2. An unambiguous prediction of behavior may require the comparison of deviations. This is the case, for example, when the net effect of opposing deviations has to be considered or two competing deviations contribute to the system behavior. A higher initial displacement x of the spring, e.g., leads to a higher velocity v. Because of the linearity of Hooke's law (F=k*x), spring force equals spring constant times displacement, and since F=m*a, (force equals mass times acceleration), x and v are always too high by the same factor, so that the period of oscillation does not change (see 10,11). This can be deduced, if a comparison of the deviations of x and v is possible and specific properties of linear relationships can be represented and exploited.

3. Deviations with an LGTN character can have effects with a non-LGTN character, i.e. drastic effects like a change of direction or a different order of events. For example, if a tank, initially partly filled with water, is being completely filled by a pump, a low pump pressure would lead to a higher duration of the filling process - provided that the pump pressure is still higher than the water pressure in the tank. But if not, the water level in the tank would decrease until the pump pressure is reached. That is, when the pump pressure is too low, the direction of the water flow can change. In the heat exchanger of Fig. 2, hot oil is cooled down. If normally the oil reaches the equilibrium temperature somewhere inside the heat exchanger and then leaves the heat exchanger completely cooled down, a

---

1. This research was supported by the Bundesminister für Forschung und Technologie under contract 01 IW 203 D-3, joint project Behavior.

2. Our techniques have been used for more complex systems like a steering control loop or a ballast system. To facilitate a better comparison to existing approaches we use well-known systems of the qualitative physics literature in this paper. Most examples stem from (11).

too high oil velocity could prevent the equilibrium temperature to be reached. Weld calls such drastic effects *changes in the behavioral topology* (10) because they involve a structural change of the behavior description.

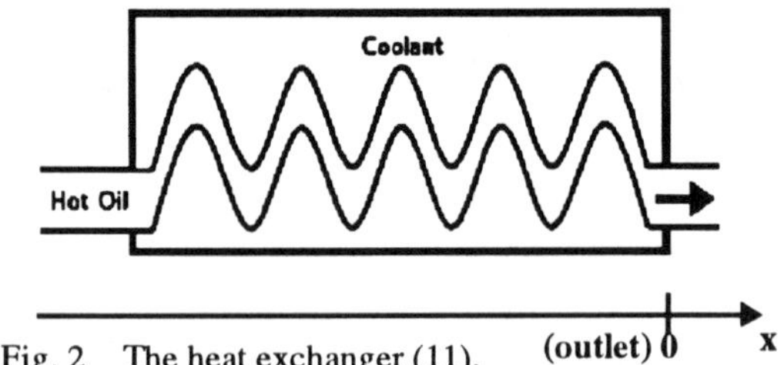

Fig. 2   The heat exchanger (11).

The first problem has sufficiently been solved by Weld's concept of *perspective* (10), i.e. deviations of parameters are described with respect to other parameters than time. The latter two problems, however, have not been solved in a satisfying way by the existing approaches: In qualitative simulation, usually, linear, underlinear, and overlinear dependencies are not distinguished. Instead, they are covered by the more general monotonic dependency. A comparison of deviations is not provided. In (10), Weld gives a proof that there does not exist a useful perspective to handle the case of the too high amplitude. In this paper, we present a theory of comparative descriptions where

- behaviors can be synchronized in order to allow a sensible comparison of corresponding parts,
- parameter values can be classified as too low, too high or normal,
- deviations of parameter values can be compared with each other,
- properties of special monotonic relationships can be represented, (This includes linear, overlinear and underlinear relationships as well as "faulty" monotonic relationships like a relationship that is too steep or too flat in comparison to the reference system.)
- changes of the behavioral topology can be handled.

This theory is realized by the RSIM+ simulator. RSIM+'s input and output and parts of the simulation technique are oriented towards QSIM (7). In fact, RSIM+ can be viewed as an extension of QSIM where QSIM's (absolute) parameter and state descriptions are refined by relative descriptions. These relative descriptions are based on the concept of P values which relate deviations to absolute values (8). In Section 2 we summarize the essential definitions concerning P values and deviations. Section 3 explains RSIM+'s modeling properties. In Section 4 it is demonstrated how RSIM+ works, and our example problems are solved. Section 5 compares RSIM+ to related approaches, and Section 6 gives a summary.

2 Describing Deviations

As it is required in QSIM, each physical quantity, called parameter, is taken to be a "reasonable" function of time, i.e. a continuously differentiable function of time with a finite number of "critical points" (where the derivative is 0)

in any bounded interval. We distinguish between a parameter in the disturbed system and the same parameter in the reference system by indexing the latter with "ref".

Def. 2.1: The deviation of a parameter value $f(t)$ from a reference value $f_{ref}(t)$ is called a **continuous** deviation with regard to a basis landmark l_a if $f(t)$ is on the same side of l_a as $f_{ref}(t)$, that is $(f(t) < l_a \wedge f_{ref}(t) < l_a) \vee (f(t) > l_a \wedge f_{ref}(t) > l_a)$. Otherwise it is called a **discontinuous** deviation wrt l_a.

The idea of this definition is to distinguish between deviations that can be described as less or greater than normal and deviations where this is not adequate due to drastic behavior changes. The border between continuous and discontinuous deviations is determined by the basis landmark which also separates "+" and "-" in the sign quantity space.

Weld calls arbitrarily small changes in the value of a parameter *differential*, and more drastic changes *non-differential* (11). The essential property of a differential change is that it could be arbitrarily small without falling into a qualitatively different area, i.e. no landmark value may lie between the deviating value and the normal value. Following Weld we call deviations that lie in the same qualitative area, i.e. have the same absolute description as the normal value, **differential**, and deviations that lie outside this area **non-differential**.

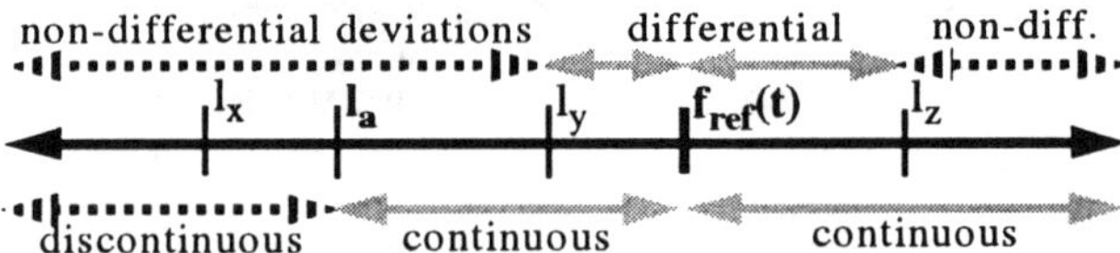

Fig. 3   Differential, non-differential, continuous and discontinuous deviations from a reference value $f_{ref}(t)$ wrt l_a.

Differential and continuous deviations are very similar. For quantity spaces with only one landmark like $\{-, 0, +\}$ both classes are identical. In general, each differential deviation is a continuous deviation and each discontinuous deviation is a non-differential deviation (Fig. 3). The way and the extent $f(t)$ differs from $f_{ref}(t)$ can be described by the quotient of the distances of $f(t)$ and $f_{ref}(t)$ from the basis landmark. We call this quotient the P value of $f(t)$.

$$\underline{Def.\ 2.2}: \quad P(f,t) = \frac{f(t) - l_a}{f_{ref}(t) - l_a}$$

Note, that P values are relative, but not qualitative. However, we are only interested in qualitative properties of P values. Therefore, we don't need exact values for the function P. We are working with two different kinds of qualitative information about P values. First, we distinguish different areas of P values. The relevant distinctions are captured by the function PQ:

Def. 2.3:
$PQ(f,t) = too\text{-}low \qquad ::= 0 < P(f,t) < 1$
$PQ(f,t) = normal \qquad ::= P(f,t) = 1 \vee f(t)\text{-}l_a = f_{ref}(t)\text{-}l_a = 0$
$PQ(f,t) = too\text{-}high \qquad ::= P(f,t) > 1$
$PQ(f,t) = discontinuous ::= P(f,t) < 0 \vee (f(t) - l_a = 0 \wedge f_{ref}(t) - l_a <> 0) \vee (f(t) - l_a <> 0 \wedge f_{ref}(t) - l_a = 0)$

Second, we use the relations <, =, and > to compare positive P values. This gives us a handle to refine qualitative system descriptions and behaviors, to distinguish more specific classes of constraints between system parameters, and to diminish some unwanted spurious behaviors. For example, system properties like the linear dependency between two parameters can be described in terms of P values, since the P values of such parameters are equal as well as the P values of their derivatives.

In addition to a QSIM-type description where the amount of a parameter is described by an interval or a landmark, and its derivative is described by a sign, in RSIM+, amount and derivative can also be described by a PQ value and relations between P values. Thus we have four description layers providing both absolute and relative descriptions: sign layer, qval layer (intervals or landmarks), PQ layer, and P layer.

3 Modeling Systems

An RSIM+ model is given by a set of constraints just as a model in QSIM. In general, every RSIM+ model is a specialized QSIM model because aside from "exact" constraints, like SUM or PRODUCT (Table 2), it comprises specializations of QSIM's qualitative constraints. These specializations concern monotonic relationships between two parameters: On the one hand, linear, overlinear and underlinear relationships can be distinguished. On the other hand, it can be expressed that a monotonic relationship in the disturbed system is steeper or flatter than in the reference system. Table 1 shows the following three specializations of QSIM's M_0^+ constraint. The definitions are equivalent under qualitative absolute descriptions, but they differ under relative descriptions.

$$\text{LINEAR}_0^+(f,g) \quad :\Leftrightarrow f(t)=H(g(t)) \;\wedge\; f_{ref}(t)=H(g_{ref}(t)) \;\wedge\; H(0)=0 \wedge H'(x)>0 \wedge H''(x)=0$$

$$\text{OVERLINEAR}_0^+(f,g):\Leftrightarrow f(t)=H(g(t)) \;\wedge\; f_{ref}(t)=H(g_{ref}(t)) \;\wedge\; H(0)=0 \wedge H'(x)>0 \wedge H''(x)>0$$

$$\text{TOO-FLAT}_0^+(f,g) \quad :\Leftrightarrow f(t)=H(g(t)) \wedge f_{ref}(t)=H_{ref}(g_{ref}(t)) \;\wedge\; H(0)=0 \wedge H'(x)>0 \wedge H_{ref}(0)=0 \wedge H_{ref}'(x)>0 \wedge \forall x,y: H'(x)<H_{ref}'(y)$$

Table 1: PQ tupels and P Relationships for Some Special M_0^+ Constraints (L: too-low, N: normal, H: too-high, D: discont.)

Constraint(f,g)	LINEAR_0^+	OVERLINEAR_0^+	TOO-FLAT_0^+
Possible PQ tupels: ((PQ(f),PQ(g))	{(L,L),(N,N), (H,H),(D,D)}	{(L,L),(N,N), (H,H),(D D)}	{(L,L),(L,N), (L,H),(N,H), (H,H),(D,D)}
P relationships between amounts (for positive P values)	P(f) = P(g)	If (L L) then P(f) < P(g) If (N N) then P(f) = P(g) If (H H) then P(f) > P(g)	P(f) < P(g)
P relationships between derivatives (for positive P values)	P(f') = P(g')	If PQ(g)=L then P(f')<P(g') If PQ(g)=N then P(f')=P(g') If PQ(g)=H then P(f')>P(g')	P(f') < P(g')

Table 2: Part of the Definition of the PRODUCT Constraint: h=f*g

PQ(h)	PQ(g)=L	PQ(g)=N	PQ(g)=H	PQ(g)=D
PQ(f)=L	L ∧ P(h)<P(f) ∧ P(h)<P(g)	L ∧ P(h)=P(f)	(L ∧ P(h)>P(f)) ∨ N ∨ (H ∧P(h)<P(g))	D
PQ(f)=N	L ∧ P(h)=P(g)	N	H ∧ P(h)=P(g)	D
PQ(f)=H	(L ∧ P(h)>P(g)) ∨ N ∨ (H ∧ P(h)<P(f))	H ∧ P(h)=P(f)	H ∧ P(h)>P(f) ∧ P(h)>P(g)	D
PQ(f)=D	D	D	D	L∨N∨H∨D

Fig. 4 shows the RSIM+ models of our example systems. It is required that a model and the corresponding reference model may only differ in the specializations of monotonic constraints (i.e. the deviating and the reference system must have the same QSIM model).

```
(create-model *spring/block*
  :quantity-spaces ((x-qs (x2* x1* 0)))   ;(qs-name landmarks)
  :variables ((x x-qs) v vv a f ke pe)
  :constants (m k te)
  :constraints ((deriv v x) ;the block's velocity is the
                            ;derivative of its position
    (deriv a v)             ;acceleration is the derivative of velocity
    (product f m a)         ;force equals mass times acceleration
    (product f k x)         ;force equals spring constant
                            ;times position
    (square vv v)           ;vv is the square of v.
    (product ke m vv)       ;Kinetic energy depends on the product
                            ;of mass and the square of velocity
    (square pe f)           ;Weld calls it a "cheating definition
                            ;of potential energy" (11, p.159).
    (sum te pe ke)))        ;Total energy is the sum of
                            ;kinetic and potential energy.
(create-model *heat-exchanger*
  :variables (x f q)
  :constants (v)
  :constraints ((deriv v x) ;velocity is the derivative of position
    (deriv f q)             ;heat flow is the derivative of heat
    (non-negative q)        ;heat cannot become negative
    (linear0- f q)))        ;heat flow is a linearly decreasing
                            ;function of the heat
```

Fig. 4   Models for spring/block system and heat exchanger.

4 Describing Behaviors

As in most qualitative simulators, RSIM+'s simulation mechanism is a cyclic process consisting of an intrastate analysis and an interstate analysis. The intrastate analysis takes an incomplete description of a system state as input and generates one or - because of ambiguities - several complete state descriptions. The interstate analysis takes a complete state description and generates an incomplete description of the successor state(s).

4.1 Intrastate Analysis

Fig. 5 shows the initial information we have for the spring/block system with a) too high mass, and b) too high initial displacement. Deviations from the reference system may not only concern the model (via special monotonic constraints) but additionally the initial state. Intrastate analysis in RSIM+ is done by constraint propagation. On the PQ layer, constraint propagation is based on the sets of allowed PQ value tupels for each constraint relation (Table 1, first line, Table 2). On the P layer, constraint propagation assigns relations to pairs of P values, so that a consistent graph of P values is generated. Since RSIM+ uses the relations <, =, >, the graph represents a partial order of sets of P values. Each set consists of P values of the same magnitude. Propagating constraints on the P layer means increasing the order between the P values of all parameters. The additional information on the P layer helps to avoid spurious behavior on the PQ layer. That is, if a system state is completely described on the PQ layer, it may happen that the corresponding P relationships are inconsistent, for example because of cycles in a path of < relationships.

	qval(x)	:x1*	pq(x) :N		qval(x)	:x2*	pq(x) :H
	sign(v)	:0	pq(v) :N		sign(v)	:0	pq(v) :N
	sign(k)	:-	pq(k) :N		sign(k)	:-	pq(k) :N
a)	sign(m)	:+	pq(m):H	b)	sign(m)	:+	pq(m):N

Fig. 5　Initial information about the deviating spring/block systems with a) too high mass and b) too high displacement.

Constraint propagation on the P layer is governed by two sources: On the one hand, there are relationships between the P values of the amounts of the constraint parameters and between their derivatives (Table 1, lines 2,3, Table 2). For example, in a linear relationship the P values of the parameter amounts are always equal. On the other hand, one can exploit dependencies between the relationships between amount and derivative of the constraint parameters. If, for example, (PRODUCT h f g), and $P(f) > P(f')$ and $P(g) > P(g')$, and $sign(f) = sign(f') = sign(g) = sign(g') = +$, then $P(h) > P(h')$.

4.2 Describing Behaviors - Interstate Analysis

RSIM+'s interstate analysis is realized by so-called transition rules in a similar way as in QSIM. Two types of transitions are distinguished: point transitions and interval transitions. A point transition is applied to states that describe the system at a certain time point. It infers information about the following time interval. An interval transition works in the corresponding way. In contrast to absolute transitions, a relative interval transition can infer information about the duration to reach the next event. PQ transitions, like QSIM transitions, cover all possible combinations of values that amount and derivative of a parameter can take. On the P layer an exhaustive treatment of all possible combinations of P values does not seem necessary. Instead, some special but very useful transitions have been formulated. RSIM+ uses 12 point transitions and 19 interval transitions for PQ values and 2 point transitions and 14 interval transitions for relations between P values. The following sections describe how particular aspects of system behavior are solved by RSIM+ for our example problems and they present some typical transitions.

4.2.1　Synchronization. A spring/block system with a too high mass has a longer period of oscillation. That is, the deviating and the reference system get out of phase. A strict pointwise comparison of both behaviors makes no sense. Instead, corresponding events and intervals should be compared with each other, i.e. the initial states, the intervals of approaching the rest position, the events of reaching the rest position, and so on. Therefore, a pointwise comparison must stop when the "faster" behavior reaches the next event. At this point, RSIM+ synchronizes both behaviors. This is done by interval transitions which infer information about the next event with a synchronization (the duration to reach the event is too low or too high) and without a synchronization (duration=N). In order to prevent discontinuous deviations, synchronization is triggered everytime when a parameter or its derivative reaches the basis landmark. The transition IAHDLN1 (an attempt of a systematic acronym: Amount High, Derivative Low or Normal), for example, describes the case where a parameter is too high, i.e. too far away from 0, and is approaching 0 with a too low or just a normal velocity. Therefore, the duration to reach 0 is too high.

$$\textbf{IAHDLN1:}\quad PQ(f,(t_i,t_j))=H \land sign(f,(t_i,t_j))=- \land$$
$$PQ(f',(t_i,t_j))\in \{L,N\} \land sign(f',(t_i,t_j))=+$$
$$\Rightarrow (duration(t_i,t_j+\Delta t)=H \land ((sign(f,t_j+\Delta t)=0 \land PQ(f,t_j+\Delta t)$$
$$=N) \lor (sign(f,t_j+\Delta t)=- \land PQ(f,t_j+\Delta t)\in \{L,N,H\})))$$
$$\lor (sign(f,t_j)=- \land ((duration(t_i,t_j)\in \{L,N\} \land PQ(f,t_j)=H)$$
$$\lor (duration(t_i,t_j)=N \land PQ(f,t_j)=D)))$$

Fig. 6a shows the first quarter of a period of RSIM+'s simulation output for the spring/block system with too high mass (concerning position, velocity, and acceleration of the block). It is deduced that reaching the rest position costs more time than normally. The interval transition IAHDLN1 could be used for parameter x in both intervals. Notice, that in comparison to a pure absolute simulation, (as done by QSIM,) we have the additional event that the acceleration reaches "normal". The behaviors of Fig. 6 can be derived unambiguously. In general, however, the degree of ambiguity of an RSIM+ simulation is significantly higher than that of the corresponding QSIM simulation. The projection of an RSIM+ behavior tree to absolute values results in the corresponding QSIM tree.

4.2.2　Comparison of deviations. A spring/block system with a too high amplitude would have the same period as the reference system because of the linear dependency of position and acceleration. Without a comparison of deviations, it cannot be decided what happens if the block has to cover a higher distance with a higher velocity. With RSIM+, it can be deduced, that the period of oscillation does not change because of the equality of the P values of position, velocity and acceleration (Fig. 6b).

The intrastate analysis for the initial state deduces that the P values of position, x, force, f, and acceleration, a, all are equal, i.e. they are too high by the same factor. The P value of the velocity, v, is not defined, since v and v_{ref} are both 0. The P transition P== deduces that in the following time interval the P values of x, v, and a must all be equal, if the P values of x and a are still equal:

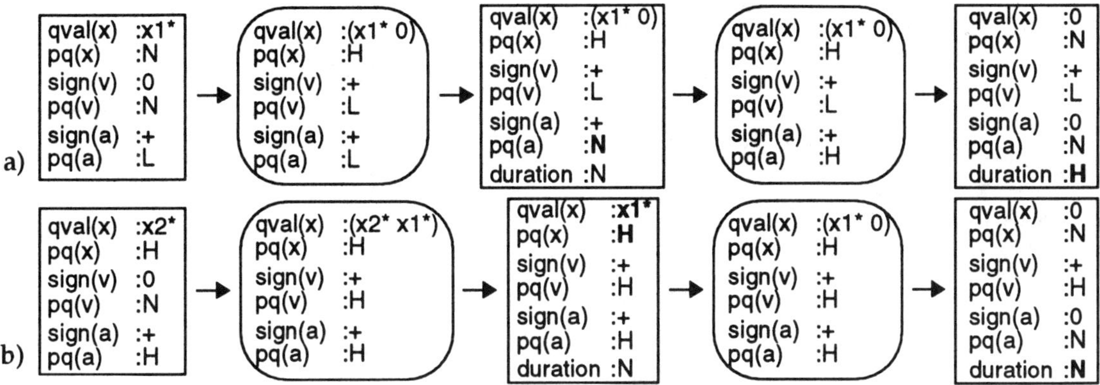

Fig. 6 Two deviating behaviors for the spring/block system, produced by RSIM+: a) the behavior for a too high mass b)the behavior for a too high amplitude. Events are indicated by rectangles, intervals by ovals.

P== : $(P(f,t_i)=P(f',t_i) \vee (PQ(f',t_i)=N \wedge sign(f',t_i)=0)) \wedge$
$\quad P(f,t_i)=P(f'',t_i)$
$\Rightarrow P(f,(t_i,t_j))=P(f',(t_i,t_j))=P(f'',(t_i,t_j)) \vee$
$\quad P(f',(t_i,t_j)) \neq P(f,(t_i,t_j)) \neq P(f'',(t_i,t_j))$

While the equality of the P values of x and a always can be determined in the intrastate analysis, the equality of $P(x)$ and $P(v)$ is propagated from state to state by transition rules like P==. A more general interval transition states that if two P values are equal in a time interval (t_i, t_j) they must still be equal at t_j. The information that the position must reach 0 in normal time is finally deduced by the interval transition IAHDH=-. This rule belongs to a group of 12 similar transitions that describe the case where a parameter is approaching 0 and both, amount and derivative, are too high or too low. In IAHDH=-, 0 is reached at the same time as normally because amount and derivative are too high by the same factor.

IAHDH=-:$PQ(f,(t_i,t_j))=PQ(f',(t_i,t_j))=H \wedge sign(f,(t_i,t_j))=-$
$\quad \wedge sign(f',(t_i,t_j))=+ \wedge P(f,(t_i,t_j))=P(f',(t_i,t_j))$
$\Rightarrow (sign(f,t_j)=0 \wedge duration(t_i,t_j)=N \wedge PQ(f,t_j)=N) \vee$
$\quad (sign(f,t_j+\Delta t)=- \wedge duration(t_i,t_j+\Delta t)=H) \vee$
$\quad (sign(f,t_j)=- \wedge duration(t_i,t_j) \in \{L,N\} \wedge PQ(f,t_j)=H)$

4.2.3 Changes in the Behavioral Topology.

A behavior can be characterized by a sequence of absolute transitions $\gamma_0, ..., \gamma_k$, i.e. the time points when a parameter reaches (or leaves) a landmark or its derivative reaches (or leaves) 0 (compare 10). Especially, we are interested in those absolute transitions $\beta_0, ..., \beta_l$, $\{\beta_j\} \subseteq \{\gamma_i\}$, where a parameter or its derivative reaches (or leaves) the basis landmark. We call the β_j basis transitions. Every behavior has a time function, T, which takes transitions to the time points when they occur.

Weld defines the behaviors of two systems, S and S_{ref}, as topologically equal if they have the same sequence of absolute transitions, $\gamma_0, ..., \gamma_k$, and for $0 \leq i \leq k$, $QS(S,T(\gamma_i))=QS(S_{ref},T_{ref}(\gamma_i))$, i.e. the absolute qualitative states of both systems are identical (corresponding parameters have identical absolute values).

If this is not the case, Weld speaks of changes in the behavioral topology. According to our discrimination of continuous and discontinuous deviations we distinguish continuous and discontinuous changes in the behavioral topology. We call a change in the behavioral topology *continuous*, if the behaviors still have the same sequence of basis transitions, $\beta_0, ..., \beta_l$, and for $0 \leq j \leq l$ all deviations of $QS(S,T(\beta_j))$ with respect to $QS(S_{ref},T_{ref}(\beta_j))$ are continuous. Otherwise we call it *discontinuous*.

The qualitative behavior of the heat exchanger is characterized by two transitions: the heat reaches the equilibrium temperature and the oil reaches the outlet. A certain reference order of these transitions can change if the oil is passing the heat exchanger with a too high velocity. Both transitions are basis transitions, hence this is an example for a discontinuous change of topology. RSIM+'s output for the heat exchanger with too high velocity is given by Fig. 7. As reference behavior, RSIM+ takes all possible absolute behaviors of the reference system. (Since deviating and reference system have the same absolute description, these behaviors are generated implicitly.) With additional model information about the reference system, a special reference behavior and thus the corresponding deviating behaviors can be determined. Discontinuous changes of parameters are marked by a PQ value of D. This means: "Normally this parameter has a different sign for this time point/interval." By a comparison with the other paths of the tree, it can be deduced which of them correspond (in their absolute descriptions) to possible reference behaviors. That is, possible changes of the absolute behavior (topology changes), resulting from an LGTN deviation, can exactly be determined. This includes an absolute description of the deviating and the reference behavior and relative (PQ and P) information for the deviating behavior.

The deviating behavior of the spring/block system with too high amplitude (Fig. 6), on the other hand, is an example for continuous topology changes. The deviating behavior has a different set of transitions (e.g. landmark x2* is reached/left only in the deviating behavior), but it has the same order of basis transitions (reaching the rest position and the return positions). All deviations at basis transitions are continuous.

5 Related Work

Relative descriptions are used in various approaches. (9) reasons about orders of magnitude, in (2) these concepts

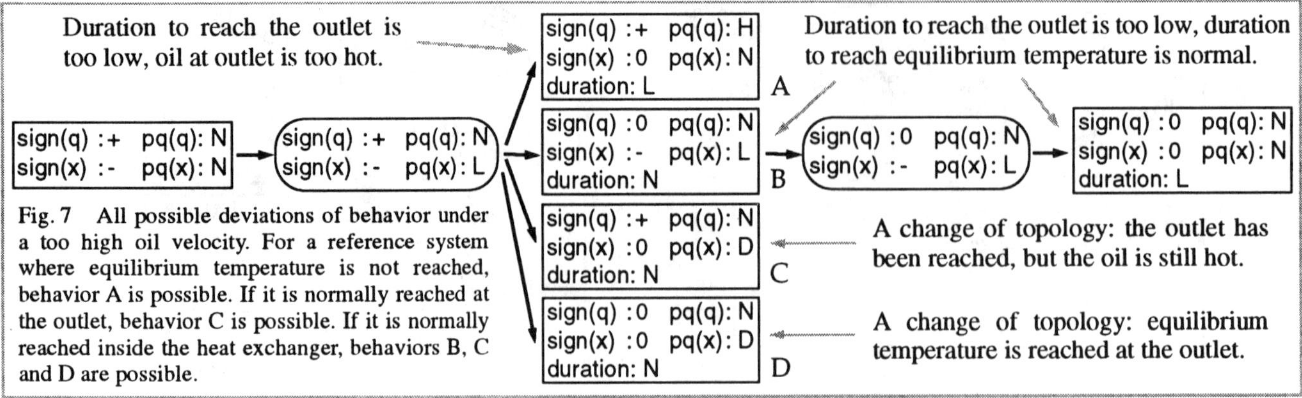

Fig. 7   All possible deviations of behavior under a too high oil velocity. For a reference system where equilibrium temperature is not reached, behavior A is possible. If it is normally reached at the outlet, behavior C is possible. If it is normally reached inside the heat exchanger, behaviors B, C and D are possible.

are used for fault diagnosis. The *IQ analysis* of (3) is a qualitative sensitivity analysis of a system's steady state. Similar techniques that aim at fault diagnosis can be found in (4,5,6). Dynamic systems, on the other hand, are analysed in Weld's *DQ analysis* and *exaggeration* (11). Both techniques predict the effects of differential changes as RSIM+ does. Input and output of RSIM+ and DQ analysis are similar, but DQ analysis cannot answer questions that require a comparison of deviations. Inferences in DQ analysis are based on the concept of *perspective*, i.e. parameter deviations are not only described with respect to time but additionally relative to other parameters. In this way, a comparison of intervals of different length is possible. In RSIM+, this problem is solved by interval transitions that perform a synchronization. DQ analysis sometimes produces no output. Due to this fact, topology changes can only be handled in an unsatisfying way (see 10, Section 4). RSIM+ always makes a prediction that contains all possible behaviors including changes in the behavioral topology. In (1) it is demonstrated how the comparative analysis problems that can be treated by DQ analysis can instead be solved by algebraic and qualitative manipulation of equations. Exaggeration answers concrete questions about the effects of a certain differential deviation on a target parameter. For this purpose it first exaggerates the given deviation, then simulates the exaggerated system and finally rescales the exaggerated behavior by comparing it to a simulated normal behavior. Exaggeration always gives an answer that unfortunately can be wrong if not all relationships between parameters are monotonous. The idea of an exaggeration conflicts with a comparison of deviations because all deviations are mapped into the same set of extreme values. RSIM+'s simulation techniques are similar to those of QSIM. But RSIM+'s inferences have a more constructive character. RSIM+ does not use Waltz filtering.

6 Summary

Relative descriptions are necessary to characterize certain kinds of system deviations and the resulting behavior. RSIM+ is a simulator that works with relative descriptions and is able to compare deviations with each other. The physical systems that can be described by RSIM+ corre-

spond to those of QSIM. In RSIM+, the special properties of linear, overlinear and underlinear relationships between parameters are exploited to gain more accuracy in the prediction of system behavior. Additionally, faulty M^* relationships like TOO-FLAT$_0^+$ can be expressed. RSIM+ predicts all changes to system behavior that can follow from LGTN deviations, i.e. changes in the behavioral topology are included.

References

(1) Chiu, C.; Kuipers, B. 1992. Comparative Analysis and Qualitative Integral Representations. In Faltings, B.; Struss, P. eds. *Recent Advances in Qualitative Physics*. The MIT Press.
(2) Dague, P.; Devès, P.; and Raiman, O. Troubleshooting: When Modeling is the Trouble, AAAI-87, Seattle (1987) 590-595
(3) de Kleer, J.: Causal and Teleological Reasoning in Circuit Recognition, TR-529, AI-Lab., MIT, Cambrigde (1979)
(4) Downing, K. L.: Diagnostic Improvement Through Qualitative Sensivity Analysis and Aggregation, AAAI-87, Seattle (1987) 789-793
(5) Gallanti, M.; Stefanini, A.; and Tomada, L.: ODS: A Diagnostic System Based on Qualitative Modelling Techniques, Conference on Artificial Intelligence Applications, Miami (1989) 142-149
(6) Kockskämper. S.; Neumann, B.; Josub, A.; and Müller, H.: Die Anwendung modellbasierten Schließens bei der Diagnose schiffstechnischer Anlagen, in F. Puppe, A. Günter (eds.) Expertensysteme 93, Springer Verlag (1993) 14-27
(7) B. J. Kuipers: Qualitative Simulation, *Artificial Intelligence* 29 (1986) 289-338
(8) Neitzke, M.: Modeling Physical Systems with Relative Descriptions of Parameters, in B. Neumann (ed.) ECAI-92, Vienna (1992) 683-684
(9) Raiman, O.: Order of Magnitude Reasoning, AAAI-86, Philadelphia (1986) 100-104
(10) Weld, D. S.: Comparative Analysis, *Artificial Intelligence* 36 (1988) 333-374
(11) Weld, D. S.: *Theories of Comparative Analysis*. (the MIT Press, Cambridge, 1990)

Qualitative Reasoning
for Automated Exploration for Chaos

Toyoaki Nishida
Graduate School of Information Science
Nara Institute of Science and Technology
8916-5 Takayama, Ikoma, Nara 630-01, Japan
nishida@is.aist-nara.ac.jp

Abstract

Chaos is ubiquitous in our everyday life and even a simple system may manifest chaotic behaviors. Chaos has been a challenge to the methodology of qualitative reasoning as well as classic science and engineering, due to unpredictability and complexity of behavior.

In this paper, I claim that associating continuous domain with symbolic representation, a basic principle of qualitative reasoning, is vital for automating analysis of chaos, as long as it is properly formalized. As an empirical support to this claim, I present a computer program called PSX3 that can semi-automatically explore for chaotic behavior of a given system of piecewise linear ordinary differential equations with three unknown functions. The power of PSX3 originates from an ability of reasoning about smooth surfaces that implicitly exist in the phase space. PSX3 is implemented using Common Lisp and Mathematica^{TM}.

Introduction

Chaos is ubiquitous in everyday life. Theoretically, it is known that even a simple system may exhibit chaos. Chaos has been a challenge to classic science. The source of difficulty is twofold: unpredictability due to sensitive dependence on initial conditions and complexity of geometry resulting from fractal structure.

Huberman and Struss (Huberman and Struss, 1989) have taken chaos as a serious challenge to the whole methodology of qualitative reasoning, for the existence of chaos severely limits applicability of various filtering techniques and effect of landmark-based representation, that have been popularly used in qualitative reasoning systems. They propose to regard chaos rather a peculiar phenomenon and carefully separate them from commonsense and qualitative reasoning.

In this paper, I show that associating continuous domain with symbolic domain, a basic principle of qualitative reasoning, is vital for analysis of chaos, as long as it is properly formalized. I claim that qualitative reasoning techniques, with adequate generalization, provide a powerful means for automating analysis of chaos.

As an empirical support to this claim, I present a computer program called PSX3 that can semi-automatically explore for chaotic behavior of a certain class of ordinary differential equations (ODEs) and generate structural description of the behavior. The power of PSX3 originates from an ability of reasoning about smooth surfaces that implicitly exist in the phase space. PSX3 is implemented using Common Lisp and Mathematica^{TM}.

In what follows, I take a system of piecewise linear ODEs that exhibits chaotic behavior and discuss issues related to analysis of chaos. Secondly, I describe how PSX3 analyzes chaotic behaviors. Thirdly, I characterize reasoning about smooth surfaces as a generalization of conventional qualitative reasoning techniques. Finally, I discuss the strength and limitation of the current technique and suggest future direction.

A Glimpse of Chaos

In dynamical systems theory (Guckenheimer and Holmes, 1983), it is known that even a simple dynamical system manifests chaotic behavior. For example, Matsumoto and Chua (Matsumoto et al., 1985) have shown that a simple continuous dynamical system consisting of three subsystems of linear ODEs with three unknown functions:

$$\begin{cases} \dfrac{\mathrm{d}x}{\mathrm{d}t} = \begin{cases} -1.8x + 6.3y - 2.7 & (x < -1) \\ 0.9x + 6.3y & (-1 \leq x \leq 1) \\ -1.8x + 6.3y - 2.7 & (1 < x) \end{cases} \\ \dfrac{\mathrm{d}y}{\mathrm{d}t} = 0.7x - 0.7y + z \\ \dfrac{\mathrm{d}z}{\mathrm{d}t} = -7y \end{cases} \tag{1}$$

exhibits chaotic behavior.

Applied mathematicians study chaotic behavior, by investigating geometric and topological features of trajectories in the phase space spanned by a given set of unknown functions (or *state variables*). In the case of (1), Matsumoto and Chua have found that trajectories (or *orbits*) tend towards a chaotic attractor with a "double scroll" structure, two sheet-like thin rings curled up together into spiral forms.[1] Orbits approach

---

[1] Roughly, an attractor is a dense collection of orbits that nearby orbits approach as $t \to \infty$. The reader is referred to (Guckenheimer and Holmes, 1983) for complete definition and detailed discussion.

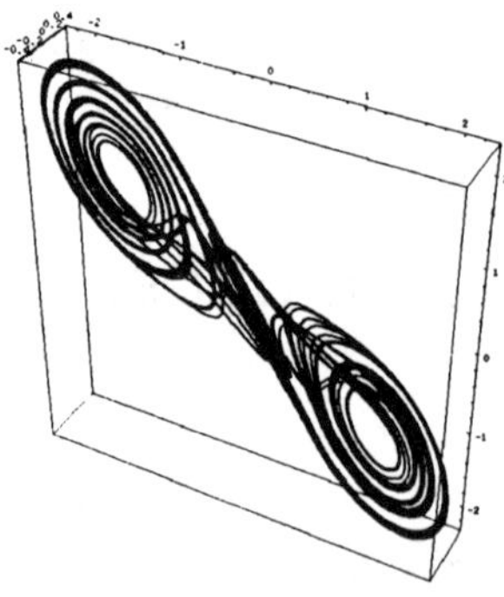

Figure 1: A trajectory of Matsumoto-Chua's equations (1) near the double scroll attractor reported in (Matsumoto *et al.*, 1985)

the attractor as time goes and manifest chaotic behavior as they irregularly transit between the two rings, as illustrated by a sample trajectory shown in Figure 1.

Investigation of chaos can be roughly divided into three stages. The first stage is search for a condition under which a given dynamical system exhibits an interesting behavior. The second stage is qualitative analysis whose purpose is to identify the structure of the behavior in focus. The third stage is quantitative analysis, by applying known measurements such as Lyapunov exponents or fractal dimension (Moon, 1987) to obtain quantitative support of findings.

Generally, as one proceeds to the later stages, the more well-studied, sophisticated mathematical techniques are available, some of which have been automated. In contrast, the earlier stages depend on more general capability of humans, such as visual perception and spatial reasoning, as pointed out in (Yip, 1991b). Even mathematicians have to go through trial and errors in early stages of analysis. It is worth developing a computational model of earlier stages of dynamical systems analysis, for (a) automated search does help both applied mathematicians in search for interesting phenomena and engineers who do not have ample knowledge about chaos, and (b) analysis and modeling of experts' intellectual behavior as an integration of various cognitive processes are an important subject of AI research.

Critical issues here are, (a) high-level representation of information such as topology and geometry of orbits, and (b) its application to intelligently controlling numerical analysis. In (Nishida, 1993), I proposed flow mappings as a solution to the first issue. In this papers, I show that qualitative analysis of chaos can in fact be automated, using flow mappings as central representation. I have implemented my theory as a program called **PSX3**. In the next section, I describe how **PSX3** works. Then, I characterize my theory as an advanced formalization of a qualitative reasoning principle.

Exploration for Chaos by PSX3

PSX3 takes a specification of system of piecewise linear ODEs with three unknown functions and a region of analysis, and produces a qualitative and quantitative description of the behavior ranging from the regular to the chaotic, which can be used as a prescription for quantitative measurements.

The procedure incorporated into **PSX3** is roughly divided into local analysis, global analysis, and prescription generation for detailed quantitative measurements.

Local Analysis

In local analysis, **PSX3** classifies trajectories in each intersection (*cell*) of region of analysis and a linear region, into coherent bundles of orbit intervals. Roughly, a coherent bundle of orbit intervals is a collection of orbit intervals from/to a singly connected region of a cell surface or the same fixed point (Nishida, 1993). Figure 2a shows[2] how **PSX3** partitions the collection of orbit intervals contained in a cell **cell-1**: $(-3 \leq x \leq -1, -2 \leq y \leq 2, -3 \leq z \leq 3)$ made by intersecting a linear region $(x \leq -1)$ and a given region of analysis $(-3 \leq x \leq 3, -2 \leq y \leq 2, -3 \leq z \leq 3)$. Figure 2b shows subsidiary partitioning on the surface of the cell, where each region of the cell surface is identified by the attached number. Figure 2c shows several bundles of orbits that **PSX3** has identified in **cell-1**. Orbits running through regions #83, #95, and #87 on the right side plane $(x = -1)$ of **cell-1** are qualitatively different with respect to this cell in the sense that they are running out of the cell from different sides of the cell (#77 on top plane $(z = 3)$, #66 on the rear plane $(x = -3)$, and #94 on the right side $(x = -1)$, respectively).

PSX3 represents the result of partitioning as

- $\{\phi_i\}$, where ϕ_i stands for either a fixed point or a two-dimensional region of the cell surface; and

- a set of *flow mappings* $\{\phi_i \rightarrow \phi_j\}$ which represents the structure of *flow* (the collection of orbits), where a flow mapping $\phi_i \rightarrow \phi_j$ means that ϕ_i (a two-dimensional region on the cell surface or a fixed point) is mapped to ϕ_j (another two-dimensional region or a fixed point) by the flow underlying the cell.

Figure 2d shows a set of flow mappings for **cell-1**. Figure 3 shows results of local analysis for the remaining two cells in the given region of analysis. In order to obtain the partitioning, nontrivial amount of qualitative and quantitative analysis is needed as described in (Nishida, 1993).

Global Analysis

After it has generated a set of flow mappings for each cell, **PSX3** proceeds to global analysis and takes a col-

---

[2] Although each surface partitioning bundles of orbit intervals is approximated by triangulation, they are only for demonstration purpose and not used for reasoning. In order to reason about the flow, PSX only refers to regions on the cell surface such as region #95 in Figure 2b.

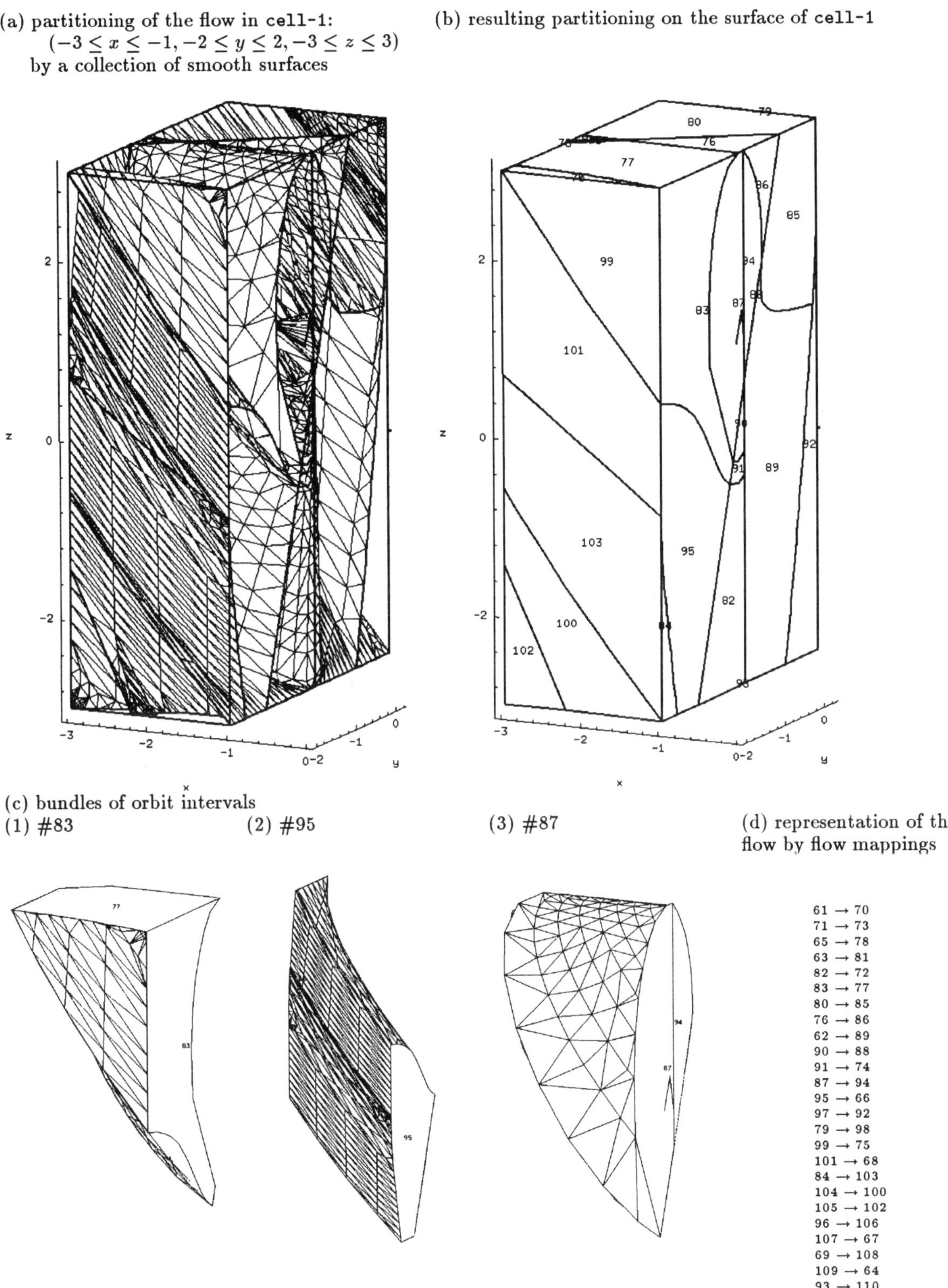

Figure 2: Local analysis PSX has produced for cell-1

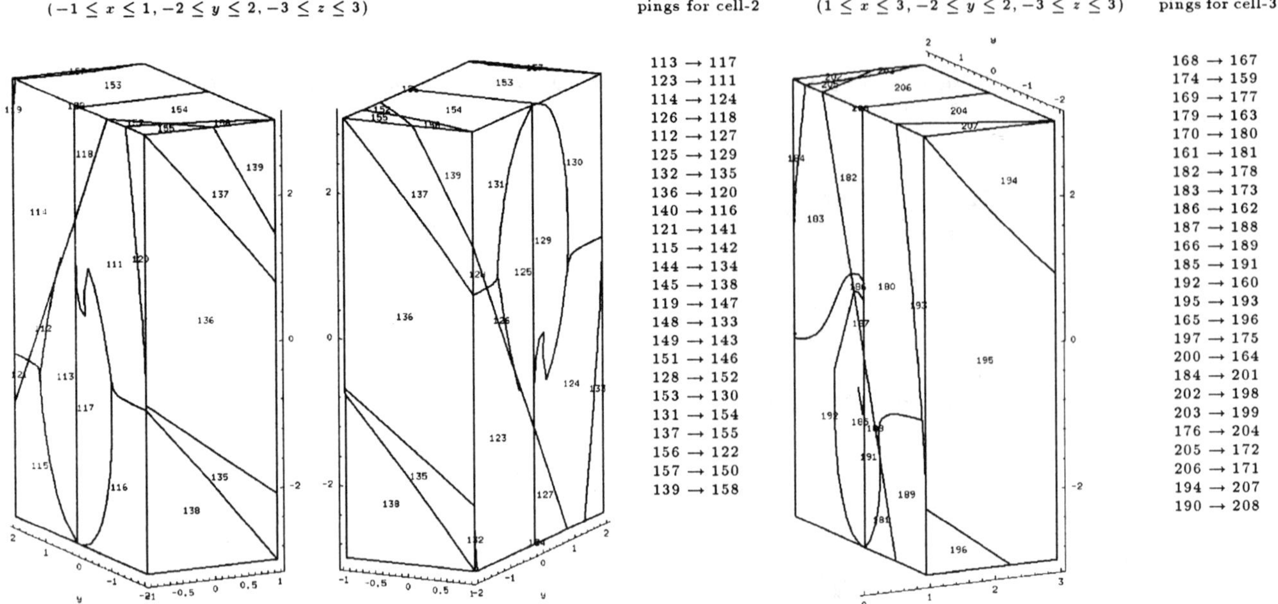

Figure 3: Result of local analysis for `cell-2` and `cell-3`

lection of flow mappings for each cell and looks for minimal sets of mutually transitioning flow mappings defined below.

Definition 1 *Given a set of flow mappings $\{\phi_i \to \phi_j\}$ and intersection relations $\{\langle \phi_m, \phi_n \rangle \mid \phi_m \cap \phi_n \neq$ empty$\}$, an extended set of flow mappings $\{\phi_p \to^* \phi_q\}$ is defined as follows:*

$(1)\ \phi_i \to \phi_j \Rightarrow \phi_i \to^* \phi_j$
$(2)\ \phi_i \to \phi_j \wedge \phi_k \to \phi_m \wedge \phi_j \cap \phi_k \neq$ empty $\Rightarrow \phi_i \to^* \phi_m.$

Definition 2 *Given a set of flow mappings $\{\phi_i \to \phi_j\}$ and intersection relations $\{\langle \phi_m, \phi_n \rangle \mid \phi_m \cap \phi_n \neq$ empty$\}$, $\Phi = \{\phi_i \to \phi_j\}$ is a minimal set of mutually transitioning flow mappings iff*
$$\forall (\phi_i \to \phi_j) \in \Phi\ [\phi_j \to^* \phi_i].$$

An algorithm for searching for a minimal set of mutually transitioning flow mappings is implemented using a simple graph search algorithm.

In the case of Matsumoto-Chua equations, PSX3 has found a minimal set of mutually transitioning flow mappings, as shown in Figure 4a. The predicted set of mutually transitioning flow mappings suggests that it is likely that the attractor is a composition of several recurrnt cycles, rather than a single cycle.

As long as the phase space is partitioned into cells in such a way that each non-point attractor intersects more than one cell, mutually transitioning flow mappings tell the approximate location and structure of the attractor. In other words, the surface of the union of bundles of orbit intervals corresponding to a minimal set of mutually transitioning flow mappings serves an envelope wrapping a candidate of a non-point attractor, as shown in Figure 4b.

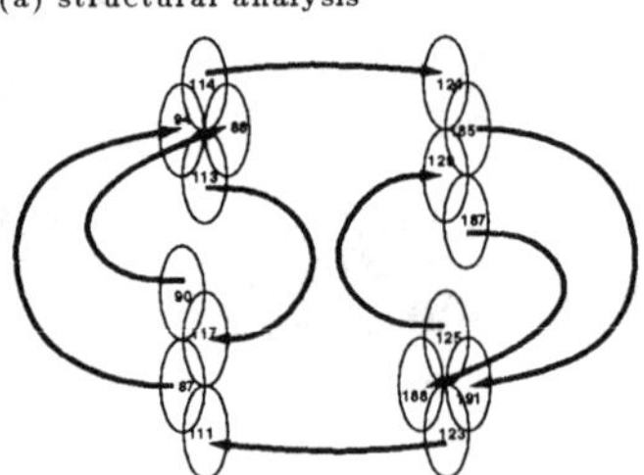
(a) structural analysis

(Transition 90 → 88 and 187 → 188 will eventually be removed at the prescription generation stage)

(b) envelope of the candidate of an attractor

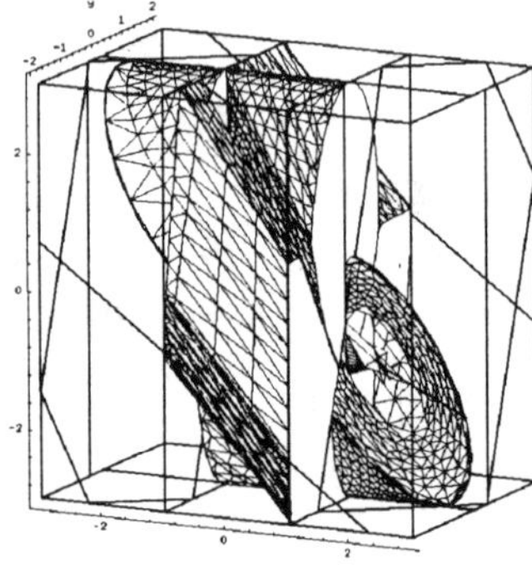

Figure 4: Result of global analysis produced by PSX3

Prescription Generation for Quantitative Measurement

Finally, PSX3 assembles a structured report on its findings as a prescription for further quantitative analysis.

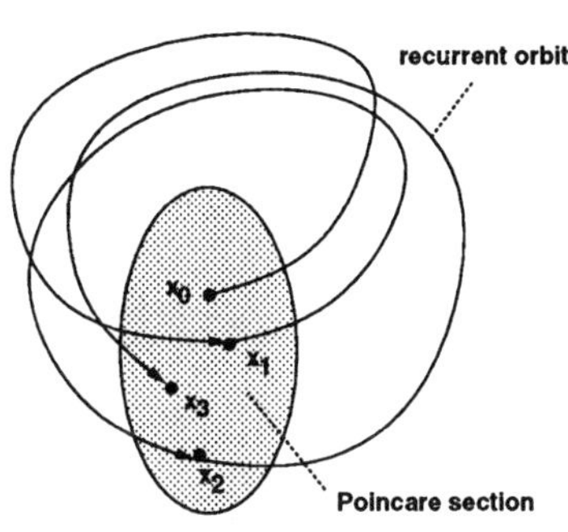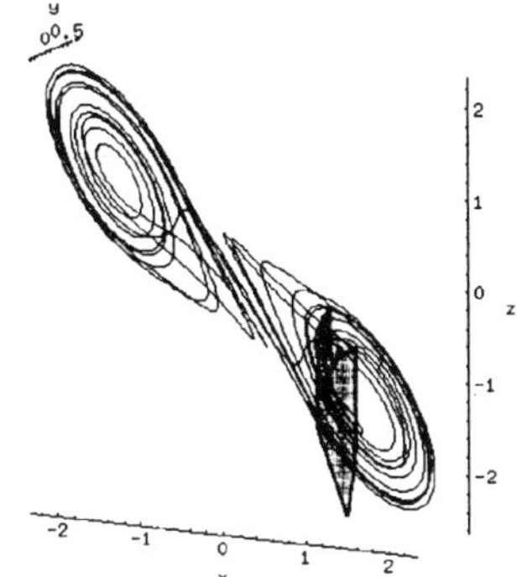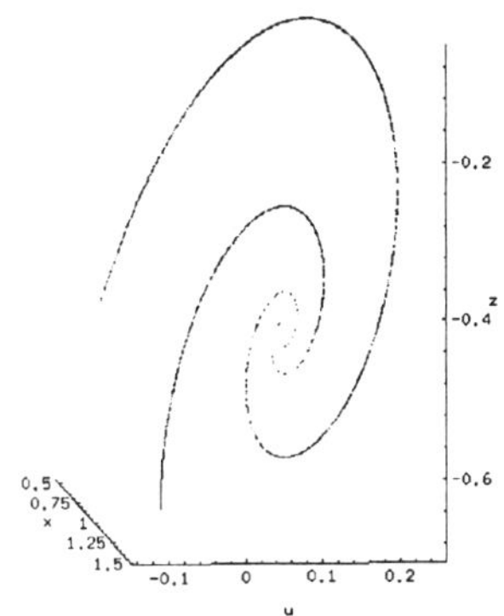

Figure 5: Prescription generation

A critical information added at this stage is a Poincaré section and mappings, which are popularly used by applied mathematicians as a basis of quantitative analysis. Poincaré section is a plane that cuts across a recurrent orbit, as illustrated in Figure 5a. A Poincaré map is represented as $x(t) = x_t \mapsto x(t+1) = x_{t+1}$, where x_i is the i-th point at which the recurrent orbit penetrates the Poincaré section. It is possible to make preliminary diagnosis of a given recurrent orbit by examining the shape of a Poincaré map as a collection of points. The more diverged and fuzzier the Poincaré map becomes, the more likely the orbit in question is chaotic.[3] PSX3 automatically generates a Poincaré section by analyzing critical section of a minimal set of mutually transitioning flow mappings. PSX3 determines where to start tracking an orbit, by intersecting the proposed Poincaré section and the internal region delimited by an envelope wrapping a candidate of a non-point attractor. Figure 5b shows a Poincaré section and an orbit that PSX3 has actually proposed and computed. Figure 5c shows a resulting Poincaré map, which conforms to the one reported in (Matsumoto *et al.*, 1985).

Reasoning about Smooth Surfaces

One of the fundamental principles of qualitative reasoning is associating continuous domain with symbolic representation by aggregating coherent objects. The techniques embodied by PSX3 fit this schema. PSX3 aggregates orbit intervals (continuous geometric objects) into bundles based on coherency relations defined with respect to a cell, associates each bundle with a flow mapping (symbolic representation), and uses the resulting set of flow mappings to set up a plan for more detailed quantitative measurements. PSX3 integrates qualitative and quantitative analysis for doing these. In particular, the success of PSX3 can be attributed

to its ability of constructing representation of smooth surfaces implicitly existing in the phase space, by intelligently controlling numeric and symbolic computation. PSX3 combines numerical analysis and reasoning about smooth surfaces to establish delimiting surfaces in a cell. For example, when encountered with a set of fragmentary observations, PSX3 will consult a library of smooth surface interaction patterns (Nishida, 1993), set up a hypothesis about the underlying geometric structure, and try to verify it in subsequent analysis.

Techniques incorporated into PSX3 can be regarded as an extension of conventional qualitative reasoning techniques in which real numbers are associated with a set of symbols, such as $\{-, 0, +\}$, by a set of landmarks. Although it has made various AI techniques such as GDE (de Kleer and Williams, 1987) applicable to continuous domains, the approach has flawed in several ways, especially in the case of reasoning about chaos.

In contrast, my formalization is based on partitioning the continuous domain by smooth surfaces. Reasoning about smooth surfaces is more sophisticated and powerful, while more computationally expensive.[4]

Related Work and Discussion

This work is considered to be an effort of developing a computational model of dynamical systems theory (Guckenheimer and Holmes, 1983). Previous work in this direction involves: POINCARE (Sacks, 1991), PSX2NL (Nishida and Doshita, 1991; Nishida *et al.*, 1991), Kalagnanam's system (Kalagnanam, 1991), MAPS (Zhao, 1993), and Perfect Moment(Bradley, 1992). KAM (Yip, 1991b) is one of the frontier work, though it is for discrete systems (difference equations), as opposed to continuous systems addressed in this paper. Unfortunately, the techniques used in these systems except MAPS (Zhao, 1993) and Perfect Moment

---

[3]I have not yet automated the evaluation of Poincaré map. Automation could be possible using techniques pioneered by Yip (Yip, 1991a).

[4]However, it should be noted that the amount of redundant computation is significantly reduced for the sake of its expressive power.

(Bradley, 1992) are severely limited to two-dimensional flows whose geometry is significantly simpler than those in three dimensional phase spaces. Indeed, continuous flow in two-dimensional Euclidean phase space never exhibits chaos.

In MAPS, the flow pipe model is used. A flow pipe represents a homotopy equivalence class of orbits and hence is essentially equivalent to a bundle of orbit intervals,[5] despite some differences at the implementation level.[6] MAPS constructs the information structure in a bottom-up fashion. Unfortunately, this is not enough for exploring for chaos. A guideline is needed to plan numerical computation for constructing a critical flow pipe which may serve as an envelope of a chaotic attractor. The method incorporated into PSX3 is a kind of exhaustive search. PSX3 partitions a given region of analysis into a set of bundles of orbit intervals and searches for a candidate of an envelope of a chaotic attractor. **Perfect Moment** handles chaos with adaptive grids, which causes several problems due to discretization.

Current implementation of PSX3 is limited in a couple of ways. Firstly, PSX3 is specialized to flow in three-dimensional phase space. This is a rather serious limitation, for most applications of practical interest are defined in higher dimensional phase spaces. The limitation might be overridden either by developing a method of extracting a lower dimensional dynamics from a given system of ODEs, or by taking a direct step towards generalizing the current method. The latter direction requires substantial efforts on reducing computational cost.

Secondly, the subsystem for reasoning about smooth surfaces is "hard wired": there is no separation between a knowledge-base and a general reasoning engine. In developing PSX3, I have manually classified geometric interactions among smooth surfaces and hand-crafted a reasoning algorithm. However, the same approach is intractable for more general classes of problems, namely hyper-surfaces in n-dimensional space. An interesting open problem is to develop a meta system which can generate a computational theory of reasoning about smooth surfaces in general n-dimensional spaces.

Conclusion

In this paper, I have shown that automated analysis of chaos can in fact be possible, and I have described PSX3 as an empirical support of the claim. The power of PSX3 originates from an ability of reasoning about smooth surfaces that implicitly exist in the phase space.

---

[5] These two models were independently developed and widely published in the summer of 1991.

[6] The flow pipe model is implemented using (a) polyhedral approximation for representing the shape of flow pipes and (b) relational graph representation for representing the topology of the phase portrait.

Acknowledgments
I am grateful to Feng Zhao for useful comments.

References

Bradley, Elizabeth 1992. *Taming Chaotic Circuits.* Ph.D. Dissertation, M.I.T.

de Kleer, Johan and Williams, Brian C. 1987. Diagnosing multiple faults. *Artificial Intelligence* 32:97–130.

Guckenheimer, John and Holmes, Philip 1983. *Nonlinear Oscillations, Dynamical Systems, and Bifurcations of Vector Fields.* Springer-Verlag.

Huberman, Bernard A. and Struss, Peter 1989. Chaos, qualitative reasoning and the predictability problem. presented at 3rd International Workshop on Qualitative Physics, Stanford.

Kalagnanam, Jayant 1991. Integration of symbolic and numeric methods for qualitative reasoning. Technical Report CMU-EPP-1991-01-01, Engineering and Public Policy, CMU.

Matsumoto, Takashi; Chua, Leon O.; and Komuro, Motomasa 1985. The double scroll. *IEEE Transactions on Ciruits and Systems* CAS-32(8):798–818.

Moon, Francis C. 1987. *Chaotic Vibrations — An Introduction for Applied Scientists and Engineers.* John Wiley & Sons.

Nishida, Toyoaki and Doshita, Shuji 1991. A geometric approach to total envisioning. In *Proceedings IJCAI-91.* 1150–1155.

Nishida, Toyoaki; Mizutani, Kenji; Kubota, Atsushi; and Doshita, Shuji 1991. Automated phase portrait analysis by integrating qualitative and quantitative analysis. In *Proceedings AAAI-91.* 811–816.

Nishida, Toyoaki 1993. Generating quasi-symbolic representation of three-dimensional flow. In *Proceedings AAAI-93.* 554–559.

Sacks, Elisha P. 1991. Automatic analysis of one-parameter planar ordinary differential equations by intelligent numeric simulation. *Artificial Intelligence* 48:27–56.

Yip, Kenneth Man-kam 1991a. *KAM — A System for Intelligently Guiding Numerical Experimentation by Computer.* The MIT Press.

Yip, Kenneth Man-kam 1991b. Understanding complex dynamics by visual and symbolic reasoning. *Artificial Intelligence* 51(1-3):179–222.

Zhao, Feng 1993. Computational dynamics: Modeling and visualizing trajectory flows in phase space. *Annals of Mathematics and Artificial Intelligence* 8:285–300.

Activity Analysis:
The Qualitative Analysis of Stationary Points for Optimal Reasoning

Brian C. Williams
Xerox Palo Alto Research Center
3333 Coyote Hill Road,
Palo Alto, CA 94304 USA
bwilliams@parc.xerox.com

Jonathan Cagan
Department of Mechanical Engineering
Carnegie Mellon University
Pittsburgh, PA 15213 USA
cagan+@cmu.edu

Abstract

We present a theory of a modeler's problem decomposition skills in the context of *optimal reasoning* — the use of qualitative modeling to strategically guide numerical explorations of objective space. Our technique, called *activity analysis*, applies to the pervasive family of linear and non-linear, constrained optimization problems, and easily integrates with any existing numerical approach. Activity analysis draws from the power of two seemingly divergent perspectives – the global conflict-based approaches of combinatorial satisficing search, and the local gradient-based approaches of continuous optimization – combined with the underlying insights of engineering monotonicity analysis. The result is an approach that strategically cuts away subspaces that it can quickly rule out as suboptimal, and then guides the numerical methods to the remaining subspaces.

Introduction and Example

Our goal is to capture a modeler's tacit skill at decomposing physical models and its application to focusing reasoning. This work is ultimately directed towards the contruction of "self modeling" systems, operating in embedded, real time situations. This article explores the modeler's decompositional skills (Williams & Raiman 1994) in the context of *optimal reasoning* — the use of qualitative modeling to strategically guide gradient-based and other numerical explorations of objective spaces. Optimal reasoning is crucial for embedded systems, where numerical methods are key to such areas as estimation, control, inductive learning and vision. The technique we present, called *activity analysis*, applies to the pervasive family of linear and non-linear, constrained optimization problems, and easily integrates with any existing numerical approaches.

Activity analysis is striking in the way it merges together two styles of search that are traditionally viewed as quite disparate: first is the more strategic, conflict-based approaches used in combinatorial, satisficing search to eliminate finite, inconsistent subspaces (e.g., (de Kleer & Williams 1987)). The second is the rich suite of more tactical, numeric methods(Vanderplaats 1984) used in continuous optimizing search to climb locally but monotonically towards the optimum. Activity analysis draws from the power of both perspectives, strategically cutting away subspaces that it can quickly rule out as suboptimal, and then guiding the numerical methods to the remaining subspaces.

The power of activity analysis to eliminate large suboptimal subspaces is derived from *Qualitative KT*, an abstraction in *qualitative vector algebra* of the foundational Kuhn-Tucker (KT) condition of optimization theory. The underlying algorithm achieves simplicity and completeness, by introducing the concept of generating *prime implicating assignments* of linear, qualitative vector equations. This process of ruling out feasible, but suboptimal subspaces in a continuous domain, nicely parallels the use of conflicts and prime implicant generation for combinatorial, satisficing search. The end result is a method that achieves parsimonious descriptions, guarantees correctness, and maximizes the filtering achieved from QKT.

Finally, activity analysis can be thought of as automating the underlying principle about monotonicity used by the simplex method to examine only the vertices of the linear feasible space. It then generalizes and automatically applies this principle to nonlinear programming problems.

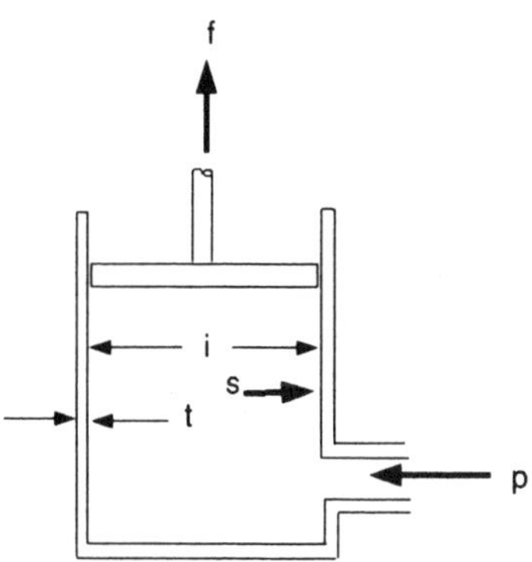

Figure 1: Hydraulic Cylinder

To demonstrate the task consider the design of a hydraulic cylinder, a classic optimization problem, introduced by Wilde (Wilde 1975) to demonstrate the related technique of monotonicity analysis. The cylinder (figure 1) delivers force f, through input pressure p. Weight is modeled as inside diameter (i) plus twice the cylinder thickness (t), force (f) as pressure (p) times cylinder area, and hoop stress (s) as pressure times diameter acting across the thickness. The task is to find a parametric solution that minimizes cylinder weight, while satisfying constraints including positivity of variables ($i, s, t, p, f > 0$), maximum pressure (P) and stress (S), and minimum force (F) and thickness (T) (design variables are in lowercase, fixed parameters in uppercase, and equality and inequality constraints are labeled h_i and g_i, respectively): Minimize $i + 2t$,

subject to:

$$
\begin{array}{rclllrcll}
s - \frac{pi}{2t} & = & 0, & (h_1 = 0): & T - t & \leq & 0, & (g_2 \leq 0) \\
f - \frac{\pi i^2}{4} p & = & 0, & (h_2 = 0): & p - P & \leq & 0, & (g_3 \leq 0) \\
F - f & \leq & 0, & (g_1 \leq 0): & s - S & \leq & 0, & (g_4 \leq 0)
\end{array}
$$

Given this symbolic formulation, activity analysis uses qualitative arguments to classify regions of the design space where optima might lie and where they cannot. After eliminating suboptimal regions, each remaining region identifies the solution as possibly lying on the intersection of one or more constraint boundaries. Each region reduces the dimensionality of the problem by the number of intersecting boundaries, thus significantly increasing the ease with which a solution can be found. In particular, for the cylinder problem activity analysis concludes there are two subspaces of the design space that could contain the optima, one subspace in which g_1 and g_4 become strict equalities, and a second in which all but g_4 become strict equalities. The new problem formulation finds the optima of the two spaces and combines the results as follows (where "arg min" returns a set of optima):

Given: vector $\mathbf{x} = (istpf)^T$,

1. Let $\mathbf{Y} = \arg\min_{\mathbf{x}}(i + 2t)$, subject to:

$$
\begin{array}{lll}
(h_1 = 0) & (g_1 = 0) & (g_3 \leq 0) \\
(h_2 = 0) & (g_2 \leq 0) & (g_4 = 0).
\end{array}
$$

2. Let $\mathbf{Z} = \arg\min_{\mathbf{x}}(i + 2t)$, subject to:

$$
\begin{array}{lll}
(h_1 = 0) & (g_1 = 0) & (g_3 = 0) \\
(h_2 = 0) & (g_2 = 0) & (g_4 \leq 0).
\end{array}
$$

3. Return $\arg\min_{\mathbf{x}}(i + 2t)$, subject to:

$$
\mathbf{x} \in \mathbf{Y} \cup \mathbf{Z}.
$$

Originally, the problem has a 3 dimensional space to be explored (3 degrees of freedom – DOF) resulting from 5 variables, 2 equality constraints. The reformulated problem rules out the interior and boundaries, except some intersections. The first remaining subspace corresponds to a *line* (1 DOF) produced by the intersection of the g_1 and g_4 constraint boundaries with the h_i. The

second remaining space is a *point* (0 DOF) produced by the intersection of g_1, g_2, g_3 and the h_i. Thus finding a solution to the first problem involves a single, one dimensional line search, and the second involves solving the system of equalities to find the unique solution. Using parameter values F=1000 lbf, T=.05 in, S=30000 psi, T=1000 in, applying matlab to the original problem took 46.3 seconds. The optimal solution lies in $\mathbf{Z}$, which took only 8.1 seconds to run; no feasible solution exists in Y for these parameter values.

Activity analysis draws inspiration from monotonicity analysis (MA) (Papalambros & Wilde 1979; Papalambros 1982). Monotonicity analysis began as a set of principles and methods used by modelers to identify ill-posed problems and to partially solve them, based on monotonic arguments alone. These principles were encoded in several rule-based implementations (Azram & Papalambros 1984; Choy & Agogino 1986; Rao & Papalambros 1987; Hansen, Jaumard, & Lu 1989), presented informally as heuristic methods.

The problem activity analysis addresses is similar in spirit to that of MA; nevertheless, the approach is quite different. First, activity analysis operates directly on an abstraction (QKT) of the Kuhn-Tucker (KT) conditions of optimization theory. While much easier to apply, QKT and KT are equivalent for the task, given only knowledge of monotonicities. Second, activity analysis provides a precise formulation of the problem in terms of *minimal pstationary coverings*, that guarantees the solution is parsimonious, maximizes the filtering derived from QKT, and insures correctness. Finally, a mapping to *prime assignments* and the introduction of a simple but complete prime assignment engine guarantees that these three properties are achieved.

Stationary Points and Kuhn-Tucker

For a point $\mathbf{x}*$ to be an optimum it is necessary that the point be *stationary*, that is any "down hill" direction is blocked by the constraints. Activity analysis exploits this fact to eliminate sets of points that can quickly be proven to be *nonstationary*, using a condition we call *Qualitative Kuhn-Tucker* (QKT). This section introduces the optimization problem, the concept of stationary point, and the traditional algebraic (Kuhn-Tucker) condition for testing stationary points. Activity analysis applies to the pervasive family of linear and non-linear, constrained optimization problems $OP = \langle \mathbf{x}, f, \mathbf{g}, \mathbf{h} \rangle$:

$$
\begin{array}{rll}
\text{Find} & \mathbf{x}* = \arg\min & f(\mathbf{x}) \\
& \text{subject to:} & \mathbf{g}(\mathbf{x}) \leq \mathbf{0} \\
& & \mathbf{h}(\mathbf{x}) = \mathbf{0},
\end{array}
$$

where column vectors are denoted in bold (e.g., $\mathbf{x}$, $\mathbf{x}*$, $\mathbf{g}(\mathbf{x})$ and $\mathbf{h}(\mathbf{x})$), $f(\mathbf{x})$ is the *objective function*, $\mathbf{g}(\mathbf{x})$ is a vector of *inequality constraints* and $\mathbf{h}(\mathbf{x})$ is a vector of *equality constraints*. A point $\mathbf{x} \in \Re^n$ is *feasible* if it satisfies the constraints, and *feasible space* $\mathcal{F} \subseteq \Re^n$

denotes all feasible points (represented $\mathcal{F} = \langle \mathbf{g}, \mathbf{h} \rangle$). A *feasible direction* $\vec{s}$ from a feasible point is one through which a non-zero distance can be moved before hitting a constraint boundary. $f(\mathbf{x})$ is *decreasing* at $\mathbf{x}$ in direction $\vec{s}$ if $\nabla f(\mathbf{x}) \cdot \vec{s} < 0$. Finally, *a point is stationary (denoted $\mathbf{x}*$) if any direction that decreases the objective is infeasible.* The Kuhn-Tucker (KT) conditions (Kuhn & Tucker 1951) provide a set of vector equations that are satisfied for a feasible point $\mathbf{x}*$ exactly when that point is stationary:

$$\nabla f(\mathbf{x}*) + \lambda^T \nabla \mathbf{h}(\mathbf{x}*) + \mu^T \nabla \mathbf{g}(\mathbf{x}*) \;=\; \mathbf{0}^T \quad \text{(KT1)}$$

subject to

$$\mu^T \mathbf{g}(\mathbf{x}*) \;=\; \mathbf{0}^T, \qquad\qquad \text{(KT2)}$$
$$\mu \;\geq\; \mathbf{0}. \qquad\qquad\qquad \text{(KT3)}$$

μ^T transposes column vector μ to a row. Gradients ∇f, $\nabla \mathbf{g}$ and $\nabla \mathbf{h}$ denote Jacobian matrices. ∇f is a row vector $\left(\frac{\partial f}{\partial x_1} \ldots \frac{\partial f}{\partial x_n} \right)$. $\nabla \mathbf{g}$ and $\nabla \mathbf{h}$ are matrices $\left(\frac{\partial g_i}{\partial x_j} \right)$ and $\left(\frac{\partial h_i}{\partial x_j} \right)$, respectively, where (a_{ij}) denotes a matrix whose element in the ith row and jth column is a_{ij}, for all i and j. For example, KT1 and KT2 are equivalences between row vectors, and KT3 is a relation between column vectors.

In KT1 the $-\nabla f$ term denotes directions of decreasing objective from $\mathbf{x}*$, the term $(\lambda^T \nabla \mathbf{h}(\mathbf{x}*) + \mu^T \nabla \mathbf{g}(\mathbf{x}*))$ denotes infeasible directions from $\mathbf{x}*$, and the equality says the decreasing directions are all infeasible; hence, $\mathbf{x}*$ is stationary. More specifically, $\vec{s}$ decreases the objective if it has a component in the $-\nabla f$ direction ($\vec{s} \cdot \nabla f < 0$). A direction is infeasible with respect to inequality constraint $g_i(\mathbf{x}*)$ if $\mathbf{x}*$ lies on the constraint boundary ($g_i(\mathbf{x}*) = 0$) and it has a component in the $+\nabla g_i(\mathbf{x}*)$ direction. A direction is infeasible with respect to equality constraint $h_j(\mathbf{x}*)$ if it has a component in either the $-\nabla h_j(\mathbf{x}*)$ or $+\nabla h_j(\mathbf{x}*)$ direction. Most importantly, if $\mathbf{x}*$ lies on multiple constraint boundaries, then an infeasible direction has a component which is a linear, weighted combination of the above gradients for these constraints. The weights are μ and λ, (called *Lagrange multipliers*), and the combination is $\mu^T \nabla \mathbf{g} + \lambda^T \nabla \mathbf{h}$ subject to KT2 and KT3. Hence all decreasing directions are infeasible when $-\nabla f$ equals one of these linear combinations (KT1). Figure 2 shows an example of ∇f and $\nabla \mathbf{g}$ gradient vectors, and the combined weighted vector, which exactly cancels ∇f.

A key property of KT is that it identifies *active* inequality constraints. Intuitively, a constraint $[g_i]$ is active at a point $\mathbf{x}$ when $\mathbf{x}$ is *on* the constraint boundary and the direction of decreasing objective, ∇f, is pointing into the boundary. When this is true μ_i is positive. The basis of our approach is to conclude, by looking at signs of μ, that the stationary points lie at the intersection of the constraint boundaries. One or more constraints have been identified as active, hence the name *activity analysis*.

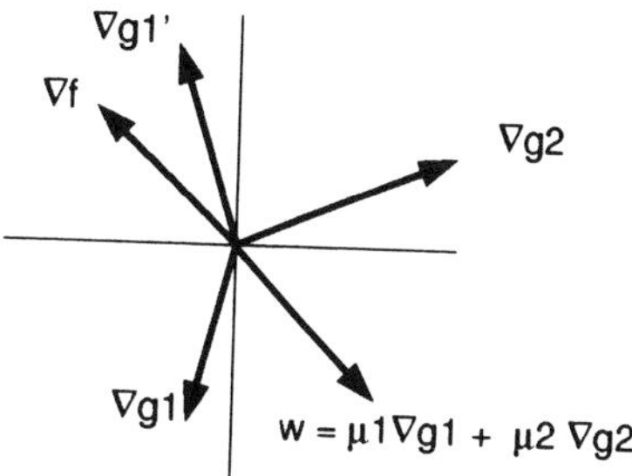

Figure 2: Example gradient vector diagram for KT.

Qualitative KT Conditions

Qualitative KT (QKT) is an abstraction of KT that is a necessary, but insufficient, condition for a point being stationary. It is the means by which activity analysis quickly rules out suboptimal subspaces. Qualitative properties used by QKT to test a point $\mathbf{x}$ include whether each constraint is active at $\mathbf{x}$, and the quadrant of the coordinate axes each gradient ∇f, $\nabla \mathbf{g}$ and $\nabla \mathbf{h}$ lies within. These properties can be extracted quickly and hold uniformly for large subsets of the feasible space, and parameterized families of optimization problems. QKT, its proof (see (Williams 1994)), and manipulations by activity analysis rely on a matrix version of SR1 – a hybrid algebra combining signs and reals. This algebra behaves as one expects given a familiarity with (scalar) sign algebra and traditional matrix algebra (see (Williams 1994; 1991)). Derived from KT, QKT states that a feasible point $\mathbf{x}*$ is stationary only if (QKT1):

$$[\nabla f(\mathbf{x}*)] + [\lambda]^T [\nabla \mathbf{h}(\mathbf{x}*)] + [\mu]^T [\nabla \mathbf{g}(\mathbf{x}*)] \supseteq \mathbf{0}^T,$$

subject to

$$[\mu]^T [\mathbf{g}(\mathbf{x}*)] \;=\; \mathbf{0}^T, \text{ and} \quad \text{(QKT2)}$$
$$[\mu_i] \;\neq\; \hat{-}, \qquad\qquad \text{(QKT3)}$$

where $[\mathbf{v}]$, called a *sign vector*, denotes the signs of the elements of $\mathbf{v}$, such that $[v_i] \in \{\hat{-}, 0, \hat{+}\}$. Recall KT said that to be stationary there must exist a weighted sum $(\vec{\mathbf{w}})$ of $\nabla \mathbf{g}$ and $\nabla \mathbf{h}$ that exactly cancels ∇f (note $\vec{\mathbf{w}}$ is a row vector). QKT says a point is *nonstationary* unless there exists a $\vec{\mathbf{w}}$ that lies in the *quadrant diagonal* from that which contains ∇f. For example, in figure 2 ∇f lies in the upper left quadrant; thus, a $\vec{\mathbf{w}}$ must exist that lies in the lower right. The sign vector $[\mathbf{v}]$ denotes the quadrant containing a vector $\mathbf{v}$, and each component $[v_i]$ describes where $\mathbf{v}$ lies relative to the $v_i = 0$ plane. For example, $[\vec{\mathbf{w}}] = (\hat{+} \;\; \hat{-})$ indicates that $\vec{\mathbf{w}}$ is in the lower right. Using this algebraic representation, the condition on diagonal quadrants becomes $-[\nabla f] = [\vec{\mathbf{w}}]$.

Using only knowledge of the quadrant each constraint's gradient lies within and whether each constraint is active (indicated by the signs of the lagrange multipliers $[\mu]$ and $[\lambda]$), we know from KT that the quadrants $\vec{\mathbf{w}}$ may lie within are a subspace of those described by $[\mu]^T[\nabla\mathbf{g}] + [\lambda]^T[\nabla\mathbf{h}]$. Thus, $-[\nabla f] = [\vec{\mathbf{w}}] \subseteq [\mu]^T[\nabla\mathbf{g}] + [\lambda]^T[\nabla\mathbf{h}]$ (i.e., QKT1). For example, in figure 2 since $\nabla g_1\ (= (\ \hat{+}\quad \hat{+}\ ))$ lies in the upper right and $\nabla g_2\ (= (\ \hat{-}\quad \hat{-}\ ))$ lies in the lower left, it is possible for a $\vec{\mathbf{w}}$ to lie in the lower right; thus, any $\mathbf{x}$ satisfying these conditions may be stationary. But suppose ∇g_1 is replaced with $\nabla g_1'$, which lies in the upper left for points in some subspace $\mathcal{F}1 \subseteq \mathcal{F}$. Then $\vec{\mathbf{w}}$ may lie in the upper or lower left, but not the lower right; thus, all points in $\mathcal{F}1$ must be nonstationary. That is, evaluating $-[\nabla f] = [\mu]^T[\nabla\mathbf{g}]$ for ∇g_1 and then $\nabla g_1'$:

$$(\ \hat{+}\quad \hat{-}\ ) \ \subseteq (\ ?\quad ?\ ) \ = (\ \hat{+}\quad \hat{+}\ )\begin{pmatrix} \hat{+} & \hat{+} \\ \hat{-} & \hat{-} \end{pmatrix} \ \text{but}$$

$$(\ \hat{+}\quad \hat{-}\ ) \ \not\subseteq (\ \hat{-}\quad ?\ ) \ = (\ \hat{+}\quad \hat{+}\ )\begin{pmatrix} \hat{-} & \hat{+} \\ \hat{-} & \hat{-} \end{pmatrix}.$$

It is this second type of conclusion, made from only qualitative properties, that activity analysis uses to eliminate feasible subspaces of nonstationary points.

Next, to instantiate QKT1 on optimization problem $OP \equiv \langle \mathbf{x}, f, \mathbf{g}, \mathbf{h}\rangle$:

1. Compute Jacobians ∇f, $\nabla\mathbf{g}$ and $\nabla\mathbf{h}$ by symbolic differentiation.

2. Compute signs of Jacobians. For each element,

   (a) replace real operators with sign operators, using properties $[a+b] \subseteq [a] + [b]$, $[ab] = [a][b]$, $[a/b] = [a]/[b]$ and $[-a] = -[a]$.

   (b) Substitute for sign variables $[a]$ using positivity conditions ($[a] = \hat{+}$), and perform sign arithmetic (e.g., $[5] \Rightarrow \hat{+}$, $(\hat{-}) + (\hat{-}) \Rightarrow \hat{-}$).

3. Expand QKT1 by expanding matrix sums and products.

Returning to the hydraulic cylinder problem from the introduction, recall that $\mathbf{x}$ is the vector $(it\,f\,sp)^T$, the objective $f(\mathbf{x})$ is $i + 2t$, and the constraint vectors are:

$$\mathbf{h} = \left(\ s - \tfrac{pi}{2t}\quad f - \tfrac{\pi i^2}{4}p \ \right)^T,$$

$$\mathbf{g} = (\ F - f\quad T - t\quad p - P\quad s - S\ ).^T$$

The following shows $[\nabla\mathbf{h}]$ after steps 2a (middle) and 2b (right):

$$[\nabla\mathbf{h}] = \begin{pmatrix} \frac{-[p]}{[2][t]} & \frac{[p][i]}{[2][t]^2} & 0 & [1] & \frac{-[i]}{[2][t]} \\ \frac{-[\pi][i]}{[2]}[p] & 0 & [1] & 0 & \frac{-[\pi][i]^2}{[4]} \end{pmatrix}$$

$$= \begin{pmatrix} \hat{-} & \hat{+} & 0 & \hat{+} & \hat{-} \\ \hat{-} & 0 & \hat{+} & 0 & \hat{-} \end{pmatrix}.$$

Repeating for $[\nabla f]$ and $[\nabla\mathbf{g}]$, and inserting into QKT:

$$\mathbf{0}^T \subseteq \begin{pmatrix} \hat{+} \\ \hat{+} \\ 0 \\ 0 \\ 0 \end{pmatrix}^T + \lambda^T \begin{pmatrix} \hat{-} & \hat{+} & 0 & \hat{+} & \hat{-} \\ \hat{-} & 0 & \hat{+} & 0 & \hat{-} \end{pmatrix}$$

$$+ \mu^T \begin{pmatrix} 0 & 0 & \hat{-} & 0 & 0 \\ 0 & \hat{-} & 0 & 0 & 0 \\ 0 & 0 & 0 & 0 & \hat{+} \\ 0 & 0 & 0 & \hat{+} & 0 \end{pmatrix}.$$

Expanding matrix operations for step 3 results in equations QKT1(1)-(5):

0	$\subseteq$	$(\hat{+}) - [\lambda_1] - [\lambda_2]$	(1)	0	$\subseteq$	$[\mu_4] + [\lambda_1]$	(4)
0	$\subseteq$	$(\hat{+}) - [\mu_2] + [\lambda_1]$	(2)	0	$\subseteq$	$[\mu_3] - [\lambda_1] - [\lambda_2]$	(5)
0	$\subseteq$	$-[\mu_1] + [\lambda_2]$	(3)				

Note that the computation of sign matrices in step 2 is extremely simple, but suprisingly adequate for many problems. The symbolic algebra system Minima (Williams 1991) provides a general tool for deducing the signs of sensitivities (e.g., $\left[\frac{\partial f(\mathbf{x})}{\partial x_i}\right]$) subject to $\mathbf{x}$ satisfying the equality and inequality constraints. Having achieved an easily evaluable condition that is sufficient for testing the suboptimality of infinite subspaces, we turn to its use for strategically focussing optimization.

Activity Analysis and Prime Assignments

Activity analysis reduces an optimization problem to a set of simpler subproblems by "cutting" out feasible subspaces that are suboptimal. These subspaces contain all and only those points that are provably nonstationary by QKT (see (Williams 1994)). The output of activity analysis is a concise description of the remainder, called a *minimal pstationary covering* ("p-" stands for "possible" according to QKT). It is a set of feasible subspaces (and corresponding optimization problems), at least one of which is guaranteed to contain the true optimum. What is key is that the descriptions are parsimonious, they maximize the "filtering" achievable from QKT, and are always correct (these three properties are theorems, stated precisely in (Williams 1994)). This section states and demonstrates the activity analysis problem, and a sound and complete solution algorithm. The core is a mapping between *minimal pstationary subspaces* and *prime assignments*, and a general prime assignment engine for arbitrary *systems of linear sign equations*.

To start we say a *point is pnonstationary* if it follows from QKT that it is nonstationary; otherwise, it is *pstationary*. A *feasible subspace is pstationary* if all its points are pstationary, and *pnonstationary* if all its points are pnonstationary. Activity analysis maximizes its use of QKT while preserving correctness by eliminating exactly the pnonstationary subspaces from its description of the feasible space. This description is built from a set Σ whose elements result from strengthening one or more of the inequality constraints $g_i \leq 0$ to strict equalities $g_i = 0$; that is, Σ is the powerset of constraint boundary intersections. The description (called a *minimal pstationary covering*), covers the pstationary points by collecting all pstationary subspaces that are maximal under superset. These cover every pstationary subspace. The activity analysis problem is then: *given optimization problem $OP = \langle \mathbf{x}, f, \mathbf{g}, \mathbf{h} \rangle$ and instantiation of QKT (=QKT(OP)), construct the minimal pstationary covering C.*

Mapping QKT(OP) to C relies on two observations: First, from QKT2 ($\equiv [\mu_i(\mathbf{x})][g_i(\mathbf{x})] = 0$) it follows that $[\mu_i(\mathbf{x})] = \hat{+} \rightarrow g_i(\mathbf{x}) = 0$ (denoted R1). That is, any point where $[\mu_i] = \hat{+}$ must be on the $g_i = 0$ constraint boundary. Thus, when activity analysis shows that a subspace of pstationary points makes $[\mu_i] = \hat{+}$ for one or more g_i's, it concludes that these points lie along the intersection of the g_i boundaries. Second, a particular set of variable assignments for QKT1, called *prime (implicating) assignments*, directly maps to the minimal pstationary covering by applying the first observation. The key here is that achieving parsimony, maximum filtering and correctness reduces to generating complete prime assignments.

The following properties, stated informally here, are given as definitions and theorems in (Williams 1994). First, a *(partial) assignment to* $[\mathbf{x}]$ is a set α which assigns each $[x_i]$ at most one value, $\alpha \subseteq \{[x_i] = s \mid [x_i] \in \mathbf{x}, s \in \{\hat{-}, 0, \hat{+}\}\}$. We are interested in the *consistent assignments to QKT1*, where the $[\mathbf{x}]$ to be assigned is a vector of lagrange multipliers $([\mu]^T [\lambda]^T)^T$. Additionally, the consistent assignments must also satisfy the restriction of QKT3 ($[\mu] \neq \hat{-}$). Note that each consistent assignment C has a corresponding subset S of feasible space, produced by applying R1 to the assignment and then adding the resulting active constraints to the original constraint set. S has the property that every point in S satisfies C.

Next, an *implicating assignment* γ is a consistent assignment to QKT1, such that whenever an extension to γ satisfies restriction QKT3, it also is consistent with QKT1. That is, assignment γ *implies* QKT1 under restriction QKT3. An implicating assignment has the important property that every point in its corresponding subspace S satisfies QKT. Thus S is a pstationary subspace.

Finally, a *prime assignment* P is an implicating assignment no proper subset of which is also an implicating assignment. Thus P's corresponding S is a maximal pstationary subspace. Conversely, every maximal pstationary subspace is the corresponding subspace of some prime assignment. Thus the set of subspaces corresponding to all prime assignments is a minimal pstationary covering.

To produce all primes for QKT1, our prime assignment engine first computes the primes P_i of each scalar equation in QKT1, then combines them using minimal set covering. Pulling this all together, the activity analysis algorithm is:

Given problem $OP = \langle \mathbf{x}, f, \mathbf{g}, \mathbf{h} \rangle$:

1. Instantiate QKT1 (given earlier) $\rightarrow QKT1(OP)$,

2. Compute prime assignments P_i of each $QKT1_i(OP) \in QKT1(OP)$,

3. Compute minimal set covering of $P_i \rightarrow P$, deleting inconsistent assignments,

4. Extract minimal sets of $[\mu_i] = \hat{+}$ assignments from $P \rightarrow U$,

5. Map each element of U to a maximal pstationary subspace by applying $[\mu_i(\mathbf{x})] = \hat{+} \rightarrow g_i(\mathbf{x}) = 0$, producing a covering.

6. Formulate and return a new optimization problem from this covering.

Step one was demonstrated in the previous section. For steps two and three we note that QKT1 is an instance of a linear system of sign equations (denoted $\mathbf{L}([\mathbf{x}])$) and solve the prime assignment problem for arbitrary $\mathbf{L}([\mathbf{x}])$. That is, $\mathbf{L}([\mathbf{x}])$ in vector form is $\mathbf{0} \subseteq [\mathbf{B}] + [\mathbf{A}][\mathbf{x}]$, with $[\mathbf{A}]$ and $[\mathbf{B}]$ being sign constant matrices, $[\mathbf{x}]$ an n vector, $[\mathbf{A}]$ an n by m matrix and $[\mathbf{B}]$ an m vector. The ith scalar equation of $\mathbf{L}([\mathbf{x}])$ (denoted $L_i([\mathbf{x}])$) is of the form:

$$L_i([\mathbf{x}]) \equiv 0 \subseteq [b_i] + \sum_{j=1}^{m} [a_{ij}] [x_j] .$$

For QKT1, $\mathbf{x}^T$ is $\left(\mu^T \lambda^T\right)^T$, $[\mathbf{B}] = [\nabla f]$, and $[\mathbf{A}]$ is the matrix $(\nabla \mathbf{g} \ \nabla \mathbf{h})$. Additionally, we generalize the set of restrictions given by QKT3 (i.e., $[\mu_i] \neq \hat{-}$), to arbitrary sets of restrictions $\mathbf{R}([\mathbf{x}]) \subseteq \{[x_i] \neq s \mid x_i \in \mathbf{x}, s \in \{\hat{-}, 0, \hat{+}\}\}$. For the cylinder (table, end of QKT section), QKT1 has 5 $L_i([\mathbf{x}])$'s, with $\mathbf{x} \equiv (\mu_1 \mu_2 \mu_3 \mu_4 \lambda_1 \lambda_2)^T$. For ease of reading we wrote terms $\hat{+}[x_i]$ as $[x_i]$, $\hat{-}[x_i]$ as $-[x_i]$, and eliminated terms $0[x_i]$. The cylinder $\mathbf{R}([\mathbf{x}])$ is $\{[\mu_1] \neq \hat{-}, [\mu_2] \neq \hat{-}, [\mu_3] \neq \hat{-}, [\mu_4] \neq \hat{-}\}$.

For step 2, the prime assignments of each $L_i([\mathbf{x}])$ are constructed from three sets of scalar assignments, consistent with $\mathbf{R}([\mathbf{x}])$: those restricting one of the equation's terms ($[a_{ij}][x_j]$) to be positive (P_i), those making a term zero (Z_i), and those making a term negative (N_i), respectively:

$$\begin{aligned}
P_i &\equiv \{[x_j] = [a_{ij}] \mid [a_{ij}] \neq 0, \ ([x_j] \neq [a_{ij}]) \notin \mathbf{R}([\mathbf{x}])\}, \\
Z_i &\equiv \{[x_j] = 0 \mid [a_{ij}] \neq 0, \ ([x_j] \neq 0) \notin \mathbf{R}([\mathbf{x}])\} \text{ and} \\
N_i &\equiv \{[x_j] = -[a_{ij}] \mid [a_{ij}] \neq 0, \ ([x_j] \neq -[a_{ij}]) \notin \mathbf{R}([\mathbf{x}])\}.
\end{aligned}$$

Justifying P_i, for example, we know in general that $[c] \neq 0 \rightarrow [c]^2 = \hat{+}$. Thus $[a_{ij}][x_j] = \hat{+}$ if $[x_j] = [a_{ij}]$ and $[a_{ij}] \neq 0$. The derivation of Z_i and N_i is similar. Constructing the prime assignments for the cylinder $L_i([\mathbf{x}])$ uses:

i	N_i	Z_i	P_i
1	$[\lambda_1] = \hat{+}, [\lambda_2] = \hat{+}$	$[\lambda_1] = 0, [\lambda_2] = 0$	$[\lambda_1] = \hat{-}, [\lambda_2] = \hat{-}$
2	$[\lambda_1] = \hat{-}, [\mu_2] = \hat{+}$	$[\lambda_1] = 0, [\mu_2] = 0$	$[\lambda_1] = \hat{+}$
3	$[\lambda_2] = \hat{-}, [\mu_1] = \hat{+}$	$\lambda_2 = 0, \mu_1 = 0$	$[\lambda_2] = \hat{+}$
4	$[\lambda_1] = \hat{-}$	$\lambda_1 = 0, \mu_4 = 0$	$[\lambda_1] = \hat{+}, [\mu_4] = \hat{+}$
5	$[\lambda_1] = \hat{+}, [\lambda_2] = \hat{+}$	$\lambda_1 = 0, \lambda_2 = 0, \mu_3 = 0$	$[\lambda_1] = \hat{-}, [\lambda_2] = \hat{-}, [\mu_3] = \hat{+}$

Next, recall that the prime (implicating) assignments for $L_i([\mathbf{x}])$ must imply $L_i([\mathbf{x}])$. That is, they guarantee that it holds, given $\mathbf{R}([\mathbf{x}])$, independent of additional consistent assignments. This is true if the right hand side of $L_i([\mathbf{x}])$ is guaranteed to be a superset of 0 (i.e., it is either 0 or $\hat{?}$). The form of the assignments that achieve this for some $L_i([\mathbf{x}])$ depends on the value of $[b_i]$, where $[b_i] = \left[\frac{\partial f}{\partial x_i}\right]$ for QKT1. Suppose $[b_i] = \hat{+}$, then the right hand side must become $\hat{?}$. This holds exactly when at least one of the $[a_{ij}][x_j]$ terms is negative (since $0 \subseteq (\hat{-}) + (\hat{+}) = \hat{?}$). For example, in the cylinder QKT equation (2), $\lambda_1 = \hat{-}$ guarantees that the equation is satisfied. The only other assignment that guarantees this is $\mu_2 = \hat{+}$. Thus the prime assignments for (2) are $\{\lambda_1 = \hat{-}\}$ and $\{\mu_2 = \hat{+}\}$. The treatment of $[b_i] = \hat{-}$ is analogous.

Next, suppose $[b_i] = 0$, then to imply $L_i([\mathbf{x}])$ the prime assignment can make the right hand side either 0 or $\hat{?}$. The first holds exactly when all terms are 0. The second holds when at least one term is positive and the other is negative. For example, $\left[\frac{\partial f(\mathbf{x})}{\partial x_i}\right] = 0$ in cylinder $QKT1(3): 0 \subseteq -[\mu_1] + [\lambda_2]$. Thus, the prime assignments are $\{\lambda_2 = 0, \mu_1 = 0\}$ and $\{\lambda_2 = \hat{+}, \mu_1 = \hat{+}\}$. Note that $\{\lambda_2 = \hat{-}, \mu_1 = \hat{-}\}$ is not acceptable, since by restriction $[\mu_i] \neq \hat{-}$. *To summarize, the prime assignments of $L_i([\mathbf{x}])$ are 1) N_i if $[b_i] = \hat{+}$, 2) P_i if $[b_i] = \hat{-}$, and 3) $\{Z_i\} \cup \{\{p, n\} | p \in P_i, n \in N_i\}$ if $[b_i] = 0$ (where p and n in $\{p, n\}$ do not contradict each other).* Completing step two for the table of cylinder equations QKT1(1) - (5) produces:

$$
\begin{array}{ll}
\{\lambda_1 = \hat{+}\}, \{\lambda_2 = \hat{+}\} & P(1) \\
\{\lambda_1 = \hat{-}\}, \{\mu_2 = \hat{+}\} & P(2) \\
\{\lambda_2 = 0, \mu_1 = 0\} \, \{\lambda_2 = \hat{+}, \mu_1 = \hat{+}\} & P(3) \\
\{\lambda_1 = 0, \mu_4 = 0\}, \{\lambda_1 = \hat{-}, \mu_4 = \hat{+}\} & P(4) \\
\{\lambda_1 = 0, \lambda_2 = 0, \mu_3 = 0\}, & \\
\quad \{\lambda_1 = \hat{+}, \lambda_2 = \hat{-},\} \, \{\lambda_1 = \hat{+}, \mu_3 = \hat{+}\} & \\
\quad \{\lambda_1 = \hat{-}, \lambda_2 = \hat{+}\}, \{\lambda_2 = \hat{+}, \mu_3 = \hat{+}\} & P(5)
\end{array}
$$

The third step, constructing the composite primes for $\mathbf{L}([\mathbf{x}])$, is based on:

$$
\bigvee_{p \in P(\mathbf{L}([\mathbf{x}]))} \left(\bigwedge_{a \in p} a\right) \equiv \bigwedge_{i=1}^{n} \left(\bigvee_{p \in P(L_i([\mathbf{x}]))} \left(\bigwedge_{a \in p} a\right)\right).
$$

The left hand side is a disjunction of the $\mathbf{L}([\mathbf{x}])$ prime assignments, and the right hand side is an expression in terms of the primes of $L_i([\mathbf{x}])$, just computed. Thus, the desired primes result from reducing the expression on the right to minimal, disjunctive normal form. For this specialized case, this step is equivalent to computing minimal set covering of the $P(L_i([\mathbf{x}]))$ and then removing inconsistent assignments (see a standard algorithm text, or (Williams 1994) for our algorithm). For the cylinder, the minimal covering of P(1) - (5) produces just two prime assignments,

$$
\begin{array}{l}
\{\{[\lambda_1] = \hat{-}, [\lambda_2] = \hat{+}, [\mu_1] = \hat{+}, [\mu_4] = \hat{+}\}, \\
\{[\lambda_1] = 0, [\lambda_2] = \hat{+}, [\mu_1] = \hat{+}, [\mu_2] = \hat{+}, [\mu_3] = \hat{+}, [\mu_4] = 0\}\}.
\end{array}
$$

The fourth step, extracting the minimal sets of $[\mu_i] = \hat{+}$ assignments results in $\{[\mu_1] = \hat{+}, [\mu_4] = \hat{+}\}$ and $\{[\mu_1] = \hat{+}, [\mu_2] = \hat{+}, [\mu_3] = \hat{+}\}$. The fifth step uses $[\mu_i] = \hat{+} \rightarrow g_i(\mathbf{x}) = 0$ to map these sets to the equivalent minimal pstationary covering. The sets tell us that g_1 and g_4 must be active, or g_1, g_2 and g_3. The resulting cover is:

$$
\begin{array}{l}
\mathcal{F}_1 \equiv \langle \{g_2, g_3\}, \{h_1, h_2, g_1, g_4\} \rangle \text{ and} \\
\mathcal{F}_2 \equiv \langle \{g_4\}, \{h_1, h_2, g_1, g_2, g_3\} \rangle,
\end{array}
$$

where $\langle \mathbf{g}, \mathbf{h} \rangle$ is a space defined by inequality $\mathbf{g}$ and equality $\mathbf{h}$ constraints. $\mathcal{F}_1$ and $\mathcal{F}_2$ denote the line and point highlighted in the introduction to the cylinder example. The final step, formulating a new optimization problem, produces:

Given: $\quad S \equiv \{\mathbf{x}* \mid \mathbf{x}* = arg \min_{\mathbf{x} \in \mathcal{F}} f(\mathbf{x}), \mathcal{F} \in \{\mathcal{F}_1, \mathcal{F}_2\}\},$
Find: $\quad \min_{\mathbf{x} \in S} f(\mathbf{x})$.

The first part finds the minimum of each subspace in the covering. The second part selects from these the global minimum. A more expanded form was given in the introduction. Thus through this example we have demonstrated activity analysis' capability of partially solving constrained optimization problems from monotonicity constraints, and for synthesizing special purpose optimization codes.

Discussion

As we mentioned in the introduction, activity analysis builds upon a large body of work from the mechanical engineering community on monotonicity analysis(Wilde 1975; Papalambros & Wilde 1979; Papalambros 1982), a method that uses derivative information to address the boundedness and global optimality of optimization problems. Monotonicity analysis provides two rules that test the boundedness of a formulation:

Rule 1: If the objective function is monotonic with respect to a variable, then there exists at least one active constraint that bounds the variable in the direction opposite of the objective function.

Rule 2: If a variable is not contained in the objective function then it must be either bounded from both above and below by active constraints or not actively bounded at all (i.e., in the latter case any constraint that is monotonic with respect to that variable must be inactive or irrelevant).

Both of these rules can be derived from the Kuhn-Tucker Conditions. They also follow as an instance of QKT and are embodied within activity analysis.

The result of monotonicity analysis (exhaustive application of the rules) are several sets of constraints one of which must be active for a problem to be well bounded. Various levels of rule-based implementations of monotonicity analysis have been described in (Michelena & Agogino 1988; Rao & Papalambros 1987; Azram & Papalambros 1984; Hansen, Jaumard, & Lu 1989), which guide numerical optimization codes. Choy and Agogino (Choy & Agogino 1986) and Agogino and Almgren (Agogino & Almgren 1987) incorporate symbolic algebraic methods to aid in the evaluation of monotonicities and the solution of the optima. Cagan and Agogino (Cagan & Agogino 1987) apply monotonicity analysis to identify topological changes to designs that improve performance. While these systems address the optimal reasoning problem, they do not present algorithms proven to be sound and complete (each of these implementations has been described as "heuristic" (Rao & Papalambros 1987; Hansen, Jaumard, & Lu 1989)).

Activity analysis provides the following contributions: it formalizes the strategic way in which a modeler focuses optimization, as the process of generating minimal pstationary coverings. It introduces QKT as a powerful condition for quickly eliminating large, suboptimal subspaces. Finally, it exploits this condition through a novel problem reformulation based on the prime, implicating assignments of linear sign equations. The activity analysis algorithm is sound and complete with respect to classifying the design space into pstationary and pnonstationary subspaces. The method of pruning suboptimal subspaces provides a continuous analog to the conflict-based approaches prevalent in combinatorial satisficing search (such as those used in model-based diagnosis (de Kleer & Williams 1987)). Activity analysis automates the intuitions about monotonicity exploited by the simplex method to examine only the vertices of the linear feasible space, most importantly, extending its application to nonlinear problems.

Activity analysis has been demonstrated on several engineering problems. The implementation is in Franz Lisp running on a Sparc 2. The problem reformulation is passed to Matlab's Optimization toolbox, where a wide variety of nonlinear gradient methods are available. (Williams 1994) describes an extension to activity analysis for cases where monotonicities are only partially known. Activity analysis is currently being pursued in the context of visual 3D matching problems and other embedded, realtime problems. Activity analysis can also be extended to provide explainable optimizers, ones that use QKT to provide commonsense explanations about optimality. Activity analysis is one of several techniques being developed that capture a modeler's expertise at strategically guiding numerical codes.

References

Agogino, A. M., and Almgren, A. S. 1987. Techniques for Integrating Qualitative Reasoning and Symbolic Computation in Engineering Optimization. *Engineering Optimization* 12:117–135.

Azram, S., and Papalambros, P. 1984. An Automated Procedure for Local Monotonicity Analysis. *Trans. ASME, Journal of Mechanisms, Transmissions, and Automation in Design* 106:82–89.

Cagan, J., and Agogino, A. M. 1987. Innovative Design of Mechanical Structures from First Principles. *AI EDAM* 1(3):169–189.

Choy, J. K., and Agogino, A. M. 1986. SYMON: Automated SYMbolic MONotonicity Analysis System for Qualitative Design Optimization. In *Proceedings of ASME 1986 International Computers in Engineering Conference*, 305–310.

de Kleer, J., and Williams, B. C. 1987. Diagnosing Multiple Faults. *Artif. Intell.* 32:97–130.

Hansen, P.; Jaumard, B.; and Lu, S. H. 1989. An Automated Proceedure for Globally Optimal Design. *Trans. of the ASME, Journal of Mechanisms, Transmissions, and Automation in Design* 361–367.

Kuhn, H. W., and Tucker, A. W. 1951. Nonlinear Programming. In Neyman, J., ed., *Proceedings of the Second Berkeley Symposium on Mathematical Statistics and Probability.* Berkeley, CA: University of California Press.

Michelena, N., and Agogino, A. M. 1988. Multiobjective Hydraulic Cylinder Design. *Journal of Mechanisms, Transmission and Automation in Design* 110:81–87.

Papalambros, P., and Wilde, D. J. 1979. Global Non-Iterative Design Optimization Using Monotonicity Analysis. *Trans. ASME, Journal of Mechanical Design* 101(4):645–649.

Papalambros, P. 1982. Monotonicity in Goal and Geometric Programming. *Transactions of the ASME, Journal of Mechanical Design* 104:108–113.

Rao, J. R., and Papalambros, P. 1987. Implementation of Semi-Heuristic Reasoning for Bounded Analysis of Design Optimization Models. In *Advances in Design Automation, proceedings of the ASME Design Automation Conference*, 59–65.

Vanderplaats, G. N. 1984. *Numerical Optimization Techniques for Engineering Design With Applications.* New York: McGraw-Hill.

Wilde, D. J. 1975. Monotonicity and Dominance in Optimal Hydraulic Cylinder Design. *Trans of the ASME, Journal of Engineering for Industry* 94(4):1390–1394.

Williams, B. C., and Raiman, O. 1994. Decompositional Modelling through Caricatural Reasoning. In *AAAI*.

Williams, B. C. 1991. A theory of interactions: unifying qualitative and quantitative algebraic reasoning. *Artif. Intell.* 51.

Williams, B. C. 1994. Characterizing Activity Analysis. in progress.

Intelligent Automated Grid Generation for Numerical Simulations

Ke-Thia Yao
Computer Science Department
Rutgers University
New Brunswick, NJ 08903, USA
kyao@cs.rutgers.edu
(908) 932-5263

Andrew Gelsey
Computer Science Department
Rutgers University
New Brunswick, NJ 08903, USA
gelsey@cs.rutgers.edu
(908) 932-4869

Abstract

Numerical simulation of partial differential equations (PDEs) plays a crucial role in predicting the behavior of physical systems and in modern engineering design. However, in order to produce reliable results with a PDE simulator, a human expert must typically expend considerable time and effort in setting up the simulation. Most of this effort is spent in generating the grid, the discretization of the spatial domain which the PDE simulator requires as input. To properly design a grid, the gridder must not only consider the characteristics of the spatial domain, but also the physics of the situation and the peculiarities of the numerical simulator. This paper describes an intelligent gridder that is capable of analyzing the topology of the spatial domain and predicting approximate physical behaviors based on the geometry of the spatial domain to automatically generate grids for computational fluid dynamics simulators. Typically gridding programs are given a *partitioning* of the spatial domain to assist the gridder. Our gridder is capable of performing this partitioning. This enables the gridder to automatically grid spatial domains of arbitrary configurations.

Introduction

Numerical simulation of physical systems plays a crucial role in engineering design. Unfortunately, getting simulation results with acceptable accuracy is a time-consuming and labor-intensive process. Although the amount of computational time needed to execute the numerical code is considerable, it may not be the dominant factor. In PDE simulations of physical systems with complicated geometries, the most time consuming portions are rather setting up the numerical simulation, verifying the correctness of the simulation results, and modifying the setup if the results are not within expect tolerances.

Partial differential equation solvers require a grid, a discretization of the spatial regions of interest. Usually in computational fluid dynamics, the spatial regions of interest are the areas of the surface that contact the fluid. The quality of the grid strongly affects the accuracy and the convergence properties of the resulting simulation. Generating a proper grid involves reasoning about the geometry of the regions of interest, the physics of the situation and the peculiarities of the numerical analysis code. To deal with the complexities of gridding, the current trend in the gridding field is toward interactive gridding (Remotique, Hart, & Stokes 1992, Kao & Su 1992). Interactive gridding more readily taps into the spatial reasoning abilities of the human user through the use of a graphical interface with a mouse. However, this approach is not acceptable for automated design systems.

We are working in the physical domain of fluid dynamics, in particular potential flows modeled by Laplace's partial differential equation. The potential flow solver we use is PMARC, a product of NASA Ames Research Center. The input PMARC requires is a panelization — a discretization of an object's wetted surface as a grid of *surface patches*, where each surface patch is an array of approximately planar quadrilateral panels. This array of panels is represented in PMARC as a matrix of corner points. See Figure 1 for a grid of a yacht automatically generated for PMARC by our gridding program.

The yacht in Figure 1 consists of three input components: an ellipsoid hull, the *Star & Strips* keel, and the *Star & Strips* winglet.[1] The wake sheets attached to the rear of the yacht are the vortices shed by the yacht. Discussions on how to attach wakes and how to determine the shape of the wakes are beyond the scope of this paper. The *Star & Strips* winglet attached to the bottom of keel is considered a major innovation in the field of racing yachts, and the success of the *Star & Strips* was in part due to its winglet. Current automated gridding programs should be but are not able to handle this kind of innovative *topological* change in design without human assistance. In this paper we describe an automated gridder that is capable of gridding geometries of arbitrary topological configurations.

The input to the gridder is expressed in a language we have developed called Boundary Surface Representation (BSR). Figure 2 graphically depicts the BSR input for this yacht example. We shall use this yacht

---

[1]The *Star & Strips* is the yacht that won the 1987 America's Cup Competition.

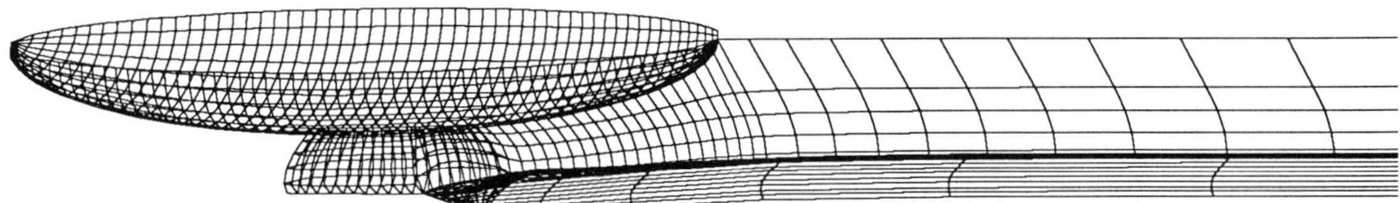

Figure 1: Yacht (consisting of three components hull, keel, and winglet) with wake sheets.

example throughout this paper. Both BSR and the input will be discussed in much more detail later. For now we'll point out that BSR input consists of two major parts: *geometrical* and *topological*. The geometrical part represents the detailed features of the yacht, which are the three input surface mappings (*shape*) in the figure. The *topological* part contains information on the adjacency of the input surfaces. The adjacency information is represented by dotted lines in the figure.

Why is automated gridding hard?

Steps to gridding

We divide gridding into three steps. The first step is to *partition* the input surface into griddable *surface patches*. That is, this step finds the appropriate boundary lines (or *partitioning lines*) for the surface patches. As we'll see this step is often the most difficult, because it involves significant physical and geometrical reasoning.

Step two, for each surface patch, *reparametrize* it by defining two families of approximately orthogonal grid lines. A formal definition will be given later when BSR is defined. But, intuitively suppose a surface patch is laying on the xy-plane, then $\{x = constant, y = constant\}$ is one possible parameterization, and $\{x + y = constant, x - y = constant\}$ is another.

The last step is to determine how many grid lines to lay down on each of the surface patches, and in particular where to lay them down. This step corresponds to picking the constants to instantiate the equations in step two. The intersections of these grid lines form corner points of the array of panels, which is the input to PMARC. This step we shall call the grid line *distribution* step. The distribution of grid lines can make grids with the same reparametrization look different and may make the numerical simulator behave differently. For example, using the *equal-distance* distribution scheme, $x = i/10$, where $i = 0, \ldots, 10$, may make the numerical simulator converge slower than a *cosine* distribution scheme, $x = (1 - \cos \pi i/10)/2$, where $i = 0, \ldots, 10$.

Evaluation criteria

Gridding as defined by the three steps above is unconstrained. The ultimate test for a grid is to check how sound the resulting simulation is, and how well it resolves the physical features of the domain. Short of feeding the grid to a simulator, there are ways of checking the goodness of a grid.

Through our discussion with hydrodynamicists we have formulated a list of grid evaluation criteria and constraints. On the basis of the geometric properties of the grid, these evaluation criteria attempt to predict the soundness of PMARC's output. We divide this list into four levels, ranging from constraints that absolutely must be satisfied to heuristic advice based on experiences of our experts.

1. Simple connectedness constraint: surface patches must be simply connected, i.e., no holes.
2. Coverage constraint: patches must not overlap or leave gaps.
3. Planarity criterion: panels must be approximately planar.
4. Heuristic criteria:
   - following streamlines: grid lines should follow the streamlines of the fluid flowing over the body.
   - orthogonality: grid lines should intersect at right angles.
   - expansion ratio: the area of the adjacent panels should not increase by more than a fixed ratio.

Difficulties of partitioning

Much work has been done on the problem of automated gridding (Thompson, Warsi, & Mastin 1985), and many gridding programs have been developed. However, most of these efforts concentrate on developing new methods of reparametrization and new distribution schemes. The choices of which reparametrization method and which distribution scheme to use are usually left to the human expert. Almost no work has been done on automated partitioning.

Most of the programs rely exclusively on the human expert to do the partitioning. He is expected to do the partitioning by either writing batch commands, or more recently by using an interactive graphical interface. In either case, the partitions created only apply to the one particular problem at hand. More recently, (Schuster 1992) has been trying to revive batch mode gridding by writing more general batch commands. However, his program is only able to grid a small, fixed set of airplane topologies.

One of the fundamental problems with the current gridding programs is that they do not make use of topology. All the topological information has been distilled away by either having the user provide the partitions or by fixing the possible topologies. The programs can only work on individual surface patches. Another problem is that programs have neither the

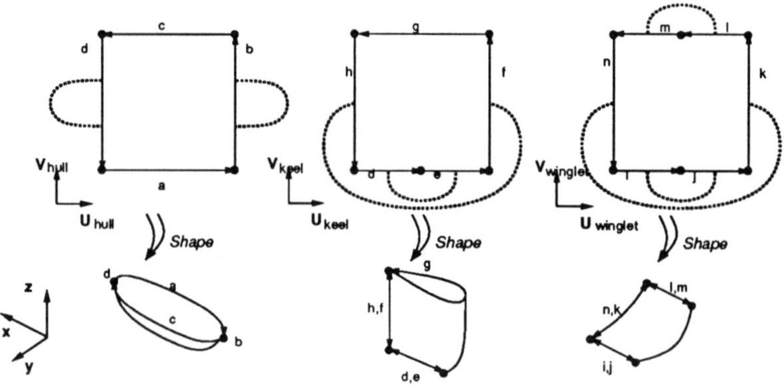

Figure 2: BSR input

knowledge of physics nor the knowledge of numerical analysis needed to generate grids that will lead to good simulations.

One manifestation of the lack of physical knowledge is as follows. A closer examination of the surface area near where the hull and keel meet reveals that the keel actually protrudes into the hull, and the hull has an extra surface area where the keel is. Surfaces given to the gridding program often contain *fictional surface areas*, areas that should not be gridded. Fictional surface areas are useful because they allow the hull and keel to be modified independently while still remaining in contact. However, an automated gridding program must be able to distinguish between the real and fictional areas in order to satisfy the *coverage* constraint.

Recall that PMARC represents each patch by a matrix of corner points. This type of representation does not allow for holes in patches, i.e., the patches must be *simply-connected*. If the gridding program has knowledge of the underlying numerical analysis program, it would realize that once it removes the fictional surface area from the hull, it must break the hull in half to "cut" out the hole. This cut can be performed in limitless ways, but how it is done affects how easily the reparametrization and distribution steps can be performed to satisfy the evaluation criteria.

In the following sections we present a geometric language, Boundary Surface Representation (BSR), which is capable of representing geometrical information, topological information as well as associating attributes of the physical domain to the geometry. Also, we present a principled method of solving the partitioning, reparametrization, and distribution problems based on reasoning about physics of the flow domain. We call this method streamline-based gridding.

Boundary Surface Representation(BSR)

Surfaces are basically two dimensional objects that reside in three dimensional space. So they are naturally represented parametrically as a mapping from parametric space, $(u, v) = ([0, \ldots, 1], [0, \ldots, 1])$, to 3D Cartesian space, (x, y, z). Our gridding system pro-

vides a mapping facility to represent this *shape* mapping, see Figure 2. No assumption is made about what mathematical form the mappings may take. Each mapping is treated as a "black box". The advantage of using a black box representation is that it provides greater flexibility by hiding the implementation details from the gridder. In our example, the hull is defined using algebraic formulae, and the keel and winglet are defined using B-spline surfaces.

This mapping facility is not limited to defining shapes. Other geometric and physical values may also be defined. For example, the outward normals of a surface may be defined as a *normal* mapping from the parametric space, (u, v), to 3D vector space. Then in turn based on the *shape* and *normal* mappings, our gridding program can approximate the stream vectors on the surfaces as a *flow* mapping by projecting the *free stream vector*, $(1, 0, 0)$, onto the surface. The free stream vector is the direction the water would flow if the yacht were not present.

Notice the boundaries of each surface are represented explicitly by directed edges, *arcs*. The arcs in turn are bounded by nodes. Explicit representation of the boundary is useful in that it allows for implicit representation of surfaces. That is, a closed sequence of arcs in parametric space can be used to denote the portion of the surface it encloses. The program adopts the *counter-clockwise rule*. A counter-clockwise, closed sequence of arcs denotes the area bound by the arcs. A clockwise, closed sequence of arcs denotes the area outside of the arcs. This implies the area on the "left-hand side" of an arc is "inside," and area on the "right-hand side" is "outside."

Arcs are also useful in expressing topological information. In our notation two arcs are connected by a dotted line if they are the same line when mapped using *shape* into xyz-space, even though they are distinct in parametric space. For example, in Figure 2 the keel parametric arcs h ($u_{keel} = 0$) and f ($u_{keel} = 1$) are connected by a dotted line, because both of these arcs map to the trailing edge of the keel. Thus in xyz-space it is possible to travel just in the direction of increasing

u_{keel} and end up at your starting point. This dotted line together with the dotted line connecting arcs d ($u_{keel} = [0, \ldots, 0.5]$) and e ($u_{keel} = [0.5, \ldots, 1]$) implies the topology of the keel is similar to that of a cylinder with one end closed or a "cup."

Notice that the hull parametric arcs b ($u_{hull} = 1$) and d ($u_{hull} = 0$) are connected to themselves. This is used to show that arcs b and d are degenerate, i.e., they each map to one point in xyz-space. The arc d maps into the trailing point of the hull; the arc b maps into the leading point of the hull.

Also, notice each of the arcs on the winglet is connected to some other arc. This means that in xyz-space the winglet surface does not have any boundaries. Of the three components the winglet is the only one that actually encloses some finite volume in xyz-space.

BSR provides a set of surface patch manipulation operations, such as intersection of surfaces, and division of patches into sub-patches. Figure 4 depicts the patches after the partitioning step. Reparametrization and distribution operations also are supported, see Figure 5. Now, we can formally define reparametrization as a mapping from a unit square, defined in a new parametric space, say (s, t), to a surface patch in (u, v) parametric space.

Streamline-based reasoning

The solution to Laplace's equation depends neither on the current state of the flow nor on time, so the geometry of the object determines the solution. Since streamlines are key characteristics of the solution, analyzing how streamlines interact with geometry provides key insights to qualitative behaviors of Laplace's equation. These insights enable us to determine the topology of streamlines. In turn this topology provides natural boundaries for patches in grids.

The most immediate reasoning problem we encounter in streamline-based reasoning is how to get the initial set of streamlines, since we have not yet run PMARC to generate the solution from which streamlines are extracted. We have experimented with various methods of predicting the streamlines *a priori*. However, we have found the simple projection of the *free stream* vector onto the body surface to be a good approximation of the true streamlines. This the *flow* mapping defined earlier.

Object classification

Analyzing the pattern of streamlines on the surface of different objects, we define two object classes. This first is the *source/sink node* class. Streamlines on objects from this class all originate from one point on the surface, the source node, and all flow to and terminate at another point on the surface, the sink node. Spheres, ellipsoids and other simple bodies of revolution are objects of this class. These objects have axial-symmetry, so there can only be one source node and one sink node.

The second is the *source/sink line* class. This class is like the previous class, except that the streamlines appear to originate and terminate at lines instead of nodes. For instance, the leading edge of a keel is *source line*, and the trailing edge is *Sink line*. All the streamlines flow from the leading edge to the trailing edge. Any wing shaped object belongs to this class.

Using only these two object classes, one can already construct complex, geometric objects, such as the yacht in this paper. The yacht consists of a source/sink node object (hull), and two source/sink line objects (keel and winglet). New classes can always be defined as the need arises.

Application to gridding

Based on the *following-streamline* heuristic for gridding, it is reasonable to grid a source/sink node object as a single surface patch, since all the streamlines are flowing in one direction, from the source node to the sink node. A source/sink line object should be gridded as two surface patches with the source line and sink line acting as partitioning lines. Although the streamlines still flow from the source line to the sink line, the streamlines take two different routes. For example, one set of streamlines flows to the sink from the right side of the keel ($u > 0.5$), and the other set flows from the left side ($u < 0.5$). The source/sink lines separate these two flow regions.

Streamlines are also useful in reparametrization. Streamlines can be defined as one family of grid lines. Lines orthogonal to the the streamlines can be defined as the other family. For example, on a sphere these two families correspond to the two spherical coordinate directions, θ and ϕ, where $x = \cos\theta, y = \sin\phi\cos\theta, z = \sin\phi\sin\theta$. Streamlines have constant θ and the orthogonal lines have constant ϕ.

The sources and sinks provide guidelines on how to distribute the grid lines. The key to distributing grid lines is to highlight the physical features of the domain. That is, put more grid lines in regions where interesting physical changes occur. In the flow domain, the most interesting change is the change in direction and velocity of the flow. This change typically occurs most dramatically around the sources and sinks. So, the grid lines should be distributed more densely around them.

The above discussion deals with idealized objects. In the yacht example, there is a keel attached to the hull, and a winglet attached to the keel. The following sections show how to deal with the topological changes in these idealized objects by going through the three gridding steps in more detail.

Partitioning

We break the partitioning step into three sub-steps: 1) Determine the surface partitioning lines, 2) Partition surfaces into surface patches, and 3) Determine real surfaces patches.

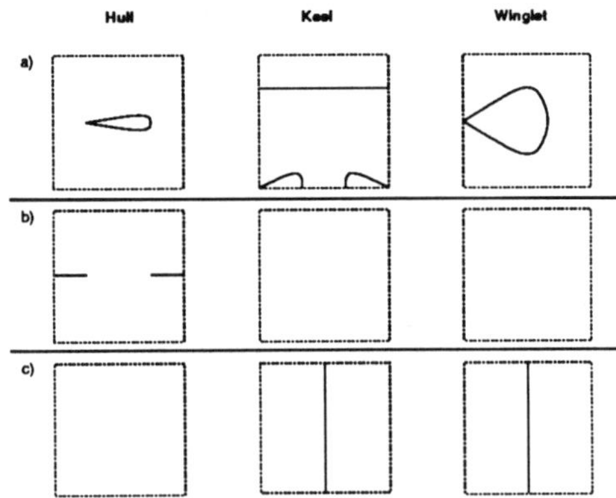

Figure 3: Partition lines: a) intersection lines, b) streamlines to "cut" holes out, and c) source/sink lines.

partitioning lines

The partitioning lines that we use can be divided into three categories: surface intersection lines, streamlines, and source/sink lines. Intersection lines provide the boundary between real and fictional surface areas, so they must be present. See Figure 3a for examples.

Notice that the hull-keel intersection line introduces a hole on the hull surface. This hole needs to be cut out, because of the *simply-connected* constraint. Using streamline-based reasoning, the logical way to "cut" out the hole is by cutting along streamlines. We search for a leading point and a trailing point along the intersection. From the leading point we trace a streamline *backward* along the hull surface. From the trailing point we trace a streamline *forward* along the hull surface. These two streamlines are shown in Figure 3b.

Source and sink lines are definitely needed, but all the sink lines turn out to be redundant. The source lines are shown in Figure 3c. Notice that source/sink nodes in *xyz*-space may become source/sink lines in *uv* parametric space, as in the hull.

partition the surface patches

We shall not go into detail on how BSR accomplishes the actual partitioning. Basically BSR 1) gathers all the partition lines of a particular surface, 2) intersects the partition lines with each other and with the boundary lines of the surface, 3) breaks all the lines at intersections, 4) forms a wire frame from the broken lines, and 5) forms the surface patches based on the wire frame. The surface patches after partitioning are shown in Figure 4. BSR updates the topological information after the partitioning process. The shaded surface patches are fictional and will not be gridded.

determine the real surface patches

Real and fictional surface patches can be distinguished by reasoning using the outward *normal* mappings, the *counter-clockwise* rule, and intersection lines. For example, the surface patch *Keel*1, Figure 5, has intersection lines in common with the hull surface (arc 6)

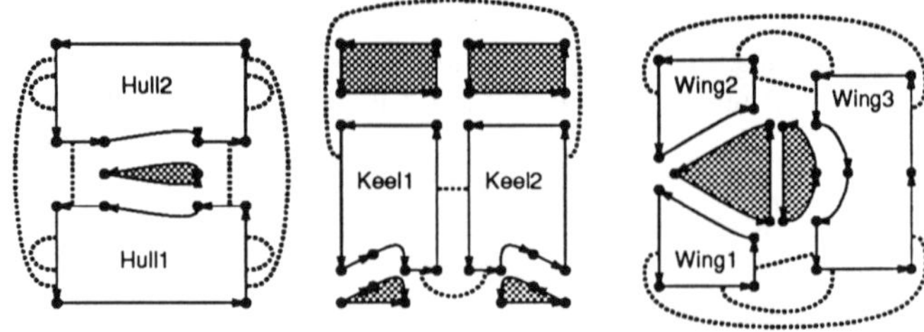

Figure 4: Surface patches after partitioning. Dotted lines across *uv*-space are not drawn to reduce clutter. Omitted dotted lines would show Keel1 connected to Hull1, Wing1 and Wing3, and would show Keel2 connected to Hull2, Wing2 and Wing3.

and the winglet surface (arcs 2 and 3). The hull outward *normals* along the hull-keel intersection generally point in the negative z-direction. The inward direction of arc 6 as defined by the counter-clockwise rule is in the negative V_{keel} direction, which corresponds to the negative z-direction in *xyz*-space. This implies that *Keel*1 is outside of the hull. Similar reasoning using arcs 2 and 3 shows *Keel*1 is outside of the winglet. Since *Keel*1 is on the outside of all its neighbor surfaces, *Keel*1 is a real surface patch. If a surface patch is on the inside of one or more of its neighbors, then it is a fictional patch.

Reparametrization

Our gridding program uses two reparametrization methods, but here we only discuss *transfinite interpolation*. Given a quadrilateral, transfinite interpolation is a well known mathematical technique that maps a unit square on to a quadrilateral by interpolating against opposite edges of that quadrilateral. This method requires the surface patch to be reparametrized to have exactly four sides. But, surface patches tend to have more than four boundary edges. In order to use transfinite interpolation, we describe a heuristic, streamlined-based method of grouping the boundary arcs of the surface patches into four groups. See Figure 5.

We can classify each arc as either parallel or orthogonal with respect to the streamlines. For example, the patch *Keel*1 is bounded by six arcs. Arc 1 is a sink line. Arc 5 is a source line. So, by definition they are orthogonal to the streamlines. Arc 4 is a boundary arc from the original input surface. Arcs 2, 3 and 6 are intersection lines. These four arcs are neither completely parallel nor completely orthogonal to the streamlines. But, by sampling different segments of these arcs we can approximately classify arcs 2, 4 and 6 as parallel, and arc 3 as orthogonal. So, six groups are formed, $\{(1), (2), (3), (4), (5), (6)\}$. But, unlike the graphical depiction in Figure 5, arc 3 is very short when compared to its neighbors, arc 2 and 4. So, heuristically merging arc 3 with its neighbors, we get four groups, $\{(1), (2, 3, 4), (5), (6)\}$.

Our grouping method works well, because the

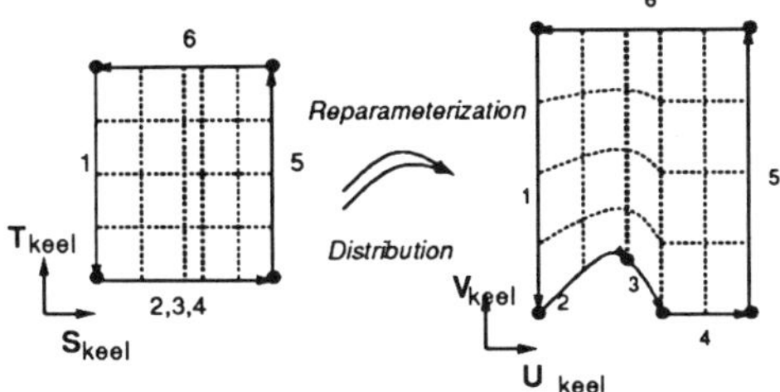

Figure 5: Reparametrization and Distribution

boundary arcs of the surfaces patches tend to be partitioning lines: intersection lines, streamlines, and source/sink lines. Classification of streamlines and source/sink lines are straightforward. In practice intersection lines tend always to be parallel, because an orthogonal intersection line causes too much drag, and would not be used in properly designed yachts.

This heuristic method may fail to group the boundary arcs into four groups. Failure indicates that the geometry of the surface patch is too complicated, and additional partitioning lines may be needed. So far we have not encountered such a case.

Distribution

According to streamline-based reasoning, grid lines should be concentrated more densely around sources and sinks. Sources and sinks tend to be at the ends of the surface patches (in Figure 5 arc 1 and arc 5) in our streamline-based gridding method. So, complicated distribution schemes usually are not needed. We have experimented with *cosine* and *hyperbolic tangent* schemes, which distribute more grid lines at the ends and yet distribute them smoothly enough as not to violate the *expansion ratio* constraint. Both schemes work well, but if many grid lines are laid out, *cosine* tends to place grid lines too densely at the ends. This leads to numerical truncation error.

Beside resolving physical features, distribution must also resolve geometric features. For example, one $S_{keel} = constant$ grid line must be laid out at the intersection of arc 2 and arc 3, and another one grid line at the intersection of arc 3 and arc 4. Grid lines that must be laid out are shown as heavy, dotted lines in Figure 5. The node at the intersection of arc 3 and arc 4 touches three surface patches, $Keel1$, $Keel2$, and $Wing3$. Not laying a grid line at that node would create a gap there so the three patches would not meet.

Computational Results

Our gridding algorithms have been implemented in a working program. Figure 6 shows the results of a convergence study in which our gridding program generated a series of grids for PMARC. A convergence study is a series of simulations using grids with the same partitioning and reparametrization, but with increasingly denser grid lines. As the grid becomes denser and

grid spacing decreases, output quantities computed by PMARC should converge to their correct values. The output quantity we are most interested in is effective draft, a measure of the efficiency of a sailing yacht's keel. Figure 7 shows how effective draft converges as grid spacing is reduced in our convergence study.

Other values in Figure 6 can also be used as checks on the soundness of the simulation. For example, the maximum C_p (pressure coefficient) should approach 1 as the grid is refined, and the minimum C_p should not become too negative, as very large negative values usually indicate flaws in the grid. (Gelsey 1992) discusses automated evaluation of simulation output quality.

Panels	Lift	Drag	Draft	min C_p	max C_p
100	2.014	0.198	1.805	-1.655	0.527
362	2.081	0.242	1.688	-1.126	0.640
1378	2.202	0.283	1.651	-1.798	0.831
5460	2.230	0.308	1.604	-2.632	0.918

Figure 6: Convergence study

Effective Draft

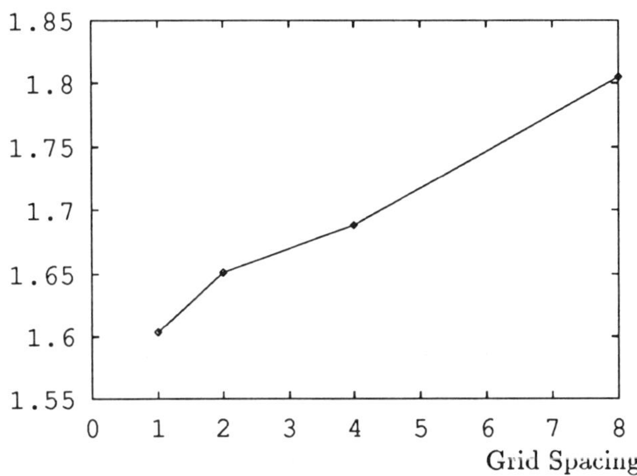

Figure 7: Convergence as spacing is reduced

Future Work

This work can be extended in various directions. One is to add feedback and local refinement capabilities to the gridder. The streamlines predicted by PMARC may be fed back into the gridder to improve the grid. Also, the gridder can be extended to detect and correct local flaws in the grid based on intermediate values, such as the coefficient of pressure. Another direction is to extend the gridder to other physical domains where PDE simulators are needed. We believe our methodology of identifying key physical features of the domain and of reasoning about how they interact with the geometry is quite general and extensible. For example, in the ingot casting problem of heat transfer the temperature profile seems to be the key feature (ky Ringo Ling, Steinberg, & Jaluria 1993). Temperature profiles tend to change the fastest near sharp corners and in appendages (regions where the surface area to volume ratio is large). This suggests that isotherms should be useful as grid lines, and they should be distributed more densely near corners and appendages.

Related Work

Using streamlines is a natural idea. (Chung, Kuwahara, & Richmond 1993) defines a 2D finite-difference method based on streamline-coordinates, instead of Cartesian coordinates. (Chao & Liu 1991) applies streamline-based gridding to 2D flow problems consisting of a single patch. Many geometric modeling systems have been developed, such as Alpha1 by (Riesenfeld 1981) and SHAPES by (Sinha 1992). (Requicha 1980) provides a good survey. Most of these systems are intended for modeling mechanical components, and provide little support for gridding, like representation of parametric space objects for reparametrization and distribution, and algorithms to manipulate these objects. Previous AI work in gridding includes (Dannenhoffer 1992), and (Santhanam *et al.* 1992). In the 2D planar flow domain, Dannenhoffer's program is able to do partitioning by merging *templates* of previously-solved cases. So, the set of shapes it can handle is limited. Santhanam identifies several key parameters to modify and improve grids in 1D Euler domain. (Gelsey 1994) describes automated setup of numerical simulations involving *ordinary* differential equations.

Conclusion

Numerical simulation of partial differential equations is a powerful tool for engineering design. However, human expertise and spatial reasoning abilities are needed in order to form the spatial grids which PDE solvers require as input. We have developed a geometric modeling language, BSR, capable of expressing geometrical, topological, and physical aspects of the gridding problem, and we have used BSR as a basis for an intelligent automated system for generating the grids required for numerical simulation. The grid generation process involves analyzing the topology of the spatial domain, predicting and classifying the interactions of physics and geometry, and reasoning about the peculiarities of the numerical simulator.

Acknowledgments

The research was done in consultation with Rutgers Computer Science Dept. faculty member Gerard Richter. We worked with hydrodynamicists Martin Fritts and Nils Salvesen of Science Applications International Corp., and John Letcher of Aero-Hydro Inc. Our research benefited significantly from interaction with the members of the Rutgers AI/Design group. Thanks to Ringo Ling, Steven Norton, and Mark Schwabacher for proofreading and commenting on the paper. This research was partially supported by NSF grant CCR-9209793, ARPA/NASA grant NAG2-645, and ARPA contract ARPA-DAST 63-93-C-0064.

References

Chao, Y. C., and Liu, S. S. 1991. Streamline adaptive grid method for complex flow computation. *Numerical Heat Transfer, Part B* 20:145–168.

Chung, S. G.; Kuwahara, K.; and Richmond, O. 1993. Streamline-coordinate finite-difference method for hot metal deformations. *Journal of Computational Physics* 108:1–7.

Dannenhoffer, J. F. 1992. Automatic block-structured grid generation — progress and challenge. In Kant, E.; Keller, R.; and Steinberg, S., eds., *AAAI Fall Symposium Series: Intelligent Scientific Computation*, 28–32.

Gelsey, A. 1992. Modeling and simulation for automated yacht design. In *AAAI Fall Symposium on Design from Physical Principles*, 44–49.

Gelsey, A. 1994. Automated reasoning about machines. *Artificial Intelligence.* to appear.

Kao, T. J., and Su, T. Y. 1992. An interactive multi-block grid generation system. In Smith, R. E., ed., *Software Systems for Surface Modeling and Grid Generation*, number 3143 in NASA Conference Publication, 333–345.

Ling, S. R.; Steinberg, L.; and Jaluria, Y. 1993. MSG: A computer system for auotmated modeling of heat transfer. *AI EDAM* 7(4):287–300.

Remotique, M. G.; Hart, E. T.; and Stokes, M. L. 1992. EAGLEView: A surface and grid generation program and its data management. In Smith, R. E., ed., *Software Systems for Surface Modeling and Grid Generation*, number 3143 in NASA Conference Publication, 243–251.

Requicha, A. A. G. 1980. Representations for rigid solids: Theory, methods, and systems. *Computing Surveys* 12(4):437–464.

Riesenfeld, R. F. 1981. Using the oslo algorithm as a basis for CAD/CAM geometric modeling. In *Proc. NCGA National Conf.*, 345–356.

Santhanam, T.; Browne, J.; Kallinderis, J.; and Miranker, D. 1992. A knowledge based approach to mesh optimization in CFD domain: 1D Euler code example. In Kant, E.; Keller, R.; and Steinberg, S., eds., *AAAI Fall Symposium Series: Intelligent Scientific Computation*, 115–118.

Schuster, D. M. 1992. Batch mode grid generation: An endangered species? In Smith, R. E., ed., *Software Systems for Surface Modeling and Grid Generation*, number 3143 in NASA Conference Publication, 487–500.

Sinha, P. 1992. Mixed dimensional objects in geometric modeling. In *New Technologies in CAD/CAM*.

Thompson, J. F.; Warsi, Z. U. A.; and Mastin, C. W. 1985. *Numerical grid generation : foundations and applications.* North-Holland, Amsterdam.

Robotics

Structured Circuit Semantics
for Reactive Plan Execution Systems

Jaeho Lee and **Edmund H. Durfee***
Department of EE and CS
University of Michigan
Ann Arbor, MI 48109
{jaeho,durfee}@eecs.umich.edu

Abstract

A variety of reactive plan execution systems have been developed in recent years, each attempting to solve the problem of taking reasonable courses of action fast enough in a dynamically changing world. Comparing these competing approaches, and collecting the best features of each, has been problematic because of the diverse representations and (sometimes implicit) control structures that they have employed. To rectify this problem, we have extended the circuit semantics notion of teleo-reactive programs into richer, yet compact semantics, called structured circuit semantics (SCS), that can be used to explicitly represent the control behavior of various reactive execution systems. By transforming existing systems into SCS, we can identify underlying control assumptions and begin to identify more rigorously the strengths and limitations of these systems. Moreover, SCS provides a basis for constructing new reactive execution systems, with more understandable semantics, that can be tailored to particular domain needs.

Introduction

The realization that agents in dynamic, unpredictable environments should consider the evolving state of the environment when making decisions about actions to take to pursue their goals, has led to a plethora of systems for reactive plan execution, including PRS (Ingrand, Georgeff, & Rao 1992), Universal Plans (Schoppers 1987), Teleo-Reactive Programs (Nilsson 1992; 1994), and RAPs (Firby 1989; 1992), among others. The challenge faced by a researcher who needs to incorporate a reactive plan execution system into a larger endeavor is determining how to decide among these candidate systems. For example, in a project to develop a system for controlling and coordinating outdoor robotic vehicles (Lee *et al.* 1994), which reactive plan execution system is right for the job?

A primary difficulty in answering this question is that many of the fundamental capabilities of and assumptions behind reactive plan execution systems are

---

*This work was sponsored, in part, by ARPA under contract DAAE-07-92-C-R012.

not easily discernible, being tied up in descriptions of procedures and interpreters, which are in turn expressed in system-specific ways. One goal of the work we describe here, therefore, is to develop a means for formally specifying reactive plan execution systems so as to cast a variety of these systems into a single framework, thereby allowing us to more readily identify and compare the capabilities and assumptions of each. With such tools in hand, moreover, we are working toward devising an interpreter for our formalism that will allow us to easily implement appropriate reactive plan execution systems with precisely the characteristics needed by a particular domain.

Our new formalism, called *Structured Circuit Semantics* (SCS), extends the Circuit Semantics of Teleo-Reactive Programs to be powerful enough to encompass the representation capability of many reactive planning systems. In this paper, we briefly review circuit semantics as a starting point for our extensions, and point out some limitations of circuit semantics that make it inappropriate for a task like that of controlling outdoor robotic vehicles. We then present our SCS formalism to overcome these limitations, and demonstrate the power of SCS through a simple assembly problem that demands reactive and robust plan execution. Finally, we analyze SCS as a general reactive plan specification language by comparing SCS with other reactive plan execution systems. We conclude this paper with discussions on implementation issues and extensions to applications involving multiple agents.

Circuit Semantics

When executing on a computational system, a program is said to have *circuit semantics* when it produces (at least conceptually) electrical circuits that are in turn used for control (Nilsson 1992). In particular, a teleo-reactive (T-R) sequence is an agent control program based on circuit semantics, combining notions of continuous feedback with more conventional computational mechanisms such as runtime parameter binding and passing, and hierarchical and recursive invocation structures. In contrast with some of the behavior-based approaches, T-R programs are re-

"

sponsive to stored models of the environment as well as to their immediate sensory inputs (Nilsson 1994). In its simplest form, a T-R program consists of an ordered set of production rules (from (Nilsson 1994)):

$$K_1 \rightarrow a_1; \ K_2 \rightarrow a_2; \ \cdots; \ K_i \rightarrow a_i; \ \cdots; \ K_m \rightarrow a_m;$$

The K_i are conditions, and the a_i are actions. The interpreter scans the T-R sequence from the top until it finds a satisfied condition, and then executes the corresponding action. However, executing an action in this case might involve a prolonged activity instead of a discrete action. While the condition is the first true one, the action continues to be taken, so the T-R program can be continuously acting and evaluating whether to continue its current action (if it still corresponds to the first true condition) or to shift to another action (if the current action's condition is no longer satisfied or a condition earlier in the program becomes satisfied).

The actions, a_i, of a T-R sequence can be T-R sequences themselves, allowing hierarchical and recursive nesting of programs, eventually leading to actions that are primitives. In an executing hierarchical construction of T-R programs, note that a change of action at any level can occur should the conditions change. That is, all T-R programs in a hierarchy are running concurrently, in keeping with circuit semantics, rather than suspending while awaiting subprograms to complete.

Limitations of the T-R programs

While T-R programs capture circuit semantics for reactive control in a very compact way, their compactness comes at the cost of representativeness for other domains. For example, in the outdoor robotic vehicle domain, suitable reactive execution appears to require a language with a richer circuit semantics than is embodied in T-R programs (or in many other reactive execution systems, for that matter).

Execution Cycle

In an ideal reactive system with circuit semantics, the conditions are *continuously* being evaluated and, when appropriate, their associated actions are *continuously* being executed. Real electrical circuits, however have a natural, characteristic frequency that leads to cycles of execution, and these same cycles occur in reactive execution systems, corresponding to the perception-cognition-action cycle. Traditionally, reactive systems have concentrated on increasing this frequency by, for example, reducing the time needs of cognition, but this cycle cannot be completely eliminated.

Circuit semantics represents two different kinds of actions— *energized* and *ballistic*. Energized actions are those that must be sustained by an enabling condition to continue operating; ballistic ones, once called, run to completion (Nilsson 1992). We argue that the energized actions can be implemented using ballistic actions by making the perception-cognition-action frequency higher than or equal to the characteristic frequency of the agent's environment. In fact, if the agent

is to be implemented using conventional computer systems, the energized actions *must* be mapped down to the ballistic actions anyway. Our definition of atomic actions to be described later is based on this argument.

Clearly defining an execution cycle, therefore, goes hand-in-hand with defining atomic actions. Without a characteristic execution cycle, a continuously running system could take control from any of its actions, even if those actions are incomplete. For example, consider a T-R program whose conditions are to be evaluated both against sensory input and on stored internal state information. While executing an action that is supposed to make several changes to the internal state, an earlier condition in the T-R program is satisfied, and the original action is abandoned, possibly rendering the internal state inconsistent. In pathological cases, the system could become caught in an oscillation between zero (when "wedged") or more actions. Of course, such interruptions could be avoided by augmenting the conditions such that they will not change truth value at awkward times, but this implicitly institutes an execution cycle and atomicity, which should be more efficiently and explicitly represented.

Non-Deterministic Behavior

In a T-R program, the condition-action pairs are ordered strictly and statically. However, generating a total ordering on the actions at design time might be difficult and can lead to overly rigid runtime performance. For example, actions that appear equally good at design time will have an order imposed on them nonetheless, possibly forcing the system into repeatedly taking one action that is currently ineffective because it happens to appear earlier than a peer action. Instead, the system should be able to leave collections of actions unordered and try them non-deterministically.

The **do any** construct in our formalism to be described in the following section can specify multiple equally good actions for the situation. One of the actions is chosen nondeterministically at run time and executed. If the chosen action fails, another action within the construct is again nondeterministically selected and tried until one of them succeeds. We can imagine a circuit component with one input and n outputs, which energizes one of its outputs whenever the component is energized. Note that, with work, this nondeterminism can be forced into T-R programs by, for example, having the condition of each equally good action include a match against some randomly assigned state variable that is randomly reassigned upon each action failure. However, once again, such machinations serve to implicitly implement a capability that should be explicit.

Best-First Behavior

One of the reasons for demanding reactivity is to be sensitive to the way utilities of actions vary with specific situations and to choose the applicable action that is best *relative* to the others. Since which action is best relative to the others depends on the runtime situation, the selection cannot be captured in the static ordering of actions. Let's consider a simple three line example T-R program:

available(airplane) → fly;
available(car)   → drive;
True   → walk;

Suppose that the airplane is not available initially. The agent thus chooses to rent a car and drive. After driving 10 hours, the agent needs to drive only 30 more minutes to get to the destination; however, it discovers that it is passing an airport which has a plane available. According to the above T-R program, the agent switches to the flying action, even though it could be that, between dropping off the rental car, boarding the plan, taxiing, and so on, flying from here will take much longer than just completing the drive.

If the agent is to accomplish its goal in a timely way, the T-R program above needs additional conditions for taking the airplane to avoid this inappropriate transition. The question is *where* to put *what* conditions. For this three line program, it is not terribly hard to devise additional conditions. If we assume, for simplicity, that the function tt (travel-time) returns the time needed to get to the destination from the current situation, the T-R program becomes:

available(airplane) ∧ tt(airplane) < tt(car)
                    ∧ tt(airplane) < tt(foot) → fly;
available(car) ∧ tt(car) < tt(foot)   → drive;
True   → walk;

But what if there are ten different ways to get to the destination? The lefthand side conditions of the T-R program might have to mention all the ways of traveling. Moreover, if a new way to travel were discovered, it could not be introduced into this T-R program without possibly affecting the conditions for other actions.

A more general answer is to introduce a *decision layer* above the *circuit layer*. The decision layer dynamically makes utility-based (cost based in dual) selections among candidate actions, conceptually energizing the "best" circuit. In SCS, the **do best** serves this purpose. Each action in the **do best** construct has an associated utility function as well as an energizing condition. Each action with a satisfied condition competes (or bids) by submitting its (expected) utility, and the highest bidder is selected.[1] This scheme is very similar to blackboard control mechanisms where each knowledge source proposes its utility, but differs from many blackboard systems in that the conditions and utilities for the actions are checked every cycle, as dictated by the circuit semantics. Using the **do best** construct,

---

[1]Tie-breaking is done similarly to the nondeterministic selection of actions. In fact, the **do any** construct is just a special case of the **do best** where the utility calculations always return identical values.

the above example will be represented as follows where ttu is a utility function of the travel time.

do best { available(airplane) [ttu(airplane)] → fly;
              available(car)   [ttu(car)]   → drive;
              True   [ttu(foot)]   → walk; }

Note that, in keeping with circuit semantics, we can map the decision layer into real circuitry as well, being realized as a circuit that controls other circuits which evaluate themselves dynamically. By having some number of decision layers (about decision layers), we can get the meta-levels of other reactive systems such as PRS.

Failure Semantics

The success of an action can be measured in terms of whether it had the desired effect at the desired time on the environment. As was argued previously, because of the characteristic frequency of the system, even sustained actions (such as keeping a vehicle centered on the road) can be viewed as sequences of atomic actions (such as repeatedly checking position and correcting heading). Thus, since an atomic action might have a desired effect on the environment, determining whether that effect was achieved is important in controlling the execution of further actions. Effects can be checked for in the energizing conditions associated with an action, such that failure naturally leads to the adoption of a different action. However, because there might be a variety of subtle effects on the environment that an action would cause that would indicate failure, and because embedding these in the energizing condition could be inefficient and messy (non-modular), it is useful to allow actions to return information about success and failure.

In T-R programs, if an action fails without changing any of the program's energizing conditions, the same action will be kept energized until the action eventually succeeds. If actions can return failure information, constructs can respond to this information, allowing a broader range of reactive (exception handling) behavior. In SCS, several different constructs encode different responses to action failures to provide a variety of reactive execution behaviors.

Structured Circuit Semantics

The basic unit in the structured circuit semantics is an *action*, a_i. Every action is atomic; it is guaranteed to terminate within a bounded time and cannot be interrupted. As argued previously, sustained actions are typically repetitions of an atomic action.

Once all actions are defined, we can limit the (upper and lower) bound for the *perception-cognition-action* cycle. Atomic actions can also be grouped to form other atomic actions, as in $(a_1; \cdots; a_n)$. In this case, all actions in the group are executed in sequence without being interrupted. Execution of an action usually changes the environment and/or internal state (including the world model) and returns either *success* or *failure*. The semantics of success and failure are important in some constructs such as **do any**, **do best**, and **do all**.

For generality, we can loosely define a *condition* as a function which returns true of false, and when true can generate bindings for variables expressed in the condition.[2] We can then define various control constructs and their semantics. Some concepts are borrowed from the semantics of the Procedural Reasoning System (PRS) and a PRS implementation (UM-PRS (Lee *et al.* 1994)). Because of space limitations, we cannot describe the PRS architecture in detail here, but interested readers can refer to (Ingrand, Georgeff, & Rao 1992). The purpose of most of the constructs is to wrap the actions and attach energizing conditions to collections of actions, corresponding to the conditions (K_i) in T-R programs. As in the T-R programs' circuit semantics, the conditions are *durative* and should be satisfied during the execution of the wrapped actions. The difference is that the conditions are checked only between atomic actions rather than continuously, providing us with clear semantics for the execution and feedback cycles, and avoiding the potential oscillation problems mentioned previously.

The constructs can be nested, and the attached conditions are dynamically stacked for checking. Whenever an atomic action is finished, the stack of conditions is checked from top to bottom (top conditions are the outmost conditions in the nested constructs). If any condition is no longer satisfied, new choices of action at that level and those below are made.

A *step* is defined recursively as follows. In the construct descriptions below, $K_i, a_i, S_i, U_i, 1 \leq i \leq n$ are conditions, actions, steps, and utility functions, respectively.

⋄ a_i is an step composed of a single atomic action. An action returns either success or failure and so does the step.

⋄ $(a_1; \cdots; a_n)$ is an atomic step composed of atomic actions. The step fails if any of the actions fails.

⋄ **do** $\{S_1; S_2; \cdots; S_n\}$ is a step that specifies a group of steps that are to be executed sequentially in the given order. The overall **do** step fails only as soon as the one of the substeps fails. Otherwise it succeeds. **do*** $\{\cdots\}$ has the same semantics as those of **do** except that, whenever a substep fails, it retries that substep until it succeeds. Thus **do*** itself never fails. This construct allows us to specify *persistent* behavior, and is particularly useful within the **do all** and **do any** constructs explained below.

⋄ **do all** $\{S_1; S_2; \cdots; S_n\}$ is a step which tries to execute all steps in parallel (at least conceptually). If the agent can do only one step at a time, it nondeterministically chooses among those as yet unachieved. If any one of the steps fails, the whole **do all** fails immediately. This is similar to the semantics of the AND branch of the Knowledge Area in PRS. **do*** **all** is a variation of **do all** which tries failed substeps persistently, yet nondeterministically until all of them have succeeded.

⋄ **do any** $\{S_1; S_2; \cdots; S_n\}$ is a step which selects nondeterministically one S_i and executes it. If that step fails, it keeps trying other actions until any of them succeeds. If every step is attempted and all fail, the **do any** step fails. This construct corresponds to the OR branch of the Knowledge Area in PRS. **do*** **any** is a variation of **do any** which keeps trying any action including the already failed steps until any of them succeeds.

⋄ **do first** $\{K_1 \rightarrow S_1; \cdots; K_n \rightarrow S_n\}$ is a step which behaves almost the same as a T-R program. That is, the list of condition–step pairs is scanned from the top for the first pair whose condition part is satisfied, say K_i, and the corresponding step S_i is executed. The energizing condition K_i is continuously checked (at the characteristic frequency) as in T-R programs. The difference is that, if a step fails, the whole **do first** fails. To persistently try a step with satisfied conditions even if it fails (as in T-R programs), the **do*** **first** construct can be used.

⋄ **do best** $\{K_1 [U_1] \rightarrow S_1; \cdots; K_n [U_n] \rightarrow S_n\}$ is a step which evaluates U_i for each TrueK_i ($1 \leq i \leq n$), and selects a step S_i which has the highest utility. If several steps have the highest utility, one of these is selected by the **do any** rules. The failure semantics is the same as that of the **do any** construct. The **do*** **best** step is similarly defined.

⋄ **repeat** $\{S_1; S_2; \cdots; S_n\}$ works the same way as **do** does, but the steps are repeatedly executed. The **repeat*** step is also similarly defined.

The **do, do all, do any, do first, do best, repeat**, and their ***-ed constructs may have following optional modifiers

⋄ **while** K_0 : specifies the energizing condition K_0 to be continuously checked between each atomic action. The associated step is kept activated only while K_0 is true. For example, **do while** K_0 $\{\cdots\}$ does the **do** step as long as K_0 is true. Note that K_0 is an energizing condition of the associated step. Thus, if the energizing condition is not satisfied, the step does *not* fail, but just becomes deactivated. **until** K_0 is shorthand for **while** $\neg K_0$.

⋄ **when** K_0 : specifies that the condition K_0 must be true before the associated step is started. That is, K_0 is only checked before execution, but not checked again during execution. For example, **do*** **all when** K_0 **while** K_1 $\{\cdots\}$ is a step which can be activated *when* K_0 is true, and *all* substeps of which will be *persistently* tried *while* K_1 is true. **unless** K_0 is shorthand for **when** $\neg K_0$.

---

[2]More specifically, for our implementation we assume a pattern matching operation between condition patterns and specific relational information in the world model. The details of this are beyond the scope of this paper.

free(1) $\land$ free(2) $\land$ available(B) $\rightarrow$ Lplace(B,2);
free(3) $\land$ free(2) $\land$ available(B) $\rightarrow$ Rplace(B,2);

free(1) $\land$ free(3) $\land$ available(A) $\rightarrow$ place(A,1);
free(3) $\land$ free(1) $\land$ available(C) $\rightarrow$ place(C,3);

free(1) $\land$ $\neg$free(2) $\land$ available(A) $\rightarrow$ place(A,1);
free(3) $\land$ $\neg$free(2) $\land$ available(C) $\rightarrow$ place(C,3).

Figure 1: T-R Program

We have described SCS as a general semantics for re-active plan execution systems. As a matter of fact, the semantics can be directly transformed into SCS Language (SCSL) which is interpreted and executed by an interpreter. We are currently implementing the *SCS Reactive Plan Execution System* in C++. The system consists of the SCSL interpreter and the world model. The SCSL has numerous other built-in actions including arithmetic operations, world model match and update, etc. In the SCSL, a step can be defined using the construct **define** with a list of arguments (local variables) that are bound when the step is called: **define** step-name(x_1, x_2, $\cdots$, x_m) step. The defined step can be called, and expanded accordingly at run time.

Example: BNL Problem

To briefly illustrate how SCS can help clarify the implicit control semantics of a plan execution language, we here consider a simpler example than what we have encountered in the robotic vehicle domain, but which still exemplifies concerns in reactive and robust plan execution. In the BNL (B Not Last) problem (Drummond 1989), we are given a table on which to assemble three blocks in a row: block A on the left, at location 1; block B in the middle, at location 2; and block C on the right, at location 3. The blocks are not initially available for placement, and each block can be placed on the table once available (the exact means for moving blocks is immaterial). The only constraint on assembly is that *block* B *cannot be placed last:* once A and C are down, there is not enough room to squeeze in B since it must be swept in from the left or the right. We assume that a block, once placed, cannot be moved away again.

As in (Drummond 1989), we assume three predicates: free, at, and available; and four actions: place(A,1) (place block A at location 1), place(C,3) (place block C at location 3), Lplace(B,2) (sweep B in from the left), and Rplace(B,2) (sweep B in from the right). The example in Figure 1 is an T-R program that we generated to solve this problem.[3] This program solves the problem, but contains some implicit ordering preferences for placing B from the left and placing A first when A and C are both available. By translating the T-R

---

[3]In (Nilsson 1992), a similar T-R program is presented, but it is for a simpler variation of the BNL problem.

do* first {
    free(1) $\land$ free(2) $\land$ available(B) $\rightarrow$ Lplace(B,2);
    free(3) $\land$ free(2) $\land$ available(B) $\rightarrow$ Rplace(B,2);
    free(1) $\land$ free(3) $\land$ available(A) $\rightarrow$ place(A,1);
    free(3) $\land$ free(1) $\land$ available(C) $\rightarrow$ place(C,3);
    free(1) $\land$ $\neg$free(2) $\land$ available(A) $\rightarrow$ place(A,1);
    free(3) $\land$ $\neg$free(2) $\land$ available(C) $\rightarrow$ place(C,3) }

Figure 2: Direct Translation to SCS

repeat while free(1) $\lor$ free(2) $\lor$ free(3) {
  do any {
    do while free(2) $\land$ available(B) {
      do any { **do when** free(1) { Lplace(B, 2) };
              do when free(3) { Rplace(B, 2) }; }}
    do while free(1) $\land$ free(3) {
      do any { **do when** available(A) { place(A, 1) };
             do when available(C) { place(C, 3) }; }}
    do while $\neg$free(2) {
      do any { **do when** available(A) { place(A, 1) };
             do when available(C) { place(C, 3) }; }}}}

Figure 3: SCS Program for the General BNL Problem

program into SCS (figure 2), and comparing it to our own solution in SCS (figure 3), the implicit control ordering of T-R programs is explicitly seen,[4] highlighting how T-R programs cannot capture, in an explicit way, nondeterminism, which has been captured in the richer semantics of SCS.

Related Work and Future Work

Because SCS embodies circuit semantics, previous comparisons (Nilsson 1992; 1994) between T-R programs and reactive plan execution systems such as SCR (Drummond 1989), GAPPS (Pack Kaelbling 1988), PRS (Ingrand, Georgeff, & Rao 1992), and Universal Plans (Schoppers 1987), are applicable here as well. In this section, therefore, we concentrate on comparisons more specifically with SCS.

As illustrated in the previous section, the **do first** construct and the capability of defining a step covers the circuit semantics of T-R programs. Universal Plans also fit easily within SCS through the nested use of the **do when** construct. The real power of SCS over T-R programs or Universal Plans are manifested when the simple SCS constructs interact in various ways.

Situated Control Rules (SCR) are constraints for plan execution that are used to inform an independently competent execution system that it can act without a plan, if necessary. The plan simply serves to increase the system's goal-achieving ability. In other words, SCR alone is *not* a plan execution system, and its rules are not executable. This does not preclude, however, developing an integrated system where one

---

[4]The SCS constructs can often allow multiple such mappings. Thus, while program equivalence cannot always be detected syntactically, the implicit control information can be captured and compared explicitly.

component generates SCRs which, in turn, are automatically compiled into a SCS program to execute on another component. The semantics of SCS would make such compilation possible, although the SCR formulation has weaknesses that must be overcome, such as (1) it does not consider variable binding, (2) it has no hierarchical execution structure (function call or recursion), and (3) it has no run-time reasoning.

The RAP system (Firby 1989; 1992) is very similar in flavor to SCS. RAP's intertwined conditional sequences enable the reactive execution of plans in a hierarchical manner. As with other systems, its basic difference with SCS is that it lacks circuit semantics, as well as several features of SCS including: failure semantics (when a RAP method fails, it assumes the robot is in the same state as before the method was attempted) and the ability to enter a method from the method's middle. SCS has clear failure semantics and specifies what to do and where to start. Another limitation of the RAP interpreter is that methods lack run-time priority information, which is expressed by utility functions in SCS **do best**. RPL (McDermott 1992) extends RAPs by incorporating *fluents* and a FILTER construct to represent durative conditions, but these are much more compactly and intuitively captured in SCS.

The central system of Sonja (Chapman 1990) uses a circuit description language, MACNET and arbitration macrology. Although it supports circuit semantics at the (boolean) gate level, the arbitration macrology allows only compilation time arbitration in a non-structured manner because it compiles down into MACNET circuitry just before the system runs. SCS can more generally capture reactive behavior required for applications such as playing video games (Sonja (Chapman 1990) and Pengi (Agre & Chapman 1987)) and for the traffic world scenario (CROS (Hendler & Sanborn 1987)).

PRS deserves special mention, because a major motivation in developing SCS has been our need for formally specifying the PRS plan representation and its execution model. A formal specification of a reactive plan is essential for us to be able to generate it, reason about it, and communicate about it among multiple agents. In the PRS perspective, SCS can be interpreted as a formalism for the PRS execution model using circuit semantics. In particular, the meta-level reasoning capabilities of PRS introduce a wide variety of possible execution structures. So far, we have been able to express much of PRS's utility-based meta-level decision making in SCS using the **do best** construct. Note that these constructs can be nested to arbitrary depth, corresponding to multiple meta-levels in PRS choosing the best method for choosing the best method for achieving a desired goal. Decisions at lower levels can affect higher-level decisions through failure semantics and changes to the internal state, while utility calculations guide choices from higher to lower levels.

Encouraged by the ability of SCS to capture explicitly the control structures of various plan execution systems, we are implementing *SCS Reactive Plan Execution System* in C++. This effort is directed at supplanting our previous implementation of PRS with a more general execution system that can be tailored to the control needs of our application domain. Toward this end, we are currently working on rigorously capturing in SCS the content of PRS meta-level knowledge areas. With this modified system, not only will we have a more flexible plan execution system, but also one with clear semantics to support inter-agent communication and coordination in dynamic environments.

References

Agre, P. E., and Chapman, D. 1987. Pengi: An implementation of a theory of activity. In *AAAI-87*, 268–272.

Chapman, D. 1990. Vision, instruction and action. Tech. Report 1204, MIT AI Laboratory.

Drummond, M. 1989. Situated control rules. In *KR'89*, 103–113.

Firby, R. J. 1989. Adaptive execution in complex dynamic worlds. Tech. Note YALE/DCS/RR #672, Dept. of Computer Science, Yale University.

Firby, R. J. 1992. Building symbolic primitives with continuous control routines. In Hendler, J., ed., *Artificial Intelligence Planning Systems: Proc. of the First International Conference*, 62–68.

Hendler, J. A., and Sanborn, J. C. 1987. A model of reaction for planning in dynamic environments. In *Proc. of the DARPA Knowledge-Based Planning Workshop*, 24.1–24.10.

Ingrand, F. F.; Georgeff, M. P.; and Rao, A. S. 1992. An architecture for real-time reasoning and system control. *IEEE Expert* 7(6):34–44.

Lee, J.; Huber, M. J.; Durfee, E. H.; and Kenny, P. G. 1994. UM-PRS: an implementation of the procedural reasoning system for multirobot applications. In *Conference on Intelligent Robotics in Field, Factory, Service, and Space (CIRFFSS '94)*, 842–849.

McDermott, D. 1992. Transformational planning of reactive behavior. Tech. Note YALEU/CSD/RR #941, Dept. of Computer Science, Yale University.

Nilsson, N. J. 1992. Toward agent programs with circuit semantics. Tech. Report STAN-CS-92-1412, Dept. of Computer Science, Stanford University.

Nilsson, N. J. 1994. Teleo-reactive programs for agent control. *Journal of Artificial Intelligence Research* 1:139–158.

Pack Kaelbling, L. 1988. Goals as parallel program specifications. In *AAAI-88*, 60–65.

Schoppers, M. J. 1987. Universal plans for reactive robots in unpredictable environments. In *IJCAI-87*, 1039–1046.

Estimating Reaction Plan Size

Marcel Schoppers

Robotics Research Harvesting, PO Box 2111, Redwood City, CA 94063

Abstract

The Shannon/Ginsberg circuit size estimate, by assuming independence of Boolean inputs, is not usable as a plan size estimate. By re-estimating circuit size as a function of the number of *combinations* w of Boolean inputs, I show that a reaction plan over w world states should grow as $\mathbf{O}(w/\log w)$, on average. However, in a Blocks World containing N blocks and $w \approx N^N$ world states, actual Universal Plans grow only as $\mathbf{O}(N^3)$. This difference is shown to be attributable to the Universal Plans' use of dynamically bound object variables. Finally I obtain the general domain-independent result that for a domain containing w world states, the expected size of a reaction plan *with variables* is $\mathbf{O}((w/\log w)^{1/\log_p(p+(b-1)v)})$ where p is the number of preconditions per operator, v is the number of those preconditions that introduce an unbound variable, and b is the number of possible bindings per variable. The exponent is < 1 and allows this formula to predict plan size reductions of many orders of magnitude.

Review of Plan Size Arguments

Reaction plans are a relatively new representation for controlling embedded agents. As argued in (Schoppers 1989b), they mitigate the cost of run-time replanning by functioning as caches of responses to possible situations, thus trading time against space. Predictably, the increased space requirements have led to criticisms that for domains of any "reasonable size", a reaction plan could only prescribe reactions to arbitrary situations by being a "very large" plan indeed. This argument was made most forcibly by (Ginsberg 1989), who formalized domain size as the number of atomic propositions (or ground literals) in the vocabulary of the domain's representation, formalized plan size as the number of gates in a hardware implementation of a reaction plan, and employed a version of (Shannon 1949)'s circuit size estimate to argue that the vast majority of reaction plans for domains having n ground literals would require $\mathbf{O}(2^n/4n)$ gates for their hardware implementation, thus implying that reaction plans would in general be too large to be practical — unless they contained a reaction that invoked a planner, in which case a reasonable plan size would be obtainable only if the reaction

plan "passed the buck" to planning nearly all the time (so why have the reaction plan at all).

Ginsberg's arguments were accompanied by two rebuttals. (Chapman 1989) exhibited a reaction plan of fixed size that was capable of building block towers of arbitrary height (without resorting to planning). (Schoppers 1989b) argued from common sense: Ginsberg's arguments imply also that production systems[1] are "impractical in general" because needing an exponential number of rules. Yet the AI field deems the hand-building of production systems a worth-while effort; how then can the automatic building of similar functionality be deemed impractical? Although those rebuttals should have cast some doubt on Ginsberg's argument, many subsequent papers have cited him as proving conclusively that reaction plans are "impractical in general" (Doyle & Wellman 1990, p.34) (Ingrand & Georgeff 1990, p.284) (Kaelbling 1990a, p.437) (Drummond & Bresina 1990) (Christensen 1990, p.1006) (Godefroid & Kabanza 1991, p.640) (Chrisman & Simmons 1991, p.761) (Bonasso 1991, p.1225) (Lyons & Hendriks 1992, p.154).

Before proceeding with the main argument, we must clarify the meaning of "all possible situations" as the range of situations a reaction plan should have reasonable responses for. It might mean "all physically possible situations" but then, if one cannot expect SIPE (for example) to build a plan that pushes a meddlesome baby out of the way when SIPE's domain model does not distinguish meddlesome babies, neither can one fault reaction plans for having the same limitation. If one replies that domain models must be dynamically refinable and that SIPE, given a refined model that includes meddlesome babies, could simply build new plans that deal with such babies, then similarly, both (Kaelbling 1988) and (Schoppers 1989a) describe how to automatically (re)construct reaction plans from do-

---

[1] In a production system the choice of rule to be fired amounts to a reaction to the contents of the system's working memory. If the rule firing engine carries any "state" from one firing to the next, that state exists solely for efficiency purposes, and makes no difference to the rule/reaction selected.

main models. From this point, the only fair arguments about reaction plan size are those that hold even under fixed domain models. Said differently, fair size arguments will hold even when "all possible situations" is reduced to "all situations distinguishable within a given domain model."

This paper

- isolates a false assumption that invalidates Shannon's circuit size estimate as a predictor of reaction plan size;
- develops an improved predictor of reaction plan size;
- exhibits a small reaction plan that defies even the improved predictor;
- mathematically attributes the unexpectedly small plan size to the plan's use of dynamically bound object variables;
- finds an expression for the expected size of reaction plans containing dynamically bound object variables;
- tests the expression on reaction plans for block stacking, and gets results that are many orders of magnitude better than previous estimates.

Importance of the Independence Assumption

The circuit size argument proceeds as follows. 1) There are 2^{2^n} Boolean functions of n Boolean variables; 2) With $g = 2^n/4n$ gates it is possible to build at most $2^{2^n/2}/n^{2g}$ ($\ll 2^{2^n}$) Boolean functions (Shannon 1949; Ginsberg 1989); hence 3) The vast majority of Boolean functions on n inputs require more than $2^n/4n$ to gates to implement them. This argument presupposes (and Ginsberg explicitly requires) that the n Boolean inputs are independent. If they are not independent, then there are $< 2^n$ possible combinations of input values, hence there are $\ll 2^{2^n}$ Boolean functions on those n inputs, hence $2^n/4n$ gates may be more than enough, hence the argument collapses. It follows immediately that the circuit size argument cannot be used to predict reaction plan size unless the independence assumption holds of the ground literals being tested by the plan.

There are not many planning domains in which the independence assumption is satisfied. In particular, fluents give rise to as many ground literals as the fluent has possible values, but those ground literals are not independent. To see how quickly fluents invalidate size estimates, observe that in an N-Blocks World, each block can sit on N things, thus generating at least N^2 ground literals, and leading to the naive conclusions that the number of world states is 2^{N^2} and the number of gates needed is $> 2^{N^2}/4N^2$. With $N = 10$ this predicts 10^{30} world states and $> 3 \times 10^{27}$ gates when in fact there are only 6×10^7 world states (see Derivation 1 of the Appendix). This huge discrepancy arises solely from the fact that what's-on(Block) and what's-under(Block) are fluents.

Hence, we can now conclude that the Shannon/Ginsberg argument works only in domains that contain no fluents. Common examples of fluents include the amount of fuel remaining, the distance travelled, the positions of things, and the current time. Since the world is full of fluents, the circuit size estimate is generally worthless as an estimate of plan size.

We can however salvage something of the circuit size estimate as follows:

- There are 2^w Boolean functions on w *combinations* of Boolean values.
- With g binary gates it is possible to build at most $(16(g+n+2)^2)^g$ Boolean functions on n inputs (Shannon 1949; Ginsberg 1989).
- If we happen to set $g = w/(2\log_2 w)$ and use $n \ll g$ we can build circuits for at most

$$
(2^4(w/2\log_2 w)^2)^g = \frac{(2w)^{2g}}{(\log_2 w)^{2g}}
$$

$$
= \frac{(2^{\log_2 2w})^{2g}}{(\log_2 w)^{2g}} = \frac{2^{(\log_2 w + 1)(w/\log_2 w)}}{(\log_2 w)^{(w/\log_2 w)}}
$$

$$
= \frac{2^{w+(w/\log_2 w)}}{(\log_2 w)^{(w/\log_2 w)}} = 2^w \times (2/\log_2 w)^{w/\log_2 w}
$$

Boolean functions, which provides for less than half of the 2^w possible functions whenever $w \geq 7$. Consequently, a planning domain containing $w \geq 7$ world states will (on average) require a reaction plan of size $\geq w/(2\log_2 w)$.

The Appendix (Derivation 2) shows that in the N-Blocks World w is $\mathbf{O}(N^N)$, so our improved plan size estimate is $\mathbf{O}(N^{N-1}/\log N)$. This estimate is shown in Table 1 under the heading "improved number of gates". Also shown, under the heading "size of random partition," is a size estimate based on the expected number of equivalence classes in a randomly selected partition on w world states (see Derivation 3). This estimate too is $\mathbf{O}(w/\log w)$ (Haigh 1972). These estimates of plan size are already much less devastating than Ginsberg's, but might still be interpreted as damaging to the (fully-explicit) reaction plans enterprise. However, the next section undermines the circuits analogy completely.

Importance of Object Variables

I begin by calculating the actual size of a Universal Plan needed to build a tower of N blocks from any initial configuration of N blocks.

Two action descriptions are required for a Blocks World that does not model the robot arm:

```
puton(X,Y) --
    on(X,Y) <+ clear(X), clear(Y).

putoff(Y,X) --
    clear(X), ontable(Y)
            <+ on(Y,X) ? clear(Y).
```

The action name comes first, followed by "--", then the action's postconditions, then "<+", and finally the action's preconditions. The preconditions preceding a "?" are filters or qualifiers on the applicability of the

blocks	number of world states	Ginsberg number of gates	improved number of gates	size of random partition	actual UP size w/o vars	actual UP size w vars	estim. UP size w vars
3	13	14	3.7	6.4	10	9	6.1
4	73	1024	12.2	23	35	22	9.6
5	501	3.36×10^5	58.2	107	192	45	16.0
6	4051	4.77×10^8	352	629	1393	81	26.0
7	37633	2.87×10^{12}	2576	4480	11834	133	40.8
8	394353	7.21×10^{16}	22078	37450	112635	204	62.5
9	4596553	7.46×10^{21}	216136	359000	1181120	297	94.0
10	5.89×10^7	3.17×10^{27}	0.22×10^7	0.39×10^7	1.35×10^7	415	140
15	6.56×10^{13}	5.99×10^{64}	1.48×10^{12}	2.30×10^{12}	8.03×10^{12}	1485	958
20	3.28×10^{20}	1.61×10^{117}	0.50×10^{19}	0.75×10^{19}	2.09×10^{19}	3630	6324
25	5.10×10^{27}	5.57×10^{184}	0.58×10^{26}	0.85×10^{26}	1.72×10^{26}	7225	41581

Table I: Sizes of Blocks World Reaction Plans.

action: If they are false, the action does not apply, and its other preconditions should not be achieved. The preconditions that come after a "?" should be achieved if they are false and the action applies. When there is no explicit "?" there is no applicability filter.

These action descriptions, when fed into a Universal Plans planner, cause the planner to autonomously discover the goal conflict associated with the Sussman Anomaly problem, and to resolve that goal conflict by generating "confinement" rules. How that is done for the 3-blocks world is described in (Schoppers 1989a). The most general confinement rule is

```
on(Y,Z) < above(X,Y) <++ ¬above(Z,X)
```

(where the **above(X,Y)** relation is defined as the transitive closure of the **on(X,Y)** relation). This rule informs the Universal Plans interpreter that whenever there exist bindings of **X**, **Y** and **Z** such that **on(Y,Z)**∧**above(X,Y)** is implied by the current goals and **on(Y,Z)** is false, then we must first make ¬**above(Z,X)** true, after which the two goals can be achieved in the given order.

The above three rules are sufficient to drive a Universal Plans interpreter. They may also be fed into a Universal Plans compiler, to produce a fully explicit Universal Plan for a given number of blocks, as follows. For convenience, let blocks be designated by numbers rather than letters, and consider a conjunctive goal of the form **on(1,2)** ∧ **on(2,3)** ∧...∧ **on(N-1,N)** . The confinement rule reorders the conjuncts as **on(N-1,N)** < ... < **on(2,3)** < **on(1,2)** and further requires that the achievement of each conjunct should be "confined" to circumstances in which each block yet to be placed is not under the tower being built. Thus, the compiled Universal Plan would be a decision tree that has the confinement rule built in as follows (J, X, Y and Z are block numbers):

```
subplan TWR-READY(J)
{ J≤2 ?
    t: — finish top 2 blocks —
      on(1,2) ?
      t: NO-OP
      f: ACHIEVE-ON(1,2)
    f: — tower is ready from base to J —
      on(J-1,J) ?
      t: — J-1 is in place too, go up —
        TWR-READY(J-1)
      f: — J-1 not in place, unbury 1..J-2 —
        cr1-ready(J-2,J-1,J) ?
        t: cr1-ready(J-3,J-1,J) ?
        .  t: ...
        .      t: cr1-ready(1,J-1,J) ?
        .         t: — not burying 1..J-2 —
        .            ACHIEVE-ON(J-1,J)
        .            — unbury each of 1..J-2 —
        .            f: ACHIEVE-NOT-ABOVE(J,1)
        .      f: ...
        . f: ACHIEVE-NOT-ABOVE(J,J-3)
        f: ACHIEVE-NOT-ABOVE(J,J-2)
}

condition cr1-ready(X,Y,Z)
{ on(Y,Z)              — confinement not needed —
  or not above(Z,X)    — confinement achieved —
}

subplan ACHIEVE-NOT-ABOVE(Z,X)
{ ACHIEVE-CLEAR(X)
}

subplan ACHIEVE-CLEAR(X)
{ NEW VAR Y;
  Y := the-block-on X;

  clear(Y) ?
  t: PUTOFF(Y,X)
  f: ACHIEVE-CLEAR(Y)
}
```

subplan ACHIEVE-ON(X,Y)
{ clear(X) ?
    t: clear(Y) ?
      t: PUTON(X,Y)
      f: ACHIEVE-CLEAR(Y)
    f: ACHIEVE-CLEAR(X)
}

An important point: while `above(Z,X)` is a relatively complex test whose presence might allow an unfair size reduction, it turns out to be dispensible: this plan would work even if `NOT above(Z,X)` was replaced with `clear(X)`.

Observe that the plan is encoded as a few functions which invoke each other recursively; the Summary section comments further. For now we treat the above as macros and pretend that they generate a monolithic Universal Plan. The size of this plan is calculated in the Appendix (Derivation 4), and comes out to be $(N-1)^3 + N$ for N blocks. This size is shown in Table 1 under the heading "actual UP size with vars".

Let us put this size in context. The Shannon/Ginsberg circuit size estimate was $O(2^{N^2}/N^2)$. My improvement thereon, allowing for dependence among literals, was $O(N^{N-1}/\log N)$ (taking $w \approx N^N$ from Derivation 2). The actual plan size is $O(N^3)$.

I claim that the actual Universal Plan is so much smaller than the predicted sizes because it uses variables to refer to "whatever block is on top of the block to be moved". To verify this, Derivation 5 calculates how big the plan would have been if block-variables had been disallowed, and comes out with the sizes shown in Table 1 under the heading "actual UP size without vars". Observe that replacing block-variables with block-constants makes the plan larger than both my improved circuit size estimate and the partition size estimate. Consequently it is safe to say that the remarkably small size of the Universal Plan with variables can be completely attributed to the utility of the block-variables.

Expected Size of Plans Containing Variables

In this section I obtain a general domain-independent result: the size of a reaction plan containing variables as a function of the size of an equivalent plan without variables. Throughout, the size of a plan is equated with the number of leaves of the equivalent binary decision tree (which is one greater than the number of decision nodes). The expected size of the decision tree is calculated using a recurrence relation on a number of construction operations r, where each operation adds an action operator/schema instance to the tree.

Let the "average" operator instance have $p(\geq 1)$ preconditions, of which $v(\geq 0, \leq p)$ contain exactly one unbound variable (other preconditions containing none) and let all unbound variables range over $b(> 1)$ possible bindings. For simplicity we assume that the subplans being used to achieve each of a given operator instance's preconditions all have the same size, and conceptually we assemble the decision tree from its leaf nodes toward its root. Then the expected size of the decision tree is given by

$$S_v(r) = \begin{cases} 1 : r = 0 \\ p\, S_v(r-1) + 1 : r > 0 \end{cases}$$

because for each tested precondition (with or without variables) a false outcome leads to the subplan of size $S_v(r-1)$ for achieving the precondition, and a true outcome leads to testing the next precondition, until all p preconditions come out true; then the last 1 is for executing the operator instance's primitive action. Thus,

$$S_v(r) = \begin{cases} r : p = 1 \\ (p^{r+1} - 1)/(p - 1) : p > 1 \end{cases}$$

Now suppose that the v variables in the average operator's preconditions can not be bound dynamically. Then the decision tree must explicitly test each possible binding to see if it matches the actual situation. Figure 1 shows an example from the Blocks World: the `on(X,a)` test, applied when block towers are dismantled, expands into one case in which `a` is already clear (no binding for `X`) and multiple cases in which `a` is under one of a number of possible blocks, with each block now requiring a separate subplan for its removal.

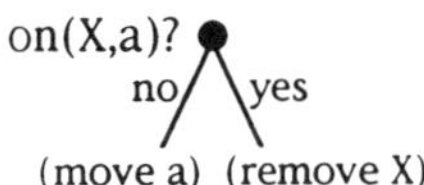

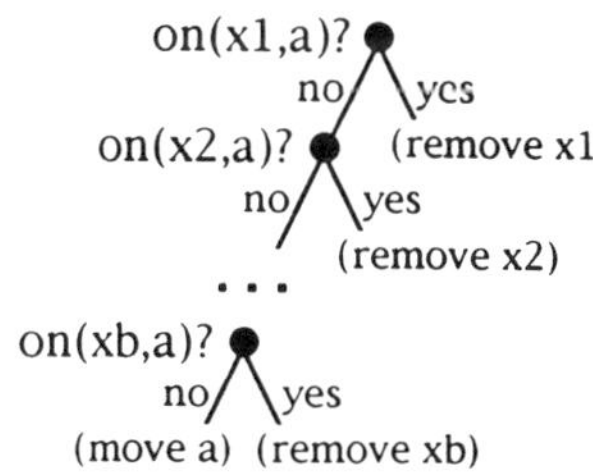

Figure 1: Plan Expansion to Eliminate Variables.

Accordingly, the size of an equivalent decision tree without variables is

$$S(r) = \begin{cases} 1 : r = 0 \\ \{v\,b + (p-v)\}\, S(r-1) + 1 : r > 0 \end{cases}$$

(wherein S has no subscript). Writing the term in braces as κ and simplifying:

$$S(r) = \begin{cases} r : \kappa = 1 \\ (\kappa^{r+1} - 1)/(\kappa - 1) : \kappa > 1 \end{cases}$$

Since $\kappa = 1$ requires both $1/b \le p \le 1$ and $v = (1-p)/(b-1)$, we ignore this case in what follows.

If the reaction plan *without* variables should distinguish S classes of world states, the appropriate number of tree construction operations is

$$r = \log_\kappa\{(\kappa-1)S + 1\} - 1 \quad (\kappa > 1).$$

Using this same number of construction operations to build the equivalent decision tree *with* variables:

$$S_v = \begin{cases} \log_\kappa\{(\kappa-1)S + 1\} - 1 : p = 1, \kappa > 1 \\ (p^{\log_\kappa\{(\kappa-1)S+1\}} - 1)/(p-1) : p > 1, \kappa > 1 \end{cases}$$

The case $p = 1$ (one precondition per operator) reveals clearly that variables can reduce a reaction plan's size to the logarithm of of its variable-free magnitude. For the case $p > 1$ we use $\log_\kappa x = \log_p x / \log_p \kappa$ to simplify:

$$S_v = \frac{\{(\kappa-1)S + 1\}^{1/\log_p \kappa} - 1}{p - 1} : p > 1, \kappa > 1$$

Let us check this last formula numerically. For S we use the known sizes of Universal Plans without variables. (In other domains, estimate w, then estimate S from $S^S \approx e^{w-1}$, see Derivation 3.) Assuming that the Universal Plan consists of equal numbers of the **puton** and **putoff** operators shown in Section 3, we find $p = 1.5$ and $v = 0.5$, and we set $b = N - 1$, so $\kappa = (N+1)/2$. The resulting plan size estimates are shown in Table 1 under "est. UP size with vars". The results reveal that our general formula is inaccurate, under-estimating for small N and over-estimating for large N. Indeed, a little algebra (with $w \approx N^{0.8N}$, $S \approx 2w/\log_2 w$, and $1/\log_p \kappa \rightarrow \log_N p$) shows that S_v is $\mathbf{O}(p^{0.8N})$ and hence remains exponential, where the actual plan grows as N^3. Nevertheless, our formula is clearly a very large improvement on previous plan size estimates.

It is worth noting that, using the values of p and v just given, the the exponent simplifies to

$$0.585/\log_2\{(N+1)/2\}.$$

When $N = 25$ this is ≈ 0.158 and is responsible for reducing the estimated plan size from 10^{26} to 10^4. While the exact reduction clearly depends on the values of p, v and b being used, the example demonstrates the power of a fractional exponent and promises similar effectiveness in other domains, since the general form of the exponent is domain-independent.

Summary

This paper has demonstrated that Shannon's circuit size estimate cannot be used as an estimate of reaction plan size, for two reasons. First, Shannon's circuit size estimate relies on an assumption that the inputs to the circuit are independent. The penalty for failing to observe the independence assumption is a massive over-estimate; the reward for observing it is the realization that virtually all planning domains contain fluents, which falsify the assumption. Second, most approaches to building reaction plans allow the plans to contain variables that are bound at execution time — a feature for which the circuit size estimate has no analog.

To drive the point home in a constructive way, I showed that the small size of a Universal Plan for Blocks Worlds was completely accounted for by the presence of dynamically bound variables in the plan, and found that in any domain, the expected size of reaction plans containing variables was $\mathbf{O}((w/\log w)^{1/\log_p(p+(b-1)v)})$, where w is the number of world states and the exponent encodes the power of dynamically bound variables. The new formula was empirically tested on Blocks World plan sizes and improved on previous estimates by many, many orders of magnitude. More generally, the new formula's fractional exponent was shown to be very effective indeed at keeping plan size under control. (Whether the new formula accurately predicts actual plan sizes is less important than the fact that the formula is based on domain-independent considerations and shows variables to be very effective.)

The fully explicit block-stacking circuits produced by other approaches will be even smaller than the sizes estimated for fully explicit Universal Plan. Those savings are generally obtained by one of two means: (1) the hand-coded "plans" may be iterative because they are built by hand, whereas Universal Plans are recursive because they are built automatically; (2) the hand-coded plans may use internal data ("state bits") to control reaction plan execution, whereas the Universal Plan analyzed above was assumed to be completely sensor-driven.

Finally, bear in mind that reaction plans are usually not fully explicit. The Universal Plans interpreter, given just the three rules required for block stacking (see Section 3), can back-chain recursively (without searching) to dynamically construct exactly the same decision sequence as the plan analyzed above. The PRS (Georgeff et al 1987) and RAPS (Firby 1987) interpreters similarly back-chain recursively to dynamically instantiate arbitrarily large plans implicit in a small number of "knowledge sources". The GAPPS compiler (Kaelbling & Rosenschein 1990b, sec 3.3.2), when made part of a situated automaton, could dynamically instantiate only the relevant parts of GAPPS programs. When fast execution-time re-assembly and disassembly of relevant plan parts is supported, the size of fully explicit reaction plans becomes entirely irrelevant.

Beyond combating an ugly rumor about reaction plans, this paper also contributes to analyses of the space complexity of solutions to entire problem domains. Such solutions include production systems and many ordinary hand-written programs — the latter may be construed as reacting to input data and the states of CPU and memory.

Appendix: Derivations

Derivation 1: Number of World States

The number of ways N blocks can be stacked is calculated in three steps:

1. find all possible combinations of tower sizes, under the assumption that blocks are identical and interchangeable,

2. for each allowed combination of tower sizes, make blocks non-interchangeable and find all ways of permuting them such that the resulting world states are distinct,

3. find the sum, over all possible combinations of tower sizes, of the number of distinct block permutations.

Step #1 is an instance of the famous "integer partition" problem (Knuth 1968, p.12). To clarify the nature of the partitions, here are the partitions for the first few integers.

N	list of partitions
1	1
2	2, 1+1
3	3, 2+1, 1+1+1
4	4, 3+1, 2+2, 2+1+1, 1+1+1+1
5	5, 4+1, 3+2, 3+1+1, 2+2+1, 2+1+1+1, 1+1+1+1+1

To generate the partitions of N+1 from those of N, add 1 to each component of each partition of N, store the resulting partition if it has not been encountered before, and finally add a partition consisting of N+1 1s.

For Step #2 we represent each partition as consisting of n_i is (e.g. a partition of 5 as 1 3s and 2 1s), then count $N!/\prod_i n_i!$ distinct states under the given partition. The denominator factors out states that differ only by a positional interchange of towers of the same size. Step #3 sums the results of Step #2 over all the partitions of N.

The above calculation was implemented as a C program. The results for $N \leq 25$ are shown in Table 1 under the heading "actual world states".

Derivation 2: Approximate Number of States

$N!$, which appears in Derivation 1, is a lower bound on the number of N-Blocks World states. A loose upper bound may be found by noting that the N things possibly under a given block can be distinguished with $\log_2 N$ bits, so that it takes only $N \log_2 N$ bits to encode what's actually under each of the N blocks in a given state, thus allowing at most $2^{N \log_2 N} = N^N$ possible states in the N-Blocks World. Empirically we find that $(N^N)^{0.8}$ is a very good approximation.

Derivation 3: Size of Random Partition

Let $\mathcal{S}_m^{(w)}$ denote a "Stirling number of the second kind" (Knuth 1968, p.65); these numbers indicate how many ways w objects can be partitioned into m non-empty subsets. Let $\mathcal{B}(w)$ be a "Bell number"; these numbers indicate how many ways a set of w objects can be partitioned. Let $c(w)$ be the cardinality of a randomly chosen partition of w objects. Then, using a well-known identity,

$$c(w) = \frac{\sum_{i=0}^{w} i\, \mathcal{S}_i^{(w)}}{\mathcal{B}(w)}$$

$$\mathcal{B}(w+1) = \sum_{i=0}^{w+1} \mathcal{S}_i^{(w+1)} = \sum_{i=0}^{w+1} (i\, \mathcal{S}_i^{(w)} + \mathcal{S}_{i-1}^{(w)})$$

$$= (c(w) + 1)\, \mathcal{B}(w). \qquad (1)$$

An alternative formulation of $c(w)$ is

$$c(w) = \frac{1}{\mathcal{B}(w)} \sum_{i=0}^{w-1} \binom{w-1}{w-1-i} (c(i) + 1)\mathcal{B}(i).$$

Here we define $c(w)$ by adding the new wth element to any subset out of a partition on $w-1$ elements. A set of $w-1$ elements contains $\binom{w-1}{w-1-i}$ possible subsets of size $w-1-i$. For each such subset, the remaining i elements can be partitioned in $\mathcal{B}(i)$ ways, and for each such partition the expected number of equivalence classes is $c(i)+1$ (the additional 1 accounts for the class containing the new wth element). Now, making heavy use of Equation 1, we obtain

$$c(w) = \sum_{i=0}^{w-1} \binom{w-1}{w-1-i} \frac{\mathcal{B}(i+1)}{\mathcal{B}(w)}$$

$$= \sum_{j=0}^{w-1} \binom{w-1}{j} \frac{\mathcal{B}(w-j)}{\mathcal{B}(w)}$$

$$= 1 + \sum_{j=1}^{w-1} \frac{1}{j!} \frac{w-1}{c(w-1)+1} \frac{w-2}{c(w-2)+1} \cdots \frac{w-j}{c(w-j)+1}$$

$$< 1 + \sum_{j=1}^{w-1} \frac{1}{j!} \left(\frac{w-1}{c(w-1)+1} \right)^j$$

$$< e^{(w-1)/c(w-1)+1}$$

Raising both sides to the power $c(w-1) + 1$, using $c(w) < c(w-1) + 1$, and taking logarithms:

$$c(w)^{c(w-1)+1} < e^{w-1}$$
$$c(w)^{c(w)} < e^{w-1}$$
$$c(w) \ln c(w) < w - 1$$

An over-estimate $\hat{c}$ of $c(w)$ can now be obtained very efficiently by iterating $\hat{c} = (w-1)/\ln \hat{c}$.

Derivation 4: Size of Actual U.P.

The size of the monolithic Universal Plan (with variables) for building a tower of N blocks is the number of decision nodes, which (in any binary tree) is one less than the number of outcomes. To get that number we need to replace the macros "ACHIEVE-<goal>" with explicit decision trees containing only the `puton()` and `putoff()` actions.

- The plan for constructing a tower of N blocks numbered from 1 (at the top) to N (at the bottom) is just an instance of `TWR-READY(N)`, which incorporates an instance of `TWR-READY(N-1)`, and so on recursively, down to `TWR-READY2`.

- For J $\geq$ 3 `TWR-READY(J)` incorporates J-2 instances of `ACHIEVE-NOT-ABOVE(Z,X)`, to ensure that the tower is not being built on top of blocks 1 through J-2. Unrolling the plan recursively as in the previous item, the plan incorporates N-2 + N-3 + ... + 1 = (N-1)(N-2)/2 instances of `ACHIEVE-NOT-ABOVE(Z,X)`. Similarly, the plan incorporates N-1 instances of `ACHIEVE-ON(J-1,J)`.

- In general, `ACHIEVE-NOT-ABOVE(Z,X)` could be achieved by dismantling the tower on top of Z, then moving Z to the table. Since the plan must provide for the worst case in which Z is directly on top of X and *all* the other blocks are stacked on top of Z,

`ACHIEVE-NOT-ABOVE(Z,X)` must be prepared to dismantle the whole tower on top of X. Moreover, everything above X must be dismantled in any case, prior to moving X. Hence we simplify the analysis by equating `ACHIEVE-NOT-ABOVE(Z,X)` with `ACHIEVE-CLEAR(X)`. Then each occurrence of `ACHIEVE-NOT-ABOVE(Z,X)` unfolds as a series of calls to `PUTOFF(Y)`, one for each next higher block in the tower. Since there can be at most N-1 blocks on top of X, the $(N-1)(N-2)/2$ occurrences of `ACHIEVE-NOT-ABOVE(Z,X)` select from a total of $(N-1)*(N-1)(N-2)/2$ outcomes.

- By virtue of the structure of `TWR-READY(J)` we know that the `ACHIEVE-ON(J-1,J)` subplan only occurs when the tower below J has been completed. Therefore, the `ACHIEVE-CLEAR(J-1)` and `ACHIEVE-CLEAR(J)` subplans incorporated within `ACHIEVE-ON(J-1,J)` need only cope with the J-2 and J-1 blocks (respectively) that are not already in the partially completed tower. Consequently, to dismantle the worst-case towers above blocks J-1 and J, each `ACHIEVE-ON(J-1,J)` subplan must unfold as $(J-2)+(J-1)$ calls to `PUTOFF()`, plus one call to `PUTON(J-1,J)`. Summing over J from 2 to N we find a total of $N\times(N-1)$ outcomes within the `ACHIEVE-ON` subtrees.

Thus the total number of outcomes of the decision tree is

$$(N\text{-}1)(N\text{-}1)(N\text{-}2)/2 + N(N\text{-}1) + 1 = (N\text{-}1)^3 + N.$$

(The last 1 is for the NO-OP in `TWR-READY(2)`.) This number is shown in Table 1 under the heading "actual UP size with vars".

Derivation 5: Size of U.P. Without Variables

Recall that the actual block-stacking plan incorporated $(N-1)(N-2)/2$ instances of `ACHIEVE-NOT-ABOVE(Z,X)`, each of which may have to remove up to N-1 blocks. Inability to use variables would force each such instance to cope with $(N-1)!$ possible permutations of blocks in each tower, for a combined size of $(N-1)!\times(N-1)(N-2)/2$ outcomes. Similarly, the N-1 instances of `ACHIEVE-ON(J-1,J)` each incorporate two subplans `ACHIEVE-CLEAR(J)` and `ACHIEVE-CLEAR(J-1)`, which may have to remove all permutations of J-1 or J-2 blocks, respectively. From those subplans we get a size contribution of

$$\sum_{J=2}^{N}\left((J-1)!+(J-2)!\right) = 1 + (N-1)! + 2\sum_{k=1}^{N-2}k!.$$

Adding a further N-1 cases in which `ACHIEVE-ON(J-1,J)` does *not* require block-removal, and the 1 case in which no action at all is necessary, we get the total sizes shown in Table 1 under the heading "est. size of UP without vars".

References

Bonasso, R.P. 1991. Integrating reaction plans and layered competences through synchronous control. Proc 12th IJCAI: 1225–1231.

Chapman, D. 1989. Penguins can make cake. *AI Magazine* 10(4): 45–50.

Chrisman, L. & Simmons, R. 1991. Sensible planning: focusing perceptual attention. Proc AAAI Nat'l Conf on AI: 756–761.

Christensen, J. 1990. A hierarchical planner that generates its own hierarchies. Proc AAAI Nat'l Conf on AI: 1004–1009.

Doyle, J. & Wellman, M. 1990. Rational distributed reason maintenance for planning and replanning of large-scale activities (preliminary report). Proc DARPA Workshop on Innovative Approaches to Planning, Scheduling and Control: 28–36.

Drummond, M. & Bresina, J. 1990. Planning for control. Proc 5th IEEE International Symposium on Intelligent Control: 658–662.

Firby, R.J. 1987. An investigation into reactive planning in complex domains, Proc AAAI Nat'l Conf on AI: 202–207.

Georgeff, M., Lansky, A. & Bessiere, P. 1987. A procedural logic. Proc 9th IJCAI: 516–521.

Ginsberg, M. 1989. Universal planning: an (almost) universally bad idea. *AI Magazine* 10(4): 40–44.

Godefroid, P. and Kabanza, F. 1991. An efficient reactive planner for synthesizing reactive plans. Proc AAAI Nat'l Conf on AI: 640–645.

Haigh, J. 1972. Random equivalence relations. *Journal of Combinatorial Theory (A)* 13: 287–295.

Ingrand, F. & Georgeff, M. 1990. Managing deliberation and reasoning in real-time systems. Proc DARPA Workshop on Innovative Approaches to Planning, Scheduling and Control: 284–291.

Kaelbling, L. 1988. Goals as parallel program specifications. Proc AAAI Nat'l Conf on AI: 60–65.

Kaelbling, L. 1990a. Specifying complex behavior for computer agents. Proc DARPA Workshop on Innovative Approaches to Planning, Scheduling and Control: 433–438.

Kaelbling, L. and Rosenschein, S. 1990b. Action and planning in embedded agents. In Maes, P. (ed) *Designing Autonomous Agents*. Elsevier.

Knuth, D. 1968. *The Art of Computer Programming I: Fundamental Algorithms*. Addison-Wesley, Reading, MA.

Lyons, D. and Hendriks, A. 1992. A practical approach to integrating reaction and deliberation. Proc 1st Conference on AI Planning Systems: 153–162.

Schoppers, M. 1989a. *Representation and Automatic Synthesis of Reaction Plans*. PhD thesis, Dept of Computer Science, University of Illinois at Urbana-Champaign.

Schoppers, M. 1989b. In defense of reaction plans as caches. *AI Magazine* 10(4): 51–60.

Shannon, C. 1949. The synthesis of two-terminal switching circuits. *Bell Systems Technical Journal* 28(1): 59–98.

Results on Controlling Action with Projective Visualization

Marc Goodman[*]

Cognitive Systems, Inc.
234 Church Street
New Haven, CT 06510

Computer Science Department
Brandeis University
Waltham, MA 02254

Abstract

A projective visualizer learns to simulate events in the external world through observation of the world. These simulations are used to evaluate potential actions on the basis of their probable outcomes. Results are given that indicate, 1). the error rate for projective visualization is sub-linear as the system projects farther into the future, 2). the error rate is inversely proportional to the number of cases, 3). a simple domain model can be used to reduce the effect of compounding error, and 4). projection can be used to increase the performance of an agent, even when this projection is imperfect.

Introduction

Projective visualization is a technique for controlling action. A system built with projective visualization learns to project situations into the future based on past experience. Potential actions are selected and rejected based on an evaluation of the projected state. Previous work (Goodman 1993) presents the basic model for projective visualization and results indicating that a limited form of projection can be used to build a system that performs as well as a reactive system, based on observation of the reactive system. It also offers preliminary results on the accuracy of projection for increasing windows of projection.

Projective visualization starts with a concrete representation of an observed process or activity. These observations are organized as a set of temporally linked cases. The system induces a large number of decision trees, using an algorithm akin to ID3 (Quinlan 1986), CART (Brieman *et al.* 1984), or Automatic Interaction Detection (Hartigan 1975). Each decision tree is responsible for projecting an individual feature of a situation one step forward into the future. During projection, a new, hypothetical case is created using these decision trees, and this hypothetical case serves as the basis for further projection.

[*]Thanks to David Waltz and Richard Alterman for useful discussion. This work was supported in part by ARPA under contract no. DAAH01-92-C-R376.

Other work on the direct application of previous experience to prediction has been presented (Rissland & Ashley 1988; Klein, Whitaker, & King 1988). Both of these works use a very restricted notion of prediction, however. It is assumed that there is only one value to be predicted and that that value is directly associated with the retrieved case (i.e. there is no notion of a projection window, or of projecting an entire situation). Rather, prediction in this sense is akin to a classification task). Prediction in Battle Planning has also been treated as a classification task (Goodman 1989).

The issues addressed in this paper are closely related to issues of simulation. Simulation has been framed in terms of a qualitative model of a domain (Kuipers 1986). The SIMGEN system (Forbus & Falkenhainer 1990) uses both qualitative and quantitative information to drive simulation of a physical systems, and introduces the notion of self-explanatory simulations. Both of these techniques require significant knowledge of the domain, in the form of qualitative relationships. One of the issues addressed by this paper is to what extent such models can be used to guide the induction process.

This paper extends previous results (Goodman 1993). This paper presents details on the inductive algorithm used to generate the projectors used by the system and evaluates their performance. This paper also compares the accuracy of projection with and without *interpretations*, and with and without a simple domain model to guide induction. Finally, the effect of projecting farther and farther into the future on the ability of the system to act is evaluated.

The Target Domain

The target domain discussed in this paper is a simulation of personal combat between two gladiators armed with axes and shields, based on the video game *The Bilestoad*. The perceptual system of the agent in the combat simulation includes a visual system, a pain sense, a kinesthetic sense, a haptic sense, a sense of joint stress, and awareness of motor control signals which control the agent's body.

The personal combat simulation is a good domain for

evaluating projection because: 1). a large amount of
data can be automatically created to test the limits of
the system, 2). the domain is inherently real-time, focusing on very small changes in the state of the world
at each time step, 3). the system must project relatively large distances into the future to evaluate the
effectiveness of its actions, and 4). there are relatively
large number of different actions that the agent can
take at each step, which allows this work to examine
both the accuracy of projection as well as the effects
of projection on performance.

How Projective Visualization Works

Projective visualization manipulates a representation
of a process or activity called a *case*. A case is defined
as a snapshot of the state of the world, along with
temporal links to previous and next cases. In effect, a
case is like a single frame of a motion picture. In the
personal combat domain, cases are gathered every $\frac{1}{6}$th
of a second. Throughout this work, this paper will use
the following terms:

Field: A case is a collection of fields, each field defining a particular value in the case. For example, in
the personal combat domain, there is a field for the
amount of damage to the left elbow of the agent,
a field for the angle of the agent's left elbow, and
so on. **Match fields** are used to build a set of inductive indices for projecting individual features of
a situation. Different sets of indices may have different match fields. **Outcome fields** are used as a
classifications or predictions by the system. Different sets of indices will have different sets of outcome
fields. For example, one set of indices may be useful
for projecting the angle of the agent's elbow, while
another set of indices is useful for projecting whether
the agent will continue walking.

Field value: A field value of a case is the value of a
particular field for that case. For example, the field
value for the angle between the agent's head and its
opponent's axe might be 30°.

Feature projector: A feature projector is a set of indices that is responsible for predicting the value of
one or more outcome fields.

Projector: A projector is a collection of feature projectors that can be used to predict an entire future
state of the combat simulation from current and previous states of the combat simulation.

Building and using the personal combat projector
consists of two separate phases. In the first phase, individual feature projectors are built off-line. In the
second phase, the resulting projector is used to rapidly
predict future states of the combat simulation. There is
no reason, in principle, why learning and action could
not be integrated. However, the computation resources
required to perform learning and the real-time requirements of action in the domain have mandated this separation.

How the Projector is Built

A projector consists of a large number of feature projectors, each of which is an inductively formed discrimination tree that indexes a set of cases. The algorithm
for generating these indices, called **PVClus**, is summarized below:

1. The Spearman's Rho correlation between pairs of
   fields is used to cluster these fields into groups that
   have high correlation using a Leader algorithm (a
   variation of the K-means clustering algorithm (Hartigan 1975)). Each group of correlated fields will
   serve as a set of outcome fields for an individual feature projector. The reason for grouping such fields
   is that highly correlated fields may have common
   underlying factors that govern their behavior.

2. The set of fields describing the combat simulation
   is enhanced by adding interpretations that capture
   temporal and other relationships between fields and
   values. For example, the system creates new fields
   that capture the first and second discrete derivatives
   of the existing fields.

3. Each feature projector with associated outcome
   fields is used to build a discrimination tree. The
   leaves of this tree are sets of cases with similar values for their outcome fields. The internal nodes of
   the tree are binary decisions. For example, an internal node might check whether the agent's shield is
   between the agent and its opponent's axe. Such an
   internal node might separate cases where the agent
   was protected from damage from other situations.
   These discrimination trees are built as follows:

(a) The set of field values associated with the outcome fields for the feature projector, the discrete
   first derivatives of these outcome fields, and the
   discrete second derivatives of these outcome fields
   are compared. The set of fields that minimizes the
   following equation is selected:

$$Error = \sum_{i=0}^{n} \left(\frac{|f_i|}{|f|}\right)^2$$

   Where each f_i is the cardinality of the subset of
   cases that all have the ith field value for their outcome field, and f is the cardinality of the set of
   cases as a whole. This measure gives an indication of the *a priori* error rate if the system were
   to use this set of fields as outcome fields. A more
   accurate measure of such error would be:

$$Error = \sum_{i=0}^{n} \sum_{j=0}^{n} \frac{FieldValue(c_i) - FieldValue(c_j)}{n^2}$$

   Where c_i represents the ith case in the set. There
   are two drawbacks to this form, however. First,
   it takes $O(n^2)$ time to compute whereas the first
   form is $O(n)$, and second, it is only appropriate for
   comparing numerical values. The set of fields with

minimum *a priori* error are used as the outcome
fields for the discrimination tree.

The purpose of this computation is to try and reduce the complexity of the decision tree needed to
accurately project a value. For example, consider
a rocket tracking domain. Before firing, the rocket
is at rest and the easiest way to predict its location
at the next time step is to use its current location.
When the rocket begins firing, its acceleration will
be constant and easy to predict, whereas its velocity and location start changing and become more
difficult to predict. After the rocket engine cuts
out, its X location will change, whereas its velocity
will be constant (barring air resistance). Meanwhile, its Y location and velocity will change, but
its acceleration will still be constant due to gravity. A natural approach to solving this problem
is to find some way for a given cluster of cases to
predict which of these representations for the future state of the rocket is easiest to predict and
to use this as the outcome for building the set of
indices inductively.

(b) The algorithm gathers all the fields that describe
the previous state of the combat simulation, and
associated interpretations. For each such field,
given a set of associated cases, all field values
for that field are tested as possible discrimina-
tors. Each discrimination divides the cases into
two sets, those whose field values are less than
or equal to the candidate field value, and those
whose field values are greater than the candidate
field value. The field value for a particular field
that accounts for the largest degree of variance
in the outcome fields for that feature projector is
found.

(c) The winning field value is tested for statistical significance using the Mann-Whitney U Test. If the
field value passes this test, the associated field is
saved as a match field. If not, the field is ignored. The Mann-Whitney U Test is an appropriate test for statistical significance because it is
non-parametric, and, in general, the system cannot make assumptions about the distribution of
values in particular fields.

(d) The best field value overall is used as an initial discrimination. The discrimination, A, is enhanced
as follows:

  i. For each match field and its associated field values, each field value is used to form a candidate
  discrimination, B.

  ii. Boolean conjunctions of features $A\&B$, $\bar{A}\&B$,
  $A\&\bar{B}$ and $\bar{A}\&\bar{B}$ are tested. The conjunction of
  features that best accounts for variance in the
  outcome fields of the feature projector is selected.
  If the variance accounted for by the conjunction is greater than the variance accounted for
  by A, then the addition of B is checked for statistical significance using the Mann-Whitney U

Test. If adding B passes this test for statistical
significance, then A is set to the conjunction of
features, and the process repeats at item 3(d)i.
If adding B fails the test for statistical significance, then the next best candidate discriminator is tried. If no discriminator passes the test
for statistical significance, or no discriminator
improves the variance accounted for by A, then
A is used as the basis for a parent node in the
tree. This technique is essentially hill climbing
to improve the discriminations in the tree. The
chief advantage of such a technique is that it con-
serves data. With all such discrimination tree
learning algorithms, the more examples that are
available at any given point, the more accurate
is the credit assignment on individual features.
By grinding as much information out of each discrimination in the tree, the system ends up with
a short tree with relatively few leaves, measures
that have been argued are particularly important
(Fayyad & Irani 1990).

(e) The set of cases are partitioned based on the internal node. The process repeats for each subset of cases at item 3a. The algorithm terminates
when no new, statistically significant discriminations can be added that improve the variance in
outcome fields.

How the Projector is Used

At run-time, a case is created that describes the current state of the combat simulation. For each feature
projector, this case is used to traverse the associated
discrimination tree of the feature projector. The mean
values for the outcome field values in the leaf cluster are used to set the corresponding fields in a fresh
case buffer. When each feature projector has been traversed, the system has a hypothetical case that describes the predicted state of the combat simulation.
This predicted state can then serve as the basis for
further projection.

Traversing each discrimination tree takes roughly
$O(\log n)$ where n is the number of cases. The total
time complexity for projection is therefore $O(pm \log n)$
where p is the projection window, or how far into the
future the situation is projected, m is the number of
feature projectors (which is effectively constant for any
given system), and n is the number of cases. It is,
therefore, possible to do projection very quickly.

Learning with Domain Knowledge

There are two primary sources of domain knowledge
available to the system. The first source of domain
knowledge is a set of *interpretations* that can be derived from the raw case representation. For example,
in the personal combat domain, the system may automatically create representations of the spatial relationships between objects in the world (such as the
joints of the bodies of the agent and its opponent)

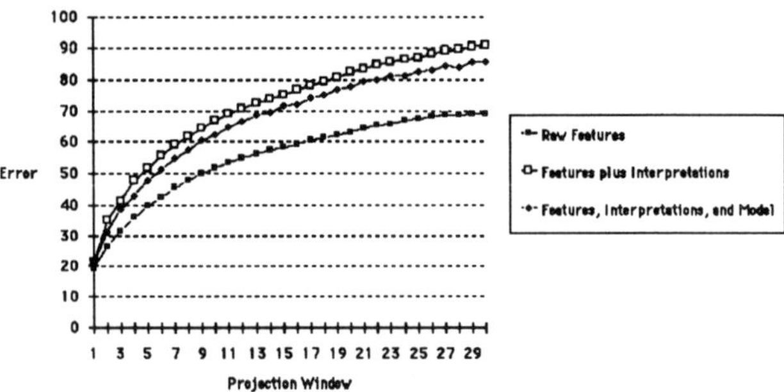

Figure 1: Error VS. Projection Window for Systems with and without Domain Knowledge

based on Cartesian, deictic, and landmark reference systems (Miller & Johnson-Laird 1976). Automatically deriving new representations is similar to constructive induction (Callan & Utgoff 1991). The effect of these new, derived representations is two-fold. On the positive side, it reduces the *hypothesis space bias*, defined as being a component of inductive bias that defines the space of hypotheses that are being searched (Buntine 1990). On the negative side, since the number of possible discriminations is drastically increased, the chance of beta error (accepting a discrimination as statistically significant because the confidence interval is too loose) is also increased. This can actually decrease the overall performance of the system (Almuallim & Dietterich 1991).

The second source of domain knowledge is a simple model of qualitative influences between fields (or *qualitative model* (Kuipers 1986)). The system uses such a model in conjunction with the inductive algorithm described in Section as follows: 1). the system determines the set of fields that are directly relevant to the outcome field using the qualitative model. 2). This subset of fields is used as the set of initial match fields by the inductive algorithm. The inductive algorithm terminates when it is unable to add any more discriminations that are statistically significant, based on these match fields. 3). The system determines the set of fields that are directly relevant to the previous set of match fields. Another pass of induction is performed. 4). The system continues to expand the set of match fields and perform additional induction phases until no new match fields can be added. At that point, a final pass of induction is performed with all available match fields.

Hence, the model is used to create an *application-specific bias* (Buntine 1990). There is some similarity between this technique and the use of primary and secondary features for indexing cases in Explanation Based Indexing (Barletta & Mark 1988).

Results

Figure 1 shows the effect of the projection window (or how far the system projects into the future) on the error rate for projection. The data points in the chart were generated as follows:

- Three projectors were built using 16K cases from observation of two reactive agents battling each other in the combat simulation. The trend labeled "Raw Features" was built with only raw fields (164 different fields) and first and second discrete derivatives used as match fields (for a total of around 500 fields). The trend labeled "Features plus Interpretations" was built using interpretations as well as raw case fields (for a total of around 2000 fields). The trend labeled "Features, Interpretations, and Model" was built using both interpretations and a simple qualitative model of the domain.

- One at a time, each projector was integrated with the combat simulation. Whenever a combat situation was detected, the system would begin projecting. These projections were saved. At the next time step, the actual state of the world was compared to the previously projected states of the world. For each of the 164 fields describing the current situation, the sum of the absolute value of the difference between the actual and projected situations was calculated. For each of the three projectors, 1,000 simulations were observed, amounting to approximately 50,000 comparisons for each graphed point.

- The maximum mean error for each field over the entire projection window was found. The corresponding field values for each of the error logs was then normalized by dividing the actual error over the maximum error. Hence, all errors for each field were normalized to the interval [0..1]. This was done so that the composite error for the projector overall would not be dominated by individual fields where the range of projection was much larger than other fields. For example, the value of a distance field could be anywhere from 0 to 4000, whereas the value of a pain field might only be in the range of 0 to 4.

- the datapoints in the trends are the sum of the normalized error rates for all of the fields in the projector. Hence, the maximum possible error rate is 164.

Note that the error rate forms a kneed-over curve with respect to the projection window. This is because as the system projects farther and farther, more and more of its projections become no better than a guess based on the *a priori* distribution of values in the set of cases. As more and more of these projections "top off," the sum of their errors becomes a kneed-over curve.

As shown in Figure 1, the projector built without interpretation or model was the most accurate over all. This result is in keeping with other work (Almuallim & Dietterich 1991). However, as shown in Figure 2, projectors built with interpretations were more accurate for complex or difficult to explain features. Figure 2 shows the results of projecting the angle of movement

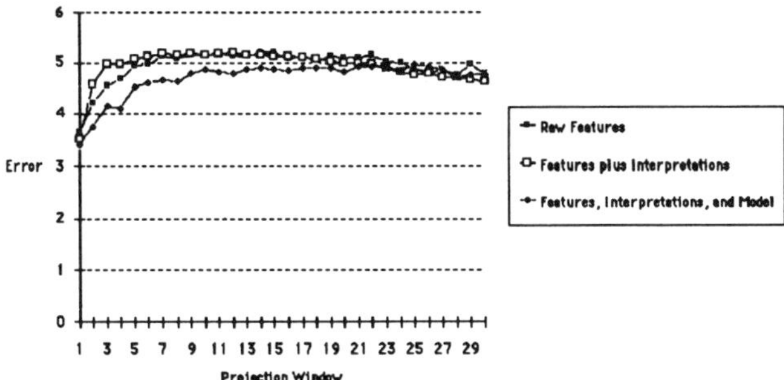

Figure 2: Error VS. Projection Window on a Complex Concept for Systems with and without Domain Knowledge

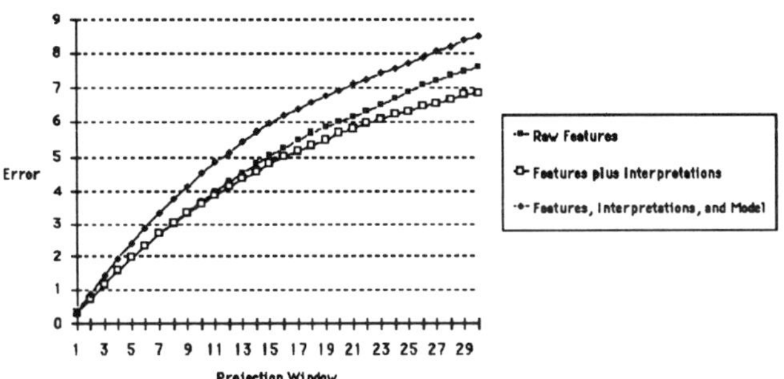

Figure 3: Error VS. Projection Window on a Complex Concept with Inadequate Model

of the agent, opponent, and devices in the simulation (a total of 18 different features). These features are particularly difficult to project accurately, because of interactions between the bodies of the agent and opponent (which may obstruct each other in a variety of complicated ways). Explaining these fields adequately requires the system to make use of higher-level interpretations. Also note that due to the difficulty in projecting this field accurately, the error rate tops off rather quickly.

In both Figure 1 and Figure 2, the accuracy of the projector built with a simple model was greater than the performance of the system with interpretation but without a model. This is because the model helps the system to reduce the effects of compounding errors. Such a situation isn't, however, guaranteed. Figure 3 shows the accuracy of the three projectors on how much pain the agent and opponent will be feeling in the future. Such a projection is very difficult to model directly, because it requires the model to explain when and under what circumstances the axe will come into contact with the agent's body in the future. A complete model would involve virtually every field of the situation description. In this case, allowing the system

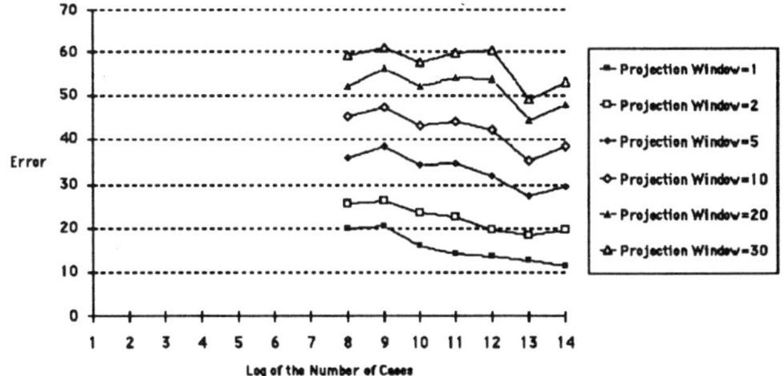

Figure 4: Error VS. Size of Training Set for Different Projection Windows

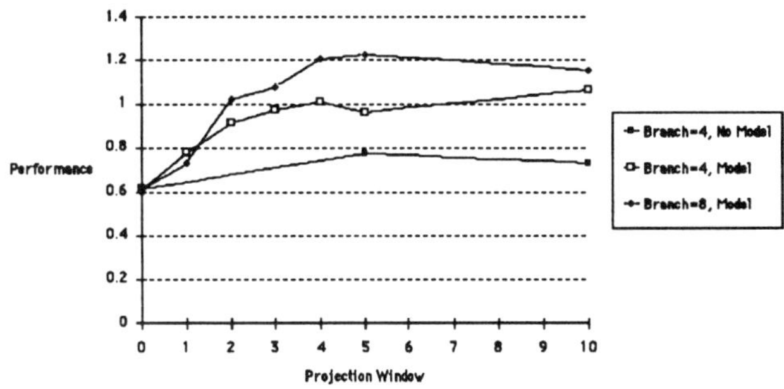

Figure 5: Performance of the Agent VS. Projection Window

to select its discriminations purely on a statistical basis is more effective than guiding induction with a model.

Figure 4 shows the effect of training set size on error rate for different projection windows. Separate projectors were built with 256, 512, 1024, ..., 16384 cases (these projectors were built with interpretations, but without a model). Error rates for each projector were generated as above. For small projection windows, the error rate falls roughly linearly in relation to the log of the number of cases in the training set. On the other hand, for larger projection windows, the effects of compounding error in projection (which can be considered a form of noise) grow to dominate the accuracy of the system. This supports the importance of reducing the effect of compounding error by using a model of the domain.

Figure 5 shows the effect of projection on one facet of the performance of the agent, namely how much damage the agent is able to inflict on its opponent in each game. These trends were generated as follows:

- The *branching factor* defines how many randomly generated patterns of control signals were evaluated (see (Goodman 1993) for a discussion of generating more accurate control signals using *action generators*). So, for a branch factor of 4, four different patterns of control signals are randomly generated, evaluated, and selected from.

- For each pattern of control signals, the system projects forward k steps.
- An evaluation of the projected situation k steps in the future is performed. For these tests, the simple difference between the sum of the damage to different parts of the agents body and the sum of the damage to the opponent's body was computed.
- The pattern of control signals with the best evaluation was determined and executed.
- At the end of the simulation, the total amount of damage to the agent's and opponent's bodies were logged. The mean values of the damage to the opponent's body are shown in the graph.

Three trends were generated. The first trend, "branch=4, no model" was generated using a projector without either a model or interpretations. The second trend, "branch=4, model" was generated using a projector built with both interpretations and a simple qualitative model, using a branch factor of 4. The third trend, "branch=8, model" was generated using the same projector as the previous trend, but with a branch factor of 8.

Note that a projection window of 0 will result in the system evaluating all patterns of control signals as being identically effective. Hence, with a projection window of 0, the system is acting completely randomly. The significant result shown in this graph is that projection does, in fact, help the system to perform more effectively, even when this projection is imperfect. Also note that the performance of the system continues to increase as the system projects farther into the future, until around 5 steps into the future where the performance levels off. This increase in performance is in spite of the compounding error shown in Figure 1.

The performance of the system with a projector that was built using both interpretations and a model was significantly higher than the performance of the system without such domain knowledge. This may seem surprising, given Figure 1 which shows that the projector without domain knowledge was more accurate overall. However, most of the fields that are most directly relevant to controlling action, such as projecting damage, rely heavily on such domain knowledge.

Figure 5 also shows that the performance of the system can be significantly increased by increasing the branching factor. Such a result, while not surprising, is good support for the usefulness of projection in selecting among actions. It also reaffirms the need for high-quality action generation (Goodman 1993).

Conclusions

This paper has demonstrated that it is possible to build systems that can project situations into the future using previous experience. It has also demonstrated that the usefulness of such projections may be increased through the judicious use of domain knowledge (specifically interpretations of raw data and simple qualitative models). Finally, it has shown that projection, even imperfect projection, can be used to improve the performance of an agent taking action in the world.

References

Almuallim, H., and Dietterich, T. 1991. Learning with many irrelevant features. In *Proceedings of the Ninth National Conference on Artificial Intelligence*.

Barletta, R., and Mark, W. 1988. Explanation based indexing of cases. In *Proceedings of the First DARPA Workshop on Case-Based Reasoning*.

Brieman, L.; Friedman, J.; Olshen, R.; and Stone, C. 1984. *Classification and Regression Trees*. Wadsworth.

Buntine, W. 1990. Myths and legends in learning classification rules. In *Proceedings of the Eighth National Conference on Artificial Intelligence*.

Callan, J., and Utgoff, P. 1991. Constructive induction on domain information. In *Proceedings of the Ninth National Conference on Artificial Intelligence*.

Fayyad, U., and Irani, K. 1990. What should be minimized in a decision tree? In *Proceedings of the Eighth National Conference on Artificial Intelligence*.

Forbus, K. D., and Falkenhainer, B. 1990. Self-Explanatory Simulations: An integration of qualitative and quantitative knowledge. In *Proceedings of the 1990 American Association for Artificial Intelligence*, 380–387. Lawrence Erlbaum Associates.

Goodman, M. 1989. CBR In Battle Planning. In *Proceedings the Second DARPA Workshop on Case Based Reasoning*, 312–326.

Goodman, M. 1991. A Case-Based, Inductive Architecture for Natural Language Processing. In *AAAI Spring Symposium on Machine Learning of Natural Language and Ontology*.

Goodman, M. 1993. Projective visualization: Learning to act from experience. In *Proceedings of the Eleventh National Conference on Artificial Intelligence*.

Hartigan, J. 1975. *Clustering Algorithms*. John Wiley and Sons.

Klein, G.; Whitaker, L.; and King, J. 1988. Using Analogues to Predict and Plan. In *Proceedings of the First DARPA Workshop on Case-Based Reasoning*, 250–259.

Kuipers, B. 1986. Qualitative simulation. *Artificial Intelligence* 29:289–338.

Miller, G. A., and Johnson-Laird, P. N. 1976. *Language and Perception*. Cambridge, Massachusetts: The Belknap Press of Harvard University Press.

Quinlan, J. R. 1986. Induction of decision trees. *Machine Learning* 1:81–106.

Rissland, E., and Ashley, K. 1988. Credit Assignment and the Problem of Competing Factors in Case-Based Reasoning. In *Proceedings of the First DARPA Workshop on Case-Based Reasoning*, 250–259.

Learning to Select Useful Landmarks

Russell Greiner
Siemens Corporate Research
Princeton, NJ 08540
greiner@learning.siemens.com

Ramana Isukapalli
Department of Computer Science
Rutgers University
ramana@cs.rutgers.edu

Abstract

To navigate effectively, an autonomous agent must be
able to quickly and accurately determine its current
location. Given an initial estimate of its position (perhaps based on dead-reckoning) and an image taken of
a known environment, our agent first attempts to locate a set of landmarks (real-world objects at known
locations), then uses their angular separation to obtain an improved estimate of its current position. Unfortunately, some landmarks may not be visible, or
worse, may be confused with other landmarks, resulting in both time wasted in searching for invisible landmarks, and in further errors in the agent's estimate of
its position. To address these problems, we propose a
method that uses previous experiences to learn a selection function that, given the set of landmarks that
might be visible, returns the subset which can reliably
be found correctly, and so provide an accurate registration of the agent's position. We use statistical techniques to prove that the learned selection function is,
with high probability, effectively at a local optimal in
the space of such functions. This report also presents
empirical evidence, using real-world data, that demonstrate the effectiveness of our approach.

1. Introduction

To navigate effectively, an autonomous agent R must
be able to quickly and accurately determine its current location. R can obtain fairly accurate estimates
of its position using dead-reckoning; unfortunately, the
errors in these estimates accumulate over long distances, which can lead to unacceptable performance
(read "bumping into walls" or "locating the wrong office"). An obvious way to reduce this problem is to
observe the environment, and use the information in
these observations to improve our estimate of R's position; $cf.$, the work using Kalman filters (Kosaka &
Kak 1992; Cox & Wilfong 1990) and other techniques
(Smith & Cheeseman 1987; Kuipers & Levitt 1988;
Fennema et $al.$ 1990; Engelson 1992) We will model the
environment using only a set of "landmarks", each a
(potentially visible) real-world object at a known location; these objects could be doors, corners and pictures
when specifying the hallways within building, or major

buildings, junctions and prominent signs when specifying the streets within a city.[1] Given an initial estimate of its position (perhaps based on dead-reckoning)
and an image taken of a known environment, R can
first attempt to locate a set of possibly visible landmarks, then use their angular separation to obtain an
improved estimate of its current position.

Landmark-based position estimation is a popular
technique in robot navigation (Case 1986; Sugihara
1988; 1987; Levitt & Lawton 1990). Many of these
landmark-based methods assume that all landmarks
can be found reliably. Unfortunately, some landmarks
may not be visible; for example, certain corners may
always be in shadow and so are difficult to see, or
some hanging pictures may have been removed after
the floor-plan was released. These can force R to waste
time, searching in vain for invisible landmarks. Worse,
some landmarks may be easily confused with others;
$e.g.$, door A may be mistaken for door B, or some landmark A (say the convex corner of two walls) may be
occluded by another object B (say the convex corner
of filing cabinet) that looks sufficiently similar that R
might think that B is A. As this can cause R to believe
that A is located at B's position, these mis-identified
objects can produce further errors in R's estimate of
its position.[2]

It therefore makes sense to search for only the subset
of the potentially visible landmarks that can be found

---

[1] Notice this information is essentially the same as the
information required for the navigation task itself, to specify the destination or some required intermediate points.
$N.b.$, we assume that this set of all possible landmarks is
known initially; this contrasts with other systems that also
attempt to learn the set of landmarks from the observations; $cf.$, (Kuipers & Byun 1988) and others.

[2] Another possible complication is that R may identify a
wide landmark correctly, but mistakenly refer to the wrong
position within that landmark. Also, R uses a set of identified landmarks to locate its position; depending on the geometric positions of these landmarks, small errors in landmark location may lead to quite large errors in R's positional estimate. We of course prefer landmarks sets that
provide position estimates that are relatively insensitive to
errors in landmark identification.

reliably, which are not confusable with others, etc. Unfortunately, it can be very difficult to determine this good subset *a priori*, as (1) the landmarks that are good for one set of R-positions can be bad for another; (2) the decision to seek a landmark can depend on many difficult-to-incorporate factors, such as lighting conditions and building shape; and (3) the reliability of a landmark can also depend on unpredictable events; *e.g.*, exactly where R happens to be when it observes its environment, how the building has changed after the floor-plan was finalized, and whether objects (perhaps people) are moving around the area where R is looking. These factors make it difficult, if not impossible, to designate the set of good landmarks ahead of time.

This report presents a way around this problem: Section 2 proposes a method that learns a good "selection function" that, given the set of landmarks that may be visible, returns the subset which can usually be found correctly. We also use statistical techniques to prove that this learned selection function is, with high probability, effectively at a local optimum in the space of such functions. Section 3 then presents empirical results that demonstrate that this algorithm can work effectively. We first close this section by presenting a more precise description of the performance task, showing how R estimates its position:

Specification of Performance Task: At each point, R will have an estimate $\hat{x}$ of its current position x and a measure of the uncertainty (here the covariance matrix). R uses the `LMs( x )` algorithm to specify the subset of the landmarks that *may* be visible from each position x; we assume `LMs( `$\hat{x}$` )` is essentially the same as `LMs( x )`. (*I.e.*, we assume that R's estimate of its position is sufficient to specify a good approximation of the set of possibly appropriate landmarks.) R also uses an algorithm `Locate( `$\hat{x}$`, `$\hat{\sigma}$`, img, lms )` that, given R's estimate of its position $\hat{x}$ and uncertainty $\hat{\sigma}$, an image `img` taken at R's current position and a set of landmarks `lms`, returns a new estimated position (and uncertainty) for R.

To instantiate these processes: In the current RAT-BOT system (Hancock & Judd 1993), the `LMs` process uses a comprehensive "landmark-description" of the environment, which is a complete list of all of the objects in that environment that could be visible, together with their respective positions. This could be based on the floor-plan of a building, which specifies the positions of the building's doors, walls, wall-hangings, etc.; or in another context, it could be a map of the roads of a city, which specifies the locations of the significant buildings, signs, and so forth. The `Locate( `$\hat{x}$`, `$\hat{\sigma}$`, img, lms )` process first attempts to find each landmark $l_i \in$ `lms` within the image `img`; here it uses $\hat{x}$ and $\hat{\sigma}$ to specify where in the image to look for this l_i. It will find a subset of these landmarks, each at some angle (relative to a reference landmark). `Locate` then uses simple geometric reasoning to obtain a set of

new estimates of R's position; perhaps one from each set of three found landmarks (Hancock & Judd 1994), or see (Gurvits & Betke 1994). After removing the obvious outliers, `Locate` returns the centroid of the remaining estimates as its positional-estimate for R, and the variance of these estimates as the measure of uncertainty; see (Hancock & Judd 1993).

As our goal is an *efficient* way of locating R's position, our implementation uses an inexpensive way of finding the set of landmarks based on simple tests on the visual image; *n.b.*, we are not using a general vision system, which would attempt to actually identify specific objects and specify particular qualities from the visual information.[3]

2. Function for Selecting Good Landmarks

While many navigation systems would attempt to locate *all* of the landmarks that might be visible in an image (*i.e.*, the full set returned by `LMs( `$\hat{x}$` )`), we argued above that it may be better to seek only a subset of these landmarks: By avoiding "problematic" landmarks (*e.g.*, ones that tend to be not visible, or confusable), R may be able to obtain an estimate of its location more quickly, and moreover, possibly obtain an estimate that is more accurate.

We therefore want to identify and ignore these bad landmarks. We motivate our approach by first presenting two false leads: One immediate suggestion is to simply exclude the bad landmarks from the catalogue of all landmarks that `LMs` uses, meaning `LMs(·)` will never return certain landmarks. One obvious complication is the complexity of determining which landmarks are bad, as this can depend on many factors, including the color of the landmark, the overall arrangement of the entire environment (which would specify which landmarks could be occluded), the lighting conditions, etc. A more serious problem is the fact that a landmark that is hard to see from one R position may be easy to see, and perhaps invaluable, from another; here, R should be able to use that landmark when registering its location from some positions, but not from others.

We therefore decided to use, instead, a selection function Sel that filters out the bad landmarks from the set of possibly visible landmarks, `lms = LMs( `$\hat{x}$` )`: Here, each selection function Sel_i returns a subset $\text{Sel}_i(\text{lms}, \hat{x}, \hat{\sigma}) = \text{lms}_i \subseteq \text{lms}$; R then uses this subset to compute its location, returning `Locate( `$\hat{x}$`, `$\hat{\sigma}$`, img, `lms_i` )`. We want to use a selection function Sel_i such that `Locate( `$\hat{x}$`, `$\hat{\sigma}$`, img, `lms_i` )` is reliably close to R's true position, x. To make this

---

[3] Figure 3 shows, and describes, the actual "images" we use. Also, this articles does not provide pseudo-code for either `LMs` or `Locate`, as our learning algorithm regards these process as black-boxes.

more precise, let

$$\text{Err}(\text{Sel}_i, \langle \mathbf{x}, \hat{\mathbf{x}}, \hat{\sigma}, \text{img} \rangle) =$$
$$\| \mathbf{x} - \text{Locate}(\hat{\mathbf{x}}, \hat{\sigma}, \text{img}, \text{Sel}_i(\text{LMs}(\hat{\mathbf{x}}), \hat{\mathbf{x}}, \hat{\sigma})) \|$$

be the error[4] for the selection function Sel_i and any "situation" $\langle \mathbf{x}, \hat{\mathbf{x}}, \hat{\sigma}, \text{img} \rangle$, and let

$$\text{AveErr}(\text{Sel}_i) =$$
$$E_{\langle \mathbf{x}, \hat{\mathbf{x}}, \hat{\sigma}, \text{img} \rangle}[\text{Err}(\text{Sel}_i, \langle \mathbf{x}, \hat{\mathbf{x}}, \hat{\sigma}, \text{img} \rangle)]$$

be the expected error, over the distribution of situations $\langle \mathbf{x}, \hat{\mathbf{x}}, \hat{\sigma}, \text{img} \rangle$, where $E[\cdot]$ is the expectation operator. Our goal is a selection function Sel_{opt} that minimizes this expected value, over the set of possible selection functions.

The second false lead involves "engineering" this optimal selection function initially. One problem, as observed above, is the difficulty of determining "analytically" which landmarks are going to be problematic for any single situation. Worse, recall that our goal is to find the selection function that works best *over the distribution of situations*; which depends on the distribution of R's actual positions when the function is called, the actual intensity of light sources, what other objects have been moved where, etc. Unfortunately, this distribution of situations is not known *a priori*.

We are therefore following a third (successful) approach: of *learning* a good selection function. Here, we first specify a large (and we hope, comprehensive) class of possible selection functions $\mathcal{S} = \{\text{Sel}_i\}$. Then, given "labeled samples" — each consisting of R's position and uncertainty estimates, the relevant landmark-set and image, and as the label, R's actual position — identify the selection function Sel_i which minimizes $\text{AveErr}(\text{Sel}_i)$.

Space of Selection Function: We define each selection function $\text{Sel}_k \in \mathcal{S}$ as a conjunction of its particular set of "heuristics" or "filters"; $\text{Filters}(\text{Select}_k) = \{f_1, \ldots, f_m\}$, where each filter f_i is a predicate that accepts some landmarks and rejects others. Hence, the `Select`$_k$(`lms`, $\hat{\mathbf{x}}$, $\hat{\sigma}$) procedure will examine each $\ell \in$ `lms` individually, and reject it if *any* f_i filter rejects it; see Figure 1.

While we can define a large set of such filters, this report focuses on only two parameterized filters:

$$\text{BadType}_{K_3}(\ell, \hat{\mathbf{x}}, \hat{\sigma}): \quad \text{Reject } \ell \text{ if Type}(\ell) \notin K_3$$

$$\text{TooSmall}_{k_1, k_2}(\ell, \hat{\mathbf{x}}, \hat{\sigma}): \text{Reject } \ell \text{ if } \|\text{Posn}(\ell) - \hat{\mathbf{x}}\| > k_1$$
$$\text{and AngleWidth}(\ell, \hat{\mathbf{x}}) < k_2$$

---

[4] As we are also considering the efficiency of the overall process, we will actually use the slightly more complicated error function presented in Section 3 below. This is also why we did not address the landmark-selection task using robust analysis: Under that approach, our system would first spend time and resources seeking each landmark, and would then decide whether to use each possible correspondence. As our approach, instead, specifies which landmarks should be sought, we will gather less data, and so expend fewer resources.

```
Sel_j( lms: landmarks, x̂: pos'n, σ̂: var.): landmarks
  OK_LMs ← {}
  ForEach ℓ ∈ lms
    KeepLM ← T
    ForEach f_i ∈ Filters( Sel_j )
     If [ f_i(ℓ, x̂, σ̂) ≡ Ignore ]  Then KeepLM ← F
    End (inner) ForEach
    If [ KeepLM ≡ T ]    Then OK_LMs  ← OK_LMs + ℓ
  End (outer) ForEach
  Return( OK_LMs )
End Select
```

Figure 1: PseudoCode for Sel_j Selection Function

where $\text{Type}(\ell)$ refers to the type of the landmark ℓ, which can be "Door", "BlackStrip", etc.[5] The parameter K_3 specifies the subset of landmark-types that should be used. Using "$\text{Posn}(\ell)$" to refer to ℓ's real-world coördinates and "$\text{AngleWidth}(\ell, \hat{\mathbf{x}})$" to refer to the angle subtended by the landmark ℓ, when viewed from $\hat{\mathbf{x}}$, $\text{TooSmall}_{k_1, k_2}(\ell, \hat{\mathbf{x}}, \hat{\sigma})$ rejects the landmark ℓ if ℓ is both too far away (greater than k_1 meters) and also too small (subtends an angle less than k_2 degrees), from R's estimated position $\hat{\mathbf{x}}$.

Using these filters, $\mathcal{S} = \{\text{Sel}_{k_1, k_2, K_3}\}$ is the set of all selection functions, over a combinatorial class of settings of these three parameters. As stated above, we want to find the best settings of these variables, which minimize the expected error $\text{AveErr}[\text{Sel}_{k_1, k_2, K_3}]$.

Hill-Climbing in Uncertain Space: There are two obvious complications with our task of finding this optimal setting: First, as noted above, the error function depends on the distribution of situations, which is not known initially. Secondly, even if we knew that information, it is still difficult to compute the optimal parameter setting, as the space of options is large and ill-structured (*e.g.*, K_3 is discrete, and there are subtle non-linear effects as we alter k_1 and k_2).

We use a standard hill-climbing approach to address the second problem, based on a set of operators $\mathcal{T} = \{\tau_k\}$ that each map one selection function to another; *i.e.*, for each $s \in \mathcal{S}$, $\tau_k(s) \in \mathcal{S}$ is another selection function. We use the obvious set of operators: τ_1^+ increments the value of k_1 and τ_1^- decrements k_1's value; hence $\tau_1^+(\text{Sel}_{5, 8, \{t1, t3, t7\}}) = \text{Sel}_{6, 8, \{t1, t3, t7\}}$ and $\tau_1^-(\text{Sel}_{5, 8, \{t1, t3, t7\}}) = \text{Sel}_{4, 8, \{t1, t3, t7\}}$. Similarly, τ_2^+ and τ_2^- respectively increment and decrement the k_2 value. There are 9 different τ_3^i operator, each of which "flips" the ith bit of K_3; hence $\tau_3^{t1}(\text{Sel}_{5, 8, \{t1, t3, t7\}}) = \text{Sel}_{5, 8, \{t3, t7\}}$ and $\tau_3^{t8}(\text{Sel}_{5, 8, \{t1, t3, t7\}}) = \text{Sel}_{5, 8, \{t1, t3, t7, t8\}}$.

To address the first problem — *viz.*, that the distribution is unknown — we use a set of observed examples

---

[5] The current system contains nine different types: Miscellaneous, Black_Strip, Concave_Corner, Convex_Corner, Dark_Door, Light_Door, Picture, FireExtinguisher and Support_between_Windows.

LEARNSF(Sel_1 : select_fn, $\epsilon : \Re^+$, $\delta : \Re^+$) : select_fn

 For $j \leftarrow 1..\infty$ **do**

  $\mathcal{T}[\text{Sel}_j] \leftarrow \{\tau_k(\text{Sel}_j)\}_k$

  Take $n \leftarrow m(\frac{\epsilon}{2}, \frac{\delta 6 |\mathcal{T}[\text{Select}_j]|}{j^2 \pi^2})$ samples,

  $\mathcal{U} \leftarrow \{u_1, \ldots, u_n\}$ $[\text{Each } u_i = \langle \mathbf{x}_i, \hat{\mathbf{x}}_i, \hat{\sigma}_i, img_i \rangle \,]$

  If $\exists \text{Sel}' \in \mathcal{T}[\text{Sel}_j]$ such that

   $\hat{E}^{(\mathcal{U})}[\text{Sel}_j] - \hat{E}^{(\mathcal{U})}[\text{Sel}'] \geq \frac{\epsilon}{2}$

  then Let $\text{Sel}_{j+1} \leftarrow \text{Sel}'$

  else $\left[\text{Here}, \forall \text{Sel}', \, \hat{E}^{(\mathcal{U})}[\text{Sel}_j] - \hat{E}^{(\mathcal{U})}[\text{Sel}'] < \frac{\epsilon}{2} \right]$

   Return Sel_j

 End For

End LEARNSF

Figure 2: (Simplified) PseudoCode for LEARNSF

to estimate the relevant information: Let

$$\hat{E}^{(\mathcal{U})}_{k_1,k_2,K_3} = \hat{E}^{(\mathcal{U})}[\text{Err}(\text{Sel}_{k_1,k_2,K_3})]$$
$$= \frac{1}{|\mathcal{U}|} \sum_{u_i \in \mathcal{U}} \text{Err}(\text{Sel}_{k_1,k_2,K_3}, u_i)$$

be the empirical average error of the selection function Sel_{k_1,k_2,K_3} over the set of training samples $\mathcal{U} = \{ \langle \mathbf{x}_i, \hat{\mathbf{x}}_i, \hat{\sigma}_i, img_i \rangle \}_i$, which we assume to be independent and identically distributed. We then use some statistical measure to relate the number of samples seen, to our confidence that $\hat{E}^{(\mathcal{U})}_i$ will be close to the real mean $\mu_i = E_{u_j}[\text{Err}(\text{Sel}_i, u_j)] = \text{AveErr}(\text{Sel}_i)$ value. In particular, we need a function $m(\cdots)$ such that, after $m(\epsilon, \delta)$ samples, we can be at least $1 - \delta$ confident that the empirical average $\hat{E}^{(\mathcal{U})}$ will be within ϵ of the population mean μ; i.e., $|\mathcal{U}| \geq m(\epsilon, \delta) \Rightarrow Pr[\, |\hat{E}^{(\mathcal{U})} - \mu| > \epsilon \,] \leq \delta$. If we can assume that the underlying distribution of error values is close to a normal distribution, then we can use

$$m_{Norm}(\epsilon, \delta) = \left(\frac{\lambda}{\epsilon} z^{-1}\left(1 - \frac{\delta}{2}\right) \right)^2$$

where the $z(p) = \frac{1}{\sqrt{2\pi}} \int_{-\infty}^{p} e^{-\frac{x^2}{2}} dx$ function computes the pth quantile of the standard normal distribution $\mathcal{N}(0, 1)$ (Bickel & Doksum 1977).

The LEARNSF algorithm, sketched in Figure 2,[6] combines the ideas of hill-climbing with statistical sampling: Given an initial selection function $\text{Sel}_1 = \text{Sel}_{k_1,k_2,K_3} \in \mathcal{S}$, and the parameters ϵ and δ, LEARNSF will use a sequence of example situations $\{u_i\}$ to climb from the initial Sel_1 through successive neighboring selection functions $(\text{Sel}_1, \text{Sel}_2, \text{Sel}_3, \ldots)$ until reaching, and returning, a final Sel_m. With high probability, this Sel_m is essentially a local optimum. Moreover, LEARNSF requires relatively few samples for each climb. To state this more precisely:

---

[6] We actually use much more efficient, but more complex, algorithm that, for example, decides whether to climb to a new $\text{Sel}_{j+1} \leftarrow \text{Sel}'$ after observing each image, (rather than a batch of n images); see (Greiner & Isukapalli 1994; Greiner 1994).

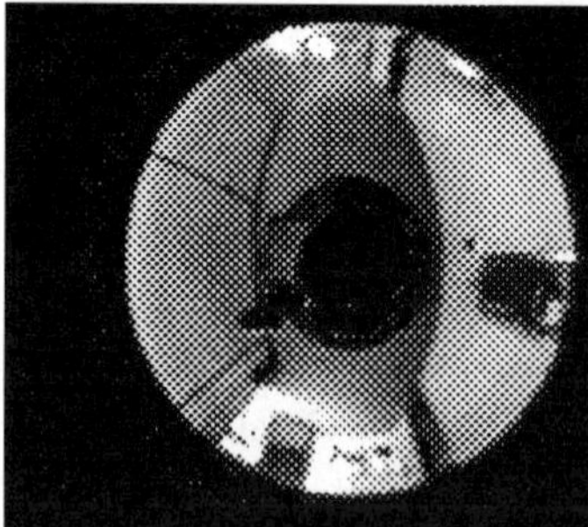
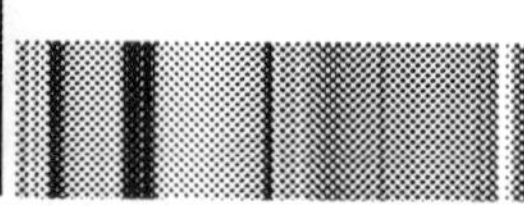

Figure 3: RATBOT's view (looking up at tree ornament), and "strip", corresponding to annulus in image

Theorem 1 (from (Greiner & Isukapalli 1994))
The LEARNSF(Sel_1, ϵ, δ) *process incrementally produces a series of selection functions* $\text{Sel}_1, \text{Sel}_2, \ldots, \text{Sel}_m$, *such that each* $\text{Sel}_{j+1} = \tau_j(\text{Sel}_j)$ *for some* $\tau_j \in \mathcal{T}$ *and, with probability at least* $1 - \delta$,

1. the expected error of each selection function is strictly better than its predecessors i.e.,
$$\forall 2 \leq j \leq m: \quad \text{AveErr}(\text{Sel}_{j-1}) < \text{AveErr}(\text{Sel}_j); \quad and$$

2. the final selection function (returned by LEARNSF*), Sel_m, is an "ϵ-local optimum" — i.e.,*
$$\neg \exists \tau \in \mathcal{T}: \text{AveErr}(\tau(\text{Sel}_m)) < \text{AveErr}(\text{Sel}_m) - \epsilon.$$

given the statistical assumption that the underlying distribution is essentially normal. Moreover, LEARNSF *will terminate with probability 1, and will stay at any* Sel_j *(before either terminating or climbing to a new* Sel_{j+1}*) for a number of samples that is polynomial in* $\frac{1}{\epsilon}$, $\frac{1}{\delta}$, $|\mathcal{T}|$ *and* $\lambda = \max_{\tau \in \mathcal{T}, \, \text{Sel} \in \mathcal{S}, u} |\text{Err}(\text{Sel}, u) - \text{Err}(\tau(\text{Sel}), u)|$, *which is the largest difference in error between a pair of neighboring selection functions for any sample.* □

3. Empirical Results

To test the theoretical claims that a good selection function can help an autonomous agent to register its position efficiently and accurately, and also that LEARNSF can help find such good selection functions, we implemented various selection functions and the LEARNSF learning algorithm, and incorporated them within the implemented autonomous agent, RATBOT, described in (Hancock & Judd 1993). This section describes our empirical results.

We first took a set of 270 "pictures" at known locations within three halls of our building. Each of these pictures is simply an array of 360 intensity values, each corresponding to the intensity at a particular angle, in a plane parallel to the floor; these are shown on right-hand side of Figure 3.[7] We have also identified 157 different landmarks in these regions, each represented as

---

[7] These were obtained using a "NOMAD 200" robot with a CCD camera mounted on top, pointing up at a spherical mirror (which is actually a christmas tree ornament); see left-hand side of Figure 3. We then extract from this image a 1-pixel annulus, which corresponds to the light intensity at a certain height; see right-hand side of Figure 3.

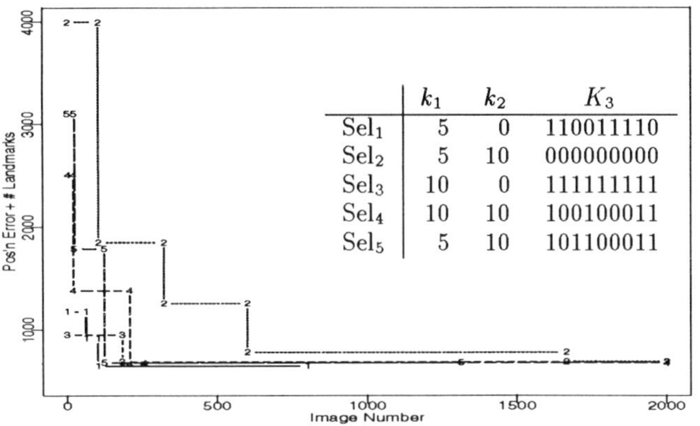

Figure 4: LEARNSF's Hill-Climbs, for different initial Selection Functions

	k_1	k_2	K_3
Sel$_1$	5	0	110011110
Sel$_2$	5	10	000000000
Sel$_3$	10	0	111111111
Sel$_4$	10	10	100100011
Sel$_5$	5	10	101100011

simply an object of a specified type (one of the nine categories), located between a pair of coördinates $\langle x_1, y_1 \rangle$ and $\langle x_2, y_2 \rangle$; where, once again, this $\langle x, y \rangle$ plane is parallel to the floor and goes through the center of the bulb.

Each experiment used a particular initial selection function, error function, values for ϵ and δ, way of estimating R's position, and statistical assumption. We first describe one experiment in detail, then discuss a battery of other experiments that systematically vary the experimental parameters.

Experiment#1 Specification: LEARNSF began with the Sel$_1$ selection function shown in Figure 4. This function rejects a landmark if either it is more than 5 meters away from our estimated position and also subtends an angle less than 0 degrees,[8] or if the landmark's type is one of Concave_Corner, Convex_Corner, or Support_between_Windows (these are the second, third and ninth types, corresponding to the bits that are 0 in the Sel$_1$ row of Figure 4). We used $\delta = 0.05$, meaning that we would be willing to accept roughly 1 mistake in 20 runs. The $\epsilon = 0.1$ setting means that we do not care if the average error of two selection functions differs by less than 0.1m; as we allowed errors as large as 4m, this corresponds to an allowable tolerance of only 2.5%.

As our goal is to minimize both positional error and computational time, we use an error function that is the weighted sum of the positional error (which is the difference between the obtained estimated position and the real position) and "#landmarks–to–pos'n-error ratio" times the number of landmarks that were selected. Here, we set the ratio to 0.01, to mean, in effect, that each additional landmark "costs" 0.01m.

Finally, while *we* know that image img$_i$ is taken at location $\mathbf{x}_i$, it unrealistic to assume that RATBOT will know that information; in general, we assume that RATBOT will instead see an approximate $\hat{\mathbf{x}}_i$. We

---

Sample #	Selection Function	$E[$ LM-Err $]$
0	Sel$_1$ = $\langle \langle 5, 0 \rangle; [110011110] \rangle$	1.171
62	Sel$_{1:1}$ = $\langle \langle 5, 0 \rangle; [110111110] \rangle$	0.916
102	Sel$_{1:2}$ = $\langle \langle 5, 2 \rangle; [110111110] \rangle$	0.647

Table 1: Data for LEARNSF's Climbs from Sel$_1$

model this by setting $\hat{x}_i = x_i + \nu_i^{(\sigma)}$, where each $\nu_i^{(\sigma)}$ is a normally-distributed random value with mean zero and variance σ. Here, we used $\sigma = 0.3$m. Recall also that the `Locate` function needs a value for $\hat{\sigma}$ to constrain its landmark-location process; we also set $\hat{\sigma}$ to be σ.

Experiment#1 Results: Given these settings, LEARNSF observed 62 labeled samples before climbing to the new selection function Sel$_{1:1}$ = $\langle \langle 5, 0 \rangle; [110111110] \rangle$, which differs from Sel$_1$ only by *not* rejecting all `Convex_Corners`.[9] It continued using this selection function for 40 additional samples, before climbing to the Sel$_{1:2}$ = $\langle \langle 5, 2 \rangle; [110111110] \rangle$ selection function, which rejects landmarks that are both more than 5m from R's estimated position and also less than 2°. It continued using this Sel$_{1:2}$ function for another 700 samples before LEARNSF terminated, declaring this selection function to be a "0.1-local optimum" — *i.e.*, none of Sel$_{1:2}$'s neighbors has a utility score that is more than $\epsilon = 0.1$ better than Sel$_{1:2}$. (We found, in fact, that Sel$_{1:2}$ is actually a *bona fide* local optimum, in that none of its neighbors is even as good as it is.)

The solid line (labeled "1") in Figure 4 shows LEARNSF's performance here. Each horizontal line-segment corresponds to a particular selection function, where the line's y-value indicates the "average test error" of its selection function, which was computed by running this selection function through all 270 images.[10] These horizontal lines are connected by vertical lines whose x-value specify the sample number when LEARNSF climbed. Table 1 presents a more detailed break-down of this data.

Other Variants: Our choice of Sel$_1$ = $\langle \langle 5, 0 \rangle; [110111110] \rangle$ was fairly arbitrary; we also considered the four other reasonable starting selection functions shown in Figure 4. Notice that Sel$_2$ = $\langle \langle 5, 10 \rangle; [000000000] \rangle$ rejects *every* landmark; and Sel$_3$ = $\langle \langle 5, 0 \rangle; [111111111] \rangle$ accepts *every* landmark. Figure 4 also graphs the performance of these functions. Notice that LEARNSF finds improvements in all five cases.

We also systematically varied the other parameters: trying values of $\epsilon = 1.0, 0.2, 0.1, 0.05, 0.02, 0.01, 0.005$; $\delta = 0.005, 0.01, 0.05, 0.1$; $\sigma =$

---

[8] As nothing can subtend an angle strictly less than 0°, this first clause is a no-op — *i.e.*, it will not reject *any* landmark.

[9] Sel$_{i:j}$ refers to the selection function reached after j climbs, when starting from Sel$_i$. Hence, Sel$_{i:0} \equiv$ Sel$_i$.

[10] To avoid testing on the training data, we computed this value using a *new* set of randomly-generated positional estimates, $\{\hat{x}_i' = x_i + \nu_i^{(\sigma)\prime}\}$, where again $\nu_i^{(\sigma)\prime}$ is a random variable drawn from a 0-mean σ-variance distribution.

0, 0.3, 0.5, 1.0; and the "#landmark–to–pos'n–error ratio" of 0, 0.02, 0.05, 0.1, 0.2. (The 0 setting tells LEARNSF to consider only the accuracy of a landmark set, and not the cost of finding those landmarks.) We also used LEARNSF$_{HI}$, a variant of LEARNSF that replaces the $m_{Norm}(\cdot)$ function with the weaker

$$m_{HI}(\epsilon, \delta) \;=\; \tfrac{1}{2}\left(\tfrac{\lambda}{\epsilon}\right)^2 \ln \tfrac{2}{\delta}$$

function, which is based on Hoeffding's inequality (Hoeffding 1963; Chernoff 1952), and so does *not* require the assumption that the error values are normally distributed. All of these results are reported, in detail, in (Greiner & Isukapalli 1994).

Summary of Empirical Results: The first obvious conclusion is that selection functions are useful; notice in particular that the landmarks they returned enabled R to obtain fairly good positional estimates — within a few tenths of a meter. Notice also that the obvious degenerate selection function, Sel$_3$ which accepted all landmarks, was *not* optimal; *i.e.*, there were functions that worked more effectively. Secondly, this LEARNSF function works effectively, as it was able to climb to successively better selection functions, in a wide variety of situations. Not surprisingly, we found that the most critical parameter was the initial selection function; the values of ϵ, δ, σ and even the "#landmark–to–pos'n–error ratio" had relatively little effect. We also found that this LEARNSF$_{Norm}$ system seemed to work more effectively than the version that did not require the normality assumption, LEARNSF$_{HI}$: in almost all instances, both systems climbed through essentially the same selection functions, but LEARNSF$_{Norm}$ required many fewer samples — by a factor of between 10 and 100! (In the numerous different runs that used $\delta = 0.05$, LEARNSF$_{Norm}$ climbed a total of 84 times and terminated 24 times, and so had $84 + 24 = 108$ opportunities to make a mistake; it made a total of only 3 mistakes, all very minor.) Finally, LEARNSF's behavior was also (surprisingly) insensitive to the accuracy of R's estimated position, over a wide range of errors; *e.g.*, even for non-trivial values of $|x - \hat{x}|$.

4. Conclusion

While there are many techniques that use observed landmarks to identify an agent's position, they all depend on being able to effectively find an appropriate set of landmarks, and will produce degraded or unacceptable information if the landmarks are not found, or mis-identified. We can avoid this problem by using only the subset of "good" landmarks. As it can be very difficult to determine this subset *a priori*, we present an algorithm, LEARNSF, that uses a set of training samples to *learn* a function that selects the appropriate subset of the landmarks, which can then be used robustly to determine our agent's position. We then prove that this algorithm works effectively — both theoretically and empirically, based on real data obtained using an implemented robot.

Acknowledgments

We gratefully acknowledge the help we received from Thomas Hancock, Stephen Judd, Long-Ji Lin, Leonid Gurvits and the other members of the RatBOT team.

References

Bickel, P. J., and Doksum, K. A. 1977. *Mathematical Statistics: Basic Ideas and Selected Topics*. Oakland: Holden-Day, Inc.

Case, M. 1986. Single landmark navigation by mobile robots. In *SPIE*, volume 727, 231–38.

Chernoff, H. 1952. A measure of asymptotic efficiency for tests of a hypothesis based on the sums of observations. *Annals of Mathematical Statistics* 23:493–507.

Cox, I., and Wilfong, G., eds. 1990. *Autonomous Robot Vehicles*. Springer-Verlag.

Engelson, S. P. 1992. Active place recognition using image signatures. In *SPIE Symposium on Intelligent Robotic Systems, Sensor Fusion V*, 393–404.

Fennema, C.; Hanson, A.; Riseman, E.; Beveridge, J.; and Kumar, R. 1990. Model-directed mobile robot navigation. *IEEE Transactions on Systems, Man and Cybernetics* 20(6):1352–69.

Greiner, R., and Isukapalli, R. 1994. Learning to select useful landmarks. Technical Report SCR-LS94-473.

Greiner, R. 1994. Probabilistic hill-climbing: Theory and applications. Technical report, SCR.

Gurvits, L., and Betke, M. 1994. Robot navigation using landmarks. Technical Report SCR-94-TR-474, SCR/MIT.

Hancock, T., and Judd, S. 1993. Ratbot: Robot navigation using simple visual algorithms. In *1993 IEEE Regional Conference on Control Systems*.

Hancock, T., and Judd, S. 1994. Hallway navigation using simple visual correspondence algorithms. Technical Report SCR-94-TR-479, SCR.

Hoeffding, W. 1963. Probability inequalities for sums of bounded random variables. *Journal of the American Statistical Association* 58(301):13–30.

Kosaka, A., and Kak, A. C. 1992. Fast vision-guided mobile robot navigation using model-based reasoning and prediction of uncertainties. *Computer Vision, Graphics, and Image Processing* 56(3):271–329.

Kuipers, B. J., and Byun, Y.-T. 1988. A robust, qualitative method for robot spatial learning. In *AAAI-88*, 774–79.

Kuipers, B. J., and Levitt, T. S. 1988. Navigation and mapping in large-scale space. *AI Magazine* 9(2):25–43.

Levitt, T. S., and Lawton, D. T. 1990. Qualitative navigation for mobile robots. *Artificial Intelligence* 44:305–60.

Smith, R., and Cheeseman, P. 1987. On the representation and estimation of spatial uncertainty. *International Journal of Robotics Research* 5(4):56–68.

Sugihara, K. 1987. Location of a robot using sparse visual information. *Robotics Research: The Fourth International Symposium*, 319–26. MIT Press.

Sugihara, K. 1988. Some location problems for robot navigation using a single camera. *Computer Vision, Graphics and Image Processing* 42(1):112–29.

Agents that Learn to Explain Themselves

W. Lewis Johnson
USC / Information Sciences Institute
4676 Admiralty Way
Marina del Rey, CA 90292-6695
johnson@isi.edu

Abstract

Intelligent artificial agents need to be able to explain and justify their actions. They must therefore understand the rationales for their own actions. This paper describes a technique for acquiring this understanding, implemented in a multimedia explanation system. The system determines the motivation for a decision by recalling the situation in which the decision was made, and replaying the decision under variants of the original situation. Through experimentation the agent is able to discover what factors led to the decisions, and what alternatives might have been chosen had the situation been slightly different. The agent learns to recognize similar situations where the same decision would be made for the same reasons. This approach is implemented in an artificial fighter pilot that can explain the motivations for its actions, situation assessments, and beliefs.

Introduction

Intelligent artificial agents need to be able to provide explanations and justifications for the actions that they take. This is especially true for computer-generated forces, i.e., computer agents that operate within battlefield simulations. Such simulations are expected to have an increasingly important role in the evaluation of missions, tactics, doctrines, and new weapons systems, and in training (Jones 1993). Validation of such forces is critical—they should behave as humans would in similar circumstances. Yet it is difficult to validate behavior through external observation; behavior depends upon the agent's assessment of the situation and its changing goals from moment to moment. Trainees can greatly benefit from automated forces that can explain their actions, so that the trainees can learn how experts behave in various situations. Potential users of computer-generated forces therefore attach great importance to explanation, just as potential users of computer-based medical consultation systems do (Teach & Shortliffe 1984).

Explanations based on traces of rule firings or paraphrases of rules tend not to be successful (Davis 1976; Swartout & Moore 1993; Clancey 1983b). They contain too many implementation details, and lack information about the domain and about rationales for the design of the system. More advanced explanation techniques encode domain knowledge and problem-solving strategies and employ them in problem solving either as metarules (Clancey 1983a) or in compiled form (Neches, Swartout, & Moore 1985). In the computer-generated forces domain, however, problem-solving strategies and domain knowledge representations are matters of current research. An intelligent agent in such a domain must integrate capabilities of perception, reactive problem solving, planning, plan recognition, learning, geometric reasoning and visualization, among others, all under severe real-time constraints. It is difficult to apply meta-level or compilation approaches in such a way that all of these requirements can be met at once.

This paper describes a system called Debrief that takes a different approach to explanation. Explanations are constructed after the fact by recalling the situation in which a decision was made, reconsidering the decision, and through experimentation determining what factors were critical for the decision. These factors are critical in the sense that if they were not present, the outcome of the decision process would have been different. Details of the agent's implementation, such as which individual rules applied in making the decision, are automatically filtered out. It is not necessary to maintain a complete trace of rule firings in order to produce explanations. The relationships between situational factors and decisions are learned so that they can be applied to similar decisions.

This approach of basing explanations on abstract associations between decisions and situational factors has similarities to the REX system (Wick & Thompson 1989). But while REX requires one to create a separate knowledge base to support explanation, Debrief automatically learns much of what it needs to know to generate explanations. The approach is related to techniques for acquiring domain models through experimentation (Gil 1993), except that the agent learns to model not the external world, but itself.

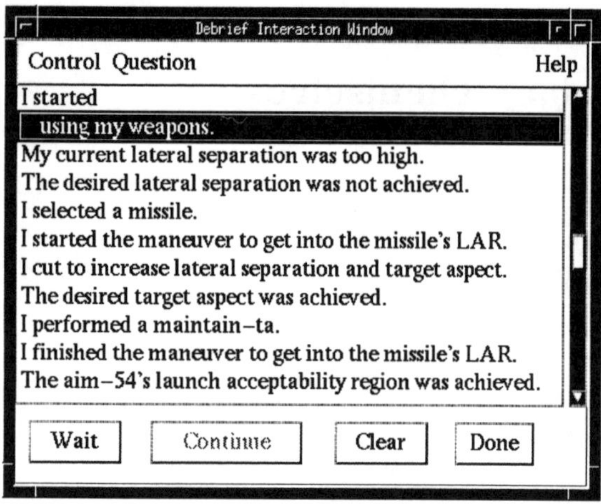

Figure 1: Part of a an event summary

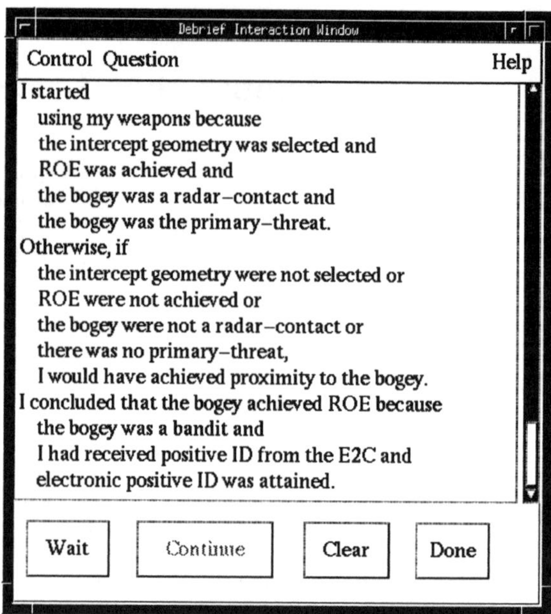

Figure 2: Explanations of the agent's decisions

Debrief is implemented as part of the TacAir-Soar fighter pilot simulation (Jones *et al.* 1993). Debrief can describe and justify decisions using a combination of natural language and diagrams. It is written in a domain-independent fashion so that it can be readily incorporated into other intelligent systems. Current plans call for incorporating it into the REACT system, an intelligent assistant for operators of NASA Deep Space Network ground tracking stations (Hill & Johnson 1994).

An Example

Consider the following scenario. A fighter is assigned a Combat Air Patrol (CAP) mission, i.e., it should fly a loop pattern, scanning for enemy aircraft. During the mission a bogey (an unknown aircraft) is spotted on the radar. The E2C, an aircraft whose purpose is to scan the airspace and provide information to the fighters, confirms that the bogey is hostile. The fighter closes in on the bogey, fires a missile which destroys the bogey, and then resumes its patrol.

After each mission it is customary to debrief the pilot. The pilot is asked to describe the engagement from his perspective, and explain key decisions along the way. The pilot must justify his assessments of the situation, e.g., why the bogey was considered a threat.

TacAir-Soar is able to simulate pilots executing missions such as this, and Debrief is able to answer questions about them. TacAir-Soar controls a simulation environment called ModSAF (Calder *et al.* 1993) that simulates the behavior of military platforms. TacAir-Soar receives information from ModSAF about aircraft status and radar information, and issues commands to fly the simulated aircraft and employ weapons. After an engagement users can interact with Debrief to ask questions about the engagement.

The following is a typical interaction with Debrief.

Questions are entered through a window interface, by selecting a type of question and pointing to the event or assertion that the question refers to. The first question selected is of type Describe-Event, i.e., describe some event that took place during the engagement; the event chosen is the entire mission. Debrief then generates a summary of what took place during the mission. The user is free to select statements in the summary and ask follow-on questions about them.

Figure 1 shows part of a typical mission summary. One of the statements in the summary, "I started using my weapons," has been selected by the user, so that a follow-on question may be asked about it. Figure 2 shows the display at a later point in the dialog, after follow-on questions have been asked. First, a question of type Explain-Action was asked of the decision to employ weapons, i.e., explain why the agent chose to perform this action. The explanation appears in the figure, beginning with the sentence "I started using my weapons because the intercept geometry was selected and..." Debrief also lists an action that it did not take, but might have taken under slightly different circumstances: flying toward the bogey to decrease distance.

One can see that the agent's actions are motivated largely by previous assessments and decisions. The bottom of Figure 2 shows the answer to a follow-on question relating to one of those assessments, namely "ROE was achieved,"[1] Debrief lists the following fac-

---

[1] ROE stands for Rules of Engagement, i.e., the conditions under which the fighter is authorized to engage the enemy.

tors: the bogey was known to be hostile (i.e., a "bandit"), the bogey was identified through electronic means and confirmation of the identification was obtained from the E2C.

In order to answer such questions, Debrief does the following. First, it recalls the events in question and the situations in which the events took place. When summarizing events, it selects information about the intermediate states and subevents that should be presented, selects appropriate media for presentation of this information (the graphical display and/or natural language), and then generates the presentations. To determine what factors in the situation led to the action or conclusion, Debrief invokes the TacAir-Soar problem solver in the recalled situation, and observes what actions the problem solver takes. The situation is then repeatedly and systematically modified, and the effects on the problem solver's decisions are observed. Beliefs are explained by recalling the situation in which the beliefs arose, determining what decisions caused the beliefs to be asserted, and determining what factors were responsible for the decisions.

Implementation Concerns

Debrief is implemented in Soar, a problem-solving architecture that implements a theory of human cognition(Newell 1990). Problems in Soar are represented as goals, and are solved within problem spaces. Each problem space consists of a state, represented as a set of attribute-value pairs, and a set of operators. All processing in Soar, including applying operators, proposing problem spaces, and constructing states, is performed by productions. During problem solving Soar repeatedly selects and applies operators to the state. When Soar is unable to make progress, it creates a new subgoal and problem space to determine how to proceed. Results from these subspaces are saved by Soar's chunking mechanism as new productions, which can be applied to similar situations.

The explanation techniques employed in Debrief are not Soar-specific; however, they do take advantage of certain features of Soar.

- The explicit problem space representation enables Debrief to monitor problem solving when constructing explanations.

- Since Soar applications are implemented in production rules, it is fairly straightforward to add new rules for explanation-related processing.

- Learning enables Debrief to reuse the results of previous explanation processing, and build up knowledge about the application domain.

The current implementation of Debrief consists of thirteen Soar problem spaces. Two are responsible for inputing questions from the user, three recall events and states from memory, four determine the motivations for actions and beliefs, three generate presentations, and one provides top-level control. The follow-ing sections describe the system components involved in determining motivations for decisions and beliefs; other parts of the system are described in (Johnson 1994).

Memory and Recall

In order for Debrief to describe and explain decisions, it must be able to recall the decisions and the situations in which they occurred. In order words, the agent requires an episodic memory. Debrief includes productions and operators that execute during the problem solving process in order to record episodic information, and a problem space called Recall-State that reconstructs states using this episodic information.

The choice of what episodic information to record is determined by a specification of the agent's working memory state. This specification identifies the state attributes that are relevant for explanation, and identifies their properties, e.g., their cardinality and signature, and how the attribute values may change during problem solving. In order to apply Debrief to a new problem solver, it is necessary to supply such a specification for the contents of the problem solver's working memory, and indicate which operators implement decisions what should be explainable. However, it is not necessary to specify how the problem solver uses its working memory in making decisions—that is determined by Debrief automatically.

When the problem solver applies an operator that as marked as explainable, Debrief records the operator application in a list of events that took place during the problem solving. It also records all attribute values that have changed since the last problem solving event that was recorded.

Debrief then builds chunks that associate the state changes with the problem solving event. Once these chunks are built, the state changes can be deleted from working memory, because the chunks are sufficient to enable Debrief to recall the working memory state. During explanation, when Debrief needs to recall the state in which a problem solving event occurred, it invokes the Recall-State problem space. This space reconstructs the state by proposing possible attribute values; the chunks built previously fire, selecting the value that was associated with the event. Recall-State aggregates these values into a copy of the state at the time of the original event, and returns it. This result is chunked as well, enabling Debrief immediately to recall the state associated with the event should it need to refer back to it in the future. This process is an instance of data chunking, a common mechanism for knowledge-level learning in Soar systems (Rosenbloom, Laird, & Newell 1987).

Debrief thus makes extensive use of Soar's long term memory, i.e., chunks, in constructing its episodic memory. In a typical TacAir-Soar run several hundred such chunks are created. This is more economical than simply recording a trace of production firings, since over

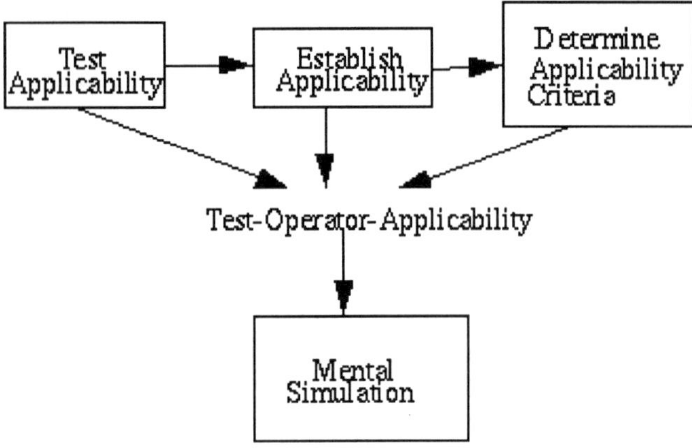

Figure 3: The process of evaluating decisions

6000 productions fire in a typical TacAir-Soar run. Since Soar has been shown be able to handle memories containing hundreds of thousands of chunks (Doorenbos 1993), there should be little difficulty in scaling up to more complex problem solving applications.

Explaining Actions and Conclusions

Suppose that the user requests the motivation for the action "I started using my weapons." Debrief recalls the type of event involved, operator that was applied, the problem space in which it was applied, and the problem solving state. In this case the event type is Start-Event, i.e., the beginning of an operator application, the operator is named Employ-Weapons, and the problem space is named Intercept. The situation was one where the agent had decided to intercept the bogey, and had just decided what path to follow in performing the intercept (called the intercept geometry).

Analysis of recalled events such as this proceeds as shown if Figure 3. The first step, testing applicability, verifies that TacAir-Soar would select an Employ-Weapons operator in the recalled state. An operator called Test-Operator-Applicability performs the verification, by setting up a "mental simulation" of the original decision, and monitoring it to see what operators are selected.

This initial test of operator applicability is important for the following reasons. State changes are not recorded in episodic memory until the operator has already been selected. The operator might therefore modify the state before Debrief has a chance to save it, making the operator inapplicable. This is not a problem in the case of Employ-Weapons, but if it were Debrief would attempt to establish applicability, which involves recalling the state immediately preceding the state of the event, and trying to find an interpolation of the two states in which the operator would be selected. But even when recalling the precise problem solving state is not a problem, verifying applicability

is useful because it causes chunks to be built that facilitate subsequent analysis.

After a state has been found in which the recalled operator is applicable, the next step is to determine applicability criteria, i.e., identify what attributes of the state are responsible for the operator being selected. This also involves applying the Test-Operator-Applicability operator to construct mental simulations.

Mental simulation

Given the problem space Intercept, the recalled state, the operator Employ-Weapons, and the decision Start-event(Employ-Weapons), Test-Operator-Applicability operates as follows. It creates an instance of the Intercept problem space as a subspace, and assigns as its state a copy of the recalled state. The working memory specification described above is helpful here: it determines which attributes have to be copied. This state is marked as a simulation state, which activates a set of productions responsible for monitoring mental simulations. Test-Operator-Applicability copies into the simulation state the event and the category of decision being evaluated. There are three such categories: perceptions, which recognize and register some external stimulus, conclusions, which reason about the situation and draw inferences from it, and actions, which are operations that have some effect on the external world. Employ-Weapons is thus an action. The Intercept problem space is disconnected from external sensors and effectors (the ModSAF simulator), so that mental simulation can be freely performed. Execution then begins in the problem space. The first operator that is selected is Employ-Weapons. The monitoring productions recognize this as the desired operator, return a flag to the parent state indicating that the desired event was observed, and the mental simulation is terminated. If a different operator or event had been selected instead, Debrief would be checked to see if it is of the same category as the expected operator, i.e., another action. If not, simulation is permitted to continue; otherwise simulation is terminated and the a description of the operator that applied instead is returned.

Whenever a result is returned from mental simulation, a chunk is created. Such chunks may then be applicable to other situations, making further mental simulation unnecessary. Figure 4 shows the chunk that is formed when Debrief simulates the selection of the Employ-Weapons operator. The conditions of the chunk appear before the symbol $\rightarrow$ and actions follow. Variables are symbols surrounded by angle brackets, and attributes are preceded by a carat ($\wedge$). The conditions include the expected operator, Employ-Weapons, the problem space, Intercept, and properties of the state, all properties of the bogey. If the operator is found to be inapplicable, a different chunk is produced, that indicates which operator is selected instead of the expected one.

```
(sp chunk-230 :chunk
  (goal <g1> ^operator <o1> ^state <s1>)
  (<o1> ^name test-operator-applicability
        ^expected-operator employ-weapons
        ^expected-step *none*
        ^problem-space intercept)
  (<s1> ^simulated-state <r1>)
  (<r1> ^local-state <l1>)
  (<l1> ^bogey <b1>)
  (<b1> ^intention known-hostile
        ^roe-achieved *yes*
        ^intercept-geometry-selected *yes*
        ^contact *yes*)
  (<l1> ^primary-threat <b1>)
-->
  (<s1> ^applicable-operator employ-weapons))
```

Figure 4: An example chunk

These chunks built during mental simulation have an important feature—they omit the details of how the operator and problem space involved is implemented. This is an inherent feature of the chunking process, which traces the results of problem solving in a problem space back to elements of the supergoal problem space state. In this case the state recalled from episodic memory is the part of the supergoal problem space state, so elements of the recalled state go into the left hand side of the chunk.

Determining the cause for decisions

At this point it would be useful to examine the chunks built during mental simulation in order to proceed to generate the explanation. Unfortunately, productions in a Soar system are not inspectable within Soar. This limitation in the Soar architecture is deliberate, reflecting the difficulty that humans have in introspecting on their own memory processes. It does not a serious problem for Debrief, because the chunks built during mental simulation can be used to recognize which attributes of the state are significant.

The identification of significant attributes is performed in the Determine-Applicability-Criteria problem space, which removes attributes one by one and repeatedly applies Test-Operator-Applicability. If a different operator is selected, then the removed attribute must be significant. If the value of a significant attribute is a complex object, then each attribute of that object is analyzed in the same way; the same is true for any significant values of those attributes. Meanwhile, if the variants resulted in different operators being selected, the applicability criteria for these operators are identified in the same manner. This generate-and-test approach has been used in other Soar systems to enlist recognition chunks in service of problem solving (Vera, Lewis, & Lerch 1993), and is similar to Debrief's mechanism for reconstructing states from episodic memory.

Since the state representations are hierarchically organized, the significant attributes are found quickly.

If chunking were not taking place, Debrief would be performing a long series of mental simulations, most of which would not yield much useful information. But the chunks that are created help to ensure that virtually every mental simulation uncovers a significant attribute, for the following reason. Subgoals are created in Soar only when impasses occur. Test-Operator-Applicability instantiates the mental simulation problem space because it tries to determine whether the recalled operator is applicable, is unable to do so, and reaches an impasse. When chunks such as the one in Figure 4 fire, they assert that the operator is applicable, so no impasse occurs. Mental simulation thus occurs only in situations that fail to match the chunks that have been built so far. In the case of the Employ-Weapons operator, a total of seven mental simulations of variant states are required: two to determine that the bogey is relevant, and five to identify the bogey's relevant attributes.

Furthermore, even these mental simulations become unnecessary as Debrief gains experience explaining missions. Suppose that Debrief is asked to explain a different Employ-Weapons event. Since most of the significant features in the situation of this new event are likely to be similar to the significant features of the previous situation, the chunks built from the previous mental simulations will fire. Mental simulation is required for the situational features that are different, or if the operator was selected for different reasons.

Two kinds of chunks are built when Determine-Applicability-Criteria returns its results. One type identifies all of the significant features in the situation in which the decision was made. The other type identifies an operator that might have applied instead of the expected operator, and the state in which the operator applies. These chunks are created when mental simulation determines that an operator other than the expected one is selected. Importantly, the chunks fire whenever a similar decision is made in a similar situation. By accumulating these chunks Debrief thus builds an abstract model of the application domain, associating decisions with their rationales and alternatives. The problem solver's performance-oriented knowledge is reorganized into a form suited to supporting explanation.

Performing mental simulation in modified states complicates mental simulation in various respects. The result of deleting an attribute is often the selection of an operator in mental simulation to reassert the same attribute. Debrief must therefore monitor the simulation and detect when deleted attributes are being reasserted. The modified state may cause the problem solver to fail, resulting in an impasse. Mental simulation must therefore distinguish impasses that are a normal result of problem solving from impasses that suggest that the problem solver is in an erroneous state.

There is one shortcoming of the analysis technique described here. Chunking in Soar cannot always backtrace through negated conditions in the left hand sides of productions. Therefore if the problem solver opted for a decision because some condition was *absent* in the situation, Debrief may not be able to detect it. Developers of Soar systems get around this problem in chunking by using explicit values such as *unknown* to indicate that information is absent. This same technique enables Debrief to identify the factors involved.

Relationship to other exploratory learning approaches

The closest correlate to Debrief's decision evaluation capability is Gil's work on learning by experimentation (Gil 1993). Gil's EXPO system keeps track of operator applications, and the states in which those operators were applied. If an operator is found to have different effects in different situations, EXPO compares the states to determine the differences. Another system by Scott and Markovich (Scott & Markovich 1993) performs an operation on instances of a class of objects, to determine whether it has different effects on different members of the class. This enables it to discover discriminating characteristics within the class.

Some exploratory learning systems, such as Rajamoney's systems (Rajamoney 1993), invest significant effort to design experiments that provide the maximum amount of information. This is necessary because experiments can be costly and can have persistent effects on the environment. Debrief's chunking-based technique filters out irrelevant experiments automatically, without significant effort. Side events on the environment are not a concern during mental simulation.

Explaining Beliefs

Explaining beliefs, e.g., that ROE was achieved, involves many of the same analysis steps used for explaining decisions. Debrief starts by searching memory for the nearest preceding state in which the belief came to be held. It determines what operator was being applied during that state, and uses Establish-Applicability if necessary to make sure that the operator applies in the recalled state. If the belief had to be retracted in order to make Test-Operator-Applicability succeed, then the operator was responsible for asserting the belief. Such is the case for the belief that ROE is achieved, which is asserted by an operator named ROE-Achieved. Otherwise, Debrief would remove the belief and attempt mental simulation again; if the belief is asserted in the course of applying the operator, the operator is probably responsible for the belief.

Summary of the Effects of Learning

Learning via chunking takes place throughout the Debrief system. The following is a summary of the different types of chunks that are produced:

- Episodic memory recognition chunks: event + attribute value → recognition;

- State recall chunks: event → state;

- Mental simulation chunks: event + problem space + state → applicable or inapplicable + alternative operator;

- Applicability analysis chunks: event + problem space + state → significant state attributes; event + problem space + state → alternative operator + alternative state;

- Natural language generation chunks: case frame → list of words; content description → list of utterances;

- Presentation chunks: content description + user model → utterances + media control commands + user model updates.

The presentation mechanisms that yield the latter two types of chunks are described in (Johnson 1994). Altogether, these chunks enable Debrief to acquire significant facility in explaining problem solving behavior. These chunks result in speedups during the course of explaining a single mission. Future experiments will determine the transfer effects between missions.

Evaluation and Status

The implementation of Debrief comprises over 1700 productions; in a typical session these are augmented by between 500 and 1000 chunks. Debrief currently can describe and/or explain a total of 66 types of events in the tactical air domain. Its natural language generation component has a vocabulary of 259 words and phrases. Debrief can explain a range of one-on-one and one-on-two air-to-air engagements.

Formative evaluations of Debrief explanations have been performed with US Naval Reserve fighter pilots. These evaluations confirmed that explanations are extremely helpful for validating the agent's performance, and building confidence in it. They also underscored the importance of having the agent justify its beliefs—the evaluators frequently wanted to ask questions about assertions made by Debrief during the course of the explanation. This motivated the development of support for the Explain-Belief question type. There was immediate interest on the part of the subject matter experts in using Debrief to understand and validate the behavior of TacAir-Soar agents.

The weakest point of the current system is its natural language generation capability. However, this was found not to be a major concern for the evaluators. Their primary interest was in understanding the thinking processes of TacAir-Soar, and to the extent that Debrief made that reasoning apparent it was considered effective.

Conclusion

This paper has described a domain-independent technique for analyzing the reasoning processes of an intelligent agent in order to support explanation. This technique reduces the need for extensive knowledge acquisition and special architectures in support of explanation. Instead, the agent can construct explanations on its own. Learning plays a crucial role in this process. Next steps include extending the range to questions that can be answered, improving the natural language generation, and making greater use of multi-media presentations. There is interest in using the mental simulation framework described here to improve the agent's problem solving performance, by discovering alternative decision choices with improved outcomes.

Acknowledgements

The author wishes to thank Paul Rosenbloom, Milind Tambe, and Yolanda Gil for their helpful comments. Dr. Johnson was supported in part by the ARPA and the Naval Research Laboratory under contract number N00014-92-K-2015 (via a subcontract from the University of Michigan). Views and conclusions contained in this paper are the author's and should not be interpreted as representing the official opinion or policy of the U.S. Government or any agency thereof.

References

Calder, R.; Smith, J.; Courtemanche, A.; Mar, J.; and Ceranowicz, A. 1993. ModSAF behavior simulation and control. In *Proceedings of the Third Conference on Computer Generated Forces and Behavioral Representation*, 347–359. Orlando, FL: Institute for Simulation and Training, University of Central Florida.

Clancey, W. 1983a. The advantages of abstract control knowledge in expert system design. In *Proceedings of the National Conference on Artificial Intelligence*, 74–78.

Clancey, W. 1983b. The epistemology of a rule-based expert system: A framework for explanation. *Artificial Intelligence* 20(3):215–251.

Davis, R. 1976. *Applications of Meta-Level Knowledge to the Construction, Maintenance, and Use of Large Knowledge Bases*. Ph.D. Dissertation, Stanford University.

Doorenbos, R. 1993. Matching 100,000 learned rules. In *Proceedings of the National Conference on Artificial Intelligence*, 290–296. Menlo Park, CA: AAAI.

Gil, Y. 1993. Efficient domain-independent experimentation. Technical Report ISI/RR-93-337, USC / Information Sciences Institute. Appears in the Proceedings of the Tenth International Conference on Machine Learning.

Hill, R., and Johnson, W. 1994. Situated plan attribution for intelligent tutoring. In *Proceedings of the National Conference on Artificial Intelligence*.

Johnson, W. 1994. Agents that explain their own actions. In *Proc. of the Fourth Conference on Computer Generated Forces and Behavioral Representation*. Orlando, FL: Institute for Simulation and Training, University of Central Florida. World Wide Web access: http://www.isi.edu/soar/debriefable.html.

Jones, R.; Tambe, M.; Laird, J.; and Rosenbloom, P. 1993. Intelligent automated agents for flight training simulators. In *Proceedings of the Third Conference on Computer Generated Forces and Behavioral Representation*, 33–42. Orlando, FL: Institute for Simulation and Training, University of Central Florida.

Jones, R. 1993. Using CGF for analysis and combat development. In *Proceedings of the Third Conference on Computer Generated Forces and Behavioral Representation*, 209–219. Orlando, FL: Institute for Simulation and Training, University of Central Florida.

Neches, R.; Swartout, W.; and Moore, J. 1985. Enhanced maintenance and explanation of expert systems through explicit models of their development. *IEEE Transactions on Software Engineering* SE-11(11):1337–1351.

Newell, A. 1990. *Unified Theories of Cognition*. Cambridge, MA: Harvard University Press.

Rajamoney, S. 1993. The design of discrimination experiments. *Machine Learning* 185–203.

Rosenbloom, P.; Laird, J.; and Newell, A. 1987. Knowledge level learning in Soar. In *Proceedings of the Seventh National Conference on Artificial Intelligence*, 618–623. Menlo Park, CA: American Association for Artificial Intelligence.

Scott, P., and Markovich, S. 1993. Experience selection and problem choice in an exploratory learning system. *Machine Learning* 49–68.

Swartout, W., and Moore, J. 1993. Explanation in second generation expert systems. In David, J.-M.; Krivine, J.-P.; and Simmons., R., eds., *Second Generation Expert Systems*. Springer-Verlag. 543–585.

Teach, R., and Shortliffe, E. 1984. An analysis of physicians' attitudes. In Buchanan, B., and Shortliffe, E., eds., *Rule-Based Expert Systems: The MYCIN Experiments of the Stanford Heuristic Programming Project*. Reading, MA: Addison-Wesley. 635–652.

Vera, A.; Lewis, R.; and Lerch, F. 1993. Situated decision-making and recognition-based learning: Applying symbolic theories to interactive tasks. In *Proceedings of the Fifteenth Annual Conference of the Cognitive Science Society*, 84–95. Hillsdale, NJ: Lawrence Erlbaum Associates.

Wick, M., and Thompson, W. 1989. Reconstructive explanation: Explanation as complex problem solving. In *Proceedings of the Eleventh Intl. Joint Conf. on Artificial Intelligence*, 135–140. San Mateo, CA: Morgan Kaufmann.

Learning to Explore and Build Maps*

David Pierce and Benjamin Kuipers
Department of Computer Sciences
University of Texas at Austin
Austin, TX 78712
dmpierce@cs.utexas.edu, kuipers@cs.utexas.edu

Abstract

Using the methods demonstrated in this paper, a robot with an unknown sensorimotor system can learn sets of features and behaviors adequate to explore a continuous environment and abstract it to a finite-state automaton. The structure of this automaton can then be learned from experience, and constitutes a *cognitive map* of the environment. A generate-and-test method is used to define a hierarchy of features defined on the raw sense vector culminating in a set of continuously differentiable *local state variables*. Control laws based on these local state variables are defined for robustly following paths that implement repeatable state transitions. These state transitions are the basis for a finite-state automaton, a discrete abstraction of the robot's continuous world. A variety of existing methods can learn the structure of the automaton defined by the resulting states and transitions. A simple example of the performance of our implemented system is presented.

Introduction

Imagine that you find yourself in front of the control console for a teleoperated robot (Figure 1). The display at the left of the console is your only sensory input from the robot. The joystick on the right can be used to move the robot through its environment. You do not know how the joystick affects the robot's motion, but you do know that the robot does not move when the joystick is in its zero position. The robot could be a mobile robot in an office building or laboratory or it could be a submarine in the ocean. Your mission is to develop a model of the robot's environment as well as its sensorimotor interface to that environment.

We present a solution to this learning problem by showing how an autonomous agent can learn a discrete model of its continuous world with no *a priori* knowledge of the structure of its world or of its sensorimo-

---

*This work has taken place in the Qualitative Reasoning Group at the Artificial Intelligence Laboratory, The University of Texas at Austin. Research of the Qualitative Reasoning Group is supported in part by NSF grants IRI-8904454, IRI-9017047, and IRI-9216584, and by NASA contracts NCC 2-760 and NAG 9-665.

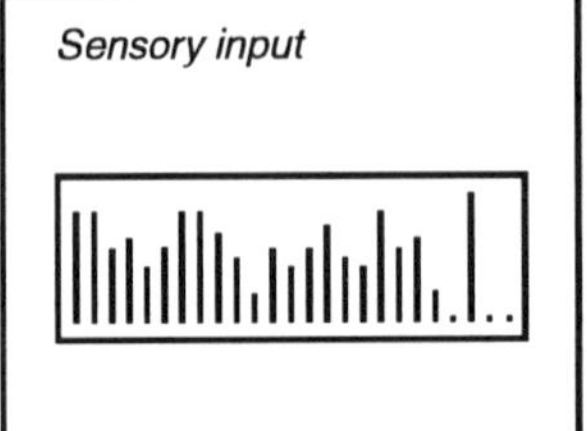
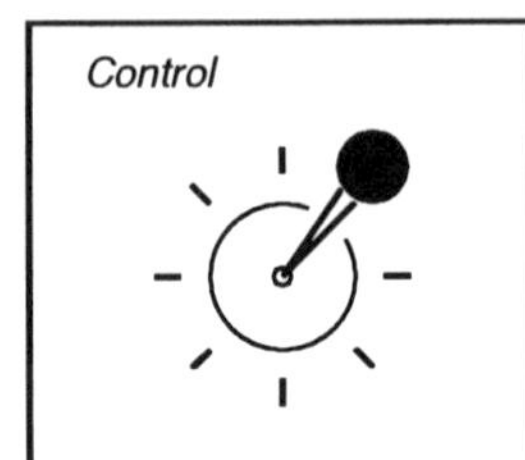

Figure 1: The *tabula rasa* learning problem is illustrated by this interface to a teleoperated robot with an uninterpreted sensorimotor apparatus in an unknown environment. The problem is to develop a practical understanding of the robot and its environment with no initial knowledge of the meanings of the sensors or the effects of the control signals.

tor apparatus. The solution is composed of two steps: 1) learning an abstraction of the continuous world to a finite-state automaton and 2) inferring the structure of the finite-state automaton. The second step has been studied extensively (e.g., Angluin 1978, Gold 1978, Kuipers 1978, Angluin 1987, Rivest & Schapire 1993). In this paper, we focus on the first step. The rest of the paper gives the details of the abstraction-learning method illustrated with an example from the world of mobile robotics.

Overview: From continuous world to finite-state automaton

The details of the method for learning a discrete abstraction of a continuous world are given below and are illustrated in Figure 2.

Given: a robot with an uninterpreted, well-behaved sensorimotor apparatus, in a continuous, static world. The definition of "well-behaved" is given in a later section.

Learn: a discrete abstraction of the continuous world, specifically, a finite-state automaton.

The solution method involves three stages.

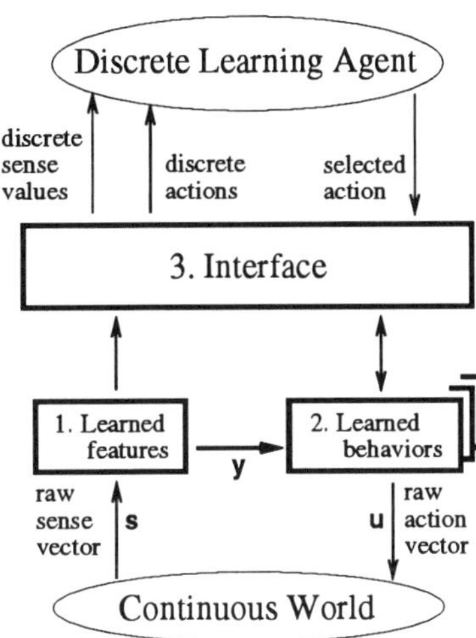

Figure 2: The continuous world is abstracted to a finite-state automaton thereby reducing the task of modeling a continuous world to the well-understood task of modeling a finite-state world. The abstraction is created by 1) learning a set of smooth features **y** defined as functions of the raw sense vector **s**, 2) learning reliable path-following behaviors based on those features, and 3) defining an interface that provides the discrete sense values and actions of the finite-state automaton. The *discrete learning agent* is any learning mechanism that can infer the structure of a finite-state automaton.

1. Feature learning

- Learn a set of almost-everywhere smooth (continuously differentiable) *features*, defined as functions on the raw sensory input. A generate-and-test method is used.

2. Behavior learning

- Learn a model of the motor apparatus, specifically, a set of *primitive actions*, one per degree of freedom. A typical mobile robot has two degrees of freedom: translation and rotation.

- Learn a model (called the *static action model*) for predicting the context-dependent effects of primitive actions on features.

- Use the static action model to define a set of behaviors for finding paths using hill-climbing, and an initial set of open-loop behaviors for following paths.

- Learn a model (called the *dynamic action model*) for predicting the effects of actions while path-following.

- Use the dynamic action model to define closed-loop behaviors for following paths more reliably.

3. Defining the abstraction

- Define an interface to the robot's sensorimotor apparatus that abstracts the continuous environment to a finite-state automaton. The learned path-following behaviors produce state transitions; their terminations define states.

The abstraction-learning method has been applied to a simulated mobile robot. Its sensory system consists of a ring of 16 distance sensors giving distances to nearby objects up to a maximum distance of two meters away. It has a tank-style motor apparatus with two real-valued control signals in the range [-1,1] specifying the speeds of the left and right treads respectively. The robot can turn in place, move forward, move backward, or do a combination of both. The robot is placed in a simple environment consisting of a single room roughly ten meters square.

Feature learning

A *feature*, as defined in this paper, is any function over time whose current value is completely determined by the history of current and past values of the robot's raw sense vector. Examples of features are: the raw sense vector itself (an example of a *vector* feature), the components of that vector (each an example of a *scalar* feature), the average value of those components, and the derivatives with respect to time of those components.

Local state variables

The state of a robot in a continuous world is represented by a state vector **x** whose components are called *state variables*. For example, a mobile robot's state can be described by the state vector $\mathbf{x} = (x_1, x_2, \theta)$ where x_1 and x_2 give the robot's position and θ its orientation. The *tabula rasa* robot does not have direct access to its state variables, but it can use learned scalar features as *local state variables*. A local state variable is a scalar feature whose gradient (its vector of derivatives with respect to the robot's set of state variables) is approximately constant and nonzero over an open region in state space. When the robot is in that region, a local state variable provides one coordinate of information about the state of the robot: constraining that feature to have a specific value reduces the dimensionality of the world by one. With enough independent features (i.e., features whose gradients are not collinear), the state of the robot can be completely determined, and hence the values of *all* of its features can be determined.

The catch is that the robot cannot directly measure feature gradients since it does not have direct access to its state. However, if the world is static and the effects of the actions can be approximated as linear for a local open region R, then the robot can recognize features suitable as local state variables by analyzing the effects of the actions on the features as is shown below. In the following, **x** is the unknown state vector for the robot, y is a scalar feature, $\dot{y}$ is the derivative of y with respect to time, and **u** is the robot's vector of motor control signals. The first equation is the general formulation for a dynamical system.

$$
\begin{aligned}
(1) \quad & \dot{\mathbf{x}} & = & \; f(\mathbf{x}, \mathbf{u}) & \\
(2) \quad & f(\mathbf{x}, 0) & = & \; 0 & \{\text{static world}\} \\
(3) \quad & f(\mathbf{x}, \mathbf{u}) & \approx & \; F_R \mathbf{u} & \{2, \text{linearity assumption}\} \\
(4) \quad & \dot{y} & = & \; \frac{\partial y}{\partial \mathbf{x}} \dot{\mathbf{x}} & \{\text{chain rule}\} \\
(5) \quad & \dot{y} & \approx & \; \frac{\partial y}{\partial \mathbf{x}} F_R \mathbf{u} & \{1, 3\}
\end{aligned}
$$

Here F_R is a matrix used to approximate function f as a linear function of $\mathbf{u}$ for states in open region R containing $\mathbf{x}$. The conclusion from equation (5) is that $\dot{y}$ is a nonzero, linear function of the action vector $\mathbf{u}$ if and only if the gradient $\frac{\partial y}{\partial \mathbf{x}}$ is nonzero and approximately constant. Therefore in order to recognize a local state variable (a feature with a nonzero, approximately constant gradient), the robot need only demonstrate that the feature's derivative can be estimated as a linear function of the action vector. This is the basis of the test portion of the generate-and-test feature-learning algorithm. A feature y is a *candidate* local state variable if its derivative is small for small actions. It is a *bona fide* local state variable, for a region R, if its derivative can be estimated by $\dot{y} = W_R \mathbf{u}$ where W_R is a matrix. Learning and representing this matrix is the job of the static action model. A sensorimotor apparatus is *well-behaved* if the following is almost-everywhere true: Given state $\mathbf{x}$ there exists an open region R containing $\mathbf{x}$ such that the dynamics of the sensorimotor apparatus can be approximated by $\dot{\mathbf{s}} = W_R \mathbf{u}$ where $\mathbf{s}$ is the raw sense vector and W_R is a matrix that depends on the region. This is not as restrictive as it first appears, since nonlinear and discontinuous functions can often be approximated by piecewise linear functions.

A generate-and-test approach

A robot's raw sensory features may not be very suitable as local state variables. For example, sonar sensors have discontinuities due to specular reflection. Their values are smooth for small regions in state space, but it is preferable to have features usable over larger regions. Fortunately, by applying the *min* operator to a set of sonar values, a new feature is obtained that is smooth over a much larger region and thus more suitable as a local state variable. This example illustrates the principle that, if a sensory system does not directly provide useful features, it may be possible to define features that are useful. This principle is the foundation for a generate-and-test approach to feature learning, implemented with a set of *generators* for producing new features and *testers* for recognizing useful features.

The following set of generators, when applied to a sensory system with a ring of distance sensors, are instrumental in discovering features corresponding to minimum distances to nearby objects. The first two, the *group* and *image* generators, are useful for analyzing the structure of a sensory system and defining features that are the basis for higher-level features such as motion detectors.

- The *group* generator splits a vector feature into subvectors, called group features, of highly correlated components. When applied to a sensory system with distance sensors and compass, the distance sensors are collected into a single group.

- The *image* generator takes a group feature and associates a position with each component thus producing an image feature whose structure reflects the structure of the group of sensors. A relaxation algorithm (Figure 3) is used to assign positions to components so that the distance between two components s_i and s_j in the image is proportional to the measured dissimilarity $d(i, j) = \sum_t |s_i(t) - s_j(t)|$. The image generator is based on the principle that sensors that are physically close together will, on average, produce similar values (Pierce 1991).

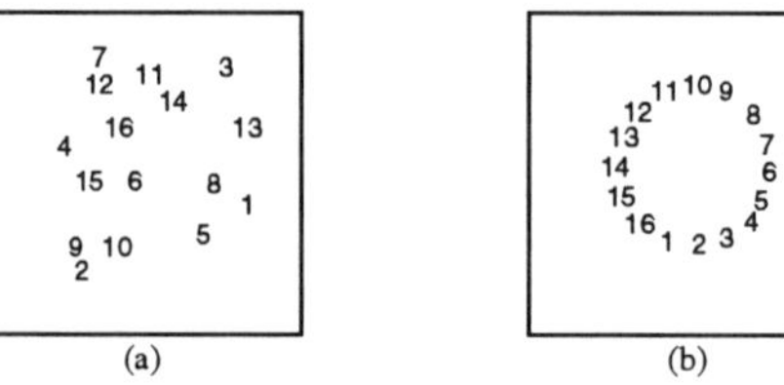

Figure 3: A relaxation algorithm is used to define an image feature for the group feature containing the 16 distance sensors. a) The components are randomly assigned to positions in a two-dimensional plane. b) The components self-organize into a ring in which components with similar values appear close together in the image.

- The *local-minimum* generator takes an image feature and produces a "blob" image feature. A blob image feature provides a mechanism for focus of attention by associating a binary strength with each component. Each component in the image whose value is less than that of its neighbors is given strength 1. Figure 4a illustrates the application of this generator to the image feature of distance values.

- The *tracker* generator takes a blob image feature and monitors the blobs (components with strength equal to 1) within it. The output is a list of blob features giving the value and image-relative position of each input blob. Figure 4b illustrates the application of this generator.

The generators are typed objects: the type of a generator is given by the type of feature to which it applies and the type of feature that it creates. For example, the image generator applies to group features and creates image features.

The only tester needed for finding potential local state variables is the *smoothness* tester. A feature is considered smooth if the standard deviation of its derivative with respect to time is less than a certain value. The generate-and-test approach was applied to the robot with 16 distance sensors. None of the distance sensors were identified as smooth, but the

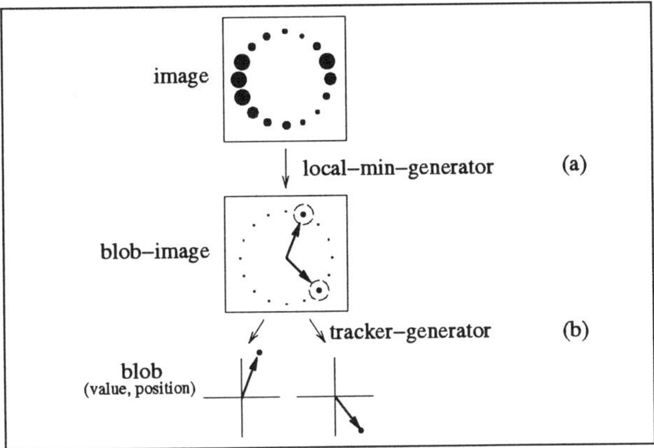

Figure 4: The *local-min* and *tracker* generators are applied to the learned image feature to produce new scalar features that will serve as local state variables. (In this diagram, sense values are represented by the sizes of the disks.) From the robot's perspective, these features are local minima of a sensory image formed by organizing an unstructured, uninterpreted sense vector into a structured ring whose organization reflects intersensor correlations. From our perspective, the features are minimum distances to nearby objects.

learned blob value features were. The size of the search space is kept reasonable by the typing of the feature generators which makes the search space deep but not wide.

Behavior learning

With a good set of features that can serve as local state variables, the problem of abstracting from a continuous world to a finite-state automaton is half solved. The features can be used to express constraints of the form $\mathbf{y} = \mathbf{y}^*$ that define paths. By following such a path until it ends, the robot executes a behavior that can be viewed as an atomic state transition by the discrete learning agent. What remains is to learn behaviors for following paths reliably.

A *behavior* has four components. The *out* component is an action vector used to directly control the motor apparatus. The *app* signal tells whether the behavior is applicable in the current context. The *done* signal tells when the behavior has finished. The *init* input signal is used to begin execution of a behavior. The *out* and *app* components will be defined using the *static* and *dynamic* action models that predict the effects of the robot's actions on the local state variables used to define the path's constraints. A path-following behavior is done when its constraint is no longer satisfied or when a new path-following behavior becomes applicable indicating that the discrete learning agent has a new action to consider.

Primitive actions

The first step toward learning the action models is to analyze the robot's motor apparatus to discover how many degrees of freedom it has and to learn a set of action vectors for producing motion for each degree of freedom. Since the effects of actions are grounded in the sensory features (the only source of information the robot has), we can analyze the motor apparatus by defining a space of action effects and then applying principal component analysis (PCA) to that space in order to define the dimensions of that space and a basis set of effects. See Mardia et al. (1979) for an introduction to PCA.

For example (see Figure 5), characterizing action effects as motion vectors and applying PCA can be used to diagnose the set of primitive actions for a mobile robot with a ring of distance sensors and a motor apparatus that affords rotation and translation actions. For the robot of our running example, this method discovers the primitive action vectors $\mathbf{u}^1 = (-1, 1)$ for one degree of freedom (rotating) and $\mathbf{u}^2 = (1, 1)$ for the second degree of freedom (advancing). The action vector used to control the motor apparatus is a linear combination of the primitive actions, written $\mathbf{u} = \sum_i u_i \mathbf{u}^i$. This method has been successfully applied to both a ring of distance sensors and a small retina (Pierce 1991).

The static action model

The purpose of the static action model is to tell how the primitive actions affect the features that serve as local state variables. Knowing how to take a feature to a target value is necessary for satisfying a constraint, i.e., moving to a path. Knowing how to keep a feature at its target value while moving is necessary for following a path.

In the simplest case, the effect of an action is constant. In general, however, the effect of an action on a feature is context-dependent, meaning that the static action model will have to take context information into account when making its predictions. For example, the advance action will decrease a minimum-distance feature's value when the robot is facing toward a wall; it will increase the value if the robot is facing away from the wall; and it will leave the value invariant if the robot is facing parallel to the wall. The orientation of the robot with respect to the wall is the context that determines the action's effect on the feature.

A brute-force way to define contexts is to break sensory space up into a large set of boxes (cf. Michie & Chambers 1968). In the current example, a more elegant solution is possible. The learned blob features have associated context information, namely the positions of the features in the image from which they are produced (see Figure 4). This information, which encodes the angle of the object whose distance is given by the feature's value, turns out to be sufficient to discriminate the different regions.

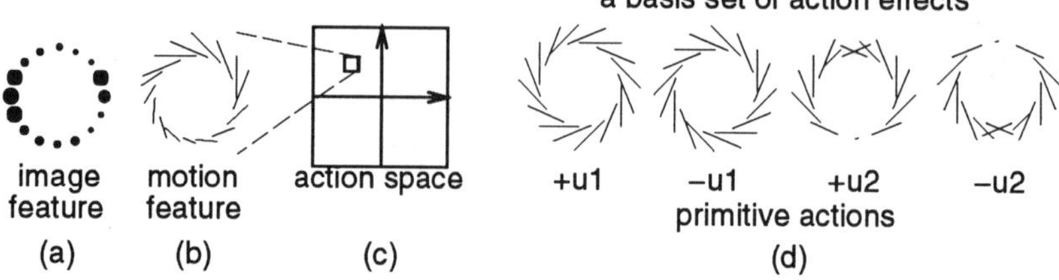

Figure 5: The diagnosis of primitive actions. A *motion* generator is applied to the learned image feature (a). The resulting motion feature (b) is used to characterize actions in terms of average motion vectors (c). Principal component analysis is used to characterize this space of motion vectors to determine a set of actions for motion in each degree of freedom (d).

$$
\begin{aligned}
&\textbf{for each primitive action } u_i \\
&\quad \textbf{for each feature } y_j \\
&\qquad \textbf{for each context } c \\
&\qquad\quad \text{find the best value of } w_{ji} \text{ in} \\
&\qquad\qquad \dot{y}_j \approx w_{ji}\, u_i \\
&\qquad\quad \text{and the associated correlation, } r.
\end{aligned}
$$

Figure 6: Learning the static action model, i.e., the elements of the context-dependent matrix W_c in $\dot{\mathbf{y}} \approx W_c\,\mathbf{u}$. Linear regression is used to find the values of w_{ji} and r. The correlation between u_i and $\dot{y}_j$ determines the goodness of fit, i.e., the validity of the hypothesis that, for a given context, the relationship is approximately linear.

The learning of the static action model is summarized in Figure 6. While the robot explores by randomly executing one primitive action at a time, linear regression is used to find the best values for w_{ji} in the equation $\dot{y}_j = w_{ji}\, u_i$ as well as a correlation that tells how good the fit is. With this information, it is possible to tell when an action has an effect on a feature (namely, when the correlation associated with the feature's current context is large) and how large that affect is. This is necessary for defining hill-climbing behaviors. It is also possible to tell when (i.e., in what context) an action leaves a feature's value invariant. This is necessary for defining path-following behaviors.

Hill-climbing behaviors. The purpose of hill-climbing behaviors is to move the robot to a state where a path-following behavior is applicable. For each primitive action $\mathbf{u}^i$ and feature y_j, a behavior for hill-climbing to the goal $y_j = y_j^*$ is defined as shown in Figure 7. It is applicable when the static action model predicts that the action is capable of moving the feature toward its target value. It is done when it has succeeded in doing so. Its output is given by a simple control law.

Open-loop path-following behaviors. The static action model does not have enough information to define closed-loop path-following behaviors with error correction to keep the robot on the path, but by using the static model, it is possible to define *open-loop* path-

$$
\textbf{Given: } \dot{y}_j \approx w_{ji}\, u_i \text{ with correlation } r \text{ for context } c.
$$
$$
\begin{aligned}
app(c) &\equiv |r| \gg 0 \\
out(c) &= u_i\,\mathbf{u}^i \\
done(c) &\equiv e_j \approx 0 \text{ where} \\
u_i &= \frac{2\zeta\omega}{w_{ji}}\, e_j + \frac{\omega^2}{w_{ji}} \int e_j\, dt \\
e_j &= y_j^* - y_j.
\end{aligned}
$$

Figure 7: A hill-climbing behavior is defined for each primitive action $\mathbf{u}^i$ and feature y_j to achieve the goal $y_j = y_j^*$. A simple proportional-integral (PI) control law is used with parameters $\zeta = 1.0$, $\omega = 0.05$ (see Kuo 1982).

following behaviors. For each primitive action and feature, an open-loop behavior is defined (Figure 8) that is applicable in contexts where, according to the static action model, the action leaves the value of the feature invariant. A signal is superimposed on top of this action that will be used in learning the dynamic action model (next section). After the dynamic action model is learned, a small error-correcting component will be added to keep the robot on the path (i.e., to keep the feature y at the desired value y^*).

$$
\begin{aligned}
app(c) &\equiv (y_j \approx y_j^*) \wedge (\dot{y}_j(\mathbf{u}^\beta, c) \approx 0) \\
out &= u_\beta\,\mathbf{u}^\beta + \sum_{\delta \neq \beta} u_\delta\,\mathbf{u}^\delta
\end{aligned}
$$

Figure 8: An open-loop path-following behavior is defined for each primitive action $\mathbf{u}^\beta$ and feature y_j. The output has two components: a base action and a small orthogonal component used in learning the dynamic action model. Only one of the u_δ's is nonzero at a time. The behavior is applicable when the constraint is satisfied and the action $\mathbf{u}^\beta$ does not change the feature's value. It is done when the constraint is no longer satisfied or a new behavior becomes applicable.

The dynamic action model

The dynamic action model is used to define *closed-loop* (i.e., error-correcting) versions of the path-following behaviors. Specifically, this model will tell, for each path-following behavior, the effect of each orthogonal action (each primitive action other than the path-following behavior's base action), on every feature that is used in the definition of the path-following behavior's constraint.

To learn the dynamic action model, an exploration behavior is used that randomly chooses applicable hill-climbing and open-loop path-following behaviors. An open-loop path-following behavior works by producing the action $\mathbf{u} = u_\beta \mathbf{u}^\beta + \sum_\delta u_\delta \mathbf{u}^\delta$ where u_β is constant, u_δ is much smaller than u_β, and only one u_δ is nonzero at a time. The behavior runs until it is no longer applicable, it no longer satisfies its constraint, or a new path-following behavior becomes applicable. While it is running, linear regression is used to learn the relationships between the orthogonal actions and the features in the context of running the open-loop path-following behavior. The learning of the dynamic action model is described in Figure 9[1].

for each primitive action $\mathbf{u}^\beta$
   for each feature y_j
      for each orthogonal action u_δ
         for each context c
            find the best values of $n \in \{1, 2\}$, k in
$$y_j^{(n)} \approx k\, u_\delta$$
            when $\mathbf{u} = \mathbf{u}^\beta + u_\delta \mathbf{u}^\delta$.

Figure 9: Learning the dynamic action model. Here, $y^{(n)}$ is the nth derivative of y. Linear regression is used to find the best value of k. The correlation between u_δ and $y_j^{(n)}$ is used to discover which derivative of the feature is influenced by the action. It is assumed that for a given context, the relationship will be approximately linear.

Closed-loop path-following behaviors. For each primitive action $\mathbf{u}^\beta$ and each feature vector $\mathbf{y}$ (i.e., each possible combination of features), a closed-loop path-following behavior is defined. It is applicable when $\mathbf{u}^\beta$ leaves $\mathbf{y}$ invariant according to the static action model. It is analogous to an open-loop path-following behavior except that it uses the orthogonal actions for error correction. Since each orthogonal action may affect each feature, there will be one term in the control law for each feature-action pair. The details are given in Figure 10.

---

[1]For the dynamic action model, it is necessary to consider both first and second derivatives of the features. Informally, this is because $\mathbf{u}^\delta$ may affect the derivative of k_β in the equation $\dot{y} = k_\beta u_\beta$, that is, $\dot{k}_\beta = k_\delta u_\delta$. Together, these give $\ddot{y} = \dot{k}_\beta u_\beta = k_\delta u_\delta u_\beta = k\, u_\delta$, using the fact that u_β is constant for a path-following behavior.

$$app(c) \equiv (\mathbf{y} \approx \mathbf{y}^*) \wedge (\dot{\mathbf{y}}(\mathbf{u}^\beta, c) \approx 0)$$
$$out(c) = \mathbf{u}^\beta + \sum_\delta u_\delta\, \mathbf{u}^\delta$$

where

$$u_\delta = \sum_j u_{\delta j}$$
$$u_{\delta j} = \frac{2\zeta\omega}{k} e + \frac{\omega^2}{k} \int e\, dt \quad \text{if } \dot{y}_j \approx k\, u_\delta,$$
$$u_{\delta j} = \frac{\omega^2}{k} e + \frac{2\zeta\omega}{k} \dot{e} \quad \text{if } \ddot{y}_j \approx k\, u_\delta,$$
$$e_j = y_j^* - y_j.$$

Figure 10: Definition of a closed-loop path-following behavior for constraint $\mathbf{y} = \mathbf{y}^*$. Here, $\mathbf{u}^\beta$ is the base action for the behavior and j is the index ranging over the features that comprise vector $\mathbf{y}$. Simple PI and PD (proportional-derivative) controllers are used. Again, ζ=1.0, ω=0.05.

Defining the discrete abstraction

Once the features are learned and the corresponding behaviors are defined, all that remains is to define an interface that presents the continuous world to the discrete learning agent as if the world were a finite-state automaton. A finite-state automaton (FSA) is defined as a tuple $(Q, B, \delta, q_0, \gamma)$ where Q is a finite set of states, B is a set of actions, δ is the next-state function mapping state-action pairs to next states, q_0 is the start state, and γ is the output function determining the sense value associated with each state.

The abstraction we propose involves using a set of learned path-following behaviors that constrain the motion of the robot to a connected network of one-dimensional loci in state space. State transitions correspond to motions resulting from the execution of the path-following behaviors. A state, $q \in Q$, is identified with the point where a path-following behavior ends. At a state, the set of actions $B_q \subset B$ is the set of applicable path-following behaviors. The output $\gamma(q)$ is a symbol that identifies the robot's sensory input at state q. If two states have the same sense vectors, they will have the same output symbol. The next-state function δ is defined by the set of all possible (q, b, q') triples where action b takes the robot from state q to q'. The start state q_0 is taken to be the first state that the robot encounters.

For a path-following behavior to implement a state transition, it must be sufficiently constrained so that the start state determines the termination state — in other words, the path's constraints must limit the robot's motion to one degree of freedom. A constraint $\mathbf{y} = \mathbf{y}^*$ and action $\mathbf{u}^\beta$ define a 1-dof path-following behavior if $\mathbf{u}^\beta$ maintains the constraint (according to the static action model) but does not maintain the constraint when combined with any other action (according to the dynamic action model). Moreover, since the other actions all have an effect on the feature vector $\mathbf{y}$ while action $\mathbf{u}^\beta$ is being taken, they can all be used as error-correcting actions in the closed-loop path-following behavior. For example, suppose the robot is facing parallel to a wall at a distance $y = y^*$. The constraint $y = y^*$ and action $\mathbf{u}^1$ (advance) define a 1-dof path-following behavior: Advancing maintains the constraint, but turning and advancing together do not. Turning can be used to provide error correction.

The interface between the continuous world and the discrete learning agent works as follows. The discrete learning agent is given the list B_q of currently applicable 1-dof path-following behaviors. It selects one which then executes until it ends. At this point, the process repeats. If, at a given state, no 1-dof path-following behaviors are applicable, then the discrete learning agent is given a set of underconstrained path-following behaviors. If no path-following behaviors are applicable, it is given a set of hill-climbing behaviors. If no hill-climbing behaviors are applicable, then it is given a single behavior that randomly wanders until another behavior becomes applicable. With this definition of the interface, the discrete learning agent's actions are kept as deterministic as possible, simplifying the task of inferring the structure of the finite-state automaton that the interface defines.

We are currently working to implement a discrete learning agent based on the map-learning approach used by the NX robot (Kuipers & Byun 1988, 1991; Kuipers et al. 1993) which provided the original motivation for this work. For now, a stochastic exploration behavior is used to demonstrate the interface. It operates by randomly choosing an applicable hill-climbing or path-following behavior and executing it until it is done or no longer applicable, or a behavior becomes applicable that previously was not. An example interaction with the interface is demonstrated in Figure 11 for a simple environment.

Related Work

Inferring the structure of finite-state worlds

The task of inferring the structure of a finite-state environment is the task of finding a finite-state automaton that accurately captures the input-output behavior of the environment. In the case that the learning agent is passively given examples of the environment's input/output behavior, it has been shown that finding the smallest automaton consistent with the behavior is NP-complete (Angluin 1978, Gold, 1978). With active learning, in which the agent actively chooses its actions, the problem becomes tractable. Kuipers (1978) describes the TOUR model, a method for understanding discrete spatial worlds based on a theory of cognitive maps. Angluin (1987) gives a polynomial-time algorithm using active experimentation and passively received counterexamples. Rivest & Schapire (1993) improve on Angluin's algorithm and give a version that does not require the reset operation (returning to the start state after each experiment).

Dean et al. (1992) have extended Rivest and Schapire's theory to handle stochastic FSA's. They assume that actions are deterministic but that the output function mapping states to senses is probabilistic. Their trick is "going in circles" until the uncertainty washes out. Dean, Basye, and Kaelbling (1993) give a good review of learning techniques for a variety of stochastic automata. Drescher's schema mechanism (1991) employs a statistical learning method called marginal attribution. The set of learned schemas fills the role that δ and γ play in the FSA model. Schemas emphasize sensory effects of actions rather than state transitions and are ideal for representing partial knowledge in stochastic worlds.

Inferring the structure of continuous worlds

Applying the previous learning methods to the real world or a continuous simulation of it requires an abstraction from a continuous environment to a discrete representation. Kuipers and Byun (1988, 1991) demonstrate an engineered solution to the continuous-to-discrete abstraction problem for the NX robot. NX's *distinctive places* correspond to discrete states and its *local control strategies* correspond to state transitions. These constructs have to be manually redesigned in order to apply to a robot with a different sensorimotor apparatus. Kortenkamp & Weymouth (1994) have engineered a similar solution on a physical robot that exploits visual as well as sonar information. Lin and Hanson (1993) are using reinforcement learning to teach a robot a predefined set of local control strategies such as hall following. A difference between their approach and ours is that our robot must discover and then learn path-following behaviors on its own. It has no concept of "hall" or "hall-following."

To summarize our position, we are developing methods for *learning* from *tabula rasa* the interface that is *engineered* by Kuipers & Byun (1988) and Kortenkamp & Weymouth (1993), and is being *taught* by Lin and Hanson (1993).

Results and Conclusions

The method for diagnosing primitive actions has been successfully applied to a variety of sensory systems: distance sensors, a 5x5 grid of photoreceptors; and to a variety of motor apparatuses: turn-and-advance, tank, translate, turn-advance-slide (having 3 degrees of freedom: rotation, forward-backward, and left-right). The method for discovering local state variables has been successfully applied to the ring of 16 distance sensors. The learning of action models and path-following behaviors has been demonstrated on the simulated robot

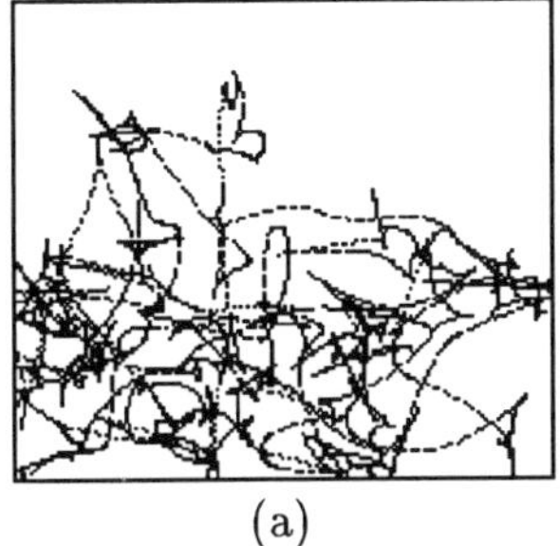
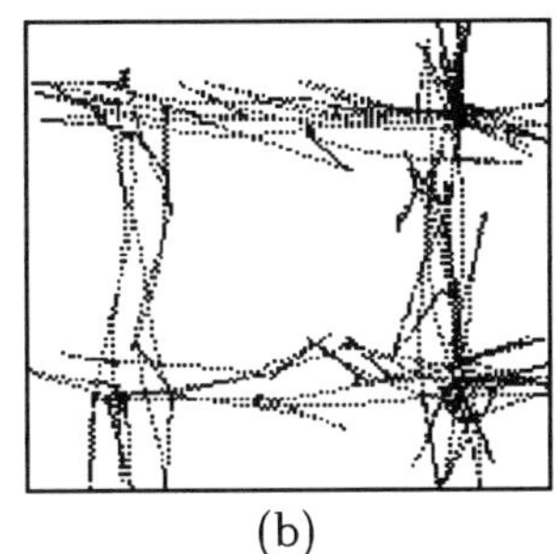
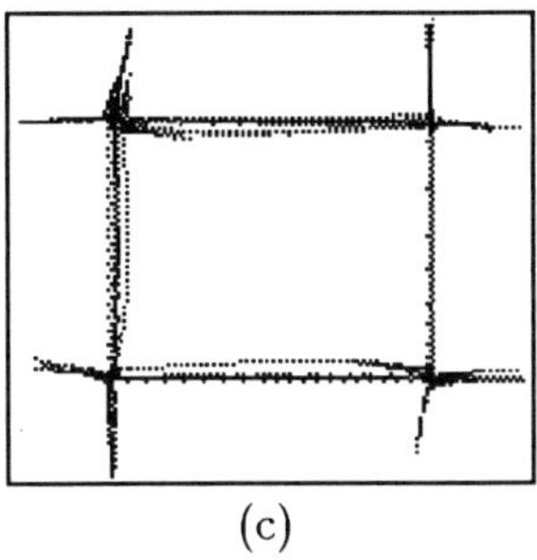

(a)   (b)   (c)

Figure 11: Exploring a simple world at three levels of competence. (a) The robot wanders randomly. (b) The robot explores by randomly choosing applicable hill-climbing and open-loop path-following behaviors based on the static action model. (c) The robot explores by randomly choosing applicable hill-climbing and closed-loop path-following behaviors based on the dynamic action model.

with distance sensors and turn-and-advance motor apparatus.

We have presented a method for learning a cognitive map of a continuous world in the absence of *a priori* knowledge of the learning agent's sensorimotor apparatus or of the structure of its world. By choosing the finite-state automaton as the target abstraction, we inherit a powerful set of methods for inferring the structure of a world. In the process of developing this abstraction, we have contributed methods for modeling a motor apparatus, for learning useful features, and for characterizing the effects of actions on features in two ways: The static action model captures first-order effects useful for defining hill-climbing behaviors and for deciding when an action leaves a feature invariant. The dynamic action model captures second-order effects useful for error correction in robust path-following control laws.

References

Angluin, D. 1987. Learning regular sets from queries and counterexamples. *Information and Computation* 75:87–106.

Dean, T.; Basye, K.; and Kaelbling, L. 1993. Uncertainty in graph-based map learning. In Connell, J. H., and Mahadevan, S., eds., *Robot Learning.* Boston: Kluwer Academic Publishers. 171–192.

Dean, T.; Angluin, D.; Basye, K.; Engelson, S.; Kaelbling, L.; Kokkevis, E.; and Maron, O. 1992. Inferring finite automata with stochastic output functions and an application to map learning. In *Proceedings, Tenth National Conference on Artificial Intelligence,* 208–214. San Jose, CA: AAAI Press/MIT Press.

Drescher, G. L. 1991. *Made-Up Minds: A Constructivist Approach to Artificial Intelligence.* Cambridge, MA: MIT Press.

Kortenkamp, D., and Weymouth, T. 1994. Topological mapping for mobile robots using a combination of sonar and vision sensing. In *Proceedings of the Twelfth National Conference on Artificial Intelligence (AAAI-94).*

Kuipers, B. J., and Byun, Y.-T. 1988. A robust, qualitative method for robot spatial learning. In *Proceedings of the National Conference on Artificial Intelligence (AAAI-88),* 774–779.

Kuipers, B. J., and Byun, Y.-T. 1991. A robot exploration and mapping strategy based on a semantic hierarchy of spatial representations. *Journal of Robotics and Autonomous Systems* 8:47–63.

Kuipers, B.; Froom, R.; Lee, W.-Y.; and Pierce, D. 1993. The semantic hierarchy in robot learning. In Connell, J. H., and Mahadevan, S., eds., *Robot Learning.* Boston: Kluwer Academic Publishers. 141–170.

Kuipers, B. J. 1978. Modeling spatial knowledge. *Cognitive Science* 2:129–153.

Kuo, B. C. 1982. *Automatic Control Systems.* Englewood Cliffs, N.J.: Prentice-Hall, Inc., 4 edition.

Lin, L.-J., and Hanson, S. J. 1993. On-line learning for indoor navigation: Preliminary results with RatBot. In *NIPS93 Robot Learning Workshop.*

Mardia, K. V.; Kent, J. T.; and Bibby, J. M. 1979. *Multivariate Analysis.* New York: Academic Press.

Michie, D., and Chambers, R. A. 1968. BOXES: An experiment in adaptive control. In Dale, E., and Michie, D., eds., *Machine Intelligence 2.* Edinburgh: Oliver and Boyd. 137–152.

Pierce, D. M. 1991. Learning a set of primitive actions with an uninterpreted sensorimotor apparatus. In Birnbaum, L. A., and Collins, G. C., eds., *Machine Learning: Proceedings of the Eighth International Workshop (ML91),* 338–342. San Mateo, CA: Morgan Kaufmann Publishers, Inc.

Rivest, R. L., and Schapire, R. E. 1993. Inference of finite automata using homing sequences. *Information and Computation* 103(2):299–347.

High Dimension Action Spaces in Robot Skill Learning

Jeff G. Schneider *

Department of Computer Science
University of Rochester
Rochester, NY 14627
schneider@cs.rochester.edu

Abstract

Table lookup with interpolation is used for many learning and adaptation tasks. Redundant mappings capture the important concept of "motor skill," which is important in real, behaving systems. Few robot skill implementations have dealt with redundant mappings, in which the space to be searched to create the table has much higher dimensionality than the table. A practical method for inverting redundant mappings is important in physical systems with limited time for trials. We present the "Guided table Fill In" algorithm, which uses data already stored in the table to guide search through the space of potential table entries. The algorithm is illustrated and tested on a robot skill learning task both in simulation and on a robot with a flexible link. Our experiments show that the ability to search high dimensional action spaces efficiently allows skill learners to find new behaviors that are *qualitatively* different from what they were presented or what the system designer may have expected. Thus the use of this technique can allow researchers to seek higher dimensional action spaces for their systems rather than constraining their search space at the risk of excluding the best actions.

Introduction

Memory-based models such as table lookup with interpolation have been used for many robotic learning tasks [Raibert 77, Atkeson 88, Atkeson 91, Mukerjee & Ballard 85, Moore 90, Moore 91]. The block diagram for a general learning task, and a specific task example (throwing a ball) are shown in Fig. 1. A table residing in the box marked "Skill" holds values for a mapping from a task parameter space to a plant command space. The plant command space is all possible vectors that could be stored in the table. The task parameters are used to index into the table. In the 1-d throwing task, the plant command space is the set

---

*This material is based on work supported by DARPA contract MDA972-92-J-1012. The government has certain rights in this material.

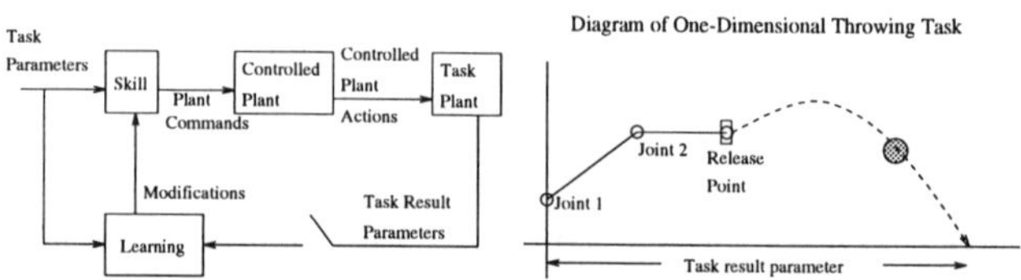

Figure 1: Skill learning system and 1d throwing task

of possible joint velocity sequences that can be sent to the robot controller and the single task parameter is the distance the ball travels.

We assume that our learning system operates in two modes: training and operational. It may train first and then remain in operational mode, or it may switch between the two frequently. In either case our goal is one of optimization: to minimize the amount of time required in training to attain a certain performance level in operation, or to maximize the performance level given a certain amount of training time. Performance may be measured with respect to accuracy, range of operation achieved, or a control effort metric.

Often, memory-based learning systems have relied on random search to fill in the table with the necessary information. This works when: the action space is inherently the same size as the task result space, the system designer has explicitly constrained the action space to be of moderate size using partial task models, or despite the size of the action space the system is interested in learning the results of all possible actions. Robot kinematic and dynamic learning systems often fall into the first and/or last categories. Skill learning systems often fall into the second category. In these kinds of system configurations random search is acceptable. Moore [Moore 90] considered tasks whose action space is of moderate size, but whose desirable actions make up a small portion of the space. He proposed an efficient search strategy for these tasks.

We consider tasks whose space of task parameters has low dimensionality (a small table), but whose space of plant commands has high dimensionality (large vectors stored in the table slots). Tasks of this type arise with open-loop control or planning, when an entire sequence of actions is derived from a single current state or goal. Each action in the sequence makes up a dimension of the space of possible action sequences, and different sequences can achieve the goal at different costs: there is redundancy in the mapping. Discrete closed-loop control avoids high-dimensional action spaces by choosing a single action at each time step. Three reasons for open-loop control are: 1) the action is fast with respect to sensor or control time constants. This problem could also be addressed by increasing sensing, computation, and control bandwidth. 2) there is a lack of sensors or controls for state during the task (e.g. during the flight of a thrown ball). 3) delay, which can destabilize a feedback system [Brown & Coombs 91]. The "Guided Fill In" algorithm given here addresses the problem of high-dimensional search to fill a small table. We test the algorithm with an open-loop robot throwing task both in simulation and on a real system.

In addition to standard table lookup methods, local function approximation methods like Kohonen maps [Ritter et al. 92], CMACs [Albus 75, Miller et al. 89], radial basis functions [Poggio & Girosi 89], and back propagation neural networks [Rumelhart et al. 86] store, retrieve, and interpolate between given data points. [Mel 90] combines a neural network approach with a depth first search of possible reaching strategies. Each method develops an efficient representation once a suitable set of input-output pairs has been found. However, none of these addresses the problem of efficiently obtaining the data to be learned. Often, the method is to let the system execute random plant commands and observe the results, which works well when the space of possible plant commands is not unreasonably large.

There is other work that attempts to perform the types of robot skills used to test the "Guided Fill In" algorithm. The use of global function approximation methods for robot skill learning was reported in [Schneider & Brown 93]. Work on throwing and juggling is reported in [Schaal & Atkeson 93, Rizzi 92]. In contrast to our work the task is usually constrained to remove redundancy or accurate models are used to approximate the desired mapping.

Guided Table Fill In

The Guided table Fill In algorithm is a modification of the SAB controller in Moore's thesis [Moore 90]. He was concerned with the efficient search of action spaces, but did not specifically address the issue of inverting a redundant action to task result mapping. Because of time constraints in real systems, it is often impractical to search the entire plant command space. Therefore, skills with redundant mappings have an increased need for search efficiency during training.

The unique inversion of a redundant mapping from some m-space of plant commands to an n-space of task parameters ($m > n$) requires a penalty function to optimize. For example, our 1-d ball throwing robot has

Fields of a Table Entry			
p^{act}	p^{res}	p^{eff}	p^{good}
action	task results	control effort	goodness value

Table 1: Table entry for skill learning

1. Initialize table using approximate task model, teacher, or random choice.
2. Evaluate each point in memory according to its control effort. Assign a "goodness" value based on a comparison of a point's control effort value to its neighbors'
3. Randomly choose goal from desired portion of task parameter space.
4. Generate candidates from plant command space using these methods:
   - Find the table entry whose penalty function is lowest for the desired goal (considering accuracy of task result and control effort). Make random modifications to the action sequence of that entry.
   - For a n-d task space choose $n+1$ "good" samples from the table and interpolate or extrapolate to produce an action for the new goal.
5. Evaluate the probability of success for each of the candidate points.
6. Execute the action with the highest probability of success and store the results in the table (Optionally, readjust the desired range of performance). Goto 2.

Figure 2: See text for a detailed explanation

two joints controlled via a sequence of six joint velocity settings ($m = 12$, $n = 1$). The penalty function measures the accuracy of the throw and the control effort (sum of squared joint accelerations). The goal of the system is to find the n-subspace of the plant command space that optimally maps onto the n-dimensional task parameter space.

The result of each system execution is stored in a table. The fields of each entry are listed in Table 1. P^{act} is the action sequence tried and p^{res} the result in task space. P^{eff} is a measure of the control effort required by the action sequence. P^{good} is a goodness value for the entry (its computation is described below).

Guided table Fill In is summarized in Fig. 2. In the first step existing models or teachers can determine points from the plant command space to become the first entries into the table. Random choice is a worst case, but possible. There are two parts to a table entry's evaluation. First (done only once): given a point in plant command space, the system executes the corresponding action (p^{act}) and observes the output (p^{res}) and its control effort value (p^{eff}). The task output parameters determine where the point is recorded in the table. Second (executed once each iteration): compare each point against its neighbors in the table (nearest points in the output space). A point's goodness (p^{good}) is the percentage of neighbors whose effort value is worse than its own.

Step 3 randomly chooses a goal from part of the task space. There are several ways the desired portion of the task space may be specified (discussed later). Step 4 generates candidate actions to accomplish the goal task result. Some of the actions are generated by local random modifications to existing "good" points. The table is searched for the entry that best accomplishes the desired goal considering both accuracy and control effort. The action for that entry is altered with small random changes. Several alterations are done to produce a set of candidate actions.

Moore advocates generating some actions from a uniform distribution over the entire space of actions. The purpose of these candidates is to keep the learner from converging to local minima. Experiments with redundant mappings showed that these candidates were not useful. The probability of a random action in a high dimensional space being useful proved to be too small. However, it is still necessary to generate candidate actions far from the existing set of actions in the table. This is done by using linear combinations of existing "good" points in the table. Several sets of points are chosen randomly with the "best" points having a higher probability of being chosen. Interpolation or extrapolation is done from the chosen points to generate new actions. These actions may be in completely unexplored regions of the action space, but are likely to be more useful than completely random actions because of the way they are generated.

Step 5 evaluates the probability of success as Moore suggests. For each candidate action, p^{act}, the table entry whose action, p^{act}_{near}, is nearest the candidate action is determined and used to estimate this probability. When several task result dimensions are considered, a probability is computed for each dimension and the product of them is the probability for the whole task result. When considering redundant mappings, reducing control effort is also a goal. Therefore, a goal effort is selected (usually a constant, unattainable, low value) and control effort is considered to be another dimension in the above computation. Finally, the candidate with the highest probability of success is executed at step 6. The results of the execution are recorded and a new table entry is made. Steps 2-6 are iterated during the training process.

Simulation Experiments

The table filling and lookup algorithms were tested on robot skill learning and performance on the task of throwing a ball. The results of these experiments are summarized in Table . The skill goal is a vector describing the position of a target and its output is sequences of joint velocities for a throwing robot. Here, the robot is the controlled plant and the forces affecting the ball's flight after it leaves the robot make up the uncontrolled plant. Skills are called n-dimensional where n is the number of parameters in the output space of the task: thus a 2-d throwing task has a target lying in a plane, such as the floor.

Experiments were simulated for 1-d and 2-d throwing tasks. For the 1-d task the robot consists of two joints in a vertical plane (Fig. 1). The control signal is a sequence of joint velocities to be executed over 6 time steps (also called a trajectory), thus making a total of 12 input command parameters. The single output dimension is the distance the ball lands from the base of the robot. In the terms of table lookup, a 12-d space must be searched to fill in a 1-d table. The 2-d throwing task is done with a three joint robot configured like the first 3 joints of a PUMA 760; a rotating base is added to the 1-d thrower. The additional joint yields an 18-d search space. The two task parameter dimensions are the x and y coordinates of the ball's landing position on the floor.

The penalty function includes the approximate amount of energy required to execute the throwing trajectories and the average task output error. The approximate energy measure has a second purpose. Robots have limits on their joint velocities and the metric tends to prefer trajectories that stay away from those limits. Later, the average value of the penalty function over the task parameter space will be referred to as the *performance* and the two terms will be referred to separately as *error* and *effort*.

Standard Table Lookup with Interpolation

Standard table lookup with interpolation using a Random Fill In (RFI) learning strategy was implemented to provide a baseline from which to compare the new algorithms. The fill in procedure is random. At each step a new random trajectory is formed by choosing ending joint velocities and positions from a random, uniform distribution over the range of valid values. The new command sequence is executed and recorded in the table. Retrieval from the table is done by finding two (three) points for linear interpolation in the 1-d (2-d) case. Extrapolation is never used for data retrieval. If no points can be found for interpolation, the nearest point in the task parameter space is chosen. When interpolation is possible, a scalar value is given to each possible pair (triple) of points to determine which should be used. It includes terms for the distance of the points from the goal in task parameter space, the average effort associated with each point's command sequence, and the distribution of the points about the goal point.

Fig. 3 shows some sample results of using RFI for 1-d throwing tasks. The desired range of operation is

1300-5000 mm (the robot's arm has a length of 1000 mm). The graphs represent averages over 20 runs. The x axis is the number of robot executions, or the number of trajectories that can be placed in the table. The y axis is an evaluation of the robot's progress learning the skill. To evaluate the robot's ability, ten targets evenly spaced in the desired range are attempted and the average effort and accuracy are recorded.

One characteristic of the graph is that effort appears to grow as the learning progresses. That happens because the robot is capable only of short throws initially (it is given the same sample short-throw trajectories that are given to the GFI algorithm in the next section). It uses those trajectories when long throws are requested and pays the penalty in accuracy (because it refuses to extrapolate). As it finds trajectories to throw greater distances, it uses them and accuracy is improved. These trajectories require greater effort thus causing the average effort to look worse. This initial decreasing error and increasing effort is a characteristic of many of the graphs presented here.

Results with Guided Table Fill In

The 1-d throwing experiments of the previous section were repeated with Guided table Fill In (GFI). The evaluation and trajectory retrieval methods are the same as for RFI. Five initial trajectories capable of throwing distances from 1370 to 1450 were given in Step 1 (for fair comparison, the same five were given to the learners using RFI). Fig. 4 shows some sample results. The GFI execution attains a value of 254 after 200 iterations compared to 818 in the RFI run.

Improvements can be made when using GFI for longer distances. Automatic range expansion is a modification that allows the algorithm to choose its range of attempts according to its current abilities. Step 6 updates the current range of operation achieved by the system. Step 3 calls for choosing goal task parameters within some desired range. That range is set to be the current range of achieved results plus some distance farther. A parameter controlling how much farther trades off how quickly the range of operation will be increased with how many trials will be spent searching for low-effort actions within the current range. Fig. 5 shows standard GFI for a range of 10000 and Fig. 6 shows the results of using automatic range expansion to a distance of 10000. The additional set of points represent the maximum distance attained (divided by 10 to fit in the graph). Shorter distance throws are easier (there are more trajectories in the command space for them). The algorithmic modification allows the robot to learn the easy part first and then move on to more difficult throws. As the graph shows, it reaches a distance of 10000 after 200 iterations and attains a final performance value of 1072 (compared to 1448 with standard GFI). Traditional engineering practice calls for the range of operation to be pre-specified for

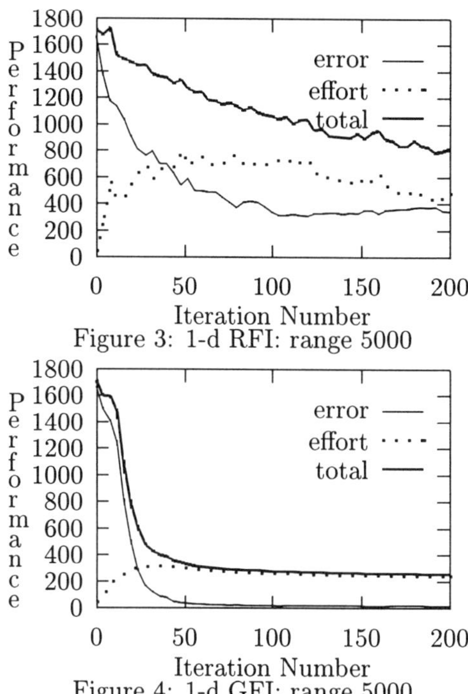

Figure 3: 1-d RFI: range 5000

Figure 4: 1-d GFI: range 5000

Task	Opt. value	GFI 200 tries	RFI 200 tries	RFI tries to catch up
1d 2.5k	24.4	55.0	267.6	over 100k
1d 5k	164.6	254.4	817.7	10k
1d 10k	467.1	1072.3	2443.8	10k
2d 2.5,1.2k	39.2	155.5	1246.9	over 100k

Table 2: Summary of experimental results: Optimal is numerically estimated. GFI is the performance of the new algorithm after 200 iterations using automatic range expansion when it produces improved results. RFI is from traditional table lookup with random trials. The last column indicates how many trials RFI needs to equal GFI's performance.

system design. However, when dealing with complex plants this may be difficult. Therefore, this modification is also important when a system designer does not know the range of performance that can be achieved, but wishes to maximize it.

A 2-d throwing experiment was also done comparing SFI with GFI. The x distance was 2500 mm and the y distance was 1200 mm. GFI is significantly better than RFI for the 2-d task. It gets a final value of 155 compared to 1247 for RFI. This result is important because it shows that performance gains can also be seen in tasks of higher dimensionality.

A revealing statistic is the number of runs RFI requires to reach the performance attained by GFI. For a 1-d range of 2500 RFI requires an average of over 100000 iterations to reach the level GFI attains after only 200. For a 1-d range of 10000, RFI requires 10000 iterations to match 200 of GFI with automatic range

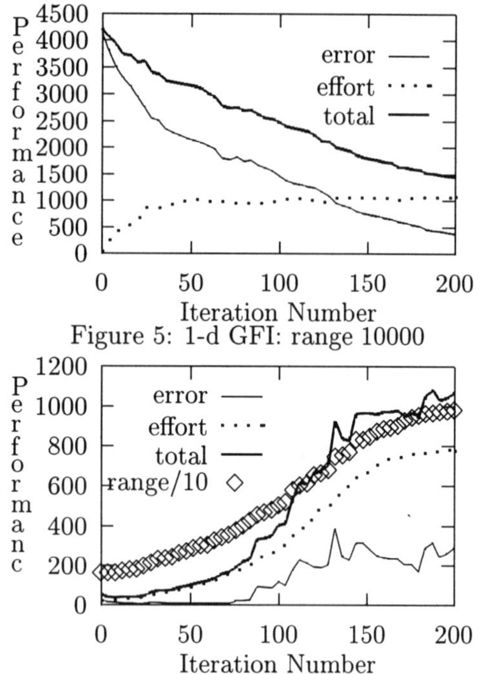

Figure 5: 1-d GFI: range 10000

Figure 6: 1-d GFI: automatic range expansion

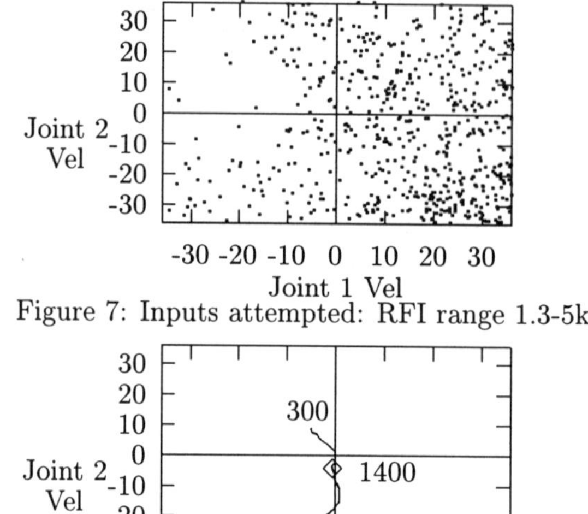

Figure 7: Inputs attempted: RFI range 1.3-5k

Figure 8: Input space points: Optimal 0.3-5k

desired range.

expansion. The larger discrepancy between RFI and GFI on the shorter task shows the benefits of using a fill in algorithm that is guided by desired range of performance vs one that randomly tries valid trajectories. GFI is able to concentrate its trials on the portion of the space that throws in the range 1300-2500. Similarly, RFI for the 2-d case required over 100000 iterations to equal the GFI performance with 200 iterations. When skill learning is attempted on real robots, the number of executions required becomes important.

The actions attempted during 1-d GFI and RFI learning show how the algorithm works. Since the search space contains the velocities of two joints, the skill learner is looking for a curve through a 12-d space. Figs. 7 through 10 are projections of the space onto the plane defined by the ending joint velocities. Fig. 7 shows that the distribution of attempted points is fairly uniform throughout the search space when using RFI. The lower density at the left is caused by a higher number of invalid trajectories there. Fig. 8 shows a projection of the optimal curve for a range of 300-5000. A description of how the optimal curve was numerically estimated is in [Schneider & Brown 92].

Figs. 9 and 10 show the points attempted by GFI at different ranges. The figures show that the GFI concentrates its trials in a small part of the search space. The optimal curve verifies that GFI trials are concentrated in a good portion of the space. The dark spot near the center of the two GFI graphs is where the five initial points are located. A comparison of the two GFI graphs shows the algorithm starting from the initial points and working toward the optimal for the

Experiments on a PUMA

The algorithms presented here were tested on a PUMA 760 with a flexible link attached (a metal meter stick). At the end of the meter stick a plastic cup is attached to hold a tennis ball for throwing experiments. The release point of the ball is not directly controlled. It comes out whenever it is moving faster than the cup. A CCD camera watches the landing area and determines where the ball landed with respect to the base of the robot. Most of the parameters of the experiment were set the same as the 1-d throwing done in simulation. Two joints of the robot are controlled by specifying joint velocities over six 200 ms time steps. The low-level controller, RCCL, interpolates to produce a smooth velocity profile. As in the simulation, the effort function prefers trajectories that are far from the robot's physical limits.

The GFI algorithm was given three sample actions that resulted in throws ranging from 143 cm to 164 cm. Automatic range expansion was used because that option performed the best for 1-d throwing in simulation and because it was not possible to determine the robot's range of capability beforehand. After 100 iterations the robot had learned to throw accurately out to a range of 272 cm (a comparison execution of Moore's algorithm attained a maximum distance of 211 cm). Its accuracy is good enough that it consistently hits a 2 cm screw placed upright anywhere within its learned range of performance. The same cameras that watch the landing position of the ball during learning locate the target during performance mode.

The most interesting result of the learning was the

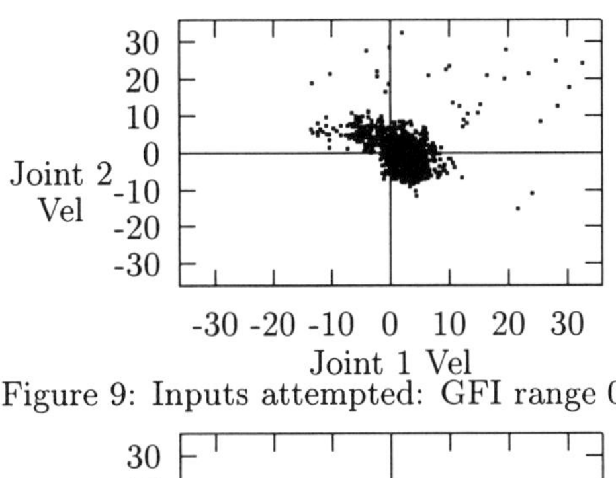

Figure 9: Inputs attempted: GFI range 0-1.5k

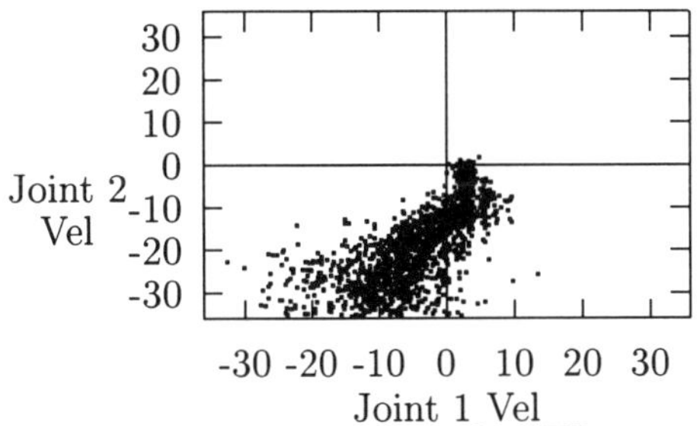

Figure 10: Inputs attempted: GFI range 1.3-5k

type of action found to produce long throws. The three sample actions smoothly accelerate both joints forward. It seems reasonable that longer throws can be obtained by accelerating more quickly. The learning algorithm tried this and it worked up to a distance of approximately 210 cm (this is also what Moore's algorithm did). It was unable to produce longer throws with that type of velocity profile, though, because of the joint velocity limits on the PUMA. It finally learned to do the following "whipping" motion (shown in fig. 11): The joints are moved forward until the meter stick begins to flex forward. Then the robot reverses the direction of its joints so that the stick is pushed forward past its flat state. Just as the stick begins to fall back again, the joints accelerate forward. This causes a large bend in the stick. Finally, the uncoiling of the stick combines with the large forward acceleration of the robot to produce a much higher ball release velocity than could be achieved by simple accelerating the joints forward.

The significant aspect of the long throws that are learned is that they are *qualitatively* different from any given to the system at the start. The sequence of events that led to the robot trying the action in Fig. 11 illustrates the GFI algorithm at its best. At iteration 15 the system was shooting for a goal of less than 200 cm (within its current range of operation). It chose an action created as a local random modification in step 3. That action had a significantly lower velocity at time step 2 for joint 3. The result was a throw for a distance of 164 cm with considerably lower control effort than any previous action for that distance. Later, at iteration 30, a similar thing happened with time step 3 of joint 5. The result was a low effort throw of 176 cm. Following that, the algorithm chose

several actions that were generated by linear combinations of these unique actions. Large extrapolations from the new points created velocity profiles with the "whipping" motion shown in fig. 11. The penalty function, small random modifications, and extrapolation all worked together to find new, useful actions in unexplored portions of a high dimensional space without having to resort to brute force search.

Discussion and Conclusions

There are many important tasks with highly redundant plant command to task parameter mappings. When inverting redundant mappings it is necessary to optimize according to additional cost functions. This poses a problem for standard table lookup methods, which require a random or brute force search of the plant command space to optimize performance.

The Guided table Fill In algorithm extends lookup table learning methods to redundant mappings. It uses data already stored in the table to select plant command space candidates that are more likely to produce good data to add to the table. Linear interpolation and extrapolation between existing good points in the table will yield more good points if the mapping is reasonably smooth. The algorithm also allows natural modifications to learn the easy parts of a task first since it explicitly includes a desired range of task parameters in its decision process.

Experiments with robot skill learning show that Guided table Fill In can yield significant improvements in the number of training trials required to attain given levels of performance. They also demonstrate how GFI may be used to learn the easy part of a task first and the performance benefits of doing so. Many sequential task learners [Watkins 89] must operate closed-loop because of the exponential explosion of action possibilities that occurs when a sequence of actions is considered. The results presented here demonstrate one way to deal with the large number of potential actions and thus offer an open loop alternative for these problems. The gains can be significant when the cost of perception is considered or feedback delay in a real-time system becomes a problem.

Experiments using a flexible manipulator for throwing demonstrate the power of the new learning algorithm. Previously, researchers applying learning to robotics attempted to constrain the action space to make the problem tractable. With efficient techniques for searching high dimensional spaces that step may not be necessary. More importantly, the ability to handle high dimensional spaces enables the learner to generate *qualitatively* different behaviors. Often these are the behaviors that the researcher would have eliminated by applying constraints based on poor intuition.

One of the disappointing aspects of work in learning is that it is often applied to tasks where the system designer "already knows the answer." In these situations

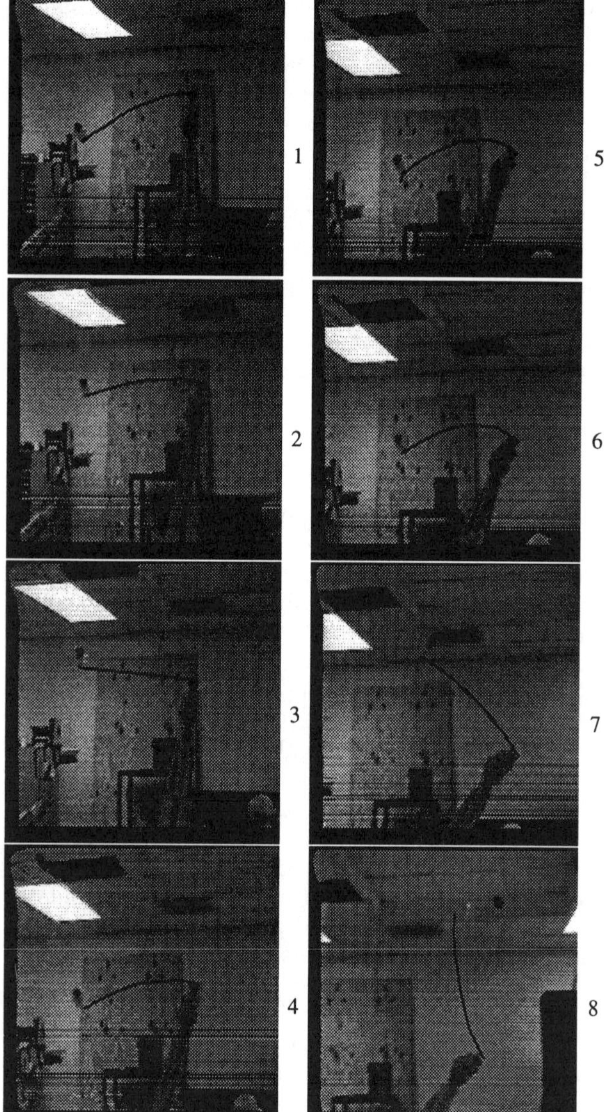

Figure 11: Learned whipping motion for long throws

learning functions more as a fine-tuner to improve accuracy or to fit model parameters. In the throwing experiments presented here, we had speculated that improvements could be made by storing energy in the manipulator. However, it was assumed that this would be done by making an initial backward motion, followed by a forward motion. Only through the use of the GFI algorithm was it revealed that a forward-backward-forward motion was the way to attain a high release velocity, given the constraints on joint velocity, the length of time allocated for the throwing motion, and the natural frequency of the meter stick.

References

[1] J. Albus. A new approach to manipulator control: The cerebellar model articulation controller (cmac). *Journal of Dynamic Systems, Measures, and Controls*, 1975.

[2] C. Atkeson. Using associative content addressable memories to control robots. In *Proceedings of the 27th Conference on Decision and Control*, December 1988.

[3] C. Atkeson. Using locally weighted regression for robot learning. In *Proceedings of the 91 IEEE Int. Conference on Robotics and Automation*, April 1991.

[4] C. Brown and D. Coombs. Notes on control with delay. Technical Report 387, University of Rochester, 1991.

[5] B. Mel. *Connectionist Robot Motion Planning: A Neurally Inspired Approach to Visually Guided Reaching*. Academic Press, 1990.

[6] W. Miller. Real-time application of neural networks for sensor-based controlof robots with vision. *IEEE Trans on Systems, Man, and Cybernetics*, July 1989.

[7] A. Moore. *Efficient Memory-Based Learning for Robot Control*. PhD thesis, University of Cambridge, November 1990.

[8] A. Moore. Variable resolution dynamic programming: Efficiently learning action maps in multivariate real-valued state-spaces. In *Proceedings of the 8th International Workshop on Machine Learning*, 1991.

[9] A. Mukerjee and D. Ballard. Self-calibration in robot manipulators. In *Proceedings of the 85 IEEE Int. Conference on Robotics and Automation*, 1985.

[10] T. Poggio and F. Girosi. A theory of networks for approximation and learning. Technical Report 1140, MIT AI Lab, 1989.

[11] M. Raibert. Analytical equations vs table look-up for manipulation: a unifying concept. In *Proceedings of the IEEE Conference on Decision and Control*, 1977.

[12] H. Ritter, T. Martinetz, and K. Schulten. *Neural Computation and Self-Organizing Maps*. A-W, 1992.

[13] A. Rizzi and D. Koditschek. Progress in spatial robot juggling. In *Proceedings of the 92 IEEE Int. Conference on Robotics and Automation*, 1992.

[14] D. Rumelhart, G. Hinton, and R. Williams. *Learning Internal Representations by Error Propagation*. MIT Press, 1986.

[15] S. Schaal and C. Atkeson. Open loop stable control strategies for robot juggling. In *Proceedings of the 93 IEEE Int. Conf. on Robotics and Automation*, 1993.

[16] J. Schneider and C. Brown. Robot skill learning and the effects of basis function choice. Technical Report 437, University of Rochester, September 1992.

[17] J. Schneider and C. Brown. Robot skill learning, basis functions, and control regimes. In *Proceedings of the 93 IEEE Int. Conf. on Robotics and Automation*, 1993.

[18] C. Watkins. *Learning from Delayed Rewards*. PhD thesis, Cambridge University, 1989.

Robot Behaviour Conflicts:
Can Intelligence Be Modularized?

Amol Dattatraya Mali and Amitabha Mukerjee

Center for Robotics, IIT Kanpur
Kanpur 208016, INDIA
e-mail:amit@iitk.ernet.in

Abstract

In this paper, we examine the modularity assumption of behaviour-based models: that complex functionalities can be achieved by decomposition into simpler behaviours. In particular we look at the issue of conflicts among robot behaviour modules. The chief contribution of this work is a formal characterization of temporal cycles in behaviour systems and the development of an algorithm for detecting and avoiding such conflicts. We develop the mechanisms of stimulus specialization and response generalization for eliminating conflicts. The probable conflicts can be detected and eliminated before implementation. However the process of cycle elimination weakens the behaviour structure. We show how (a) removing conflicts results in less flexible and less useful behaviour modules and (b) the probability of conflict is greater for more powerful behaviour systems. We conclude that purely reactive systems are limited by cyclic behaviours in the complexity of tasks they can perform.

1   Introduction

Complex robot interactions are conveniently modeled in terms of stimulus-response sequences often called behaviours. It is easier to model and debug the *behaviour modules* as opposed to the larger and more integrated centralized controllers. Impressive results have been achieved using this strategy in a can collection robot (Connell 1990), navigation of mobile robot (Arkin 1992), a prototype airplane controller (Hartley & Pipitone 1991), office rearrangement robot in AAAI-93 robot competition etc. This behaviour-based intelligence paradigm propounded by Brooks and others has challenged the role of representation in AI. In a sense, these approaches treat the world as an external memory from which knowledge can be retrieved just by perception. Brooks argues that when intelligence is approached in such an incremental manner, reliance on representation disappears (Brooks 1991).

In response, traditional AI researchers such as Kirsh have argued that control cannot serve as a complete substitute for representation (Kirsh 1991). At the same time, behaviour systems have also been moving away from the purely reactive paradigm. A well-known extension of the Brooks' approach includes the SONAR MAP (Brooks 1986) which is a module that learns what looks suspiciously like a central representation. Some researchers (Gat 1993) are beginning to propose that the internal state be used, but only for modeling highly abstract information.

All modular designs (databases, architectures, factories) face the problem of intermodular conflict. In robot behaviour implementations, conflicts which do not result in cycles can be removed by prioritization schemes (e.g. suppressive links), but this is usually *ad hoc*, with the primary objective of demonstrating success in the current task objectives. Brooks stresses that additional layers can be added without changing the initial system - our results show that such a claim is most probably not tenable. Then how does one put the behaviour modules together and get useful performance? This depends on identifying the possible sources of inter-modular conflicts that are likely to arise in behaviour chains.

This paper is one of the first formal investigations on the issue of combining behaviours and inter-behaviour conflicts. Despite the attention such models have been receiving, the issue of inter-behaviour conflict, which challenges the fundamental assumption of modularity, has not been investigated. For example, if the consequence of a behaviour a triggers the stimulus for behaviour b and b precedes a, then we have an unending cycle. Such conflicts are also beginning to show up in the more complex behaviour implementations. For example, Connell records an instance where a can collecting robot attempts to re-pick the can it has just deposited in the destination area as shown (Figure 1); this conflict was detected only after a full implementation (Connell 1990). Cyclical wandering and cyclic conflict of going back and forth between two obstacles have been reported (Anderson & Donath 1990) (Miller 1993). Can behaviour systems be constructed so that such conflicts can be detected beforehand? How can one modify the structure so as to avoid such conflicts? These are some of the questions we set out to answer.

Our analysis in this paper is dependent on a crucial observation regarding the temporal structure of purely reactive systems. The conflicts we are addressing are not control conflicts but temporal sequence conflicts for which it is necessary to define the temporal structure of behaviours, which is usually sequential since one behaviour usually provides the stimulus for another, so that there is often a clear temporal sequence in which behaviours are executed. In this paper we show that cycles occuring in this temporal sequence can be avoided only by modifying the behaviours themselves, and we introduce two such modifications, based on specializing the stimulus or restricting the action of a behaviour. One of the key results of the paper is that any such modification reduces the usefulness of the behaviour structure and makes it less flexible.

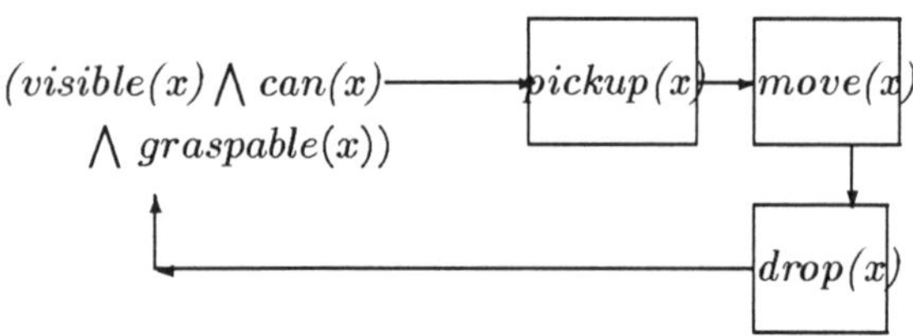

Figure 1. *Conflict in picking and placing the can.*

2 What Is a Behaviour?

AI researchers, psychologists, cognitive scientists, ethologists and roboticists, all use the term behaviour in senses that are related but are fundamentally different. At one end of the spectrum is Brooks who looks upon behaviours as a type of intelligent module, an input-output relation to solve small problems (Brooks 1986). Hopefully these modules can be combined to solve larger problems. There is no shared global memory. The stimulus to a behaviour is boolean and is tested by an *applicability predicate*. This is the model of behaviour investigated in this paper.

Minsky suggests thinking about goal directed behaviour as an output of a difference engine that measures the differences between the world state and the goal state and takes actions to reduce these differences (Minsky 1986). On the other hand, Simon feels that complex behaviour need not necessarily be a product of an extremely complex system, rather, complex behaviour may simply be the reflection of a complex environment (Simon 1969). Arkin proposes the *motor schema* as a model of behaviour specification for the navigation of a mobile robot (Arkin 1992).

Notation

Maes models a behaviour as a *4-tuple* <c, a, d, α> which represent pre-conditions, add list, delete list and level of activation respectively (Maes 1990). In this work we have followed the behaviourists and adopted a *3-tuple* model of behaviour: stimulus, action, consequence. An elemental behaviour module β takes the form <s, a, c>, although the action a is not directly referred to by us, and we sometimes abbreviate the notation to <s, c>. Both the stimulus s and the consequence c are commonly defined in terms of a predicate. We define the *dominant period* of a behaviour as that period when the behaviour is active. In most behaviour implementations, behaviours become dominant in a temporal sequence. We use the symbol ":" *(precedes)* to denote this. $\beta_1 : \beta_2$ implies that behaviour β_2 becomes dominant following behaviour β_1.

Behaviour Chain

We define a *behaviour chain* as a sequence of behaviour modules $\{ \beta_1 : \beta_2 : \beta_3 : ... : \beta_n \}$. Here the action of the earlier module changes the situation in such a way that the newly changed part of the situation is in turn a stimulus for the next module in the sequence. If the consequence and stimulus include a finite universal state as well, then we can say that the stimulus s_{i+1} of the behaviour module β_{i+1} is logically implied by the consequence of the module β_i i.e. $(c_i \Rightarrow s_{i+1})$. What we mean by the finite universal state can be clarified by an example. Let $Universe = X \wedge Y \wedge Z$ and $c_1 = A$ and $s_2 = X \wedge A$. Then β_1 leads to β_2 but $(c_1 \not\Rightarrow s_2)$. Thus when we say that $(c_1 \Rightarrow s_2)$ we mean that a part of s_2 was true in the Universe and some literals in c_1 cause the rest of s_2 to come true. Thus in order for $(c_1 \Rightarrow s_2)$ to be true, both stimulus and consequence should always contain the "state of the universe predicate." This allows us to develop the argument effectively, skirting the philosophical debate on the frame problem (Georgeff 1987).

We define a *behaviour space B* as a set of behaviour modules. A temporal chain of behaviours C is said to be composable from B (written as $C \prec B$), if and only if $(C = ordered\ set\{\beta_i\} \wedge (\forall i)\beta_i \in B)$. A *stimulus space* Σ of a behaviour space B is the union of the stimuli of all behaviour modules in B.

Power, Usefulness and Flexibility of Behaviours

To compare different behaviour systems, we define a few relative measures.

Definition 1

• **Power :** A behaviour $(\beta := $ <s, a, c>$)$ is more powerful than $(\beta' := $ <s', a', c'>$)$ iff $(s' \Rightarrow s) \wedge (c \Rightarrow c')$. In other words, it can be triggered at least as frequently as a less powerful behaviour and results in at least as strong a consequence. A behaviour space B is more powerful than the behaviour space B' if B' can be obtained from B by replacing some module $\beta \in B$ by less powerful module β'.

- **Usefulness:** A behaviour space B spans the task space τ if and only if $\{\forall\,(t \in \tau)\;(\exists\,(C \prec B)\,fulfills\,(C, t))\}$. The *greatest fulfillable task space* $\tau_G(B)$ is the largest task space that is spanned by the behaviour space B. The *usefulness* of a behaviour space is defined as the ratio $\frac{|\tau_G(B)|}{|B|}$.
- **Flexibility:** A behaviour space B is at least as flexible as behaviour space B' if $\{\forall t \in (\tau_G(B) \cap \tau_G(B'))\,\exists\,(C \prec B)\{fulfills\,(C,t) \bigwedge \forall (C' \prec B')\,\{fulfills\,(C',t) \Rightarrow |\,C\,| \leq |\,C'\,|\}\}\}$.

3 Detection of Conflicts

In the broad sense of the word conflict, any behaviour chain leading to non-fulfillment of the desired objectives can be said to have a conflict. Let a chain $C = \{\beta_1 : \beta_2 : ... : \beta_n\}$ be the desirable behaviour sequence that achieves a desirable outcome. There are three types of conflicts that can cause the chain C from not being executed, by breaking the sequence $\beta_i : \beta_{i+1}$.

Definition 2

(a)**Extraneous behaviour Conflict:** $\beta_i : \beta'$, $\beta' \notin C$.
(b)**Cyclic Conflict:** $\beta_i : \beta_k$, $\beta_k \in C$, $k \leq i$. (discussed later)
(c) **Skipping Conflict:** $\beta_i : \beta_k$, $\beta_k \in C$, $k > (i+1)$. This type of conflict can be treated in a manner analogous to extraneous behaviour conflicts.

The type of behaviour that we are investigating is the *cyclic conflict*, where, both β_{i+1} and β_k may be triggered and clearly the triggering of β_k would lead to a cycle (Figure 2).

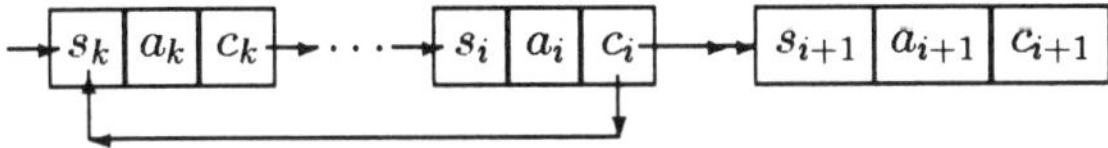

Figure 2. *Cycle in a temporal chain of behaviours.*

Terminated Cycles

All cycles do not result in a conflict. Let us say that a large block of butter needs to be cut into a number of smaller pieces. A module *cut* achieves it. Let $s_{Cut} = butter(x) \bigwedge cuttable(x) \bigwedge breadth(x,b) \bigwedge (b \geq 2\lambda)$. We specify the smallest acceptable size of the piece of butter by specifying the limit λ, which introduces the termination condition.

Prioritization

There are three types of prioritization used in robot behaviour control. If $\alpha : \beta$ is a possible but undesirable sequence of behaviours, the sequence can be modified. In *suppression*, a module γ suppresses the output of β, and instead of $\alpha : \beta$, $\alpha : \gamma$ occurs. In *inhibition* the action of β may take place, but only after γ is no longer dominant. Here the chain $\alpha : \beta$ has the module γ inserted, so $\alpha : \gamma : \beta$ may occur, if the stimulus for β is not affected by γ. *Delayed action* is a special case of inhibition, where the inhibitive link remains effective for some time t_{delay} even after the inhibiting module is no longer dominant. Connell uses the term *retriggerable monostable* to capture this sense (Connell 1990). These mechanisms are not guaranteed to kill the stimulus of β_k, hence β_k may be active after dominant period of the suppressing module is over. Thus within the scope of the three prioritization schemes discussed here, it is not possible to guarantee that cyclic conflicts will be avoided.

Detecting Cycles in Behaviour Graphs
Representing a behaviour chain as a graph, we present without proof the following lemmas:
Lemma 1(a). Whenever there is a cyclic conflict, there is a cycle in the temporal graph of behaviours.
Lemma 1(b). Whenever there is a cycle in the temporal graph of behaviours that is not terminated by a recursive condition, there is a cyclic conflict.
Thus detecting conflicts in a behaviour chain is equivalent to detecting cycles in the corresponding graph.

4 Behaviour Refinement

From definition 2, whenever there is a cycle in a behaviour chain $C = \{\beta_1 : \beta_2...\beta_k...\beta_i : \beta_{i+1}...\beta_n\}$, there must be a triggering of the kind $\beta_i : \beta_k$, where $k \leq i$. Then both $\beta_i : \beta_{i+1}$ and $\beta_i : \beta_k$ are possible at this point. Our objective is to break the $\beta_i : \beta_k$ link without disturbing the $\beta_i : \beta_{i+1}$ or $\beta_{k-1} : \beta_k$ triggerings which are essential to the successful execution of the chain. We have seen that priority based methods are not guaranteed to achieve this, so we look for behaviour modification approaches which will maintain $(c_i \Rightarrow s_{i+1})$ whereas $(c_i \Rightarrow s_k)$ would be negated. We develop two methods for achieving this: in stimulus specialization, s_k is specialized, and in response generalization, c_i is generalized.

Stimulus Specialization

Let us consider the conflict in picking up the soda cans, where the freshly deposited can is picked up. If we were to add the condition "not-deposited-just-now (x)" to the stimulus predicate for pickup, then we would only need a small recency memory (recently dropped can). Thus the stimulus for β_k becomes more specialized. However, in doing this, one must be careful so as not to disturb the rest of the chain, i.e. $(c_{k-1} \Rightarrow s_k)$ should still hold but $(c_i \Rightarrow s_k)$ must be broken. Clearly this will not be possible where $(c_i \Rightarrow c_{k-1})$, then any changes we make in s_k such that $\neg(c_i \Rightarrow s_k)$ will also result in $\neg(c_{k-1} \Rightarrow s_k)$. Thus stimulus specialization can be used only if $(c_i \Rightarrow c_{k-1})$ is not true. One model for this is to say that there must be a literal γ such that $(c_{k-1} \Rightarrow s_k \wedge \gamma)$ but $\neg(c_i \Rightarrow s_k \wedge \gamma)$. The conjunction of all such literals $\Gamma = (\gamma_1 \wedge \gamma_2 \wedge ... \gamma_m)$ is called the maximal difference between c_{k-1} and c_i. Stimulus specialization works only when $\Gamma \neq \emptyset$, and involves modifying s_k to $(s_k \wedge \gamma)$, $\gamma \in \Gamma$. It is advisable not to specialize it more than necessary (e.g. by adding more than one literal), since this adversely affects the power of the behaviour. A simpler understanding of the process is obtained if both c_i and c_{k-1} are in conjunctive form. Then Γ is nothing but the difference $(c_{k-1} - c_i)$ and s_k is modified by conjunction with one of the literals that is in c_{k-1} but not in c_i. Note that since the stimulus is specialized, any stimuli that are required by the action are still available to it.

Response Generalization

Here the action is modified so that the consequence of the action is weaker i.e. if the old consequence was c and the new one is c' then $(c \Rightarrow c')$ but $\neg(c' \Rightarrow c)$. For example, we can modify the action of the module *drop* so that while dropping the can on the ground, the robot puts it in an inverted position which prevents the robot from detecting that the object is a can. The original consequence was *(visible(x) $\wedge$ can(x) $\wedge$ graspable(x))* and the modified consequence is *(visible(x) $\wedge$ graspable(x))*, assuming the sensors cannot identify cans that have been inverted. Otherwise, we may modify the consequence by covering the can to make the predicate *visible(x)* false, then this leads to addition of a new behaviour module or modifying the action part of the original module, both of which require considerable re-programming, and are expensive. In response generalization, $(c_i \Rightarrow s_k)$ must be negated, while $(c_i \Rightarrow s_{i+1})$ must hold. Hence response generalization can be used only when $(s_{i+1} \Rightarrow s_k)$ does not hold. In fact, one could characterize the process of response generalization by saying that there must exist σ s.t. $(c_i \vee \sigma) \Rightarrow s_{i+1}$ but $\neg(c_i \vee \sigma) \Rightarrow s_k$. The disjunction of all such σ's is Σ. Again, if s_k and s_{i+1} are in conjunctive form, then a simpler understanding is obtained, since $\Sigma =\sim (s_k - s_{i+1})$ i.e. the negation of all the conjunctions that appear in s_k and not in s_{i+1}. This negation is a disjunction of many negative literals $(\sim \gamma)$. In this instance, modifying c_i is better understood as dropping the literal γ already appearing in c_i, written as $(c_i - \gamma)$. Since stimuli/consequences are often conjunctive, this difference notion is a useful concept in practice. Thus c_i is modified to $(c_i - \gamma)$, where $\gamma \in (s_k - s_{i+1})$.

Stimulus specialization is easier to do than response generalization, as response generalization requires that the action should be modified. However, stimulus specialization may not always be possible; e.g. with "not-deposited-just-now(x)" the robot may still pick up an older deposited can. Better solutions to this, such as "never-deposited-before(x)" or "not-at-depository(x)" would require considerable global memory. Therefore, stimulus specialization, while cheaper to implement, may not be available in many instances, since the actions require a minimum stimulus, and specializing it without memory may be counter-productive.

Effects Of Behaviour Refinement

Let us now investigate the effects of stimulus specialization and response generalization.

Lemma 2. Removing a cycle from chain C by stimulus specialization or response generalization cannot introduce a cycle in any other chain C', that did not have a cycle before.

Proof :- Let β_k be the behaviour that was specialized. Now to introduce cycles when no cycles existed before, some link $\beta' : \beta_k$ must have become possible, i.e. $(c' \Rightarrow s_k)$ has become true. This is not possible since c' is the same and s_k is more specific. Similarly, since c_k has not been modified, no new links $\beta_k : \beta'$ could have been created. Hence no new cycle will be initiated. Similarly it can be shown that response generalization does not introduce new cycles. $\square$

Lemma 3. Whenever a behaviour space is modified to eliminate cyclic conflicts by response generalization and/or stimulus specialization, either the flexibility or usefulness of the behaviour space decreases.

Proof :- Let Σ be the stimulus space and $s \subset \Sigma$ and s is a conjunction of its members. Now let s be specialized to s' so that $s' \subset s$. Now tasks or subsequent behaviours requiring the predicates in $(s - s')$ will no longer be attended to by B. Thus we need a new behaviour β'' such that $(s'' \cup s') = s$, so that β and β'' together serve the stimulus set s which implies that $|B|$ increases and the usefulness of B decreases. Similarly, if the response of β is generalized so that c has more literals than c'. Thus $(c - c')$ is not being performed by β. Hence other new behaviours are needed to complete tasks requiring $(c - c')$ which increases $|B|$, and also increases the chain lengths for performing tasks, reducing flexibility. Otherwise, some tasks requiring $(c - c')$ cannot be performed which implies that $|\tau'| < |\tau|$ which again means that the usefulness of the behaviour space decreases. $\square$

Let us say that we have a behaviour β whose consequence $c = p \wedge q$ leads to a cycle. If we use response generalization, we may have to design two behaviours β' and β'' such that $c' = q$ and $c'' = p$. If β has a stimulus $s = p \vee q$ which is triggered leading to a cycle and if we use stimulus specialization, we may have to design two more behaviours β' and β'' such that s' = p and $s'' = q$. In some cases, it may not be possible to design an action such that it will fulfill these conditions. This discussion brings us to our most important results, which have to do with the power and usefulness of behaviour spaces.

Behaviour Modification Theorem. Given two behaviour spaces B and B' such that B is more powerful than B' (i.e. B' can be obtained from B by replacing some behaviours β of B by the less powerful ones β') then:
(a) The greatest fulfillable task space for behaviour space B' is less than that for B, i.e.
$$|\tau_G(B')| \leq |\tau_G(B)|$$
(b) Usefulness of B is greater than that of B' i.e.
$$\frac{|\tau_G(B)|}{|B|} \geq \frac{|\tau_G(B')|}{|B'|}.$$
(c) Probability of a cycle is also greater in B.
Proof (a) :- First, let us consider the case where a single behaviour β has been replaced by the less powerful β'. The set of chains of behaviours composable from a behaviour space represents a tree with initial point corresponding to the availability of the right initial stimulus and each node in this tree represents a world state which may correspond to the desired task. The greatest fulfillable task space is proportional to the total size of this tree of behaviour chains. Now, either the behaviour β will have more applicability due to smaller stimulus length as compared to the behaviour β', or the behaviour β will have stronger consequences resulting in more behaviours being triggerable. In terms of the task tree, either β will have more parent nodes, or it will have more children. In either case, the branching factor is higher in B than in B' and the size of the task tree will be as large or larger. Since $|B|$ has not changed, the usefulness of the behaviour space, $\frac{|\tau_G(B)|}{|B|}$ has decreased which proves part (b). This treatment can be extended to multiple instances of replacing a strong behaviour by a weak one. $\square$
Proof (c) :- Let $\beta_i \in B$ and $\beta_i' \in B'$ be two behaviours s.t. β_i is more powerful than β_i', i.e. $(s_i' \Rightarrow s_i)$ or s_i is weaker than s_i'. Now consider any chain composable in B and B' of n modules, which differ only in that the module β_i is replaced by β_i'. Now consider all behaviours $\beta_j \in C$, $j \geq i$, with consequence c_j. The probability of a cycle *prob-cycle (B)* is $\sum_{j\geq i}^{n} prob(c_j \Rightarrow s_i)$ and *prob-cycle (B')* is $\sum_{j\geq i}^{n} prob(c_j \Rightarrow s_i')$. Clearly, since $(s_i' \Rightarrow s_i)$, $\{\forall j[prob(c_j \Rightarrow s_i) \geq prob(c_j \Rightarrow s_i')]\}$. Similarly $(c_i \Rightarrow c_i')$ for which similar analysis can be carried out. Thus *prob-cycle (B)* $\geq$ *prob-cycle (B')*. $\square$

Corollary :- If B and B' have the same greatest fulfillable task space τ_G, but $\exists (\beta \in B) \wedge \exists (\beta' \in B') \{\beta$ is more powerful than $\beta'\}$, but $\sim [\exists (\beta \in B) \wedge \exists (\beta' \in B') \{\beta'$ is more powerful than $\beta]$, then $|B| \leq |B'|$.

Residual

In this section we consider the parsimony of the logical chain underlying the behaviour chain. If $\beta_i : \beta_{i+1}$, then $(c_i \Rightarrow s_{i+1})$. There may be some literals in c_i which are not necessary in this implication, or there may be some disjunctive literals in s_{i+1} not referred to by c_i. We call this difference between c_i and s_{i+1}, the *residual*. If c_i and s_{i+1} are identical, then their residual is null. If θ is the most general matching string between c_i and s_{i+1}, i.e. θ is the most general construct for which $c_i \Rightarrow \theta$ and $\theta \Rightarrow s_{i+1}$, then we can write $c_i = \theta \wedge \gamma, s_{i+1} = \theta \vee \sigma$, then the residual consequence = γ, the remedial stimulus = σ and the total residual between (β_i, β_{i+1}), R_i, is defined as $\gamma \wedge \neg\sigma$. Residuals are a measure of the degree of *coupling* in a behaviour chain. The intuition behind this is that as the residual increases, the flexibility as well as probability of cycles increase. Stimulus specialization as well as response generalization decrease the residual.

Lemma 4. If two chains C and C' have identical residuals except for some residuals R in C which are stronger than corresponding R' in C', then the probability of a cycle is greater in C.
Proof :- Consider two behaviour chains C and C' where C' is formed from C by replacing the single behaviour β_i by β_i'. Then all residuals in the two chains are also identical except R_{i-1} and R_i. If the residuals in C are stronger, then $(\gamma_i \Rightarrow \gamma_i')$ and $(\sigma_{i-1}' \Rightarrow \sigma_{i-1})$, i.e. behaviour β is more powerful than β'. Hence by part (c) of the behaviour modification theorem, probability of a cycle is greater in C than in C'. The same arguments can be extended for multiple behaviour changes between C and C'. $\square$

Conclusion

In this paper we have focussed on the *temporal* relations between behaviours as opposed to the control relations. This has highlighted an important similarity between behaviour-based modeling and the classical models of planning in AI. The effect of actions, which become new stimuli is similar to the postcondition - precondition structure in means ends planners such as STRIPS (Georgeff 1987). One of the approaches used to avoid cyclic conflicts in planning is the meta-level reasoner, idea which has also been used in behaviour systems such as in (Arkin 1992). But purists would not consider these to be true reactive behaviour systems. However, behaviour models differ from planning in some crucial aspects. Locality of behaviour programming makes opportunistic plan-generation automatic, since the relevant behaviour is triggered automatically when stimulus becomes very strong. Also, cycles are much more of a problem in behaviour models since unlike planners, a behaviour does not "switch-off-and-die" after execution; if the stimulus reappears, it may re-execute, causing a cycle.

One of the benefits of this work is that by testing for cycles, the designers will not have nasty surprises awaiting them after implementation. We also show that approaches such as prioritization will not avoid cycles. Thus the only guaranteed method for avoid cycles is to modify the behaviour itself, and this can be done either by specializing the stimulus or generalizing the response of some behaviour module. Unlike learning, which makes the behaviours more powerful, this reduces the usefulness of the behaviour module. If a robot can pick up a soda can, it should be able to pick up a coffee cup or other similar object. Using stimulus specialization, such a general behaviour would be split into many separate behaviour for picking up separate objects. The principal insight to be gained from this discussion is that in behaviour design, there is a trade-off between the power of a behaviour and the likelihood of cycles. The crucial task of the behaviour designer is to achieve just the right amount of refinement, without involving conflicts and without sacrificing too much flexibility.

Can conflicts be avoided by using alternate architectures such as fuzzy logic (which allows behaviour designers to model *strength of stimulus*), meta-level reasoning (Yamauchi & Nelson 1991), or connectionist architectures (Payton, Rosenblatt & Keirsey 1990)? If we ported the can-pickup example into any of these representations, the conflict does not go away, since the conflict arises at the knowledge level and not at the representation level. Using internal state would not, in itself, be able to remove this type of conflict, although it would make it easier to modify the behaviours so that the conflict can be avoided. Another issue related to internal state is the intention of the robot (psychologists read *will*). Knowing the intention at some meta-level, it may be possible to construct tests for detecting conflicts, and even possibly of avoiding them. At the same time, models involving will or intention (as in Searle) are one of the most debated and difficult quagmires in AI today. Is there then some limit on the complexity of a system of behaviours before self-referential cycles develop? A deeper question raised by the presence of such cycles in behaviour based robotics, as well as in other branches of AI, is that of its significance to the entire search for artificial intelligence. Is there some bound on the complexity of *any* system claiming intelligence, before it begins to develop cyclic conflicts? This paper is a beginning of the search for these answers which are sure to affect the future of the behaviour-based robot modeling paradigm in particular and that of models for intelligence in general.

References

[1] Anderson, T. L.; Donath, M. 1990. Animal Behaviour As A Paradigm For Developing Robot Autonomy, Robotics and Autonomous Systems, 6(1 & 2): 145-168.

[2] Arkin, R. C. 1992. Behaviour-Based Robot Navigation for Extended Domains, Adaptive Behaviour 1(2): 201-225.

[3] Brooks, R. A. 1986. A robust layered control system for a mobile robot, IEEE transactions on robotics and automation, 2(1): 14-23.

[4] Brooks, R. A. 1991. Intelligence without representation, Artificial Intelligence, 47(1-3): 139-159.

[5] Connell, J. 1990. Minimalist mobile robotics, A colony style architecture for an artificial creature, Academic press Inc.

[6] Gat, E. 1993. On the Role of Stored Internal State in the Control of Autonomous Mobile Robots, AI Magazine, 14(1): 64-73.

[7] Georgeff, M. P. 1987. Planning, Annual Review of Computer Science, 2: 359-400.

[8] Hartley, R.; Pipitone, F. 1991. Experiments with the subsumption architecture, In Proceedings of the IEEE Conference on Robotics and Automation, 1652-1658.

[9] Kirsh, D. 1991. Today the earwig, tomorrow man?, Artificial Intelligence, 47(1-3): 161-184.

[10] Maes, P. 1990. Situated Agents Can Have Goals, Robotics and Autonomous Systems, 6(1-2): 49-70.

[11] Miller, D. P. 1993, A Twelve-Step Program to More Efficient Robotics, AI Magazine, 14(1): 60-63.

[12] Minsky M. L. 1986. The Society of Mind, Simon and Schuster.

[13] Payton, D.W.; Rosenblatt J. K.; and Keirsey, D. M. 1990. Plan guided reaction, IEEE Transactions on Systems, Man and Cybernetics, 20(6): 1370-1382

[14] Simon, H. A. 1969. The Sciences of the Artificial, The MIT Press.

[15] Yamauchi, B.; Nelson, R. 1991. A behaviour-based architecture for robots using real-time vision, Proceedings of the IEEE Conference on Robotics and Automation, 1822-1827.

Merging Path Planners and Controllers through Local Context

Sundar Narasimhan

MIT Artificial Intelligence Laboratory, Room 826
Cambridge, MA 02139
sundar@ai.mit.edu

Abstract

This paper presents an implemented approach to robotic tasks involving intermittent contact and changing dynamics in uncertain environments. The approach is to use global planning to find paths in a tesselated representation of the environment, and a set of local controllers to take into account possibly time varying dynamics. The important difference from conventional path-planning in robotic tasks is how this approach uses local sensory information, and the important difference from reactive or behavior-based approaches is that the local controllers are learnt from simulation models or actual trials and are not programmed in a-priori.

Introduction

Consider a scene as shown in Figure 1. This scene shows a number of polygonal objects resting on the plane. Also shown is a rod (which is a simplified form of a robot) which can move in the plane. While so doing, this rod contacts and pushes the objects in the environment. To simplify what follows, we will assume that the objects in the environment are fixed and only one of them beside the robot can move in the environment. The task is, stated very simply, to move a specified shape from a starting configuration s_i to a specified ending configuration s_g.

This task looks simple. Yet it shares a number of important features with other tasks:

1. It requires interacting with the environment, especially with the object the robot intends to move. In this particular task, because of the lack of a gripper, contact is intermittent.

2. The environment is filled with uncertainty. The positions of the objects are known only to within a certain accuracy, and the effect of actions cannot be predicted with arbitrary precision. More importantly, the pressure distribution at the object's surface in contact with the table underneath is unknown.

3. While moving the object in its environment, the robot and the moving object can come into contact

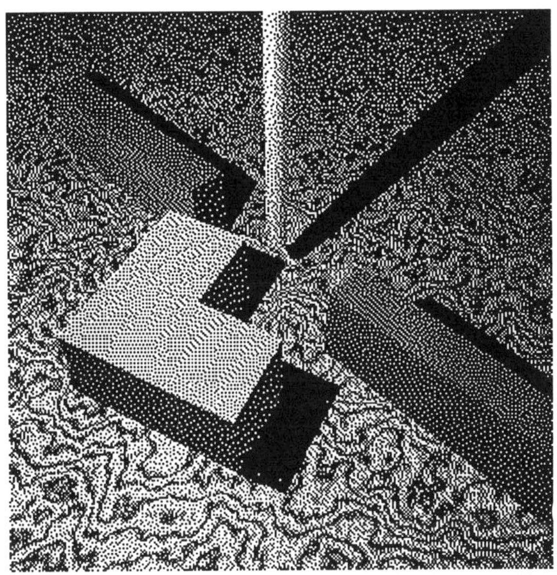

Figure 1: The Robot and its Environment

with obstacles in the environment. The dynamics of predicting the evolution of the object's state through such contact situations is difficult if not impossible (see Mason & Wang 1988, Erdmann 1984 and more recently Baraff 1993 about inconsistencies that can arise when one tries to apply models of Newtonian mechanics along with the Coulomb model of friction).

Previous Work

Given the nature of this problem, how can one program a robot to carry out this task? There have been many approaches to this fundamental problem of a robot's interaction with its uncertain environment. However, one can classify almost all of these into two broad categories. In what follows, we will instantiate the two approaches in our pushing domain, in order to illustrate their main characteristics.

The first approach relies on a rather clean separation

of a *planning* component from the *execution* unit. In this approach, a geometric model of the environment is acquired and a path for the object to be pushed is planned. A highly abstract description of an example program for such a task might look like:

```
environment = sense
path = findpath (object, s-i, s-g, env)
push-object (object, path)
```

The last line in the above program suggests where the execution component is utilized. This execution unit is saddled with the task of actually pushing the object along the path in an uncertain and possibly changing environment.

This basic idea has been explored for a wide variety of robot tasks. By separating the planning problem from execution, one could optimize and study them independently. The output of the planner is a sequence of actions. Its input comes from the sensors. However, the raw sensor values are usually pre-processed and merged into a world model.

In contrast to this approach stands the *reactive* and *behavior-based* approach for programming robot tasks[1]. The behavior-based technique was originally suggested to address problems in robot navigation (Brooks 1986) and has been extended by a number of researchers (Connell 1990, Brooks 1991). To program a robot to push an object using this approach, one would construct a series of behaviors that map sensory values to actions. Each of these behaviors can be thought of as finite-state machines in the behavior-based approaches or as simple table-lookups in purely reactive systems. Many such behaviors are hooked up in a topology predetermined by the programmer. Examples have been presented for the navigation task (Mataric 1990), the grasping task (Brock 1993) and numerous others.

Conventional planners are brittle in the sense that they cannot handle uncertain or changing environments. They also have to face the problem of sensor fusion in order to merge different sensing inputs into a common world model. Reactive and behavior-based systems on the other hand require careful construction and anticipation, at design time, of the consequences of entire sequences of actions.

Approach

As has been recognized by many researchers, a framework that provides for both global geometric planning and local sensory interaction in order to take uncertain dynamics into account would be extremely useful. In what follows, we describe our approach to this problem and illustrate how it works in the pushing domain. Our approach is a hybrid one that has planning and reactive components. While we have explored issues

---

[1]We acknowledge the distinction between purely *reactive* and *behavior-based* systems. The latter retain state, can use internal representations and are often implemented on distributed systems.

related to the retention of state in our reactive component, this paper does not present those results.

In our pushing domain, the state of an object can be parametrized by three variables $s = (x, y, \theta)$, and consequently the configuration space (see Lozano-Pérez 1983) of the moving object in its environment is three dimensional. Our model for the dynamics will be quasi-static because it allows the *state* space to be identified with the configuration space of the moving object. It should be noted that our model for $\mathcal{S}$ is infinite (i.e. $s \in \mathcal{S} = \mathcal{R}^2 \times \mathcal{SO}^1$).

Our model for an action will be a tuple $A_i = (x, y, dx, dy)$ where the first two numbers quantify a point on the pushed object where the robot starts to push the moving object, and the last two specify the length and direction of the push in a co-ordinate system fixed on the moving object. This model of actions is object-centered and comprises the set of linear one-step pushing actions. It should be noted that our model for $\mathcal{A}$ is also infinite.

Our approach will be to use a geometric planner to plan feasible paths for the pushed object *without* taking into account any model of uncertainty. This assumption makes the planning problem tractable. An execution unit that attempts to push the object along this path will be presented. Both these components are assumed to be running in parallel. The information that is communicated from the planner to the execution unit is the set of geometric parameters that specifies the next segment along a path to the goal configuration.

We rely on feedback loops to ensure disturbance rejection and robustness. We will present a controller that can deal with the varying pressure distributions at the support surface quite effectively, when the environment contains no obstacles. To deal with the fact that the dynamics of pushed objects can change quite drastically upon contacting these obstacles, we present an approach that relies on switching controllers based on sensed local configurations.

Global Path Planning

We assume that a model of the environment exists and that a global path planner operates on this environment to produce a path. In our experiments, such a model is sensed and built from a vision system that uses a camera mounted beneath the plane in which the objects move. All our objects are assumed to be polygonal. In this paper, we do not address the algorithms used in the perceptual component. Furthermore, in the following sections, we will consider the task of moving only *one* object from a specified starting configuration to a specified goal configuration.

The configuration space of the environment characterizes all legal positions for the moving object where no collisions exist between the moving object and the stationary obstacles. Obstacles in the configuration space consist of configurations where the moving object would collide with one or more of the stationary obstacles. Our planner constructs these configuration space obstacles using the *trace* algorithm (Guibas, et al. 1983) extended to handle rotations. We then search a discretized representation of this configuration space to find paths connecting start and goal configurations.

Two views of the constructed configuration space for the example in Figure 1 are shown in Figure 2.

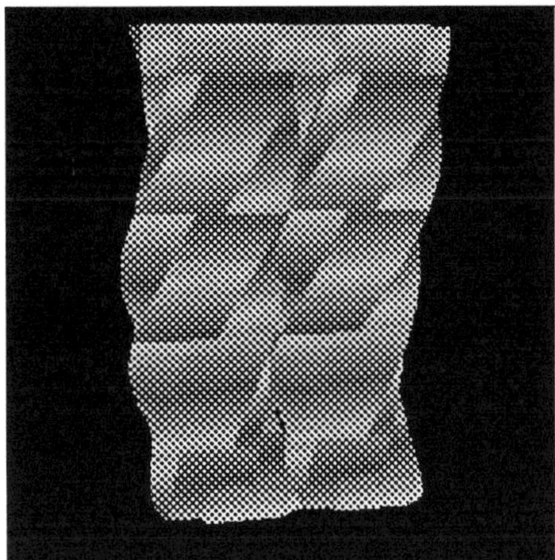

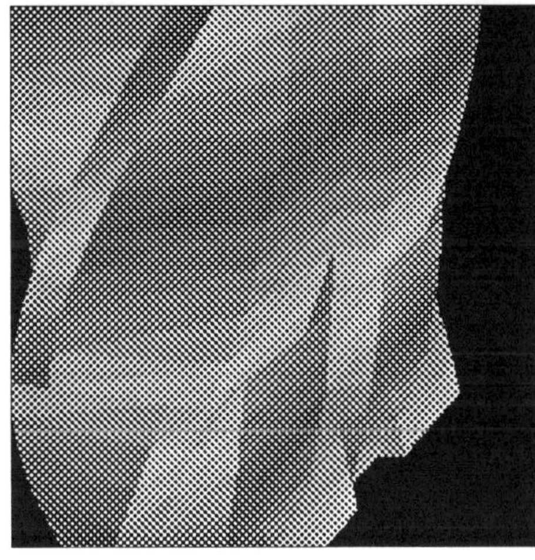

Figure 2: Two views of 2+1D C-space

Paths found in the tesselated configuration space can be displayed graphically. In Figure 3 we show two such paths found by the planner, the second of which contains many more segments involving rotations than the first.

The path-planner's output is encoded by a series of configurations $P = x_i, y_i, \theta_i$.

Local Control

Even though we now have a desired path for the pushed object, we have not yet specified how the robot is to effect the motion of a pushed object along this specified path.

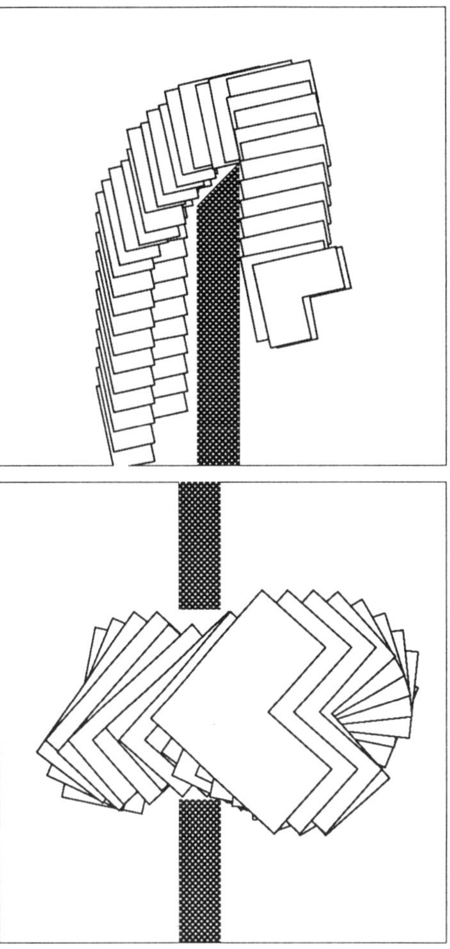

Figure 3: Paths found by FindPath

We have explored three alternatives for specifying local controllers.

1. The first approach hand-codes specific behaviors intended to effect particular object-relative motion. For example, we wrote behaviors tuned to translate the object along the path, and other behaviors that sought to rotate the object clock-wise or counter clock-wise.

2. The second approach was to apply the principles of traditional feedback control to the problem. The idea can best be illustrated graphically. In Figure 4 we illustrate the L-shaped object's initial and final configuration at some stage along the path. A line Ol is drawn opposite the line segment connecting the positions occupied by the center of mass of the object as it moves along the path. This line intersects the line segments comprising the polygon in a number of places. The segment that contains the furthest point from O is chosen as the segment on which the pushing action will be applied. Since the direction of rotation desired is counter-clockwise, we use *Mason's*

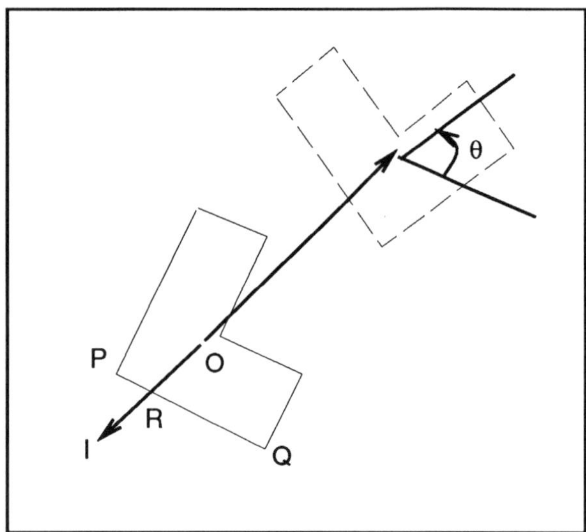

Figure 4: Geometrical Control Rule

rule (Mason 1986) to find a point along the segment RQ and use a small incremental push dx, dy along the translation direction indicated. If no such point can be found, then we choose another edge adjacent to PQ and retry.

3. The third approach uses a local controller that relies on a simulated model of the physics of the domain. The model is based on a randomly varying 3-point pressure distribution. We implemented a 2-d minimization procedure (similar to Mason 1982) that takes as input an executed robot motion A_i and produces as output $ds = (\delta x, \delta y, \delta\theta)$ which is the predicted object motion if that action were to be executed. Using this, we produce a forward map from actions to changes in state by repeatedly executing this simulation procedure for various values of the action tuple.

   To implement the local controller, we invert this table using particular choices for distance functions.

The last approach uses a table which could be built from actual trials (Christiansen et al. 1991). Other work that is also relevant includes work on bounding loci of possible centers of rotation (Peshkin & Sanderson 1988) and estimating friction parameters of pushed objects (Lynch 1993).

The last approach has proven to be robust in carrying out the required motions in simulations and in actual experiments. In Figure 5 we illustrate the performance of this controller in two different trials where the L-shaped object is moved from $(40, 40, 0.8)$ and $(40, 40, 1.57)$ to $(0, 0, 0)$.

We choose a particular sampling of the action space based on performance metrics. The parameters we attempt to choose are k, the number of pushing points

along an edge of the object, d the length of the push and l the number of directions along which the pushing action is exerted. Values for these parameters are chosen by measuring the performance of the controller on a set of sample tasks. First a set of k equally spaced points are chosen along each edge of the pushed object. This specifies the first two values x, y of the action tuple. To derive values for the next two values, directions of pushes are sampled into l values in the range $[\hat{n} + \theta_{max}, \hat{n} - \theta_{max}]$ about this point. $\hat{n}$ denotes the normal to the edge and θ_{max} was set to 60 degrees. The length of pushes d, is at present held constant to 2 cm. By considering the number of pushes, length travelled between pushes, and the ratio of successful pushes to failures in a specified time period on a set of previously chosen pushing tasks, the algorithm chose $k = 4$, and $l = 5$ in the examples shown below. This results in the size of $\mathcal{A}$ being 120 in this case for the L-shaped object.

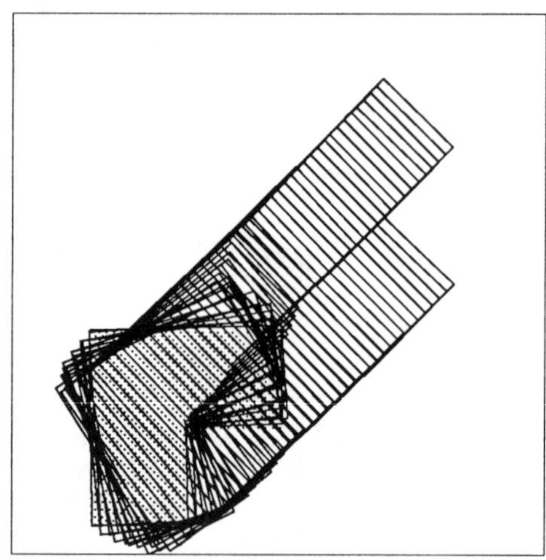

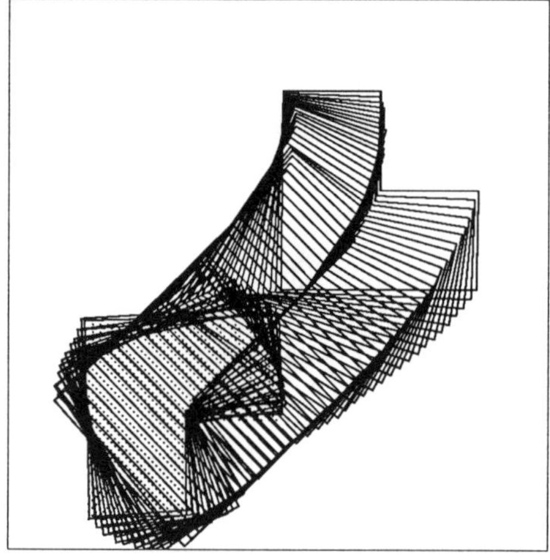

Figure 5: Two execution trails produced by local controller

Adding Context

If the environment had been sensed accurately, and if our model of control is perfect, and if indeed our path-planner produces collision-free paths, we would be done. Unfortunately, reality is rarely this forgiving. Control, sensing and model error all conspire against perfect executions of our nominal paths.

The most obvious failures occur because of interactions between the pushed object and other obstacles in the environment. Failures include limit cycling on segments of the path, chattering about certain points, and getting into *trap* states. In such states, the set of applicable actions that produce a noticeable effect reduces to zero.

One approach to handling this difficulty would be to attempt to model the dynamics of such interactions and include in the planner the ability to plan paths that take into account these explicit models of dynamics.

However, we will describe an approach that we have implemented that seems to work quite well. It presently cannot handle **trap** states. The approach is motivated by the observation that when collisions happen and contact occurs to change the dynamic behavior of the pushed object from what the controller expects it to do, what really matters is the locally sensed geometry of the environment. The basic idea is to generate a number of simple controllers to handle *each* of these local configurations much like the first level controller handles object motion in free-space.

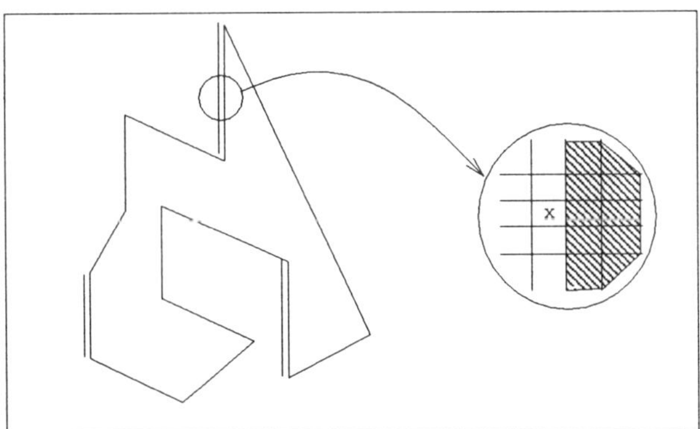

Figure 6: Illustration of Local Similarity

To illustrate the idea, consider Figure 6. Here we show a 2-D representation of a configuration space obstacle. The double lines indicate locations where the local contact geometry is similar. The expanded view indicates how if the robot is in a configuration cell marked x, its local view of the configuration space is identical if 4 or 8 neighbouring cells are considered. The reason for defining locality in configuration space should now be obvious. Since one can essentially view the pushed object as having been reduced to a point in this space, tests for locality can be much simpler even for objects of complicated shapes. If we use only orthogonal neighbours in a tesselated representation of the configuration space to define locality, then in an n-dimensional space we have 2^{2n} possible local configurations. For each one of these, our approach attempts to learn a local control rule that applies, much like the first level controller was learnt in free-space. It is this local configuration that we label *context*.

The planning, control and learning algorithm for the pushing task now looks like:

```
push-object (object, segment)
    context = sense-local-context
    controller = find-control (context)
    if ( controller = NIL )
        learn-rule (context)
    find-action (controller, object, segment)
```

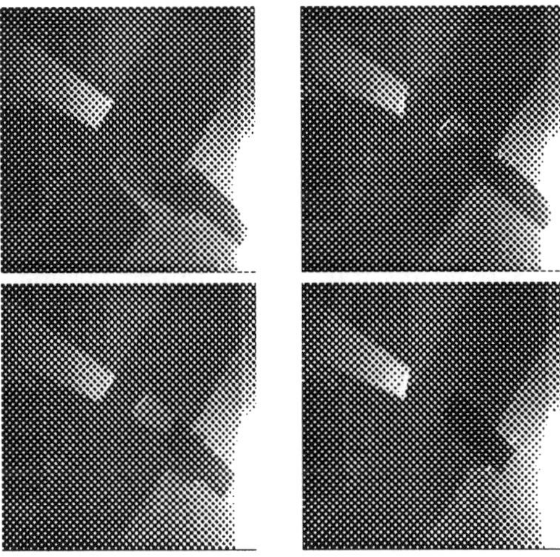

Figure 7: Peg-In-Hole Assembly by Pushing

Such a decomposition of the task-level strategy using local context has been the key to deriving robust strategies (see Figure 7 for four intermediate frames from the vision system during an assembly task). This approach has been the first one to solve all our examples we have thus far tested it on[2]. In our simulated examples, with a library of 30 part shapes on 20 tasks this approach is the only one that solves some of the complicated examples, and the only one not to exhibit significant limit cycling or chatter.

It should be noted that:

1. The locally sensed configuration space allows us to implement robot relative control loops extremely easily. Reactive behaviors that attempt to follow a moving object can be expressed quite easily in this framework.

---

[2]Control and angular error in our similations have been $[-10, 10]$ degrees in the direction of the push, and position sensing error has been a ball of 1 cm.

2. We do not seek to compute a single controller to handle the entire task, but settle for a set of controllers instead. We thus tread a path that is midway between approaches that seek a single sequence of actions, and approaches that attempt to derive a single map from sensed states to actions.

3. In practice, we do not actually need 2^{2n} controllers. Our examples seem to require about 2^n controllers on average. This is still exponential and a more precise bound would be desirable.

4. There is no inherent restriction that we only plan the path once. In fact, in domains where fast path planning can be implemented easily, we can envision the path to be the output of an any-time planner that is in continous operation.

5. At present, we do not change the different controllers once they are built. However, the framework does not prevent controllers whose parameters are changeable over time, or choosing actions using different algorithms than the ones we have presently implemented.

Conclusion

We have presented an approach that solves the problem of pushing objects around in the plane from configuration to configuration in a robust fashion. The approach's strength lies in the combination of a global path planner along with a set of local control laws or feedback rules that are activated depending upon the local context the pushed object is in.

The global path planner can be viewed to be continually in operation, while the local controllers can be derived automatically from simulation models or actual trials. In certain domains, geometry crucially affects dynamics especially when objects interact. The success of manipulator operations hinges on taking into account such geometrical effects. Our approach relies on a decomposition which allows the planner to operate in configuration space while ignoring the dynamics and the evolution of a set of controllers to deal with local dynamics. We expect such an approach to be more successful than others that attempt to take all of the dynamics into account at planning time, and others that rely entirely on local controllers.

References

1. Baraff, D., 1993. Issues in Computing Concact Forces for Non-Penetrating Rigid Bodies, *Algorithmica*, 10 : 292-352.

2. Brock, D. L., 1993. A Sensor Based Strategy for Automatic Robotic Grasping, Ph. D. Thesis, Department of Mechanical Engineering, Massachusetts Institute of Technology.

3. Brooks, R. A., 1986. A Robust Layered Control System for a Mobile Robot, *IEEE Journal of Robotics and Automation*, RA-2 (1) : 14-23.

4. Brooks, R. A., 1991. Intelligence Without Reason, *Proceedings of the International Joint Conference on Aritifical Intelligence*, 569-595.

5. Connell, J., 1990. A Colony Architecture for an Artificial Creature, MIT AI-TR-1151, Artificial Intelligence Laboratory, Massachusetts Institute of Technology.

6. Christiansen, A. D., Mason, M. T. and Mitchell, T. M., 1991. Learning Reliable Manipulation Strategies Without Initial Physical Models, *Robotics and Autonomous Systems*, 8 : 7-18.

7. Erdmann, M. E., 1984. On Motion Planning with Uncertainty, S. M. Thesis, Department of Electrical Engineering and Computer Science, Massachusetts Institute of Technology.

8. Guibas, L., Ramshaw, L., and Stolfi, J., 1983. A Kinetic Framework for Computational Geometry, *Proc. of the 24'th Annual IEEE Conference on the Foundations of Computer Science*, 100-111.

9. Lozano-Pérez, T., 1983. Spatial Planning: A Configuration Space Approach, *IEEE Transactions on Computers*, C-32 (2) : 108-120.

10. Lynch, K., 1993. Estimating the Friction Parameters of Pushed Objects, *IEEE/RSJ International Conference on Intelligent Robots and Systems*, 186-193.

11. Mason, M. T., 1982. Manipulator Grasping and Pushing Operations, Ph. D. Thesis, Dept. of Electrical Engg. and Computer Science, Massachusetts Institute of Technology.

12. Mason, M. T., 1986. Mechanics and Planning of Manipulator Pushing Operations, *International Journal of Robotics Research*, 5 (3) : 53-71.

13. Mason, M. T. and Wang, Y., 1988. On the inconsistency of rigid-body frictional planar mechanics, *Proc. IEEE Conference on Robotics and Automation*, 524-528.

14. Mataric, M., 1990. A Distributed Model for Mobile Robot Environment Learning and Navigation, AI-TR-1228, Artificial Intelligence Laboratory, Massachusetts Institute Of Technology.

15. Peshkin, M. A. and Sanderson, A. C., 1988. The Motion of a Pushed, Sliding Workpiece, *IEEE Journal of Robotics and Automation*, 4 (6) : 569-598.

Teleassistance: Contextual Guidance for Autonomous Manipulation*

Polly K. Pook and Dana H. Ballard
Computer Science Department
University of Rochester
Rochester, NY 14627-0226 USA
pook|dana@cs.rochester.edu

Abstract

We present *teleassistance*, a two-tiered control structure for robotic manipulation that combines the advantages of autonomy and teleoperation. At the top level, a teleoperator provides global, *deictic* references via a natural sign language. Each sign indicates the next action to perform and a relative and hand-centered coordinate frame in which to perform it. For example, the teleoperator may point to an object for reaching, or preshape the hand for grasping. At the lower level autonomous servo routines run within the reference frames provided. Teleassistance offers two benefits. First, the servo routines can position the robot in relative coordinates and interpret feedback within a constrained context. This significantly simplifies the computational load of the autonomous routines and requires only a sparse model of the task. Second, the operator's actions are symbolic, conveying intent without requiring the person to literally control the robot. This helps to alleviate many of the problems inherent to teleoperation, including poor mappings between operator and robot physiology, reliance on a broad communication bandwidth, and the potential for robot damage when solely under remote control. To demonstrate the concept, a Utah/MIT hand mounted on a Puma 760 arm opens a door.

Introduction

Autonomous servo control and teleoperation have complementary advantages and disadvantages as robotic control schemes. Servo control of robotic manipulation has benefited from the development of compliant manipulators with rich position and force sensing capabilities. When situated in a local context, fast distributed servo feedback enables a robot to react quickly and appropriately [Brooks 1986][Connell 1989]. Servo control currently suffers, however, from a poor ability to perceive and plan according to global state. Teleoperation addresses this weakness by putting a person

in the loop, one who can provide more global guidance. But teleoperation eliminates local servo control, resulting in slow jerky movement that is quite tedious for the teleoperator. Local reactivity is lost. What is needed is a two-layer control strategy: a high level to select a context in which low-level behaviors situate

Consider the advantages of each control mechanism for the hypothetical task of planing a board. A teleoperator can more easily set up the task by locating and positioning the planer on the board, than an autonomous robot can. Once context is established the servo controller more readily maintains a smooth, sliding contact with the board. It moves along the central axis of the planer, independent of world coordinates, while tightly monitoring force feedback on an orthogonal axis, independent of the orientation of the board. Feedback is interpreted within the context of planing to adjust force and position. The teleoperator provides a high-level reference context that low-level servo behaviors could exploit.

Setting up a reference frame for subsequent relative actions is an example of a *deictic*, or pointing, strategy [Agre & Chapman 1987]. We propose a *teleassisted* controller for robotic manipulation that interfaces high-level deictic strategies with context-sensitive servo behaviors. A person wearing a master teleoperation device provides the deictic references. Rather than literally teleoperate the robot and bear the concomitant problems of delayed and limited feedback, the operator uses a gestural sign language to select successive contexts for low-level autonomous force and position control.

Deictic strategies

Studies suggest that animals use high-level deictic strategies to bind low-level perceptual and motor behaviors to the current context [Kowler & Anton 1987][Ballard et al. 1992]. Visual fixation is an example of a deictic strategy that binds motor behavior to a relative coordinate frame. For example, an object can be grasped by first looking at it and then directing the hand to the center of the image coordinate frame. In depth, the hand can be servoed relative to

*This work was supported by NSF research grant no. IRI-8903582 and by a research grant from the Human Science Frontiers Program.

the horopter using binocular cues. This strategy is invariant to agent movement and task locale.

Like visual fixation, the act of grasping an object provides a framework for interpreting the associated kinesthetic feedback. For example, bi-manual animals often use one hand as a vise and the other for dexterous manipulation. We hypothesize that the vise hand marks a reference frame and that the dexterous motions are made relative to that frame. Similarly, body position creates a reference for motor actions. Studies of human hand-eye coordination have found head movements to often be closely associated with hand movements. [Pelz et al. 1994] found that most subjects square their head with respect to the site of a complex manipulation action and then hold it very still during the manipulation, even when the eyes are looking elsewhere. This fits our hypothesis if we consider head position as a reference frame for relative hand motion. To make this more concrete as a control strategy, we assign a deictic strategy two roles: to make a *temporal* and a *spatial* binding to the world.

Temporal binding

The intended action, such as reaching or grasping, binds the servo controller to the *temporal context*. Without a detailed model of the world, many interpretations of feedback are possible; temporal context can allow the controller to select the correct one. Earlier studies demonstrate the importance of temporal context in reducing the complexity of robot motor tasks. In [Pook & Ballard 1992], a Utah/MIT dexterous manipulator autonomously grasps a spatula, positions it in a pan and flips a plastic egg without relying on precise positioning or force information. Each successive action is controlled by interpreting qualitative changes in force feedback within the current context. For example, identifying force contact can be done by simply noting a significant change in tension on any hand joint, regardless of the particular hand or task configuration. To determine what event is associated with a qualitative change in force, whether it be from grasping the spatula, placing it in the pan or sliding it under the egg, the controller can refer to the current context. In deterministic sequential tasks, this context is implicit in the control program. This approach has parallels with the behavioral approach of [Salganicoff & Bajcsy 1991] but relies on local feedback.

Spatial binding

A *spatial binding* defines a relative coordinate frame for successive perceptual and motor behaviors. Deictic bindings avoid world-centered geometry that varies with robot movement. For fixation the reference is gaze-centered. To open a door, for instance, looking at the doorknob defines a relative servo target. [Crisman & Cleary 1994] demonstrate the computational advantage of target-centered frames for mobile robot navigation.

Pointing and preshaping the hand create hand-centered spatial frames. Pointing defines a relative axis for subsequent motion. In the case of preshaping, the relative frame attaches within the *opposition space* [Arbib, Iberall, & Lyons 1985] of the fingers. With adequate dexterity and compliance, simply flexing the fingers toward the origin of that frame coupled with a force control loop suffices to form a stable grasp. Since the motor action is bound to the local context, the same grasping action can be applied to different objects, a spatula, a mug, a doorknob, by changing the preshape.

A teleassisted control strategy

In teleassistance, the operator, wearing a master device, guides the robot with natural gestures that correspond to the task at hand. These gestures form a sign language. The signs are deictic in that they define a spatial and temporal context for subsequent robot behaviors. A sign is recognized by monitoring the operator's finger positions and matching them to stored models. On recognition of a hand sign, the controller calls the servo behaviors, with the current spatial context as a parameter. In this way, a person motions the robot through a complex and possibly non-deterministic task.

Each sign can be mapped to a high-level state in a non-deterministic finite state machine (FSM), as shown in Figure 1. At top are the deictic states, marked with dashed lines. From each high-level state, control is passed to the appropriate low-level servo routines, shown at bottom, that perform the intended action. The two state classes are separated in the figure for clarity. In practice, all states belong to a single FSM for the task. The topology encodes the task context.

We will illustrate teleassistance through the task of opening a door. A simple scheme for door-opening is to reach for the handle, then grasp and turn it. Under teleassistance, the task might be performed as follows. The operator steers the robot to the door handle by pointing and shapes the hand and wrist for the handle type. The robot in turn moves along the given direction until it bumps into the door, copies the operator's hand shape, moves to contact the handle, then grasps and turns it. These behaviors are described in detail in the next section.

The non-determinism of the FSM affords the operator some flexibility. The operator may choose to compose task actions arbitrarily when order is not crucial. Or the operator may wish to take emergency action when an error is detected. The FSM topology can be designed to support such deviations. In our simple examples, the operator can rest or stop at intermediate points in the task. It is worth noting that the topology must be pre-specified for each task and so this flexibility is restricted.

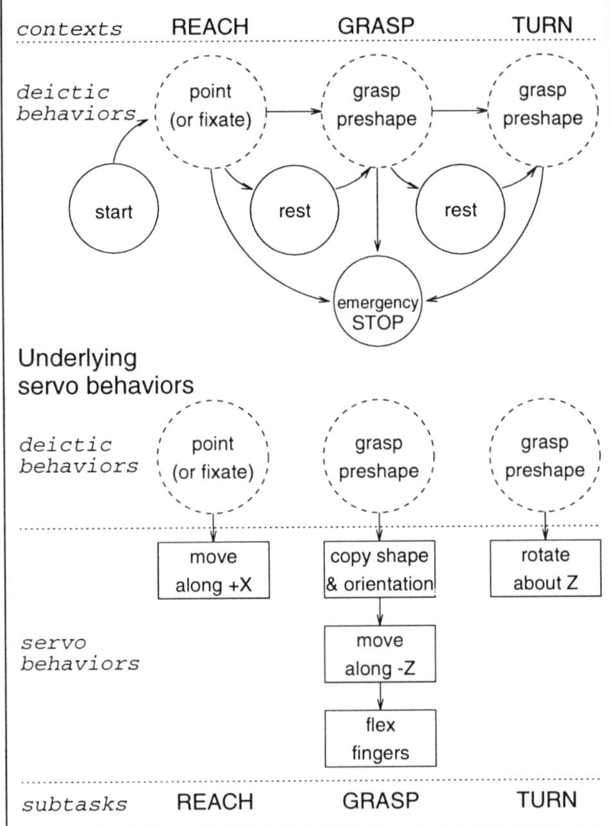

Figure 1: A FSM for opening a door. The flow of control among high-level states is shown at *top*. Each deictic gesture, marked with a dashed line, defines a relative coordinate frame and a task context (REACH, GRASP, TURN). From a deictic state, control is passed to appropriate low-level robot behaviors that perform the sub-task (shown at *bottom*). Each low-level action moves within its relative frame, servoing on guard conditions such as force contact.

Example: Opening a door

To illustrate the two-tiered control strategy, a robot manipulator opens a small door equipped with a lever handle. The door is placed arbitrarily within the working space of the hand. Each high-level deictic routine, ties a temporal context (REACH, GRASP, TURN) and a relative coordinate frame to subsequent low-level actions. In this example, all coordinate frames are hand-centered.

The low-level servo routines are a sequence of guarded moves. The direction of each move (of the fingers and/or the arm) is implicit in the context of the task and is made relative to the current frame. Feedback consists of finger position error, i.e., the difference between the actual and commanded finger joint angles. A change in the position error is interpreted within the current context of REACHING, GRASPING, etc., to control the action appropriately. Each routine is described in greater detail below.

Lab Setup

Hardware The manipulator is a sixteen degree-of-freedom Utah/MIT hand mounted on a six degree-of-freedom PUMA 760 arm. The hand has four fingers with four joints apiece. A pair of pneumatically driven agonist-antagonist tendons actuates each joint. Hall effect sensors monitor each joint angle. The hand is both dexterous and compliant so its control strategy can ignore many inessential variations in the task configuration, such as the precise shape and orientation of a door handle [Pook & Ballard 1992].

The teleoperator wears an EXOS Dexterous Hand Master (TM) that measures four joint angles on each of four fingers. Additionally, an Ascension Bird (TM) polhemus sensor mounted on the back of the teleoperator's hand measures the position and orientation of the operator's arm and wrist in lab coordinates.

Coordinate frame mapping The teleoperator and the robot each have their own relative coordinate systems with a mapping between them. For arm motion, only the orientation of the teleoperator's polhemus sensor is mapped to the corresponding robot frame. For finger motion, only the joint angles are mapped. In either case, translation is ignored.

The sign language The sign language for this task consists of six signs: point, preshape, rest, emergency stop, speedup, and slow down. Previously, we empirically derived a range of permissible joint angles for the operator's hand and arm for each sign. To recognize a sign on-line, the program monitors the joint angles on the EXOS and polhemus devices and identifies a match when it occurs. We are currently working on learning new signs automatically, rather than through empirical determination. See the last section, *Future Work*, for details.

The program

REACHING for the door. The teleoperator commences action by pointing the robot arm toward the door, as shown in the upper left of Figure 2. This provides a temporal launching point for the program and defines a spatial coordinate frame centered on the back of the robot hand. While the operator points, the PUMA moves in the direction of the pointing axis, independently of world coordinates. Thus the robot reach is made relative to a deictic axis which the teleoperator can easily adjust.

The autonomous move monitors the guard condition of a change in position error on any of the Utah/MIT finger joints. In the context of REACHING, the change in robot finger position is interpreted as contact with a non-compliant surface and the reach halts and backs off a small distance from the point of contact. So, when the hand bumps into the door, the arm stops.

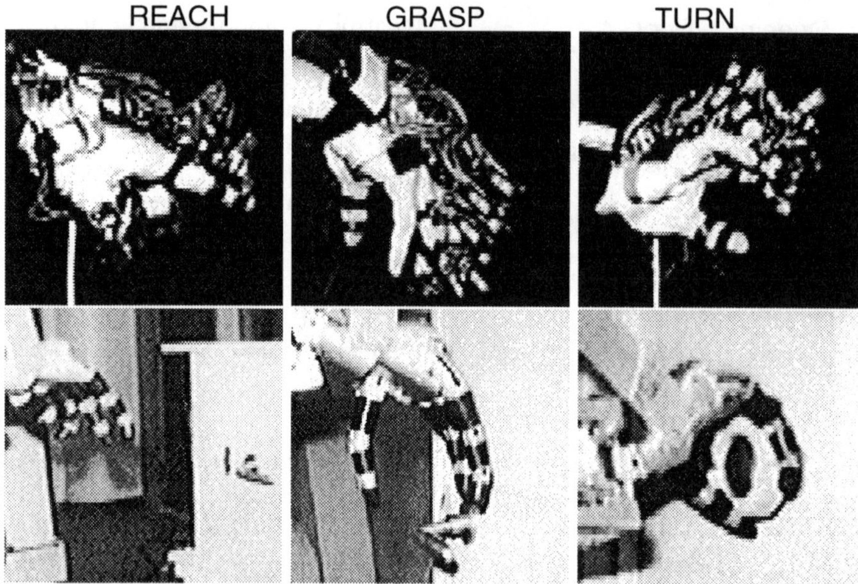

Figure 2: At top are the teleoperator reference poses to REACH, GRASP and TURN the door handle. For illustrative purposes both a lever and a knob are shown, although only the lever is used. Snapshots of subsequent robot behavior are shown at bottom. In REACHING, the context of a pointing index finger signifies that only the x-direction of the polhemus sensor is important. In GRASPING the overall shape of the three fingers and the thumb define a preshape for the particular handle. In TURNING, the grasp shape reveals the handle type and, by extension, its pivot point. Notably, the robot hand itself could provide the deictic reference for TURNING, by noting its current pose.

The FSM has self-loops in each deictic behavior so that the operator can successively point in new directions to accurately place the robot hand. In a typical trial, the operator points the robot arm toward the door. When the robot reaches the door by sensing contact, the operator repeatedly points anew to position the hand over the door handle. Each movement halts when the operator changes the pointing axis, stops pointing, or the hand detects contact. A new pointing axis initiates a new movement. When satisfied, the teleoperator adopts a grasp preshape. The FSM recognizes the new sign and shifts context to that of GRASPING.

GRASPING the door handle. A grasp preshape defines a new spatial frame centered on the palm of the hand. The robot mimics the preshape using a linear, joint to joint mapping between the EXOS and the robot hand [Speeter 1993]. The middle column of Figure 2 shows the preshape for turning the door lever. Subsequent servo routines find the handle and grasp it.

In the new spatial context, the negative Z-axis points out of the palm. To find the handle, the robot hand moves along this axis until it senses contact. The advantage of a deictic framework can be seen by comparing this action for different door handles. For the door *lever*, the hand-centered Z-axis points downward. For a *knob*, the Z-axis is horizontal. The move is independent of world coordinates, however, because it is made relative to the hand frame.

A change in position error, resulting from contact with the doorhandle, stops the motion.[1] In either case, the controller interprets the error as contact and so, within the current context, proceeds to grasp.

To grasp the door handle, the robot flexes the finger joints until they are all either fully flexed or maintaining a position error. The preshape set the fingers in opposition to one another as needed to grasp the particular door handle. Because the grasp is performed within the context of that preshape this strategy applies to either door handle.

TURNING the handle. The robot pose (or the human preshape) defines whether the context is one of grasping a knob or a lever. The rightmost column of Figure 2 shows the hand grasping the door knob. In this case the pivot point of the handle is set to the center of the palm (i.e., the origin of the current deictic frame). If the hand shape corresponds to a wrap grasp, then the pivot is about a point alongside the grip, i.e., offset along the current Y-axis which corresponds to the axis of the lever. A new spatial frame is attached to the pivot point and the arm rotates about the new Z-axis. Such a rotation is much simpler than computing an equivalent trajectory in lab space.

---

[1]The hand must be positioned fairly accurately over the lever, such that one or more of the finger links makes contact with it. A better solution is to have a contact sensor on the palm or a force sensor in the wrist.

The arm continues its rotation until a position error is sensed. In this context, the controller interprets the error to mean the handle's mechanical stop has been reached.

Results

Four different operators each performed ten trials of the task under teleoperation control and ten trials under teleassistance. For each controller, the operators trained until they were comfortable: 10 to 15 minutes for teleoperation and 2 to 10 minutes for teleassistance. Twice during each 10-trial set, the door was moved to a new position selected arbitrarily within the workspace.

The results are shown in Table 1, along with the results of a completely autonomous controller. Teleassistance required about the same amount of time as the autonomous controller, and both are, on average, 33% faster than teleoperation. The time is occupied differently by each controller, however. 60% of the time spent under teleassistance is in fact under autonomous control. Thus, the operator actually spent only 8 seconds, on average, controlling the robot via hand signs. The teleoperator, in contrast, spent more than treble the time (29 sec.) in literal master-slave control of the robot.

The teleoperator, however, is able to avoid failures that other two controllers cannot. In the case of teleassistance, all failures were due to not turning the door handle far enough to free the catch. The servo controller did not detect the mechanical stop correctly. The autonomnous controller failed due to its reliance on hard-coded position information. Thus, changing the doors position twice during the trials resulted in the controller failing (not finding the door or the handle) two-thirds of the time. This figure is not generalizable as it depends entirely on the degree of certainty in the task. In a structured, static environment, the autonomous controller would work very well. In an unstructured world, however, teleassistance is preferable.

Conclusion and related work

The idea of combining traditional teleoperation and autonomous servo controllers has been suggested in various forms by several researchers. [Sayers, Paul, & Mintz 1992] at the University of Pennsylvania Grasp Lab allows the teleoperator to select among a menu of geometric targets. The teleoperation apparatus (the master) is then constrained to motions along the selected geometry. [Yokohoji et al. 1993] suggest building a manual control box which the teleoperator can pre-set to a desired strategy as needed: full teleoperation, full autonomy, or one of two combinations . [Kuniyoshi, Inaba, & Inoue 1992], [Ikeuchi & Suehiro 1992], and [Kang & Ikeuchi 1994] visually recognize teleoperator motions to guide the robot.

Our approach is to make the transfer of control between teleoperator and robot implicit in the context of the task. A task specific FSM encodes the context

in its topology. The teleoperator, rather than being responsible for direct control of the robot, guides the robot with gestures and supplies the spatial and temporal frameworks in which to situate the autonomous servo behaviors[2]. The behavior can then operate in a relativistic constrained domain and perform with computational efficiency. This method of providing for local interpretation of feedback compares with the qualitative vision strategies made possible with gaze control vision systems [Ballard 1991][Ballard & Brown 1992] . Given the task context, these methods can rely on a very sparse model of the world. Such strategies are common to animal systems [Bower 1982][Twitchell 1970] but are a notable departure from traditional robot control schema that rely on precise force and position models.

Future work: acquiring and recognizing new hand signs

The transfer of control between high and low-level behaviors, implicit in the task, requires explicit recognition of the sign language used by the operator. Currently, we provide an *a priori* empirical model of each hand sign. This method has at least two drawbacks. One is that the models must be robust to different operators and to the non-linearities of the EXOS device. We have handled this by defining the models quite loosely. However, as more signs are added to the lexicon, overlap will occur and ambiguity will arise. A more accurate, but still robust, method is needed. Secondly, it would be useful to learn signs dynamically, allowing for operator preference.

Earlier studies suggest a remedy to these drawbacks. These studies demonstrate the ability to learn and recognize manipulation primitives from temporal features in the robot state [Pook & Ballard 1993]. (see also [Hannaford & Lee 1991]). In this experiment, several teleoperators performed samples of each primitive while we recorded the finger joint tensions and velocities. By applying Learning Vector Quantization (LVQ) [Kohonen 1990] to these recordings we could create canonical patterns for each primitive. Using these learned patterns we could segment a compound manipulation task, flipping an egg, into its recognizable primitives, although with numerous errors. However these errors, in the form of ambiguities and spurious misclassifications, could be eliminated by performing the segmentation within the context of the task. The context was encoded in the topology of a hidden markov model (HMM), just as the context of opening a door is encoded in an FSM. An HMM is a probabilistic finite state machine that models a markov process; i.e., it accommodates natural variation and is sensitive only to the current state[see Rabiner & Juang 1986].

---

[2]If other deictic inputs are available, such as a computer vision system with gaze control, they could replace the teleoperator where desired.

Controller	Avg. Time (sec.)	Mean Time (sec.)	% Time under		Failure Rate
			Operator control	Auto control	
Teleoperation	29	24.5	100%	0%	0%
Teleassistance	20	19.0	40%	60%	13%
Autonomy	20	20.0	0%	100%	66%*

*see text

Table 1: Results for the task of opening a door under the three controllers.

The probabilistic contextual constraint provided by the HMM makes matching considerably easier.

This method of pattern-matching within a known context was robust to the vagaries of different operators and changes in the task configuration. We are now investigating the use of this method to dynamically and automatically learn the deictic sign language. Preliminary results are promising and address the drawbacks of our present empirical scheme.

Acknowledgments

The authors wish to thank Ray Frank, Tim Becker and Luid Bukys for their technical assistance and forbearance and John Lloyd and Vincent Hayward for the RCCL Puma controller.

References

[1] P. E. Agre and D. Chapman. Pengi: An implementation of a theory of activity. In *Proceedings of the Sixth National Conference on Artificial Intelligence*, pages 268–272. Morgan Kaufmann, Los Altos, CA, 1987.

[2] M. Arbib, T. Iberall, and D. Lyons. Coordinated control programs for movements of the hand. Technical report, COINS Dept. of Comp. and Inf. Science, University of Massachussetts, 1985.

[3] D. H. Ballard. Animate vision. *Artificial Intelligence*, pages 57–86, February 1991.

[4] D. H. Ballard and C. M. Brown. Principles of animate vision. *CVGIP: Image Understading*, July 1992.

[5] D.H. Ballard, M.M. Hayhoe, F. Li, and S.D. Whitehead. Hand-eye coordination during sequential tasks. *Proc. of the Phil. Trans. Royal Soc. of London*, 1992.

[6] T. G. R. Bower. *Development in Infancy*. New York: W.H. Freeman and Co., 1982.

[7] R. Brooks. A layered intelligent control system for a mobile robot. *IEEE Journal of Robotics and Automation*, pages 14–23, April 1986.

[8] J. Connell. A colony architecture for an artificial creature. Tech. Report 1151, MIT AI Lab, 1989.

[9] J. Crisman and M. Cleary. Deictic primitives for general purpose navigation. *Proc. of the AIAA Conf. on Intelligent Robots in Factory, Field, Space, and Service (CIRFFSS)*, March 1994.

[10] B. Hannaford and P. Lee. Hidden markov model analysis of force/torque information in telemanipulation. *International Journal of Robotics Research*, pages 528–538, October 1991.

[11] K. Ikeuchi and T. Suehiro. Towards an assembly plan from observation. *Proc. of the IEEE International Conference on Robotics and Automation*, May 1992.

[12] S.B. Kang and K. Ikeuchi. Grasp recognition and manipulative motion characterization from human hand motion sequences. *Proc. of the IEEE International Conference on Robotics and Automation*, May 1994.

[13] T. Kohonen. Improved versions of learning vector quantization. *Proc. of the International Joint Conference on Neural Networks*, June 1990.

[14] E. Kowler and S. Anton. Reading twisted text: Implications for the role of saccades. *Vision Research*, pages 27:45–60, 1987.

[15] Y. Kuniyoshi, M. Inaba, and H. Inoue. Seeing, understanding and doing human task. *Proc. of the IEEE Int'l Conf. on Robotics & Automation*, May 1992.

[16] J. Pelz, M. M. Hayhoe, D. H. Ballard, and A. Forsberg. Separate motor commands for eye and head. *Submitted, Investigative Ophthalmology and Visual Science, Supplement 1994*, 1993.

[17] P. K. Pook and D. H. Ballard. Sensing qualitative events to control manipulation. *Proceedings of the SPIE Sensor Fusion V Conference*, November 1992.

[18] P. K. Pook and D. H. Ballard. Recognizing teleoperated manipulations. *Proc. of the IEEE International Conference on Robotics and Automation*, May 1993.

[19] L.R. Rabiner and B.H. Juang. An introduction to hidden markov models. *IEEE ASSP Magazine*, Jan. 1986.

[20] M. Salganicoff and R. Bajcsy. Sensorimotor learning using active perception in continuous domains. *AAAI Fall Symposium Series: Sensory Aspects of Robotic Intelligence*, November 1991.

[21] C. Sayers, R. Paul, and M. Mintz. Operator interaction and teleprogramming for subsea manipulation. *4th IARP Workshop on Underwater Robotics*, 1992.

[22] T. H. Speeter. Transforming human hnad motion for telemanipulation. *Presence: Teleoperators and Virtual Environments*, 1992.

[23] W. Twitchell. Mechanisms of motor development. In *Reflex Mechanisms and the Development of Prehension*. New York: Academic Press, 1970.

[24] Y. Yokohoji, A. Ogawa, H. Hasanuma, and T. Yoshikawa. Operation modes for cooperating with autonomous functions in intelligent teleoperation systems. *Proc. of the IEEE International Conference on Robotics and Automation*, May 1993.

Automatically Tuning Control Systems for Simulated Legged Robots

Robert Ringrose
MIT Leg Lab
MIT Artificial Intelligence Laboratory
545 Technology Square
Cambridge, MA 02139
ringrose@ai.mit.edu

Abstract

Rather than create a control system from scratch each time we build a new robot creature, we would like to generate control systems automatically. I have implemented an algorithm which, given a control system that works well for one creature, automatically tunes it to work for a new, similar creature. Using this approach, the control system for a horse might be adjusted for use with elephants, giraffes, and dogs. The adjustment is accomplished by gradually altering the original creature to make it like the new one and repeatedly tuning the control system as these changes are made. Because the creature's alteration is gradual, the control system can be tuned using a local search such as gradient descent. In simulation tests, the tuning algorithm has successfully tuned the control system of a planar quadruped simulation to accommodate a reduction in leg length by a factor of two, an increase in body mass by a factor of three, and changes in the commanded speed while trotting.

Introduction

Within the domain of actively balanced legged locomotion, it is necessary to tune control systems to reflect physical alterations of the robot. I have designed and implemented a tuning algorithm which will tune an existing control system to control a different robot, or to exhibit different behavior. This algorithm has successfully tuned the control system of a planar quadruped simulation to accommodate a reduction in leg length by a factor of two, an increase in body mass by a factor of three, and changes in the commanded speed while trotting.[1]

Any control system has some set of control parameters, numbers which determine how it performs. For example, a parameter might control how rapidly it tries to accelerate to a desired speed or how much energy it injects at each step. For a complicated system, the

appropriate values for these control parameters are not obvious. There are several advantages to having a computer search for a set of parameters which minimizes an evaluation function rather than having a human tune the control system directly. Automatically tuning the control system does not require that a human with experience tuning invest a large amount of time. One can also specify the desired behavior without considering the interactions between any specific input parameters to the control system. Additionally, it is easier for a computer to optimize for something which is not obvious to a human, such as minimal energy consumption. Properly specifying the desired behavior is not a trivial task, but it seems easier than manually tuning the control system.

Other work on self-tuning controllers (Helferty, Collins, & Kam 1988), which frequently used searching techniques such as spacetime constraints (Witkin & Kass 1988) or genetic algorithms (Pearse, Arkin, & Ram 1992), has addressed similar problems. Tuning controllers for dynamically balanced legged systems is particularly challenging because there is typically only a small "sweet spot" near the global minimum where one can effectively evaluate the robot's behavior. A parameter set outside this sweet spot will generally make the robot fall over or not take any steps, while a parameter set inside the sweet spot will make the robot run well enough that its performance can be evaluated objectively. The vast majority of the possible parameter sets for dynamically balanced legged locomotion lie outside of the sweet spot. As a consequence, general search methods like genetic algorithms and simulated annealing will take a long time to find any working solution, and searches which follow a local slope will only find a useful minimum if they start in the sweet spot. A frequently used method for getting around this challenging search space is to simplify the problem so as to drastically increase the sweet spot's size (for example, one can add constraints to the model that prevent the robot from falling over). Instead of modifying the search space to suit my algorithm, however, I have attempted to adjust my algorithm to fit the search space.

In the event that there is a parameter set which is

---

[1]This material is based upon work supported under a National Science Foundation Graduate Research Fellowship. Any opinions, findings, conclusions, or recommendations expressed in this publication are those of the author and do not necessarily reflect the views of the National Science Foundation.

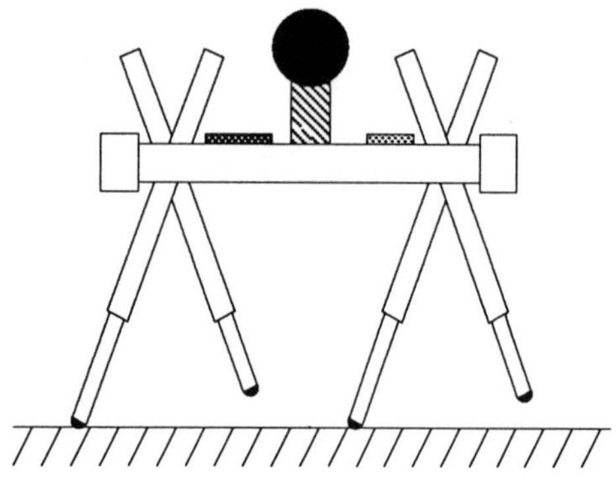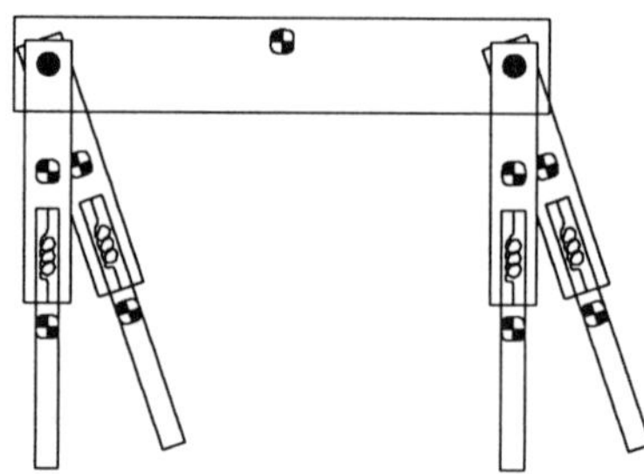

Figure 1: Illustration of the simulated quadruped and the associated model. The actuators at the hips are implemented as torque sources. The leg actuator is implemented as a spring with controllable rest length and different constants in compression and extension. The simulation is a planar rigid-body model.

in the sweet spot, a simple gradient descent search can find a local minimum. Additionally, most of the time a small change in the robot's configuration will result in only a small change in the sweet spot. The tuning algorithm presented here uses this characteristic to break the search for a new set of parameters into a series of smaller searches for which minima are easier to find. For example, assume the control system for a quadruped running simulation has been tuned to run with legs of a particular length. To find a set of control parameters for a quadruped running with legs half as long, the tuning algorithm gradually reduces the leg length and optimizes at several leg lengths between full and half length. As the leg length changes, the location of the sweet spot will change. For small changes the sweet spot's motion will usually be slight enough that the control parameters for the unchanged leg length will still be within the new sweet spot. The tuning process may fail if gradient descent cannot find a local minimum (the sweet spot might not be continuous), if the sweet spot changes dramatically with a small alteration in the robot, or if there is no way for the given control system to control the robot.

To find appropriate values for the control parameters, the tuning algorithm described in this paper starts with an existing control system, simulation, and parameter set. It finds out how far it can modify the simulation and still get acceptable behavior, makes that modification, and then uses a gradient descent search to improve the performance of the modified simulation. This process of modifying the simulation and re-tuning the control system is repeated until you have the desired final simulation.

The Simulation

I have used a planar quadruped simulation to test the tuning algorithm. It retains enough complexity to illustrate most of the problems that come up, but is simple to visualize and easy to explain. The simulation is based on a physical robot described by Raibert (Raibert, Chepponis, & Brown 1986)(Raibert 1990).

The simulation is a rigid body simulation, the dynamics of which are generated using a commercial dynamic modeling program (Rosenthal & Sherman 1986)(Ringrose 1992a). Simulation creation is automated so that it is possible to change and re-create any simulation as part of the tuning process. The planar quadruped which I used is illustrated in figure 1.

The simulated robot is controlled by a planar variation of the finite state controller for the Raibert trotting quadruped (Raibert *et al.* 1992). The control system uses measurements which could be sensed or calculated on a physical robot, such as position, velocity, actuator lengths, and ground contact. The control system's behavior can be modified through 20 parameters, including maximum acceleration, desired speed, spring constants, and desired leg length during different running phases. Some previous investigations into robotic running are described in references (Hodgins & Raibert 1989)(Hodgins & Raibert 1991)(Playter & Raibert 1992)(Raibert *et al.* 1992). Further details of the controller and model are available in (Ringrose 1992b).

Searching for Solutions

In order to search for an appropriate set of control parameters, you need a way to compare the behavior generated by different sets of control parameters. I use the results from an evaluation function which simulates the creature and returns an objective measure of the creature's performance. Most evaluation functions for dynamically stable running motions result in a search space whose structure makes global searching algorithms ineffective. However, once you have a reasonably good solution, a gradient descent search (Press *et al.* 1988) modified to take into account local minima (Ringrose 1992b) will frequently be able to find a better solution.

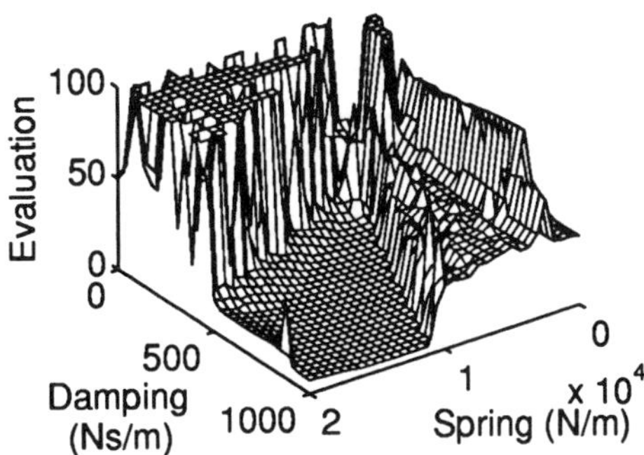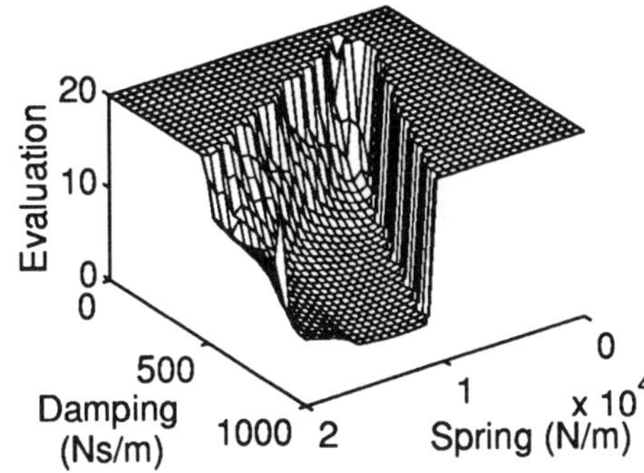

Figure 2: Graph of evaluation results over changes in leg spring and damping constants for the planar quadruped, using the evaluation function described in the text. The noisy, high-valued regions are outside the sweet spot. The right graph is the same as the left, with a lower maximum value imposed to emphasize the structure of the sweet spot.

Most evaluation functions for legged locomotion have a nearly pathological search space because if the parameters are out of a small sweet spot around the good solutions the simulated creature fails catastrophically, usually by falling over or not taking any steps. When such a failure occurs, a meaningful evaluation of performance is difficult since the causes of the simulation's failure to trot are difficult to determine. The creature could fall over if it stubs its toe, the leg springs are not strong enough, the swing legs do not come forward fast enough to catch the robot, or some other reason. It is not difficult to make an evaluation function which recognizes when it is out of the sweet spot, but it is difficult to ensure that when outside the sweet spot the gradient of the evaluation function leads towards the sweet spot.

Because of the inherent difficulty evaluating a catastrophic failure, most evaluation functions only have a useful section near the global minimum and the rest is noise. Evaluation functions usually have more dimensions than can be readily visualized, but cross sections can give an idea of the search space's general structure. A two dimensional cross-section of the evaluation function is somewhat like a smooth canyon (the sweet spot) in noise, with the noise being uniformly higher-valued than the sweet spot. There are many parameter sets that do not generate information except to indicate that the creature failed (in the noisy section) and there is a smaller number of parameter sets where the creature may actually run well. Figure 2 illustrates the general shape of evaluation functions, using data from the simulated quadruped.

Evaluating Performance

In order to evaluate the performance of a set of control parameters, I created an evaluation function which reflects the fact that a control algorithm for a trotting quadruped needs to do more than propel the quadruped forward. Raibert's experimentation in quadruped control suggests that it should (Raibert 1990):

- control the forward velocity.
- regulate the body attitude.
- put reasonable constraints on the forces and torques applied.
- limit the vertical motion of the body.
- keep the running cycle stable.

The evaluation function I used is the integration of the departures from these goals over the course of seven simulated seconds (Ringrose 1992b). Seven seconds, the length of time over which the behavioral error is integrated, is several times the length of the step cycle, allowing transients to die out. This evaluation function does not guarantee that the running cycle is stable beyond the seven seconds of running actually simulated. In practice, however, if the simulation successfully trots for that length of time it is stable enough that it is unlikely to fail later.

Getting a Close Solution

A goal of this work is to be able to automatically tune the control system when there are large changes in the physical characteristics of the creature. When the simulation changes by a small amount, a good parameter set may no longer be locally optimal, but it may still be within the sweet spot. Figure 3 shows a cross section of a sample evaluation function and how it changes as the simulation is altered. If the simulation's change is small enough that the new location of the sweet spot still overlaps the old set of control parameters, those original control parameters can be used with a local search such as gradient descent to find a new set of acceptable control parameters. Generally, if there is a large physical change, the control parameters which were originally acceptable give poor results because the sweet spot moves too far. However, by splitting the large change into a series of smaller changes one can follow the motion of the sweet spot as the simulation changes.

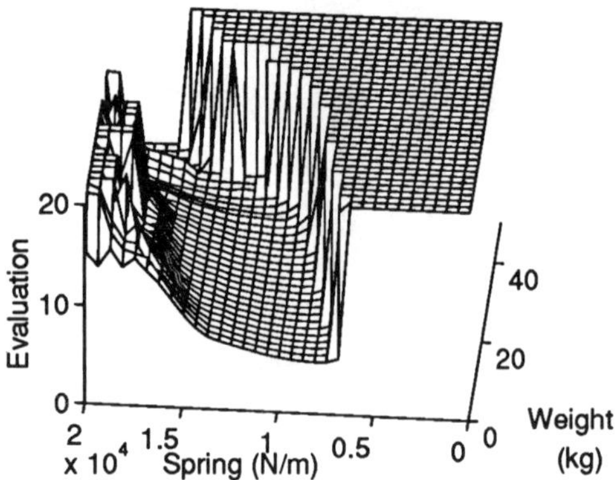

Figure 3: Leg spring constant in compression as weight on the quadruped increases. Note how by staying in the minimum as weight is added to the quadruped's trunk it is possible to find a spring constant for 50 kg which is within the sweet spot. Parameters other than the leg spring constant in compression are optimized for the appropriate weight.

In order to have the tuning process work efficiently, it is desirable to take large steps when possible. I use a divide-and-conquer algorithm which splits large changes in half if necessary and recursively solves each half. Set up the simulation with a fraction f which goes from 0 to 1, where 0 is the original configuration and 1 is the final configuration. Let $F_a(P)$ represent running the simulation with the fraction $f = a$ and the parameter set P, applying the evaluation function to the run, and returning the result. Let a and b be numbers between 0 and 1. Let P_a be a parameter set such that $F_a(P_a)$ is "acceptable" (less than a user-defined constant). The algorithm used to find some P_b, a parameter set such that $F_b(P_b)$ is acceptable, is:

- If $F_b(P_a)$ is "good enough" (less than a constant supplied by the user), $P_b = P_a$.

- Otherwise, if $F_b(P_a)$ is "acceptable", P_b is the set of parameters arrived at by a gradient descent search with P_a as a starting point and using the model with fraction b until the result $F_b(P_b)$ is "optimized" (less than another user-defined constant).

- Let $c = (a + b)/2$.

- Recursively use this algorithm to find P_c, a parameter set such that $F_c(P_c)$ is acceptable, from P_a, a, and c.

- Recursively use this algorithm to find P_b from P_c, c, and b.

Setting the constants "optimized", "good enough" and "acceptable" requires some care. If the level at which the simulation is considered "optimized" is too low, the gradient descent search will take a long time finding a good parameter set (recall that low evaluation results correspond to desired behavior). On the other hand, if "optimized" is too high, the gradient descent search could return a parameter set which is close to the edge of the sweet spot, reducing efficiency. The constant "good enough" corresponds to the point at which the control system performs well and does not need further optimization. This means that the conditions for beginning optimization are less rigorous than the conditions for ending optimization, so that each time the gradient descent search is used it is required to perform a non-trivial amount of work. Finally, "acceptable" corresponds to the edge of the sweet spot. If the result of the evaluation is too high, it is considered to be in the area where the evaluation function is essentially useless.

Note that the fractions at which the gradient descent search is used increase monotonically from 0, and the only time the parameter set P is modified is when the gradient descent search is used.

There are restrictions to this procedure. It must be possible to gradually change the parameter set and configuration from the initial parameter set and configuration to the final one, without leaving the sweet spot. Also, the control system must be able to control the new configuration. For example, the person designing the control system might neglect one of the moments of inertia, and in a new configuration that moment could be extremely important for stability. Since this tuning method will not alter the control system, it will not be able to address this type of problem. Additionally, the behavior for the initial configuration must be similar to the behavior required in the final configuration. If there is a drastic change in strategy involved, such as a change in gait, it may not be able to find suitable parameters. Finally, if the global minimum is on the edge of the sweet spot, this type of tuning will be inefficient, although still functional.

Results

In order to evaluate the algorithm described in the previous chapters, I applied it to adjusting the control of the simulated quadruped running machine shown in figure 1. I used a planar quadruped simulation because it allowed the solution of interesting problems with a reasonable amount of processing time. I tested the algorithm for variations in leg length, body weight, and desired speed; it performed well on all of these. Due to space considerations, only the data on variations in leg length is included here.

The tuning algorithm was used to reduce the leg length to half its initial value, while maintaining the trotting gait. Interestingly, the problem of getting the quadruped to trot with half-length legs was more difficult than expected because of the very short travel allowed for the leg actuators.

The initial configuration was the quadruped simulation and control system mentioned earlier. The final

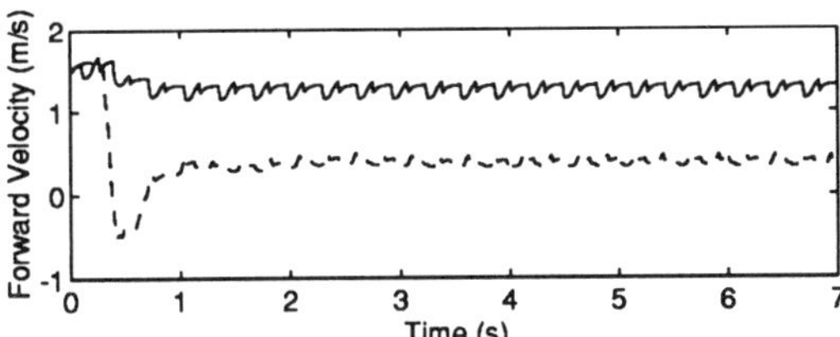
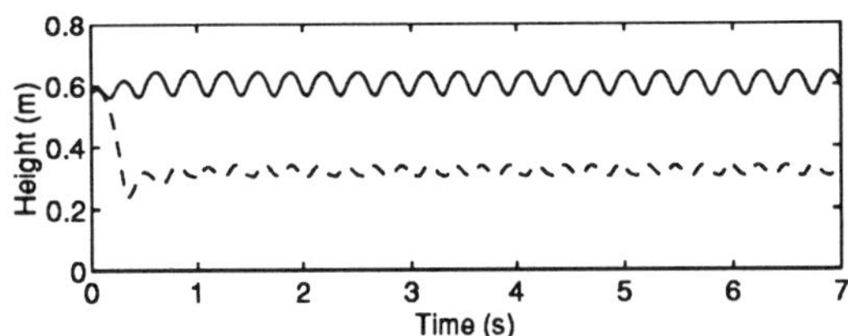

Figure 4: Height above ground and forward velocity over time, included to illustrate that the trotting achieved is stable before and after tuning. Solid lines indicate original leg length and original parameter set and dashed lines indicate half leg length and the corresponding tuned parameter set. Note that the initial conditions remain the same, so the quadruped with shorter legs actually falls to the ground, stops, and begins trotting.

Parameter	*Initial*	*Final*	*Units*
Maximum acceleration	0.31284	0.36085	m
Leg spring constant, compression	7803.57	8731.33	N/m
Leg damping coefficient, compression	471.971	630.748	Ns/m
Leg spring constant, extension	21183.7	19637.5	N/m
Leg damping coefficient, extension	462.931	1071.51	Ns/m
Stance leg length	0.62217	0.35498	m
Stance leg length increase	0.08635	0.07645	m
Swing leg length	0.45252	0.28027	m
Increase in swing hip torque with speed	-0.0042	-0.0058	N/s
Acceleration rate	0.65024	0.05992	s
Hip servo	282.093	182.354	Nm
Hip damping	21.3930	17.0266	Nms
Desired forward speed	1.50000	0.34164	m/s

Table 1: Parameters modified while decreasing the quadruped leg length.

configuration was the same quadruped simulation and control system, with legs half as long and leg moments of inertia and masses scaled as cylinders. The tuning experiment took three and a half days on an IBM RS/6000 model 550 to find the result listed in table 1. Figure 4 illustrates the stable running elicited by the original and final parameter sets when used with their respective simulations. Figure 5 shows the leg lengths at which the optimization occurred. Note that that the original control parameters for full length legs will not work on the final quadruped.

Conclusions

The tuning algorithm presented here has successfully solved several optimization problems relating to dynamically stable legged locomotion. All of these problems involve a planar trotting quadruped simulation and vary the amount of weight on the body, the leg length, or how closely it tracks a desired speed. I have also used this tuning algorithm to increase the amount of weight on the quadruped's feet and to increase the running speed of a kangaroo-like robot.

Many searching methods fail when dealing with dynamically balanced legged locomotion because easily created evaluation functions tend to result in a search space which is only tractable near a solution. The

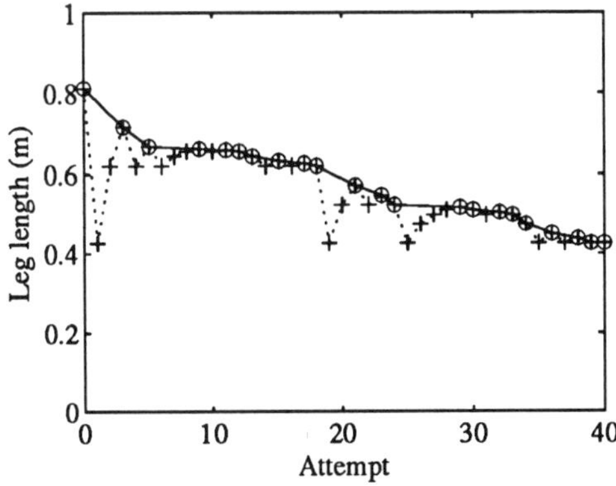

Figure 5: Leg lengths where the tuner tried to optimize (dotted line) and leg lengths where it succeeded (solid line).

tuning algorithm presented here succeeds because it makes the simplifying assumption that the tractable area moves slowly as the simulation is altered. This simplification allows the use of a fairly simple search within the tractable area.

Because of the assumptions behind it, there are limitations to the usefulness of this tuning algorithm. It must be possible to gradually change the parameter set and configuration from the initial parameter set and configuration to the final one, without leaving the sweet spot. If there is a drastic change in strategy involved, such as a change in gait, it may not be possible to gradually change the control parameters. Also, the control system must be capable of controlling the new configuration, as the tuning algorithm will not alter the structure of the control system. Finally, if the global minimum is on the edge of the sweet spot, this tuning algorithm will be inefficient. Some of these limitations can be overcome by carefully constructing the evaluation function.

Even with its limitations, this tuning method will prove useful for modifying simulations and eliciting desired behaviors. I believe that tuning methods such as the one presented here will turn the art of tuning a simulation into the art of constructing an evaluation function—still an art, but one which is a little easier.

Acknowledgments

The author would like to thank Marc Raibert for his guidance during the course of this research.

References

Helferty, J. J.; Collins, J. B.; and Kam, M. 1988. A learning strategy for the control of a mobile robot that hops and runs. In *Proceedings of the 1988 International Association of Science and Technology for Development*. IASTED.

Hodgins, J. K., and Raibert, M. H. 1989. Biped gymnastics. *International Journal of Robotics Research*.

Hodgins, J. K., and Raibert, M. H. 1991. Adjusting step length for rough terrain locomotion. *IEEE Transactions on Robotics and Automation* 7(3).

Pearse, M.; Arkin, R.; and Ram, A. 1992. The learning of reactive control parameters through genetic algorithms. *Proc. IEEE/RSJ International Conference on Intelligent Robots and Systems* 1:130–137.

Playter, R. R., and Raibert, M. H. 1992. Control of a biped somersault in 3d. In *IFToMM-jc International Symposium on Theory of Machines and Mechanisms*.

Press, W. H.; Flannery, B. P.; Teukolsky, S. A.; and Vetterling, W. T. 1988. *Numerical Recipes in C*. Cambridge University Press. chapter 10, 290–352.

Raibert, M. H.; Hodgins, J. K.; Playter, R. R.; and Ringrose, R. P. 1992. Animation of maneuvers: Jumps, somersaults, and gait transitions. In *Imagina*.

Raibert, M. H.; Chepponis, M.; and Brown, Jr., B. 1986. Running on four legs as though they were one. *IEEE Journal of Robotics and Automation* RA-2(2).

Raibert, M. H. 1990. Trotting, pacing and bounding by a quadruped robot. *Journal of Biomechanics* 23.

Ringrose, R. 1992a. The creature library. Unpublished reference guide to a C library used to create physically realistic simulations.

Ringrose, R. 1992b. Simulated creatures: Adapting control for variations in model or desired behavior. Master's thesis, Massachusetts Institute of Technology.

Rosenthal, D. E., and Sherman, M. A. 1986. High performance multibody simulations via symbolic equation manipulation and kane's method. *Journal of Astronautical Sciences* 34(3):223–239.

Winston, P. H., and Shellard, S. A., eds. 1990. *Artificial Intelligence at MIT: Expanding Frontiers*, volume 2. Cambridge, MA: MIT Press. 149–179.

Witkin, A., and Kass, M. 1988. Spacetime constraints. In *Computer Graphics*, 159–168.

Reactive Deliberation: An Architecture for Real-time Intelligent Control in Dynamic Environments

Michael K. Sahota
Laboratory for Computational Intelligence
Department of Computer Science
University of British Columbia
Vancouver, B.C., Canada, V6T 1Z4
sahota@cs.ubc.ca

Abstract

Reactive deliberation is a novel robot architecture that has been designed to overcome some of the problems posed by dynamic robot environments. It is argued that the problem of action selection in nontrivial domains cannot be intelligently resolved without attention to detailed planning. Experimental evidence is provided that the goals and actions of a robot must be evaluated at a rate commensurate with changes in the environment. The goal-oriented behaviours of reactive deliberation are a useful abstraction that allow sharing of scarce computational resources and effective goal-arbitration through inter-behaviour bidding. The effectiveness of reactive deliberation has been demonstrated through a tournament of one-on-one soccer games between real-world robots. Soccer is a dynamic environment; the locations of the ball and the robots are constantly changing. The results suggest that the architectural elements in reactive deliberation are sufficient for real-time intelligent control in dynamic environments.

Introduction

A robot operating within the real-time constraints of the external environment must answer the question: "What to do now?" It is not sufficient for a robot to react and interact with its environment; it must act in goal-oriented ways to produce externally observable intelligent behaviour (Brooks, 1991) and not just any behaviour. The importance of real-time control is identified by the following quote: "An oncoming truck waits for no theorem prover." (Gat, 1992) The moral is that robots operating in dynamic domains must keep pace with changes in the environment. This point has been argued more formally by Maes (Maes, 1990).

Robot architectures specify the organizing principles of a robot controller. Key issues are: the computational model used, locus of control, response time, and action selection mechanism. Depending on trade-offs made in design, architectures may only be appropriate for specific classes of problem domains. This paper argues that the challenges posed for robots in complex dynamic domains have not been adequately addressed by extant architectures and describes one possible solution.

Related Work

The Good Old Fashioned AI and Robotics (GOFAIR) (Haugeland, 1985; Mackworth, 1993) research paradigm has shaped the area of robotics since the time of the robot Shakey (Nilsson, 1984). Some of the fundamental assumptions made of the world in the pure form of GOFAIR were that there is only one agent, that the environment is static, that actions are discrete and are carried out sequentially, and that the world can be accurately and exhaustively modeled by the robot. Under these assumptions, the problem of robot control is reduced to generating a plan (a sequence of actions that will, if executed, achieve a goal) and monitoring the execution of the plan. These assumptions are invalid in complex dynamic environments where it is no longer possible to accurately predict the outcome of a sequence of actions. More recent planning-based architectures (Firby, 1992; Gat, 1992) allow for local adaptation to changes in the environment, but still commit the robot to the nearly blind pursuit of arbitrary length plans. AT-LANTIS (Gat, 1992) is a notable exception since it allows the consideration of alternate plans, but the commitment to the plans-as-communication view (Agre & Chapman, 1990) prevents specific plan details from being computed until they are needed, thus resulting in a greater latency in response time.

The failure of GOFAIR has led to the development of architectures that provide a direct coupling of perception to action in order to provide highly reactive behaviour. The most notable of these is the Subsumption architecture (Brooks, 1986), where the control system of a robot is composed of a hierarchy of task-achieving behaviours in which higher levels of behaviour can subsume lower levels. The concrete-situated approach (Agre & Chapman, 1987; Chapman, 1991) formulates the control system for a robot as a collection of action proposing modules. Conflicts between proposals for external actions are resolved through a fixed priority scheme. In the situated automata approach (Kaelbling & Rosenschein, 1990), a fixed ranking of goal priorities and a set of goal reduction rules are compiled into a set of condition-action pairs so that an appropriate action can be selected at each time step. All of these approaches allow the robot to react immediately to changes in the environment, but are based on a fixed ranking of actions (or equivalently behaviours or goals). With a fixed ranking, the designer of a robot is limited in adapting the controller to the environment. A key feature of these approaches is the ability to compile the specification for a robot controller into circuits or augmented finite state machines for fast execution. A potential drawback is that controllers based on the concrete-situated and situated automata approaches cannot perform the search-type algorithms needed for planning. Although the subsumption architecture supports arbitrary computations, the subsumption mechanism and the commitment to avoid representations seems to be a significant hinderance in the development of more sophisticated robots. Some evidence for this point is given with the discussion of experimental results.

Maes proposed action selection mechanism for dynamic domains is a network consisting of goals, input predicates, and competence modules that represent actions (Maes, 1990). Activation energy flows about the network according to the dependencies and conflicts among the elements. Global parameters allow the network to be tuned to an environment; these can be learned automatically (Maes, 1991). Possible drawbacks of this mechanism are that inputs are restricted to predicates and all goals are of equal weight. The use of predicates forces potentially useful information about the environment to be discarded, while the equal weighting of goals does not reflect the likely possibility that some goals are more important than others.

Overview

The bulk of this paper is divided into two sections. The first introduces the *reactive deliberation* architecture while the second describes the experiments used to test it. The architectural elements and the motivations for reactive deliberation — a robot architecture targeted towards dynamic domains — are discussed. A tournament of one-on-one soccer games has been conducted using real-world robots to demonstrate the utility of the proposed architecture. The use of soccer is motivated, the experimental testbed is briefly described, and the results are discussed. This paper ends with conclusions and future work.

The Reactive Deliberation Architecture

Reactive deliberation is a robot architecture that integrates reactive and goal-directed activity. Even deliberation must be to some extent reactive to respond to changes in the environment. Although the name is apparently an oxymoron, it is consistent with Artificial Intelligence nomenclature (cf Reactive Planning).

Under reactive deliberation, the robot controller is partitioned into a deliberator and an executor; the distinction is primarily based on the different time scales of interaction. Informally, the deliberator decides what to do and how to do it, while the executor interacts with the environment in real-time. These components run asynchronously to allow the executor to interact continuously with the world and the deliberator to perform time consuming computations. This partition is inspired by recent architectures that attempt to integrate planners with more reactive components (Firby,

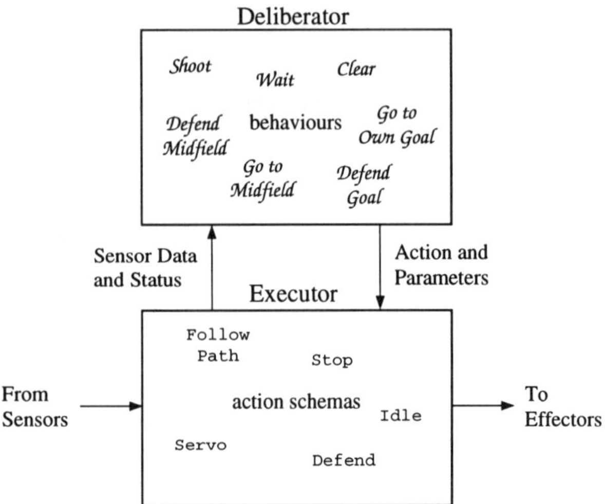

Figure 1 The Reactive Deliberation Controller

1992; Gat, 1992) A structural model illustrating the partition with examples of a soccer-playing robot can be seen in Figure 1.

The Executor

The executor is composed of a collection of action schemas. An *action schema* is a robot program that interacts with the environment in real-time to accomplish *specific* actions. Action schemas exhibit the same level of complexity as controller modules in RAP (Firby, 1992) and primitive actions in ATLANTIS (Gat, 1992). They are designed in the spirit of behaviour-based approaches, where each schema is experimentally verified. All the schemas together define the capabilities of the robot and are independent of the robot's goals.

The deliberator enables a single action schema with a set of run-time parameters that fully defines the activity. Only one action schema is enabled at a time and it interacts with the environment through a tight feedback loop. In the world of real-time control there is no room for time consuming planning algorithms. Computations in action schemas are restricted to those that can keep pace with the environment, so lengthy computations are performed in the deliberator.

Several examples of action schemas applicable to the soccer domain are shown in Figure 1. The *follow path* schema follows a path that consists of circular arcs and straight line segments to within a certain tolerance measured in absolute position and heading errors. The *servo* schema tries to servo the robot into the ball by driving to the predicted future location of the ball that is computed using an internal model of the ball's dynamics. The *defend* schema alternates between two modes. Normally, the robot stays between the ball and the center of the net. However, if the projected motion of the ball will carry it past the line the robot is defending, the robot moves to intercept it in an effort to keep the ball away from the net.

The Deliberator

The focus of the deliberator is on an effective mechanism for selecting actions or goals in a timely manner. A central feature of reactive deliberation is that the deliberator is composed of concurrently active modules called *behaviours* that represent the goals of the robot. The notion of a behaviour is used in the sense of Minsky's mental proto-specialists (Minsky, 1986). The examples given in Figure 1 illustrate the goals of a simple soccer-playing robot. These include goals of achievement such as *shoot* or *clear* the ball and goals of prevention such as *Defend Goal* where goals are prevented from being scored by the other robot.

A *behaviour* is a robot program that computes an action that may, if executed, bring about a specific goal. Behaviours propose actions whereas action schemas perform actions. Each behaviour must perform the following: 1) select an action schema, 2) compute run-time parameters for the schema (plan the action), and 3) generate a bid describing how appropriate the action is. The most appropriate behaviour, and hence action, is determined in a distributed manner through inter-behaviour bidding.

Each bid is an estimate of the expected utility and is based on the current state of the world as well as the results of planning. Currently, the criteria for generating the bids are hand coded and tuned so that the most appropriate behaviour is active in each situation. This approach requires the designer of a system to explicitly state the conditions under which certain behaviours are suitable or favourable. A simplified version of this appears in architectures with fixed ranking schemes. For example, the concrete-situated approach uses binary preference relations to establish an ordering of proposers or actions.

Modularity   The principal advantage of behaviour-based bidding is modularity. Since bids are calibrated to an external measure of utility, behaviours can be added, modified or deleted without changing the bidding criteria of the established system. A new behaviour must, of course, be tuned to be compatible with existing ones. Behaviours are independent, so they can have different representations and approaches to generating actions. For instance, a behaviour could incorporate a traditional planner and generate a bid that reflects the utility of the current step of the plan. There is no central decision maker that evaluates the world and decides the best course of action, so behaviours can be run concurrently on different processors (instead of timesharing a single processor), thus improving the speed of the system. In our approach, there is no negotiation between behaviours, unlike in systems such as contract nets (Smith, 1980). As a result, it is not possible to combine the preferences of multiple behaviours, and this remains an open problem.

Real-time computations   In a real robot there is more to the problem of action selection than just deciding what to do. In dynamic environments, a robot needs to quickly decide what to do and how to do it. The deliberator must keep pace with changes in the environment to produce intelligent behaviour. Each behaviour is responsible for computing a bid and planning the action. Fixed computational resources (processor cycles) need to be distributed among the behaviours, since it is typically the case that there is too much computation to be done.

The exact mechanism for distributing computational resources is left unspecified as it is strongly dependent on the real-time requirements of the system, the number of behaviours, and the resources needed by each behaviour. However, the basic principle is to divide the available computational resources among the behaviours such that the ruling behaviour receives more resources. This allows behaviours that perform minimal computations to respond quickly, while those that perform lengthy computations will respond slowly. It might be appropriate to allocate resources according to the importance and needs of each behaviour, but there are no provisions for this in the current implementation. There is no perfect architectural solution to the problem of limited computational resources: if the computations are slow, then the robot will be slow too. The only possible solutions are to get more computers, faster computers, better algorithms, or switch to simpler tasks.

Why this partition?

Reactive deliberation, like GOFAIR approaches, partitions the controller for a robot into a deliberator and executor. One difference is the level of abstraction at which the split between reasoning and execution monitoring occurs; our claim is that the reactive deliberation split is more suitable for dynamic environments.

The deliberator is responsible for answering the questions: "What to do now?" and "How should it be done?" Believers in the theory of plans-as-communication (Agre & Chapman, 1990) argue that these questions can and should be resolved independently (Gat, 1992). In this case a planner decides what to do based on an abstract world model, while the problem of resolving how each action should be performed is postponed until it is to be executed. In a dynamic environment, however, these questions are usually interrelated. Before committing to an action, it is important to verify that the action is both feasible and more appropriate than other actions. Architectures that follow the planning paradigm check to see if an action is feasible, but not if there is a better action.

Answering the question "How should it be done?" provides information about the utility of an action. For example, detailed planning may show that one action is impossible, while another can be accomplished quickly. This suggests that generating plans at a high level of abstraction may not provide an effective solution for the problem of action selection. Unless all actions of the robot are feasible and the outcomes can be predicted at design time, the question "What to do now?" cannot be intelligently answered without also answering "How should it be done?"

Another advantage of reactive deliberation is that the deliberator is responsible for generating a single action (schema), whereas other planning-based architectures generate a complete plan (i.e. sequences of actions). This distinction allows behaviours to focus on either the immediate situation or some interval of time depending on what is appropriate.

The boundary between appropriate and inappropriate computations in the executor is a function of the computing power of a particular system and specific environmental constraints. Any computations that can be performed within the time constraints of the environment are suitable for use in the executor. All other computations are relegated to the deliberator to avoid degrading the ability of the robot to interact in real-time. Regardless of advances in computing power, there will likely be interesting algorithms that do not run in real-time. This suggests that the partition between the executor and the deliberator is indicative of a technology-independent need to partition computations.

Soccer-playing Experiments

This section links theory to practice through a robot controller that has been constructed using reactive deliberation. The controller has been designed so that the robot can compete with another robot in a one-on-one game of soccer. In this section, the use of soccer is motivated as an appropriate domain for robotic experiments in dynamic domains. The testbed used to perform the experiments is briefly described. The experimental results are presented and their implications for robot architectures are discussed.

Why soccer?

Soccer has characteristics prevalent in the real-world that are absent from typical robot problem domains (Sahota & Mackworth, 1994). Soccer-playing is a dynamic environment because the ball and the cars are all moving. A robot must deal with cooperating agents on the robot's team, competing agents on the other team, and neutral agents such as the referee and the weather. The world is not completely predictable: it is not possible to predict precisely where the ball will go when it is kicked, even if all the relevant factors are known. Continuous events such as a player running to a position and the ball moving through the air occur concurrently add further complexity.

One advantage of the soccer domain is that there are objective performance criteria; the ability to score and prevent goals and the overall score of the game allow explicit comparisons of alternative controller designs. The ability to compare controller designs and draw conclusions from their strengths and weaknesses is a central feature of this domain.

One problem with a direct comparison of robot controllers is that differences in performance may be the result of technical details (such as the length of time the designer spent tuning the controller) that may have nothing to do with the underlying architectures. However, implemented systems can provide a lower bound on the utility of an architecture since limitations in the architecture are often reflected in the functionality of a robot. For the experiments described in this paper, the problem is avoided by using the same program fragments in each controller with different organizational principles.

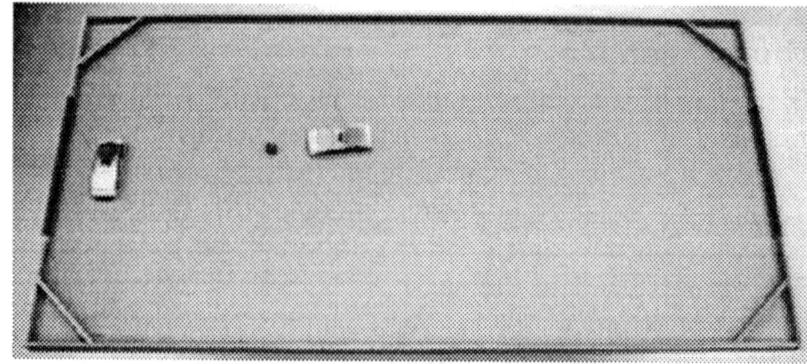

Figure 2 Robot Players on the Soccer Field

The Dynamite Testbed

A facility called the Dynamite testbed has been designed to provide a practical platform for testing theories in the soccer domain using multiple mobile robots (Barman *et al.*, 1993). It consists of a fleet of radio controlled vehicles that perceive the world through a shared perceptual system. In an integrated environment with dataflow and MIMD computers, vision programs can monitor the position and orientation of each robot while planning and control programs can generate and send out motor commands at 60 Hz. This approach allows umbilical-free behaviour and very rapid, lightweight fully autonomous robots.

The mobile robot bases are commercially available radio controlled vehicles. We have two controllable 1/24 scale racing-cars, each 22 cm long, 8 cm wide, and 4 cm high excluding the antenna. The testbed (244 cm by 122 cm in size) with two cars and a ball is shown in Figure 2. The cars have each been fitted with two circular colour markers allowing the vision system to identify their position and orientation. The ball is the small object between the cars.

A feature of the Dynamite testbed is that it is based on the "remote brain" approach to robotics. The testbed avoids the technical complexity of configuring and updating on-board hardware and makes fundamental problems in robotics and artificial intelligence more accessible. We have elected not to get on-board the on-board computation bandwagon, since the remote (but untethered) brain approach allows us to focus on scientific research without devoting resources to engineering compact electronics.

A physics-based graphics simulator for the Dynamite world has been used for testing and developing reasoning and control programs.

Results

Several controllers based on reactive deliberation have been implemented to allow robots to compete in one-on-one games of soccer. Current functionality includes various simple offensive and defensive strategies, motion planning, ball shooting and playing goal. The robots can drive under accurate control at speeds up to 1 m/s, while simultaneously considering alternate actions. We have produced a 10 minute video that documents these features.

A series of experiments, soccer games, called the Laboratory for Computational Intelligence (LCI) Cup were performed using the Dynamite testbed (Sahota, 1993). The

Controller	No- wit	Half-wit	Reactive Deliberation
Reactive Deliberation	11 - 1	7 - 4	3 - 3
Half-wit	6 - 3	5 - 5	
No-wit	8 - 2		

Table 1   Final Scores in the Soccer Tournament (11 – 1 means that the reactive deliberation controller scored 11 goals while the no-wit controller scored only 1.)

most elaborated reactive deliberation controller competed with subsets of itself to provide, through the scores of the games, an objective utility measure for some of the architectural features of reactive deliberation. The results of the soccer tournament that has been conducted in our laboratory can be seen in Table 1. The versions of the controller used were:

- **Reactive Deliberation**: the controller performs concurrent deliberation and execution, as is intended of the architecture.
- **Half-wit**: the executor yields control to the deliberator only when an action (activity) has been completed or a time-out occurs; this is equivalent to a GOFAIR controller.
- **No-wit**: the controller alternates between offensive and defensive behaviours according to a fixed timer regardless of the current world state.

There is an element of chance in these soccer games: the scores are a result of a complex set of interactions between the robots and their environment. These results are partially repeatable because the same general results will emerge, but the actual scores will be different. For a better estimate of the results, the duration of the soccer game could be extended from the current time of 10 minutes. Playing multiple games is equivalent to extending the duration of a single game.

The rank of the controllers from best to worst is: reactive deliberation, half-wit, and no-wit. This ranking is probably reliable since the better controllers scored nearly twice as many goals (7–4 and 6–3 are the scores) as the controller ranked beneath it. The results of the games played with the same controller indicate that the better two controllers (reactive deliberation, half-wit) generate fairly constant performance, while the no-wit controller produces somewhat random performance. The scores (5–5 and 3–3) should be interpreted as close scores, rather than identical. They really do not show the underlying randomness that *is* present as might be shown by a listing of when the goals were scored. The score 8–2 in the no-wit vs. no-wit game is a result of the almost random playing strategy of that controller.

The reactive deliberation controller performs better than a human controlling the opposing robot. This is, however,

somewhat of an unfair comparison since excellent motor skills are needed to even shoot the ball.

Discussion

The difference in score between the reactive deliberation and half-wit controllers is significant. The only difference between these two controllers is that reactive deliberation considers alternate actions all the time, while the half-wit controller does so only when an action schema terminates. The reactive deliberation controller selects goals as frequently as possible and can interrupt actions. The half-wit controller is like the traditional planning-based architectures: alternate actions are considered only when the current action has terminated. This is evidence that the frequent evaluation of goals and actions is critical to success in dynamic worlds.

The level of performance that the robots were able to achieve is partially due to the use of internal world models. An internal model of the dynamics of the robot is used to provide feed-forward control. This is not a superfluous element; it really is necessary for the robots to operate at speeds of 1 m/s. Brooks argues that "the world is its own best model" and that internal models are inappropriate (Brooks, 1991). Experiences with these soccer-playing robots suggest that Brooks' slogan is misleading and that either explicit or implicit models are needed.

The performance of the robots is largely a function of the action selection mechanism. It has been fine-tuned through an iteration cycle with observations of soccer games followed by incremental changes to the behaviours. A useful abstraction that helps with this is the *routines* of action from the concrete-situated approach (Agre & Chapman, 1987). The central idea is that the agent (or robot) interacts with the environment in a routine or typical way. One routine in soccer is: clear the ball, defend red line, shoot, etc. In the case of soccer-playing, the construction of successful robots does involve careful attention to patterns of activity. This is an emergent (and surprising) result of our experiments.

The reactive deliberation controller plays a nice, although not flawless, game of soccer. The competitive nature of soccer places very strict time constraints on the robots and allows different controllers to be easily compared. The dynamic and unpredictable nature of one-on-one robot soccer favours approaches that are concerned with the immediate situation and reactive deliberation takes advantage of this.

Reactive deliberation is not a panacea for robotic architectural woes. A further disclaimer is that it is an incomplete robot architecture since it focuses on the issues related to dynamic domains and ignores a number of issues such as perceptual processing and the development of world models. The proposal is orthogonal to those issues.

Conclusions

The theoretical contributions of reactive deliberation to the design philosophy of robot architecture for dynamic environments are the following:

- A new split between reasoning and control is proposed

since utility and hence action selection cannot always be suitably determined without detailed planning.

- Goal-oriented *behaviours* are a useful abstraction that allow sharing of scarce computational resources and effective goal-arbitration through inter-behaviour bidding.

A series of one-on-one soccer games have been conducted with real-world robots to evaluate reactive deliberation. The score of a soccer game provides an objective criterion for evaluating the success of a robot controller. The experimental results suggest that the architectural elements in reactive deliberation are sufficient for generating real-time intelligent control in dynamic environments. Further, it has been experimentally demonstrated that the goals and actions of a robot need to be evaluated at a rate commensurate with changes in the environment.

Future Work

Future work can be classified as either testing or extensions. Possible testing procedures include comparing reactive deliberation with other architectures and testing it in other problem domains. It is not clear how general reactive deliberation is and it remains to be determined in which domains this style of architecture is preferable. One limitation of this research is that the experiment, from proposed solutions to testing, has been performed by the author; a more hands-off or double-blind procedure is needed to provide greater scientific rigour. It still remains to be demonstrated that our architecture is more appropriate than others even in the particular soccer-world that has been used.

Some possible extensions to reactive deliberation are as follows:

- incorporation of perceptual processing and world modeling into the architecture.
- development of a more formal, yet practical, mechanism for estimating utility.
- learning utility estimates and models of the robot's dynamics.
- ability to combine the preferences of different behaviours.
- support for inter-robot cooperation.

Acknowledgments

I am grateful to Rod Barman, Keiji Kanazawa, Stewart Kingdon, Jim Little, Alan Mackworth, Dinesh Pai, Heath Wilkinson and Ying Zhang for help with this. In particular, Alan has provided deep insights and help revising drafts. This work is supported, in part, by the Canadian Institute for Advanced Research, the Natural Sciences and Engineering Research Council of Canada and the Institute for Robotics and Intelligent Systems Network of Centres of Excellence.

References

Agre, P., and Chapman, D. 1987. Pengi: An implementation of a theory of activity. In *AAAI-87*, 268–272.

Agre, P., and Chapman, D. 1990. What are plans for? In Maes, P., ed., *Designing Autonomous Agents: Theory and Practice from Biology to Engineering and Back*. M.I.T. Press. 17–34.

Barman, R.; Kingdon, S.; Little, J.; Mackworth, A. K.; Pai, D.; Sahota, M.; Wilkinson, H.; and Zhang, Y. 1993. Dynamo: real-time experiments with multiple mobile robots. In *Proceedings of Intelligent Vehicles Symposium*, 261–266.

Brooks, R. A. 1986. A robust layered control system for a mobile robot. *IEEE Journal of Robotics and Automation* RA-2:14–23.

Brooks, R. A. 1991. Intelligence without reason. In *IJCAI-91*, 569–595.

Chapman, D. 1991. *Vision, Instruction, and Action*. MIT Press.

Firby, R. J. 1992. Building symbolic primitives with continuous control routines. In *First International Conference on Artificial Intelligence Planning Systems*, 62–69.

Gat, E. 1992. Integrating planning and reacting in a heterogeneous asynchronous architecture for controlling real-world mobile robots. In *AAAI-92*, 809–815.

Haugeland, J. 1985. *Artificial Intelligence: The Very Idea*. Cambridge, Mass.: MIT Press.

Kaelbling, L. P., and Rosenschein, S. J. 1990. Action and planning in embedded agents. In Maes, P., ed., *Designing Autonomous Agents: Theory and Practice from Biology to Engineering and Back*. M.I.T. Press. 35–48.

Mackworth, A. 1993. On seeing robots. In Basu, A., and Li, X., eds., *Computer Vision: Systems, Theory, and Applications*. World Scientific Press. 1–13.

Maes, P. 1990. Situated agents can have goals. In Maes, P., ed., *Designing Autonomous Agents: Theory and Practice from Biology to Engineering and Back*. M.I.T. Press. 49–70.

Maes, P. 1991. Learning behaviour networks from experience. In *Proceedings of the First European Conference on Artificial Life*. M.I.T. Press.

Minsky, M. 1986. *The Society of Mind*. Simon & Schuster Inc.

Nilsson, N. 1984. Shakey the robot. Technical Report 323, SRI International. Collection of Earlier Technical Reports.

Sahota, M. K., and Mackworth, A. K. 1994. Can situated robots play soccer? In *Proceedings of Canadian AI-94*. Forthcoming.

Sahota, M. K. 1993. Real-time intelligent behaviour in dynamic environments: Soccer-playing robots. Master's thesis, University of British Columbia.

Smith, G. 1980. The contract net protocol: High-level communication and control in a distributed problem solver. *IEEE Transactions on Computing* 29(12).

Search and Genetic Algorithms

Exploiting Problem Structure in Genetic Algorithms

Scott H. Clearwater and Tad Hogg

Xerox Palo Alto Research Center
3333 Coyote Hill Road
Palo Alto, CA 94304, U.S.A.
clearwat@parc.xerox.com, hogg@parc.xerox.com

Abstract

Recent empirical and theoretical studies have shown that simple parameters characterizing the structure of many constraint satisfaction problems also predict the cost to solve them, on average. We apply these observations to improve the performance of genetic algorithms. In particular, we use a simple cost measure to evaluate the likely solution difficulty of the different unsolved subproblems appearing in the population. This is used to determine which individuals contribute to subsequent generations and improves upon the traditional direct use of the underlying cost function. As a specific test case, we used the GENESIS genetic algorithm to search for the optimum of a class of random Walsh polynomials. We also discuss extensions to other types of machine learning and problem solving systems.

Introduction

Several recent studies of NP-hard search problems have shown that easily computable characteristics of their structure determine, on average, their *hardness*, i.e., the cost to solve them with a variety of heuristic search methods [Cheeseman et al., 1991, Mitchell et al., 1992, Williams and Hogg, 1992a, Williams and Hogg, 1992b]. While these results provide insight into the nature of NP-hard problems, there remains the issue of whether they can also be used to improve search methods. If possible, an improvement based on these results would be a significant domain-independent heuristic. At first sight this might appear difficult since the relation between problem structure and hardness only holds on average: the large observed variances indicate that any individual problem instance can deviate significantly from the average behavior. Thus these results cannot be expected to give detailed guidance for sophisticated domain-specific heuristics.

However, some search methods, such as genetic algorithms [Holland, 1975, Goldberg, 1989, Forrest, 1993] (GAs), rely on a statistical sample of search states. Evaluating these states with respect to the overall goal is then used to guide the selection of further states. To the extent that the selection method is able to focus the search toward solution states, on average, these methods can be effective. Such methods are natural candidates for exploiting an improved understanding of average problem hardness.

The novel contribution of this paper is using a theory relating problem structure to hardness to help select individuals within the context of a genetic algorithm, and comparing this improvement with the traditional approach. We do this for a particular class of constraint satisfaction problems. We also discuss how this specific example may be generalized to learning programs and other search problems. Our results suggest that the relation between problem structure and hardness can indeed be exploited to give improved domain-independent heuristics.

Genetic Algorithms for Constraint Satisfaction

Genetic algorithms are a general optimizing search method. They use analogs of evolutionary operators on a population of states in a search space to find those states that minimize the value of a given cost function. Equivalently, they can be viewed as maximizing a fitness function. We used the search space consisting of bit-strings of length μ, commonly employed with GAs. Each particular search problem was defined by a cost function on these states, with a known optimal state. By contrast, the studies of problem structure and hardness have focused mainly on constraint satisfaction problems (CSPs). In these problems, one is given a set of constraints and attempts to find a state in a search space that satisfies all of them (i.e., a solution to the CSP), or prove no such state exists. In our work, we used a simple class of optimization problems that can also be viewed as CSPs, thus allowing for the most direct use of the hardness theory.

Specifically, our cost function can be expressed as a type of Walsh polynomial, i.e., a sum of discrete Walsh functions with coefficients. The Walsh functions form a basis set for functions defined on bit-strings. These polynomials, which are thus much like Fourier series, have been studied previously with GAs [Forrest and Mitchell, 1993]. Each such Walsh function is specified by a bit-string β and maps bit-strings b in the search space to ± 1 as:

$$\psi_\beta(b) = \begin{cases} 1 & \text{if } b \wedge \beta \text{ has even parity (even no. of 1's)} \\ -1 & \text{otherwise} \end{cases}$$

$$(1)$$

where $\wedge$ is the bitwise AND operator. The number of 1's in β is referred to as the *order* of the Walsh function. Example values for an order-2 function are $\psi_{1100}(1110) = 1$ and $\psi_{1100}(1010) = -1$. A function defined on bit-strings of length μ is expressed as a Walsh polynomial as:

$$F(b) = \sum_{\beta=0}^{2^{\mu}-1} \omega_\beta \psi_\beta(b) \qquad (2)$$

where ω_β are real coefficients. Here the sum is over all possible bit-strings β of length μ. The *number of terms* in $F(b)$ is defined to be the number of nonzero coefficients ω_β appearing in the sum.

For our experiments, we defined a class of optimization problems by selecting the Walsh polynomials randomly according to specified parameters to correspond to the simplest CSPs studied with the theory. First, we only included Walsh functions of a specified order k. And among these, we selected randomly exactly n terms to include in the Walsh polynomial, i.e., from among the $\binom{\mu}{k}$ Walsh functions of order k, we randomly selected n to use. Second, for each problem we selected a random bit-string B and chose the sign of each coefficient so that $\omega_\beta \psi_\beta(B) > 0$, with the magnitude of the coefficient a random integer in the range $[1, 5]$. With this choice of signs, the maximum value of F is:

$$F_{max} \equiv \max_b \left(F(b) \right) = \sum |\omega_\beta| \qquad (3)$$

and is achieved by the state B. Finally, the optimization problem presented to the GA in our experiments was to find a bit-string b which minimized the cost function

$$c(b) = F_{max} - F(b). \qquad (4)$$

The minimum of this cost is zero, so we can readily determine how close to optimal the GA gets.

The optimization problem defined this way can also be viewed as a constraint satisfaction problem (CSP) with a prespecified solution. Specifically, we can view each position in the bit-string as a variable which can be assigned one of two values (0 or 1). Moreover, each term $\omega_\beta \psi_\beta$ in the Walsh polynomial corresponds to a constraint. A given bit-string b satisfies the constraint if and only if $\omega_\beta \psi_\beta(b) > 0$. By our choice of signs for the ω_β the minimum value of the cost function is achieved only when all terms are positive, so a minimum cost state corresponds to a solution to the CSP, i.e., a state in which all constraints are satisfied. In particular, the state B is a solution.

Theory

By viewing the optimization problem as a CSP, we can apply recently developed theories [Williams and Hogg,

μ	number of variables and bits in the state
k	size of constraints = order of Walsh functions
n	number of constraints and terms in Walsh polynomial
m	number of minimized nogoods, $n2^{k-1}$

Table 1. Mapping between theory parameters and the experimental testbed.

1992b] to characterize the difficulty of searching for a solution. In this work, a CSP is characterized by the number of variables (μ), the domain size of each variable (2 for our case of binary variables), and the number and size of the *minimized nogoods* of the constraints. These nogoods are simply those smallest subsets of all possible states in the problem that violate at least one constraint. Their *size* is just the number of variables involved.

For example, consider a Walsh polynomial with one term, $F(b) = 2\psi_{1100}(b)$. The corresponding CSP has μ=4, k=2, and n=1. Since only the non-zero bits are important in determining the value of the Walsh polynomial there are at most two variables we need to be concerned about, in this particular example the first and second positions. For these two variables there are two ways to obtain $\psi_{1100} = +1$ and hence a positive contribution to F since $\omega_{1100} = 2$ is positive (the "goods"), $\{b_1 = 0, b_2 = 0\}$ and $\{b_1 = 1, b_2 = 1\}$. There are also two ways to obtain a -1 (the "nogoods"), $\{b_1 = 1, b_2 = 0\}$ and $\{b_1 = 0, b_2 = 1\}$ where $b_i = s$ denotes the assignment of value s to variable i, i.e., value s appearing at position i in the bit-string b.

More generally, a Walsh function of order k will involve exactly k variables, so the corresponding nogoods will have size k. Moreover, of the 2^k possible assignments to these variables, exactly half will have even parity giving $\psi_\beta(b) > 0$. Thus, for either choice of the sign of the coefficient ω_β, exactly half the assignments will violate the constraint associated with this term, i.e., will be nogood. So each term in the Walsh polynomial will contribute 2^{k-1} minimized nogoods. Moreover, these will be distinct from those contributed by other terms since each term has a distinct subset of the variables in the problem. From this argument we see that our CSP's, in which the Walsh polynomial has n terms, have $n2^{k-1}$ minimized nogoods, all of size k. This mapping between the parameters in the theory and our problem class is summarized in Table 1.

For simple backtrack search, the theory [Williams and Hogg, 1992a, Eq. 10] estimates that the search cost, on average, as a function of μ, k and n is

$$C_{theory} = \frac{\sum_{i=0}^{\mu} e^{g_i}}{\max\left(1, e^{g_\mu}\right)} \qquad (5)$$

with

$$g_i = i \ln 2 + n 2^{k-1} \ln \left(1 - \left(\frac{i}{2\mu} \right)^k \right). \qquad (6)$$

Note that g_i decreases as more terms are added, i.e., as n increases, and this decrease is more rapid for larger values of i. This means that, for fixed μ and k, C_{theory} first increases with n, eventually reaches a peak at a value $n = n_{crit}$ (which depends on μ and k), and then decreases, as shown in Fig. 1 for parameter values used in some of our experiments.

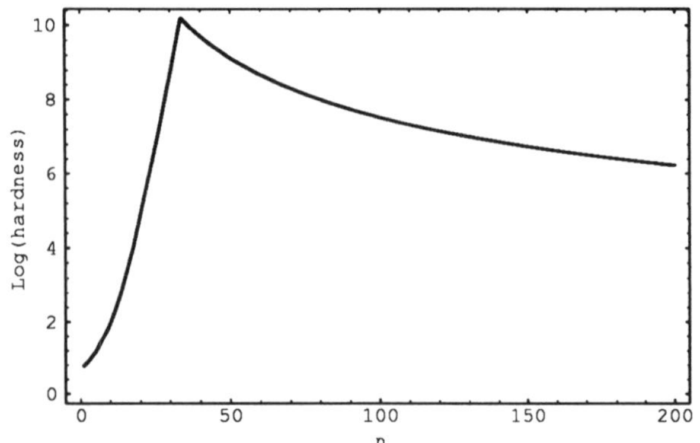

Fig. 1. $\ln (C_{theory})$ versus n, the number of constraints, for $\mu = 25$ and $k = 4$. The maximum hardness occurs for $n = 34$.

A Hardness-Based Cost Measure

As it stands, this theory evaluates the expected search difficulty of an entire problem. Applied in the context of a GA, we need to evaluate the usefulness of different individual states in the population. That is, some states are more likely than others to lead readily to a solution, and hence should have an enhanced number of offspring in the next generation. The traditional fitness function approach simply equates usefulness of a state with the value of the function to be optimized applied to that state, where the function to be optimized may be either maximized or minimized.

We now describe how we applied the theory to evaluate individual states and used this evaluation to define a new cost measure for use with the GA. For an individual state b some constraints in the problem will be satisfied while others are violated. Thus one way to apply the problem hardness measure of Eq. 5 is to view the violated constraints as forming a subproblem and use this subproblem's hardness measure as the hardness associated with the state b. While there are several specific ways one could do this, our particularly simple approach is to replace the value of n in Eq. 5 with the number of constraints (i.e., terms in the Walsh polynomial) that are violated by the state.

The potential advantage of using hardness-based cost is that we can exploit hard and easy parts of the search space and either seek out or avoid those areas as necessary. When applied to GAs this implies we can bias the population in one direction or the other via reproduction operations. For example, if a particular individual had a cost to the right of the maximum hardness peak of Fig. 1 and the next generation had a cost to the left, then we would want to exploit that discovery by heavily increasing that individual's number of offspring for the next generation. Note that this is the case even if the hardness to the left of the maximum is *higher* than the hardness to the right. This is because a problem becomes easier very rapidly to the left of the peak. Thus, in our experiments we sought to decrease the number of violated terms, without considering the weights given to the various terms by the coefficients, unlike the traditional approach.

To do this within the context of a GA, we need to relate the hardness measure we defined for an individual state to an appropriate cost function. In this context we note that the standard cost measure of Eq. 4 monotonically decreases as the state gets close to the optimum. The situation is more complicated for the non-monotonic hardness function of Eq. 5. The region to the left of the maximum peak is monotonically decreasing as n decreases, which is fine. The problem is that the hardness function is monotonically *increasing* to the right of the maximum hardness peak as n decreases. Instead, we need to find a function of hardness which decreases even though hardness itself increases. There are a plethora of ways to define an appropriate cost function. One way that systematically produces better results is as follows. If the state b, with n violated constraints, is "to the right" of the maximum hardness peak, i.e., $n > n_{crit}$, then reducing the cost requires first solving harder problems closer to the peak on the way towards the steeply dropping part of the hardness curve "to the left" of the peak. Thus, to encourage the GA to reduce the number of violated constraints, a function inversely proportional to the hardness can be used. Similarly, when $n < n_{crit}$ a function proportional to the hardness can be used. Moreover, to stress the importance of states to the left of the hardness peak, a rescaling of hardness is done to cause a "stampede" across the hardness peak that might otherwise take a long time. Since the hardness theory is an approximation, the exact location of the peak is uncertain, but on the average it should, like the GA procedure itself, lead to better performance. The cost function we chose was one based on simplicity, namely:

$$c_{hard}(\mu, k, n) = \begin{cases} \ln (C_{theory}) & \text{if } n < n_{crit} \\ 400/\ln (C_{theory}) & \text{otherwise} \end{cases} \qquad (7)$$

Finally, the cost for given bit-string b was $c_{hard}(b) = c_{hard}(\mu, k, n)$ where n was the number of constraints that conflict with the state b. This cost is minimized when all constraints are satisfied, i.e., when $n = 0$, corresponding to a solution. To distinguish this use of n for a state b, we use n_0 to denote the total number of terms in the Walsh polynomial of the problem. This remains fixed while the n values associated with a population of states varies as states are modified by the GA.

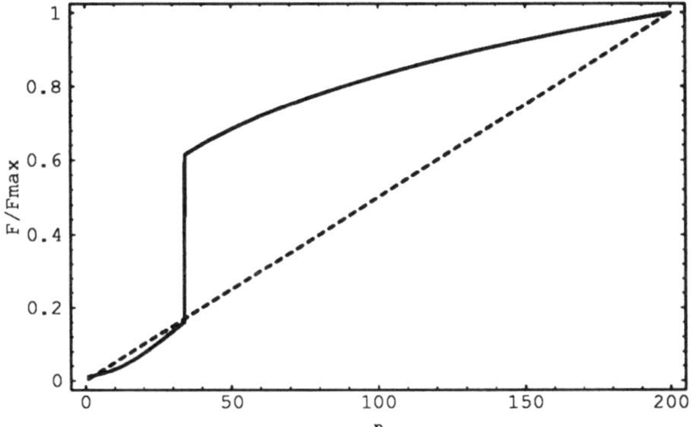

Fig. 2. Comparison of standard (dashed) and hardness-based (solid) cost measures as a function of the number of violated constraints n for $\mu = 25$ and $k = 4$. Both values are normalized to their maximum value in the range considered. Note that the standard measure depends on the values of the coefficients and hence the line represents a hardness averaged over many problems with this structure. Note the abrupt change in the hardness at the transition point $n_{crit} = 34$ which acts to initiate a stampede of individuals across the critical region.

To illustrate our application of the theoretical measure to individual states, we can examine the number of constraints that are violated by individual randomly chosen initial states. It is important to realize that most such states will already satisfy many constraints. Thus, if we assume the constraints are independent, one would expect that the number of terms in conflict with a random initial state would be $n = \frac{1}{2}n_0$. In fact, we observe somewhat more initial conflicts, and further, there is a wide variation in the initial number terms to be solved. This of course leads to a spread in the initial hardness of the problem to be solved.

Experimental Setup

We used a publicly available genetic algorithm called GENESIS for GENEtic Search Implementation System version 5.0 [Grefenstette, 1990]. The program provides a standard genetic algorithm implementation with bit-string or floating point vector representation. The user provides an evaluation function for determining the fitness of the individuals in the population. The user also provides the crossover and mutation rates. There is also an elitist mechanism for guaranteeing that a number of the fittest individuals from one generation will survive to the next. In all the experiments reported here a fitness proportionate reproduction was used where the number of offspring from an individual was proportional to its fitness (which means how well it minimizes cost) in the overall population.

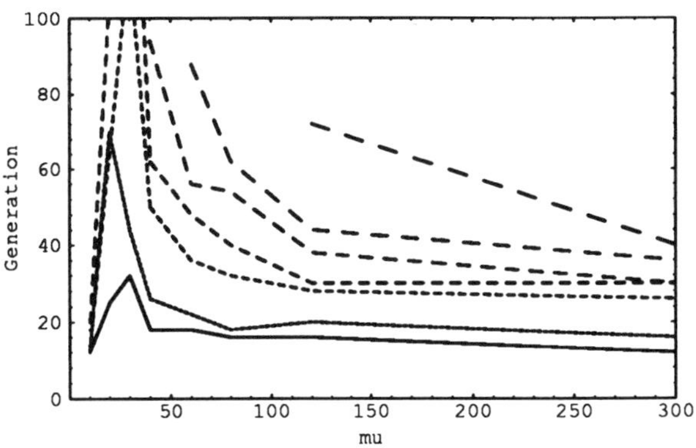

Fig. 3. Generation versus μ with $k=4$, $n=3$, using the standard cost measure. The lowest curve (solid black) is the distribution of time to reach 80% of the optimal solution averaged over 10 runs, i.e., the time required to first find a state with $F(b)/F_{max} \geq 0.8$. Similar curves follow upward and become more dashed are for 85%, 90%, 92%, 94%, 96%, and 98%. Curves that do not have certain μ values did not reach the specified level of optimum within 100 generations. This is in qualitative agreement with the theory which states that the hardest problems are in the regions of intermediate μ. A similar easy-hard-easy pattern of problems is seen when n is varied at a fixed value of μ, in qualitative agreement with the behavior shown in Fig. 1.

All of the experiments used 250 individuals with a mutation rate of .02 per bit and a crossover rate of 0.5 per individual. At each generation, the best 10 individuals were guaranteed to survive. Typically 100 runs were made under the same conditions. Each run ran for 100 generations. With our choice of parameters μ, k and n describing the class of problems, the initial hardness was in the overconstrained part of the space. Thus, the individual had to move through the maximum hardness peak to solve the problem. Further, the polynomials were easy enough to be solved in a reasonable amount of time so that decent statistics could be obtained. Still, not every problem was solved within the allotted time. Thus we have a choice of performance metrics: fraction of time the problem was solved within a given number of generations, and fraction of the optimal solution found at a given generation.

Does the Theory Apply to GAs?

Before presenting our evaluation of the new fitness function, we first used the standard GA to see whether the theory applies at all to GAs. Although a relation between problem structure and hardness has been observed for a variety of search methods, it is important to check that it also applies to our problems solved by GAs. More generally, instead of examining the time required to reach an optimal state, we considered near-optimal states as well. Fig. 3 shows how the search cost varies with problem size and closeness to optimality. We see the development of a peak indicating a region of particularly hard problems, in qualitative agreement with the theoretical prediction and empirical observations of other search methods. This generalizes and "explains" more generally

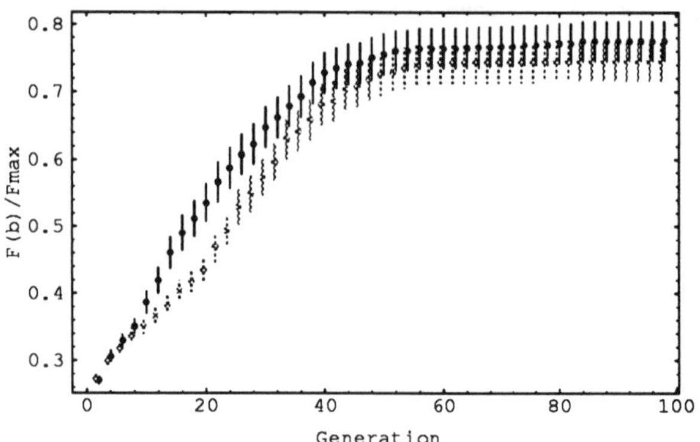

Fig. 4. Fraction of optimum as a function of generation, i.e., the largest value of $F(b)/F_{max}$ for states b in the population. For this plot $\mu = 25$, $k = 4$, $n_0 = 150$. Black points are the hardness-based cost results and the gray points are the standard fitness results. The error bars are the standard error of the mean for the generation. All 100 runs are plotted. Much of the displayed variance is due to the different problem instances. A more precise comparison of the two algorithms is given by Hotelling's multivariate paired T test [Johnson and Wichern, 1992]. This test on the differences in the two methods on 400 problems, rejects the hypothesis that they have the same behavior at a significance level of less than 10^{-4}.

two observations [Forrest and Mitchell, 1993] where what naively seems to be a harder problem (since it involves more variables) is actually easier.

Search Performance

We compare the hardness-based cost measure with a standard measure in Fig. 4. Note that in the figure the hardness-based cost led to superior performance. Additionally, the hardness-based cost found the optimum on 63 out of 100 runs versus 58 with the standard fitness. Each run consisted of a randomly generated Walsh polynomial, which was used with both the hardness–based and standard cost functions. By using the same problem instances with both methods we obtain a more discriminating comparison between the methods than if we had used separate random samples for each case.

It is also worthwhile looking at the finishing time of the runs that actually finished, shown in Fig. 5. As can be seen from the figure the hardness based fitness measure is significantly faster at finishing than the standard fitness. Thus not only is the hardness measure better at finding solutions, it is also finds those solutions faster.

Finally, we mention the computational resources required for our new method. There is no extra storage cost incurred using this implementation. Further, although the hardness computation is not optimized, its use adds only about 13% to the CPU time to evaluate each generation on a SUN SparcStation 2. This modest increase is more than offset by the large reduction in the problem solving steps, from an average of 49±1 generations using the standard fitness measure to 28±1 using the hardness-based measure (where the ± is the standard error of the mean), so that

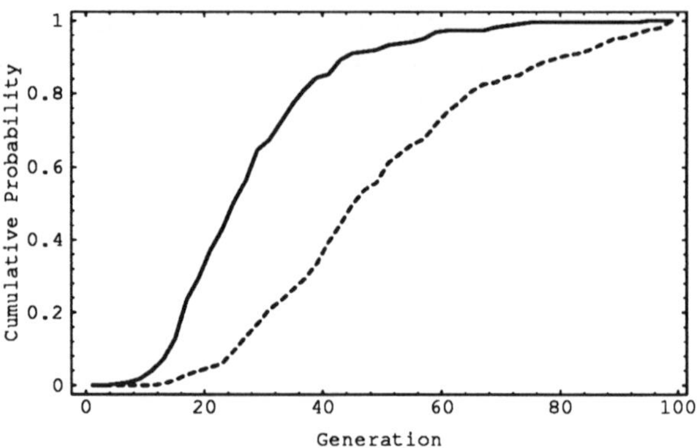

Fig. 5. Probability of finishing as a function of generation averaged over 400 runs. For this plot $\mu = 25$ and $k = 4$, $n_0 = 150$. The solid line the hardness-based fitness results (224 finishers) and the dotted line is the standard fitness results (201 finishers). The chance that the two distributions are the same is rejected at a significance level of a few parts per million using the Kolmogorov-Smirnov test [Press et al., 1986].

our method uses 1.75 times fewer generations, on average, and thus runs 1.52 times faster in CPU time.

Diversity

One important characteristic of GAs is the diversity of the individuals in the population. The mutation rate is a force acting to increase diversity and the crossover operation is a force acting to reduce diversity. Diversity can be a good or bad depending on when it occurs during problem solving. During the early part of a search we would like to have a high diversity so as to reap the benefits of having many individuals exploring different parts of the search space. On the other hand, once a promising region of the space has been found we would like to focus our resources on that area which necessitates a reduction of the diversity.

We defined the diversity of the GA as the average over the population of the fraction of the least prominent value for a particular bit location in the state, averaged over all the locations. Thus, the maximum diversity of 0.5 means that 0's and 1's are evenly distributed, and the minimum diversity of 0 means that each member of the population is identical at each location. The evolution of diversity is shown in Fig. 6. As seen in the figure the diversity for the hardness-based runs is lower than for the standard runs in the region where the hardness-based runs typically finish. This means that the hardness switchover that occurs at maximum theoretical hardness is having the desired effect of focussing the individuals into easier regions of the problem and thereby speeding problem solving.

Extensions

In this paper we have shown how the simple use of a theoretically motivated measure of problem difficulty provides a useful heuristic for evaluating a population of search states. Within this context there are a variety of extensions that could also be tried. For instance, instead of focusing on how hard the remaining part of the problem

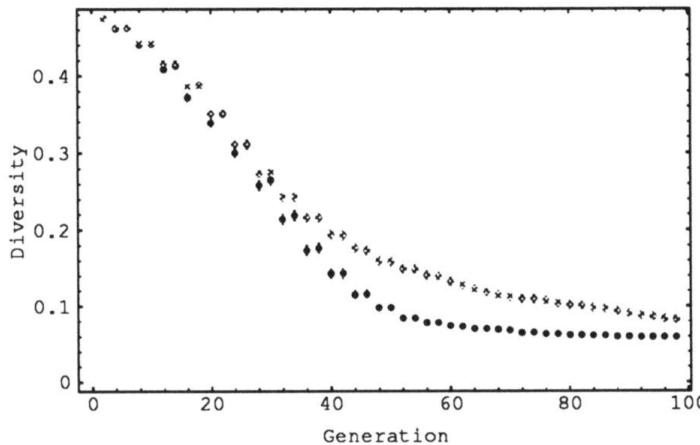

Fig. 6. Diversity as a function of generation for 400 runs. For this plot $\mu = 25$ and $k = 4$, $n_0 = 150$. The black points are for the hardness-based fitness result and the gray points are for the standard fitness result.

is to solve (favoring easier cases), we could also examine how hard a subproblem has already been solved. There are also more sophisticated ways to define the subproblem hardness. In particular, one could vary not only the number of constraints as we did, but also the number of variables. That is, only count those variables that are involved in at least one conflicting constraint. This would focus more precisely on the remaining subproblem, but ignores any interaction with the remaining constraints, which are already satisfied by the given state. If these remaining constraints greatly restrict the allowed choices for solving the subproblem, that subproblem will in fact be much more difficult than it appears on its own. This can be addressed to some extent by including the overlap of the remaining constraints with the subproblem as additional constraints for the subproblem. Including this level of detail requires using an extension of the basic theory that applies to minimized nogoods of differing sizes [Williams and Hogg, 1992a].

The idea of using general statistical knowledge of the problem may be extended to other types of problem solving techniques. For example, we may be able to use the hardness criteria to better adjust the cooling schedule in simulated annealing [Kirkpatrick et al., 1983]. Neural network learning may also benefit by using a hardness measure to automatically adjust the learning rate of the network as it learns. Heuristic search, such as beam search or heuristic repair [Minton et al., 1990] may also benefit.

A more intriguing possibility exploits the diversity behavior we found using the "stampede" across the critical region. In nature, this kind of high diversity to low diversity activity is seen with ants who initially forage over a wide area but become highly localized once a food source has been found. Similarly, one could imagine a collection of mobile robots [Brooks, 1991] trying to solve some kind of constraint satisfaction problem. Initially the robots would be highly dispersed but would become much more

clustered as one of them informed the others that it had found something interesting to investigate. This would correspond to the genetic stampede we have observed.

References

Brooks, R. A. (1991). New approaches to robotics. *Science*, 253:1227–1232.

Cheeseman, P., Kanefsky, B., and Taylor, W. M. (1991). Where the really hard problems are. In Mylopoulos, J. and Reiter, R., editors, *Proceedings of IJCAI91*, pages 331–337, San Mateo, CA. Morgan Kaufmann.

Forrest, S. (1993). Genetic algorithms: Principles of natural selection applied to computation. *Science*, 261:872–878.

Forrest, S. and Mitchell, M. (1993). What makes a problem hard for a genetic algorithm? Some anomalous results and their explanation. *Machine Learning*, 13:285–319.

Goldberg, D. E. (1989). *Genetic Algorithms in Search, Optimization and Machine Learning*. Addison-Wesley, NY.

Grefenstette, J. (1990). A User's Guide to GENESIS Version 5.0. *Navy Center for Applied Research in AI, Naval Research Laboratory*.

Holland, J. H. (1975). *Adaptation in Natural and Artificial Systems*. University of Michigan Press, Ann Arbor, MI.

Johnson, R. A. and Wichern, D. W. (1992). *Applied Multivariate Statistical Analysis*. Prentice Hall, Englewood Cliffs, NJ, 3rd edition.

Kirkpatrick, S., Gelatt, C. D., and Vecchi, M. P. (1983). Optimization by simulated annealing. *Science*, 220:671–680.

Minton, S., Johnston, M. D., Philips, A. B., and Laird, P. (1990). Solving large-scale constraint satisfaction and scheduling problems using a heursitic repair method. In *Proceedings of AAAI-90*, pages 17–24, Menlo Park, CA. AAAI Press.

Mitchell, D., Selman, B., and Levesque, H. (1992). Hard and easy distributions of SAT problems. In *Proc. of 10th Natl. Conf. on Artificial Intelligence (AAAI92)*, pages 459–465, Menlo Park. AAAI Press.

Press, W. H., Flannery, B. P., Teukolsky, S. A., and Vetterling, W. T. (1986). *Numerical Recipes*. Cambridge Univ. Press, Cambridge.

Williams, C. P. and Hogg, T. (1992a). Exploiting the deep structure of constraint problems. Technical Report SSL92-24, Xerox PARC, Palo Alto, CA.

Williams, C. P. and Hogg, T. (1992b). Using deep structure to locate hard problems. In *Proc. of 10th Natl. Conf. on Artificial Intelligence (AAAI92)*, pages 472–477, Menlo Park, CA. AAAI Press.

Increasing The Efficiency of Simulated Annealing Search by Learning to Recognize (Un)Promising Runs *

Yoichiro Nakakuki
C&C Research Laboratories, NEC Corp.
4-1-1 Miyazaki, Miyamae-ku
Kawasaki 216, JAPAN
nakakuki@swl.cl.nec.co.jp

Norman Sadeh
The Robotics Institute, Carnegie Mellon University
5000 Forbes Avenue
Pittsburgh, PA 15213, U.S.A.
sadeh@cs.cmu.edu

Abstract

Simulated Annealing (SA) procedures can potentially yield near-optimal solutions to many difficult combinatorial optimization problems, though often at the expense of intensive computational efforts. The single most significant source of inefficiency in SA search is its inherent stochasticity, typically requiring that the procedure be rerun a large number of times before a near-optimal solution is found. This paper describes a mechanism that attempts to learn the structure of the search space over multiple SA runs on a given problem. Specifically, probability distributions are dynamically updated over multiple runs to estimate at different checkpoints how promising a SA run appears to be. Based on this mechanism, two types of criteria are developed that aim at increasing search efficiency: (1) a *cutoff criterion* used to determine when to abandon unpromising runs and (2) *restart criteria* used to determine whether to start a fresh SA run or restart search in the middle of an earlier run. Experimental results obtained on a class of complex job shop scheduling problems show (1) that SA can produce high quality solutions for this class of problems, if run a large number of times, and (2) that our learning mechanism can significantly reduce the computation time required to find high quality solutions to these problems. The results further indicate that, the closer one wants to be to the optimum, the larger the speedups.

1   Introduction

Simulated Annealing (SA) is a general-purpose search procedure that generalizes iterative improvement approaches to combinatorial optimization by sometimes accepting transitions to lower quality solutions to avoid getting trapped in local minima (Kirkpatrick 83; Cerny 85). SA procedures have been successfully applied to a variety of combinatorial optimization problems, including Traveling Salesman Problems (Cerny

85), Graph Partitioning Problems (Johnson et al. 89), Graph Coloring Problems (Johnson et al. 91), Vehicle Routing Problems (Osman 92), Design of Integrated Circuits, Minimum Makespan Scheduling Problems (Matsuo et al. 88; Osman & Potts 89; Van Laarhoven et al. 92) as well as other complex scheduling problems (Zweben et al. 92), often producing near-optimal solutions, though at the expense of intensive computational efforts.

The single most significant source of inefficiency in SA search is its inherent stochasticity, typically requiring that the procedure be rerun a large number of times before a near-optimal solution is found. Glover et al. developed a set of "Tabu" mechanisms that can help increase the efficiency of SA and other neighborhood search procedures by maintaining a selective history of search states encountered earlier during the *same run* (Glover & Laguna 92). This history is then used to dynamically derive "tabu restrictions" or "aspirations", that guide search, preventing it, for instance, from revisiting areas of the search space it just explored. This paper describes a complementary mechanism that attempts to learn the structure of the search space *over multiple runs* of SA on a given problem. Specifically, we introduce a mechanism that attempts to predict how (un)promising a SA run is likely to be, based on probability distributions that are refined ("learned") over multiple runs. The distributions, which are built at different checkpoints, each corresponding to a different value of the temperature parameter used in the procedure, approximate the cost reductions that one can expect if the SA run is continued below these temperatures. Two types of criteria are developed that aim at increasing search efficiency by exploiting these distributions:

- *A Cutoff Criterion*: This criterion is used to detect runs that are unlikely to result in an improvement of the best solution found so far and, hence, should be abandoned;

- *Restart Criteria*: When completing a run or abandoning an unpromising one, these criteria help determine whether to start a fresh SA run or restart search in the middle of an earlier promising run.

*This research was supported, in part, by the Defense Advanced Research Projects Agency under contract F30602-91-C-0016 and, in part, by an industrial grant from NEC. The research was carried out while the first author was a visiting scientist at Carnegie Mellon University.

The techniques presented in this paper have been applied to a class of complex job shop scheduling problems first described in (Sadeh 91)[1]. Problems in this class require scheduling a set of jobs that each need to be completed by a possibly different due date. The objective is to minimize the sum of tardiness and inventory costs incurred by all the jobs. This class of problems is known to be NP-complete and is representative of a large number of actual scheduling problems, including Just-In-Time factory scheduling problems (Sadeh 91; 93). Experimental results indicate (1) that SA can produce high quality solutions for this class of problems, if run a large number of times, and (2) that our learning mechanism can yield significant reductions in computation time. The results further indicate that, the closer one wants to be to the optimum, the larger the speedups.

The remainder of this paper is organized as follows. Section 2 quickly reviews fundamentals of SA search. Section 3 analyzes the behavior of typical SA runs and introduces a mechanism that aims at learning to recognize (un)promising runs on a given problem, using the concept of *Expected Cost Improvement Distributions* (*ECID*). In Section 4, we use *ECID* distributions to develop a *cutoff criterion* to determine when to abandon unpromising runs. Section 5 presents three *restart criteria* based *ECID* distributions. Experiments obtained on a set of benchmark job shop scheduling problems with tardiness and inventory costs are reported in Section 6. A summary is provided in Section 7.

2 Simulated Annealing Search

Figure 1 outlines the main steps of a SA procedure designed to find a solution $x \in S$ that minimizes a real-valued function, $cost(x)$. The procedure starts from an initial solution x_0 (randomly drawn from S) and iteratively moves to other neighboring solutions, as determined by a neighborhood function, $neighbor(x)$, while remembering the best solution found so far (denoted by s). Typically, the procedure only moves to neighboring solutions that are better than the current one. However, the probability of moving from a solution x to an inferior solution x' is greater than zero, thereby allowing the procedure to escape from local minima. $rand()$ is a function that randomly draws a number from a uniform distribution on the interval $[0, 1]$. The so-called temperature, T, of the procedure is a parameter controlling the probability of accepting a transition to a lower quality solution. It is initially set at a high value, T_0, thereby frequently allowing such transitions. If, after N iterations, the best solution found by the procedure has not improved, the temperature parameter T is decremented by a factor α $(0 < \alpha < 1)$. One motivation for progressively lowering the temper-

---

[1]These optimization problems should not be confused with the set of Constraint Satisfaction problems also introduced in this dissertation.

ature is to obtain convergence. Additionally, as the procedure slowly moves towards globally better solutions, accepting transitions to lower quality solutions becomes increasingly less attractive. When the temperature drops below a preset level T_1, the procedure stops and s is returned (not shown in Figure 1).

```
T = T_0; x = x_0 (∈ S); min = ∞;
while (T > T_1)   {
    for i = 1, N    {
        x' = neighbor(x);
        if (cost(x') < cost(x));
            x = x';
        else if (rand() < exp{(cost(x) − cost(x'))/T});
            x = x';
        if(cost(x) < min)   min = cost(x), s = x;
    }
    if (Min was not modified in the above loop);
        T = T * α;
}
```

Fig. 1 Basic Simulated Annealing Procedure.

Fig. 2 depicts the cost distribution of the best solutions returned by 300 SA runs on a typical combinatorial optimization problem − a job shop scheduling problem from a set of benchmarks to be described in Section 6.

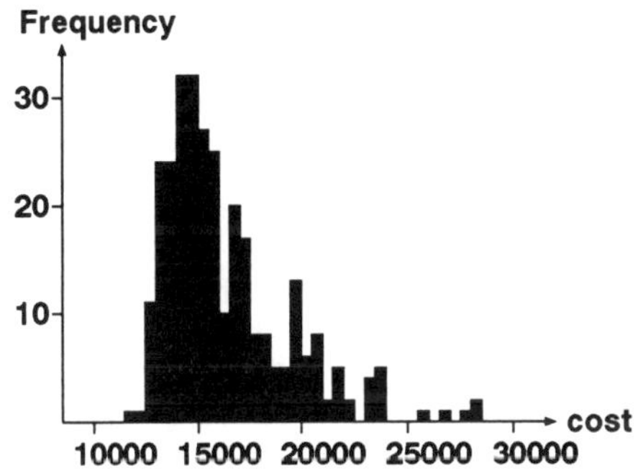

Fig. 2 Cost Distribution of the Best Solutions Found by 300 SA Runs.

The optimal solution for this problem is believed to have a cost around $11,500$ − the value in itself is of no importance here. Figure 2 indicates that, if run a large number of times, SA is likely to eventually find an optimal solution to this problem. It also shows that, in many runs, SA gets trapped in local minima with costs much higher than the global minimum. For instance, 60% of the runs produce solutions with a cost at least 30% above the global minimum. This suggests that, if rather than completing all these unsuccessful runs, one could somehow predict when a run is likely to lead to a highly sub-optimal solution and abandon it, the efficiency of SA could be greatly enhanced. The following section further analyzes the behavior of typical SA runs and proposes a mechanism which, given a problem, aims at learning to recognize (un)promising SA runs.

3 Learning To Recognize (Un)Promising SA Runs

Figure 3 depicts the behavior of a SA procedure on two different scheduling problems (from the set of benchmarks used in Section 6). For each problem, the figure depicts five SA runs, plotting the cost of the best solution, s, as the temperature of the procedure is progressively lowered — temperatures are shown in log scale, which is almost equivalent to computation time in linear scale. SA behaves very differently on these two problems. For instance, in Problem #1, the range of final solutions is relatively narrow, while in Problem #2 it is much wider. Another differentiating factor is the behavior of the procedure at low temperatures. It seems that for Problem #1, the quality of a run can already be estimated quite accurately at $T = 50$ (e.g. the best run at $T = 50$ remains best at lower temperatures), while this is less so for Problem #2.

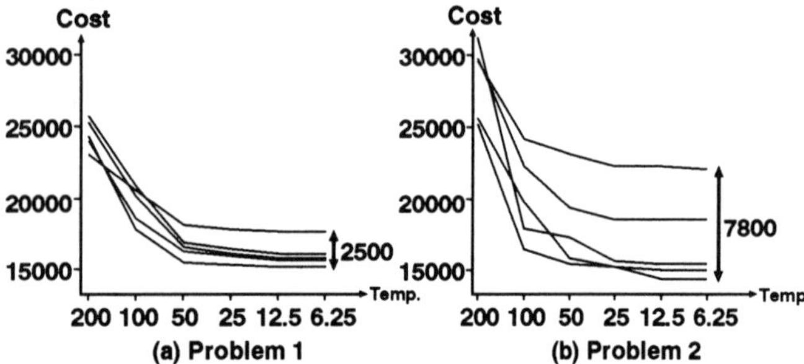

Fig. 3 Cost reductions in five SA runs on two different problems.

Clearly, such properties are not intrinsic to a problem itself. They could change if a different neighborhood structure or a different cooling profile was selected, as these parameters can affect the types of local optima encountered by the procedure and the chance that the procedure extricates itself from these local optima below a given temperature. While, in general, it may be impossible to find a SA procedure that reliably converges to near-optimal solutions on a wide class of problems, we can try to design adaptive SA procedures which, given a problem, can learn to recognize (un)promising runs and improve their performance over time. Below, we present a mechanism, which, given a problem, attempts to "learn" at different checkpoint temperatures the distribution of cost improvements that one can hope to achieve by continuing search below these temperatures.

Specifically, we postulate that, given a problem and a checkpoint temperature $T = t$, the distribution of the cost improvement that is likely to be achieved by continuing a run below t can be approximated by a normal distribution. Using performance data gathered over earlier runs on a same problem, it is possible to approximate these *Expected Cost Improvement Distributions* (*ECID*) for a set C of checkpoint temperatures and use these distributions to identify (un)promising runs.

Formally, given a combinatorial optimization problem and a SA procedure for that problem, we define c_i^t as the cost of the best solution, s, at check point t in the i-th run and c_i^0 as the cost of s at the end of the same run (i.e., at temperature $T = T_1$) When the $(n+1)$-st run reaches a checkpoint temperature t, the *ECID* below t is approximated as a normal distribution $N[\mu_n^t, \sigma_n^t]$, whose average, μ_n^t, and standard deviation, σ_n^t, are given by:

$$\mu_n^t = \frac{\sum_{i=1}^n (c_i^t - c_i^0)}{n}, \quad \sigma_n^t = \sqrt{\frac{\sum_{i=1}^n \{(c_i^t - c_i^0) - \mu_n^t\}^2}{n-1}}$$

By incrementally refining these estimators over multiple runs, this mechanism can in essence "learn" to recognize (un)promising SA runs. The following sections successively describe a cutoff criterion and three restart criteria based on *ECID* distributions.

4 A Cutoff Criterion

Suppose that, in a sixth run on Problem #1, the best solution obtained at checkpoint $T = 100$ is solution **A** — Figure 4(a). At this checkpoint, the distribution of c_6^0 — the cost of the best solution that will have been found if the run is completed — can be approximated by the normal distribution $N[c_6^{100} - \mu_5^{100}, \sigma_5^{100}]$. This distribution, represented in Fig. 4(a), suggests that, if continued, the current run has a good chance of improving the current best solution, **x**.

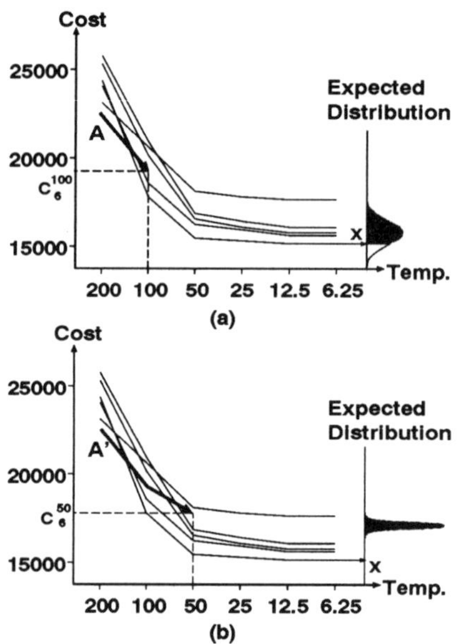

Fig. 4 Expected Cost Improvement Distributions at T=100 and T=50.

Suppose that based on this analysis, the run continues until the next checkpoint, $T = 50$, and that the best solution found by the run when it reaches that temperature is **A'**. At this point, a new distribution of c_6^0 can be computed to check how the run is doing. This distribution, $N[c_6^{50} - \mu_5^{50}, \sigma_5^{50}]$ is shown in Figure

4(b). It appears much less promising than the one at $T = 100$. Now, the chances of improving the current best solution, $\mathbf{x}$, appear remote: it probably does not make sense to continue this run.

Formally, when the $(n+1)$-st run reaches a checkpoint temperature t, a cutoff criterion is used to determine whether or not to continue this run. In the study reported in Section 6, we use a cutoff criterion of the form:

$$\frac{(c_{n+1}^t - \mu_n^t) - x_n}{\sigma_n^t} > threshold$$

where x_n is the cost of the best solution found during the previous n runs and $threshold$ is a threshold value. If the inequality holds, the current run is abandoned. For example, if $threshold = 3$ (the value used in our experiments) and the cutoff inequality holds at a given checkpoint temperature t, the probability of improving x_n by continuing the run below t is expected to be less than 1% (Beyer 87).

5 Three Restart Criteria

Whenever a run is completed or abandoned, two options are available: either start a fresh new annealing run *or*, instead, restart an earlier (promising) run, using a different sequence of random numbers ("reannealing"), i.e. restart from an intermediate temperature, using the solution x obtained at that temperature in an earlier run. In total, if reannealing is constrained to start from one of the checkpoint temperatures, there are up to $n \cdot |C| + 1$ possible options, where n is the number of earlier runs and $|C|$ the number of checkpoints in set C. Below, we describe three "restart criteria" that aim at selecting among these options so as to maximize the chances of quickly converging to a near-optimal solution.

5.1 Maximum Cost Reduction Rate Criterion

When considering several points from which to restart search, two factors need to be taken into account: (1) the likelihood that restarting search from a given point will lead to an improvement of the current best solution and (2) the time that it will take to complete a run from that point. Restarting from a low temperature will generally bring about moderate solution improvements, if any, while requiring little CPU time. Starting fresh new runs or restarting from higher temperatures can lead to more significant improvements, though less consistently and at the cost of more CPU time. In general, the cost improvements that can be expected from different temperatures will vary from one problem to another, as illustrated in Figure 3 (and as formalized by $ECID$ distributions).

A natural restart criterion is one that greedily picks the restart point expected to maximize the rate at which the cost of the current best solution will improve. For each restart candidate O_k (fresh annealing or reannealing), this can be approximated as the expected cost reduction (in the best solution), if search is restarted from O_k, divided by the expected CPU time required to complete a run from that restart point. Below, we use $R(O_k)$ to denote this approximation of the expected cost reduction rate, if search is restarted from O_k:

$$R(O_k) = \frac{expected\text{-}reduction(O_k)}{expected\text{-}CPU(O_k)}$$

where $expected\text{-}reduction(O_k)$ is the expected cost reduction at the end of a run starting from O_k and $expected\text{-}CPU(O_k)$ is the CPU time that this run is expected to require. $expected\text{-}CPU(O_k)$ can be approximated as the average time required to complete earlier runs from O_k's temperature. $expected\text{-}reduction(O_k)$ can be evaluated using $ECID$ distributions, as detailed below.

Given a reannealing point O_k at checkpoint temperature t and n earlier SA runs completed from t or above, $expected\text{-}reduction(O_k)$ can be approximated as:

$$expected\text{-}reduction(O_k) = \int_{LB}^{x_n} \{P_{nk}^t(x) \cdot (x_n - x)\}dx$$

where $P_{nk}^t(x)$ is the density function of the normal distribution $N[c_k - \mu_n^t, \sigma_n^t]$, c_k is the cost of O_k's best solution[2], x_n is the cost of the best solution obtained over the first n runs, and LB is a lower-bound on the optimal solution[3]

If O_k is a fresh SA run, $expected\text{-}reduction(O_k)$ can similarly be approximated as:

$$expected\text{-}reduction(O_k) = \int_{LB}^{x_n} \{P_n(x) \cdot (x_n - x)\}dx$$

where $P_n(x)$ is the density function of the normal distribution $N[\mu_n^0, \sigma_n^0]$, with

$$\mu_n^0 = \frac{\sum_{i=1}^n c_i^0}{n}, \quad \sigma_n^0 = \sqrt{\frac{\sum_{i=1}^n \{c_i^0 - \mu_n^0\}^2}{n-1}}.$$

5.2 Randomized Criterion

One possible problem with the above criterion is its high sensitivity to possible inaccuracies in approximations of $ECID$ distributions (e.g., when the number of earlier runs is still small). When inaccurate $ECID$ distributions lead the criterion to choose a poor restart point, the procedure may take a long time before it improves the quality of the current best solution. In the meantime, it may keep on coming back to the same poor restart point. For this reason, it is tempting to use a randomized version of the criterion. One such variation involves randomly picking from a set of promising restart points, $H = \{O_l | R(O_l) > \beta \cdot Max\{R(O_k)\}\}$, while assuming that each element in H has the same probability, $1/|H|$, of being selected. β is a constant whose value is between 0 and 1.

---

[2]To be consistent, if O_k corresponds to the i-th SA run, $c_k = c_i^t$, as defined in Section 3.

[3]In the experiments reported in this paper, LB was simply set to 0.

5.3 Hybrid Criterion

A third alternative involves keeping some level of stochasticity in the restart criterion, while ensuring that more promising restart points have a higher chance of being selected. This can be done by selecting restart points in H according to a Boltzmann distribution that assigns to each element $O_l \in H$ a probability

$$p(O_l) = \frac{exp(R(O_l)/\tau)}{\sum_{O_k \in H} exp(R(O_k)/\tau))}$$

Here, τ is a positive constant. If τ is very large, this method becomes equivalent to the randomized criterion described in subsection 5.2. If $\tau \approx 0$, this criterion becomes similar to the criterion of subsection 5.1. A similar distribution is used in the Q-learning algorithm described in (Watkins 89).

6 Performance Evaluation

6.1 The Job Shop Scheduling Problem with Tardiness and Inventory Costs

To evaluate performance of our cutoff and restart criteria, we consider a set of complex job shop scheduling problems first introduced in (Sadeh 91). The problems assume a factory, in which a set of jobs, $J = \{j_1, j_2, \cdots, j_n\}$, has to be scheduled on a set of resources, $RES = \{R_1, R_2, \cdots, R_m\}$. Each job requires performing a set of operations $O^l = \{O_1^l, O_2^l, \cdots O_{n_l}^l\}$ and, ideally, should be completed by a given due date, dd_l, for delivery to a customer. Precedence constraints specify a complete order in which operations in each job have to be performed. By convention, it is assumed that operation O_i^l has to be completed before operation O_{i+1}^l can start ($i = 1, 2, \cdots, n_l - 1$). Each operation O_i^l has a deterministic duration du_i^l and requires a resource $R_i^l \in RES$. Resources cannot be assigned to more than one operation at a time. The problem is to find a feasible schedule that minimizes the sum of tardiness and inventory costs of all the jobs ("Just-In-Time" objective). This problem is known to be NP-complete (Sadeh 91) and is representative of a large number of actual factory scheduling problems where the objective is to meet customer demand in a timely yet cost effective manner.

Experimental results reported below suggest that a good neighborhood function for this problem can be obtained by randomly applying one of the following three operators to the current schedule[4]:

- SHIFT-RIGHT: randomly select a "right-shiftable" operation and increase its start time by one time unit[5].
- SHIFT-LEFT (mirror image of SHIFT-RIGHT): randomly select a "left-shiftable" operation and decrease its start time by one time unit.
- EXCHANGE: randomly select a pair of adjacent operations on a given resource and permute the order in which they are processed by that resource. Specifically, given two consecutive operations, A and B on a resource R, with A preceding B in the current solution, the exchange operator sets the new start time of B to the old start time of A and the new end time of A to the old end time of B [6].

In our experiments, the probability of picking the EXCHANGE operator was empirically set to 3/7 while the probabilities of picking SHIFT-RIGHT or SHIFT-LEFT were each set to 2/7. Additionally, the values of parameters in the SA procedure (see Figure 1) were set as follows: $T_0 = 700$, $T_1 = 6.25$, $N = 200,000$ and $\alpha = 0.85$.

The performance of this SA procedure has been evaluated in a comparison against 39 combinations of well-regarded dispatch rules and release policies previously used to assess the performance of the Sched-Star (Morton 88) and Micro-Boss (Sadeh 91; 93) systems on a set of 40 benchmark problems similar to the ones described in (Sadeh 91). The 40 benchmarks consisted of 8 problem sets obtained by adjusting three parameters to cover a wide range of scheduling conditions: an average due date parameter (tight versus loose average due date), a due date range parameter (narrow versus wide range of due dates), and a parameter controlling the number of major bottlenecks (in this case one or two). For each parameter combination, a set of 5 scheduling problems was randomly generated, thereby producing a total of 40 problems. Each problem involved 20 jobs and 5 resources for a total of 100 operations. On average, when compared against the best solution found on each problem by the 39 combinations of dispatch rules and release policies, SA reduced schedule cost by 22% (average over 10 SA runs). When comparing the best solution obtained in 10 SA runs against the best solution obtained on each problem by the 39 combinations of dispatch rules and release policies, SA produced schedules that were 30% better. However, while running all 39 combinations of dispatch rules and release policies on a given problem takes a few CPU seconds, a single SA run takes about 3 minutes

---

[4]In the scheduling jargon, the Just-In-Time objective considered in this study is known to be irregular(Morton & Pentico 93). Prior applications of SA to job shop scheduling have only considered regular objectives such as Minimum Makespan. It can be shown that the neighborhoods used in these earlier studies are not adequate to deal with irregular objectives such as the one considered here (Sadeh & Nakakuki 94).

[5]An operation is said to be "right(left)-shiftable" if its start time can be increased (decreased) by one time unit without overlapping with another operation.

[6]In our implementation, exchanging two operations is allowed even if a precedence constraint is violated in the process. Precedence constraint violations are handled using large artificial costs that force the SA procedure to quickly get rid of them (Sadeh & Nakakuki 94).

(on a DECstation 5000/200 running C). Additional details on these experiments can be found in (Sadeh & Nakakuki 94).

6.2 Empirical Evaluation of Cutoff and Restart Criteria

We now turn to the evaluation of the cutoff and restart criteria presented in this paper and compare the performance of five variations of the SA procedure presented in 6.1:

- **N-SA**: regular SA, as described in 6.1 (no learning).

- **P-SA**: SA with cutoff criterion.

- **B-SA**: SA with cutoff and Maximum Cost Reduction Rate restart criteria.

- **R-SA**: SA with cutoff and randomized restart criteria ($\beta = 0.5$).

- **H-SA**: SA with cutoff and hybrid restart criteria ($\beta = 0.5$ and $\tau = 1$).

When running P-SA, B-SA, R-SA, and H-SA, the cutoff and/or restart criteria were only activated after 5 complete SA runs to allow for the construction of meaningful $ECID$ distributions. All four of these procedures used the same set of checkpoints, $C = \{200, 100, 50, 25, 12.5\}$.

The five procedures were compared on the same 40 benchmark problems described in subsection 6.1. Each SA procedure was run for 2 hours on each benchmark problem.

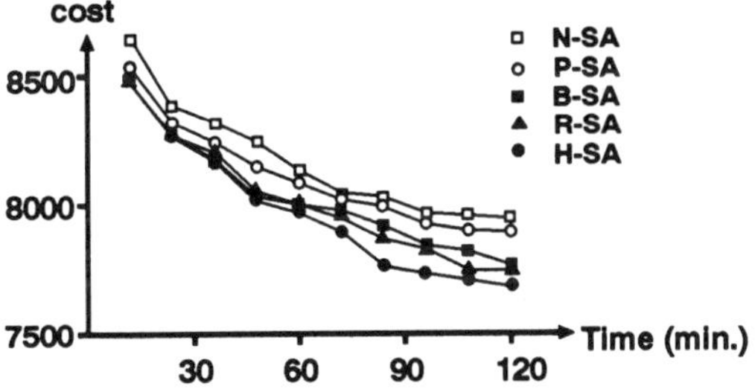

Fig.5 Improvement of the best solution over time.

Fig. 5 depicts the performance of the five SA procedures on a typical benchmark problem. It shows that throughout its run, N-SA was dominated by the other four procedures. It also indicates that both the cutoff criterion and the restart criteria contributed to this performance improvement. Among the three restart criteria, H-SA appears to perform best. Figure 5 further suggests that the restart criterion in H-SA improves performance through the entire run, as the gap between H-SA and N-SA widens over time. These observations are confirmed by results obtained on the 8 problem sets of the study, as depicted in Figure 6. Fig. 6(a) shows the average cost reductions yielded by P-SA, B-SA, R-SA and H-SA over N-SA at the end of the two-hour runs. Figure 6(b) gives the average CPU time reductions obtained by each of these four procedures (over N-SA), when required to produce a

solution of quality equal to or better than that of the best solution found by N-SA in 2 hours. It can be seen that H-SA requires between 25% and 70% less CPU time than N-SA.

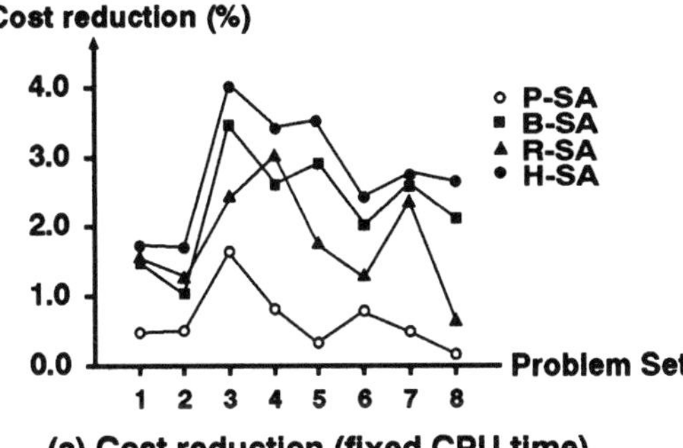

(a) Cost reduction (fixed CPU time)

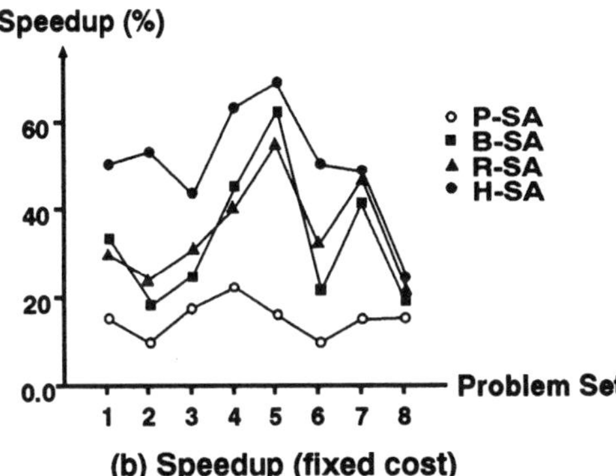

(b) Speedup (fixed cost)

Fig. 6 Empirical comparison.

A finer analysis indicates that performance improvements produced by our cutoff and restart criteria increase as one requires higher quality solutions. Figure 7, compares the average CPU time of each of the five procedures as the required quality of solutions is increased. While all five procedures take about as long to find a solution with cost below 9000 or 8800, the time required to find a solution below 8500 varies significantly (e.g. H-SA can find such a solution in 3500 seconds while N-SA requires close to 10,000 seconds).

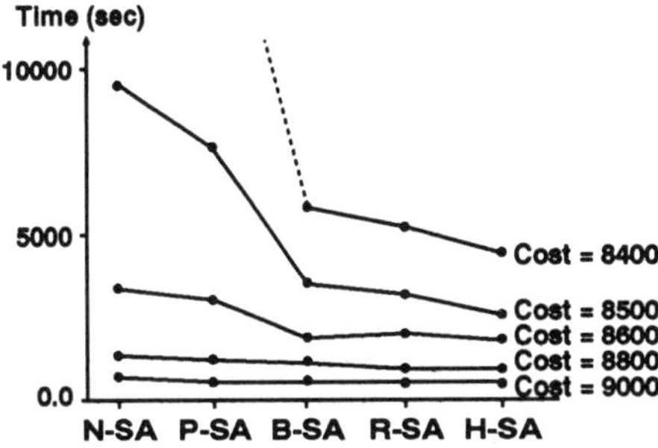

Fig. 7 Speedups as a function of required solution quality.

As already indicated in Section 5, the difference in performance between B-SA, R-SA and H-SA suggests that a deterministic use of $ECID$ distributions to decide where to restart search can be tricky, as these distributions may not be accurate, especially when only a small number of runs has been completed. By injecting non-determinism in the restart criterion, R-SA and H-SA ensure that the procedure will not always restart from the same point. The procedure is forced to sample a wider area and in the process gets a chance to refine $ECID$ distributions. From this point of view, B-SA is a procedure that places more emphasis on using existing knowledge of the search space than on acquiring new one, while R-SA places more emphasis on learning and less on exploiting already acquired information. H-SA appears to provide the best compromise between these two requirements.

Finally, it should be obvious that the CPU time and memory overheads of our cutoff and restart criteria are very moderate. All in all, in our experiments, the CPU time required to learn $ECID$ distributions and apply the cutoff and restart criteria was well under 1% of total CPU time.

7 Summary

In summary, we have developed a mechanism that learns to recognize (un)promising SA runs by refining "Expected Cost Improvement Distributions" ($ECID$s) over multiple SA runs, and have developed search cutoff and restart criteria that exploit these distributions. These mechanisms can be applied to any SA procedure and have been validated on complex job shop scheduling problems with tardiness and inventory costs, where they have been shown to dramatically reduce the computational requirements of a competitive SA procedure. Experiments presented in this paper further indicate that the closer one seeks to be to the optimum, the larger the speedups.

Acknowledgments

The first author would like to thank Masahiro Yamamoto, Takeshi Yoshimura and Yoshiyuki Koseki of NEC Corporation for giving him the opportunity to spend a year at Carnegie Mellon University.

References

Cerny, V., "Thermodynamical Approach to the Traveling Salesman Problem: An Efficient Simulation Algorithm," *J. Opt. Theory Appl.,* Vol. 45, pp. 41–51, 1985.

Beyer, W.H. "CRC Standard Mathematical Tables, 28th Edition," CRC Press, Inc., Boca Raton, FL, 1987.

Garey, M. R. and Johnson, D. S. "Computers and Intractability: A Guide to the Theory of NP-Completeness," Freeman and Co., 1979

Glover, F. and Laguna M. "Tabu Search," Chapter in *Modern Heuristic Techniques for Combinatorial Problems*, pp. 70–150, Colin Reeves (Ed.), Blackwell Scientific Publications, Oxford, 1993

Graves, S. C. "A Review of Production Scheduling," *Operations Research* Vol. 29 no. 4, pp. 646–675, 1981

Johnson, D. S., Aragon, C. R., McGeoch, L. A. and Schevon, C. "Optimization by Simulated Annealing: Experimental Evaluation; Part I, Graph Partitioning" *Operations Research* Vol. 37 no. 6, pp. 865–892, 1989

Johnson, D. S., Aragon, C. R., McGeoch, L. A. and Schevon, C. "Optimization by Simulated Annealing: Experimental Evaluation; Part II, Graph Coloring and Number Partitioning" *Operations Research* Vol. 39 no. 3, pp. 378–406, 1991

Kirkpatrick, S., Gelatt, C. D., and Vecchi, M. P., "Optimization by Simulated Annealing," *Science,* Vol. 220, pp. 671–680, 1983.

Matsuo H., C.J. Suh, and R.S. Sullivan "A Controlled Search Simulated Annealing Method for the General Jobshop Scheduling Problem" Tech. Report, "Dept. of Management, The Univ. of Texas at Austin Austin, TX, 1988.

Morton, T.E. and Pentico, D.W. "Heuristic Scheduling Systems," *Wiley Series in Engineering and Technology Management,* 1993

Morton, T.E. "SCHED-STAR: A Price-Based Shop Scheduling Module," *Journal of Manufacturing and Operations Management,* pp. 131–181, 1988.

Osman,I.H., and Potts, C.N., "Simulated Annealing for Permutation Flow-Shop Scheduling," *OMEGA Int. J. of Mgmt Sci.,* Vol. 17, pp. 551–557, 1989.

Osman, I.H. "Meta-Strategy Simulated Annealing and Tabu Search Algorithms for the Vehicle Routing Problem" Technical Report, Institute of Mathematics and Statistics, University of Kent, Canterbury, Kent CT2 7NF, UK 1992.

Palay, A. "Searching With Probabilities" PhD thesis, Department of Computer Science, Carnegie Mellon University, Pittsburgh, PA 15213, July 1983.

Sadeh, N. and Nakakuki Y. "Focused Simulated Annealing Search: An Application to Job Shop Scheduling" *Annals of Operations Research*, To appear, 1994.

Sadeh, N. "Micro-Opportunistic Scheduling: The Micro-Boss Factory scheduler" Ch. 4, *Intelligent Scheduling*, Zweben and Fox (Ed.), Morgan Kaufmann Publishers, 1994.

Sadeh, N. "Look-ahead Techniques for Micro-Opportunistic Job Shop Scheduling" PhD thesis, School of Computer Science, Carnegie Mellon University, Pittsburgh, PA 15213, March 1991.

Van Laarhoven, P.J., Aarts, E.H.L., and J.K. Lenstra "Job Shop Scheduling by Simulated Annealing," *Operations Research,* Vol. 40, No. 1, pp. 113–125, 1992.

Vepsalainen,A.P.J. and Morton, T.E. "Priority Rules for Job Shops with Weighted Tardiness Costs," *Management Science,* Vol. 33, No. 8, pp. 1035–1047, 1987.

Watkins, C. J. C. M., "Learning with Delayed Rewards" PhD thesis, Cambridge University, Psychology Department, 1989.

Wefald, E.H. and Russel, S.J. "Adaptive Learning of Decision-Theoretic Search Control Knowledge" *Sixth International Workshop on Machine Learning*, Ithaca, NY, 1989.

Zweben, M., Davis E., Daun B., Deale M., "Rescheduling with Iterative Repair" Technical Report FIA-92-15, NASA Ames Research Center, Artificial Intelligence Research Branch, Moffett Field, CA 94025 April, 1992.

Improving Search through Diversity

Peter Shell
Center for Machine Translation
Carnegie Mellon University
5000 Forbes Avenue
Pittsburgh, PA 15213
pshell@cmu.edu

Juan Antonio Hernandez Rubio
Gonzalo Quiroga Barro
Union Fenosa
Capitán Haya, 53
28020 Madrid (Spain)
gquiroga@uef.es

Abstract

Adding diversity to symbolic search techniques has not been explored in artificial intelligence. Adding a diversity criterion provides us with a powerful new mechanism for finding global maxima in complex search spaces and helps to alleviate the problem of premature convergence to local maxima. A theoretical analysis is presented of issues in diversity searching which previously haven't been addressed, and a domain-independent diversity-search algorithm for practical breadth-first searching is developed. Empirical results of an implementation in the CRESUS expert system for intelligent cash-management confirm that diversity can significantly improve the solution quality of symbolic searchers.

Introduction

This paper presents a new symbolic technique for tackling a fundamental problem found in all search techniques used in complex domains: converging to a local maximum at the expense of not finding a global optimum. In large and complex search problems where it is impossible to visit a significant fraction of the possible states, heuristic evaluation functions must be used to decide which intermediate solutions to reject and which to pursue. This can cause pruning of locally suboptimal intermediate states even though they may have led to a better global solution. This recurring problem has not been studied in depth and thus there are not many good solutions to it.

This problem manifests itself in all heuristic search paradigms. In genetic algorithms (Holland 1975) one of the main problems affecting search performance is "premature convergence", where most of the members of the "population" end up being very similar to each other and many potentially useful "genes" are lost. This results in suboptimal solutions when the best solution included one of the lost genes. A similar problem occurs in breadth-first search as we will see.

In depth-first search such as game-trees, there is a similar problem called the "horizon effect". The evaluation function gives an inaccurate estimation of the cost of a state because it was at an unstable local maximum or minimum (for example threatening the king in chess), thereby misleading the search to prefer that state even though it may not ultimately lead to an optimum.

This paper develops and evaluates a method I call "diversity search". Diversity search maintains the uniqueness of intermediate states and operators in order to increase the coverage of the space searched. It promises to improve the performance of many types of searchers by alleviating the local-minimum problem. Although it can augment most search techniques, it has received little attention in artificial intelligence. The idea has been used in genetic algorithms (Mauldin 1984) and simulated annealing (Kirkpatrick, Gelatt & Vecchi 1983) but hasn't been attempted in symbolic search methods such as depth-first or breadth-first search. This paper reports work which has combined ideas found in genetic algorithms and simulated annealing with symbolic search techniques. I address some issues surrounding diversity search which haven't previously been considered, then develop a domain-independent algorithm for diversity-search in a breadth-first searcher. An implementation is presented in CRESUS (Shell et al. 1992), a working expert-system in the complex domain of cash-management, with empirical results that show that diversity search can significantly improve global search performance.

Related Work

Here we consider related solutions to the local maximum problem in different search formalisms and contrast them to diversity search. Although diversity search hasn't been addressed in symbolic search, it has been addressed in genetic algorithms. Genetic algorithms simulate natural evolution to optimize an evaluation function. They are analogous to breadth-search where the intermediate states are called "genomes"; sets of states correspond to populations; and the evaluation function corresponds to the physical environment. New states are generated by applying genetic operators such as crossover or mutation to single or pairs of parent genomes. Genomes with the highest evaluation function have the best probability of "reproducing." Search proceeds by reproducing and replacing genomes for typically several thousands of generations, and picking the most fit genomes from the resulting population. Genetic algorithms are mostly used in machine learning (DeJong 1990).

DeJong (DeJong 1975) recognized early on that premature convergence in genetic algorithms adversely affected performance and attempted to alleviate it. He employed probabilistic reproduction and operator mutation so that the locally favored genes wouldn't dominate the pool. Although this increased the diversity of the population it didn't significantly improve performance. Adding a "crowding factor", which limited the number of genotypes similar to the favored genotype, helped his system on his hardest test case (F5). Mauldin (Mauldin 1984) later introduced an explicit diversity criterion into genetic search and showed that diversity significantly improved performance using DeJong's 5 polynomial test functions. Booker (Booker 1987) developed several new crossover strategies (such as using two crossover points and strategically varying the crossover rate) which gave similar improvement without explicitly introducing diversity.

For several reasons, diversity in genetic algorithms doesn't transfer easily to symbolic search methods. Genetic algorithms usually require several thousand iterations to find an optimized solution. This works well for the simple polynomial functions used in much of the genetic-algorithms literature where the evaluation is fast and states are represented in few bits, but isn't feasible in knowledge-rich systems where the evaluation function takes longer to compute and the states are more complex. Furthermore, the two orthogonal criteria of diversity and primary evaluation cannot be combined in the same way by symbolic searchers, as we will see. Finally, the metric used to evaluate diversity in genetic algorithms is simply the "Hamming distance" between the bit-strings representing each genome. Since symbolic search methods don't usually use a bit-string representation this metric is not transferrable.

Simulated annealing (Kirkpatrick, Gelatt & Vecchi 1983) is a stochastic search technique designed to find minimum-cost solutions to large optimization problems without converging to a local minimum. It is based on an analogy with statistical mechanics. It has been used in such tasks as graph bisection (Jerrum & Sorkin 1993) and connectionistic networks such as the Boltzman machine (Ackley, Hinton & Sejnowski 1985) However, simulated annealing is a slow process which requires fast evaluation and generation functions (Davis & Steenstrup 1987) and so wouldn't be feasible for most knowledge-based expert-systems. Furthermore, as Mauldin (Mauldin 1984) pointed out, it is not intrinsically parallel like genetic algorithms.

Techniques have been developed for alleviating a similar problem in depth-first search. Quiescence search (Beal 1990), used largely in game programs to handle the horizon effect, identifies local maxima with respect to the (sometimes inaccurate) evaluation function by situations of instability such as checking a king in chess. Such situations are likely to "fool" the evaluation function into giving an inaccurate cost. When they occur the algorithm continues searching until a stable, or quiescent, state is reached. Depth-first searchers can't incorporate the diversity of states into their algorithms because they only retain one state at a time, and they need to compare the states to determine their diversity.

Berliner (private communication) has experimented with increasing the diversity of operators in depth-first searchers by grouping operators by similarity and ensuring that several different groups of operators are generated at each step in the search. This may encourage diversity at the operator-generation level but lacks the ability to ensure diversity among states.

Motivation

The introduction described the need for a technique to avoid convergence to a local maximum in order to find the global maximum, and noted the lack of research into diversity search in symbolic domains. Here we examine the behavior of a specific breadth-first searcher which will motivate introducing diversity into searching techniques.

Our breadth-first searcher is part of CRESUS (Shell et al. 1992), a cash-management expert-system used by the treasury department of Union Fenosa, an electric company serving greater Madrid in Spain. This expert system could be used by any medium or large-sized company to automate and improve their treasury. The task of the treasurer is to manage the daily cash-flow and cover the company's financial needs by borrowing money from some subset of the numerous company credit lines, balance several bank accounts, allocate payments and collections and invest any excess funds. Each such operation involves commissions and interest payments which vary depending on the amount of money and the associated financial instrument (e.g., check or wire), credit-line or bank-account. The goal is to minimize the global cost of all of these operations.

An artificial intelligence approach was developed after it was realized that non-heuristic algorithms such as linear programming couldn't find a solution in a reasonable amount of time due to the large number of variables in the problem. In the CRESUS searcher, an *operator* is a cash-management operation such as moving \$1000 from account A to account B using a wire transfer. A *state* is defined by the current balance of all the bank accounts and amounts available in the credit lines. The evaluation function computes the total cost of the current operations plus the estimated cost of the remaining operations. A *solution* is a sequence of operations which balance all of the bank accounts. CRESUS is implemented in Common-Lisp and currently runs on Sun Sparcstations. It uses the PARMENIDES (Shell & Carbonell 1988) frame language as its knowledge representation and FRULEKIT (Shell & Carbonell 1986) for the inference engine.

An experienced treasurer requires several hours to manually complete the task. The searcher automates the decision-making and performs it in about 5 minutes with a hybrid beam-search (Newell 1978) algorithm. Further, the searcher usually outperforms the treasurer, finding solutions which cost about 20% less than the treasurer's.

The cash-management task is extremely complex. For each state in the search space, about 100 operators may apply, and solutions typically consist of a sequence of about 100 operators. Thus the search space contains about 10^{200} states. Furthermore, it is multi-modal, of high dimensionality and has a high degree of "epistasis": one part of a solution can be inhibited or modified by another part. This space is made tractable by encoding expert knowledge into the operator evaluation and generation functions, and by partitioning it into minimally interacting subspaces. These subspaces correspond to the daily solution versus the global, or period, solution of 2 to 4 weeks and the space of operators of a particular type.

Although the beam-searcher usually finds solutions which the human expert can't improve, occasionally it constructs suboptimal solutions corresponding to local maxima. It is important to avoid such solutions because the treasury department has started to rely on the searcher on a daily basis; and since the searcher usually finds good solutions, the expectations of the users have been raised. Furthermore, the company plans to market the system and would like it to perform consistently well.

Examining the states at which the searcher arrived at the end of the search illustrates the problem. The final states are extremely similar to each other. Table 1 shows the average number of operators constituting each state which are unique to that state, i.e. which don't appear in any other state. For example, if state 1 were created by the application of operators $\{A,B,C\}$ and state 2 by operators $\{B,D,A\}$ then those states would each have two unique operators, C and D, respectively (the computation of operator uniqueness is discussed in more detail in the next section). The beam-searcher was run over 5 days in October 1993 with a beam-width of 20. Similar results are obtained when the intermediate states are examined, for example after 10 or 20 iterations.

Table 1: Average number of unique and common operators in the beam searcher states

Day	1	2	3	4	5	Average
# unique ops	*1.7*	*1*	*1*	*1*	*2*	*1.34*
Operators in common	*95.9%*	*97.8%*	*97.1%*	*98.3%*	*96.7%*	*97.2%*

Intuition explains the high similarity between the states. When any type of searcher tries to find an optimal state in a large search space it will only be able consider a tiny subset of those nodes. For example a beam searcher might keep a set of on the order of the 20 best states and generate 10 potential successors to each state. If the average depth of a space is 100, then the searcher will only have considered $20 \times 10 \times 100$ or 20,000 states. Because the number of states visited by the searcher is so small compared to the number in the space (10^4 versus 10^{200}), intuition tells us that the states which have the highest evaluation will end up being very similar to each other. This is because the states which only differ from the preferred state by one operator or by a small change in an operator, will likely have one of the highest evaluations as well. This isn't due to an inaccurate evaluation function because the evaluation function had been finely tuned – it performs miniature searches of its own to accurately estimate the cost of the remaining operations. These observations led me to develop the diversity search algorithm.

The Diversity-search Algorithm

The heuristic of diversity search is that by increasing the "diversity" of the intermediate states in a breadth-first searcher, we may be able to improve the final results. By retaining some states not only because they have a desirable primary evaluation (such as cost) but also because they are sufficiently different from the other states, we can avoid converging on local maxima which can mislead the global searcher. A formalization of the standard beam-search algorithm is presented, followed by the diversity-based algorithm. Next two issues in diversity searching which haven't been sufficiently considered are addressed: how to define diversity of states and how to combine the primary evaluation with the diversity evaluation.

The Standard Beam-search Algorithm

To compare diversity-search with a more traditional algorithm and to introduce notation, the standard beam-search algorithm used in CRESUS is first presented.

a. Initialize set-of-states to a set containing one state which is the current problem's state.

b. REPEAT until no more states can be expanded:

  1. Expand set-of-states using generation function G.

  2. Evaluate the expanded states using primary evaluation function E.

  3. Pick the K highest-evaluated states as the next set of states.

The generation and evaluation functions are as follows:

$$G: State_0 \implies \{State_1, State_2, \ldots State_n\}$$

$State_i$ is derived by applying an operator to $State_0$.

$$E: State \implies Evaluation$$

Evaluation is the estimated cost of the given state. $\underline{K}$, the beam width, is the number of states retained at each step.

The Diversity Beam-search Algorithm

The diversity beam-search algorithm augments steps b.2 and b.3 to include an evaluation of the diversity of states as well as primary evaluation:

```
a. Initialize set-of-states to a set
   containing   only   the   current
   problem's state.

b. REPEAT until no more states can be
   expanded:

 1. Expand    set-of-states    using
    generation function G.

 2. Evaluate the expanded states using
    primary evaluation function E.

 2'. Evaluate the diversity of the
     expanded states using diversity
     evaluation function D.

 3. Pick  the  K  highest-evaluated
    states into the next set of states.

 3'. Add the K' states which maximize
     the function C(E,D) to the next set
     of states.
```

Where:

```
D: State ⟹ Diversity-evaluation
```

where *Diversity-evaluation* is the estimated diversity of the given state relative to the other states and:

```
C: Cost-eval, Diversity-eval ⟹
   Combined-eval
```

$\underline{K}'$ is the diversity beam width, i.e., the number of states to keep at each step based on their diversity in addition to the $\underline{K}$ cost-wise best states.

The diversity-computation function **D** and combination function **C** are discussed next.

Computing the Diversity

Because diversity search hasn't previously been attempted in symbolic search techniques, the issue of computing the diversity of states hasn't been adequately addressed. An intuitive method would be to compare states directly using domain-specific functions. For example, in the cash-management domain, one might compare how many bank accounts are balanced and how much

money is available in each credit-line. However, this requires domain-specific comparison functions and doesn't take into account that different sequences of operators with different costs could have led to the same state.

A more accurate way to compare states is to count how many constituent operators – independent of order – that they have in common, since it is the constituent operators which comprise the solution. In symbolic searchers where operators are applied to generate new states, the sequence of operators leading to each state can be associated with each state. To calculate the closeness between two states S_1 and S_2, we will define *State-match(S_1,S_2)* to be:

$$\sum_{i=1}^{Len(S_1)} \text{Op-state-match}\,(\text{Op-num}\,(i, S_1), S_2) \qquad \textbf{(EQ 1)}$$

where *Op-state-match(Op,S)* is defined as:

$$\text{Max(Op-match(Op,Op-num}\,(i, S))\,)\ \ \forall i < Len\,(S) \qquad \textbf{(EQ 2)}$$

where *Op-num(i,S)* returns the ith operator in state S.

Note that if the search technique compared states at different depths, such as A^*, *State-match* would have to return a percentage instead of a count of matches.

The function *Op-match* should return a number 0 through 1, where 0 means that the operators are completely different and 1 means that they are identical. To simplify and to make the comparison domain-independent, we can define *Op-match* to return 1 only if the operators are identical and to otherwise return 0. Under this definition, *State-match(S_1,S_2)* tells us how many operators associated with S_1 are also associated with S_2.

Finally, to compute the degree of match of a state relative to a set of states, a logical method would be to compute the maximum match between the state in question and the rest of the states in the state-set. Thus *Match-in-Set(S,Set)* is:

$$\text{Max(State-match(S,State-num(i,Set)))}\ \ \forall i < Len(S) \qquad \textbf{(EQ 3)}$$

State-num(i,Set) gives the ith state in the set of states Set.

The *diversity* of a state is then the number of operators in the state minus the *Match-in-Set* of that state.

Combining Primary and Diversity Evaluation

A harder question is how to combine the orthogonal criteria of primary cost-evaluation and diversity evaluation. We want to retain some states because of their diversity, but we should also retain some of the best cost-evaluated states so that the search proceeds towards the global minimum. In genetic algorithms, Mauldin (Mauldin 1984) limited the population size by requiring that all intermediate states have a minimum diversity from the others, and probabilistically "reproduced" the state with the highest cost-evaluation. However, these two steps are merged in beam search and there is no analog to "reproduction" in symbol search, so a different technique is needed.

A simple method would be to maintain two different sets of states: one for the states which minimize the cost and one for the states which maximize the diversity function. This would cause combination function **C** to simply return the diversity and ignore the cost-evaluation. The heuristic is that if a state from the diversity-set becomes qualified it would "jump" to the cost-evaluation set.

A disadvantage of the "simple" approach is that the states in the diversity-set are not selected for cost-evaluation and so may stray towards extremely diverse but high-cost solutions. Thus a more sophisticated algorithm was developed which maintains multiple "bands" of diversity sets, each containing states within a given range of diversities. Within each band, the lowest-cost states are retained. Since states only compete with other states within the same band, high-diversity but higher cost states won't replace medium-diversity but lower cost states. Note that diversity is always computed by comparing to all states, not just the ones sharing the same band. The idea is that some of the high-diversity states will turn into medium-diversity states which in turn may eventually jump into the cost-evaluation set.

The parameters to the band searcher are the number and size of the bands and the minimum diversity. For example, if the minimum diversity were 2, the number of bands were 3 and the band-size were 2 then the first band would contain states with diversity 2 and 3, the second would contain states with diversity 4 and 5, and so on. The next section measures the effect of these diversity techniques on the global searcher.

Empirical Results

The standard CRESUS beam-searcher and 3 variations of the diversity searcher were run on 4 separate weeks of 1993 company treasury data. The total cost for each weekly solution is computed by summing the costs of credit-line dispositions, funds-movement and payment and collection commissions, and overdrawn-account fees. For the standard beam-searcher, the beam-width $\underline{K}$ of 10 was used; for the diversity searchers, the cost-eval beam-width $\underline{K}$ was 5 and the diversity-eval $\underline{K}'$ was 5. In this way we can determine if the 5 additional states are most effectively used as cost-eval states or diversity-eval states.

The Y axis in Figure 1 plots the cumulative total cost of solutions found by each search strategy. The simple diversity searcher, *simple*, and two variants of band-searching are shown. In the first variant, *band(4,1)*, there were 4 bands and the band-size was 1; in *band(3,2)*, the number of bands was 3 and the band-size was 2. The minimum diversity in both band searchers was 2.

All three diversity algorithms did better than standard beam-searching. Week 1 saw the largest improvement. It contained many local maxima because it contained a holiday and there were more constraints on funds-movements. In the standard search all of the states converged to a situation where idle funds were stuck in unusable accounts. In *simple* and *band(3,2)*, some funds had still been allocated to accounts which were affected by the holiday; in *band(4,1)*, all money had been correctly allocated. *Simple* also did surprisingly well on week 2 but worse than standard search on week 4. *Band(4,1)* did the best overall because of consistently good performance (see Table 2). *Band(4,1)* did better than *band(3,2)* because the latter suffers from the same problem as *simple*: within each band of size 2, slightly lower-cost states will be selected over more diverse states. Thus bands should probably always be of size 1. The reason that *band(4,1)* did slightly worse than *simple* on week 4 may be that that week didn't contain many local maxima which fooled *simple;* or that the local maxima fooled the diversity approaches as well as *simple*. In this case the benefits of using diversity weren't used and the space devoted to diversity states was wasted.

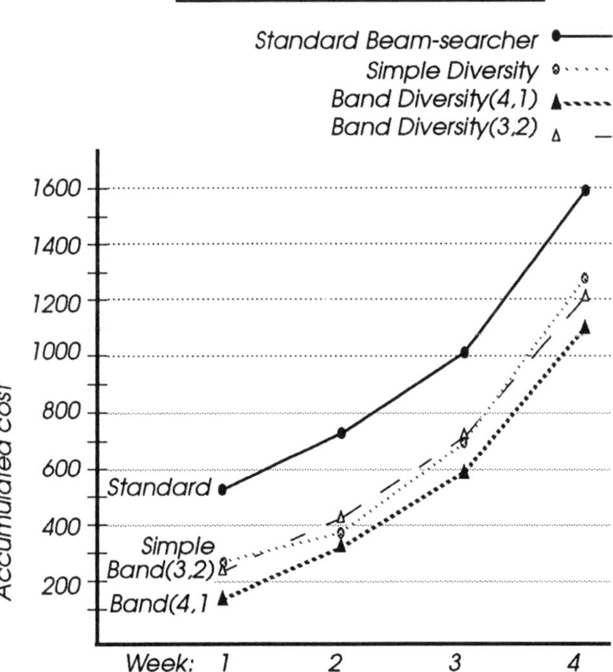

Figure 1: *Total cost of the standard beam-search and diversity searchers in the* CRESUS *expert system.*

References

Ackley, D.H., Hinton, G.E. and Sejnowski, T.J. 1985. A Learning Algorithm for Boltzmann Machines. *Cognitive Science.* 9(1):147-169.

Beal, Don F. 1990. A Generalized Quiescence Search Algorithm. *Artificial Intelligence.* 43(1):85-98, April.

Booker, L. 1987. Improving Search in Genetic Algorithms. *Genetic Algorithms and Simulated Annealing.* In Davis, L., Morgan Kaufmann Publishers, Los Altos, California, pages 61-73.

Davis, L. and Steenstrup, M. 1987. Genetic Algorithm and Simulated Annealing. *Genetic Algorithms and Simulated Annealing.* In Davis, L., Morgan Kaufmann Publishers, Los Altos, California, pages 1-11.

DeJong, K.A. 1975. *Analysis of the Behavior of a Class of Genetic Adaptive Systems.* Ph.D. thesis, University of Michigan, Ann Arbor.

DeJong, K.A. 1990 Special Issue on Genetic Algorithms. *Machine Learning.* 5(4).

Holland, J. 1975. *Adaptation in Natural and Artificial Systems.* University of Michigan Press.

Jerrum, M., and Sorkin, G.B. 1993. *Simulated Annealing for Graph Bisection.* Technical Report, University of Edinburgh, Dept. of Computer Science.

Kirkpatrick, S., Gelatt, C.D. and Vecchi, M.P. 1983. Optimization by Simulated Annealing. *Science.* (220):671-680.

Mauldin, M.L. 1984. Maintaining Diversity in Genetic Search. *Proceedings of the National Conference on Artificial Intelligence*, pages 247-250.

Newell, Allen. 1978. *Harpy, Production Systems and Human Cognition.* Pittsburgh, PA: Carnegie Mellon University.

Shell, P. and Carbonell, J. G. 1988. *The Parmenides Reference Manual.* CMU Computer Science Department internal paper.

Shell, P. and Carbonell, J. G. 1986. *The FRuleKit Reference Manual.* CMU Computer Science Department internal paper.

Shell, P., et al. 1992. CRESUS: An Integrated Expert System for Cash Management. Scott, A. and Klahr, P. (editor), *Innovative Applications of Artificial Intelligence 4.*

Table 2: Percentage cost of diversity searchers compared to standard beam searcher

Week	1	2	3	4	Average
Standard	*100%*	*100%*	*100%*	*100%*	*100%*
Simple	*52%*	*48%*	*98%*	*112%*	*81%*
Band(4,1)	*28%*	*94%*	*79%*	*102%*	*71%*
Band(3,2)	*50%*	*83%*	*87%*	*98%*	*78%*

Conclusions

Diversity searching is a step towards extending knowledge-based searchers to obtain the benefits of genetic search while retaining the advantages of the symbolic approach. Although the idea of diversity has been investigated in genetic algorithms and simulated annealing, this is the first time that maintaining diversity during a symbolic search has been attempted. This paper addressed the issues involved and presented a framework for diversity search. A domain-independent algorithm was shown and empirical results from a working expert-system show that diversity search can substantially improve knowledge-based searchers.

Diversity search will be most useful in complex domains that are not amenable to genetic algorithms or simulated annealing. These include problems which require a fast response and those which exhibit a high degree of epistasis. It may be that symbolic diversity search will occupy a useful middle-ground between knowledge-rich systems that need to do much search and genetic algorithms and simulated annealing which are not feasible in complex, knowledge-rich domains.

Diversity search shows promise; it warrants more exploration. It should be evaluated with different parameters and combination functions. A simulated-annealing technique of decreasing the diversity as the search progresses according to a schedule may further enhance the search results. It would also be interesting to try applying it to different problems and with different searchers in order to determine how broadly applicable it is.

Acknowledgments

I would like to thank Jaime Carbonell, Michael Mauldin, Ben MacLaren, Rick Chimera and Alex Franz for helpful comments on earlier drafts of this paper, and the rest of the CRESUS team: Javier Berbiela, Maria José Moro Martín, Paloma Bilbao and Lorenzo Tello.

Genetic Programming and AI Planning Systems[1]

Lee Spector

School of Communications and Cognitive Science
Hampshire College, Amherst, MA 01002
lspector@hamp.hampshire.edu

Abstract

Genetic programming (GP) is an automatic programming technique that has recently been applied to a wide range of problems including blocks-world planning. This paper describes a series of illustrative experiments in which GP techniques are applied to traditional blocks-world planning problems. We discuss genetic planning in the context of traditional AI planning systems, and comment on the costs and benefits to be expected from further work.

Introduction

Genetic programming (GP) is an automatic programming technique developed by Koza that extends the genetic algorithm framework of Holland (Holland 1992). Whereas the conventional genetic algorithm uses evolution-inspired techniques to manipulate and produce fixed-length chromosome strings that encode solutions to problems, GP manipulates and produces computer programs. Koza shows how programs can be "evolved" to solve a wide range of otherwise unrelated problems (Koza 1992).

Several of the problems that Koza describes are of interest to AI planning research. These include control programs for artificial ants, box-moving robots, wall-following robots, and block-stacking systems. The block-stacking problems are closest to the classic problems in the literature of AI planning systems, but Koza uses an unusual variant of blocks-world, making it difficult to relate his results to those of mainstream AI planning research (Tate et al. 1990).

In this paper we apply GP to the block-stacking problems that have been central in the literature of AI planning. In particular, we describe experiments in using GP techniques to 1) find a plan to achieve a single goal from a single initial state, 2) find a "universal plan" for achieving a single goal from a range of initial states, 3) find a domain-dependent planning program, capable of producing action sequences to achieve different sets of goals from a variety of initial states. We conclude that while GP has much to offer to AI planning research, more work must be done to determine exactly how it can be best applied.

Genetic Programming

GP works with a large population of candidate programs and uses the Darwinian principle of "survival of the fittest" to produce successively better programs for a given problem. To use GP one must choose the primitive elements (*functions* and *terminals*) out of which the programs will be constructed.[2] Every terminal in the terminal set and every value that may be returned by any function in the function set must be acceptable as an input for every argument position of every function in the function set; this is called the *closure* property.

The programmer wishing to employ GP must also produce a problem-specific fitness function. This function must take a program as input, producing a number that indicates the "fitness" of the program as output. This describes "how good" the program is at solving the problem under consideration, and determines the likelihood that the program and its offspring will survive to subsequent generations. In this paper all fitness values are "standardized fitness" values, for which *lower* fitness values indicate *better* programs (Koza 1992, p. 96).

Fitness is normally assessed by running the program on some number of *fitness cases,* each of which establishes inputs to the program and describes the corresponding output that the individual program should produce. One is often interested in producing a program that works over a very large, perhaps infinite, set of inputs; but the fitness of individual programs is assessed only with reference to a usually small, finite set of fitness cases. A program is said to be *robust* if it produces proper results for inputs that were not used in assessing fitness during the GP process.

The GP process starts by creating a random initial population of programs. The closure property ensures that each of these programs, unfit though it may be, will execute without signalling errors. Each of the programs is assessed for fitness, and fitness-sensitive *genetic operations* are then used to produce the subsequent generation. These may include reproduction, crossover, mutation, permutation, and others (Koza 1992); we use only reproduction and crossover here. The reproduction operator selects a highly fit individual and simply copies it into the next generation. Selection for re-

[1]The author acknowledges the support of the Dorothy and Jerome Lemelson National Program in Invention, Innovation, and Creativity.

[2]The description of genetic programming that follows covers only the simplest variant of the technique. See (Koza 1992) for more sophisticated variants.

production is random but biased toward highly fit programs. The crossover operation introduces variation by selecting two highly fit *parents* and by producing from them two *offspring*. The crossover operation selects random fragments of each of the two parents and swaps them; the resulting programs are copied to the next generation.

If GP is "working" on a given run then the average fitness of the population will tend to improve over subsequent generations, as will the fitness of the best-of-generation individual from each generation. After a preestablished number of generations, or after the fitness improves to some preestablished level, the best-of-run individual is designated as the result and is produced as the output from the GP system.

GP appears to be a powerful technique with wide applicability. It is CPU intensive, but there are ample opportunities for parallelism (e.g., in the assessment of fitness across a large population). We believe that it has great promise, but as Dewdney wrote of genetic algorithms more generally, "The jury is still out on a method that (a) claims to solve difficult problems and (b) is suspiciously painless." (Dewdney 1993, p. xiii) In order to understand the strengths and weaknesses of the technique we must apply it to areas in which prior research has mapped the computational territory. This strategy is being pursued by many, and is evident in (Koza 1992); in the remainder of this paper we endeavor to lay the foundations for such work in the mainstream of AI planning.

Genetic Planning

One can apply the techniques of GP to AI planning problems in a variety of ways.[3] GP systems produce programs; AI planning systems produce plans. Insofar as a plan is a program for an execution module, one can use a GP system *as* a planning system—one can use a GP system to evolve a plan which, when executed in the context of a given initial state, achieves a given set of goals.

A traditional AI planning system takes as input an initial state, a goal description, and a set of operator schemata, and produces as output a sequence of operator schemata, along with any necessary variable bindings. One can use a GP system in a similar way; given an initial state, a goal description, and a description of the actions that the execution module can perform, one can produce a program for the execution module that will achieve the goals from the initial state. The first of the experiments described below uses GP in this way.

The parallel between the traditional planning system and the genetic planning system need not be exact; whereas most planning systems require that the available actions be described declaratively (using, e.g., STRIPS operators

(Fikes & Nilsson 1971)), purely procedural "operators" will suffice for the genetic planning system.[4] This is because the genetic planning system can assess the utility of action sequences by *running* them in simulation, rather than by analyzing declarative structures that describe operator effects. The cost of simulation can be high, both in runtime and in simulation development time, but the simulation approach obviates the need for declarative action representation. Since declarative action representation is an active research area with many outstanding problems (Ginsberg 1990), the availability of a planning methodology that does not require such representations is interesting for this reason alone. In addition, the way that simulation is used in GP is clearly parallelizable; the fitness of each program can be assessed in an independent simulation.

A more ambitious approach to genetic planning is to evolve control programs that can achieve some given set of goals from a variety of initial conditions. If one augments the function set to allow for decision-making and iteration in the evolved plans, one can actually evolve such "universal plans" (in the sense of (Schoppers 1987)). Koza's work on blocks-world planning takes this approach, as does the second of the experiments described below.

A third approach to genetic planning is to evolve complete domain-dependent planners. The function set must in this case include functions that access the system's current goals; given such a function set one can evolve programs that can achieve a range of goal conditions from a range of initial states. The third of the experiments described below uses GP in this way.

A fourth approach to genetic planning is to evolve complete domain-*independent* planners. The function set would in this case presumably include functions that have proven to be useful in existing domain independent planners; e.g., functions for constructing partial orders of plan steps. We have not yet conducted any experiments using this ambitious approach.

Koza's Genetic Blocks-World Planner

Koza has described the use of GP for a set of planning problems in a variant of blocks-world (Koza 1992, sec. 18.1). In this domain the goal is always to produce a single stack of blocks. The domain never contains more than one stack; every block is always either part of the stack or on the table (and clear). He considers the example of producing the 9-block stack that spells "**UNIVERSAL**" from a variety of initial configurations. Note that this is an instance of the second approach to genetic planning outlined above; we seek a single program that transforms a range of initial states to satisfy a single, prespecified goal condition.

Koza's blocks-world is unusual both because it is limited to a single stack of blocks and because it uses an unusually powerful set of functions and terminals (defined by (Nilsson 1989)). The terminal set consists of the following "sensors": **CS**, which dynamically specifies the top block of the stack; **TB** ("Top Correct Block"), which specifies the highest block on the stack such that it and all blocks below it are in the correct order; and **NN** ("Next Needed"), which

---

[3]Note, however, that although Holland's seminal work on genetic algorithms (Holland 1992) contains much of interest to planning researchers, its use of the phrase "genetic plan" has no relation to "planning" as used in the literature of AI planning systems.

[4]Some "traditional" planners use operators that include procedural components as well, e.g. NOAH (Sacerdoti 1975).

specifies the block that should be on top of **TB** in the final stack. The functions are: **MS** ("Move to the Stack"), which takes a block as its argument and, if it is on the table, moves it to the stack and returns **T** (otherwise it returns **NIL**); **MT** ("Move to the Table"), which takes a block as its argument and, if it is *anywhere* in the stack, moves the *top* block of the stack to the table and returns **T** (otherwise it returns **NIL**); **DU** ("Do Until"), which is actually a macro that implements a control structure—it takes two bodies of code, both of which are evaluated repeatedly until the second returns non-**NIL**; **NOT**, which is the normal LISP boolean negation function; and **EQ**, which is the normal LISP equality predicate.

Note that the function and terminal sets are carefully tailored to the specialized nature of the domain (O'Reilly & Oppacher 1992). **CS** would not generalize in any obvious way to a domain with multiple stacks. **TB**, though described as a "sensor," depends on the goal and must perform computation to match several elements in the world to components of the goal. Goal-sensitivity in the function and terminal sets is not necessarily to be avoided; indeed, in some cases it is necessary, and we use goal-sensitive functions below. But it is important to note that **TB** is goal-sensitive in a highly specialized, domain-dependent way. **TB** also depends on the fact that the domain can contain only one stack. **NN** is domain-specific in much the way that **TB** is. **MS** and **MT** make sense only in a single-stack world.

Koza ran his GP system on the "**UNIVERSAL**" problem for 51 generations with a population size of 500 individuals. He assessed fitness with respect to 166 of the millions of possible initial configurations. Fitness for an individual program was calculated as 166 minus the number of fitness cases for which the stack spelled "**UNIVERSAL**" after the program was run. A 100% correct program emerged in generation 10. It was: **(EQ (DU (MT CS) (NOT CS)) (DU (MS NN) (NOT NN)))**

Although this program is correct, it is not particularly efficient. It used 2,319 block movements to handle the 166 fitness cases, whereas it is possible to use only 1,641. By factoring the number of block movements into the fitness function Koza was able to produce a correct and maximally efficient program. That program, however, was longer than it needed to be. By factoring the number of symbols in the program into the fitness function (a "parsimony" measure) he was able to produce a correct, maximally efficient, and maximally parsimonious program.

Blocks-World Experiment #1

We have performed several experiments to assess the applicability of GP techniques to more traditional AI planning domains. The three that we describe here are all blocks-world experiments. Koza's GP code was used in all cases.[5]

Our first experiment was to use GP to produce a single correct plan that achieves a particular (conjunctive) goal condition from a particular initial state. We chose the problem known as the Sussman Anomaly as a representative

---

[5]Koza's code can be found in the appendix to (Koza 1992), and can also be obtained by anonymous FTP.

problem from the blocks-world domain. The goal in this problem is to start with a world in which **C** is on **A**, and in which **A** and **B** are both on the table, and to produce a state in which **A** is on **B**, **B** is on **C**, and **C** is on the table. We will refer to the resulting state as an {**ABC**} tower.

We built a simple blocks-world simulation environment and wrote **NEWTOWER** and **PUTON** functions that are procedural versions of the following **STRIPS**-style operators. In these operators distinctly named variables must bind to distinct blocks:

Operator: (NEWTOWER ?X) ;; move X to the table if clear
Preconditions: (ON ?X ?Y) (CLEAR ?X)
Add List: ((ON ?X TABLE) (CLEAR ?Y))
Delete List: ((ON ?X ?Y))

Operator: (PUTON ?X ?Y) ;; put X on Y if both are clear
Preconditions: (ON ?X ?Z) (CLEAR ?X) (CLEAR ?Y)
Add List: ((ON ?X ?Y) (CLEAR ?Z))
Delete List: ((ON ?X ?Z) (CLEAR ?Y))

Our functions check that the required preconditions hold and change the world according to the add and delete lists if they do. Each function returns its first argument (the top of the resulting stack) upon success, or **NIL** if passed **NIL** or if the preconditions do not hold. We used a function set consisting of **NEWTOWER**, **PUTON**, and two sequence-building functions, **PROGN2** and **PROGN3**, which are versions of LISP's **PROGN** that take 2 and 3 arguments respectively. The resulting programs may have a hierarchical structure since the functions in the function set can be nested in many ways. The terminals used for this experiment were the names of the blocks: **A**, **B** and **C**.

We calculated fitness with respect to a single fitness case:

INITIAL: ((ON C A) (ON A TABLE) (ON B TABLE) (CLEAR C)
        (CLEAR B))
GOALS: ((ON A B) (ON B C) (ON C TABLE))

Our fitness function had three components: a correctness component, an efficiency component, and a parsimony component. The correctness component was calculated as 70 times the number of achieved goals divided by the total number of goals (in this case 3). This produces a number between 0 and 70, with higher numbers indicating better programs. The efficiency component was calculated from the number of **NEWTOWER** and **PUTON** actions actually executed in running the program. All executions were counted, even if the action was not successful. The number of actions was scaled to produce a number between 0 and 15, with higher numbers indicating more efficient programs. The parsimony component was calculated from the number of symbols in the program, scaled to produce a number between 0 and 15, with higher numbers indicating more parsimonious programs. The values of the correctness, efficiency, and parsimony clauses were summed and subtracted from 100, producing an overall fitness value between 0 and 100, with lower numbers indicating better programs.

Following a suggestion of Koza, we staged the introduction of the efficiency and parsimony components into the

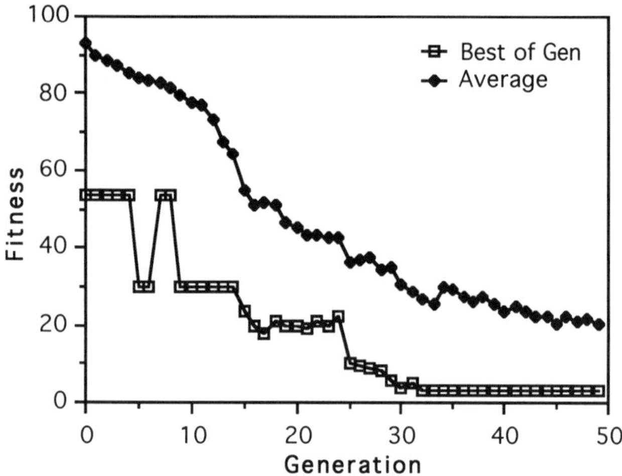

Figure 1. Best-of-generation and average fitnesses for exp. #1.

fitness function. In generations 0–14 only the correctness component of the fitness function was used. The efficiency component was introduced at generation 15 and was used thereafter. The parsimony component was introduced at generation 25 and was used thereafter.

We ran the GP system for 50 generations with a population size of 200. The overall performance of the GP system on this problem is summarized in Figure 1. In the initial generation of random programs the average fitness was 92.88. The best individual program of the population had a fitness measure of 53.33. It was: **(PUTON (PROGN2 C B) (NEWTOWER C))**. This gets **C** on the table and **B** on **C**, achieving 2 of the 3 goals. The average fitness of the population improved over the subsequent generations, but there was no improvement in the best-of-generation program until generation 5, when the following program was produced with a fitness measure of 30.0:

```
(PROGN3 (PROGN2 (NEWTOWER C)
               (NEWTOWER (NEWTOWER A)))
        (NEWTOWER (PROGN2 B B))
        (PROGN3 (PUTON B C) (PUTON B C) (PUTON A B)))
```

This program solves the Sussman Anomaly, but it is neither efficient nor elegant. The average fitness of the population continued to increase through the subsequent generations, although no improvement of best-of-generation individual was possible until generation 15, when the efficiency component of the fitness function became effective and allowed for differentiation among the correct plans. At generation 25 the parsimony clause became effective as well, and by generation 32 a maximally efficient, parsimonious, and correct plan had evolved with a fitness measure of 3.15: **(PROGN3 (NEWTOWER C) (PUTON B C) (PUTON A B))**.

Blocks-World Experiment #2

The best-of-run plan from experiment #1 solves the Sussman Anomaly, but it is not useful in many other cases. In our second experiment we wanted to evolve a "universal plan" for achieving a single goal condition from a range of initial states. To achieve greater generality we changed the terminal and function sets:

FUNCTION SET: (NEWTOWER PUTON PROGN2 PROGN3 TOP-OVER DO-ON-GOALS)
TERMINAL SET: (TOP BOTTOM)

The **TOPOVER** function takes one argument, a block, and returns the top of the stack of which that block is a part. It returns its argument if it is something that is currently clear, or **NIL** if it is **NIL**. **DO-ON-GOALS** is actually a macro that implements a limited iteration control structure. It takes one argument, a body of code, that it evaluates once for each of the system's unachieved "ON" goals. During each iteration the variables **TOP** and **BOTTOM** are set to the appropriate components of the current goal. Note that we have removed **A**, **B** and **C** from the terminal set; programs can refer to blocks only via **TOP** and **BOTTOM**. **TOP** and **BOTTOM** are both **NIL** outside of any calls to **DO-ON-GOALS**, and calls to **DO-ON-GOALS** can be nested. The **DO-ON-GOALS** macro was developed for experiment #3, below, in which the need for access to the system's goals is more obvious.

We used 20 fitness cases and averaged their results; they were constructed from the following lists by pairing each initial state with each goal list:

INITIAL:
1. ((ON A TABLE)(ON B TABLE)(ON C TABLE)
   (CLEAR A)(CLEAR B)(CLEAR C))
2. ((ON A B)(ON B C)(ON C TABLE)(CLEAR A))
3. ((ON B C)(ON C A)(ON A TABLE)(CLEAR B))
4. ((ON C A)(ON A B)(ON B TABLE)(CLEAR C))
5. ((ON C A)(ON A TABLE)(ON B TABLE)(CLEAR C)(CLEAR B))
6. ((ON A C)(ON C TABLE)(ON B TABLE)(CLEAR A)(CLEAR B))
7. ((ON B C)(ON C TABLE)(ON A TABLE)(CLEAR B)(CLEAR A))
8. ((ON C B)(ON B TABLE)(ON A TABLE)(CLEAR C)(CLEAR A))
9. ((ON A B)(ON B TABLE)(ON C TABLE)(CLEAR A)(CLEAR C))
10. ((ON B A)(ON A TABLE)(ON C TABLE)(CLEAR B)(CLEAR C))

GOALS:
1. ((ON A B)(ON B C)(ON C TABLE))
2. ((ON B C)(ON A B)(ON C TABLE))

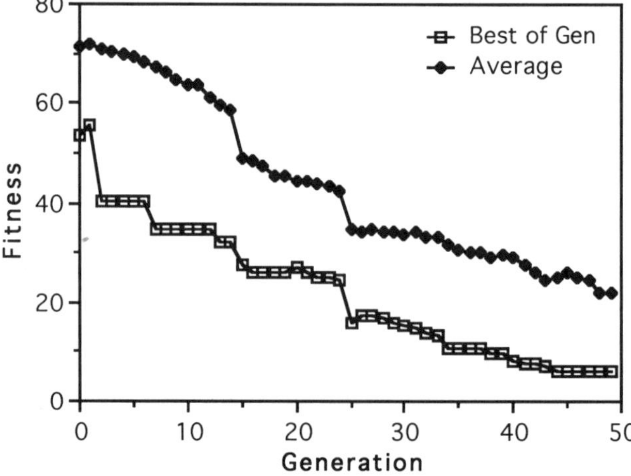

Figure 2. Best-of-generation and average fitnesses for exp. #2.

Note that the 10 fitness cases using goal list 2 are duplicates of the those using goal list 1 but with the order of the goal clauses changed; since **DO-ON-GOALS** loops through the goals in the order that they are presented, this helps to ensure that the resulting program is not overly dependent on goal ordering. All other GP parameters were set to the values used in experiment #1. The overall performance of the GP system in this experiment is summarized in Figure 2. In the initial generation of random programs the average fitness was 71.20. The best individual program of the population had a fitness measure of 53.33 and correctly handled 6 of the 20 fitness cases. It was:

(NEWTOWER (DO-ON-GOALS
        (PROGN3 (PUTON TOP BOTTOM)
             (PUTON BOTTOM BOTTOM)
             (DO-ON-GOALS TOP))))

The best-of-run individual program for this run was found on generation 48. It had a fitness measure of 5.91 and correctly handled all 20 fitness cases. It was:

(PROGN2
  (DO-ON-GOALS
   (DO-ON-GOALS
     (PROGN3 (NEWTOWER (DO-ON-GOALS
                 (TOP-OVER TOP)))
          (PROGN2 (TOP-OVER TOP) TOP)
          (PUTON TOP BOTTOM))))
  (DO-ON-GOALS (PUTON TOP BOTTOM)))

Note that the program is robust over initial states that were not in the set of fitness cases. The program correctly builds an {**ABC**} tower from all three of the possible configurations that were not used as fitness cases: the towers {**CBA**}, {**BAC**}, and {**ACB**}. Because many problems are isomorphic, the use of function and terminal sets that refer to blocks only by their positions in goals, and not by their names, is helpful in achieving this robustness.

The robustness of the solution program does not extend to changes in goal sets. For example, the program will not achieve the unary goal list (**(ON B A)**) from an initial state consisting of a {**BCA**} tower.

Blocks-World Experiment #3

Our third experiment was an attempt to evolve a blocks-world planner capable of achieving a range of goal conditions from a range of initial conditions. We used the same terminal and function sets as in experiment #2. We increased the population size to 500 and the number of generations to 201, with efficiency introduced into the fitness function at generation 33 and parsimony introduced at generation 66. We used 40 fitness cases, constructed by pairing each of the initial states from experiment #2 with each of the following goal lists:

1. **((ON A B) (ON B C) (ON C TABLE))**
2. **((ON B C) (ON A B) (ON C TABLE))**
3. **((ON C B) (ON B TABLE))**
4. **((ON B A))**

All other GP parameters were set to the values used in experiment #1. The performance of the GP system in this experiment is summarized in Figure 3. In the initial generation of random programs the average fitness was 77.02. The best individual program of the population had a fitness of 59.17 and correctly handled 14 of the 40 fitness cases. It was:

(TOP-OVER
   (PROGN3 (PUTON (NEWTOWER (DO-ON-GOALS BOTTOM))
              (DO-ON-GOALS (PUTON TOP BOTTOM)))
     (DO-ON-GOALS
       (TOP-OVER (DO-ON-GOALS BOTTOM)))
     (DO-ON-GOALS
       (NEWTOWER (PROGN2 BOTTOM BOTTOM)))))

The first 100% correct solution emerged at generation 25. It had a fitness of 30.0, contained 49 symbols, and was messy; we do not show it here. The efficiency and parsimony components of the fitness function, introduced at generations 33 and 66 respectively, helped to improve the programs considerably. The best-of-run individual program was found on generation 168 and had a fitness of 6.54. It was:

(PROGN3
  (TOP-OVER
    (DO-ON-GOALS
      (NEWTOWER (DO-ON-GOALS (TOP-OVER TOP)))))
    (DO-ON-GOALS (NEWTOWER (TOP-OVER BOTTOM)))
    (DO-ON-GOALS
      (DO-ON-GOALS (PROGN2 (NEWTOWER (TOP-OVER TOP))
                (PUTON TOP BOTTOM)))))

The planner evolved in experiment #3 is considerably more robust than that evolved in experiment #2. In fact, although it was evolved with only 40 fitness cases, it correctly solves all 13x13=169 possible 3-block problems. It even solves some 4-block problems: for example, it will correctly produce both an {**ABCD**} tower and a {**DCBA**} tower from an initial state containing an {**ABC**} tower and the additional block **D** on the table. We have not yet fully analyzed the program's robustness for 4-block and larger problems.

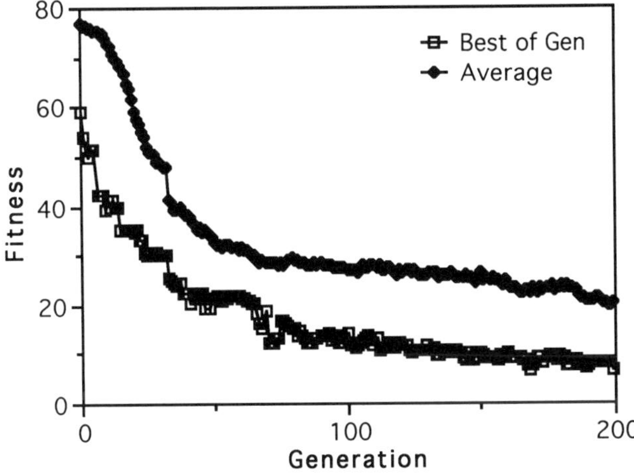

Figure 3. Best-of-generation and average fitnesses for exp. #3.

Discussion

In experiment #1 we wanted to see how well a GP engine could function in place of a traditional planner, which is generally invoked to produce a single plan that achieves a particular set of goals from a particular initial state. While we were able to evolve a correct, efficient, and parsimonious plan, one is lead to ask why a genetic technique should used in this case; traditional AI planning algorithms can solve such problems more reliably and more efficiently. Further, we should note that single blocks-world problems, at least with our fitness function (based on number of goals achieved), are not well suited to solution by genetic programming. This is because the coarseness of the fitness function provides little guidance to the evolutionary process. This can be seen in the first 10 generations of Figure 1, in which the coarseness of the fitness metric leads to large jumps in the best-of-generation fitness. We succeeded because the combinatorics of a 3-block world are manageable even with minimal guidance, especially with a program population size of 200. A more complex domain would demand a more informative fitness function. But GP may nonetheless be a good choice for solving some single-initial-state/single-goal planning problems. In particular, it can be appropriate when we have trouble representing the system's actions declaratively, or when the dynamics of the domain are best represented via simulation.

GP seems better suited, overall, to the construction of universal planners of the sort produced in our experiment #2, or complete domain-dependent planners of the sort produced in our experiment #3. There will always be problems in achieving robustness, however, and the genetic programming of universal planners is necessarily an iterative, experimental process. The success of a particular run of GP is highly sensitive to seemingly minor changes of parameters. Population size, crossover parameters, details of the terminal and function sets, choice of fitness cases, and variations in fitness metrics may all have large, difficult to predict effects. For example, we tried variations of blocks-world experiment #3 with identical parameters except for minor variations in the function and terminal sets (e.g., substituting a **DO-UNTIL** for **DO-ON-BLOCKS**, and providing other functions to access the goals). Many of these variations failed to produce fit programs. O'Reilly and Oppacher discuss the sensitivity of GP to this kind of variation and suggest modifications to the technique that they believe will lessen this sensitivity (O'Reilly & Oppacher 1992). But GP is an inherently experimental technique, and the resulting orientation may actually be quite welcome in some segments of the AI planning community; several planning researchers have recently called for just the sort of experimental framework that GP allows, and indeed requires (Hanks et al. 1993).

Genetic methods may also provide so-called "anytime" behavior (Dean & Body 1988), another feature of interest to the planning community: As can be seen in the fitness graphs in this paper, genetic programming starts by producing poor programs, and gradually improves the quality of its programs over time. The process can be stopped at any point to provide the current best-of-run program.

Conclusions

We conclude that GP has much to offer as an AI planning technology: freedom from declarative representation constraints, a methodology for building fast, domain-specific systems, a welcome experimental orientation, and anytime behavior during evolution. It also has many shortcomings: it is CPU-intensive, it is sensitive to minor changes in parameters, and it does not yet reliably produce robust results. Further work is clearly indicated.

Bibliography

Dean, T.; and Boddy, M. 1988. An Analysis of Time-Dependent Planning. In *Proceedings of the Sixth National Conference on Artificial Intelligence, AAAI-88*, 49–54.

Dewdney, A. K. 1993. *The New Turing Omnibus*. New York: W. H. Freeman and Company.

Fikes, R.E.; and Nilsson, N. 1971. STRIPS: A New Approach to the Application of Theorem Proving to Problem Solving. In *Artificial Intelligence* 2: 189–208.

Ginsberg, M.L. 1990. Computational Considerations in Reasoning about Action. In *Proceedings of the Workshop on Innovative Approaches to Planning, Scheduling and Control*, K. P. Sycara, ed. Defense Advanced Research Projects Agency (DARPA).

Hanks, S.; Pollack, M.E.; and Cohen, P.R. 1993. Benchmarks, Test Beds, Controlled Experimentation, and the Design of Agent Architectures. *AI Magazine* 14 (Winter): 17–42.

Holland, J.H. 1992. *Adaptation in Natural and Artificial Systems*. Cambridge, MA: The MIT Press.

Koza, J.R. 1992. *Genetic Programming*. Cambridge, MA: The MIT Press.

Nilsson, N. 1989. Action Networks. In *Proceedings from the Rochester Planning Workshop: From Formal Systems to Practical Systems*, J. Tenenberg, ed., Technical Report 284, Dept. of Computer Science, University of Rochester.

O'Reilly, U.; and Oppacher, F. 1992. An Experimental Perspective on Genetic Programming. In *Parallel Problem Solving from Nature, 2*, Männer, R.; and Manderick, B., eds. Amsterdam: Elsevier Science Publishers.

Sacerdoti, E.D. 1975. The Nonlinear Nature of Plans. In *Advance Papers of the Fourth International Joint Conference on Artificial Intelligence, IJCAI-75*, 206–214.

Schoppers, M.J. 1987. Universal Plans for Reactive Robots in Unpredictable Environments. In *Proceedings of the Tenth International Joint Conference on Artificial Intelligence, IJCAI-87*, 1039–1046.

Tate, A.; Hendler, J.; and Drummond, M. 1990. A Review of AI Planning Techniques. In *Readings in Planning*, Allen, J.; Hendler, J.; and Tate, A., eds., 26–49. San Mateo, California: Morgan Kaufmann Publishers, Inc.

Hierarchical Chunking in Classifier Systems

Gerhard Weiß

Institut für Informatik, Technische Universität München
D-80290 München, Germany
weissg@informatik.tu-muenchen.de

Abstract

Two standard schemes for learning in classifier systems have been proposed in the literature: the bucket brigade algorithm (BBA) and the profit sharing plan (PSP). The BBA is a local learning scheme which requires less memory and lower peak computation than the PSP, whereas the PSP is a global learning scheme which typically achieves a clearly better performance than the BBA. This "requirement versus achievement" difference, known as the locality/globality dilemma, is addressed in this paper. A new algorithm called hierarchical chunking algorithm (HCA) is presented which aims at synthesizing the local and the global learning schemes. This algorithm offers a solution to the locality/globality dilemma for the important class of reactive classifier systems.

The contents is as follows. Section 1 describes the locality/globality dilemma and motivates the necessity of its solution. Section 2 briefly introduces basic aspects of (reactive) classifier systems that are relevant to this paper. Section 3 presents the HCA. Section 4 gives an experimental comparison of the HCA, the BBA and the PSP. Section 5 concludes the paper with a discussion and an outlook on future work.

Motivation

The foundations for classifier systems (CSs for short) were laid by Holland (1975) and Holland and Reitman (1978). CSs are parallel, message-passing, rule-based systems that are capable of environmental interaction and of reinforcement learning through credit assignment and rule modification. Up to now two different learning schemes for credit assignment in CSs have been proposed: the *bucket brigade algorithm* (BBA for short, e.g. Booker, 1982; Holland, 1985, 1986; Riolo, 1988) and the *profit sharing plan* (PSP for short, e.g. Grefenstette, 1988; Holland & Reitman, 1978). These two schemes significantly differ from each other in that the BBA is a local learning scheme which incrementally assigns credit whenever the CS interacts with its environment, whereas the PSP is a global learning scheme which episodically assigns credit only when the CS receives a reinforcement signal from its envi-

ronment. A consequence of this difference, known as the *locality/globality dilemma*, is that the BBA requires less memory and less peak computation than the PSP, but the PSP typically achieves a better performance level than the BBA. Roughly, this is because the PSP needs to maintain detailed information about the past activities carried out by the CS, whereas the BBA has difficulties in generating long activity sequences that are both useful and stable.

There is a lot of work centered around the locality/globality dilemma in the context of the BBA and the PSP; for instance, see the performance comparisons of the BBA and the PSP described in (Grefenstette, 1988; Weiß, 1992) and the investigations and considerations on the formation and maintenance of activity sequences presented e.g. in (Holland, 1985; Riolo, 1987, 1989; Robertson & Riolo, 1988; Wilson, 1987). However, despite this work it is still an open and challenging research issue to develop a local algorithm like the BBA that possesses the learning abilities of a global algorithm like the PSP. This issue has been addressed by the work reported in this paper. A new learning algorithm called hierarchical chunking algorithm is presented which offers a solution to the locality/globality dilemma for the important class of reactive CSs, that is, CSs whose activity is, at each time, exclusively triggered by the information they have about the actual environmental state.

An Introduction to Classifier Systems

This section gives a brief introduction to basic aspects of CSs. For a more comprehensive introduction the reader is referred to (Booker, Goldberg, & Holland, 1989; Goldberg, 1989; Wilson & Goldberg, 1989).

The prototypical organization of a CS can be described as follows. Structurally, a CS is composed of four *major components*:

- An input interface which consists of at least one detector providing information about the environment in the form of messages.

- An output interface which consists of at least one effector enabling the system to interact with the environment.

- A classifier list which consists of *condition/action* rules called classifiers. The condition part specifies the messages that satisfy the classifier, and the action part specifies the messages to be sent when the classifier is activated. Associated with each classifier is a quantity called its strength.

- A message list which contains the messages sent by the detectors and the classifiers.

Functionally, the overall activity of a CS results from the repeated execution of the following *major cycle*:

1. Activation of the input interface: The actual detector messages are added to the message list.
2. Activation of the classifier list: The system decides which classifiers are allowed to produce new messages. This is done by running a strength-based competition between all satisfied classifiers.
3. Activation of the output interface: The system interacts with its environment in dependence on the contents of the message list.
4. Credit assignment: Strength-update rules are applied to adjust the classifier strengths such that they reflect the classifiers' relevance to goal attainment.
5. Rule modification: Some classifiers are modified by a genetic algorithm.

An important class of restricted CSs is that of *reactive CSs*. In these systems only a single classifier is selected during each major cycle, and this selection is guided only by the actual detector messages (and not by internal messages). Reactive CSs have been extensively used for theoretical and experimental studies (e.g., see Wilson, 1985; Grefenstette, 1988), and they are also taken as a basis for the work described in this paper.

As mentioned in section 1, the BBA and the PSP have been proposed as *credit assignment schemes*. In its elementary form, the BBA locally updates the classifier strengths as follows. Whenever a competition runs, each satisfied classifier C_j makes a bid Bid_j,

$$Bid_j = b \cdot Str_j \cdot Spec_j \qquad (1)$$

where b is a small constant called risk factor, Str_j is C_j's strength (initialized with a constant Str^{init} for all classifiers) and $Spec_j$ is C_j's specificity (a quantity expressing the classifier's relevance to particular environmental situations). The probability that a bidding classifier C_j wins the competition is given by

$$\frac{Bid_j}{\sum_{C_l \in \mathcal{B}} Bid_l} \qquad (2)$$

where $\mathcal{B}$ is the set of all bidding classifiers. A winning classifier reduces its strength by the amount of its bid, and hands this amount back to its predecessors, that is, to those classifiers whose preceding activities enabled it to become active. (The winning classifiers pay for the privilege of being active, and the predecessors are rewarded for appropriately setting up the environment.) Formally, if C_j is a winning classifier and $\mathcal{P}_j$ is the set of its predecessors, then the strengths are modified according to the following rules:

$$Str_j \;=\; Str_j - Bid_j \qquad \text{and} \qquad (3)$$

$$Str_i \;=\; Str_i + \frac{Bid_j}{|\mathcal{P}_j|} \quad \forall\, C_i \in \mathcal{P}_j \;. \qquad (4)$$

Additionally, if an external reward is received from the environment, then it is equally distributed among the classifiers that sent the effector-activating messages. The idea underlying the BBA is to internally reward classifiers that are useful in achieving specific goals but that are not active when the external reward is obtained.

The PSP in its elementary form updates the classifier strengths as follows. Bidding and selection of the winning classifiers is done according to (1) and (2), respectively. In contrast to the BBA, the PSP globally rewards sequences of active classifiers. At the end of each episode (i.e., whenever an external reward Ext is received) the strength Str_j of each classifier C_j that was active at least one time during this episode is modified according to rule

$$Str_j = Str_j - Bid_j + b \cdot Ext \qquad (5)$$

where b is the risk factor used in bid calculation.

There are many variants of the BBA – e.g., see (Dorigo, 1991; Huang, 1989; Riolo, 1990; Weiß, 1991; Wilson, 1985, 1987) – as well as of the PSP – e.g., see (Grefenstette, 1988; Holland & Reitman, 1978; Weiß, 1992). However, none of these variants solves the locality/globality dilemma.

The Hierarchical Chunking Algorithm

Chunking is an experience-based learning mechanism which was originally proposed within the frame of a psychological model of memory organization (Miller, 1956). According to this model, chunking refers to the process of correlating pieces of knowledge or sensory input in such a way that they can be treated and used as a single memory unit or "chunk" on its own. If it is explicitly assumed that already existing chunks can be used for building new ones, then this process is referred to as *hierarchical* chunking. Hierarchical chunking has received much attention in psychology as well as in artificial intelligence; for instance, see (Chase & Simon, 1973; Chi, 1978; Newell & Rosenbloom, 1981; Rosenbloom, 1983; Rosenbloom & Newell, 1986). In the following, a new algorithm called *hierarchical chunking algorithm* (HCA for short) is described which was designed to solve the locality/globality dilemma for reactive CSs; this algorithm synthesizes the local (BBA-type) and the global (PSP-type) learning paradigms by applying the mechanism of hierarchical chunking to successful sequences of active classifiers.

Under the HCA each classifier C_j is assumed to be of the *generalized form* $Cond_j/Act_j$, where

$$Cond_j = \langle c_{j1}, \ldots, c_{jr_j} \rangle \qquad (6)$$

specifies the tuples $(m_1, \ldots, m_{r_j})$ of messages m_k that satisfy C_j and

$$Act_j = \langle a_{j1}, \ldots, a_{js_j} \rangle \qquad (7)$$

specifies the sequence $(m_1, \ldots, m_{s_j})$ of messages m_k to be sent when C_j wins the competition ($r_j, s_j \in \mathbb{N}$ for all j). Each message sent within a sequence of messages is immediately processed by the effectors; with that, a CS is able to carry out several environmental interactions (instead of just a single interaction) within one major cycle.[1] In the following, the length of Act_j of a classifier C_j is called the level of C_j, and is denoted by L_j; furthermore, if $L_j = 1$, then C_j is said to be an elementary classifier, and if $L_j > 1$, then C_j is said to be an extended classifier or macro-classifier or a chunk. As an illustration of this generalized view of classifiers, consider a CS which has to navigate from the start state S to the goal state G in the maze shown in figure 1. Assuming that the CS is able to interact with its environment by moving, in each location, to one of the neighbouring locations, an elementary classifier might represent the behavioral rule "If the current location is in the upper-left area, then move one step to the right", and an extended classifier might represent the rule "If the current location is in the middle area, then first move one step to the left and then one step down".

The HCA arranges a *hierarchical competition* between the classifiers for the right to produce new messages. Among all satisfied classifiers, only the highest-level classifiers are allowed to make bids and to compete against each other. More exactly, if S is the set of all satisfied classifiers (in the actual cycle), then only the classifiers being contained in the set $\mathcal{B}$,

$$\mathcal{B} = \{C_j : C_j \in \mathcal{S} \text{ and } L_j \geq L_l \; \forall \; C_l \in \mathcal{S}\}, \quad (8)$$

are allowed to participate in the competition. Each classifier $C_j \in \mathcal{B}$ calculates a bid according to (1), and the probability that C_i wins the competition is given by (2).

The HCA modifies the classifier strengths similar to the implicit BBA proposed by Wilson (1985). Compared to the general BBA described in section 2, the HCA takes a simplified point of view of a classifier's predecessor which bases on the assumption that the temporal order of active classifiers is imposed by the environment. If the classifiers C_i and C_j won the competition in the previous and the actual cycle, respectively, then C_i is considered to be the only predecessor of C_j (i.e., $\mathcal{P}_j = \{C_i\}$), and their strengths are adjusted according to (3) and (4). In this way a linkage is established between time-adjacent classifiers.

At the beginning (i.e., before learning takes place), the classifier list is assumed to contain only elementary classifiers. The extended classifiers are dynamically formed and dissolved under the HCA in the course of environmental interaction. The formation and dissolution of extended classifiers correspond to the formation and dissolution of chunks, respectively, and make up the core of the HCA. The *criteria* used for triggering formation and dissolution are conceptually similar to (and, in fact, have been inspired by) the group-development criteria proposed by Weiß (1993a, 1993b) in the context of BBA-based multi-agent learning. Formally, the formation and dissolution criteria are as follows. Let C_i be the preceding winning classifier, C_j

the actual winning classifier, $\mathcal{B}$ the set of all actual bidding classifiers, and $\mu = \frac{1}{|\mathcal{B}|} \sum_{C_l \in \mathcal{B}} Str_l$ the average strength of all classifiers contained in $\mathcal{B}$. A new (extended) classifier $Cond_i/Act_i \circ Act_j$ with

$$Act_i \circ Act_j = \langle a_{i1}, \ldots, a_{is_i}, a_{j1}, \ldots, a_{js_j} \rangle \quad (9)$$

is formed out of C_i and C_j, if and only if

$$Str_j \geq \mu + \sigma \cdot \sqrt{\frac{1}{|\mathcal{B}|} \sum_{C_l \in \mathcal{B}} (Str_l - \mu)^2} \quad (10)$$

where σ is a constant called formation factor. The strength of the new classifier is initialized with Str_j. Conversely, an (extended) classifier $C_k \in \mathcal{B}$ is dissolved and removed from the classifier list, if and only if

$$Str_k \leq \mu - \rho \cdot \sqrt{\frac{1}{|\mathcal{B}|} \sum_{C_l \in \mathcal{B}} (Str_l - \mu)^2} \quad (11)$$

where ρ is a constant called dissolution factor. With equations (10) and (11), formation as well as dissolution take place if the strength of a classifier is not within the "standard range" that can be expected given the average strength and the strength deviation of the bidding classifiers. Because both criteria are defined over the strength values, extended classifiers are formed and dissolved in an experience-based and goal-directed manner. Furthermore, because strength adjustment, formation and dissolution are strongly interrelated and mutually influence each other, the HCA endows a reactive CS with highly dynamic adaptation and learning abilities. (It should be noted that the HCA does not require more information for realizing learning than the BBA; in particular, the HCA forms and dissolves classifiers on the basis of local information and, in contrast to the PSP, without the need of an episodical trace of all – useless and useful – winning classifiers.)

Experimental Analysis

As an initial learning domain a navigation task first introduced by Sutton (1990) has been chosen. This type of task captures the essential features of the locality/globality dilemma, and it is well suited for experimentally comparing the HCA, the BBA and the PSP. Subsequently experiments on the task of learning to navigate through the maze shown in figure 1 are described.[2] The maze is a 10 by 7 grid of locations, where the shaded locations are obstacles that cannot be entered. In each location the CS can move to each of the neighbouring locations, except where such a movement would take the system into an obstacle or outside the maze. The CS has to learn to move from each possible location of the maze to a fixed location called goal

---

[1] The definition of $Cond_i$ corresponds to the traditional notion of a classifier's condition part. Against that, the definition and interpretation of Act_i establishes a rather unconventional notion of a classifier's action part which opens up new possibilities in the coupling between a CS and its environment.

[2] A number of experiments with other mazes has been performed, varying the grid size, the directions in which the system can move, and the number of possible starting states, the position of the goal state, and the number and positions of the obstacles. The results of these experiments are qualitatively similar to those presented below.

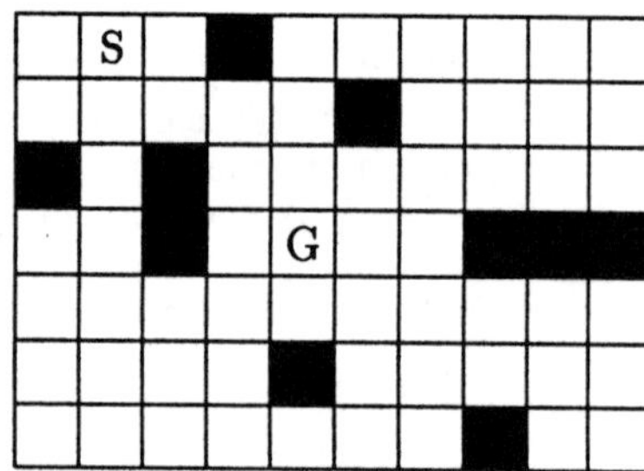

Figure 1: Maze.

state (G). If and only if the goal state is reached, then a non-zero external reward is provided, a new location called start state (S) is randomly chosen and the next episode starts.

Some implementational details. A problem of every system that works with an internal representation of its environment is the mapping problem, that is, the problem that the system can produce discontinuous mappings from input to output even if the environment is continuous (and vice versa). This problem also exists for CSs (Wilson & Goldberg, 1989), and in order to avoid or at least strongly reduce it, the following domain-specific *decimal coding* is used. If the CS is in the location (x, y), then the actual detector message simply is of the form (x, y). Furthermore, each classifier is of the form $\langle u, v \rangle / \langle w_1, \ldots, w_s \rangle$, with $\langle u, v \rangle$ being its condition part and $\langle w_1, \ldots, w_s \rangle$ being its action part ($u \in \{1, \ldots, 10\}$, $v \in \{1, \ldots, 7\}$ and $w_i \in \{0, \ldots, 7\}$). Associated with each classifier C_j is an integer M_j called its matching radius. M_j is randomly chosen from the integer interval $[0, \ldots, M^{max}]$, and is used to define C_j's specificity as $Spec_j = \frac{1}{1+M_j}$. (The smaller a classifier's matching radius, the higher is its specificity, and reversely.) A classifier C_j having $\langle u, v \rangle$ as its condition part matches each detector message (x, y) with $x \in [u - M_j, \ldots, u + M_j]$ and $y \in [v - M_j, \ldots, v + M_j]$. A classifier having $\langle w_1, \ldots, w_s \rangle$ as its action part codes the activity sequence "First go to direction w_1, then to direction w_2, …, and finally to direction w_s", where direction "0" is interpreted as "north", "1" as "northeast", "2" as "east", and so on. (As an illustration, consider the classifier $C_j = \langle 9, 6 \rangle / \langle 5, 6, 4 \rangle$, and assume that $M_j = 1$. This classifier matches the detector messages (8,5), (8,6), (8,7), (9,5), (9,6), (9,7), (10,5), (10,6), and (10,7), and codes for the activity sequence "First go one step southwest, then one step west, and finally one step south".)[3]

In order to guarantee the system's capacity to act, a variant of Wilson's (1985) *create operation* has been implemented as follows. Whenever the system enters a location (x, y) whose associated detector message is

---

[3]Traditionally, a tertiary coding over the alphabet $\{0, 1, \#\}$ is used, where # acts as a don't-care symbol. Obviously, this is a very problematic, discontinuous coding for the task domain under consideration, because in this case the condition part of a classifier can match detector messages that represent completely different, non-adjacent locations.

not matched by any classifier, then a new elementary classifier $C_j = \langle u, v \rangle / \langle w_1 \rangle$ is created, where u is randomly chosen from the interval $[x - M_j, \ldots, x + M_j]$, v is randomly chosen from $[y - M_j, \ldots, y + M_j]$, and w_1 is randomly chosen from $\{0, \ldots, 7\}$. With that, the system never stops moving around and searching for the goal state.

In the experiments a slightly modified, more *"reactive"* PSP has been used: instead of adjusting the strengths of all classifiers that won during an episode, only the strengths of the last 4 winning classifiers are adjusted according to (5). This modification is consistent with the general notion of a reactive system; in particular, it is realistic to assume that a purely reactive CS is only "aware" of the last few actions, no matter when the last external reward was received.

Finally, some details on the implemented *genetic algorithm*. The genetic algorithm is applied with probability 0.04 at the end of each episode. If applied, 5 percent of the classifiers, which are selected with probability proportional to the inverse of their strengths, are replaced by new classifiers. The new classifiers are created as follows. Until no further classifier is required, a classifier C_j is selected with probability proportional to its strength and mutated, resulting in a new classifier C_j'. If C_j is of the form $\langle u, v \rangle / \langle w_1, \ldots, w_s \rangle$ and M_j is its matching radius, then C_j' is of the form $\langle u', v' \rangle / \langle w_1', \ldots, w_s' \rangle$ with $u' = u + a$, $v' = v + b$ and $w_k' = (w_k + c_k) \bmod 8$ for all $k \in \{1, \ldots, s\}$, where a and b are randomly chosen from the integer interval $[-M_j, \ldots, +M_j]$ and c_k is randomly chosen from $[-1, 0, +1]$. The matching radius of C_j' is randomly chosen from $[0, \ldots, M^{max}]$. No crossover operator is applied. (In other experiments not described in this paper we found that the standard crossover operators are rather inefficient for the learning domain under consideration, since they typically produce classifiers which represent illegal moves.)

Figure 2 shows the performance profiles of the PSP, the HCA, the BBA and a random-walk algorithm (i.e., an algorithm which randomly and with uniform probability selects, in each location, a legal direction and moves one step in this direction). The parameter setting was as follows: $b = 0.1$, $Str^{init} = Ext = 1000$, $\sigma = \rho = 2$, and $M^{max} = 3$. (The classifier system turned out to robust over a broad range of the parameters, and the learning effects reported here are not restricted to exactly this setting.) Each curve shows, averaged over 100 runs, for each of the episodes 1 to 1000 the number of decisions (cycles) required to reach the goal state. In each run the CS was initialized with a set of 100 randomly generated classifiers. At the beginning of learning, each learning algorithm started at the random performance level. Each of the three learning curves rapidly falls within the first 30 episodes. (Interestingly, with that the PSP, the HCA and the BBA led to an early behavioral improvement much like the dynamic-programming approaches investigated by Sutton (1990) did for the same type of task.) After about episode 40, the curves of the PSP and the HCA continuously decrease; the curve of the BBA requires a longer period to become smooth,

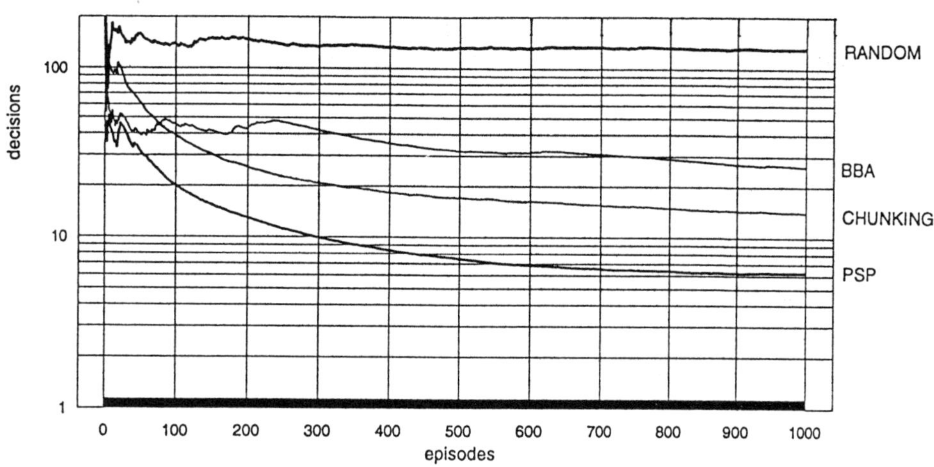

Figure 2: Performance Profiles.

namely about 230 episodes. Averaged over the last 100 episodes, the mean episode length achieved by the PSP, the HCA, the BBA and the random-walk algorithm is 6.2, 15.4., 27.3 and 142.8, respectively. (The behavior of the learning algorithms was observed up to episode 5000. After episode 1000 the performance levels of the three learning algorithms did not further improve and remained almost constant.) Obviously, each of the three learning algorithms performed significantly better than the random-walk algorithm. In particular, after about 85 episodes, the curve of the HCA runs between the curves of the BBA and the PSP: the HCA clearly outperformed the BBA and, at the same time, remained below the performance level of the PSP. This illustrates that hierarchical chunking is an appropriate mechanism for synthesizing local and global learning principles, and that the HCA successfully combines BBA-type and PSP-type learning.

(It is worth to note that even the best performing algorithm, the PSP, left room for improvement, since the minimal episode length, averaged over all legal positions, is 3.0. This shows that CSs, after more than 15 years of existence, still establish an open and challenging area of research on machine learning.)

Conclusion

The HCA attacks the locality/globality dilemma in the context of reactive CSs by bringing together local and global learning principles known from the BBA and the PSP, respectively. On the one side, the HCA retains the local strength adjustment rules of the BBA. On the other side, by introducing the concept of extended classifiers or chunks and by providing mechanisms for their formation and dissolution, the HCA achieves global adjustment qualities much like the PSP does. As a consequence, the HCA approaches to both the lower computational requirements of the BBA and the higher performance level of the PSP.

Wilson and Goldberg (1987) proposed to introduce higher organizational units in the learning and per-

formance processes of a CS in order to cope with the *chaining problem* (i.e., the problem of generating and maintaining long chains of active classifiers) as well as with the *cooperator/competitor dilemma* (i.e., the dilemma that classifiers being active in a chain are cooperative w.r.t. strength adjustment but competitive w.r.t. the selection mechanism of the genetic algorithm). The HCA is much in the spirit of this proposal: the chunks formed and dissolved under the HCA act as such organizational units, since they eliminate (or at least greatly reduce) the need for long chains of elementary classifiers.

Like the standard PSP, the HCA in its present form is not applicable to general CSs. This is an important objection because general CSs, compared to reactive ones, allow multiple winning classifiers per cycle as well as the processing of internal messages, and, with that, achieve a higher degree of parallelism and cognitive plausibility. We think, however, that the HCA can be fully extended towards general CSs. In particular, in artificial intelligence there is a plenty of work on learning by chunking in rule-based systems and production systems (e.g., see (Laird, Rosenbloom & Newell, 1986) and the references therein), and this work is likely to be very stimulating and useful for constructing such an extension.

The work described in this paper shows new perspectives of several issues of current CS research, including the locality/globality dilemma, the cooperator/competitor dilemma, the chaining problem, the mapping problem, and the system-environment interaction. However, further investigations are needed in order to fully understand the merits and limitations of hierarchical chunking in CSs.

Acknowledgements

I want to thank Armin Wirth and Martin Eldracher for many stimulating and fruitful discussions on learning in classifier systems.

References

Booker, L.B. 1982. Intelligent behavior as an adaptation to the task environment. Ph.D. diss., Dept. of Computer and Communication Sciences, Univ. of Michigan.

Booker, L.B., Goldberg, D.E., and Holland, J.H. 1989. Classifier systems and genetic algorithms. *Artificial Intelligence* 40: 235–282.

Chase, W.G., and Simon, H.A. 1973. Perception in chess. *Cognitive Psychology* 4: 55–81.

Chi, M.T.H. 1978. Knowledge structures and memory development. In R.S. Siegler ed. *Children's thinking: What develops?* Hillsdale, NJ: Erlbaum.

Dorigo, M. 1991. New perspectives about default hierarchies formation in learning classifier systems. Technical Report, No. 91-002. Dipartimento di Elettronica, Politecnico di Milano.

Goldberg, D.E. 1989. *Genetic algorithms in search, optimization, and machine learning.* Reading, MA: Addison-Wesley.

Grefenstette, J.J. 1988. Credit assignment in rule discovery systems based on genetic algorithms. In *Machine Learning* 3: 225–245.

Holland, J. H. 1975. *Adaptation in natural and artificial systems.* Ann Arbor, MI: Univ. of Michigan Press.

Holland, J.H. 1985. Properties of the bucket brigade algorithm. In Proceedings of the First International Conference on Genetic Algorithms and Their Applications, 1–7. Pittsburgh, PA: Erlbaum.

Holland, J.H. 1986. Escaping brittleness: The possibilities of general-purpose learning algorithms to parallel rule-based systems. In R.S. Michalski, J.G. Carbonell, and T.M. Mitchell eds. *Machine learning: An artificial intelligence approach*, 593–632. Los Altos, CA: Morgan Kaufmann.

Holland, J.H., and Reitman, J.S. 1978. Cognitive systems based on adaptive algorithms. In D.A. Waterman and F. Hayes-Roth eds. *Pattern-directed inference systems*, 313–329. New York: Academic Press.

Huang, D. 1989. The context-array bucket-brigade algorithm: An enhanced approach to credit-apportionment in classifier systems. In Proceedings of the Third International Conference on Genetic Algorithms, 311–316. Fairfax, VA: Morgan Kaufmann.

Laird, J.E., Rosenbloom, P.S., and Newell, A. 1986. Chunking in Soar: The anatomy of a general learning mechanism. *Machine Learning* 1: 11–46.

Miller, G.A. 1956. The magic number seven, plus or minus two: Some limits on our capacity for processing information. *Psychological Review* 63: 81–97.

Newell, A., and Rosenbloom, P.S. 1981. Mechanisms of skill acquisition and the law of practice. In J.R. Anderson ed. *Cognitive skills and their application.* Hillsdale, NJ: Erlbaum.

Riolo, R.L. 1987. Bucket brigade performance: I. Long sequences of classifiers. In Proceedings of Second International Conference on Genetic Algorithms, 184–195. Hillsdale, NJ: Erlbaum.

Riolo, R.L. 1988. CFS-C: A package of domain independent subroutines for implementing classifier systems in arbitrary, user-defined environments. Technical Report. Division of Computer Science and Engineering, Univ. of Michigan.

Riolo, R.L. 1989. The emergence of coupled sequences of classifiers. In Proceedings of the Third International Conference on Genetic Algorithms, 256–264. Fairfax, VA: Morgan Kaufmann.

Riolo, R.L. 1990. Lookahead planning and latent learning in classifier systems. In J.-A. Meyer and S. Wilson eds. *From Animals to Animats 1*. Cambridge, MA: The MIT Press.

Robertson, G.G., and Riolo, R.L. 1988. A tale of two classifier systems. *Machine Learning* 3: 139–159.

Rosenbloom, P.S. 1983. The chunking of goal hierarchies: A model of practice and stimulus-response compatibility. Technical Report, No. 83–148. Computer Science Institute, Carnegie–Mellon Univ.

Rosenbloom, P.S., and Newell, A. 1986. The chunking of goal hierarchies: A generalized model of practice. In R.S. Michalski, J.G. Carbonell, and T.M. Mitchell eds. *Machine learning: An artificial intelligence approach* (Vol. 2). Los Altos, CA: Morgan Kaufmann Publ.

Sutton, R.S. 1990. Reinforcement learning architectures for animats. In J.-A. Meyer and S. Wilson eds. *From Animals to Animats 1*, 288–296. Cambridge, MA: MIT Press.

Weiß, G. 1991. The action–oriented bucket brigade. Technical Report, FKI-156-91. Institut für Informatik, Technische Univ. München.

Weiß, G. 1992. Learning the goal relevance of actions in classifier systems. In Proceedings of the 10th European Conference on Artificial Intelligence, 430–434. Baffins Lane, Chichester: Wiley.

Weiß, G. 1993a. Action selection and learning in multi-agent environments. In J.-A. Meyer, H.L. Roitblat, and S.W. Wilson eds. *From Animals to Animats 2*, 502–510. Cambridge, MA: MIT Press.

Weiß, G. 1993b. Learning to coordinate actions in multi-agent systems. In Proceedings of the 13th International Joint Conference on Artificial Intelligence, 311–316. San Mateo, CA: Morgan Kaufmann.

Wilson, S.W. 1985. Knowledge growth in an artificial animal. In Proceedings of the First International Conference on Genetic Algorithms and Their Applications, 16–23. Pittsburgh, PA: Erlbaum.

Wilson, S.W. 1987. Hierarchical credit allocation in a classifier system. In L. Davis ed. *Genetic algorithms and simulated annealing*, 104–115. Los Altos, CA: Morgan Kaufmann.

Wilson, S.W., and Goldberg, D.E. 1989. A critical review of classifier systems. In Proceedings of the Third International Conference on Genetic Algorithms, 244–255. Fairfax, VA: Morgan Kaufmann.

Exploiting Algebraic Structure in Parallel State Space Search

Jonathan Bright[*] Simon Kasif[†] Lewis Stiller[‡]

Department of Computer Science
The Johns Hopkins University
Baltimore, MD 21218

Abstract

In this paper we present an approach for performing very large state-space search on parallel machines. While the majority of searching methods in Artificial Intelligence rely on heuristics, the parallel algorithm we propose exploits the algebraic structure of problems to reduce both the time and space complexity required to solve these problems on massively parallel machines. Our algorithm runs in $O(N^{1/4}/P)$ time using $O(N^{1/4})$ space with P processors where N is the size of the state space and P is the number of processors. The technique we present is applicable to several classes of exhaustive searches. Applications include the knapsack problem and the shortest word problem in permutation groups which is a natural generalization of several common planning benchmarks such as Rubik's Cube and the n-puzzle.

Introduction

The best-known algorithm for finding optimal solutions for general planning problems on sequential computers is IDA* developed by R. Korf (Korf 1985a; 1985b). IDA* has an exponential worst-case complexity and its efficiency heavily depends on the ability to synthesize good heuristics. There are many attempts to parallelize state space search (Evett *et al.* 1990; Powley & Korf 1991; Powley, Ferguson, & Korf 1991; Powley & Korf 1988; Rao & Kumar 1987). In this paper we examine several problems for which the computational cost of exploring the entire space of possible states may be prohibitive and derivation of good heuristics is difficult. Exploitation of the algebraic structure of the problems we are considering substantially reduces the time and space complexity of the algorithm. For example, we consider problems that have brute-force $O(k^n)$ solutions (where n is the size of the input to the algorithm) and suggest parallel solutions whose time complexity is $O(k^{n/2}/P)$ (where P is

[*]Supported by the 1993 CESDIS Cray Research Earth and Space Science Fellowship

[†]Supported in part by NSF/DARPA Grant CCR-8908092

[‡]Supported by U.S. Army Grant DAAL03-92-G-0345

the number of processors) and whose space complexity is $O(k^{n/4})$. While the time-space complexity remains exponential, these algorithms are capable of solving problems that were not tractable for conventional architectures. There are several examples where reducing the time complexity of an algorithm from $O(k^n)$ to $O(k^{n/2})$ has resulted in significant progress. Chess is one such example since it is known that alpha-beta at best accomplishes this type of complexity reduction. Thus our main goal is to double the depth of the search current technology can perform. We feel that this class of problems seem to be particularly well matched with massively parallel machines such as the CM-2 or CM-5 (Thinking Machines Corporation 1992; Hillis 1985).

Our approach is influenced by the elegant sequential algorithm proposed by Schroeppel and Shamir and the later generalization by Fiat, Moses, Shamir, Shimshoni and Taros, which we will review in the next section (Schroeppel & Shamir 1981; Fiat *et al.* 1989). We view our work as a direct parallel implementation of this algorithm.

In this paper we describe parallel algorithms using the shared memory (CREW PRAM) model of parallel computation. This model allows multiple processors to read from the same location and therefore hides the cost of communication. While this assumption is unrealistic in practice it allows us to simplify the description of a relatively complex algorithm. Detailed analysis of our algorithms suggests that they can be expressed by efficient composition of computationally efficient primitives such as sorting, merging, parallel prefix and others (Stiller 1992).

Review of the Schroeppel and Shamir Algorithm

In this section we consider the knapsack (decision) problem to illustrate this approach. This is a canonical NP-complete problem of the "monotonic and decomposable" genus proposed by Schroeppel and Shamir. The knapsack problem has also been used as the basis for certain cryptographic schemes and other applications (Merkle & Hellman 1978; Diffie & Hellman 1976;

Tarjan & Trojanowski 1977). The input to the algorithm is a list of integers S and a number x. The output is a sublist of S, call it S', such that the sum of the elements in S' is equal to x. This problem has applications in scheduling, cryptography, bin packing and other combinatorial optimization problems. For example, we can use solutions to this problem to minimize the total completion time of tasks of fixed duration executing on two processors.

Let n the size of S. We will introduce some helpful notation. Let A and B to be sets of integers. Define $A + B$ to be the set of integers c such that $c = a + b$ where $a \in A$ and $b \in B$. Define $A - B$ to be the set of integers c such that $c = a - b$ where $a \in A$ and $b \in B$.

Observation 1:

The knapsack problem can be solved in $O(n2^{n/2})$ time and $O(2^{n/2})$ space.

Proof: We partition S into disjoint lists S_1 and S_2 such that the size of S_1 is $n/2$. Let G_1 and G_2 be the lists of all sums of sublists of elements in S_1 and S_2 respectively. Clearly, our problem has a solution iff the list G_1 has a non-empty intersection with $\{x\} - G_2$. However, note that we can sort both lists and find the intersection by merging. Thus, the time complexity of this algorithm can be seen to be $O(n2^{n/2})$ using any optimal sorting algorithm and noting the trivial identity $2\log(2^{n/2}) = n$. Unfortunately, the space complexity is also $O(2^{n/2})$ which makes it prohibitive on currently available machines for many interesting problems. This approach was first suggested by Horowitz and Sahni (Horowitz & Sahni 1974). However, in the AI literature the algorithm has a strong similarity to bi-directional search studied by Pohl (Pohl 1971). The next observation allows us to reduce the space complexity to make the algorithm practical.

Observation 2: (Schroeppel and Shamir 1981)

The knapsack problem can be solved in $O(n2^{n/2})$ time and $O(2^{n/4})$ space.

Proof: We partition S into four lists, S_i, $1 \leq i \leq 4$. Each set is of size $n/4$. Let G_i, $1 \leq i \leq 4$ be the lists of all possible sublist sums in S_i respectively. Clearly, the partition problem has a solution iff $G_1 + G_2$ has a non-empty intersection with the list $(\{x\} - G_4) - G_3$.

This observation essentially reduces our problem to computing intersections of $A + B$ with $C + D$ (where A, B, C and D are lists of integers each of size $n/4$). To accomplish this we utilize a data structure that allows us to compute such intersections in $O(n2^{n/2})$ time without an increase in space. The main idea is to create an algorithm that generates the elements in $A + B$ and $C + D$ in increasing order, which allows us to compute the intersection by merging. Since we will use a very similar data structure to the one proposed in (Fiat *et al.* 1989) we review their implementation in the next section.

A Parallel Solution to Intersecting $A + B$ with $C + D$

We will first review how to generate elements in $A + B$ in ascending order sequentially. First, assume without loss of generality that A and B are given in ascending sorted order. During each phase of the algorithm, for each element a_k in A we keep a pointer to an element b_j such that all the sums of the form $a_k + b_i$ $(i < j)$ have been generated. We denote such pointers by $a_k \rightarrow b_j$. For example, part of our data structure may look similar to the figure below:

$$
\begin{array}{ccc}
a_1 & \rightarrow & b_{10} \\
a_2 & \rightarrow & b_7 \\
a_3 & \rightarrow & b_6 \\
a_4 & \rightarrow & b_4
\end{array}
$$

Additionally, we will maintain a priority queue of all such sums. To generate $A + B$ in ascending order we repeatedly output the smallest $a_k + b_j$ in the priority queue, and insert the pointer $a_k \rightarrow b_{j+1}$ into the data structure and also insert $a_k + b_{j+1}$ into the priority queue. It is easy to see that, if A and B are of size $2^{n/4}$ we can generate all elements in $A + B$ in ascending order in $O(n2^{n/2})$ time. However, this algorithm is strictly sequential as it generates elements in $A + B$ one at a time.

Our algorithm is based on the idea that instead of generating the elements of $A + B$ one at a time we will in parallel generate $2^{n/4}$ elements at a time. To simplify our presentation, we describe the algorithm assuming that we have $2^{n/4}$ processors (which is of course unfeasible). By applying Brent's theorem (Brent 1974) we obtain speed-up results for any number of processors less than or equal to $2^{n/4}$. This is important since $2^{n/4}$ in practice will be far larger than the number of processors in the system.

The main idea of the algorithm is as follows. Each element a_k in A points to the smallest element of the form $a_k + b_j$ that has not been generated yet. Our algorithm works as follows. We first insert these $2^{n/4}$ elements in an array $TEMP$ of size $2 * 2^{n/4}$ which will keep track of the elements that are candidates to be generated. The reader should note that we cannot just output these elements. We call those a_k such that $a_k + b_j$ is in $TEMP$ alive (this notion will be clarified in step 5 below). We execute the following procedure:

1. *offset*=1.

2. Repeat 3–6 until *offset* equals $2 * 2^{n/4}$.

3. Each a_k that is alive and points to b_j $(a_k \rightarrow b_j)$ inserts all elements of the form $a_k + b_{j+m}$, where $m \leq offset$ in the array $TEMP$.

4. Find the $2^{n/4}$th smallest element in $TEMP$ and delete all elements larger than it.

5. If the element of the form $a_k + b_{j+offset}$ remains in $TEMP$ we will call a_k alive. Otherwise, a_i is called

dead, and will not participate in further computations.

6. Double the offset (i.e., *offset* := 2***offset*).

Note that the number of elements in *TEMP* never exceeds $2 * 2^{n/4}$. This is true for the following reason. Assume that at phase t the number of live elements a_k is L. Each of these L elements contributes exactly *offset* pairs $a_i + b_j$ to *TEMP*. In the next phase, each such a_k will contribute $2 \times$ *offset* pairs, doubling its previous contribution. Thus, we will add *offset*$\times L$ new pairs to *TEMP*. Since *offset* $\times L \leq 2^{n/4}$, the number of pairs in *TEMP* never exceeds $2 \times 2^{n/4}$.

It is easy to see that the procedure above terminates in $O(\log(2^{n/4}))$ iterations since we are doubling the offset at each iteration. Therefore, the entire process of generating the next $2^{n/4}$ elements can be accomplished in $O(\log^2(2^{n/4})) = O(n^2)$ time using $O(2^{n/4})$ storage. We use the procedure above repeatedly to generate the entire set $A + B$ in ascending order.

Parallel Solution to KNAPSACK

Using our idea above we can obtain significant speedups in the implementation of each phase of the knapsack algorithm. We provide informal analysis of each phase indicating the speed-up that is possible in each phase.

1. We partition S into four lists, S_i, $1 \leq i \leq 4$. Each list is of size $n/4$.

2. We generate the lists G_i, $1 \leq i \leq 4$, i.e., the lists of all possible subset sums S_i, $1 \leq i \leq 4$. Each set is of size $2^{n/4} = M$. It is trivial to obtain M/P time complexity for this problem for any number of processors $P \leq M$. We sort G_1, G_2, G_3 and G_4. Parallel sorting is a well studied problem and is amenable to speedup.

3. We invoke our algorithm for computing the next M elements in the set $A+B$ as described in the previous section to generate G_1+G_2 and G_3+G_4 in ascending order. This phase take M/P time.

4. We intersect (by merging) the generated sets in M phases, generating and merging M elements at a time. Merging can be accomplished in $M/P + O(\log \log P)$ time by a known parallel merge algorithm. Since at least M elements are eliminated at each phase, and the number of possible sums is M^2, the total time to compute the desired intersection is $O(M^2/P)$ time.

The algorithm we sketched above provides a framework to achieve speed-up without sacrificing the good space complexity of the best known sequential algorithm. The novel aspect of the algorithm is step 3 where we suggest an original procedure. There are many details missing from the description of the algorithm above.

There have been a variety of approaches to parallelizing this problem (Chen & Jang 1992; Chen, Chern, & Jang 1990; Teng 1990; Lee, Shragowitz, & Sahni 1988; Lin & Storer 1991). Dynamic programming is efficient in certain cases. Karnin (Karnin 1984) proposes a parallel PRAM algorithm that takes $O(2^{n/2})$ time and uses space $O(2^{n/6})$ but it requires $O(2^{n/6})$ processors. Ferreira (Ferreira 1991) gives an $O(2^{n/4})$ time algorithm with $O(2^{n/4})$ processors but which uses $O(2^{n/2})$ space. Since the space requirements are quadratic in the time and in the number of processors, space becomes a bottleneck on most machines. An open question he posed, therefore, was to find an algorithm with $O(2^{n/4})$ space complexity(Ferreira 1991). This paper provides such an algorithm. Furthermore, our methodology can be applied to the taxonomy of problems presented in (Schroeppel & Shamir 1981) to parallelize of monotonically decomposable problems along a range of time-space tradeoffs, although we feel that the $S = O(2^{n/4})$, $T = O(2^{n/4})$, $P = O(2^{n/4})$ is the simplest and most useful.

Parallel Planning

It turns out that the algorithm sketched above has applications to a variety of problems which on the surface appear different from the knapsack problem. In particular, it is possible to adapt the approach to versions of planning problems. The idea was first outlined in a paper by Fiat, Moses, Shamir, Shimshoni and Tardos on planning in permutation groups (Fiat *et al.* 1989). We give a very informal description of their idea and then show how to use the parallel algorithm we discussed in the previous section, with some modifications, to implement the approach on massively parallel machines. A planning problem we consider may be stated as follows. Let S be a space of states. Typically, this space is exponential in size. Let G be a set of operators mapping elements of S into S. We denote composition of g_i and g_j by $g_i \circ g_j$. As before, by $G_i \circ G_j$ we denote the set of operators formed by composing operators in G_i and G_j respectively. We assume that each operator g in G has an inverse denoted by g^{-1}.

The planning problem is to determine the shortest sequence of operators of the form $g_1, g_2, \ldots$ that maps some initial state X_0 to a final state Y. Without loss of generality assume the initial and final states are always some state 0 and E respectively. In this paper we make the planning problem slightly simpler by asking whether there exists a sequence of operators of length n that maps the initial state into the final state. Assume k is the size of G. Clearly, the problem can be solved by a brute force algorithm of time complexity $O(k^n)$. We can also solve it with $O(n)$ space by iterative-deepening depth-first search. We are interested in problems for which k^n time is prohibitive but $\sqrt{k^n}$ as the total number of computations is feasible.

Let us spell out some assumptions that make the approach work. We assume that all the operators have inverses. We refer to G^{-1} as the set of all inverses of operators in G. We also assume that it is possible to induce a total order $<$ on the states of S. For example, in the example above the states are sums of subsets ordered by the $<$ relation on the set of integers. In the case of permutation groups considered in (Fiat *et al.* 1989), permutations can be ordered lexicographically. There are several additional mathematical assumptions that must be satisfied, some of which are outlined in the full version of our paper.

Let $G_1 = G_2 = G_3 = G_4 = G \circ G \circ \cdots \circ G$, (G composed with itself $l/4$ times). To determine whether there exists a sequence $g_1, ,\ldots, g_l$ that maps 0 into E (i.e., $g_1\ldots g_l(0) = E$), we instead ask the question whether E is contained in $G_1 \circ G_2 \circ G_3 \circ G_4(0)$.

But since the operators have inverses we can ask the question of whether $G_2^{-1} \circ G_1^{-1}(E)$ has a non-empty intersection with $G_3 \circ G_4(0)$.

However, this naturally suggests the very similar scenario that we considered in the discussion on the knapsack problem. If the sizes of G_1, G_2, G_3 and G_4 are M, we can solve this intersection problem in time $O(M^2/P)$ and space $O(M)$. This assumes that we can generate the states in $A \circ B$ (where $\circ$ is now a composition on operators) in increasing order.

To illustrate this approach let us consider a very simple problem. Let $f_1(x) = x + 5$ and $f_2(x) = 3 * x$ be two functions (operators). Given integers c_1 and c_2 we want to find whether there is a sequence of applications of either f_1 or f_2 to c_1 that yield c_2. E.g., $(10+5)*3)+5 = 50$, that is 50 is reachable from 10 by $f_1(f_2(f_1(10) = 50$. To find out whether c_2 is reachable from c_1 in 40 applications of our operators we first create a set F of all possible functions of the form $f(x) = a * x + b$ that can be created by composing f_1 and f_2 with each other ten times. This set is of size 2^{10}.

Now consider the two inverses of f_1 and f_2, namely $h_1(y) = y - 5$ and $h_2(y) = y/3$. We create a set H of all possible functions of the form $h(y) = y/c - d$ that can be generated by composing h_1 and h_2 ten times. This set is also of size 2^{10}. Now we need to find out whether $F \circ F(c_1)$ has a non empty intersection with $H \circ H(c_2)$. The reader can verify that we can produce a monotone order on the operators in F and H that allows us to apply the approach we sketched above. Therefore, we can solve this problem sequentially in time proportional to roughly $20 * 2^{20}$ with 2^{10} storage. The brute force bidirectional search requires 2^{20} storage. Using the algorithms we developed in this paper we can parallelize this approach without increase in storage.

As another application of this approach, we can obtain a parallel algorithm for problems such as Rubik's Cube and other similar problems. The implementation of the algorithm sketched above becomes somewhat more involved because composition of operators is not necessarily monotonic, as defined later. We, nevertheless, can modify the algorithms sketched above to obtain efficient parallel implementations with reduced space.

To describe the algorithm, we assume that our operators are members of a permutation group Π. The *degree* of Π is defined to be the number of points on which Π acts. We set this to be q. We can suppose without loss of generality that each permutation P is a bijection from the set of integers $[1, 2, \ldots, q]$ to itself. The notation for P will be the vector $\langle P(1), P(2), \ldots, P(q) \rangle$. For example, $\langle 4, 3, 2, 1 \rangle$ is the reversal permutation of degree 4 that sends 1 into 4, 2 into 3, 3 into 2, and 4 into 1. If P and Q are permutations then we define their product $P \circ Q$ by $(P \circ Q)(i) = Q(P(i))$. This order of multiplying permutations is customary in much contemporary group-theoretic literature, so we will retain it. Let G be a subset (not a necessarily a subgroup) of k permutations in Π. The elements of G are our basic operators. Given an integer n and a group element γ we ask if γ can be written as the product of n elements from G. We have seen that this problem is reducible to the following: Given 4 sorted lists of permutations A, B, C, D, each of size $O(k^{n/4})$, does $A \circ B$ intersect $C \circ D$? This problem in turn reduces to the problem of generating the elements of $A \circ B$ in sorted order. We order permutations lexicographically. (Remark: the number of elements in A, B, C, D may be smaller, in certain cases, than $O(k^{n/4})$ because the same group element may be written in many different ways as words in G of length $k/4$.) We apply our earlier parallel algorithm for the knapsack problem to generate the elements of $A \circ B$ in batches of $k^{n/4}$ at a time.

A problem arises because our algorithm requires, given an $a_i \in A$ and a $b_j \in B$, the generation of the next *offset* elements of the form $a_i \circ b, b \in B$. When $\circ$ was the $+$ operator, we could simply let these elements be $a_i + b_{j+1}, a_i + b_{j+2}, \ldots, a_i + b_{j+offset}$. This works because sum is a monotonic operator: $b < b' \iff a + b < a + b'$. This monotonicity fails in the case of permutations, however. For example, $\langle 1, 3, 2, 4 \rangle < \langle 1, 3, 4, 2 \rangle$, but

$$
\begin{aligned}
\langle 4, 3, 2, 1 \rangle \circ \langle 1, 3, 2, 4 \rangle &= \langle 4, 2, 3, 1 \rangle \\
&> \langle 2, 4, 3, 1 \rangle \\
&= \langle 4, 3, 2, 1 \rangle \circ \langle 1, 3, 4, 2 \rangle
\end{aligned}
$$

Thus, each a will induce a new ordering of B, and B will have to be traversed in this ordering, in parallel, for all a.

As in the sequential case, a list of permutations will be stored in a trie, a depth q tree whose leaves correspond to permutations in the list and whose unused branches are pruned. Each edge is labeled and the labels encountered when traversing the tree from root to leaf are the images of $[1, 2, \ldots, q]$ of the permutation that is represented by that leaf (see Figure 1).

If the edges emanating from any node in the tree are arranged in increasing order, then the leaves of the tree will be in lexicographically increasing order from

Figure 1: Tree representing the list of 6 permutations $\langle 1, 2, 3, 4 \rangle$, $\langle 1, 3, 2, 4 \rangle$, $\langle 1, 3, 4, 2 \rangle$, $\langle 2, 4, 1, 3 \rangle$, $\langle 2, 4, 3, 1 \rangle$, $\langle 4, 3, 2, 1 \rangle$. Each leaf represents a permutation and the leaves are in lexicographically increasing order from left to right. The leftmost leaf is the identity permutation $\langle 1, 2, 3, 4 \rangle$ and the rightmost leaf is the reversal permutation $\langle 4, 3, 2, 1 \rangle$.

Figure 2: Reordered tree of Figure 1. Each interior node has been reordered according to the permutation $\langle 4, 3, 2, 1 \rangle$. If leaf b is to the left of leaf b' then the permutation $\langle 4, 3, 2, 1 \rangle \circ b$ is lexicographically less than the permutation $\langle 4, 3, 2, 1 \rangle \circ b'$.

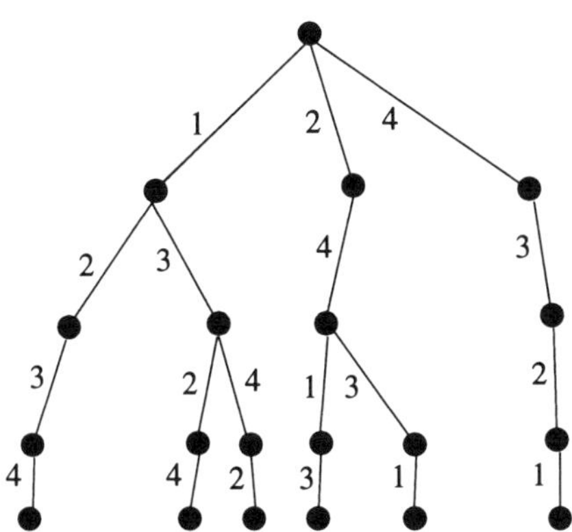

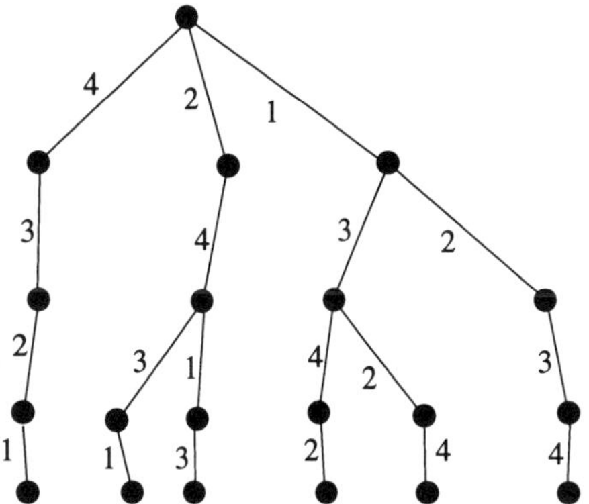

left to right. Given a permutation a, we can rearrange the order of edges emanating from each node to reflect their order in a. The leaves of the new tree, reading from left to right, are increasing with respect to the order induced by a. If the leaf b is to the left of the leaf b' in the new order, then $a \circ b < a \circ b'$ (see Figure 2).

In order for the earlier algorithm to go through, it is necessary, given a_i and b_j to find the b such that there are precisely m leaves between b_j and b in the order induced by a_i. This is done by initially storing the number of leaves in the rooted tree at each node of B with that node. In addition to the pointer from a_i to b_j, a_i also stores the index of b_j in the ordering it introduces. A top down search starting at the root can then find b by performing a prefix sum on the number of leaves in the subtrees of the children of each node in the a_i ordering. This requires only time linear in q, and from this information the child of the node in whose subtree b resides can be inferred. This requires $O(q^2)$ work, as in the sequential algorithm. Note that the step at each node can be performed in parallel with only q extra processors because in the algorithm we use we only need a subinterval of B so that nodes to the left of b are all generated. However, because q is usually fairly small it would almost certainly be a waste of time in practice to perform the prefix sum of the q values in parallel due to communication and synchronization overheads.

This method gives a complexity of $T = O(V/P)$, $S = O(\sqrt{V})$, for $P \leq \sqrt{V}$ up to logarithmic factors and multiplicative factors in q for finding a length n shortest word on k generators, where $V = k^{n/2}$, and

the time complexity of the best sequential algorithm is O(V). This parallelizes the method of Fiat et al. efficiently with respect to work on a CREW PRAM when $P \leq sqrtV$ without asymptotic space utilization greater than the sequential method. Other time space tradeoffs, though possible, are not as useful. Although this technically only applies to a group of operators it is easy to modify the algorithm to apply to a groupoid of operators such as arises in the 15-puzzle.

The CREW PRAM model is unrealistic for current parallel architectures and was used here only for simplicity of exposition. A direct implementation of the algorithm we described would be slow on real machines because of its extensive reliance on complex communication and synchronization patterns. We have developed a slightly more complex algorithm with the same asymptotic time/space complexity (up to logarithmic factors) which is better suited to implementation because of its greater reliance on local memory accesses and should also perform better when $P \ll \sqrt{V}$. In general there are many implementation-dependent parameters that can affect the performance of parallel permutation group manipulation algorithms such as whether to perform permutation composition itself locally (York 1991). Although fundamental permutation group operations are theoretically parallelizable, their practical implementation remains challenging (Babai, Luks, & Seress 1987; Cai 1992; Stiller 1991).

Discussion

We presented an approach for massively parallel state-space search. This approach is a parallel implementation of the sequential algorithm proposed in (Fiat *et al.* 1989) for finding shortest word representations in permutation groups. Our implementation relies on a new idea for computing the k-smallest elements in the set $A + B$. This idea is used to parallelize a key part of the algorithm.

As future work we would like to apply compression techniques such as binary decision diagrams to this state space (Clarke, Filkorn, & Jha 1993; Burch, Clarke, & McMillan 1992).

References

Babai, L.; Luks, E.; and Seress, A. 1987. Permutation groups in NC. In *STOC 87*, volume 19, 409–420.

Brent, R. P. 1974. The parallel evaluation of general arithmetic expressions. *Journal of the ACM* 21(2):201–206.

Burch, J. R.; Clarke, E. M.; and McMillan, K. L. 1992. Symbolic model checking: 10^{20} states and beyond. *Information and Computation* 98(2):142–170.

Cai, J.-Y. 1992. Parallel computation over hyperbolic groups. In *24'th Annual STOC*, 106–115. ACM.

Chen, G.-H., and Jang, J.-H. 1992. An improved parallel algorithm for 0/1 knapsack problem. *Parallel Computing* 18(7):811–821.

Chen, G.-H.; Chern, M.-S.; and Jang, J.-H. 1990. Pipeline architectures for dynamic programming algorithms. *Parallel Computing* 13(1):111–117.

Clarke, E. M.; Filkorn, T.; and Jha, S. 1993. Exploiting symmetry in temporal logical model checking. In *Proceedings of the Fifth Workshop on Computer-Aided Verification*, 450–462.

Diffie, W., and Hellman, M. 1976. New directions in cryptography. *IEEE Trans. Information Theory* IT-22:644–654.

Evett, M.; Hendler, J.; Mahanti, A.; and Nau, D. 1990. PRA*: A memory-limited heuristic search procedure for the Connection Machine. In *Third Symposium on the Fontiers of Massively Parallel Computations*, 145–149.

Ferreira, A. G. 1991. A parallel time/hardware trade-off $T \cdot H = O(2^{n/2})$ for the knapsack problem. *IEEE Transactions on Computers* 40(2):221–225.

Fiat, A.; Moses, S.; Shamir, A.; Shimshoni, I.; and Tardos, G. 1989. Planning and learning in permutation groups. In *30th Annual Symposium on Foundations of Computer Science*, 274–279. IEEE Computer Society Press. Los Alamitos, CA, USA.

Hillis, D. 1985. *The Connection Machine*. MIT Press.

Horowitz, E., and Sahni, S. 1974. Computing partitions with applications to the knapsack problem. *Journal of the Association for Computing Machinery* 21(2):277–292.

Karnin, E. D. 1984. A parallel algorithm for the knapsack problem. *IEEE Trans. Comput.* C-33:404–408.

Korf, R. E. 1985a. Depth-first iterative-deepening: an optimal admissible tree search. *AI* 27:97–109.

Korf, R. E. 1985b. Iterative-deepening-A*: an optimal admissible tree search. In *International Joint Conference on Artificial Intelligence*.

Lee, J.; Shragowitz, E.; and Sahni, S. 1988. A hypercube algorithm for the 0/1 knapsack problem. *Journal of Parallel and Distributed Computing* 5(4).

Lin, J., and Storer, J. A. 1991. Processor-efficient hypercube algorithms for the knapsack problem. *Journal of Parallel and Distributed Computing* 13(3):332–337.

Merkle, R., and Hellman, M. 1978. Hiding information and receipts in trap door knapsacks. *IEEE Transactions on Information Theory* IT-24:525–530.

Pohl, I. 1971. Bi-directional search. In Meltzer, B., and Michie, D., eds., *Machine Intelligence 6*. Edinburgh: Edinburgh University Press. 127–140.

Powley, C., and Korf, R. E. 1988. SIMD and MIMD parallel search. In *Proceedings of the AAAI Symposium on Planning and Search*.

Powley, C., and Korf, R. E. 1991. Single-agent parallel window search. *IEEE Transactions on Pattern Analysis and Machine Intelligence* 13(5):466–477.

Powley, C.; Ferguson, C.; and Korf, R. E. 1991. Parallel tree search on a SIMD machine. In *Third IEEE Symposium on Parallel and Distributed Processing*.

Rao, V. N., and Kumar, V. 1987. Parallel depth-first search, part i. Implementation. *International Journal of Parallel Programming* 16(6):479–499.

Schroeppel, R., and Shamir, A. 1981. A $T = O(2^{n/2})$, $S = O(2^{n/4})$ algorithm for certain NP-complete problems. *SIAM Journal on Computing* 10(3):456–464.

Stiller, L. 1991. Group graphs and computational symmetry on massively parallel architecture. *Journal of Supercomputing* 5(2/3):99–117.

Stiller, L. 1992. An algebraic paradigm for the design of efficient parallel programs. Technical Report JHU-92/26, Dept. of Computer Science, Johns Hopkins University, Baltimore, MD 21218.

Tarjan, R., and Trojanowski, A. 1977. Finding a maximum independent set. *SIAM Journal on Computing* 6:537–546.

Teng, S.-H. 1990. Adaptive parallel algorithms for integral knapsack problems. *J. Parallel and Distributed Computing* 8(4):400–406.

Thinking Machines Corporation. 1992. *Connection Machine CM-5 Technical Summary*. 245 First St., Cambridge, MA 02142–1264: Thinking Machines Corporation.

York, B. W. 1991. Implications of parallel architectures for permutation group computation. In Finkelstein, L., and Kantor, W., eds., *Proceedings of the Workshop on Groups and Computation*, 293–313. Rutgers, NJ: DIMACS.

The Trailblazer Search:
A New Method for Searching and Capturing Moving Targets

Fumihiko Chimura and **Mario Tokoro***
Department of Computer Science,
Faculty of Science and Technology, Keio University
3–14–1 Hiyoshi, Kohoku–ku, Yokohama 223, Japan
{chimura, mario}@mt.cs.keio.ac.jp

Abstract

This paper proposes a new search algorithm for targets that move. Ishida and Korf presented an algorithm, called the *moving target search*, that captures a target while deciding each search step in constant time (Ishida & Korf 1991). However, this algorithm requires many search steps to solve problems, if it uses a heuristic function that initially returns inaccurate values. The *trailblazer search* stores path information of the region it has searched and exploits this information when making decisions. The algorithm maintains a *map* of the searched region, and chases the target once it falls on a path found on the map. We empirically show that the algorithm's map function can significantly reduce the number of search steps, compared with the moving target search. We also discuss the efficiency of the trailblazer search, taking the maintenance cost of the map into consideration.

Introduction

Heuristic search for moving targets models the case where the location of the goal changes dynamically. This assumption is realistic because there are many applications in which the goal moves before the search reaches the original location. Search for moving targets is a real-time task that interleaves decision and execution of search steps (Korf 1990). The search is illustrated intuitively when you try to meet someone in a crowd. You have to be careful in performing the search: there is a possibility that you and the person will cover the same ground many times before you actually meet. We study the search in an abstract search space as multiple paths finding to every possible location of the goal.

Ishida and Korf proposed the *moving target search* (MTS) algorithm (Ishida & Korf 1991). MTS tries to learn the exact distance to the target, while exploring the search space. It starts with an initial heuristic estimate of the distance. After the exact distance to the target is known, the search is just the process of catching the target up. The distinctive characteristic of MTS is that it makes decisions in constant time. The major concern in MTS is that it requires many search steps to solve a problem, if the initial heuristic estimate of the distance to the target greatly differs from the exact value.

This paper investigates an underlying intelligence that reduces the number of search steps, in the search for moving targets. We propose the *trailblazer search*: a method that stores path information of the region it has searched, and exploits this information when making decisions.[1] Information of the searched region is organized into a *map* that contains paths and associated costs to every site in the region from the current location of the algorithm. The trailblazer search uses a heuristic function, in an algorithm that conducts a systematic search and avoids exploring the same region twice. Once the target crosses a path on the map, the algorithm follows the path to catch the target up. Under the assumption of moving faster than the target, the trailblazer search captures the target.

The trailblazer search makes decisions using a map that gets larger as the algorithm steps further. We will discuss the efficiency of the trailblazer search, taking the maintenance cost of the map into consideration.

Search for Moving Targets

We study the search for moving targets in an abstract search space: a connected and undirected graph with a unit cost on each edge. A problem solver searches for a target representing the goal. At any point during search, both the problem solver and the target are assigned nodes in the graph that represent their states, or simply denote their locations. They can move to any node adjacent to their current locations. We assume that they move on alternate turns. The problem solver and the target are assigned initial nodes at the beginning of the search; the search ends when their locations coincide. We say a node is *explored* if it has been the location of the problem solver.

We make three assumptions to assure a solution to the search. The first is that the problem solver always

---

*Also with   Sony Computer Science Laboratory Inc., 3-14-13 Higashigotanda, Shinagawa–ku, Tokyo 141, Japan.

[1]We use the term "trailblazer" in the sense of a guide or pathfinder since it uses a map.

knows the location of the target. The second is that the problem solver has a heuristic function that returns an estimated distance between any two nodes in the search space. We further assume that the heuristic function is initialized to return non-overestimated values, that is the function is *admissible* (Pearl 1984). The last assumption is that the problem solver moves faster than the target. In the particular search space defined above, we realize this by eventually skipping the turn of the target.

Search for moving targets is a real-time task that interleaves decision and execution of search steps. This is the result of practical resource limitations that do not allow a method to first find a sequence of steps that leads to the goal, and then execute the sequence. Korf presented the *learning real-time A** (LRTA*) algorithm that reaches the goal while making decisions in constant time (Korf 1990). Basically, LRTA* starts with an initial heuristic estimate of the distance from a node in the search space to the goal and, while exploring the search space, tries to find the exact distance. In the learning step, the heuristic distance $h(x)$ between node x and the goal is updated to the value of $min_i\{c(x, x_i) + h(x_i)\}$, where x_i is a node adjacent to x, $c(x, x_i)$ is the actual distance from x to x_i, and $h(x_i)$ is the heuristic distance between x_i and the goal. This update is done to ensure that $h(x)$ is not smaller than the estimated length of the path from x to the goal that goes through a node adjacent to x.

Ishida and Korf extended the learning method of LRTA* to tackle the search problem for moving targets (Ishida & Korf 1991). Their algorithm, the *moving target search* (MTS), learns the exact distance between any pair of nodes in the search space. This capacity is added because both the problem solver and the target can move to any location in the search space. Once the problem solver knows the complete set of exact distance values, the search task is reduced to moving to the adjacent nodes that are closer to the target. MTS is guaranteed to reach the target if the search problem follows the above assumptions. The worst case time complexity of MTS is $O(N^3)$, and the worst case space complexity is $O(N^2)$, where N is the number of nodes in the search space.

The major concern of LRTA* and MTS is that they require a significant number of search steps to reach the goal, if their heuristic functions initially return inaccurate values. In MTS, excessive search steps is typically shown using a target on a plane with randomly placed obstacles. When trapped in dead ends, the problem solver moves back and forth because the obstacles prevent direct movement to the target placed just beyond the obstacles. Ishida presented an extension to MTS that conducts a *lookahead* search in order to get out of dead ends fast (Ishida 1992). His algorithm, the *Intelligent Moving Target Search* (IMTS), considers the tradeoff between the increased computation cost to explore nodes with the lookahead search,

and the reduced execution cost to reach the target with fewer steps. The learning method in LRTA* and that in MTS is a sort of *reinforcement learning*; learning from positive and negative rewards of executing search steps. Whitehead, and also Koenig and Simmons studied the issue of excessive search steps in the context of reinforcement learning (Whitehead 1991; Koenig & Simmons 1993).

The Trailblazer Search

We propose a new search algorithm for targets that move. We aim at reducing the number of search steps, yet guaranteeing the accomplishment of the task. The basic idea is to store path information of the region where the algorithm has searched, and exploit this information for the task. The information of the searched region is especially useful when the target is moving because, as the region expands, there is a good chance that the target will cross a path that the problem solver has already used for search.

The problem solver records every search step it takes by remembering an undirected edge connecting the departure and arrival nodes of the step. This record is organized into a graph called the **trail**. The **map** is a table calculated from the trail and it contains the information of minimum cost paths from the current location of the problem solver to any node it has explored. The map is a partial map of the whole search space, and is relative to the search steps that the problem solver has taken so far. Thus we consider it as a relative search tree rooted at the current location of the problem solver. In the following, we describe how we maintain the map.

Let p_n be the node the problem solver reaches after n steps, where n is a non-negative integer. We assume that p_n takes values from a set of integers that identify the actual nodes in the search space. Let V_{p_n} and E_{p_n} be the sets of accumulated nodes and edges at location p_n. Weighted and undirected edges are denoted by triplets, $(p_n, p_{n+1}, c(p_n, p_{n+1}))$, where $c(p_n, p_{n+1})$ is the actual cost to traverse the edge.

Definition 1 (The Trail) *Let p_0 be the initial node of the problem solver. The trail of the problem solver at location p_0 is a weighted and undirected graph $G_{p_0} = (V_{p_0}, E_{p_0})$, where the set of nodes V_{p_0} is $\{p_0\}$ and the set of edges E_{p_0} is $\{\ \}$.*

Assume that the problem solver moves from p_{n-1} to p_n on its nth step with actual cost $c(p_{n-1}, p_n)$, where n is a positive integer. The trail of the problem solver at location p_n is a weighted and undirected graph $G_{p_n} = (V_{p_n}, E_{p_n})$, where the set of nodes V_{p_n} is $V_{p_{n-1}} \cup \{p_n\}$ and the set of edges E_{p_n} is $E_{p_{n-1}} \cup \{(p_{n-1}, p_n, c(p_{n-1}, p_n))\}$.

We assume that the problem solver is able to record the trail of the target and to maintain the map of the target. This means that the location of the target is regarded as a sort of explored node for the problem solver. Using the above procedure, we define the trail of the target at location q_m to be a graph $G'_{q_m} = (V'_{q_m}, E'_{q_m})$, where q_m is the node the target reaches after m steps, where m is a non-negative integer. The problem solver is able to refer to a graph $G = (V_{p_n} \cup V'_{q_m}, E_{p_n} \cup E'_{q_m})$ at location p_n as the total trail of the search.

We use Dijkstra's *shortest path algorithm*, a *routing algorithm*, to calculate the map. Dijkstra's algorithm has a time complexity of $O(N^2)$ when the number of nodes in the search space is fixed to N (Aho, Hopcroft, & Ullman 1974). Let $C(x, y)$ be the cost of the minimum cost path from the current location x of the problem solver to some node y in the trail. The path goes only through nodes in the trail, and the cost of the path is the sum of the costs of the edges that constitute it. The routing algorithm calculates a *routing table* that holds the value for $C(x, y)$, and the node x' succeeding x on the path to y.[2] The value of $C(x', y)$ is simply $C(x, y) - c(x, x')$, where $c(x, x')$ is the cost of the edge between x and x'. The value of $C(x, y)$ is ∞ if there is no path between x and y. In other words, we know that there is a path from x to y if $C(x, y)$ has a finite value. The map is nothing else than the routing table calculated from the trail by the routing algorithm.

We use **trailblazer search** to refer generally to algorithms that maintain a map to perform a search. A trailblazer search has two distinct phases: (1) a *search phase* in which the map has no path to the target, and the search space is heuristically searched, and (2) a *chase phase* in which the map has a path to the target that is deterministically followed to catch the target up. The phases are characterized by the evaluation functions they use to determine which adjacent node to move to next. In the search phase, decisions arc made using the heuristic estimates of the distances from the adjacent nodes to the goal. In the chase phase, decisions are made using the costs on the map that indicate the best known paths from the adjacent nodes to the goal. We describe a particular instance of the trailblazer search that uses hill-climbing in the search phase.

The Trailblazer Search with Hill-Climbing

Let x and y be the locations of the problem solver and the target. Let $h(x, y)$ be the heuristic estimate of the distance between x and y, and $C(x, y)$ be the cost of the minimum cost path between x and y. To eliminate unnecessary re-exploration of the same node, we assume that the problem solver holds the set of explored nodes. We also assume that the problem solver records, for each explored node, the *parent* node from which it has arrived to the node for the first time.

---

[2]We applied some minor modification to Dijkstra's algorithm to avoid repeated calculation for known paths.

Procedures of the problem solver when it is its own turn to move.

Update the routing table according to the location x of the problem solver. For each node x' adjacent to x, read $C(x', y)$ to find if there is a path from x' to y. If there is no path on the map, enter the search phase. Otherwise, enter the chase phase.

- *In the search phase*:
  For each non-explored node x' adjacent to x, calculate $h(x', y)$, move to the node x' with minimum $h(x', y)$. If all of the adjacent nodes have been explored, move to the node x' that is the parent node of x. Assign the value of x' to x as the new location.

- *In the chase phase*:
  Move to the adjacent node x' with minimum $C(x', y)$, and assign the value of x' to x as the new location.

- *In both the search phase and the chase phase*:
  Record the move of the problem solver in the trail.

Procedures of the problem solver when it is the target's turn to move.

- *In both the search phase and the chase phase*:
  Record the move of the target in the trail.

If a tie occurs such that two node evaluations return the same cost, the tie is broken randomly.

The algorithm is *complete* in the sense that it never fails to capture the target if the search problem follows the assumptions in the previous section. As a short proof, consider first the search phase. Since the search space is finite, the algorithm must either find the target or the trail of the problem solver and the target must overlap before all the search space is explored. If the trails overlap, the algorithm enters the chase phase because there is now a path to the target on the map, whatever steps the target may take. The cost of the path never increases when the problem solver and the target alternate turns. Hence, under the assumption that the problem solver moves faster than the target, it will eventually reach the target.

We will now analyze the complexity of the algorithm. Let N be the number of nodes in the search space, and M the number of search steps. The time complexity of the trailblazer search is the number of search steps plus the time complexity of map maintenance. The time complexity of map maintenance on the Mth step of the problem solver is $O((2 * M)^2) = O(M^2)$. Although we omit a formal proof, this can be seen intuitively because the total number of steps of the problem solver and the target, and thus the number of nodes in the total trail, is at most $2 * M$ when the problem solver moves M steps. The algorithm re-calculates the map every time the problem solver moves. Thus the time complexity of map maintenance is $O(\sum_{i=0}^{M} i^2)$ when the problem solver moves M steps. Since this value is bounded by $O(M^3)$, the time complexity of the trailblazer search is $O(M + M^3)$ when the problem solver moves M steps.

In the search phase, the steps of the problem solver are along a search tree that grows to exhaust the search space. Since this tree has at most $N - 1$ edges and it takes $2 * (N - 1)$ steps to traverse the whole tree, in the search phase, the worst case of the number M of search steps is $2 * (N - 1)$. In the chase phase, the steps of the problem solver are along a path found on the map. Since the initial cost of this path is at most $N - 1$, in the chase phase, the worst case of M is $(N - 1)/\alpha$, where α is the difference in speed between the problem solver and the target; it takes $(N - 1)/\alpha$ steps to catch the target up. In each phase of the search, M is bounded by $O(N)$, if we assume α is a constant.

Consequently, the algorithm's worst case time complexity is $O(N + N^3)$ that is bounded by $O(N^3)$. The worst case space complexity is $O(N^2)$ because this is the size of the complete routing table. Note that these values are the same as those for MTS. However, the factor that determines the worst case time complexity of the trailblazer search differs from that of MTS. In MTS, the determining factor is the number of search steps. In the trailblazer search, it is the time complexity of map maintenance, since the worst case of the number of search steps reduces from $O(N^3)$ to $O(N)$, compared with MTS. This indicates that the trailblazer search considers the tradeoff between the computation cost to maintain the map, and the execution cost of the search steps.

Performance of the Trailblazer Search

We empirically evaluate the performance of the trailblazer search. We also discuss its efficiency, while considering the maintenance cost of the map. The search space of our problem is a rectangular grid with randomly placed obstacles. The problem solver and the target move along the grid from junctions to adjacent junctions, but not to those occupied by obstacles. Logically, increasing the number of obstacles changes the regularity of the search space and causes the heuristic function to return an increasing number of errors. The grid is a square of 50 junctions on each side, organized as a torus.

We implemented the trailblazer search with hillclimbing (denoted by TBS), and, for comparison, the moving target search algorithm by Ishida and Korf (denoted by MTS). The problem solver uses the Manhattan distance as its heuristic function. We performed four experiments, using for each, a different movement strategy of the target. (1) *Avoid*: the target moves to the furthest adjacent junction from the problem solver, estimated by the Manhattan distance, (2) *Stationary*: the target does not move, (3) *Random*: the target moves randomly, (4) *Meet*: the target moves to meet the problem solver, i.e., searches for the problem solver. With the *Avoid* strategy, the target executes the same learning method as MTS in the hope to flee from the

problem solver cleverly. With the *Meet* strategy, the target uses the same search method as the problem solver (TBS matches TBS, MTS matches MTS). We set the speed of the target to 4/5 that of the problem solver by skipping the turn of the target once every five turns. The problem solver and the target are initially separated diagonally on the square grid at a distance of 50 junctions in the Manhattan distance.

We set the obstacle ratio between 0% and 40% at intervals of 5%, and randomly created 100 sample grids for each obstacle ratio. Both TBS and MTS solved the same samples, and we averaged the total number of search steps of the problem solver over the 100 samples. For TBS, we also measured the actual complexity of map maintenance while solving the samples. The actual complexity is calculated by counting the number of references to entries on the routing table for each time the map is updated. We do this because references to entries are the actual operations that decide the complexity of map maintenance. We will briefly mention some results of the actual complexity of map maintenance.

Figure 1 shows the number of search steps when we change the obstacle ratio. We obtained similar results for problem sizes ranging from 20 to 50 junctions on each side of the grid. TBS and MTS show almost the same performance when there are few obstacles. However, as the obstacle ratio increases and the heuristic function begins to return inaccurate values, TBS significantly reduces the number of search steps, compared with MTS. When the obstacle ratio is 40% and when the target strategy is *Avoid*, *Stationary*, *Random*, *Meet*, the proportion of the number of search steps of MTS to that of TBS is $3475/405 \simeq 8$, $1586/444 \simeq 3$, $6313/376 \simeq 16$, $20981/180 \simeq 100$, respectively. The reason for the gain is that TBS can use the map to detour walls of obstacles, and get out of dead ends fast.

By the nature of their movements, targets with the *Random* strategy do not move far from their initial locations. When the obstacle ratio is high, targets with the *Avoid* strategy get trapped in dead ends and do not move far either. Thus, for a systematic search like TBS and a high obstacle ratio, targets with the *Random* and the *Avoid* strategies are as easy (takes as much search steps) to capture as targets with the *Stationary* strategy. Actually, with a high obstacle ratio, there is a slight tendency that moving targets will be easier (takes less search steps) to capture. The fact that TBS collects more information of the search space from the movements of the target, explains the result. We predict that these results will hold, even if we change the speed ratio between the problem solver and the target because change in speed does not affect the target's strategy.

As seen in figure 1, when there are many obstacles, MTS shows a counterintuitive behavior in that targets with the *Meet* strategy are far more difficult to capture than those using the *Avoid* strategy, even though tar-

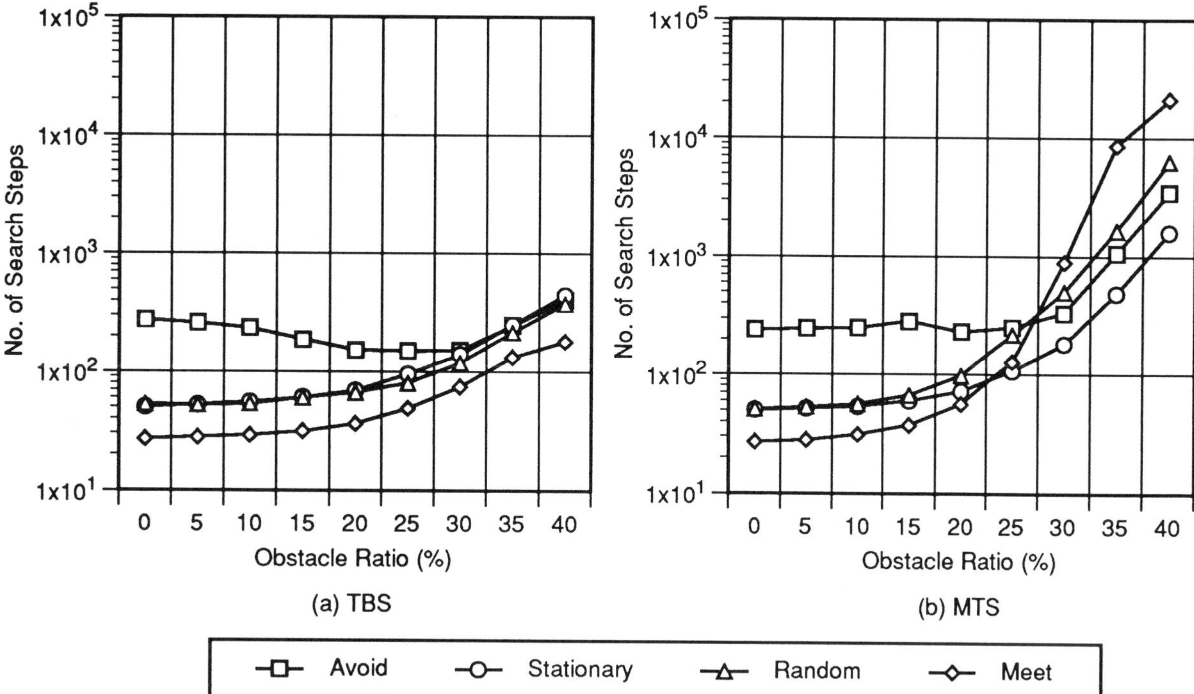

Figure 1: Results of the number of Search Steps

gets with the *Meet* strategy cooperate with the problem solver. Ishida and Korf pointed out this result in their paper (Ishida & Korf 1991). This doesn't happen in TBS; in TBS, targets with the *Meet* strategy are the easiest to capture, regardless of the obstacle ratio. Increasing the target's speed increases the efficiency of TBS, reducing the number of search steps. As we decrease the target's speed, the number of search steps approaches that TBS needs to capture targets with the *Stationary* strategy.

An interesting characteristic of TBS is that it does not take the optimal path even if there are no obstacles (and hence the Manhattan distance gives the correct distance to the target). When the obstacle ratio is 0% and the target executes the *Avoid* strategy, TBS takes 275 steps to capture the target while MTS takes the optimal path of 239 steps. This happens because the current implementation of TBS is completely *faithful* to the map, in the sense that the problem solver always follows the map whenever a path is found, even if the distance to the target in the Manhattan distance is smaller than the cost of the path.

Evaluating the Real Efficiency of the Trailblazer Search

For TBS, the drastic reduction of search steps is due to the benefit of the map. Here we estimate the total cost of search, and discuss the real efficiency of TBS, while considering the maintenance cost of the map.

We emphasize that, from the viewpoint of the worst case time complexity, TBS and MTS have identical efficiency. Compared with IMTS (the extended form of MTS), TBS exchanges the cost to explore information with a lookahead search, for the cost to exploit information of the searched region. The total cost of search is the sum of the cost to make decisions on search steps and the cost to execute them. We simply assume that the decision cost is proportional to its time complexity, and that the execution cost is proportional to the number of search steps. We further assume that the search steps are decided in a computer and are executed in the real world. That is, we weight the decision cost by $1/\beta$, where β is a large number. Formally, this makes the total cost for TBS, $T_{TBS} = M_{TBS} + M_{TBS}^3/\beta$, and for MTS, $T_{MTS} = M_{MTS} + M_{MTS}/\beta$, where M_{TBS} and M_{MTS} are the numbers of search steps that each algorithm requires to solve a problem. The fact that TBS maintains a map to make decisions, and that MTS makes a constant time decision, justifies the difference between T_{TBS} and T_{MTS}.

For example, we set β to 10^6. This is a plausible figure because, in the real world, search steps usually take seconds of time to execute, while, in current computers, the unit operation of map maintenance takes on the order of microseconds. When the obstacle ratio is over 30% and the target is moving, the empirical results of the actual complexity of map maintenance ranges from $4.8*10^3$ (30% obstacles, *Meet* strategy target) to $6.7 * 10^4$ (40% obstacles, *Random* strategy target). These values have small impact on T_{TBS}, when we weight them by 10^{-6}. Thus, in our empirical search space, when the obstacle ratio is high and the target is moving, T_{TBS} is smaller than T_{MTS} because, as we observe in figure 1, M_{TBS} is smaller than M_{MTS} by a factor of 10 in average. This indicates the applicability of TBS to real domain problems that have the same size ($50*50 = 2500$ nodes) as our empirical search space. For large scale problems, however, the maintenance cost of the map increases the time TBS uses to make decisions, and this becomes an issue for TBS if we look at its ability to react to the real world.

Currently, TBS maintains a full size map in the sense that it includes information concerned with all the explored nodes. The aim is to utilize plenty of alternative paths to efficiently and intelligently reach the target. The idea of limiting the size of the map, while preserving efficiency, is extremely important for two reasons: to improve the ability of TBS to react to the real world, and to reduce the average space complexity.

Conclusion

We dealt with search for moving targets, and proposed an efficient method to capture moving targets. The *trailblazer search* maintains a map of the searched region and uses this for the search. We compared the properties of the trailblazer search with those of the *moving target search* (Ishida & Korf 1991). Formally, the two algorithms have the same worst case time complexity of $O(N^3)$ where N is the number of nodes in the search space. However, the determining factors of the values are different. For the moving target search, the number of search steps determines its worst case time complexity. For the trailblazer search, this value is determined by the maintenance of the map, since the number of search steps reduces from $O(N^3)$ to $O(N)$ when compared with the moving target search.

To examine this difference, we tested the performance of the algorithms on a grid-like search space with randomly placed obstacles. We showed that when the algorithms use inaccurate heuristic functions, the trailblazer search significantly reduces the number of search steps, when compared with the moving target search. In a square grid with 50 junctions on each side and an obstacle occupation ratio of 40%, where the problem solver and the target searched for each other, we obtained a 100–fold reduction. We also estimated the impact of map maintenance on the total cost of the trailblazer search. We made an assumption that the map is maintained in a computer and the search steps are executed in the real world, and hence weighted the cost to maintain the map by a plausible factor. In our empirical search space, the impact of map maintenance is small when compared with the execution cost of search steps. This indicates the applicability of the trailblazer search to real domain problems. For large scale problems, a parallel implementation of the map maintenance method decreases the cost to maintain the map (Chandy & Misra 1982).

As a consequence, we showed that, for the purpose of efficient search, we can tradeoff the execution cost of search steps for the computation cost to maintain a map. When memory is limited, it is useful to consider a mixed strategy that uses the heuristic function while it returns accurate values, and maintains the map only if necessary. We plan to research this strategy further.

Acknowledgements

We had a fruitful discussion with Toru Ishida of Kyoto University. Members of Sony Computer Science Laboratory helped to improve initial concepts and colleagues at Keio University supported us invaluably. Finally, F. Chimura would like to express his deepest gratitude to his family for their support.

References

Aho, A. V.; Hopcroft, J. E.; and Ullman, J. D. 1974. *The Design and Analysis of Computer Algorithms.* Reading, Mass.: Addison-Wesley.

Chandy, K. M., and Misra, J. 1982. Distributed Computation on Graphs: Shortest Path Algorithms. *Communications of the ACM* 25(11):833–837.

Ishida, T., and Korf, R. E. 1991. Moving Target Search. In *Proceedings of the Twelfth International Joint Conference on Artificial Intelligence*, 204–210.

Ishida, T. 1992. Moving Target Search with Intelligence. In *Proceedings of the Tenth National Conference on Artificial Intelligence*, 525–532.

Koenig, S., and Simmons, R. G. 1993. Complexity Analysis of Real-Time Reinforcement Learning. In *Proceedings of the Eleventh National Conference on Artificial Intelligence*, 99–105.

Korf, R. E. 1990. Real-Time Heuristic Search. *Artificial Intelligence* 42:189–211.

Pearl, J. 1984. *Heuristics: Intelligent Search Strategies for Computer Problem Solving.* Reading, Mass.: Addison-Wesley.

Whitehead, S. D. 1991. A Complexity Analysis of Cooperative Mechanisms in Reinforcement Learning. In *Proceedings of the Ninth National Conference on Artificial Intelligence*, 607–613.

ITS: An Efficient Limited-Memory Heuristic Tree Search Algorithm*

Subrata Ghosh
Department of Computer Science
University of Maryland
College Park,MD 20742
subrata@cs.umd.edu

Ambuj Mahanti
IIM, Calcutta
Calcutta 700 027
India
iimcal!am@veccal.ernet.in

Dana S. Nau
Dept. of Computer Science, and
Institute for Systems Research
University of Maryland
College Park, MD 20742
nau@cs.umd.edu

Abstract

This paper describes a new admissible tree search algorithm called Iterative Threshold Search (ITS). ITS can be viewed as a much-simplified version of MA* [1], and a generalized version of MREC [12]. We also present the following results:

1. Every node generated by ITS is also generated by IDA*, even if ITS is given no more memory than IDA*. In addition, there are trees on which ITS generates $O(N)$ nodes in comparison to $O(N \log N)$ nodes generated by IDA*, where N is the number of nodes eligible for generation by A*.

2. Experimental tests show that if the node-generation time is high (as in most practical problems), ITS can provide significant savings in both number of node generations and running time. Our experimental results also suggest that in the average case both IDA* and ITS are asymptotically optimal on the traveling salesman problem. not common enough

Introduction

Although A* is usually very efficient in terms of number of node expansions [2], it requires an exponential amount of memory, and thus runs out of memory even on problem instances of moderate size. This problem led to Korf's development of IDA* [6]. IDA*'s memory requirement is only linear in the depth of the search, enabling it to solve larger problems than A* can solve in practice. However, when additional memory is available, IDA* does not make use of this memory to reduce the number of node expansions. This led to the development of several other limited-memory heuristic search algorithms, including MREC and MA*. In this paper, we present the following results:

1. We present a new admissible tree search algorithm called Iterative Threshold Search (ITS). Like IDA*, ITS maintains a threshold z, expands each path until its cost exceeds z, and then revises z. But if given additional memory, it keeps track of additional nodes, and backs up path information at parents when nodes

get pruned. ITS can be viewed as a much simplified version of MA*, and a generalized version of MREC. ITS's node selection and retraction (pruning) overhead is much less expensive than MA*'s.

2. We have proved (for proofs, see [4]) that ITS dominates IDA*; i.e., even if ITS is given no more memory than IDA*, every node generated by ITS is also generated by IDA*. In addition, we present example trees in which ITS expands $O(N)$ nodes in comparison to $O(N \log N)$ nodes expanded by IDA* where N is the number of nodes eligible for expansion by A*.

3. We present extensive experimental tests on ITS on three problem domains: the flow-shop scheduling problem, the 15-puzzle, and the traveling salesman problem. Our results show that if the node-generation time is high (which is the case for most practical problems), ITS can provide significant savings in both number of node generations and running time.

4. Our experiments suggest that in the average case both IDA* and ITS are asymptotically optimal on the traveling salesman problem. Although Patrick *et al.* [8] showed that there exists a class of traveling salesman problems in which IDA* is not asymptotically optimal, our experimental results suggest that such problems are not common enough to affect IDA*'s average performance over a large number of problem instances.

Background

The objective of many heuristic search algorithms is to find a minimum cost solution path in a directed graph G. To find such a path, these algorithms use a node evaluation function $f(n) = g(n) + h(n)$, where $g(n)$ is the cost of a minimum cost path currently known from the start node s to n, and $h(n) \geq 0$, the heuristic value of node n, is an estimate of $h^*(n)$. $h^*(n)$ is the cost of a minimum cost path from n to a goal node. In this paper, we assume that the heuristic function h is admissible, i.e $\forall n \in G$, $h(n) \leq h^*(n)$. The cost of an edge (m, n) in G is denoted by $c(m, n)$.

Algorithm ITS

Most heuristic search algorithms maintain a search tree T containing data about each node n that has been

*Supported in part by NSF Grants NSFD CDR-88003012, IRI-9306580, and CMDS project (work order no. 019/7-148/CMDS-1039/90-91).

installed in the tree. Nodes of G are generated one at a time and installed into T, until a solution path is found in T that duplicates the least-cost solution path of G. Usually the branches of T are represented only as links among the data structures representing the nodes. However, in the search tree T maintained by ITS, ITS maintains heuristic information not only for each node of the tree, but also for each branch of the tree. Thus, rather than considering a branch (p, q) merely to be a link between the node p and its child q, we consider it as a separate entity in T.

Conceptually, ITS installs (p, q) into T at the same time that it installs p into T, even though ITS has not yet generated q. It is possible to implement such a scheme without incurring the overhead of generating all of p's children, by creating one branch $(p, R(p))$ for each operator R applicable to p without actually invoking the operator R. A *tip branch* of T is a branch (p, q) in T such that q is not in T. A *tip node* of T is a node p of T such that every branch (p, q) in T is a tip branch. Such nodes are eligible for *retraction* by ITS. Retracting p consists of removing from T the node p and every branch (p, q).

For each branch (p, q) in T a variable B is maintained, which stores an estimate of the cost of the minimum cost solution path containing the branch (p, q). $B(p, q)$ is initialized to $f(p) = g(p) + h(p)$, when the node p is installed in T. However, unlike f-value of a node, $B(p, q)$ is updated every time the node q is retracted.

S is the amount of storage (number of nodes) available to ITS.

Procedure ITS:

1. Call Install$(s, 0)$.

2. Do the following steps repeatedly:

   (a) Set $z := \min\{B(p, q) : (p, q) \text{ is a tip branch}\}$.

   (b) Do the following steps repeatedly, until $B(p, q) > z$ for every tip branch (p, q):

   i. Select the leftmost tip branch (m, n) such that $B(m, n) \leq z$.

   ii. If m is a goal node then EXIT, returning $g(m)$.

   iii. If $n = \text{DUMMY}$, then set $B(m, n) := \infty$. Otherwise, do the following:

   A. If T contains $\geq S$ nodes and has at least two tip nodes, then retract a node, as follows. If there is a tip node x such that $B(x, y) > z$ for every branch (x, y), then let q be the leftmost such node. Otherwise, let q be the rightmost tip node of T. Set $B(p, q) := \min_r B(q, r)$, where p is q's parent in T. Remove q and every branch (q, r) from T.

   B. Call Install$(n, g(m) + c(m, n))$.

Procedure Install(n, g):

   1. Put n into T.

2. If no operators are applicable to n, then put a dummy branch (n, DUMMY) in T. Else for each operator R applicable to n, put a branch $(n, R(n))$ in T.

3. Set $g(n) := g$.

4. For each branch (n, r), set $B(n, r) := g(n) + h(n)$.

Basic Properties of ITS

For $i = 1, 2, \ldots$, the i'th *instant* in the operation of ITS is the i'th time that Step 2(b)i is executed, i.e., the i'th time that ITS selects a tip branch for expansion. ITS's j'th *iteration* is the j'th iteration of the outer loop in Step 2. ITS's j'th *threshold value* is the value of z during this iteration.

In Theorem 1 below, we prove that no node is generated more than once by ITS during iteration j, and from this it follows that the number of instants in iteration j equals the number of nodes generated in iteration j. At each instant i, ITS either exits at Step 2(b)ii or generates a node n_i at Step 2(b)iiiB. In the latter case, either n_i is a new node (i.e., a node that has never before been generated), or else it is a node that was previously generated and retracted.

Theorem 1 ITS satisfies the following properties:

1. A tip branch (m, n) of T will be selected during an iteration iff $B(m, n) \leq z$ during that iteration.

2. The value of ITS's threshold z increases monotonically after each iteration.

3. For each instant i, for each branch (m, n) of T, $g(m) + h(m) \leq B(m, n) \leq \text{cost}(P)$, where P is the least costly solution path containing (m, n).

4. Let i be any instant in iteration j, and suppose that at instant i, ITS selects some branch (m, n) and generates n. Let (n, p) be the leftmost branch from n. Then unless $B(n, p) > z$, (n, p) will be selected at instant $i + 1$.

5. No node is generated more than once during each iteration.

Theorem 2 ITS terminates and returns an optimal solution.

Comparison of ITS with IDA*

Theoretical Results

In this section we show the following:

1. ITS never generates a node more times than IDA*. As a consequence, ITS generates every node generated by IDA*, and that for every node n, ITS generates n no more times than IDA* does.

2. There are classes of trees on which ITS will have better asymptotic time complexity than IDA*, even when given no more memory than IDA* (i.e., $S = 0$). The main reason for this is that when ITS retracts nodes, it backs up path information, which allows it to avoid re-generating many subtrees.

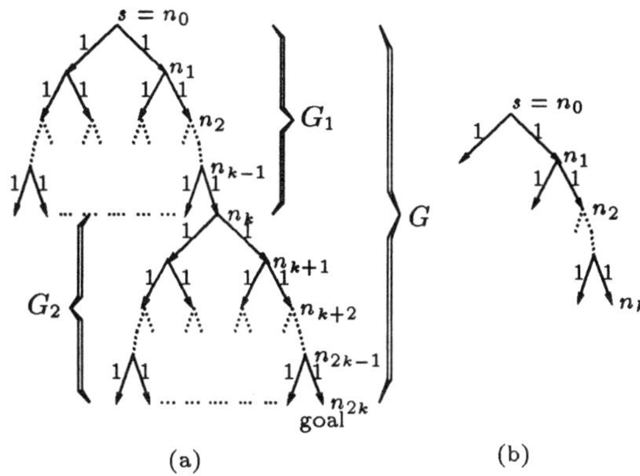

(a)   (b)

Figure 1: A tree G on which IDA* is $O(N \log N)$ and ITS is $O(N)$

Theorem 3 IDA* and ITS do the same number of iterations, and for every j,

{nodes generated in IDA*'s j'th iteration} = {nodes generated in ITS's iterations $1, 2, \ldots, j$}.

Theorem 4 Let G be any state space, and n be any node of G. If IDA* and ITS expand nodes from G in left-to-right order following the same sequence of operators, then

1. ITS and IDA* generate exactly the same set of nodes;

2. For every node n, ITS generates n no more times than IDA* does.

The above theorem shows that ITS's time complexity is never any worse than IDA*'s. Below, we show that there are classes of trees on which ITS does only $O(N)$ node expansions compared to IDA*'s $O(N \log N)$ node expansions on the same trees. The same result also holds for node generations. In the tree in Example 1, it is simpler to count the number of node expansions, and therefore we present the result in terms of node expansions.

Example 1. In the search tree G shown in Figure 1(a), each non-leaf node has a node-branching factor $b = 2$, and each arc has unit cost. G consists of two subtrees G_1 and G_2 where each one is a full binary tree of height k. G_2 is rooted at the right most node of G_1. Every leaf node, except the one labeled as goal, is a non-terminal. For each node n in G, $h(n) = 0$.

Clearly G_1 and G_2 each contain $N' = \lceil N/2 \rceil$ nodes, where N is the number of nodes eligible for expansion by A*. The cost of the solution path is $2k = 2[\log_2(N' + 1) - 1]$. Let $N_0 = b^k + 2b^{k-1} + 3b^{k-2} + \ldots + kb$. Then the total number of node expansions by IDA* in the worst-case is

$$N_0 + kN' + N_0 \geq kN' + N' = k(N' + 1) = O(N \log N).$$

Now we count the total number of node expansions by ITS on G. As in the case of IDA* no node of G_2 will

be expanded prior to the expansion of all the nodes of G_1 at least once. Using the theorem 4, we can infer that the total number of node expansions by ITS on G_1 is $O(N)$. Once ITS begins expanding nodes of G_2, the portion of G_1 that will be retained in memory is shown in Figure 1(b). The branches of G_1 which do not lead a goal node (all left branches) will have B value of ∞. Therefore no node of G_1 will be reexpanded while expanding nodes of G_2. Since G_1 and G_2 are symmetric, by the same argument as in case of G_1, ITS will not make more than $O(N)$ node expansions on G_2. Thus the worst-case time complexity of ITS on trees like G will always be $O(N)$.

Experimental Results

In the example above, we have shown that there are classes of trees on which ITS's asymptotic complexity is better than IDA*'s. In this section we report results of our experiments on three problem domains namely flow-shop scheduling, traveling salesman and 15-puzzle. These problems were selected mainly to encompass a wide range of node generation times. While the node generation time for the 15-puzzle is very small, it is significant for the traveling salesman problem. The node generation time for flow-shop scheduling problem is also small but higher than that of 15-puzzle. All the programs were written in C and run on a SUN sparcstation. We describe the problems and our results in the following sections.

One purpose of our experiments was to compare ITS with IDA*, and another purpose was to see how giving ITS additional memory would improve its performance in terms of both node generation and running time. For the latter purpose, we ran ITS with varying amounts of memory. The definition of ITS includes a parameter S which gives the total amount of memory available to ITS for storing nodes. If $S = 0$, then ITS retracts all nodes except those on the current path. For each problem instance p, let ITS(v) be ITS with $S = vM$, where M is the number of distinct nodes generated by ITS on p. Thus, $v = S/M$ is what fraction ITS gets of the amount of memory it would need in order to avoid doing any retractions.[1] For example, ITS(1) is ITS with enough memory that it doesn't need to retract any nodes, and ITS(1/4) is ITS running with 1/4 of the amount of memory as ITS(1).

Flow-Shop Scheduling Problem The flow-shop scheduling problem is to schedule a given set of jobs on a set of machines such that the time to finish all of the jobs is minimized. In our experiments, we selected the

---

[1] If we had expressed S as an absolute number rather than a fraction of M, this would not have given useful results, because the number of distinct nodes generated by ITS on each problem instance varies widely. For example, with 100,000 nodes, on some problem instances ITS would have exhausted the available memory very quickly, and on others, it would not even have used the whole memory.

Table 1: IDA* and ITS′(0) on the 10-job
3-machine flow-shop scheduling problem.

algorithm	node generations	time (sec)
IDA*	211308.76	3.93
ITS′(0)	210842.96	4.43

Table 2: ITS(v) on the 10-job 3-machine
flow-shop scheduling problem.

v	node generations	time (sec)
0	210842.96	23.22
1/4	123764.71	13.64
1/2	61690.79	6.92
3/4	28174.31	3.32
1	17663.28	1.80

number of machines to be 3. We used a search-space representation and admissible node evaluation function of Ignall and Schrage [5].

For ITS(0), there is a special case to consider. In the flow-shop scheduling problem, it is very easy to generate the successor n' of a node n. Thus, since IDA* and ITS(0) will need to keep track of only one successor of n at a time, both IDA* and ITS(0) can generate n' by modifying the record for n (and undoing this modification later when retracting n'), rather than generating an entirely new record For the flow-shop scheduling problem, we used this technique to improve the efficiency of both IDA* and ITS(0). To distinguish between the normal version of ITS(0) and the improved version, we call the latter ITS′(0).

We ran IDA* and ITS′(0) on 100 problem instances with 10 jobs in the jobset. The processing times of the jobs on the three machines were generated randomly from the range [0,100] using a uniform distribution. Table 1 presents the average node generation and running time figures for IDA* and ITS′(0) on these problem instances. As can be seen, ITS′(0) generated fewer nodes than IDA*. However, ITS′(0) took slightly more time than IDA*. This is primarily because the node generation time for this problem is small, and therefore the smaller number of nodes generated by ITS′(0) did not compensate for its slightly higher overhead than IDA* in node selection and retraction.

We also ran ITS(v) on the same problem instances, with various values of v. The average node generation and running-time figures for ITS(v) are given in Table 2. The table shows that as the amount of available memory increases, ITS improves its performance in terms of both node generations and running time.

Traveling Salesman Problem The traveling salesman problem is as follows: given a set of K cities with nonnegative cost between each pair of cities, find the cheapest tour. A tour is a path that starting at some initial city visits every city once and only once, and returns to the initial city. We chose the well known method of Little et al. [7] to represent the search space and the lower bound heuristic for the traveling salesman problem.

The technique that we used to improve the efficiency of IDA* and ITS(0) in the flow-shop scheduling problem cannot be used in the traveling salesman problem, because in this problem it is much more difficult to generate the successors of a node.

We ran our experiments with the number of cities K equal to 5, 10, 15, 20, 25, 30, 35 and 40. For each value of K, one hundred cost matrices were generated, taking the cost values $c(i, j)$ at random from the interval [0,100] using a uniform distribution (except when $i = j$, in which case $c(i, j) = \infty$). Thus, in general the cost matrices were not symmetric and did not satisfy the triangle inequality.

The results of our experiments are summarized in Figures 2 through 5, which graph the performance of IDA*, ITS(0), ITS(1/4), ITS(1/2), and ITS(1). From figures 2 and 3, it can be seen that on this problem, ITS(0) makes fewer node generations and runs slightly faster than IDA*. This is because the node generation time is large enough that the extra overhead of ITS over IDA* becomes relatively insignificant, and therefore the reduction in number of node generations does reduce the running time. Furthermore, the additional memory used by ITS significantly reduces the number of node generations as well as the running time.

In order to study how IDA*'s average-case asymptotic behavior compares to ITS's, in figures 4 and 5 we have plotted ratios of node generations and running time of IDA* and ITS. The interesting point to be noted about these graphs is that in each case, the ratio first goes up and then goes down. If ITS's asymptotic performance were strictly better than IDA*'s, we would have expected the ratios to keep going up. Since Theorem 4 shows that ITS's asymptotic performance is at least as good as IDA*'s, that both algorithms have the same asymptotic performance on this problem. Since this behavior also occurs for ITS(1), which is essentially a version of A*, this suggests that both ITS and IDA* are asymptotically optimal on the traveling salesman problem (at least in the case when the costs between cities are generated uniformly from a fixed range).

15-Puzzle The 15-puzzle problem consists of a 4×4 frame containing fifteen numbered tiles and an empty position usually known as the "blank". The valid moves slide any tile adjacent to the blank horizontally or vertically to the adjacent blank position. The task is to find a sequence of valid moves which transform some random initial configuration to a desired goal configuration. The manhattan distance function was used as the heuristic in our experiments.

In the 15-puzzle, we made the same efficiency-improving modification to IDA* that we made in the flow-shop scheduling problem. We considered making the same modification to ITS(0), but decided not to run ITS(0) at all on this problem, for the following reason. In the 15-puzzle, with the manhattan distance heuristic, the threshold in every iteration of IDA* and

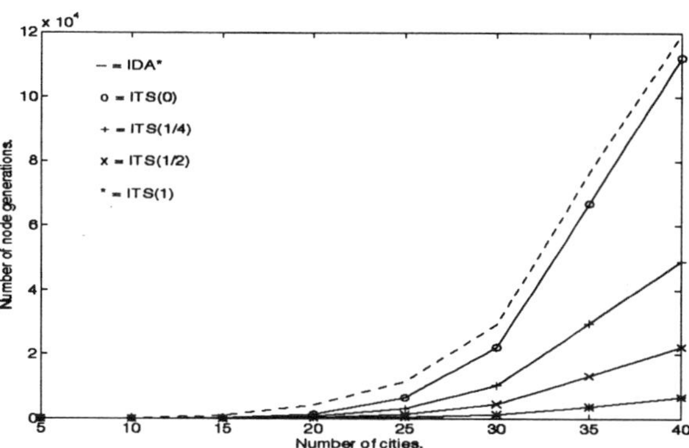

Figure 2: Nodes versus no. of cities.

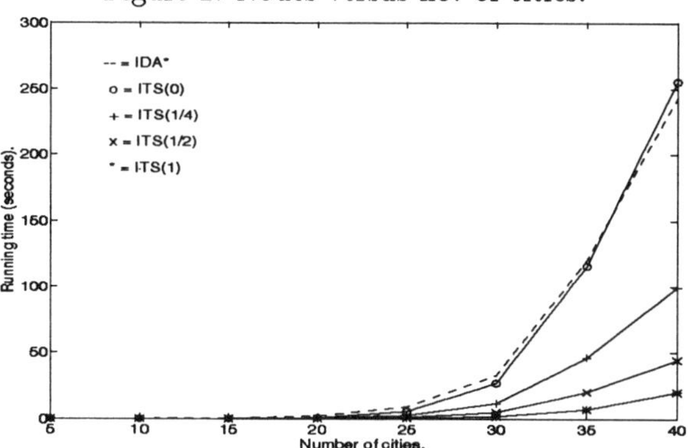

Figure 3: Time versus no. of cities.

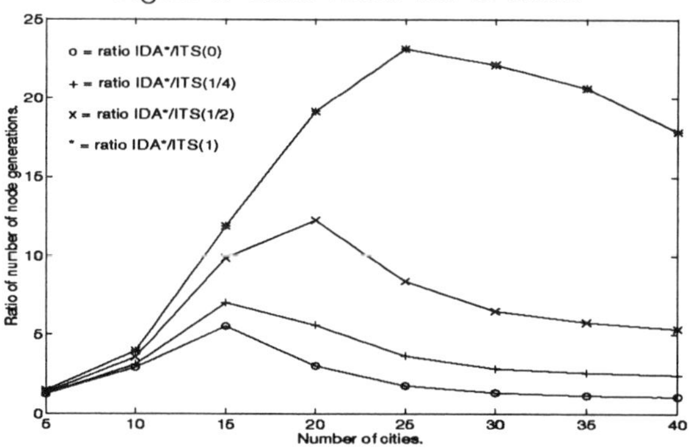

Figure 4: IDA* to ITS nodes, versus no. of cities.

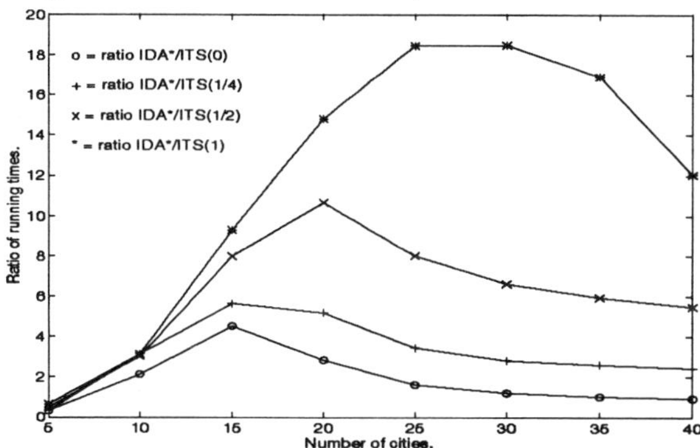

Figure 5: IDA* to ITS time, versus no. of cities.

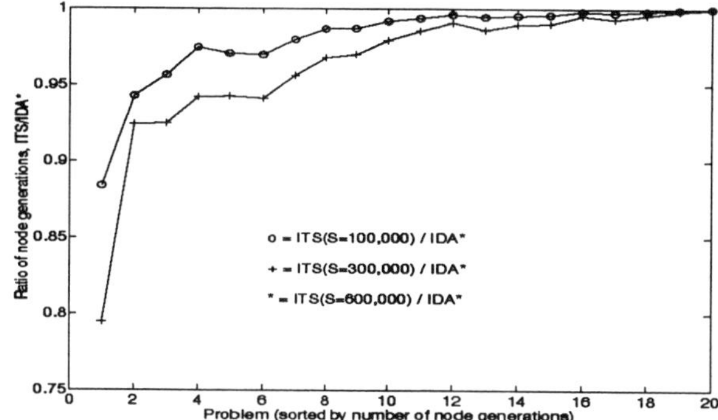

Figure 6: ITS to IDA* nodes on 20 problem instances.

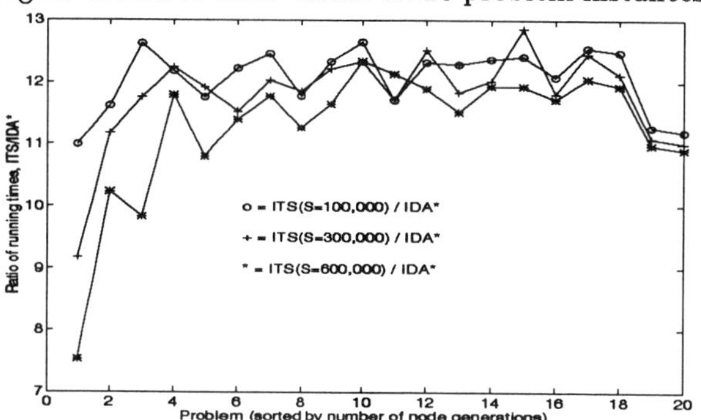

Figure 7: ITS to IDA* time on 20 problem instances.

ITS increases by exactly two. Also, if z is the threshold during the current iteration, every tip branch (p, q) whose B value exceeds z has $B(p, q) = z + 2$. This makes it useless to back-up B values during retraction, because every node that is retracted in iteration i must be regenerated in iteration $i + 1$. Thus, in order to improve the efficiency of ITS(0) on this this problem, we should not only simplify the node-generation scheme as described in the flow-shop scheduling problem, but should also remove the back-up step. But that makes ITS(0) essentially identical to IDA*.

The same reasoning suggests that on the 15-puzzle, even if $S \neq 0$, ITS will not reduce the number of node generations very much in comparison with IDA*. If IDA* makes I iterations on a problem, then ITS with S amount of memory will save at most $S * I$ number of node generations. Since I is usually small for 15-puzzle (between 5 and 10), the actual savings is expected to be relatively small. Thus, since ITS has higher overhead than IDA*, we would expect ITS to take more time than IDA* on this problem.

To confirm these hypotheses, we ran ITS and IDA* with $S = 100,000$, $300,000$, and $600,000$ on the twenty problem instances on which Chakrabarti *et al.* ran MA*(0). We could not run ITS(v) on these problem instances because the number of distinct nodes is so large on some of the problem instances that they exceed the available memory. Therefore, we had to run ITS with fixed values for S. The results are summarized in Figures 6 and 7. As expected, ITS did not achieve a significant reduction in the number of node generations, and took significantly more time than IDA*.[2] Thus, for the 15-puzzle, IDA* is the preferable algorithm.

Related Work

Following IDA*, several other limited-memory algorithms have been designed to reduce the number of node generations compared to IDA*. These algorithms can be categorized into two classes: (1) the first class uses additional memory to store more nodes than IDA*, and thereby reduce regeneration of some nodes. The algorithms which belong to this class are MREC, MA*, RA* [3], SMA* [10], and ITS, and (2) the second class of algorithms attempts to reduce node regenerations by reducing the number of iterations, by increasing the threshold more liberally than IDA*. IDA*_CR [11], DFS* [9], and MIDA* [13] belong to this class.

Like IDA*, MREC is a recursive search algorithm. The difference between MREC and other algorithms in its class is that MREC allocates its memory statically, in the order in which nodes are generated. Algorithm MA* makes use of the available memory in a more intelligent fashion, by storing the best nodes generated so far. MA* does top-down and bottom-up propagation of heuristics and generates one successor at a time. RA* and SMA* are simplified versions of MA*, with some differences.

Although algorithms MA*, RA*, and SMA* are limited-memory algorithms, their formulation is more similar to A*'s than IDA*'s. They all maintain OPEN and CLOSED, select the best/worst node from OPEN for expansion and pruning. Therefore, their node generation/pruning overhead is much higher than IDA*'s. As a result, even if they generate fewer nodes than IDA*, they do not always run faster than IDA*. ITS's formulation is similar to IDA*'s and therefore has a low node-generation overhead than any of them.

Algorithms IDA*_CR, MIDA*, and DFS* work similar to IDA* except that they set successive thresholds to values larger than the minimum value that exceeded the previous threshold. This reduces the number of iterations and therefore the total number of node generations. However, unlike IDA*, the first solution found by these algorithms is not necessarily optimal and therefore to guarantee optimal solution, these algorithms revert to depth-first branch-and-bound in the last iteration.

Finally, it should be noted that the techniques used in the two classes of algorithms can be combined.

Conclusion

We have presented a new algorithm called ITS for tree search in limited memory. Like IDA*, ITS has low

node-generation overhead—and like MA*, it makes dynamic use of memory. Our theoretical analysis shows that, ITS never does more node generations than IDA* and there are trees where it generates fewer nodes than IDA*. Our experimental results indicate that with additional memory, ITS can significantly reduce the number of node generations and run faster on problems for which the node-generation time is sufficiently high.

References

[1] P. P. Chakrabarti, S. Ghosh, A. Acharya, and S. C. De Sarkar. Heuristic search in restricted memory. *Artif. Intel.*, 47:197–221, 1989.

[2] R. Dechter and J. Pearl. Generalized best-first search strategies and the optimality of A*. *JACM*, 32(3):505–536, 1985.

[3] M. Evett, J. Hendler, A. Mahanti, and D. Nau. PRA*: A memory-limited heuristic search procedure for the connection machine. In *Frontiers'90: Frontiers of Massively Parallel Computation*, 1990.

[4] S. Ghosh. *Heuristic Search with Limited Resources*. PhD thesis, Department of Computer Science, University of Maryland, 1994 (forthcoming).

[5] E. Ignall and L. Schrage. Applications of the branch and bound technique to some flowshop scheduling problems. *Operations Research*, 13(3):400–412, 1965.

[6] R. E. Korf. Depth first iterative deepening: An optimal admissible tree search. *Artif. Intel.*, 27:97–109, 1985.

[7] J. D. Little, K. G. Murty, D. W. Sweeney, and C. Karel. An algorithm for the traveling salesman problem. *Operations Research*, 11:972–989, 1963.

[8] B. G. Patrick, M. Almulla, and M. M. Newborn. An upper bound on the complexity of iterative-deepening-A*. In *Symposium on Artif. Intel. and Mathematics*, Fort Lauderdale, FL, 1989.

[9] V. N. Rao and V. Kumar R. E. Korf. Depth-first vs. best-first search. In *AAAI-1991*, pages 434–440, Anaheim, California, 1991.

[10] S. Russell. Efficient memory-bounded search methods. In *ECAI-1992*, Vienna, Austria, 1992.

[11] U. K. Sarkar, P. P. Chakrabarti, S. Ghose, and S. C. De Sarkar. Reducing reexpansions in iterative deepening search by controlling cutoff bounds. *Artif. Intel.*, 50(2):207–221, 1991.

[12] A. Sen and A. Bagchi. Fast recursive formulations for best-first search that allow controlled use of memory. In *IJCAI-89*, pages 274–277, 1989.

[13] B. W. Wah. MIDA*, an IDA* search with dynamic control. Technical Report UILU-ENG-91-2216, University of Illinois at Urbana, Champaign-Urbana, IL, 1991.

---

[2]Oddly, Figure 7 shows a relative improvement for ITS at the two largest problem sizes. However, we suspect that these data are spurious, because on these two problem instances, we exceeded the maximum integer size of some of our counters and also encountered thrashing.

Memory-Bounded Bidirectional Search

Hermann Kaindl
Siemens AG Österreich
Geusaugasse 17
A–1030 Wien, Austria — Europe
e-mail: kaih@siemens.co.at

Aliasghar Khorsand
Huglgasse 13-15/6
A–1150 Wien
Austria — Europe

Abstract

Previous approaches to bidirectional search require exponential space, and they are either less efficient than unidirectional search for finding *optimal* solutions, or they cannot even find such solutions for difficult problems. Based on a memory-bounded unidirectional algorithm for trees (SMA^*), we developed a graph search extension, and we used it to construct a very efficient memory-bounded bidirectional algorithm. This bidirectional algorithm can be run for difficult problems with bounded memory. In addition, it is much more efficient than the corresponding unidirectional search algorithm also for finding optimal solutions to difficult problems. In summary, bidirectional search appears to be the best approach to solving difficult problems, and this indicates the extreme usefulness of a paradigm that was neglected for long.

Notation

s, t	Start node and goal node, respectively.
$\Gamma_1(n)$	Successors of node n in the problem graph.
$\Gamma_2(n)$	Parents of node n in the problem graph.
d	Current search direction index; when search is in the forward direction $d = 1$, and when in the backward direction $d = 2$.
d'	$3 - d$; it is the index of the direction opposite to the current search direction.
$g_i^*(n)$	Cost of an optimal path from s to n if $i = 1$, or from t to n if $i = 2$.
$h_i^*(n)$	Cost of an optimal path from n to t if $i = 1$, or from n to s if $i = 2$.
$g_i(n), h_i(n)$	Estimates of $g_i^*(n)$ and $h_i^*(n)$, respectively.
$f_i(n)$	Static evaluation function.
$F_i(n)$	Revised evaluation after pathmax or backup.
C^*	Cost of an optimal path from s to t.
C	Cost of a solution path from s to t found.
$L_{\min}$	Cost of the best (least costly) complete path found so far from s to t.
TREE_1	The forward search tree.
TREE_2	The backward search tree.
OPEN_i	The set of open nodes in TREE_i.
CLOSED_i	The set of closed nodes in TREE_i.
$p_i(n)$	Parent of node n in TREE_i.

Introduction

Originally, bidirectional heuristic search did not work as expected. Although the bidirectional approach was shown to be more efficient than its unidirectional counterpart when heuristic knowledge is unavailable, the inverse result was found in experiments with *BHPA* using a heuristic evaluation function (Pohl 1971). BS^* (Kwa 1989) improved *BHPA* technically, but its performance was only nearly as good as the unidirectional A^* (Hart, Nilsson, & Raphael 1968). There was consensus that bidirectional heuristic search is afflicted with the problem of search fronts missing each other. Consequently, *wave-shaping* techniques were investigated (de Champeaux & Sint 1977; de Champeaux 1983; Davis, Pollack, & Sudkamp 1984; Politowski & Pohl 1984). This work showed that bidirectional heuristic search can be rather efficient in terms of the number of expanded nodes. However, these algorithms are either excessively computationally demanding, or they have no restriction on the solution quality.

Recent results show that the missing of the search fronts is not the central problem (Köll & Kaindl 1993). In fact, the fronts typically meet rather early. However, when aiming for *optimal* solutions, much effort has to be spent for subsequently improving the solution quality, and finally for proving that there is indeed no better solution possible. Therefore, only slightly relaxing the requirements on the solution quality yields strong improvements in efficiency.

In fact, the algorithms presented in (Köll & Kaindl 1993) proved that the bidirectional paradigm is efficient in terms of node expansions when searching for ε-admissible solutions, without using computationally very demanding wave-shaping techniques.[1]

However, while efficient *linear-space* algorithms like IDA^* (Korf 1985) and $RBFS$ (Korf 1993) have been developed for the unidirectional case, classical bidirectional search typically requires exponential space. (Usually, two classical *best-first* searches like A^* are used for the opposing search fronts.) In fact, is seems impossible to implement bidirectional search

---

[1] A search algorithm is called ε-*admissible* if it guarantees that solution costs are bounded by $(1 + \varepsilon)C^*$, i.e., a factor of the cost of an optimal solution (Pearl & Kim 1982; Pearl 1984). This is the same approach as the one of an ε-*approximate* algorithm (Horowitz & Sahni 1978) which shall find approximate solutions to NP-hard problems.

with linear-space requirement, since at least part of one of the search fronts must be in memory in order to recognize meeting of these fronts. Therefore, it would seem that bidirectional search cannot be used for problems of the same difficulty as solvable by linear-space algorithms due to its apparently inherent memory requirement.[2]

In this paper, we show how bidirectional search can be performed very efficiently using *bounded* memory. The key idea is to use a unidirectional algorithm that is memory-bounded by it own — instead of best-first algorithms with exponential memory requirements like A^*. From several such approaches existing today (MA^* (Chakrabarti *et al.* 1989), $MREC$ (Sen & Bagchi 1989), the approach of using certain tables for IDA^* (Reinefeld & Marsland 1991), and ITS (Mahanti *et al.* 1992)), we selected the first one, since it grows the search tree dynamically. Unfortunately, there are several technical problems with the algorithm MA^*. Therefore, we used the improved SMA^* by Russell (Russell 1992) as a basis for our bidirectional algorithms. Actually, we extended it first for directed acyclic graphs (which is not trivial due to its strategy of deleting and re-generating nodes).

While our bidirectional algorithm does not contain additional new techniques, it is a rather complicated integration of several approaches. This integration is necessary for showing an important result: bidirectional heuristic search can be performed efficiently with bounded memory, and it can be more efficient than corresponding unidirectional search also for finding optimal solutions.

First, we describe the development of an ε-admissible graph search extension of SMA^* — we named it $WSMAG^*$ (weighted simplified memory-bounded A^* for graphs). Based on it, we show our construction of bidirectional search with bounded memory — the algorithm we present here is called $MBBS$ (memory-bounded bidirectional search). Then we illustrate the key results and compare them to related work. Finally, we discuss *why* our approach works well.

An ε-Admissible Graph-Search Extension of SMA^*

A short review of SMA^*

SMA^* is a direct successor of MA^*. A key idea of these algorithms is to tradeoff the number of nodes generated and the number of nodes saved. They retain as many nodes as possible, and prefer to retain the most promising ones. As soon as the given memory limit is reached, MA^* prunes all but the ones with the best evaluation (f-cost). In contrast to A^*, these algorithms only partially-expand nodes, generating the successors one at a time.

---

[2]A bidirectional algorithm sketched in (Korf 1985) utilizes *depth-first iterative-deepening* (without using heuristic knowledge). Still, its space requirement is $O(b^{d/2})$.

Unfortunately, MA^* is quite complicated and very difficult to implement efficiently (Korf 1993). Even worse, it is not correct in the sense that it can return suboptimal solutions (Mahanti *et al.* 1992), although Chakrabarti *et al.* claimed its *admissibility*.

SMA^* improves MA^*, since it preserves information using "pathmax" with the backed-up f-costs (see line 9 in the pseudocode of $WSMAG^*$ in Appendix A), while MA^* loses this information. Moreover, SMA^* maintains fewer f-cost quantities (making it simpler), and it backs up values once per fully-expanded node, rather than once per node generated (reducing the overhead). Finally, SMA^* adds and prunes only one node at a time (saving re-generations of nodes).

Unfortunately, the pseudocode in (Russell 1992) contains some few bugs.[3] An improved (and more formal) pseudocode of SMA^* can be found in Appendix A, when omitting lines 10 and 11, and using $\varepsilon = 0$ in line 8. Moreover, SMA^* as presented in (Russell 1992) only deals with the case of finding *optimal* solutions and *tree* search.

ε-admissibility

The extension of SMA^* to an ε-admissible version is analogous to the corresponding extensions of IDA^* to $WIDA^*$ or of A^* to WA^* (which we call HPA^* for historic reasons) (Korf 1993). It is just necessary to multiply the heuristic component h of the usual A^*-type evaluation by a weight. According to the notation in (Pearl & Kim 1982), we use the weight $(1 + \varepsilon)$ (see line 8 of $WSMAG^*$ in Appendix A). We named this ε-admissible algorithm $WSMA^*$.

Graph search

The extension of SMA^* from searching trees to dealing with directed acyclic graphs is less trivial. In A^*, this issue is usually dealt with by simply moving a repeatedly found node from CLOSED back to OPEN. Such simple attempts for a straight-forward solution can lead to infinite loops due to SMA^*'s strategy of deleting and re-generating nodes (Khorsand 1994). The best way to solve this issue that we found uses a technique we call *blocking* (see the pseudocode of GRAPH-CONTROL in Appendix A). Whenever a new path to a node already stored is found, a distinction is made whether the new path is better than the old one. If this is not the case, the arc from the parent on the new path

---

[3]*best* ← deepest least-f-cost leaf in OPEN;
should be ... node ... instead of ... leaf ..., since each partially expanded node should be selectable for further expansion;
delete shallowest, highest-f-cost node in OPEN;
should be ... leaf ... instead of ... node ..., since only nodes without any generated successor can be deleted safely;
the procedure BACKUP should have the structure given in Appendix A; otherwise no backup of the value could occur to the root.

is permanently deleted, otherwise the one from the parent on the old path. Moreover, when the new path is better, the subtree previously grown from this node is pruned. In both cases it must be checked whether the other successors of the respective parent of the common node are also blocked. If this is the case and this parent node is already completed, then also this node is deleted, and the blocking mechanism is performed recursively (see SUCC-CHECK in Appendix A).

We call the resulting (ε-admissible) algorithm for directed acyclic graphs $WSMAG^*$ (for details see (Khorsand 1994)). The complete pseudocode is given in Appendix A.

Bidirectional Heuristic Search with Bounded Memory

The classical approaches to implementing bidirectional search typically use A^*- or HPA^*-type search from both sides concurrently. On a single processor, of course, only one direction can be followed at a time. For the selection of search direction, (Pohl 1971) proposed the so-called cardinality criterion (see line 4 of $MBBS$ in Appendix B).

Since this approach runs into trouble when the memory is limited, we use instead the memory-bounded $WSMAG^*$ algorithm from both sides. In the following, we sketch the development of an efficient memory-bounded bidirectional algorithm based on this idea.[4]

First, the two search fronts using $WSMAG^*$ must meet each other. Since both these dynamically grown trees are stored, this meeting can be efficiently checked using hashing. However, meeting just means that any solution was found. Therefore, it may be necessary to continue the search until a solution of required quality is detected. Even if that is the case, the search may not yet know it.

The *termination condition* of a heuristic bidirectional search is usually based on the best heuristic estimates in both search fronts. When dealing with ε-admissible search, an improved termination condition as introduced in IBS_ε^* (Köll & Kaindl 1993) can be used (see line 3 of $MBBS$ in Appendix B). Since for checking this termination condition the $g+h$-values are needed (in addition to the F-costs used by SMA^*), the backup procedure was extended accordingly.

Moreover, it is useful to consider whether and how the technical improvements of BS^* (Kwa 1989) to $BHPA$ are also applicable in our approach.[5] Because

---

[4] Actually, we developed several bidirectional algorithms along the lines of (Köll & Kaindl 1993), but we focus on the most efficient one in this paper. The other algorithms and details are described in (Khorsand 1994).

[5] These improvements are the following:
(i) *nipping*: When a node is selected for expansion which is already closed in the opposite search tree, it can just be closed *without* expansion.
(ii) *pruning*: In the same situation, descendants of this node in the opposing OPEN list can be removed.
(iii) *trimming*: Open Nodes (in both directions) whose f-

of the partial-node-expansion strategy of SMA^* as well as its method of deleting and re-generating nodes, there are significant differences to BS^* that do not allow the use of its *nipping* and *pruning* technique in our approach. However, *trimming* and *screening* are very useful especially for the task of finding optimal solutions, and these techniques fit well into the paradigm of deleting nodes by SMA^* (see lines 14–16 and 31–33 of $MBBS$ in Appendix B). However, similar to the extension of dealing with graphs, it is necessary here to use the blocking technique described above. The parents of the currently best node (in the case of screening) or of all the trimmed nodes must be checked whether their other successors are also blocked (see lines 16 and 33).

The pseudocode of $MBBS$ is given in Appendix B. Its subroutines are analogous to those of $WSMAG^*$.

Results

Given an admissible heuristic h, both $WSMAG^*$ and $MBBS$ are ε-admissible, i.e., if a path exists from s to t, they terminate with a solution whose cost does not exceed the optimal cost by more than a factor $(1 + \varepsilon)$. Due to lack of space we cannot include here the formal proofs (see (Khorsand 1994)).

Below we summarize the empirical results of extensive experiments on an NP-complete problem (finding optimal solutions to the 15-Puzzle) and on the relaxed problem of finding near-optimal solutions (with a guaranteed worst-case bound). Fig. 1 compares $WSMAG^*$ and $MBBS$ (storing 256k nodes) with several algorithms.[6] The x-axis represents various values of ε, the given worst-case bound as guaranteed by these algorithms. The comparison is in terms of generated nodes as, e.g., in (Köll & Kaindl 1993; Korf 1993), and the y-axis shows the average number of node generations on the 15-Puzzle on a logarithmic scale.

This figure and statistical tests (for details see (Khorsand 1994)) demonstrate the following key results:

- *Significant superiority of $MBBS$ to (unidirectional) linear-space search in terms of generated nodes*
  On the whole range, $MBBS$ generates much fewer nodes than $WIDA^*$ and $RBFS$. Therefore, $MBBS$ makes excellent use of the modest amount of memory given — 256k nodes: 2 orders of magnitude more

---

values are $\geq L_{min}$ can be removed.
(iv) *screening*: Nodes whose f-values are $\geq L_{min}$ need not to be stored in the OPEN lists.

[6] We have used the set of 100 instances from (Korf 1985). The data in the figure currently lack the results of the 11 most difficult problems, since these experiments are for some of the algorithms still running at the time of this writing. Since HPA^* and IBS_ε^* cannot solve all these instances for all values of ε even when storing millions of nodes, their corresponding lines are not complete in this figure.

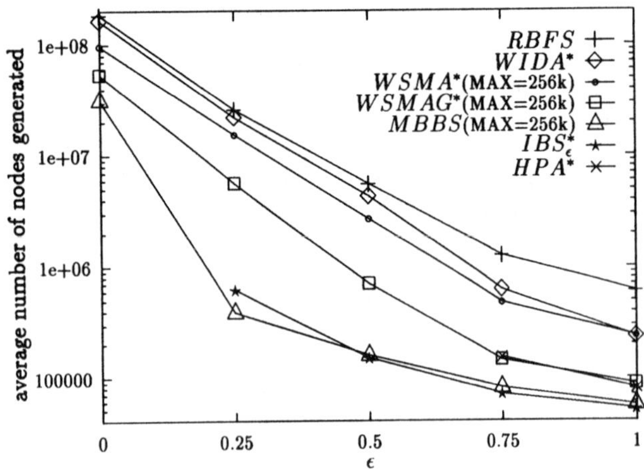

Figure 1: Comparison on the 15-Puzzle.

nodes are generated in the average for finding optimal solutions. However, for the task of finding optimal solutions ($\varepsilon = 0$), $WIDA^*$ is still faster on this puzzle (see below).

- *Significant superiority of the novel bidirectional approach to the corresponding unidirectional one (using the same amount of memory)*
  Also for finding optimal solutions $MBBS$ is significantly better than both $WSMA^*$ and $WSMAG^*$. Generally, the improvement is even slightly stronger comparing the run time, since instead of one priority queue the bidirectional algorithm uses two shorter ones.

- *Significant superiority of the memory-bounded bidirectional search to classical (unidirectional) best-first search (HPA*)*
  The improvement in terms of node generations is statistically significant, although $MBBS$ stores much fewer nodes. For $\varepsilon \leq 0.5$, HPA^* cannot even find solutions to all the problems even when storing millions of nodes.

- *Comparable results of the memory-bounded to more classical bidirectional search (IBS_ε^*), that uses much more memory*
  The memory-bounded approach is even significantly better for $\varepsilon = 0.25$ due to its partial node expansions.

Despite Russell's improvements to MA^*, an efficient implementation of these memory-bounded algorithms is non-trivial (see (Khorsand 1994) for the data structures used instead of the binary trees of binary trees suggested by Russell, which are not efficient for the (usual version of) the sliding-tile puzzles with uniform-cost evaluation). Unfortunately, it strongly depends on the domain and also the efficiency of implementation, whether the overhead of maintaining the priority queues is deteriorating the performance or not. In particular, the importance of the overhead depends on the effort for computing heuristic values. Even the machine architecture can influence the relative running time when there are differences in the size of memory used. While node generation and evaluation is very efficient for the sliding-tile puzzles (Korf 1993), we primarily wanted to compare the algorithms on a basis that is more independent of such factors.

Compared to the worst-case bound ε, the *average* solution quality is much better for all the algorithms compared here. For $\varepsilon = 0.25$, e.g., the cost C of a solution found must be ≤ 1.25 times the cost of an optimal solution C^*. In the average, $MBBS$ finds solutions of quality $C = 1.04C^*$ here, i.e., they are only 4 percent worse than optimal ones, which require about eighty times more node generations to be found.

Related Work

Apart from the genesis of $MBBS$ based on the unidirectional A^*, MA^* and SMA^*, as well as the bidirectional $BHPA$, BS^* and IBS_ε^*, there are some relations to other *unidirectional* search algorithms with reduced space requirements. We focus here on their results on the sliding-tile puzzles:

- $MREC$ (Sen & Bagchi 1989) did not achieve a real improvement over IDA^*, partly because they used a *tree* version; (Korf 1993) reports that the number of node generations of a *graph* version storing 100k nodes reduced the number of node generations by 41 percent compared to IDA^* on the 15-Puzzle;

- ITS (Mahanti *et al.* 1992) generated the same number of nodes as IDA^* on the 15-Puzzle;

- the best version of the approach of using certain tables for IDA^* (Reinefeld & Marsland 1991) examined 45.82 percent of the nodes generated by pure IDA^*, storing 256k nodes.

In summary, all these algorithms are less efficient than our bidirectional search algorithm $MBBS$ even for finding *optimal* solutions (at least on the difficult 15-Puzzle and in terms of node generations). Moreover, $MBBS$ can find near-optimal solutions with a guaranteed worst-case bound, a task on which it is even much more efficient.

Discussion

An interesting question is how this bidirectional approach can be better than its unidirectional counterpart. In an exponential search space, bidirectional search has the potential to divide the exponent by 2. However, the first results with bidirectional *heuristic* search were bad (Pohl 1971), and the explanation given there in terms of the *missile metaphor* was misleading. The primary issue appears to be that after the first meeting especially a bidirectional algorithm aiming for *optimal* solutions has to spend much effort for subsequently improving the solution quality, and finally for proving that no other open node can give a better solution (Köll & Kaindl 1993). Therefore, only a slight relaxation of solution quality already leads to strong improvements in efficiency, and in particular to even more than in the unidirectional case. Actually, the results of $MBBS$ for $\varepsilon = 0.25$ are relatively much better than those for $\varepsilon = 0$.

However, Kwa (Kwa 1989) already noted the relative improvement of BS^* versus A^* with increasing problem difficulty (in the context of finding optimal solutions). This tendency was also observed in the case of finding near-optimal solutions (Köll & Kaindl 1993). Consequently, the dynamic memory utilization of $MBBS$ (based on SMA^*) allows it to perform the bidirectional search efficiently for problems that are difficult enough to make it better than its unidirectional counterpart.

Conclusion

In summary, we developed a graph search extension of SMA^*, and we used this unidirectional algorithm to construct a very efficient memory-bounded bidirectional algorithm. This algorithm can use as much memory as there is available (a constant amount).

The construction of this algorithm uses primarily known techniques (apart from the graph search extension with its novel blocking mechanism). However, this combination is necessary for showing an important result: bidirectional heuristic search can be performed efficiently with bounded memory, and it can be more efficient than its unidirectional counterpart also for finding *optimal* solutions.

If problems are too difficult for finding optimal solutions within reasonable time, finding near-optimal (ε-admissible with a small ε) solutions may help. For this task the bidirectional approach is even better.

Acknowledgments

We would like to thank Dennis de Champeaux, Gerhard Kainz, and Ira Pohl for comments on earlier versions of this paper. Our implementations are based on the code of WA^* provided by Richard Korf.

APPENDIX A: Pseudocode of WSMAG*

```
procedure WSMAG*(s, t);
 1. OPEN ← {s}; CLOSED ← ∅; USED ← 1;
 2. while ( OPEN ≠ ∅ ) and (no solution found) do
        /* select deepest node with lowest F-value : */
 3.     B ← {x | (x ∈ OPEN) ∧ (∀y ∈ OPEN: F(x) ≤ F(y))};
                    /* set of nodes with lowest F-value */
 4.     select best ∈ {x | x ∈ B ∧ (∀y ∈ B: g(x) ≥ g(y))};
                    /* deepest node from B */
 5.     if best ≠ t then    /* best is not goal */
 6.         succ ← next-successor ∈ Γ(best);
 7.         g(succ) ← g(best) + c(best, succ);
 8.         f(succ) ← g(succ) + (1+ε)·h(succ);
 9.         F(succ) ← max(F(best), f(succ));    /* pathmax */
10.         if succ ∈ TREE then    /* succ already stored */
11.             GRAPH-CONTROL;
            else
12.             MEM-CONTROL;
13.             OPEN ← OPEN ∪ {succ}; USED ← USED + 1;
                            /* insert succ in OPEN */
14.             S(best) ← S(best) ∪ {succ};
                            /* insert succ in best's successor list */
            endif
15.         if completed(best) then
16.             BACKUP(best);
            endif
17.         if Γ(best) all in memory then
18.             OPEN ← OPEN \ {best};
19.             CLOSED ← CLOSED ∪ {best};    /* close best */
            endif
        endif
    endwhile
endprocedure

procedure MEM-CONTROL;
    /* if memory is full, delete a node */
 1. if USED = MAX then
        /* delete shallowest, highest- F-value leaf in OPEN ,
           a leaf node has no successor either in OPEN or CLOSED : */
 2.     W ← {x | (x ∈ OPEN) ∧ (∀y ∈ OPEN: F(x) ≥ F(y))};
 3.     select worst ∈ {x | x ∈ W ∧ (∀y ∈ W: g(x) ≤ g(y)) ∧ (S(x) = ∅)};
 4.     delete worst;
 5.     USED ← USED - 1; /* remove worst from its parent's succ. list */
 6.     S(p(worst)) ← S(p(worst)) \ {worst};
 7.     if p(worst) ∈ CLOSED then
 8.         CLOSED ← CLOSED \ {p(worst)};
 9.         OPEN ← OPEN ∪ {p(worst)};
        endif
    endif
endprocedure

procedure BACKUP(n)
    /* back up F-values */
 1. if completed(n) then
        /* least F-value of all successors: */
 2.     newF ← F(x) | x ∈ Γ(n) ∧ (∀y ∈ Γ(n): F(x) ≤ F(y));
 3.     if newF > F(n) then
 4.         F(n) ← newF;
 5.         reorder OPEN according to new F-value;
 6.         if n has a parent then
 7.             BACKUP(p(n));
            endif
        endif
    endif
endprocedure

procedure GRAPH-CONTROL;
    /* deal with directed acyclic graphs */
 1. old ← old node which is equal to succ ;
 2. if g(succ) ≥ g(old) then    /* new path is not better */
 3.     block succ in best's successor list;
 4.     SUCC-CHECK(best);
    else    /* a better path to old has been found */
 5.     prune subtree(old);
        /* remove all nodes which are in subtree with root old */
 6.     block old in p(old)'s successor list;
 7.     USED ← USED - |subtree (old)|;
 8.     SUCC-CHECK(p(old));
 9.     OPEN ← OPEN ∪ {succ}; USED ← USED + 1;
                            /* insert succ in OPEN */
10.     S(best) ← S(best) ∪ {succ}; /* insert succ in best's succ. list */
    endif
endprocedure

procedure SUCC-CHECK(n)
    /* checks whether the other successors are also "blocked" */
 1. if completed(n) and n has only "blocked" successors then
 2.     delete n; USED ← USED - 1;
 3.     block n in p(n)'s successor list;
```

4.   if n has a parent **then**
5.   SUCC-CHECK(p(n));
        endif
    else
6.   BACKUP(n);
    endif
endprocedure

APPENDIX B: Pseudocode of MBBS

procedure MBBS(s, t);
1. $OPEN_1 \leftarrow \{s\}$; $OPEN_2 \leftarrow \{t\}$; $CLOSED_1 \leftarrow CLOSED_2 \leftarrow \varnothing$;
2. $USED_1 \leftarrow USED_2 \leftarrow 1$; $L_{min} \leftarrow \infty$;
3. **while** $(OPEN_1 \neq \varnothing)$ **and** $(OPEN_2 \neq \varnothing)$
        and $(L_{min} > (1+\varepsilon) \cdot \max(ghmin_1, ghmin_2))$ **do**
4.   **if** $|OPEN_1| \leq |OPEN_2|$ **then**   /* cardinality criterion */
5. $d \leftarrow 1$; **else** $d \leftarrow 2$;
        endif
6. $d' \leftarrow 3 - d$;   /* set the opposite search direction */
7.   Trimflag $\leftarrow$ **false**;
        /* select deepest node with lowest F-value : */
8. $B \leftarrow \{x \mid (x \in OPEN_d) \wedge (\forall y \in OPEN_d : F_d(x) \leq F_d(y))\}$;
                        /* set of nodes with lowest F-value */
9.   *select* best $\in \{x \mid x \in B \wedge (\forall y \in B : g_d(x) \geq g_d(y))\}$;
                        /* deepest node from B */
10.   succ $\leftarrow$ next-successor $\in \Gamma_d(best)$;
11. $g_d(succ) \leftarrow g_d(best) + c(best, succ)$;
12. $f_d(succ) \leftarrow g_d(succ) + (1+\varepsilon) \cdot h_d(succ)$;
13. $F_d(succ) \leftarrow \max(F_d(best), f_d(succ))$; /* pathmax */
14.   **if** $g_d(succ) + h_d(succ) \geq L_{min}$ **then**   /*screening */
15.   *block* succ in best's successor list;
16.   SUCC-CHECK(best);
        else
17.   **if** succ $\in TREE_d$ **then**   /* succ already stored */
18.   GRAPH-CONTROL;
            else
19.   MEM-CONTROL;
20. $OPEN_d \leftarrow OPEN_d \cup \{succ\}$; $USED_d \leftarrow USED_d + 1$;
                        /* insert succ in OPEN */
21. $S_d(best) \leftarrow S_d(best) \cup \{succ\}$;
                        /* insert n succ best's successor list */
            endif
22.   **if** succ $\in TREE_{d'}$ **and** $g_1(succ) + g_2(succ) < L_{min}$ **then**
                        /* better solution found */
23. $L_{min} \leftarrow g_1(succ) + g_2(succ)$;   /* update L_{min} */
24.   MeetingNode $\leftarrow$ succ;
25.   Trimflag $\leftarrow$ **true**;
            endif
        endif
26.   **if** *completed*(best) **then**
27.   NEW-BACKUP(best);
        endif
28.   **if** $\Gamma_d(best)$ all in memory **then**
29. $OPEN_d \leftarrow OPEN_d \setminus \{best\}$;
30. $CLOSED_d \leftarrow CLOSED_d \cup \{best\}$;   /close best */
        endif
31.   **if** Trimflag **then**   /* trimming */
32.   *remove* from $OPEN_1$ and $OPEN_2$ those nodes n with
            $g(n) + h(n) \geq L_{min}$ and which have no successors and
            are not source or meeting nodes; block them in their
            parent's successor list;.
33.   SUCC-CHECK(p(n));   /* parents of all removed nodes */
        endif
    endwhile
endprocedure

References

Chakrabarti, P.; Ghose, S.; Acharya, A.; and DeSarkar, S. 1989. Heuristic search in restricted memory. *Artificial Intelligence* 41(2):197–221.

Davis, H.; Pollack, R.; and Sudkamp, T. 1984. Towards a better understanding of bidirectional search. In *Proc. of AAAI-84*, 68–72. Austin, TX: Los Altos, CA.: Kaufmann.

de Champeaux, D., and Sint, L. 1977. An improved bidirectional heuristic search algorithm. *J. ACM* 24:177–191.

de Champeaux, D. 1983. Bidirectional heuristic search again. *J. ACM* 30:22–32.

Hart, P.; Nilsson, N.; and Raphael, B. 1968. A formal basis for the heuristic determination of minimum cost paths. *IEEE Transactions on Systems Science and Cybernetics (SSC)* SSC-4(2):100–107.

Horowitz, E., and Sahni, S. 1978. *Fundamentals of Computer Algorithms*. New York: Springer-Verlag.

Khorsand, A. 1994. Heuristische Graph-Suche mit begrenzbarem Fehler und Speicherbedarf sowie Einheitskosten. Diplomarbeit, Technische Universität Wien.

Köll, A., and Kaindl, H. 1993. Bidirectional best-first search with bounded error: Summary of results. In *Proc. Thirteenth International Joint Conference on Artificial Intelligence (IJCAI-93)*, 217–223.

Korf, R. 1985. Depth-first iterative deepening: An optimal admissible tree search. *Artificial Intelligence* 27(1):97–109.

Korf, R. 1993. Linear-space best-first search. *Artificial Intelligence* 62(1):41–78.

Kwa, J. 1989. BS*: An Admissible Bidirectional Staged Heuristic Search Algorithm. *Artificial Intelligence* 38(2):95–109.

Mahanti, A.; Nau, D.; Ghosh, S.; and Kanal, L. 1992. An efficient threshold heuristic tree search algorithm. Technical Report UMIACS TR 92-29, CS TR 2853, Computer Science Department, University of Maryland, College Park, Md.

Pearl, J., and Kim, J. 1982. Studies in semi-admissible heuristics. *IEEE Transactions on Pattern Analysis and Machine Intelligence (PAMI)* 4(4):392–399.

Pearl, J. 1984. *Heuristics: Intelligent Search Strategies for Computer Problem Solving*. Reading, MA: Addison-Wesley.

Pohl, I. 1971. Bi-directional search. In *Machine Intelligence 6*, 127–140. Edinburgh: Edinburgh University Press.

Politowski, G., and Pohl, I. 1984. D-node retargeting in bidirectional heuristic search. In *Proc. of AAAI-84*, 274–277. Austin, TX: Los Altos, CA.: Kaufmann.

Reinefeld, A., and Marsland, T. 1991. Memory functions in iterative-deepening search. Technical Report FBI-HH-M-198/91, Fachbereich Informatik, Universität Hamburg, Hamburg, Germany.

Russell, S. 1992. Efficient memory-bounded search methods. In *Proc. Tenth European Conference on Artificial Intelligence (ECAI-92)*, 1–5. Vienna, Austria: Chichester: Wiley.

Sen, A., and Bagchi, A. 1989. Fast recursive formulations for best-first search that allow controlled use of memory. In *Proc. Eleventh International Joint Conference on Artificial Intelligence (IJCAI-89)*, 297–302.

Best-First Minimax Search: Othello Results

Richard E. Korf and David Maxwell Chickering
Computer Science Department
University of California, Los Angeles
Los Angeles, Ca. 90024
korf@cs.ucla.edu

Abstract

We present a very simple selective search algorithm for two-player games. It always expands next the frontier node that determines the minimax value of the root. The algorithm requires no information other than a static evaluation function, and its time overhead per node is similar to that of alpha-beta minimax. We also present an implementation of the algorithm that reduces its space complexity from exponential to linear in the search depth, at the cost of increased time complexity. In the game of Othello, using the evaluation function from Bill (Lee & Mahajan 1990), best-first minimax outplays alpha-beta at moderate depths. A hybrid best-first extension algorithm, which combines alpha-beta and best-first minimax, performs significantly better than either pure algorithm even at greater depths. Similar results were also obtained for a class of random game trees.

Introduction and Overview

The best chess machines are competitive with the best humans, but generate millions of positions per move. Their human opponents, however, only examine tens of positions, but search much deeper along some lines of play. Obviously, people are more selective in their choice of positions to examine. The importance of selective search was first recognized by (Shannon 1950).

Most work on game-tree search has focussed on algorithms that make the same decisions as full-width, fixed-depth minimax. This includes alpha-beta pruning (Knuth & Moore 1975), fixed and dynamic node ordering (Slagle & Dixon 1969), SSS* (Stockman 1979), Scout (Pearl 1984), aspiration-windows (Kaindl, Shams, & Horacek 1991), etc. We define a selective search algorithm as one that makes different decisions than full-width, fixed-depth minimax. These include B* (Berliner 1979), conspiracy search (McAllester 1988), min/max approximation (Rivest 1987), meta-greedy search (Russell & Wefald 1989), and singular extensions (Anantharaman, Campbell, & Hsu 1990). All of these algorithms, except singular extensions, require exponential memory, and most have large time overheads per node expansion. In addition, B* and meta-greedy search require more information than a single static evaluation function. Singular extensions is the only algorithm to be successfully incorporated into a high-performance program.

We describe a very simple selective search algorithm, called best-first minimax. It requires only a single static evaluator, and its time overhead per node is roughly the same as alpha-beta minimax. We describe an implementation of the algorithm that reduces its space complexity from exponential to linear in the search depth. We also explore best-first extensions, a hybrid combination of alpha-beta and best-first minimax. Experimentally, best-first extensions outperform alpha-beta in the game of Othello, and on a class of random game trees. Earlier reports on this work include (Korf 1992) and (Korf & Chickering 1993).

Best-First Minimax Search

The basic idea of best-first minimax is to always explore further the current best line of play. Given a partially expanded game tree, with static evaluations of the leaf nodes, the value of an interior MAX node is the maximum of its children's values, and the value of an interior MIN node is the minimum of its children's values. There exists a path, called the *principal variation*, from the root to a leaf node, in which every node has the same value. This leaf node, whose evaluation determines the minimax value of the root, is called the *principal leaf*. Best-first minimax always expands next the current principal leaf node, since it has the greatest affect on the minimax value of the root.

Consider the example in figure 1, where squares represent MAX nodes and circles represent MIN nodes. Figure 1A shows the situation after the root has been expanded. The values of the children are their static values, and the value of the root is 6, the maximum of its children's values. Thus, the right child is the principal leaf, and is expanded next, resulting in the situation in figure 1B. The new frontier nodes are statically evaluated at 5 and 2, and the value of their MIN parent changes to 2, the minimum of its children's values. This changes the value of the root to 4, the maximum of its children's values. Thus, the left child of the root is the new principal leaf, and is expanded next, result-

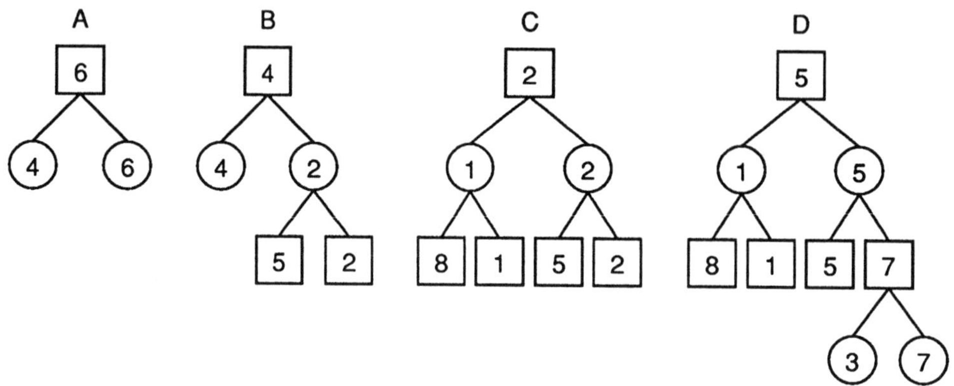

Figure 1: Best-first minimax search example

ing in the situation in figure 1C. The value of the left child of the root changes to the minimum of its children's values, 1, and the value of the root changes to the maximum of its children's values, 2. At this point, the rightmost grandchild is the new principal leaf, and is expanded next, as shown in figure 1D.

By always expanding the principal leaf, best-first minimax may appear to suffer from the exploration of a single path to the exclusion of all others. This does not occur in practice, however. The reason is that the expansion of a node tends to make it look worse, thus inhibiting further exploration of the subtree below it. For example, a MAX node will only be expanded if its static value is the minimum among its brothers, since its parent is a MIN node. Expanding it changes its value to the maximum of its children, which tends to increase its value, making it less likely to remain as the minimum among its siblings. Similarly, MIN nodes also tend to appear worse to their MAX parents when expanded, making it less likely that their children will be expanded next. This *tempo* effect adds balance to the tree searched by best-first minimax, and increases with increasing branching factor. Surprisingly, while this oscillation in values with the last player to move is the reason that alpha-beta avoids comparing nodes at different levels in the tree, it turns out to be advantageous to best-first minimax.

While in principle best-first minimax could make a move at any point in time, we choose to move when the length of the principal variation exceeds a given depth bound, or a winning terminal node is chosen for expansion. This ensures that the chosen move has been explored to a significant depth, or leads to a win.

The simplest implementation of best-first minimax maintains the current tree in memory. When a node is expanded, its children are evaluated, its value is updated, and the algorithm moves up the tree updating the values of its ancestors, until it reaches the root, or a node whose value doesn't change. It then moves down the tree to a maximum-valued child of a MAX node, or a minimum-valued child of a MIN node, until

it reaches a new principal leaf. A drawback of this implementation is that it requires exponential memory, a problem that we address below.

Despite its simplicity, best-first minimax has apparently not been explored before. The algorithm is mentioned as a special case of AO*, a best-first search of an AND-OR tree, in (Nilsson 1969). The chess algorithm of (Kozdrowicki & Cooper 1973) seems related, but behaves differently on their examples. Best-first minimax is also related to conspiracy search (McAllester 1988), and only expands nodes in the conspiracy set. It is also related to Rivest's min/max approximation (Rivest 1987). Both algorithms strive to expand next the node with the largest affect on the root value, but best-first minimax is much simpler. All four related algorithms above require exponential memory.

Recursive Best-First Minimax Search

Recursive Best-First Minimax Search (RBFMS) is an implementation of best-first minimax that runs in space linear in the search depth. The algorithm is a generalization of Simple Recursive Best-First Search (SRBFS) (Korf, 1993), a linear-space best-first search designed for single-agent problems. Figure 2 shows the behavior of RBFMS on the example of figure 1.

Associated with each node on the principal variation is a lower bound Alpha, and an upper bound Beta, similar to the bounds in alpha-beta pruning. A node will remain on the principal variation as long as its minimax value stays within these bounds. The root is bounded by $-\infty$ and ∞. Figure 2A shows the situation after the root is expanded, with the right child on the principal variation. It will remain on the principal variation as long as its minimax value is greater than or equal to the maximum value of its siblings (4). The right child is expanded next, as shown in figure 2B.

The value of the right child changes to the minimum of its children's values (5 and 2), and since 2 is less than the lower bound of 4, the right child is no longer on the principal variation, and the left child of the root is the new principal leaf. The algorithm returns to the

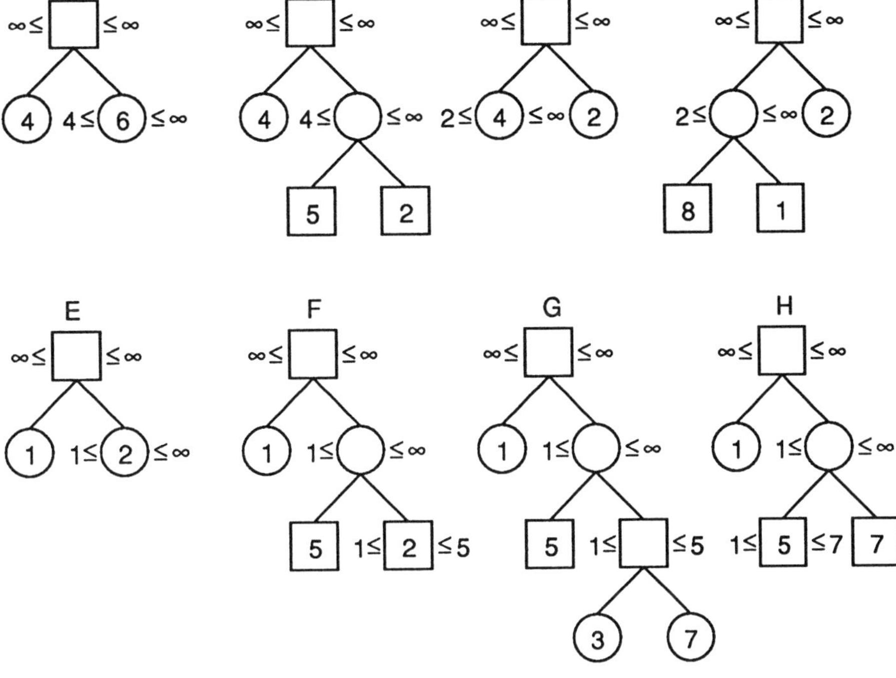

Figure 2: Recursive best-first minimax search example

root, freeing memory, but stores with the right child its new minimax value of 2, as shown in figure 2C. This method of backing up values and freeing memory is similar to that of (Chakrabarti et al. 1989).

The left child of the root will remain on the principal variation as long as its value is greater than or equal to 2, the largest value among its siblings. It is expanded, as shown in figure 2D. Its new value is the minimum of its children's values (8 and 1), and since 1 is less than the lower bound of 2, the left child is no longer on the principal variation, and the right child of the root becomes the new principal leaf. The algorithm returns to the root, and stores the new minimax value of 1 with the left child, as shown in figure 2E. Now, the right child of the root will remain on the principal variation as long as its minimax value is greater than or equal to 1, the value of its best sibling, and is expanded next. The reader is encouraged to complete the example. Note that the values of interior nodes on the principal variation are not computed until necessary.

RBFMS consists of two recursive and entirely symmetric functions, one for MAX and one for MIN. Each takes three arguments: a node, a lower bound Alpha, and an upper bound Beta. Together they perform a best-first minimax search of the subtree below the node, as long as its backed-up minimax value remains within the Alpha and Beta bounds. Once it exceeds those bounds, the function returns the new backed-up minimax value of the node. At any point, the recursion stack contains the current principal variation, plus the siblings of all nodes on this path. Its space complexity is thus $O(bd)$, where b is the branching factor of the tree, and d is the maximum depth.

The children of a node are generated and evaluated one at a time. If the value of any child of a MAX node exceeds Beta, or the value of any child of a MIN node is less than Alpha, that child's value is immediately returned, without generating the remaining children.

```
BFMAX (Node, Alpha, Beta)
FOR each Child[i] of Node
 M[i] := Evaluation(Child[i])
 IF M[i] > Beta return M[i]
SORT Child[i] and M[i] in decreasing order
IF only one child, M[2] := -infinity
WHILE Alpha <= M[1] <= Beta
 M[1] := BFMIN(Child[1],max(Alpha,M[2]),Beta)
 insert Child[1] and M[1] in sorted order
return M[1]

BFMIN (Node, Alpha, Beta)
FOR each Child[i] of Node
 M[i] := Evaluation(Child[i])
 IF M[i] < Alpha return M[i]
SORT Child[i] and M[i] in increasing order
IF only one child, M[2] := infinity
WHILE Alpha <= M[1] <= Beta
 M[1] := BFMAX(Child[1],Alpha,min(Beta,M[2]))
 insert Child[1] and M[1] in sorted order
return M[1]
```

Syntactically, recursive best-first minimax appears very similar to alpha-beta, but behaves quite differently. Alpha-beta makes its move decisions based on the values of nodes all at the same depth, while best-first minimax relies on node values at different levels.[1]

Saving the Tree

RBFMS reduces the space complexity of best-first minimax by generating some nodes more than once. This overhead is significant for deep searches. On the other hand, the time per node generation for RBFMS is less than for standard best-first minimax. In the standard implementation, when a new node is generated, the state of its parent is copied, along with any changes to it. The recursive algorithm does not copy the state, but rather makes only incremental changes to a single copy, and undoes them when backtracking.

Our actual implementation uses the recursive control structure of RBFMS. When backing up the tree, however, the subtree is retained in memory. Thus, when a path is abandoned and then reexplored, the entire subtree is not regenerated, While this requires exponential space, it is not a major problem, for several reasons.

The first is that once a move is made, and the opponent moves, we only save the remaining relevant subtree, and prune the subtrees below moves that weren't chosen by either player, releasing the corresponding memory. While current machines will exhaust their memories in minutes, in a two-player game, moves are made every few minutes, freeing much of the memory.

The second reason that memory is not a serious constraint is that only the backed-up minimax value of a node, and pointers to its children must be saved. The actual game state, and alpha and beta bounds, are incrementally generated from the parent. Thus, a node only requires a few words of memory.

If memory is exhausted while computing a move, however, there are two options. One is to complete the current move search using the linear-space algorithm, thus requiring no more memory than for the recursion stack. The other is to prune the least promising parts of the current search tree. Since all nodes off the principal variation have their backed-up minimax values stored at all times, pruning is simply a matter of recursively freeing the memory in a given subtree.

Since best-first minimax spends most of its time on the expected line of play, it can save much of the tree computed for one move, and apply it to subsequent moves, particularly if the opponent moves as expected. Saving the tree between moves improves the performance considerably. In contrast, the standard depth-first implementation of alpha-beta doesn't save the tree from one move to the next, but only a subset of the

nodes in a transposition table. Even if alpha-beta is modified to save the tree, since it searches every move to the same depth, relatively little of the subtree computed during one move is still relevant after the player's and opponent's moves. In the best case, when alpha-beta searches the minimal tree and the opponent moves as expected, only $1/b$ of the tree that is generated in computing one move is still relevant after the player's and opponent's moves, where b is the branching factor.

Othello Results

The test of a selective search algorithm is how well it plays. We played best-first minimax against alpha-beta in the game of Othello, giving both algorithms the same amount of computation, and the same evaluation function from the program Bill (Lee & Mahajan 1990), one of the world's best Othello players.

The efficiency of alpha-beta is greatly affected by the order in which nodes are searched. The simplest ordering scheme, called fixed ordering (Slagle & Dixon 1969), fully expands each node, statically evaluates each child, sorts the children by their values, and then searches the children of MAX nodes in decreasing order, and the children of MIN nodes in increasing order. We use fixed ordering on newly generated nodes until one level above the search horizon. At that point, since there is no advantage to further ordering, the children are evaluated one at a time, allowing additional pruning. To ensure a fair comparison to best-first minimax, our alpha-beta implementation saves the relevant subtree from one move to the next. This allows us to order previously generated nodes by their backed-up values rather than their static values, further improving the node ordering and performance of alpha-beta.

Each tournament consisted of 244 pairs of games. Different games were generated by making all possible first four moves, and starting the game with the fifth move. Each game was played twice, with each algorithm moving first, to eliminate the effect of a particular initial state favoring the first or second player to move. An Othello game is won by the player with the most discs at the end. About 3% of the games were tied, and are ignored in the results presented below.

When alpha-beta can search to the end of the game, both algorithms use alpha-beta to complete the game, since alpha-beta is optimal when the static values are exact. In Othello, the disc differential is the exact value at the end of the game. Since best-first minimax searches deeper than alpha-beta in the same amount of time, however, it reaches the endgame before alpha-beta does. Since disc differentials are not comparable to the values returned by Bill's heuristic function, best-first minimax evaluates endgame positions at $-\infty$ if MAX has lost, ∞ if MAX has won, and $-\infty + 1$ for ties. If the principal leaf is a winning terminal node for best-first, it stops searching and makes a move. If alpha-beta makes the expected response, the principal leaf doesn't change, and best-first minimax will make

---

[1] While Recursive Best-First Search (RBFS) is more efficient than Simple Recursive Best-First Search (SRBFS) for single-agent problems (Korf 1993), the minimax generalizations of these two algorithms behave identically.

AB depth	1	2	3	4	5	6	7
BF depth	1	4	8	12	15	19	23
BF wins	50%	67%	78%	69%	57%	58%	51%

Table 1: Pure best-first vs. alpha-beta on Othello

AB depth	1	2	3	4	5	6	7	8
BF depth	1	4	7	10	14	18	21	24
BF wins	50%	67%	83%	81%	67%	72%	67%	68%

Table 2: Best-first extension vs. alpha-beta on Othello

its next move without further search. Conversely, if the principal leaf is a loss or tie, best-first minimax will continue to search until it finds a win, or runs out of time. While this endgame play is not ideal, it is the most natural extension of best-first minimax.

For each alpha-beta search horizon, we experimentally determined what depth limit caused best-first minimax to take most nearly the same amount of time. This was done by running a series of tournaments, and incrementing the search horizon of the algorithm that took less time in the last tournament. Node evaluation is the dominant cost, and running time is roughly proportional to the number of node evaluations.

Table 1 shows the results of these experiments. The top line shows the alpha-beta search depths, and the second line shows the best-first search depth that took most nearly the same amount of time as the corresponding alpha-beta depth. The third line shows the percentage of games that were won by best-first minimax, excluding ties. Each data point is an average of 244 pairs of games, or 488 total games.

Both algorithms are identical at depth one. At greater depths, best-first searches deeper than alpha-beta, and wins most of the time. Its winning percentage increases to 78%, but then begins to drop off as the gap between the alpha-beta and best-first horizons becomes very large. At greater depths, we believe that best-first will lose to alpha-beta.

Best-First Extensions

One explanation for this performance degradation is that while best-first minimax evaluates every child of the root, it may not generate some grandchildren, depending on the static values of the children. In particular, if the evaluation function grossly underestimates the value of a node, it may never be expanded. For example, this might occur in a piece trade that begins with a sacrifice. At some point, it makes more sense to consider all grandchildren of the root, rather than nodes 23 moves down the principal variation.

To correct this, we implemented a hybrid algorithm, called best-first extension, that combines the uniform coverage of alpha-beta with the penetration of best-first minimax. Best-first extension performs alpha-beta to a shallow search horizon, and then executes best-first minimax to a greater depth, starting with the tree, backed-up values, and principal variation generated by the alpha-beta search. This guarantees that every move will be explored to a minimum depth, regardless of its evaluation, before exploring the most promising moves much deeper. This is similar to the

idea of principal variation lookahead extensions (Anantharaman 1990).

Best-first extension has two parameters: the depth of the initial alpha-beta search, and the depth of the subsequent best-first search. In our experiments, the alpha-beta horizon of the initial search was set to one less than the horizon of its pure alpha-beta opponent, and the best-first horizon was whatever depth took most nearly the same total amount of time, including the initial alpha-beta search, as the pure alpha-beta opponent. Even in this case, most of the time is spent on the best-first extension. Table 2 shows the results for Othello, in the same format as table 1. At alpha-beta depths greater than two, best-first extension performs significantly better than both alpha-beta and pure best-first minimax. At increasing depths the results appear to stabilize, with best-first extension defeating alpha-beta about two out of three games.

Random Game Tree Results

As a separate test of our results, we also experimented with a class of random game trees (Fuller, Gaschnig, & Gillogly 1973). In a uniform random game tree with branching factor b and depth d, each edge is independently assigned a random cost. The static heuristic evaluation of a node is the sum of the edge costs from the root to the node. Since real games do not have uniform branching factors, we let the number of children of any node be a random variable uniformly distributed from one to a maximum branching factor B. In order not to favor MAX or MIN, the edge-cost distribution is symmetric around zero. Our edge-cost distribution was uniform from -2^{15} to 2^{15}.

Different random games were generated from different random seeds. Each game was played twice, with each algorithm moving first. A random game ends when a terminal position is reached, 100 moves in our experiments, and returns the static value of the final position as the outcome. Given a pair of random games, and the corresponding terminal values reached, the winner is the algorithm that played MAX when the larger terminal value was obtained. Each random game tournament consisted of 100 pairs of games.

In random games with maximum branching factors ranging from 2 to 20, we obtained results similar to those for Othello (Korf & Chickering 1993). In particular, pure best-first outplayed alpha beta at shallow depths, but tended to lose at greater depths, while best-first extension outplayed alpha-beta at all depths.

Conclusions and Further Work

We presented a very simple selective search algorithm, best-first minimax. It always expands next the frontier node at the end of the current principal variation, which is the node that determines the minimax value of the root. One advantage of the algorithm is that it can save most of the results from one move computation, and apply them to subsequent moves. In experiments on Othello, best-first minimax outplays alpha-beta, giving both algorithms the same amount of computation and evaluation function, up to a given search depth, but starts to lose beyond that depth. We also presented a hybrid combination of best-first minimax and alpha-beta, which guarantees that every move is searched to a minimum depth. This best-first extension outperforms both algorithms, defeating alpha-beta roughly two out of three games. While memory was not a limiting factor in our experiments, we also showed how to reduce the space complexity of the algorithm from exponential to linear in the search depth, but at significant cost in nodes generated for deep searches. Finally, we performed the same experiments on a class of random games, with similar results.

Since pure best-first minimax performs best against relatively shallow alpha-beta searches, it is likely to be most valuable in games with large branching factors, and/or expensive evaluation functions. These are games, such as Go, in which computers have been least successful against humans. Current research is focussed on implementing singular extensions in an attempt to improve our alpha-beta opponent, and implementations on other games.

Acknowledgements

Thanks to Kai-Fu Lee for the sources to Bill, to Judea Pearl, Joe Pemberton, and Weixiong Zhang for many helpful discussions, and to Hermann Kaindl for comments on an earlier draft. This work was supported by NSF Grant No. IRI-9119825, and a grant from Rockwell International.

References

Anantharaman, T.S., A statistical study of selective min-max search in computer chess, Ph.D. Thesis, Dept. of Computer Science, Carnegie-Mellon Univ., Pittsburgh, Pa. 1990.

Anantharaman, T., M.S. Campbell, and F.-H. Hsu, Singular extensions: Adding selectivity to brute-force searching, *Artificial Intelligence*, Vol. 43, No. 1, 1990, pp. 99-109.

Berliner, H.J., The B* tree search algorithm: A best-first proof procedure, *Artificial Intelligence*, Vol. 12, 1979, pp. 23-40.

Chakrabarti, P.P., S. Ghose, A. Acharya, and S.C. de Sarkar, Heuristic search in restricted memory, *Artificial Intelligence*, Vol. 41, No. 2, 1989, pp. 197-221.

Fuller, S.H., J.G. Gaschnig, and J.J. Gillogly, An analysis of the alpha-beta pruning algorithm, Technical Report, Dept. of Computer Science Carnegie-Mellon University, Pittsburgh, Pa., 1973.

Kaindl, H., R. Shams, and H. Horacek, Minimax search algorithms with and without aspiration windows, *IEEE Transactions on Pattern Analysis and Machine Intelligence*, Vol. 13, No. 12, 1991, pp. 1225-1235.

Knuth, D.E., and R.E. Moore, An analysis of Alpha-Beta pruning, *Artificial Intelligence*, Vol. 6, No. 4, 1975, pp. 293-326.

Korf, R.E., Best-first minimax search: Initial results, Technical Report, CSD-920021, Computer Science Dept., University of California, Los Angeles, 1992.

Korf, R.E., Linear-space best-first search, *Artificial Intelligence*, Vol. 62, No. 1, 1993, pp. 41-78.

Korf, R.E., and D.M. Chickering, Best-first minimax search: First results, *Proceedings of the AAAI Fall Symposium on Games: Planning and Learning*, Raleigh, NC, Oct. 1993, pp. 39-47.

Kozdrowicki, E.W., and D.W. Cooper, COKO III: The Cooper-Koz chess program, *C.A.C.M.*, Vol. 16, No. 7, 1973, pp. 411-427.

Lee, K.-F. and S. Mahajan, The development of a world-class Othello program, *Artificial Intelligence*, Vol. 43, No. 1, 1990, pp. 21-36.

McAllester, D.A., Conspiracy numbers for min-max search, *Artificial Intelligence*, Vol. 35, No. 3, 1988, pp. 287-310.

Nilsson, N.J., Searching problem-solving and game-playing trees for minimal cost solutions, in *Information Processing 68, Proceedings of the IFIP Congress 1968*, A.J.H. Morrell (Ed.), North-Holland, Amsterdam, 1969, pp. 1556-1562.

Pearl, J. *Heuristics*, Addison-Wesley, Reading, Mass., 1984.

Rivest, R.L., Game tree searching by min/max approximation, *Artificial Intelligence*, Vol. 34, No. 1, 1987, pp. 77-96.

Russell, S., and E. Wefald, On optimal game-tree search using rational meta-reasoning, *Proceedings of the Eleventh International Joint Conference on Artificial Intelligence (IJCAI-89)*, Detroit, MI, 1989, pp. 334-340.

Shannon, C.E., Programming a computer for playing chess, *Philosophical Magazine*, Vol. 41, 1950, pp. 256-275.

Slagle, J.R., and Dixon, J.K., Experiments with some programs that search game trees, *J.A.C.M.*, Vol. 16, No. 2, 1969, pp. 189-207.

Stockman, G., A minimax algorithm better than Alpha-Beta? *Artificial Intelligence*, Vol. 12, No. 2, 1979, pp. 179-196.

Evolving Neural Networks to Focus Minimax Search *

David E. Moriarty and Risto Miikkulainen
Department of Computer Sciences
The University of Texas at Austin, Austin, TX 78712
moriarty,risto@cs.utexas.edu

Abstract

Neural networks were evolved through genetic algorithms to focus minimax search in the game of Othello. At each level of the search tree, the focus networks decide which moves are promising enough to be explored further. The networks effectively hide problem states from minimax based on the knowledge they have evolved about the limitations of minimax and the evaluation function. Focus networks were encoded in marker-based chromosomes and were evolved against a full–width minimax opponent that used the same evaluation function. The networks were able to guide the search away from poor information, resulting in stronger play while examining fewer states. When evolved with a highly sophisticated evaluation function of the Bill program, the system was able to match Bill's performance while only searching a subset of the moves.

Introduction

Almost all current game programs rely on the minimax search algorithm (Shannon 1950) to return the best move. Because of time and space constraints, searching to the end of the game is not feasible for most games. Heuristic evaluation functions, therefore, are used to approximate the payoff of a state. Unfortunately, heuristics create errors that propagate up the search tree, and can greatly diminish the effectiveness of minimax (Korf 1988). Minimax also assumes that the opponent will always make the best move. It does not promote risk taking. Often in losing situations the best move may not be towards the highest min/max value, especially if it will still result in a loss. Knowledge of move probabilities could guide a search towards a more aggressive approach and take advantage of possible mistakes by the opponent.

Recently, several algorithms have emerged that are more selective than the standard fixed-depth minimax search (Korf and Chickering 1994; McAllester 1988;

---

*Thanks to Kai-Fu Lee and Richard Korf for providing the source code for Bill's evaluation function.

Rivest 1987). These algorithms allow moves that appear more promising to be explored deeper than others, creating nonuniform-depth trees. While these techniques have lead to better play, they still allow minimax to evaluate every unexplored board and are therefore vulnerable to errors in the evaluation function.

Most game programs overcome weak evaluation functions by searching deeper in the tree. Presumably, as the search frontier gets closer to the goal states, the heuristic evaluations become more accurate. While this may be true, there is no guarantee that deeper searches will provide frontier nodes closer to the goal states. Hansson and Mayer (1989) have shown that without a sound inference mechanism, deeper searches can actually cause more error in the frontier nodes. A more directed search, therefore, seems necessary.

An alternative to deeper searches is to decrease the errors in the evaluation function. Bayesian learning has been implemented to combine several heuristic estimates (Lee and Mahajan 1990) and to adjust the heuristic values based on values of other nodes in the tree (Hansson and Mayer 1989). The new estimates represent a measure of belief in the heuristic value. These methods have provided stronger play, although they do not address problems inherent in minimax such as no risk taking.

This paper presents a novel approach using evolutionary neural networks that can compensate for problems in the evaluation function as well as in the minimax algorithm. Artificial neural networks have proven very effective in pattern recognition and pattern association tasks, which makes them a good candidate for recognizing undesirable board situations. Genetic algorithms provide a powerful, general training tool for neural networks. Like natural evolution, artificial evolution is very good at discerning problems and finding ways to overcome them. Our approach is based on a marker-based encoding of neural networks which has been shown particularly effective in adapting to new challenges in complex environments (Fullmer and Miikkulainen 1992; Moriarty and Miikkulainen 1993).

Genetic algorithms were used to evolve *Focus networks* to direct a minimax search away from poor infor-

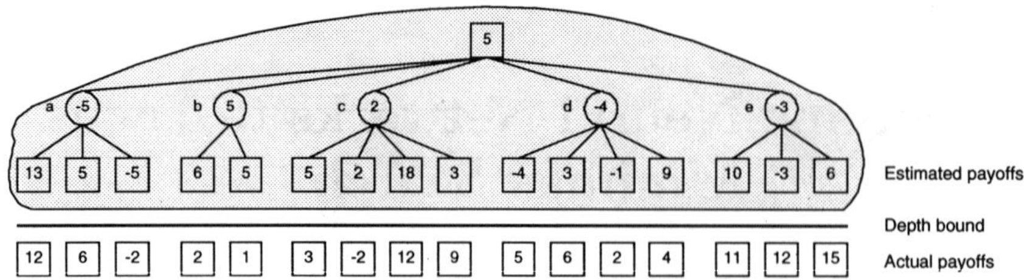

Figure 1: A full-width minimax search to level 2. All nodes in the shaded area are evaluated. The actual payoff values of the leaf states are listed below the depth bound. Their heuristic estimates are shown inside the leaf nodes. Min (circles) selects the lowest payoff and max (squares) the highest of min's choices. As a result, move *b* is selected for the root.

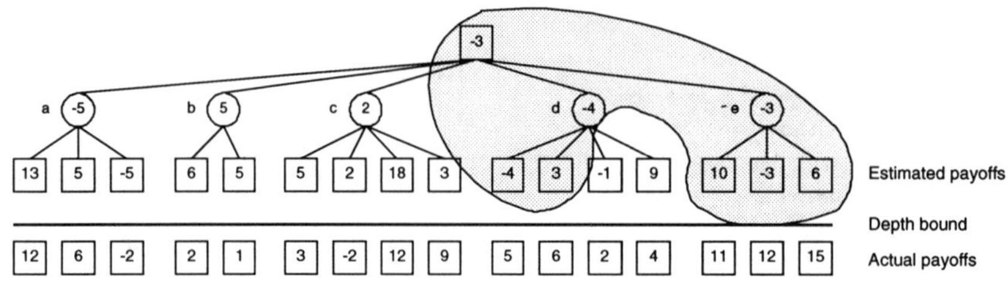

Figure 2: A focused minimax search. Only the states in the focus window (the shaded region) are evaluated. As a result, move *e* appears to be max's best choice.

mation. At each state in the search, the focus network determines which moves look promising enough to be further explored. The focus network is able to control which moves the minimax search can see, and can evolve to overcome limitations of the evaluation function and minimax by focusing the search away from problem states.

A population of focus networks was evolved in the game of Othello. The results show that the focus networks are capable of stronger play than full–width minimax with the same evaluation function, while examining fewer positions. Also, when evolved with the highly sophisticated evaluation function of the Bill program (Lee and Mahajan 1990), the focus networks were able to maintain Bill's level of play while searching through fewer states.

The next section describes the basic idea and implementation of the focus networks. Section 3 describes marker-based encoding and the specifics of the evolution simulations. The main experimental results are presented in section 4, and discussed in section 5.

Focus Networks

Selecting Moves for Minimax

Focus networks decide which moves in a given board situation are to be explored. At each level, the network sees the updated board and evaluates each move. Only those moves that are better than a threshold value will be further explored. This subset of moves can be seen as a window to the search tree returned by the focus network. The .search continues until a fixed depth bound is reached. A static evaluation func-

tion is applied to the leaf states, and the values are propagated up the tree using the standard minimax method. The α-β pruning algorithm (Edwards and Hart 1963; Knuth and Moore 1975) is used as in a full–width search to prune irrelevant states.

To illustrate how such control of minimax might be beneficial, consider the following situation. Two moves, A and B, are considered in the current board configuration. Although move A returns, through minimax search, a higher evaluation value than move B, both moves appear to lead to losing situations. Move B, however, can result in a win if the opponent makes a mistake. By assuming that the opponent will always make the best move, minimax would choose A over B resulting in a sure loss. Focus networks, however, could learn that a win can sometimes be achieved by selecting move B, and they would thus not include A in their search window.

More generally, restricting the number of moves explored has two advantages: (1) the branching factor is reduced which greatly speeds up the search. As a result, searches can proceed deeper on more promising paths. (2) The focus networks are forced to decide which moves the minimax search should evaluate, and in order to play well, they must develop an understanding of the minimax algorithm. It is possible that they will also discover limitations of minimax and the evaluation function, and learn to compensate by not allowing minimax to see certain moves.

Figures 1 and 2 illustrate the focused search process. The current player has a choice of 5 moves (*a* through *e*). Figure 1 shows a basic minimax search with a depth bound of 2. The leaf states are evaluated according to

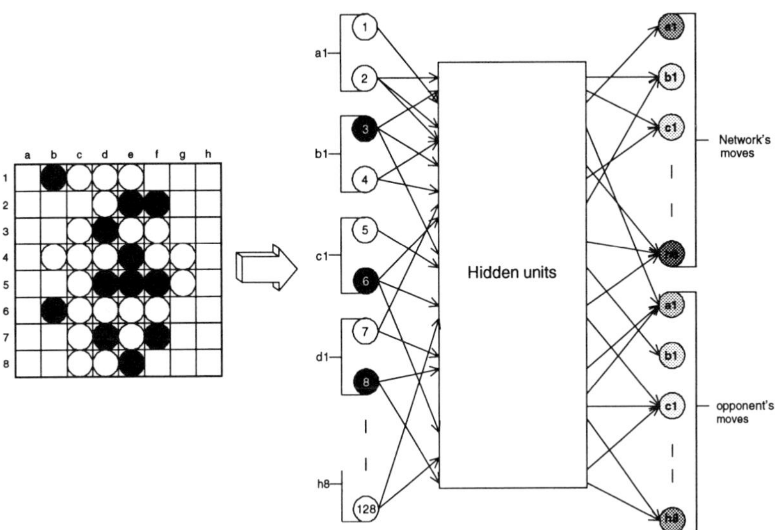

Figure 3: The architecture of the focus networks for Othello. Two inputs are used to encode each position on the board. The encoding of the first four spaces (a1, b1, c1, d1) for the given board with the network playing black are shown in the input layer. Both input nodes 1 and 2 are off since a1 is empty. Node 3 is on (i.e. dark) since b1 has the network's piece in it, and nodes 6 and 8 are on since the opponent has pieces in c1 and d1 (both nodes for the same position are never on simultaneously). The activation of the output layer is shown by the shading. The corners (such as a1 and h8) have high activations since corners are almost always good moves. Only the input and output encoding was prespecified for the network. The input and output connectivity and the number and connectivity of the hidden nodes were all evolved using genetic algorithms.

a static evaluation function. The actual payoff value of each leaf is shown below the depth bound. The difference between these values is the error or misinformation generated by the evaluation function. The best move is e, as it will generate a payoff of at least 11. Because of the misinformation, however, full-width minimax would choose move b. Figure 2 shows the same search tree but with the addition of a focus window. Only the nodes in the window are evaluated. By focusing the search away from the poor information, the best move (e) would be selected. The question is, how can we reliably form such a search window?

The evolutionary approach is attractive because no previous knowledge of minimax or the evaluation function is needed. The usual neural network learning algorithms such as backpropagation (Rumelhart et al. 1986) would require exact target values to be specified for each training example. Such information is very difficult to establish in the search focus task. In the neuro-evolution approach, however, evolutionary pressures will guide the networks toward providing good windows for the search. Networks will discover misinformation by associating certain board situations with winning and losing. Networks that prune out problem states will win more games, allowing them to survive and propagate their genes to future networks.

Implementation in Othello

Othello is a board game played on an 8×8 grid (figure 3). Each piece has one white and one black side.

Players ("white" and "black") take turns placing pieces on the board with their own color facing up until there are no further moves. For a move to be legal, it must cause one or more of the opponent's pieces to be surrounded by the new piece and another of the player's pieces. All surrounded pieces are subsequently flipped to become the player's pieces. Several world championship-level Othello programs have been created using full-width minimax search (Lee and Mahajan 1990; Rosenbloom 1982). Like most advanced game programs, they achieve high performance through examining millions of positions per move.

In our implementation of focus networks, two input units were used to represent the type of piece in each board space. Each output unit corresponded directly to a space on the board. The activation of an output unit determined how strongly the network suggested moving to that position. Separate output units were used for the two players. Thus, the ranking for the network's moves may differ from the ranking of the opponent's moves. This distinction is beneficial since an aggressive player should not assume his opponent is equally aggressive and should take a more conservative approach when predicting his opponent's moves. Similarly, a defensive player should not presume defensive play from his opponents. The separation of player and opponent's output units allows offensive and defensive strategies to develop.

The number of hidden units and connections between them were determined through evolution. Each

$< start >< label >< value >< key_0 >< label_0 >< w_0 > \ldots < key_n >< label_n >< w_n >< end >$

$< start >$	- Start marker.
$< label >$	- Label of the node.
$< value >$	- Initial value of the node.
$< key_i >$	- Key that specifies whether connection is from an input unit/to an output unit or from another hidden unit.
$< label_i >$	- Label of the unit where connection is to be made.
$< w_i >$	- Weight of connection.
$< end >$	- End marker.

Figure 4: The definition of a hidden node in marker–based encoding.

hidden unit used a linear threshold of 0 to determine it's output (either 0 or 1). Usually the networks contained about 120 hidden nodes and 600 connections with a large amount of recurrency. For each state to be explored in a search tree an activation was propagated through the network. The legal moves with activation greater than or equal to 0 were included in the search window.

Evolution

Each focus network's genetic representation was based on a marker–based encoding (Fullmer and Miikkulainen 1992) of the architecture and weights. The encoding is inspired by markers in DNA that separate protein definitions. Artificial markers in the chromosome are used to separate neural network node definitions. Alleles serve as start markers if their absolute value MOD 25 equals 1 and end markers if their absolute value MOD 25 equals 2. Any integer between a start marker and an end marker is always part of the genetic code. The interpretation of non-marker alleles depends on their location with respect to a start or an end marker. Figure 4 summarizes the structure of the hidden node definition in marker-based encoding.

Each chromosome consisted of 5000 8-bit integers ranging from -128 to 127. Two 8-bit integers were used for the connection definitions. The *key* integer specifies whether the connection is to be made with the input/output layers or with another hidden unit. If the key is positive, the second integer, *label*, specifies a connection from the input layer (if the label is ≥ 0) or to the output layer (if the label is < 0). If the key is negative, the label specifies an input connection from another hidden unit. Figure 5 shows an example gene and the network information it encodes.

The chromosome is treated as a continuous circular entity. A node may begin on one end of the chromosome and end on the other. The final node definition is terminated, however, if the first start marker is encountered in the node definition. The hidden nodes were evaluated in the order specified in the chromosome.

A population of 50 networks was evolved using standard genetic algorithms (Goldberg 1988; Holland 1975). A two point crossover (figure 6) was used to produce two offspring per mating. Only the top 15 net-

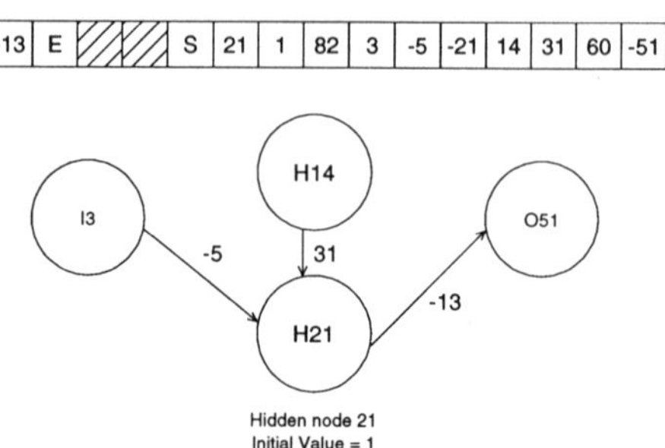

Figure 5: An example node definition in a marker-based gene. The first connection has $key = 82$, $label = 3$, $w = -5$. The key and label are both positive so the connection is to be made from input unit 3.

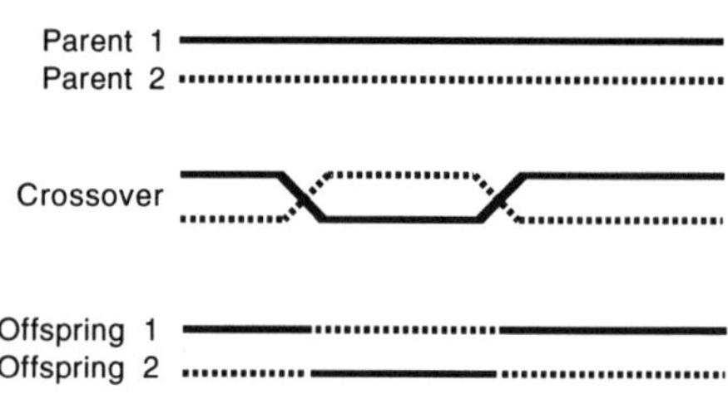

Figure 6: Two point crossover. Each offspring receives the front and rear part of one parent's chromosome and the middle of the other parent's chromosome.

works were allowed to mate with each other, creating 30 new offspring per generation. The new offspring replaced the least fit networks in the population. Traits that previously led to high fitness levels were passed to future generations, whereas traits that led to poor performance were selected against. Mutation, at the rate of 0.4%, was implemented at the integer level by adding a random value to an integer allele. The top 3 networks were not mutated.

To determine a network's fitness, it was inserted into an α-β search program and played against a full-width, fixed-depth minimax-α-β search. Both players were allowed to search through the second level. To optimize α-β pruning, node ordering was implemented based on the values of the evaluation function (Pearl 1984).

Both players always used the same evaluation function. One population was evolved based on the positional strategy of Iago (Rosenbloom 1982), one of the first championship-level Othello programs. Such an evaluation function is relatively weak as it only considers the merits of single spaces without taking mobility into account[1]. The goal was to see how well the focus networks could evolve to make use of weak heuristic information, and also to provide enough errors so that the effect of focus networks would be easily seen.

A separate population was evolved using the evaluation function from the Bill program (Lee and Mahajan 1990). Bill's evaluation has been optimized through Bayesian learning and is believed to be one of the best in the world. The goal was to see if the focus networks could achieve any improvement over such an already strong heuristic.

To create different games, an initial state was selected randomly among the 244 possible board positions after four moves. To prevent networks from expecting certain moves, the opponents moved randomly 10% of the time. The random moves also make risk taking a viable option in a losing situation since the opponent will not always make the best move. If the opponent's evaluation function returned the same value for two or more moves, a random selection was made between the equal-valued moves, further discouraging expectations. The number of wins over ten games determined each network's fitness.

Results

The networks were evolved for 1000 generations, which took about four days on a Sun Sparcstation 1. After evolution, the best focus network was again played against the full–width search program, but this time the program made no random moves. The performance was measured by the percentage of games won over all 244 opening games.

In the first test (figure 7), the focused search level was fixed at 2, and the full–width opponent's was varied. As a control, a 2-level, full–width minimax search was also played against the full–width opponent. Note that the focused (shaded bars) and full–width (white bars) searches are not playing against each other, but against another full–width opponent. The results show that a focused search to level 2 appears to be as strong as a full–width search to level 4.

In the second test (figure 8), the focused search level was increased with the full–width opponent's. The control full–width search (white bars) performs consistently at 50% because it is simply playing itself at each level. The results show that the focused search consistently outplays the full–width search even as the search level increases far beyond its training. The performance is strongest at level 2, where the focused network was actually trained, and is otherwise approximately constant at 65%. This result is important

---

[1]Iago also included a complex mobility strategy.

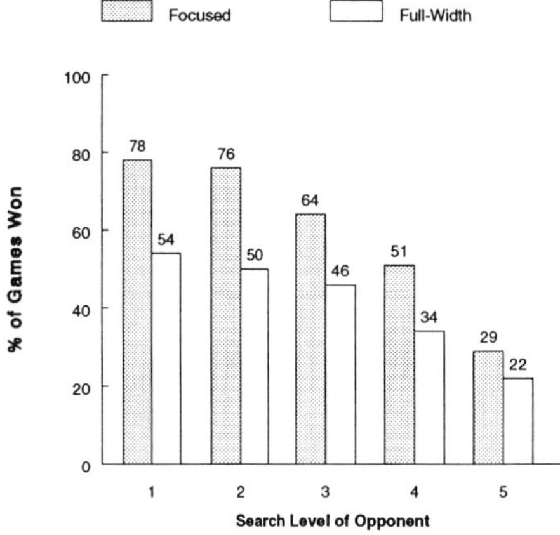

Figure 7: The winning percentage of two level search with and without a focus network against a variable-level full–width opponent.

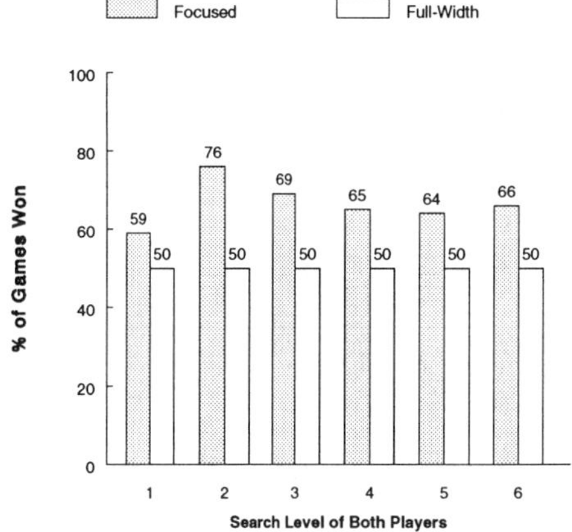

Figure 8: The winning percentage of a variable-level search with and without a focus network against a variable-level full–width opponent.

because it suggests that the focus network could be trained at any level, and would generalize well to other search depths.

It is also important to note that the focused searches were winning while looking at only a subset of the states that the full-width searches are examining. Figure 9 shows the average number of board positions examined per game for each search bound. Of all available legal moves, only 79% were included in the focus window. The full-width search must be receiving poor information from minimax, causing it to choose bad moves. Since the focused search is using the same evaluation function and is searching to the same depth, it appears that the focus network is shielding the root from this misinformation.

To better understand how the stronger play was achieved, the moves included in the focus window were further analyzed. 100 test games were played against a full-width search using the same evaluation function.

	1	2	3	4	5	6
Focus	189	662	3440	12172	63304	230487
Full	226	842	4042	16684	75696	330453

Figure 9: The average number of states examined per game for each depth bound.

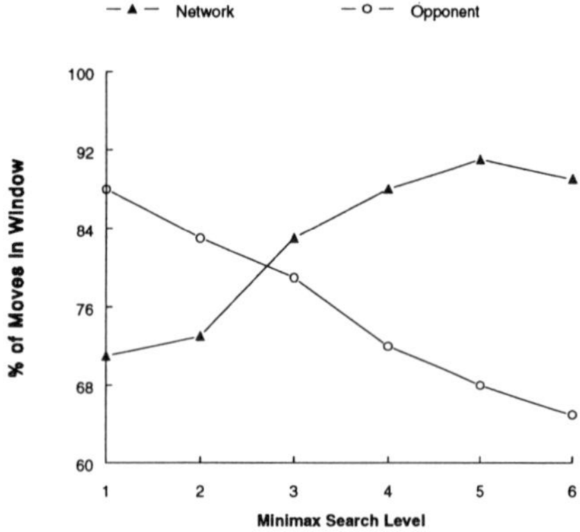

Figure 10: The percentage of moves returned by minimax as its choice that the focus network considers.

At each board position the moves in the focus window were compared with the move a full–width minimax search would return at the same position. Figure 10 shows the percentage of full–width minimax's moves that were included in the focus network's window. The graph thus reflects how often the focus network agrees with full–width minimax. The results show that the focus network is effectively looking far ahead. The moves in the network's window are similar to moves that a deep–searching, full–width minimax would return (black triangles in figure 10). However, since the network has only been evolved against a shallow-searching opponent, its predictions of the opponent's moves become less accurate as the opponent searches deeper (white circles in figure 10). The focus network's moves are strong because they are not tied to the moves that a full–width minimax search would choose. Instead, they reflect moves that have led to wins. It is this strong offense that allows the networks to scale with the search level. It is conceivable that eventually the network's diminishing defense will leave it vulnerable to a powerful opponent, however that was never observed in our experiments.

In the second population, evolved using the evaluation function from Bill, the best focus networks achieved a winning percentage of 51% over the full–width searches to the same level. Apparently, since Bill's evaluation function has very few errors, the focus networks were not able to improve the play very much. However, it is significant that the focused searches achieved this performance while examining only 84% of the moves that full-width Bill evaluated. It seems the focus networks were able to discover and prune unnecessary nodes even with a Bayes-optimized heuristic. In

a game playing setting where time constraints must be taken into account, such an improved efficiency translates directly to better performance.

Discussion and Future Work

The results show that better play can be achieved through more selective search. Much like humans, focus networks selectively dismiss moves that have previously led to adverse situations. Whereas full-width minimax is very sensitive to inconsistencies in the evaluation function, focused searches can actually discover and discard unreliable information. The approach will be most useful in improving performance in domains where it is difficult to come up with good evaluation functions. The evolution system can take a weak heuristic and discover how to best use the information it provides. In this sense, the approach is similar to other recent improvements in game playing such as Bayesian optimization of evaluation functions (Hansson and Mayer 1990; Lee and Mahajan 1990). A comparison of these techniques and a study of how they perhaps could be combined would be most interesting.

In an earlier implementation of focus networks, a fixed-size focus window that always included the three best moves was used (Moriarty and Miikkulainen 1994). This strategy achieved performance comparable to the threshold-based window with an even more dramatic reduction in the number of states evaluated. However, the fixed window system was not able to generalize well to better opponents such as Bill. When evolved with Bill's evaluation function, the fixed window pruned too many nodes and performed very poorly. On the other hand, the threshold-based window allows the system to adjust the extent of pruning according to how much reliable information there is in the tree.

It seems to make little difference how deep the system is allowed to search during training (figure 8). The focus networks should therefore perform well in real game-playing situations where the search depth may vary significantly depending on the available time. However, the training opponent's search depth (and evaluation function) may have a significant effect on performance. It might be possible to evolve better play by improving the opponent gradually during training. If the opponent gets stronger as the networks evolve, the networks would have to compensate by improving their defensive strategy, and superior overall play should result.

In our implementation, focus networks searched only through uniform–depth trees. Focus networks could also be implemented with algorithms such as best–first minimax (Korf and Chickering 1994), where the tree is grown in non-uniform depths allowing more promising moves to be searched deeper. Whereas the standard best–first minimax considers all unexplored board positions in the decision of where to explore next, a selective window of the most important positions could be maintained to focus the search.

Another application of neuro-evolution to game playing is to evolve networks to serve as the evaluation function. Interestingly, the results have been discouraging so far. Whereas the focus networks' output values only need to indicate above or below a threshold, the evaluation networks' output units must reflect an absolute value comparable to other board evaluations. It has proven very difficult for the networks to discover such global values.

While focus networks may be well suited for Othello, their implementation in more complex games like chess is not as straightforward. In our implementation, the output layer represented the entire move space. This is feasible in Othello, since there are only 60 possible moves. It is unrealistic to try to represent the entire move space of a game such as chess in a single output layer. A possible solution is to use two focus networks in the decision process. The first network's output layer would represent each piece and would decide which pieces to consider. The second network's output layer would represent each space on the board (as in the Othello networks). Given the current board and the piece to be moved, the second network could decide which moves of a given piece to consider. Such an extension constitutes a most interesting direction of future research.

Conclusion

Artificial evolution of neural networks is a promising paradigm for developing better search strategies. It is possible to identify unreliable information in the search tree and find ways to avoid it. Focus networks can overcome not only errors in the evaluation function but flaws inherent in minimax itself. Focused searches are cognitively more appealing since they produce more human-like search rather than systematic exhaustive search. In Othello, a focused search consistently outplayed full–width minimax while examining a subset of the moves. Even with a highly sophisticated evaluation function, the focus networks were able to create a more efficient search by pruning irrelevant nodes. Applications to more complex domains are more challenging, but not infeasible.

References

Edwards, D., and Hart, T. (1963). The alpha-beta heuristic. Technical Report 30, MIT.

Fullmer, B., and Miikkulainen, R. (1992). Evolving finite state behavior using marker-based genetic encoding of neural networks. In *Proceedings of the First European Conference on Artificial Life*. Cambridge, MA: MIT Press.

Goldberg, D. E. (1988). *Genetic Algorithms in Search, Optimization and Machine Learning*. Reading, MA: Addison-Wesley.

Hansson, O., and Mayer, A. (1989). Heuristic search as evidential reasoning. In *Proceedings of the Fifth Workshop on Uncertainty in AI*.

Hansson, O., and Mayer, A. (1990). Probabilistic heuristic estimates. *Annals of Mathematics and Artificial Intelligence*, 2:209–220.

Holland, J. H. (1975). *Adaptation in Natural and Artificial Systems: An Introductory Analysis with Applications to Biology, Control and Artificial Intelligence*. Ann Arbor, MI: University of Michigan Press.

Knuth, D. E., and Moore, R. W. (1975). An analysis of alpha-beta pruning. *Artificial Intelligence*, 6:293–326.

Korf, R. E. (1988). Search: A survey of recent results. In Shrobe, H. E., editor, *Exploring Artificial Intelligence*. San Mateo, California: Morgan Kaufmann.

Korf, R. E., and Chickering, D. M. (1994). Best-first minimax search: Othello results. In *Proceedings of the Twelfth National Conference on Artificial Intelligence*.

Lee, K.-F., and Mahajan, S. (1990). The development of a world class Othello program. *Artificial Intelligence*, 43:21–36.

McAllester, D. A. (1988). Conspiracy numbers for minmax search. *Artificial Intelligence*, 35:287–310.

Moriarty, D. E., and Miikkulainen, R. (1993). Evolving complex Othello strategies using marker-based genetic encoding of neural networks. Technical Report AI93-206, Department of Computer Sciences, The University of Texas at Austin.

Moriarty, D. E., and Miikkulainen, R. (1994). Improving game tree search with evolutionary neural networks. In *Proceedings of the First IEEE Conference on Evolutionary Computation*.

Pearl, J. (1984). *Heuristics: Intelligent Search Strategies for Computer Problem Solving*. Reading, MA: Addison-Wesley.

Rivest, R. L. (1987). Game tree searching by min/max approximation. *Artificial Intelligence*, 34:77–96.

Rosenbloom, P. (1982). A world championship-level Othello program. *Artificial Intelligence*, 19:279–320.

Rumelhart, D. E., Hinton, G. E., and Williams, R. J. (1986). Learning internal representations by error propagation. In Rumelhart, D. E., and McClelland, J. L., editors, *Parallel Distributed Processing: Explorations in the Microstructure of Cognition, Volume 1: Foundations*, 318–362. Cambridge, MA: MIT Press.

Shannon, C. E. (1950). Programming a computer for playing chess. *Philisophical Magazine*, 41:256–275.

A Strategic Metagame Player
for General Chess-Like Games

Barney Pell
RIACS, NASA Ames Research Center
AI Research Branch, Mail Stop: 269-2
Moffett Field, CA 94035–1000
pell@ptolemy.arc.nasa.gov

Abstract

This paper introduces METAGAMER, the first program designed within the paradigm of Meta-Game Playing (Metagame) (Pell 1992a). This program plays Metagame in the class of symmetric chess-like games (Pell 1992b), which includes chess, Chinese-chess, checkers, draughts, and Shogi. METAGAMER takes as input the *rules* of a specific game and analyses those rules to construct for that game an efficient representation and an evaluation function, for use by a generic search engine. The strategic analysis performed by META-GAMER relates a set of general knowledge sources to the details of the particular game. Among other properties, this analysis determines the relative value of the different pieces in a given game. Although METAGAMER does not learn from experience, the values resulting from its analysis are qualitatively similar to values used by experts on known games, and are sufficient to produce competitive performance the first time METAGAMER actually plays each new game. Besides being the first Metagame-playing program, this is the first program to have derived useful piece values directly from analysis of the rules of different games. This paper describes the knowledge implemented in METAGAMER, illustrates the piece values META-GAMER derives for chess and checkers, and discusses experiments with METAGAMER on both existing and newly generated games.

1   Introduction

Virtually all past research in computer game-playing has attempted to develop computer programs which could play existing games at a reasonable standard. While some researchers consider the development of a game-specific expert for some game to be a sufficient end in itself, many scientists in AI are motivated by a desire for generality. Their emphasis is not on achieving strong performance on a particular game, but rather on understanding the general ability to produce such strength on

a wider variety of games (or problems in general). Hence additional evaluation criteria are typically placed on the playing programs beyond mere performance in competition: criteria intended to ensure that methods used to achieve strength on a specific game will transfer also to new games. Such criteria include the use of learning and planning, and the ability to play more than one game.

However, even this generality-oriented research is subject to a potential methodological bias. The human researchers know at the time of program-development which specific game or games the program will be tested on, and therefore it is possible that they import the results of their own understanding of the game directly into their program. In this case, it is difficult to determine whether the subsequent performance of the program is due to the general theory it implements, or merely to the insightful observations of its developer about the characteristics necessary for strong performance on this particular game. An instance of this problem is the *fixed representation trick* (Flann & Dietterich 1989), in which many developers of learning systems spend much of their time finding a representation of the game which will allow their systems to learn how to play it well.

This problem is seen more easily when computer game-playing with known games is viewed schematically, as in Figure 1. Here, the human researcher or programmer is aware of the rules and specific knowledge for the game to be programmed, as well as the resource bounds within which the program must play. Given this information, the human then constructs a playing program to play that game. The program then plays in competition, and is modified based on the outcome of this experience, either by the human, or perhaps by itself in the case of experience-based learning programs. In all cases, what is significant about this picture is that the human stands in the centre, and mediates the relation between the program and the game it plays.

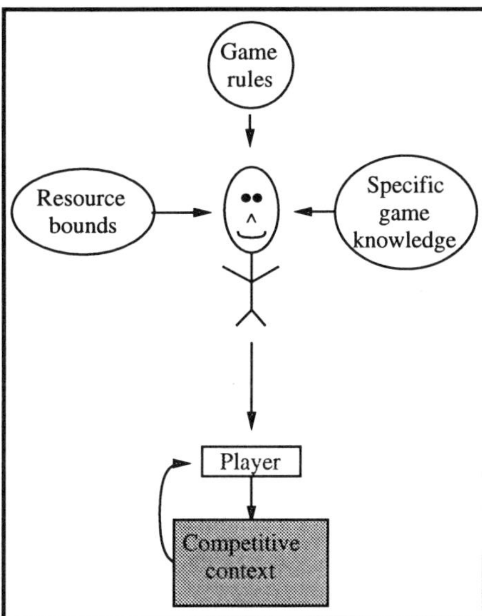

Figure 1: Computer Game-Playing with existing games: the human programmer mediates the relation between the program and the game it plays.

1.1 Metagame

Most AI games researchers, when pressed, will confess that their real interest is not in writing an expert-level chess program or checkers program. Their interest is in understanding general principles that are best tested by play at these well-understood games. This introduces the possibility of experimental bias. An experimenter can design a program that takes advantage of peculiar features of a single game, or uses a tuned representation to permit the program to learn features that the experimenter is well aware of.

The concept of *Meta-Game Playing* (Pell 1992a), shown schematically in Figure 2, is an attempt to reduce the possibility of such bias. Rather than designing a program to play an existing game known in advance, we design a *metagamer* to play a large but well-defined *class* of games. A metagamer takes as input only the rules of a new game (as produced by an automatic game generator and encoded in a well-specified language), and then produces a specialised program (a *player*) to play that game. Different metagamers are evaluated in the context of a *Metagame-tournament*, in which a set of new games are generated, the game rules are provided directly to the programs, and the programs then play the games against each other without human intervention. As only the *class* of games is known to the human developer in advance, metagamers are required to perform any game-specific optimisations with-

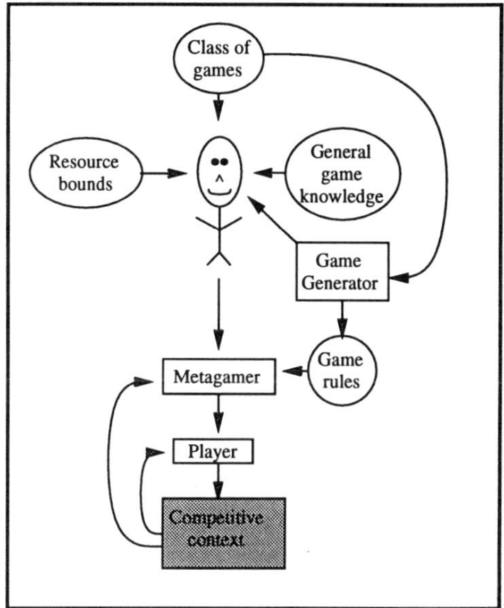

Figure 2: Metagame-playing with new games.

out human assistance. The challenge is to produce the metagamer which receives the highest overall score across all game instances and opponents in the tournament. In contrast with the discussion on existing games above, the human no longer mediates the relation between the program and the games it plays, instead she mediates the relation between the program and the *class* of games it plays. By making the class explicit, we are able to quantify the level of generality achieved. Moreover, we can begin with classes which represent only moderate generalisations over tasks we have already looked at, and gradually move to more general classes of problems as scientific understanding develops.

1.2 SCL-Metagame

SCL-Metagame (Pell 1992b) is a Metagame research problem based around the class of symmetric chess-like games. The class includes the games of chess, checkers, noughts and crosses, Chinese-chess, and Shogi. An implemented game generator produces new games in this class (some of which are objects of interest in their own right (Pell 1992b)).

Symmetric Chess-Like Games A *symmetric chess-like game* is a two-player game of perfect information, in which the two players move pieces along specified directions, across rectangular boards. Different pieces have different powers of movement, capture, and promotion, and interact with other pieces based on ownership and piece type. Goals involve eliminating certain types of pieces (*eradicate goals*), driving a player out of moves (*stalemate goals*), or getting certain pieces to occupy specific squares (*arrival goals*). Most importantly, the games are *symmetric* between the two players, in that all the rules can be presented from the perspective of one player only, and the differences in goals and movements are solely determined by the direction from which the different players view the board. For a formal definition and analysis of this class of games, see Pell (1992b).

Game Generation The goal of game generation is to produce a wide variety of games, all of which fall in the class of games as described by a *grammar*. Pell (1992b) implemented a statistical game generator for this class, and Pell (1993c) analysed the complexity and variety of games it produces.

Structure of Paper With the provision of the class definition and generator, Pell (1992b) formally defined the Metagame research problem of SCL-Metagame. This paper extends that work by constructing the first program to play games in this class, and by evaluating this program within the Metagame paradigm. The rest of this paper is organised as follows. Section 2 discusses the general architecture and the class-specific knowledge implemented in METAGAMER. Section 3 illustrates the analysis performed by METAGAMER to determine piece values for the games of chess and checkers, when presented with only the rules of those games. Section 4 discusses experiments with METAGAMER on those existing games and on newly generated games. Section 5 compares METAGAMER to other work on general game-playing programs and on automatic methods for determining feature values in games. Section 6 concludes the paper.

2   Constructing a Metagame-player

The main intention of Metagame is to serve as a test-bed for learning and planning. One obvious test of a testbed is to compute lower bounds: how well do existing techniques perform on the challenges of the testbed. In this section, we engineer a metagamer using existing game-playing techniques.

Search Engine To this end, the search engine used incorporates many standard game-playing search techniques (see Levy & Newborn (1991)). It is based on the *minimax* algorithm with *alpha-beta pruning*, *iterative deepening*, and the *principal continuation heuristic*. More details of the Metagame search engine are given by Pell (1993c).

Automated Efficiency Optimisation This powerful search engine should allow a playing program to search deeply. However, search speed is linked to the speed with which the primitive search operations of move-generation and goal detection can be performed. For a game-specific program, these issues can be easily hand-engineered, but for a program which is to play an entire class of games, the excess overhead of such generality initially caused the search to be unbearably slow. This problem was overcome by using a *knowledge-compilation* approach. We represent the semantics of the class of games in an extremely general but inefficient manner, and after receiving the rules of a given game the program automatically *partially evaluates* the general theory with respect to it, thus compiling away both unnecessary conditionality and the overhead of interpretation (Pell 1993a). In addition to the partial evaluation techniques discussed by Pell (1993a), METAGAMER contains a set of pre-computation methods which produce *static-analysis tables*. These tables speed up position evaluation by caching compute-intensive properties, in some cases providing approximate versions of knowledge which would be too expensive to compute correctly at runtime (Pell 1993c).

2.1   Meta-Level Evaluation Function

With the search engine in place, using the optimised primitive operations, we have a program which can search as deeply as resources permit, in any position in any game in this class. The remaining task is to develop an evaluation function which will be useful across many known and unknown games.

Following the approach used in HOYLE (Epstein 1989), we view each feature as an *advisor*, which encapsulates a piece of advice about why some aspect of a position may be favourable or unfavourable to one of the players. This section briefly explains some of the advisors currently implemented for METAGAMER. It should be noted that this list is incomplete due to space limitations, the set is still growing, and there are several important general heuristics which are not yet incorporated (such as *distance* and *control* (Snyder 1993)). Motivation and more detailed descriptions of all advisors were provided by Pell (1993c; 1993b). The advisors can be categorised into four groups, based on the general concepts from which they derive.

Mobility Advisors The first group is concerned with different indicators of *mobility*. These advisors were inspired in part by Church & Church (1979) and Botvinnik (1970), and by generalising features used for game-specific programs (Pell 1993c).

- `capturing-mobility`: counts the captures each piece could make in the current position.

- `dynamic-mobility`: counts the squares to which a piece can move directly from its current square on the current board, using a *moving* ability.[1]

- `static-mobility`: a static version of the above, this counts the squares to which a piece could move directly from its current square on an otherwise empty board.

- `eventual-mobility`: measures the total value of all squares to which a piece could move eventually from its current square on an otherwise empty board, using a *moving* ability. The value of each square decreases with the number of moves required for the piece to get there.[2]

Threats The second group of advisors deals with threats and conditions enabling threats. The advisors come in two types, *local* and *global*. Local advisors assess each threat separately, and return the sum of the values of all threats in a position. Global advisors determine the most important of these threats, and return only the maximum value of the local advisors. To determine the value of a threat, these advisors make use of the other advisors to determine, for example, the contribution a threatened piece makes to the present position.

Goals and Step Functions The third group of advisors is concerned with goals and regressed goals for this class of games.

- `vital`: Measures dynamic progress by both players on goals to eradicate sets of pieces.

- `arrival-distance`: this is a decreasing function of the abstract number of moves it would take a piece to *move* (i.e. without capturing) from its current square to a goal *destination* on an otherwise empty board, where this abstract number is based on the minimum distance to the destination plus the cost/difficulty of clearing the path.

- `promote-distance`: for each *target-piece* that a piece could promote into, this measures both the value and difficulty of achieving such a promotion.

- `possess`: This advisor handles games involving *placements*, in which a player can place a piece down on any of a set of squares. The value in such a situation is related to value the piece would have on the maximum available square.[3]

---

[1] Pieces in this class (e.g. checkers pieces) may move and capture in different ways (see Section 1.2).

[2] Thus while a bishop has 32 eventual moves and a knight has 64 from any square, the bishop can reach most of its squares more quickly, a fact captured by this advisor.

[3] Examples of such placement games are Shogi and Nine-Men's Morris.

Material Value The final group of advisors are used for assigning a fixed material value to each type of piece, which is later awarded to a player for each piece of that type he owns in a given position. This value is a weighted sum of the values returned by the advisors listed in this section, and does not depend on the position of the piece or of the other pieces on the board.

- `max-static-mob`: The maximum static-mobility for this piece over all board squares.

- `avg-static-mob`: The average static-mobility for this piece over all board squares.

- `max-eventual-mob`: The maximum eventual–mobility for this piece over all board squares.

- `avg-eventual-mob`: The average eventual-mobility for this piece over all board squares.

- `victims`: Awards 1 point for each type of piece this piece has the ability to capture (i.e. the number of pieces matching one of its *capture-types*).[4]

- `eradicate`: Awards 1 point for each opponent goal to eradicate this piece, and minus one point for each player goal to eradicate this piece.

- `stalemate`: This views the goal to stalemate a player as if it were a goal to eradicate all of the player's pieces, and performs the same computation as *eradicate* above.

- `promote`: This is computed in a separate pass after all the other material values. It awards a piece a fraction of the material value (computed so far) of each piece it can promote into. This advisor is not fully implemented yet, and was not used in the work discussed in this paper.

Section 3 provides concrete examples of the application of these advisors to the rules of different games discussed in this paper.

2.2 Weights for Advisors

The last major issue concerning the construction of the strategic evaluation function involves assigning weights to each advisor. While this issue is already difficult in the case of existing games, it is correspondingly more difficult when we move to unknown games, where we are not even assured of the presence of a strong opponent to learn from. However, the construction of some advisors provides one significant constraint on their possible values. For advisors which anticipate goal-achievement (such as `promote-distance` and the threat advisors), it would seem that their weight should not exceed 1. The reason is that they return some fraction of the

---

[4] A more sophisticated version of this feature, not fully implemented yet, takes into account the value of each victim, as determined by other static advisors.

value derived from achieving their anticipated goal. If such an advisor were weighted double, for example, the value of the threat would exceed the anticipated value of its execution, and the program would not in general choose to execute its threats.

Beyond the above constraint on such advisors, this issue of weight assignment for Metagame is an open problem. One idea for future research would be to apply temporal-difference learning and self-play (Tesauro 1994) to this problem. It would be interesting to investigate whether the "knowledge-free" approach which is so successful in learning backgammon transfers to these different games, or whether it depends for its success on properties specific to backgammon. In the meantime, we have been using METAGAMER with all weights set to 1.[5]

3   Examples of Material Analysis

One important aspect of METAGAMER's game analysis, which was discussed in Section 2.1, is concerned with determining relative values for each type of piece in a given game. This type of analysis is called *material analysis*, and the resulting values are called *material values* or *static piece values*. This section demonstrates METAGAMER's material analysis when applied to chess and checkers. In both cases, METAGAMER took as input only the rules of the games. In conducting this analysis, METAGAMER used the material advisors (Section 2.1) all with equal weight of one point each.

Checkers Table 1 lists material values determined by METAGAMER for the game of checkers, given only an encoding of the rules as an instance of the class of symmetric chess-like games (Pell 1992b).[6] In the table, K stands for *king*, and M stands for *man*. For compactness, advisors which do not apply to a game (and thus have value of 0 for all pieces) are not listed in material analysis tables for that game.

METAGAMER concludes that a king is worth almost two men. According to expert knowledge,[7] this is a gross underestimate of the value of a man. The reason that men are undervalued here is that METAGAMER does not yet consider the static value

---

[5]It should be noted that this is not the same as setting all piece values for a given game to equal value. The general knowledge still imposes constraints on the relative values of individual pieces in a game. For example, even a random setting of weights will cause METAGAMER to value queens above rooks in chess (Pell 1993c).

[6]The game definition for the entire rules of checkers as an instance of this class requires under 250 words and fits on one column of a page. It has been omitted due to space limitations.

[7]I am thankful to Nick Flann for serving as a checkers expert.

Material Analysis: checkers		
	Piece	
Advisor	K	M
max-static-mob	4	2
max-eventual-mob	6.94	3.72
avg-static-mob	3.06	1.53
avg-eventual-mob	5.19	2.64
eradicate	1	1
victims	2	2
stalemate	1	1
Total	23.2	13.9

Table 1: Material value analysis for checkers.

of a piece based on its possibility to promote into other pieces (see Section 2.1). When actually playing a game, METAGAMER does consider this, using the dynamic **promote-distance** advisor.

Chess Table 2 lists material values determined by METAGAMER for the game of chess, given only an encoding of the rules similar to that for checkers (Pell 1993c). In the table, the names of the pieces are just the first letters of the standard piece names, except that N refers to a knight.

Material Analysis: chess						
	Piece					
Advisor	B	K	N	P	Q	R
max-static	13	8	8	1	27	14
max-eventual	12	12.9	14.8	1.99	23.5	20.2
avg-static	8.75	6.56	5.25	0.875	22.8	14
avg-eventual	10.9	9.65	11.8	1.75	22.4	20.2
eradicate	0	1	0	0	0	0
victims	6	6	6	6	6	6
stalemate	1	1	1	1	1	1
Total	51.7	45.1	46.9	12.6	103	75.5

Table 2: Material value analysis for chess.

As discussed for checkers above, pawns are here undervalued because METAGAMER does not consider their potential to promote into queens, rooks, bishops, or knights. According to its present analysis, a pawn has increasingly less eventual-mobility as it gets closer to the promotion rank. Beyond this, the relative value of the pieces is surprisingly close to the values used in conventional chess programs (queen=9, rook=5, bishop=3.25, knight=3, and pawn=1) (Botvinnik 1970; Abramson 1990), given that the analysis was so simplistic.

4 Summary of Results

An evaluation of the game-playing performance of METAGAMER was carried out by Pell (1993c) across a set of existing and generated games.

4.1 Known Games

Performance in the games of chess and checkers demonstrated that the knowledge encoded in METAGAMER endows it with a modest level of competence against highly specialised programs, which was still impressive given that METAGAMER plays these games in effect from first-principles.

Checkers The performance of METAGAMER in checkers was assessed by playing it against Chinook (Schaeffer *et al.* 1991). Chinook is the world's strongest computer checkers player, and the second strongest checkers player in general. As it is a highly optimised and specialised program, it is not surprising that METAGAMER always loses to it (at checkers, of course!). However, to get a baseline for METAGAMER's performance relative to other possible programs when playing against Chinook,[8] we have evaluated the programs when given various handicaps (number of men taken from Chinook at the start of the game).

The primary result from the checkers experiments was that METAGAMER is around even to Chinook, when given a handicap of one man. This is compared to a deep-searching greedy material program which requires a handicap of 4 men, and a random player, which requires a handicap of 8. In fact, in the 1-man handicap positions, METAGAMER generally achieves what is technically a winning position, but it is unable to win against Chinook's defensive strategy of hiding in the double-corner.

On observation of METAGAMER's play of checkers, it was interesting to see that METAGAMER "rediscovered" the checkers strategy of not moving its back men until late in the game. It turned out that this strategy emerged from the `promote-distance` advisor, operating defensively instead of in its "intended" offensive function. In effect, METAGAMER realized from more general principles that by moving its back men, it made the promotion square more accessible to the opponent, thus increasing the opponent's value, and decreasing its own.

Chess In chess, METAGAMER played against Gnu-Chess, a very strong publicly available chess program.[9] GnuChess is vastly superior to META-GAMER (at chess, of course!), unless it is handicapped severely in time and moderately in material. The overall result of the experiments was that METAGAMER is around even to GnuChess on its easiest level,[10] when given a handicap of one knight. For comparison, a version of METAGAMER with only a standard hand-encoded material evaluation function (queen=9, rook=5, bishop=3.25, knight=3, and pawn=1) (Botvinnik 1970; Abramson 1990) played against METAGAMER with all its advisors and against the version of GnuChess used above. The result was that the material program lost every game at knight's handicap against Gnu-Chess, and lost every game at even material against METAGAMER with all its advisors. This showed that METAGAMER's performance was not due to its search abilities, but rather to the knowledge in its evaluation function.

On observation of METAGAMER's play of chess, we have seen the program develop its pieces quickly, place them on active central squares, put pressure on enemy pieces, make favourable exchanges while avoiding bad ones, and restrict the freedom of its opponent. In all, it is clear that METAGAMER's knowledge gives it a reasonable *positional* sense and enables it to achieve longer-term strategic goals while searching only one or two-ply deep. This is actually quite impressive, given that none of the knowledge encoded in METAGAMER's advisors or static analyser makes reference to any properties specific to the game of chess—METAGAMER worked out its own set of material values for each of the pieces (see Section 3), and its own concept of the value of each piece on each square. On the other hand, the most obvious immediate limitation of METAGAMER revealed in these games is a weakness in *tactics* caused in part by an inability to search more deeply within the time constraints, in part by a lack of quiescence search, and also by the reliance on full-width tree-search. These are all important areas for future work.

4.2 New Games

Pell (1993c) carried out an experiment in the form of a *Metagame tournament*. In the experiment, several versions of METAGAMER with different settings of weights for their advisors played against each

---

[8]In our experiments, Chinook played on its easiest level. It also played without access to its opening book or endgame database, although it is unlikely that the experimental results would have been much altered had it been using them.

[9]GnuChess was the winner of the C Language division of the 1992 Uniform Platform Chess Competition.

[10]In the experiments, GnuChess played on level 1 with depth 1. This means it searches 1-ply in general but can still search deeply in quiescence search. METAGAMER played with one minute per move, and occasionally searched into the second-ply.

other and against baseline[11] players on a set of generated games which were *unknown* to the human designer in advance of the competition. The rules were provided directly to the programs, and they played the games without further human intervention. The most significant result of the experiment was that the version of METAGAMER which made use of the most knowledge clearly outperformed all opponents in terms of total score on the tournament. This was true despite the added evaluation cost incurred when using more knowledge. This result is evidence that the knowledge implemented in METAGAMER provides it with competitive strength across the entire class of games, at least relative to more limited versions of itself and to a set of baseline programs.

5   Related Work

This section compares METAGAMER to other work on general game-playing programs and on automatic methods for determining feature values in games.   There have been many efforts to develop general game-playing programs which have been tested on more than one game (Epstein 1989; Williams 1972; Tadepalli 1989; Collins *et al.* 1991; Callan, Fawcett, & Rissland 1991; Gherrity 1993). However, none of these programs have been evaluated within the context of Metagame, which poses several unique challenges.   First, the human designer cannot influence the representation of specific games (as they are input directed to the metagamers). Second, there is no existing body of knowledge or game records for newly generated games, which poses difficulties for approaches which rely on learning concepts or weights from textbooks or large amounts of existing games. Finally, there are no existing experts against which programs can train, which suggests that stronger programs will be based on self-play (Tesauro 1994) or more active forms of rule analysis (such as that performed by METAGAMER).

Despite its simplicity, METAGAMER's analysis produced useful piece values for a wide variety of games, which agree qualitatively with the assessment of experts on some of these games. This appears to be the first instance of a game-playing program automatically deriving material values based on active analysis when given only the rules of different games. It also appears to be the first instance of a program capable of deriving useful piece values for games unknown to the developer of the program

---

¹¹

(Pell 1993c). The remainder of this section compares METAGAMER to previous work with respect to determination of feature values.

Expected Outcome and Self-Play Abramson (1990) developed a technique for determining feature values based on predicting the *expected-outcome* of a position in which particular features (not only piece values) were present. The expected-outcome of a position is the fraction of games a player expects to win from a position if the rest of the game after that position were played randomly. He suggested that this method was an *indirect* means of measuring the mobility afforded by certain pieces. The method is statistical, computationally intensive, and requires playing out many thousands of games. Similar considerations apply to work on self-play (Tesauro 1994; Epstein 1992). On the other hand, the analysis performed by METAGAMER is a *direct* means of determining piece values, which follows from the application of general principles to the rules of a game. It took METAGAMER under one minute to derive piece values for each of the games discussed in this section, and it conducted the analysis without playing out even a single contest.

Automatic Feature Generation There has recently been much progress in developing programs which generate features automatically from the rules of games (de Grey 1985; Callan & Utgoff 1991; Fawcett & Utgoff 1992). When applied to chess such programs produce features which count the number of chess pieces of each type, and when applied to Othello they produce features which measure different aspects of positions which are correlated with mobility. The methods operate on any problems encoded in an extended logical representation, and are more general than the methods currently used by METAGAMER. However, these methods do not generate the *weights* of these features, and instead serve as input to systems which may learn their weights from experience or through observation of expert problem-solving. While METAGAMER's analysis is specialised to the class of symmetric chess-like games, and thus less general than these other methods, it produces piece values which are immediately useful, even for a program which does not perform any learning.

Evaluation Function Learning There has been much work on learning feature values by experience or by observation of strong players (e.g. (Samuels 1967; Lee & Mahajan 1988; Levinson & Snyder 1991; Callan, Fawcett, & Rissland 1991; Tunstall-Pedoe 1991)). These are all examples of passive analysis (Pell 1993c), and would not seem likely to produce a strong program in a Metagame-tournament until later rounds, after which the program would have had significant experience with stronger players.

6 Conclusion

The results on existing and generated games establish METAGAMER as a competent competitor for SCL-Metagame. At present, a number of challenger Metagame-playing programs are under development by independent researchers in the games and learning communities. This raises the possibility of a large-scale Metagame-tournament in the near future, which is an exciting prospect.

7 Acknowledgements

Thanks to Jonathan Schaeffer for permitting me to use Chinook, and to Stuart Cracraft for making GnuChess available. Thanks also to Othar Hansson, Robert Levinson, Pandu Nayak, Manny Rayner, and the anonymous reviewers for useful comments on drafts of this work. Parts of this work have been supported by the British Marshall Scholarship, the American Friends of Cambridge University, Trinity College (Cambridge), and the Cambridge University Computer Laboratory.

References

Abramson, B. 1990. Expected-outcome: A general model of static evaluation. *IEEE Transactions on Pattern Analysis and Machine Intelligence* 12(2).

Botvinnik, M. M. 1970. *Computers, chess and long-range planning.* Springer-Verlag New York, Inc.

Callan, J. P., and Utgoff, P. 1991. Constructive induction on domain knowledge. In *Proceedings of AAAI-91.*

Callan, J. P.; Fawcett, T. E.; and Rissland, E. L. 1991. Adaptive case-based reasoning. In *Proceedings of IJCAI-91.*

Church, R. M., and Church, K. W. 1979. Plans, goals, and search strategies for the selection of a move in chess. In Frey, P. W., ed., *Chess Skill in Man and Machine.* Springer-Verlag.

Collins, G.; Birnbaum, L.; Krulwich, B.; and Freed, M. 1991. Plan debugging in an intentional system. In *Proceedings of IJCAI-91.*

de Grey, A. 1985. Towards a versatile self-learning board game program. Final Project, Tripos in Computer Science, University of Cambridge.

Epstein, S. 1989. The Intelligent Novice - Learning to Play Better. In Levy, D., and Beal, D., eds., *Heuristic Programming in Artificial Intelligence - The First Computer Olympiad.* Ellis Horwood.

Epstein, S. 1992. Learning Expertise from the Opposition: The role of the trainer in a competitive environment. In *Proceedings of AI 92.*

Fawcett, T. E., and Utgoff, P. E. 1992. Automatic feature generation for problem solving systems. In Sleeman, D., and Edwards, P., eds., *Proceedings of the Ninth International Workshop on Machine Learning.*

Flann, N. S., and Dietterich, T. G. 1989. A study of explanation-based methods for inductive learning. *Machine Learning* 4.

Gherrity, M. 1993. *A Game-Learning Machine.* Ph.D. Dissertation, University of California, San Diego.

Lee, K.-F., and Mahajan, S. 1988. A pattern classification approach to evaluation function learning. *Artificial Intelligence* 36.

Levinson, R. A., and Snyder, R. 1991. Adaptive, pattern-oriented chess. In *Proceedings of AAAI-91.*

Levy, D., and Newborn, M. 1991. *How Computers Play Chess.* W.H. Freeman and Company.

Pell, B. 1992a. Metagame: A New Challenge for Games and Learning. In van den Herik, H., and Allis, L., eds., *Heuristic Programming in Artificial Intelligence 3 - The Third Computer Olympiad.* Ellis Horwood.

Pell, B. 1992b. Metagame in Symmetric, Chess-Like Games. In van den Herik, H., and Allis, L., eds., *Heuristic Programming in Artificial Intelligence 3 - The Third Computer Olympiad.* Ellis Horwood.

Pell, B. 1993a. Logic Programming for General Game Playing. In *Proceedings of the ML93 Workshop on Knowledge Compilation and Speedup Learning.*

Pell, B. 1993b. A Strategic Metagame Player for General Chess-Like Games. In *Proceedings of the AAAI Fall Symposium on Games: Planning and Learning.*

Pell, B. 1993c. *Strategy Generation and Evaluation for Meta-Game Playing.* Ph.D. Dissertation, Computer Laboratory, University of Cambridge.

Samuels, A. L. 1967. Some studies in machine learning using the game of Checkers. ii. *IBM Journal* 11.

Schaeffer, J.; Culberson, J.; Treloar, N.; Knight, B.; Lu, P.; and Szafron, D. 1991. Reviving the game of checkers. In Levy, D., and Beal, D., eds., *Heuristic Programming in Artificial Intelligence 2 - The Second Computer Olympiad.* Ellis Horwood.

Snyder, R. 1993. Distance: Toward the unification of chess knowledge. Master's thesis, University of California, Santa Cruz.

Tadepalli, P. 1989. Lazy explanation-based learning: A solution to the intractable theory problem. In *Proceedings of IJCAI-89.*

Tesauro, G. 1994. TD-Gammon, A Self-Teaching Backgammon Program, Achieves Master-Level Play. *Neural Computation* 6(2).

Tunstall-Pedoe, W. 1991. Genetic Algorithms Optimizing Evaluation Functions. *ICCA-Journal* 14(3).

Williams, T. G. 1972. Some studies in game playing with a digital computer. In Siklossy, and Simon, H., eds., *Representation and Meaning.* Prentice-Hall.

An Analysis of Forward Pruning *

Stephen J. J. Smith
Department of Computer Science
University of Maryland
College Park, MD 20742
sjsmith@cs.umd.edu

Dana S. Nau
Department of Computer Science, and
Institute for Systems Research
University of Maryland
College Park, MD 20742
nau@cs.umd.edu

Abstract

Several early game-playing computer programs used *forward pruning* (i.e., the practice of deliberately ignoring nodes that are believed unlikely to affect a game tree's minimax value), but this technique did not seem to result in good decision-making. The poor performance of forward pruning presents a major puzzle for AI research on game playing, because some version of forward pruning seems to be "what people do," and the best chess-playing programs still do not play as well as the best humans.

As a step toward deeper understanding of forward pruning, we have set up models of forward pruning on two different kinds of game trees, and used these models to investigate how forward pruning affects the probability of choosing the correct move. In our studies, forward pruning did better than minimaxing when there was a high correlation among the minimax values of sibling nodes in a game tree.

This result suggests that forward pruning may possibly be a useful decision-making technique in certain kinds of games. In particular, we believe that bridge may be such a game.

Introduction

Much of the difficulty of game-playing is due to the large number of alternatives that must be examined and discarded. One method for reducing the number of nodes examined by a game tree search is *forward pruning*, in which at each node of the search tree, the search procedure may discard some of the node's children before searching below that node. On perfect-information zero-sum games such as chess, forward pruning has not worked as well as approaches that do not use forward pruning [4, 24]. This presents a major puzzle for AI research on game playing, because some version of forward pruning seems to be "what people do," and the best chess-playing programs still do not play as well as the best humans. Thus, it is important to try to understand why programs have been unable to utilize forward pruning as effectively as humans have done, and whether there are ways to utilize forward pruning more effectively.[1]

As a step toward deeper understanding of how forward pruning affects quality of play, in this paper we set up a model of forward pruning on two abstract classes of game trees, and we use this model to investigate how forward pruning affects the probability of choosing the correct move. Our results suggest that forward pruning works best in situations where there is a high correlation among the minimax values of sibling nodes. Since we believe that bridge has this characteristic, this encourages us to believe that forward pruning may work better in the game of bridge than it has worked in other games.

Forward-Pruning Models

Consider a zero-sum game between two players, Max and Min. If the game is a perfect-information game, then the "correct" value of each node u is normally taken to be the well known *minimax value*:

$$
mm(u) = \begin{cases}
\text{the payoff at } u \\
\quad \text{if } u \text{ is a terminal node;} \\
\max\{mm(v) : v \text{ is a child of } u\} \\
\quad \text{if it is Max's move at } u; \\
\min\{mm(v) : v \text{ is a child of } u\} \\
\quad \text{if it is Min's move at } u.
\end{cases}
$$

Due to the size of the game tree, computing a node's true minimax value is impractical for most games. For this reason, game-playing programs usually mark some non-terminal nodes as terminal, and evaluate them using some static evaluation function $e(u)$. The simplest version of this approach is what Shannon [16] called "Type A" pruning: choose some arbitrary cutoff depth d, and mark a non-terminal node u as terminal if and only if u's depth exceeds d. A more sophisticated version of this is *quiescence search*: mark a non-terminal

---

*This work supported in part by an AT&T Ph.D. scholarship to Stephen J. J. Smith, Maryland Industrial Partnerships (MIPS) grant 501.15, Great Game Products, and NSF grants NSFD CDR-88003012 and IRI-9306580.

[1]In particular, we are developing a forward-pruning search technique for the game of bridge [17, 18], by extending task-network planning techniques [22, 23, 13, 20] to represent multi-agency and uncertainty.

node u as terminal if and only if u's depth exceeds d and u is "quiet" (i.e., there is reason to believe that $e(u)$ will be reasonably accurate at u).

To further decrease the number of nodes examined, game-tree-search procedures have been developed such as alpha-beta [5], B* [2], or SSS* [21]. These procedures will ignore any node v below u that they can prove will not affect u's minimax value $mm(u)$.

This approach has worked well in games such as chess [3, 7], checkers [15, 14], and othello [6]. A more aggressive approach is *forward pruning*, in which the procedure deliberately ignores v if it believes v is *unlikely* to affect $mm(u)$, even if there is no proof that v will not affect $mm(u)$. Although several early computer chess programs used forward pruning, it is no longer widely used, because chess programs that used it did less well than those that did not [4, 24].

Our Model of Forward Pruning

In the game trees investigated in this paper, the value of each leaf node is either 1, representing a win for Max, or 0, representing a win for Min. Our model of a forward-pruning algorithm works as follows. At each node u where it is Max's move, u has three children, u_1, u_2, and u_3. The forward-pruning algorithm will choose exactly two of these three nodes to investigate further. Normally, it will make this choice by applying a static evaluation function $eval(.)$ to the three nodes, and discarding the node having the lowest value—and this is what we do in the "Statistical Studies" section. For our mathematical derivations, we assume fixed probabilities for which nodes will be chosen and which node will be discarded, as described below. There are three possible cases:

1. Two of the nodes, say u_1 and u_2, have minimax values representing wins for the current player. One of the nodes, say u_3, has a minimax value representing a loss for the current player. Then the *correct* two children to investigate further are the ones whose minimax values are the same as the minimax value of u, in this case u_1 and u_2. Thus, for a Max node, the correct children have value 1; for a Min node, the correct children have value 0. If the algorithm does not choose both of the correct children, then the algorithm will search only one of u_1 and u_2. Thus, it will continue part of its search down an incorrect branch, in this case the branch leading to u_3. This may result in an error in the algorithm's computation of u's minimax value.

   In our mathematical derivations, we assume that the probability of choosing the correct two children is p, where p is constant throughout the tree. The algorithm's probability of choosing one correct child and the incorrect child is thus $(1 - p)/2$ for each correct child.

2. One of the nodes, say u_1, has a minimax value representing a win for the current player. Two of the

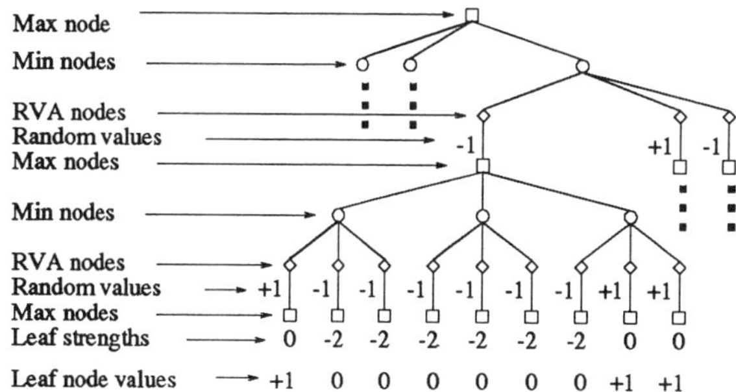

Figure 1: Example of an N-game-like tree.

nodes, say u_2 and u_3, have minimax values representing losses for the current player. In this case, the correct child is u_1. If the algorithm chooses the two incorrect nodes, it will continue the rest of its search down incorrect branches, those leading to u_2 and u_3. This is likely to result in an error in the algorithm's computation of u's minimax value.

In our mathematical derivations, we assume that the probability of choosing the two incorrect nodes is r, where r is constant throughout the tree. The algorithm's probability of choosing the correct child and one incorrect child is thus $(1 - r)/2$ for each incorrect child. (For the rest of this paper, we will set $r = (1 - p)^2$ and define $q = 1 - (p + r)$.)

3. All of the nodes have the same minimax value. In this case, all children are equally correct; the algorithm's probability of choosing any given pair of branches is $1/3$.

Game-Tree Models

In this section, we define two different classes of game trees. In later sections, we will investigate how forward pruning behaves on these trees.

N-Game trees and N-Game-Like Trees

An *N-game-like tree* is a complete tree that contains the following types of nodes (for example, see Fig. 1):

1. *Max* nodes, where it is Max's move. Each Max node is either a leaf node or has three children, all of which are Min nodes.

2. *Min* nodes, where it is Min's move. Each Min node has three children, all of which are RVA nodes.

3. *RVA* (random-value addition) nodes, which have numeric values assigned to them at random. The numeric value of each RVA node is chosen independently from the set $\{-1, 1\}$ with probability p_N being the probability of choosing 1. (For the rest of this paper, we will set $p_N = 0.61803$, the golden ratio, so that in the limit, there is still a nonzero probability of each player having a forced win in the game tree.) Each RVA node has a single child, which is a Max node.

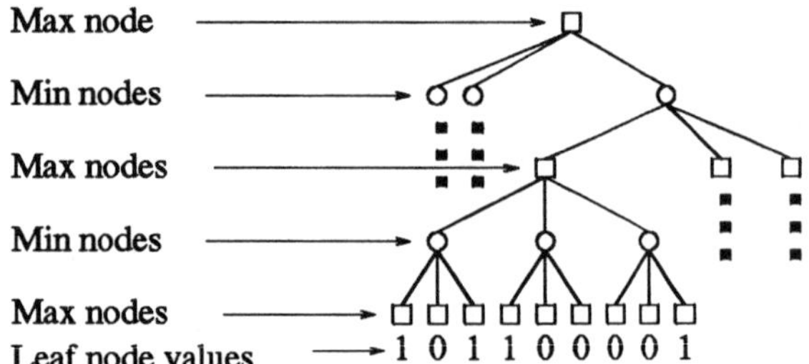

Figure 2: Example of a P-game tree.

The tree's *Max-height*, h, is one less than the number of Max nodes on any path from the root to a leaf node.[2] The *strength* of each leaf node u is the sum of the values of the RVA nodes on the path from the root to u. If the strength of a leaf node is nonnegative, it is classified as a win; otherwise, it is classified as a loss.

An N-game tree, as defined in [9, 10], is similar to the N-game-like trees defined above, except that N-game trees have no RVA nodes. Instead, a value of 1 or -1 is randomly assigned to each arc, with a probability of 0.5 of choosing 1. In this paper, we study N-game-like trees in the "Mathematical Derivations" section, and N-game trees in the "Statistical Studies" section.

Comparison with Bridge

In the game of bridge, the basic unit of play is the trick. After each side has made a move, one side or the other wins the trick. At each point in a bridge hand, the *trick score* for each side is the number of tricks that side has scored so far. The outcome of the hand depends on each side's trick score at the end of the hand.

This trick-scoring method gives bridge a superficial resemblance to the N-game-like trees defined above. To see this, consider a node v in a bridge game tree, and suppose that v represents a bridge deal in which n tricks are left to be played. If T is the subtree rooted at v, then the trick scores of the leaves of T cannot differ from one another by any more than n. A similar situation occurs in an N-game-like tree of height h: if a Max node v has a Max-height of n, and T is the subtree rooted at v, then the strength of the leaves of T cannot differ from one another by any more than $2n$.

P-Game Trees

A *P-game tree* [9, 10, 12] is a complete tree that contains the following types of nodes (an example appears in Fig. 2):

1. *Max* nodes, where it is Max's move. Each Max node is either a leaf node or has exactly three children, all of which are Min nodes.

---

[2]This is analogous to the height of a complete tree (which is one less than the number of nodes on any path from the root to a leaf node), except that here we only count Max nodes.

2. *Min* nodes, where it is Min's move. Each Min node has exactly three children, which are both Max nodes.

As before, the tree's *Max-height*, h, is one less than the number of Max nodes on any path from the root to a leaf node. Since the tree is complete, each leaf node has the same height, and thus the same Max-height. The value of each leaf node u is randomly, independently chosen from a the set $\{0, 1\}$, with probability p_P of choosing 1. (For the rest of this paper, we will set $p_P = 0.68233$, in order to guarantee that in the limit, there is still a nonzero probability that each player will have a forced win in the game tree [1, 11, 9].) Because u's value does not depend on the path from the root to u, there is no need for RVA nodes.

Mathematical Derivations

Forward Pruning on N-Game-Like Trees

We want to compute the probability that the forward-pruning algorithm estimates a value of s and the actual value is t for an N-game-like tree T whose Max-height is h. That is, we want Pr[estimated value s, actual value $t \mid T$'s Max-height is h]. We can compute this from the node strengths, as follows. Let

$$e_{h,x,y} = \text{Pr[estimated strength } x\text{, actual strength } y \mid \text{Max-height } h\text{, root is a Max node]};$$

$$f_{h,x,y} = \text{Pr[estimated strength } x\text{, actual strength } y \mid \text{Max-height } h\text{, root is an RVA node]};$$

$$g_{h,x,y} = \text{Pr[estimated strength } x\text{, actual strength } y \mid \text{Max-height } h\text{, root is a Min node]}.$$

These probabilities depend on p and p_N (recall that $p_N = 0.61803$). The base case is $e_{0,x,y} = 1$ if $x = y = 0$, and $e_{0,x,y} = 0$ otherwise. The recurrence for $f_{h,x,y}$ is

$$f_{h,x,y} = p_N e_{h,x-1,y-1} + (1 - p_N)e_{h,x+1,y+1}.$$

The recurrences for $g_{h,x,y}$ and $e_{h+1,x,y}$ are too complicated to include here; see [19]. Now, let

$$\bar{e}_{h,s,t} = \text{Pr[estimated value } s\text{, actual value } t \mid \text{Max-height } h\text{, root is a Max node]};$$

$$\bar{f}_{h,s,t} = \text{Pr[estimated value } s\text{, actual value } t \mid \text{Max-height } h\text{, root is an RVA node]};$$

$$\bar{g}_{h,s,t} = \text{Pr[estimated value } s\text{, actual value } t \mid \text{Max-height } h\text{, root is a Min node]}.$$

Then

$$\bar{e}_{h,1,1} = \sum_{x:x \geq 0} \sum_{y:y \geq 0} e_{h,x,y};$$

$$\bar{e}_{h,1,0} = \sum_{x:x \geq 0} \sum_{y:y < 0} e_{h,x,y};$$

$$\bar{e}_{h,0,1} = \sum_{x:x < 0} \sum_{y:y \geq 0} e_{h,x,y};$$

$$\bar{e}_{h,0,0} = \sum_{x:x < 0} \sum_{y:y < 0} e_{h,x,y}.$$

For $\bar{f}$ and $\bar{g}$, the equations are similar.

Forward Pruning on P-Game Trees

Since there are no strengths in P-game trees, we can compute the probabilities for the values directly. We define

$$e'_{h,x,y} = \Pr[\text{estimated value } x, \text{ actual value } y \\ \mid \text{Max-height } h, \text{ root is a Max node}];$$

$$g'_{h,x,y} = \Pr[\text{estimated value } x, \text{ actual value } y \\ \mid \text{Max-height } h, \text{ root is a Min node}].$$

The base case is $e_{0,x,y} = p_P$ if $x = 1$ and $y = 1$; $(1-p_P)$ if $x = 0$ and $y = 0$; and 0 otherwise. As shown in [19], the recurrence for $g'_{h,x,y}$ is identical to that for $f_{h,x,y}$, except that each occurrence of $e_{h,m,n}$ is replaced by $e'_{h,m,n}$. The recurrence for $e'_{h+1,x,y}$ is identical to that for $e_{h+1,x,y}$, except that each occurrence of $f_{h,m,n}$ is replaced by $f'_{h,m,n}$.

Probability of Correct Decision

We can use the above recurrences to measure the *probability of correct decision*. This is the probability that the forward-pruning algorithm, given a choice between two alternatives that have different minimax values, will choose the correct one.[3] In particular, consider an N-game-like tree T of Max-height h, whose root is a Max node u with children u_1 and u_2 such that the value of u_1 is greater than the value of u_2. Then

$$
\begin{aligned}
D_h &= \Pr[\text{estimated value of } u_1 > \\
&\qquad \text{estimated value of } u_2] \\
&\quad + \frac{1}{2}\Pr[\text{estimated value of } u_1 = \\
&\qquad \text{estimated value of } u_2] \\
&= [\bar{g}_{h-1,1,1}\bar{g}_{h-1,0,0} + \\
&\quad \frac{\bar{g}_{h-1,0,1}\bar{g}_{h-1,0,0}/2 + \bar{g}_{h-1,1,1}\bar{g}_{h-1,0,1}/2]}{[(\bar{g}_{h-1,1,1} + \bar{g}_{h-1,0,1}) \times (\bar{g}_{h-1,1,0} + \bar{g}_{h-1,0,0})]}.
\end{aligned}
$$

Similarly, for P-game trees,

$$
\begin{aligned}
D'_h &= [g_{h-1,1,1}g_{h-1,0,0} + \\
&\quad \frac{g_{h-1,0,1}g_{h-1,0,0}/2 + g_{h-1,1,1}g_{h-1,0,1}/2]}{[(g_{h-1,1,1} + g_{h-1,0,1}) \times (g_{h-1,1,0} + g_{h-1,0,0})]}.
\end{aligned}
$$

Results and Interpretations

To derive closed-form solutions for the recurrences described in the "Mathematical Derivations" section would be very complicated. However, since we do have exact statements of the base cases and recurrences, we can compute any desired value of $e_{h,x,y}$ or $e'_{h,m,x,y}$, and thus any desired value of D_h or D'_h. We have computed D_h and D'_h for trees of height $h = 1, 2, \ldots, 15$. The results are shown in Fig. 3, along with the probability

---

[3]We have also investigated the probability of correct decision among three alternatives; the formulas [19] are too complicated to present here, but the results are similar.

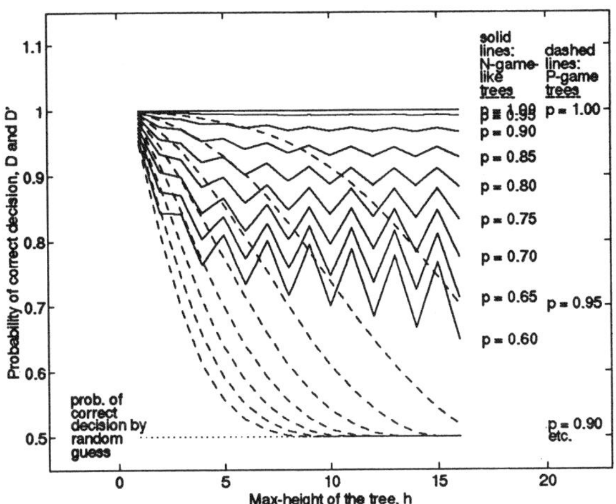

Figure 3: D_h and D'_h versus h for various values of p.

of correct decision by random guess, included for comparison purposes. Our interpretation of these results is as follows:[4]

1. The higher the value of p, the more likely it is that the forward-pruning algorithm will choose the correct two nodes to investigate at each level of the tree, and thus the more likely it is that the algorithm will return a good approximation of the tree's minimax value. As shown in Fig. 3, this occurs in both P-game trees and N-game-like trees.

2. In N-game-like trees, there is much stronger correlation among the values of sibling nodes than there is in P-game trees. Therefore, in N-game-like trees, even if the forward-pruning algorithm chooses the wrong node, the minimax value of this node is not too far from the minimax value we would compute anyway. Thus, as shown in Fig. 3, for each value of p, the forward-pruning algorithm returns more accurate values in N-game-like trees than in P-game trees.

Statistical Studies

The results in the "Mathematical Derivations" section suggest that minimax with forward pruning does better when there is a high correlation among the minimax values of sibling nodes in a game tree. Previous studies [9, 10] have shown that ordinary minimaxing also does better when there is a high correlation among the minimax values of sibling nodes in a game tree. Thus, the next question is whether minimax with forward

---

[4]The probability of correct decision for N-game-like trees exhibits a "manic-depressive" behavior similar to that observed in [8], that is, it is higher for odd Max-heights than it is for even Max-heights. We believe this is because our RVA nodes are only put below Min nodes. Standard N-game trees have the equivalent of our RVA nodes below both Min and Max nodes.

pruning would do better than ordinary minimaxing—
for otherwise, it wouldn't make sense to use forward
pruning for actual game playing.

To answer this question, we computed the probabilities of correct decision at various search depths on
P-game trees and N-game trees, for minimax with and
without forward pruning. For this study, we wanted to
use a real evaluation function rather than a mathematical model of one. This made it impossible to do an
analysis similar to the one in the "Mathmetical Derivations" section, so instead we did a statistical study.

For $h = 2, \ldots, 6$, we generated 5000 ternary N-game
trees and P-game trees of Max-height h. The trees
were generated at random, except that if a tree's root
did not have at least one forced-win child c_{win} and
one forced-loss child c_{loss}, we discarded the tree and
generated another. For each tree T, we did a depth
d minimax search of T,[5] using the same evaluation
function used in [9, 10]:

$$eval(u) = \frac{\text{winning leaf-descendants of } u}{\text{all leaf-descendants of } u}.$$

We did this for $d = 1, \ldots, 2h - 2$.[6] To get a statistical
approximation of the probability of correct decision,
we averaged the following over all 5000 N-game trees
or P-game trees:

$$\text{quantity averaged} = \begin{cases} 1 & \text{if } mm(c_{win}, d-1) > \\ & \quad mm(c_{loss}, d-1), \\ 1/2 & \text{if } mm(c_{win}, d-1) = \\ & \quad mm(c_{loss}, d-1), \\ 0 & \text{otherwise.} \end{cases}$$

We then repeated the same experiment, using minimax
with forward pruning.

The results are shown in Figures 4 and 5, which
graph the probability of correct decision for minimaxing both with and without forward pruning. To indicate how good a decision each approach could produce
given the same amount of search time, these figures
graph the probability of correct decision as a function

---

[5]The depth-d minimax value of a node is

$$mm(u, d) = \begin{cases} eval(u) \text{ (the payoff at } u) \\ \quad \text{if } d = 0 \text{ or } u \text{ is a terminal node,} \\ \max\{mm(v, d-1) : v \text{ is a child of } u\} \\ \quad \text{if it is Max's move at } u, \\ \min\{mm(v, d-1) : v \text{ is a child of } u\} \\ \quad \text{if it is Min's move at } u. \end{cases}$$

where $eval(u)$ is u's evaluation function value. A depth d
minimax search from a node u means computing the depth
$d - 1$ minimax values of u's children.

[6]We did not search to depths $2h - 1$ and $2h$ because
the comparison would not have been fair. At these depths,
ordinary minimaxing applies $eval(u)$ only to nodes within
one move of the end of the game. For such nodes, $eval(u)$
produces perfect results, hence so does ordinary minimaxing.

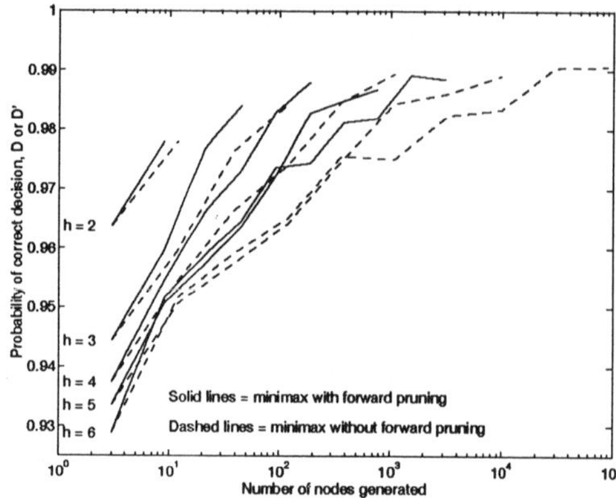

Figure 4: Probability of correct decision on N-games,
versus number of nodes generated, for minimax with
and without forward pruning. The data is averaged
over 5000 game trees.

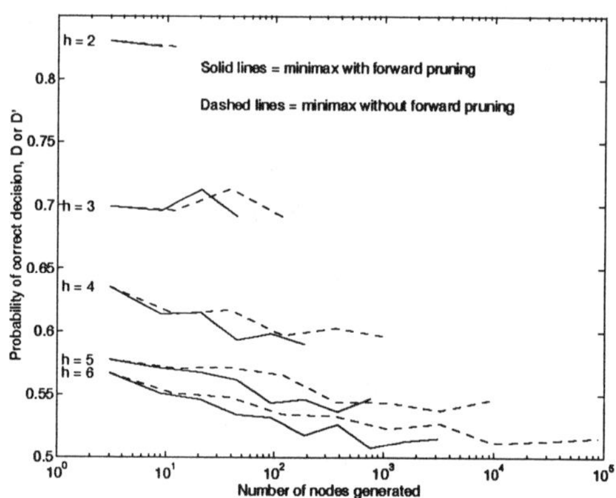

Figure 5: Probability of correct decision on P-games,
versus number of nodes generated, for minimax with
and without forward pruning. The data is averaged
over 5000 game trees.

of the number of nodes generated by the search.[7] As
can be seen, minimaxing with forward pruning generally does better than ordinary minimaxing on N-
games, and slightly worse than ordinary minimaxing
on P-games.

Conclusion

In this paper, we set up models of forward pruning on
ternary N-game-like game trees, and ternary P-game
trees. We used these models to compute the probabil-

---

[7]For ternary game trees, the number of nodes generated
by a ordinary minimax search is $3^1 + \ldots + 3^n = (3^{n+1} - 3)/2$.
The number of nodes generated with forward pruning is
$3(2^0 + \ldots + 2^{n-1}) = 3(2^n - 1)$. This is without alpha-beta
pruning. With alpha-beta pruning, there would have been
a different number of nodes generated in each game tree,
making it difficult to obtain meaningful averages over our
5000 games.

ity of correct decision produced by minimax with and without forward pruning.

In our studies, minimax with forward pruning did better than ordinary minimaxing in cases where there was a high correlation among the minimax values of sibling nodes in a game tree. Thus, forward pruning may possibly be a viable decision-making technique on game trees having the following characteristics:

first characteristic: there is generally a high correlation among sibling nodes;

second characteristic: when there are exceptions to the first characteristic, one can accurately identify them.

To extend our work, we intend to do an empirical study of forward pruning on the game of bridge. We are interested in bridge for the following reasons:

- Bridge is an imperfect-information game, because no player knows exactly what moves the other players are capable of making. Because of this, the game tree for bridge has a large branching factor, resulting in a game tree containing approximately 6.01×10^{44} nodes in the worst case. Ordinary minimax search techniques do not do well in bridge, because they have no chance of searching any significant portion of the game tree.

- Our preliminary studies on the game of bridge show that by using forward-pruning techniques based on task-network planning, we can produce search trees of only about 1300 nodes in the worst case [17]. Thus, forward pruning will allow us to search all the way to the end of the game. Thus, we will not need to use a static evaluation function, and thus will not have to deal with the inaccuracies produced by such functions.

- We believe that bridge has the two characteristics described above, primarily because of the trick-scoring method used in bridge. Thus, we believe that forward pruning techniques may produce reasonably accurate results in bridge.

References

[1] Baudet, G. M. 1978. On the branching factor of the alpha-beta pruning algorithm. *Artif. Intel.* 10:173–199.

[2] Berliner, H. J. 1979. The B* tree search algorithm: A best-first proof procedure. *Artif. Intel.* 12:23–40.

[3] Berliner, H. J.; Goetsch, G.; Campbell, M. S.; and Ebeling, C. 1990. Measuring the performance potential of chess programs. *Artif. Intel.* 43:7–20.

[4] Biermann, A. W. 1978. Theoretical issues related to computer game playing programs. *Personal Computing* 86–88.

[5] Knuth, D. E. and Moore, R. W. 1975. An analysis of alpha-beta pruning. *Artif. Intel.* 6:293–326.

[6] Lee, K.-F. and Mahajan, S. 1990. The development of a world class othello program. *Artif. Intel.* 43:21–36.

[7] Levy, D. and Newborn, M. 1982. *All About Chess and Computers.* Computer Science Press.

[8] Nau, D. S. 1982. The last player theorem. *Artif. Intel.*, 18:53–65.

[9] Nau, D. S. 1982. An investigation of the causes of pathology in games. *Artif. Intel.* 19:257–278.

[10] Nau, D. S. 1983. Pathology on game trees revisited, and an alternative to minimaxing. *Artif. Intel.* 21(1, 2):221–244.

[11] Pearl, J. 1980. Asymptotic properties of minimax trees and game-searching procedures. *Artif. Intel.* 14:113–138.

[12] Pearl, J. 1984. *Heuristics.* Addison-Wesley, Reading, MA.

[13] Sacerdoti, E. D. 1977. *A Structure for Plans and Behavior.* American Elsevier Publishing Company.

[14] Samuel, A. L. 1967. Some studies in machine learning using the game of checkers. ii–recent progress. *IBM Journal of Research and Development* 2:601–617.

[15] Schaeffer, J.; Culberson, J.; Treloar, N.; Knight, B.; Lu, P.; and Szafron, D. 1992. A world championship caliber checkers program. *Artif. Intel.* 53:273–290.

[16] Shannon, C. 1950. Programming a computer for playing chess. *Philosophical Magazine* 7(14):256–275.

[17] Smith, S. J. J.; Nau, D. S.; and Throop, T. 1992. A hierarchical approach to strategic planning with non-cooperating agents under conditions of uncertainty. In *Proc. First Internat. Conf. AI Planning Systems.* 299–300.

[18] Smith, S. J. J. and Nau, D. S. 1993. Strategic planning for imperfect-information games. In *AAAI Fall Symposium on Games: Planning and Learning.*

[19] Smith, S. J. J.; Nau, D. S. Formal and statistical analysis of forward pruning. Forthcoming.

[20] Stefik, M. 1981. Planning with constraints (MOLGEN: Part 1). *Artif. Intel.* 16:111–140.

[21] Stockman, G. C. 1979. A minimax algorithm better than alpha-beta? *Artif. Intel.* 12:179–196.

[22] Tate, A. 1976. Project planning using a hierarchic non-linear planner. Technical Report 25, Department of Artif. Intel., University of Edinburgh.

[23] Tate, A. 1977. Generating project networks. In *Proc. 5th IJCAI.*

[24] Truscott, T. R. 1981. Techniques used in minimax game-playing programs. Master's thesis, Duke University, Durham, NC.

Spatial
Reasoning

Basic Meanings of Spatial Relations:
Computation and Evaluation in 3D Space

Klaus-Peter Gapp
Cognitive Science Program, Dept. of Computer Science
Universität des Saarlandes
D-66041 Saarbrücken, Germany
gapp@cs.uni-sb.de

Abstract

Spatial relations play an important role in the research area of connecting visual and verbal space. In the last decade several approaches to semantics and computation of spatial relations in 2D space have been developed. Presented here is a new approach to the computation and evaluation of basic spatial relations' meanings in 3D space. We propose the use of various kinds of approximations when defining the basic semantics. The vagueness of the applicability of a spatial relation is accounted for by a flexible evaluation component which enables a cognitively plausible continuous gradation. For validating the evolved methods we have integrated them into a workbench. This workbench allows us to investigate the structure of a spatial relation's applicability region through various visualization methods.

Introduction

An important part of research in artificial intelligence deals with connecting visual and verbal space, that is, the translation of visual information into natural language descriptions. The advantage of linguistic descriptions in certain situations is based on the more compact possibilities of language for the transmission of information, compared to a graphical representation with the same content of information (cf. (Wahlster 89)). For generating a scene description in natural language a correct treatment of the *spatial relations* is essential. Spatial relations are independent from a particular language and act on a higher abstract level as a connecting link between visually perceived data and natural language. The linguistic representatives for the spatial relations are prepositions in their spatial meanings (cf. (Retz-Schmidt 88)). Prepositions combined with descriptions of placement, an *object to be localized* (*LO*) and a *reference object* (*REFO*), build the class of *localization expressions* (Herskovits 86).

Today, research and applications in 3D space are increasing in importance. Thus the old definitions of spatial relations, which were mainly for 2D space, need to be extended. For example, a localization expression like *"the car in front of the house"* implies not necessarily that the car is at exactly the same height as the house.

A purely geometrical representation of the semantics of spatial relations is not appropriate (cf. (Miller & Johnson-Laird 76)), because functional dependencies and pragmatic principles are not considered. We therefore propose the use of a multilevel model (cf. (Gapp 93)). On a low level, just the geometrical properties of the objects (*basic meanings*) are considered. The higher levels provide the possibility to include functional dependencies and pragmatic aspects. Our objective here is to present a computational model for the basic meanings of spatial relations which propositionally describes the relationships between geometrical objects in 2D and 3D space.

In the definition of the basic semantics of spatial relations we agree with the thesis of (Landau & Jackendoff 93), that if people are applying spatial relations they do not account for every detail of the objects involved. We are therefore able to use an *approximative* algorithm, which considers only the essential shape properties of an object. The evaluation of a spatial relation's applicability differs from one person to another (cf. (Kochen 74)). This phenomenon is accounted for by integrating a flexible evaluation component. The exact specification of the gradation functions will be determined through psychological experiments, which are currently in progress.

To obtain a validation of the developed algorithms they have been integrated into a workbench. This allows us to investigate the structure of a spatial relation's applicability region through various visualization methods (Gapp 94). The workbench is part of the *VITRA* (VIsual TRAnslator) project which deals with the relationship between vision and natural language (cf. (André et al. 89)).

Related work

Hanßmann (Hanßmann 80) developed in the SWYS project (Hußmann & Schefe 84) a module which answers queries about a 2D scene in German. To express the vagueness of the spatial relations, he uses the functions *SFUNK* and *PFUNK* of Zadeh's Fuzzy-Set Theory (Zadeh 65). Carsten and Janson (Carsten & Janson 85) developed a component in the NAOS project (Neumann 82) for classifying spatial prepositions in 3D traffic scenes. They used a hierarchy for each preposition to generate more specified localization expressions like *exactly behind*. The range of applicability of a spatial relation was fixed, therefore no gradation was supported. Systems which used differentiated values for the applicability of spatial prepositions were the CITYTOUR and the SOCCER system of the VITRA project (André et al. 88). Both systems worked in a 2D environment. A local coordinate system, which depends on the outline of the reference object, is initially defined. The distance between the object to be localized and the referent measured on the local coordinate system is then mapped to a fixed evaluation function ($e^{-\frac{vh}{d_1}}$). (Abella & Kender 93) presented a framework for a system that describes qualitatively 2D objects using spatial prepositions. They define a preposition by a set of inequalities. A fuzzification procedure using Monte Carlo Simulation was used to account for the vagueness of prepositions. Some prerequisites for the prepositions applicability appear to be too restrictive, for example, the applicability of *near* requires an intersection of the objects' bounding boxes.

In the approach presented here, we use an extended local coordinate system to approximate the reference object's extension. Furthermore, we assign high priority to the possibility of a cognitively plausible evaluation of the spatial relations' applicability.

Before turning to the computation, we briefly describe the input of the algorithms — the objects' shape descriptions — and the hierarchy of idealizations used for calculating the basic semantics.

Object representation and idealization

We need a geometrical representation of the observed objects in order to establish spatial relationships between them. The object descriptions we use as input for our algorithms are described in terms of their surface boundaries, i.e., they are specified as collections of faces. The geometrical representation is currently restricted to the following types of faces: planar polygon, box, disc, ring, cylinder, and sphere. The geometrical model can have a hierarchical structure for grouping objects into a new object. The definition of types of objects, which might be instantiated several times, is also supported.

In (Herskovits 86) Herskovits proposed employing various kinds of object idealizations, e.g., object approximations to a point, a line, a surface, a horizontal plane, etc. Landau and Jackendoff also confirm that spatial relations depend mainly on boundedness, surface, or volumetric nature of an object and its axial structure (Landau & Jackendoff 93, p. 226).

Therefore it seems reasonable to consider only approximated shape properties of an object when computing spatial relations. In most cases, it is sufficient to approximate the object to be localized with its center of gravity, since only position is required for the applicability of the spatial relation. In our system the following idealizations are used:

(1) *Center of gravity.* (2) *Bounding rectangle (BR)*: The bounding rectangle of an object with respect to a direction vector $\vec{v}$ is the minimal rectangle which is aligned to $\vec{v}$ and contains the 2D representation of the object. (3) *2D representation*: The base of each object (Necessary when perceiving objects from a bird eye's view, e.g., maps). (4) *Bounding right parallelepiped (BRP)* (5) *3D representation*: The complete geometrical description of an object.

Computation of spatial relations

Three distinct classes of spatial relations are considered, the topological relations, the projective relations, and the relation *between*, which takes an exceptional position in the group of spatial relations. Their basic meanings with respect to their use in the German language, are described first, followed by explanations of the computational procedures. Accounting for the vagueness of the applicability of spatial relations, the result of a computation always lies in the interval [0..1]; the endpoints stand for *not* and *fully* applicable respectively.

Topological relations

The topological prepositions in German considered are *an* (engl. *at*) and *bei* (engl. *near*) in their local use.[1]

The semantics of "at" and "near" The topological relations *at* and *near* both refer to a region proximal to an object. Their range of applicability therefore often overlaps. Differences appear mainly on the pragmatic level. If one has the choice between *near* and *at* to describe a spatial constellation, *near* is never preferred to describe a spatial situation with a direct contact between two objects. Therefore the following definition of the basic semantics is used:

At localizes an object in the proximal exterior of a *REFO*. Contact is not necessary. For the applicability of the relation *near* contact between objects is explicitly prohibited.

But note, in a question like *"Is object A located near object B?"*, it is still possible that contact between A and B exists.

The computational procedure The computational procedure for the topological relations *at* and *near* attempts to reflect the definitions as described above. Depending on the prevailing dimension, the *REFO* is approximated by either its *BR* or *BRP*,

---

[1] In the sequel only the English expressions for the German prepositions are used. Slight differences between the German and the English may appear.

aligned to its intrinsic front and the *LO* by its center of gravity $CG(LO)$. If the *REFO* has no intrinsic front it may acquire an *accidental front* by virtue of its location (cf. (Miller & Johnson-Laird 76)). If a contextual induced accidental front is also not available, then the deictic orientation is used. In the following, only the 3D case is considered. The 2D case can be treated analogously.

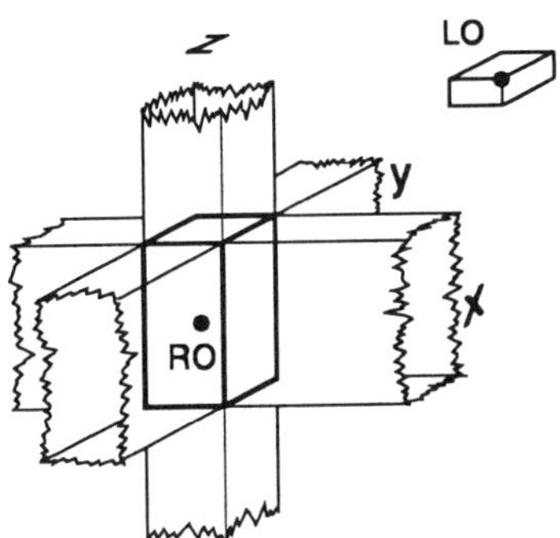

Figure 1: Definition of the *local coordinate system*

Based on the *BRP* of the *REFO*, a *local coordinate system*, as shown in Figure 1, is defined. The intrinsic orientation of the *REFO* $\vec{v}_{REFO}$, projected onto the plane orthogonal to gravitational force (*horizontal*), and the direction of gravity (*vertical*), determine the *BRP's* alignment. Thus, the *REFO* should be in its intrinsic vertical position. If this is not the case at the time of calculation, a transformation of the object relative to its vertical alignment is necessary. The scaling along a single axis corresponds to the extension of the *REFO* along the prevailing dimension. To find the local coordinates of the *LO*, the *BRP* is aligned to the positive y-axis of the *world coordinate system* with the help of a rotation ROT_z around the z-axis and then shifted to the origin. Expressing the rotation and the translation in matrix notation, the transformation matrix $M_{Transform}$ yields:

$$M_{Transform} := M_{Translation} * M_{Rot_z}(\vec{v}_{REFO})$$

Applying the matrix of transformation $M_{Transform}$ to $CG(LO)$ results in the transformed center of gravity $CG_{transf}(LO)$ and thus, the *local* distance $DIST_{loc}$ between *LO* and *REFO* with respect to the local reference system.

$$CG_{transf}(LO) := M_{Transform} * CG(LO)$$

$$DIST_{loc}(LO) := \|CG_{transf}(LO)\|_{loc}$$

The local coordinate system therefore ensures a scaling of the distance between *LO* and *REFO* depending on the prevailing external dimensions of the *REFO*. The approximation of the *LO* by its center of gravity provides a appropriate evaluation if the two *LOs* have different sizes. Therefore, two buildings would typically not stand as near as a building and a fire hydrant.

Using this method, topological relations can be computed in the 2D as well as 3D. Even instances in different dimensions, e.g., the *LO* is a parking lot and the *REFO* is a building, can be handled appropriatly.

The local distances of different *REFOs* are comparable, i.e., object-independent, and this is a requirement for defining a evaluation function, which maps the distances to the interval [0..1] of the degrees of applicability. The evaluation functions used here are cubic spline functions $Spline_{Rel}$. They ensure a continous evaluation and, furthermore, a flexible definition of the graph. Figure 2 shows a possible definition of the evaluation functions for *at* and *near*. In partially instantiated queries incontiguity between regions of objects involved is necessary for a successful evaluation. This is taken into account by the definition of the evaluation function $Spline_{near}$. If the query is fully specified (see the note above), then a curve shape like the one of *at* must be used. By means of modification, addition, and deletion of spline footings the evaluation can be adapted to the prevailing user's perception.

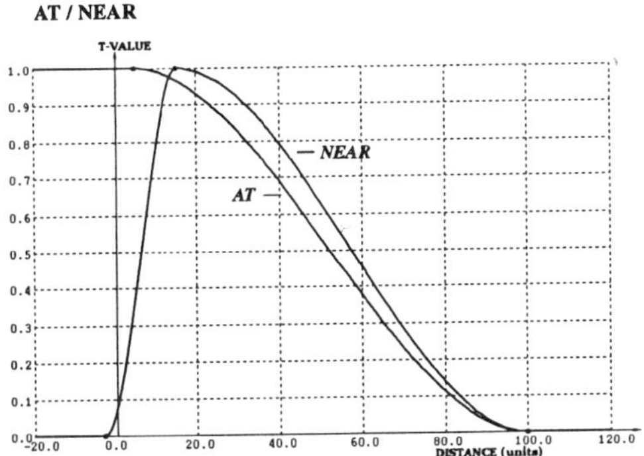

Figure 2: Evaluation functions of the proximal region concerning *at* and *near*

Given two objects *LO* and *REFO*, the function $DA_{Rel_{topo}}$, which computes the degree of applicability $Rel(LO, REFO)$, can now be specified as:

$$DA_{Rel_{topo}} : (LO, REFO) \mapsto SPLINE_{Rel_{topo}}(DIST_{loc}(LO)),$$

with $Rel_{topo} \in \{at, near\}$

For the case local distance equal to 0, i.e., the *LO* is inside the *BRP* or *BR*, but not inside the *REFO*, a special scaling factor is applied to the evaluation function, which is also dependant on the extension of the *REFO*. More details concerning the handling of the so-called *critical areas* can be found in (Gapp 93).

Projective relations

The relations considered are *in front of*, *behind*, *right*, *above*, *below*, and as a special case the relation *beside*, which can be viewed as the disjunction of the relations *right* and *left*. First a description of the basic meanings is given.

The semantics of projective relations To evaluate spatial relations with respect to the projective

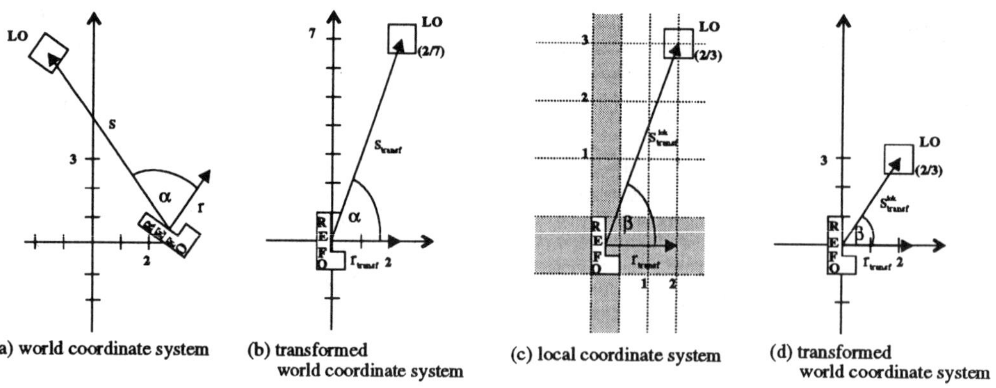

Figure 3: Role of the the coordinate system in angle calculation

prepositions, the computational procedure described above must be extended. The algorithm developed thus far can be used as a basis because using a projective relation as well as topological ensures a localization of an object proximal to a reference object.[2] Consequently, there is an initial requirement for the structure of a projective relation's region of applicability: If the distance from the *LO* to the *REFO* increases, then the degree of applicability decreases. Additionally the factor *direction* must be accounted for in the evaluation. This yields a further segmentation of the proximal region into relevant areas, i.e., areas in which the *LO* reaches a degree of applicability greater than zero. The reference system, which is necessary for the computation, depends on the different ways of looking at the *REFO* (intrinsic, extrinsic or deictic use).

In summary, basic meanings of projective relations localize, with respect to a reference system, an object depending on the proximal region of the *REFO* and the canonical direction implied by the relation. The larger the direction deviation or distance, the smaller the applicability of a projective relation.

The relation *beside* is the only projective relation with an orientation involving two opposite directions, which correspond to relations *right* and *left*. Because the use of *beside* always implies an alignment of the *REFO* it is reasonable to define the region of applicability for *beside* as the union of the applicability regions of the relations *right* and *left*.

The extended evaluation procedure As mentioned before, the existing method for evaluating topological relations can also be used for getting the proximal region of the *REFO* depending on its extension in each dimension. Additional requirements for projective relations are the determination of a reference system (depending on the perspective used), and the

---

[2]This holds in any case for questions using *where*. If the query is fully specified it is possible that the requirement of proximity is not necessary. But this will have to be determined in future research.

inclusion of the canonical direction implied by the prevailing relation. The conceptual system must determine which perspective is to select in a specific case. In intrinsic use, every transformation that has already been applied to the *REFO*, must be reversed and then applied to the *REFO* and the *LO*. This is very important producing the correct result, e.g., using this procedure the computation of *"the thigh is above the knee"* still holds even if the person is sitting on a chair, with the thighs in a horizontal position.

To calculate a reference system for extrinsic/deictic use, the gravitational force determines the vertical axis and the horizontal part of the extrinsic/deictic orientation vector $\vec{v}$ determines arrangement of the two horizontal axes. Dependant on this reference system, the local coordinate system is built up as described above. With respect to this reference system the local distance $DIST_{loc}^{\vec{v}}$ is computed from the local coordinates of the center of gravity and mapped to the evaluation function $SPLINE_{proj}$. In contrast to the evaluation of topological relations, the deviation of the *LO* from the canonical direction, implied by the projective relation, is taken into account. Therefore, let $\vec{r}$ be the direction vector implied by the projective relation and $\vec{s} = CG(LO) - CG(REFO)$. Then $\alpha = \angle(\vec{s}, \vec{r})$ denotes the deviation of *LO* from the canonical direction $\vec{r}$ referring to the world coordinate system (Figure 3a).

Let $\vec{r}_{transf} = M_{transf}(\vec{r})$ and $\vec{s}_{transf} = M_{transf}(\vec{s})$, the transformed vectors of $\vec{r}$ and $\vec{s}$ are referring to the local reference system. The angular deviation is not affected by the transformation (Figure 3b).

Let $\vec{s}_{transf}^{loc} = CG_{transf}(LO) - CG_{transf}(REFO)$ be the vector between the two transformed centers of gravity (referring to the *local* coordinate system). Hence, $\beta = \angle(\vec{s}_{transf}^{loc}, \vec{r}_{transf})$ is the *local angular deviation*, referring to the local reference system, and $\beta \neq \alpha$. This is important because the angles referring to the world coordinates do *not* consider the extension of the *REFO*. However, computing the angle using the local coordinates, as shown in Figure 3c, includes the reference system in the evaluation of the direction deviation. The distinction between the two variants will be obvious when the local coordinates are transferred to the world coordinate system (Figure 3d). Like the local distance, the angle is mapped to a spline function $SPLINE_{angle}$, which results in a value between 0 and 1.

The inclusion of the direction, with the help of the direction deviation, can be applied to 2D as well as to 3D data. In the 3D instance, the angular deviation β increases, corresponding to a larger or smaller z-coordinate of the vector $\vec{v}$ and hence the value of $SPLINE_{angle}(\beta)$ also increases. Given two objects, LO and $REFO$, and an orientation vector $\vec{v}$, the degree of applicability $DA_{Rel_{proj}}$ of a projective relation Rel_{proj} can now be defined as:

$$DA_{Rel_{proj}} : (LO, REFO, \vec{v}) \mapsto$$
$$SPLINE_{prox}(DIST^{\vec{v}}_{loc}(LO)) \cdot SPLINE_{angle}(\beta))$$

with $Rel_{proj} \in \{behind, left, above, ...\}$

Figure 4 is a visual example of the 3D applicability structure of *above* (a) and *right* (b) using a building as $REFO$. The darker the grey areas of the relation's region of applicability are, the higher is the degree of applicability.

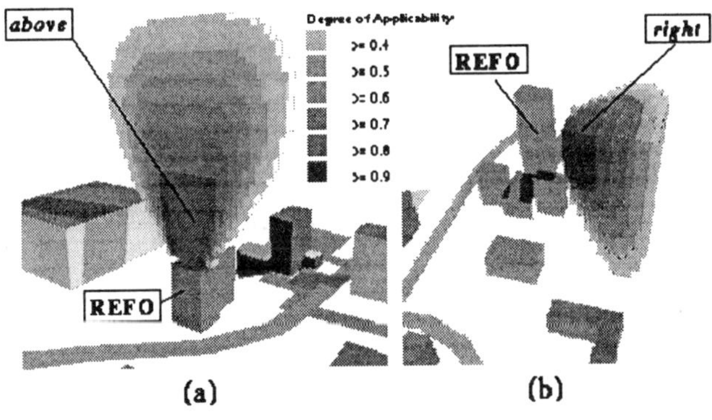

Figure 4: Cross-sections of the 3D applicability structure of *above* and *right*

The relation "between"

The relation *between* occupies an exceptional position among the static relations considered because it refers to two reference objects.

The semantics of "between" The basic meaning of *between* is defined by the structure of its region of applicability. The location with the highest degree of applicability is normally exactly midway between the two $REFOs$ (provided no other object lies inside the interspace) Increasing the distance to this location decreases the applicability, depending on the extension of the $REFOs$. This dependence on the $REFO$ is expressed by a displacement of the region of applicability towards the $REFO$ with the smaller extension. The

structure of the region of applicability is specified pictorially in Figure 5.

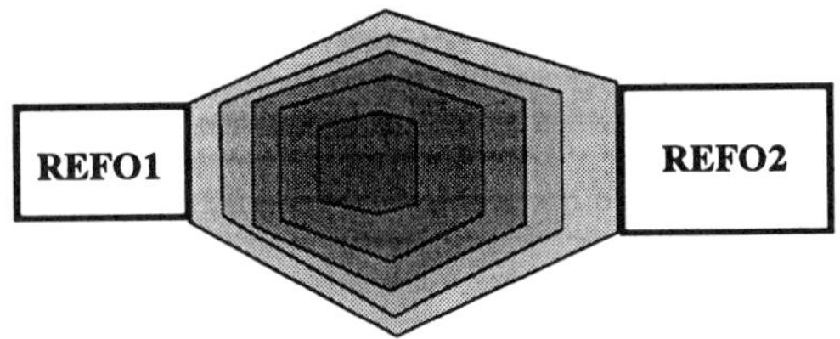

Figure 5: 2D Applicability structure of *between*

The computational procedure Approaches for computing the applicability of *between* can be found in (Hanßmann 80; Habel 89). A cognitively plausible gradation was not supported by these approaches. Because of this, we use a new method to compute the applicability of *between*; it is as follows: Four essential variables need to be considered:

1. The distance between the two $REFOs$
2. The angle $\angle(\overline{CG_{LO}\ CG_{REFO1}}, \overline{CG_{REFO1}\ CG_{REFO2}})$
3. The angle $\angle(\overline{CG_{LO}\ CG_{REFO2}}, \overline{CG_{REFO2}\ CG_{REFO1}})$
4. The extension of the $REFOs$.

Neglecting the second $REFO$ in the requirements given above and taking into account the vector which results from building the difference of the $REFOs$' center of gravity, there are the same requirements that have to be met by the evaluation of the projective relation *in front of*. So it is natural to make use of the computation *in front of* to obtain the semantics of *between*. Hence *between* is defined as:

An object LO is located *between* two reference objects $REFO1$ and $REFO2$, provided it is extrinsic *in front of* $REFO1$, using $REFO2$ as point of view, and vice versa.

Mathematically such a double dependency can be expressed by taking the arithmetic mean of both degrees of applicability:

$$DA_{between} : (LO, REFO1, REFO2) \mapsto$$
$$\frac{DA_{infrontof}(LO, REFO1, \vec{v}_1) + DA_{infrontof}(LO, REFO2, \vec{v}_2)}{2}$$

with $\vec{v}_1 = CG(REFO1) - CG(REFO2)$
and $\vec{v}_2 = CG(REFO2) - CG(REFO1)$

Figure 6 shows that the 2D structure of applicability for the relation *between* fulfills the exact requirements of the semantics above.

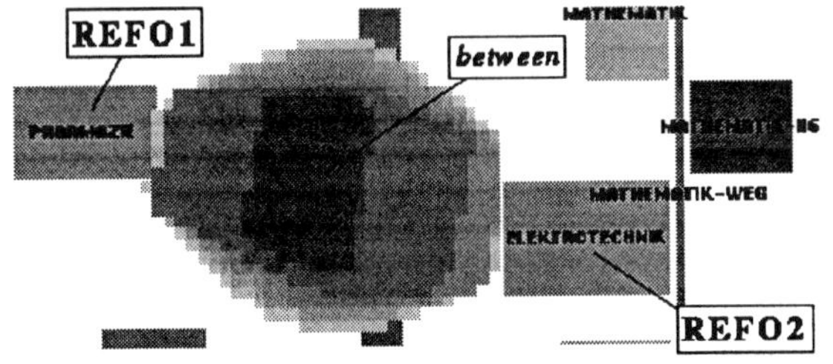

Figure 6: The structure of applicability of *between*

Implementation

The presented computational model was fully implemented and tested. For validation purposes different visualization methods (cf. (Gapp 94)) are used to get an idea of the spatial relations' region of applicability (Figure 4 and 6). The system proceeds from a geometrical scene description and answers questions in natural language about the constellation of the objects involved in a cognitively plausible manner. Using an object indexing method permits an immediate object access to accelerate answering partially instantiated queries. Presently every possible applicable spatial relation has been generated. The construction of a component which decides what spatial relation or compositions in a certain situation should be used is currently under investigation.

The computational model is integrated in a workbench which serves as a basis for the incremental event recognition component of the *VITRA* project.

Conclusion and future work

In this paper methods were developed for computing the basic meanings of spatial relations with respect to geometrical object properties. We have proposed an approximative algorithm which represents a reasonable compromise between simplification and necessary exactness. The described methods for computing the relations between objects in 2D and 3D space consider the extension of the *REFO* and permit a plausible evaluation dependant on the user's perception. The evaluation procedures are applicable to 2D as well as 3D scene data. Even the application of a spatial relation to objects with different dimensions, e.g., a parking lot and a house, is supported.

The next step is to acquire psychological evidence of the applicability of basic spatial relations' meanings. For this purpose, empirical studies have been designed. Subsequently further phenomena can be considered, e.g., the influence of intervening objects or borders.

Acknowledgements

I would like to thank Gerd Herzog for his support, advice, and criticism. Thanks also to Anthony Jameson, Amy Norton, and Dagmar Schmauks for improving the readability of this paper.

References

A. **Abella** and J. R. **Kender**. *Qualitatively Describing Objects Using Spatial Prepositions*. In: Proc. of AAAI-93, pp. 536–540, Washington, DC, 1993.

E. **André**, G. **Herzog**, and T. **Rist**. *On the Simultaneous Interpretation of Real World Image Sequences and their Natural Language Description: The System SOCCER.* In: Proc. of the 8 [th] ECAI, pp. 449–454, Munich, 1988.

E. **André**, G. **Herzog**, and T. **Rist**. *Natural Language Access to Visual Data: Dealing with Space and Movement.* In: F. Nef and M. Borillo (eds.), Proc. of the 1 [st] Workshop of Logical Semantics of Time, Space and Movement in Natural Language. Hermès, 1989.

I. **Carsten** und T. **Janson**. *Verfahren zur Evaluierung räumlicher Präpositionen anhand geometrischer Szenenbeschreibungen.* Diplomarbeit, FB Informatik, Univ. Hamburg, 1985.

K.-P. **Gapp**. *Berechnungsverfahren für räumliche Relationen in 3D-Szenen.* Diplomarbeit, FB Informatik, Univ. des Saarlandes, Saarbrücken, 1993. Auch als: Memo 59, SFB 314, 1993.

K.-P. **Gapp**. *Einsatz von Visualisierungstechniken bei der Analyse von Realweltbildfolgen.* In: Proc. of the 1 [st] Workshop of Visual Computing, Darmstadt, 1994.

C. **Habel**. *Zwischen-Bericht.* In: C. Habel, M. Herweg, and K. Rehkämper (eds.), Raumkonzepte in Verstehensprozessen: Interdisziplinäre Beiträge zu Sprache und Raum, pp. 37–69. Tübingen: Niemeyer, 1989.

K.-J. **Hanßmann**. *Sprachliche Bildinterpretation für ein Frage-Antwort-System.* Ifi-hh-m-74/80, FB Informatik, Univ. Hamburg, 1980.

A. **Herskovits**. *Language and Spatial Cognition. An Interdisciplinary Study of the Prepositions in English.* Cambridge, London: Cambridge University Press, 1986.

M. **Hußmann** and P. **Schefe**. *The Design of SWYSS, a Dialogue System for Scene Analysis.* In: L. Bolc (ed.), Natural Language Communication with Pictorial Information Systems, pp. 143–201. München: Hanser/McMillan, 1984.

M. **Kochen**. *Representations and Algorithms for Cognitive Learning.* Artificial Intelligence, 5:199–216, 1974.

B. **Landau** and R. **Jackendoff**. *"What" and "where" in spatial language and spatial cognition.* Behavioral and Brain Sciences, 16:217–265, 1993.

G. A. **Miller** and P. N. **Johnson-Laird**. *Language and Perception.* Cambridge, London: Cambridge University Press, 1976.

B. **Neumann**. *Bildverstehen.* In: W. Bibel und J. Siekmann (Hrsg.), Künstliche Intelligenz, pp. 285–355. Berlin, Heidelberg: Springer, 1982.

G. **Retz-Schmidt**. *Various Views on Spatial Prepositions.* AI Magazine, 9(2):95–105, 1988.

W. **Wahlster**. *One Word Says More Than a Thousand Pictures. On the Automatic Verbalization of the Results of Image Sequence Analysis Systems.* Computers and Artifial Intelligence, 8:479–492, 1989.

L. A. **Zadeh**. *Fuzzy Sets.* Information and Control, 8:338–353, 1965.

Spatial Reasoning in Indeterminate Worlds

Janice Glasgow *
Department of Computing and Information Science
Queen's University, Kingston, Ontario
Canada K7L 3N6
janice@qucis.queensu.ca

Abstract

A possible worlds semantics for model-based spatial reasoning is presented. In this semantics, worlds are characterized by the alternative states that result from indeterminacy or partial knowledge. A world is represented as a set of symbolic arrays, where symbols in the array map to entities in the world and the relative locations of symbols correspond to the relative locations of entities. Deduction is carried out using a model-theoretic approach in which array representations are "inspected" using primitive array functions. Nonmonotonic reasoning using array representations is also discussed.

Introduction

Psychologists have acknowledged that mental models are fundamental to human problem solving, particularly for their predictive and explanatory power in understanding human interactions with the environment and with others. Just as mental models are pervasive to human problem solving, computational models for spatial reasoning provide a foundation for problem solving in AI.

This paper is concerned with the development of a computational methodology for spatial reasoning with models. A knowledge representation scheme is presented in which symbolic array data structures are used, in conjunction with imagery inspection and transformation operations, to reason about the spatial properties of a world. Figure 1 illustrates a symbolic array representation for a map of Europe.[1] Symbols in the array correspond to the entities in the geographic domain and the relative locations of symbols in the array denote the relative directions among these entities. Each dimension in an array defines a linear order relation among entities in the domain. The order may correspond to relative location (e.g. left-of), geographic

(e.g. north-of), temporal (e.g. before) or conceptual (e.g. taller-than) relations. In particular, we are concerned with transitive relations — i.e., relations r such that if $r(x, y)$ and $r(y, z)$ then $r(x, z)$. Topological relations, such as *touching, contained-in, bonded-to*, etc., can also be represented in an array. For the array representation of Europe in Figure 1, the *adjacent-to* relation in the array maps to the *borders-on* relation for the world.

The formalism presented in this paper borrows from previous research in the area of computational imagery (GP92; Gla93), which involves the study of AI knowledge representation and inferencing techniques that correspond to the representations and processes for mental imagery. In computational imagery, a mathematical theory of arrays provides a basis for representing and reasoning about visual (e.g. shape) and spatial (e.g. relative location) properties of entities in the world. Although results of cognitive studies offered initial motivation for the representations and functionality of the formalism, the ultimate concerns of research in computational imagery are expressive power, inferential adequacy and efficiency; whenever possible, the limitations of the human information processing system are overcome.

The research described in this paper extends work in computational imagery by presenting a formal semantics for spatial reasoning with array representations of worlds. The proposed formalism provides a foundation for deductive reasoning, where inferences are based on a semantic theory of relational deductions, rather than on a syntactic theory that depends on rules of inference. Incomplete or uncertain knowledge may result in worlds with multiple possible interpretations, where each consistent interpretation is represented by a unique array representation. In the remainder of the paper we present a model-theoretic approach to spatial reasoning with array representations. An ongoing issue in AI is how to effectively update a knowledge base as new information is added or the world is transformed. The paper addresses this issue by demonstrating how nonmonotonic reasoning is achieved in the formalism.

---

*This research was supported by the Natural Science and Engineering Research Council (NSERC) of Canada and the Information Technology Research Corporation (ITRC) of Ontario.

[1] Note that adjacent cells in the array that contain identical symbols (e.g. Germany) are denoted by a single symbol with multiple indexes.

<table>
<tr><td></td><td></td><td></td><td></td><td>Norway</td><td>Sweden</td><td>Finland</td></tr>
<tr><td></td><td></td><td></td><td></td><td>Denmark</td><td></td><td></td></tr>
<tr><td>Ireland</td><td>Britain</td><td></td><td>Holland</td><td rowspan="2">Germany</td><td>Poland</td><td></td></tr>
<tr><td></td><td></td><td></td><td>Belgium</td><td>Czech Republic</td><td>Slovakai</td></tr>
<tr><td></td><td></td><td rowspan="2">France</td><td></td><td>Switzerland</td><td>Austria</td><td>Hungary</td></tr>
<tr><td></td><td></td><td></td><td rowspan="2">Italy</td><td colspan="2">? Yugoslavia ?</td></tr>
<tr><td>Portugal</td><td>Spain</td><td></td><td></td><td>Greece</td></tr>
</table>

Figure 1: Array representation of Europe

Deductive Reasoning with Spatial Models

Reasoning by deduction is the process of logically inferring a conclusion from a given set of premises. For example, from the premises:

left-of(a,b), *left-of(b,c)*, and
left-of(X,Y) $\wedge$ *left-of(Y,Z)* $\rightarrow$ *left-of(X,Z)*,

one can deduce *left-of(a,c)*. This form of reasoning, where conclusions are derived using the iterative application of syntactic inference rules, is referred to as *proof-theoretic*. Alternatively, the validity of an argument can be demonstrated using a *model-theoretic* approach. Given the above premises, an array representation (model) – $\boxed{a\ |\ b\ |\ c}$ – can be constructed in which *left-of* in the array corresponds to the *left-of* relation in the world being described. From this representation we can logically deduce the valid conclusion *left-of(a,c)* through the process of model inspection (also referred to as model checking).

Existing computational systems generally employ proof-theoretic deduction: reasoning is carried out by applying rules that manipulate syntactic forms of expressions. The proposed system for spatial reasoning, however, relies on semantics, or the mapping between the representation and the domain of interest. Conclusions are derived by applying functions that map to the relevant spatial relations in the world. Thus, reasoning with array representations can be thought of as a restricted form of model-theoretic deduction, one which is limited to the spatial inferences that are made explicit by array inspection functions (GP92). In addition, the system is useful for reasoning about the indeterminate worlds resulting from uncertainty or incomplete information. This section describes how symbolic arrays can be used to represent worlds, including indeterminate worlds, consisting of entities and spatial relationships among the entities. A possible worlds semantics for deductive reasoning is also presented.

Array Representations

An *array representation* for a determinate world consists of a symbolic array, containing constant symbols corresponding to the entities in the world, and a set of array functions, which are used to determine the spatial relations among entities in the world. For example, a world described as:

The ball and the lamp are on the table and the lamp is to the right of the ball.

could be represented as the symbolic array

$$\mathcal{A} = \begin{array}{|c|c|} \hline ball & lamp \\ \hline \multicolumn{2}{|c|}{table} \\ \hline \end{array},$$

where the symbols *lamp*, *ball* and *table* in array $\mathcal{A}$ are mapped to the corresponding entities in the world.

Truth of an atomic formula for an array representation is defined using primitive functions that "inspect" an array data structure. Assume that p is an n-ary spatial predicate symbol corresponding to a relation w_p in the world and $c_1, ..., c_n$ are constant symbols that denote entities in the world. Then the atomic formula $p(c_1, ..., c_n)$ is true for an array representation if and only if the function application $f_p(c_1, ..., c_n, \mathcal{A})$ evaluates to true, where f_p denotes the array function that inspects the array $\mathcal{A}$ to determine if the relation w_p holds for symbols $c_1, ..., c_n$. For example, in the previous array representation a function application *left-of(ball,lamp,$\mathcal{A}$)* would evaluate to *true*, whereas the expression *on-top(ball,lamp,$\mathcal{A}$)* would evaluate to *false*. A symbolic array $\mathcal{A}$ is said to represent a world w if and only if for all atomic formula $\phi = p(c_1, ..., c_n)$ in a specified language:

$$f_p(c_1, ..., c_n, \mathcal{A}) = \text{true} \ \text{ if and only if } \ (c_1, ..., c_n) \in w_p.$$

In such a case, we say that world w is *representable*.

An individual array representation models a determinate world in which all the spatial relations for the entities are explicitly specified or implied. However, a world may be indeterminate in the sense that its set of spatial relations is underspecified, resulting in ambiguity concerning the relative locations of certain entities. Indeterminacy generally implies the existence of alternative possible worlds, each of which is an extension of the indeterminate world (by adding more facts), and each of which is representable as an array. For example, a world described as – *The spoon is to the right of the fork and the knife is to the right of the fork* – suggests two consistent extensions, represented by the arrays:

$$\boxed{fork\ |\ spoon\ |\ knife}\quad\text{and}\quad\boxed{fork\ |\ knife\ |\ spoon}\,.$$

An indeterminate world can be characterized by its complete (representable) extensions – i.e., those that have array representations. We say that world w' is an *extension* of world w, denoted $w \preceq w'$ if and only the two worlds consist of the same entities and all relations that hold in w also hold in w'. A world w is considered *possible* if there a representable world w' such that $w \preceq w'$. In general, we say an array $\mathcal{A}$ represents an indeterminate world w if and only if it represents a determinate extension of w.

Possible Worlds Semantics

Following, we present a possible worlds semantics for spatial reasoning based on a modal logic that accounts for the *necessity* and *possibility* of truth of a proposition. A well-formed formula (wff) is necessarily true in a given world if it is true in all representable extensions of the world; a wff is possibly true if it is true in some representable extension of the world. Truth of a wff in a world w is defined recursively in terms of the truth of the atomic wffs and truth in the worlds that are extensions of w. In the following definition, a statement of the form $\models_w \phi$ denotes that the wff ϕ is true in world w.

Definition. Given a world w, we define truth of a wff ϕ in w as follows:

- If $\phi = p(c_1, ..., c_n)$ is an atomic wff then $\models_w \phi$ if and only if $(c_1, ..., c_n) \in w_p$, where w_p is the relation in w corresponding to predicate symbol p.
- $\models_w \phi \wedge \psi$ if and only if $\models_w \phi$ and $\models_w \psi$.
- $\models_w \phi \vee \psi$ if and only if $\models_w \phi$ or $\models_w \phi$.
- $\models_w \neg\phi$ if and only if not $\models_w \phi$.
- $\models_w \Box\phi$ if and only if $\models_{w'} \phi$ for all worlds w' such that $w \preceq w'$ and w' is representable.
- $\models_w \Diamond\phi$ if and only if $\models_{w'} \phi$ for some world w' such that $w \preceq w'$ and w' is representable.

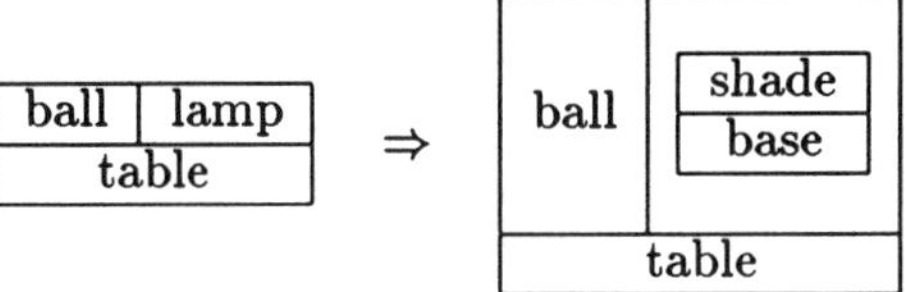

Figure 2: Embedded array representation

The proposed model theory assumes the principle of compositionality: the meaning of a wff in a possible world is determined totally by the meaning of its entities and their atomic relations. Possible worlds semantics is a version of model theory where truth of a wff in one world may depend on its truth in other possible worlds. Computationally, the possibility and necessity of truth for a wff in a world w can be determined by inspection of the array representations for the world.

Theorem: An atomic wff $\phi = p(c_1, ..., c_n)$ is necessarily true for a world w ($\models_w \Box\phi$) if and only if for all array representations $A_i = <S, \mathcal{A}_i, F>$ for w, $f_p(c_1, ..., c_n, \mathcal{A}) = $ true for array function f_p.

Theorem: An atomic wff $\phi = p(c_1, ..., c_n)$ is possibly true for w ($\models_w \Diamond\phi$) if and only if for some array representation $A_i = <S, \mathcal{A}_i, F>$ for w, $f_p(c_1, ..., c_n, \mathcal{A}) = $ true for array function f_p.

The proposed formalism for model-based reasoning was designed to capture and reason about the relevant spatial and structural qualities of a world. Although the examples presented are two-dimensional, the array theory on which the formalism is based (JG89) is not restricted – array functions have been developed for generating, transforming and inspecting arrays of any dimensionality. Ongoing research in this area involves several extensions to the formalism. One such extension involves the representation and inspection of structured worlds; results of cognitive studies suggest that mental models may be hierarchically organized and that reasoning takes place at varying levels of structural decomposition based on a *part-of* relation. Reasoning at multiple levels of a parts hierarchy can be achieved using nested array representations where array symbols may define subarrays that correspond to the subworlds for the structured entities in the world. Figure 2 illustrates a representation where the symbol *lamp* denotes a subarray that represents the world corresponding to a structured entity.

The scheme is also being extended to model temporal worlds, where a temporal model is represented as a one-dimensional array consisting of discrete "snapshots" of worlds at progressive time steps. As well, inferences in the formalism need not be restricted to deductions. A model-based approach to analogical reasoning is also being developed using array representations.

Nonmonotonic Reasoning

Many current reasoning systems, such as first-order predicate logic, were designed for monotonic reasoning: if knowledge is added to a system then everything that was previously derivable is still derivable. Hoever, the domains that involve spatial reasoning often face the problems posed by uncertain or constantly changing knowledge where the property of monotonicity does not hold. A variety of representation schemes have been developed in an attempt to accommodate nonmonotonic reasoning. These systems typically extend existing logics to include axioms and rules of inference that make it possible to reason in indeterminate worlds. Reiter's (Rei80) *default logic* allows inference rules of the form: *If A is provable and it is consistent to assume B then conclude C.* McDermott and Doyle (MD80) alternatively state defaults as sentences of the form: *If A holds and B is not disprovable then B.* Concepts such as "it is consistent to assume" and "is not disprovable" can be expressed and validated using the the concept of "possibility" in our formalism, i.e., B is not disprovable in w if B is true in some array representation for w. Two issues that have to be addressed by nonmonotonic reasoning systems are:

> *How can inferences be made in the presence of incomplete knowledge?* In the previous section we presented a formalism for making inferences in the presence of spatial indeterminacy. These inferences are achieved by constructing and inspecting symbolic arrays that represent the alternative interpretations arising from uncertainty.

> *How is the knowledge base updated when new information is added?* A knowledge base for spatial reasoning can be defined as the set of array representations for a given world. In the remainder of this section, we address the question of how such a knowledge base can be modified as the world is transformed by acquiring new knowledge or by modifying the existing spatial relations.

Knowledge Acquisition

In spatial reasoning systems, knowledge acquisition generally involves extending the spatial constraints for the world. Updating the array representations to accommodate such information is straightforward: the new world is modeled by eliminating from the knowledge base those representations that are inconsistent with the added information. Consider the indeterminate world described by the atomic wffs *left-of(a,b)*, *left-of(a,c)*, *left-of(a,d)* and *left-of(b,d)*. This description suggests three representable extensions, corresponding to the following arrays:

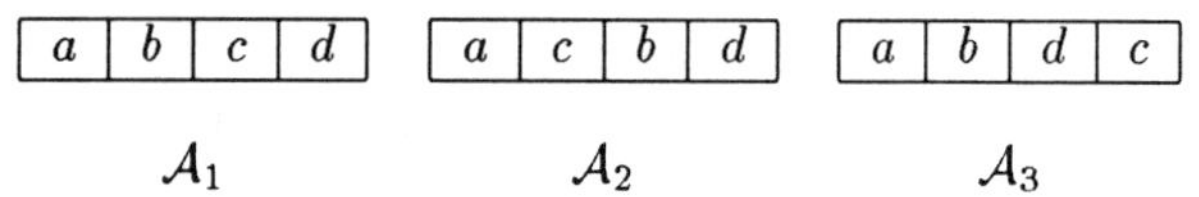

$$\mathcal{A}_1 \qquad \mathcal{A}_2 \qquad \mathcal{A}_3$$

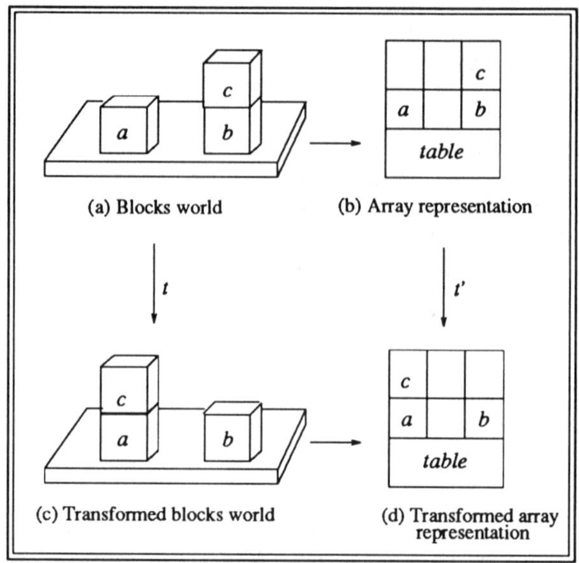

Figure 3: Representation of a blocks world

If the world is modified to include the spatial relation *left-of(c,d)*, then the array representation containing structure $\mathcal{A}_3$ would be eliminated from the knowledge base, since it is not consistent with the added spatial relationship.

Transforming a World

Spatial reasoning may involve applying transformations that result in changes to the relative locations of entities in the world. Reasoning in the presence of such change is problematic in traditional reasoning systems, since it is necessary to consider the implications on the current state of affairs. In the proposed scheme for model-based reasoning, however, the inferences arising from transformations on a world can be derived by applying analogous array functions to the representation. Thus, if t is a transformation that can be applied to a world w resulting in a world w', then we define a function t' such that if t' is applied to an array representation for w it would result in an array that represents w'.

To illustrate how the effects of transformations can be modeled, consider the blocks world in Figure 3(a) and its array depiction $\mathcal{A}$ in Figure 3(b). The blocks world resulting from the transformation $t = move\ block$ *c to the top of block a* is illustrated in Figure 3(c). This change is modeled by applying a primitive array operation $t' = move\_rel$ to the parameter list $(c, a, \mathcal{A}, above)$. This function application results in an array that represents the transformed world, as depicted in Figure 3(d).

Array transformation functions may be complex and involve knowledge of the physical model for the entities in the domain. For example, the transformation operation for *push* in the blocks world would have to take into account that if the block being pushed is supporting other blocks, then the locations of the supported blocks are also changed by the transformation.

In summary, modifying a world by adding knowledge or by applying spatial transformations results in a new world, which can subsequently be used for reasoning about the validity of wffs. Note that it is not necessary to examine any previous deductions to determine whether relationships need to be deleted from the knowledge base, since the modified spatial relations are determined directly from inspection of the transformed array representations. Thus, the model-based approach to spatial reasoning addresses the *frame problem* (Rap71), which is concerned with what relations are withdrawn or remain valid as change occurs in a world. This information is implicit in the transformation functions for the array.

Control Strategies for Model-based Reasoning

Model-based deduction can be carried out as a three step process: 1) a knowledge base array representations is constructed to represent the possible states of affairs (representable extensions) for the world; 2) transformations are performed on the representations in the knowledge base, corresponding to the transformations that occur in the world (this step is optional); and 3) conclusions are formed by applying inspection functions to the array representations. Alternative strategies can also be developed for model-based reasoning, depending on the form of the desired conclusion. Deductions that involve the possibility of a wff can be achieved by constructing a single model, corresponding to a possible world in which the premises and wff are true. Similarly, proving a wff invalid requires the construction of a single model in which the premises are true and the putative conclusion is false.

Model-based reasoning, as an alternative to theorem proving, has also been considered by Halpern and Vardi (1991). In this work, an agent's knowledge is represented using a semantic model, where model checking is used to determine validity of a formula. For cases where the number of possible worlds grows exponentially, they suggest that heuristics could be used to focus attention on those worlds that are "most relevant" or "most likely".

Cognitive studies suggest that humans reason with a single model, even in situations that imply multiple states of affairs (JL93). If it is discovered that the current model does not correspond to the situation that is described then it is changed. A similar control strategy could be developed for a computational approach to model-based reasoning, where an alternative model is generated if the current model becomes inconsistent.

Although the representation scheme was motivated by our understanding of cognitive processes, it was not intended to be model of cognition. The proposed computational approach to model-based reasoning can overcome some of the limitations of human information processing. Human errors occur in model-based deduction by failing to consider all possible interpretations compatible with a given set of facts (JL93). In domains where the amount of indeterminacy is restricted, all possible array representations for a world can be generated and checked. Thus, no consistent interpretations are left unconsidered. The inferencing process for spatial representations also facilitates parallel implementations: multiple array representations can be constructed, transformed and inspected concurrently (GP92).

In conclusion, the proposed representation scheme for model-based reasoning provides an effective tool for performing spatial inferences. Alternative control strategies can be constructed for carrying out deductions by generating, transforming and inspecting array representations. For cases where the number of array models is unmanageable, heuristic or backtracking strategies can be developed.

Discussion

The concept of constructing knowledge representations that mirror the structure of the world is not unique to the proposed array representation. Hayes (Hay74) discusses *direct* representations in which there exist similarities between what is being represented and the medium of the representation. Sloman (Slo93) has also argued the pros and cons of analogical representations, and has concluded that a variety of representation formalisms, including those specialized for spatial reasoning, are important to AI problem solving. Other hybrid approaches have been suggested for visual-spatial and model-based reasoning. Barwise and Etchemendy (BE92) proposed a system called *Hyperproof* which integrates diagrammatic reasoning with sentence-based logics. Myers and Konolige (MK92) treat model-based manipulations as a form of inference within a classical logic system. More specifically, they store partially interpreted sensor data using an analogical representation that interacts with a general-purpose sentential language.

Although interest and activity in spatial and diagrammatic reasoning is escalating, most of the research in this area is focussed on logic or analogical representations. What the array formalism offers is an intermediate representation that is less specific than a visual representation, yet less abstract than a logic representation. A characteristic of the array representation for model-based reasoning is that it brings relevant spatial properties to the forefront. The entities and spatial relations in the world are explicitly denoted as symbols and relations in a multi-dimensional array. This representation provides for a simplified model of the world — one that captures salient spatial features and suppresses unnecessary or irrelevant details.

The array representation for spatial reasoning has measurable computational advantages over proof-theoretic logic systems. In particular, array models can be used to develop *vivid* knowledge bases. Levesque (Lev86) defines a vivid knowledge base as one that is structured so that there is a one-to-one correspondence between the entities in the world and the symbols in the knowledge base, and for each simple relationship of interest in the world – in our case spatial relationships – there exists a corresponding connection among symbols in the knowledge base. Levesque argues that the main advantage of vivid knowledge bases is that they provide for efficient worst case reasoning behavior, since calculating what is logically implicit generally reduces to retrieving what is explicit.

Assuming that the array representations correctly model the world, the proposed knowledge representation scheme provides a complete and sound reasoning system that can perform under conditions of uncertainty or incomplete information. A model-theoretic formalism is used to make inferences about indeterminate worlds, using a three step process of constructing, transforming and inspecting array representations for the world. Thus, the process of generating syntactic proofs to derive spatial information is replaced by the process of model checking. The non-existence of a proof can be determined by finding an exception — i.e., an array representation in which the formula is refuted. The scheme provides a framework for integrating model-theoretic deduction with nonmonotonic reasoning in which representations are updated and reinterpreted as new information is acquired or as transformations are performed.

The proposed model-based approach to reasoning can be motivated and justified by human needs. Simon (Sim78) has proposed criteria for assessing and selecting representations based on information content and on ease of programming. These criteria are task dependent and partially rely on the ability of the programmer to represent the state of knowledge in the world and the transformations and inferences that may occur. Experimental results in cognitive psychology suggest that humans apply model-based reasoning for problem solving in a variety of domains. Certainly a formalism that captures the representations and processes associated with model-based reasoning would facilitate the implementation of computational reasoning systems in such problem solving domains. Although our scheme was motivated by human needs, it can overcome inherent limitations of the cognitive system.

In a recent debate, which was concerned with the advantages/disadvantages of descriptive versus depictive (model-based) representations, Levesque and Reiter (LR93) state that a reason to prefer descriptive (logic) representations is that they are "blessed with a *semantics*". Although logic-based representations can be advocated for their semantic clarity, we have shown that an intuitive semantics for model-based reasoning with array representations also exists.

References

J. Barwise and J. Etchemendy. Hyperproof: Logical reasoning with diagrams. In *Proceedings of the AAAI Spring Symposium on Reasoning with Diagrammatic Representations*, 1992.

J.I. Glasgow. The imagery debate revisited: A computational perspective. *Computational Intelligence*, 9(4):309–333, 1993. Taking issue paper.

J.I. Glasgow and D. Papadias. Computational imagery. *Cognitive Science*, 16(3):355–394, 1992.

P. Hayes. Some problems and non-problems in representation theory. In *Proceedings of AISB Summer Conference*, pages 63–79, University of Sussex, 1974.

J.H. Halpern and M.Y. Vardi. Model checking vs. theorem proving: a manifesto. In J.A. Allen, R. Fikes, and E. Sandewall, editors, *Principles of Knowledge Representation and Reasoning: Proceeding of the Second International Conference (KR '91)*, pages 325–334, 1991.

M.A. Jenkins and J.I. Glasgow. A logical basis for nested array data structures. *Programming Languages Journal*, 14(1):35 – 49, 1989.

P.N. Johnson-Laird. *Human and Machine Thinking*. Lawrence Erlbaum Assoc: Hillsdale, NJ, 1993.

H.J. Levesque. Making believers out of computers. *Artificial Intelligence*, 30:81–108, 1986.

H.J Levesque and R. Reiter. A counterexample is worth a thousand words. *Computational Intelligence*, 9(4):394–397, 1993. Commentary on taking issue paper.

D.V. McDermott and J. Doyle. Non-monotonic logic. *Artificial Intelligence*, 13:41–72, 1980.

K. Myers and K Konolige. Reasoning with analogical representations. In *Proceedings of the Conference on Principles of Knowledge Representations and Reasoning*, Los Altos, CA, 1992. Morgan Kaufmann.

B. Raphael. The frame problem in problem-solving systems. In Findler and Meltzer, editors, *Artificial Intelligence and Heuristic Programming*, pages 159 – 169. Edinburgh University Press, 1971.

R. Reiter. A logic for default reasoning. *Artificial Intelligence*, 13, 1980.

H.A. Simon. On the forms of mental representations. In W.C. Savage, editor, *Minnesota Studies in the Philosophy of Science, Vol. IX: Perception and Cognition: Issues in the Foundations of Psychology*. University of Minnesota Press: Minneapolis, 1978.

A. Sloman. Varieties of fomalisms for knowledge representation. *Computational Intelligence*, 9(4):413–423, 1993.

Automatic Depiction of Spatial Descriptions*

Patrick Olivier
Centre for Intelligent Systems
University of Wales
Aberystwyth
Dyfed, SY23 3DB, UK
plo@aber.ac.uk

Toshiyuki Maeda
Central Research Laboratories
Matsushita Electric Ind. Co. Ltd.
3-4, Hikaridia, Seika-cho
Soraku-gun, Kyoto 619-02, Japan
maechan@crl.mei.co.jp

Jun-ichi Tsujii
Centre for Computational Linguistics
University of Manchester
Institute of Science and Technology
Manchester, M60 1QD, UK
tsujii@ccl.umist.ac.uk

Abstract

A novel combination of ideas from cognitive linguistics and spatial occupancy models in robotics has led to the WIP (Words Into Pictures) system. WIP automatically generates depictions of natural language descriptions of indoor scenes. A qualitative layer in the conceptual representation of objects underlies a mechanism by which alternative depictions arise for qualitatively distinct interpretations, as often occurs as a result of deictic/intrinsic reference frame ambiguity. At the same time, a quantitative layer, in conjunction with a potential field model of the semantics of projective prepositions, is used in the process of capturing the inherently fuzzy character of the meaning of natural language spatial predications.

Introduction

People often relate their visual experiences to one another by means of verbal descriptions. Relying on a commonality of perceptual experience of the world about us. For example, the size and orientation of objects can be captured using dimensional predications such as "the pole is high". The relative positions of objects are communicated by, amongst other means, static spatial predications such as "a chair is in front of the desk".

Adequate representation of the meaning of spatial prepositions and dimensional adjectives must be grounded in our cognitive model of three-dimensional space, which in turn is structured based on the functionality of our perceptual system. Such a representation should distinguish qualitative ambiguities (eg. the deictic, intrinsic and extrinsic interpretations of a preposition (Retz-Schmidt 1988)), but also quantitative differences (for example, that certain regions in space are more typically "in front of" a reference object than others). Further, the qualitative and quantitative components of meaning are dependent on the entities that are the objects of the spatial predications.

Drawing on the work of Lang (Lang 1993) (Lang, Carstensen, & Simmons 1991) (Bierwisch & Lang

---

*This research was kindly funded by the Matsushita Electric Industrial Company Limited.

1989) and incorporating ideas originating in the field of robot manipulator path planning (Khatib 1986), the WIP (Words Into Pictures) system automatically generates such a representation for natural language scene descriptions in English, and produces depictions of quantitatively likely, but qualitatively distinct, interpretations.

The Domain

The WIP system addresses the problem of understanding and generating depictions of room descriptions. As such, it is a prototype application under the umbrella of research into natural language interaction with multi-media systems. Users are initially required to specify the type of room and their vantage point (ie. their position and orientation within the room). They can then specify the room's contents and the locations of the contents using dimensional and prepositional expressions. In this paper we restrict ourselves to describing the semantic representation and processing of spatial prepositions, in particular projective prepositions.

Spatial Prepositions

Projective prepositions place a constraint on the proximity of the located object and the reference object. Predications such as "the chair is in front of the desk" constrain the "desk" and "chair", to some degree, to be proximal to each other. Conversely projective prepositions such as "away from" predicate a distal relationship between the located and reference object. Further, the degree of the proximity expressed in any projective prepositional predication varies according to a number of considerations including: the spatial context (the spatial extent and content of the scene described); and the absolute and relative sizes of the located object and reference object. This last consideration can be illustrated by contrasting the the predications: "a car is to the left of a lorry" and "an apple is to the left of the orange ". Whilst the preposition used here is the same in both cases, the pieces of fruit will be closer to each other than will the "car" and "lorry".

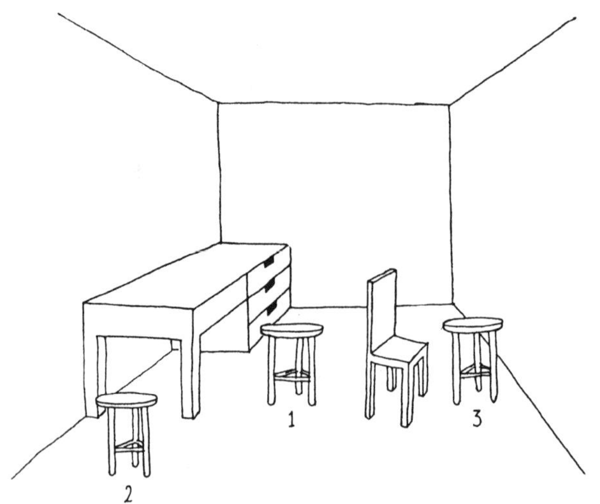

Figure 1: Intrinsic, deictic and extrinsic ambiguity

In addition to the constraint on the proximity of the located object and reference object, projective prepositions place a constraint on the position of the located object relative to a particular side of the reference object. In the case of the intrinsic interpretation of a predication such as "the stool is in front of the desk", the "stool" is located in some spatial region defined by the half-plane that is the intrinsic front of the "desk". Intuitively, the closer the "stool" is to the region defined by the projection of the desk's dimensions, the more the spatial arrangement conforms to the prototypical interpretation of the predication.

Intrinsic, deictic and extrinsic interpretations of projective prepositions qualitatively differ according to the reference frame with respect to which the directional constraint is characterized (Retz-Schmidt 1988). In the intrinsic case the reference frame is centered at the reference object and adopts the intrinsic orientation of the reference object. In figure 1, stool number 1 is intrinsically "in front of the desk". The reference frame for a deictic interpretation is centered at the speaker and adopts the speaker's orientation; deictic readings can be invoked explicitly with qualifications such as "from where we are standing"; when the reference object has no intrinsic or extrinsic sideness relating to the preposition used; or when intrinsic or extrinsic interpretations are ruled out on other grounds (eg. the impossibility of spatially arranging the objects as required by the interpretation). In figure 1 stool number 2 is deictically "in front of the desk".

Extrinsic readings can occur when the reference object has no intrinsic sides relating to the locative preposition (eg. trees) but is in close proximity to another object that is *strongly sided* (such as a house); in which case the reference frame capturing the intrinsic orientations of the stronger sided object can be adopted by

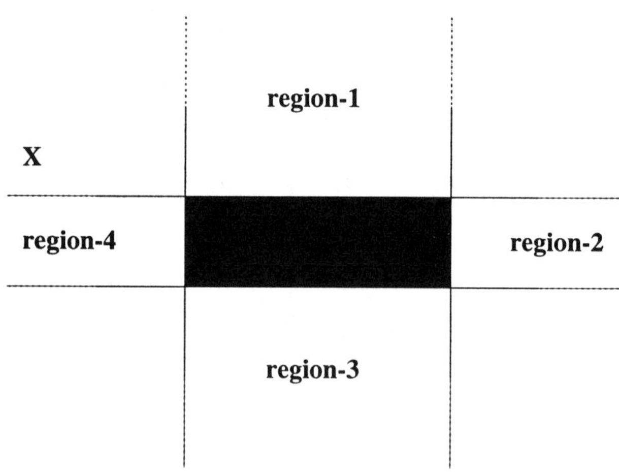

Figure 2: A qualitative model of space

the reference object. Referring to figure 1 the chair is extrinsically "in front of stool number 3"; the stool has inherited an extrinsic front from the right wall.

Typically an object is located with respect to more than one reference object by the means of multiple spatial predications. Consequently, a requirement on meaning representation for spatial predications is that they must being easily combined to giving rise to a cumulative meaning.

Related work

Past work has failed to construct a computational semantics rich enough to capture the phenomena mentioned so far, due to a concentration either on a purely qualitative model or an overly simplistic quantitative model of spatial predicates. Early efforts such as (Winograd 1972) and (Waltz & Boggess 1979) are deficient as a result of their commitment to a purely qualitative model of constraint, though in the case of (Waltz & Boggess 1979) the resulting representation is analog (quantitative).

More recently, Kalita (Kalita & Badler 1991) uses Talmy's geometric-relation schema (Talmy 1983) and Douglas' qualitative spatial model (Douglas & Novick 1987). Spatial predications specify inclusions in rectangular regions that are outward projections of the extents of the reference object.

Figure 2 depicts the two-dimensional case for such an approach, inclusion in regions 1 to 4 corresponds respectively to "in front of", "right of", "behind" and "left of" predications. In addition to being too restrictive (clearly point X is "left of" the object), intrinsic and deictic sides are not distinguished, and any point within a particular region, regardless of its distance from the reference object, equally satisfies the constraint. Lang (Lang, Carstensen, & Simmons 1991), (Lang 1993) uses a similarly qualitative model but distinguishes deictic and intrinsic sides in his object schema representation of objects, with reference to which the corresponding competing interpretations are captured.

Yamada uses the concept of a potential field to capture North-South and East-West directional constraints (Yamada, Nishida, & Doshita 1988). For example, if object A is North of B, this spatial constraint is modeled using a torsion spring-like function. Any further constraint on A (which might cause it to be located other than due North of B) is similarly modeled with a potential function. The most likely interpretation is computed as the minimum energy configuration of the objects and springs. Schirra uses the inversely related concept of a normalized typicality field in which the potential is highest for more prototypical configurations (Schirra & Stopp 1993). Whilst Schirra's typicality fields can capture both direction and proximity constraints, only intrinsic interpretations are catered for. Both Schirra and Yamada idealize reference objects as points and fix the magnitude of fields for particular prepositions, regardless of the reference object's dimensions.

Conceptual Representation

The WIP system represents spatial predications as either geometric or potential field constraints over two layered conceptual representations of objects consisting of a qualitative spatial and perceptual representation, coupled to a quantitative object model. This allows it to differentiate between interpretations relative to different reference frames, and also to vary the degree of constraint depending on the reference and located objects concerned. The resulting representation facilitates the depiction of the 'most plausible' interpretations.

Qualitatively modeling objects

The qualitative layer of the object representation is based on Lang's object schemata (Lang 1993). The desk of figure 3(a) is represented as in figure 3(b). In this first schema a, b and c label three orthogonal axes centered at the object, each of which is instantiated by one or more dimensional assignment parameters (DAPs)[1]; a1-a2, b1-b2 and c1-c2 are corresponding half-axes. Each half axis is labelled either `nil` or with an intrinsic side (eg. `i-front`). If the object has been constrained in the scene as a result of some spatial predication, WIPS infers the object's deictic side assignment. For example, if the desk of figure 3(a) is against a wall in a room to the left of the observer then its object schemata will be as given in figure 3(c).

The explict representation of deictic and intrinsic sides allows the identification of the actual face of an

---

[1]DAPs are not of direct interest here although they are fundamental to the process of dimensional designation and where dimensional assignment might result in a reorientation of the conceptual object (eg. assigning verticality in the process of interpreting "the pole is high").

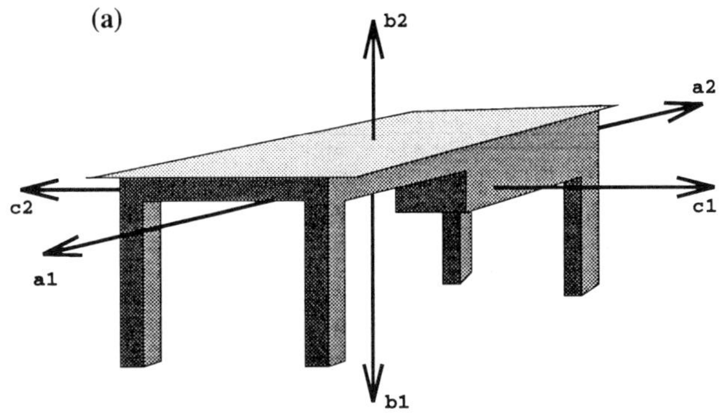

(b)

a:	max	b:	vert	c:	obs
a1:	i-left	b1:	i-bottom	c1:	i-front
a2:	i-right	b2:	i-top	c2:	i-back

(c)

a:	max	b:	vert	c:	obs
a1:	i-left	b1:	i-bottom	c1:	i-front
	d-front		d-bottom		d-right
a2:	i-right	b2:	i-top	c2:	i-back
	d-back		d-top		d-left

Figure 3: Object schemata

object relative to which a spatial constraint is constructed.

Quantitatively modeling objects

The quantitive model of the objects in WIP is comprised of:

- the graphical description of the parts (GDP), constructed from a finite set of geometric primitives

- the mapping from the geometric axis system to the qualitative axis system

The set of graphical primitives in the WIP system is currently restricted to lines and quadrilaterals, which are specified relative an object's geometric axis system (GAS). The mapping between the GAS and the qualitative axis system is specified in terms of the alignment of the x, y and z axes of the GAS and the qualitative half-axes a1-a2, b1-b2 and c1-c2. The GDPs for each object are located relative to the speaker/viewer as a result of intepreting spatial predictions over the object, although the elements of the background scene (the internal walls) are located in the process of defining the speaker's vantage point on the scene. The magnitudes of the extents of an object can be calculated from the configuration of the GDPs that comprise the object.

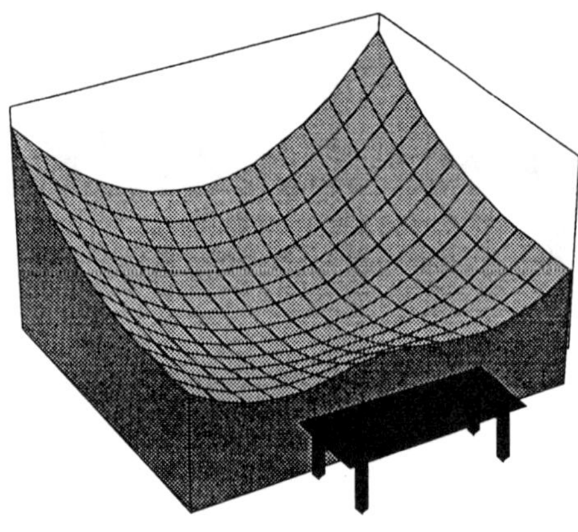

Figure 4: Field for intrinsic "in front of the desk"

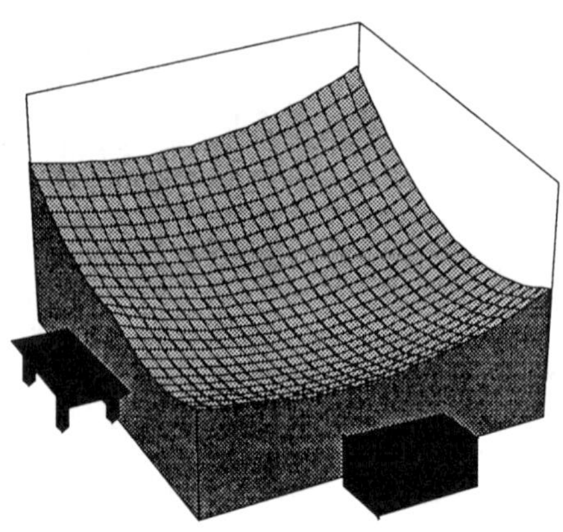

Figure 5: Combined potential fields

Potential Fields

Spatial predications are interpreted as constraints on the orientation and the position of the located object relative to the reference object. The qualitative distinction corresponding the use of either the deictic and intrinsic reference frames is captured by identifying the different deictic and intrinsic sides of the qualitative conceptual representation of the object. Having identified any ambiguity, a potential field (originating from the half-plane relevant to the particular interpretation) is used to capture the fuzzy character of the constraint imposed by spatial prepositions.

Originating in robot manipulator path planning (Khatib 1986), we use the potential field model (PFM) to capture the proximity and direction components of the spatial constraint imposed by certain prepositions, particularly projective prepositions. In general, for a preposition that imposes a projective constraint relative to the face of a reference object, the normal of which extends in the x-direction, we use a potential function $P(x, y)$, where:

$$P(x, y) = P_{prox}(x, y) + P_{dir}(x, y) \qquad (1)$$

$$P_{prox}(x, y) = \frac{K_{prox}}{2}\left(\sqrt{d_x^2 + d_y^2} - L_{prox}\right)^2 \qquad (2)$$

$$P_{dir}(x, y) = \frac{K_{dir}}{2}d_x^2 \qquad (3)$$

$$d_x = (x - x_0) \qquad (4)$$

$$d_y = (y - y_0) \qquad (5)$$

The y axis when combined with the x axis defines the plane in which the constraint applies; (x_0, y_0) is the Cartesian coordinate of the reference object relative to the speaker/viewer. The lower the value of $P(x, y)$ for a point (x, y), the *better the spatial constraint is satisfied*. The minimum for the field can be easily computed by gradual approximation (Yamada, Nishida, & Doshita 1988). Figure 4 shows a region of the field corresponding to the intrinsic interpretation of "in front of the desk".

Quantitative variations in proximity and directional constraints are dependent on reference object and located object dimensions. Modifying the potential function constants on the basis of object dimensions is the mechanism by which this dependency can be captured. The the shape and extent of the potential field $P(x, y)$ is governed by the three constants:

1. K_{prox}
   Directly proportional to the proximity localisation of the minimum energy configuration.

2. L_{prox}
   The distance of the minimum energy configuration from the reference object.

3. K_{dir}
   Directly proportional to the directional localisation of the minimum energy configuration.

In WIP values for K_{prox}, L_{prox}, and K_{dir} are linearly dependent on the dimensions of the reference object and located object, which gives rise to intuitively more plausible depictions for the same preposition with different reference and located objects.

Multiple spatial predications over an object are simply accommodated by the linear addition of the component fields. Figure 5 illustrates the cumulative potential field resulting from the expression "in front of the desk and near the cabinet".

An Overview of WIP

WIP has been implemented using Prolog and Smalltalk/Objectworks. After specifying the dimensions of the room and the speaker/viewer's vantage

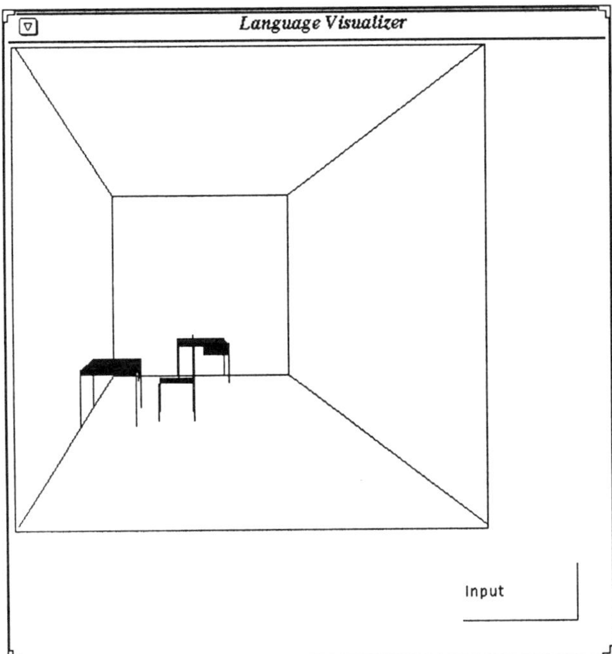

Figure 6: Intrinsic interpretation of "a chair is in front of the left desk"

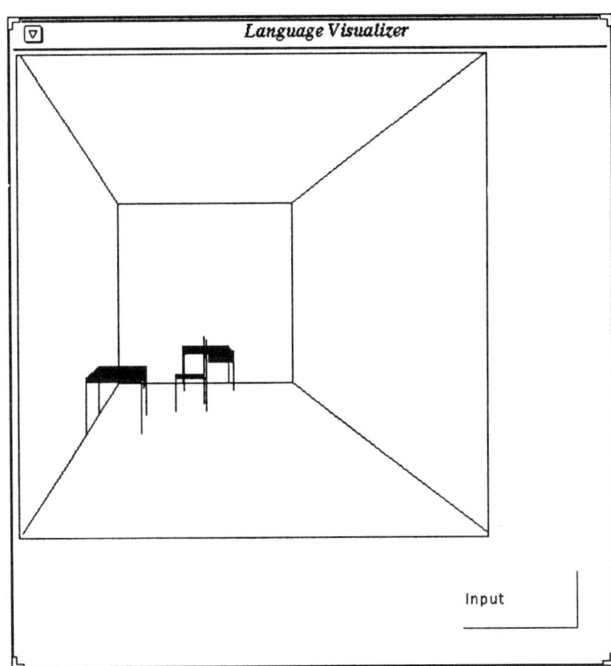

Figure 7: Adding the predication "the chair is near the back desk"

point, natural language descriptions are parsed to logical forms. Spatial predicates and their arguments instantiate potential field specifications and the two-layer models of objects from the conceptual lexicon; and the cumulative potential fields for a description are constructed. Where qualitative ambiguities arise (such as competing deictic and intrinsic interpretations of a preposition) parallel intepretations are generated.

Unconstrained degrees of freedom are set on the basis of default assumptions, for example, if a chair is described as being "in front of" a desk, then the vertical position of the chair is constrained to keep its bottom on the floor. Lastly the minima of the potential fields for each interpretation are computed and the now fully constrained graphical model of the objects used to render the depictions.

Figures 6 and 7 illustrate example outputs from WIP. In figure 6 the chair in the scene is only constrained to be in front of the left desk. In figure 7 the constraint that the chair is near the back desk has been added.

Concluding Remarks

Past attempts at addressing the problem of relating natural language description of spatial scenes to physical referents (through depiction or otherwise) have been deficient in one or more of the following:

- the ability to distinguish competing deictic and intrinsic interpretations

- a probabilistic model of the possible location denoted by projective prepositions.

- an automatic tuning of the degree of proximity and directional constraint imposed by prepositions, in accordance with the dimensions of the reference and located objects.

WIP encompasses all of these, and generates intuitively reasonable depictions of natural language descriptions of scenes. Deictic and intrinsic interpretations are distinguished by the qualitative representation; the potential field model provides the ability to assign a likelihood to the different possible locations of a located object; and by making the constants of the PFM dependent on the extents of the reference and located objects automatic tuning of the PFM is guaranteed. The preposition processing component of WIP is currently being developed to account for more subtle effects, such as, extrinsic interpretations and disallowing interpretations for which a located object is obscured in the resulting depiction.

References

Bierwisch, M., and Lang, E. 1989. *Dimensional Adjectives: Grammatical Structure and Conceptual Interpretation*. Berlin Heidelberg New York: Springer-Verlag.

Douglas, S., and Novick, D. 1987. Consistency and variance in spatial reference. In *Proceedings of the Ninth Annual Cognitive Science Society Meeting*, 417–426.

Kalita, J., and Badler, B. 1991. Interpreting prepositions physically. In *Proceedings AAAI-91*, 105–110.

Khatib, O. 1986. Real-time obstacle avoidance for manipulators and modile robots. *The International Journal of Robotics Research* 5(1):90–98.

Lang, M.; Carstensen, K.; and Simmons, G. 1991. *Modelling Spatial Knowledge on a Linguistic Basis.* Berlin Heidelberg: Springer-Verlag.

Lang, E. 1993. A two-level approach to projective prepositions. In Zelinsky-Wibbelt, C., ed., *The semantics of prepositions: from mental processing to Natural Language processing.* Berlin: Mouton de Gruyter.

Retz-Schmidt, G. 1988. Various views on spatial prepositions. *AI Magazine* 9(2):95–105.

Schirra, J. R. J., and Stopp, E. 1993. Antlima — a listener model with mental images. In *Proceedings of IJCAI*, 175–180.

Talmy, L. 1983. How language structures space. In Pick, H., and Acredolo, L., eds., *Spatial Orientation: Theory, Research, and Application.* New York: Plenum Press. 225–282.

Waltz, D. L., and Boggess, L. 1979. Visual analog representations for natural language understanding. In *Proceedings of IJCAI*, 926–934.

Winograd, T. 1972. *Understanding Natural Language.* New York: Academic Press.

Yamada, A.; Nishida, T.; and Doshita, S. 1988. Figuring out most plausible interpretation from spatial descriptions. In *Proceedings of the 12th International Conference on Computational Linguistics*, 764–769.

A Model for Integrated Qualitative Spatial and Dynamic Reasoning about Physical Systems *

Raman Rajagopalan
Artificial Intelligence Laboratory
Department of Computer Sciences
University of Texas at Austin
Austin, Texas 78712
raman@cs.utexas.edu

Abstract

Qualitative spatial reasoning has many applications in such diverse areas as natural language understanding, cognitive mapping, and reasoning about the physical world. We address problems whose solutions require integrated spatial and dynamic reasoning.

In this paper, we present our spatial representation, based on the extremal points of objects, and show that this representation is useful for modeling the spatial extent, relative positions, and orientation of objects, and in reasoning about changes in spatial relations and orientation due to the translational and rotational motion of objects. Our theory has been implemented to support a magnetic fields problem solving application using the QPC and QSIM systems for qualitative modeling. The issues encountered in integrating spatial and dynamic reasoning in the context of these systems are also discussed.

Introduction

Spatial reasoning has been studied in Artificial Intelligence from many perspectives, including natural language understanding [Freksa 92, Mukerjee and Joe 90, Retz-Schmidt 88], cognitive mapping [Kuipers and Levitt 88], and qualitative reasoning about physical systems [Forbus, et. al. 91, Joskowicz and Sacks 91, Nielsen 88, Weinberg, Uckun, and Biswas 92]. A fundamental starting point for spatial reasoning is the representation of the spatial extent of an object. Problems which require knowledge of the exact shapes of objects, such as determining whether two gears will mesh together, will require a numerically precise spatial representation, such as the configuration space [Forbus, et. al. 91, Joskowicz and Sacks 91].

For many problems, knowledge of the *approximate extent* of objects is sufficient, or that could be only information available. Several spatial reasoning methods, based on the use of simplifying abstractions to approximate the actual extents of objects [Abella and Kender 93, Cui, Cohn, and Randell 92, Mukerjee and Joe 90], have been developed to address these cases. None are sufficiently rich to simultaneously model all of the following properties: the spatial extents, relative positions, and orientations of objects, and the effects of translational or rotational motion on the spatial state.

For example, Cui, Cohn, and Randell [1992] use convex hulls as an abstraction method. They present techniques for reasoning about the relative positions of objects, but do not discuss the orientation of objects. They also do not provide a *qualitative* method to describe the convex hull itself, or how to compute its changing location or orientation if the underlying object translates or rotates. They assume that an external function will provide this information.

We consider problems whose solutions require integrated spatial and dynamic reasoning. Specifically, we are implementing a magnetic fields problem solver, which, given a diagram to describe the initial spatial state and text to describe any dynamic changes taking place, solves the problem through qualitative simulation. An input processing specialist, The Figure Understander [Rajagopalan and Kuipers 94], is used to integrate the information in the text and diagram input into a unified model of the initial state. A library of model fragments, for spatial reasoning and for the magnetic fields domain, is used by the QPC [Crawford, et. al. 90, Farquhar 94] qualitative modeling system to detect spatial configurations that could lead to dynamic processes. The effects of any active processes are determined using the QSIM [Kuipers 86] qualitative simulation system.

Our problems cover the operation of such commonly used devices as motors, generators, and transformers. Relative position and orientation information is used to study the effects of changing the magnetic flux passing through a closed conducting object. The change in flux can be due to a time-varying magnetic field (transformer), or to the translational or rotational motion of the conducting object (motor, generator).

Forbus, Neilsen, and Faltings [1991] and Joskowicz and Sacks [1991] also address the issue of integrated

---

*This work has taken place in the Qualitative Reasoning Group at the Artificial Intelligence Laboratory, The University of Texas at Austin. Research of the Qualitative Reasoning Group is supported in part by NSF grants IRI-8904454, IRI-9017047, and IRI-9216584, and by NASA contracts NCC 2-760 and NAG 9-665.

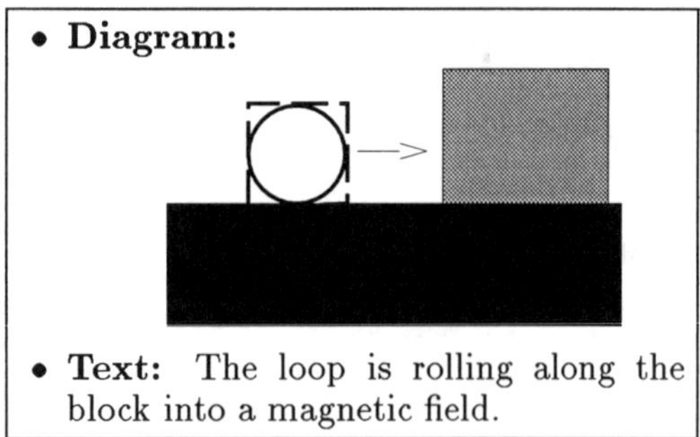

Figure 1: A magnetic fields problem involving translational motion: What happens as the conducting loop (white) rolls across the magnetic field (gray)? The rectangular bounding box abstraction shown for the loop is not included in the input to the problem solver.

spatial and dynamic reasoning, but the characteristics of our problems are not well suited for the configuration space-based approach they have adopted. They work with domains where objects cannot share the same physical space, and objects cannot be dynamically created or destroyed. In such cases, the configuration space must be computed only once, and the boundaries of the forbidden regions can be used to detect the points at which two objects are in contact. In our problem set, the most interesting spatial relation is overlap between objects, and since magnetic fields can be created simply by establishing a current flow in a wire, we must allow for the dynamic creation and destruction of spatial objects.

In the following sections, we describe our spatial representation and its use in reasoning about the relative positions between objects and the orientation of convex objects, particularly in dynamically changing worlds. We will also discuss the issues encountered in integrating spatial and dynamic reasoning in the context of the QPC and QSIM systems.

Example Magnetic Fields Problems

Consider the scenarios in Figures 1 and 2. In Figure 1, a conducting loop is rolling into a magnetic field. In Figure 2, a conducting loop is rotating inside a magnetic field. The problem is to describe what happens as the specified motions take place.

We have to recognize changes in the *relative position* (figure 1) or *orientation* (figure 2) of the loop relative to the field to determine when the magnetic flux through the loop is changing. During those periods, an induced emf will be established in the loop such that the resulting current flow will produce a magnetic field that opposes the change in flux through the loop. Magnetic forces can then act on the loop, and orientation information can be used to determine the net magnetic force/torque and its effects (e.g., the loop in Figure 1 will slow down as it enters and exits the field).

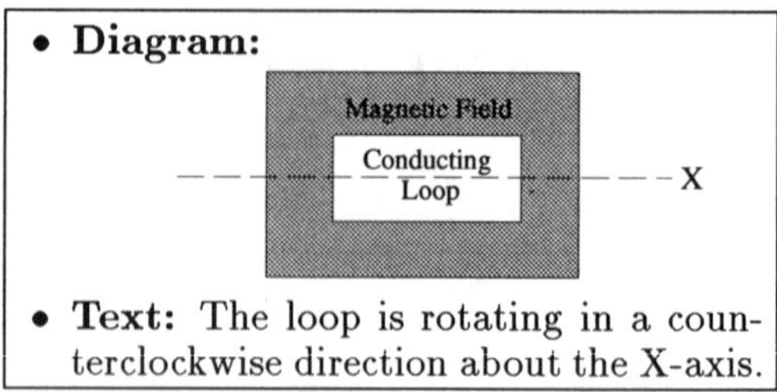

Figure 2: A magnetic fields problem involving rotational motion: A rudimentary generator.

The Figure Understander

The Figure Understander works with text input and a numerical description of a diagram, a PostScript file produced by the InterViews drawing editor, to output a qualitative, constraint-based description of the initial state. A picture description language is used to define a semantics for diagram objects, greatly simplifying the task of processing the input. For example, for Figure 2, given that white objects are conducting loops, The Figure Understander easily associates the direction of rotational motion with the smaller rectangular object.

The diagram-based input method serves two purposes. First, it is a more natural and less error-prone method of entering the initial spatial state than using a special purpose text form. Second, it allows numerically-precise spatial data to be extracted for solving problems where such information is necessary. For example, The Figure Understander includes heuristics for selecting frames of reference, and when appropriate, numerically rotates the diagram before extracting the initial spatial state. The Figure Understander corrects minor human errors in drawing the diagram by assuming that coordinate values within a given epsilon measure are equal.

The Spatial Representation

When an abstraction is used to *approximate* the actual spatial extent of an object, there can exist real distinctions that can no longer be reasoned about without additional case-specific information. If a maximally covering abstraction is used, such as a convex hull, one can *guarantee* non-intersection conclusions based on examining only the approximate shapes, but not intersection conclusions. For example, if the convex hulls of two objects are not intersecting, then the underlying objects cannot be intersecting. However, it's possible that the underlying objects do not intersect even if the convex hulls intersect. Similarly, if an abstract shape is fully contained within the actual shape, then one can guarantee intersection conclusions, but not non-intersection conclusions.

Our problems require reasoning about what can happen *if* two objects are intersecting or *if* one object is fully enclosed inside another. We enforce the constraint that a shape abstraction should fully enclose an underlying object at all times, to guarantee when it is at all possible for two objects to be intersecting.

We also wish to minimize the need for quantitative information in describing the initial spatial state and to maintain the spatial state as objects translate and rotate. The goal is that a qualitative solution should apply to any physical scenario that fits the initial state description. The generality of the solution will degrade with the requirement for precise numerical information in describing the initial spatial state or in determining subsequent spatial states.

Modeling Spatial Extent

We describe the spatial extent of an object qualitatively in terms of its **extremal points**: the `topmost` (tm), `rightmost` (rm), `bottommost` (bm), and `leftmost` (lm) points [Rajagopalan 93]. To reason about three dimensional objects, we add the frontmost and rearmost points.

We use two abstractions, **a rectangular bounding box** drawn around the extremal points of an object, and a **bounding circle**, as described below, to approximate the region occupied by the object. For problems in three-dimensional space, we use a **bounding cube** and a **bounding sphere** respectively. In Figure 3, we illustrate our abstraction method on two polygons. We draw a bounding circle around object A and a rectangular bounding box around object B. The radius of the bounding circle is the maximum distance from the center of gravity of an object to any point on its perimeter.

The bounding box abstraction is sufficient for reasoning about problems involving static worlds or only translational motion. The bounding circle/sphere abstraction is used for problems involving rotation about the center of gravity. The latter abstraction provides the guarantee that an underlying rotating object will always remain within the bounding abstraction, and that the abstractions will have a fixed shape.

The bounding circle/sphere abstraction is, in general, weaker than the bounding box abstraction. Consider the real possibilities that a rotating object could come into contact with another object, and that rotation could remove an existing contact. If two bounding spheres are not intersecting, we can conclude with certainty that the underlying objects cannot come into contact after any rotation of either object about its center of gravity. If two bounding spheres intersect, they will continue to intersect after any rotation of the underlying objects. Additional information, such as the distances between the objects, their sizes, and relative orientations, will be required in that case to determine with certainty if rotation can create or remove contacts between the underlying objects.

Modeling Relative Positions/Orientation

We describe the relative positions of objects through *inequality relations* between their extremal points. If

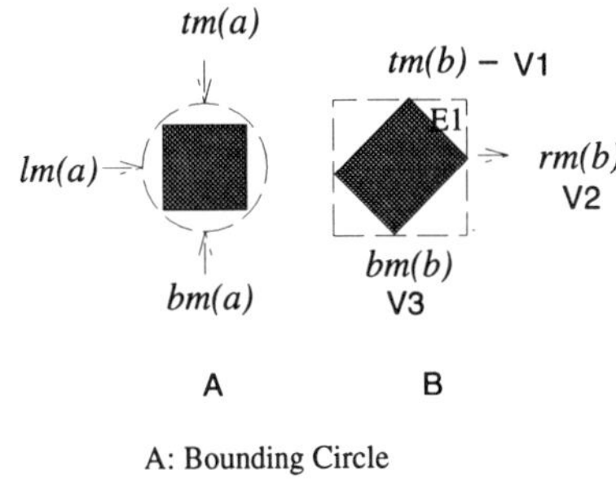

Figure 3: Examples of the rectangular bounding box and bounding circle as methods of shape abstraction for two polygons.

the rectangular/cubic bounding box abstraction is used, the extremal points of the shape abstraction and the underlying object are the same. If the bounding circle/sphere abstraction is used, the extremal points used are those of the bounding abstraction, and not the underlying object. For example, for the objects in Figure 3, the inequality relation $rm(A) < lm(B)$, represents the fact that A is to the left of B.

Although we can conclude that objects are intersecting with certainty in some special cases (such as overlap across an extremal edge), in general, for relations involving intersections between objects, we can prove only the weaker relation that the bounding abstractions of the objects satisfy the desired property. For example, object A `bounding-abstraction-encloses` object B if $(lm(A) \leq lm(B)) \wedge (rm(A) \geq rm(B)) \wedge (tm(A) \geq tm(B)) \wedge (bm(A) \leq bm(B))$.

We define the `orientation` of a surface of an object with respect to a global Cartesian frame of reference through its surface normal direction, as used by Nielsen [1988]. In our representation, this may be obtained through knowledge of the identities of the extremal points between which a surface lies. For example, the orientation vector of edge E1 for object B in Figure 1 has positive X and Y components since it lies between Vertices V1 and V2, the topmost and rightmost points.

Rectangular bounding boxes and bounding circles are powerful abstractions for qualitative spatial reasoning: numerically precise information is not required, even in a dynamically changing world, to maintain the bounding boxes and bounding circles. All we need are the inequality relationships between the extremal points of the bounding abstractions that are used. The use of circular/spherical abstractions for rotating objects ensures that only translational motion can change the position of the extremal points of the shape abstractions and thus, the relative positions of objects (assuming that objects have fixed shapes).

Orientation information, as required to determine the direction of current flow in an edge of a conducting loop, may be obtained if the connectivity of an object and its extremal points are known. Only rotational motion can change the identities of the vertices and edges that form the extremal points of an object, and thus, its orientation.

Translational Motion

Our model of relative positions, based on inequality relations between the extremal points of objects, allows us to recognize that a qualitatively interesting event will occur when the inequality relation changes (e.g., when $rm(A) = lm(B)$ in Figure 3). This can be used to study the effects of translational motion.

The values of the rightmost and leftmost points of an object will change over time if the X-velocity of the object is non-zero, and the values of the topmost and bottommost points will be affected by the Y-velocity. In Figure 3, if the X-velocity of object A is positive, the coordinate value of its rightmost point will increase over time, and we can recognize that a qualitatively interesting state will occur once $rm(A) = lm(B)$.

Rotational Motion

To maintain the orientation of a rotating object, we must determine the changes in the identities of the vertices and edges that form its extremal points as it rotates. Currently, we only consider the rotation of two dimensional objects about an axis that passes through their center of gravity. Rotation can also change the projected area of an object onto another object in a different plane, a property of great interest for the generator problem described in Figure 2.

The projected area of an object rotating about the X or Y axis onto another object in the XY plane is a function of the area of overlap between the two objects (as if both were in the XY plane) and the cosine of the angle between the plane of the rotating object and the XY plane. We independently model the effects of rotation about the X and Y axes, and use qualitative addition to determine the net change in the projected area. We model the extent of rotation about the X and Y axes, respectively, through two angles measured counterclockwise from the XY plane to the plane of the object: θ_Y, the angle between the plane of the object and the Y axis, and θ_X, the angle between the plane of the object and the X axis.

When θ_X or θ_Y is equivalent to 90 or 270 degrees, the projected area of an object onto the XY plane is zero. These angles also mark the point at which the orientation of the object changes. During counterclockwise rotation about the X-axis, when θ_Y is in the interval 90 degrees to 270 degrees, the identities of the topmost and bottommost points will be reversed. During rotation about the Y-axis, the identities of the leftmost and rightmost points can be reversed. In Figure 3, considering object B, if the object has a value for θ_Y in the interval 90 to 270 degrees, then the orientation of edge E1 would have a positive X-component and a negative

Y-component since vertex V1 would be a bottommost point instead of a topmost point.

Rotation in the XY Plane Rotation about the Z-axis can only change the orientation of an object, and not the projected area onto the XY plane. Given, as in Figure 3, that vertex V1 is the topmost point of an object rotating in the counterclockwise direction, and that vertex V2 follows V1, V2 will be the next topmost point. The difficult problem is to determine which extremal point will change first. Given that V2 is the rightmost point and that V3 follows V2, the question now becomes will V2 become the topmost point before V3 becomes the rightmost point? Since the bottommost and leftmost points may also change, there is always a four-way race condition.

For a general polygon, we would require quantitative knowledge (e.g., the internal angles of the polygon) to avoid intractable branching during a qualitative simulation. However, for such commonly encountered special shapes as circles, rectangles and parallelograms, qualitative solutions do exist. For example, rectangles have the property that all four extremal points change simultaneously, eliminating the race condition.

Integrating Spatial and Dynamic Reasoning

We have implemented our spatial reasoning methods using the QPC [Crawford, et. al 90, Farquhar 94] qualitative modeling system, which in turn uses the QSIM [Kuipers 86] qualitative simulation system. We encountered two difficulties in integrating spatial and dynamic reasoning in the context of these systems - the need to model piecewise continuous variables, and the need to model variables with circular quantity spaces.

Modeling Piecewise Continuous Variables

Several qualitative modeling tools, such as QPC and QPE [Forbus 90], require model variables to be continuous. In problems involving both spatial and dynamic reasoning, it's possible for certain model variables to be piecewise-continuous. Figure 1 shows a conducting loop, whose abstracted shape is a rectangle, moving into a rectangular field. As the loop enters, the derivative of the area of overlap between the two objects is positive and is proportional to the X-velocity of the loop. Once the loop is enclosed in the field, the derivative of the area of overlap drops discontinuously to zero. This derivative is a *piecewise-continuous* variable - one whose value is continuous within a given world model, but which may change discontinuously at a transition point, when a new world model is computed to reflect a qualitatively significant change in the world state.

QPC inherits the values of model variables from the previous model when determining the new model after a transition point. Discontinuous changes in the values of variables could lead to contradictions in the new model. In our implementation, we allow the QPC model builder to explicitly declare that a variable is piecewise-continuous within a QPC model fragment description, and prevent their values and any inequality relations involving such variables from being inherited at a transition point. This technique may be used for any dependent variable, since the new value for the variable may be recomputed in a subsequent model, or for any independent variable whose new value is explicitly given in the subsequent model. Variables that are dependent on piecewise continuous variables must also be modeled as piecewise continuous since their values could also change discontinuously.

Modeling Circular Quantity Spaces

A second modeling restriction imposed by the existing qualitative reasoning systems is that the range of values for a model variable is given through a *linear* quantity space. For modeling such phenomena as rotation, it is beneficial to model some variables through a circular quantity space to directly model the fact that the behavior of the system is cyclic.

Consider the variable θ_Y for the example of Figure 2. This measures the extent of rotation around the X-axis. The qualitatively significant values for θ_Y include 0, 90, 180, 270, and 360 degrees. We would like to directly state that the value of 360 degrees is functionally equivalent to zero degrees (resulting in a circular quantity space), instead of having to model, in a linear quantity space, that 450, 540, etc., are also significant values. We cannot model this fact in a linear quantity space since we would have that $(0 < 270)$, $(270 < 360)$, and $(0 = 360)$, which leads to a contradiction.

We use the circular-quantity-space declaration -

```
(circular-qspace-quantity
    theta-y convex-2-d-objects
    (theta-y-0 theta-y-90 theta-y-180 theta-y-270))
```

to define the variable theta-y as a quantity for the domain class convex-2-d-objects. It has a circular quantity space with four qualitatively significant values represented by theta-y-0, theta-y-90, theta-y-180, and theta-y-270. After theta-y-270, the quantity space wraps back to theta-y-0. Note that each of these values actually represents a set. We maintain the inequality relationships between θ_Y and each of θ_{Y0}, θ_{Y90}, θ_{Y180}, and θ_{Y270} to model the relative value of θ_Y. The same inequality relations, $(\theta_Y > \theta_{Y0})$ and $(\theta_Y < \theta_{Y90})$, are used to capture the fact that θ_Y is between 0 and 90 degrees or 360 and 450 degrees.

We avoid contradictions in the model by asserting only a linear subset of the circular quantity space into each QPC model. Assuming that each of the qualitatively significant values in a circular quantity space is associated with a model transition condition, in any QPC model, we only have to consider the relationship between the circular-valued variable (θ_Y) and three of those values. For example, in the initial state of the

problem described in Figure 2, we have that θ_Y is equal to θ_{Y0}, is less than θ_{Y90}, and is greater than θ_{Y270}. We may model θ_Y to be greater or less than θ_{Y180}, and not both, to linearize the circular quantity space since we know that θ_Y cannot equal θ_{Y180} without first crossing through θ_{Y90} or θ_{Y270}, when a model transition is required to occur.

We use the piecewise-continuous variable feature to model the fact that the inequality relationships between θ_Y and any of θ_{Y0}, θ_{Y90}, θ_{Y180}, and θ_{Y270} can change discontinuously at a transition point. The appropriate inequality relations are automatically asserted into the subsequent model. For example, in Figure 2, the loop is rotating in a counterclockwise direction about the X-axis and the next qualitatively significant change occurs when θ_Y equals θ_{Y90}. Then, we ignore all previous inequality relations between θ_Y and its possible values, and insert into the model that $(\theta_Y = \theta_{Y90})$, $(\theta_Y < \theta_{Y180})$, and $(\theta_Y > \theta_{Y0})$. The relationship between θ_Y and θ_{Y270} is insignificant, and may be modeled as '<' or '>' since the relationship in the previous model (>) will not have been inherited.

Qualitative Behavior for the Examples in Figures 1 and 2

To illustrate both solutions, we have artificially combined the problems in Figures 1 and 2 into a single problem: *As in Figure 1, the loop moves to the right until it is entirely enclosed in the magnetic field. At that point, its translational motion stops, and it rotates around the X-axis as in Figure 2.* This was done by treating translational and rotational velocity as piecewise continuous variables, and resetting their values once the loop was enclosed in the field.

During translational motion (denoted by time points t0, t1, and t2), as the loop enters the field (t1 to t2), the area of overlap, and thus, the magnetic flux through the loop, increases steadily (steady due to the use of the rectangular bounding box abstraction for the conducting loop). During this period, an induced emf is established in the loop, which results in a steady current flow. The current flow is negative to show that it opposes the increase in the flux through the loop. The direction of current flow may be either clockwise or counterclockwise depending on the direction of the magnetic field, a property we ignore for the purposes of this example.

The variables `DIF-<F.LM-XVAL>-<L.RM-XVAL>` and `DIF-<F.LM-XVAL>-<L.LM-XVAL>` are generated by QPC to encode the inequality relations between the rightmost and leftmost points of the loop and the leftmost point of the field. Note that a qualitatively interesting change occurs in the *relative positions* of the loop and the field whenever one of the `DIF` terms is zero (i.e., an inequality relation changes). When the former `DIF` variable is zero, the loop begins to *enter* the field. When the latter is zero, the loop is fully *enclosed* in the field. Note also that the value of the derivative of the

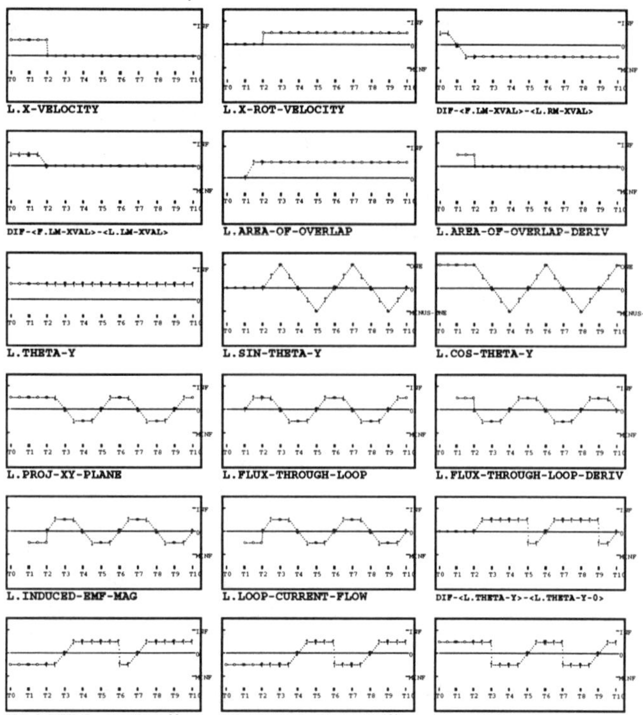

Figure 4: Qualitative behavior produced by QPC/-QSIM for the problems in Figure 1 (up to time t2) and Figure 2 (after time t2). The shape abstraction for the loop is assumed to be rectangular in the models for translational motion, and is assumed to be circular in the models of rotational motion. The values of **L.AREA-OF-OVERLAP** (constant after t2) and **L.AREA-OF-OVERLAP-DERIV** (constant during t1-t2) reflect these assumptions.

area of overlap between the loop and the field changes discontinuously from a positive value to zero at time t2. The variables dependent on this derivative, such as the derivative of the flux passing through the loop, the magnitude of the induced emf, and the current flow in the loop, also change discontinuously.

At time point t2, translational motion stops and rotational motion begins. We show the output for two complete, counterclockwise rotations of the loop. Each time interval after t2 corresponds to an additional 90 degree increment in the value of θ_Y. Theta-Y has a positive value equivalent to zero in the initial state (I.e., the actual value may be 360, 720, etc.). It is continuously increasing after time t2 since the rotational velocity of the loop is positive and constant.

The magnetic flux through the loop is proportional to the projected area of the loop onto the magnetic field, which is given by $Proj\text{-}Area = (Area\text{-}Loop)(\cos \theta_Y)$. The rate of change of flux through the loop, $d\Phi/dt$, is proportional to the rate of change of the projected area of the loop onto the field, which

is given by $dProj\text{-}Area = (Area\text{-}loop)(-\sin \theta_Y)(d\theta_Y)$. The induced emf in the loop is proportional to $-d\Phi/dt$.

The simulation output shows the sinusoidal behavior of the model variables as the loop rotates around the field. The last four **DIF** variables encode the inequality relationships between theta-Y and its possible values. The qualitatively interesting changes (in orientation) occur whenever one of the **DIF** terms crosses zero. Note that at time t3, when the value of theta-Y is equivalent to 90 degrees (the difference term dif-<l.theta-y>-<l.theta-y-90> is zero), the projected area of the loop onto the XY plane becomes zero. The projected area is then negative through time point t5, when theta-Y becomes equivalent to 270 degrees (the difference term dif-<l.theta-y>-<l.theta-y-270> is zero). This represents the period when the orientation of the loop is reversed due to the identities of the topmost and bottommost points being reversed.

Note the discontinuous changes in the values of the last four **DIF** variables. These occur when a newly asserted inequality relation (after a transition) between theta-Y and any of θ_{Y0}, θ_{Y90}, θ_{Y180}, and θ_{Y270} is different from that in the previous model. This demonstrates not only the operation of the circular quantity space mechanism, but also the usefulness of the ability to model piecewise continuous variables.

Summary and Conclusions

Forbus, Nielsen, and Faltings [1991] have conjectured that there exists no purely qualitative, general purpose, representation of spatial properties. Their conclusions are based on the need to reason about the *exact shapes* of objects in reasoning about mechanical devices, a spatial property that is indeed difficult to describe in a qualitative fashion.

Many qualitative formalisms have since been developed to support spatial reasoning [Mukerjee and Joe 90, Cui, Cohn, and Randell 92, Abella and Kender 93]. They share the property that *simplifying abstractions* are used to *approximate* the actual shapes of objects. The authors describe how abstractions such as the convex hull, collision parallelograms, or inertia tensor-based bounding boxes may be used for qualitative spatial reasoning, but do not describe how these abstractions can be represented internally in a qualitative fashion, or how to *qualitatively compute* the changes in the positions and orientations of the abstractions as the underlying objects translate or rotate.

We discussed the advantages and fundamental limitations of using shape abstractions for spatial reasoning, and presented an *extremal point-based* spatial representation that requires little information to compute and maintain even as objects translate and rotate. With this method, we can describe the relative positions of objects through inequality relations between their extremal points, and easily determine the effects of translational motion on the spatial state. We showed that the orientation of a convex object with respect to a global Cartesian frame of reference could be determined given just the connectivity of the object and the identities of its extremal points, and discussed methods for maintaining the orientation if the object rotates about an axis passing through its center of gravity.

We are applying our spatial reasoning methods in a problem solver for the magnetic fields domain. The remaining work in this ongoing project will cover the use of orientation information to compute and reason about the effects of magnetic forces, and will address methods for modeling dynamically created spatial entities, such as magnetic fields due to current flow in a wire. We have also tested the utility of our spatial representation for use in natural language understanding, including reasoning about objects with intrinsic fronts, by considering problems involving the use of spatial reasoning to isolate objects in a complex scene to name them [Rajagopalan 94].

Acknowledgements

I thank Professor Benjamin Kuipers for his many suggestions in developing the ideas presented in this paper, and Bert Kay, James Lester, Toyoaki Nishida, Sowmya Ramachandran, and Lalitha Rajagopalan for providing valuable comments on earlier drafts.

References

[Abella and Kender 93] Abella, A. and J. Kender. Qualitatively Describing Objects Using Spatial Prepositions. In: AAAI-93, Washington, DC, 1993.

[Crawford, et. al. 90] Crawford, J., A. Farquhar, and B. Kuipers. QPC : A Compiler from Physical Models into Qualitative Differential Equations. In: AAAI-90, Boston, MA, 1990.

[Crawford and Kuipers 91] Crawford, J. and B. Kuipers. Algernon - A Tractable System for Knowledge-Representation. AAAI Spring Symposium on Implemented Knowledge Representation and Reasoning Systems, Palo Alto, CA 1991.

[Cui, et. al. 92] Cui, Z., A. G. Cohn, and D. Randell. Qualitative Simulation Based on a Logical Formalism of Space and Time. In: AAAI-92, San Jose, CA, 1992.

[Egenhofer and Al-Taha 92] Egenhofer, M. and K. Al-Taha. Reasoning about Gradual Changes in Topological Relationships. In: A. Frank, I. Campari, and U. Formentini, Eds., *Theories and Methods of Spatio-Temporal Reasoning in Geographic Space*, Springer-Verlag, Berlin, 1992.

[Farquhar 94] Farquhar, A. A Qualitative Process Compiler. In: AAAI-94, Seattle, WA, 1994.

[Forbus, et. al. 91] Forbus, K., P. Nielsen, and B. Faltings. Qualitative Spatial Reasoning: the CLOCK Project. *Artificial Intelligence* **51**, 1991.

[Forbus 90] Forbus, K. The Qualitative Process Engine. In Weld, D., and de Kleer, J., eds., *Readings in Qualitative Reasoning about Physical Systems*. Morgan Kaufman, Los Altos, CA, 1990.

[Freksa 92] Freksa, C., Using Orientation Information for Qualitative Spatial Reasoning. In: A. Frank, I. Campari, and U. Formentini, Eds., *Theories and Methods of Spatio-Temporal Reasoning in Geographic Space*, Springer-Verlag, Berlin, 1992.

[Galton 93] Galton, A., Towards an Integrated Logic of Space, Time, and Motion. In: IJCAI-93, Chambery, France, 1993.

[Joskowicz and Sacks 91] Joskowicz, L., and E. Sacks. Computational Kinematics. *Artificial Intelligence* 51, 381-416, 1991.

[Kuipers 86] Kuipers, B. Qualitative Simulation. *Artificial Intelligence* 29, 289-338, 1986.

[Kuipers and Levitt 88] Kuipers B., and T. Levitt. Navigation and Mapping in Large-Scale Space. AI Magazine, 9(2), 25-43.

[Mukerjee and Joe 90] Mukerjee, A. and G. Joe. A Qualitative Model for Space. In: AAAI-90, Boston, MA, 1990.

[Nielsen 88] Nielsen, P. A Qualitative Approach to Mechanical Constraint. In: AAAI-88, Saint Paul, MN, 1988.

[Rajagopalan 93] Rajagopalan, R. A Model of Spatial Position Based on Extremal Points. In Proceedings: ACM Workshop on Advances in Geographic Information Systems, Arlington, VA, 1993.

[Rajagopalan 94] Rajagopalan, R. Integrating Text and Graphical Input to a Knowledge Base. In Working Notes: AAAI Workshop on Integration of Natural Language and Vision Processing, Seattle, WA, 1994.

[Rajagopalan and Kuipers 94] Rajagopalan, R. and B. Kuipers. The Figure Understander: A System for Integrating Text and Diagram Input to a Knowledge Base. In Proceedings: The Seventh International Conference on Industrial and Engineering Applications of Artificial Intelligence and Expert Systems (IEA/AIE-94), Austin, TX, 1994.

[Resnick and Halliday 88] Resnick J. and D. Halliday. *Fundamentals of Physics*, 3rd. Edition, John Wiley and Sons, 1988.

[Retz-Schmidt 88] Retz-Schmidt, G. Various Views on Spatial Prepositions. *AI magazine*, 9(2).

[Weinberg, et. al. 92] Weinberg, J., S. Uckun, G. Biswas, and S. Manganaris. Qualitative Vector Algebra. In: B. Faltings and P. Struss, Eds., *Recent Advances in Qualitative Physics*, pp. 177-192, The MIT Press, Cambridge, MA, 1992.

A Theory for Qualitative Spatial Reasoning Based on Order Relations

Ralf Röhrig

Laboratory for Artificial Intelligence
University of Hamburg
Vogt-Kölln-Str. 30
22527 Hamburg, Germany
email: roehrig@informatik.uni-hamburg.de

Abstract

What is needed for an analysis of the existing approaches to qualitative spatial reasoning and for a deeper understanding of the domain of space is a unifying theory that explains all of the concepts used for the representation of the different aspects of space by some primitive but well understood relations. In order to provide such primitive relations it will be shown that the concepts used in the existing approaches can be explained by simple order relations between points on some low-dimensional structures. One of the properties of an order relation is transitivity. It will be shown that this property alone is sufficient to explain all the inferences described in the various approaches to qualitative spatial reasoning.

Motivation

Several approaches to qualitative spatial reasoning have been developed recently. A major problem with these approaches is the lack of comparability between them. One difficulty is that the approaches deal with different aspects of the spatial domain. Each of them provides some concepts for spatial relations, but most of the concepts differ in a substantial way. An overview of the dimensions of qualitative spatial reasoning is given in (Freksa & Röhrig 1993). Another difficulty in the comparison of the various approaches is that most of them use look-up tables for the explication of possible inferences instead of using the properties of the concepts involved. Even though look-up tables may have computational advantages, they include only very specialised rules that are not likely to be compared with properties of concepts from other approaches.

What is needed for an analysis of the existing approaches and for a deeper understanding of the domain of space is a unifying theory that explains all of the concepts used for the representation of the different aspects of space by some primitive, but well understood, relations. In order to provide such primitive relations it will be shown that the concepts used in the approaches to qualitative spatial reasoning can be explained by simple order relations between points on some low-dimensional structures. For some of the approaches these low-dimensional structures are one-dimensional axes to which the spatial scenes are projected. For other approaches, those using orientation relations as basic spatial concepts, the low-dimensional structures are circles around the objects, and other objects are projected to those circles. Since it is not possible to define a binary order relation on a circle, a ternary relation with similar algebraic properties will be introduced. This relation is a sort of a cyclic order, and will therefore be called CYCORD. For the approaches using topological relations the low-dimensional structure is a system of subsets of space that is partially ordered by set inclusion. One of the properties of an order relation is transitivity. It will be shown that this property alone is sufficient to explain all the inferences described in the various approaches to qualitative spatial reasoning.

The Theory

Although the existing approaches to qualitative spatial reasoning differ substantially, they have some aspects in common: they deal with objects in 2, 3, or n-dimensional space, they refer to spatial scenes by spatial relations between those objects, and they use composition of spatial relations for doing inferences. The thesis of this paper is that for all approaches, 1) objects can be projected to points on some low-dimensional structures that are ordered by an order relation 2) spatial relations can be expressed in terms of these order relations, 3) transitivity can be used to do inferences, and 4) the inferred facts can be translated back into the original terms, ending up in exactly the same inferences as are described in the approaches. The low-dimensional structures are axes, circles, and, for the topological approaches, partially ordered systems of subsets of space. There is a limitation to this theory: in some approaches, spatial relations require a theory of equality of points on the low-dimensional structures. For the sake of simplicity, and because the introduction is straightforward, equality is not included here.

Order relations

In this section, the algebraic properties of a binary order relation are recalled to provide a basis for the definition of a ternary order relation on cyclic structures. An order relation is known to be *asymmetric, non-reflexive,* and *transitive.* Now, a relation with similar properties will be defined on the points of a circle. There is a problem defining a binary order relation on a circle, even when committing to a clockwise orientation for example; if any point A appears on a circle before a point B, then it is also true that B appears before A, when starting between A and B (cf. Figure 1). This problem can be fixed by defining a starting point for each pair of points and adding this point as a third argument to the order relation. The resulting relation will be called CYCORD, which is short for CYClic

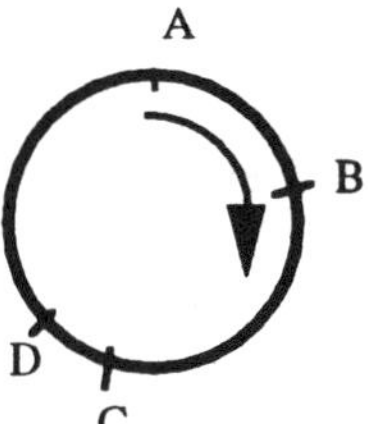

objects: points on a circle
relation: CYCORD : point X point X point

Properties
Asymmetry   A-B-C ==> ¬ (A-C-B)
Non-Reflexivity   ¬ (A-B-A)
bounded Transitivity A-B-C, A-C-D ==> A-B-D
Revolving   A-B-C ==> B-C-A

Figure 1:   Properties of a cyclic order relation

ORDer. The interpretation of CYCORD (A, B, C) (or A-B-C for short) is that in a clockwise direction, B appears before C when starting at A. Another valid interpretation of A-B-C is that B is between A and C, when committing to a clockwise direction. There is no restriction regarding additional points between A and B or B and C. Still another view of CYCORD is that the circle is cut in A, resulting in an open interval from A to A on which a normal binary order is defined for any two points that are unequal to A.

Each of the algebraic properties of a binary order relation has a correspondence in a property of the cyclic order. CYCORD is *asymmetric*: if B is between A and C, then B should not be between C and A. CYCORD is *non-reflexive*: A-B-A holds for no A, B; this property ensures that CYCORD does not collapse into a binary order. CYCORD is transitive, but not in the expected way, which would be: if A-B-C and B-C-D, then A-B-D. Even though this property seems to hold in Figure 1, it does not hold in the general case. This may be verified by the same picture in Figure 1: A-C-D holds, and C-D-B holds too, but it is not the case that A-C-B holds. The problem is that the circle must not be traversed more than once, when transitivity is applied. Therefore, a property called *bounded transitivity* is imposed here, which is a more conservative form of transitivity, based on a constant starting point: if A-B-C and A-C-D, then A-B-D, in words, if B is before C when starting from A, and C is before D when starting from the same point A, then also B is before D when starting from that point A. This property is very intuitive and is valid, because it is guaranteed that the circle is not traversed more than once.

There is one additional property that holds for CYCORD: since CYCORD is a relation over three arbitrary points on a circle, the three points may change places in a *revolving* manner: if B is between A and C, then also is C between B and A. The revolving property offers some very intuitive enhancements to the other properties of CYCORD. First, in combination with asymmetry it ensures that no two arguments of the CYCORD relation may be switched. Second, in combination with non-reflexivity it ensures that no two arguments of the CYCORD relation are the same. Third, in combination with bounded transitivity, it allows for other transitivity schemes, where the bound is not necessarily the first argument. And fourth, applying the revolving property more than once makes the arguments of a CYCORD relation a cyclic list.

Applications

In this section, the theory will be supported by several examples. Approaches to qualitative spatial reasoning are divided into three major classes, those using orderings, those using orientation information, and those using topological relations for the description of spatial relations between objects.

Ordering approaches

In some of the approaches, such as (Jungert 1988), (Güsgen 1989), or (Mukerjee & Joe 1991), the projection step is done explicitly: objects are projected to multiple one-dimensional axes. Since there is no interaction between the axes, an inference calculus can be applied on each axis independently. Projection of objects results in intervals on each axis, and spatial relations are represented by interval relations. Since intervals are defined by their start and end points, it is straightforward to translate the interval relations to relations between points. For example, an *A before B* becomes a simple *end(A) < start(B)*, while *B overlaps C* becomes a more complex formula: *start(B) < start(C) and start(C) < end(B) and end(B) < end(C)*, where "start" and "end" are functions from intervals to their start points and their end points, respectively. Using transitivity of "<" it can be inferred from the two facts above, that *end(A) < start(C)* . The inferred fact can be translated back into terms of interval relations as *A before C*. This inference corresponds to the one Güsgen stated in his composition table (Güsgen 1989). Since there is no loss of information, when translating intervals to points and interval relations to order relations on points, all inferences valid in one formalism have to be valid in the other one.

Orientation approaches

Some of the approaches, such as (Frank 1991) and (Hernández 1992), use sector models for a description of orientation relations between objects. In these approaches, objects are considered to be points, and each object induces several sectors around it which are each bounded by two globally oriented lines (cf. Figure 2). Information about a

point being on either side of a straight line can be reduced to an order relation on a one-dimensional axis perpendicular to that line, where the point and the line itself are projected to points on that axis. Since each orientation relation in the approaches corresponds to one sector, it can without loss of information be translated to order relations on each of the axes perpendicular the bounds of that sector.

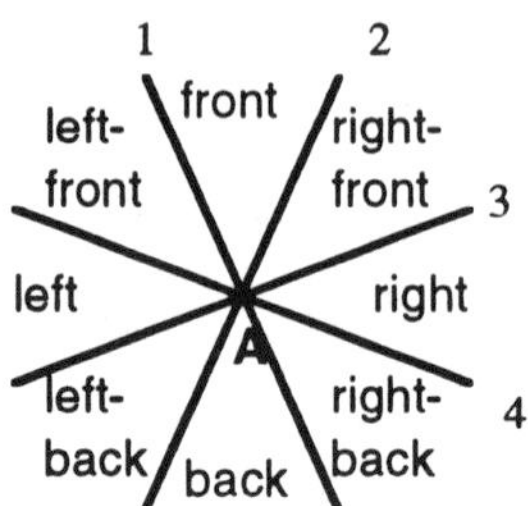

Figure 2:   Representation of orientations in (Hernández 1992)

For example, in the sector model of (Hernández 1992), *A front B* becomes *A < B* on the axis perpendicular to bound 1, and *B < A* on the axis perpendicular to bound 2. In the same manner, *B front C* becomes *B < C* on the axis perpendicular to bound 1, and *C < B* on the axis perpendicular to bound 2. Since a global system of orientations is used, the bounds are oriented in the same way in every object. Hence, the axes perpendicular to the bounds are the same for any bound with the same index. Using transitivity, from the facts above we can conclude *A < C* on axis 1, and *C < A* on axis 2. These inferred facts correspond to *A front C* in terms of orientations, which is one type of inference included in the composition table in (Hernández 1992).

Some other approaches, such as (Schlieder 1992), (Freksa 1992), and (Latecki & Röhrig 1993), use locally oriented sector systems for the description of orientation relations. Since the orientation of the bounds of the sectors is determined locally by another object instead by a global reference orientation as before, the corresponding axes are distinct for most orientation relations, and hence, transitivity cannot be applied here. Instead of global axes, locally defined structures can be used for the projection step: on a circle around an object, the projection of any other object results in a point on that circle. Additional points are induced by each object depending   on the theory in the corresponding approach. In (Schlieder 1992), for example, a *complementary view* is induced, and in (Freksa 1992) and (Latecki & Röhrig 1993), a model of four sectors induces four points on the circle, one for each bound between the sectors (cf. Figure 3).

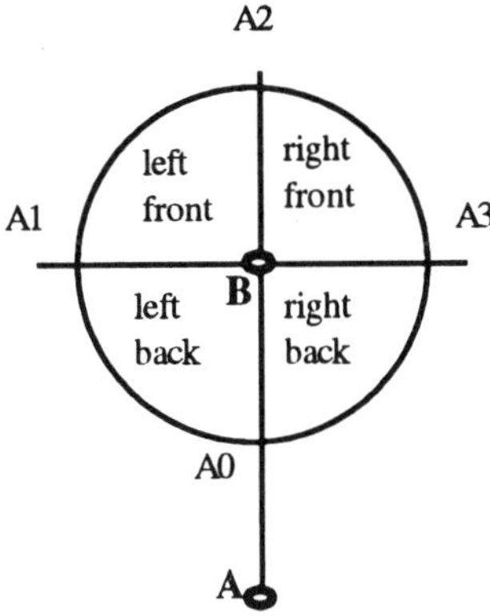

Figure 3:   In a local sector model with four sectors, an object A induces four points on a circle around another object B.

An orientation relation in these approaches corresponds to one sector defined by two objects, i.e. a third object is between the corresponding bounds, which can be expressed by a CYCORD relation on the circle. In Figure 3, for example, Object A induces four points A0, A1, A2, and A3 on a circle around B, and an orientation relation *C right-front B w.r.t. A* can be translated to A2-C0-A3. Accordingly, *D right-front B w.r.t. C* can be translated to C2-D0-C3. Using bounded transitivity, one of the properties of CYCORD, A0-D0-A2 can be inferred from the two facts above, which in the example in Figure 3 corresponds to *D left B w.r.t. A*, which in turn is short for the disjunction *D left-front B w.r.t. A or D left-back B w.r.t. A*. This type of inference can be found in the composition tables of (Freksa 1992), or can be calculated by the inference rule in (Latecki & Röhrig 1993).

Topological approaches

Some of the approaches to qualitative spatial reasoning are based on topological considerations. The basic assumption is that objects are embedded in a given space of any dimension. Each object separates the space into disjoint regions. (Egenhofer 1989), for example, uses the boundary of an object to distinguish its interior, boundary and exterior. The same division of space is used by

(Hernández 1992), whereas (Cohn et al. 1993) use a cling film to establish the convex hull of the space occupied by an object. From that they get a further subdivision of the space: the interior of an object is separated into the space that is properly inside the object, and that which is inside the convex hull, but not inside the object.

Spatial relations between objects are represented by comparison of the subsets of space induced by the objects. While in some of the topological approaches the empty or non-empty intersection of each pair of subsets is used for the definition of spatial relations, set inclusion is equally well suited for the same definitions. Figure 4 shows for the relation *A disjoint B* a complete transformation from the 9-intersection model of (Egenhofer 1989) into a representation using set inclusion.

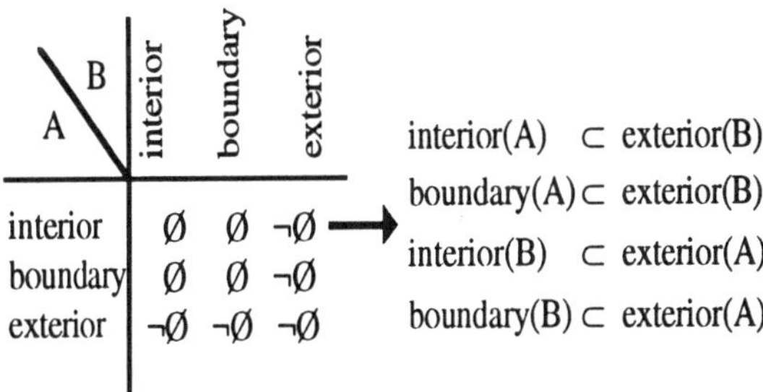

Figure 4:   Representation of the disjoint relation in the 9-intersection model of (Egenhofer 1989), and transformation of a 9-intersection into set inclusions

The set of subsets of space induced by the objects together with set inclusion forms a lattice, where the empty set is the bottom element, and the whole space is the top element. Even though this lattice is not a proper one-dimensional structure, it is still the case that all spatial relations can be expressed by a binary order relation, set inclusion, and transitivity is the only property needed to explain the inferences in the topological approaches. For example, if *A disjoint B* and *B includes C*, then *interior(B) ⊂ exterior(A)*, and *interior(C) ⊂ interior(B) and boundary(C) ⊂ interior(B)*, so *interior(C) ⊂ exterior(A) and boundary(C) ⊂ exterior(A)* can be inferred. These facts can be translated back to topological terms as *A disjoint C*, which is one of the inferences in (Egenhofer 1989) and in (Hernández 1992).

Comparison of existing approaches

Even though the various approaches to qualitative spatial reasoning deal with different aspects of space, all of their spatial concepts can be expressed in terms of simple order relations. While it is hard to see the differences and the common ground of the spatial relations when analysing composition tables, the new theory offers a way of a direct comparison of spatial concepts on the level of the basic structures. Existing as well as new approaches can be classified by the structure on which of their concepts can be expressed in terms of order relations. One class of approaches can be explained by linear axes, such as, of course, approaches using orderings for the definition of spatial concepts, but also the orientation approaches of (Frank 1991) and (Hernández 1992). Approaches in this class can be compared by analysing the axes and the possible interaction between the axes. While in the approaches of (Jungert 1988) and (Güsgen 1989) the axes are totally independent, in the approach of (Hernández 1992), information about order relations on two axes may be used to infer information about orderings on the other axes: in Figure 2, for example, if an object B is to the right of bound 1, and is to the left of bound 2, then it is also above bound 3 and above bound 4. It is also easy to see how different approaches of the same class may be combined: by the identification of axes. If, for example, it happens to be that one of the bounds in the approach of (Hernández 1992) is pointing to the north, then two of the axes are the same as in the approach of (Jungert 1988), and so, information given in one system can be used by the other. Also some differences become obvious: although in both approaches, that of (Jungert 1988) and that of (Frank 1991), the cardinal directions north and east are used for the definition of spatial concepts, the axes are different; while in the first approach the distinction whether some object is to the north or to the south of another object is made by an axis heading exactly to the north, the same distinction is done in the latter approach by a sector model consisting of two axes, one heading north-west, and the other heading north-east.

In another class of approaches, the basic structure for the expression of spatial concepts in terms of order relations is a set of circles around every object. On this level it can be observed, for example, that the concepts in the approach of (Latecki & Röhrig 1993) are expressed by the same CYCORD relations as the concepts in (Freksa 1992), and therefore, a direct translation can be given: if, for example, *ABC forms a positively oriented obtuse angle* in (Latecki & Röhrig 1993), the information is the same as *C left-front AB* in (Freksa 1992).

Still another class of approaches requires a system of subsets as their basic structure for the expression of spatial concept in terms of set inclusion. Since this system is not a spatial structure, there will not be any flow of information between concepts from this class and concepts of either of the other classes. In (Hernández 1992), for example, his concepts *projection* and *orientation* are disintegrated because they refer to basic structures from different classes, namely, spatial axes and systems of subsets of space.

Discussion

From a knowledge representation theoretic point of view, any inference rule can be seen as a property of the concepts involved. Since composition tables, as they are found in most of the approaches to qualitative spatial reasoning, are a collection of inference rules, these approaches formally describe their spatial concepts by a lot of properties. There have been attempts to reduce the amount of properties by compacting the composition tables using symmetry and redundancy (Freksa 1992b). The theory described in this article provides a single property, transitivity, which is not applied to the original spatial concepts in the approaches, but is applied to concepts that are a result of a transformation from the original concepts. Since this transformation can be done without loss of information, the properties of the transformed concepts can be seen also as properties of the original concepts. Describing spatial concepts by a single property is not only useful for a comparison of the various approaches, but also provides a simple mechanism for all of the inferences included in the calculi of the approaches.

While for the description of these inferences a single property, *transitivity*, is sufficient, there are two more properties of an order relation, *asymmetry* and *non-reflexivity*. These properties can be used to introduce negation and to infer negative facts. For example, if *A before B* in (Güsgen 1989), then end(A) < start(B), and since start(X) < end(X) holds for any interval X, using transitivity we can infer start(A) < end(B). Now, asymmetry can be used to infer ¬ end(B) < start(A), which corresponds to *not B before A* in terms of the original concepts. For another example, in (Hernández 1992) non-reflexivity can be used to infer ¬ A<A on any axis. This negative fact can be used in the back transformation step to conclude *not A front A*, *not A right A*, and so on, for every orientation relation used in Hernández' theory. These negative facts can be very useful in large spatial data bases, and are necessary for natural language understanding.

Acknowledgement

I would like to thank Christian Freksa and Geoff Simmons for a critical review of the final version of this paper and for correcting my English. I would also like to thank the anonymous referees for their detailed comments on the first version of this paper.

References

Allen, J.F. 1983: Maintaining Knowledge about Temporal Intervals, *CACM* 26 (11): 832-843.

Cohn, A.G., Randell, D.A., Cui, Z. 1993: A Taxonomy of Logically Defined Qualitative Spatial Relations. In Proceedings of International Workshop on formal Ontology, Padova, Italy

Egenhofer, M. 1989: A Formal Definition of Binary Topological Relationships. In W. Litwin and H.-J. Schek eds. *Third International Conference on Foundations of Data Organisation and Algorithms*, vol. 367 of Lecture Notes in Computer Science, 457-472. Springer, Berlin.

Frank, A.U. 1991: Qualitative Spatial Reasoning With Cardinal Directions. In Proc. Seventh Austrian Conference on Artificial Intelligence, Wien, 157-167, Springer, Berlin.

Freksa, C. 1992: Using Orientation Information for Qualitative Spatial Reasoning. In: A. U. Frank, I. Campari, U. Formentini eds. 1992 Theories and Methods of Spatio-Temporal Reasoning in geographic space, Springer, Berlin.

Freksa, C. 1992b: Temporal reasoning based on semi-intervals. *Artificial Intelligence* 54: 199-227

Freksa, C. & Röhrig, R. 1993: Dimensions of Qualitative Spatial Reasoning. In Piera Carreté, N., Singh, M.G. eds. 1993 *Qualitative Reasoning and Decision Technologies*, Proc. QUARDET'93, CIMNE Barcelona.

Güsgen, H.W. 1989: Spatial Reasoning Based on Allen's Temporal Logic. Technical Report, TR-89-049, International Computer Science Institute, Berkeley.

Hernández, D. 1992: Qualitative Representation of Spatial Knowledge. Doctoral Dissertation, Technische Universität München.

Jungert, E. 1988: Extended Symbolic Projections as a Knowledge Structure for Spatial Reasoning. *Pattern Recognition*, Kittler, J. ed. 1988, Cambridge, U.K.

Latecki, L. & Röhrig, R. 1993: Orientation and Qualitative Angle for Spatial Reasoning. In Proceedings of the 13th International Joint Conference on Artificial Intelligence, 1544-1549. Chambery, France.

Mukerjee, A. & Joe, G. 1991: A Qualitative Model for Space. In Proceedings of AAAI-90, 721-727.

Schlieder, C. 1992: Anordnung und Sichtbarkeit. Eine Charakterisierung unvollständigen räumlichen Wissens. Doctoral Dissertation, Universität Hamburg.

Student
Abstracts

Classification of noun phrases into concepts or individuals

Saliha Azzam
CRIL Ingénierie - CAMS - Paris-Sorbonne
174, rue de la République 92817 Puteaux France
e-mail : azzam@cril-ing.fr

Abstract

We tackle here the problem of discrimination between instances of the language representation and concepts. This procedure is necessary according to the aim of the application that uses the conceptual structures. We propose linguistic rules for doing this discrimination inside natural language texts, and indicate how these rules are combined to build an accurate procedure.

Introduction

The problem we address here deals with the automatic discrimination inside a natural language (NL) text between instances (i.e., individuals) and concepts. The procedure is integrated into a semantic parser and implemented in the context of COBALT project (CEC/LRE project). The terms that are substituted by concepts are noun phrases (NPs) and the problem is that of classifying the NPs as instances or concepts. The necessity of this classification (of NPs), depends on the aim of the application that uses the conceptual structures. It may be worth noticing that, even if this problem is very general and not restricted to the natural language (NL) processing domain, it is very difficult to find useful suggestions in the literature, at least in a knowledge engineering context. We will only mention here a well-known paper (Brachman *et al.* 1991) about the CLASSIC system, in which the differentiation about concepts and individuals is essential. In this paper, indications about the rules we suggest for a systematic classification are given (Azzam 1993).

How rules are applied

The rules are ordered and exclusive, i.e., given a rule numbered i: if condition i then <classification-i>, means if (not condition i-1 and condition i) then <classification-i>. If a given rule succeeds on a NP, the latter is suppressed from the list of NPs to be classified and the next NP is considered. The algorithm has an empirical nature and some rules are incremental, i.e., as soon as a given NP is classified, the result is taken into account for the next NP. The procedure is then reapplied at the end of a rules session, on the unclassified NPs and stops when no rule can be applied.

The classification rules

The main features taken into account and involved in the rule conditions, are: 1) **The NP type**, e.g. if it corresponds to a proper noun it is an instance. In order to find the location of the concept which subsumes this instance, semantic and syntactic patterns are checked out 2) **The type of the recognized concept**: for example the concepts of 'abstract qualities' sub-hierarchy do not have any instances 3) **The syntactic structure of the NP** 4) **The determiner type of the NP** (possessive , demonstrative, ...) 5) **The mark of punctual situation** in the sentence, as the temporal adverbs that favor instances 6) **The expressions introducing general context** that favor concepts, e.g., "in general" or conditional assertions like "in default of" 7) **The semantic category of the verb** 8) **The syntactic role of other classified NPs**.

Conclusion

The rules use linguistics knowledge, without involving any additional world knowledge. There are expressed under the form of syntactic and semantic constraints which are tested on the syntactic tree and using the associative knowledge of the representation language. Applied on COBALT corpus extracted from Reuters news, the rules succeed in 90 percent of cases, i.e., rules classify 90 percent of NPs in a correct way. The cases of failure are cases of unclassified NPs and not incorrect classification". Therefore, future works address the extension of rules to process more cases and also, the rules refinement to avoid any hazardous results.

References

Azzam, S. 1993. Classification of NPs. Technical report, COBALT report ST/06/93 STEP:Paris.

Brachman, R.; McGuinness, D.; Patel-Schneider; P.F., R. L.; and Borgida. 1991. Living with classic : When and how to use a kl-one-like language. In Sowa, J., ed., *Principles of Semantic Networks*. San Mateo (CA): Morgan Kaufmann.

Regression Based Causal Induction With Latent Variable Models

Lisa A. Ballesteros

Experimental Knowledge Systems Laboratory
University of Massachusetts/Amherst
Box 34610
Amherst, MA 01003-4610
balleste@cs.umass.edu
(413) 545-3616

Scientists largely explain observations by inferring causal relationships among measured variables. Many algorithms with various theoretical foundations have been developed for causal induction e.g., (Spirtes, Glymour, & Scheines 1993; Pearl & Verma 1991), but it is widely believed that regression is ill-suited to the task of causal induction. Multiple regression techniques attempt to estimate the influence that regressors have on a dependent variable using the standardized regression coefficient, β. Assuming the relationship among variables is linear, β_{YX} measures the expected change in Y produced by a unit change in X with all other predictor variables held constant.

Arguments against using regression methods for causal induction rest on the fact that the error in estimating β_{YX} can be large, particularly when unmeasured or latent variables account for the relationship between X and Y, or when X is a common cause of Y and another predictor (Mosteller & Tukey 1977; Spirtes, Glymour, & Scheines 1993). In fact, β may suggest X has a strong influence on Y when it has little or none. We have developed a regression-based causal induction algorithm called FBD (Cohen *et al.* 1994) which performs well in these situations.

The heuristic that is primarily responsible for making FBD less sensitive to the above problems is the ω score. Let r_{XY} be the correlation between X and Y, and $\omega = (r_{YX} - \beta_{YX})/r_{YX}$. ω measures the proportion of r_{YX} not due to the direct effect of X on Y. If ω_{YX} exceeds a threshold, X is pruned from the set of candidate predictors. This threshold is set arbitrarily by the user, but we are exploring the use of clustering algorithms to set it by partitioning the ω values of the predictor variables.

Spirtes et al. describe four causal models (1993, p. 240) for which their studies showed regression methods performed poorly by always choosing predictors whose relationship to the dependent variable is mediated by latent variables or common causes. One model is reproduced in Figure 1. The difficulty with this model is that the error in the estimate for $\beta_{X_2 Y}$ may be large due to X_2's relationship to X_3 via the latent variable T_1.

To determine the susceptibility of FBD to latent variable effects, we tested the performance of FBD[1] on latent variable models, and ran stepwise regressions as a control. Twelve sets of coefficients for the structural equations for

---

[1] In comparison studies among FBD, Pearl's IC, and Spirtes's PC, FBD performed better on all of our measures of performance (Cohen *et al.* 1994; Gregory & Cohen 1994).

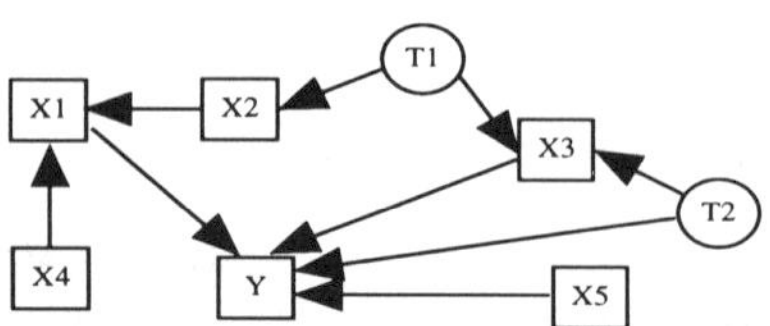

Figure 1: Latent Variable Model

each of Spirtes's models were generated, as were data sets for each, having 100 to 1000 variates. Each sample was given to FBD and to MINITAB's stepwise procedure. Performance was measured by the number of times the algorithm incorrectly chose predictors related via latent variables and the number of times it chose correctly. FBD chose 88% of the correct predictors, while MINITAB chose 93% of them. On the other hand, FBD rejected variables whose relationships to the dependent variable were due to latent or common causes 82% of the time, while MINITAB rejected them only 25% of the time. Thirty nine percent of FBD's rejections were due to ω. Although MINITAB got a slightly higher hit rate for correct predictors than did FBD, FBD got fewer false positives. These results suggest that ω makes FBD less susceptible to latent variable effects than standard regression techniques. FBD's ability to avoid the problems described above make it a promisng causal induction algorithm.

References

Cohen, P. R.; Ballesteros, L.; Gregory, D.; and St.Amant, R. 1994. Regression can build predictive causal models. Submitted to the Tenth Annual Conference on Uncertainty in AI. Technical Report 94-15, Dept. of Computer Science, University of Massachusetts/Amherst.

Gregory, D., and Cohen, P. R. 1994. Two algorithms for inducing causal models from data. Submitted to Knowledge Discovery in Databases Workshop, Twelfth National Conference on Artificial Intelligence.

Mosteller, F., and Tukey, J. W. 1977. *Data Analysis and Regression, A Second Course in Statistics.* Addison-Wesley Publishing Company.

Pearl, J., and Verma, T. 1991. A statistical semantics for causation. *Statistics and Computing* 2:91–95.

Spirtes, P.; Glymour, C.; and Scheines, R. 1993. *Causation, Prediction, and Search.* Springer-Verlag.

Probabilistic Knowledge of External Events in Planning

Jim Blythe

School of Computer Science
Carnegie Mellon University
Pittsburgh, PA 15213
blythe@cs.cmu.edu

My research tries to improve the robustness of plans by using limited knowledge about external events. These are events that are not directly caused by the planning agent. I use a discrete-time model and assume that the probability of occurrence for a particular type of event in a given situation is known, but the specific occurrence of such an event cannot be predicted with certainty. For example, when a bicycle is left outside a building, there is some probability p that it will be stolen at each time point. The probability that the bicycle is still outside the building after n time units is then $(1 - p)^n$, neglecting the effects of other possible events.

"Reactive" planners, that create plans in response to exceptions during execution, are subject to severe time constraints that limit their performance. My aim is to create contingent plans off-line that have a higher probability of success than could be achieved under these constraints and without considering external events. Stochastic techniques such as policy iteration are not yet tractable for realistic planning problems, so I concentrate on classical planning systems.

Most other planning systems that reason about uncertainty deal with non-deterministic effects and/or incomplete knowledge of the state of the world, e.g. (Kushmerick, Hanks, & Weld 1993; Pryor & Collins 1993). However, these models cannot easily be used to represent uncertainty about external events. There are two main reasons for this, both related to the frame problem and stemming from the fact that uncertainty about events depends on the actions being performed only through the state. Firstly, uncertainty about the occurrence of an event while an action is performed would have to be modelled by probabilistic effects for every action that could be performed at the same time as the event. For instance, every action that can be performed while the bicycle is outside would have to include the bicycle being stolen as a possible effect. Thus, the number of distinct possible outcomes for each action is exponential in the number of event types that could simultaneously occur. This is a misleading representation, as well as very cumbersome. Secondly, consider a planning agent that leaves a bicycle outside a building, performs some actions inside the building and then returns to cycle away. The probability that the bicycle is outside the building, as required, upon the agent's return depends on the length of time spent inside the building, but this fact could not be modelled in the situation calculus using non-deterministic actions alone.

I have designed a planner based on Prodigy 4.0 that considers external events in order to increase the expected utility of a plan, and applied it to a transportation domain. I represent events in a STRIPS-like fashion, with preconditions specifying when events are possible, add and delete lists specifying their effects, and with a probability attached to each event (Blythe 1994). When the preconditions are satisfied, the event may occur with the given probability. The planner first produces a plan without considering external events, and may then use three different routines to find possible sequences of events that would cause the plan to fail: a Monte Carlo simulation, a Markov chain analysis and an exhaustive search for single event instances that can defeat the plan. There is no exhaustive search for sequences of events that would defeat the plan, as this would in general take far longer than the planning phase.

Once sequences of events are found that can cause the plan to fail, the system considers three different ways to repair each one: (1) Conditional steps can be added that address the "bad" situations that arise, for example hailing a cab if the bicycle is stolen. (2) Steps can be added to make bad events inapplicable or less likely, for example by locking the bicycle. (3) The existing steps can be re-ordered or moved along a timeline to reduce the probability of bad events, for example re-ordering the plan to spend as little time as possible inside the building. Since some events have zero duration, this method can sometimes eliminate problems entirely. In experiments, these techniques improve the probability of plan success greatly. I plan to improve plan projection, using techniques such as Bayes nets to relax independence assumptions, and study various domains. I also aim to prove convergence of the algorithm to plans of maximal utility.

References

Blythe, J. 1994. Decision-theoretic subgoaling in goal-directed search. AAAI Spring Symposium on Decision-Theoretic Planning.

Kushmerick, N.; Hanks, S.; and Weld, D. 1993. An algorithm for probabilistic planning. Technical Report 93-06-03, Department of Computer Science and Engineering, University of Washington.

Pryor, L., and Collins, G. 1993. Cassandra: Planning for contingencies. Technical Report 41, The Institute for the Learning Sciences.

DANIEL: Integrating Case-Based and Rule-Based Reasoning in Law

Stefanie Brüninghaus
Lehrstuhl für Praktische Informatik I
Universität Mannheim
D - 68131 Mannheim, GERMANY
steffi@pi1.informatik.uni-mannheim.de

Motivation

This paper introduces DANIEL,[1] an architecture for the integration of case-based reasoning and rule-based reasoning for legal interpretation. Rather than interleaving the reasoners and assuming their complementarity, like in previous approaches, they are applied concurrently. Conflicting interpretations are handled explicitly, based on domain knowledge and on the notion of redundancy.

The principal problems of legal interpretation are the lack of deep models for legal reasoning, the existence of inherently ill-defined predicates and the frequent use of open-textured concepts, as pointed out in (Rissland & Skalak 1991). A hybrid approach to representing the legal sources and the use of meta-knowledge seems to be appropriate to solve these problems. The scope of DANIEL is not limited to this particular domain, since the noted difficulties do not occur exclusively, but prototypically in the law.

Architecture and Function of DANIEL

The main knowledge sources in the legal domain are legislation and case law. It has been shown comprehensively in (Rissland & Skalak 1991) that case law and legislation are best mapped on a case base and a rule base, respectively.

In the proposed architecture, the reasoners are integrated via a blackboard, which allows an easy exchange of data and a hierarchical integration of multiple statutes. Since in a given case each knowledge source is likely to contribute to the solution and can be assumed to obtain a result on its own, the problem solvers are applied concurrently and autonomously. Their local results are evaluated by a *rule-based coordination component*, whose meta-knowledge is derived from general legal doctrine, and from the capabilities of the problem solvers. In case of differing local results, the most probable solution is chosen according to the legally determined binding force of the respective legal source, the degree of open-texturedness of the predicates, and the similarity between the given and the retrieved case.

The function of DANIEL can be illustrated by a simplified example: From the statutes, it can be derived that built-in laundry facilities belong to a building, and that therefore the

---

[1] Distributed Architecture for the kNowledge-based Integration of Expert systems in Law

respective expenses must be manufacturing cost. The German Supreme Tax Court, however, decided that a washing machine fixed to the concrete is an extra asset not included in the manufacturing cost of the building. Since the definition of the manufacturing cost is rather open-textured, while the cited case is an exact match, case law has to be applied.

Related Work and Discussion

For space limitations, only the most prominent and obviously very similar system, CABARET (Rissland & Skalak 1991) will be discussed here. It is a domain-independent reasoning shell that incorporates a case-based and a rule-based reasoner via a blackboard. While CABARET uses control heuristics to *interleave* the two reasoners, the reasoners in DANIEL are applied *concurrently*. Also, the coordination component does not work heuristically, but rather it contains domain specific knowledge, in order to overcome the lack of a deep domain model. In other approaches, from various domains, cases are generally considered complementary to rules, and applied accordingly. Even though it can be demonstrated that cases cannot be transformed to rules and vice versa without loss of information, the mutual influence of rules and cases is not explicitly modeled.

Merging the reasoning chains of a case-based and a rule-based reasoner is generally not advisable for the following reasons:

- different binding force/validity of the knowledge sources,
- incompatible partial results of the problem solvers due to their different internal representations and semantics,
- redundant and contradictory knowledge in the problem solvers (only part of it is complementary and disjunct),
- interdependency of the legal sources (existing case law influences future legislation and vice versa).

Apart from avoiding these problems by separating the reasoners, the concurrent application enables their mutual control and takes advantage of their complementarity. In this way, the solution quality can be increased considerably.

References

Rissland, E., and Skalak, D. 1991. CABARET: Rule Interpretation in a Hybrid Architecture. *International Journal on Man-Machine Studies* 34(1):839–887.

Decision-Theoretic Plan Failure Debugging and Repair

Lisa J. Burnell[1]

Department of Computer Science Engineering
The University of Texas at Arlington, Box 19015, Arlington, Texas 76019
burnell@cse.uta.edu

A number of strategies exist for the recovery from execution-time plan failures. One manner in which these strategies differ is the degree of dependence on the reliability and availability of the planner's knowledge. The best strategy, however, may be dependent on a number of considerations, including the type of plan failure, the criticality of the failure, the availability of resources, and the reliability and availability of the knowledge involved in a given plan failure instance. We are examining a decision-theoretic approach to diagnose plan failures and to dynamically select from multiple failure recovery strategies when an execution-time plan failure occurs.

Existing failure recovery strategies generally classify, with assumed or proven certainty, the type of error that occurred during plan execution and then select a fixed strategy to recover from that error. Assumptions regarding the accuracy and completeness of the planner's domain model vary. On one end are approaches that use deterministic heuristics or purely syntactic analyses to debug and repair. These approaches are efficient and require limited knowledge, but generally are limited in the level of diagnosis and repair they can perform. On the other end are logic-based approaches, that are robust, but are knowledge and resource intensive. Such approaches are not always feasible.

Incomplete or uncertain knowledge of previous planning actions, as in multi-agent planners, precludes a complete logical analysis. Even when possible, the costs of collecting and reasoning with complete information may be intractable, especially given time pressures and other resource constraints. The goal of our work is the development of an approach that can intelligently select and apply failure recovery strategies that are appropriate to the situation and that can cope with uncertainty.

There are three primary components of our research: diagnosis of plan failures, plan repair and planner modification. When a failure is detected, we use a

probabilistic method for determining the error class and the source(s) of the error. This method has already proven effective in debugging programs (Burnell & Horvitz 1993), and is being adapted for debugging generated plans. Plan repair strategies are selected using a decision theoretic approach similar to (Howe & Cohen 1991), with the added feature of dealing with potential uncertainties in the error classification and resource constraints. Finally, machine learning methods are employed, when warranted, to correct and refine the planner itself.

Our approach uses probabilistic models, represented as belief networks, to construct an ordering over classes of errors, to identify the likely source(s) of the error and to recommend an appropriate repair strategy. The belief networks model the uncertain relationships about the nature and structure of planning actions and the likelihood of types of errors. Value of information calculations recommend which computationally complex logical analyses are worth undertaking collect evidence. Also modeled is the decision problem of selecting a preferred repair strategy, which may include planner modification, based on the likely error class, failure criticality and resource availability, as in (Horvitz 1988). For example, in a multi-agent planner, repair strategies may include local selection of a reactive failure-recovery action or requesting replanning from a more sophisticated planner.

References

Burnell, L. J. and Horvitz, E. J. 1993. A Synthesis of Logical and Probabilistic Reasoning for Program Understanding and Debugging. Proc. of the 9th Conf. on Uncertainty in AI, 285-291. San Mateo, CA: Morgan Kaufmann.

Horvitz, E.J. 1988. Reasoning under varying and uncertain resource constraints. Proc. of the 7th National Conf. on Artificial Intelligence, 111-116. San Mateo, CA:Morgan Kaufmann.

Howe, A. and Cohen, P. 1991. Failure Recovery: A model and Experiments. Proc. of the 9th National Conf. on Artificial Intelligence, 801-808. Menlo Park, CA: AAAI.

[1] This work is supported in part by the Advanced Research Projects Agency, State of Texas Advanced Technology Projects and the National Science Foundation.

Decidability of Contextual Reasoning

Vanja Buvač
HB 455, Dartmouth College
Hanover, New Hampshire 03755.
vanja@dartmouth.edu.

Contexts were first suggested in McCarthy's Turing Award Paper, (McCarthy 1987), as a possible solution to the problem of generality in AI. McCarthy's concern with the existing AI systems has been that they can reason only about some particular, predetermined task. When faced with slightly different circumstances they need to be completely rewritten. In other words, AI systems lack generality. Cyc (Guha & Lenat 1990), a large common-sense knowledge-base currently being developed at MCC, is one example of where contexts have already been put to use in attempt to solve the problem of generality. Because of the complexity of the problem of generality, it has been speculated that any reasoning system which would be able to solve this problem would itself be computationally unacceptable. The purpose of this paper is to show that propositional contextual reasoning is decidable.

Propositional logic of context extends classical propositional logic with a new modality, $\mathtt{ist}(c, \phi)$, used to express that the sentence, ϕ, is true in the context c. We first give a short sketch the syntax and the semantics of the language of context, as proposed in (McCarthy 1993) and formalized in (Buvač & Mason 1993).

To define the syntax, we begin with two distinct countable sets: $\mathbb{K}$ the set of all contexts, and $\mathbb{P}$ the set of propositional atoms. The set, $\mathbb{W}$, of well-formed formulas is built up from the propositional atoms, $\mathbb{P}$, using the usual propositional connectives (negation and implication) together with the $\mathtt{ist}$ modality:
$$\mathbb{W} = \mathbb{P} \cup (\neg \mathbb{W}) \cup (\mathbb{W} \to \mathbb{W}) \cup \mathtt{ist}(\mathbb{K}, \mathbb{W}).$$

To define the semantics we first need to introduce some mathematical notation. If X is a set then $\mathbf{P}(X)$ is the set of subsets of X. X^* is the set of all finite sequences, and we let $\bar{x} = [x_1, \ldots, x_n]$ range over X^*. The infix operator $*$ is used for appending sequences. Drawing on the intuition that a context describes a state of affairs, and that the nature of the context may itself be context dependent, i.e. that a context may appear different when viewed from different contexts, a model, $\mathfrak{M}$, is defined to be a function which maps a context sequence to a set of truth assignments. Formally, $\mathfrak{M} : \mathbb{K}^* \to \mathbf{P}(\mathbb{P} \to 2)$. Satisfaction is a relation on $<\mathfrak{M}, \nu, \bar{c}, \phi>$, written as $\mathfrak{M}, \nu \models_{\bar{c}} \phi$, and defined inductively by:

$\mathfrak{M}, \nu \models_{\bar{c}} \rho$ iff $\nu(\rho) = 1, \quad \rho \in \mathbb{P}$

$\mathfrak{M}, \nu \models_{\bar{c}} \mathtt{ist}(c_1, \phi)$ iff $\forall \nu_1 \in \mathfrak{M}(\bar{c} * c_1) \quad \mathfrak{M}, \nu_1 \models_{\bar{c} * c_1} \phi$

The clauses for $\neg$ and $\to$ are defined in the usual way. We write $\mathfrak{M} \models_{\bar{c}} \phi$ iff $\forall \nu \in \mathfrak{M}(\bar{c}) \quad \mathfrak{M}, \nu \models_{\bar{c}} \phi$; we say that ϕ is valid in $\bar{c}$ iff $\forall \mathfrak{M} \quad \mathfrak{M} \models_{\bar{c}} \phi$.

We proceed to define some notation, needed for the decidability results. The *vocabulary* of a sentence ϕ in given in $\bar{c}$, $\mathrm{Vocab}(\bar{c}, \phi)$, is a relation on a context sequence and the atoms which occur in the scope of that context sequence:

$$\mathrm{Vocab}(\bar{c}, \phi) = \begin{cases} \{<\bar{c}, \phi>\} & \phi \in \mathbb{P} \\ \mathrm{Vocab}(\bar{c}, \phi_0) & \phi \text{ is } \neg \phi_0 \\ \mathrm{Vocab}(\bar{c} * c, \phi_0) & \phi \text{ is } \mathtt{ist}(c, \phi_0) \\ \mathrm{Vocab}(\bar{c}, \phi_0) \cup \mathrm{Vocab}(\bar{c}, \phi_1) & \phi \text{ is } \phi_0 \to \phi_1 \end{cases}$$

The restriction of a truth assignment, ν, with respect to $\mathrm{Vocab}(\bar{c}_0, \phi)$ is defined to be the unique truth assignment ν' such that

$$\nu'(p) = \begin{cases} \nu(p) & <\bar{c}, p> \in \mathrm{Vocab}(\bar{c}_0, \phi) \\ 0 & <\bar{c}, p> \notin \mathrm{Vocab}(\bar{c}_0, \phi). \end{cases}$$

The definition extends in the natural way to $\mathfrak{M}_{\mathrm{Vocab}(\bar{c}_0, \phi)}$, the restriction of the model $\mathfrak{M}$ with respect to the vocabulary $\mathrm{Vocab}(\bar{c}_0, \phi)$.

Theorem (Finite Model Property): $\mathfrak{M} \models_{\bar{c}_0} \phi$ iff $\mathfrak{M}_{\mathrm{Vocab}(\bar{c}_0, \phi)} \models_{\bar{c}_0} \phi$.
The theorem is proved by induction on the structure of the formula ϕ.

Corollary (Decidability): There is an effective procedure which will determine whether or not a formula given in some context is valid.

References

Buvač, S., and Mason, I. 1993. Propositional logic of context. In *AAAI 93*.

Guha, R. V., and Lenat, D. B. 1990. Cyc: A midterm report. *AI Magazine* 11(3):32–59.

McCarthy, J. 1987. Generality in artificial intelligence. *Comm. of ACM* 30(12):1030–1035.

McCarthy, J. 1993. Notes on formalizing context. In *IJCAI 93*.

Simplifying Bayesian Belief Nets while Preserving MPE or MPGE Ordering

YaLing Chang

Computer Science Dept., Graduate Center,
City Univ. of New York, 33 W. 42 St., NYC 10036
Email: lay@cunyvms1.gc.cuny.edu

The abstraction of probability inference is a process of searching for a representation in which only the desirable properties of the solutions are preserved. Simplification is one of such abstraction which reduces the size of large databases and speeds transmission and processing of probabilistic information[Sy & Sher, 94].

Given a set of evidence S_e, human beings are often interested in finding the few Most Probable Explanations (MPE) or Most Probable General Explanations (MPGE) in a Bayesian belief network, i.e., to identify and order a set of H_is or L_is (for MPGE), $P(H_1|S_e) \geq ... \geq P(H_n|S_e)$, or $P(L_1|S_e) \geq ... \geq P(L_n|S_e)$, where H_i is an instantiation of all non-evidence variables and L_i is an instantiation of a subset of all non-evidence variables. Furthermore, the ordering is often more important than the quantitative probability values in certain domain such as in diagnosis and prediction.

The complexity of deriving MPEs or MPGEs is exponential if straight forward computation is employed. Various algorithms have been developed to reduce the computational complexity. Yet, so far no attemp has been made to explore the idea of simplification which is based on searching an alternative representation, i.e., a different Bayesian belief network which preserves the MPE or MPGE ordering relevant to queries of particular interests. This approach will try to reduce the connectivity of the network so that it is more sparse but has a probability distribution which preserves the orders of MPEs or MPGEs.

Our idea is to relax the probability constraints so that only the orders of MPEs or MPGEs are preserved. Since many probability distributions may preserve the desired orders, different belief networks may be realized because a belief network is uniquely defined by its topological structure and probability distribution. Ideally, we hope to find a network whose structure has only few connections (i.e., a network which manifests many independency relations). If such a network can be found, one can discard irrelevant information and reduce the size of the Bayesian belief network. Consequently, the complexity of deriving MPEs and MPGEs is reduced.

One can conceptualize the abstraction process as a search which attempts to find appropriate network structures and probability distributions. In finding the structure of a simplified network, the MDL (minimum description length) principle can be used. The idea is to define a cost function whose value is proportional to the sparsity of a network [Lam and Bacchus, 93]. In finding the probability distributions, one may use a measure which can quantify the independency relations represented by the network. Cross entropy is one such measure proposed by Chow and Liu.

So far all the research for automated learning or construction of the Bayesian belief network are taking the approach that attempts to recover the original probability distribution as much as possible. Our approach is different in the sense that deviation is allowed and encouraged as long as the probability distribution preserves the orders of MPEs or MPGEs and a simple structure of a network can be obtained. A heuristic method, which is reported elsewhere [Sy 94a], has been developed to achieve the construction of a network with a simple structure.

An experimental study will be conducted on a set of multiply connected Bayesian belief networks. Each of this network consists of eight variables and has a high interconnectivities among the variables. After the new network with a simpler structure is generated, comparisons will be made between the orders generated by using the original belief network and the *simplified* network generated by the heuristic algorithm. The particular questions to be addressed in this expreimental study are listed below:

(1) Although it is theoretically possible to have networks which preserve the orderings of all possible MPE and MPGE, it is still unknown the level of complexity involved in finding these networks. We would like to know the possible ways of characterizing the complexity.

(2) If the networks mentioned in (1) are found, we would like to know whether there are any networks whose structure are simple such as singly connected configuration. If the singly connected configuration does not exist, we would like to know which one, among these multiply connected networks, is the best in terms of the fators affecting the computation and also, which one is more spare and preserving more independency assumptions ?

(3) If we can get a belief network which preserves all possible MPE and MPGE ordering, then this new Bayesian belief network is a new representation of the underlying probability inference system. This network is considered as a summary of the original network within the context of the abstraction theory proposed by Bon and Sher [94b]. Otherwise this network is considered as a simplification. When a network is only a simplification, we would like to know the percentage of the orderings being preserved.

Acknowledgments

This work is part of the on going Ph.D research under the supervision of Pf. Bon K. Sy.

References

[Lam and Bacchus, 1993] "Using Causal Information and Local Measure to Learn Bayesian Networks," *Proc. of the 9th Conference of Uncertainty in AI*, 1993.

[Sy B.K. 1994a] "Abstract Belief Networks with Preserved Probabilistic Ordering," submitted to the *10th Conf. of Uncertainty in Artificial Intelligence*, 1994.

[Sy B.K. and Sher D.B. 1994b] "An Abstraction Theory for Probabilistic Inference," submitted to the *Journal of Artificial Intelligence Research*.

Abstract of the Forest Management Advisory Systems

Yousong Chang and **Donald Nute**

Artificial Intelligence Programs
University of Georgia
Athens, GA 30602
E-mail:ychang@ai.uga.edu

Expert system technology is a powerful tool for enhancing the decision making capabilities of nonexperts with reasonable knowledge of a domain to expert level in that domain. U.S.D.A. Forest Service has been working on forest management expert systems for several years. However, building different expert systems for each kind of forest is a demanding task.

To develop a complete expert system in a high level language, we think the best approach to take is the toolkit approach. The idea is to develop separate modules for different kinds of inferencing, different kinds of user interaction, and different kinds of explanatory facilities. So we developed a toolkit mostly in Prolog for building expert systems for forest management. The first components of the toolkit were developed in Visual Basic, Hypertxt for Windows, Windows Notepad, and LPA Prolog for Windows to support development of a management system for red pine forests. This first system is called Red Pine Forest Management Advisory System (RPFMAS). The same tools used in RPFMAS were then used to develop a system for aspen forests .

Our toolkit architecture includes three logical levels: a domain level, a tactical level, and a strategic level.

The domain level should support as many different knowledge representation schemes as possible. We now support three structures.
(1) facts and rules with or without MYCIN-like certainty factors
(2) Prolog databases
(3) procedures

The tactical level includes the inference engines and the user interface. We now have:
(1) backward chaining
(2) forward chaining
(3) mixed backward and forward chaining
Backward and forward chaining will support reasoning with incomplete or uncertain information using either MYCIN-like certainty factors or defeasible rules. The RPFMAS supports incomplete but certain information. The user interface provides a variety of methods for collecting task-specific information from the user and for communicating conclusions to the user. The user interface of RPFMAS allows reasonable opportunity for the user to review and to change responses without the need to restart the consultation. The explanatory facility, controlled by Visual Basic through DDE to Hypertxt for Windows, provides explanations for questions asked and for conclusions offered.

The strategic level includes tools combining different components of the tactical level to produce a consultation driver suitable for a particular application. It is at this level that the control structure for an entire system is developed. This level includes a variety of tools to help the developer test and tune systems at the domain, the tactical, and the strategic levels.

The basic architecture for our toolkit is a blackboard system implemented in Prolog. Each module reads the blackboard and becomes active when appropriate. Non-Prolog modules are activated by Prolog demons which read the blackboard for them.

The major modules in the RPFMAS are shown below. All the modules are written in Prolog except "Growth simulator" in Visual Basic, "Explanatory facilities" in Visual Basic and Hypertxt, "Trace" in Windows Notepad.

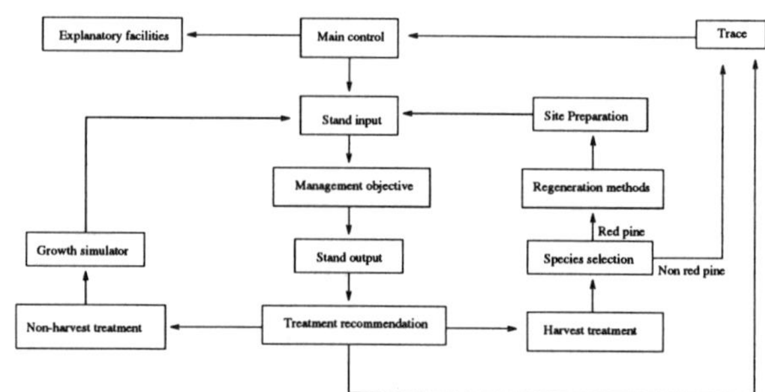

Figure 1: RPFMAS architecture

References

Rauscher, H. M., and Benzie, J.W. (1990) A Red Pine Management Advisory System: Knowledge Model and Implementation. *AI Applications* 4(3):27-43.

SodaBot: A Software Agent Environment and Construction System

Michael H. Coen*

MIT Artificial Intelligence Laboratory
545 Technology Sq. NE43-823
Cambridge, MA 02139
mhcoen@ai.mit.edu

Much of the work done in the area of software agents can be placed into one of two categories: (1) highly theoretical treatment of agents' intentions and capabilities; and (2) applied construction of specific agents. However, determining for what (and if) software agents are actually useful requires building many of them, and the agent construction process poses difficult technical challenges.

Building agents generally involves a multi-layered approach ranging from low-level "system-hacking" (e.g. of mailers, networks, etc.) to high-level application development (e.g., a meeting scheduler) and everything in between. Each of these layers can require a substantial amount of independent implementation and debugging time. Additionally, it can be difficult to distribute new agents; they tend to be site-specific in intricate ways and disconnecting them from their local dependencies can be technically involved; for similar reasons, they can be difficult to install.

This abstract describes SodaBot, a general-purpose software agent user-environment and construction system. In SodaBot, each user is given a personal *basic software agent* (BSA) which typically runs in the background on her home workstation. The BSA is an *agent operating system*. By this, we mean that it is a generic (in the sense of universal) computational framework for implementing and running specific agent applications. The BSA is programmed in the SodaBot *agent programming language* (SodaBotL).[1] As a quick sanity check, see if the following (rough) analogy makes sense:

SodaBotL is to SodaBot the way C Language is to Unix.

A BSA simultaneously (via a time-sharing algorithm) runs multiple SodaBotL programs provided both by its owner and by other people. The BSA architecture *disconnects* agent programs from the specific computational environment in which they run. They

---

*The research described here was conducted at the Artificial Intelligence Laboratory of the Massachusetts Institute of Technology. Support for the laboratory's artificial intelligence research is provided in part by the Advanced Research Projects Agency of the Department of Defense under Office of Naval Research contract N00014–85–K–0124.

[1] Pronounced "Soda-Bottle."

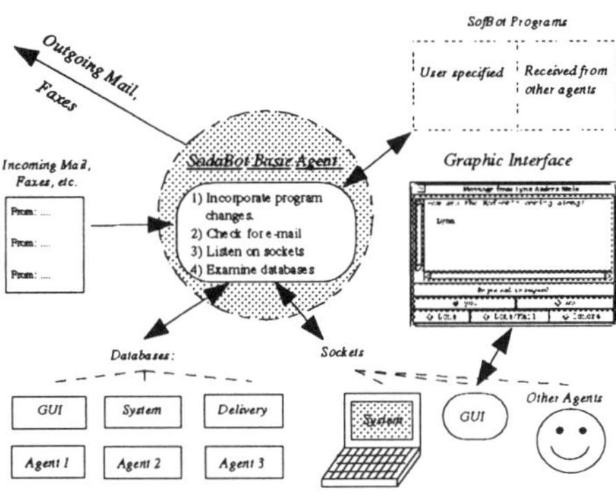

Figure 1: The SodaBot Basic Software Agent architecture

no longer need to be "hard-coded" with specific parameters for particular activities.

The SodaBot agent programming language (SodaBotL) offers high-level primitives and control-structures designed around human-level descriptions of agent activity. *In SodaBotL, users can easily implement a wide-range of typical software agent applications*, e.g. personal on-line assistants and meeting scheduling agents. SodaBotL abstracts out the low-level details of agent implementation. In a typical Unix environment, for example, agent creators are freed from the bother of dealing with system calls, mail servers, sockets, and X-windows. It is therefore much easier, for example, to have an agent:

- Interact with the user:
    Get Response {prompt "And what's your opinion?"; timeout in 10 minutes}
    $pollster_query;
                            or
- Handle time:
    Wait until Tuesday before $date: {
    Display "Reminder, you have an appointment with $person on $date";}

Additional features of SodaBot include *automatic distribution of user-created agents* and a graphical user-interface. SodaBot has been built and tested, and it is in current development and use at the MIT AI Lab.

Empirical knowledge representation generation using n-gram clustering

Robin Collier

Department of Computer Science, University of Sheffield

Regent Court, 211 Portobello Street, Sheffield

England, S1 4DP

r.collier@dcs.shef.ac.uk

Background

The work discussed below enables the automatic generation of structures similar to the key templates which are predefined in information extraction/retrieval conferences - this would be a significant development.

The motivation is similar to that of AutoSlog (Riloff 1993) which generates a domain-specific dictionary of concepts, although the approach is quite different.

System Overview

The approach acquires a domain-specific semantic representation by carrying out stochastic analysis of a corpus. Sets of conceptually similar paragraphs are utilised.

The corpus and semantic representation are used to generate schematic structures. These are used to concisely store the knowledge contained within existing texts.

New texts are processed to dynamically update the knowledge base. Any novel concepts encountered are analysed and a new structure added to the representation.

A more comprehensive explanation of this system and references to related work are presented in (Collier 1994).

Paragraph Clustering

The fundamental stage is the representation generation. The approach identifies *useful* (i.e. frequently occurring and widely distributed) clusters of n-grams within paragraphs, which correlate with other paragraphs within the corpus. Six steps are carried out, utilising five structures.

Structures

The first structure is an array containing a unique numeric entry for each unique word in the corpus.

The remaining structures have the same format; identical words are grouped together in an array and ordered by group size, this causes the loss of the word order.

The second structure defines the word order, it contains pointers to the next word in the text.

The third structure contains the unique integer representing the next word pointed to in the text.

The fourth structure contains the length of the phrase associated with each word.

The final structure is related to the fourth. Each corresponding entry is a pointer to the next identical phrase.

Algorithm

The six steps of the algorithm are:

1. Word/integer generation: creates an associative array containing a numeric entry for each unique word.

2. Integer conversion: translates the text into a numeric representation, and generates structures two and three.

3. Generate phrase lengths: each of the groups of similar words are processed and the longest phrases which occur a multiple number of times are identified. This information is stored in structures four and five.

4. Identify useful n-grams: sets of phrases with similar lengths are ordered by their frequency of occurrence and the n-best are identified amending structures four and five.

5. Paragraph weight parse: each paragraph is assigned a weight representing the number, size, frequency, distribution, etc. of n-grams existing in that paragraph.

6. Identify useful paragraph clusters: sets of paragraphs containing correlating n-grams are identified, and the n-best extracted by considering the quantity of paragraphs which they exist in, and quality of the n-grams.

Conclusions

An application developed using this process has the potential to be invaluable for domain specialists who wish to identify documents containing similar conceptual information within extremely large knowledge bases.

It is necessary to evaluate the scope and quality of the representations generated. One possibility is to compare, using an identical corpus, the representation generated by a group of experts with that of the system.

References

Collier, R. 1994. N-gram cluster identification during empirical knowledge representation generation. In Proceedings of the Fifteenth International Conference on Computational Linguistics. Kyoto, Japan: Forthcoming.

Riloff, E. 1993. Automatically constructing a dictionary for information extraction tasks. In Proceedings of the Eleventh National Conference of Artificial Intelligence. Washington, D.C.: MIT Press, Cambridge, MA.

Case-Based Introspection*

Michael T. Cox

College of Computing
Georgia Institute of Technology
Atlanta, GA 30332-0280
cox@cc.gatech.edu

To effectively reason about one's own knowledge, goals, and reasoning requires an ability to explicitly introspect. A computational model of introspection is a second-order theory that contains a formal language for representing first-order processes and that processes instances of this representation. The reasoning algorithm used to perform such processing is similar to the algorithm used to reason about events and processes represented in the original domain: case-based reasoning.

Case-based understanding 1) takes as input some event in its domain along with its context, 2) based on salient cues in the input, retrieves a prior case to interpret the input, then 3) adapts the old solution to fit the current situation, and finally 4) outputs the result as its understanding of the domain. Similarly, case-based introspection 1′) takes as input a representation of some prior reasoning [e.g., an instance of case-based understanding] 2′) based on salient cues in the input, retrieves a prior case of reflection to interpret the input, then 3′) adapts the old case to fit the current situation, and finally 4′) outputs the result as its self-understanding. Here, the system's domain is itself.

We have extended the notion of an explanation pattern (XP) from Schank (1986) and Ram (1991). A *meta-explanation pattern* (Meta-XP) is an explanation of how and why an explanation goes awry in a reasoning system. We have developed two classes of Meta-XPs that facilitate a system's ability to reason about itself and to assist in selecting a learning algorithm or strategy. A *Trace Meta-XP* (TMXP) explains how a system generates an explanation about the world or itself, and an *Introspective Meta-XP* (IMXP) explains why the reasoning captured in a TMXP fails. The TMXP records the structure of reasoning tasks and the reasons for decisions taken in processing in a chain of decide-compute nodes. The IMXP is a causal structure composed of primitive, network structures that represent various failure types from a failure taxonomy. They are retrieved and applied to instances of reasoning captured in TMXPs and guide learning-goal formation after failure occurs.

Case-based introspection has proved useful during blame-assignment in a multistrategy learner called Meta-AQUA. Failure analysis cannot always look to the external world

for causes. Often the assignment of blame is with the knowledge and reasoning of the system itself. Therefore, when Meta-AQUA encounters a reasoning failure while reading drug-smuggling stories, it uses case-based introspection to explain why it failed at its reasoning task. The system uses this analysis as a basis to form learning goals and subsequently to construct a learning plan to repair its memory. Figure 1 specifies the algorithm in some detail.

```
0. Perform and Record Reasoning in TMXP
1. Failure Detection on Reasoning Trace
2. If Failure Then
       Learn from Mistake:
         • Blame Assignment
             Compute index as characterization of failure
             Retrieve Introspective Meta-XP
             Apply IMXP to trace of reasoning in TMXP
             If Successful XP-Application then
                 Check XP-ASSERTED-NODES
                 If one or more nodes not believed then
                     Introspective questioning
                     GOTO step 0
                 Else GOTO step 0
         • Create Learning Goals
             Compute tentative goal priorities
         • Choose Learning Algorithm(s)
             Expand subgoals
             Build learning plan
             Compute data dependencies
             Order plans
         • Apply Learning Algorithm(s)
```

Figure 1: Introspective Multistrategy Learning Algorithm
(from Ram et al. 1993)

References

Schank, R. C. 1986. *Explanation Patterns: Understanding Mechanically and Creatively.* Hillsdale, NJ: LEA.

Ram, A. 1991. A Theory of Questions and Question Asking. *The Journal of the Learning Sciences*, *1*(3&4), 273-318.

Ram, A., Cox, M. T., & Narayanan, S. 1993. Goal-Driven Learning in Multistrategy Reasoning and Learning Systems. In A. Ram & D. Leake (eds.), *Goal-Driven Learning*, Cambridge, MA: MIT Press. Forthcoming.

---

*This research was done with the author's advisor, Ashwin Ram.

Time Units and Calendars

Diana Cukierman and James Delgrande
School of Computing Science
Simon Fraser University
Burnaby, BC, Canada V5A 1S6
{diana,jim}@cs.sfu.ca

Abstract

We are investigating a formal representation of *time units* and *calendars*, as restricted temporal entities for reasoning about activities. We examine characteristics of time units, and provide a categorization of the hierarchical relations among them. Hence we define an abstract hierarchical unit structure (a *calendar structure*) that expresses specific relations and properties among the units that compose it. Calendar structures subsume systems that can be based on discrete units together with a repetitive containment relation.

The motivation for this work is to (ultimately) be able to reason about schedulable, *repeated activities*, specified using calendars. Examples of such activities include going to a specific class every Tuesday and Thursday during a semester, attending a seminar every first day of a month, and going to swim every other day. Defining a precise representation and developing or adapting known efficient algorithms to this domain would provide a valuable framework for scheduling systems.

In a representation scheme for such activities, one would ideally be able to determine consistency among several repeated activities, find a minimal set of potential ways repeated activities may interact, convert between time units, etc. Such a structure would be a restriction of, for example, the general algebra of intervals (Allen 1983); hence one might hope that the resulting restricted structure would have good computational properties. Work has been done around repeated activities, for example (Poesio & Brachman 1991), where a main concern is the implementation of variants of constraint propagation algorithms to detect overlapping repeated activities. We search for a different (more general and formalized) representation of the temporal entities. We explore further the *date* concept, used in their work as a reference interval, building a structure that formalizes dates in calendars.

Human, schedulable activities are based on conventional systems called *calendars*. Examples of calendars include the Gregorian calendar as well as university calendars and a business calendar, where the latter calendars are defined in terms of the Gregorian. Calendars are repetitive, cyclic temporal objects. We define an abstract structure that formalizes calendars as composed of time units which are related by a *decomposition* relation, which is a containment relation involving repetition and other specific characteristics. Time units decompose into contiguous sequences of other time units in various ways. For example, the expressions *year* $\unrhd$ *month*, with *Cons(year,month,12)* and *Alig(year,month)* indicate that the time unit *year* decomposes into *month* in a constant and aligned way, with a repetition factor of 12.

We have studied transitivity properties of *constancy* and *alignment* in the decomposition relation. The decomposition relation is defined as a partial order on the set of time units. A *calendar structure* is a hierarchical structure based on the decomposition of time units and expresses relationships that hold between them in several calendars.

At this point in the research, the formalism is under systematic study, particularly regarding its mathematical properties. Representation of specific temporal objects based on the formalism are under study also. Still to be addressed are considerations about algorithms that would best fit with this formalism, so that we may obtain efficient inferences when reasoning about single and repeated activities. Algorithms developed for temporal constraint satisfaction problems, or variations, will be considered in this matter. We believe also that the hierarchy defined represents a generic approach, appropriate to represent any measurement system based on discrete units that relate with a repetitive containment relation, such as the Metric or Imperial measurement systems.

References

Allen, J. F. 1983. Maintaining knowledge about temporal intervals. *Communications of the ACM* 26(11):832–843.

Poesio, M., and Brachman, R. J. 1991. Metric constraints for maintaining appointments: Dates and repeated activities. In *Proc. of the AAAI-91*, 253–259.

Local Search in the Coordination of Intelligent Agents[*]

Daniel E. Damouth and Edmund H. Durfee
Artificial Intelligence Laboratory
1101 Beal Avenue
The University of Michigan
Ann Arbor, MI 48109-2110
{damouth, durfee}@engin.umich.edu

In a world inhabited by numerous agents pursuing distinct goals, conflicts are inevitable. To succeed in the environment, an agent must explicitly reason about the behaviors of other agents as well as itself, and be prepared to find new behaviors that are more coordinated. Because traditional AI has had great success viewing problem solving as a *search* in a *problem space*, we have chosen to represent the process of coordination as a distributed search (Durfee *et al.* 1994). In searching through a joint behavior space for coherent coordination patterns, an agent must observe three kinds of constraints: its abilities, its goals, and the activities of other agents in the environment.

The nature of the third constraint is dependent on the abilities and goals of the other agents in the environment. Knowledge of other agents' planned actions is often sufficient for conflict avoidance; however, the ability to reason about alternative activities not only for oneself but for *other* agents requires deeper modeling of them. Our concept of the *behavior* as a modeling structure contains not only spatial and temporal information about agents' actions but also represents their goals and capabilities. With this modeling information an agent can reason from other agents' goals and capabilities to arrive at likely alternative behaviors for them and itself. We call this *local search*. Depending on the distribution of knowledge among the agents, local search might occur at any number of agents. Our approach complements the distributed search process of (Durfee & Montgomery 1991), which emphasized the efficient propagation of information among agents rather than the local search of an individual agent.

We are investigating local search in the **producer-consumer-transporter** (PCT) domain, by implementing a search for coordination patterns for solving package delivery problems. In a PCT problem, "producers" create objects that must be delivered by "transporters" to "consumer" agents, who cause the objects to disappear. Representing coordination schemes as a hierarchy of behaviors, we have been able to generate many different agent organizations by decomposing according to agent *goals* and agent *capa-*

[*]Supported, in part, by NSF grant IRI-9158473.

bilities, respectively. Using the former decomposition we arrive at an analog to "product hierarchies", in which agents are grouped according to the products they help make. Using the latter decomposition gives rise to "functional hierarchies", in which agents are grouped according to their capabilities. Our use of taxonomic knowledge of capabilities and goal-subgoal relationships also allows us to represent *hybrid* organizations that incorporate features of both kinds of hierarchies. We have identified instances in which a hybrid organization outperforms any "pure" form. Our ongoing analysis is focusing on the evaluation of organizational forms in terms of coordination costs (the amount of run-time communicating and thinking), production costs (overall throughput), and vulnerability costs (the effect on performance if some agent breaks down).

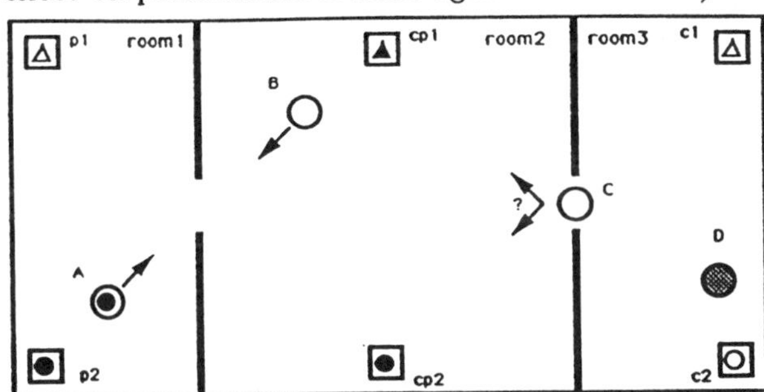

We are working to characterize these factors with the aim of automating the generation and search of a behavior space for this coordination task. In a broader context, we hope to shed light on issues such as the effect of different task decompositions on the complexity of local processing, and the effects that different coordination costs have on effective agent organization.

References

Durfee, E. H., and Montgomery, T. A. 1991. Coordination as distributed search. *IEEE Transactions on Systems, Man, and Cybernetics* 21(6).

Durfee, E.; Damouth, D.; Huber, M.; Montgomery, T.; ; and Sen, S. 1994. The search for coordination. In *Decentralized AI*. Springer-Verlag, Lecture Notes in Artificial Intelligence.

GKR: A Generic Model of Knowledge Representation

Angélica de Antonio, Jesús Cardeñosa, Loïc Martínez Normand

Laboratorio de Inteligencia Artificial.
Facultad de Informática. Campus de Montegancedo.
28660 Boadilla del Monte. Madrid (Spain)
E-Mail:lia@fi.upm.es

Extended Abstract

In the 1956 Darmouth College conference two aspects of the definition of AI were emphasized: a) the separation between the knowledge and the procedures using it and b) the equivalence of the different knowledge representation (KR) formalisms. Taking the last concept as an origin, an idea arose in Knowledge Engineering: Building generic KR's that could allow to represent any Knowledge Base (KB) developed using any formalism, to work with it without worrying about the actual formalism used in the construction of the KB. This is an objective that has not yet been reached, although research in this area continues as shown in the following examples:

- In the area of Validation and Verification (V&V) of Knowledge Based Systems (KBS) we can mention the VALID project (ESPRIT II number 2148 project [CARD-93]). This project was based on the idea of building a generic model of KR called CCR (Common Conceptual Representation) in which the formalism of any system could be translated to apply a set of V&V tools to the translated KB.

- In the Knowledge Acquisition area this idea has been used, for example, in the ACKNOWLEDGE project (ESPRIT II number 2576 project [ACK-88]). The main objective of this project was to develop a Knowledge Engineering Workbench integrating several knowledge acquisition methods, techniques and tools. In order to integrate the knowledge acquired by each of those, it was necessary to use a generic KR called CKR (Core KR).

- Finally, this idea has also been used in Automatic Translation. This idea is de basis of the INTERLINGUA representation (used in project PIVOT [NEC-86]) which is a representation of the natural language knowledge independent of the actual language (Spanish, English, etc.) used.

We show in this paper a proposal for a new generic model of KR called GKR (Generic Knowledge Representation). This model has been developed as a result of the analysis of the models described in the preceding examples. The study of the successes and shortcomings of these models helped us to define GKR with several properties that improve its representation ability:

- We have divided the representation of a KBS into three parts: 1) a static part that represents the knowledge that has the system about its problem domain (that is, the KB), 2) a dynamic part that represents, using traces of the execution, how does work the KBS faced to a problem (or test case) and 3) some information referring to design particularities of the KBS. This part represents why does the static part work as shown by the dynamic part. This part of the systems represents control information.

- We have chosen frames [MINS-75] and rules [MATÉ-88] as KR formalisms for the static part. These formalisms are defined in GKR with characteristics that were not implemented in the other models, such as: representation of user-defined facets, explicit representation of inheritance rules, representation of non hierarchical relations between frames and the representation of conditions and actions allowing rules to access or modify any part of the KB.

The above properties make possible to represent in GKR things that would not be able to represent in the other models. The definition of the GKR design is composed by a set of structures that cannot be described in this abstract. Although GKR can be used in other AI areas, it is being used in the definition of a Validation environment based in this representation model. This environment will apply several V&V tools to KBS represented in GKR and it is being developed by the Validation Group of the AI Laboratory of the Universidad Politécnica of Madrid.

References

[ACK-88] ACKnowledge Project. "ACKnowledge Technical Annex." 1988.

[CARD-93] Cardeñosa, J. and Juristo, N. "General Overview of the Valid Project." Proceedings of the European Symposium on the Validation and Verification of KBS, EUROVAV'93. Palma de Mallorca. Spain. 1993.

[MATÉ-88] Maté, J.L. and Pazos, J. "Ingeniería del Conocimiento: diseño y construcción de sistemas expertos." Ed SEPA. 1988.

[MINS-75] Minsky, M.. "A framework for Representing Knowledge" en "The Psychology of Computer Vision." P. H. Wilson (ed.) McGraw-Hill. 1975.

[NEC-86] Nec. "Overview of Pivot". C&C systems researchs laboratory. NEC Corporation. Japan. 1986.

Experiments Towards Robotic Learning By Imitation

John Demiris
Department of Artificial Intelligence
University of Edinburgh
80 South Bridge, Edinburgh, Scotland
email: johnde@aifh.ed.ac.uk

Learning by imitation is a form of learning, which despite the fact it has been widely studied by ethologists, has not been fully understood yet. In fact, there is a considerable disagreement even on the terminology used despite attempts to clarify it (Davis,1973; Galef, 1988;). We believe that by building robots which instantiate the mechanisms hypothesised to underlie these types of behaviour, those mechanisms will be illuminated with explanatory adequacy. Our investigation into imitative learning begins with the construction of an appropriate experimental testbed and the design of a suitable architecture which would enable one robot (the learner) to imitate another one (the teacher) which is performing a task, and learn to perform the task while imitating the teacher. Initially, the idea was to have one robot to perform a sequence of moves ("dance"), while the other robot would learn dancing by imitating the first one. Such an experiment however, does not satisfy our need to be able to evaluate whether the robot has actually learned anything. Instead, we choose to have as a testbed a maze, where the robot learner would imitate the actions that the robot teacher is performing during its maze negotiation strategy. After the learning phase, we could ask the second robot to navigate itself through a new (different) maze, which would provide us with a more evident demonstration that learning has taken place.

The architecture that was devised has five distinct modules, largely independent from each other:

Maze negotiation How is the teacher dealing with the maze? This can take various forms, from simple dead reckoning to complex maze following behaviours.

Teacher following This can also take various forms of increasing complexity. In the simplest form, the learner keeps a fixed distance behind the teacher, regardless of the teacher's motion; more sophisticated implementations would have the learner follow only when the teacher is moving purposively and ignore "loitering".

Significant event perception The learner robot recognises when and where the teacher robot is performing an action it deems significant. Ways of doing so include detecting changes in direction of movement or the orientation of the teacher, or even having the

teacher emitting a sound ("watch me, this is important").

Environment perception Depends on the sensing capabilities of the learner; we use both simulated robots, and mobile robots equipped with a vision system, ultrasonic, and infra-red sensors.

Finally, in order to successfully learn, the robot learner has to associate the enviroment's configuration perceived with the appropriate action. Thus, we also need a mechanism for :

Derivation of appropriate action We make use of the fact that the learner is performing a teacher-following behaviour all the time. The difference in the states of the robot-learner just before and after the significant event (for example, a 90-degrees change in direction of movement) is associated with the enviroment's configuration perceived. The form of association can also range from simple if-then rules, to connectionist solutions.

The architecture described has been successfully implemented in simulation and the results so far are encouraging. The robot learner successfully learns to traverse increasingly complicated mazes, indicating that this architecture is promising in dealing with simple learning situations. Currently, we are implementing the architecture on mobile robots. The next step will be to increase the complexity of each module, and continue the research into more complex tasks (for example, imitative learning of obstacle avoidance behaviours). We believe that, in addition to the contribution that our findings may have in the field of ethology, this research will result to new versatile forms of robotic learning.

The assistance of my supervisor, Dr. Gillian Hayes, is acknowledged, and highly appreciated.

- (Davis, 1973) J.M. Davis, "Imitation: a review and critique", in Perspectives in Ethology, P.G. Bateson and P.H. Klopfer (eds.), Plenum Press, 1973.
- (Galef, 1988) Bennett G. Galef, Jr., "Imitation in animals: history, definition, and interpretation of data from the psychological laboratory", in Social Learning: Psychological and Biological Perspectives, T.R. Zentall and B.G. Galef, Jr. (eds.), Lawrence Erlbaum Associates, 1988.

Goal-Clobbering Avoidance in Non-Linear Planners

Rujith de Silva
Carnegie Mellon University
5000 Forbes Avenue
Pittsburgh, Pennsylvania 15213-3891
desilva+@cmu.edu

A central issue in non-linear planning is the ordering of operators so as to avoid undesirable interactions between their effects. The Modal Truth Criterion (Chapman 1987) states the conditions under which these interactions will occur. Non-linear planners use the Criterion, directly or indirectly, to promote or demote operators, or to co-designate variables, so as to avoid interactions.

This abstract describes a method, called *Goal Clobbering Avoidance* (GCA), to avoid some interactions in a partially-ordered plan by promoting or demoting a sequence of operators, rather than individual operators. Effectively, it simultaneously applies the Modal Truth Criterion to all operators in the sequence, using pre-compiled information about the domain.

GCA will be illustrated in the familiar Blocksworld domain, with the operators

⟨put-down ?block⟩	on table
⟨pick-up ?block⟩	from table
⟨stack ?blockA ?blockB⟩	
⟨unstack ?blockA ?blockB⟩	

Consider the following problem, related to Sussman's Anomaly, in which Block C has been unstacked from Block A.

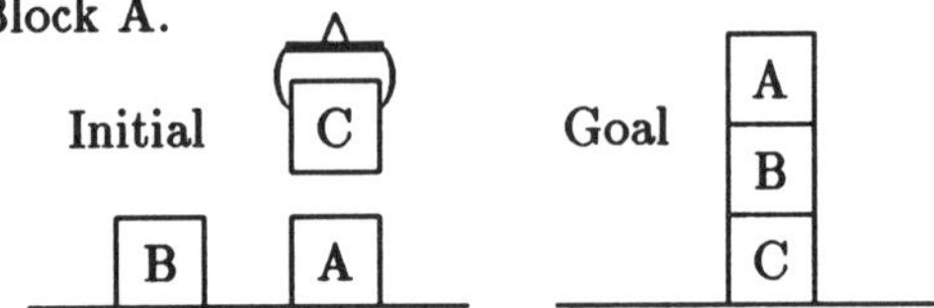

Furthermore, suppose a partially-ordered plan has been built as shown towards solving the problem.

(on A B)	(on B C)
⟨stack A B⟩	⟨stack B C⟩
(holding A)	(holding B)
⟨pick-up A⟩	⟨pick-up B⟩
(arm-empty)	
⟨put-down C⟩	

This plan has a large number of interactions involving (arm-empty), (clear B) and (clear C), and it is not immediately clear how to promote or demote the operators to achieve the desired goals.

Consider the goals and operators under (on A B) in relation to the sibling goal (on B C). If (on A B) is achieved first, then *any* plan that achieves (on B C) will dis-achieve (on A B). Similarly, any such plan will also dis-achieve (holding A).

Hence applying ⟨pick-up A⟩ before ⟨stack B C⟩ is pointless, as its effects will be clobbered by the later achievement of (on B C). However, applying ⟨put-down C⟩ is not pointless, as (arm-empty) is *not* dis-achieved by (on B C). Therefore the planner can split the left-hand branch by constraining ⟨pick-up A⟩ and ⟨stack A B⟩ to occur after the achievement of (on B C). Furthermore, it can do this *before* even deciding how to achieve (on B C), as it makes use of the following judgements expressing properties of *all* possible ways of achieving (on B C):

Goal-clobbering by (on ?B ?C) of (on ?A ?B)
Goal-clobbering by (on ?B ?C) of (holding ?A)

The first states that any plan, justified or not, whose final operator achieves (on ?B ?C) must result in a final state in which (on ?A ?B) is not true. Similarly for the second. Conditional goal-clobberings that constrain the initial states in which they are applicable also exist.

GCA has yielded large savings in planning-time in numerous domains on the totally-ordered non-linear planner PRODIGY(Etzioni 1991). I am currently evaluating its performance in partially-ordered planners. In addition, I am automating the derivation of goal-clobbering judgements, which explicitly state provable properties of the domain, by extending the work done by (Etzioni 1991).

References

Chapman, D. 1987. Planning for conjunctive goals. *Artificial Intelligence* 32:333–377.

Etzioni, O. 1991. STATIC: A problem-space compiler for PRODIGY. In Proceedings of the Eighth National Conference on Artificial Intelligence, 533–540.

Dynamically Adjusting Categories
to Accommodate Changing Contexts

Mark Devaney and **Ashwin Ram**
College of Computing
Georgia Institute of Technology
Atlanta, GA 30332-0280
E-mail: {markd,ashwin}@cc.gatech.edu

Context

Concept formation is the process by which generalizations are formed through observation of *instances* from the environment. These instances are described along a number of *attributes*, which are selected according to their *relevance* to the problem or task for which the concepts will be used. The *context* of a concept learning problem consists of the goals and tasks of the learner, as well as its background knowledge and domain theories and the external environment in which it operates. Context is essential to inductive concept learning for it determines which *attributes* to use for a given problem out of the infinitely many available, providing a *bias* for the learner (Mitchell, 1980). Furthermore, context is not a static entity, but is constantly changing, especially in the types of learning tasks faced by humans (e.g. Seifert 1989, Barsalou 1991). As concept formation systems are employed in tasks more typical of natural domains and "real-world" problems, the ability to respond to changing contexts becomes increasingly important.

Attribute-incrementation

Toward this end, we introduce the notion of *attribute-incrementation*, the dynamic incorporation and removal of attributes from existing concepts. This ability allows a concept learner to accommodate changing contexts by altering the set of attributes used to describe instances in a problem domain while retaining its prior knowledge of that domain. This capability has been implemented in a concept formation system called AICC (Attribute Incremental Concept Creator), an extension of an existing concept learner, COBWEB (Fisher, 1987). AICC is capable of both adding new attributes and removing existing ones from a COBWEB concept hierarchy and restructuring it accordingly.

Performance

We have performed extensive evaluations of AICC and compared its performance along several dimensions to that of COBWEB. One of the conclusions of this research is that AICC is able to construct concept hierarchies by incrementally incorporating attributes in significantly less time than COBWEB. These hierarchies achieve comparable predictive accuracy and classification efficiency to those produced by COBWEB. In additional experiments, AICC has been used to remove attributes from existing concept hierarchies as well as add new attributes to hierarchies constructed with varying numbers of initial attributes. These experiments have been replicated with a wide variety of data, with similar results.

Conclusions

Current concept learners are referred to as incremental if they incorporate *instances* one-at-a-time into their concept hierarchies. However, the attribute set used to describe these instances is an integral part of the concept formation problem. The ability to incorporate *attributes* incrementally allows concept learners to dynamically modify their bias and respond to a wider variety of changes in context without discarding prior domain knowledge. This ability is important given the trend toward creating systems that must face real-world tasks and their corresponding constraints.

References

Barsalou, L. W. 1991. Deriving categories to achieve goals. In G. H. Bower (Ed.), *The psychology of learning and motivation: Advances in research and theory*, (Vol. 27). New York: Academic Press.

Fisher, D. H. 1987. Knowledge acquisition via incremental conceptual clustering. *Machine Learning*, 2, 139-172.

Mitchell, T. M. 1980. The need for biases in learning generalizations (Tech. Rep. CBM-TR-117). New Brunswick, NJ: Rutgers University Department of Computer Science.

Seifert, C. M. 1989. A retrieval model using feature selection. *Proceedings of the Sixth International Workshop on Machine Learning*, 52-54). Ithaca, NY: Morgan Kaufmann.

Substructure Discovery Using Minimum Description Length Principle and Background Knowledge

Surnjani Djoko

Department of Computer Science and Engineering
University of Texas at Arlington
Box 19015, Arlington, TX 76019
djoko@cse.uta.edu

Abstract

Discovering conceptually interesting and repetitive substructures in a structural data improves the ability to interpret and compress the data. The substructures are evaluated by their ability to describe and compress the original data set using the domain's background knowledge and the minimum description length (MDL) of the data. Once discovered, the substructure concept is used to simplify the data by replacing instances of the substructure with a pointer to the newly discovered concept. The discovered substructure concepts allow abstraction over detailed structure in the original data. Iteration of the substructure discovery and replacement process constructs a hierarchical description of the structural data in terms of the discovered substructures. This hierarchy provides varying levels of interpretation that can be accessed based on the goals of the data analysis.

The structural data is represented as a labeled graph. A substructure is a connected subgraph within the graphical representation. An instance of a substructure in an input graph is a set of vertices and edges from the input graph that match, graph theoretically, to the graphical representation of the substructure. The substructures are evaluated by their ability to describe and compress the original data set using the domain's background knowledge and the minimum description length (MDL) of the data. Once interesting substructures are discovered, they can be replaced by a single representative node in the original graph, and can be used as part of another substructure definition in a hierarchy of discovered structures.

The minimum description length principle states that the best theory to describe a set of data is the theory which minimizes the description length of the entire data set. The minimum description length of a graph is defined to be the number of bits necessary to completely describe the graph. The theory that best accounts for a collection of data is the one that minimizes $I(S) + I(G|S)$, where S is the discovered substructure, G is the input graph, $I(S)$ is the number of bits required to encode the discovered substructure, and $I(G|S)$ is the number of bits required to encode the input graph G with respect to S.

Although the principle of minimum description length is useful for discovering substructures that maximize compression of the data, scientists often employ knowledge or assumptions of a specific domain to the discovery process. To make the discovery process more powerful across a wide variety of domains, the background knowledge have been added to guide the discovery process. This background knowledge is entered in the form of rules for evaluating substructures. Because only the most-favored substructures are kept and expanded, these rules control the discovery process of the system.

For example, in the CAD circuit domain, circuit components can be classified according to their passivity. A component which is not passive is said to be active. The active components are the main driving components. Identifying the active components is the first step in understanding the main function of the circuit. The component rule assigns relatively higher values to the active components, and assigns lower values to the passive components. Once the active components are selected, attention can be focused on the passive components. Similarly, the loop analysis rule favors subcircuits containing loops. Since the components in the closed path are generally a part of the subcircuit or the subcircuit itself. Furthermore, the component complexity rule prefers minimum number of distinct component in the substructure.

The approch has also been applied to the domains of chemical compound analysis, scene analysis, CAD circuit analysis, and analysis of artificially-generated graphs. The results demonstrate the applicability and significance of the approcah in the above domains.

References

J. R. Quinlan and R. L. Rivest. Inferring decision trees using the minimum description length principle. *Information and Computation*, 80:227-248, 1989.

P. Cheeseman, J. Kelly, M. Self, J. Stutz, W. Taylor, and D. Freeman. Autoclass: A bayesian classification system. In *Proceedings of the Fifth International Conference on Machine Learning*, 54-64, 1988.

Exploiting the Ordering of Observed Problem-solving Steps for Knowledge Base Refinement: an Apprenticeship Approach

Steven K. Donoho and **David C. Wilkins**
Department of Computer Science, University of Illinois
Urbana, IL 61801
donoho@cs.uiuc.edu, wilkins@cs.uiuc.edu

Apprenticeship is a powerful method of learning among humans in which a student refines his knowledge by observing and analyzing the problem-solving steps of an expert. In this paper we focus on knowledge base (KB) refinement for classification problems and examine how the *ordering* of the intermediate steps of an observed expert can be used to yield leverage in KB refinement. In the classical classification problem, the problem-solver is given an example consisting of a set of attributes and their corresponding values, and it must put the example in one of a pre-enumerated set of classes.

Consider a slightly different situation, though, in which the problem-solver is not given *all* the attribute/value pairs from the outset but rather must request attributes one at a time and make his classification decision once sufficient evidence is gathered. This situation would arise when it is too costly or otherwise unreasonable to simply be given all the attribute values. When a mechanic is troubleshooting a malfunctioning car, he does not run every test possible and then stop to examine his data and make his decision. Rather he checks one thing, and based on the result of that, he decides what to check next. Thus the order in which attributes are requested reflects the internal problem-solving process going on in the mind of the observed expert. By watching the order in which a superior problem-solver requests attributes, we should be able to refine the KB of a weaker problem-solver.

The ordering of attribute requests can be used to detect KB shortcomings because it allows the analysis of an attribute request with respect to what was and what was not known at the time of the request. As an example from the audiology domain, if the expert requests the attribute *history_noise* after *age_gt_60* is known to be *true*, it can be assumed that knowing *history_noise* is important to know even when *age_gt_60* is *true*. If in the KB we are refining, *history_noise* is not worth knowing given that *age_gt_60* = *true*, then our KB contradicts the actions of the expert indicating a KB shortcoming. Using our KB, we cannot explain why the expert would ask *history_noise* given what he already knew; thus, the expert must have some knowledge which our KB lacks.

Once a KB shortcoming has been detected, an attempt is made to repair it by adding a rule of the form: $condition_1 \wedge \ldots \wedge condition_N \longrightarrow class_i$ where each condition is an attribute/value pair such as *history_dizziness* = *true*. The repair is built by starting with an initial single-condition rule and greedily adding conditions. The condition in the initial rule consists of the **unexplained attribute** (*history_noise* in the above example) and one of its possible values. The class of the initial rule is any class that has not been ruled out by the attribute requests preceding the unexplained attribute (with respect to a set of training examples). Since there may be multiple feasible classes and multiple values for the unexplained attribute, multiple initial rules may have to be explored. The conditions which are greedily added each consist of an attribute requested before the unexplained attribute and its known value — this is because knowledge of these attributes gave rise to the request of the unexplained attribute; therefore, they may be related to the unexplained attribute and to the shortcoming. Conditions are added until the purity of the set of training examples covered by the rule no longer improves.

The principles explored have been implemented, and experiments were run using the audiology dataset. In a test with a training set of size 100, an initial KB was created using C4.5 which achieved an accuracy of 67.9%. This initial KB was refined, and the final KB achieved an accuracy of 82.1%, a net improvement of 14.2%. The ordered sequences of requested attributes were generated by C4.5 using all 226 audiology examples. The power of the attribute ordering method of apprenticeship is that it does not rely solely on empirical calculations to discover attribute/class relationships. Rather, these attribute/class relationships are suggested by attribute ordering and are only *verified* empirically requiring less empirical evidence.

The KM/KnEd System: An Integrated Approach to Building Large-scale Multifunctional Knowledge Bases*

Erik Eilerts
Department of Computer Science
University of Texas
Austin, Texas 78712-1188
(512) 471-9565
eilerts@cs.utexas.edu

1   Background

In 1987, Dr. Bruce Porter began work at the University of Texas at Austin on the Botany Knowledge Base Project. The goal of the project is to develop a large-scale multi-functional knowledge base in the area of Botany. This Botany Knowledge Base (BKB) is used to support research projects in question answering, automated modeling, and intelligent tutoring. Due to the size and complexity of the BKB, a decision was made in 1990 to begin construction of a new knowledge representation language and interface to support the knowledge base. The knowledge representation language was named KM, for Knowledge Manager, and the interface was named KnEd, for Knowledge Editor. The KM/KnEd system is similar to Doug Lenat's CYC project and Doug Skuce's CODE4 system.

2   KM/KnEd

KM is a frame-based knowledge representation language that uses slot-and-filler structures. KM's most important feature is that it allows the *annotation* of values with extra details.

Value annotations are used to represent information contextually. Consider the assertion "Texas Bluebonnets secrete nectar that contains a low concentration of sugar." This problem could be solved by creating the frame **The-Sugar-contained-in-the-Nectar-secreted-by-a-Texas-Bluebonnet** and adding the "concentration Low" attribute to it. But, this removes all contextual information about the frame. Instead, KM allows the user to retain contextual information by recursively nesting annotations (KM is one of the few languages with this feature). Figure 1 shows how this assertion is represented using KM's value annotation mechanism. In this figure, the (Texas-Bluebonnet secretes Nectar contains Sugar) address is connected to the "concentration Low" attribute.

---

*Support for this research was provided by a grant from the National Science Foundation (IRI-9120310), a contract from the Air Force Office of Scientific Research (F49620-93-1-0239), and donations from the Digital Equipment Corporation. This work was conducted at the University of Texas at Austin.

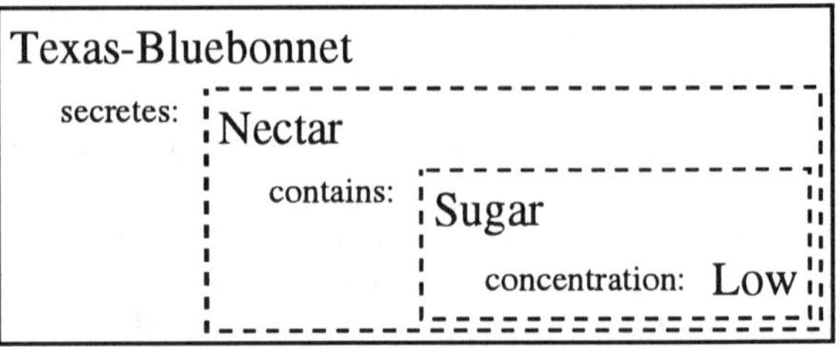

Figure 1: Value Annotation

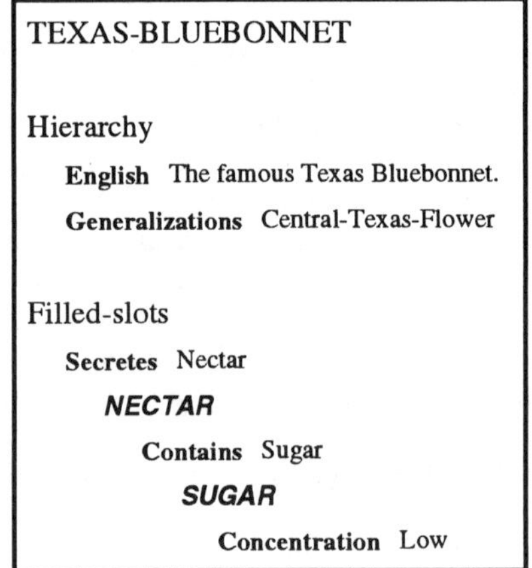

Figure 2: KnEd Text Pane

KnEd is a graphical user interface for viewing and editing large-scale knowledge bases. The basic display mechanism used is the text pane. It displays all the relations associated with a frame. Figure 2 is an example of a text pane display of the Texas-Bluebonnet frame. KnEd provides several tools to aid the user in adding, removing, changing, and copying values in the knowledge base. KnEd also supports navigation around the knowledge base and distributed editing.

With the help of KM and KnEd, the BKB has successfully grown to contain more than 150,000 facts. The complexity added by the annotation mechanism of KM made KnEd's viewing and editing capabilities indispensable. As knowledge bases increase in size, tools such as KM's annotation mechanisms and the KnEd interface will become essential.

Situated Agents Can Have Plans

Mark Fasciano
Department of Computer Science
University of Chicago
Chicago, IL 60637
fasciano@cs.uchicago.edu

Much of our everyday activity is not made up of solving isolated problems with single clear-cut goals, but rather dedicated to the ongoing maintenance of many goals or policies such as eating when hungry and maintaining a comfortable personal space. Furthermore, in many complex, dynamic worlds, an agent must maintain many goals at the same time and be able to act quickly and flexibly, because some decisions are time critical and the world is not perfectly predictable.

The domain of SimCity requires this kind of behavior. In the simulation, you are never finished repairing the roads or fighting crime, because disasters and evolution will always require more work in the future. Survival depends on deciding what you should work on now, and by what you will allow yourself to be interrupted. In short, playing SimCity requires a robust theory of attention.

Situated agents are built to address problems of timely activity in complex, dynamic worlds. (Maes) Such systems stress that competent behavior can arise out of continually selecting primitive actions based on information about the environment. Situated activity theories propose that resource conflicts can be avoided by noticing conflicts at compile time. Most situated agents, however, are not required to accomplish long-term activities such as building an industrial complex.

Memory-based planning (Hammond), on the other hand, contends that in some interesting worlds an episodic memory of plans can adequately cover the longer-term problems an agent will face, thus providing an alternative to the intractability of exhaustive search.

How do we arbitrate between memory-based, long-term behavior, and reactive, short-term maintenance?

The Problem of Interruption in SimCity

Imagine that in response to the problem of unemployment in the city, you decide to build an industrial park on the outskirts of town. You develop a plan for this, and you have the funds to execute it. Such a project could take three simulator months, but during the execution of this plan, an earthquake strikes. If you continue to carry out your plan, half the city may be destroyed by fires. Since you can only do one thing at a time, you must interrupt your industrial development plan and deal with the earthquake.

The MAYOR Project

The goal of the MAYOR project is to build a planner which will be sensitive to long-term abstract goals such as increasing population or generating income and long-term activity such as building a suburb outside the city center. At the same time, MAYOR must react to unpredictable phenomena such as earthquakes, and the continual maintenance of the infrastructure of the city (roads, power lines, etc.).

The main point of the planner is to provide a model for how attention may be focused in a complex world like SimCity.

Inspired by (Minsky), MAYOR consists in a network of agents called advocates, each of which are dedicated to working on specific tasks. Some advocates are designed to monitor certain conditions in the world, and develop plans to address their task or purpose. Other advocates are designed not to monitor the world, but to monitor other advocates, settling disputing claims to the same resources.

Some conflicts between goals are settled at compile time; advocates which address the same goals inhibit each other. For example, while the Urban-Planner advocate is building an industrial complex to increase employment, the Roadworker is blocked from maintaining roads while the complex is being constructed, because the Urban-Planner's plan addresses this goal. On the other hand if a fire breaks out, since the Urban-Planner does not handle fires, the Urban-Planner may be interrupted by the Firefighter advocate. Instead of attempting to foresee all the possible conflicts, MAYOR proposes that such activity conflicts should be handled at run time, with a set of task arbitration strategies. An example of an implemented strategies is "seize-cheap-opportunity" which stops work on an long-term task in favor of an inexpensive, local, short-term plan.

Currently MAYOR attempts to service the long-term goal of maintaining a minimum income while handling problems of crime, fire protection and fires, and pollution control. At this stage of development, however, it is clear that success hinges on a robust theory of attention.

References

Hammond 1989. *Case-Based Planning,: Viewing Planning as a Memory Task.* Academic Press.

Maes, P. 1990. Situated Agents Can Have Goals. *Robotics and Autonomous Systems* 6: 49-70.

Minsky, M. 1985. *The Society of Mind.* New York, NY: Simon&Shuster.

Introspective Reasoning in a Case-based Planner

Susan Fox and **David Leake**
Lindley Hall 215
Indiana University
Bloomington, IN 47405
(812) 855-8702
sfox@cs.indiana.edu and leake@cs.indiana.edu

Many current AI systems assume that the reasoning mechanisms used to manipulate their knowledge may be fixed ahead of time by the designer. This assumption may break down in complex domains. The focus of this research is developing a model of *introspective reasoning and learning* to enable a system to improve its own reasoning as well as its domain knowledge. Our model is based on the proposal of (Birnbaum *et al.* 1991) to use a model of the ideal behavior of a case-based system to judge system performance and to refine its reasoning mechanisms; it also draws on the research of (Ram & Cox 1994) on introspective failure-driven learning.

This work examines introspection guided by expectation failures about reasoning performance. We are developing a vocabulary of failures for the case-based system, an introspective reasoner which uses a hierarchical model of system behavior, and a method of reusing CBR for parts of the case-based planner itself.

The system we are developing combines a model-based introspective reasoner with a case-based planning system. The planner generates high-level plans for navigating city streets, and is similar in structure to the planner CHEF (Hammond 1989). However, we implement components of the planner using the case-based reasoning mechanisms of the planner as a whole. Our primary interest in this approach is the advantage it offers for developing the model for introspective reasoning. We can reuse expectations that apply to the planner as a whole for its case-based parts.

During the planning process, the introspective reasoner compares the planner's reasoning to its assertions about ideal behavior. When a failure is detected, for instance if the system judges that the retrieved case is not the "best" case in memory, the introspective reasoner considers related assertions to pinpoint the source of the failure and to suggest a solution. In this case our system creates a new index to distinguish the true best case from the bad retrieved case.

Determining what information to include in the model and how to structure it are central issues. Birnbaum's model is a set of high-level assertions applicable to many case-based planners (Birnbaum *et al.* 1991).

While such assertions cover a wide range of failures, they are too general to easily specify causes or repairs for failures. We propose as an alternative a hierarchical model including highly abstract assertions as well as assertions specific to this planner. Low-level assertions help to notice failures and pinpoint repairs, while high-level assertions provide connections between assertions for finding the root causes of failures. By using a hierarchy, the general structure of the model will apply to other systems while we retain the ability to detect and repair specific failures of our system.

We are developing a vocabulary of failure types to guide our choice of assertions to include in the model. For example, identifying the failure "failing to complete adaptation" leads to assertions about how to gauge the progress of adaptation in this planner. We also include higher level failure types as are described in (Ram & Cox 1994); some such failures recurred for different components of the planner, leading us to use CBR to implement components themselves.

We have constructed a skeletal hierarchical model and have begun testing the case-based planner with and without introspective corrections. Initial experimental results indicate that introspectively re-indexing memory alone improves the planner's efficiency in retrieval and allows it to succeed more often than without introspection. We are currently in the process of fleshing out the model and expanding the scope of possible repairs.

References

Birnbaum, L.; Collins, G.; Brand, M.; Freed, M.; Krulwich, B.; and Pryor, L. 1991. A model-based approach to the construction of adaptive case-based planning systems. In *Proceedings of the DARPA CBR Workshop*, 215–224. Morgan Kaufman.

Hammond, K. 1989. *Case-Based Planning: Viewing Planning as a Memory Task*. Academic Press.

Ram, A., and Cox, M. T. 1994. Introspective reasoning using meta-explanations for multistrategy learning. In Michalski, R., and Tecuci, G., eds., *Machine Learning: A Multistrategy Approach, Vol. IV*. Morgan Kaufman.

A Statistical Method for Handling Unknown Words

Alexander Franz
Computational Linguistics Program and Center for Machine Translation
Carnegie Mellon University
5000 Forbes Avenue
Pittsburgh, PA 15213
amf@cs.cmu.edu

Robust Natural Language Processing systems must be able to handle words that are not in their lexicon. We created a classifier that was trained on tagged text to find the most likely parts of speech for unknown words. The classifier uses a contingency table to count the observed features, and a loglinear model to smooth the cell counts. After smoothing, the contingency table is used to obtain the conditional probability distribution for classification.

A number of features, determined by exploration (Tukey 1977), are used. For example, is the word capitalized? Does the word carry one of a number of known suffixes? We maximize the conditional probability of the proposed classification given the features to achieve minimum error rate classification (Duda & Hart 1973).

The baseline results are provided by using only the prior probabilities $P(c)$ (column **Prior**). (Weischedel *et al.* 1993) describe a probabilistic model with four features that are treated as independent, which we reimplemented (column **4 Indep**). For comparison, we created a statistical classifier with the same four features (column **4 Class**). Our best model was a classifier with nine features (column **9 Class**).

Measure	Prior	4 Indep	4 Class	9 Class
Overall Accuracy	28%	61%	69%	73%
Overall Res. Amb.	7.6	1.7	2.8	3.4
2-best Accuracy	53%	77%	87%	87%
2-best Res. Amb.	2.0	1.5	1.6	1.8
0.4-beam Accuracy		66%	81%	86%
0.4-beam Res. Amb.		1.2	1.4	1.6
0.4-beam Size		1.2	1.6	1.8

(*n*-best) Accuracy:	Percentage that the correct POS was among the *n* most likely POSs.
F-beam Accuracy:	All POSs with probability within beam factor F of the most probable POS.
Residual Ambiguity:	Mean perplexity for the POS tags in the answer set.
F-beam Size:	Mean number of tags in an answer set derived using beam factor F.

The graph below shows the accuracy of the simple probabilistic model versus the statistical classifier using one to nine features. The accuracy of the classifier is always higher and increases as more features are added, but does not decrease with nuisance features.

The simple probabilistic model, on the other hand, peaks a four features, and then degrades.

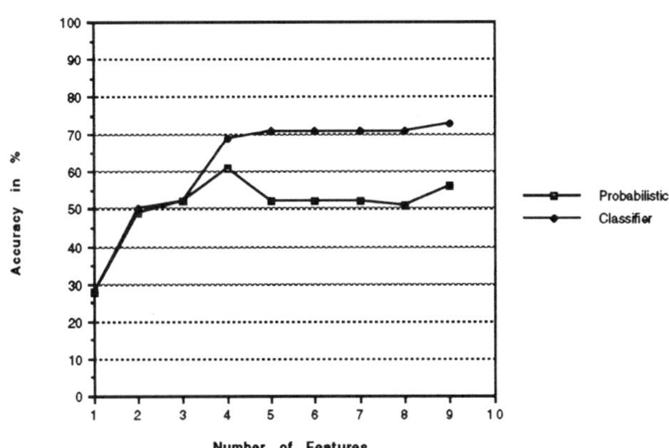

In future work, we will apply this method to other ambiguity resolution problems that require a combination of a number of categorial disambiguating features, such as POS tagging and PP attachment.

Acknowledgments: I would like to thank Jaime Carbonell, Ted Gibson, Michael Mauldin, Teddy Seidenfeld, and Akira Ushioda.

References

Agresti, A. 1990. *Categorical Data Analysis.* New York: John Wiley & Sons.

Duda, R. O., and Hart, P. E. 1973. *Pattern Classification and Scene Analysis.* New York: John Wiley & Sons.

Franz, A. 1994. Ambiguity resolution via statistical classification: Clasifying unknown words by part of speech. Tecnical Report CMU-CMT-94-144, Center for Machine Translation, Carnegie Mellon University.

Tukey, J. 1977. *Exploratory Data Analysis.* Reading, MA: Addison-Wesley.

Weischedel, R.; Meteer, M.; Schwartz, R.; Ramshaw, L.; and Palmucci, J. 1993. Coping with ambiguity and unknown words through probabilistic models. *Computational Linguistics* 19(2):359–382.

Low Computation Vision-Based Navigation For a Martian Rover

Andrew S. Gavin

Massachusetts Institute of Technology Artificial Intelligence Laboratory
Department of Electrical Engineering and Computer Science
545 Technology Square NE43-737, Cambridge Massachusetts 02139
(617) 253-8837 agavin@ai.mit.edu

Abstract[1]

In the design and construction of mobile robots vision has always been one of the most potentially useful sensory systems. In practice however, it has also become the most difficult to successfully implement. At the MIT Mobile Robotics (Mobot) Lab we have designed a small, light, cheap, and low power Mobot Vision System that can be used to guide a mobile robot in a constrained environment. The target environment is the surface of Mars, although we believe the system should be applicable to other conditions as well. It is our belief that the constraints of the Martian environment will allow the implementation of a system that provides vision based guidance to a small mobile rover.

The purpose of this vision system is to process realtime visual input and provide as output information about the relative location of safe and unsafe areas for the robot to go. It might additionally provide some tracking of a small number of interesting features, for example the lander or large rocks (for scientific sampling). The system we have built was designed to be self contained. It has its own camera and on board processing unit. It draws a small amount of power and exchanges a very small amount of information with the host robot. The project has two parts, first the construction of a hardware platform, and second the implementation of a successful vision algorithm.

For the first part of the project, which is complete, we have built a small self contained vision system. It employs a cheap but fast general purpose microcontroller (a 68332) connected to a Charge Coupled Device (CCD). The CCD provides the CPU with a continuous series of medium resolution gray-scale images (64 by 48 pixels with 256 gray levels at 10-15 frames a second). In order to accommodate our goals of low power, light weight, and small size we are bypassing the traditional NTSC video and using a purely digital solution. As the frames are captured any desired algorithm can then be implemented on the microcontroller to extract the desired information from the images and communicate it to the host robot. Additionally, conventional optics are typically oversized for this application so we have been experimenting with aspheric lenses, pinholes lenses, and lens sets.

As to the second half of the project, it is our hypothesis that a simple vision algorithm does not require huge amounts of computation and that goals such as constructing a complete three dimensional map of the environment are difficult, wasteful, and possibly unreachable. We believe that the nature of the environment can provide enough constraints to allow us to extract the desired information with a minimum of computation. It is also our belief that biological systems reflect an advanced form of this. They also employ constant factors in the environment to extract what information is relevant to the organism.

We believe that it is possible to construct a useful real world outdoor vision system with a small computational engine. This will be made feasible by an understanding of what information it is desirable to extract from the environment for a given task, and of an analysis of the constraints imposed by the environment. In order to verify this hypothesis and to facilitate vision experiments we have build a small wheeled robot named Gopher, equipped with one of our vision systems.

---

1. This research has been graciously funded by JPL and occurred at the MIT AI Lab, which is partially funded by ARPA.

Learning About Software Errors Via Systematic Experimentation

Terrance Goan   Oren Etzioni

Department of Computer Science and Engineering, University of Washington
Seattle, WA 98195
`{goan, etzioni}@cs.washington.edu`

Classical planners assume that their internal model is both correct and complete. The dynamic nature of real-world domains (e.g., multi-user software environments) makes these assumptions untenable. Several new planners (e.g.,XII [2]) have been designed to work with incomplete information, and strides have been made in planning with potentially incorrect information. But, efficient operation in the presence of incorrect information is highly dependent on a planner's ability to detect errors. Failing to recognize errors can result in unexpected and potentially destructive effects, as well as further corruption of the world model.

This abstract describes ED (the Error Detective) which automatically generates error detection functions for a software robot (softbot). In addition to error detection, the functions generated by ED accurately *diagnose* the cause of the errors. The *automatic* generation of these functions is important due to the large number of conditions that can affect the success of command execution. In addition, the ability to diagnose the cause of an error can greatly reduce the number of preconditions which need to be checked/resatisfied prior to a successful execution of the operator. In tackling this problem we utilize three key insights:

(1) If an operator is completely specified, every error is due to some subset of the preconditions being unsatisfied.
(2) Software error messages generally signal only one error. For example, in UNIX, if you execute the `diff` command on two files x and y, where both files are **not** readable, the error message would be `"diff:  x: Permission denied."` It provides no information about the status of file y. More formally: error-msg(~p1 **and** ~p2) = (error-msg(~p1) **or** error-msg(~p2)), where ~p1 and ~p2 represent unsatisfied preconditions.
(3) Since software errors do not interact, errors can be fixed incrementally (the decomposable fault assumption). This means we need not assume just a single fault has occurred, rather we assume that if error-msg(~p1 **and** ~p2) = error-msg(~p2) and we re-execute the operator (after achieving p2), we will now get error-

msg(~p1) which can be handled in turn.

ED "learns" the error diagnosis functions via a decision tree. The attributes which compose the training instances are: error message length (number of tokens) and a binary (present or not present) attribute for every token seen in the collected error messages. And the classes are sets of preconditions which may be at fault.

We compared the accuracy of the decision tree with two other methods: (1) our current hand-crafted error detection functions which rely on the presence of colons in error messages and makes no attempt to diagnose the cause of the error and (2) a simple string match method which looks for an exact match (except for command arguments).

The rate of correct diagnosis for the three methods were hand-crafted (57%), string match (71.6%), and decision tree (90.4%). In addition, both the string match and decision tree methods resulted in a significant decrease (50.5 and 63.6 respectively) in the number of preconditions which must be checked/resatisfied prior to re-executing an operator (i.e., the number of preconditions which can be rejected as the cause of the given error).

ED is complementary to "The Operator Refinement Method" presented in [1]. Where we assume correct operator models while developing error detectors, Carbonell and Gil assume accurate error detection while augmenting operator models.

Accurate error diagnosis allows yet another set of potentially fruitful experiments—finding the "optimal" set of operator preconditions. By "optimal" we mean the set of preconditions which best balance the cost of operator execution with the cost of error recovery. For example, it seems reasonable to execute `pwd` without verifying that all ancestor directories are readable. Simply execute the operator and handle the errors which will occasionally occur.

[1] Carbonell and Gil. Learning by Experimentation: The Operator Refinement Method. *Machine Learning: An Artificial Intelligence Approach* vol. III. 1990.
[2] Golden et al. XII: Planning for Universal Quantification and Incomplete Information. *AAAI* 1994.

Reasoning About What to Plan

Richard Goodwin

School of Computer Science, Carnegie Mellon University
5000 Forbes Ave. Pittsburgh, Pennsylvania 15213-3890
rich@cs.cmu.edu

Agents plan in order to improve their performance. However, planning takes time and consumes resources that may in fact degrade an agents performance. Ideally, an agent should only plan when the expected improvement outweighs the expected cost and no resources should be expended on making this decision. To do this, an agent would have to be omniscient. The problem of how to approximate this ideal, without consuming too many resources in the process, is the meta-level control problem for a resource bounded rational agent.

There are two central questions that have to be addressed for meta-level control: Where to focus planning effort and when to start executing the current best plan. These questions are interrelated. To start execution, the beginning of the plan must be elaborated to a level where it is operational. Even then, execution should only begin when the expected improvement due to further planning is outweighed by the cost of delaying execution. Once the agent has committed to executing some action, the planner can then disregard any plans inconsistent with this action and can concentrate on elaborating and optimizing the rest of the plan.

In my thesis research, I am exploring the use of sensitivity analysis based meta-level control for focusing computational effort. The object level problem of deciding which actions to perform is modeled as a standard decision problem and an approximate sensitivity analysis is performed. To facilitate the sensitivity analysis, actions, both abstract and operational, are augmented with methods for estimating their resource and time requirements. Methods are also needed to estimate the likelihood of events and action outcomes. All estimates include both the expected value and the expected range or variance. Information about the precision of estimates is critical when deciding whether to commit to a particular plan or whether to refine estimates through further computation or sensing.

When presented with a new task, the planner generates abstract plans for accomplishing the new and existing tasks. A sensitivity analysis identifies which of these plans are potentially optimal and non-dominated. Dominated and never-optimal plans are discarded. The sensitivity analysis also identifies which estimates the choice between plans is most sensitive to. Estimates that affect all plans more or less equally need not be refined. For instance, the occurrence of an earthquake may adversely affect all plans equally.

Determining the probability of an earthquake more exactly would not help in selecting between plans. Other factors may have differing affects. For instance, the likelihood of rain would help to choose between a plan to walk and a plan to drive somewhere. The sensitivity of a plan to particular estimates can also suggest ways of making the plan more robust. For instance, carrying an umbrella helps to reduce sensitivity to the likelihood of rain for the plan to walk.

When there are a number of plans that are potentially optimal and non-dominated and when the potential opportunity cost of selecting the wrong plan is significant, the meta-level controller directs the efforts of the planner to refine critical estimates. Estimates of resource use and action times can be improved by elaborating abstract operators into more operational operators or by simulated execution. Other object level estimates can be refined by adding more sensing to the plan or by additional computation using techniques such as temporal projection (Hanks 1990). Estimating computation time for complex planners is problematic. Further research is needed to determine how to best estimate and characterize expected plan improvement as a function of computation time.

Information from the sensitivity analysis and estimates of the cost of improving the current plan are used to make the tradeoff between the cost of delaying execution and the expected improvement in the plan for doing additional planning. Often systems that make this tradeoff ignore the fact that execution and planning can be overlapped in many situations. The DTA* algorithm is one example (Russell and Wefald 1991). In related work, I show how taking into account overlapping of planning and execution can improve performance (Goodwin 1994).

References

Richard Goodwin. Reasoning about when to start acting. In K. Hammond, editor, *Proceedings of the Second International Conference (AIPS94)*. Artificial Intelligence Planning Systems, June 1994.

Steve Hanks. Practical temporal projection. In *Proceedings, Eighth National Conference on Artificial Intelligence*. AAAI, July 1990.

Stuart Russell and Eric Wefald. *Do the Right Thing*. MIT Press, 1991.

The Crystallographer's Assistant

Vanathi Gopalakrishnan, Daniel Hennessy, Bruce Buchanan, Devika Subramanian*
Intelligent Systems Laboratory, University of Pittsburgh, Pittsburgh, PA 15260, USA
{vanathi, hennessy, buchanan, devika}@cs.pitt.edu

The only routinely used technique available today for obtaining the 3-D structure of a protein or DNA molecule is by X-ray diffracting a crystal of the macromolecule. The rate limiting step in structure determination is the process of growing a crystal of the macromolecule. This process is not very well understood, and can take a few weeks to several years. Crystallographers, therefore, are in great need of tools to aid them in the process of designing and performing experiments. There is a great deal of experiential data in this domain, in the form of scientific notebooks with graphical and textual representations of previous experiments.

We are in the process of collecting, analyzing and applying the knowledge available in this domain in order to design and develop the Crystallographer's Assistant (CA). The CA is an intelligent electronic assistant that will: help crystallographers record and maintain experimental context, offer suggestions as to experimental conditions that are likely to be successful for the current experiment (based on previously recorded successes and failures), and provide rationale for explaining failures (based upon theories that capture the significant relationships that exist in the data).

A set of about twenty-five parameters (e.g., pH, temperature) have been identified that affect the process of macromolecular crystallization[1]. Crystallographers systematically search this parameter space to find the optimal set of conditions under which a well diffracting crystal of the new macromolecule can be obtained. There exists only a preliminary understanding of the relationships that exist between two or more of these parameters.

In order to convince ourselves that it is indeed possible to find relationships among the various crystallization parameters from existing data, we have applied RL[2], an inductive learning program, to the data available in the Biological Macromolecular Crystallization Database (BMCD). The data in the BMCD is sparse, noisy, and represents only successful instances of crystal growth. In spite of the noisy nature of the data, RL has produced rules (and correlations) which have been considered significant by our domain experts. The limiting factor in the BMCD data is its lack of negative instances.

The Crystallographer's Assistant is based upon a case-based reasoning approach, and involves, as a first step, creating a database (from both existing experiment notebooks and on-going experiments), of about 1000 examples of crystallography experiments. These examples will provide us with both successful as well as failed experiments, and will be used both by RL as well as the case-based reasoner. Given the significant complexity and weak theory of the relationships between the features of the experiments, a case-based approach is being taken for similarity assessment. Experiential data concerning how the domain experts define pairs of cases to be similar and different will be used to guide the indexing and selection of cases. The result will be an experimenter's assistant which, given the results of the latest set of experiments, will remind the user of previous experiments with similar conditions and make suggestions based upon what was done in both cases of success and failure.

The results from applying RL to the BMCD data have yielded possibly significant new empirical relationships, as evaluated by our expert crystallographers. We are now in the process of applying RL to the newly created database of crystallography experiments. The next step will be to make the database available to researchers at other sites in order to expand the database to hold 100,000 or more cases. This will provide sufficient data to develop a more complete domain theory with the aid of modeling and machine learning techniques.

*Dr. Subramanian is affiliated with Department of Computer Science, Cornell University, Ithaca, NY 14853. This research is supported in part by funds from the W.M. Keck Center for Advanced Training in Computational Biology at the University of Pittsburgh, Carnegie Mellon University and the Pittsburgh Supercomputing Center.

References

[1] McPherson, A. Current approaches to macromolecular crystallization. *European Journal of Biochemistry*, 189 (1990), 1-23.

[2] Clearwater, S., and Provost, F. 1990. RL4: A Tool for Knowledge-Based Induction. In Proceedings of the Second International IEEE Conference on Tools for Artificial Intelligence, 24-30. IEEE CS. Press.

Time-Critical Scheduling in Stochastic Domains

Lloyd Greenwald   **Thomas Dean**
Department of Computer Science
Brown University, Box 1910, Providence, RI 02912
lgg@cs.brown.edu   tld@cs.brown.edu

In this work we look at extending the work of (Dean *et al.* 1993) to handle more complicated scheduling problems in which the sources of complexity stem not only from large state spaces but from large action spaces as well. In these problems it is no longer tractable to compute optimal policies for restricted state spaces via policy iteration. We, instead, borrow from operations research in applying bottleneck-centered scheduling heuristics (Adams *et al.* 1988). Additionally, our techniques draw from the work of (Drummond and Bresina 1990).

Consider the problem of scheduling planes and gates at a busy airport. A stochastic process describes the arrival of planes at the airport and is affected by uncontrollable events such as weather. Stochastic processes also govern the processing requirements for unloading and loading passengers at arrival and departure gates. Deadlines for theses operations are determined by pre-specified desired arrival and departure times. Other sources of uncertainty include gate closings. The optimization problem is to assign planes to gates at each time step to minimize some global measure of tardiness. In any given state there is, in general, one action for every possible assignment of planes to gates.

The work of (Dean *et al.* 1993) introduces a general approach to planning and scheduling in stochastic domains in which a two-phase iterative procedure is employed. The first phase determines a restricted subset of the state space on which to focus (called the *envelope*) and the second phase constructs a policy for this envelope. Deliberation scheduling is employed to allocate on-line computation time between the anytime algorithms that make up each phase and across iterations of both phases. This approach directly addresses uncertainty by modeling the environment as a stochastic automaton and constructing policies to account for alternative trajectories reachable from a given start state. Restricting policy construction to a given envelope addresses the large state space issue.

Our work addresses the additional combinatorial explosion of large action spaces by focusing processing on *time windows* rather than envelopes of specific states, and by selectively exploring the space described by the window rather than exhaustively exploring the space via policy iteration. While planning domains such as robot navigation may adhere to a restricted neighborhood of states over time, states solved for prior time steps in scheduling domains with large action spaces do not remain relevant as the process progresses. Additionally, alternative actions from any given state lead to disjoint state spaces with little chance that the trajectories will merge on a common envelope of specific states. By partitioning the state space along the time dimension we capture the appropriate context in scheduling domains.

We generate policies by selectively exploring the state space described by the time window. For any given state we use dispatch scheduling rules such as earliest deadline first to select an action. We then employ Monte Carlo simulation on a stochastic model of the domain to determine the most probable reachable states. This process is repeated for a fixed amount of time to determine a partial policy. A second phase attempts to improve the expected value of the policy by detecting bottlenecks and constraining associated actions in further iterations of policy generation. By using greedy dispatch rules on unconstrained actions, we avoid exhaustively searching large action spaces. This procedure is augmented with default reflexes for low probability states not explicitly simulated. We employ deliberation scheduling to allocate on-line processing time across time windows and phases based on anticipated quality-time tradeoffs.

References

Adams, J.; Balas, E.; and Zawack, D. 1988. The shifting bottleneck procedure for job shop scheduling. *Management Science* 34(3):391–401.

Dean, Thomas; Kaelbling, Leslie; Kirman, Jak; and Nicholson, Ann 1993. Planning with deadlines in stochastic domains. In *Proceedings AAAI-93*. AAAI. 574–579.

Drummond, Mark and Bresina, John 1990. Anytime synthetic projection: Maximizing the probability of goal satisfaction. In *Proceedings AAAI-90*. AAAI. 138–144.

Planning for Component-based Configurations*

Gail Haddock

University of Texas - Arlington
Department of Computer Science and Engineering
416 Yates, Arlington, Texas 76019
haddock@csr.uta.edu

Abstract

The Scenario-based Engineering Process (SEP) is a novel approach to developing complex systems (Haddock & Harbison 1994). SEP builds new application systems through a selection process that groups primitive components into application specific components. The selection of primitive components and the construction of interfaces among components in an application system is currently a tedious manual undertaking. The automation of this process will require a configuration system that can support the complex interactions of the components, the dynamic requirements of users, and the capabilities of providing multiple viewpoints and managing extensive domains.

The University of Michigan Procedural Reasoning System, UM-PRS (Lee et al. 1993), is a reactive reasoning and planning system based on PRS (Georgeff & Lansky, 1990). UM-PRS is currently being used in the autonomous vehicle domain. Its ability to continually consider the real-time dynamic environment and access plans accordingly fits well into military applications, where plans have already been generated in the form of standing operating procedures and reactions to the quickly changing environment are paramount. Our SEP domain does not require the hard real-time speed of a reactionary system. However, much of the UM-PRS architecture maps readily to the configuration problem in the SEP domain.

The Scenario-based Engineering Procedural Reasoning System, SEPRS, will use the architecture of UM-PRS to implement a configuration system for SEP. Primitive components will take the place of plans and will be selected according to the application requirements and the application architecture in progress.

The interpreter will use the application requirements as goals to satisfy by accessing the primitive components. Components previously selected for an application architecture will be in the in-process area. They are accessed by the interpreter to determine which goals are not yet satisfied. The interpreter will activate relevant primitive components that are maintained by the intention structure. The intention structure will release the chosen primitive component to the component integrator. The

component integrator will employ Adaptive Semantic Language techniques (Hannon 1994) to build the interfaces and messages necessary for adding the primitive component to the application architecture. The grouping of primitive components into components remains a manual task, as this grouping can be done from a variety of viewpoints. For example, some groupings may be done solely for marketing purposes. The environment area of UM-PRS then becomes our system engineer. The system engineer's modifications are added back to SEPRS through a component monitor, who sends the component determinations to the in-progress area, thus completing the cycle.

Since requirements are continually accessed by the interpreter, user modifications can be interjected at any point in the architecture creation cycle. These modifications may immediately cause primitive components to be deselected and their interfaces disconnected, which may then require an extensive reconfiguration of the architecture. SEPRS also supports the expansion of primitive components. As new technologies are invented that result in new components, those components can be added to the system.

We are building a configuration system, SEPRS, for component-based architecture methodologies by adapting the UM-PRS reactive planning system. We expect it to fit well in our system engineering environment that includes scenario modeling, object-oriented analysis and design, and simulation systems.

References

Georgeff, M. and Lansky, A. 1990. Reactive Reasoning and Planning. Allen, J., Hendler, J., and Tate, A., eds., *Readings in Planning*, San Mateo, Ca: Morgan Kaufmann.

Haddock, G., and Harbison, K. 1994. From Scenarios to Domain Models; Processes and Representations. In Proceeding of Knowledge-based Artificial Intelligence Systems in Aerospace and Industry. Bellingham, Wa: International Society for Optical Engineering.

Hannon, C. 1994. An n-Towers Model for the Knowledge Representation of an Adaptive Semantic Language. Master's thesis, Dept. of Computer Science Engineering, University of Texas at Arlington.

Lee, J., Huber, M., Durfee, E., Kenny, P. 1993. UM-PRS: An Implementation of the Procedural Reasoning System. Technical Report, University of Michigan.

*This research has been partially supported by the National Science Foundation, the National Center for Manufacturing Sciences, the Advanced Research Projects Agency and the State of Texas.

The Epistemology of Physical System Modeling

Kyungsook Han and **Andrew Gelsey**
Department of Computer Science
Rutgers University
New Brunswick, NJ 08903
{kshan, gelsey}@cs.rutgers.edu

Modeling and simulation have been typically pursued in isolation. When a model of a complex system is reported in the literature, there is a considerable emphasis on the end result, the model. On the other hand, many works on simulation assume the existence of models, and focus on developing representations and reasoning about the models in the representations. However, not every physical system has its models ready to use for problem-solving tasks and constructing adequate models is not trivial. Choosing a simulation method is also dependent on the kinds of models available, the creation of which in turn depends on the knowledge available and its representation. A model of a physical system is normally created by the person studying the system with considerable time and effort spent. But a hand-crafted model is often error-prone and difficult to modify to solve a similar problem about other physical systems.

Our work is motivated by three goals: (1) examining the process of model-building and simulation, as well as the types of knowledge and their representation required to perform the process or to evaluate the process and its results; (2) automating the process of model-building and simulation to reason about moving objects; and (3) making the modeling process as general as possible so that common knowledge can be shared and reused instead of being duplicated.

Consider, for example, a spring with one end attached to a fixed point and the other end attached to a block. If the block is pulled from its equilibrium position and released, it shows oscillatory motion on a straight line. This harmonic oscillator is a common textbook example which is frequently used in qualitative physics research. It is well known that the oscillator has one degree of freedom, i.e., displacement of the block from its equilibrium position. However, if the block is pulled *and* rotated from its equilibrium position before being released, predicting its behavior is not as simple as before. Is the motion going to be still oscillatory? More interesting questions include: (1) What if a spring is attached to a corner of a block instead of the center of the face? (2) What if a block attached to a spring is put in arbitrary position and orientation before being released? (3) What if two blocks are connected by a spring? (4) What if multiple blocks connected by multiple springs are put in arbitrary positions and orientations?

Different forms of these problems require spatial reasoning to formulate equations of motion, in particular the ability to reason explicitly about vector quantities and moving frames of reference. Many qualitative physics approaches which can solve the linear harmonic oscillator problem cannot handle the more complex problems we describe above because they lack this spatial reasoning ability.

We have developed an automated modeling and simulation system called ORACLE. Knowledge is represented with general model fragments in a purely declarative, neutral, algorithm-independent form; most of the knowledge is just the same fundamental equations that appear in any standard text on the subject, with their implied semantics of vectors and frames of references. Starting with the basic, simple knowledge, ORACLE generates a powerful model and simulator which can be used to predict the motion of a physical system with multiple moving objects in arbitrary configurations. Evidence of the generality of the ORACLE approach across different types of physical systems was demonstrated by the experimental results of testing it on spring-block systems in a variety of configurations, sailboats in fluids, and composite objects of rigid bodies. ORACLE can also model many other types of physical systems with no or minor changes, including multiple rigid bodies connected by springs, propeller-driven airplanes, and spinning balls. This extensibility to a broad class of physical systems is possible for several reasons. First, knowledge is represented in a general form and instantiated later for particular situations so that common knowledge can be shared and reused. Second, instead of using a special purpose method intended to handle a certain class of physical systems only, a general method is used to construct and simulate models; model fragments relevant to a physical system being modeled are identified and composed to formulate a model, and the model is applied to solve a problem.

Testing a KBS using a conceptual model

Corinne Haouche
DIAM-SIM & LAMSADE, Paris IX Dauphine
91, Bd de l'Hôpital – 75634 Paris Cedex 13 – France
Tel: 45 83 67 28 - Fax: 45 86 56 85 - haouche@biomath.jussieu.fr

Abstract

We propose a KBS testing procedure that uses a KADS conceptual model (CM). The set of *Valid Inference Paths* is derived from the inference structure, and, a "high level" trace, representing the *Current Inference Path*, is built using the links established between the CM and the KBS. The comparison of this trace to the VIP can lead to modify either the code or the CM.

Introduction

The lack of specifications while developing a knowledge-based system (KBS) makes the KBS validation a hard task. We investigate the use of an *inference structure*, which is part of a KADS (Knowledge Acquisition and Design Support (Wielinga, Schreiber, & Breuker 1992)) conceptual model (CM), as a set of specifications in order to conduct parts of the validation process. An inference structure describes existing links between *roles* through *inferences*. A role is a class of concepts that have the same behavior in a given problem. An inference is a reasoning step. We focus on **testing the KBS behavior** using this structure. The white box approach to test KBS uses a structural description of the system under test (e.g. (Preece *et al.* 1993)) and studies whether the test cases permit to "cover" all the parts of a KB. Our approach is close to this approach in the sense that we use a description of the KBS, but it is different regarding the nature of this description and the way we use it. In fact, we use an implemented representation of the inference structure of a KADS CM of a KBS, to validate this KBS. We assume that this CM is valid but that it can still evolve. The set of *Valid Inference Paths* is derived from the inference structure and, a "high level" trace, representing the *Current Inference Path*, is built using the links established between the CM and the KBS. The comparison of this trace to the VIP can lead to modify either the code or the CM.

Testing with an inference structure

We describe hereafter our procedure to use the inference structure during the testing phase. All the infer-ence paths between initial roles, *ie* roles that are not outputs for any inference, and final roles, *ie* roles that either are not inputs for an inference or are specified as final roles, are derived automatically. These paths are correct from a syntactic point of view. Clearly, that means that each time an inference follows another, it is added to the path that is being built. However, these paths have to be checked for semantic correctness. This step is done in cooperation with the domain expert and provides the VIP.

- All the *Valid Inference Paths* (VIP) are derived from the inference structure.
- When the KBS is used on a set of data, the links between the code and the inference structure are used to build the *Current Inference Path* (CIP).
- *If* CIP $\in$ VIP *then* the process is applied on another data case, *else* either the KBS or the CM have to be modified by the expert and the knowledge engineer.

Discussion and perspectives

This procedure is currently being tested on a real world KBS for which we developed a CM (Haouche 1993). Testing a system using its CM becomes easier because, on the one hand, we have access to a trace which is easily understood, and on the other hand, the errors made are more easily localized thanks to the explicited links that are established between the CM and the KBS. Furthermore, we think that this CM is valuable to address the classical "coverage" problems and to provide criteria to stop the testing process.

References

Haouche, C. 1993. Using a Conceptual Model to Validate KBSs. In *Proceedings of the European Workshop on Validation and Verification of KBSs*.

Preece, A.; Chander, P.; Grossner, C.; and Radhakrishnan, T. 1993. Modeling rule base structure for expert system quality assurance. In *IJCAI93 Workshop on Validation of KBSs*.

Wielinga, B.; Schreiber, A.; and Breuker, J. 1992. KADS: a modeling approach to knowledge engineering. *Knowledge Acquisition* 4(1):5–53.

A Dynamic Organization in Distributed Constraint Satisfaction

Katsutoshi Hirayama, Seiji Yamada, and Jun'ichi Toyoda

ISIR, Osaka University,
8-1 Mihogaoka,
Ibaraki, Osaka 567, JAPAN
{hirayama, yamada, toyoda}@ai.sanken.osaka-u.ac.jp

Abstract

We present a novel dynamic organization to solve DC-SP(Distributed Constraint Satisfaction Problem). DCSP provides a formal framework for studying cooperative distributed problem solving[Yokoo 92]. To solve DCSP, we have developed a simple algorithm using iterative improvement. This technique has had great success on certain CSP(Constraint Satisfaction Problems)[Minton 90][Selman 92]. In our algorithm each agent performs iterative improvement and also plural agents can do in parallel. However, one drawback of this technique is the possibility of getting caught in local minima(which are defined specifically in our algorithm). LMO is a technique for escaping from local minima. It is summarized as follows:

When an agent(A1) gets caught in a local minimum,
(*step 1*) A1 sends its CSP(variables, domains and constraints) to an agent(A2). A1 selects A2 such that it shares violated constraints at that time. Ties are broken randomly.
(*step 2*) A2 puts its CSP and A1's CSP together and searches for all possible assignments with simple backtracking. After that, A2 performs iterative improvement.

Besides escaping from local minima, LMO prevents agents from getting caught in the same local minima as before. Therefore our algorithm for DCSP is complete.

LMO is also the algorithm for a dynamic organization since agents reassign the responsibilities of solving CSP based on a developing view of the problem. As a dynamic organization, LMO is characterized by grouping in response to the conflicts(i.e., local minima) that arise during problem solving. This produces the effect that the organization with LMO(we call it the LMO organization) makes groups depending on the number of local minima. That is, when there are few local minima in a problem, the LMO organization solves it in a distributed manner, and when there are many, it does in a centralized manner.

To evaluate the performance of LMO, we have compared the LMO organization with the following ones.

1. Distributed organization: This organization always solves problems in a distributed manner. In this organization each agent performs iterative improvement. When one agent gets caught in a local minimum, all agents change their assignments randomly and continue to perform iterative improvement.
2. Centralized organization: This organization always solves problems in a centralized manner. In this organization, to begin with agents have to solve the leader election problem. Then all agents(but the leader) send their CSP to the leader. Finally the leader searches for one solution with simple backtraking(the method used in LMO). Note that agents solve the leader election problem and send their CSP regardless of the possibility of distributed problem solving.

In our experiments, for the problems with few local minima the LMO organization solves them faster than the Centralized organization(because the cost of leader election exceeds that of distributed problem solving), and for the problems with many local minima it solves them faster than the Distributed organization.

Finally, in LMO, we use backtracking as a method to help iterative improvement. We believe that this approach will be applicable to non-distributed CSP. That will be our future work.

References

[Minton 90] Minton, S., Johnston, M. D., Philips, A. B. and Laird, P., Solving Large-Scale Constraint Satisfaction and Scheduling Problems Using a Heuristic Repair Method, *AAAI-90*, 17-24, 1990.

[Selman 92] Selman, B., Levesque, H. and Mitchell, D., A New Method for Solving Hard Satisfiability Problems, *AAAI-92*, 440-446, 1992.

[Yokoo 92] Yokoo, M., Durfee, E. H., Ishida, T. and Kuwabara, K., Distributed Constraint Satisfaction for Formalizing Distributed Problem Solving, *12th IEEE International Conference on Distributed Computing Systems*, 614-621, 1992.

Tractable Anytime Temporal Constraint Propagation

Louis J Hoebel
Department of Computer Science
University of Rochester
Rochester, NY 14627
hoebel@cs.rochester.edu

1 Introduction

A major concern when reasoning about time in artificial intelligence problems is computational tractability. We present a method for applying temporal reasoners to large scale dynamic problems. We present a partitioning of the temporal database and means of constraint propagation that presents an efficient approach for producing tractable systems. Our goal is not to enhance underlying reasoners but to develop mechanisms by which reasoning about time can be practically applied to certain problems. Tractable computation is the basic consideration.

In reasoning with time a relation exists between expressibility and tractability. In real and complex problems, increased expressibility requires tractability to be more than a theoretical concern [Allen92]. Approaches to intractability include restricted expressiveness and using fragments of an algebra; or using organizational and heuristic approaches for a particular application. We provide a method for temporal reasoners to be invoked on large sets of dynamic assertions and constraints while providing an adequate inference mechanism within the computational constraints of the class of problems of interest.

Our approach to controlling computation comes from the conjecture that time and temporal relations have a structure that can be exploited. The intimate relation of time and space also provide a basis for the heuristic propagation of constraints. Assertions and constraints may have limited, although not necessarily only local, effects. In dynamic problems it is infeasible and perhaps unnecessary to compute a complete minimal network upon every invocation of a temporal reasoner.

2 Approach

We provide a framework and mechanisms for controlling computation costs. The mechanisms are based on the heuristic propagation and compiling of constraints. The framework is based on a reference hierarchy and partitioning of time and space. No restrictive assumption is made on the underlying representation or reasoner. In addition to tractability, the solution developed is *anytime* [Dean&Boddy 88] and as *theoretically complete* as the underlying temporal reasoner permits. The trade-off required is a necessary *incompleteness* at anytime and a relaxed or bounded definition of *consistency*.

The approach taken here is to provide a flexible system that can operate: in a trivial manner of only recording constraints; in an efficient manner, considering only those constraints necessary; and, as an anytime algorithm. This last method of operation is required as efficient (near optimal) may still be intractable in practice.

This approach includes developing a structure of reference hierarchy intervals based on a partitioning of time; and by analogy applicable to spatial data also. This approach and its pitfalls has been suggested in [Allen83]. In order to preserve the hierarchy we create non-strict reference intervals, removing restrictions on intervals being strictly during a reference interval

Using the reference hierarchy structure, an anytime algorithm is implemented, partitioning inference and restricting the size of any call to the core inference procedure. This procedure is called on individual reference intervals. The procedure is restricted to operate on the constraints and intervals of a single reference interval at any one time. Limiting the size of reference intervals and associated inference computation time provides halting and resumption for anytime performance.

3 Results

We implement propagation and inference schemes using an expressive temporal reasoner, MATS [MATS90], that provides tractable reasoning and anytime operation. We provide methods for control of propagation and inference based locality and on spatio-temporal relations.

Application to a small problem has yielded encouraging results, exhibiting locality of effects. The implementation, with caching and propagation overhead and repeatedly invoking the reasoner on smaller interval sets, is nearly as fast as a single batch application. MATS does not scale well, while our approach has been developed for scaling to large, dynamic problems.

4 References

[Allen83] J.F. Allen. "Maintaining Knowledge about Temporal Intervals" *Communications of the ACM,*26(1)

[Allen92] J. F. Allen "Getting Serious about Simultaneous Actions" *1st Inter. Planning Conf.*, Silver Springs MD

[Dean &Boddy 88]T. Dean, M. Boddy "An Analysis of Time -Dependent Planning" *Proc. AAAI-88* Seattle WA

[MATS91] H. Kautz "MATS Documentation" *AT&T Bell Laboratories*, 1991

Processing Pragmatics for Computer-Assisted Language Instruction

Keiko Horiguchi
Computational Linguistics Program and Center for Machine Translation
Carnegie Mellon University
5000 Forbes Avenue
Pittsburgh, PA 15213
keiko@cs.cmu.edu

Computer-assisted language instruction systems that only perform syntactic processing of input sentences are not able to offer advice on pragmatic aspects of language use, and they cannot handle the variability generally afforded by natural languages to express a given propositional content.

This paper describes a solution to this problem implemented as an extension to the existing Japanese tutorial system ALICE-chan (Evans & Levin 1993). We designed the *p-structure* to represent pragmatic information as well as the propositional content of a sentence. The pragmatic content is encoded in terms of the speech situation, the speaker's attitude toward the addressee, and the felicity conditions for the intended speech act. Linguistic features that express the speaker's uncertainty are interpreted as reducing factors that weaken felicity conditions of the intended speech act of the sentence.

We implemented a p-structure mapping program that generates p-structures from syntactic structures. As an example, the p-structure for the sentence *Tegami-wo kaite itadakenai darou ka to omou n desu ga* ("I wonder if you might be able to write a letter for me") is shown below.

SPEECH-ACT	requesting-action		
FEATURE	receive-favor-potential		
ACTION	ACTEE		手紙を (tegami-wo)
			SENSE "letter"
	書いて (kaite)		
	SENSE "write"		
BELIEF			
DESIRE			
EXPECTATION	FEATURE		receive-favor-potential
	REDUCING-FACTOR		
	EXTENDED-		
	PREDICATE		んです (n desu)
	CONJUNCTION		が (ga)
	THINK		と思う (toomou)
	NEGATIVE		+
	TENTATIVE		だろう (darou)
	INTERROGATIVE		か (ka)
	FAVOR		頂けない
			(itadakenai)
PLACEMENT-			
OF-ADDRESEE	higher		
SPEECH-			
SITUATION	formal		

The system stores the pragmatic analysis template. The error analysis matcher compares this template with the student input. It then reports any features that are missing or different, as well as error features that are inserted during the analysis. Based on this, the error matcher then formulates appropriate feedback. For example, if a student used the verb *sashiagerarenai* instead of *itadakenai* for the above sentence, the system would respond as follows:

```
You seem to have used the giving verb with
the wrong direction.  You should have used
the verb with inward direction.
```

Our computer assisted instruction system benefits from adopting *p-structure* in two ways. First, the system allows students flexibility for expressing propositions in different ways, since the system can accept similar information expressed in different structures. Second, the system is able to detect errors and give finer feedback on pragmatic usage of the language. Students can now express the required proposition more freely without burdening the teacher with the task of typing in all possible correct answers and incorrect answers with appropriate feedback.

Acknowledgments: I am grateful to Lori Levin, David Evans, Martin Thurn, and Steve Handerson for their help and guidance.

References

Allen, J. F. 1983. Recognizing intentions from natural language utterances. In Brady, M., and Berwick, R., eds., *Computational Models of Discourse*, 107–166. Cambridge, MA: MIT Press.

Evans, D. A., and Levin, L. S. 1993. Intelligent computer-asisted language learning theory and practice in ALICE-chan. In *Army Research Institute Workshop on Advanced Technologies for Language Learning*.

Kogure, K.; Iida, H.; Yoshimoto, K.; Maeda, H.; Kume, M.; and Kato, S. 1988. A method of analyzing Japanese speech act types. In *Prceedings of the 2nd International Conference on Theoretical Methodological Issues in Machine Translation of Natural Languages*.

Generating Rhythms with Genetic Algorithms

Damon Horowitz

MIT Media Laboratory, 20 Ames St. E15-488, Cambridge, MA 02139
damon@media.mit.edu

Abstract

My system uses an interactive genetic algorithm to learn a user's criteria for the task of generating musical rhythms. Interactive genetic algorithms (Smith 91) are well suited to solving this problem because they allow for a user to simply execute fitness functions (that is, to choose which rhythms or features of rhythms he likes), without necessarily understanding the details or parameters of these functions. As the system learns (develops an increasingly accurate model of the function which represents the user's criteria), the quality of the rhythms it produces improves to suit the user's taste. This approach is largely motivated by Richard Dawkins, who succinctly summarizes the attraction of IGAs for artistic endeavors in stating: "Effective searching procedures become, when the search space is sufficiently large, indistinguishable from true creativity" (Dawkins 86).

In the context of this project, rhythms are one measure long sequences of notes and rests occurring on natural pulse subdivisions of a beat; I only deal with a specific subset of the enormous class of rhythms, in order to provide a well-defined domain for the application of the learning algorithm. The benefit of this reduction of the domain is that a rhythm phenotype can now be viewed as a simple vector. Thus, the set of rhythms satisfying the user's criteria could be represented by a Boolean formula. I actually use a slightly more complex representation for the rhythm genotype, motivated by the benefits of using a diploid genetic structure, consisting of several short array templates; the order of the layering of these templates in creating the phenotype effectively determines the dominance hierarchy between the genes.

The simplest mode of interaction is for the user to playback each of the rhythms in a randomly generated population, and then subjectively assign them fitness values based upon their satisfaction of his criteria. The system then uses standard GA selection (with fitness scaling), reproduction (with crossover monitors), and mutation operators. In order to deal with the difficulties resultant from the subjectivity and variability of the user's criteria, there are also several objective functions with which the system can automatically evolve generations of rhythms: syncopation, density, downbeat, beat repetition, cross rhythm, and cluster functions are currently included. Each of these functions represents an axis in a feature space which is useful for distinguishing rhythms. While these are only a few of the many possible objective functions that could be implemented, they provide a richset of possibilities with which to begin exploring. The user can specify the ideal target value for each of these fitness functions, and also their relative importance (weighting of coefficients) in determining the overall fitness of a rhythm. The system then automatically evolves the indicated number of successive generations, using the objective fitness values to determine selection.

The system also makes use of a meta-level genetic algorithm designed to evolve populations of parameters (target values and weights) to the objective fitness functions defined above. This is motivated by the research done in the application of genetic algorithms to the k-nearest-neighbor technique of classification (Punch et al. 93); each meta-level individual represents a warping of K-NN space, such that the fitness of each individual is determined by how well its warping of the feature-space helps to discriminate useful features, and thus correctly perform classifications. Evolving populations of meta-individuals allows a user to quickly reduce the search space by subjective evaluation of the rhythms generated by the meta-individuals, without having to directly specify values for the objective functions.

This combination of methods proves to be a powerful hybrid approach to the subjectivity problem, one which allows for greater coverage of the search space than would have been possible ordinarily using a small population (which is necessitated by most IGA's, and is particularly important when dealing with sequential acoustic data), and more efficient convergence on a satisficing solution. The system is able to converge on near-optimal solutions (acceptable to test users) after about fifty user-evaluations of rhythms. While the GA itself is mechanically quite simple, it is important to note that the implementation of appropriate fitness functions is difficult, and largely determines the musicality of the output. The major future improvement will involve adding the capacity for the system to learn to design its own fitness functions to represent features characteristic of rhythms selected by users in past sessions.

References

Dawkins, R. 1986. "Accumulating Small Change," in The BlindWatchmaker. New York: W.W. Norton and Co.

Punch, W. et al 1993. Further Research on Feature Selection and Classification Using Genetic Algotihms. In Proceedings of the Fifth International Conference on Genetic Algorithms.

Smith, J. 1991. Designing Biomorphs with an Interactive Genetic Algorithm. In Proceedings of the Fourth International Conference on Genetic Algorithms.

The Automated Mapping of Plans for Plan Recognition[*]

Marcus J. Huber   Edmund H. Durfee   Michael P. Wellman

Artificial Intelligence Laboratory
The University of Michigan
1101 Beal Avenue
Ann Arbor, Michigan 48109-2110
{ marcush, durfee, wellman } @engin.umich.edu

To coordinate with other agents in its an environment, an agent needs models of what the other agents are trying to do. When communication is impossible or expensive, this information must be acquired indirectly via plan recognition. Typical approaches to plan recognition start with specification of the possible plans the other agents may be following and develop special techniques for discriminating among the possibilities. These structures are not the direct nor derived output of a planning system. Prior work has not yet addressed the problem of how the plan recognition structures are (or could be) derived from executable plans as generated by planning systems. Furthermore, concerns about building models of agents' actions in all possible worlds lead to a desire for dynamically constructing belief network models for situation-specific plan recognition activities. As a step in this direction, we have developed and implemented methods that take plans, as generated by a planning system, and creates a belief network model in support of the plan recognition task.

We start from a language designed for plan specification, PRS (Ingrand, Georgeff, & Rao 1992).[1] From a PRS plan, we generate a belief network model that directly serves plan recognition by relating potential observations to the candidate plans. Our methods handle a large variety of plan structures such as conditional branching, subgoaling, and alternative goals. Furthermore, our application domain is coordinated autonomous robotic teams, where sensor-based observations are inherently uncertain. The methodology we have developed handles this uncertainty through explicit modeling, something not necessary in other plan recognition domains (Charniak & Goldman 1993; Goodman & Litman 1990) where observations are certain. An example of a belief network generated by the mapping methods from a set of simple plans for performing a "bounding-overwatch" surveillance task can be seen in Figure 1. Results from early experiments have shown the dynamically constructed belief

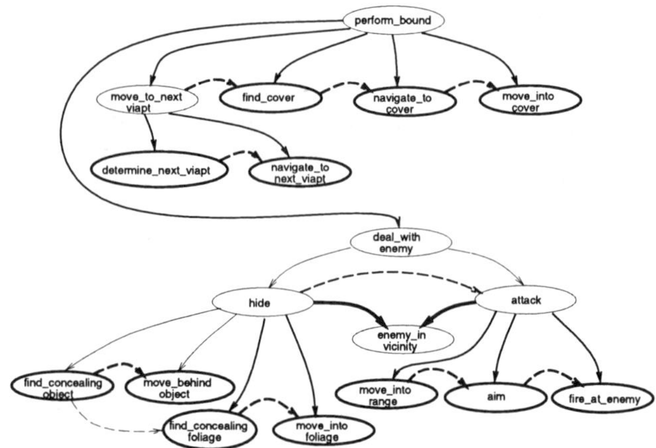

Figure 1: Belief network representation.

network to be a useful mechanism for inferring the observed agent's plans based solely upon observations of its actions.

This research is novel in that the plan recognition model is derived *directly* from a plan as represented by a planning system, instead of being built from a specially constructed database. Our explicit modeling of the uncertainty associated with observations is also unique. Our future research includes extending the methodolgy to incorporate iteration and recursion and in more extensive evaluation of the utility of using plan recognition for coordination of multiple robotic agents.

References

Charniak, E., and Goldman, R. P. 1993. A Bayesian model of plan recognition. *Artificial Intelligence* 64(1):53–79.

Goodman, B. A., and Litman, D. J. 1990. Plan recognition for intelligent interfaces. In *Proceedings of the Sixth Conference on Artificial Intelligence Applications*, 297–303.

Ingrand, F.; Georgeff, M.; and Rao, A. 1992. An architecture for real-time reasoning and system control. *IEEE Expert* 7(6):34–44.

[*]This research was sponsored in part by NSF grant IRI-9158473, and by DARPA contract DAAE-07-92-C-R012.

[1]Although any plan language would serve as well.

Preliminary Studies in Agent Design in Simulated Environments

Scott B. Hunter
Department of Computer Science
Cornell University
Ithaca, NY 14853
E-mail: hunter@cs.cornell.edu

It is known that, in general, the point along the purely-reactive/classical-planning axis of the controller spectrum that is most appropriate for a particular environment/task (E/T) pair will be determined by characteristics of the environment, the agent's perceptual and effectual capabilities, and the task. Instead of proposing another hybrid architecture, we want to determine criteria for determining which architectural compromise is best suited for a given E/T. Our goal is to understand relationships between E/T pairs and the agent architecture, so that we can predict the performance of the architecture under parametric variations of the environment and/or the architecture. This is a first step toward constructing methods for automatic synthesis of agents as in (Ros89).

Our example of a domain where the choice of architectural basis is not so clear is the game of XChomp (programmed by Jerry J. Shekhel), a close relative of the commercial game PacMan. This domain allows for easy change of parameters to simulate a number of discrete combinatorial problem domains.

Interesting characteristics of the game that make it different from the E/Ts considered in (AC87), (Bro86), (Cha91), (Sch87) among others, are:

There are non-local tasks. By non-local, we refer to not only spatial and temporal extents, but also universal quantification of parameters of the task.

Hostile aspects of the environment may be temporarily made not only benign, but positive concrete goals; these conversions are under the control of the player. Classification of objects changes over time, complicating the decision of how to respond to such objects, as these are based on projections of possible futures.

There is not much flexibility with respect to movement. Not only is movement within this environment restricted to the four cardinal directions, but it is a maze, so that in most locations, only two of those four may be used. When the cost of making mistakes is high, the extra effort to get it right the first time is (possibly) justified.

There are multiple conflicting objectives. While having multiple objectives is not particularly novel, those in this environment have a nasty habit of pulling their acquisitions at cross purposes.

Any designer must answer the following questions:

On what informational basis does an agent make its action selection choice? What aspects of the world does it perform forward projection on, what aspects does it sense, and what is the map from external and internal state of the agent to an action (or sequence) that maximizes the objective function of the agent? We need to be able to construct a solution and justify it using methods other than pointing to the constructed solution as an existence proof. This follows in the spirit of work done in (Hor93) for a mobile robot.

To enable us to study these questions, we isolate a range of E/T combinations based on the XChomp game. We implement a range of controllers that exploit the information needed for "optimal" play and test their task performance experimentally. We then vary the performance requirements and environmental specifications in a form of perturbation analysis to determine how robust the agents are; and how to modify them to be effective in new situations.

In addition, starting from a very simplified version of this E/T, we are developing a theoretical basis upon which to justify the agents we develop. This basis is expected to not only be used in determining how an agent should behave, but also what a designer should not be concerned about.

References

P. Agre and D. Chapman. Pengi: an implementation of a theory of activity. In *Proceedings of AAAI-87*. Morgan Kaufmann, 1987.

R.A. Brooks. A robust layered control system for a mobile robot. *IEEE Journal of Robotics and Automation*, 2(1), 1986.

D. Chapman. *Vision, Instruction and Action.* PhD thesis, MIT AI Lab, 1991.

I. Horswill. Poly: A vision-based artificial agent. In *Proceedings of AAAI-93*. Morgan Kaufmann/MIT Press, 1993.

S.J. Rosenschein. Synthesizing information-tracking automata from environment descriptions. In *Proceedings of KR-89*. Morgan Kaufmann, 1989.

M.J. Schoppers. Universal plans for reactive robots in unpredictable domains. In *Proceedings of IJCAI-87*. Morgan Kaufmann, 1987.

Dempster-Shafer and Bayesian Networks for CAD-based Feature Extraction: A Comparative Investigation and Analysis

Qiang Ji, Michael M. Marefat, and Paul J. A. Lever*

Dept. of Electrical and Computer Engineering, and Dept. of Mining and Geological Engineering*
The University of Arizona
Tucson, Arizona 85721
qiangji@ece.arizona.edu

Introduction

Information pertaining to real world problems often contains noises and uncertainties. This has been a major challenge faced by the contemporary AI researchers. Of various paradigms developed for handing uncertainties, the Dempster-Shafer theory (DS) and the Bayesian Belief Networks (BBN) have received considerable attention in the AI community recently. They have been successfully applied to problems in medical diagnosis, decision-making, image understanding, machine vision, etc.. Despite their obvious success, blindly using them without understanding their limitations may result in computational difficulty and unsatisfying inference results. The aim of this paper is to analyze and compare the performance of the two paradigms in extracting manufacturing features from the solid model descriptions of objects. Such a comparison will serve to identify their strengths, weakness, and appropriate application domains.

Problem Domain and Formulation

A major difficulty faced by the previously proposed methods for feature extraction has been the interaction between features. Feature interaction introduces uncertainties to feature representation, making their recognition very difficult [Ji, 1993]. We propose to recognize interacting features by identifying a set of correct virtual links, based on generating and combining geometric and topological evidences.

A DS approach was developed in this research that can correctly identify multiple virtual links simultaneously by overcoming the mutual exclusiveness assumption. The approach constructed a frame of discernment consisting of the subsets of all potential virtual links. Domain-specific knowledge was used to prune the original frame to a manageable size. A key component of this approach is the *principle of association* we developed for interpreting evidences and for assigning bpas to proper hypothesis sets. Virtual links were determined through evidence aggregation. An approximate method was developed to reduce the evidence aggregation from exponential to linear time by replacing the newly-generated focal elements with their existing nearest supersets.

A hypothesis space consisting of subsets of potential virtual links was used to construct an initial BBN. The casual-consequence relationship between any two connected nodes was represented by the whole-part relationship. Heuristic knowledge was then applied to prune the initial network into a singly-connected BBN for effective belief propagation. To identify multiple virtual links, the belief revision algorithm [Pearl, 1988] was employed for belief propagation, resulting in an optimal state for each node in the network that best explained the observed evidences. Virtual links were subsequently determined from the optimal state of each hypothesis.

Comparison and Conclusion

The measures used for comparison include informational complexity, time complexity, and robustness. Informational complexity study reveals that BBNs require a complete probabilistic model to initiate an inference while DS can function under incomplete model. Furthermore, the auxiliary information required by BBNs may sometimes prove to be difficult and expensive to obtain. In time complexity, both mechanisms are NP-hard in general. While linear time may be achieved for special cases, approximate methods are normally employed for general cases. The robustness study indicates that BBNs tolerate large deviations in prior probability and link matrices. DS, on the other hand, is very sensitive to input data change and conflicting evidences.

This research concludes that while both mechanisms can overcome the mutual exclusiveness assumption to identify multiple virtual links, the BBNs are well suited to applications where probabilities are known or can be acquired, and where human subjective opinions are important. On the other hand, the DS theory is a good choice for applications where uncertainty is best thought of as being distributed in power sets, and where no prior knowledge is available. One disadvantage with DS is that it still stays in lifeless number manipulation while the BBNs use intuitively meaningful semantic networks. In certain fields however, both algorithms can be applied, and the qualities of the results often depend on the skill of the users in adapting the basic theories to their particular problems.

References

Q. Ji, 1993. Bayesian Methods for Machine Understanding of CAD Models. MS thesis, Dept. of Electrical and Computer Eng., Univ. of Arizona.
Pearl, J., 1988. *Probabilistic Reasoning in Intelligent System*, Morgan Kaufmann Publishers, INC.

Finding Multivariate Splits in Decision Trees Using Function Optimization

George H. John[*]
Computer Science Department
Stanford University
Stanford, CA 94305
gjohn@cs.Stanford.EDU

We present a new method for top-down induction of decision trees (TDIDT) with multivariate binary splits at the nodes. The primary contribution of this work is a new splitting criterion called soft entropy, which is continuous and differentiable with respect to the parameters of the splitting function. Using simple gradient descent to find multivariate splits and a novel pruning technique, our TDIDT-SEH (Soft Entropy Hyperplanes) algorithm is able to learn very small trees with better accuracy than competing learning algorithms on most datasets examined.

The process of finding a splitting function at a node of a decision tree is a search problem, and we choose to view it as unconstrained parametric function optimization over the space of hyperplane weight vectors $w \in R^n$. Our objective function is soft entropy, a new continuous approximation to the entropy measure (Quinlan 1986). Soft entropy was chosen for two reasons. First, it is well-established that *entropy* is a good splitting criterion (Buntine & Niblett 1992). Second, *softness* is important to get good generalization in continuous spaces, as shown in Figure 1. Related work is similar overall, but the OC1 algorithm of Murthy *et al.* (1993) uses entropy as a criterion, and Brodley and Utgoff (1992) describe algorithms using error, also a hard splitting criterion.

Figure 1: All four splits shown on the left have equivalent entropy and error. On the right we show the split found by minimizing soft entropy.

The overall learning algorithm is simply the standard TDIDT method (Quinlan 1986). To choose a split at a node, it uses gradient descent to find the hyperplane with minimal soft entropy. To prune the resulting tree, it uses a new pruning technique which

Dataset	Vote	Vote1	Monks2	Monks3
See	Buntine & Niblett		Thrun et al.	
#Train/Test	200/135	200/135	135/432	122/422
SEHpr	**98.5 (3)**	**94.8 (3)**	**100 (9)**	90.7 (3)
SEHp	**98.5 (3)**	90.4 (13)	**100 (9)**	91.2 (5)
SEH	96.3 (15)	85.9 (29)	**100 (9)**	93.8 (9)
OC1p*	95.6 (11)	92.6 (17)	97.9(5)	92.6 (3)
C4.5p*	97 (7)	92.6 (27)	75.9(39)	**100 (9)**
C4.5*	94.8 (12)	92.6 (33)	75.5 (135)	97.2 (17)

Table 1: Test set accuracy and number of nodes (in parentheses) in the induced decision tree for several datasets. "p" indicates use of pruning, "r" indicates re-filtering. "*" indicates several versions were run with different parameter settings, and the best results for each dataset are presented.

we call *iterative re-filtering*, a general regularization algorithm that we are investigating further.

Table 1 shows results on various datasets. SEH achieves the best test-set accuracy on all datasets except for Monks3, which was difficult because the algorithm pruned away four of the data points which turned out not to be noise. On the rest of the domains, SEH was able to achieve high accuracy using very small trees.

References

Brodley, C. E., and Utgoff, P. E. 1992. Multivariate versus univariate decision trees. Technical Report COINS TR 92-8, Department of Computer Science, University of Massachusetts, Amherst, MA, 01003.

Buntine, W., and Niblett, T. 1992. A further comparison of splitting rules for decision-tree induction. *Machine Learning* 8:75–85.

Murthy, S.; Kasif, S.; Salzberg, S.; and Beigel, R. 1993. OC1: randomized induction of oblique decision trees. In *AAAI-93: Proceedings, Eleventh National Conference on Artificial Intelligence*, 322–327. MIT Press.

Quinlan, J. R. 1986. Induction of decision trees. *Machine Learning* 1:81–106.

Thrun, S. B., et al. 1991. The monk's problems – a performance comparison of different learning algorithms. Technical Report CMU-CS-91-197, CMU School of Computer Science.

[*]Inquiries are welcome. This material is based upon work supported under a National Science Foundation Graduate Research Fellowship.

When the Best Move Isn't Optimal: Q-learning with Exploration

George H. John*
Computer Science Department
Stanford University
Stanford, CA 94305
gjohn@cs.Stanford.EDU

The most popular delayed reinforcement learning technique, Q-learning (Watkins 1989), estimates the future reward expected from executing each action in every state. If these estimates are correct, then an agent can use them to select the action with maximal expected future reward in each state, and thus perform optimally. Watkins has proved that Q-learning produces an optimal policy (the function mapping states to actions) and that these estimates converge to the correct values given the optimal policy.

However, often the agent does not follow the optimal policy faithfully – the agent must also *explore* the world, taking suboptimal actions in order to learn more about its environment. The "optimal" policy produced by Q-learning is no longer optimal if its prescriptions are only followed occasionally. In many situations (*e.g.*, dynamic environments), the agent never stops exploring. In such domains Q-learning converges to policies which are suboptimal in the sense that there exists a different policy which would achieve higher reward when combined with exploration.

A bit of notation: $Q(x, a)$ is the expected future reward received after taking action a in state x. $V(x)$ is the expected future reward received after starting in state x. $\widehat{Q}$ and $\widehat{V}$ are used to denote the approximations kept by the algorithm. Each time the agent takes an action a moving it from state x to state y and generating a reward r, Q-learning updates the approximations according to the following rules:

$$\widehat{Q}(x, a) \leftarrow \beta(r + \gamma\widehat{V}(y)) + (1 - \beta)\widehat{Q}(x, a)$$
$$\widehat{V}(x) \leftarrow \max_a \widehat{Q}(x, a) \qquad (1)$$

where β is the learning rate parameter and γ is the discount rate parameter.

We propose replacing the $\widehat{V}$ update equation by

$$\widehat{V}(x) \leftarrow \sum_a P(a)\widehat{Q}(x, a) \ . \qquad (2)$$

That is, update $\widehat{V}(x)$ with the *expected*, not the *maximal*, future reward, taking into account the exploration

*This material is based upon work supported under a National Science Foundation Graduate Research Fellowship.

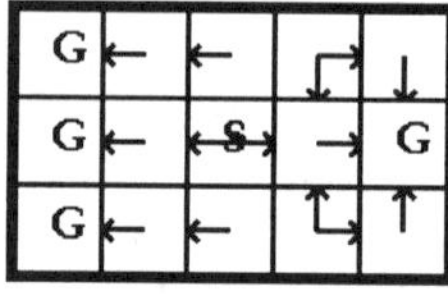 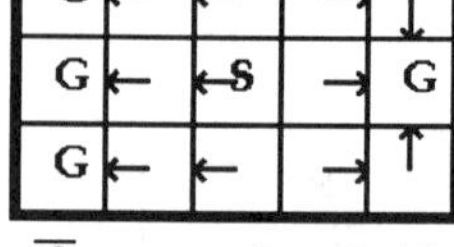

Q: reward = 3.35 $\overline{Q}$: reward = 3.44

Figure 1: Policies and average reward produced by Q and $\overline{Q}$-learning. "S" is the starting state and "G" indicates goal states which give a reward of 9 units. The algorithms were run for 10^6 steps. Here *random walk* exploration was used, where 30% of the time the agent took a random action instead of the policy-recommended action. $\gamma = .9$, $\beta = .5$.

policy when calculating the expected reward. We call this new algorithm $\overline{Q}$-learning. When the agent always takes the best action, Equations 1 and 2 are equivalent. For some exploration strategies $P(a)$, the probability of taking action a, might be estimated using sample statistics if it is not possible to calculate in closed form. In our experiments this did not degrade performance.

Figure 1 shows an example motivating our approach. The agent begins in the middle of the world and must choose whether to approach the wall of goals on the left, or the single goal on the right. Q-learning is indifferent as to which action should be performed, because with no exploration either action is optimal – a goal is only two steps away in either direction. $\overline{Q}$ prefers to move left towards the wall of goals because it knows that the agent will explore, and because of this it is better to move left since a goal is still close if exploration causes it to move up or down. By thus taking exploration into account, $\overline{Q}$ achieves higher reward.

The results in Figure 1 are typical of our experiments. $\overline{Q}$-learning always generates policies giving greater average reward, but the improvement over Q-learning depends on the domain and the amount of exploration.

References

Watkins, C. J. C. H. 1989. *Learning from Delayed Rewards*. Ph.D. Dissertation, Cambridge University. Psychology Department.

"

HIPAIR: Interactive Mechanism Analysis and Design Using Configuration Spaces

Leo Joskowicz
IBM T.J. Watson Research Center
P.O. Box 704
Yorktown Heights, NY 10598
E-mail: josko@watson.ibm.com

Elisha Sacks
Computer Science Department
Princeton University
Princeton, NJ 08544
E-mail: eps@cs.princeton.edu

We present an interactive problem solving environment for reasoning about shape and motion in mechanism design. Reasoning about shape and motion plays a central role in mechanism design because mechanisms perform functions by transforming motions via part interactions. The input motion, the part shapes, and the part contacts determine the output motion. Designers must reason about the interplay between shape and motion at every step of the design cycle.

Reasoning about shape and motion is difficult and time consuming even for experienced designers. The designer must determine which features of which parts interact at each stage of the mechanism work cycle, must compute the effects of the interactions, must identify contact transitions, and must infer the overall behavior from this information. The designer must then infer shape modifications that eliminate design flaws, such as part interference and jamming, and that optimize performance. The difficulty in these tasks lies in the large number of potential contacts, in the complexity of the contact relations, and in the discontinuities induced by contact transitions.

Current computer-aided design programs support only a few aspects of reasoning about shape and motion. Drafting programs provide interactive environments for the design of part shapes, but do not support reasoning about motion. Simulation programs, which compute and animate the motions of the parts of mechanisms, reveal only one of many possible behaviors. Commercial simulators only handle linkages: mechanisms whose parts interact through permanent surface contacts, such as hinges and screws. Other packages handle specialized mechanisms, such as cams and gears. They cannot handle mechanisms whose parts interact intermittently or via point or curve contacts. Yet these *higher pairs* play a central role in mechanism design. Our survey of 2500 mechanisms in an engineering encyclopedia shows that 66% contain higher pairs and that 18% involve intermittent contacts.

We have developed a problem solving environment, called HIPAIR, for reasoning about shape and motion in mechanisms. The core of the environment is a module that automates the kinematic analysis of mechanisms composed of linkages and higher pairs. This module provides the computational engine for a range of tasks, including simulation, behavior description, and parametric design. It is comprehensive, robust, and fast. HIPAIR handles higher pairs with two degrees of freedom, including ones with intermittent and simultaneous contacts. This class contains 90% of 2.5D pairs and 80% of all higher pairs according to our survey.

HIPAIR computes and manipulates configuration spaces. The configuration space of a mechanism is a geometric representation of the configurations (positions and orientations) of its parts. Configuration spaces encode the relations among part shapes, part motions, and overall behavior in a concise, complete and explicit format. They simplify and systematize reasoning about shape and motion by mapping it into a uniform geometrical framework.

The videotape explains configuration spaces and illustrates how HIPAIR supports mechanism design and analysis. HIPAIR has been tested on over 100 parametric variations of 25 kinematic pairs and on dozen multipart mechanisms, including a Fuji disposable camera with ten moving parts.

References

1. "Mechanism Comparison and Classification for Design", L. Joskowicz, in *Research in Engineering Design*, Springer-Verlag, Vol 1. No. 2, 1990.

2. "Computational Kinematics", L. Joskowicz and E. Sacks, *Artificial Intelligence*, Vol. 51, Nos. 1-3, North-Holland, 1991.

3. "Automated Modeling and Kinematic Simulation of Mechanisms", E. Sacks and L. Joskowicz, *Computer-Aided Design*, Vol. 25, No. 2, 1993.

4. "Configuration Space Computation for Mechanism Design", E. Sacks and L. Joskowicz, *Proc. of the IEEE Int. Conference on Robotics and Automation*, IEEE Computer Society Press, 1994.

5. "Mechanism Analysis and Design Using Configuration Spaces", E. Sacks and L. Joskowicz, submitted, *Communications of the ACM*, 1994.

Learning Sorting Networks By Grammars

Thomas E. Kammeyer and **Richard K. Belew**
CS&E Department (0114)
University of California, San Diego
La Jolla, CA 92093
{tkammeye,rik}@cs.ucsd.edu

Definitions and Previous Work

A compare-exchange network, or CMPX-net, is a sequence of operations of the form $[i : j]$, each of which operates on an array, D, of length N. The network is said to have *width* N. The *length* of the network is the number of CMPX's in the network. For each $[i : j]$, we have $i < j$ and $i, j \in [0, N - 1]$. To apply a CMPX-net to an array, swap $D[i]$ and $D[j]$ if $D[i] > D[j]$ for each $[i : j]$ in the sequence. A *sorting network*(SNet) is a CMPX-net which will sort D's contents into nondecreasing order no matter how D's contents are ordered initially. A *merging network* (MNet) is a pair containing a CMPX-net of even width, N, and a partition of the indices into two equal-size sets or "sides." If the data on each side of the partition are sorted initially then the output will be sorted. The space of CMPX-nets with n_c CMPX's and width N is large, of size $C(N; 2)^{n_c}$. With MNets, the space is still bigger, since we must multiply the number of networks by the number of partitions, $C(N; N/2)$.

We use a genetic algorithm(GA) to search for CMPX-nets which are SNets or MNets. The GA repeatedly samples the space of potential solutions in a series of "generations," each using the relative "fitness" of the previous generation's samples to apportion more samples in promising regions. Mutation and especially cross-over operators are applied to generate similar but novel new sample points; this process is iterated until some stopping criterion is achieved. Hillis has had encouraging success using a GA to evolve sorting networks(Hillis 1991).

In our work, we represent CMPX-nets by grammars which describe CMPX-nets. Terminals define particular CMPX sequences and nonterminals specify ways in which larger networks are built from smaller ones.

Merging Networks — Recent Results

Our most recent experiments have involved MNets for several reasons. MNets can be fully tested in polynomial time using $(N/2 + 1)^2$ input sequences; exhaustively testing SNets is much more expensive, requiring 2^N input sequences. In addition, our random MNet generation experiments have shown that despite this

reduction in the cost of exhaustive testing, the problem is still very difficult. Some MNets are "log-sequential" sorters. That is, if we cycle the output of the network back to its input $log_2 N$ times, then the data will be sorted.

Recent analytic work has produced two log-sequential MNets(Dowd *et al.* 1989; Canfield & Williamson 1991). The network due to Canfield and Williamson is particularly interesting because it is "log spectrum" (The number of distinct $j - i$ over all $[i : j]$ in the network is $O(log_2 N)$) and "log delay" (it can be parallelized to execute in time $O(log_2 N)$). Both of these characteristics can provide critical advantages in hardware implementation.

Using our GA and grammar representation, we have found an interesting network similar to but distinct from the Canfield-Williamson network. The grammar which generates our network requires only two rules and generates an entire family of networks, one for each $N = 2^i, i >= 2$. It appears to be a log-sequential sorter, and has log spectrum and log delay. This network embeds the Canfield-Williamson network of half as many inputs several times and in an overlapping fashion.

Acknowledgements

We gratefully acknowledge many useful conversations with S. Gill Williamson.

References

Canfield, E. R., and Williamson, S. G. 1991. A sequential sorting network analogous to the batcher merge. *Linear and Multilinear Algebra* 29:43–51. Patent applied for March 1991, University of California as Assignee.

Dowd, M.; Perl, Y.; Rudolph, L.; and Saks, M. 1989. The periodic balanced sorting network. *J. Assoc. Computing Machinery* 36(4).

Hillis, W. D. 1991. Co-evolving parasites improve simulated evolution as an optimization procedure. In *Artificial Life II*. Addison-Wesley Publishing Company.

The Formation of Coalitions Among Self-Interested Agents

Steven Ketchpel

Stanford University
Computer Science Department
Stanford CA, 94305
ketchpel@cs.stanford.edu

The Problem

Researchers in the multi-agent systems community of DAI assume that agents will have to interact with others agents that were designed by different designers for different goals. These diverse agents could benefit each other by collaborating, but they will do so only if the resulting deal is beneficial from each agent's point of view. One useful definition of beneficial is that of economic rationality, maximizing the agent's expected payoff in terms of a utility function.

An open problem in this area is to design a protocol that allows a large pool of agents to determine which of the subsets among them can profit by working together. A solution to a coalition problem is a partition of the agents into subsets (**coalitions**), such that each agent in every coalition receives the most utility it can expect.

Objectives

The coalitions that are formed must be **stable** in the sense that none of the agents would leave their current coalitions to form a new one yielding all of the agents in that new coalition a higher utility than they obtain from their previous coalitions. Formally, the agents $a_1,...,a_N$ are divided into a partition P containing coalitions $C_1,...,C_N$ such that every agent is a member of exactly one coalition. The payoff to an agent is a function $u(P, a)$ of both the partition and the agent. For P to be stable, there must not be any other partition P' forming $C'_1,..., C'_N$ such that $\exists C'_i \in P' \, \forall a_j \in C'_i$ with $u(P', a_j) > u(P, a_j)$. If there were such a C'_i, the agents of that coalition would desert their current coalitions and form C'_i.

Since the agents have different abilities, they may be making different contributions to the final outcome. Therefore, splitting the joint reward equally among the included agents might not be equitable. Finally, there are computational considerations. In addition to efficiency, decentralization is desirable, with more robustness in case of node failures and fewer communication bottlenecks.

Methods and Results

Although the idea of coalition formation is relatively new to the field of artificial intelligence, it has been studied by economists working in game theory. Their solutions cannot be directly applied to problems in computer science, however, since different assumptions are made and different phenomena are modeled. One approach to solving the coalition problem is to integrate work from game theory with traditional computational methods. In fact, this approach is being taken by a number of researchers [(Ketchpel 1993), (Shechory & Kraus 1993), (Zlotkin & Rosenschein 1993)]. One greedy algorithm based on the solution to the stable marriage problem (Gusfield & Irving 1989) meets the criteria of being decentralized and efficient, though may yield results which are not stable (Ketchpel 1993). Agents pair off in coalitions that improve their utility the most, then re-enter as a single "agent". The process continues until no new coalitions are formed. A modification to the algorithm (Ketchpel 1994) proposes a "two agent auction" mechanism for cases where the value of collaboration is uncertain. Many questions in this area still need to be addressed. For example, some problems have no stable solution, others have several. Giving the agents more information about each other could introduce strategic behavior that requires more game theoretic analysis.

References

Gusfield, Dan and Irving, Robert W. 1989. *The Stable Marriage Problem: Structure and Algorithms.* Cambridge, MA: MIT Press.

Ketchpel, Steven P. 1993. Coalition Formation Among Autonomous Agents. In Pre-Proceedings of the 5th European Workshop on "Modeling Autonomous Agents in a Multi-Agent World" Supplement. Neuchâtel, Switzerland: Institut d'Informatique et Intelligence artificielle, Université de Neuchâtel. [MAAMAW-93].

Ketchpel, Steven. 1994. Forming Coalitions in the Face of Uncertain Rewards. In Proceedings of the Twelfth National Conference on Artificial Intelligence. Menlo Park, CA: AAAI Press.

Shechory, On and Kraus, Sarit. Coalition Formation Among Autonomous Agents: Strategies and Complexity. In [MAAMAW-93].

Zlotkin, Gilad and Rosenschein, Jeffrey S. 1993a. One, Two, Many: Coalitions in Multi-agent Systems. In [MAAMAW-93].

Learning From Ambiguous Examples

Stephen V. Kowalski
University of Southern California
Department of Electrical Engineering Systems
EEB 232, MC 2562
Los Angeles, California 90089–2562
skowalsk@pollux.usc.edu

Current inductive learning systems are not well suited to learning from ambiguous examples. We say that an example is ambiguous if it has multiple interpretations, only one of which may be valid. Some domains in which ambiguous learning problems can be found are natural language processing (NLP) and computer vision. An example of an ambiguous training instance with two interpretations is shown below, where $\oplus$ is the Exclusive-OR function and each interpretation is a conjunction of attribute values.

$$
\begin{aligned}
E_1 &= i_1 \oplus i_2 \\
i_1 &= [(\text{cat} = \text{verb}) \wedge (\text{agree} = \text{n3sg})] \\
i_2 &= [(\text{cat} = \text{noun}) \wedge (\text{num} = \text{singular})]
\end{aligned}
$$

Our first thought is to transform this example into disjunctive normal form (DNF). Each conjunction would then become a new example described in a representation that can be understood by most existing inductive learners. There are several problems with this approach, two of which are described below.

First, there would be a combinatorial explosion in the number of training examples and thus the complexity of the learning algorithm. A second problem arises from the introduction of negated attribute values[1] in the training instances which some learners (e.g. ID3 (Quinlan 1986)) are ill-equipped to handle. We also note that an ambiguous example may take multiple paths down a decision tree during classification. These paths may terminate at leaf nodes that are labeled with different classes.

A system that could learn directly from ambiguous examples would broaden the use of inductive learning in the previously mentioned domains.

One problem in NLP is sentence classification. Each word in a sentence has multiple interpretations corresponding to different dictionary meanings. For example, E_1 might be a representation for the word *plant*. A sentence could then be represented as a list of these expressions, one for each word.

Our approach to learning from ambiguous examples is to represent the training instances and the hypotheses with the same language. This language, at its highest level, employs a form of regular expression to match patterns of text. This expression consists of an ordered list of *items* which are either Kleene stars or expressions that consist of an exclusive disjunction[2] of interpretations. Each interpretation is a conjunction of attribute values, and internal disjunctions are permitted (e.g. category = noun $\vee$ verb). An example hypothesis is shown below.

$$
\begin{aligned}
H_1 &= \{*, t_1\} \\
t_1 &= [(\text{cat} = \text{noun}) \wedge (\text{num} = \text{singular})] \oplus \\
&\quad [(\text{cat} = \text{adverb})]
\end{aligned}
$$

This hypothesis, H_1, would match any sentence where the last word can be interpreted as either a singular noun or an adverb.

Our inductive learning algorithm performs a beam search from general to more specific expressions and relies heavily on a formal definition of subsumption. Since we are using the same language for the training examples and the hypotheses that are learned, we say that a hypothesis *matches* a training example if the expression for the hypothesis *subsumes* the expression for the example. A subsumption operator is a binary Boolean operator that takes as arguments two expressions, and evaluates true if the expression on the left is more general or has the same generality as the expression on the right, and false otherwise.

Experiments have been conducted in one of the domains of the Message Understanding Conference (MUC). Text sentences were classified by the type of information that they contained, and a dictionary-based pre-processor was used to generate the ambiguous representation. The learning algorithm was shown to successfully learn concepts that could be used to form information extraction rules. Our current work is on integrating the learning system with a performance element which is a rule-based information extraction system.

References

Quinlan, J. R. 1986. Induction of Decision Trees. *Machine Learning* 1:81–106.

---

[1] $a \oplus b = (a \wedge \neg b) \vee (\neg a \wedge b)$.

[2] An exclusive disjunction is of the form $a \oplus b \oplus c$.

Exploiting the Environment: Urban Navigation as a Case Study

Nicholas Kushmerick

Department of Computer Science & Engineering   University of Washington Seattle

nick@cs.washington.edu

The Situated Action approach to AI emphasizes the role of the environment in the generation and control of behavior; see (Norman 1993) for an introduction. Work to date has focused mainly on activity within spatially and temporally localized environments such as kitchens and video games (Agre & Chapman 1987; Agre & Horswill 1992). How useful is this perspective when larger-scale activities are considered? I attempt to answer this question by considering some issues related to navigation in urban environments. I identify several constraints on the structure of street grids that make navigation much easier than arbitrary graph search. The ultimate goal is a theory of the relationship between features of an urban environment and the computational complexity of navigation. This work extends the sort of analysis advocated by (Agre & Horswill 1992; Horswill 1993).

Navigation is an attractive task for studying the ways agents might exploit the structure of their environment. There is no doubt that people make and use elaborate mental representations when they navigate. But city street grids are constrained in ways that make navigational problems relatively simple, and these constraints are poorly understood. The constraints take a variety of forms, ranging from the physical structure of space to cultural phenomena such as neighborhoods. • Street grids are *physically stable*. New buildings and streets are constructed, but the time scale at which street grids change is several orders of magnitude slower than the scale at which navigation occurs. • Navigation is much simpler than arbitrary graph search because streets are *topologically sensible*. It is impossible to drive along a street and suddenly end up on the other side of town; *culs-de-sac* are relatively rare, so hill-climbing tends to work; one-way streets never completely isolate regions. • Navigation occurs in a *topographically translucent* environment: some information is available by virtue of the 3-D nature of the environment, although not all. Often one can see more than just the immediate surroundings. Deciding which highway exit to take can involve simply looking at the buildings in the distance to decide when the correct exit is approaching. • Some cities are *coherently labeled*. Streets might be numbered, alphabetized or follow some other regular pattern. • Most cities are *informatively labeled*. Downtown Seattle is filled with signs guiding one to Interstate 5; dead-end streets have signs so indicating; freeway exits indicate the places the exit serves; fast-food restaurant billboards guide one to the nearest franchise. • Most street grids *facilitate optimization*. Arterials are easily recognizable and uniformly distributed. Near-optimal navigation is thus simplified because a simple policy of using the nearest arterial is easy and effective. • Finally, cities are composed of *neighborhoods*, with just a few major streets running through each. It is often sufficient to identify a goal location by neighborhood; navigation within the neighborhood can then be done with a combination of visual and exhaustive physical search.

I take navigation to be physical search over a highly constrained graph. Environmental features map directly to constraints on the graph, thereby illuminating each feature's computational significance. Thus, physical stability means that the graph is static, while topological sensibility requires that the graph be strongly connected and nearly planar. Street signs and topographic constraints are especially interesting; they are treated as node labels informing the agent about remote parts of the graph. Further research will clarify the relationship between the environmental and graph constraints. Ultimately, I seek a formal theory of the relationship between the complexity of navigation and graph constraints derived from the environment. The following cases illustrate that the complexity of the agent and the environment are in some sense equivalent: an agent with a complete street map can navigate in an arbitrarily complicated city; an agent with a compass but no map can navigate if all streets are numbered. A theory describing these tradeoffs will help elucidate the general principles governing interactions between agents and environments in a wider variety of circumstances. To validate my analysis I have begun to formally model a complete street map of Seattle.

References

Agre, P., and Chapman, D. 1987. Pengi: An implementation of a theory of activity. In *Proc. 6th Nat. Conf. on A.I.*

Agre, P., and Horswill, I. 1992. Cultural support for improvisation. In *Proc. 10th Nat. Conf. on A.I.*

Horswill, I. 1993. Analysis of adaptation and environment. *Artificial Intelligence*. To appear.

Norman, editor, D. 1993. Special issue on Situated Action. *Cognitive Science* 17(1).

Quantitative Evaluation of the Exploration Strategies of a Mobile Robot

David Lee*and Michael Recce
Computer Science Department, University College,
Gower Street,
London WC1E 6BT, U.K.
davidlee@cs.ucl.ac.uk

How should a mobile robot explore its environment in order to build a high-quality world model as efficiently as possible? We address this question through experimentation with a sonar-equipped mobile robot.

The robot is taken to be a delivery robot, such as could be used in an office, hospital or home. Its objective is to execute efficient collision-free paths between user-specified locations. A grid-based free-space map is generated for this purpose. This map is derived from a feature-based map, built using techniques similar to those of (Leonard & Durrant-Whyte 1992).

Before starting to evaluate an exploration strategy, it is vital to have a clear definition of map quality. Previous map-building research has typically judged map quality either by visual inspection or by measuring the robot's success in achieving its goals with a *completed* map. Neither approach provides an objective quality measure *during* map construction. There is therefore a need for a quantitative measure which can be applied during exploration. We solve this problem by defining a small number of numeric measures which together *predict* the robot's efficiency if it were to use its current world model to achieve its objectives.

The quality of the robot's map is measured by comparing its performance in a set of tasks using either the robot's map or an ideal map. The set of benchmark tasks is created by selecting pairs of locations such that there is an executable path between them, according to the ideal map. For each pair of locations, an attempt is then made to plan a path between them, using the robot's map. Counts are kept of the numbers of these paths which fall into each of three categories; "Impossible", "Collision" or "Feasible". A path is "Impossible" if the current map shows either that one of the endpoints is occupied or that the path is blocked. A path is a "Collision" if the current map shows the route to be possible, but in fact the planned route would cause a collision with an obstacle. A path is "Feasible" if the planned route is possible without collision. In this case, we compare the cost of executing the planned route with the "ideal" cost from the true map. The categorisation of the paths and the ef-

ficiency of the feasible paths measure different aspects of the map quality. The relative significance of these aspects can be assessed in the context of the robot's application.

These measures were used to fine-tune the map construction process. Parameter values were selected and design choices were made to maximise the map quality obtained from given sensor data. Objective quality measures were essential during this process.

We report the results of the evaluation and comparison of a number of exploration strategies by monitoring the quality measures as the robot explores a set of test environments. The first strategy tested was wall-following, a completely reactive navigation strategy in which all decisions are made on the basis of immediately available sensory data. The map is not used to control the exploration. In sparse environments the map quality increases rapidly at the start of the exploration but reaches a plateau when, for example, the robot is following a wall which has already been observed from elsewhere. An immediate challenge in designing an exploration strategy is to use the information gathered so far to eliminate such redundant movements.

We also report the results of a "Visit All" behaviour (Zelinsky 1992), which directs the robot systematically towards unknown regions, and a "Seed-Spreader" technique (Lumelsky, Mukhopadhyay, & Sun 1989), which is theoretically guaranteed to find all obstacles in the environment.

*Supported by a SERC grant

References

Leonard, J. J., and Durrant-Whyte, H. F. 1992. *Directed Sonar Sensing for Mobile Robot Navigation*. MIT: Kluwer Academic Publishers.

Lumelsky, V. J.; Mukhopadhyay, S.; and Sun, K. 1989. Sensor-based terrain acquisition: a "seed spreader" strategy. In *IEEE/RSJ International Workshop on Intelligent Robots and Systems*, 62–67. Academic Press.

Zelinsky, A. 1992. A mobile robot exploration algorithm. *IEEE Transactions on Robotics and Automation* 8(6):707–717.

Everyday Reasoning Meets Geometry Theorem-Proving

Thomas F. McDougal

University of Chicago Computer Science
1100 E. 58th St.
Chicago, IL 60637
email: mcdougal@cs.uchicago.edu

In an earlier paper [McDougal and Hammond 1993], we reported on POLYA, a computer program which proves high school geometry theorems. POLYA is a memory-based problem-solver in the case-based planning tradition [Hammond 1989, Kolodner 1993]. It uses features of the problem (mostly from the diagram) to index into a library of plans. Some of those plans are solutions to entire problems; others apply a single inference. The plans are indexed in memory by the features which predict the relevance of the plan without necessarily guaranteeing it.

POLYA's domain is the set of problems which occur in a high school textbook (in particular, [Rhoad, Whipple and Milauskas 1988]). This domain is interesting because of the ways in which the textbook authors have structured it to help the student: problems build on earlier problems, common idioms recur, and diagrams are drawn to suggest particular ways of thinking. By using ideas from case-based planning, POLYA recognizes and exploits the regularities in the domain to avoid the NP-complete problem of proving theorems from scratch.

POLYA can reuse proofs for similar problems, where similarity is defined in terms of the diagram and the goal. POLYA does not directly apply the proof, but uses it to focus attention on those objects in the diagram which were important previously. Features in the diagram enable POLYA to determine the specific inferences to apply.

Many of the idioms that help POLYA figure out the specific steps in the proof are similar to the diagram configuration schema described in [Koedinger and Anderson 1990], except that there is an emphasis in POLYA on capturing the details of specific problems in the text. The details make it possible to choose specific inferences without going through a second stage of inference chaining, as Koedinger and Anderson's system does.

An important part of POLYA's task is to extract features from the problem, and many of its plans (called *search plans*) are for that purpose alone. For example, if POLYA detects a triangle which appears to be isosceles (based on the numerical coordinates of the vertices), an isosceles-triangle-search-plan computes descriptions of the legs and base angles.

Several issues have come up in this project which are basic to planning in general:

Plan selection. POLYA often has a choice of several plans, some of which will result in finishing the proof more quickly than others. POLYA uses proofs from past problems to determine which plans are most likely to lead to the solution.

Flexibility. The proof for one problem rarely applies exactly to another. POLYA adapts proofs flexibly by establishing a sequence of goals based on the proof, then relying on features of the problem to trigger the appropriate plans for achieving those subgoals.

Interrupts. While in the middle of one plan, POLYA will sometimes trigger a plan that would complete the proof immediately. The current algorithm does not allow plans to be interrupted.

These issues come up in many other planning domains. Plan selection is important when an agent has multiple goals. Flexibility is important whenever the planner has imperfect knowledge about the world. Interrupts are important if disaster strikes, demanding immediate action. As we address these issues in the geometry domain we hope to contribute to a general theory of planning and action in regular domains.

References

Hammond, K. 1989. *Case-Based Planning: Viewing Planning as a Memory Task.* Academic Press.

Koedinger, K. R. and Anderson, J. R. (1990). "Abstract planning and perceptual chunks: Elements of expertise in geometry." *Cognitive Science,* **14**, 511-550.

Kolodner, J. 1993. *Case-Based Reasoning.* Morgan Kaufmann.

McDougal, T. F. and Hammond, K. J. (1993). "Representing and using procedural knowledge to build geometry proofs." *Proceedings of the Eleventh National Conference on Artificial Intelligence.* M.I.T. Press.

Rhoad, R., Whipple, R., and Milauskas, G. 1988. *Geometry for enjoyment and challenge.* McDougal, Littell.

Determination of Machine Condition using Neural Networks

John MacIntyre, Professor Peter Smith, John Tait
School of Computing and Information Systems, University of Sunderland,
Tyne & Wear, England. e_mail: jmacintyre@sunderland.ac.uk

Condition monitoring is a developing discipline in machinery maintenance. Data such as vibration levels, temperatures, oil analysis values etc, are acquired from plant, and analyzed to determine the condition of the plant at the time of measurement. Software packages are currently available to allow graphical display of the data, with varying levels of diagnostic tools available to assist engineers in performing data analysis. This abstract outlines the development of a condition monitoring system at Blyth Power Station, owned by National Power, the major electricity generating company in the United Kingdom. The abstract goes on to describe research into the development of a data analysis system employing neural networks trained to recognise machinery defects.

Blyth Power Station is located on North East coast of England, with a generating capacity of 1,180MW, and is one of the oldest coal-fired sites in the United Kingdom. The Station recognised the requirement to move away from traditional, manpower-intensive strategies of planned or breakdown maintenance, towards a condition-based maintenance policy for critical areas of auxiliary plant [1]. To achieve this, the Station entered into a collaborative agreement with the University of Sunderland to develop and implement a condition monitoring system for use within the Station, and to investigate the use of artificial intelligence in data analysis.

Figure 1 below shows a typical frequency spectrum acquired from a Cooper rolling element bearing. The spectrum is obtained by performing a Fast Fourier Transform on the time domain vibration signal, after a band pass filter and envelope filter have been applied to it. In this spectrum, a large peak is visible at the frequency specific to an outer race defect (ORD).

This clear and well-defined spectra shows distinct characteristics relating to the bearings. The plant is readily accessible, and the transducer can be placed close to the bearing being monitored. In many cases, the picture is far more vague, through background noise, difficulty of access, low frequency applications etc; for example, data collected from coal mill gearboxes is a much more complex problem for analysis [2].

Neural Networks for Data Analysis

Initial work employed the well-documented multi-layer perceptron using back-propagation [2]. This network topology was applied to the analysis of data from rolling

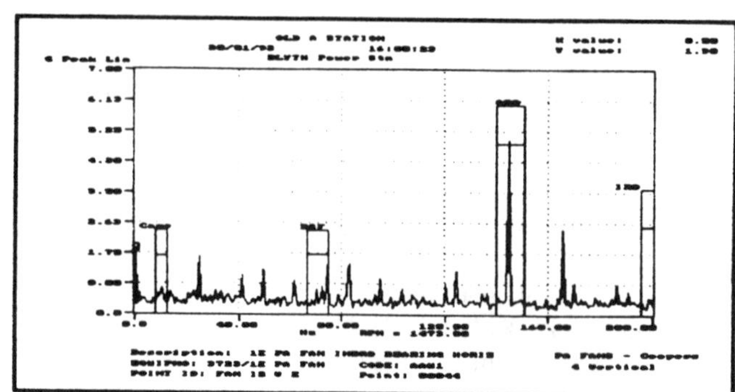

Figure 1 - FFT spectrum from a Cooper bearing

element bearings, similar to that shown in Figure 1. Whilst this problem domain is not particularly complex, the amount of data collected makes an automated system desirable. Two versions of the Neural Bearing Analyzer (NBA) were developed; first, one which took a limited amount of information from the frequency spectrum as its inputs, and had as its output classes degrees of severity of defect in each individual bearing component, and second, one which took the whole of the frequency spectrum (400 datum points) as its inputs, and had a simplified output class set for overall bearing condition. The second system proved difficult to train, with problems in achieving convergence to within a suitable RMS error threshold. However, once convergence was achieved, its performance in classification of live data was very good when compared to the diagnosis of a consultant condition monitoring engineer, agreeing in 93% of test cases. This network topology is now being used to analyze more complex data, and other topologies such as Self-Organising Maps are also being investigated [2].

References

1. MacIntyre, J.; Smith, P.; Wiblin, C. 1993. Development of a Condition Monitoring System for Off-Line Monitoring of Auxiliary Plant for National Power. In Proceedings of 5th International Congress on Condition Monitoring and Diagnostic Engineering Management, University of the West of England, United Kingdom.

2. MacIntyre, J.; Smith, P.; Harris, T.; Brason, A. 1993. Application of Neural Networks to the Analysis and Interpretation of Off-Line Condition Monitoring Data. In Proceedings of the 6th International Symposium on Artificial Intelligence, Monterrey, Mexico.

Building a Parser That can Afford to Interact with Semantics

Kavi Mahesh

College of Computing
Georgia Institute of Technology
Atlanta, Georgia 30332-0280 USA
mahesh@cc.gatech.edu

Natural language understanding programs get bogged down by the multiplicity of possible syntactic structures while processing real world texts that human understanders do not have much difficulty with. In this work, I analyze the relationships between parsing strategies, the degree of local ambiguity encountered by them, and semantic feedback to syntax, and propose a parsing algorithm called *Head-Signaled Left Corner Parsing* (HSLC) that minimizes local ambiguities while supporting interactive syntactic and semantic analysis. Such a parser has been implemented in a sentence understanding program called COMPERE (Eiselt, Mahesh, & Holbrook 1993).

A parser could quickly eliminate many possible syntactic structures for a sentence by using (a) the grammar to generate syntactic expectations, (b) structural preferences such as Minimal Attachment or Right Association, (c) feedback from semantic analysis (d) statistical preferences based on a corpus, or (e) case-based preferences arising from prior texts about stereotypical situations. None of the above strategies suffices by itself for handling real text.

In this work, I assume that (a) we must strive to design parsing strategies capable of analyzing general, real life text, (b) it is beneficial to produce immediate, incremental interpretations ('meanings') of incoming texts, and (c) semantic (and pragmatic) analysis can provide useful feedback to syntax without requiring unbounded resources. Given these, my objective is to design a parsing strategy that makes the best use of linguistic preferences–both grammatical and structural, and also semantic and conceptual preferences, while minimizing local ambiguities. Strong cognitive motivations for devising such a solution were presented earlier in (Eiselt, Mahesh, & Holbrook 1993).

The question this leads to is: When should the parser interact with the semantic analyzer? It should interact only when such interaction is beneficial to one or both, that is, when one can provide some information to the other to help reduce the number of choices being considered. Parsing strategies can be distinguished along a dimension of "eagerness" depending on when they make commitments to a syntactic unit and are ready for interaction with semantics. At one end of the spectrum lies pure bottom-up parsing, being too circumspect and precluding the use of syntactic expectations. Pure top-down parsing, at the other end, is too eager and leads to unwarranted backtracking. Such nondeterminism is a problem for incremental interaction with semantics. A combination strategy called Left Corner (LC) Parsing has been shown to be a good middle ground for using top-down expectations as well as avoid unnecessary early commitments (Abney & Johnson 1991).

LC Parsing captures the best of both bottom-up and top-down parsing by processing the leftmost constituent of a phrase bottom-up and predicting subsequent constituents top-down from the parent constituent proposed using the leftmost. LC parsing however defines a range of strategies in the spectrum depending on the arc enumeration strategy employed—an important distinction between different LC parsers. In Arc Eager LC (AELC) Parsing, a node in the parse tree is linked to its parent without waiting for all its children. Arc Standard LC (ASLC) Parsing, on the other hand, waits for all the children before making attachments.

In this work, I propose an intermediate point in the LC Parsing spectrum between ASLC and AELC strategies and argue that the proposed point, that I call Head-Signaled LC Parsing (HSLC), turns out to be the optimal point for efficient interaction with semantics. In this strategy, a node is linked to its parent as soon as a particular required child of the node is analyzed, without waiting for other children to its right. This required unit is predefined syntactically for each phrase; it is not the same as the standard 'semantic head'. (E.g., N is the required unit for NP, V for VP, and NP for PP.) HSLC makes the parser wait for essential units before interacting with semantics but does not wait for optional adjuncts (such as PP adjuncts to NPs or VPs).

In conclusion, while LC Parsing affords incremental parsing and optimizes memory requirements, pure LC parsing does not generate syntactic units in an order suitable for incremental semantic processing. HSLC, being a hybrid of LC and head-driven parsing strategies yields the right mix to enable incremental interaction with semantics and reduce the number of interpretations explored. Empirical evaluation of the HSLC algorithm in the COMPERE system is currently in progress.

References

Abney, S. P.; Johnson, M. 1991. Memory Requirements and Local Ambiguities of Parsing Strategies. *Journal of Psycholinguistic Research*, 20(3):233-250.

Eiselt, K. P.; Mahesh, K.; and Holbrook, J. K. 1993. Having Your Cake and Eating It Too: Autonomy and Interaction in a Model of Sentence Processing. In Proceedings of AAAI-93, 380-385.

Using Errors to Create Piecewise Learnable Partitions

Oded Maron
M.I.T. Artificial Intelligence Lab
545 Technology Square, #755
Cambridge, MA 02139
oded@ai.mit.edu

After a learning system has been trained, the usual procedure is to average the testing errors in order to obtain an estimate of how well the system has learned. However, that is tossing away a lot of potentially useful information. We present an algorithm which exploits the distribution of errors in order to find where the algorithm performs badly and partition the space into parts which can be learned easily. We will show a simple example which gives the intuition of the algorithm, and then a more complex one which brings forth some of the details of the algorithm. Let us suppose that we are trying to learn the absolute value function. Almost all learning algorithms perform well along the arms of the function, but do badly around the cusp. If we notice th 'hill' of errors around $x = 0$, then we can partition the space which we are trying to learn into two parts which fall on either side of the hill. Those two partitions have the property of not only being linear, but of being learnable. Each partition can be trained separately, and when tested separately gives a better answer since irrelevant and misleading training points from other partitions have not been included.

Now let us take a more complex example of trying to learn the function shown in Figure 1. It is made up of constant parts for simplicity's sake, but in fact the parts can be anything learnable. The discontinuities cannot be learned easily by the particular learning algorithm which we are using (local weighted regression which looks at 10% of the nearest points). Figure 2 shows the error distribution gotten by cross validation. The problem of finding 1-d 'hills' of errors for one dimensional functions now becomes a problem of finding multi-dimensional 'ridges'. This is equivalent to the vision problem of edge detection. While techniques exist for two or three-dimensional edge detection, it is a difficult problem for arbitrary dimensions. Therefore, we make the assumption that the ridges occur in axis-parallel hyperplanes. While this is a big assumption, it makes the problem tractable, and this assuption is used in other well known partitioning algorithms such as CART. The algorithm now proceeds as follows: for each dimension, we scan across that dimension, looking for ridges which are parallel to our scan line. If we find such a ridge, then all points before that are put in one partition, and we continue scanning. After going through all of the dimensions this way, we have partitioned the space into pieces which are independently learnable.

The question which remains is: how do we detect these hills? The hill must be high enough so that noisy data will not cause over-partitioning. In addition, the hill must be wide enough so that a few outliers will not cause over-segmentation of the training set. Unfortunately, there is no rigorous answer to this question. We used the heuristics of detecting hills which are higher than the average error and wider than $\sqrt{n}$ if there are n points in the current partition. Once the partitions are created, we need to assign a learner to each one. The choice of how to do this is up to the particular implementation. The same learning architecture can be used for every partition, or we can try to find the best learner for each piece of the domain. Each partition also has a hyper-rectangle associated with it which encompasses the points in that partition. For a new query point, we find which hyper-rectangle in which it falls and use the learner associated with that partition to answer the query. The main differences between this algorithm and other decision-tree algorithms is that the partitions are not necessarily constant or linear — they are learnable, and that ridges of error are used to decide where to break the space.

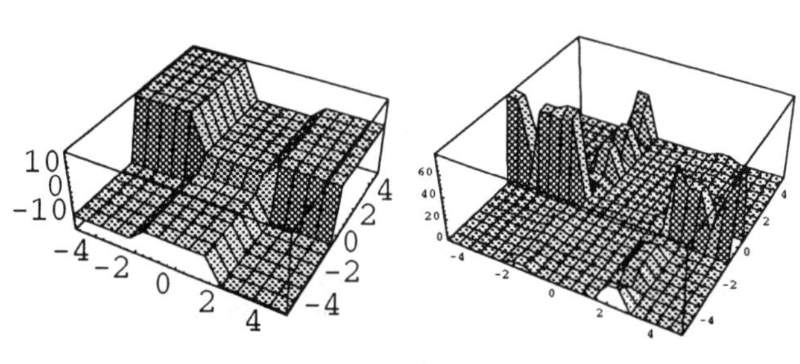

Figure 1:   Figure 2:

Development of an Intelligent Forensic System For Hair Analysis and Comparison*

C. Medina   **L. Pratt**
Department of Mathematical and Computer Sciences
Colorado School of Mines
Golden, CO 80401

C. Ganesh
Division of Engineering
Colorado School of Mines
Golden, CO 80401

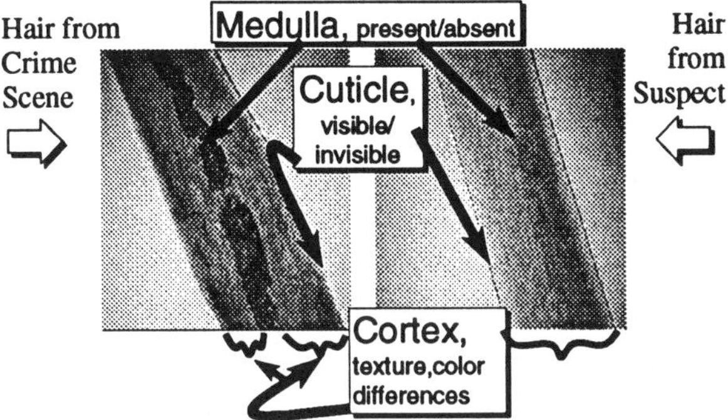

Figure 1: Microscopic images from two different hairs

The Problem: An important forensic task is to analyze and compare hair evidence in criminal cases. A forensic expert compares sets of hair images from a crime scene to a set from a suspect. Under a microscope, hairs are fairly distinctive, as shown in Figure 1. The *medulla*, which runs along the center of the hair, can take on a variety of different shapes. The *cortex* material outside the medulla has different textures and colors. The *cuticle*, which is located on the exterior of the hair, can be either visible or invisible.

Forensic analysis is a tedious procedure. The forensic expert must manually compare hundreds of hair samples to determine whether or not two sets of samples came from the same person.

The Solution: Neural networks have been used for several problems involving interpretation of images. In forensic hair analysis, a neural network can be used as a preprocessor to extract important features from a microscopic image of a hair. This can facilitate the comparison process.

Project Description: This project explores the automation of hair analysis. We are working with the Colorado Bureau of Investigation to develop a system to aid in the hair comparison process. Our system will take as input a microscopic image of hair and produce classification decisions about features like visibility of the cuticle, presence or absence of a medulla, and cortical texture and color.

The database for this project contains 725 microscopic hair images from 8 different people. To gather the images, a color video camera was connected to a microscope. The video images were sent to a computer-based image viewer. The image was finally captured using a frame-grabber and saved as a TIFF graphic file. 600 of the images were taken from 3 people corresponding to "suspect" hairs. 125 images were taken from 5 people corresponding to "crime scene" hairs.

Each image was segmented into a number of pieces appropriate for classification of different features. We used a variety of image processing techniques to enhance this information in advance of neural network classification. Statistical tests will be used to determine the degree of match between the resulting collection of hair feature vectors.

Analysis of Results: An important issue in the automation of any task used in criminal investigations is the reliability and understandability of the resulting system. To address this concern, we are doing rigorous empirical analysis of our networks. In addition, we are developing methods to facilitate explanation of a neural network's behavior.

One way to better describe the internal decision process of a neural network is to interpret hidden unit hyperplanes as a decision tree. Each node of the decision tree represents a decision made at a particular point of the classification process. The leaves represent a classification choice. This method provides both a graphical and more readily interpretable description of the means by which the neural network classification is made.

*This research is supported under a grant from the Colorado Advanced Software Institute (CASI). CASI is sponsored by the Colorado Advanced Technology Institute (CATI), an agency of the state of Colorado. CATI promotes advanced technology education and research at universities in Colorado for the purpose of economic development.

Model-Based Sensor Diagnosis: When Monitoring Should Be Monitored

Joël MILGRAM

Électricité De France, DER-IMA-TIEM
1, avenue du Général De Gaulle
92141 Clamart Cedex FRANCE
Joel.Milgram@der.edf.fr

Abstract

A complex industrial plant, such as a nuclear power plant, is monitored thanks to a number of sensors. The instrumentation may be itself a complex system liable to failures. We propose a model-based sensor diagnosis system which relies on the topological description of the plant and on a set of component models. This model implicitly conceals relations involving only sensor data. Such relations must always be verified if components behave normally; thus, the detection task consists of verifying these relations. So, this work is a first step in extending the scope of model-based diagnosis, since we question here the information stemming from the plant and normally considered as safe. As further studies, we wish to monitor this detection system itself; i.e., whenever the instrumentation is supposed to behave correctly, non-verified constraints point out to errors in the plant model.

Questioning the model-based diagnosis

A model-based diagnosis (Reiter 1987) relies on structural and behavioural knowledge and on observations. Observations in a plant stem from sensors. Since the instrumentation is liable to failures, sensor data are questionable. On the other hand, component models in a thermohydraulic circuit are very crude and the topological database describing the plant must be updated after each human intervention on the plant. So, when a model-based reasoning system provides a result, three assumptions must be taken into account: there is no sensor failure, component models are accurate enough, and the topological database rigorously describes the plant.

Sensor failure in a thermohydraulic circuit

Fluid behaviour is described by a set of equations of different kinds stemming from the plant model. As some of the variables are measured by sensors, we seek to exhibit, when they exist, algebraic relationships between them by eliminating the variables which are not measured. Such constraints should be verified at each step if every component behaves properly. Constraint violation is equivalent to a malfunction and is seen as a sensor failure.

Constraints can be found in two steps. First, a qualitative model of constraint existence is set up by means of structural analysis. Secondly, models are formally handled as according to the structural analysis results in order to establish the constraints on sensor data.

The set of equations is turned into a structural matrix (Iwasaki & Simon 1986) in which each variable v is characterized with respect to each equation E by only two pieces of information: whether v is involved in E and whether E can be solved with respect to v. Constraints are found by triangulation of a part of this matrix.

Further research direction

Whereas the operator may check the installation thanks to the instrumentation, the present system aims at providing a diagnosis on the instrumentation itself, rather than on the installation. We wish to check the sensors with their own values. Sensor data, thus validated, may be used in other monitoring systems. Sensor diagnosis may be seen as a part of the diagnosis of a monitoring system. On the other hand, this sensor diagnosis system may itself be faulty, and should also be monitored. This system is based on four sources of knowledge and data, namely: the topological database describing the installation (TDB), the models library (ML), the research and generation algorithm (A), and sensors data. If no sensor is assumed to be faulty, then constraints violation is seen as a set of malfuctions of (TDB), (ML), or even (A).

Conclusion

The system proposed here relies on structural analysis and generates constraints on sensor data. Presently, for each circuit, a monitoring program is automatically generated from the model. This application uses resources which must themselves be monitored. When the sensors behave normally, we wish to diagnose the topological data base or the component model; this is still under study.

References

Reiter, R. 1987. A theory of diagnosis from first principles. *Artificial Intelligence*, 32:57-95.

Iwasaki, Y., and Simon, H. A. 1986. Causality in device behavior. *Artificial Intelligence*, 29:3-32.

Theoretical and Experimental Studies of Temporal Constraint Satisfaction Problem

Debasis Mitra
Center for Advanced Computer Studies
University of Southwestern Louisiana, P.O. Box 44330
Lafayette, Louisiana 70504-4330
dm@cacs.usl.edu

Reasoning with time is embedded in many application domains than we are often aware of. For example, understanding a parallel program involves how each unit of the program is temporally related to the other unit through dependency. There is a growing awareness about the importance of understanding *time* in any dynamic or evolving situation. Within last twenty years different dimensions of reasoning have been identified, such as, qualitative reasoning versus quantitative reasoning, point-based representation versus interval-based representation, propositional expression versus first order expression. My work concentrates on interval-based qualitative propositional reasoning. The representation scheme and a polynomial approximate algorithm were proposed by James Allen. The problem of detecting global consistency has been subsequently proved to be NP-complete. Practical reasoning systems have been developed based on Allen's 3-consistency algorithm. This algorithm checks for consistency over constraints between each subset of 3 temporal entities of the full set of temporal assertions in the system (rather than checking for complete consistency between all constraints, which is called global-consistency). There has been very little systematic study on either the 3-consistency problem, or the global-consistency problem.

We have hypothesized that the hardness of the problem, measured by the average-case time-complexity of 3-consistency algorithm, is a well-behaved function of the initially generated constraints, parameterized with two distributional coefficients (average, and second moment) of (1) initially constrained arcs (with a constraint network representation) for each node (temporal entities), and (2) the degree of constraints on each initially constrained arc. We are doing rigorous statistical analyses to find a predictable behavior of the time-complexity with respect to those structural parameters of the input problem. Our work is in line with the current experimental research on NP-complete problems. But a richer problem structure in TCSP demands a more rigorous data analyses technique than have been

attempted so far. We have developed a statistical regression model for predicting time-complexity of the algorithm. The model can be used for the purpose of theoretical explanation of empirical results, thus providing with a better insight into the problem of temporal consistency. We have also identified easy-hard zones of the problem[1].

I have also developed a heuristic-based global-consistency algorithm to find all consistent temporal scenarios. Ladkin et al has recently shown that the problem of detecting global-consistency is not as hard, on an average, as is suggested by its property of being NP-complete. Our algorithm has been implemented. Current experiments with the implementation is producing promising results from the point of view of efficiency. One of our results shows that, on randomly generated network, the growth rate of the number of temporally consistent models is not as explosive as intuition suggests. The algorithm has some importance from application points of view, specially in temporal data base[1]. However, apart from having its applied significance, we hope to do some fundamental experimental studies on global-consistency problem with this algorithm in future. This result, along with the statistical studies of 3-consistency algorithm, is likely to produce a better understanding of the temporal constraint satisfaction problem. Hopefully, this study will also lead to a better insight in relating NP-complete problems and P-class problems. Such a study involving approximate algorithms for temporal reasoning are also part of the project.

References

[1] Debasis Mitra and Rasiah Loganantharaj. Some experimental works with 3-consistent temporal constraint propagation algorithm. In *IJCAI-93 Workshop on Spatial and Temporal Reasoning*, 1993.

---

[1]Our implementation is in C++. We hope to extend it to a practical reasoning system in future.

A Theory of Reading[*]

Kenneth Moorman and Ashwin Ram

Georgia Institute of Technology
College of Computing
Atlanta, GA 30332-0280
{kennethm,ashwin}@cc.gatech.edu

Introduction

Reading has been studied for decades, yet no theories exist which completely explain it. In particular, a type of knowledge intensive reading, creative reading, has been practically ignored. *Creative reading* is the reading of texts which contain novel concepts. Nearly all reading will be creative to some degree; thus, any theory which overlooks this will be incomplete. By combining results from psychology, artificial intelligence, and education, we have produced a functional theory of the complete reading process, aimed at explaining creative reading.

Reading supertasks

In order to produce a functional theory of reading, we need to identify the *tasks* which the *process* must perform in order to produce the desired behavior. Related tasks are then grouped into *supertasks*. The supertasks presented below are the result of functional analyses of our own reading processes, backed up by extensive prior research in the areas of psycholinguistics (e.g., van Dijk & Kintsch 1983), reading comprehension (e.g., Black & Seifert 1981), story understanding (e.g., Rumelhart 1977), memory (e.g., Schank 1982), and metacognition (e.g., Flavell 1976).

Metacontrol integrates the other supertasks and includes focus control, which manages the depth of reading; time management; and suspension of disbelief, which enables a reader to accept a text which violates her/his world view. *Sentence processing* is responsible for low-level understanding, and includes tasks such as pronoun reference, syntactic parsing, and punctuation analysis. The *story structure understanding* supertask handles story structure details, including character and setting identification, plot description, and genre identification. The tasks making up the *scenario understander* are the event parser, which identifies agents, actions, states, objects, and locations; the agent modeler, which maintains models of the agents; and the device modeler, which forms models of objects. The *explanation and reasoning* supertask performs high-level reasoning and learning through the tasks of creative understanding, which attempts to understand novel concepts; interest management; belief management, responsible for managing the beliefs of the characters and the reader; explanation, which builds inferences; and metareasoning, which reflects on the reader's own actions. Finally, the *memory management* supertask handles memory storage and retrieval.

Conclusions

Our theory is implemented in ISAAC, a system which creatively reads science fiction stories. ISAAC deals with real stories and currently possesses the knowledge and processes to successfully understand *Men Are Different* (Bloch 1963), which contains novel concepts (sentient robots, the death of Mankind, space travel, etc.). Future work is focused on the addition of stories, as well as exploring issues in evaluation of both reading and creative performance.

Reading is a complex cognitive ability; through understanding the process, we gain a window into understanding general cognition. By making extensive use of the knowledge which exists within a story and by relying on a close interaction between the various reading supertasks, our theory is capable of modeling the reading process in a way which allows creative reading issues to be dealt with, a research goal not reached with earlier theories and models.

References

Black, J. B., and Seifert, C. M. 1981. The psychological study of story understanding. Technical Report 18, Yale.

Bloch, A. 1963. Men Are Different. In Asimov, I., and Conklin, G., eds., *50 Short Science Fiction Tales*. New York: MacMillan Publishing Co.

Flavell, J. H. 1976. Metacognitive aspects of problem solving. In Resnick, L., ed., *The Nature of Intelligence*. Hillsdale, NJ: Lawrence Erlbaum Associates.

Rumelhart, D. E. 1977. Understanding and summarizing brief stories. In Berge, D. L., and Samuels, J., eds., *Basic processes in reading and comprehension*. Hillsdale, NJ: Lawrence Erlbaum Associates.

Schank, R. 1982. *Dynamic Memory: A Theory of Learning in Computers and People*. New York: Cambridge University Press.

van Dijk, T. A., and Kintsch, W. 1983. *Strategies of Discourse Comprehension*. New York: Academic Press.

---

[*]This work was supported by a Fannie and John Hertz Foundation fellowship and by the Georgia Institute of Technology.

A Hybrid Parallel IDA* Search *

Shubha S. Nerur
Computer Science and Engineering
University of Texas at Arlington
Box 19015, Arlington, TX 76019
nerur@cse.uta.edu

ABSTRACT

Heuristic search is a fundamental problem-solving method in artificial intelligence. The main limitation of search is its computational complexity which can be overcome by parallel implementation of the algorithms. Distributed tree search and Parallel window search are two of the approaches to parallelizing search algorithms.

We are developing an algorithm called HyPS (Hybrid Parallel Search) which is a combination of distributed tree search (RKR87) and parallel window search (PK91). In the HyPS, the set of processors is divided into clusters. Each cluster searches the same space, but uses a unique cost threshold. Within each cluster, processors are given unique portions of the search space to expand. Each cluster, adopts the rule of parallel windows, but distributed tree search is performed within a cluster. First, the initial state is expanded generating distinct subtrees. The number of distinct subtrees generated is equal to the number of processors in a cluster. Each processor in a cluster receives a subtree on which IDA* search is performed. The first cluster is given the heuristic estimate to reach the goal. All remaining clusters are given incrementally larger thresholds. The algorithm finds a first solution or an optimal solution. Many of the processors will be idle when searching for an optimal solution. Load balancing within a cluster will overcome the idling of processors within a cluster. HyPS is implemented on Connection Machine 5. The parallel algorithm is tested for different cluster sizes to find the first solution and the optimal solution. We are interested in finding which cluster size yields the best solution.

Test to Find	Clusters	Speedup	Efficiency
First Sol.	1	19.07	0.30
	2	22.02	0.34
	4	45.69	0.71
First Sol. with	1	14.65	0.23
operator ordering	2	27.53	0.43
	4	108.03	1.69
Optimal Sol.	1	7.9	0.12
	2	6.7	0.10
	4	2.2	0.03
Optimal Sol. with	1	9.36	0.14
load balancing	2	6.16	0.10
	4	2.93	0.05
Optimal Sol. with	1	13.20	0.21
Load balancing	2	6.10	0.10
& operator ordering	4	5.27	0.08

Test to Find	Clusters	Speedup	Efficiency
Optimal Sol. with	1	57.70	0.90
Load balancing	2	106.82	1.67
& operator ordering	4	36.71	0.57

The domain of testing is the Fifteen Puzzle problem and the robot path planning problem. The average speedup and efficiency for the Fifteen Puzzle Problem instances are shown in the first table. Also the average speedup and efficiency for the Robot Planning Problem instances are shown in the second table. The initial testing shows marked improvement over serial and parallel algorithms.

References

Curt Powley and Richard E Korf. Single-agent parallel window search. *IEEE Transactions on Pattern Analysis and Machine Intelligence*, 13(5), 1991.

V N Rao, V Kumar, and K Ramesh. A parallel implementation of Iterative-Deepening-A*. In *Proceedings of AAAI*, pages 178–182, 1987.

*Supported by the National Science Foundation grant IRI-9308308 and by grant TRA93029N from the National Center for Supercomputing Applications.

Time-situated reasoning within tight deadlines and realistic space and computation bounds

Madhura Nirkhe
Dept. of EE and Dept. of CS
University of Maryland, College Park, MD 20742
madhura@cs.umd.edu
advisor: Donald Perlis (perlis@cs.umd.edu)
collaborator: Sarit Kraus (sarit@bimacs.cs.biu.ac.il)

We develop an effective representational and inferential framework for *fully* deadline-coupled, time-situated problem solving. Our effort is to model an agent in a tight and rigid deadline situation, in need of successfully formulating and executing a deadline-feasible plan of action as the world around the agent continues to change. We highlight the severe time-pressure under which the agent must operate with a paradigmatic problem scenario : Nell & Dudley and the railroad tracks. Nell is tied to the railroad tracks as a train approaches. Dudley, our agent, must formulate a plan to save her and carry it out before the oncoming train reaches her. He must deliberate (plan) in order to decide this, yet as he does so, the train draws nearer to Nell.

While meta-planning is the usual proposal for reasoning about the reasoning process, few formalisms acknowledge that it takes time, and none to date account for *all* the time spent in the reasoning within the same framework. We cite here some key related works: (Dean & Boddy 1988) formulate an algorithmic approach to time-dependent planning problems by introducing "anytime algorithms" which capture the notion that utility is a monotonic function of deliberation time. (Pollack & Ringuette 1990) explore the relation between agent design and environmental factors. (Rosenschein & Kaelbling 1989) provide a situated automata theory highlighting the role of logic, complexity and information in situated agents. (Russell & Wefald 1991) offer an optimal design for a limited rational agent using utility-based search. Our *fully* deadline-coupled planner has an important qualification that these efforts fail to meet: in addition to determining the current time, estimating the expected execution time of partially completed plans and being able to discard alternatives that are deadline-infeasible, it also has a built-in way of accounting for all the time spent as a deadline approaches. The underlying framework is that of Step-logics (Elgot-Drapkin & Perlis 1990) (now renamed active logics) which is a mechanism for reasoning situated in time.

We have demonstrated the generality of the formal methods employed by our formalism by solving some real-time versions of canonical temporal projection problems such as the Yale Shooting Problem. While an agent under severe time-pressure may spend substantial amount of the available time in reasoning toward and about a plan of action, in a realistic setting, the same agent must also measure up to two other crucial resource limitations as well, namely space and computation bounds. We address these concerns and offer improvements by introducing a limited short term memory combined with a primitive relevance mechanism and a limited capacity inference engine. We propose heuristics to maximize the agent's chances of meeting the deadline in this enhanced framework with additional space and computation constraints.

We provide a modal semantics for active logics which serves as a link between active logics and existing logic approaches that deal with time. Logical omniscience, and in particular inferential closure is a computational impossibility for an agent in the real-world. We have constructed a variation on active-logics for which there is a sound and complete modal semantics. It overcomes the key obstacle of closure under consequence, and restricts closure under *valid* consequence. It illustrates important comparisons between active logic work and previous modal approaches to knowledge and belief.

References

Dean, T., and Boddy, M. 1988. An analysis of time-dependent planning. In *Proceedings, AAAI-88*, 49–54.

Elgot-Drapkin, J., and Perlis, D. 1990. Reasoning situated in time I: Basic concepts. *Journal of Experimental and Theoretical Artificial Intelligence* 2(1):75–98.

Pollack, M. E., and Ringuette, M. 1990. Introducing the tileworld: Experimentally evaluating agent architectures. In *Proceedings, AAAI-90*, 183–189.

Rosenschein, S., and Kaelbling, L. 1989. Integrating planning and reactive control. In *Proceedings of NASA Telerobotics conference*. Pasadena, CA.

Russell, S., and Wefald, E. 1991. *Do the right thing*. The MIT press, Cambridge, Mass.

Integrating Induction & Instruction: Connectionist Advice Taking

David C. Noelle and **Garrison W. Cottrell**
Department of Computer Science and Engineering
University of California, San Diego
La Jolla, CA 92093-0114
dnoelle@cs.ucsd.edu and gary@cs.ucsd.edu

Humans improve their performance by means of a variety of learning strategies, including both gradual statistical induction from experience and rapid incorporation of advice. In many learning environments, these strategies may interact in complementary ways. The focus of this work is on cognitively plausible models of multistrategy learning involving the integration of inductive generalization and learning "by being told". Such models might be developed by starting with an architecture for which advice taking is relatively easy, such as one based upon a sentential knowledge representation, and subsequently adding some form of inductive learning mechanism. Alternatively, such models might be grounded in a statistical learning framework appropriately extended to operationalize instruction. This latter approach is taken here. Specifically, connectionist back-propagation networks (Rumelhart, McClelland, & the PDP Research Group 1986) are made to instantaneously modify their behavior in response to quasi-linguistic advice.

Many of the previous approaches to the instruction of connectionist networks have involved the encoding of symbolic rules as initial connection weights which may be later refined by inductive learning (Giles & Omlin 1993) (Tresp, Hollatz, & Ahmad 1993). A major drawback of this approach is that advice may only be given *before* inductive training begins. This is an unreasonable constraint for a cognitive model of instructed learning. Instead, a connectionist network is needed which may have its behavior altered by a stream of encoded instructions without a delay period for lengthy retraining.

The approach which is examined here focuses on encoding the receipt of instruction as motion in a network's activation space. In short, advice is presented to such an instructable network as a temporal sequence of instruction tokens, where each token is encoded as an input activation pattern. The network is trained to appropriately modulate its behavior based on input of such advice sequences. The correct interpretation and operationalization of input instruction sequences is learned inductively, but, once this initial learning is complete, instruction following proceeds at the speed of activation propagation. This focus on activation space dynamics allows instructional learning and standard connectionist inductive learning to function in tandem.

This strategy has been successfully applied to a simple discrete mapping task and to the learning of natural number arithmetic. In this latter domain, the connectionist adder of Cottrell and Tsung (Cottrell & Tsung 1993), which is capable of systematically operating on arbitrarily large natural numbers, was augmented to receive instruction in various methods of addition and subtraction. The resulting network tackles arithmetic problems by examining one column of digits at a time and sequentially performing actions such as writing a resultant digit for the column, announcing a carry or borrow, and shifting attention to the next digit column. The network's behavior is determined by the most recently presented sequence of instruction tokens. Future experiments will extend these multistrategy learners to include auto-associative memories containing *articulated attractors* in activation space which will facilitate systematic generalization to novel advice sequences. These later experiments will abandon arithmetic and will focus instead on simple planning tasks in a "blocks world" environment.

References

Cottrell, G. W., and Tsung, F.-S. 1993. Learning simple arithmetic procedures. *Connection Science* 5(1):37–58.

Giles, C. L., and Omlin, C. W. 1993. Rule refinement with recurrent neural networks. In *1993 IEEE International Conference on Neural Networks*, 801–806. San Francisco: IEEE Neural Networks Council.

Rumelhart, D. E.; McClelland, J. L.; and the PDP Research Group. 1986. *Parallel Distributed Processing: Explorations in the Microstructure of Cognition*, volume 1. Cambridge: The MIT Press.

Tresp, V.; Hollatz, J.; and Ahmad, S. 1993. Network structuring and training using rule-based knowledge. In Hanson, S. J.; Cowan, J. D.; and Giles, C. L., eds., *Advances in Neural Information Processing Systems 5*. San Mateo: Morgan Kaufmann.

A Comparison of Reinforcement Learning Methods for Automatic Guided Vehicle Scheduling

DoKyeong Ok*
Department of Computer Science
Oregon State University
Corvallis, OR 97331
okd@research.cs.orst.edu

Automatic Guided Vehicles or AGVs are increasingly being used in manufacturing plants for transportation tasks. Optimal scheduling of AGVs is a difficult problem. A learning AGV is very attractive in a manufacturing plant since it is hard to manually optimize the scheduling algorithm to each new situation.

In this paper we compare four reinforcement learning methods for scheduling AGVs. Q-learning[Watkins and Dayan 92] and R-learning[Schwartz 93] do not use action models. Q-learning optimizes the discounted total reward, while R-learning optimizes the average undiscounted reward per step. ARTDP[Barto et al. to appear] is a discounted method that uses action models. H-learning[Tadepalli and Ok 94] is an undiscounted version of ARTDP based on an algorithm of Jalali and Ferguson[Jalali and Ferguson 89].

In our domain(see Figure 1), there are two queues generating jobs, an AGV, a moving obstacle and two lanes. Queue 1 generates jobs for lane 2 half the time and Queue 2 always generates lane 1 jobs. The task of AGV is to move jobs from the queues to their destination lanes while avoiding collisions with the obstacle, which randomly moves up and down. There are a total of 540 states. At any time an AGV may do nothing, load, unload, or move up, down, left or right. The goal is to maximize the average reward per step.

An experiment compared Q-learning, R-learning, ARTDP and H-learning in our AGV domain. The reward is -5 when the AGV collides with the obstacle, +5 when it unloads a job to lane 1, and +1 when it unloads a job to lane 2. Figure 1 shows the medians of average reward per step over 30 trials evaluated separately after turning off learning at various stages. To enable exploration, 50% of the time a randomly chosen action was excuted during learning. The parameters of ARTDP, Q-learning, and R-learning were tuned to this domain by trial and error. ARTDP with discount factor γ=0.9 and Q-learning could not converge to the optimal policy even after 2 million steps. Even though R-learning and ARTDP with high γ converged to the

*This research was supported by the National Science Foundation under grant number IRI:9111231. I thank my advisor Prasad Tadepalli for his help and guidance.

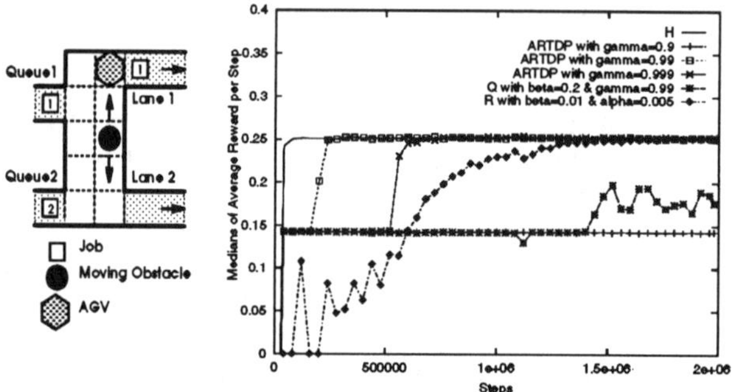

Figure 1: An AGV domain(left); average reward per step for the four learning methods(right)

optimal policy, they converged slower than H-learning. The results show clearly that H-learning converges to the optimal policy fastest without any parameter tuning, while the other three methods are very sensitive to the parameters.

The future research will explore extensions to H-learning that scale for larger state spaces.

References

Barto, A. G., Bradtke, S. J., and Singh, S. P. To appear. Learning to Act using Real-Time Dynamic Programming. *Artificial Intellignece.*

Jalali, A. and Ferguson, M. 1989. Computationally Efficient Adaptive Control Algorithms for Markov Chains. In IEEE proceedings of the 28th Conference on Decision and Control, Tampa, FL.

Schwartz, A. 1993. A Reinforcement Learning Method for Maximizing Undiscounted Rewards. In proceedings of the Tenth International Machine Learning Conference, 298–305. San Mateo, CA.:Morgan Kaufmann.

Tadepalli, P. and Ok, D. 1994. H-learning: A Reinforcement Learning Method to Optimize Undiscounted Average Reward, Technical Report, 94-30-1. Dept. of Computer Science, Oregon State Univ.

Watkins, C. J. C. H. 1989. Learning from Delayed Rewards. Ph.D. Thesis, Cambridge univ., Cambridge, England.

Making the Most of What You've Got: using Models and Data to Improve Learning Rate and Prediction Accuracy

Julio Ortega
Computer Science Dept., Vanderbilt University
P.O. Box 1679, Station B
Nashville, TN 37235
julio@vuse.vanderbilt.edu

Abstract

Prediction and classification in areas such as engineering, medicine, and applied expert systems often relies on two sources of knowledge: actual data and a model of the domain. Recent efforts in machine learning (Ourston 1991) (Towell, Shavlik, & Noordewier 1990) have developed techniques that take advantage of both sources, but the methods are often tied to particular types of models and induction techniques. We propose two general techniques that allow induction methods, C4.5(Quinlan 1993) in our case, to take advantage of an available model(Ortega 1994).

Our first technique exploits the implicit information in the model, which is used as a feature generator for induction. In particular, "model" simulation on input data computes many intermediate and output values which can serve to extend the features that describe the data. For example, in models expressed as propositional theories, we generate extended features from the proofs of the intermediate concepts in the theory. As the number of extended features proliferates quickly, we use feature selection techniques borrowed from the statistical recognition literature (Kittler 1985) to reduce the number of features considered during induction. The original data is re-expressed in terms of the selected features, and induction (i.e. C4.5) is run over this set of data.

Our second technique is motivated by the observation that the reliability of both the available model and the available data may vary widely from one domain (or situation) to another. Our approach consists of evaluating the effectiveness of the model as a predictor using the available data. The data set available for training is divided in two categories: data on which the model is accurate, and data on which the model is inaccurate. This divided data set is used to a build a "Model Reliability" predictor (using our default inductive method, i.e. C4.5) that provides a mechanism for deciding in which situations the model should be chosen for the prediction of future instances. Another predictor, the "Data" predictor is built using induction on the available data. This predictor is used on future instances where the "Model Reliability" predictor indicates that the model is unreliable.

We have conducted experiments using some databases (recognizing DNA promoter sequences, soybean and audiology diseases) which are often used in the Machine Learning community as a benchmark. The results show that the combined use of our techniques compare favorably to existing approaches, both in terms of efficiency and accuracy. However, unlike other techniques for combining inductive and deductive learning, the techniques we are developing are quite general and can be adapted to apply in non-propositional domains. We are also implementing our techniques in a domain where the model is of a mathematical nature (prediction of diabetes glucose levels), and a domain where the model is of a qualitative nature (Reaction Control System of the Space Shuttle).

References

Kittler, T. 1985. Feature selection and extraction. In Young, T. Y., and Fu, K. S., eds., *Handbook of Pattern Recognition and Image Processing*. Orlando, FL: Academic Press. 59–83.

Ortega, J. 1994. Making the most of what you've got: using models and data to improve learning rate and prediction accuracy. Technical Report TR-94-01, Computer Science Dept., Vanderbilt University.

Ourston, D. 1991. *Using Explanation-Based and Empirical Methods in Theory Revision*. Ph.D. Dissertation, University of Texas, Austin, TX.

Quinlan, J. R. 1993. *C4.5: Programs for Machine Learning*. San Mateo, CA: Morgan Kaufmann.

Towell, G. G.; Shavlik, J. W.; and Noordewier, M. O. 1990. Refinement of approximate domain theories by knowledge-based neural networks. In *Proceedings of the Eighth National Conference on Artificial Intelligence*, 861–866.

Acknowledgments

This research is supported by NASA Ames grant NAG 2-834 to D.H. Fisher.

Learning Quality-Enhancing Control Knowledge

M. Alicia Pérez *

School of Computer Science
Carnegie Mellon University
Pittsburgh PA 15213-3891
aperez@cs.cmu.edu

Generating production-quality plans is an essential element in transforming planners from research tools into real-world applications. However most research on planning so far has concentrated on methods for constructing sound and complete planners that find *a* satisficing solution, and on how to find such solution in an efficient way. Similarly most of the work to date on automated control-knowledge acquisition has been aimed at improving the *efficiency of planning*; this work has been termed "speed-up learning". Our work focuses on how control knowledge may guide a planner towards *better plans*, and how such control knowledge can be learned. "Better" may be defined in a domain-dependent way and vary over time. (Pérez & Carbonell 1993) contains a detailed taxonomy of plan quality metrics. We have concentrated on metrics related to plan execution cost, expressed as an evaluation function additive on the cost of the individual operators. These functions are linear and do not capture the existence of tradeoffs between different quality factors.

Our goal is to have a system that improves over experience the quality of the plans it generates by acquiring in a fully automated fashion control knowledge to guide the search. Figure 1 shows the architecture of the current system, fully implemented on top of the PRODIGY nonlinear planner (Carbonell et al. 1992).

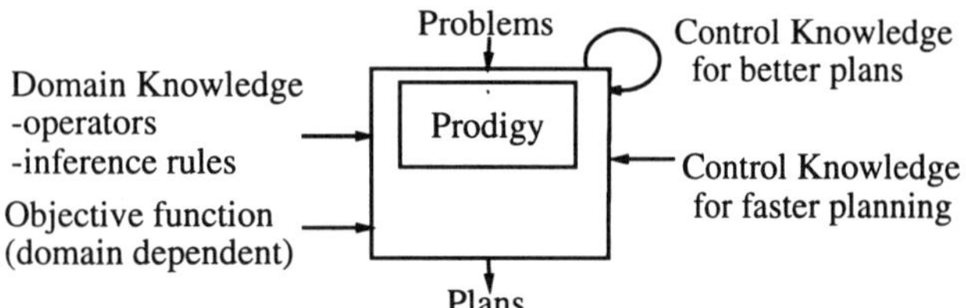

Figure 1: Architecture of a system to learn control knowledge to improve plan quality (Pérez & Carbonell 1994).

*Thanks to Jaime Carbonell for his suggestions and support in this work. This research is sponsored by the Wright Laboratory, Aeronautical Systems Center, Air Force Materiel Command, USAF, and the Advanced Research Projects Agency (ARPA) under grant number F33615-93-1-1330. Views and conclusions contained in this document are those of the authors and should not be interpreted as necessarily representing official policies or endorsements, either expressed or implied, of Wright Laboratory or the United States Government. The author holds a scholarship from the Ministerio de Educación y Ciencia of Spain.

The learning algorithm is *given* a domain theory (operators and inference rules) and a domain-dependent objective function that describes the quality of the plans. It is also given problems to solve in that domain. The algorithm analyzes the problem-solving episodes by comparing the search trace for the planner solution given the current control knowledge, and another search trace corresponding to a better solution (*better* according to the evaluation function). The latter search trace is obtained by letting the problem solver search further until a better solution is found, or by asking a human expert for a better solution and then producing a search trace that leads to that solution. The decision points where control knowledge failed to guide the planner to the better plan are used as learning opportunities. From the comparison of the two traces the algorithm *explains* why one solution is better than the other using the evaluation function, and its *output* is search control knowledge that leads future problem solving towards better quality plans. Two points are worth mentioning:

- Learning is driven by the existence of a better solution and a failure of the current control knowledge to produce it.
- There is a change of representation from the knowledge about quality encoded on the objective function into knowledge that the planner may use at problem solving time, as the plan and search tree are only partially available when a decision has to be made.

We do not claim that this control knowledge will necessarily guide the planner to find optimal solutions, but that the quality of the plans will incrementally improve with experience, as the planner sees new interesting problems in the domain.

We have obtained good preliminary results using randomly-generated problems in a process planning domain. We plan to explore different domains and types of evaluation functions.

References

Carbonell, J. G., and The PRODIGY Research Group. 1992. PRODIGY4.0: The manual and tutorial. TR CMU-CS-92-150, Carnegie Mellon University.

Pérez, M. A., and Carbonell, J. G. 1993. Automated acquisition of control knowledge to improve the quality of plans. TR CMU-CS-93-142, Carnegie Mellon University.

Pérez, M. A., and Carbonell, J. G. 1994. Control knowledge to improve plan quality. Proceedings AIPS 94.

Database Learning for Software Agents

Mike Perkowitz   Oren Etzioni
Department of Computer Science and Engineering, FR–35
University of Washington, Seattle, WA   98195
{map, etzioni}@cs.washington.edu

With the amount of information available rapidly outstripping the ability of individuals to use it, we wish to explore how a software agent can learn a description of an information resource (such as a database on the internet) in order turn it into a well-understood tool at the agent's disposal. An agent who could do this would have access to all the information it could find without having to cache the internet.

As the agent makes queries to an information resource, it will generalize from those queries and generate hypotheses about the structure and content of the database. We therefore formulate this problem as a learning problem in which the input is (1) the agent's *model* – its representation of the world; and (2) a series of queries to and responses from a database. The output is a mapping from fields in the information resource to predicates in the model.

Our approach to this learning problem relies on overlap between the agent's model and the information in the database. The agent will use its own knowledge to form hypotheses about the structure of the records. We have developed the *correspondence heuristic*, which states that a correspondence of tokens between the agent's world model and the information resource indicates a correspondence between types. The agent matches the values of the fields in the database against facts in its model. The relationships that hold among these facts in the model are assumed to correspond to relationships in the database.

Suppose that the agent makes a query to `staffdir`, the UW personnel directory, and gets back "`Oren Etzioni 206`". The agent would have facts in its model like (`lastname person37 Etzioni`) and (`office person37 206`). From this query and this knowledge, the agent could conclude that the second field of the output is `lastname` and the third field is `office`.

Our work has many similarities to structure-mapping work (Falkenhainer, Forbus, & Gentner 1986). Both approaches rely on discovering correspondences between separate domains. Structure-mapping, however, seeks correspondence between underlying structure, while the correspondence heuristic relates tokens in order to make inferences about the structure.

The correspondence heuristic is an inductive bias which can be formalized as a *determination*:

$$\forall(x,y)[T(x) \wedge T(y) \wedge (S(x) = M(x)) \rightarrow S(y) = M(y)]$$

T is a *type* predicate such as "on the UW faculty". S is a *syntactic* predicate like "the first field in the output of `staffdir x`". M is a *semantic* predicate (i.e. from the agent's model) such as "the first name of x".

This formalization clearly indicates three areas for work. Learning T could be handled by standard inductive learning algorithms. We assume a syntactic model of ordered fields to account for S. Future work may pursue other kinds of syntax, such as keyword-based syntax. The focus of our work is learning the appropriate M predicate.

In particular, we have been exploring the problem of *Predicate mismatch*, which occurs when instances of one type in the database are instances of a different type in the model, or when relations in the database do not correspond to primitive relations in the model. For example, imagine that the agent gets back "`Oren Etzioni FR-35`" from a query. `FR-35` is actually the mail stop of Etzioni's department and so there is no fact to link the person `Etzioni` to the string `FR-35` directly. Instead, the agent must realize that the entry in the database corresponds to a chain of predicates in its model linking `Etzioni` to `Computer Science` and `Computer Science` to `FR-35`. We have devised a way of doing this using a method reminiscent of spreading activation, in which a link between two tokens is found by exploring outward from the tokens until an intersection is found.

Given simplifying assumptions about the syntax, our implemented algorithm has learned `staffdir` as well as `ls` and `finger` (UNIX commands with tabular output can be treated as query/response databases). In the future, we will extend this to be able to handle information resources found on the World Wide Web by programs that traverse the web automatically.

References

Falkenhainer, B., Forbus, K., and Gentner, D. 1986. The structure-mapping engine. In *Proc. 5th Nat. Conf. on A.I.*

Diagnosing Multiple Interacting Defects with Combination Descriptions

Nancy E. Reed

Computer Science Department, University of Minnesota
4-192 EE/CS Bldg., 200 Union St. S.E., Minneapolis, MN 55455
reed@cs.umn.edu

Cases with multiple defects can be difficult to diagnose because the defects can interact, meaning that the observable cues are not a sum of the cues for the component defects. Diagnostic methods that use cue-to-defect relationships fail when interactions between defects change the observable cues. The primary alternative, model-based methods, are limited to domains with accurate and complete models, along with initialization data. Using these traditional methods, when defects interact and models aren't available, each possible defect combination must be included in the knowledge base. This results in an explosion of possible alternatives, greatly increased knowledge acquisition effort, slower processing, and increased maintenance effort.

This research develops a computational diagnostic model that can diagnose multiple defects, even when cues are altered or missing, by using descriptions of cue combinations. We develop a description and classification of the ways cues change when defects interact. Each type of cue may combine in a different way, so each type has a separate description. The combination methods use the expectations of component defects to diagnose multiple interacting defects, instead of requiring a description of each possible defect combination.

In a medical domain (diagnosis of congenital heart defects), we found that cues combine with one another in a small number of ways: all cues may appear *(union)*, the values of the cues may be *added* (quantitatively or qualitatively), or *dominant* cues may mask other cues present. Cues of each type combine in one of these basic ways, or use a combination of a few of the basic ways, depending on characteristics of the cues, case, or domain.

Figure 1 shows two types of cues, murmurs and heart sounds, for an example case. The case has two defects, atrial septal defect (ASD) and aortic stenosis (AS).

The cues are different than expected because the defects interact. Two murmurs are expected, a loud systolic ejection murmur in the pulmonary area for ASD, and a moderate systolic ejection murmur in the aortic area for AS. Only one murmur is observed. Loud murmurs mask softer ones occurring at the same time, so the absence of the (softer) expected murmur for AS is explained. The observed murmur supports ASD alone or ASD+AS. The observed heart sound S2 is normal, while both defect expectations are abnormal. ASD produces a wide, fixed split S2 while AS produces a narrow, variably split S2. The wide and narrow widths combine additively to explain a normal width, while the variable and fixed expectations combine additively to a variable split, which is a normal S2. Neither ASD nor AS is supported alone, but ASD+AS is supported by the normal S2 cue.

If we had used cue-to-defect relationships and matching on this case, we would have explained only the observed murmur (with one of the component defects), leaving three missing abnormal expectations unexplained.

The diagnostic model is tested by constructing a program with a knowledge base in pediatric cardiology (Fallot) and testing it on cases of single and multiple defects from hospital files. Fallot uses a combination of recognition-based reasoning (Thompson et al. 1983) and the cue combination descriptions. This program correctly diagnoses cases with multiple interacting defects for which conventional methods fail.

References

W. B. Thompson, P. E. Johnson, and J. B. Moen. 1983. Recognition-based diagnostic reasoning. In *Proceedings of the Eighth International Joint Conference on Artificial Intelligence*, pages 236–238.

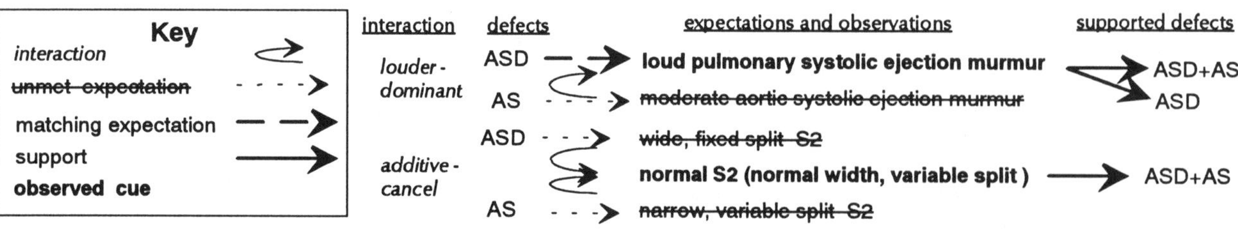

Figure 1: Explanation for murmur and heart sound cues for a case

Building Emotional Characters for Interactive Drama

W. Scott Reilly
Computer Science Department, Carnegie Mellon University
5000 Forbes Avenue
Pittsburgh, PA 15213-3891
scott.reilly@cs.cmu.edu

Goals and Methodology

The Oz project is developing tools to create interactive, dramatic stories (Bates 1992).[1] An important aspect of this work is to develop technology for creating the characters for these stories. We feel it's critical that these characters appear emotional; just as characters in novels and movies that are unemotional are called "flat" and aren't very believable, we expect the same applies to computer controlled drama as well.

We're developing an agent architecture, Tok (Bates, Loyall, & Reilly 1992), and an emotion subsystem, Em (Reilly & Bates 1992), that will allow artists to build emotional characters for their particular interactive stories. This goal places a number of constraints on the architecture. First, the architecture must be *usable*. That is, it must not be overly complicated to develop emotional characters, especially simple ones. Second, the architecture must be *flexible* enough to create idiosyncratic characters. We're willing to pass up psychological reality for the usablility and flexibility needed to create believable, artistic characters.

Emotions in Em are generated by a flexible set of generation rules. We make emotion generation usable by providing a default set of rules based on the cognitive emotion system of (Ortony, Clore, & Collins 1988). For example, Em will generate *joy* whenever an important goal of the character succeeds. Using similar rules, Em generates: distress, fear, hope, like, dislike, pride, shame, admiration, reproach, anger, gratitude, gratification, remorse, satisfaction, disappointment, relief, and fears-confirmed. Also planned are: happy-for, pity, gloating, resentment, and frustration.

The emotions, once generated, are mapped into Behavioral Features (BFs) which, in turn, affect other Tok processes. For example, anger will often result in an aggressive BF being generated. This BF then affects other Tok subsystems. The BFs allow for a bit of individualism in the characters. So, not all characters must act aggressively when angry. It is just as simple to create a character who acts withdrawn when angry

---

[1]This work is supported in part by Fujitsu Laboratories, Ltd.

or aggressively when frightened.

We're exploring how to model the effects of emotions (via BFs) on the rest of Tok. Emotions currently affect goal processing by creating new goals, altering plan choices, rearranging goal priorities, and affecting the style of actions (e.g., stomping instead of walking). These effects are presently hand-coded, but we plan to create a useful set of behavioral features that will map automatically into these kinds of effects.

Results

The best way to test such a system is to build agents. One Tok/Em agent is Lyotard the cat (Bates, Loyall, & Reilly 1992). Lyotard was the first demonstration that Em and Tok can be used to create reasonably believable, albeit somewhat simple, agents. A second set of agents are the Woggles: three ellipsoidal creatures who live in a real-time graphical world (Loyall & Bates 1993). Informal evidence from hundreds of users indicates that the Woggles are believable, engaging characters. We're also developing a gunman and a cashier for use in a hold-up story.

References

Bates, J.; Loyall, A. B.; and Reilly, W. S. 1992. Integrating reactivity, goals, and emotion in a broad agent. In *Proceedings of the Fourteenth Annual Conference of the Cognitive Science Society*.

Bates, J. 1992. Virtual reality, art, and entertainment. *PRESENCE: Teleoperators and Virtual Environments* 1(1):133–138.

Loyall, A. B., and Bates, J. 1993. Real-time control of animated broad agents. In *Proceedings of the Fifteenth Annual Conference of the Cognitive Science Society*.

Ortony, A.; Clore, G.; and Collins, A. 1988. *The Cognitive Structure of Emotions*. Cambridge University Press.

Reilly, W. S., and Bates, J. 1992. Building emotional agents. Technical Report CMU-CS-92-143, School of Computer Science, Carnegie Mellon University, Pittsburgh, PA.

ON THE COMPUTATION OF POINT OF VIEW

Warren Sack

MIT Media Laboratory, 20 Ames St., E15-487, Cambridge, MA 02139
email: wsack@media.mit.edu *phone*: 617/253-9497 *fax*: 617/258-6264

Abstract

Previous work in AI story understanding has largely been used to build tools which can summarize stories and categorize them according to the events they describe (e.g., the technologies developed for the Message Understanding Conferences). These sorts of technologies are built around the assumptions that (1) events reported as facts in news stories should be "understood" as facts; (2) the style of a story, i.e., the way in which a story is told, is not of interest; and, (3) the source of a story should not influence its analysis. These assumptions are obviously unrealistic. Everyone knows that one should not believe everything in the news. But, by making these simplifying assumptions most existing story understanding systems function as gullible "readers." [1] The focus of my current research is to build a less gullible story understander by encoding in it a means to recognize *point of view*. The techniques that I am developing will be useful, not only for information retrieval tasks which demand a search for credible stories, but also in future entertainment technologies which will be capable of finding and then assembling together into a unified presentation a set of texts or video clips to tell a story from an ensemble of points of view.

It is often possible, upon reading the first sentence or two of a news story, to determine the storyteller's point of view. For example, consider the following lead sentences from two different news reports about two different events:

1. Clandestine, 30 Mar 89 (Radio Venceremos) -- A report from San Miguel Department states that FMLN antiaircraft units ambushed a Salvadoran Air Force helicopter in Arenales canton at 1700 GMT on 29 March, as it was traveling from Usulutan to San Miguel department. Our unit's effective antiaircraft fire hit and damaged the helicopter. [MUC3-0096]

2. San Salvador, 9 Jan 90 (DPA) -- The Salvadoran Army today prevented the occupation of cities in the eastern part of El Salvador, waging strong clashes between midnight and dawn, according to reports by military sources. [MUC3-0006]

One does not need to know about Salvadoran news agencies nor much about the past civil war in El Salvador to notice clues which give away the storytellers' points of view: In story 1 the author notes the actions of the FMLN's antiaircraft units and then refers to the antiaircraft units as "ours." Clearly the use of the possessive shows that the first story is told from the point of view of the FMLN. In story 2 the point of view is less clear, but can be identified nonetheless. First of all, "military sources"

are said to be the main source of the story. Secondly, and more subtly, it was said that the Army "prevented the occupation of cities" instead of, for example, "prevented the liberation." Together, these two clues mark story 2 as one told from the Salvadoran Army's point of view.

SpinDoctor is a system which identifies a news story's point of view using mechanisms which are built on the following observation: News products with significantly different points of view habitually cast the same news actors in different roles (e.g., the American press will cast Hussein as the villain, whereas the Iraqi press will cast Hussein as the hero). The current system has a database of fairy-tale-like roles described by linguist George Lakoff as those employed by American journalists to describe actions and actors in the Gulf War (Lakoff .1991).

> Under orders from President Bush, U.S. and allied troops moved into defensive positions, ready to shoot if attacked but otherwise content to let President Saddam Hussein's conquered warriors *slink* [my emphasis] home, leaving their tanks and artillery behind them.
>
> (p. 1, *San Jose Mercury News*, February 28, 1991)

SpinDoctor's analysis process is as follows: (1) it parses the news story; (2) notes which sorts of roles are evoked by various words and phrases (e.g., that "slink home" connotes a serpentine or animal-like activity by comparing the verb phrase to the part of the role definition of serpent which describes typical and unique actions for a serpent); (3) uses a set of heuristics to determine which actors are assigned to which sorts of roles (e.g., that the conquered warriors are being compared, metaphorically, to a snake, via the verb "slink"); (4) resolves various relations of anaphora (e.g., the fact that "President Saddam Hussein's conquered warriors" is a reference to the Iraqi Army) by chaining together actor-role assignments (e.g., if role(a1) = r1, role(a2) = r1, then a1 might be equal to a2); and, (5) outputs the name of one or more news sources (as the recognized point of view) which use actor-role assignments consistent with the actor-role assignments identified.

Most contemporary story understanding systems are built for data extraction and text categorization tasks and so are designed to answer the standard questions of news *reporting*: Who? What? When? Where? Why? How? In contrast SpinDoctor has been designed to help explore the issues of news *filtering* and *editing*, namely, Whose point of view, whose interests, are represented in the news? SpinDoctor is now being scaled up to analyze the corpus of news stories used in the MUC3 competition.

References

Lakoff, G. 1991. Metaphor and War: The Metaphor System Used to Justify the War in the Gulf. *Journal of Urban and Cultural Studies* 2(1): 59-72.

---

[1] There are some early exceptions (e.g., Abelson and Carroll, 1966) and this neglect has not been complete in closely related areas (in dialog and argument understanding,, e.g., Allen and Perrault 1980, Birnbaum Flowers and McGuire 1980, Alvarado 1990; intelligent tutoring systems, e.g., Farrell and Bloch 1988; and, in the field of language generation, e.g., Hovy 1988).

Multi-agent Learning in Non-cooperative Domains

Mahendra Sekaran and **Sandip Sen**
Department of Mathematical & Computer Sciences
University of Tulsa
600 South College Avenue, Tulsa OK 74104-3189
mahend@euler.mcs.utulsa.edu

Motivation

Previous work in *coordination* (Bond & Gasser 1988) on multi-agent systems are specific either to cooperative or non-coperative problem domains. Previous work in *learning* in multi-agent systems have considered agents operating to solve a cooperative task with explicit information sharing and negotiations (Weiß 1993, Tan 1993). In a companion paper (Sen, Sekaran, & Hale 1994) we describe a general purpose system which describes a cooperative domain in which two agents work together on a joint task without explicit sharing of knowledge or information. The focus of this poster is to extend this approach to a non-cooperative domain, where the agents have conflicting goals. The strength of this work lies in the fact that there is no explicit knowledge exchange between the agents and no dependencies on agent relationships.

Problem description

The problem we consider is the "Block pushing" problem in which two autonomous agents with different capabilities and no knowledge of the domain are to push a block from a initial position to individual goal positions in Euclidean space. At each step, each agent applies a force and angle and the block is transferred to the next state by a combination of the actions. A trial ends when the block reaches either one of the goal positions or when it is out of the playing field. Each agent through repeated trials learns a optimal policy to reach (as close as possible) its goal position. The feedback received after each action is an exponentially decreasing function of the current distance of the block from the optimal path to their respective goals. Based on the received feedback the agents update their individual policies using a well-known reinforcement learning scheme , the Q-learning algorithm (Watkins 1989). Convergence of policy matrices (there is no significant update in the individual policies over a set of trials) is used as the stopping criteria for experiments.

Experiments and Results

We found that when the force range for one agent is greater than the other agent, it is able to overpower the other agent and drag the block to its goal. The number of trials to convergence increases as the force range for the weaker agent is increased (because it offers more resistance). When the two agents possess equal capabilities, neither of them are able to push the block to their goal and they manage to push the block to a position in between the goals. As the strength of the weaker agent increases the final block position moves away from the goal of the stronger agent. This phenomenon is accentuated when the number of discrete options available to the weaker agent is increased. This is because the stronger agent coverges to a sub-optimal policy and can be avoided by choosing a probabilistic action scheme instead of a deterministic one (though policy convergence will be much slower).

We show that agents can use reinforcement learning schemes to achieve their goal even when working against a non-benevolent agent without requiring a model of the latter. Currently, we are investigating resource sharing between multiple agents using the same approach.

References

A. H. Bond and L. Gasser. *Readings in Distributed Artificial Intelligence*. Morgan Kaufmann Publishers, San Mateo, CA, 1988.

C. Watkins. *Learning from Delayed Rewards*. PhD thesis, King's College, Cambridge University, 1989.

G. Weiß. Learning to coordinate actions in multi-agent systems. In *Proceedings of the International Joint Conference on Artificial Intelligence*, pages 311–316, August 1993.

M. Tan. Multi-agent reinforcement learning: Independent vs. cooperative agents. In *Proceedings of the Tenth International conference on Machine Learning*, pages 330-337, June 1993.

S. Sen, M. Sekaran and J. Hale. Learning to coordinate without sharing information. In *Proceedings of the twelfth national conference on Artificial Intelligence*, August 1994

Coalition formation methods in multi-agent environments *

Onn Shechory
Department of Mathematics and Computer Science
Bar Ilan University Ramat Gan, 52900 Israel
shechory@bimacs.cs.biu.ac.il
Tel: +972-3-5318863 Fax: +972-3-5353325

Autonomous agents are designed to reach goals that were pre-defined by their operators. An important way to execute tasks and to maximize utility is to share resources and to cooperate on task execution by creating coalitions of agents. If the agents are individually rational, such coalitions will take place if, and only if, each member of a coalition gains more if it joins the coalition than it could gain previously. There are several ways of creating such coalitions and dividing the joint payoff among the members. Variation in these methods is due to different environments, different settings in a specific environment, and different approaches to a specific environment with specific settings (Zlotkin & Rosenschein 1993).

In this research we develop methods for coalition-formation and utility distribution in various environments, we discuss their advantages and suggest occasions when each is most suitable (Shechory & Kraus 1993). The algorithms are developed with reference to different approaches. Some approaches are based on theoretical concepts from game theory (Shapley & Shubik 1973). Other approaches are based upon negotiation (Kraus & Wilkenfeld 1991), and the use of methods and concepts from distributed AI. The algorithms require communication and computation operations. These operations are either distributed among the agents or performed all by one agent. There are algorithms that can be halted in the middle of processes but still give reasonable results, i.e., any-time algorithms (Dean & Boddy 1988), while others, if were stopped before they end will give no results.

We use a new concept of *polynomial* Kernel-stability based on the original Kernel-stability (Davis & Maschler 1965), to develop a Coalition Negotiation polynomial Algorithm (CNA), on which we focus. The CNA consists of steps in which coalitions are formed, where each step is constructed as follows:

1. Each coalition ranks the other coalitions according to the expected utility from forming a joint coalition.

2. Each coalition designs proposals to be offered to other coalitions, transmits the proposals and waits for response.

3. Each coalition that receives proposals accepts or rejects them according to an evaluation done with respect to the polynomial-kernel-stability of the offer.

The CNA leads to distribution of calculations and communications and to a vast reduction of the calculational complexity, although it partially employs computational methods that were developed for the exponential problem, e.g., the Stearns transfer scheme (Stearns 1968). It is an anytime algorithm: if halted after any negotiation step, it provides the agents with a set of formed polynomial K-stable coalitions. The advantages of our algorithm are that the average expected utility of the agents is an increasing function of the time and effort spent by the agents performing the CNA steps, and is always better than when cooperation is avoided.

References

Davis, M., and Maschler, M. 1965. The kernel of a cooperative game. *Naval research Logistics Quarterly* 12:223–259.

Dean, T., and Boddy, M. 1988. An analysis of time-dependent planning. In *Proceedings, AAAI88*, 49–54.

Kraus, S., and Wilkenfeld, J. 1991. Negotiations over time in a multi agent environment: Preliminary report. In *Proc. of IJCAI-91*, 56–61.

Shapley, L. S., and Shubik, M. 1973. *Game Theory in economics*. Santa Monica, California: Rand Corporation.

Shechory, O., and Kraus, S. 1993. Coalition formation among autonomous agents: Strategies and complexity. In *Proc. of MAAMAW-93*.

Stearns, R. E. 1968. Convergent transfer schemes for n-person games. *Transactions of the American Mathematical Society* 134:449–459.

Zlotkin, G., and Rosenschein, J. 1993. One,two,many: Coalitions in multi-agent systems. In *Proc. of MAAMAW-93*.

*The author is indebted to Sarit Kraus for her support and for her helpful advice. The material in this research is based upon work supported in part by the NSF under Grant No. IRI-9123460.

Integrating Specialized Procedures in Proof Systems

Vishal Sikka

Computer Science Department
Stanford University
Stanford, CA - 94305
vishal@cs.stanford.edu

Introduction

We present the outline of a simple but powerful scheme for describing procedures that can be used by an automatic theorem prover. Our approach is to *describe* specialized procedures to a theorem prover by adding procedure description axioms to its set of facts, instead of *building in* these procedures by using attachments. Our work can be viewed as an extension of the hybrid reasoning techniques based on attachments (Myers91).

In this abstract we briefly describe our approach and state some of its advantages. In (Sikka94), we present this work in detail and formally show how the full expressibility of attachment-like approaches can be achieved in a simple logic-theoretic way. The work described here is part of the author's Ph.D. thesis research in collaboration with Prof. Michael Genesereth.

A Simple Integration Scheme

We treat a programming environment as a 3-tuple $\Im : \langle \mathcal{P}, \mathcal{D}, \mathcal{E} \rangle$, of procedures ($\mathcal{P}$), data structures ($\mathcal{D}$), and an evaluation function $\mathcal{E} : \mathcal{P} \times \mathcal{D}^* \to \mathcal{D}$. We integrate procedures from such an environment into a first order deductive calculus. Here we briefly describe its syntax and semantics. The language $\mathcal{L}_\mathcal{M}$ is a construction from a standard first order language $\mathcal{L}$, a set P_N of procedure names (of $\mathcal{P}$ in $\Im$), and an n-ary function symbol *apply*.

We can use $\mathcal{L}_\mathcal{M}$ to describe procedures in a programming environment and their relationship to functions and relations. For example, the sentence
$\forall x . \forall y . \, plus(x, y) = apply(+, x, y)$
relates the procedure $+$ to the function *plus*.

Every expression containing the function symbol *apply* has the following semantics:
$apply(p, t_1, t_2, \ldots, t_n)^\Im = \mathcal{E}(\phi, \tau_1, \tau_2, \ldots, \tau_n)$
where $p^\Im = \phi$, and $t_i^\Im = \tau_i$ for every i, $1 \leq i \leq n$. Every other expression in $\mathcal{L}_\mathcal{M}$ has standard first order semantics. We add to the deductive machinery an inference rule that allows us to replace a ground term containing the function symbol *apply* with the result of applying the associated procedure on the corresponding argument terms. This framework allows us

to prove the following result. It is formally described and proved in (Sikka94).

Theorem 1 *For every set of attachments, there is a set of sentences in $\mathcal{L}_\mathcal{M}$ that entail the same deductions.*

Summary

There are four principal advantages to using this approach for integration:

1. Attachments are principally *substitutional* in nature. Our scheme can be used to describe and use specialized procedures that perform more complex types of reasoning.
2. Attachment-based approaches are limited in the kinds of conditions that can be imposed on the invocation of procedures. With our scheme the language of representation, i.e. $\mathcal{L}_\mathcal{M}$ itself can be used to prescribe any conditions on the use of the attached procedures.
3. Sentences with the function symbol *apply* can be used to reason about the attached procedures. Since sentences containing the function symbol *apply* are ordinary sentences, composition axioms for attached procedures can be described and reasoned with ordinarily.
4. Describing attached procedures to a theorem prover is much easier, from an implementational viewpoint, than building in the attachment for every function and relation symbol that has an associated procedure.

References

Myers, K.L. 1991, Universal Attachments: A Logical Framework for Hybrid Reasoning, Ph.D. Thesis, Dept. of Computer Science, Stanford University, 1991.

Sikka, V.I., and Genesereth, M.R. 1994. Integrating Specialized Procedures in Proof Systems. Logic Group Technical Report LOGIC-94-3, Dept. of Computer Science, Stanford University. Also to appear in the Workshop on Metatheoretic Extensibility of Automated Reasoning Systems, *CADE-12*, Nancy, France.

Towards Situated Explanation

Raja Sooriamurthi and **David Leake**
Computer Science Department
Indiana University, Bloomington, IN 47405
{raja,leake}@cs.indiana.edu

In AI research on explanation, the mechanisms used to construct explanations have traditionally been neutral to the environment in which the explanations are sought. Our view is that the explanation process cannot be isolated from the situation in which it occurs. Without considering the intended use for an explanation, the explanation construction process cannot be properly focussed; without considering the situation the process cannot act effectively to gather corroborating information. The emphasis of this research is to view explanation as a means to an end and in this work the end is the successful functioning of the system requesting explanation. We develop a model of explanation as a situated, utility-based, hierarchical, goal-driven process.

Explanation is viewed as a memory process of adapting prior explanations of similar problems to fit the current situation. By using case-based reasoning we incorporate prior experience during the explanation process and also generate an initial set of hypotheses in a relatively inexpensive way. The system under development consists of a planner, acting in a simple simulated world, integrated with a case-based explainer. The over-arching goal of the explanation system is to aid the formulation and execution of plans. The occurrence of a planning or execution failure triggers explanation. Given the goals of the planner the explanation system has to decide when to explain, what to explain and how to explain in a dynamic environment. Related to earlier work on goal-directed diagnosis (Rymon 1993), a major issue being addressed in this research is how contextual changes influence the ongoing explanation process.

As an example of the issues to address consider the following scenario implemented in our system. The planner is trying to achieve the goal of catching a plane and generates two possible plans: driving to the airport or taking a taxi. Choosing the option of driving, the plan steps are executed in a simulated world and it is detected that the car does not start. In trying to determine why the car will not start our model of the ensuing explanation process involves:

- **Situated reasoning.** The explanation process responds to two types of situational changes:

1. *Changes in the external environment:* For example, due to time constraints the explanation effort could be curtailed and the system might choose the alternative plan of taking a taxi. But if the system becomes aware of a delay in the flight it opportunistically uses the extra available time for continuing with the explanation effort.

2. *Changes in the system goals:* The system will be able to produce explanations for three explanation purposes (Leake 1992): anomaly resolution, recovery and prevention. Changes in these explanation goals might produce explanations at levels of detail ranging from "something is wrong with the engine" to "drained-battery".

- **Knowledge planning.** An important facet of situated explanation is that all the information necessary to formulate an explanation might not be initially available to the system. The explainer has to determine what type of additional information is needed and how to procure it by planning to acquire knowledge (Hunter 1990). Prior cases help to package such knowledge planning actions that guide the information search.

- **Utility-based and hierarchical reasoning.** The utilities of the alternatives the explainer considers change with changes in the external environment. Our model of explanation allows the system to switch its focus to those alternatives that look most worthwhile in the current situation. The utilities of the alternatives also help to adjust the depth of the explainer's exploratory efforts. Case-based reasoning forms an effective mechanism to determine and update the situational utility of the alternative explanations.

References

Hunter, L. 1990. Planning to learn. In *12th Annual Conference of the Cognitive Science Society, Cambridge, Massachusetts*, 261–268. Lawrence Erlbaum Associates, Inc., Hillsdale, New Jersey.

Leake, D. B. 1992. *Evaluating Explanations: A content theory.* Lawrence Erlbaum Associates, Inc., Hillsdale, New Jersey.

Rymon, R. 1993. *Diagnostic Reasoning and Planning in Exploratory-Corrective Domains.* Ph.D. Dissertation, University of Pennsylvania.

Reflective Reasoning and Learning

Eleni Stroulia *

College of Computing

Georgia Institute of Technology

Atlanta, GA 30332-0280

eleni@cc.gatech.edu

The capability of learning is a prerequisite for autonomy. Autonomous intelligent agents, who solve problems in a realistic environment need to learn in order to extend the classes of problems they can solve, to improve their performance on these problems, and to improve the quality of the solutions they produce.

One way in which an intelligent agent may effectively use its experiences to learn, is by reflection upon its own problem-solving process. To do that, the agent needs to have an explicit meta-model of its own reasoning and knowledge. This work takes a functional stance towards reflective learning. This stance gives rise to a specific computational model which is based on three major hypotheses: (i) agents can be viewed as abstract devices, (ii) their reasoning can be understood in terms of structure-behavior-function (SBF) models, and (iii) learning can be viewed as a self-redesign task in which the agent uses its understanding of its own reasoning to improve its subsequent performance.

Modeling Reasoning in terms of SBF Models Intelligent agents accomplish their problem-solving tasks through the internal information-processing behaviors of their functional architecture. The SBF model describes the agent's reasoning as a non-deterministic sequence of information transformations, through which the output information of the agent's task is produced from its input.

Each information transformation corresponds to some subtask of the agent. The SBF model explicitly specifies the interactions among subtasks in terms of information and control flow. For each subtask, the model also specifies the role it plays to the accomplishment of the overall task in terms of the information it consumes, the information it produces, and a set of "correctness relations" between its input and output. Further, the SBF model specifies the representational and organizational assumptions on which the agent's world knowledge is based, and they ways in which this knowledge is used by the agent to select among its reasoning methods and accomplish its tasks.

Reflection If an agent has such a model of its own reasoning, it can use it to

1. *monitor* its own behavior. The SBF model of the problem solver provides a language for the agent to interpret its own reasoning steps in terms of its current goals and to generate expectations regarding their outcomes.

2. *assign blame* when it fails. The SBF model of the problem solver along with the record of its reasoning on the failed problem-solving episode, enables the agent to localize the cause of its failure to some element of its task structure.

3. *redesign* itself appropriately. The semantics of the SBF language enable the the agent to modify itself in a way that maintains the overall consistency of its reasoning.

This reflection process enables problem solvers, to some extent, to redesign themselves and adapt their problem-solving behavior to meet new requirements. Therefore, it is especially useful when the agent's tasks are complex and when the requirements imposed by the the environment upon the agent regarding its processing and the quality of the solutions it produces can change. If, on the other hand, the environment is stable and the task structure is close to optimal, it may be less cost efficient.

Discussion AUTOGNOSTIC (Stroulia and Goel 1993) is a system that implements and evaluates this theory of reflective reasoning and learning. Given the SBF model of a problem solver, AUTOGNOSTIC monitors its reasoning, and when it fails, assigns blame to some of its elements and redesigns it appropriately. AUTOGNOSTIC presently operates in two widely different task domains: on top of ROUTER, in the domain of navigational planning, and on top of KRITIK2, in the domain of engineering design. Both ROUTER and KRITIK2 are autonomous multistrategy systems developed independently of AUTOGNOSTIC, and since they solve widely different tasks in widely different domains, the success of AUTOGNOSTIC's reflection process suggests that its SBF models of problem solving and reflection process are quite general. AUTOGNOSTIC is capable of identifying and correcting errors

1. in the representation scheme of the world knowledge,

2. in the organization of the world knowledge,

3. in the content of the world knowledge itself,

4. in the assumptions on the applicability and utility of different reasoning methods, and

5. the role of a subtask in the overall reasoning process.

References

[Stroulia and Goel 1993] Stroulia, E; and Goel, A. 1993. Functional Representation and Reasoning for. Reflective Systems. *Applied Artificial Intelligence: An International Journal* Forthcoming.

*This research was conducted under the advice of Dr. Ashok Goel. It has been supported by the NSF (grant IRI-92-10925), the ONR (contract N00014-92-J-1234), the Advanced Projects Research Agency, and an IBM graduate fellowship.

Case-Based Reasoning for Weather Prediction

C. Vasudevan
AUV Group, Department of Ocean Engineering,
Florida Atlantic University,
500, NW 20th St., Boca Raton, FL 33431.
email: vasu@transquest.oe.fau.edu

Abstract

Computer-based forecasting of weather was first experimented in 1950 at Princeton University. Since then, there have been newer and more accurate methods to predict the incoming climate. One common practice of weather prediction is by using the general circulation models which are based on the laws of physics (J.M.Moran & M.D.Morgan 1986). These models are highly complex and computational intensive limiting their use for only short range predictions and that too needing supercomputers. The accuracy of forecasting deteriorates rapidly for periods longer than 48 hours and it often becomes minimal beyond 10 days due to imperfections in the models. The *analog* technique of weather forecasting is another approach which searches for periods in the past when the current conditions were similar and use the past spatial patterns as analogs (J.T.Houghton, G.J.Jenkins, & J.J.Ephraums 1990). Long term trends and recurring events guide the decisions. This is more relevant for long range predictions as well as in single station predictions. The *analog* method is relatively simple compared to the complex processes of development, validation, use, and maintenance of numerical models.

The *analog* technique closely resembles the principles of case-based reasoning (CBR) (Kolodner 1993; Hammond 1989). The CBR scheme attempts to identify a solution by searching a historical database of solutions. Rather than performing statistical computations on past records, CBR attempts to retrieve one or a few best matching cases from its casebase and modifies them to fit the current scenario. The CBR approach often results in a faster synthesis of solutions compared to rule-based reasoning or reasoning from first principles.

This paper discusses the relevance of CBR in weather forecasting and outlines an indexing and evaluation scheme for prediction. The major issue is the task of identifying a set of indices to retrieve matching past case records and interpret them in the current context. For *weather cases*, the indices are typically the observations of relevant atmospheric parameters such as *cloud amount, cloud altitude, cloud water content, wind direction and speed, sea and land surface temperatures, location and density of heat islands, atmospheric pressure*, and *water vapor content*. In addition to matching individual records, the variational patterns of these factors are also to be considered in assessing the situation. There are a number of rules of thumb derived from past experience that should be reflected in the case indices. Some examples are: *Falling air pressure may indicate the approach of a stormy weather. A wind shift from northwest to west to southwest is usually accompanied by warm air advection.* Building the casebase for weather prediction benefits from the archives already maintained by various meteorological agencies. The 'repair' or adaptation of matching case(s) is based on the immediate past information and the interpretation of mismatches in the observed data with the past case data.

The case-based reasoning scheme naturally suits weather prediction based on historical records. Although recurrence of climatic patterns may not be always dependable, this approach provides a simpler and faster method to predict the future weather conditions than the complex numerical models. Moreover, this scheme establishes a baseline for a detailed and more accurate scheme based on the physics of the system. This project is in a preliminary stage and a detailed knowledge engineering of weather patterns and prediction skills is needed to build the case library.

References

Hammond, K. 1989. *Case-Based Planning: Viewing Planning as a Memory Task.* Academic Press.

J.M.Moran, and M.D.Morgan. 1986. *Meteorology.* Macmillan Publishing Company.

J.T.Houghton; G.J.Jenkins; and J.J.Ephraums. 1990. *Climate Change: The IPCC Assessment.* Cambridge University Press.

Kolodner, J. 1993. *Case-based Reasoning.* Morgan-Kaufmann.

Agent Modeling Methods Using Limited Rationality

José M. Vidal and **Edmund H. Durfee** *
Artificial Intelligence Laboratory, University of Michigan.
1101 Beal Avenue, Ann Arbor, Michigan 48109-2110
jmvidal@umich.edu

To decide what to do in a multiagent world, an agent should model what others might simultaneously be deciding to do, but that in turn requires modeling what those others might think that others are deciding to do, and so on. The Recursive Modeling Method (RMM) [1] provides representations and algorithms for developing these nested models of beliefs and using them to make rational choices of action. However, because these nested models can involve many branches and recurse deeply, making decisions in time-constrained multiagent worlds requires methods for inexpensive approximation and for metareasoning to balance decision quality with decisionmaking cost.

RMM represents an interaction as a payoff matrix that specifies an agent's payoffs for different combinations of agents' actions. To predict others' actions, an agent will similarly model how it believes they see the interaction as matrices specifying their payoffs. The agent can model how the others see others as another layer of payoff matrices, and so on. When uncertain of how others will model the interaction, an agent associates probabilities with alternative models. We thus define a *situation* as a 4-tuple which includes the matrix (M) that corresponds to the agent's expected payoffs in this interaction, a probability density function (f) over the possible strategies that it should play, an estimate of the number of nested levels (l) of belief to which it has expanded this situation, and the set of situations that it thinks the other agents are in:

$$s = (M, f, l, \{(p, r)| \sum p = 1, r \in S\}) \in S \qquad (1)$$

The set of all situations is denoted as S. p is the probability with which the agent believes that some other agent is in the situation r.

The recursive definition of a situation makes it possible for loops to exist. That is, an agent might be in a situation s and believe, with some probability, that all the other agents are in the same situation s, and so on recursively. If the probability associated with these models is one, this can be interpreted as "all agents have common knowledge that they are in situation s." Such situations could lead RMM into infinitely deep recursion but, fortunately, game theory can provide alternative algorithms for identifying solutions in common knowledge situations. In fact, in some cases these algorithms can be substantially more efficient than reasoning about nested beliefs as RMM does. Thus, even when common knowledge does not exist, it might be more cost effective for an agent to assume that it does and converge on an approximate solution quickly, than to compute an exact solution using RMM.

In time-constrained cases where RMM should be employed, meta-reasoning can be used to selectively expand the recursive nesting of situations. We borrow some of Russell's notation [2] for limited rationality in turn-taking games (examining future game states), and apply it to RMM (examining more deeply-nested beliefs in the current state). The time cost to examine a situation s is denoted by $TC(s)$. Limiting ourselves to only two agents, we denote our top-level strategy as α and our counterpart's as β. The payoff we, as an agent, expect is $P(\alpha, \beta)$. If a situation s is not the top-level one, then we define our strategy, after expanding s and propagating a strategy back up the tree, as α_s. Similarly, our counterpart's is β_s. When we do not have time to fully expand a situation, we use the situation's function f to predict what strategy it is likely to return. In these cases, the associated strategies are $\hat{\alpha}_s$ and $\hat{\beta}_s$. We can now define the value of a situation $V(s)$ in terms of it's utility $U(s) = P(\alpha_s, \beta_s)$, and do the same for its expected value $E(V(s))$. Our expected gain in expanding a situation is $G(s)$.

$$V(s) = U(s) - TC(s) = P(\alpha_s, \beta_s) - TC(s) \qquad (2)$$

$$E(V(s)) = E(U(s)) - TC(s) = P(\hat{\alpha}_s, \hat{\beta}_s) - TC(s) \qquad (3)$$

$$G(s) = P(\hat{\alpha}_s, \hat{\beta}_s) - P(\alpha, \hat{\beta}_s) - \epsilon \cdot TC(s) \qquad (4)$$

We have designed an algorithm that uses these concepts to determine which parts, if any, of the RMM hierarchy could be gainfully expanded. We are working on its implementation and improving its ability to learn expected strategies.

[1] P.J.Gmytrasiewicz, E.H.Durfee, and D.K.Wehe. A decision theoretic approach to coordinating multiagent interactions. *IJCAI*, 1991.

[2] S.Russell and E.Wefald. *Do The Right Thing*. The MIT Press, Cambridge, Massachusetts, 1991.

*Supported, in part, by NSF grant IRI-9158473.

Learning by Observation and Practice:
A Framework for Automatic Acquisition of Planning Operators

Xuemei Wang *

School of Computer Science
Carnegie Mellon University
Pittsburgh PA 15213-3891
wxm@cs.cmu.edu

The knowledge engineering bottleneck is a central problem in the field of Artificial Intelligence. This work addresses this problem in the context of planning systems. It automatically learns planning operators by observing expert agents and by subsequent knowledge refinement in a learning-by-doing paradigm. Our learning method is implemented on top of the PRODIGY architecture(Carbonell *et al.* 1992).

The learning system is given at the outset the description language for the domain, which includes the types of objects and the predicates that describe states and operators. The observations of an expert agent consist of: 1) the sequence of actions being executed, 2) the state in which each action is executed (*pre-state*), and 3) the state resulting from the execution of each action (*post-state*). Our planning system uses STRIPS-like operators and the goal of this work is to learn the preconditions and the effects of the operators. We assume that the operators have conjunctive preconditions and no conditional effects, everything in the state is observable, and there is no noise in the state.

The architecture for learning by observation and practice in planning includes *the observation module, the learning module, the planning module*, and *the plan execution module*, as illustrated in Figure 1.

Operators for the domain are learned from these observation sequences in an incremental fashion utilizing a conservative specific-to-general inductive generalization process. When an operator is observed for the first time, the system creates the corresponding operator such that its precondition is the complete *pre-state* and its effect is the difference between the *post-state* and *pre-state*. Operators thus learned may have extra preconditions that correspond to the irrelevant features in the state. These extra preconditions are removed incrementally if they are not present in the *pre-states* of the new observations. In order to further refine the new operators to make them correct and complete, and to evaluate the new operators, the system uses them to solve practice problems. The system first generates an appoximate plan to solve the practice problem using the par-

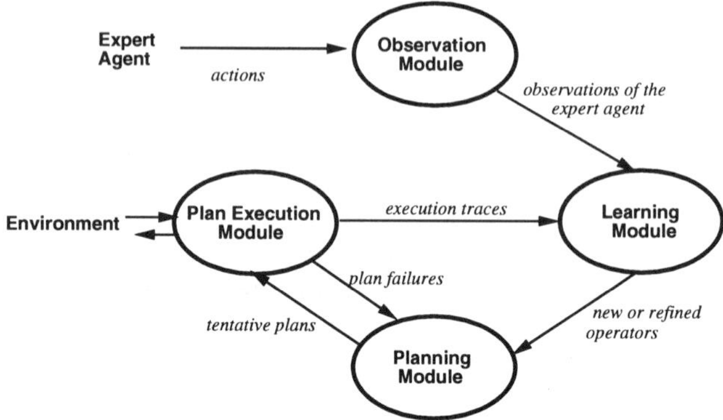

Figure 1: Overview of the data-flow among different modules of the learning system. The observation module provides the learning module with observations of the expert agent. The learning module formulates and refines operators in the domain. The planning module is essentially the PRODIGY planner modified to use some heuristics for planning with incomplete and incorrect operators as well as for plan repair, it generates tentative plans to solve practice problems. The plan execution module executes the plans, providing the learning module with the execution traces, and passing the plan failures to the planning module for plan repair.

tially incorrect and incomplete operators, then it executes the plan. When an operator fail to apply, it repairs the plan and continues execution, until the problem is solved or a resource bound is exceeded. The system also refines operators based on the executions. oIn summary, operators are refined through a process which integrates learning, planning, plan repair, and execution. See (Wang 1994) for more details of this research. This learning method has been partially demonstrated in the extended-strips domain and the process planning domain. We are currently performing more extensive tests in these domains. We plan to extend the algorithm to handle situations when part of the state is not observable, and there is noise in the state.

References

Carbonell, J. G., and The PRODIGY Research Group. 1992. PRODIGY4.0: The manual and tutorial. TR CMU-CS-92-150, Carnegie Mellon University.

Wang, X. 1994. Learning Planning Operators by Observation and Practice. In *Proceedings of the Second International Conference on AI Planning Systems*.

*Thanks to Jaime Carbonell for his suggestions and support in this work. This research is sponsored by the Wright Laboratory, Aeronautical Systems Center, Air Force Materiel Command, USAF, and the Advanced Research Projects Agency (ARPA) under grant number F33615-93-1-1330. Views and conclusions contained in this document are those of the authors and should not be interpreted as necessarily representing official policies or endorsements, either expressed or implied, of Wright Laboratory or the United States Government.

A Modular Visual Tracking System

Mike Wessler*
MIT Artificial Intelligence Laboratory
545 Technology Sq. NE43-803
Cambridge, MA 02139
wessler@ai.mit.edu

I am currently building an active visual tracking system for a real world robot. The hardware is being built at MIT under the supervision of Professors Rod Brooks and Lynn Andrea Stein, and is humanoid in form. The software is also humanoid: I am basing its organization on models of early vision in the human brain. Most of the software is still in the design phase; what I describe here is the part of the system that is already up and running.

The robot, named Cog, has roughly the same degrees of freedom in the waist, neck, arms and eyes as a human and is designed with similar proportions in mind. The eyes sport a simulated fovea – each eye consists of two cameras mounted in the same plate, one with a wide field of view, and one with a much narrower view. Both cameras produce 128×128 gray scale images. The narrow one is used for tracking, and can be used for object recognition, while the wider view will be used for motion detection and peripheral vision.

I have written a visual tracking system that will eventually be hooked up to the motors in Cog's neck and eyes. For now, tracking is simulated by moving a small 16×16 "attention window" around the larger image from one of the cameras. On startup, the system memorizes the 16×16 segment in the center of the full image as a "reference" image. For the rest of the run, the system moves the window around to maintain whatever was initially present within its view.

The tracking system runs as follows. Once a new frame is grabbed, the system makes a guess about where the new window location should be, based on its previous velocity. Next, a portion of the image slightly larger than the attention window is selected, and the derivative of this region is computed.[1] Finally, a simple correlation is performed between the memorized reference image and the nine 16×16 windows centered around the pixel position nearest the guess. The one with the best correlation becomes the new center of the attention window. The entire sequence of grab, process, and correlate runs at 15 Hz on one of the Motorola 68332 processors that make up Cog's "brain".

The system can track anything that accelerates less than one pixel (0.15 degrees for the narrow-angle camera) per frame per frame. This becomes a problem only for objects that jerk suddenly; the system does very well with objects like hands and faces moving at normal speeds. Furthermore, by examining the result of the best correlation, the tracker knows exactly when it has "lost" the image, and should request the coordinates of a new region to track.

The tracking routines form the heart of a much larger system that models Stephen Kosslyn and Olivier Koenig's view of early vision in human brains. Instead of tracking whatever happened to be in the center of the camera view on startup, the full architecture will have an attention shift module to direct the gaze from one object to another. This module receives inputs from other modules that detect motion, faces or other "popouts" in the field of view. An opposing forces model, described by Marcel Kinsbourne, implements the decision of when to switch attention: if one of the "watchers" detects a very strong stimulus, or when the tracking system has lost the image or has gotten "bored" with the image, the attentional system will prompt a tracking change.

Further up the line, information from the tracking window will be fed to a system that keeps a representation of location. This system gradually builds up a map of the world as attention is yanked from one object to another. Furthermore, by watching its hands and arms, Cog can learn to associate certain arm positions with certain locations in space, in effect learning hand-eye coordination.

Finally, because the image within the tracking window is relatively constant, a moving background can be segmented out simply by averaging one image with the next. This yields extremely useful data for an object recognition system, which can then put "labels" on the locations that the location system is recording. Information from the object recognition system can also be used to guide attention around the image, for example from a face to the eyes or mouth.

---

*This research is supported by an NSF Graduate Fellowship and by ARPA ONR contract N00014–91–J–4038. Any opinions, findings, conclusions or recommendations expressed in this material are those of the author and do not necessarily reflect the views of the NSF.

[1] Originally, I had taken two derivatives in the x and y directions, but it turns out that a single derivative runs twice as quickly, with very little decrease in reliability.

Utility-Directed Planning

Mike Williamson   Steve Hanks
Department of Computer Science and Engineering, FR–35
University of Washington, Seattle, WA   98195

Classical AI planning has adopted a very narrow notion of plan *quality*, namely that a plan is good just in case it achieves a specified *goal*. Goals provide a valuable point of computational leverage: despite the fact that planning is intractable in the worst case, goal-satisfying planning algorithms can effectively solve classes of problems by using the goal to focus the search for a solution (using backward-chaining techniques), and by exploiting domain-specific heuristic knowledge to control search.

But as the sole description of a planning problem, goals are in several regards inadequate. Goals provide neither a means of representing partial satisfaction (either a plan succeeds in achieving the desired world state or it does not), nor a way of describing the value of the specified world state relative to the cost of achieving it. In short, goals provide insufficient information to measure plan quality in any satisfying way.

Decision theory has been proposed as a solution to this problem. It provides a rich theoretical framework for the construction of utility models capturing precisely the notion of partial satisfaction and the cost-benefit tradeoff mentioned above. But the planning community has been slow to adopt utility models for the description of planning problems, since planning with utility models requires optimization, commonly thought to be less tractable and less amenable to heuristic control than classical goal satisfaction.

We claim that optimal planning can be made heuristically tractable for a class of utility models that is significantly more expressive than simple goal formulas. We extend the definition of plan quality to take into account partial satisfaction of the goal and the cost of resources used by the plan, while at the same time building an effective planning algorithm by exploiting classical planning techniques like backward chaining and knowledge-based search control rules.

We have adopted a *goal-directed* utility model similar to proposals by (Haddawy & Hanks 1993). This utility model allows the description of *soft deadline* goals whose value is a function of the time when the goal is satisfied. A goal is represented by a propositional goal formula, a *temporal decay function*, and a *goal-value coefficient*. The temporal decay function must be uniformly 1.0 until the deadline, and decrease monotonically thereafter. The goal-value coefficient determines the relative value of achieving the goal. The cost of the plan is captured with a *residual utility function*, a function of the resources consumed by a plan. Like temporal decay, the residual utility must be monotonically decreasing with respect to increased consumption of any given resource.

We have implemented PYRRHUS, a planning algorithm which finds optimal plans for the utility model described above. PYRRHUS is a synthesis of branch-and-bound optimization with a least-commitment, plan-space planner. The underlying planning mechanism is based on the UCPOP planning system (Penberthy & Weld 1992), with extensions to provide support for time and metric resources. In addition to the sort of search control knowledge employed by classical goal-satisfying planners, PYRRHUS uses the structure of the utility model to compute an upper bound on the utility of partial plans, possibly allowing them to be pruned from the search space.

Our initial empirical results are encouraging. We have conducted a number of experiments in a simulated transportation domain, comparing classical goal-satisfying planning to optimal planning with various utility models. PYRRHUS is able to employ the same heuristic search control knowledge as a classical planner to solve problems that would be intractable otherwise. We found the difficulty of optimal planning depends strongly on the nature of the utility model; in some cases the additional structure of the utility model makes optimal planning much easier than simple goal-satisfying planning, while in other cases it is more difficult. We are in the process of developing a formal characterization of the relationship between the structure of the utility function and the difficulty of optimal planning.

References

Haddawy, P., and Hanks, S. 1993. Utility Models for Goal-Directed Decision-Theoretic Planners. Technical Report 93–06–04, Univ. of Washington, Dept. of Computer Science and Engineering. Submitted to *Artificial Intelligence*.

Penberthy, J., and Weld, D. 1992. UCPOP: A sound, complete, partial order planner for ADL. In *Proc. 3rd Int. Conf. on Principles of Knowledge Representation and Reasoning*, 103–114.

Fuzzy Irrigation Decision Support System

Hong Xiang
AI Programs
The University of Georgia
Athens, GA 30602
xhong@ai.uga.edu

Brahm P. Verma
Department of Biological
and Agricultural Engineering
The University of Georgia
Athens, GA 30602
bverma@gamma.bae.uga.edu

Gerrit Hoogenboom
Department of Biological
and Agricultural Engineering
The University of Georgia
Griffin, GA 30223
ghoogen@gaes.griffin.peachnet.edu

Water is a limiting factor in agriculture and when improperly managed reduces the yield potential of crops. The objective of this study is to develop a Fuzzy Irrigation Decision Support System (FIDSS) to optimize water management for soybean production.

Management of irrigation systems for greatest benefit requires an understanding of many physical, biological and chemical processes, and economical factors. Such processes are very complicated and involves many uncertainties. During the last 20 years, considerable progress has been made in developing computer crop growth simulation models. These models are developed with the desire to incorporate quantitatively the fundamental mechanisms controlling the above processes. However, this objective has been compromised by simplifying the mechanisms' representations by general process descriptions which use empirical relationships determined from experimental data. In most cases, it is not possible to collect and correlate data for all conditions due to the nature of these processes. For example, variables such as soil water uptake by roots, soil water content at various depths and water lost by evapotranspiration interact with each other in a complex way making it hard to determine fundamental quantitative relationships among these variables.

This study is therefore undertaken to begin the development of a mechanistic model using qualitative rather than quantitative relationships of the most important variables for making irrigation decisions. The Fuzzy set theory introduce by Lofti Zadeh in 1965 provides the framework to cope with ambiguity and unnaturalness of the traditional crisp method in this domain. Fuzzy expert systems utilize human experience and decision methods, and they have proven to be valuable when dealing with non-linear and complex relationships.

In FIDSS we have developed membership functions for 21 important variables of three primary components: 1) variables for plant, such as, leaf area index (LAI) and evapotranspiration (EP); 2) variables for water status and flow in soil, such as, soil-water content in a layer (θ_L) and infilteration (IN); and 3) variables for weather, such as, maximum temperature (TM) and solar radiation (RAD). FIDSS has 163 rules in its knowledge base specified as follows:

IF　(LAI IS HIGH)　*AND*　(RAD IS HIGH)
AND　(TM IS HIGH)　**THEN**　(EP IS HIGH)

FIDSS is organized to receive crisp daily values of all state variables from an existing crop model, fuzzify the received inputs, perform evaluation with the knowledge base to give a fuzzy output, defuzzify the output to a crisp value which is then compared to a predetermined threshold condition for irrigation decision.

The existing soybean crop growth simulation model SOYGRO V5.42 developed at the University of Florida by James Jones et al. was used to update state variables. SOYGRO also has an irrigation management model in it which provided us an opportunity to compare decisions made by FIDSS with the ones of SOYGRO. The important additions in FIDSS are that it includes two days' predicted weather data for estimating soil water content and more additional variables for making decisions.

At this early stage of FIDSS development, only limited attempts have been made to tune the rules. However, the following comparison of FIDSS output with the outputs of SOYGRO shows promise for this approach. The output shown below is for soybean (cultivar 'Bragg') grown in Millhopper Fine Sandy soil for 1978 weather condition (for which field data is available). A further tuning of rules and a systematic evaluation of FIDSS is planned.

Table 1: Irrigation Outputs of SOYGRO and FIDSS

MODEL	Irrigation days (from planting) and final resultes
SOYGRO	$73, 77, 82, 87, 93, 98, 115$ $Yield = 3386.6(kg/ha)$ Total $Water = 211(mm)$
FIDSS	$8, 15, 68, 72, 76, 80, 84, 88, 92, 96, 110$ $Yield = 3406.8(kg/ha)$ Total $Water = 275(mm)$

Synthetic Robot Language Development

Holly A. Yanco*
MIT Artificial Intelligence Laboratory
545 Technology Square, Room 741, Cambridge, MA 02139
holly@ai.mit.edu   (617)253-7884

Cooperating robots can benefit from communication. Our robots create their own adaptable synthetic robot languages (ASRLs). We have shown that robots can develop "basic", context dependent, and compositional ASRLs using reinforcement learning techniques. (See (Yanco 1994) for a complete description of this work.)

We have demonstrated that the robots are able to develop ASRLs using two different reinforcement schemes: task-based reinforcement and individual reinforcement. In task-based reinforcement, the robots only receive positive reinforcement when the task is completed properly. This reinforcement method is preferable in situations where it can not be determined who performed the correct actions to reach the goal, but it is clear that the goal was reached. Individual reinforcement is better suited to tasks where it is clear which of the robots helped to reach the goal. This determination is used to give the robots that helped reach the goal good reinforcement while penalizing the robots that did not contribute toward the group goal. In our model, the robots are able to learn more quickly using the individual reinforcement, but at the expense of convergence. However, most tasks can not easily be decomposed to determine which members of the group acted correctly, and even for those tasks that can be easily decomposed, the overhead necessary to make the determination is often costly. While task-based reinforcement results in longer learning times, it only requires a one-bit decision in allocating reinforcement.

The basic ASRL is a simple one-to-one mapping of robot signals to robot actions. The development of this ASRL in simulation and with robots demonstrated that robots could learn to communicate and could adapt their language to changing circumstances.

Simulated robots have also created a context dependent ASRL. In a context dependent language, robot words can have different meanings depending on the state of the world as perceived through sensor readings. For example, the robots could learn a command for *DO*, where they should *DO recharge* in the presence of a charging station, *DO gather* when sensors indicate that objects are present that should be collected, or *DO sleep* when the lights are turned out. The context dependent language requires shorter learning times than the basic experiment because the robots need to learn fewer ASRL signals.

The simulated robots have also developed a compositional ASRL. A compositional language combines words with ways for the words to be put together to form higher level concepts. For example, you have probably never read a sentence exactly like this one before; however, you are able to understand the sentence because you know the meanings of the words in this sentence and understand English grammar. In the basic ASRL, whenever the robots encounter a new sentence (or concept), they must start the learning process from scratch, even if the concept only varies slightly from a previously learned concept. In compositional ASRLs, the robots can use what they have already learned as they encounter new sentences containing old words. Therefore, the learning times for the compositional ASRL are dramatically faster than for both the basic ASRL and the context dependent ASRL.

Adaptable synthetic robot languages developed by the robots themselves have several advantages. They allow the robots to create languages that will be well-suited to specific tasks and to the capabilities of the robot hardware. ASRLs require less human involvement than pre-programmed robot languages. The robots are able to adapt to changing circumstances without outside assistance. In a dynamic environment where robots must work continuously without human assistance, adaptable synthetic languages are the communication method of choice.

References

Yanco, H. A. 1994. Robot communication: issues and implementations. Master's thesis, Massachusetts Institute of Technolgy. Also available as MIT-AI-TR 1478.

---

*This research is supported by the NSF under Professor Lynn Andrea Stein's NSF Young Investigator Award No. IRI–9357761, Digital Equipment Corporation, the Gordon S. Brown Fund, and ARPA ONR contract N00014–91–J–4038. Any opinions, findings, conclusions or recommendations expressed in this material are those of the author and do not necessarily reflect the views of the NSF.

Computer Simulation of Statistics and Educational Measurement
StatSim: An Intelligent Tutoring System for Statistics

Liu Zhang

Artificial Intelligence
University of Georgia
Athens, GA 30602
lzhang@ai.uga.edu

Donald Potter

Artificial Intelligence
University of Georgia
Athens, GA 30602
dpotter@ai.uga.edu

The purpose of this research is to develop an adaptive tutoring system which uses AI techniques to explore how to diagnose student's misconceptions in problem solving and generate relevant instructions from the context. The system is called StatSim.

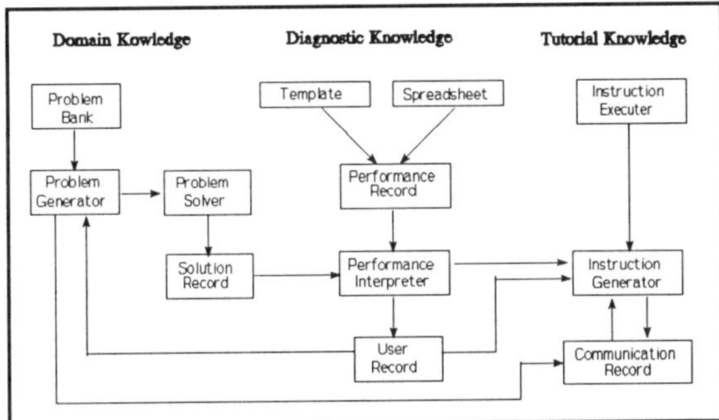

StatSim is an expert system for teaching basic concepts of statistics such as standard deviation, normal distribution and standard scores. It simulates three types of knowledge: statistics domain knowledge, diagnostic knowledge and tutorial knowledge to guide students in problem solving. At the beginning of the tutorial, the student is given a case as a statistics problem to solve, produced by the problem generator based on the student's record. The consultation program (domain expert) solves the problem first and saves the results and reasoning process in working memory. The diagnosis program (diagnosis expert) interprets the student's behavior by comparing the student's behavior in solving the same problem with the expert's behavior. The tutoring program (teaching expert) responds to the student's behavior on the basis of what the student knows and his goals for the tutorial session. It can take the initiative by offering orientation when a new concept is introduced or by interrupting a student when it finds some explanation is necessary. The purpose of this tutorial is to use the context of an actual problem to make the student aware of gaps and inconsistency in his knowledge and to correct these deficiencies.

The whole tutoring process consists of two sessions: a consultation session and a tutorial session. During the consultation session, the Problem Solver program applies domain knowledge production rules to derive a solution. It reads in a problem text, converts it into a set of keywords in the form of attribute-value pairs and saves them in working memory. The rule interpreter fires all the rules whose conditions are satisfied and saves the results as a text file.

During the tutorial session, the Tutor program maintains and updates a student model and a record of the communication between the tutor and student. A set of tutorial rules are used to control what to teach and how to teach on the basis of what the student knows. A template-based user interface is designed to keep track of the student's mental activity. It serves both as an external memory and a source of input to the system. The student's problem-solving behavior is recorded in performance history.

A special module (performance interpreter) which simulates the diagnostic expertise of a teacher is developed to reconstruct the student's model of domain knowledge on the basis of the student's performance history. The input to the performance interpreter comes from the generic template and working spreadsheet. Each move in the student's behavior on the screen is recorded whenever an input textbox is out of focus. The interpreter keeps its observations until it collects enough information to update the student model. Interpretation rules are employed to decide when to intervene and how to intervene, one of the major issues in ITS. The system is sensitive to every step in the student's problem solving process but at the same time lets him explore the solution to the problem.

StatSim has four major features: 1) it uses multiple faulty diagnosis techniques to locate student's misconceptions; 2) it employs graphics, animation, menus, windows and other interactive techniques in instruction delivery to enhance understanding and motivation; 3) it uses production rules to control the intervention so that the user has enough control of the system; 4) it uses planning to refine the explanations and instructional acts to maximize the teaching effects.

Video
Program

Guardian: A Prototype Intelligent Agent for Intensive-Care Monitoring

Barbara Hayes-Roth[1]   **Serdar Uckun**[1]   **Jan Eric Larsson**[1]
David Gaba[2]   **Juliana Barr**[2]   **Jane Chien**[2]

[1] Knowledge Systems Laboratory, Stanford University
701 Welch Road Bldg. , Palo Alto, CA 94304
[2] Stanford University School of Medicine and Department of Veterans Affairs
3801 Miranda Ave., Palo Alto, CA 94304
{hayes-roth, uckun, larsson, gaba} @KSL.Stanford.Edu

A surgical intensive care unit (ICU) is a challenging monitoring environment. The multitude of monitored variables, the high frequency of alarms, and the severity of likely complications and emergencies can overload the cognitive skills of even experienced clinicians. ICU monitoring is also complicated by changes in clinical context. Over the course of a few days, a patient may evolve from a high-vigilance immediate post-operative state to a convalescent state that involves entirely different sets of monitoring principles, problems, and treatments.

Guardian is an experimental intelligent agent for monitoring patients in a surgical ICU (Hayes-Roth et al. 1992). Guardian is based on the BB1 blackboard control architecture and is under development in a laboratory environment using simulated and recorded patient data. Guardian has a number of advantages over existing real-time intelligent monitoring architectures. These include multiple reasoning skills, configuration of available knowledge and skills based on context, data reduction based on the availability of computational resources, and dynamic selection of reasoning skills under time pressure. Guardian is composed of a variety of software modules organized in two levels. At the lower level, Guardian has modules that perform data reduction and abstraction tasks. At the higher level, various reasoning skills exist and cooperate under the guidance of BB1. Domain knowledge bases for Guardian are coordinated through a shared ontology for intelligent monitoring and control. These knowledge bases are available to any of Guardian's problem solving components that wish to use them. Incremental knowledge acquisition continues in parallel with the development for Guardian.

This videotape focuses on the dynamic and context-sensitive aspects of reasoning in Guardian. In the demonstration, Guardian starts monitoring a simulated patient who has had open heart surgery and has just been taken from the operating room to the surgical ICU. This situation is defined as the "early postoperative" situation. Later in the demonstration, the patient improves to a more stable situation. Since the domain knowledge bases are extensive, Guardian selects different subsets of problems for which to prepare short-latency reactions as appropriate for these different contexts. Its choices reflect consideration of several features of known contingencies, such as criticality, side effects, and likelihood – in the given context (Dabija 1994).

During normal operation, over a hundred channels of data flow into Guardian at regular intervals or on demand. A data reduction and dynamic filtering component reduces the incoming data rate based on dynamic attention focusing decisions and also on the dynamic global rate at which Guardian can process incoming data. A temporal fuzzy pattern recognition component classifies incoming data in terms of clinically-relevant signs and symptoms.

Two component reasoning skills are demonstrated. In the immediate postoperative situation, a reactive diagnosis skill (Ash et al. 1993) utilizes action-based hierarchies to provide short-latency diagnosis and therapeutic response to one of the selected subset of context-relevant clinical problems. Later, a probabilistic causal reasoning skill (Peng & Reggia 1990) performs associative diagnosis based on clinical signs and symptoms for a non-time-stressed problem. These examples illustrate Guardian's ability to make runtime choices among alternative reasoning methods based on problem characteristics and the availability of data, knowledge, and real-time computational resources.

References

Hayes-Roth, B., et al. 1992. Guardian: a prototype intelligent agent for intensive-care monitoring. *Artificial Intelligence in Medicine* 4 (2): 165-185.

Dabija, V. 1994. Deciding whether to plan to react. Ph.D. diss., Dept. of Computer Science, Stanford University.

Ash, D.; Gold, G.; Seiver, A.; and Hayes-Roth, B. 1993. Guaranteeing real-time performance with limited resources. *Artificial Intelligence in Medicine* 5(1): 49-66.

Peng, Y.; and Reggia, J. 1990. *Abductive inference models for diagnostic problem-solving*. New York, NY: Springer-Verlag.

The Guardian project is sponsored by ARPA/NASA grant NAG2-581 under ARPA order 8607.

Dynamic Generation of Complex Behavior

Randolph M. Jones
Artificial Intelligence Laboratory
University of Michigan
1101 Beal Avenue
Ann Arbor, Michigan 48109–2110
rjones@eecs.umich.edu

Simulation can be an effective training method if the simulation environment is as realistic as possible. An important part of the training for Navy pilots involves flying against computer-controlled agents in simulated tactical scenarios. In order for such a situation to be realistic, the computer-controlled agents must be indistinguishable from human-piloted agents within the simulated environment. The primary goal of the Soar-IFOR project (Jones et al. 1993; Rosenbloom et al. 1994) is to provide such believable agents for flight training simulations.

To achieve this goal, we have constructed the TacAir-Soar system.[1] Developing this system requires us to address a number of core research issues within artificial intelligence, including reasoning about interacting goals, situation interpretation, communication, explanation, planning, learning, natural language understanding and generation, temporal reasoning, and plan recognition.

This report focuses on two particular issues required to function reasonably within the tactical air domain: a system must be able to generate behavior in response to complex goals and situations, and it must be able to do so dynamically, in response to extremely rapid changes in the agent's situation. On the surface, these two capabilities seem to be at odds to each other. Approaches to real-time or reactive behavior have generally not been used within complex domains, and systems that focus on complex goals do not usually do so in real time. Our solution has been to encode knowledge within the Soar production architecture (Rosenbloom et al. 1991) in order to take advantage of state-of-the-art matching algorithms to provide real-time, reactive behavior. In addition, the knowledge is represented at a fine grain size, capturing a deep representation of the first principles involved in the tactical flight domain. This representation allows reactive rules to combine in a fashion that leads to appropriate responses to complex goal and situation combinations.

The current version of TacAir-Soar has been flown in simulated exercises against other computer-controlled agents, as well as human-controlled flight simulators. The agent exhibits a wide variety of complex behaviors, and it meets the real-time requirements of the task. In addition, the agent provides realistic, human-like behavior in a number of tactical scenarios.

References

Jones, R. M., Tambe, M., Laird, J. E., & Rosenbloom, P. S. 1993. Intelligent automated agents for flight training simulators. In *Proceedings of the Third Conference on Computer Generated Forces and Behavioral Representation* (pp. 33–42). Orlando, FL.

Rosenbloom, P. S., Johnson, W. L., Jones, R. M., Koss, F., Laird, J. E., Lehman, J. F., Rubinoff, R., Schwamb, K. B., & Tambe, M. 1994. Intelligent automated agents for tactical air simulation: A progress report. In *Proceedings of the Fourth Conference on Computer Generated Forces and Behavioral Representation*. Orlando, FL.

Rosenbloom, P. S., Laird, J. E., Newell, A., & McCarl, R. 1991. A preliminary analysis of the Soar architecture as a basis for general intelligence. *Artificial Intelligence, 47*: 289–325.

---

[1] This research involves the efforts of John E. Laird, Randolph M. Jones, Paul E. Nielsen, and Frank Koss at the University of Michigan; Paul S. Rosenbloom, Milind Tambe, W. Lewis Johnson, and Karl B. Schwamb at the University of Southern California, Information Sciences Institute; and Jill E. Lehman and Robert Rubinoff at Carnegie Mellon University. The members of BMH, Inc. have also provided invaluable assistance as subject-matter experts. The research is supported by contract N00014-02-K-2015 from the Advanced Systems Technology Office of the Advanced Research Projects Agency and the Naval Research Laboratory.

HIPAIR: Interactive Mechanism Analysis and Design Using Configuration Spaces

Leo Joskowicz
IBM T.J. Watson Research Center
P.O. Box 704
Yorktown Heights, NY 10598
E-mail: josko@watson.ibm.com

Elisha Sacks
Computer Science Department
Princeton University
Princeton, NJ 08544
E-mail: eps@cs.princeton.edu

We present an interactive problem solving environment for reasoning about shape and motion in mechanism design. Reasoning about shape and motion plays a central role in mechanism design because mechanisms perform functions by transforming motions via part interactions. The input motion, the part shapes, and the part contacts determine the output motion. Designers must reason about the interplay between shape and motion at every step of the design cycle.

Reasoning about shape and motion is difficult and time consuming even for experienced designers. The designer must determine which features of which parts interact at each stage of the mechanism work cycle, must compute the effects of the interactions, must identify contact transitions, and must infer the overall behavior from this information. The designer must then infer shape modifications that eliminate design flaws, such as part interference and jamming, and that optimize performance. The difficulty in these tasks lies in the large number of potential contacts, in the complexity of the contact relations, and in the discontinuities induced by contact transitions.

Current computer-aided design programs support only a few aspects of reasoning about shape and motion. Drafting programs provide interactive environments for the design of part shapes, but do not support reasoning about motion. Simulation programs, which compute and animate the motions of the parts of mechanisms, reveal only one of many possible behaviors. Commercial simulators only handle linkages: mechanisms whose parts interact through permanent surface contacts, such as hinges and screws. Other packages handle specialized mechanisms, such as cams and gears. They cannot handle mechanisms whose parts interact intermittently or via point or curve contacts. Yet these *higher pairs* play a central role in mechanism design. Our survey of 2500 mechanisms in an engineering encyclopedia shows that 66% contain higher pairs and that 18% involve intermittent contacts.

We have developed a problem solving environment, called HIPAIR, for reasoning about shape and motion in mechanisms. The core of the environment is a module that automates the kinematic analysis of mecha-

nisms composed of linkages and higher pairs. This module provides the computational engine for a range of tasks, including simulation, behavior description, and parametric design. It is comprehensive, robust, and fast. HIPAIR handles higher pairs with two degrees of freedom, including ones with intermittent and simultaneous contacts. This class contains 90% of 2.5D pairs and 80% of all higher pairs according to our survey.

HIPAIR computes and manipulates configuration spaces. The configuration space of a mechanism is a geometric representation of the configurations (positions and orientations) of its parts. Configuration spaces encode the relations among part shapes, part motions, and overall behavior in a concise, complete and explicit format. They simplify and systematize reasoning about shape and motion by mapping it into a uniform geometrical framework.

The videotape explains configuration spaces and illustrates how HIPAIR supports mechanism design and analysis. HIPAIR has been tested on over 100 parametric variations of 25 kinematic pairs and on dozen multipart mechanisms, including a Fuji disposable camera with ten moving parts.

References

1. "Mechanism Comparison and Classification for Design", L. Joskowicz, in *Research in Engineering Design*, Springer-Verlag, Vol 1. No. 2, 1990.

2. "Computational Kinematics", L. Joskowicz and E. Sacks, *Artificial Intelligence*, Vol. 51, Nos. 1-3, North-Holland, 1991.

3. "Automated Modeling and Kinematic Simulation of Mechanisms", E. Sacks and L. Joskowicz, *Computer-Aided Design*, Vol. 25, No. 2, 1993.

4. "Configuration Space Computation for Mechanism Design", E. Sacks and L. Joskowicz, *Proc. of the IEEE Int. Conference on Robotics and Automation*, IEEE Computer Society Press, 1994.

5. "Mechanism Analysis and Design Using Configuration Spaces", E. Sacks and L. Joskowicz, submitted, *Communications of the ACM*, 1994.

ALIVE: Artificial Life Interactive Video Environment

Pattie Maes, Trevor Darrell, Bruce Blumberg, Sandy Pentland

MIT Media-Laboratory
20 Ames St.
Cambridge Ma. 02139
pattie/trevor/bruce/sandy@media.mit.edu

Abstract

In this video we demonstrate a novel system which allows wireless full-body interaction between a human participant and a graphical world inhabited by autonomous agents. The system is called "ALIVE", an acronym for Artificial Life Interactive Video Environment. The goal of ALIVE is to present a virtual environment in which a user can interact, in natural and believable ways, with autonomous semi-intelligent agents whose behavior is equally natural and believable.

In ALIVE, a single CCD camera is used to obtain a color image of a person which is composited into a 3D graphical world. The composite world is projected onto a large video wall in a world-centered reference frame, which faces the user and acts as a type of "magic mirror". No goggles, gloves, or wires are needed for interaction with the world: agents and objects in the graphical world can be acted upon by the human participant through the use of domain-specific computer vision techniques that analyze the silhouette and gestures of the person.

The agents inhabiting the world are modeled as self-contained autonomous systems with internal needs and motivations which are embodied in a dynamic world: they sense the world via sensors, and move in, and act on the world in real time in response to the user's gestures and actions. As a result of the presence of these semi-intelligent entities, the system does not just allow for the obvious direct-manipulation style of interaction, but also a more powerful, indirect style of interaction in which gestures can have more complex meanings, which may vary according to the situation in which the agents and user find themselves.

The video presents a specific implementation of the ALIVE system which was demonstrated as part of SIGGRAPH-93's Tomorrow's Realities show. Approximately 500 attendees interacted with the ALIVE system over the course of 5 days. The video footage was taken during that time.

More information on the ALIVE system in general may be found in [Maes93] and [Darrell94]. Information on the details of the behavior and agent model used in ALIVE may be found in [Blumberg94]. More information on details of the visual routines may be found in [Darrell94].

References

Blumberg, B. 1994. Action-Selection in Hamsterdam: Lessons from Ethology. In: The Proceedings of the Third International Conference on the Simulation of Adaptive Behavior, Brighton. Forthcoming

Darrell, T., Maes, P., Blumberg, B. and Pentland, S. 1994. Situated Vision and Behavior for Interactive Environments, Technical Note No. 261. M.I.T. Media Laboratory Perceptual Computing , M.I.T.

Maes, P. 1993. ALIVE: An Artificial Life Interactive Video Environment. In: Visual Proceedings, The Art and Interdisciplinary Programs of Siggraph 93. ACM, NY.

A Reading Coach that Listens: (Edited) Video Transcript

Jack Mostow, Alex Hauptmann, Steven F. Roth, Matt Kane, Adam Swift, Lin Chase, Bob Weide

Project LISTEN, Carnegie Mellon Robotics Institute, 215 Cyert Hall, 4910 Forbes Avenue, Pittsburgh, PA 15213-3890

At Carnegie Mellon University, Project LISTEN[1] is taking a novel approach to the problem of illiteracy. We have developed a prototype automated reading coach that listens to a child read aloud, and helps when needed. The coach provides a combination of reading and listening, in which the child reads wherever possible, and the coach helps wherever necessary -- a bit like training wheels on a bicycle. Let's see how the automated coach responds to various things a child might do. The output of the automatic speech recognizer is displayed at the bottom of the screen.

Help when needed: The coach recues a misread word by rereading the words that lead up to it, just like the expert reading teachers whom the coach is modelled after. This context often helps the reader correct the word on the second try:

Text: `The cow lives on the farm.`
Reader: "The cow lives on the farm."
Text: `She eats grass all day long.`
Reader: "She eats good all day long."
Coach: SHE EATS
Reader: "grass"
Coach: GRASS. PLEASE CONTINUE.

Support comprehension: The coach is designed to emphasize comprehension and ignore minor mistakes, such as repeated words. However, the word "very" is important to the meaning of the sentence, so the coach asks the reader to reread it. The coach rereads the sentence to help the reader comprehend it:

Text: `At night she is very tired.`
Reader: "At night ... at night she is tired."
Coach: READ THIS WORD AGAIN. [flashes `very`]
Reader: "tired?"
Coach: VERY. AT NIGHT SHE IS VERY TIRED.

Maintain flow: When the reader gets stuck, the coach jumps in, enabling the reader to complete the sentence:

Text: `Then she slowly comes home.`
Reader: "Then she then she s ... s ... "
Coach: SLOWLY
Reader: "slowly comes home."

---

[1]**Note:** For acknowledgements, further references, and technical details, please see (Mostow et al, 1994).

This research was supported primarily by the National Science Foundation under Grant Number MDR-9154059 and by the Advanced Research Projects Agency, DoD, through DARPA Order 5167, monitored by the Air Force Avionics Laboratory under contract N00039-85-C-0163. Lin Chase is supported by a Howard Hughes Doctoral Fellowship from the Hughes Research Laboratory. The views and conclusions contained in this document are those of the authors and should not be interpreted as representing the official policies, either expressed or implied, of the sponsors or of the United States Government.

Minimize disruption: Since short function words like "to" and "be" do not usually affect comprehension, the coach refrains from interrupting the reader to correct this omission:

Text: `I want to be milked, she says.`
Reader: "I want milked she says"

We're having children try out this prototype coach to help us improve it. [Show children using coach].

Clicking for help: To get help with a word, the child can click on it. [Coach speaks word.] This feature is very useful, but children often don't realize when they need help. [Child misreads `democratic` as "dramatic," even after coach recues it.]

Tolerate recognizer inaccuracy: We're working to make the coach recognize children's speech more accurately, and behave reasonably even when the speech recognizer is inaccurate. [Coach misrecognizes "slowly," causing it to reread the sentence.]

In an earlier study we compared how well second graders read with and without similar assistance. Without assistance, they missed one word in eight, which is considered overly frustrating. With assistance, they missed fewer than one word in forty, enabling them to read and comprehend material more than six months beyond their independent reading level.

Children can't read to learn until they learn to read -- whether it's a science passage or anything else. We need to find out how the coach can help children learn over time, and explore how the coach can help in ways that human teachers cannot -- for example, by modifying the text dynamically, and by tapping into the motivational power of computers. [Child comments on coach.]

Project LISTEN builds on years of previous government-funded research in basic speech technology. It has the potential to pay back many times over for the cost of that research, since illiteracy costs the United States over 225 billion dollars every year (Herrick, 1990).

Moreover, this work applies to several important areas in addition to children's reading instruction, including adult literacy, English as a second language, and foreign language learning. It opens the door to a new generation of intelligent tutoring systems that can listen to their students.

References

E. Herrick. (1990). *Literacy Questions and Answers.* Pamphlet. P. O. 81826, Lincoln, NE 68501: Contact Center, Inc.

J. Mostow, S. Roth, A. G. Hauptmann, and M. Kane. (August 1994). A Prototype Reading Coach that Listens. *Proceedings of the Twelfth National Conference on Artificial Intelligence (AAAI94).* Seattle, WA, American Association for Artificial Intelligence.

Machine Rhythm

David Rosenthal

International Media Research Foundation
TOHMA Building B1, 2-14-1 Nishi-Waseda
Shinjuku-ku,Tokyo, 169, JAPAN
dfr@media.mit.edu

The video discusses *Machine Rhythm,* a program which emulates human rhythm perception. Given a musical performance represented as a MIDI stream, the program determines the program's rhythm — that is, it decides the meter of the performance, the rhythmic value of each note, and the location of barlines. The basic orientation of the video is to demonstrate applications of the program; more theoretical aspects are treated in (Rosenthal 1992).

Machine rhythm-finding is a difficult problem for several reasons. First, the timing of downbeats, which are heard by human listeners as a regular pulse, actually varies quite wildly; in certain cases the period can vary by a factor of two in adjacent beats. This can happen even when tempo variation is not being used as an expressive device. Second, not all downbeats correspond to actual musical events — in other words, one sometimes taps to a beat that doesn't correspond to a note in the music. Syncopations are particularly difficult instances of this, but the problem occurs even in unsyncopated music. Third, there is no straightforward method by which the location of downbeats can be extracted from a performance; downbeats are not reliably louder than other notes, for example. Finally, the rhythm of a piece of music is not a single pulse, but rather an interlocking hierarchy or pulses with periods of different sizes; hence the nomenclature of "measure," "half-note," "quarter-note," and so on.

Despite these apparent difficulties, human listeners have little trouble arriving at an unambiguous interpretation; in this sense rhythm finding is as well-defined a problem as, say, speech understanding. Humans apparently compensate for the problems mentioned in the last paragraph by integrating a variety of acoustic and musical cues, such as texture, melodic pattern, relative time between onsets, length of notes, and others. Humans also have the ability to fluently change their interpretations, either because of an initial interpretation is incorrect or because of a change in the music. Humans apparently track the various-size periods simultaneously, and use them to confirm each other.

In an effort to build a machine rhythm tracker with performance approaching that of a human, we integrated many of these methods into our system: The system integrates evidence from a variety of cues, some of which involve subtle analyses of the music from the MIDI data. The system achieves the flexibility to handle difficult situations by maintaining a hierarchy of hypotheses. The system tracks several "levels," or different-sized periods simultaneously, using them as checks on each other.

The first section of the video uses an animation to explain the problem of rhythm parsing, and briefly outlines our approach.

The next section shows the program parsing various live performances, and demonstrates an application — automatic transcription. This section also demonstrates the program's ability to handle somewhat more challenging situations, such as varying tempo and triplets.

The final section of the video shows another kind application, which we call automatic synchronization. In this section we take a piece written for four hands and record each pianist's part separately. We then demonstrate that the two parts need to be synchronized in order to be played together. Furthermore, they cannot be synchronized by globally altering their tempos; local adjustment of the tempo is necessary. To do this, the program must make use of the rhythmic parsing that the Machine Rhythm program produces. When the two parts are synchronized in this way, the piece sounds as it should.

References

Rosenthal, D. 1992. Machine Rhythm: Computer Emulation of Human Rhythm Perception. Ph.D. diss., The Media Laboratory, Massachusetts Institute of Technology.

Acknowledgments

This video was produced while I was a doctoral student at the MIT Media Lab. I'd like to thank Stuart Cody and Greg Tucker, both of the Media Lab, for their help.

Index